REFERENCE

Melton's Encyclopedia *of*
American Religions

Eighth Edition

Melton's Encyclopedia *of*
American Religions

Eighth Edition

J. GORDON MELTON

James Beverley, *Associate Editor*

Constance Jones, *Assistant Editor*

Pamela S. Nadell, *Assistant Editor*

Foreword by **Rodney Stark**

GALE
CENGAGE Learning·

Detroit • New York • San Francisco • New Haven, Conn • Waterville, Maine • London

Melton's Encyclopedia of American Religions, eighth edition

J. Gordon Melton

James Beverley, Associate Editor

Constance Jones, Associate Editor

Pamela S. Nadell, Associate Editor

For product information and technology assistance, contact us at Gale Customer Support, 1-800-877-4253

For permission to use material from this text or product, submit all requests online at www.cengage.com/permissions Further permissions questions can be emailed to permissionrequest@gale.cengage.com

Since this page cannot legibly accommodate all copyright notices, the acknowledgments constitute an extension of the copyright notice.

Cover photographs reproduced by permission of Corbis (pictures of teenagers praying, mega church, young woman praying), Shutterstock (church steeple, young African Muslim woman, Indian woman, Yemenite shofar, replica statue of Jesus Christ known as The Christus, design on hands, praying hands), Digital Stock (bowl of communion wafers, Christian man praying, crucifix and Bible, Muslims facing Mecca to pray, Muslim boy praying, nuns, new age, Amish carriage on rural road, protrait of Buddhist monk, mosaic/religious art), Image Works (Sikh man).

While every effort has been made to ensure the reliability of the information presented in this publication, Gale, a part of Cengage Learning, does not guarantee the accuracy of the data contained herein. Gale accepts no payment for listing; and inclusion in the publication of any organization, agency, institution, publication, service, or individual does not imply endorsement of the editors or publisher. Errors brought to the attention of the publisher and verified to the satisfaction of the publisher will be corrected in future editions.

Gale
27500 Drake Rd.
Farmington Hills, MI, 48331-3535

LIBRARY OF CONGRESS CATALOGING-IN-PUBLICATION DATA

Melton's encyclopedia of American religions/ J. Gordon Melton, editor in chief ; James Beverley, Constance Jones, Pamela S. Nadell, associate editors. — 8th ed.
    p. cm.
  Includes bibliographical references and index.
  ISBN 978-0-7876-9696-2 (hardcover : alk. paper) — ISBN 978-1-4144-1039-5 (ebook)
1. Sects—United States. 2. Cults—United States. 3. Sects—United States—Directories. 4. Cults—United States—Directories. 5. United States—Religion. I. Melton, J. Gordon. II. Beverley, James A. III. Jones, Constance M. IV. Nadell, Pamela Susan. V. Title: Encyclopedia of American religions.
  BL2525.M449 2009
  200.973'03—dc22
                                         2008037465

ISBN-13: 978-0-787-69696-2
ISBN-10: 0-78-769696-X

This title is also available as an e-book.
ISBN-13: 978-1-414-41039-5 ISBN-10: 1-41-441039-5
Contact your Gale sales representative for ordering information.

Printed in the United States of America
4 5 6 7 13 12 11 10

Editorial and Production Staff

Project Editors	*Shawn Corridor*
	Carol Schwartz
Editorial Technical Support	*Luann Brennan*
	Mark Drouillard
Researchers	*Heidi Bright-Parales*
	Judy Clinebell
	Pamela S. Dear
	Lisa DeShantz-Cook
	Kathy Droste
	Nancy Dziedzic
	Margaret Haerens
	Amanda Iles
	John Krol
	Matthew May
	John Mumm
	Sean Paul
	Heather Price
	Christine Przyblo
	David Shave
	Christopher Soltis
Copyeditors	*Deborah Baker*
	Judy Clinebell
	Tony Coulter
	Judy Culligan
	Anne Davidson
	Ellen Henderson
	Jessica Hornik-Evans
	Peter Jaskowiak
	Peg Knight
	William Kaufman
	Christine Kelley
	Eric Linderman
	Laurie Malashanko
	Linda Sanders
	Darcy Thompson
	Ken Wachsberger
Proofreaders	*John Krol*
	Eric Lowenkron
Indexer	*Laurie Andriot*
Product Design	*Pamela A.E. Galbreath*
	Patricia A. Hudepohl

Graphic Art	*GGS Book Services PMG*
	XNR Productions
Composition	*Evi Seoud*
Manufacturing	*Rita Wimberley*
New Product Development	*Erin Podolsky Walker*
Publisher	*Jay Flynn*

Contents

Contents

One morning in 1978, when I opened my mail I found a flyer for something called the *Encyclopedia of American Religions*, in two volumes. According to the ad copy, these two books would provide details on about 1,200 different faiths currently operating in the United States. It sounded much too good to be true. I remember saying to my wife that if these volumes were half as complete as they claimed to be, it would be a work of monumental value to scholars. But for that very reason it was probably all hype. As I should have anticipated, she replied, "Rod, its only 90 bucks. Why not buy it?" So I did.

When the books arrived I was stunned. They were far more complete, far better organized, and far more sophisticated than the ad had claimed. For one thing, every effort had been made to provide *comparable* information on each of the groups. Since nearly all American religions groups originated in this country, most of them having broken away from a 'parent' body, great care had been taken to organize religious bodies in lineages on the basis of the denominational 'family' within which they had originated. In addition, critical historical details were provided as to the specific origins of each group, its growth and spread over time, and subsequent splits and conflicts that had developed. Equally careful attention was devoted to basic doctrines and special practices. The pattern of growth/decline of each group since its first days in America also was sketched. Of course, it would not have been difficult to provide this information for the twenty or thirty major Christian bodies. The incredible achievement was to have gathered surprisingly complete data for each of the hundreds of small Christian sects.

An even greater achievement was to have done all of this for the hundreds of non-Christian groups—New Thought, Spiritualist, Witchcraft, Theosophical, and the like. At the time, very few of us were more than dimly aware that these groups also formed lineages (or families) as most of them too had broken off from another group or had been founded by a leader with a prior background in another group. Moreover, most of these groups were (and are) tiny and many of them were (and are) extremely secretive and somewhat hostile to outsiders. Yet there they were, all assembled into families, their origins and history revealed, and with plausible membership figures.

Within the first hour of examining my new books I recognized their value for doing quantitative comparative studies and within the year I had created and analyzed a data set of 417 American-born Christian sects and 501 American-born non-Christian religious groups. The published results continue to inform scholars. Since then, of course, there has been an immense amount of scholarship making use of the *Encyclopedia of American Religions*.

My next response to my new books was: Who was this guy J. Gordon Melton anyway? I had good reason to wonder since I thought I knew all of the significant players in the history and sociology of American religion. I concluded that Melton must be someone about 80 years old who had devoted an obscure life of effort to amassing this incredible assembly of material. The dust jacket located him in Evanston, Illinois, so I got his phone number and called him. Surprise! He was quite young, supported himself as a Methodist pastor, and had devoted himself to collecting data on American religious groups since his teens. He told me that one day during high school he had come across Elmer T. Clark's *Small Sects in America* and had gone home, sold his baseball cards, and started collecting sects. His achievement was all the more extraordinary considering that he had done it without any assistants and without any financial support. That's why soon after the second edition appeared, the late Jeffrey K. Hadden began to characterize Gordon as "a national treasure." And so he is.

We now have the eighth edition and it comes with all sorts of valuable new features. For the first time, this edition is illustrated and includes many maps, tables, charts, and graphs. It also is available as an e-book. Amazingly, the number of entries has grown from about 1,200 in the first edition to more than 2,300 independent religious groups as of 2008.

How is it possible for the number of groups to increase in every edition? The primary reason is that the number of religious groups in America keeps growing. A second reason is that Gordon keeps finding tiny groups here and there that he had missed. Consider this example of his constant scrutiny.

A few years ago I organized a conference on new religious movements bringing Gordon Melton and a dozen other well-known scholars to Orcas Island, Washington. This is a small resort community located in Puget Sound, famous locally for the several pods of killer whales (orcas) that frequent the area. Everyone flew into Seattle and then we took a chartered yacht to the island. Shortly after we arrived at the hotel, Gordon excused himself and said he had arranged to see a psychic practitioner on the other side of the island. "This guy has been trying to start a group and I want to see if he has any followers." About two hours later Gordon returned. No followers. No new entry for the *Encyclopedia*, but another lead followed up. At the end of the conference we returned to Seattle in four single-engine float planes that picked us up on the beach and landed on Lake Union in downtown Seattle. Most of the other participants then took cabs to the Seattle/Tacoma Airport. Not Gordon. There were four possible new groups in Seattle he wanted to check out first. He never stops. And that's why, as superb as the first edition was, the eighth is far, far better.

Rodney Stark
Distinguished Professor of the Social Sciences &
Co-Director of the Institute for Studies of Religion
Baylor University

As a high school student, I found a copy of Elmer T. Clark's pioneering study, *The Small Sects of America*, in a bookstore. Fifty years later I can still remember the sense of fascination I had as I read through the volume and discovered the many ways my neighbors did religion. Birmingham, Alabama, was not the most religiously pluralistic city in the country, but it had an amazing array of churches from Eastern Rite Catholic to Spiritualist along with representative congregations of most of the Holiness and Pentecostal groups. There was quite enough to start me looking for any groups that Clark had missed, and by the time I finished college in 1964, I had found several hundred. Moving on to Chicago for seminary and graduate school, I was able to witness the great expansion that America was undergoing following the 1965 change in immigration laws. At the beginning of the 1970s, when it came time to write my dissertation, I was totally focused on trying to understand the development of the unique American religious environment.

At first glance, the religious situation in America appears somewhat chaotic with all the different religions vying for attention and a following, some very successfully, some all but ignored. The first task was making sense of a bewildering array of belief. This task was somewhat accomplished by the emergence in my research and the subsequent designation of the religious families. Each family consists of a set of religious denominations that were bound together by their sharing the same history, engaged each other in like theological discourse, and followed similar behavior patterns. From looking at the families, I concluded that there was an interesting variety of ways to do religion, but not a huge infinite number. There are actually a relatively small number of basic religious myths that have captured the attention of the world's billions and a relatively limited number of ways that communities have found to successfully embody the myth. Meanwhile, the words and actions used to express those myths still seem endless.

In the modern secular world (where the separation of religion and government is in effect) people group themselves around these basic religious formats that have proved most viable in following them. Subsequently, they will construct the long-term, more-or-less stable organizations that facilitate an ongoing organized religious life. In the United States, we generally use the term *denomination* (a word first used in the Christian context) to designate these long-term organizations that are the basic structure of religious life. That term works well in North America, where some 80 percent of the public identify as Christians. It does not work so well with other religious communities. At the Institute for the Study of American Religion, we use the term *primary religious group*. A primary religious group is a religious organization or association that organizes individuals into local centers for regular worship (or its equivalent) and then organizes these centers of like-minded individuals in regional and national associations (the denominations). Overwhelmingly, these regional and national associations are legally established as corporations.

Primary religious groups are to be distinguished from secondary religious groups (association of denominations—such as ecumenical and interfaith groups) and tertiary religious groups (organizations that engage in religious activity but lack the full range of communal worship and related congregational life of a denomination). Tertiary groups, often called para-churches, usually specialize in a single task which they perform for multiple denominations—education, publication, evangelism, etc. Para-churches include everything from independent Bible schools to advocacy groups to large publication houses to overseas missionary organizations.

Once in place, the primary religious groups become the basic building blocks of religious life in a (relatively) free society. They make the basic rules that govern their own life.

They set the boundaries of belief that will be articulated by the group's religious functionaries and determine the strictness with which belief will be held. They decided on the type of worship that will be conducted and how often. They decide on the looseness or tightness of the organizational structure, who will own the property, and how authority will be exercised. They will raise and distribute money to further the overall group program. Most importantly, they will provide space and opportunity for the regular (daily, weekly, or other) gathering of the group for the affirmation of group's values and belief, the acknowledgement of the super-mundane realm, and the development and maintenance of community.

The primary religious groups form the stable structures that one can expect to be present week in and week out. They persist though the ups and downs of group life. Religious enthusiasms, theological fads, and spiritual excitements come and go; the primary groups react to these events, but continue on. Since the early nineteenth century, various religious visionaries have perceived the divisive nature of denominations and have articulated the hopes of a united Christianity or even a single religious community open and available to all, and have taken steps to bring their vision into reality. Such visions have always fallen short of understanding the function of denominations in a free society where knowledge is limited and religious communities serve a variety of functions for its members.

While some might hope for a post-denominational world or a united religion, no one has yet found a better way to serve the religious needs of a free and diverse people exercising their freedom on issues of the religious life as with every other area of life. Because so many disagreements on matters of belief, worship, organization, and ways to deal with new issues exist, sectarian differences as structured into the different denominations will remain with us for the foreseeable future. Post-denominational and interdenominational churches simply become new denominations and united religious communities become new religions. It is to be noted the only places where denominational differences have disappeared are in lands where the coercive power of the state is used to privilege one religious tradition while suppress all competition and dissent.

In the United States, understanding the meaning of separation of church and state has come to include strict limitations on government interference in the religious life of its people. That noninterference policy has also come to include strictures against government agencies compiling basic information about religion. Prior to World War II, the U.S. government gathered data from all of the different religious bodies functioning in America and issued a decade-by-decade census. That valuable report was discontinued in 1936. The federal and later the National Council of Churches attempted to fill the gap partially by the *Yearbook of American Churches*, however, that volume was very much limited. It only reported on groups it considered worthy, and was then further limited to information that groups supplied to it. Given the role of the *Yearbook* as an expression of the National Council of Churches, many large religious groups ideologically refused to report to it. At the same time, the Council felt unable to recognize some groups, for example the many Western Esoteric organizations, as members of the larger religious community.

As I became aware of the many religious groups in America that received no attention from my scholarly colleagues and about which no material existed in standard reference books, I saw the need for an organization that would research and systematically provide information on the many different religious organizations in (North) America. This need led to the founding of the Institute for the Study of American Religion (ISAR) in the fall of 1968. At that time I was just beginning my graduate program at Garrett Evangelical Theological Seminary and Northwestern University. I carried out the primary gathering of a basic collection of material on all of the different religious groups then functioning in North America, pursued a graduate degree, and wrote my dissertation on the shape and structure of American religion (denominationalism) simultaneously with the early development of ISAR. Finally, in the late 1970s, I was able to write the first edition of the *Encyclopedia of American Religions*, utilizing the solutions to the problems of distinguishing and understanding the basic religious structures in my dissertation.

Since its initial appearance in 1979, the *Encyclopedia of American Religions* has been the only reference book that has provided basic data on the growing number of different religious groups in the United States and Canada, and thanks to the publisher, ISAR has been given the opportunity to regularly update the material and add entries on new religious bodies as they form. In the period that the eight editions have appeared, several of the largest religious groups in America (Evangelical Lutheran of America, Presbyterian Church [U.S.A.]) have formed and the number of known religious groups in the United States has grown from some 800 to more than 2,300. Together, the various editions have chronicled the changing scene of religious life for a generation and thereby filled a major gap in information about one of the most important aspects of North American culture. Meanwhile, ISAR has supplemented the findings of the *Encyclopedia* in the more than 300 monographs it has seen into publication.

In this new edition of the *Encyclopedia*, I have been particularly aided by three people: James Beverley, Pamela S. Nadell, and Constance Jones. Beverley, a professor at Tyndale Seminary in Toronto, Ontario, became the associate director of the Institute for the Study of American Religion in 2000. With this edition, he also assumes additional duties in the preparation of the Institute's most important publication. For this edition he took on responsibility especially for the editing and updating of the introductory essay on religion in Canada and the two chapters on the Baptists and Islam. It is assumed that he will take on a greater proportion of the work in future editions.

As the coverage of the *Encyclopedia* has expanded, no single person can now hope to stay current on the ever-growing number of religious bodies it covers. Just the task of gathering updated material on the more than 2,000 religions in America is impossible for ISAR's small staff, even with the assistance of the large network of cooperating scholars who periodically call our attention to important developments. In previous editions we reached out for help on Catholicism and Shinto. In this edition we were able to secure two scholars to assist in the revisions on Judaism and Hinduism. Pamela S. Nadell is the Patrick Clendenen Professor of History and Director of the Jewish Studies Program at American University in Washington, and after working with her on the many needed revisions to the Jewish chapter in the *Encyclopedia*, I understand fully why she was recently named her university's Scholar/Teacher of the Year (2007–2008). She not only knew her stuff, she was kind and patient in her criticisms as we worked our way through the introductory material and individual entries. I am most grateful for her assistance.

Dr. Constance Jones is a sociologist with whom I have worked on a variety of projects for the last two decades. She is a sociologist and a professor of Transformative Studies at the California Institute for Integral Studies in San Francisco, and recently completed the *Encyclopedia of Hinduism* (Facts on File, 2007). It was only natural to twist her arm to assist in revising the material on Hinduism for the *Encyclopedia*. As I have come to expect of her, she did an excellent job of offering suggestions for revision.

With my own work on Buddhism, Dr. Beverley's help with Islam, and the efforts of Drs. Nadell and Jones, the major chapters on the Eastern and Middle Eastern religions in America have been most thoroughly revised and updated. This work represents one of the major features of this eighth edition of the *Encyclopedia*. At the same time, it has been my growing belief over the past decade that the chapters listed in previous editions as the Ancient Wisdom, Spiritualism and the New Age, and Magical families should be reorganized to reflect their common roots and continuing interaction. This reorganization has been accomplished in this edition with the designation of a new family, "Western Esotericism," and the reordering of the material in the three chapters. This reordering reflects the larger act of defining Esotericism as a long-standing tradition in Western religion by an emerging community of scholars specializing in Western Esotericism, and acknowledges their accomplishments over the last two decades. In this effort I am particularly reliant on the work of European scholars such as Antoine Faivre, Wouter Hanegraaff, and Massimo Introvigne, and especially North American scholars such as Joscelyn Godwin, Robert Ellwood, and Arthur Versluis.

With the assistance from the several scholars who review specific chapters and the support of a team of editorial assistants supplied by the publisher, I was able for the first time since the early editions of the *Encyclopedia* to do a thorough revision (and in places major rewriting) of its entire text and to review every one of the more than 2,000 entries. With this edition, we also for the first time introduce maps and graphic materials. It is hoped that these will assist in illustrating some of the important aspects of the religious scene from the continuing role of older structures such as the ancient Episcopal sees of the Mediterranean Basin to the radical growth of some religions in the twentieth century.

As with earlier editions, we also offer coverage of what some are surprised to find in a reference work devoted to religion: entries on what I term the religiously irreligious—atheists, humanists, and rationalists. I do so because I have found groups such as American Atheists, Inc., and the Council on Secular Humanism to fit into a community of theological dissent from older religious communities and who now fulfill for their constituencies the roles that have traditionally been filled by religions—ritual acknowledgement of important events, moral guidance, expressions of community, and affirmations of ultimate concerns. These groups not only help us understand the boundaries of the larger religious community but represent the ferment as the cutting edge of religious development.

The continued growth of the American population, the arrival of tens of thousands new immigrants annually, and the concentration of people in large urban complexes has meant that the number of new religious options has continued to expand and, while some religious groups disappear, the net increase in the number of new religious bodies grows at a more-or-less steady pace (following the population curve). These new religions represent the merger of previous existing groups, schisms from older groups, new organizations brought to the country by immigrants, and innovative religious expressions created by the country's residents. Each edition of the *Encyclopedia of American Religions* has grown to reflect the growth of these new religions. With this edition, we have adopted a format change to accommodate the addition of more than 200 newly formed groups; we have decided to remove all the entries on defunct religious bodies from the main body of the *Encyclopedia* and place that material in a Defunct Appendix.

I am continually amazed by the developments in the North American religious community, though by now I should be used to seeing the changes in old religions and the seeming need for the new to emerge. I am also amazed the way that a seemingly small project begun as a grad student went on to grow into the dominating work of a lifetime. I have the greatest of appreciation for the many many people who have in ways great and small, in ways visible and invisible, contributed to making the *Encyclopedia of American Religions* a reality. I could not have done it without all of the assistance I have received. Hopefully, the new edition will continue to serve the information needs of its many users.

J. Gordon Melton
January 2009

Introduction

to the Eighth Edition

Melton's *Encyclopedia of American Religions* (*MEAR*), now in its eighth edition, provides a comprehensive survey of religious and spiritual groups in North America. The *Encyclopedia* continues in its role as "an indispensable guide to the confused landscape of American Religion" (*Choice*) by providing both a historical perspective and current information on the many groups that constitute America's religious life.

MEAR covers currently functioning religious groups and, in the Defunct Appendix, groups that are no longer active. Most groups covered meet the following criteria:

- seeks the chief religious loyalty of its members
- promotes its particular view
- satisfies one of the following conditions of size:
  - if the group is organized into congregations, has two or more congregations, or has one congregation with more than 2,000 members who make a measurable impact on the country through mass media
  - if not organized into congregations, membership is drawn from more than one state and from beyond a single metropolitan area

Several groups that do not meet the size requirements outlined above have been included. These groups, such as satanists, espouse beliefs that are at odds with those of most people in the United States and Canada. Despite their limited numbers, these groups have been included to illustrate the religious complexity and diversity of America.

NEW IN THIS EDITION. The eighth edition of the *Encyclopedia* contains over 2,300 descriptive entries on religious bodies, including over 200 new to this edition, and represents a complete revision and expansion of the previous edition. For the first time, the *Encyclopedia* will have illustrations such as maps and charts. Defunct entries have been removed from the directory listings and placed in a Defunct Appendix. This edition also features:

Master Name, Subject, and **Keyword Indexes** have been consolidated to created one Index, providing a one-stop listing of all key details mentioned in this edition.

CONTENT AND ARRANGEMENT. The eighth edition of the *Encyclopedia* now consists of two parts, which are followed by two appendices and an index:

- Three **Introductory Essays** trace the development of religion in America and Canada.

- Twenty-four **Religious Family Historical Essays** discuss the growth and development of the major religious families and traditions in North America. Following each essay are the directory listings for that religious family. They provide contact and descriptive information on the various groups that comprise the 24 families and traditions. Two remaining directory sections—Unclassified Christian Churches and Unclassified Religious Groups—include those groups that cannot be classified within any of the distinct religious families.

The **Defunct Appendix** lists organizations that have become defunct. The **Geographic Appendix** and **Index** facilitate access to information provided in this edition.

For additional details on the content, arrangement, and indexing of *MEAR*, consult the **User's Guide,** following the introductions.

COMPILATION METHODS. The information contained in the entries has been assembled from material obtained directly from the religious bodies listed. Each group was asked to update and return a revision form containing information on their organization, and the majority of organizations graciously complied. In some cases, follow-up telephone conversations were held.

AUTHOR BRINGS UNIQUE PERSPECTIVE. Dr. J. Gordon Melton has been studying America's religious landscape for more than thirty-five years. A graduate of Garrett Evangelical Theological Seminary in Evanston, Illinois, with a Ph.D. from Northwestern University in the History and Literature of Religions, Dr. Melton is nationally recognized as a leading authority on religion, particularly the newer, small groups. He serves as the Director of the Institute for the Study of American Religion based in Santa Barbara, California, and is a research specialist with the Department of Religious Studies at the University of California—Santa Barbara. He has authored a number of articles, text books, and reference works on American religion. Among the many Gale titles authored by Melton are the *New Age Encyclopedia, Religious Leaders of America,* and *The Churches Speak Series.*

For additional details on the author and the impetus for undertaking the *Encyclopedia,* see Selections from the Introduction to the First Edition following this introduction.

***MEAR* ALSO AVAILABLE IN ELECTRONIC FORMATS.** *Melton's Encyclopedia of American Religions* is also available online through the Gale Virtual Reference Library and Gale Directory Library. Information on ordering these versions can be found at www.gale.com. *MEAR* is available for licensing. The complete database is provided in a fielded format and is deliverable on such media as disk or CD-ROM. For more information, contact Gale's Business Development group at 1-800-877-GALE, or visit our website at http://gale.cengage.com/bizdev/.

COMMENTS AND SUGGESTIONS WELCOMED. Comments, suggestions, and information on new organizations or organizations not currently listed are welcomed. Please contact:

Dr. J. Gordon Melton
Institute for the Study of American Religion
Box 90709
Santa Barbara, CA 93190-0709

or

Gale, Cengage Learning
27500 Drake Rd.
Farmington Hills, MI 48331-3535
Telephone (248) 699-GALE
Toll-Free (800) 347-GALE

from the Introduction to the First Edition

The *Encyclopedia of American Religions* explores the broad sweep of American religions and describes over 1,200 [now 2,300] churches. Some churches in the *Encyclopedia*, such as certain Hindu and Jewish bodies, follow a tradition several thousand years old. Others were born yesterday, like Garner Ted Armstrong's Church of God International, formed in the summer of 1978. With few exceptions, if a church existed in the United States in 1976 [now 2009], it is discussed in the *Encyclopedia*.

In my years of study of American religion I discovered three kinds of religious institutions: primary religious bodies (i.e., churches), secondary organizations that serve the primary bodies, and tertiary organizations that strive to change the primary bodies. The *Encyclopedia* treats only the primary religious bodies, but it does refer to the two other kinds of institutions, so some comment on all three types is necessary here.

In defining primary religious bodies (a church, denomination, sect, or cult), I established certain criteria. First, a church seeks the chief religious loyalty of its members. Second, it meets requirements of size. If it is organized into congregations, it has at least two congregations, or it has one congregation of more than 2,000 members who make a measurable impact on the country through the mass media. If a church is not organized into congregations, it meets the size requirement when its members come from more than one state and from beyond a single metropolitan area. The third criterion concerns faith: a primary religious body tends to promote its particular views. For instance, it may encourage belief or disbelief in the Trinity. Or it may try to discourage the wearing of neckties; some holiness churches consider wearing neckties ostentatious.

I waived the size requirement for primary religious bodies whose beliefs are at odds with those of most people in our culture. For example, some satanic groups are discussed in the *Encyclopedia* although they do not have enough members to meet my size criterion for primary religious bodies. The vast majority of churches in the *Encyclopedia* do, however, meet my three criteria.

Most primary religious bodies share other traits. Their leaders "marry and bury," as the saying goes. The churches usually hope to expand: they plan to make converts and form additional congregations. Finally, a number of primary religious bodies, though under-represented in America, have large foreign branches.

Much of the money and time given to religious enterprises in the United States is channeled not into the primary religious bodies, but into secondary and tertiary religious institutions. Secondary religious organizations, service agencies, perform tasks for one or more primary body. The tasks include missionary work, the education of seminarians, the publication of church materials, the sale of religious articles, and care for orphans and the aged.

Tertiary organizations try to change a number of primary religious bodies by promoting one special issue. For example, ecumenical organizations seek the unity of churches. However, few churches supporting the ecumenical organizations have specific plans to merge with other churches, so ecumenists try to change the attitudes of the churches. Among the country's ecumenical groups are several that draw members from various religious families (e.g., the National Council of Churches and the National Association of Evangelicals) and many more whose members are limited to one family (e.g., the Christian Holiness Association, the Pentecostal Fellowship of North America, the World Baptist Alliance, the International New Thought Alliance, the American Council of Witches, the Midwest Pagan Council, and the Buddhist Council of Hawaii).

Tertiary organizations have been formed to promote peace (the Fellowship of Reconciliation), a belief in creation instead of evolution (the Bible Science Association, Inc.), the psychic (the Spiritual Frontiers Fellowship), spiritual healing (the International Order of St. Luke, the Physician), Pentecostalism (the Full Gospel Businessmen's Fellowship, International), and Sabbatarianism (the Bible Sabbath Association).

Because the country is virtually flooded with secondary and tertiary organizations, the primary religious bodies form only a small percentage of American religious institutions. It is to the primary bodies, though, that the secondary and tertiary organizations look for members and support.

In describing America's 1,200 [2,300] primary religious bodies, I am departing from the church-sect-cult categories of Ernst Troeltsch. He pioneered in describing various Christian bodies, not in doctrinal, but in social terms, treating churches as far more than defenders of certain beliefs. In the latter part of his work, *The Social Teachings of the Christian Churches* (New York: Macmillian, 1931), Troeltsch examined the Christian churches of post-Reformation Europe. He discovered three types of groups: the dominant state churches, the sect groups (schismatic groups that broke away from the state churches), and the mystical groups (the latter came to be called cults). Unfortunately, American sociologists applied Troeltsch's categories to American religions. With time, the popular media attached pejorative connotations to the words "sect" and "cult," connotations Troeltsch never intended. To understand Troeltsch properly, one must remember that he described only Christian religions. Furthermore, he studied countries with Christian state churches, to which all citizens were expected to belong. The United States has no state church and has far more non-Christian churches than Europe had before 1800, the terminal point of Troeltsch's study.

American religions do not yield to so simplistic a set of categories as the church-sect-cult triad. Instead of using those three classifications, I examined religions family by family and have found 17 [now 18] distinct families. This approach, I hope, does justice to the amazing variety found within the American religious experience. Ten [12] of the 17 [18] religious families in the United States basically follow Christian beliefs and practices; seven [6] do not.

Within the 17 [18] families of American religions, the member bodies of each family share a common heritage, thought world (theology in its broadest sense), and lifestyle. These three features define each individual religious body and illuminate its relationship to other churches in the family.

It has become fashionable to use other characteristics in classifying religious bodies, characteristics such as ethnicity, class, racial composition, type of leadership (priest? guru? pastor?), and the degree of acceptance of or hostility to the world. While these characteristics provide useful information, they are entirely inadequate in explaining the formation, development, relationships, and continuing life of the broad spectrum of America's religious bodies. Elements of ethnicity are, for example, most helpful in identifying sub-groups within the older European church traditions brought to America in the eighteenth and nineteenth centuries. Lutheran, Reformed, and Pietist churches split along ethnic lines, each sub-group using its own language. But as language barriers disappeared, the ethnic orientation of the churches diminished. Thus Swedish Baptists in America are more likely to develop joint programs, to merge, or to share missionary concerns with German or English or even black Baptists than with Swedish Lutherans or Swedish Pentecostals. The strength of family relationships overrides ethnic considerations.

In order to understand any family or its members, it is necessary to understand the family's heritage, thought world, and lifestyle. In many families, one of the three features—heritage, thought world, and lifestyle—is dominant. For the Lutheran family and those churches within the liturgical family, heritage is the feature setting them apart from other churches. Lifestyle is the key feature for four families in particular: the Communal, Holiness, Pentecostal, and Psychic families. Group ownership of property and certain self-imposed disciplines put communes into a class of their own. A day-to-day striving for perfect love dominates holiness preaching and teaching, with worldly activities prohibited. Pentecostals seek certain gifts of spirit, such as speaking in tongues, prophesying, and healing, so Pentecostals have a distinctive lifestyle in both their worship and their daily lives. Finally, the psychics are set apart from other religious groups because of their interest in extrasensory perception, psychokinesis, and communication with spirits through seances and visions.

If heritage and lifestyles distinguish certain families so does the thought world for other families. For fundamentalists and for the Protestant churches, especially those that follow John Calvin's Reformed theology, the features distinguishing them from each other is their thought world. They hold divergent views on these topics in particular: sacrament, ecclesiology, the sovereignty of God, perfection, and the nature of the end of time. But even where there is agreement, sharing a thought world does not necessarily mean holding identical views. Rather, it means sharing some beliefs that set the context for constant debate over specifics. Adventists, for example, expect Christ to return soon, but violently argue among themselves about the nature of his return, the possibility of pinpointing the date of his return, and the significance of certain world events as signs of his return.

Of particular interest to me are the families of "hidden religions" outside the country's religious mainstream. The spiritualists who hold seances are within the hidden families; so are the Buddhists, the Sufis, and the witches in their covens. Such groups are invisible to many Americans, but often they have large national followings. Several congregations that belong to these sizable but hidden families meet within a few blocks of my home in Evanston, Illinois. But had I not searched hard for these congregations, I would never have found them.

Many years of searching have gone into my study of America's religions. I might be better qualified to study the country's religions if I were a detective instead of a Methodist minister. I have examined endless printed material and interviewed countless church founders and leaders—all with the aim of understanding the heritage, lifestyle, and thought world of the religions. To say the least, the task has had its challenges. Some churches exaggerate or deny aspects of their lifestyle or history. Many Pentecostals say their church was founded at Pentecost, in 33 C.E., and hide their recent origins. Other churches try to gloss over the career their founder led before establishing their church. Among such founders, David Berg (of the Children of God), L. Ron Hubbard (of the Church of Scientology), A. A. Allen (of the Miracle Revival Fellowship), and Sun Myung Moon (of the Unification Church) have followed or still follow vocations quite different from that of a spiritual leader. For example, Hubbard was an undercover agent for the Los Angeles Police Department, a fiction writer, and an explorer before founding his church.

Some religious bodies function as such but deny their religious nature. One such organization is the World Plan Executive Council, popularly called Transcendental Meditation. Others dislike denominational labels and refuse to list themselves in the phone book or give brochures to non-members. The Cooneyites, also called the Two-by-Two's, have developed the shunning of publicity into a fine art.

To paint a picture of America's religious bodies in 1978 is not to describe them as they will be in 1988 [or 2018]. Families dwindle and expand. The major church in a family (one that claims more than half the family's members) may divide in half in a decade, torn by schism. Smaller churches in a family may consolidate—e.g., through merging all-black and all-white churches. Lutherans, once divided according to European ethnic origins and language, have consolidated in this century and then redivided over doctrinal issues. The Eastern religious bodies in this country—originally composed of Hindu and Buddhist immigrants—have attracted young American devotees, thereby blending the West with the East. Despite changes within families, however, the identity of the families remains the same. An intense conservatism governs religious bodies; they would rather lose dissident members than change. Further, churches rarely jump from one family to another. Theological and organizational patterns tend to perpetuate themselves. True, institutions adjust to the changing society, but only begrudgingly. The division of religions into families (denominationalism) is fundamental to religious life in the United States. We do not live in a post-denominational age. The ideals of ecumenism have swept through American Christianity, firing imaginations, creating cooperation structures, and breaking down walls of intolerance and hostility between religions. But if ecumenism has illustrated anything, it has been this: the religious family is strong. It will endure.

J. Gordon Melton

User's Guide

Melton's Encyclopedia of American Religions consists of the following sections:

- Introductory Essays
- Religious Family Historical Essay Chapters, with Directory Listings
- Defunct Appendix
- Geographic Appendix
- Index

Each section is fully described below.

INTRODUCTORY ESSAYS. Three essays, "The Development of American Religion: An Interpretive View," "Religion in Canada: A Historical Survey, 1500 to the Present," and "American Religion in the Twenty-first Century," provide an overview of American and Canadian religion as well as the latest religious trends for the future. Together these introductory essays present a comprehensive picture of the evolution of North American religion and project some trends for the immediate future. These essays also place the historical essays covering each denominational family into a larger context.

RELIGIOUS FAMILY HISTORICAL ESSAY CHAPTERS, WITH DIRECTORY LISTINGS. This portion of the *Encyclopedia* contains 24 general essays that trace historically the rise of the 24 major religious families and traditions, as outlined on the "Contents" pages, into which most U.S. and Canadian bodies can be classified. A select list of bibliographic source materials appears at the end of each essay. Directory listings of individual religious groups that fall into each of the 24 religious families immediately follow the narrative for that chapter. The remaining two directory sections—Unclassified Christian Churches and Unclassified Religious Groups—include those groups that cannot be classified within any of the distinct religious families.

Whenever available or appropriate, a directory listing typically contains the following categories of information in the order listed.

Organization Name and Acronym. The official name of the organization and, if available, acronym.

Address. The street location and/or mailing address of the organization appears directly under its name. If the organization's current address could not be located for the current edition, it is noted here.

Alternate Address. Provides, if applicable, the address of an organization's Canadian or international headquarters, or an alternative address at which the organization may be contacted.

Description. A discussion of the organization's history, beliefs, organization, and leaders, generally paraphrased from information obtained from the organization itself. This data preserves, as closely as possible, the original wording from a questionnaire response, website, etc., in order to avoid any misinterpretation of the organization's beliefs.

Membership. Most recent statistics as reported by the group, including, as appropriate, number of members, centers, congregations, churches, and ministers. The geographic location of the various congregations, churches, or other groups may also be provided. If no membership statistics are provided, the phrase "not reported" appears.

Educational Facilities. An alphabetical listing of post-secondary educational institutions sponsored and/or supported by the group. Each listing includes the city and state/province in which the institution is located.

Periodicals. Periodicals and newsletters issued by the group. Unless otherwise noted, publications are available from the address provided at the beginning of the entry.

Remarks. Includes additional information not applicable to the basic headings listed above. It could include comments or interpretation by those outside the organization.

Sources. Provides complete bibliographic citations, arranged alphabetically, of selected source materials used to develop the entry as well as sources for further reading. When known, URLs for the organizations' primary websites have been added as the first item.

DEFUNCT APPENDIX. Provides information on organizations that have become defunct, listed according to their religious family in the order in which those chapters appear in the *Encyclopedia*. Entries include the organization name and a brief synopsis of the group's history, beliefs, organization, and leaders.

GEOGRAPHIC APPENDIX. Offers geographical arrangement of the organizations included in Directory Listings. Entries are arranged by country (with the U.S. first), then listed alphabetically by state and then by city. Canadian entries follow the U.S. listings, with entries arranged alphabetically by province and then by city. Entries outside the U.S. and Canada are listed last, alphabetically by country, then by city Entries include organization name and address.

INDEX. Provides an alphabetic arrangement of all religious organizations, acronyms, individuals, educational facilities, periodicals, and other significant details mentioned in the historical essays, the directory listings, and the defunct appendix. The index also includes inversions on significant keywords appearing in the names of organizations, periodicals, and other entities. (Due to their prevalence, keyword inversions are not provided for "Church," "Religion," and similar terms.) The index also includes *see* and *see also* references. Periodical titles are rendered in *italic* type. The leading articles "A," "An," and "The" are disregarded for filing purposes within the index; thus, "The Prayer of Peace" will be found filed under "P" and not "T." A **boldface** number following an organization name indicates that organization's main entry in a directory section.

Key to Abbreviations

&	and	Co.	Company	Hon.	Honorary	MS	Mississippi
A.B.	Bachelor of Arts	Col.	Colonel	Hwy.	Highway	Msgr.	Monsignor
AB	Alberta	Coord.	Coordinator	IA	Iowa	MSW	Master of Social Work
A.M.	Master of Arts	Corp.	Corporation	ID	Idaho	MT	Montana
Abp.	Archbishop	Corr.	Corresponding	IHM	Sisters of the Immaculate	Mt.	Mount
Admin.	Administrative, Administrator	CSA	Sisters of the Congregation of		Heart of Mary	Mus.B.	Bachelor of Music
AK	Alaska		St. Agnes	IL	Illinois	Mus.D.	Doctor of Music
AL	Alabama	CSC	Congregation of the Holy	IN	Indiana	N.	North
Apt.	Apartment		Cross	Inc.	Incorporated	Natl.	National
AR	Arkansas	CSJ	Congregation of St. Joseph	Intl.	International	NB	New Brunswick
Assoc.	Associate	CSP	Paulists	J.C.B.	Bachelor of Canon Law,	NC	North Carolina
Asst.	Assistant	CT	Connecticut		Bachelor of Civil Law	ND	North Dakota
Ave.	Avenue	Ct.	Court	J.C.D.	Doctor of Canon Law, Doctor	NE	Nebraska, Northeast
AZ	Arizona	Cust.	Customer		of Civil Law	NF	Newfoundland
b.	born	CZ	Canal Zone	J.D.	Doctor of Jurisprudence,	NH	New Hampshire
B.A.	Bachelor of Arts	d.	died		Doctor of Law	NJ	New Jersey
B.D.	Bachelor of Divinity	D.D.	Doctor of Divinity	J.U.D.	Doctor of Both Laws (i.e.	NM	New Mexico
B.L.	Bachelor of Laws, Bachelor of	D.Th.	Doctor of Theology		Canon and Civil)	No.	Number
	Literature, Bachelor of Letters	DC	District of Columbia	Jr.	Junior	NS	Nova Scotia
B.S.	Bachelor of Science	D.D.S.	Doctor of Dental Science	KS	Kansas	NT	Northwest Territories
B.Theo.	Bachelor of Theology	DE	Delaware	KY	Kentucky	NV	Nevada
BC	British Columbia	Dir., Dirs.	Director, Directors	L.Th.	Licentiate in Theology	NW	Northwest
Bd.	Board	Div.	Division	LA	Louisiana	NY	New York
Bldg.	Building	Dom.	Domestic	LL.B.	Bachelor of Laws	OAR	Order of the Augustinian
Blvd.	Boulevard	Dr.	Doctor, Drive	Ln.	Lane		Recollects
Bp.	Bishop	E.	East	Ltd.	Limited	OCD	Order of Discalced
Brig.	Brigadier	Ed.D.	Doctor of Education	M.A.	Master of Arts	Ofc.	Officer
Bro.	Brother	Exec.	Executive	M.Div.	Master of Divinity	OFM	Order of Friars Minor
Bus.	Business	Expy.	Expressway	M.R.E.	Master of Religious Education	OH	Ohio
c.	circa	FL	Florida	M.Re.	Master of Religion	OK	Oklahoma
c/o	care of	Fl.	Floor	M.S.	Master of Science	OMI	Oblats de Marie Immaculee
CA	California	For.	Foreign	M.Th.	Master of Theology	ON	Ontario
CAE	Certified Association Executive	Fr.	Father	MA	Massachusetts	OP	Ordo Praedicatorum
Card.	Cardinal	FSC	Fratres Scholarum	Maj.	Major	OR	Oregon
CEO	Chief Executive Officer		Christianarum	MB	Manitoba	OSA	Order of St. Augustine
Chm.	Chairman	FSE	Brothers of the Holy Eucharist	MD	Doctor of Medicine, Maryland	OSB	Ordo Sancti Benedicti
Chwn.	Chairwoman	FSP	Pious Society of the Daughters	ME	Maine	OSC	Order of St. Clare
CM	Congregatio Missioni Sancti		of St. Paul	Mgr.	Manager	OSF	Order of St. Francis
	Vicentiia Paulo, Congregatio	Ft.	Fort	MI	Michigan	OSU	Order of St. Ursula
	Mariae	Fwy.	Freeway	MIC	Missionary Sisters of the	PA	Pennsylvania
Cmdr.	Commander	GA	Georgia		Immaculate Conception	PE	Prince Edward Island
CMF	Congregation of Missionary	Gen.	General	Min.	Minister	Ph.B.	Bachelor of Philosophy
	Sons of the Immaculate Heart	GU	Guam	Mktg.	Marketing	Ph.D.	Doctor of Philosophy
	of the Blessed Virgin Mary	HI	Hawaii	MN	Minnesota	Pkwy.	Parkway
CO	Colorado			MO	Missouri		

Pl.	Place	Rte.	Route	SM	Sisters of Mercy	Tpke.	Turnpike
PO	Post Office Box	S.	South	SND	Sisters of Notre Dame	Treas.	Treasurer
PR	Puerto Rico	S.S.L.	Licentiate of Sacred Scripture	Sq.	Square	TX	Texas
Pres.	President	S.T.B.	Bachelor of Sacred Theology	Sr.	Senior, Sister	U.S.	United States
Prod.	Producer	S.T.D.	Doctor of the Science of Theology, Doctor of Sacred Theology	SSCC	Congregation of the Sacred Hearts of Jesus and Mary	U.S.A.	United States of America
Prof.	Professor					UT	Utah
Prog.	Program			SSE	Sisters of St. Carmelites Elizabeth	V.P.	Vice President
Prop.	Proprietor	S.T.L.	Reader in Sacred Theology, Licentiate in Sacred Theology	SSJ	Sisters of St. Joseph	VA	Virginia
QC	Quebec			St.	Saint, Street	ven.	Venerable
Rd.	Road	S.T.M.	Master of Arts in Theology	Sta.	Station	VI	Virgin Islands
RD	Rural Delivery	SC	South Carolina	STD	Doctor of the Science of Theology	VPM	Voix du Peuple Murundi
Reg.	Regional	SD	South Dakota			VT	Vermont
Rep.	Representative	SE	Southeast	Ste.	Sainte, Suite	W.	West
Rev.	Reverend	Sec.	Secretary	SW	Southwest	WA	Washington
RFD	Rural Free Delivery	Serv.	Service	Ter(r).	Terrace, Territory	WI	Wisconsin
RI	Rhode Island	SJ	Societas Jesu	Th.B.	Bachelor of Theology	WV	West Virginia
Rm.	Room	SHCJ	Society of the Holy Child Jesus	Th.D.	Doctor of Theology	WY	Wyoming
RR	Rural Route	SK	Saskatchewan	Th.M.	Master of Theology	YT	Yukon Territory
RSCJ	Society of the Sacred Heart	SL	Sisters of Loretto at the Foot of the Cross	TN	Tennessee		
RSM	Sisters of Mercy						

The Development of American Religion: An Interpretive View

Essay 1

The United States is currently home to more than 2,000 different primary religious organizations—churches, sects, cults, temples, societies, missions—each seeking to be the place of expression of the religious allegiances and sentiments of its members and adherents. The majority of these organizations are Christian churches, and the overwhelming majority of Americans who engage in any outward religious activity are members of one of the more than 1,000 Christian denominations. Prior to the 1880s, the Christian churches had little competition, except from the Native American religions, which Christians saw at best as dying faiths soon to be replaced by Christianity. The Christian churches enjoyed the favor of the influential elite of society. They had the support of the government, the approbation of the press, and the control of education at all levels. At the same time, however, the churches also faced a public, the majority of which regarded religion with attitudes that varied from indifference to open hostility. Simply expressed, the church existed as an instrument of the state, another element in the overall system of social control.

That situation began to change dramatically at the time of the American Revolution (1775–1783). With the exception of several New England states, formal ties between church and state were cut, and each succeeding decade brought an end to more and more of the numerous informal ties. For many congregations, the Revolution included the loss either temporarily or completely of their buildings. The Anglican Church lost the most, and its situation was made all the more severe by the sudden departure of the majority of its ministers to England and the loss of its legal status.

After the war, the groups that had assumed the controlling positions in American religious life began to take second place to groups that had played little prior role. The changes became evident during the Second Great Awakening, a period marked by the rise of the Methodists, Baptists, Disciples of Christ, and Cumberland Presbyterians and the evangelistic endeavor that led to their churching of the western frontier. From the beginning of the nineteenth century, the church has moved from a position of disestablishment in the midst of an indifferent public to the creation of what amounts to a powerful new religious establishment through its ownership of ever-increasing sums of real estate and stock and its steady penetration of the indifferent public, the majority of which it has finally won to its membership. Every decade of the last two centuries has seen Christian church

membership increase in both numbers and percentage of the population. Since 1900, while the nation's population increased three and a half times, church membership grew sevenfold. At the same time, the church has step-by-step relinquished control of education, lost its favored status in the press, and must fight for its right to criticize the government or lobby for what it considers just laws. The church has also been rent with schism (from 20 denominations in 1800 to more than 1,000 in 1988), while at the same time having to face competition from the hundreds of different varieties of the great world religions and an imposing assortment of innovative new American faiths, including a revived and assertive Native American spirituality.

This encyclopedia covers the story of American religion, from the entrance in the sixteenth century of Europeans determined to convert Native Americans, to the pluralistic religious situation of the early twenty-first century. It is a story of religious conquests and losses, the search for simply a place to be alone, the rise and fall of utopian dreams, and the attempts by different religions to find ways to exist in close proximity with constant war and rumor of war.

NATIVE AMERICANS IN 1500: THE FIRST SETTLERS.

Ten thousand years ago, 40,000 years ago, or even more than 100,000 years ago, depending on which source is consulted, the first human settlers arrived in what today is called North America. They may have walked, or they may have built a crude boat, but they crossed the Bering Strait (periodically in the past a land bridge) and moved across the continent to establish their residences, learn the arts of survival and culture, and generally claim the land for their people. Over the years they differentiated themselves as separate peoples (clans, tribes, nations, etc.), emphasizing hunting, agriculture, trading, or fishing in their conquests of the very different environments, climates, and resources the land provided. They also developed religion, which took at least as many forms as there were tribes.

Possibly 30 million Native Americans inhabited North America in 1500. They were divided into groups that spoke more than 200 languages. They also showed such immense variation in religion as to make it improper to speak of an Indian *religion*; rather, there were a number of Indian *religions*.

Native American religion was distinct relative to the faith later brought to North America by the Europeans. Religion was embedded in the close communal life of fairly small

1

groups. Native American life was organized in such a way that the distinctive realms of life so characteristic of modern society—sacred-secular, work-leisure, political-economic—did not operate. Life within a single Native American group maintained a holistic cast so that those elements we commonly think of as religion permeated every segment of existence. It was a common European activity to observe Native life and pick out the "religious" elements and describe in the abstract a particular Native people's religion, an act that in itself pulled Native life into the European world.

However, the white people who began their conquest of North America in the sixteenth century paid little attention to the Native Americans' religions. Beyond the writing up of accounts of them by a few missionaries (later superseded by ethnographers) with varying levels of sophistication, the European program was to totally replace the Native Americans' religions with the observance of Christianity. For this reason, the religions of the Indians and the faiths of European origin, until recently, rarely interacted. Once the Europeans took control, Indian religions were offered no role in the conquering culture and to a large extent were eradicated, either by the deaths of their adherents or their conversion to some form of Christianity.

MAJOR THEMES IN THE DEVELOPMENT OF AMERICAN RELIGION.
In the movement from the religious situation in 1500 to that of the late nineteenth century, four factors arise as dominant elements in the shaping of American religious patterns: *immigration, religious freedom, proselytism,* and *denominationalism.* Of the more than 2,000 religious groups that presently exist in the United States, the overwhelming majority originated by the direct immigration of their members or practitioners to the United States. These immigrants established centers for worship and for the recruitment of new members among the general population. Most of the remaining groups are schisms of those immigrant groups. The actual number of new religions that have developed in America, apart from Native American faiths, is small, and such indigenous American religions are all the more noteworthy for that fact: Adventism (which includes both Seventh-day Adventists and Jehovah's Witnesses), Spiritualism, the new metaphysical religions (Christian Science and New Thought), the new forms of esotericism (from Theosophy to Scientology), and Pentecostalism.

IMMIGRATION. Understanding immigration as the first of the four factors shaping American religious life also underscores the role of ethnic-national settlements in setting the initial patterns of American religious life during the colonial period. Spanish Catholics came to Florida, New Mexico, and California. French Catholics settled the Gulf Coast from Mobile to New Orleans and the Mississippi River Valley north to St. Louis and St. Paul. The British settled New England and the southern colonies. The Dutch came into New York (formerly New Netherlands), the Swedes colonized Delaware, and the Germans made up a substantial portion of the colony established by William Penn (1644–1718). In the nineteenth century, the patterns of immigration would again change the

face of American religion as, for example, Germans and Scandinavians moved into the area north and west of Chicago to create the still-dominant Lutheran belt from Milwaukee to Butte. Newly arrived Italians and Irish would take control of New England from British Congregationalists and place it in the hands of Roman Catholics. The influx of Hispanics into the area north of the Rio Grande would return that area lost to Protestants at the time of the gold rush to Roman Catholic hegemony.

Immigration laws, especially after 1882, also helped shape religious patterns in America. For example, the normal growth of Asian religions, which were being established among immigrants in the last half of the nineteenth century, was thwarted by the imposition of a series of immigration laws from 1882 to 1924. The 1924 law, which all but stopped immigration from Asia, also blocked the flow of immigrants from southern and eastern Europe. Thus, while the law slowed the growth of Eastern religions, it also strongly affected the growth of Judaism, Eastern Orthodoxy, and Islam. In like measure, the lifting of the 1924 restrictions in 1965 contributed directly to the massive expansion of these religions since then, completely altering the overall shape and structure of the American religious community.

RELIGIOUS FREEDOM. Religious freedom, both in concept and practice, has expanded in America. Credit for the first accomplishments in that direction must go to the early colonists in New York, Rhode Island, Pennsylvania, and Maryland. An early expression of that expanded freedom was the colonists' reception of Jewish settlers. Generations before most Europeans were thinking about religious toleration, the Dutch had become the most religiously tolerant nation in Europe. In their American colonies, that tolerance was demonstrated by the welcome given to fleeing Brazilian Jews, who established the first synagogue in North America in New York. Rhode Island, which had been founded by Roger Williams (c. 1603–c. 1683) after he fled the intolerance of the Massachusetts Puritans, welcomed the second congregation of Jews. It is not surprising to find one of the other colonial congregations in Philadelphia.

Religious liberty was, of course, greatly advanced by the American Revolution and the Bill of Rights to the U.S. Constitution. That the 1787 Constitutional Convention refused to grant any group, in this case any Christian church, the power, prestige, and privilege of being the nation's established religious body was both an important experiment and a significant act of infidelity. As an experiment, it tested a major axiom of European thought: that a nation needed one religious body (i.e., a state church) as a necessary force in uniting the population and assisting in social control. America's post-Revolutionary success proved the untruth of the assumption. At the same time, America's experiment in religious liberty would not have been possible had not the delegates to the Constitutional Convention also recognized both that no religious group served more than a small fraction of the population, and that the great majority of the public did not support any religious organization. This twofold observation was amply verified in the decades after the Revolution when, in total, American churches could only claim on their roles somewhere between 10 and 20 percent of the now-free people.

The freedom guaranteed by the First Amendment has been steadily broadened during the last two centuries. Within a few decades, all of the states dropped the last remnants of their formal religious establishments. The implications of the First Amendment for unpopular religions have gained increasing attention and clarity. And the society itself tolerates an ever-increasing variety of religious beliefs and practices. The heightened toleration experienced during the twentieth century was disseminated from the large impersonal urban complexes, which both permitted divergent religious groups to develop apart from the watchful and critical eyes of small-town society and provide a concentrated pool of the potential recruits needed by any new religion in its critical first years of existence.

PROSELYTISM. The freedom to practice a new religion includes the freedom to *proselytize* (i.e., to invite someone to convert to one's faith). From 1800 to the present, no activity apart from immigration has so altered the pattern of American religion as the evangelical efforts of religious groups. Following the American Revolution, the older colonial churches dominated religious life. However, they were prepared neither in theology nor organization to respond to the irreligious public that confronted them at the end of the eighteenth century. The Methodists and Baptists, both of whom were evangelically oriented, were prepared, and by the middle of the nineteenth century, they replaced the Congregationalists, Presbyterians, and Episcopalians as the dominant church bodies, a position they have never relinquished.

At the same time, in the religiously free situation, innovative religious movements, movements that would have been suppressed by the government under a state-church regime, were permitted to grow and proselytize as well. Thus, early in the nineteenth century, new Christian churches, such as the Cumberland Presbyterian Church and the Disciples of Christ, broke from older bodies, and representatives of completely new ways of doing religion appeared, from Swedenborgians to Latter-day Saints (Mormons), from Spiritualists to Transcendentalist free religionists. The number of new religious gestalts multiplied decade by decade. Soon after each new religious movement organized, if it showed signs of popular success, it further divided, producing an array of similar organizations and eventually new religious denominational families. Throughout the nineteenth century, almost all of the major new divergent religious thrusts were Christian. However, during the last two decades of the nineteenth century, Hinduism, Buddhism, and Islam were introduced into American life and looked for converts among a public only 35 percent of whom had joined a church.

During the twentieth century, the role of proselytizing activity was spectacular. As the nation's population multiplied three and a half times (from 75 million to 250 million),

Christian church membership multiplied seven times, and the percentage of church members doubled from slightly more than 30 percent to more than 65 percent. Religious affiliation climbed even higher as the Jewish, Muslim, Buddhist, Hindu, and occult-metaphysical communities, minuscule at the turn of the century, each developed constituencies numbering in the millions.

DENOMINATIONALISM. The dual effect of freedom of religion and proselytizing activity leads directly to the consideration of denominationalism. In a religiously free society, denominations—voluntary religious associations of like-minded (and like-spirited) people—are the basic form of religious life. In spite of the various predictions of the fading of denominations (through the ecumenical movement) or the decline of their importance (through increasing individualized religion), they remain, and for the foreseeable future will remain, the bedrock of American religion. Denominations are the stable primary religious associations formed in those societies that do not impose a single dominant religious structure. In a state-church society, for example, there is one "religion" and may be a number of dissenting "sects." In a free society, there are a number of more or less competing religious organizations, no one of which has a majority of the population in its membership. Some organizations, because of such factors as their many years in existence, their inherent appeal, or their aggressive programs for conversion, have many members. Others, primarily because they are new, lack substantial appeal, or limit proselytizing efforts, remain small.

Denominations, whatever their size, provide the primary religious identification for most religious people. They offer regular times and facilities for the affirmation of beliefs in group activity, worship, study, and service. Often associated with and supported by the denominations are a variety of what might be termed secondary or paradenominational religious organizations. These organizations usually specialize in one limited task in relation to one or a small group of similar primary religious organizations. Thus, while large denominations may support several seminaries for the training of ministers, smaller denominations may send their ministerial candidates to an independent seminary or Bible college whose perspective is supportive or compatible with their theological outlook. Included among the paradenominational organizations are independent publishers, missionary organizations, evangelical ministries, and social service agencies. On occasion, a secondary or paradenominational structure (especially evangelical ministries engaged in the conversion of individuals) will begin forming congregations and make the transition into a new primary group. It will subsequently enlarge its services to include all of those normally provided by a primary religious group. Within an evangelical group, such a transformation can be noted when the group stops sending its recruits to the supporting denominational structures and begins forming congregations of its converts. Such a transformation occurred in the 1970s among some Jewish-

Christian evangelical groups, which began to form ethnic Jewish-Christian synagogues.

Within the pluralistic environment of the early twenty-first century, the formation of so many new competing religious groups has eroded the exclusive and dominant positions of some of the older and more-established religious organizations. This erosion of position has been most evident in the major defeats suffered by conservative Christian groups on such issues as abortion legislation, the ban on corporate prayer in public schools, the display of religious symbols in government-owned facilities, and the elimination of the Christian facade that had been placed over many facets of public and social life. Interpreted by many as signs of secularization, the defeats are more adequately understood when seen as manifestations of (1) the growing seriousness with which dissenting religious positions are treated, and (2) an increasing sensitivity toward religious concerns that has developed within the public sphere. Coupled with this new sensitivity is the loss of ability by even the most powerful religious bodies to enforce their own ideas in the populace at large, especially at the national level. What power remains is largely a veto power.

With these forces in mind, we can now turn to a brief consideration of the movement of religion from the arrival of the Spanish conquistadors and padres to the complex pluralistic religious environment of today. That development will be considered in six overlapping periods. The Native American period began in prehistory and extends to the nineteenth century. The Catholic era began around 1500 and continued in parts of the country until the nineteenth century. The period of western European (primarily British) conquest began around 1600, with the arrival of settlers in Virginia. The Revolutionary era began with the disruptions of the 1770s and carried through the transitions into the new religious environment established by the Constitution. The period of the churching of the nation can be said to begin in 1801 and to continue to this day. The period of transition from Christian dominance into a pluralistic society of shared religious hegemony began in the 1880s and has also continued to the present.

NATIVE AMERICANS TO 1800.

The first human settlers came into North America during the prehistoric past and moved across the continent, eventually settling almost every niche. By the time of the coming of the Europeans, the differing peoples manifested a wide variety of governmental structures, economic systems, and family forms. The structure of their religious life was equally varied, and there are few threads that run through all the Indian religions. As is true of most religions prior to the segregation of life into the modern distinction between secular and sacred, Native American religions tended to be at one with the whole life of the people. Religion was intimately tied to tribal survival, the self-identity of individuals as tribal members, and the organization of tribal routine.

Just as the religious aspect of life was integrated into other aspects of tribal life, so tribal life was integrated into the natural environment chosen by the tribe for its home, including the climate, terrain, and the animal and plant life. Indians took the land seriously and lived by its seasonal changes. Survival demanded an intense and intimate relationship with nature, which appeared to be permeated with life power, sometimes viewed as one force but often differentiated into many particular powers.

Some Europeans thought of the Indians as being without religion, an opinion that highlights some essential truths about Native American spirituality. There was, for example, no word in any Indian language that could be translated "religion." There was also, generally speaking, a lack of what might be considered worship, since in most Indian religions, ceremonies and actions were not a matter of supplication of a deity so much as the development of a working relationship with the sacred realm. Ceremonies and actions created a matrix within which life moved, and that movement tended to be circular, following the coming, going, and return of the seasons. The sacred realm was the realm of the pervasive powers.

Living with the powers that existed in and sustained the world led many tribes to develop forms of magic—the art and practice of manipulating the spirit powers. Most tribes had functionaries who practiced the arts of magic and used them for good or ill. These "religious" leaders were among those most threatened by the arrival of Christianity and its priests.

The life and beliefs of the different tribes were articulated in a variety of *myths* that described in story format the underlying structure of reality. These verbal expressions of life, which ranged from the sacred to the mundane, embodied the Indians' sophisticated understandings of both the immediate environment and the larger world, gave a rationale for the accepted behavioral standards for the tribe, and supplied the answers to the basic religious questions.

The coming of the Europeans had little immediate impact for the great majority of Indian tribes, who encountered white people only with the push to settle the interior of the continent in the nineteenth century. However, those tribes located on the lands first colonized frequently faced disaster. Not an insignificant amount of damage was done by the spread of new diseases, in defense of which the Native American had no weapons of immunity or medicine. Measles and smallpox were especially deadly. At the very least, those Indians residing in close proximity to the new settlements became the targets of missionary efforts. Almost every church group, soon after its arrival in the New World and its establishment of a stable presence among the white settlers, turned its attention to missionary activity among the Indians. The most extensive missions were established by Roman Catholics in the St. Lawrence River Valley, Florida, the Gulf Coast, and across the Southwest from Texas to California. John Eliot (1604–1690) is remembered as the primary missionary supported by the New England Puritans. The desire to support his work inspired the formation in England in 1649 of one of the first of the voluntary missionary societies, soon to become so popular in evangelical circles. Anglican missions to the Indians were promoted by one of these societies, the Society for the Propagation of the Gospel (SPG) in Foreign Parts.

Despite the dedication of the missionaries, their efforts often fell victim to seemingly unrelated forces that tended not only to destroy the missions but the Native American's entire culture. For example, King Philip's War (1675–1676) led to the destruction of the towns of the "Praying Indians" established by Eliot's converts. Other missions were destroyed when the lands upon which they were established changed hands from one nation to another, usually after a war. In such a manner, many of the Catholic missions were lost as French domains were taken over by the British.

However, the missions themselves tended to intrude in most destructive ways into the Indians' culture. Typical of the disruption of Indian life caused by the Europeans was the Spanish movement into the land of the Chumash Indians who inhabited the California coast from present-day Malibu to San Luis Obispo. The Spanish found the Chumash organized into numerous villages, each ruled by a chief, termed a *wots*, who provided moral authority and general guidance. The wots was assisted by a *paha*, who presided at the principal festivals and ceremonies. The Chumash had established a hunting-fishing-gathering-trading economy, which had in turn produced an artistic culture of high standards. When the Spanish first arrived in 1769, the Chumash welcomed the new settlers and provided them needed items from their abundant supply.

The missionaries who accompanied the Spanish explorers discovered that the Chumash saw themselves as living in a larger universe permeated with power that had been scattered through the world at the point of creation. Individuals were allowed to use the power, if they possessed the proper knowledge. They could also gain access to the powers through a dream helper, a personified form of a natural reality, such as a bear, an eagle, or even a plant such as datura. Important to Chumash "religion" was the balancing of all the powers that existed. Special people, *antaps*, knew the secret knowledge to keep the powers balanced.

However, with the arrival of the Spanish, the village organization, the economy, and the religious tradition were attacked at the core. The Indians were invited to convert to the Roman Catholic faith and to abandon the villages for the mission. At the mission, an alternative economy was established that included candle making, agriculture, ironworking, and masonry. The missions and pueblos provided a new economy that soon involved enough Indians that it undercut the older economy still maintained by those who refused to accept mission life. But those Indians who did move to the pueblo were often blocked in their participation in the new economy. They were trapped between the long-term goals of the missionaries and the immediate objectives of the colonial government. In the 60-plus years of their existence, the missions completely obliterated the old village life of the Chumash. The mission period ended in 1833 with secularization—the removal of the missions from the control of the

Franciscans and the redistribution of their lands to Mexican settlers. The Chumash were thus left with neither the villages of their ancestors nor the new life forced upon them by the missions. Those who survived retained but a remnant of their original beliefs and practices.

Other Indian peoples in those lands first invaded by Europeans in the seventeenth century reacted in a variety of ways toward their new neighbors. Most at first accepted the Europeans and allowed Christian priests to move among them. Others, some following an initial acceptance, found themselves at war with both the white settlers and their ministers. The settlers increasingly wanted the Indians' territory and resources, and the ministers wanted to change their religious perspective (which implied altering almost every aspect of their lives). As the Indians fought the encroachments of Christianity, the churches counted the victims of such fighting as martyrs.

In the end, however, the Indians were forced to seek some means of accommodating the reality of a permanent European presence. Some accepted the settlers, even to the point of taking sides in the periodic wars, while at the same time resisting the missionaries' pressure to change their thoughts and ways. They signed treaties and gave concessions. But the trends were against them, and gradually they were forced into designated parcels of land and targeted for conversion by the various churches. As the dust of the American Revolution settled, there was still hope that the Indians' life and religions could survive to some extent, but the new nation on the East Coast of the continent had caught a vision of the West and eagerly rushed to claim it as its own. In the process, it was quite willing to push the Indian out of the way.

THE CATHOLIC ERA: THE COMING OF THE SPANISH. The largest religious body in the United States today and throughout the twentieth century has been the Roman Catholic Church. Its members were also the first to arrive, conquer, and colonize parts of the land now making up the United States. Shortly after the discovery of the New World by Christopher Columbus (1451–1506), the rulers of Spain appealed to Pope Alexander VI (1431–1503) to settle the dispute between Spain and Portugal over their claims to the new lands. In 1493 the pope drew a line in the middle of the Atlantic, east of which Portugal would have hegemony and west of which Spain would operate. The line would have left Portugal with Africa and the islands off the Atlantic Coast, but without any access to the New World. In 1494 the line was moved farther west, and as a result Portugal received Brazil. From Cuba and then Mexico, Spain began a program of conquest and settlement that included North America. The governmental drive to develop the Spanish Empire and the church's desire to convert and Christianize the native populations often came into conflict. While the church won many smaller victories in its attempts to champion the cause of humane treatment, in the end the government usually dominated the situation.

The actual movement of Spain into what is now the United States was occasioned by the settlement in Florida of a group of French Huguenots (Protestants) along the St. Johns River (near present-day Jacksonville) in 1564. Having previously claimed Florida as its own, the offended Spanish established a settlement at St. Augustine and quickly moved to destroy the St. Johns River colony. From there, Spanish missionaries established missions that at one point reached as far north as South Carolina and briefly the Chesapeake Bay area. The missions in Florida, in spite of their ups and downs, were most successful through several generations.

The second movement of Spain into what is now the United States was from Mexico in the Southwest. In 1540 Francisco Vasquez de Coronado (c. 1510–1554) began his famous trek that took him from New Mexico to central Kansas. In his easternmost exploration, he came upon the village of Quivera. Returning to his advance base in New Mexico, Coronado ordered his expedition members home. The Franciscans, however, decided to stay. Two of their number, Brother John of the Cross and Brother Luis Descalona, settled in the Bernalillo-Pecos area of New Mexico. Father Juan de Padilla journeyed back to Quivera. Brother John and Brother Luis were successful to the point of angering the Indians' own religious functionaries. They eventually disappeared and are believed to have been killed. Father de Padilla was successful at Quivera, but was killed when he tried to extend his work to other tribes.

Further movement into the Southwest was to wait a generation. In 1598 an expedition headed by Juan de Oñate (c. 1550–1626) moved into New Mexico and established a settlement along the Rio Grande. The church built at this settlement, called San Juan and later San Gabriel, was the second oldest church in America. The site now is in ruins, for in 1609 a new capital for the territory was established at Santa Fe, and San Gabriel was abandoned. Missionary work led to the founding of some 11 missions by 1617 and 43 by 1625. The work of the missions was not without its problems. There was much resistance by many of the New Mexico tribes to the missionary efforts, and a number of priests were killed. The Indians' resentment of both the efforts to destroy their culture and the cruelty of the Spanish rulers boiled over in 1680. Led by a medicine man, Popè, the Indians revolted and drove the Spanish south of El Paso. Twelve years later, the Spanish moved back into New Mexico and established a permanent presence. About this time, a Jesuit priest, Father Eusebio Kino (c. 1644–1711), was traveling through northern Mexico and Arizona. In 1697 he founded San Xavier del Bac, the beginning of a small but continuous Roman Catholic presence in the territory.

The Spanish government and the Franciscan missionaries moved into Texas in 1691 but abandoned the work in 1693, after an Indian revolt. A permanent presence was established in 1703 at a mission along the Rio Grande. In 1715, following the development of a plan to conquer the land and convert the Indians, the original missions were again occupied, and under the capable leadership of Father Antonio Margil de

Jesus (1657–1726), the missionary work extended throughout the territory.

THE ARRIVAL OF THE FRENCH.

While Spain and Spanish Roman Catholicism were occupying Florida and establishing their hegemony from Texas to California in the Southwest, France was moving from its original settlements in the St. Lawrence River Valley of Canada to claim territory along the Atlantic Coast, in the Great Lakes region, through the Mississippi Valley, and along the Gulf Coast west of Florida. Actually, the first Roman Catholic chapel in the New World was erected on an island off the coast of Maine in 1604, though the colony on the island soon failed. The French initiated their more permanent settlement in 1608 at Quebec, which they used as a base for Jesuit missionaries who fanned out to work among the tribes in the land along what is now the Canada–United States border, primarily the Mohawk, Iroquois, Algonquin, and Huron. The Indian mission became famous more for the martyrs it produced than the numbers it converted. In the 1640s, a number of priests, including Isaac Jogues (1607–1646) and Jean de Brébeuf (1593–1649), were tortured and killed. The work was lost in the 1700s as the British took over the territory from the French.

In 1669 a Jesuit priest, Jacques Marquette (1637–1675), began the French push into the Great Lakes region. His initial exploratory trip was followed by a career working among the Indians of Illinois and Wisconsin, the first mission being established in 1684. Marquette was followed by others. The work initiated by Marquette was balanced by exploration and settlement along the Gulf Coast as early as 1685 when Renè-Robert Cavalier Sieur de La Salle (1643–1687), who had followed Marquette's explorations by some of his own in the Great Lakes in 1678 and in the Mississippi Valley in 1682, sailed into the Gulf of Mexico in 1685 and founded Fort St. Louis on the coast of what is now Texas. His actions also established Spain and France as competitors in east Texas. Following La Salle's short-lived experiment, others established Biloxi (1697), Mobile (1702), and New Orleans (1718). New Orleans would become the major dissemination point for Catholicism northward along the Mississippi River. In New Orleans, the New World's first religious institute for women, the Ursuline Convent, was built, and from there the missionary work among the southern Indians was launched.

The progress of the Roman Catholic work in North America, indeed of religion in general, was greatly altered in the 1760s by events on the other side of the world. The Seven Years' War (1756–1763), which involved the three major powers in North America, was concluded, and on February 10 the Treaty of Paris was signed. Britain received most of the territory claimed by France, including Canada and all of France's American territory east of the Mississippi River (except New Orleans). From Spain, Britain received Florida, in partial exchange for Cuba. Except for Quebec, Catholic influence was radically curtailed for several generations in the colonies ceded to Britain. The ceding of Louisiana to Spain in 1769 did little to assist the spread of Catholicism there, which continued with a predominantly French constituency. Spanish Catholicism was expanding in only one place—California. While the first Spanish expedition led by Juan Rodrìguez Cabrillo (d. 1543) had sailed along the California coast in 1542, it was not until 1769, that settlement and the opening of a mission in California began at San Diego. Following the establishment of Spanish towns, Father Junìpero Serra (1713–1784) founded nine missions along the coast of California, the first of 21 such missions opened as far north as Sonoma. Unfortunately, the push into California came just as Spain was weakening at home; hence it was unable to properly exploit the new colony.

The Catholic work west of the Mississippi grew slowly through the arrival of new settlers and the conversion of the Indians, but was increasingly thwarted by the westward push of the new American nation. First, in 1800 France again took control of Louisiana, but sold it to the United States three years later. Further westward expansion climaxed in the Treaty of Guadalupe Hidalgo (1848), in which Mexico ceded Texas, New Mexico, most of Arizona, and California to the United States. With quick and massive movement of predominantly non-Catholic settlers into the formerly Catholic Southwest, the Catholic era can be said to have come to an end.

THE BRITISH ERA: ANGLICANS AND CONGREGATIONALISTS.
The movement of western and northern Europeans and their religions into the North American continent, apart from the Viking explorations, began in the late fifteenth century with the arrival of John Cabot (c. 1450–c. 1499). On his first voyage (1497), he probably reached as far south as Maine, and on his second (1499), he seems to have sailed along the coast from Maine to Maryland. However, it was not until 1584 that exploitation of the American coast began with the attempted settlement of a colony on Roanoke Island and the more important and subsequently successful colony at Jamestown in 1606. With the establishment of Jamestown, the Church of England came to North America (though previously services had been held by chaplains assigned to the explorers' ships). To a largely unknown priest of the Church of England, Robert Hunt (c. 1568–c. 1608), goes the honor of having been the first non-Catholic Christian minister to reside and pastor in North America. He came to Jamestown in the spring of 1607. His career was short and the date of his death never recorded, although he died along with the majority of the early Jamestown settlers. The more substantial career of Alexander Whitaker (1585–1617), who arrived in 1611 to serve the church at the new settlement of Henrico, is more illustrative of the progress of the Church of England. Whitaker served the colony for several years and actively promoted increased migration by Britons.

Virginia became the first of the British settlements along the Atlantic Coast. In 1620 a group of Puritan Separatists, popularly called the Pilgrims, landed at Plymouth, Massachusetts. They were followed a decade later by a second group, this time non-Separatists, called simply the Puritans, who founded the Massachusetts Bay Colony and began to spread out across Massachusetts, Connecticut, and most of New England. The range of opinions represented by the Pilgrims, the Puritans, and the Church of England is the product of a whole era of post-Reformation church life in Great Britain.

England had gone through the Protestant Reformation of the sixteenth century in a much different manner from most of the countries on the continental mainland. England had emerged during the reign of Elizabeth I (r. 1558–1603) with a church that drew major components from both Roman Catholicism and Protestantism. The Church of England, Anglicanism, was the inheritor of Elizabeth's *via media*. However, there were Protestants who were not content with anything less than a fully Protestant church. The union of Scotland and England strengthened their cause in 1607 with the ascension of James I (r. 1603–1625) to the throne. Scotland had gone through a reformation and established Presbyterianism.

Puritanism is the name given to the movements whose goal was to purge the Church of England of its remaining unwanted Romanish elements. The different Puritan sects disagreed as to the priorities for a purification of the church. One group looked for minor changes, mostly of a pietistic and worshipful nature within the Church of England, but sought no basic changes in its government. Others looked to the Presbyterians of Scotland for their model. They sought the establishment of Presbyterianism as the state church of England. The most radical of all, the Separatists, wished to separate from any state church and to call only committed disciples of Christ into a visible and voluntary fellowship. Alexander Whitaker was a mild Puritan, loyal to the established church, but with definite Presbyterian tendencies. The Pilgrims of Plymouth were Separatists. The Puritans of Massachusetts and Connecticut were neither Presbyterians nor Separatists. In their new setting, they developed an innovative form of Puritanism: Congregationalism. Like the Separatists, these Puritans wanted a congregation of converted believers; they also wanted to place authority for the governance of the church in the local congregation. Unlike the Separatists, however, they wished to remain in close association with the state, to be the established church for their colonies, to identify as much as possible church membership with membership in the political community. Only church members could vote or hold government office. Puritans sought to possess all of the prerogatives of the Church of England, since they were but its purified branch, not a separate schismatic body. And the Puritans in at least one important aspect copied the church of the homeland: They were as intolerant of those who deviated from the Puritan path as the Elizabethan bishops in England had been of the Puritans.

THE OTHER COLONIES.
While Anglicanism was spreading from its base in Virginia and Congregationalism was spreading through New England, other colonies were being formed with quite different religious bases. Early in the seventeenth century, the Dutch had begun to explore the

coast of America. In 1609 Henry Hudson (c. 1570–c. 1611) sailed up the river that now bears his name as far as the present city of Albany, New York, and staked a Dutch claim for the area. The Dutch established the colony of New Netherlands in 1624, and two years later founded New Amsterdam on Manhattan Island. As tolerant as the Dutch were, they still retained a state church that, since the overthrow of the Spanish, had been reformed. Thus, at the beginning of the colony's life, two lay officers, called in the Dutch Reformed structure "comforters of the sick," were among the earliest settlers. Peter Minuit (1580–1638), director general of the colony, famous for his purchase of Manhattan, was a French Reformed lay elder who led services until 1628, when Jonas Michaelius (b. 1577), an ordained Reformed minister, arrived in the New World to begin a three-year pastorate. Michaelius immediately organized a congregation, still in existence today and known as the Marble Collegiate Church, the oldest continuously existing Protestant church in North America. The term *collegiate* referred to the collegial relationship that developed among the early Reformed congregations in New Netherlands. Reformed congregations spread to Long Island and northward along the Hudson River. In 1642 the church at Fort Orange (now Albany) was organized by Johannes Megapolensis (1603–1670).

The colony enjoyed its most prosperous period during the governorship from 1646 to 1664 of Peter Stuyvesant (c. 1612–1672). Stuyvesant administered the company's religious policies, which included both discouraging the establishment of competing worship centers and encouraging very diverse groups to migrate to the colony. Thus, Stuyvesant recognized the chaos created by the adherents of so many different churches in his colony, but continually refused to let them organize. For example, in 1649, when a group of Lutherans called a minister from Holland, Stuyvesant forbade him to preach and eventually forced him to return to Europe. Interestingly, the company took a different perspective on Jews, who, over Stuyvesant's protests, were welcomed as refugees in 1654 from the former Dutch colonies in Brazil. In New Netherlands, they organized the first Jewish congregation and built the first synagogue.

In 1638 Swedes founded Fort Christiana (now Wilmington, Delaware), and the following year Reorus Torkillus (d. 1643), the first Lutheran minister in America, arrived to establish true and befitting worship in the Lutheran mode. Lutheranism spread among the Swedish and Finnish settlers until 1655, when the Dutch overran the colony and took control. They permitted one Lutheran pastor to remain and Lutheran worship to continue.

Conditions changed considerably in 1664 when the British took over New Netherlands and changed its name to New York. While opening an Anglican chapel, the government was forced to adopt a policy of liberal toleration toward a variety of forms of worship among its new predominantly non-Anglican subjects. A generation later, the government imposed an Anglican establishment on the colony, although the Dutch were allowed to continue their distinctive worship and survive today as the Reformed Church in America.

A new life for Roman Catholicism began in Maryland. Two Jesuits arrived in 1634 with the first colonists that included both Catholics and Protestants. Struggling with the problems of continued actions against the Catholic community (the Jesuits were expelled in the early 1640s), the colony passed a Toleration Act in 1649, which granted freedom of worship to all Christian sects. That act stayed in effect until 1692, when the Church of England was officially established. However, by that time the presence of so many dissenters kept the establishment weak and allowed the strong Catholic presence to remain largely unmolested.

Rhode Island originated in the dissenting views of Roger Williams, a teacher in the Congregational Church in Massachusetts. Unhappy with Williams's Separatist tendencies, in 1635 the authorities banished him from the colony. Finding temporary shelter among the Pilgrims at Plymouth, he moved on in 1636 to found Rhode Island. Drawing on his experience with Puritan intolerance and on his Separatist views, he established a colony and society far ahead of its time. Government and religion were separated, and persecuted sects, such as the Quakers, were welcomed. Like many who adopted a Separatist perspective, Williams became a Baptist and is generally credited with founding the first Baptist congregation in America, though he soon withdrew from the Baptists and thereafter labeled himself a mere "seeker."

As important as Williams is to Rhode Island and Baptist history, his real import is in the development of the sectarian tradition of church-state relations. Williams is the ultimate source and Rhode Island the ultimate example for the perspective on religious freedom that would eventually come to the fore in America. In 1644 Williams authored one of the great classics of religious liberty, *The Bloody Tenant of Persecution*, which would voice in full the ideals of religious freedom, far earlier than those Puritan voices in the next century who would begin to grapple with the breakdown of Congregationalist authority among New Englanders. In 1663 his ideals would be written into the Rhode Island charter.

Following the example of Williams, William Penn created Pennsylvania as a haven for Quakers and other religious minorities. The first settlers into Penn's colony were Welshmen who arrived in 1682, but they were soon followed by the Quakers and representatives of numerous German groups, Penn having recruited heavily among Germany's persecuted sects. As a result, Pennsylvania not only became the originating point for groups such as the Mennonites, Amish, German Rosicrucians, and the Church of the Brethren, but also for the German Lutheran and Reformed churches.

Thus, by the last decades of the seventeenth century, the southern and middle colonies (except for Pennsylvania) had an Anglican establishment, and the New England colonies (except for Rhode Island) were still dominated by Congregationalism. Throughout the 1600s, the Congregational establishment remained strong enough to deal with (banish, imprison, or execute) most dissidents. In contrast, the Church of England's establishment was weak in most areas, there being no bishop in the colonies and many parishes lacking priests. This weakness was due primarily to the presence in significant numbers of both the irreligious and the dissenting sects, especially the Presbyterians and the Baptists, and in Maryland the Roman Catholics, none of which had anything to gain from a strong Church of England presence.

THE EIGHTEENTH CENTURY.

Toward the end of the seventeenth century, changes in England were causing people to look more positively at the church in what was emerging as the British Empire and to promote means to strengthen it. Initial efforts were made to extend the church into areas where it had little or no presence. King's Chapel was forced upon Boston in 1692. The next year, New York passed an establishment act, even though there had been no call for Anglican worship. The minuscule Anglican community of Philadelphia organized Christ Church in 1694.

The most important step in the revival and extension of the Church of England in the colonies followed the appointment of Thomas Bray (c. 1656–1730) as commissary for Maryland in 1696. Bray, unable to travel to America immediately, devoted his time to the organizing of the Society for the Promotion of Christian Knowledge, which began sending libraries to the New World. After a brief sojourn in the colonies in 1699, Bray returned to England and organized the Society for the Propagation of the Gospel (SPG) in 1701. With backing at the highest levels of the church, the society recruited priests for America and sent more than 300 men to staff the churches during the next three-quarters of a century. The SPG put the Church of England in a position to compete with the other churches, but much of its gains were countered by the growth of Presbyterians, Baptists, and, later in the century, the influx of Pietism.

Presbyterians had been coming into the colonies throughout the seventeenth century but had been overwhelmed and in many cases, especially in New England, absorbed by the Congregationalists. Scattered Presbyterian churches were formed in New Jersey as early as 1667, but it was not until the arrival of Francis Makemie (1658–1708) in 1683 that the church began to assume a significant presence. Makemie traveled through the middle colonies organizing churches among the Scottish, Irish, and British settlers. The first presbytery was organized in Philadelphia in 1706 and included churches in Virginia, Maryland, and Delaware. It soon reached out to congregations in New York and New Jersey, and by 1716 was able to divide into four presbyteries and form a synod. The continued immigration from Scotland and Ireland promoted the rapid increase of the church's membership during the first half of the century and its spread throughout the colonies.

The development of Presbyterianism in the American colonies coincided with the emergence of a new movement in Germany. Philip J. Spener (1635–1705), a Lutheran minister at Frankfurt, began to appeal for a deeper Christian life through prayer, Bible study, loving service, and the informal gatherings of Christians. These issues were addressed in his 1675 dissertation, *Pia Desideria*, out of which the Pietist movement was born. Forced out of Frankfurt, he found his way to Berlin, where he received the support in 1694 to found the University at Halle, which became the institutional center of the movement. The movement received a considerable boost in the early 1700s when Moravian refugees, Czechoslovakian Protestants, settled on the estate of Count Nicolaus Ludwig von Zinzendorf (1700–1760), which they renamed Herrnhut.

Pietism was spread to America primarily by the correspondence of American ministers with the Pietist leaders and became visible through the development of an evangelistic thrust among Presbyterians. The beginnings of this "revival" party is usually attributed to German-born Theodore J. Frelinghuysen, (c. 1691–1748), who came to America as a Dutch Reformed minister, and William Tennent (1673–1746), founder of the "log cabin" college in Bucks County, near Philadelphia. Among his most capable students were his three sons, Gilbert (1703–1764), John (1707–1732), and William Jr. (1705–1777). The development of the Presbyterian revivalists began to split the Presbyterians over the acceptance and rejection of the new emphases.

Moravian Pietism was brought to the United States in 1735 by a group under the direction of Bishop August G. Spangenberg (1704–1792). On the voyage across the Atlantic, Spangenberg had a most important encounter with a young Anglican minister, John Wesley (1703–1791). The event led Wesley to worship with the Moravians upon his return to London and became integral to the series of events leading to his spiritual awakening in 1738. Wesley would go on to lead the most important phase of the Pietist Movement in England, Methodism. Among Wesley's close friends and associates from college days was George Whitefield (1714–1770). In 1739 Whitefield called Wesley to Bristol, England, to take charge of his ministry among the miners. The move was, for Wesley, an important step in the development of Methodism. Whitefield's trip to America became a major event in the development of American religion.

George Whitefield began his evangelistic tour of the American colonies in Georgia. As he moved northward he rallied his support and each stop involved more people in what became a national revival of religion. It would later be called the Great Awakening. By the time he reached New England in the fall of 1740, the revival had drawn many unconverted into the churches; it sparked the Presbyterian and Baptist membership, which soared at a spectacular rate between 1740 and 1780. But the Awakening would also lead directly to major splits among the Presbyterians, Congregationalists, and even the Baptists, many of whom rejected what they saw as the emotional excesses of the meetings led by Whitefield and his imitators. People would often react in seemingly uncontrolled fits in the process of responding to the preacher's call to turn from sin. There is evidence that rejection of revivalism was strongest among the wealthier and educated classes in the cities, and the most acceptance was found among the poorer and less-educated peoples in the countryside.

In 1741 the Presbyterians divided into New School (accepting of revivalism) and Old School. The Congregationalists of New England experienced measurable losses as a new wave of Separatist congregations was formed by those persons most affected by the revival. The Separatists insisted on a converted regenerate membership and tended to accept adult baptism as a sign of the regeneration. While some would eventually return to the Congregationalist fold, most of these congregations would become Baptist. Meanwhile, the Regular Baptists also split, as new Separate Baptists demanded that church members give clear evidence of a conversion experience. In their enthusiasm for the revival, they developed what seemed to the older Baptists to be an informal and noisy worship style, led by preachers who spoke in a distinctive, shrill, singsong manner.

As the revival progressed among the English-speaking colonists, at least one new group that was to take on some importance in the next century appeared. German Lutherans began to filter into New Jersey, Pennsylvania, and New York in the first half of the century. The first congregation was organized in Hackensack, New Jersey, around 1704. By 1750 there was a string of congregations along the Hudson River through New Jersey into southeast Pennsylvania.

Attempts to organize were stifled in New York by the Dutch regime (which favored the Reformed church) and slowed in New Jersey and Pennsylvania, where German settlers were slow to adapt to a government that would supply tax money for neither the building of churches nor the support of the ministry. The most prominent minister among the Lutherans was Henry Muhlenberg (1711–1787). Muhlenberg arrived in 1742 from the Pietist center at Halle, and brought some of that spirit with him. In 1748 he organized the Evangelical Lutheran Ministerium of Pennsylvania, regarded as the first Lutheran synodical organization in America. The second synod, the New York Ministerium, was not created until after the Revolutionary War, in 1786.

All churches were assisted by the attention given religion by the Great Awakening, and those who most readily adopted the revivalistic techniques began a generation of growth. By the beginning of the American Revolution, though almost totally confined to New England, the Congregationalists retained their status as the largest church in the colonies, with approximately 675 congregations. They were followed by the Presbyterians with 450, the Anglicans and Baptists with approximately 400, and lesser numbers of Lutherans (more than 200), Quakers (190), Reformed (180), and Roman Catholics (50). Had it not been for the American Revolution, there is every reason to believe that the churches in the American colonies might have developed much as they did in Canada. Because of the Revolution, a different course would be taken.

And because of the Revolution, it is important to make note of Methodism, the main organization in the British phase of the eighteenth-century evangelical awakening. In the 1750s, Methodism spread through England and reached Wales, Ireland, and Scotland. At about the same time, Methodists began to migrate to the American colonies, and by 1766 the first Methodist chapel was established by Robert Strawbridge (d. 1781) at Leesburg, Virginia. In 1769 Methodist founder John Wesley sent the first two preachers to oversee and promote the work in America. While centers were being established in the cities and at a few plantations along the coast, Methodism had barely begun when its work was interrupted by the Revolution. No one was aware of the difference in American religion the war was to make once peace returned.

REVOLUTION AND TRANSITION. The churches in the colonies had gone through wars before. After each war, they had merely resumed their work and returned to normal. But the American Revolution was different. It was not just another war. It destroyed a whole way of life and produced a new society. Religiously considered, the new nation that arose out of the success of the Revolution provided a distinct way of structuring religion, in which religious bodies became voluntary associations cut off both from official state support and public revenues. Each church would have to adjust to the new ways, and as might be expected, some would do it with far greater acumen than others. Necessary to the coming of this new world was a new religious-philosophical element that began to intrude upon the thinking of America's social and literary elites in the decades prior to the fight with the British homeland.

THE DEVELOPMENT OF DEISM. Nurtured within the bosom of Anglicanism as the Revolution approached was a new philosophy that denied the major affirmations of orthodox Christianity and set itself against the churches' leadership role. The new perspective was called *deism*, and its importance lay not so much in the number of its adherents (which seems to have been small), but in: (1) its acceptance by many of the men who were to provide the theoretical framework for the Revolution and the Constitution of the new nation; (2) the compatibility of its major affirmations with the irreligious elements of the American public; and (3) the role it played in further diluting the strength of the Church of England.

Such leading figures as Thomas Jefferson (1743–1826), Benjamin Franklin (1706–1790), George Washington (1732–1799), and James Madison (1751–1836), while retaining their formal affiliation with the established church, had left it in their hearts and begun to speak against it. Striking at the heart of Anglican control in the colonies, they opposed the designation of the Church of England (or any church) as the established church in the new nation.

Deists undergirded their attack on established religion with a general attack on traditional Christianity. They derided theologians for creating complicated and speculative cosmologies beyond the comprehension of the people. They focused especially on the concept of particular revelation, that God revealed certain truths to one person and not everyone, and the dogmas (such as the Trinity) that were derived from those claims of revelation. They argued that real religion was centered on issues of reason and morality. They elevated reason above all religious speculation and demanded a rational Christianity.

The passing of the First Amendment with its clauses on religious freedom, though hammered through by the deists, represents the coming together of the sectarian Protestant arguments for religious liberty that had developed out of persecution, and the deist arguments that had developed out of their theological speculations and general anticlericalism. While Roger Williams had argued for freedom from persecution and the creation of a free environment for proselytization of unbelievers, the deists bemoaned the evils of speculative systems imposed by clerics on an unwilling public. They had despaired of finding theological truth around which to unify amid the variety of opinions everywhere espoused. Such religious speculation was of little consequence. All religions agreed on the need for moral behavior, and a rational moral code included most everything that was important religiously. Given the deist stance, no reason remained for persecuting people or even for demanding conformity on matters of mere religious opinion and speculation.

THE EFFECT OF DISESTABLISHMENT. The Revolution, or more directly, the resulting Constitution of the new nation, served to free religion within the republic. While apologists for state-established religion have argued for its role in promoting religion in general and have cited disestablishment as a sign of societal secularization, religious establishments have done as much to suppress religious expression as they have to support it. Established religions, such as colonial Congregationalism in New England, were organized in accord with the wishes of the social elite. Through the state religion, the government controlled, regulated, and limited religious expression, and discouraged the formation and expression of religion, especially among those most alienated from the ruling class. It thus kept or drove many otherwise potentially religious people into a state of irreligion, by limiting their choice to a religion in which they did not believe or no religion at all.

In situations dominated by a state religion, only the most committed (in New England's case, the Quakers) persisted in their religious alternative as the state attempted to bring them into conformity. The volumes on religious persecution are filled with accounts of those who did resist, and American colonial history has its chapters in such volumes.

In freeing those formerly persecuted for their religious impulses, the First Amendment also created a situation in which new innovative religious gestalts could emerge. And as new varieties of religion became available, greater numbers became involved with the religious life. In the United States, the long-term result of religious freedom has been the steady growth of the percentage of the population who claim membership in a religious group (beginning with little more than 15 percent in 1790) and, in the last half of the twentieth century and after, the voluntary movement of the overwhelming majority of Americans into religious organizations (more than 85 percent by 2008). The destruction of government-backed religious controls has produced the most religious nation on earth.

AFTERMATH OF THE REVOLUTION. The American Revolution, significant battles of which occurred in every part of the colonies, thoroughly disrupted the entire country. For the churches, it meant disruption of services, confiscation, and even destruction of church buildings and loss of members. Congregations were divided by conflicting loyalties, though interestingly enough, no new church bodies appeared as a result of the war.

In one sense, the Congregationalists were least affected by the war. A number of ministers were identified with the Patriots' cause, and in spite of the church's identification with the state prior to the Revolution, its conflicts with the British government (such as its resistance to the planting of a Church of England congregation in Boston) left it in good standing when peace returned. Congregationalism did not, however, remain unscathed. First, it suffered an immediate loss of membership and a membership drain through the remainder of the century as British Loyalists left New England to resettle in Canada. Also, even though Congregationalism was the country's largest church body and had its membership concentrated in New England, it had to recognize that the majority of New Englanders were not church members. Out of that recognition, Connecticut passed a Toleration Act in 1784, a prelude to complete disestablishment in 1818. Massachusetts, the last to separate church and state, disestablished the church in 1833.

In the long run, Congregationalism suffered more severely from the spread of the deistic religious spirit in New England. Harvard had already become infected with anti-Trinitarian thought, and by the time Massachusetts disestablished, the church was in the midst of the Unitarian controversy that would result in the loss of many of its most prominent parishes. In spite of the losses to Canada and to the Unitarians, Congregationalism continued to grow at a slow pace, but it steadily fell in the ranking of Protestant churches. It continued to exert a significant influence for another century primarily through its educational leadership and the allegiance of New England's elite to its ranks.

As the war ended, there was some doubt as to whether Anglicanism could ever find a place in American life. Identified as the church of the enemy, it existed in an extremely hostile atmosphere. The SPG missionaries deserted it. Of the few who remained, many were not allowed to serve their parishes because of their Loyalist sympathies. The rector at Boston's King's Chapel defected to the Unitarian cause and took the church with him.

Disestablishment also came swiftly and harshly to the Church of England in the colonies. The church had been so intricately tied to secular structures, disestablishment destroyed both its financial base and legal status. Formerly somewhat dependent on the leadership of bishops, of which it now had none, it lost almost a decade in the search for episcopal authority. The need for a bishop led the Connecticut parishes to reorganize and select one of their number,

Samuel Seabury (1729–1796), as their bishop-elect. He was able to obtain apostolic orders from the nonjuring Scottish bishops (bishops whose church rejected the established Presbyterian church of Scotland), but the ministers and parishes in the southern and middle colonies did not want Scottish orders. They reorganized and elected William White (1748–1836), Samuel Provoost (1742–1815), William Smith, and David Griffith as their bishops-elect and waited for an opening in England. White and Provoost were finally able to obtain orders in London in 1787. They proceeded to organize the Protestant Episcopal Church in the U.S.A. and rebuild its work among the still-loyal members located primarily in southeastern Pennsylvania, Delaware, Maryland, and Virginia. They also were able to bring the work under Seabury in New York and Connecticut into the larger fellowship. Like the Congregationalists, the new church kept the allegiance of many of the new nation's more wealthy citizens.

Entering the country in the 1760s, the number of Methodists was almost too small to count as the Revolution began. However, they were solidly identified with the Church of England, having constituted themselves as a religious society within that church. Because of Wesley's political tracts, they were also identified with the Tory cause. Like the Anglican priests, the Methodist preachers, except for Francis Asbury (1745–1816), returned to England as a result of the Revolution. Methodism was largely shut down, and Asbury was forced to live in retirement during the war years. After the war, the Methodists were the first to greet Washington with protestations of loyalty, and then quickly turned to the task of reorganizing in the light of the changed situation. In 1784 the American preachers met at Barrett's Chapel in rural Maryland to organize the Methodist Episcopal Church. They elected Asbury their first bishop and began to develop their organization now free of the Church of England. They were, along with the Baptists, to receive the greatest benefits from the changes that occurred.

Presbyterians, primarily identified with the Revolution, lost little, considering that their churches, concentrated in New Jersey, Pennsylvania, and Delaware, were in close proximity to much of the fighting. They benefited greatly from the continued influx of Scottish and Scottish-Irish immigrants, and membership grew substantially from 1770 through the end of the century.

Few groups so benefited from the Revolution as did the Baptists. They had been the most vocal of the two major dissident churches in colonial America, especially on the issues of religious freedom and disestablishment, and had become as a whole strong supporters of the Revolution. After the war, they led the fight in New England for disestablishment and when it occurred, they were quick to claim the spoils.

Like the Baptists, the Quakers held their own during the war years. As a group, the pacifist Society of Friends did not participate, a perennial source of community hostility during wartime, but the war did not seem to stop their growth. They began the nineteenth century as one of the larger colonial bodies.

The Dutch Reformed and the German groups (Lutheran, Reformed, Mennonite, etc.) of Pennsylvania were basically dependent on immigration for growth. The war seemed but a momentary pause in the slow growth of the Dutch and the rapid growth of the German groups, with the Reformed and Lutherans receiving the most increase. The German Lutherans had begun to arrive in the colonies early in the eighteenth century. They came from all sections of the still divided nation-to-be and were only beginning to be organized as the war began. Leading spokespersons represented a wide spectrum of opinion on the Revolution, from those opposed to the colonists' cause to those who defended the German king who sat on the British throne. When the war ended, the Lutherans resumed their basic task of learning to build churches, print religious literature, and provide pastoral leadership in a land that refused to support their church in ways they had been taught to expect.

THE CHURCHING OF THE WEST: CHANGE THROUGH IMMIGRATION AND PROSELYTISM.

By the turn of the century, all of the churches had recovered from the war and reorganized for work in the new United States. The new country presented them with a monumental task. Within the first generation, the geographical area of the United States greatly expanded, first to the Mississippi River and then by the Louisiana Purchase to the Rockies and beyond. Along with the geographical expansion, the population exploded due to immigration. Beginning with almost four million in 1790 (when the first census was taken), the population tripled by 1830 and almost doubled again by the time of the Civil War (1861–1865). After the war, the numbers increased even more dramatically, growing by more than 12 million in each of the last two decades of the century.

Throughout the century, no religious group was able to adequately cope with the massive population growth. Few, other than the Roman Catholics, could cross the language barrier from the English majority to the German minority (the only significant minority through the early nineteenth century). In their attempts, however, religious groups could essentially adopt one of three programs. First, some religious groups sought out those immigrants who shared their Old World country of origin and defined their basic task as providing them with the American version of the same familiar church that they had left at home. Many groups, mostly the non-English-speaking ones, such as the Lutherans, received most of their growth in this manner, the Roman Catholic Church being most successful.

Second, many immigrant groups, both English-speaking and not, brought their religion with them and established a new branch of the church of their homeland in America. Thus the number of new denominations increased steadily as most of the European sects were transplanted to America. In the establishment and growth of the predominantly immigrant/ethnic churches and religions lies half the story of American religion in the next century.

Third, the majority of the population had left behind a situation in which church membership and citizenship were largely synonymous, and in their new free situation they chose to support no religion, profess no religious affiliation, and join no church. Churches could begin massive efforts to bring the population into the religious life they offered. Most churches engaged in evangelism, some limited to one language or ethnic group. In the success of their evangelistic endeavors lies the other half of the story of the next phase in American religion.

THE SECOND GREAT AWAKENING. Symbolic of the changes that were to occur in the new nation was a conference of Methodist ministers in Lexington, Kentucky, on April 15–16, 1790. Though still establishing itself along the eastern seaboard, Methodism was already reaching out to the new settlers on the other side of the mountains. Under Bishop Asbury's direction, 12 preachers departed the conference to ride their circuits throughout Kentucky and into Tennessee. Six years later, the church had recruited enough members and preachers to justify formally designating the area as a new conference, and in so doing, the general conference further enlarged the new conference to include all of the yet-unchurched territory to the west and north.

While Methodists were directing their circuit riders into the newly settled land, the lay-oriented Baptists were migrating in large numbers, setting up worship in private homes, and establishing chapels led by part-time farmer preachers. By 1800 they had no less than ten associations (of congregations) west of the mountains.

Like the Methodists and the Baptists, the Presbyterians and Congregationalists felt the responsibility to plant Christian churches in the West. To some extent they had been influenced by the revivalistic fervor that had been present throughout the eighteenth century. Very soon after the war they began to form missionary societies and recruit ministers to pastor among their members who had migrated westward, to gather new converts, and to establish missions among the Indians. At least theoretically realizing the scope of the growing task, in 1801 the two theologically similar groups laid aside their organizational differences to unite efforts to convert the West. Missionaries were recruited and sent west to establish congregations, build colleges, and civilize the wilderness.

In the expanding frontier, measures as dramatic as the expanding country were needed. Some means of attracting the attention of the scattered and irreligious populous had to be found. The program of the Plan of Union led to the establishment of some churches among groups of transplanted easterners. These new congregations called the available seminary-trained pastors, and developed the familiar forms of parish life. Following such a plan, both Congregational and Presbyterian churches began to appear in the new population centers in the West. Because of their more efficient organizational structure, the Presbyterians were better equipped to plant congregations systematically, and soon turned the earlier situation around and received many of the scattered Congregational churches into their membership.

The program of the Presbyterians and the Congregationalists was simply inadequate for the West. They could not train ministers fast enough to serve the growing population. They could not move fast enough to keep up with the expanding frontier. Most importantly, they could not adapt fast enough to the new society being created in the West. The two churches, especially the Congregationalists, began to be left behind.

In contrast, the Methodists and the Baptists seemed perfectly suited to the new land. They were extremely mobile. Since they emphasized their preachers' willingness and ability to preach apart from any formal educational credentials, they could train and deploy new circuit riders with great speed. They gave revivalistic and evangelistic activity their highest priority. They stood ready to exploit a wide variety of tools to winning the unsaved.

The first new tool for churching the frontier was the camp meeting. The idea grew out of a sacramental conference among Presbyterian churches under the leadership of James McGready (c. 1758–1817) in the Red River area of Kentucky. McGready was a graduate of the "log cabin" college and an enthusiastic preacher. At a four-day sacramental meeting held for the Red River church he served in 1800, emotions flowed freely, and many were converted, especially by the unplanned exhortations of a visiting Methodist, John McGee. McGready, noting the excitement, publicized the next meeting, and news of the events at Red River spread across the region. The next summer, more than 10,000, including preachers of a variety of denominations, attended the gathering at Cane Ridge, Kentucky. The event became a turning point. The camp meeting combined entertainment, a break in the loneliness of farm life, and religion.

The Methodists and Baptists, and those Presbyterians associated with McGready, lost no time in integrating the camp meeting into their regular program. In 1801 alone, the Methodists organized more than 400 of them. But the Presbyterians in the East were not as enthusiastic. They condemned the excesses of the camp meetings in 1805, and rejected McGready's work in the newly formed Cumberland Presbytery. In no small part, the church simply could not supply ministers fast enough to keep up with the new churches created out of the evangelistic efforts of McGready. Unable to reconcile his differences with the church, McGready and his colleagues formed the Cumberland Presbyterian Church.

The Cane Ridge meeting also changed the thinking of Presbyterian minister Barton Stone (1772–1844), who came away not only with a revivalistic mission but a conviction that the churches that gathered at Cane Ridge should put away their differences and unite in the task of converting the frontier. Stone and his followers left the Presbyterian Church and assumed the simple designation of Christian. In a similar action, Thomas Campbell (1763–1854) and Alexander Campbell (1788–1866) withdrew from the Baptists in western Pennsylvania and took the name Disciples of Christ. Finally discovering each other, the two groups united in 1832.

Thus, present on the frontier were four groups ready to evangelize the land, and evangelize they did. The Baptists, already among the larger church bodies due to their revivalistic efforts in the previous century, quickly moved to become the largest church body in America during the decades immediately after the Revolution. However, the Methodists moved even more quickly. From a few thousand members in 1784, they jumped ahead of the Baptists in the 1820s and during the rest of the century never looked back. The Cumberland Presbyterians were able to keep pace for most of the time, and after the 1832 merger of the Stone and Campbell movements, the Disciples of Christ enjoyed spectacular growth.

About the same time that Methodist membership surpassed the other churches, a new phase of revivalism began with the introduction of the "new measures." Developed by Congregationalist evangelist Charles G. Finney (1792–1875), the new measures were designed to create a climate for revival and to promote the crisis of decision, and in the hands of Finney and those who learned his techniques they brought millions into the churches. The techniques included the use of protracted meetings in the form of community-wide evangelistic campaigns with no announced ending date; testimony meetings in which people (even women) told of their conversion experience; the anxious bench, a place to counsel with individuals wrestling with a decision; and cottage prayer meetings. The new measures, rejected by Finney's church, but adopted with great success by Baptists and Methodists, institutionalized revivalism.

IMMIGRATION IN THE NINETEENTH CENTURY. While the evangelistic endeavors of the Methodists and Baptists were altering the shape of the religious community, immigration was having an equal effect. Of the millions that immigrated prior to the Civil War, the single largest group was Irish, followed by the Germans. The Irish were predominantly Roman Catholic, and while most Germans were Lutheran, many were also Roman Catholic. In addition, with the purchase of Louisiana, the French Roman Catholics of the territory were brought into the American Church. By midcentury, Roman Catholic membership rivaled that of the Methodists and Baptists. By the end of the century, with additional immigration from Poland and Italy, the church had jumped out ahead of both and emerged as the largest religious group in America.

The growth of the church is easily traced through the development of its hierarchy. Following the Revolution, John Carroll (1735–1815) was appointed in 1784 as superior of the American mission, and in 1790 he was consecrated as the first bishop for the United States with his see in Baltimore. In 1808 Baltimore was made an archdiocese, and New York City, Philadelphia, Boston, and Bardstown, Kentucky, received bishops. In 1846, 1847, and 1853 respectively, archdioceses were named in Oregon City (later Portland) for the American Northwest, St. Louis, and San Francisco. During the second half of the century, the sites of the early bishops on the East Coast would be elevated to metropolitan (arch-

diocese) status, as would Chicago, Dubuque, St. Paul, and Milwaukee.

Second only to Roman Catholicism in receiving positive results from immigration were the Lutherans. First from massive German immigration in the first half of the nineteenth century and then from Scandinavian immigration in the last half, the Lutherans grew in spite of their overall rejection of revivalism. The impact of Lutheranism on the country was, however, severely limited by the splintered condition of the church. As groups of Lutherans flocked to the country and settled in the frontier, they retained their linguistic and national boundaries, tended to organize separate synods in each region of the country, and were further split by internal doctrinal discord. Of major concern for the German community were issues of pan-Germanism (i.e., union with the German Reformed Church) and the confessional-doctrinal emphasis championed by Charles P. Krauth (1823–1882), who was opposed to the Pietist-experiential emphasis supported by Samuel S. Schmucker (1799–1873). By midcentury, the Lutherans were divided into more than 100 autonomous bodies. Since the end of the Civil War, they have pursued a process of union that has seen that number reduced to fewer than 20, with the overwhelming majority now in one denomination, the Evangelical Lutheran Church in America, established in 1988.

The Presbyterians, apart from the Cumberlands, were able to hold their own in the growing nation because of significant immigration from Scotland and Northern Ireland. Like the Lutherans, the Scots brought with them the problems of the homeland, and in America the Presbyterians split into a number of bodies reflective of the Scottish divisions.

During the nineteenth century, the Quakers received no significant immigrant support, faced a major schism just as the western movement came to the fore, and abandoned growth in the South over the slavery issue. Most importantly, Quakers quickly discovered that aggressive revivalism conflicted with their emphasis on the inner light. Early in the century, they simply ceased to grow in real numbers. They remain as a small body whose importance lies in its idealistic dissent on a number of issues, such as peace and social justice, which has placed the Quakers outside the mainstream of American life but given them a remarkable role as an agent for change in society.

SLAVERY AND THE DEVELOPMENT OF THE AFRICAN-AMERICAN CHURCH. In the nineteenth century, one issue seriously split the American religious community: slavery and its accompanying racial attitudes. The slavery issue, considered in its broadest aspect, had two overarching influences on the development of religious life in America. First, it split several of the older predominantly white denominations so deeply that the divisions have yet to be healed. Second, it led to the development of a number of separate, predominantly black, denominations.

As the division between the white people of the North and South widened over the institution of slavery, the churches that included those people felt the same tension.

The largest of the Protestant groups, the Methodist Episcopal Church, divided first. It had originally tried to keep the peace in the family by pushing the abolitionists out into the Wesleyan Methodist Church in 1843. But the next year, it opened the general conference with the scandal of a bishop from Georgia who had inherited slaves. Bishop James O. Andrew (1794–1871) refused to move from his home state, was unable by Georgia law to free his slaves, and planned to continue as an active traveling bishop. The church, unable to resolve the issue, voted to divide itself into two jurisdictions. The outcome was a division of the church into the Methodist Episcopal Church and the Methodist Episcopal Church, South.

The Baptists faced a similar problem precipitated by the refusal of the American Baptist Foreign Missionary Convention to accept slaveholders for positions as missionaries. In 1844 the Alabama and Georgia state conventions had forced the issue. After their rebuff in 1845, the southerners formed the Southern Baptist Convention. The Presbyterians waited until the war began, but in 1861, they too split into two bodies.

The issues raised by the slavery debates in the middle of the nineteenth century had been argued by the Methodists in the northern states soon after the formation of the Methodist Episcopal Church. Staunchly abolitionist at its beginning, African Americans had been a significant part of its membership since the 1860s. After the formal organization of the church, however, step by step it backed away from its original position as it grew in the South. Northern congregations that had been integrated instituted segregationist policies. Blacks were relegated to balconies, were the last to be served communion, and were generally treated as second-class citizens. Only a few were admitted to ministerial orders. Through the 1790s, black members from Charleston to Boston walked out and formed all-black congregations. Then, early in the nineteenth century, some congregations of free black people in the North left the Methodist Episcopal Church to found three African-American denominations: the African Union Church (1813), the African Methodist Episcopal (AME) Church (1816), and the African Methodist Episcopal Zion (AMEZ) Church (1820). Richard Allen (1760–1831), the first bishop of the AME Church, became one of the most prominent American black leaders through the 1820s.

The first black Baptist churches in the North were organized in Boston (1804), New York (1808), and Philadelphia (1809). It was not until the 1830s that the first associations were formed: the Providence Baptist Association in Ohio and the Wood River Association in Illinois. Missionary work by blacks led to the formation of the most substantial organizations. The American Baptist Missionary Convention, formed by blacks in 1840, not only sent foreign missionaries, but directed the organization of Baptist freedmen after the Civil War.

In the South, black Baptists appeared as the church spread among slave owners. The first congregations of Baptists were not organized until just before the American Revolution, however, as most slave owners were reluctant to allow independent organizations, including religious ones, among the slaves. The Methodists were the primary church that systematically approached slave owners on behalf of their slaves and recruited members from among the slave population. This effort was institutionalized in the South in the 1830s, and over the last years of the slavery era, some 200,000 African Americans joined the Methodist Episcopal Church, South. After the Civil War, most of these members joined the AME Church, the AMEZ Church, or the newly formed Colored (now Christian) Methodist Episcopal (CME) Church.

After the Civil War, the black Baptist and Methodist churches enjoyed a period of growth as they expanded their work among the freedmen. Neither the AME or AMEZ Church, under the control of northern freed blacks, had been allowed to recruit in the South, and quickly made up for lost time. With the addition of the CME Church, the African-American Methodists enjoyed an unprecedented period of growth and several million former slaves became Methodists. The problem of slavery was succeeded by that of widespread poverty and segregation, the need for education, and the imposition of a spectrum of Jim Crow laws. Black Baptists, lacking the organizations of the Methodists, were slower to get started after the war, but soon made up for the slow start. They quickly formed a number of regional and national organizations that merged in the 1890s to become the National Baptist Convention. By the end of the century, they approached the Methodists in membership and soon surpassed them. Today, most African Americans are Baptists—approximately 60 percent according to some estimates—with the several million Methodists forming the second largest bloc.

In lesser numbers, African Americans have been proselytized by and have responded to most religious traditions found in America, and have formed religious organizations representative of those different religious families. After the Civil War, most of the larger denominations established missions among the freedmen. Unfortunately, apart from their views toward slavery, northerners exhibited the same racial attitudes concerning black people that were prevalent in the South. Even so, some African Americans became (northern) Methodists, Presbyterians, Congregationalists, Episcopalians, and Roman Catholics. While welcoming black members as a whole, these churches instituted a pattern of racial segregation at the congregational and regional levels. On the other hand, in joining the predominantly white denominations, black church members brought into the African-American community all of the diverse religious commitments, theological tensions, and variation in worship of white society. As in the white community, the black denominational structures became the stable organizational units that shaped the larger religious community and set the pattern of belief and action at the congregational level. The varying response to issues facing the black community—the Ethiopianism of the 1930s, the civil rights movement in the 1960s (which split the Baptists), and the attempt to identify a common black religious experience in the 1970s—has largely followed denominational biases.

THE NATIVE AMERICAN RESPONSE TO THE WESTERN SPREAD OF CHRISTIANITY.

Originally, the policy of the newly formed United States focused on the "civilization" of Native Americans and envisioned the Christian churches as the main agent in that process. In 1819 the government passed a measure creating a "Civilization Fund," through which it subsidized church missions that aimed not only at conversion but Americanization of the Native Americans. Even prior to the 1819 legislation, pressures were mounting for the removal of Native Americans to the far west. A major step in that program followed the discovery of gold in Georgia, and the subsequent passing of the Removal Act of 1830 that pushed most of the members of Five Tribes out of the Southeast.

Following the Civil War, as serious settlement west of Independence, Missouri, expanded, the settlers' demands for Indian lands led to a series of Indian wars and the confinement of Native Americans to designated reservations. The pressures on Native Americans in the face of the overrun of the land by whites and the development of the dependency of the Indian people on the government and the churches had two significant religious consequences. First, many Native Americans responded to the evangelical efforts of the hundreds of missions established by Christian churches and converted to Christianity.

Almost all of the larger church bodies have Native American members, the result of missions established in the nineteenth or early twentieth centuries. In recent years, the majority of the older Christian churches have also moved to remove the Native American congregations from any stigma as a mission and to integrate them into the total life of the denomination. However, many smaller churches and independent missionary agencies continue to support "missions" on or near the reservations and have, since World War II (1939–1945), developed additional missions in the urban centers where many Indians migrated.

As Native American life was disrupted by the westward rush of white society, some who did not accept Christianity developed alternatives that attempted to go beyond the tradition of any particular tribe and reach all Native Americans with a combination of religious fervor and political protest. Of the several movements that developed, the Ghost Dance movement was by far the most important. Born among the Paiute in the 1870s, the movement found its great prophet in Wovoka (c. 1858–1932), a Paiute who lived most of his life in Nevada. Near his thirtieth birthday, he had a revelation during a solar eclipse. To those who practiced the distinctive circular dance already a part of the movement, the revelation promised a return of the Indian dead, the eradication of sickness, and a time of prosperity. A date during 1891 was set for the change. In the meantime, he urged followers to drop any overt hostility to the whites and become "civilized." The prophecy found immediate support among the Plains peoples, especially among the Oglala Sioux (the Lakota). They introduced the holy shirt, the design of which had been received in a vision, which would protect the wearer from any harm, even the bullets of the U. S. Army.

The Ghost Dance movement climaxed at Wounded Knee in South Dakota, where 300 Ghost Dance participants were killed by the U.S. Army in 1890, a clear demonstration of the inability of the shirts to provide the promised protection. While the dance survived into the middle of the twentieth century, it lost its mass appeal and left a vacuum soon to be replaced with another movement developed in Mexico. The peyote religion spread as the Ghost Dance receded, and offered a mystical alternative to the earlier apocalyptic movement. Drawing on both Christian and Native American themes, it added the strong psychological impact of peyote's ability to alter consciousness. While preaching many of the values that the white culture wished to spread among Native Americans, the peyote religion, in addition, offered a note of defiance in its use of a hallucinogenic drug. After the formal incorporation of the movement as the Native American Church in 1918, it spread among numerous Indian tribes and became a powerful force in building an identity among Native Americans as one people. The Native American church also enjoyed an interesting history in the courts as it established its right to use the sacred substance.

THE POSTWAR SCHISM OF AMERICAN PROTESTANTS.

In the last half of the nineteenth century, the major North American Protestant groups were rent with controversy. Tensions became evident as a new set of issues that demanded a response confronted the churches. The challenges of the new issues were qualitatively different from those at the beginning of the century that had demanded an increase in activity and endeavor. These issues appeared in the form of new ideas that carried the force of scientific and academic backing. They also demanded acceptance of a totally new worldview.

From Germany came a new way of looking at the Bible. Critical scholars had begun to question the accuracy of the biblical texts in several ways. Some challenged the legitimacy of the miracle stories in the name of science. What could not happen within the boundaries of the known laws of the universe, probably did not happen. Others challenged the integrity of the texts, especially the first five books of the Bible. They denied the Mosaic authorship and suggested that these books were a complex edited narrative created by combining into a single text several older texts that had been written by different people in different circumstances. The new scholarship was seen by many as defying the authority of the Bible, which most Christians understood literally.

For many, the challenge to biblical authority by the German critics seemed to resonate with the new claims in the sciences of geology and biology. Geologists studying the nature of various earth-building processes, such as volcanoes, concluded that the earth was not a few thousand years old, but hundreds of thousands, even millions of years old. Charles Darwin (1809–1882) and his colleagues concluded that not only had life forms evolved from one species to another but that even humanity was a product of evolution from other primates. The new sciences presented a complete alternative to the literal biblical account of God creating the species and separately creating the first man and woman.

Also, as the overseas mission programs of the churches expanded, interest in and information about religions in foreign lands grew. To some, it became evident that Buddhism, Hinduism, Islam, and the other great world religions offered a sophisticated spirituality and would not simply capitulate in the face of the presentation of the Christian message. Some voices arose to suggest that Eastern religions could possibly teach the West something vital and important. The impact of the other religions was brought home at the 1893 World's Parliament of Religions where Hindu Swami Vivekananda (1863–1902), Theosophist Annie Besant (1847–1933), and Buddhist Anagarika Dharmapala (1864–1933) drew huge audiences.

While new ideas challenged church leaders' thoughts, immigration was producing unprecedented growth in American urban centers, which were ill-equipped to deal with sudden heavy population increases. Industrialists looking for cheap labor exploited the new urbanites. Slums appeared as many immigrants were crowded into inadequate housing. Drunkenness was common. Churches could not (or would not) expand fast enough to serve the immigrants (many of whom spoke no English or came from Roman Catholic countries). Scholars and activists began to suggest that older solutions to social problems, usually directed toward reforming individuals through hygiene, education, and hard work, were inadequate. What America needed was a change in the system that allowed slums and exploited workers to exist. Answers were suggested by the new science of sociology, which suggested that social problems could be solved by human manipulation of social structures. Among the most popular overall solution was some form of socialism.

Church leaders responded to these intellectual and social challenges in two ways. A growing number of them suggested a positive response to the new ideas and began to seek ways of reconciling Christianity to biblical criticism, evolution, the existence of sophisticated world religions, and the crises in the cities. Those who took such a positive stance, yielding to the demands of the modern age, came to be called *modernists*. Other church leaders saw in the modernist revisions of the faith not just an adaptation to a new situation but the destruction of traditional Christianity and its replacement by a different gospel. They responded by calling their ministerial colleagues and the churches of the land to once again affirm the nonnegotiable fundamentals of the faith, and in so doing they became known as *fundamentalists*.

Modernism, the progenitor of contemporary liberal Protestantism, came to be identified with a variety of opinions. Modernists accepted biblical criticism and redefined the nature of biblical authority. In the process, they discarded the literal interpretation of the early chapters of Genesis and the biblical miracle stories and emphasized instead the eternal lessons to be drawn from them. Modernists accepted the opinions of geologists and biologists about the age of the universe and the evolutionary origin of humanity. However, they suggested that evolution was not a process without obvious purpose, that it did not follow natural selection but derived from the constant action of God, drawing life and humanity to higher levels of attainment. This perspective was called *theistic evolution*.

In their encounter with world religions, modernists such as James Freeman Clarke (1810–1888), a Unitarian professor teaching at the University of Chicago, attempted to make the case for the superiority of Christianity, not as the true religion over against the falsehood of all other religions, but as the most true religion in a world of religions of partial truths. Each religion contains elements recognized as good and noble, but only Christianity contains goodness and truth in their fullness. As a major expression of this approach, the League of Liberal Clergymen in Chicago organized the World's Parliament of Religions in 1893.

In their response to the cities, modernists borrowed well-known biblical symbols that they identified with the socialist program of radical changes in late nineteenth-century society. They spoke of building the kingdom of God and ushering in a millennium of peace and justice through the reorganization of social patterns. They called their message the *social gospel*.

Modernist theology was optimistic in the extreme and based on a positive view of human nature. Humanity, in the opinion of modernists, had evolved beyond its animal nature over many thousands of years. The human condition was not so much due to sin and human depravity. It was an effect of the continued presence of the animal past. Humans had evolved out of the animal world, and they could now evolve mentally and spiritually; they inevitably must evolve into the life of the kingdom of God. Progress became the watchword of modernist perspectives, and a utopian hope for humanity's future undergirded every action.

Fundamentalists claimed that modernism undercut biblical authority in the name of science and replaced Christian commitments with a new religion, hardly recognizable as Christian. As the nineteenth century moved to its close, they began to see seminary professors spreading modernism in their classrooms and ministers voicing it from prominent pulpits. The most visible erosion appeared in the Baptist, Presbyterian, and Congregationalist churches, those older churches with a strong Calvinist confessional heritage. In the first stage of the battle, the conservatives charged individuals with deviating from confessional standards. Beginning in the 1870s, the public was treated to a series of heresy trials, the most famous being the Presbyterian actions against David Swing (1830–1894), Charles Briggs (1841–1913), and Henry Preserved Smith (1847–1927). A variety of denominations took official action (from censoring to dismissal) against instructors in their schools who voiced modernist opinions.

At first, the conservatives showed their strength, but by the turn of the century, sentiment turned against them. The denominations showed a new reluctance to condemn modernists who were filling more and more denominational posts. Sensing a loss of control, the conservatives began to organize. Interdenominational conferences, the most famous being the annual gatherings at Niagara Falls, provided places for conservatives to find strength, strategize, and organize. Out of the Niagara conferences came a series of statements of faith affirming "fundamental" beliefs. The conservatives also began to establish independent schools where fundamental doctrines would be upheld and taught. Among the first were Moody Bible Institute in Chicago and the Philadelphia College of the Bible.

The conservative cause received a significant boost in the first decade of the twentieth century when California oilman Lyman Stewart (1840–1923), a Presbyterian, began to divert money to the conservative cause. In 1906 he helped establish the Bible Institute of Los Angeles, which became the nexus for West Coast fundamentalists. He brought R. A. Torrey (1856–1928) from Moody to be the dean of the college. Withdrawing from Immanuel Presbyterian Church, he donated the initial endowment for the independent Church of the Open Door, the pulpit of which Torrey also assumed. Lyman gave money toward the production of the Scofield Reference Bible (published in 1909), whose notes, written by lawyer turned pastor C. I. Scofield (1843–1921), systematically presented the fundamentalist position. In 1909 Lyman gave the money to produce a series of booklets, *The Fundamentals*, which were mailed to pastors across the country. These booklets, which gave the conservatives their name, launched a new assertive phase of the conservative cause. That new phase took organizational form immediately after World War I (1914–1918) with the formation of the World Christian Fundamental Association.

Fundamentalism and modernism represent two distinctly different ways of viewing the world and Christianity. The battles of the nineteenth century set the issues and created two camps within each of the affected denominations. In the decades between the world wars, the growing hostility between the camps would lead to showdown battles that finally divided the Presbyterians and Baptists, and left the modernists firmly in control of most of the older denominations. The fundamentalists were pushed out into new denominations, the formation of which permanently institutionalized the fundamentalist-modernist controversy and has kept it alive to this day. The cleavage within the Protestant camp in North America between conservative evangelical Protestants and liberal Protestants shows no sign of being resolved, even as issues have shifted. Both sides have strong support from large denominational bodies.

METHODISTS DIVIDE.
While Presbyterians and Baptists launched their fights over doctrinal issues, the Methodists had little time for the debate. They believed that heartfelt religion and the living of the Christian life were more important than doctrinal purity. When the early Niagara conferences began to produce doctrinal statements, the Methodists had little sympathy for the emphasis the conservatives placed on human depravity. They championed the

possibility of human perfection and the need for sanctified holy living.

After the Civil War, the church had been swept by a revival as evangelists promised the born-again Methodists the possibility of a second encounter with the Holy Spirit as dramatic and almost as important as the first born-again experience. This encounter, this *second blessing*, as it was termed, would go beyond justifying the sinner and guaranteeing a place in heaven; it would actually make the Christian blessed in perfect love. This theme of Holiness and perfection had been present, with varying emphases, throughout Methodist history. But as it reached a new peak in its acceptance, numerous Holiness camp-meeting associations were established throughout the several Methodist denominations.

In the 1880s, Methodists began to back away from the Holiness emphasis. Prominent leaders championed the cause of gradual growth in grace over a single critical event such as the second blessing. Critics also charged that the associations were placing too much emphasis on the minutiae of the personal habits of Christians. District superintendents struggled to control the otherwise independent Holiness associations. The tension reached a climax in Illinois, where Holiness leaders began to call for members to "come out" of the indifferent and often hostile Methodist church and form independent Holiness congregations. While never leaving in large enough numbers to slow the steadily climbing Methodist membership figures, many Holiness people did separate to found congregations that would soon band together in small regional Holiness associations. A few of these remain today, but most merged into the older schismatic Methodist churches that had retained a Holiness emphasis (the Wesleyans and the Free Methodist Church) or combined with other regional bodies to form national denominations, such as the Church of the Nazarene.

Even before the independent Holiness groups had consolidated their gains, the movement was swept with a new teaching that originated in a Holiness Bible school in Topeka, Kansas, under the leadership of Charles Fox Parham (1873–1929). The teaching promised that not only was there a second blessing available to Christians, there was a third: the baptism of the Holy Spirit. While the second blessing cleansed the heart, the third filled the believer with power. Accompanying Spirit baptism and confirming its truth, proponents asserted, were supernatural manifestations, the gifts of the Spirit, the first and most important being the individual's miraculously speaking in a foreign language that, under normal circumstances, he or she did not understand. They saw speaking in tongues as a revival of the events of Pentecost described in the biblical book of Acts.

Pentecostalism was taken from Topeka to Houston by Parham and from Houston to Los Angeles by Parham's student, William J. Seymour (1870–1922), an African-American Holiness preacher. In Los Angeles, Pentecostal manifestations created a sensation, and for over three years Seymour led daily meetings in a building on Azusa Street to which visitors flocked from around the continent. Within those three years, the Pentecostal movement spawned congregations across North America and around the world.

The Holiness and Pentecostal movements attracted the most conservative Methodists, just as fundamentalism would later attract the most conservative Baptists and Presbyterians. By the time of the major schisms in the 1920s, Methodism had already lost many of those who would possibly have aligned themselves with the fundamentalists, especially in their affirmations of biblical authority and creationism. Methodism passed through the heat of the fundamentalist battles with only minor skirmishes. But just as fundamentalism created a major schism in Protestantism, so too did the Holiness and Pentecostal movements, both now claiming millions of adherents in America and still growing.

HOMEGROWN RELIGION.

In the midst of the expansion of religion as the nation was being churched in the nineteenth century, new religious impulses arose among New Englanders who were being subjected to the efforts of revivalists. Though often beginning with issues raised by older religious groups, these groups provided new solutions and in the process created genuinely new gestalts of the religious life. Among the first was the Church of Jesus Christ of Latter-day Saints, popularly called the Mormons. Sharing many common roots with the equally indigenous Disciples of Christ, the Latter-day Saints sought a unity of religions of the frontier, and found such unity in a new revelation given to Joseph Smith Jr. (1805–1844). Spiritualism grew up in reaction to scientific critiques of religious hopes for an afterlife. Accepting the critiques, Spiritualists utilized scientific models to claim that Spiritualist phenomena provided "proof" that life after death is real. New England Transcendentalism, centered on the community at Brook Farm in Massachusetts, was among the first American religious movements to draw on Asian wisdom.

While Mormonism and Spiritualism emerged in the countryside, the important late nineteenth-century groups, Theosophy, Christian Science, and New Thought, started their work in the cities, especially New York, Boston, and Chicago. Over the years, each movement produced numerous splinter groups (more than 100, for example, can be traced to Theosophy) that would result in the formation of a new family of religions. Each would also build its own agenda without particular reference to the continuing life of the Christian churches and the ideas deemed important in their centers of learning.

The impulse that produced the nineteenth-century sectarian movements was similar to impulses that had sought expression in previous centuries. Only in the nineteenth century, the promise of religious freedom allowed these groups to emerge, proselytize, and, to a relative degree, prosper. In previous centuries, their founders would possibly have been outlawed and the groups hounded out of existence. In nineteenth-century America, they had only to withstand the press of popular opinion.

IMMIGRATION, 1880–1924.

By 1880 the population of the United States had reached more than 50 million. During the next 25 years, before the brakes were applied to immigration, the population would double. People from many nationalities, previously represented by only scattered individuals, now came in large numbers. In colonial times, immigration had brought those religious groups that still dominate the patterns of American religious life. After the American Revolution and through most of the nineteenth century, immigration would continually add members to the older groups and steadily bring new groups, most of which were variations of the older groups. The spurt of immigration between 1880 and 1924 would substantially alter America's religious landscape (already bulging with the indigenous innovative religions) by markedly increasing the variety of religious expression. Greeks, Romanians, Bulgarians, and Serbians brought all the variations of Eastern Orthodoxy. Russian and Polish Jews overwhelmed and recreated the small German-dominated Jewish community. The Japanese added their expressions of Buddhism to the Chinese forms. Indians brought Sikhism and Hinduism.

Eastern Orthodoxy had been introduced into California in the early nineteenth century and into Alaska even earlier. However, it remained small and the few parishes of the Russian Orthodox Church housed believers of every national-ethnic group. In the late nineteenth century, immigration brought people from predominantly Orthodox lands in such numbers that each was in turn able to organize separate parishes and eventually form separate dioceses. Some groups, such as the Ukrainians, were able to create autonomous jurisdictions for the first time in the free climate of North America. After the Russian revolution of 1917, and again after World War II, the Orthodox churches would further divide along political lines, creating even more new church groups.

Jews had come to America in three waves. In the seventeenth century, a small number of Sephardic Jews (Jews with a Spanish background) emigrated to the colonies. The first synagogue, Congregational Shearith Israel, was organized in New York in 1728. The second synagogue, in Newport, Rhode Island, still stands, but its members were driven out by the British capture of the city during the Revolutionary War. There were approximately 3,000 Jews in America as the colonial era ended.

During the nineteenth century, enough German Jews came to the United States to dominate the small colonial Jewish community. By 1840 there were approximately 15,000 Jews. Most importantly, the new immigrants were heirs of a liberalizing influence that had grown among German synagogues. They wanted revision of the traditional forms of Jewish life and worship, stripping away nonessential items that tended to alienate the non-Jewish community. By the middle of the century, in religiously free America, they created a new way of doing Judaism: Reform Judaism. In response, the more traditional Jews organized to defend their traditional ways; traditionalists became known as Orthodox Jews.

The wave of Eastern European Jews that began in the 1880s would in turn overwhelm the German Jewish community as completely as German Jews had attained hegemony over the colonial community. More than three million came, and both Orthodox and Reform communities vied for the immigrants' allegiance. In the midst of this tension, a new form of Judaism that attempted to mediate between the two camps appeared. Conservative Jews respected the tradition, but made mild reforms of what were considered less-essential items. Over several decades, each group attained approximately the same number of adherents, and each organized both rabbinical and congregational associations on a national level.

Religiously, the Jewish community is built around the three ways of doing Judaism: Reform, Conservative, and Orthodox. Equally important, standing outside of these three groups, were the large number of Jews who adhered to none of the three. As with the settled Gentile community, approximately one-half of the Jewish immigrants acknowledged no religious affiliation. Over the years, in the pluralistic climate of the United States, many of those unattached Jews found their way into the wide variety of non-Jewish religions, especially Hinduism, Buddhism, and even Islam, and some became prominent leaders. Others created Jewish versions of non-Jewish religions, such as Christian Science and humanism.

No groups were so affected by the immigration laws as were the Asians. In the 1850s, the Chinese began to arrive in America in large numbers. While many were Christians, a large number followed the several Chinese faiths, especially Buddhism. After anti-Chinese feeling led to the passage of an exclusion act in 1882, Japanese and Filipinos began to move into the West Coast to replace the Chinese as cheap labor. These new immigrants brought their Buddhism and Catholicism respectively. However, public opinion began to turn against the Japanese, and in 1908 a "gentleman's agreement" was reached with Japan to limit further immigration. During the first decade of the twentieth century, East Indians, mostly Punjabi, also came into Washington, Oregon, and California. Like the Japanese, they found themselves the object of public hostility. In 1917 Congress passed an Asian Exclusion Act that largely stopped immigration from all of Asia, except Japan. Prior to the 1917 act, several forms of both Hinduism and Buddhism had been introduced into America and had attracted non-Asian converts. After the 1917 act, that growth, now slowed considerably, continued through the development of non-Asian Hindu and Buddhist groups, most of which were small, with membership limited to a single urban center. They often existed quietly for years, relatively unknown even by their immediate neighbors.

However, in 1924 an omnibus immigration quota act, which assigned strict limits to the number of immigrants from each country, stopped significant immigration not only from Asia, including Japan, but also from southern and eastern Europe. Thus, not only was the spread of Buddhism and Hinduism stifled, but the growth of the Eastern Orthodox and Jewish communities slowed. Since each of these communities possessed strong ethnic bonds that prevented evangelism outside of the ethnic group, further growth depended on the community's birthrate.

PLURALISM: A NEW PATTERN FOR THE TWENTIETH CENTURY.

At the beginning of the twentieth century, between 30 and 40 percent of the American population was affiliated with a church or religious group. The majority of Americans remained unchurched, but tremendous growth had been experienced by religion in general and the Christian churches in particular. The percentage of the population that was religiously affiliated doubled. While the population had grown by three and a half times, church membership had grown by more than double that rate. In the process, the number of different religious denominations also expanded greatly. There were fewer than 40 denominations in 1800. By the beginning of the twentieth century, some 200 different religious bodies representing 16 different denominational families could be found. By 1990 there were more than 2,000.

Most religious people were affiliated with one of the major Christian bodies, the largest of which was the Roman Catholic Church. Over against Catholicism, the major Protestant churches found unity and saw themselves collectively as the majority party in the land. In 1908 they gave expression to that unity by creating the Federal Council of Churches. The creation of the Federal Council occurred as the churches were facing the great conservative-liberal split between fundamentalists and modernists and between Methodism and the Holiness and Pentecostal churches. The council became the forum of liberal Protestantism. Among its first acts was the adoption of a slightly altered version of the Methodist Social Creed, an early statement of social concerns that incorporated important elements of the social gospel.

The council became the first successful expression of the ecumenical movement. Holding aloft the ideal of the unity of Christianity, in stark contrast to the numerous denominational divisions of the church, especially in America, ecumenists expressed the desire for the organic unity of Protestantism. The movement generated periodic waves of enthusiasm throughout the twentieth century, and can claim major accomplishments in the uniting of churches within the several Protestant families, highlighted by the formation of the Evangelical Lutheran Church in America through mergers in 1918, 1930, 1960, and 1988; the United Methodist Church through mergers in 1939 and 1968; the Presbyterian Church (USA) through mergers in 1906, 1958, and 1983; and the United Church of Christ through mergers in 1931 and 1948.

Rejection of the council and the liberal ecumenical movement became an additional affirmation for the fundamentalists as they pulled out of the larger denominations. In their place, fundamentalists organized two councils—the American Council of Christian Churches (1941) and the National Association of Evangelicals (NAE) (1942)—the former being the more conservative of the two. Fundamentalist Christians limited their ecumenical activity to those with whom they were in essential doctrinal agreement. Pentecostals gave outward expression both to their growth and their distinctive presence in the American community by the organization of the Pentecostal Fellowship of North America (disbanded and reformed as the Pentecostal/Charismatic Churches of North America in 1994). Years earlier, at the beginning of the Holiness revival, a National Holiness Camp Meeting Association for the Promotion of Holiness had been created. During the twentieth century, it went through a process of reorganization to emerge as a council of Holiness churches, and in 1970 the organization took the name Christian Holiness Association (now the Christian Holiness Partnership).

The first half of the twentieth century continued the pattern of growth for the various religious groups, in the midst of which liberal Protestants extended the ecumenical ideal to open contacts and build bridges of understanding with the Roman Catholic and Jewish communities. Those contacts were fruitful enough in the public sphere that by the middle of the century, sociologist Will Herberg (1901–1977) could rightfully speak of America's three faiths—Protestantism, Catholicism, and Judaism.

But other groups were also growing. The nineteenth-century religious groups whose members spoke a language other than English went through a process of Americanization and were ready to interact with the larger community. Eastern Orthodox leaders formed the Standing Council of Orthodox Bishops in 1960. The International New Thought Alliance formed earlier in the century had grown up with the metaphysical churches.

DEVELOPMENTS SINCE 1965.
The gradual restructuring that had been occurring throughout the twentieth century was given a new impetus in 1965. That year, the U.S. Congress rescinded the Asian Exclusion Act and redistributed immigration quotas, allowing Asian, Eastern European, and Middle Eastern countries to send immigrants as never before. In the decades since its passing, this single act has done more to readjust the religious community in America than any other force. This action once again allowed the flow of immigrants from countries that had been excluded in 1917 and 1924. The result has been twofold.

First, American religious communities with roots in eastern and southern Europe have been strengthened. Second, immigration from Islamic countries has for the first time occurred in significant numbers, with believers from throughout the diverse Muslim world settling in America. Eastern religions have extended their presence in America through both first-generation immigrant organizations and the unexpected conversion of thousands of young adult Americans to both Buddhism and guru-led Hindu religions. More than 100 different Hindu "denominations" have been planted in America since 1965, and more than 75 forms of Buddhism currently exist. Each community now claims between three and five million adherents. Their rate of growth continues to be among the highest in the country.

During the twentieth century, the New Thought metaphysical churches (Religious Science, Divine Science, and the Unity School of Christianity) became a familiar sight on American street corners. Now with hundreds of thousands of adherents, their influence has permeated the mainstream of American culture through the spread of their literature. Unity material, especially its devotional monthly, *Daily Unity*, enters millions of homes. Even more noticeable was the spread of metaphysical thought through the extensive ministry of such preachers as Norman Vincent Peale (1898–1993) and more recently Robert Schuller (b. 1926) and Oral Roberts (b. 1918), all of whom have been heavily influenced by New Thought ideas.

Esoteric religions, among the least understood religious options, have broken out of the small esoteric groupings that were so typical at the beginning of the twentieth century. Spiritualism, often thought of as merely a nineteenth-century fad, experienced noticeable periods of revival after every war, and perpetuated itself in all of the major urban complexes. Theosophy, based on teachings delivered to Helena Petrovna Blavatsky (1831–1891) by what she maintained were ascended masters of wisdom, while never claiming more than a few tens of thousands of members, multiplied its influence through the more than 100 organizations it spawned. Esotericism can now claim more adherents that either Buddhism or Hinduism, and can point to the twentieth century as a period of esoteric revival. Astrology also reaches a steadily growing segment of the public. One needs no better indicator of the penetration of public consciousness by esoteric (as well as related Eastern) ideas than the late twentieth-century surveys that revealed that almost one-fourth of Americans believe in the concept of reincarnation, the idea that human souls inhabit a series of physical bodies over several lifetimes.

While the number of people attracted to metaphysics and the occult has increased with each generation, the distrust of organization that permeates both movements has stymied the growth of metaphysical groups to the extent that the spread of metaphysical ideas would seem to warrant. To perpetuate itself, the community must rely on periods of revival of its major concerns within the larger secular community, as it has yet to develop structures that can pass its teachings to the next generation through more traditional family structures, and has yet to form schools for the training of leaders. The New Age movement of the 1980s was the latest period of revival. It raised public awareness of metaphysical and esoteric ideas, brought millions into the previously established esoteric and metaphysical fellowships, led to the formation of many new fellowships, and supported the emergence of a network of metaphysical bookstores across North America.

AMERICAN RELIGIOUS GROUPS IN THE NEW MILLENNIUM.
At the turn of the new century, American religion can be seen as divided into 10 recognizable groups of denominations, each of which claims a substantial number of adherents. Each group is united by common beliefs and commitments, and separated from other groups by adherence to a distinct way of doing religion. Six of these groups are Christian and together can claim both a majority of American citizens and the bulk of America's religious

adherents. The Christian community is divided into Roman Catholic, Eastern Orthodox, liberal Protestant, conservative evangelical, Holiness, and Pentecostal-charismatic.

There are more than 60 million Roman Catholics in America, making the group three times larger than its closest competitor, the Southern Baptist Convention. The American Roman Catholic Church exists both as a single organization, and as an inclusive mixture of ethnic parishes, religious orders, and diverse theologies. The church assumed an important role in the nineteenth century. It grew to become the nation's largest religious body in the 1840s, and in many cities claimed the allegiance of the majority of citizens. Its earlier attempts to integrate into the American fabric and become an active participant in shaping social policy were thwarted by strong anti-Catholic sentiments, one of the few concerns around which competing Protestant sects could unite. In addition, at the end of the nineteenth century, prominent Catholic leaders proposed a program for realigning the church in America with certain important American values. They called on the church to emphasize its similarities with Protestantism, rather than its differences. Unfortunately, this program, which became known in Europe as *Americanism*, was denounced in a papal encyclical in 1899, and the American church pulled back from what appeared to be a new era of broad cultural engagement in favor of concentration on more internal concerns. Only since World War II, with the generation of new leadership, the changes wrought at the Second Vatican Council (1962–1965), and the election of John F. Kennedy (1917–1963), a Catholic, as U.S. president, has the church enjoyed a more positive image and been accepted as a stable and legitimate part of the American religious landscape. Its new role in American society is manifest in the thoughtful attention now given the regular pronouncements on public policy made by the United States Conference of Catholic Bishops.

Similar to, but in many ways essentially distinct from, Roman Catholicism, is Eastern Orthodoxy. Emerging to prominence in America in the early twentieth century, the Orthodox groups have been committed to the preservation of both the Orthodox faith and the ethnic heritage of their constituencies. After the Russian revolution of 1917, and with the spread of communism following World War II, they were united by the problems resulting from the emergence of governments hostile to religion in many of their ethnic homelands. In the wake of World War II, they have emerged as vocal participants, as well as a force with which to be reckoned, in the wider debates and ecumenical discussions. Many of the Orthodox groups, besides uniting in the Standing Conference of Orthodox Bishops, have extended their influence through affiliation with the National Council of Churches (NCC).

In the late nineteenth and early twentieth centuries, Protestantism split into at least four major camps, each united enough and distinct enough from the others to be considered a separate religious grouping. Aligned within the NCC (which superseded the Federal Council of Churches)

are the major liberal Protestant denominations. They include the Protestant Episcopal Church, the Evangelical Lutheran Church in America, the Presbyterian Church (USA), the United Church of Christ, the United Methodist Church, the American Baptist Church in the U.S.A., and the six major black Protestant groups (three Methodist churches and three Baptist conventions). As a whole, these are the older and larger Protestant bodies, the most socially oriented, the most accepting of contemporary scholarship (both secular and sacred), and the most visible religious bodies in America.

One measure of the prominence of religious groups in a society is the role given particular religious groups in a public setting, and during most of American history, Protestantism's leadership in religiously shaping the nation was unchallenged. Liberal Protestantism assumed the leadership position as it took control of the older, larger church organizations. Through the NCC and its constitutive bodies, liberal Protestantism continues that tradition of leadership and guidance to the nation on important national and international social issues. Slowly, the liberal Protestant churches have acknowledged that they now share leadership with, at least, the Roman Catholic Church and the Jewish community.

In the last decades of the twentieth century, that primal leadership role was actively challenged, especially by the three dissenting conservative Protestant groups: the evangelical conservatives (whose most conservative element is fundamentalism), the Holiness churches, and the Pentecostals (including the newer charismatic churches). These conservatives have rejected the leadership of the older Protestant groups. Counting the 16-million-member Southern Baptist Convention as a part of the evangelical-conservative grouping (as its most liberal wing), this group claimed a constituency of some 40 million, equal in size to the combined membership of the affiliates of the NCC. Based on that assessment of support, evangelical conservatives emerged in the 1980s as a group claiming the Protestant heritage of leadership against that of the NCC and their member organizations. Evangelical conservatives have claimed additional support from the membership of the liberal Protestant churches, which has been repeatedly shown to be out of step with their churches' public pronouncements. Liberal Protestantism has also been unique in its steady loss of members since the 1960s. Evangelicals claim, with some justification, that those members have been lost to evangelical churches, which in fact adhere more closely to the American Protestant tradition.

As the new century begins, some softening of attitudes between the churches supportive of the NAE and those holding membership in the NCC has emerged. In 2000 the NAE abandoned its long-standing rule against member churches also holding membership in the NCC. There have also been talks between NAE and NCC leaders looking toward possible cooperation and even merger (though a merger seems unlikely as of 2008). This dialogue has become possible as NAE leadership has recognized the wide variance of theologies that have appeared among evangelical spokespersons.

The Holiness and Pentecostal churches have been identified with the conservative-evangelical camp on basic issues such as the mutual affirmation of the authority of the Bible, and on important public positions such as opposition to abortion, support of prayer and the teaching of creationism in public schools, and support for the state of Israel. While some churches have joined the NAE, the Holiness and Pentecostal groups have remained distinct bodies within the evangelical consensus due to intense doctrinal differences, such as their support for a female ministry. Both Holiness and Pentecostal groups grew throughout the twentieth century, but since the mid-1980s Pentecostalism has made spectacular strides. It has, for example, come to dominate the airtime given religion on radio and television. The Church of God in Christ, with more than five million members, has led Pentecostalism in overtaking Methodism in the number of African-American adherents. The Assemblies of God claims more than two million adherents, and both the United Pentecostal Church and the Church of God (Cleveland, Tennessee) have more than a half a million members.

The various major groups of Christians follow what are described in the chapters of this *Encyclopedia* as denominational families. But among Anglicans, Lutherans, Presbyterians, Congregationalists, Methodists, and Baptists, the split between liberal and conservative groupings rivals the denominational family structures in importance. That split, however, relates to a limited (though important) number of theological and social issues, which together constitute only a small part of the churches' religious life. Conservative and liberal Lutherans, for example, still agree on the majority of issues that make them Lutheran. The same could be said for the other denominational families. And while they align on certain issues along liberal and conservative lines, they also participate in family traditions that have both national and international organizational expression. In that regard, liberals and conservatives will join together to support fellowship groups such as the Lambeth Conference of bishops of the Anglican Communion, the Lutheran World Federation, the World Alliance of Reformed Churches (Presbyterian and Congregational), the World Methodist Council, and the Baptist World Fellowship.

The larger denominational communities still have responsibility for congregational life, worship, pastoral care, the production of educational materials, and the continuing of the family traditions. The family traditions remain very much alive, and attempts to unite groups across family lines in either liberal or conservative Protestant churches have failed time and again because of strongly held denominational differences. The Consultation on Church Union, so promoted in the 1970s, is merely the most recent example of such failure. The commitment to denominational distinctions provides stability amid shifting perspectives on various social issues and ephemeral ecumenical enthusiasms.

The American Jewish community is the most prominent religious community in America apart from the several Christian groups, and the only community with a continuous presence since the colonial period. In the public sphere, George Washington acknowledged the Jewish presence after the Revolution, and Jewish chaplains served on both sides during the Civil War. During the twentieth century, Jewish rabbis were invited to preside equally with Protestant and Catholic leaders in public religious celebrations, such as Thanksgiving.

New openness toward the Jewish community came in the wake of the Holocaust (a reference to the six million Jews killed in Europe during the Nazi era), the establishment of the state of Israel, and the new position toward the Jewish community articulated by the Roman Catholic Church during the Second Vatican Council. The Vatican statement, promulgated in 1965, refuted a once-popular Christian position that blamed the Jews for Christ's death, and it has created a new basis for Jewish-Christian dialogue. That dialogue has focused on two issues: the Middle East and the evangelization of Jews by Christians. In the last generation, Roman Catholics and liberal Protestants have largely withdrawn support for missionary activities directed toward the Jewish community, but have been most supportive of Palestinians in the Middle East. Evangelical Christians, on the other hand, have continued to increase support for Jewish missionary endeavors, while at the same time supporting the U.S. government's complete backing of Israel.

In the new dialogue, the major speakers for the Jewish community have been the American Jewish Committee and the now-defunct Synagogue Council of America. The former provides a meeting ground for both secular and religious Jews, and the latter represented the different Jewish congregational and rabbinical associations in a manner similar to the NCC. Since the dissolution in the late 1990s of the Synagogue Council, its cooperative voice has been picked up by the North American Board of Rabbis.

Arising to challenge the Jewish position in America, the Islamic community has, since World War II, paralleled the spectacular growth of Methodism after the American Revolution. It now nearly equals the Jewish community in size and has emerged as a potent political force balancing the Jewish-allied support for Israel in public debates on the Middle East. Awareness of the size of the American Islamic community was low until recently because of public images that identified it solely with the Arab world. In fact, the Islamic world stretches from Indonesia through China and India, through the Arab world, and across the African continent. In America, it is strongly represented in the Indo-Pakistani community and has received the additional support of a significant number of black Americans (who now constitute more than 20 percent of its total). Only in the 1970s did impressive mosques (the Islamic houses for prayer and worship) become visible in most American cities.

The Islamic community gained a heightened presence in the American consciousness following the attacks on the World Trade Center and the Pentagon on September 11, 2001, by individuals identified as Muslim extremists. Following an immediate and hostile reaction by Americans toward their Muslim neighbors, a process of getting to know the Muslim community and the life of Muslim believers who also participate in American life has occurred—a process strongly supported by government policy.

Though trends suggest that Islam will soon stand beside Judaism as the second-largest religious community in America, it shows no sign of challenging Christianity in size. However, its growth is taking place within a new understanding of religious pluralism, and Islam's agenda will be taken with increasing seriousness by the general public and politicians, a fact that is already becoming manifest in public statements from both the Christian community and the U.S. government.

The presence of Buddhists and Hindus in significant numbers in America is leading to an additional shift in American religion. Accommodation to the presence of Jews in an otherwise Christian-dominated society was made from an appeal to a shared heritage as the children of Abraham and Moses. Islam is also a product of that heritage. However, Hinduism and Buddhism provide the most complete alternative to the basic perspective of Christianity. Dismissed for many decades as "cults," Hindu and Buddhist groups began to rise above that negative label as large Asian immigrant communities emerged following the change in immigration laws in 1965. Asians can now be found at every level and in every power center in American culture, and they are forcing the encounter of Asian and non-Asian Americans at every level of society.

The Buddhist community matured the quickest. Two signs of that maturity appeared in 1987 with the naming of the first Buddhist chaplain in the armed forces and the formation of the American Buddhist Congress. Operating much like the NCC, the American Buddhist Congress provides a vehicle for Buddhism's engagement with American society, actively works for a more adequate understanding of Buddhists and Buddhism in American life, and gives voice to the Buddhist community's opinions on matters of public policy. Less organized nationally, American Hindus have been represented by a chapter of the Vishwa Hindu Parishad, an international Hindu intrafaith organization, but are in the process of forming additional pan-Hindu organizations without the political identifications of the Vishwa Hindu Parishad.

Not to be forgotten in the massive pluralism so evident in contemporary American life is the continuance and revival of Native American religions and religious traditions. While most Native Americans are now members of Christian churches, the traditional religions were never totally abandoned, and in many tribes a core of people who practice the old religions survives into the present. In the 1970s, along with the spread of numerous young-adult-oriented new religions, a variety of new Native American religions, drawing heavily on traditional themes and traditionalist movements within particular tribes, arose. These new movements have a double importance. Not only have they given new life to traditional faiths, they have produced the first influx of tradi-

tional Native American religion into the white culture. During the 1980s, non–Native Americans who identified with environmental concerns, the occult, and transpersonal psychology found parallel concerns in Native American themes of oneness with the sacred land, shamanism, and the transformative power of Native American rituals.

Besides the large families of religious groups described above, America is home to a number of other diverse religious groups, from the five-million-member Church of Jesus Christ of Latter-day Saints to the small Wicca and Pagan covens of 10 to 15 members. There is also a small but vocal atheist humanist community—the religiously irreligious, so to speak—important far beyond its size because of its strong support within the academic world. While the relative sizes of the individual communities vary, America, and to a lesser extent Canada, have become microcosms of world religion. Every major world religious community is now present in strength. While a majority of Americans have become Christian (and the community as a whole shows no evidence of declining), the climate of mutual respect and honor demanded by pluralism in a free religious society has given the world religions and interfaith issues the highest priority on the agenda of the older Christian bodies, which had until a generation ago largely limited interfaith contact to Jewish-Christian dialogue. The results of this new pluralism are only beginning to be discerned.

SOURCES

Further listings related to each religious family group are given at the end of each chapter. Besides including some of the latest and best general works on American religion, the sources listed below include some of the more prevalent books produced during the past the seventy years.

Albanese, Catherine L. *America: Religions and Religion.* 4th ed. Belmont, CA: Thomson/Wadsworth, 2006. 326 pp.

Baer, Hans, and Merrill Singer. *African American Religion: Varieties of Protest and Accommodation.* 2nd ed. Knoxville: University of Tennessee Press, 2002. 328 pp.

Butler, Jon, Grant Wacker, and Randal Balmer. *Religion in American Life: A Short History.* Rev. ed. New York: Oxford University Press, 2008. 496 pp.

Carmody, John Tully, and Denise Lardner Carmody. *Exploring American Religion.* Mountain View, CA: Mayfield, 1990. 376 pp.

Carroll, Bret E. *The Routledge Historical Atlas of Religion in America.* New York: Routledge, 2000. 143 pp.

Corbett, Julia Mitchell. *Religion in America.* 4th ed. Upper Saddle River, NJ: Prentice-Hall, 1999. 344 pp.

Corrigan, John, and Winthrop S. Hudson. *Religion in America: An Historical Account of the Development of American Religious Life.* 7th ed. Upper Saddle River, NJ: Pearson/Prentice Hall, 2004. 450 pp.

Eck, Diana L. *A New Religious America: How a "Christian Country" Has Become the World's Most Religiously Diverse Nation.* San Francisco: HarperSanFrancisco, 2001. 416 pp.

Forbes, Bruce David, and Jeffrey H. Mahan, eds. *Religion and Popular Culture in America.* Rev. ed. Berkeley: University of California Press, 2005. 339 pp.

Gaustad, Edwin Scott. *Dissent in American Religion.* Rev. ed. Chicago: University of Chicago Press, 2006. 190 pp.

Gaustad, Edwin Scott, and Leigh Schmitt. *A Religious History of America.* Rev. ed. San Francisco: HarperSanFrancisco, 2002. 464 pp.

Gaustad, Edwin Scott, with Mark A. Noll. *A Documentary History of Religion in America.* 3rd ed. 2 vols. Grand Rapids, MI: Eerdmans, 2003.

Griffith, R. Marie. *American Religions: A Documentary History.* New York: Oxford University Press, 2007. 672 pp.

Handy, Robert T. *A Christian America: Protestant Hopes and Historical Realities.* 2nd ed. New York: Oxford University Press, 1984. 269 pp.

Hutchinson, William R. *The Modernist Impulse in American Protestantism.* Cambridge, MA: Harvard University Press, 1976. 347 pp.

Johnson, Douglas W., Paul R. Packard, and Bernard Quinn. *Churches and Church Membership in the United States: An Enumeration by Region, State, and County, 1971.* Washington, DC: Glenmary Research Center, 1974. 237 pp.

Johnson, Paul E., ed. *African American Christianity: Essays in History.* Berkeley: University of California Press, 1994. 189 pp.

Marsden, George M. *Religion and American Culture.* 2nd ed. Fort Worth, TX: Harcourt, 2000. 337 pp.

———. *Fundamentalism and American Culture.* 2nd ed. Oxford: Oxford University Press, 2006. 351 pp.

Marty, Martin E., ed. *Our Faiths.* Royal Oak, MI: Cathedral, 1975. 236 pp.

———. *Pilgrims in Their Own Land: Five Hundred Years of Religion in America.* Boston: Little, Brown, 1984. 500 pp.

———. *Protestantism in the United States.* New York: Scribner's, 1986. 290 pp.

Mead, Sidney E. *The Lively Experiment: The Shaping of Christianity in America.* New York: Harper & Row, 1963. 220 pp.

———. *The Nation with the Soul of a Church.* New York: Harper & Row, 1975. 158 pp.

Melton, J. Gordon. *Religious Leaders of America.* 2nd ed. Detroit, MI: Gale, 1999. 724 pp.

———. *American Religions: An Illustrated History.* Santa Barbara, CA: ABC-Clio, 2000. 316 pp.

———. *A Will to Choose: The Origins of African American Methodism.* Lanham, MD: Rowman and Littlefield, 2006. 315 pp.

———. *Nelson's Guide to Denominations.* Nashville, TN: Thomas Nelson, 2007. 620 pp.

Morris, Richard R. *Encyclopedia of American History.* New York: Harper & Brothers, 1953. 776 pp.

Moyer, Elgin S., with Earle Cairns. *The Wycliffe Biographical Dictionary of the Church.* Chicago: Moody Press, 1982. 449 pp.

Murphy, Larry G., Jr., J. Gordon Melton, and Gary L. Ward, eds. *Encyclopedia of African American Religions.* New York: Garland, 1993. 926 pp.

Myers, Gustavus. *History of Bigotry in the United States* (1943). New York: Capricorn, 1960. 474 pp.

Noll, Mark, et al., eds. *Eerdmans' Handbook to Christianity in America.* Grand Rapids, MI: Eerdmans, 1983. 507 pp.

Noll, Mark A., and Luke E. Harlow. *Religion and American Politics: From the Colonial Period to the Present.* 2nd ed. New York: Oxford University Press, 2007. 520 pp.

Penn, Anthony B. *The African American Religious Experience in America.* Gainesville: University Press of Florida, 2007. 384 pp.

Piepkorn, Arthur C. *Profiles in Belief: The Religious Bodies of the United States and Canada.* 3 vols. New York: Harper & Row, 1977–1979.

Quinn, Bernard, et al., eds. *Churches and Church Membership in the United States, 1980: An Enumeration by Region, State, and County, Based on Data Reported by 111 Church Bodies.* Atlanta, GA: Glenmary Research Center, 1982. 321 pp.

Smith, H. Shelton, Robert T. Handy, and Lefferts A. Loetscher. *American Christianity: An Historical Interpretation with Representative Documents.* 2 vols. New York: Scribner's, 1960.

Sweet, William Warren. *Religion in Colonial America.* New York: Scribner's, 1942. 367 pp.

———. *The Story of Religion in America.* 2nd ed. New York: Harper, 1950. 656 pp.

Wentz, Richard E. *Religion in the New World: The Shaping of Religious Traditions in the United States.* Minneapolis, MN: Fortress Press, 1990. 370 pp.

Williams, Peter. *America's Religions: Traditions and Culture.* New York: Macmillan, 1990. 478 pp.

———. *America's Religions: From Their Origins to the Twenty-first Century.* 3rd ed. Urbana: University of Illinois Press, 2008. 800 pp.

Religion in Canada:
A Historical Survey, 1500 to the Present

THE INITIAL CONQUEST OF CANADA: NATIVE AMERICANS IN CANADA. For centuries before the invasion and conquest by Europeans of what is today known as Canada, the vast territory was, like the United States, inhabited by many native tribes. The population density was not great, there being an estimated 220,000 persons living in Canada in 1500. The tribes that inhabited the shores of the St. Lawrence River, such as the Huron, were most affected by the first European settlements, but eventually almost every tribe felt the impact of European culture and governmental rule. The establishment of the dominance of the European settlers did away with the self-sufficient cultures of the Indians and eventually made them dependent on the larger resources developed by the newly arrived Europeans.

While much of the religious life of the tribes was either destroyed or transformed as tribal members responded to Christian missionary efforts, the story of North American Indian religion, especially as it continues in its contemporary forms, is integral to the story of Canadian religion. As with the Native Indian tribes in what is now the United States, the Indians of Canada exhibited a significant variation of religious belief and practice, from the Huron and Algonquin in the east, to the Blackfoot of the plains, to the Eskimo of the Arctic reaches, to the Kwakiutl and the other tribes of British Columbia known so widely for their totem poles. Native Canadians also shared with Native Americans the characteristic of integrating religion into their tribal self-identity and survival. Because of the harsher climate, the religion of the Canadian Indians reflected their ties to the land and the needs of survival even more than was the case with tribes farther south.

The initial settlement of Europeans in Canada in the 1600s had its primary impact on the tribes of the St. Lawrence Valley. Both the Huron and the Iroquois became entangled in the wars of the British and French for control of Canada, and were the target of missionary activities. The first Jesuits arrived in 1611, and many of them worked among the Huron and Iroquois. It is also among these tribes, quite apart from the missionaries, that the most destructive influence of the European intrusion became manifest. The Jesuits became trapped in the war that developed between the two tribes over the supply of beaver fur, which was being rapidly exhausted through the early decades of the seventeenth century. The Indians had become dependent on the European goods that they purchased with fur. In the resultant hostilities, the Huron were annihilated.

With the exception of a few European traders who began to enter the interior of Canada, the majority of Canadian Indians did not have to deal with whites until the nineteenth or even the twentieth century. The British initiated the penetration of the west through fur-trading companies that established settlements along the coast of Hudson Bay. During the 1700s, traders began the serious push inland that led to the fur companies' control of the western half of Canada, a situation that persisted until the fur traders gave way to the new Dominion of Canada in the last half of the nineteenth century.

After the French era, as European Canadians moved into Indian lands and gradually took possession of most of them, the level of hostilities proved to be far lower than in the United States. Canada established a pattern of making treaties with the Indians that included land grants and, with few exceptions, honoring those treaties. Canada also pursued a policy of punishing violations of the treaties by non-Indians.

The relatively peaceful nature of the long-term relationship between the Canadian government and the Indian tribes allowed for the development of Christian missions and the conversion of the majority of Indians to Christianity. The Roman Catholic Church, the Anglican Church, and the churches now comprising the United Church of Canada all developed strong missions, especially in western Canada. On the other hand, traditional Indian religions have survived and can be found among tribes in all sections of the country.

Especially notable among the surviving tribal religions of Canada are the Eskimo religions, which had been dominated by shamans, the ubiquitous leaders in Eskimo religious matters. The shamans, much like modern mediums, entered a trance state, during which they allowed various spirits to take possession of their consciousness and use their body to speak and dance. Integral to the shaman's work, and characteristic of shamanism as compared to common mediumship, was soul *flight*, in which the shaman was believed to send his or her soul to the spirit realm on some errand, such as obtaining advice on an important question that had arisen in the tribe.

The practice of shamanism was also seen as integral to the survival of Eskimo tribes, for which starvation was a frequent problem. Eskimo shamans would predict (and even try to control) the weather and the supply of game. They would send their souls to placate a goddess such as Sedna, believed to control the sea mammals, or to locate the caribou and entice its appearance for the hunters. It was their job to spot violations of taboos that were believed to inhibit the luck of the hunt. They also attempted to improve fertility in the tribe using their special powers to aid infertile females. The practice of shamanism has been significantly limited by the inroads of Christianity, secular education, and the modern technological world in general. Its future is unclear, given the current rebirth of shamanism in other areas of the culture.

THE ARRIVAL OF EUROPEANS IN CANADA.

Most historians assume that the first sighting of North America by a European occurred around 986 C.E. when Bjarni Herjulfson and his crew of Norse sailors were blown off course while sailing in the waters off Greenland. Some 15 years later, Leif Eriksson explored the coast of North America, though scholars disagree as to the exact area described in the early accounts of his trips. Several other voyages followed, but scholarly knowledge of the full extent of Norse exploration has been hindered by the production of a number of fraudulent artifacts purporting to be relics of Norse explorers.

For the purposes of later history, however, the exploration of Canada began with the arrival of John Cabot (c. 1450–1499) off Newfoundland in the summer of 1497. Cabot was followed by other explorers looking for the Northwest Passage, as well as French ships that began exploitation of the fishing grounds off Newfoundland. Both the British and French established early claims to Canadian territory. Then, in 1534, Jacques Cartier (1491–1557) arrived at the mouth of the St. Lawrence River to confirm the claim on New France made by Giovanni da Verrazano (c. 1485–1527) in 1523. Further British claims to present-day Canada would be delayed until the 1570s and the three voyages of Martin Frobisher (c. 1535–1594), followed by John Davis (c. 1550–1605), George Weymouth, and John Knight (d. 1606).

During the sixteenth century, the economic pursuits of the explorers and their financial backers overrode any religious goals that might have been expressed for the New World that was being discovered. The first settlers were not particularly religious people. Nevertheless, both Roman Catholicism and Anglicanism were introduced, though no permanent structures were created. Cartier included among his crew a priest who celebrated the first mass in Canada when the ship docked at Gaspe Peninsula. Anglican services were first held by a Master Wolfall, chaplain on Frobisher's third voyage. The first communion service in Canada, according to the rite of the Church of England, was held in 1578 in Baffinland. During the sixteenth century, French efforts were concentrated on the St. Lawrence Valley, to be joined by the British settlement of Newfoundland after Frobisher's voyages.

In the late 1500s, the French settled and began to develop the trading business in the St. Lawrence. Though the companies were responsible for supplying and supporting Roman Catholic priests in their Canadian centers, they did little to further the cause of religion during the remaining years of the sixteenth century. One must look to England for the public emergence of the religious impulse. In 1583 Sir Humphrey Gilbert (c. 1539–1583) was sent to claim Newfoundland for England, and in the establishment of the colony he proclaimed that worship according to the Church of England should prevail. However, he was lost at sea on his return voyage home, and the colony soon dissolved.

Finally, early in the seventeenth century, a permanent religious structure was created with the founding first of Acadie (1603–1613) in Nova Scotia and subsequently of Quebec (1608) by Samuel de Champlain (c. 1570–1635). Champlain not only introduced Roman Catholic worship into his settlements, but seems to have been the first forcefully to articulate the desire to convert the indigenous residents of the surrounding lands. To that end, in 1615 he introduced the Roman Catholic Order of Recollects (one of several Franciscan orders), and when they proved ineffective, in 1625 he invited the Jesuits to begin work. Arriving with the first wave of Jesuits was Father Jean de Brèbeuf (1593–1649), who authored a number of reports that provide some of the best observations on French Canada during the 15 years between the first report and Brèbeuf's death by torture in 1649 at the hands of those he was attempting to convert. During Brèbeuf's Canadian career, the French territory expanded, new towns such as Montreal (1642) were founded, and more priests arrived (the Sulpicians joined the first two orders in the 1640s).

The success of the Catholic missionaries was demonstrated clearly in 1659 when François de Montmorency-Laval (1623–1708) was appointed vicar apostolic for Canada. That appointment was connected to the increased interest in New France expressed by King Louis XIV (1638–1715), who designated the region an official colony by royal decree four years later. Further growth of the church led to Laval being named the first bishop of Quebec in 1674.

The unfruitful Protestant efforts to colonize Canada continued in the 1600s, when a group of Danish Lutherans established a short-lived settlement on Hudson Bay. Their minister was among the first settlers to die of scurvy, which ravaged the colony shortly after it was settled. Meanwhile, under James I (1566–1625), the British renewed their interest in Canada. In 1610 James issued a charter for a colony in Newfoundland. John Gay of Bristol responded by establishing a "plantation" on Conception Bay, and in 1627 brought Erasmus Stourton (1603–1658), an Anglican priest, to the colony. Stourton thus became the first resident non–Roman Catholic clergyman to reside in Canada. Stourton remained in Canada for 15 years, his stay being made possible by the charter for Scottish (Presbyterian) settlement issued by James I (1622) on the lands formerly settled by the ill-fated colony in Acadie. The new colony, however, was no sooner established on a permanent basis than war broke out between France and England. In the treaty settling the conflict in 1632, Nova Scotia was returned to France and the settlers moved to Newfoundland. In 1633 King Charles I (1600–1649) chartered the colony of Newfoundland and decreed in the document that worship according to the prayer book of the Church of England should be conducted (by ship's officers in the absence of clergymen) each Sunday.

THE BRITISH ERA IN CANADA: THE END OF FRENCH DOMINANCE.

During the rest of the century, both British and French colonization of Canada continued, though the French expansion into the upper reaches of the St. Lawrence and Great Lakes region far outstripped British efforts. As colonization proceeded, British and French Canadians also found themselves in ongoing conflict as the worldwide interests of their home countries continually overlapped. The intermittent hostile actions periodically disrupted their lives and altered the development of Canada. During the seventeenth century, the French were able to continue their expansion in spite of the conflict, but after 1698 the trend of world events began to favor the British in Canada. In that year, the Anglican Society for the Promotion of Christian Knowledge began to actively support the Reverend John Jackson (d. 1717), the minister in St. John's, Newfoundland (and the only Church of England priest in the territory). Three years later, the society turned its commitment over to a new missionary organization, the Society for the Propagation of the Gospel (SPG), which began to send missionaries into Canada. The British position and that of the Church of England were greatly improved in 1713 when the Treaty of Utrecht ended French-British hostilities for a generation. The British moved to build and consolidate their strength in Canada.

The beginning of the end of French power can be more clearly seen with the reopening of war in 1744. Britain's successful action against the French stronghold of Louisburg in Nova Scotia, and its subsequent return with the peace treaty signed in 1748, forced the British to further strengthen their position in Nova Scotia. In 1749 they founded the city of Halifax as a military stronghold to counter Louisburg. The establishment of Halifax became a signal event in Canadian religious history, for it was here that the religious patterns that dominated subsequent Canadian history initially became apparent. Immediately after the founding of the community, non–Roman Catholic Christianity in all of its variety emerged in eastern Canada.

Responding to government action, the SPG promised six ministers and six schoolmasters to Halifax, and shortly after their arrival, on June 13, 1750, the foundation stone of St. Paul's Church was laid. (Today's St. Paul's congregation worships in the oldest church building in Canada.) And, since King George II (1683–1760) of England was also king of Hanover, he encouraged his German subjects to emigrate. German Lutherans became a significant percentage of the early population of the new town, and they erected St. George's Lutheran Church. A German Reformed congregation also arose, and St. Matthew's Church (which served both Congregationalists and Presbyterians and was filled by British subjects from Ireland, Scotland, and New England) rounded out the religious life of the community.

The stabilization of life in Halifax was accomplished just as war returned. In 1755 the British moved against Acadie and removed the French settlers (an episode later immortalized in Henry Wadsworth Longfellow's 1847 poem "Evangeline: A Tale of Acadie"). In 1758 Louisburg fell, and the following year Quebec fell. With the capture of Quebec, the British effectively ended French control of Canada, though further action continued into the next year. Following the fall of Quebec, the first Anglican service in the city was conducted in the chapel of the Ursuline Convent by a former Roman Catholic priest, Michel Houdin, chaplain for the British forces.

UNDER BRITISH RULE.

The Treaty of Paris of 1763, which made official the accomplishments of the war, also necessitated the altering of relations between the French Canadians and the now-hostile government. While the treaty guaranteed religious freedom, the British government moved to replace the Roman bishop with an Anglican one and to subvert the stability of the Catholic community by sending all the children to Anglican schools. When a new bishop was selected, the government refused to permit his consecration. The property of the Recollects and the Jesuits was confiscated, and both orders, as well as the Sulpicians, were forbidden to receive new members from abroad. This trend was reversed in 1774 when the Act of Quebec granted a high degree of tolerance. Local suspicion toward the Catholic community lessened when the French not only refused to support American efforts to gain them as allies during the American Revolution (1775–1783), but joined efforts to repel an attempted invasion by the rebels.

Meanwhile, as soon as the war ended, more Protestant groups made their way to Canada, though most came not to the newly conquered territory but to the Maritime Provinces, where so many Protestant firsts occurred. The first truly Presbyterian church in Canada was founded at Londonderry, Nova Scotia, in 1761 by a group of Irish Presbyterian immigrants. The growth of both Congregationalism and Presbyterianism throughout the decade led in 1770 to a unique occurrence brought about by the inability of the German Reformed congregation in Halifax to obtain a minister from Pennsylvania. They decided to ordain one of their own members, Bruin Romkes Comingo (1723–1820), after two Congregationalist ministers joined two Presbyterian ministers to constitute a presbytery for purposes of the ordination.

Around 1760, the first Baptists arrived to take possession of land abandoned by the Acadians. The arrival of the small Baptist community in Nova Scotia coincided with the expansion of the Congregationalists, both groups migrating from New England. Many of the Congregationalists were partial to the Newlight position, which accepted the theology and practices of the Great Awakening. Many Newlights found themselves more at home with the Baptists than with their more staid Oldlight Congregationalists. The issue was raised by Henry Alline (1748–1784), a talented Newlight preacher who forced a division among Congregationalists. Alline had an eccentric theology, but this was obscured by his preoccupation with revivalism and his evangelical fervor. Alline's followers soon drifted into the Baptist camp and provided the initial substance out of which a significant Canadian Baptist church would emerge.

Finally, around 1775, as Alline's influence was reaching its peak, the first Methodists appeared from among a group of Cornish immigrants in Nova Scotia. William Black Jr. (1760–1834) later emerged as their leader and traveled the communities of the province both establishing Methodism and opposing Alline. After the American Revolution, Black looked to Methodists in the United States for assistance. He traveled to Maryland in 1784 to attend the organizational session of the Methodist Episcopal Church. For a number of years, he attached himself to the American church, by which he was eventually ordained, and from which he was assigned assistants to extend his missionary endeavors. Eventually, however, the Canadians grew to resent American leadership, and Black turned to the Wesleyan Methodists in England, who accepted responsibility for the now-growing work.

Of more than passing interest was the development in Nova Scotia of both Methodist and Baptist work among Africans. During the American Revolution, many African Americans, most former slaves, were promised freedom and a stake if they remained loyal to Britain. After losing the war, the British transported many of these African people to Nova Scotia, particularly to towns along the southeastern coast. Among them were both Baptist and Methodist preachers, who led the congregations formed in the several African Canadian communities. William Black regularly visited the Methodists. Over the next few years, the Africans waited on the British government, which never gave them the promised stake. Finally, British abolitionists raised the money to transport them to Freetown, Sierra Leone, where they became the seed from which the Baptist and Methodist churches of that country were to grow.

In the generation after the founding of Halifax, the major religious pattern to be developed in the next centuries of Canadian history was established. The Church of England (or the Anglican Church) and those Protestant churches introduced into Nova Scotia during the 1750s and 1760s joined the Roman Catholic Church in creating a dominant consensus in Canadian religious life and thus initiated the major factor in the emerging Canadian religious story. Any account of Canadian religion must center on the movement of the Roman Catholics, Anglicans, Presbyterians, Congregationalists, Methodists, Lutherans, and Baptists in their efforts to church the sprawling nation, on their successes and failures in relating to one another, and on their ability to adjust to the growing ethnic and religious pluralism of twentieth-century Canadian life. The focus on these groups does not deny or diminish the important contributions of the hundreds of other Canadian religious groups. It merely recognizes that due to the simple appeal of these groups to the masses of Canadian citizens, they set the pace to which the others had to relate.

At least two other groups found their way into Canada during this initial period and opened their own niches in the religious community. As early as 1762, American Quakers arrived in Nova Scotia from Nantucket, Rhode Island. Though their original effort to settle did not last many years, it heralded a more permanent Quaker thrust into Canada a few years later. Second, the missionary-minded Moravian Church, directing their attention farther north, arrived in Canada in 1771 when missionary Jens Haven (1724–1796) established work in Nain, Labrador. The Moravians pioneered both Christian missionary and educational work among the Eskimo population. While never extensive, it was the forerunner of later efforts.

THE SETTLEMENT OF LOWER AND UPPER CANADA (QUEBEC AND ONTARIO). Even as the settlement and development of the church in Nova Scotia and the Maritime Provinces proceeded, the new British administration had to deal with the 70,000 French-speaking residents living in Canada proper, over which they now had governmental control. The British showed every intent of replacing Roman Catholic authority with the complete establishment of the Church of England. They confiscated the properties of the Jesuits and Recollects and forbade all orders to accept novices, and they initiated plans to educate all Catholic children in Anglican schools. Loyal Catholics in both Canada and France registered their opposition in every way possible. Assisted by the unrest in the colonies to the south, a decade of protest met with measurable success. Not needing a second revolt on their hands, the British moved to pacify the French by passing the Quebec Act of 1774. Although it returned some measure of religious toleration to the Catholic community, antagonism continued for many years while the Church of England pursued other means of cutting into Catholic support. However, the Roman Catholic community continued to grow, and by 1784 it numbered 130,000, aided substantially by the immigration of Catholics from the Highlands of Scotland during this period.

Though the British took control of eastern Canada and the St. Lawrence River Valley in 1763, growth of the Church of England was slow, at least for several decades. The colonies to the south attracted more immigrants from Europe due to the warmer climate. Thus a population favorable to Anglicanism did not arrive in great numbers until after the American Revolution sent waves of Loyalists north to escape rebel rule. Most of these were Loyalist Protestants, and many were Anglicans. The growth provided by the Loyalists justified the establishment of the first see for British North America, and Charles Inglis (1734–1816) was consecrated as the first bishop in 1787 with his seat in Halifax, Nova Scotia. Six years later, Jacob Mountain (1749–1825) was consecrated as the first bishop of Canada, with his seat in Quebec City.

Faced with the continued resistance of the French Canadians to proselytizing actions and to ensure that they remained peaceful and loyal British subjects, the Parliament in England passed the Constitutional Act of 1791. It divided Canada by setting off Upper Canada (Quebec), where most of the French lived, from Lower Canada (Ontario), where most of the British lived. Ontario was just beginning to receive the first waves of Loyalists. Each province had a separate parliament but was administratively under a single governor-in-chief. Important for the churches, the legislation also set aside land for the support of the clergy of the Church of England and made specific provisions for the support of Anglican clergy and the construction of rectories. The provisions of the 1791 act greatly assisted the Anglican Church in its spread and development across Canada. Parishes were established, churches and schools erected, and new ministries initiated. While not leading to success in Quebec, the expansion of the church in Ontario was demonstrated by the necessity of placing a bishop in Toronto in 1839. Government support undoubtedly gave the Anglicans an immense advantage for several decades, but also seriously hindered the church's long-term development. The bishop's attempt to administer the Canadian church's affairs from England discouraged local development of active lay commitment. Thus, when the government withdrew financial support several generations later, the church had to quickly create a new ecclesiastical structure equipped to mobilize member loyalty and voluntary financial support.

Lower Canada, now known as Ontario, was soon to become the most densely populated section of Canada, and religiously the most diverse. The Loyalists brought with them the great variety of religions previously established in the American colonies. And, as Lower Canada was opened, new settlers directly from the British Isles brought the profusion of sects that arose as Protestant dissenters proliferated both in numbers and factions.

Presbyterians were among the most numerous of the new settlers. As early as 1791, Presbyterian congregations started by American ministers had formed on the Niagara Peninsula and by 1833 had founded the Niagara Presbytery. Growth was assisted by the movement into the church of many former Congregationalists. They were soon joined by immigrants directly from Scotland who established congregational outposts of the Church of Scotland and of the dissenting groups that had been created through protests over the loyalty oath and the church's patronage system. Each group established its own synod, leaving the Presbyterians with the task of reconciling their differences, most of which were nondoctrinal and irrelevant to the Canadian environment.

Methodism, having gotten its Canadian start in Nova Scotia, found a second unrelated beginning in Lower Canada in the settlements of the war veterans in the 1780s. In 1791 Methodist Bishop Francis Asbury (1745–1816) directed Reverend William Losee (1757–1832) from New York to go to Lower Canada, where he oversaw the construction of the first Methodist chapel in the region on Paul Huff's farm near the Bay of Quinte. Most influential in the development of the church were the Ryersons, originally an Anglican family who settled near Lake Erie in 1799. The sons all became Methodists, and Egerton Ryerson (1803–1882), in particular, manifested an ability as an educator and apologist for the family's new faith, as they became frequent targets of Anglican critics. Originally trained for the legal profession,

Egerton Ryerson joined the ministry in the 1820s and rose to prominence as the first editor of the Methodist periodical *The Christian Guardian*. Among his many accomplishments, he fought to break the hold of the Anglicans on university education, and eventually became the first principal of Victoria College.

The original work of the Methodists in Lower Canada occurred under the care of the Methodist Episcopal Church, which had been organized in the United States in 1784. During the early nineteenth century, Methodists from the several factions in England—the Wesleyans, the Primitive Methodists, and the Bible Christians—established competitive work and taunted those who were still attached to the disloyal former colonies. The War of 1812 demonstrated the problem of any church organization attempting to hold a membership across the American-Canadian border. After the war, Canadian Methodists initiated a break with their American comrades, and merged with the British Wesleyan Connection in 1833.

Because of the very visible support for the colonists by prominent Congregationalist ministers in the American Revolution, the equally important existence of many Congregationalist Loyalists is frequently overlooked. While most of these Loyalists left the United States via the short sea route from New England to Nova Scotia, by the first decade of the 1800s Congregationalist groups emerged in Quebec among settlers who simply walked across the border from Vermont. The greatest Congregationalist expansion occurred during the ministry of Henry Wilkes (1805–1886), for more than fifty years the pastor of a church in Montreal. He established Canadian ties with British Congregationalists and received funds from the London Missionary Society for the establishment of congregations in both Upper and Lower Canada. Wilkes did much to change the negative image of Congregationalists, whose identification with the Revolution had caused many of their number to become Presbyterians.

Lutherans led a migration of people of German background into Canada in the late eighteenth century. The Lutherans were accompanied in their migrations by members of other German groups, with whom they had to compete to gain and even hold members. While many of these settlers were dedicated to keeping the German language alive, the inevitable process of assimilation took its toll, and they lost members to the English-speaking Anglicans and the evangelistically oriented Methodists. The first wave of Lutherans, war veterans, received grants of land in Dundas, Lennox, and Addington counties in the 1780s. A decade later, responding to an invitation for Germans to settle in Ontario, a group of unhappy New York residents received a grant of 64,000 acres, upon which the town of Markham was built.

In spite of their early and continued establishment of new congregations throughout the first half of the nineteenth century, the Lutherans suffered from a dire lack of clerical leadership and a resultant isolation of one organization from another. Only in the middle of the century, as Lutherans in the Synod of Pittsburgh learned of the state of the Ontario Lutherans, were qualified ministers sent to their aid. A Canadian Conference was finally created in 1853.

Baptists entered Upper and Lower Canada in three waves, the first coming into the Niagara area just as the Revolution commenced. Baptists filtered into Quebec in the 1790s and were joined in 1815 by a group migrating from Scotland. Once settled, the Baptists spread quickly. An association formed in 1816 became the precursor of many more. However, the Baptists were hesitant to unite in larger efforts beyond the associational level. Inherently independent, they were further divided over the question of the admission of non-Baptists to communion. Only in 1851, when the issue of the disposal of the government's clergy reserves (in which the Baptists by principle never participated) became significant, did the Baptists finally form the Regular Baptist Missionary Convention of Canada West.

MORE NEW CHURCHES. During the initial settlement of Lower Canada, various new church groups were introduced into the country. The encouragement of German immigration, for example, brought not only Lutherans but Mennonites and United Brethren as well. The first Mennonites came into the Niagara Peninsula in 1786, and during the next three decades approximately 2,000 migrated into Ontario. Many were a part of the predominantly Lutheran settlement at Markham. Others founded Ebytown, now the city of Kitchener. In 1824 the first congregation of Amish settled in Waterloo County.

Early in the nineteenth century, Germans from two groups heavily influenced by the Methodists—the United Brethren in Christ and the Evangelical Association—began to preach and build churches among the German-speaking settlements. In 1816 John Dreisbach (1789–1871) of the Evangelical Association traveled in Ontario, but he did not establish any congregations. However, four years earlier, United Brethren had been among German immigrants who moved from Pennsylvania into the Waterloo area. By 1825 a circuit had been established, and the Ontario Conference was created in 1856. Permanent Evangelical Association work had an unusual beginning. Several Waterloo families who had returned to the United States encountered association members in Ohio. Informed of the Canadian situation, ministers began to travel to Chippewa and the Waterloo area, and later to other German-speaking communities. The first German-language Sunday school in Canada was founded by Evangelical Association ministers in what is now Kitchener.

Among the migrants into Lower Canada after the Revolution were members of the Church of the Brethren, a pacifist group. The Brethren did not assume any permanent presence, however, as some of the families soon returned to the United States.

The great movement to church the western United States (then the area from the Appalachians to the Mississippi River), usually termed the Second Great Awakening, spawned several new denominations, among them the Christian Church (Disciples of Christ). Very soon after its formation,

this highly evangelical group, loosely organized and, except for a few peculiar emphases, doctrinally close to the Baptists, moved into Canada. In 1807 Thomas Campbell (1763–1854) formed the first rudimentary organization, the Christian Association, and by 1810 work had spread to the Maritime Provinces. A few years later, centers could be found at Poplar Hill and Norval in Upper Canada.

During the first half of the nineteenth century, Ontario also became home to a number of groups that had broken from the mainstream of the Western Christian tradition. Most of these groups were imported from the United States, where they had originally emerged. As early as 1832, Unitarians under the leadership of Benjamin Workman (1794–1878) began to gather in Montreal. His efforts would become the basis for a strong congregation, but not before he had moved on to Toronto, where in 1845 he formed the first Unitarian congregation in Canada. While the Church of Jesus Christ of Latter-day Saints did not move into Canada in a substantial fashion until late in the century, it did make an important incursion in 1842. Missionaries in Toronto that year converted John Taylor (1808–1887). Taylor left Toronto for Nauvoo, Illinois, and became a close associate of Mormon leader Joseph Smith Jr. (1805–1844). Taylor, who was one of the two men to survive the attack in which Smith was murdered, eventually became president of the church. He is remembered today as one of the last Mormon leaders to vigorously defend the practice of polygamy.

THE JEWISH PRESENCE IN CANADA TO 1850. Though an occasional Jew will make a brief appearance at odd moments in Canadian history, the French ban on Jews in New France served to keep them out of Canada until the middle of the eighteenth century. In 1749 a small group of Sephardic Jews (of Spanish-Portuguese origin) organized in Halifax and bought a cemetery, but their community was short-lived. A decade later, Samuel Jacobs, who settled near Montreal, became the first of a number of prominent Jewish merchants in Upper and Lower Canada. He was joined the next year by Samuel Hart (d. 1810), who established his headquarters in Three Rivers. As other Jews arrived, several of whom prospered in business, Congregation Shearith Israel, modeled on the congregation of the same name in New York City, was formed. Though most of the members were of English background (and thus would seem to favor the Ashkenazic worship forms), they adopted the Sephardic ritual of their New York brethren, and in 1777 they erected a building. Congregation Shearith Israel was one of two Canadian synagogues during the next several generations. Records also speak of the "Hart synagogue" in Three Rivers. By 1825 there were still fewer than 100 Jews in Canada. This lack of members did not keep them in 1828 from petitioning for full recognition as a religious community (which would allow them to maintain their own records of births, marriages, and deaths), which was granted the next year. In 1832 Canadian Jews were granted equal rights as British subjects (which removed any barriers to their holding public office or serving as officers in the military), a privilege not granted British Jews until 1858.

Though still small in comparison to the total population, the Jewish population in Upper Canada grew perceptibly during the middle nineteenth century. A Jewish community emerged in Toronto in the 1840s. Following a general pattern in new Jewish communities, first, in 1849 a cemetery was purchased, and then a congregation, the Sons of Israel, was organized in 1856. In 1859 a second congregation, following the Ashkenazic ritual, was opened in Montreal. By 1860 there were approximately 1,200 Jews in Canada.

THE CANADIAN ERA BEGINS: MIDCENTURY CHANGES.

During the mid-nineteenth century, the major issue affecting all Christian churches in Canada was the changing relationship between the Canadian government and the Anglican Church. By the action of the British government in the decades after the fall of Quebec, the Church of England became the established church of Canada. By law and with the backing of public funds, worship and education in the tradition of the Church of England were developed, encouraged, and maintained. Canada's ministers were directly responsible to the Lord Bishop of London. In 1787 the British Crown appointed the first bishop for British North America, and the governors of Nova Scotia and Quebec were given orders to assist him in the exercise of his jurisdictional duties. The church, in spite of local episcopal authority, remained in a missionary situation and developed no synodical structures.

In 1791, integral to the action that separated the region into Upper and Lower Canada, the government set aside lands for the support of the clergy and the church. As the church expanded, the government provided revenue to create new dioceses and appoint bishops. Decade by decade, however, forces grew in favor of unifying the separated Canadian provinces into a single governmental entity under a form of home rule that would be largely autonomous of England without breaking completely with the empire. The growing autonomy in the Canadian government forced significant shifts in the relations between the Anglican Church in Canada, the Church of England, and the governments. The crux of the changes centered on the disposition of the clergy reserves.

Vocal opposition to the 1791 provisions for clergy land grants had arisen from the beginning. Secular interests demanded the use of the revenues from the lands (which consisted of some 2.5 million acres) for other purposes, such as nonsectarian public education. Churches joined the battle from their varying perspectives. Some opposed the unfair advantage given the Anglicans (especially the Presbyterians, who wanted their share in light of their establishment in Scotland), while some, such as the Canadian branch of the Free Church of Scotland, opposed government support of churches on principle. The Anglicans were heavily dependent on these lands, which directly supplemented financial support from the church in England and the Society for the Propagation of the Gospel, the foreign missionary structure

of the Church of England. The loss to the church would be significant. By midcentury, however, it was clear that the loss would occur, and in 1853 all of the clergy land reserves in Canada were secularized. The drawn-out battle over the clergy reserves had also created an unwanted side effect for the Anglicans. By focusing opposition on the Anglican's favored status, the issue united the Protestant churches against the Church of England in Canada.

Financial concerns thrust a second issue on the Canadian Anglicans: the development of self-government. Because of their status as a missionary arm of the Church of England, the Anglicans in Canada had not been free to develop internally. Each diocese worked as a separate unit, directly responsible to authorities in England. In 1851, as the land reserves issue was reaching a climax, five of the seven Canadian bishops met and called for the creation of a province of Canada under a metropolitan (archbishop) and the formation of diocesan synods that would include lay participation. These new structures would facilitate the transformation of the church into a voluntary association that relied on its own membership for its major financial support. The first synod, that of the Diocese of Toronto, met in 1857. Four years later, the bishop of Montreal was appointed metropolitan of the Canadian province, and an initial provincial synod was held for what was termed the Church of England in Canada. The province did not include Manitoba and the territories to the west, which developed as a separate province, as did British Columbia. Eventually, in 1893, the several provinces were united into an autonomous General Synod under a Primate of All Canada. Thus, by the end of the century, the Anglicans in Canada had emerged as another independent member of the developing worldwide Anglican Communion.

RELIGION MOVES INTO THE CANADIAN WEST: WHERE IS RUPERT'S LAND?

Chartered in 1670, the Hudson's Bay Company had been given exclusive rights to the land north and west of Ontario. During the last half of the nineteenth century, the company's monopoly collided with the needs of Canada for expanded territory. Land was becoming scarce, immigration was increasing, and population was exploding. At the same time, a new sense of Canadian nationalism emerged with some degree of support from the British homeland. The completion in 1869 of the transcontinental railroad across the United States merely highlighted the advantages of such a railroad across Canada.

Thus, in 1867, when the four Canadian provinces (Ontario, Quebec, Newfoundland, and the Maritime) united in a confederation, they immediately looked west. In 1870 the confederation took in Rupert's Land, today known as Manitoba, and in 1871, on the condition that a transcontinental railroad be built, it added British Columbia. Railroad construction began soon afterward, and the line to Winnipeg was finished in 1881. It took only four more years to complete the track to the Pacific Coast. Though Alberta and Saskatchewan would not become provinces until 1905, the completion of the railroad effectively opened them to massive immigration. The older churches, which had already established initial centers, quickly moved in with the new immigrants, and just as importantly, numerous new religious groups found a home in the newly opened territory.

In 1812 Thomas Douglas, the fifth earl of Selkirk (1771–1820), with the cooperation of the Hudson's Bay Company, founded Kildonan, a community of Scottish immigrants, on the Red River near present-day Winnipeg. In order to protect the settlers from the rival North West Company, he hired German mercenaries. Concerned for the religious life of the soldiers, many of whom were Roman Catholic, he requested a priest, and in 1818 the Diocese of Quebec sent Father Joseph-Norbert Provencher (1787–1853). Besides serving the immediate community, he began to expand work to neighboring sites and to Indian and Eskimo missions. He soon received the aid of the Oblates of Mary, who took special responsibility for the missionary work. The growth of the work initiated by Provencher led in 1844 to his being named vicar apostolic, and in 1847 he became the first bishop of St. Boniface (Manitoba). During the first half of the nineteenth century, Provencher provided the foundation for Roman Catholic expansion in western Canada through the conversion of the native population, the immigration of Catholics from around the world, and the recruitment of members from among the new (but previously non-Catholic) settlers.

Anglican work in the west was initiated by Reverend John West (1778–1845), who served at Kildonan in the absence of a Presbyterian minister. With Anglican funds, West built two schools, one for the colonists' children and one for the Indians. His missionary endeavors produced one priest, Henry Budd (c. 1812–1875), from among the Indian parishioners. West's efforts were bolstered in 1822 when the Church Missionary Society decided to take responsibility for Indian missions and began to send clergymen from England. By 1849, two years after the naming of a Roman Catholic bishop, David Anderson (1814–1885) was consecrated the first Anglican bishop of Rupert's Land. In 1865 Robert Machray (1831–1904) became bishop of Rupert's Land, a post he held for the rest of the century. During this period, operating independently of the province (limited to the dioceses to the east until the creation of the General Synod in 1893), Machray developed Rupert's Land into a separate province that included nine dioceses between Manitoba and the Rocky Mountains.

THE OTHER CHURCHES COME TO MANITOBA.
The Methodists' movement into the northwest followed a series of unusual events in England. The Canadian Methodist preacher Egerton Ryerson had an Indian friend, Peter Jones (also known as Sacred Feathers, 1802–1856), who traveled to England. Jones's speeches before a variety of Methodist audiences excited them over the possibilities of missionary work among the Indians of Upper Canada. Learning of Jones's work, Hudson's Bay Company officials, possibly looking for a way to gain social control (through religion) over the Indians, invited the Methodists into their territory. To the company, Jones seemed a living demonstration that the Methodists could deal with the native population.

Within a few years, the Wesleyan Methodist Connection, bypassing the Canadian Methodists, sent James Evans (1801–1846), Thomas Hurlburt (1808–1873), and Peter Jacobs (c. 1807–1890) to establish work on Manitoulin Island. Evans soon broke with the Hudson's Bay Company and established Norway House in northern Manitoba. Among his major contributions was the development of a syllabic system for printing the Cree Indian language, a system that was easily adapted to other languages. Evans's career overlapped that of Robert Rundle (1811–1896), who moved among the tribes farther west from his base in Edmonton, Alberta.

The Wesleyans supported the missions around Norway House and Edmonton for several decades, but in 1853 turned the work over to the Canadian Methodists. The following year, John Ryerson (1800–1878) made a trip through the territory and noted 18 Protestant missionaries, of which 13 were Anglican, four Methodist, and one Presbyterian.

That one Presbyterian was John Black (1818–1882), a graduate of Knox College in Toronto, who had settled in Kildonan to serve the Scots who had waited 20 years for a Presbyterian minister. Black stayed in Kildonan for more than 30 years. The Presbyterian work expanded in the 1860s through James Nisbet (1823–1874), who went out from Kildonan to found the town of Prince Albert, Saskatchewan, and initiate Presbyterian work in that future province.

By midcentury, settlers began to trickle into western Canada in increasing numbers, and the other churches soon came to provide their spiritual nurture. In 1873 the first Baptist missionary arrived in Winnipeg, and throughout the decade Baptist churches were started in Saskatchewan and Alberta. The Baptists turned their attention to the various non-English-speaking immigrants who began to pour into the area, and soon raised a number of ethnic churches. Early churches tended to be located along the railroad routes that brought the immigrants to their new homes.

ACROSS THE ROCKIES: EVEN FARTHER WEST.
British Columbia developed somewhat independently of the steady western movement of Canadian life. In like measure, the stream of both Roman Catholic and Anglican development flowed along an independent course, only to be merged at the end of the nineteenth century. In British Columbia, two paths to the farthest reaches of Canada converged. Many of the earliest settlers trekked northward from California along the Pacific Coast. Then, in 1792, Alexander MacKenzie (1764–1820) made it over the mountains to the coast and initiated the rich fur trade that was started by the North West Company in 1806. The west coast remained the territory of the North West Company (and then, after 1821, the Hudson's Bay Company) until British Columbia joined the confederation in 1871. In addition, until the settlement of the boundary between Canada and the United States in 1846, the entire Pacific Coast north of California was disputed territory. As a result, the progress of the Roman Catholic missionary work in the region, begun in 1838, was delayed almost a decade when the bishop of Quebec, who had initiated work in the Oregon Territory, questioned his

prerogative in sponsoring the mission because the territory seemed to also belong to the bishop of St. Louis in the United States.

The Oregon Mission included not only Oregon and Washington, but Fort Vancouver and all of British Columbia. Soon after their arrival, the first priests, Francis Norbert Blanchet (1795–1883) and Modeste Demers (1809–1871), began to envision the possibility of bringing the Indian population into the church. They saw a bright future if only a bishop, with authority to recruit a cadre of priests and religious workers, could be sent to the northwest. In 1843 Rome responded by appointing Blanchet as vicar apostolic for the territory. Blanchet, somewhat overwhelmed, requested that the vast territory under his authority be further divided. Then, immediately after the border between the United States and Canada was established by treaty in 1846, the Holy See named Blanchet bishop of Oregon, as well as archbishop of the new province of Oregon City. Four days later, his brother, Augustin-Magloire Blanchet (1797–1887), was named bishop of Walla Walla (Washington), and the next year Demers became bishop of Vancouver, as part of the Oregon City province.

The work prospered for several years, only to be ravaged by the California gold rush. By 1855 only seven priests were left in the province, the rest having followed their flocks south. Three years later, the diocese's fortunes reversed with the discovery of gold on the Fraser River in British Columbia, and the town of New Westminster emerged quickly as a new population center. With the completion of the railroad in the 1880s, the number of residents of British Columbia steadily increased, and the work of the church stabilized into a pattern of growth that followed the population trends.

The Church of England in Canada was much slower to respond to the needs on the Canadian Pacific Coast than was the Roman Catholic Church. In part, the Church of England in Canada was distracted by its midcentury problem of building a new financial base and redefining itself independently of the bishops in England. Also, being a national church, the settlement of the boundary dispute with the United States had much more severe implications for the extension of the ministry.

Following the 1846 treaty, the Hudson's Bay Company abandoned its major post on the Columbia River and in 1849 founded Fort Victoria on Vancouver Island. An Anglican priest, R. J. Staines (c. 1820–1854), was appointed priest and schoolmaster of the new settlement. He worked alone for the rest of his life. He would later be succeeded by a lay teacher in 1857 and a missionary to the Indians in 1858. Then in the wake of the discovery of gold and the influx of thousands into the area, an urgent request for assistance in British Columbia fell into the hands of a wealthy and devout heiress in London. She endowed a bishopric for British Columbia, and in 1859 the Reverend George Hills (1816–1895) was consecrated for the new diocese. Hills recruited men and raised funds before his arrival in Victoria in 1860. With initial financial backing from the Church of England, he was able to organize the

work without financial support from the Canadian government, and he put it on a firm and stable foundation from the beginning. The dioceses of New Westminster (at the mouth of the Fraser River) and Caledonia (centered on the headwaters of the Fraser), created in 1879, become the backbone of the province of British Columbia in the next century.

The initiation of Congregationalist work in British Columbia grew out of concern in Great Britain for slaves who had escaped the United States and found their way to the Vancouver area. In 1859 the Colonial Missionary Society sent a minister to Victoria to create a church and serve the black residents. His interracial efforts met strong opposition from the larger community of white residents and the work collapsed when the society withdrew the missionary. A decade later, a second missionary was sent, and he organized two congregations, one each in 1879 and 1881. But Congregationalism had trouble competing with the more aggressive Presbyterians and Methodists, and made little progress in western Canada as a whole.

The other Protestant churches lagged in their movement to the coast. A Presbyterian minister arrived at Fort Camosun on Vancouver Island in 1861. Beginning in the courthouse, he established what was the only Presbyterian congregation west of Kildonan. A Baptist, John Morton, arrived in 1862 to homestead some 600 acres of what is now downtown Vancouver. A generation later, enough Baptist churches had been formed to justify the formation of the Baptist Convention of British Columbia in 1897.

With the formation of the Roman Catholic and Anglican dioceses in western Canada and the movement of the older churches into the territory, especially after the completion of the railroad, the initial churching of Canada could be said to have been completed. All of the churches continued to grow and spread as the population grew, but that growth consisted of the spreading of the already dominant structure. In the process, a number of issues came to the fore, to which the churches would have to give their time and energy. Like their sister churches south of the border, all the Canadian churches were forced to respond to the new ideas and realities that emerged so forcefully in the late nineteenth century—biblical criticism, the biological and geological sciences, urbanization, and historical consciousness—out of which grew an embittered phase of the fundamentalist-modernist controversy. By the end of the century, the Protestants were focused on the possibility of building a united church from the multitude of sectarian and regional church bodies.

OTHER GROUPS IN WESTERN CANADA.

Dating largely from the opening of the West by the railroad, Canada became home to a wide variety of ethnic groups and an even wider variety of new (at least for Canada) religions. Among the first new groups to arrive in the West, Mennonites from Russia settled along the Red River south of Winnipeg in 1874. A second wave after World War II (1939–1945) settled on farms in Alberta, Saskatchewan, and Manitoba. In the United States, these Mennonites split into several factions, the largest being the General Conference Mennonite Church.

After the Mennonites, other churches also representative of the European free church tradition found western Canada a suitable place for settlement. Possibly the most controversial of these groups is the Doukhobors, who began to arrive in 1899. Controversy followed their attempts to keep their religious practices intact in the face of Canadian laws (such as those dictating educational standards). One group has been accused of staging violent protests (at least against property), and some fame has come to certain groups for their practice of disrobing in public as a means of protest.

Following their inability to reach a suitable accord with the U.S. government after its entry into World War I, the pacifist, communally organized Hutterite Brethren systematically sold their American farms and relocated in western Canada. Though many later returned to the United States, the Hutterites retain a strong Canadian presence.

Eastern Europeans also began to move into western Canada prior to the turn of the century and continued after immigration restrictions were imposed in the United States in 1924. For example, more than 8,000 Romanians, mostly farmers, migrated to Alberta, Saskatchewan, and Manitoba prior to World War I (1914–1918). The first church, St. Nicholas, was built in Regina, Saskatchewan, in 1902. Canadian Ukrainians, now headquartered in Winnipeg, were present in numbers when the struggle for Ukrainian independence led them to organize separately from the Russian Orthodox Church. Their first congregation was formed in Saskatoon, Saskatchewan.

Scandinavian ministers entered Manitoba as early as the 1870s to begin work among the Swedes. An Evangelical Covenant Church was organized in Winnipeg in 1904, about which time ministers of the Evangelical Free Church arrived to initiate work among the Norwegians and Danes. The first Evangelical Free Church was organized in 1913.

Members of the Church of Jesus Christ of Latter-day Saints also entered Canada during this period. In 1887 a group of 41 led by Charles Ora Card (1839–1906) migrated north from Salt Lake City to what is today the province of Alberta. At that time, Canada had no laws against polygamy. Card's group founded the town of Cardston, about 40 miles from Lethbridge, where a temple was built and from which the church has spread throughout Canada. At a later date, members of the Reorganized Church of Jesus Christ of Latter-day Saints would also begin to colonize Canada.

As with the United States, Asian immigration into Canada commenced on the West Coast following the gold rush. Of the Chinese who flocked to the gold fields, many stayed and introduced Buddhism to Canada. By the end of the nineteenth century, Indians, primarily Punjabis, migrated to British Columbia and brought their Sikh faith with them. The construction of the first house of worship, a *gurudwara*, was initiated in 1906 in Vancouver.

The churches described above represent only a few of the many ethnic church groups that were established in western Canada. These were later joined by new indigenous churches that split from the older church bodies. Together, they have given western Canada the same pluralistic flavor so evident in the large urban centers in the eastern half of the nation.

A NEW CONSCIOUSNESS FOR A NEW CENTURY: THE GROWTH OF MODERNISM AND FUNDAMENTALISM.

Modernism, a theological perspective that accepted and even celebrated the changing world of the late nineteenth and early twentieth centuries, blossomed in Canada as it did throughout the West. Responding to the scholarly community, modernists embraced the new "scientific" approach to history (as exemplified in critical methodologies) and society (through the new discipline of sociology), and the radical new assertions of biology and geology. British scholars exposed Canadian churchmen to the historical-critical methods of Bible study as early as 1860 through the publication of the book *Essays and Reviews*, which attempted to inform the British public about the new German scientific critique of scripture. In Canada, the book initiated a continuing debate over the authority of the Bible, the integrity of the biblical text, and the nature of miracles. The debate led to the adoption of both historical and textual criticism in Bible classes in most Canadian seminaries. In like measure, Charles Darwin's *Origin of the Species* (1859) and *The Descent of Man* (1871) provoked extended and heated debate over the supernatural origins of humanity, a debate that still divides. The issues raised by Darwin were given added weight by new discoveries in the geological sciences that called for pushing back the age of the earth by hundreds of thousands of years. Modernists accepted the new discoveries and developed a theology that placed humanity within the unfolding process of evolution.

Canadians also responded to the social displacements of urbanization, especially as Toronto and Montreal grew with the late nineteenth-century influx. By the 1890s, Canadian voices had arisen to address the social implications of Christianity and build new urban ministries. In 1890, for example, Presbyterian Daniel James MacDonnell (1843–1896), pastor of St. Andrew's Church in Toronto, opened mission houses near the slums in Toronto and began night classes for the education of working women. Closely tied to the social gospel was a new belief in the goodness and perfectibility of humans, a view that saw the race progressing into the kingdom of God. Given a new view of their long history on earth, thinkers began to project the future in almost utopian terms.

Among the leading Canadian modernists was Presbyterian George Monro Grant (1835–1902), author of the best-selling book *Ocean to Ocean*, an optimistic look at the Canadian future first published in 1873. First at Dalhousie University and then at Queen's Theological College, Grant championed the modernist cause, demanding that all religious teaching become intellectually respectable. He was joined by professors John Watson (1847–1939) and George Paxton Young (1818–1889).

The progress of modernist thought was not always smooth. Methodist George Workman (1848–1936) was forced to resign his post at Victoria University in 1899 after his public denial of the "dictation theory" of biblical inspiration, a frequent step in the acceptance of biblical critical methodology. Finding a post at another school, he was again forced out in 1907. Daniel James MacDonnell, though acquitted, was forced to stand trial by the General Assembly of the Canadian Presbyterian Church for a comment denying the doctrine of everlasting hell.

Possibly the most disturbed by the growth of the new theological perspectives were the Baptists. Shortly after the turn of the century, charges were leveled at McMaster University, the Baptist's university in Toronto, with the primary target being Professor Isaac G. Matthews (1871–1959). Matthews was accused of attacking the integrity of the book of Genesis. Rising to lead the attack on McMaster was Thomas T. Shields (1873–1955), the pastor of Jarvis Avenue Baptist Church in Toronto, soon to become an internationally known spokesperson for fundamentalism, the conservative theological perspective based on a defense of the unique divine authority of the Bible and the traditional Christian affirmations (the "fundamentals"). Fundamentalists vigorously fought the growing acceptance of critical methods of Bible study, as well as the social gospel and evolution. After an examination, the Baptist Convention of Ontario and Quebec exonerated Matthews, which led Shields and his supporters to break with the convention. Several new Baptist groups eventually emerged from that schism, most notably the Fellowship of Evangelical Baptist Churches.

By World War II, the issues raised by the controversy had been settled in the modernists' favor, and the majority of the mainline churches had gone on to other matters. In Canada, fundamentalism did not retain the power it has held in the United States, though most of Canada's denominations outside of the mainline are evangelical in doctrine.

THE MOVE TO UNIFY.
At the same time that modernism emerged within the larger churches, a drive to unite the scattered sects of Protestantism gathered strength. While there had been no schisms among Canadian Protestants like those that rent the U.S. churches during the American Civil War (1861–1865), the Canadian churches in the late nineteenth century existed in a disunited state because of sectional divisions over the vast Canadian territory, as well as the establishment of many similar but organizationally separate churches by each new wave of immigrants. Efforts to unify led to the formation of the United Church of Canada in 1925 and the Canadian Council of Churches in 1944.

The work of uniting the churches began as individual denominations identified likeminded groups and began a process of denominational family cooperation. For example, in the early nineteenth century, the Methodists sought out means to bring together the non-episcopal British Wesleyans with those who were episcopally led. The process of a merger culminated in 1864 when the Canadian branches of all the various British Methodists merged into a single Methodist body for the country. The even larger number of Presbyterian bodies followed a similar pattern between 1817 and 1879.

The Congregationalists had two major unions in 1906 and 1907.

While the Methodists, Presbyterians, and Congregationalists were merging their denominational families, as early as the 1860s serious proposals for unions across denominational lines were entertained by Methodists and Presbyterians. Similar proposals were considered in the 1870s by Congregationalists and Presbyterians and a decade later by Anglicans with all three denominations. However, nothing came of these discussions prior to the turn of the century.

In 1902 an idea originally suggested by George Monro Grant in 1874 of a united "Church of Canada" began to bear fruit. That year the Methodist general conference issued an overture to its sister denominations to appoint committees to plan for union. The overture was received favorably by the Presbyterians and Congregationalists at their gatherings during the next two years, and the three initiated work on a "basis of union" document in December 1904. After four years, an agreement was reached and passed on to the three churches. The main topics of discussion included doctrine (which led the Baptists to decline participation) and polity (over which the Anglicans ultimately withdrew). A variety of names were proposed and discussed. Once submitted to the denominations, a lengthy struggle to gain commitment to the plan and the proper enabling legislation to have the plan adopted and implemented ensued. Finally, in 1925, the Methodist, Presbyterian, and Congregationalist churches merged to form the United Church of Canada, which immediately assumed its place as the third major church body in the country.

By the time of the formation of the United Church of Canada, the spirit of Christian cooperation and unity, at least on the councilor level, was growing. In the United States, the Federal Council of Christian Churches was fruitfully functioning. On the international level, the conferences that were to lead to the formation of the World Council of Churches were underway. The idea of a council to facilitate communication, prevent duplication of efforts, coordinate ministries, and provide fellowship seemed a practical step toward unity. Thus, in 1944, 12 denominations came together to form the Canadian Council of Churches. It included both Protestant and Eastern Orthodox bodies. Over the years, the Lutherans, one of the few major Christian bodies not among the charter members, joined, while the Baptist Federation of Canada withdrew (even though its major component, the Baptist Convention of Ontario and Quebec, immediately joined). In more recent years, the Canadian Conference of (Roman) Catholic Bishops has become an associate member. The council now includes the overwhelming majority of Canadian Christians among its member organizations.

The trend to unity also played out in Canada's evangelical churches. In 1964 Harry Faught, pastor of Danforth Gospel Temple in Toronto, worked with Oswald J. Smith (founding pastor of the Peoples Church) and Arthur Lee (Calvary Church, Toronto) to form the Evangelical Fellowship of Canada. The organization appointed Brian

Stiller its first full-time director in 1983, followed by Gary Walsh in 1997 and Bruce Clemenger in 2003. As of 2008, the fellowship comprised 41 denominations. Since Stiller's time, the fellowship has sought to influence the social fabric of Canada and has had a significant impact through political connections in the nation's capital.

JUDAISM FROM 1850 TO THE PRESENT.
Though always a small minority, the Jewish community of Canada spread as the country grew. Jews were among the first settlers in the west. A synagogue was established in Victoria, British Columbia, in the 1860s. The first informal congregational service was held in Winnipeg in 1882, and Congregation Beth El was organized two years later. A congregation is noted in Regina, Saskatchewan, in 1913.

Beginning in the late nineteenth century, Jews migrated to Canada in large numbers. More than 80,000 arrived between 1900 and the beginning of World War I. Most of the new arrivals were Orthodox, and even though Reform Judaism arose among Canadians quite early, it never gained the support it had in the United States. During the period between the wars, the religious segment of the community aligned itself with the three main Jewish groups (Conservative, Reform, and Orthodox), with both Sephardic and Ashkenazic Orthodox congregations in existence. Most of the congregations also aligned with one of the several congregational associations headquartered in New York City.

Immediately after World War II, Canadian Jewry experienced a second major wave of immigration, as survivors of the war and the Holocaust poured into the country. Since then, the community has grown to approximately 300,000. Again, the new arrivals tended to be Orthodox and included members of several Hasidic groups (such as the Lubavitchers), though the growth of Conservative congregations has been noticeable and a few Reconstruction synagogues have been established.

THE OTHER RELIGIONS.
Throughout Canada, since the middle of the nineteenth century, the larger church bodies have been faced with the organizational splintering of Christendom. While finding some unity in the formation of the United Church of Canada and the Canadian Council of Churches, such efforts have always been countered by schisms in Canadian church bodies. For example, a large minority of members of the Presbyterian Church refused to join the United Church of Canada, and remains today as a separate organization, though a member of the Canadian Council of Churches. In addition to the schisms, Canada has seen the arrival of new churches from Europe and, most importantly, the constant importation of the hundreds of sectarian bodies that have formed in the United States and that view Canada as a mission field.

During the 1850s, for example, Spiritualism, which started in New York, spread from Ontario to the Maritime Provinces, and letters attesting to the power of Spiritualist phenomena regularly filled the pages of early Spiritualist periodicals. During the twentieth century, Canadians formed several national Spiritualist associations. In the 1860s, Seventh-day Adventists arrived in eastern Canada, spreading their message of the Second Coming, Sabbath observance, and trust in Ellen G. White's (1827–1915) prophetic status. The Holiness movement came to Canada in the 1800s and produced several new churches, the most prominent being that led by Ralph Cecil Horner (1854–1921), a former Methodist. He organized and led the Holiness Movement Church, but when asked to retire as its bishop in 1919, he left to found the Standard Church of America.

Pentecostalism spread quickly to Canada from the 1906 revival on Azusa Street in Los Angeles. Canadians later initiated two of the important teachings in Pentecostalism, which led to the development of two new subgroups, producing a score of new denominational organizations. Possibly the first Canadian Pentecostal was Robert Edward McAlister (1880–1953). At a camp meeting in Los Angeles in 1913, he preached on water baptism in the name of "Jesus only," thus initiating what was to become the apostolic or non-Trinitarian Pentecostalism. In 1948 in western Canada, at an independent Bible school, the Sharon Orphanage and School at North Battleford, Saskatchewan, a Pentecostal revival began and swept across North America. The Latter Rain revival brought to Pentecostalism a new emphasis on prophecy and the laying-on-of-hands. Though considering itself a nondenominational movement, the Latter Rain revival produced more than 20 new denominations in North America.

In 1994 the Toronto Airport Vineyard Church, part of the Association of Vineyard Churches, became the site of a major charismatic renewal known as the Toronto Blessing. The church (later renamed the Toronto Airport Christian Fellowship), pastored by John and Carol Arnott, became a spiritual tourist destination as millions arrived in the mid-1990s to experience alleged supernatural manifestations, including holy laughter.

The Church of Christ, Scientist, came to Canada during the life of its founder, Mary Baker Eddy (1821–1910). In 1906 to 1907 Canada became the location of two important court cases involving Christian Scientists. In both cases, parents who had used Christian Science treatment in the place of standard medical assistance were convicted of manslaughter in the deaths of their children.

While a growing number of Christian sects found their way to Canada prior to World War II, in more recent decades Canada has faced the same rapid proliferation of new and diverse groups, especially in its major cities, as has the United States. Many of these groups have been imported from the United States, but many have also come directly from Asia and the Middle East (usually by way of Europe or Australia). For example, the Baha'i faith was brought to Canada in 1903 when Canadian architect William Sutherland Maxwell (1874–1952) married an American Baha'i practitioner. However, it was not until 1949 that the work grew to a point that it could be set apart under its own National Spiritual Assembly.

Included among the recently arrived are not only teachers seeking to convert Canadians, but also a new wave of Asian immigrants who are building Buddhist and Hindu temples. Besides the well-known new religions, such as the Unification Church and the International Society for Krishna Consciousness, Canada is the headquarters of the Zen Lotus Society, the Yasodhara Ashram Society, and the Sivananda Vedanta Yoga Centers, as well as of Kabalarian philosophy. In addition, British Columbia is home to the largest Sikh community outside of India. Though the first Sikhs came to Canada in 1897, their numbers remained small until the loosening of Canada's immigration laws in the 1960s.

CANADIAN RELIGION: A CONTEMPORARY OVERVIEW.

Canada's current religious makeup reflects the whole of Western society. While Christianity shows every sign of continuing as the faith of the majority of Canadians for the foreseeable future, the country has become home to an ever-increasing number of the world's faiths.

Two contradictory trends have emerged in Canadian religion since the late twentieth century. Canada has become home to the same kind of diverse religious life that characterizes the contemporary West in general. Thus, to leave one of the older churches is not necessarily to drop out of the religious life altogether, and the decline of the dominant liberal Protestant faiths should not be interpreted as a sign of the secularization of society so much as a readjustment in the face of an increasingly diverse religious economy.

In the 1980s and 1990s, Canadian sociologist Reginald Bibby tracked the negative side of recent Canadian religious history, both the decline of church membership over the previous generation and the startling decline in church attendance. All of the major denominations, including Roman Catholicism, showed a membership increase in the decades immediately following World War II, but the numbers peaked in the late 1960s and began to decline in the 1970s. The decline has not been reversed. During this period, the population increased, and thus the percentage of people affiliated with a religious organization declined decade by decade. Equally important, the percentage of church members attending services regularly dropped dramatically, by almost 50 percent for Roman Catholics and more than 50 percent for Protestants.

The interpretation of these trends varies considerably, but most observers suggest that Canada offers an open and fluid religious situation as it enters the twenty-first century. Bibby has adopted an optimistic view, arguing for a renaissance in religion. However, a reversal of the increasingly entrenched direction that religion is taking may be difficult to achieve.

As the new century begins, Canada is home to well over 600 different religious bodies. Most are affiliates of bodies based in the United States or around the world. In the entries below, for churches whose main headquarters is in the United States, an effort has been made to also list the address of the Canadian headquarters. The next largest group is constituted by autonomous bodies that became independent of groups based in the United States, with whom they retain a fraternal relationship. There are also a small number of groups that originated in Canada.

SOURCES

General Sources

Beverley, James, and Barry M. Moody, eds. *The Life and Journal of the Rev. Mr. Henry Alline.* Hantsport, NS: Lancelot Press, 1982. 268 pp.

Bibby, Reginald W. *Fragmented Gods: The Poverty and Potential of Religion in Canada.* Toronto, ON: Irwin, 1987. 319 pp.

———. *Unknown Gods: The Ongoing Story of Religion in Canada.* Toronto, ON: Stoddart, 1993.

———. *Restless Gods: The Renaissance of Religion in Canada.* Toronto, ON: Novalis, 2004.

Crysdale, Stewart, and Les Wheatcroft, eds. *Religion in Canadian Society.* Toronto, ON: Macmillan of Canada, 1976. 498 pp.

Grant, John Webster. *The Canadian Experience of Church Union.* Richmond, VA: John Knox Press, 1967. 106 pp.

———. *The Church in the Canadian Era.* Toronto, ON: McGraw-Hill Ryerson, 1972. 241 pp.

Kilbourn, William. *Religion in Canada: The Spiritual Development of a Nation.* Toronto, ON: McClelland and Stewart, 1968. 128 pp.

Marshall, David B. *Secularizing the Faith: Canadian Protestant Clergy and the Crisis of Belief, 1850–1940.* Toronto, ON: University of Toronto Press, 1992.

Masters, Donald C. *A Short History of Canada.* Princeton, NJ: van Nostrand, 1958. 191 pp.

McInnis, Edgar. *Canada: A Political and Social History.* Toronto, ON: Rinehart, 1959. 619 pp.

Melton, J. Gordon, and James A. Beverley. *International Directory of the World's Religions: Canada, 1998–99.* Chicago: Institute for World Spirituality, 1998. 151 pp.

Menendez, Albert J. *Church and State in Canada.* Amherst, NY: Prometheus, 1996. 140 pp.

Moir, John S. *The Church in the British Era: From the British Conquest to Confederation.* Toronto, ON: McGraw-Hill Ryerson, 1972. 230 pp.

Murphy, Terrence B., ed. *A Concise History of Christianity in Canada.* Toronto, ON: Oxford University Press, 1996. 456 pp.

Noll, Mark. *The Old Religion in a New World: The History of North American Christianity.* Grand Rapids, MI: Eerdmans, 2001. 340 pp.

Silcox, Claris Edwin. *Church Union in Canada: Its Causes and Consequences.* New York: Institute of Social and Religious Research, 1933. 493 pp.

van Die, Marguerite. *Religion and Public Life in Canada: Historical and Comparative Perspectives.* Toronto, ON: University of Toronto Press, 2001.

Wilson, Douglas J. *The Church Grows in Canada.* Toronto, ON: Canadian Council of Churches, 1966. 224 pp.

Major Religious Bodies in Canada

Airhart, Phyllis. *Serving the Present Age: Revivalism, Progressivism, and the Methodist Tradition in Canada.* Montreal, QC: McGill-Queen's University Press, 1992.

Bryant, M. Darrol. *Canadian Anglicanism at the Dawn of a New Century.* Lewiston, NY: Mellen Press, 2001.

Brym, Robert J., William Shaffir, and Morton Weinfeld, eds. *The Jews in Canada.* Toronto, ON: Oxford University Press, 1993. 446 pp.

Card, Brigham Y., ed. *The Mormon Presence in Canada.* Logan: Utah State University Press, 1990.

Carrington, Philip. *The Anglican Church in Canada: A History.* Toronto, ON: Collins, 1963. 320 pp.

Centennial of Canadian Methodism. Toronto, ON: Briggs, 1891. 339 pp.

Cronmiller, Carl R. *A History of the Lutheran Church in Canada.* Toronto, ON: Evangelical Lutheran Synod of Canada, 1961. 288 pp.

Epp, Frank H. *Mennonites in Canada, 1920–1940.* Toronto, ON: Macmillan of Canada, 1982. 640 pp.

Fay, Terence J. *A History of Catholics in Canada.* Montreal, QC: McGill-Queen's University Press, 2002.

Guenter, Jacob G. *"Men of Steele": Life Style of a Unique Sect.* Saskatoon, SK: Author, 1981. 261 pp.

Hayes, Alan L. *Anglicans in Canada: Controversy and Identity in Historical Perspective.* Urbana: University of Illinois Press, 2004.

Penton, M. James. *Jehovah's Witnesses in Canada.* Toronto, ON: University of Toronto Press, 1985.

Quiring, Walter, and Helen Bartel. *Mennonites in Canada: A Pictorial Review.* Altona, MB: Friesen, 1961. 208 pp.

Regehr, Ted D. *Mennonites in Canada, 1939–1970: A People Transformed.* Toronto, ON: University of Toronto Press, 1996.

Reimer, Margaret Loewen. *One Quilt, Many Pieces: A Guide to Mennonite Groups in Canada.* Waterloo, ON: Herald Press, 2008. 140 pp.

Renfree, Harry A *Heritage and Horizon: The Baptist Story in Canada.* Mississauga, ON: Canadian Baptist Federation, 1988. 380 pp.

Rosenberg, Stuart E. *The Jewish Community in Canada.* Toronto, ON: McClelland and Stewart, 1970. 231 pp.

Sanderson, J. E. *The First Century of Methodism in Canada.* 2 vols. Toronto, ON: Briggs, 1908–1910.

Semple, Neil. *The Lord's Dominion: The History of Canadian Methodism.* Montreal, QC: McGill-Queens University Press, 1996.

Walker, J. U. *History of Wesleyan Methodism in Halifax.* Halifax, NS: Hartley and Walker, 1834. 279 pp.

Zeman, Jarold K., ed. *Baptists in Canada: Search for Identity amidst Diversity.* Burlington, ON: Welch, 1980. 282 pp.

American Religion in the Twenty-first Century

The *Encyclopedia of American Religions* has assumed a unique role in American religious studies. When it first appeared in 1979, it filled a vacuum in providing basic information on each and every religious group operating in the United States, the first attempt to do so since the last *Census of Religious Bodies* in 1936. As it turned out, religious life had entered a significant growth phase, and subsequent editions, simply by documenting that growth, created a record of the major trends undergirding the marked increase in religious affiliation during the last decades of the twentieth century and the first decade of the new millennium. This essay attempts to summarize these trends, which have come to the fore since 1979.

If one were examining the state of American religion a century ago, it would, at first glance, appear to be prosperous. The country's religious groups increased steadily through the nineteenth century, with an additional spurt of growth at the end of the century. Though church membership was still below 50 percent of the American population, the gap was closing.

At the same time, however, voices had arisen with a contrary perspective. New tools of analysis were emerging that offered a different perspective. A set of new thinkers about social processes, most operating in Europe in the context of a single dominant state church, was suggesting that religion was in a severely wounded condition and was prophesying that its decline would be the story of the next century. These voices included some of the most quoted observers of human society—social analyst Karl Marx (1818–1883), pioneering sociologists Émile Durkheim (1858–1917) and Max Weber (1864–1920), psychotherapist Sigmund Freud (1856–1939), and biologist Charles Darwin (1809–1882). Through their lifetimes in Europe, the dominant Christian churches had taken a number of palpable hits, and church establishments were being dismantled. The separation of church and state had been instituted in France, and the idea would gain popularity in other countries, though it would be the middle of the twentieth century before most countries would act on it. The most dramatic exception would be Italy, where the Papal States that once dominated the central part of the peninsula were reduced to the miniscule Vatican City as the country unified under a secular head.

Intellectually, numerous scholars abandoned any idea of a continuing significant role for religion in the broad culture. The emergence of a new view of the world from the study of biological evolution (and geological processes) was seen as an attack on the literal understanding of the Bible narrative, especially the book of Genesis. If one destroyed the idea of a literal Garden of Eden, global flood, and Exodus miracles, could the destruction of the whole Christian worldview be far behind? Simultaneously, sociologists suggested that as religion was wrenched from its place of power in the political-social structure, it would lose its relevance and become merely a personal fantasy for the less educated. Freud's opinion of religion, now that psychotherapy had created a new map of the subconscious, was summarized in his 1927 book, *The Future of an Illusion.*

Through the twentieth century, especially in the decades since World War II, the children of Marx, Durkheim, and Weber would develop much more nuanced perspectives on secularization, They would move away from a primary concentration on religious membership to issues of separation of religion from official ties to and support by the state, the visibility of religion in the public square, the permeation of the arts by religious language, images, and sentiments and the rise of science as a general authority for societal decision making, However, especially among observers based in Europe, the decline of public support for the older religious institutions remained the foundation for belief in the steady advance of secularizing tendencies, while at the same time religion in America and the rest of the world were looked upon as exceptions.

At the same time that the older state churches were leading an apparent decline of religion across Europe, religion in America continued to grow well ahead of population growth, but found itself embattled. The wealth of European ideas quickly found their way across the ocean into the halls of learning, including the churches' seminaries. The larger denominations were all, at various levels, struggling with how to respond to the new intellectual currents. One group of professors, slowly gaining the upper hand, advocated a more positive response to the plethora of new ideas. They suggested that the new perspectives could be appropriated and turned to good use by churches. While the new approach to the first books of the Bible altered the way religious people saw biblical history, it did not destroy Christianity. These thinkers suggested that God operated through evolutionary processes to create the world. The early books of the Bible could best be understood as Hebrew myths, stories that possibly lacked literal truth but nevertheless conveyed true ideas about the nature of humanity and its relationship with divine realities.

As they absorbed new understandings of social processes, Christian social thinkers suggested that sociological insights could be used to bring in the kingdom of God on earth, a more just and loving society. Usually their suggestions took the form of socialism. They called this approach the *social gospel* and launched a new era of religious activism at the legislative level with calls for society to respond to its social problems.

Still other thinkers saw the exploration of the human psyche as uncovering truths that spiritual perspectives on the individual had earlier highlighted. New psychological tools could aid the spiritual life, shed new life on spiritual conflict. Pioneers in what would become known as *pastoral counseling* arose to bring psychological insights into the pastor's office and make ministers more proficient in responding to the concerns of parishioners.

This modernist approach gained ground in the generation prior to World War I (1914–1918) and became the dominant approach among scholars associated with most of the larger Protestant churches by 1920. But not all agreed. A large group of religious scholars saw the modernist camp as abandoning the tradition. These more conservative thinkers chose to reject the new intellectual trends. In their opinion, the Bible was literally true, the more familiar theological approach was basically sound, and biology and geology were misinterpreting the evidence. The traditional thrust of the church toward individuals rather than society as a whole was still the better option to change the world. Religion was not an illusion, psychology was. These traditionalists took their stand on what they saw as the "fundamentals" of Christian faith and branded the modernists as heretics. In the decades between the world wars, these fundamentalists fought modernists for control of the major denominations. In the 1930s, the fundamentalists lost major battles in the Presbyterian and northern Baptist churches.

The fundamentalists withdrew, and some voiced their anger at being pushed aside and reduced to an increasingly marginalized minority. Not recognized at the time, the more important group, the Evangelicals, formed a coalition of conservatives among the many who stayed in the larger denominations, those who left, and those who had formed conservative denominations in the nineteenth century. This Evangelical coalition began quietly to rebuild all they had lost—the needed seminaries, a fresh leadership, and a means of bypassing the large denominations and reaching the public directly. In 1947 they founded a new seminary in Pasadena, California, Fuller Theological Seminary, named for radio evangelist Charles Fuller (1887–1968). They also found a new leader in evangelist Billy Graham (b. 1918), and discovered the means of reaching the public through radio and television. By the 1970s, they had rebuilt and were ready to reassert their presence in American religion. Some of their new denominations had grown large, and one that never fell into the modernist camp, the Southern Baptist Convention,

had become the largest Protestant denomination in America. At the same time, they could also claim the allegiance of significant minorities in many of the large liberal (modernist) Protestant churches.

As late as the 1970s, most social scientists were still emphasizing the secularization story, seeing religious life going on around them as remnant of the past rather than herald of the future. Secularization seemed clearly evident in Europe. In Eastern Europe, the state churches had been dismantled by antireligious governments, and in Western Europe, the state churches were losing public support decade by decade. The European decline seemed to be manifesting in America, where the mainline Protestant churches were facing slowing growth rates, a leveling off, and then an actual decline in membership. The Jewish community remained a 50-50 situation, with only half of the community attached to a synagogue. Evolutionary theory seemed relatively unchallenged, and psychotherapy had developed a massive presence. Few were prepared for what was now about to occur.

AN OVERVIEW OF AMERICAN RELIGION.

Overviews of American religion in the 1970s operated from a depleted data base. In the early decades of the twentieth century, the U.S. Department of Commerce had gathered data on religion, and each decade the department published a summary of the data. The last of these appeared in 1936; future government-sponsored data gathering and reports were stopped in the face of challenges based on separation of church and state. The work of reporting on the development of religious groups then fell to the Federal Council of Churches (soon to be superseded by the National Council of Churches), which put out an expanded council membership handbook as the *Yearbook of American Churches* in the 1950s. While providing vital information on most (but not all) of the larger American churches, the *Yearbook* limited its coverage to groups that on the one hand it could approve, and on the other would report to it. Of the more than 450 groups operating in America in the 1930s, it reported on fewer than 150. By the 1970s, the number of groups included in the *Yearbook*, mostly Christian denominations, had grown to around 200, while in the meantime more than 300 new denominations had formed. While aware of the crisis that was developing in the churches that made up the councils' membership, the *Yearbook* largely missed the growth that was taking place in the "other" Christian churches and that was beginning to occur outside of the Christian community.

Although the liberal Protestant community was experiencing a decline, and the Jewish community remained stable, the more conservative elements of Christianity were developing new and innovative theologies based in spirituality (Pentecostalism, new forms of devotion), a new public image based in televangelism, and a new, more-positive assessment and appreciation of secular culture. Evangelical leaders replaced previous simplistic dismissals of the evil culture with attempts to discover God's presence and action in the world quite apart from the church. Then, due in large part to a change in immigration law, the miniscule Asian and Middle

Eastern religious communities, which included the whole spectrum of the world's religions from Advaita Hinduism to Zoroastrianism, began to grow at an unprecedented rate. This growth initially impacted the West Coast and several large metropolitan areas (New York, Chicago, Atlanta, Houston), but by the 1990s it was evident across the United States. In addition, integrating itself into multiple social openings was the older "occult" community, which experienced a monumental revival in the 1980s in the form of the New Age movement, a diverse decentralized movement that swept millions into what was being recast as the Western esoteric tradition.

Growth on every front reshaped American religion. The country had now become home to all of the world's major religious traditions, each of which was able to form one or more national associations or centers. The major traditions were able to organize pandenominational associations that moved to normalize the tradition's presence in the secular culture and the political community. By the end of the twentieth century, even smaller, newer religious groups, such as the neopagan and Wiccan community, could project a future of participation in the religious world as a substantive minority voice.

The spectacular rise of different religious groups—the Church of Jesus Christ of Latter-day Saints being an additional notable success story—could easily suggest to some operating from within those groups the imminent arrival of a new religious establishment, one that would displace the dominant role of mainstream Christianity. Such visions were at best premature, for even as the world's religions were establishing their beachheads, the Christian community continued to grow. The Roman Catholic Church, the largest religious body in the country, for a period grew beyond its ability to recruit a sufficient number of priests. The second largest denomination, the Southern Baptist Convention, enjoyed significant growth for several decades as it expanded from its base in the Deep South to become a national denomination. Over all, Christian growth in the last decades of the twentieth century was greater than that of all the other religions combined. The development of the world religions on American soil did not occur at the expense of the Christian community, but of the religiously unaffiliated community.

The single most significant trend in American religion from 1900 to the present has been the steady and spectacular decline in the percentage of religiously unaffiliated people in the American population.

THE MOBILE RELIGIOUS.
The decline in the numbers of religiously unaffiliated and the parallel growth of American religion through the twentieth century to the present leads to several observations. The emergence of hundreds of never-before-seen religious groups, marked initially by the growing number of Christian denominations, revealed an increasingly mobile religious public. Religious movement is somewhat correlated with family mobility, with most nuclear families moving several times over the course of their life, and high divorce rates, with family units being the major

focus of many groups. That being the case, Americans have increasingly shown a willingness to leave older denominations and join new ones both as a group and individually. To a lesser extent, Americans have been willing to leave Christianity for non-Christian religions. At the same time, the older churches, even those showing net membership losses, have received new members both from sister churches and from the larger religious culture. From another perspective, the willingness of individuals and families to change religions means that the boundaries between religious groups have become increasingly porous.

THE PERSISTENCE OF DENOMINATIONS.
The 1960s, in the wake of the founding of the World Council of Churches (1948) and the Second Vatican Council (1962–1965), saw the Christian community experience a massive wave of ecumenical enthusiasm. During the era of good feeling that grew from the very real accomplishments of Catholic-Protestant dialogue, a forward-looking group of theologians envisioned a united Christian church or, at the very least, a united Protestant church. Prophetic voices declared the issues that had divided Christendom to have been overcome, and argued that the new challenges facing the churches demanded a united front reoriented around present priorities. Denominations were obsolete, and Christians should welcome the new postdenominational era.

Plans for church mergers proliferated, and significant mergers culminated in, for example, the creation of the Presbyterian Church (U.S.A.) and the Evangelical Lutheran Church in America. Meanwhile, a more ambitious project, the Consultation on Church Union, sought to unite Methodists, Episcopalians, and Presbyterians into a model united Protestant church. A generation of negotiations crashed against the reality of denominational life, however, and church leaders set aside the more utopian vision of ecumenism.

By the 1990s, it had become evident that successful church mergers continued the pattern of mergers from the previous century. They were limited to church bodies that already shared close family attraction. Mergers were possible among denominations from what in this encyclopedia are termed *family groups*—churches that share the same history, that are united in theology, and that have a similar polity. Members of merging groups must also possess a strong belief that the merger, with its loss of prior denominational identity, will produce very real and positive gains.

Second, the attempts to unite across family lines demonstrated that the older denominational issues were still very much alive. Although a variety of resolutions to differences in theology and polity were available, negotiators showed an inability to avoid, or in some cases understand, the larger, often unspoken, implications of the doctrinal and organizational differences. Episcopalians, Methodists, and Presbyterians share a sixteenth-century Protestant doctrinal heritage with a high degree of consensus. Methodist bishops resemble Episcopal bishops, and Methodist conferences act very much like presbyteries. However, the seemingly slight differences of emphasis signal very different ways of structuring the Christian life. They provide a different feel to Sunday worship, signal different ways of reacting to problem situations, and represent different values relative to such key concerns as liturgy, piety, and managing a local parish.

Thus, while denominations fell out of favor in some circles, they persisted as the single stable structure amid all the changes of the last decades of the twentieth century. Denominations remained important in that they are the way that religious life is shaped in a free society. Denominations provide different ways to give form to a larger religious tradition. One cannot, for example, form simply a "Christian" church (or Islamic mosque, or Hindu temple, or Jewish synagogue). A Christian congregation, or association of congregations, has to make a host of decisions that ground it in the particularity of a Christian life (just as a synagogue or mosque must make basic decisions about Jewish or Islamic life). In Christianity, crucial decisions must, for example, be made about the sacraments. How shall one baptize (immersion, pouring, or sprinkling) and who will one baptize (adults only or infants)? How many sacraments will one have—seven, two, none? Who will be admitted to the sacraments—only adult believers, all baptized Christians, anyone? While every group is free to decide among the options, it is not free to avoid making a decision. It is also the case that in making some of these decisions, the group is also making a set of additional decisions about the nature of the Christian life and how the church relates to society as a whole. Similarly, one must decide about leadership. Will there be bishops? Will they have an apostolic lineage? Will they have real power? Will they be permitted to marry? Each decision one makes about episcopal leadership is a simple decision about organization, but carries with it a set of implications about how members think about the church and its role in the world. Anyone opening a new synagogue or mosque must make similar decisions about the variety of ways one could structure Jewish or Islamic life.

Every church must make decisions about its beliefs and practices that set it within a denominational tradition or, on rare occasions, make it the pioneer of a new denominational family. The older denominational groups persist in that they have found workable ways to structure the Christian life and have already experimented with many options that have proved less workable. They have also developed efficient methods of serving parishioners and supplying them with a means to express their faith. Thus, while within a free society many different denominations can arise, no one has yet found a better way to provide for the week-in, week-out communal life of religious people. They may call "denominations" by different names (pagan *traditions*, Buddhist *sects*, esoteric *currents*), but denominations are the persistent reality of contemporary religion wherever a high degree of religious freedom prevails.

PLURALISM AND THE NEW CONSENSUS.

Given the persistence of denominations, the subsequent major reality of American religious life has been its ever-increasing pluralism. The United States was founded with fewer than 20 different religious communities, all Christian except for the small Jewish community. By 1900, that number had grown to more than 300, mostly Christian, denominations. By the end of the twentieth century, there were more than 2,000 denominations in the United States; by that time, however, only about half were Christian. At the beginning of the twentieth century, Buddhism, Hinduism, and Islam had minimally made their presence felt. In the last half of the twentieth century, the number of Buddhist, Hindu, and Islamic options in America represented most forms of the world's religions that were present globally in any strength. In addition, there was a host of new, uniquely American, variations.

The pluralistic scene means that almost every American, especially any urban dweller, now has almost the full spectrum of the world's religions from which to choose, and one can pursue that faith at any level of commitment, from participating in a full-time ordered community to making casual visits on important holidays. The immediate presence of a community that more closely conforms to one's religious wants and needs further increases the likelihood that one will actually join a new religious group.

The larger Christian denominations in the United States include (membership figures have been rounded off to the nearest 100,000):

···

Roman Catholic Church	67,200,000
Southern Baptist Convention	16,400,000
United Methodist Church	8,200,000
Church of God in Christ	5,400,000
National Baptist Convention, U.S.A., Inc.	5,000,000
Evangelical Lutheran Church in America	4,900,000
National Baptist Convention of America, Inc.	3,500,000
Presbyterian Church (U.S.A.)	3,200,000
Assemblies of God	2,700,000
African Methodist Episcopal Church	2,500,000
National Missionary Baptist Convention of America	2,500,000
Progressive National Baptist Convention	2,500,000
Lutheran Church—Missouri Synod	2,400,000
Episcopal Church	2,300,000
Churches of Christ	1,500,000
Greek Orthodox Archdiocese of America	1,500,000
Pentecostal Assemblies of the World, Inc.	1,500,000
American Baptist Churches in the U.S.A.	1,400,000
African Methodist Episcopal Zion Church	1,400,000
United Church of Christ	1,200,000
Baptist Bible Fellowship International	1,200,000
Christian Churches and Churches of Christ	1,000,000
Orthodox Church in America	1,000,000

···

Together, these 23 denominations include half of all religiously affiliated people in the United States. They represent the primary traditions of Christianity, inclusive of the Catholic, Protestant, and Eastern Orthodox communities, and range from the most conservative (the Baptist Bible Fellowship International) to the most liberal (the United Church of Christ). While differing on a host of issues, they share some common understandings of the Christian symbols and some boundaries defining who is inside and who is outside the Christian community. Together they carry the mainstream of the Christian heritage in America.

In the 1950s, sociologist Will Herberg (1901–1977), out of his observations of postwar American religion, suggested that a new framework for understanding could be constructed around three foci: the Protestant, the Catholic, and the Jewish communities. At the time, he could not perceive the Eastern Orthodox community, then keeping a very low profile, nor could he foresee the changes about to transform America's religious world through the last decades of the twentieth century (from the rise of African Americans and Pentecostals to the emergence of other Middle Eastern and Asian religions). His thesis did, however, point to the important role that a few groups have above and beyond the Roman Catholic Church and the several larger Protestant denominations.

Herberg would probably not, for example, have made some of the distinctions that are found within the Christian community. Together, the Catholic, Protestant, and Eastern Orthodox churches recognize each other, to a large degree, as sharing a single Christian tradition. Some post-Protestant groups are deemed by these same Catholic, Orthodox, and Protestant churches as having, to some degree, stepped outside the mainstream of that tradition. (The term *post-Protestant* refers to groups that have their beginnings in the larger Protestant community, from which they take a great deal, but that have adopted elements of belief and behavior that have alienated them from the larger Protestant community. Though continuing to utilize the major Christian symbols, post-Protestant groups would not be recognized as fellow believers by Protestant churches.) Several of these post-Protestant groups have grown quite large and now play an important role in shaping the culture, most notably:

• • •

Jehovah's Witnesses	2,230,000
Church of Jesus Christ of Latter-day Saints	5,770,000

• • •

While to an outside observer like Herberg, both the Jehovah's Witnesses and the Latter-day Saints might appear to be simply additional Christian variations, neither have been accepted into ecumenical relationships within the larger Christian community, and both groups (along with numerous small post-Protestant groups) are continually having to redefine and reassert their vision of their place relative to Christianity. The Jehovah's Witnesses and the Church of Jesus Christ of Latter-day Saints are the largest dissenting groups on the edge of the dominant Christian establishment in the United States.

Because of Judaism's role as the parent religion to Christianity, it holds a special place in American religion. The Jewish faith, though having only around 4.5 million adherents in the United States, is the religious tradition with the second largest number of adherents. (An uncounted number of people who would be defined as of Jewish ethnicity now follow one of the many non-Jewish religions operating in the United States; both the Hindu and Buddhist communities, for example, include prominent leaders who were born and raised in Jewish homes.) In the American context, three forms of Judaism have emerged, each gaining a sizeable following. A product of a century of Jewish-Christian dialogue, the Jewish community has now attained a meaningful place as part of the American religious establishment.

• • •

Conservative Judaism	1,500,000
Orthodox Judaism	1,000,000
Reform Judaism	1,500,000

• • •

An estimate of the size of the Orthodox Jewish community is difficult because it is a splintered community with many divisions, including over a dozen Hasidic groups. The figure presented above is limited to the estimated number of adherents of the Union of Orthodox Jewish Congregations of America, by far the largest of the several Orthodox groups. Another half million believers would be attached to Reconstructionist Judaism and various smaller Orthodox (including Hasidic) groups.

Together, the 28 religious bodies mentioned above (along with some 70 additional Christian churches that have as many as 100,000 members) constitute the American religious establishment, in the sense that together they largely control the religious environment in which most Americans operate. At the same time, other religious groups must, to some degree, react to and adjust to the environment these larger groups have created and maintain. The approximately 900 smaller Christian denominations and Jewish synagogue associations have dissented from these groups on one or more issues.

Their very size and connectedness means that every community of any size in America will have a representative congregation of these few groups, and, while admitting of regional differences, these congregations will offer much the same religious atmosphere to congregants as found in like congregations elsewhere in the country. These denominations set the backdrop for emergent theologies and new approaches to the spiritual life. Their members form the public to be organized for interdenominational social movements, and to be wooed and won as controversies swell. And while theologies, spiritualities, movements, and controversies come and go, these denominations and their congregations persist, awaiting the emergence of the next theologies, spiritualities, movements, and controversies.

REVITALIZING CHRISTIANITY THROUGH PENTECOSTALISM. Many commentators on religion see Pentecostalism as the most definitive movement of the twentieth century. Founded in 1901, it experienced a sudden national and even international expansion during the years of the Azusa Street revival in Los Angeles (1906–1909). Denounced for decades as a realm of overemotional, primitive religious experiences attracting the mentally unstable, Pentecostalism nevertheless grew through the first half of the

twentieth century and took its initial steps toward acceptance by the larger Christian community when several of its denominational structures joined the National Association of Evangelicals (NAE). A variety of psychological studies in the 1960s and 1970s dispelled any suggestion of a connection between Pentecostal spirituality and mental disorders (the case appearing to be quite the opposite). Meanwhile, the continued acceptance of Pentecostals in the NAE has led to their dominance of the organization. Like Evangelicals in general, Pentecostals found in religious broadcasting a major tool that greatly assisted the movement's growth during the last half of the twentieth century.

In the 1960s, the Pentecostal experience of speaking in tongues and the other charismatic gifts of the spirit (described in I Corinthians 12), especially spiritual healing, moved anew into the larger churches. Through the 1970s, almost all non-Pentecostal Christian denominations of any size developed a charismatic movement. Collectively, the charismatic community quickly spread through the denominations internationally. During the last decades of the twentieth century, Pentecostal churches developed as large international bodies, though their growth was small relative to the spread of the charismatic movement within otherwise non-Pentecostal denominations. This latter spread has made Pentecostalism an international movement with which to be reckoned.

The growth of Pentecostalism in the United States is seen in the addition of three Pentecostal churches among the 23 largest churches in the United States. Among the more noteworthy religious discoveries of the 1990s was that the Church of God in Christ, an African-American church that had previously never done a membership count, was among the five largest churches in America. As the older Pentecostal churches have grown, the charismatic movement has continued and a third-wave, neo-charismatic movement has made its presence felt. The charismatic movement, which has become the dominant face of Pentecostalism in most countries, peaked in North America in the 1980s as each of the major denominations took positions of mild opposition. Church leaders opposed the charismatics' tendency to treat their noncharismatic fellow members as second-class Christians, and a set of new charismatic denominations were formed by people disappointed at the larger churches reluctance to embrace the charismatic renewal.

The neo-charismatic movement, which finds its historical base in the Latter Rain movement of the 1940s and which has taken charismatics in a different direction through its apostolic and prophetic leadership, developed in North America but has found its major success in South America and Africa. Because of an uneven level of leadership in the neo-charismatic movement, the possibility of straying into questionable areas doctrinally (as with the positive confession movement), and the competition neo-charismatic groups offer to older Pentecostal denominations, the third-wave groups have been marginalized in North America, though a few have developed strong national organizations.

PERSISTING RACIAL BARRIERS.

Even as the civil rights movement was taking the lead in changing American behavior relative to race, 11 a.m. on Sunday morning, when most congregations meet for worship, was described as the most segregated hour in American life. Since the Civil War (1861–1865), segregated worship has been the norm in American religion, the few exceptions being congregations that self-consciously decided to integrate. One church stands out in this regard, the Pentecostal Assemblies of the World. As Pentecostalism arose out of the revival of a African-American congregation in Los Angeles under the leadership of an African-American preacher, it attempted to evolve as an integrated movement, and early on had prominent African-American leaders, including C. H. Mason (1866–1961) and G. T. Haywood (1880–1931). However, the segregation patterns throughout American culture, enforced by law in the South, led the emerging denominations to become either all white or all black.

The Pentecostal Assemblies of the World, one of the first of the Pentecostal denominations to take shape (1906), was hit with the full force of the arguments for segregation, backed by a significant schism of white members. The organization nonetheless kept its ideals and was able to retain a measurable white minority membership. It manifested its interracial commitments by periodically electing white leaders to top posts, one symbol of the effort the organization made to live beyond the racism within the larger culture.

Beginning at the time of the civil rights movement, a number of the larger, predominantly white denominations with a black minority moved to end segregated structures, passed statements repenting of past racist attitudes and deeds, backed measures that empowered black members, and in general created an atmosphere that would allow racial harmony to increase. Black church members responded overwhelmingly with acceptance, forgiveness, and pledges to cooperate with the new attitudes that were being generated. Through the 1970s, segregated structures were largely eliminated at the national and regional levels, and soon afterward desegregation began to occur at the state and local jurisdictional levels.

Less noticeable has been the emergence of functionally integrated congregations even in those areas where the local community is segregated. The integration of local congregations has proved far more complex an issue than that envisioned in the 1960s, and for a variety of reasons, the arrival of the stated ideal, a time when race is no longer an issue in determining membership in congregations, may be slow in being realized.

WORLD RELIGIONS IN AMERICA.

Paralleling the persistence of Christian denominations through the last half of the twentieth century to the present has been the emergence and institutionalization of the world's religions. Included within this larger picture of American religion are a variety of "Christian" groups that, because of their distinctive beliefs and practices, have developed apart from the mainstream of the Christian community, what we have termed the *post-Protestant* groups. Though some of these Christian groups have taken their place on the American religious scene and integrated into the culture, they are still viewed as significantly different by most Christians. Among these marginalized Christian groups, as mentioned above, are two of some size, the Church of Jesus Christ of Latter-day Saints, which claims over 5.7 million members in the United States, and the Jehovah's Witnesses, with between 1.5 and 2.3 million members. Both groups are now visible in every part of the United States (even though 20 percent of all Latter-day Saints reside in the state of Utah), and their houses of worship are found in every community of any size. The Witnesses have developed a systematic program that attempts to reach every home in the United States every five years. Both groups have also parented a set of splinter groups, and a few, such as the Christian Community (formerly the Reorganized Church of Jesus Christ of Latter-day Saints), have enjoyed some success regionally.

Following the changes in immigration law in 1965, Eastern religions began to grow in the United States. One of the smaller groups, the International Society for Krishna Consciousness, became a very visible Asian religion as its members engaged in public chanting and dancing on the streets of most urban centers and in fundraising and book distribution at the nation's airports. Similarly, Buddhism gained a high profile from large numbers of Anglo converts, including many scholars. Although groups that converted non-Asians were given more attention, real growth resulted from the quiet movement of hundreds of thousands of Asians into the United States. Asian-American Buddhists and Hindus raised their profile slowly, as they built their often-elaborate temples, which have proliferated on the edges of major urban complexes. The Buddhist community in America received an additional lift from the honors heaped on the fourteenth Dalai Lama of Tibet, though the actual number of Tibetan Buddhist adherents in the United States remains small.

Though both the Buddhist and the Hindu communities in the United states now number in the millions, their visibility nationally has been blunted by their uneven distribution across the country. Some 40 percent of both communities reside in southern California, with an additional strong presence in the San Francisco Bay area. In addition, the Buddhist community is divided into more than one hundred "sects," analogous to Christian denominations, with no single group having more than a few hundred thousand members. Hinduism is likewise divided, with the more visible segments affiliated with one of the nearly 100 organizations built around a contemporary living teacher (*guru*). Most Hindu groups are associated with the immigrant community and thus are organized geographically, each temple serving those Indian Americans within driving distance of it. Temples are locally autonomous but basically divided along geographical lines (serving southern Indian or northern Indians) and the two major communities (*sampradayas*) in each area

(Vaishnava or Shaiva). Some of the new Hindu temples in the United States are replicas of famous temples in India.

Most non-Asian converts to Hinduism are associated with one of the many guru groups headed by a living spiritual teacher. Such groups became popular in the 1970s; however, in the twenty-first century, a new wave of younger teachers has arisen to fill the vacuum as the original teachers who came to America in the 1970s have retired or passed away. These teachers are among the most difficult religious leaders to locate and document because their presence on the landscape is virtually invisible. They often operate out of rented facilities or in members' homes, and have few stable worship centers relative to their size, though their profile rises during the summer when nomadic Hindu teachers make American tours.

THE RISE OF ISLAM. Most visible of all the newly arrived world religions in America is Islam. American Muslims, like Hindus and Buddhists, have become concentrated in southern California, but they are more evenly spread across the country and appear to have more adherents, though the actual number of Muslims in America is a matter hotly contested among those who try to count. This encyclopedia has taken the more conservative approach and considers a practicing Muslim community of some four to five million. They are divided into a variety of subcommunities along lines of national origin (Middle Eastern, Asian, African) and differences in belief and practice (Sunni, Shi'a, Ismaili, Sufi, etc.).

The terrorist attacks on the Pentagon and World Trade Center in 2001 lifted the profile of the American Muslim community and made its neighbors aware of the mosques that had been quietly operating in almost every American urban center. (The attacks also raised the profile of the American Sikh community, after turban-wearing Sikhs were frequently confused with Muslims in the period following the attacks.) By 2008, with the United States involved in wars in Afghanistan and Iraq, and making strong diplomatic moves involving China, Pakistan, and Iran (to name only a few prominent examples), the issues involving religion in foreign policy have given the American Muslims a place in the national consciousness that they would not have had otherwise. Even as the major newspapers and electronic media gained sophistication in separating the two realities, some commentators (including those speaking from a specifically religious position) consciously associated the terrorist acts with the American Muslim community, ignoring the facts that those responsible for the attacks were not Americans (they were aliens, primarily from Saudi Arabia), nor were they active in any American Muslim circles.

Prior to the 1960s, the American Muslim community was based in the country's relatively small Middle Eastern population, with most Muslims residing in the Midwest. After 1965, immigration from India and Pakistan took the lead (in the same wave of immigration that laid the foundation for the expansion of Hinduism), coupled with the parallel development of Islam within the African-American community. Indo-

Pakistani Muslims now make up the largest segment of the American Muslim community, which has its organizational center in the Islamic Society of North America, headquartered in suburban Indianapolis, Indiana.

The growth of Islam within the African-American community is an artifact of Jim Crow legislation. Early in the nineteenth century, the discrimination directed against African Americans was embedded in the U.S. legal structure and reflected in the attitudes of many Christians. This situation led many African Americans to seek a new path in Islam and the related Black Nationalist movement. When a new Indo-Pakistani movement, Ahmadiyya, arose in the 1920s, African Americans flocked to it, and throughout most of the twentieth century formed the largest segment of its membership. Today, quiet apart from sectarian Islamic movements such as the Nation of Islam led by Louis Farrakhan, African Americans make up more than 25 percent of the American Muslim community.

Though demographers and sociologists are continually improving their approaches, the size, as well as the best means of measuring the size, of the American Muslim community remains one of the most contested issues in American religious studies. In the 1990s, some suggested that the number of Muslims in America might be as high as six million (a figure derived from adding up all the immigrants from predominantly Muslim communities). That figure was immediately contested, and a census of all the mosques in America could identify only about 1.5 million attendees. While some continue to advocate even larger figures (as high as 10 to 12 million), most estimate there to be 4 to 5 million American Muslims in 2008 (a figure more in line with the developing Buddhist and Hindu communities), including many people who self-identify as Muslim even though they are not currently active in any organized religious activities. The exact figure has become more important as Muslims press their case for changes in government policies toward the Middle East and try to resolve issues of discrimination experienced by their members. American Muslims also look to the day when their growing community will overtake the American Jewish community in size (a development likely to occur in the 2020s if present growth rates continue).

Meanwhile, Islam has assumed a very public presence. Mosques can now be found in American cities of any size. At the same time, Muslim leaders, conditioned by Muslim culture to participate in public life, moved more quickly than their Buddhist and Hindu neighbors to exercise their role in cultural and political affairs through organizations such as the Muslim Public Affairs Council, with headquarters in both southern California and Washington, D.C., and the Council on America-Islamic Relations, also based in Washington, D.C.

The rapid growth and heightened profile of the Muslim community has had ambiguous results for Judaism. The Jewish community is still the largest non-Christian religious community in America, and continues to enjoy widespread benefits from the century-long growth of amiable relations between Jews and Christians that were fed by the decisions of Vatican II and a vigorous ongoing Jewish-Christian dialogue. Jews maintain their unique place in America life, a status deriving in part from the Christian use of the Jewish Bible and from widespread revulsion over the culmination of anti-Semitism in the Holocaust.

At the same time, the Jewish community has begun to feel the impact of competing religions and the persistence of attitudes in the still-overwhelmingly dominant Christian community that views Jews as but one among many other religions. Jewish leaders have also begun to anticipate a date in which the Muslim American community will overtake the Jewish community in size, the former being in a growth phase that dates to the 1970s. A variety of possibilities remain open for both groups.

GLOBALIZATION OF THE RELIGIOUS COMMUNITY.

The pluralistic religious environment emerging in the United States is now the common experience of the majority of the world's countries, with important differences in some countries where an older single religion, once the privileged faith, remains favored in many areas of life. In Malaysia, for example, there is broad religious pluralism, but among native Malaysians, religious pluralism is limited to various sects of Islam, while many varieties of Hinduism, Buddhism, and Christianity flourish among that half of the population of Chinese, Indian, and European background.

The amazing pluralism that became so visible in the late twentieth century can be traced to the global mission undertaken by Christianity during the colonial era. By the middle of the nineteenth century, most Christian denominations in North America and Europe were expending sizeable portions of their funds sending missionaries around the world. They succeeded in planting all of the Western denominations in new contexts where, as they took on an indigenous cast, they developed new histories and new variations on denominational forms. As colonial establishments came to an end, most mission churches became autonomous bodies with local leadership. Thousands of new churches came into existence as Western churches cut their international members free.

The country-by-country development of so many new churches meant that new forms of association and fellowship had to be developed, and plans for such structures—ecumenical councils—were already in the formative stages as the new independent governments arose. The new councils provided for a reordering of former relationships between mission-sending and mission-receiving churches into partnerships in mission. The process of forming such councils accelerated after World War II (1939–1945), with the newly formed World Council of Churches becoming a model for regional, national, and more local councils. At the same time, older organizations that attempted to unite churches within a single denominational family (the World Methodist Council, the World Alliance of Reformed Churches, the Lutheran World Federation, etc.) were given new life and developed rapidly as former mission churches assumed their new roles on the global stage. Whenever serious divisions appeared within family groups, multiple parallel family-based ecumenical organizations would form to serve distinctive constituencies within different communions. Most would arise within the Reformed Presbyterian family, where fine distinctions would be drawn between separatist fundamentalists, Evangelicals, and more liberal Presbyterians, and between those of continental Reformed, British Presbyterian, and Congregationalist traditions.

The international ecumenical organizations that became so evident within Christian circles were mirrored in other faiths as well. Internationally, such organizations as the Muslim World League and the World Fellowship of Buddhists sought to bridge gaps that had arisen by the global spread of the religions, the rise of national states, and the different demands placed upon believers in varying contexts. Even a relatively small tradition like Judaism, which had developed distinctive denominational communities, formed international structures (such as Masorti Olami, the World Council of Conservative/Masorti Synagogues, and the World Union for Progressive Judaism) that tie international groupings within Judaism together.

Together, the global conciliar structures developed by the major religious communities serve as an important counter to the continued splintering of the religious scene. Because all of the major world religions have developed large worshipping constituencies in North America, the United States has become an important nexus for the global conciliar organizations—all of which have a national or continental office in the United States, and many of which have their international headquarters there.

NEW RELIGIOUS MOVEMENTS.
Among the religious controversies of the last decades of the twentieth century, few reached the intensity of the "cult wars." As a result of the convergence of the 1965 changes in immigration law and the coming of age of the baby-boom generation, a new set of religions found a ready audience. Several hundred new and unfamiliar religious organizations founded in the 1950s and 1960s were joined by several hundred additional groups launched in the 1970s. These groups enjoyed a period of rapid growth among young adults unable to find a place in a society not ready to receive them. While most of these new religions assumed a low profile in the culture, several dozen, due in large part to their aggressive recruitment tactics and the high level of demands they made on the time and energy of their members, became embedded in controversy.

The controversy surrounding new religions began fading during the 1970s, but suddenly burst forth with new energy following the deaths of more than 900 members of the Peoples Temple at Jonestown in Guyana in November 1978. The Peoples Temple was an unusual group in that it was a congregation of a large America denomination, the Christian Church (Disciples of Christ), a member of the National Council of Churches. In the mid-1970s, members of the Peoples Temple were active in the California ecumenical scene, and its social-action work received high praise in liberal Protestant circles. Following the deaths of its members in

Guyana, however, the Peoples Temple went from controversial congregation to "cult" overnight, and became the catalyst for a spectrum of state and federal legislation and the organization of a national cult-awareness movement. Unable to get legislation passed, the cult-awareness movement operated in civil courts where, through the 1980s, it backed a number of former "cult" members who claimed that the religion they had left had brainwashed them. The coercive control implied in the brainwashing accusation not only formed the foundation for the court action but also justified the accompanying practice of kidnapping group members and subjecting them to "deprogramming" in an attempt to convince them to renounce their faith.

Both the civil suits, which netted a number of multimillion-dollar judgments, and the practice of deprogramming came to an end following a series of reversals in court beginning in 1990 when a federal court declared that the expert witnesses who spoke of brainwashing did not meet the court's standards for scientific testimony. Previously, several academic organizations, most notably the American Psychological Association, had declared the case proposed by its members for psychological brainwashing to be methodologically flawed. In 1995, following a countersuit brought by a victim of an unsuccessful deprogramming, the main cult-awareness organization, the Cult Awareness Network, was forced into bankruptcy.

The "cult wars" essentially ended in 1995, after which most of the new religions, including the more controversial ones, saw a significant drop in the level of tension they experienced relative to the larger society and the more established religious community. At the same time, the newer groups, those founded after 1990, found a higher level of initial acceptance within the American culture and avoided the period of trials prior to being integrated into the larger religious landscape.

WESTERN ESOTERICISM.
Among the many noteworthy national and international movements of the last half of the twentieth century was the New Age movement, a millennial movement that in the 1970s proposed the emergence of a new age of love and light (wisdom) to arrive early in the twenty-first century. As the movement underwent analysis, it was seen as a revitalization within the older "occult" community. The New Age movement was originally generated within and derived its initial support from several independent British Theosophical groups.

Utilizing older occult practices, the New Age movement called people's attention, in a new and different context, to the possibility of healing and transforming their individual lives, while at the same time projecting a vision of broad social renovation. From England, the movement traveled to the United States and found popular support from a wide range of alternative religious groups, most relatively small. However, year by year the movement grew and through the 1980s began to count its adherents in the hundreds of thousands and then in the millions. As the New Age movement peaked toward the end of the 1990s, it is estimated that as many as 2 to 3 percent of the population were attracted to it, and many times that number at least minimally affected by it. Some 25 percent of the American population, for example, now professes a belief in some form of reincarnation.

The New Age movement transformed the older, miniscule, occult community into what in the 1990s began to be called the Western Esoteric community—a new name denoting the new level of respectability that these earlier berated beliefs and practices had attained. The new name also came as the culmination of a generation of scholarship that had been done on esoteric groups, redefining them as part of a third religious tradition whose origins rivaled that of the more dominant Christian community. The Esoteric tradition is a broken tradition whose adherents were, like the Jews, frequently the object of persecution, but which had since the seventeenth century been able to find an increasing space in Western cultural life.

The Esoteric Tradition has supplied an alternative to the mainstream orthodox Christian tradition since the emergence of the Gnostics in the patristic era (the exact origins of the Gnostics being another significantly contested issue in contemporary scholarship). Once Christianity became the dominant religious community in the West, groups with strong resemblance to the Gnostics regularly reappeared and were just as regularly hounded out of existence. However, in the growing atmosphere of religious freedom, Gnostic-like groups, some even assuming that name, have once again returned in force, and now are taking their place on the larger religious landscape, and furthering its pluralism.

SUMMARY. As American religion enters the twenty-first century, it faces a very positive environment. With few exceptions, religious communities are experiencing a growth trajectory. Given the size of the country and its increasing population, the growth of one religious group is not dependent on the growth (or decline) of others and often accomplished without awareness of the rise and fall of religious neighbors. Given the country's projected population growth and current immigration policies, the continued growth of most religious communities appears to be the story that will dominate in the religious community. Those groups that lose members will be the exception, and their losses in such a context will be a matter for serious reflection.

While non-Christians groups will continue to grew during the next generation, there is nothing on the horizon to suggest a loss of Christian hegemony in the American religious community as a whole, nor any groups that will even begin to challenge that hegemony. At the same time, religious leaders reflecting on the global situation appear ready to offer other religions a level of freedom and respect (significantly beyond mere tolerance) that would not have been imaginable even a century ago. This heightened religious pluralism even reaches out to the new humanist-atheist community, the religiously irreligious, whose observations are now welcomed into discussions on basic religious concerns.

SOURCES

Bacher, Robert, and Kenneth Inskeep. *Chasing Down a Rumor: The Death of Mainline Denominations.* Minneapolis, MN: Augsburg, 2005. 192 pp.

Barrett, David, George T. Kurian, and Todd M. Johnson. *World Christian Encyclopedia: A Comparative Survey of Churches and Religions in the Modern World.* 2nd ed. 2 vols. New York: Oxford University Press, 2001.

Butler, Jon, Grant Wacker, and Randall Balmer. *Religion in American Life: A Short History.* Rev. ed. New York: Oxford University Press, 2008. 596 pp.

Eck, Diana L. *A New Religious America: How a "Christian Country" Has Become the World's Most Religiously Diverse Nation.* San Francisco: HarperSanFrancisco, 2001. 416 pp.

Herberg, Will. *Protestant—Catholic—Jew: An Essay in American Religious Sociology.* With a new Introduction by Martin E. Marty. Chicago: University of Chixcago Press, 1955, 1960, 1983. 326 pp.

Kim, Jun Ha, and Pyonmg Gap Min. *Religions in Asian America: Building Faith Communities.* Walnut Creek, CA: AltaMira Press, 2002. 224 pp.

Lazerwitz, Bernard, J. Alan Winter, Arnold Dashefsky, and Ephram Tabory. *Jewish Choices: American Jewish Denominationalism.* Albany: State University of New York Press, 1998. 209 pp.

Lindner, Eileen W., ed. *Yearbook of American and Canadian Churches, 2008.* Nashville, TN: Abingdon Press, 2008. Issued annually under the auspices of the National Council of Churches.

Mead, Frank S., Samuel S. Hill, and Craig D. Atwood. *Handbook of Denominations in the United States.* 12th ed. Nashville, TN: Abingdon Press, 2005. 430 pp.

Mead, Sidney E. *The Lively Experiment: The Shaping of Christianity in America.* New York: Harper & Row, 1963. 220 pp.

Melton, J. Gordon. *American Religions: An Illustrated History.* Santa Barbara, CA: ABC-Clio, 2000, 316 pp.

———. *Nelson's Guide to Denominations.* Nashville, TN: Thomas Nelson, 2007. 620 pp.

Mullin, Robert Bruce, and Russell E. Rickey, eds. *Reimagining Denominationalism: Interpretive Essays.* Religion in America. New York: Oxford University Press, 1994. 336 pp.

Noll, Mark A., and Luke E. Harlow. *Religion and American Politics: From the Colonial Period to the Present.* 2nd ed. New York: Oxford University Press, 2007. 502 pp.

Pew Forum on Religion and Public Life. U.S. Religious Landscape Survey. 2008. religions.pewforum.org.

Roozen, David A., and James R. Nieman, ed. *Church, Identity, and Change: Theology and Denominational Structures in Unsettled Times.* Grand Rapids, MI: Eerdmans, 2005. 656 pp.

Williams, Peter. *America's Religions: From Their Origins to the Twenty-first Century.* 2nd ed. Urbana: University of Illinois Press, 2001. 800 pp.

"World's Youth More Religious Than Reputed: Bertelsmann Stiftung's Study on Religion Reveals Contradictory Trends Worldwide." Bertelsmann Stiftung press release. July 10, 2008. www.bertelsmann-stiftung.org/.

Interfaith and Ecumenical Family of Organizations

1

INTERFAITH ACTIVITY. Amid the variety of long-term trends noticeable in the religious life of Western culture since the sixteenth-century Reformation, the move toward religious diversity has been most evident. With the breakup of the Roman Catholic dominance of religious expression and the assumption of control in large areas of Europe by Anglican, Lutheran, and Calvinist churches, not only was Roman Catholic hegemony limited, but the loose control at the boundaries of the newly established communities invited further diversity and disruption of what unity remained. At the same time that Europe was expanding across the Atlantic into a new world, ideas supportive of broad freedoms of religious expression were circulating among settlers who had already cut major social ties to the homeland.

Through the nineteenth century, Europe continued its expansionist ways. The leading nations established colonies in Africa, the South Seas, the mainland of Asia, and the Middle East. The United States and Canada pushed their ambitions for territorial expansion across North America. Everywhere the Europeans and Americans went, they found new and diverse religions, radically different from the beliefs and practices of the Christianity and Judaism with which they were most familiar. A few scholars began to study these new faiths and to share their findings first with colleagues back home, and then as the century came to an end, with the public at large. A small but significant minority of these early students of the world's religions found in these newly discovered faiths what had been lacking in their own religious upbringing, and they became the first modern Western converts to Islam, Buddhism, and Hinduism.

By the second half of the nineteenth century, the major Protestant churches of Europe and North America were gearing up for a worldwide missionary endeavor that would literally carry them to every country of the world, to many areas that had yet to be mapped. Through the last decades of the century, books, from superficial travelogues to scholarly texts, would document what the missionaries found. From this time forward, the theological task would include the incorporation of knowledge of the presence of many different religions outside of the Abrahamic lineage (i.e., neither Judaism, Christianity, nor Islam). Eastern intellectual leaders would confront the learned centers of the West with the subtleties of Indian philosophy, the Buddhist parallels to Christianity, and the imperial power behind Shintoism.

While there were many shades of opinion, two essential approaches emerged that would dominate the Western religious community's response to the ever-increasing levels of religious pluralism through the twentieth century. One group of leaders saw in the existence of the world's different religions an opportunity, if not a moral imperative, to learn and understand. Each of these leaders possessed an appreciation for the accomplishments, ethical integrity, and spiritual life of at least one of the world's religious communities and could by analogy extend that appreciation to the other communities. In the beginning of the twentieth century, almost all westerners saw Christianity as superior to other religions; they also could not deny the many likenesses each of the different faiths shared with one another and with Christianity. Such an approach undergirded the organization and furtherance of interfaith activities.

A second group of leaders saw the existence of the world's different religions as a challenge to their Christian faith. Foreign lands dominated by Buddhists, Hindus, Muslims, and other smaller (in number of adherents) faiths led these leaders first to create and then back the international missionary enterprise. However, the reaffirmation of Christianity's superiority and uniqueness accompanying the missionary enterprise also highlighted the scandal of Christianity's many divisions, especially when a heated debate from home was carried to the mission field and became focused in the rival recruitment activities of two mission stations in the same community. Christian leaders were spurred to cooperative and coordinated activity by the necessity of presenting a united front on the mission field (which in the nineteenth century included the American West) and making the most of their missionary dollars.

Those who saw the world primarily as a target for evangelism tended to move toward Christian ecumenical endeavors. While many arguments based in abstract theological ideals could and would be made for Christians to put aside their sectarian differences, to find their oneness in their common affirmation of the same Christ, and to cooperate in what all saw as important endeavors, the argument from the missionary field would remain dominant for many decades.

INTERFAITH BEGINNINGS: THE WORLD'S PARLIAMENT OF RELIGIONS. Unitarian James Freeman Clarke (1810–1888), while a professor at Harvard Divinity School, pioneered the study of what he termed *comparative theology*. As

Interfaith and Ecumenical Family Chronology

1846 At a conference held in London, some 800 people from 52 churches in eight countries launch modern ecumenical movement by forming the Evangelical Alliance.

1893 A generation of the study of the world's religion in the West leads to the gathering of representatives from around the globe in Chicago for the first World's Parliament of Religions.

1908 Most of the larger Protestant churches join in the formation of the Federal Council of Churches.

1910 Edinburgh Missionary Conference initiates new effort at international ecumenical cooperation.

1914 Philanthropist Andrew Carnegie gives two million dollars for the work of the Church Peace Union which is to include Protestant, Roman Catholic and Jewish leadership.

1920 Preparatory Conference on Faith and Order meets in Geneva.

1921 John R. Mott is named chairman of the International Missionary Council.

1925 Conference on Life and Work gathers in Stockholm, Sweden.

1927 The first international Conference on Faith and Order meets at Lausanne, Switzerland.

1930 The Universal Christian Council for Life and Work meets at Chexbres, Switzerland.

1934 An early attempt by African American Christians to raise their level of cooperation results in the formation of the National Fraternal Council of Negro Churches. Its work led to the formation of the Interdenominational Theological Center in Atlanta, Georgia.

1937 Second World Conference on Faith and Order.

1941 Separatist fundamentalists found American Council of Christian Churches.

1942 Moderate fundamentalists (who had come to be known as Evangelicals) form National Association of Evangelicals.

1944 Canadian Council of Churches founded.

1947 America and Canadian Lutheran churches join in formation of the Lutheran World Fellowship which immediate turns its attention to the rebuilding of post-war Europe.

First World Pentecostal Conference gathers in Zurich, Switzerland.

1948 Representatives of 147 Protestant and Eastern Orthodox churches form the World Council of Churches with headquarters in Geneva, Switzerland.

1950 National Council of Churches of Christ in the U.S.A. supersedes the Federal Council of Churches.

1951 Evangelicals establish the World Evangelical Fellowship.

World Methodist Council formed to continue work of the Ecumenical Methodist conference.

1957 The World Conference of All Religions organized by Jain Master H. H. Acharya Sushil Kumarji Maharaj meets in Delhi and leads to the founding of the World Fellowship of Religions.

1960 Pope John XXIII forms Secretariat for Promoting Christian Unity to administer a new effort to dialogue with the Christian churches not in communion with Rome.

1962–65 Second Vatican Council creates new opportunities within Catholicism for ecumenical and interfaith relationships. Protestants attend as official observers.

1970 A decade of work for peace led to the first World Conference on Peace in Kyoto and the organization of the World Conference on Religion and Peace as a continuing organization.

The International Congregational Council and the World Alliance of Reformed Churches unite to form the World Alliance of Reformed Churches (Presbyterian and Congregational).

1973 Conversations between Lutheran and Reformed churches aimed at reaching enough agreement to allow formal communion and pulpit fellowship culminates in the formation of the Leuenberg Church fellowship.

1988 Pope John Paul II recognizes accomplishments of the Secretariat for Promoting Christian Unity by renaming it the Pontifical Council for Promoting Christian Unity.

1993 The Council for a Parliament of the World's Religions hosts the centennial celebration of the first Parliament.

1990 Episcopal bishop William E. Swing leads in formation of United Religions Initiative.

1997 The National Holiness Association, originally formed in 1867 as the National Camp Meeting Association for the Promotion of Holiness, changes its name to Christian Holiness Partnership.

1999 Parliament of the World's Religions gathers in Cape Town, South Africa.

2001 World Pentecostal Conference meets in Los Angeles in anticipation of the centennial of the Azusa Street revival that launched the movement in 1906.

2004 Some 8,900 people attend the third Parliament of the World's Religions gathering in Barcelona, Spain.

2006 Pentecostals gather in Los Angeles to celebrate the centennial of the Apostolic Faith Mission established on Azusa Street and the resultant revival that launched their global movement.

2009 Parliament of the World's Religions to gather in Melbourne, Australia.

---

defined by him, the field's first problem was "analytical, being to distinguish each religion from the rest." He compared different religions to see wherein they agreed and wherein they differed. But the next problem, he added, "is synthetical, and considers the adaptation of each system to every other, to determine its place, use, and value, in reference to universal or absolute religion" (*Ten Great Religions* [1868] 1895). As information about different religions filtered back to the West, the early students of world religion began the task of sketching out the upward evolutionary trend they discerned in religious life and thought. This trend led directly to the crown and pinnacle of Christianity in its liberal Protestant form. Tying all of the religions together was an ideal and absolute religion to which any particular faith more or less conformed and by which it could be measured.

Such a perspective fit in nicely with the positive evolutionary thought of the day with its intense faith in human progress. As Clarke further noted of his intellectual discipline, the study of comparative religion "shows the relation of each particular religion to human civilization and observes

World Map of Prevailing Religions

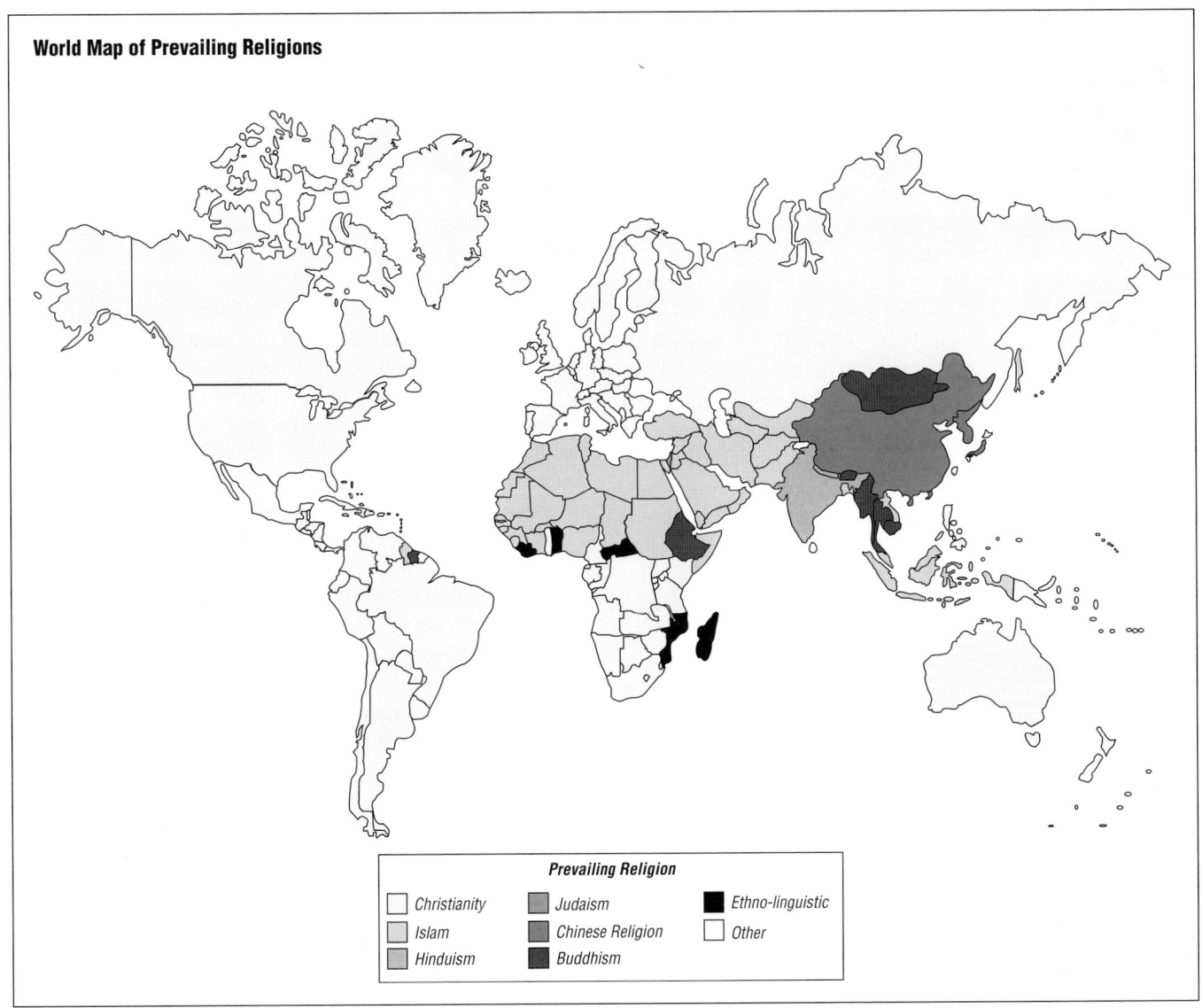

Prevailing Religion

- Christianity
- Islam
- Hinduism
- Judaism
- Chinese Religion
- Buddhism
- Ethno-linguistic
- Other

how each religion of the world is a step in the progress of humanity. It shows that both the positive and negative side of a religion make it a preparation for a higher religion, and that the universal religion must root itself in the decaying soil of partial religions. Christianity was superior to the other religions as it was a post-tribal faith capable of serving all humankind and an ever-evolving faith as shown by the appearance of Protestantism out of Catholicism (or Papal religion)."

While one would be hard pressed to defend Clarke's position today, it was shared by his scholarly colleagues and by many liberal religious leaders. It also supported the first great interfaith effort, the World's Parliament of Religions, held in Chicago in the fall of 1893. The parliament actually grew out of another event, the Columbian Exposition, a massive celebration of the 400th anniversary of Christopher Columbus's discovery of America. As congresses were created to give expression to each area of human knowledge, the question of religion arose, and in 1891 Presbyterian minister John Henry

Barrows (1847–1902) was chosen to chair a committee to consider the question of the appropriateness of a congress of religion.

Barrows's committee quickly reached a consensus that such a congress was a worthy enterprise and that it should consist of representatives of all of the world's major religions. In reaching that decision, the committee set off a debate over the form that such a meeting could have and the relationship of different religions to each other implicit in such a gathering. It was the hope of the committee in issuing a call for cooperation in the holding of such a congress that it would be an expression of mutual respect and not sow any additional seeds of discord (as many who opposed the idea feared).

Once the conference was set, representatives of many different Christian churches and all of the major non-Christian religious groups chose to participate, but for a variety of very different reasons. The more idealistic groups believed that in coming together to talk about the overriding concerns of the era, the great truths that they believed permeated all religions would come to the fore and point to a direction for the uplifting of humankind and the solving of its major problems. Many of the smaller groups saw the parliament as a platform from which they could state their case to a large audience. Some of the Eastern religions seized the opportunity to refute what they considered to be misrepresentations of them in Christian literature. In the end, some joined in simply to avoid being left out.

The World's Parliament of Religions was a magnificently staged production; the building presently housing the Art Institute of Chicago was constructed especially for its sessions. It opened to a full house of 4,000 in the main hall on September 11, 1893, and continued for 17 days. While each of the represented religions had ample opportunity to sing its own praises (and a number of groups held special sessions for adherents), the program of the parliament centered upon the discussion of various social issues, from the status and role of women to the imperative for religions to assist the rise of African Americans. Crime, labor relations, international arbitration, and general social reform received the attention of a cadre of presenters.

Interestingly enough, the stars of the parliament were not the famous preachers and orators of the day, but two virtual unknowns: British Theosophical leader Annie Besant (1847–1933) and Indian teacher Swami Vivekananda (1863–1902). Besant, well-known in England for her oratorical skills, received an enthusiastic response for her talk to the Theosophists' denominational congress. Whenever Swami Vivekananda spoke, the large hall had to be used to accommodate the crowd that flocked to hear the charismatic young teacher who so articulately and vigorously defended his homeland and his Hindu faith.

The parliament's planners were unable to predict the major consequences of their establishing the series of meetings. The gathering became an unprecedented opportunity for representatives of Buddhism, Hinduism, and Islam to present their teachings to a virgin audience. Capable speakers from each community, to the surprise of their audience, demonstrated that their religion was sophisticated enough to stand beside anything the West had to offer, and a few members of the audience decided that these new foreign faiths offered a valid alternative to the Christianity or Judaism in which they had been raised. Plans emerged to follow up on what they had heard at the parliament. Swami Vivekananda stayed in the United States to teach, and he eventually organized the first Hindu center in the country, the Vedanta Society of New York. Muslim leader Alexander Russell Webb (1846–1916) also moved to New York City, where he opened the first mosque in the country and midwifed the emergence of the Muslim community. Buddhists had already established a presence in the United States; though generally confined to ethnic communities in California during the gold rush, Buddhists now made arrangements not only to accept Western converts, but to actively offer their faith to westerners.

The primary motivating force behind the World's Parliament of Religions—liberal Protestant leaders like James Freeman Clarke—believed in the moral and ideological superiority of Christianity as the particular religious expression that most closely approached their ideal of a universal and absolute religion. This view did not fare as well at the congress as other perspectives, but following the congress, they were able to institutionalize their program of promoting liberal Protestantism when Caroline E. Haskell endowed the Barrows Lectures through the University of Chicago. The lectures were named in honor of John Henry Barrows, the university's professor who served as president of the parliament. The endowment called for a set of lectures to be given annually in Calcutta, India, and other cities in India as appropriate, on the relationship of Christianity to other religions. In this manner, the case for Christianity could be regularly presented before an audience of educated Hindus with the hope that they would come to see the convincing claims of the Christian faith. Barrows himself delivered the first set of lectures, collectively titled "Christianity, the World Religion." The series continued for several years, but there was no report of any converts, especially among influential Indians, from the presentations.

Possibly the most substantial fruit of the parliament was the more formal organization of the most liberal wing of American religion into a cooperative organization, the American Congress of Liberal Religious Societies. Even before the establishment of the congress, Unitarian and Universalist church leaders, primarily in the Midwest, had been cooperating in the production of a Chicago-based periodical, *Unity*. The parliament inspired them to take the additional step of creating a national organization that would bring together not only liberal Christians but Reform Jews, Ethical Culturists, and other liberal religious voices for cooperative endeavors. Some 200 people attended the organizational meeting in 1894 at Chicago's prominent Sinai Temple, the Reform Jewish synagogue on the shores of Lake Michigan.

The new American Congress of Liberal Religious Societies emerged around the ideal of what it termed "undogmatic" religion. The congress looked for the organization of nonsectarian churches and societies based upon absolute religious liberty. Members included not only churches and synagogues belonging to older denominations (including one Quaker congregation), but several new independent churches, such as Jenken Lloyd Jones's All Souls Church in Chicago. The congress went through several name changes, emerging in 1900 as simply the Congress of Religion.

Changes in the religious alignment of the major supporters of the Congress of Religion made it increasingly obsolete after the turn of the century. But in the meantime, Unitarian leaders in New England (where liberal religion actually enjoyed its greatest strength) founded a cooperative organization with the ponderous name of International Congress of Unitarian and other Liberal Religious Thinkers and Workers. This congress drew support from the center of both the

Unitarian and Universalist movements, as opposed to the older Congress of Religion, which had claimed the most liberal and radical religionists among its key supporters. At its meeting in Boston in 1907, the International Congress proposed the formation of a national federation of religious liberals, somewhat like the newly formed Federal Council of Churches (see below) then in the process of formation, and among the major Protestant organizations. Thus, as the Congress of Religion faded, the new Federation of Religious Liberals of America arose to take its place.

The federation was unburdened by the "nonsectarian" language of the older congress and did not threaten established denominational interests. Using the Federal Council of Churches model, leaders avoided the antidenominational activity of calling for the formation of independent unaligned congregations. Approximately 1,000 attended the first gathering in Philadelphia in 1909. Its establishment orientation was clearly demonstrated in 1913, when the entire social program of the Federal Council of Churches was adopted as its own. The organization's National Council met regularly until the early 1930s, when it fell victim to the Great Depression.

In the meantime, the international body (which, following a series of name changes, finally emerged as the International Congress of Religious Liberals) had its ups and downs, especially through the period following World War I (1914–1918). In 1930 the weakening organization was superseded by the International Association for the Promotion of Liberal Christianity and Religious Freedom, with a secretariat located in Amsterdam. World War II (1937–1945) again disrupted the organization, and the headquarters returned to the United States. More recently, it revived as the International Association for Religious Freedom and reestablished its European presence with a secretariat in Frankfurt, Germany. It is currently the oldest international interfaith organization in existence, and in the last generation has built a vital program focused in its triennial congresses.

The devastation of World War I gave birth to visionaries who saw the role that a unified world religious community could play in the postwar recovery. Among them were such very different people as Charles Frederick Weller (1870–1957) and Jane Addams (1860–1935) in Chicago, Francis Younghusband (1863–1942) in England, and the Maharaja Gaekwar of Baroda (1863–1939) in Gujarat, India. Their vision merged with the aspirations of others, and in 1924 led three American groups—the League of Neighbors, the Union of East and West, and the Fellowship of Faiths—to unite their efforts in the formation of what would become the World Fellowship of Faiths. Beginning in 1925, the new fellowship held an initial meeting in New York City, followed by additional gatherings across the United States, in London, and in India. Affiliated meetings soon took place across Europe and into the West Indies.

As news was received that a world's fair would be held in Chicago in 1933, suggestions for a meeting analogous to the 1893 World's Parliament of Religions began circulating and plans for a gathering of a World Fellowship of Faiths got underway. Two important steps beyond the parliament of 1893 were suggested for the 1933 event: First, greater emphasis would be placed upon religious communities applying their faith to solving human problems with a resulting de-emphasis upon their simply restating their positions on various issues. Second, the term *faiths*, rather than *religions*, would be used so that fellowship leaders would understood that their conversation was not limited to members of formally organized religions; all types of spiritual consciousness and conviction would be included in the dialogue established by the fellowship.

In the end, the fellowship moved faster than the world's fair, and thus, in the summer of 1933, 83 sessions of the World Fellowship of Faiths were convened in an effort that surpassed the original parliament in both size and scope. More than 250 key religious and secular leaders from around the world participated, from Methodist bishop Francis McConnell (1971–1953), who served as national chairman of the 1933 gathering, to Professor John Dewey (1859–1952), a humanist, to Duke Kwei Nyamikye Kuntu of the Gold Coast, a leader of the Ashanti African religion. Following the meeting, Charles Frederick Weller collected the papers and published them in a massive volume.

Out of the 1933 meeting, Francis Younghusband took the lead and a second congress was held in London in 1936. Earlier in his life, while in Tibet in 1903, Younghusband had a mystical experience of what he described as "a mighty joy-giving power" that was at work in the world. His religious experience also led him to a belief in the mystical sense of the unity of all people. He saw in his interfaith work the task of making religious leaders aware of the mystical unity that transcended their religious differences. Among his early attempts at spreading his message, apart from his several books, was an address he gave to the Religions of the Empire Conference, a more scholarly informational meeting held in London in 1924.

Younghusband used his aristocratic connections to bring a set of speakers to the 1936 congress that were as eminent as those assembled by Francis McConnell three years previously. Younghusband also did some innovative programming by setting up dialogues and discussions between the participants as part of the program. Previously, such events had simply consisted of paper presentations without the public interaction that held the possibility of open conflict. In Younghusband's presence, such potentially disastrous discussions were carried out in an atmosphere of respect and even good humor.

The contacts leading up to the 1936 meeting nurtured the new consensus reached by the interfaith leadership in the mid-1930s concerning the insufficiency of religious *tolerance* as an ideal. Tolerance carried the notion of condescension, with the more powerful, established Western religions acting graciously toward what they viewed as their inferior religious counterparts in the rest of the world; while better than religious persecution and suppression, it was inadequate for reaching the goals of the fellowship. Thus leaders began to give vocal support to ideals of mutual appreciation, of each participant in the dialogue being able to honor the faith of others. As the implications of this position were slowly understood, people engaged in dialogue with the adoption of an attitude of listening and openness to others as they spoke out of their faith commitments. This view would come to dominate interfaith dialogue, and on occasion involved a radical and personal shift in perspective by people of deep religious commitment who also engaged in such dialogue over a period of time.

Immediately after the 1936 meeting, a continuation committee with Younghusband as chairman was established. Annual congresses were held for the next three years, but were cut short due to the outbreak of World War II and Younghusband's death in 1942. The fellowship continued in the decades after the war, and has done a monumental job in the United Kingdom of keeping alive the interfaith vision. After the war, the fellowship responded to the full resistance of a Christian movement that arose in war-torn Europe and was unwilling to consider interfaith concerns in the midst of its own intrafaith enthusiasms. However, slowly, the fellowship's work has born fruit, as England's own religious diversity has been recognized.

INTERFAITH ACTIVITY SINCE WORLD WAR II. World War II disrupted most of the fragile interfaith ties that had been built during the 1920s and 1930s. By the time the world recovered, many of the leaders active in the prewar interfaith movement had retired from the scene, and the war itself released forces that were to reorder political and social relationships internationally. Colonialism's days were numbered. Beginning with the loss of colonies by the losing countries in the war, and the move toward Indian independence, the entire colonial system began to be dismantled. For religions, this change meant a significant shift in power relationships between the religious leaders of the colonial powers and the religious leaders of once-conquered nations. Buddhists, Hindus, and Muslims around the world tolerated no implications of second-class status in dialogues that were to take place with their European and North American counterparts.

Along with the political shifts came the formation of the United Nations and the adoption in 1948 of the Universal Declaration of Human Rights. The very existence of such a body gave status to the different religions that dominated the member nations of the United Nations. The declaration specifically empowered those religions in its statement that read, "Every one has the right to freedom of thought, conscience and religion; this right includes freedom to change his religion or belief, and freedom, either alone or in community with others and in public or private to manifest his religion or belief in teaching, practice, worship and observance." The Universal Declaration largely embodied the understanding of the secular state inherent in Western thought, which suggested that in the eyes of the state, all religions are equal and that the state is not to choose among them so much as to protect the right of each to exist in the larger social community.

In such a situation, religion relinquishes its use of the state's coercive power to spread its message.

Increasingly, with the independence of India, the changes wrought by the Chinese revolution, the travel privileges afforded residents of the British Commonwealth, and the new openness to immigration expressed by the United States after 1965, representatives of and adherents to the world's religions moved to the West and established worshipping communities. And, like the Christian missionaries of the nineteenth century, they moved to gather converts from among those who had been born and raised in Europe and the Americas. As those communities grew, related institutions such as colleges, seminaries, monasteries, and publishing houses slowly appeared. Building interfaith relationships was no longer necessarily tied to international travel and global gatherings. Any of the world's urban centers was now home to the spectrum of the world's religions.

At least in the West, interfaith activity and contact dipped to its lowest point since before 1893 in the decade immediately after World War II. Amid other pressing recovery needs, interfaith activity tended to be pushed aside. When it did reemerge in strength, it did so in the service of a vital human interest—world peace. Occasioned by the 1962 Cuban missile crisis, which brought the United States and the Soviet Union to the brink of war, Dr. Dana McLean Greeley (1908–1986), Methodist bishop John Wesley Lord (1902–1989), Rabbi Maurice N. Eisendrath (1902–1973), and Bishop (later Cardinal) John Joseph Wright (1909–1979) met to discuss the possibility of creating an international structure involving religious leaders working for peace. An initial conference to this end was held in New York City in 1964, and a National Inter-Religious Conference on Peace was held two year later in Washington, D.C. Early in 1967, Homer Jack (1916–1993) and an associate made a world tour to test the waters on convening an international conference. The positive reception they encountered led to the formation of the first International Inter-Religious Symposium on Peace in New Delhi, India, in 1968, by which time many of the American delegates were deeply involved in the anti–Vietnam War (1957–1975) protest movement.

The work of the conference in New Delhi was continued two years later by an international conference on peace held in Kyoto, Japan, at which more than 300 delegates from some 40 countries established the World Conference on Religion and Peace (WCRP). Since that time, the WCRP has held world assemblies every five years, spawned numerous national and local affiliate groups to advocate the organization's peace concerns, and developed a variety of social programs, especially some responding to the needs of refugees of war.

The WCRP has had a vital international program with concern focused on a single issue: peace. The other type of successful interfaith organization has been built around a very different kind of focus: the dialogue between two (or on occasion, three) religions aimed at resolving problems between the differing communities or responding to the mutual threats faced by the communities. During the twentieth century, the most fruitful of such dialogues were carried out between Jewish and Christian leaders. While wandering broadly through religious, social, and political issues common to the two groups, the bedrock of the conversation has been the elimination of anti-Semitism and, by extension, the eradication of all forms of ethnic, racial, and religious prejudice.

No interfaith activity has commanded the time and energy that characterizes the Jewish-Christian dialogue, and efforts were only increased as the severe damage done to the Jewish community during the Nazi Holocaust became more generally known. The statement on the Jews by the Roman Catholic Church's Second Vatican Council (1962–1965), followed by similar statements from various Protestant church bodies, created new openings around which dialogue could proceed.

Beginning with initial organizations in the 1920s, today the cause of Christian-Jewish understanding is served by a set of organizations that function from the international and national levels to local congregations. Through the last half of the twentieth century, the Middle Eastern situation continued to boil, even as Muslims developed a significant presence in North America and the United Kingdom. In the shifting context, three-party dialogues between Christians, Jews, and Muslims have emerged, though they have not yet had the measurable impact on public consciousness that the Christian-Jewish dialogues have generated.

A SECOND WORLD'S PARLIAMENT, 1993. The approaching centennial of the original World's Parliament of Religions occasioned reflection by the leaders of the religious community in Chicago, some of whom began early in the 1980s to suggest that an appropriate moment was approaching to consider what had occurred as a result of the forces released at the first parliament, and to initiate a new effort at interfaith dialogue and activity. Twenty years of immigration had transformed the religious outlines of the Chicago metropolitan area, which by then was home to substantial communities of Buddhists, Hindus, and Muslims, with smaller assemblies of Zoroastrians, Sikhs, Ismaili, and Shintoists. The North American headquarters of the Baha'is was located there, and the area had congregations of most of the world's new religions.

In spite of a slow start and at times doubts as to whether the meeting would actually be held, the Centennial Parliament of the World's Religions was finally convened with more than 6,000 in attendance. The Parliament drew speakers as establishment-oriented as a Roman Catholic cardinal, as questionable as a Neopagan priestess, and as controversial as African-American leader Louis Farrakhan. The attendees adopted a lengthy ethical statement, and various continuing efforts have been initiated.

It is yet to be seen what may grow out of the 1993 parliament, but initially, even in the planning (led by the Hindu, Buddhist, and Muslim communities) and later in observing the participants, a distinct difference between 1893 and 1993 was evident. Non-Christian groups not present at the 1893 gathering saw the parliament as a time to assert their pres-

ence in the West, and the newer religions seized the opportunity to inform the older religious community of their desire to be recognized and to participate as partners in any ongoing dialogue.

Paralleling the efforts of the new parliament, a second continuing effort at interfaith dialogue emerged as part of the global activities of Korean evangelist Sun Myung Moon (b. 1920) to unite the world's people. Moon, founder and leader of the controversial Unification Church, encouraged the formation of the Global Congress of the World's Religions—originally suggested by a professor at the Unification Seminary—and poured a considerable amount of the church's resources into bringing religious leaders from around the world into both regional meetings and occasional large international gatherings. In 1985 the Global Congress was superseded by the Assembly of the World's Religions. The congress and assembly provided the most stable continuing international interreligious dialogue from the 1960s to the 1990s, but they were hampered by the boycotting of their meetings by many key religious figures who rejected any association with Moon.

Both the 1993 Parliament of the World's Religions and the activities of the Assembly of the World's Religions point to the overwhelming problem faced by those who would engage in interfaith dialogue. Such activity is usually done without the backing of the community of faith of the participants and often by people who do not have the ear of the decision-making leadership of their own faith community. Such interfaith gatherings have no direct impact upon the larger religious community, and accomplishments must be measured in other terms—in the insights, discoveries, and agreements reached by participants who then return to the larger religious community to exercise leadership informed by their interfaith experience. Slowly, a community of people deeply committed to their own faith and traditions, and also committed to the "appreciation" of the faith and spiritual wisdom of people of other faiths, has emerged, and a global context, at least in principle, in which dialogue can be nurtured has been set in place.

The new efforts at interfaith dialogue in the 1990s pioneered by the Unification Church and the new Parliament of the World's Religions were followed up by two additional efforts: the United Religions Initiative and more recently the World Council of Religious Leaders. The United Religious Initiative, founded with the backing of Episcopal bishop William Swing, bishop of San Francisco from 1979 to 2006, has dedicated its efforts to the ending of violence and the promotion of peace. It had developed as a grassroots organization and has spread through the formation of cooperation circles that by 2002 numbered 170 based in more than 60 countries. The World Council of Religious Leaders grew out of the Millennium World Peace Summit, a gathering of religious leaders held at the United Nations in August 2000. It held its first meeting in June 2002 in Bangkok, Thailand. Both organizations are still in the process of solidifying their organizational structure, and neither has been active long enough to have a list of accomplishments. The new World Council, including as it does the administrative leaders of many large religious bodies, has great potential, but has yet to demonstrate that it can overcome the entrenched interests of its constituent communities.

Following its initial meeting in Chicago, the leadership of the Parliament of the World's Religions formed the Council of the Parliament of the World's Religions as a permanent continuing structure to plan and administer future gatherings, which it was agreed would be held every five years. Successful events were held in Cape Town, South Africa (1999), and Barcelona, Spain (2004), and a fourth gathering is planned for Melbourne, Australia, in 2009.

THE PLACE OF ISLAM. The growth of Islam in the West in general and North America in particular had through the 1990s generated calls for greater Christian-Muslim dialogue to parallel the very active Christian-Jewish dialogue that by consensus was dubbed a great success. There were even some voices calling for a Christian-Jewish-Muslim dialogue. All of the developments relative to the Muslim community were called into question and then immediately gained great urgency with the September 11, 2001, attacks on the Pentagon and World Trade Center. As an environment of fear and hostility developed with the war in Afghanistan and the subsequent invasion of Iraq by U.S. Armed Forces, religious leaders began an intensive effort at Christian-Muslim dialogue. A variety of dialogues continue at both national and local levels, though their impact is yet to be felt.

INTRAFAITH ECUMENISM.

In the West, the splitting of the Christian movement into warring factions had become a constant element of Christian life to which accommodation had to be made. The churches in the easternmost nations, Syria and beyond, followed what, from the standpoint of the Western churches, were heretical paths. Eastern Orthodoxy and Roman Catholicism went their separate ways at the end of the first Christian millennium. Then the West was traumatized in the sixteenth century by the splitting of Christian Europe into Roman, Anglican, Lutheran, and Reformed territories, with bothersome Anabaptists popping up in various unexpected locations. Still, depending upon where one stood to look around, the number of factions immediately available was limited. Even the threat of Lutheranism and Anglicanism seemed to pale for papal authorities in light of the incursions of Muslim Turkish forces up the Danube Valley beyond Budapest to the gates of Vienna.

The number of actual religious competitors (i.e., different churches) remained small until the seventeenth century, when Pietism and Puritanism sent shock waves through Protestantism, and the rise of deism and free thought challenged the whole Christian enterprise as then constituted. Numerous new movements began to appear, some harshly suppressed, but most finding havens of tolerance, even if they had to flee across the Atlantic to the New World.

As Christendom splintered, counter-voices calling for the unity of the Christian movement arose, along with theologies that affirmed the unity of the church, even in the face of the obvious administrative factionalism. These voices, however, expressed the minority point of view. Even into the twentieth century, it was often difficult for Protestants and Catholics to put aside the bitter events of the Reformation era and to forgive each other for the excesses and deaths in the religious wars and persecutions. Open hostilities ceased, only to be replaced with the harshest of polemics. And even among the various Protestant groups, harsh rhetoric could be heard as each proclaimed its superiority to rivals and championed its peculiar insight into the gospel message.

In the nineteenth century, with the major Reformation and Puritan Protestant groups gaining solid organizational power and stabilizing their position in the larger society, Protestant leaders began to think in terms of some kind of understanding that might lead to their engagement in cooperative endeavors in the face of common goals and tasks. Much of that commonality came from the opportunity for global expansion, as Europeans began their explorations of the rest of the world and as North Americans moved across the continent to claim it and settle it for the United States and Canada.

The churches' responses to the forces operating on them at the beginning of the nineteenth century can be seen in the Plan of Union of 1801 and the emergence of the Disciples of Christ movement. By the beginning of the nineteenth century, westward migration was seen as a major theme in American life, and it was obvious to the leaders of the two largest Protestant churches of New England that they were expending much energy in taking their quarrel over church polity into the newly opened territories west of the Appalachian Mountains. Hence, in 1801, they worked out an agreement by which they cut their competition in the American West and divided the rest of the world into exclusive missionary areas. The plan worked for more than a generation, until the Congregationalists perceived that it gave the Presbyterians a distinct advantage in the west, and pulled out in 1852.

The Disciples of Christ was a new denomination that arose in the American West, partially in response to the sectarian bickering between the various Presbyterian, Baptist, and Methodist churches. The Disciples of Christ refused to accept a "denominational" name, though its doctrine was largely a Baptist-Calvinist theology, including the Baptist free-church perspective that eschewed any sacraments (in favor of the ordinances of baptism and the Lord's Supper) and radically limited any organization above the congregational level. While opposing sectarianism, the founders failed to perceive that sectarianism or denominationalism was the form of religious life in a free secular society. Where the physical coercion of the state did not operate, religious debate never resolved issues, and only made each party more resolute in its position. In such a setting, the nonsectarian ideal became simply another sectarian perspective held by the group denominated as the Disciples of Christ.

Thus it was that a more realistic attempt to unite Christians across denominational lines, to present a common front, to work on mutual tasks that could be done most effectively by cooperation, and to avoid denominational bickering emerged in the early nineteenth century with the suggestion of the formation of an international alliance of Protestant (or Evangelical) churches. The original suggestion seems to have come from several European church leaders, but four Americans quickly emerged as champions of the cause: Leonard W. Bacon (1802–1881), Robert Baird (1798–1863), William Patton (1798–1879), and Samuel Schumacher. Their initial efforts culminated in the formation in 1839 of the Society for the Promotion of Christian Unity, one of a variety of voluntary societies supported primarily by the Congregationalists and the older Lutheran and Reformed churches in nineteenth-century America. The effectiveness of the organization, however, was hampered by the divisions that were then occurring in the larger Protestant bodies due to the slavery crisis.

In the midst of the conflicting tensions of organization breakups and calls for union, British leaders issued a call for a conference in London in August 1846 for the purpose of forming an international Evangelical Alliance. Given the participation of leaders from the Church of England, the new alliance had to handle the question of denominationalism carefully. The alliance structured itself as a coalition of individual Christians, not denominations, and made clear that no intentions of creating a new super church or world church administratively existed.

The conference was able to reach some agreement on essential beliefs, and affirmed common Christian doctrines of the authority of the Bible, the Trinity, the deity of Christ, the sanctifying work of the Holy Spirit, and future life in heaven and hell. In distinction from Roman Catholicism, general assent was given to the doctrine of justification by faith alone. It was also obvious that Roman Catholicism was seen as the major presence to which some response was necessary. The conference struggled with the issue of making defining affirmations, but in such a way as to not override the equally important belief in the right of private judgment on the reading and interpretation of scripture. Issues of predestination, election, and free will (the issues that divided Anglicans and Methodists from Presbyterians and Congregationalists) were avoided entirely. Unitarians and Universalists (nontrinitarians) were defined as outside the Evangelical camp.

The conference considered two plans for its governance. One plan would have had the British firmly in control, with various national affiliates. However, a more acceptable plan for governing the proposed alliance offered a confederation model established around six national units. Each national unit would be the equal of the others and would carry out its program and send delegates to an international conference that would gather periodically. The adoption of this plan, however, floundered on the subsequent controversy that arose over American slavery and the unwillingness of the Europeans to enter into any union with slaveholders. While

some progress toward an international alliance was reached, in the end it fell apart as the Americans withdrew.

As a result of the London meeting, an international Evangelical Alliance continued to exist in the weakest sense, and meetings were held regularly in Europe through the remainder of the century. Britain dominated the movement and on a more practical level took the lead in spreading the Evangelical gospel worldwide. Meanwhile, the American delegates returned home and in 1846 formed an Evangelical Alliance for the United States, but it soon disbanded as the Civil War (1861–1865) approached. It was reorganized after the war in 1867, though strength was initially concentrated in the northern urban centers. The life of the alliance in America was placed in the hands of theologian Philip Schaff (1819–1893), businessman William E. Dodge (1805–1883), and general secretary Josiah Strong (1847–1916). Emphasis was placed on social work, organization at the community level, and evangelism of the unchurched.

The alliance era, both nationally and internationally, forms the first chapter in the modern ecumenical movement. The work of the prospering alliance was continually undercut, however, in the face of denominational growth programs that led to increasing competition for members by denominations, and in the regular emergence of new denominations that were often bitter foes of the group from which they had just departed. The alliance's most noticeable continuing contribution to American religious culture was the annual Week of Prayer for Christian Unity. During the late nineteenth century, however, the alliance had significant success in promoting religious liberty and protecting Protestant missionaries from oppressive governments around the world.

Also competing with the world Evangelical movement was the movement by various denominational families to pull together and reaffirm their common roots. The first were the Anglicans, who in 1865 called the initial Lambeth Conference at the Church of England's headquarters, Lambeth Palace in London. While initially dealing with internal issues of the national bodies in communion with the Church of England, it expanded its program to provide a focus for defining relationships with likeminded churches around the world and to set policy on the nature of such relationships.

Reformed and Presbyterian churches held an initial gathering of what was called the Alliance of Reformed Churches throughout the World Holding the Presbyterian System in 1873. Three years later, the General Conference of the Methodist Episcopal Church issued the call for what eventually evolved into the first Methodist Ecumenical Conference in London in 1881. That conference met every decade for more than half a century until it was superseded by the present World Methodist Council. In 1889 the Old Catholic Churches of Europe formed the Union of Utrecht. Following the suggestion of Canadian Congregationalists in 1885, an International Congregational Council assembled in London in 1891. The Baptist World Alliance grew out of the gathering of Baptists from 23 countries in London in 1905.

These denominational family structures outwardly cooperated fully with the pandenominational organizations and generally saw themselves as an extension and expression of such ecumenical work. However, at the practical level, these family groups presented additional competition for the time and resources of individuals and churches for ecumenical endeavors. As calls for church union arose in the pandenominational organizations, the practical effect was the union of members of the denominational families. Unions across denominational lines were the rarest of occurrences in American Christianity, and in fact were only effective in countries where Protestant Christians were a distinct and somewhat beleaguered minority.

THE FEDERAL COUNCIL ERA. Astute observers of the Protestant Christian community at the beginning of the twentieth century could see looming signs of radical change and the prospect of trouble ahead. Intense debates were moving forward on issues that had embedded themselves into the religious community—the new sciences of biology and geology were challenging biblical authority just as the new insights of the historical (higher or destructive) criticism of the Bible were coming out of Germany. The social gospel was suggesting a marked redirection of church life away from evangelism toward social planning and the building of a more just society. Immigration was beginning to reshape city life. Ever-increasing knowledge of world religions on the one hand and a growing atheist movement on the other were challenging the theological framework of traditional Christianity.

However, few were prepared at the turn of the century to see in these forces the rationale for radically altering church life. In fact, the larger Protestant denominations were enjoying an era of growth and had just come to see themselves as functionally constituting America's established religions in a country with no official establishment. Over against the religions of the world, over against a Roman Catholic Church (by this time by far the largest single church body in the United States), and over against the still significant number of unchurched citizens, the Protestant churches reigned supreme in the religious community.

Through the decade following the Civil War, the Evangelical Alliance had been the primary organizational expression of that Protestant establishment, but with the passing of its initial core of powerful leadership in the 1890s, the alliance was left a shell of its former self. In its stead, a new prophet arose in the person of Elias B. Sanford (1843–1932). A Congregationalist with Methodist roots, Sanford proposed the formation of a delegated Federal Council of Churches. It would go beyond the Evangelical Alliance, an organization of individual members, but would stay away from ideas aimed at creating a single super church or amalgamation with the Roman Catholics.

The Federal Council would allow the Protestant churches to speak with a united voice on those many issues in which they in fact had agreement and to exert greater influence on the moral climate and social conditions of the day. Without

initially adopting the social gospel perspective, the council did represent a positive response to the demands for more attention to the social context than had previously been given by the churches. At the time of the council's formation, it adopted a revised form of the social statement adopted a few years earlier by the Methodist Episcopal Church, South. Rather than develop the full program that some might expect, the Federal Council chose instead to nurture a variety of other independent ecumenical groups that had already established hegemony over particular areas of concern.

The formation in 1908 of the Federal Council of Churches in the United States coincided with the need felt by Christians internationally to provide for more coordinated activity on the mission field. Working in areas where Christianity was a new religion and where the Christian community was small and represented an intrusion into a traditional culture, missionaries felt drawn to fellowship with their colleagues from other churches. In such settings, denominational particularities inherited by them from another century faded in importance and a more common witness to the faith emerged. Missionaries became the new champions of the notion that the division of Christianity into warring factions was the great hindrance to their work. These divisions were of even less concern to recent converts who saw the European and American churches importing a foreign history into their countries that not only did not help new converts become better Christians but actively slowed their progress.

John R. Mott (1865–1955), a Methodist layman with a strong sense of Christian unity and missionary zeal, organized a delegated conference with official representatives from the different missionary societies, both independent and denominationally affiliated. Out of this conference came a new organization in 1921, the International Missionary Council, which provided a continuing opportunity for ecumenical relationships to grow.

The Edinburgh Missionary Conference, which met in 1910, supplied some impetus for the formation of a sister movement to begin the discussion of the relationships of Christians to fellow Christians of other denominations. In the years following Edinburgh, proposals were made to begin conferences discussing issues of what was then termed "faith and order." Though slowed by the outbreak of World War I, the first international Conference on Faith and Order convened in Lausanne, Switzerland, in 1927. It too established a body to insure that deliberations were pursued on an ongoing basis, the Continuation Committee, and agreed to meet again a decade later. The International Missionary Council, and the Continuation Committee on Faith and Order, spawned an international ecumenical discussion of immense importance both for the consensus it slowly built, at least among liberal Protestants, and the relationships it created among the leaders of various denominations. Their work would be carried on through World War II and the new era signaled by the 1948 formation of the World Council of Churches.

Back in the United States, the major churches were slowly becoming battlegrounds as fundamentalists, the more conservative branch of the church, and the modernists, the more liberal branch, divided into two camps. The modernists were defined by their embracing of many of the new elements of twentieth-century society: the critical approach to the biblical text, the progressive view of human society undergirded by the belief in evolution, a desire to reorganize society into a more just social order, and the understanding that other religions had some truth in them. Each of these ideas carried immense potential for affecting the life of the Christian church from the highest international office to the local congregation. Collectively, modernists tended to undermine biblical authority, challenge traditional understandings of sin and grace, and focus upon social and political issues rather than membership recruitment and evangelism. They carried great intellectual appeal and gradually came to dominate many of the leading seminaries.

As World War I, a decidedly uniting factor in churches, came to an end, fundamentalist and conservative voices were raised against the growing visible presence of modernists in key denominational positions, especially the denominational staff, mission boards, and seminary faculties. The debate heated to a boiling point through the 1920s, especially in the northern Presbyterian and Baptist churches. By the early 1930s, it was evident to the fundamentalists that they had delayed too long and had lost control of the denominational apparatus and the seminaries (where the great majority of future leaders would be trained). Thus a series of schisms began to occur in which many of the conservative leaders resigned and formed a series of new denominations with such names as the Orthodox Presbyterian Church, the Bible Presbyterian Church, the Conservative Baptist Association, and the General Association of Regular Baptist Churches.

As the schisms occurred, fundamentalists were divided into three distinct camps. Many of the fundamentalists refused to participate in the schisms and remained in the older denominations. They became the core of continuing conservative caucuses in most of the large liberal Protestant bodies. Those who did split divided primarily over the issue of separatism. Some fundamentalists argued for complete separation from modernists and from those who associate with modernists (i.e., the fundamentalists who remained in the larger denominations). Others simply withdrew from what they felt had become an apostate denomination but kept ties to individuals inside those denominations whom they knew otherwise to be sound doctrinally. As World War II began, the separatist fundamentalists became a group unto themselves, while the nonseparatists and those still within the denominations made common cause and became the core of a new movement, Evangelicalism.

ECUMENISM SINCE WORLD WAR II. Through the 1940s, forces unleashed during the first half of the century would coalesce, organize, and reorganize to produce the essential ecumenical establishment as it exists at present. The United States would exert tremendous leverage on the world scene as the nation that came out of the war not only victorious, but among the least damaged. It would lead in the postwar reconstruction efforts and its churches would play a prominent role. There would also be the attempt to carry the issues that split the American church in the 1930s to the rest of the world and, in effect, impose the divisions on Christians.

In 1941 the separationists among the fundamentalists, now largely confined to several relatively small denominations, organized the American Council of Christian Churches. It had as its standard of membership the agreement on a very conservative Protestant theological position and opposition to all forms of liberalism as represented by the Federal Council of Churches. As relations with the Soviet Union soured and the Cold War began, the organization was articulate in the cause of anticommunism.

The American Council found capable leadership in the person of Carl McIntire (1906–2002), a Presbyterian leader who had aligned himself with the conservative J. Gresham Machen (1881–1937) at Princeton, but then split with Machen over premillennialism and separatism. A talented speaker, McIntire pastored a large congregation in Collinswood, New Jersey, and for many decades hosted a national radio show, *The Twentieth-Century Reformation Hour*.

Having built a viable American organization, as news of the impending organization of the World Council of Churches spread, McIntire mustered what international support he could and formed the International Council of Christian Churches. The International Council chose Amsterdam in 1948 as its place and time of organization, the exact spot chosen by the World Council of Churches. The confusion that ensued among reporters who little understood, in many cases, the difference between the two organizations, gave the International Council an immediate boost, and it would frequently be accused of attempting to disrupt the World Council by deliberately creating confusion and spreading the false image that it represented a much larger constituency than it actually did.

Eventually, at the end of the 1960s, McIntire had a falling out with a number of his colleagues in the United States and was removed from his position with the American Council of Christian Churches. McIntire, and those who supported him, regrouped as the American Christian Action Council. The split in what was already a small group largely silenced the American Council's voice as a viable alternative on the national religious scene. In the meantime, the International Council continued, though without the bulk of its American support. It found some strength among older missionary churches that had consistently been more conservative than their European and American parent bodies. Out of the International Council also came a set of denominational family intrafaith groups that paralleled the larger liberal Protestant denominational family structures.

Spurred along by the formation of the American Council, nonseparatist conservative leaders—primarily among Presbyterian, Congregationalist, and Baptist Churches—also sought a means of uniting their voices and of creating a struc-

Symbols of Major Faiths

Faith	Symbol	Faith	Symbol
Christian Cross		Community of Christ	
Buddhist (Wheel of Righteousness)		Sufism Reoriented	
Judaism (Star of David)		Tenrikyo Church	
Presbyterian Cross		Seicho-no-ie	
Russian Orthodox Cross		Church of World Messianity (Izunome)	
Lutheran Cross		United Church of Religious Science	
Episcopal Cross		Christian Reformed Church	
Unitarian Church/Unitarian Universalist Association		United Moravian Church	
United Methodist Church		Eckankar	
Aaronic Order Church		Christian Church	
Mormon (Angel Moroni)		Christian & Missionary Alliance	
Native American Church of North America		United Church of Christ	
Serbian Orthodox		Humanist Emblem of Spirit	
Greek Cross		Presbyterian Church (USA)	
Bahai (9 Pointed Star)		Izumo Taishakyo Mission of Hawaii	
Atheist		Soka Gakkai International—USA	
Muslim (Crescent and Star)		Sikh (Khanda)	
Hindu		Wicca (Pentacle)	
Konko-Kyo Faith			

Adapted from U.S. Department of Veterans Affairs.

ture that would speak to their unique situation. First, they wanted to speak as conservative Protestants against liberal Protestantism, but they distinguished themselves from the separatist fundamentalists. While some were in new denomi-

nations, such as the Orthodox Presbyterians and Conservative Baptists, many, if not the majority, of conservative leaders were still in the larger denominations. They needed a name to distinguish themselves and found it in the term *Evangelical*, at times using the designation of *neo-Evangelical*. They needed an organization that would unite both those Evangelicals still in the older denominations and those in the newer Evangelical denominations. They found the solution in the National Association of Evangelicals (NAE), established in 1942, which provided for membership by denominations, organizations, local congregations, and individuals. Thus a conservative pastor and his congregation, though officially a member of a liberal Protestant denomination, could also affiliate with the NAE.

Conservative leaders who remained within the older denominations had the problem of access to a seminary. Because most of the seminaries had been captured by liberals, they had nowhere to send ministerial candidates who could form a continuing source of conservative leadership for the next generation. They saw the possibility of the Evangelical perspective simply dying out in the older churches. That problem was partially solved by the formation in 1947 of Fuller Theological Seminary, an independent seminary firmly rooted in the traditional Calvinist theology shared by Baptists, Congregationalists, and Presbyterians. The formation of Fuller, located in Pasadena, California, also served as an announcement that Evangelicals were prepared to continue to confront their liberal counterparts on the academic level.

As the National Association of Evangelicals grew, it had to come to grips with the new alignments within conservative Protestantism as a whole, arguably the most important factor in that reordering being the spectacular success of Pentecostalism in the wake of the charismatic movement of the 1970s. Frequently derided through the first half of the twentieth century, Pentecostals grew to strength by midcentury, founded their own family intrafaith organization, the Pentecostal Fellowship of North America (since 1994 the Pentecostal and Charismatic Churches of North America), and in 1947 began holding the World Pentecostal Conferences. Pentecostals came out of World War II with a distinctly ecumenical stance that found embodiment in the ministry of David DuPlessis (1905–1987), a South African who wandered the world introducing the Pentecostal movement to any and all Christians who would listen. Equally important were organizations like the Full Gospel Businessman's Fellowship International, which brought lay people of all denominations together in their common experience of the Pentecostal gifts of the Holy Spirit. Pentecostals soon found a national hero in Oral Roberts (b. 1918), the first successful televangelist.

As Pentecostals gained a new level of success in the 1970s, and as they sought entrance into the National Association of Evangelicals, all of whose formal entrance and fellowship requirements they fully met, gradually the barriers between Evangelicals from a Calvinist theological background and those from Methodist backgrounds (i.e., Holiness and Pentecostal) began to crumble. The NAE emerged as the voice of this much larger reordered Evangelical movement, and its influence in making public policy (an arena once left entirely to the Federal and National Councils of Churches) steadily grew.

FROM FEDERAL TO NATIONAL COUNCIL. Some of the most important changes to come out of World War II were the cooperative efforts of the American and European churches in the rebuilding of Europe. These efforts provided an agenda by which the interfaith trends that had been projected so strongly prior to the war could be revived and could reach culmination. Ecumenical ideals, left on hold during the war, were revived and took on visible form in the creation of the World Council of Churches. The essential outlines of a plan to bring the various ecumenical groups together into a single international organization had been put together as early as 1937, and a specific proposal for a World Council of Churches was developed over the next year. Only the war stood between the promulgation of that plan and its implementation.

The World Council of Churches was formed in Amsterdam in 1948 and brought together many of the larger churches of North America and Europe. While a modest number of churches from Africa, Asia, and South America were included from the beginning, much of the subsequent history of the Council has been built around its expanding perspective on world Christianity and its gradual incorporation of, especially, Asian and African churches in its membership and leadership.

Through the council, a series of national and regional ecumenical councils were organized. In the United States, the immediate effect of the council's formation was the added impetus it gave to the creation of a more effective ecumenical body serving the larger denominations. While the Federal Council of Churches had worked for half a century, by the 1940s its manifold limitations were visible to all. In name it was a council of churches, but in fact the logical workload of such an organization was parceled out to more than a dozen specialized agencies. This segregation of concern had hindered American participation in the various discussions that led to the formation of the World Council.

Not least among the factors underlying the cry for a more effective council, however, was the vision projected by a few for a united Protestant church for America. Such a church had come into existence in Canada in 1925. Also, in the years prior to World War II, a number of intrafamily mergers among the Methodist, Lutheran, and Reformed churches seemed a possible preliminary stage for the merger of churches across denominational family lines. The existence of a more effective council of churches would facilitate such mergers.

Thus it came about that a massive reorganization of American ecumenical structures occurred in 1950. The new National Council of the Churches of Christ in the U.S.A. brought together the older Federal Council with a number of specialized agencies, such as the United Council of Church Women and the International Council of Religious Education, many of which survived as divisions of the

National Council. New offices were opened on Riverside Drive in Manhattan.

The National Council of Churches (NCC) has been, for more than half a century, the most important cooperative religious organization functioning in the United States. Representing more than 40 million Christians, it has been effective in providing a united voice for the liberal Christian community. It has been especially effective in providing consultation to legislators in Washington, D.C., on a host of social concerns, such as support for the poor and needy and separation of church and state, to more organizational matters, such as chaplains for the armed services and the federal prison system.

During the years of its existence, the National Council, like the Federal Council before it, has been the center of controversy, especially as it involved itself in controversial social issues, such as the civil rights movement and the Middle East conflict. It took a leading role in reintegrating Eastern Orthodox leadership into the ecumenical scene in the post-Stalinist era, and was deeply involved in peace efforts during the Vietnam War.

The vision of a united Protestant church, however, has not been realized. During the 1960s and 1970s, interest in the possibility of such a united church rose to new heights, especially in the wake of Vatican II. One promising plan, popularly called COCU (for Consultation on Church Union), would have brought together nine churches, including the United Methodist Church, several of the African-American Methodist churches, the Episcopal Church, and the United Presbyterian Church. While COCU gained some initial support, it soon experienced difficulties both on sacramental issues (about which the Episcopalians were the least compromising) and from a general lack of broad support among the lay constituencies of participating denominations. Those most interested in the proposed united church were unable to communicate any real benefits it would bring. COCU continues as the Church of Christ Uniting (since 2002), which is attempting to negotiate agreements of full communion between the various participating bodies—an important step of mutual recognition, but not involving any merger. At the same time, the several Methodist bodies that had participated in COCU have joined together in the Commission on Pan-Methodist Cooperation and Union, looking for closer working relationships between the larger Methodist bodies across racial lines.

The failure of COCU vividly demonstrated the trend against religious groups merging across their denominational family lines. During the last century of ecumenical endeavor in the United States, only one such merger has occurred, the 1931 merger of the Christian and Congregational churches (though in fact many of the Christian Church congregations were later lost as they one-by-one pulled out of the merged body).

By the 1980s, few were left to rally liberal Protestants around a vision of a united Protestant church, though officially the COCU plan is still alive. Most members of the National Council see the future as one of cooperative endeavor but not organizational unity. In the meantime, they and their member churches face the problem of eroding support. All of the leading liberal Protestant churches have been steadily losing members since the 1960s and, given the growth of population, even more rapidly losing their relative position in the society. However, given the lack of any other religious coalition with a similarly large constituency, the National Council remains a significant organization in American religious life.

The 1990s saw a major development in Christian ecumenical relations. After a half-century of hostility, the National Association of Evangelicals and the National Council of Churches began dialogue and searched for common ground for possible cooperation on issues of mutual concern. These efforts became apparent in 1996 when the former president of NAE, Donald Argue, addressed the general assembly of the NCC. Then, in 2000, the NAE voted to drop a rule preventing member organizations from holding joint NAE-NCC membership. While the relationship between the two organizations is warming, it cost the NAE its long-term relationship with the National Religious Broadcasters, which withdrew its support in protest of the liberalizing trend.

The changes in the National Association of Evangelicals signaled not only Evangelical Protestantism's growth but its desire to claim a position within the mainstream of Christianity in America. The NAE vote in 2000 had immediate repercussions—the following year Evangelical leaders, including Pentecostal representatives, met with liberal Protestant, Roman Catholic, and Orthodox leaders to talk about a larger coalition of American Christians than that provided by existing ecumenical organizations. The initial talks led to the 2006 formation of Christian Churches Together in the USA. Initially, 34 denominations affiliated with the new organization, and others joined in the months following. Still others are in the process of considering the new organization. It is yet to be seen if Christian Churches Together will ultimately create a new Christian center in the United States.

THE ROMAN CATHOLIC CHURCH. The Roman Catholic Church is the largest single religious organization in the world. It is also the largest church body in both the United States and Canada. While twice as many people in America identify themselves as Protestant, they are scattered in hundreds of denominations, the largest being the Southern Baptist Convention, which is less than half the size of the American Roman Catholic Church. Traditionally, the Roman Catholic Church has called for the reunion of Christendom but has seen as the norm for that reunion the return of all other churches to a state of communion with the bishop of Rome.

Even the largest of non-Roman Christian churches appears minuscule when compared to the Roman Catholic Church, and until the twentieth century, no church or related group of churches provided what could be thought of as international competition to the Roman Catholic Church.

The formation of the World Council of Churches changed that situation. The subsequent making of common cause between many divergent elements of non-Roman Christianity also provided a symbolic point of dialogue between Rome and the thousands of "other" churches scattered around the globe. As negotiations proceeded between the members of the World Council, dialogue could open between the World Council and Rome. Individuals on both sides of that dialogue proposed a variety of means by which agreement on many issues, acknowledgment of each other's legitimacy, and even some degree of eventual union could be reached.

The first step in that dialogue was greatly influenced by what some see as the fruition of the work of many, and what others see as happenstance (or in theological terms, a miracle, the work of providential grace). It came in the form of a new bishop in Rome, Pope John XXIII (1881–1963), a man many said was elected because no compromise could be reached between the supporters of the "real" candidates for the office. He was initially thought of as an interim pope.

But Pope John XXIII (r. 1958–1963) caught the imagination of a generation with his spirituality, sense of humor, and graciousness. He was loved by Protestants as much as Roman Catholics, and it was he who called the first church council in almost a century, a council that would bring numerous changes to the church internally, among them the rewriting of the rules for Catholic/non-Catholic relationships. By far the most significant statement affecting interreligious relationships was the one denying the guilt of the Jews collectively for the death of Jesus. That statement came to symbolize a new era for all Christians (not just Roman Catholics) assuming responsibility for the persecution of Jews through the centuries, culminating with the Holocaust. It has been the starting point and a large percentage of the substance of all Jewish-Christian dialogue ever since.

The World Council of Churches sent official observers to the Second Vatican Council (1962–1965), and their presence undoubtedly affected the final wording of the document that opened a new era in Protestant and Orthodox contact. Harsh language was gone and Roman Catholics everywhere were encouraged to build relationships with the "separated brethren." Through the 1970s and into the 1980s, ecumenical contacts flourished, an era of good feeling was launched, and a new base of familiarity and trust was erected between Christians and Jews that now provides the foundation for ongoing discussions on a myriad of issues.

POST–VATICAN II CHANGES IN AMERICA. During the euphoria that accompanied the flurry of ecumenical contacts during the post–Vatican Council era, few noticed that even as the Christian community was drawing together, the shape of the religious landscape was changing dramatically. Beginning in 1965, large numbers of Muslims, Buddhists, and Hindus began flowing into the United States. While all three communities had been present in the United States for many decades, the new immigrants turned these once isolated ethnic enclaves into significant participants in the larger religious community. With annual growth in the tens of thousands from both immigration and conversion, the Hindu, Buddhist, and Muslim presence will play an expanding role in the creation of public policy. Each is now served by organizations analogous to the National Council of Churches.

One cannot fully understand the shifting story of contemporary interfaith and ecumenical relationships without returning to consideration of the Jewish community. Jews have been in America from early in its history, but their numbers grew greatly due to massive immigration between 1880 and 1924, when highly restrictive immigration laws that blocked Jews as well as Asians from entering the country were passed. In the American context, the Jewish community, like the Christian community, experienced both the freedoms of a modern secular society and the pressures from contemporary intellectual concerns; and, also like the Christian churches, the synagogues become divided along linguistic lines and by the extent of their Americanization. By the mid-twentieth century, three major communities were discernible—Orthodox, Conservative, and Reform—and a number of additional divisions were on the horizon.

Thus, internal pressures, such as the need to speak with a united voice on issues not related to those that divided religious Jews, along with external pressures, such as continuing anti-Semitism and, more recently, the desire to support the state of Israel, led Jewish leaders to develop cooperative structures between congregational and rabbinical associations. The most important of these associations is the Synagogue Council of America, founded in 1926 as the coordinating body for Orthodox, Conservative, and Reform rabbinical and congregational organizations. After more than a half-century of cooperation, the Synagogue Council became victim to the deterioration of relationships between the Orthodox segment of the Jewish community (the dominant element almost everywhere except the United States) and non-Orthodox religious Jews. This deterioration was most noticeable in Israel, where Reform and Conservative forms of Judaism were denied legal recognition. The Synagogue Council of American formally disbanded in 1994.

Overall, the trend in Western religion is toward greater organizational splintering and theological diversity. Ecumenical and interfaith organizations will not reverse that trend, but do provide a vital function in reducing the social tension created by the loss of religious consensus. Such organizations create a forum in which different religions can gain knowledge and understanding of each other; a vehicle by which the religious concerns of a select community can be communicated to the society as a whole; an organization in which people with very different religious perspectives can discover their common aspirations and learn to work together for the common good; and a social setting in which people, having been introduced to their neighbors of a different religious background, can discover their common humanity.

SOURCES

Interfaith Activities

Beversluis, Joel, ed. *A Sourcebook for the Community of Religions.* Chicago: Council for a Parliament of the World's Religions, 1994. 240 pp.

Braybrooke, Marcus. *Inter-Faith Organizations, 1893–1979: An Historical Directory.* New York: Mellen Press, 1980. 213 pp.

Bryant, M. Darrol, and Frank Flinn, eds. *Interreligious Dialogue: Voices from a New Frontier.* New York: Paragon, 1989. 234 pp.

Clark, Francis, ed. *Interfaith Directory.* New York: International Religious Foundation, 1987. 178 pp.

Clarke, James Freeman. *Ten Great Religions: An Essay in Comparative Theology* (1868). Boston: Houghton, Mifflin, 1895.

Cobb, John B., Jr., Leonard Swidler, Paul F. Knitter, and Monica K. Hellwig. *Death or Dialogue? From the Age of Monologue to the Age of Dialogue.* Philadelphia: Trinity Press, 1990.

Cobb, John B., Jr., and Christopher Ives, eds. *The Emptying God: A Buddhist-Jewish-Christian Conversation.* Maryknoll, NY: Orbis, 1990.

Dirks, Jerald. *The Cross & the Crescent: An Interfaith Dialogue between Christianity and Islam.* Beltsville, MD: Amana, 2001.

Gort, Jerald D., et al., eds. *On Sharing Religious Experiences: Possibilities of Interfaith Mutuality.* Grand Rapids, MI: Eerdmans, 1992.

Magida, Arthur J., and Stuart M. Matlins, eds. *How to Be a Perfect Stranger: A Guide to Etiquette in Other People's Religious Ceremonies.* Rev. ed. 2 vols. Woodstock, VT: Skylight Paths, 1999.

Miller, John W. *Interfaith Dialogue: Four Approaches.* Waterloo, ON: University of Waterloo Press, 1986. 99 pp.

Shafiq, Muhammad, and Mohammad Abu-Nimer, eds. *Interfaith Dialogue: A Guide for Muslims.* Herndon, VA: International Institute of Islamic Thought, 2007. 142 pp.

Smith, Jane I. *Muslims, Christians, and the Challenge of Interfaith Dialogue.* New York: Oxford University Press, 2007. 200 pp.

Weller, Charles Frederick, ed. *World Fellowship: Addresses and Messages by Leading Spokesmen of All Faiths, Races, and Countries.* New York: Liveright, 1935. 986 pp.

Christian Ecumenism

Bilheimer, Robert S. *Breakthrough: The Emergence of the Ecumenical Tradition.* Grand Rapids, MI: Eerdmans, 1989. 238 pp.

Burgess, Joseph A., ed. *In Search of Christian Unity: Basic Consensus, Basic Differences.* Minneapolis, MN: Fortress Press, 1991. 259 pp.

Carpenter, Joel A., ed. *A New Evangelical Coalition: Early Documents of the National Association of Evangelicals.* New York: Garland, 1988. 63 pp.

Cavert, Samuel McCrea. *The American Churches in the Ecumenical Movement, 1900–1968.* New York: Association Press, 1968. 288 pp.

———. *Church Cooperation and Unity in America: A Historical Review, 1900–1970.* New York: Association Press, 1970. 400 pp.

Desseaux, Jacques. *Twenty Centuries of Ecumenism.* Trans. Matthew J. O'Connell. New York: Paulist Press, 1984. 103 pp.

Fey, Harold, ed. *A History of the Ecumenical Movement, 1948–1968.* Vol. 2. Philadelphia: Westminster Press, 1970. 524 pp.

Ford, John T., and Darlis J. Swan, eds. *Twelve Tales Untold: A Study Guide for Ecumenical Reception.* Grand Rapids, MI: Eerdmans, 1993.

Jordan, Philip D. *The Evangelical Alliance for the United States of America, 1847–1900: Ecumenism, Identity, and the Religion of the Republic.* New York: Mellen Press, 1982. 277 pp.

Kinnamon, Michael. *Truth and Community: Diversity and Its Limits in the Ecumenical Movement.* Grand Rapids, MI: Eerdmans, 1988. 118 pp.

———. *The Vision of the Ecumenical Movement and How It Has Been Impoverished by Its Friends.* Indianapolis, IN: Chalice Press, 2002. 192 pp.

Kinnamon, Michael, and Brian Cope, eds. *Ecumenical Movement: An Anthology of Key Texts and Voices.* Geneva, Switzerland: World Council of Churches, 1997.

Lossky, Nicolas, et al., eds. *Dictionary of the Ecumenical Movement.* 2nd ed. Geneva, Switzerland: World Council of Churches; Grand rapids, MI: Eerdmanns, 2002. 1196 pp.

McDonnell, John J. *The World Council of Churches and the Catholic Church.* New York: Mellen Press, 1985. 467 pp.

Meyer, Harding, ed. *That All May Be One: Perceptions and Models of Ecumenicity.* Trans. William G. Rusch. Grand Rapids, MI: Eerdmans, 1999.

Murphy, Francesca A, and Christopher Asprey. *Ecumenism Today: The Universal Church in the 21st Century.* Aldershot, U.K.: Ashgate, 2008. 238 pp.

Rouse, Ruth, and Stephen Charles Neill, eds. *A History of the Ecumenical Movement, 1517–1948.* 2nd ed. Vol. 1. Philadelphia: Westminster Press, 1967. 838 pp.

Wengart, Timothy J., and Charles W. Brockwell Jr., eds. *Telling the Churches' Stories: Ecumenical Perspectives on Writing Christian History.* Grand Rapids, MI: Eerdmans, 1995.

✺ Interfaith Groups

Berkeley Area Interfaith Council

2340 Durant Ave., Berkeley, CA 94704

Although the Berkeley Area Interfaith Council is a local organization designed to serve the needs of the Berkeley/Oakland area of the San Francisco Bay community in California, the wide publicity generated by its very active program has given it an unusual status and recognition in interfaith work in North America. It grew out of the former Berkeley Council of Churches, which had become known in the years immediately following World War II for its political activism but which began to dwindle by the beginning of the 1970s. In 1971 the idea was placed before the council to become more inclusive.

The idea of a new council became a reality in 1973 with the hiring of a full-time director, the Rev. William Shive, whose desire to live a simple life coincided with the minuscule salary the council could afford. He began the task of visiting all of the different churches and religious groups of the community. The council met each month in a different center, the host taking the lead in explaining what his or her group was all about as part of a program that would include a discussion on some topic of widespread interest. By the end of the 1970s the council had become involved in religious freedom controversies, advocacy of gay rights (including the right to marry), and various local issues.

In spite of ups and downs, the council survived. Its projects in the 1990s included working on the follow-up to the World's Parliament of Religions meeting held in Chicago in 1993. The council is part of the San Francisco Bay Area Interfaith Coalition.

Membership: Not reported.

Sources:

Magalis, Elaine. "Methodists, Moonies, and Mormons." *New World Outlook* (May 1979): 1620.

Canadian Ecumenical Action

1420 West 12th Ave., Vancouver, BC, Canada V6H 1M8

Canadian Ecumenical Action is described as a multifaith community-services society. It was founded in 1973 as the People's Opportunity in Ecumenical Mission by a group of Christians under the leadership of the Rev. Val Anderson. In 1975 the group began the *Canadian Ecumenical News.* Gradually people of other faiths were included and the group emerged as an interfaith work. The group operates primarily in western Canada.

Canadian Ecumenical Action seeks to promote interfaith understanding, provide information and resources on world religions to the community and encourage interfaith dialogue on community issues, and promote community service programs. *Canadian Ecumenical News* carried announcements of interfaith activities across Canada, though it no longer publishes as a separate entity. Canadian Ecumenical Action is headed by a planning board of 15 people. Board members serve as interested individuals rather than official representatives of their religious communities.

Membership: Participants in Canadian Ecumenical Action come from the many different religious communities represented in Canada.

Inter Religious Federation for World Peace

481 8th Ave., New York, NY 10011

Devoted to the relationship between religion and peace, the Inter Religious Federation for World Peace (IRFWP) has been involved in international negotiations such as those of the First Gulf War and its aftermath, the Ayodhya Mosque controversy, the Eritrea-Ethiopia border clashes, the battles of the former Yugoslavia, and many other areas of life-and-death confrontation. IRFWP's root organizations include the New Ecumenical Research Association (New ERA), the Council for the World's Religions, the International Religious Foundation, the Religious Youth Service (RYS), the Assembly of the World's Religions, and many others. These organizations have maintained vigorous programs, some for decades, and often have played central roles in world affairs where issues of religion and peace are prevalent.

The IRFWP, formally established in 1991, grew out of an older organization, the Global Congress of the World's Religions, which developed from an initial proposal for a centennial celebration of the World's Parliament of Religions, originally held in 1893 in Chicago. The proposal was made by Dr. Warren Lewis, a professor of church history at the Unification Theological Seminary. It received the backing of the seminary, which sponsored several exploratory meetings in the late 1970s. The Global Congress was formally organized in 1980 and during the next few years sponsored a regular series of consultations around the world.

In the mid-1980s the Global Congress acquired the sponsorship of the International Religious Foundation, one of the arms of the Unification Church, which had supplied it with financial and personal resources. Its activity was then divided between two structures: the Council for the World's Religions, which promoted worldwide faith meetings, and the Assembly of the World's Religions, which met every few years. The assembly, which involves the leadership of the council, also draws upon the resources of the International Religious Foundation. At its 1990 assembly meeting, Rev. Sun Myung Moon (b. 1920) announced the formation of the Inter-Religious Federation for World Peace. The IRFWP has peace as its general goal, which includes peace within one's self and one's family, peace within societies and among nations, peace within and among religions, peace within and among cultures, and peace between the human and natural worlds.

In addition to the investment of massive resources into post–9/11 programs to restore and reconcile interreligious and international relations, especially within Islam and between Muslim and Christian world cultures, the IRFWP is active on other fronts such as India-Pakistan, the Middle East, and the Muslim-Christian encounters in Southeast Asia and in the countries of the former Soviet Union. The IRFWP acts as a watchdog and often criticizes those Protestant and Catholic organizations and institutions it views as critical of Islam. Services of the IRFWP include shuttle diplomacy, international programs, conferences/events, and periodical and literary publications. Such structures are used for special weekday ceremonial work rather than being centers for the weekly gathering of worshippers. The four main services performed in the temple are the baptism for the dead, in which the living are baptized as proxies for those who died in generations past; the temple endowments; temple marriage; and sealings, which establish family structures in the life beyond earthly existence.

The leadership of the federation believes that inter-religious peace is essential for world peace and that respect for religious pluralism is a key element of modern life. The federation is headed by an interfaith presiding council assisted by a board of advisers composed of a large number of religious leaders and scholars. An executive staff administers the day-to-day work of the federation.

Membership: Not reported.

Periodicals: *IRFWP Newsletter*. • *Dialogue and Alliance*.

Sources:

Inter Religious Federation for World Peace. www.irfwp.org.

Bryant, M. Darrol, John Maniatus, and Tyler Hendrics, eds. *Assembly of the World's Religions, 1985: Spiritual Unity and the Future of the Earth.* New York: International Religious Foundation, 1985.

Lewis, Warren, ed. *Towards a Global Congress of the World's Religions.* Barrytown, NY: Unification Theological Seminary, 1978.

Thompson, Henry O. *The Global Congress of the World's Religions: Proceedings, 1980–82.* Barrytown, NY: Unification Theological Seminary, 1982.

Walsh, Thomas G., ed. *Assembly of the World's Religions, 1990: Transmitting Our Heritage to Youth and Society.* New York: International Religious Foundation, 1992.

National Conference for Community and Justice (NCCJ)

328 Flatbush Ave., PO Box 402, Brooklyn, NY 11217

Alternate Address: International Council of Christians and Jews, Martin Buber House, PO Box 11 29, D-64629, Heppenheim, Germany; Canadian Council of Christians and Jews, 4211 Yonge St., PO Box 17, Toronto, Ontario, Canada M2P 2A9.

The National Conference for Community and Justice (NCCJ), founded in 1927 as the National Conference of Christians and Jews, is a human relations organization dedicated to fighting bias, bigotry, and racism in America. The NCCJ promotes understanding and respect among all races, religions, and cultures through advocacy, conflict resolution, and education.

The NCCJ was founded by Charles Evans Hughes, Newton D. Baker, S. Parkes Cadman, Roger W. Straus, and Carlton J. H. Hayes. The work extended to Canada in 1940 with the formation of the Canadian Council of Christians and Jews and to Europe in 1950 with the formation of the World Brotherhood (now embodied in the International Council of Christians and Jews).

Through the years, NCCJ has promoted interreligious dialogue, especially between Jewish and Christian leaders, and in the 1980s moved into the needful area of Jewish-Christian-Muslim dialogue. It has also initiated dialogues between African Americans, the Jewish community, and the larger non-Jewish white population. In the aftermath of the September 11, 2001, terrorist attacks against the United States the NCCJ hosted various conferences and workshops in an effort to combat perceived discrimination against Muslims and other Arab communities.

NCCJ focuses on the multiple manifestations of discrimination and oppression based on religion, race, gender, sexual orientation, economic and social class, age, or physical ability status. Through its programming strategies, research, and public policy initiatives, NCCJ works to transform communities so that they are more whole and just and to promote understanding and respect across groups by preparing and supporting faith, economic opportunity, education, youth, news and advertising media, and government leadership to build inclusive institutions.

Membership: In 2008 the NCCJ reported more than 55 regional offices in 32 states and the District of Columbia and more than 400 full- and part-time staff members.

Sources:

National Conference for Community and Justice. www.nccj.org.

Braybrooke, Marcus. *Inter-Faith Organizations, 1893–1979: An Historical Directory.* New York: Edwin Mellen Press, 1980.

North American Interfaith Network (NAIN)

4910 Valley Crest Dr., St. Louis, MO 64128-1829

Alternate Address: Canadian Office: c/o Rev. David A. Spence, Multifaith Action Society, 33 Arrowwood Pl., Port Moody, BC, Canada V3H 4J1; Mexican Office: c/o Jonathan Rose, Mexican Interfaith Council, Calle Matameros 4, Tepaztlan, Marleas, CP 62525, Mexico.

North American Interfaith Network (NAIN) was established in 1988 out of a gathering in Wichita, Kansas, of some 350 people from across North America representing the spectrum of the world's religious faiths. NAIN emerged from that meeting as a network of participating member organizations. It has been successful in involving local interfaith councils and groups representative of traditions other than Christian.

NAIN sponsors an annual conference, during which it awards several scholarships to students. Through the affiliated Interfaith Voices for Peace & Justice, it publishes a directory of more than 800 faith-based and interfaith organizations.

Membership: In 2008 NAIN reported approximately 100 member organizations.

Periodicals: *NAINews & Interfaith Digest*.

Sources:

North American Interfaith Network. www.nain.org/.

Temple of Understanding

211 E 43rd St., Ste. 1600, New York, NY 10017

The Temple of Understanding grew out of the vision of Juliet Hollister for a center for the promotion of understanding among the world's religions, recognition of the oneness of the human family, and ultimately the organization of a spiritual United Nations. The ideas as put forth in the 1950s were warmly received by a number of prominent leaders around the globe, from Eleanor Roosevelt to Albert Schweitzer, who in 1960 became "founding friends" of the temple.

The temple is headed by a president, a board of directors, an advisory board, and an international committee. Over the years the temple has held a number of Spiritual Summit Conferences. Plans have existed for many years to create a permanent home for the temple on land near Washington, D.C., but financial resources to construct the facility have not as yet been forthcoming.

The temple is a nongovernmental organization (NGO) in consultative status with the United Nations Economic and Social Council, as well as an active entity within the United Nations itself. The temple also offers programs in interfaith education for students at the secondary level and beyond. These programs include seminars, community visits, and immersion experiences.

Sources:

Temple of Understanding. www.templeofunderstanding.org/.

Braybrooke, Marcus. *Inter-Faith Organizations, 1893–1979: An Historical Directory.* New York: Edwin Mellen Press, 1980.

United Religions Initiative

PO Box 29242, San Francisco, CA 94129-0242

The United Religions Initiative (URI) dates to 1990, when Rt. Rev. William E. Swing, the Episcopal bishop of California, conceived of a global interfaith community that could work toward ending religiously motivated violence by putting in place new structures based on healing, peace, and justice. He began to share his vision with colleagues, and its ideals generated a response internationally. In 1996 the first of what has become an annual Global Summit Conference gathered in San Francisco.

As the idea of a United Religions Initiative, the name attached to the vision, took shape, the group sponsored the 72 Hours of Peace program to promote the idea of a transition to the year 2000 in a prayerful and spiritual context. Subsequent conferences initiated a spectrum of projects internationally that drew the support of prominent religious leaders to its cause. The international work led to the formation of local groups ("cooperation circles"), the appointment of an interim Global

Council, the formation of regional (continental) assemblies, and the establishment of an office and executive staff in San Francisco. Staffing was being established on each of the six major continents.

In June 2000 an inaugurating conference was held in Pittsburgh, Pennsylvania, at which the URI was formally organized. The ceremony was highlighted by people from 39 different religious traditions and 44 countries penning their names to the charter. The URI's program initiatives are based upon a belief/hope that daily interfaith cooperation can lead to the end of violence caused by religious conflict and the establishment of a new culture characterized by peace, justice, and healing. To implement its ideal, it promotes a variety of training and pilot projects aimed at creating a new paradigm for peace building through the twenty-first century.

Membership: In 2008 the initiative reported 398 cooperation circles in 67 countries representing over 100 religions.

Periodicals: *URI Update*.

Sources:

United Religions Initiative. www.uri.org/.

World Conference of Religions for Peace (WCRP)

Religions for Peace International, 777 United Nations Plz., New York, NY 10017

The World Conference of Religions for Peace (WCRP; originally named the World Conference on Religion and Peace) grew out of an initiative to bring religious resources to bear on world situations threatening to lead to war. It calls upon people of different faiths to unite in a common effort for world peace.

The work that led to the founding of WCRP can be traced to 1962 and to the Unitarian-Universalist leader Dr. Dana McLean Greeley (1908–1986), who brought together Rabbi Maurice N. Eisendrath (1902–1973), Bp. John Wesley Lord (Methodist; 1902–1989), and Bp. John Wright (Roman Catholic; 1909–1979). The occasion for their first gathering was the Cuban Missile Crisis of that year. Their informal gatherings led to an initial conference in New York in 1964 and a National Inter-Religious Conference on World Peace in Washington, D.C., in 1966. The next year, two representatives of the National Conference made a round-the-world tour to ascertain support for an international meeting.

An initial International Inter-Religious Symposium on Peace in 1968 led directly to the first World Assembly held in Kyoto, Japan, in 1970, at which time the WCRP was formally established. The founding of WCRP occurred in the wake of the heightened war effort in Vietnam. Since that time, WCRP has been given status as a United Nations nongovernmental organization. It has carried on a regular program of relief to the victims of war and speaking to nations either at war or threatening to go to war. The WCRP convenes a World Assembly every five years, bringing together hundreds of representatives of the world's religions to discuss global issues. The Eighth World Assembly of August 2006, meeting once again in Kyoto, had as its theme "Confronting Violence and Advancing Shared Security."

Periodicals: *Mosaic*.

Sources:

World Conference of Religions for Peace. www.wcrp.org/.

Braybrooke, Marcus. *Inter-Faith Organizations, 1893–1979: An Historical Directory.* New York: Edwin Mellen Press, 1980.

Jack, Homer. *WCRP: A History of the World Conference on Religion and Peace.* New York: World Conference on Religion and Peace, 1993.

World Conference on Religion and Peace. *Religions for Peace: Action for Common Living.* Maryknoll, NY: Orbis Books, 2000.

World Fellowship of Religions

Current address not obtained for this edition.

The World Fellowship of Religions was founded in the 1950s in India and later established branches in more than 30 countries. It was founded by Jain master H.

H. Acharya Sushil Kumarji Maharaj (1926–1994), who presented an initial proposal for the fellowship in 1955. This led to the World Conference of All Religions held in Delhi in 1957, following which the World Fellowship of Religions was formally inaugurated. Subsequent world conferences have been held, primarily in India.

WFR set as its goals the promotion of peace, the establishment of right human relationships, and the building of right human relationships through love, equality, compassion, and friendship. Stressing nonviolence as essential to its mission, it created a number of projects to directly help suffering people, such as the setting up of medical facilities and development of nutrition programs.

Sources:

Clark, Francis, ed. *Interfaith Directory*. New York: International Religious Foundation, 1987.

Christian Ecumenical Organizations

Alliance of Confessing Evangelicals

1716 Spruce St., Philadelphia, PA 19103

The Alliance of Confessing Evangelicals was formed by a group of Protestant leaders and churches as an association to speak to the contemporary world self-consciously from the perspective of the Ancient and Reformation creeds. As a guiding perspective, the Alliance seeks to recover for the Christian church an emphasis on the landmarks of the Reformation: Scripture as the sole norm of faith, grace as the sole cause of God's salvation, Christ as the sole and sufficient Savior, and faith as the sole instrument by which God saves the sinner. The alliance exists as a broad coalition of Protestant Evangelical leaders from a number of different denominations—Baptist, Lutheran, Presbyterian, Reformed, and others.

The alliance has supported a wide variety of conferences for theologians and ministers.

Membership: Among the churches whose members are supportive of the alliance are the Associate Reformed Presbyterian Church, Bible Presbyterian Church, Free Presbyterian Church, Orthodox Presbyterian Church, Presbyterian Church in America, Presbyterian Reformed Church, Reformed Presbyterian Church of North America, Protestant Reformed Churches, United Reformed Churches, Reformed Episcopal Church, Traditional Protestant Episcopal Church, Evangelical Lutheran Synod, Lutheran Church–Canada, Lutheran Church–Missouri Synod, Wisconsin Evangelical Lutheran Synod, Confederation of Reformed Evangelicals, and the Reformed Ecumenical Council.

Periodicals: *Reformation 21*. Available from www.reformation21.org/.

Sources:

Alliance of Confessing Evangelicals. www.alliancenet.org/.

American Council of Christian Churches

PO Box 5455, Bethlehem, PA 18015

The American Council of Christian Churches was founded in 1941 as an expression of not only the fundamentalist-modernist split in American Protestantism but also the growing split among conservative Christians into fundamentalist separatists and evangelicals. The American Council represented the most conservative wing of Protestant thought, generally characterized by an affirmation of the infallibility and inerrancy of the Bible and by a desire to separate fully from the heresy and apostasy that it saw gaining control of liberal Protestantism, then embodied in the Federal Council of Churches of Christ in America. The American Council has also rejected as unacceptable the willingness of some conservative Christians, with whom it agrees theologically, to cooperate on programs with or be a part of otherwise liberal Protestant projects and groups.

The leading figure in the formation of the council was Carl McIntire (1906–2002), founder of the Bible Presbyterian Church. McIntire had left the Presbyterian Church in 1936 during the fundamentalist controversy, but because of his acceptance of premillennial eschatology he was at odds with other conservative fundamentalists such as J. Gresham Machen and the Orthodox Presbyterian Church. Thus in 1941 McIntire became the first president of the American Council of Christian Churches (ACCC), dominated it for a quarter of a century, and led it through a series of controversies.

In 1948 McIntire led in the founding of the International Council of Christian Churches, which held its first meeting in Amsterdam, the Netherlands, shortly before the inaugural meeting of the World Council of Churches in that same city. McIntire was accused of deliberately trying to interfere with the World Council and mislead the public. In 1950 he sponsored a project to send Christian literature into Eastern Europe and the Soviet Union via balloons. Such actions began to cost him the allegiance of many leading conservative Christians who had originally given the ACCC their support. Then in 1956 the Bible Presbyterian Church split after a majority repudiated McIntire. Three years later the ACCC itself acted to remove McIntire from its board, and it moved on to a new phase of its existence.

The ACCC remains in opposition to the Ecumenical movement as embodied in the World Council of Churches and the National Council of the Churches of Christ in the USA and regularly assumes a position in opposition to those bodies it feels are contrary to biblical doctrine. In like measure, the ACCC is opposed to the National Association of Evangelicals and prohibits members from holding joint membership. In 1987 the ACCC supported the formation of the Council of Bible Believing Churches International, now the World Council of Biblical Churches, a worldwide fellowship association of fundamentalist churches.

Membership: In 2008 the ACCC reported as members the Bible Presbyterian Church, Evangelical Methodist Church of America, Fellowship of Fundamental Bible Churches, Free Presbyterian Church of North America, Fundamental Methodist Church, Independent Baptist Fellowship of North America, and Independent Churches Affiliated. In addition, an unreported number of independent congregations are affiliated with the ACCC.

Periodicals: *Fundamental News Service*.

Sources:

American Council of Christian Churches. www.amcouncilcc.org/.

Mayer, F. E. *The Religious Bodies of America*. St. Louis, MO: Concordia Publishing House, 1956.

Roy, Ralph Lord. *Apostles of Discord*. Boston: Beacon Press, 1953.

Canadian Council of Churches

47 Queen's Park Crescent E, Toronto, ON, Canada M5S 2C3

The Canadian Council of Churches (also known as Le Conseil canadien des Eglises) was founded in 1944, a product of the ecumenical movement that would soon lead to the formation of the World Council of Churches and the immediate necessity for coordinated action by churches both during and after World War II. Member churches are required to confess Jesus Christ as Lord and Savior according to the Bible and seek to fulfill their common calling to the glory of God. The council seeks to give visible expression to the unity of its member bodies in Jesus Christ.

The council attempts to further ecumenism, to speak to social problems of the day, to facilitate the encounter of Christians of different denominations, and to respond creatively to social change. It operates through the leadership of a president, a general board, a general secretary, and commissions on world concerns and Canadian concerns. Its assembly meets triennially. The council cooperates with the World Council of Churches and nurtures the development of regional and local church councils throughout Canada. The council also has accreditation with the United Nations as a nongovernmental organization.

Membership: In 2008 member denominations included the General Synod of the Anglican Church of Canada, Archdiocese of Canada of the Orthodox Church in America, Armenian Holy Apostolic Church—Canadian Diocese, Baptist Convention of Ontario and Quebec, Baptist Union of Western Canada, British Methodist Episcopal Church of Canada (Associate Member), Canadian Conference of Catholic Bishops, Canadian Yearly Meeting of the Religious Society of Friends (Quakers), Christian Church (Disciples of Christ) in Canada, Christian Reformed Church in North America—Canada, Coptic Orthodox Church of Canada, Ethiopian Orthodox Tewahedo Church of Canada, Evangelical Lutheran Church in Canada, Greek Orthodox Metropolis of Toronto (Canada), Mennonite Church Canada, Old Catholic Church Union of Utrecht, Presbyterian Church in Canada, Regional Synod of Canada—Reformed Church in America, Salvation Army, Ukrainian Orthodox Church of Canada, and United Church of Canada.

Sources:

Canadian Council of Churches. www.ccc-cce.ca/.

Directory of Christian Councils. Geneva: World Council of Churches, 1985.

Evangelical Fellowship of Canada

MIP Box 3745, Markham, ON, Canada L3R 0Y4

The Evangelical Fellowship of Canada was founded in 1964 and serves conservative Protestant denominations, organizations, congregations, and individuals. It has a doctrinal stance like that of the National Association of Evangelicals (NAE), which emphasizes the Bible as the infallible Word of God and the necessity of salvation by faith in Jesus Christ. Like the NAE, it is a member of the World Evangelical Alliance. It provides Protestant Christians with an alternative to the Canadian Council of Churches.

The fellowship reports on religious persecution in China, supports anti-abortion causes and organizations, and advocates for a religious presence in public affairs.

Membership: Not reported. In prior years membership has included 32 Protestant denominations, 150 church-affiliated organizations, 1,000 local church congregations, and more than 15,000 supporting individuals.

Periodicals: *Faith Today*.

Sources:

Evangelical Fellowship of Canada. www.evangelicalfellowship.ca.

International Council of Christian Churches

c/o Rev. Andy Jenkins, North American Regional Council ICCC, PO Box 2453, Collins, MS 39428-2453

Alternate Address: c/o ICCC General Secretariat, 3 & 5 Tavistock Ave., Singapore 555108.

The International Council of Christian Churches (ICCC) was founded in 1948 by a number of conservative Protestant Christians, the most prominent being Dr. Carl McIntire (1906–2002), also the founder of the Bible Presbyterian Church in Collingswood, New Jersey. The ICCC was the international counterpart of the American Council of Christian Churches (ACCC), founded in 1941 also by McIntire, although in 1969 McIntire and the ACCC went their separate ways and McIntire founded the American Christian Action Council (ACAC). At that time, the ICCC recognized the ACAC, now known as the ICCC in America.

The ICCC grew out of the split within twentieth-century Protestantism between fundamentalists and modernists, and represents the continuing allegiance to fundamentalist positions. Also, in the 1940s, as fundamentalists split into two factions, the ICCC was aligned with the more conservative faction. It upholds the inerrancy and infallibility of the Bible and calls Christians to separate themselves from all evil, especially heresy and apostasy.

The major target of the ICCC is the modern ecumenical movement as represented in the World Council of Churches and the National Council of the Churches

of Christ in the U.S.A. The ICCC often has been criticized for holding its meetings in the same cities and around the same dates as the World Council's meetings.

Membership: At its fiftieth anniversary in Amsterdam in 1998, the ICCC reported 700 denominations from more than 100 countries in its membership.

Sources:

International Council of Christian Churches. www.iccc.org/sg/.

ICCC–USA. www.pointsouth.com/icccna/.

Harden, Margaret C., comp. *A Brief History of the Bible Presbyterian Church and Its Agencies*. Privately published, 1968.

Mayer, F. E. *The Religious Bodies of America*. St. Louis, MO: Concordia Publishing House, 1956.

Leuenberg Church Fellowship

Jebensstrasse, 3 D-10623 Berlin, Germany

The Leuenberg Church Fellowship is an alliance of more than 100 (mostly European) Protestant Christian denominations that share an understanding on a number of key points of Christian belief. Based upon that understanding, they can share complete pulpit and table fellowship, meaning that ministers of any group in the fellowship may be allowed to preach in the congregations of the other churches, and that members recognize and may receive the sacraments of the other churches. The agreement grew out of conversations initiated between the Lutheran and Reformed churches following World War II, later expanded to include the Waldensian Church (Italy) and the Church of the Czech Brethren (Czechoslovakia).

In 1973 the Leuenberg Church Fellowship was formed following the publication of a lengthy agreement that participating churches had reached. The agreement affirms the Christian faith centered in the affirmation of the triune god and salvation in Jesus Christ. Essential to the agreement were the paragraphs on the sacraments, the major doctrine dividing Protestants at the time of the Reformation in the sixteenth century.

In language that bypasses the disagreements of Martin Luther and John Calvin, the agreement affirmed that in the Lord's Supper, "the risen Jesus Christ imparts himself in his body and blood, given up for all, through his word of promise with bread and wine." This formulation laid aside a host of creedal statements issued through the centuries by the Reformation churches. It also allowed a variety of different churches to sign the agreement, and the fellowship soon included the Methodists, though neither the Baptists (who have a nonsacramental view of the Lord's Supper) nor the Anglicans affiliated. Most fellowship members are also members of the World Council of Churches.

Membership: Among the 103 churches of the fellowship is the U.S.-based United Methodist Church, which has congregations scattered across Europe.

Sources:

Leuenberg Church Fellowship. www.leuenberg.net/.

National Association of Evangelicals

Box 28, Wheaton, IL 60187

The National Association of Evangelicals (NAE) grew out of the reorganization of conservative Protestants following the most eventful phase of the fundamentalist-modernist controversy of the 1920s and 1930s. Through the first decades of the twentieth century, conservative Protestants had seen many of the major denominations, especially the Methodists, Baptists, and Presbyterians in the northern states, become dominated by what the conservatives considered to be approaches to Christianity that abandoned essential beliefs and placed an undue emphasis on social reform, with a resulting de-emphasis on missions and evangelism.

The battle between conservatives (the fundamentalists) and the liberals (the modernists) led to the liberals taking control of most of the denominational leadership, and increasingly in the 1930s, to many conservatives leaving to form new schools, mission-sending agencies, and denominations. By the end of the 1930s fundamentalists seemed to have divided into two mutually exclusive camps. In this context many conservatives began to reevaluate their situation. They were in agreement with the conservative theological emphasis of the fundamentalists of the 1920s, but were upset at what appeared an unwarranted separatism and fear of the modern world. These conservatives wanted to embrace modern learning, which they felt could be accommodated to their theological commitments. Also, many did not want to separate from the denominational heritage in which they had grown up, and wanted to be able to work with their modernist colleagues in areas not relating directly to their doctrinal conflicts. This position became known as neoevangelicalism.

The National Association of Evangelicals emerged as one of the organizational expressions of neoevangelicalism. It included among its leaders representatives from those churches that had resisted the pull of modernism, new churches formed out of the fundamentalist controversy, and conservative pockets that remained in most of the older liberal Protestant denominations. Liberal Protestant denominations had previously organized into the Federal Council of the Churches of Christ in America. In 1941 separatist fundamentalists had organized the American Council of Christian Churches in opposition to the Federal Council at every point.

Thus in 1942 evangelicals effected a national organization. Direct inspiration for the National Association was given by the successes of the regional New England Evangelical Fellowship that had formed in the late 1930s. Not limited to denominational membership, it allowed denominations, individual congregations, and various organizations and schools to become members. Members are united by a seven-point confession of faith that affirms belief in the Bible as the authoritative and infallible Word of God, the Trinity, the divinity of Christ, the human need of salvation, the ministry of the Holy Spirit, the resurrection of humans, and the spiritual unity of believers.

The NAE has developed a broad program to serve its members, the most important being to provide a united witness for evangelical Christians. It assists mission agencies in their interactions with foreign governments, has developed a relief arm to assist the needy around the world, and interacts with the armed forces on the matter of chaplaincies for member organizations. It also reaches out through National Religious Broadcasters, the National Sunday School Association, and its Evangelism and Spiritual Life Commission. As the NAE has matured, it also has issued opinions on a variety of social issues and has established an Office of Public Affairs in Washington, D.C.

The National Association is a member of the World Evangelical Fellowship, whose North American headquarters are located in the NAE headquarters building in Wheaton, Illinois.

Membership: Membership in the NAE is held by a number of denominations, who provide the bulk of its support, and several hundred evangelical organizations. Denominational members include the following: Advent Christian Church; Assemblies of God; Baptist General Conference; Brethren Church (Ashland, Ohio); Brethren in Christ Church; Christian and Missionary Alliance; Christian Catholic Church (Evangelical Protestant); Christian Church of North America; Christian Reformed Church of North America; Christian Union; Church of Christ in Christian Union; Church of God (Cleveland, Tennessee); Church of God of the Mountain Assembly; Church of the Nazarene; Church of the United Brethren in Christ; Congregation Holiness Church; Conservative Baptist Association of America; Conservative Congregational Christian Conference; Elim Fellowship; Evangelical Christian Church; Evangelical Church of North America; Evangelical Congregational Church; Evangelical Free Church of America; Evangelical Friends International/North America; Evangelical Mennonite Church; Evangelical Methodist Church; Evangelical Presbyterian Church; Evangelistic Missionary Fellowship; Fire-Baptized Holiness Church of God of the Americas; Free Methodist Church of North America; General Association of General Baptists; International Church of the Foursquare Gospel; International Pentecostal Church of Christ; International Pentecostal

Holiness Church; Mennonite Brethren Churches, USA; Midwest Congregational Christian Fellowship; Missionary Church; Open Bible Standard Churches; Pentecostal Church of Christ; Pentecostal Free Will Baptist Church; Presbyterian Church in America; Primitive Methodist Church, USA; Reformed Episcopal Church; Reformed Presbyterian Church of North America; Salvation Army; Wesleyan Church; World Confessional Lutheran Association; Worldwide Churches of God; and Vineyard Christian Fellowship. In addition, members and congregations of many other denominations are also related to the NAE.

Periodicals: *NAE Washington Insight.*

Sources:

National Association of Evangelicals. www.nae.net.

Carpenter, Joel A., ed. *A New Evangelical Coalition: Early Documents of the National Association of Evangelicals.* New York: Garland, 1988.

NAE Resolutions. Wheaton, IL: National Association of Evangelicals, 1985.

Shelley, Bruce L. *Evangelism in America.* Grand Rapids, MI: Eerdmans, 1967.

National Black Evangelistic Association

5736 N Albina Ave., Portland, OR 97217

The National Black Evangelistic Association was founded in 1963 as the National Negro Evangelical Association, a cooperative organization for conservative African-American ministers and churches. Most of the founding members were Baptist. In 1970 the association attracted 1,500 delegates to the first African-American conference on evangelism, which met at St. Stephen Baptist Church in Kansas City, Missouri. The building of lines of communication among African-American evangelicals and the development of local evangelistic programs have provided a focus for the association. In 1988 the association founded the Institute of Black Evangelical Thought and Action.

Membership: Not reported.

Periodicals: *NBEA Outreach.* • *Journal.*

National Council of Churches of Christ in the U.S.A.

475 Riverside Dr., New York, NY 10115-0050

The National Council of Churches of Christ in the U.S.A. is the largest of the several Christian ecumenical councils operating in the United States. It includes among its member organizations most of the older liberal Protestant churches and many of the U.S. branches of the Eastern and Oriental Orthodox churches.

The National Council was founded in 1950 by representatives of 29 Protestant, Anglican, and Orthodox communions who met in Cleveland, Ohio. The council represented the merger of 12 previously existing national ecumenical organizations, the most important being the Federal Council of the Churches of Christ in America, which it superseded. The 11 remaining bodies included the Foreign Missions Conference of North America, Home Missions Council of North America, International Council of Religious Education, Missionary Education Movement of the United States and Canada, National Protestant Council on Higher Education, United Council of Church Women, United Stewardship Council, Church World Service, Interseminary Committee, Protestant Film Commission, and the Protestant Radio Commission. Three years later, the Student Volunteer Movement merged into the council.

In its formation, the National Council followed the example previously set by the World Council of Churches (founded in 1948), and many of its leaders also served as American representatives in World Council work. The council was established to manifest the churches' oneness in Christ, to continue the work of the predecessor agencies, to renew the life of the church, to foster cooperation, and to speak as a single voice on important public and social issues. In this last function, like the former Federal Council of Churches, the National Council has a history of controversy that peaked during the civil rights movement of the 1960s, to which it gave its full support.

The council is headed by its president, a general assembly (representative of the member churches), and a general secretary. It maintains work in the areas of faith, justice, and education. Through its various units and subunits, the council speaks to its constituency and the general public. Policy statements are issued by the general assembly, which meets annually.

Membership: Most members of the National Council are also members of the World Council of Churches, though some are represented through their international headquarters, which may be in another country. The members include:the African Methodist Episcopal Church; African Methodist Episcopal Zion Church; the Alliance of Baptists; American Baptist Churches in the U.S.A.; the Antiochian Orthodox Christian Archdiocese of North America; Armenia Church of America; Christian Church (Disciples of Christ); Christian Methodist Episcopal Church; Church of the Brethren; Coptic Orthodox Church in North America; the Episcopal Church; Evangelical Lutheran Church in America; Friends United Meeting; Greek Orthodox Archdiocese of America; Hungarian Reformed Church in America; International Council of Community Churches; Korean Presbyterian Church in America; Malankara Orthodox Syrian Church; Mar Thoma Syrian Church of India; Moravian Church in America (Northern Province, Southern Province); National Baptist Convention of America; National Baptist Convention, U.S.A., Inc.; National Missionary Baptist Convention of America; Orthodox Church in America; Patriarchal Parishes of the Russian Orthodox Church in the USA; Philadelphia Yearly Meeting of the Religious Society of Friends; Polish National Catholic Church of America; Presbyterian Church (USA); Progressive National Baptist Convention, Inc.; Reformed Church in America; Serbian Orthodox Church in the USA and Canada; the Swedenborgian Church; Syrian Orthodox Church of Antioch; Ukrainian Orthodox Church of America; United Church of Christ; and the United Methodist Church. Membership has remained fairly stable over the years, though a few churches have left and others have joined. Approximately 50 million Christians belong to the council's 36 member communions.

Periodicals: *Yearbook of American Churches*. • *Eculink*.

Sources:

National Council of the Churches of Christ in the U.S.A. www.ncccusa.org/.

Cavert, Samuel McCrea. *The American Churches in the Ecumenical Movement, 1900–1968*. New York: Association Press, 1968.

World Council of Biblical Churches

c/o American Council of Christian Churches, PO Box 5455, Bethlehem, PA 18015

The World Council of Biblical Churches, founded in 1987 as the Council of Bible Believing Churches International, is an association of Fundamentalist Christian churches affiliated with the American Council of Christian Churches (ACCC). From 1948 to 1969 the American Council had an international affiliate, the International Council of Christian Churches (ICCC). However, in 1969 the ACCC removed Carl McIntire (1906–2002) from its board, and the International Council of Christian Churches, which McIntire had been instrumental in founding, had sided with him. The ICCC and the ACCC discontinued their relationship. The council sees itself as an issue-oriented body whose members have come together to speak to the major concerns of Fundamentalist Christians worldwide.

Like the ACCC, with whom it shares its headquarters facilities, the council is a conservative Protestant body affirming the infallibility and inerrancy of the Bible and the need for complete separation from heresy and apostasy such as the council believes is manifest in the World Council of Churches and the National Council of the Churches of Christ in the USA. To council members, separation includes militant opposition to Romanism, ecumenism, materialism, communism, and every other thing that is contrary to sound doctrine. Members of the council cannot be affiliated with, or represented in any manner by, the World Council of Churches or any of its affiliates, the World Evangelical Alliance (WEA) or any of its affiliates, the International Council of Christian Churches (ICCC) or any of its affiliates, the modern Charismatic movement, or the Ecumenical movement.

The council is governed by an executive committee that includes representatives from each member body.

Membership: North American members of the council are the same as those in the American Council of Christian Churches. In 2008 these included Bible Presbyterian Church, Evangelical Methodist Church of America, Fellowship of Fundamental Bible Churches, Free Presbyterian Church of North America, Fundamental Methodist Church, Independent Baptist Fellowship of North America, and Independent Churches Affiliated.

Sources:

American Council of Christian Churches. www.amcouncilcc.org/main.asp

World Council of Churches

425 Riverside Dr., New York, NY 10115

Alternate Address: International Headquarters: Box 66, 150 route de Ferney, 1211 Geneva 20, Switzerland.

The World Council of Churches, the primary organization representing the Christian community outside of the Roman Catholic Church, grew out of and is the major expression of the ecumenical movement of the twentieth century. There had been international cooperation of Anglican and Protestant churches through the first half of the century by three distinct bodies, each concerned with a special area of Christian church life: the Universal Christian Council for Life and Work, the Continuation Committee of the World Conference of Faith and Order, and the International Missionary Council. In 1933 William Adams Brown (1865–1943) suggested to Anglican Abp. William Temple (1881–1944) that representatives of these organizations, along with the World Alliance for International Friendship and the Student Christian Movement, begin conversations about their common future.

Archbishop Temple initiated informal discussions, which led in 1937 to a proposal to form a world council of churches. Work began on a constitution in 1938. The council was to include those churches that accepted Jesus Christ as God and Savior. Deliberations were slowed by the advent of World War II; however, the American members of the provisional committee opened an office in New York City and created an American Committee for the World Council of Churches. The provisional committee resumed its work in 1946.

The inaugural Assembly of the World Council was held in Amsterdam, the Netherlands, in 1948. The desire for the council was spurred by the formation of the United Nations and the perceived need for a means of staying in contact with it. The council seeks to be a visible symbol of the unity of the individual Christian churches, to encourage their common witness for Christ, and to support their worldwide missions. The council assigned itself the tasks of facilitating common action by its member bodies, promoting cooperation among various churches, and promoting the growth of ecumenical conferences.

The council carries out its program through regular meetings of its General Assembly and a continuing program centered upon its headquarters in Geneva, Switzerland. There is a full-time general staff that operates under the guidance of the general secretary. Along with the general secretariat, there are three program units: Faith and Witness, Justice and Service, and Education and Renewal.

Integral to the carrying out of the council's work are the many regional and national councils, which in North America include the National Council of the Churches of Christ in the U.S.A. and the Canadian Council of Churches. Individual churches may be members of the World Council of Churches irrespective of their membership in one of the national councils.

Membership: The World Council of Churches currently consists of more than 300 member churches, including from North America the following: African Methodist Episcopal Church; African Methodist Episcopal Zion Church; American Baptist Churches in the U.S.A.; Anglican Church of Canada; Apostolic Catholic Assyrian Church of the East; Canadian Yearly Meeting of the Society of Friends; Christian Church (Disciples of Christ); Christian Methodist Episcopal Church; Church of the Brethren; Evangelical Lutheran Church in America; Evangelical Lutheran Church of

Canada; Friends General Conference; Friends United Meeting; Hungarian Reformed Church in America; International Council of Community Churches; International Evangelical Church; Moravian Church in America; National Baptist Convention of America; National Baptist Convention, U.S.A., Inc.; Orthodox Church in America; Polish National Catholic Church of America; Presbyterian Church of Canada; Presbyterian Church (U.S.A.); Progressive National Baptist Convention, Inc.; Reformed Church in America; United Church of Canada; United Church of Christ; and United Methodist Church. In addition, many international churches with members in North America, including the various Orthodox bodies, are represented through their international headquarters.

Periodicals: *The Ecumenical Courier*. • *The Ecumenical Review*. • *One World International Review of Missions*.

Sources:

World Council of Churches. www.oikoumene.org

Cavert, Samuel McCrea. *The American Churches in the Ecumenical Movement, 1900–1968*. New York: Association Press, 1968.

Directory of Christian Councils. Geneva, Switzerland: World Council of Churches, 1985.

"Toward a Common Understanding and Vision of the World Council of Churches." Available from www.wcc-coe.org/wcc/who/cuv-e.html.

Van der Bent, Ans J., ed. *Handbook of Member Churches: World Council of Churches*. Geneva, Switzerland: World Council of Churches, 1982.

Vanelderen, Marlin, and Martin Conway. *Introducing the World Council of Churches*. Geneva, Switzerland: Consul Oecumenique, 2002.

World Council of Independent Christian Churches (WCICC)
Bowling Green Station, PO Box 76, New York, NY 10274-0076

The World Council of Independent Christian Churches (WCICC) is an Evangelical Christian fellowship of churches, pastors, ministries, and schools that, though not limited to Jewish evangelism, is very much based in Jewish Messianism. The council professes belief in the divine inspiration of the Bible, the Triune God, the fallen nature of humanity, and salvation through Jesus Christ/Yeshua. It further professes belief in a premillennial dispensational view of salvation history that begins with God's progressively revealed Self through successive ages (or dispensations), during each of which humanity was tested in obedience to some specific revelation of the will of God, and that the next event in that history will be, at any moment, the Rapture of the saved, which will happen when the Lord descends from heaven to take his people to meet him in the air. His people compose the Church of Jesus Christ that had its beginning at Pentecost and is composed solely of believers.

Since 1992 the council has provided ordination to otherwise independent believers, a practice designed to meet the needs of individuals who have not found a place in other Evangelical and Messianic organizations. Prospective ministers must obtain the required education needed to sustain the call (all forms of education considered), show a knowledge of the Bible, and be a member of the council. For otherwise qualified individuals, gender, age, or marital status is no hindrance to ordination.

The council has developed a special interest in the issues of religious freedom in the world and has become an activist organization calling for the end of all forms of religious persecution and racism. In this cause it has worked with the U.S. Department of State and various United Nations agencies. The council is recognized by the United Nations as a nongovernmental organization (NGO) with consultative status.

Membership: In 2008 the WCICC reported work in 76 countries and a membership of more than 350,000.

Sources:

World Council of Independent Christian Churches. www.wcicc.org.

World Evangelical Alliance
Box WEF, Wheaton, IL 60189-8004

The World Evangelical Alliance, formerly known as the World Evangelical Fellowship, was founded in 1951 but sees itself as the continuation of the Evangelical Alliance, which was founded in England in 1846 and had a vital life through the rest of the nineteenth century. The alliance suffered greatly from the rise of liberal Protestantism and its capture of most of the leading Protestant denominations in the early twentieth century.

The alliance serves as a coordinating and fellowship agency for all evangelical groups, which have attained a growing presence around the world. It has a representative national organization in more than 110 countries. Regional organizations serve Asia, Europe, Africa, Latin America, and the Caribbean.

Membership: In North America the World Evangelical Fellowship operates through the Evangelical Fellowship of Canada and the National Association of Evangelicals (with whom it shares headquarters space). Worldwide, in 1997 WEF reported that its 110 national and regional organizations represented some 150 million believers in 60,000 congregations. In 2008 the Alliance spoke for 420 million Evangelical Christian in 128 countries.

Periodicals: *Evangelical World*. • *Evangelical Review of Theology*.

Sources:

World Evangelical Fellowship. www.worldevangelical.org.

Fuller, W. Harold. *People of the Mandate—The Story of World Evangelical Fellowship*. Grand Rapids, MI: Baker Book House, 1996.

Howard, David M. *The Dream That Would Not Die: The Birth and Growth of the World Evangelical Fellowship, 1846–1986*. Exeter, U.K.: Paternoster Press, 1986.

Western Liturgical Family, Part I: The Western Catholic Tradition

2

PROLOGUE: THE EARLY CHRISTIAN MOVEMENT. The fourth century C.E. proved to be a decisive turning point for the Christian movement. Before the reign of the emperor Constantine (r. 306–337), Christianity was an outlaw faith throughout the Roman Empire. During Constantine's reign, Christianity would be decriminalized, then legalized, then elevated to a most-favored status. Certainly from the time of the Great Fire in 64 C.E., which destroyed much of Rome during the reign of the emperor Nero (r. 54–68 C.E.), Roman authorities had looked upon Christians as a disturbing force in the empire. Periodically the church's members were targeted for persecution, some of the most violent occurring during the reigns of Decius (r. 249–251) and Diocletian (r. 284–305), whose reign ended shortly before Constantine's rise to power.

Christianity had spread through the Roman Empire from Spain to Syria and beyond its borders to the east in the first century C.E. Given its far-flung existence and its status as a marginalized faith, it developed as a somewhat decentralized movement with local patriarchal leaders (the bishops) emerging as authorities in the larger cities and the territory surrounding them. The leading bishops in the largest cities tended to gain authority over nearby dioceses; the most prominent bishops could be found in such places as Jerusalem, Antioch, Alexandria, and Edessa in the East, and Lyon, Rome, and Arles in the West.

Research on the early Christian movement has been greatly affected by the discovery of caches of relevant documents in the mid-twentieth century—the Dead Sea scrolls and the library at Nag Hammadi, Egypt, being the most important. The Dead Sea scrolls have help clarify the existence of a variety of groups and intellectual currents flowing within the Jewish community in the first century B.C.E. Christianity originally emerged as an additional Jewish way in first-century Palestine. Like all of Judaism, it was significantly disturbed by the Jewish revolt in 66 C.E. and the subsequent destruction of Jerusalem and its temple four years later.

As the Christian movement grew, it accepted Gentiles into membership and then leadership, and it would outpace its Jewish origins and find itself in competition with a variety of religious movements that had been able to spread throughout the empire, such as Mithraism and the healing temples of Asclepius. In good time, Christianity was able to blend into its environment and thus escape the attention of potentially hostile rulers.

The Christian movement was also diverse. From the writings of Irenaeus, the second-century bishop of Lugdunum, Gaul (Lyons, France), we learn of a group of teachers who had gained a following within the larger Christian movement and whom Irenaeus condemned as heretics. We know less about how widely Irenaeus's *Against Heresies* circulated during the several decades after he penned it, or how his fellow bishops reacted to his condemnations. We do know that he had little authority to enforce his views beyond his diocese and that the followings of some of the teachers he mentioned (such as Valentinus) were noticeable into the third and fourth centuries. Even within those elements of the movement that would find favor in the post-Constantinian world, a level of diversity existed around various traditions that dated to the founding of the church in distinct locations by what reputedly were different apostles or their close associates.

When one looks around the early church, certainly through the second and third centuries, one would be hard-pressed to find what might be called Bible-believing Christians. The Bible was yet to be assembled. The Jewish Bible was revered, and various books that were to be included in the New Testament were copied and recopied and circulated among the local congregations. Few congregations were able to reference all of those pieces of writing, and different books were assigned varying levels of authority. Some books that were not ultimately included in the Bible were popular, widely read, and freely circulated through the congregations. The letters of Paul were among the most widely honored, and the Apocalypse (book of Revelation) was possibly the most questioned. A book called the Didache, or the Teachings of the Twelve Apostles, is among the popular texts that did not finally make it into the canon.

The informal and marginalized existence of the church was to change dramatically in the 320s. Most symbolic of that change was the calling of the first of the great ecumenical councils that met at Nicea in 325 C.E., with the emperor's support and approbation. While sometimes compared to the first-century gathering of church leaders at Jerusalem, described in Acts 15:4–22, the Council of Nicea was a gathering of official leaders of what had become a large international movement on the verge of attaining a level of power few could have imagined just a decade previously.

Western Liturgical Family Chronology

1492	Christopher Columbus brings Catholicism to the Americas.
1494	The Treaty of Tordesillas stated that Portugal was entitled to lands in the New World east of a line drawn 370 leagues west of the Azores and Cape Verde (i.e. Brazil). Spain was given hegemony over the lands west of that line. Pope Julius II confirmed the treaty in 1506.
16th century	Organizational unity of Christianity in Europe shattered by Protestant Reformation.
1634	Maryland founded. Roman Catholic Church planted in British North America.
1776	Charles Carroll become the only Roman Catholic who signs the Declaration of Independence.
1790	John Carroll is consecrated as the first bishop for the United States.
1810	John Carroll is named the first archbishop in the United States.
1844	The Methodist Episcopal Church, the largest church in America, divides into two jurisdictions, allowing the Roman Catholic Church to assume its place.
1869	Fr. Junipero Serra founds the first of a string of Franciscan missions along the coast of California.
1870	Papal States annexed by Italy, a major step to formal unification the next year. First Vatican Council defines the doctrine of the infallibility of the Pope as dogma.
1871	Opponents of the doctrinal "innovation" at Vatican I meet in Munich and launch Old Catholic Movement.
1875	James Augustine Healy, an African American able to pass as white, becomes the Roman Catholic bishop of Maine. He is now recognized as the first African American recipient of a Ph.D. and the first African American president of a predominantly white university.
	Abp. John McCloskey of New York is named the first American cardinal.
1881	Catholic laborers form Knights of Columbus fraternal organization, which promotes catholic interests.
1886	Augustus Tolton becomes the first African American recognized as such by his contemporaries ordained to the priesthood.
1897	Polish National Catholic Church founded by Roman Catholics unappreciative of Irish and German bishops and priests.
1895	Pope Leo XIII voices opposition to "Americanism," a view championing Catholic co-existence with the separation of church and state and demands the resignation of Bps. Joseph J. Keane and Denis J. O'Connell.
1928	Al Smith, governor of New York, is the first Roman Catholic to run for president on a major party ticket.
1946	Mother Francis X. Cabrini becomes the first American to be canonized as a saint.
1951	Msgr. Fulton J. Sheen begins successful prime-time national television show *Life Is Worth Living*.
1960	John F. Kennedy becomes the first Roman Catholic in the White House.
1962	Pope John XXIII calls Second Vatican Council (1962–1965), which creates new positive atmosphere within Catholicism for ecumenical and interfaith relationships.
1965	Pope Paul VI and Patriarch Athenagoras I of Constantinople rescind the excommunications of 1054.
1969	Pope Paul VII condemns abortion in his encyclical *Humanae Vitae*.
	Following the decrees of Vatican II, Pope Paul Vi promulgates the new mass which replaces the Tridentine Latin mass and quickly goes into vernacular languages.
1970	A traditionalist movement forms to oppose the replacement of the Latin Mass.
1975	Elizabeth Ann Seton becomes the first person born in what is now the United States to be canonized as a Roman Catholic saint.
1977	Supporters of women in the priesthood organize the Women's Ordination Conference.
1979	Pope John Paul II become the first pope to visit the United States.
1984	Card. Joseph Ratzinger issues critique of the liberation theology and disciplines several of its leading exponents.
1985	Vatican removes Fr. Charles Curran's license to teach catholic theology due to his advocacy of artificial birth control.
1988	Conservative French archbishop Marcel Lefebvre, the leading voice of the traditionalist movement, is excommunicated after consecrating four priests to the episcopacy.
	Abp. Eugene A. Marino is the first African American named as an archbishop.
	Pope John Paul II beautifies Fr. Junipero Serra.
1994	Pope John Paul II ends post–Vatican II debate over admitting women to the priesthood in the encyclical *Ordinatio Sacerdotalis*.
2000	Pope John Paul II canonizes Mother Katherine Mary Drexel, founder of the Sisters of the Blessed Sacrament.
2002	Conviction of Fr. James F. Geoghan of child molestation brings issue of pedophilia among American catholic priests to the forefront leading to numerous court cases, prompting a major study of the problem by the U.S. Conference of Catholic Bishops, and forcing the resignation of Cardinal Bernard Law, Archbishop of Boston.
	Catholic dioceses begin paying settlements that amount to a billion dollars or more by 2007.
	Seven women on a boat on the Danube River become the first modern women publicly ordained to the Roman Catholic priesthood. Bp. Romulo Braschi of Argentina performed the ordinations.
	Card. Joseph Ratziner becomes Pope Benedict XVI.
2006	South African bishop Patricia Fresen brings new female ordination movement to the United States.

The calling of the council was a sign of the church's new status, but also manifested the theological diversity that had been part of the developing thought-world of the decentralized church. For the first time, the church's leaders from around the Mediterranean Basin had the opportunity to gather and the power to make decisions that could be enforced throughout the movement. The council's first decision would be reached over the conflicting opinions of two bishops—Arius (c. 250–336) and Athanasius (c. 293–373). The issue was important, and both approached the council with substantial support. In the end, Athanasius's opinion prevailed and became the orthodox position. The Nicene Creed that was promulgated after the meeting contains specific anti-Arian language. Certainly, had Arius's position won, Christian theology would have taken a significantly different direction.

Arius's widespread following did not, of course, disappear, and the broad acceptance of the Nicene Creed came with the use of the state's power. The controversy periodically reemerged over the next century, and Arianism attained some power at the fringes of the empire, the very places to which leaders supportive of Arius's views were often exiled. Arianism was particularly favored by the Goths and Vandals of central Europe, the Visigoths having been initially converted to Christianity by Arians in 376. It would be Arian Christians who would sack Rome in 410 C.E., and for several centuries Arian kingdoms in western Europe would play an important role in Western Christianity.

THE EMERGENCE OF CHRISTIANITY.

In the several centuries following the reign of Constantine, Christianity would be shaped and reshaped as it adjusted to its new status as the privileged religion of the Roman Empire. Its worship life would continue to evolve, its organization would assume responsibility for the empire's entire population, and its doctrinal conflicts would find a means of resolution in successive church councils. Given the church's alignment with government authorities, a loss in a church conflict now carried significant consequences. Outspoken bishops and their followers would immediately lose favor. Bishops could lose their position, be exiled, arrested, or even executed. At the same time, the Christian movement had spread beyond the borders of the Roman Empire, especially eastward into what is now Armenia and Iraq. In these lands, neither Greek nor Latin were the primary languages for liturgy or daily life, and the church leaders were beyond the reach of Roman authorities.

LITURGY. As the church evolved from the fourth century forward, a strong liturgical life became one of its most distinguishing features, and this rich liturgical tradition would retain center stage in the older Christian churches that maintain an organizational continuity to the present day. Although these churches have other distinguishing characteristics—creeds, orders, sacraments, language, culture—liturgy is the realm where these characteristics find their expression, so it is appropriate to group these churches that trace their origins into the pre-Constantinian era together as the liturgical family. In this family are to be found the many church bodies of the four major traditions: the Eastern Orthodox churches, the non-Chalcedonian Orthodox traditions, the Western Roman Catholic tradition, and the Anglican tradition.

Most of the liturgical churches celebrate seven sacraments: baptism, the Eucharist, holy orders, unction, marriage, confirmation, and penance. Among contemporary Christians in North America and western Europe, few topics exist about which there is such a variety of thinking as the number and nature of the sacraments. Sacramental life came to the fore in the debates surrounding the origin of Protestantism in the sixteenth century. Most Protestant groups, such as the Lutherans and Presbyterians, celebrate only two sacraments—baptism and holy communion—while many free churches, from the Mennonites to the Baptists,

have no sacraments. Free churches practice baptism and holy communion, but as ordinances not sacraments. Some add a third ordinance, foot washing. A fully developed sacramental system, however, characterizes the members of the liturgical family. The exception is the Anglican tradition. Formed in the crucible between Catholics and Protestants, it developed a liturgical life with a slightly Protestantized cast. The via media allowed for the central role of the Sunday liturgy and an almost Catholic understanding of the sacraments, but limited the number of sacraments to two.

APOSTOLIC SUCCESSION. The churches of the liturgical family are generally led by bishops who believe that they exercise their authority from a lineage of bishops that can be traced back to Christ's original twelve apostles. Though that lineage is slightly different in each jurisdiction, each church professes that it inherits an unbroken line of authority from the apostles who founded the Christian church at Pentecost.

Speaking of this unbroken line, for example, Bishop Sion Manoogian (1906–1991) says of the Armenian Church: "The Armenian Church was founded by two of the Apostles of Our Lord, St. Thaddeus and St. Bartholomew, in the first century. This is the reason for its sometimes being called the Armenian Apostolic Church" (*The Armenian Church and Her Teachings*, 1951(?), pp. 2, 15). Dean Timothy Andrews (1914–2007) says of the Greek Orthodox Church: "It is the church founded by Christ, received its mission on Pentecost, propagated throughout the world by the Holy Apostles" (*What Is the Orthodox Church?* 1964, p. 7). The Church of the East traces its conversion, establishment, and apostolic succession to the 70 disciples (Luke 10:1) and the 12 apostles, but more particularly to Mar Shimun Koopa (St. Simon Peter), Mar Tooma (St. Thomas), Mar Addai (St. Thaddeus), Mar Mari (St. Mari, one of the 70 disciples), and Mar Bar Thulmay (St. Bartholomew). The Roman Catholic Church traces its origins to St. Peter, the first bishop of Rome.

THE CHURCH COUNCILS. Beginning in the fourth century, the church was frequently able to call church councils to settle controversies. Most councils were local or regional affairs, but controversies that affected the entire church could be referred to an international council that included the majority of bishops from around the Mediterranean Basin and to some extent from beyond the Roman Empire. During what is termed the conciliar era, a time of debate and discussion from 325 C.E. to 787 C.E., seven councils of the entire church, called ecumenical councils, were held.

What is considered the First Ecumenical Council was called almost immediately after the church attained its new status, in 325 C.E. at Nicea, near Constantinople (Istanbul), in present-day Turkey, to deal with the issues raised by Bishop Arius. The council turned its attention to the relationship of God the Father and God the Son in Christian thinking. Arius argued that the Son is not of the same "substance" as the Father, thus denying the essential full divinity of Jesus Christ. Rather, Arius contended, the Son was created by the Father as an agent for creating the world. In the end, the council condemned Arius and declared his teaching heretical.

Arius and his supporters, however, did not go away. The promulgation of the Nicene Creed, for example, caused an immediate defection in the church in Egypt, where Arius resided. In various places around the edge of the Roman Empire, Arian Christians remained in some force for several centuries, especially in lands north and west of the Italian Peninsula. Since the sixth century, a beautiful Arian baptistery has stood near the Orthodox baptistery in Ravenna, Italy, a symbol of the town's location on the boundary between the Orthodox and Arian communities.

The council at Nicea promulgated the creedal statement that embodied a summary of the basic affirmations of what would now become "orthodox" Christianity. The creed affirmed a transcendent deity who related to humanity as a parental creator, salvation through the atoning work of Jesus Christ, the sustaining work of the Holy Spirit, the church as the organizational expression of the faith, and continued existence after death for Christians in a heavenly state. The Nicene Creed would set the basic perspective of the faith accepted by almost all Christians since the fourth century, and laid a foundation for the next stage of theological discussion, focused on questions left open by the new creedal statement. The Nicene statement, more than any other document, defines orthodox Christianity, and its basic position would provide the consensus that was never questioned when the various schisms occurred over the centuries. Even most of the modern "noncreedal" churches basically accept the decisions of the Council of Nicea in their definition of Christian belief.

The Second Council met at Constantinople in 381 C.E. and continued the development of the doctrine of the Trinity. Christianity affirms the existence of one God who is manifest as a Trinity of Father, Son, and Holy Spirit. Those who gathered at Constantinople affirmed that the three—Father, Son, and Holy Spirit—are coeternal and consubstantial.

The Third Council met at Ephesus in 431 C.E. This council met to discuss the opinions of Nestorius (d. c. 451), who had been made patriarch of Constantinople three years earlier, concerning the relationship of the divine and human in Jesus Christ. Nestorius argued that Christ was not the Son of God, but that God was living in Christ. The two natures, said Nestorius, were separable. The debate centered upon the use of the word *Theotokos* (Greek for "Mother of God"). The Nestorians rejected the term, saying that Mary bore Christ, not God.

Though the youngest of the five patriarchal sees, Constantinople had gained power because of its proximity to the emperor's court. When the council ruled against Nestorius and deposed him as patriarch, he did not go down immediately. A few days after the Ephesian Council adjourned, Nestorius's followers organized another council and deposed the opposition. Subsequently, the secular authorities supported the majority, and Nestorius was imprisoned and eventually banished to Egypt. His followers still did not go away, but formed a strong church in Syria and Persia,

to the east of Constantinople's reach. Later missionary activity carried the Nestorians even further east, into India and China. They are represented today by the Church of the East, one of the churches of the non-Chalcedonian Orthodox tradition (meaning they did not participate or accept the rulings of the next council).

The Fourth Council met at Chalcedon in 451 C.E. It drafted what came to be known as the Chalcedonian Creed, which stated:

> *Therefore, following the holy Fathers we all with one accord teach men to acknowledge one and the same Son, our Lord Jesus Christ, at once complete in Godhead and complete in manhood, truly God and truly man, consisting also of a reasonable soul and body; of one substance with the Father as regards his Godhead, and at the same time of one substance with us as regards his manhood; like us in all respects, apart from sin; as regards his Godhead, begotten of the Father before the ages, but yet as regards his manhood begotten, for us men and for our salvation, of Mary the Virgin, the God-bearer; one and the same Christ, Son, Lord, Only-begotten, recognized in two natures, without confusion, without change, without division, without separation [emphasis added]; the distinction of natures being in no way annulled by the union, but rather the characteristics of each nature being preserved and coming together to form one person and subsistence, not as parted or separated into two persons, but one and the same Son and Only-begotten God the Word, Lord Jesus Christ; even as the prophets from earliest times spoke of him, and our Lord Jesus Christ himself taught us, and the creed of the Fathers has handed down to us.*

This creed, an expanded statement of the position embodied in the Nicene Creed, is considered the "orthodox" solution to the various theological (primarily Christological) problems considered by the early church and now agreed upon by the Roman Catholic, Anglican, and Eastern Orthodox churches, as well as most Protestant churches. While representing the consensus of the majority, the Nicene Creed continued to be the favored creed for use in the liturgy.

Most important for the development of Christianity, some Christian communities rejected the creed's emphasis on the two natures of Christ. The non-Chalcedonian Orthodox tradition, so named for its rejection of the Chalcedonian Creed, emerged over the next century as one of the four main traditions of the liturgical family. These churches continue to use the creedal statement promulgated by the Council of Nicea in 325 C.E., but not the Chalcedonian statement. Many non-Chalcedonians were called Monophysites because they felt the human and divine in Christ constituted only one nature. Today, the Armenian Church and the Coptic Church represent part of the non-Chalcedonian Orthodox tradition.

The first four councils—at Nicea, Constantinople, Ephesus, and Chalcedon—served to separate and isolate the non-Chalcedonian Orthodox tradition from the Eastern Orthodox and Western Roman traditions. The Eastern Orthodox tradition developed centers of authority in

Antioch, Alexandria, and Constantinople. The Western branch's center of authority was in Rome. This East-West division was originally more a cultural than a doctrinal separation, but over time, culture and politics would lead them toward an eventual break in fellowship. When the official division came in 1054 with mutual excommunications, the churches were declaring to the world what had already been a reality for some time. This explanation is not to say that there are no important differences of doctrine, rites, or ecclesiastical practices between the two churches, or to deny that these differences have grown stronger since 1054. It is merely to show how even these pale into insignificance when set against the glaring differences caused by rival cultures, conflicting empires, and several centuries of miscommunication.

Of the three oldest traditions of the liturgical family—the Eastern Orthodox tradition, the non-Chalcedonian Orthodox tradition, and the Western Roman tradition—only the third failed to remain fairly stable from the end of the conciliar era to the nineteenth century. The Eastern Orthodox Church split jurisdictions along national and cultural lines and was able to preserve unity by granting local autonomy to the various national groups. Like the Eastern Orthodox centers at Jerusalem, Antioch, and Alexandria, the churches of the non-Chalcedonian Orthodox tradition in the Middle East— the Coptic Church and the Nestorian Church of the East—fell under the rule of rising Islam after the sixth century. The force of an overpowering enemy served to keep them both relatively small and united. In the Western Roman tradition, however, the Roman Catholic Church attempted to provide a religious blanket covering all of Western culture. Consequently, it was to suffer when secular power deserted it. Not only did the various Protestant and post-Protestant groups break off from it in the sixteenth century, but the fourth major liturgical tradition, Anglicanism, emerged from it.

The Church in England had been at odds with the see of Rome as early as Thomas à Becket (c. 1120–1170), the twelfth-century archbishop of Canterbury. In the sixteenth century, the financial and marital marriage problems of King Henry VIII (r. 1509–1547) led to the break with Rome. With few immediate changes in the church beyond confiscation of church property by Henry, the Church of England had to wait for the radical Protestantizing of Edward VI's (r. 1547–1553) reign and the subsequent mediating position articulated by Queen Elizabeth I (r. 1558–1603) for a genuinely new orientation. The development and spread of the Elizabethan prayer book alone is reason to look upon the Anglicans, discussed more fully in chapter three, as a separate liturgical tradition.

Each of the four major liturgical traditions was brought to the United States by immigration of its Old World disciples. The traditions came as structures to preserve the Old World customs and cultures in the secular environment of the United States. Churches were founded wherever a significant group of immigrants or their descendants resided. These churches remained under the supervision of ancient sees and kept much closer contact with the sees than with neighboring American churches. There was little attempt to evangelize beyond the boundaries of the immigrants' particular ethnic group. Schism would wait until the twentieth century for most groups, when Americanization and the desire for bishops born and raised in America would become major issues.

ROMAN CATHOLICISM. In the postconciliar era, the Roman Catholic Church emerged as the single ecclesiastical body dominating the life of Western Europe from Italy and Spain to Ireland and Scandinavia. As such, it came to have a special and unique role in shaping Western European history. It held sway, with only minor competition from relatively small dissenting groups, until the sixteenth century. Taking an inclusive view of its role in society, it was able to absorb and provide space for a variety of religious enthusiasts and divergences through the development and sponsoring of religious orders, and the allowances for a wide variety of local practices peculiar to a particular region. It also had considerable room for those who broke its rules to reconcile themselves and come back into the good graces of the ecclesiastical authorities.

While many of the peculiarities of Roman Catholicism will be discussed below, it is fruitful at this point to note some aspects of the medieval church that characterized it in its relationship to Western society. For example, in the chaos that followed the collapse of the Roman Empire, as the ancient world made the transition to the medieval period, the Roman Catholic Church emerged as an integrating element in Western Europe, and came to provide a variety of services that allowed some semblance of order to return as the transition to the synthesis of the Middle Ages developed.

Most importantly for later theological development, the Church developed through its sacramental system a theological worldview that encompassed all of the stages of human life. Across Europe, the land was laid out in parishes, and a church building was placed in each parish for the gathering of the community. Ideally, church membership and community membership overlapped completely, and the church frequently kept the vital records of the surrounding territory. Thus the operation of the sacramental world of the church would begin even before someone was born, because the individual's parents would live in the community and participate in the church. A short time after birth, the baby would be presented for baptism, a ritual that welcomed the child into membership in the church. As the child grew, it would be taught Christian doctrine and practice, and at some point intensively so, through the memorizing of the catechism. The catechism presented the Church's doctrine in the form of an ordered series of questions and answers. When the child was deemed of age, he or she would be passed through the sacrament of confirmation, and immediately afterward, for the first time, receive the sacrament of the Eucharist, the ritually offered body and blood of Christ. The Eucharist is the most holy of Christian sacraments.

From the time of confirmation, the individual was considered an adult by the church. Regularly, usually once a week, but minimally once a year, the individual went through the sacrament of penance in which sins were verbally confessed to a priest who, as a representative of the church and of God, pronounced forgiveness and set some actions that were to be done by the individual as recompense for the wrong. After the priest pronounced forgiveness of sin and the individual participated in the rite of penance, he or she was ready to receive the Eucharist. In general, the Eucharist was only to be received after a period of hours during which food had not been consumed and, as such, the Eucharistic service was usually held the first thing in the morning, after which a meal breaking the fast (i.e., breakfast) would be eaten.

The Eucharist provided a week-by-week and even day-by-day means of both building a moral society and continually reintegrating individuals as they deviated, broke the moral rules, and sought to right themselves in the eyes of the community and the divine order. It became the means of reconciling neighborly quarrels and restoring those guilty of gross crimes. One's eternal destiny depended upon being in fellowship with God and the church. The right to receive the Eucharist was a primal sign of the existence of that fellowship. To break fellowship, by unrepentant sin or heresy (espousing incorrect belief on an essential issue of doctrine), was a serious matter, and could lead to a formal act of a denial of the sacraments, that is, excommunication. Excommunication was not a denial of membership in the church so much as a public statement that someone was out of communion with God and the church and hence not fit to receive its primary sacrament.

After one became an adult (and in the Middle Ages one was recognized as an adult at a much younger age than at present), a set of special sacraments would become available. One could, for example, choose a mate and find the church's sanction through the sacrament of marriage. For most, that was a one-time occurrence (unless of course a spouse died, at which time one was free to marry a second time or to pursue other options). One could also choose to enter the priesthood or a monastic life, and thus become one of the people set aside to keep the sacramental system and perform the sacramental acts. In the priesthood, one would pass through the sacrament of ordination to holy orders. Within the Roman Catholic Church, there were multiple levels to holy orders, but three became important—deacon, priest, and bishop. By the Middle Ages, the priesthood was celibate and, hence, holy orders and marriage did not mix (a characteristic that would come to distinguish Roman Catholicism from Eastern Orthodoxy). Those who entered holy orders were, in effect, married to the church. Females who entered a convent were seen as married to Christ.

The church was also present to oversee the last hours of life and to ease the movement into the afterlife. The goal of the Christian was heaven, the place where God resided. Those who died outside of the state of grace, with a serious sin that had not been repented and forgiven, were destined for eternal separation from God, that is, hell. Hell became the object of numerous speculations, and many employed their imaginations vividly to describe the horrors of separation from God, often in the most excruciating language.

Average Christians who died in a state of grace were destined for heaven, but usually had yet to make amends for all of the sins they had committed; to enter heaven one had not only to be forgiven but holy. Thus purgatory was posited as a place where one could finish the process of paying back (in suffering) for one's sins and thus reach a state of holiness to enter heaven.

A few persons were seen to have become so holy in this life as to be ready to enter heaven directly at the moment of their death. They were also possessed of an abundance of sanctity that could be supernaturally applied to assist the average sinful Christian. It was an act of piety to pray for the abundance of the saints to be applied to lessen the suffering of someone, possibly a beloved parent or family member, in purgatory.

It might be obvious how the teachings on purgatory, designed to account for the need to satisfy justice, could become corrupted. In general, one affected one's stay or another's stay in purgatory by acts of prayer and piety. Among the acts of piety would be the giving of one's income or possessions to aid the poor or to assist the church in its mission. It did not take long for some church authorities to see the financial possibilities of manipulating the fear of purgatory to raise money. In fact, it was the charge of the reformers of the sixteenth century that the Roman Catholic Church was selling guarantees of freedom from purgatory to people who contributed to the building of Saint Peter's, the headquarters church now located in Vatican City.

To insure that one was in a state of grace at the moment of death, as it approached, ideally, a priest would be present to anoint the body with oil and pronounce forgiveness, the sacrament of extreme unction. The church then oversaw the funeral services and the burying of the body in ground especially consecrated for that purpose.

The church had by the Middle Ages developed a holistic theology and practice that was totally integrated into the secular order. In practical use, that powerful system was prone to significant corruption at all levels, and through the fourteenth and fifteenth century, many people agreed that a reformation was necessary. However, the church proved difficult to reform, the developing tradition proving a powerful barrier to the needed systemic changes. For many, cleaning up the corruption became identified with questioning doctrines, even questioning the very basis of the church's authority, which emanated from Rome, and the close relationship of that authority with the coercive powers of the state.

The questioning of the authority of the Roman Catholic Church would, in the sixteenth century, lead to the splitting of the Roman church and the emergence of the Anglican (chapter 3), Lutheran (chapter 5), and the Reformed-Presbyterian (chapter 6) churches, each establishing itself in a territory over which it had hegemony. Also emerging were the European free church bodies (chapter 10), which renounced any tie to the state governmental system. The sixteenth-century churches would then, century by century, become the parents of subsequent new traditions. Most important for North America, a second reforming tradition, Puritanism (which attempted various programs to "purify" the Anglican Church in Great Britain) gave birth to the Baptists (chapter 11) and the Congregationalists (chapter 6). Later calls for reformation and renewal would bring forth the Methodist (chapter 7), Holiness (chapter 8), Pentecostal (chapter 9), Fundamentalist (chapter 12), and Adventist (chapter 13) churches.

Emerging within the Western liturgical tradition and retaining the basic liturgical life that dominated the medieval church were the Church of England, the parent church of the worldwide Anglican Communion (the subject of chapter 3), and the Old Catholic Church. Both have major representative bodies in North America, and both have, since the mid-twentieth century, given birth to numerous smaller schismatic bodies.

THE ROMAN CATHOLIC CHURCH IN THE TWENTIETH CENTURY.

The loss of territory in the sixteenth century, and the secularization of European society in the nineteenth century (punctuated by the separation of church and state in many countries) placed the Roman Catholic Church in a somewhat defensive position. As one might expect, the church opposed the loss of its position and power, and various popes railed against the unchristian direction they saw culture taking. The history of the Roman Catholic Church in the twentieth century, however, has been marked by the gradual reversal of its defensive stance toward the emerging democratic culture in western Europe and North America. That process led to and was accelerated by the Second Vatican Council (1962–1965), two long pontifical careers by Pope Pius XII (r. 1939–1958) and John Paul II (r. 1978–2005), and notable global expansion that has seen the Roman Catholic Church emerge as the single largest religious organization in the world.

The nineteenth century was marked by a significant loss of temporal power, with the Roman Catholic Church being disenfranchised in France and its territory in Italy being reduced by the unification of the country under secular rule. The embattled stance adopted by the Vatican was most evident in the United States by the church's rejection of Americanism, the program articulated by American church leaders looking toward a positive adjustment of the American church to the realities of life in a democratic society. The initial turn in Vatican politics is usually dated from the encyclical *Rerum novarum* (1891), issued by Pope Leo XIII (1878–1903), which tackled questions of Christian relations toward capital and labor and encouraged the development of Christian Democratic political parties. The effects of this positive stance toward labor was somewhat blunted in North America following the pope's denunciation of Americanism in 1898. The American church consequently stopped much of its dialogue with American culture and noticeably turned inward until World War II (1937–1945).

The growing willingness of the Vatican to deal with the now recognizable and irreversible wave of democracy that was sweeping away the previous monarchical governments of Europe became evident in its policies with post–World War I (1914–1918) Europe and finally with the approval given to the formation of a United Nations after World War II. The changes in the church culminated in the Second Vatican Council's widespread and forward-looking policies that reformed the church in many ways unpredictable even at midcentury. The Catholic Church opened dialogue with both Jews and Protestants and developed a new stance toward the striving of the world's people for liberation and expression.

The long pontificate of Pope Pius XII (1876–1958) was marked by the church's attempt (now widely criticized) to deal with Adolf Hitler (1889–1945), and the massive effort to rebuild Europe after World War II. Disagreement over who was to succeed the popular Pius XII led to the election of the virtually unknown John XXIII (r. 1958–1963). Many saw him as someone to hold the papal chair briefly until a more consensus candidate could emerge. John XXIII, now described in the most glowing terms by Catholics and non-Catholics alike, surprised everyone both for his outgoing demeanor and his calling of a church council to review church policy and teachings on the widest variety of subjects. The changes were left to his successor, Pope Paul VI (r. 1963–1978), to consolidate and implement. His significant career was followed by the short pontificate of Pope John Paul I (1912–1978), who died a month after his election in August 1978.

Pope John Paul II (1920–2005), whose pontificate extended more than three decades, enjoyed a popularity approaching that of John XXIII. The first Polish pope, he spoke eight languages, a skill he put to use in his globetrotting travels. While Pius XII was the first pope to visit the United States, John Paul II visited on several occasions and frequently spoke directly to the American situation. At the beginning of the twenty-first century, he set a new tone for Catholicism as he publicly confronted the history of the church's questionable actions toward many indigenous people and the tensions that existed between Catholicism, an evangelizing faith, and the other world religions. His talks on these issues regularly culminated in public apologies and the request for forgiveness. While forward-looking on some issues, John Paul II was a traditionalist in most areas. He survived an assassination attempt in 1981, and he attributed his survival to the intervention of the Blessed Virgin Mary. During his many years in office, he had appointed the majority of the cardinals holding office at the time of his death. They selected the very conservative Joseph Cardinal Ratzinger (b. 1927), prefect of the Congregation for the Doctrine of the Faith, as John Paul's successor. He took office as Pope Benedict XVI in 2005.

Pope Benedict XVI oversees the largest religious body in the world. The Roman Catholic Church now claims more than one billion members worldwide, approximately 17.5 percent of the world's population and slightly more than half of all the world's Christians. There are almost as many

Catholics as Muslims, and the Catholic community is larger than the world's Buddhist and Hindu communities. It is strongest in South America (more than 80 percent of the population) and Europe (almost 40 percent). Catholicism claims 22 percent of the population in North America. It is weakest in Asia, with only 3 percent.

INDEPENDENT CATHOLICISM.

Following the disruption of the sixteenth century, the Roman Catholic Church responded with what was termed the Counter Reformation, which included important elements such as reforms instituted by the Council of Trent (1545–1563) and efforts of revitalization by several orders, such as the Carmelites in Spain. As a result, the church recovered some lands that could have been lost to the Protestants, including Poland, some German states, and some Swiss cantons. For several centuries, no new schisms occurred, even though calls for additional reforms continued to be heard. The major voices calling for reform were conservative, asking for resistance to the secularism arising from the Enlightenment of the eighteenth century. The calls for consideration of new action would lead to a church council, the first since Trent, to meet at the Vatican in 1870.

Some dissidents in Holland had been hoping for a council as a means of redress for their grievances that Rome seem to be ignoring. Others, exponents of a new wave of devotion directed toward the Blessed Virgin Mary, saw a chance for support, and the council did open on the anniversary of the Feast of the Immaculate Conception, a belief recently declared as dogma. The Immaculate Conception refers to the belief that the Virgin Mary was born free of sin and thus was a fit vessel to bear the sinless messiah. Still others clamored for a new assertion of papal authority, and they were the group most rewarded when the council issued a declaration on the infallibility of the pope. This precisely defined position affirmed that "the Roman Pontiff, when he speaks ex cathedra—that is, when in discharge of the office of pastor and teacher of all Christians, by virtue of his supreme apostolic authority, he defines a doctrine regarding the faith or morals to be held by the universal church, by the divine assistance promised to him in Blessed Peter, is possessed of that infallibility with which the divine redeemer willed that his Church should be endowed in defining doctrine regarding faith and morals; and therefore such definitions are irreformable of their own nature and not in virtue of the Church's consent"

This new dogma proclaimed by the council would become the occasion of a significant schism, and would prepare the way for a set of schisms that would afflict the church into the twenty-first century. The first of the schisms was the Old Catholic movement that immediately opposed the dogma of papal infallibility. It began in Germany, quickly gained adherents in Switzerland, Austria, and Holland, and then, decade by decade, spread through most of the countries of Europe and North America.

THE OLD CATHOLICS. The Old Catholic movement dates from the 1870s but has its roots in a disturbance in the seventeenth century in Port Royal, France. At Port Royal, Jansenists—members of a mystical movement that carried on the work of Dutch theologian Cornelius Jansen (1585–1638)—found themselves in opposition to the Jesuits, priests of a religious order obedient to the pope. Jansenists believed that the human will was not free and that redemption was limited to only some of humankind. Thus Jansenists were condemned by the pope and opposed by the Jesuits. The Jesuits accused the Jansenists of being Protestants, hence heretics; the Jansenists accused the Jesuits of despotism and laxity in doctrine and discipline. In alliance with the French monarchy, the Jesuits began a persecution that eventually broke the power of the Jansenists, many of whom fled to Holland, where Catholics were a minority, in the territory of the see of Utrecht.

As the Jansenists moved into Holland from Port Royal, Utrecht's newly consecrated bishop, Peter Codde (r. 1689–1710), entered into relations with them. When the pope demanded that Codde subscribe to the condemnation of the Jansenists, he refused and was himself accused of Jansenism. Rival parties developed—one behind Codde and another behind Theodore de Cock, whom the pope favored to replace Codde. For various reasons, the Dutch government stepped in and banished de Cock from Holland. The Vatican subsequently deposed Codde, and he ceased exercising his functions.

Without episcopal functionaries, the see soon began to wither, as no ordinations or confirmations could occur. This problem was somewhat alleviated by the unexpected stop in Amsterdam of Dominique Marie Varlet (1678–1742), newly consecrated bishop of Babylon, on his way to Persia in 1719. In Amsterdam, he confirmed more than 600 children, the first confirmed in 17 years. For this act he was suspended from office. He returned to Europe and settled in Amsterdam. In 1724 Varlet consented to consecrate a new archbishop of Utrecht, Cornelius van Steenoven (r. 1723–1725). When van Steenoven died shortly thereafter, Varlet consecrated Cornelius Wuytiers (r. 1725–1733). Several other consecrations for the neighboring dioceses of Harlem and Deventer followed, insuring that the apostolic succession would not be lost. For approximately 150 years the Church of Utrecht, commonly called the Old Catholic Church, continued in a local contested situation, with only the matter of approved episcopal supervision, not an unimportant issue, as the dividing line between it and Rome.

OLD CATHOLICS AND VATICAN I. Though the Old Catholic movement traces its history back to the see of Utrecht in Holland in 1702, it dates officially from the 1870s and the reaction to the declaration of papal infallibility at the First Vatican Council. In 1870 the First Vatican Council declared the pope infallible when speaking on matters of faith and morals. A number of Roman Catholics saw this position as a new doctrine, a deviation from the tradition, and many Roman Catholics left their church and sought communion with the Church of Utrecht. Even before the council, opposition in anticipation of the declaration arose, particularly in Germany. In 1871 in Munich, a congress of opponents, led by Johann Friedrich von Schulte (1827–1914), a professor of canon law, was held. Three hundred delegates, including representatives from the Church of England, attended. Even the church in Utrecht, now having lost hope that the larger Roman Catholic Church would ever review and resolve its situation, sent representatives. The attendees organized the Old Catholic Church, dividing jurisdictions along national lines. In 1873 Joseph Hubert Reinkens (1821–1896), a professor of church history at Breslau, was elected bishop and was consecrated by the bishop of the church at Deventer. The episcopal authority that continued in the Dutch dioceses now provided the apostolic succession for the new Old Catholic Church. A constitution was adopted the next year that recognized national autonomy and established an international Synod of Bishops. The archbishop of Utrecht now presides over the episcopal conference.

The Old Catholic Church retained most of the doctrines of Rome but rejected ecclesiastical unity under the pope. In 1874 the Old Catholic Church dropped the compulsory fasting and auricular confession of the Roman Catholic Church, and feast days were reduced. By 1880 vernacular Mass began to replace the Latin. The seven sacraments were continued, but baptism and the Eucharist were elevated to prime importance. The Roman Catholic Church has recognized the validity of Old Catholic (Utrecht) orders, though it considers the exercise of the episcopal powers illegal.

In the United States, the primary ally the Old Catholics acquired was the Polish National Catholic Church, a new jurisdiction organized in 1904 by several independent parishes that wished to keep their Polish heritage alive. Their bishop, Francis Hodur (1866–1953), was consecrated in Holland by the Old Catholic bishops. The Polish National Catholic Church was the only American body recognized by the Old Catholics before their coming into communion with the Anglicans.

OLD CATHOLICISM IN ENGLAND AND THE UNITED STATES. Because the Church of England (the Anglican Church) was so similar to the Old Catholic Church on the European continent, no attempt was made to introduce the latter church into England. However, through the nineteenth century, men emerged who wished to function as bishops outside of either the Roman or Anglican communions. In some cases, these were former priests who had left one of the older communions. A few represented ethnic communities that expressed desires to maintain nationalistic particularities.

At the same time, the independent movement developed an antiauthoritarian character. Most of its bishops were self-appointed and maintained relatively miniscule followings. They have pressed for recognition of orders while demanding an independence of jurisdiction from those who granted orders. As an attempt at legitimization, they have sought recognition or reconsecration by bishops of one of the Eastern Orthodox or non-Chalcedonian churches (often

after being rebuffed by the archbishop of Utrecht, the head of the Old Catholic Church). Thus, what began as a specific protest against the pope's authority turned into a drive by independent bishops to set up schismatic dioceses. With the growth of independent dioceses and recognition by various Eastern and Western churches, the variation in ritual and doctrine within the liturgical tradition has increased tremendously.

As the Old Catholic movement developed in America, a chaotic episcopal scene emerged. Many bishops claim dioceses that exist only on paper and ordinations by bishops whose existence cannot be verified. A few churches were created specifically to serve the homosexual community. A small number have been confidence schemes.

In the United States, most of the independent Catholic and Old Catholic churches derive their orders through two lines of succession, that of Arnold Harris Mathew (1852–1919) or Joseph René Vilatte (1854–1929). A third faction traces its lineage to miscellaneous Eastern and Western orders through Hugh George de Willmott Newman (1905–1979). Neither Vilatte's nor Mathew's churches remained in communion with the European Old Catholic churches, which entered into full communion with the Church of England in 1932 and with most of the churches of the Anglican Communion by 1936.

ARNOLD HARRIS MATHEW. The Old Catholic Church came to England through the person of Arnold Harris Mathew, a former Roman Catholic priest. After serving several parishes, Mathew became a Unitarian. He flirted with the Church of England for a while, changed his name, and married. Eventually, he made peace with Rome and settled down as a layman and author. He penned a number of items, including a collaboration in editing the third edition of H. C. Lea's (1825–1909) *History of Sacerdotal Celibacy in the Christian Church* (1907). Then, in September 1907, he began corresponding with Bishop Eduard Herzog (1841–1924), an Old Catholic bishop in Switzerland. In these letters, and later ones to Bishop J. J. Van Thiel of Harlem, he made a case for expanding the Old Catholic Church to England.

Mathew had in the years previous to his correspondence become associated with a group of disgruntled ex-Catholics, led by Father Richard O'Halloran. Under O'Halloran's urging, Mathew was selected as the bishop for these former Catholics, who now saw themselves as the Old Catholic Church in England. The problem was how to get valid orders. The church at Utrecht, the central see of the Old Catholic Church, was initially very hesitant, but finally on April 22, 1908, Mathew was consecrated in Utrecht by the archbishop, under protest from the Anglicans.

Mathew returned to England to find that O'Halloran had lied to him and that the community that had selected him as their bishop was virtually nonexistent. To Mathew's credit, he immediately wrote the archbishop of Utrecht informing him of the deceit and offered his resignation. When his resignation was refused, Mathew accepted his new office as the head of a mission diocese. He found initial support from Reverend

W. Noel Lambert (d. 1954), who turned over the independent chapel in his possession. It became Mathew's headquarters, renamed St. Willibrord's Procathedral.

In 1910 Mathew broke his agreement with Utrecht and secretly consecrated two ex-Roman Catholic priests as bishops. He did not inform Utrecht of his actions, and performed the ceremony without the assistance of other validly consecrated bishops (the usual number seen as necessary for a valid consecration being three). Mathew subsequently declared himself and his work independent of Utrecht. Over the next years, he succeeded in building a small jurisdiction, but in the end died in lonely poverty. Just before his death, Mathew set the stage for Old Catholicism in America.

Among Bishop Mathew's significant consecrations were those of Prince de Landas Berghes et de Rache, Duc de St. Winock (1873–1920), who brought Mathew's lineage to the United States, and Frederick Samuel Willoughby, who would found the Liberal Catholic Church. Mathew's consecrations also included that of John Kowalski of the Polish Mariavite Church.

The Duc de Landas Berghes was an Austrian nobleman consecrated by Bishop Mathew of the Old Catholic Church on June 28, 1913, probably with the idea of setting up an independent church in Austria. De Landas Berghes was prevented from returning to Austria from England because of World War I, however, and fled to the United States to escape arrest as an enemy alien. During his short career, before his submission to Rome in 1919, he consecrated as bishops W. H. Francis Brothers (1887–1979) and Henry Carfora (1895–1958), the direct sources of most Old Catholic bodies in America to date because of the many men that they consecrated as bishops.

JOSEPH RENÉ VILATTE. The man who first brought the Old Catholic Church to America was Joseph René Vilatte. French-born, Vilatte appeared in Wisconsin in the 1880s preaching Old Roman Catholic doctrines among French and Belgian immigrants. He had a checkered religious education under an ex-Roman Catholic priest, Father Charles Chiniquy (1809–1899), and had come to believe both Roman Catholic and Protestant positions invalid. After marked success in Wisconsin, Vilatte went to Berne and obtained ordination from Bishop Herzog, but a protest from the Anglicans prevented his obtaining consecration from Utrecht, the central see of the Old Catholic Church. After a long search, though keeping his old Catholic stance, he accepted consecration as archbishop of the archdiocese of America on May 29, 1892, from Archbishop Alvarez of Ceylon, who had received his orders from the non-Chalcedonian Syro-Jacobite Church of Malabar.

Vilatte briefly returned to Roman Catholicism in 1899 to 1900, but soon became frustrated, resumed his independent work, and for the next 20 years operated as an archbishop for the American Catholic Church. Given his Roman background and his Orthodox orders, it is not surprising that both Old Catholic and independent Eastern Orthodox jurisdictions sprang from his activity. Also, because the Syro-

Jacobite Church of Malabar refused to recognize the various consecrations he performed, even for leaders in his own church, he became further removed from the mainstream of American church life. Finally, in 1925, he again returned to the Roman Catholic Church and, renouncing his separatist and independent course of action, died in the arms of *Mater Ecclesia*. His own American Catholic Church, after the death of Archbishop Frederick E. J. Lloyd (1859–1933), Vilatte's successor, was taken over by bishops with Theosophical leanings and moved totally into the Liberal Catholic Church community.

HUGH GEORGE DE WILLMOTT NEWMAN. Among the most colorful bishops in the independent Catholic community, Hugh George de Willmott Newman can be credited with introducing an increasingly common practice among the autonomous bishops, that of seeking numerous reconsecrations in order to legitimize an otherwise minuscule ecclesiastical jurisdiction by having its bishop embody a wide variety of lines of apostolic succession, both East and West. Such jurisdictions would symbolize the ecumenical church.

Newman was originally consecrated in 1944 by Dr. William Bernard Crow (1895–1976), whose orders derived from Luis Mariano Soares (Mar Basilius) of the small Syro-Chaldean Church in India, Ceylon, Socotra, and Messina. However, within the next decade Newman received no less than nine additional consecrations, usually in ceremonies in which he in turn reconsecrated the other bishop (thus passing along the apostolic lineages he had already received). Of the several consecrations swapped by Newman, that with W. D. de Ortega Maxey (1902–1992) of the Apostolic Episcopal Church was most important for the American scene, as Maxey not only established an American branch of Newman's Catholicate of the West, but became the prime source for American bishops to receive Newman's lineages.

Episcopally led churches have traditionally based their legitimacy on their ability to trace their line of succession from the original 12 apostles. That is, for a bishop to be validly consecrated, and thus able to validly ordain priests, that bishop must himself be consecrated by a validly consecrated bishop. Thus, the story of the independent Old Catholic jurisdictions in America is the story of the search for legitimacy through ever more valid consecrations. In the 1980s, it became common for independent bishops to receive multiple consecrations, especially after changing allegiance to a different jurisdiction.

By the 1990s, the several lines of apostolic succession had become well established in the person of a large number of the independent bishops; thus the need for reconsecration services of newer bishops, so notable in the 1980s, became unnecessary. The different lineages were passed simultaneously, and the practice of multiple consecrations has largely disappeared.

The importing of Eastern orders for a Western church, and the intermingling of Eastern and Western lineages in bishops such as Newman, also initiated a complex mixing of liturgies. The independent jurisdictions have felt free to

U.S. Roman Catholic Provinces and Dioceses

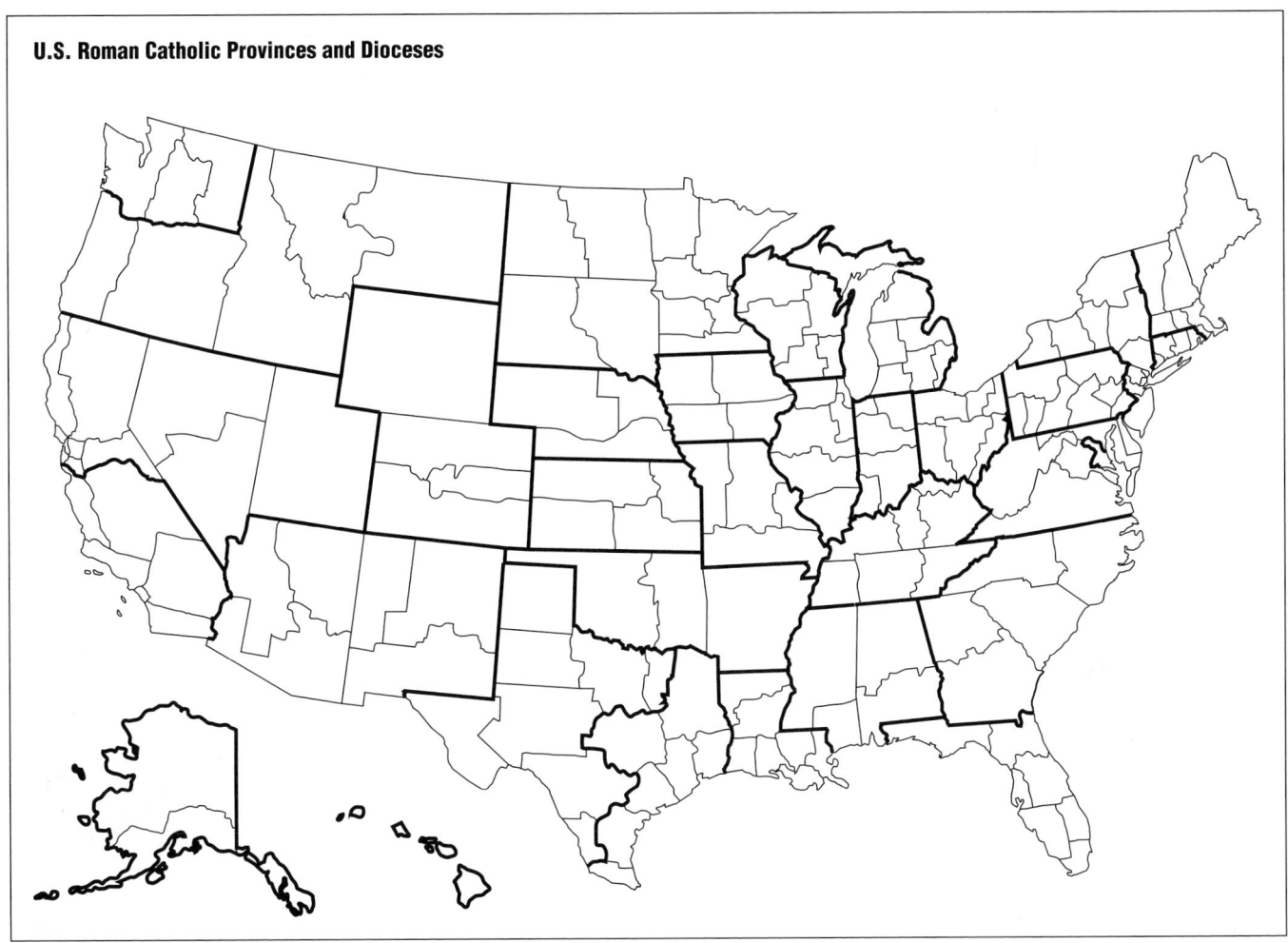

adopt, regardless of the practices of the body from which they received their apostolic succession, any number of liturgies—Roman, Anglican, Eastern, or even Theosophical—while some have written their own. Since many of the American jurisdictions are quite small, with an unpaid clergy and property owned by the local congregations, one of the few real decisions the bishop can make is in regard to the liturgies that the congregations may use.

Adopting the practice introduced by Bishop Mathew of having an unpaid clergy, the Old Catholic (and independent Orthodox) Church has splintered into more than 100 jurisdictions. Priests and bishops, since they have no financial tie to any given jurisdiction, can leave at will, and frequently do. The constant flux within the jurisdictions has made the problem of straightening out the line of succession extremely complex; however, the work begun in this area by H. R. T. Brandweth, Peter Anson, and Arthur C. Piepkorn was later expanded by bishops Karl Prüter, Bertil Persson, and Alan Bain.

BRAZILIAN APOSTOLIC CATHOLIC CHURCH. Possibly the most substantial schism experienced by the Roman Catholic Church since the sixteenth century occurred in Brazil. In the 1930s, Carlos Duarte Costa (1888–1961), the Roman Catholic bishop of Botucatu, emerged as a prominent

advocate of the poor. He complained loudly about the neglect of the poor by both the state and his own church, and his analysis of the situation led to his blaming the problem on the inequality of the distribution of wealth in the country. He also began to speak out about the collaboration of the church with Adolf Hitler. In 1937 Duarte Costa was forced out of office. At the end of the war, he protested the church's role in helping Nazis, many accused of war crimes, escape to Brazil.

In 1945 Duarte Costa also left the Roman Catholic Church and founded the Brazilian Catholic Apostolic Church. The new jurisdiction did not have an easy road. Toward the end of the decade, a hostile Brazilian government moved in and forced it to abandon public worship. Authorities claimed that because of the similarity of the Mass, people would be confused and possibly think that they were attending a Roman Catholic Church instead of the Brazilian church. The action proved a catalyst for change. Alterations were made to the Mass, and the priests adopted a new gray clerical attire.

In the wake of the reopening of the parishes for worship, the church also abolished the requirement for celibacy among its clergy, translated the liturgy into Portuguese, and instituted a system of worker-priests as a means of further

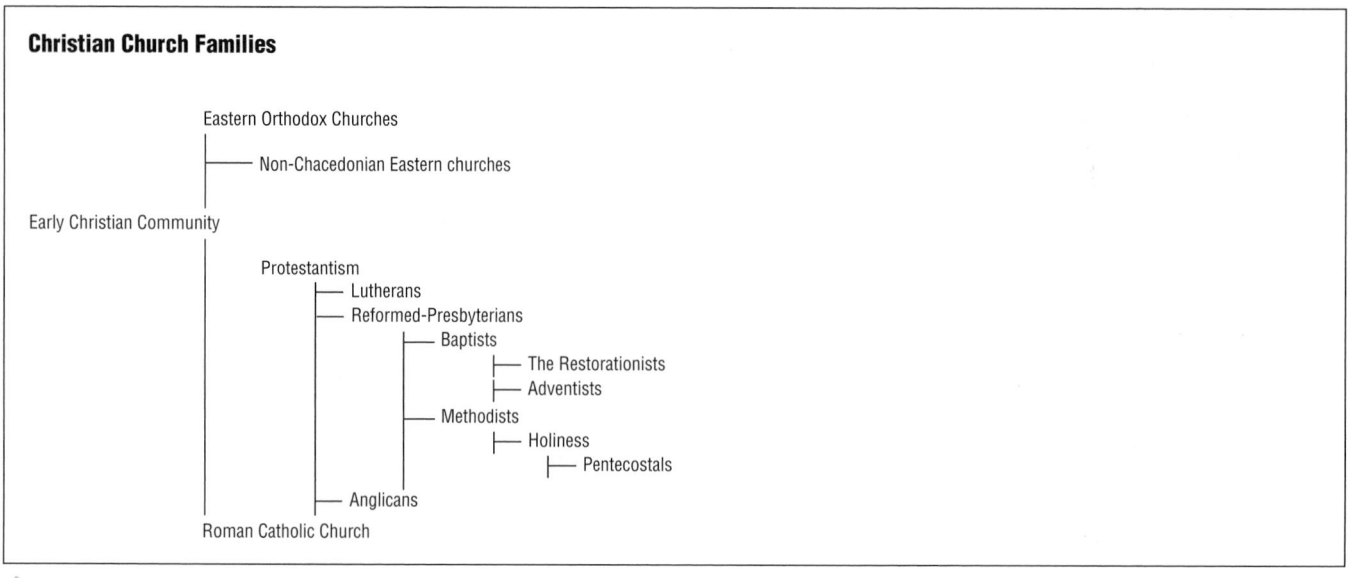

Christian Church Families

J. Gordon Melton

identifying with the poor. The church grew steadily decade by decade. By 1995, the church had some three million adherents and had been exported to North America and Europe, though the attempts of Americans to duplicate the success in Brazil have been blunted by the instability of the larger independent Catholic Church scene.

TRADITIONAL ROMAN CATHOLICISM. In the 1960s, the Second Vatican Council made a number of sweeping changes in the life of the Roman Catholic Church; changes that were implemented over the next decades. Many of the more conservative leaders opposed the changes, especially the dropping of the Latin liturgy in favor of the spoken languages of individual worshipping communities. Two archbishops, Ngo Dinh Thuc (1897–1984) of Vietnam and Marcel LeFebvre (1905–1991) of Switzerland, became vocal critics. Both sought a conservative alternative within the post–Vatican II church, and eventually both, without papal approval, consecrated bishops to lead the communities that had been excommunicated by the Roman Catholic Church. The Thuc bishops have in turn consecrated other bishops, and reconsecrated bishops who had previously received Old Catholic orders; from their hands, several independent jurisdictions have flowed.

Archbishop LeFebvre resisted consecrating any new bishops, and through the 1980s made repeated attempts to negotiate a means by which traditionalists could remain and function openly within the present church authority, but he was rebuffed by the highest church authorities in the Vatican. In 1987, in the realization that he was growing old and reaching the end of his life, he asked that a commission for traditionalist Catholics be established and that he be allowed to consecrate three bishops to carry on his work. These negotiations fell through in the spring of 1988. On June 30, 1988, assisted by Brazilian bishop Antonio de Castro Mayer (1904–1991) of the Duarte Costa lineage, LeFebvre consecrated four bishops. As a result, all participants were excom-

municated; the Roman Catholic Church branded them as schismatics.

Traditionalists associated with the Society of St. Pius X, the organization founded by LeFebvre, consider themselves good Roman Catholics, as do members of some of the other traditionalist groups, even though they have their own bishops and worship in separate local congregations headed by priests assigned by these bishops. They pray for the pope by name at every Mass, as well as the Roman Catholic bishop in whose diocese the services of the society are held. They adhere to all the Roman Catholic dogma and maintain a celibate priesthood. The society's seminaries adhere to all of the provisions for seminaries as found in the documents of the Second Vatican Council. They have refused to associate with the Old Catholics, who deny papal authority, or with the Mass of independent jurisdictions (many of which they consider heterodox) now found in Europe and North America.

FEMALE PRIESTS AND BISHOPS. While both the Old Catholics and traditionalist Catholics represented conservative schisms from Roman Catholicism, the most recent efforts to reform the church came from liberal Catholics who accepted all the changes wrought by Vatican II, but also advocated an important further (and seemingly logical) change, the admission of females into the priesthood. In 2002 seven Roman Catholic women accepted ordination from Rûmulo Antonio Braschi, an independent Catholic bishop. Braschi, an Argentinean, is the founder of what is now known as the Catholic Apostolic Charismatic Church of "Christ the King." He had in turn been consecrated by bishops Roberto Garrido Padin, of the Brazilian Catholic Apostolic Church, and Hilarios Karl-Heinz Ungerer, of the Free Catholic Church.

The seven women ordained in 2002, known as the Danube Seven because they were ordained while on a boat on the Danube River, were Christine Mayr-Lumetzberger, Adelinde Theresia Roitinger, Gisela Forster, Iris Muller, Ida Raming, Pia Brunner, and Angela White. For their action, they were excommunicated from the Roman Catholic Church.

In 2004 Christine Mayr-Lumetzberger and Gisela Forster were consecrated as bishops and began to ordain additional women. They would be joined in the episcopal office by Patricia Fresen (2005), Ida Raming (2006), and Dana Roberts (2008). The source of the episcopal orders of the women has not been publicly announced, though the women claim that they come directly from Roman Catholic bishops.

The women work through Roman Catholic Womenpriests, an organization dedicated to the training and ordination of Catholic women as priests and working for the day when they will be fully accepted into an inclusive Roman Catholic Church. They have rejected the excommunication placed upon them by the Vatican and cite various authorities to indicate that they are merely refusing to obey an unjust law.

SOURCES

The study of Roman Catholicism in America is focused by the American Catholic Historical Association, c/o Mullen Library, Catholic University of America (CUA), Washington, D.C. 20064. It publishes the *Catholic Historical Review*. In addition to CUA, significant archives of Roman Catholic materials can also be found at St. Charles Borromeo Seminary (Philadelphia), Notre Dame University (Notre Dame, Indiana), St. Mary's Seminary and University (Roland Park, Maryland), Georgetown University (Washington, D.C.), and St. Louis University (St. Louis, Missouri). On Canadian Roman Catholic history, contact the Research Center in Religious History in Canada, c/o St. Paul University, 223 Main Street, Ottawa, Ontario K1S 1C4.

The Western Liturgical Tradition

Aland, Kurt. *A History of Christianity*. Trans. James L. Schaaf. Philadelphia: Fortress Press, 1985. 474 pp.

Algermissen, Konrad. *Christian Denominations*. Trans. Joseph W. Grundner. St. Louis, MO: Herder, 1946. 1051 pp.

Bowden, John, ed. *Encyclopedia of Christianity*. London: Oxford University Press, 2005. 1406 pp.

Frankforter, A. Daniel. *A History of the Christian Movement: The Development of Christian Institutions*. Chicago: Nelson-Hall, 1978. 317 pp.

Johnson, Paul. *A History of Christianity*. London: Weidenfeld and Nicolson, 1976. 556 pp.

McGonigle, Thomas D., and James F. Quigley. *A History of the Christian Tradition: From Its Jewish Origins to the Reformation*. New York: Paulist Press, 1988. 218 pp.

McManners, John, ed. *The Oxford Illustrated History of Christianity*. New York: Oxford University Press, 1990. 724 pp.

Mirgeler, Albert. *Mutations of Western Christianity*. Trans. Edward Quinn. New York: Herder and Herder, 1965. 158 pp.

Sheldon, Henry C. *Sacerdotalism in the Nineteenth Century: A Critical History*. New York: Abingdon, 1909. 461 pp.

Thompson, Baird. *Liturgies of the Western Church*. Cleveland, OH: Meridian, 1961. 434 pp.

Roman Catholicism

Allen, John L., Jr. *The Rise of Benedict XVI: The Inside Story of How the Pope Was Elected and Where He Will Take the Catholic Church*. Garden City, NY: Doubleday, 2005. 245 pp.

Bokenkotter, Thomas. *A Concise History of the Catholic Church*. Rev. ed. Garden City, NY: Doubleday, 2004. 431 pp.

Brantl, George, ed. *Catholicism*. New York: Washington Square Press, 1962. 277 pp.

Collinge, William J. *Historical Dictionary of Catholicism*. Metuchen, NJ: Scarecrow Press, 1996.

Flinn, Frank K. *Encyclopedia of Catholicism*. New York: Facts on File, 2007. 670 pp.

Foy, Felician A. *Catholic Almanac*. Huntington, IN: Our Sunday Visitor. Issued annually.

———. *A Concise Guide to the Catholic Church*. Huntington, IN: Our Sunday Visitor, 1984. 158 pp.

Frederic, Catherine. *The Handbook of Catholic Practices*. New York: Hawthorn, 1964. 320 pp.

Hillerbrand, Hans J., and Jon Woronoff. *Historical Dictionary of the Reformation and Counter-Reformation*. New York: Routledge, 2000. 304 pp.

James, Theodore, ed. *The Heart of Catholicism: Essential Writings of the Church from St. Paul to John Paul II*. Huntington, IN: Our Sunday Visitor, 1997.

McBrien, Richard P., ed. *HarperCollins Encyclopedia of Catholicism*. San Francisco: HarperSanFrancisco, 1995. 1349 pp.

———. *Inside Catholicism: Rituals and Symbols Revealed*. San Francisco: HarperSanFrancisco, 1995. 112 pp.

———. *Lives of the Popes*. San Francisco: HarperSanFrancisco, 2000. 528 pp.

McKenzie, John L. *The Roman Catholic Church*. New York: Holt, Rinehart and Winston, 1969. 288 pp.

McNeil, Brian. *Dictionary of Popes and the Papacy*. New York: Herder & Herder, 2001. 352 pp.

The Roman Catholic Church in North America

Catholicism in America: A Series of Articles from the Commonweal. New York: Harcourt, Brace, 1954. 242 pp.

Carey, Patrick W. *The Roman Catholics*. Westport, CT: Greenwood Press, 1993. 375 pp.

Dolan, Jay P. *The American Catholic Experience: A History from Colonial Times to the Present*. Garden City, NY: Doubleday, 1985. 504 pp.

Ellis, John Tracy. *Documents of American Catholic History*. Rev. ed. 2 vols. Chicago: Regnery, 1967.

———. *American Catholicism*. 2nd ed. Chicago, University of Chicago Press, 1969. 322 pp.

Gallup, George, and Jim Castelli. *The American Catholic People: Their Beliefs, Practices, and Values*. Garden City, NY: Doubleday, 1987. 206 pp.

Gillis, Chester. *Roman Catholicism in America*. New York: Columbia University Press, 2000. 366 pp.

Hennesey, James. *American Catholics*. Oxford: Oxford University Press, 1981. 397 pp.

Kelly, George A. *The Battle for the American Church*. Garden City, NY: Doubleday, 1979. 513 pp.

Massa, Mark A. *Catholics and American Culture: Fulton Sheen, Dorothy Day, and the Notre Dame Football Team*. New York: Crossroad, 1999. 278 pp.

Maynard, Theodore. *The Story of American Catholicism*. New York: Macmillan, 1941. 694 pp.

Morris, Charles. *American Catholic: The Saints and Sinners Who Built America's Most Powerful Church*. New York: Vintage, 1998. 528 pp.

Walch, Timothy. *Catholicism in America: A Social History*. Melbourne, FL: Krieger, 1989. 239 pp.

Roman Catholic Thought

Abbott, Walter, ed. *The Documents of Vatican II*. New York: Guild Press, 1966. 793 pp.

Abell, Aaron I. *American Catholic Thought on Social Questions*. Indianapolis, IN: Bobbs-Merrill, 1968. 571 pp.

Berkouwer, G. C. *Recent Developments in Roman Catholic Thought*. Grand Rapids, MI: Eerdmans, 1958. 81 pp.

Bokenkotter, Thomas. *Essential Catholicism.* Garden City, NY: Doubleday, 1985. 437 pp.

Burghardt, Walter J., and William F. Lynch. *The Idea of Catholicism.* New York: Meridian, 1960. 479 pp.

A Catholic Catechism. New York: Herder and Herder, 1958. 448 pp.

Fremantle, Anne. *The Papal Encyclicals.* New York: New American Library, 1956. 317 pp.

O'Brien, John A. *Understanding the Catholic Faith.* Notre Dame, IN: Ave Maria Press, 1955. 281 pp.

O'Carroll, Michael. *Corpus Christi: A Theological Encyclopedia of the Eucharist.* Wilmington, DE: Glazier.

———. *Theotokos: A Theological Encyclopedia of the Blessed Virgin Mary.* Wilmington, DE: Glazier, 1986.

Trese, Leo J. *The Creed: Summary of the Faith.* Notre Dame, IN: Fides, 1963. 155 pp.

Roman Catholic Liturgy

Dalmais, Iréné Henri. *Principles of the Liturgy.* Trans. Matthew J. O'Connell. Collegeville, MN: Liturgical Press, 1987. 301 pp.

Lefebvre, Gaspar. *The Spirit of Worship.* Trans. Lance Sheppard. New York: Hawthorn, 1959. 127 pp.

Martimort, Aimé Georges. *The Church at Prayer: An Introduction to the Liturgy.* Trans. Matthew J. O'Connell. 4 vols. Collegeville, MN: Liturgical Press, 1986–1988.

Segundo, Juan Luis. *The Sacraments Today.* Trans. John Drury. Maryknoll, NY: Orbis, 1974. 154 pp.

The Treasures of the Mass. Clyde, MO: Benedictine Convent of Perpetual Adoration, 1957. 128 pp.

Roman Catholic Polity

McKnight, John P. *The Papacy: A New Appraisal.* London: McGraw-Hill, 1953. 400 pp.

Reese, Thomas. *Inside the Vatican: The Politics and Organization of the Catholic Church.* Cambridge, MA: Harvard University Press, 1996.

Scharp, Heinrich. *How the Catholic Church Is Governed.* Trans. Annelise Derrick. New York: Herder, 1960. 128 pp.

Tillard, J. M. R. *The Bishop of Rome.* Trans. John de Satgé. Wilmington, DE: Glazier, 1983. 242 pp.

Eastern Rite Roman Catholicism

Andrews, Timothy. *What Is the Orthodox Church?* Pamphlet. 1964.

Attwater, Donald. *Eastern Catholic Worship.* New York: Devin-Adair, 1945. 224 pp.

———. *The Christian Churches of the East.* Milwaukee: Bruce, 1948. 232 pp.

Liesel, Nikolaus. *The Eastern Catholic Liturgies: A Study in Words and Pictures.* Westminster, MD: Newman Press, 1960. 168 pp.

Manoogian, Sion. *The Armenian Church and Her Teachings.* Detroit, MI: Armenian Church, 1951(?).

National Conference of Catholic Bishops, Committee on the Relationship of the Eastern and Latin Catholic Churches. *Eastern Catholics in the United States of America.* Washington, DC: Author, 1999. 38 pp.

Roberson, Ronald G. *The Eastern Christian Churches: A Brief Survey.* 6th ed. Rome: Edizioni Orientalia Christiana, Pontificio Istituto Orientale, 1999.

Anti-Catholicism

Billington, Ray Allen. *The Protestant Crusade.* New York: Macmillan, 1938. 514 pp.

Chiniquy, Charles. *Fifty Years in the Church of Rome* (1885). Grand Rapids, MI: Baker Book House, 1958. 597 pp.

de la Bedoyere, Michael. *Objections to Roman Catholicism.* Philadelphia: Lippencott, 1965. 185 pp.

Massa, Mark A. *Anti-Catholicism in America: The Last Acceptable Prejudice.* 2nd ed. New York: Crossroad, 2005. 288 pp.

McLoughlin, Emmett. *Famous Ex-Priests.* New York: Stuart, 1968. 224 pp.

Independent Catholicism

Anson, Peter F. *Bishops at Large.* London: Faber and Faber, 1964. 593 pp.

Bain, Alan. *Bishops Irregular: An International Directory of Independent Bishops.* Bristol, U.K.: Author, 1985. 256 pp.

Brandreth, Henry R. T. *Episcopi Vagantes and the Anglican Church.* 2nd ed. London: S.P.C.K., 1961. 140 pp.

Clarke, Boden. *Lords Temporal & Lords Spiritual: A Chronological Checklist of the Popes, Patriarchs, Katholikoi, and Independent Archbishops and Metropolitans of the Monarchical Autocephalous Churches of the Christian East and West.* San Bernardino, CA: Borgo Press, 1985. 136 pp.

Conger, Yves. *Challenge to the Church: The Case of Archbishop Lefèbvre.* Trans. Paul Inwood. Huntington, IN: Our Sunday Visitor. 1976. 96 pp.

Davies, Michael. *Pope Paul's New Mass.* Dickinson, TX: Angelus Press, 1980. 673 pp.

Ford, James Ismael. *Episcopi Vagantes and the Challenge to Catholic Ministry.* M.A. thesis. Berkeley, CA: Pacific School of Religion, 1992.

Groman, E. Owen, and Jonathan E. Trela. *Three Studies in Old Catholicism.* Scranton, PA: Savonarola Theological Seminary Alumni Association, 1978. 37 pp.

Huelin, Gordon, ed. *Old Catholics and Anglicans, 1931–1981.* Oxford: Oxford University Press, 1983. 177 pp.

Moss, C. B. *The Old Catholic Movement: Its Origins and History.* 2nd ed. London, S.P.C.K., 1964. 362 pp.

Plummer, John L. *The Many Paths of the Independent Sacramental Movement: A National Study of Its Liturgy, Doctrine, and Leadership.* Berkeley, CA: Apocryphile Press, 2006. 236 pp.

———, and John R. Mabry. *Who Are the Independent Catholics?* Berkeley, CA: Apocryphile Press, 2006. 100 pp.

Prüter, Karl, ed. *A Directory of Autocephalous Bishops of the Apostolic Succession.* 15th ed. San Bernardino, CA: Borgo Press, 2007. 100 pp.

Prüter, Karl, and J. Gordon Melton. *The Old Catholic Sourcebook.* New York: Garland, 1983. 254 pp.

Ward, Gary L., Bertil Persson, and Alan Bain, eds. *Independent Bishops: An International Directory.* Detroit, MI: Apogee, 1990. 524 pp.

✿ Intrafaith Organizations

Augustana Evangelical Catholic Communion

c/o St. Michael's House, 1200 NE 81st Terr., Kansas City, MO 64118-1361

The Augustana Evangelical Catholic Communion is an association of episcopally led jurisdictions from Lutheran and Anglican and ideally Western Roman traditions. They are affiliated together because they share the desire for visible, corporate reunion of their jurisdictions with the Roman Catholic Church. They are open to a variety of options as to how that reunion (and reestablishment of communion) might take place. In the meantime the communion has brought the several member churches together for shared worship, service, the proclamation of the Gospel, and work toward reunion.

The communion is currently led by Archbishop Irl A. Gladfelter who serves as its Metropolitan Archbishop. Gladfelter is also the metropolitan-Archbishop of the Anglo-Lutheran Catholic Church.

Membership: Not reported. At present, the Anglo-Lutheran Catholic Church is the only church directly affiliated with the communion; however, it is in communion with three other jurisdictions of like mind: the Association of Independent

Evangelical Lutheran Churches, the Traditional Church of England, and the Evangelical Marian Catholic Church

Sources:

Augustana Evangelical Catholic Communion.
www.geocities.com/littledogs2424/ALCC.html.

Council of Old Roman Catholic Bishops

704 Old Harrods Creek Rd., Louisville, KY 40223

Following the death of Archbishop Carmel Henry Carfora (1878–1958), who had pioneered the Old Catholic movement in North America, the North American Old Roman Catholic Church that he founded split into several independent churches. These were the Old Roman Catholic Church in North America–Diocese of Michigan and the Central States, the Western Regionary Diocese (Evangelical Orthodox Catholic Church in America) Church, the North American Old Roman Catholic Church, and the Old Roman Catholic Church–Diocese of Florida within the Historic See of Caer Glow.

In 1981 the Diocese of Michigan and the Central States sent its then vicar general, Right Rev. Donald R. Currie, to Holland with the purpose of informing the Church of Utrecht on developments in North America and to probe the possibilities of a renewed dialogue between the North American leadership and the see of the Utrecht Union of Churches.

The archbishop of Utrecht, Marinus Kok, noted that before a dialog could begin, an entity that was representative of the various Old Catholic bodies would need to be identified. Taking their cue from the Archbishop's observation, the Diocese of Michigan and the Central States initiated a dialogue among the groups that carried an unbroken lineage from Archbishop Carfora. An initial gathering of prelates was held in September 1982, and the attending bishops formed the Council of Independent Catholic Bishops, which later changed its name to Council of Old Roman Catholic Bishops (1999). Abp. Frederick L. Pyman of the Western Regionary Diocese and Abp. James H. Rogers, the Old Roman Catholic archbishop of New York, served as the first and second chairmen of the Council, respectively. Members of the council share common Catholic beliefs and practices and a documented apostolic succession from Archbishop Carfora.

The Council has as its goals the fostering of communication between the member churches, in order to lead their prelates into a greater experience of unity, and to expand the Old Catholic movement in North America. It does not interfere with the internal workings of its member jurisdictions. The members have agreed not to contribute to the proliferation of the episcopacy, an ongoing problem within the larger Old Catholic movement. A major accomplishment of the Council has been the development of an Old Catholic seminary.

Most Rev. John J. Humphreys, bishop of Florida, presently serves as chairman of the Council, and Most Rev. Francis P. Facione, bishop of Michigan and the Central States, is the executive director.

Membership: The Council includes the six bishops of the Council's several founding bodies.

Educational Facilities:

Thomas Aquinas Old Roman Catholic Seminary, St. Petersburg, Florida.

Sources:

Council of Old Roman Catholic Bishops. www.orccna.org/ourfaith/indbishops.htm.

Ecumenical Communion of Catholic and Apostolic Churches

c/o The American Old Catholic Church, 14100 E Jewell Ave., Aurora, CO 80012

As its name implies, the Ecumenical Communion of Catholic and Apostolic Churches (ECCAC) is an ecumenical fellowship of churches of the Christian tradition. It was founded in the mid-1990s to bear witness through worship, ministry, and life to the essential unity that already spiritually exists among all the branches of the historic Catholic faith. It recognizes that the one true Holy Catholic Church includes equally the Roman Catholic communion and all those in communion with it, all of the autocephalous communions and jurisdictions of the Eastern Orthodox Church, those provinces of the worldwide Anglican Communion which hold to orthodox, historic apostolic faith and order (including the "Continuing Church" movements within Anglicanism), and the orthodox, valid communions of the Old Catholic Church and other valid and orthodox branches or autocephalous communions with true apostolic succession, faith and worship. It considers all ecclesial communions that can clearly trace their lines of apostolic succession and hold to historic, apostolic, and Catholic order and practice in their faith and worship (as defined by the ancient and undivided church and reflected in the teaching of the first seven Ecumenical Councils of the early Christian Church) as valid and orthodox.

In practical terms, it supports unity while embracing a diversity of historic, orthodox Catholic liturgies, as used by the major branches of Catholic and Orthodox Christianity from the beginning. These would include the Divine Liturgy of St. John Chrysostom, the Novus Ordo of the Roman Catholic Church, Anglican liturgies, Western Rite Orthodox liturgies, and others recognized as expressions of rites used historically within the broad scope of orthodox, Catholic Christianity worldwide.

The ECCAC believes that Christian unity can best be restored by the return of all Christian communions to the principles of unity exemplified by the undivided Catholic Church during the first stages of its existence that includes as an inherent component the affirmation of:

1. The Holy Scriptures of the Old and New Testaments as the revealed word of God, "containing all things necessary to salvation" and as being the rule and ultimate standard of faith.

2. The creeds, i.e., the Apostles' Creed, as the baptismal symbol; the Nicene Creed, as the sufficient statement of the Christian faith; and the Athanasian Creed, or Quicunque Vult, as of great value in articulating the essentials of true Catholic and orthodox Christian faith.

3. The sacraments as outward signs that confer the very grace they signify. These sacraments were ordained by Christ and are at least seven in number: baptism, anointing the sick, confirmation, matrimony, the Holy Eucharist, holy orders, and reconciliation.

4. The Historic Episcopate, locally adopted in the methods of its administration to the varying needs of the people.

5. The Seven General or Ecumenical Councils only, which are recognized by the whole of Catholic Christendom, held respectively in Nicea (325 c.e.), Constantinople (381), Ephesus (430), Chalcedon (451), Constantinople (553), Constantinople (680), and Nicea (787).

At a meeting in Brooklyn, New York, in 1995, all of the bishops of the Ecumenical Communion consecrated each other, and subsequent newly affiliating bishops are free to mingle lines of apostolic succession with all members of the communion. At a meeting in San Antonio, Texas, in 1996, ECCAC members accepted a set of protocols or agreements by which the communion is governed. All members of the communion are considered to be in communion with all the other members. Intercommunion does not require members of the communion to accept all doctrinal opinions, sacramental devotions, or liturgical practices of the other, but each accepts the others as holding to all the essentials of the Christian faith.

Membership: Members of the ECCAC in 1998 were the American Old Catholic Church, the American Catholic Orthodox Church, Saint Matthew American Catholic Church, the Anglican Church of the United States, the Communion of Evangelical Episcopal Churches, the Ecumenical Catholic Church, the Free Catholic Communion, and the Diocese of St. Paul the Apostle.

Sources:

Ecumenical Communion of Catholic and Apostolic Churches.
    www.aocc.org/ECCAC.htm

Barrett, David B. *World Christian Encyclopedia*. New York: Oxford, 1982.

Independent Catholic Clergy Association

PO Box 6903, Glendale, CA 91205

The Independent Catholic Clergy Association is a fellowship of clergy from various Independent and Old Catholic jurisdictions. It was founded in 1986 to promote the spread of Christianity, to provide fellowship, to establish a forum for discussion of present issues, and to advance the cause of the Independent Orthodox and Old Catholic tradition. Among its first accomplishments was the attainment of television air time for one of its members during Pope John Paul II's visit to Los Angeles, California, in 1987.

The association holds monthly meetings in Southern California and promotes the formation of similar gatherings in other parts of the United States.

Periodicals: *The Independent*.

Old Catholic Communion in North America

c/o Bp. Michael Nesmith, 181 Baywood Ln., Monticello, AR 71655

Alternate Address: Bp. David Kocka, PO Box 6542, Louisville, KY 40206-0542

The Old Catholic Communion in North America was formed in the first decade of the twenty-first century as a coalition of several small Old Catholic dioceses and churches. Affiliating dioceses share the common history of the Old Catholic Movement beginning in the 1870s and the common stance of Old Catholicism centered in pre—Vatican I beliefs and practices. Since their break with the Roman Catholic Church, Old Catholics have moved to vernacular worship and have accepted women and married people into the ordained ministry. The churches of the Old Catholic Communion are opposed to abortion, but have welcomed into active membership people who are divorced.

Bishops who affiliate with the Communion are asked to sign a concordat based upon the 1931 Bonn Agreement, by which the European Old Catholics came into a relationship with the Anglican Communion, and must be able to show that they exist as more than paper organizations. The concordant requires the signing bishops to recognize the legitimacy and independence of the other bishops and their dioceses. It also calls for some tolerance of variant liturgies and rites. Member groups agree not to ordain homosexuals, not to allow priests to officiate in same-sex unions, not to reject any parts of the Nicene Creed, and not to use the rites of non-Christian religions.

At present, the Old Catholic Communion is built around two dioceses, the Diocese of the Holy Spirit headed by Bp. Michael Nesmith of Monticello, Arkansas, and the Ecumenical Catholic Church + USA headed by Bp. David Kocka of Louisville, Kentucky. Both bishops possess multiple lineages of apostolic succession. Bishop Nesmith was originally consecrated by Most Rev. Paul Combs of the Old Catholic Church of North America. The Ecumenical Catholic Church operates the Vilatte Theological Seminary, a distance-learning school.

Membership: In 2008 the Diocese of the Holy Spirit included five parishes, and the Ecumenical Catholic Church had six parishes and missions.

Educational Facilities:

Vilatte Theological Seminary, O'Fallon, Missouri.

Sources:

Old Catholic Communion in North America. www.oldcatholicchurch.net/.

Union of Independent Catholic Churches of the North American Old Catholic Church

c/o The Rt. Rev. Bill Peckenpaugh, OSFL, 135 Fiske St., Silverton, OR 97381-2012

Alternate Address: Most Rev. Diana Dale, Presiding Bishop, ACOC, 2311 Fountainview, No. 64, Houston, TX 77057.

The Union of Independent Catholic Churches of the North American Old Catholic Church (UICC) is a cooperative fellowship established in the fall of 1993. Its existence was formalized by a Concordat of Intercommunion between the Apostolic Catholic Orthodox Church, the Agape of Jesus Independent Catholic Church (now the Independent Catholic Church of America (ICCA)), and the Apostolic Independent Catholic Church. The union attempts to strengthen its members in their unity of service to Christ, while allowing each to keep its separate identity. It promotes the sharing of resources (such as liturgical, educational, and pastoral materials and opportunities) and responsibilities for some projects (such as chaplaincy training and clinical pastoral education training) among members.

Each of the bishops, representing their own jurisdictions, have also affirmed mutual intercommunion among their churches. The specifics of this affirmation follow the form published by the Old Catholic Church of the Netherlands, as follows:

> 1. Each Communion (jurisdiction) recognizes the catholicity and independence of the others and maintains its own.
>
> 2. Each jurisdiction agrees to admit members of the other signing jurisdictions to participate in the sacraments.
>
> 3. Intercommunion does not require from the jurisdictions the acceptance of all doctrinal, sacramental devotion, or liturgical practices characteristic of the others, but implies that each believes the others to hold all the essentials of the apostolic Christian faith.

Membership: In 1997 the union included the Apostolic Catholic Orthodox Church, the Independent Catholic Church of America, the Apostolic Independent Catholic Church, the United Catholic Church (UCC), and several independent Catholic and Orthodox bishops as members.

Union of Traditional Apostolic Churches (UTAC)

1718 Moseley Dr., Hopkinsville, KY 42240

The Union of Traditional Apostolic Churches was founded in 2001 by Archbishop Maximilian-Anthony (Gregory Godsey, b. 1979), presiding bishop of the Continuing Apostolic United States Episcopacy. His goal was to unite all Old Catholics, Continuing Anglicans, and Orthodox groups to teach and preach the undivided faith, which includes affirmation of the teaching of the seven historic ecumenical councils; Christ's true presence in the Eucharist (though the exact formulation of that presence is left open); apostolic succession; and a priesthood exercised exclusively by heterosexual males (meaning that women and gay and lesbian people are excluded).

All jurisdictional members must give their adherence to the Old and New Testaments as the Revealed will of God; The Three Ecumenical Creeds; *The Apostles Creed, The Nicene Creed* (with or without the Filoque Clause), *The Athanasian Creed*, The Historic Episcopate; and the Liturgical Forms of Public Worship which are shared in common.

Original signatories to the Union's charter were Archbishop Maximilian-Anthony, Most Rev. Brendan-Michael Hammacher of the Orthodox Catholic Church of America, Most Rev. Pauli Pereira of the Vetro-Catholic Church in Brazil, and Rev. Oscar Joseph Rivest of the Cistercian Order of the Holy Cross.

Leadership in the union is divided between the House of Bishops and a Council of Bishops. The House of Bishops consists of the presiding bishops of each participating jurisdiction. All matters concerning the UTAC must pass through this house. The Council of Bishops is made up of the other bishops in the participating jurisdictions who advise the house on all matters before it.

Membership: Not reported.

Sources:

Union of Traditional Apostolic Churches. www.forministry.com/USNYNONDEUOTAC/

United Catholic Church

5017 Bellflower Ct., Melbourne, FL 32940

Despite what its name might suggest, the United Catholic Church is not a new denomination. A free association of denominations, various interchurch fellowships, independent churches, and individuals, it does not form new parishes or ordain ministers. Rather, it maintains a clearinghouse for the exchange of worship materials, liturgies, music, newsletters, press releases, and so on; provides assistance to churches by arranging clergy exchanges; directs travelers to churches in the areas they are visiting; and facilitates contact between member groups.

The genesis of the United Catholic Church can be traced to 1996 and the consecration to the bishopric of Robert M. Bowman, after his long and varied career as a United States Air Force officer, space industry executive, and churchman. He was consecrated by five bishops including William Donovan and John Reeves, through whom he received various lines of apostolic succession now available in the independent Catholic world.

At about the same time, a group of independent Catholic bishops from different jurisdictions meeting in synod asked Bowman to create a prospectus for their common life around the concept of inclusivity. They asked him to deal with a range of questions such as: What is it that makes us Catholic? What are our core beliefs? How can unity be expressed given the differences of the various jurisdictions? How can unity exist without uniformity? The result was a lengthy paper, "What Does It Mean to Be Catholic? (A Call to Unity)," which spelled out such essentials as the authority of Scripture, faith in Jesus Christ, apostolic succession, the unity of the church, and the Great Commandment to love God and to love one's neighbor. He also cited a number of nonessentials, including beliefs about such issues as the Virgin Mary, abortion, praying to the saints, birth control, and homosexuality. Bowman concluded that, though these may be important issues, they do not hold salvation in the balance. Thus, he argued, concerning such nonessentials diversity should be allowed, and charity should operate in all matters.

The fellowship is open to Roman Catholics, Old Catholics, independent Catholics, Orthodox Catholics, Anglican Catholics, and Protestant Catholics. The United Catholic Church ordains without regard to gender, sexual orientation, or marital status; however, it does not tolerate pedophiles or promiscuous and abusive clergy.

Membership: The church reports fifteen affiliated churches and ministries (including one each in Canada and American Samoa) and a number of additional churches and ministers. It considers as sister organizations the Ecumenical Communion of Catholic and Apostolic Churches, the American Association of Independent Catholic Bishops, and the Old Catholic Church of Canada.

Educational Facilities:

The church recommends two seminaries for ministerial training: Sanctus Theological Institute in Mesa, Arizona; and St. Willibrord's Seminary in Ontario, Canada.

Sources:

United Catholic Church. www.rmbowman.com/catholic/.

World Bishops Council

339 State St., PO Box 2302, Springfield, MA 01101

The World Bishops Council, formed in 1997, describes itself as the "Largest Ecumenical Council of Christian Bishops Contending for Unity in the Faith." It was formed both to serve as a forum through which Christian bishops globally could meet together and share their experiences and as a structure for the dissemination of information on primary issues of education, governmental affairs, ecclesiastical endorsements, and educational, theological, and humanitarian efforts.

The council is led by its Holy Synod, the council's presidents, and the Executive College of Bishops with its seven standing committees: the Executive Committee, the Humanitarian Committee, the Governmental Affairs Committee, the Education Committee, the Economic Development Committee, the Ecclesiastical Endorsement, and the Program Committee. The synod includes representatives from all the member churches.

The council has brought together bishops both from churches that lay claim to a formal apostolic succession and from churches that have episcopal leadership, but no apostolic success (including many Pentecostal churches). The president of the council is His Beatitude Timothy Paul Baymon, metropolitan archbishop of the International Communion of the Holy Christian Orthodox Church. Baymon is assisted by two vice-presidents: Abp. Peter Paul Brennan—primate of the Order of Corporate Reunion—and Bp. Michel Milner of the International Free Catholic Communion.

In 2002 the World Bishops Council formed the World Federation of Churches (WFC) to address the needs of small and independent congregations, specifically to distinguish legitimate small churches from those deemed less than legitimate. The WFC investigates small churches when they apply for membership, and upon accepting them into membership issues to them a "certificate of authenticity." At present, Bp. William P. Brown is founder and chief pastor of Mt. Zion Full Gospel Cathedral, located in Stafford, Virginia, and the founder and primate of the Fellowship of Independent and Global Churches and Ministries, Inc.

Membership: In 2008 the Council drew membership from 37 churches, most based in the United States, but with representative in more than 20 other countries. It claims to represent more than 23 million Christians worldwide.

Sources:

World Bishops Council. www.worldbishopscouncil.org/.

Roman Catholic Church

Armenian Catholic Church

c/o Mgr. Mikael Nerses Setian, 110 E 12th St., New York, NY 10003

Alternate Address: International headquarters: Rue de l'Hopital Libanais, Jeitaoui, 2400 Beirut, Lebanon.

The Armenian Catholic Church, an Eastern-rite church in full communion with the Roman Catholic Church, emerged in the eighteenth century as a result of several centuries of missionary activity among members of the Armenian Apostolic Church residing in Lebanon. The ancient church of Armenia became alienated from both the Roman church and the Eastern Orthodox churches after its bishops refused to affirm the teachings promulgated by the Council of Ephesus, which in 431 C.E. had made theological decisions concerning the nature of Christ. The Armenian position, traditionally termed *monophysitism*, held that Christ had only one nature, the divine; in contrast, church leaders at Ephesus affirmed that Christ had both a human and divine nature. The argument remained an important issue over the centuries, and the majority of Christians considered the Armenians to be heretics.

During the Middle Ages, members of the Armenian Church met the Crusaders who passed through Lesser Armenia (Cilisia), an Armenia land on the southern coast of what is now Turkey. As a result, an alliance of the church in Cilesia and the Church in Rome was established in 1198. But the union proved unacceptable to most Armenians, and the Tatar conquest of the region in 1375 occasioned its end. However, some Roman Catholics kept the ideal alive and convinced the Council of Florence in 1439 to publish a decree affirming the former union.

As opportunities arose, Catholic priests pursued efforts at evangelism, and a few Armenian congregations affiliated with Rome. Then in 1742, an Armenian bishop, Abraham Ardzivan (1679–1749), converted to Catholicism, and Pope Benedict XIV established the Armenian Catholic Church with Ardzivan as their first patriarch under the name Abraham Pierre I. His successors included "Pierre" as part of their Episcopal title. With some minor adjustments, the church continued to use the Armenian liturgy with which they were familiar.

The new church came into immediate conflict with the Ottoman Empire, because government authorities wanted to relate to their Armenian subjects through a single church, the Armenian Apostolic Church, and its bishop in Constantinople. It took more than 80 years (1829) before the government would recognize the Armenian Catholic Church. Finally, the government allowed the appointment of a second bishop who would have his seat in Constantinople, where the Ottoman Empire was headquartered. In 1867 the two diocese united into a single patriarchate in Constantinople.

The church prospered through the late nineteenth century, but was decimated during the Turkish massacre of Armenians as World War I came to an end. It lost more than 100,000 members, seven bishops, and a number of priests and nuns. In 1928 the patriarch moved to Lebanon.

The Turkish massacre spurred the relocation of many Armenians around the world, including North America. Subsequently, the American diocese was established in 1981. The diocese was headed by His Excellency Mgr. Mikael Nerses Setian. Most Rev. Hovhannes Tertzakian succeeded Bishop Setian; in 2008 the current apostolic exarch for North America was Bishop Manuel Batakian, appointed November 30, 2000.

Membership: Not reported. There are an estimated 150,000 members worldwide. Dioceses are found in France, Argentina, Turkey, Iran, Iraq, and Egypt.

Educational Facilities:

The church supports a seminary in Lebanon and a college in Rome.

Sources:

Armenian Catholic Church. www.armeniancatholic.org.

Liesel, N. *The Eastern Catholic Liturgies: A Study in Words and Pictures*. Westminster, MD: Newman Press, 1960.

Roberson, Ronald G. *The Eastern Christian Churches—A Brief Survey*. 5th ed. Rome: Edizioni Orientalia Christiana, Pontificio Istituto Orientale, 1995.

Chaldean Catholic Church

St. Thomas the Apostle Chaldean Catholic Diocese Chancery, 25603 Berg Rd., Southfield, MI 48034

Alternate Address: International headquarters: PO Box 6112, Baghdad, Iraq.

The Chaldean Catholic Church, an Eastern-Rite church in full communion with the Roman Catholic Church, was founded in Iraq in the 1550s. The church traces it origins to the fifth century when the Iraqi Christian community separated from Eastern Orthodoxy over an unwillingness to affirm the statements of the Council of Ephesus (351), one of the international gatherings of bishops of the Christian church at which decisions on essential Christian doctrines were made. The resulting Apostolic Catholic Assyrian Church of the East rejected the Orthodox formulations concerning the personhood of Christ. That church survived through the centuries in spite of the rise of Islam to dominance in Iraq.

In the thirteenth century, Roman Catholic missionaries began to proselytize within the Iraqi Christian community (proselytizing among Muslims being against the law). The missionaries happened to be on the scene in the 1550s, when a problem developed over the appointment of a new Patriarch. The Assyrian church had traditionally passed the office of Patriarch from uncle to nephew within a single family. Occasionally, this practice resulted in the selection of an untrained youth as the new Patriarch. Such a youth was selected in 1552. In reaction, a group of the church's bishops declined to acknowledge the new Patriarch and instead turned to Rome. They selected a new Patriarch from among the adult clergy, and in 1553 the pope inserted himself into the situation by consecrating him as Patriarch Simon VIII of the Chaldean Catholic Church. The new church accepted Catholic doctrine, especially its understanding of the person and work of Christ, but retained its own rite,

the ancient East Syrian liturgy of Addai and Mari (with the few changes needed to bring it in line with Catholic belief and practice). The new church faced an immediate crisis when after only two years in office the new Patriarch was arrested and executed by Iraqi authorities. However, the church survived.

At the request of the Chaldean Patriarch Mar Paulus II Cheikho (1906–1989), Pope John Paul II established the Apostolic Exarchate (protodiocese) for the Chaldean faithful residing in the United States. Rev. Ibrahim N. Ibrahim was named the first Apostolic Exarch (a patriarch's deputy) in 1982. Three years later the pope elevated the Apostolic Exarchate for the Chaldeans to the rank of Epachy (diocese) and appointed Bishop Ibrahim as the first ordinary of the diocese.

Membership: As of 2008, there were some 419,000 members worldwide. There are 10 dioceses in Iraq, four in Iran, and seven additional dioceses in the Middle East. Outside the Middle East, there are two dioceses, the Diocese of St. Thomas the Apostle and the diocese of St. Peter the Apostle in the United States. The latter was created in 2002 by Pope John Paul II, and includes 19 states:, Arizona, Alaska, California, Colorado, Hawaii, Idaho, Kansas, Montana, Nebraska, Nevada, Oklahoma, New Mexico, North Dakota, South Dakota, Oregon, Texas, Utah, Washington, and Wyoming. The diocese has seven parishes and two missions. The Diocese of St. Thomas the Apostle has seven parishes, five in Michigan and two in Illinois.

Sources:

Liesel, N. *The Eastern Catholic Liturgies: A Study in Words and Pictures*. Westminster, MD: Newman Press, 1960.

Roberson, Ronald G. *The Eastern Christian Churches: A Brief Survey*. Rome: Edizioni Orientalia Christiana, Pontificio Istituto Orientale, 5th ed., 1995.

Coptic Catholic Church

St. Mary Coptic Catholic Church, 2701 Newell St., Los Angeles, CA 90039

Alternate Address: International Headquarters: BP 69, Rue Ibn Sandar, Pont de Koubbeh, Cairo, Egypt. Canadian Mission: Danforth Ave., Toronto, ON, Canada M4J 1M5.

The Coptic Catholic Church, an Eastern-Rite Catholic church in full communion with the Roman Catholic Church, traces its origin to 1741 and the conversion of a bishop of the Coptic Orthodox Church to Roman Catholicism.

In the fifth century, the majority of Egyptian Christians separated themselves from both the Eastern Orthodox churches and the Roman Catholic Church by refusing to affirm the promulgations of the Council of Chalcedon (451) concerning the nature of Christ. The orthodox Christian formulation taught that the divine and human natures were present in the one person of Christ. Egyptian Christian tended to follow a position called *monophysitism*, which affirmed Christ's divine nature but not His human nature. The larger world of Christianity considered the Coptic Church to be heretical.

A millennium later, representatives of the Coptic Orthodox Church attended the Council of Florence (1442), where they signed a document of reconciliation with Rome. However, the church in Egypt refused to support their representatives' action. Roman Catholic missionaries moved into Egypt in the 1600s, but met with little success until the 1741 conversion of a Coptic bishop. This bishop was subsequently appointed vicar apostolic of what became the Coptic Catholic Church. The church adopted Catholic doctrine, but continued to use the Coptic liturgy with some minor changes.

In 1824, Pope Leo XIII established an Egyptian Patriarchate, but it remained inoperative until 1899 when Cyril Makarios was named Patriarch of Alexandria of the Copts. He retained the office until 1908, when he resigned. The office was again vacant until 1947, when a new patriarch was named. By the end of the 1990s, the patriarchate was larger than the Latin-Rite Catholic Church in Egypt. Membership is divided into nine dioceses. The church supports six religious orders, an extensive parochial school system, a set of medical facilities, and St. Leo's Theological Seminary in Maadi (a Cairo suburb).

Membership: The Coptic Catholic Church has approximately 190,000 members, the great majority of whom reside in Egypt. As of 2001 there were about 10,000 Coptic Catholics in the Egyptian Diaspora, served by six parishes located in Paris (France), Montreal (Canada), Sydney and Melbourne (Australia), and Brooklyn and Los Angeles (USA), all under the care of local Latin bishops. There is also a mission in Toronto, Canada.

Sources:

Coptic Catholic Church (unofficial). www.opuslibani.org.lb/copticmenufr.html.

St. Mary Coptic Catholic Church. www.stmarycopticcatholicchurch.com.

Liesel, N. *The Eastern Catholic Liturgies: A Study in Words and Pictures*. Westminster, MD: Newman Press, 1960.

Roberson, Ronald G. *The Eastern Christian Churches: A Brief Survey*, 5th ed. Rome: Edizioni Orientalia Christiana, Pontificio Istituto Orientale, 1995.

Ethiopian Catholic Church

c/o Kidane-Mehret Ge'ez Catholic Church, 415 Michigan Ave. NE, Ste. 65, Washington, DC 20017

Alternate Address: International Headquarters: Catholic Archbishop's House, PO Box 21903, Addis Ababa, Ethiopia.

Prior to the twentieth century, Ethiopian Christianity was first aligned with the Egyptian church, and then largely isolated. The Ethiopian Orthodox Tewahado Church, which originated from the Coptic Orthodox Church (Egypt), followed its parent body in refusing to affirm the doctrine promulgated by the several Councils of the fifth century. The Chalcedonian Creed (451), for example, affirmed that Christ existed as one person with both a human and divine nature. The Monophysites who predominated in Egypt held that Christ had only a divine nature. In the centuries following Islam's coming to dominance in Egypt and across North Africa, Ethiopia was separated from the larger Christian world. European Christians rediscovered Ethiopia in the fifteenth century and representatives of the Roman Catholic Church initiated efforts to bring the Ethiopian Church into union with Rome.

In 1622, the king of Ethiopia declared his allegiance to Catholicism and designated the nation a Catholic state. The following year, the pope named Affonso Mendez, a Portuguese Jesuit, to become the first patriarch of a new Ethiopian Catholic Church. He was installed in 1626, but soon lost popular support when he tried to alter the liturgy (after the model of the Latin Rite). His actions led to his banishment and the end of the union of the Ethiopian Church and Rome.

Catholic missionaries did not reenter the country until the end of the nineteenth century and did not expand significantly until the years of the Italian occupation (1935–1941). Finally, in 1961, an Episcopal see, headquartered at Addis Ababa, was erected. Additional suffragan dioceses were established in Asmara and Adigrat. In 1993, Eritrea became independent of Ethiopia. Approximately half of the Ethiopian Catholic membership resided in the new country; as a result, two additional dioceses (Keren and Barentu) were created.

As Ethiopians and Eritreans migrated to the United States during the last several decades of the twentieth century, parishes of expatriates, attached to Latin-Rite dioceses, began to emerge. The existence of these parishes was given a primary acknowledgement in the mid-1980s by the formation of the Ethiopian and Eritrean Catholic Apostolate in the United States. However, as of the beginning of 2002, the apostolate (association) did not have a national office. The church in Washington, D.C., offers informal national coordination, but it has, as of 2001, no permanent parish building (though it has an expansive Internet site). Other congregations are found in Dallas, Boston, Denver, Chicago, New York City, the Bay Area of California, and Columbus, Ohio.

Membership: In 2001, the church had approximately 190,000 members, most of whom reside in either Ethiopia or Eritrea. In that year there were approximately 300,000 Ethiopians and Eritreans in the United States, of whom about 3 percent (or 9,000 people) were estimated to be Catholic.

Sources:

Kidane-Mehret Ge'ez Catholic Church. www.kidane-mehret.org/.

Liesel, N. *The Eastern Catholic Liturgies: A Study in Words and Pictures*. Westminster, MD: Newman Press, 1960.

O'Mahoney, Fr. Kevin. *The Ethiopian (Ge'ez) Catholic Rite: 1840–1979*. Gaba, Ethiopia: MECEA Pastoral Institute, 1980.

Roberson, Ronald G. *The Eastern Christian Churches: A Brief Survey*, 5th ed. Rome: Edizioni Orientalia Christiana, Pontificio Istituto Orientale, 1995.

Italo-Albanian Catholic Church

51 Redgrave Ave., Staten Island, NY 10306

Alternate Address: International headquarters: c/o Mt. Rev. Vescovado, Corso Skanderberg 54, 87010 Lungro, Italy.

The Italo-Albanian Catholic Church is a relatively small Eastern-rite Catholic church in full communion with the Roman Catholic Church that developed among people of Greek heritage who came to reside in southern Italy and Sicily. In this area, Christianity developed with a Greek rather than Latin liturgical form, even though the church was included under the authority of the bishop of Rome. Through the centuries the process of Latinization in the area began, but before it was completed, in the eighth century the region was transferred from Rome's jurisdiction to Byzantium's. Subsequently, the process of introducing the Latin rite was reversed, and there was a revival of Greek Christianity. Then, in the eleventh century, the Normans (Roman Catholics) conquered the region. The area returned to the Roman jurisdiction, and the process of Latinization was reintroduced.

The Greek Byzantine rite seemed destined to disappear in southern Italy, but the process of Latinization was slowed considerably by the immigration of Albanians in the 1400s. Their persistence was rewarded in 1595 when a bishop was appointed for them. Although they were a relatively small community, their numbers declined over the next centuries, the Vatican began to nurture the group, and in the nineteenth century it recognized the group's equality within the church. In 1732 a seminary was founded in Calabria, and two years later a second opened in Palermo. In 2008 the church was served by two dioceses and three bishops, one of whom served as abbot of the monastery of Santa Maria de Grottaferrata (founded in the eleventh century and the oldest structure in the church).

The Italo-Albanians have no parishes in the English-speaking world, but the identity of the small immigrant communities there has been preserved through groups such as the Italo-Albanian Byzantine Rite Society of Our Lady of Grace, based in Staten Island, New York, which has at its goal the reestablishment of the Italo-Greek and Italo-Albanian rite in the United States. The society is heir to a parish society of what had been the only Italo-Greek church in the North America. The society sponsors the monthly celebration of an Italo-Greek Divine Liturgy in different churches in the New York metropolitan area.

Membership: At the end of the 1990s there were about 62,00 members in the church.

Periodicals: *Quarterly Newsletter of the Italian Byzantine Rite Catholic Society of Our Lady of Grace.*

Sources:

Our Lady of Grace Mission. www.byzantines.net/OurLadyofGrace/.

Roberson, Ronald G. *The Eastern Christian Churches: A Brief Survey*. 5th ed. Rome: Edizioni Orientalia Christiana, Pontificio Istituto Orientale, 1995.

Maronite Catholic Church

Eparchy of St. Maron of Brooklyn, 109 Remsen St., Brooklyn, NY 11201

Alternate Address: Eparchy of Our Lady of Lebanon of Los Angeles, 931 Lebanon Dr., St. Louis, MO 63104.

The Maronite Catholic Church, an Eastern-rite church in full communion with the Roman Catholic Church and under the authority of the papal see, traces it history to St. Maron (d. 410 C.E.), a charismatic figure who converted followers in what is today Syria. They in turn created a monastery west of Antioch (in present-day Turkey). Following the advent of Islam in the region, the Maronites relocated to the mountainous region in Lebanon, where they survived as an isolated community. From among their bishops, they elected their own leader, who assumed the title of Patriarch of Antioch and All the East.

In the twelfth century the Maronite leadership made contact with bishops of the Roman Catholic Church who had been brought to the Middle East by the Crusades. In 1182 the Maronites affiliated with the Catholic Church and were allowed to retain their Syriac liturgy, slightly modified to align them with Roman belief and practice (as distinguished from the Eastern Orthodox churches). The Maronites, who had existed in isolation through the period of the break between the Roman Catholics and Eastern Orthodox, saw themselves as never having been out of communion with Rome, though no active relationship had existed since the Islamic move into the region.

Then, in the sixteenth century, the Maronite homeland was incorporated into the rising Ottoman Empire, and in spite of periodically suffering persecution from the Turkish authorities, it has survived to the present. A particularly horrendous incident, the massacre of thousands of Maronites in 1860, caused the French to intervene and eventually establish French control over Lebanon following World War I. The patriarch of the Maronite Catholic Church still resides in Bkerke, a small community near Beirut, Lebanon. The church sponsors two seminaries and a college in Rome. The University of the Holy Spirit at Kasnik offers advanced theological training.

The 1860 massacre also led Maronites to begin migrating from their homeland, and by the end of the century they had founded expatriate communities in North and South America and Australia. The establishment of an independent Lebanon in 1944 and the civil war that began in 1975 has encouraged further migration.

In the United States, the first congregations of Maronite believers were founded in the late nineteenth century and integrated as parishes into Latin-rite dioceses. Finally, in 1966, by papal decree, the Maronite congregations were regrouped into the Maronite Apostolic Exarchate (proto-diocese). Mt. Rev. Francis Mansour Zavek (b. 1920) was selected as the first exarchate (bishop). His episcopal see was in Detroit, and he served as the suffragan bishop for the Latin-rite archdiocese. The exarchate was elevated to the status of eparchy (diocese) in 1971 and named the Eparchy of Saint Maron of Detroit. In 1977 the eparchy moved to Brooklyn, New York, and the name changed accordingly. A second eparchy was created in 1994, and Mt. Rev. John George Chedid (b. 1923) selected as the first bishop of the Eparchy of Our Lady of Lebanon of Los Angeles.

In 1996 Abp. Francis M. Zayek retired and was succeeded by Hector Doueihi (b. 1927), the current bishop for the Eparchy of Saint Maron of Brooklyn. Bishop Chedid was succeeded by Robert Shaheen as second bishop of the Eparchy of Our Lady of Lebanon of Los Angeles (headquartered in St. Louis). In 2008 the bishop for the Eparchy of Saint Maron of Brooklyn is Bp. Gregory John Mansour, enthroned April 27, 2004.

Membership: At the end of the 1990s the church claimed some three million members internationally. There are ten dioceses in Lebanon and six dioceses in neighboring countries. Additional dioceses exist in Cyprus, Greece, Argentina, Brazil, Mexico, Canada, and Australia, with scattered congregations across Europe. There are 72 parishes in the two eparchies in the United States.

Periodicals: *The Maronite Voice*, a monthly newsletter.

Educational Facilities:

Maronite Seminary, Washington, D.C.

Sources:

"Eparchy of St. Maron of Brooklyn." www.stmaron.org/.

Liesel, N. *The Eastern Catholic Liturgies: A Study in Words and Pictures*. Westminster, MD: Newman Press, 1960.

"Maronite Catholic Church." www.bkerke.org.lb/.

Roberson, Ronald G. *The Eastern Christian Churches: A Brief Survey*. 5th ed. Rome: Edizioni Orientalia Christiana, Pontificio Istituto Orientale, 1995.

Melkite Catholic Church

158 Pleasant St., Brookline, MA 02446

Alternate Address: International Headquarters: Melkite Catholic Church, BP 22249, Damascus, Syria.

The Melkite Catholic Church is a Greek Catholic church that originated in Syria and Lebanon. Its liturgy is derived from the Greek liturgy developed by the Eastern Orthodox churches and widely utilized by a variety of churches around the eastern end of the Mediterranean Sea. It is in full communion with the Roman Catholic Church and under the authority of the Papal See.

The church emerged in the eighteenth century in Syria following a schism within the Syrian Orthodox Church of Antioch. Antioch, an ancient center of Christianity (see Acts 11:26), is the home of one of the four ancient jurisdictions of Eastern Orthodoxy; however, in 1724 the Syrian church split into two parties, each of which elected their own patriarch. The Ecumenical Patriarch in Istanbul (the nominal head of Eastern Orthodoxy) declared the candidate of the party based at Aleppo to be the new Patriarch of Antioch. The other candidate, Cyril VI, who resided in Damascus, was deposed and forced into exile in Lebanon. Then, in 1729, Pope Benedict XIII intervened and declared Cyril the new Patriarch of Antioch. Cyril led his followers into communion with the pope and formed the Melkite Catholic Church.

The new church retained its Eastern liturgy and traditions (including the ordaining of married priests), but adopted Roman Catholic doctrine, especially concerning those matters about which the Roman Catholic Church and Eastern Orthodoxy had disagreed since the eleventh century.

The majority of the church's members reside in Syria and Lebanon, but members have spread to Palestine and Egypt, and the patriarch was given additional titles as Patriarch of Jerusalem and Alexandria (the two sites of the other ancient Christian patriarchates). In 1848 the church was granted recognition by the authorities of the Ottoman Empire, and its headquarters were moved to Damascus from the original site in Sidon (Lebanon). Beginning late in the nineteenth century, Melkite Christians joined in the dispersion of Syrians and Lebanese around the world. Communities were established in Brazil, Venezuela, Mexico, Canada, and the United States, all of which evolved into new dioceses.

Through the twentieth century, Melkite parishes were founded in the United States and, as occurred with other Eastern-Rite congregations, were incorporated into the Latin-Rite diocese. During his years as archbishop of Boston (1944–1970), Richard Cardinal Cushing (1895–1970) took a particular interest in the Melkite faithful and lobbied for a separate diocese for them. That diocese (or eparchy) was established in 1966 under the leadership of its first bishop, Kyr Justin Najmy. It is currently led by Mt. Rev. John A. Elya.

Membership: The Melkite Catholic Church has approximately one million members worldwide. In 2002, the American eparchy had 36 parishes scattered throughout 20 states.

Educational Facilities:

St. Basil's Greek Melkite Catholic Seminary, Methuen, Massachusetts.

St. Gregory the Theologian Seminary, Brookline, Massachusetts.

Periodicals: *Sophia Wisdom Magazine.*

Sources:

Eparchy of Newton. www.melkite.org.

Melkite Catholic Church (Australian). www.melkiteorg.au/.

Melkite Greek Catholic Church Information Center United States. www.mliles.com/melkite/newtonvocationspriest.shtml.

Descy, Serge. *The Melkite Church: An Historical and Ecclesiological Approach*. Newton, MA: Sophia Press, 1993.

Liesel, N. *The Eastern Catholic Liturgies: A Study in Words and Pictures*. Westminster, MD: Newman Press, 1960.

Roberson, Ronald G. *The Eastern Christian Churches: A Brief Survey*, 5th ed. Rome: Edizioni Orientalia Christiana, Pontificio Istituto Orientale, 1995.

Zoghby, Elias. *A Voice from the Byzantine East*. Yonkers, NY: Educational Services, 1992.

————. *We Are All Schismatics*. Yonkers, NY: Educational Services, 1996.

Roman Catholic Church

United States Conference of Catholic Bishops, 3211 4th St. NE, Washington, DC 20017-1194

[Introductory note: The Roman Catholic Church is by far the largest ecclesiastical community in the United States, more than three times as large as the Southern Baptist Convention, its closest rival. That fact, coupled with its position as the largest Christian body in the world and as such, the bearer of much of the Christian tradition, gives it a special position in any survey of religious bodies. Overwhelmingly, western Christian churches can trace their origins to dissent from Roman Catholicism, on one or more points. Even within a predominantly Protestant country such as the United States, the Roman Catholic Church provides a measuring rod by which other Christian groups (approximately two-thirds of those treated in this encyclopedia) can locate themselves. Understanding the lives of these groups presupposes some knowledge of their variation from Catholicism. The Roman Catholic Church was also one of the first churches to come to America, bringing with it the long history of western Christianity. The matter of the origin of the Roman tradition and of the emergence of the see of Rome as the dominant body in the west is a matter of intense debate among ancient-church historians. Most agree, however, that by the fifth century Rome was the ecclesiastical power in the west, and Rome's bishop was the leading episcopal authority. Further, for the next millennium, the story of Christianity in the west is largely the story of Rome. The detailing of this story and the elaboration of this developing tradition is far beyond the scope of this volume. Interested readers are referred to the volumes cited at the end of this entry for a sample of books that treat those topics. This volume merely provides a summary of basic material about the church and its historical development in the west, the emergence of religious orders, its history in the United States, its basic beliefs and practices, and its organization. The long history of the church and some of its sanctioned but less than universal practices (e.g., Eastern-rite liturgies, localized forms of piety, etc.) is treated primarily as background for understanding those groups that have dissented from the church.]

HISTORY. The Roman Catholic Church is that Christian religious community whose members are "baptized and incorporated in Christ, profess the same faith, partake of the same sacraments and are in communion with and under the government of the successor of St. Peter, the pope, and the bishops in union with him" (Foy 1984). The rise of the Roman Catholic Church to a position of dominance within the Christian community can be traced through a series of steps beginning with the geographical spread of the church throughout the Roman Empire and beyond and the emergence of an authority structure built around bishops (who are mentioned in the New Testament, but hardly as the figures of authority that exist today). Then the conversion of the Emperor Constantine pulled the church out of its role as just another religion competing in the Roman forum.

In 303 C.E. Diocletian initiated a plan designed to stabilize the vast empire he ruled. He divided it into eastern and western sections, and over each section he placed a senior emperor assisted by a junior emperor with the right of succession. Diocletian then voluntarily resigned and the four appointees took his place: the senior emperor Constantius Chlorus and his junior partner, Severus, in the west; and Galerius and his junior partner, Maximinus, in the east. However, upon the death of the emperor in the west, his son Constantine usurped the power and Severus, the rightful successor, was killed.

In the midst of his rise to power Constantine identified himself with what was at the time a very small Christian community (only much later was he baptized). According to the Christian historian Eusebius, Constantine saw a vision over the Milvian bridge where he was to meet his rival. The vision was of a cross in the sky surrounded by the words "In this sign you will conquer." Constantine ordered this sign painted on the shields of his soldiers, defeated his rival, and emerged as sole ruling power in the west. One of his first acts was to free Christianity by granting it legal status equal with paganism. In the east, Galerius followed Constantine's lead. Under Constantine, the idea that Christianity flourished best under the protection of the empire began its ascendancy, along with its corollary—that the empire and the emperor not only were capable, but in fact were divinely appointed to rule and to render that protection. The centuries of intimate union between the "Christian" state and the Christian church, and the church-state theory based upon that union, were initiated at that time, even before the church became the dominant religious power in the empire.

Then in 330 C.E., Constantine transferred his capital from Rome to Byzantium (now Istanbul) in the east. He renamed it Constantinople and over the next decades initiated a whole new thrust in culture, but in so doing, he abandoned Rome and created a severe power vacuum throughout the west. The church and the bishop of Rome, the pope, emerged as the organization with both the will and the ability to accommodate to the new situation. Christian bishops took up temporal authority and, given the emperors' acceptance of their role, became an elite ruling class. The bishops in the more important towns of the empire came to be known as archbishops, and those in the major cities, such as Antioch, Alexandria, Constantinople, and Rome, were known as patriarchs. The Roman patriarch assumed some preeminence both as successor to Peter, who died in Rome, and patriarch of the significant urban center in the west.

But while the bishop of Rome claimed a primacy of honor and privilege, the eastern patriarchs claimed a similar prestige. The emperor resided in the east. The ecumenical councils were held there. Most Christians lived there, where Christianity had begun and had its longest history. However, the western church had an opportunity for growth and development that it would not miss.

Pope Gregory the Great, elected in 590, in a very real sense the founder of the modern papal structure, began the process of centralizing upon Rome the entire western church, which was at that time loosely organized into a set of dioceses. He brought a vision, discipline, missionary instinct, and sense of order and rule to the church. The pope's power of jurisdiction and supremacy had been ill defined previously, and it was Gregory who sharpened the definition. A high civil official before becoming a monk, he used his organizational ability to reorganize church finances, thus making it financially independent. He consolidated and expanded the church's power. He exercised hegemony for the church throughout the west and sent forth missionaries (usually monks) to claim lands for the faith. He took major steps to convert the Germanic tribes, end Arianism in Spain, and gain the loyalty of the Irish church. Gregory sent St. Augustine to England, where he converted the king and established the see at Canterbury. The papacy emerged as the international center of the western church in power as well as prestige. The church that emerged under Gregory's successors looked to Rome, not to the emperor in Constantinople nor to his representative at Ravenna.

Two centuries after Gregory, the emperor Charlemagne (742–814) consolidated secular political rule in almost all of Europe and reestablished an empire to match the spiritual realm delineated by the church. A bond was forged, and the marriage between the western church and the western empire took place. The eastern emperor became a mere figurehead to the west.

The dissipation of Charlemagne's empire into the hands of numerous local monarchs set the stage for Pope Gregory VII, elected in 1073, the founder of the papal monarchy. By Gregory's time, western Christendom had grown "larger" than the territory of any empire. Gregory, the monarch of his own country, but more importantly, the representative of a religion that transcended the boundaries of both his country and the empire as it then existed, began to assume more universal powers—full political and spiritual supremacy. He encouraged remote territories such as Spain, Denmark, and Hungary to accept the protection of the Holy See, implying that he, the pope, rather than any emperor, was the real universal center of things. He insisted that the pope could be judged by none; that the pope alone could depose, move, and/or restore bishops. He took authority to depose rulers or to absolve subjects from their allegiance to their rulers. Under Gregory and his successor, the papacy exercised its greatest temporal authority in the west. The extensive corruption of that power, felt throughout the church at every level, created the need for reform and set the stage for Martin Luther (1483–1546), John Calvin (1509–1564), and the Protestant and Radical Reformers.

The Reformation can best be seen as the convergence of numerous historical and political factors on northern and western Europe in the sixteenth century. The church was beset with internal problems and also was filled with voices calling for its reform and a new emphasis upon spirituality in place of its preoccupation with political involvement. Several centuries of reform efforts had coincided with the rise of strong national states, which further stripped the Holy Roman Emperor of real power to hold structures together in the west. Once Luther's cause gained support, other independent reform efforts proceeded, ranging from those of Calvin in Switzerland and Henry VIII in England to the more radical Swiss Brethren (Mennonites) and Unitarians. Once the political power supporting the Roman Catholic Church was broken, the establishment of various independent and locally controlled churches became possible.

The Reformation divided the west among five Christian traditions (Roman, Lutheran, Reformed, Anglican, and Free Church) and fostered the further division of the non-Roman traditions into many individual organizations with linguistic, political, nationalistic, and doctrinal divergences, leading to the establishment of numerous churches in the sixteenth century. Although Rome remained in control of the largest block of territory, it had to devise new ways of relating to religiously divided societies, especially in those countries that had both a Roman Catholic presence and a hostile Protestant ruler.

The Reformation occurred at the same time as the discovery, exploration, and settlement of the Americas. Roman Catholicism settled in most parts of South and Central America and became the dominant religious force. In North America, with the early settlers, the church found a much different situation—a predominantly Protestant society moving quickly toward a religious freedom and pluralism not hinted at since the days of the Roman Empire.

The forces of reform that disrupted the church in the sixteenth century were not new to western Christianity. Reform had been expressed and acted upon by numerous movements throughout the church's history. Some reformers founded rival movements that are remembered today as the great heretical movements (e.g., Gnosticism, Montanism, etc.). When the church gained access to political power, it turned upon those movements and left a record of persecution that haunted it in later centuries. However, with reformist, mystical, and enthusiastic movements that were not defined as heretical (but nevertheless as potentially schismatic) the church had a more creative solution in the formation of ordered religious communities. The schismatic tendencies of, for example, Protestantism and the Free Church families, led to the formation of new sects. In Roman Catholicism, however (and to a lesser extent in Eastern Orthodoxy), these tendencies resulted in the formation of various orders of monks, nuns, and lay brothers and sisters. Many such orders show all of the characteristics of sectarian bodies, including liturgical and theological peculiarities, distinctive dress, and special mis-

sional emphases; but all these groups remain in allegiance to the bishop of Rome. Many orders operate outside of local diocesan control, effectively, reporting directly to the orders' officials, who in turn report directly to the pope or curia. Of course, by accepting new religious movements as ordered communities, the church is able both to nurture genuine religious enthusiasms and to control their excesses.

From the fifth to the twelfth centuries, there was practically only one religious order in the church: the Benedictines. Then, in the twelfth century, a variety of new types of religious communities appeared on the scene, with many derivative branches. The Benedictine Order no longer was held to be the only safe road to heaven, and in fact, by the twelfth century, a noticeable decline had set in. Some monasteries had become socially exclusive and fossilized into great symbols of stability from which no innovations could be expected. New orders were needed. First, there were the Augustinians (Luther's order), an informal group compared to the structured Benedictines, who were dedicated to practical service to others (rather than self-perfection) and to survival in a world of change. The Cistercians, in contrast, wanted to flee change, flux, and the world, and return to pristine Benedictine rigor and purity. They moved into the some of the uninhabited lands of Europe, first growing rapidly, then like the Benedictines before them, succumbing to success.

The new town culture of the late Middle Ages brought into being the two most influential orders of the time, the Franciscans and Dominicans. Founded by middle-class men (Francis of Assisi was the son of a merchant) as an order of brothers (*fratello* in Italian) or friars, they were not to withdraw from the world, as older orders did, but to penetrate it. They gave to the age the common spectacle of the traveling friar and itinerant preacher.

ROMAN CATHOLICISM IN AMERICA. The Roman Catholic Church came to America with the early Spanish and French explorers. Priests accompanied Hernando de Soto and Francisco Coronado, and some, like Jacques Marquette and Junipero Serra, became explorers in their own right. The first missions were begun in Florida after the founding of St. Augustine in 1565. Spanish priests and (after 1573) Franciscans developed the missions. The settlement of large segments of America by European Catholic countries largely determined the earliest religious development of America. Florida, the Gulf Coast of present-day Alabama and Mississippi, California, and the Southwest were Spanish territory. The French settled Canada, Louisiana, and the Mississippi Valley. The early Catholic hegemony is reflected in the many towns named for the saints they revered.

Under the leadership of an English Catholic convert, George Calvert (who became the first Baron of Baltimore), a small band of British Catholics settled on the East Coast and in 1634 founded the colony of Maryland. In stark contrast to their neighbors in Pennsylvania, many of whom had come to America fleeing Roman Catholic persecution, these Catholics had come fleeing Protestant attacks. In 1649 Calvert issued the famous Act of Toleration offering the "free exercise" of religion to residents. Unfortunately, Catholic control of the colony was soon lost, and in 1654 the act was repealed and Catholicism prohibited. Four Catholics were executed and the Jesuits driven out. Not until 1781 were Catholics allowed to participate in public life.

Catholicism existed in America for more than two centuries without a bishop. There were no confirmations, and all clergy were ordained abroad. Beginnning in 1757 the colonies were nominally under the bishop in London, but after the American Revolution a resident bishop was needed. The person chosen for the task was John Carroll, a member of the most prominent Catholic family in the colonies and a cousin to Charles Carroll, one of the signers of the Declaration of Independence. By the end of the eighteenth century Carroll had approximately 50,000 Catholics under his care.

During the nineteenth century several factors shaped the life of the church. First, the dominance of people of British and German ancestry, both of whom had a strong anti-Catholic bias from the days of the Reformation, meant that Catholics lived in a frequently hostile environnment. (This reached its height in the mid-nineteenth century during the so-called Know Nothing era.) Secondly, the church grew massively as literally millions of immigrants from predominantly Roman Catholic countries poured into the United States. At the same time, the church became divided internally into many ethnic groupings, as Catholics from different countries and with different languages settled into their own homogeneous communities, mostly in pockets in the cities where they recreated (as much as possible) life in the old country. To this day, many of the nation's leading cities retain a large Catholic element, and many neighborhoods retain remants of these immigrant communities. The many ethnic groups also contrasted strongly with the predominantly Irish clergy and hierarchy. Attempts to play down ethnicity and "Americanize" parishes (in part by assigning priests from outside the predominant ethnic group in a parish) caused considerable friction; indeed, it was the cause of the only major schism within the church in the United States, which produced the Polish National Catholic Church. The parochial school system, mandated in 1884, was originally established to assist Catholic immigrants as they adjusted to life in non-Catholic America.

Growth of the church during the nineteenth century (which lasted until immigration from mostly Catholic countries was curtailed in 1921) was spectacular. By 1822 Baltimore had been designated an archepiscopal see. Bishops resided in Boston; New York; Philadelphia; Norfolk, Virginia; New Orleans; and Bardstown, Kentucky. By 1900 there were more than twelve million Catholics in the United States (eclipsing by far the population of the largest Protestant church), and by 1930 there were more than twenty million. During the next half-century, church membership more than doubled in size.

BELIEFS. The Roman Catholic Church bases its beliefs on the revelation of God as given through the Bible, and on tradition handed down from the apostles through the church. The essential beliefs have come to be summarized in several creedal statements, especially those developed by the early ecumenical councils: the Apostles Creed, Nicene Creed, and Athanasian Creed. Until recently, new converts to the church were asked to sign a "Profession of Faith" that included a rejection of a number of false doctrines, a promise of obedience to the church, and a statement of belief. Though no longer required, the statement of belief remains an authoritative guide to the church's essential belief:

> *One only God, in three divine Persons, distinct from and equal to each other, that is to say, the Father, the Son, and the Holy Ghost; the Catholic doctrine of the Incarnation, Passion, Death, and Resurrection of our Lord Jesus Christ; the personal union of the two natures, the divine and the human; the divine maternity of the most holy Mary, together with her spotless virginity; the true real and substantial presence of the Body and Blood, together with the Soul in the Eucharist; the seven Sacraments instituted by Jesus Christ for the salvation of mankind, that is to say, Baptism, Confirmation, Eucharist, Penance, Extreme Unction, Orders, and Matrimony; Purgatory, the Resurrection of the Dead, Everlasting Life; the primacy, not only of honor, but also of jurisdiction, of the Roman Pontiff, successor of St. Peter, prince of the apostles, Vicar of Jesus Christ, the veneration of the saints and their images; the authority of the Apostolic and Ecclesiastical traditions, and of the Holy Scriptures, which we must interpret and understand, only in the sense which our holy mother, the Catholic Church, has held, and does hold; and everything else that has been defined, and declared by the Sacred Canons, and by the General Councils, and particularly by the holy Council of Trent and delivered, defined and declared by the General Council of the Vatican, especially concerning the primacy of the Roman Pontiff and his infallible teaching authority.*

Defined by the first Vatican Council, the doctrine of papal infallibility remains the most controversial of Roman Catholic beliefs. It grows out of and is an expression of the church's long held belief that it is kept from error by the power of the Holy Spirit. The pope's words are considered infallible only when he is speaking *ex cathedra*, that is, in his office as pastor and doctor of all Christians, and when defining doctrine on matters of faith or morals to be held by all Christians. More often than not, papal statements do not fall into this category. However, Catholics are enjoined to give heed to papal messages as part of their obedience to the church's teaching authority.

Two relatively recent papal statements in which the pope has been deemed to have spoken *ex cathedra* concerned what is possibly the second most controversial area of Roman Catholic doctrine (at least to most Protestant Christians): the understanding of the Virgin Mary. During the nineteenth century the veneration of the Virgin Mary took on a new importance within Roman Catholicism, and it found expression in numerous new pietistic forms and practices, many built around the several apparitions, such as those at Lourdes (France) and Fatima (Portugal). In 1854 the doctrine of the Immaculate Conception (the sinless birth of Mary) was defined as dogma by Pope Pius IX. In 1950 her bodily assumption into heaven was defined.

Supplementing the beliefs of the church are the moral precepts that are considered binding upon church members. They are required to do the following:

1. Participate in Mass on Sundays and specified holy days and abstain from work and business concerns that impede worship;
2. Fast and abstain on appointed days (primarily during the Lenten season);
3. Confess their sins at least annually;
4. Receive the Eucharist during the Easter season (for American Catholics, between the first Sunday of Lent and Trinity Sunday);
5. Contribute to the support of the church;
6. Observe the laws of the church concerning marriage.

Worship in the Catholic Church is centered upon the liturgy, the major components being the following: the Eucharist (the Mass) and the other six sacraments; sacramentals (signs such as holy water, rosaries, holy medals, etc.); sacred art; sacred music; the prayer cycle of the Liturgy of the Hours (the Divine Office); and the designation of the liturgical year and calendar.

Individuals are brought into the church through baptism, by which original sin is washed away. The Mass, instituted by Christ at the Last Supper, is a real sacrifice of Christ using the elements of bread and wine. During the liturgy of the Mass, the church teaches that the bread and wine change ("transubstantiate") into the body and blood of Christ. The Eucharist is the major sacramental expression encountered by church members on a regular basis. Confirmation, usually given to youths or adult converts immediately after a period of instruction in the faith, is generally conferred by the bishop, and it empowers individuals with the force of the Holy Spirit. Penance is the means by which the faithful confess and receive forgiveness for present sin. Holy Orders sets aside Catholic males (unmarried and celibate) for specified priestly functions. The anointing of the sick (unction) is performed when an individual is in danger of death, either in hopes of improving his or her health, or to ask forgiveness of sins at the time of death. Matrimony binds two people together in God's eyes.

Over the years, supplementing the sacramental life, the church has broadly defined the life and structure of faith through the liturgical calendar. The calendar focuses attention on the essentials of the faith and commemorates the lives of the Virgin Mary and the saints. The liturgical year begins with Advent and includes as its high points Christmas, Lent, Easter, and Pentecost. Worship is further enhanced by the promotion of a variety of devotional practices, including prayers said using the rosary, novenas, and meditation on the stations of the cross (picturing Christ's passion and death).

ORGANIZATION. The Roman Catholic Church derives its authority as the church founded by Christ through the apostles. The signs of Christ's church are its oneness in doctrine, worship, and practice; its holiness by the indwelling of the Holy Spirit; its apostolic nature; and its catholicity, or universal aspect. The apostolic authority has been passed, generation by generation, through the bishops of the church, especially the pope—the successor to Peter and the first bishop of Rome. The pope resides in Vatican City, a small sovereign state outside of Rome, Italy. The curia, where the College of Cardinals meets, is located there.

The pope, the Supreme Pastor of Christians, is elected by the College of Cardinals. The College, which evolved out of the synod of the clergy of the diocese of Rome, includes the principal advisors and assistants to the pope who help administer the affairs of the church. It was officially constituted in 1150, and 29 years later the selection of its members was left to the reigning pope. Members of the College are of three types: cardinal bishops, the bishops of dioceses geographically neighboring the diocese of Rome; cardinal priests, bishops of dioceses away from Rome who have been assigned to a church in Rome; and cardinal deacons, bishops assigned to administrative offices in the Roman curia. Generally, the archbishops of the most important sees in the United States are appointed cardinal priests.

The offices of the Roman Catholic Church that administer its affairs worldwide are called the *curia*. It includes the Secretariat of State, the Council for the Public Affairs of the Church, and numerous other departments, congregations, tribunals, and secretariats. Worldwide, the church is divided into a number of dioceses. The largest and most important are designated archdioceses, with an archbishop who generally has some supervisory rights over the neighboring dioceses. Dioceses are grouped into provinces, provinces into regions, and regions into conferences. In 1966 bishops in the United States were formed into the National Catholic Conference in the United States. The church as a whole is governed according to canon law, the rules of the church. A revised edition of that law, written during the Second Vatican Council, was issued in 1981. The 1,752 canons cover all aspects of church life, from the nature and structure of the church to the rights and obligations of the faithful.

In the years after the split between the Roman Catholic Church and the Eastern Orthodox churches in the eleventh century, communities that were historically Eastern Orthodox were converted to Catholicism, and they came under the jurisdiction of the pope. In many cases these churches were allowed to keep their Eastern liturgical life. There are six patriarchs who preside over nongeographical dioceses of the faithful of their respective rites, wherever in the world they might be found. Some of these churches have married priests. Eastern-rite Catholics began to emigrate to the United States in the late 1700s, and parishes were founded in the nineteenth century. The presence of Eastern Catholic and Eastern Orthodox parishes so close together in the relatively free environment of the United States facilitated the movement of members (and sometimes even whole parishes) from one church to another.

Membership: In 1989 there were 57,019,948 members, 53,111 priests, and 23,500 parishes in the United States. In Canada there were 11,375,914 members, 11,302 priests, and 5,922 parishes. There are more than 851 million Roman Catholics worldwide.

Educational Facilities:

For a complete list of institutions of higher learning supported by the Roman Catholic Church see the latest edition of either the *Official Catholic Directory* or the *Catholic Almanac*. Both are regularly revised and updated.

Periodicals: There are more than 500 church-related newspapers and 300 magazines published in the United States. For a complete list, see the latest edition of either the *Catholic Almanac* or the *Official Catholic Directory*.

Sources:

Roman Catholic Church. www.usccb.org.

Daughters of St. Paul. *Basic Catechism with Scripture Quotations*. Boston: St. Paul Editions, 1984.

Dolan, Jay. *The American Catholic Experience: A History from Colonial Times to the Present*. Notre Dame, IN: University of Notre Dame Press, 1992.

Ellis, John Tracy. *American Catholicism*. Garden City, NY: Doubleday, 1965.

————, ed. *Documents of American Catholic History*. 2 vols. Chicago: Henry Regnery, 1967.

Foy, Felician A. *A Concise Guide to the Catholic Church*. Huntington, IN: Our Sunday Visitor, 1984.

Frederic, Sister M. Catherine. *The Handbook of Catholic Practices*. New York: Hawthorn Publishers, 1964.

Greeley, Andrew M. *The Catholic Myth: The Behavior and Beliefs of the American Catholics*. Old Tappan, NJ: Macmillian, 1991.

Hennesey, James. *American Catholics*. Oxford, U.K.: Oxford University Press, 1981.

Kohmescher, Matthew F. *Catholicism Today*. New York: Paulist Press, 1980.

Steinfels, Peter A. *A People Adrift: The Crisis of the Roman Catholic Church in America*. New York: Simon and Schuster, 2004.

Tillard, J. M. R. *The Bishop of Rome*. Wilmington, DE: Michael Glazier, 1983.

Vidmar, John. *The Catholic Church through the Ages: A History*. Mahwah, NJ: Paulist Press, 2005. 384 pp.

Romanian Greek Catholic Church

Eparchy of Canton, Chancery Office, 1121 44th St. NE, Canton, OH 44714

Alternate Address: International Headquarters: Str, P. P. Aron 2, RO-3 175, Blaj AB, Romania.

The Romanian Greek Catholic Church is an Eastern-Rite church in full communion with the Roman Catholic Church. It appeared at the end of the seventeenth century following the retreat of the Turks from Transylvania in 1687. The new Hapsburg rulers of the Austro-Hungarian Empire encouraged the Orthodox majority in Transylvania to transfer their spiritual allegiance to Rome. A combination of pressures, including the denial of full civil rights to Orthodox believers, persuaded the head of the Orthodox Church in Transylvania to agree to a union of his church with Rome in 1698, an agreement approved at a synod two years later.

In 1744 a devout Orthodox monk began a revival of Eastern Orthodoxy, and in 1759 a new Orthodox bishop was consecrated for Transylvania. When the dust settled, two communities of about equal strength emerged. Continued bitter feeling between the two groups was heightened at the end of World War I when Transylvania was taken from Catholic Hungary and annexed to Orthodox Romania. By the end of the 1930s, the Romanian Catholic Church had five dioceses serving some 1.5 million believers.

In the 1940s the new Marxist government forced the Greek Catholics to break their ties to Rome, and in 1948 the church was officially dissolved. Its property was turned over to the officials of the Romanian Orthodox Church. Shortly thereafter, all of the Catholic bishops were arrested. Five died in jail and the sixth died in 1970 under house arrest.

The Romanian Greek Catholic Church was not able to revive itself until after the fall of the Ceausescu government. In 1990, the 1948 dissolution decree was rescinded. Suddenly, three bishops who had been operating underground appeared on the scene, and Pope John Paul II appointed bishops for all the remaining vacant dioceses. The reemergence of the church has ignited new conflict with the Orthodox Church. Greek Catholics have demanded the return of all the property seized in 1948. Despite Orthodox opposition, through the 1990s the church has recovered most of its former property, though some parish property remains in dispute. The church is led by Lucian Muresan (b. 1931), the Archbishop of Fagaras and Alba Julia and Metropolitan of the Romanian Greek-Catholic Church, United with Rome.

Romanian Catholics came to the United States along with other Romanians beginning late in the nineteenth century. Their parishes were first included in the Latin-Rite diocese, but in 1982 they were set apart in the Exarchate (protodiocese) of Canton, which five years later was elevated to become the Eparchy (diocese) of Canton. Most Rev. John Michael Botean is the current Bishop of the Eparchy.

Membership: According to the latest government statistics (1992), there are 223,327 adherents in Romania. The church itself reports, as of the end of 1998,

1,420,000 members in Romania. The only diocese/eparchy outside of Romania is in the United States. It reports 15 parishes for 5,300 faithful as of 2000.

Sources:

Romanian Catholic Dioceze of Canton. www.romaniancatholic.org.

Romanian Greek Catholic Church (unofficial). 198.62.75.1/www2/greek-catholic/menu_e.html.

Branzea, Nicolae I., and Stefan Lonita. *Religious Life in Romania*. Bucharest: Editura Paideia, 1999.

Cuciuc, Constantin. *Atlasul Religiilor si al Monumentelor Istorice Religi case din Romania*. Bucharest: Editura Onosis, 1996.

Roberson, Ronald G. *The Eastern Christian Churches: A Brief Survey*, 5th ed. Rome: Edizioni Orientalia Christiana, Pontificio Istituto Orientale, 1995.

Ruthenian Catholic Church

c/o Eparchy of Pittsburgh, Chancery Office, 66 Riverview Ave., Pittsburgh, PA 15214-2253

Alternate Address: International headquarters: Ruthenian Catholic Church, Zakarpatska 18, 294017 Uzhorod, Ukraine.

The Ruthenian Catholic Church (also known as the Byzantine Catholic Church) is a Greek Catholic church that uses a Greek liturgy derived from the one popularized in the several Greek Orthodox jurisdictions but modified to be in conformity with the beliefs and practices of the Roman Catholic Church. The Ruthenian Church is in full communion with the Roman Catholic Church and under the authority of the Papal See (the authority and governmental functions associated with the papacy). The church originated in the Carpathian Mountains where southwestern Ukraine, Slovakia, and southeastern Poland converge. Ruthenians speak a Ukrainian dialect, but identify ethnically as Rusyns, not Ukrainians. Christianity entered the region in the ninth century under the preaching of Saints Cyril (d. 869) and Methodius (d. 885). Although Cyril and Methodius were Greek (from Thessalonika), and represented the Ecumenical Patriarchate in Constantinople, they used the Slavonic language in worship. Following the break between the Roman Catholic Church and the Eastern Orthodox Church in 1054, the Rusyn church adhered to Eastern Orthodoxy.

About the same time that the Rusyn church opted for Eastern Orthodoxy, the land of the Ruthenian people was incorporated into Hungarian territory. Once Hungary, a Roman Catholic nation, established its control, Catholic priests entered the region and began to agitate for the Orthodox to come into communion with Rome. In 1646, 63 priests, mostly from Slovakia, transferred to the Catholic Church. The act of receiving them, the Union of Uzhorod, occurred at a town on the Ukrainian-Slovakian border. After two similar acts of returning that occurred in the Ukraine in 1664 and 1713, Eastern Orthodoxy largely disappeared from the region.

Through the eighteenth century, the issue in the region centered upon a battle for control of the Ruthenians between local bishops who followed the Latin Rite, and those priests who represented the Orthodox converts and continued to use the Slavonic Rite. Then in 1771, a Ruthenian bishop was elected and made the head of a Ruthenian eparchy (diocese). A Ruthenian seminary was established in 1778 at Uzhorod. Thus, the Ruthenian Catholic Church emerged as a distinctive ethnic church that continued a variety of Eastern Orthodox traditions (including a married priesthood) that strongly identified with the Rusyn people of Transcarpathia.

Following World War I, with the breakup of the Hungarian Empire, the region was incorporated into the new nation of Czechoslovakia, and in the 1920s one group left the church and returned to Orthodoxy. Then following World War II, the area east of Uzhorod became part of the Soviet Union. Pressure was made in the Ukraine to force the church back into Orthodoxy and its parishes were placed under the Russian Orthodox Church and its patriarch in Moscow. In like measure, an effort was made to destroy the church in Poland and Czechoslovakia. However, a revival of the Ruthenian Church began with the fall of the Soviet Union. In January 1991,

the Vatican reestablished the Eparchy of Mukachevo (Ukraine) and appointed a new bishop. An estimated 500,000 Rusyn Catholics could still be found. A seminary was opened in Uzhorod in 1992. The status of the church in what is now the Ukraine remains open. Both the Ukrainian Catholic Church and the Ukrainian Orthodox Church have been reestablished in the independent nation.

Beginning in the nineteenth century, more than half a million Rusyns had migrated to the United States. However, they found that the hierarchy of the Catholic Church in America was unsympathetic to the continuance of the Ruthenian Church, and the majority reverted to Orthodoxy. In 1905, Father Andrew Hodobay was sent to America as an Apostolic Visitor (appointed by the Vatican) to care for Ruthenians, but, being a Hungarian, he proved unsuitable. Rome then sent Fr. Gabriel Martyak (1859–1934). He founded parishes primarily in Pennsylvania, New Jersey, Ohio, and various states in the Northeast United States. In 1924 Rome authorized the creation of an American Exarchate (proto-diocese) with Bishop Basil Takach (1879–1948) as its first exarch (bishop). There are now four American eparchies (dioceses) with national leadership provided by the metropolitan (archbishop) who resides in Pittsburgh, Pennsylvania. Additional eparchies are at Passaic (New Jersey), Parma (Ohio), and Van Nuys (California). Ruthenian Catholics also reside in Australia and Western Europe, but are largely integrated into the Ukrainian Catholic Church.

Membership: Some 200,000 Ruthenian Catholics reside in the United States. In 2008 there were 60 parishes in the United States.

Educational Facilities:

Saints Cyril and Methodius Byzantine Catholic Seminary, Pittsburgh, Pennsylvania.

Periodicals: *Byzantine Catholic World*.

Sources:

Ruthenian Catholic Church. www.catolicos.org/ritosruthenianbizcathchindex.htm

Liesel, N. *The Eastern Catholic Liturgies: A Study in Words and Pictures*. Westminster, MD: Newman Press, 1960.

Roberson, Ronald G. *The Eastern Christian Churches: A Brief Survey*, 5th ed. Rome: Edizioni Orientalia Christiana, Pontificio Istituto Orientale, 1995.

Roccasalvo, John. *The Eastern Catholic Churches: An Introduction to Their Worship and Spirituality*. American Essays in Liturgy Series. Collegeville, MN: Liturgical Press, 1992.

Syrian Catholic Church

502 Palisade Ave., Union City, NJ 07087-5213

Alternate Address: International headquarters: Rue de Danms, BP 116-5087, Beirut, Lebanon.

The Syrian Catholic Church is an Eastern Rite Catholic church in full communion with the Roman Catholic Church. It is a product of missionaries operating in the vicinity of Aleppo, in northwest Syria in the seventeenth century. The majority of Syrian Christians were traditionally members of the Syrian Orthodox Church of Antioch, the so-called "Jacobite" church, which had not affirmed the teachings of the Ecumenical Council held at Ephesus (431 C.E.) concerning the nature of Christ as both human and divine. The Syrians generally held the Monophysite position that Christ had only a divine nature.

The Catholic mission experienced some success in the 1650s, but then in 1662, Andrew Akhidjan, a priest with Catholic leanings, was elected as the new patriarch of the Syrian Church. All was well during his reign; following his death, the two factions emerged (one pro-Rome and one independent of Rome), each of whom elected a patriarch. The authorities of the Ottoman Empire (into which Syria had been incorporated) supported the Orthodox faction. The Catholic bishop died out.

Those Syrian priests and congregations that continued to use the Syrian-Antiochene liturgy but were inclined to accept the authority of the bishop of Rome found themselves increasingly harassed and through much of the eighteenth century had to operate underground. Then in 1782 the new Syrian patriarch declared his allegiance to Rome, fled to Lebanon, and established a new monastic community, Our Lady of Sharfeh Monastery. He also initiated a new line of Syrian Catholic patriarchs. A generation later, in 1828, the Ottoman government dropped its opposition to the Catholic community and granted recognition to the Syrian Catholic Church. In 1850, the headquarters of the church was moved to Mardin, in southwestern Turkey.

The church prospered through the rest of the century, but met disaster during World War I when thousands of Syrians were massacred. As a result of those massacres, many Syrian Catholics fled to Lebanon, and in the 1920s the Patriarchate moved its headquarters to Beirut. The current patriarch, Ignatius Musa I Daud, like each patriarch during the last two hundred years, added "Ignatius" to his patriarchal name.

The events of World War I also began the migration of Syrian Catholics to the United States and Canada. Through most of the twentieth century, they were included within the Latin-Rite dioceses, though increasingly Syrian parishes were established. In 1995, Pope John Paul II authorized the creation of Our Lady of Deliverance Syriac Catholic Diocese (Eparchy) for Syriac Catholics in the United States and Canada. Mar Ephrem Joseph F. Younan became the small diocese's first bishop.

Membership: There are some 100,000 Syrian Catholics, most residing in Lebanon, Syria Turkey, Egypt, and Iraq. Our Lady of Deliverance Syriac Catholic Diocese in the United States and Canada is composed of nine parishes—seven in the United States and two in Canada.

Sources:

Liesel, N. *The Eastern Catholic Liturgies: A Study in Words and Pictures*. Westminster, MD: Newman Press, 1960.

Roberson, Ronald G. *The Eastern Christian Churches: A Brief Survey*. Rome: Edizioni Orientalia Christiana, Pontificio Istituto Orientale, 5th ed., 1995.

Syro-Malabar Catholic Church

c/o St. Thomas Syro-Malabar Catholic Diocese of Chicago, 372 S Prairie Ave., Elmhurst, IL 60126

Alternate Address: International headquarters: Major Archbishop's House, PB No. 2580, Kochi, Kerala, India 682 031.

The Syro-Malabar Catholic Church is an Eastern Rite Catholic church in full communion with the Roman Catholic Church. and is under the authority of the Papal See. The faithful who belong to St. Thomas Syro-Malabar Diocese of Chicago are the Catholics of the Syro-Malabar Rite who have immigrated to the United States and Canada. They trace their heritage of faith to the preaching of St. Thomas, one of the apostles of Jesus Christ. Tradition holds that he came to India in 52 C.E. and established seven Christian communities, and was martyred in Mylapore, India, in 72 C.E. The Catholics of the Syro-Malabar Rite are also known as St. Thomas Christians along with those who have broken away from them and established themselves as Jacobites and Marthomites. The Syro-Malabar Rite belongs to the Chaldean liturgical family and used Aramaic (Syriac) in their liturgical celebrations until the end of the Vatican Council. Until the Synod of Diamper, which was held in 1599 by the archbishop of Goa, St. Thomas Christians were under the spiritual jurisdiction of the Chaldean Church. After the death of the last Chaldean bishop, Mar Abraham, in 1597, the archbishop of Goa took the spiritual control of St. Thomas Christians.

The first Latin bishop after the Synod of Diamper was Francis Rox, S. J., who was appointed in 1599 and consecrated as bishop in 1601. A few of the faithful under the leadership of Archdeacon Thomas took an oath in a church in Mattancherry, Kerala, not to obey the Portuguese bishop in 1653. Twelve priests among them laid hands on the archdeacon and made him their bishop. He took the title Mar Thoma 1. The breakaway group later came under the influence of the Syrian Orthodox Patriarchate and began to sue the Antiochian Rite in their liturgy.

The major part of the community of St. Thomas Christians came under the jurisdiction of the Latin bishops. In response to the constant appeals of the faithful for a native hierarchy, the Holy See in 1887 created a new hierarchy with two vicariates, Kottayam and Trichur. In 1896 it was reorganized under three vicariates, Ernakulam, Changancherry, and Trichur. In 1923 Enrakulam was raised to the status of a Metropolitan See, and in 1956 Changancherry was raised as a Metropolitan See. In 1992 the Syro-Malabar Church was raised to the status of Major Archiepiscopal *sui juris* Church with the title of Ernakulam-Angamaly. There are now five archdioceses: Ernakulam, Changanacherry, Trichur, Tellicherry, and Kottayam, eleven eparchies within the proper territory of the Major Archiepiscopal Church, and eleven outside. The liturgical language remained Aramaic until the end of the Second Vatican Council, although the liturgy carried some changes introduced by the archbishop of Goa at the Synod of Diamper.

In 1934 Pope Pius XI appointed a commission for the restoration of the liturgy. In 1957 a new text for the Mass was published with the approval of Pius XII. In 1962 the text for the Ordinary Mass was introduced with Malayalam as the language of the Mass. Later, the ancient form of the liturgy was restored, and it began to be used in the Syro-Malabar Church from 1985.

St. Thomas Syro-Malabar Diocese of Chicago is the only diocese of the Syro-Malabar Rite outside of India. It was erected in 2001 with Mar Jacob Angadiath as the bishop. The bishop is a member of the Syro-Malabar Bishops' Synod as well as a member of the Bishops' Conference of the United States.

Membership: The Syro-Malabar Catholic Church has an estimated 4,300,000 members, approximately 100,000 of whom are in the United States and Canada.

Sources:

Syro-Malabar Catholic Church. www.thesyromalabarchurch.org/.

Hoke, Donald, ed. *The Church in Asia*. Chicago: Moody Press, 1975.

Moffett, Samuel Hugh. *A History of Christianity in Asia*. Vol. 1: *Beginnings to 1500*. San Francisco: Harper San Francisco, 1992.

Neill, S. C. *A History of Christianity in India*. 2 vols. Cambridge, U.K.: Cambridge University Press, 1984, 1985.

Syro-Malankara Catholic Church

c/o Mt. Rev. Isaac Mar Cleemis, Apostolic Visitor for Europe, 670 Hulses Corner Rd., Howell, NJ 07731

Alternate Address: International Headquarters: Archbishop's House, Trivandrum 695 004, Kerala, India.

The Syro-Malankara Catholic Church is an Eastern-Rite Catholic church in full communion with the Roman Catholic Church and under the authority of the Papal See. Its origins date back to its 1926 split from the Malankara Orthodox Syrian Church.

The Malankara Church traces its beginning to the ministry of the Apostle Thomas, who it believes came to Kerala, India, soon after the resurrection of Christ. With the arrival of the Portuguese in India in the fifteenth century, Roman Catholic missionaries initiated efforts to integrate the Indian Christians into the Roman Catholic Church. While initially agreeing to such an arrangement, in 1653 the majority of the Indian faithful rejected Roman authority and returned to the Syriac liturgy that they had previously used.

During the nineteenth century, the Church of England, which came to India with British rule, exerted its influence on the Indian church. The attempt to deal with various reform proposals led to the church's splitting into two branches: the Mar Thoma Syrian Church of Malabar and the Malankara Orthodox Syrian Church. The Mar Thoma Church accepted the reforms suggested by the Anglicans and established formal communion with the Church of England, whereas the Malankara Church continued with its traditional practice and its communion with the Syrian Orthodox Church of Antioch.

In the 1880s, a dispute emerged between the patriarch of the Syrian Orthodox Church and the Malankara Church. That dispute continued into the middle of the twentieth century. Meanwhile, in 1926 five Malankara bishops opened negotiations with Rome. In return for transferring their allegiance, they asked that their liturgy be retained and that they remain as bishops of their dioceses. The first two made their profession of faith on September 30, 1930. The next day, two additional bishops joined them. The four and their diocese constituted the Syro-Malankara Catholic Church. In 1932 Bishop Ivanios (1882–1953) visited Rome, where he was named archbishop of Trivandrum and the Archeparchy of Tiruvalla was established. By 1960 the new church claimed more than 68,000 members.

Members of the Syro-Malankara Catholic Church have joined the migration of Indians to North America in the years since 1965 and various North American congregations have been formed that remain connected to the Latin-Rite diocese in which they are located. There are also Malankara priests who are working in the United States to serve Indian Catholics in areas where no parish currently exists. Some attachment to the church in India is provided by apostolic visitors from the subcontinent.

Membership: The Syro-Malankara Church has 408,725 members worldwide, the majority in India. In 2001 there were 10 Malankara congregations in the United States and one in Canada (in Toronto).

Sources:

Syro-Malankara Catholic Church. www.malankara.net/.

Roberson, Ronald G. *The Eastern Christian Churches: A Brief Survey*, 5th ed. Rome: Edizioni Orientalia Christiana, Pontificio Istituto Orientale, 1995.

Ukrainian Catholic Church

c/o Ukrainian Archeparchy of Winnipeg, 233 Scotia St., Winnipeg, MB, Canada R2V 1V7
Alternate Address: International Headquarters: Ploscha Sviatoho Jura 5, 290000 Lviv, Ukraine; Archeparchy of Philadelphia, Chancery Office, 827 N. Franklin St., Philadelphia, PA 19123.

The Ukrainian Catholic Church is an Eastern-Rite Catholic church that is in full communion with the Roman Catholic Church and under the authority of the Papal See. It traces its history to the advent of Christianity in what is now Ukraine at the end of the first millennium C.E. Following the division between the Roman Catholic Church and the Eastern Orthodox Church in 1054, the Ukrainians adhered to Eastern Orthodoxy. The church was under the jurisdiction of the Ecumenical Patriarchate residing in Constantinople. In the fourteenth century, Lithuania, a Roman Catholic nation, invaded the region. Ukrainians developed a much stronger sense of their own national and ethnic identity in opposition to the Lithuanian authority.

Then in 1439 the Orthodox Metropolitan of Kiev, Isidore, attended the Council of Florence, a gathering of the bishops of the Roman Catholic Church, and agreed to the union of the Ukrainian Church with Catholicism. While many accepted the union, many others rejected it and continued in their Orthodox faith. Then in 1569, following the union of Lithuania and Poland, Poland took control of the region, and Polish Catholic leaders pursued a united Catholic/Orthodox structure in order to block further growth of Protestantism.

In this context, Orthodox leaders saw a union with Rome as a means of preserving their Eastern Church from full absorption into the expanding Latin-Rite church. Thus in 1596, at a gathering of Orthodox bishops, a new union of Ukrainian Orthodoxy with Rome was proclaimed. Over the next century the majority of Ukrainians accepted this union. It survived until the nineteenth century, when Russia expanded its control in the region. Russian authorities suppressed the Roman Catholic Church and incorporated both the Ukrainian Catholic Church and the Ukrainian Orthodox Church into the Russian Orthodox Church. The Ukrainian Catholic Church survived in Galicia, western Ukraine, which had by this time come under Austrian control.

During the years after World War II and following the Soviet annexation of Galicia, Poland deported most Ukrainians in Poland to the Soviet Union, and the Soviet government suppressed the Ukrainian Catholic Church. All of the bishops were arrested and all but one died in prison. Believers were forced to choose between the Russian Orthodox Church and the Latin-Rite Roman Catholic Church, though in fact the Ukrainian Catholic Church survived as an underground church. As the Soviet Union began to fall apart in the late 1980s, a distinctive Ukrainian Catholic Church began to reemerge; it was formally reestablished in 1989 when a new bishop of Przemysl was named. In 1991 Myroslav Cardinal Lubachivsky (1914–2000) was able to move into his residence in Lviv. By the end of the year, seminaries were established at Lviv and Ivano-Frankivsk and religious orders were revived.

Because Ukrainians have migrated worldwide since the late-nineteenth century, Ukrainian Catholic parishes are found in the United States, Canada, South America, Australia, and Western Europe. These parishes served an important role in keeping Ukrainian identity alive. In the United States, the first parish (St. Michael the Archangel) was established in 1884 in Shenandoah, Pennsylvania. It and other early parishes were under the authority of the Latin-Rite bishops until 1907, when a Ukrainian Catholic exarchate (diocese) was established in Philadelphia. By 1916 there were 152 parishes, but it was not until 1956 that a second diocese was created, in Stamford, Connecticut. In 1961, the diocese of Chicago was established, followed in 1983 by the diocese of St. Josaphat (in Parma, Ohio). The original exarchate evolved into the archeparchy (metropolitan see) in Philadelphia.

Winnipeg, in the Canadian province of Manitoba, became the leading site for Ukrainian settlement and the center of church development in Manitoba and then in Canada overall. Parishes also emerged in the provinces of Alberta and Saskatchewan. In 1902 Rev. W. Zholdak was appointed the Apostolic Administrator for the Ukrainian Catholics in Manitoba and all of northwestern Canada. In 1910 Metropolitan Sheptytsky (1865–1944) visited Canada and met with both Roman Catholic and government officials to discuss the Ukrainian people having their own church leadership and jurisdiction. In 1912 Nykyta Budka (1877–1949), the first bishop of the Ukrainian Catholics in Canada, arrived to take up his official duties. By that time there were some 150,000 Ukrainians in Canada and approximately 80 churches and chapels.

In 1948, the single exarchate (protodiocese) of the Ukrainian Catholic Church of Canada was divided into three exarchates: the eastern exarchate in Toronto, the western exarchate in Edmonton, and the central exarchate in Winnipeg, which continued under the directorship of Bp. Basil Ladyka (d. 1956). In 1951, Bishop Ladyka was raised to the status archbishop. Five years later, Pope Pius XXII set up the Ukrainian Catholic Metropolitinate (archdiocese) in Canada and named Bp. Maxim Hermaniuk (1911–1996), formerly the auxiliary bishop for Archbishop Ladyka, as the Metropolitan of Canada. The existing exarchates were raised to eparchies (dioceses). In 1974, the western eparchy was divided and a new eparchy was established, headquartered in New Westminster, British Colombia.

There are five eparchies in Canada and four in the United States. There are also eparchies in Australia, Brazil, and Argentina. Apostolic exarchates have been appointed for France, Germany, and the United Kingdom. Ukrainian Catholic seminaries are located in Washington, D.C.; Ottawa, Canada; and Curitiba, Brazil.

Membership: Not reported.

Educational Facilities:

Holy Spirit Seminary, Ottawa, Ontario, Canada.

St. Basil College Seminary, Stamford, Connecticut.

Periodicals: *Ukrainian Catholic News Progress.*

Sources:

Ukrainian Catholic Eparchy of Stamford. www.stamforddio.org/

Ukrainian Catholic Archeparchy of Winnipeg. www.archeparchy.ca.

Ukrainian Catholic Church. www.ugkc.lviv.ua/.

Dyrud, Keith P. *The Quest for the Rusyn Soul: The Politics of Religion and Culture in Eastern Europe and in America, 1890–World War I.* Philadelphia: Balch Institute Press, 1992.

Himka, John-Paul. *The Greek Catholic Church and Ukrainian Society in Austrian Galicia.* Cambridge, MA: Ukrainian Studies Fund, Harvard University, 1986.

Kowcz-Baran, Anna Maria. *Ukrainian Catholic Churches of Winnipeg Archeparchy: History of Ukrainian Catholic Churches in Canada.* Saskatoon, Saskatchewan, Canada: Archeparchy of Winnipeg, 1991.

Liesel, N. *The Eastern Catholic Liturgies: A Study in Words and Pictures.* Westminster, MD: Newman Press, 1960.

Roberson, Ronald G. *The Eastern Christian Churches: A Brief Survey*, 5th ed. Rome: Edizioni Orientalia Christiana, Pontificio Istituto Orientale, 1995.

❋ Independent and Old Catholic Churches

African-American Catholic Congregation

c/o Most Rev. George A. Stallings Jr., 10911 194th St., Ct. E, Graham, WA 98338-8142

The African-American Catholic Congregation was founded in 1989 by George A. Stallings Jr. (b. 1948), a former priest of the Roman Catholic Church. Raised a Roman Catholic, Stallings began his education for the priesthood at the age of 16. He completed his education in Rome and was ordained in 1974. In 1976 he was assigned to the parish church of St. Teresa of Avila, a predominantly black congregation in Washington, D.C. He served as a lecturer at both St. Mary's Seminary in Emmitsburg, Maryland, and the Washington Theological Union. He also emerged as an activist in the black community in Washington.

Although he was successful as a parish priest, Stallings became increasingly critical of the Roman Catholic Church and charged it with a deep-seated racism. In 1988 Abp. James Hickey removed Stallings from St. Teresa and made him an archdiocesan evangelist with the special task of evangelizing in the black community. However, relations between Stallings and Hickey worsened; Stallings withdrew and Hickey moved to excommunicate him and those who supported the new congregation he formed, Imani Temple. Imani is a Swahili word for "faith." Stallings subsequently established new churches in Philadelphia, Norfolk, and Baltimore, and a second congregation in Washington, D.C.

Following his break with the Roman Catholic Church, Stallings turned to the independent Catholic movement, and on May 12, 1990, was consecrated by Abp. Richard W. Bridges of the American National Catholic Church (formerly the American Independent Catholic Church). Stallings also adopted some of the distinctive perspectives of the Old Catholic Church: allowing priests to marry, accepting divorced and remarried individuals into full membership, and allowing artificial birth control. The church also allows women to make their own decisions about abortion, and has organized a variety of social outreach ministries.

Membership: Not reported. There are five congregations.

Sources:

African-American Catholic Congregation. www.ind-movement.org/demons/aacc_imani.html.

Grogan, David. "A Black Catholic Priest's Renegade Church Stirs Up an Unholy Furor." *People* 32, no. 5 (July 31, 1989): 26–28.

Historical and Doctrinal Digest of the African-American Catholic Congregation. Washington, DC: African-American Catholic Congregation, 1990.

American Apostolic Catholic Church

c/o Bishop Vincent Lavieri, 124 S Lafayette, Greenville, MI 48838

The American Apostolic Catholic Church is a small independent Old Catholic jurisdiction founded in 1996.

Membership: Not reported.

Sources:

American Apostolic Catholic Church. www.americanchurch.org.

Pruter, Karl. *The Directory of Autocephalous Bishops of the Apostolic Succession.* San Bernardino, CA: Brogo Press, 1906. 104 pp.

Ward, Gary. *Independent Bishops: An International Directory.* Detroit: Apogee Books, 1990. 524 pp.

American Catholic Church (Hampton Bays, New York)

c/o Reverend Sharon DiSunno, PO Box 725, Hampton Bays, NY 11946

Alternate Address: Divine Mercy Parish, 861 Seneca Creek Rd., West Seneca, NY.

The American Catholic Church was formed in the mid-1990s following the consecration of Robert Joseph Allmen to the episcopacy in 1995 by William Donovan, a bishop in the lineage of Herman Adrian Spruit, the late patriarch of the Church of Antioch. The church sees itself as a post–Vatican II church that emphasizes the best of contemporary Catholic thought. It offers its ministry to those who have been alienated by their earlier contacts with the church, especially those who have been denied the sacraments because they have been divorced, or because the church disapproves of their sexual orientation or gender.

The church does not wish to be identified as Roman Catholic, Eastern Orthodox, or Protestant. It has an apostolic succession that has several lineages to the ancient church. It ascribes to the Nicene Creed and the Apostles Creed and practices the seven traditional sacraments of the western church. In its desire to overcome barriers to serving people, it offers baptism to any infants or children whose parents desire it, it welcomes married clergy and women to all levels of the priesthood, and it serves the Eucharist to divorced individuals and to gay men and lesbians.

The American Catholic Church has been the source of other similar bodies with which it is not to be confused—the American Catholic Church International, the American Catholic Church in the United States, and the American Catholic Church in New England.

Membership: Not reported.

Sources:

American Catholic Church. www.geocities.com/WestHollywood/4136/shepherd.htm.

American Catholic Church in the United States

PO Box 119, Frederick, MD 21705-0119

The American Catholic Church in the United States is an independent jurisdiction under the leadership of its archbishop, Mt. Rev. Lawrence J. Harms. The church has its roots in the American Catholic Church (founded in 1995), through whom its orders are derived. Formed in the late 1990s, the American Catholic Church in the United States, like its parent body, considers itself a post-Vatican II church that is guided through the "sense of the faithful" as it seeks to transform the church into an institution that can provide a credible witness in the modern world. It also seeks to provide a special ministry to those who have been alienated from their prior contact with the Christian church, especially those who have been denied the sacraments due to their gender, due to being divorced, or due to sexual orientation. The church does not wish to be identified as either Roman Catholic, Eastern Orthodox or Protestant, and possesses an apostolic succession that has several lineages to the ancient church. It ascribes to the Nicene Creed and the Apostles' Creed and practices the seven traditional sacraments of the western church. In its desire to overcome the past barriers to serving individuals, it offers baptism to any infants or children whose parents desire it, it welcomes married clergy to the priesthood, and provides the Eucharist to divorced individuals and those of gay/lesbian orientation.

The American Catholic Church is divided into four Provinces, each headed by a bishop. They are the province of St. Mark (northwest), Province of St. Francis (southwest), Province of St. Luke (Midwest and northeast), and the Province of the Holy Cross (southeast). Work outside of the 50 states is directly under the presiding archbishop who is also the ordinary for the Province of the Holy Cross.

The clergy of the American Catholic church are secularly employed and operate in their clerical office apart from their gainful employment. While offering the common parish life of worship and pastoral care, the majority are engaged in non-parish ministries with the church's Ministerial Outreach Program to nursing homes and hospitals, an internet ministry with outreach to people all over the world, and a ministry to people with HIV-AIDS. Clergy from other jurisdictions are welcomed into the church if otherwise qualified.

Membership: Not reported.

Educational Facilities:

ACCUS Theological Institute, Frederick, Maryland.

Sources:

American Catholic Church in the United States. www.accus.us.

American Catholic Church International

c/o Mt. Rev. Sharon DiSunno, 38 Prince St., Elizabeth, NJ 07208

American Catholic Church International (also known as the American Catholic Church of Nevada) was founded in the late 1990s as an alternative to the Roman Catholic Church. The church has its roots in the American Catholic Church (founded in 1995), through whom its orders are derived. While generally accepting the Roman Catholic perspective growing out of Vatican II, the American Catholic Church International continues the emphases of its parent body on issues of gender and sexual orientation. It practices the seven sacraments, but sees itself as the bearer of a progressive trend in Catholic thought.

The church believes that gay and lesbian relationships are not sinful, and it is willing to bless gay and lesbian unions. It also affirms that birth control is not a sin and that parents have the right to determine the number of children they will bring into the world. Women may be admitted to all levels of the ordained ministry (deacon, priests, bishop) and ordained clergy may marry or be united in gay or lesbian unions.

The apostolic succession of the American Catholic Church International is derived from the Church of Antioch and its late partriarch, Herman Adrian Spruit (1911–1994). Abp. Robert Joseph Allmen, the presiding bishop of the American Catholic Church, was consecrated in 1995, and he consecrated the present (2008) archbishop, Sharon DiSunno, in 1997.

Membership: Not reported. The church has parishes or missions in seven states.

Sources:

American Catholic Church International. www.americancatholicchurch.net.

Ind-Movement.org. www.ind-movement.org/denoms/acci_disunno.html.

American Catholic Church—Old Catholic

Church of the Good Shepherd, 5230 Clark Ave., Ste. 9, Lakewood, CA 90712

The American Catholic Church—Old Catholic was established in 1986 by the Most Rev. E. Paul Raible (b. 1933). Raible was consecrated on April 24, 1988, by Bp. Forest Barber of the Brazilian Catholic Apostolic Church and Bp. Joseph H. Palumbo. He was consecrated *sub conditione* two months later by Abp. Francisco Pagtakhan (b. 1916) of the Philippine Independent Catholic Church, assisted by Abp. Emile Federico Rodriguez y Fairfield (b. 1912) of the Mexican National Catholic Church, Bp. Forest Barber, Abp. Bertil Persson of the Apostolic Episcopal Church, and Bp. Paul G. W. Schultz (1931–1995) of the Philippine Independent Catholic Church.

The American Catholic Church—Old Catholic is Catholic in faith and practice. It follows conventional Roman Catholicism, with a full sacramental ministry, but does not believe that infallibility can exist exclusively within the papal ministry. It allows priests and bishops to marry, welcomes remarried Catholics into membership, and allows the use of artificial contraceptives. Women are encouraged to take a more active role in the church's lay ministry. The church is opposed to the ordination of women.

Membership: Eight priests serve 150 parishioners in a single parish in Lakewood, California. Several parishes recently withdrew from the jurisdiction.

Sources:

Good Shepherd American Catholic Church. www.goodshepherd-church.org/.

Hackman, Peter. *A Way of Being Catholic in Today's World.* Orange, CA: Saint Matthew Old Catholic Church, [1990].

American Old Catholic Church

3138 S Parker Rd., Aurora, CO 80014

The American Old Catholic Church is an independent Old Catholic body that was founded in the 1990s and closely identifies with other Catholic communities that have become independent of the Roman Catholic Church. It considers itself to be an authentic Catholic community in that it possesses a leadership with apostolic succession back to the original apostles; maintains a faithful adherence to the apostolic tradition; and actively participates in the sacramental ministry of the historic Catholic Church.

The church believes that Jesus commissioned his apostles to be the first leaders of his church. Before they died, they appointed others to lead the church. These leaders were called bishops. This appointment was a sacrament called ordination. The Holy Apostles ordained the first bishops to be their successors. These bishops in turn ordained others to succeed them. This sacred line of leadership is called apostolic succession. The American Old Catholic Church derives its apostolic succession through the independent Catholic archbishop of Utrecht. The archbishop of Utrecht traces his apostolic succession back to the Holy Apostles.

The apostolic tradition began with the apostles who proclaimed and taught the message of Jesus. The tradition was passed on in the apostles' written letters, which were collected into what we now call the New Testament and in an "oral tradition" that is to be found in the community. The Liturgy (the Mass and the sacraments) embodies both the written and oral traditions of the apostles.

The American Old Catholic Church practices the seven sacraments of the historic Catholic Church, including baptism, confirmation, the Holy Eucharist, reconciliation, the sacrament of the sick, marriage, and holy orders. The American Old Catholic Church does not accept papal infallibility and exists independently of papal jurisdiction. Both priests and bishops are permitted to marry. Women are encouraged to be more fully involved in the ministry of the church. Divorced people who remarry are able to be reconciled to the church through the grace of God and therefore are not excluded from the sacraments. A divorced person may remarry with the blessing of the church. Artificial contraception is considered an issue of conscience between husband and wife and God. Since each Catholic is seen as an equal part of the church, lay people are encouraged to play a prominent role in the church. No Christian is excluded from the sacramental ministry. All baptized Christians are invited to participate in the worship and sacraments of the church.

The church is led by Bp. Dan Gincig and is a member of the Ecumenical Communion of Evangelical Episcopal Churches.

Membership: Not reported.

Sources:

American Old Catholic Church. www.aocc.org.

Pruter, Karl. *The Directory of Autocephalous Bishops of the Apostolic Succession.* Springfield, MO: Author, 2006. 78 pp.

American Orthodox Catholic Church–Western Rite Mission, Diocese of New York

318 Expressway Dr. S, Medford, NY 11763

Joseph J. Raffaele, a Roman Catholic layperson, founded St. Gregory's Church, an independent traditionalist Latin-rite parish, in Sayville, New York, on August 28, 1973. Three months later he was ordained by Bp. Robert R. Zaborowski of the

Archdiocese of the American Orthodox Catholic Church in the U.S. and Canada (now called the Mariavite Old Catholic Church). Raffaele developed a congregation among traditionalists who felt spiritually alienated from the post–Vatican II Roman Catholic Church. The parish grew slowly, and Raffaele and his assistants continued to work in secular jobs, devoting evenings and weekends to the church. The parish moved from Sayville to Shirley to Ronkonkoma, New York. During the mid-1970s Bishop Zaborowski insisted upon the acceptance of Mariavite (i.e., Polish) liturgical patterns by the congregations under his jurisdiction. Both St. Gregory's and Father Raffaele left the Mariavite Old Catholic Church. Shortly after, Archbishop Zaborowski issued an excommunication decree.

Raffaele joined the Mount Athos Synod under Bp. Charles R. McCarthy (a bishop in the American Orthodox Catholic Church under Abp. Patrick J. Healy). On July 18, 1976, McCarthy consecrated Raffaele and raised his associate priest, Gerard J. Kessler, to the rank of monsignor. Six months later, in December 1976, St. Gregory's and Raffaele, due to some personal disagreements with McCarthy, left the Mount Athos Synod and became an independent jurisdiction, the American Orthodox Catholic Church–Western Rite Mission, Diocese of New York.

The new jurisdiction continues as a traditionalist Latin Rite Catholic Church, though Eastern Rite usage is allowed. The jurisdiction accepts the Baltimore Catechism (minus the papal references) as a doctrinal authority and uses the 1917 Code of Canon Law (again minus the papal references). Clerical celibacy is not demanded, but female priesthood is rejected. No collection is taken on Sunday at worship services. Communion is open to all.

In 1978 St. Matthias Church, in Yonkers, New York, was begun as the first mission parish. In 1979 St. Gregory's moved into a newly purchased building in Medford, New York. That same year, Raffaele consecrated Elrick Gonyo as an independent Uniate bishop in Stuyvesant, New York, and Raffaele and Gonyo consecrated Kessler as the auxiliary bishop for the jurisdiction.

The church sponsors three religious orders: the Society of St. Gregory the Great (for priests, brothers, and nuns); the Benedictine Order of St. Michael the Archangel, a community for Benedictine nuns in Colorado; and the Oblates of the Blessed Sacrament, a community of priests headquartered in Trenton, New Jersey.

In 1986 the church reported a significant spiritual renewal within the jurisdiction that led to the production of a new contemporary liturgy. The new mass was first used at the parish at Medford on Pentecost Sunday 1986 and now coexists with the Tridentine Rite. The renewal also launched an exploration of new nonparochial forms of ministry to extend the missionary outreach, including an intercessory prayer circuit, a healing ministry, and the use of lay ministers. Glad Tidings Ministries, a multimedia spiritual outreach, also arose out of the renewal.

Membership: In 1997 the church reported 987 members (including clergy). Besides the main parish in Medford, New York, there were ministry centers in Florida, New Jersey, Arizona, and Colorado.

Periodicals: *Glad Tidings*.

Sources:

The American Orthodox Catholic Church–Western Rite. www.aoccw.org.

The Inquirers Handbook. Medford, NY: American Orthodox Catholic Church–Western Rite Diocese of New York, n.d. 18 pp.

"Milestones," *American Orthodox Catholic Church*. Medford, NY: St. Gregory's Church, 1983.

American Traditional Catholic Church (ATCC)

104-11 95th Ave., Ozone Park, NY 11416-1808

The American Traditional Catholic Church (ATCC) is an independent Old Catholic/Anglican jurisdiction. The church follows the teachings and traditions of Holy Scripture as expressed in the Seven Ecumenical Councils, and the teachings and traditions of the Old Catholic Movement as presented in the Treaty of Utrecht, the Treaty of Bonn, the 14 Theses of the Old Catholic Union, and the Lambeth

Quadrilateral. The Statement of Faith and Belief of the ATCC is expressed confessionally through the three ancient creeds: The Athanasian Creed (c. 296–373 C.E.), the Nicene Creed (c. 325 C.E.), and the Apostles' Creed (second century C.E.). The ATCC is not in communion with Rome; it is subject neither to the jurisdiction of the pope nor the Roman Catholic Magesterium. However, it recognizes that the pope is "primus et patris," that is "first among equals" among all bishops of all Catholic traditions. Pronouncements from the Vatican and the Holy Father are only binding on members of the ATCC provided that those pronouncements do not contradict the teachings and traditions of Holy Scripture and the Ecumenical Councils of the undivided church. The ATCC follows Old Catholic tradition in promoting the exercise of individual conscience. However, the exercise of conscience must be in accord with the teachings and traditions referenced above and must not bring scandal to either the church or its membership. This church, with a few exceptions, follows the canons of the Roman Rite of 1917, those exceptions being addressed in the documents of the Old Catholic Movement.

The ATCC is headed by the presiding bishop although no directive is issued without the concurrence of the church's board of directors. The presiding bishop may, with board concurrence, appoint or entertain the nomination of a candidate as suffragan (auxiliary) bishop or vicar to oversee new missional enterprises. The ATCC follows the traditional practice of ordination of an eligible candidate to the four minor orders (Porter, Lector, Exorcist, and Acolyte) and the three major orders (Subdeaconate, Deacon, and Priest). The American Traditional Catholic Church does not provide for the ordination of women to Holy Orders, although recognizing that women have a viable role in the life of the church. The ATCC does not discriminate based on race, creed, color, lifestyle orientation, marital status, age, or national origin, and with exception of the ordination of women, does not discriminate based on sex/gender.

The church administers the seven sacraments of baptism, confession, Holy Communion, confirmation, holy matrimony, holy orders, and extreme unction. Of those seven, the administration of holy orders and confirmation is reserved to the bishop.

The ATCC sponsors an ordered community, the Discalced Carmelite Servants of Mercy-Disciples of the Blessed Sacrament, which exists as an Episcopal institute (i.e., accountable to the presiding bishop rather than a suffragan bishop or vicar forraine).

Membership: In 2002 the ATCC reported six missionary congregations worldwide with approximately 933 members including clergy.

Apostolic Catholic Church in America

425 23rd Ave. S, Ste. A204, Seattle, WA 98144

The Apostolic Catholic Church in America was founded as the African Orthodox Church of the Moors in 1984 by Frs. Paul David Strong, Robert Neuman, and Christopher Reynolds. It was originally designed to meet the particular needs of African Americans. Fr. Strong was elected bishop and consecrated in November 1994 by Bp. Tedi Weber, operating under the authority of Abp. Joseph Vredenburgh of the Mar Thoma Orthodox Church. The church was renamed the Orthodox Catholic Church of the Moor in 1995 and then adopted its present name in 1996, a reflection of its emergence as a multiethnic and multicultural body. Bp. Robert Withrow was elected bishop of the Apostolic Catholic Church in America on August 18, 2007, succeeding Bp. David Strong-Primate.

The Apostolic Catholic Church in America is an inclusive, multicultural, and gay-friendly church. It welcomes the divorced and remarried, and assumes that all baptized Christians are entitled to the sacraments of Christ's church. The church accepts the teachings of the Seven Ecumenical Councils and the ancient creeds. It adheres to the Bible and Tradition. The church is organized with deacons, priests, and bishops. It practices the seven sacraments and allows both Eastern and Western rites, though the archbishop has published the church's own liturgy, which is widely utilized throughout the church. The church also practices foot washing.

The church supports several ordered communities including the Servants of Saint Benedict the Moor, the Franciscan Order of Saint Benedict the Moor, and the Order of Saint John the Divine.

Membership: In 1997 the church reported six congregations worldwide with 70 members. There was one congregation in Milan, Italy, and one in Canada.

Periodicals: *Quarterly Newsletter*.

Sources:

Apostolic Catholic Church in America. www.apostoliccatholicchurchinamerica.org.

Strong, Paul David, with Anthony P. Begonja. *The Order of Mass*. Seattle, WA: Apostolic Catholic Church in America, 1996. 33 pp.

Apostolic Catholic Orthodox Church

1900 St. James Pl., Ste. 880, Houston, TX 77056

The Apostolic Catholic Orthodox Church is a small independent jurisdiction founded in 1990 by its presiding bishop, Diana C. Dale. It sponsors the St. Francis of Assisi Worship Community and the Institute of Worklife Ministry Center for Industrial Chaplaincy, both in Houston. It is a member of the Union of Independent Catholic Churches of the North American Old Catholic Church.

Membership: Not reported.

Sources:

Apostolic Catholic Orthodox Church. www.apostoliccatholic.org.

Apostolic Episcopal Church

80-46 234th St., Queens, NY 11427

The Apostolic Episcopal Church was founded in 1925 by Arthur Wolfort Brooks (1898-1948), a former Episcopal Church clergyman. Brooks was succeeded as presiding bishop by Wallace de Ortega Maxey (1902–1992), Harold F. Jarvis, John More-Moreno (d. 1958), Robert Ramm, and, most recently, Archbishop Bertil Persson, who resides in Sweden. Archbishop Ramm also served as Archbishop of the Province of the West. Upon his retirement, he was succeeded by Archbishop Paul G. W. Schultz, who passed away in 1995.

In the meantime, in 1992, Fr. Francis C. Spataro (b. 1936) was consecrated as a bishop by Archbishop Persson and designated as the Episcopal leader of the Western Rite Vicariate of New York City and the Hudson Valley, New York. The following year he became the rector of the New York chapter of the Order of Corporate Reunion, an organization formed in 1874 and dedicated to the reunion of the many jurisdictions of the Anglican and Eastern Orthodox Churches. Bishop Spataro also has been named a Bishop Emeritus of the Association of Independent Evangelical Lutheran Churches.

On September 23-24, 2000, in New York City, the Apostolic Episcopal Church signed Concordats of Intercommunion with the following Christian Churches: The Anglican Independent Communion, The Ethiopian Orthodox Coptic Archdiocese of North and South America, The Uniate Western Orthodox Catholic Church, and the Byelorussian Orthodox National Church in Exile. In effect, the Apostolic Episcopal Church thus became a Uniate Western Rite of the Orthodox Church of the East, using the 1928 book of Common Prayer. In 1905, under the guidance of Archbishop Tikhon Bellavin (later Patriarch of Moscow), the Holy Synod in St. Petersburg approved the use of the Anglican Liturgy for Western Rite Orthodox Christians. Today this usage is called the Rite of St. Tikhon and is in use among many Orthodox Western Rite Jurisdictions.

This pilgrimage to Orthodoxy among Anglicans began in 1712 with the Non-Jurors Anglican Hierarchy and faithful. These Non-Jurors were Anglican clergy who in 1689 refused allegiance to King William III and Queen Mary, the usurpers who had overthrown King James II. In 1712 Metropolitan-Bishop Arsenios of the Alexandrine Patriarchate visited England and received many of these "British Katholicks" into the Orthodox Church.

Membership: In 2002 the church reported a membership of 12,000.

Educational Facilities:

Extension Seminary.

Periodicals: *The Tover of St. Cassian*.

Sources:

Apostolic Episcopal Church. www.cinemaparallel.com/AECSynod.html and www.cinemaparallel.com/HolyOrthodoxChurch.html.

Apostolic Episcopal Church, Diocese of California/Nevada

1933 73rd Ave., Oakland, CA 94621

The Apostolic Episcopal Church, Diocese of California/ Nevada, traces its history to the founding of the United Catholic Conference in 1973 by Bp. Donald Pierce Weeks, who was at that time the vicar general of the Old Roman Catholic Church (then led by Abp. Richard A. Marchenna [1911–1982]). Bishop Weeks served an Anglo-Catholic parish that wanted to withdraw from the Old Roman Catholic Church, which used primarily a Tridentine Roman liturgy. In 1976 Weeks was consecrated by Abp. Wallace David de Ortega Maxey (1902–1992), assisted by Abp. Ramon Verostek and Bp. Dwayne Houser, and established the Diocese of California/Nevada. The United Catholic Conference merged into the Ancient Christian Fellowship.

In 1993 Weeks established Holy Angels Christian Community of the Ancient Christian Fellowship to reach out to people affected by AIDS/HIV and those addicted to drugs and alcohol. In 1995 Weeks came under the jurisdiction of the Apostolic Episcopal Church International, headed by Swedish Abp. Bertil Persson, and the Diocese of California/Nevada was designated the church's western province, with authority over the western United States. Included in the diocese are the Oratory of Saint Ambrose, Holy Angels Catholic Church; the Sanctuary of East Oakland, the Sanctuary of West Contra Costa County; and the Daniel Brockman House for Men, the Bishop Maxey House, and the Doris Powell Home for Women, all in the Greater San Francisco Bay Area. Plans have been made for expansion into Nevada and southern California.

The Apostolic Episcopal Church was founded in 1925 in New York by Bp. Arthur Wolfort Brooks, formerly an Episcopal church clergyman. Over the years leadership of the church moved to England and eventually to Sweden when Archbishop Persson became the presiding bishop following the retirement of Abp. Robert Ramm.

The Diocese of California/Nevada has adopted a set of Thirty-nine Articles of Religion derived from those of the Church of England.

Membership: Not reported.

Sources:

Weeks, Donald Pierce. *The Apostolic Episcopal Church*. Oakland, CA: Diocese of California/Nevada, 1997.

Apostolic Episcopal Church–Order of Corporate Reunion

PO Box 2401, Apple Valley, CA 92307

The Apostolic Episcopal Church grew out of a missionary movement by a group of American churchmen in the state of New York to provide spiritual ministrations for the scattered adherents of the Near Eastern churches. The movement began in 1922, but it was not until 1924 that a group succeeded in forming the Anglican Universal Church of Christ in the United States of America (Chaldean). In 1925, through canonical authority, Mar Antoine Lefberne, as a special commissariat of the patriarch of the Chaldean Catholic Church, consecrated Arthur Wolfort Brooks (1888–1948), who took the ecclesiastical name Mar John Emmanuel. Brooks, a clergyman of the Episcopal Church who at his own request had resigned in 1926, left the Anglican Universal Church in 1927, and formed his own jurisdiction, the Apostolic Episcopal Church (Holy Eastern Catholic and Apostolic Orthodox Church).

The new church initially spread by absorbing other independent missionary congregations such as the African-American parish in Manhattan headed by Fr.

John More-Moreno (d. 1958). As the church grew, other bishops were added. In 1934, Brooks consecrated Harold F. Jarvis and Charles W. Keller. In 1946, he elevated Wallace D. de Ortega Maxey (1902–1992) to the office of archbishop. At the time Maxey was serving as the superintendent of the Caribbean Episcopal Church of the British Isles; chaplain of Scandinavia for the Patriarchal Order of the Holy Cross of Jerusalem of the Melkite-Greek Catholic Church under Patriarch Maximos V. Hakim; metropolitan bishop of Scandinavia of the Western Orthodox Catholic Church in America; and bishop of Ordo Supremus Militaris Templi Hierosolymitani.

Following Brooks's death in 1948, he was succeeded by Maxey, who resigned in 1951. His successor, Lowell Paul Wadle, served for two years and, following his resignation, was succeeded by Metropolitian Abp. Hugh George de Willmott Newman (1905–1979), the patriarch of Glastonbury. Newman, commonly known as Mar Georgius, headed the church until his death in 1979. He was succeeded by William Henry Hugo Newman-Norman (Mar Seraphim) who served as patriarch of Glastonbury from 1979 to 1994. In 1994 he was consecrated as a bishop of the Coptic Orthodox Church and resigned all affiliation with the Apostolic Episcopal Church. In the interim following his death the Most Rev. Paul G. W. Schultz, also at the time the apostolic administrator of the American Archdiocese of the Philippine Independent Catholic Church, assumed leadership. He passed away on September 13, 1995, and was succeeded by Abp. Donald E. Hugh, who has moved to reorganize and revive the American work.

The church is also intimately associated with the Order of Corporate Reunion (OCR), originally founded in 1874 in London, England, to confer valid apostolic orders on individuals it considered qualified with a particular emphasis on the union of Anglican and Eastern Orthodoxy. Today the OCR emphasizes the reunion of the various independent orthodox catholic groups. Rt. Rev. Francis C. Spataro is the current rector pro-provincial of the OCR.

The Apostolic Episcopal Church considers itself a conservative body in the Chaldean Orthodox tradition. It is guided by the Holy Scripture, the Apostolic Constitution, Teachings, and Creed. It accepts the rulings of the initial three Ecumenical Councils and recognizes the spirit of the remaining four. It accepts the seven sacraments and possesses an apostolic succession through the Order of Corporate Reunion.

At the time Archbishop Hugh succeeded to the leadership of the AEC, it was the American branch of the Apostolic Episcopal Church International headed by Swedish Abp. Bertil Persson. However, Hugh soon rejected the archbishop's leadership and in 1995 reincorporated the Apostolic Episcopal Church and the Order of Corporate Reunion as a single entity, the Apostolic Episcopal Church–Order of Corporate Reunion. At that time, the church severed its relationship with Abp. Persson and Bp. Donald Pierce Weeks, whom Persson had consecrated as archbishop of California-Nevada.

In 1997 Bp. Francis Spataro, who headed the church's Western Vicariate in New York, decided to return to Archbishop Persson's jurisdiction. The Apostolic Episcopal Church–Order of Corporate Reunion now exists as a small jurisdiction under Hugh's leadership. It has also established a concordat with its sister church, the Holy Celtic Church, also headed by Hugh.

Membership: Not reported.

Remarks: Almost immediately after his consecration in 1946, Bp. Herman Abbinga returned to his native Holland and established the Apostolic Episcopal Church in that country. However, little more than a month after his original consecration, he accepted consecration from Hugh George de Willmott Newman (Mar Georgius), who had consecrated Mar David I. Over the next six years, his tendencies toward theosophy and the Liberal Catholic Church (in which he had been a priest) reasserted themselves, and he gradually drifted from the Apostolic Episcopal Church. In 1952, following his excommunication by Mar Georgius, he founded an independent jurisdiction, the Oosters Apostolisch Episcopale Kerk.

Sources:

The Apostolic Episcopal Church. www.celticsynod.org/aec.htm.

The Divine Liturgy, Holy Eucharist. Queens, NY: Apostolic Episcopal Church, 1943.

Persson, Bertil. *An Apostolic Episcopal Ministry: Archbishop Arthur W. Brooks and Christ's Church By-the-Sea. In Memory and Inspiration.* Phoenix, AZ: St. Michael's Press, 1992.

————. *Aramaic Idioms of Eshoo (Jesus) Explained.* Solna, Sweden: St. Ephrem's Institute, 1978.

————. *A Collection of Documentation on the Apostolic Succession of Joseph Rene Vilatte with Brief Annotations.* Solna, Sweden: Author, 1974.

Archdiocese of the Antiochian Catholic Church in America / St. Demetrios Antiochian Catholic Church

2001 Middlebrook Pke., Knoxville, TN 37921

The Archdiocese of the Antiochean Catholic Church in America was founded in 1991 when the former Diocese of Lexington, Kentucky, of the Church of Antioch was granted autocephaly and became an independent jurisdiction. The Diocese of Lexington had been created in 1986 when the Most Rev. H. Gordon Hurlburt, a bishop of the Church of Antioch, moved to rural Compton, Kentucky, from Wichita, Kansas. Hurlburt, who assumed the ecclesiastical name Mar Peter, had been consecrated in 1981 by Abp. Herman Adrian Spruit, then primate of the Church of Antioch. In 1990 Hurlburt consecrated Victor C. Herron of Knoxville, Tennessee, as his coadjutor. Herron, who took the name Mar Michael, became the Antiochian Catholic Church in America's *metran*, or archbishop, when Mar Peter retired in 1996.

The Archdiocese of the Antiochian Catholic Church in America largely embraces the theology and much of the practice of the Oriental Orthodox Western Syriac tradition. It accepts the Councils of Nicea (325 C.E.), Constantinople (381 C.E.), and Ephesus (431 C.E.) as being fully ecumenical; the pronouncements of these councils, including the so-called Nicene Creed and the status of the Blessed Virgin Mary as Theotokos ("God-Bearer"), are therefore dogma for the church. However, it is not in full communion with the mainstream Oriental Orthodox churches because it ordains women and because it allows married clergy members to serve as bishops. The church's approach to theology and practice is a process of "critical reappropriation" that is open to all sectors of Christendom but is, simultaneously, firmly rooted in the Western Syriac tradition, particularly with regard to such basic issues as Christology, soteriology, ecclesiology, and ethics. The church's liturgy, which remains a work in progress, is a redaction of the West Syriac Rite.

The See City of the Archdiocese is Knoxville, Tennessee. Its primate, the Most Rev. Victor Mar Michael Herron, presides at St. Demetrios Antiochian Catholic Church, whose pastor is Avva (Fr.) Zakkai Patrick Pardee. While attendance at the Sunday Qurbana (Eucharist) at St. Demetrios is small, averaging around 13 people (including three clergy members), the congregation, located in the inner city, operates a food bank that serves more than 50 persons weekly. Another small congregation, St. Elias, worships in nearby Kodak, Tennessee; its pastor is Chorepiscopus Andreas Richard Turner, chancellor and suffragan bishop-elect. Avva Andreas is slated to be raised to the episcopate in October 2008 at the annual clergy convocation.

Father Gregory Ned Blevins, the archdiocese's ecumenical and social concerns representative, offers the Qurbana weekly at the Chapel of SS Perpetua and Felicity in his home near Columbia, South Carolina, for a small congregation. Amma (Mother) Caitlin Turner is an itinerant missionary throughout the southeastern United States. Avva Andreas and Avva Greg also conduct an annual three-day training event for junior clergy during Holy Week at St. Demetrios.

In 2007 the Cloistered Heart Franciscans, an ecumenical sisterhood headed by Mother Shirley Raper of Sparta, Tennessee, reorganized within the archdiocese as the Cloistered Heart Myrrh-Bearers. Mother Shirley, a deaconess, conducts weekly services for about 20 people at a small facility called Holy Adoration Chapel in the absence of a priest. Sister Jacqueline Dierring of Black Mountain, North Carolina, also a deaconess, conducts similar services at Holy Trinity Chapel, an oratory in her home. Priests occasionally offer the Qurbana in these venues when available. As of April 2008, the order had begun to accept brothers, called Cloistered Heart God-Bearers, under the patronage of St. Ignatios of Antioch.

Sources:

The Antiochian Catholic Church in America.
www.geocities.com/Athens/Forum/7951/index.html.

Antiochian Catholic Church. www.myspace.com/orthoknox.

Blevins, Fr. Gregory Ned. "Vagante Priest: Life on the Ecclesiological/Ecclesiastical Margins." vagantepriest.blogspot.com.

The Publications of the Antiochian Catholic Church in America.
www.geocities.com/rik_turner.

Army of Mary (Armee de Marie) / Centre International de l'Armee de Marie Spiri-Maria

626 Rte. du Sanctuaire, Lac-Etchemin, QC, Canada G0R 1S0

The Army of Mary, an independent community in the Roman Catholic tradition, was founded by Marie-Paule Giguere (b. 1921). Marie-Paule was born in Sainte-Germaine-du-Lac-Etchemin (Quebec) and later married and became the mother of five children. At the request of four different authorities, among them her spiritual director and social worker, she separated from her husband in 1957 in order to protect her children from his unhealthy influence.

Her deeply religious formation opened her to the love of Jesus and Mary, the church and the Eucharist, and especially the sublime priesthood. At the age of twelve Marie-Paule offered herself as a soul-victim, and this marked the beginning of her life of intimate union with Jesus and Mary. After several years of progression along this path of intimate union and mystical formation, her spiritual director asked her to write her spiritual autobiography, which appeared as the 15-volume series *Vie d'amour* (*Life of Love*), published in 1979–1980. Five additional volumes entitled *Vie d'amour, Appendice*, which carried on with the history of the Army of Mary, were published between 1992 and 1994.

In 1954 the name "Army of Mary" was revealed to her. It was at the end of a day of prayer with a group of friends known as the Marian Group, on August 28, 1971, that Heaven informed her: "Today saw the founding of the Army of Mary." A Catholic priest, Father Philippe Roy (1916–1988), joined the movement in 1972 and became its general director. Subsequently, in 1975, the archbishop of Quebec, Maurice Cardinal Roy (1905–1985; not a relative of Fr. Roy) recognized the Army of Mary as a Catholic lay association. The following year, a popular French author of books on prophecy, Raoul Auclair (1906–1997), become a member of the group. He moved to Quebec and served as the editor of the movement's magazine between 1979 and 1982. The Army of Mary membership soon numbered in the thousands in Canada and hundreds in Europe.

The Army of Mary's goal being the sanctification of souls, it promotes the spiritual renewal of its members through personal interior reform in accordance with the precise directives of Pope Paul VI and through its devotion to the Eucharist, Mary, and the pope. Over the years it has sought to promote renewal in other sectors of daily life. So it was that other works were born of the Army of Mary: the Family of the Sons and Daughters of Mary, a lay organization founded in 1981, for the renewal of family; the Oblate-Patriots, established in 1986, for the renewal of society through spreading Catholic social teaching; and the Marialys Institute, created in 1992, with the twofold mission of promoting the fidelity of priests to the Holy Father and coming to the aid of young people.

The Community of the Sons and Daughters of Mary, a religious order including both priests and nuns, was established in 1981. Pope John Paul II personally ordained the first Son of Mary to the priesthood in 1986. After her husband's death in 1997, Marie-Paule formally became a Daughter of Mary and was subsequently elected superior general of the community following a unanimous vote of the sisters.

While having official support, the Army of Mary continually found itself in conflict with elements of the Catholic hierarchy. More liberal bishops in Quebec were suspicious of whether this movement was faithful with respect to Vatican II, and Cardinal Roy's successor, Louis-Albert Cardinal Vachon, was hostile to Marie-Paule's visions and revelations, some of which he regarded as theologically questionable. He was also critical of Army member Marc Bosquart, who wrote two books claiming that the Immaculate was now mystically inhabiting Marie-Paule. Vachon withdrew the recognition of the Army of Mary as an official Catholic organization. In 1987 the Congregation for the Doctrine of Faith (at the Vatican) judged Bosquart's opinions to be "seriously erroneous." Then, on March 31, 2000, the Vatican's Congregation for the Doctrine of Faith informed all of the Canadian bishops that Marie-Paule's *Vie d'amour* contained doctrinal errors. In 2001 the National Conference of Canadian Bishops published a statement saying that the Army of Mary should no longer be regarded as a Roman Catholic organization, without mentioning the congregations of the Sons and Daughters of Mary, who as priests and nuns remain in an ambiguous relationship to the Roman Catholic Church. They are both members of the Army of Mary, whose orthodoxy has been questioned, and highly praised Catholic workers scattered in many dioceses.

Membership: Because anyone is free to enter or leave the Army of Mary, there is no membership list.

Periodicals: *Le Royaume*.

Sources:

Army of Mary. www.communaute-dame.qc.ca.

Giguere, Marie-Paule. *The Community of the Lady of All Peoples*. Quebec: Editions Co. Dame, 1998. 120 pp.

———. *Vie d'amour*. 15 vols. Limoilou, Quebec: Vie d'Amour, 1979–1980. English edition as *Life of Love*. Limoilou, Quebec: Vie d'Amour, 1979–1987.

———. *Vie d'amour, Appendice*. 5 vols. Limoilou, Quebec: Vie d'Amour, 1992–1994.

Introvigne, Massimo. "En Route to the Marian Kingdom: Catholic Apocalypticism and the Army of Mary." In Stephen Hunt, ed., *Christian Millenarianism: From the Early Church to Waco*. London: Hurst, 2001, pp. 149–165.

Catholic Apostolic Church International

c/o Bp. Joseph J. Gouthro, The Chancery Office, 925 Felix Palm Ave., North Las Vegas, NJ 89032

The Catholic Apostolic Church International was founded in the first decade of the twenty-first century by Most Rev. Joseph J. Gouthro, who continues to serve as its presiding bishop. Gouthro was originally consecrated as a bishop for the Independent Catholic Church by Robert Joseph Allmen, Lawrence J. Harms, and Sharon Di Sunno, bishops of the American Catholic Church, who were assisted by three bishops of the Catholic Apostolic Church in North America: Willard Schultz, Donald Buttenbusch, and Joseph Anderson Johnson. It was the lineage of the three latter bishops, which could be traced to Carlos Duarte Costa, a former Roman Catholic bishop in Brazil, that Gouthro emphasized when founding the Catholic Apostolic Church International. He identifies the Catholic Apostolic Church International with Duarte's relatively successful Catholic Apostolic Church of Brazil, though there is not an official organizational connection.

The Catholic Apostolic Church International is very close to the post–Vatican II Roman Catholic Church in belief and practice. Its major difference is its allowing of a married priesthood.

The Catholic Apostolic Church International has parishes in New Jersey, New Hampshire, Kansas, Maryland, and Florida.

Membership: Not reported. In 2008, the Church reported two bishops, and three priests ministering from five locations in five states.

Remarks: On September 24, 2006, Joseph J. Gouthro joined three other independent Catholic bishops in a ceremony held in Washington, D.C., in which they were reconsecrated to the episcopal office by Abp. Emmanuel Milingo, the former Roman Catholic bishop of Zambia. Archbishop Milingo, a well-known figure in Roman Catholic episcopal life, had become controversial in the 1990s after he became associated with Rev. Sun Myung Moon of the Unification Movement, and eventually, in violation of his long-standing vows of celibacy, married a woman in one of the mass weddings conducted by Reverend Moon. This act led to a continuing series of events that have cost Milingo his standing within the Roman Church.

Widely misunderstood by the press, Milingo acted as a person with an indisputable lineage of succession from the Apostles and passed that lineage to four men who had previously been consecrated as bishops with apostolic lineages from different churches. Through the centuries, reconsecration has occurred in circumstances in which there was some doubt concerning the correctness of an earlier consecration. Because of the many questions that have been raised about Independent Catholic and Old Catholic lineages, independent bishops have at times been reconsecrated several times in order to receive multiple lineages of apostolic succession passed through both the Eastern and Western churches. It appears that Archbishop Milingo had developed a desire to pass the Roman Catholic lineage to the Old Catholics and by so doing force Rome to recognize them. For his actions, he was excommunicated.

Two months after the ceremony, the four bishops—Gouthro, Peter Paul Brennan, Patrick E. Trujillo, and George Augustus Stallings—joined Archbishop Milingo in addressing a letter to Pope Benedict XVI calling on him to solve the problem of the shortage of Roman Catholic priests by allowing married men to be ordained.

Sources:

Catholic Apostolic Church International.

www.catholicapostolicchurchinternational.com/.

Catholic Apostolic National Church

7030 W. Diversey Ave., Chicago, IL 60707

The Catholic Apostolic National Church was founded in 1980 as the Apostolic Catholic Church of America, and in 1999 changed its name to the Old Catholic Church of the United States. In 2005, the church was received into the Worldwide Communion of Catholic Apostolic National Churches (ICAN) under the Catholic Apostolic Church of Brazil (Igreja Catolica Apostolica Brasileira), and changed its name to the Catholic Apostolic National Church. The church derives its apostolic succession from Roman Catholic Bishop Carlos Duarte Costa of Brazil, who founded the Catholic Apostolic Church of Brazil. The Most Reverend Robert M. Gubala, SCR, served as its current Archbishop-Metropolitan in 2008.

The Catholic Apostolic National Church is a community of Christians committed to Jesus Christ and his teaching. They accept and believe the testimony of his apostles, eyewitnesses of his life, death, and resurrection from among the dead. The faith of the Catholic Apostolic National Church is that the Ecumenical Councils clearly express their beliefs, and they affirm the ancient creeds of faith, the Athanasian Creed, the Apostles' Creed, and the Nicene Creed. The church traces their apostolic succession through the ancient churches back to the apostles, and participates in the full sacramental ministry. The Rule of Faith of the Catholic Apostolic National Church is faithful adherence to sacred scripture and apostolic tradition, as protected by the teaching Magisterium of the church.

Bishop Carlos Duarte Costa was consecrated as the Roman Catholic Diocesan Bishop of Botucatu, Brazil, on December 8, 1924, and was the most outspoken Brazilian bishop in defending the poor. In 1937, at the insistence of the Getúlio Vargas régime in Brazil, the Vatican forced Bishop Duarte Costa to retire as Bishop of Botucatu, and he was appointed as Titular Bishop of Maura. Nonetheless, he continued in speaking out on behalf of the poor and, in 1944, was imprisoned for several months. Finally, in 1945, after protesting the Vatican's helping several Nazis

and Nazi sympathizers find refuge in Brazil, Bishop Duarte Costa broke with Rome and founded the Igreja Católica Apostolica Brasileira (ICAB). The Brazilian Church suffered persecution at the hands of hostile governments and others, even as it established educational and social programs designed to feed, clothe, house, and educate those in need. Bishop Duarte Costa died on March 26, 1967; he is revered by the Brazilian Church and her daughter churches as St. Carlos of Brazil.

In matters of discipline, administration, and procedure, the Catholic Apostolic National Church, which is not under papal jurisdiction, differs from the Roman Catholic Church. Clerical celibacy is optional in the Catholic Apostolic National Church: Married men may be ordained, as in the Eastern Orthodox Churches, and in many dioceses clergy may, with prior Episcopal consent, be married after ordination. Liturgical expression is also a matter of discipline determined by the local bishop. Consequently, many communities have adopted the liturgical renewal promulgated following the Second Vatican Council while still maintaining Tridentine liturgy, in Latin or direct translation into classical or modern English, in those parishes that desire it. Eastern Rite parishes exist as well. Catholic Apostolic National Church communities are small, and adhere to the Ignatian model of the Church. The Catholic Apostolic National Church describes itself as an understanding of the Western and Eastern traditions in one complete tradition. It promises to support Catholic faith without excessive institutionalism, promote full participation in the life and sacraments of the church, and provide a viable alternative and allow a person to be a part of Christ's church, and be at peace with his/her conscience.

The church sponsors an order, the Society of Christ the King, which has responsibility for overseeing the church's nonresident seminary program.

Membership: Not reported.

Educational Facilities:

Christ the King Theological Seminary, Chicago, Illinois.

Sources:

The Catholic Apostolic National Church. www.catholic-ican.org.

Catholic Charismatic Church

c/o Patriarch Michael, St. Jude Catholic Charismatic Church, 240 School St., Berlin, NH 03570

The Catholic Charismatic Church is a Western liturgical church that integrates the gifts of the Holy Spirit, including speaking in tongues, into its worship life. It accepts the traditional creeds of Christianity (Apostles, Nicene, Athanasian) as authoritative statements of belief and affirms the authority of the Bible as the written Word of God. It administers the seven sacraments of the Western church. It considers itself as the charismatic branch of the one true church of Christ. A variety of rites are used by the different priests in the church. The church accepts married priests, but does not admit either women or practicing homosexuals to the ordained priesthood. Priests are not permitted to officiate at same-sex unions.

The church is led by its patriarch, Most Rev. J. Paul A. Boucher, better known by his religious name, Patriarch Michael. The church reports nine dioceses functioning in the United States, each led by a bishop. In addition, the church reports work in Puerto Rico, the Congo, Rwanda, Kenya, Tanzania, Cameroon, Germany, Pakistan, India, and Bangladesh. The expansive work in Cameroon is in cooperation with the Communauté Catholique Charismatique Saint Mathieu de Yaounde and the Autonomous Fraternity of the Holy Spirit. The work in Europe is in cooperation with the Autonomous Society of Saint George, which has six dioceses scattered across Western Europe.

The Catholic Charismatic Church emphasizes its independent existence and its lack of ties to other similarly named jurisdictions, such as the Catholic Charismatic Church of Canada or the Charismatic Catholic Church of America.

Membership: Not reported.

Educational Facilities:

St. James the Elder Theological Seminary.

Sources:

Catholic Charismatic Church. mysite.verizon.net/M-boyle/CCChurch.html.

Catholic Charismatic Church of Canada

La Cite de Marie Ste. Scholastique, 11,141 Rte. 148, RR 1, Mirabel, QC, Canada J0N 1S0

The Catholic Charismatic Church of Canada was founded in 1957 by the Mt. Rev. Andre Barbeau (1912–1994), the church's archbishop, also known as Patriarch Andre the First, a former Roman Catholic priest in the Diocese of Montreal. In 1968, he was consecrated by Bp. Charles Brearly of the Old Holy Catholic Church, a small British Old Catholic jurisdiction. The purpose of founding the church was "to assist the Roman Catholic Church in its mission as a supplemental rite." Since his consecration, Patriarch Andre has responded to statements in the reports of Vatican II inviting new rites and the formation of new patriachates as they are needed. The Catholic Charismatic Church is conceived as such a new venture, "a new stem, spouting out of the Church, a progressive-conservative sort of Patriarchate." Immediately after its establishment, Archbishop Barbeau petitioned the pope concerning the status of the rite.

The church follows the teachings and practices of Roman Catholicism. It observes the seven sacraments and supports the papacy in all matters. It has offered the Roman Catholic Church its new rite, one written by the patriarch, which obligates itself only to the essentials of the Catholic faith. It seeks to preserve a proper freedom. Also, limiting itself to the essentials, the church sees itself as being a ready avenue for reconciling former Catholics to the church. The rite is also charismatic, meaning that it is a mystical liturgy.

The church is headed by its archbishop. Patrick Barbeau died in 1994. He was succeeded by Patriarch Andre II (a.k.a. Archbishop Andre Le Tellier), who had served as Coadjutor Bishop. There are other bishops and a number of priests. Though there are several parishes, such as the Holy Wisdom Community in San Diego, California, most priests are worker priests and are encouraged to create household sanctuaries. As mysticism and religious experience is emphasized over scholastic endeavors, priests are not required to have the seminary education usually expected of a Roman Catholic priest. Priests are not committed to celibacy, and may marry. Individuals not wishing to assume priestly duties are invited to become part of the permanent deaconate. While the church has not accepted women priests yet, it remains open to the possibility. The church's headquarters, La Cite de Marie (the City of Mary), established in rural Quebec, was in part inspired by *The City of God*, a mystical classic written by Mary of Agreda.

Membership: Not reported.

Remarks: Over the years, for purposes of establishing ecumenical relations, Archbishop Barbeau has received a number of reconsecrations, a common practice among independent Catholic jurisdictions. In 1973 he was consecrated by G. R. Armstrong (of unknown affiliation). In 1976 he was consecrated by Robert S. Zeiger, then of the Apostolic Catholic Church of the Americas, assisted by Gordon I. DaCosta. That same year he was consecrated by German Bishop Joseph Maria Thiesen of L'Eglise Catholique Apostolique Primitive D'Antioche et le Tradition Syro-Byzantine. In 1980 he was consecrated by Patrick McReynolds of the American Orthodox Catholic Church, assisted by Andre Letellier and J. Letellier.

Sources:

Bethany Charismatic Church of Canada/USA. www.bethanyccc.org/index.html

Barbeau, Archbishop Andre. *Liturgie des Saints Mysteres*. Montreal, QC: La Cite de Marie, 1971.

Catholic Church of the Apostles of the Latter Times

290 7e Rang, PO Box 4478, Mont-Tremblant, QC, Canada J8E 1A1

The Catholic Church of the Apostles of the Latter Times, also known as the Apostles of Infinite Love of the Order of the Mother of God, has as its members followers of the Order of the Mother of God, which was requested by the Blessed Virgin Mary in her apparition at La Salette, France, in 1846. The order was founded in France in 1935 with ecclesiastical approval by the French priest Fr. Michel Collin (d. 1974). In 1960 he declared himself to be Pope Clement XV, the mystical pope named in the Third Secret of Fatima, the final, secret part of the message received by the children who communicated with the Blessed Virgin at Fatima, Portugal, in 1917. His followers, and those of Fr. John of the Trinity after him, frequently have been referred to as the Renewed Church of Jesus Christ.

Father Collin named Fr. John of the Trinity superior general of the order in 1962. In the 1940s Father John, then a young religious brother with the Hospitaler Brothers of St. John of God in Montreal, had several visions in which he was told to establish a community of new apostles to preach the Gospel as the biblical apostles had; he also saw the future Clement XV. Thus the Brothers of Jesus Mary came into being in 1952 near Montreal, and were granted a decree of foundation signed by Pope Pius XII in 1953. The brothers merged with the Apostles of Infinite Love in 1962, when Father John was ordained and consecrated a bishop by Clement, and the Mother House of the order of the Mother of God was transferred to St. Jovite, Quebec. The rule given by the Virgin at La Salette was adopted. Since then, the community has founded mission houses throughout Canada, and in the United States, Europe, the West Indies, Latin America, and South Africa. Members from all these regions have joined the order, taking traditional vows or becoming tertiary or lay members.

A crises occurred in 1967 when Father John was attacked by Canadian Roman Catholic priests because of his association with Clement. In 1968 he had visions in which he was chosen as Servant of the Church of Jesus Christ with the name Gregory XVII. Several mystics in Canada had confirmatory revelations. On May 9, 1969, Clement confirmed in writing that Father John was his successor with the name of Gregory XVII; Gregory concurred with Clement in saying that the official Church of Rome had fallen into aspotasy.

The faith, doctrine, tradition, and practices of the church are Catholic; in its desire to return to the evangelical simplicity and purity of early Christianity, it maintains a doctrinal unity with the traditional Catholic Church. A particular goal of the order is the preservation of the Deposit of Faith by religious teaching in all its forms to adults and children. Another specific goal is the struggle against all the abuses that have brought about the decadence of the clergy, the religious state, and Christian society. Besides perpetual adoration of the Most Blessed Sacrament, prayer, study, and work of all kinds, the order lends itself to all the spiritual and corporal works of mercy. It also labors toward the Christian unity so desired by Jesus Christ and His true disciples: unity in Truth.

The Order of the Apostles exists as a nonprofit corporation. In addition to its monthly magazine, the *Magnificat*, it publishes many books and brochures as one important means of apostolate.

Membership: In 2008 the Order of the Mother of God included approximately 300 religious brothers and sisters who had taken vows, and several hundred followers in North and South America, Latin America, French West Indies, Europe, and Africa, where there are several convents and monasteries.

Educational Facilities:

Monastery of the Magnificat, Mont-Tremblant, Quebec, Canada.

Periodicals: *Magnificat*.

Remarks: There is one other movement that derives from Clement XV (Collin), the Church of St. Joseph in Cicero, Illinois, which is not connected to the church led by Gregory XVII (Fr. John of the Trinity). Clemente Gomez, the leader of a movement based in Spain, also claimed to be Gregory XVII. That group has no connection at all with the Apostles.

Sources:

Catholic Church of the Apostles of the Latter Times. www.magnificat.ca/english.

Barette, Jean-Marie. *The Prophecy of the Apostles of the Latter Times*. St. Jovite, QC: Editions Magnificat, 1988.

Cote, Jean. *Prophet without Permit—Father John of the Trinity*. N.p.: Pro Manscripto, 1988.

Cuneo, Michael. "The Vengeful Virgin." In *Millennium, Messiahs, and Mayhem: Contemporary Apocalyptic Movements*, ed. Thomas Robbins and Susan J. Palmer. New York: Routledge, 1987.

de la Trinite, Fr. Jean-Gregory. *Escaping the Shipwreck*. St. Jovite, QC: Editions Magnificat, 1976.

The Eclipse of the Church. St. Jovite, QC: Editions Magnificat, 1971.

Gregory XVII. *Peter Speaks to the World: Universal Encyclical for Christian Unity*. St. Jovite, QC: Magnificat, 1989.

Gregory XVII. *Universal Encyclical for Christian Unity*. St. Jovite, QC: Editions Magnificat, 1975.

John Gregory of the Trinity, Fr. *Escaping the Shipwreck*. St. Jovite, QC: Editions Magnificat, 1976.

————. *Questions and Answers on the Apostles of Infinite Love*. St. Jovite, QC: Monastery of the Magnificat of the Mother of God, 1989.

————. *When Bad Faith Hides Behind the Law*. St. Jovite, QC: Magnificat, 1968.

St. Pierre, Catherine. *Thou Art Peter*. St. Jovite, QC: Magnificat, 1994.

When Prophecy Comes True. St. Jovite, QC: Editions Magnificat, 1972.

Catholic Church (Pope Michael I)

PO Box 74, Delia, KS 66418-0074

Pope Michael I is the leader of a small group of former Roman Catholics who feel that, after the death of Pope Pius XII in 1958, the church moved into a state of apostasy that has invalidated the authority of all subsequent popes and bishops. Pope Michael I was born in 1959 as David Bawden. As a young aspirant to the priesthood, he became dissatisfied with the changes in the church following Vatican II and came to the conclusion, as had other Catholic Traditionalists, that the church was seriously committed to errors of doctrine and practice. He affiliated with the Society of St. Pius X, one of the leading organizations of the larger Traditionalist movement, and moved to Switzerland, where the society had a seminary. He transferred to the society's seminary then in Armada, Michigan. However, he was dismissed without cause from the seminary. He then moved to St. Mary's College, where he worked in various positions through 1980 until his resignation from the society in March 1981. He had concluded that the society and the whole Traditionalist movement was heretical.

On December 26, 1983, he issued a letter asserting that Traditionalist priests had no right to operate chapels or to confer the sacraments. He expanded upon this letter in a 16-page treatise, "Jurisdiction during the Great Apostasy," in 1985. He teamed up with Teresa Stanfill Benns from Denver, Colorado, to produce a book, *Will the Catholic Church Survive the Twentieth Century?*, published in 1990. It included the 1985 treatise and additional material written in response to that treatise. The book argued that the majority of masses, baptisms, and confessions within the Roman Catholic Church are invalid due to the reform of Vatican II and the leadership of an invalid pope, and true Catholics should cease attendance at English-language masses. He also argued that the present day was the time of the Antichrist, whom he identified as Pope Paul VI. Paul died, but his authority was passed to John Paul I and John Paul II, thus giving the appearance of being slain, recovering, and living anew. Bawden suggested that in 1958 Cardinal Alfredo

Ottavani may have been elected pope, but his place was usurped by Pope John XXIII.

Bawden further suggested that a precedent had been established for the election of a pope apart from the action of the College of Cardinals. Thus on July 16, 1990, six people, including Bawden's parents, gathered in Belvue, Kansas, and elected Bawden as the new pope. A chapel and papal headquarters was initially established in their resale shop, The Question Mark, in Belvue. On November 1, 1993, Pope Michael I moved his papal office to its present location in Delia, Kansas.

Michael I is not ordained to the priesthood and thus does not say mass. He is awaiting the emergence of a bishop unaffected by the post–Vatican II changes to ordain him and believes that some such bishops have survived either in Russia or China. Meanwhile, he conducts Sunday services of prayer and preaching to those who have accepted his authority.

In the fall of 2001, Gordon Bateman of Australia called for a council to bring together all those who are of the sedevacantist view. This view was that John Paul II was not pope. He also contacted several of the claimants to the Papacy, including Pope Michael and Antipope Linus II, who resides in England. Following the precedent set at the Council of Constance, this effort to call a council was endorsed by Pope Michael, provided that all make the Professions of Faith, renunciation of any heresy they may have held, and take the Oath Against the Errors of Modernism.

Membership: In 2002 the group reported 59 members.

Sources:

The Vatican in Exile. www.vaticaninexile.com.

Bawden, David (Pope Michael I). *Truth Is One*. E-book, 2005. www.vaticaninexile.com/downloads/truthisone.html.

Benns, Teresa Stanfill, and David Bawden. *Will the Catholic Church Survive the Twentieth Century?* Privately published, 1987.

Crumbo, Christine. "The Thrift Store Pope." *Wichita Eagle* (July 19, 1990).

Pope Michael Web site. www.popemichael.homestead.com/index.html.

Celtic Anabaptist Communion

266 Tallaha Rd., Rte. 1, Box 114-E, Tillatoba, MS 38961

The Celtic Anabaptist Communion (CAC) is a diverse fellowship of ministers and churches founded by Michael Wrenn, the Communion's presiding archbishop. Wrenn was consecrated as a bishop by Abp. Rodney P. Rickard of the Reformed Catholic Church, from whom he inherited several Old Catholic and Eastern Orthodox lines of succession. He defines the Communion as a combination of Celtic and Anabaptist ways, which shared, among a variety of characteristics, a less authoritarian approach to church life and a lack of division between the sacred and the secular. Furthermore, according to Wrenn, these traditions affirmed the spiritual equality of women and men, reflected a belief in the closeness of God to this world, and were missionary-minded. The CAC ardently advocates for the principle of "soul liberty," or freedom of conscience. Wrenn conceives of his own role as archbishop in an anti-hierarchical fashion, in keeping with the Anabaptist and Celtic traditions. Archbishops are to serve as a pastor to the bishops, while bishops should be a pastor to the ministers in their dioceses.

Since being consecrated, Wrenn has been very active in recruiting men and women to the ministry and in locating experienced ministers to serve as bishops in his jurisdiction. He has been especially open to people who, like himself, seek both ordination and a new church home. Celtic Anabaptist Communion affirms the autonomy of the local church. Affiliated local churches own their own property and are allowed to call and ordain their own ministers. While Wrenn possessed a traditional lineage in apostolic succession, he does not require it of ministers licensed through the CAC, though he makes it available to them.

The church is in communion with the Reformed Catholic Church and the Christian Missionary Anglican Communion. Archbishop Wrenn sits in the House of Bishops of the Christian Missionary Anglican Communion. The CAC allows its clergy to maintain dual affiliations with other Christian communions whose teachings are not diametrically opposed to those of the CAC. It rejects churches that ordain practicing homosexuals or perform same-sex unions.

Membership: Not reported.

Educational Facilities:

The CAC does not have a seminary of its own, but approves a variety of schools supported by other Christian bodies.

Sources:

Celtic Anabaptist Communion. www.celtic-anabaptist-ministries.com/.

Charismatic Catholic Church: Independent Rite of America
Current address not obtained for this edition.

The Charismatic Catholic Church: Independent Rite of America is a small jurisdiction founded in 1981 by Bp. Daniel C. Braun. It is a Western Rite church which is open to and encourages the charismatic gifts of the Spirit, including speaking in tongues, healing, and prophecy. The jurisdiction is based in the St. Francis of Assisi Church in Rocky Point, New York.

Membership: Not reported.

Sources:

Ward, Gary L. *Independent Bishops: An International Directory*. Detroit, MI: Apogee Books, 1990.

Christ Catholic Church
c/o Most Rev. Karl Pruter, 405 Kentling Rd., Highlandsville, MO 65669

Christ Catholic Church was founded in 1965 by the Rev. Karl Pruter (1920–2007), a Congregationalist minister deeply involved in the liturgically oriented Free Catholic movement, a fellowship among ministers and lay people of the Congregational and Christian Churches. The movement did not fare well after the 1957 merger of the Congregational-Christian Churches with the Evangelical and Reformed Church to form the United Church of Christ. The subsequent splintering found leaders of the movement in different denominations. In despair, in 1965 Pruter made a pilgrimage to Europe, where he met with many Old Catholic leaders. Returning to the United States, he settled in Boston and searched for a Free Catholic Church or bishop. Finding neither, he turned to independent Orthodox Abp. Peter A. Zhurawetsky (1901–1994), and under his authority began a church in Boston's Back Bay area. He emphasized the contemplative life, mysticism, and an experiential faith. The growing congregation soon opened a mission in Deering, New Hampshire.

In 1967 Archbishop Peter, assisted by Abp. Uladyslau Ryzy-Ryski of the American World patriarchs, consecrated Father Pruter to the episcopacy as bishop of the Diocese of Boston. The next year, he designated the diocese as an independent communion. The two jurisdictions met in synod and accepted the constitutions and canons given to the new body by Archbishop Peter.

The church's headquarters moved from Boston to New Hampshire to Scottsdale, Arizona, to Chicago, and finally to Highlandsville, Missouri, in the early 1980s. There Bishop Pruter served as pastor of the Cathedral Church of the Prince of Peace, a small chapel described as the smallest cathedral in the world. In 1989 Christ Catholic Church received into membership the Ontario Old Catholic Church, consisting of a single parish in Toronto, Ontario. The church's pastor, Bp. Frederick P. Dunleavy, had been consecrated by Archbishop Pruter in 1988. In 1991 Dunleavy was elected to succeed Pruter as the new presiding bishop of Christ Catholic Church.

Under Archbishop Dunleavy, the church adopted an expansionist policy. The immediate fruit of that policy was the merger, approved in December 1992, with the Liberal Catholic Church of Ontario (LCCO). The merged body became known as Christ Catholic Church International (CCCI), and the presiding bishop of the former Liberal Catholic Church of Ontario became the new presiding bishop of the merged

church. CCCI continued to grow in both Canada and the United States. However, Archbishop Pruter and the priests of the Christ Catholic Church began to question some of the actions of their new Canadian members, including their joining the Fellowship of Independent Orthodox Churches led by Matriarch Meri Louise Spruit of the Church of Antioch. This affiliation, though short-lived, seemed to indicate both a tolerance of heterodox theosophical ideas and an openness to females in the priesthood. Archbishop Pruter, by then retired, also objected to the use by many of the Canadian parishes of the St. Francis Liturgy, which contained controversial selections from the post–Vatican II Roman Catholic liturgy.

As complaints mounted, in 1995 Archbishop Pruter called for a dissolution of the merger between Christ Catholic Church and the former Liberal Catholic Church of Ontario. He came out of retirement and reorganized the former parishes under his leadership as Christ Catholic Church. Those who did not agree with Pruter continued as Christ Catholic Church International.

St. Willibrord's Press, founded by Archbishop Pruter, is the major publisher of Old Catholic literature in North America. Pruter is the author of many tracts and pamphlets, as well books such as *The Teachings of the Great Mystics* (1969) and *A History of the Old Catholic Church* (1973). He also operates Tsali Bookstore, which specializes in Native American literature, and Cathedral Books, which specializes in peace literature.

Christ Catholic Church is Old Catholic in faith. It adheres to the Holy Scriptures, the ecumenical creeds, the seven ecumenical councils, and the Confession of Utrecht. The church uses the vernacular liturgy "The Christ Catholic Mass," which follows the Old Catholic pattern.

Membership: Not reported.

Educational Facilities:

Bishop Varlet School of Theology, Highlandsville, Missouri.

St. George Theologate, Highlandsville, Missouri.

Periodicals: *St. Willibrord Journal*.

Remarks: On April 17, 1988, Bishop Pruter consecrated Frederick P. Dunleavy of the Ontario Old Roman Catholic Church to the episcopacy, and the two jurisdictions united.

Sources:

Christ Catholic Church. www.christcatholicchurch.com.

Pruter, Karl. *Bishops Extraordinary*. Highlandville, MO: St. Willibrord's Press, 2003.

———. *The Directory of Autocephalous Bishops in the Apostolic Succession*. Highlandville, MO: St. Willibrord Press, 2005.

———. *A History of the Old Catholic Church*. Scottsdale, AZ: St. Willibrord's Press, 1973.

———. *The Story of Christ Catholic Church*. Chicago: St. Willibrord's Press, 1981.

———. *The Teachings of the Great Mystics*. Goffstown, NH: St. Willibrord's Press, 1969.

———, and J. Gordon Melton. *The Old Catholic Sourcebook*. New York: Garland, 1983.

Christ Catholic Church International
c/o St. Lukes Cathedral, 5165 Palmer Ave. Niagara, Falls, ON, Canada L2G 1Y4

Christ Catholic Church International (CCCI) was formed in 1993 by the merger of several Old Catholic jurisdictions and has subsequently grown through further mergers and individual evangelistic outreach.

Among the constituent bodies of CCCI was the Liberal Catholic Church of Ontario (LCCO), which began in the 1930s with an independent Old Catholic parish, the Church of St. Francis of Assisi, in Hamilton, Ontario, organized by a former Anglican priest, William H. Daw (1902–1986). Daw was consecrated in 1955 by Edward M. Matthews (1898–1985) and installed as the presiding bishop of the autonomous LCCO. Bp. John Henry Vincent Russell (1920–1985) succeeded Daw in 1974.

Russell had been consecrated in 1960 and, along with several priests, had founded and established Blessed Trinity parish in Hamilton. During Russell's term, oratories were established in Brantford, Ontario, and North Hero, Vermont, and a parish opened in Niagara Falls, Ontario. Bp. Thomas D. J. McCourt succeeded Russell in 1985, and was succeeded the following year by Bp. Donald William Mullan.

A second constituent body of CCCI was Christ Catholic Church, in 1993 head-quartered in Toronto. Christ Catholic Church came into Canada in 1989 when the Ontario Old Catholic Church merged into the Christ Catholic Church based in the United States. The Ontario Old Catholic Church dates to 1962 with the consecration of William Pavlik by Abp. Richard A. Marchenna (1911–1982) of the Old Roman Catholic Church. In 1963 Pavlik created a separate jurisdiction and consecrated his successor, Nelson D. Hillyer (1912–1987). Hillyer was eventually succeeded by Frederick P. Dunleavy. Dunleavy was consecrated in 1988 by Bp. Karl Pruter (1920–2007) of the Christ Catholic Church and in 1991 succeeded him.

In 1992, negotiation between the Liberal Catholic Church of Ontario and Christ Catholic Church began and resulted in Dunleavy's bringing his jurisdiction into what became Christ Catholic Church International. An election for bishop of the new church resulted in the selection of Most Rev. Donald W. Mullan.

The period immediately following the merger included further expansion. Rt. Rev. Gerard La Plante and the Old Catholic Church of British Columbia Society joined the CCCI and four former priests of the Mercian Orthodox Catholic Church were granted "Episcopal protection" by the CCCI.

The Old Catholic Church of British Columbia Society dates to the mid-1920s and the establishment of an independent Catholic parish in Vancouver under the leadership of Fr. J. P. Kirk. Kirk was succeeded by Fr. H. J. Barney, who served the parish for over 30 years. He was succeeded by Fr. Gerard LaPlante in 1975. In 1978 the church, finding itself no longer in full agreement, became independent, and Fr. LaPlante was consecrated as bishop. While autonomous, the church remained in full communion with the LCCO.

Issues that came to the fore in the early years of Christ Catholic Church International included some objections to the church's St. Francis Liturgy that contained selections from the post-Vatican II Roman Catholic liturgy. The actions of the College of Bishops were questioned by several clergy who felt that the consecration of three of the Mercian priests had been premature.

The new church also affiliated with the ecumenical Fellowship of Independent Orthodox Churches. Bishop Pruter led the opposition to membership, which he saw as a major mistake by the church's leadership. Pruter came out of retirement and reorganized Christ Catholic Church. CCC and CCCI have continued in dialogue, and hope for eventual reconciliation is high.

CCCI is both Old Catholic and Orthodox Catholic in faith and practice. CCCI holds to the teachings of the first seven Ecumenical Councils, the Declaration of the Old Catholic Union of Utrecht, and the creeds of the undivided church. As part of the mystical Body of Christ, CCCI affirms and teaches an apostolic succession vested in the bishops of the Catholic Church and passes that succession through Holy Orders. The holding of such Holy Orders is a prerequisite for the valid celebration of the sacraments. The CCCI further believes that each bishop has the teaching/administrative authority granted to the apostles by Jesus Christ, and that this authority is not limited to a single bishop regardless of office or position, but is equally and jointly held by all bishops.

Matters of faith and morals may be defined for the church only by the College of Bishops in light of Sacred Scripture and Apostolic Tradition.

CCCI is a founding member of the Federation of Orthodox Catholic Churches United Sacramentally (FOCUS), and during the period of its membership has been led to emphasize the Orthodox element of its faith and practice.

Membership: In 2002 the church reported more than 7,800 members worldwide of which 2,960 were in the United States, 3,880 in Canada, and 1,000 in Europe and Australia.

Educational Facilities:

St. Mary's Seminary, Niagara Falls, Ontario.

Periodicals: *St. Luke Magazine.*

Sources:

Christ Catholic Church International. www3.sympatico.ca/dwmullan/HOME.HTM

Christ Catholic Orthodox Church

St. Francis House, 2079 Harkness Ave., Cincinnati, OH 45225

Christ Catholic Orthodox Church, an American Orthodox Christian church, originally the Western Orthodox Church in America, was founded by then Rev. James F. Mondok, who was given a mandate to build the church. It was granted a charter in January 1984 by the state of Ohio. Reverend Mondok was consecrated in June 1984 in Pittsburgh, Pennsylvania, by Abp. Charles David Luther, assisted by Bps. Alan Bain and Paul Brennan. He established his seat in Euclid, Ohio. The church traces its lineage through Carlos Duarte Costa and Stephen Meyer Corradi-Scarella, as well as the African Orthodox Church, among other lines of episcopal succession. The church's name change occurred in 1988.

Christ Catholic Orthodox Church uses a modern Orthodox Divine Liturgy. Seminarians are trained at St. Seraphim's Center for Theological Studies. Associated with the church is an Orthodox branch of the Secular Order of St. Francis and the Minor Order of Paduans, an order devoted to St. Anthony of Padua. The church sees itself as following the intention of Abp. Aftimios Ofiesh in building a broad American Orthodox church (as opposed to an ethnically based Orthodox church operating in the United States). The church teaches that in extreme cases, women may become ordained priests. Clergy may be married.

The church is headed by a council of bishops that includes Presiding Bp. James Mondok and Abps. Frank Vandeventer and Most Rev. Michael Hembree. They lead the church in participation in a variety of ecumenical outreach programs, including work in hospitals and in chaplaincies throughout the world.

Membership: Not reported.

Educational Facilities:

St. Seraphim's Center for Theological Studies, Cleveland, Ohio.

Periodicals: *The Voice of the Fisherman.*

Sources:

Christ Catholic Orthodox Church. www.ind-movement.org/denoms/ccoc_mondok/index.html.

Christian Catholic Church (Old Catholic) in the United States of America

1205 Thomas Blvd., Springdale, AR 72762

The Christian Catholic Church (Old Catholic) in the United States of America is an independent Old Catholic jurisdiction founded on July 9, 1988, by its present presiding bishop, Mt. Rev. Raymond E. Sawyer (b. 1946), assisted by Mt. Rev. Albert W. Smith, who serves as the church's suffragan bishop. On May 10, 1988, the Synod of the Old Catholic Diocese of Salt Lake City and Dependencies (now part of the Christian Catholic Church) named Sawyer bishop-elect, and he was consecrated in the Cathedral Church of Saint Luke the Evangelist on July 9, 1988, with immediate canonical release, by Abps. Andre Barbeau and Andre Letellier of the Catholic Charismatic Church of Canada. In 1990 he received consecration, *sub conditione* (with conditions), from Bp. Karl Pruter of Christ Catholic Church. Bishop Smith (b. 1951) was consecrated by Bishop Sawyer on July 3, 1989.

The Christian Catholic Church accepts the authority of the first Seven Ecumenical Councils of the undivided Church; the ancient creeds, and the traditional mysteries or sacraments (seven) of the Church. It also accepts the Orthodox proscription against modification to the Nicene Creed (and hence does not include the filioque clause) in the text of the creed as repeated in the Mass. Western Rite liturgies are utilized, though with special permission; Anglican or Episcopal parishes that are admitted into the jurisdiction may use the Liturgy of St. Tikkhon (an amended liturgy of the *Book of Common Prayer* used by canonical Orthodoxy for that same purpose). Women may not be admitted to the priesthood.

The church is a member of the Federation of Independent Catholic and Orthodox Bishops.

Membership: Not reported.

Christian Orthodox Catholic Church

United States Chancery Office, 795 La Playa St., No. 1, San Francisco, CA 94121-3258

The Christian Catholic Church was founded in 1988 by Most Rev. Richard P. Lane, its presiding bishop. Lane had previously served for 16 years as a priest in the North American Old Roman Catholic Church-Utrecht Succession and two years as Episcopal vicar to Abp. E. R. Verostek, the church's presiding bishop. Verostek consecrated Lane in 1987. The Christian Orthodox Catholic Church was formed the same year that Verostek retired. It was Lane's opinion that the more traditional approaches of the Church did not meet the needs of the people and he has taken the lead in developing an updated liturgy and offering contemporary forms of spirituality while remaining in the basic orthodox Old Catholic theological structure of the North American Old Roman Catholic Church.

The church adheres to the Apostles' and Nicene Creeds and the doctrines promulgated by seven Ecumenical Councils. It practices an open communion to which all baptized Christians, of any denomination, may participate. Seven sacraments are celebrated. Married men are admitted to the priesthood.

The church is headed by Bishop Lane. There is one diocese (California), two districts (Illinois and Arizona), and a protectorate (Florida).

Membership: Not reported.

Educational Facilities:

St. Ignatius School of Theology, San Francisco, California.

Christ's Apostolic Church of North America

c/o Most Rev. Ronald D. Nowlan, D.D., Chancery Office, 316 Hullett St., Long Beach, CA 90805-3424

Christ's Apostolic Church of North America is a small Old Catholic jurisdiction whose primate, Most Rev. Ronald D. Nowlan, holds lines of apostolic succession derived from the Roman Catholic Church, the Old Catholic Church of Utrecht, and the Brazilian National Catholic Church. The church was founded with the intention of establishing independent ministries, most operating out of private homes, throughout the United States.

The church uses an Old Catholic liturgy, but others are acceptable. Archbishop Nowlan is assisted by the Vicar General for North America, Most Rev. Irwin Young, and the diocese's chancellor, Rt. Rev. Msgr. Harvey Beagle. The church has good relations with the Independent Catholic Church of America headed by Most Rev. Maurice McCormick.

Membership: Not reported.

Church of St. Joseph

2307 S. Laramie, Cicero, IL 60650

The Church of Saint Joseph began as an independent traditionalist Catholic parish in the 1960s by Fr. Henry Lovett, a former associate of Fr. Gommar A. DePauw (1918–2005), head of the Catholic Traditionalist Movement. Lovett moved to Illinois from New Jersey with the intention of creating a parish to be aligned with DePauw's efforts, but disagreements with him led to the founding of St. Joseph's as a completely independent effort. Lovett looked at several other traditionalist groups (i.e., those opposed to the innovations of Vatican II), but rejected affiliation with any. In 1970 he met John Higgins, who had recently been consecrated as a bishop by Pope Clement XV, the traditionalist French priest who claimed to be the true pope. Higgins was consecrated soon after Bp. Jean de la Trinite, head of the Order of the Mother of God and Clement's major North American supporter, had

broken away from Clement's jurisdiction. Lovett invited Higgins to come to Cicero as the episcopal leader for the parish.

Higgins first heard of Michael Collin, the French papal claimant, while studying in Rome. Higgins traveled to Clemery, Lorraine, where he concluded he had discovered the secret of Fatima. In 1917 at Fatima, Portugal, three children claimed to have seen the Blessed Virgin. Among the several messages she gave was one "secret," which was supposed to be revealed in 1960. As of 1986, that secret, written down by one of the three children who saw the Virgin, is the private possession of the Vatican and has never been revealed. Speculation on its content has been a major object of speculation by Marian devotees. Higgins believed that the content of the message was that beginning in 1960, "There shall be no more conclaves for the election of the Pope." Instead, each pope will choose his successor. Pope John XXIII, it is claimed, chose Clement XV.

Higgins saw Clement as the instrument by which the Roman Catholic Church could be returned to its pre-Vatican II state. However, following Clement's death in 1974, Higgins broke with the French followers and refused to accept any of the several claimants to his position. The parish follows pre-Vatican belief and practice, except for its belief in Clement's authority.

Membership: There is but a single congregation affiliated with Bishop Higgins, with several hundred members.

Sources:

Blei, Norbert. "Catholics Reborn." *Chicago Sunday Sun-Times, Midwest Magazine* (November 30, 1975).

Church of Utrecht in America

2103 S. Portland St., Los Angeles, CA 90007

HISTORY. The Church of Utrecht in America, formerly known as the American Prelature, continues the ministry begun by Abp. Richard A. Marchenna (1932–1982) as the Old Roman Catholic Church. Marchenna's consecration to the bishopric in 1941 by Abp. Carmel Henry Carfora (1916–1958) began a tumultuous career in Carfora's North American Old Roman Catholic Church culminated in his deposition and excommunication in 1952. With several clergy and four parishes, he organized the Old Roman Catholic Church and entered into communion with Gerard George Shelley, originally consecrated by Marchenna. Shelley, while serving as bishop in England, had received the lineage of B. M. Williams, and claimed the direct succession of Abp. Arnold Harris Mathew, who had founded the Old Catholic Church in England.

Following Carfora's death, Marchenna laid claim to Carfora's succession through Cyrus A. Starkey (1932–1965). Starkey, Carfora's coadjutor, who left the North American Old Roman Catholic Church after Carfora's death, had asked Marchenna to become the supreme primate of the Old Roman Catholic Church.

Marchenna slowly put together one of the larger of the Old Catholic jurisdictions. Then, in 1974, he consecrated an openly homosexual priest, Fr. Robert Clement, head of the Eucharistic Catholic Church. That action led to his break with Shelley and the loss of many of his priests. Following Marchenna's death, Derek Lang, formerly Episcopal vicar for Nicaragua and regionary bishop for North America at the time of Marchenna's death, assumed the leadership of the now decimated jurisdiction. Among other offices, Marchenna had appointed Lang Titular Bishop of Middleburg (a sixteenth-century diocese that had ceased to exist). He began to reorganize it into the American Prelature, thus "replacing the less modest titles and structures used by his predecessors." He also moved the headquarters to the West Coast. More recently, the American Prelature became the Church of Utrecht in America.

BELIEFS. The Church of Utrecht in America follows the belief and practices of pre-Vatican I Roman Catholicism and the North American Old Roman Catholic Church, differing only in matters of administration. It accepts the decrees promulgated by the Council of Trent (1565) but does not accept the infallibility of the pope or other documents related to the excessive powers inherent in the pope's teaching office.

ORGANIZATION. The Church of Utrecht in America is headed by its archbishop. He oversees work in Los Angeles, California, and a hospital, seminary, and mission in Nicaragua.

Membership: In 1988 the church reported approximately 2,000 members (and some 20,000 constituents), mostly in Nicaragua. There were two centers in Los Angeles.

Educational Facilities:

St. Martin's Seminary, La Esperanza, Zelaya, Nicaragua.

Sources:

Old Catholic Church (Utrecht Succession). Chicago: Old Catholic Press of Chicago [1980].

Church Universal and Global

PO Box 7512, Alexandria, VA 22307

The Church Universal and Global was founded in 2002 by Bp. Daniel Clay. Ordained in 1980 in a Pentecostal church by Reverend Paul Dixon, Clay then obtained ordination from the Calvary Grace Church of Faith. He subsequently founded the divine assembly of the holy prophets. During the 1990s, he grew close to the Old Catholic tradition and was consecrated as bishop for that United Catholic Church's Diocese of Virginia on July 22, 2001. He later left the UCC and founded the small independent body that currently serves as a vehicle for his widespread ministry.

Though an Old Catholic bishop, Clay is best known for his many prophecies, several of which were delivered in July 1996 and later compiled into a book, *The Prophecies of His Divine Grace Daniel Clay* (1997). According to the book, as a young child Clay had extraordinary healing and clairvoyant abilities. According to Clay, the prophecies were given so that people may have knowledge of forthcoming events and may use this information to advantage as the events occur. The prophecies are extensive and cover a host of topics. There is a set of prophecies specifically aimed at the various nations of the world. He also predicts a giant earthquake that will split the United States into two parts.

Clay also notes that all prophecies can be altered by the changing consciousness of humanity.

Membership: Not reported.

Sources:

Clay, Daniel. *The Fables and Parables of His Divine Grace Daniel Clay.* Vincentown, NJ: Haas Publications, 1993.

———. *Prophecies of His Divine Grace Daniel Clay.* Vincentown, NJ: Haas Publications, 1997.

Community of Catholic Churches

Current address not obtained for this edition.

The Community of Catholic Churches is a small jurisdiction formed in 1971 as a result of a group of Old Catholic priests and bishops deciding to abandon the traditional Catholic hierarchical structure. They removed the purely administrative functions from their ecclesiastical offices and formed a fellowship of clergy and parishes. Priests kept their sacerdotal functions and provided priestly leadership for the parishes, most of which are house churches. The group is led by Sr. Bp. Thomas Sargent and Convenor, the Most Rev. Lorraine Morgenson.

The Community generally follows Catholic doctrine and practice, but sets no particular doctrinal standard for members. It also allows the option of dual membership in other churches. It differs from other Old Catholic groups in its willingness to ordain both females and homosexuals to the priesthood.

Membership: Not reported.

Continuing Apostolic United States Episcopacy

1718 Moseley Dr., Hopkinsville, KY 42240

The Continuing Apostolic United States Episcopacy was founded in 2001 by Abp. Maximilian-Anthony (Gregory Godsey, b. 1979). The future archbishop was raised a Roman Catholic. However, in 1998, he joined the Independent Catholics movement and was ordained as a priest by Bishop Ford of the Independent Catholic Church in 1999. Later that year he was consecrated as a bishop, also by Ford.

In June 2001, he left the Independent Catholics and affiliated with the Continuing Anglican Movement, specifically with the Diocese of the Holy Spirit, headed by Bp. Steven Murrell. However, four months later he left Murrell's jurisdiction to found the Continuing Anglican United States Episcopacy. The Episcopacy assumed its present name in 2002.

The Episcopacy is a conservative Anglican body that affirms Christ's true presence in the Eucharist, apostolic succession, a priesthood exercised exclusively by heterosexual males, and the teaching of the seven historic ecumenical councils. Outside of holy orders, women as lay people may exercise the office of deaconess as a form of ministry. The clergy are allowed to marry.

Through the Union of Traditional Apostolic Churches, the Episcopacy has relations with the Orthodox Catholic Church of America, the Vetro-Catholic Church in Brazil, and the Cistercian Order of the Holy Cross.

Membership: Not reported.

Diocese of Ecumenical and Old Catholic Faith Communities

c/o Saint Matthew Church, 1111 W. Town and Country Rd., Orange, CA 92868

The Diocese of Ecumenical and Old Catholic Faith Communities traces its history to 1985 and the founding of Saint Matthew Old Catholic Mission Church of Tustin, Orange County, California, by Fr. Peter Hickman. The original congregation consisted of six people. The following year, the church relocated to Huntington Beach and growth continued at a slow pace, highlighted by the adherence of Fr. Jim Faris, a former Roman Catholic priest. In 1989 the parish relocated a second time, to Orange, California. Several other former priests associated with the church, and in 1992 Fr. Dan Gincig was sent by the church to Aurora, Colorado (a Denver suburb), to found a mission affiliated with St. Matthew's. Later that year another parish was begun in Lakewood, California. In 1993 St. Matthew's became a co-founder of Xela-Aid, a humanitarian relief organization assisting people in Guatemala, and continues that support.

In 1995 the congregation at St. Matthew's voted to support Hickman's consecration as a bishop. The idea was presented to the Ecumenical Communion of Catholic and Apostolic Churches (ECCAC) whose bishops approved of his candidacy. In the meantime, Gincig had been consecrated by R. Augustin Sicard, and his mission in Colorado had grown into the independent American Old Catholic Church. In 1996 he consecrated Hickman.

The diocese shares a common theology and liturgical tradition with the Roman Catholic Church, but identifies with the Old Catholic rejection of Papal infallibility. It also does not accept Roman Catholic canon law. It places a particular emphasis on the role of the laity symbolized by its polity of lay participation in the selection of bishops and pastors of congregations. The diocese allows priests to marry, allows couples the use of tools for birth control, and is open to the remarriage of the divorced. Women may be ordained to the priesthood and the church affirms "the dignity of all human persons regardless of race, national origin, religious affiliation, gender, or sexual orientation."

The new diocese has grown both by the addition of older parishes and by opening new ones. Included among its parishes is a Lithuanian parish in Minnesota and a Spanish-speaking parish in Huntington Beach, California.

Membership: Not reported. As of 2002, the diocese had nine churches scattered across the United States.

Sources:

Diocese of Ecumenical and Old Catholic Faith Communities. www.saint-matthew.org/.

Ecclesia Catholica Traditionalis "Conservare et Praedicare"

PO Box 26414, San Francisco, CA 94126-6414

The Ecclesia Catholica Traditionalis "Conservare et Praedicare" is an independent Catholic Church community whose mission is "to preserve and to proclaim" the traditional Catholic faith. It holds all the truths, doctrines, and dogmata of the Catholic Church since its Apostolic beginnings and subscribes to all seven Ecumenical Councils of the Church, as well as subsequent councils in accord with the tradition of the church, the early fathers, and sacred Scripture.

The community is jurisdictionally independent of the Holy See, although it acknowledges the Bishop of Rome (the Pope) as the successor of St. Peter and spiritual head of the Church. The community received an Apostolic Blessing from Pope John Paul II on July 13, 1985.

The community undertakes as its special vocation to preserve and practice the traditional liturgy of the church as a living liturgy. The western rite of the community preserves in full the traditional Latin ("Tridentine") rite, in addition to the Dominican rite. The eastern rite of the community preserves the East Syriac rite. The community preserves and administers the seven sacraments and sacramentals in their traditional form.

Originally founded on May 22, 1983, by the Most Rev. Thaddeus B. J. Alioto as the Ancient Tridentine Catholic Church, the community changed its legally registered name on May 29, 1990, to Ecclesia Catholica Traditionalis "Conservare et Praedicare." The community's Archbishop Primate Thaddeus was consecrated on May 22, 1983, by His Beatitude Mar David I (Wallace David de Ortega Maxey, 1902–1992), whose apostolic succession descends through His Eminence Antonio Cardinal Barerini, nephew of Pope Urban VII, and through additional Eastern lines.

Membership: In January 1992 the overall community consisted of five activity centers: the secular western-rite community of Sts. Dominic and Francis (San Francisco) and four religious communities: The Franciscan Mariavite Monastery of St. Mary of the Angels of the Little Portion (Kelseyville, California); the eastern-rite Mt. Izla Monastery (Curlew, Washington); the eastern-rite Valley Mission of St. Thomas (Fall City, Washington); and the western-rite third Order of St. Dominic (Glendale, Oregon). The community is served by a total of nine priests and eight other clergy and religious.

Remarks: Mar David I's career has carried him through a variety of ecclesiastical organizations and positions. In 1951 he resigned his position with the Catholicate of the West and joined the Universalist Church. In 1970 (at a time when the Catholicate had no American parishes or priests in the United States) he resumed his Episcopal role and consecrated Alan S. Stanford, with whom he founded the Catholic Christian Church. A few years later, however, he disassociated himself from Stanford.

Ecumenical Catholic Church USA

c/o Rt. Rev. Senia Fix, 23 Atrium Way, Englishtown, NJ 07726

Ecumenical Catholic Church USA (not to be confused with the Ecumenical Catholic Church) was founded in the mid-1990s. Its presiding bishop, Carl Thomas Swaringim, was consecrated in 1996 by Bp. William Dennis Donovan, assisted by Grant Cover and Maurice McCormick as co-consecrators, who together represent several Old Catholic and Orthodox lines of succession.

The church is at one in doctrine and practice with the Western Old Catholic tradition, adhering to the seven sacraments and the creeds of the ancient church. It upholds the practice of the liturgy of the mass, the invocation of the saints, and the veneration of the Blessed Virgin Mary. It differs in that it welcomes women to the priesthood and episcopacy and allows priests to marry. No attempt is made to define the nature of the real presence in the Eucharist (such as the Roman Catholic doctrine of transubstantiation). In the tradition of British Old Catholic bishop Arnold Harris Mathew, the church leadership is largely in the hands of worker priests, meaning that during the week, the priests work at secular jobs from which they make their living.

In the matter of issues currently under discussion among various independent catholic churches, the Ecumenical Catholic Church USA allows the practice of artificial birth control and will offer the sacraments to divorced persons. In addition, while recognizing that celibacy may be the preferred state of life for a divorced person, the church acknowledges that few have the gift for such a life. Hence the church will marry previously divorced persons with its blessings. The church draws the line at homosexuality. It will neither ordain homosexuals nor perform weddings or union services for homosexual couples. The church practices open communion and allows any baptized person to participate fully in the service of the Mass, and to receive the eucharistic elements regularly.

The church is divided into two dioceses, one of which, serving the eastern states, is headed by a female. There are also a number of ministries supported by the church, including several ordered communities and an Internet correspondence seminary, Sanctus Theological Institute, a school jointly sponsored by a spectrum of independent Catholic jurisdictions. David Mark Kocka serves as the presiding bishop.

Educational Facilities:

Sanctus Theological Institute, Mesa, Arizona

Vilatte Theological Seminary, O'Fallon, Missouri

Sources:

Ecumenical Catholic Church USA. www.ecc-usa.org.

Ecumenical Catholic Diocese of America

151 Regent Pl., West Hemstead, NY 11552

In 1984 a number of former priests of the Roman Catholic Church formulated a plan for responding to the unresolved problems of Vatican II. Growing out of a number of renewal groups, the priests sought a means to implement a practical ecumenism that would bring Christians together across denominational lines: equal rights for females; a more pastoral approach to divorce and remarriage; and a role for married priests. Many of the leaders of the new movement were themselves married. The priests called for an alternative church-like organization characterized by all of the features of institutionalized Catholicism, but flexible enough to respond to the major unresolved problems. Such an organization would provide a place for those not served by the Roman Catholic Church, such as married priests, former nuns, and dissatisfied Catholics who were having difficulty forming their spiritual lives.

Plans for the new diocese were implemented at a gathering in Chicago in August 1984 by representatives of four Catholic renewal groups: The Federation of Christian Ministries, Women Church Speaks, CORPUS, and Maryknoll-in-Diaspora. Prior to the gathering, Fr. Peter Brennan of West Hempstead, New York, received Old Catholic Episcopal orders and was chosen the diocese's first bishop.

The Ecumenical Catholic Diocese of America considers itself a progressive Roman Catholic Church attempting to move the church in a progressive, rather than conservative, direction. Except for those issues that brought it into existence, the Ecumenical Catholic Diocese of America is in basic agreement with the Roman Catholic Church. It considers itself under the wider pastoral care of the pope and views the papacy as the center of Christian unity. While respecting the pope, the Ecumenical Catholic Diocese of America is jurisdictionally independent.

Membership: Not reported.

Ecumenical Old Catholic Church

c/o Grace House, 7451 NW 23 St., Margate, FL 33063

The Ecumenical Old Catholic Church was founded by its bishop, John Hardy. Hardy had been raised as a Roman Catholic and later attended King's College London and the London School of Economics. As a lecturer with the Faculty of Monastic Studies at Ealing Abbey he became familiar with the Western mystical traditions and as an editor for George Allen & Unwin he came to know Eastern traditions. At one point he spent half a year in Korea as a guest of the Chogye Buddhist Order. He was ordained a priest in the 1980s and consecrated a bishop on February 23, 1992, in the lineage of the Liberal Catholic Church through James Ingall Wedgewood.

The new church sees itself as a radical Christian community that is attempting to respond to the need some have expressed to move beyond denominational religion and its structures. It identifies with eastern orthodox mysticism, but rejects the allegiance to ethnic and political concerns.

The church perpetuates a traditional sacramentalism, but at the same time respects intellectual freedom and encourages members to think for themselves. The church attempts to respond to the post-modern world and speak to the present conditions of modern humanity. It also attempts to be global in its approach. The church identifies itself as Catholic in that it proclaims that we are what we are meant to be when we are "in Christ." At the same time, it sees itself as a reformed community, hence Protestant, meaning that nothing must be allowed to come between the individual and God. In this light, the role of the Church is primarily therapeutic—to assist in the development of insights for growth and to help one overcome life's obstacles.

The church differs from the Christian tradition in its belief that all the great religions of the world express God's presence. The effect of that belief is an openness to looking for God's presence in a multitude of contexts, not specifically Christian. The church also allows married priests, is open to female ordination, and has created a welcoming atmosphere for gay and lesbian members.

The single American congregation, in southern Florida, is headed by Henry Breitenkam.

Membership: In 2002 there were two congregations, one in London and one in the Greater Fort Lauderdale area in Florida.

Evangelical Catholic Church

PO Box 26824, Scottsdale, AZ 85255-0160

The Evangelical Catholic Church began as a movement to promote liturgical piety within the Lutheran Church—Missouri Synod in Michigan and Indiana. In 1965 a small group founded the Order of the Servants of the Holy Cross. That society withdrew from the Missouri Synod in the early 1970s and in 1977 affiliated as a monastic order with the newly formed Evangelical Catholic Church under the leadership of Rev. Karl Julius Barwin. Barwin was consecrated in 1989 by the bishops Bertil Persson, Emilio Federico Rodriguez y Fairfield, Arthur J. Garrow, Carroll Lowery, and Howard Van Orden. Barwin's apostolic lineage is Orthodox and, through Perrson, can be traced to Patriarch Alexy of Moscow.

Barwin affirms roots within the Lutheran community, and the Evangelical Catholic Church is seen as representative of those Lutherans who most closely affirm their place within the larger Catholic world. The church's emblem incorporates Martin Luther's coat of arms within it, and the *Book of Concord* is accepted as a doctrinal standard. The church has a high Lutheran understanding of the Eucharist. It is unique in its belief that the Eucharist should be given to infants and children who are confirmed at the time of baptism.

During the 1980s the Order of the Servants of the Holy Cross disbanded. The Confraternity of the Holy Sacrament of the Sacred Body and Most Precious Blood of Our Lord Jesus Christ is currently associated with the church. The confraternity is a devotional society that advocates a return to Catholic piety and the adoration of Christ in the Eucharist. It is headed by its secretary-general, Ronald A. Cross. In 1993 the Center for Christian Arts and Iconography in Republic, Missouri, affiliated with the ECC.

Membership: In 1995 the church reported three congregations serving 18 families.

Periodicals: *The Intercession Paper.*

Sources:

Evangelical Catholic Church. members.aol.com/EvCathCh/index.HTML.

The Church. Phoenix, AZ: Evangelical Catholic Church, n.d. Brochure.

Infant Communion. Phoenix, AZ: Evangelical Catholic Church, n.d. Brochure.

Federation of Christian Ministries

1709 W 69th St. #3, Cleveland, OH 44102-2957

The Federation of Christian Ministries began in 1968 as the Society for Priests for a Free Ministry, an organization that lobbied for a role for married priests in the Roman Catholic Church. The Roman Catholic Church had refused to provide an opening for married priests within its Latin Rite, in which the overwhelming majority of priests functioned, though some married priests were present in the several Eastern rites.

Participation in that debate and reaction to the church's refusal to accept married priests led the group to reconsider its position, reflected in its name changes in 1971 (Fellowship of Christian Ministries) and 1981 (Federation of Christian Ministries). Clergy members of the organization began to see their ministry as based in Christian communities, and saw the legitimacy of their ministry as based in their call to ministry and community in baptism, rather than in the formal ordination from church authorities. As the group evolved it began to sanction an inclusive sacramental ministry under the leadership of both married and unmarried priests, and to accept female priests.

Today the Federation has emerged as a renewal community and coalition of small faith communities that offers training and ordination to candidates for the ministry and sacramental services (including baptisms, weddings, and funerals). The Federation continues to use a Roman Catholic theological and sacramental format, and welcomes those who feel otherwise rejected and alienation by the church.

Among the best known of the priests associated with the Federation is Bridget Mary Meehan, one of eight women ordained as priests on July 31, 2006, in Pittsburgh, Pennsylvania, by three women bishops who had been ordained by Roman Catholic male bishops. All involved in the original consecrations of the three women and in their subsequent ordinations were excommunicated from the Roman Catholic Church, but their ordinations are considered valid, if irregular.

Membership: In 2008 the Federation reported 32 faith communities served by some 33 priests scattered across the United States. There is also an outpost in Peru, headed by Bp. Sean M. Walsh.

Sources:

Federation of Christian Ministries. www.federationofchristianministries.org/.

Meehan, Bridget Mary, and Mary Beben. *Walking the Prophetic Journey: Eucharistic Liturgies for Twenty-first Century Small Faith Communities*. Sofia, 2007.

Meehan, Bridget Mary, and Regina Madonna Oliver. *A Promise of Presence*. Sofia, 2007.

Fellowship of Independent and Global Churches and Ministries

PO Box 112, Garrisonville, VA 22463

The Fellowship of Independent and Global Churches and Ministries is an association made up of independent Christian congregations and parachurch ministries that wish to find partnerships in their pilgrimage of faith and service while retaining a high degree of local independence. The Fellowship affords such freedom to members, but at the same time creates a degree of accountability toward those churches with which members partner.

The Fellowship was founded in 2002 by Bishop William P. Brown, a former Baptist minister who founded a church in Stafford, Virginia, that grew to become the Mt. Zion Full Gospel Cathedral, a Pentecostal congregation. Through the 1990s, Bishop Brown had worked widely in ecumenical circles and headed several ecumenical organizations.

In January 2003, Bishop Brown was received into the World Bishops Council, whose president, Abp. Timothy Paul Baymon, is also the metropolitan bishop of the International Communion of the Holy Christian Orthodox Church. Baymon passed his lineage of apostolic succession to Bishop Brown in August 2003. Brown now also serves as prelate for the Fredericksburg, Virginia, diocese and as the titular bishop for North America of the Christian Orthodox Church.

The Fellowship is led by a College of Bishops, which is split into two boards (or houses). All of the bishops in the Fellowship together constitute the General Board. From them are drawn the Executive Board of Bishops, which includes the first presiding bishop (currently Bishop Brown), the first and second vice—presiding bishops, the general secretary bishop, and the ecumenical liaison bishop. The work of the Fellowship is currently divided into twelve dioceses and one archdiocese.

Membership: Not reported.

Educational Facilities:

Faith University and Schools.

American Bible College of Oklahoma.

Sources:

Fellowship of Independent and Global Churches and Ministries. web.mawebcenters.com/fig/about.ivnu.

Evangelical Orthodox (Catholic) Church in America (Non-Papal Catholic)

c/o Most Rev. Perry Sills, 1213 N San Pedro St., San Jose, CA 95110-1436

The Evangelical Orthodox (Catholic) Church in America (Non-Papal Catholic) was originally founded as the Protestant Orthodox Western Church in 1938 by Bp. Wilhelm Waterstraat in Santa Monica, California. When he retired in 1940 he chose as his successor Fr. Frederick Littler Pyman (d. 1993). In 1943 Pyman was consecrated bishop by Abp. Carmel Henry Carfora (1878–1958), of the North American Old Roman Catholic Church (Rogers). Under Bishop Pyman the Protestant Orthodox Western Church remained an integral part of Archbishop Carfora's jurisdiction until 1948, when Pyman withdrew and changed the name of the church to the Evangelical Orthodox (Catholic) Church in America (Non-Papal Catholic).

Bishop Pyman had hoped to create a "bridge church," and he led his small denomination in adopting the Leipsic Interim of 1548, a document drawn up as part of a sixteenth-century process to reconcile Protestant and Catholic differences. But the twentieth-century promulgation under Bp. Wilhelm Waterstraat and Bishop Pyman drew no reaction from either Protestants or Catholics.

In most respects the church adheres closely to the Old Catholic position. The church recognizes the office and authority of the Supreme Pontiff, but only Christ is considered infallible. Clerical celibacy is optional. Oral confession is not required. Both the Latin and vernacular mass is said.

Upon Bishop Pyman's retirement in the 1970s, the leadership of the church passed to Abp. Perry R. Sills, who had been enthroned as Bishop Pyman's successor and Second Regionary Bishop on June 30, 1974. On the previous day he had been consecrated by Archbishop Pyman and Bps. Larry L. Shaver, William Elliot Littlewood, and Basil. In 1984 Sills affiliated with the Patriarchial Synod of the Orthodox Catholic Church of America, an association of independent bishops.

Membership: In the early 1980s the church reported six parishes and 10 clergy, but gave no membership figures.

Sources:

Evangelical Orthodox (Catholic) Church in America (Non-Papal Catholic). www.evangelicalorthodoxcatholic.org/.

The Evangelical Orthodox (Catholic) Church. Santa Monica, CA: Committee on Education, Regionary Diocese of the West, 1949.

For My God and My Country

W5703 Shrine Rd., Neceda, WI 54646-7916

For My God and My Country is an organization which developed as a result of the visions of the Blessed Virgin Mary by Mary Ann Van Hoof (1909–1984) and the subsequent establishment of the Queen of the Holy Rosary Mediatrix of Peace Shrine, an independent Catholic shrine at Necedah, Wisconsin. Van Hoof had her first apparition of the Virgin on November 12, 1949, one year after a reported apparition in Lipa City, Philippines. Then on April 7, 1950 (Good Friday), a series of apparitions were announced by the Virgin and,as promised, occurred on May 28 (Pentecost), May 29, May 30, June 4 (Trinity Sunday), June 16 (Feast of the Sacred Heart), and August 15 (Feast of the Assumption). As word of the apparitions spread, crowds gathered. More than 100,000 people attended the events of August 15, 1950.

On June 24, 1950, the chancery office of the Diocese of La-Crosse (Wisconsin) released information that a study of the apparitions had been initiated. In August, Bp. John Treacy (1891–1964) announced that preliminary reports had questioned the validity of the apparitions, and he placed a temporary ban on special religious services at Necedah. He temporarily lifted the ban for the announced event on August 15. An estimated 30,000 people attended a final apparition on October 7, at which it was claimed that the sun whirled in the sky just as at the more famous site of Marian apparitions at Fatima, Portugal in 1917. On October 18, the group that had grown around Van Hoof published an account of the visions and announced that a shrine was to be built and completed by May 28, 1951, the anniversary of the first public apparition.

In spite of the negative appraisal by Bishop Treacy and an editorial in the Vatican's newspaper in 1951 condemning the visions, the activity at Necedah continued, and people attended the public events at which Van Hoof claimed to be conversing with the Virgin Mary. Finally, in June 1955, Treacy issued a public statement declaring the revelations at Necedah false and prohibiting all public and private worship at the shrine. Approximately 650 pilgrims attended the August 15, 1955 (Feast of the Assumption), apparition in defiance of Treacy's ban. In September, details of the exhaustive study of the shrine (by then operating under the corporate name For My God and My Country, Inc.) were released. The report attacked Van Hoof as a former spiritualist who had never been a practicing Roman Catholic. While the report of the diocese lessened support, worship at the shrine continued, and efforts were made to have a second study conducted. Finally, in 1969, Bp. F.W. Freking, Treacy's successor as bishop of LaCrosse, agreed to reexamine the case. For a time during the study, the shrine was closed to visitors. In 1970 the commission again produced a negative report, and in June 1972, Freking warned the corporation officers to cease activities or face church sanctions. Such sanctions were invoked in May 1975, when seven people were put under an interdict. In spite of the interdict, the work at the shrine has continued although there were several problems in the intervening years. In 1979, leaders of the shrine affiliated it with the small independent North American Old Catholic Church, Ultrajectine Tradition. In the wake of the resignation of the bishops and priests of that church, it dissolved (see Remarks). Then on May 18, 1984, Mary Ann Van Hoof died. In spite of these setbacks, the group that has developed around the shrine, many of whose members had moved into the immediate area, have continued to pursue the program initiated under the direction of the visions. In line with a strong anti-abortion polemic, the Seven Sorrows of Our Sorrowful Mother Infant's Home has been opened to assist unwed mothers and unwanted children. The construction of the St. Francis Home for Unfortunate Men has also continued, and work on the House of Prayer constructed at the Sacred Spot of the Apparitions has been initiated.

In the years since Van Hoof's death, a large "House of Prayer" has been built over the site where the apparitions were said to have appeared. It sits in the midst of the shrine grounds that contain numerous statues of different saints, a replica of the Van Hoof home, and a God and Country Shrine featuring figures of George Washington, Abraham Lincoln, and Jesus together. The shrine has developed its own annual liturgical calendar built around major church holidays and anniversaries of seminal events in Van Hoof's career.

Membership: Not reported.

Periodicals: *Shrine Newsletter.*

Remarks: For several years the shrine was affiliated with the now defunct North American Old Roman Catholic Church, Ultrajectine Tradition. That affiliation was formally acknowledged in May 1979, with the presentation to the shrine's supporters of Old Catholic Bishop Edward Michael Stehlik as archbishop and metropolitan of the church. On May 28, 1979, Stehlik dedicated the shrine, 29 years after the first public apparition. The church was at one in doctrine with the Roman Catholic Church, except in its rejection of the authority of the papal office. Stehlik has been consecrated by Bishop Julius Massey of Plainfield, Illinois, pastor of an independent Episcopal Church. Massey had been consecrated by Denver Scott Swain of the American Episcopal Church.

The North American Old Catholic Church, Ultrajectine Tradition faced one crisis after another. During 1980 Stehlik and the priests he brought around him came under heavy attack in the press for falsifying their credentials. Stehlik's assistant, Bishop David E. Shotts, formerly of the Independent Ecumenical Catholic Church, was arrested for violation of parole from an earlier conviction of child molestation. Then in January 1981, Stehlik quit the church, denounced the apparitions as a hoax, and returned to the Roman Catholic Church. He was succeeded by Francis diBenedetto, whom he had consecrated. However, on May 29, 1983, diBenedetto, in the midst of a service at the shrine, announced his resignation, further labeled the shrine a hoax, and returned to the Roman Catholic Church. In the wake of diBenedetto's departure, a large number of adherents also quit and returned to communion with the Roman Catholic Church.

Sources:

Queen of the Holy Shrine. www.queenoftheholyrosaryshrine.com/

Swan, Henry H. *My Work at Necedah.* 4 vols. Necedah, WI: For My God and My Country, 1959.

Van Hoof, Mary Ann. *The Passion and Death of Our Lord Jesus Christ.* Necedah, WI: For My God and My Country, 1975.

———. *Revelations and Messages.* 2 vols. Necedah, WI: For My God and My Country, 1971–1978.

Free Catholic Church

c/o St. Thomas the Doubter Free Catholic Church, 1010 University Ave., No. 158, San Diego, CA 92103

The Free Catholic Church was founded in the early 1980s by Most Rev. Thomas Charles Clary (b. 1927). In the early 1990s Clary had joined the Free Catholic Church International, an independent jurisdiction founded by Most Rev. Michael Sherwood Daigneault, formerly of the Church of Antioch. Clary founded and pastored the Free Catholic Church of SS. Mary Magdalene & Thomas, Apostles, in Washington, D.C. Then, on April 30, 1994, he was consecrated by Bps. Brian G. Turkington, Martha Teresa Schultz, and Judy Carolyn Adams. He subsequently moved to San Diego, California, and founded the Free Catholic Church.

The church is similar in faith and practice to the Church of Antioch. It keeps fraternal relationships with other Free Catholic jurisdictions, many of whom also have their roots in the Church of Antioch, and is affiliated with the International Council of Community Churches.

Membership: In 1997 the church reported 105 congregations and 20,000 members in the United States and an additional 5,000 members overseas in congregations in Germany, Southeast Asia, and Latin America.

Educational Facilities:

Free Catholic Seminary.

Periodicals: *The Free Catholic.*

Sources:

The Free Catholic Church. www.freecatholic.org.

Constitution, By-Laws, and Statues. San Diego. CA: Free Catholic Church, 1995. 52 pp.

Heartland Old Catholic Church

c/o Rt. Rev. James R. Judd, St. Ignatius Center, 1624 Luella St. N., St. Paul, MN 55119-3017

The Heartland Old Catholic Church is a new Old Catholic jurisdiction founded by Rt. Rev. James R. Judd, who was consecrated as a bishop in 1999 by Most Rev. Donald William Mullan, the archbishop of Christ Catholic Church International. He is assisted by Rt. Rev. Charles F. Braun, who was consecrated in 2001 by Bps. William Harrison and Lawrence J. Harms. Like other Old Catholic jurisdictions, the church is based on the Gospel of Jesus Christ, apolistic tradition and succession, the (seven) sacraments, the unanimously accepted decisions of the Seven Ecumenical Councils of the ancient church, and guidance from the Holy Spirit. Worship is conducted using either the Roman Missal (which includes both the English and Latin liturgies), the Old Catholic Missal promulgated by Bp, Arnold H. Mathew (1852–1919) in England in the early twentieth century, or the American edition of the Anglican Missal.

The church welcomes both women and married men to the ordained priesthood. The church is described as affirming and inclusive, and offers the sacraments to all Christians baptized in a trinitarian faith.

Membership: In 2008 the church reported seven parishes in Minnesota and greater Washington, D.C.

Sources:

Heartland Old Catholic Church. www.heartlandoldcatholic.org/.

Fundamental Evangelistic Association

1476 W Herndon, Ste. 104, Fresno, CA 93711

The Fundamental Evangelistic Association was founded in 1928 as the result of a controversy at the Bible Institute of Los Angeles (BIOLA), a bastion of fundamentalist thought. In 1927 John MacInnis was appointed BIOLA's dean. Immediately thereafter, one of the professors, M. H. Reynolds Sr., charged MacInnis with being a purveyor of liberal theology in his book, *Peter the Fisherman Philosopher: A Study in Higher Fundamentalism*, which had been published BIOLA that same year. Reynolds was, at the time, also the pastor of the San Gabriel Union Church and one of the pioneer radio ministers.

Reynolds circulated a 30-page analysis of MacInnis's work, "Is 'Peter the Fisherman Philosopher' True to the Scriptures?" In response, BIOLA fired him, and he founded the Fundamental Evangelistic Association to continue what he saw as the straightforward, unyielding testimony to biblical fundamentalism. The incident also led to the split between Reynolds and radio colleague Charles Fuller (who sat on the BIOLA board). Reynolds went on to champion the fundamentalist cause on the West Coast against the development of neo-evangelicalism as it came to be represented in the National Association of Evangelicals, Fuller Theological Seminary (Pasadena, California), and the evangelist Billy Graham. Reynolds was succeeded as president of the association by his son, M. H. Reynolds Jr.

The association affirms the authority of the Bible as inspired, inerrant, and infallible. However, it goes further to affirm that the "initial miracle of divine inspiration of the original autographs also extends to the divine preservation of a pure text to this day. We have, therefore, the very Word of God preserved through the Hebrew Masoretic Text and the Greek Textus Receptus. In the English language, the only Bible translated from the aforementioned texts is the King James Version." A literal interpretation of scripture is noted in the belief that "God created all things in a time frame of six literal, twenty-four hour days."

It affirms the major doctrines of orthodox Christianity, including the Trinity, salvation by the atoning work of Christ, and justification by faith. The association also holds to a fundamentalist position on separation from the world that includes separation from worldly and sinful practices, from apostasy and unbelief (that is, not identified with unbelief in, for example, joint religious activities), and from disobedient brethren and doctrinal compromise with respect to all ministry and service.

The association further holds that ministry is based in autonomous local churches. Its base is the Fundamental Bible Church in Los Osos, California, pastored by M. H. Reynolds Jr. until his death in 1997. The church and association continue to be engaged in a national ministry that includes the radio broadcasts *What Does the Bible Say?*; a periodical, *Foundation*; and the publication of a number of booklets and pamphlets dealing with issues of the decline of conservative Protestantism into apostasy. Pastor Reynolds expressed particular concern for the movement of fundamentalists into neo-evangelicalism, Pentecostalism, and cooperation with Roman Catholicism.

Membership: The association is not a membership organization.

Periodicals: *FOUNDATION: A Magazine of Biblical Fundamentalism.*

Sources:

Fundamental Evangelistic Association. www.feasite.org.

Hispanic-Brasilian Confraternity of Christian Doctrine, Saint Pius X
Current address not obtained for this edition.

The Hispanic-Brasilian Confraternity of Christian Doctrine, Saint Pius X, can be traced to December 8, 1958, when Fr. Hector Alejandro Roa y Gonzalez formed the Puerto Rican National Catholic Church as a Spanish-speaking Old Catholic body for the Commonwealth. The original intentions and hope were to affiliate with the Polish National Catholic Church (PNCC) and the new church adhered strictly to the Declaration of Utrecht of September 24, 1889, one of the definitive documents of Old Catholicism. Gonzalez opened negotiations with the primate of the Polish National Catholic Church in 1959.

The PNCC withdrew from the negotiations in 1960, in part due to the presence of the Protestant Episcopal Church (with whom, at that time, it was in full communion) on the island. Gonzalez then turned to Eastern Orthodoxy and in 1961 was received into the Patriarchial Exarchate of the Russian Orthodox Church in the Americas. The next year his church was registered as La Santa Iglesia Catolica Apostolica Orthodoxa de Puerto Rico Inc. (The Holy Catholic Apostolic Church of Puerto Rico). The church for a time kept its revised Tridentine ritual, with a few necessary Orthodox alterations. However, within a short time, the Orthodox liturgy was translated into Spanish and introduced into the Puerto Rican parishes. Gradually other changes were introduced, and some members began to feel that the church had lost its identity and was being totally absorbed into Russian Orthodoxy, as its Spanish Western Rite Vicariate.

Gonzalez led the fight against the Russification of the vicariate, but after the replacement of Abp. John Wendland as head of the Exarchate, he found that he had lost his major support within the jurisdiction. In 1968, with his followers, Gonzalez withdrew and reestablished the Western Rite Vicariate. Parishes and missions were organized in the Dominican Republic, the United States, and Brazil. In 1977, for the sake of the future of the movement, the clergy and laity together decided to seek the episcopacy for Gonzalez. As a bishop, however, strict restrictions were imposed upon him. He was allowed to perform the minor episcopal functions, especially the rite of confirmation, and in some extreme cases the ordination of men to the diaconate and priesthood. However, he was not allowed to consecrate or assist in the consecration of anyone to the episcopal office.

Gonzalez received episcopal consecration from the hands of the Portuguese bishop Dom Luis Silva y Vieria. Bishop Vieria's apostolic succession comes from a dissident Roman Catholic group in Brazil (the Independent Catholic Church in Brazil) formerly headed by Msgr. Salomao Ferraz. Ferraz was received as a bishop in the Archdiocese of Sao Paulo by order of Pope Pius XII. Pope John XXIII appointed him auxiliary of Sao Paulo. Later Pope Paul VI appointed him to one of the commissions working on Vatican II. Before his reception into the Roman Catholic Church, however, he had been consecrated a bishop by Dom Carlos Duarte Costa, leader of

the Catholic Apostolic Church in Brazil and former Roman Catholic bishop of Botucatu. In 1979, in recognition of the geographical spread of the movement, its name changed to the United Hispanic Old Catholic Episcopate. The term "Old Catholic" created enormous confusion for the movement. The term was chosen to indicate its adherence to pre–Vatican II doctrine and practice and in no way implied the group's association with the Old Catholicism that had appeared in protest of papal infallibility after Vatican I. Therefore, Msgr. Gonzalez and the jurisdiction's clergy, with the approval of the laity, moved to change the official name to more accurately reflect its position. The episcopate became the Confraternity of Christian Doctrine with the name of its patron saint, Pope Pius X, added as a means of honoring the virtues of the late pope, known as a true defender of the faith and a champion against modernism.

The confraternity continued to use the Roman Tridentine Rite liturgy of Pope Pius V and the revised liturgy of Pope John XXIII. It accepts the seven traditional sacraments of the Roman Catholic Church and all the councils of the church including Vatican II. It recognizes the pope as the Vicar of Christ and bishop of Rome and acknowledges the See of Rome as the center of Catholic Christianity. Since the total separation from Eastern Orthodoxy, the church demands clerical celibacy. Many of the currently active clergy were ordained in the Roman Catholic Church in the years prior to Vatican II.

Membership: In 1992 the Confraternity reported 32,432 members in the Western Hemisphere. In the United States the confraternity was served by one bishop and 14 priests. There were 27 priests and members of religious orders serving overseas in Argentina, Brazil, Chile, Colombia, Costa Rica, Puerto Rico, and Spain.

Sources:

Actual Facts about the Russian Orthodox Church. Brooklyn, NY: Hispanic-Brasilian Confraternity of Christian Doctrine, Saint Pius X, 1988.

Boyle, Terrence J. "Costa Consecrations." www.tboyle.net/Catholicism/Costa_Consecrations.html.

The Hispanic-Brasilian Confraternity of Christian Doctrine. Brooklyn, NY: Confraternity Publications, 1989.

Welcome to Our Chapel. Brooklyn, NY: Confraternity Publications, n.d.

Holy Catholic Church (Western Rite)
c/o Fr. Arthur Barrymore, St. Edward's House, 4851 Anacacho St., San Antonio, TX 78217

Alternate Address: International headquarters: Bishop Michael Wright, 18 Frenchfield Rd., Peasedown St. John, Bath, UK BA2 8SL.

The Holy Catholic Church (Western Rite) is a church in the Roman Catholic tradition consisting of a number of congregations scattered around the world who found some fellowship in the 1990s. It affirms the Western Christian tradition and therefore accepts the faith of the Seven Ecumenical Councils and Western catholic tradition and practice, and the Bible as the Word of God. It recognizes seven sacraments and holds to the Apostles, Nicene, and Athanasian creeds. It does not use the filioque clause added by the Roman Catholic Church to the Nicene Creed in the eleventh century concerning the origin of the Holy Spirit. Devotion to the Virgin Mary is promoted.

The church is currently led by the metropolitan archbishop and ordinary of the Archdiocese of Europe, Most Rev. Leslie Hamlett, who resides in the United Kingdom. Its bishop stands in a lineage of apostolic succession. Additional bishops are found in India, South Africa, and New Zealand. The members and congregations view themselves as "refugees" from other churches and exist today as a number of small congregations scattered widely in different countries. The statement of Faith and Canons of the church was adopted in 2002. Work in the United States is concentrated in the state of Texas (El Paso and San Antonio). The church has a working relationship with the Holy Catholic Church (Anglican Rite).

Membership: Not reported. The church lists congregations in Spain, Sweden, the United Kingdom, South Africa, Korea, Colombia, New Zealand, and the United States. There is one parish in Point Edward, Ontario, Canada.

Sources:

Holy Catholic Church (Western Rite). www.holycatholicchurch-wr.org.

Holy Catholic Church (Western Rite) Supplemental site.
  netministries.org/churches/ch15301/.

Holy Palmarian Church

El Palmar de Troya, Archidona, Malaga, Spain

The Holy Palmarian Church began after apparitions of the Blessed Virgin Mary were reported to have been seen by Clemente Dominguez Gomez (1946–2005) of Palmar de Troya, Spain. Gomez began seeing the Virgin and having accompanying prophetic visions in 1968. The content of these visions, which included predictions of a number of cataclysmic events (a schism in the Catholic Church following the death of Pope Paul VI and a Communist revolution in Spain after the death of General Francisco Franco), was soon circulated internationally. In 1970 the Roman Catholic archbishop of Seville denounced Gomez's visions as lacking any validity. During the 1970s, the messages were circulated in the United States and trips to America were sponsored by St. Paul's Guild in Orwell, Vermont, and the Mount Carmel Center in Santa Rosa, California, though neither center was ever given formal status in the Holy Palmarian Church.

Other claims of Marian apparitions contemporaneous to those at Palmar de Troya took a decidedly traditionalist stance against the innovations introduced by Vatican II. In the face of continued rebuff by the Catholic hierarchy, Gomez's followers formed the Carmelite Order of the Holy Face. Gomez came into contact with the retired Vietnamese archbishop Pierre Martin Ngo-Dinh-Thuc, formerly archbishop of Hue. Thuc was also a traditionalist, then living in Italy. On December 31, 1975, Thuc traveled to Spain and ordained Gomez and four of his associates. On January 11, 1976, he consecrated Gomez to the episcopacy, along with one of the other recently ordained priests and three additional priests from other dioceses. During 1976 Gomez and his associated bishops ordained and consecrated other priests and bishops. In September 1976, Thuc, Gomez, and all the affiliated priests and bishops were formally suspended from performing their priestly offices and excommunicated. Almost immediately Thuc repented his action, and the excommunication (though not the suspension) was lifted.

After the death of Pope Paul VI in 1978, Gomez was declared the new pope by his supporters and took the name Pope Gregory XVII. By this time the Palmarian Church had spread throughout the Roman Catholic world, particularly in the Spanish-speaking part. Following the death of Gregory XVII in 2005, Manuel Alonso Corral, one of the Palmarian bishops, was selected as his successor and took the name Pope Peter II.

Membership: Not reported. It appears that any previous work in North America has dissolved.

Sources:

Holy Palmarian Church, Archidona, Malaga, Spain.
  www.geocities.com/palmardetroyaarchidona/1ingles.htm.

Inclusive Orthodox Church (IOC)

1750 Kalakaua Ave., No. 103-183, Honolulu, HI 96826-3795

The Inclusive Orthodox Church (IOC), formerly known as the New Catholic Communion (NCC), is an autonomous orthodox Christian jurisdiction established in Hawaii in December 1994 by Most Rev. Daniel J. Dahl (b. 1944). It has churches and clergy in the United States (Hawaii and California), and Mexico and provincial bishops in Honolulu by Most Rev. Randolph J. Sykes (b. 1951), and Veracruz, Mexico, by Most Rev. Daniel de Jesus Ruiz Flores (b. 1971). Bishop Dahl is the bishop and apostolic president.

The Inclusive Orthodox Church holds that eminent definition of the Christian faith is found in the Nicene-Constantinopolitan Creed and recognizes as ecumenical the first seven councils held between 325 and 787. It prays for and acknowledges as equals the six patriarchs of the East and West: the patriarch of Jerusalem, the patriarch of Antioch and All the East, the patriarch of Alexandria and the See of Saint Mark, the patriarch of the Lateran and pope of Rome, the archbishop of Constantinople and ecumenical patriarch, and the patriarch of Moscow and All Russia. The IOC recognizes the pope of Rome as *primus inter pares* among patriarchs. The apostolic succession of the bishops of the IOC is traced through four primary lines: Russian Orthodox, Greek Orthodox, Roman Catholic, and Episcopal. IOC clergy and members come from a mixed background of Eastern Orthodox, Roman Catholic, and Episcopalian heritages. The IOC holds a particular devotion to Theotokos, the Mother of God in the icon of Our Lady of Guadalupe as patroness of the Americas.

The Rite of the America—the IOC's Service Book—incorporates essential elements of the Divine Liturgies of Saint John Chrysostom and Saint Basil, the Novus Ordo of the Roman Catholic Church and the Book of Common Prayer. The IOC administers the seven sacraments in accordance with the rubrics of the Rite of the Americas in conformity with the substance of Apostolic Tradition. The Rite of the Americas is available and services are conducted in both English and Spanish languages.

The inclusive nature of the IOC supports the diversity of liturgical practice as well as recognition of the responsibilities of one holy, catholic, and apostolic church to address systemic injustice as a result of poverty, illiteracy, health care, and discrimination against anyone for any reason. The IOC advocates unity among the Christian churches and respects the traditions of Hindus, Jews, Buddhists, Moslems, and the indigenous religions of all peoples. It holds that unity among the Christian churches is God's will and the solution to the wars, genocide, mass starvation, discrimination, politics, and waste typical of the behavior endorsed by many. Separation of church and state is strongly supported by the IOC.

Ministries of the IOC emphasize spiritual and physical healing, education (especially literacy training), and publishing. Clergy hold advanced degrees in theology, philosophy, education, and foreign languages. While it accepts donations, the church has been self-supporting in having nonstipendiary clergy who personally finance their ministries through nonchurch employment. Deacons, deaconesses, and priests may be conjugal; bishops are celibate. Clergy are either monastic or independent, as their status befits.

Membership: In 2002 the IOC reported 1,250 congregants and 12 clergy and monastics.

Educational Facilities:

Apostolic College of the Pacific.

Sources:

Inclusive Orthodox Church. www.inclusiveorthodox.org.

Independent African American Catholic Rite

c/o The Most Rev. Bruce E. Greening, 4105 Alton St., Capitol Heights, MD 20731

The Independent African American Catholic Rite grew out of the movement led by Rev. George A. Stallings who, in January 1990, established the African-American Catholic Congregation in Washington, D.C. During the years immediately prior to his excommunication by the Roman Catholic Church and his organizing his following in an independent jurisdiction, Stallings had developed a network of support which included Fr. Bruce E. Greening. Greening formed the second congregation of the African-American Catholic Congregation, the Umoja Temple, also in Washington, D.C.

In February 1990, Greening and the Umoja Temple left Stallings's jurisdiction and attempted to reconcile with the Roman Catholic Church. They asked only that they be allowed a five-year period to experiment with the liturgy and that their pastor, Father Greening, be reinstated in the church's priesthood. They were unable to obtain a response to their overtures.

The Umoja Temple then changed its name to the Church of St. Martin de Porres, the Black saint from Peru canonized in 1963. On June 15, 1990, it declared its independence from Rome and elected Father Greening its bishop. He was consecrated on September 28, 1990, by Abp. Stafford Sweeting, the present Patriarch of the African Orthodox Church. The church is committed to the empowerment of African Americans through the development of institutional ownership, the nurturance of an indigenous clergy and lay leadership, and the encouragement of Black-owned businesses. The church sees itself redressing the inability of the Roman Catholic Church to be inclusive by ministering to those who have been neglected.

Membership: Not reported.

Sources:

Payne, Wardell J., ed. *Directory of African American Religious Bodies: A Compendium by the Howard University School of Divinity*. Washington, DC: Howard University Press, 1991.

Independent Catholic Church of America

c/o Bp. Maurice McCormick, 8701 Brittany Dr., Louisville, KY 40220

The Independent Catholic Church of America (ICCA) is an independent, sacramental church continuing the teaching and fellowship of the apostles through the particular tradition of the Old Catholic Church of Utrecht. The ICCA respects the Roman Catholic Church and also the pope as the bishop of Rome and the first among equals, but it does not adhere to a belief in the infallibility of the pope nor his universal authority. Although papal infallibility and jurisdiction were the two primary doctrinal reasons for the separation of the Old Catholic churches, since then several other doctrinal differences have arisen (such as the ordination of women).

The ICCA adheres to the essentials of faith and doctrine as expressed in the traditional creeds of the church (viz., Nicene, Apostles'), in various declarations, and in the doctrinal formulations of the ecumenical councils held prior to the Great Schism (between Rome and the Orthodox Church) of 1054.

While no one person is the "head" of the ICCA, Abp. George Le Mesurier serves as the primate, and Abp. Maurice McCormick is primate emeritus. Every bishop in the ICCA is considered an equal among equals. The ICCA recognizes that those who are married may receive a call to sacerdotal ministry, and that those who received a call to ministry while single may also be called to a life of marriage. There are no restrictions (such as married people being allowed to serve only as permanent deacons, or bishops being chosen only from unmarried celibate priests). The ICCA also ordains qualified women to all ranks of the clergy.

The ICCA does not consider divorce, or remarriage after divorce, a legitimate barrier to the reception of any sacraments. It does not prohibit using contraceptive devices. The ICCA abhors abortion, which it sees as the ending of a potential human life. It strongly encourages women with unwanted pregnancies to consider options to abortion but will not turn a woman who has had an abortion away from the church. The ICCA also accepts gays and lesbians as children of God and welcomes them into participation in church life and worship, but it will not ordain them. The ICCA is a member of the Union of Independent Catholic Churches of the North American Old Catholic Church.

Membership: The church reported 120 clergy and 4,000 members in 2002.

Educational Facilities:

Agape of Jesus Seminary, Clearwater, Florida; Ottawa, Ontario; and Louisville, Kentucky.

Heed University School of Theology, Hollywood, Florida.

Sources:

Independent Catholic Church of America. www.independentoldcatholicchurch.com.

Independent Catholic Church of America (Cronin)

Current address not obtained for this edition.

The Independent Catholic Church of America is a small Old Catholic jurisdiction founded by Mt. Rev. Patrick M. Cronin. Cronin was consecrated as a bishop of the Western Orthodox Church in America on June 4, 1988, by Luis Fernando Castillo-Mendez of the Igreja Catolica Apostolica Brasileira assisted by Richard J. Ingram of the Western Orthodox Church in America and Walbert Rommel Coelho of the Igreja Catolica Apostolica Brasileira. Cronin withdrew from the Western Orthodox Church five months after his consecration and subsequently formed the Independent Catholic Church in America. It is similar in belief and practice to its parent body, the issues leading to its formation being administrative, not doctrinal.

Membership: Not reported.

Independent Catholic Churches

3460 Powerline Rd., Fort Lauderdale, FL 33309

The Independent Catholic Churches is a small independent Old Catholic jurisdiction founded by Mt. Rev. Richard E. Drews. Drews had been consecrated in 1969 by William Andrew Prazsky of the Autocephalous Slavonic Orthodox Catholic Church (in Exile) and soon afterwards formed the Reformed Orthodox Church in America. The Independent Catholic Churches (also known as the Independent Catholic Archdiocese of Florida) superseded the Reformed Orthodox Church. Most recently, Archbishop Drews has been succeeded by Abp. Robert Caudill.

The church is Old Catholic in faith and practice and independent in administration. Included is an outreach to the Hispanic community of Florida where most of its congregations are located.

Membership: In 1997 the jurisdiction reported 600 members.

Sources:

Barrett, David B. *World Christian Encyclopedia*. New York: Oxford, 1982.

Independent Evangelical Catholic Church

PO Box 178388, Chicago, IL 60617-8388

Alternate Address: Evangelical Catholic Diocese of the Southwest, PO Box 20744, Albuquerque, NM 87154-0744.

The Independent Evangelical Catholic Church is a sacramental liturgical church in the Western Roman tradition founded in 1997. It is currently led by David J. Doyle, its presiding bishop. The apostolic succession in the church is derived from various lines of succession currently available in the independent Catholic world that have been passed to it primarily by Most Rev. Mark Steven Shirilau, the archbishop and primate of the Ecumenical Catholic Church.

The Independent Evangelical Catholic Church adheres to the teachings and practice of the seven Ecumenical Councils (that includes those summarized in the Nicene Creed) and continues the celebration of the traditional seven sacraments in the Western Catholic Church.

The church differs with the tradition in that it does not require a vow of celibacy from its priests and bishops, both being allowed to marry. It has also opened holy orders and religious life to all regardless of gender, orientation, marital status, or racial/ethnic background. The church is open to divorced people and allows them to be remarried without the lengthy process of obtaining a statement of dissolution (as required in the Roman Catholic Church). The church also encourages family planning and sanctions the use of various birth control measures.

At its founding, the church divided the country into four regions, each designated a mission diocese. Work has begun in two dioceses: the Southwest, headed by Bishop Doyle; and the Northwest, headed by Bp. James Alan Wilkowski.

The church has defined itself as an open and affirming church, and in that regard it seeks to invite under its ministry those who have previously been condemned or injured by the Roman Catholic Church and unite with them in a quest for equality and justice. Bishop Wilkowski has especially called attention to the plight of women, gays and lesbians, and racial and ethnic minorities.

Membership: There are three centers of activity in the church: Chicago, Illinois; Albuquerque, New Mexico; and Hammond, Indiana.

Sources:

Independent Evangelical Catholic Church. www.iecca.org/.

Independent Old Roman Catholic Hungarian Orthodox Church of America

PO Box 290261, Weatherfield, CT 06129-0261

The Independent Old Roman Catholic Hungarian Orthodox Church of America was founded in 1970 as the Independent Catholic Church by Bp. Edward C. Payne. Payne was consecrated in 1969 by Abp. Hubert A. Rogers (1887–1976) of the North American Old Roman Catholic Church (NAORCC) (Rogers). Originally, he rejected the liturgy used by the NAORCC and decreed that the Anglican Rite be used by his congregations as it most nearly corresponded to the Scriptural norm of St. Paul's First Letter to the Corinthians.

Soon after the establishment of the Independent Catholic Church, Payne was attracted to Eastern Orthodoxy. He met Abp. Peter A. Zhurawetsky (1901–1994), who was in communion with Payne's consecrator, and through Zhurawetsky he met Abp. Uladyslau Ryzy-Ryski (1925–1978), who was consecrated by Zhurawetsky and who had been constructing the American World Patriarchs. It was Ryzy-Ryski's goal to establish an international association of ethnic Orthodox jurisdictions by appointing archbishops over each national group. In 1972, he elevated Payne to be archbishop of New England, in an archdiocese affiliated with the American World Patriarchs. Three years later he elevated Payne to be metropolitan of Ugro-Finnic Peoples and patriarch of the Orthodox Catholic Autocephalous Church of Hungary in Dispersion.

At that time, Payne, who was Hungarian by birth, had about 20 Hungarian families in his Connecticut congregation, and other families in his archdiocese in Pennsylvania and Florida. During the intervening years, Payne has asserted the Hungarian roots of the church, both through the orders that can be traced through the NAORCC to the Austro-Hungarian Archbishop, the Duc de Landas Berghes, and the role assigned by Ryzy-Ryski. This heritage led to adoption of the jurisdiction's present name in 1984.

The church is Old Catholic in doctrine and practice and accepts the Declaration of Utrecht. It rejects papal infallibility as well as the universal pastorship of the pope. It also rejects the recent doctrinal statements on the Immaculate Conception and Bodily Assumption of the Virgin Mary. Open communion is practiced. No ordination of homosexuals or women is allowed.

Membership: Not reported.

Educational Facilities:

Independent Catholic Seminarium, Hartford, Connecticut.

Periodicals: *The Independent Catholic.* Send orders to 171 Colby, Hartford, CT 06106.

Infant Jesus of Prague Traditional Roman Catholic Chapel and Shrine

3442 W. Woodlawn St., San Antonio, TX 78228

The Infant Jesus of Prague Traditional Roman Catholic Chapel and Shrine was founded in 1979 by Msgr. John Gabriel (b. 1948). Gabriel was ordained in 1979 by Bishop Paul Gilbert Russell of the Holy Orthodox Catholic Church. On June 11, 1983, Bishop Raymond E. Hefner, Archbishop Paul Gilbert Russell, and Bishop Thomas T. Peters consecrated Msgr. John Gabriel to Abbot Ordinary for the Religious Order of the Gabriel Fathers). The order was dedicated to Pope John Paul II.

Bp. John Gabriel claims the Apostolic line of succession from Dom. Carlos Duarte Costa and the present Patriarch of Brazil, Dom. Luis Fernando Castillo-Mendez. To lay to rest all doubts of the validity of John Gabriel's consecration, Castillo-Mendez came to San Antonio and re-consecrated Bp. John Gabriel at the Infant Jesus of Prague Traditional Roman Catholic Chapel and Shrine on October 30, 1999. The

Patriarch of Brazil is expected to return to San Antonio to elevate Bishop Gabriel to archbishop. Gabriel will continue to represent the Patriarch of Brazil in Texas and throughout the United States.

Membership: In 2002 the church reported 600 members.

Sources:

Pruter, Karl. *The Directory of Autocephalous Bishops of the Apostolic Succession.* San Bernadino, CA: Brogo Press, 1906. 104 pp.

Ward, Gary. *Independent Bishops: An International Directory.* Detroit: Apogee Books, 1990. 524 pp.

The Inter-American Old Catholic Church

c/o Juergen Bless, Presiding Bishop, Diocese of Los Angeles, 7561 Center Ave., Ste. 49, Huntington Beach, CA 92647

The Inter-American Old Catholic Church was founded by Rt. Rev. Juergen Bless, who was consecrated to the episcopacy in 1986 by Abp.p Paul G. W. Schultz of the Philippine Independent Catholic Church. Though possessed of orders that come through the Episcopal lineage, Bless identifies the church he leads with the Old Catholic tradition of continental Europe.

Bless holds that a valid Christian church must teach and practice the historic faith as passed by Christ to His Apostles (and as summarized in the historical creeds of the ancient church) and must maintain a free fellowship of Christians who believe because they may. The Inter-American Church attempts to serve those who have found obstacles to church relations in other bodies that adhere either to a "rigid dogmatism or a vapid liberalism." The church claims its "catholic" designation as it follows the practice of the traditional seven Sacraments of the Western Church.

The church has one diocese, in southern California. Services are conducted in its single parish for German-, English-, and Spanish-speaking parishioners.

Membership: Not reported.

International Communion of the Holy Christian Orthodox Church

The Grand Cathedral, 207 Main St., Indian Orchard, MA 01151

The International Communion of the Holy Christian Orthodox Church was founded by His Eminence Timothy Paul Baymon, who serves as its metropolitan archbishop. A resident of Springfield, Massachusetts, Baymon served as pastor of the Praise and Glory Church of God in Christ in that city. In the 1990s he became involved in what is known as the *convergence movement*, a movement among people who expressed a desire to experience the best of what the three major traditions— the liturgical/sacramental, the Evangelical/Reformed, and the Pentecostal/ Charismatic—could offer when brought together. His own pilgrimage led him in 1999 to be consecrated as a bishop by several independent Catholic bishops (Carl Jimenez, Peter Paul Brennan, James Lagona, and Joseph Grenier). While Baymon inherited several lines of success, the primary line derives from Carlos Duarte Costa (1888–1961), the Brazilian Catholic bishop who founded the Catholic Apostolic Church of Brazil. Baymon subsequently founded the Holy Christian Orthodox Church and then the World Bishops Council, an ecumenical organization.

Originally directing its attention to peoples of color—African Americans, Hispanics, Native Americans, Indians (in India)—the International Communion of the Holy Christian Orthodox Church (ICHCOC) grew to comprise approximately 230 parishes and missions, over 350 clergy, and approximately 500,000 faithful (its own estimates) by 2004, at which time it declared itself an autocephalous community of faith.

His Eminence Timothy Paul had developed a program of coalition-building as the center of the Communion and the World Bishops Council. He has brought a number of African-American Pentecostal leaders into the World Bishops Council, and through the Communion offered them apostolic succession as bishops and invited them to sit on the Communion's board of bishops. Most notable of these new bishops are William Brown of the Fellowship of Independent and Global

Churches and Ministries and Harris Clark of the Kingdom Life Fellowship International.

In 2007 the Communion purchased a former Masonic temple in Springfield, Massachusetts, which now serves as its headquarters.

Membership: Not reported.

Educational Facilities:

Springfield Christian College and Theological Seminary, Springfield, Massachusetts.

Remarks: As the twenty-first century began, His Eminence Timothy Paul's rise in the religious world was signaled by two seemingly contradictory events. First, in 2001, Paul accepted the invitation of the Unification Church to introduce Rev. Sun Myung Moon at the beginning of one of Moon's expansive lecture tours. Then, two years later, he led the World Bishop's Council to condemn prominent Pentecostal minister Carlton Pearson as a heretic for his Universalist views.

Sources:

International Communion of the Holy Christian Orthodox Church.
    www.ichcoc.org/Institutions.dsp.

Kingdom Life Fellowship International
1221 Good Hope Church Rd., Starr, SC 29684

Kingdom Life Fellowship International is a Trinitarian Pentecostal denomination founded by its bishop, Harris E. Clark. In 1995, Clark became the pastor of Holly Creek Baptist Church in Starr, South Carolina. Two years later, Clark, who had a Pentecostal background, led the church to join the Full Gospel Baptist Church Fellowship then led by Bp. Paul S. Morton. Clark rose quickly in the organization and became district overseer a mere two years later. He also joined the Lord's Churches, Fellowships, and Ministries International, and was consecrated a bishop by that organization in 2002. Two years later, Clark left the Full Gospel Baptist Church Fellowship and founded the Kingdom Life Fellowship International.

The new fellowship is an expression of what is generally termed the *convergence movement*, a movement that began to appear in the 1980s among people who expressed a desire to experience the best of what the three major traditions—the liturgical/sacramental, the Evangelical/Reformed, and the Pentecostal/Charismatic—could offer when brought together. The Fellowship has become a notable manifestation of that movement within the African-American community. As part of that manifestation, Bishop Clark was reconsecrated as a bishop, this time with a formal lineage of apostolic succession, by Abp. Timothy Paul Baymon and the synod of the International Communion of the Holy Christian Orthodox Church.

During its short existence, the Kingdom Life Fellowship International has grown to include more than 20 congregations. The church is led by its council of bishops and dioceses have been established in Georgia and South Carolina.

Membership: Not reported. In 2008, there were 22 congregations.

Sources:

Kingdom Life Fellowship International. www.klfii.org.

Latin-Rite Catholic Church
PO Box 16194, Rochester, NY 14616

The Latin-Rite Catholic Church is the American branch of the church aligned to Abp. Pierre Martin Ngo-Dinh-Thuc (1897–1984), the traditionalist leader of an international Roman Catholic movement that rejects the authority of the current pope, Pope Benedict XVI. Thuc was formerly archbishop of Hue, Viet Nam, who retired to Italy during the papacy of Pope Paul VI and the sessions of Vatican II. He was strongly opposed to the innovations introduced by the church council and in December 1975 ordained a group of men associated with the claimed apparitions of the Blessed Virgin Mary at Palmar de Troya, Spain. The following month he consecrated five priests to the episcopacy. Thuc, and all those whom he consecrated,

were suspended from exercising their office and excommunicated by the papacy. Thuc repented, and his excommunication was lifted. However, Thuc's suspension from his bishop's office was not lifted. The other bishops and priests did not recant their actions but went on to form the Holy Palmarian Church.

Thuc remained in retirement until April 1981, when he again exercised his office of bishop by consecrating George J. Musey, head of the Servants of the Sacred Heart of Jesus and Mary, Friend-wood, Texas. In October 1981, Thuc secretly consecrated two traditionalist priests from Mexico, Moises Carmona and Adolfo Zamora. Formerly supporters of traditionalist Abp. Marcel Lefebvre (1905–1991), they rejected his leadership when reports surfaced of negotiations with the Vatican. After their consecration, Carmona and Zamora established the Union Catolica Trento (Tridentine Catholic Union), referring to the allegiance to the canons of the Council of Trent prior to Vatican II. In May 1982, he consecrated Fr. Gerard des Lauriers (d. 1988), a former supporter of traditionalist Archbishop Lefevre, who in turn consecrated Gunther Storch of Munich, Germany (1985); Robert McKenna of Connecticut (1986); and Franco Munari of Italy (1987).

Soon after the establishment of the church in Mexico, Thuc's lineage was further extended in the United States with the consecration of Louis Vezelis, head of the Order of St. Francis of Assisi in Rochester, New York. Vezelis was consecrated in 1982 by Carmona, assisted by Zamora and Musey.

Soon after Vezelis's consecration, the Latin-Rite Church was founded at Coeur d'Alene, Idaho, by Abp. Francis K. Schuckardt (1937–2006) who had been consecrated in 1971 by traditionalist Bp. Daniel Q. Brown. Schuckhardt believed and taught that Pope John XXIII was neither a true nor false pope, but an interim pope, but he believed John XXIII's successors (Paul VI, John Paul I, and John Paul II) to be false popes. This position was based on an underlying premise that the Vatican had been taken over by Freemasons who had murdered Pope Pius XII in order to complete their infiltration of the Curia. John Paul II was seen to be an instrument of the Freemasons. By introducing the New Mass and the false pope, the Roman Catholic Church had moved into apostasy. Schuckhardt and seven people broke with the Roman Catholic Church in 1968 and began a new organization promoting traditionalist life and values. Within a short time the Tridentine Latin-Rite Church had grown to more than 800 members, and by 1980 there were approximately 3,000. Schuckhardt established the Congregation of the Mary Immaculate Queen, "and through it the Our Lady of Fatima Cell Movement," the prime structure through which it reached out to traditionalist Roman Catholics around the United States. In 1978 the congregation bought Mount Saint Michael, a former Jesuit center in Spokane, which became its main headquarters. The 350-acre tract now houses the congregation, a seminary, the cell movement, two parochial schools, and several related organizations. The movement encountered stiff opposition from the Roman Catholic Church in the Northwest, which officially condemned the group. Former members accused it of cult-like practices and filed lawsuits, one of which resulted in a substantial judgment against the group. However, in 1984, Schuckhardt split with the remaining leadership of the Tridentine Latin-Rite Catholic Church and he, with a small number of followers, left. The Tridentine Latin-Rite Church then came under the episcopal authority of Bishop Musey.

Meanwhile, the Orthodox Roman Catholic Church Movement (ORCM), founded by Fr. Francis E. Fenton and led through the early 1980s by Fr. Robert McKenna, had developed some irreconcilable differences with McKenna who was moving into the influence of the movement developing around Thuc. After his consecration in 1986, the ORCM dissolved and McKenna took those who were willing into the Latin Rite Catholic church. In 1987 McKenna consecrated two other bishops, J. Vida Elmer of New York and Richard Bedingfeld, British-born leader of a traditionalist movement among the Zulus of South Africa. Musey consecrated Conrad Altenbach (d. 1986) of Milwaukee, Wisconsin, in 1984 and in 1987 consecrated a French priest, Michael Main, head of an Augustinian order in Thiviers, France.

Membership: Not reported. In 1986 centers were to be found in most of the United States, Canada, and New Zealand.

Educational Facilities:

Mount St. Michael Seminary, Spokane, Washington.

Periodicals: *The Seraph.* • *The Reign of Mary.* • *Salve Regina.*

Mariavite Old Catholic Church–Province of North America

c/o Most Rev. Archbishop Robert R. J. M. Zoborowski, O.M., D.D., 2803 10th St., Wyandotte, MI 48192-4994

Mariavitism is a characteristically Polish confession emanating from the Father Honorat movement and was inaugurated within the bosom of the Roman Catholic Church. In the late eighteenth century, in the portion of Poland that had been partitioned by Russia, there began to arise numerous monastic congregations, based in the III Rule of St. Francis of Assisi. The initiator of these congregations, especially the female ones, was Fr. Honorat Kozminski of the Congregation of Capuchin Fathers. The principal aim of these monastic communities, which led a hidden life fearing the persecutions and repressions of the tsarist authorities, was the maintenance of the religious life, especially the monastic, as well as a widespread and understandable apostolate of social work among male laborers.

The Roman Catholic sister and foundress of the Plock Congregation of the Poor Sisters of St. Clare was Feliksa Magdalena (religious name Maria Franciszka) Kozlowska, later called Mateczka (Little Mother) by the Mariaviates. She came to Plock in 1886 at the recommendation of Fr. Honorat, as a visiatrix of the hidden congregations. She was occupied there with the factory sisters and organized a Congregation of the Clarisses (that is, a congregation of sisters based on the stricter Rule of St. Clare, known as the II Rule of St. Francis of Assisi).

The Congregation of the Poor Sisters of St. Clare was initiated on August 8, 1887. It comprised six sisters who later adopted the name Congregation of Mariavite Sisters of Perpetual Suppliant Adoration. Initially subsiding on voluntary contributions, the congregation later began making church linens and paraments and eventually artistically embroidered chasubles, copes, baldachinos, stoles, and pictures of religious and country scenes, some of which remain on permanent exhibit at the Plock Motherhouse in Poland.

The initiation and propagation of the Mariavite movement is strictly linked with the person of Maria Franciszka and is the inspired Divine Revelation given the foundress on August 2, 1893, known as the Work of Great Mercy. The purposes of both Mariavite congregations is demonstrated in the revelation transcribed by the foundress: "In the year 1893, on the second day of August, after hearing Holy Mass, I was suddenly separated from my thoughts and placed before the Divine Majesty. An unfathomable light encompassed my soul and I was then shown: the universal ruination of the world and the last times then the loosening of the morals within the clergy and the sins to which the priests subject themselves to. I saw the Divine Justice measured for the punishment of the world and the Mercy given to the perishing world, as a final salvation, the adoration of the Most Blessed Sacrament and the help of Mary." After a moment of silence the Lord spoke: "As the means of propagating this adoration, I want that there would arise a Congregation of Priests under the name Mariavite, their standard: 'Everything for the greater glory of God and the honor of the Most Blessed Virgin Mary,' they will remain under the protection of the Mother of God of Perpetual Help, since as there are perpetual efforts against God and the Church, so is there necessary the Perpetual Help of Mary" (*The Work of Great Mercy*, p. 5). From that time the number of Mariavite priests grew, particularly within the Dioceses of Plock and Lublin as well as in the Archdiocese of Warsaw.

In August 1903 a delegation, including Maria Franciszka, went to Rome and presented Pope Pius X with a petition for the legalization of the congregation. They received papal promises of approval, but meanwhile the Polish hierarchy of the Roman Catholic Church sent numerous documents concerning the Mariavites to Rome, with the purpose of no less than the complete liquidation of the Mariavite movement. In September 1903 the Congregation of the Holy Office issued a decree ordering that the society of Mariavite Priests be completely suppressed. Despite further attempts by the Mariavite delegation for legalization in 1905 and early

1906, on April 5, 1906, Pius X published the encyclical *Tribus circiter*, in which he confirmed the decisions of the Congregation of the Holy Office in 1904 and recognized the Mariavite society as illegal and invalid and one that should be suppressed and condemned; further, that it should be excommunicated if the decision was not honored. In response, the Mariavites relinquished their obedience to the diocesan church authorities.

In Poland, churches that had been built by Mariavites were confiscated; clergy and people were the target of ambushes; medals, scapulars, and pictures of Our Lady of Perpetual Help were taken from Mariavites; tens were killed and hundreds wounded. However, in December 1906 the Mariavites were recognized as a confession by the Russian tsar, and the Mariavites began forming their own hierarchy, eventually adopting the name Old Catholic Church of the Mariavites.

After the death of Maria Franciszka Kozlowski, the administration within the church was taken by Archbishop J. M. M. Kowalski, who initiated a series of volcanic innovations: marriage of priests with the sisters (1922–1924), Holy Communion under both species (1922), priesthood of the sisters (1929), universal priesthood of the people (announced 1930 and initiated in the Felicianow branch in 1935), suspension of auricular confession (1930), Holy Communion to children after baptism (1930), suspension of religious titles and forms of orders (1930), suspension of the religious state (1930), simplification of ceremonies and liturgical prescriptions of Lent and others (1931–1933), mitigation of the Eucharistic fast and reform of other fasts (1933), and other radical changes. The controversy caused by these actions resulted in several priests resigning from the church, and Archbishop Kowalski was deposed by the General Chapter of the Mariavite Priests in 1935. Kowalski rejected the chapter's decisions and withdrew, creating a schism within the church. Three priests, approximately 80 sisters, and 25 percent of the faithful followed Archbishop Kowalski, who created a separate church in Felicianow near Plock and called it Catholic Church of the Mariavites. The remaining 30 priests, 280 religious sisters, and 75 percent of the faithful formed the Old Catholic Church of the Mariavites, with its historic seat of central authority in Plock. The schism continues to this day.

Many Mariavites emigrated to North America because of the partitioning of Poland by Russia, Germany, and Austria in the latter years of the nineteenth century and the outbreak of the World War I. Initially without their own parishes and clergy, some organized domestic oratories or chapels and strove to preserve their faith despite the obstacles; others associated themselves with the Old Roman Catholic Church of North America. In 1930 Francis Ignatius Boryszewski was consecrated as the church's first bishop in North America by Bp. Roman Maria Jacob Prochniewski of Poland, assisted by Abp. Frederick E. J. Lloyd, Abp. Gregory Lines, and Bp. Daniel C. Hinton. With its own bishop and respective clergy, the Mariavite movement quickly spread among large and small communities within the United States and Canada, erecting churches, chapels, and domestic chapels. The strength of Mariavitism remained steadfast despite the contempt and animosity toward the movement by elements within the Polish National Catholic Church, the Roman Catholic Church, and diverse "Old Catholic" sects that began to appear across North America. Francis Boryszewski died in 1975 after 45 years as a bishop and was succeeded by Abp. Robert R. J. M. Zaborowski, who continues as second prime bishop of the Mariavites in North America.

The Mariavite Old Catholic Church–Province of North America bases itself on the ancient Catholic principles of faith and morals contained in the canonical books of the Old and New Testaments. It also bases itself on the Work of Divine Mercy received by Maria Franciszka Kozlowska, which teaches that the salvation for the world perishing in sins is in Christ as present in the Most Blessed Sacrament as well as in the invocation of the Perpetual Help of the Most Blessed Virgin Mary. The church does not promulgate new dogmas and does not accept dogmas that were promulgated by the church after the separation of Christianity in the year 1054. It recognizes that only an ecumenical or universal council representing all Christianity can implement new dogmas that obligate all Christians. Clerical celibacy is mandatory except in individual cases of married clergy accepted and received into the church from the Anglican, Eastern Orthodox, or other licit communions. Although it is accepted that God authors miracles in the soul of an individual, the church does not recognize so-called miraculous relics and iconography, though it does not reject the great respect that should surround iconography of religious content as well as relics and remembrances of the saints. Auricular confession before a priest is obligatory for children and youth to age 18. The church recognizes seven sacraments, distributes Holy Communion under both single species and both species, retains the use of liturgical Latin, and does not issue condemnations and interdictions.

Membership: The Mariavite Old Catholic Church has reported a spectacular rate of growth. From its modest beginnings (it reported only 487 members, in eight centers and 32 clergy in 1972), it claimed, by 1980, to have 301,009 members in 117 churches served by 25 clergy in the United States. An additional 48,990 members were claimed for the 58 churches in Canada and several hundred members were claimed for churches in France and West Germany. By 1990 the church claimed 357,608 members and affiliates, 48 clergy, and 159 parishes in the United States as well as an additional 31,104 members in several congregations in Paris, France, and Germany. In 1995 the church reported 356,034 members and affiliate, 48 clergy and 157 parishes in the United States and Canada as well as 1 bishop, 6 clergy, and 29,105 members in France and Germany.

Educational Facilities:

Mariavite Academy of Theological Studies, Wyandotte, Michigan.

Periodicals: *The Mariavita Monthly* • *The Mariavita Bulletin* • *The Mariavite Newsletter*.

Remarks: A number of factors have raised doubt about the accuracy of the facts and figures reported by the Mariavite Old Catholic Church. In spite of its reported growth from 1972 to 1980, observers have been unable to locate any of the congregations affiliated with the church except the small chapel in Archbishop Zaborowski's residence in Wyandotte, Michigan. Zaborowski has consistently refused to share with inquirers the names and addresses of any of the claimed parishes or their priests. Doubts have also been raised about Archbishop Zaborowski's ordination and consecration. During the early 1970s he circulated copies of his ordination (1968) and consecration (1972) certificates. They bore the names of Bps. Francis Mazur and Ambrose as prime officiants, and they were on forms bearing the title "Antiqua Ecclesia Romanae Catholicae" (i.e., Old Roman Catholic Church). It was supposed by observers (and claimed by Zaborowski) that he had been ordained by the same Bp. Francis Mazur who had been consecrated by Abp. Carmel Henry Carfora of the North American Old Roman Catholic Church. Later, Zaborowski circulated a different set of certificates bearing the title of the Mariavite Old Catholic Church—Province of North America (a name not used until two years after his consecration) and bearing signatures of Abp. (not bishop) Francis A. Mazur and Abp. Francis Ignatius Boryszewski as prime officiants. The signatures on the two ordination certificates do not resemble each other in the least. (Archbishop Zaborowski had claimed that he himself had confused the Bishop Mazur consecrated by Carfora and Archbishop Mazur of the Old Catholic Church of Poland.) The earlier ordination certificate also carries no signatures of any other bishops who might have assisted in the ordination. In like measure, Zaborowski claims that Archbishop Boryszewski wished his role in the consecration service suppressed until his death, and hence it was not revealed until 1975. However, the signatures of those bishops whose names appear on both consecration certificates vary in great detail. It should also be noted that even a third ordination certificate exists which claims that Zaborowski was ordained in 1965 by a Roman Catholic bishop, the Most Rev. G. Krajenski (living in exile) and signed by the Most Rev. Cardinal Wojtyla, ordinary of the Diocese of Krakow, who became of course none other than Pope John Paul II.

Sources:

Peterkiewicz, Jerzy. *The Third Adam*. London: Oxford University Press, 1975.

Zaborowski, Robert R. *Catechism*. Wyandotte, MI: Ostensoria Publications, 1975.

———. *The Sacred Liturgy*. Wyandotte, MI: Ostensoria Publications, 1975.

———. *What Is Mariavitism?* Wyandotte, MI: Ostensoria Publications, 1977.

Mexican National Catholic Church

4011 E. Brooklyn Ave., East Los Angeles, CA 90022

During the presidency of General Plutarco Elias Calles (1924–1928), Mexico put into effect provisions of the 1917 Constitution aimed at curbing the political power of the Roman Catholic Church. With Calles's tacit consent, a rival Mexican-controlled Catholic body free from any connection to foreign interests was formed. The leaders turned to Abp. Carmel Henry Carfora (1878–1958) of the North American Old Roman Catholic Church (Rogers) for episcopal orders. On October 17, 1926, Carfora consecrated successively Jose Joaquin Perez y Budar, Antonio Benicio Lopez y Sierra, and Macario Lopez y Valdez. Perez y Budar became primate and patriarch.

Before returning to Mexico, Bishop Lopez y Valdez visited his family in Los Angeles, California, and contacted Bp. Roberto T. Gonzalez, pastor of El Hogar de la Verdad, an independent spiritualist church operating within the Mexican community in East Los Angeles. Lopez developed a friendly relationship with Gonzalez. Gonzalez died in 1928, and two years later, Lopez consecrated Gonzalez's successor, Alberto Luis Rodriguez y Durand. By this act the Mexican National Catholic Church was able to extend its territory into southern California. El Hogar de la Verdad gradually became known as the Old Catholic Orthodox Church of St. Augustine of the Mystical Body of Christ.

Over the next decades, as church-state relations improved in Mexico, the National Church, which by 1928 had claimed 120 priests and parishes in 14 Mexican states, began to dissolve. The largest remnant united with the Orthodox Church in America and became its Mexican exarchate in 1972. Its bishop, Jose Cortes y Olmas, was named exarch. The Los Angeles parish survived as the single U.S. outpost of the church. In 1955 Bishop Rodriguez, who was in poor health, consecrated Emilio Federico Rodriguez y Fairfield (b. 1912) as his successor.

In 1962 Fairfield decided to affiliate with the Canonical Old Roman Catholic Church, the U.S. branch of the Old Roman Catholic Church headed by British Abp. Gerard George Shelley. Following Shelley's death, Fairfield joined Bp. John Humphreys in consecrating a new archbishop in 1982. When Shelley's successor, Michael Farrell, resigned a month after his consecration, Fairfield emerged as the senior bishop of the church. Then in 1983, with the death of Jose Cortes y Olmas, Fairfield became the sole possessor of episcopal orders from the Mexican National Catholic Church. On September 13, 1983, he was installed as archbishop primate of the Iglesia Ortodoxa Catolica Apostolica Mexicana.

Membership: Only one parish of the Mexican National Catholic Church remains, in East Los Angeles, California. It has fewer than 100 members.

Sources:

Mexican National Catholic Church. www.mncc.net

Adherents.com. www.adherents.com/Na/Na_452.html.

Schultz, Paul. *A History of the Apostolic Succession of Archbishop Emile F. Rodriguez-Fairfield from the Mexican National Catholic Church, Iglesia Ortodoxa Catolica Apostolica Mexicana*. Glendale, CA: Author, 1983.

North American Old Roman Catholic Church (Rogers)

c/o James H. Rogers, 118-09 Farmers Blvd., St. Albans, NY 11412

The North American Old Roman Catholic Church (Rogers) dates to October 4, 1916, when the Duc de Landas Berghes (1873–1920), in the United States to escape confinement in England during World War I, consecrated the Rev. Carmel Henry Carfora (1878–1958) at Waukegan, Illinois. The Italian-born Carfora had come to the United States to do Roman Catholic mission work among the immigrants in West Virginia, but by 1911 had broken with Rome. In 1912, he sought consecration from Bp. Paolo Miraglia Gulotti, who had been consecrated by Abp. Joseph Rene Vilatte (1854–1929) and proceeded to form several independent Old Catholic parishes. After his second consecration, he broke with Bp. W. H. Francis Brothers (1887–1979), also consecrated by Landas Berghes, settled in Chicago, Illinois, and began to organize his own jurisdiction, which he named the North American Old Roman Catholic Church. (Brothers organized the Old Catholic Church in America.) During his lengthy life, Carfora was able to build a substantial church that may have had as many as 50,000 members. He absorbed numerous independent parishes, many of an ethnic nature. He also consecrated numerous bishops (at least 30) most of whom left him to found their own jurisdictions, both within the United States and outside of it. In the mid-1920s, a short-lived union with the American Catholic Church was attempted under the name The Holy Catholic Church in America.

Even before Carfora's death in 1958 the North American Old Roman Catholic Church (NAORCC) began to collapse, and remnants of what was once a growing ecclesiastical unit now exist as several small jurisdictions. Most have simply disappeared. Splintering began with Samuel Durlin Benedict, who left Carfora a few years after his 1921 consecration to found the Evangelical Catholic Church of New York, a small group that did not survive his death in 1945. In 1924 Carfora consecrated Edwin Wallace Hunter, who in 1929 assumed the title of archbishop of the Holy Catholic Church of the Apostles in the Diocese of Louisiana. This church also died with its founder in 1942. In 1931 Carfora consecrated James Christian Crummey, who, with Carfora's blessing, founded the Universal Episcopal Communion, an ecumenical organization that attempted to unite various Christian bodies (with little success). Crummey broke relations in 1944 and died five years later. The Communion did not continue into the 1950s. This pattern continued throughout Carfora's lifetime. More then 20 jurisdictions trace their lineage to Carfora.

The pattern of Carfora's consecrating priests beyond any ecclesiastical substance to support them, followed by their leaving and taking their meager diocese to create an independent jurisdiction, continued throughout Carfora's life. The major loss of strength by Carfora's NAORCC, however, came in 1952 when 30 parishes under Bp. Michael Donahue moved, with Carfora's blessing, into the Ukrainian Orthodox Church. Donahue was received as a mitered archpriest.

Carfora was succeeded as head of the North American Old Roman Catholic Church by Cyrus A. Starkey (1932–1965), his coadjutor, but before the year was out, the synod met and set aside Starkey's succession. It elected Hubert A. Rogers (1887–1976) who had served for five years as coadjutor but had been deposed by Carfora just a few months before his death. Rogers, while proving a most capable leader, was a West Indian. Most of the nonblack priests and members refused to accept his position and withdrew. This final splintering of the church left it a predominantly African-American membership, which it remained for the next years. H. A. Rogers was succeeded as head of the church by his son James H. Rogers (r. 1972–1990). Rogers was succeeded by Archbishop Herve Lionel Quessy (r. 1990–1991), Archbishop Edward J. Ford (r. 1991–2002), and Archbishop Edmund F. Leeman (r. 2002–2006). In 2006 Archbishop Ford assumed the leadership of the church for a second time and remains in that office to the present

The NAORCC advocates a faith in complete agreement with pre-Vatican I Roman Catholicism: "The Old Roman Catholic Church has always used the same ritual and liturgy as the early Church practiced, abiding by the same doctrines and dogmas; following the exact teaching given by the Apostles of Christ, and continuing through valid historical succession down to the present time." In one point it follows Old Catholic rather than Roman Catholic practice: Carfora married, and a married priesthood is allowed at all levels in the NAORCC. The practice has been passed on to those churches that derived from it.

Membership: In 2008, the Church reported eight parishes in the United States, five in Canada and three in Haiti.

Periodicals: *The Augustinian*. Send orders to Box 021647, G.P.O., Brooklyn, NY 11202.

Sources:

North American Old Roman Catholic Church. www.naorcc.org/

Trela, Jonathan. *A History of the North American Old Roman Catholic Church*. Scranton, PA: The Author, 1979.

North American Old Roman Catholic Church (Schweikert)
4200 N. Kedvale, Chicago, IL 60641

The North American Old Roman Catholic Church (Schweikert) is one of several Old Catholic jurisdictions that claims to be the legitimate successor to the North American Old Roman Catholic Church (NAORCC) formed by Abp. Carmel Henry Carfora (1878–1958). Abp. John E. Schweikert (d. 1988) based his claim upon his consecration by Bp. Sigismund Vipartes (d. 1961), a Lithuanian bishop who had served in Westville, Illinois, under Bishop Carfora beginning in 1944.

Archbishop Carfora died in 1958 and was succeeded by Cyrus A. Starkey (1932–1965), his coadjutor. However, the synod of the NAORCC. put aside his succession in favor of Hubert A. Rogers, who had been coadjutor until a few months before Carfora passed away. Starkey left the NAORCC. in 1960, and Richard A. Marchenna (1911–1982) claimed that Starkey named him as his successor. According to the records of the NAORCC, Schweikert was consecrated by Marchenna on June 8, 1958.

Following Starkey's death in 1965, Schweikert asserted a claim to be his successor against that of Marchenna. He also claimed that Vipartes, not Marchenna, consecrated him in 1958. Through Vipartes (consecrated by Carfora in 1944) and Starkey, Schweikert claimed to be Carfora's legitimate successor.

Headquarters for the church are in Chicago, Illinois, in a building complex that also houses a sisterhood of nuns: the Order of Our Most Blessed Lady, Queen of Peace. The sisters operate a school for mentally disabled children. Belief and practice follow that of the North American Old Roman Catholic Church, though Bishop Schweikert discontinued the practice of an unpaid clergy and promoted a more democratic church structure. In 1962 Schweikert consecrated Robert Ritchie (1907–1999) as bishop of the Old Catholic Church of Canada, founded in 1948 by the Rt. Rev. George Davis. The two jurisdictions remain in communion.

Membership: In 1986 the North American Old Roman Catholic Church (Schweikert) reported 133 parishes and missions, 62,611 members, and 150 clergy, figures that reflect the continuing increase in numbers reported during the last decade.

Remarks: It must be noted that during the past decade researchers have been unable to locate any parishes under Archbishop Schweikert's jurisdiction other than the single parish and affiliated mission, both in the Chicago area, over which he serves as pastor. Archbishop Schweikert consistently refused to reveal the names of any priests or the addresses of any parishes under his jurisdiction.

North American Old Roman Catholic Church–Utrecht Succession
19230 Mallory Canyon Rd., Salinas, CA 93907

The North American Old Roman Catholic Church–Utrecht succession dates to 1936, when Bp. A. D. Bell, who had been consecrated in 1935 by Abp. W. H. Francis Brothers of the Old Catholic Church in America, accepted reconsecration from Abp. Carmel Henry Carfora of the North American Old Roman Catholic Church. In 1938 Bell consecrated his successor, Edgar Ramon Verostek. In 1943 Carfora commissioned Elsie Armstrong Smith (d. 1983) as abbess of a new order, the Missionary Sister of St. Francis, and he was succeeded by Archbishop Verostek, who in turn was succeeded by Abp. Joseph Andrew Vellone in 1994. Abp. Chris Hernandez of Detroit is coadjutor archbishop with rights of succession. The church is an independent autocephalous church. As an independent order, the sisters have conducted a ministry of visiting the sick, offering intercessory prayers, and serving the church by making vestments and publishing pamphlets and prayerbooks. Over the years the congregation separated from the main body of the North American Old Roman Catholic Church, though it continues to follow its lead in theology and practice. The Missionary Sisters are headquartered in Mira Loma, California, where they maintain a chapel.

Membership: In the early 1980s the church reported six parishes with fewer than 200 members.

Sources:

North American Old Roman Catholic Church–Utrecht Succession. www.naorc.org/.

Old Catholic Church (Anglican Rite)

Most Rev. John Charles Maier, 489 Jasmine St., Laguna Beach, CA 92651

The Old Catholic Church (Anglican Rite) was founded in 1951 as the Old Catholic Episcopal Church by Jay Davis Kirby (d. 1989), a chiropractor and priest. Kirby had been consecrated in 1970 by Abp. Herman Adrian Spruit of the Church of Antioch. Affiliated to the church is an order community open to people of other similar church jurisdictions, the Old Catholic Order of Christ the King (Ordo Christus Rex). The order was founded by Fr. Alban Cockeram of Leeds, England, and brought to the United States by Bp. E. Vance Harkness of Atlanta, Georgia. Kirby brought the charter for the order to California. Both the church and the order follow traditional Catholic Christian values and doctrines. During the 1980s, because of its more ecumenical position, the order was the more active structure, developing a ministry through social service in hospitals and other care-providing facilities.

In 1978 Kirby consecrated John Charles Maier as his suffragan. In 1988 Kirby retired and entrusted the work to Maier.

Membership: In 2002 there were 638 members, four congregations, eight priests, and two sisters. There are two congregations in Mexico, served by one priest.

Educational Facilities:

Chapman College, Orange, California.

Cambridge Hall Theological Seminary, Webb City, Missouri.

Periodicals: *Old Catholic Church (Anglican Rite) Newsletter*. Send orders to Box 367, Laguna Beach, CA 92652-0367.

Sources:

Old Catholic Church (Anglican Rite). www.aicamericas.org.

Old Catholic Church in America (Brothers)

c/o Metropolitan Hilarion, 1905 S. 3rd St., Austin, TX 78704

The Old Catholic Church in America is one of the oldest independent Catholic bodies in the United States, founded in 1917 by W. H. Francis Brothers (1887-1979). Brothers, prior of a small abbey under the patronage of the Protestant Episcopal Church, began to move under the umbrella of several independent Catholic bishops. He was ordained in 1910 by Abp. Joseph Rene Vilatte (1854–1929) and the next year took the abbey into the Polish Old Catholic Church headed by Bp. J. F. Tichy (d. 1951). Tichy resigned due to ill health, and in 1914, Brothers became bishop-elect of a miniscule body that had lost most of its members to the Polish National Catholic Church. Then Brothers met the Duc de Landas Berghes (1873–1920), the Austrian Old Catholic bishop, spending the war years in the United States. He consecrated Brothers and then Carmel Henry Carfora (later to found the North American Old Roman Catholic Church) on two successive days in October 1916.

Brothers broke with both Landas Berghes and Carfora, renamed the Polish Old Catholic Church, and assumed the titles of archbishop and metropolitan. He began to build his jurisdiction by appointing bishops to work within ethnic communities. He consecrated Antonio Rodriguez (Portuguese) and attracted Bishops Stanislaus Mickiewicz (Lithuanian) and Joseph Zielonka (Polish) into the church. Most important, former Episcopal Bp. William Montgomery Brown (1873–1920) joined his college of bishops. The church grew and prospered, and in 1927, the Episcopal Synod of the Polish Mariavite Church gave Brothers oversight of the Mariavites in the United States. In 1936, the church reported 24 parishes and 5,470 members.

By the 1950s, the once prosperous church began to suffer from the Americanization of its ethnic parishes and the defection of its bishops. In 1962, Brothers took the remnant of his jurisdiction into the Russian Orthodox Church and accepted the title of mitred archpriest. However, five years later he withdrew from the Russian Church and reconstituted the Old Catholic Church in America. He consecrated Joseph MacCormack as his successor. Brothers retired in 1977, and MacCormack organized the synod that administers the affairs of the church. He also began the slow process of rebuilding the jurisdiction. An important step was the acceptance of the Old Catholic Church of Texas, Inc., an independent jurisdiction formerly associated with the Liberal Catholic Church International, and its leader Robert L. Williams, Metropolitan Hilarion, into the church in 1975. Archbishop MacCormack died in 1990 and has been succeeded by Metropolitan Hilarion.

Metropolitan Hilarion serves as resident leader of Holy Name of Mary Old Catholic Church and Saint Hilarion's Monastery in Austin, Texas. The monastery has three resident members and follows the rules of Saint Benedict. The liturgical use is that of Sarum, the restored and historically accurate text which has been published along with its Gregorian music, by the monastery. The Texas church stresses Western Orthodoxy, in remembrance of Abp. Arnold Harris Mathew's union with Antioch in 1911 and in honor of Metropolitan Hilarion's visit with Elias IV, Patriarch of Antioch, in Oklahoma City in 1977.

The Old Catholic Church in America follows the Old Catholic tradition passed to it from Bishop Mathew. The Julian calendar is used and kept in publication by the monastery in Texas.

In 1984, Metropolitan Hilarion consecrated Ivan Divalakov as Archbishop of Belgrade (Yugoslavia).

Membership: In 1992 the church claimed four congregations, 500 members, and 12 clergy. Affiliated congregations in Yugoslavia have approximately 2,000 members. In 1992 the parish in Austin reported a membership of 55 and an additional 20 constituents.

Sources:

Brothers, William H. F. *Concerning the Old Catholic Church in America*. N.p. 1925.

————. *The Old Catholic Church in America and Anglican Orders*. N.p. 1925.

LoBue, John. "An Appreciation, Archbishop William Henry Francis Brothers, 1887–1979." *The Good Shepherd* (1980).

Old Catholic Church in North America (Catholicate in the West)

Current address not obtained for this edition.

The Old Catholic Church in North America was established in 1950 by Grant Timothy Billet (d. 1981) and several Old Catholic bishops. Billet had been consecrated by Earl Anglin James of Abp. Carmel Henry Carfora's North American Old Roman Catholic Church. Billet established headquarters in York, Pennsylvania, and organized the interdenominational American Ministerial Association, which attracted a wide variety of clergy under its umbrella. During the 1970s he reported a membership of the church at approximately 6,000, a highly inflated figure. Billet died in 1981. He was succeeded by Abp. and Patriarch Charles V. Hearn, a psychotherapist and noted counselor on alcoholism. He reorganized the church and reincorporated both it and the American Ministerial Association in California. The church generally follows Roman Catholic doctrine and practice. However, celibacy is not a requirement for the priesthood. Dr. Orlando Hyppolitus Francis Dominic Lima now serves as archbishop patriarch.

Membership: Not reported.

Educational Facilities:

Trinity Hall College & Seminary, Denver, Colorado.

Sources:

The Old Catholic Church in North America (Catholicate in the West). www.danielclayministries.org/OCCNAHome.htm.

Old Catholic Church of British Columbia

715 E. 51st Ave., Vancouver, BC, Canada V5X 1E2

The Old Catholic Church of British Columbia was established in Vancouver in 1921. That year Bishop Irving Cooper (1882–1935) from Los Angeles, while returning from Australia, celebrated Holy Mass, baptisms, and other liturgical and social functions.

Rev. J. P. Kirk, ordained by Bishop Cooper in 1925, served until 1930. The mission grew under the leadership of Rev. Fr. H. J. Barney, O.M.I., a Roman Catholic priest of the Oblate of Mary Immaculate order. He opened St. Raphael's Old Catholic Church in 1934. Fr. Barney died in 1964 and was succeeded by Fr. John Carey, who had been an assistant since 1956. Fr. Carey retired in 1975, and that same year Bp. Ernest R. Jackson ordained Rev. Fr. Gerard LaPlante, who continued St. Raphael's Old Catholic Church and was consecrated as bishop on September 30, 1979, by Bp. Joseph H. V. Russell and Bp. Donald M. Berry. The Rt. Rev. L. M. McFerran, an ordained Anglican Church of Canada priest for more than 40 years, was consecrated auxiliary bishop for the Old Catholic Church by Bishop LaPlante, Rt. Rev. Donald William Mullan, Rt. Rev. John Brown, and Rt. Rev. Seraphim MacLennan in 1998 at Blessed Trinity Cathedral, Niagara Falls, Ontario.

The Old Catholic Church of British Columbia has two bishops, six priests, and two deacons. Church history has been featured in local, provincial, and national newspapers, publications, and television and radio programs. In October 1993 the National Film Board of Canada filmed a documentary on the church and Bishop LaPlante for the 1994 Year of the Family.

The church is Old Catholic in faith. It adheres to the Holy Scriptures, ecumenical creeds, seven ecumenical councils, and the Confession of Utrecht, and uses an Old Catholic liturgy. An autonomous body, the church does not receive funds or grants from any government branch, yet it has provided room and board for more than 250 people in need over the past three decades. Clergy hold outside employment and are not paid by the church. The majority of its members are ethnically, socially, and religiously diverse. The Lord's Prayer is recited in five to eight languages every week.

Membership: In 2002 the church reported a membership of 2,000. Parishes and missions are located in the Greater Vancouver area in British Columbia and Montreal, Quebec, in Canada; and Bellevue, Washington, in the United States.

Sources:

The Old Catholic Church of BC. www.oldcatholicbc.com.

Old Catholic Church of Canada

Mississauga, ON, Canada

The Old Catholic Church of Canada was founded in 1948 by the Rt. Rev. George Davis. In 1962, Davis's successor, Robert Ritchie (1907–1999), was consecrated by Abp. John E. Schweikert (d. 1988) of the North American Old Roman Catholic Church. The church follows Old Catholic doctrine, rejecting papal infallibility and such recent additions to the Roman Catholic Church dogma as the Immaculate Conception of the Virgin Mary. An English-language translation of the Latin rite is used in worship. Celibacy is optional for all clergy. Most Rev. David Thomson, archbishop, retired in June 2001 and was appointed presiding bishop emeritus. The Most Rev. Dr. Arthur Keating was elected third presiding bishop that year.

Membership: Not reported.

Sources:

Old Catholic Church of Canada. www.netministries.org/see/churches/ch05841.

Old Catholic Church of North America

c/o Most Rev. Paul Combs, PO Box 260473, Tampa, FL 33685

The Old Catholic Church of North America is an Old Catholic jurisdiction formed in the first decade of the twenty-first century by its current presiding bishop, Most Rev. Paul Combs. The church sees itself as continuing the Old Catholic movement that began in the 1870s. It rejected the dogma of papal infallibility. Old Catholics continued with the doctrines and practice of the pre–Vatican I Roman Catholic Church, but subsequently developed worship in the vernacular and welcomed married men to the priesthood. More recently, most Old Catholic jurisdictions have accepted women into the priesthood and even into the office of bishop.

The Old Catholic Church of North America accepts women into the priesthood, and in 2007 consecrated its first female bishop. The church stops short of ordaining homosexuals to the ministry. The church does not view divorce and remarriage as a sufficient reason to exclude individuals from the sacraments, most notably the Eucharist.

Bishop Combs possesses multiple line of apostolic success, which he has passed to the two bishops who now assist him in leading the diocese: Rt. Rev. Pamela "Pam" LeClerc and Rt. Rev. Ted William "Will" Smith. The Old Catholic Church of North America is primarily based in Florida and Texas, where all of its parishes are located.

Membership: In 2008 the church reported seven parishes and missions.

Sources:

Old Catholic Church of North America. www.oldcatholicchurch.org/index.html. 2008.

Old Catholic Churches

1307 Bethany Ln., Gloucester, ON, Canada K1J 8P3

Formerly known as the Old Roman Catholic Church, the Old Catholic Churches was originated with Earl Anglin James who had been consecrated as bishop of Toronto by Abp. Carmel Henry Carfora (1878–1958) of the North American Old Roman Catholic Church in 1945. The following year, however, he associated himself with Hugh George de Willmott Newman (Mar Georgius) of the Catholicate of the West. During the summer of 1946, Mar Georgius had extended the territory of the Catholicate to the United States through Wallace David de Ortega Maxey. In November, by proxy, he enthroned James as exarch of the Catholicate of the West in Canada. James was given the title Mar Laurentius and became archbishop and metropolitan of Acadia.

Mar Laurentius led a colorful career as an archbishop of the Old Roman Catholic Church. He claimed a vast following, at times in the millions. He collected degrees, titles and awards, and as freely gave them out to those associated with him. He became affiliated with a wide variety of international associations. In 1965, he consecrated Guy F. Hamel and named him his coadjutor with right of succession. After James's retirement in 1966, Hamel was enthroned as the Universal Patriarch and assumed the title of H.H. Claudius I. Hamel became one of the most controversial figures in Old Catholic circles. He was ordained in 1964 by Bp. William Pavlik of the Ontario Old Roman Catholic Church. However, before the year was over, he went under Mar Laurentius. After becoming head of the Old Roman Catholic Church, Hamel began to appoint an international hierarchy, a list of which was published in the April 1968 issue of *C. P. S. News*, the church's periodical. The list included not only most of the Old Catholic bishops in the United States and Canada (many of whom have taken pains to denounce Hamel) but also many people who were never associated with him—the Rev. Arthur C. Piepkorn (Lutheran theologian), Archbishop Irene (Orthodox Church in America), and Bp. Arthur Lichtenberger (Protestant Episcopal Church). After the publication of this list, which enraged many whose names were listed and amused others who recognized the names of many long-dead prelates, Hamel continued to lead the Old Roman Catholic Church, more recently renamed Old Catholic Churches.

The Old Catholic Churches follow the creeds of the early Christian Church and the Pre-Vatican II rituals. All seven sacraments are administered, and devotion to the Virgin Mary, as well as the veneration of images and relics of the saints is espoused.

Membership: Not reported.

Periodicals: *C. S. P. World News*.

Sources:

Disciplinary Canons and Constitutions of the Old Roman Catholic Church (Orthodox Orders). Havelock, ON: C.S.P. News, 1967.

Hamel, Guy F. Claude. *Broken Wings.* Cornwall, ON: Vesta Publications, 1980.

————. *The Lord Jesus and the True Mystic.* Toronto: Congregation of St. Paul [1968].

Old Catholic Orthodox Church

c/o Most Rev. Jorge Rodriguez-Villa, PO Box 3221, Montebello, CA 90640

The Old Catholic Orthodox Church, formerly known as Apostolic Orthodox Old Catholic Church, is a Spanish-speaking Old Catholic Church founded in 1985 in Chicago, Illinois, by Rt. Rev. Jorge Rodriguez. Rodriguez was born in Colombia, then moved to Chicago, where he was raised a Roman Catholic and decided to go into the priesthood. He came to oppose what he saw as a common problem in Latin America—the dominance of much of the Roman Catholic Church by repressive, right-wing bishops.

Rodriguez was consecrated in 1985 by Most Rev. Victor Herard of the Haitian Eglese Apostoloque, assisted by Abp. Roberto Toca of the Catholic Church of the Antiochine Rite and Abp. Carl St. Clair. Since its founding, the Old Catholic Orthodox Church has established a ministry to the elderly in Chicago and a mission to Latin America, where the church, known as the Ecclesia Catholica Apostolica Orthodoxa, establishes congregations as alternatives to the less progressive dioceses of the Roman Catholic Church. The church has 50 bishops throughout South America, Europe, Africa, and the United States. Their laity is in excess of 25,000.

Membership: Not reported.

Educational Facilities:

St. Moses, the Black, Theological Seminary, West Monroe, Louisiana.

Old Holy Catholic Church of the Netherlands

Current address not obtained for this edition.

The Old Catholic movement began in the Netherlands in the former Roman Catholic dioceses of Utrecht, Deventer, and Haarlam. The Old Holy Catholic Church of the Netherlands (Oud Heilig Katholieke Kerk van Nederland) is one in faith with the Old Catholic Church, but administratively is distinct and is not recognized by the Old Catholic Church of Utrecht. It was founded by Abp. Theodorus P. N. Groenendijk. Groenendijk was ordained as a priest in 1971 by A. J. A. Materman of the Liberal Catholic Church International. He was consecrated five years later by Abp. Josef Maria Theissen of the Alt Romanisch Katholische Church (Old Roman Catholic Church), an independent jurisdiction in Germany.

The Old Holy Catholic Church of the Netherlands was established in North America in the mid-1970s by Abp. Rainer Laufers, a French-Canadian whose headquarters are in Montreal. The church operated as the Old Holy Catholic Church of Canada. Under Laufers's direction a United States vicariate, The Vicariate of Colorado, was established by William H. Bushnell, who had been ordained by Laufers in 1979. Bushnell administered the vicariate for two years before moving to the Philippines for a year. Bushnell was consecrated in 1988 as bishop for the Diocese of Pennsylvania, currently the only diocese in North America.

Membership: Not reported.

Sources:

Ward, Gary L. *Independent Bishops: An International Directory.* Detroit, MI: Apogee Books, 1990.

Old Roman Catholic Church (English Rite)

1722 N 79th Ave., Elmwood Park, IL 60635-3505

A single church body with two corporate names, the Old Roman Catholic Church (English Rite) was headed by Bp. Robert W. Lane (d. 1999). Lane, a priest in the Old Roman Catholic Church (English Rite) headed by Abp. Robert A. Burns (d.1974),

was consecrated by Howard Fris on September 15, 1974. Both Burns and Lane perceived that Fris had failed to follow the correct form for the ceremony, and later that same day, Burns reconsecrated Lane.

Burns died two months later. Lane left Fris's jurisdiction and placed himself under Abp. Richard A. Marchenna of the Old Roman Catholic Church. It then became clear that during the last year of his life, Burns had allowed the corporation papers of his jurisdiction to lapse; when Lane learned of the situation, he assumed control of the corporate title. He was at that time serving as pastor of St. Mary Magdelen Old Catholic Church in Chicago.

According to Lane, in 1978 Marchenna offered him the position of coadjutor with right of succession. He had, however, developed some disagreements with Marchenna, and both men refused the position and left the Old Roman Catholic Church. Lane had previously incorporated his work for Marchenna in Chicago as the Roman Catholic Church of the Ultrajectine Tradition. Upon leaving the Old Roman Catholic Church, Lane formed an independent jurisdiction that continues both former corporations.

The Old Roman Catholic Church (English Rite) and the Roman Catholic Church of the Ultrajectine Tradition are thus two corporations designating one community of faith that maintains a Catholic way of life. It is like the Roman Catholic Church in most of its beliefs and practices. It retains the seven sacraments and describes itself as "One, Holy, Catholic, Apostolic, and Universal." It differs from the Roman Catholic Church in that it uses both the Tridentine Latin mass (in both Latin and English translation) and the Ordo Novo. It has also dropped many of the regulations that govern Roman Catholic clergy, most prominently the provision prohibiting the marriage of clergy.

During the mid-1980s Lane established six vicariates that function as proto-missionary dioceses. Within each vicariate are one or more quasi-parishes, that is, communities of the faithful that have not yet attained parish status. Vicariates are located in Racine, Wisconsin; St. Charles, Missouri; Elmwood Park, Illinois; and Carlsbad, California. In 1992 most Rev. Floyd Anthony Kortenhof was named bishop coadjutor of the jurisdiction with right of succession to Bishop Lane.

Membership: In 2002 there were three congregations.

Educational Facilities:

Seminary of St. Francis of Assisi, Chicago, Illinois.

Old Roman Catholic Church in North America

1207 Potomac Pl., Louisville, KY 40214

The Old Roman Catholic Church in North America is an ecclesiastical descendent of the North American Old Roman Catholic Church (the Old Roman Catholic Diocese of America). It was organized by Abp. Robert A. Burns (d. 1974) in 1963 during the period of fragmentation of the parent body after the death of its metropolitan primate, Abp. Carmel Henry Carfora (1878–1958). Bishop Burns, ordained in 1948 by Archbishop Carfora, served as vicar general to the Mt. Rev. Richard A. Marchenna (1911–1982), archbishop of the North American Province of the Old Roman Catholic Church under the jurisdiction of the Mt. Rev. G. George Shelley (d. 1980), archbishop of Caer Glow and primate of the Old Roman Catholic Church. Bishop Burns was elected bishop-auxiliary to the metropolitan during the Second Synod of Hamilton on May 22, 1961, and consecrated in Chicago on October 9 of the same year by Archbishop Marchenna, assisted by Bp. Emile Rodriguez-Fairfield (b. 1912) and Bp. John Skikiewicz.

Bishop Burns departed the jurisdiction of Archbishop Marchenna in 1963 and affiliated with the English Rite, Old Roman Catholic Church in Great Britain. He was elevated to metropolitan of the Midwestern Province (USA) of that ecclesiastical body by Abp. W. A. Barrington-Evans. Archbishop Burns died in 1974, and the Mt. Rev. Andrew G. Johnston-Cantrell was elected to succeed him. That same synod, held in Chicago on November 1, 1974, elected the Mt. Rev. Francis P. Facione as suffragan bishop. Archbishop Cantrell consecrated Facione on November 30 in Toronto. In early 1975 Johnston Cantrell resigned due to health reasons and the

Synod of the Midwestern Province elected Facione titular archbishop of Devon and presiding bishop. The same synod, held on April 12, 1975 in Detroit, voted to terminate its affiliation with the English Rite, Old Roman Catholic Church in Great Britain and change the corporate title of the jurisdiction to the Old Roman Catholic Church in North America, adopting North Old Roman Catholic Church as a subsidiary title. The synod also created the Diocese of Michigan and the Central States and elected Bishop Facione as first ordinary of the diocese.

At the synod of the Diocese of Michigan and the Central States held on December 3, 1988, the Right Rev. Raphael J. Adams, vicar-general of the diocese, was elected suffragan bishop with the title of bishop of Selsey. He was consecrated on February 4, 1989, by Archbishop Facione, assisted by Abp. John J. Humphreys, archbishop of Caer Glow and primate of the Old Roman Catholic Church, and Abp. James H. Rogers, archbishop of New York of the North American Old Roman Catholic Church.

In addition to the Diocese of Michigan and the Central States, two other dioceses are part of the Old Roman Catholic Church in North America: the Western Regionary Diocese, whose ordinary, the Mt. Rev. Patrick H. King, was consecrated on June 5, 1993, by Archbishop Facione and Bishop Adams to succeed Abp. Frederick Littler Pyman (d. 1993); and the Diocese of the French Caribbean (French West Indies), under the jurisdiction of the Mt. Rev. William Francis Luke Amadeo Izzi, who was consecrated to the episcopacy by the Mt. Rev. Joseph Vellone, archbishop of California, North American Old Roman Catholic Church.

Membership: In 2002 the church reported 1,100 members, 10 parishes, and 12 clergy.

Educational Facilities:

St. Thomas Aquinas Old Roman Catholic Seminary, St. Petersburg, Florida.

Periodicals: *New Perspectives.* • *Journal of the Old Roman Catholic Church.*

Sources:

Old Roman Catholic Church in North America. www.orccna.org.

Old Roman Catholic Church (Shelley/Humphreys)

5501 62nd Ave., Pinellas Park, FL 33565

The Old Roman Catholic Church (Shelley/Humphreys) emerged out of a dispute between Abp. Gerard George Shelley (d. 1980), primate of the Old Roman Church in England and America, and Abp. Richard A. Marchenna (1911–1982), head of the jurisdiction in the United States. In 1974, Marchenna consecrated Fr. Robert Clement (b. 1925) as bishop of the Eucharistic Catholic Church, an openly homosexual jurisdiction. As a result, Shelley, acting as Marchenna's superior, excommunicated him and those who followed his leadership.

Both those who followed Shelley and those who stayed with Marchenna continued to use the name Old Roman Catholic Church. Following Shelley's death, Fr. Michael Farrell of San Jose, California, was chosen as the new primate. On June 13, 1981, he was consecrated by Bp. John Humphreys, formerly the church's vicar general in the United States, who had been consecrated by Shelley soon after the split with Marchenna. Farrell resigned after only a brief time in his office, and in 1984 Humphreys was elected the new primate.

The church follows the doctrine and practice of the Roman Catholic Church prior to the changes of Vatican II.

Membership: In 1997 the church reported eight parishes.

Remarks: In the 1960s Archbishop Humphreys had briefly worked with Fr. Anthony Girandola, one of the early married Roman Catholic priests. Girandola, who had become somewhat of a celebrity after his founding of an independent parish in St. Petersburg, Florida, interested Humphreys in sharing leadership of the parish so that he could respond to media appearances.

Sources:

Humphreys, John J., ed. *Questions We Are Asked.* Chicago: Old Roman Catholic Information Center, 1972.

Old Roman Catholic Church–Utrecht Succession

c/o Roy G. Bauer, 21 Aaron St., Melrose, MA 02176

Abp. Roy G. Bauer was consecrated in 1976 by Bp. Armand C. Whitehead of the United Old Catholic Church and Bp. Thomas Sargent of the Community of Catholic Churches, but served as a bishop under Abp. Richard A. Marchenna (1911–1982) of the Old Roman Catholic Church. In 1977, he, along with Bps. John Dominic Fesi (b. 1940), of the Traditional Roman Catholic Church in the Americas, and Andrew Lawrence Vanore, accused Marchenna of usurping authority, and resigned their positions in the church. Bauer, together with Vanore, went on to found the Old Roman Catholic Church–Utrecht Succession, following the faith and practice of the parent body. Bauer was elected presiding archbishop in 1979.

The church accepts the Baltimore Catechism and, in general, pre-Vatican II Roman Catholic theology with the exception of the dogmas of papal infallibility, the Immaculate Conception, and the Bodily Assumption of the Virgin Mary. The doctrines on the Virgin Mary are acceptable as pious belief. The church is headquartered in Boston, and parishes are located in Denver, Colorado; Orlando, Florida; Pennsylvania; California; Texas; and several locations in Massachusetts. In 1984 Bishop Bauer affiliated with the Patriarchal Synod of the Orthodox Catholic Church of America, an association of independent Orthodox and Catholic bishops. Archbishop Bauer is assisted by two auxiliaries: Bishop Andros (Andrew Lawrence Vanore) and Bp. Patrick Callahan.

Membership: In 1995 the church reported approximately 900 members in nine congregations. The archbishop is assisted by two bishops and 16 priests.

Orthodox Catholic Church in America

Chancery Office, 409 N Lexington Pky., DeForest, WI 53532

The Orthodox Catholic Church in America, until recently known as the Archdiocese of the Old Catholic Church of America, began in 1941 when Bishop Francis Xavier Resch (d. 1975), who had been consecrated by Abp. Carmel Henry Carfora (1878–1958) of the North American Old Roman Catholic Church, broke with that jurisdiction and began the independent Diocese of Kankakee, centered upon his parish in Kankakee, Illinois. In a short time he had parishes in Illinois, Indiana, Michigan, and Wisconsin. However, these parishes, consisting primarily of first-generation Eastern European immigrants, developed a more broadly based constituency as the second generation became Americanized. In 1963 Resch consecrated Father Walter X. Brown (b. 1931) to the episcopacy. Brown moved the headquarters to Milwaukee, where the church developed a seminary, several programs for the treatment of alcoholism and drug abuse, and several new parishes.

During the 1980s, under Brown's leadership, the church moved steadily from an Old Catholic to an Eastern Orthodox position. The church accepts both the Eastern and Western Orthodox tradition of the seven ecumenical councils and the unanimous opinion of the fathers of the Christian Church. The faith, practices, and discipline of the Eastern Orthodox churches have been adopted. The seven sacraments are practiced, and the Nicene Creed is followed in the church's own statement of faith. Individual parishes may use either the Western Gregorian or Eastern Byzantine rites.

In 1997 Brown retired and was succeeded by Most Rev. James E. Bostwick (b. 1949). Bostwick had been ordained by Brown in 1976 and consecrated to the bishopric in 1992, at which time he was also named bishop coadjutor with the rite of succession.

The church supports two monastic communities, one Eastern and one Western, in Milwaukee.

Membership: Not reported. In 1988 the church reported 2,100 members, 10 congregations, and 16 clergy in the United States. In 2008, the church was led by four bishops, with 16 priests in the United States, two in Canada, and one in Peru.

Educational Facilities:

Holy Cross Theological Seminary, Milwaukee, Wisconsin.

Priestly Fraternity of Saints Peter and Saint Paul House of Studies, Galloway, New Jersey.

Periodicals: *The Messenger*.

Remarks: In 1986 the Orthodox Catholic Church in America entered into an agreement of intercommunion with the Orthodox Catholic Church of America, headed by Abp. Alfred Louis Lankenau. The two jurisdictions jointly formed the Holy Orthodox Synod of America, a confederation of independent Orthodox bishops for the purposes of sharing and fellowship.

Sources:

Orthodox Catholic Church in America. www.oldcatholic.org/.

Holman, John Cyprian. *The Old Catholic Church of America*. Milwaukee, WI: Port Royal Press, 1977.

Resch, Francis X. *Compendium Philosophiae Universae*. Lake Village, IN: The Author, 1950.

Orthodox Roman Catholic Movement

c/o Our Lady of Rosary Chapel, 15 Pepper St., Monroe, CT 06468

Among the first efforts to organize traditionalist members of the Roman Catholic Church was the Orthodox Roman Catholic Movement (ORCM), founded by Fr. Francis E. Fenton. Fenton began holding traditional Latin masses in a private home in Sandy Hook, Connecticut, in 1970. In 1972 the group was large enough to purchase a chapel in Brewster, New York. Later they purchased another chapel in Monroe, Connecticut, which has been the headquarters of the movement ever since. Fr. Robert McKenna was installed as pastor of the Monroe church in 1973. Four additional priests joined the ORCM in the fall of 1975, and with the aggressive outreach of the movement, the church began to grow, with congregations emerging in Florida, Colorado, and California, as well as in a number of locations in the Northeast.

The movement was controversial even among traditionalists who shared the opinion that the new mass was unsound. Father Fenton was a vocal member of the John Birch Society and was continually criticized for this affiliation. Leaders and members approved of his anticommunist stance but not of his membership in a non-Catholic organization. When disagreement among the OCM priests arose over its administration, Fenton and four others left the movement to found the Traditional Catholics of America 1978. Fenton died in Colorado in 1995.

The departure of Fenton and his supporters essentially destroyed the Orthodox Roman Catholic Movement as a national organization. Only the single congregation at Our Lady of Rosary Chapel in Monroe, Connecticut, remained. In 1986 its pastor, Father McKenna, was consecrated as a bishop by Gerard des Lauriers, a bishop in the lineage of Apb. Pierre Martin Ngo-Dinh-Thuc (1897–1984). McKenna has continued to be active in the circle of traditionalists in the Thuc lineage, primarily through the sporadic publication of a newsletter, *Catholics Forever*.

Periodicals: *Catholics Forever*.

Sources:

Orthodox Roman Catholic Movement. www.rosarychapel.net.

The Essential Roman Catholic Catechism. Monroe, CT: Orthodox Roman Catholic Movement, 1973.

Fenton, Francis E. *The Roman Catholic Church: Its Tragedy and Its Hope*. Stratford, CT: Orthodox Roman Catholic Movement, 1978.

Gasquet, Francis Aidan. *Breaking with the Past*. [1914]. Stratford, CT: Orthodox Roman Catholic Movement, n.d.

Our Lady of the Roses, Mary Help of Mothers Shrine

Box 611052, Bayside, NY 11361

Our Lady of Roses, Mary Help of Mothers Shrine emerged from the visionary experiences of Veronica Vera Lueken (1923–1995), a Bayside, Queens, New York,

housewife and mother of five. Lueken experienced her first heavenly manifestation on June 6, 1968. St. Therese of Lisieux made many appearances preparing Lueken for a visit from the Blessed Virgin Mary, which occurred on April 7, 1970. Lueken was told that Our Lady would appear on the grounds of the parish church, the old church of St. Robert Bellarmine, on the eve of designated feast days. Our Lady requested a sanctuary on this spot and gave directives for the first vigil, June 18, 1970, but clergy who had been notified at the request of Our Lady ignored her requests. Our Lady announced that she would return on the eve of the major feast days of the church, especially those dedicated to her. She requested a shrine and basilica be erected on the grounds occupied by St. Roberts. She revealed herself as "Our Lady of the Roses, Mary Help of Mothers" and Veronica was to be her "voice-box" to disseminate future messages.

More than 300 messages were relayed from 1970 to 1995 through Lueken and recorded on audiotape. Many of the messages focused on trends in modern life: abortion, euthanasia, surrogate motherhood, artificial life and experimentation in all forms, the disintegration of parenthood and family life, immodesty and impurity, homosexuality, and the practice of the occult and witchcraft. Some messages predicted the seating of an anti-pope in Rome.

The messages denounced the taking of communion in the hand, changes in the Bible and catechism, and the watering-down of faith teachings, and they predicted the eventual loss of the sacraments and the closing of churches. They predicted a chastisement comparable to Sodom and Gomorrah or Noah's flood, which consist of World War III and a fiery comet colliding with earth.

As the apparitions continued, Lueken's following grew. The neighborhood was incited against pilgrims attending the vigils, and by a court order in May 1975 they were moved to Flushing Meadows Park on the site of the Vatican Pavilion. The vigils continue today. Unknown clerics of the Roman Catholic Diocese of Brooklyn took offense at the messages and sent two monsignors and a seminarian to evaluate the situation. No investigation was ever carried out, but the diocese of Brooklyn printed an unfavorable report in their newspaper, citing expensive publication as proof of "spurious" events. When the pilgrim who had offered the publication came forward, the diocese printed a buried retraction. The Blessed Mother predicted opposition among the clergy, and requested Sunday Holy Hours on the Sacred Grounds for the clergy, which she promised to attend. The monsignor who blocked the investigation of the apparition and messages died suddenly and unexpectedly on the Feast of St. Michael.

Messages from Our Lady declared that the bishop will receive a sign that the basilica will be built on the grounds of St. Robert Bellarmine, that both sites of prayer vigils will be future sites of pilgrimages, that miraculous waters will erupt on the grounds of St. Roberts, and that the clergy will try to cap it. The vigils continue, and although many pilgrims are unable to attend physically, they do join in the vigil times with prayers from their homes.

Many groups that had supported the shrine split upon the death of Lueken, refusing to accept her husband as legitimate successor. A court battle ensued, and Arthur Lueken was recognized as the legitimate one to carry on the work of the shrine, as Veronica Lueken had requested. Several groups refused to obey the court order and began to carry on their own vigils, claiming that theirs was the legitimate shrine and causing much confusion. These groups were ordered not to use the titles and properties of Our Lady of the Roses, Mary Help of Mothers, by constraint of the same court order.

Our Lady of the Roses produces a series, *The Urgent Message from Bayside*, on public-access cable channels in various cities.

Membership: International. Formal membership is not required. As of April 7, 2008, membership was reported at 35,000. All are invited to attend and pray for world peace; religious affiliation is immaterial. Vigil schedules are available by mail from the above address or from the organization's website.

Educational Facilities:

Our Lady identified the Bayside Vigils as her seminary. Books and messages can be ordered through the shrine. Secondary institutions are expected to be established through the Roman Catholic Church, to include two religious orders: Our Lady of the Roses (cloistered nuns and a lay order) and the Order of St. Michael.

Sources:

Our Lady of the Roses. www.ourladyoftheroses.org.

De Paul, Vincent. *The Abominations of Desolations: AntiChrist Is Here Now.* St. Louis, MO: Author, 1975.

Grant, Robert. "War of the Roses." *Rolling Stone* no. 113 (February 21, 1980): 42–46.

Our Lady of the Roses, Mary Help of Mothers. Lansing, MI: Apostles of Our Lady, 1980.

Polish National Catholic Church

1006 Pittston Ave., Scranton, PA 18505

In the last decades of the nineteenth century, nationalistic enthusiasms engulfed the Polish communities in the United States. Tension developed because of the assignment of non-Polish priests to predominantly Polish parishes, and movements for autonomy developed in Chicago, Buffalo, and Scranton. In Chicago an independent Polish parish, All Saints Catholic Church, had been established under Father Anthony Kozlowski (d. 1907). In Buffalo an independent congregation was formed and later called Fr. Stephen Kaminski (d. 1911) as its priest. Other independent parishes developed in Cleveland and Detroit.

All of these churches were autonomous. On November 21, 1897, Kozlowski was consecrated a bishop by Bishop Herzog of the Old Catholic Church in Switzerland. Kaminski was elected bishop and sought consecration from Abp. Joseph Rene Vilatte. Vilatte consecrated Kaminski on March 20, 1898, and two factions, often bitterly rivalrous, developed.

A third group of Polish nationals emerged in Scranton, Pennsylvania, where the issue was local control of church property. In consultation with Fr. Francis Hodur (1866–1953), their former priest, the Poles constructed an independent church, and in 1897 Father Hodur accepted the pastorate. After unsuccessfully attempting to remain within the Roman Catholic Church, Hodur was excommunicated in September 1898. A second church was founded in nearby Dickson City.

Other independent congregations followed, and in 1904 a synod met in Scranton. At that time the Polish National Catholic Church of America (PNCC) was organized and Hodur was elected bishop. On January 14, 1907, Bishop Kozlowski died. The Old Catholic bishops consented to consecrate Father Hodur; the consecration was held in St. Gertrude's Old Catholic Cathedral in Utrecht on September 19, 1907. Most of Bishop Kozlowski's followers aligned themselves with Bishop Hodur and the Scranton movement. Bishop Kaminski died in Buffalo on September 19, 1911, and three years later, the cathedral parish entered into communion with the Polish National Catholic Church.

The Polish National Catholic Church of America differed little from the Roman Catholic Church because its establishment predated the changes brought about by the Second Vatican Council of the 1960s. It added some feast days and teaches that the preaching and hearing of the Word of God has sacramental power. Bishop Hodur emphasized the love of God, and the church hopes and prays that all will be saved. There is local control of property and the congregation does have some say in naming its pastor. The liturgy, which for many years was said in Polish, has been translated into English. Today English is used in most parishes for the church services.

In 1914 Hodur helped to establish a Lithuanian National Catholic Church, and in 1924 he consecrated Fr. John Gritenas as its bishop. The body became independent but was eventually reabsorbed. The Polish National Catholic Church of America grew steadily through the first half of the twentieth century. It became the only official Old Catholic jurisdiction in communion with the Union of Utrecht in the United States. For many years it was in intercommunion with the Episcopal Church, but broke communion after the Episcopalians decided to ordain female priests.

During the last two decades the Polish church has suffered greatly from Americanization, especially the abandonment of the Polish language by younger members, and the mobility of its members, many of whom have moved into areas not served by a PNCC parish.

The PNCC is organized into four American dioceses: Central (Scranton, Pennsylvania); Eastern (Manchester, New Hampshire); Western (Chicago, Illinois); and Buffalo-Pittsburgh (Lancaster, New York). There is also a Canadian diocese with its see in Toronto. An active mission begun after World War I produced a national church in Poland, the Polish Catholic Church. A bishop was appointed in 1924. In 2008 there were three dioceses in Poland, in Warsaw, Krakow, and Wroclaw. The PNCC is a member of both the World Council of Churches and the National Council of Churches, and is in ecumenical dialogue with the Roman Catholic Church and the Episcopal Church. Bishop Robert M. Nemkovich was elected as sixth prime bishop in 2002.

Membership: In 1998 the church reported a membership of approximately 60,000. There were about 150 parishes and missions in the United States and Canada. An Anglican parish and several Hispanic parishes came into communion during the 1990s.

Educational Facilities:

Savonarola Theological Seminary, Scranton, Pennsylvania.

Periodicals: *God's Field (Rola Boza)* • *Polka* • *PNCC Studies*

Sources:

Polish National Catholic Church. www.pncc.org.

A Catechism of the Polish National Catholic Church. Scranton, PA: Mission Fund Polish National Catholic Church, 1962.

Fox, Paul. *The Polish National Catholic Church.* Scranton, PA: School of Christian Living, [1955].

Grotnik, Csasimir J., ed. *The Polish National Catholic Church of America: Minutes of the Supreme Council, 1904–1969.* New York: East European Monographs, 2004.

Janowski, Robert William. *The Growth of a Church, A Historical Documentary.* Scranton, PA: Author, 1965.

Orzell, Laurence. *Rome and the Validity of Orders in the Polish National Catholic Church.* Scranton, PA: Savonarola Theological Seminary Alumni Association, 1977.

Wielewinski, Bernard. *Polish National Catholic Church: Independent Movements, Old Catholic Church, and Related Items: An Annotated Biography.* New York: Columbia University Press, 1989.

Wlodarski, Stephen. *The Origin and Growth of the Polish National Catholic Church.* Scranton, PA: Polish National Catholic Church, 1974.

Reformed Catholic Church of America

c/o Archbishop Rodney P. Rickard, PO Box 3165, Pinellas Park, FL 33780

Alternate Address: 58 Aqua Cir., Parkersburg, WV 26104

The Reformed Catholic Church was founded and is led by its present archbishop, Rodney P. Rickard, who in 1997 was consecrated to the episcopacy by Maurice McCormack of the Independent Catholic Church of America. McCormick passed to Rickard multiple lines of apostolic succession, most of which pass through Abp. Adrian Spruit of the Church of Antioch.

The church places itself firmly within the Western Catholic liturgical tradition, but adds strong elements of reform from the Lutheran tradition. It accepts the 1530 Augsburg Confession as a guiding document for church life. The church administers the seven sacraments of Baptism, Confession, Eucharist, Chrismation/Confirmation, Anointing of the Sick, Ordination, and Marriage, but accepts the Lutheran emphases on the scripture as the primary, sufficient, and reliable written source of belief; on salvation by grace through faith; and on the belief that all things are made new by the Holy Spirit.

The church differs from the Roman Catholic Church in its acceptance of women and married men into the ordained ministry. Priests in the church will not perform same-sex unions or marriages, nor ordain or license practicing homosexuals to the ministry. Priests may remarry members who have been divorced.

Membership: Not reported.

Sources:

Reformed Catholic Church of America. www.reformed-catholic.net/.

Servant Catholic Church

50 Coventry Ln., Central Islip, NY 11722

The Servant Catholic Church first convened on the Feast of All Saints in 1978 and finalized its polity in January 1980 with the election of its first Bishop-Primate, Robert E. Burns, SSD (d. 1994). Burns was consecrated on July 13, 1980, by Abp. Herman Adrian Spruit (1911–1994) of the Church of Antioch. A second bishop, Patricia duMont Ford, served the church from 1980 through 1986, at which time she retired from active ministry to pursue feminist theological studies. In 1993 Ford resumed active ministry due to the failing health of Burns, and succeeded him as Primate the following year when he died. The core teaching of the church, termed "eleutheric theology," is rooted in the perception that the essence of the Christian *kerygma* (preaching of the gospel of Christ) lies in the proclamation of freedom. All the church's ministries—liturgical, pastoral, sacramental, and social action—reflect this belief system. The church's three-year theological training curriculum centers upon the study of eleutherics. Resonances of this teaching are found in the church's liturgy and in its code of canon law. The church recognizes the sacraments of initiation (baptism), restoration (penance and healing), union (holy, Eucharist), instruction (proclamation and teaching), and holy orders. Confirmation and matrimony are designated as sacramental rites.

Though receiving orders from Liberal Catholic sources, the College of Bishops of the Servant Catholic Church has rejected theosophy as "inauthentic teaching." The Servant Catholic Church reaches out ecumenically to other ecclesiastical bodies that share its commitment to peace, justice, effective pastoral ministry, sound theological education, and the admission of women to the three-fold, Catholic-ordained ministry. As of August 2000, the Servant Catholic Church signed an Agreement of Affiliation with the American Catholic Church of New England.

Membership: Not reported.

Educational Facilities:

Vilatte Institute, Margate, Florida.

Sources:

The Sacramentary and Daily Office of the Servant Catholic Church. Central Islip, NY: Theotokos Press, 1981.

Slaves of the Immaculate Heart of Mary

Saint Benedict Center, 282 Still River Rd., PO Box 1000, Still River, MA 01467

The Slaves of the Immaculate Heart of Mary emerged in the 1940s as one of the first groups to protest the growing accommodation of the Roman Catholic Church to liberal ideas, particularly the acceptance of the possibility of salvation outside of the Roman Catholic Church. The leader of the group was Fr. Leonard Feeney (1897–1978), a Jesuit priest who had become a popular Catholic writer in the 1930s. Feeney taught at Weston College in Cambridge, Massachusetts.

Trouble began in the late 1940s when Feeney began to attack the Jesuits who sat in classes taught by openly atheistic professors at Harvard University. He broadened his attack to include the liberalism of the church. Feeney charged that some were moving away from the traditional Catholic position that outside the (Catholic) church there was no salvation. Fortified by Feeney's rhetoric and leadership, his followers became a committed group of dedicated conservative Catholics. The church moved to quiet Feeney by ordering him to take a position at the College of the Holy Cross.

Tension increased when four teachers associated with Feeney, who also taught at Boston College (a Jesuit institution), accused some of the faculty colleagues of the General of the Society of Jesus of heresy. The college fired the four for promoting intolerance and bigotry. When Feeney defended them, Abp. Cardinal Richard Cushing silenced him and then forbade Catholics to associate with the Cambridge center. Feeney and his followers interpreted Cushing's actions as another blow to traditional Catholic faith.

Feeney was dismissed from the Society of Jesus and in 1953, excommunicated. His excommunication marks the establishment of the Slaves of the Immaculate Heart of Mary as a group independent of the Roman Catholic Church. They saw themselves as a small remnant still holding to the true faith. The group established a residence compound, purchasing several adjacent homes and erecting a high fence around the property. The school lost its accreditation, and thus its funding from the post–World War II G.I. Bill, and eventually it closed. The Slaves made money by publishing a series of popular books on Catholic themes and selling them door-to-door in the Boston area. They generally spent their Sundays in Boston Commons defending their position within the heavily Catholic community.

In 1958 the Slaves moved from Cambridge to a farm near Still River, Massachusetts. There they followed an ascetic lifestyle, and eventually all of the adults accepted a vow of celibacy. Children, who made up half the community's membership, were raised collectively.

After a period of relative quiet, the community went through a series of changes that ended its life as a separated community. In 1974 Feeney led 29 men and women of the community back into communion with the Roman Catholic Church. In 1988 the 14 remaining sisters of the group were formally received back into communion and the order regularized. The Slaves of the Immaculate Heart of Mary began a new life as an order recognized by the Roman Catholic Church.

Periodicals: *From the House Tops.*

Sources:

Slaves of the Immaculate Heart of Mary. www.catholicism.org.

The Communion of Saints. Still River, MA: Slaves of the Immaculate Heart of Mary, 1967.

Connor, Robert. *Walled In.* New York: New American Library, 1979.

Feeney, Leonard. *The Gold We Have Gathered: Selections From the Writings of Father Leonard.* Stillwater, MA: The Center, 1989. 122 pp.

The Holy Family. Still River, MA: Slaves of the Immaculate Heart of Mary, 1963.

Our Glorious Popes. Still River, MA: Slaves of the Immaculate Heart of Mary, 1955.

Society of St. Pius V

8 Pond Pl., Oyster Bay Cove, NY 11771

Fr. Clarence Kelly (b. 1941) was among the first American priests to graduate from the seminary established by traditionalist Abp. Marcel Lefebvre (1905–1991) at Econe, Switzerland. In 1973 Lefebvre ordained Kelly, who returned to the United States with four other priests to found the U.S. branch of the Society of St. Pius X. Kelly served as U.S. superior of the society and as superior of the Northeast District, when the territory was divided in 1978. In the early 1980s Kelly and Fr. Donald J. Sanborn, superior of St. Thomas Aquinas Seminary in Ridgefield, Connecticut, became concerned about Lefebvre's contacts with Pope John Paul II and his attempts to accommodate the innovations introduced since Vatican II, innovations that had led to the formation of the seminary and the society.

In March 1983 nine society priests, including Sanborn and Kelly, sent a letter to Lefebvre calling his attention to their objections on a number of issues, including:

1. The introduction of liturgical changes at St. Thomas Aquinas Seminary;

2. The use of doubtfully ordained priests in missions in the Southwest;

3. The archbishop's desire to introduce the liturgical changes of Pope John XXIII throughout the society;

4. The improper dismissal of priests;

5. The society's usurpation of teaching authority;

6. The need to subordinate loyalty to the fraternity to loyalty to the church; and

7. The liberal acceptance of marriage annulments by Lefebvre.

Lefebvre responded to the letter by dismissing Sanborn from his post at the seminary and dismissing all the priests from the society.

Despite disagreements with Lefebvre, the society continued its activities as before, publishing its two periodicals and performing services at its churches and missions. In 1984 four priests previously ordained by Lefebvre joined the society, further expanding it. That same year, Father Kelly founded a congregation of sisters in Round Top, New York, known as the Daughters of Mary, Mother of Our Savior. In 1988, the community had 22 members. The society also operates four elementary schools and two high schools.

The society operated under its founding name until the fall of 1987, when it adopted its present name.

Membership: Not reported.

Periodicals: *The Bulletin.* • *The Roman Catholic.*

Sources:

Society of St. Pius V. www.sspv.net.

Society of St. Pius X

c/o Regina Coeli House, 11485 N Farley Rd., Platte City, MO 64079

Of the several groups of traditionalist Roman Catholics, the Society of St. Pius X claims the largest number of adherents. Prior to the 1980s, the society was the only traditionalist group that had orders from, and the support of, a Roman Catholic bishop with undisputed episcopal orders—Archbishop Marcel Lefebvre.

Marcel Lefebvre (1905–1991) was raised in a pious Catholic family and spent much of his adult life in Africa as a missionary. After World War II he steadily rose in the African hierarchy as vicar-apostolic of Dakar (1947) and then apostolic delegate for French-speaking Africa (1948). In 1955 Pope Pius XII appointed him archbishop of Dakar. Pope John XXIII appointed Lefebvre to serve on the Central Preparatory Commission of Vatican II. The Council's rejection of all the work prepared by that commission, and the initiation of a number of changes and reforms, disturbed Lefebvre. In 1962 he was appointed by Pope John XXIII as bishop of Tulle (France) and shortly thereafter was elected superior general of the Holy Ghost Fathers, the religious order of which he was a member. However, Lefebvre found the ruling elite of that order quite accepting of the liberal decisions of Vatican II, and in 1968 he resigned his post and retired from public life.

Lefebvre's retirement was soon interrupted by several theological students who, knowing of the archbishop's opposition to the decisions of Vatican II, sought his assistance. There was no seminary where they could receive traditional Catholic training in theology and spiritual formation. Reluctantly Lefebvre responded to their overtures for help and in 1969 opened the Fraternite Sacerdotale de Saint Pius X, attached to the University of Fribourg. Fribourg was like other universities, and the Fraternite soon moved to Econe, Canton of Valais, Switzerland, to create a full seminary curriculum. In this venture Lefebvre had the full approval of local bishops. As word spread that a seminary built on pre–Vatican II patterns existed, enrollment increased and growth was rapid.

In 1974 the official attitude toward Econe changed; in November the French bishops issued a joint statement against adherents of the Latin mass. Informally, the statement was tied to a policy of no longer accepting graduates from Econe into the French dioceses. On May 6, 1975, official approval for Econe was withdrawn by the bishop of Fribourg, charging that the seminary opposed the teachings of Vatican II and the authority of Pope Paul VI.

In the wake of the new attitude toward his work, Lefebvre continued his efforts, frequently staying but one step from excommunication. The next major battle

began in the spring of 1976 as Lefebvre prepared to ordain some graduates of his seminary. Paul VI publicly rebuked him, but Lefebvre persisted with his plans and ordained 13 seminarians in June. On July 22 Paul VI suspended him from exercising any further priestly functions. Lefebvre responded by traveling to Lille, France, on August 29, 1976, and publicly celebrating mass and denouncing some of the "uncatholic" practices of the Roman Catholic Church. His actions led to a personal meeting with Paul VI the following month, which lessened, but did not end, the tension between the two.

Shortly after the meeting with the pope, Lefebvre traveled to England for his first mass there, and the next year he went to the United States. His continued activity inspired the outstanding French theologian Yves Conger to write a book attacking Lefebvre and led Paul VI to threaten excommunication. After Paul VI's death, Lefebvre continued to promote the Society of St. Pius X and to negotiate with Pope John Paul II, viewed by many as a conservative pope. Those negotiations, which produced concessions from Lefebvre, led some to reject his leadership of the movement.

The Society of St. Pius X had its origin in the United States when several Americans traveled to Econe to study. Upon returning to America, they established centers in East Meadow, New York; Houston, Texas; and San Jose, California. They were soon joined by Fr. Anthony Ward, ordained at Econe in 1975, who founded St. Joseph's Seminary at Armada, Michigan. Fr. Clarence Kelly, one of five Americans ordained in 1973 by Lefebvre, began a periodical entitled *For You and For Many*. It tied together traditionalist supporters around the United States.

By the end of 1975 there were more than 50 congregations served by the priests of the society, and the search for permanent chapel sites was begun. In March 1978 Frs. Kelly, Donald J. Sanborn, and Hector Bolduc met with Lefebvre and decided to divide the work into two districts. Kelly remained superior of the Eastern and Northern Districts and Bolduc was appointed head of the new Western and Southern, headquartered in Houston, Texas. In the Houston suburb of Dickinson, Bolduc founded Angelus Press, which became the major source for literature about Lefebvre and the work of the society.

That same year the society was split by a bitter conflict over the relationship between Lefebvre and the pope. Since the beginning of the society, Lefebvre had continually acknowledged the pope to be the leader of the church and tried to obtain the freedom to keep the traditional liturgy and doctrine within the Roman Catholic Church. However, some of his followers in America, including nine priests led by Frs. Kelly and Sanborn, took a more conservative stance. They tended to reject all changes since Vatican II and even some liturgical adjustments made by Pope Pius XII. In 1983 they outlined their complaints in a seven-point letter that included a request for independence from Lefebvre, superior general of the order. In response, Lefebvre, who interpreted their action as evidence of constant disobedience, expelled them from the order. The following year Father Bolduc also left the society. A court suit ensued, in which the expelled priests tried to retain the property of the Northeast District of the society, over which they had previously had control, and bring it into their new organization, the Society of St. Pius X. In 1986 the court returned all the major property, including the seminary, to the society.

In 1987 Archbishop Lefebvre, realizing his aging condition, made a last approach to the authorities in the Vatican and initiated negotiations looking toward the formation of a commission of traditional Catholics that included a provision for him to consecrate three traditionalist bishops to care for the members of the society around the world. These negotiations continued through the winter of 1987–1988 but gradually fell apart. Unwilling to delay further, Lefebvre informed the pope of his intention to consecrate four auxiliary bishops, which he, assisted by Bp. Antonio de Castro Meyer of Brazil, did on June 30, 1988. The four bishops were Bernard Fellay, Alfonso de Galarreta, Bernard Tissier de Mallerais, and the American Richard Williamson. Both the consecrating and consecrated were immediately excommunicated.

The four bishops were not assigned jurisdictions and there has been no attempt to establish dioceses or to give the appearance of establishing a rival church.

Although Roman Catholic officials consider the bishops and members of the Society of St. Pius X to be in schism, the members of the society consider themselves good Roman Catholics and acknowledge the authority of the pope conflicts with church authorities they believe to be in error following the "reforms" of Vatican II. The society adheres to all Roman Catholic dogma. At each mass said by the society, prayer is offered by name for the pope and the local diocesan bishop. The society's seminaries follow all of the regulations for seminaries as handed down by Vatican II.

The society has avoided all connections with the Old Catholics who deny papal infallibility. They affirm that the pope is infallible when speaking *ex cathedra* but is not inerrant (protected from errors of judgment) or impeccable (protected from committing sin). The society also avoids contact with those independent Catholic and Orthodox jurisdictions that deny various tenets of Catholic dogma or traditional practice (such as the ordination of females to the priesthood).

The American District of the society is headquartered in Kansas City, where Angelus Press is also located. There are two seminaries in the United States and a number of elementary and secondary schools. There is also a separate Canadian district.

Membership: Not reported.

Educational Facilities:

St. Thomas Aquinas Seminary, Winona, Minnesota.

Jesus and Mary Seminary, El Paso, Texas.

St. Mary's Academy and College, St. Mary's, Kansas

Periodicals: *The Angelus • Si Si No No.*

Sources:

Conger, Yves. *Challenge to the Church.* Huntington, IN: Our Sunday Visitor, 1976.

Davies, Michael. *Apologia Pro Marcel Lefebvre Part I, 1905–1976.* Dickinson, TX: Angelus Press, 1979.

———. *Pope Paul's New Mass.* Dickinson, TX: Angelus Press, 1980.

Hanu, Jose. *Vatican Encounter: Conversations with Archbishop Lefebvre.* Kansas City, KS: Sheel, Andrews and McMeel, 1978.

Lefebvre, Marcel. *Liberalism.* Dickinson, TX: Angelus Press, 1980.

———. *Open Letter to Confused Catholics.* Dickinson, TX: Angelus Press, 1999.

Thee Orthodox Old Roman Catholic Church

Box 49314, Chicago, IL 60649

Thee Orthodox Old Roman Catholic Church is one of several bodies that claims to carry on the work of the Old Roman Catholic Church (English Rite) headed by the late Abp. Robert A. Burns (d. 1974). It was founded by Peter Charles Caine Brown, generally known by his ecclesiastical title, Archbishop Simon Peter. Brown was originally ordained in 1972 by Bp. Anthony Vruyneel of the Orthodox Old Roman Catholic Church of Bellgarden, California. In 1973 he met Mar Markus I (Leo Christopher Skelton) and was consecrated by him. On August 14, 1973, he was enthroned as archbishop. On December 18, 1974, he was appointed chancellor of the jurisdiction headed by Burns. He succeeded to the role of metropolitan on December 31, 1974.

Membership: Not reported.

Traditional Catholic Church—Conservare et Praedicare

Current address not obtained for this edition.

The Traditional Catholic Church was founded in 1983 by Thaddeus B. J. Alioto (b. 1934) as the Ancient Tridentine Catholic Church (Catholicate of the West) with the aim of preserving Tridentine Latin liturgy and Gregorian chant, practices then under attack with the spread of changes in the Roman Catholic liturgy following the precepts of Vatican II. The present name was adopted in the late 1980s. The church follows conservative Roman Catholic pre-Vatican II beliefs and practices.

Alioto, the brother of San Francisco's former mayor, had been ordained by Wallace D. Ortega Maxey (1902–1992), who carried orders from both Arthur Wolfort Brooks (1898–1948) and the Apostolic Episcopal Church, and Hugh George de Willmott Newman (1905–1979) of the Catholicate of the West. Bp. Robert Ramm, who carried a similar lineage, assisted Ortega Maxey when he consecrated Alioto in 1983.

In 1987, Alioto consecrated Ignatius Mack, who heads an ordered community within the Traditional Catholic Church, the Order of the Holy Spirit.

Membership: Not reported.

Sources:

Pruter, Karl. *The Directory of Autocephalous Bishops of the Apostolic Sucession.* San Bernadino, CA: Brogo Press, 1906. 104 pp.

Ward, Gary. *Independent Bishops: An International Directory.* Detroit: Apogee Books, 1990. 524 pp.

Traditional Roman Catholic Church in the Americas

425 E. 11th Ave., Apt. 215, Vancouver, BC, Canada V5T 4K8

HISTORY. The Traditional Roman Catholic Church in the Americas was formed in June 1978 by John Dominic Fesi (b. 1940), a bishop consecrated by Damian Hough, head of the Old Roman Catholic Church in the U.S. Fesi had begun his ecclesiastical career as a Franciscan friar in the Franciscan Provine of Christ the King, a community within the Archdiocese of the Old Catholic Church in America (now known as the Orthodox Catholic Church in America) under the leadership of Archbishop Walter Xavier Brown (b. 1931). In 1972, Brown created the Vicariate of Illinois and consecrated Msgr. Earl P. Gasquoine as its bishop. Gasquoine in turn appointed Fesi as Vicar of Religious with the title of reverend monsignor. As part of his duties, Fesi managed Friary Press, which printed a quarterly periodical, The Franciscan, and pamphlets for the Archdiocese. The community dissolved shortly after Fesi's leaving the Archdiocese in 1973.

After his departure from Brown's jurisdiction, Fesi was approached by Damian Hough, with whom he became associated. On June 30, 1974, Hough, assisted by Bishops Joseph G. Sokolowski (1903–1989) and John Skikiewicz (1893–1983), consecrated Fesi as a bishop. During this time, Fesi also worked at the Church of St. Mary Mystical Rose, an independent Polish Catholic parish in Chicago. It had originally been founded in 1937 in response to a vision of Maria Kroll, a young Polish immigrant. The parish was, in effect, an independent Catholic jurisdiction headed by Skikiewicz, who had pastored the church for many years. During the 1970s, as his health failed and he could no longer handle the parish work, Fesi was appointed his successor. Though once a strong congregation, support had dwindled and services were being held in the rectory basement hall. After Skikiewicz's death, support further dwindled until the church's board sold the property (which is today the site of a parish of the Polish National Catholic Church). Fesi founded the Traditional Roman Catholic Church a short time later.

BELIEFS. The Traditional Roman Catholic Church follows the doctrine and liturgy of the pre-Vatican II Roman Catholic Church. The Tridentine Latin mass is celebrated, and the Baltimore Catechism is used in teaching. The seven sacraments are kept, and baptism is considered essential for salvation. Veneration of the images and pictures of the saints is promoted. Abortion is condemned.

Bishops Sokolowski and Hough consecrated Fesi on June 30, 1974. Fesi took his friars into the Old Roman Catholic Church headed by Richard Marchenna (1911–1982). Though The Franciscan was discontinued, Friary Press became the church's major publishing arm.

During his years with Brown and Marchenna, Fesi and the Franciscans assisted at the Church of St. Mary Mystical Rose, an independent Old Catholic parish in Chicago. Bishop Skikiewicz pastored the congregation that had been founded in 1937 in response to a vision of Maria Kroll, a young Polish immigrant. The church was in effect an independent Old Catholic jurisdiction. Eventually, Fesi was appointed associate pastor. Marchenna appointed Fesi head of the Vicariate of

Illinois and eventually the Church of St. Mary Mystical Rose became part of the vicariate. Though a strong congregation, after Skikiewicz's death the support dwindled and the building was sold.

The Traditional Roman Catholic Church in the Americas follows the Old Catholic tradition. It keeps the seven sacraments and teaches that baptism is essential for salvation. Veneration of images and pictures of the saints (who are present in a mystical manner in their image) and especially the Blessed Virgin Mary (whose intercession is essential to salvation) is promoted. Abortion is condemned. The church is organized hierarchically. Under the bishop is an ecclesiastical structure which includes priests, deacons, subdeacons, acolytes, exorcists, lectors, and doorkeepers. Priests are allowed to marry. The priests are organized into a synod that meets annually.

Membership: In 1987 the church reported 14 parishes, 26 priests, and 981 members.

Educational Facilities:
Our Lady of Victory Seminary, Chicago, Illinois.

Periodicals: *The Larks of Umbria*.

Sources:

Fesi, John Dominic. *Apostolic Succession of the Old Catholic Church*. Chicago: Friary Press [1975].

———. *Canonical Standing of Religious in Regards to the Sacred Ministry*. Chicago: Friary Press, 1975.

———. *Reasons for Divorce and Annulment in Church Law*. Chicago: Friary Press, 1975.

Tridentine Catholic Church Traditional Catholic Archdiocese in America

1740 W. 7th St., Brooklyn, NY 11223-1301

HISTORY. In the 1960s Archbishop Thomas Fehervary (1917–1984), a Hungarian exile in Montreal, Canada, established the Traditional Christian Catholic Church there. In 1974 the archbishop moved to extend the jurisdiction of the Canadian-based church to the United States by ordaining Fr. Leonard J. Curreri and two other priests. In 1975 the archbishop ordained Fr. Peter Seghizzi to the priesthood to work with Fr. Curreri. On that occasion he also chose to convene a synod, at which it was decided to call the American branch of the jurisdiction the Tridentine Catholic Church because it best symbolized the affirmations for which the church stands. However, within two years the American clergy, their correspondence with the archbishop having gone unanswered, assumed that he wished no further communication with them. It was then decided that, either the jurisdiction would seek Episcopal oversight elsewhere, or one of the three priests would be chosen to provide this oversight by accepting Episcopal consecration.

Fr. Curreri was consecrated by Abp. Francis Joseph Ryan (d. 1987) of the Ecumenical Orthodox Church of Christ on April 23, 1977, thus bestowing on Fr. Curreri the Old Calendar Greek Orthodox Succession. His co-consecrators were Bishops H. Bennett Dayhoff and John Basilo. Because of Abp. Ryan's unwillingness to sign the consecration documents and for the sake of lineal continuity with the Roman Catholic Church, Bishop Curreri was consecrated *sub conditione* (with conditions) by Abp. Andre Barbeau of the Charismatic Catholic Church and three other bishops, including Abp. Rainer Laufers of the Old Holy Catholic Church (of Canada), thus bestowing on him the Brazilian Roman Catholic line of apostolic succession. In January 1991 new articles of incorporation were drawn up and filed, thus establishing the church as the Traditional Catholic Archdiocese in America. However, some requested a return to the original name. A compromise was reached with the combination of the two names into one. Thus the church is known as the Tridentine Catholic Church Traditional Catholic Archdiocese in America.

BELIEFS. The Tridentine Catholic Church follows the doctrines and practices of the pre–Vatican II Roman Catholic Church. It rejects the Novus Ordo Missae (the New Order of Mass that developed from the changes initiated by the Second Vatican Council) as invalid. The church accepts infallibility as an article of Divine and Catholic Faith, as proclaimed by the First Vatican Council. It rejects the ordination of women in toto. Clerical celibacy is the rule, but exceptions are made.

The church views birth control as a matter requiring the response of a well-formed conscience, keeping in mind the constant teaching of the Catholic Church pertaining to conjugal relations and the responsibilities stemming from them. Contraceptives or willful sterilization are not valid measures for the prevention of unwanted children. By "birth control" the church means "self–control," affirming that if a couple does not want more children than they can reasonably afford to support and educate they should agree to abstain from conjugal relations for a period of time to be determined by them.

The church teaches that abortion is the willful killing of a human fetus, an act that is never allowable for any reason whatever. It does not recognize divorce, but it does recognize that for a variety of reasons a couple may not want to cohabit and may seek a church annulment. The Tridentine Catholic Church does not feel it has the authority to grant such annulments; however, if a couple has obtained a canonically valid annulment it will be recognized.

Membership: In 2002 the church reported four priests in the United States.

Sources:

Tridentine Catholic Church. www.mrtrid.com.

Curreri, Leonard J. *De Sacramentis*. Brooklyn, NY: n.d.

———. *More Questions and Answers on the Tridentine Catholic Church*. Brooklyn, NY: n.d.

———. *Questions and Answers on the Tridentine Catholic Church*. Brooklyn, NY: n.d.

———. *Seccessio Apostolica*. Brooklyn, NY: 1984.

Tridentine Old Roman Community Catholic Church (Jones)

c/o Most Rev. Jacque A. Jones, Fisherman Orthodox Catholic Church, 10446 Highland Ave., Bellflower, CA 90706-4123

The Tridentine Old Roman Community Catholic Church was organized in 1976 by Fr. Jack Alwin Jones, generally known by his church name Jacque A. Jones. Jones was consecrated as a bishop in 1980 by Bishops Lawrence E. Carter of the North American Old Roman Catholic Church—Utrecht Succession and Thomas Sargent of the Community of Catholic Churches. In the mid-1980s, however, Jones resigned his leadership of the single parish of the jurisdiction, St. John the Apostle Church in Bellflower, California, and turned the corporation over to Bishop Charles T. Sutter, who had recently moved to southern California from Ohio.

Sutter, founder of the American Orthodox Catholic Church, Archdiocese of Ohio, was consecrated in 1979 by Mar Apriam I (Abp. Richard B. Morrill), head of the Holy Orthodox Catholic Church, Eastern and Apostolic. During the early 1980s Sutter's jurisdiction included parishes and a religious order in Florida and a school in Arkansas. However, in the summer of 1982 the corporation was dissolved, at which point Sutter moved to the West Coast.

Membership: In 1988 there was one small parish in Long Beach, California.

True Catholic Church

c/o Papal Office of the TCC, PO Box 133, Springdale, WA 99173

The True Catholic Church is among a spectrum of groups that have at one time declared the office of pope of the Roman Catholic Church vacant. Many of the more conservative groups considered the office vacated by the death of Pope Pius XII (1876–1958); for them, the death of the cardinals whom Pius XII had named put an end to the possibility that the College of Cardinals could elect a new valid pope. Invoking the rule that a lapse from the faith carries with it resignation from the office, those who constitute the True Catholic Church believe that Pope John XXIII (1881–1963) was not a true pope because of his membership in Freemasonry and his promotion of the teachings of Vatican II, especially the new liturgy. He and the subsequent popes, in this view, have all promulgated heresies.

As the True Catholic Church sees it, the Papal Office was vacant from 1958 until 1998. In that year the College of Electors, a worldwide body of the faith with the assumed authority and duty to elect the pope in the absence of a valid College of Cardinals, elected Earl Pulvermacher (b. 1918), a Capuchin priest ordained in 1946, to the office as Pope Pius XIII. In the absence of the cardinals, "natural law" is invoked to elect the pope, using a remnant of loyal Catholics (the remnant church) as the electorate.

The electors submitted their votes electronically to a central committee, which administered the conclave. Pulvermacher was elected on the first ballot as a result of his receiving two-thirds of the total plus one vote. When informed of the results, he accepted the election and became the Pope of the Holy Catholic Church, with all the powers therein. He was consecrated in July 1999 in services led by Gordon Cardinal Bateman of Victoria, Australia, held in Kalispell, Montana. After his election every attempt was made to announce the new pope's existence; but his residence, as a matter of security, has not been published.

During the mid-1970s, Pulvermacher had associated with a variety of priests who supported the continuance of the Latin mass, but he concluded that most were not truly Catholic. In August 1976 he withdrew from participation in the Traditional movement. He worked alone until the 1990s, when he began to associate with those who would eventually create the conclave that elected him to the Papacy.

The new pope set as his priorities the reestablishment of the pre-Vatican Church, the reinstitution of the Latin mass, and the appointment of new cardinals (who can elect his successor). He has invited Catholics to associate with the one parish that now exists, headed by the one pastor, the pope. Further, he has suggested that all true Catholics should write to him, and upon recognition he will send them a letter recognizing their association (an encyclical).

Membership: Not reported. As of 2002, one bishop and one priest had professed obedience to Pius XIII.

Sources:

True Catholic Church. www.truecatholic.org/.

United American Catholic Church

612 Crows Nest Ct., Virginia Beach, VA 23452

The United American Catholic Church was founded in 2002 by the Most Rev. Anthony Hash, its presiding archbishop. Hash was consecrated to the episcopacy in 1995 by Bp. Catherine Adams of the Friends Catholic Communion, who passed to him several lines of apostolic succession that reach back through Bp. Martha Schultz of the New Order of Glastonbury to Abp. Adrian Spruit of the Church of Antioch.

The church is an independent Catholic church, free of the jurisdiction of the Roman Catholic Church. While respecting other Christian churches and even other religions with a positive message, it has chosen the Catholic tradition as it wishes to preserve apostolic succession and perpetuate the Gospel of Christ and its call for love, forgiveness, and healing. The church accepts the Bible as the Living Word of God and administers the seven sacraments. The church also values individual freedom and wishes to allow all to grow with God as they feel led to by the Holy Spirit.

The Church is led by its bishops and national synod, which together oversee a number of semi-autonomous ministries. Men and women are welcomed into the church's ordained ministry without regard to gender, marital status, ethnic origin, social status, sexual orientation, or upper age.

The United American Catholic Church is in communion with the Catholic Apostolic Church in North America, the Contemporary Catholic Church, and the Independent Catholic Christian Church.

Membership: Not reported.

Sources:

United American Catholic Church. www.uacatholicchurch.org/.

United Catholic Church

PO Box 603, Cheshire, CT 06410

The United Catholic Church (UCC) is a nonpapal Catholic jurisdiction whose apostolic succession derives from the Old Catholic Church and other lineages. It was founded by Most Rev. Dr. Robert M. Bowman, retired; the Presiding Bishop, Most Rev. Rose Tressel, was elected in March 2006. The UCC's mission is threefold: first, to serve those who seek a church that holds that worship and the sacraments must be validly apostolic in terms of historical belief and succession; second, to serve the increasing number of Christians who seek both a Catholic and an ecumenically driven church home; and third, to serve isolated individuals who are unable, or feel they are unable, to reach out to participate in a traditional faith community. In pursuit of this healing mission the UCC welcomes all people seeking to come closer to God and actively sponsors both congregations where people can grow in Christ and specialty outreach missions and chaplaincies.

In addition to being a denomination, the United Catholic Church is also an interchurch fellowship that strives to offer a source of unity to other churches in the independent Catholic movement. UCC Associate Churches and their clergy are full members of the United Catholic Church while also maintaining their own identities, canons, and means of organizing. Through the established Associate Church covenant relationship, responsibilities and rights are both given and received, by each church to the other, enabling all the churches to work together as a family to build up the Body of Christ.

The UCC is an Orthodox Christian body in the Western tradition that recognizes the importance of the Sacraments and affirms the Real Presence of Christ in the Eucharist. It relies on the Scriptures and the early creeds of the church as its authority but does not recognize the canonicity of the Apocrypha, or require belief in any doctrine lacking biblical support. Similarly, it does not require belief in purgatory, indulgences, and prayers for the dead. The UCC also utilizes the pre-1054 form of the Nicene Creed, without the "filioque clause" ("and the son"), out of respect for the churches of the East.

Membership: In August 2006 the church reported approximately 2,300 members, 57 clergy, 14 churches, 3 cross-denominational pastorates, and 7 chaplaincies.

Sources:

United Catholic Church. www.united-catholic-church.org/index.html.

United Reform Catholic Church International

PO Box 1058, Kane'ohe, HI 96744-1058

The United Reform Catholic Church International was founded and is led by its archbishop, M. J. Kimo Keawe. Raised a Roman Catholic in Hawaii, Keawe began a ministry after being ordained in the Church of Gospel Ministry. Over the next years, while managing the Christian Life Ministry, Keawe attended a local Catholic parish church, where he was an active member. He acquired a master's degree from the St. Luke Evangelical School of Biblical Studies, sponsored by the First International Church of the Web. In 2001 he was accepted into the United Catholic Church, ordained, and appointed vicar of that church's newly formed Hawaii Diocese, which was drawn to include all of Hawaii, California, Samoa, and Tahiti, and the entire Polynesian Rim. Keawe also served as the pastor of the United Reform Catholic Church of Honolulu. In the latter part of 2001, he was consecrated by Abp. Robert Bowman as bishop of the Hawaii Diocese of the United Catholic Church.

In 2002 Keawe led in the formation of the United Reform Catholic Church International, as a new jurisdiction independent of the United Catholic Church. An initial synod was held in 2003 at which time Articles of Faith, a Code of Canon, a Mission Statement, and liturgy were approved. As it has developed, the United Reform Catholic Church International (URCCI) is a Western Catholic church but differs from a Roman Catholic church in several important regards. It is administratively independent of the Roman Catholic Church and does not accept the notion of papal infallibility.

The church accepts the traditional three levels of ministry, but permits priests to marry and welcomes women to all levels of the ordained ministry. The church has opened its sacraments to divorced persons who have remarried and does not ban contraceptives for use by married couples.

The new church moved to establish intercommunion with the Open Episcopal Church of Great Britain, headed by Bp. Richard Palmer, and the Ecumenical Catholic Church of Australia, headed by Bp. Ron Langham. In 2005 the United Reform Catholic Church International merged with these two churches and the new united church took the name United Ecumenical Catholic Church. After working within the United Church for a year, Archbishop Keawe and the North American work decided to withdraw amicably and once again become the United Reform Catholic Church International. Since then, the United Reform Catholic Church International has developed cordial relationships with several American-based jurisdictions and has created a college of bishops with their leaders. That college of bishops now includes Bp. Mark Newman of the Catholic Apostolic Church of Antioch-Malabar Rite, Bp. William Wettingfeld of the National Catholic Church of North America, and Bp. Rusty Clyma of the Inclusive Celtic Church, as well as Bps. Ron Langham and Terry Fynn, and Br. Jack Isbell of the United Ecumenical Catholic Church.

Membership: Not reported.

Sources:

United Reform Catholic Church International. www.urcci.net/index.html.

Universal Christian Apostolic Church
Current address not obtained for this edition.

In 1947 the Universal Christian Apostolic Church was founded in Vancouver, British Columbia by William F. Wolsey. Wolsey received apostolic succession eight years later when he was consecrated by British Old Catholic bishops Hugh George de Willmott Newman (Mar Georgius) of the Catholicate of the West and Harold Percival Nicholson (Mar Joannes), who had left Mar Georgius to found the Ancient Catholic Church. Wolsey claimed a degree in Bio-Psychology from the Taylor School of Bio-Psychology, out of which he claimed to have developed a psychiatric method compatible with Christianity.

The Universal Christian Apostolic Church believes in the "usefulness" of the original Christian doctrine, but attempted to be nonsectarian in its interpretation. Unique to its perspective are beliefs in Christian doctrine as a living philosophy best manifested in the work of the Christian Ministry and in Jesus as a perfect manifestation of the "Christos," the Christ-Spirit. The Christ-Spirit is thought of as enthusiasm plus, "that something more." Those who are anointed with it reveal the actual presence of Jesus that gives life to worship and ritual.

Membership: Since Wolsey's death in the 1980s, there has been no sign of the church's continuance. It may be defunct.

Remarks: Wolsey became known during his career as a collector of degrees and a member in a number of honorary societies and orders. These, along with a number of open membership organizations which he had joined, were duly noted on his lengthy curriculum vitae.

Sources:

Shyam Sundar Agarwal Sarad. *The World Jnana Sadhak Society and Its Founder*. Jalpaiguri, W. Bengal, India: The Author, 1966.

Somanah, Meernaidoo T. *Mahatma Gandhi and Other Dedicated Souls*. Port Louis, Mauritius: 1968.

———. *The Philosophy and Spiritual Teachings of the Modern Saint, Patriarch-Archbishop Dr. William F. Wolsey*. Port Louis, Mauritus: Standard Printing Establishment, 1971.

Wolsey, William Franklin. *Vivesco*. North Burnaby, BC: Universal Life Foundation, 1957.

White Robed Monks of St. Benedict
c/o Most Rev. Robert M. Dittler, OSB, Box 27536, San Francisco, CA 94127

The White Robed Monks of St. Benedict is an Old Catholic ordered community that functions as an independent ecclesiastical jurisdiction. It was founded and is led by its abbot, the Most Rev. Robert M. Dittler, who was consecrated a bishop on November 19, 1991, by Bishop Carlos A. Florida of the Orthodox Catholic Church. Dittler was granted the title of Titular Bishop of Bodhgaya, India.

Members of the order follow the Zen Rule of St. Benedict. The White Robed Monks include clerical and lay monks, affiliates, and associates. As a jurisdiction, the White Robed Monks formally accept ordained (generally Roman) Catholic clerics who are currently without a bishop and who wish to serve. The group has developed a ministry of providing the traditional Catholic sacraments and the Word to all who seek them. Members have attempted to remove any obstacles in their adherents' spiritual path and have found a particular calling to those Roman Catholics who for whatever reason are no longer able to receive the sacraments or a spiritual presence from the church of their origin.

The White Robed Monks envision their mission as letting the world be a more compassionate place. They have adopted a monastic practice of Soto Zen meditation, as they consider the Earth, rather than a building, their monastery. They teach meditation to any who wish to learn. Their motto is the first word of the Rule of St. Benedict, "Listen"; by practicing listening they aim to shed their allusions, delusions, and illusions so as better to appreciate God's message as offered.

Membership: In 2002 they reported a membership of approximately 3,800, of which 3,690 reside in the United States, 21 in Canada, and 89 in Central and South America, Europe, Eastern Europe, Asia, Africa, and the Middle East.

Sources:

White Robed Monks of St. Benedict. www.whiterobedmonks.org.

Western Liturgical Family, Part II: Anglicanism

 3

Christianity probably entered the British Isles in the second century, as there was an organized church among the Celtic tribes by the third century. In the fifth century, the Romans withdrew and the southern half of what became England was invaded by a Germanic people (Angles, Saxons, and Jutes) who pushed the Celts westward. Though initially resistant, the Anglo-Saxon tribes were evangelized both by Celts under St. Aidan (d. 651) (Ireland and Wales had been Christianized in the fifth century) and Roman Catholics under St. Augustine (d. 604). In the seventh century, the British formalized their incorporation into Roman Catholicism.

The eastern shore was subject to Danish invasions through the eighth and ninth centuries, adding a new element into the church's membership. In the eleventh century, a singularly new element was added to the mix with the conquest of England by Norman forces under William the Conqueror (c. 1028–1087). The coming of the Normans also strengthened British ties to the church in Rome. Over the next centuries, the British church served as a unifying force among the various tribal strains significantly present in the emerging nation. However, there were also repeated controversies over the extent of papal authority and its intrusion into British affairs both secular and ecclesiastical.

Had the continental Reformation under Martin Luther (1483–1546) not occurred, there is reason to believe England would have continued as a branch of the Roman Church that, like the French, German, or American church, has its own characteristics. However, the challenges to church authority across northern Europe provided an environment in which England could challenge Rome's hegemony, though it moved in a very different direction from that articulated by the continental reformers.

England, of course, had its own prophets of reform. John Wycliffe (c. 1330–1384) challenged the church's abuse of wealth and power, and he attacked the church's doctrine of transubstantiation, the idea that the elements in the Mass actually change substantively into the body and blood of Christ. He believed that this kind of magical notion merely assisted the clergy in holding onto unscriptural authority. To back his arguments he translated, published, and preached from a new edition of the scripture in the vernacular.

THE EMERGENCE OF INDEPENDENT ANGLICANISM. Under King Henry VIII (1491–1547), the Church of England came into open conflict with papal authority. The conflict did not concern doctrinal problems, however, as Henry (r. 1509–1547) was a staunch Catholic and anti-Protestant. In fact, in 1521 Henry had taken the time to author a refutation of one of Martin Luther's writings, and as a result of his volume, *Assertion of the Seven Sacraments against Luther*, the pope awarded him the title "Defender of the Faith." But two issues of central importance to him as the king of England would undo his cordial relationship with Rome: his desire for a male heir and his financial needs.

The pope had sanctioned Henry's marriage to his brother's widow, Catherine of Aragon (1485–1536), who also happened to be the daughter of Spanish rulers Ferdinand II (1452–1516) and Isabella (1451–1504), and her relatives ruled both Spain and the Holy Roman Empire. When Henry became concerned that she had produced no male heir, he moved against Catherine. Of the six children she bore, only one, Mary (1516–1558), survived. Henry asked for a divorce, an act that would call the papacy's relationships with Catherine's powerful relatives into question, and the pope refused. Eventually, the Church of England renounced allegiance to the pope and accepted Henry's supremacy over ecclesiastical law. The church backed its position by withholding money that was traditionally paid annually to Rome. In 1533 Henry forced the selection of Thomas Cranmer (1489–1556) as the new archbishop of Canterbury (the most powerful office in the Church of England), and Cranmer in turn declared the marriage with Catherine null and void. Anne Boleyn (1507–1536) became Henry's new wife.

Though the pope threatened excommunication, the British Parliament passed a series of acts that finalized the independence of the Church of England. The initial measure forbade payment to Rome, denied appeals to Rome, and placed powers heretofore exercised by the pope into the hands of the archbishops of Canterbury and York. The Act of Succession (1534) declared Mary illegitimate and named Elizabeth (1533–1603), Anne Boleyn's daughter, as heir. Later that year, the Act of Supremacy made it a crime punishable by death to not accept the Act of Succession or to fail to acknowledge the supremacy of the king.

Having already taken steps to separate from Rome, Henry also saw in the church, which possessed great wealth through its extensive landholdings, a means of supplementing his always tenuous treasury. Henry ordered the new archbishop of Canterbury to survey the many monasteries across the

Western Liturgical Family: Anglicanism Chronology

1533	British King Henry VIII marries Anne Boleyn following Abp. Thomas Cranmer's declaration of his marriage to Catherine of Aragon null and void. As a result of his marriage, Pope Clement VII excommunicates him.
1534	British Parliament passes the Act of Supremacy that names the king the "Protector and only Supreme Head of the Church and Clergy of England." In the wake of the abrogation of Papal authority, the clergy are obliged to swear allegiance to Henry as the new head of the Church of England.
1547–53	During the brief reign of Edward VI, every effort is made to Protestantize the Church in England. The Book of Common Prayer (1549) supplies the new outline for worship, and the Catholic Mass abandoned.
1553	Mary Tudor becomes Queen of England and attempts to return England to the Roman Catholic fold.
1559–63	Following her coronation, Elizabeth I outlines a *via media* between Puritanism and Roman Catholicism by issuing the Act of Uniformity (1559), publishing a new edition of the Prayer Book (1559), and promulgating a revised doctrinal statement, the Thirty-nine Articles of Religion (1563).
1583	Episcopal priest Erasmus Stourton settles in St. John's, Newfoundland.
1587	First Anglican services in British American colonies are held at the Roanoke Colony in Virginia.
1588	Defeat of the Spanish Armada.
1692	The Church of England forces the opening of King's Chapel in Puritan-dominated Boston, Massachusetts.
1696	Bishop of London appoints Thomas Bray commissary for the American colonies. He subsequently founds the Society for Promoting Christian Knowledge (1698) and the Society for the Propagation of the Gospel in Foreign Parts (1701).
1776	As the American Revolution begins, Anglican establishments exist, at least formally, in New York, New Jersey, Delaware, Maryland, Virginia, North Carolina, South Carolina, and Georgia.
1774	The Continental Congress chooses Rev. Jacob Duche to open its sessions with prayer.
1781	With the British defeat in the Revolution, most Anglican priests return to England.
1784	Samuel Seabury consecrated by bishops of the Episcopal Church of Scotland.
1787	Charles Inglis of Halifax, Nova Scotia, consecrated as the Anglican bishop of Canada.
	The bishop of London consecrates William White and Samuel Provost as bishops for the new Protestant Episcopal Church of the United States of America.
1789	The U.S. Senate elects Episcopal bishop Samuel Provost as its first chaplain.
	George Washington is inaugurated as President of the United States, the first of 12 Episcopalians to hold that office.
1816	Archbishop of Canterbury launches a mission in the Hawaiian Islands.
1855	Bishop of Maryland sets apart two women as deaconesses.
1873	Low-church dissidents leave to found the Reformed Episcopal Church.
1886	Episcopal Church's House of Bishop approves four-point statement of essential beliefs which includes the Holy Scriptures as the word of God, the Apostles' and Nicene Creeds as the rule of Faith, the two commonly accepted Sacraments (baptism and Holy Communion), and the historical episcopate. Later approved by the 1888 Lambeth conference, the statement becomes known as the Chicago-Lambeth Quadrilateral.
1928	Episcopal Church issues new edition of the *Book of Common Prayer*.
1958	Episcopal Theological School admits women to ministerial studies program.
1965	Deaconess Phyllis Edwards recognized as deacon by Bp. James Pike, San Francisco.
1970	Women admitted to General Convention as lay deputies.
1972	House of Bishops votes 74–61 in favor of ordaining women priests.
1974	Eleven women deacons ordained to priesthood by two retired and one resigned bishop in Philadelphia on July 29.
1975	Anglican Church of Canada approves ordaining women.
	House of Bishops censures all bishops who have participated in the ordaining of women.
1976	General Convention approves the ordination of women to the priesthood and episcopate.
	Conservative members of the Episcopal Church gather in St. Louis in opposition to the proposed new edition of the *Book of Common Prayer* (ultimately adopted in 1979) and the admission of women to the priesthood. The St. Louis Congress leads to the formation of the first of several dozen new small denominations representing the Continuing Anglican movement.
1989	Barbara C. Harris, an African American woman, is consecrated as an Episcopal bishop.
2003	Gene Robinson, an openly gay man, was elected bishop-designate of New Hampshire. Outraged conservative Anglican Churches around the world begin still as-yet-unresolved multi-level controversy threatening unity of the Anglican Communion.
2006	The Episcopal Church elects Dr. Katharine Jefferts Schori as Presiding Bishop and Primate.

country. Cranmer reported that extensive corruption was found, and in 1536 Henry closed most of the monasteries and pocketed the income from the sale of their lands.

Through the 1540s Henry married several more times, finally had a son, Edward (1537–1553), and ended his reign by moving against the Protestants who had begun to surface. While breaking with Rome under Henry, the Church of England retained its structure, with bishops, clergy, church buildings, and congregations, but it continued under the archbishop of Canterbury rather than the pope. The church

was also still completely Roman in doctrine, liturgy, and organization.

Under Edward VI (r. 1547–1553), who ascended the throne at the age of ten, England began to align outwardly with the reformers. The Council of Regency, appointed to administer the country until Edward came of age, was dominated by people with Protestant leanings. Cranmer published a thoroughly Protestant *Book of Common Prayer* for use in all the churches, and Parliament passed a series of decrees that changed the face of the church over the next three years.

Exponents of the Reformed Church were brought to England to teach, and Cranmer authored a doctrinal statement, the Forty-two Articles, that embodied the Reformed position.

England might have come into the Reformed camp at that point had it not been for the sickliness of Edward, who passed away before reaching adulthood. He was succeeded by his older sister Mary (r. 1553–1558), a devout Roman Catholic with a memory of the indignities heaped upon her mother. She married a Spaniard, abolished Cranmer's prayer book, and moved against the Protestant church leaders. The extensive nature of her persecutions, which included a number of executions at the stake, earned her the long-term enmity of Protestants and the label "Bloody Mary." The country was on the verge of revolution when Mary died after only five years on the throne.

Mary's death brought Elizabeth I (r. 1558–1603) to the throne. Her half-century of rule is remembered as one of the great eras in England's history. It was during this time that the distinctions of the Anglican tradition were developed. Seeking to create a strong and peaceful nation, she forced a compromise of the positions of the two warring factions. A new *Prayer Book* was issued, and a set of Thirty-nine Articles, derived from the Forty-two Articles, was promulgated. Some of the articles, which continued to embody the Reformed theological perspective, condemned specific Roman Catholic practices. Purgatory, indulgences, venerating saints' relics, and celebrating the liturgy in any tongue other than the vernacular were among the Roman elements condemned. However, Elizabeth retained the traditional episcopal structure.

Elizabeth I, aware that Edward and Mary had strong support for their choices of religions, adopted what became known as the *via media* (middle way), blending Roman Catholic and Protestant elements.

Opposition to the compromises came from both sides, but Elizabeth was affected most by the objections of the Roman Catholics. In 1570 she was excommunicated by the pope. She uncovered several plots to have her assassinated and replaced with Mary Queen of Scots (1542–1587). She gradually gave up any hope of reconciling with the pope, who in 1588 supported the building and launching of the Spanish Armada against England. The defeat of the armada remains one of the crucial turning points of European history. In one of the final acts against Elizabeth, in 1596 the pope declared that the Anglican's episcopal orders were seriously flawed and hence were not valid.

Early in Elizabeth's reign, a number of Roman Catholic bishops resigned. In response, Archbishop Matthew Parker (1504–1585) moved to fill the vacant seats, a major point in Rome's conclusion that the Anglicans had lost their apostolic succession. This action soured Anglican/Roman Catholic relations into the twentieth century. They have yet to be fully resolved, but initial steps at healing the Roman-Anglican split were taken in the atmosphere of goodwill generated by the Second Vatican Council (1962–1965).

The Book of Common Prayer, the Anglican liturgical book that replaced the Roman missal, has gone through several editions. The edition published during Elizabeth's reign is crucial: it makes concrete the distinctive character of Anglicanism that has continued to this day. That edition includes the Thirty-nine Articles of Religion, the ancient Christian creeds, a church calendar, and texts of liturgical services. Material on the sacraments in that edition is somewhat vague, thus allowing various interpretations of the Eucharist. Anglicans recognize only two sacraments: baptism and the Lord's Supper. Anglican doctrine on the church shifted from the Roman emphasis on the bishop to the Calvinist emphasis on the congregation. *The Book of Common Prayer* asserts that the church exists where the Word of God is preached, the sacraments are duly administered, and the faithful are gathered.

A certain Anglophilia characterizes the Church of England. When Rome commissioned St. Augustine to be a missionary in England in 597, he found Christians already in England. Over the centuries, since the final break with Rome, many Anglicans have insisted that their church was not formed by Rome and that the Anglican Church in England predates the arrival of the Roman Catholic Church to the British Isles. Anglicanism is thus a tradition separated from Roman Catholicism by its liturgical differences, its condemnation of some Roman beliefs and practices, and its alignment with this pre-Roman British Christian "Celtic" tradition. With the expansion of England in the seventeenth century, the Anglican tradition spread throughout the world.

ENGLAND AFTER ELIZABETH I. The development of the Church of England did not cease with the imposition of the *via media*, and Elizabeth's long reign and ability to triumph over her enemies did much to set it firmly in place. Elizabeth never married, and hence had no children to succeed her. She was succeeded by James I (1566–1625), the son of Mary Queen of Scots. During his two decades on the throne (1603–1625), James's Catholic tendencies were stymied by the discovery of plots to assassinate him. Instead of giving in to the demands of his Roman Catholic subjects, he supported the new Puritan translation of the Bible, and a series of laws restricting Roman Catholic participation in various activities. He then tested the Puritan strength with a refusal to allow further revisions of the *Prayer Book*.

The reign of James's successor, Charles I (1600–1649), saw the rise to power of Archbishop William Laud (1573–1645). Charles was a champion of Anglicanism and initiated policies that infuriated the Puritans (Protestants in the Reformed tradition), so-called for their desires to further "purify" the Church of England of its Roman remnants. Protestants largely controlled Parliament, with whom Charles found himself in a continuing contest of wills. Matters came to a head when the Scots (who had by this time established Presbyterianism as the country's faith) revolted. Parliament used the situation to assert its control. In the end, Parliament called for an assembly of Puritan clergy to meet at Westminster and advise the Parliament. They proceeded to write what were to become the defining documents of British Presbyterianism, the Westminster Confession of Faith, the Directory of Worship, and the Catechism. In 1645 Parliament forbade the continued use of the *Prayer Book* and outlawed Anglicanism with its Catholic remnants.

The civil war that followed brought Oliver Cromwell (1599–1658) to power. He articulated a policy of religious toleration (Roman Catholics and Anglicans excepted), and then through a Commission of Triers he began to systematically move the British church toward the austere Reformed faith demanded by the Puritan leaders. But a number of his reforms went against the heart of the popular exercise of faith. For example, he outlawed dancing and Christmas and other festivals. He also saw to the dismantling of numerous ornate church altar areas. Each act cost him valuable support. He was able to hold the country together while alive, but his son was driven from power, and Charles II (1630–1685), a Roman Catholic, ascended the throne.

Under Charles II (r. 1660–1685), the Anglican Church resumed its place as the national Church of England, a position it has not since relinquished, and the real struggle among the Christians of the British Isles shifted to finding some means of accommodating the many dissenting groups that were present in the culture. A major landmark was the Toleration Act of 1689, which granted liberty of worship to all the various Protestant dissenting groups, though it did not yet expand that toleration to Roman Catholics, Jews, and Unitarian Christians (who did not affirm the Christian doctrine of the Trinity).

THE WORLDWIDE ANGLICAN COMMUNION.

While Britons were trying to decide who would rule and what kind of government would direct the country, they were also pursuing an expansionist policy in regard to the New World across the Atlantic. Beginning in the eighteenth century, the British actively settled the East Coast of the North American continent. Some Anglicans responded in 1649 by founding the Society for the Propagation of the Gospel in New England. The society picked up the support of John Eliot (1604–1690), already in Massachusetts working among the Native Americans. Its efforts were supplemented by the Society for Promoting Christian Knowledge (SPCK), founded in 1698, and the Society for the Propagation of the Gospel in Foreign Parts (SPG), founded in 1701. The majority of the Anglican clergy operating in North America prior to the American Revolution (1775–1783) was sent through the SPG.

The American Revolution had a marked effect on the spread of Anglicanism. The missionary societies withdrew from the new United States, and redirected their efforts elsewhere. By that time, England was establishing the first centers of what would become its vast colonial empire of the nineteenth century. Joined by the Church Missionary Society and the London Missionary Society, both founded in 1795, the SPG set to the tasks of providing church life for British colonists (and expatriates around the world in noncolonial

settings) and evangelizing non-Christian populations that came under the hegemony of the British government.

The nineteenth century was the era for the massive expansion of Christianity in all parts of the world, carried in large part by the European colonial enterprise. Anglicanism became a worldwide faith centered upon the colonists that responded to the efforts of the missionaries in setting up the Church of England everywhere the British erected settlements. Given the extensive nature of the British Empire, it is not surprising that by the beginning of the twentieth century Anglicanism had established itself throughout the Orient, across India and Africa, and to a lesser extent in South America.

Just as the previous two centuries had seen the vast expansion of the British colonial empire, the twentieth century saw a major change in England's relationships with colonial states, signaled in 1931 by the formation of the British Community (or Commonwealth) of Nations. Among the first acts of the Commonwealth was the reordering of relations through the granting of independence to Canada, New Zealand, Australia, and South Africa. India and Pakistan gained independence in 1947, and during the next decade most of the former colonies also either gained independence through armed conflict or were granted it. Most recently changing status was Hong Kong, which in 1997 again became part of China. Many former colonies chose to remain part of the Commonwealth, but others went their own ways.

The dismantling of the empire was in some cases anticipated by the reordering of the relationships within the Church of England internationally. Beginning in the middle of the nineteenth century, church names began to change; for example, the Church of England in Canada became the Anglican Church in Canada, which was later granted independent status and joined the worldwide Anglican Communion as a sister church. Such changes were most frequently accompanied by the development of an indigenous leadership, the organization of dioceses and archdioceses, and the naming of a primate (leading bishop) from among the country's citizens.

The Protestant Episcopal Church (now known simply as the Episcopal Church) in the United States was the first church granted recognition as an independent body, a decision made after and in light of the success of the American Revolution. The first Anglican bishop outside of the British Isles was named for Canada in 1787: Charles Inglis (1734–1816), bishop of Halifax, Nova Scotia. Through the next century, missions were established and grew into dioceses, but each diocese operated autonomously and reported directly to England. Finally, in 1861, the first provincial synod for the Church of England in Canada met. That church continued to evolve, and finally emerged in 1897 as an autonomous body.

Around the world, the story of the emergence of the various independent jurisdictions that now comprise worldwide Anglicanism is distinct for each nation or region. The first to attain independent status was New Zealand (1857), but the overwhelming majority of the autonomous provinces were created after World War II (1937–1945). Many arose not only in the rush to end colonialism, but in the euphoria of the mid-twentieth-century ecumenical movement. In a variety of countries where Christianity was a minority movement, Anglicans joined Congregationalists, Methodists, and Presbyterians to create national Protestant churches, the most prominent being the Church of North India, the Church of South India, the Church of Pakistan, and the Church of Bangladesh.

Of particular interest because of its intrusion into Anglican affairs in the last generation is the church in the Philippines. The Philippine Independent Church (PIC) emerged out of the Spanish-American War (1898) in which the United States took over the island nation; the indigenous PIC created a schism between it and the Roman Catholic Church. The PIC founder led the church into Unitarianism, a trend that was checked by his successor, and in 1947 the church officially accepted a Trinitarian creed and was accepted by the Episcopal Church (in the United States) as a sister church. In the meantime, a Philippine Episcopal Church had been established in the common pattern to service British expatriates and missionize the indigenous population. Both churches continue to the present.

WOMEN AND ANGLICANISM.
In the last decades of the twentieth century, possibly the most significant issue before Anglicanism worldwide was the admission of females to the ordained ministry—an issue squarely placed before the worldwide communion by the ordinations of women in Hong Kong in 1971 and in the American Episcopal Church in 1974. A few churches followed suit in the early 1980s, and by the time of the meeting of the Lambeth Conference in 1988, it had become the single most divisive issue before the international gathering of Anglican bishops. They established a commission to deal with any potential schisms resulting from the spreading acceptance of women in the ministry.

By the next meeting of the Lambeth Conference in 1998, the issue had been largely settled. Not only have additional provinces around the world moved to ordain women, but in 1989 the American church consecrated its first female bishop, Barbara Harris (b. 1930), an African American. There were eleven female bishops in attendance at the 1998 Lambeth Conference. They came from the United States (eight), Canada (two), and New Zealand (one). The vote of the church in Korea that same year to ordain women meant that the majority of provinces now accepted women into the ministry. This trend culminated in 2006 when the Episcopal Church elected Katharine Jefferts Schori (b. 1954) as its presiding bishop.

While the majority of the Anglican Communion has shifted in favor of the ordination of females, it is by no means unanimous, and the growing presence of women in the hierarchy has raised repeated threats of schism. In 2000 the bishops of Singapore and Rwanda consecrated Chuck Murphy and John Rodgers as bishops to lead what has been termed the Anglican Mission to America. The pair has been vigorous in setting up congregations and dioceses by drawing conservatives who oppose not only female ordination but other

actions resulting from positions assumed by the Episcopal Church.

ANGLICANISM IN AMERICA.
The Anglican tradition entered North America with the coming of the British explorers in the sixteenth century. Worship according to the Church of England was established at St. John's, Newfoundland, in 1583, where the Reverend Erasmus Stourton (1603–1658) became the first Anglican minister to reside in North America, though Anglican services had been held for the first time in what is now the United States on August 13, 1587, at the ill-fated Roanoke colony in Virginia. Anglican services were permanently established in 1607 in Jamestown. The first minister at Jamestown was Robert Hunt (1568–1608), who died soon after his arrival in America. His efforts were followed by the more substantive career of Alexander Whitaker (1585–c. 1614), who served the colony as pastor of Henrico, the second church in Virginia.

Throughout the 1600s, the Church of England spread through British North America, finally entering Puritan Boston in 1692. It was given a significant boost in 1701 by the establishment of the SPG as the foreign missionary arm for the Church of England, and by the arrival of society founder Thomas Bray (1658–1630). Appointed commissioner, with some of the powers of a bishop, Bray settled in Maryland and directed the missionary endeavor. The work in Canada expanded immensely in the late eighteenth century, following a series of events beginning with the British seizure of Quebec (1759) and the subsequent Treaty of Paris (1763), which gave Canada to the British. The American Revolution then sent large numbers of British loyalists northward. The growth is no better symbolized than by the placing of Charles Inglis, a former parish priest from New York, in Halifax as the first bishop of the Church of England in Canada in 1787.

While aiding church growth in Canada, the American Revolution almost destroyed Anglicanism in the American colonies. Identified as antipatriotic by the public, the Church of England in America also lost its legal status, most of its priests (who returned to England), and its financial base. The church was virtually cut off from the homeland because the bishops in England initially refused to pass along episcopal orders. Samuel Seabury (1729–1796), elected bishop by the remaining priests in Connecticut, was consecrated by Scottish bishops in 1784. It was not until 1787, the same year a bishop was placed in Nova Scotia, that William White (1748–1836) and Samuel Provost (1742–1815) were consecrated in London and a working accord was reached between the new Protestant Episcopal Church in the United States and the Church of England.

While the church in America grew as an independent body, the church in Canada prospered as a missionary branch of the Church of England and was officially designated as the Church of England in Canada; it changed its name to the Anglican Church in Canada in 1955.

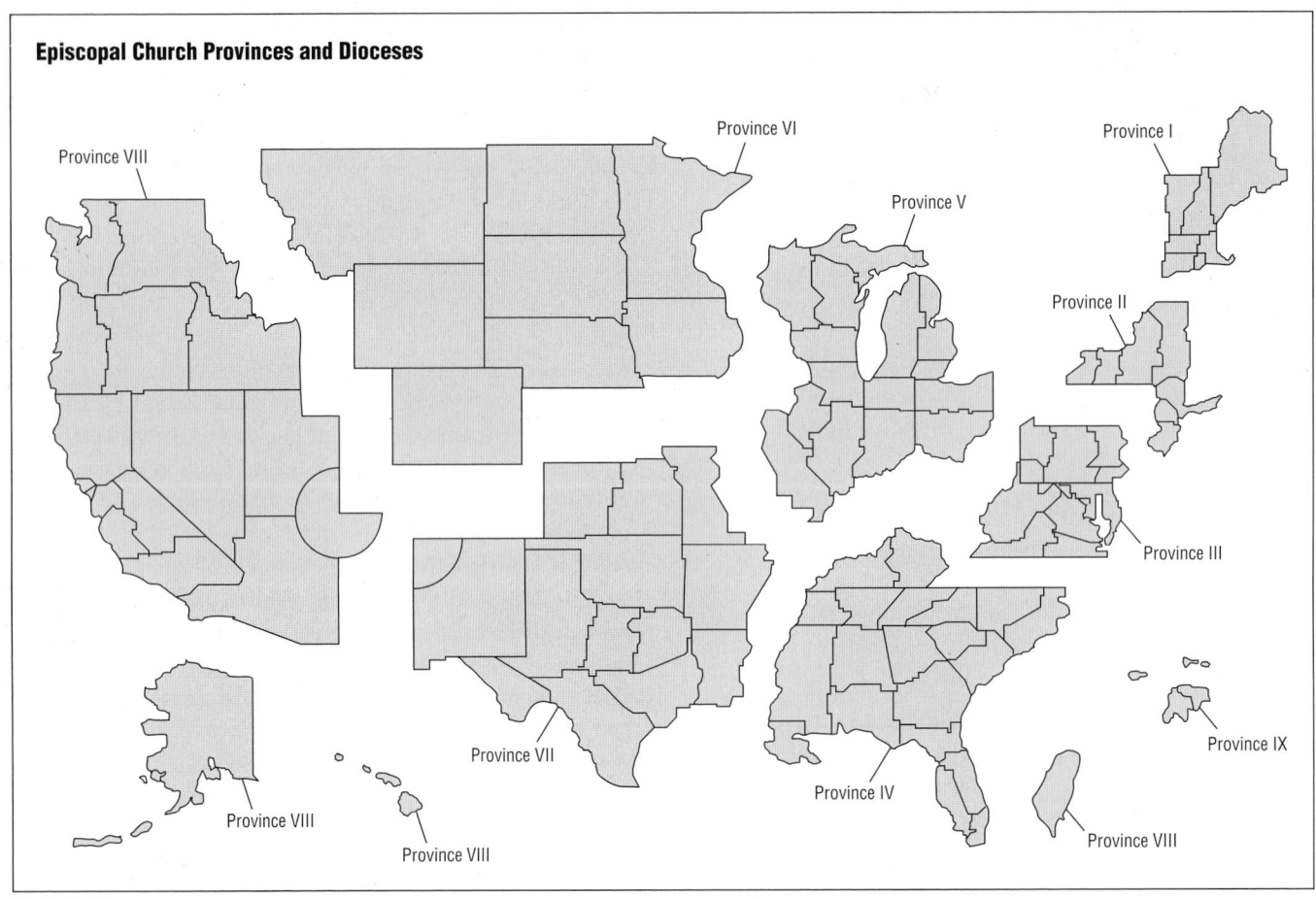

Episcopal Church Provinces and Dioceses

TRADITIONALIST ANGLICANISM. The Protestant Episcopal Church, the Anglican Church in Canada, the Reformed Episcopal Church (a nineteenth-century evangelical splinter group), and a few congregations of the Philippine Independent Church provided the main substance of the Anglican tradition for North America until the mid-1960s. There had been several smaller schisms, but not until the 1960s did the Episcopal Church suffer its first widespread losses from members withdrawing in protest over modernist changes in the church. It was primarily related to a shifting moral code (manifest in new attitudes toward sexuality), revisions of the *Prayer Book*, and the acceptance of females into the priesthood. The initial schism of 1964 and the subsequent formation of the Anglican Orthodox Church brought widespread unrest that heightened in 1976 after women were ordained in both Canada and the United States.

The Anglican Catholic Church (ACC) and the Anglican Catholic Church in Canada (ACCC) are the two largest bodies of the 20 or more churches formed among dissenting Anglicans. As they were formed, each of the new jurisdictions faced the problem of apostolic succession. The Anglican Orthodox Church had accepted old Catholic and independent Orthodox orders. In the 1970s, ACC and ACCC leaders turned to the international Anglican Communion for support, and found it in the Philippine Independent Church.

Bishop Francisco Pagtakhan, the PIC missionary bishop whose jurisdiction covered North America, performed the initial consecrations. As additional new Anglican jurisdictions were established, Pagtakhan was joined by two colleagues, Bishops Sergio Mondala and Lupe Rosete, and together they performed a series of consecrations during the early 1980s. As a result of these and other actions, Pagtakhan faced severe disagreements with the church in the Philippines in the mid-1980s, and eventually left to form the Philippine Independent Catholic Church, which has now established parishes in North America.

The independent Anglicans who emerged in the 1970s have been the most conservative wing of Anglicanism. While most are concentrated in the few larger churches that grew out of the 1976 meeting in St. Louis, Missouri (especially the Anglican Catholic Church and the Anglican Catholic Church in Canada), the number of new jurisdictions has continued to increase and the overall situation remains in flux.

A new phase of the controversy opened in 2000, when two conservative Anglican bishops, one from Rwanda and one from Singapore, consecrated two American Episcopalians, Chuck Murphy and John Rodgers, as bishops of new Anglican work in the United States. The act of setting up the Anglican Mission to America severely strained relationships in the worldwide Anglican Communion with the invasion of personnel authorized by one bishop in the jurisdictions of another.

Implicit in the action was the questioning of the legitimacy of the Episcopal Church by the leadership of other provinces. While the Anglican Mission to America has yet to draw the various jurisdictions founded since 1976 into it, it has that potential, as well as drawing conservative congregations still within the Episcopal Church.

HOMOSEXUALITY.

While the issue of woman as bishops was disturbing the Anglican Communion globally, the growing acceptance of homosexuality among members and clergy hovered in the background. As early as 1957, England had taken the lead in decriminalizing homosexual activity. Even earlier, homosexual men had found a haven within the all-male clergy of the Church of England, a fact that was periodically acknowledged when individual actions became the focus of public scandal. As the gay movement came to prominence in the Christian world in the 1970s, American Episcopalian lesbians and gay men founded Dignity, an organization to foster their presence within the church.

The Episcopal Church began to address the issues raised by Dignity as early as 1988 when a group of the church's bishops issued a statement recognizing the presence and contributions of homosexuals who had served in the priesthood and declaring their opposition to the church's recently stated position of refusing to ordain anyone who was having sexual relations outside of a heterosexual marriage. Through the 1990s, the subject of homosexuality was widely debated, and the church's official position was often honored by being ignored. A number of homosexuals and a few lesbians were quietly ordained. Many parishes accepted priests living openly with a gay partner.

The ongoing debate within the Episcopal Church reached a peak in 2003 when V. Gene Robinson, an openly gay priest, was elected bishop of the Episcopal Diocese of New Hampshire on June 7, 2003. He had previously served for some 17 years as the bishop's assistant. His consecration set off an intense debate within the church, with those who had been opposed to women in the priesthood gaining significant strength. Not only did a number of parishes take steps to withdraw from the church (with the issue of who retains the deed to parish property remaining in doubt), but several bishops threatened to withdraw their dioceses from the church.

While debate raged within the American church, Robinson's election also evoked responses from Anglican churches internationally. Bishops from around the world, especially central Africa, demanded that the American church be cast out of the Anglican Communion, or they would take their churches out of it. The ongoing situation has placed the diplomatic skills of the archbishop of Canterbury at the center of the international crisis, the resolution of which remains elusive.

SOURCES

Anglican historical studies are brought together by the Historical Society of the Episcopal Church, PO Box 2247, Austin, TX 78768. The Historical Society publishes the quarterly journal *Anglican and Episcopal*

History. In addition to the society's archives in Austin, other significant archival deposits are found at the Berkeley Divinity School at Yale in New Haven, Connecticut; the General Theological Seminary of the Episcopal Church in New York City; and the Episcopal Church headquarters in New York City.

Church of England and the Worldwide Anglican Communion

Avis, Paul. *The Identity of Anglicanism: Essentials of Anglican Ecclesiology.* Edinburgh, U.K.: Clark, 2008. 201 pp.

Chapman, Mark. *Anglicanism: A Very Short Introduction.* New York: Oxford University Press, 2006. 168 pp.

Dart, J. L. C. *The Old Religion: An Examination into the Facts of the English Reformation.* London: S.P.C.K., 1956. 210 pp.

Flindall, R. P., ed. *The Church of England, 1815–1948.* London: S.P.C.K., 1972. 497 pp.

Hardy, E. R., Jr., ed. *Orthodox Statements on Anglican Orders.* New York: Morehouse-Gorham, 1946. 72 pp.

Holloway, Richard, ed. *The Anglican Tradition.* Wilton, CT: Morehouse-Barlow, 1984. 129 pp.

Neill, Stephen. *Anglicanism.* Rev. ed. London: Mowbrays, 1977. 421 pp.

Wand, J. W. C. *What the Church of England Stands For: A Guide to Its Authority in the Twentieth Century.* London: Mowbray, 1951. 131 pp.

Whale, John. *The Anglican Church Today: The Future of Anglicanism.* London: Mowbray, 1988. 102 pp.

Wingate, Andrew, et al. *Anglicanism: A Global Communion.* London: Mobray, 1998. 416 pp.

Anglicanism in North America

Addison, James Thayer. *The Episcopal Church in the United States, 1789–1931.* New York: Scribner's, 1951. 400 pp.

DeMille, George E. *The Episcopal Church since 1900: A Brief History.* New York: Morehouse-Gorham, 1955. 223 pp.

Hein, David, and Gardiner H. Shattuck Jr. *The Episcopalians.* Westport, CT: Praeger, 2004. 361 pp.

Herklots, H. G. G. *The Church of England and the American Episcopal Church.* London: Mowbray, 1966. 183 pp.

Katerberg, William H. *Modernity and the Dilemma of North American Anglican Identities, 1880–1950.* Montreal, Quebec: McGill-Queen's University Press, 2001.

Kew, Richard, and Roger J. White. *New Millennium, New Church: Trends Shaping the Episcopal Church for the 21st Century.* Cambridge, MA: Cowley, 1992. 177 pp.

Konolige, Kit, and Frederica Konolige. *The Power of Their Glory: America's Ruling Class, the Episcopalians.* New York: Wyden, 1978. 408 pp.

Lewis, Harold T. *Yet with a Steady Beat: The African American Struggle in the Episcopal Church.* Valley Forge, PA: Trinity Press International, 1996. 253 pp.

Manross, William W. *A History of the American Episcopal Church.* 2nd ed. New York: Morehouse-Gorham, 1950. 415 pp.

Sumner, David E. *The Episcopal Church's History, 1945–1985.* Wilton, CT: Morehouse-Barlow, 1987. 221 pp.

Sydnor, William. *Looking at the Episcopal Church.* Wilton, CT: Morehouse-Barlow, 1980. 142 pp.

Webber, Christopher L., and Frank T. Griswold III. *Welcome to the Episcopal Church: An Introduction to Its History, Faith, and Worship.* Harrisburg, PA: Morehouse, 1999. 133 pp.

Woolverton, John Frederick. *Colonial Anglicanism in North America.* Detroit, MI: Wayne State University Press, 1984. 331 pp.

New Anglicans

Armentrout, Donald S. *Episcopal Splinter Groups.* Sawanee, TN: School of Theology, University of the South, 1985.

Bess, Douglas. *Divided We Stand: A History of the Continuing Anglican Movement.* Berkeley, CA: Apocryphile Press, 2006. 292 pp.

Dibbert, Roderic B. *The Roots of Traditional Anglicanism.* Akron, OH: DeKoven Foundation of Ohio, 1984. 13 pp.

A Directory of Churches of the Continuing Anglican Tradition. Eureka Springs, AK: Fellowship of Concerned Churchmen, 1983–1984.

Hassett, Miranda K. *Anglican Communion in Crisis: How Episcopal Dissidents and Their African Allies Are Reshaping Anglicanism.* Princeton, NJ: Princeton University Press, 2007. 320 pp.

Joseph, Murray. *Priests Forever.* Valley Forge, PA: Brotherhood of the Servants of the Lord, 1975. 16 pp.

Opening Addresses of the Church Congress at St. Louis, Missouri, September 14–16, 1977. Amherst, VA: Fellowship of Concerned Churchmen, 1977.

A Retired Priest. *The Broken Body.* 1980. 38 pp.

❊ Intrafaith Organizations

Anglican Consultative Council

The Anglican Communion Office, St Andrew's House, 16 Tavistock Crescent, London, W11 1AP U.K.

The Anglican Consultative Council is the continuing organizational arm of the worldwide Anglican Communion, those Anglican churches around the world in communion with the Church of England. Most member churches were at one time an integral part of the Church of England but have since become autonomous national churches. Traditionally, the unity of the Anglican Communion was expressed through the periodic conferences of bishops that met at Lambeth Palace, the headquarters of the Church of England in London. The Lambeth Conference of 1968, in light of the growing number of independent Anglican jurisdictions, suggested the formation of the council.

The council meets every three years, and each member church may send up to three representatives. The council has no legislative authority but facilitates communication and consultation. It may make recommendations and on occasion speak for the Anglican Communion. It also encourages the participation of member churches in the larger ecumenical movement. It conducts ecumenical discussions with similar international organizations of other church groups.

Membership: In North America the council members include the Anglican Church of Canada and the Episcopal Church.

Sources:

Anglican Consultative Council. www.anglicancommunion.org/communion/acc/.

Whale, John. *The Anglican Church Today: The Future of Anglicanism.* London: Mowbray, 1988.

Wingate, Andrew, et al., eds. *Anglicanism: A Global Communion.* London: Mowbray; and New York: Church Pub., 1998.

American Anglican Council

2296 Henderson Mill Rd. NE, Ste. 406, Atlanta, GA 30345-2739

The American Anglican Council is a fellowship of congregations and church leaders who have united to affirm a traditional Christian witness in the face of the issues currently affecting the Episcopal Church. Most of the member congregations remain affiliated with the Episcopal Church, though many are former Episcopal congregations now affiliated with Anglican Provinces based in other parts of the world (especially Africa and South America) or with one of the newer independent Anglican jurisdictions.

The American Anglican Council grew out of a meeting in 1995 at the Briarwood Conference Center in suburban Dallas, Texas, attended by a cadre of prominent conservative Episcopal leaders (including five bishops). The group informally adopted a statement of belief and concern entitled "A Place to Stand: A Call to Mission" and called for a second gathering to be held in 1996 that would assemble a larger and more representative group of people interested in renewal within the church. That gathering, called Briarwood II, met at Techny, Illinois, and led to the incorporation of the American Anglican Council. The Council was conceived as a focal point for those bishops, parishes, and specialized ministries who wish to present to the larger society a visible, tangible community that demonstrates God's Kingdom in a manner faithful to the Anglican tradition. The ACC began to network with concerned bishops, parishes, and ministries in the United States and then with like-minded Anglican worldwide. Those affiliated with the ACC affirm the Lambeth Quadrilateral, which finds the essentials of Christian faith in the Holy Scripture, the Nicene Creed, the Sacraments of Baptism and Holy Communion, and the Historic Episcopate.

The ACC emphasizes its role in networking, advocacy, and otherwise serving the needs of its members (including offering legal advice as regards property). It does not conduct ordinations or consecrations, and has no official role in either the Episcopal Church or the Anglican Communion. While somewhat energized into opposition by the Episcopal Church's election of a gay bishop, the ACC is tolerant of females in the ministry; it affirms the sanctity of life (and generally opposes abortion), and does not advocate for any particular edition of the Prayer Book. Members see the essential issue to be their opposition to what is termed *revisionism* or *progressive Christianity*—that is, views of Christianity that reject the authority of Scripture and the uniqueness of Jesus Christ as the only means of human salvation.

In general, the ACC is in accord with a resolution on sexuality passed at the 1998 Lambeth Conference. Generally known as Lambeth 1.10, this affirms marriage as the union of a man and a woman in a lifelong relationship, endorses sexual abstinence for those not married, and declares homosexual practice "incompatible with Scripture." While the resolution rejects same-sex unions in principle, and ordination of any involved in such unions, it declares a commitment to "minister pastorally and sensitively" to all, including those who practice homosexuality.

Membership: By 2008, chapters of the ACC had been started in more than 25 dioceses of the Episcopal Church, and three dioceses (Dallas, Texas; Fort Worth, Texas; and Quincey, Illinois) had officially affiliated. The ACC reported some 330 affiliate parishes scattered across some 40 states. The ACC cooperates with several other organizations with similar purposes, such as Common Cause Partners, the Anglican Communion Network, and the Anglican Network in Canada.

Sources:

American Anglican Council. www.americananglican.org/.

Traditional Anglican Communion

PO Box 746, Blackwood, SA, Australia 5051

The Traditional Anglican Communion is the international ecumenical organization serving the Continuing Church movement that swept through Anglican churches in the 1970s. Following a convention held at St. Louis, Missouri, in 1977, conservative members and priests began to organize traditionalist congregations, establish new jurisdictions, and, with the help of bishops of the Philippine Independent Church, have bishops consecrated. Through the 1980s, independent jurisdictions were established in Canada, Australia, and New Zealand as it became evident that as a whole, Anglican jurisdictions worldwide were either approving or tolerant of liturgical experimentation and the ordination of females to the priesthood. Thus, in February 1992, the Anglican Catholic Church, the Anglican Catholic Church of Canada, the Anglican Catholic Church—Australia, and related traditional churches in New Zealand, Hong Kong, and Central America, formed the Traditional Anglican Communion, a traditionalist counterpart of the jurisdictions in communion with the Church of England.

Membership: North American members include the Anglican Catholic Church and the Anglican Catholic Church of Canada.

Sources:

Traditional Anglican Communion. www.acahome.org/tac/index.htm.

 # Anglican Churches

American Anglican Church

680 Albany Post Rd., Scarborough, NY 10510

The American Anglican Church emerged out of the larger Continuing Church movement, which began in the mid-1970s among former Episcopalians who rejected the direction the Episcopal Church was taking in the revision of traditional worship and the ordination of females to the priesthood. It represents the high church or Anglo-Catholic wing of Anglicanism, which places great emphasis on the affinity of Anglicanism to Roman Catholicism. The church's constitution and canons were adopted in 1996. Bp. Donald Perschall was elected as the first presiding bishop.

In the late 1990s, Perschall became a leading figure in conversations between some of the bishops in the Continuing Church movement and traditionalists who chose to remain within the Episcopal Church. At two meeting held at St. Benedict's Abbey in Bartonville, Illinois, a set of Articles of Ecclesiastical Fellowship were agreed upon. However, as conversations continued, in 2003 Bp. Perschall left the American Anglican Church and joined the Episcopal Church, in which he was named rector of Holy Trinity Episcopal Church in Mount Vernon, Illinois. The new presiding bishop of the American Anglican Church is Rt. Rev. John A. Herzog (b. 1932).

The Anglican American Church was a signer to the 1999 statement of "Ecclesiastical Fellowship" that placed them in relationship with the Anglican Church in America, the Anglican Province of America, the Anglican Rite Synod in the Americas, the Episcopal Missionary Church, and the Episcopal Orthodox Church. The statement assumes a common adherence to the Bible as the Word of God, the ancient Ecumenical Creeds, the historic episcopate (and an understanding of apostolic succession), and the historic Anglican liturgies, primarily those preserved in the 1928 Book of Common Prayer. The church also affirmed its adherence to the 39 Articles of Religion of 1801, and to both the Chicago (1886) and Lambeth (1888) statements of the Lambeth Quadrilateral.

The American Anglican Church has accepted the 1928 Book of Common Prayer as its official prayer book. It specifically affirms traditional standards of marriage and the limitation on sexual relations outside of marriage. The church has also agreed to not alter liturgical texts merely to accommodate current trends.

The Order of St. Andrew, an ordered community founded in 1986 and based in Scarborough, New York, is associated with the church. The church is also in communion with the Traditional Church of England, a conservative jurisdiction with parishes in the United Kingdom.

Membership: In 2008 there were 11 parishes in the United States and one in Canada.

Educational Facilities:

Saint Andrew's Institute of Theology.

Sources:

American Anglican Church. www.americananglicanchurch.org/seminary.html.

Nones, Jane, ed. *1994/95 Directory of Traditional Anglican and Episcopal Parishes*. Tulsa, OK: Fellowship of Concerned Churchmen, 1995.

Anamchara Celtic Church

432 W High St., Wills Point, TX 75169

The Anamchara Celtic Church was founded in 1996 in Wills Point, Texas, by its presiding bishop, Thomas J. Faulkenbury. He was consecrated by Bp. Ivan MacKillop of the Church of the Culdees (formerly the Servant Catholic Church). The church views itself as an association of people who follow the prayer and Eucharist in the tradi-tion of the ancient Celtic Church (the pre-Roman Catholic Church of the ancient British Isles). Celtic Christianity is distinguished, in part, by an emphasis on community over institutional religion and recognition of gender equality. The theological work of St. Morgan of Wales (354–418 C.E.) and St. John Scotus Erigena (810–877 C.E.) are especially appreciated.

The church affirms the truth of the Holy Scriptures (including the intertestament writings known as the Apocrypha), the Nicene Creed, and the seven ecumenical councils. It affirms the unity of the church as exemplified by the undivided Catholic Church during the first ages of its existence rather than an enforced organizational unity. The church recognizes all of life to be sacramental, but also practices the two major sacraments of baptism and Holy Communion in addition to the following five minor sacraments: confirmation, penance (or reconciliation), matrimony, holy orders, and unction. The church is headed by an episcopate in the apostolic lineage, though leadership tends toward an attitude of service rather than autocracy.

The church practices open Communion and invites all Christians to partake of the Holy Eucharist. Worship varies from congregation to congregation, but some use the contemporary Celtic-inspired Desert Missal still in the process of development. The Celtic calendar is followed as are the feast days of the saints (with special emphasis on Celtic saints). Some congregations mark the seasonal changes at Samhain (October 31), Imbolc (February 2), Beltaine (May 1), and Lammas (August 1).

The church is headed by a bishop, but congregations are organized into a loosely affiliated fellowship. The Anamchara Celtic Church is a member of the Celtic Christian Communion and is in communion with the Church of the Culdees and St. Ciaran's Fellowship of Celtic Christian Communities.

Membership: In 1997 the church reported 300 members in 11 congregations served by 10 priests in the United States. There was a single congregation in Canada and one each in Scotland and Japan.

Periodicals: *Celtic Fire Newsletter*.

Anglican Catholic Church

c/o The Most Reverend Mark Haverland, PO Box 5223, Athens, GA 30604-5223

Prior to 1974 dissent over what many felt was theological and moral drift in the Protestant Episcopal Church had led to the formation of several small protesting bodies. However, large-scale dissent occurred only after a series of events beginning in 1974 gave focus to the conservative protest. In that year four Episcopal bishops (in defiance of their colleagues and the church) ordained 11 women to the priesthood. The following year, the Anglican Church of Canada approved a provision for the ordination of women. Then in 1976, with only a token censure of the bishops, the Protestant Episcopal Church regularized the ordinations of the 11 women. It also approved the revised *Book of Common Prayer*, which replaced the 1928 edition most Episcopalians had used for half a century.

The events of the mid-1970s led to the calling of a Congress of Episcopalians to consider alternatives to the Protestant Episcopal Church and to find a way to continue a traditional Anglican Church. In the months leading up to the congress, several congregations and priests withdrew from the Episcopal Church and formed the provisional Diocese of the Holy Trinity. They designated James O. Mote (1922–2006) as their bishop elect. In September 1977 1,800 people gathered in St. Louis, where they adopted a lengthy statement, the "Affirmation of St. Louis," calling for allegiance to the Anglican tradition of belief (as expressed in the ancient creeds and the teachings of the church fathers) and practice (as exemplified in the 1928 edition of the Book of Common Prayer). It specifically denounced the admission of women to the priesthood, the liberal attitudes to alternative sexual patterns (especially homosexuality), and both the World Council of Churches and the National Council of Churches. It affirmed the rights of congregations to manage their own financial affairs and expressed a desire to remain in communion with the See of Canterbury.

Throughout 1977 more congregations left the Protestant Episcopal Church, and others were formed by groups of people who had left as individual members.

Following the September congress, three more provisional dioceses were established and bishops elected. The Diocese of Christ the King elected Robert S. Morse; the Diocese of the Southwest elected Peter F. Watterson (d. 1996); and the Diocese of the Midwest elected C. D. Dale Doren. Bishops were sought who would consent to consecrate the new bishopselect, and four finally agreed. Of the four Paul Boynton, retired suffragan of New York, was the first to withdraw from the consecration service, due to illness. Then Mark Pae of the Anglican Church of Korea, a close friend of Dale Doren, withdrew under pressure from his fellow bishops, though he did send a letter of consent to the consecration. On January 28, 1978, with Pae's letter to confirm the action, Albert Chambers (1907–1993), former bishop of Springfield, Illinois, and Francisco Pagtakhan, of the Philippine Independent Church, consecrated Doren. Doren in turn joined Chambers and Pagtakhan in consecrating Morse, Watterson, and Mote.

Having established itself with proper episcopal leadership, the new church, unofficially called the Anglican Church of North America, turned its attention to the task of ordering its life. A national synod meeting was held in Dallas in 1978. Those present adopted a name, the Anglican Catholic Church, and approved a constitution, which was sent to the several dioceses (by then seven in number) for ratification. In May 1979 the bishops announced that five of the seven dioceses had ratified the actions of the Dallas synod; thus the Anglican Catholic Church had been officially constituted.

The early 1980s was a period of flux for the Anglican Catholic Church. It emerged as the single largest body of the St. Louis meeting, claiming more than half of the congregations and members. But along the way it lost two of its original dioceses and three of its original bishops. The dioceses of Christ the King and the Southeast and their bishops (Morse and Watterson) refused to ratify the constitution. They instead continued under the name Anglican Church of North America. The Diocese of the Southeast soon broke with the Diocese of Christ the King and became an independent jurisdiction. Then, in 1984, Watterson resigned as bishop and joined the Roman Catholic Church. His action effectively killed the diocese, and member churches were absorbed by the other Anglican bodies, primarily the Anglican Catholic Church.

While dealing with the loss of the dioceses of Christ the King and the Southeast, the church continued to grow as new and independent congregations joined; additions more than made up for losses. Bishop Doren resigned in 1980, but only two congregations followed him. In 1981 several priests and parishes left to form the Holy Catholic Church, Anglican Rite Jurisdiction of the Americas. The largest schism occurred in 1983, when the Diocese of the Southwest under Bishop Robert C. Harvey withdrew and took twenty-one congregations in Arkansas, Texas, Oklahoma, New Mexico, and Arizona. Later that year they joined the American Episcopal Church.

The Anglican Catholic Church describes itself as the continuation of the traditional Anglicanism as expressed in the Nicene and Apostles' Creeds, and it holds to the liturgy of the Book of Common Prayer, 1928 edition. It rejects women in the priesthood and holds to traditional standards of moral conduct, condemning specifically "easy" divorce and remarriage, abortion on demand, and homosexual activity.

At its national convention in 1983, Louis W. Falk, bishop of the Diocese of the Missouri Valley, was elected as the ACC's first archbishop. Falk was succeed by Mt. Rev. William O. Lewis (d. 1997) and Mt. Rev. M. Dean Stephens (1990–1998), who died after less than a year in office. In 2008 the Most Revered Mark Haverland was the metropolitan and archbishop.

Internationally, the church is in communion with the equally conservative Anglican Catholic Church–Australia, which is under Canadian oversight. In what is termed its Original Province, the church has parishes in Puerto Rico, Colombia, and Guatemala. In 1984 a Province for India was created. It has five dioceses and 3,000 members; in 2008 the Most Reverend John Augustine served as metropolitan for the province. The American church has also developed direct oversight of a new conservative Anglican movement developing in New Zealand.

Membership: In 1988 the church reported 12,000 members, 200 parishes, and 200 priests in the United States. Worldwide membership included an additional 8,000 members. There are seven dioceses in the United States and missionary dioceses in Haiti, India, Australia, South America, South Africa, and the United Kingdom.

Periodicals: *The Trinitarian*.

Sources:

Anglican Catholic Church. www.anglicancatholic.org/.

A Directory of Churches of the Continuing Anglican Tradition. Eureka Springs, AK: Fellowship of Concerned Churchmen, 1983–84.

Laukhuff, Perry. *The Anglican Catholic Church.* Eureka Springs, AK: Fellowship of Concerned Churchmen, 1977.

Opening Addresses of the Church Congress at St. Louis, Missouri, 14–16 September 1977. Amherst, VA: Fellowship of Concerned Churchmen,1977.

Anglican Catholic Church of Canada

The Diocesan Office of the Anglican Catholic Church of Canada, Unit 4, 190 Colonnade Rd., Nepean, ON, Canada K2E 7J5

The Anglican Catholic Church of Canada grew out of the same movement against changes in the Anglican Church of Canada that had occurred within the Episcopal Church in the United States. In Canada, changes included the allowance of new liturgical forms of questioned orthodoxy, including new sacramental rites, the loosening of the regulations of the marriage canons, and, most important, the ordination of female priests. The unrest in the church came to a head in 1980 when Carmino J. deCatanzaro, an eminent Anglican scholar who had participated in the 1977 congress of traditionalist Episcopalians in St. Louis, Missouri, left the Anglican Church of Canada and was consecrated by Bp. Lupe Rosete of the Philippine Independent Catholic Church, assisted by a number of other bishops of the Continuing Church Movement. As with its sister church in the United States, the Anglican Catholic Church, the Anglican Catholic Church of Canada considers itself the continuing Anglicanism in Canada, believing that the Anglican Church of Canada has departed from the faith.

The Anglican Catholic Church of Canada was shaken shortly after its founding by deCatanzaro's sudden death in 1983. Alfred Woolcock, who had recently affiliated with the new jurisdiction, succeeded him and on January 27, 1984, was consecrated by Bp. Louis W. Falk of the Anglican Catholic Church, assisted by Bps. James O. Mote and William O. Lewis. Woolcock died in 2003 and was succeeded by Peter D. Wilkinson.

The Anglican Catholic Church of Canada follows the traditional Anglican liturgy and belief. It uses the *Book of Common Prayer* (1962, Canadian revision). It is a part of the Traditional Anglican Communion, an association of national Anglican churches in the United States, Australia, New Zealand, Hong Kong, and Central America. Association with the World Council of Churches and the Canadian Council of Churches has been renounced.

Membership: Not reported.

Periodicals: *The Diocesan Circular*.

Sources:

Anglican Catholic Church of Canada. www.anglicancatholic.ca/.

Nones, Jane, ed. *1994/95 Directory of Traditional Anglican and Episcopal Parishes.* Tulsa, OK: Fellowship of Concerned Churchmen, 1995.

Anglican Church in America

PO Box 37635 #54594, Philadelphia, PA 19101-0635

The Anglican Church in America was founded in 1991 following merger talks between the American Episcopal Church and the Anglican Catholic Church (ACC). In the end, leadership of the Anglican Catholic Church was in disagreement with the merger plan and the majority withdrew its support. However, a large segment of the church under Abp. Louis W. Falk did approve, and they subsequently separated from their colleagues in the ACC and merged with the American Episcopal Church. Falk was elected primate of the merged church. Abp. Anthony F. M. Clavier, the leader of the American Episcopal Church, continued as head of the diocese covering the eastern states.

The American Episcopal Church was founded in 1968 by a group of former clergy and members of the Episcopal Church and the Anglican Orthodox Church. They sought a more loosely organized structure than that offered by the Anglican Orthodox Church and formed the new jurisdiction with a congregational polity. The church turned to James Charles Ryan, better known by his Indian name, Joseph K. C. Pillai (1901–1970), of the Indian Orthodox Church, for episcopal orders. Pillai then became the first primate of the new church and merged the Indian Orthodox Church into it. In December 1968, Pillai consecrated James George as Bishop of Birmingham. Bishop George succeeded Pillai as primate following the latter's death in 1970.

On February 11, 1970, George consecrated Clavier as suffragan bishop. Having found the very loose structure of the church unworkable, the pair spearheaded a reorganization plan that led to the adoption of a more centrally organized polity. To accomplish the reorganization, it proved necessary for all of the clergy to resign and to reconstitute the structure. Then the new American Episcopal Church, meeting in a general convention in April 1970, ratified a constitution and canon more in keeping with Anglican tradition. After the reorganization, George resigned as primate and Bishop Clavier succeeded him. In 1981 the bishops of the American Episcopal Church received conditional reconsecration from Bp. Francisco Pagtakhan, assisted by Bps. Sergio Mondala and Lupe Rosete, three bishops of the Philippine Independent Church who chose to become involved in the emergence of the Continuing Church Movement in the United States.

In 1982 the American Episcopal Church grew with the addition of two dioceses from the Anglican Episcopal Church, which merged into it. In 1986 churches that had formed in Mexico in the late 1970s were recognized as a diocese. The Rt. Rev. Roberto Martinez-Resendiz, formerly suffragan bishop of Central Mexico of the Episcopal Church, became the first bishop of the new diocese In addition, the church also entered into communion with the Anglican Church in India and the Anglican Diocese of Pakistan.

The Anglican Catholic Church was one of two bodies that came directly out of the 1977 conference of Episcopalians who met at St. Louis, Missouri, to protest the direction of the Episcopal Church and discuss alternatives for those who adhered to the conservative stance regarding the Anglican tradition. After the formation of the church, originally under the name of the Anglican Church of North America, retired Episcopal bishop Albert Chambers and Francisco Pagtakhan of the Philippine Independent Church consecrated the bishops of the new jurisdiction. In 1983 Louis W. Falk, bishop of the Diocese of the Missouri Valley, was elected the ACC's first archbishop.

BELIEFS: The Anglican Church in America is theologically conservative and follows the 1928 *Book of Common Prayer* in its liturgy and teachings. It acknowledges the authority of the ancient creeds of Christendom, the teachings of the seven Ecumenical Councils, and the Chicago-Lambeth Quadrilateral of 1886–88. The 1801 text of the Anglican Thirty-nine Articles of Religion are accepted.

ORGANIZATION: The Anglican Church in America is episcopal in that it is headed by a bishop, but democratic in that laity share in the decision-making process at every level of church life. The church is governed by a General Synod consisting of the House of Bishops, the House of the Clergy, and the House of the Laity. The General Synod meets biannually.

Archbishop Falk resides in Iowa. He is assisted by seven other bishops whose territory covers the United States and the several foreign dioceses. Four of the eight bishops were reconsecrated conditionally by Bps. Robert Mercer, Robert Mize, and Charles Boynton, thereby providing them with an undisputed Anglican succession

of orders and erasing any lingering doubts about the orders that had been earlier passed to the Continuing Church Movement.

Internationally, the Anglican Church in America is the American Jurisdiction within the Traditional Anglican Communion. Other countries represented by the communion include Canada, Australia, England, Ireland, India, Pakistan, South Africa, Mexico, Puerto Rico, Colombia, and Guatemala. In 1992 Archbishop Falk was elected the primate of the Traditional Anglican Communion.

Membership: Not reported.

Educational Facilities:

Traditional Anglican Theological Seminary, Spartanburg, South Carolina.

St. Mary's Theological College, Los Angeles, California.

Periodicals: *Ecclesia*, Box 368, Ivy, VA 22945-0368. • *Anglican Herald*, 4807 Aspen Dr., West Des Moines, IA 50265.

Remarks: In 1995 Archbishop Clavier was charged with sexually abusing several female members of his diocese and subsequently resigned his position. The church quickly moved to minister to the abused women while reaffirming its allegiance to its traditional ethical stance on sexual matters. Clavier left the Anglican Church in America and served as an Episcopal priest in the diocese in Arkansas.

Sources:

Anglican Church in America. www.acahome.org/.

Falk, Louis W. *The Anglicans: Who Are They? What Is Their Faith?* West Des Moines, IA: Anglican Church in America, n.d.

Nones, Jane, ed. *1994/95 Directory of Traditional Anglican and Episcopal Parishes*. Tulsa, OK: Fellowship of Concerned Clergymen, 1995.

Anglican Church of North America
1906 Forest Green Dr. NE, Atlanta, GA 30329

The Anglican Church of North America traces its origin to the Independent Anglican Church founded in Canada in the 1930s by William H. Daw (1902–1987), who was originally a priest of the Church of England in Canada (now the Anglican Church of Canada). Later he led his jurisdiction into the Liberal Catholic Church headed by Bp. Edward M. Matthews (1898–1985), who would consecrate Daw in 1955. In 1964 Daw and Bp. James Pickford Roberts left Matthews to found the Liberal Catholic Church International. Daw assumed the role of primate, but retired because of severe health problems. He resumed the primacy in 1979.

In 1981 Daw participated in the formation of the Independent Catholic Church International, which brought together a number of independent Old Catholic, Anglican, and Liberal Catholic jurisdictions in both North America and Europe. Meanwhile, the Liberal Catholic Church International and Daw reasserted its Anglican roots in the wake of the increased liberalization of the national Anglican churches. The Liberal Catholic Church International repudiated all non-Orthodox theology and practice and changed its name to the North American Episcopal Church. In 1983 Peter Wayne Goodrich Reynold became primate of the North American Episcopal Church. Goodrich had originally been consecrated by Daw as bishop for the small Independent Catholic Church of Canada.

Goodrich's leadership of the North American Episcopal Church was temporary, however, and within a year Archbishop Daw again resumed the primacy. Daw died in 1987. Two bishops, Rt. Rev Robert T. Shepherd and Rt. Rev. M. B. D. Crawford, were consecrated to administer the work of the church in America and Canada, respectively. In 1985 Crawford retired to lay life and abandoned his office, which was resumed by Goodrich. The first American parish was established in Atlanta, Georgia, in 1983. In June 1984, the church's name was changed to the Anglican Church of North America.

The Anglican Church of North America, as other continuing Anglican bodies, accepts the 1977 affirmation of St. Louis and follows the practices of the Protestant Episcopal Church and the Anglican Church of Canada prior to the changes of the 1970s. It differs from other continuing Anglican bodies in that it believes that small independent churches, even at the diocesan level, are preferable to a single jurisdiction for all of North America. It also stresses the collegiality of all levels of the clergy and the laity.

Membership: Not reported.

Educational Facilities:

St. Matthew's Cathedral Seminary, Niagara Falls, Ontario, Canada (a correspondence school).

Anglican Church of Virginia
582 Simons Way, Front Royal, VA 22630

The Anglican Church of Virginia was founded in February 2001 by Bp. Larry W. Johnson and other conservative Anglicans. Johnson had previously served in the Anglican Catholic Church, in which he was ordained in 1984. He was consecrated as a bishop on February 27, 2001, by Bp. Wayne E. Ellis of the Anglican Church Diocese of the Southwest, and Bp. Lafond Lapointe and Bp. Luther Pierre Toussaint, both of the Orthodox Apostolic Anglican Church of Haiti. After working to found the Anglican Church of Virginia, Johnson then took the lead in November 2001 in creating the Anglican Church International Communion, an ecumenical association of independent Anglican jurisdictions; he was joined in this work by both Lapointe and Toussaint.

The Anglican Church in Virginia adheres to traditional Anglican affirmations in the authority of the Bible, the Apostles' and Nicene Creeds, the two sacraments of baptism and Holy Communion, and the trifold ministry of deacon, priest, and bishop. It used the 1928 edition of the Prayer Book.

The Anglican Church of Virginia is in full communion with the Orthodox Anglican Church of Haiti, which was founded in 1987 by the Rt. Rev. Lafond Lapointe (d. 2001). Shortly before his death, Lapointe asked the newly consecrated Bp. Johnson to provide oversight for the work in Haiti and to organize parishes in Virginia. It was this commission that led to the founding of both the Anglican Church of Virginia and the Anglican Church International Commission.

Membership: In 2008 the church reported three parish churches and four missions under its jurisdiction.

Educational Facilities:

Anglican Seminary of Virginia and Counseling Institute, Front Royal, Virgina.

Periodicals: *The Anglican* • *The Anglican Voice* (via email).

Sources:

The Anglican Church of Virginia. theanglicanchurch.net/.

Anglican Churches of America and Associates
2402 Usery Pass Rd., Mesa, AZ 85207

The Anglican Churches of America and Associates is a confederation of churches founded in 1968. Though jurisdictionally separate, in belief and practice it is at one with the Continuing Church movement, which rejects the liturgical changes that have occurred within the Episcopal Church in the last generation and does not believe in the ordination of females to the priesthood. The current presiding bishop is Rt. Rev. Ronald Johnson.

Membership: Not reported.

Sources:

St. Paul's Anglican Church.

www.stpaulsanglicanchurch.org/custom.cfm?CustomLinkID=2.

Nones, Jane, ed. *1994/95 Directory of Traditional Anglican and Episcopal Parishes.* Tulsa, OK: Fellowship of Concerned Churchmen, 1995.

Anglican Diocese of Arizona
c/o Saint Luke's Church, PO Box 870, Sedona, AZ 86339-0870

The Anglican Diocese of Arizona is an independent Anglican jurisdiction in the Anglo-Catholic (high-church) tradition. It was founded by Bp. David Gregory McMannes, who was consecrated by Bp. Robert S. Morse of the Anglican Province of Christ the King, assisted by Bps. James Pollard Clark and Edward LaCour, of the province's diocese of the southern states. Originally known as the Diocese of the Blessed Sacrament, the diocese was renamed Anglican Diocese of Arizona by Bishop McMannes out of the belief that the Continuing Church movement needs to strive for greater unity and less focus on theological differences.

McMannes cited as the rationale for the new diocese what he perceived as the "instability and conflict" existing within many Christian denominations that hold the apostolic ministry. Those churches misunderstand the call to corporate worship, especially the call to "worship and adore Christ Jesus in the sacramental setting of the Holy Eucharist," variously known as the Mass, Holy Communion, or the Divine Liturgy. Many neglect the duty to worship on Sunday, clearly prescribed in the 1928 Book of Common Prayer (which is used in the diocese). Thus, lack of attendance at church on Sunday has become the norm in contemporary America, and when attendance does occur it is often marked by a lack of spirit and interest.

The diocese's doctrine is derived from the Bible and the ancient Christian creeds. It has set as its fourfold mission: (1) the proclamation of biblical truth; (2) the preaching of God's Word and administration of the Sacraments; (3) showing the love of Christ through works of charity; and (4) the upholding of Christian family values that includes the passing along of Christian faith and morality to the next generation.

Membership: Not reported.

Sources:

Anglican Diocese of Arizona. www.episcopalnet.org/.

Anglican Diocese of the Great Lakes
2415 McCann Rd., Hastings, MI 49058

The Anglican Diocese of the Great Lakes was established in 1998 through the merger of two previously existing jurisdictions, the Independent Anglican Diocese of Ontario and the Independent Anglican Missionary District of the USA. These jurisdictions trace their history to a number of independent Anglican churches that came into existence in the 1930s, but took on new life due to the controversy that arose in Canadian Anglicanism in the 1970s with the ordination of the first women to the priesthood, a development rejected by the Diocese. The bishops of the former jurisdictions, Rt. Rev. Julius A. Neeser and Rt. Rev. Jackson D. Worsham Jr., served as the first diocesan bishop and suffragan respectively. The Diocese was temporarily part of the Anglican Church, Inc., until the latter was dissolved. The current bishop ordinary is David Thomas Hustwick and the current suffragan bishop is John M. Pafford. The Diocese has established intercommunion with the United Episcopal Church of North America.

Like the other churches of the Continuing Church movement, the Diocese rejects revisions to the traditional Prayer Book made by the Anglican Church of Canada and the Episcopal Church in the United States, and is committed to the use of the King James Version of the Bible and the 1928 Book of Common Prayer. It affirms the succession pattern of Episcopal leadership, which it sees as part of a lineage of bishops that can be traced to the Apostles, and supports the three traditional levels of ordained ministry: bishop, priest, and deacon. It affirms the 39 Articles of Religion common to the Anglican tradition.

Membership: Not reported. The diocese has five congregations: four in Ontario, Canada, and one in Michigan.

Sources:

Anglican Diocese of the Great Lakes. netministries.org/see/churches/ch03356.

Anglican Independent Communion

Mt. Calvary Southern Episcopal Church, PO Box 262, Lothian, MD 20711

The Anglican Independent Communion is a small independent jurisdiction that considers itself as part of the larger Continuing Church movement that grew out of a convention of traditionally oriented Episcopalians who met in St. Louis in 1976. The communion was founded in the later 1990s and held its first annual meeting in 1999. At that time, the Rev. Peter A. Compton-Caputo (d. 2000) was named the first presiding bishop. He was succeeded by Rt. Rev. Robert Samuel Loiselle, who currently leads the church. In 2000 Loiselle was consecrated as a bishop by Bp. Paget E. J. Mack of the Apostolic Episcopal Church, who was joined by Bps. Emigidiusz J. Ryzy and Compton-Caputo. Bishop Mack had been consecrated by Abp. Bertil Persson of the Apostolic Episcopal Church, who was assisted by Bps. Francis C. Spatero and Edwin Caudill.

Among the highlights of the church's short history was the participation of Bishop Compton-Caputo and other clergy in the meeting at Brandenburg, Maryland, at which traditional Anglican leaders called for the Episcopal Church to return to its authentic Catholic roots. Speakers centered their remarks around their affirmation that as Anglicans, they had no faith except that of the fathers of the church and of the undivided councils (from which they believed the Episcopal Church had departed). Also participating was Abp. Louis W. Falk and Bp. Louis Compese of the Anglican Church in America.

In 2000 the communion also adopted a Statement of Doctrine that accepts the 1928 Book of Common Prayer, the 39 Articles of Religion (of traditional Anglicanism), and the authority of the Holy Scriptures. Clergy must accept the St. Louis Affirmation and the Bladensburg Call. The communion accepts only males to the ordained priesthood.

The communion sponsors the Atlantic Orthodox and Anglican Seminary, which was cofounded by the communion and Most Rev. E. J. Ryzy, the Primate of American World Patriarchs.

Membership: Not reported. The Anglican Independent Communion has two congregations, both in Maryland.

Educational Facilities:

Atlantic Orthodox and Anglican Seminary, Lothian, Maryland.

Sources:

Anglican Independent Communion. www.cinemaparallel.com/anglican.html.

Anglican Mission in the Americas

PO Box 3427, Pawleys Island, SC 29585

The Anglican Mission in the Americas began in 2000 following three years of negotiation among members of the conservative Continuing Church movement in the United States and several bishops of the worldwide Anglican Communion. The mission was born in Amsterdam, Holland, in August 2000 following three years of preparation. In 1997, the Association of Anglican Congregations on Mission (a nonprofit corporation), claiming to represent a wide spectrum of conservative Episcopalians, petitioned the Episcopal Church hierarchy concerning what they saw as a case of exceptional emergency caused by the rejection of the authority of the Bible, the undermining of the orthodox Anglican faith, and the approval given to sexual relations outside of marriage (especially homosexuality). The association professed belief in the Anglican tradition and commitment to the historic creeds of the Christian church and the traditional prayer book. It affirmed the 39 Articles of Religion and the Chicago-Lambeth Quadrilateral. Earlier that year, several bishops of the worldwide Anglican Communion had protested the ordaining of practicing homosexuals and the blessing of same-sex unions by Anglican bishops.

Then, in January of 2000, Abps. Emmanuel Kolini of Rwanda and Datuk Yong Ping Chung of Southeast Asia consecrated Revs. Charles H. Murphy and John H. Rodgers as missionary bishops to the United States, representing Rwanda and Southeast Asia, respectively. This action sent shock waves through the communion. It represented the entrance of bishops from two Anglican provinces into the territory assigned to another Anglican jurisdiction with whom they were in full communion. The Archbishop of Canterbury, the chief spokesman for the Anglican Communion, has refused to recognize the missions, and the issue remains unresolved. The mission has seen a precedent for its existence in other less than strictly geographical dioceses. In 2001, four additional bishops were consecrated for the mission.

However, the American Mission, founded subsequently to the consecration, began immediately to receive congregations that wished to leave the Episcopal Church and to plant new congregations across the United States in the belief that a parallel Anglican communion/province in America was the future. The mission sees itself as an Anglican missionary effort in the United States from countries that were in the last century the objects of the missionary thrust. As such, it is not believed to be a new church, but a mission to the American church accountable to the Archbishops of Rwanda and Southeast Asia.

While adhering to traditional Anglican belief and practice, the new mission has been open to the wide range of traditions of belief and practice within Anglicanism, including the charismatic, the low-church evangelical, and the high-church Anglo-Catholic. It also accepts females into the priesthood, unlike most churches of the Continuing Church movement.

The mission has developed a working agreement with the Reformed Episcopal Church and the Anglican Province of America, and has developed an association with the Anglican Evangelical Church. While disagreeing with many of the conservative Anglican churches on female priests, it seeks to bring together the various Anglican splinter jurisdictions.

The church sponsors the Institute for Christian Leadership, Pawleys Island, South Carolina, for the training of clergy. The institute has an academic partnership with Columbia International University, Columbia, South Carolina.

In 2007, the Anglican Rite Synod of the American completed a process of merging into the Anglican Province of America. The synod had originally been founded in 1989 under the leadership of Abp. Lawrence Shaver. And bishops William C. Thompson and David Marion Davis. Through the early year of the first decade of the new century, the synod affiliated with the Anglican Province of America as the non-gropgraphical Diocese of St. Augustine. Then in 2007, it completed a merger with the Missionary Society of Saint John, an ordered community that had begun establishing Anglican congregations, and emerged as the Province's Diocese of the Midwest.

Membership: Not reported. As of 2001, the mission had 37 affiliated congregations and was in a growth phase, with every month bringing clergy, individual members, and congregations into the membership.

Educational Facilities:

Institute for Christian Leadership, Pawleys Island, South Carolina.

Periodicals: Newsletter.

Sources:

Anglican Mission in the Americas. www.theamia.org/.

Anglican Orthodox Church

National Headquarters, PO Box 128, Statesville, NC 28687

Rev. James Parker Dees (1915–1990), a priest in the Protestant Episcopal Church, was the first of the modern spokespersons to call the members of that church who opposed the changes in liturgy and program to come out and separate themselves from apostasy. A low-church Episcopalian, he had trouble both with liberalism, which he felt denied biblical authority, and sacerdotalism among high-church members. He therefore left the Episcopal Church and in 1963 formed the Anglican Orthodox Church. The following year he received episcopal orders from the autocephalous Ukrainian bishop Wasyl Sawyna and the Old Catholic bishop Orlando J. Woodward (who later joined the United Episcopal Church of America). Formed in the southern United States in the early 1960s, the North Carolina–based group found its greatest response among Episcopalians who rejected the Protestant Episcopal Church's departure from scriptural teaching and sound biblical doctrine.

The Anglican Orthodox Church follows the low church in a very conservative manner. It adheres to the Thirty-Nine Articles and uses the 1928 edition of the Book of Common Prayer. The polity is episcopal, but local congregations are autonomous and own their own property. Much power has been placed in the hands of the presiding bishop in order to provide a strong center of leadership and reduce the opportunity for error.

The Anglican Orthodox Church was able to bring together many pockets of dissent, however, and has created a strong church. By 1972 it had 37 congregations, though some were lost to other Anglican splinters as the decade progressed. Dees established Cramner Seminary, which in 1977 had four full-time students. He also has brought the church into communion with like-minded churches in Pakistan, South India, Nigeria, the Fiji Islands, Rhodesia (Zimbabwe), the Central African Republic, Madagascar, Colombia, South Africa, the Philippines, Japan, and Liberia.

As other Anglican groups formed, Dees was pressed to draw sharp lines of distinction. He argued against the doctrinal "looseness" and high-church tendencies found in other groups of Anglicans. He continued his campaign against the growing "apostasy" he saw within the Protestant Episcopal Church, and concentrated his attention on building the Anglican Orthodox Church into a viable and continuing denomination. Bishop Dees died in 1990. The present bishop is Rt. Rev. Jerry L. Ogles.

Membership: In 2002 the church reported congregations and members in most of the 50 states. Foreign work, both missionary and with other jurisdictions in communion with the church, has given it a worldwide constituency of over 100,000. There are members in Liberia, Madagascar, South Africa, the Philippines, Pakistan, the Central African Republic, India, Canada, Kenya, and Haiti.

Educational Facilities:

Cramner Seminary, Statesville, North Carolina.

Periodicals: The Anchor of Faith.

Sources:

Anglican Orthodox Church. www.anglicanorthodoxchurch.org/.

Dees, James P. *Reformation Anglicanism.* Statesville, NC: Anglican Orthodox Church, 1971.

Anglican Province of America
c/o Saint Alban's Anglican Cathedral, 3348 W State Rd. 426, Oviedo, FL 32765

The Anglican Province of America is a traditional Anglican jurisdiction. It emerged in 1995 from the failed union of the American Episcopal Church and the Anglican Church in America. The Most Rev. Walter H. Grundorf serves as its presiding bishop. It follows the Anglican tradition as passed from the Church of England to the Episcopal Church in the United States, and, at one with other churches of the Continuing Church movement who have left the Episcopal Church in the last three decades, it uses the 1928 *Book of Common Prayer.* The church is led by its bishops and adheres to the faith as summarized in the creeds and in the teachings defined by the early church in its councils.

Though headed by bishops, the church has developed a democratic structure that involves laity in all levels of ongoing decision-making (other than the doctrinal). Local church property is owned by the congregation.

Membership: In 2002 the organization reported 4,000 baptist members and 40 congregations.

Educational Facilities:

Cranmer Theological House, Houston, Texas.

Sources:

Anglican Province of America. www.anglicanprovince.org/.

Anglican Province of Christ the King
2725 Sacramento St., San Francisco, CA 94115

The Anglican Province of Christ the King shares the history of that larger conservative movement which participated in the 1977 congress at St. Louis, where delegates adopted the Affirmation of St. Louis The Province was one of the four original provisional dioceses that were formed. Its bishop-elect, Robert S. Morse, was consecrated along with the other new Anglican bishops in Denver, Colorado, on January 28, 1978, by Bishops Albert Chambers (1907–1993), Francisco Pagtakhan, and C. D. Dale Doren. However, Bishop Morse and other members of his diocese were among those most opposed to the new constitution adopted by the synod at Dallas in 1978 by the group which took the name Anglican Catholic Church. Neither the Diocese of Christ the King (as it was then called) nor the Diocese of the Southeast ratified the constitution, preferring instead to work without such a document. They called a synod meeting for Hot Springs, Arkansas, on October 16–18, 1978, two days prior to the opening of the Anglican Catholic Church synod at Indianapolis, Indiana. Those gathered at Hot Springs decided to continue informally to use the name Anglican Church of North America. They adopted canons (church laws) but no constitution.

The new jurisdiction immediately faced intense administrative pressures. In response to the "Anglican Church of North America" claiming many congregations in California and the South, the Anglican Catholic Church established a new structure, the patrimony, to facilitate the movement of existing congregations into the church and to assist the formation of new congregations in areas not covered by existing diocesan structures. Both Bishop Morse and Bishop Peter F. Watterson (d. 1996) viewed the patrimony as an attempt to steal the congregations under their jurisdiction.

The pressure from the Anglican Catholic Church did not keep the two dioceses in the Anglican Church of North America from facing crucial internal issues. Bishop Watterson argued for a strict division of the Anglican Church of North America into geographical dioceses with the understanding that neither bishop would attempt to establish congregations or missions in the other's diocese. The Diocese of Christ the King rejected Watterson's suggestions, and the Diocese of the Southeast became a separate jurisdiction. The Diocese of Christ the King proceeded to initiate work in the South.

Once separated, the Diocese of the Southeast experienced continued internal problems. In 1980 nine congregations withdrew with the blessing of Bishop Pagtakhan (who was becoming increasingly dissatisfied with the Anglican Catholic Church) and formed the Associated Parishes, Traditional Anglo-Catholic. Pagtakhan named Fr. J. Bruce Medaris as archdeacon. This new jurisdiction quickly dissolved and merged back into the Anglican Catholic Church. Finally, in 1984 Bishop Watterson resigned his office and joined the Roman Catholic Church. His jurisdiction dissolved and the remaining congregations realigned themselves with the other Anglican bodies. The dissolution of the Diocese of the Southeast left the Diocese of Christ the King the only diocese in the Anglican Church of North America.

At its synod meeting in 1991, the Diocese of Christ the King voted to completely reorganize as the Anglican Province of Christ the King. The congregations were divided into three dioceses. At subsequent meetings of the new dioceses, George Daniels Stenhouse was elected bishop of the Diocese of Eastern States and James Pollard Clark of the Diocese of Southern States. Morse became bishop of the new Diocese of Western States. In 2007 James Eugene Provence was elected archbishop, the second since the founding of the Province.

The Anglican Province of Christ the King is at one in faith and practice with the other Anglican bodies, holding to the faith of the undivided primitive church to which Episcopalians have always belonged, as spelled out in the Affirmation of St. Louis. It rejects both the National Council of Churches and the World Council of Churches. It differs from the Anglican Catholic Church on several matters of canon law and in its insistence that its clergy be trained at seminary.

Membership: In 2007 the Anglican Province of Christ the King reported 70 congregations.

Educational Facilities:

Saint Joseph of Arimathea Anglican Theological College, Berkeley, California.

Periodicals: *The Province*.

Sources:

Anglican Province of Christ the King. www.anglicanpck.org/.

A Directory of Churches in the Continuing Anglican Tradition 1983–84. Eureka Springs, AK: Fellowship of Concerned Churchmen, 1983–84.

Anglican Rite Catholic and Orthodox Church in America

9 Abaco St., Toms River, NJ 08757-3736

The Anglican Rite Catholic and Orthodox Church in America was founded in 1997 by Abp. James N. Meola (b. 1938). Meola had been consecrated in 1986 by Bp. John Rifenbury, then with the United Anglican Church of North America. He has served as a bishop with the Free Protestant Episcopal Church, the Southern Episcopal Church, and the Independent Philippine Catholic Church (IPCC). In 1996 he became the secretary general of the American branch of the IPCC, a position he held until the founding of the Anglican Rite Catholic and Orthodox Church.

Membership: Not reported.

Sources:

Barrett, David B., ed. *World Christian Encyclopedia: A Comparative Study of Churches and Religions in the Modern World, AD 1900–2000*. New York: Oxford University Press, 1982.

Anglican Rite Old Catholic Church

PO Box 5787, San Antonio, TX 78201

The Anglican Rite Old Catholic Church is an independent Old Catholic jurisdiction founded in Houston, Texas, in 1994 by its Metropolitan Abp. William Champion, pastor of St. Albans Catholic Church–Anglican Rite in Houston. He is assisted by Most Rev. Louis Bernhardt, Bishop of South Texas and Mexico, who is also executive director of the Internet Catholic Church. The church uses the 1928 edition of the Prayerbook.

The church is a member of the Holy Patriarchate of the Americas and the Federation of Independent Catholic and Orthodox Bishops. It is in communion with the Patriarch of the American Orthodox Church (Russian Orthodox) and the Byzantine Independent Catholic Church of North America.

Membership: Not reported.

Sources:

Anglican Rite Old Catholic Church. netministries.org/see/churches/ch01331/.

Anglo-Lutheran Catholic Church

c/o Office of the Metropolitan Archbishop, St. Michael's House, 1200 NE 81st Terr., Kansas City, MO 64118-1361

The Anglo-Lutheran Catholic Church (also known as the Evangelical Community Church—Lutheran, and the Athanasian Catholic Church of the Augsburg Confession) is an episcopally led Lutheran church that emphasizes the Catholic tradition within Lutheran thought and looks forward to eventual reunion with the Roman Catholic Church. Its bishops have their apostolic succession from several independent Catholic lineages, most notably that of Brazilian Bp. Carlos Duarte Costa (1888–1961). The current archbishop metropolitan is Most Rev. Irl A. Gladfelter.

In emphasizing its Catholic heritage, the Anglo-Lutheran Catholic Church emphasizes its liturgical worship over the ministry of the Word, and its worship, though vernacular, resembles more closely that of the pre–Vatican II Roman Catholic Church than that of other Lutheran churches. The church is also theologi-

cally conservative, and affirms the traditional Lutheran belief in salvation by grace through faith. It also affirms that the Bible is the written Word of God, and accepts several recent Roman Catholic statements in that regard. The church largely accepts the Lutheran Book of Concord, which includes the early church creeds and a set of sixteenth-century documents including the Augsburg Confession, the Apology of the Augsburg Confession, the Small Catechism of Martin Luther, and the Large Catechism of Martin Luther. The church dissents from the Book of Concord primarily on organizational matters, taking its perspective on episcopal leadership from the Lutheran Church of Sweden and the Oxford Movement (which led a number of British Anglicans into the Roman Catholic Church). It does not admit women to the ordained ministry.

Joining Archbishop Gladfelter in leading the church are six additional archbishops. Together they oversee the four geographical archdioceses that include parishes in seven states, and two nongeographical archdioceses serving Vietnamese and Sudanese parishes. Missions have been developed in Canada, Kenya, and the Sudan.

The Anglo-Lutheran Catholic Church has joined with the Holy Cross Anglican Communion and the Evangelical Marian Catholic Church in the Augustana Evangelical Catholic Communion, and is a member of the Sudanese Council of Churches USA (a coalition of U.S. congregations serving recent immigrants from the Sudan). Additionally, the church is in full communion with the Association of Independent Evangelical Lutheran Churches, the Evangelical Marian Catholic Church, and the Traditional Church of England.

Membership: In 2008 the church reported 13 parishes in the United States.

Educational Facilities:

Wittenberg Lutheran Seminary, Kansas City, Missouri.

Alcuin Institute of the Trans-Pecos, Alpine, Texas.

Sources:

Anglo-Lutheran Catholic Church. www.ecclnet.org/.

Augustana Evangelical Catholic Communion. home.sprintmail.com/~gallups/id2.html.

Apostles Anglican Church

1375 Syvania Ave., Toledo, OH 43612

The Apostles Anglican Church is a conservative Anglican Church founded by its bishop, Most Rev. Lawrence Michael Cameron. Cameron had been consecrated in 2004 by Bp. Robert M. Bowman of the United Catholic Church. Bowman passed his multiple lines of apostolic succession to Cameron, and the church describes itself as drawing on various traditions—Catholic, Anglican, Evangelical, Celtic, Pentecostal, and Reformed. The Pentecostal element separates it from many of its Anglican brothers and sisters.

The church has affiliated with both Forward in Faith and the American Anglican Council, two organizations that unite congregations both inside and independent of the Episcopal Church who oppose the church's accepting women into the ordained ministry.

The Apostles Anglican Church is led by its presiding bishop; the House of the Clergy, which includes all the ordained clergy in the church; and the Episcopal Council, which includes all the church's bishops, the vicar general, and two lay people. Currently, the church has only one bishop.

Membership: Not reported. In 2008 the church had twelve priests. Parishes were located in Ohio, Michigan, and Pennsylvania.

Sources:

Apostles Anglican Church. http://oneholychurch.org.

Celtic Christian Church

c/o Most Rev. Dr. Joseph A. Grenier, PO Box 299, Canadensis, PA 18325-0299

The Celtic Christian Church, formerly known as St. Ciaran's Fellowship of Celtic Christian Communities, is a contemporary independent Catholic and Orthodox church inspired by the ancient Celtic Church. It adheres to the Seven Ecumenical Councils of the undivided Christian church and the Nicene Creed. It celebrates the seven sacraments (also called Mysteries) of this church, and believes in the real presence of Christ in the Eucharist.

Although contemporary Celtic Christian spirituality has held a special appeal to persons of Celtic heritage, the Celtic Christian Church is not an ethnic fellowship and welcomes all who are attracted to the Christian life it offers. The church is composed of small faith communities, some meeting as "house churches" or in small chapels. It stresses small communities based on kin and friends, not in an exclusive way but rather hospitably. Priesthood is open to both men and women, married or celibate. The bishops are elected by the church's members.

Most Rev. Joseph A. Grenier, founder and bishop of the Celtic Christian Church, was ordained a priest in 1958 in Rome, and has a Ph.D. in theology from Fordham University in New York City. He was employed as a family therapist.

Membership: The church reports about 100 members.

Sources:

Celtic Christian Church. www.celticchristianchurch.org/.

Celtic Evangelical Church

PO Box 90880, Honolulu, HI 96835-0880

The Celtic Evangelical Church is a small Anglican body formed in 1981 by its presbyter-abbot, Wayne W. Gau, and others who had formerly been members of the Celtic Catholic Church. Numerous inquisitions about the background of the episcopal credentials of that church's bishop, Dwain Houser, had remained unanswered.

At its first general synod in November 1981, the church adopted a nine-point doctrinal statement. It is evangelical in its approach and regards the teachings and liturgy of the original Celtic Church as authoritative. There are seven sacraments: baptism and the Eucharist, necessary for all Christians; and confirmation, penance, holy orders, matrimony, and unction, warranted by Scripture but not mandatory. It acknowledges the presence of Christ in the bread and wine of the Holy Eucharist. The filioque ("and the son") clause in the Nicene Creed is rejected, following the practice of the Eastern Orthodox churches. Worship is conducted in Latin following the ancient Celtic rite.

The church has nurtured one religious order for men: the Community of St. Columba. Members are engaged in research in the ancient liturgies of Christianity, with special emphasis upon Celtic- and Gallican-type rites. The order's work is directed by Can. James H. Donalson. It accepts associate members from other denominations.

In 1983 the church signed a concordant of intercommunion with the Catholic Apostolic Church of America, a small Anglican jurisdiction with parishes in the southwestern United States. The concordant was terminated in 1985, when the Catholic Apostolic Church united with the Holy Catholic Church, Anglican Rite Jurisdiction of the Americas. However, in 1987 Msgr. James B. Gillespie left the Anglican Rite Jurisdiction and reorganized the Catholic Apostolic Church of America as an independent jurisdiction. The Celtic Evangelical Church reinstituted the concordant with the revived church. In 1992 the church signed a concordant of intercommunion with the Independent Anglican Church in Canada Synod, followed by a similar agreement with the Episcopal Missionary Church in 1993 and the Igreja Catolica Apostolica Ortodoxa do Brasil in 1997.

Membership: In 2002 the church had one congregation in Hawaii.

Educational Facilities:

The Iona Institute, Honolulu, Hawaii.

Periodicals: *The Celtic Evangelist.*

Christian Church–Synod of St. Timothy

c/o All Saints Community, Bp. Paul Stanley, PO Box 1592, Rome, GA 30162

The Christian Church–Synod of St. Timothy is an independent Catholic Anglican jurisdiction constituted by the coming together of several congregations and ministries under a common life that includes both an Episcopal polity and a wide latitude for local divergences. The synod has adopted a polity from its reading of St. Ignatius, one of the earliest postbiblical Christian writers. It has noted that in the second century there was a bishop in nearly every city, and the normative method of celebrating communion was to be in the presence of the bishop on the Lord's Day. Thus it is that each congregation of the synod normally is led by a bishop.

Unity throughout the Synod is supplied by each congregation's acceptance of *The Book of Common Life*, a volume that outlines the beliefs generally held by the membership. It contains the various creeds of the ancient church, a modified version of the Church of England's Articles of Religions, and a doctrinal position statement derived from the Chicago Lambeth Quadrilateral. The latter provides a presentation of the essentials of Christianity as a basis for relations with other Christian churches, and acknowledges that "as essential to the restoration of unity among the divided branches of Christendom, we account the following, to wit:

> 1. The Holy Scriptures of the Old and New Testaments as the revealed Word of God.
>
> 2. The Nicene Creed as the sufficient statement of the Christian Faith.
>
> 3. The Mysteries of Baptism and the Eucharist, ministered with unfailing use of Christ's words of institution and of the elements ordained by Him.
>
> 4. The Succession of Faith and Order (commonly called the Apostolic Succession or Historic Episcopate), locally adapted in the methods of its administration to the varying needs of the nations and peoples called of God into the unity of His Church."

The Synod consists of three congregations—one each in LaPorte, Texas, Rome, Georgia, and southeast Indiana; an ordered community, the Desert Companions of Saint Anthony; and a chaplaincy ministry in Indianapolis. It episcopal leadership is provided by Bps. Paul Stanley, Craig Davis, and Michael Joe Thannisch.

The Synod of St. Timothy is in communion with the several jurisdictions of the Orthodox Catholic Communion.

Membership: Not reported.

Sources:

Christian Church–Synod of St. Timothy. www.christiansynod.org/.

Christian Episcopal Church of Canada

4300 Corless Rd., Richmond, BC, Canada V7C 1N2

In 1992 some traditionalists within the Anglican Church of Canada who had hoped that the church would reverse what they saw as a growing tolerance for teachings contrary to the Christian faith concluded that their situation had become hopeless. It also became clear to them that the church would not only remain on its present course but would provide no haven for traditionalists within the church community. Their major complaints against the church included its support of Third World liberation movements, the ordination of female priests and bishops, new liturgical and hymn books which they saw as theologically flawed, and the presence (with official approval) of rites, under the guise of feminist and Native spirituality, which they deemed "pagan" and highly offensive.

Meanwhile in the United States, traditionalists within the Episcopal Church had reached a similar conclusion, and with leadership provided by Rt. Rev. A. Donald Davies, formerly a bishop in the Episcopal Church, they formed the Episcopal Missionary Church. Bishop Davies, who had emerged as a conservative leader in the Episcopal Church while serving as the bishop of Dallas–Fort Worth (Texas), also assisted the traditionalists in Canada in the creation of the Christian Episcopal Church of Canada. Through Davies and the Episcopal Missionary Church, they received apostolic orders. In 2008 Davies was the Archbishop and Primate of Canada.

The church is theologically conservative and has accepted as its doctrinal standards the Bible, the three creeds of the early Church (Apostles, Nicene, and Chalcedonian Creeds), the Solemn Declaration of 1893, the 1562 Thirty-nine Articles of Religion, and the *Book of Common Prayer*. The church uses the 1962 Canadian edition of the *Book of Common Prayer* and the Canadian *Book of Common Praise*. Women are welcomed into the order of deacon but are barred from the priesthood.

Membership: Not reported.

Sources:

Christian Episcopal Church of Canada. www.christianepiscopal.ca/.

Christian Missionary Anglican Communion

c/o Most Rev. James A. Groover, Presiding Archbishop, PO Box 228, Slatington, PA 18080

Alternate Address: International Headquarters: Christian Missionary Anglican Communion in Canada, c/o Most Rev. Aaron R. Orr, Archbishop, 305-598 Fennel Ave. E., Hamilton, ON, Canada L8V 1T1.

The Christian Missionary Anglican Communion (CMAC) is a new Anglican jurisdiction founded in 2006, which sees itself as operating within the Anglican and Evangelical Reformed Catholic Tradition. It considers itself open to Anglican, Episcopalian, Lutheran, and Catholic perspectives on community and worship. The church is a charismatic body, and affirms its belief that subsequent to conversion each believer should become filled with the Holy Spirit, a process that is both a crisis and a progressive experience. It also emphasizes the reality of divine healing. The church additionally teaches that the second coming of Jesus Christ will be imminent, personal, visible, and premillennial.

The Church is led by its presiding archbishop, the Most Rev. James A. Groover. Groover was consecrated by Bp. Kenneth Denski, who passed to him a number of episcopal lineages, all of which the CMAC affirms. Archdioceses currently exist in Canada, Pennsylvania, the Northeast states, South Carolina, Florida, Oklahoma, the Southwest (provisionally), Arkansas (provisionally), Japan, and Rwanda. There are dioceses in Colorado and Tennessee. The Church is in intimate communion with the Celtic Anabaptist Communion, whose presiding archbishop sits in the CNAC House of Bishops, as does a bishop of the Reformed Catholic Church. Provisional archdioceses have also been established in Africa, Pakistan, and Germany. Intercommunion is shared with the Fellowship of Christ International, the World Natural Health Organization, and the Celtic Anabaptist Communion.

Membership: Not reported. The Church has parishes and ministries scattered across the United States.

Educational Facilities:

International Faith Theological Seminary, Burlington, Washington; Nairobi, Kenya.

Sources:

Christian Missionary Anglican Communion. www.orgsites.com/pa/cmac/.

Church of North India

Rev. Dr. Enos Das Pradhan, General Secretary, CNI Synod, 16, Pandit Pant Marg, New Delhi, 110 001 India

The Church of North India, formed in 1970, was the product of more than four decades of merger negotiation among various churches that had grown out of nineteenth-century Protestant Christian missions. The Church of England entered India through the Church Missionary Society in 1813, and within a few decades its work was thriving in such places as Benares, Lucknow, Meerrut, and Allahabad. The Society for the Propagation of the Gospel in Foreign Parts supplemented the church's efforts. British Methodists entered in 1819, after beginning work in Sri

Lanka prior to their being allowed into India proper. Although their work was concentrated in the south, it eventually moved into Bengal, Benares, and Lucknow.

The Baptists initiated their world missionary enterprise in India with the formation of the Baptist Missionary Society in London in 1792. William Carey and John Thompson landed in Bengal the next year and established their headquarters at Serampore. The work expanded greatly in the 1820s after a college to train Indian national leadership was established in 1818. One of the larger bodies to grow out of the original mission was the Council of Baptist Churches in North India.

The American Board of Commissioners for Foreign Missions (supported by American Congregationalists, now a part of the United Church of Christ) sent missionaries to Sri Lanka in 1818. Missionary Dr. John Scudder (1793–1855) arrived in Madura in 1835. From there, the work spread across India to include a variety of educational and social service institutions, the most notable being a medical college at Ludhiana, in the north. Ludhiana had been the site of the original mission station established by the Presbyterians from the United States in 1834. In 1924 the Presbyterian and Congregational missions merged their efforts and formed the United Church of North India.

The Moravians did not intend to initiate work in India, but when their missionaries were unable to enter Tibet, they settled at Kyelang, India, and worked among the Tibetan-speaking residents there. Work expanded to include the Ladakh people along the China-Tibet border, though few converts were made. World War I spurred the drive to develop indigenous leadership. In 1953 the congregation at Leh, the capital of Ladkh, affiliated with the United Church of North India.

The Church of the Brethren launched its mission in India in 1895, concentrating on the Gujarati-speaking region in northwest India. It expanded in the early twentieth century to include stations in the Marathi-speaking area along the coast north of Mumbai (Bombay). The Christian Church (Disciples of Christ) began its work in India at Harda (northeast of Mumbai) in 1882. From the initial station, missionaries established centers primarily in the central part of the country.

Negotiations toward the union of missions in North India began early in the twentieth century, and were further spurred by the formation of the Church of South India. However, the northern groups faced additional theological and organizational problems before a merger could be accepted by the participants. The Plan of Union was completed in 1970 and found approval with seven groups: the Council of Baptist Churches in North India, the Church of the Brethren, the Disciples of Christ, the Methodist Church, the United Church of North India, and the Church of India, Pakistan, Burma, and Ceylon, as the Anglicans were then known.

The new church adopted an episcopal polity, thus making it acceptable to the worldwide Anglican Communion. The church also retained membership in the World Methodist Council and the World Alliance of Reformed Churches; it cooperates with Global Ministries, the combined world ministries agency for the United Church of Christ and the Christian Church (Disciples of Christ). The church developed its own ecumenical statement of faith included in the "Basis of Union" document promulgated in 1970. In 1978 it developed full communion with the Church of South India and the Mar Thoma Syrian Church of Malabar. The three churches accept the validity of each other's sacraments and ministerial credentials.

The church is led by its bishops and the General Synod, its highest legislative body, which meets every three years.

Through the twentieth century, but especially since 1965, members of the Church of North India have moved to the United States. There is as yet no central headquarters for the church in North America, and the Episcopal Church has assumed some responsibility for their care.

Membership: In 2001 the church reported 1.25 million members worldwide, with 26 dioceses in India.

Periodicals: *North India Church Review*, 16 Pandit Pant Marg, New Delhi 110001.

Sources:

Church of North India. www.cnisynod.org/.

Marshall, W. J. *A United Church: Faith and Order in the North India/ Pakistan Unity Plan: A Theological Assessment*. New Delhi: I.S.P.C.K.,1987.

Neill, Stephen C. *A History of Christianity in India*. 2 vols. Cambridge, U.K., and New York: Cambridge University Press, 1984–85.

Webster, J. C. B. *The Christian Community and Change in Nineteenth Century North India*. Delhi: Macmillan, 1976.

Church of South India

c/o Shibu Kurian, Church of South India of North America, PO Box 40278, Glen Oaks, NY 11004

Alternate Address: International headquarters: CSI Centre, No. 5 Whites Rd., PO Box 688, Royapettah, Madras 600 014, India.

The Church of South India was founded in 1947 by the merger of the Anglican, Methodist, Congregationalist, and Presbyterian mission churches that had been founded in the southern half of the Indian subcontinent early in the nineteenth century. India was one of the first countries targeted by Protestant groups as they began the missionary movement that, by the end of the twentieth century, turned Protestantism into a global reality. The original Indian mission was begun by two graduates of the University of Halle (Germany) in 1706. Representatives of the Church of England later assumed care for that work. The real beginning of the Church of South India was the arrival in 1798 of Nathaniel Forsyth, of the Congregational Church-based London Missionary Society. His initial work in Calcutta soon expanded to Madras (1814) and Travancore (1818). In 1813 Abdul Masih, an Anglican convert from the Middle East, began missionary work for the Church Missionary Society (associated with the Church of England) in the United Province. Previously, the East India Company, which controlled European access to most of India, had blocked missionary expansion; but in 1813 Parliament forced the company to open the land. British Methodists also took advantage of the new policy and sent its first group of missionaries to India. Though initially held up in Sri Lanka, one of their number made it to the Indian mainland in 1817.

Missionaries from the Scottish Missionary Society (Presbyterians affiliated with the Church of Scotland) began work in Bombay (now Mumbai) in 1823. In 1833 American Presbyterians and Congregationalists moved into India with missionaries arriving under the sponsorship of the American Board of Commissioners for Foreign Missions. The American Board, like the Methodists, had been working in Sri Lanka.

Efforts to end competition and extend cooperation led to a series of mergers that began in 1901 when the American and Scottish Presbyterian missions merged to form the South India United Church. Four years later, the British and American Congregationalists united to form the Congregational General Union of South India. The United Church and the General Union merged in 1924 as the United Church of South India.

In the years after World War I, negotiations began to create a broad union that would include the Anglican and Methodist churches. For such a merger to occur, the issues of the form of government of the new church and the nature of ministerial orders would have to be resolved. The Anglicans insisted on the institution of a threefold ministry of bishop, priest, and deacon, which in the end was accepted, as was the idea of an episcopacy in apostolic lineage reaching back to Christ's twelve Apostles. The Church of South India, formed in 1947, accepted as its doctrinal position the Lambeth Quadrilateral, the historic statement of Anglican agreement.

Today, the congregations are divided among 16 dioceses (including one diocese in Sri Lanka). The synod, the highest legislative body, meets biennially, at which time the presiding bishop is designated. The church is a member of the World Council of Churches, the Anglican Communion, the World Alliance of Reformed Churches, and the World Methodist Council. In 1972 the Church of England's General Synod finally voted full communion.

A number of the CSI members have moved to the United States, especially after immigration was eased in 1965. At first many worshipped in parishes of either the Episcopal Church or one of the Indian Orthodox churches, but they gradually began to form groups that evolved into churches. In 1981 the diocese of Kerala recognized the existence of these several parishes and began to include them in their pastoral concern. In 1988 the CSI Synod placed all of the parishes of the church outside of the country directly under the presiding bishop. These congregations have a cordial relationship with the Episcopal Church.

Membership: In 2000 the church reported 3,800,000 members in 14,000 congregations worldwide, the great majority in India. In 2008 the church listed 31 congregations in the United States, one in Canada, and one each in Sri Lanka, the United Arab Emirates, Bahrain, Kuwait, and Australia.

Sources:

Church of South India. www.csichurch.com/.

The Church of England Yearbook. London: Church Publishing House, 2002.

Kane, J. Herbert. *A Global View of Christian Mission*. Grand Rapids, MI: Baker Book House, 1971.

Van der Bent, Ans J., ed. *Handbook/Member Churches/World Council of Churches*. Geneva: World Council of Churches, 1985.

Wingate, Andrew, et al., eds. *Anglicanism: A Global Communion*. London: Mowbray, 1998.

Church of the Culdees

Saint Brendan Church Office, 2665 C St., Springfield, OR 97477

The Church of the Culdees was founded in the mid-1990s by the Most Rev. Ivan B. D. G. MacKillop, who was consecrated in 1984 by Bp. Robert E. Burns of the Servant Catholic Church and served as the bishop of its western diocese. While still associated with the Servant Catholic Church, MacKillop founded the Order of the Celtic Cross, which continues as part of the independent Church of the Culdees.

The early Culdee Church was monastic in character. Parishes were normally connected to monasteries, sometimes composed of both men and women, which were the training grounds for clergy. Ordained monastics were not required to take vows of celibacy.

The contemporary Church of the Culdees is organized in much the same way. Men and women are eligible for the Order of the Celtic Cross so long as they are 18 years old, have maintained active membership in the church, and pass an entrance exam. Members of the Order are not required to take vows of celibacy, but do take vows of moral purity, apostolic poverty, obedience, and stability (that is, the vow not to leave the jurisdiction of one's presiding abbot or abbess without approval). They continue their secular lives but must pray the seven daily Offices and attend all church functions unless specially released by the abbot or abbess.

The Church of the Culdees has a leadership composed of deacons, priests, and bishops. It is associated with the Celtic Christian Communion.

Membership: Not reported.

Sources:

Church of the Culdees. www.peak.org/~culdee/.

Communion of Evangelical Episcopal Churches

Current address not reported.

The Communion of Evangelical Episcopal Churches (CEEC) is one of the products of the "convergence movement," the term referring to the "convergence" of various streams of renewal that shared an understanding of the church as one body with a variety of diverse but contributing parts. Following the lead of Swedish Bishop Leslie Newbigin, the convergence movement affirmed the threefold essence of the church as Catholic, Protestant, and Orthodox/Pentecostal. The church is Catholic as it relates to the emphases of "incarnation and creation," Protestant with an emphasis on "biblical proclamation and conversion," and Orthodox/ Pentecostal in relation to "the mystical and the Holy Spirit."

In the 1970s, drawing on insights from the ecumenical, charismatic, and Liturgical Renewal movements, Robert Webber, a professor of theology and biblical studies at Wheaton College, began to articulate the convergence theme as he sought to promote ecumenical and evangelical renewal. His book *Common Roots* (1978) highlighted the resources from the second-century church for renewal and in a second volume, *Evangelicals on the Canterbury Trail: Why Evangelica Christians Are Attracted to the Liturgical Church* (1985), he told of his own pilgrimage to Anglicanism.

Webber's initial voice led to the formation of the Fellowship of St. Barnabas, which sponsored the 1993 conference in Oklahoma City, Oklahoma, on the "Treasures Old and New: The Convergence of the Streams of Christianity." Attending were a variety of people on a journey to liturgical life, many from a Pentecostal/ charismatic background, including some of the founders of the Charismatic Episcopal Church. Also in attendance were the future founders of the Communion of Evangelical Episcopal Churches.

The CEEC was formally inaugurated in 1995, at which time the first bishops were consecrated, and the name Evangelical Episcopal church was chosen. The previously consecrated Michael D. Owen, who presided over the ceremony, was asked to become the first presiding bishop of the new jurisdiction and its initial five congregations. The church experienced spectacular growth in its first year, and, in 1996, missionary bishops were consecrated to respond to inquiries for affiliation from outside the United States.

In 1997 the church decided to completely reorganize and began anew as the Communion of Evangelical Episcopal Churches. The new corporation allowed for the formation of new provinces overseas. Affiliated work began in the Philippines, India, Canada, England, Romania, and Hungary.

In 2000, the CEEC received Archbishop Gilbert McDowell and churches and clergy that were formerly a part of the Traditional Episcopal Church. McDowell now heads the extraterritorial Province of the Holy Spirit, overseen with the CEEC.

As of 2002 a diocese has been established in the Philippines and work is expanding into Indonesia and other nearby countries. An archdiocese exists in the Caribbean that includes congregations in churches in the West Indies, Haiti, Mexico, and Guyana. In the United States there are two provinces: the Provincial Diocese of Christ the Good Shepherd, with three missionary dioceses, and the Province of the USA that includes eight dioceses. In 2008 Archbishop Duraisingh James was elected the Presiding Bishop for the CEEC.

Doctrinally, the CEEC accepts the Chicago-Lambeth Quadrilateral of 1886, which cites the authority of the Holy Scriptures of the Old and New Testaments, The Apostle's Creed, the Nicene Creed, two sacraments (baptism and the supper of the Lord), and the historic episcopate. The CEEC ordains women to the diaconate, the only exception being in those countries where it is believed that cultural differences would present an obstacle to the church's witness within a given culture. Ordination of women to the priesthood is left to the discretion of the bishop of each diocese.

The CEEC has established intercommunion agreements with the Anamchara Celtic Church, the International Communion of Christian Churches (led by Archbishop Daniel Williams), and the American Old Catholic Church (with headquarters in Aurora, Colorado, under the leadership of Archbishop Daniel Gincig).

Membership: In 2002 the CEEC reported 46 congregations and 145 clergy in the United States. Worldwide, there are 240 congregations in full affiliation with the CEEC and an additional 1100 congregations/missions in association with the CEEC through their bishops/leaders. There are affiliated churches, missions, and clergy in 22 nations (Canada, England, Romania, India, Philippines, Kenya, Uganda, Tanzania, Rwanda, Sudan, Burundi, Malawi, Angola, Ghana, Italy, Colombia, Mexico, Haiti, Barbados, S. Vincent, Tobago, and Guyana).

Educational Facilities:

Theological College of St. Alcuin, St. Paul, Minnesota.

Evangelical Episcopal University and Theological Seminary, Memphis, Tennessee.

St. Jude's Seminary, Phoenix, Arizona.

St. Patrick's Diocesan School of Theology, Tulsa, Oklahoma.

Laud Hall Seminary, Clearwater, Florida.

Sources:

Communion of Evangelical Episcopal Churches. www.theceec.org/

Webber, Robert. *Common Roots*. Waco, TX: Word Publishing, 1978.

————. *Evangelicals on the Canterbury Trail: Why Evangelical Christians Are Attracted to the Liturgical Church*. Waco, TX: Word Publishing, 1985.

Continuing Anglican United States Episcopacy

Current address not reported.

The Continuing Anglican United States Episcopacy was founded in September 2001 by Bp. Gregory Wayne Godsey (b.1979), formerly a priest and bishop with the Independent Catholic Church. Raised as a Roman Catholic, Godsey joined the Independent Catholics in 1998. He was ordained in January 1999 and consecrated to the episcopacy in June 1999 by its bishops. He left the Independent Catholic Church complaining of its "departure from the moral values of the Bible."

In September 2001, Bishop Godsey formed the Continuing Anglican United States Episcopacy. He adopted a conservative Anglican approach to belief and practice that included affirmation of the 39 Articles of Religion. In October 2001, Godsey created All Saints Anglican Church in Hopkinsville, Kentucky, and ordained Rev. Fr. David S. Jennings as the church's first priest. He consecrated two bishops for the church, William E. Conner and Jeffrey L. Cottingame, as the Bishop of the Church's Central Diocese. (Both Connor and Cottingame have subsequently left the Episcopacy and formed the independent Holy Cross Anglican Communion. Godsey also opened Holy Cross Seminary for the training of future priests.

Membership: Not reported.

Educational Facilities:

Holy Cross Seminary, Hopkinsville, Kentucky.

Continuing Episcopal Church (CEC™)

PO Box 50824, Colorado Springs, CO 80949-0824

The Continuing Episcopal Church (CEC™) was founded in 1984 by former members of the Episcopal Church who opposed a series of actions taken by the leadership. These included the church's participation with other churches in the Consultation on Church Union, the ordination and consecration of women as priests and bishops, and the new liturgy of 1979. On June 2, 1984, Colin James III and Henry C. Robbins were consecrated as bishops for the Continuing Episcopal Church by Abp. Dismas F. G. Markle of the Eastern Orthodox Catholic Church in America. James was selected presiding bishop. Holy Orders came through the Russian Orthodox Church before 1917. The Continuing Episcopal Church is in communion by necessity with the Holy Eastern Orthodox Catholic and Apostolic Church in North America.

The Continuing Episcopal Church is a conservative Anglican body. It accepts the traditional Thirty-nine Articles of Religion as a doctrinal standard and the Lambeth Quadrilateral of 1888–1889 as authoritative statements of catholicity. It uses the 1928 edition of the *Book of Common Prayer* and the King James Version of the Bible.

Membership: Not reported. In 2002 the church reported three congregations, one retired deacon and three retired priests (including the two bishops), and about 100 members.

Educational Facilities:

The Anglican Institute of Theology (AIT).

Sources:

Continuing Episcopal Church. www.the-episcopal-church.org/.

Ecumenical Catholic Church of America

Ecumenical Catholic Church Communion, 98-1277 Kaahumanu St. PMB 345, Honolulu, HI 96701

The Ecumenical Catholic Church of America (ECCA) is the North American Diocese of the Ecumenical Catholic Church Communion. The ECCA was formed in 2004 by priests and congregations who had left several denominations, but especially the Episcopal Church, due to the ordination of homosexuals to the ministry. The ECCA is a theologically conservative organization and offers episcopal oversight to independent congregations seeking a larger church fellowship. In general, member congregations are allowed to maintain worship as they see fit; however, they are required to utilize the *Book of Common Prayer* in all sacraments and sacramental ceremonies—marriage, ordination of priests, burial, and so on. The ECCA is working on a revised version of the *Book of Common Prayer* (begun in 1979) which it intends to place into service in the near future.

Soon after its formation, the ECCA developed ties internationally with similar congregations that had also rejected ties to homosexual ministers and bishops. Thus, it moved to form an international jurisdiction, the Ecumenical Catholic Church Communion (ECCC), and to reorganize the ECCA as the communion's North American diocese.

Leading both the ECCA and the ECCC is Abp. R. C. Anderson, the church's patriarch. Anderson was consecrated a bishop in 1998 by Bps. Marcus Cummins, John Clayton, and Martin Bowers, who passed to him multiple lines of apostolic succession, the primary ones derived from Hugh George de Willmott Newman (1905–1979) and Walter Propheta (1912–1972).

The ECCA is organized into eight geographical regions (dioceses), each under the authority of a bishop. Bishops have been assigned to three of the eight regions. Internationally, the ECCC is organized into seven archdioceses, one per continent. Archbishops have been assigned to five of the seven continents.

Membership: Not reported.

Sources:

Ecumenical Catholic Church Communion. www.eccconline.com/.

Ecumenical Catholic Church of America. www.ecca.us/.

Episcopal Church

815 2nd Ave., New York, NY 10017

The Church of England came into the American colonies with the first British settlers. The first church was established at Jamestown in 1607, and in 1619 an act of the Virginia legislature formally declared Virginians to be members of the Church of England. By the time of the American Revolution, more than 400 Anglican parishes were spread along the coast from Georgia to New Hampshire.

The American Revolution created a crisis for the church in the new nation because, in spite of the large number of parishes, the church in the colonies had no bishop. War with England meant England would not be sending a bishop to America, so there was no way to ordain new priests or consecrate future bishops. Further, many priests (already in short supply) sided with England during the Revolution and returned to England. Thus, the war left Anglican congregations highly disorganized. In 1783, the Connecticut churches sent Samuel Seabury (1729–1796) to England to be consecrated. But, because he would not swear allegiance to the British Crown, he could not be consecrated. He was finally consecrated by the Nonjuring Church of Scotland in 1784. Upon Seabury's return in 1785, the Connecticut priests held a convocation to organize their parishes.

Meanwhile, a second movement to reorganize the American parishes was undertaken in the Middle Colonies (mainly in Pennsylvania and Virginia) under the leadership of William White (1748–1836). A series of meetings over the next several years resulted in the adoption of the "Ecclesiastical Constitution of the Protestant Episcopal Church in the United States." William White and Samuel Provoost (1742–1815) were chosen as bishops. They sailed for England and were consecrated by the archbishop of Canterbury in 1787, after Parliament had rescinded the requirement of an oath of loyalty to the Crown for any consecrated bishop from "foreign parts." In 1789 the new constitution was adopted by all the American churches (including Bishop Seabury's diocese). The Protestant Episcopal Church, the church that represents the Anglican tradition in the United States, was born.

The Protestant Episcopal Church, popularly called the Episcopal Church, grew and became a national body during the nineteenth century. Within its membership three informally organized but recognizable groups developed: the high church of the Anglo-Catholic group; the low-church evangelicals; and the broad church party (the group between the high-church and low-church groups). The differences between these groups were largely based on their approach to liturgy and the Eucharist. Episcopalians have followed the liturgy of the Prayer Book, which is built upon a belief in the Real Presence of Christ in the Eucharist. The Church of England passed to American Episcopalians a repudiation of the particular explanation of that doctrine of the Real Presence called *transubstantiation*. High-church Episcopalians have tended to emphasize the forms and ceremonies associated with the Roman tradition and have tended toward a Roman explanation of the Real Presence. In contrast, low-church Episcopalians have emphasized the "Puritan" element introduced into the Anglican Church after the Reformation. They have opposed the emphasis on outward ceremony, and center their attention on the reading and preaching of the Word.

During the 1840s the American Church began to be influenced by the Oxford Movement, a high-church revival in the Church of England. Among the personages identified with the movement was John Henry Newman (1801–1890), who later joined the Roman Catholic Church. In the wake of the revival, church architecture and sanctuary furnishings began to change. The Gothic church became common. The typical arrangement of furniture in the sanctuary centered upon a table, and the pulpit was replaced with a center altar, the common arrangement today.

The broad-church party, which reached into both high-church and low-church camps, was identified mostly by its liberalism in matters of discipline, doctrine, and biblical interpretation. Broad churchmen generally avoided too much emphasis on ceremony and identified themselves through their inclusive spirit. They were open to a variety of creedal interpretations and would often open their pulpits and altars to non-Episcopalians.

During the mid-twentieth century new issues began to become prominent in the church, and these led to new lines of division that cut across the older groupings. Dissent within the church sprung up around a number of issues: laxity in church moral standards (especially, acceptance of sexual immorality), the ordination of women priests, the reported use of funds contributed to the National Council of Churches and World Council of Churches for "far-left" political causes, and the church's involvement in various social crusades (from civil rights and women's liberation to gay liberation). In addition, disagreements evolved over the introduction of extensive revisions to the 1928 edition of the *Book of Common Prayer*, made available in a revised prayer book. These issues came to a head in 1976 when the General Convention of the church approved the ordination of women and the revised *Book of Common Prayer*. Several thousand who disapproved of the changes left the church in the late 1970s. (Following the movement out of the Episcopal Church, the Anglicans, as the conservatives called themselves, tended to split along the older party lines).

Membership: Not reported.

Educational Facilities:

Seminaries

Berkeley Divinity School at Yale, New Haven, Connecticut.

Bexley Hall–Colgate-Rochester, Rochester, New York.

Church Divinity School of the Pacific, Berkeley, California.

Episcopal Divinity School, Cambridge, Massachusetts.

Episcopal Theological Seminary of the Southwest, Austin, Texas.

General Theological Seminary, New York City, New York.

Nashotah House, Nashotah, Wisconsin.

Seabury-Western Theological Seminary, Evanston, Illinois.

Virginia Theological Seminary, Alexandria, Virginia.

Colleges and Universities

Bard College, Annandale-on-the-Hudson, New York.

Hobart and William Smith Colleges, Geneva, New York.

Kenyon College, Gambier, Ohio.

St. Augustine's College, Raleigh, North Carolina.

St. Paul's College, Lawrenceville, Virginia.

Trinity College, Hartford, Connecticut.

University of the South, Sewanee, Tennessee.

Voorhees College, Denmark, South Carolina.

Periodicals: *The Episcopalian*. Available from 1930 Chestnut St., Philadelphia, PA 19103. • *The Living Church*. Available from 407 E Michigan St., Milwaukee, WI 53202. • *Historical Magazine*. Available from Box 2247, Austin, TX 78705.

Remarks: In 1967 the General Convention adopted the designation "Episcopal Church" as an official alternative name.

Sources:

Episcopal Church. www.ecusa.anglican.org/.

Gray, William, and Betty Gray. *The Episcopal Church Welcomes You*. New York: Seabury Press, 1974.

Holmes, David L. *A Brief History of the Episcopal Church*. Harrisburg, PA: Trinity Press International, 1994.

Kew, Richard, and Roger J. White. *New Millennium, New Church: Trends Shaping the Episcopal Church for the 21st Century*. Cambridge, MA: Cowley Publications, 1992.

Konolige, Kit, and Frederica Konolige. *The Power of Their Glory*. New York: Wyden Books, 1978.

Manross, William W. *A History of the American Episcopal Church*. New York: Morehouse-Gorham, 1950.

Pittenger, W. Norman. *The Episcopalian Way of Life*. Englewood Cliffs, NJ: Prentice-Hall, 1957.

Prichard, Robert W. *A History of the Episcopal Church*. Harrisburg, PA: Morehouse Publications, 1987.

Summer, David C. *The Episcopal Church's History, 1945–1985*. Harrisburg, PA: Morehouse Publications, 1987.

Synder, William. *Looking at the Episcopal Church*. Wilton, CT: Morehouse-Barlow, 1980.

Webber, Christopher L. *Welcome to the Episcopal Church: An Introduction*. Harrisburg, PA: Morehouse Publishing, 2000.

Episcopal Missionary Church

Box 1294, Aiken, SC 29802

The Episcopal Missionary Church was founded in 1992 by Rt. Rev. A. Donald Davies, formerly a bishop in the Episcopal Church. Bishop Davies had emerged as a conservative leader in the Episcopal Church, and while serving as the bishop of Dallas—Fort Worth (Texas) had founded the Episcopal Synod, still the organization of traditionalists within the Episcopal Church. In 1992, having concluded that the Episcopal Church would never be a welcome environment for traditionalists, he left and founded the Episcopal Missionary Church. Initially, several congregations affiliated with it. Then in 1994 the Holy Catholic Church, Anglican Rite Jurisdiction of the Americas (ARJA), dissolved and united with the Episcopal Missionary Church.

ARJA brought Los Hermanos Franciscanos de la Providencia, a Franciscan order headquartered in Puerto Rico, into the new church.

The Episcopal Missionary Church follows the traditional Anglican practice and belief. It uses the 1928 edition of the Book of Common Prayer. It rejects the liturgical changes of the Episcopal Church and does not accept the ordination of females to the priesthood. The church's name includes the word "missionary" because of members' belief that missionary work is central to the Christian life, whether conducted abroad or at home when sharing the gospel with one's neighbors.

Membership: In 2008 the church listed 34 affiliated congregations in 19 states.

Sources:

Episcopal Missionary Church. www.emchome.org/.

Nones, Jane, ed. *1994/95 Directory of Traditional Anglican and Episcopal Parishes*. Tulsa, OK: Fellowship of Concerned Churchmen, 1995.

Evangelical Anglican Church in America (EACA)

Office of the Presiding Bishop 1379, Park Western Dr., Ste. 329, San Pedro, CA 90732

The Evangelical Anglican Church in America (EACA) was founded in 1993 when Rev. Craig S. Bettendorf, formerly of the Philippine Independent Church, opened All Saints Parish in Los Angeles. Bettendorf, a gay priest, had contact over the years with a number of marginalized clergy (both gay and non-gay) and developed the Anglican Institute for Affirmative Christian Studies to unite them through study of a curriculum based on liberation theology. After his election as the first bishop, Bettendorf was consecrated in December 1994 by Abp. Gary Stephen Trivoli-Johnson of the Central Orthodox Synod. The church has grown out of the high-church traditions of the Anglican Communion and affirms Holy Scripture, believes in tradition, and utilizes reason. It offers the sacraments of baptism and the Eucharist and the rite of confirmation, marriage (and holy union), housewarming blessings, anointing, memorial services, and ordination.

The distinctive role of the EACA, in relation to other Anglican and Old Catholic jurisdictions, is its inclusivity. The church welcomes all people without reference to gender, marital status, sexual orientation, race, or physical challenges. It welcomes gay men, lesbians, and bisexual people to the ordained ministry, but describes itself as inclusive rather than primarily gay/lesbian. It also advocates the use of inclusive language in its worship and affirms God as Creator, Redeemer, and Giver of Life.

During the Second Triennial General Convention held in Tulsa, Oklahoma, in May 2001, the passing of a constitutional amendment written and approved for a vote during the previous convention (Tampa, Florida, 1998) created a new system of church governance. A Three House system (consisting of the House of Laity, House of Clergy, and House of Bishops, all with equal voice and vote) was established to replace the former Episcopal system. An executive committee comprising two individuals from each House manages all daily aspects of the church in between triennial conventions (when all members of the Three Houses meet). The positions of chief financial officer, chief administrative officer, and chief operating officer were also established and filled by election during the Second Convention. Bps. Rusty Smith and Carmen Valenzuela are the current co-presiding bishops.

Membership: In 2000 there were 13 missions/parishes and 850 communicant members, 16 priests, 6 transitional deacons, and 2 permanent deacons.

Educational Facilities:

Anglican Institute for Affirmative Christian Studies, San Diego, California.

Periodicals: *Kaleidoscope*.

Sources:

Evangelical Anglican Church in America. www.eaca.org/.

Evangelical Episcopal Church (GRIDER)

17275 E Goshawk Rd., Colorado Springs, CO 80908

The Evangelical Episcopal Church was founded on May 26, 1993, by a core group of charismatic and renewal movement participants, with the additional participation of liturgical and sacramental leaders involved in the convergence movement. The Evangelical Episcopal Church is an international network of churches, ministries, and leaders who are affiliated on the basis of spiritual bond, not merely a shared theological perspective or form of worship.

The bishops, priests, deacons, and lay leaders are required to affirm and uphold the international doctrinal statement of Christian unity: the Lausanne Covenant.

The Evangelical Episcopal Church is inclusive, liturgical, sacramental, evangelical, charismatic, and concerns itself with compassion-based evangelism, church planting, and world missions. Canterbury Seminary is a ministry of the Evangelical Episcopal Church that provides parish-based ministry training, professional networking, and apostolic ministry team building in local congregations.

The Evangelical Episcopal Church affirms and recognizes all evangelical denominations, leadership networks, and professional ministerial associations that support and defend, in word and deed, the great (or first) commandment and the great commission (i.e., to spread the teachings of Christ). Men and women clergy, from around the world, serve in all levels of the church. The Evangelical Episcopal Church maintains all the signs, symbols, and structure of a denomination, yet strives to maintain freedom, flexibility, collegiality, and a professional standard of excellence. The clergy of the Evangelical Episcopal Church are encouraged to maintain dual affiliation with other Christian groups as an expression of unity, inclusiveness, and a shared ministry among the communities they are invited into and serve.

Membership: Not reported.

Sources:

Ward, Gary L., Bertil Persson, and Alan Bain, eds. *Independent Bishops: An International Directory*. Detroit, MI: Apogee Books, 1990. 524 pp.

Evangelical Old Catholic Communion

c/o St. Martin's Old Catholic Church, 1420 S. Catalina Ave., Springfield, MO 65804

The Evangelical Old Catholic Communion is a new Old Catholic jurisdiction founded and headed by Most Rev. Francis John Sahuque, its presiding bishop. Sahuque was consecrated as a bishop in 2006 by Bp. Brian E. Brown and Abp. Rodney Rickard. They passed to him their multiple line of apostolic succession, the most important of which traces back to Carmel Henry Carfora (1878–1958), who pioneered the Old Catholic movement in the United States. The new jurisdiction describes itself as Catholic, apostolic, and liturgical. The church uses its own biblically based rituals and draws its doctrine from the Seven Ecumenical Councils (325–787 C.E.).

It welcomes married persons and women to the priesthood, but will not knowingly accept practicing homosexuals to the ordained ministry

Membership: Not reported. In 2008 the church reported two congregations, one in Missouri and one in Nebraska.

Sources:

Evangelical Old Catholic Communion. evangelicaloldcatholiccommunion.net/.

Free Church of Scotland on Prince Edward Island

c/o Rev. William R. Underhay, Box 4907, Crapaud, PE, Canada C0A 1J0

The present Free Church of Scotland on Prince Edward Island dates to 1954 when the Church of Scotland congregations were received into the Free Church of Scotland as the Presbytery of Prince Edward Island.

The history of these congregations dates to pioneer times. Rev. Donald MacDonald, a minister of the Church of Scotland, arrived in Prince Edward Island in 1826; about two years later, following a transforming spiritual experience, his preaching became very effective and bore much fruit. He preached over a large part of the island, mostly to Scottish immigrants. At the time of his death in 1867 he had about 5,000 followers. While ministers of the Church of Scotland increased in number MacDonald's ministry became largely independent of them, although officially MacDonald and his followers always considered themselves Church of Scotland.

With the Disruption in Scotland in 1843, a large section of the Established Church (including nearly 500 ministers) withdrew in a protest against the practice of partronage, which interfered with the independence of the church. Chiefly at stake was the induction of ministers against the will of the people. The new body became the Church of Scotland Free. The split in the church also took place in the colonies, including Prince Edward Island. However, Donald MacDonald and his followers, as well as a number of others in Prince Edward Island and elsewhere in the Lower Provinces, did not join the Free Church movement. During the following years, several church unions occurred among the Presbyterians in British North America, culminating in the Presbyterian Church of Canada in 1875. By this time, Donald MacDonald had died. The Orwell Head congregation, the main center of MacDonald's followers in the eastern part of the island, was received into the Presbyterian Church of Canada in 1896 and eventually became part of the United Church of Canada. A little over half a century after the union of 1875 more congregations entered the Presbyterian Church of Canada. Thus a significant number of the congregations connected with the ministry of MacDonald and his successors had departed, leaving a much reduced Church of Scotland population.

However, in 1954, when the Church of Scotland on Prince Edward Island was received into the Free Church of Scotland, there were still at least 10 church buildings in use. In addition, services were being held in several halls. The congregations were divided into three pastoral charges by the Free Church. At present, there are seven churches where regular services are held. In two others, there are occasional services. Each of the pastoral charges has a pastor.

In the latter part of the nineteenth century and the early part of the twentieth century many people from Prince Edward Island emigrated to Massachusetts, and a Church of Scotland congregation was formed there. This congregation continued until recent years but never became part of the Free Church.

There are other Free Church congregations in North America, located in Livonia, Michigan, and Toronto, Ontario. Together they form the Presbytery of the Great Lakes and Western Canada. The history of the formation of these congregations is distinct from that of the congregations on Prince Edward Island. The two presbyteries together make up the Free Church of Scotland of North America. Each presbytery may appoint commissioners to the general assembly that meets in Edinburgh, Scotland.

The Free Church is conservative in faith, holding to the inerrancy and infallibility of the Bible. It adheres to the Westminister Confession of Faith as its secondary standard to which all ordained office bearers are required to subscribe. The Westminster Large and Shorter Catechisms are also officially recognized. The material for congregational praise is the Scottish Psalter, sung without instrumental accompaniment. The Free Church of Scotland does not participate in the World Council of Churches but is a member of the International Council of Reformed Churches (ICRC).

Membership: In 2008 the church's total membership in the three pastoral charges including adherents and children was approximately 180, with seven congregations and two clergy. Former mission centers in Peru, South Africa, and India have been formed into separate denominations, but financial support is still provided and, in the case of South Africa and Peru, missionaries are still sent.

Educational Facilities:

Free Church College, Edinburgh.

Sources:

Free Church of Scotland on Prince Edward Island. www.islandfreechurch.org.

Collins, G. N. M. *Heritage of My Fathers*. Edinburgh, U.K.: Knox Press.

Graham, Clement, ed. *Crown Him Lord of All*. Edinburgh, U.K.: Knox Press, 1993.

MacLeod, Donald, ed. *Hold Fast Your Confession*. Edinburgh, U.K.: Knox Press, 1978.

Free Episcopal Church

c/o The Rt. Rev. Sherrie Albrecht, 2100 Manchester Rd., Ste. 900, Wheaton, IL 60187

The origins of the Free Episcopal Church date back to 1999, when discussions began among a group of ministers and laypeople searching for a church based around the idea of servanthood. Through these discussions, the idea of a church outside of a traditional parish model emerged, as well as the desire for a ministry that would reach out to those who tended to be overlooked by the larger denominations. The result was the creation of the Free Episcopal Church in 2001. The new church found its place within the larger Anglican tradition, with its affirmation of the Scriptures, the Apostolic Church, and the early Church Fathers and Mothers.

Being Anglican, the church utilizes the Book of Common Prayer, from which it emphasizes proclamation of the Word and the celebration of the life, death, and resurrection of Christ Jesus through the bread and wine. The church also affirms the historical three-fold ministry of bishop, presbyter, and deacon; the priesthood of all believers; and the Via Media or "middle way" between Roman Catholics and Anglicans, which doctrinally is spelled out in the Thirty-Nine Articles of Religion. The Church has chosen the 1979 edition of the Book of Common Prayer, developed by the Episcopal Church.

Integral to the life of the Free Episcopal Church is its policy of inclusivism. The church had declared itself to be inclusive, open, and affirming. Without regard to race, ethnicity, social or economic status, gender, age, sexuality, or physical ability, both men and women are eligible to attend its worship, participate in its programs, and be admitted to ordained and unordained leadership positions.

Leadership of the church is vested in its bishops: Rt. Rev. Rob Angus Jones, its founding bishop; and Rt. Rev. Sherrie Albrecht, its present presiding Bishop. The apostolic lineage of the church is traced to the Syrian Church in Antioch and in India by way of Joseph René Vilatte. Jones was consecrated to the episcopacy by Abp. Joseph Laverne Vredenburgh (Mar Narsai), patriarch of the Federation of St. Thomas Christians, in 2001. In 2004 Jones, assisted by Most Rev. Sharon Hart of the Contemporary Catholic Church and Rt. Rev. Rusty Clyma of the New Church—Inclusive Anglican Reform (now the Inclusive Celtic Church), consecrated Bishop Albrecht.

Membership: Not reported.

Sources:

Free Episcopal Church. www.free-episcopal.org/.

Free Protestant Episcopal Church

Cathedral District Post Office, PO Box 33079, Regina, SK, Canada S4T 7X2

The Free Protestant Episcopal Church was established in 1897 through the union of three small British episcopates: the Ancient British Church (founded 1876/1877), the Nazarene Episcopal Ecclesia (founded in 1873), and the Free Protestant Church of England (founded in 1889). Leon Checkemian (1848–1920), an Armenian who became the first primate of the new church, was supposedly consecrated by Bp. A. S. Richardson of the Reformed Episcopal Church in 1890, though more recently it has been claimed that he was consecrated in 1878 by an Abp. Leon Chorchorunian (1822–1897). In either case, no papers have been produced, and the validity of the consecration is questioned by many. In 1952, Charles D. Boltwood (1889–1985) became the fifth person to hold the post of primate.

The faith of the Free Protestant Episcopal Church is the same as that of the Protestant Episcopal Church. The Thirty-Nine Articles are accepted. There are, however, seven doctrines condemned as contrary to God's word:

1. That the church exists in only one order or form of polity;
2. That ministers are "priests" in any other sense than that in which all believers are part of a "royal priesthood";
3. That the Lord's table is an altar on which the oblation of the body and blood of Christ is offered anew to the Father;
4. That Christ is present in the elements of bread and wine in the Lord's Supper;
5. That regeneration and baptism are inseparably connected;
6. That the law should punish Christians with death;
7. That Christians may wear weapons and serve in war when aiding the wounded or assisting in civil defense.

In these seven objections, the sacramentalism of Anglo-Catholicism is explicitly denied and conscientious objection to carrying arms in war is elevated to dogma.

The Free Protestant Episcopal Church came to America in 1958 when Boltwood, on a trip to Los Angeles, consecrated Emmet Neil Enochs as archbishop of California and primate of the United States. On the same trip, John Marion Stanley (b. 1923) was consecrated bishop of Washington; subsequently four additional bishops were consecrated for the United States. The primate was directly responsible to the bishop primus in London.

In 1966 Boltwood consecrated Albert John Fuge Sr. (1911–1982), a Lutheran pastor in New York City, as the new bishop of the church for New York State. At that time, the Free Protestant Episcopal Church reported 23 congregations plus a number of affiliated missions, and there were an estimated 2,000 members in the United States and Canada. Two years later Boltwood replaced Enochs, who had become an Old Catholic bishop, as archbishop of New York and metropolitan of the United States. He operated out of the Boltwood Chapel at 177 West Broadway in Manhattan.

At the age of 89, Boltwood retired as the church's primus and nominated Fuge as his successor. Boltwood handed over the deed of succession to the office of bishop primus to Fuge in 1978. Bps. Horst K. F. Block (1936–2008), the missionary bishop for Germany and France, and Emmanuel Samuel Yekorogha (d. 1983), the archbishop of West Africa, did not accept Fuge and subsequently formed another church, called the International Free Protestant Episcopal Church.

In 1982 Archbishop Fuge died and was succeeded as archbishop of the United States by Rt. Rev. Robert Randolph Rivette (1916–2004), who had been consecrated in 1971 by Bps. Fuge and Boltwood. Dr. Charles K. S. S. Moffatt (1907–1989), the archbishop of Canada, became the new international primus. In 1989 Archbishop Moffatt died without naming a successor as primus. In 1994 it was determined that by default, Bp. Dr. Edwin Dwane Follick (b. 1935), on account of his being the senior-most cleric at that moment, would be accepted as the legal primus.

The church is currently led by Archbishop Follick; Rev. Melvin Frederick Larson (b. 1920), the archbishop of the Pacific Northwest; and Rev. Matthew John Carles Tuz (b. 1951), the archbishop of Canada.

Membership: Not reported.

Sources:

Free Protestant Episcopal Church. netministries.org/see/churches/ch18802.

Holy Catholic Church (Anglican Rite)

c/o Rt. Rev. Thomas Kleppinger, 44 S. 8th St., Quakertown, PA 18951-5334

The Holy Catholic Church (Anglican Rite) is the result of a schism in the Anglican Catholic Church, the major body representing the Continuing Church Movement that emerged in the 1970s among conservative members of the Episcopal Church who rejected the direction the church was taking. Essential to the dissent was the church's ordination of females to the priesthood. Leading the Holy Catholic Church is Rt. Rev. Thomas Kleppinger who previously served in the United Episcopal Church. He followed that church's merger into the Anglican Episcopal Church and subsequently the Anglican Catholic Church. The 1997 schism appears to be primarily administrative, as non-doctrinal issues appear to divide the Holy Catholic Church and the Anglican Catholic Church.

The church is similar in belief and practice to the Anglican Catholic Church. It places special emphasis upon its adherence to the seven Ecumenical Councils of the ancient Christian Church. The church's congregations are divided into dioceses including the Diocese of the Resurrection (in the Eastern states), the Diocese of the Holy/ Trinity and Great Plains, and the Diocese of the Pacific and the Southwest. There is a mission in Mexico. The church sponsors St. Gregory's House of Theological Studies, a combined residential and distance learning program for theological instruction under the administration of the church's Diocese of the Resurrection. It has a working relationship with the Holy Catholic Church (Western Rite).

Membership: Not reported.

Educational Facilities:

Saint Gregory's House of Theological Studies, Tampa, Florida.

Sources:

Holy Catholic Church (Anglican Rite). www.anglicaneducationcentre.net/

Holy Celtic Church

c/o Most Rev. Donald E. Hugh, Presiding Bishop, PO Box 2401, Apple Valley, CA 92307

The Holy Celtic Church traces its history to the ancient Celtic church that preceded the imposition of Roman authority in Celtic lands. Documentation concerning the Celtic church has been lacking because of the destruction of its records and artifacts beginning with the Roman conquests. The modern Holy Celtic Church was reestablished in the 1990s with orders derived from the Order of Corporate Reunion. The Order had been founded in 1874 in London, England, to confer valid apostolic orders on individuals who were working for the unity of Anglican and Eastern Orthodox churches. In more recent years, it has focused on unifying the many independent Anglican and Orthodox jurisdictions.

The Holy Celtic Church is conservative and adheres closely to basic Christian teachings and the Holy Scripture as expressed in the Apostolic Constitution, Teachings, and Creed. It recognizes the spirit of the Seven Ecumenical Councils, especially the first three, which were attended by Celtic bishops. The church has a particular affinity with the Coptic Church, especially the spirit of the ancient Desert Fathers who carried Christianity to the fringes of the their known world. The church""s clergy work to visit those unable to attend church services, and to establish small missions, priories, and cell groups.

Membership: Not reported.

Sources:

Holy Celtic Church. www.celticsynod.org/celtic.htm.

Holy Cross Anglican Communion

c/o Rev. Canon Larry A. Hoyt, 6 Jefferson, Castile, NY 14427

The Holy Cross Anglican Communion is a small new jurisdiction of the Continuing Church movement, the conservative movement of former members of the Episcopal Church who, beginning in the mid-1970s, rejected what they saw as liberal trends in the Episcopal Church and left to found independent dioceses. The Communion, originally known as the Holy Cross Episcopal Church, traces its existence to the March 6, 2001, consecration of the Rev. William E. Conner to the office of bishop. In August 2001 Conner consecrated Rev. Jeffrey Cottingame as the church's second bishop. The service was held at the Parker College of Chiropractic Chapel in Dallas, Texas. Following the consecration ceremony, the new Bishop Cottingame laid his hands on Bishop Conner in an act to elevate him to the office of archbishop for the Communion. The new jurisdiction brought together several previously existing ministries in Texas and elsewhere. Its present name was adopted in September 2001.

At the beginning of 2002 the Communion merged with the Continuing Anglican United States Episcopacy, which was founded in September 2001 by Bp. Gregory Wayne Godsey. Godsey had been the original consecrator of Bishop Conner. However, at the beginning of February 2002, the bishops of Holy Cross

Anglican Communion voted overwhelmingly to dissolve the merger. They reorganized the Communion and created a new logo using the shield of St. George. The Communion affirms the authority of the 39 Articles of Religion and the Nicene Creed, both of which are affirmed unanimously in the larger Anglican world, and uses the 1928 Book of Common Prayer. Although they affirm the vital role of female leadership in the church, the Communion rejects the entrance of women into the ordained ministry.

Membership: In 2008 the Communion reported two parishes in the United States and one in Canada.

Educational Facilities:

Holy Cross Seminary, New Rochelle, New York.

Sources:

Holy Cross Anglican Communion. hcac2.tripod.com/.

Independent Episcopal Church (Anglican Rite, Old Catholic Church)

5414 W Pierson St., Phoenix, AZ 85031

The Independent Episcopal Church (Anglican Rite, Old Catholic Church), also known as the Independent Episcopal Church, International, was founded in 1987 by Rev. Steven Styblo, its primate bishop. Styblo was consecrated in 1985 by Bp. John Michael Dale, the bishop abbot of the Missionaries of Saint John the Beloved and the Western Orthodox Church (ordinariates within the Evangelical-Eucharistic Catholic observance). He is assisted by the Church by Bishop Protestant Episcopal Church but has added insights from the Orthodox and Old Catholic traditions. It accepts the Thirty-nine Articles of Religion common to Anglicanism and the Lambeth Quadrilateral, which were approved by the Episcopal Church (1886) and the Church of England (1888) as their standard of doctrine. The quadrilateral establishes four foundational points of church unity: the Bible, the ancient creeds (Apostles' and Nicene), the two sacraments of baptism and the Lord's Supper, and the historic episcopate. The Independent Episcopal Church deviates from the quadrilateral in its acceptance of seven sacraments (rather than the two accepted by Anglicans).

The church is centered in the Diocese of Arizona and the Christ the King Cathedral Mission in Phoenix, Arizona.

Membership: Not reported. There are three clergy members and a single parish in Phoenix.

Periodicals: Christ Work: Independent Episcopal Newsletter.

Sources:

Ward, Gary L., Bertil Persson, and Alan Bain, eds. *Independent Bishops: An International Directory*. Detroit, MI: Apogee Books, 1990. 524 pp.

International Communion of the Charismatic Episcopal Church

50 St. Thomas Pl., Malverne, NY 11565

The International Communion of the Charismatic Episcopal Church, founded in 1992, is a conservative Anglican church that differs from other jurisdictions of the Continuing Church Movement by its acceptance and support for the charismatic experience. Members of the church are encouraged to participate in the manifestation of the gifts of the Holy Spirit as mentioned in I Corinthians 12. Such gifts include speaking in tongues, divine healing, and prophecy. The charismatic movement spread through the Episcopal Church in the 1970s, but some charismatics found themselves alienated from the directions being pursued by the church as a whole.

Rev. Randolph Adler was consecrated as the first bishop and primate of the International Communion of the Charismatic Episcopal Church on June 26, 1992. He survived an early challenge to his authority in that his episcopal orders derived from Archbishop Bishop Adrian Spriuit (1911–1994), known for his theosophical approach to Christianity. Subsequently, the Charismatic Episcopal Church spread across the United States and gained some significant following in Africa and Asia.

Then in 2006, allegations were raised against some ICCEC leaders, which led to the withdrawal of nearly a third of its clergy and congregations.

Adler retired in 2007, and the Most Rev. Craig W. Bates was elected patriarch in 2008.

Membership: In 2008 the church reported 107 congregations in the United States organized into five diocese and five congregations in Canada. In addition, there are some 200,000 members and 1,700 congregations outside the United States, in the Philippines, Brazil, Europe and Africa.

Sources:

International Communion of the Charismatic Episcopal Church. www.iccec.org/.

Nones, Jane, ed. *1994/95 Directory of Traditional Anglican and Episcopal Parishes*. Tulsa, OK: Fellowship of Concerned Churchmen, 1995.

Old Protestant Episcopal Church

PO Box 33079, Cathedral District Post Office, Regina, SK, Canada S4T 7X2

The Old Protestant Episcopal Church, one of the newer Anglican bodies, was founded in August 2001 in Regina, Saskatchewan, by Bp. Darrel Hockley. Hockley originally saw his effort as a revival of the missionary work in western Canada of the Free Protestant Episcopal Church, in whose name his work was incorporated. However, as he investigated the church further, he learned of its factionalism and withdrew. He reorganized his work as the Old Protestant Episcopal Church, and he structured it to function exclusively in the Canadian province of Saskatchewan and to operate as a house church body.

The church bases its teachings on five sets of documents:

1. Holy Scripture;

2. The Creed of Nicaea-Constantinople;

3. The Dogmatic Decisions of the first four Ecumenical Councils;

4. The Canadian edition of the *Book of Common Prayer* (1962); and

5. The 39 Articles of Religion (1571).

The 1962 *Book of Common Prayer* is the authorized liturgical text for the new church.

The church recognized the threefold ministry of bishop, priest, and deacon. Although Hockley did not go through a formal consecration ceremony, on April 24, 2001, Abp. Joseph L. Vredenburgh, patriarch of the Federation of St. Thomas Christians, sent Hockley a letter confirming his status as a bishop in the Federation's lineage of apostolic succession (the Federation has several different lines of apostolic succession). Unlike the Federation, the Old Protestant Episcopal Church does not ordain women to the ministry. Women are invited to its Order of Deaconess.

The Old Protestant Episcopal Church is in communion with the Free Episcopal Church, formerly known as the Free Protestant Episcopal Church—USA.

Membership: Not reported. The Old Protestant Episcopal Church has one mission, St. Matthias the Apostles Missions, in Regina.

Sources:

Old Protestant Episcopal Church. netministries.org/see/churches/ch08923.

Oratory of Saint Jerome

114 Deluxe Cir., Thomaston, GA 30286

Most Rev. D. Ceabron Williams was consecrated as a bishop in 1999 by Most Rev. Howard E. Stark, the presiding bishop of the Ecumenical Anglican Catholic Church. For the next few years Williams served as the general secretary for the church. However, he subsequently left the Ecumenical Anglican Catholic Church and founded the Oratory of St. Jerome as an independent Anglican-Catholic jurisdiction. The Oratory exists as a sacramental, ecumenical, evangelical, and charismatic community and ministry. It locates itself in the center of the western Christian tradition and affirms the beliefs stated in the Apostles', Athanasian, and Nicene Creeds.

Membership: Not reported.

Sources:

Oratory of Saint Jerome. www.georgiachurch.org/.

Orthodox Anglican Church

464 N. County Home Rd., Lexington, NC 27292

The Orthodox Anglican Church was incorporated in 1964 as the Anglican Orthodox Church. In 1998 a schism occurred when several relatives and others who had worked with founder Bp. James Parker Dees (1915–1990) broke with the church's leadership. They purchased the headquarters in Statesville, North Carolina, and were given the old name Anglican Orthodox Church, which in 2005 was changed to Orthodox Anglican Church. The congregation from which they had split changed its name to the Episcopal Orthodox Christian Archdiocese of America.

The Orthodox Anglican Church was the first of several contemporary groups to reject the departures from traditional doctrinal perspective by some of the Episcopal Church's bishops. Dees received episcopal consecration from Wasyl Sawyna of the Holy Ukrainian Autocephalic Orthodox Church of North and South America and Orlando J. Woodward, a bishop in the Old Catholic tradition. The Orthodox Anglican Church champions the 1928 *Book of Common Prayer*, emphasizes Christian orthodoxy, and insists on high moral standards.

Following Dees's death in 1990, he was succeeded by Mt. Rev. Dr. George Schneller, a 1973 graduate of the archdiocese's Cranmer Seminary (now named St. Andrew's Theological College and Seminary). Schneller was consecrated in 1991 by Rt. Rev. Laione Q. Vuki of the Anglican Orthodox Church of Polynesia. Soon after taking office, Schneller fell ill and had to retire. In 1995 Robert J. Godfrey was consecrated by Hesbon O. Njera of the Anglican Orthodox Church in Kenya. He was subsequently named archbishop of the church in the United States and metropolitan of what had become a worldwide Orthodox Anglican Communion. He led the church through the time of the schism in 1998 and the subsequent name change.

During his episcopacy, Godfrey developed friendly relations with the leadership of the Anglican Rite Synod in the Americas. In 1999, when the new auxiliary bishop for the church, Rev. Scott McLaughlin, was to be consecrated, Godfrey asked Mt. Rev. Dr. Herbert Groce of the Anglican Rite Synod to be the chief consecrator. He was assisted by Larry L. Shaver, also of the synod. Shortly thereafter, Godfrey and McLaughlin led the Orthodox Anglican Church into full communion with the Anglican Rite Synod in the Americas.

Archbishop Godfrey retired in April 2000, and Bishop McLaughlin succeeded him as archbishop of the Orthodox Anglican Church and metropolitan of the Orthodox Anglican Communion. The church, communion, and seminary have grown tremendously under McLaughlin's leadership.

Dees also founded the Orthodox Anglican Communion in 1967 as a worldwide fellowship of conservative Anglicans. Members vow allegiance to the doctrine, discipline, and worship of the classic Anglican formularies, especially the various editions of the *Book of Common Prayer*—the 1662 English, 1928 American, 1929 Scottish, and 1962 Canadian editions. The presiding bishop of the U.S. branch of the communion, the Orthodox Anglican Church, serves as metropolitan for the communion. Under McLaughlin, the communion has grown to include member churches in Australia, Brazil, Colombia, the Congo, Ghana, Honduras, India, Italy, Kenya, Latvia, Madagascar, Mexico, Slovakia, and Tanzania.

The church owns St. Andrew's Theological College and Seminary, which was established in 1971 (its name was changed in 2002 from Cranmer Seminary). Today, the seminary has branches in the United States, Italy, and India, and offers nine degree programs.

A religious order, the Cathedral Priory of St. Stephen the Protomartyr, is affiliated with the Orthodox Anglican Church.

Membership: In 2008 the church reported 750,000 worldwide members, including 1,000 in the United States.

Educational Facilities:

St. Andrew's Theological College and Seminary, Lexington, North Carolina.

Periodicals: *The Orthodox Anglican Herald.*

Sources:

Orthodox Anglican Church. www.orthodoxanglican.net.

Dees, James P. *Reformation Anglicanism*. Statesville, NC: Anglican Orthodox Church, 1973.

Philippine Independent Catholic Church in the Americas

14373 Shady Hollow Ln., Chino Hills, CA 91709

During the 1980s, the Philippine Independent Church, the representative of the worldwide Anglican Communion in the Philippine Islands, was shaken by severe internal disputes. A major issue focused on the church's refusal to reelect Marcario V. Ga as *Obispo Maximo*, Supreme Bishop. Ga had served in that position for several four-year terms. Refusing to accept the decision of the church, he reorganized his following and began what has become an ongoing court fight for recognition in the Philippines. The split in the Philippine Independent Church has had significant repercussions in the United States where several of Ga's close associates have involved themselves since the late 1970s.

In January 1978, Abp. Francisco Pagtakhan took center stage at the consecration of C. Dale D. Doren, Robert S. Morse, James O. Mote, and Peter F. Watterson as bishops for the new church being formed by the conservative Anglicans who had recently left the Episcopal Church. His active participation in the event projected the Philippine Independent Church directly into the affairs of a sister communion by providing legitimacy to a breakaway group.

During the 1980s, Pagtakhan and two other bishops, Sergio Mondala and Lupe Rosete, performed consecrations for several independent Anglican groups, each time further straining relations between the Episcopal Church and the Philippine Independent Church. Following the split in the Philippines, Pagtakhan moved to establish the Ga branch of the Philippine Independent Church in North America. (All of the previous consecrations had been for independent American Anglican jurisdictions.) In April 1986, Pagtakhan consecrated Thomas Gore, an Episcopal minister who was a psychiatrist in Lubbock, Texas. Gore moved to incorporate the church as the Eglesia Filipina Independente, the Philippine Independent Catholic Church in the Americas, as a Texas corporation. Pagtakhan was named president and Gore vicar-general. Pagtakhan and Gore consecrated George Martinus as the church's bishop for Mexico in 1988.

In the few years of the church's existence, it has grown through the addition of independent bishops who have sought association with it. These include Bp. Paul G. W. Schultz (Glendale, California), Bp. Charles Boulton (Texas), and Bp. Charles S. J. White (Washington, D.C.) In 1987, Pagtakhan named Abp. Bertil Persson, primate of the Apostolic Episcopal Church, as his apostolic representative for Scandinavia and Europe.

Membership: Not reported.

Sources:

Philippine Independent Catholic Church in the Americas. www.ifi.ph/

Ward, Gary L. *Independent Bishops: An International Directory*. Detroit, MI: Apogee Books, 1990.

Philippine Independent Church

c/o Rt. Rev. Raul C. Tobias, 14373 Shady Hollow Ln., Chino Hills, CA 91709

The Philippine Independent Church emerged from the political struggles of the nineteenth century that led to full independence of the Philippine Islands. Following the defeat of the Spanish in 1898, the United States took control of the Philippines rather than grant it full governmental autonomy, and as a result, a revolt led by Emilio Aguinaldo developed against U.S. rule. In that area of the country briefly controlled by Aguinaldo, a military vicar general, Gregorio Aglipay

(1860–1940), was appointed to head the Roman Catholic Church. In 1899 the Roman Catholic archbishop of Manila excommunicated Aglipay, and the church under his control reorganized as the Iglesia Filipina Independiente.

As a guerrilla general, Aglipay became a hero to many, and was the last of the revolutionary leaders to surrender. He retained the loyalty of the members of the new church, and spent the remainder of his life guiding it. The progress of the church was checked by a 1906 ruling of the country's supreme court that awarded most of the church's property to the Roman Catholic Church. Early in the century Aglipay became influenced by Unitarian views that deny the doctrine of the Trinity, and he led the church to accept them. The extent of the theological drift was clearly demonstrated by the 1939 appointment of Dr. Louis C. Cornish, president of the American Unitarian Association, as the honorary president of the church.

The dominance of Unitarian thought was ended after Aglipay's death by his successor as supreme bishop, Isabelo de los Reyes Jr. A Trinitarian, Reyes led the church in 1947 to adopt a strong Trinitarian Declaration of Faith that included acceptance of the Apostles' and Nicene Creeds. Concurrently, the Protestant Episcopal Church recognized the Philippine Independent Church. The following year the supreme bishop and two other bishops of the Philippine Independent Church were consecrated by the Protestant Episcopal Church, giving them the Anglican lineage of apostolic succession.

The Philippine Independent Church began work in the United States during the years of negotiation, which led to the establishment of full intercommunion with the Protestant Episcopal Church in 1961. With the blessing of the Episcopal bishop in Hawaii, a mission among Filipino-Americans was initiated in 1959. By the mid-1970s three parishes, meeting in Episcopal churches, had been established. Services were held in both the English and Ilocano languages. The church subsequently established congregations in other states. Eventually enough parishes were created to justify the organization of the Diocese of the United States and Canada, which in 2008 was led by Bp. Raul C. Tobias.

The Philippine Independent Church established communion with the Protestant Episcopal Church, the Philippine Episcopal Church, and other Anglican bodies through the terms of the Bonn Agreement of 1931, which brought the Church of England and the Old Catholic Church into accord. In 2008 it maintained communion with a number of Anglican bodies, the Old Catholic Churches in Europe, the Polish National Catholic Church, and the Lusitanian Catholic–Apostolic Evangelical Church. It is a member of the World Council of Churches. The world leader of the church in 2008 was Obispo Maximo XI.

Membership: In 2008 the church reported 12 parishes in the United States and three in Canada.

Periodicals: *Aglipayian Review*. Send orders to Box 2484, Manila, Philippines.

Remarks: During the 1970s relations between the Protestant Episcopal Church and the Philippine Independent Church were strained due to the participation of several Philippine bishops in the consecration of bishops for independent conservative Anglican jurisdictions established by former Episcopalians. In 1978 Francisco Pagtakhan, bishop secretary of missions for the Philippine Independent Church, participated in the consecration of several bishops for what became the Anglican Catholic Church, the Diocese of Christ the King, and the United Episcopal Church of North America. Then in 1980 Pagtakhan led in the founding of the Holy Catholic Church, Anglican Rite Jurisdiction of the Americas, and with Bps. Sergio Mondala and Lupe Rosete consecrated three bishops for the new church. In 1982 he broke relations with that jurisdiction and established rival work in a new Anglican Rite Diocese of Texas.

The tension was reduced somewhat following the 1981 schism in the Philippines in which between one third and one half of the members withdrew under the leadership of former Obispo Maximo Ga, who continued as the leader of what became the Philippine Independent Catholic Church. Pagtakhan and his fellow bishops in the United States adhered to the new Philippine jurisdiction, which has a minute existence in North America.

Sources:

Philippine Independent Church. www.ifi.ph/.

Anderson, Gerald H., ed. *Studies in Philippine Church History*. Ithaca, NY: Cornell University Press, 1969.

Deats, Richard L. *Nationalism and Christianity in the Philippines*. Dallas, TX: Southern Methodist University Press, 1967.

Reformed Episcopal Church

260 Second Ave., Blue Bell, PA 19422

The Reformed Episcopal Church was founded on December 2, 1873, in New York City at the call of the Rt. Rev. George David Cummins (1822–1876), formerly the assistant bishop of Kentucky in the Protestant Episcopal Church in the U.S.A. As an evangelical, Cummins viewed with alarm the influence of the Anglo-Catholic movement and certain excesses that it had produced within the Episcopal Church. He had come to believe that it had fatally compromised the Protestant character of Anglican doctrine and worship and that it had bred intolerance to evangelical preaching and worship. Furthermore, he believed its lack of regard for the Articles of Religion and the rubrics in the prayer book was paving the way for liberalism to take over the Protestant Episcopal Church.

Throughout the 1860s, factions within the Episcopal Church had been clashing over ceremonial and doctrinal issues, especially concerning the meaning of critical passages of the *Book of Common Prayer*. These clashes reached a climax for Cummins in October 1873, when he was publicly attacked by his fellow bishops for participating in an ecumenical communion service under the aegis of the Evangelical Alliance in New York City. On November 10, 1873, he resigned his office of assistant bishop and on November 15 issued the call to other evangelical Episcopalians to join him in organizing a new, re-formed Episcopal church for the "purpose of restoring the old paths of the fathers. . . ."

At the organization of the new church, a declaration of principles was adopted along with the Thirty-nine Articles of Religion of 1801, and the Rev. Charles E. Cheney (1836–1916) was elected bishop to serve with Cummins (Cheney was consecrated by Cummins on December 14, 1873, using the ordinal of 1662). In May 1874 the Second General Council approved a constitution and canons for the church and a slightly amended version of the *Book of Common Prayer* of 1785 (later revised in 1932 and again in 1966). During the 1990s the general council began a process of prayer book revision based on the 1662 *Book of Common Prayer*. The revised prayer book is now complete, and includes communion services based on the 1662 and 1928 prayer books. Certain modern-language rites for morning and evening prayer and Holy Communion have also been approved for use. The constitution and canons of the church were revised, expanded, and approved in 2005.

The church has grown to six dioceses in the United States and Canada. Although the was little growth in the early 1900s, the Reformed Episcopal Church has nearly doubled in the number of parishes since 1990. It now comprises four dioceses in the United States and two in Canada (Diocese of the North East and Mid-Atlantic, Diocese of the South East, Diocese of Mid-America, Diocese of Eastern Canada, Diocese of Western Canada, and the Missionary Diocese of Central States). It maintains three theological seminaries, in Philadelphia, Summerville, South Carolina, and Houston, Texas. Each seminary offers a three-year curriculum and houses a library and archival resources.

The church is governed by a triennial general council and elects a presiding bishop from among its serving bishops to be executive head of the church, but most authority lies at the diocesan and parish levels. It has maintained in its doctrine the principles of episcopacy (in historic succession from the apostles) and Anglican liturgy. The doctrine of the church is found in the three ancient creeds of the church, commonly known as the Nicene Creed, the Apostles' Creed, and the Creed of Athanasius, and in the dogmatic definitions of the first four ecumenical councils of the undivided church. The church "holds the following documents to comprise the received and unalterable body of its doctrine: 1) The Thirty-nine Articles of Religion in their 1801 form, 2) The Declaration of Principles of 1873 as adopted by the first General Council of this Church, 3) The Chicago-Lambeth Quadralateral of 186–1888."

In its practice, it recognizes certain nonepiscopal orders of evangelical ministry, but requires that they are regularized through the laying on of hands to maintain historic succession. The church was briefly a member of the Federal Council of Churches at its inception. It has participated in dialogue in response to invitations from the Episcopal Church in 1920, 1931 to 1941, 1987 to 1988, and 2003 to 2006 It is a member of the Federation of Anglican Churches in the Americas and the Common Cause Partner Federation of Anglican Churches in North America. In addition, it, along with the Anglican Province of America, is now in Covenant Union Concordat with the Anglican Church of Nigeria (Anglican Communion).

Membership: In 2005 the church reported 13,463 members in 137 congregations and missions, and about 350 ministers.

Educational Facilities:

Theological Seminary of the Reformed Episcopal Church, Philadelphia, Pennsylvania.

Cummins Memorial Theological Seminary, Summerville, South Carolina.

Cranmer Theological House, Houston, Texas.

Sources:

Reformed Episcopal Church. rechurch.org/recus/recus/index.html.

The Book of Common Prayer. Philadelphia: Reformed Episcopal Publication Society, 2005.

Carter, Paul A. "The Reformed Episcopal Schism of 1873: An Ecumenical Perspective." *Historical Magazine of the Protestant Episcopal Church* 33, no. 3 (September 1964).

Cheney, Charles Edward. *What Reformed Episcopalians Believe*. Philadelphia: Reformed Episcopal Church, 1961.

Guelzo, Allen C. *The First Thirty Years: A Historical Handbook for the Founding of the Reformed Episcopal Church, 1873–1903*. Philadelphia: Reformed Episcopal Publication Society, 1986.

Platt, Warren C. "The Reformed Episcopal Church: The Origins and Early Development of its Theological Perspective." *Historical Magazine of the Protestant Episcopal Church* 61 (1983).

Southern Episcopal Church

c/o Most Reverend Huron C. Manning, Jr., Presiding Bishop, 234 Willow Ln., Nashville, TN 37211

The Southern Episcopal Church was formed in 1953 by 10 families of All Saints Episcopal Church in Nashville, Tennessee. Its constitution was ratified in 1965. The presiding bishop for its first quarter-century was Rt. Rev. B. H. Webster. Webster died in 1991 and was succeeded by Bp. Huron C. Manning, Jr. He is assisted by fellow bishops William Green, Jr., and Henry L. Atwell. The church is governed by the National Convention composed of all bishops (House of Bishops) and the lay and clerical delegates. The 1928 *Book of Common Prayer* is standard for worship. The church sponsors an American Indian mission as well as foreign work in four countries, including a mission in India started in the mid-1980s. American parishes can be found in Alabama, the Carolinas, Florida, Georgia, Indiana, New York, Ohio, Oklahoma, and Tennessee.

Membership: Not reported.

Educational Facilities:

Holy Trinity College, Nashville, Tennessee.

Periodicals: *The Southern Episcopalian*, 4513 Park Ave., Nashville, TN 37209.

Sources:

Southern Episcopal Church. www.angelfire.com/biz/Southern/.

Traditional Protestant Episcopal Church

St. Francis at the Point, PO Box 916, Scenic Hwy 98, Point Clear, Alabama 36564-0916

The Traditional Protestant Episcopal Church was founded in 1986 by Bp. Charles Edward Morley, who had attended Roman Catholic schools while a member of the Protestant Episcopal Church. He became a candidate for ordination in the Protestant Episcopal Diocese of New York in 1976. He attended General Seminary in New York before being ordained to the diaconate in 1979 by Bishop Anthony Clavier in the American Episcopal Church. In 1981 he was ordained to the priesthood by C. D. Dale Doren in the United Episcopal Church U.S.A. Consecrated to the episcopate in 1984 by Abp. Richard C. Acker of the United Episcopal Church of America, he succeeded Bp. Acker as head of the UEC after Acker's death.

Instead of continuing the United Episcopal Church, Morley founded a new church. To avoid the confusion of multiple jurisdictions with similar names, the church incorporated as the Traditional Protestant Episcopal Church in 1986. It has one diocese, the Missionary Diocese of the Advent. Morley was consecrated *sub conditione* in 1989 by Abp. Francisco Pagtakhan of the Philippine Independent Catholic Church, Rt. Rev. E. H. Marshall, and Bp. Larry L. Shaver. As its name implies, the Traditional Protestant Episcopal Church is a conservative Anglican body. It adheres to the 39 Articles of Religion of the Episcopal Church and uses the 1928 *Book of Common Prayer* and the King James Version of the Bible. The church also affirms the inerrancy of the Bible. It is evangelical and low church (less liturgical) in its practice of Anglicanism and rejects Anglo-Catholic approaches to understanding the tradition. In 2008 the Rt. Rev. Delbert R. Murray of Pensacola, Florida, was assistant bishop in the Diocese of the Advent.

Membership: In 2006 the church reported 14 clergy in three parishes or missions in Alabama, Delaware, and Massachusetts.

Sources:

The Protestant Alliance: An Outreach Ministry of the Traditional Protestant Episcopal Church. www.reformer.org/.

United Anglican Church

c/o Most Rev. Dr. Robert D. Parlotz, Archbishop, Diocese Office, 1640–167th Ave. NE, Bellevue, WA 98008-2909

The United Anglican Church (not to be confused with two other Anglican jurisdictions of the same name) was formed at the end of the twentieth century through the union of the Anglo-Catholic Church in the Americas (ACTA) and the Traditional Episcopal Church. The Traditional Episcopal Church was founded in 1991 by Mt. Rev. Richard G. Melli, its presiding bishop. In the mid-1970s Melli was a lay reader at the St. Edward the Confessor Episcopal Church in Mt. Dora, Florida, a congregation of the Episcopal Church. Following the formation of the Anglican Catholic Church, a conservative body of former Episcopal priests and lay people, he assisted in the founding of new congregations in central Florida. He was ordained a deacon in 1980 and the following year a priest by Bp. Frank Knutti.

Melli initially served as the dioceasan administrative officer and soon was named canon. During these years the Anglican Catholic Church largely established itself as an Anglo-Catholic high church and developed some intolerance for the evangelical wing of the conservative Continuing Church movement. Following Bishop Knutti's death, Melli left the church and joined the Anglican Episcopal Church of North America under Bp. Walter Hollis Adams. Melli found himself in charge of four parishes and a mission; an ordered community, the Order of Oblates of the Holy Spirit (founded in 1983); and Laud Hall Seminary, an in-house school providing training for the church's clergy.

When Adams died and the Anglican Episcopal Church of North America moved into a period of instability, Melli and the parishes under his leadership began to seek another jurisdiction that was like them—nonpolitical, Christ-centered, Spirit-filled, and serving God. They could find no jurisdiction to their liking within the Continuing Church movement, and so in 1991 formed the Traditional Episcopal Church. To insure the validity of his orders, Melli sought consecration by bishops in

three different lineages: Bps. Howard Russell (Anglican), Peters (Orthodox), and Roberto Toca (Old Catholic).

The Anglo-Catholic Church in the Americas was reactivated as a province in February 1997, building upon the foundation of two earlier but disbanded provinces, the Anglo-Catholic Church in America and of the Anglican Rite Jurisdiction in America (ARJA), of which they were the logical successors. In 2008 the bishops, the Rt. Rev. Jose Delgado and the Rt. Rev. Norman Strauss, were in succession from the bishops consecrated in Denver in 1978 (in response to the Episcopal Church's adoption of the extension of the ordained ministry to women). Their consecration marked an important juncture in the Continuing Church movement. The two bishops also had orders from the Philippine Independent Catholic Church, whose bishops were directly involved in the beginning of ARJA.

As a Continuing Church organization, the United Anglican Church affirms the 39 Articles of Religion that present the traditional Anglican position and the Affirmation of St. Louis. The church limits the ordained ministry of bishops, priests, and deacons to men. Worship is conducted from the Book of Common Prayer of 1928, the 1662 Book of Common Prayer, and other approved liturgical texts, including the Anglican, American, and English Missals.

The church has two dioceses in the United States: the Diocese of the Transfiguration, based in New York and headed in 2008 by the Rt. Rev. Barry Eugene Yingling; and the Diocese of the West, based in Washington state and headed in 2008 by Rt. Rev. Robert D. Parlotz. The primary foreign mission is in the Caribbean by the Franciscan Brothers of Divine Providence, under the leadership of Jose Delgado, bishop of Puerto Rico and the Americas. It includes several houses in Puerto Rico and a companion order of sisters in Tanzania (Africa). The friars work in the poorest areas of Puerto Rico and the Caribbean. Education work is pursued through Laud Hall Seminary, formerly an institution of the Traditional Episcopal Church.

The Traditional Episcopal Church has moved toward union with the Anglican Church in America. Intercommunion has been approved, and steps toward possible merger have begun.

Membership: In 2008 the church reported seven parishes in the United States, two missions in Puerto Rico, and two parishes in Canada.

Educational Facilities:

Laud Hall Seminary, York, Pennsylvania.

Periodicals: *The Word* (newsletter). Available from Rt. Rev. Barry E. Yingling, 505 N George St., York, PA 17404-2702.

Sources:

United Anglican Church. www.unitedanglicanchurch.org/.

United Episcopal Church (1945) Anglican/Celtic

PO Box 1931, Tucson, AZ 85702

HISTORY. The United Episcopal Church (1945) Anglican/Celtic (UEC) was formed in 1945 in Plainfield, Illinois, by Bps. Julius Massey, Albert Sorensen, and Hinton Pride. They envisioned a restored church of Anglican and Celtic heritage. St. Paul's Catherdral was designed and built in Plainfield. During the process of its early growth, several previously founded churches affiliated with the UEC, including the Norwegian Seaman's Mission in Chicago, Illinois. In the mid-1950s, Bp. James E. Burns, who had previously founded several Anglican churches, brought his jurisdiction into the United Episcopal Church. Burns had originally been consecrated by William H. Schneider, who, like Massey, had been consecrated by Denver Scott Swain of the American Episcopal Church (1940s). Burns also persuaded the Rev. Orlando J. Woodward (d. 1990), pastor of the independent Bethany Presbyterian Church in Fort Orlethorpe, Georgia, to bring his congregation into the jurisdiction. Woodward had been ordained by Abp. W. H. Francis Brothers of the Old Catholic Church in America, but had introduced the congregation he served to the Episcopal prayer book and led it to adopt the Thirty-nine Articles of Religion of the Protestant Episcopal Church in the U.S.A. as its standard of doctrine.

After a period of growth between 1961 and 1965, during which time Woodward served as presiding bishop, the church entered a period of decline. Woodward suffered a near-fatal illness, several of the priests retired, and bishops Massey and Sorensen died. With the church nearly moribund, Bishop Burns consecrated Richard C. Acker, who founded the United Episcopal Church of America. However, in the 1980s, Woodward was able to resume his duties as presiding bishop and began reviving the UEC. New parishes were created and in 1988, with the assistance of Karl Pruter (1920–2007), head of the Christ Catholic Church, Woodward consecrated Ted D. Kelly as coadjutor bishop with might of succession and bishop of the Southwest. In 1990 Archbishop Woodward died and was succeeded by Bishop Kelly. As of 2008, Rev. Michael R. Porter is the church's chancellor.

BELIEFS. The UEC accepts the Thirty-nine Articles of Religion common to Anglicanism and uses the 1928 edition of the *Book of Common Prayer*. It considers the traditional teachings of the Anglican faith to be binding and not subject to alteration or debate. It also accepts as valid those practices and the liturgical worship as introduced into the ancient British Isles by the Celtic and Gallic monks and missionaries, which, when integrated into the traditions of St. Augustine of Canterbury (d. 604 C.E.), produced the Anglican tradition. The church recognizes two greater sacraments, baptism and the Holy Eucharist, and five lesser ones: confirmation, confession, holy orders, marriage, and unction. It retains the spectrum of high (more liturgical), low (less formal), and broad church emphases in the expression of worship.

ORGANIZATION. The church follows an episcopal polity. The governance is invested in their national convention, consisting of all the bishops (the College of Bishops) and all of the priests and lay delegates from each parish (the House of Delegates). The presiding bishop presides at the convention meetings. In 1987 Bishop Woodward and Bishop Kelly founded the Missionary Order of St. Jude, dedicated to the assistance of the poor and needy. The church is opposed to the admission of women into the priesthood.

Membership: Not reported.

Educational Facilities:

The School of Theology, Tucson, Arizona; The School of Clinical Counseling, Nashville, Tennessee.

Periodicals: *The Celt*.

United Episcopal Church of North America
614 Pebblestone Ct., Statesville, NC 28677

In 1980 C. Dale David Doren, senior bishop of the Anglican Catholic Church and head of its mid-Atlantic diocese, resigned. He contended that the Anglican Catholic Church was becoming exclusively "high-church" or "Anglo-Catholic" in its stance. With only two congregations, he formed the United Episcopal Church of the U.S.A. (known since 1985 as the United Episcopal Church of North America). This church adheres to the traditional beliefs and practices of the Protestant Episcopal Church as exemplified in the 1928 *Book of Common Prayer* and the Thirty-Nine Articles of Religion.

The United Episcopal Church tends to the "low-church" end of the Anglican spectrum. Each parish is independent and holds title to properties and control over temporal affairs. The jurisdiction adopted the 1958 Protestant Episcopal Church Constitution and Canons (with specific changes in relation to church properties) as its own. The presiding bishop was given the title of archbishop, but the church vested little power in the office. In 1984, Archbishop Doren consecrated Albion W. Knight as a missionary bishop to assist him in leadership of the jurisdiction's affairs. In the 1980s, Doren retired and was succeeded by Knight. The Most Rev. Steven C. Reber is the current archbishop.

Membership: Not reported.

Periodicals: *Glad Tidings*. Available from 7162 Soft Wind Ln., Mechanicsville, VA 23111-5623.

Sources:

United Episcopal Church of North America. united-episcopal.org/.

Eastern Liturgical Family

4

THE EASTERN ORTHODOX TRADITION.

The Eastern Orthodox Church continues the church established in the apostolic era, the first generation of Christianity, in the eastern Mediterranean Basin. The Eastern Church and the Western Roman Church formally coexisted as two branches of the same church for centuries. However, cultural differences, politics, and doctrinal disagreements finally led to official division and mutual excommunication in 1054. By that time, the Eastern Church dominated the eastern Mediterranean Basin, spreading through Greece, Egypt, Asia Minor, some of the Arab countries, and the Balkans. It would later spread northward through Eastern Europe and become the dominant faith in Romania, the Ukraine, and Russia. Then, in the early Middle Ages, its dominance would be weakened by the loss of the "heretical" churches (the non-Chalcedonian Orthodox churches) and most thoroughly by the Muslim conquests.

In each area it came to dominate, the Eastern Church developed an episcopal structure of national autonomous sees. Certain older sees were more prominent and had been designated patriarchates. They included Alexandria, Antioch, Jerusalem, and Constantinople. In more recent years, patriarchates have been designated in Bulgaria, Serbia, Russia, and Romania. Autocephalous churches, headed by a bishop but without a patriarchate, exist in the Ukraine, Cypress, Albania, Greece, Poland, and Georgia. Autonomous churches, headed by a bishop, self-governing on internal matters but dependent on a patriarchate for the appointment of a primate (head bishop) and relations with other churches, exist in Finland, Estonia, Czechoslovakia, Latvia, and Lithuania, and at the monastic community at Mt. Sinai.

The Eastern Church finds its spiritual unity in the office of the ecumenical patriarchate headquartered at Istanbul (formerly known as Constantinople and the lead city of the eastern Byzantine Empire), though his position of primacy is one of honor, not power. All of the patriarchs are of equal authority and none has the right to interfere with the work in another's territory. The patriarchates and leaders of various national churches have expanded their authority into the West as parishioners have moved into Europe and the Americas. Jurisdiction for the Greek-speaking Orthodox in the West has been placed under the authority of the ecumenical patriarchates, though the Church of Greece now has a small number of parishes in North America. The various

Orthodox churches are "in communion" with each other, and in the United States the bishops of the churches who directly relate to the ecumenical patriarch work together as the Standing Conference of Canonical Orthodox Bishops in the Americas. Most Orthodox Christians in America are members of these churches.

THE SPREAD OF ORTHODOXY.

During the first century C.E., the Christian movement established centers around the Mediterranean Basin. As the movement grew, Jerusalem, Alexandria, Antioch, and Constantinople became the leading centers from which the movement emanated through the eastern half of the Roman Empire. Jerusalem was the ancient biblical center. Antioch was the place mentioned in the book of Acts where the followers of Jesus were first called Christians. Alexandria, the Egyptian city, was the center of Orthodoxy in the face of the refusal of the majority of Egyptian Christians to accept the promulgations of the Council of Chalcedon in 451. Constantinople was, of course, the capital of the empire established by Constantine (r. 306–337). In 451 it was named second only to Rome in importance.

During the years of the Byzantine Empire, the Christian movement had already begun the thrust into the east that would see the establishment of Christian movements as far east as India and strong Christian nations in such places as Armenia. Most of the work to the east would, like Egypt, be lost during the conciliar era, as different national churches refused to accept the latest promulgation of one council or another. Also, contact with these churches would be additionally hindered by the rise of Islam, which decimated their ranks in many areas.

The loss of the Eastern churches would be compensated by the movement of Christianity northward into the Balkans, Romania, and Russia. These lands, which today are thought of as traditionally Orthodox, only began to be reached by missionaries in the ninth century. Christianity was introduced into Bulgaria around 854 when Boris I (r. 852–889), the ruler, accepted the new faith and imposed it upon the people. A short time later, Christians from Moravia came into the country and introduced the Old Slavonic liturgy, which had been developed by the missionaries Cyril (c. 827–869) and Methodius (c. 826–885). The church adhered to Constantinople when the Christian movement split in 1054. A bishop resided in Okhrida (or Akrida) in western Bulgaria

---

Eastern Liturgical Family Chronology

325–787	Concilior Era. The decisions of the Seven Ecumenical Councils define Christian Orthodoxy. By the fourth council, the Eastern Orthodox churches are separated from the dissenting Arian, Monophysite, and Nestorian churches.
1054	Roman Catholic and Eastern Orthodox churches go their separate ways following mutual excommunication by the Pope and the Archbishop of Constantinople.
1743	First resident of the Aleutian Islands is baptized as a Christian.
1768	Greek Orthodox lay people settle in New Smyrna, Florida.
1794	Saint Herman leads mission to Paul's Harbor, Alaska.
1815	First Orthodox parish church built in Sitka, Alaska.
1848	Saint Innocent of Alaska is consecrated as North America's first Orthodox bishop.
1864	Greek Orthodox parishes are founded in New Orleans and St. Augustine.
1872	The Russian Orthodox Church's American diocese moves to San Francisco.
1904	Raphael Hawaweeny, the first bishop consecrated in North America, is appointed to head the Syrian Mission of the Russian Orthodox Church.
1916	Russian Bp. Alexander become first Orthodox bishop to reside in Canada.
1918	The Greek Orthodox Archdiocese in North and South America organized under the authority of the Ecumenical Patriarchate.
1921	Former African American Episcopal priest George Alexander McGuire is consecrated as an independent bishop and founds the African Orthodox Church.
	Metropolitan Platon of Odessa is appointed Metropolitan of North America for the Russian Orthodox Church Outside of Russia.
1924	North American Russian Church declares its autonomy from Moscow at its second Sobor (synod) in Detroit, Michigan.
1927	Metropolitan Platon appoints Bp. Aftimios Ofiesh to head an American Orthodox Church for English-speaking Orthodox believers. The rejection of this new jurisdiction by the Episcopal Church and other Orthodox jurisdictions leads to the development of multiple independent orthodox jurisdictions.
1930	Bp. Fan Noli organizes Albanian Orthodox parishes into the Albanian Orthodox Archdiocese in America.
1937	The first diocese of Orthodox Bulgarians is formed by Bp. Andrei Velichky.
1945	Soviet hegemony is extended over Bulgaria and Romania and atheist Communist governments arise in Albania and Serbia (as part of Yugoslavia). Reacting to the new political situation, new anti-Communist branches of the Bulgarian, Romanian, Serbian, and Albanian Orthodox churches emerge.
1946	Unity of Russian Orthodox in America is broken when the leadership of the Russian Orthodox church outside of Russia disagree with the Russian Orthodox Greek Catholic Church of America's desire to reestablish ties with the Patriarch of Moscow.
1950	Various Orthodox jurisdictions become charter members of the National Council of Churches of Christ in the U.S.A.
1959	American Greek archbishop Iakovos meets with Pope John XXIII, the first such meeting in 350 years.
1960	Abp. Iakovas leads in founding of the Standing Conference of Canonical Orthodox Bishops in the Americas.
1961	Abp. Iakovos elected one of the presidents of the World Council of Churches.
1965	Pope Paul VI and Patriarch Athenagoras I of Constantinople mutually nullify the excommunications of 1054.
1991	Soviet Union is dissolved and replaced with Commonwealth of Independent States. The end of Soviet power (and control over the Russian Orthodox church) makes possible the realignment of relationship between Orthodox churches in Central Europe and their related jurisdictions in North America.
1992	Two jurisdiction of Serbian Orthodox in America merge.
2003	Russian Orthodox Church severs relations with the Episcopal Church over its consecration of the openly gay bishop.
2005	Antiochian Orthodox Christian Archdiocese of North America withdraws from National Council of Churches over its relatively liberal stance on issues of sexuality. As part of an effort to strengthen ties to its Orthodox members, the National Council of Churches General Assembly elects Armenian Orthodox bishop Vicken Aykazian as its president-elect.

---

and in Tirnova in the east. The Bulgarian bishops existed autonomously until the Turkish conquest of the land in 1393, when Tirnova was absorbed into Okhrida.

Christianity was introduced among the Serbian people as early as the seventh century, but effective evangelization efforts did not occur until the end of the ninth century. It was not until the last half of the twelfth century that the Serbians were united into a single state, and finally in 1219 a bishopric was established. A synod in 1346 declared the church autonomous. While leaning toward Rome for many years, the Serbian church gradually shifted allegiance to the East.

Romanians, a Latin people living in a land surrounded largely by Slavic peoples, received Latin/Western Christianity as early as the third century. In the ninth century, the Bulgarians conquered the area and imposed their Eastern Slavonic ways on the Christian community. Their Orthodoxy became an issue in their continuing conflict with their Hungarian neighbors (Roman Catholics) to the north, and

Orthodoxy became integral to the emerging national identity. The Romanian church made some gain after the land was overrun by the Turks and was able to attain a degree of independence from the Bulgarian authorities.

Crucial for the future of the church in the southern Balkans was the fall of Constantinople in 1453. The conquest of the capital of the old Eastern Roman Empire ended any hope of its comeback. The conquest also brought the "headquarters" of Eastern Christianity under the thumb of a Muslim government. In the eighteenth century, the Turkish Empire would attempt to organize all the Christians in its empire under the authority of the patriarch in Constantinople, an action that would be greatly resented by many.

A notable gain for Orthodoxy occurred toward the end of the tenth century when Prince Vladimir I of Kiev (Ukraine) (c. 956–1015) invited missionaries from Constantinople into his land. In 988 he "gave" Christianity to his people, and it is from that year that later generations would date the conversion of the land to Christianity. Entirely dependent upon Constantinople, the church in Russia adhered to Eastern Orthodoxy during the schism of 1054. Several centuries later, after Kiev fell to the Mongol invasion, the center of Russian Orthodoxy moved to Moscow, and the Moscow patriarchate ruled over the lands controlled by the Russian government. Included in these lands were the Ukrainians and the Byelorussians, both people with a separate language and culture who have periodically attempted to exist as an autonomous church body.

The Turkish invasion of the lands of the southern Balkans had a telling effect upon the churches under its control. In the eighteenth century, the Turks imposed the idea that all Christians were under Constantinople. In 1767 the government suppressed the independent bishoprics, and the Greek church, headquartered at Constantinople, followed with a period of hellenization. The most important effect was the imposition of the Greek language in the worship of all monasteries and the larger churches. Old Slavonic, which had existed as primarily a liturgical language, was slowly forgotten. The Turkish government reversed its policy in 1856 and declared the freedom and equality of the Christians residing in the empire. That new policy, and the accompanying gradual disintegration of the Ottoman Empire through the nineteenth century, allowed autonomous national churches to reemerge.

Romania emerged as an independent nation by several steps in the nineteenth century. Under the reign of Alexandru Ioan Cuza (1820–1873), which began in 1864, a fully independent country allowed the emergence of a Romanian church independent of Constantinople. Constantinople formally recognized the new situation in 1885.

The Serbian church also lost its autonomy in 1767 and went through a period of hellenization. Like Romania, Serbia gained its independence in stages through the nineteenth century. It was declared an autonomous state in 1879, and the independent status of the church immediately followed. The Serbian church gained from the establishment of Yugoslavia following World War I (1914–1918), suffered from the rise of a secular Marxist government after World War II (1937–1945), and has yet to rebound from the war that followed the breakup of the country in the early 1990s.

The Bulgarian church began to lobby for independence from Constantinople as part of an overall effort by Bulgarians to free themselves from Turkish control. This finally occurred in 1878. Ecclesiastical independence, however, was gained in 1870. The patriarch in Constantinople excommunicated the Bulgarian bishops two years later and considered the Bulgarian church schismatic until 1945, when it was finally recognized as an autonomous body.

The Orthodox churches of the southern Balkans have experienced great ups and downs through the twentieth century as various boundaries changed, often radically, and successive governments adopted different policies toward Christianity. Some formerly independent jurisdictions have disappeared altogether. Through the twentieth century, the Orthodox churches saw the disappearance of the Ottoman Empire; the emergence of communism and its dominance for many decades in Russia, Romania, Serbia, and Bulgaria; and the overthrow of communist governments. After World War II, those Eastern Orthodox churches in countries under communist control experienced schisms among members outside of the country. Many members argued that the leadership had departed from the faith by becoming puppets of the communist governments.

Throughout this period, Greece has a unique and interesting history. It stood on the border between East and West with a background of orientation toward Rome, but was later assigned to the territory of the Eastern Roman Empire. It eventually leaned toward the Eastern Church, and its ecclesiastical life came directly under Constantinople. Greece was conquered by the Turks in the fifteenth century, but as it was already part of the land under the Patriarchate in Constantinople, little change in church structure occurred. Then, in the nineteenth century, a successful civil war freed much of the land from Turkish control. In 1831 the Greek church declared itself free of the control of the patriarchate, who still resided in territory controlled by the hated Turks. The territory of the Church of Greece grew in stages, but has suffered periodically due to government instability.

One particularly grievous event was the adoption of the Western calendar early in the twentieth century. The abandonment of the old Julian calendar became a symbol of unwanted change, and the Old Calendar conservatives have been a small but vocal group that has formed independent episcopal jurisdictions and has continually caused problems for the Orthodox Church ever since.

Since World War II, the Eastern churches have also become involved in the worldwide ecumenical movement and have developed friendly relationships with Western Protestant churches through structures such as the World Council of Churches. This new openness to non-Orthodox Christians brought many charges that the church was changing and adopting un-Orthodox practices. Ecumenical structures became important in supplying Orthodox churches formerly in the Soviet Union or in those countries under its hegemony. The World Council of Churches was a force in reintroducing the world to the Russian Orthodox Church in the post-Soviet era, and other churches from Bulgaria, Romania, Moldavia, and Georgia also affiliated. In the decades since their initial involvement, the Orthodox churches have been among the most vocal critics of what they have seen as questionable interference into tense political situations and, more recently, the advocacy of rights for homosexuals.

The World Council of Churches moved in 1998 to address the concerns articulated by its Orthodox members by setting up a special commission to deal with a wide range of issue, such as the council's process for making decisions and the scope of its public statements. This action was a response, in part, to the withdrawal of the Orthodox Church of Georgia. Subsequently, in 2005, the Orthodox Church of

The Seven Ecumenical Councils

Council	Place and Date	Decision
First Ecumenical Council	Nicea, Asia Minor, 325 A.D.	Formulated the First Part of the Creed. Defining the divinity of the Son of God.
Second Ecumenical Council	Constantinople 381 A.D.	Formulated the Second Part of the Creed, defining the divinity of the Holy Spirit.
Third Ecumenical Council	Ephesus, Asia Minor 431 A.D.	Defined Christ as the Incarnate Word of God and Mary as Theotokos.
Fourth Ecumenical Council	Chalcedon, Asia Minor 451 A.D.	Defined Christ as Perfect God and Perfect Man in One Person.
Fifth Ecumenical Council	Constantinople II 553 A.D.	Reconfirmed the Doctrines of the Trinity and Christ.
Sixth Ecumenical Council	Constantinople III 680 A.D.	Affirmed the True Humanity of Jesus by insisting upon the reality of His Human will and action.
Qinisext Council (Trullo)	Constantinople 692 A.D.	Completed the 5th and 6th Ecumenical Councils.
Seventh Ecumenical Council	Nicea, Asia Minor 787 A.D.	Affirmed the propriety of icons as genuine expressions of the Christian Faith.

Adapted from www.atl.americanchurch.org

America publicly called its membership in both the World Council of Churches and the National Council of Churches of Christ in the U.S.A. into question. Although as of 2008, the Orthodox Church of America remains a member, the Antiochian Christian Orthodox Archdiocese of North America did withdraw. In response, like its international partner, the National Council of Churches has instituted several structures to become more sensitive to the Orthodox perspective on ecumenical dialogue.

THE DOCTRINAL POSITION OF EASTERN ORTHODOXY.
To most Americans, familiar with only the Roman and Anglican traditions, the Eastern Orthodox tradition presents several distinctive features. The celibate priesthood of the Roman Catholic Church is not demanded. In the East, priests may marry (though they must do so before ordination). Monks do not marry. Bishops are drawn from the ranks of the monks. Priests who are not monks are not eligible for the episcopacy. The Eastern Church does not recognize the authority of the bishop of Rome over the various patriarchs of the Eastern Church.

The Eastern churches recognize only the seven ecumenical councils held between 325 and 787 because no further councils occurred at which the bishops of Rome and the Eastern patriarchs worked together. In their acceptance of these councils, the Eastern Church is doctrinally at one with Roman Catholicism and the churches of the Western tradition. This doctrinal consensus has been illustrated since the later twentieth century by the meetings of the ecumenical patriarch and the pope, and the Eastern churches' membership along with Protestant and free churches in the World Council of Churches and other regional and national ecumenical bodies.

After the formal split between the Roman Catholic Church and the Eastern churches, the Roman Church continued to hold councils at which new doctrinal positions were promulgated. Several of these remain unacceptable doctrines to the Eastern Church, which, for example, rejects the *filioque* doctrine as popularized in the Western Church beginning in the fifth century. Filioque is the Latin word for "and the Son," added to the Western version of the creed to assert the equality of the Father and the Son by suggesting that the Holy Spirit proceeds from both the Father and the Son. Some theologians of the Eastern Church insisted that the Holy Spirit proceeds from the Father through the Son. The Eastern Church rejected the filioque doctrine partly on biblical grounds, in that John 15:26 makes no mention of the Son and instead speaks of "the Spirit of truth who proceeds from the Father."

The Greek Liturgy of St. Chrysostom is used throughout the Eastern Church. The various national bodies have translated it into their native tongues, and in America, English translations are being increasingly used.

Those areas where Orthodoxy exists only as a small minority religion, geographically removed from the ancient centers, are designated Orthodoxy in diaspora. The single largest diaspora community is the more than three million Orthodox Christians in the United States.

ORTHODOXY IN NORTH AMERICA.
Orthodoxy entered the United States in the eighteenth century following the discovery of Alaska by Russians in 1741. In 1743 an Aleutian by the name of Andreu Islands was baptized. The Russian Orthodox Church was firmly established in 1794 when seven monks came to Paul's Harbor and consecrated the first church. By 1841 a seminary was in operation in the Aleutian Islands. The first diocese, created after Alaska was purchased by the United States, was moved to San Francisco in 1872.

Sporadic movement of Orthodox Christians into North America began in the first part of the nineteenth century, but did not become significant until the 1890s. Prior to 1891, the only parishes were those in Alaska and a single church in San Francisco. At this time, the Russian Orthodox Church included members from all ethnic backgrounds and had all of North America under its hegemony. Then, the movement of people from the Middle East and from eastern and southern Europe increased significantly because of growing tension in Russia, Turkish and Russian expansion, and the general suffering occasioned by World War I. This wave of immigration was all but stopped by the immigration quota limitations imposed in 1924. Immigrants settled in the northern and eastern urban centers but found their way to the prairies of western Canada and the farmlands of California. As significant numbers of each national group arrived, they began efforts to form their own unique parishes and then to organize separate dioceses. By the early twentieth century, the Russian church began to lose its ethnic parishes, and the various ethnic branches of the Orthodox Church formed.

As these new branches were formed one by one, most were severely tested by two outside forces. First, the inevitable process of Americanization—the demands of conformity, especially in language—divided the generations, and on occasion led to schism. Of more concern, however, was the Russian Revolution and the spread of atheist regimes in predominantly Orthodox countries. Because Orthodox churches have tended to align with the state, the loss of state support was devastating. The actual hostility of a government that appeared ready to either destroy or subvert the church to its own purposes called into question the relationship of American and Canadian churches to the patriarchal headquarters caught in the revolutionary situations. Some Americans demanded loyalty to the patriarchs and accommodation to the new regimes, while others with equal strength demanded autonomy from the homeland. Beginning in the 1920s with the Russians and accelerating after World War II, schism rent almost every branch of Eastern Orthodoxy in North America.

The structure of American Orthodoxy was dramatically changed in 1970 with the creation of the Orthodox Church in America by the merger of several of the Russian churches. Russian Orthodoxy, by reason of its early arrival date, has always had primacy in America. Many of the currently existing independent Orthodox bodies were formed under its care. The growth of the Greek Orthodox Church in America led to challenges to Russian primacy, challenges based on the claims of the ecumenical patriarch in Istanbul as the first among equals in world Orthodoxy. The argument was somewhat academic, since each American church was directly related to a different overseas see. The Orthodox Church in America, unattached to a foreign see, was authorized by Patriarch Alexis (1877–1970) in Moscow, whose right to grant such status has been questioned by the Greek Orthodox Church.

The new body, the Orthodox Church in America, hoped to become the point of unity for Orthodox bodies of all ethnic groups, the goal being the union of all into a single American Orthodox body. This ideal has been championed by several bishops, most notably Archbishop Philip Saliba (b. 1931) of the Antiochean Church. The Orthodox Church in America is the only Orthodox church that has all of the structures necessary to continue without outside help—seminaries, monasteries, and charitable institutions. However, in spite of vocal support from several influential individuals, no sign of a move toward unity has become manifest. American Orthodoxy remains divided into a spectrum of churches serving individual ethnic constituencies.

THE EMERGENCE OF INDEPENDENT ORTHODOXY IN THE TWENTIETH CENTURY.

During the nineteenth century, Orthodox believers from many of the European national churches migrated to America. A few, such as the Greeks, remained autonomous and eventually formed their own ethnic church. Others, such

as the Syrians, began as an ethnic group under the care of the Russian church, which, because it was the first Orthodox church to establish work, had a special hegemony within the United States. Once in the United States with its multiethnic atmosphere, geographically removed from its homeland, the Orthodox Church became subject to a variety of forces that split its community into a number of ecclesiastical factions. The first major splinter began as a movement to unite American Orthodoxy.

Aftimios Ofiesh (1890–1971) came to America in 1905 to work among Syrians, then a part of the Russian Orthodox Church. In 1917 he was consecrated bishop for the Syrian work, succeeding Bishop Raphael Hawaweeny (1860–1915). On February 2, 1927, the Russian bishops gave him the duty of caring for the American-born Orthodox, especially the English-speaking parishes, not otherwise being given proper attention. By their action they created a new jurisdiction, the American Orthodox Church, as an autonomous body with a filial relationship to the Russian church.

The project met immediate opposition. The non-Russian bishops were not supportive of a united American Orthodoxy as proposed and the ecumenical patriarch, the nominal head of all Orthodox churches, denounced the project as schismatic. The Greeks were angered by Ofiesh's publication of a magazine, *Orthodox Catholic Reporter*. Especially offended were the Episcopalians, who considered themselves the American form of Orthodoxy and who were providing the Russians with large amounts of financial support. They applied pressure on Metropolitan Platon (Rozhdestvensky) (r. 1907–1914, 1921–1934) to abandon Ofiesh. Even though soon abandoned by the Russians, Ofiesh continued in his project and, beginning with Emmanuel (Rizkallah Abo-Hatab) (1890–1933) in 1927 and Sophronius Bishara (1888–1940) the following year, he consecrated four bishops to head his independent work.

The problem with Ofiesh was not the only trouble to disturb the Russian church during the 1920s. As a result of the Russian Revolution and the coming to power of an antireligious regime, the close allegiance of the church to the Russian government was called into question, especially after the imprisonment of the patriarch of Moscow in 1922. Soviet supporters within the Russian church in 1924 organized a sobor (convention) of what came to be called the Living Church faction. They voiced support of the Soviet government and elected the only American at the sobor, John Kedrowsky, bishop of America. He came to America with his sons, Nicholas (later his successor as bishop of America) and John, and through court action took control of St. Nicholas Cathedral in New York City. However, he was rejected by a synod of the American Russian Church in 1924 that declared its autonomy in administrative matters from the church in Russia.

While the Russians were splintering into several factions, the Greeks, never under Russian control, were having their own problems. In 1908 the Greek parishes in America were transferred from the direct authority of the ecumenical patriarch to the holy synod of the church in Greece. That arrangement did not provide the necessary leadership for the burgeoning American church, so in 1918 the ecumenical patriarch began the process of establishing the American church as an archdiocese, a task finally accomplished in 1922. However, that arrangement also did not resolve the leadership question, and in 1930 the ecumenical patriarch reasserted his hegemony in America by appointing a representative to go to the United States and take over leadership of the archdiocese.

Meanwhile, as organizational trouble plagued the church, it was further divided by internal problems in Greece. A faction of the American membership opposed the transfer of the allegiance of the American church from the church in Greece to the ecumenical patriarch. In the 1930s, they removed themselves from the archdiocese and sought consecration of a new bishop by the church in Greece. Thus, in 1934, Christopher Contogeorge (1894–1950), with the blessing of the church in Greece, was consecrated the archbishop of Philadelphia by Albanian bishop Fan Stylin Noli, assisted by Bishop Sophronius Bishara. Archbishop Christopher was the consecrator of Bishop John Kedrowsky's son and successor, Nicholas Kedrowsky.

By the mid-1930s, Archbishop Christopher and bishops Sophronius, Nicholas (Kedrowsky), and Fan constituted a group of independent Orthodox bishops both organizationally and emotionally separated from the larger body of Orthodox bishops and faithful. These four participated in a number of consecrations of new bishops, both in their several jurisdictions and in other independent Orthodox churches. From their lineage came bishops Joseph Klimowicz (1880–1961), Walter A. Propheta (1912–1972), and Peter A. Zhurawetsky (1901–1994), who in turn consecrated most of the men who head the next generation of independent Orthodox churches.

There is one strain of independent Orthodoxy that has a history independent of the bishops discussed above, that which derives from Archbishop Joseph Renè Vilatte (1854–1929) of the American Catholic Church (discussed in chapter 2 as one of the founders of Old Catholicism in America). Vilatte's episcopal orders came from a small Orthodox body in India, and during the later years of his life he consecrated individuals who adopted an Orthodox stance, most notably George A. McGuire (1866–1934), founder of the African Orthodox Church. Also, at least one person from the Vilatte lineage participated in the consecration of Propheta.

Finally, it should be noted that just as both Orthodox and Catholic jurisdictions derived from the work of Vilatte, so too have they both derived from the independent Orthodox bishops. Most notably, the Christ Catholic Church derived as an Old Catholic body from the previous jurisdiction of Peter Zhurawetsky.

In the 1980s, Orthodox bishops who carried lineages from several lines of apostolic succession (including Catholic and Anglican lines) emerged, and in the 1990s it became common for bishops leading Orthodox jurisdictions to note the various lines of apostolic succession they offer. The bishops holding these several lineages passed them to any persons they consecrated.

THE NON-CHALCEDONIAN ORTHODOX CHURCHES.
Separating during the years of the great ecumenical councils, the Christian churches of Egypt, Armenia, and the Middle East, for a variety of reasons, refused to ratify one or more of the creeds, primarily the Chalcedonian Creed of 451, which most of the Eastern Orthodox world accepted as a standard of Orthodox Christian faith. Both the Roman Catholic Church and the Eastern Orthodox churches have branded these churches as heretical in faith, though the Armenian church has vigorously protested such labeling as a misunderstanding of its position both theologically and relationally to the Council of Chalcedon.

THE NESTORIANS. The monk Nestorius (d. c. 451), who became patriarch of Constantinople in 428, believed that Christ was not the Son of God, but that God was living in Christ. The two natures of Christ—divine and human—were separable, said Nestorius. Further, he said Mary bore the human Christ, not God. Thus she was not *Theotokos*, the God-bearer. And it was not God who suffered and died. Nestorius preached his doctrines throughout the Eastern Church. In 431 the Third Council of the early church met at Ephesus to treat the teachings of Nestorius. The council ruled that Mary was Theotokos, and that the human and divine natures are inseparably bound together in the one person of Christ. The council condemned Nestorius, declared his teachings heretical, and deposed him as patriarch of Constantinople. These actions began a four-year battle of ecclesiastical and imperial politics. The result was Nestorius's banishment and the burning of his books.

The Nestorians continued to spread Nestorius's beliefs. They conducted missionary work in Persia, India, and China and won followers in Arabia and Egypt. Under the Mohammedans they were essentially free from persecution until the modern era. They survive to this day as the Church of the East. Their largest losses have been to proselytizing efforts by Roman Catholics, Jacobites (to whom they lost much of the church in India), and more recently, Protestants.

The Church of the East belongs to the non-Chalcedonian Orthodox tradition in the sense that it opposes the statement of the Council at Chalcedon that Christ was "begotten . . . of Mary the Virgin, the God bearer."

When the Nestorians were rediscovered in the 1830s by Protestant missionaries, their preservation of an old Aramaic dialect also became news. They have since made this dialect the language of their scriptural translation. The seven sacraments they observe are baptism, ordination, the Holy Eucharist, anointing, remission of sins, holy leaven, and the sign of the cross. The holy leaven refers to the belief that a portion of the bread used at the Last Supper was brought to the East by the apostle Thaddeus, and every Eucharist in the Church of the East is made from bread continuous with that meal. The sign of the cross is considered a sacrament, and a specific formula is prescribed for its rubric.

As with all of the Eastern churches, relation with a particular apostle is assumed. The Church of the East claims a special relationship with the apostle Thaddeus, who visited the kingdom of Oshroene soon after Pentecost, and with Mari (one of the 70 disciples). Supposedly there was correspondence between Abgar, the ruler of Oshroene, and Christ, in which the former invited Jesus to settle at Edessa, the capital city.

The liturgy of the Church of the East is that of the "Holy Apostles Addai and Mari" (saints Thaddeus and Mari), who brought it from Jerusalem. The leadership of the church is found in the patriarchate, which has since 1350 been hereditary in the family of Mar Shimun. Since the patriarch is celibate, the office passes from uncle to nephew. Under the patriarch are the metropolitans and bishops. The priests are allowed to marry at any time, even after their ordination.

THE MONOPHYSITES. The Monophysite churches, like the Eastern Orthodox and Roman Catholic, emphasize liturgy in their church life; they believe strongly in an apostolic succession, and they derive their doctrinal position from the ancient creeds. Their distinctiveness comes from the content of their creed, which differs more from both Constantinople and Rome than the latter two differ from each other. The Monophysite churches are united on doctrine, but have lines of succession and liturgy with a national flavor.

The distinct Monophysite doctrines derive from the fifth-century discussions on the nature of Christ. It was the Monophysite position that Christ was one person of one (mono) nature (physis), the divine nature absorbing the human nature. In the context of the debate, Monophysitism was opposed to Nestorianism, which said that Christ had two natures but that they were separable.

Monophysitism was condemned by the Fourth Council of the early church, held at Chalcedon in 451. The council formulated what came to be called the Chalcedonian Creed, which says that Christ is "of one substance with the Father as regards his Godhead, and at the same time of one substance with us as regards his manhood." Rejecting this creed, most of the Armenian, northern Egyptian, and Syrian churches broke away from the main body of the Christian church. In general, the Monophysite churches accept only the first three councils of the early Christian church (those at Nicea, Constantinople, and Ephesus) as valid and binding.

Theologians continue to debate Monophysite Christology. Some writers contend that the Monophysite churches are Eutychean, that is, that they follow the teaching of Archimandrite Eutyches, a monk of Constantinople, who asserted the unity of nature in Christ in such a way that the human nature was completely fused and absorbed in the divine. Others, however, assert that the Monophysite churches (at least some of them) are not Eutychean, but Orthodox with an "undeveloped terminology." The Armenian, Syrian, and Coptic churches represent the *Monophysite* tradition, but they

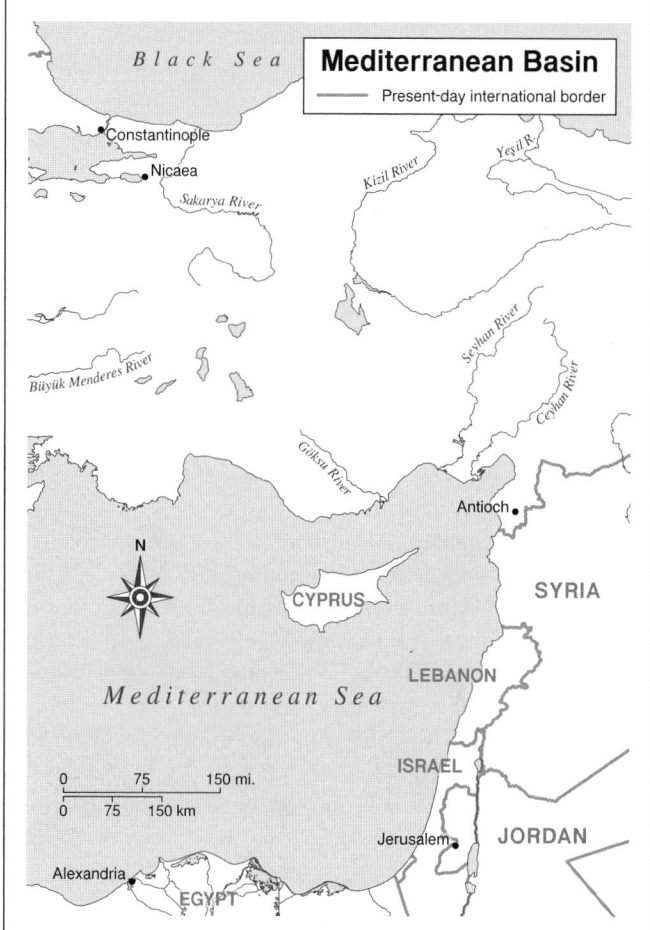

XNR Productions

deny the label Monophysite and deny that they teach any submergence of Christ's human nature.

THE ARMENIAN CHURCHES. According to tradition, Christianity was brought to Armenia by Thaddeus and Bartholomew, two of the original 12 apostles. By 260, a bishopric had been established in Armenia and was referred to in Eusebius's *Ecclesiastical History*. In 301 Tiridates II, the king of Armenia (r. c. 197–238), became the first Christian monarch. St. Gregory the Illuminator (c. 257–c. 331), who converted Tiridates, worked with the king's blessing to organize the Armenian church. Through the church, a written language was developed and a literate Armenian culture emerged. As is common with Monophysite churches, the Armenian church accepted only the first three ecumenical councils (those at Nicea, Constantinople, and Ephesus), and uses the Nicene Creed. Members of the Armenian church did not attend the Council of Chalcedon in 451 and rejected its decisions.

Ecclesiastical authority in the Armenian church was invested in the catholicos who originally resided at Vagharshapat in central Armenia. There, close to the palace, Gregory built Etchmiadzin, the great cathedral. Because of changing political fortunes, the catholicos was frequently forced to move, first to Dovin (484), then, among other places, to Argina (944), Tauplour (1054), Domnplov (1065), and finally Sis, in the kingdom of Lesser Armenia or Cilicia (1293). In 1441 an assembly was held at Etchmiadzin, and a catholicos was installed. The catholicos at Sis at that time took the title Catholicos of Cilicia. Both sees—Etchmiadzin and Cilicia—have functioned until the present.

There are several minor peculiarities in the Armenian church's sacraments, distinguishing it from other churches in the liturgical family. Holy communion is customarily celebrated only on Sunday and on special occasions and cannot be celebrated twice in the same day. Pure wine (without water) and unleavened bread are used, and the laity receive the Eucharist by intinction. The Eucharist is served to infants immediately after baptism by touching the lips with the elements.

Armenians in America. During the last 1,500 years, Armenia has suffered foreign domination and persecution by Muslims and Russians. The most terrible of these persecutions were the ones begun by the Turks in 1890 and carried on intermittently for the next 30 years. The effect was practically to destroy and scatter the Armenian nation. The arrival of Armenians in America dates from the immigration begun as a result of the massacres. The antireligious persecution by the Russians after World War I followed the Turkish onslaughts.

Armenians in America began to form churches in the late nineteenth century. The first was organized in 1891 in Worcester, Massachusetts. After 1921, American Armenians began to divide politically into two factions. One group remained intense nationalists, loyal to an independent Armenia and its symbols. The other group, often described as pro-Soviet, accommodated themselves to and then supported the inevitable Russian dominance of Armenia. The political division was deeply felt throughout the entire American Armenian community, including the church.

Though practically autonomous, the Armenian church in America recognized the authority of the catholicos of Etchmiadzin. Archbishop Levon Tourian (d. 1933) was designated by the see of Etchmiadzin as the supreme prelate of the Armenian Apostolic Church in America. Shortly after his arrival he managed to offend both political parties with contradictory statements concerning the nationalist flag. The continued polarization of the two factions led in 1933 to a split in the church itself.

The split occurred during the annual meeting of the national church council. Pro-Soviet lay delegates began to hold rump sessions, and from their meeting a second church was, in effect, begun. While there was little doubt of the legal continuance through the church council, Archbishop Tourian recognized the pro-Soviet group and declared some of the nationalist priests "unfrocked." A few months later, Bishop Tourian was assassinated during High Mass in New York City. So deep was the split in the Armenian community that, as one writer observed, "Armenians have come to hate one another with a passion that has exceeded at times even a hatred for the Turks" (Atamian, *The Armenian Community,* 1955, p. 358).

THE SYRIAN CHURCHES. Antioch, an ancient city of Syria, is the place where the followers of Jesus were first called Christians (Acts 11:26). In the early centuries, Antioch was the center of a large Christian movement rent by the Monophysite controversy concerning whether Christ had two natures, human and divine, or one (mono) nature (physis). Jacob Baradeus (r. 542–578), a resident of Antioch though bishop of Edessa, was both a favorite of Empress Theodora (c. 500–548) and a fervent Monophysite. After his consecration in 542, he toured all of the area from Turkey to Egypt, organizing churches. Those churches under his authority were to take his name in later years.

The evangelical zeal of the Jacobites was hindered and many of their gains destroyed by the conquests of Islam. In 1665 the Jacobites gained strength in India and Ceylon when the Nestorian Malabar Christians came under the Antiochean patriarch. This action more than doubled the size of the church, and today makes up more than 60 percent of its worldwide membership of 100,000.

The Jacobites have several distinctive practices. Baptism is by triune infusion (pouring). Auricular confession to the priest is not used. During the Eucharist, the priest waves his hand over the elements to symbolize the operation of the Holy Spirit. The action is also used in ordination ceremonies.

THE COPTIC CHURCHES OF EGYPT AND ETHIOPIA. At one time, the church in Egypt, the Coptic church, was among the largest in Christendom. But in 451 Dioscurus (d. 454), the patriarch of Alexandria, was deposed by the Council of Chalcedon, the fourth of the general councils in the early centuries of Christianity. There began an era of persecution of the Copts, first by their fellow Christians and then after 640 by Arab conquerors. Beginning with heavy taxes, the persecutions became bloody toward the end of the first millennium C.E. By the end of the Middle Ages, the Coptic church had shrunk from six million to 15,000 members. Growth since that time has been slow, but religious toleration in the nineteenth century helped, and by the middle of the twentieth century, there were three to five million members.

The Coptic church developed its own traditions. Its members are proud of Egypt as the childhood home of Jesus and the location of the ministry of St. Mark, who traditionally is credited with Egypt's initial evangelization. Several liturgies are used, but the most popular is the Liturgy of St. Basil, written by St. Basil the Great (b. 330). There is particular veneration of the Virgin, manifest in the 32 feasts in her honor during the ecclesiastical year. In 1971 she is said to have appeared over the Coptic Cathedral in Cairo.

The head of the Coptic church is the patriarch of Alexandria, with his see at Cairo. In 1971 this office was assumed by Pope Shenouda III (b. 1923). On May 6, 1973, Pope Shenouda greeted Pope Paul VI (1897–1978) with a kiss of peace on a visit to St. Peter's Basilica in Rome.

Ethiopia accepted Christianity in the fourth century and the first bishop, Frumentius, was consecrated by Athanasius, who was the patriarch of Alexandria. The Ethiopian church came under the jurisdiction of the Coptic church in Egypt, and followed its theological lead. Isolated by its mountains, Ethiopia withstood the advances of Islam but was cut off from the rest of Christendom. It reached its heights of glory in the thirteenth century under King Lalibela, who gave his name to a city of churches, 10 of which were hewn from solid rock. Modern history for this church began when Catholic missionaries sought to bring the Abyssinians under the Roman pontiff. They almost succeeded in the seventeenth century, when for a few years Roman Catholicism was accepted by the ruler.

The Ethiopian church differs from the Coptic church in that it has absorbed strong Jewish traits. It accepts the apocrypha as scripture, venerates the Sabbath along with Sunday, recognizes Old Testament figures as saints, and observes many Old Testament regulations on food and purification.

IN THE MODERN WORLD. Since the mid-twentieth century, the non-Chalcedonian churches have received some recognition from the larger Christian community. Most are now members of the World Council of Churches along with their Protestant and Orthodox sister churches. In the United States, many have joined the National Council of Churches of Christ in the U.S.A. Included in this latter body are the Diocese of the Armenian Church of America, the Coptic Orthodox Church in North America, the Malankara Orthodox Church, the Mar Thoma Church, and the Syrian Orthodox Church of Antioch.

SOURCES

Prominent archives of the Eastern Orthodox tradition in North America are located at the Department of Archives and History (Orthodox Church in America), Syosset, NY; Logos Mission Center (Greek), PO Box 4319, St. Augustine, FL 32085; and the headquarters of the Ukrainian Orthodox Church of the U.S.A., PO Box 495, South Bound Brook, NJ 08880. The Greek Orthodox Archdiocese of America created its Department of Archives in the 1980s. It is located at the church's New York headquarters. The Standing Conference of Canonical Orthodox Bishops in America has sponsored the Orthodox Theological Society in America, which provides for both theological and historical inquiry.

Eastern Orthodoxy

Adeney, Walter F. *The Greek and Eastern Churches*. New York: Scribner's, 1908. 634 pp.

Attwater, Donald. *The Dissident Eastern Churches*. Milwaukee: Bruce, 1937. 349 pp.

Benz, Ernst. *The Eastern Orthodox Church: Its Thought and Life*. Trans. Richard and Clara Winston. Garden City, NY: Doubleday, 1963. 230 pp.

Bogolepov, Alexander. *Toward an American Orthodox Church: The Establishment of an Autocephalous Orthodox Church*. Crestwood, NY: St. Vladimir's Seminary Press, 2002. 1991. 130 pp.

Bulgakov, Sergius. *The Orthodox Church*. London: Centenary Press, 1935. 224 pp.

FitzGerald, Thomas E. *The Orthodox Church*. Westport, CT: Greenwood Press, 1995.

Handbook of American Orthodoxy. Cincinnati, OH: Forward Movement, 1972. 191 pp.

Harakas, Stanley S. *Orthodox Church: Four Hundred and Fifty-Five Questions and Answers*. Indianapolis, IN: Light & Life Communications, 1988.

Lau, Robert Frederick, Wm. Chauncey Emhardt, and Thomas Burgess. *The Eastern Church in the Western World*. Milwaukee: Morehead, 1928. 149 pp.

Le Guillou, M. J. *The Spirit of Eastern Orthodoxy*. Trans. Donald Attwater. Glen Rock, NJ: Paulist Press, 1964. 121 pp.

Meyendorff, John. *Orthodox Church: Its Past and Its Role in the World Today*. Trans. John Chapin. Crestwood, NY: St Vladimir's Seminary Press, 1996.

Michalopulos, George C., and Herb Ham. *The American Orthodox Church: A History of Its Beginnings*. Salisbury, MA: Regina Orthodox Press, 2003. 234 pp.

Oleska, Michael. *Orthodox Alaska: A Theology of Mission*. Crestwood, NY: St. Vladimir's Seminary Press, 1992. 252 pp.

Orthodoxy: A Faith and Order Dialogue. Geneva, Switzerland: World Council of Churches, 1960. 80 pp.

Prokurat, Michael, Alexander Golitzin, and Michael D. Peterson. *Historical Dictionary of the Orthodox Church*. Metuchen, NJ: Scarecrow Press, 1996.

Roberson, Ronald G. *The Eastern Christian Churches: A Brief Survey*. 6th ed. Rome: Pont. Institutum Studiorum Orientalium, 1999. 276 pp.

Schmemann, Alexander. *The Historic Road of Eastern Orthodoxy*. New York: Holt, Rinehart and Winston, 1963. 343 pp.

Serafim, Archimandrite. *The Quest for Orthodox Church Unity in America: A History of the Orthodox Church in North America in the Twentieth Century*. New York: Saints Boris and Gleb Press, 1973. 195 pp.

Taft, Robert F. *The Oriental Orthodox Churches in the United States*. Washington, DC: Secretariat, Bishops Committee on Ecumenical and Interreligious Affairs, National Conference of Catholic Bishops, 1986. 28 pp.

Zernov, Nicolas. *The Church of Eastern Christians*. London: Society for Promoting Christian Knowledge, 1942. 114 pp.

Orthodox Liturgy

Dalmais, Irénée-Henri. *Eastern Liturgies*. Trans. Donald Attwater. New York: Hawthorn, 1960. 144 pp.

The Orthodox Liturgy. London: Society for Promoting Christian Knowledge, 1964. 110 pp.

Sokolof, Dimitri, comp. *A Manual of the Orthodox Church's Divine Service*. Jordanville, NY: Holy Trinity Russian Orthodox Monastery, 1968. 166 pp.

Wybrew, Hugh. *The Orthodox Liturgy: The Development of the Eucharistic Liturgy in the Byzantine Rite*. London: S.P.C.K., 1989. 189 pp.

Orthodox Theology

Allen, Joseph J., ed. *Orthodox Synthesis: The Unity of Theological Thought*. Crestwood, NY: St. Vladimir's Seminary Press, 1981. 231 pp.

Lossky, Vladimir. *The Mystical Theology of the Eastern Church*. London: Clarke, 1957. 252 pp.

Maloney, George A. *A History of Orthodox Theology since 1453*. Belmont, MA: Nordland, 1976. 388 pp.

Platon, Metropolitan. *The Orthodox Doctrine of the Apostolic Eastern Church* (1857). New York: AMS Press, 1969. 239 pp.

Independent Orthodoxy

Anson, Peter F. *Bishops at Large*. London: Faber and Faber, 1964. 593 pp.

Bain, Alan. *Bishops Irregular: An International Directory of Independent Bishops*. Bristol, U.K.: Author, 1985. 256 pp.

Brandreth, H. R. T. *Episcopi Vagantes and the Anglican Church*. London: S.P.C.K., 1961. 140 pp.

Clark, Boden. *Lords Temporal & Lords Spiritual: A Chronological Checklist of the Popes, Patriarchs, Katholikoi, and Independent Archbishops and Metropolitans of the Monarchical Autocephalous Churches of the Christian East and West*. San Bernardino, CA: Borgo Press, 1985. 136 pp.

Morris, John W. "The Episcopate of Aftimios Ofiesh." *The Word*: Pt. I: 25, 2 (February 1981) 5–9; Pt. II: 25, 3 (March 1981): 5–9.

Prüter, Karl, and J. Gordon Melton. *The Old Catholic Sourcebook*. New York: Garland, 1983. 254 pp.

Tillett, Gregory. *Joseph René Vilatte: A Bibliography*. Sydney, Australia: Vilatte Guild, 1980. 23 pp.

Ward, Gary L., Bertil Persson, and Alan Bain, eds. *Independents Bishops: An International Directory*. Detroit, MI: Apogee, 1990. 524 pp.

Non-Chalcedonean Orthodoxy

Atamian, Sarkis. *The Armenian Community*. New York: Philosophical Library, 1955.

Butler, Alfred J. *The Ancient Coptic Churches of Egypt*. 2 vols. Oxford: Clarendon Press, 1884.

Elmhardt, William Chauncey, and George M. Lamsa. *The Oldest Christian People: A Brief Account of the History and Traditions of the Assyrian People and the Fateful History of the Nestorian Church* (1926). New York: AMS Press, 1970. 141 pp.

Fortescue, Adrian. *The Lesser Eastern Churches*. London: Catholic Truth Society, 1913. 468 pp.

Issac, Ephraim. *The Ethiopian Church*. Boston: Sawyer, 1968. 59 pp.

McCullough, W. Stewart. *A Short History of Syriac Christianity to the Rise of Islam*. Chico, CA: Scholars Press, 1982. 197 pp.

Meinardus, Otto F. A. *Christian Egypt: Faith and Life*. Cairo, Egypt: American University in Cairo Press, 1970. 513 pp.

Ramban, Kadavil Paul. *The Orthodox Syrian Church: Its Religion and Philosophy*. Puthencruz, Syria: Pathrose, 1973. 167 pp.

St. Mark and the Coptic Church. Cairo, Egypt: Coptic Orthodox Patriarchate, 1968. 164 pp.

Sarkissian, Karekin. *The Council of Chalcedon and the Armenian Church*. New York: Armenian Church Prelacy, 1965. 264 pp.

———. *The Witness of the Oriental Orthodox Churches*. Artelias, Lebanon: Author, 1970. 91 pp.

 # Intrafaith Organizations

Federation of Independent Catholic and Orthodox Bishops

32378 Lynx Hollow Rd., Creswell, OR 97426

The Federation of Independent Catholic and Orthodox Bishops (FICOB) emerged in the 1990s as an ecumenical body serving as a meeting ground for Old Catholic, Anglican, Orthodox, and Liberal Catholic bishops. While united by their separation from the older and larger historical liturgical churches, the independent jurisdictions have disagreed with each other on a variety of issues from the ordination of female priests and acceptance/rejection of homosexuals, to various doctrinal and liturgical matters. It has been the suggestion of Archbishop Meri Louise Spruit, matriarch of the Church of Antioch and director of the federation, that FICOB unites people only in Christ's Law of Love. The federation came about in part as a result of independent bishops across North America coming into contact through the Internet.

The federation promotes the idea that all of the churches share in a portion of God's truth and that much is to be gained by a promotion of tolerance, understanding, and an acceptance of diversity. There is also an auxiliary organization, the Friends of FICOB.

Membership: At the start of 1996, FICOB had 93 episcopal members.

Periodicals: *FICOB & Friends*.

Federated Orthodox Catholic Churches International

407 Donovan Rd., Brushton, NY 12916

The Federated Orthodox Catholic Churches International (FOCUS) (formerly known as the International Federation of Orthodox Churches United Sacramentally) is a federation of sacramental churches that considers itself to be based on the evangelizing Holy Scriptures and empowered by the Holy Spirit. It is the desire of FOCUS to establish a body that is loving (as commanded by Jesus), forgiving, and united to the glory of God. FOCUS serves as synod of synods, and individual members do not relinquish their own internal structure and governance. Dioceses without a synod may affiliate and FOCUS will provide oversight and function as their synod.

FOCUS grew out of a felt need among Orthodox Catholic jurisdictions of the world for a central body for recognition and succor. Members recognize the need to come together in Christ's Holy Name to seek and follow the will of God. It is the stated goal of FOCUS to provide a meeting place where each expression of the ancient Orthodoxia can "come together" and still not fear the loss of individual identity. (The "Orthodox" in the title does not refer to "Eastern" Orthodoxy but rather to the true teachings or Orthodoxia, and the "Catholic" refers to the fullness thereof [Jesus Christ], the original meaning as found in the creeds.) Member jurisdictions are in sacramental communion with each other and can thus provide the sacraments for those individual members of other FOCUS communions who do not reside close to a church or priest of their own jurisdiction.

FOCUS jurisdictions have a wide variety of approved liturgies available for their use, including the Sarum Rite, the Roman Rite (so-called Tridentine Mass) and its revised version of the Novus Ordo, the Liturgy of St. John Chrysostomos, the Liturgy of St. Basil, the Liturgy of St. James, the Western Rite (Sarum) adapted by St. Tikhon, the Gregorian Rite, the Celtic Rite, the Qurbana (conforming to the Councils), and the Gallican Rite.

FOCUS jurisdictions agree that the Holy Church was founded by Jesus Christ who empowered the apostles to bring the church into the world. In the early centuries, the church grew around five historic centers, the Patriarchates, whose bishops were honored and given special positions as "first among equals." Thus, the church developed as a collegial institution in which the bishops could not exercise jurisdiction or authority beyond their own boundaries or dioceses. The government of the church was conciliar as was demonstrated in the Seven Ecumenical Councils that defined the Christian Faith between the years 325 and 787 C.E.

At present, the Eastern Churches are primarily national churches as manifested in their particular ethnic customs, liturgies, and culture. The great flood of immigrants to America brought this heritage with them, a heritage which in North America has led to a multiplicity of church names, the fragmentation of Orthodoxy, and its isolation into ethnic enclaves. FOCUS affirms the sacramental unity of all Orthodox Catholic jurisdictions that hold to the Faith of Holy Orthodox Catholic Christian Tradition, i.e. Holy Scriptures and the teaching of the Seven Ecumenical Councils and the Holy Fathers. Member jurisdictions regard as sinful the denial and refusal of the Holy Sacraments to believing and practicing Orthodox Catholic Christians. Further, they hold that these individuals are victims of separation imposed at hierarchical levels.

Member communions may use either the Julian Calendar or the Gregorian Calendar. FOCUS recognizes a hierarchy of spiritual leadership: the bishops, the presbyters, and the deacons. The highest spiritual office in the church is that of the bishop, and all the FOCUS bishops are equal in authority. Above each bishop is the authority of all the bishops in Council (Synod) under the guidance of the Holy Spirit. While one bishop may preside, such as a metropolitan or archbishop, there is no universal "bishop of bishops."

Membership: The International Federation of Orthodox Catholics United Sacramentally includes the Holy Orthodox Catholic Church, the Apostolic Orthodox Catholic Church, and Christ Catholic Church International. The ministry of FOCUS members is carried out by 17 bishops and more than 150 clergy and religious among their many ministries.

Sources:

Federated Orthodox Catholic Churches International. www.jesusfocus.org/focus2.htm

Orthodox Catholic Church in North America

Current address could not be obtained for this edition.

The Orthodox Catholic Church in North America (THEOCACNA), formerly known as the Holy Eastern Catholic and Apostolic Church in North America, is an ecumenical fellowship of various Eastern Orthodox churches. It was founded in 1927 and renamed in the 1970s as the Ecumenical Orthodox Catholic Church by Abp. Francis Joseph Ryan (d. 1987). Reportedly, Ryan was consecrated in 1969 by Abp. Walter A. Propheta of the American Orthodox Catholic Church. Originally incorporated as the Ecumenical Orthodox Catholic Church—Autocephalous, the synod continued under that name until 1985 when Ryan was succeeded as primate-metropolitan by Abp. Dennis Garrison. It assumed its present name in 1997. Garrison led the synod through a period of expansion. In 1986 he consecrated Renee Bergeron to develop the church in Canada under the name Église Écuménique Orthodoxe Occidentale au Canada. In 1988 Garrison was succeeded by Paul Vincent Dolan.

The Holy Synod of THEOCACNA consists of the bishops of the affiliated churches. Member churches include the American Orthodox Church, the Celtic Orthodox Catholic Church, the Tridentine Orthodox Catholic Church, the Église Écuménique Orthodoxe Occidentale au Canada, the Orthodox Catholic Church—Nigeria, and the Église Orthodoxe du Benin.

Membership: Not reported.

Sources:

Orthodox Catholic Church in North America. www.angelfire.com/journal/occna/.

Orthodox Catholic Patriarchate of America

66 N Brookfield St., Vineland, NJ 08360

The Orthodox Catholic Patriarchate of America began in 1950 as the Provisional Orthodox Synod of America by the associating together of a number of independent Orthodox jurisdictions. The provisional synod in turn authorized the formation of the patriarchate and elected Bp. Joseph Klimovich (1880–1961) as its first patriarch. The patriarchate is a coalition of churches joined in faith to the older patriarchal churches headquartered in Antioch, Alexandria, Constantinople (Istanbul), and Jerusalem, but completely separate administratively and not recognized by the older patriarchates. The group was later joined by Abp. Joseph K. C. Pillai of the Indian Orthodox Church.

The driving force in the creation of the patriarchate was Archbishop Klimovich of the American Holy Orthodox Catholic Eastern Church and representatives of the African Orthodox Church, the Autonomous Greek Orthodox Church, the Polish Old Catholic Church in America, and several other small Orthodox bodies, including one Canadian Ukrainian jurisdiction. Klimovich died in 1961 and was succeeded by Abp. John Cyril Sherwood (1895–1969), who as patriarch took the name and was thereafter known as Clement I. Following Clement I's death in 1969, Abp. George A. Hyde (b. 1923) of the Orthodox Catholic Church of America became the patriarch. He served only until a synod could be called, at which time Archimandrite Pangratios Vrionis was named the new patriarch. Early in 1970 Vrionis was consecrated as archbishop of the Greek archdiocese of Vasiloupolis and began his reign as head of the patriarchate. While his church had grown, the patriarchate largely remained an inactive body.

Among the founders of the patriarchate was Peter A. Zhurawetsky (1901–1994), a priest consecrated by Klimovich in 1950. In the 1960s he had a dispute with Clement I, whom he accused of stealing the patriarchate. He organized a rival Holy Synod of the Orthodox Catholic Churches of the Americas and Europe. Then in 1975, he discovered that the original charter of the patriarchate had become inactive (as had the patriarchate under Hyde), and he seized the opportunity to take over the corporation, at which time he dissolved his rival body.

Zhurawetsky continued to head the minuscule patriarchate, whose member groups were largely paper organizations until his death in 1994. In 1993, he turned over his patriarchal authority to the synod of bishops.

Membership: Not reported.

Periodicals: *Our Missionary*.

Sources:

Hyde, George Augustine, ed. *Protocol: The Holy Synod of Bishops, the Orthodox Catholic Patriarchate of America*. Belleair, FL: Author, 1984.

Standing Conference of Canonical Orthodox Bishops in the Americas

10 E 79th St., New York, NY 10075

The Standing Conference of Canonical Orthodox Bishops in the Americas was founded in 1960 to express the unity of Orthodoxy in America and to facilitate cooperative possibilities among the various ethnic Orthodox communions represented in the United States and Canada. It includes those churches in direct communion with the Ecumenical Patriarchate of Constantinople.

The conference has achieved some measure of success in coordinating activities and reducing duplication of services between member churches in areas such as campus work, Christian education, military and hospital chaplaincies, ecumenical relationships, foreign mission work, and humanitarian aid. The hierarchs hold semiannual meetings to discuss ecumenical issues, review its past work, and plan for the future.

Membership: Membership in the conference includes the Greek Orthodox Archdiocese of America, Serbian Orthodox Church in the USA and Canada, Orthodox Church in America, Romanian Orthodox Archdiocese in America and Canada, Albanian Orthodox Diocese of America, Antiochian Orthodox Christian Archdiocese of North America, Carpatho Russian Orthodox Diocese in the USA, Bulgarian Eastern Orthodox Church, and Ukrainian Orthodox Church of the USA.

Educational Facilities:

St. Vladimir's Seminary, Crestwood, New York.

Holy Cross Theological School, Brookline, Massachusetts.

Hellenic College, Brookline, Massachusetts.

Sources:

Standing Conference of Canonical Orthodox Bishops in the Americas. www.scoba.us/.

Orthodoxy

African Orthodox Church, Inc.

122 W 129th St., New York, NY 10023

The African Orthodox Church was founded in 1921 following the consecration of George Alexander McGuire (1866–1934) as a bishop by Abp. Joseph Rene Vilatte (1854–1929) of the American Catholic Church. The ceremony culminated a long search by McGuire, an African American, for recognition for his ministry.

McGuire, an immigrant from the West Indies, had joined the Episcopal Church in 1895 and was ordained two years later. Like all American denominations with both episcopal leadership and a significant black membership, the Episcopal Church faced problems and pressures related to electing and elevating their first black member to the bishopric. Within the Episcopal Church the cries for a bishop drawn from among black members grew even louder after the Civil War. The leadership refused these demands, arguing that, since the church did not recognize racial distinctions, it could not elevate a man to the bishopric just because he was black. A step toward the solution came in 1910 with the creation of black "suffragan" bishops, bishops without right to succession and without vote in the house of bishops. Among those who complained that suffragans were not enough was Dr. McGuire.

McGuire served parishes in Cincinnati, Ohio; Richmond, Virginia; Philadelphia; and Cambridge, Massachusetts, before becoming the archdeacon for the Commission for Work Among the Colored People under William Montgomery Brown, the bishop of Arkansas. In 1911 McGuire became field secretary for the

American Church Institute, but two years later he left the country for his native Antigua, where he remained for five years serving as a pastor. Then, in 1918, McGuire moved to New York City to participate in the movement led by Marcus Garvey, the United Negro Improvement Association. Working with Garvey only strengthened McGuire's dissatisfaction with serving a church where black people were systematically denied positions of leadership, and he became determined to pursue an independent course. In 1919 he left the Episcopal Church to found his own congregation, the Good Shepherd Independent Episcopal Church.

McGuire seems to have settled on the idea of a separate black church with a recognized apostolic succession. On September 2, 1921, in the Church of the Good Shepherd in New York City, a meeting of independent black clergy resolved itself into the first synod of the African Orthodox Church and designated McGuire as its bishop-elect. The synod then entered into negotiations with the Russian Orthodox Church in America in its search for episcopal orders for its newly elected bishop. The Russians indicated a willingness to consecrate McGuire, but only if they controlled the newly created jurisdiction. The idea of nonblack control had no appeal to either McGuire or his followers. They then turned to the American Catholic Church, headed by Abp. Joseph Rene Vilatte, who was willing to confer orders and asked little or nothing in the way of control. On September 29, 1921, Abp. Vilatte, assisted by Carl A. Nybladh, consecrated Dr. McGuire in the Church of Our Lady of Good Death in Chicago. Upon his return from his consecration, McGuire was enthroned as the first bishop of the new African Orthodox Church.

The new jurisdiction grew quickly, and within two years had parishes in Brooklyn, New York; Pittsburgh, Pennsylvania; New Haven, Connecticut; and outside the country in Nova Scotia, Canada; Cuba; and Santa Domingo in the Dominican Republic. Soon afterward, congregations in Philadelphia, Boston, Florida, and the Bahamas were added. McGuire also initiated an order of deaconesses. Its major appeal was to African Americans of West Indian heritage.

McGuire died in 1934 and was succeeded by William E. J. Robertson (1875–1962). In the wake of the passing of the original leadership, the church went through a period of turmoil and several schismatic churches, all now defunct, emerged as bishops left or were suspended from office. However, the time of trouble passed and Robertson remained in the archbishop's throne until his death in 1962. He was succeeded by Richard Grant Robinson (served 1962–1967), who adopted the patriarchal name Peter IV. Among Robinson's major accomplishments was the reunion he effected with the last remaining group that had left a generation before, the Holy African Church, then under the leadership of Gladstone St. Clair Nurse. Nurse succeeded Robinson as the archbishop of the reunited African Orthodox Church. Nurse was succeeded in turn by William R. Miller (served 1976–1981) and Stafford J. Sweeting. The current archbishop is George Walter Sands.

Membership: Not reported.

Educational Facilities:

Endich Theological Seminary, New York, New York.

Sources:

African Orthodox Church Inc. www.netministries.org/see/churches.exe/ch26904.

Burkett, Randall K. *Garveyism as a Religious Movement*. Metuchen, NJ: Scarecrow Press, 1978.

The Divine Liturgy and Other Rites and Ceremonies of the Church. Chicago: African Orthodox Church, 1945.

Newman, Richard. "The Origins of the African Orthodox Church." In *The Negro Churchman*. Millwood, NY: Krause Reprint Co., 1977.

Terry-Thompson, Arthur C. *The History of the African Orthodox Church*. Author, 1956. 139 pp.

Trela, Jonathan. *A History of the North American Old Roman Catholic Church*. Scranton, PA: Author, 1979. 124 pp.

Albanian Orthodox Diocese of America

6455 Silver Dawn Ln., Las Vegas, NV 89118

In 1950 Bp. Mark I. Lipa came to the United States with authority from the ecumenical patriarch in Constantinople to organize the Albanian faithful. The following year he formed the Albanian Orthodox Diocese of America, which is a member of the Standing Conference of Canonical Orthodox Bishops in the Americas. Bishop Mark died on March 23, 1982. Rt. Rev. Ilia Katre is his current successor.

Membership: In 2001 the diocese reported 2 parishes, 1,300 members, and 2 clergy.

Sources:

Albanian Orthodox Diocese. www.goarch.org/en/otherpatriarchal/alb.asp.

American Carpatho-Russian Orthodox Greek Catholic Church

312 Garfield St., Johnstown, PA 15906

The American Carpatho-Russian Orthodox Greek Catholic Church was founded in the 1930s by a group of former members of the Roman Catholic Church who had migrated to the United States from Carpatho-Russia. Carpatho-Russia had been forcefully converted from Eastern Orthodoxy to the Roman Catholic Ruthenian Rite by a series of rulers who basically followed the Latin Rite. Once the church was established in the United States, a process of further latinizing the Ruthenian Rite parishes began. Among other things, attempts were made to curtail the assignment of married priests to American parishes.

As early as 1891, a Carpatho-Russian Catholic parish sought to return to Eastern Orthodoxy. It was soon joined by others. Then in 1936, approximately 40 parishes that had left Roman jurisdiction organized and selected Orestes P. Chornock (1883–1977) as their leader. The next year they designated him their bishop-elect and turned to the ecumenical patriarch in Constantinople for recognition. In 1938 the patriarch consecrated Chornock and authorized the American Carpatho-Russian Orthodox Diocese as an independent body. In 1966 the patriarch elevated Chornock to the dignity of a metropolitan. The present ruling bishop is Metropolitan Nicholas Smisko.

The American Carpatho-Russian Orthodox Greek Catholic Church is an independent autonomous body directly under the authority of the ecumenical patriarch. It has a working relationship with the Greek Orthodox Archdiocese of North and South America, whose archbishop is the exarch of the patriarch. The archbishop intercedes when the appointment of a new bishop is requested by the church and has the task of consecrating him. The church is at one with Eastern Orthodox faith and practice, though its liturgy still retains a few minor peculiarities reflective of its Roman Catholic history. The church is a member of the Standing Conference of Canonical Orthodox Bishops in the Americas.

Membership: In 2008 the church reported 82 parishes being served by 132 priests.

Educational Facilities:

Christ the Savior Seminary, Johnstown, Pennsylvania.

Periodicals: *Cerkovny Vistnik—Church Messenger*. • *A.C.R.Y. Annual*. Available from 211 W Grand Ave., Rahway, NJ 07065.

Sources:

American Carpatho-Russian Orthodox Diocese. www.acrod.org/.

Barringer, Lawrence. *Good Victory: Metropolitan Orestes Chornock and the American Carpatho-Russian Orthodox Greek Catholic Diocese*. Brookline, MA: Holy Cross Orthodox Press, 1985.

Roman, Jaroslav. "The Establishment of the American Carpatho-Russian Orthodox Greek Catholic Diocese in 1938: A Major Carpatho-Uniate Return to Orthodoxy." *St. Vladimir's Theological Quarterly* 20 (1976): 158.

American Exarchate of the True (Old Calendar) Orthodox Church of Greece

c/o Center for Traditionalist Orthodox Studies, St. Gregory Palamas Monastery, PO Box 398, Etna, CA 96027-0398

Alternate Address: International Headquarters: c/o His Eminence, the Most Reverend Cyprian, Metropolitan of Oropos and Fili, Bishop-Abbot of the Holy Monastery of Saints Cyprian and Justina, T Th. 46006, 133 10 Ano Liosia, Greece.

The Old Calendar movement in the Greek Orthodox Church had its inception in 1924, when the state church of Greece, which had hitherto followed the Old or Julian Calendar—a calendar that continues to be followed by the overwhelming majority of Orthodox Christians throughout the World—adopted the Gregorian Calendar. Refusing to accept this innovation, hundreds of thousands of the faithful walled themselves off from communion with the state (new calendar) church, in the hope that they might thereby exert pressure on the hierarchy to restore the traditional calendar.

One issue that has divided the movement since its separation from the state church is whether any saving Grace (i.e., the efficacious Mysteries) remains in the Church of Greece. The Old Calendarists under Metropolitan Cyprian are the only group acknowledging that such Grace does exist in the state church, in spite of the fact that, in their view, this church has seriously compromised its integrity by actively participating in what the Old Calendarists see as relativistic excesses that characterize much of the contemporary ecumenical movement.

The monastery founded and headed by Metropolitan Cyprian had originally belonged to the state church, but returned to the Julian Calendar in 1967 and broke communion with the New Calendar church two years later, accepting the authority of the Old Calendarist hierarchy. Metropolitan Cyprian was consecrated to episcopacy in 1979. The Old Calendar movement in Greece was disrupted in the early 1980s, and the various factions reorganized themselves into independent groups. The more moderate groups accepted Metropolitan Cyprian as their leader. The synod of bishops under Metropolitan Cyprian, the Holy Synod in Resistance, hopes for a future reunion with the state church, viewing a return on the part of the latter to the Julian Calendar and a decisive withdrawal from the ecumenical movement as necessary conditions for the restoration of ecclesiastical communion.

The Church is organized into five dioceses: two in Greece, two in Italy, and the diocese of Etna, which includes the parishes and monastic centers in North America. Along with the parishes, there is one monastery and one convent in Etna, California, and one convent in Bluffton, Alberta, Canada.

Membership: In 2008, the Diocese of Etna reported 11 parishes in the United States and 2 in Canada.

Educational Facilities:

Center for Traditionalist Orthodox Studies, Etna, California.

Periodical: *Orthodox Tradition*.

Sources:

Orthodox Church of Greece, Holy Synod in Resistance. www.synodinresistance.org/.

Chrysostomos, Archimandrite, with Hieromonk Ambrosios and Hieromonk Auxentios. *The Old Calendar Orthodox Church of Greece.* Etna, CA: Center for Traditionalist Orthodox Studies, 1991.

"Greek Old Calendarists in the U.S.A.: An Annotated Directory." *Orthodox Tradition* 2, no. 2 (1985): 49–61.

American Orthodox Catholic Church (Kochones)

810 E Walnut St., Pasadena, CA 91101

The American Orthodox Catholic Church was founded in 1969 as the Church of God in the Lord Jesus Christ by Bp. Steven A. Kochones (b. 1931). Kochones was raised as a member of the Greek Orthodox Archdiocese of North and South America, but left the jurisdiction as a young man. In 1956 he was ordained as a minister in the

Independent Assemblies of God, a Protestant church of Pentecostal faith, after he had experienced the baptism of the Holy Spirit as evidenced by speaking in tongues. After some years as a Pentecostal minister, Kochones was drawn back to his Orthodox heritage and in 1967 accepted ordination as an Orthodox priest by Abp. Walter A. Propheta (1912–1972) of the American Orthodox Catholic Church (Propheta).

In 1969 he established the Church of God in the Lord Jesus Christ, an independent church in fellowship with the American Orthodox Catholic Church (Propheta). It combined Orthodox faith with Pentecostal piety and some insights from messianic Judaism. Kochones developed a system of seven sacraments and seven sacramentals. The seven sacraments were baptism and confirmation, confession and absolution, Holy Eucharist and Holy Communion, ministry and priesthood, marriage, private and public prayer, and preaching and teaching. The seven sacramentals were bowing or kneeling to pray and praise; singing choruses, hymns, and psalms; clapping or uplifted hands in prayer; dancing and singing in the Holy Spirit; music and drama; making the sign of the cross and smiting the breast; and speaking in tongues, prophecy, and interpretation. The church used Jewish symbols, such as the Star of David, in its iconography, and speaks of God as Yahweh. It acknowledged the continuing validity of the Seventh-Day Sabbath, and services are held on both Saturday and Sunday.

The church observes the biblical dietary laws as found in Leviticus. Women, otherwise meeting ordination requirements, may be ordained to the priesthood.

In 1979, following a burglary at the church's headquarters in Pasadena, California, at which time the corporation papers and seal were stolen, the church's name was changed (for legal reasons) to the Catholic Church of God. The church's symbol combined a latin cross, the Star of David, and the Jewish seven-stemmed candelabra. The name chosen also reflected a trend within the church to bring it more in line with the perceptions of the historical and ancient church being made by Kochones. Included in this trend was a new emphasis on apostolic succession, and Kochones began to seek consecration as a bishop. He was consecrated in 1980 by Bp. David Baxter of the Orthodox Church of America.

In 1989 The Catholic Church of God changed its name to the American Orthodox Catholic Church, though it remains separate from the jurisdiction of the same name of late founded by Archbishop Propheta.

Membership: Not reported.

Periodicals: *Orthodox Messenger.*

Sources:

The Christian Liturgy. Pasadena, CA: Church of God in the Lord Jesus Christ, 1977. 9 pp.

The Feast of Passover. Pasadena, CA: Church of God in the Lord Jesus Christ, n.d. 8 pp.

Ward, Gary L., Bertil Persson, and Alan Bain, eds. *Independent Bishops: An International Directory.* Detroit, MI: Apogee Books, 1990. 524 pp.

American Orthodox Catholic Church (Propheta)

c/o Metropolitan Samuel, 2004 Esprit Glade, Baldwinsville, NY 13027

The American Orthodox Catholic Church was incorporated in 1965 by Walter M. Propheta (1912–1972), a former Ukranian Orthodox priest. In 1964 he was consecrated to the episcopacy by Abp. Peter Zhurawetsky (1901–1994), exarch in the United States for the Greek Patriarchate of Alexandria, assisted by Abp. Joachim Souris, metropolitan primate of the Autocephalous Greek Orthodox Church in America, and Abp. Theodotus DeWitow, metropolitan primate of the Holy Orthodox Church in America. In 1966 he was consecrated as archbishop by Abp. Theoklitos Kantaris of the Old Calendar Greek Orthodox Jurisdiction, Greece, and Archbishop DeWitow.

Propheta continued the task of building an independent and indigenous American Orthodoxy, which had been initiated by his direct predecessor, the Most Rev. Aftimios Ofiesh (1889–1966) of Brooklyn, who in 1927 received canonically and formally from the synod of bishops of the American dioceses of the Russian Orthodox Church the mandate to initiate an American Orthodox Catholic Church. As Archbishop and Patriarch Wolodymir I (as Propheta was ecclesiastically known), he ordained and consecrated a number of clergymen who became part of his jurisdiction. Some of them left the jurisdiction and founded their own autonomous groups, and others were received into different jurisdictions as a result of the struggle for control of the church after Propheta's death.

Abp. Francis Joseph Ryan (d. 1986), successor to Abp. Propheta and Abp. John A. Christian (d. 1984), was consecrated to the episcopacy in 1969 by Abps. Propheta, Christian, and Uladislau Ryzy-Rysky. His successor was Abp. Jeremiah, (David William Worley), consecrated to the episcopacy in 1972 by Abps. LaVon Miguel Haithman (Gabre Kristos Mikael), Francis Ryan, Jamed Edward Burns, and Anthony Everhart.

Archbishop Samuel, the current patriarch of yhe American Orthodox Catholic Church, was consecrated to the episcopacy in 2004 by Archbishop Jeremiah. The American Orthodox Catholic Church Holy Synod in 2005 ratified and approved this appointment and confirmed him as patriarch of the church.

The American Orthodox Catholic Church is Orthodox in doctrine and follows the decrees of the Seven Ecumenical Councils. It adheres to the Nicene Creed and requires only adherence to the traditional Orthodox text. A variety of preschismatic rites are allowed, though the Eastern, or Byzantine, is most frequently used.

The church follows an episcopal polity and is governed by the patriarch and the Holy Synod.

Membership: In 2008 the church reported congregations and more than 100 monastics in the United States, Africa, and Great Britain. Membership is estimated to be 1,200.

Educational Facilities:

Holy Mother Theotokos Seminary, Baldwinsville, New York.

Northern University and Seminary, Lusaka, Zambia.

St. Columba of Iona Institute, Flint, Michigan.

Sources:

American Orthodox Catholic Church (Propheta).

   www.forministry.com/USNYAMOCCNOCCN.

Patriarch Samuel and Bishop Daniel. *Renewing American Orthodoxy: The History of The American Orthodox Catholic Church*. New York: Archdiocese of Baldwinsville, 2007.

Propheta, Walter M. *Divine Liturgy for 20th Century Christians*. New York: American Orthodox Church, 1966.

American World Patriarchates
c/o Chancellery of Church, 19 Aqueduct St., Ossining, NY 10562

Uladyslau Ryzy-Ryski (1925–1978), a Belarusian priest, was consecrated in 1965 by Abp. Walter A. Propheta of the American Orthodox Catholic Church as the Bishop of Laconia, New Hampshire and the New England States. During this period he also met Abp. Peter A. Zhurawetsky (1901–1994) of the Old Orthodox Catholic Patriarchate of America, who on November 4, 1967, in the presence of a congregation of four, elevated him to the status of Archbishop. Without leaving Propheta's jurisdiction, Ryzy-Ryski began to create archbishops-patriarchs for each national/ethnic group and—quite apart from any laity demanding leadership—to build a hierarchy which he envisioned as international in scope. The World Patriarchate was very loosely structured, and established in large part by the elevation to patriarchal status of other independent bishops not otherwise required to recognize Ryzy-Ryski's authority or come under his jurisdiction. In 1972, as one of the last acts before his death, Propheta excommunicated Ryzy-Ryski from the American Orthodox Catholic Church, an action that merely spurred the growth of the American World Patriarchates, who established patriarchs for Canada, Hungary, Germany, Puerto Rico, Colombia, Haiti, Santo Domingo, Brazil, Peru, Argentina, El Salvador, Nigeria, the West Indies, Norway, Sweden, Formosa, and the Ukraine.

Only rarely were new congregations established as a result of a patriarch being named. Occasionally, the new patriarch could claim a small following.

In connection with the American World Patriarchates, Ryzy-Ryski organized the Peoples University of the Americas, an educational center designed to meet the needs of various ethnic and immigrant groups in the Bronx, New York. A well-educated man, with a good academic background, he led a faculty that offered a wide variety of courses in the humanities, and especially in English as a second language. The school also provided the World Patriarchates with a seminary.

Since the death of Patriarch Uladyslau Ryzy-Ryski in 1978, the work has continued under his brother, Abp. Emigidius J. Ryzy, who holds the title of Apostolic Administrator of All American World Patriarchates. He is assisted by Abp. Adam Bilecky, Patriarch II of the American World Patriarchate, Abp. Frank Barquera, and Bp. Piot Huszoza.

Membership: In 1997, the church reported 19,457 members, 17 congregations, and 54 priests in the United States. There were also one congregation and three priests in Canada. Affiliated work was to be found in 17 foreign countries. The newest work was in Ryzy-Ryski homeland, Belarus. There are a reported 54,542 members worldwide.

Educational Facilities:

Peoples University of the Americas, American College and Seminary, Bronx, New York.

Universidad de los Pueblos de las Americas, San Juan, Puerto Rico.

Sources:

American World Patriarchates. members.aol.com/AmWorldpat/

Antiochian Orthodox Christian Archdiocese of North America
358 Mountain Rd., Englewood, NJ 07631

In 1895 the Russian Orthodox Church began a Syrian Mission in the United States to provide spiritual guidance for Orthodox Christians from the Eastern Mediterranean basin. In 1904 the first Orthodox bishop ever consecrated in North America, Archimandrite Raphael Hawaweeny (1860–1915), became the bishop of the Syrian Mission of the Russian Orthodox Church. Metropolitan Germanos came to the United States in 1914 and began organizing Syrian churches. These two efforts paralleled each other until 1925, when an independent church was created. In 1936 Archimandrite Anthony Bashir (1898–1966) was elected and consecrated bishop by the American Syrian churches. He became metropolitan of New York and all North America in 1940 and provided leadership for 30 years.

In the 1936 election, in which Bashir was elected to the bishopric, Archimandrite Samuel David of Toledo, Ohio, polled the second-highest number of votes. On the same day that Archbishop Bashir was consecrated in New York, Russian bishops consecrated Samuel David as archbishop of Toledo. Abp. Samuel David was condemned and excommunicated in 1938 but then recognized the following year. The Antiochian Orthodox Archdiocese of Toledo, Ohio, and Dependencies that he led existed as a separate body until 1975.

In 1966 the Mt. Rev. Philip Saliba succeeded Bashir and became primate of the Antiochian Orthodox Christian Archdiocese of New York and All North America. Archbishop Philip was a leader in promoting the use of English in the liturgy. He gave priority to missions and emphasized the cause of Orthodox unity in North America and abroad.

In 1958 Archbishop David died, and hope for reunion of the two Antiochian churches emerged. Abp. Michael Shaheen succeeded Archbishop Samuel and conducted talks toward union, which were finally consummated in 1975. The new Antiochian Orthodox Christian Archdiocese of North America selected Archbishop Philip as head of the church with the title of metropolitan. There are four auxiliary bishops: Bishop Antoun, Bishop Joseph, Bishop Basil, and Bishop Demetri.

In February 1987 the former Evangelical Orthodox Church (EOC) was received as a body into the Antiochian Orthodox Christian Archdiocese of North America, thus ending for its members a pilgrimage that began almost two decades earlier. The

Evangelical Orthodox Church had its roots in the late 1960s, when a number of the staff of Campus Crusade for Christ left their positions. Some launched independent ministries; some affiliated with various independent evangelical churches. In the early 1970s several of these leaders—Peter Gillquist, John Braun, Dick Ballew, Ken Berven, and Jack Sparks—banded together as the New Covenant Apostolic Order (NCAO).

The formation of the NCAO afforded a context for study that led to a concentrated reappraisal of a common view of Evangelical Protestant Christians, that the first-century church had become corrupted over the centuries until restored by Evangelicals in relatively modern times. Gathering in Chicago in 1979, the leaders of the movement announced the formation of the Evangelical Orthodox Church to supercede the NCAO and to call Evangelicals back to their historic roots. Special emphasis was placed on ritual, a subject largely neglected in Evangelical circles. The new church immediately turned its attention to a search for valid Orthodox episcopal orders. Initial talks were held with the Orthodox Church in America. Although a major obstacle was overcome when the leaders of the EOC professed their belief in the Blessed Virgin Mary as *theotokos*, the Mother of God, the talks eventually reached a stalemate. Finally, the EOC was able to work out an arrangement with the Antiochian Church by which the leaders dropped their designation as bishops and were reordained by Archbishop Philip.

Over the years the leaders of the EOC have written a number of books that received wide circulation within Evangelical circles. Most of these were published by Thomas Nelson, where Gillquist worked as an editor, and included Gillquist's *Why We Haven't Changed the World* and *It Ain't Gonna Reign No More* by Jon Braun. Most notable among them was *The Mindbenders*, by Jack Sparks, an anticult book that led to a lawsuit for libel by the Local Church, one of the groups treated in the volume, and its eventual withdrawal by the publishers.

In October 2003, the Holy Synod of the Antiochian Orthodox Church allowed the Archdiocese to proceed under autonomous rule in an effort for more efficient self-government, internal organization, and effective outreach ministries.

On July 28, 2005, the Archdiocese voted unanimously to withdraw its membership from the National Council of Churches (NCC), becoming the first Orthodox jurisdiction to leave the NCC. The Archdiocese cited the increased politicization of the NCC and irrelevancy of its relationship as the main reasons for the withdrawal.

Membership: In 2002 the archdiocese reported 240 parishes and missions, 350,000 members, and 400 priests and deacons.

Periodicals: *The Word*. 1777 Quigg Dr., Pittsburgh, PA 15241-2071. • *Again*. Box 106, Mt. Hermon, CA 95041.

Sources:

Antiochian Orthodox Christian Archdiocese. www.antiochian.org/.

Aydin, Edip. *The History of the Syrian Orthodox Church of Antioch in North America: Challenges and Opportunities*. M.Div. thesis. Crestwood, NY: St. Vladimir Orthodox Seminary, 2000.

Braun, Jon E. *It Ain't Gonna Reign No More*. Nashville, TN: Thomas Nelson, 1978.

Corey, George et al., eds. *The First One Hundred Years: A Centennial Anthology Celebrating Antiochian Orthodoxy in North America*. Englewood, NJ: Antakya Press, 1995.

Gabriel, Antony. *The Ancient Church on New Shores: Antioch in North America*. San Bernardino: St. Willibrord's Press, 1996.

Gillquist, Peter E. *Becoming Orthodox: A Journey to the Ancient Christian Faith*. Ben Lomond, CA: Conciliar Press, 1992.

Apostolic Catholic Church of the Americas
Current address not obtained for this edition.

The Apostolic Catholic Church of the Americas was founded as the American Orthodox Catholic Church in Colorado in 1962, with Robert S. Zeiger as its Archbishop of Denver and Primate. He was consecrated in 1961 by Archbishop Peter A. Zhurawetsky (1901–1994) as an Orthodox bishop for Westerners.

The Anglican Church of the Americas was founded by Gordon A. Da Costa (d. 1991) in Indiana in 1971. In 1976 a synod was held at Marion, Indiana, at which Da Costa and others became members of the American Orthodox Catholic Church. At that time, the American Orthodox Catholic Church, in order to avoid confusion with Archbishop Walter A. Propheta's church in New York, took an alternative official name, the Apostolic Catholic Church of the Americas, which became its most commonly used designation.

Da Costa was elected Archbishop Primate of the Apostolic Catholic Church of the Americas. Zeiger, who had resigned as head, was elected chancellor. There was no actual merger of the American Orthodox Catholic Church and the Anglican Church of the Americas. However, Da Costa continued parallel activities as head of the Anglican Church of the Americas for some time in order to carry out responsibilities for those of his clergy who wished to continue as members of that church.

In 1977 Zeiger resigned and submitted to the jurisdiction of the Roman Catholic Church. As a condition for union with Rome, he was required to agree not to exercise his office as bishop or priest. In 1981 Zeiger returned to Orthodoxy. At that time, he became a cofounder of the Holy Synod of Denver in 1984. This venture floundered after a dispute in 1986. At that time, Zeiger returned to the Apostolic Catholic Church of the Americas as Archbishop *ad personam* of Lakewood, Colorado. Zeiger has since been arrested twice in connection with pro-life activities.

Archbishop C. F. Quinn of Dallas, Texas, was elected Archbishop Primate Coadjutor with the right of succession to Da Costa in 1986. Quinn succeeded as primate in 1988, when Da Costa could no longer serve. Quinn continued as Archbishop Primate after Da Costa's death.

The Apostolic Catholic Church of the Americas employs Western liturgy, accepts as the rule of faith the Sacred Scriptures and Divine Tradition as expressed in the writings of the church Fathers and the dogmatic degrees of the Seven Ecumenical Councils. The church makes clerical celibacy optional, even for bishops. It rejects females as candidates for the priesthood. Church property is held in lay trusteeship. The church is in the Apostolic succession; Catholic, not Protestant; Orthodox, not Roman; and American, not a foreign mission.

Membership: Not reported.

Periodicals: *The Door*. Send orders to 4201 Fairmount St., Dallas, TX 75219.

Sources:

The Order of Daily Prayer. Dallas: Diocese of Texas, Apostolic Catholic Church, n.d.

Zeiger, Robert S. *The Independent Catholic Orders Valid? The Understated Case*. Lakewood, FL: St. David's Press, 1994.

Apostolic Orthodox Catholic Church
PO Box 1834, Glendora, CA 91740

The Apostolic Orthodox Catholic Church was founded by Bps. Richard J. Ingram and Charles Ingram, both former bishops in the Western Orthodox Church in America (WOCA). Richard J. Ingram had been consecrated on June 17, 1984, by Charles David Luther, assisted by Bps. Peter Brennan and Alan Maxwell Bain. He was also consecrated *sub conditione* in 1988 by Bp. Luis Fernando Castillo-Mendez, assisted by several of his fellow bishops in the Igreja Catolica Apostolica Brasileira, Josivaldo Pereira de Oliveira, Galvao Barros, and Walbert Rommel Coelho. Richard Ingram consecrated Charles Ingram on September 10, 1989; before the end of the month, both had resigned from the WOCA. The Apostolic Orthodox Catholic Church is like its parent body in faith and practice, the differences leading to its founding being primarily administrative.

Membership: Not reported.

Association of Occidental Orthodox Parishes

Current address not obtained for this edition.

The use of the Western Rite in Orthodox Churches experienced a revival during the twentieth century as Eastern Orthodoxy flourished in the West. It has a long history, though little noticed because of the predominance of the Roman Rite. Some held the view, verified by such examples as the Western Rite Vicariate within the Antiochian Orthodox Church, that Western Rite parishes do not remain Western within a predominantly Eastern Rite church body. The Orthodox Church of France is a Western Rite diocese founded in 1953 by Fr. Evgraph Kovalevsky (1905–1970) and several other priests who withdrew from the Russian Orthodox Church. As priests in Lithuania they had followed a Western Rite, and Father Kovalevsky had pastored a Western Rite parish opened in 1944 in Paris. That parish became the source of several others.

After leaving the Russian Orthodox Church, the priests and their parishes affiliated with the Russian Orthodox Church Outside of Russia. Bishop John Maximovitch (1896–1966) ordained several new Western Rite priests and saw to the publication of the liturgy, the old Gallican Rite according to Saint Germain, Bishop of Paris (555–576), not to be confused with the eighteenth-century occultist of the same name. The death of Bishop John led to a break with the Russian Church, and, as relations worsened, Kovalevsky, who had been consecrated in 1964, led his followers in forming an autonomous diocese. But he died in 1970 without having a successor consecrated. Finally, in 1972, the Patriarch of Romania agreed to consecrate Pere Gilles Hardy as the new bishop of the Orthodox Catholic Church of France. He was known as Bishop Germain. The Western Rite was reintroduced to America by Fr. Stephen Empson, who founded a parish in New York City. In 1981 he organized the Association of Occidental Orthodox Parishes to further promote Western Rite Orthodoxy.

Membership: Not reported.

Periodicals: Unofficial: *Axios*. 800 S Euclid St., Fullerton, CA 92632.

Autocephalous Orthodox Catholic Apostolic Church

Current address not obtained for this edition.

The Autocephalous Orthodox Catholic Apostolic Church is an independent Orthodox jurisdiction founded by Mt. Rev. Paul W. Seese, formerly with the Western Orthodox Church in America. He had been consecrated in 1989 as a bishop by Mt. Rev. Richard J. Ingram of the Western Orthodox Church in America, assisted by Mt. Rev. Patrick M. Cronin of the Independent Catholic Church of America and Timothy W. Browning of the Byzantine Orthodox Catholic Church. The Western Orthodox Church, though an Orthodox body, follows a Western Rite, and Seese, wishing to follow an Eastern Rite, withdrew in 1991.

Membership: Not reported.

Sources:

Bogolepov, Alexander A. *Toward an American Orthodox Church: The Establishment of an Autocephalous Orthodox Church*. New York: Morehouse-Barlow Company, 1963.

Pruter, Karl. *The Directory of Autocephalous Bishops of the Apostolic Sucession*. San Bernadino, CA: Brogo Press, 1906. 104 pp.

Ward, Gary. *Independent Bishops: An International Directory*. Detroit: Apogee Books, 1990. 524 pp.

Autocephalous Traditional Orthodox Catholic Church

PO Box 17105, St. Bernard, OH 45217

The Autocephalous Traditional Orthodox Catholic Church is a small Orthodox jurisdiction founded in 1963. It is headed by the Mt. Rev. Athanasius K. Armstrong.

Membership: Not reported. The church reported priests in the United States and Canada. Missionary branches are reported in Japan, the Philippines, Russia, Poland, Singapore, Mexico, and in Africa.

Sources:

Bogolepov, Alexander A. *Toward an American Orthodox Church: The Establishment of an Autocephalous Orthodox Church*. New York: Morehouse-Barlow, 1963.

Belarusan Autocephalous Orthodox Church in the U.S.A.

c/o Archbishop Mikalay, Primate, St.Cyril's of Turau Cathedral, 401 Atlantic Ave., Brooklyn, NY 11217

Belarus, which achieved independence after the dissolution of the Soviet Union, is west of Russia, north of Ukraine, east of Poland, and south of Latvia and Lithuania. During the Soviet era the region was called Byelorussia. A national church, called the Metropolia of Kiev, under Greek jurisdiction, was established in Belarus in 1291. At that time the city of Kiev was under the authority of the Grand Duchy of Lithuania. Subsequent elected church heads, or Metropolitans, were Belarusans.

The church eventually came under the control of the Moscow head of the Russian Orthodox Church. In 1922 the Bishop of Miensk, Metropolitan Melchizedeck, called a council of clergy and laity under his leadership, and attempted to organize a Belarusans Church independent of Moscow. This action was met with the furious disapproval of both the communist government and the leadership of the Russian Orthodox Church. Over time the government arrested all the pro-Belarusan leaders, bishops, priests, and laity and sent them to Siberia; the church reverted to its dependent status. During the German occupation of Belarus in 1942, the church again attempted to organize independently, but this effort ended with the defeat of the German forces.

The Belarusan Autocephalous Orthodox Church, which emerged among refugee Belarusans in Germany after the war, is one of two Orthodox groups serving Belarusan immigrants. Their own bishops had turned to the Russian Church, while the clergy and laity followed the Ukrainian Church. Metropolitan Palikarp not only blessed the reorganization of the church among the Belarusans, but in 1948 granted permission for one of his bishops, Siarhej, to leave his jurisdiction and join the new church. In 1949, accompanied by his former Ukrainian colleagues, Siarhej consecrated a second bishop for the church, Bishop Vasil. As the church spread among immigrants worldwide, two more bishops, Andrej (Alexander Kryt) and Mikalay (Michael Macukievic) were consecrated in 1948.

Archbishop Mikalay was elected primate of the church in 1984, serving until his death in 2007. He was succeeded by Metropolitan Iziaslau (b. 1926).

Periodicals: *Carkouny Paslaniec* (Church Messenger), the quarterly bulletin of the Parish Council of St. Cyril's of Turau Cathedral.

Membership: In 2007 the church reported four parishes in the United States, two in Canada, three in the United Kingdom, and two in Australia.

Bulgarian Eastern Orthodox Church (Diocese of North and South America)

519 Brynhaven Dr., Oregon, OH 43616

The reestablishment of relations between the Orthodox Church in Bulgaria and the Bulgarian Eastern Orthodox Church (Diocese of North and South America and Australia) and the resultant manifestation of that accord in the joint visitation of North American parishes in 1963 by Bishop Andrey Velichky (d. 1972), metropolitan of the American church, and Bishop Preiman, metropolitan of Nevrokop, Bulgaria, led to major protests throughout the Church. Bishop Andrey was accused of violating the declaration made in 1947 that the Bulgarian Church in America would not accept any orders from the Church in Bulgaria. In March 1963 protesting leaders representing 18 churches and missions met in Detroit, Michigan, and reconstituted themselves as the Bulgarian Eastern Orthodox Church (Diocese of the United States of America and Canada) and elected Archimandrite Kyrill Yonchev (1927–2007) as their bishop.

They turned to the Russian Orthodox Church Outside of Russia for support. The Russians, also cut off from their homeland by a hostile communist regime, gave the new Bulgarian jurisdiction their canonical protection, and their bishops consecrated bishop-elect Yonchev in 1964 at their monastery in Jordanville, New York.

The Bulgarian Eastern Orthodox Church differs from its parent body only in matters of administration. It lays claim to all properties belonging to the undivided Church in America though it has not been able to take control of them. It was staunchly anti-Communist during the Soviet era.

Membership: In the mid-1970s the church reported 21 parishes and missions.

Bulgarian Eastern Orthodox Diocese of the USA, Canada, and Australia

550-A W 50th St., New York, NY 10019

Bulgarians arrived in the United States throughout the nineteenth century and by 1907 were numerous enough to begin establishing congregations. The first parish was formed in Madison, Illinois. Soon, the Holy Synod in Sofia established a mission to oversee their American members. In 1937 a diocese was created, and Bishop Andrey Velichky (d. 1972) came from Bulgaria as its head. Bishop Andrey returned to Bulgaria during World War II and worked on various projects, among which was the handling of negotiations between the ecumenical patriarch in Istanbul and the Bulgarian patriarch, which helped repair a 70-year-old broken relationship.

Soon after the war ended, Archbishop Andrey returned to America. In 1947 he incorporated the Bulgarian Eastern Orthodox Diocese of the USA, Canada, and Australia. The constitutional assembly meeting in March of that year realigned its relationship to the Church in Bulgaria by declaring that while it saw itself as part of the whole of Bulgarian Orthodoxy, it could not accept orders from the church leaders in Sofia as long as a Communist regime ruled their homeland. They then proceeded to formally elect Andrey as their leader. The Holy Synod reacted by declaring the election null and void. The American diocese ignored the Synod, and for the next 15 years the diocese operated independently of the church leaders in Sofia. In 1962 the church in Bulgaria recognized the Metropolia and reestablished a working relationship. In 1969 the jurisdiction was divided into two dioceses, and in 1972 Bp. Joseph Znepolski succeeded Archbishop Andrey as Metropolitan. In 1989, the year the communist government fell in Bulgaria, the two dioceses were again merged into one under Metropolitan Joseph.

The Bulgarian Eastern Orthodox Diocese follows standard Orthodox faith and practice. It is a member of the Standing Conference of Canonical Orthodox Bishops in the Americas.

Membership: In 2008 the diocese reported 22 parishes in the United States, 4 in Canada, and 3 in Australia.

Sources:

Bulgarian Eastern Orthodox Diocese of the USA, Canada, and Australia. www.bulgariandiocese.org/.

Byelorussian Orthodox Church

Current address not obtained for this edition.

When refugees and immigrants from Byelorussia came to the west after World War II, some organized as the Byelorussian Autonomous Orthodox Church and elected their own bishops. Others formed independent congregations and sought the canonical blessings of other Orthodox bishops. The Byelorussian Orthodox Church consists of three congregations that placed themselves under the jurisdiction of Archbishop Iakovos, head of the Greek Orthodox Archdiocese of North and South America, in his role as exarch in America for the ecumenical patriarch. Besides the congregation in South River, New Jersey, parishes are found in Chicago and Toronto.

Membership: Not reported.

The Byzantine Catholic Church, Inc. (Independent Jurisdiction)

19818 Hart St., Winnetka, CA 91306

The Byzantine Catholic Church, Inc., assumed its present form in 1984 through a merger of the Byzantine Old Catholic Church (BOCC), Inc., and the Holy Orthodox Catholic Church, Eastern and Apostolic (HOCCEA). The BOCC, originally an Old Catholic jurisdiction and now an Orthodox Catholic jurisdiction, has a history that is intimately tied to the career of its leader, Mar Markus I, who was elected patriarch in 1967.

Mar Markus I was born Mark I. Miller in 1927. In the early 1960s, he joined the North American Orthodox Catholic Church, in which he was ordained in 1964 after completing his seminary training. Miller was consecrated by Christopher Maria Stanley (1902–1976), who was assisted by Bp. John Joseph Frewen, in Kentucky in 1965. The church itself was incorporated in 1964.

In 1966, in an attempt to engender an expansion of the church, Stanley commissioned Miller to work with the Orthodox Old Catholic Church headed by Bp. Claude Hamel (b. 1935), but Miller's objections to aspects of Hamel's leadership led to a myriad of problems. Thus, after Stanley fell ill and died, Miller separated his work from Hamel and changed the name of the jurisdiction to the Orthodox Old Roman Catholic Church II, to try to salvage some of the work for expansion in 1967. Miller then moved to Los Angeles, California, and in 1967 the synod of bishops unanimously elected him to succeed Stanley as patriarch, naming him Mar Markus I.

In the mid-1970s, Mar Markus reorganized the church and changed the name back to the North American Orthodox Catholic Church, as it was called when he was originally consecrated. During this period he was moving both theologically and liturgically away from the Old Catholicism toward Eastern Orthodoxy.

In 1981 the church reorganized again, the result being the formation of the Byzantine Old Catholic Church, Inc. The reorganization occurred during a period of great flux in the congregations. After the new church was formed, Mar Apriam I (Abp. Richard B. Morrill, d. 1994), who headed the Holy Orthodox Catholic Church, Eastern and Apostolic (HOCCEA), joined with Abp. Mar Markus in the formation of a Sacred Synod of Bishops. Mar Apriam became president of the synod and Mar Markus became vice president of the synod and chief justice of the Spiritual Court of Bishops, in addition to maintaining his own jurisdiction.

A further merger in mid-1984 united the BOCC and the HOCCEA and led to the formation of the Byzantine Catholic Church, Inc. However, before the year was out, Morrill withdrew with approval and reconstituted the HOCCEA. Mar Markus remained as head of the Byzantine Catholic Church, Inc., which came into full communion with the reconstituted HOCCEA, their differences being purely administrative.

The possible merger of Morrill's jurisdiction with the Byzantine Catholic Church, Inc. was again raised and in 1991 a synod was called with that idea on the agenda. However, before it could meet, Mar Apriam died. When the synod did meet, it agreed to unite the various segments of the church previously under Mar Apriam under Mar Markus.

BELIEFS. The Byzantine Catholic Church, Inc. is Orthodox Catholic in faith and practice. It celebrates the Liturgies of St. John Chrysostom and St. Basil in the vernacular of its various jurisdictions. The church also has a growing Western Rite vicariate that is Orthodox Catholic in creed and tridentine in liturgical practice.

Membership: In 1997 the patriarchate reported over 500 congregations worldwide. Affiliated congregations are spread throughout the United States. Outside the United States, affiliated congregations are found in Great Britain, France, Italy, Congo, Nigeria, Liberia, Haiti, and South America and together have a reported membership of over 100,000.

Educational Facilities:

St. John's Theological Seminary, Los Angeles, California.

L'Institute Orthodoxe Ecumenique de St. Jean Chrysostome, Port au Prince, Haiti.

Byzantine Orthodox Catholic Church (Armstrong)

Current address not obtained for this edition.

The Byzantine Orthodox Catholic Church is a small Orthodox jurisdiction founded in the 1980s by Bp. Harry C. Armstrong. On December 3, 1988, assisted by bishops of the Western Orthodox Church in America, Timothy W. Browning was consecrated as a second bishop for the church.

Membership: Not reported.

Byzantine Orthodox Catholic Church (St. Peters)
6329 E 55th Pl., Indianapolis, IN 46226-1647

The Byzantine Orthodox Catholic Church is a small Orthodox jurisdiction founded in 1986 in Cincinnati, Ohio, by Most Rev. Donald St. Peters.

Membership: In 2002 the church had 12 congregations served by 32 priests. There are foreign congregations in Germany and the West Indies.

Sources:
Pruter, Karl. *Directory of Autocephalous Bishops of the Apostolic Succession*. Springfield, MO: Author, 2006.

Ward, Gary. *Independent Bishops: An International Directory*. Detroit, MI: Apogee Books, 1990.

Catholic Apostolic Church in North America
Current address could not be obtained for this edition.

Though officially reconstituted in 1983, the Catholic Apostolic Church in America has had an unbroken existence since 1950, the year in which Stephen Meyer Corradi-Scarella (1912–1979) established an American outpost of the Catholic Apostolic Church in Brazil. The Catholic Apostolic Church in Brazil was formed in 1946 by Dom Carlos Duarte Costa (1888–1961), a former bishop of the Roman Catholic Church who had been excommunicated by Pope Pius XII because of his criticism of the church during World War II. Among those whom Costa consecrated was Dom Luis F. Castillo-Mendez, who succeeded him as patriarch of the church in 1949. Corradi-Scarella was consecrated by Mendez in 1949 and established the church as an exarchate with headquarters in New Mexico. During the 1960s, following the death of Costa, Corradi-Scarella lost touch with the Brazilian group and began to associate with the various Old Catholics in the United States. By 1970 he called his jurisdiction the Diocese of the Old Catholic Church in America.

The church grew slowly until the 1970s. In 1973 Corradi-Scarella was joined by Francis Jerome Joachim (1928–1997), a priest ordained by Abp. Bartholomew Cunningham of the Holy Orthodox Church, Diocese of New Mexico. Joachim brought an Eastern Orthodox perspective with him, in contrast to Corradi-Scarella's Catholic tradition, but soon became Corradi-Scarella's chief associate. Corradi-Scarella arranged for Joachim's consecration by Abp. David M. Johnson of the American Orthodox Church, Diocese of California, on September 28, 1974. Two months later, on December 1, 1974, Corradi-Scarella, then almost 70 years old, resigned in favor of Joachim.

Under Joachim the small jurisdiction grew, at one point having almost 100 clergy, but over time it lost significant strength due to the defections of many to other independent jurisdictions. In 1980 Joachim renamed his jurisdiction the Western Orthodox Church in America. At the request of Mendez, Joachim changed the name of the church back to the Catholic Apostolic Church of North America. In 1985 Joachim was named primate of all North America and the church was recognized as the Autocephalous Catholic Apostolic Church in Brazil in North America.

The church believes in the Nicene Creed, the Apostle's Creed, and the Athanasian Creed and practices sacraments such as the Eucharist, baptism, matrimony, and anointing of the sick. Membership is open to anyone who wishes to join and the church makes a point of reaching out to individuals who may not feel welcome elsewhere. The church recognizes the pope as the bishop of Rome but not as the supreme leader of Catholics throughout the world.

The church is currently led by Abp. Rev. Anthony Santore, who succeeded Mt. Rev. Willard E. Schultz, the presiding bishop emeritus and now the church's historian. Bishop Santore is also assisted by Bps. Francisco Betancourt and Carl Purvenas-Smith.

Membership: In 2008 the church reported 10 parishes in the United States.

Educational Facilities:

St. John Chrysostom Theological Seminary, San Francisco, California.

St. Charles Academy of Theology, San Francisco, California.

Periodicals: *Journal Apostolica*.

Sources:
Catholic Apostolic Church in North America. www.cacina.org/home.php?flag=1.

Celtic Orthodox Christian Church
c/o Deaconess Elizabeth, Cele De, Box 72102, Akron, OH 44372

The Celtic Orthodox Christian Church, founded in the 1990s, is one product of the revival of interest in Celtic religious life, especially in the Christian community toward the end of the twentieth century. The church sees itself as continuing the faith and practice of the Christian Church in the West prior to 1000 and traces its history to Saint Irenaeus of Lyon (c.115–c. 202 C.E.), who resided in Gaul (modern France). Irenaeus was a student and disciple of Polycarp of Smyrna, and St. Polycarp was reputedly a student of the Apostle John. The church uses the Liturgy of the Lorrha "Stowe" Missal in its worship, the only surviving Celtic liturgy. It is also the only surviving Eucharistic liturgy according to the form used by churches of the British Isles, France, Germany, Switzerland, and northern Italy prior to 900 C.E.

Celtic churches were largely replaced by the Roman Catholic (Latin-Rite) by 1172. The suppression of the Celtic church began in England during the seventh century and was continued by Charlemagne in the ninth century. Suppression followed in Scotland, Wales, and Cornwall in the tenth and eleventh centuries. The last stronghold, Ireland, gave way in the twelfth century following the synod of Cashel in 1172. The suppression meant that no line of apostolic succession through Celtic bishops survived into the modern era. The revived church received its apostolic succession through independent bishops representing the lineage of the Antiochian Orthodox Church and the Russian Orthodox Church.

In using the term Orthodox, the Church does not, however, identify with Eastern Orthodoxy; rather, the term *Celtic Orthodox* is interpreted to mean that the church is committed to the belief and practice of the undivided church (which split into Roman and Eastern in the eleventh century). That belief and practice is believed to have been held by the saints of the Celtic churches, whose writings are especially valued.

The church follows the belief promulgated by the seven ecumenical councils. It stands apart from both Eastern Orthodoxy and the Roman Catholic Church in its understanding of original sin that is expressed in its understanding of Mary, Jesus' mother. It uses the term Theotekos (Birthgiver of God), and understands that Mary was free from both the stain of a sinful life and the guilt inherited from Adam. In that respect, she is like all people. Original guilt is seen as an error attributed to St. Augustine (354–430 C.E.). The idea of original guilt requires the further error of the Immaculate Conception, which posits Mary's freedom from the stain of original guilt. In contrast, the Celtic Church teaches that although original sin is a deficiency that causes individuals to tend toward sin, it does not impart guilt nor does it cut people off from God's grace. Guilt follows from sin committed by an individual.

The church does not admit women to the priesthood; however, it offers females the opportunity in the ordered religious life as a Celi De (or Culdee), a Companion or Servant of God. The Celi De serve through prayer, teaching, and/or service. They may be male or female, married or monastic. Contemporary Celi De look to St. Maelruain, who in 755 C.E. established a monastery at Tallaght. The writings of that monastery have survived, including the Rule of St. Maelruain.

The church is currently led by Abbot-Bishop Maelruain, Cele De, Metropolitan and Archbishop of Armagh. He is assisted by Bishop Timothy, Cele De, of Nashville and Glasgow, and Bishop Photius, Cara Cele De, of Iona.

Membership: In 2008 the church reported two parishes in Akron, with a third forming in Nashville, Tennessee.

Periodicals: *Celtic Orthodox Christian Quarterly*.

Sources:

Celtic Orthodox Christian Church. www.celticchristianity.org/.

Celtic Rite Orthodox Diocese

c/o The Order of the Servants of Jesus, PO Box 350, Clarkdale, GA 30020

The Celtic Rite Orthodox Diocese is a rite of the Holy Orthodox Catholic Church that wishes to bring the strength of Celtic spiritual expression into the twenty-first century. The diocese considers itself Christian, Orthodox, and Celtic—that is, Christian in love and mission; Orthodox in theology, beliefs, and practices; and Celtic in the expression of spirituality and heritage. The diocese uses the vernacular in worship and freely experiments with an array of ancient and modern music. The Order of the Servants of Jesus is a small ordered community affiliated with the diocese. The church is a member of the International Federation of Orthodox Catholics United Sacramentally (FOCUS).

Membership: Not reported.

Sources:

Pruter, Karl. *The Directory of Autocephalous Bishops of the Apostolic Succession*. San Bernadino, CA: Brogo Press, 1996.

Ward, Gary. *Independent Bishops: An International Directory*. Detroit: Apogee Books, 1990.

Charismatic Orthodox Church

110 Masters Dr., St. Augustine, FL 32086

The Charismatic Orthodox Church was founded in 1989 by Bishop Symeon John I. Born Mark D. Kersey into a family who were members of the Jehovah's Witnesses, as a young man the future bishop began a spiritual search that led him to become a Baptist pastor. From there he became influenced by Pentecostalism, especially its teachings on the baptism of the Holy Spirit and modern activity of the gifts of the spirit (as mentioned by the Apostle Paul in I Corinthians 12). He also was led to Eastern orthodoxy by his study of church history, but found that no church accepted both his belief in charismatic gifts and Orthodoxy.

After receiving consecration as a bishop in a lineage of apostolic succession, Bishop Symeon John I founded the Charismatic Orthodox Church in 1998. The new church attempts to continue the Eastern orthodox tradition while being thoroughly charismatic. It affirms the Nicene and Apostles' Creed. It is Eastern in theology and spiritual focus while allowing both Eastern and Western practice, including worship formats. It attempts to blend three streams of what some call the Convergence Movement, meaning that it is orthodox (faith), charismatic/liturgical (in style), and evangelical (practice). Women may serve as deacons (evangelists, prophets, and teachers), but not as priests or bishops.

The church has its primary presence on the Internet, and its bishops travel around the United States to oversee the needs of the scattered faithful. The Transformation Theological and Rabbinical Institute, the church's training school, operates primarily by correspondence through e-mail. Men may apply for ordination as a priest, bishop, monastic, or deacon.

The church is divided into four dioceses, including one in West Africa. Missions are supported in China, the Czech Republic, and Belgium. The cathedral congregation in St. Augustine is currently meeting in a church-owned building erected in 2005.

Membership: In 2008 the church reported six parishes, missions, and works in the United States, and one in Sierra Leone, West Africa.

Educational Facilities:

Theosis Christian College & Seminary, Fort Wayne, Indiana.

Holy Cross Academy (kindergarten through fifth grade), St. Augustine, Florida.

Sources:

Charismatic Orthodox Church. userpages.aug.com/~mdkersey/wizzg.html.

Church of Greece

c/o Metropolitan Demetrios, Holy Cross Church, 50 Goddard Ave., Brookline, MA 02140

Alternate Address: International Headquarters: c/o His Beatitude Serephim, Archbishop of Athens and All Greece, Ag Philotheis 21, GR-10556 Athens, Greece.

The Church of Greece refers to those ancient churches in the Orthodox tradition that used Greek as their dominant language and continued a Greek heritage. The church operated on a territorial basis from the old patriarchates at Alexandria, Jerusalem, Antioch, and Constantinople (now Istanbul). Over the centuries, each of these churches assumed jurisdiction in different territories and relinquished territories as new autonomous national churches and patriarchates were created. In the twentieth century, with the massive movements of people, the lines between jurisdictions blurred.

In 1850 the Church of Greece was granted autonomy, and the Ecumenical Patriarchate relinquished jurisdiction over most of the country. However, he retained jurisdiction over the Americas. Thus the Greek Orthodox Archdiocese of North and South America, to which most Americans who are Greek Orthodox belong, is affiliated with the Ecumenical Patriarchate. However, Greek immigrants in the twentieth century who wished to remain attached to the Church of Greece organized a diocese in America. It is at one in faith and belief with all of Orthodoxy, but administratively separate.

Membership: Not reported.

Sources:

Church of Greece. www.ecclesia.gr.

Orthodoxy. Regensburg: Ostkirchliches Institute, 1996.

Tomkinson, John L. *Between Heaven and Earth: The Greek Church*. Athens: Anagnosis, 2004.

Church of the True Orthodox Christians of Greece (Synod of Bishop Gregory)

c/o Church of the Holy Protection of the Holy Theotokos, 26-37 12th Street, Astoria, NY 11102-3723

Alternate Address: International headquarters: The Holy Synod of the Prelacy, 22 Constantinoupoleos St., Athens 11854, Greece.

The Church of the True Orthodox Christians of Greece considers itself the one, holy, Catholic and Apostolic Church of Christ, alone in preserving the unadulterated Apostolic Faith, continuing unbroken the Apostolic Succession, and preserving all the sacred traditions without adding to or subtracting from them. One such tradition is the church calendar, used by the church from the beginning of its history.

On March 10, 1924, supported by the revolutionary military government, the state church of Greece replaced the Old (Julian) calendar with the New papal (Gregorian) calendar. This change was implemented without the consensus of the whole church, and against prior consensus of the church reached in 1583, 1587, and 1593, at the Pan-Orthodox Synods, which forbade, condemned, and anathematized any change to the church calendar. However, the calendar change was mandated by a 1920 Encyclical of the Patriarchate of Constantinople, as a first step toward the ecumenical communion of all Christian denominations and the amalgamated unification of Orthodoxy and, in the church's view, all the heresies.

Because of this change, the new-calendar state church of Greece became schismatic and cut itself off from the Orthodox Church. The Greek Orthodox who respectfully abided by the historical church decisions regarding the calendar, and whose conscience militated against the schismatic innovation, refused all communion with the state church. In 1935 they gained episcopal oversight when three Church of Greece bishops accepted the Orthodox Confession of Faith. The three bishops quickly ordained four new bishops, among whom was Bishop Matthew of VresTheni. However, within a few months a significant difference of opinion arose among the Old Calendar bishops concerning the status of the state church. Metropolitan Chrysostomos released a statement saying that, by adopting the

Gregorian Calendar, the state church was in a position of potential schism and that, if no other heretical moves were made, it retained the grace of the Holy Spirit and valid sacraments.

Bishop Matthew steadfastly rejected Metropolitan Chrysostomos's position and cut the latter off from the main body of the Old Calendarists. He argued that the Church of Greece was in schism and that grace was no longer present in its sacraments. In 1948, two years before his death, Bishop Matthew consecrated four more bishops. The other Old Calendar factions did not recognize these consecrations, arguing that it takes more than one bishop to perform the ceremony. Nevertheless, Metropolitan Chrysostomos, who had three more bishops on his side, refused to ordain new bishops and left no successors when he died in 1955; this was seen as proof that he recognized the state church as orthodox. Moreover, two of the bishops aligned with him entered into full communion with the state church.

In 1971 Bishop Matthew's successors attempted to unite with the Russian Orthodox Church Outside of Russia, on the basis of an Orthodox confession of faith, but their communion broke down when the latter violated this confession. The issue of the position of the state church continued to divide the several Old Calendar factions, and even though various bishops of the other Old Calendar groups moved toward the Matthew position, the fragmentation was not overcome.

In 1995 the Church of the True Orthodox Christians of Greece defrocked Archbishop Andreas and two other bishops because of their views regarding the veneration of icons. The church is currently led by His Beatitude Archbishop Nicholas of Athens and All Greece, and in the United States by the Very Rev. Archpriest Anthony Gavalas, who serves as the Episcopal deputy.

Membership: In 2008 the church reported 10 parishes scattered across the United States.

Sources:

Church of the Genuine Orthodox Christians in the United States. orthodox-christianity.net/.

Chysostomos, Archimandrite, with Hieromonk Ambrosios, and Hieromonk Auxentios. *The Old Calendar Orthodox Church of Greece.* Etna, CA: Center for Traditionalist Orthodox Studies, 1986.

"Greek Old Calendarists in the U.S.A.: An Annotated Directory." *Orthodox Tradition* 2, no. 2 (1985): 49–61.

Community of St. James the Just

c/o Most Rev. Clyde Ramon Allee, PO Box 92497, Long Beach, CA 90809-2497

The Community of St. James the Just is an autonomous Orthodox jurisdiction formed in 1960 in Los Angeles by then Fr. Clyde Ramon Allee to serve the spiritual needs of those who could not attend a regularly scheduled Divine Liturgy because of incapacity, location, or vocation. In 1988, after Fr. Allee's consecration by Bp. Alan Bain (assisted by Bsps. John Lester Peace and Morris Saville), the community became fully self-governing. Mar Ramon traces his apostolic succession through the lineages of his consecrators from Antioch (Melkite Greek Catholic and Syrian Orthodox), Constantinople (Ukrainian and Russian Orthodox), and Rome (Utrecht Old Catholic).

Bishops, priests, and deacons now serve in Texas, California, Tennessee, Great Britain and the Philippines. Their ministries include hospitals, convalescent homes, and hospices; prisons, military, and veterans organizations; and also parish congregations. English-language translations of Eastern and Western Orthodox liturgies are used as the pastoral needs require. Dialogue with other Orthodox and Catholic jurisdictions seeking reciprocal communion is ongoing.

Membership: Not reported.

Sources:

Ward, Gary L. *Independent Bishops: An International Directory.* Detroit, MI: Apogee Books, 1990.

The Eastern Orthodox Catholic Church, North American Synod (EOCC)

c/o John Paul the Great Eastern Orthodox Catholic Monastery, PO Box 15302, San Antonio, TX 78212-8502

The Eastern Orthodox Catholic Church, North American Synod (EOCC) was originally founded in the 1980s as an Eastern Rite Division of the Independent Catholic Church (based in Nashua, New Hampshire), and incorporated separately in Texas in 1989 as the Independent Byzantine Catholic Church (IBCC). When the Independent Catholic Church disbanded, the IBCC affiliated with The Holy Eastern Orthodox Catholic and Apostolic Church of North America (THEOCACNA) based in Denver, Colorado, and took its present name. When the Denver jurisdiction also disbanded, the EOCC formed as a new jurisdiction, independent of any other group. Most Rev. George Michael Jachimczyk was named the first bishop.

The church is at one in faith and practice with the other Eastern Orthodox churches. The founders saw the EOCC as having a special ministry to open a path of spirituality to those disenfranchised from their native (ethnic) churches without losing the tradition embodied in the rites of the church. They tried to incorporate different practices from different churches (including the Roman Catholic) into the liturgical life. The church also adopted the Gregorian calendar (as opposed to the Julian calendar used by the more conservative Orthodox churches).

In practice, clergy are allowed to marry. The church has instituted a female deaconate. Candidates for the clergy are considered apart from their sexual orientation. However, the church has strict rules concerning anyone accused of molesting a minor. The church is led by its presiding bishop and administered by its board of directors with the presiding bishop serving as president. The church is based in John Paul the Great Eastern Orthodox Catholic Monastery in San Antonio, where the religious order it supports, the Community of Divine Charity, is based. There is also a mission in Miami, Oklahoma.

Membership: Not reported.

Sources:

The Eastern Orthodox Catholic Church, North American Synod. www.geocities.com/Athens/Thebes/5793/.

Ecumenical Orthodox Christian Church

Current address not obtained for this edition.

The Ecumenical Orthodox Christian Church was founded in 1991 with orders from the Russian and Albanian Orthodox Churches. Its leader is His Beatitude, the Most Blessed Sergius (Quilliams), who is assisted by Bps. Yuri Spaeth Jr. (Florida) and Ignatius Cash (Erie, Pennsylvania). The Ecumenical Orthodox Christian Church is an Old Calendar church adhering to the Julian Calendar in its liturgical practice. It is strictly Orthodox, accepts the teachings of the Seven Ecumenical Councils of the third through seventh centuries, and uses an English translation of the Divine Liturgy of St. John Chrysostom in its celebrations. As with most Orthodox, it rejects the Filioque addition to the Nicene Creed made by the Roman Catholic Church in the Middle Ages.

The church has separated itself from most independent Roman, Old Catholic, High Anglican, and Orthodox jurisdictions in which it finds unacceptable doctrine and practice. It does not allow Western Rites within the church, and priests must wear the proper vestments, including a hat indicative of their marital status. The church's Synodical Statutes offer detailed instruction on the proper dress of a priest and furnishing of a sanctuary in which the liturgy is to be celebrated. It rejects the doctrines of papal infallibility, papal supremacy, and purgatory. It also rejects the idea of using unleavened bread in the Eucharist. The church adheres to the idea of Mary as Theotokos (birth giver of God) and affirms Mary's holy (but not immaculate) conception, her assumption into heaven, and her role as one who can make supplication for the believer, but it rejects the title of Mary as co-redemtrix.

Membership: Not reported.

Educational Facilities:

Holy Wisdom Correspondence Seminary, Tuscaloosa, Alabama.

Ecumenical Orthodox Church

Current address not obtained for this edition.

The Ecumenical Orthodox Church is a small jurisdiction founded by Bp. Stanley J. Anjulis, who was consecrated in 1986 by Bp. Denise Mary Michele Garrison of the American Orthodox Church (now the Holy Eastern Orthodox Catholic and Apostolic Church in North America). He remained in Garrison's jurisdiction for only a year, although he was appointed vicar general of the church. In 1987 he left to found his independent work.

Membership: Not reported.

Sources:

Ward, Gary L. *Independent Bishops: An International Directory*. Detroit, MI: Apogee Books, 1990.

Estonian Orthodox Church

Current address not obtained for this edition.

In 1944 the Union of Soviet Socialist Republics gained political hegemony over Estonia. Primate of the Estonian Orthodox Church Archbishop Alexander fled to Sweden, where he organized the Estonian Orthodox Church in Exile. The church is under the Greek Orthodox Church's ecumenical patriarch in Constantinople and at one in faith and worship with the Greek Orthodox Church.

In 1949 the V. Rev. Sergius Samon established the first congregation of the Estonian Church in North America at Los Angeles. Large numbers of Estonians had come to the United States and Canada following World War II. Congregations were subsequently established in San Francisco, Chicago, and New York City. Canadian parishes were established in Vancouver, Toronto, and Montreal.

Estonians were surprised by the fall of the Soviet Union and the establishment of a free and independent Estonia in 1991. Subsequently the autonomous Estonian Orthodox Church was reestablished and in 1996 the Patriarchate of Constantinople formally acknowledged the autonomous church as being under its jurisdiction. Archbishop John of Finland was named to head the church until a episcopal election could be held. This action led the Moscow Patriarchate to sever relations with the Ecumenical Patriarchate (there still being an Orthodox church in Estonia under the Moscow Patriarchate). The events in Estonia signaled the end of the period of exile for Estonians abroad, though otherwise their lives continued much as in previous decades.

Membership: In 2008 there were several thousand Estonians of the Orthodox faith in North America.

Evangelical Apostolic Church of North America

Current address not obtained for this edition.

The Evangelical Apostolic Church of North America, formerly known as the Autocephalous Syro-Chaldean Church of North America, derives from the Ancient Holy Apostolic Catholic Church of the East through the Metropolitan of India, Mar Basilius, who in 1902 consecrated Mar Jacobus (Ulric Vernon Herford) bishop to bring the line to England. In 1952 Mar Georgius (Hugh George de Willmott Newman) was brought into the episcopal lineage by Mar Paulus (William Stanley McBean Knight), successor to Mar Jacobus.

Mar Georgius consecrated Charles D. Boltwood (1889–1985) bishop in 1952. In 1959 Bishop Boltwood was elevated to archbishop of the Free Protestant Episcopal Church in England. That same year, Archbishop Boltwood consecrated John Marion Stanley (b. 1923) bishop of Washington State. Bishop Stanley subsequently withdrew from the Free Protestant Episcopal Church and formed the Syro-Chaldean

Archdiocese of North America, taking the name of Mar Yokhannan. In 1969 Mar Yokhannan received into the archdiocese Mar Jacobus (James A. Gaines), who had received consecration in the Ukranian Orthodox succession.

The series of events that led to the formation of this body began at a meeting of the Holy Synod of the Syro-Chaldean Archdiocese, December 13–14, 1974. The synod designated Archpriest Bertram S. Schlossberg as bishop-elect with the task of organizing a Diocese of New York. By that action, Father Schlossberg came under the direct authority of Mar Jacobus, who had received authority from the Archdiocese for the Eastern half of the United States. Together, on April 16, 1976, they incorporated their new work as the Autocephalous Syro-Chaldean Archdiocese of the Eastern United States of America. On October 31, 1976, Mar Jacobus and Mar Yokhannan consecrated Father Uzziah bar Evyon (Schlossberg). In December, the diocese of the Northeast was erected with Mar Uzziah as bishop.

On April 2, 1977, Mar Yokhannan released Mar Jacobus and Mar Uzziah from "all canonical obedience" and then withdrew from the Syro-Chaldean Archdiocese to join the Patriarchal See Holy Orthodox Catholic Church, Eastern and Apostolic, located in California. Mar Jacobus and Mar Uzziah then recognized all the work within the Eastern Archdiocese and in October 1977 incorporated the Autocephalous Syro-Chaldean Church of North America. Mar Jacobus was archbishop and metropolitan. Mar Uzziah was bishop of the Northeast. Upon his retirement in 1978, Mar Jacobus elevated Mar Uzziah to be metropolitan of North America.

Since 1978 the church has grown slowly, concentrating on proclaiming the Gospel to the unsaved and ministering to the broken and wounded in the spirit of Isaiah 61. The Northeastern Diocese was erected as a mission diocese with the expectation that smaller local dioceses would be carved out of it. The intention was that the church would be organized along small diocesan lines, each diocese being a city or county. In the years since, the Diocese of Fairfield in Connecticut and the Diocese of Westchester in New York have been created. In addition to New York and New England, the church has work in Florida, a mission parish in the Philippines, and a mission in the Middle East.

In 1992 the Episcopal Synod agreed to change the name to the Evangelical Apostolic Church of North America. The church follows the Orthodox theology of the Church of the East. It affirms the Bible as the Word of God and both the Apostles' and Nicene Creeds. It keeps seven sacraments: baptism, confirmation or chrismation, holy communion, reconciliation, annointing for healing, holy matrimony, and holy orders. Its official liturgy is a simplified English-language version of the Liturgy of Mar Addai and Mar Mari, but it allows parishes freedom in their use of the liturgy. Several alternative forms are also authorized. The church is evangelical, believing that all persons need to repent and be converted to Christ; catholic, stressing the historical doctrines, sacraments, and practices of Christianity; and charismatic, emphasizing the ministry of the Holy Spirit. It is strongly opposed to the acceptance of homosexuality and other forms of sexual liberalism that it considers to be a sin. The church stands opposed to the practice of abortion. Women are ordained to the diaconate, but not to the priesthood.

Membership: Not reported. In 1991 the church reported 1,000 members. There were 16 clergy, including three active bishops in three dioceses with five parishes altogether.

Educational Facilities:

Christ the King Seminary and School of Discipleship, Rockville, Connecticut.

Sources:

Evangelical Apostolic Church of North America. www.eacna.org.

Finnish Orthodox Church

Current address not obtained for this edition.

The first Orthodox missionaries reached Finland in the tenth century and founded Valamo Monastery. While the church has remained small, it has persisted. Finland gained independence from Russia in 1919 and a wave of nationalism swept the church. In 1923 the church was given autonomy under the Greek Orthodox Church's ecumenical patriarch in Constantinople. The following year a non-Russian bishop was named primate. The church is Orthodox in faith and practice and uses the Finnish and Russian languages. The selection of archbishops must be submitted to Constantinople for approval.

In 1955 the first attempts to call together Orthodox Finns residing in the United States found most already attached to Russian congregations, but a small mission chapel was established in the Upper Peninsula of Michigan. It was not able to minister to the 1,300 Orthodox Finns and ceased to exist in 1958. In 1962 Fr. Denis Ericson implemented a new plan, which entailed traveling from his home base of Lansing, Michigan, to four worship stations, conducting services in English but preserving Finnish hymns and customs.

Membership: Not reported.

Sources:

Finnish Orthodox Church. www.ort.fi/en/index.php.

Purmonen, V., ed. *Orthodoxy in Finland: Past and Present.* 2nd ed. Kuopio, Finland: Orthodox Clergy Association, 1984.

Venkula-Vauraste, L. "800 Years of Orthodox Faith in Finland." *Look at Finland* 5 (1977): 42–47.

Free Orthodox Church International
Current address not obtained for this edition.

The Free Orthodox Church International, formerly known as the Greek Orthodox Eparchy of Lincoln, was founded in 1984 by the Most Rev. Dr. Melchizedek, the archbishop-metropolitan. Trained as a Roman Catholic, the future archbishop converted to Orthodoxy in 1983. He affiliated with the Holy Orthodox Synod for Diaspora and Hellas, a free Holy Synod which had been organized in Greece in 1950, and began to work within its jurisdiction. He moved to Lincoln, Nebraska, in 1986 and the following year became the pastor of St. Tikhon's Orthodox Church. He was consecrated in 1993. In 1994 the American work became autocephalous as a step in adjusting to the American situation.

As a free jurisdiction, the church is not affiliated with either the Church of Greece (or any other national jurisdiction) or any of the ancient patriarchates. Archbishop Melchizedek believes that since society has abandoned patriarchal structures, the church has no scriptural mandate to continue them. It is, however, at one with the Orthodox world in faith and practice and accepts the authority of the Holy Scriptures and the Seven Ecumenical Councils. It recognizes any jurisdiction that teaches and practices the Orthodox faith in nonjudgmental Christian love. Members of the church are encouraged to devote their lives to the service of Christ according to their own life experience.

The church has some opinions that differ from the main body of Orthodoxy. It accepts the authority of the intertestament books commonly called the Apocrypha. It denies the doctrine of original sin. The church allows bishops to marry. Baptism is by triple immersion in the name of the Father, the Son and the Holy Spirit. The church retains the power to pronounce the forgiveness of sin through the sacrament of forgiveness (confession, penance, and counseling). Life is sacramental but focused in holy baptism, crismation, absolution of sins, the Eucharist, holy anointing of the sick, priesthood, and matrimony.

Various rites have been approved for workshop in the several parishes including the Sarum Rite, the Tridentine Roman Rite, the Liturgy of St. Chrysostomos, the Qurbana, and the Gallican Rite. Worship in the vernacular is recommended but Greek and Latin allowed. Among the structures sponsored by the church is the noncommunal Oblate Order of the Blessed Virgin Theotokos, whose members offer themselves to the life of the Blessed Virgin in the spirit of the Magnificat (Luke 1:46–55). When received, the new member is given a blue robe and matching scapular which is worn on special occasions, though on a day-to-day basis members do not dress in special clothing. They are also assigned an individual obedience, in most cases a specific daily prayer to follow.

The church has formal communion with the Diocese of Emmaus, Christ Catholic Church International, the Free Orthodox Catholic Church of Germany, and the Holy Eastern Orthodox Catholic and Apostolic Church in North America, and fraternal relations with the Federation of St. Thomas Christian Churches, the Holy Catholic Apostolic Orthodox Church, and the Shekinah Glory Mar Thoma Orthodox Church.

Membership: Not reported.

Educational Facilities:

St. Elias School of Orthodox Theology, Lincoln, Nebraska.

Periodicals: *The Pilgrim.*

Greek Orthodox Archdiocese of America
8-10 E 79th St., New York, NY 10021

As early as 1767 Greek Orthodox Christians settled in New Smyrna, Florida. Greek merchants in New Orleans established Holy Trinity, the first Greek Orthodox Church in America, in 1864. Other parishes sprang up across the country. No attempt was made to organize the parishes until 1918 when the Greek Orthodox Archdiocese of North and South America, as it was initially named, was organized. Archbishop Alexandros headed the archdiocese from 1922. He began the extensive work of bringing the many Greek parishes under his jurisdiction. The greatest progress in this direction was made by his successor, Metropolitan Athenagoras Spirou (1886–1972), who became the ecumenical patriarch in 1948.

The Greek Orthodox Archdiocese has over the years become the largest in the United States. It has ten districts, each headed by a bishop. Archbishop Iakovos (1911–2005), as chairman of the Standing Conference of Canonical Orthodox Bishops and exarch for the ecumenical patriarch, was a recognized spokesman of the Greek Orthodox community to the outside world for much of the latter half of the twentieth century.

Currents of change that have flowed through the Orthodox world made Archbishop Iakovos a subject of intense controversy as he emerged as a founding father of the modern ecumenical movement. Much of the criticism was directed against the growing openness of Patriarch Athenagoras toward Rome and the World Council of Churches, while Archbishop Iakovos was criticized for approving this openness and initiating contact on his own in the United States with various Protestant and Catholic bodies. Ultratraditionalists see such ecumenical activity as compromising Orthodox faith. Mt. Athos, the most famous Orthodox monastery, has become a center of traditionalism and at times has been critical of Archbishop Iakovos and of changes in the contemporary church, which has always been done under the aegis of the mother church and headquarters of the Ecumenical Patriarchate in Istanbul, Turkey.

Archbishop Iakovos retired in 1996 (amid rumors that it had been forced). He was succeeded by Archbishop Spyridon (b. 1944), whose short three-year tenure was filled with controversy. He resigned in 1999 and was succeeded by Archbishop Demetrios (b. 1928).

Liturgy being the most important aspect of Orthodox church life, changes affecting liturgy have been met with extreme resistance when not in conformity to early church tradition and the ecclesiology of the Eastern Orthodox Church. In 1922 the Greek Orthodox Archdiocese of North and South America, following the mandate of the Ecumenical patriarchate, accepted the Gregorian calendar. Some other patriarchates continue to use the Julian calendar. For the canonical Orthodox Churches, the calendar controversy has been a nonissue.

Membership: In 2004 the archdiocese reported 563 churches, with 834 clergy serving 1.5 million members.

Educational Facilities:

Holy Cross School of Theology and Hellenic College, Brookline, Massachusetts.

Periodicals: *Orthodox Observer.*

Sources:

Greek Orthodox Archdiocese of America. www.goarch.org.

Constantelos, Demetrios J. *The Greek Orthodox Church*. New York: Seabury Press, 1967.

———. *An Old Faith for Modern Man*. New York: Greek Orthodox Archdiocese, 1964.

The Divine Liturgy of St. John Chrysostom. Brookline, MA: Greek Orthodox Theological Institute, Press, 1950.

Geanakoplos, D. *A Short History of the Ecumenical Patriarchate of Constantinople (330–1990): "First Among Equals" in the Eastern Orthodox Church*. Brookline, MA: Holy Cross Orthodox Press, 1990.

Litsas, Fotios K. *A Companion to the Greek Orthodox Church*. New York: Department of Communication, Greek Orthodox Archdiocese of North and South America, 1984.

Poulos, George. *A Breath of God*. Brookline, MA: Holy Cross Orthodox Press, 1984.

Greek Orthodox Church of America
Current address not obtained for this edition.

The Greek Orthodox Church of America (not to be confused with the other church of the same name) was established in the mid-twentieth century as the outpost of the Eastern Orthodox Patriarchate of Alexandria (Egypt). In the first century C.E., Christianity spread among the Greek-speaking residents of Egypt and from them to the Coptic-speaking peoples. In the fifth century C.E., the Patriarch of Alexandria became a monophysite, a position denounced by the Council at Ephesus in 451, and a new Patriarch, Proterios, was installed in his place. The mass of Coptic-speaking peoples followed the deposed patriarch, but a small minority stayed with the Patriarch of Alexandria, whose jurisdiction extended across North Africa. It was substantially reduced by the Muslim conquest of the territory but has survived to the present. The American exarchate was organized among Greek-speaking migrants to North America from North Africa.

In 1964 the exarchate received a young priest into its jurisdiction by the name of Makrogambrakis (1919–2005). He had migrated to America in the previous year and served under Bishop Petros of the Hellenic Orthodox Church. In 1983 Makrogambrakis was consecrated as Bishop Dionysios and named Exarchate of the Greek Orthodox Church of America. Several years later, the exarchate was granted autonomy, and as Archbishop Dionysios he became primate of the new church.

Membership: Not reported.

Sources:

Clarke, Boden. *Lords Temporal and Lords Spiritual*. San Bernardino, CA: Borgo Press, 1985.

Greek Orthodox Diocese of New York
Current address not obtained for this edition.

The Greek Orthodox Diocese of New York was formed in 1964 at Philadelphia, Pennsylvania, by priests and laity formerly under the jurisdiction of Archbishop Iakovos (1911–2005) of the Greek Orthodox Archdiocese of North and South America, to whose administration they objected. As the only Orthodox body in the West that allows the laity the sole right to elect bishops and to keep the monies of the church under the control of the members they were able to select new leaders. Oxford-educated Bishop Photios was elected archbishop, and Theocletos of Salimis, auxiliary bishop. Photios has gathered the largest group of Greek Orthodox followers not under Archbishop Iakovos. The installation of the archbishop took place in St. George's Greek Orthodox Church in Memphis, Tennessee, where Archbishop Photios resided for several years.

In 1965 jurisdiction was extended to Australia. Archbishop Photios was in communion with the late Bishop Dionisije of the Serbian Orthodox Free Diocese of the United States and Canada and Bishop Alexis of Adelaide, Australia, of the Byelorussian Autocephalic Church.

Membership: Not reported.

Sources:

Spasovic, Stanimir. *The History of the Serbian Orthodox Church in America and Canada, 1941–1991*. Trans. Nedeljko Lunich. Belgrade, Yugoslavia: Printing House of the Serbian Patriarchate, 1998.

Greek Orthodox Missionary Archdiocese of Vasiloupolis
44-02 48th Ave., Sunnyside/Woodside, NY 11377

The Greek Orthodox Missionary Archdiocese of Vasiloupolis was founded in 1970 when Archimandrite Pangratios Vrionis was elected and consecrated by Romanian Bp. Theofil Ionescu, Russian Patriarch Dositheus Ivanchenko, and Albanian Apb. Christoforus Rado to serve among the Greek-Americans who had migrated to Long Island from Albania, Romania, and parts of Russia. The name Vasiloupolis ("royal city") refers to Queens, New York, where Metropolitan Pangratios was consecrated. The church grew out of a refugee program started by the late Fr. Alexander Tzulevitch, pastor of St. Nicolas Russian Orthodox Church in New York City. At a "Synod of the Diaspora," Archimandrite Pangratios was chosen to be the archbishop over those people who had declared their desire for a leader who was traditionalist with a multicultural background, an American citizen, and missionary-minded. In addition, he would have to be approved by the exiled royal families of Greece and Romania.

Through the 1970s, Metropolitan Pangratios moved to build the archdiocese, which had grown primarily through the addition of conservative ethnic parishes. He is assisted by five titular bishops: Michael Pangratios (Rouse) of New Carthage, Kyrill Esposito of Taormina, Elias Milazzo of Apollonia, George Dimitre Pias of Palation and Metropolitan, and Leontios de Noronhos of Brazil and Argentina. Together with Metropolitan Pangratios they constitute the Hierarchical Consistory.

In 1999 the archdiocese was accepted fully as a sister church by the Old Calendar and Traditionalist Church of Greece, under the jurisdiction of Abp. Maximos Vallianatos (Auxentios).

The archdiocese is Orthodox in faith and takes a traditionalist stance, although it does accept and maintain, in a canonical Orthodox manner, Western Rite Orthodox parishes. It is an Old Calendarist group, meaning its liturgical life follows the Julian rather than the Gregorian calendar. It opposes what it considers to be the modernist trends and attempts at liturgical reform represented in the churches that make up the Standing Conference of Orthodox Bishops in America.

Membership: In 2008 the archdiocese reported 42 parishes and 8 monasteries.

Remarks: One of Metropolitan Pangratios's consecrators was Abp. Christoforus Rado, who around 1958 had founded the Independent Albanian Orthodox Church of St. Paul. Archbishop Christoforus died in 1974. While some of his parishes joined the Orthodox Church of America, some came under Pangratios, who consecrated Stavros Skembi to lead them. Pangratios also inherited the following of Greek-Romanian Bishop Theofil. In 1981 Pangratios consecrated Stephen Degiovanni to minister to a group of Italo-Greek immigrants located on Long Island, New York, and New Jersey.

Sources:

Blighton, Paul. *Memoirs of a Mystic*. San Francisco: Holy Order of MANS, 1974.

Book of the Master Jesus. 3 vols. San Francisco: Holy Order of MANS, 1974.

The Golden Force. San Francisco: Holy Order of MANS, 1967.

Lucas, Philip Charles. *The Odyssey of a New Religion: The Holy Order of MANS from New Age to Orthodoxy*. Bloomington, IN: Indiana University Press, 1995.

Spasovic, Stanimir. *The History of the Serbian Orthodox Church in America and Canada, 1941–1991*. Trans. Nedeljko Lunich. Belgrade, Yugoslavia: Printing House of the Serbian Patriarchate, 1998.

Hellenic Orthodox Traditionalist Church of America: Holy Diocese of Astoria

St. Markella of Chios, 22-68 26th St., Astoria, NY 11105

At the time the state Church of Greece adopted the Gregorian calendar in place of the Old (Julian) Calendar it had followed for centuries, pockets of opposition began to arise immediately. Continued adherence to the Old Calendar also emerged among Greek Orthodox believers in the United States. In 1952 Bishop Petros, then a monk from Mt. Athos, arrived in the United States from Greece as the representative of the Old Calendarists to pull together the scattered American believers. In 1962 he was consecrated as bishop of Astoria (New York), where he had established his headquarters, and Exarch of the American work. He was consecrated by two bishops of the Russian Orthodox Church Outside of Russia.

Throughout the years of its existence, the Old Calendar Movement had been split by an ongoing controversy over the presence of grace in the state Church of Greece, given its abandonment of the traditional liturgical calendar. The moderate faction held to the position that grace remained in the state church. In 1974, however, Archbishop Auxentios, the head of the synod of the moderates, issued a statement (seemingly in an attempt to placate the more extreme group, which denied the presence of grace in the state church) in which he accepted the essence of the extreme position.

As a result of Archbishop Auxentios's action, Petros left his jurisdiction and reorganized his work independently as the Hellenic Orthodox Church in America. He followed the traditional belief and practice of Orthodoxy. By 1967 he had five churches and some 9,000 members. St. Sincletike Convent is located in Farmingdale, New York. He started a newsletter, *The Voice of Orthodoxy*, and a radio show of the same name. Membership in the jurisdiction is centered among Greek Americans on Long Island.

Membership: In 1985 there were parishes in Astoria, Bethpage, and Hensonville, New York.

Periodicals: *The Voice of Orthodoxy*.

Sources:

Chrysostomos, Archimandrite, with Hieromonk Ambrosios, and Hieromonk Auxentios. *The Old Calendar Orthodox Church of Greece*. Etna, CA: Center for Traditionalist Orthodox Studies, 1986.

"Greek Old Calendarists in the U.S.A.: An Annotated Directory." *Orthodox Tradition* 2, no. 2 (1985): 49–61.

Holy Eastern Orthodox Catholic and Apostolic Church in North America

733 Tick Rd., Mountain View, AZ 72560

The Holy Eastern Orthodox Catholic and Apostolic Church in North America was canonically established on February 2, 1927, with the approval of the Russian Patriarch. Archbishop Aftimios Ofiesh (1889–1966) was appointed first archbishop of this church and headed it until his death in 1966. The church was incorporated in February 1, 1928, and continues as the same church and same corporation. It is a Western Rite jurisdiction but includes some Eastern Rite clergy and liturgies.

Prior to the death of Archbishop Aftimios the church had only one bishop after the deaths of Dr. Joseph Zuk (d. 1934) and Bishop Sophronios Bishara (1888–1934), leaving only Archbishop Aftimios. Upon the death of Aftimios the church continued "in locum tenens" until its clergy were able to obtain consecration in acceptable lines. Metropolitan Victor Prentice was corporate vice president under locum tenens prior to his election in 1997 as Metropolitan President of the Church.

The church reports that its name, over the years, has been used by others in the independent movement who have claimed to be this church or related to it, as a "status symbol" because of the 1927 charter. However, because the charter was issued to Archbishop Aftimios, who subsequently incorporated the church, and the church has continued without cessation, the church asserts that these claims are untrue and misleading.

Membership: In 2002 the church reported a membership of 4,274.

Sources:

The American Orthodox Patriarchate: Holy Eastern Orthodox Catholic and Apostolic Church in North America. www.geocities.com/theocacna/index.html.

Italo-Greek Orthodox Archdiocese of the Americas and Canada

c/o Cathedral of the Theotokos of Great Grace, South Street at Howard Avenue, Utica, NY 13201

Orthodoxy established itself in southern Italy and Sicily in the Greek communities that had established themselves in ancient times. Most of these Greek churches came under the authority of the Roman Catholic Church after the Synod at Bari in 1097. Only two bishops refused to submit, and they led their Orthodox followers into what became an increasingly underground church. The church survived in spite of severe measures to convert its members to Catholicism. Cut off from mainline Orthodoxy, however, it developed several peculiarities, including a married bishopric. The church also has a mobile episcopacy, in part due to the persecution it felt, and began to designate its bishops as being "in" a See location rather than "of" a See City. The Church became fully autonomous in 1428. The first Italian Orthodox priests came to America in 1904 and established parishes in Brooklyn, New York; Newark, New Jersey; and Philadelphia. Progress was slow until 1979, when Emilio Rinauldi and Luciano Gaudio were elected bishop in Newark and Las Vegas respectively. They were consecrated by a deputation of bishops from Italy headed by the late Primate Constantino, Bishop in Catania.

In the United States, Sicilian immigrants organized the first community in 1902 in Philadelphia, Pennsylvania. The first Italian Orthodox priests came to America in 1904 and led in the funding of additional parishes in Brooklyn, New York, and Newark, New Jersey. Progress was slow until 1979, when Emilio Rinauldi and Luciano Gaudio were elected bishop in Newark and Las Vegas respectively. They were consecrated by a deputation of bishops from Italy headed by the late Primate Constantino, Bishop in Catania. They worked through the 1980s but then the church entered another period in which they existed for two decades without Episcopal leadership. Recently a bishop, Metropolitan Stephen, has been appointed. He is assisted by four priests and two deacons.

Membership: Not reported.

Holy Eastern Orthodox Church of the United States

Current address not obtained for this edition.

The Holy Eastern Orthodox Church of the United States (Orthodox Catholic Archdiocese of Philadelphia, Metropolitan See) dates itself to 1927 and the establishment of the American Orthodox Church under Bp. Aftimios Ofiesh (1889–1966), as authorized by the American bishops of the Russian Orthodox Church. In 1971 Abp. Trevor Wyatt Moore and the priests under his jurisdiction incorporated the Orthodox Catholic Archdiocese of Philadelphia. Moore had been consecrated in the Ofiesh lineage, on July 11, 1971, by Abps. Peter A. Zhurawetsky (1901–1994) and Uladyslau Ryzy-Ryski (1925–1978). A month later Ryzy-Ryski, head of the American World Patriarchs, in his plan to establish a hierarchy of patriarchs representing the various ethnic groups, elevated Moore to archbishop with jurisdiction for the English-speaking world. In 1972 he designated Moore a metropolitan.

From the very beginning the archdiocese was incorporated independently as a self-protective measure against any irregularities, heterodoxy, or heresy that might develop within the American World Patriarchs. Within a few years, Metropolitan Trevor saw a significant and unacceptable drift within the American World Patriarchs as evidenced by its following a pan-ecumenism, developing anti-Russian attitudes, espousing the use of a self-created Western liturgy, and most important, failing to perpetuate the necessary conditions set forth by the synod of Russian bishops in 1927 for the American Orthodox Church. Metropolitan Trevor had rigorously followed those conditions in theology, liturgy, and otherwise.

As a result of the irregularities, the archdiocese severed all connections with the American World Patriarchs in 1976, when the official name became the Holy Eastern Orthodox Church of the United States, an abridgement of the original name given to Ofiesh's jurisdiction, the Holy Eastern Orthodox Catholic and Apostolic Church in North America.

Metropolitan Trevor asserted that his jurisdiction was the only remnant of the original jurisdiction headed by Archbishop Ofiesh in that it was the only one that adhered to all of the conditions set forth in the original charter and constitution. It has remained truly Orthodox in all aspects of its life and, though independent, has acknowledged the primacy of the Russian jurisdiction, preserving a filial relationship to the Orthodox Church of Russia by the Patriarchal Authority of Moscow and All Russia. (Note: In Orthodox practice, the first Orthodox Church to initiate work in a new country is generally acknowledged to have canonical primacy for that country. In the case of the United States, the Russian Orthodox Church was present for a century prior to any other Orthodox jurisdiction's establishment of a parish.)

The church is strictly Eastern Orthodox in faith and practice and adheres to the Byzantine rite. It holds to the Nicene Creed and follows its Eastern text.

The church is episcopal in polity. It is organized into the Metropolitan See of Philadelphia, the Orthodox-Greek Catholic Missionary Eparchy of Trenton and All New Jersey, and the Orthodox-Greek Catholic Diocese of Providence and All New England. Congregations can be found in Pennsylvania, New Jersey, Rhode Island, Massachusetts, Virginia, Florida, Illinois, and Nebraska. There is a mission church in Puerto Rico.

The church has been most attuned to the issues that have dominated the established churches in the United States, particularly in matters of social concern. It has spoken out forcefully on peace and nonviolence. It operates a social service center in Philadelphia, Pennsylvania, and through its affiliated Society of the Helpers of Saint Herman of Alaska, a mental health ministry in Florida. It has been active in civil rights and interracial and intercultural efforts, particularly in Spanish-speaking communities. Metropolitan Trevor was one of only a few independent Orthodox leaders to gain some recognition from the larger Christian community, through his authorship of several books and service as an editor-at-large for the *Christian Century* magazine.

Membership: Not reported.

Periodicals: *Tserkobnost.*

Holy Orthodox Catholic Church

c/o Paul Gilbert Russell, 5831 Tremont, Dallas, TX 75214

Formed in 1965 as the American Orthodox Church, this body changed its name in 1972 to the Holy Orthodox Catholic Church. It was headed by Bishop Paul G. Russell, who was consecrated on August 22, 1976, by Bishops David Baxter and William Henry. The church accepts the idea of female priests and the ordination of homosexuals to Holy Orders, but in all other respects it holds to the Orthodox-Catholic faith.

Membership: Not reported.

Holy Orthodox Church, American Jurisdiction

c/o St. Basil's Cathedral, 355 Tusculum Rd., Nashville, TN 37211-6101

HISTORY. The Holy Orthodox Church, American Jurisdiction, though restructured in 1974, was originally established as the American Orthodox Church by the Russian Orthodox Archdiocese of Brooklyn in 1932 under the episcopacy of Archbishop Aftimios Ofiesh (1889–1966) for the communicants of Western Rite Orthodoxy. Aftimios's mission, assigned him by the Moscow Patriarchate, was to unite the various ethnic-Orthodox jurisdictions in America into a single American jurisdiction. The unification effort failed because of both foreign and domestic influences, and the Russian Church directed Aftimios to abandon the mission, dis-

band the diocese of Brooklyn, and turn over its cathedral and assets to the Syrian Orthodox Church.

Aftimios had established the orthodox Western (Gregorian) Rite in America in January 1932 and ordained the former Episcopal Church priest William Albert Nichols (1867–1947) to the Orthodox priesthood. With the understanding that he would follow the Gregorian rite, Aftimios assigned him as pastor of the very first canonical Orthodox Western Rite parish in America, located in New York City.

As directed, Aftimios began closing down the affairs of the Brooklyn Archdiocese. Among his last actions before turning over the archdiocese to the Syrian Orthodox Church, Aftimios, assisted by Bishops Joseph Zuk (d. 1934) and Sophronios Bishara (1888–1934), consecrated Nichols to the episcopacy on September 30, 1932. They named him archbishop of the newly established Western Rite archdiocese under the identity of the American Orthodox church. Nichols took the name Ignatius as his episcopal name.

The Society of Clerks Secular of St. Basil, commonly known as the Basilian Fathers, was founded by Aftimios and Nichols as the missionary arm of the newly formed Western Rite apostolate, with Nichols as the superior general. Eventually, as Nichols's health failed, Fr. Tyler Turner (1905–1971), S.S.B., was elected superior-general of the Order and was subsequently consecrated in 1939. Taking the religious name Alexander, he succeeded Ignatius as head of the Western Rite archdiocese of the American Orthodox Church.

In 1960, of the 19 then active members of the Order of Basilian Fathers, four were incardinated as priests in the Antiochian Orthodox Christian Archdiocese of North America, then led by Metropolitan Archbishop Anthony Bashir (1898–1966). Two years previously, the Syrian Orthodox Patriarch of Antioch had authorized Bashir to establish a Vicariate for the Western Rite communicants.

The Basilian Order, as such, did not become part of the Syrian Vicariate. It remained an autonomous entity unto itself committed to the Western Rite apostolate. Nearly two years after Alexander's death, Fr. William Francis Forbes, S.S.B., was elected a superior general of the Order in 1973. In the summer of 1974, following a tenure of 15 years with the Syrian jurisdiction, Father Forbes withdrew from the Vicariate to give full time to the Western Rite apostolate of the Basilians. On October 20, 1974, two bishops within the Aftimios-Ignatius line of succession, Abp. Thomas Jude Baulmer and Bp. John Chrysostom Martin, consecrated Forbes to the episcopacy, thus restoring the original line of apostolic succession to the Basilians and the American Orthodox Church. Shortly thereafter, Bishop Forbes restructured both the Basilian Order and the American Orthodox Church. He sold the Basilian Motherhouse in New York and moved the entire operation of the Order and the church to Antioch, a suburb of Nashville, Tennessee, where the Cathedral of St. Basil is located.

BELIEFS. The church is thoroughly Orthodox in faith and sacramental practice. It accepts the original Nicene Creed and the doctrinal affirmation of the seven Ecumenical councils. The majority of the parishes are Western Rite. Though the Eastern Rite is allowed, few choose to follow it.

ORGANIZATION. The ecclesiastical order of the church is vested in its Synod of Bishops, which has five members. The Synod has authority over its Metropolitan-Archdiocese of Nashville, the Archdiocese of Boston (Bridgewater) Massachusetts, and the Dioceses of Philadelphia, Louisiana (New Orleans), and Montreal-Quebec.

Membership: Not reported.

Educational Facilities:

St. Basil's Seminary, a tutorial structure for preparing priests.

Periodicals: *The Communicator.* • *The Reconciler.* c/o Emmaus House, 27 N Walker, Taunton, MA 02780.

Sources:

St. Basil's Cathedral—Holy Orthodox Church, American Jurisdiction. www.stbasilscathedral.org/home.cfm/sid/146.

Samuchin, Michael. *A Brief History of the Holy Orthodox Church (American Jurisdiction)*. Antioch, TN: Society of Clerks Secular of St. Basil, 1992.

Holy Orthodox Church in America

PO Box 192-B, Preston Hollow, NY 12469

The Orthodox Church in America grew out of the early interest in Christian Mysticism of Rosicrucian George Winslow Plummer (1876–1944). Plummer had been one of the founders of the Societas Rosicruciana in America (SRIA) in 1907 and became its leader when Sylvester Gould died two years later. In the 1920s Plummer's particular interest in mysticism led him to found the Seminary of Biblical Research, through which he issued lessons on Christian mysticism. About this same time he founded the Anglican Universal Church and sought consecration from a Puerto Rican bishop, Manuel Ferrando.

In 1934 Plummer was reconsecrated by Bishop William Albert Nichols (1867–1947) of the American Orthodox Church, originally founded by Lebanese Orthodox bishop Aftimios Ofiesh (1889–1966), and took the religious name Mar Georgius. Following his consecration, he reconsecrated three of his bishops of the Anglican Universal Church and incorporated as the Holy Orthodox Church in America. The Holy Orthodox Church in America (Eastern Catholic and Apostolic) accepted through Nichols the mandate of Bishop Ofiesh to develop an American Eastern Orthodoxy.

The Holy Orthodox Church, while endorsing the canons of the Seven Ecumenical Councils, has remained intimately connected to the Rosicrucian organization that Plummer headed. The original episcopal leadership was drawn from the SRIA, and the original parishes were all located in cities with an SRIA group. The liturgy of the church is that of St. John Chrysostom; however, the church places special emphasis on spiritual healing and holds weekly special services for that purpose.

Plummer died in 1944 and was succeeded by Abp. Theodotus Stanislaus DeWitow (formerly Witowski; d. 1969). When Dewitow died, the church was without a bishop from 1969 to 1981. The work was carried on by three deaconesses, two of whom, Mrs. G. E. S. DeWitow (aka Mother Serena), widow of the last archbishop, and Lucia Grosch were consecrated in 1981 by Abp. Herman Adrian Spruit (1911–1994) of the Church of Antioch. Mother Serena died in 1989. She was succeeded by Abp. Matriarch Lucia Grosch, who in 2008 was the presiding bishop.

Membership: In 2008 the church reported that it had two churches, one chapel, and a membership of approximately 100.

Periodicals: *Mercury*.

Holy Orthodox Church in North America

c/o The Holy Orthodox Metropolis of Boston, 1476 Centre St., Roslindale, MA 02131-1417

The Holy Orthodox Church in North America is the American branch of the Church of the True Orthodox Christians of Greece (the Synod of Archbishop Maximos). The church was established as a result of the problem that emerged in the State Church of Greece in 1924 when the Gregorian Calendar replaced the older Julian Calendar and ecumenical events between the state church and non-Orthodox bodies began to occur. Rejecting these developments, the old calendar faithful saw a need to organize separately. In 1963 Archbishop Auxentios (1912–1994) became their leader. The old calendar movement had also found some response in America, and parishes began to emerge there in the 1930s. The State Church of Greece, in the meantime, declared the sacraments of the Old Calendarists invalid and instituted a persecution by which the faithful were killed and their churches destroyed or confiscated.

In 1974 Archbishop Auxentios issued an encyclical in which he declared that the sacraments of the State Church of Greece were devoid of grace, hence invalid. This encyclical earned him the animosity of the State Church; in the Western Hemisphere, his American Exarchate, under the leadership of Bishop Petros, left him. In 1987 Archbishop Auxentios's jurisdiction in America was again augmented

by the addition of a number of parishes that had withdrawn from the Russian Orthodox Church Outside of Russia.

Since its formation following the Russian Revolution, the Russian Orthodox Church Outside of Russia had become the bastion of conservative traditionalist eastern orthodoxy. It stood against the subversion of the Russian Church under the hostile antireligious regime and opposed changes in the Orthodox community that had entered into the post–World War II spirit of dialogue and ecumenical accommodation with both Protestants and Roman Catholics. In the United States, priests and believers from a variety of ethnic backgrounds were drawn to this church. Among the issues disturbing twentieth-century Orthodoxy were the increasing ecumenical activities and statements and joint prayers that were contrary to centuries-old Orthodox Church traditions. Many saw the involvement in ecumenism as a serious compromise of the Orthodox faith, and the Russian church opposed these developments.

In 1986 clergy within the Russian Church, some of whom were Greek-Americans, leveled a series of charges concerning the Russian Church's change of course and its failure to discipline clergy who had participated in extracanonical ecumenical events. This protest was brought to a head by encyclicals, published by the Russian bishops, which confirmed the charges made by these clergy. As a result, in December 1986 a group of 17 congregations, 25 clergy, and 2 monasteries left the Russian Church and placed themselves under Bishops Akakios and Gabriel, two Greek Old Calendar bishops. That arrangement did not work out administratively, and in the fall of 1987 the group placed itself under Archbishop Auxentios.

In June 1988 Auxentios made his first visit to the United States to meet with his new following. At the church's Holy Synod in July 1988, Hieromonk Ephrem of Transfiguration Monastery was elected to the Episcopate; he was consecrated on August 17. In 1991 the Diocese of Toronto was created and Bishop Markarios (consecrated in Greece in January 1991) was placed in charge. Following the death of Archbishop Auxentios in 1994, Archbishop Maximos was selected to succeed him.

Membership: In 2008 the church reported 62 congregations, 100 clergy, and 9 monastic establishments in the United States and Canada with over 6,000 members. The church is the largest of the Greek Old Calendar Orthodox churches. Affiliated branches are found in Switzerland, Russia, Ukraine, Australia, Italy, and France.

Periodicals: *Orthodox Christian Witness* • *Orthodox Ligh* • *The True Vine* • *The Struggler*

Sources:

Sister Churches: Five Hundred Years after Florence. Boston: Holy Orthodox Church in North America, 1994.

Holy United Orthodox Catholic and Apostolic Church

PO Box 703, Browns Mills, NJ 08015

The Holy United Orthodox Catholic and Apostolic Church traces its history to 901 C.E. and the founding of the Holy Eastern Orthodox Catholic and Apostolic Church, Order of Saint Gregory of Nyssa by Father Jakot of Worms and Father Hugo of Cologne. The occasion for the founding of this Orthodox church in what was nominally Roman Catholic territory was the recovery of the lost writings of Gregory of Nyssa (a fourth-century bishop). In 1065, eleven years after the Great Schism between the Orthodox and Roman Catholic churches, envoys from Constantinople arrived in Cologne and consecrated Bishop Johann as the German Orthodox bishop. The lineage of Bishop Johann was passed on through the centuries.

The relatively small church suffered greatly through the Reformation era (sixteenth century) but survived to the present. The German Orthodox bishops participated in several conferences following the establishment of the Old Catholic Church in the 1870s. In 1873 Abp. Wilhelm Von Strom (1840–1928) was the co-consecrator of German Old Catholic bishop Joseph Hubert Reinkens (1821–1896). He was succeeded by Abps. Otto Stefan Von Strom and Hansel Johann Von Strom;

the latter consecrated James Stroms as archbishop and enthroned him as Patriarch of the Order of Saint Gregory of Nyssa in 1988. Following Archbishop Hansel's death in 1996, Archbishop Paul II (James Stroms) moved the headquarters to the United States and the following year brought Saint Gregory Seminary from Cologne to Saint Paul Cathedral in Hyder, Alaska. In 1997 he was formally enthroned as Archbishop of the Holy United Orthodox Catholic and Apostolic Church of America (German-American Rite).

The church is Orthodox in faith and practice. The church operates through seven regional divisions, four archdioceses, and three dioceses. The church has been active ecumenically. In 1995 Archbishop Paul II was consecrated into the Order of Saint Gregory of the West African Rite by Patriarch Behazin Optat of Lagos, Nigeria. In 1996 he brought the church into the Holy Patriarchate of the Americas. Archbishop Paul II also served as the commander in chief of the United Chaplains Service and Association.

Membership: In 2008 the church reported over 70,000 members in 38 congregations worldwide (including Germany, Poland, and Nigeria), and 20,000 members in five congregations served by 14 priests in the United States. There were over 200 members in two congregations in Canada.

Educational Facilities:

Saint Gregory Seminary, Hyder, Alaska.

Periodicals: *Orthodox Newsletter*.

Sources:

Barrett, David B. *World Christian Encyclopedia*. New York: Oxford University Press, 1982.

Independent Greek Orthodox Church of the United States

1814 Slate NW, Albuquerque, NM 87104-1320

The Independent Greek Orthodox Church of the United States is a small Eastern Orthodox jurisdiction under the leadership of Rt. Rev. Elias, the bishop of San Francisco. As a group, the church members see themselves as being at odds with the mainline Orthodox institutions and as moving into the modern world. At the same time, the church believes that Eastern Orthodoxy as the true way, unclouded by what it considers to be heresies promulgated by western Christianity. The church adheres to the eternal truths put forth by the ancient church concerning the nature of God, the incarnation of His Son, the position of the Holy Spirit, the believers' relationship to the Theotokos (Mary, the God Bearer), and her relationship to her Son. These truths are set forth in the Nicene Creed and the affirmations of the Seven Ecumenical Councils. Many of the later canons promulgated by the Orthodox Church were of a more temporal nature, more suited to medieval rural life than to modern urban existence. They do not have the significance of the ancient canon that defined the faith.

The church supports a small monastic community, Protection of the Holy Theotokos Skete in New Mexico.

Membership: In 2008 the diocese reported two parishes and a monastic community: Sts. Theodore Tiro and Theodore Stratilates Parish in San Francisco; St. Elijah the Prophet Parish in Los Angeles; and the Protection of the Holy Theotokos Skete in Albuquerque, New Mexico.

Sources:

Independent Greek Orthodox Church of the United States. www.orthopraxis.org/.

Independent Greek Orthodox Holy Archdiocese of North and South America

Current address not obtained for this edition.

The Independent Greek Orthodox Holy Archdiocese of North and South America was started in 1975 by Abp. Dorotheos Flengas. Archbishop Dorotheos was born in Greece, and after completing his studies at the University of Athens, he became a priest in the Greek Orthodox Church. He came to America in 1953. He left the Greek

Orthodox Church and in 1958 was consecrated as a bishop. He died in 1981. He was succeeded by Metropolitan Andreas. The archdiocese is aligned with other independent bishops and churches in Greece.

Membership: Not reported.

Educational Facilities:

St. Fanourios Greek School, Elizabeth, New Jersey.

Macedonian Orthodox Church

American-Canadian Macedonian Orthodox Diocese, Eastern American Deanery, 5073 Onondaga Rd., Syracuse, NY 13215

A schism in the Serbian Church occurred in 1947 when, under pressure from Marshall Tito's Communist government, a new church was created to serve the geographic area of Macedonia, which extended through parts of Yugoslavia, Greece, and Bulgaria, though its strength was in South Serbia. In 1959 the patriarchate was "forced" to recognize it as autonomous but under the Belgrade patriarch, and Bishop Dositej was placed at its head. In 1967 Dositej proclaimed separation and independence, an act not recognized by the patriarch (or by anyone but Tito) and thus became schismatic.

In the United States the Macedonian Church was begun in Gary, Indiana, in 1961 during a visit of Rev. Spiridon Tanaskovski. Other parishes were established in Syracuse, New York, and Columbus, Ohio. In 1972 a schism developed in the Sts. Peter and Paul Macedonian Orthodox Church in Gary. As a result of disputes, Reverend Tanaskovski left and founded a new church, St. Clement Ohridski, which he claimed was loyal to the American flag and not to Tito.

Since the dissolution of Yugoslavia and the end of Communist control and repression in the church, the Macedonian Orthodox Church has clashed with the Serbian Orthodox Church over the former's recognition from the Ecumenical Patriarchate of Constantinople and the method used to gain autocephaly. While the two groups have attempted to reconcile, no settlement has been reached.

The Macedonian Orthodox Church is headed by Archbishop Stephen of Ohrid and Macedonia. There are seven dioceses in Macedonia and six outside the country. The American and Canadian diocese is headed by Mt. Rev. Metropolitan Metodij.

Membership: In 2008 the church reported 22 churches in the United States and 10 in Canada.

Sources:

Macedonian Orthodox Church. www.m-p-c.org/History/history.htm.

Macedonian Churches in North America (USA and Canada). faq.macedonia.org/religion/.

Orthodox American Church

Cathedral of the Holy Mother of God, 33-11 89th St., Jackson Heights, NY 11372

Orthodox American Church is a small Orthodox jurisdiction that focuses upon the inner teachings of Orthodoxy but does so apart from the monastic tradition (where such inner teachings are usually found). It recognizes that there are a variety of mystical traditions within Orthodoxy, each of which contribute to the fullness of the body of Christ. The church offers a step-by-step program that leads from fundamental and foundational concepts to the most advanced teachings of the inner life. This program is based on the mystical interpretation of the New Testament supplemented by prayerful reading of and meditation on the Psalms. At the same time, members are introduced to spiritual exercises based on the practice of the Cross of Light and the Tree of Light (Kabbalah), along with the set feasts of the Orthodox Church. In addition, the church strives to follow The Way of the Holy Cross, and the iconographic representations known as the "twenty-two holy pictures" (tarot) are seen as depicting the way of the Eternal Life. Meditation and prayer on the tarot are seen as a means of opening the consciousness to eternal truth and eventually full illumination.

Members are invited to participate in the mystical lesson and the church's worship services. Devotion and reception of Holy Communion in and at the Divine Liturgy is a sine qua non of this spiritual path. This mystical path does not involve the disciplined practice of the Jesus Prayer, one of the more famous Orthodox practices.

The church lays claim to a line of apostolic succession from the Russian Orthodox Church Outside of Russia, though it emphasizes that it is completely independent of the older Russian jurisdictions. It is also an English-speaking church. The church is led by Metropolitans John Schneyder and James Johnson.

Membership: Not reported. There are parishes in New York, Texas, and Connecticut.

Sources:

Orthodox American Church. orthodoxamericanchurch.com.

Orthodox Catholic Autocephalous Church

Current address not obtained for this edition.

The Orthodox Catholic Autocephalous Church was founded in the 1980s by Bp. James E. Henderson. Henderson had been consecrated by Abp. Trevor Wyatt Moore of the Holy Eastern Orthodox Church in the United States, and for a number of years Henderson functioned as a bishop in that church. The Orthodox Catholic Autocephalous Church resembles its parent body; the occasion for the split was primarily administrative.

Membership: Not reported.

Sources:

Ward, Gary L. *Independent Bishops: An International Directory*. Detroit, MI: Apogee Books, 1990.

Orthodox Catholic Church

c/o Most Rev. Carlos A. Florido, Presiding Bishop, 544 Oak St., San Francisco, CA 94127

The Orthodox Catholic Church was founded in the mid-1980s by Carlos A. Florido. Florido was born in Cuba and became a priest in 1961. He subsequently moved to the United States. In 1983 he was consecrated as a bishop by Lewis S. Keizer of the Independent Church of Antioch and shortly thereafter founded the Independent Catholic Church headquartered at the St. Francis of Assisi Church in San Francisco. At a later date that church became known as the Orthodox Catholic Church. In 1990 Florido consecrated Katherine Kurtz as a bishop in charge of an order community, the Third Order of St. Michael, based in Kilmacanogue, County Wicklow, Ireland.

Membership: Not reported.

Sources:

Ward, Gary L. *Independent Bishops: An International Directory*. Detroit: Apogee Books, 1990.

Orthodox Catholic Church in America (Verra)

c/o Michael Edward Verra, 238 Mott St., New York, NY 10012

The Orthodox Catholic Church, known through the mid-1980s as the American Catholic Church, Archdiocese of New York, was established in 1927 by Fr. James Francis Augustine Lashley. Father Lashley, himself an African American, was moved to establish a Catholic jurisdiction to serve those African Americans who were drawn to the Roman Catholic faith but felt rejected by the Roman Catholic Church. He also fostered the religious vocation of African-American men called to the priesthood who were refused admission to Catholic seminaries because of their race.

In 1932 Bp. William F. Tyarks, of the American Orthodox Catholic Church, consecrated Father Lashley in the lineage of Abp. Joseph Rene Vilatte, an episcopal lineage originating in the Syrian Patriarchate of Antioch and the East. Lashley built a substantial jurisdiction, which in the mid-1960s reported 20 congregations (nine

in the United States and 11 in the West Indies). Lashley died in the mid-1980s and was succeeded by Bishop Verra.

The Orthodox Catholic Church in America does not consider itself independent but a part of the Body of Christ, the One, Holy, Catholic, and Apostolic Church. The church takes as its standards of faith the Sacred Tradition, the accumulated teachings of the fathers of the Christian Church; the Holy Bible; the truths of the Seven Ecumenical Councils; and the Synod of Jerusalem of 1692, all believed to be inspired by the Holy Spirit. It specifically rejects the universal episcopal jurisdiction and infallibility of the pope, the Filioque clause in the Apostles' Creed; purgatory; indulgences; the immaculate conception of the Virgin Mary; limbo; and the use of unleavened bread in the Divine Liturgy. The church uses a Western Rite liturgy in conformity with its Orthodox Catholic beliefs concerning the procession of the Holy Spirit from the Father and the changing of the bread and wine into the body and blood of Christ by the Holy Spirit in the Eucharist. Both icons and statues are used. Clergy may marry.

Membership: Not reported. In 2002 the church reported two parishes and three priests in the United States and two parishes and two priests in Trinidad.

Orthodox Catholic Church of America

c/o Metropolitan Skip Carsten, Crosswood Centre, 5355 CR 35, Auburn, IN 46709-9717

Several jurisdictions derive their orders from Abp. Joseph Rene Vilatte (1854–1929), founder of the American Catholic Church through the orders given to the African Orthodox Church. In 1926 William F. Tyarks, a priest in the American Catholic Church who had been ordained in 1916 by Vilatte's successor, Abp. Frederick E. J. Lloyd (1859–1933), left Lloyd's jurisdiction and with other priests and members formed the American Catholic Orthodox Church. The group applied to the African Orthodox Church for orders, and Abp. George A. McGuire (1866–1934) consecrated Tyarks in 1928.

In 1930 Tyarks consecrated one of the priests who had come from the American Catholic Church with him, Clement John Cyril Sherwood (1895–1969). Sherwood soon left Tyarks and was reconsecrated by McGuire in 1932. The next year he formed the American Holy Orthodox Catholic Apostolic Eastern Church. Sherwood's career overlapped that of Abp. Aftimios Ofiesh's activity, and Sherwood became acquainted with his vision of a united American Orthodoxy. He incorporated it in an ecumenical organization, the Orthodox Catholic Patriarchate of America.

Among Sherwood's bishops was George A. Hyde, whom the patriarch consecrated in May 1957. Hyde had formed the Eucharistic Catholic Church in Atlanta, Georgia, in 1946. This first exclusively gay ministry in America continued until 1959 when Hyde moved to Washington, D.C., and formed the Society of Domestic Missionaries of St. Basil the Great, an order of priests. The following year, he left Sherwood and formed the Orthodox Catholic Church of America. He believed that Sherwood was too narrowly Eastern in his approach to liturgy and theology and wanted to restructure the church making it open to Western Rite Orthodox practice. In spite of leaving Sherwood's jurisdiction, Hyde continued to participate in the ecumenical Orthodox Catholic Patriarchate of America.

In 1969 Sherwood died. At a meeting of the Synod the next year, Hyde was elected to succeed him as head of the Patriarchate, and the Holy Orthodox Catholic and Apostolic Eastern Church voted to become the Eastern Rite Diocese of the Orthodox Catholic Church of America. Thus Archbishop Hyde took control of all the work begun by Sherwood.

Doctrinally, the Orthodox Catholic Church of America follows the teachings of the Seven Ecumenical Councils and rejects doctrinal innovations such as purgatory, papal infallibility, the immaculate conception, communion in one kind only, and an unmarried clergy. The church uses both the Eastern and Western rites in its liturgy. Under Hyde's administration, the church was active in promoting a ministry to homosexuals and is the ultimate source of the present Eucharistic Catholic Church. After Hyde's retirement in 1983, this and other special ministries were discontinued in favor of work directed to all people.

Hyde's elected successor was Alfred Louis Lankenau, bishop of the Diocese of Indianapolis and Chicago. Under the new archbishop, the Orthodox Catholic Patriarchate of America, which had ceased to function during the 1970s, was revived, and several Catholic and Orthodox jurisdictions affiliated. In 1983 the Holy Orthodox Church, American Jurisdiction, headed by Abp. James Francis Miller, which had broken from the church of the same name headed by Abp. William Francis Forbes, merged into the church. Bp. Perry Sills of the Western Rite Orthodox Church was incardinated in 1988.

Archbishop Lankenau's tenure of leadership was marked by the church's expansion into sixteen states and movement into Canada. He also opened the ordained ministry to women. The first woman was ordained to the priesthood in 1995. Archbishop Lankenau retired in 1999. He was succeeded by Abp. E. Paul Brian Carsten, who had been consecrated as a bishop the previous year. Archbishop Carsten had led the church into further growth at all levels. He also reinstated the church's Synod of Bishops.

Membership: In 2008 the church reported communities and missions in California, Illinois, Indiana, Iowa, Kentucky, Maine, Massachusetts, Michigan, Minnesota, Nebraska, New Mexico, New York, North Carolina, Rhode Island, South Carolina, Texas, Wisconsin, and Hidalgo, Mexico. There are 35 priests and over 1,000 members.

Remarks: In 1986 the Orthodox Catholic Church of America entered into an agreement of intercommunion with the Orthodox Catholic Church in America led by Abp. Walter X. Brown and jointly formed the Holy Orthodox Synod of America. The synod is a confederation that independent Orthodox bishops may join.

Sources:

Orthodox Catholic Church of America. www.orthodoxcatholicchurch.org.

Bernard, R. J. *A Faith for Americans*. Anderson, SC: Ortho, 1974.

The Divine Liturgy. Elberton, GA: Orthodox Catholic Church of America, 1966.

Hyde, George Augustine., ed. *The Courage to Be Ourselves*. Anderson, SC: Ortho-Press, 1972.

————. *The Genesis of the Orthodox Catholic Church of America*. Indianapolis, IN: Orthodox Catholic Church of America, 1993.

Orthodox Catholic Church of North and South America
PO Box 1213, Akron, OH 44309

The Orthodox Catholic Church of North and South America was inspired by the ideal of the American Orthodox Church founded by Abp. Aftimios Ofiesh under the guidance of Patriarch Tikhon of the Russian Orthodox Church. A new attempt to bring this into reality began with Bp. Joseph W. Alisauskas Jr. (d. 1980), who had been consecrated in 1968 by Abp. W. H. Francis Brothers (1887–1979) of the Old Catholic Church in America. Early in the 1960s Brothers had taken his jurisdiction into the Russian Orthodox Church, but in 1967 he withdrew and reconstituted the Old Catholic Church in America. Alisauskas left Brothers's jurisdiction in 1969 and formed the Orthodox Catholic Diocese of Connecticut and New England, a name selected to designate accurately its geographic extent. In choosing the name, he was also drawing upon the impulse of Abp. Joseph Rene Vilatte (1854–1929), who had ordained Brothers in 1910 and consecrated him in 1913. The church adopted a new constitution in 1976, at which time it assumed its present name.

Associated with Alisauskas was the Holy Protection of the Mother of God Monastic Community of Cleveland cofounded by Roman Bernard, a layman. Bernard was ordained by Alisauskas and in 1978 was consecrated bishop of Ohio City and Cleveland. The same year, Alisauskas was elevated to the rank of metropolitan and, upon his death on August 26, 1980, was succeeded by Archbishop Roman.

The Orthodox Church of North and South America is Orthodox in faith and practice but follows a variety of liturgical rites including the Orthodox-Byzantine, the Ambrosian-Milanese, a modified (de-protestantized) Anglican, the Gallican (but only in the van der Mensbrugghe translation, approved by the 1985 synod meeting), and the Roman Tridentine.

This jurisdiction grew significantly in 1988 when the Catholic Orthodox Church of Guatemala and Latin America, some 200,000 strong, affiliated with it, bringing several parishes and priests plus a seminary with 46 students. At the 1990 synod held at Akron, Ohio, a bishop (Jose Imre of Tiquisate, Guatemala) was consecrated by Archbishop Roman and Bishop Emanuel of Montreal, Quebec, for Central America.

In addition to its spiritual activities, this independent Orthodox body has a strong consciousness. Father Andres Giron, once a member of the Guatemalan Parliament, has been a member of the United Nations Human Rights Commission for quite some time. He is also the president and founder of ANACAMPRO, a collective farm system for poor and disenfranchised peasants without land. In the United States two facilities care for the homeless (St. James House in Philadelphia and Holy Cross Home in Cleveland), while N.T.S./St. Paul's Mission in Glassport (Pittsburgh area), Pennsylvania, locates jobs, free of charge, for the unemployed.

Membership: Not reported. In 1997 the church reported 28 parishes and missions and 11 mission stations, two of which are in the United States (Warren, Ohio, and Pittsburgh, Pennsylvania), semi-monastic communities (in Pittsburgh, Pennsylvania; Phoenix, Arizona; and Barberton, Ohio), and a Shrine of St. Jude, also in Barberton. Among the personnel are two bishops, 13 priests, three subdeacons, three seminarians in the United States, and nine members of religious communities (including monastics) with a total membership of approximately 214,300.

Educational Facilities:

St. Nicholas Seminary, Akron, Ohio.

Seminario de San Jose, Nueva Conception, Escuintla Province, Guatemala.

Periodicals: *The Orthodox Catholic Voice* (5/year). • *The Image* (monthly). Send orders to 594 5th Ave. NE, Barberton, OH 44203. • *The Western Orthodox Catholic* (periodic). Send orders to Box 27-406, Willow Station, Cleveland, OH 44127. • *The Clarion*. Available from St. Michael's Monastery, PO Box 8219, Phoenix, AZ 85066.

Remarks: According to Archbishop Roman, Archbishop Brothers had always considered himself head of the Western Orthodox Catholic Church of America and had a large, oval, episcopal ring (used for sealing official documents) which bore that designation. Vilatte, consecrated by the Oriental Orthodox Patriarchate of Antioch, had been permitted to use the title Exarch of the Old Catholic Church in America, a tacit admission of the Patriarchate's equation of "Old Catholic" and "Western Orthodox." Since that time the name "Old Catholic" has taken on a variety of meanings not envisioned by the Patriarchate in 1892.

Orthodox Catholic Church of the Americas
Current address not obtained for this edition.

The Orthodox Catholic Church of the Americas is a small independent Catholic jurisdiction founded in 1986 by Msg. Antonio Fuoco. Most of its work is among French Canadians, and it is also known by its French name, Eglise Catholique Orthodoxe des Ameriques. Fuoco was consecrated in 1983 by Abp. Andre Barbeau (1912–1994) of the Catholic Charismatic Church of Canada, assisted by Andre Letellier and Jean-Marie Breault. He assumed the ecclesiastical name Mar Petros Johannes. In 1985 Fuoco founded the Religious Order of Saint Michael (Communaute Ecclesiale Oecumenique de Saint-Michel), over which he serves as superior general.

Membership: Not reported.

Orthodox Christian Fellowship of Mercy
PO Box 1107, Thonotosassa, FL 33592

The Orthodox Christian Fellowship of Mercy is a relatively new independent Catholic jurisdiction that emerged out of the dissolution of the American Orthodox Catholic and Apostolic Church, Holy Synod of the Americas. The Holy Synod had formerly existed as the Diocese of Florida of the American Catholic Church but had become independent as an Eastern Orthodox body, though keeping the American Catholic Church's stance toward an inclusive ministry that opened its doors to women and to gay and lesbian people in all areas of ecclesiastical life. On November 4, 2000, Fr. John Missing, a tonsured Stavrophore monk with the church, was consecrated as a bishop. Less than two months later (December 31, 2000), Metropolitan Abp. Vladimir Sergius II resigned as primate and appointed the new bishop to assume the primacy. However, he also dissolved the corporation, and in 2001 he reorganized his own ministry as the Pride Church International, which developed a primary relationship to the gay/lesbian/bisexual/transgendered community.

In the wake of the events at the end of 2000, Bishop John reorganized the church as a separate jurisdiction, the Orthodox Christian Fellowship of Mercy. He has developed a ministry to the "neglected" elements of society—the aged and AIDS patients in nursing homes, alcoholics and addicts, and the imprisoned. He envisions the opening of a hospice that will combine elements of a home environment with the spirituality of a monastic community. It would combine healthy diet, some gardening, prayer and meditation, and modern and alternative medical care into a healing environment. Through his life, the bishop moved from a Baptist to an Eastern Orthodox perspective; his current perspective is one shaped by an appreciation of Gnosticism, Buddhism, Theosophy, and Creation Spirituality. He is also working with the teachings of famed British Spiritualist healer Harry Edwards (1893–1976).

The ministries of the small jurisdiction are limited to supplying religious services at meetings of the Society for Creative Anachronism, providing prayer and counseling at nursing homes and assisted living facilities, intercessory prayer for healing, and spiritual counseling over the Internet.

Membership: Not reported.

Sources:

Orthodox Christian Fellowship of Mercy. churches.net/userpages/Mercy.html.

Orthodox Church in America

Chancery Administration Offices, 6850 N Hempstead Turnpike, PO Box 675, Syosset, NY 11791

The Orthodox Church in America is the oldest continuously existing Eastern Orthodox body in North America in general and the United States in particular. As the first Orthodox church began to arrive, it assumed a hegemony over what became in the nineteenth century a multiethnic Orthodox community, and many of the presently existing independent Orthodox churches in America began as parishes and/or a diocese within what is today known as the Orthodox Church in America.

The OCA began in Alaska with the arrival of missionaries of the Russian Orthodox Church. In 1794 eight monks and two novices arrived on Kodiak Island to follow up on the work of converting the Native Americans already begun by a generation of Russian lay people in the Aleutians. Among these ten was Father Herman, later canonized by the church. In 1824 John Veniaminov (1787–1879), a married priest, was sent to the Aleutians. After the death of his wife, he was consecrated the first bishop of a missionary diocese. Bishop Innocent had an outstanding career in Alaska, building the first cathedral at Sitka, among other accomplishments. He was called in 1868 to be the metropolitan of Moscow, the highest office in the church, and in 1977 was canonized.

The sale of Alaska to the United States left the missionary diocese on its own. It moved its headquarters to San Francisco in 1872 and changed its name to the Russian Orthodox Church, Diocese of the Aleutian Islands and North America. The period during the episcopacy of Bishop Nicolas (d. 1915) beginning in 1891 was a time of noted growth. The Alaskan mission was expanded, and the work in Canada and the eastern United States began.

In 1905 the diocese moved its headquarters from San Francisco to New York City. Its growth was recognized by its elevation to the rank of archdiocese. Under the archbishop was a bishop for Alaska and an Arabic-speaking bishop, Raphael Hawaweeny (1860–1915), who as bishop of Brooklyn had oversight of Orthodox from the Middle East. Two additional bishops in Cleveland and Pittsburgh were soon added. The church progressed steadily until disrupted by events in Russia during World War I.

The Russian Revolution proved a disaster for the American Russian church. Russian Orthodox Christians had always carried a special loyalty for the royal family, which had been executed by the new government in Moscow. Also, money from Russia, which had always assisted in the support of the archdiocese, was abruptly curtailed, only to be followed almost immediately by a wave of immigration by refugees looking to the church for spiritual guidance and support. The patriarch of Moscow was arrested and the American church split over loyalty to him versus acceptance of the new government. Representatives of what was termed the "Living Church" (those supportive of the Communist regime) arrived in the United States in 1923. At a synod of the Russian Church in 1924 in Detroit the credentials of the Living Church were rejected and the church asserted its administrative, judicial, and legislative independence from Russia. It assumed a new name, the Russian Orthodox Greek Catholic Church of America, and declared the imprisoned Archbishop Platon "Metropolitan of All America and Canada," an action that led the church to be popularly called the "Metropolia." However, before the church was able to validate legally its separation from Moscow, the Living Church representatives were able, through a court ruling, to win the transfer of the title of St. Nicolas Cathedral in New York City into their hands.

In 1925 Archbishop Platon died. He was succeeded by Archbishop Sergius (1867–1944), who in 1927 issued a declaration calling for loyalty and cooperation with the new Russian government. Prior to this declaration, the bishops of the Russian Orthodox Greek Catholic Church of America had cooperated with other Russian bishops around the world caught outside of Russia and also cut off by the Revolution. Following the declaration, Metropolitan Platon declared his loyalty to Sergius but specifically denied him any power to make administrative decisions concerning the American church. In spite of the challenges of competing branches of Russian Orthodoxy—one branch staunchly opposed to any cooperation with the church under Communist domination (Russian Orthodox Church Outside of Russia) and the other administratively tied to the patriarch of Moscow (the American Exarchate of the Russian Orthodox Catholic Church)—the Russian Orthodox Greek Catholic Church in America retained the support of most American believers.

During the years following the turmoil of the Russian Revolution, the Metropolia assumed the position that it would give recognition to the spiritual authority of the patriarch in Moscow if he would recognize its administrative autonomy. However, the church in Russia continued its support of those parishes in the exarchate who recognized his complete authority. Finally, in 1970, the separation of the Metropolia from the church in Russia ended when the patriarch of Moscow, His Holiness Alexis (1877–1970), granted autonomous status to the Russian Orthodox Greek Catholic Church of America, renamed the Orthodox Church in America. The exarchate was dissolved and most of its parishes moved into the OCA.

For quite different reasons, the creation of the Orthodox Church in America created a controversy within the larger American Orthodox community. For many years there had been various attempts to move away from the ethnic divisions within American Orthodoxy. In creating the Orthodox Church in America, the Russian community asserted its status as the oldest Orthodox church in North America and as such the most fitting focus of Orthodox unity. Other Orthodox groups, particularly the Greek Archdiocese, saw the emergence of the OCA as a unilateral effort not deserving of recognition.

The OCA is headed by its archbishop, Metropolitan Herman (Swaiko), whose jurisdiction extends throughout the western hemisphere. There are nine dioceses in the United States, one in Canada, and an exarchate in Mexico. Also under its canonical jurisdiction are the autonomous Albanian Orthodox Archdiocese and the Romanian Orthodox Episcopate of America. The latter places the OCA in a peculiar position, having a relationship with the Romanian Episcopate while holding membership in the Standing Conference of Canonical Orthodox Bishops which includes the rival Romanian Orthodox Church of America.

Membership: Not reported.

Educational Facilities:

St. Tikhon's Orthodox Theological Seminary, South Canaan, Pennsylvania.

St. Vladimir's Orthodox Theological Seminary, Tuckahoe, New York.

Periodicals: *The Orthodox Church* • *The Canadian Orthodox Messenger*

Sources:

Orthodox Church in America. www.oca.org.

Koulomzin, Sophie. *The Orthodox Christian Church through the Ages*. New York: Russian Orthodox Greek Catholic Church of America, 1956.

The Orthodox Liturgy . . . According to the Use of the Church of Russia. London: Society for Promoting Christian Knowledge, 1964.

Tarasar, Constance. *Orthodox America, 1794–1976: Development of the Orthodox Church in America*. Syosset, NY: Orthodox Church in America, Department of Archives and History, 1975.

Orthodox Church of America

Current address not obtained for this edition.

The Orthodox Church of America was formed on June 29, 1970, by Bp. David Baxter. Bishop Baxter had been consecrated the previous year by Abp. Walter Propheta of the American Orthodox Catholic Church, assisted by Bps. John A. Christian and Foster Gilead. The church uses the Western Rite, but places emphasis upon its Eastern orders and Eastern spirituality. Its faith is based on the Nicene Creed, the seven sacraments, and the necessity of orders in the apostolic succession.

Membership: Not reported.

Orthodox Church of Canada–Orthodox Church of the East and West (Canada & USA)

Archeparchy of Edmonton & All Canada & North American Missions–Eastern Rite, 5824-118 Ave., Edmonton, AB, Canada T5W 1E4

The Orthodox Church of Canada is an autocephalous metropolia in the apostolic lineage of the Ukrainian Autocephalous Orthodox Church. As a daughter church of the UAOC it remains rooted in those traditions both canonically and historically. It also describes itself as an Orthodox church with both Eastern and Western components and maintains a broader jurisdictional affiliation with several churches in the United States as the Orthodox Church of the East and West (Canada & USA). Since 2004 the church has been led by Metropolitan Archbishop Joseph Royer.

Membership: Not reported. In 2008 the church was headquartered at All Saints Orthodox Cathedral in Edmonton, Alberta, where it also had a mission; affiliated U.S. churches were in Hartly, Delaware; Camden, South Carolina; and Rockdale, Texas.

Sources:

Orthodox Church of Canada. www.orthodoxchurchofcanada.org.

Orthodox Church of the East and West. www.holyspiritorthodox.com.

Orthodox Church of the West—USA

W. Henry Ave., Tampa, FL 33604

The Orthodox Church of the West—USA is an autonomous Orthodox jurisdiction established in 1996. It grew out of the career of its founder, Bishop Gabriel, who spent three decades as a monk in several jurisdictions connected with the Russian

Orthodox Church outside of Russia. In 1978 he founded the St. Seraphim of Sarov Monastery. In 1994 he was asked to affiliate with the Hellenic Orthodox Church in the Diaspora, one of several Old Calendar Orthodox churches based in Greece, and the following year he was consecrated as the church's bishop for Greek and American Old Calendar Greeks. In 1998 Bishop Gabriel founded the Diocese of the Assumption/Dormition of the Orthodox Church of the West—USA.

The new church and diocese were established as an expression of the belief and practice of the undivided Christian church of the first millennium C.E. It rejects changes that were introduced in the west during and after the schism between the Eastern Orthodox Patriarchates and the Roman Catholic Church. Most notably, it rejects the use of the Gregorian calendar, which largely replaced the older Julian calendar.

The church considers itself an Orthodox Catholic church. It is Orthodox in following the faith and practice of the undivided church, but it follows western formats. It has also organized a western monastic community that follows the Benedictine rule. Its uses a western liturgy, most notably the eucharistic rite of the Mass (liturgy) of St. Gregory of Rome. It honors saints of the ancient western church such as Irenaeus of Lyon, Martin of Tours, Hilary of Poitiers, and Patrick of Ireland.

The church supports the Holy Cross Benedictine community and an associated lay order, the Benedictine oblates. It hopes to found a convent for women who wish to take the Benedictine vows.

Membership: Not reported.

Sources:

Orthodox Church of the West. www.orthodoxchurchofthewest.org/.

Patriarchal Parishes of the Russian Orthodox Church in the U.S.A.

c/o St. Nicholas Patriarchal Cathedral, 15 E 97th St., New York, NY 10029

Following the Russian Revolution, the members of the Russian Orthodox Church in both Russia and the United States were split over rejecting or acknowledging the new government that had risen to power. Within the United States, especially after the arrest of the patriarch of Moscow, the sentiment was largely against any accommodation, and the American archdiocese declared itself administratively autonomous of the homeland. Meanwhile, within the Soviet Union, leaders of the so-called Living Church, those who supported accommodation to the Communist government, assumed control of the church and elected John Kedrovsky as the new bishop for the West. Kedrovsky arrived in America in 1923 prepared to take up his leadership role. However, at the same synod meeting in 1924 at which the church declared its autonomy, Kedrovsky's credentials were rejected. As the official representative of the church in Russia, however, he did find some support and in 1926 won possession of the headquarters' cathedral in New York City.

Kedrovsky's situation was further complicated in 1933 by the arrival of Metropolitan Benjamin Fedchenkov. In the years that Bishop John had lived in the United States, the church in Russia had regained some stability and the Living Church faction had died away. Metropolitan Benjamin represented a more acceptable accommodationist position and gained some support. He established the American Exarchate of the Russian Orthodox Catholic Church. However, for another decade Bishop John, succeeded by his son Nicholas Kedrovsky, whom he had consecrated, kept possession of St. Nicholas Cathedral. Finally, in 1945, after the deaths of both John and Nicolas, the Kedrovsky faction was left without either support of the church in Russia or an episcopal leader. Rev. John Kedrovsky, Bishop John's other son, signed over the cathedral to the Exarchate.

Negotiations continued sporadically in an attempt to work out differences between the church authorities and the larger autonomous Russian Orthodox Greek Catholic Church of America. These reached fruition in 1970. The Russian Orthodox Greek Catholic Church of America became the Orthodox Church in America and recognized the patriarch of Moscow as its spiritual authority. The patriarch, in turn, recognized its autonomous status. As part of the agreement, the

Exarchate was dissolved. At the time of the dissolution of the Exarchate, it was agreed that any parishes that wished to remain under the direct administrative authority of the Moscow patriarchy could remain outside of the Orthodox Church in America. These several parishes reformed as the Patriarchal Parishes of the Russian Orthodox Church in the United States and Canada. A vicar bishop was placed in charge of the approximately 40 parishes. St. Nicholas remained with the patriarchal parishes and served as its headquarters. Over the years parishes have been allowed to transfer to the OCA. The church is also a member of the National Council of Churches.

Membership: The church reported over 10,000 members in 45 parishes.

Sources:

Russian Church (Moscow Patriarchate).
www.russianchurchusa.org/index.php3?ln=en.

Russian Orthodox Church (Moscow Patriarchate). www.mospat.ru/index.php.

Pokrovshy, M. *St. Nicholas Cathedral of New York, History and Legend*. New York: St. Nicholas Cathedral Study Group, 1968.

Reformed Orthodox Catholic Church

Current address not obtained for this edition.

The Reformed Orthodox Catholic Church is a small Orthodox jurisdiction founded by Most Rev. Thomas Ephraim (the ecclesiastical name of Bishop Dennis Smith). Smith had originally been consecrated on July 1, 1971, in Miami, Florida, by Abp. Richard E. Drews, head of the Reformed (Slavonic) Orthodox Church of Florida, assisted by Abps. Mark Karras and George Erline. He later left Drews's jurisdiction.

Membership: Not reported.

Reformed (Slavonic) Orthodox Church

808 W Sunrise Blvd., Fort Lauderdale, FL 33311

The Reformed (Slavonic) Orthodox Church is a small Orthodox jurisdiction founded by Abp. Richard E. Drews. He was originally consecrated on October 4, 1969, at St. Fanourios Orthodox Church, Woodside, New York, by Abp. Lowell Paul Wadle of the American Catholic Church, assisted by Abps. Mark Karras and George Erline. He later founded the Reformed (Slavonic) Orthodox Church in Florida.

The church is Orthodox in belief and practice. The liturgy is in English.

Membership: Not reported.

Romanian Orthodox Archdiocese of America

5410 N Newland Ave., Chicago, IL 60656-2026

The Romanian Orthodox Church of America, officially known as the Romanian Orthodox Missionary Archdiocese in America and Canada, had its beginning in the formation of the first Romanian Orthodox parish in North America, formed in Regina, Saskatchewan, in 1902. Two years later a parish was formed in Cleveland, Ohio, the first in the United States. These parishes and others to follow functioned under the hegemony of the Russian Orthodox Church. A diocese was created in 1929 and a bishop assigned in 1935. Bp. Policarp Morusca (1883–1958) returned to Romania at the beginning of World War II; after the war he was detained and in 1948 involuntarily retired by the new Romanian government. A new bishop, consecrated and sent by the church in Romania, arrived in 1950. The appearance of Bishop Andrei Moldovan (d. 1963) divided the American church, which had a bylaw providing for the consecration of a bishop only after election by a diocesan congress.

The majority of the American Romanian Orthodox rejected Moldovan. The Romanian Orthodox Church in America began with the 12 parishes that accepted him. They organized as the Canonical Missionary Episcopate in the United States, Canada, and South America. The church is fully Orthodox in faith and practice, a member of the Standing Conference of Canonical Orthodox Bishops in the Americas (SCOBA), and differs from the larger Romanian Orthodox Episcopate of America in administration.

Membership: As of 2008, there were 28 churches and missions (1 monastery and 1 monastic center) in the United States; 23 churches and missions (and 1 monastery) in Canada; 1 mission in Argentina and 1 church in Venezuela.

Periodicals: *Credinta—The Faith*.

Sources:

The Romanian Orthodox Archdiocese in the Americas. www.romarch.org/.

Romanian Orthodox Episcopate of America

2535 Grey Tower Rd., Jackson, MI 49201-9120

The first Romanian Christians came to America at the end of the nineteenth century. A parish of the Romanian Orthodox Church was organized in Regina, Saskatchewan, in 1902, and two years later St. Mary's Church was founded in Cleveland. Individual congregations cooperated with Russian bishops but were related directly to the hierarchy in Romania. After a quarter of a century, a church congress was held in Detroit and in 1929 the Romanian Orthodox Episcopate (diocese) of America was organized. In 1935 the first bishop, His Grace Policarp (Morusca) (1883–1958) came to the United States and settled in Grass Lake, Michigan.

The second bishop, the Most Rev. Archbishop Valerian (Trifa) (1914–1987), was succeeded by the Most Rev. Archbishop Nathaniel Popp (b. 1940), the current ruling bishop of the episcopate. Canonically the episcopate is under the jurisdiction of the Orthodox Church in America.

Membership: In 2001 the episcopate reported 70 parishes, 100,000 members, and 120 clergy, including 18 parishes and 13 clergy in Canada.

Educational Facilities:

St. Andrew House, Detroit, Michigan.

Periodicals: *SOLIA, The Herald*. Send orders to PO Box 185, Grass Lake, MI 49240-0185. • *Lumina Lina*. • *Joyous Light SOLIA CALENDAR Annual Almanac*.

Remarks: In 1939 Bishop Polycarp went to Romania, but because of political events he could not return. After World War II he was detained by the Romanian government and in 1948 placed in retirement. The Romanian patriarchate, without the knowledge or consent of the American diocese, consecrated a new bishop, the Rev. Andrei Moldovan, a parish priest in Akron, Ohio, who had gone to Romania to be consecrated without the concurrence or support of the American parishes. His return to the United States created a major crisis as the status and bylaws of the diocese provided for ordination of bishops only after election by the diocesan congress. The majority party (48 parishes) declared themselves in full separation from the Romanian patriarchate. Later, in 1951, they elected Viorel (Valerian) D. Trifa, who had recently arrived in the United States as their bishop. Through a fraternal tie, Trifa was able to bring the episcopate under the canonical protection of the Russian Orthodox Greek Catholic Church of America (now the Orthodox Church in America), which recognized Trifa's church as a self-governing body.

The episcopate faced a second major crisis in the 1970s when Bishop Trifa was charged with concealing an alleged role in Nazi atrocities in Romania. In 1980 he surrendered his U.S. citizenship and in 1984 went into exile in Portugal. He died there in 1987 and was succeeded by Bp. Nathaniel Popp.

In 2008 the episcopate requested the initiation of talks with the Church of Romania in order to clarify a number of issues between the two organizations and seek understanding. Representatives from both organizations participated jointly in worship service. They also drafted and released a joint statement of clarification explaining the influences of communism in Eastern Europe that led to the separation while asking for mutual forgiveness for misunderstandings and past tension. The statement also made clear a mutual desire for reunification.

Sources:

Romanian Episcopate of America. www.roea.org.

Beliefs of Orthodox Christians. Jackson, MI: Romanian Orthodox Episcopate, n.d.

Bobango, Gerald J. *The Romanian Orthodox Episcopate of America*. Jackson, MI: Romanian American Heritage Center, 1979.

50th Anniversary, 1938–1988. Vatra Dedication. Jackson, MI: Publishing Department, Romanian Orthodox Episcopate in America, 1988.

Holy Liturgy for Orthodox Christians. Jackson, MI: Romanian Orthodox Episcopate, n.d.

Lascu, Traian. *Valerian, 1951–1984*. Madison Heights, MI: Knello Printing Services, 1984.

Trifa, Valerian D. *Holy Sacraments for Orthodox Christians*. Jackson, MI: Romanian Orthodox Episcopate, n.d.

Russian Orthodox Autonomous Church of America

c/o Saint Nicholas the Wonderworker Orthodox Parish, Right Rev. Andrew of Pavlovskoye, 95 Elm St., Elmwood Park, NJ 07407-1610

The Russian Orthodox Autonomous Church of America is the North American representative of the Free Russian Orthodox Church, which was formally established in 1994 in Russia. It draws on the tradition of resistance to the former Soviet Union's atheism and subversion of the Russian Orthodox Patriarchate. The church traces its history to 1920 and a decree issued by Patriarch Tikhon, calling on the church outside of Soviet control to organize separately and preserve the heritage. This decree led to the formation of the Russian Orthodox Church Outside of Russia. In the 1970s, that church assisted in the process of setting up independent underground churches in the Soviet Union and supplying them with Episcopal leadership.

During the years since the fall of the Soviet Union, the Russian Orthodox Church Outside of Russian began talks that eventually led to its reconciliation with the Moscow Patriarchate. The Free Russian Orthodox Church saw these negotiations and their culmination as a betrayal of trust. It continues to view the Moscow patriarchy as an apostate body that has not rid itself of the subversive element acquired during the Soviet years. In the wake of the actions of the Russian Church Outside of Russia, it broke fellowship and in 2000 began to establish parishes outside of Russia. Its leader, Metropolitan Valentine of Suzdal and Vladimir, had particular concern for North America, which had been a Russian missionary territory prior to the Russian Revolution (1917).

The Russian Orthodox Autonomous Church of America continues the beliefs and practice of the Russian Orthodox Church prior to the rise of the Soviet Union. It is opposed to the ecumenical endeavors of the modern Russian Orthodoxy. The American diocese is led by Bp. Andrew of Pavlovskoye, the administrator of the Russian Orthodox Autonomous Church of America.

Membership: Not reported. In 2008 there were six parishes.

Sources:

Russian Orthodox Autonomous Church of America. www.roacusa.org/.

Russian Orthodox Church in America

Monastery of Saint John the Wonderworker, 1105 W Deming St., Roswell, NM 88203

The Russian Orthodox Church in America (not to be confused with either of the large Russian Orthodox jurisdictions, the Orthodox Church in America or the Russian Orthodox Church Outside of Russia), traces it history to the career of Abp. Aftimios Ofiesh (1880–1971), who in the 1920s was part of a short-lived experiment by the then Russian Orthodox jurisdiction in America to create an American Orthodox church. Ofiesh, of Syrian ancestry, was consecrated as a bishop in 1917 and elevated to archbishop in 1923. He formed the American Orthodox Church in 1927. The church came to a crossroads when the Russian bishops withdrew support and in 1932 moved Ofiesh out of his church in Brooklyn, New York. He pushed forward with the independent effort but lost what little support remained within the larger Orthodox community in 1933 when he married. The bishops consecrated by Ofiesh would through the twentieth century become the source for a number of small Orthodox groups.

The American Orthodox church was centered upon a monastic community, the Monastery of Saint John the Wonderworker, originally founded in Wyoming in 1987 by two monks of northern European descent. The monastery later moved to Denver (1984), where a distant-learning seminary was also established.

In 1996 the church faced a crisis when its leader, Archbishop Vladimir, resigned his position and left the church altogether. At that point, a monk named Symeon, who had retired due to ill health, was the only bishop remaining in the church and was asked to assume the role of metropolitan. Two years later, now assisted by Bishop Macarius, he re-chartered the church under its present name, the Russian Orthodox Church in America, to more correctly reflect its history. In 2002, Metropolitan Symeon founded the cathedral parish of Mary Joy of the Sorrowing in Aurora, Colorado.

The church faced another crisis when Archbishop Macarius withdrew from the church in 2005, again leaving Metropolitan Symeon as the only bishop. Metropolitan Symeon subsequently invited Bishop Ioan, who headed the independent Holy Trinity Orthodox Church in western Denver to affiliate with the Russian Orthodox Church. Together, they rebuilt the church's hierarchy.

Metropolitan Symeon moved from Denver, Colorado, to Roswell, New Mexico, in 2006. He also relocated the Monastic Skete of Saint John the Wonderworker and established the parish of the Holy New Martyrs of Russia. In the summer of 2008, the seminary began classes on a new campus also in Roswell campus of the Saint Innocent of Alaska Orthodox Theological Seminary.

In 2008 Metropolitan SYMEON also received the Church of the Holy Faith of the Christian East (also known as the Orthodox Church of Columbia) into the Russian Orthodox Church in America. As part of the ceremonies, its bishop, Jairo Gonzales y Montoya, was elevated to the archepiscopacy and named Archbishop for the Western Rite in Central and South America.

Membership: In 2008 the church had parishes and missions scattered in 17 states and an affiliated archdiocese in Columbia, South America.

Educational Facilities:

Saint Innocent of Alaska Orthodox Theological Seminary, Roswell, New Mexico.

Sources:

Russian Orthodox Church in America. www.russianorthodox.org.

Russian Orthodox Church Outside of Russia

75 E 93rd St., New York, NY 10028

Following the Russian Revolution and the cutting of lines of authority and communication between the patriarch of Moscow and bishops serving Russian Orthodox communities outside of Soviet control, attempts were made to reorganize the church. In 1921 a conference of Russian Orthodox bishops in exile met at Sremski Karlovtsy, Yugoslavia. Among the participants was Metropolitan Platon (1866–1934), leader of the American archdiocese. Metropolitan Platon continued to work with the Council of Bishops Abroad until 1926 when he ran into conflict over the movement toward autocephalous status of the American church. Metropolitan Platon declared the Council of Bishops an uncanonical organization. The Council dismissed Platon and assigned Bishop Apollinary in his place.

Bishop Apollinary was elevated to archbishop in 1929 and, after a short period of leadership, died in 1933. He was succeeded by Bishop Vitaly (1910–2006). Efforts to heal the schism between the Church Abroad and the autonomous Russian Orthodox Greek Catholic Church of America (popularly called the Metropolia) led to a temporary rapproachment in 1935, which continued through the period of World War II. In the mid-1940s, however, it became evident that the larger body wished some realignment with the patriarch of Moscow, and in 1946 it broke completely with the Church Abroad. The American followers of the Church Abroad asserted their continuity with Russian Orthodoxy in America and declared the Metropolia schismatic. The Russian Orthodox Church Outside of Russia thus became the major voice of the anti-Soviet faction of Russian Orthodoxy and has tried ever since to continue the traditional practices of the Russian Church.

In 2007 the Russian Orthodox Church Outside of Russia signed the Act of Canonical Communion with the Moscow Patriarchate, reestablishing the canonical link between the churches.

Membership: In 1994 the church reported 177 parishes in the United States, 25 parishes in Canada, and 37 parishes in South America, with approximately 100,000 members in the United States. In 2008 the church reported over 400 parishes globally and over 400,000 members.

Educational Facilities:

Holy Trinity Orthodox Seminary, Jordanville, New York.

Periodicals: *Orthodox Life*. Available from Holy Trinity Monastery, Jordanville, NY 13361. • *Orthodox America*. Send orders to PO Box 3132, Redding, CA 96099.

Sources:

Russian Orthodox Church Outside of Russia.
  www.russianorthodoxchurch.ws/english/.

A Cry of Despair from Moscow Churchmen. New York: Russian Orthodox Church Outside of Russia, 1966.

Fiftieth Anniversary of the Russian Orthodox Church Outside of Russia. Montreal: Monastery Press in Canada, 1971.

Holy Transfiguration Monastery. *A History of the Russian Church Abroad and the Events Leading to the American Metropolia's Autocephaly, 1917–1971*. Seattle: Saint Nectarios Press, 1972.

Rodzianko, M. *The Truth about the Russian Church Abroad*. N.p. 1975.

Young, Alexey. *The Russian Orthodox Church Outside Russia: A History and Chronology*. San Bernardino: St. Willibrord's Press, 1993.

Russian Orthodox Church Outside of Russia (Vitaly)

c/o Bishop Vladimir, PO Box 191363, Sacramento, CA 95819

In 2001 Metropolitan Vitaly (1910-2006), the head of the Russian Orthodox Church Outside of Russia, retired and was succeeded by Metropolitan Laurus. Vitaly moved to the Transfiguration Monastery in Mansonville, Quebec, which he had built during his years as head of the church's Canadian work. However, only a few weeks after announcing his retirement, Metropolitan Vitaly rescinded his announcement and attempted to reassume his role as the church's First Hierarch. Even before this, relations with his fellow bishops had deteriorated and strongly polemical statements began to be issued by both sides. In particular, Vitaly condemned the Council of Bishop for taking hasty steps to reconcile with the Moscow Patriarchate.

Vitaly called upon his fellow bishops and all of the church's priests and members to reject Metropolitan Laurus and what he termed the "robber council." With his supporters, he formed the Russian Orthodox Church in Exile, under which name the new organization was incorporated in 2002. Two bishops and approximately a dozen priests and monks from the Russian Orthodox Church Outside of Russia aligned with him. The name Russian Orthodox Church in Exile was rejected in 2003, and the church resumed using the name Russian Orthodox Church Outside of Russia and claimed to possess and continue that church's heritage. In its present form it continues the belief and practices of the Russian Orthodox Church from the years prior to the Russian Revolution (1917)

The jurisdiction led by Metropolitan Vitaly steadily picked up the support of bishops, priests, and parishes, though it failed to match the strength of the jurisdiction led by Metropolitan Laurus. It continued a polemic his jurisdiction based on its reconciliation with the Moscow patriarchate.

Metropolitan Vitaly died in 2006. No successor has been named as of 2008. The church is currently led by its four bishops, of whom Bishop Vladimir, who heads the Diocese of San Francisco and the Western United States, is the most prominent. Dioceses cover North and South America, Russia, and Europe.

Membership: Not reported. In 2008 there were 14 parishes in the United States and 11 in Canada. Outside of North America parishes could be found in Chile, Brazil, Venezuela, France, Belgium, Holland, Norway, the United Kingdom, and Russia.

Sources:

Russian Orthodox Church Outside of Russia (Vitaly). www.rocor-v.com/rocor/engindex.html#.

Russian True Orthodox Church—Metropolia of Moscow

For information: archbishop.alexy&gmail.com

The Russian True Orthodox Church is one of several churches that arose after the fall of the Soviet Union. During the years of Soviet rule, many rejected the Russian Orthodox Church, which they felt had been subverted by the government. However, as a more religiously free climate emerged in the 1980s, those opposed to the Russian church, many of whom lacked any episcopal leadership, disagreed about which bishops to follow into the post-Soviet era.

In 1996 one group of Russian Orthodox believers turned to Patriarch Dimitry of the Ukrainian Autocephalous Orthodox Church, seeking the restoration of an acceptable hierarchy. Patriarch Dimitry gave his consent for two Ukrainian archbishops, Roman and Methody, to consecrate Hieromonk John as the first bishop of what became the Russian True Orthodox Church. Shortly thereafter, Bp. Methody joined Bp. John in consecrating Archimandrite Stefan as the second bishop for the Russian True Orthodox Church. Bps. John and Stefan consecrated additional bishops. In 2000 the Russian True Orthodox Church added "Metropolia of Moscow" to its name in order to distinguish it from other groups that were also emerging at the time. As the church grew, leadership passed to Metropolitan Vyacheslav of Moscow and Kolomensk and Abp. Mikhail of Krutitski and Bronitski.

The jurisdiction of the Russian True Orthodox Church was extended to the United States in 2003 when Abps. Vyacheslaw and Michael consecrated Bp. Alexy as the bishop of Minneapolis and Chicago. Two years later the churches synod elevated him to the office of archbishop.

The church is at one with the Orthodoxy in belief and practice.

Membership: Not reported.

Sources:

Russian True Orthodox Church. theorthodox.org/true_orthodox_church.htm.

Sacred Heart Catholic Church (Arrendale)

Current address not obtained for this edition.

The Sacred Heart Catholic Church was founded in 1980 by Abp. James Augustine Arrendale and other former members of Abp. James Francis Augustine Lashley's American Catholic Church, Archdiocese of New York. Arrendale was consecrated on August 10, 1981, by Bishop Pinachio, who was assisted by Bps. Donald Anthony and William Wren. The group adheres to the teachings of the Seven Ecumenical Councils and the three Ecumenical Creeds. Archbishop Arrendale died in 1985 and the future course of the archdiocese is in doubt.

Membership: Not reported.

Saints Cyril and Methodius Orthodox Church

260 Lauer Rd., Poughkeepsie, NY 12603

Saints Cyril and Methodius Orthodox Church was founded in the late 1990s as the Anglican Catholic Byzantine Orthodox Church by Paul Victor Verhaeren and Wayne Moore Hay. Verhaeren and Hay had been consecrated in 1997, first by Ronald D. Nowland, a bishop in the line of Carlos Duarte Costa of the Brazilian Apostolic Catholic Church, and then by Irwin R. Young, Jr., a bishop in the Old Catholic Church succession of Arnold Harris Mathew. Both bishops carried several lines of Apostolic succession. Verhaeren, now known as Stephanos I, serves as the church's patriarch and Hay as its metropolitan. Through its lines of succession the church has drawn its authority from both Eastern and Western rites. This is reflected in the several liturgies it promotes—a corrected Tridentine Mass, St. Tikhon's Mass based on the Book of Common Prayer, the Liturgy of St. John Chrysostom, and a specially approved Gallican Liturgy.

Although it draws on various traditions, the church is basically Orthodox in it use of the Nicene Creed without the Filioque clause inserted by the Roman Catholic Church in the eleventh century and its adherence to the seven ecumenical councils of the undivided church. The western church has continued to hold councils, the most recent being Vatican II (1962–1965). It accepts seven sacraments (rather than two as held by the Anglicans and Protestants) and believes in the real presence of Christ in the Eucharist. Great emphasis is also placed on church tradition from the seven councils and the early fathers of the church, which are honored as being agreeable to Holy Scripture and the church's authority. Authority in the church is placed in its bishops as Orthodox bishops in apostolic succession.In 2008 there were four bishops in the church.

In 2003 the Anglican Catholic Church (ACC), claiming that the use of "Anglican Catholic" was a violation of copyright laws, threatened legal action against the Anglican Catholic Byzantine Orthodox Church. Faced with a costly legal battle, the Anglican Catholic Byzantine Orthodox Church complied with the ACC's request to cease using the words "Anglican Catholic," and changed its name to the Saints Cyril and Methodius Orthodox Church.

Membership: In 2008 the church reported four affiliated parishes and missions in the United States and one in Mexico.

Sources:

Saints Cyril and Methodius Orthodox Church.
    whozontop.com/whozon/memberSite.asp?wsID=684&hitzone=HZ0011.

Serbian Orthodox Church in the United States of America and Canada

St. Sava Monastery, PO Box 519, Libertyville, IL 60048

Few churches have been so affected by the changes in modern Europe as the Serbian Church, which has survived centuries of shifting political division of the traditional Serbian homelands in the Balkan region. An independent Serbian Orthodox Church had been established in 1219 under Archbishop St. Sava (1169–1236). A patriarchate was established in the fourteenth century. From 1389 to 1815 Serbia was under Turkish rule and the church suffered severe persecution, but a nineteenth-century revival followed independence from Muslim control.

In 1765 Serbian autonomy ended, and the church returned to the jurisdiction of the ecumenical patriarch in Constantinople, who began a hellenization program. In 1832 the archbishop of Belgrade was given the title metropolitan, and in 1879, as a result of the Congress of Berlin, the Serbian Church regained autonomy. In 1920 it joined with the independent Serbian churches in Montenegro, Bosnia, Herzegovina, Dalmatia, and Croatia—regions that, like Serbia, were now constituent parts of the political state soon to be known as Yugoslavia—to form the Serbian patriarchate. The seat was established in Belgrade, and its independence was recognized by the ecumenical patriarch in 1922.

Immigrants from Serbia began to arrive in the United States in significant numbers in the 1890s. In 1892 Archimandrite Firmilian arrived and began to organize parishes. The first was in Jackson, California, but others soon followed in Chicago, Illinois; Douglas, Alaska; and McKeesport, Steelton, and Pittsburgh, Pennsylvania. All of these early parishes were placed under the jurisdiction of the Russian Orthodox Church in America. The Serbian Church began to seek autonomous status as early as 1913. With Russian encouragement, Serbian Father Mardary was sent to the United States to organize an independent diocese in 1917. In 1919 the Russians elevated him to archimandrite. In 1921 the Serbs separated from the Russian Orthodox Church, and Mardary became the administrator. In 1926 he was consecrated bishop for the American diocese. The Serbian Church grew slowly in this country until World War II, when a flood of refugees came into the United States. St. Sava Monastery at Libertyville, Illinois, was built soon after Bishop Mardary's consecration, and the church headquarters are currently established there.

The changes in political structure in Yugoslavia after World War II drastically altered the American diocese. In 1940 Bp. Dionisije Milivojevich was sent to the United States to assume authority for the church. Because Bishop Dionisije was a vocal defender of the Serbian monarchy and foe of Marshall Tito, the new ruler of Yugoslavia, Tito encouraged the Belgrade patriarch to release Milivojevich of his duties. At the same time, Tito moved against the church by confiscating all church property, thus placing the church under his financial control. The American Archdiocese was divided into three dioceses. Milivojevich was left in charge of the Midwest. He rejected the actions of the patriarch in Belgrade, which he interpreted as coming from an atheist government bent on absolute control of the church. He was suspended from office and excommunicated the following year. He appealed the actions of the Belgrade patriarch to the clergy and laity of the American church and individual congregations, and priests began to take sides. Each side filed suit against the other, and two churches evolved: the Serbian Orthodox Church in the United States of America and Canada and the Free Serbian Orthodox Church—Diocese for the U.S.A. and Canada.

The Serbian Orthodox Church in the United States of America and Canada was the canonical body loyal to the Mother Church with its Patriarchal See in Belgrade. In 1963 it was reorganized into three dioceses. Leading the church since 1991 is Metropolitan Christopher (Kovacevich), who heads the Metropolitanate of Midwestern America, located in Libertyville, Illinois. During the period of the 1960s and 1970s when the headquarters property of the church at St. Sava Monastery was being contested in court and under the control of Bishop Dionisije, the Midwestern Diocese erected a large church building in Chicago that served (until 1980) as its temporary headquarters. The Western American Diocese is headquartered in Alhambra, California, and the Eastern American Diocese in Edgeworth, Pennsylvania. In 1983 the Canadian parishes were separated from the Eastern Diocese and organized into a new Canadian Diocese. The Serbian Orthodox Church in the United States of America and Canada is a member of the Standing Conference of Canonical Orthodox Bishops in the Americas. Through its ties to the church in Belgrade, it is also a member of the World Council of Churches.

In 1992 major steps were taken to heal the division between the two bodies of Serbian Orthodox believers in North America. On February 15, following discussions with the patriarchate in Belgrade, bishops of the Serbian Orthodox Metropolitanate of New Gracanica, concelebrated the Divine liturgy with Patriarch Pavle. The action formally healed the schism. Only the formalities of working out the legal and administrative issues remained. By 1998 a common Constitution was being worked out for the entire Serbian Church in North America. Once agreed upon and accepted, territorial reorganization of the churches and dioceses will take place, so that administrative unity can follow.

Membership: Not reported. In 1986 the church reported 67,000 members, 68 parishes and missions, and 82 priests.

Educational Facilities:

St. Sava Serbian Orthodox Seminary, Libertyville, Illinois.

Periodicals: *The Path of Orthodoxy* • *The Clergy Messenger*

Sources:

Serbian Orthodox Church in the United States of America and Canada.
    www.serborth.org.

Dionisije, Bishop. *Patriarch Gherman's Violations of the Holy Canons, Rules and Regulations of the Serbian Orthodox Church in Tito's Yugoslavia.* Libertyville, IL: Serbian Orthodox Diocese in the U.S.A. and Canada (Free Serbian Orthodox Church in Free World), 1965.

Divine Liturgy, Prayers, Catechism. Libertyville, IL: St. Sava Seminary Fund, 1979.

Gracanica. Grayslake, IL: Serbian Orthodox Free Diocese of the United States and Canada, 1984.

A Time to Choose. Third Lake, IL: Monastery of the Most Holy Mother of God, 1981.

Todorovich, Jovan. *Serbian Patron Saint, Krsna Slava*. Merrilville, IN: The Author, 1978.

Velimirovich, Nicholai D. *The Life of St. Sava*. Libertyville, IL: Serbian Eastern Orthodox Diocese, 1951.

Standing Episcopal Conference of Orthodox Bishops

c/o The Right Reverend Mitred Archpriest Michael, Moderator, PO Box 687, New Albany, OH 43054-0687

The Standing Episcopal Conference of Orthodox Bishops (SEC), formerly the Holy Orthodox Catholic Patriarchate of America (HOCPA), traces its origin to Jesus Christ on the day of Pentecost, having survived through schisms and heresies. According to church history, Orthodox missionaries reached the North American continent via exploratory voyages long before the arrival of Columbus in 1492. By the mid-1800s various ethnic jurisdictions, predominantly the Russian Orthodox Church, were firmly planted in America. In 1921 the Holy Synod of Moscow, under the authorization of Patriarch Tikhon, gave its consent to the formation of a group of Orthodox bishops in North America. This was the first definitive act by an "old world" jurisdiction to establish an Orthodox body indigenous to the Americas.

At its earliest beginnings, the American Patriarchate bishops ordained and consecrated, even outside their ethnic boundaries, to ensure canonical clergy to serve their churches in America. The church acknowledges a tremendous debt to Archbishop Palladios Rudenko of the Holy Ukrainian Autocephalic Orthodox Church in Exile and to Archbishop Athenagoras Spyrou (1886–1972), Greek Orthodox Archdiocese of North and South America, who became the Ecumenical Patriarch in 1948.

In Orthodoxy, valid Apostolic Succession ensures heredity from the historical church of the Apostles. HOCPA's unbroken line derives from Archbishop Sophronios Bishara (1888–1934), Greek Orthodox Archdiocese of North and South America; Metropolitan Theophan Noli (1882–1965), Albanian Orthodox Archdiocese; Metropolitan Christopher Contogeorge (1894–1950), American Exarch, Greek Orthodox Patriarchate of Alexandria; and Archbishop Benjamin Fedchenkov (1880–1961), Russian Orthodox Patriarchate of Moscow.

On March 1, 1945, Archbishop Athenagoras Spyrou issued a letter, on behalf of the Ecumenical Patriarch of Constantinople, confirming the canonical character and validity of the ecclesiastical acts of Metropolitan Christopher Contogeorge. It was Contogeorge who consecrated Abp. Nicholas Kedroffsky (1902–1944) for the Moscow Patriarchate, who then consecrated Metropolitan Joseph Klymowycz (1880–1961), who would become HOCPA's first archbishop.

On October 14, 1950, canonical Orthodox bishops met at Springfield, Massachusetts, to formally break all ties with Moscow and function as an American Jurisdiction working independently of Russia. On January 15, 1951, Metropolitan Joseph Klymowycz and Abp. Peter A. Zhurawetsky (1901–1994) met in Albany, New York, to incorporate the Holy Orthodox Catholic Patriarchate of America, erected and existing under the canonical authority and blessings of the Holy Synod, inseparably joined in faith with the Great Church of Constantinople and with every other jurisdiction of the 300 million worldwide Eastern Orthodox Catholic and Apostolic Church.

In March 1951 HOPCA established the Standing Episcopal Conference of Orthodox Bishops (SEC) that bound several bodies in unity of faith and communion in the Seven Sacraments. Its founding members included canonical Orthodox bishops from the Greek, Alexandrian, Albanian, Ukrainian, and Russian jurisdictions. Member bishops continue to be "equals among equals" in all matters of church administration and discipline.

All members of HOPCA profess the Word of God as being inspired in Holy Scripture, the Didache (Teaching of the Twelve Apostles), seven Holy Mysteries (Sacraments) instituted by Christ, veneration of the Theotokos, the ever-virgin Mary as Mother of God, and intercession of saints. Absolute adherence to the dogmatic definitions of the Holy Fathers of the Seven Ecumenical Councils (325–787) is demanded. Members promise to remain faithful to the written and oral traditions that have been taught (II Thess. 2:15), including the articles of the Nicene Creed, Holy Scriptures, and the decisions of the Local, Ecumenical, and Pan-Orthodox Councils. Ordination to the priesthood has been limited to men since Apostolic times, but either the married or celibate state within all levels of sacerdotal life is permitted. Respect for the legitimate Eastern and Western Liturgical Rites of Orthodoxy is maintained; however, the co-mixing of different liturgical traditions is not tolerated.

In 1950 the HOPCA leadership gathered for a fiftieth anniversary celebration. At that time, they adopted a new name, The Standing Episcopal Conference of Orthodox Bishops, by which it has been subsequently known. The SEC is headed by the Right Reverend Mitred Archpriest Michael, whose jurisdiction extends throughout the Archdiocese of Columbus, Ohio, and Dependencies.

Membership: In 2002 the Holy Orthodox Catholic Patriarchate of America reported 14,500 members in 56 congregations with 72 ordained priests and deacons. The Standing Episcopal Conference of Orthodox Bishops reported a worldwide membership of approximately 10 million in more than 2,500 congregations.

Educational Facilities:

St. Alexis Toth Orthodox Seminary, Ontario, Canada.

Three Hierarchs Seminary, Columbus, Ohio.

Periodicals: *Our Missionary*, The Chancery, 4636 Commons Park Dr., New Albany, OH 43054. • *The Monastic Newsletter*, 4977 N. Chippewa Rd., Coleman, MI 48618.

Sources:

Standing Episcopal Conference of Orthodox Bishops. www.ourchurch.com/view/?pageID=26340.

Syro-Russian Orthodox Catholic Church

c/o Saint Mary the Theotoko Orthodox Catholic Church, 5907 Grand Avenue, Duluth, MN 55807

The Syro-Russian Orthodox Catholic Church continues the work begun by Abp. Joseph Renè Vilatte (1854-1929), one of the pioneers of independent Catholic and Orthodox groups in the United States. His lineage was carried on by, among others, Joseph Gabriel Sokolowski (1903-1989), who for many years headed St. Paul's Monastery Old Roman Catholic Church, headquartered in Rolling Prairie, Indiana. Sokolowski was associated with several jurisdictions through the years, but in 1970 he was consecrated a bishop by Joseph John Skureth of the Western Orthodox Church. Skureth had been consecrated by Bp. Konstantin N. Wendland, who for several years (1963-1967) headed the American work of the Russian Orthodox Church, before being recalled to Moscow.

In 1987 Archbishop Joseph consecrated three bishops-Stanislaus Bullock, Tage Howes, and Stephen Thomas. Bishop Thomas was subsequently elected and enthroned as sixth metropolitan archbishop and protohierarch of the lineage claimed by Archbishop Joseph. Renamed, by Archbishop Stephen, the Syro-Russian Orthodox Church sees itself as continuing the work started by Archbishop Vilattee.

The church is Eastern Orthodox in faith and practice, and its worship utilizes the liturgy of St. John Chrysostom (with other liturgies both Western and Eastern allowed for specific settings). It allows married men to enter the priesthood, but only celibate males may become bishops.

The Church is in communion with the Byelorussian Orthodox Autocephalous Church in Exile led by Archbishop Jovan. It is also a member of the Council of Canonical Autocephalous Orthodox Bishops.

Membership: In 2008 the church reported 10 parishes in the United States. Internationally, it reported 25,000 members of its Archdiocese of the Americas and

Diaspora, which includes work in Cuba, India, Nigeria, Pakistan, Kenya, Congo, Tanzania, Spain, Nicaragua, Guatemala, Mexico, and the United Kingdom.

Educational Facilities:

The church oversees St. Mark-Romano Byzantine College (Alexandria, Virginia), St. Mark-Romano Byzantine College Extension (Bolton, Ontario, Canada), St. Basil Seminary (Nicaragua), St. Nicholas Institute (Dar Es Salaam, Tanzania), St. Vasilios College (Athens, Greece), and St. Dionyssios Seminary (also Athens).

Sources:

Syro-Russian Orthodox Catholic Church. rbsocc.org/.

Traditional Orthodox Christian Church (TOCA)

306 Mendocino Ave., Apt. 314, Santa Rosa, CA 95401

Traditional Orthodox Christian Church (TOCA), also known as the Russian-Greek Orthodox Christian Archdiocese, was founded by Archbishop Seraphim, its metropolitan. A priest of a Russian Orthodox jurisdiction, he left to join the Serbian Orthodox Church. He affiliated with the Greek Orthodox Archdiocese of New Jersey in 1997 and was consecrated in 1998 as a missionary bishop by Archbishop Andreas, the head of the archdiocese. The archdiocese is an independent Old Calendar Orthodox church under the leadership of Abp. Joachim Souris. Souris, who resided in the United States in the middle of the twentieth century, was associated with Abp. Christopher Contogeorge (1894–1950) and Abp. Peter A. Zhurawetsky (1901–1994) (of the Holy Synod of the Orthodox Catholic Churches of the Americas and Europe) and the source of several lineages of independent orthodoxy. He currently resides in Athens, Greece.

TOCA follows traditional orthodox belief (Nicene Creed) and practice (in the Greek Orthodox liturgy) but has opposed the adoption in the twentieth century of the Gregorian calendar, which replaced the Julian calendar that had been used for centuries in the Eastern Orthodox churches, and by the Greek Orthodox Church that was established as an independent entity again in the nineteenth century. They also oppose the ecumenism in which the majority of the national Orthodox churches now participate. Through Archbishop Souris, TOCA asserts its own apostolic succession.

The jurisdiction is small with only a few parishes affiliated with it. Also affiliated with the church are St. John the Baptist Hermitage in Hawaii and the Holy Theotokos Community in Buena Vista, California. Assisting the metropolitan is Archbishop Ignatius.

Membership: Not reported.

Sources:

Traditional Orthodox Christian Church.

www.netministries.org/see/churches/ch03236.

Ukrainian National Autocephalous Orthodox Church in Exile

c/o Archbishop Haralambos, PO Box 7007, West Palm Beach, FL 33405

The Ukrainian National Autocephalous Orthodox Church in Exile (formerly the Holy Ukrainian Autocephalic Orthodox Church in Exile) was organized in New York City in 1951 among immigrants who had left the Ukraine, primarily that part formerly controlled by Poland, as a result of the disruptions of World War II. A diocese was formed under the guidance of Abp. Palladios Rudenko, former bishop of Krakiv, Lviv, and Lemkenland, and Abp. Ihor Huba, former bishop of Poltava and Kremenchuk, both refugees then living in the United States. The church was incorporated in 1960.

The church was briefly associated with the Standing Conference of Canonical Orthodox Bishops of America in the 1960s, but has since existed as an independent jurisdiction. In 1978, leadership of the church passed to Abp. Nikolaus Ilnyckyj (d.1998). He was consecrated as a bishop by several of the independent Orthodox bishops then active, most notably Abp. Peter A. Zhurawetsky (1901–1994), Abp. Joachim Souris, and Bp. Lavrentios Maniatakis.

Metropolitan Nikolaus served a declining jurisdiction, many of the members leaving for the larger Ukrainian jurisdictions. In 1997 he elevated Bp. Haralambos Bouchlas, whom he had previous consecrated to the episcopacy, to the office of archbishop. Upon the death of Metropolitan Nikolaus, Archbishop Haralambos succeeded to the office of metropolitan. Haralambos, of Greek heritage, is attempting to lead the church beyond its ethnic roots to serve a more inclusive American constituency. He has also assumed leadership of Saint Michael Academy, established in 1985, which a variety of ecclesiastical degree programs. The Archdiocese also has a monastic community, Holy Theotokos Monastery.

Membership: In 2008 the church reported on congregations, active missions, a monastery, a college, and a retreat house.

Periodicals: *Kýrie Eléison*

Educational Facilities:

Saint Michael Academy, West Palm Beach, Florida.

Sources:

Ukrainian National Autocephelous Orthodox Church in Exile. www.unaocinexile.org/.

Ukrainian Orthodox Church in America (Ecumenical Patriarchate)

St. Andrew's Ukrainian Orthodox Diocese, 9034 139th St., Jamaica, NY 11435

A new era in the relationship between the Ecumenical Patriarchate and Ukrainians was opened in the late nineteenth century when many immigrants, especially from western Ukraine, came to the United States and Canada. Prior to World War I, no universally recognized Ukrainian Orthodox jurisdiction existed in North America, and many Ukrainians converted back to Orthodoxy under the Russian Church hierarchs in America, with the predictable result that their ethnic heritage was once again submerged.

The movement to reestablish direct ties between the ecumenical patriarch and his Ukrainian children received a new impetus on April 9, 1929, when a church congress was held in Allentown, Pennsylvania, attended by 15 clergy and 24 laymen. At this meeting, the decision was made to form a separate Ukrainian Orthodox diocese. A second congress took place in New York in July 1931, when Fr. Dr. Joseph Zuk (d. 1934) was nominated to be the first bishop of the Ukrainian Orthodox Church of America and Canada. Bishop Zuk served the diocese until his untimely death on February 23, 1934.

A new bishop, Fr. Bohdan Shpylka (d. 1965), was consecrated on February 28, 1937, in the Greek Orthodox Archdiocesan Cathedral in New York by Archbishop Athenagoras (1886–1972), the future ecumenical patriarch. During Bishop Bohdan's tenure, many pastoral visits were made and a cathedral and adjoining building at Fourth Street and Avenue C in New York were acquired along with a monastery in Bridgeport, Connecticut. Bishop Bohdan passed away on November 1, 1965.

On January 28, 1967, Fr. Andrei Kuschak was consecrated in New York by Archbishop Iakovos (1911–2005). Through careful diligent management he was able to improve the precarious financial position of the diocese, including the acquisition of the current Cathedral of St. Andrew in Jamaica, New York. His missionary travels included meetings with His All Holiness Patriarch Dimitrios (1914–1991), Patriarch Elia IV of Antioch, Patriarch Maximos (b. 1914) of the Bulgarian Orthodox Church, Patriarch Justin (1910–1986) of the Romanian Orthodox Church, and Abp. Michael Ramsey (1904–1988) of Canterbury, England. Bishop Andrei was elevated to metropolitan in 1983 at the same time that Fr. Nicholas Smisko was consecrated as auxiliary bishop. Metropolitan Andrei passed away on November 17, 1986.

Bishop Vsevolod of Scopelos was consecrated on September 27, 1987, by His Eminence Archbishop Iakovos. His efforts aimed at generating a new spirit of respect among the members for the Orthodox faith and Ukrainian heritage. Special emphasis has been placed on a rejuvenated youth program.

Membership: Not reported. In 1977 the church reported 28 parishes, 25,000 members, and 35 priests. A 1980 survey indicated 23 parishes, 3,465 confirmed members, and an additional 2,000 adherents.

Periodicals: *Ukrainian Orthodox Herald.*

Sources:

Ukrainian Orthodox Church in America. www.uaocamerican.net.

Ukrainian Orthodox Church of Canada

9 St. John's Ave., Winnipeg, MB, Canada R2W 1G8

At the time of the Russian Revolution, the Ukrainian National Republic came into existence and Ukrainian Orthodox Christians began asserting their independence. Full separation from the Russian Orthodox Church and the proclamation establishing an autonomous national body came about in 1919. As news of the Revolution spread, immigrants to Canada acted quickly to found an independent jurisdiction. Approximately 150 delegates met in July 1918 at Saskatoon, Saskatchewan. Growth of the new jurisdiction was augmented by the movement of Eastern Rite congregations of the Roman Catholic Church into Orthodoxy. At the time, Rome was attempting to have the Eastern churches adopt the Latin Rite.

In 1919 Metropolitan Germanos of the Antiochean Orthodox Church agreed to take the new church under his jurisdiction as a temporary measure. Rev. S. W. Sawchuk became the administrator. He traveled to Europe to attempt to secure a bishop but was prevented entry to the Ukraine by Soviet officials. In 1924 Abp. John Theodorovich arrived in the United States to care for the Ukrainian Orthodox. The Canadians accepted him as their spiritual head, though Reverend Sawchuk continued to administer the church. In 1946 Archbishop Theodorovich asked to be relieved of his Canadian obligations. The Council of Bishops of the Ukrainian Autocephalous Orthodox Church in Exile suggested that Bp. Mstyslaw Skrypnyk lead the Canadian work, which was growing into the largest segment of Ukrainian Orthodoxy outside of Ukraine. He began his tenure in 1947 and retired in 1950. In 1951 Skrypnyk was succeeded by Metropolitan Ilarion Ohienko and an assistant, Abp. Michael Horoshij. In 1990 the Ukrainian Orthodox Church of Canada entered into eucharistic union with the Patriarchate of Constantinople. Since 2005 the jurisdiction has been headed by Metropolitan John Stinka.

The church also operates St. Andrew's College, affiliated with the University of Manitoba in Winnipeg. It was the only center for Ukrainian Orthodox theological education of its kind outside of the former Soviet Union and was used by other Ukrainian jurisdictions of the United States, England, and Western Europe. In recent years, several additional Ukrainian Orthodox theological institutions have been opened.

In 2008 the UOCC had only two bishops, one fewer than necessary to create a Council of Bishops.

Membership: In 2002 there were 140,000 members in 250 congregations, and 85 priests.

Educational Facilities:

St. Andrew's College, Winnipeg, Manitoba, Canada.

Periodicals: *Visnyk* • *Ridna Nyva*

Sources:

Ukrainian Orthodox Church of Canada. www.uocc.ca.

Bilon, Peter. *Ukrainians and Their Church.* Johnstown, PA: Western Penn. Branch of the U.O.L., 1953.

Ukrainian Orthodox Church of the USA

PO Box 495, South Bound Brook, NJ 08880

Ukrainian Christians, primarily Roman Catholic followers of the Uniate Eastern Rite, arrived in the United States and organized parishes in the nineteenth century. However, they soon encountered efforts of the Roman Church in America to further Latinize the Uniate parishes. In response, some left and joined the Russian Orthodox Church, in spite of what many felt were imperial designs against Ukrainians. In 1915 a Ukrainian National Church was founded. It placed itself under the independent Catholic bishop Carmel Henry Carfora (1878–1958), head of the National Catholic Diocese in North America and later primate of the North American Old Roman Catholic Church, with an understanding that it would affiliate with the Ukrainian Orthodox Church when and if it was allowed to exist in the Ukraine. In 1917, as the Russian Revolution progressed, the Ukrainian National Republic came into existence, and in 1919 it proclaimed the Ukrainian Autocephalous Orthodox Church the official church of the land. Unable to find a bishop who could give them orders, the clergy and lay leaders assembled at a church council in 1921 and consecrated several candidates for bishop by the laying on of hands of all present. In this manner Archpriests Wasyl Lypkiwsky and Nester Sharayiwsky were elevated to the office of bishop. Lypkiwsky was designated metropolitan.

The Ukrainian-Americans immediately began to establish an independent church. An initial All-Ukrainian Orthodox Council of the American Ukrainian Orthodox Church met in 1922. It petitioned for a bishop and two years later John Theodorovich, who had been consecrated by Metropolitan Lypkiwsky, arrived to head the new church. He established his see in Philadelphia in 1926.

The arrival of Bishop John (who had been consecrated in 1921 in the Ukraine by the Autocephalous Church) led other Uniate congregations to leave the Roman jurisdiction and become Orthodox. In response Rome appointed a bishop over its Ukrainian parishes. However, the new bishop soon came into conflict with many of the members. They broke with Rome and, not yet resolved to become Orthodox, formed the independent American-Ukrainian Greek-Catholic Church. During the 1920s, the parishes decided to become Orthodox and looked to Archbishop Aftimios Ofiesh (1889–1966), head of the American Orthodox Church, for episcopal leadership. In 1932 he consecrated Joseph Zuk (d. 1934) as the bishop of the Ukrainian Orthodox Church of America. He was succeeded by Bp. Bohdan Shpylka (d. 1965).

The Ukrainian Orthodox Church of the USA and the Ukrainian Orthodox Church of America existed side by side for several decades as competitors. Several attempts at union failed. However, in 1948, the Ukrainian Orthodox Church of America elected Mstyslav Skrypnyk, then head of the Ukrainians in Canada, as their new archbishop and named Bishop Bohdan as the auxiliary. Resigning from his Canadian post, Mstyslav took the lead in seeking ways to unite the two churches. Through several gatherings in which members of both churches participated, the barriers to union were removed. As agreed to in the negotiations, Archbishop John was reconsecrated in order to silence any objections to the regularity of his original consecration.

Archbishop John was elected metropolitan of the new church, Archbishop Mstyslav headed the consistory, and Archbishop Hennadij became the auxiliary bishop. Bishop Bohdan did not join the union and, with several parishes, continued to exist separately as the Ukrainian Orthodox Church of America (Ecumenical Patriarch).

Archbishop Mstyslav emerged as the most potent leader in the new church and eventually succeeded to the post of metropolitan. He developed the St. Andrews the First-Called Apostle Memorial Center, the headquarters complex in South Bound Brook, New Jersey, which now includes the seminary, St. Sophia Press (the publishing enterprise), a museum and archives, and the Home of Ukrainian Culture.

The church is at one in faith and practice with all of Orthodoxy. It accepts the Nicene Creed. It adheres closely to a rule against instrumental music and uses only vocal music in its worship.

Headed in 2008 by its primate, Metropolitan Constantine, the church comprises three eparchies in the United States: Central, Eastern, and Western. The archbishop is also designated the metropolitan of the church in diaspora. In this task he is assisted by archbishops in Paris, France and Australia. Eparchies have been established for Latin America, Great Britain, Western Europe, and Australia and New

Zealand. A sobor of bishops meets every two years. In some countries, general sobors of synods of the church meet every three years to establish general and specific administrative policies. The church is also served by the United Ukrainian Orthodox Sisterhoods and the Ukrainian Orthodox League of the USA. The church is in communion with the Ukrainian Greek-Orthodox Church in Canada.

Membership: Not reported.

Educational Facilities:

St. Sophia Ukrainian Orthodox Theological Seminary, South Bound Brook, New Jersey.

Periodicals: *Ukrainian Orthodox Word* (Ukrainian and English editions). • *Vira (Faith)*. • *UOL Bulletin*.

Sources:

Ukrainian Orthodox Church of the USA. www.uocofusa.org.

Bilon, Peter. *Ukrainians and Their Church*. Johnstown, PA: Western Pa. Branch of the U.O.L., 1953.

Ukrainian Orthodox Church–Western Rite Metropolia

PO Box 1303, Seaside, CA 93955

On May 2, 2001, in the state of Ohio, the Ukrainian Orthodox Church–Western Rite Metropolia was incorporated to serve the larger Orthodox faith community in North America and to express the faith of Americans from all cultural backgrounds and ancestry. The Metropolia traces its history to 1884 and the arrival in America of Fr. Ivan Wolansky, an Eastern Rite Roman Catholic priest from the Ukraine. At the time, the Latin Rite Roman Catholics who dominated the American church were quite hostile to the presence of Eastern Rite communities. That hostility would lead to the defection of many Ukrainians and others to Orthodoxy.

However, more important to the history of the Metropolia was the attempt early in the twentieth century made by Abp. Aftimios Ofiesh (1889–1966) to create an Orthodox church that would be truly American. His initial support from the Russian Orthodox Church ceased when the Episcopal Church, which provided substantial subsidy for the Russian Church, objected. It claimed that it was the American equivalent of the Orthodox Church. Ofiesh continued his efforts, though with little success. He did leave behind a lineage of bishops with Orthodox church orders, a lineage that included, among others, Abps. Sophronios Bashira, Christopher Contogeorge, Nicholas Kedroffsky (1902–1944), Joseph Klymowycz (1880–1961), and Peter A. Zhurawetsky (1901–1994).

Zhurawetsky was the primary consecrator (1978) of Metropolitan Nicholas Llnyckyj. In 1989 Metropolitan Nicholas, assisted by Bps. Christopher Jones and David Quilliams, consecrated Metropolitan Yuri Spaeth. On January 17, 1999, Metropolitan Yuri, assisted by Abp. Matthew McCarthy, consecrated Abp. Michael Damian-Benedict Palladino. On April 25, 2001, Metropolitan Michael Damian-Benedict, assisted by Bps. Martin-Benedict Tindall and Brendan Nuadha Donovan, consecrated Metropolitan Abp. Brian Joseph Kennedy, a Benedictine monk.

Abps. Michael Damian-Benedict and Brian Joseph Kennedy, along with Abp. Joseph Thaddeus and Archpriest-Abbot John-Sebastian, became the founding core group of the Ukrainian Orthodox Church–Western Rite Metropolia. They were further assisted by Bishop Martin-Benedict, Bishop Brendan Nuadha, and Abbot David Francis of Alberta, Canada. In forming the new church, the group was in part inspired by the example of the Orthodox Church of France, which in the 1930s had been able to create a Western Rite Orthodoxy using the Gallican Rite.

The Metropolia acknowledges the ecumenical patriarch, the honorary head of the Eastern Orthodox community, but ascribes no jurisdiction to him in the West. The church sees as its task building an Orthodox church that is at one in essentials with the Eastern churches but that may be identified with North America and the West as a cultural base. Its faith is not a different faith from that of their fathers and mothers who came to North America from ancient Scythia (Ukraine), but it is

expressed in Western terms. The Metropolia believes that there is only one holy orthodox church and that it is larger than any one nationality, culture, or tradition.

The church recognizes the teachings of the Seven Ecumenical Councils as summarized in the Nicene Creed. It has established its authority through bishops in apostolic succession. It rejects the primacy of the pope and the doctrine of papal infallibility. While having the highest respect for Mary as the immaculate, ever-virgin Mother of God, it rejects the idea of the Immaculate Conception. It also holds that the vision of the children at Fatima, Portugal, in 1917 was a deception of Satan. It does not admit females to the priesthood.

Membership: Not reported.

United American Orthodox Catholic Church

1000 Lake Maurer Rd., Excelsior Springs, MO 64024

The United American Orthodox Catholic Church is one of several independent Orthodox jurisdictions that emerged in the 1980s out of the Western Orthodox Church in America. It began in 1988 as a regional meeting of the Western Orthodox Church held at the Monastery of St. Anthony in Excelsior Springs, Missouri. Abbot David L. Jones of St. Anthony's and Fr. Michael Kilarsky were chosen as bishops, with Jones selected as presiding bishop. Jones and Kilarsky were consecrated in February 1989 by Bps. Ignatius Cash, Patrick M. Cronin, Max Broussard, and Joseph Turnage.

Early attempts at recognizing a variety of liturgical expressions served only to confuse and frustrate both the clergy and the lay people. Instead of serving to unite people under the teachings of the ancient Christian church, it served to divide. By September of 1992, the organization was reduced to only Bishop David and a handful of clergy and faithful who desired to pursue development of a truly united American Orthodox church. All subsequent activity has centered on reestablishing the work begun early in this century by Bp. Aftimios Ofiesh and Metropolitan Theophan Noli, both of whom appear in Bishop David's succession.

The group continues to practice the Eastern Orthodox faith according to the canons of the ancient and undivided Christian Church. Only the usual Eastern Rite liturgies are used, although Bishop David believes that there is room for a Western Rite liturgy. The church maintains a fraternal relationship with the Orthodox Church of France and steers those interested in Western orthodoxy to that group.

Membership: The church has one parish, St. Innocent, in Excelsior Springs, Missouri.

Educational Facilities:

The Monastery of St. Anthony coordinates a clergy training program in cooperation with local pastors.

Sources:

United American Orthodox Catholic Church.

www.orthodoxusa.org/uao/abouttheuao/index.htm.

Church Manual. Excelsior Springs, MO: United American Orthodox Catholic Church, n.d.

United Orthodox Church

202 International Ave., Hyder, AK 99923

The United Orthodox Church, headed by Abp. Gregory Robertson, is an Orthodox church with a Russian Orthodox Church heritage and lineage but believes that the church was never intended to be structured along ethnic or national lines. It is also a conservative body that rejects what it considers to be the Russian church's departure from tradition and participation in the larger ecumenical movement. The church staunchly adheres to the Nicene Creed and rejects prayer or common worship with other Christians (deemed heretics). The church also has married bishops (believing that the naming of unmarried bishops was an expedient adopted by the church that is no longer needed) and does not allow women to participate vocally (such as having membership in church choirs) in liturgical worship.

The church is a member of the Synod of Autonomous Canonical Orthodox Churches of North America.

Membership: Not reported.

Educational Facilities:

Saint Gregory Seminary, Hyder, Alaska.

Sources:

Pruter, Karl. *The Directory of Autocephalous Bishops of the Apostolic Succession*. San Bernadino, CA: Brogo Press, 1906. 104 pp.

Ward, Gary. *Independent Bishops: An International Directory*. Detroit: Apogee Books, 1990. 524 pp.

Universal Shrine of Divine Guidance

c/o Most Rev. Mark Athanasios Constantine Karras, PO Box 1771, Camarillo, CA 93011

Father Mark Karras, the American-born son of Greek parents, was consecrated in the Church of Saints Damian and Cosmas in Newark, New Jersey, on July 17, 1966, and on the following day elevated to the position of archbishop of Byzantium by Abp. Peter A. Zhurawetsky (1901–1994), patriarch of the Orthodox Patriarchate of America. He was assisted by independent Greek Apb. Joachim Souris, the American exarch of the Patriarchate of Alexandria. In the month following his consecration, Archbishop Karras founded the Universal Shrine of Divine Guidance, assisted by Veronica Perweiler (nee Szcente Janos, of the ancient noble House of Hungary), whom he consecrated as abbess the following year.

The Universal Shrine views itself as continuation of the Apostolic Church based upon Pentecost. The first stage was the regulatory period of Judaism and the second the instructional stage of Christianity. In the third stage, a period of fulfillment through enlightenment and grace will ensue. Archbishop Karras promulgates a pure philosophy of faith in God and spiritual values, a universal faith emphasizing moral achievement and merit. At the heart of the doctrine is the Christian teaching of love. To protect the church against ridicule, in 1974 Archbishop Karras moved in the American courts to counter the author, publishers, and filmmakers of the book and film *The Exorcist* for the unauthorized use of his name and work.

He is the supreme prelate of the ancient (312 C.E.) dynastic Christian Order of Saints Constantine the Great and Helen of the Byzantine House of the Lascaris Comnenus of Constantinople. Under his auspices, the Universal Shrine upholds the principle of the Americas as New Byzantium, which is the outcome of Western Christian civilization based upon the influence of the influence of Byzantium.

Membership: Not reported.

Sources:

Karras, Mark. *Christ unto Byzantium*. Miami, FL: Apostolic Universal Center, 1968.

Western Orthodox Catholic Church of California

c/o Most Rev. Martin J. Hill, 4109 Louisiana St., San Diego, CA 92104-1691

The Western Orthodox Catholic Church of California is a small Orthodox jurisdiction founded and led by Bp. Martin J. Hill. Hill was ordained to the priesthood in 1981 by Charles David Luther of the Western Orthodox Church in America and consecrated two years later by Francis Jerome Joachim. Hill subsequently established the Western Orthodox Catholic Church as an independent jurisdiction. The church is Eastern Orthodox in faith but follows a Western ritual format.

In August 1993 Hill consecrated Douglas Rees as auxiliary bishop. In 1994 Rees was installed as bishop of Camarillo and Central California and then elected to succeed Hill as the presiding bishop. Rees also serves as the superior general of the Order of the Most Holy Trinity and the director of St. Sergius Seminary. In 1996 Hill founded the interdenominational Order of Agia Sophia (Holy Wisdom Fathers) for the study and teaching of mysticism for Christians.

Membership: Not reported.

Sources:

Ward, Gary L. *Independent Bishops: An International Directory*. Detroit: Apogee Books, 1990.

Western Orthodox Church in America
Current address not obtained for this edition.

The Western Orthodox Church in America (WOCA) grew out of the Catholic Apostolic Church of Brazil founded by the former Roman Catholic Church bishop Carlos Duarte Costa (1888–1961), which had been brought to the United States by Bp. Stephen Meyer Corradi-Scarella (1912–1979), an independent bishop in New Mexico. In 1973 Corradi-Scarella gave Fr. Charles David Luther, a priest he had ordained, directions to found the Community of the Good Shepherd as a fellowship of priests and priests-in-training. In 1977 the name was changed to Servants of the Good Shepherd (SGS). The community's mission was to accept qualified men into the priesthood, train them, and assist them in starting mission churches, usually as worker priests.

In 1977 Luther was consecrated by Bp. Charles R. McCarthy, assisted by Jerome Joachim (1928–1997) and Wallace David de Ortega Maxey. In 1974 Joachim had succeeded Corradi-Scarella as head of the Catholic Apostolic Church in North America (CACINA). In 1980 he renamed his jurisdiction the Western Orthodox Church in America. After his consecration Luther brought the Servants of the Good Shepherd into Joachim's jurisdiction. He became bishop of the Diocese of Altoona and was later (1981) made archbishop. In 1983, however, Joachim and Luther decided to become independent of each other. Joachim and his following became the Catholic Apostolic Church in North America, while Luther retained the name Western Orthodox Church in America.

In 1984 Luther consecrated Richard J. Ingram as bishop of Hobart (Indiana) and James F. Mondok as bishop of Euclid (Ohio). During the next few years, the church experienced significant growth across the United States but also a series of administrative and canonical disagreements among its five synods, leading to affiliation changes and jurisdictional dissolution. In 1989 two bishops resigned and founded the Apostolic Orthodox Catholic Church in Glendale, California. In the 1990s two main jurisdictions were carrying on the WOCA name: the SGS/WOCA group under Luther and another that was incorporated as WOCA of Minnesota. After Luther's death in 2000, the Servants of the Good Shepherd eventually reorganized as an order within the Unity Catholic Church, and the Minnesota jurisdiction became the most active branch of the WOCA. Then, in 2007, the Minnesota jurisdiction, under Abp. Randolph A. Brown, was received into the Catholic Apostolic National Church as an archdiocese restored to full communion with the Catholic Apostolic (National) Church of Brazil, the mother church founded by Duarte Costa.

Membership: Not reported.

Sources:

Western Orthodox Church in America (WOCA). home.comcast.net/~woca/woca.htm.

Servants of the Good Shepherd. www.unitycatholic.org/page12.html.

A Brief Description of the Servants of the Good Shepherd. Altoona, PA, 1980.

# Non-Chalcedonian Orthodoxy

Ancient Church of the East
2064 Fifth St., San Fernando, CA 91340

Alternate Address: International Headquarters: c/o Mar Addai, Catholicos Patriarch, PO Box 2363, Baghdad, Iraq.

In the 1970s, the schism of the Ancient Assyrian Church of the East split when the Iraqi government recognized Mar Addai (b. 1950) as patriarch of the church. The larger faction, led by Mar Dinkha (b. 1935), known in the United States as the

Apostolic Catholic Church of the East, North American Diocese, is recognized by the Vatican. The smaller faction, the Ancient Church of the East, continues with the present government's blessing. The two factions of the church are identical in faith and practice, the differences being purely administrative.

In the United States, a diocese of the Ancient Church of the East that acknowledges Mar Addai was formed among America believers in the 1970s.

Membership: Not reported.

Sources:

Orthodoxy. Regensburg, Germany: Ostkirchliches Institute, 1996.

Antiochian Catholic Church in America

St. Demetrios' Antiochian Catholic Church, 2001 Middlebrook Pike, Knoxville, TN 37921

The Antiochian Catholic Church in America was founded in 1991 when the former Diocese of Lexington (Kentucky) of the Church of Antioch was granted autocephaly as an independent self-governing jurisdiction. The diocese had been under the leadership of H. Gordon Hurlburt, who was consecrated in 1981 by Abp. Herman Adrian Spruit (1911–1944), primate of the Church of Antioch. Through the 1980s Hurlburt led his clergy away from the Church of Antioch's theological perspective toward a more Orthodox position, modeled after the Syrian (Jacobite) Church (the principle source of their orders). Following the granting of independence on mutually agreeable terms, Hurlburt was elected the church's metropolitan-primate and took the ecclesiastical name Mar Peter. After his retirement in 1996 he was succeeded by Metropolitan Archbishop Victor Mar Michael Herron of Knoxville, Tennessee.

In liturgical and theological matters the church generally resembles other churches of the Syro-Antiochene tradition but prefers the term *Ephesine* to describe their Christology over the more controversial term *Monophysite* (as defined by the Council of Ephesus in 431 C.E.). Several of the clergy are engaged in Aramaic biblical and liturgical research and scholarship. The church departs from this Eastern pattern principally in the areas of ecclesiology and women's ordination. Married priests are not barred from the episcopate. The church also actively recruits former Roman Catholic priests and allows the use of the Tridentine Mass where there is an obvious pastoral need. All available clergy meet annually with the metropolitan to discuss issues, advise the metropolitan, establish pastoral goals and guidelines, and renew the bonds of fellowship. Clergy are typically bivocational.

In 2007 an ecumenical sisterhood called the Cloistered Heart Franciscans reorganized within the Antiochian Catholic Church in America; the group conducts services in Tennessee for a small group of people each week.

Membership: In 2008 the church reported one parish with two congregations, in Knoxville and Kodak, Tennessee. There is also one missionary priest who itinerates through several states in the Southeast.

Periodicals: *Chrism.*

Sources:

Antiochian Catholic Church in America. www.geocities.com/Athens/Forum/7951/index.html.

Ward, Gary L. *Independent Bishops: An International Directory.* Detroit, MI: Apogee Books, 1990. 524 pp.

Apostolic Catholic Assyrian Church of the East, North American Diocese

c/o Mar Aprim Khamis, North American Diocese, 8908 Birch Ave., Morton Grove, IL 60053

Alternate Address: His Holiness Mar Dinkha IV, Catholicos Patriarch, PO Box 3257, Sadoun, Baghdad, Iraq.

Victims of Turkish expansion, the Church of the East was dispersed in the late nineteenth century and its headquarters in northern Kurdistan abandoned. Scattered members of the church began to arrive in America in the 1890s, but for many years were without organization. Early in this century, there were several visitations by the bishops. They found a flock served by an insufficient number of priests and deacons meeting whenever space was available. All of this changed in 1940 when Mar Eshai Shimun XXIII, the 119th patriarch of the church, moved his headquarters to Chicago. A church-reorganization program was initiated. Priests and deacons were ordained; churches were purchased and built; administration was put in efficient order; and a publishing program, including a new periodical, was begun. The progress of the church has continued under the present patriarch, who has reestablished the international headquarters in Iraq.

Membership: Not reported. In 1989 the diocese reported 22 churches, 120,000 members, and 109 clergy.

Periodicals: *Voice from the East.*

Sources:

The Liturgy of the Holy Apostles Adai and Mari. London: Society for Promoting Christian Knowledge, 1893.

O'Dishoo, Mar. *The Book of Marganita (The Pearl) on the Truth of Christianity.* Kerala, India: Mar Themotheus Memorial Printing & Publishing House, 1965.

Rules Collected from the Sunhados of the Church of the East & Patriarchial Decrees. San Francisco: Holy Apostolic and Catholic Church of the East, 1960.

Yulpana M'Shikhay D'eta Qaddishta Washlikhayta O'Qathuliqi D'Mathnkha. *Messianic Teachings.* Kerala, India: Mar Themotheus Memorial Printing & Publishing House, 1962.

Apostolic Orthodox Church (Harrisburg, Pennsylvania)

Rt. Rev. James H. Hess, 2410 Derry St., Harrisburg, PA 17111-1141

The Apostolic Orthodox Church was founded in 1997 by Bp. James H. Hess. He was consecrated in 1984 by Bp. Brian G. Turkington, then affiliated with the Free Anglican Church in North America. He headed the Arian Apostolic Church (later renamed Nestorian Apostolic Church), superseded by the Apostolic Orthodox Church. The church is a traditional non-Chalcedonian jurisdiction most closely resembling the other Monophysite churches from Armenia, Egypt, and Ethiopia.

The church accepts the authority of Scripture (including the Apocrypha) and Tradition with particular reference to some of the early Christian writings (Didache, Apostolic Constitutions, the letters of Ignatius, the letters of Clement, the Shepherd of Hermes, Barnabas, and the Martyrdom of Polycarp), the pre-Chalcedonian liturgical books, and the three creeds (Apostles, Nicene, and Athanasian). The Filioque clause in the creeds (which affirms that the Holy Spirit proceeds from the Father and the Son) is accepted. It affirms the two natures (divine and human) of Jesus recognized inseparately (rather than separately as taught at Chalcedon). The church practices the traditional seven sacraments including the Unction for the Sick. It affirms the real presence of Christ in the Eucharist.

The church rejects homosexuality and abortion and does not ordain women to the priesthood. It also believes that the post-Chalcedonian Roman papacy is the Beast of Revelation, that Protestantism is the image of the Beast, that the church in union with the papacy is the whore of Babylon, that Evangelicalism is the false prophet of Revelation, and that the seven trumpets and vials represent the seven heresies of Sabellianism, Arianism, Macedonianism, Apollinarianism, Nestorianism, Diophysitism, and Iconoclasm. The phenomena of contemporary miracles and signs (including Marian apparitions and charismatic occurrences) are rejected. It is believed that the signs of the apostolic age were discontinued after the death of the last apostle.

Membership: The church has one congregation.

Armenian Apostolic Church of America

138 E 39th St., New York, NY 10016

In 1933 the Armenian Church in America split along political lines as a result of the Soviet dominance of Armenia. The Armenian Apostolic Church of America preserves the church that began to form in the 1890s among Armenian Americans and whose members were most committed to a free and independent Armenia. This church existed without official sanction until 1957 when Zareh I, the newly elected catholicos of the See of Cilicia, took it under his jurisdiction. Located in Sis, the capital of Lesser Armenia since the fifteenth century, the See of Cilicia moved to Lebanon in the twentieth century.

The Eastern Prelacy of the United States is located in New York City and is under the leadership of Abp. Oshagan Choloyan. The Western Prelacy is located in Los Angeles, California, under the leadership of Moushegh Mardirossian. The Canadian Prelacy is under Khajag Hagopian.

Membership: In 2002 the church reported 400,000 members in 37 churches with 42 priests in the United States. There were five churches in Canada. Affiliated congregations under the see of Cilicia were located in 10 countries with a reported worldwide membership of 900,000.

Educational Facilities:

Armenian Theological Seminary, Bikfaya, Lebanon.

Periodicals: *The Outreach.*

Sources:

Armenian Prelacy, Armenian Apostolic Church of America. www.armenianprelacy.org/.

Armenian Prelacy of Canada. www.armenianprelacy.ca/home.htm.

Sarkissian, Karekin. "Armenian Church in Contemporary Times." In *The Church in the Middle East*, ed. A. J. Arberry. Cambridge, U.K.: Cambridge University Press, 1969.

————. *The Council of Chalcedon and the Armenian Church*. New York: Armenian Church Prelacy, 1965.

————. *The Witness of the Oriental Orthodox Churches*. Antelias, Lebanon: The Author, 1970.

Catholic Apostolic Church at Davis

c/o Gates of Praise Center, 921 W 8th St., Davis, CA 95616

The Catholic Orthodox Church at Davis was founded in 1972 by Albert Ronald Coady. He was ordained in May 1972 by Abp. John Marion Stanley (b. 1923) of the Orthodox Church of the East. In June 1972 Stanley consecrated Coady at a service in Trichur, India. That consecration was confirmed in July 1972 in a service of enthronement conducted by Abps. Walter A. Propheta, John A. Christian, Lawrence Pierre, and C. Clark, all of the American Orthodox Catholic Church (Propheta). Stanley also participated in that ceremony. Originally known as the Christian Orthodox Church, it became the Eastern Catholic Church Syro-Chaldean Rite before taking its present name in the mid-1980s.

The church is Eastern in its liturgy and, like the Orthodox Church of the East, accepts the Nicene Creed. It is also charismatic in that it accepts the current manifestation of the gifts of the Spirit (I Corinthians 12) in its worship life.

Membership: Not reported.

Coptic Orthodox Church

Coptic Orthodox Church of St. Mark, 427 West Side Ave., Jersey City, NJ 07304

Since World War II, an increasing number of Copts have left Egypt because of Muslim discrimination. Many of these have come to the United States. In 1962 the Coptic Association of America was formed to serve the Coptic Egyptians in New York City and vicinity and to work for the establishment of regular pastoral care. The following year Bishop Samuel, bishop of public, ecumenical, and social services, was delegated to come to the United States by Pope Kyrillos VI to meet with the Coptic Association and implement pastoral care. In 1965 Fr. Marcos Abdel-Messiah was ordained in Cairo and sent as a priest to Toronto to establish the Diocese of North America. In 1967 Fr. Dr. Rafael Younan arrived in Montreal. By 1974 there were nine priests serving four churches in New York, plus other churches in Los Angeles, Houston, Detroit, Jersey City, St. Paul, Indianapolis,

Milwaukee, Chicago, and several smaller centers. An English translation of *The Coptic Orthodox Mass and the Liturgy of St. Basil* has been produced and educational literature has been initiated by Fr. Marcus Beshai of Chicago.

Membership: Not reported.

Sources:

Coptic Orthodox Church. www.coptic.org.

Abdelsayed, Gabriel. "The Coptic-American: A Current African Cultural Contribution in the United States of America." *Migration Today* 19 (1975): 17–19.

Ishak, Fayek M. *A Complete Translation of the Coptic Orthodox Mass and the Liturgy of St. Basil*. Toronto: Coptic Orthodox Church, Diocese of North America, 1973.

Isichei, Elizabeth. *A History of Christianity in Africa: From Antiquity to the Present*. Grand Rapids, MI: William B. Eerdmans, 1995.

St. Mark and the Coptic Church. Cairo: Coptic Orthodox Partriarchate, 1968.

Coptic Orthodox Church (Western Hemisphere)

Current address not obtained for this edition.

The Coptic Orthodox Church is a small African-American Orthodox jurisdiction founded in the late 1970s by Samuel Theophilus Garner. He had been associated with the American Catholic Church, Archdiocese of New York, whose archbishop, James Francis Augustine Lashley, consecrated Garner in 1976. Garner founded the Coptic Orthodox Church a short time later. The church follows Coptic belief and liturgy but is not connected with the Coptic Church in either Egypt or Ethiopia.

Membership: Not reported.

Sources:

Ward, Gary L. *Independent Bishops: An International Directory*. Detroit, MI: Apogee Books, 1990. 524 pp.

Diocese of the Armenian Church of America

Diocese of the Armenian Church of America (Eastern), 630 2nd Ave., New York, NY 10016

Alternate Address: International Headquarters: Catholicosate of All Armenians, Mother See of Holy Etchmiadzin, Vagharshapat, Republic of Armenia.

The Armenian Church of America is the American branch of the Armenian Church. It is under the jurisdiction of the See of Etchmiadzin in the Republic of Armenia. In North America there are three dioceses: Abp. Khajag Barsamian (b. 1951) is primate of the Eastern Diocese; Abp. Hovnan Derderian is primate of the Western Diocese; and Bp. Bagrat Galstanyan is primate of the Canadian Diocese.

Membership: In 2008 the church reported 63 organized and mission parishes in the Eastern Diocese, 36 in the Western Diocese, and 17 in Canada.

Educational Facilities:

St. Nersess Seminary, New Rochelle, New York.

Periodicals: *The Armenian Church*

Sources:

Diocese of the Armenian Church in America (Eastern). www.armenianchurch.net.

The Armenian Church—The Mother See of Holy Etchmiadzin. www.armenianchurch.org/.

Gulesserian, Papken. *The Armenian Church*. New York: Diocese of the Armenian Church in America, 1966.

Gurlekian, Hogop. *Christ's Religion in Every Branch of Life and the Armenians Really Alive*. Chicago: The Author, 1974.

The Handbook on the Divine Liturgy of the Armenian Apostolic Holy Church. Boston: Baikar, 1931.

Manoogian, Sion. *The Armenian Church and Her Teachings*. The Author, n.d.

Zakian, Christopher H., ed. *The Torch Was Passed. The Centennial History of the Armenian Church of America*. New York: St.Vartan Press, 1998.

Eastern Catholic Archdiocese (Chaldean-Syrian)

PO Box 610, Rancho Cordova, CA 95741-0610

Formerly known as the Holy Apostolic-Catholic Church of the East (Chaldean-Syrian), the archdiocese traces its history to the Aramaic-speaking segment of the Christian Church that emerged immediately after the resurrection of Jesus and Pentecost. It has also been known as the Eastern Catholic Church, Coptic, Syriac, and Chaldean-Syrian Rites and the Eastern Catholic Archdiocese (Chaldean-Syriac Rite). The Apostles who founded the church were St. Peter, St. Thomas, and St. Jude Thaddeus during the first century C.E. in what is present-day Iran and India. It survived through centuries that included periods of great expansion and subsequent periods of persecution that saw its almost complete destruction.

In 1934 the Eastern Catholic Church came to the United States in the person of Mar David of Edessa (Stanislaus, Graf von Czernowitz), who served as its first metropolitan. The present metropolitan of the church is Metropolitan Mar Mikhael of Edessa (Heinrich XXVI, Prinz Reuss von Plauen-Brankovic).

The belief and practice of the church is Orthodox. Like the Church of the East, it holds to the doctrines of the first two Ecumenical Councils, affirms the virgin birth of Jesus, his incarnation and sacrificial atonements, and the Holy Trinity. It holds fast to the three original creeds of the church (Athanasian, Apostles, and Nicene). The Bible, consisting of the Old and New Testaments, combined with the Oral and Sacred Traditions of the Church and the Ancient Synodus, are the authorities under which the church operates. The Peshitta, the Bible version translated directly from the ancient Aramaic texts, is utilized. The jurisdiction differs from some other Eastern Christian and other Orthodox churches in that: (1) it entered into the charismatic renewal in 1947 and continues to believe and to teach that the gifts the Holy Spirit (I Corinthians 12) are meant for today; and (2) since the seventh century, the canon laws of the church have permitted its priests to marry either before or after ordination to the priesthood.

Membership: In 2008 the church reported 2.9 million members. In 2001 the church reported 1,143 parishes, 265 missionary and medical missionary stations, hospices, nursing stations, monasteries, and two homes for AIDS babies and toddlers. There were three inpatient hospices for the terminally ill. The ecclesiastical province includes North, Central, and South America; Australia; New Zealand; and Korea as well as vicar-dioceses in Germany and Philippines.

Educational Facilities:

Holy Trinity Seminary holds state accreditation and is affiliated with the German University System (Consortium).

Remarks: *The Old Catholic Sourcebook* (Garland, 1983), authored by J. Gordon Melton and Karl Pruter, incorrectly identified Mar Mikhael with Michael A. Itkin, a bishop since deceased who also resided in the San Francisco Bay area, who had taken the same ecclesiastical name. Itkin, however, headed a church that is openly identified with the homosexual community (The Community of Love). This practice is in direct opposition to the beliefs and practices of the Eastern Catholic Archdiocese (Chaldean-Syrian) and Metropolitan Mar Mikhael.

Sources:

Eastern Catholic Archdiocese (Chaldean-Syrian). www.easterncatholicchurch.org.

Ethiopian Orthodox Church in the United States of America

Current address not obtained for this edition.

From its beginning, the Ethiopian Church was affiliated with the See of St. Mark at Alexandria, Egypt. After the death of Frumentius, the first bishop of Ethiopia, Egyptian bishops were appointed to head the Ethiopian church. This practice continued into the twentieth century. However, the changes wrought by the new century, including a new feeling of independence aroused by the leadership of Emperor Haile Selassie (1891–1975), made it desirable to have native bishops.

Negotiations began in 1926 and step by step the church moved toward an autonomous status. In 1929, for the first time, native bishops were consecrated, though they were not assigned to specific dioceses and not allowed to perform further consecrations. In 1944 the emperor established the Theological College in Addis Ababa. Immediately after World War II, in 1948, the Statute of Independence of the Ethiopian Church from the Egyptian Coptic Church was promulgated. That same year the Ethiopian Church joined the World Council of Churches. In 1959 the Ethiopian Church was granted full independence, though it remains in canonical union with the Coptic Church. In 1971 the See of Addis Ababa was raised to patriarchal status and Abuna Theophilus (1909–1977) was elevated to patriarch of Addis Ababa.

The 1970s and 1980s were difficult times for the Ethiopian Church. In 1974 Haile Selassie was overthrown and an atheist Marxist regime came to power. In 1975 church-state separation was declared and the church placed on its own. In 1976 Abuna Theophilus was removed from office and arrested. He disappeared and was never seen again.

In 1959, the same year the Ethiopian Church attained independence, Laike Mandefro joined a small group of Ethiopian priests studying in the United States. The group was originally sponsored by Abuna Gabre Kristos Mikael of the Ethiopian Coptic Church of North and South America. However, they soon removed themselves from that jurisdiction and placed themselves under Abuna Theophilus, then archbishop of Harar Province in Ethiopia. Mandefro gathered an initial congregation in Brooklyn, New York, and soon afterward led in the formation of churches in Trinidad and Guyana. As his efforts bore fruit, he was raised to the rank of archimandrite. In 1970 he moved to Jamaica and over the next seven years established the church in a number of locations across the island.

In 1972 the Diocese of the Western Hemisphere was created and Mandefro consecrated as its first bishop. He was elevated to archbishop on 1983. Branch churches of the archdiocese are located in the United States, Guyana, South Africa, and a number of the Caribbean Islands.

In 1992 American leaders of the church split with the mother church after declaring themselves independent from the hierarchy in Addis Ababa. Despite the break, Archbishop Abuna Yesehaq (1933–2005) indicated that American representatives of the church would continue to abide by the teachings, traditions, and beliefs of the Ethiopian Orthodox Church. The main reason behind the split was that Archbishop Yesehaq was among those who believed that the current patriarch of the church in Ethiopia, Abune Paulos, had been fraudulently installed and was unworthy of deference on the part of the church membership and leadership. Archbishop Yesehaq died in Newark, New Jersey, on December 29, 2005.

Membership: In 1992 the archdiocese reported 100,000 communicant members and 75 ordained priests and deacons. Congregations in the United States are located in New York City and the Bronx, New York; Boston, Massachusetts; Washington, D.C.; Atlanta, Georgia; Seattle, Washington; and Fresno, Oakland, and Los Angeles, California.

Sources:

Ethiopian Orthodox Tewahedo Church. www.eotc.faithweb.com/orth.html.

Bessil-Watson, Lisa, comp. *Handbook of Churches in the Caribbean*. Bridgetown, Barbados: Cedar Press, 1982.

Molnar, Enrico S. *The Ethiopian Orthodox Church*. Pasadena, CA: Bloy House Theological School, 1969.

Simon, K. M. *The Ethiopian Orthodox Church*. Addis Ababa, Ethiopia, n.d.

Yesehaq, Archbishop. *The Ethiopian Tewahedo Church: An Integrally African Church*. Bel Air, CA: Winston-Derek Publishers, 1997.

Ethiopian Orthodox Coptic Church, Diocese of North and South America

Current address not obtained for this edition.

The Ethiopian Orthodox Coptic Church, Diocese of North and South America, was formed by Most Rev. Abuna Mikael Gabre Kristos an Ethiopian American who established his jurisdiction under the authority of the Abp. Walter Propheta of the American Orthodox Catholic Church. In 1959 he traveled to Ethiopia, was ordained, and then was elevated to the rank of chorepiscopus by Abuna Basilios, patriarch of Ethiopia. He then served as sponsor for a group of three priests and five deacons sent by Abuna Basilios to the United States for advanced study and to develop an American branch of the Ethiopian Orthodox Church. However, the priests, led by Fr. Laike Mandefro (1933-2005), broke relations with Kristos and centered their efforts on a parish in Brooklyn, New York, later relocated to the Bronx, which was directly under the authority of the patriarch in Addis Ababa. The Ethiopian Orthodox Coptic Church remains in communion with the American Orthodox Catholic Church, from which some of the clergy were drawn.

In the few years of its existence it has established churches in Trinidad, Mexico, and Pennsylvania; in Brooklyn there are two churches, one with a Latin and one with a Coptic Ethiopian rite, the rite commonly followed by the church. The worship is in English. The priests are both celibate and married, and all bishops are celibate, the common Eastern church practice. Most of the members and clergy are black, but the church made news in 1972 by elevating a white man to the episcopate as bishop of Brooklyn.

Friction has developed between the two "Ethiopian" churches, each questioning the legitimacy of the other.

Membership: Not reported. It is estimated that several hundred members can be found in the parishes in New York and Pennsylvania.

International Alliance of Web-Based Churches

c/o Rev. David M. Ford, 4202 Windsor Spring Rd., No. 131, Hephzibah, GA 30815

The International Alliance of Web-Based Churches is a fellowship of online churches associated together in cyberspace. Membership is through mutual agreement and consent and is open to any Internet church regardless of denomination. Members share a commitment to bring the Word of God to all nations by utilizing the potential of the Internet. Founder and coordinator of the alliance is Rev. David M. Ford, who also founded the First International Church of the Web.

Member churches come from a variety of conservative Protestant perspectives, emphasizing the teachings of Jesus Christ over and above interpretive differences.

Membership: In 2008 the alliance reported 24 member churches or ministries.

Sources:

International Alliance of Web-Based Churches. www.ficotw.org/Alliance.html.

Malankara Orthodox (Syrian) Church

American Diocese, Indian Orthodox Church Center, 80-84 Commonwealth Blvd., Bellerose, NY 11426

The Malankara Orthodox (Syrian) Church dates itself to the arrival of St. Thomas, one of the disciples of Jesus, in India in 52 C.E. St. Thomas worked in southern India and was martyred on St. Thomas Mount, Madras. After existing independently for many centuries, the church developed a relationship with the Roman Catholic Church in 1599 at the Synod of Daimper. That relationship ended in 1653 in what is frequently referred to as the "Coonan Cross incident." In dramatic action, church members grasping a rope that symbolically tied them to a cross erected at Mattancherry, Cochin, renounced the Roman Catholic faith and the authority of the pope both for themselves and succeeding generations.

The Malankara Church soon affiliated with the Syrian Church of Antioch. After separating from the church, it was left without a bishop. In 1765 Archdeacon Thomas of Mar Thoma VI, who was consecrated bishop in 1761, was made metropolitan by the name Mar Dionysius I (r. 1765–1808). A century later the head of

the Indian church found himself engaged in a quarrel with another bishop claiming authority over the Indian Christians. He asked the Syrian patriarch, who had consecrated the rival, to assist him. In 1875 Patriarch Mar Peter came to India, excommunicated the rival, and reorganized the Indian Church into seven dioceses, each headed by a bishop subject to him.

The following decades were spent asserting the independent position of the church from both the Syrian patriarch (who tried to assume title to church property) and the followers of the excommunicated rival. Two decisive events ended the controversy: First, in 1912, the Syrian patriarch cooperated in the creation of the East Catholicate by declaring the defunct Catholicate of Edessa (Syria) reestablished in India. Second, the last lawsuit was settled in 1958 when the Indian courts recognized the authority of the Indian Catholics in all matters of church administration. In 1995 the Indian Supreme Court reconfirmed the decision.

The Malankara Orthodox Church was brought to the United States in the mid-twentieth century by immigrants from southern India. A diocese was created in 1979, and Thomas Mar Markarios was installed as the first diocesan metropolitan. In 1980 the first church building, Mar Gregorios Syrian Orthodox Church, Staten Island, New York, was purchased and dedicated.

The church is similar in faith and practice to the Syrian Orthodox Church of Antioch and the Syrian Orthodox Church of Malabar. The church was a charter member of the World Council of Churches. The present patriarch of the church is His Holiness Baselios Marthoma Didymos I, enthroned in 2005, whose chair is located at the Catholicate Palace at Kottayam, Kerala. In 2008 the metropolitan of the American Diocese of the Malankara Orthodox Syrian Church was H. G. Mathews Mar Barnabas.

Membership: In 2008 the American Diocese reported 83 parishes, 87 priests, 10 deacons, and 3,500 families, with churches in 25 states.

Sources:

Malankara Orthodox Syrian Church. malankaraorthodoxchurch.in.

Attwater, Donald. *The Christian Churches of the East*. Milwaukee, WI: Bruce Publishing, 1962.

Brown, Leslie. *The Indian Christians of St. Thomas*. Cambridge, U.K.: Cambridge University Press, 1956.

Mathews Mar Barnabas, Metropolitan. *Handbook for the Malankara Orthodox*. Bellerose, NY: Privately published, 1997.

Pamban, Kadavil Paul. *The Orthodox Syrian Church, Its Religion and Philosophy*. Vadayampady, Puthencruz, India: K. V. Pathrose, 1973.

Orthodox Church of the East

5068 SE Horstman Rd., Port Orchard, WA 98366

HISTORY. The Orthodox Church of the East (also known as the Church of the East in America) was founded in 1959 by Bp. John Marion Stanley (b. 1923), and is one of several churches claiming affiliation with the ancient Church of the East through the lineage of its episcopal orders. Stanley was consecrated to the bishopric in 1959 by Charles D. Boltwood (1889–1985) of the Free Protestant Episcopal Church as bishop of Washington. Boltwood also granted Stanley a mandate for an autocephalous body under Boltwood's guidance. Boltwood himself had originally been consecrated by Abp. William Hall, whom he succeeded as head of the church, but was later consecrated *subconditione* by Hugh George de Willmott Newman (1905–1979) of the Catholicate of the West. Newman passed to Boltwood the lineage of Mar Basilius Soares, head of a small body of Indian Christians who have their orders from the Church of the East.

In 1963 Boltwood withdrew from the Catholicate of the West, but remained in communion with Stanley. During this period, Stanley was elevated to metropolitan of the United States by Newman, who gave him the ecclesiastical title of Mar Yokhannan (Aramaic for "Bishop John"). Stanley then experienced the pentecostal baptism of the Holy Spirit accompanied by speaking in tongues. He in turn led his jurisdiction into acceptance of the pentecostal experience and the exercise of the gifts of the Holy Spirit as mentioned in I Corinthians 12. He also became a popular speaker at the interdenominational Full Gospel Businessmen's Fellowship International conferences.

Also in 1963, Stanley became concerned over the report on Newman in Peter Anson's study of independent bishops, *Bishops at Large*. Under the direction of Metropolitan Archbishop Howard of Portland, Oregon, and the Roman Catholic Archdiocese of Seattle, Washington, he entered into dialogue with Rome. For five years cathedrals throughout the world were opened to him to celebrate the Eastern rite.

In 1970, in the Catholic Church of the Holy Resurrection in New York City, Patriarch Woldymyr I (Walter A. Propheta, 1912–1972), founder of the American Orthodox Catholic Church, performed an economia so that Stanley could serve as his apostolic delegate for foreign missions. In 1971 Woldymyr appointed Stanley as exarch plenipotentiary, granting him full authority to deal with problems in church leadership oversees. Stanley's church and clergy remained in his jurisdiction, and he continued in the Church of the East Rite.

Bishop Stanley remained with the American Orthodox Catholic Church until October 24, 1977, when Patriarch Mar Apriam I (Richard B. Morrill, d. 1994) of the Holy Orthodox Catholic Church, Eastern and Apostolic, gave his patriarchal blessing and letter to return the Orthodox Church of the East to an autonomous and autocephalous independent status. Some of the prelates and clergy in Stanley's jurisdiction had previously been under Mar Apriam I. Since that time, the Orthodox Church of the East has remained autonomous from, though in dialogue with, the Church of the East in Iraq and the Church of the East in India. It also remains in open communion with the Free Protestant Episcopal Church.

Mar Yokhannan consecrated Mar Khananishu (Mt. Rev. Robert W. Burgess Jr.) as bishop of Washington on June 25, 1989. Bishop Burgess was elected to succeed Mar Yokhannan on October 12, 1989.

BELIEFS. The Orthodox Church of the East in America is Orthodox in faith and practice and accepts the Nicene Creed, using the Eastern text. It follows the Syro-Chaldean (Aramaic) liturgy of the Holy Apostolic Catholic Assyrian Church of the East, but uses an English text based on the archbishop of Canterbury's committee's translation of Kirbana Kadisha (Holy Eucharist), the shortened form approved by the Metropolitan of India in 1976 during his visit to Santa Barbara, California. It also follows the Church of the East's Hebraic standards prohibiting statues or pictures in the sanctuary, but does not emphasize the *malka*—that is, the tradition of preparing the Eucharist from dough kept since the Last Supper. Members make room for praising in tongues (speaking in tongues) following the ancient liturgy's words, "We make new harps in our mouths, and speak a new tongue with lips of fire."

ORGANIZATION. The Orthodox Church of the East follows an episcopal polity. It keeps the biblical practice of bishops being the husbands of one wife (which the patriarch of the Church of the East reinstated). Women are not admitted to the priesthood but many serve as deaconesses up to the rank of archdeaconess. There is no restriction as to their ministering in the gifts of the Spirit whenever it is appropriate and necessary.

Bishop Stanley also founded the Messianic Believer's Trust, a parachurch organization promoting charismatic (Pentecostal) renewal. It cooperates with the Believers Charismatic Fellowship, a similar organization, in the publication of the *Messianic Messenger*. Another organization under the church is the World Alliance for Peace, which promotes peace among the people of God, primarily by developing bridges among Christians, Muslims, and Jews. Recent efforts have included an Israeli Children's tennis match for peace before the 1988 Olympic Games in Seoul, Korea, and preparations for a Pacific Peace Conference that will include representatives from Nicaragua and Costa Rica.

The church has a bible school and hospital under its direction in India. A mission work in Pakistan cooperates with other churches in running relief programs for Afghan refugees and seeks to maintain goodwill within the Muslim government. The church is also working to develop an accredited graduate school in Pakistan.

Membership: Not reported.

Educational Facilities:

Suviseshapuram Bible and Technical School, Kerala, India.

Periodicals: *The Messianic Messenger.* • *Messiah Letter.*

Syrian Orthodox Church of Antioch (Patriarchal Vicariates of the United States and Canada) (Jacobite)

Eastern U.S. Vicariate, 260 Elm Ave., Teaneck, NJ 07666

Alternate Address: Western U.S. Vicariate, 900 N Glenoaks Blvd., Burbank, CA 91502; Canadian Vicariate, 4375 Henri Bourassa Quest, St. Laurent, QC, Canada H4L 1A5.

The Syrian Orthodox Church of Antioch (Patriarchal Vicariates of the United States and Canada) dates itself to the beginnings of Christianity in Antioch as recorded in the Acts of the Apostles in the New Testament, but it has been greatly affected by two events. In the fifth century, the church refused to accept the decisions of the Council of Chalcedon concerning the Person of Christ and as a result developed a doctrinal position identical to that of the Coptic, Ethiopian, and Armenian churches. In the following century, the church experienced a marked revival of spiritual life under St. Jacob Baradaeus (500–578), and in recognition of his work, has frequently been referred to as the Syrian Jacobite Church.

The church came to the United States through the migration of members in the late nineteenth century. In 1907 the first priest was ordained and sent to work in America. Abp. Mar Athanasius Y. Samuel (1909–1995) moved to America in 1949 and was soon appointed patriarchal vicar. The archdiocese was formally created in 1957. Archbishop Samuel received some fame in the 1950s as a result of his having purchased the first of what were to become known as the Dead Sea Scrolls. Samuel died in 1965 and was buried in the Netherlands.

In 1995 the Holy Synod of the Syrian Orthodox Church of Antioch divided the Archdiocese of North America into three separate Patriarchal Vicariates, each under a hierarch of the church.

The church adheres to the faith of the first three Ecumenical Councils. It accepts the Nicene Creed but not the Chalcedonian formula and its teaching on the two natures of Christ. There are seven sacraments: baptism, chrismation, the Eucharist, confession (and penitence), marriage, holy orders, and the anointment of the sick.

The Patriarchal Vicariates are an integral part of the Syrian Orthodox Patriarchate of Antioch and All the East, whose headquarters are located in Damascus, Syria. The church is currently headed by His Holiness Moran Mor Ignatius Zakka I Iwas (b. 1932), the patriarch of Antioch and All the East. The Patriarchate is a member of the World Council of Churches and the Middle East Council of Churches. The Patriarchal Vicariates of the United States are a member of the National Council of Churches. There is an annual convention of the Patriarchal Vicariates.

Membership: In 2008 there were 16 priests in 19 parishes in the United States. Worldwide, more than 3 million believers were related to the Patriarchate.

Periodicals: *SOAYO Speaks and Voice of the Archdiocese.* • *Tebeh.*

Sources:

Syrian Orthodox Church of Antioch, Archdiocese of the Eastern United States. www.syrianorthodoxchurch.org.

Syriac Orthodox Patriarchate of Antioch. sor.cua.edu/Patriarchate/.

Anaphora. Hackensack, NJ: Metropolitan Mar Athanasius Yeshue Samuel, 1967.

Ephrem, Mar Ignatious, I. *The Syrian Church of Antioch, Its Name and History.* Hackensack, NJ: Archdiocese of the Syrian Church of Antioch in the United States and Canada, n.d.

Ephrem Barsoun, Mar Severius. *The Golden Key to Divine Worship.* West New York, NJ, 1951.

Kiraz, George, and Thomas Joseph. *The Syriac Orthodox Church of Antioch: A Brief Overview.* Burbank, CA: Syriac Heritage Committee of the Syriac Orthodox Church, 2000.

Ramban, Kadavil Paul. *The Orthodox Syrian Church, Its Religion and Philosophy*. Vadayampady, Puthencruz, India: K.V. Pathrose, 1973.

Samuel, Athanasius Yeshue. *Treasure of Oumran*. Philadelphia: Westminster Press, 1966.

Syrian Orthodox Church of Malabar

c/o Syriac Orthodox Church of Antioch, Archdiocese of the Eastern United States, 260 Elm Ave., Teaneck, NJ 07666

From the time of the ancient church, there has existed on the southwest Malabar coast of India a people who by legend were first evangelized by the Apostle Thomas. Relations with the Roman See were established in the Middle Ages. In the fifteenth century when the Portuguese began to colonize the Malabar coast, they attempted to Latinize the church, and after a period of tension most of the church withdrew from papal jurisdiction in 1653. In 1665 the Syrian Jacobites sent their representative to the Malabar coast and eventually many of the Malabar Christians were brought under the Syrian patriarch of Antioch. A Malabar bishop was consecrated in 1772. There were approximately 1.5 million Christians in his jurisdiction at the date of last publication.

The Syrian Orthodox Church of Malabar has established a mission in the New York area directly under the patriarch of Antioch. His Eminence Mor Cyril Aphrem Karim has been the archbishop and patriarchal vicar of the Antioch archdiocese since 1996 and oversees 20 parishes in the eastern United States, many of them established since his installation.

Membership: Not reported.

Sources:

www.syrianorthodoxchurch.org.

An English Translation of the Order of the Holy Ourbana of the Mar Thoma Syrian Church of Malabar. Madras, India: Diocesan Press, 1947.

Kaniamparampil, Kurian Corepiscopa. *The Syrian Orthodox Church of India and Its Apostolic Faith*. Tiruvalla, India: N.p., 1989.

Madey, Johannes. "Background and History of the Present Schism in the Malankara Church." In *Oriens Christanus* 60 (1976): 95–112.

Paul, Daniel Babu. *The Syrian Orthodox Christians of St. Thomas*. Ernakulam, India: Cochin, 1968.

Ramban, Kadavil Paul. *The Orthodox Syrian Church, Its Religion and Philosophy*. Vadayampady, Puthencrez, India: K. V. Pathrose, 1973.

Lutheran Family

5

Lutheranism embraces the two basic precepts of Luther's writings: first, that salvation comes by grace through faith alone; and second, that the Bible is the sole rule of faith and the sole authority for doctrine. Lutheranism is distinct from other Reformation churches because of its continued emphasis on a sacramental liturgy and because of Luther's understanding of the Eucharist.

LUTHERAN DOCTRINE. Word and sacrament are the keystones of Lutheran church life. *Word* refers to the appeal to the Bible instead of to both the Bible and tradition. *Sacrament* refers to the high regard Lutherans have for the two sacraments they observe—baptism and the Eucharist—and Luther's theology of the Eucharist. Luther's belief that salvation comes by grace through faith alone finds expression in Lutherans' interpretation of the Bible and reliance on it, and in their celebration of the sacraments.

A discussion of the importance of the Word to Lutherans must start with Luther's background. He was a Bible scholar and a professor at the University of Wittenberg in Germany. He translated the Bible into German and based his theology on the Bible. Before he broke with the Roman Catholic Church, he was an Augustinian monk who strove to merit salvation through ascetic practices. In studying the Bible, however, he found that salvation does not come through human action but only by God's free gift. Thus comes the emphasis on man's sinfulness in Lutheranism: a person who breaks one law is as guilty as a person whose whole life is the breaking of laws. Luther saw that the entire point of Christ's coming was to bring salvation; human beings could not earn it by themselves.

It remains for each person to welcome grace by faith in Christ. This view contrasts with the traditional Roman Catholic emphasis on both faith and good works. Further, this emphasis contradicts a practice popular in Luther's time—the selling of indulgences (by which people paid to cancel the punishment they would receive in purgatory for their sins). Proceeds from the sale of indulgences in Germany were being used, among other things, to finance the building of St. Peter's Basilica in Rome.

Luther's discovery that the righteousness (goodness) of God is humankind's only reason for hope came during the winter of 1513 to 1514 in what is called his "tower experience," so named because it occurred while he was in the monastery tower. Among biblical passages supporting his doctrines are Romans 1:17 ("For in it [the gospel of Jesus] the righteousness of God is revealed through faith, for faith. He who through faith is righteous shall live") and Ephesians 2:8 ("For by grace you have been saved through faith. This is not your own doing, but the gift of God, not because of works, lest anyone should boast").

Because of Johannes Gutenberg's (c. 1390–1468) development of the printing press in the fifteenth century, Luther's translation of the Bible was made widely available. He published a translation of the New Testament in 1522 and the Old Testament in 1534, and they quickly became best sellers in Germany. Lutherans then and now have used the Bible as their only standard for faith and doctrine. Further, Luther used it to counter a range of traditional Catholic elements. First, Luther came to believe that only two sacraments, baptism and the Eucharist, had a biblical basis. Hence Lutherans do not consider the remaining five sacraments administered by the Roman Catholic Church to have sacramental status: penance, confession, holy orders, unction, and marriage. Second, Luther argued against a number of practices that Roman Catholics consider sanctioned by tradition if not by the Bible. For example, he argued that the celibate priesthood has no biblical basis, and he soon left the Augustinian order, in which he functioned as a priest, and married a former nun. Among the pious practices that Lutherans abandoned were monastic life, the veneration of relics, radical fasting, pilgrimages, hair shirts, scourges, and the rosary. Lutheran piety instead developed around hearing the Word in the liturgy, receiving the Eucharist, and reading the Bible. Third, Luther cited the Bible to counter the authority of the pope, and claimed the Bible as the source of his own authority to reform the church.

To discuss the importance of *sacrament* for Lutherans involves treating both Luther's understanding of the Eucharist, and other elements discussed in the next section that make Lutheran liturgy distinctive.

Luther's doctrine of the Eucharist is called *consubstantiation*, a departure from the Roman Catholic doctrine called *transubstantiation*. Luther suggested that Christ is present everywhere, but his presence is especially focused in the Eucharist. The bread and wine still exist, but under the guise of bread and wine is Christ, who is received by the believer physically. This reception occurs, said Luther, because of Christ's promise at the Last Supper that it would occur. The doctrine of transubstantiation, on the other hand, suggests

---

Lutheran Family Chronology

1517 On October 31, German monk Martin Luther posts his Ninety-five Theses concerning indulgences on the door of the Castle Church in Wittenberg.

1523 Luther defends himself before the Imperial Diet meeting at Worms. Afterwards, Emperor Charles V declares him an outlaw.

1530 Luther's supporters present the Confession of Augsburg, primarily authored by Philip Melanchthon, to Charles V in effort to reconcile with Roman Catholics.

1555 Peace of Augsburg gives first legal recognition to Lutheranism and allows each ruler throughout Germany to choose between Lutheranism and Catholicism.

1638 Swedish Lutherans establish Fort Christiana on the Delaware River.

1742 Henry Melchior Muhlenberg arrives in the British American colonies.

1748 Muhlenberg leads in the formation of the first Lutheran synod, the Ministerium of Pennsylvania.

1786 New York Ministerium formed.

1820 The first general, national Lutheran body, the General Synod, is organized in Hagerstown, Maryland.

1826 Samuel S. Schmucker takes the lead in the founding of the Lutheran Theological Seminary at Gettysburg, Pennsylvania.

1846 The Lutheran Church-Missouri Synod is founded by immigrants from Saxony who have rejected the merger of the Lutheran and Reformed churches in their homeland.

1850 Conservative German Lutherans form the Wisconsin Evangelical Lutheran Synod.

1860 Swedish Lutherans form the Augustana Synod.

1872 Conservative Lutheran synods join together in the Lutheran Synodical Conference.

1889 The Alpha Synod, the only African American Lutheran synod, is formed in North Carolina with four pastors, five congregations, and about 180 members. It will last only two years.

1890 Finnish American Lutherans form the Finnish Evangelical Lutheran church.

1917 Three ethnic Norwegian synods joined to form the Norwegian Lutheran Church of America (NLCA).

The National Lutheran Commission is formed to provide for the spiritual well-being of U.S. service personnel involved in World War I.

1918 The General Synod, the General Council, and the General Synod of the South, three predominantly German American synods, join to form the United Lutheran Church in America. The National Lutheran Council, a cooperative body of America Lutheran denominations, was formed to respond to needs growing out of World War I.

1929 Finnish Lutherans in the revivalist Laestadian tradition organize the Apostolic Lutheran Church in America.

1930 Three churches with German origins merge to form the American Lutheran Church.

1935 Walter A. Maier becomes the first speaker for the long-running radio show *The Lutheran Hour.*

1960 The American Lutheran Church (1930, German), United Evangelical Lutheran Church (Danish), and the Evangelical Lutheran Church (Norwegian) merge to form the American Lutheran Church (ALC).

1962 The United Lutheran Church in America (German, Slovak, and Icelandic) joins with the Augustana Evangelical Lutheran Church (Swedish), Finnish Evangelical Lutheran Church, and American Evangelical Lutheran Church (Danish) to form the Lutheran Church in America (LCA).

1963 The Lutheran Free Church (Norwegian) merges into the American Lutheran Church.

1970 The first women are ordained to the ministry: Rev. Elizabeth Alvina Platz (Lutheran Church in America) and Rev. Barbara Andrews (American Lutheran Church).

1976 Controversy within the Lutheran Church-Missouri Synod results in the more liberal faction, centered on Concordia Theological Seminary, withdrawing and forming the Association of Evangelical Lutheran Churches. Rev. Pamela McGee becomes the first female ordained to the Lutheran ministry in Canada.

1979 Earlene Miller is ordained as the first African American female pastor in the Lutheran Church in America.

1988 The American Lutheran Church, the Lutheran Church in America, and the Association of Evangelical Lutheran churches merge to form the Evangelical Lutheran Church in America.

---

that the essence of bread and wine are replaced by the essence of Christ, who thus becomes present physically.

The doctrine of consubstantiation allowed Lutherans to preserve their liturgical worship instead of denying the sacraments altogether. So Lutheran liturgy is distinct from that of, for example, the Anabaptists, who do not have any sacraments, although they do observe a memorial meal as an ordinance. The consubstantiation doctrine also kept Lutherans from following the Reformed tradition, which replaces belief in Christ's physical presence in the sacramental elements with belief only in his spiritual presence in the Eucharist.

LUTHERAN LITURGY. Lutheranism vies with the historic Catholic and Orthodox traditions for its emphasis on liturgy. In the early 1520s, Luther began revising the Sunday service and found himself in conflict with those reformers, such as Andreas von Carlstadt (1486–1541), who looked for radical changes in the worship. Luther developed a form of worship in Wittenberg that followed the form of the Roman liturgy but emphasized the use of the vernacular in preaching,

in the liturgy, and in hymns. Vestments, candles, and pictures became optional. The church calendar remained in use.

Luther did change the format of the service by bringing the sermon into the worship, and on days when the Eucharist was not served, a sermon substituted for it. The use of Gregorian music continued but gradually was replaced. The medieval outline that was standard for each liturgical service was also retained and remains basic in Lutheran liturgy. This outline is reflected in the Agenda, forms of worship adopted by the Lutheran churches in the United States in 1958.

No discussion of Lutheran liturgy would be complete without mention of Lutheran hymnology. All Protestants are familiar with Luther's "A Mighty Fortress Is Our God," a popular anthem that became known as the battle hymn of the Reformation. In 1524 Luther published his first hymn book and a second was published before the year was out. The popular hymns not only spread Luther's ideas on man's sinfulness and God's righteousness, but became integral to the

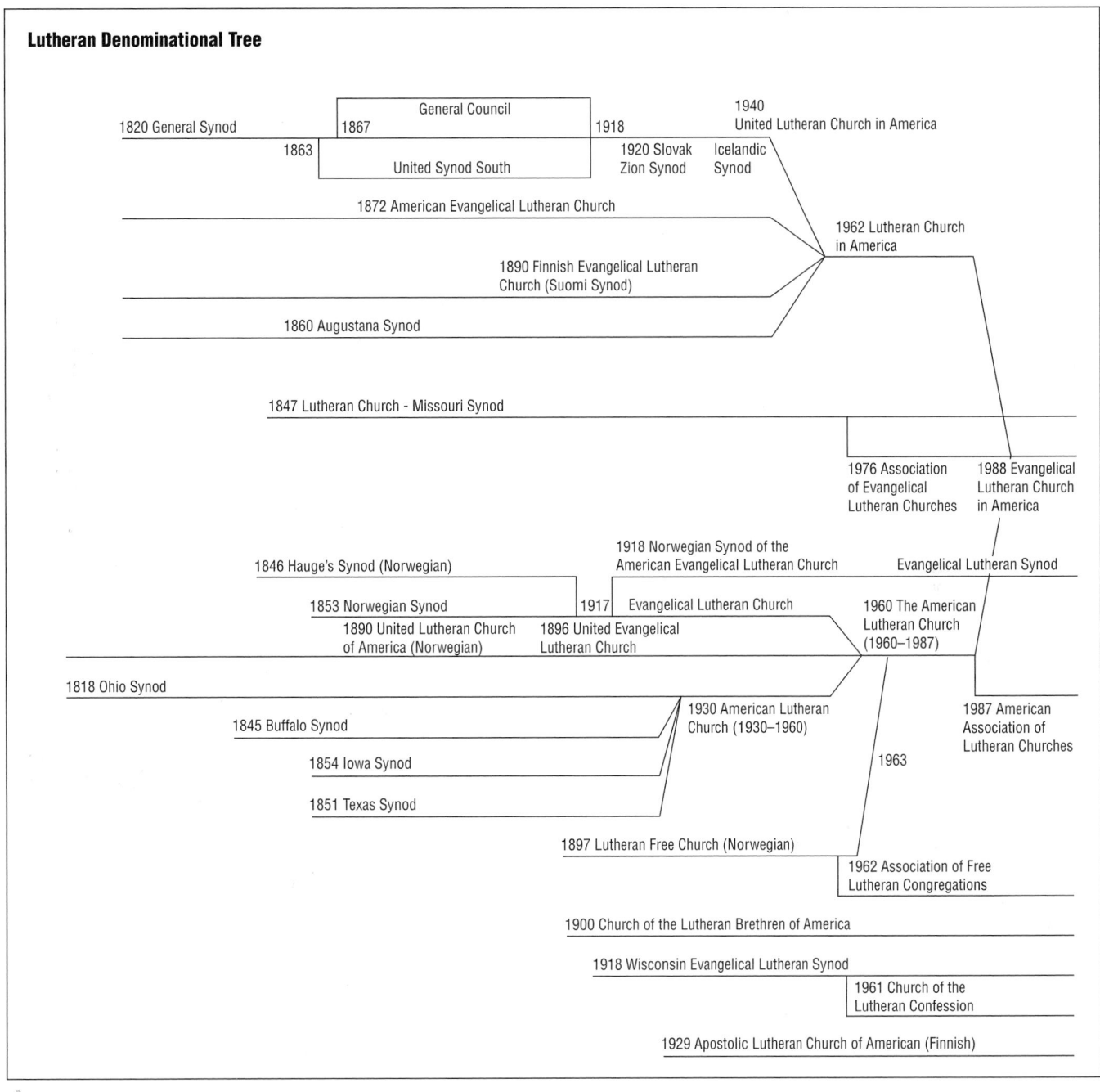

Lutheran Denominational Tree

1820 General Synod

1867 General Council — 1918

1863 — United Synod South

1940 United Lutheran Church in America

1920 Slovak Zion Synod — Icelandic Synod

1872 American Evangelical Lutheran Church

1962 Lutheran Church in America

1890 Finnish Evangelical Lutheran Church (Suomi Synod)

1860 Augustana Synod

1847 Lutheran Church - Missouri Synod

1976 Association of Evangelical Lutheran Churches — 1988 Evangelical Lutheran Church in America

1846 Hauge's Synod (Norwegian)

1918 Norwegian Synod of the American Evangelical Lutheran Church

Evangelical Lutheran Synod

1853 Norwegian Synod — 1917 — Evangelical Lutheran Church

1890 United Lutheran Church of America (Norwegian) — 1896 United Evangelical Lutheran Church

1960 The American Lutheran Church (1960–1987)

1818 Ohio Synod

1845 Buffalo Synod

1930 American Lutheran Church (1930–1960)

1987 American Association of Lutheran Churches

1854 Iowa Synod

1851 Texas Synod

1963

1897 Lutheran Free Church (Norwegian)

1962 Association of Free Lutheran Congregations

1900 Church of the Lutheran Brethren of America

1918 Wisconsin Evangelical Lutheran Synod

1961 Church of the Lutheran Confession

1929 Apostolic Lutheran Church of American (Finnish)

Adapted from Association of Religion Data Archives

worship and distinguish Lutheran liturgy from most other liturgical services.

POLITY. Polity is largely a low-priority subject among Lutherans. Bishops, though rare, have not been entirely unknown. The tendency generally, however, is for churches to operate somewhere between a congregational polity and a form of presbyterianism in which power is vested in the synod or body of ministers.

Luther advocated cooperation between church and state. He said a Christian ruler, acting in a Christian manner, should govern the secular sphere, and the church should govern the religious sphere. Thus the Christian ruler and the church, each in their respective spheres, would oversee the activities of all the people in the state.

THE "CONFESSING" CHURCH. Luther's doctrinal insights and his criticisms of Roman Catholicism were first publicly presented in the Ninety-five Theses he posted on the church door in Wittenberg in 1517, and then in the three treatises of 1521. His position did not find confessional status until 1530, with the Augsburg Confession. Princes who were following Luther and breaking the unity of the Roman Catholic Church had to account to the Holy Roman Emperor for their actions. They presented the Augsburg Confession to the emperor to explain their position. As written by Philip

XNR Productions

Melanchthon (1497–1560), a professor of Greek and a New Testament scholar at Wittenberg, it has remained the central statement of Lutheran essentials. It includes traditional Christian beliefs, those articulated during the conciliar era from the fourth to eighth centuries, such as belief in the Trinity and the resurrection of the body. But it goes further to elaborate on statements concerning humanity, specifically,

on human sinfulness, forgiveness of sin, and justification by grace through faith alone. Lutherans rallied around the Augsburg Confession, and Roman Catholics united against it. It became the standard under which Lutherans later entered the Thirty Years' War (1618–1648).

The Augsburg Confession began the practice of the "confessing" church. Typically, when pressed by a contemporary situation, Lutheran (and Reformed) churches will summarize a stance in the form of a "confession of faith" that says to the world, "Here we stand; we can do no other." In the twentieth century, for example, such statements were issued to counter Nazism and South African apartheid.

To the Augsburg Confession were added other confessions and documents that further clarified a Lutheran position as opposed to other religions. These documents include the Larger and Small Catechism (1529), written by Luther; the Smalcald Articles (1537); and the Formula of Concord (1577). These, along with the three ecumenical creeds (the Apostles' Creed, the Nicene Creed, and the Chalcedonian Creed), were collected in 1580 into the *Book of Concord*. This collection constitutes the basic body of Lutheran doctrinal writings, a clear statement of the truths Lutherans feel are taught in scripture and the starting point for other theological endeavors.

ORIGINS. At least three dates vie for the beginning of Lutheranism. The most widely accepted date is October 31, 1517, the day Luther issued his Ninety-five Theses for debate. Outside the scholarly circles of Lutheran seminaries, this date goes virtually unrivaled as the beginning date not only of Lutheranism but also of the entire Reformation. Lutheran scholars have pointed out, however, that other dates are worthy of consideration. Some cite Luther's discovery of the meaning of the righteousness of God during the winter of 1513 to 1514. This was the so-called tower experience, which supplied the theological insights inherent in the Ninety-five Theses.

The third and most valid year for the origin of Lutheranism is 1530. The years 1514 and 1517 cannot really qualify as dates of origin because no Lutheran church existed then. The year 1530 brought the publishing of the Augsburg Confession. Thereafter, what had been an almost chaotic movement had a symbolic document around which to rally. The congregations that wished to identify with Luther could be said to have become a public entity.

LUTHERANS IN AMERICA. After 1530, Lutheranism spread in Germany, Sweden, Denmark, Finland, and Norway. An independent church was established in each country. But when the Lutherans came to the United States, they entered a vast country as compared to the smaller European states. Lutherans from any one European country were scattered throughout America, seeking good farmland, especially in the Midwest and along the southern seaboard. Everywhere they spread, each linguistic group established a synod, an autonomous Lutheran church. Each group was independent of the churches of other linguistic groups, and typically was independent of the churches established by members of the same immigrant group in other American states. The rapid immigration in the nineteenth century led to the creation by 1850 of more than 150 separate independent Lutheran church bodies. Since that time, the major trend in the history of American Lutheranism has been the story of the merger of

these 150 synods into the relatively few Lutheran churches today.

For no other family of American religions does national origin make such a difference. For example, the Roman Catholics, who came to the United States from all over Europe, remained one ecclesiastical entity when they arrived. Roman Catholic immigrants from various national and linguistic groups did not create diverse denominational bodies. To give another example, most Methodists migrated to the United States from the British Isles and did not create churches divergent from the European Methodist churches (with two minor exceptions). For neither Catholics nor Methodists did national origin matter as much as for Lutherans.

Lutheranism did not enter North America by the establishment of the usual center on the Atlantic coast. It made its appearance, if briefly, in Manitoba, on Hudson's Bay. In 1619, the year before the Puritans landed in Massachusetts, Jens Munck (1579–1628), a Danish explorer, founded a colony at what is today known as Fort Churchill. Among the colonists was Rasmus Jensen (1579–1620), a Lutheran pastor. The colony prospered for several months, until in the dead of winter scurvy began to kill its residents. Only three men remained to sail back to Denmark in the spring. It would be more than 100 years before a second group of Lutherans arrived in what today is Canada, this time to a more hospitable climate in Nova Scotia.

During the 1740s Lutherans descended upon Nova Scotia from two directions. The first group arrived from Maine, where a German colony had been created in 1740 by Samuel Waldo. They were part of an expedition to capture Louisburg from the French. After the battle, a few of the Germans remained and settled in the new English city of Halifax. There they were joined in 1749 by some Germans who came with the original 4,000 settlers and in 1750 by a group of about 300 German colonists. A church, St. George's, was organized and a building was erected. The congregation, however, was continually beset by pastors who converted to Anglicanism. Eventually the church was lost, but not before a permanent Lutheran congregation was established at Lunenburg, a congregation still in place when the loyalist German subjects of King George III (1738–1820) who had been in America began to arrive in Canada after the American Revolution (1775–1783).

Lutheranism was first brought to the United States by Swedes who established a colony, Fort Christina, on the Delaware River in 1638. The Reverend Reorus Torkillus (1599–1643), the first Lutheran pastor in the New World, accompanied them. The Swedes were bolstered by the arrival of German Lutherans who began to settle in Pennsylvania in the last half of the century. By the middle of the eighteenth century, they were firmly entrenched in Pennsylvania and the surrounding territory. In March 1734 Salzburgers created a third Lutheran center in Georgia.

In 1742 Henry Melchior Muhlenberg (1711–1787) came to the colonies, and from the time of his work and ministry, organized Lutheranism in America is dated. Installed as pastor of three congregations in Pennsylvania, he began to reach out to other parishes and to write Germany for continued help. In 1748 he led in the organization of the Ministerium of Pennsylvania, the first Lutheran synod in the colonies. He also opened his home to ministerial candidates. In 1792 a new constitution was adopted. Lay persons were first allowed to come to meetings of ministers in 1796, and the organizational tie to Germany was established in that year.

The decades following the war were ones of expansion and the addition of new synods—New York (1786), North Carolina (1803), Ohio (1818), Maryland (1820), and Tennessee (1820). The General Synod (1820) was a cooperating body for the various state synods. Accompanying the growth was the emergence of tension over the issue of Americanization. Theologian Samuel S. Schmucker (1799–1873) became a leading "liberal" who advocated the use of English in worship and a strong *pietistic* emphasis (a stress on piety and religious experience instead of on rigid doctrinal conformity). Schmucker was opposed by the newly arriving immigrants who came in great numbers in the second quarter of the nineteenth century; they were orthodox and conservative.

Emerging as the leader of the "conservatives" was Carl Ferdinand Wilhelm Walther (1811–1887), who had migrated from Saxony in 1839. He published *Der Lutheraner* to argue his position and was influential in setting the form of Lutheranism for such synods as Missouri (1846), Buffalo (1845), and Iowa (1854).

During the middle of the century, the Scandinavian Lutherans began to arrive in great numbers and to form their own synods. The first Norwegian Synod was formed in 1846. The Swedes in the General Synod joined with recent immigrants to form the Augustana Synod in 1860. Lars Paul Esbjörn (1808–1870) led the Swedish schism. Other synods were formed by the Danes (1872), Icelanders (1885), Finns (1890), and Slovaks (1902).

The great strength of Lutheranism shifted away from the East Coast in the nineteenth century and became dominant in the states north and west of Chicago. Centers were established along the Mississippi River at St. Louis, Missouri; Rock Island, Illinois; and Minneapolis, Minnesota.

The large influx of immigrants who took control away from the older, liberal eastern leaders like Schmucker delayed but could not avoid the problems created by Americanization. The use of English and adaptation to "American" mores increasingly plagued the church and reached its culmination during World War I (1914–1918). There is little doubt that English-speaking churches were able to fan the flames of prohibition by attacking their German brethren who supported German brewers such as Schlitz and Anheuser-Busch.

From the last quarter of the nineteenth century until the present, the major thrust in the Lutheran family has been intrafamily ecumenism. Although Lutherans have entered ecumenical discussions with those of other faiths, these dis-

cussions have never reached the stage of definite plans for a merger. Within Lutheranism, however, there has been a century of mergers by the multitude of independent synodical bodies established in the nineteenth century. Mergers were usually preceded by the formation of cooperative councils. The more conservative Lutheran churches formed the Lutheran Synodical Conference in 1872. The conference included such synods as the Missouri Synod, the Synod of Evangelical Lutheran Churches, the Evangelical Lutheran Synod, and, until 1892, the three synods of Wisconsin, Michigan, and Minnesota. Only the Missouri Synod and the Synod of Evangelical Lutheran Churches remained in the Lutheran Synodical Conference. For all practical purposes, the conference fell apart, due to the Missouri Synod's negotiations through the 1960s with more liberal Lutheran bodies. The National Lutheran Council (1918–1966) and the American Lutheran Conference became the arena for the largest number of mergers by various linguistic traditions as they became Americanized. Major mergers in the 1960s made these obsolete, and they were replaced by the Lutheran Council in the U.S.A., in which the three larger churches participated: the Lutheran Church in America, the American Lutheran Church, and the Lutheran Church-Missouri Synod. In 1977 the Missouri Synod withdrew from the council.

The withdrawal of the Missouri Synod from the Lutheran Council in the U.S.A. occurred during an internal controversy that was to bring conservative forces to the forefront of the synod's life. It also led to the withdrawal of many of the synod's more liberal members, those generally associated with Concordia Theological Seminary. Those who left the synod in 1976 formed the Association of Evangelical Lutheran Churches. They almost immediately joined ongoing merger talks with the two larger Lutheran bodies: the Lutheran Church in America and the American Lutheran Church. That three-way merger was completed in 1987, and the new church, the Evangelical Lutheran Church in America, was officially inaugurated on January 1, 1988. The new church counts more than half of all Lutherans in the United States in its membership, though more than 2.5 million remain in the Missouri Synod. In the years immediately prior to the merger, a number of conservative theological and renewal movements appeared in the two larger Lutheran churches. At the time of the merger, several of these became the nucleus around which emerged schismatic churches that rejected the merger.

In 1997 the Evangelical Lutheran Church in America took a major step in reconciling itself to the churches that grew out of the Reformation, namely the major churches of the Reformed tradition in America. It voted to share communion and extend pulpit fellowship to the Presbyterian Church (USA), the Reformed Church in America, and the United Church of Christ. All four churches have had a long-standing mutual relationship through the National Council of Churches. A similar full communion was celebrated with the Moravian Church in America in 2000 and with the Episcopal Church on January 6, 2001. (The Evangelical

Lutheran Church in Canada and the Anglican Church of Canada also declared full communion with each other later in 2001.) In taking these actions, the Evangelical Lutheran Church in Canada has further strained its relationship with the Lutheran Church–Missouri Synod, with which it does not share either communion or pulpit fellowship.

THE APOSTOLIC LUTHERANS.

One group, the Finnish Apostolic Lutherans, has developed to a large extent outside of the main thrust of Lutheran history in America. The product of an intense pietistic movement originating in a geographically isolated region of northern Scandinavia, and centered in a relatively isolated part of the United States, the Apostolics have moved along a distinct pathway, though still very Lutheran in faith and life. Their small numbers have, due to their splintering, accounted for a large number of Lutheran church bodies.

In the 1840s, in northern Sweden in the area called Lapland, a young pastor, Lars Levi Laestadius (1800–1861), led a revival in the state church, the Swedish Lutheran Church. The movement was based on Laestadius's powerful preaching of repentance. The revival spread from Kaaresuvanto to all of northern Scandinavia. Characteristic of the revival were deep sorrow for sin, public confession of sin before the whole congregation, and the experience of deliverance. Among the leaders of the emerging revival was Juhani Raattamaa (1811–1899), a lay preacher. Raattamaa discovered the "power of the keys," the practice of absolution by which a representative of the church laid hands on the penitent and pronounced forgiveness. The penitent was to believe these words as if Christ had pronounced them. The Laestadians believed that God sent times of visitation on all peoples and that there were Christians in all churches, but they emphasized the need to follow the Bible to attain salvation.

Finns (Laplanders) and other Scandinavians from near the Arctic area began to migrate to America in the 1860s due to economic problems in Scandinavia. They settled in Minnesota and the Upper Peninsula of Michigan. Antti Vitikka began to preach among the Finns and in 1870 gathered a Laestadian group at Calumet, Michigan. The congregation called Solomon Korteniemi as their pastor, and in 1872 to 1873 organized the Solomon Korteniemi Lutheran Society. Korteniemi proved to be a poor leader, and was succeeded by John Takkinen, sent from Sweden. Under his leadership in 1879, the name "Apostolic" Lutheran was chosen.

The Apostolic Lutherans grew and prospered in their American home but quickly became rent with controversy, which splintered them into five separate churches. Each faction goes under the name of Apostolic Lutheran and is distinguished by its secondary name and its doctrine and practice. Only one group has organized formally as a church body.

The first schism in the Apostolic Lutheran movement occurred in the Calumet congregation in 1888. Members opposed to the "harsh rule" of Takkinen elected John Roanpaa and seized the church property. In 1890 Arthur Leopold Heideman arrived from Lapland to serve this new congregation.

In Europe in 1897, the Laestadians split into the Church of the First Born and the Old Laestadians. In America, the Takkinen congregation aligned with the Church of the First Born, and the followers of Arthur Heideman aligned with the Old Laestadians.

Another schism occurred in Europe when a Pietist party, called the New Awakening, left its Pietist church in Finland. In 1910 the New Awakening sent Mikko Saarenpää and Juho Pyörre to America.

These three prime groups—the Old Laestadians, the Church of the First Born, and the New Awakening—share the common Laestadian Lutheran doctrinal heritage transmitted through Raattamaa. Raattamaa had taught that justification and conversion came by hearing the gospel preached by the church of Christ. The New Awakening, however, believed that conversion could occur without hearing the Word. The New Awakening accused the Laestadians of moral laxity and emphasized a strict moral life. The New Awakening also departed from the other Laestadians on their belief in the "third use of the law," that is, that the Ten Commandments were in force for Christians. For the Old Laestadians, the only law was the law of Christ, the commandments of love. The Old Laestadians tended to believe that the church must be outwardly one. Hence they tended to be ultra-exclusivist.

A fourth schism occurred among the Old Laestadians when an emphasis on evangelism—redemption, forgiveness, and the righteousness of Christ—was opposed to an emphasis on Christian life and conduct and the repentance of sin. The evangelicals were inspired by the fervent preaching of Heideman and felt that the preaching of free grace would produce good fruit of itself.

The Apostolic Lutherans have always had a congregational government, in part a reaction to Scandinavian Lutheran episcopacy. Like other extreme congregationalists, they have resisted organization but can be distinguished by doctrinal position, periodicals, and foreign alignments.

SOURCES

The study of American Lutheranism is focused through the Lutheran Historical Conference, 801 DeMun Ave., St. Louis, MO 63105, which publishes *Lutheran Historical Conference Essays and Reports*. Major archival depositories are located at the headquarters of the Evangelical Lutheran Church in America, 8765 W. Higgins Rd., Chicago, IL 60631, and at Concordia Historical Institute, on the campus of Concordia Theological Seminary (a seminary of the Lutheran Church-Missouri Synod) in St. Louis.

Martin Luther

Bainton, Roland. *Here I Stand: A Life of Martin Luther*. New York: Abingdon-Cokesbury, 1950.

Kittelson, James M. *Luther the Reformer: The Story of the Man and His Career*. Minneapolis, MN: Fortress Press, 2003, 334 pp.

Lehman, Hartmut. *Martin Luther in the American Imagination*. Munich, Germany: Fink, 1988. 349 pp.

Lohse, Bernhard. *Martin Luther's Theology: Its Historical and Systematic Development*. Trans. Roy A. Harrisville. Minneapolis, MN: Fortress Press, 1999.

Luther, Martin. *Works.* Eds. Jaroslav Pelikan and Helmut T. Lehman. 55 vols. St. Louis, MO: Concordia Publishing House; Philadelphia: Fortress Press, 1958–1967.

———. *What Luther Says: An Anthology.* St. Louis, MO: Concordia, 1959.

———. *Three Treatises.* Philadelphia: Fortress Press, 1960. Frequently reprinted.

Ritter, Gerhard. *Luther: His Life and Work.* Trans. John Riches. New York: Harper & Row, 1963. 256 pp.

Schwarz, Hans. *True Faith in the True God: An Introduction to Luther's Life and Thought.* Trans. Mark Williams Worthing. Minneapolis, MN: Augsburg, 1996.

The Lutheran Church Worldwide

Bergendoff, Conrad. *The Church of the Lutheran Reformation: A Historical Survey of Lutheranism.* St. Louis. MO: Concordia, 1967. 339 pp.

Bodensieck, Julius, ed. *The Encyclopedia of the Lutheran Church.* 3 vols. Minneapolis, MN: Augsburg, 1965.

Gassmann, Günther, with Duane H. Larson and Mark W. Oldenburg. *Historical Dictionary of Lutheranism.* Metuchen, NJ: Scarecrow Press, 2001.

Gritsch, Eric W. *Fortress Introduction to Lutheranism.* Minneapolis, MN: Fortress Press, 1994. 172 pp.

———. *A History of Lutheranism.* Minneapolis, MN: Fortress Press, 2002. 350 pp.

Hanson, Bradley. *Grace that Frees: The Lutheran Tradition.* Maryknoll, NY: Orbis, 2004. 159 pp.

Hillerbrand, Hans J. *The Oxford Encyclopedia of the Reformation.* 4 vols. New York: Oxford University Press, 1996.

Jacobson, Arland, and James Aageson. *The Future of Lutheranism in a Global Context.* Minneapolis, MN: Augsburg Fortress, 2007. 192 pp.

Janz, Denis R., ed. *A Reformation Reader: Primary Texts and Introductions.* Minneapolis, MN: Fortress Press, 2008. 202 pp.

Lucker, Edwin L., ed. *Lutheran Cyclopedia.* St. Louis, MO: Concordia, 1975. 845 pp.

Lutheran Churches of the World. Minneapolis, MN: Augsburg, 1972. 333 pp.

Nelson, E. Clifford. *The Rise of World Lutheranism: An American Perspective.* Philadelphia: Fortress Press, 1982. 421 pp.

Vajta, Vilmos, ed. *The Lutheran Church, Past and Present.* Minneapolis, MN: Augsburg, 1977. 392 pp.

Lutherans in North America: Historical

Cronmiller, Carl R. *A History of the Lutheran Church in Canada.* Toronto, ON: Evangelical Lutheran Synod of Canada, 1961. 288 pp.

Nelson, E. Clifford, ed. *The Lutherans in North America.* Rev. ed. Philadelphia: Fortress Press, 1980. 564 pp.

Thorkelson, Wilmar. *Lutherans in the U.S.A.* Minneapolis, MN: Augsburg, 1969.

Wallace, Paul A. W. *The Muhlenbergs of Pennsylvania.* Philadelphia: University of Pennsylvania Press, 1950. 358 pp.

Weideraenders, Robert C., and Walter G. Tillmanns. *The Synods of American Lutheranism.* St. Louis, MO: Lutheran Historical Conference, 1968. 209 pp.

Wentz, Abdel Ross. *A Basic History of Lutheranism in America.* Philadelphia: Muhlenburg Press, 1964. 439 pp.

Wolf, Richard C. *Documents of Lutheran Unity in America.* Philadelphia: Fortress Press, 1966. 672 pp.

Doctrine

Allbeck, Willard Dow. *Studies in the Lutheran Confessions.* Rev. ed. Philadelphia: Fortress Press, 1968. 306 pp.

Arnold, Duane W. H., and C. George Fry. *The Way, the Truth, and the Life: An Introduction to Lutheran Christianity.* Grand Rapids, MI: Baker, 1982. 300 pp.

Bratten, Carl E. *Principles of Lutheran Theology.* 2nd ed. Minneapolis, MN: Fortress Press, 2007. 179 pp.

Gritsch, Eric W., and Robert W. Jenson. *Lutheranism: The Theological Movement and Its Confessional Writings.* Philadelphia: Fortress Press, 1976. 214 pp.

Lull, Timothy F., and Mark S. Hamson. *On Being Lutheran: Reflections on Church, Theology, and Faith.* Minneapolis, MN: Augsburg Fortress, 2005. 125 pp.

Mildenberger, Friedrich. *Theology of the Lutheran Confessions.* Trans. Erwin L. Lueker. Philadelphia: Fortress Press, 1986. 257 pp.

Schlink, Edmund. *Theology of the Lutheran Confessions.* Trans. Paul F. Koehneke and Herbert J. A. Bouman. Philadelphia: Muhlenberg Press, 1961.

Liturgy

Reed, Luther D. *The Lutheran Liturgy.* Philadelphia: Muhlenberg Press, 1947. 824 pp.

Stauffer, S. Anita, Gilbert A. Doan, and Michael B. Aune. *Lutherans at Worship.* Minneapolis, MN: Augsburg, 1978. 96 pp.

Polity

Asheim, Ivar, and Victor R. Gold, eds. *Episcopacy in the Lutheran Church? Studies in the Development and Definition of the Office of Church Leadership.* Philadelphia: Fortress Press, 1970. 261 pp.

❋ Intrafaith Organizations

International Lutheran Council

1333 S. Kirkwood Rd., St. Louis, MO 63122-7295

The International Lutheran Council (ILC) is an association of confession-oriented Lutheran bodies that was formally organized in 1993. Its roots can be traced to a gathering of leaders from several confessional Lutheran churches in Uelzen, Germany, in 1952. Seven years later a second, similar meeting was held in Oakland, California, specifically around the topic, "The Fellowship between Our Churches." A third meeting in Cambridge, England, followed shortly thereafter. At Cambridge the name International Lutheran Theological Conference was adopted for an informal series of similar gatherings that would be held over the next three decades. Churches participating in these gatherings adopted a constitution at the 1993 conference in Antigua, Guatemala, and the International Lutheran Council or a formal organization came into existence.

Member churches of the ILC accept the Holy Scriptures as the inspired and infallible Word of God; they view the Lutheran Confessions contained in the Book of Concord as the true and faithful exposition of the Word of God and take them as the basis for their relationship with each other in the council. The organization provides communication, fellowship, mutual encouragement, and mutual assistance among the member churches.

Membership: In 2008 the ILC reported 34 member churches with a combined membership of 3.4 million members on six continents. North American member churches include the Lutheran Church–Canada and the Lutheran Church–Missouri Synod.

Sources:

International Lutheran Council. www.ilc-online.org/.

Lutheran Council in Canada

1512 St. James St., Winnipeg, MB, Canada R3H 0L2

The Lutheran Council in Canada began in 1952 as the Canadian Lutheran Council to serve the churches in Canada affiliated with those Lutheran churches in the United States thatwere affiliated with the National Lutheran Council (namely the Lutheran Church in America (LCA) and the American Lutheran Church (ALC)). In the early 1960s the LCA and the ALC entered into negotiations with the Lutheran

Church–Missouri Synod that led to the discontinuance of the National Lutheran Council and the inauguration of the Lutheran Council in the U.S.A. at the beginning of 1967. In anticipation of this action in the United States, the Canadian Lutheran Council disbanded in the summer of 1966 and reformed as the Lutheran Council in Canada. It began to function officially on January 1, 1967, as did its American counterpart.

In 1967 the American Lutheran Church released its Canadian parishes, who organized as the Evangelical Lutheran Church of Canada. In 1986, in anticipation of the merger of the ALC and LCA in the United States, the Evangelical Lutheran Church merged with the three Canadian synods of the Lutheran Church in America to form the Evangelical Lutheran Church in Canada. Then in 1988 the Canadian synods of the Lutheran Church–Missouri Synod became autonomous as the Lutheran Church–Canada. The Lutheran Council in Canada serves these two Lutheran bodies.

Sources:

Wiederaenders, Robert C., and Walter G. Tillmans. *The Synods of American Lutheranism*. St. Louis, MO: Lutheran Historical Conference, 1968.

Lutheran World Federation

c/o Office of Ecumenical Affairs, Evangelical Lutheran Church, 8765 W Higgins Rd., Chicago, IL 60631

Alternate Address: International Headquarters: 150 route de Ferney, Box 2100, CH-1211 Geneva 2, Switzerland.

The Lutheran World Federation was founded in 1947 but emerged out of the prior work of the World Lutheran Convention, which first met in 1923. The convention grew out of World War I, when many American Lutherans felt the sting of having originated from Germany—the country the United States was fighting—or being closely identified with it. As soon as the war ended, they initiated plans to help those ravaged by the war and began relief efforts in 20 European countries. The desire for closer Lutheran association developed in this postwar atmosphere. In 1921 the National Lutheran Council considered the recommendation for a World Lutheran Federation, and after consideration, launched plans for an international conference of Lutherans, which met in Eisenbach, Germany, in August 1923. After its initial gathering, two more meetings of the convention were held, in Copenhagen, Denmark (1929) and Paris, France (1935). The 1940 meeting, the first scheduled for the United States, was cancelled by the beginning of World War II.

The shattered unity caused by the war was reconstituted in 1947 by the organization of the Lutheran World Federation at Lund, Sweden. Forty-nine churches from 22 countries joined in the effort. The Department of Lutheran World Service was created to aid suffering and needy Lutheran groups. However, the federation quickly turned to the broad areas of church life and thought, and created work areas for theology, world missions, student life, liturgy, theology, and others concerns. Over the years, a greater focus has been placed on Lutherans in traditionally non-Lutheran settings in the Third World.

The Lutheran World Federation has taken a lead in the modern ecumenical movement. It has its headquarters in the World Council of Churches building in Geneva, Switzerland.

Membership: The Lutheran World Federation includes the more liberal wing of Lutheranism worldwide, and in North America counts the following among its members: in Canada, the Estonian Evangelical Lutheran Church Abroad and the Evangelical Lutheran Church in Canada; in the United States, the Evangelical Lutheran Church in American and the Lithuanian Evangelical Lutheran Church in Diaspora.

Periodicals: *Lutheran Reports and Documentation.* • *LWF Information.* • *LWF Sunday.* • Department for Theology and Studies Series *Thinking It Over. . . .*

Sources:

Lutheran World Federation. www.lutheranworld.org.

Bachmann, Mercai Brenne, ed. *Lutheran Mission Directory*. Geneva: Lutheran World Federation, 1982.

Nelson, E. Clifford. *The Rise of World Lutheranism*. Philadelphia: Fortress Press, 1982.

Schjorring, Jens Holger, Prasanna Kumari, and Norman A. Hjelm, eds. *From Federation to Communion: The History of the Lutheran World Federation*. Minneapolis, MN: Fortress Press, 1997.

Wolf, Richard C. *Documents of Lutheran Unity in America*. Philadelphia: Fortress Press, 1966.

U.S. National Committee for the Lutheran World Federation

Evangelical Lutheran Church, 8765 W Higgins Rd., Chicago, IL 60631

The U.S. National Committee for the Lutheran World Federation began during World War I. Lutherans found it expedient to cooperate in caring for the spiritual needs of Lutherans serving in the armed forces, so in 1917 the National Lutheran Commission for Soldiers' and Sailors' Welfare was founded. Most Lutheran bodies cooperated, and the success of the venture led to the suggestion that a more permanent cooperative structure be created. Several meetings led to the formation of the National Lutheran Council in 1918.

The major Lutheran bodies participated in the council. Following the adoption of a constitution by the Lutheran World Federation in 1952, the National Lutheran Council was designated the National Committee for the Lutheran World Federation in the United States, and the council proceeded in 1956 to establish a Division of Lutheran World Federation Affairs. In 1967 the National Lutheran Council was superseded by the Lutheran Council in the U.S.A., which continued its support of the Lutheran World Federation. With the recent disbanding of the Lutheran Council, the work of the committee has been supported by the Evangelical Lutheran Church in America, and the committee has its headquarters in that church's Department for Ecumenical Affairs.

Membership: The Lutheran World Federation includes the more liberal wing of Lutheranism worldwide, and in North America counts the following among its members: Estonian Evangelical Lutheran Church in Exile; Evangelical Lutheran Church in America; Evangelical Lutheran Church in Canada; and Lithuanian Evangelical Lutheran Church in Exile.

Sources:

U.S. National Committee for the Lutheran World Federation. www.elca.org/.

Bonderud, Omar, and Charles Lutz, eds. *America's Lutherans*. Columbus, OH: Wartburg Press, 1955.

Wolf, Richard C. *Documents of Lutheran Unity in America*. Philadelphia: Fortress Press, 1966.

❀ Lutheran Churches

American Association of Lutheran Churches

6600 N Clinton St., Augustine Hall, #13, Fort Wayne, IN 46825-1551

Alternate Address: 921 E Dupont Rd., #920, Fort Wayne, IN, 46825.

The American Association of Lutheran Churches was founded in 1987 by former pastors and members of the American Lutheran Church (ALC) who did not wish to participate in that church's 1988 merger with the Lutheran Church in America (LCA) and Association of Evangelical Lutheran Churches. The church was organized at a gathering in Bloomington, Minnesota, in November 1987. The move by the ALC to merge occasioned the protest of more theologically conservative leaders who did not wish closer association with the more liberal LCA. A major concern was the authority of scripture, which the conservatives felt should include an affirmation of the inerrancy of the Bible.

With an emphasis upon the inerrancy of scripture, the new church accepted the position of the ALC, designating the ancient ecumenical creeds (The Apostles,

Athanasian, and Nicene), the unaltered Augsburg Confession, and Martin Luther's Small Catechism as its doctrinal statement. It also acknowledged the remaining documents of the Book of Concord as the normative presentation of its faith. It called its congregations to a program of solid Bible teaching and evangelism. It also passed strong statements against abortion (except when the mother's life is threatened) and homosexuality. The association has a congregational form of church government.

Membership: By 2008, the association had 72 congregations, 9,000 baptized members, and 80 pastors. Churches are located in Arizona, California, Colorado, Florida, Illinois, Iowa, Kansas, Maryland, Michigan, Minnesota, Montana, New Mexico, New York, North Carolina, Ohio, Oregon, Pennsylvania, South Dakota, Virginia, Washington, and Wisconsin.

Educational Facilities:

American Lutheran Theological Seminary, Fort Wayne, Indiana.

Sources:

The American Association of Lutheran Churches. /www.taalc.org.

"American Association of Lutherans Holds Constituting Convention." *The Christian News* (December 14, 1987): 1, 15.

"American Protestantism or Lutheran Orthodoxy?" *The Christian News* (September 28, 1987): 16.

Bachmann, E. Theodore, and Mercia Brenne Bachmann. *Lutheran Churches in the World: A Handbook*. Minneapolis, MN: Augsburg Press, 1989.

Apostolic Lutheran Church of America

R.R. 1, Bentley, AB, Canada T0C 0J0

The Apostolic Lutheran Church of America is the only branch of the Laestadian (Finnish Apostolic Lutheran) Movement to organize formally. Since 1908 the Old Laestadians had held an annual "big meeting" that was primarily a time for theological discussions and for affirming consensus. In 1928 the Old Laestadians announced their intention to establish a national church. In 1929 the constitution and by-laws were adopted, asserting the authority of the Bible and the *Book of Concord*. A congregational government and a mission program were established. The church body ordains ministers, establishes institutions, and helps found new congregations. The Old Laestadians practice the laying on of hands to absolve the confessor of felt sin. They also believe in the three baptisms: of water (establishing the covenant between God and his children), of the Holy Spirit (the bond of love), and of blood (godly sorrow).

The Apostolic Lutheran Church is headed by a president and a central board. There are two districts. Congregations are located in Michigan, Minnesota, the Dakotas, Massachusetts, Washington, Oregon, California, Canada, and the Carolinas. It has a foreign mission board with missions in India, Guatemala, Nigeria, and South Africa.

Membership: In 2006 the church reported 51 congregations in the United States and four in Canada.

Educational Facilities:

Inter-Lutheran Theological Seminary, Hancock, Michigan.

Periodicals: *Christian Monthly*. Available from PO Box 2126, Battle Ground, WA 98604-2126.

Sources:

Apostolic Lutheran Church of America. www.apostolic-lutheran.org.

Constitution and By-Laws. Finnish Apostolic Lutheran Church of America, 1929.

Saanivaara, Uuras. *The History of the Laestadian of Apostolic-Lutheran Movement in America*. Ironwood, MI: National Publishing Company, 1947.

Apostolic Lutherans (Church of the First Born)

Current address not obtained for this edition.

The branch of the Apostolic Lutherans, generally called the First Borns, are a continuation of the congregation headed by John Takkinen. They are aligned with the followers of Juhani Raattamaa headquarted at Gellivaara, Finland. They differ from the Old Laestadians (i.e., the Apostolic Lutheran Church) by their emphasis on the simplicity of the Christian life. They turn to the elders of Gellivaara for particular decisions on moral questions. They forbid neckties, pictures on walls, taking photographs, hats on women, Christmas trees, life insurance, and flowers at funerals.

The First Borns were among the first to introduce English in worship and to publish English books. They hold Big Meetings every summer. They print their church news in *Valvoju*, an unofficial publication circulated among Apostolic Lutherans. By the latest count (in the 1940s) there were approximately 2,000 members. Churches are located in Michigan; Wilmington, North Carolina; Wilmington, Delaware; Brush Prairie, Washington; and Gackle, North Dakota. There are approximately 25 congregations.

Membership: Not reported.

Sources:

Saanivaara, Uuras. *The History of the Laestadian or Apostolic-Lutheran Movement in America*. Ironwood, MI: National Publishing Co., 1947.

Apostolic Lutherans (Evangelicals No. 1)

Current address not obtained for this edition.

That branch of the Apostolic Lutheran Movement generally referred to as the "Evangelicals No. 1" began with the inspiration and preaching of Arthur Leopold Heideman (1862–1928), who emphasized positive evangelism. Among the Apostolic Lutherans, they put the least emphasis on confession and sanctification. They use, but do not consider important, public confession. The Evangelicals No. 1 have experienced two splits: In 1921 to 1922 a group led by Paul A. Heideman returned to the beliefs of the Old Laestadians; and in 1940 a split occurred over the place of the commands and counsels of Christ and the apostles and the use of confession. The Evangelicals No. 1 represent those who hold that the commands of Christ are necessary as a norm for Christian living. They believe themselves to be the one church of true believers.

Membership: Not reported.

Sources:

Saavinaara, Uuras. *The History of the Laestadian or Apostolic-Lutheran Movement in America*. Ironwood, MI: National Publishing Co., 1947.

Apostolic Lutherans (Evangelicals No. 2)

Current address not obtained for this edition.

Formed in 1940 and having broken from the Apostolic Lutherans (Evangelicals No. 1), the branch of the Apostolic Lutheran Movement generally called the "Evangelicals No. 2" rejects the need of the commands and counsels of Christ because, they say, the grace of God works in believers to bring about a denial of unrighteousness and worldly lusts, and it works to instill godly and righteous behavior. They reject the confession of sins as a Roman Catholic institution, and they do not emphasize absolution. The law, they believe, should be preached to unbelievers, but only the gospel of free grace to believers.

Like the Evangelicals No. 1, this group believes itself to be the one true church of Christ. Founders of the group include John Koskela, Victor Maki, John Taivalmaa, and Andrew Leskinen.

Membership: Not reported.

Apostolic Lutherans (New Awakening)

Current address not obtained for this edition.

Possibly the smallest branch of the Laestadians, or Apostolic Lutheran Movement, is the New Awakening Group. They teach the "third use of the law," that is, that Christians must abide by the Ten Commandments in addition to Christ's two laws of love of God and love of neighbor. They also teach a second experience following conversion, the "circumcision of the heart," in which one's heart is deeply broken but then experiences a fuller knowledge of Christ's redemptive work and of sanctification.

Membership: Not reported.

Sources:

Saanivaara, Uuras. *The History of the Laestadian or Apostolic-Lutheran Movement in America*. Ironwood, MI: National Publishing Co., 1947.

Apostolic Lutherans (The Heidmans)

Current address not obtained for this edition.

The Heidemans are the second largest group of Apostolic Lutherans. The group was formed in 1921 to 1922 by members of the Apostolic Lutherans (Evangelicals No. 1) who separated and returned to the Old Laestadian position. Thus they resemble the Old Laestadians group, but they remain outside of its organization. The leader of the group was Paul A. Heideman, son of Arthur Leopold Heideman, who was for many years the only ordained minister in the group. He was assisted by a number of preachers.

Membership: Not reported.

Periodicals: *Rauhan Tervehdys*. • *Greetings of Peace*.

Association of Confessional Lutheran Churches

c/o Rev. Rolf D. Preus, First American Lutheran Church, 214 Third Ave. NE, PO Box 541, Mayville, ND 58257

The Association of Confessional Lutheran Churches was formed in 2007 by seven pastors and nine congregations that either left or were dropped from membership in the Evangelical Lutheran Synod. They were representative of a movement that placed renewed emphasis on the Lutheran Confessions and their application to church life. They also complained of a certain level of apathy in the Synod. The member churches state: "We reject and condemn any approach to the Lutheran Confessions that would deny their relevance to the church today or their suitability to settle doctrinal disputes among us."

The new association differs from its parent body on matters of emphasis rather than disagreement over specific doctrines or practice. The association almost immediately entered into dialogue with several other conservative confessional Lutheran bodies, including the Orthodox Lutheran Confessional Conference and the Evangelical Lutheran Diocese of North America. It adopted a form of conferencing that allows for conversation without commitment to specific outcomes.

Membership: In 2008 the association reported nine congregations located in the Midwest and on the West Coast.

Sources:

Association of Confessional Lutheran Churches. reformationchurch.org/ACLC.htm.

Association of Free Lutheran Congregations

3110 E Medicine Lake Blvd., Plymouth, MN 55441

HISTORY. The Association of Free Lutheran Congregations was formed in 1962 by congregations that refused to enter the merger of the Lutheran Free Church with the American Lutheran Church. Among the organizers was the Rev. John P. Strand, who became president at its founding. The dissenting congregations (about 40 in number) met at Thief River Falls, Minnesota, for the organization. They opposed the American Lutheran Church's membership in the World Council of Churches; the liberal theology reflected in new attitudes toward the Bible and the Roman Catholic Church; compromises of congregational polity; high-churchism; and the lack of emphasis on personal Christianity.

BELIEFS. The Association adheres to the traditional Lutheran confessional documents, especially the Unaltered Augsburg Confession and Luther's Small Catechism. The group believes the Bible is the word of God, complete, infallible, and inerrant, and rejects all affiliations and associations that do not accept the Bible alone as definitive for life and practice. The Association specifically rejects the liberal drift of Lutheran theology that accepts modern biblical criticism. It also has refused to make any move toward Roman Catholicism unless the Roman Catholic Church first accepts the Lutheran principles of justification by faith alone and the role of the Bible as the supreme authority for humanity.

A variety of worship styles is characteristic of the Association. A variety of biblical translations are used. Simplicity in worship is encouraged and centrality is given to preaching.

ORGANIZATION. The Association continues the congregational structure of the former Lutheran Free Church. Final human authority rests in local churches, under the Word of God and the Holy Spirit. Representatives of the congregations meet annually in conference. The conference oversees the seminary and bible school; mission work in Brazil, Canada, India, Mexico, and South Africa; and a home mission program.

Membership: In 2008, the Association reported 43,000 members, 280 churches, and 252 ministers in the United States. There are seven churches and eleven ministers in Canada.

Educational Facilities:

Association Free Lutheran Theological Seminary, Plymouth, Minnesota.

Association Free Lutheran Bible School, Plymouth, Minnesota.

Periodicals: *The Lutheran Ambassador*.

Sources:

Walker, Larry, ed. *Standing Fast in Freedom*. AFLC, 1996. Booklet, available through AFLC.

Association of Independent Evangelical Lutheran Churches

c/o St. Peter and St. Paul Lutheran Church, 14th St. and 27th Ave., Astoria, NY 11102

The Association of Independent Evangelical Lutheran Churches is a small, conservative Lutheran church. It affirms the authority of the Bible as the true written Word of God and finds true declaration of its teachings in the Apostles', Nicene, and Athanasian Creeds. Theologically, it is shaped by the writings of Martin Luther and the sixteenth-century Lutheran community collected in the Book of Concord: the Augsburg Confession of 1530, the Smalcald Articles of 1537, the Small and Large Catechism of 1529 by Martin Luther, the Treatise, and the Augsburg Confession and Apology.

The church is led by its presiding bishop, the Most Rev. Dr. Pedro Bravo-Guzmán, who oversees its U.S. parishes. There are also dioceses for Haiti, South America, and South Africa. The church is in full communion with the Anglo-Lutheran Catholic Church, the Lutheran Orthodox Church, and the Lutheran Evangelical Protestant Church, all based in the United States, and several churches based in Haiti and South America.

Membership: Not reported. There are several parishes in New York and the Caribbean.

Sources:

Association of Independent Evangelical Lutheran Churches. www.associationofindependentevangelicallutheranchurches.org/.

Pastor Zip's U.S. Lutheran Web Links. homepage.mac.com/pastorzip/uslutheranlinx.html#LEPC.

Augsburg Lutheran Churches

PO Box 332, Greenfield, IA 50849

The Augsburg Lutheran Churches were formed in 2001 at a constituting meeting held at Elk Horn, Iowa, of representatives of several congregations previously belonging to the Evangelical Lutheran Churches of America (ELCA). The representatives initially formed the Augsburg Lutheran District, a nongeographical district of the ELCA and a fellowship of churches who opposed ongoing trends in the ELCA to standardize the practices of ordination in the church. In the 1990s the ELCA had entered into a number of ecumenical relationships. From their discussions with the Episcopal Church, the ELCA had accepted an imperative to unify its practice of ordination and associated church structures; the many proposals were embodied in a 2001 document, "Called to Common Mission." Among the most controversial was the move toward a bishopric with full apostolic succession.

Some within the church opposed the changes because they believed that the Augsburg Confession (1530), considered the founding document of Lutheranism, holds that ordination is not a sacrament, but a human ceremony. Thus its observance need not be uniform across the church. In 2003 the Augsburg Lutheran District reorganized as a separate denomination and adopted its present name.

The Augsburg Lutheran Churches are organized congregationally and exist as a fellowship to serve and support the member churches. The fellowship organization carries on a variety of tasks for the member churches, including publishing a bimonthly newsletter, maintaining a roster of member clergy, facilitating the efforts of member ministers to serve as military chaplains, and holding an annual convention. The annual convention is the highest legislative body among the churches, and it selects the Augsburg Council and an executive council to administer the churches' affairs between conventions. The churches accept the basic documents constituting the Lutheran theological tradition and apply a conservative interpretation to them.

The Augsburg Lutheran Churches is closely associated with the Lutheran Congregations in Mission for Christ, and some of its congregations have joint membership in both bodies.

Augsburg is a member of the National Association of Evangelicals (NAE) and the National Association of Evangelicals Chaplains Commission

Membership: Not reported.

Educational Facilities:

Augsburg Lutheran Theological Seminary.

Periodicals: *The Crux of the Matter*.

Sources:

Augsburg Lutheran Churches. www.augsburgchurches.org/.

Church of the Lutheran Brethren of America

1020 Alcott Ave. W, Fergus Falls, MN 56537

Alternate Address: PO Box 655, Fergus Falls, MN 56538-0655

The Church of the Lutheran Brethren of America was organized December 17, 1900, when five independent Lutheran congregations met in Milwaukee, Wisconsin, and adopted a constitution closely patterned after that of the Lutheran Free Church of Norway.

The spiritual awakening in the upper Midwest during the 1890s brought new concerns to pastors and laymen, particularly issues of church membership, communion, confirmation, and church polity. These concerns crystallized into convictions that led to the founding of the Church of the Lutheran Brethren.

The Church of the Lutheran Brethren is nonliturgical in worship, with central emphasis on the sermon. The primary criterion for church membership is a personal profession of faith in Jesus Christ. The communion service is reserved for those who profess personal faith in Christ. Each congregation is autonomous, and the synod serves the congregations in advisory, administrative, and cooperative capacities.

Approximately 40 percent of the synodical budget goes towards world mission ventures. A growing home mission ministry is planting new congregations in the United States and Canada. The educational mission of the synod dates back to its very beginning; a Bible school begun in 1903 continues to this day under the name of the Lutheran Center for Christian Learning. A seminary department was added during its early years, and in 1917 an academy was added. The three schools share adjacent campuses in Fergus Falls, Minnesota.

The administrative offices and Faith and Fellowship Press are located near the school campuses. Affiliate organizations operate several retirement/nursing homes, and conference and retreat centers.

Membership: The Church of the Lutheran Brethren of America (CLBA) is a family of 123 congregations in the United States and Canada, with 1,500 daughter congregations in Cameroon, Chad, Japan, and Taiwan now organized into four national churches.

Educational Facilities:

Lutheran Brethren Seminary, Fergus Falls, Minnesota.

Lutheran Center for Christian Learning, Fergus Falls, Minnesota.

Periodicals: *Faith and Fellowship*. Send orders to 704 Vernon Ave. W, Fergus Falls, MN 56537.

Sources:

Church of the Lutheran Brethren of America. www.clba.org.

Levang, Joseph H. *The Church of the Lutheran Brethern, 1900–1975*. Fergus Falls, MN: Lutheran Brethren, 1975.

Petersen, A. A. *Questions and Answers about the Church of the Lutheran Brethren of America*. Fergus Falls, MN: Lutheran Brethren, 1962.

Varberg, Dale, and Idella Varberg. *The Church of the Lutheran Brethren: Its Historical Roots and Distinctive Beliefs*. Fergus Falls, MN: Faith and Fellowship Press, 2000.

Church of the Lutheran Confession

501 Grover Rd., Eau Claire, WI 54701

The Church of the Lutheran Confession (CLC) was organized in 1960 at Watertown, South Dakota, by congregations and clergy who had formerly belonged to the various Lutheran denominations that had comprised the Synodical Conference, a Lutheran ecumenical body. With the loss of doctrinal unity within the conference, they felt compelled by their consciences to leave. At the time of their organization, there were more than 30 congregations; during a generation of growth, this conservative body has more than doubled in size.

Membership: In 2002 the church reported 75 congregations, 8,671 members, and 60 ministers. In 2008 member congregations of the CLC were located in 23 states and Canada, and the church body supported missions in 18 U.S. cities. Although it is not in fellowship with any other U.S. Lutheran body, the CLC has fellowship with three overseas church bodies it is helping to support in India and Nigeria.

Educational Facilities:

Immanuel Lutheran College and Seminary, Eau Claire, Wisconsin.

Periodicals: *The Lutheran Spokesman*. Send orders to 2750 Oxford St. N, Roseville, MN 55113. • *Journal of Theology*. Available from Immanuel Lutheran College and Seminary, 501 Grover Rd., Eau Claire, WI 54701.

Sources:

Church of the Lutheran Confession. clclutheran.org.

Bachmann, E. Theodore, and Mercia Brenne Bachmann. *Lutheran Churches in the World: A Handbook*. Minneapolis, MN: Augsburg Press, 1989.

Mark . . . Avoid . . . Origin of CLC. Eau Claire, WI: CLC Bookhouse, 1983.

Concordia Lutheran Conference

Central Ave. at 171st Pl., Oak Forest, IL 60452-4913

The Concordia Lutheran Conference was organized in 1951 as the Orthodox Lutheran Conference, chiefly by former members of the Lutheran Church—Missouri Synod who wished to "continue in the former doctrinal position of the Missouri Synod" in the face of what they held to be persistent deviations in doctrine and practice. Reorganized in 1956 under its present name and constitution, the church body holds the Bible to be the verbally inspired, inerrant Word of God and the only source and norm of Christian doctrine and life. They accept the *Book of Concord* of 1580 as a proper exposition of the Word of God in the matters that it treats, together with the Missouri Synod's Brief Statement of 1932, as confessional documents to which all their clergy and member congregations subscribe without qualification. Although it rejects indiscriminate ecumenism, the conference is non-separatist and seeks fellowship with others on the basis of unity in faith and confession. Without apologizing for its small size, it maintains a broad-based program that includes a seminary, a publishing house, and foreign missions in Russia and Nigeria.

Membership: In March 2008 there were six member congregations and six clergy/ministersin the United States. and seven congregations and ministers in fellowship abroad. They have affiliated work in Russia and Nigeria. Their publishing house, Scriptural Publications, is in Oak Forest, Illinois.

Educational Facilities:

Concordia Theological Seminary, Oak Forest, Illinois.

Periodicals: *The Concordia Lutheran* (bimonthly).

Sources:

Concordia Lutheran Conference. www.concordialutheranconf.com.

Concordia Lutheran Conference. *Articles of Incorporation: The Concordia Lutheran Conference, Inc.* Amended February 2000.

Bachmann, E. Theodore, and Mercia Brenne Bachmann. *Lutheran Churches in the World: A Handbook*. Minneapolis, MN: Augsburg Press, 1989.

Concordia Lutheran Conference. "What Is the Concordia Lutheran Conference?" Available from www.concordialutheranconf.com.

Concordia Lutheran Conference. *Constitution and Bylaws*. Oak Forest, IL: Author, 1957–2004.

Mensing, H. David. *A Popular History of the Concordia Lutheran Conference*. Oak Forest, IL: Scriptural Publications, 1981. Rpt. 2004.

Conservative Lutheran Association

3504 N Pearl St., PO Box 7186, Tacoma, WA 98407

The Conservative Lutheran Association is the name adopted by the congregations associated with the World Confessional Lutheran Association, a conservative Lutheran advocacy group founded as Lutherans Alert National in 1965 in Cedar Rapids, Iowa, by a group of conservative Lutheran pastors and laypeople concerned with the drift of the larger Lutheran bodies, all of which have now merged into the Evangelical Lutheran Church in America (1988). Chief among their concerns was what they saw as a lessening of the authority of scripture. Lutherans Alert, a nonchurch-forming group, affirmed the inerrancy of the Bible.

In 1969 Lutherans Alert participated in the founding of Faith Evangelical Theological Seminary, a cooperative project of several conservative denominations. As support for Lutherans Alert continued to grow, it changed its name to World Confessional Lutheran Association in 1984 to acknowledge its international constituency.

The lack of response to the concerns of Lutherans Alert and the move toward the 1988 merger of the larger Lutheran denominations led congregations to attach themselves to the World Confessional Lutheran Association. These merged groups were organized in a separate division called the Conservative Lutheran Association, which slowly emerged as a separate Lutheran denomination. Lutherans Alert National has survived as the apologetics division of the larger World Association. Missions and social concerns are now handled by Lutheran World Concerns.

Membership: In 2002 there were 1,267 members and 29 clergy in three churches.

Educational Facilities:

Faith Evangelical Theological Seminary, Tacoma, Washington.

Faith Evangelical Theological Seminary and Biblical Institute, Northridge, California.

Periodicals: *Lutherans Alert National.*

Sources:

Bachmann, E. Theodore, and Mercia Brenne Bachmann. *Lutheran Churches in the World: A Handbook*. Minneapolis, MN: Augsburg Press, 1989.

"Oklahoma Church Leaves LCA." *Christian News* (October 5, 1987): 1, 22.

Estonian Evangelical Lutheran Church (Abroad)

383 Jarvis St., Toronto, ON, Canada M5B 2C7

The Estonian Evangelical Lutheran Church (Abroad) was instated in 1944 as a continuation of the Estonian Evangelical Lutheran Church in the free world after the occupation of Estonia by Communist forces of the former U.S.S.R. It was to serve Estonian Lutherans who fled their country at that time. Internationally, the church is organized into seven synods. It is a member of the Lutheran World Federation, the World Council of Churches, and the Council of European Churches.

In the years following World War II Estonians scattered to North and South America and Australia, where they formed congregations and, later, synods and a unified church. This international church body is overseen by an archbishop and the consistory—previously in Stockholm, Sweden, and since 1991 in Toronto, Canada. The church is conservative, holding the Book of Concord (including the unaltered Augsburg Confession) as its standard of faith.

Since the collapse of the former U.S.S.R. in 1991, firm steps have been taken to unite the church in Estonia and that in the West.

Membership: In 2002 the church reported 24 congregations, about 5,000 members, and 18 pastors in the United States; and 15 congregations, 4,500 members, and 12 pastors in Canada.

Sources:

Estonian Evangelical Lutheran Church (Abroad). www.eelk.ee/eng__EELCabroad.html.

Bachmann, E. Theodore, and Mercia Brenne Bachmann. *Lutheran Churches in the World: A Handbook*. Minneapolis, MN: Augsburg Press, 1989.

Bachmann, Mercia Brenne. *Lutheran Missionary Directory*. Geneva, Switzerland: Lutheran World Federation, 1982.

We Bless You from the House of the Lord. The Estonian Evangelical Lutheran Church of Today. Tallinn, Estonia: Consistory of the EELC, 1997.

Evangelical Lutheran Church in America (1988)

8765 W. Higgins Rd., Chicago, IL 60631-4101

The Evangelical Lutheran Church in America (1988; ELCA) was formed January 1, 1988, by the merger of the Lutheran Church in America, the American Lutheran Church, and the Association of Evangelical Lutheran Churches. This merger created not only the nation's largest Lutheran body, but its fifth-largest denomination. Through the lineage of the Lutheran Church in America, the Evangelical Lutheran Church in America continues the work of the earliest Lutheran organizations in the United States: the Philadelphia Ministerium (1748) and the New York Ministerium (1786). It also culminates a process begun in the first half of the nineteenth century of merging diverse American Lutheran churches and synods so as to unite Lutherans.

HISTORY. The Lutheran Church in America, the largest body merging into the ELCA, was formed in 1962 by the merger of four Lutheran bodies: the United

Lutheran Church in America, the Finnish Evangelical Lutheran Church (Soumi Synod), the American Evangelical Lutheran Church, and the Augustana Evangelical Lutheran Church, which for most of its life was known simply as the Augustana Synod. The 1962 merger was the culmination of no fewer than eight previous mergers, the most significant of which was the 1918 merger of the General Synod, the General Council, and the General Synod of the South to form the United Lutheran Church in America, the largest Lutheran body through most of the twentieth century. The General Synod had in turn been created by the 1820 merger of the older Lutheran associations: the Philadelphia Ministerium, part of the New York Ministerium, and the North Carolina Synod. The membership of the churches in the United Lutheran Church in America tradition was primarily German-American.

Lutheran immigrants established the Synod of Illinois in the Midwest in 1851. Around 1860 the Swedish and Norwegian elements of that synod withdrew and formed the Scandinavian Augustana Synod. That synod joined with the remainder of the New York Ministerium in 1867 to form the very loosely associated General Council. In 1918, when the General Council merged into the United Lutheran Church in America, the Augustana Synod refused to join in the merger and remained an independent body until 1962.

The Finnish Evangelical Lutheran Church, formed in 1890 in Calumet, Michigan, used the liturgy of the Church of Finland. The American Evangelical Lutheran Church dates to 1872, when Danish-American Lutherans formed the Kirklig Missions Forening. Through the merger of these Finnish and Danish synods into the larger German, Swedish, and Norwegian bodies, the Lutheran Church in America became the most complete amalgamation of Lutherans across ethnic boundaries and heralded the Americanization of Lutheran immigrant communities (a process through which all immigrant communities in America must eventually pass).

Another body entering into the 1988 merger, the American Lutheran Church, was formed in 1960 by the merger of three Lutheran bodies: the United Evangelical Lutheran Church, the Evangelical Lutheran Church, and the American Lutheran Church (1930–1960). The merged church retained the name of the group formed in 1930 by the merger of the Ohio (1818), Buffalo (1845), Texas (1851), and Iowa (1845) synods, all of which were of German background. The United Evangelical Lutheran Church was founded in 1896 by the union of two separate synods of Danish background. Pastors seceding from the Norwegian-Danish Conference of 1870 formed the Danish Evangelical Lutheran Association in 1884; a group that had withdrawn from the Danish Evangelical Lutheran Church of America (which eventually merged into the Lutheran Church in America) created the Danish Evangelical Lutheran Church in North America in 1894. The Evangelical Lutheran Church was the result of a merger in 1917 of the different Norwegian Lutheran bodies established in America in the nineteenth century: the United Norwegian Church, the Norwegian Synod, and the Hauge Synod. The American Lutheran Church was the first major merger of Lutheran groups across ethnic lines. In 1963 the Lutheran Free Church also joined the ALC.

The Association of Evangelical Lutheran Churches, the newest and the smallest of the bodies to enter into the 1988 merger, was formed in 1976 by ministers and congregations that withdrew from the Lutheran Church–Missouri Synod. The formation of the association followed many years of increased tensions within the Missouri Synod, spurred by a series of complaints by conservative members about what was seen as a liberal drift within the church. Conservatives demanded the withdrawal of pulpit and altar fellowship from the American Lutheran Church. (Pulpit fellowship refers to the practice of exchanging ministers between congregations for Sunday morning worship. Altar fellowship refers to the acceptance of members from other church bodies during Holy Communion.) Further, conservatives asked for the end of cooperation with both the American Lutheran Church and the Lutheran Church in America in the Lutheran Council in the U.S.A. Most important, they demanded an investigation of the Concordia Theological Seminary, whose faculty, they alleged, was teaching doctrine contrary to official synod standards. Among the key items to which they objected was the teaching of

modern biblical criticism, which, some claimed, compromised belief in the inerrancy of the Bible.

The question of the synod's ability to control teaching at the seminary came to a head in 1972. J. A. O. Preus, president of the Missouri Synod, issued a report accusing some of the seminary faculty members of teaching false doctrines, singling out seminary president John Tietjen for particular criticism. This action further polarized the two visible parties in the synod, and the conservative group increased its demands that the synod enforce doctrinal standards, particularly a literal interpretation of the Bible. The liberals, whose strength centered on the seminary, insisted on greater freedom to interpret the Bible and teach theology. Following a defeat at the 1973 meeting of the synod, the liberals organized Evangelical Lutherans in Mission (ELIM). Early in 1974 Tietjen was suspended as president of Concordia. In reaction, 43 of the 47 professors went on strike; three-fourths of the student body supported them, voting to boycott classes. After leaving Concordia, the faculty and students established Concordia Seminary in Exile (popularly known as Seminex). ELIM supported the new seminary and prepared itself to remain as a liberal dissenting group within the synod.

Over the next two years polarization continued, as conservatives, then in control of the synod, pressed for total conformity with traditional doctrinal standards and threatened removal of voices of dissent. The liberals fought a defensive action until 1976, when, feeling that they could no longer remain in the fellowship, they left to form the Association of Evangelical Lutheran Churches. While retaining the formal doctrinal standards of the Missouri Synod, the new church emphasized openness, diversity, and ecumenism. It immediately established pulpit and altar fellowship with the American Lutheran Church and the Lutheran Church in America, which the church leaders saw as merely a first step to the realization of complete union.

Lutheran work began in Canada in the 1740s, and for many decades the Canadian work was affiliated with the American synods and churches. Congregations affiliated with the American Lutheran Church became an independent body in 1967, and those affiliated with the Lutheran Church in America became an independent body in 1986. (For more on the history of the Evangelical Lutheran Church in Canada, see separate entry.)

BELIEFS. The Evangelical Lutheran Church in America confesses the Triune God, Father, Son, and Holy Spirit. It also confesses Jesus Christ as Lord and Savior and the Gospel as the power of God for the salvation of all who believe. It accepts the canonical Scriptures of the Old and New Testaments as the inspired Word of God and the authoritative source and norm of its proclamation, faith, and life. It accepts the Apostles', Nicene, and Athanasian Creeds as true declarations of its faith, and it accepts the Unaltered Augsburg Confessions as a true witness to the Gospel. It accepts the other confessional writings in the Book of Concord as further valid interpretations of the faith of the Church.

ORGANIZATION. The congregations, synods, and churchwide organization are interdependent partners of the Evangelical Lutheran Church in America. The church is governed by a biennial Churchwide Assembly and, in the interim, a Church Council, which serves as the board of directors. The Evangelical Lutheran Church is headed by a presiding bishop. The church is divided into 65 synods, each headed by a bishop. The publishing ministry of the church is Augsburg Fortress, Publishers. The church is a member of the National Council of Churches, the World Council of Churches, the Lutheran World Federation, and other ecumenical and interreligious conciliar bodies.

In 1997 the ELCA voted to establish full-communion relationships, which foster joint ministries and allow the exchange of pulpits by clergy and the sharing of the sacraments by members with the Presbyterian Church (USA), the United Church of Christ, and the Reformed Church in America. In 1999 full-communion relationships were established with the Episcopal Church and the Northern and Southern Provinces of the Moravian Church. In 2007 the Eastern West Indies Province entered into a full-communion relationship with the ELCA. In 2005 a relationship of interim Eucharistic sharing was established with the United Methodist Church.

Membership: In 2006 the ELCA reported 4,774,205 baptized members, as well as 2,256,700 communing and contributing members, 10,470 congregations, and 17,655 clergy.

Educational Facilities:

Seminaries:

Lutheran School of Theology at Chicago, Chicago, Illinois.

Lutheran Theological Seminary at Gettysburg, Gettysburg, Pennsylvania.

The Lutheran Theological Seminary at Philadelphia, Philadelphia, Pennsylvania.

Lutheran Theological Southern Seminary, Columbia, South Carolina.

Pacific Lutheran Theological Seminary, Berkeley, California.

Trinity Lutheran Seminary, Columbus, Ohio.

Wartburg Theological Seminary, Dubuque, Iowa.

Luther Seminary, St. Paul, Minnesota.

Colleges and Universities:

Augsburg College, Minneapolis, Minnesota.

Augustana College, Rock Island, Illinois.

Augustana College, Sioux Falls, South Dakota.

Bethany College, Lindsborg, Kansas.

California Lutheran University, Thousand Oaks, California.

Capital University, Columbus, Ohio.

Carthage College, Kenosha, Wisconsin.

Concordia College, Moorhead, Minnesota.

Dana College, Blair, Nebraska.

Gettysburg College, Gettysburg, Pennsylvania.

Grand View College, Des Moines, Iowa.

Gustavus Adolphus College, St. Peter, Minnesota.

Lenoir-Rhyne College, Hickory, North Carolina.

Luther College, Decorah, Iowa.

Midland Lutheran College, Fremont, Nebraska.

Muhlenberg College, Allentown, Pennsylvania.

Newberry College, Newberry, South Carolina.

Pacific Lutheran University, Tacoma, Washington.

Roanoke College, Salem, Virginia.

St. Olaf College, Northfield, Minnesota.

Finlandia University, Hancock, Michigan.

Susquehanna University, Selingrove, Pennsylvania.

Texas Lutheran University, Seguin, Texas.

Thiel College, Greenville, Pennsylvania.

Wagner College, Staten Island, New York.

Waldorf College, Forest City, Iowa.

Wartburg College, Waverly, Iowa.

Wittenberg University, Springfield, Ohio.

Periodicals: *The Lutheran*. • *Lutheran Partners*. • *Lutheran Women Today*. • *Seeds for the Parish*.

Sources:

Evangelical Lutheran Church in America. www.elca.org/.

Alman, Lowell G. *One Great Cloud of Witnesses!: You and Your Congregation in the Evangelical Lutheran Church in America*. Minneapolis, MN: Augsburg Fortress, 1997.

Anderson, H. George; Herbert W. Chilstrom; and Mark S. Hanson. *Living Together as Lutherans: Unity within Diversity*. Minneapolis, MN: Augsburg Fortress, 2008.

Bachmann, E. Theodore, with Mercia Brenne Bachmann. *The History of the United Lutheran Church in America, 1918–1962*. Minneapolis: Augsburg Fortress, 1997.

Chilstrom, Herbert W. *Foundations for the Future*. Minneapolis: Publishing House of the Evangelical Lutheran Church in America, 1988.

Nichol, Todd W. *All Those Lutherans*. Minneapolis, MN: Augsburg Publishing House, 1986.

Trexler, Edgar R. *Anatomy of a Merger: People, Dynamics, and Decisions That Shaped the ELCA*. Minneapolis, MN: Augsburg, 1991.

————. *High Expectations: Understanding the ELCA's Early Years, 1988–2002*. Minneapolis, MN: Augsburg Fortress, 2003.

Evangelical Lutheran Church in Canada

302–393 Portage Ave., Winnipeg, MB, Canada R3B 3H6

Lutheranism in Canada dates to the last half of the eighteenth century, when German Lutherans began to migrate into Nova Scotia. Periodic migrations, especially from America in the nineteenth century, led to the formation of Canadian parishes attached to what became two of the three largest American Lutheran bodies, the American Lutheran Church and the Lutheran Church in America. The American Lutheran Church, formed in 1960 by a merger of several Lutheran bodies, began an immediate process of facilitating the Canadian congregations' autonomy. They became fully autonomous in 1967 as the Evangelical Lutheran Church of Canada. In 1986 that church merged with the three Canadian synods of the Lutheran Church in America to form the Evangelical Lutheran Church in Canada. This merger anticipated the 1988 merger of the American Lutheran Church, the Lutheran Church in America, and the Association of Evangelical Lutheran Churches to form the Evangelical Lutheran Church in America (1988).

The new Evangelical Lutheran Church in Canada retains a formal working relationship with the Evangelical Lutheran Church in America, providing for the exchange of pastors and complete altar and pulpit fellowship. The church meets in convention every two years. Foreign work is supported in Argentina, Colombia, Uruguay, Peru, El Salvador, and Papua New Guinea. The church is a member of the Canadian Council of Churches, the World Council of Churches, and the Lutheran World Federation. It also responds to poverty in the world through the Global Hunger and Development Appeal (GHDA) and support international community development projects and programs through Canadian Lutheran World Relief.

Membership: In 2008 the church reported 182,077 baptized members and 620 congregations.

Educational Facilities:

Lutheran Theological Seminary, Saskatoon, Saskatchewan, Canada.

Waterloo Lutheran Seminary, Waterloo, Ontario, Canada.

Augustana University College, Camrose, Alberta, Canada.

Luther College, Regina, Saskatchewan, Canada.

Lutheran Collegiate Bible Institute, Outlook, Saskatchewan, Canada.

Periodicals: *Canada Lutheran* • *E-Communique* • *Healing and Hope* • *The Steward*

Sources:

Evangelical Lutheran Church in Canada. www.elcic.ca.

Synod of Alberta and the Territories, Evangelical Lutheran Church in Canada. www.albertasynod.ca.

Cronmiller, Carl R. *A History of the Lutheran Church in Canada*. Toronto: Evangelical Lutheran Synod of Canada, 1961.

Evangelical Lutheran Diocese of North America

c/o Rt. Rev. James D. Heiser, Salem Lutheran Church, 718 HCR 3424 E, Malone, TX 76660

The Evangelical Lutheran Diocese of North America was founded in 2006 by a group of ministers who had withdrawn from the Lutheran Church—Missouri

Synod. They sought to restore and advance a "consistently Evangelical Lutheran doctrine and practice in harmony with the Sacred Scriptures and the Book of Concord (1580)." At their initial gathering they accepted the idea of episcopal leadership, and chose Pastor James Heiser as the diocesan bishop. Although they accept the leadership of a bishop, the diocese continues to follow the congregational polity of the Missouri Synod. By their definition, the diocese consists of the ministerial members. Congregations remain independent even as they are being served by the diocese's ministers.

The diocese remains a conservative Lutheran body that follows the perspective of the Missouri Synod. It had no doctrinal disagreement with the synod apart from concern about a certain lack of consistency with regard to doctrine and practice. In that regard, the diocese practices closed communion, does not allow ordination of women, and disavows altar fellowship with those churches who are members of the Lutheran World Federation. It also has sought to avoid any adoption of Eastern Orthodox practices not in agreement with the teachings of the Book of Concord.

Membership: In 2008 the diocese's nine pastors served churches scattered around the United States.

Sources:

Evangelical Lutheran Diocese of North America. web.mac.com/hunnius/ELDoNA/Welcome.html.

Evangelical Lutheran Synod

6 Browns Ct., Mankato, MN 56001

The Evangelical Lutheran Synod was formed at Lake Mills, Iowa, in 1918 by a group of 40 pastors and laymen (the conservative wing of Norwegian Lutherans) who declined to enter the merger of other Norwegian Lutherans, deciding instead to establish an independent synod. The name Norwegian Synod of the American Evangelical Lutheran Church was adopted. The present name was assumed in 1957. In 1920 it was received into the conservative-oriented Lutheran Synodical Conference, but withdrew along with the Wisconsin Evangelical Lutheran Synod in 1963. It rejects fellowship with all who deny the essence of Lutheran belief.

Doctrine is the same as the Lutheran consensus with a conservative interpretation (similar to the Wisconsin Synod), and the Evangelical Lutheran Synod has in the past used the Wisconsin and Missouri Synods' seminaries for training its ministers. It is congregational in polity. Resolutions passed by the synod are not binding until sent to the congregations for acceptance. The officers of the synod direct the work of common interest. Home missions are conducted in nine states. Foreign mission work is conducted in Peru, Chile, South Korea, India, the Czech Republic, Latvia, and the Ukraine.

Membership: In 2006, the synod reported 20,559 members, 138 congregations, and 172 ministers.

Educational Facilities:

Bethany Lutheran College, Mankato, Minnesota.

Centro Cristiano Seminary, Lima, Peru.

Periodicals: *Lutheran Sentinel.* Available from Box 185, Albert Lea, MN 56007. • *Lutheran Synod Quarterly.* Available from Bethany Lutheran Theological Seminary, 6 Browns Ct., Mankato, MN 56001.

Sources:

Bachmann, E. Theodore, and Mercia Brenne Bachmann. *Lutheran Churches in the World: A Handbook.* Minneapolis, MN: Augsburg Press, 1989.

Evangelical Marian Catholic Church

PO Box 10317, Brookville, FL 34603

The Evangelical Marian Catholic Church is a small independent Catholic jurisdiction that draws upon Western Catholic, Eastern Catholic, and Lutheran traditions. It is led by its archbishop metropolitan, Most Rev. Anthony J. M. Burns of Child Jesus. The church accepts the ancient creeds of the Christian church and affirms the teachings of the Church Fathers and the Seven Ecumenical Councils. It also accepts the Unaltered Augsburg Confession (1530) and Martin Luther's Small Catechism (from the Lutheran Book of Concord), while interpreting them in the light of what it considers authentic Catholic faith and tradition.

While recognizing the primacy of the pope, the church is administratively independent. It looks toward ultimate union with the Roman Catholic Church, and to that end has joined the Augustana Evangelical Catholic Communion. Affiliated with the church is a ordered community, the Order of St. Ninian.

Membership: In 2008 the church reported one parish in Florida and one in Missouri.

Sources:

Evangelical Marian Catholic Church. www.evmcc.org/.

Fellowship of Lutheran Congregations

320 Erie St., Oak Park, IL 60302

The Fellowship of Lutheran Congregations is a small Lutheran body founded in 1979 by former pastors and members of the Lutheran Church–Missouri Synod who objected to what they saw as liberal trends in the Synod. The group is doctrinally aligned to the Missouri Synod, but adheres to a strict conservative interpretation of the Lutheran doctrinal confessions. Churches are located primarily in Illinois, Missouri, and Minnesota.

Membership: In 1998 there were five congregations, six ministers, and approximately 600 members.

Periodicals: *The Voice.*

General Conference Evangelical Protestant Church/Lutheran Evangelical Protestant Church

PO Box 5184, West Columbia, SC 29171

The General Conference Evangelical Protestant Church/Evangelical Lutheran Protestant Church was founded in 1999 by a small group of independent Lutheran ministers and churches who saw themselves as reorganizing the Evangelical Protestant Church of North America. The Evangelical Protestant Church of North American had been organized originally in 1885 as an informal fellowship of German-American Lutheran congregations in the Ohio Valley who were opposed to the liberal trends beginning to dominate German and American Lutheran seminaries and denominational bodies. The church was more formally organized in 1912, but the association declined in the decades after World War I. It eventually ceased to exist, and its member congregations identified with other synods. The new General Conference emerged from several parishes that traced their roots to the former Evangelical Protestant Church.

The founders of the new General Conference concluded that the Lutheran denominations with which they had been affiliated previously had become theologically and morally liberal. They rejected debates concerning the gender of God, any questioning of the divinity of Jesus, and any erosion of the authority of the Bible. The General Conference accepts the writings included in the Book of Concord as its doctrinal base, and from them it has developed its Statement of Faith and Core Beliefs. The General Conference is open to ordaining women to the ministry, but is opposed to ordaining practicing homosexuals. It does not allow ministers to officiate at civil unions of gay or lesbian couples.

The General Conference is led by its presiding bishop, Most Rev. Nancy Drew, and its board of advisors and synod of bishops. The church is organized into three synods in the United States, and its international synod includes churches in Germany, Kenya, Nigeria, and Zimbabwe. The General Conference was briefly disrupted in 2004 when several of its bishops accepted the opportunity to be reconsecrated in a ceremony that would provide them with apostolic succession. The bishops of the General Conference, like most Lutheran bishops, do not have apostolic succession (as defined within Roman Catholic and Eastern Orthodox circles).

Following the ceremony, the two bishops left the General Conference and participated in the founding of the Orthodox Lutheran Church.

Membership: Not Reported.

Educational Facilities:

Concordia Theologica Institute for Biblical Studies.

Sources:

Lutheran Evangelical Protestant Church. www.orgsites.com/pa/lutheranepc/.

Illinois Lutheran Conference

No central headquarters. For information: Cross of Christ Lutheran Church, Pr. Robert E. Sempert, Jr., 2969 David Rd., Midland, MI 48640

The beginnings of the Illinois Lutheran Conference can be traced to 1970, when two pastors of the Wisconsin Evangelical Lutheran Synod, Wayne A. Popp (d. 2007) of Sauk Village, Illinois, and Richard W. Shekner of Tinley Park, Illinois, were suspended from speaking on the *Lutheran Heritage Hour* radio broadcast. They were attempting to advocate the superiority of the King James Version (1611) of the Bible relative to more recent translations. Pastor Popp subsequently resigned from the Wisconsin Evangelical Lutheran Synod (1970). Pastor Shekner remained in the synod but was finally suspended in 1974. The congregations served by the two men also withdrew from the synod. In 1971 the pair launched the *Lutheran Reformation Hour* over WYCA in Hammond, Indiana. This broadcast became the means of contacting other Lutheran ministers of like mind.

Toward the end of 1978, representatives from Gloria Dei Evangelical Lutheran Church (Tinley Park, Ill.), Our Savior's Evangelical Lutheran Church (Morris, Ill.), and St. Mark's Evangelical Lutheran Church (Sauk Village, Ill.) attended meetings that laid the foundation for what was to become the Illinois Lutheran Conference, which was organized formally in 1979. The new Conference continues the conservative Lutheran perspective of the Wisconsin synod, and is distinguished primarily by its use of the King James version of the Bible.

The *Lutheran Reformation Hour* remains the primary pan-congregational activity supported by the Conference.

Membership: In 2008 the Conference reported seven congregations located in Illinois, Missouri, Michigan, Montana, and Wisconsin, served by four pastors.

Educational Facilities:

Lutheran Theological Studies Center.

Periodicals: *Illinois Lutheran Conference Journal.*

Sources:

Illinois Lutheran Conference. www.illinoislutheranconference.org/index.htm.

International Lutheran Fellowship

c/o The Rev.d. Dr Robert W. Hotes, President/Presiding Bishop, 1124 S Fifth St., LL-C, Springfield, IL 62703

The International Lutheran Fellowship (ILF) was founded in 1967 in Fargo, North Dakota.

Following the precepts of holy scripture and the Lutheran Book of Concord, the ILF seeks to provide ministry to those who wish to maintain a Lutheran identity within the universal Christian (catholic) church. Following amendments to the ILF Constitution in 1994, under the influence of the Lutheran Church of Sweden, the ecclesiastical polity was reorganized to observe the historic apostolic succession of bishops and maintain the clerical offices of bishop, presbyter, and deacon, as a mark of the universal Christian church in the Lutheran understanding.

Membership: As of January 2008, the church reported 65 bishops, pastors, deacons, and teachers in the active directory of clergy and more than 1,000 active individual members. The organization supports active ministries in eleven countries and states worldwide including California, Florida, Indiana, Michigan, New York, North Dakota, Ohio, Pennsylvania, and Tennessee in the United States; Nova

Scotia, Ontario, and the North West Territories, Canada; India, Uganda, Liberia, Republic of Singapore, Thailand, and Venezuela. They meet monthly to fellowship within the various geographical locations of service and annually as a collective body or synod.

Sources:

Bachmann, E. Theodore, and Mercia Brenne Bachmann. *Lutheran Churches in the World: A Handbook.* Minneapolis, MN: Augsburg Press, 1989.

Laestadian Lutheran Church

279 N Medina St., Ste. 150, Loretto, MN 55357

The Laestadian Lutheran Church takes its name from Lars Levi Laestadius, a Lutheran pastor who served in northern Sweden from 1825 to 1861. In 1844 Laestadius encountered Milla Clementsdotter, a member of a revival movement, who guided him toward acceptance of the living faith. His sermons began to inspire a new fervor, and a revival movement soon spread beyond Swedish Lapland.

Finnish immigrants brought the movement to North America in the 1860s. Congregations were first formally organized in Cokato, Minnesota, in 1872 and Calumet, Michigan, in 1873. After 1890 the movement underwent several schisms over the understanding of justification, God's congregation, and the sacraments. The last division prompted the establishment of the Association of American Laestadian Congregations (AALC) on June 9, 1973. The association changed its name in 1995 Laestadian Lutheran Church (LLC) to better convey its spiritual heritage and the nature of its organization.

The teachings of Laestadianism, in accord with the Lutheran Confessions, hold that the Bible is the highest guide and authority for Christian faith, doctrine, and life. At the center is the sermon of Jesus' suffering, death, and victorious resurrection. Laestadians believe the work of Jesus Christ continues in this world as the work of the Holy Spirit in Christ's congregation. The church preaches repentance and the forgiveness of sins.

Membership: In March 2008 the church reported 2,500 members in 32 congregations served by 85 ministers. There are affiliated churches in Canada and several European countries, including Finland, Sweden, Norway, England, Germany, and Russia, as well as in Ecuador, Togo, Ghana, and Kenya. In North America the highest concentrations of members are in Minnesota, Washington, Arizona, Michigan, and Saskatchewan.

Periodicals: *The Voice of Zion.* • *Shepherd's Voice.*

Sources:

Laestadian Lutheran Church. www.laestadianlutheran.org/.

Latvian Evangelical Lutheran Church in America

1853 N. 75th St., Milwaukee, WI 53213

The Soviet occupation of the Baltic states (Latvia, Lithuania, and Estonia) after World War II placed minority Lutheran churches in a precarious position. Latvian nationals who had fled Communist rule and refugees who had left during the war and felt unable to return established a church-in-exile with headquarters in Germany. Latvian Lutherans in the United States organized in 1957 as the Federation of Latvian Evangelical Lutheran Churches in America. The churches reorganized in 1975 to become the Latvian Evangelical Lutheran Church in America. It served as the American constituent point of the Lutheran Church of Latvia in Exile; when Latvia regained independence in 1991 after the breakup of the Soviet Union, the church changed its name to the Latvian Evangelical Lutheran Church Abroad. The Latvian Evangelical Lutheran Church in America supports the School of Theology at the University of Latvia in Riga, Latvia, by providing financial support to raise faculty salaries and sponsoring guest lecturers from the United States and Canada.

The Latvian Lutheran Church follows Lutheran doctrine and affirms the three ancient creeds (Apostles, Nicean, and Athanasian), as well as the unaltered

Augsburg Confession, Luther's Small and Large Catechisms, and the other parts of the Book of Concord.

The synod, presided over by the church's president, meets every three years.

Membership: In 2007 the church reported about 7,900 members in 45 congregations served by 39 ministers in the United States; 3,100 members, 13 congregations, and 9 ministers in Canada; and, in South America, one congregation in Buenos Aires, Argentina, one in São Paulo, Brazil, and one in Caracas, Venezuela, with a total of about 150 members.

Periodicals: *Cela Bîedrs.* • *LELBA Ziņas.*

Sources:

Latvian Evangelical Lutheran Church in America. www.lelba.org/.

Bachmann, E. Theodore, and Mercia Brenne Bachmann. *Lutheran Churches in the World: A Handbook.* Minneapolis, MN: Augsburg Press, 1989.

Lithuanian Evangelical Lutheran Church in Diaspora

c/o Acting Bishop Valdas Ausra, Zion Evangelical Lutheran Church, 9000 S Menard Ave., Oak Lawn, IL 60453

Alternate Address: International address: Lithuanian Evangelical Lutheran Church, c/o Bp. Jonas Kalvanas, J. Tumo-Vaiganto 50, LT-5900 Taurage, Lithuania.

Lutheranism entered Lithuania early in the sixteenth century as the Reformation spread, and it eventually found support among the country's nobility. By the end of the sixteenth century the country had become predominantly Protestant, and then it returned to Catholicism as the Counter Reformation appeared in force. Lutheranism continued as a minority faith. In 1590 Jonas Bretkunas (Johannes Bretke) (1536–1602) completed the translation of the Bible to Lithuanian. When the country came under Russian control in the nineteenth century, the church's synod and consistory were abolished (1832) and the Lutheran parishes incorporated into a Russian-based judicatory. (Other parts of the country were under German and Polish control.) Lithuania finally regained its independence in 1918, and the northern part of Lithuania reunited five years later. However, different parts of Lutheranism remained under different jurisdictions until 1955, when the modern Evangelical Lutheran Church of Lithuania was constituted.

Because of World War II and because Lithuania had been incorporated into the Soviet Union, beginning in 1940 many Lithuanians fled to the west. After 1944 large numbers of Lutheran lay people and nearly all the pastors found asylum in the west. A constituting synod formed the Lithuanian Evangelical Lutheran Church in Exile in 1946 in Germany. Subsequently, the headquarters movement to the United States.

Meanwhile, the remnant church in Lithuania reconstituted a consistory in 1950. An initial synod was held in 1955, the first since World War II. Both the Evangelical Lutheran Church of Lithuania and the Lithuanian Evangelical Lutheran Church in Exile are members of the Lutheran World Federation and the World Council of Churches.

Membership: In 2006 the Lithuanian Evangelical Lutheran Church in Diaspora had about 1,500 members. In Lithuania, in 2001 the church had 55 parishes served by about 25 clergy.

Sources:

Ausra, Valdas. "Lithuanian Lutherans in North America." *Litunas: Lithuanian Quarterly Journal of Arts and Sciences* 42, no. 2 (Summer 1995): 5–18.

Bachmann, E. Theodore, and Mercia Brenne Bachmann. *Lutheran Churches in the World: A Handbook.* Minneapolis, MN: Augsburg, 1989.

Lutheran Church–Canada

3074 Portage Ave., Winnipeg, MB, Canada R3K 0Y2

In 1988 the former Canadian districts of the Lutheran Church–Missouri Synod were set apart as an autonomous body that took the name the Lutheran Church–Canada. The synod's ministry in Canada began with the arrival of Johann Adam Ernst (1817–1882) in Ontario in the 1850s as an outreach of the parish he was serving in Eden, New York. Among the early churches he founded was St. Peter's congregation at Rhineland and the Holy Ghost congregation near Fisherville. The work grew by the affiliation of both previously formed and new congregations, culminating in 1879 in the formation of the Canadian district, with Ernst as the first president. Work soon followed in western Canada, and by the early twentieth century four districts had been founded. In 1959 a federation of the Canadian districts was created, a step toward the autonomy granted in 1988.

The Lutheran Church–Canada is as one in doctrine with the Lutheran Church–Missouri Synod and follows its conservative perspective on the Lutheran tradition. It has a congregational polity, and a convention meets triennially.

The Lutheran Church–Canada has affiliated work in Cambodia, Costa Rica, Honduras, Nicaragua, Thailand, and Ukraine.

Membership: As of December 31, 2006, the Lutheran Church–Canada reported 74,443 members, 322 congregations, and 375 clergy.

Educational Facilities:

Concordia Lutheran Seminary, Edmonton, Alberta.

Concordia University College of Alberta, Edmonton, Alberta.

Concordia Lutheran Theological Seminary, St. Catharines, Ontario.

Periodicals: *The Canadian Lutheran*, Box 163, Sta. A, Winnipeg, MB, R3K 1A1, Canada.

Sources:

Lutheran Church–Canada. www.lutheranchurch.ca/index.html.

Bachmann, E. Theodore, and Mercia Brenne Bachmann. *Lutheran Churches in the World: A Handbook.* Minneapolis, MN: Augsburg Press, 1989.

Cronmiller, Carl Raymond. *A History of the Lutheran Church in Canada.* Toronto: Evangelical Lutheran Synod of Canada, 1961.

Threinen, Norman J. *A Religious-Cultural Mosaic: A History of Lutherans in Canada.* Vulcan, AB: Today's Reformation Press, 2006.

Lutheran Church–Missouri Synod

International Center, 1333 S Kirkwood Rd., St. Louis, MO 63122-7295

Of the largest Lutheran bodies, the Lutheran Church–Missouri Synod, often called simply the Missouri Synod, is by far the most conservative. In 1839 a group of Saxon Lutherans fleeing the rationalism that had captured the Lutheran Church in Germany arrived in New Orleans, Louisiana. They eventually settled south of St. Louis, Missouri, on a large tract of land in Perry County. They were led by the Rev. Martin Stephan (1777–1846), who had been elected bishop. Also among the group was Carl Ferdinand Wilhelm Walther (1811–1887), a young Lutheran minister. Soon after settling in Perry County, Stephan was banished when the colonists discovered he had misappropriated funds and engaged in sexual misconduct.

After Stephan's banishment, Walther became the acknowledged leader. He fought what he felt were the theological errors of Stephan's preaching, particulary the beliefs that the Lutheran Church was the one church, without which there was no salvation; that the ministry was a mediatorship between God and man, hence, ministers were entitled to obedience in all things, even matters not treated by God's Word; and that questions of doctrine were to be decided by the clergy alone. Walther helped found the small school in Altenburg, Missouri, that eventually became Concordia Seminary in St. Louis. In 1841 he went to St. Louis as pastor and in 1844 began to publish the *Lutheraner*, which, issue after issue, championed orthodox Lutheranism as opposed to rationalism (a reliance on reason instead of faith). Articles in the *Lutheraner* fought for the rights and responsibility of the congregation in the church. In 1847 the Missouri Synod was founded on the principle of the autonomy of the congregation. There were 14 congregations and 22 ministers.

The synod had been joined by some Franconians in Michigan and Hanoverians in Indiana. Over the years, they were joined by other small synods, including the

Illinois Synod (1880) and the English Synod of Missouri (1911). In 1963 the National Evangelical Lutheran Church merged into the Missouri Synod. In 1971 the Synod of Evangelical Lutheran Churches joined the Missouri Synod as one of its districts.

Doctrinally, significant differences exist between the Missouri Synod and the Evangelical Lutheran Church in America, the other large American Lutheran body, particularly concerning ordination of women. Polity is congregational. The nodical convention meets triennially. There are 35 districts represented. The convention elects a president and oversees the vast institutional and missional program. There are two seminaries (including Concordia in St. Louis) and 10 colleges and universities in the United States. A number of hospitals and homes dot the nation.

LCMS World Mission works with partner church bodies and emerging church bodies worldwide. They have active work or mission relationships in approximately 85 countries. International fields are divided into four regions, including Africa, Asia, Eurasia, and Latin America.

Membership: In 1996 the Missouri Synod reported 2,601,730 members in 6,099 congregations. There were 8,215 pastors and 8,735 teachers.

Educational Facilities:

Christ College, Irvine, California.

Concordia College, Ann Arbor, Michigan.

Concordia College, Austin, Texas.

Concordia College, Bronxville, New York.

Concordia University, Irvine, California.

Concordia University, Mequon, Wisconsin.

Concordia College, Portland, Oregon.

Concordia University, River Forest, Illinois.

Concordia College, St. Paul, Minnesota.

Concordia College, Selma, Alabama.

Concordia College, Seward, Nebraska.

Concordia Seminary, St. Louis, Missouri.

Concordia Theological Seminary, Ft. Wayne, Indiana.

Periodicals: *The Lutheran Witness. • Reporter.*

Remarks: During the 1960s the Missouri Synod was racked with doctrinal controversy that focused on differing views about how the Bible can be considered the Word of God. The conservatives believe the Bible to be the inerrant Word of God and interpret it quite literally. The more liberal members consider the Bible to bear the Word of God, that is, Jesus Christ, to the church, and, as such, to be properly the object of historical criticism.

In the end (and for the first time in the twentieth century), the conservative viewpoint prevailed, but only after a decade of discussion. As a result, 200 of the 6,100 congregations, representative of the liberal faction, left the synod to form the Association of Evangelical Lutheran Churches, which in 1988 merged with the Evangelical Lutheran Church in America.

Sources:

Lutheran Church—Missouri Synod. www.lcms.org.

Arndt, W. *Fundamental Christian Beliefs*. St. Louis, MO: Concordia Publishing House, 1938.

Graebner, A. *Half a Century of True Lutheranism*. Chattanooga, TN: J. A. Fredrich, n.d.

The Lutheran Annual 1986. St. Louis, MO: Concordia Publishing Company, n.d.

Lutheran Church—Missouri Synod. *Handbook*. St. Louis, MO: Author, n.d.

Meyer, Carl S. *A Brief Historical Sketch of the Lutheran Church—Missouri Synod*. St. Louis, MO: Concordia Publishing House, 1938.

A Week in the Life of the Lutheran Church—Missouri Synod. St. Louis, MO: Concordia Publishing House, 1996.

Lutheran Churches of the Reformation

4014 Wenonah Ln., Fort Wayne, IN 46809

In 1964, several congregations in the Midwest (formerly a part of the Lutheran Church—Missouri Synod) joined to form the Lutheran Churches of the Reformation. These congregations had protested what they considered the growing theological liberalism of the Missouri Synod. They follow the doctrine and life of their parent body but take a conservative position on doctrinal questions. The organization supports active ministries in Nigeria, Congo, Kenya, and Sri Lanka.

Membership: As of 2008, the church reported sixteen clergy serving fifteen congregations and about 1,000 members.

Educational Facilities:

Martin Luther Institute of Sacred Studies, Decatur, Indiana.

Periodicals: *One Accord. • The Faithful Word.*

Sources:

Bachmann, E. Theodore, and Mercia Brenne Bachmann. *Lutheran Churches in the World: A Handbook*. Minneapolis, MN: Augsburg Press, 1989.

Lutheran Congregations in Mission to Christ

No central headquarters. For information:, William Sullivan, Service Coordinator, 7000 Sheldon Road, Canton, MI 48187

Lutheran Congregations in Mission to Christ (LCMC) was founded in March 2001 by pastors and congregations of the Evangelical Lutheran Church in America (ELCA). Their association was prompted by their mutual rejection of the provisions of an agreement that had been hammered out by the ELCA and the Episcopal Church. The agreement embodied in a report, "Called to Common Mission," made provisions for the ELCA bishops to accept consecration (in some cases reconsecration) in a lineage with valid apostolic succession. Those who formed the LCMC rejected the idea of apostolic succession for Lutherans. They also held to a generally more conservative theological stance than the ELCA, focusing on the various Lutheran confessional documents.

The LCMC as originally conceived was to be a "postdenominational" association of churches and ministers that evolved into a new denomination with a congregational polity. In the beginning, several congregations remained within the ELCA, and the LCMC made provisions for double affiliation. Subsequently, some congregations also affiliated with the Augsburg Lutheran Churches, another new denomination founded for reasons similar to the LCMC's.

Member churches meet in an annual gathering where fellowship business is conducted. They also sponsor an annual youth gathering and leadership conference.

Membership: In 2008 LCMC reported 213 affiliated congregations, of which 153 were in the United States. The rest were scattered in seven countries.

Educational Facilities:

Schools recognized by Lutheran Congregations in Mission for Christ *are:*

Bethel Seminary, St. Paul, Minnesota.

The Independent Lutheran Theological Education Project (ILTEP), Oshkosh, Wisconsin.

The Master's Institute Seminary, St. Paul, Minnesota.

North American Baptist Seminary, Sioux Falls, South Dakota.

Salt Lake Theological Seminary, Salt Lake City, Utah.

Sources:

Lutheran Congregations in Mission for Christ. www.lcmc.net/.

Lutheran Ministerium and Synod—USA

c/o St. Matthew Lutheran Church, 2837 E. New York St., Indianapolis, IN 46201

The Lutheran Ministerium and Synod—USA originated out of the concerns of members of the American Association of Lutheran Churches (AALC, formed in

1987) that pentecostalism was seeping into the church's life. Among the most concerned were Prs. John Erickson, Christ Lutheran Church (Chetek, Wisconsin), Ralph Spears, St. Matthew Lutheran Church (Indianapolis, Indiana), and Richard Hueter, Community Lutheran Church (McAllister, Wisconsin). The three called a meeting of fellow pastors to discuss the matter.

At that meeting, held October 7, 1993, Erickson argued that the new denomination's attempt to unite Orthodox, Evangelical, and Charismatic Lutherans in a single church was not working. Shortly after the meeting, new issues arose about the charismatic influence at the AALC's seminary. This brought Pr. Donald Thorson of Christ Lutheran Church (Chippewa Falls, Wisconsin) and Rev. Roy Steward of Altoona, Pennsylvania, to the group of concerned church leaders. The 1994 AALC Convention, however, proved unresponsive to their concerns.

As a next step, the six pastors and their churches organized a conference in Indianapolis on the subject of the inerrancy of Scripture. Subsequently, in 1995, several of the congregations withdrew from the AALC. The pastors and their churches began to discuss the formation of a new church body that would be moderate to middle conservative, confessional, liturgical, and nonhierarchical. These plans bore fruit swiftly with the formation of the Lutheran Ministerium and Synod—USA (LMS–USA). Of the first group of concerned pastors, Prs. Erickson, Spears, and Steward adhered to the new church, and brought along Erickson's Christ Lutheran Church and Spears's St. Matthew Lutheran Church.

The new church adopted a conservative Lutheran theological perspective and affirmed its belief that "the Lutheran Confessions and the Apostles, Nicene, and Athanasian Creeds contained in the Book of Concord of 1580 are the correct exposition of the teaching of Holy Scripture." It adopted a congregational form of church government and affirmed that the church should be self-governing and hold title to its property. The LMS–USA is limited in its authority, but can advise and recommend. The church also adopted a lengthy statement refuting what it saw as the errors of pentecostalism.

The work of the churches collectively is carried forward by the synod, which meet annually. The pastors collective also meet annually and advise on theological matters. The highest offices in the church are the president of the ministerium and chairman of the synod.

Membership: Not reported.

Periodicals: *Table Talk*.

Sources:

Lutheran Ministerium and Synod—USA. www.lmsusa.org

Lutheran Orthodox Church
c/o St. Paul's Lutheran Orthodox Chapel, PO Box 74, Neffs, PA 18065

The Lutheran Orthodox Church (also known as the the Catholic Church—Lutheran Rite) was founded by two former bishops and some lay members of the General Conference Evangelical Protestant Church. Like most Lutheran bishops, the General Conference bishops did not have apostolic succession as generally defined in the Roman Catholic and Eastern Orthodox Churches. In 2004 several of its bishops were offered the opportunity to be reconsecrated with a valid apostolic succession in a ceremony presided over by Swedish archbishop Bertil Persson, presiding bishop of the Apostolic Episcopal Church and the Order of Corporate Reunion. Bps. Samuel Guido and Raymond Copp accepted the invitation, and along with Bp. Tan Binh Phan Nguyen of the Association of Independent Evangelical Lutheran Churches, were consecrated on July 11, 2004. Additional Orthodox, Catholic, and Anglican bishops attended and passed their lineage to the new bishops.

From that consecration ceremony, the new Orthodox Lutheran Church emerged as a small, conservative Lutheran body that continues the emphases of the General Conference Evangelical Protestant Church. It believes that most Lutheran churches have deviated from the teachings of Martin Luther to the point that they are no longer Lutheran in any recognizable sense. The Orthodox Lutheran Church is also "Catholic" in style, and seeks an eventual alignment with the Roman Catholic

Church, at least to the extent of having "communion" the pope (as the Eastern Orthodox Church currently does). The church will ordain women, but not practicing homosexuals.

The Orthodox Lutheran Church is led by its presiding bishop, Most Rev. Sam Guido, and a board of directors consisting of the thirteen archbishops who also constitute the Council of Bishops. Continuing a tradition found in many Old Catholic churches, most pastors are bivocational, drawing their income from secular jobs and serving their congregations for little or no salary. Affiliated parishes are found in the Philippines, Sri Lanka, and India. The church has signed intercommunion agreements with the Association of Independent Evangelical Lutheran Churches, the Athanasian Catholic Church of the Augsburg Confession, the Order of Corporate Reunion, and the Communion of Ante-Nicene Christian Fellowships.

Membership: Not reported.

Sources:

Orthodox Lutheran Church. www.orgsites.com/pa/lutheranorthodox/.

Orthodox Lutheran Confessional Conference of Independent Congregations
No central headquarters. For information: Augsburg Lutheran Church, 1200 N. Lily Pl., Sioux Falls, SD 57103

The Orthodox Lutheran Confessional Conference of Independent Congregations was formed in 2006 by five congregations who left the Lutheran Churches of the Reformation, which had declared that it was granting women the right to vote in congregational meetings. The pastors and members of the five congregations rejected the change as unbiblical, and sought to form a true biblical fellowship. In most respects, the new Conference resembles it parent body.

The small coalition of congregations that make up the Orthodox Lutheran Confessional Conference maintain a loose association. They have found some wider fellowship with the congregations of the Association of Confessional Lutheran Churches, whom they meet in an annual conference. These annual "free conferences" were designed to explore relationships with other congregations and synods who shared the Orthodox Lutheran Confessional Conference's beliefs and practices.

Membership: In 2008 there were five congregations scattered in five midwestern states.

Sources:

Orthodox Lutheran Confessional Conference of Independent Congregations.
    www.olccic.org/.

Norwegian Seaman's Church (Mission)
1035 Beacon St., San Pedro, CA 90731

The Norwegian Seaman's Mission was founded in 1864 in Bergen, Norway, to provide mission centers in port cities around the world. Such centers offer a Christian witness and a homelike atmosphere for Norwegian sailors in foreign lands. In many cites the missions also have developed into community and worship centers for first-generation Norwegians in foreign lands. The number of centers worldwide reached a peak in the nineteenth century, but more recently some of the centers, such as the one in Philadelphia, have closed. The one in San Pedro, California, opened in 1941. The missions provide services in accordance with the practices of the Church of Norway, the state Lutheran church.

Membership: In 1997 there were 40 Norwegian Seaman's Mission units worldwide. In 2008 the five in the United States were in San Pedro, San Francisco, Houston, New Orleans, and Miami.

Sources:

Gabriel, Judy. "A Refuge for Scandinavian Seamen." *Los Angeles Times*, December 22, 1985.

Wisconsin Evangelical Lutheran Synod

2929 N Mayfair Rd., Milwaukee, WI 53222-4398

The Wisconsin Evangelical Lutheran Synod (WELS, or popularly called the Wisconsin Synod) was established in response to calls for pastoral service from German immigrants to Wisconsin in the 1840s. Ministers answered the call, and in May 1850 the First German Evangelical Lutheran Synod of Wisconsin was organized under the direction of President John Muelhaeuser at Salem Evangelical Lutheran Church, Milwaukee (Granville), Wisconsin.

In the 1840s a Michigan Synod had also been organized among the Wuerttembergers by Stephan Koehler and Christoph Eberhardt. A Minnesota Synod was organized by "Father" J. C. F. Heyer and others in 1860. The Wisconsin, Michigan, and Minnesota Synods became conservative theologically, staunch defenders of Lutheran doctrine against the "compromises" of the larger bodies. In 1892, after all three had joined the Lutheran Synodical Conference, they federated to form the Evangelical Lutheran Joint Synod of Wisconsin, Minnesota, and Michigan. A merger in 1917 led to the formation of the Evangelical Lutheran Joint Synod of Wisconsin and Other States. The present name was adopted in 1959.

Characterized as doctrinally conservative, the Wisconsin Synod accepts the Bible as the inerrant Word of God. It maintains doctrinal fellowship with one other U.S.-based church body, the Evangelical Lutheran Synod based in Minnesota. It also is a member of the Confessional Evangelical Lutheran Conference, an organization of 20 church bodies around the world.

The synod meets biennially. It is divided into 12 districts spread across the nation, though membership is concentrated in Wisconsin and the Midwest. There is a network of 343 Lutheran elementary schools, 400 early childhood ministries, two synodical preparatory high schools, 23 area Lutheran high schools, a college, and a seminary. Northwestern Publishing House in Milwaukee publishes books, Sunday school literature, and religious materials. A vigorous mission program is supported both at home and abroad. WELS conducts cross-cultural ministry in the United States and Canada among Apache, Hispanics, Hmong, Indo-Caribbeans, Japanese, Koreans, Navajo, Sudanese, and Vietnamese. Foreign mission endeavors are supported in Albania, Brazil, Bulgaria, Cameroon, Colombia, Dominican Republic, Hong Kong, India, Indonesia, Japan, Malawi, Mexico, Mozambique, Nepal, Nigeria, Pakistan, Portugal, Puerto Rico, Russia, Taiwan, Thailand, and Zambia.

WELS has an affiliated television broadcast called *Time of Grace*, out of Milwaukee, Wisconsin.

Membership: In 2007 the Wisconsin Synod reported 394,264 members in the United States and Canada (with an additional 78,976 in foreign mission fields), in 1,276 congregations served by 1,297 ministers.

Educational Facilities:

Wisconsin Lutheran Seminary, Mequon, Wisconsin.

Martin Luther College, New Ulm, Minnesota.

Wisconsin Lutheran College, Milwaukee, Wisconsin.

Periodicals: *Forward in Christ*. • *Mission Connection*. • *Wisconsin Lutheran Quarterly*. Send orders to 1250 N 113th St., Milwaukee, WI 53226-3284.

Sources:

Wisconsin Evangelical Lutheran Synod. www.wels.net.

Braun, John A. *Together in Christ*. Milwaukee, WI: Northwestern Publishing House, 2000.

Brug, John F. *WELS and Other Lutheran: Lutheran Church Bodies in the USA*. Milwaukee, WI: Northwestern Publishing House, 1995.

Continuing in Word. Milwaukee, WI: Northwestern Publishing House, [1951].

Frederich, Edward C. *The Wisconsin Synod Lutherans*. Milwaukee, WI: Northwestern Publishing House, 1992.

This We Believe. N.p., 1967. Pamphlet.

Reformed-Presbyterian Family

6

The Lutheran Reformation, centered in Germany, provided a climate in which further efforts to reform the Western Roman Church could proceed. In Switzerland that reforming activity led to the establishment of the Reformed Church based on the work of John Calvin (1509–1564), who established himself in Geneva, Switzerland, in the 1540s. Subsequently, his thought would come to dominate Holland, Scotland, and parts of Germany, and to be received by significant minorities in France and Hungary. The various churches that trace their origins to Calvin are set apart from other Christian churches by their theology (Reformed) and church government (Presbyterian).

Calvin's theological system was shaped by his belief in God's sovereignty in creation and salvation. The other major theological tenets of Calvinism—predestination and limited atonement—are built on this belief in God's sovereignty. Strictly interpreted, predestination means that the number and identity of "the elect" (those who are saved) were ordained by the sovereign God before the beginning of the world. Christ's atonement for sin was thus limited to the elect; salvation is not possible for all humanity, but only for those predestined to be saved. The issue of a strict or lenient interpretation of predestination has divided both European and American Calvinists.

Churches in the Reformed-Presbyterian tradition perpetuated a presbyterial (rule by elders) form of church government. The presbytery is a legislative and/or judicial body composed of clergy (teaching elders) and laity (ruling elders) in equal numbers from the churches of a given region. The laity are elected by the members of the church. The word *presbytery* is also sometimes used to refer to the ruling body of the local church, but the name *Presbyterian* derives from the regional governing body.

Thus the name of this family has been designated *Reformed* for Calvin's theology (an attempt to reform the Roman Catholic Church) and *Presbyterian* for the form of church government based on the presbytery. The name for this tradition also reflects history. On the continent, Calvinists established Reformed churches. In the British Isles, predominantly in Scotland, Calvinists established Presbyterian churches. In America, both the Reformed churches and the Presbyterian churches belong to the same Reformed-Presbyterian tradition, along with the Congregational churches. In this chapter, the word *Reformed* applies to Calvinist theology, worship, and churches using Calvinist the-

ology. The word *Reformed* is not used to refer to the whole Reformation, a movement much broader than Calvinism, although Calvin played a major role in that movement.

Reformed theology involves many beliefs in addition to the distinguishing tenets mentioned above—beliefs in God's sovereignty, human depravity, predestination, and a limited atonement. Reformed churches join the Roman Catholics, Anglicans, Eastern Orthodox, and Lutherans in accepting the theological decisions reached during the conciliar era (fourth to eighth centuries). These are expressed in the creeds of the early centuries of Christianity: beliefs in the parental creator God, Christ and his atoning and salvific work, the Holy Spirit, the resurrection of the body, and the Christian's life with God after the experience of death.

Beyond these beliefs come those shared by Reformed theology with Lutherans and other Protestant theologies: the belief in salvation by grace through faith, and the reliance on the Bible as the sole authority for faith and doctrine. With the followers of Martin Luther (1483–1546) and Ulrich Zwingli (1484–1531), the leader of the Reformation in Zurich and German-speaking Switzerland, Calvinists were Protestants in that they both spoke forth their faith and disagreed with various doctrines and practices of the Roman Catholic Church during the sixteenth century. The Protestant emphasis on salvation by grace through faith stands opposed to the Roman Catholic understanding of salvation that is worked out through a life of faith and good works. Further, when Protestants claim the Bible as their sole authority for faith and doctrine, they negate the Roman Catholic dual reliance on both the Bible and tradition. Reformed churchmen were generally hostile toward practices sanctioned by tradition unless the practices could be substantiated by scripture.

Within Reformed theology, the definition of the church makes no reference to bishops or apostolic succession (the line of succession by ordination from the apostles to modern times), two elements that are crucial to churches in the liturgical traditions. Instead, Reformed theology defines the church as the place where the "pure doctrine of the gospel is preached" and the "pure administration of the sacraments" is maintained. By the "pure doctrine of the gospel" is meant the gospel preached by ordained ministers according to Calvinist emphases (e.g., the authority of the Bible, the sovereignty of God, and predestination). By the "pure administration of the sacraments" is meant the administration only of baptism and the Lord's Supper as sacraments. This practice contrasts with

Reformed-Presbyterian Family Chronology

1536	John Calvin publishes the *Institutes of the Christian Religion*, the first systematic presentation of Protestant theology.
1541	Calvin establishes the Reformed Church in Geneva.
1560	John Knox leads in establishing Presbyterianism as state religion in Scotland.
1618	A synod convenes at Dortrecht, in the Netherlands, to respond to the Remonstrants, followers of Jacob Arminius, whose theology opposed ideas of predestination and by extension other basic of Reformed Church thought. The synod suggested five basic pillars of Calvinist theology: total predestination, utter depravity, limited atonement, irresistible grace, and perseverance of the saints. The Arminian perspective would later be embodied in the Methodist movement.
1620	The Pilgrims (independent separatists) land at Plymouth, Massachusetts.
1628	Dutch reformed minister Jonas Michaelius organizes the Collegiate Church of the City of New York, now the oldest continuously existing congregation in the United States.
1630	Puritans launch settlement of New England.
1640	The first Presbyterian congregation in the British American colonies is formed at South Hampton, Long Island, New York.
1647–48	British church leaders meeting at Westminster Abbey produce the defining documents of the Presbyterian tradition, the "Westminster Confession of Faith," the "Larger Catechism," and the "Shorter Catechism."
1648	American Congregationalists define stance in the Cambridge Platform.
c.1705	Francis Makemie organizes the first Presbyterian synod in the British American colonies.
1747	German congregations in Pennsylvania form the Coetus of the Reformed Ministerium of Pennsylvania, later the Reformed Church in the U.S.
1749	Presbyterians and Congregationalists begin settlement of British Nova Scotia.
1789	The first General Assembly of the Presbyterian Church in the U.S.A. meets in Philadelphia, May 21.
	The First Congress chose Rev. William Lynn, a Presbyterian from Philadelphia, as the official chaplain of the U.S. House of Representatives.
1792	Dutch Reformed congregations organize what becomes the Reformed Church in America.
1801	Congregationalists and Presbyterians approve a Plan of Union outlining the development of congregations west of the Alleghany Mountains.
1813	Conflict within Presbyterianism over revivalism in the western states led those supportive of the revivals to form the Cumberland Synod (later the Cumberland Presbyterian Church).
1840	Saxon Germans in the Mississippi Valley organize the German Evangelical Church Society of the West, later the Evangelical Synod.
1858	Scottish American synods unite to form the United Presbyterian Church of North America.
1859	Conservative reformed congregations in the Midwest that have withdrawn from the Reformed Church in America form what would become known as the Christian Reformed Church.
1861	Southern commissioners withdraw from the main denomination to form the Confederate Presbyterian Church, later named the Presbyterian Church in the U.S.
1874	African American members of the Cumberland Presbyterian organize separately as the Cumberland Presbyterian Church in America.
1906	The Cumberland Presbyterian Church unites with the Presbyterian Church in the U.S.A.
1925	Methodists, Presbyterians, and Congregationalists in Canada merge to form the United Church of Canada. A minority of Canadian Presbyterians refuse to join the merger and continue as the Presbyterian Church in Canada.
1931	National Council of Congregationalist Churches unites with the Christian Church to form the General Council of Congregationalist Christian Churches.
1934	The Reformed Church in the U.S. and the Evangelical Synod unite to form the Evangelical and Reformed Church.
1934–36	The Fundamentalist-Modernist debate culminates in the defrocking of Princeton professor J. Gresham Machen (1934) and the formation of the Orthodox Presbyterian Church (1936).
1956	Margaret Towner becomes the first ordained female minister in the Presbyterian Church in the U.S.A.
1957	The Evangelical and Reformed Church unites with the Congregational-Christian Churches to form the United Church of Christ.
1958	United Presbyterian Church of North America and the Presbyterian Church in the U.S.A. unite to form the United Presbyterian Church in the U.S.A.
1972	Conservatives in the Presbyterian Church in the U.S. form the Presbyterian Church in America.
	Rev. William Johnson of the United Church of Christ becomes the first openly gay person ordained in a major American denomination.
1977	Anne Holmes of the United Church of Christ becomes the first openly lesbian person ordained in a major American denomination.
1983	The United Presbyterian Church in the U.S.A. and the Presbyterian Church in the U.S. merge to form the Presbyterian Church (U.S.A.).
1995	The Christian Reformed Church votes to accept women into the ordained ministry. As a result, it is forced to withdraw from the North American Presbyterian and Reformed Council.

Roman Catholicism's celebration of seven sacraments and some churches' rejection of all sacraments. (The Zwinglians and the Anabaptists serve as two examples of those rejecting all the sacraments. Zwinglians considered the Eucharist a memorial meal, not a sacrament. The Anabaptists had no sacraments but did have ordinances, including foot washing and adult baptism.)

Though not without some differences, Lutherans and Roman Catholics accepted the doctrine of the real physical presence of Christ in the sacraments. The followers of Calvin supplanted this idea with belief in the spiritual presence

apprehended by faith. In Calvin's perspective, changes in the sacrament as a special focus of Christ's presence in the world move away from the sacramental world of the liturgical churches. The Reformed world is a secular world. God is present and can be apprehended by one of faith.

Worship in a Reformed church is centered on the preaching of the sermon, which ideally combines the exposition of scripture with the ordered presentation of a great truth of the faith. While having been influenced by the emotive appeal of the Methodists in modern times, the Reformed sermon still serves primarily a teaching function. Prayers and hymns rehearse the basic tenets of the Reformed faith—confession, forgiveness, and the acknowledgement of the sovereignty of God. Hymns for many years were limited to the Psalms set to music, and the church produced many editions of Psalters. Most now use hymnbooks, though the Psalms remain important.

As spelled out in the Second Helvetic Confession (1566), the characteristics of Reformed worship are the Word of God properly preached to the people, decent meeting spaces purged of anything offensive to the church, and services conducted in order, modesty, discipline, and in the language of the people. Gone are the aesthetic/theological/sacramental appeals of worship. Gone are "offensive" elements such as statues, vestments, saints' festivals, indulgences, pilgrimages, and relics. Reformed worship is directed on a cognitive level—preaching, worship understandable to the layperson, logical thoughts and ordered behavior, and a disciplined atmosphere.

The Reformed theological position was codified in confessions in the sixteenth and seventeenth centuries. The main Reformed confessions are the First Helvetic Confession (1536), the Belgic Confession (1561), the Second Helvetic Confession (1566), the Canons of the Synod of Dort (1619), and the Westminster Confession of Faith (1647). Also helpful in understanding the Reformed faith is the Heidelberg Catechism (1693) and the two *Westminster Catechisms* (1647). The above description of Reformed theology aligns with these confessions, all of which agree on a basic doctrinal position and in addition address whatever current crisis or local debate prompted the confessions. Along with other documents written by the Westminster Assembly of Divines in the 1640s, the Westminster Confession is the confession that has had the greatest impact on English-speaking church bodies in the Reformed-Presbyterian tradition. Most Congregationalists and Baptists, which are Reformed in theology while rejecting the Presbyterian organization, have written or accepted confessions of faith derived from the Westminster documents.

Calvin developed the doctrine of two spheres of action, the secular and religious. Although his Reformed Church in Geneva was an established state church, he ended most interference of the state in church affairs, including the celebration of church festivals and the appointment of church officials. Calvin attempted to develop a theocracy, a form of government designed to have God as its head. The church defined the magistrates' authority as coming from God and the church had power over the magistrates in that magistrates were church members. Thus religion had considerable power over all social activities; for some years, Calvin was the most powerful man in Geneva. The theocracy was patterned on church life described in Calvin's monumental theological treatise, *Institutes of the Christian Religion* (1536).

The presbyterial system assumes the existence of state authority and was designed for intimate communion between the church and the secular authority. It was based on a parish system in which the country would be divided into geo-graphic areas with one congregation to a parish. All people who had been baptized would be members. The church and state together, each in its proper sphere, would keep order. The most notable example of the interworking of church and state in Geneva concerned a heretic, Michael Servetus (1511–1553). Above the technical objections to his denial of orthodox Christian doctrines, Servetus had brought great offense to Roman Catholics and Protestants alike by his comparing the Trinity to the three-headed hound of hell. Calvin condemned Servetus as a heretic, and subsequently the secular authorities in Geneva tried and executed him.

Within the presbyterial system of the Reformed-Presbyterian tradition, clergy and laypeople together rule the church. The preaching elders (ministers) are the pastors and teachers. The ruling elders (laypeople) are to assist the teaching elders in discipline and in the governance and administration of the church. Deacons collect the offering and see to its distribution. In the local congregation, the ministers and elders together make up the consistory or session, occasionally called the presbytery. In some cases, the deacons also belong to the consistory. All ministers and elders are called and elected by the other elders.

The ministers and elders form a series of judicial and legislative bodies. The local consistories (or sessions) are organized into what is variously termed a presbytery, classis, or coetus. From this body of all the ministers in a given region, plus an equal number of elected elders, comes the name for the presbyterial form of government. The presbyters, those in the presbytery, have the power within the church. Several presbyteries (usually a minimum of three) may come together to form a synod (or classis), and synods may form an even larger body, such as the General Assembly of the Presbyterian Church (U.S.A.). Each body has specific functions and usually a protest of a decision at one level can be appealed to a higher level. (In actual practice, among some Presbyterian churches, a congregational form of government prevails and the presbytery functions as an advisory forum to facilitate cooperative endeavor.)

Both Luther and Calvin established state churches, as did Zwingli. Following Zwingli's death, his church in Zurich, Switzerland, would be absorbed into Calvin's Reformed Church. The Anabaptists (discussed in chapter 10) opposed all state churches, whether Lutheran, Calvinist, or Roman Catholic, and they were persecuted by the state churches. The Reformation brought its share of bloodshed.

Calvin's doctrine, more than the doctrine of any other religion, moved with the rising mercantile society and justified secular activity in the world. By contrast, Anabaptism was a world-denying view that sheltered the elect against a hostile, sinful, secular society. The Anabaptist tradition continues in the Mennonites, the Amish, the Quakers, and the Church of the Brethren. Lutheranism retained a more sacred character than Calvinism; Lutheranism spread by refurbishing Catholic forms. Calvinism, however, rose on the emerging middle class of Western Europe.

John Calvin wrote the single most influential Protestant theological text, *Institutes of the Christian Religion,* and was the first Protestant systematic theologian. He gained a reputation for intellectual brilliance while a student in Paris. After a 1533 sermon in which he pleaded for the reform of the Roman Catholic Church, he was forced to leave Paris. In Geneva, he introduced reforms, but in 1538 he was forced to leave Geneva because of the severity of the reforms he tried to institute. (Later his church would be characterized by stern morality, austerity, and insistence on attending church services.) A noted preacher, Calvin went to Strassburg for several years and from there he maintained communication with those in Geneva. In 1541 the people of Geneva recalled him. From then on, Geneva was the headquarters for Calvin and the Reformed Church.

There the future leaders of Calvin's reform found a haven from non-Calvinist magistrates of other areas. William Tyndale (c. 1494–1536), Miles Coverdale (1488–1568), and John Knox (c. 1514–1572) exported Calvin's ideas from Geneva to the British Isles. By 1600, representatives of the Reformed faith were making themselves heard throughout all of central Europe.

THE SPREAD OF CALVINISM. As early as 1555, a Protestant congregation was organized in France by a disciple of Calvin. In 1559 the first synod of the French Reformed Church met. The next centuries for the French Reformed Church, or the Huguenots as they were popularly called, were years of persecution. In 1598 Henry IV (r. 1589–1610) issued the Edict of Nantes and began a brief period of toleration. But Louis XIV (r. 1643–1715) revoked the edict in 1685, and periods of persecution followed until the Constitution of 1795 granted religious freedom.

Reformed Church advocates entered the Netherlands very soon after Calvin's reign in Geneva began. The religious wars that followed led to revolution by the Protestants and the formation of two countries, predominantly Reformed Holland and predominantly Catholic Belgium. This separation was completed in 1579 under the Protestant leader William of Orange (1533–1584). In Holland in 1618 a major controversy that had troubled Calvinism for several decades reached a climax with the Synod of Dort. The synod was called to refute what was considered the theological heresies of Jacob Arminius (1560–1609), former professor of theology at the University of Leyden. In 1610, the year after Arminius's death, his followers summarized his theories in a five-point remonstrance, which led to his followers becoming known as the Remonstrants.

Arminius's revision of Calvin's thought affirmed: (1) a general atonement, that is, that Christ died for every person; (2) that God's foreknowledge of who would accept Christ's saving grace came before his predestination and election of them; (3) that God's grace could be resisted; (4) that humans were fallen and in need of God's grace, but were capable of responding to it; and (5) that while victory over sin was possible with God's grace, it was also possible for individuals to fall away from grace. The Synod of Dort responded by affirming

that: (1) Christ died only for those elected to salvation; (2) predestination and election to salvation constituted an act of God's sovereign will (rather than being the natural result of his foreknowledge); (3) God's grace given to an individual is irresistible; (4) humans were so depraved that they could do nothing for their own salvation; and (5) God's elect will persevere to the end.

The canons of the Synod of Dort became the official doctrine of the Dutch church and of many Reformed Church bodies. Among those in attendance at Dort were several of the British Separatists then residing in Holland who were later to travel to America as the Pilgrims. In contrast, Armenian ideas found their way to England and became the theological starting point for John Wesley (1703–1791) and the Methodists of the eighteenth century.

No other centers of Reformed faith on the continent grew as did Switzerland, France, and Holland. However, the faith did seep into the surrounding countries, and synods were formed in what is today the Czech Republic and Hungary. Also, in northern Italy the Reformed faith began to dominate the Waldensians, a group that had separated from the Roman Catholic Church in the previous century. Because of its affinity with Lutheranism, the Reformed Church moved north into Germany and, while never challenging Lutherans for control, became a large minority religion. It is from this body that the 1693 Heidelberg Catechism emerged; its teaching was to have a profound influence on the interpretation of Calvin in Reformed history.

The leading center of Reformed faith in the British Isles was Scotland. John Knox, a devout follower of Calvin, returned to Scotland in 1559 after a year and a half on a French galley and 12 years of exile in Europe. He found the country ripe for Protestantism. He quickly became the leader of the cause that in another year saw the Scottish parliament abolish Catholicism and begin to set up Presbyterianism, the name given the Reformed Church in Scotland. Despite recurrent battles with then Episcopal England, Presbyterianism was firmly settled in Scotland and became the seedbed from which the Reformed movement could spread to Ireland and England.

In 1603 James I of England (r. 1603–1625) invited the Scots to settle the rebels' land in Ulster (Northern Ireland), which had been forfeited to the crown. So many came to Ireland that soon Ulster was dominantly Protestant and, in spite of James's Catholic preferences, he reasoned that Presbyterians were better than people with no religion at all. Irish Catholics were not so quick to give in to the Protestant intruders, and religious wars ensued. By 1642 things had quieted to a point that the first presbytery in Ireland could be formed, but a stable accord has never been reached between Irish Catholics and Presbyterians.

PURITANISM. In England, Reformed-Presbyterian thinking was labeled *Puritanism.* This name came as a result of the different Reformed thinkers' uniting around the issue of "further purifying the church," as the latter stages of the Reformation brought Elizabeth I (r. 1558–1603) to the

Presbyterian Denominational Tree

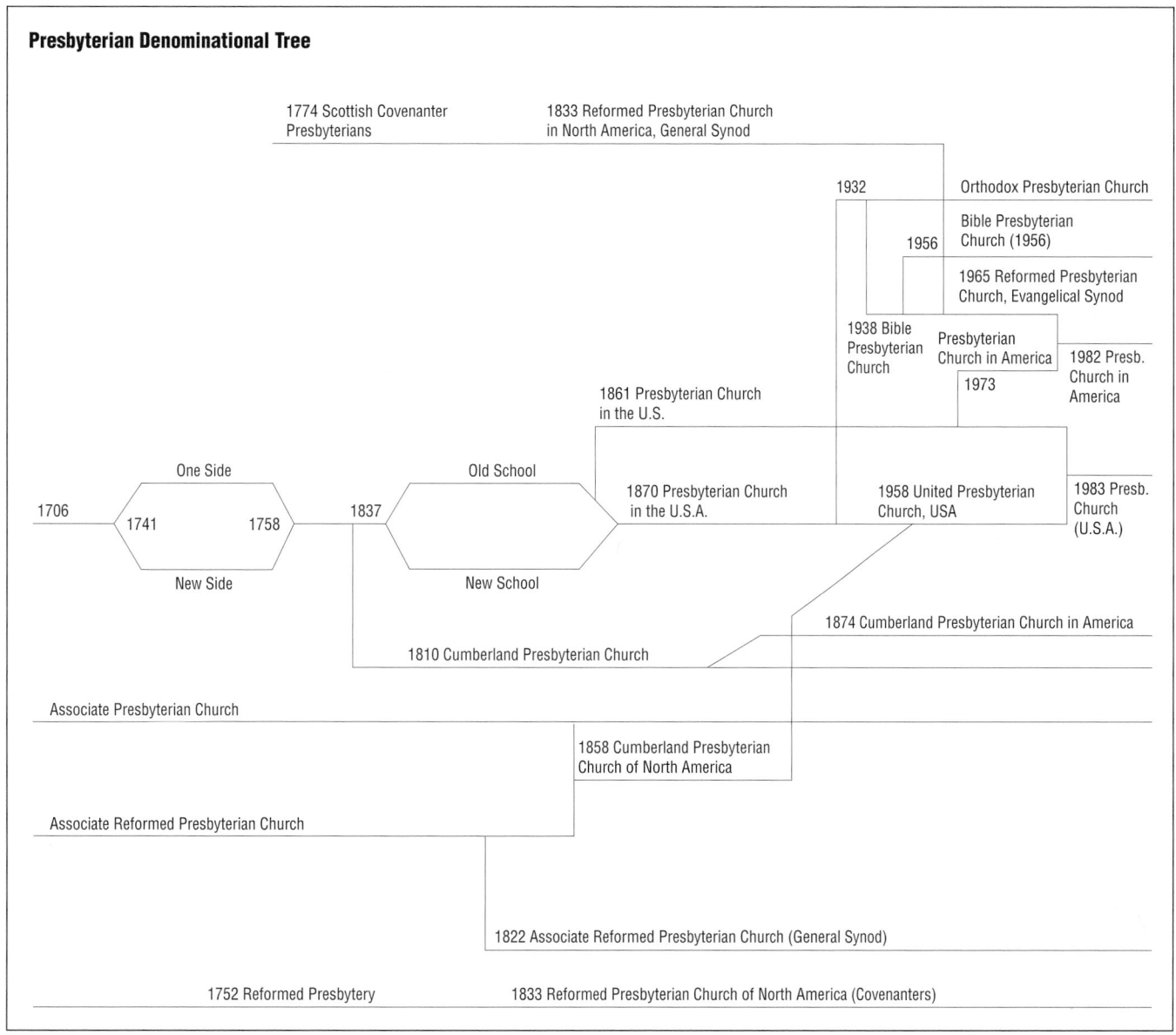

1774 Scottish Covenanter Presbyterians

1833 Reformed Presbyterian Church in North America, General Synod

1932

Orthodox Presbyterian Church

1956

Bible Presbyterian Church (1956)

1965 Reformed Presbyterian Church, Evangelical Synod

1938 Bible Presbyterian Church

Presbyterian Church in America

1982 Presb. Church in America

1973

1861 Presbyterian Church in the U.S.

One Side

Old School

1706

1741   1758

1837

1870 Presbyterian Church in the U.S.A.

1958 United Presbyterian Church, USA

1983 Presb. Church (U.S.A.)

New Side

New School

1874 Cumberland Presbyterian Church in America

1810 Cumberland Presbyterian Church

Associate Presbyterian Church

1858 Cumberland Presbyterian Church of North America

Associate Reformed Presbyterian Church

1822 Associate Reformed Presbyterian Church (General Synod)

1752 Reformed Presbytery

1833 Reformed Presbyterian Church of North America (Covenanters)

Adapted from Association of Religion Data Archives

throne in 1558 with her *via media* solution to religious strife. (For a discussion of Elizabeth's blending of both Roman Catholic and Protestant elements, see the section in chapter 3 on the Anglican tradition.) The two major groups within Puritanism were the Independents and the Presbyterians. Most Puritans were Reformed in their thinking, but beyond that they varied from those who merely wished to simplify church vestments and worship, to the Independents who wished to set up a congregationally organized church, one in which the highest authority lay within the local church instead of in a regional or national governing body.

The years 1558 to 1649 were years of struggle, persecutions, war, and on-again, off-again toleration among proponents of the various churches in England. In 1649 Puritan Oliver Cromwell (1599–1658) succeeded in his revolt against the monarchy and established the Puritan Commonwealth. Although Cromwell was an Independent, the Presbyterians were dominant in Parliament, so when Cromwell's reign began, Presbyterianism was imposed upon the established Church of England. Up to that time the Presbyterians and Independents had sustained a united front against the Episcopalian state church of the monarchy. However, once Puritanism gained the position of state church, the factions within Puritanism—Presbyterians and Independents—no longer needed to be united against Episcopalianism, and their differences with each other intensified. The Congregationalists, a group within the Independents, began to press for a state church based on a congregational system instead of on a presbyterial system. The Congregationalists wanted to remain attached to the Church of England in the sense that the Congregationalists would preach the doctrines of the Church of England but they would choose their own ministers, own their own property, and would not come under the authority of any bishops of the Church of England.

The Congregationalists were opposed by another party within the Independents, the Separatists. This latter party wished to become separate from any Episcopal entanglements.

In 1660 Presbyterianism lost its established church status. That year, the monarchy was restored to power, and the Anglican Church and its bishops again received state support. Presbyterians were reduced to simply another small English sect among a range of Christian sectarian groups. The Restoration therefore meant the end of Presbyterian ecclesiastical power, though Reformed theology remained equally dominant in most of England's Puritan bodies—Presbyterians, Congregationalists, and Separatists.

Several years before Cromwell came to power, Parliament paved the way for the establishment of Presbyterianism by abolishing the system of bishops. In 1642 Parliament convoked the Westminster Assembly of Divines to reorder the Church of England. This assembly, meeting for a number of years, produced the three most important works in Reformed history (apart from Calvin's *Institutes*, from which they derived): the Larger and Shorter Catechisms, the Westminster Confession of Faith, and the Directory of Public Worship. Even though only four Scots were in the Westminster Assembly, the Church of Scotland quickly adopted the Westminster documents. These documents remain to this day the basic works in doctrine and organization for most Presbyterian churches around the world.

With time, the Separatists, a group within the Independents, divided into Brownists and Baptists. Robert Browne (c. 1550–1633) was among the first to move toward the idea of a "sect" church of pure Christians, as opposed to a universal or state church of all baptized citizens. The Baptists were even more radical than the Brownists. The Baptists were antiliturgical and rejected even the Calvinist understanding of the sacraments. For them, baptism was an ordinance and was reserved for adults instead of being available also to children.

The various groups mentioned above existed as parties within the Puritan movement in England from the late 1500s until the 1689 Act of Toleration, which allowed them freedom to develop fully as distinct sects. The Brownists, however, gradually faded from existence as a separate group.

IN NORTH AMERICA. Among the first European Christians in the New World were members of the Reformed Church. As early as 1564, Huguenots (French Protestants), fleeing persecution, settled along the St. John's River near present-day Jacksonville, Florida. The colony was destroyed the next year by the Spanish who had already claimed the territory. During the last half of the century, others began to flee to the towns of New France along the St. Lawrence River. They continued to arrive until forbidden to migrate by Cardinal Richelieu (1585–1642) in 1628. Huguenots did not prosper, but a few did survive in Canada until the fall of Quebec in 1749. They were soon absorbed into other Protestant churches.

With the establishment of Halifax in 1749, German and Dutch members of the Reformed Church, as well as Congregationalists and Presbyterians (primarily from Scotland), became residents of the new city. At first they shared the same building. As years passed, they spread through Nova Scotia founding churches. Growth of the Reformed faith was greatly augmented by the arrival of the Loyalists, many from New England, after the American Revolution (1775–1783). The first synods were formed in 1795 and 1796 by two factions of the Scottish Presbyterians.

Dissension, already high among the Scots, increased with the arrival of the New Englanders, among whom was Henry Alline (1748–1784), a fervent disciple of Newlightism, the revival-oriented separatist Congregationalism that had been inaugurated by the First Great Awakening (1740s), prior to the American Revolution. Alline drew away many Congregationalists into independent congregations that eventually became the birthing place of the Baptists of the province.

The story of the Reformed-Presbyterian tradition in colonial America is the story of the establishment of American branches of the various European Reformed churches. As early as 1611 the Reverend Alexander Whitaker (1585–c. 1614) arrived in Virginia with his Presbyterian views. The Pilgrims and Puritans arrived in the 1620s to establish American Congregationalism. Dutch Calvinists were in New York as early as 1623. French Huguenots, who settled along the coast in a number of different communities, quickly Americanized and joined the Presbyterian Church. The backbone of American Presbyterianism was the vast migration of the Scottish-Irish Ulsterites. Between 1705 and 1775, more than 500,000 Ulsterites reached America and settled in its middle section, particularly the Carolinas. Germans began to arrive in the late 1600s and settled in Pennsylvania, where the Calvinists among them organized the German Reformed Church.

Francis Makemie (1658–1708), recognized as the father of American Presbyterianism, landed in the colonies in 1683 to begin organizing the scattered Presbyterians. About 1705 (the date is not clear), he organized the first presbytery (of Philadelphia). Makemie died early in the new century just as the great Scottish-Irish immigration was beginning. In 1717 the Synod of Philadelphia was organized with 19 ministers, 40 churches, and 3,000 members.

The Reformed traditions have displayed several interesting patterns of growth in America. The churches of the Reformed tradition (with the possible exception of Presbyterianism) are regional churches. Largely continental in their background, they are concentrated in those areas in the Northeast and Midwest where large-scale German migration occurred. The Congregationalists were located largely in the Northeast, but gained strength in the Midwest through mergers in 1931 and 1958.

Significant in the spread of the Reformed churches were the antievangelical, antirevivalistic policies of church leaders in the eighteenth and nineteenth centuries. The Reformed churches gained new members largely through groups of laymen who migrated West, formed congregations, and called a pastor.

Education has been a major contribution of the Reformed tradition to Protestantism. The churches always insisted on a college-trained clergy, and they created numerous colleges for that purpose. They have based their program on a theologically sound teaching ministry. A large number of the outstanding theologians in American history were out of this tradition—Cotton Mather (1663–1728), Jonathan Edwards (1703–1758), John Williamson Nevin (1803–1886), Horace Bushnell (1802–1886), Benjamin B. Warfield (1851–1921), Reinhold Niebuhr (1892–1971), and H. Richard Niebuhr (1894–1962).

The Plan of Union of 1801 was an agreement between Presbyterians and Congregationalists concerning their frontier congregations. (The "frontier" of the early 1800s was the area west of the Allegheny Mountains.) The Plan of Union stipulated that in those areas where small groups of Presbyterians and Congregationalists resided, the two groups would unite and be served by a minister from either church. Because more Presbyterian ministers went to the frontier than Congregationalist ministers, most of those united churches became Presbyterian.

Splintered into a number of separate denominational bodies in the nineteenth century, Presbyterians made significant strides in bringing members together into one organization during the twentieth century. The most important step in the merging process was accomplished in 1983 when the two largest Presbyterian bodies, split since before the Civil War (1861–1865), merged to form the Presbyterian Church (U.S.A.). The story of this church and its antecedents constitutes the bulk of Presbyterian history in the United States.

CONGREGATIONALISM: A VARIATION OF THE REFORMED TRADITION. Congregationalism, a form of Puritanism that lies between Presbyterianism and Separatism, is somewhat unique in that it developed in America within the Massachusetts Bay Colony and was then taken back to England. In contrast to the Presbyterians, who looked for the development of a state church modeled on the theocracy that Calvin established in Geneva and headed by a synod of elders (presbyters), the Congregationalists looked for a state church that was congregationally oriented. While agreeing with the Separatists on the issue of the local church, Congregationalists disagreed with them in that they wished to keep their supportive ties to the state. In colonial America, Separatism was first represented by the Pilgrims at Plymouth, Massachusetts. All three groups were Reformed in their theology and acknowledged the Westminster documents, but differed fundamentally on their desires for church organization and its relation to the state. Eventually, Congregationalism would absorb the Separatists of Plymouth (those not lost to Unitarianism), but a new separatist movement would emerge in the 1700s and survive as Baptists.

Congregational organization had four distinctive features. First, the church was built on the covenant of people together. A church was not formed until the people consti-

tuted it. Second, the church was tied to a place. It was the covenanted people in a specific location. Ideally, the whole countryside would be divided into parishes, geographic areas each with one congregation. The importance of place is reflected in the fact that the Mayflower Compact (a civil version of the church covenant) was not drawn up until the Pilgrims reached the New World. Third, the church was to be an established church. In New England, it had intimate ties with the government, and ministers drew their salaries from the civil authority. Finally, the church was to be the sacred institute for the society. The clergy spoke directly to issues of public morals, expected to be consulted on matters of importance to public life, and often represented the colony as political figures.

The early Congregationalists have often been confused with those Independents who desired a church totally cut off from state affiliation, control, and finance. While it is true that Congregationalism later became independent of state authority, it is well to keep in mind the movement's original aim to be a state church.

Meeting at Cambridge, Massachusetts, in 1648, representatives of the four Puritan colonies issued what came to be called the Cambridge Platform. It became the basic document of Congregational policy in New England. As stated in the Platform, "The Government of the Church is a mixed Government . . . in respect of Christ the Head and King of the Church, and the sovereign power residing in Him, it is a Monarchy; in respect of the Body of Brotherhood of the Church, and Power from Christ granted unto them, it resembles a Democracy; in respect of the Presbytery, and Power committed unto them, it is an Aristocracy." The basic unit was the visible congregation united into one body by a covenant. The care of the church was left to elders (pastors, teachers, and ruling elders) and deacons, all elected by the congregation.

Churches, though equal, were to maintain communion with one another by means of synods. Synods, though not of the essence of the church, were deemed necessary to the times, to establish truth and peace. Composed of elders and other messengers, synods were to "debate and determine controversies of Faith and Cases of Conscience; to clear from the Word holy directions for the Holy Worship of God, and good Government of the Church; to hear witness against maladministration and corruption of manners in any particular church; and to give Directions for the Reformation thereof." Churches were enjoined not to remove themselves from the communion of the other churches. In its developed form, Congregationalism was very close to Presbyterianism rather than to the independent congregational policy that later became typical of the Baptists. Developed Congregationalism was also far removed from the free church structure of the Plymouth Brethren.

A key element in Congregationalism was the power granted by the church to the secular magistrate. The magistery was encouraged to restrain and punish idolatry, blasphemy, heresy, schism, and like actions. When the power of the magistery was removed from Congregationalism by the American Revolution, the churches adopted an independent congregationalism, but always with a tendency to presbyterial forms.

Some have asserted that Congregationalism was a non-creedal church. However, when asked to prepare a creed, the same body that drew up the Cambridge Platform adopted the Westminster Confession of Faith, which placed Congregationalism doctrinally within British Calvinism (Puritanism).

The first branch of the Reformed tradition in America was Congregationalism, the church of the Massachusetts Puritans. They landed in 1620 and 1630 and established their theocracy. Their church operated as a state church until disestablished after the American Revolution. It adopted the Westminster Confession shortly after promulgation by the English believers. It was the church of the New England patriots, Harvard and Yale universities, and of famous ministers, including Thomas Hooker (1586–1647), Cotton Mather, Charles Chauncy (1592–1672), Jonathan Edwards, and Timothy Dwight (1752–1816). It also became the seedbed upon which Unitarianism, Universalism, and Christian Science were to grow. Only in the twentieth century, as it became a major force in Reformed family ecumenism, did it produce schismatic churches.

THE REFORMED-PRESBYTERIAN FAMILY IN THE TWENTY-FIRST CENTURY. As a new century began, the larger churches of the Reformed-Presbyterian tradition remain powerful forces in the American religious scene, and home to many of the tensions that have defined concerns in the decades since World War II (1939–1945). During the 1920s and 1930s, intense battles over the emergence of modernist expressions of Reformed thought divided the churches, and theologies variously labeled *liberal* or *modernist* came to dominate the larger bodies that would eventually merge to create the United Church of Christ and the Presbyterian Church (U.S.A.). Along the way, important dissenting movements arose to champion more traditional approaches to the Calvinist tradition—the Presbyterian Church in America and the Orthodox Presbyterian Church being among the more prominent. They were joined by several Korean American churches founded by very conservative Christian who migrated to America after the Korean War (1950–1953).

As might be expected, the national gatherings of the United Church of Christ and the Presbyterian Church (U.S.A.) have become occasions for the ongoing debates concerning such issues as abortion, women in the ministry, and the acceptance of homosexuals within the church. The United Church of Christ has emerged as possibly the most liberal of all the Protestant churches. Its antecedent bodies were among the first to ordain females, and it remains one of the few major Protestant bodies to ordain noncelibate gay men and lesbians. While the Presbyterian Church has yet to condone such acts, it has regularly faced intensive debates and close votes. Meanwhile, the more conservative churches

remain opposed to even considering the changes being discussed in the more liberal churches. (A similar liberal-conservative polarity has emerged between the Reformed Church in America and the Christian Reformed Church).

SOURCES

Historical work on the Reformed Church tradition is given focus through the Commission on History of the Reformed Church in America, c/o New Brunswick Theological Seminary, New Brunswick, NJ 08901. The Christian Reformed Church archives are at Calvin College, Grand Rapids, MI 49056.

Presbyterian history is coordinated by the Presbyterian Historical Association and Department of History of the Presbyterian Church (U.S.A.), 425 Leonard St., Philadelphia, PA 28757. A second center, which served the former southern Presbyterian Church in the U.S., is to be found at the Historical Foundation, Montreat, NC 28757.

Congregational history is parceled out among the surviving structures of the churches that merged to form the United Church of Christ. Both the Evangelical and Reformed Historical Society and the archives of the United Church of Christ are at the Lancaster Theological Seminary, Lancaster, PA 17603. The archives of the former Evangelical and Reformed Church are at Eden Theological Seminary, St. Louis, MO 63119. The Congregational Christian Historical Society and the Congregational Library are at 14 Beacon St., Boston, MA 02108.

The central archives of the United Church of Canada are at Victoria University in Toronto.

International

Bauswein, Jean-Jacques, and Lukas Vischer, eds. *The Reformed Family Worldwide: A Survey of Reformed Churches, Theological Schools, and International Organizations.* Grand Rapids, MI: Eerdmans, 1999. 740 pp.

Collinson, Patrick. *The Reformation: A History.* New York: Modern Library, 2006. 262 pp.

Grimm, Harold J. *The Reformation Era.* New York: Macmillan, 1954. 675 pp.

Hillerbrand, Hans J., ed. *The Oxford Encyclopedia of the Reformation.* 4 vols. New York: Oxford University Press, 1996.

Leith, John H. *An Introduction to the Reformed Tradition: A Way of Being the Christian Community.* Atlanta, GA: John Knox Press, 1977. 253 pp.

Loetscher, Lefferts A. *A Brief History of the Presbyterians.* 4th ed. Philadelphia: Westminster Press, 1983.

MacCulloch, Diarmaid. *The Reformation.* New York: Penguin, 2005. 864 pp.

McGrath, Alister E. *Life of John Calvin: A Study in the Shaping of Western Culture.* Oxford: Blackwell, 1990.

McKim, Donald K., ed. *Encyclopedia of the Reformed Faith.* Louisville, KY: Westminster/John Knox Press, 1992. 414 pp.

McNeill, John T. *The History and Character of Calvinism.* New York: Oxford University Press, 1954. 466 pp.

Parker, T. H. L. *John Calvin: A Biography.* Rev. ed. Louisville, KY: Westminster/John Knox Press, 2007. 227 pp.

Reaman, G. Elmore. *The Trail of the Huguenots in Europe, the United States, South Africa, and Canada.* London: Frederick Muller, 1964. 318 pp.

Thompson, Ernest Trice. *Through the Ages: A History of the Christian Church.* Richmond, VA: CLC Press, 1965. 480 pp.

History, North American

Armstrong, Maurice, Lefferts A. Loetscher, and Charles A. Anderson, eds. *The Presbyterian Enterprise: Sources of American Presbyterian History.* Philadelphia: Westminster Press, 1956. 336 pp.

Benedetto, Robert, Darrell L. Guder, and Donald K. McKim. *Historical Dictionary of Reformed Churches.* Lanham, MD: Scarecrow Press, 1999.

Brackenridge, R. Douglas. *The Presbyterian Church (U.S.A.) Foundation: A Bicentennial History, 1799–1999.* Louisville, KY: Westminster/John Knox Press, 1999. 168 pp.

Bratt, James D. *Dutch Calvinism in Modern America: A History of a Conservative Subculture.* Grand Rapids, MI. Eerdmans, 1984. 329 pp.

Breamer, Francis, and Tom Webster, eds. *Puritans and Puritanism in Europe and America: A Comprehensive Encyclopedia.* Santa Barbara, CA: ABC-Clio, 2005. 697 pp.

Hart, D. G., and John R. Muether. *Seeking a Better Country: 300 Years of American Presbyterianism.* Phillipsburg, NJ: P & R, 2007. 288 pp.

Lingle, Walter L. *Presbyterians: Their History and Beliefs.* Richmond, VA: John Knox Press, 1944. 127 pp.

Parker, Harold M. *Bibliography of Published Articles on American Presbyterianism, 1901–1980.* Westport, CT: Greenwood Press, 1985. 261 pp.

Slosser, Gaius Jackson, ed. *They Seek a Country: The American Presbyterians, Some Aspects.* New York: Macmillan, 1955. 330 pp.

Watts, George B. *The Waldenses in the New World.* Durham, NC: Duke University Press, 1941. 309 pp.

Theology

Beardslee, John W., III, ed. and trans. *Reformed Dogmatics: J. Wollebius, G. Voetius, F. Turretin.* New York: Oxford University Press, 1965. 471 pp.

Bratt, John H., ed. *The Heritage of John Calvin.* Grand Rapids, MI: Eerdmans, 1973. 222 pp.

Bullock, Robert H., Jr. *Presbyterians Being Reformed: Reflections on What the Church Needs Today.* Louisville, KY: Geneva Press, 2006. 133 pp.

Calvin, John. *Institutes of the Christian Religion* (1536). Ed. John T. McNeill. Trans. Ford Lewis Battles. 2 vols. Philadelphia: Westminster Press, 1960.

Cochrane, Arthur C., ed. *The Reformed Confessions of the Sixteenth Century.* Philadelphia: Westminster Press, 1966. 336 pp.

Geer, Felix B. *Basic Beliefs of the Reformed Faith: A Biblical Study of Presbyterian Doctrine.* Richmond, VA: John Knox Press, 1960. 80 pp.

Gettys, Joseph M. *What Presbyterians Believe.* Clinton, SC: Author, 1953. 128 pp.

Osterhaven, M. Eugene. *The Spirit of the Reformed Tradition.* Grand Rapids, MI: Eerdmans, 1971. 190 pp.

Schaff, Philip. *Creed Revision in the Presbyterian Churches.* New York: Scribner's, 1890. 67 pp.

Life and Worship

Mackay, John A. *The Presbyterian Way of Life.* Englewood Cliffs, NJ: Prentice-Hall, 1960. 238 pp.

Melton, Julius. *Presbyterian Worship in America: Changing Patterns since 1787.* Richmond, VA: John Knox Press, 1967. 173 pp.

Nichols, James Hastings. *Corporate Worship in the Reformed Tradition.* Philadelphia: Westminster Press, 1968. 190 pp.

Van Hoeven, James W., ed. *Word and World: Reformed Theology in America.* Grand Rapids, MI: Eerdmans, 1986.

Congregationalism

Hiemert, Alan, and Andrew Delbanco, eds. *The Puritans in America: A Narrative Anthology.* Cambridge, MA: Harvard University Press, 1985. 438 pp.

Johnson, Daniel H., and Charles E. Hambrock-Stowe, eds. *Theology and Identity: Traditions, Movements, and Polity in the United Church of Christ.* Rev. ed. Cleveland, OH: United Church Press, 2008. 201 pp.

Starkey, Marion L. *The Congregational Way: The Role of the Pilgrims and Their Heirs in Shaping America.* Garden City, NY: Doubleday, 1966. 342 pp.

Von Rohr, John. *The Shaping of American Congregationalism: 1620–1957.* Cleveland, OH: Pilgrim Press, 1992. 499 pp.

Walker, Williston. *The Creeds and Platforms of Congregationalism.* Boston: Pilgrim Press, 1960. 604 pp.

Wells, David F. *Reformed Theology in America: A History of its Modern Development.* Grand Rapids, MI: Eerdmans, 1985.

Youngs, J. William T. *The Congregationalists.* New York: Greenwood Press, 1990. 376 pp.

Intrafaith Organizations

International Association of Reformed and Presbyterian Churches
756 Haddon Ave., Collingswood, NJ 08108

The International Association of Reformed and Presbyterian Churches was founded in Amsterdam, the Netherlands, in 1962 by delegates and visiting clergymen attending the meeting of the International Council of Christian Churches (ICCC). The ICCC represents the most conservative wing of twentieth-century Protestantism, usually termed *fundamentalism*, characterized by its affirmation of the inerrancy and infallibility of the Bible and its demand for separation from all apostasy and heresy, especially as it is represented in modernist theology and embodied in liberal Protestant denominations. The ICCC received much of its early inspiration from a Presbyterian minister, Dr. Carl McIntire (1906–2002) of the Bible Presbyterian Church.

Leading in the formation of the International Association were McIntire; Dr. A. B. Dodd of Taiwan, the first moderator; and Dr. J. C. Maris of the Netherlands, the first secretary. The occasion for the formation of the International Association was the visit of the moderator of the Church of Scotland to the Vatican for a meeting with the pope. At its first gathering, the association also attacked the World Presbyterian Alliance, whom it accused of departing from the Reformed creeds and faith, and denounced its friendly relationship with the World Council of Churches. Members of the alliance are barred from membership in the association.

Meetings of the association are planned to coincide with meetings of the ICCC.

Membership: Not reported. It includes the members of the ICCC of the Reformed and Presbyterian traditions.

Sources:

Harden, Margaret C., comp. *A Brief History of the Bible Presbyterian Church and Its Agencies.* Privately published, 1968.

International Conference of Reformed Churches
8586 Harbour Heights Rd., Vernon, BC, Canada V1H 1J8

The International Conference of Reformed Churches (ICRC), founded in 1982, is a fellowship of conservative Reformed denominations. At an initial gathering held at Groningen, the Netherlands, and hosted by the Reformed Churches (Liberated), nine Reformed and Presbyterian churches were represented. The host church had been formed during World War II by former members of the state-supported Netherlands Reformed Church as a result of debates on several theological issues. As the debates culminated, the church issued several doctrinal documents, and a protest arose over the demand to adhere to the new statements. Professor K. Schilder (1890–1952) was among the church intellectuals who argued that forcing new theological positions on the church would not end the controversy. His exclusion from the church's ministry resulted in his supporters and several congregations joining to create the Reformed Churches (Liberated), which soon developed relationships with other conservative bodies in the Netherlands and then internationally.

The liberated church and others that formed the ICRC shared a feeling that they faced a concerted attack from the larger Reformed churches on the authority of the Bible and the Reformed creeds originally issued in the sixteenth century. The ICRC adopted the Bible, "Three Forms of Unity" (Belgic Confession, Heidelberg

Catechism, Canons of Dort) used by most continental European Reformed churches, and the Westminster documents (Westminster Confession, Larger and Shorter catechisms) used by most English-speaking groups, as the basis of their fellowship. Member churches are expected to be loyal to the confessional standards of the Reformed tradition.

The ICRC's first assembly gathered in Edinburgh, Scotland, in 1985. Subsequent gatherings have been held in Langley, British Columbia (1989); Zwolle, the Netherlands (1993); Seoul, Korea (1997); Philadelphia, Pennsylvania (2001); and Pretoria, South Africa (2005). The Conference promotes cooperation in missions and the presentation of a united front on the Reformed faith and related issues by its member churches.

Membership: More than 25 Reformed churches worldwide are now members of the Conference, including in North America the Orthodox Presbyterian Church, Associate Reformed Presbyterian Church, Reformed Presbyterian Church of North America, Free Reformed Churches of North America, Reformed Church in the United States, United Reformed Churches in North America, Free Reformed Churches of North America, and Canadian Reformed Churches.

Periodicals: *Newsletter of the Missions Committee of the International Conference of Reformed Churches.*

Sources:

International Conference of Reformed Churches. www.icrconline.com.

Bauswein, Jean-Jacques, and Lukas Vischer, eds. *The Reformed Family Worldwide: A Survey of Reformed Churches, Theological Schools, and International Organizations.* Grand Rapids, MI: William B. Eerdmans, 1999.

International Congregational Fellowship
Rev. Dr. Patrick Shelley, c/o Lake Country Congregational Church, 400 West Capitol Dr., Hartland, WI 53029-1921

The International Congregational Fellowship was founded in 1975 in Chrislehurst, England, to provide an international meeting ground for Congregationalists. It considers itself a successor body to the International Congregational Council, formed in 1891, which merged with the World Alliance of Reformed Churches in 1966 to form the World Alliance of Reformed Churches (Presbyterian and Congregational). Some had felt that the World Alliance did not deal sufficiently with the desires of Congregationalists for fellowship around their distinctive community lifestyle.

The fellowship has established a network of communication with Congregationalists around the world and disseminates news of interest to the community. It also provides a forum for theological discussions, has established a relief service for the needy, champions the cause of religious freedom, and promotes cooperative activities among Congregationalists.

The fellowship gathers periodically in international conferences. Regional secretaries exist for the United Kingdom, North America, the Pacific and Australia, Central and South America, and Africa and Central Europe.

Membership: The fellowship is in contact with Congregationalists in more than 50 countries. The most prominent U.S. affiliate is the National Association of Congregational Christian Churches.

Periodicals: *International Congregational Journal.*

Sources:

International Congregational Fellowship. www.intercong.org.

North American Presbyterian and Reformed Council (NAPARC)
The Orthodox Presbyterian Church, 607 N Easton Rd., Bldg. E, Box P, Willow Grove, PA 19090-0920

The North American Presbyterian and Reformed Council (NAPARC) is an association of conservative Presbyterian churches. These churches accept a conservative and strict reading of the main Reformation statements of the Reformed theological position as set forth in the Heidelberg Catechism, the Belgic Confession, the

Canons of Dordt, the Westminster Confession of Faith, and the Westminster Larger and Shorter Catechisms, and affirms the authority of the Bible as the inerrant Word of God. The intention of NAPARC is to facilitate cooperation between its member churches and suggest means of possible future unions between like-minded bodies.

Membership: In 2008 members included the Associate Reformed Presbyterian Church, the Free Reformed Churches of North America, the Heritage Reformed Congregations, the Korean American Presbyterian Church, the Orthodox Presbyterian Church, the Presbyterian Church in America, the Reformed Church in the United States, the Reformed Church of Quebec (ERQ), the Reformed Presbyterian Church of North America, and the United Reformed Churches in North America. Pending memberships include the Canadian Reformed Churches and the Presbyterian Reformed Church. Many of the member churches are also members of the International Conference of Reformed Churches.

Sources:

North American Presbyterian and Reformed Council. www.naparc.org.

Reformed Ecumenical Council
2050 Breton Rd. SE, Ste. 102, Grand Rapids, MI 49546-5547

The Reformed Ecumenical Council was founded in 1946 as the Reformed Ecumenical Synod. It unites thirty-eight Reformed and Presbyterian denominational bodies in twenty-three countries. They share the same Reformed heritage and have joined together based on a common confession of faith. These churches represent a more conservative and evangelical element in the Reformed/Presbyterian community.

The council meets in general assembly every four years. The day-to-day affairs are placed in the hands of an executive committee and permanent secretariat. Through the council, member churches speak on current world issues, coordinate mission programs, and share ideas.

Membership: The council includes one church based in North America, the Christian Reformed Church in North America. The other 39 member churches are found in 22 countries. The churches have a total of about 12,000,000 members.

Periodicals: *News Exchange.*

World Alliance of Reformed Churches (WARC)
150 route de Ferney, PO Box 2100, 1211 Geneva 2, Switzerland

The World Alliance of Reformed Churches (WARC) was formed in 1970 in a merger of the Alliance of the Reformed Churches Throughout the World Holding the Presbyterian System (1875) and the International Congregationalist Council (1891). The merger grew out of a recognition of the common heritage of the Reformed, Presbyterian, and Congregational churches in the theology of John Calvin, Ulrich Zwingli, John Knox, and others.

In 2008 WARC was involved in a merger process with the Reformed Ecumenical Council (REC) to create the World Communion of Reformed Churches (WCRC) in a uniting General Council in Grand Rapids, Michigan, in June 2010. This merger was expected to combine more than 80 million Reformed Christians into one organization.

WARC has a president, six vice-presidents, and an executive committee of 40 persons who meet every two years. Work is carried out by a small secretariat in Geneva, Switzerland, and by networks and area councils, including the Caribbean and North American Area Council (CANAAC).

Membership: In 2008 WARC reported 75 million Reformed Christians in 214 member churches in 107 countries.

Sources:

World Alliance of Reformed Churches. http://www.warc.ch

World Reformed Fellowship

430 Montier Rd., Glenside, PA 19038

The World Reformed Fellowship (WRF), an ecumenical association of churches of the Reformed and Presbyterian tradition, was established in 2000 through the merger of two older associations, the World Fellowship of Reformed Churches (WFRC) and the International Reformed Fellowship (IRF). The WFRC had been formed in 1994 by the Presbyterian Church in America and a number of sister churches throughout Latin America. The International Reformed fellowship, also founded in 1994, joined together a variety of churches in Asia.

The churches of the WRF affirm the inerrancy of the Christian scriptures and the orthodox faith of the ancient creeds—the Apostles, Nicene, and Chalcedonian. In addition, each of the member churches affirms one or more of the major confessions of the Reformed faith: the Gallican Confession, the Belgic Confession, the Heidelberg Catechism, the Thirty-Nine Articles, the Second Helvetic Confession, the Canons of Dort, the Westminster Confession of Faith, the London Confession of 1689, or the Savoy Declaration.

The fellowship engendered by the WRF is made visible in its quadrennial assemblies. The next is slated for 2010 in Scotland. Between meetings of the assemblies, the work of the fellowship is administered by the WRF executive committee, which assigns much of its work to its three commissions (theological education, theology, and missions and evangelism) and its six regional boards.

Membership: The WRF consists of 28 member churches, four of which operate in the United States and Canada: the Associate Reformed Presbyterian Church, the Evangelical Presbyterian Church, the Presbyterian Church in America, and the United Christian Church and Bible Institute. In addition, a number of individual congregations and parachurch organizations are members.

Sources:

World Reformed Fellowship. www.wrfnet.org/.

Confronting Kingdom Challenges: A Call to Global Christians to Carry the Burden Together. Wheaton, IL: Crossway Books, 2007.

 # Reformed

Association of Free Reformed Churches

c/o Shiloh Christian Church, 14030 Radcliffe Rd., Leroy Township, OH 44077
Alternate Address: c/o The Christian Statesman, PO Box 42, Geigertown, PA 16526.

The Association of Free Reformed Churches was formed in 1994 by several ministers in the Cleveland, Ohio, area, including Jeffery A. Ziegler, pastor of Shiloh Christian Church, who is the association's moderator. In 1985 Zeigler had founded the Reformation Bible Institute to train pastors and laymen in the theological opinions of the historic Reformed faith. Ziegler is a board member of the National Reform Association, whose mission is to maintain and promote the Christian principles of civil government in American life. Among other founders is Andrew Sandlin, pastor of Church of the Word in Painesville, Ohio, the editor of *Chalcedon Report* and the *Journal of Christian Reconstruction*, two influential Christian Reconstructionist periodicals founded by R. J. Rushdoony.

Both associations and the Institute generally hold to what has been termed Christian Reconstruction theology, a perspective that grows out of a reading of traditional Calvinist theology. Christian Reconstruction affirms that God's law is found in the Bible and remains as a standard of righteousness. It is to be used for three important purposes: to move the sinner to trust in Christ; as a standard of obedience for the Christian; and to maintain order in society, by restraining evil. It is the job of the Christian to build Christ's kingdom in the present time and advocate the godly taking dominion over the earth and society. Every area dominated by sin must be "reconstructed" in terms of the Bible, from the individual to the state. The goal is the building of a Christian civilization.

Reconstructionists support the separation of church and state, but affirm that no separation should exist between the state and God. They seek what they think of as a godly decentralized theocracy, or the rule of the law of God. That is distinct from rule by an institutional church.

The Reconstructionist movement has been a matter of ongoing conversations within the larger Evangelical community, in which it is a distinct minority. The association's vice-moderator, Rev. William O. Einwechter, who is also the vice-president of the National Reform Association, has been a focus of controversy as he has been widely quoted for his opinion that juvenile delinquents should be stoned per Deuteronomy 21:18–21, and that God commands the woman as wife/mother to stay at home to care for the family and manage the household.

Membership: Not reported.

Educational Facilities:

Reformation Bible Institute, Eastlake, Ohio.

Periodicals: *The Puritan Storm*, 35155 Beachpark Dr., Eastlake, OH 44095.

Sources:

Bauswein, Jean-Jacques, and Lukas Vischner, eds. *The Reformed Family Worldwide: A Survey of Reformed Churches, Theological Schools, and International Organizations.* Grand Rapids, MI: W. B. Eerdmanns, 1999.

Canadian and American Reformed Churches

PO Box 62053, Burlington, ON L7R 4K2
Alternate Address: American Reformed Churches, c/o Rev. P. Kingma, 3167 68th St., SE, Caledonia, MI 46316 American Reformed Churches, c/o Rev. P. Kingma, 3167 68th St. SE, Caledonia, MI 46316.

The Canadian and American Reformed Churches is a conservative reformed church founded in Canada in 1950. It spread to the United States in 1955. It accepts the Bible as the infallible Word of God and finds it is best summarized in the Belgic Confession of Faith (1561), the Heidelberg Catechism (1563), and the Canons of Dort (1618–19). It has a presbyterian polity.

Membership: In 2007 the churches reported 54 congregations, 16,365 members, and 68 ministers in the United Sates and Canada.

Periodicals: *Reformed Perspective.* • *The Canadian Reformed Magazine.*

Educational Facilities:

Theological College of the Canadian Reformed Churches, Hamilton, Ontario

Remarks: The group produces a radio broadcast, *Voice of the Church.*

Christian Presbyterian Church (Korean)

4741 N Glen Arden Ave., Covina, CA 91724

The Christian Presbyterian Church was founded in 1992 when a group of Korean members of the Christian Reformed Church in North America under the leadership of Dr. John E. Kim left the denomination over the issue of woman's ordination, which the Koreans strongly opposed. By 1976 Kim had built his own congregation in Los Angeles into the second largest within the Christian Reformed Church. Kim also founded International Theological Seminary, a Los Angeles–based seminary largely serving students from third-world countries. He took a leading role in 1992 in the formation of the International Reformed Fellowship (IRF), a conservative ecumenical organization that served as an alternative to the World Council of Churches, the World Alliance of Reformed Churches, and the Reformed Ecumenical Council. The Christian Reformed Church was a prominent member of the Reformed Ecumenical Council, and its leadership sharply criticized Kim for his actions.

The newly formed Christian Presbyterian Church included some 40 percent of the Korean membership of the Christian Reformed Church. During the next three years, the Los Angeles congregation almost doubled in membership, growing from 1,440 members to 2,800 members. In 1995 Kim returned to Korea to become president of Chongshin Seminary, the largest ministerial training school in the world.

The church is conservative, and acknowledges the Westminster Confession of Faith, the Belgic Confession, and the Heidelberg Catechism. It affirms the Bible as the infallible word of God.

Membership: In 1995 the church reported 20 congregations and 50 ordained clergy.

Educational Facilities:

International Theological Seminary, Los Angeles, California.

Sources:

International Theological Seminary. www.itsla.edu.

Maurina, Darrell Todd. "Dr. John E. Kim Appointed President of World's Largest Reformed Seminary in Seoul, Korea." United Reformed News Service, May 26, 1995. www.iclnet.org/pub/resources/text/reformed/archive95/nr95-042.txt.

Christian Reformed Church in North America

2850 Kalamazoo Ave. SE, Grand Rapids, MI 49560

Alternate Address: In Canada: 3475 Mainway, Box 5070 STN LCD 1, Burlington, ON L7R 3Y8, Canada.

The Christian Reformed Church began in the Netherlands in the 1830s. At that time, some members of the Reformed Church of the Netherlands resisted an attempt to bring the church under the control of the Dutch monarchy. Despite the objections of these churchmen, the church was brought under state control. This led in 1834 to the Sucession (the formation of a church independent from the monarchy). Sucession leaders were Hendrik DeCock (1801–1842), Henrik Scholte (1805–1868), and Albertus C. van Raalte (1811–1876). They saw themselves as defenders of the historical faith that was being lost because of the indifference of the main body of the Reformed Church of the Netherlands. Following religious persecution and the failure of the country's potato crop in 1846, the dissidents supporting the Sucession made plans to immigrate.

In 1847 the settlers arrived in western Michigan and by 1848 had formed the Classis Holland. Having been aided by members of the Reformed Church in America with whom they shared the same faith, they affiliated with them in 1850, becoming a classis within the Reformed Church in America. Members of the Classis Holland understood that they could leave the Reformed Church in America if the ecclesiastical connection should prove a threat to their interests. For most, it never did. However, one church that belonged to the Classis Holland did leave the classis and the Reformed Church in America in 1857, and others followed, eventually forming the Christian Reformed Church.

The background of the schism starts with Gysbert Haan (1801–1874). Within a few years of the 1850 affiliation, Haan began to criticize practices of the Reformed Church in America, and in 1857 four documents of Sucession were received by the classis, urging the classis to leave the Reformed Church in America. The documents charged the Reformed Church in America with open communion, the use of a large collection of hymns, and the neglect of catechism preaching. Further, the documents asserted that the Reformed Church in America believed the Sucession in the Netherlands had been unjustified. The classis received but did not approve these documents. Several churches left the classis beginning in 1857, and in 1859 these congregations became known as the Dutch Reformed Church. Growth was slow at first and came primarily from additional immigration from the Netherlands. Immigration and growth were particularly heavy in the closing decades of the nineteenth century. Through a series of name changes the church became the Christian Reformed Church in 1904, and it has retained that name.

Confessional subscription is required and church doctrine is based on the Belgic Confession, the Heidelberg Catechism, and the Canons of the Synod of Dort. In 1906 the church adopted the Conclusions of Utrecht, which recognized that some questions were open for disagreement. Only the children of confessing members are baptized. The church is staunchly antilodge. Worship is ordered and consistent with the practice of the Christian church through the centuries. The early hymnology was largely confined to the Psalms, but an expanded hymnology developed in the twentieth century. Catechistic instruction is stressed. Polity is presbyterial. The general synod, the broadest assembly of the church, is composed of two ministers and two elders of each of the 47 classes. There is no intermediate or particular synod between the classis and general synod. Classes meet biannually or triannually.

There is an active mission program. Home missions include an active church-planting program, an established church development program, campus ministry, and Native American missions. World mission agencies of evangelism, education, relief, and development are active in 40 countries located in North America, Central America, South America, Africa, Europe, and Asia. A media ministry (radio/TV) blanketing the globe is called the *Back to God Hour*. Other media ministries include *Kids Corner*, *Walk the Way*, and *Spotlight*.

Membership: In 2008 the church reported 300,000 members and 1,000 congregations.

Educational Facilities:

Calvin Theological Seminary, Grand Rapids, Michigan.

Calvin College, Grand Rapids, Michigan.

Periodicals: *The Banner*. • *Reformed Worship*. • *CRC Ministry Report*. • *Today* daily devotional.

Sources:

Christian Reformed Church in North America. crcna.org.

One Hundred Years in the New World. Grand Rapids, MI: Centennial Committee of the Christian Reformed Church, 1957.

Schapp, James C. *Our Family Album: The Unfinished Story of the Christian Reformed Church*. Grand Rapids, MI: CRC Publications, 1998.

Church of the Golden Rule

6507 Ranch Rd. 32, Blanco, TX 78606

The Church of the Golden Rule continues the French Huguenot tradition of the Alsatian Protestants who look to Martin Buber and the city of Strasbourg as the source of their faith. A congregation of Alsatian immigrants was formed in 1939 at Hempstead, Long Island, New York, under Pr. Alfred E. Huss. He was authorized by Pastor Boegner of the Alsatian churches. When Huss died, the congregation relocated to California. In 1971 there were four congregations with about 600 families, all in California, under the leadership of Dr. Pierre Duval. The Church of the Golden Rule is under the Unite Huguenotte Française.

Membership: Not reported.

Remarks: The Church of the Golden Rule owns Ridgewood, a working ranch in Willits, California, that was the orginal home of the legendary racehorse Seabiscuit. The ranch has been designated one of the United States's most threatened historic places by the National Trust for Historic Preservation, and the church has endeavored to be a model steward of the ranch by keeping developers at bay and by permanently protecting the historic structures that constitute Seabiscuit's legacy. The church has worked toward restoring several historic buildings and has joined the Seabiscuit Heritage Foundation, the National Trust, and others to develop an overall preservation and resource management plan and identify necessary funding sources for the effort.

Sources:

Church of the Golden Rule. www.churchofthegoldenrule.org.

Churches of God, General Conference

PO Box 926, Findlay, OH 45839

The Churches of God, General Conference was formed by John Winebrenner (1797–1860), a German Reformed pastor of four churches in and around Harrisburg, Pennsylvania. Winebrenner, though a reformer in many areas, never intended to form a new denomination. However, in attempting to reform what he perceived as the spiritual apathy in the Reformed Church, he and other Reformed pastors adopted some of the "new measures" which had become popular during the Second Great Awakening. They began to preach the importance of personal acceptance of Jesus Christ as savior; they introduced prayer meetings in the homes of those concerned about their salvation; they prayed for people by name in their services; they initiated altar calls.

The vestry of the Harrisburg congregation served by Winebrenner took exception to these new devices. Their concern was heightened by their pastor accepting invitations to preach in the local Methodist church and by his refusal to baptize the children of unbelieving parents. He was locked out of the church building in 1823, though he continued to serve other Reformed congregations and remained a member of the synod for several years.

In 1825, a Harrisburg congregation of persons loyal to Winebrenner and others attracted by his preaching was formed. The General Conference dates its beginning from this event. The name Church of God was adopted after a search of the scripture showed it to be the New Testament name of the church. The name was considered to be inclusive of all true believers. (Winebrenner's was one of several early nineteenth-century movements that attempted to return to the New Testament model of the church. It was the first of many to follow that adopted the name "Church of God" as an element in their self-reformation.)

The essential teachings of the New Testament Church were taken to be redemption and regeneration through belief in Jesus Christ, justification by faith, and free moral agency. Three "ordinances" instituted by Jesus were followed: believer's baptism by immersion, the observance of the Lord's Supper, and feetwashing. A presbyterial polity was followed, with preachers ordained as "teaching elders," assisted by "ruling elders" and deacons in the local congregation. The first organization of a group of churches into an eldership was accomplished in 1830. For many years the group was known General Eldership of the Churches of God in North America.

While pastors and elders still participate with each other in the sixteen regional annual business meetings, most are now called "conferences" rather than "elderships." The triennial meeting of ministerial, lay, and youth delegates from local conferences and elderships is called the General Conference.

An administrative council functions between the triennial meetings of the General Conference.

The General Conference has affiliated work in six countries, including Bangladesh, Brazil, Haiti, India, Moldova, and Sweden. They also have ministries to U.S. Asian Pacific, Haitian, Hispanic, and Southwestern people groups.

Membership: In 2006, the church reported 33,208 members, 319 congregations, and 451 ministers in the United States.

Educational Facilities:

The University of Findlay, Findlay, Ohio.

Winebrenner Theological Seminary, Findlay, Ohio.

Periodicals: *The Church Advocate* • *The Missionary Signal* • *The Gem*

Sources:

Churches of God, General Conference. www.cggc.org.

Kern, Richard. *John Winebrenner, 19th Century Reformer*. Harrisburg, PA: Central Publishing House, 1974.

We Believe. Findlay, OH: Churches of God Publications, 1986.

Yahn, S. G. *History of the Churches of God in North America*. Harrisburg, PA: Central Publishing House, 1926.

Confederation of Reformed Evangelical Churches

Randy Booth, Moderator, 8784 FM 226, Nacogdoches, TX 75961

The Confederation of Reformed Evangelical Churches (CREC) was formed in 1997 in reponse to a concern that the Christian church is in a period of decline, and that Christians need to return to scriptural standards and encourage others to do the same. Its member churches and leaders see the confederation as a group within the larger church from which they can work together for a reformation of the whole.

Member churches are asked to adopt as their doctrinal standard the Apostles Creed, the Nicene Creed, and the Chalcedonian Creed, as well as one or more of the following creedal statements: the Westminster Confession of Faith (1647); the American Westminster Confession of Faith (1788); the Three Forms of Unity (Belgic Confession—1561, Heidelberg Catechism—1563, Canons of Dort—1619); the London Baptist Confession (1689); the Savoy Declaration (1658); or the Reformed Evangelical Confession. The Bible is the acknowledged ultimate authority, but members believe that the aforementioned creeds rightly interpret and summarize it.

The confederation is committed to the autonomy of the local church, though it sees value in transcongregational structures insofar as they do not violate local independence. In keeping with this policy, missionaries are sent from local churches. Any two local churches may form a presbytery, and two or more presbyteries may form a church council. The council elects a moderator who becomes the spokesperson for the denomination. The council may not appoint any standing committees, and all committees must operate as a task force and disband as soon as their work is completed.

Churches applying for membership in the confederation must have existed for at least two years; those that do not meet that criterion may be accepted as mission churches. There is an annual meeting of the CREC. It is a member of the Alliance of Confessing Churches.

Membership: Not reported. During the 2005 meeting of the CREC, two presbyteries were established: Augustine Presbytery east of the Rockies, and Anselm Presbytery in the western United States. Congregations also are located in Canada, Japan, Poland, Russia, and Uganda. In 2008 there were 24 members in the Anselm Presbytery and 34 in the Augustine Presbytery.

Sources:

Confederation of Reformed Evangelical Churches. www.crepres.org/.

Free Reformed Church of North America

950 Ball Ave. NE, Grand Rapids, MI 49503

The Free Reformed Church of North America was started by post–World War II immigrants whose roots were in the Christian Reformed Churches in the Netherlands (Christelijke Gereformeerde Kerken in Nederland). The first churches of this denomination began to form in 1950, and two U.S. congregations joined in the 1960s. A synod of the churches meets annually in June, usually in Ontario, Canada, where most of the churches are located. The churches fully subscribe to three creeds (the Heidelberg Catechism, the Belgic Confession, and the Canons of Dort) that are found, together with the liturgical forms used, in the denominational songbook, *The Psalter*. A full corresponding relationship exists with the parent denomination in the Netherlands. The denomination also supports foreign mission work in Cubulco, Guatemala.

Membership: In 2008 the church had 21 congregations (18 in Canada and three in the United States) and a mission church in Guatemala.

Periodicals: *The Messenger*.

Sources:

Free Reformed Church of North America. www.frcna.org.

Heritage Netherlands Reformed Congregations

540 Crescent St. NE, Grand Rapids, MI 49503

The Heritage Netherlands Reformed Congregations resulted from a 1993 split within the First Netherlands Reformed Congregation of Grand Rapids, Michigan (affiliated with the Netherlands Reformed Congregations), which had more than 1,000 members. In July 1993 the split resulted in the dissolving of the former congregation and each group's establishing a new one. One group continued its previous denominational affiliation, whereas the other formed a new denomination. Rev. J. R. Beeke, who had led the previous congregation since 1986, continued as pastor of the new organization. Subsequently, the original Heritage Netherlands Reformed Congregation was joined by three other congregations, including two in Ontario, Canada.

Though small, the new denomination opened its own seminary in 1995. Beeke has served as a professor of theology at the seminary, whose students come from a variety of reformed groups.

Membership: In 2008 the church reported six affiliated congregations in the United States and five in Canada.

Educational Facilities:

Puritan Reformed Theological Seminary, Grand Rapids, Michigan.

Periodicals: *The Banner of Sovereign Grace Truth.* • *Sovereign Grace Truth.*

Sources:

Heritage Netherlands Reformed Congregations. www.hnrc.org/.

Heritage Netherlands Reformed Congregation, Grand Rapids, Michigan. reformed.net/hnrc/mi/gr/index.shtml.

Puritan Reformed Theological Seminary. www.puritanseminary.org/.

Hungarian Reformed Church in America

c/o Andrew Harsanyi, 220 4th St., Passaic, NJ 07055

Hungarian Reformed congregations were established in the United States in the late nineteenth century and in 1904 the Hungarian Reformed Church in America was formed under the care of the Reformed Church in Hungary. Following World War I, however, there was a series of negotiations with the Reformed Church in the United States resulting in the 1921 Tiffin Agreement. This agreement, made at Tiffin, Ohio, joined the Hungarian Reformed Church in America to the Reformed Church in the United States. The merged body is now a part of the United Church of Christ. Three congregations of the Hungarian Reformed Church did not wish to accept the Tiffin Agreement. These congregations and four new ones united to form the Free Magyar Reformed Church in America, which in 1958 adopted the name Hungarian Reformed Church in America.

Doctrinally, the church follows the Second Helvetic Confession and the Heidelberg Catechism. The constitution includes elements of both the presbyterian and episcopal systems. There is a synod headed by a bishop and a lay curator. The New York, Eastern, and Western Classes are headed by a dean and lay curator. The synod meets every four years. The church is a member of the World Alliance of Reformed Churches (Presbyterian and Congregational), the National Council of Churches, and the World Council of Churches.

Membership: In 1995 the church reported 4,195 members, 38 ministers in the United States; 275 members and 12 ministers in Canada.

Periodicals: Magyar Egyhaz (Magyar Church). Available from Mr. Stephen Szabo, Synod Chief Elder, 464 Forest Ave., Paramus, NJ 07652.

Sources:

Hungarian Reformed Church in America. www. hrca.us.

Lithuanian Evangelical Reformed Church

c/o Mrs. Halina Davis, 3542 W 66th Pl., Chicago, IL 60629

The Lithuanian Evangelical Reformed Church consists of one congregation that is an outpost of the synod of the Reformed Church in Lithuania. The Reformed Church first came to Lithuania in the middle of the fifteenth century, and the first church was formed in 1555. It was granted equal rights with Lutherans and Catholics in 1564. It survived through the centuries as the country fell under Russian and then Soviet control. (Through the twentieth century, more than 800,000 Lithuanians

migrated to the United States.) There are more than 10,000 members of the Reformed Church residing in Lithuania.

The church holds to the Apostles Creed and the Heidelberg Catechism as its standards of faith. It is led by its elders (teaching and ruling), and congregational representatives meet annually as a synod. The Lithuanian synod opened ordination to women in 1991.

The church in the United States retains fraternal relations with other Lithuania churches, especially several that are integrated into the Lutheran Church–Missouri Synod. It is a member of both the World Council of Churches and the World Alliance of Reformed Churches.

Membership: In 2008 the single congregation had approximately 50 members.

Periodicals: *Musu Srarnai* (Our Wings).

Sources:

Bauswein, Jean-Jacques, and Lukas Vischner, eds. *The Reformed Family Worldwide: A Survey of Reformed Churches, Theological Schools, and International Organizations.* Grand Rapids, MI: William B. Eerdmanns Publishing Co., 1999.

Netherlands Reformed Congregations

Current address not obtained for this edition.

The Netherlands Reformed Congregations were formed in 1907 by the merger of two Dutch Reformed denominations. The Churches of the Cross had originated in 1834 with churches that had broken with the Seccession (an earlier group that had broken with the state church). The Ledeboerian Churches had been established under the leadership of Reverend Ledeboer, who had left the state Reformed church at a later date. Doctrinal standards of the church are the Belgic Confession, the Heidelberg Catechism, and the Canons of the Synod of Dort. The church has been very active in publishing and Christian education. It operates seven high schools and elementary schools in the United States.

Membership: In 2003 the Netherlands Reformed Church (NRC) had 9,524 members in 27 congregations served by 10 clergy members.

Educational Facilities:

Netherlands Reformed Theological Seminary, Grand Rapids, Michigan.

Periodicals: *Banner of Truth.* • *Paul.* • *Insight Into NRCEA.*

Protestant Reformed Churches in America (PRC)

4949 Ivanrest SW, Grandville, MI 49418

The Protestant Reformed Churches in America (PRC) has its roots in the sixteenth-century Reformation of Martin Luther and John Calvin, as it developed in the Dutch Reformed churches. The denomination originated as a result of a controversy in the Christian Reformed Church in 1924 involving the adoption of the "Three Points of Common Grace." Three ministers in the Christian Reformed Church, the Revs. Herman Hoeksema (1886–1965), Henry Danhof (d. 1942), and George Ophoff (1891–1962), and their consistories (Eastern Avenue, Hope, Kalamazoo) rejected the doctrine. Eventually, these men were deposed, and their consistories either deposed or set outside the Christian Reformed Church. The denomination was founded in 1926 with three congregations.

The PRC follows the presbyterian form of church government as determined by the Church Order of Dordt. There is an annual synod. The synodical stated clerk and board of trustees deal with the necessary business of the church between the meetings of synod.

The PRC's doctrinal standards are the Reformed confessions: the Heidelberg Catechism, Belgic Confession of Faith, and Canons of Dordrecht. It maintains the "five points of Calvinism." The doctrine of the covenant is a cornerstone of its teaching. It maintains an unconditional, particular covenant of grace that God establishes with His elect. In practice, the Protestant Reformed Churches maintains the regulative principle of worship, rejects remarriage of divorced persons, and maintains many of its own Christian schools.

Membership: In 2008 the PRC included about 25 churches in the United States and two in Canada (Edmonton and Lacombe, Alberta), and almost 6,000 members. The denomination's seminary is in Grandville, Michigan, where the largest number of churches is located. Over the years the PRC has established numerous mission stations in North America, and has been working in Northern Ireland, United Kingdom, New Zealand, the Philippines, and Singapore.

Educational Facilities:

Protestant Reformed Theological School, Grandville, Michigan.

Periodicals: Although the PRC has no official publication, its seminary publishes the *Protestant Reformed Theological Journal*, and several organizations within the denomination publish periodicals, including *Beacon Lights*, *Perspectives in Covenant Education*, and *Standard Bearer*. Another organization, the Reformed Free Publishing Association, also publishes religious books both theological and educational.

Sources:

Protestant Reformed Churches in America. www.prca.org/prc.html.

Hoeksema, Herman. *The Protestant Reformed Churches in America*. Grand Rapids, MI: Author, 1947.

———. *Why Protestant Reformed?* Grand Rapids, MI: Sunday School of the First Protestant Reformed Church, 1949.

Reformed Church in America

475 Riverside Dr., New York, NY 10115

The first Dutch settlers in America, members of the Reformed Church in the Netherlands, brought that church to this country. The Rev. Jonas Michaelius arrived in 1628 and organized the first congregation, now known as the Collegiate Church of the City of New York. Because of a shortage of ministers, some people began to advocate ministerial training in the colonies. Queens College (now Rutgers University) was founded and a theological seminary established there. The independence of the American church was achieved in 1770 when John Livingston returned from his theological work at Utrecht with a plan of union. In 1792 a constitution was adopted, and in 1819 the church was incorporated as the Reformed Protestant Dutch Church. It took its present name, the Reformed Church in America, in 1867.

The church spread through New York and New Jersey during the colonial era. In the middle of the nineteenth century a new wave of Dutch immigrants arrived. They settled primarily in Michigan and Iowa and from there moved to other states, particularly South Dakota.

Doctrinally, the church has remained very conservative, accepting as its standard doctrine the Belgic Confession, the Heidelberg Catechism, and the Canons of the Synod of Dort. Worship is outlined in the liturgy and is supplemented by the church's hymnal, *Rejoice in the Lord*. The liturgies of the Lord's Supper, baptism, and ordination are obligatory; those for the Sunday service and marriage are not.

The polity is presbyterial. The highest authority is the General Synod, which meets annually in June. A 62-member executive committee functions between sessions. The General Synod is divided into 46 classes that are distributed in eight regional synods made up of lay and clerical members of each classes. The voting members of the classes are all the ministers and an elder from each church in the classes. The ruling body at the congregational level is the consistory, composed of the ministers and elected elders and deacons.

Education has always been given high priority by the Reformed Church, and a Board of Theological Education keeps oversight of its seminaries. The General Synod Council oversees work among American Indians; social services; and foreign work in Central America, Africa, Asia, Europe, and the Middle East. The church is a member of the National Council of Churches and the World Council of Churches.

Membership: In 1997 the church reported 304,113 members, an additional 190,000 active communicants, 957 churches, and 1,800 ministers. There were 6,535 members in Canada.

Educational Facilities:

Seminaries:

Western Theological Seminary, Holland, Michigan.

New Brunswick Theological Seminary, New Brunswick, New Jersey.

Colleges:

Hope College, Holland, Michigan.

Northwestern College, Orange City, Iowa.

Central College, Pella, Iowa.

Periodicals: *The Church Herald*. Send orders to 4500 60th St. SE, Grand Rapids, MI 49512.

Sources:

Reformed Church in America.
    www.rca.org/NETCOMMUNITY/Page.aspx?pid=183&srcid=425.

Reformed Church in the United States

407 W Main St., Grass Valley, CA 95945

In 1934 the Reformed Church in the United States merged with the Evangelical Synod. (In 1961 that merged body joined the United Church of Christ.) One classis of the Reformed Church in the United States, the Eureka Classis in South Dakota, decided not to enter the 1934 merger. So the Eureka Classis adopted the name of its parent body, the Reformed Church in the United States, and stayed separate from all the other classes that joined the 1934 merger. The present Reformed Church in the United States continues the polity and doctrines (adherence to the Heidelberg Confession) of the former Reformed Church in the United States. The classis meets annually.

Membership: In 2008 the church had 46 congregations. It has two main mission fields in Africa. They have fraternal relations with the Canadian and American Reformed Churches, Reformed Churches in the Netherlands (Liberated), Reformed Confessing Church of the Congo, Reformed Presbyterian Church of North America, and the Orthodox Presbyterian Church. They are members of the North American Reformed and Presbyterian Council and the International Conference of Reformed Churches.

Periodicals: *The Reformed Herald*. Send orders to 6121 Pine Vista Way, Elk Grove, CA 95758.

Sources:

Reformed Church in the United States. www.rcus.org/.

Reformed Church of Quebec

844, rue de Contrecoeur, Quebec, QC, Canada G1X 2X8

Reformed Church of Quebec claims a heritage that begins even before the Protestant Reformation, in the writings of Jacques Lefevre d'Etaples (c. 1450–1536), a professor of theology of the University of Sorbonne. In 1512, he authored a commentary on the biblical book of Romans that had an instrumental role in the transformation of Martin Luther and was subsequently read by leading French Reformers such as William Farel and John Calvin. Through the sixteenth and seventeenth centuries many Protestants (in France called Huguenots) migrated to Canada and several rose to positions of eminence.

In 1835 two Swiss missionaries, Louis Roussy and Henriette Feller, from the Swiss Missionary Society, arrived in Montreal. From their effort an initial parish was formed in 1837. Two years later, they formed the Franco-Canadian Missionary Society. In 1921, the congregations resulting from this effort became a part of the Presbyterian Church of Canada and then moved into the United Church of Canada. However, as Canada grew, and attention was focused on growth in the far west, the French-speaking element in the church declined. By 1975, only three congregations of some 25 remained.

In 1978 Rev. Harold Kallemeyn of the Christian Reformed Church began a new thrust into Quebec and founded a congregation in Montreal. His effort also led to the foundation of the Evangelical Reformed Alliance (Alliance Reformee evangelique [A.R.E.]) founded that same year at Montmorency. A.R.E. proposed three goals: (a) to establish Farel Institute (later Farel Reformed Theological Seminary) for the training of ministers; (b) to launch a journal; and (c) to revise and publish French Reformed books. Over the next decades with the support of Christian Reformed Church in North America, the Presbyterian Church of America, and the continuing Presbyterian Church of Canada, additional congregations were formed. In 1984 several congregations formed the Conseil des eglises Reformees du Quebec (C.E.R.Q.) as a step toward the formation of a separate French-speaking Reformed denomination. A three-year process of negotiation on structure and doctrine followed and the Eglise Reformee du Quebec was officially inaugurated on November 6, 1988.

The church accepted the Heidelberg Catechism and the Westminster Confession of Faith. Initially, nine congregations affiliated.

Membership: As of March 2008, there are five congregations and seven clergy, all in Quebec. The church reported a membership of 250.

Educational Facilities:

Farel Reformed Theological Seminary, Montreal, Quebec, Canada.

Sources:

Reformed Church of Quebec. www.erq.qc.ca.

Farel Reformed Theological Seminary. www.farel.net.

Bauswein, Jean-Jacques, and Lukas Vischner, eds. *The Reformed Family Worldwide: A Survey of Reformed Churches, Theological Schools, and International Organizations.* Grand Rapids, MI: Eerdmanns, 1999.

United Reformed Churches of North America

No central headquarters. For information, write c/o, Mr. Bill Konynenbelt, Stated Clerk of the Federation, 5824 Bowwater Cr. NW, Calgary, AB, Canada T3B 2E2

The United Reformed Church of North America (URCNA) grew out of dissatisfaction with a variety of decisions being made within the Christian Reformed Church of North America. Dissatisfaction initially manifested through the organization of a Consistorial Conference, a gathering of consistories/councils at which issues could be aired and discussed. In the early 1990s, the conference transformed into the Alliance of Reformed Churches that included both congregations that had withdrawn from the Christian Reformed Church and others that retained their formal affiliation. Over time, several congregations not previously a part of the Christian Reformed Church also affiliated with the Alliance.

In November 1995, representatives from more than 40 churches in both the United States and Canada gathered in Lynwood, Illinois, to develop a constitution and by-laws for a new federation of reformed churches. Their work led to the formation the next year of the United Reformed Churches in North America at a synod meeting also held in Lynwood.

The new federation adopted the Bible as confessed in the Heidelberg Catechism, Belgic Confession, and the Canons of Dort as their standard of faith (Three Forms of Unity). Liturgical forms based on that of the 1976 Psalter Hymnal of Christian Reformed Church were also adopted in a slightly modified form.

At its Sixth Synod (2007), the United Reformed Church gave a new committee permission to post a list of URC Churches, Synodical agendas and minutes, and similar documents on a newly developed and soon to be public web site of the federation, www.urcna.org. The next Synod meeting of the URCNA is scheduled be held in London, ON, Canada, in 2010.

The URCNA is a member of North American Presbyterian and Reformed Council (NAPARC, www.naparc.org) and The International Conference of Reformed Churches (ICRC, www.icrconline.com).

Membership: In 2008 the church reported that there were 21,832, 68 congregations in the United States and 34 congregations in Canada.

Sources:

United Reformed Churches in North America. www.urcna.org.

Presbyterian

American Presbyterian Church
1647 Dyre St., Philadelphia, PA 19124-1340

The American Presbyterian Church was founded in 1977 by persons who withdrew from the Bible Presbyterian Church then under the domination of Dr. Carl McIntire (1906–2002). In that year, McIntire had directed the dissolution of the Bible Presbyterian Church's Philadelphia Presbytery. Three congregations took the opportunity to reorganize separately as the American Presbyterian Church. The dispute was organizational, not doctrinal, and the new church retained the very conservative stance of the Bible Presbyterian Church, acknowledging the authority of the Heidelberg Catechism and the Westminster Confession of Faith. The church sings only with a psalter (the Psalms set to music) and demands that members refrain from imbibing alcohol. The church does not ordain women to the ministry.

The church has open relations with other small Presbyterian groups (such as the Reformed Presbyterian Church–Hanover Synod and the Presbyterian Reformed Church) with whom they share a basic outlook.

Membership: Not reported. In the 1990s there were some 60 members in three congregations.

Periodicals: *Katartizo*.

Sources:

American Presbyterian Church. www.americanpresbyterianchurch.org.

Bauswein, Jean-Jacques, and Lukas Vischner, eds. *The Reformed Family Worldwide: A Survey of Reformed Churches, Theological Schools, and International Organizations.* Grand Rapids, MI: William B. Eerdmanns, 1999.

American Reformation Presbyterian Church
6702 Dalrock Rd., Ste. 126 PMB 214, Rowlett, TX 75089-2662

The Reformation Presbyterian Church was formed in 1994 by several congregations, most formerly related to the Presbyterian Church in America. Among the important leaders in the new denomination is Dr. Richard Bacon, pastor of the church in Rowlett, Texas. Its members do not see themselves as part of a separatist or a protest movement, because of common agreement over the manner in which they interpret the teachings of the Bible. Basic to the denomination is a common understanding of the authority of the church. Such authority in matters of doctrine, government, and worship are carefully laid out in the Bible. As a result, the doctrine prescribed by the church is limited to what is clearly taught; its government to that which can be found described in the Bible; and worship to that commanded by God.

The church accepts the Westminster Confession of Faith and Larger and Shorter Catechisms as the most complete and accurate summaries of biblical truth. In that light it rejects the idea that God is gracious to all people, holding instead that God's grace is particular and effectual to his chosen people only. It does not accept the notion of human free will having any efficacious role in salvation. It rejects the belief that those whom God has elected may finally fall away.

The church rejects all modern methods of evangelicalism that assume the autonomy of humans. They believe that humans live in total depravity (and hence unable to do anything about their salvation). In the end, God chooses the elect based entirely on His own sovereign will.

The "Presbyterian" in the name denotes their belief that the Bible teaches the principle of church government by elders (presbyters) in a graded series of church courts.

When the Reformation Presbyterian Church met in its eleventh presbytery on November 17, 2001, the denomination's name was changed to American Reformation Presbyterian Church. This move was taken as a demonstration of their sister church status with the Myanmar Reformation Presbyterian Church.

Membership: There is one congregation in Texas, which is led by Bacon.

Periodicals: *The Blue Banner*

Sources:

American Reformation Presbyterian Church. www.fpcr.org/arpc.htm.

Faith Presbyterian Church Reformed. www.fpcr.org/fpcr.htm.

Bauswein, Jean-Jacques, and Lukas Vischner, eds. *The Reformed Family Worldwide: A Survey of Reformed Churches, Theological Schools, and International Organizations.* Grand Rapids, MI: William B. Eerdmanns Publishing Co., 1999.

Associate Reformed Presbyterian Church

c/o Associate Reformed Presbyterian Center, 1 Cleveland St., Ste. 110, Greenville, SC 29601-3646

The Associate Reformed Presbyterian Church traces its origin to the preaching of Reformer John Knox in Scotland and the establishment of the Scottish Church as the official church of all Scotland in 1560. Under King William II, in 1688 the Church of Scotland was reorganized into the Established Presbyterian Church of Scotland. In 1733 a pastor, Ebenezer Erskine (1680–1754), led a group of Christians in forming a separate Associate Presbytery. Ten years later another group of Christians who had come into conflict with the established church organized the Reformed Presbytery.

Both churches spread first to Ireland and then the United States, where the first Associate and Reformed Presbyteries were formed in the mid-eighteenth century. Formal negotiations between the Associates and Reformeds looking toward union began in 1777 and reached fruition five years later. Although some congregations did not join the union, the new church included congregations scattered from Georgia to New York.

In 1790 the Associate Reformed Presbytery of the Carolinas and Georgia was formed in Abbeville County, South Carolina, followed some years later (1803) by the division of the entire church into four synods (Carolinas, Pennsylvania, New York, and Scioto) and one General Synod. Headquarters was established in Philadelphia. In 1822 the Synod of the Carolinas was granted independent status, and by the end of the century it was the sole remaining body of the Associate Reformed Presbyterian Church because the remaining synods had been absorbed through several mergers into the former United Presbyterian Church U.S.A.

The remaining Associate Reformed Presbyteries in the Southeast continued as the Synod of the South, becoming the General Synod in 1935. In 2008 there were nine presbyteries in the United States—First (North Carolina), Second (Western South Carolina and Georgia), Northeast, Virginia, Tennessee and Alabama, Mississippi Valley, Catawba, Florida, and Pacific.

The church holds to the Westminister Confession of Faith and the Larger and Shorter Catechism. The General Synod is the church's highest authority. It is composed of all teachings elders (ministers) and least one ruling elder (lay leader) from each church. The church supports mission work in Mexico, Pakistan, Germany, Russia, and the Middle East; several retirement centers; and an assembly grounds, Bonclarken, at Flat Rock, North Carolina.

Membership: In 2008 the church reported 34,000 members in more than 200 churches. APR World Witness programs are active in Mexico, Pakistan, Germany, Russia, Turkey, Wales, and the Persian world, as well as internationals in the United States. In addition, cooperative missionaries serve in Africa, Papua New Guinea, Singapore, in Bible translation and international student ministries in the United States.

Educational Facilities:

Erskine College, Due West, South Carolina.

Erskine Theological Seminary, Due West, South Carolina, and in various other locations.

Periodicals: *ARP Magazine.*

Sources:

Associate Reformed Presbyterian Church. www.arpchurch.org/.

King, Ray A. *A History of the Associate Reformed PLresbyterian Church.* Charlotte, NC: Board of Christian Education, ARPC, 1996.

Bible Presbyterian Church

1115 Haddon Ave., Collingswood, NJ 08108

HISTORY. The Rev. Carl McIntire (1906–2002) had been a student at Princeton Theological Seminary when J. Gresham Machen left to found the independent Westminster Theological Seminary. McIntire graduated from Westminster in 1931 and became the pastor of the Presbyterian congregation in Atlantic City, New Jersey. In September 1933 he became pastor of the Presbyterian congregation in Collingswood, New Jersey. He was suspended from the Presbyterian Church in the U.S.A. along with Machen, and left with him and others to establish what became the Orthodox Presbyterian Church. In 1937, after the death of Machen, the church divided on three points. The Orthodox Presbyterians refused to take a stand against intoxicating beverages, rebuffed attempts to become distinctly premillennial in its eschatology, and declined further support of the Independent Board of Presbyterian Foreign Missions in favor of a church-controlled board. (A premillennial eschatology refers to the belief that before the millennium—Christ's predicted thousand-year reign on earth with his saints—Christ will return to earth to fight the battle of Armageddon and bind Satan.) In 1938 McIntire and his supporters formed the Bible Presbyterian Church.

At times, the personality of McIntire seemed to have been a more significant factor in the formation of the Bible Presbyterian Church than any of his three objections to the Orthodox Presbyterian Church. He led a zealous crusade against modernism, communism, and pacifism, and called for what he termed a "twentieth-century reformation" to root out apostasy and build true churches. Prime targets were the National Council of Churches and its sister organization, the World Council of Churches. McIntire called all true Christians to separate themselves from the apostasy of members of these councils.

McIntire provided followers with a variety of alternative organizations to support. In 1937, along with others, he founded Faith Theological Seminary. Four years later he was active in organizing the American Council of Christian Churches (ACCC) to bring together separatist churches from across the country. Separatist churches refuse to deal with liberal churches or with conservative churches that cooperate with liberal churches in any way. Just before the Amsterdam meeting of the World Council of Churches in 1948, McIntire joined with others to organize the International Council of Christian Churches (ICCC). Because of criticism by some outstanding conservative Presbyterian leaders, the ACCC and ICCC lost much support, and in 1956 they were repudiated by some who had been close followers of McIntire. In that same year, a faction of the synod of the Bible Presbyterian Church terminated its support of Faith Theological Seminary, the Independent Board of Presbyterian Foreign Missions, the ACCC, and the ICCC. The seminary and board, though largely supported by Bible Presbyterians, were both separate corporations. The ICCC and ACCC were both interdenominational and had been criticized for some of their activities in the early 1950s, such as the Bible balloon project to send religious literature behind the Iron Curtain by balloon. In repudiating these organizations, some of the churches also repudiated McIntire, who had been instrumental in founding the organizations as well as the church. The Bible Presbyterian Church then split into two factions. The larger group, those objecting to McIntire and the organizations, soon changed its name to Reformed Presbyterian Church, Evangelical Synod. It is now a constituent part of the Presbyterian Church in America.

The smaller group, the supporters of McIntire, included the presbyteries of New Jersey (of which he was moderator), California, and Kentucky-Tennessee. They declared themselves independent and free of the 1956 synod. At a meeting in Collingswood they created the new synod of the Bible Presbyterian Church. They returned support to ACCC, ICCC, Faith Theological Seminary, the Independent Board for Presbyterian Foreign Missions, and the Independent Board for Presbyterian Home Missions. In 1969, however, McIntire was removed from the board of ACCC, and he then helped form the American Christian Action Council, now the National Council of Bible-Believing Churches in America.

BELIEFS. Doctrinally, the Bible Presbyterian Church accepts the Westminster Confession of Faith and the Larger and Smaller Westminster Catechisms. Church members are premillennial, which means that they believe Christ will return before the millennium. Premillennialists also look for Christ to come unexpectedly in the near future to fight the battle of Armegeddon and bind Satan, thus ushering in the millennium. The Bible Presbyterians also have taken strong stands against intoxicating beverages, the new evangelicalism, the Revised Standard Version of the Bible, evolution, civil disobedience, and the United Nations.

ORGANIZATION. The polity is presbyterial, but there is a strong assertion of congregational autonomy. The church supports the Friends of Israel Testimony to Christ; the Five Civilized Tribes Ministry in Oklahoma; Reformation Gospel Publications; the *Twentieth-Century Reformation Hour*, a radio broadcast; the Christian Admiral Bible Conference; and the Cape Canaveral Bible Conference in Florida, all independent corporations. The church also supports the Bible Presbyterian Home in Delanco, Florida.

Membership: In 2008 the Bible Presbyterian Church included more than 40 local churches. There are more than 130 ministers listed on the roll. For overseas missions, the church supports work done by the Presbyterian Missionary Union and the the Independent Board for Presbyterian Foreign Missions.

Educational Facilities:

Western Reformed Seminary, Tacoma, Washington.

Periodicals: *The Christian Observer*. Available from 9400 Fairview Ave., Manassas, VA 22110.

Sources:

Bible Presbyterian Church. www.bpc.org/.

Carl McIntire's 50 Years, 1933–1983. Collingswood, NJ: Bible Presbyterian Church, 1983.

The Constitution of the Bible Presbyterian Church. Collingswood, NJ: Independent Board of Presbyterian Foreign Missions, 1959.

Harden, Margaret G. *Brief History of the Bible Presbyterian Church and Its Agencies*. N.p. 1965.

McIntire, Carl. *Modern Tower of Babel*. Collingswood, NJ: Christian Beacon Press, 1949.

————. *Servants of Apostasy*. Collingswood, NJ: Christian Beacon Press, 1955.

————. *Twentieth Century Reformation*. Collinswood, NJ: Christian Beacon Press, 1944.

Cumberland Presbyterian Church
1978 Union Ave., Memphis, TN 38104

Before the American Revolution, most of the colonies had state churches, some Congregational, many Episocpal (Anglican). All the colonists supposedly belonged to the state church established by their colony. Immediately after the American Revolution, when state churches no longer existed in America, only 15 percent of

the new nation chose to belong to a church. The remaining 85 percent had no religious affiliation. Around the turn of the nineteenth century, this situation ushered in a great drive to "save the nation," a wave of revivalism usually called the Second Great Awakening. One revivalist was the Rev. James McGready (1763–1817), who worked in Kentucky. While preparing to be a Presbyterian minister, he had a mystical conversion experience and became a strong evangelist. He was licensed by the Redstone Presbytery of the Presbyterian Church and moved to Logan County, Kentucky, where he began to preach regeneration, faith, and repentance. Through his work, revivals flourished and by 1800 spread beyond McGready's congregations. The Great Awakening in Kentucky became ecumenical, including Presbyterians, Methodists, and Baptists. Among the new practices that developed were the group meeting and the anxious seat or mourner's bench. Those in attendance at the revivals exhibited signs of emotional excess, loud, spontaneous behavior, and what today would be called altered states of consciousness (such as trances).

Religious bodies confronted the issue of using unordained men educated in alternate routes to fill leadership posts in the growing church. Some of these men were ordained by the Cumberland Presbytery, which had been formed in 1802 from the Transylvania Presbytery of the Presbyterian Church. Critics of the Great Awakening protested the ordination of ministers who were not trained at Princeton or some other seminary, and also complained that ministers did not believe in the Westminister Confession. In 1805 the Kentucky Synod judged against the ordinations of the Cumberland Presbytery and decided to examine those irregularly licensed and ordained and to judge their fitness. The Cumberland Presbytery, however, refused to submit to the Kentucky Synod's judgment. In 1806 the Synod dissolved the Cumberland Presbytery, but McGready and the ministers continued to function while appeal was made to the General Assembly of the Presbyterian Church. The efforts for appeal went unresolved and finally in 1810, in Dickson, Tennessee, three ministers—Finis Ewing (1773–1841), Samuel King (1175–1842), and Samuel McAdow (1760–1844)—constituted a new presbytery, again called the Cumberland Presbytery. In 1813, those still unable to find reconciliation with the Kentucky Synod formed two more presbyteries, Elk and Logan, and created the Cumberland Synod.

Growth was quick and the Cumberland Synod spread in every direction from its Tennessee and Kentucky base. By 1829, when the General Assembly of the Cumberland Presbyterian Church was organized, the church had reached into eight states.

Post-Civil War efforts at reunion came to fruition in 1906 when the main body of the Cumberland Presbyterian Church reunited with the Presbyterian Church in the United States of America, now an integral part of the Presbyterian Church (U.S.A.). From the Cumberland point of view, though, the union was not altogether a happy one. The union carried by only a slight majority of 60 presbyteries to 51, and a large segment of the church refused to go into the united church. They reorganized themselves as the continuing Cumberland Presbyterian Church, and took that name.

The theology of Cumberland Presbyterianism is derived from the Westminster Confession and is described as the middle ground between Calvinism and Arminianism, a theology that defends free will and opposes the belief in strict predestination. The Cumberland Presbyterians deny the five points of Calvinism with the exception of the perseverance of the saints. (The other four points of Calvinism, which this church rejects, are the utter depravity of man, total predestination, limited atonement, and irresistible grace.) The Cumberland Presbyterians have a presbyterian polity. Their General Assembly meets annually.

After 1906 Cumberland Presbyterian missions emerged in Colombia, Hong Kong, Liberia, and Japan. These missions developed into five presbyteries that exist as integral parts of the church. Domestic work includes a Choctaw Indian mission in Oklahoma, and new church developments, some of which are union congregations with the Presbyterian Church (U.S.A.). The church participates in ecumenical Christian education curriculum development.

Membership: In 2006 the church reported 81,034 members, 721 churches, and 831 ministers in the United States. There were an additional 7,980 members in Colombia, Hong Kong, Japan, and Korea, and affiliated work in Brazil and Zambia.

Educational Facilities:

Bethel College, McKenzie, Tennessee.

Memphis Theological Seminary, Memphis, Tennessee.

Periodicals: The Missionary Messenger. • The Cumberland Presbyterian.

Sources:

Cumberland Presbyterian Denominational Headquarters. www.cumberland.org.

Barrus, Ben M.; Milton L. Baughn; and Thomas H. Campbell. *A People Called Cumberland Presbyterians*. Memphis, TN: Frontier Press, 1970.

Campbell, Thomas J. *Good News on the Frontier*. Memphis, TN: Frontier Press, 1965.

Confession of Faith for Cumberland Presbyterians. Memphis, TN: Frontier Press, 1984.

Hughey, John H. *Lights and Shadows of the C. P. Church*. Decatur, IL: Author, 1906.

Irby, Joe Ben. *This They Believed*. Memphis, TN: Cumberland Presbyterian Resource Center, 1997.

Reagin, E. K. *We Believe So We Speak*. Memphis, TN: Department of Publication, Cumberland Presbyterian Church, 1960.

Cumberland Presbyterian Church in America

1978 Union Ave., Memphis, TN 38104

In the early years of the Cumberland Presbyterian Church, ministers of the church established a mission to African Americans in the South, many of whom were slaves. Many congregations had black members, and some all-black congregations were formed. By the time of the Civil War, there were some 30,000 black members on the roll of the church. After the war, steps were taken to train black ministers, and separate synods were established as a means of organizing (and segregating) African Americans. Between 1871 and 1874 synods were set up in Tennessee, Kentucky, and Texas.

On May 14, 1874, black members of the Cumberland Presbyterian Church met at Murfreesboro, Tennessee, and organized separately what was for many years called the Second Cumberland Presbyterian Church. For many years, the Cumberland Presbyterian continued some financial support of the new denomination.

Over the years, the church spread across the South and into the Midwest. During the early 1980s it completed a process of revising its statement of faith and church polity, which it originally had inherited from its parent body. That process was finished in 1984, and a new Confession of Faith was issued at that time. Soon after, it entered into merger negotiations with the Cumberland Presbyterian Church, but in 1991 voted against the plan of union.

The church is organized into four synods and 16 prebyteries. The general assembly meets annually. The church is a member of the World Alliance of Reformed Churches.

Membership: In 2008 the church listed 19 congregations on its Web site. The denomination also listed churches in Brazil, China, Colombia, Hong Kong, Japan, Liberia, and Macau.

Educational Facilities:

Bethel College, McKenzie, Tennessee.

Memphis Theological Seminary, Memphis, Tennessee.

Periodicals: *The Cumberland Presbyterian*.

Sources:

Cumberland Presbyterian Church in America. www.cumberland.org.

Burrus, Ben M.; Milton L. Baughn; and Thomas H. Campbell. *A People Called Cumberland Presbyterians.* Memphis, TN: Frontier Press, 1972.

Campbell, Thomas H. *Good News on the Frontier*. Memphis, TN: Frontier Press, 1965.

Evangelical Presbyterian Church

Office of the General Assembly, 17197 N Laurel Park Dr., Ste. 567, Livonia, MI 48152-7912

The Evangelical Presbyterian Church (EPC), established in March 1981, in St. Louis, Missouri, is a conservative denomination of 11 geographical presbyteries (10 in the United States and one in Argentina). From its inception with 12 churches, the EPC has grown to more than 200 churches. In 1991 the General Assembly approved the formation of the newest presbytery, the Presbytery of Mid-America, located in the heartland of the nation. It held its first meeting in October 1991.

Planted firmly within the historic Reformed tradition, presbyterian in polity, evangelical in spirit, the EPC places high priority on church planting and development along with world missions. Missionaries serve in 20 countries. Working together with the Presbyterian Church of Brazil (IPB), a Joint Committee on Missions was established in 1986. It meets annually in November in alternating sites to formulate strategies for supporting each other in mission outreach and theological preparation.

Based on the truth of Scripture and adhering to the Westminster Confession of Faith and its own Book of Order, the denomination is committed to the "essentials of the faith." Its historic motto, "In essentials, unity; in nonessentials, liberty; in all things, charity," illustrates the spirit of the EPC, along with the New Testament theme of "truth in love." The EPC is made up of churches where worship styles range from traditional to contemporary to charismatic (but not Pentecostal). Some churches choose to ordain women as ruling elders, others do not. The particular church owns and governs its own property.

The EPC does not advocate taking political positions, but does believe that the church has an obligation to speak its mind on matters of importance. The General Assembly has adopted position papers on the subjects of abortion, the value of and respect for human life, homosexuality, capital punishment, the ordination of women, and the Holy Spirit.

The Evangelical Presbyterian Church is a member of the World Alliance of Reformed Churches, National Association of Evangelicals, World Evangelical Fellowship, and the Evangelical Council for Financial Accountability. In addition, observers annually attend the North American Presbyterian and Reformed Churches (NAPARC), though they are not members.

Membership: According to their Web site, in 2008 the EPC had more than 200 churches and 85,000 members. Missionaries are serving in about 20 countries.

Sources:

Evangelical Presbyterian Church. www.epc.org/.

Free Presbyterian Church

Current address not obtained for this edition.

The Free Presbyterian Church, popularly identified with conservative Presbyterian minister Ian Paisley (b. 1926), began in 1951 when a group of Presbyterians at Crossgar (County Down) in Northern Ireland came into conflict with the leadership of the local Presbyterian congregation. A decision that prohibited them from using the church for a gospel mission became the occasion for their withdrawal from a church they felt had departed too much from what they saw as traditional gospel standards. At that time, Paisley was already pastor of an independent congregation, and the group in Crossgar called him to assist in their forming a new congregation. With the assistance of George Stears, a former missionary in Brazil, a new denomination emerged, the Free Presbyterian Church. Within a few months two other congregations joined the new effort. Over the next decades, the church would become identified with opposition to the Roman Catholic community in Northern Ireland.

The church is presbyterian in theology and organization and holds to the Reformed positions articulated in the sixteenth century. The church basically holds to the Westminster standards (Confession of Faith and the Larger and Shorter Catechisms) but also has its own Articles of Faith. It accepts a conservative interpretation of traditional Presbyterian beliefs but differs at two main points. It allows both views on baptism, namely one that allows infant baptism and one that limits it to confessing adults. Second, it allows divergent views on eschatology, issues regarding last things.

It views true Presbyterianism as focused on the all-sufficiency of Christ and refuses to deal with such philosophical topics as predestination, particular redemption, or human moral responsibility. It accepts these as an element of God's revelation in the Bible and does not find value in speculation as to how they operate. The church attempts to keep a theology that is evangelically warm as well as biblically orthodox.

The Free Presbyterian Church has called for conservative Protestants to separate from liberal and ecumenical ideals. While recognizing the history of Protestant participation in interdenominational activities, the Free Presbyterians believe that such movements have evolved into an effort to create a single church and eventually lead all Protestants back into the Roman Catholic Church. Present-day participation in the ecumenical movements, especially the World Council of Churches, necessarily involves one in a compromise of faith.

Based upon its conservative reading of the Bible, the church maintains a variety of opinions that set it apart from many of the larger church bodies. It believes that no women may be appointed to or ordained for any preaching, pastoral, or governmental office in the church. It has determined that males should not attend to worship with their heads covered, and females without their heads being covered. It also holds that no divorced person or anyone married to a divorced person can be elected to the office of deacon or elder in the church. It prohibits the use of any Free Presbyterian church building for a marriage service that includes a divorced person and does not allow any Free Presbyterian minister to officiate at such a ceremony.

Through the 1960s the Free Presbyterian Church spread across Northern Ireland, and its conservative stance found support in other parts of the world. Many identified with Paisley's political activities through the last decades of the twentieth century in the conflicts that beset Northern Ireland. In the 1980s separatist congregations began to appear in North America that identified with his work. They are now found across the continent.

Although the church has no central headquarters, the list of local congregations and contact persons is posted on its expansive Web site. *Let the Bible Speak* is the worldwide radio broadcast ministry of the Free Presbyterian Church.

Membership: In 2002 the church reported 15 congregations in the United States and 10 in Canada. It also has churches in India, Jamaica, Kenya, Northern Ireland, Republic of Ireland, and Spain.

Educational Facilities:

Whitefield College of the Bible, Banbridge, Northern Ireland, with extensions in Greenville, South Carolina, and Toronto, Canada.

Geneva Reformed Seminary, Theological Seminary of the Free Presbyterian Church of North America, South Carolina.

Periodicals: *The Burning Bush.* Available from www.ivanfoster.org/main.asp.

Sources:

Free Presbyterian Church. www.freepres.org/main.asp.

General Assembly of the Korean Presbyterian Church
17200 Clark Ave., Bellflower, CA 90706

The General Assembly of the Korean Presbyterian church was founded in 1976. It grew out of the migration of numerous Koreans to the United States, especially since the end of the Korean War. Many of these Koreans were Presbyterians, and many chose to align themselves with one of the older American Presbyterian denominations. However, still others found themselves unwilling to affiliate, either

because of the barrier created by language or their conservative theology. The General Assembly represents one such group that specializes in serving the Korean American community.

It is conservative in theology and accepts the Westminster Confession as its doctrinal standard. It has a presbyterian form of government.

Membership: In 2003 the church reported 302 churches, 55,000 members, and 583 ministers.

Educational Facilities:

KPCA Presbyterian Theological Seminary, Santa Fe Springs, California.

Sources:

Association of Religion Data Archives. www.thearda.com/Denoms/D_930.asp.

Korean American Presbyterian Church
8500 Bolsa Avenue, Westminster, CA 92683

Many of the Koreans who migrated to the United States in the years following the Korean War were conservative Presbyterians. Once in America, they began to form independent Korean-speaking presbyteries. In 1978 five such presbyteries that had formed in California, the Midwest, New York, Pennsylvania, and Canada came together to create the Korean American Presbyterian Church. The meeting that formed the church was held on February 8–9, 1978, at Westminster Theological Seminary (the school of the Orthodox Presbyterian Church), in Philadelphia, Pennsylvania. Thirty-two ministers attended, and the eldest among them, Rev. Jae Lee, was elected to the office of moderator. Immediate needs were the formation of a seminary and the establishment of relationships with both the General Assembly of the Presbyterian Church in Korea and contact with the numerous unaffiliated congregations of Korean Presbyterians known to exist throughout the Western Hemisphere. The church grew quickly from both the adherence of previously formed congregations and the organization of new ones.

The church is staunchly conservative in its theological perspective. It acknowledges an inerrant Bible, the authority of the Westminster Confession of Faith, and both the Larger and Shorter Westminster Catechisms as the most correct interpretations of scripture.

The church is organized into regional presbyteries. A general assembly of the whole church meets annually.

Membership: In 1990 there were 186 ordained ministers serving approximately 12,000 communicant members in the United States and Canada. There is also a Presbytery of Central South America with congregations in Brazil, Paraguay, Argentina, and Chile.

Educational Facilities:

International Reformed University & Seminary, Los Angeles.

Sources:

Korean American Presbyterian Church. www.kapc.org/gb/.

Orthodox Presbyterian Church
607 N Eastern Rd., Bldg. E, Box P, Willow Grove, PA 19090-0920

In the early years of the twentieth century the Presbyterian Church in the United States of America became a major focus of the fundamentalist-modernist controversy. Conservatives felt that liberals were leading the church into compromise with the world and away from the witness to the gospel. Conservatives traced liberalism to the Plan of Union of 1801 between Presbyterians and Congregationalists. The Conservatives said the plan aligned Presbyterians with Congregationalists infected with the "New School" theology of Samuel Hopkins (1721–1803). Late in the nineteenth century the issues of compromise with the world and lack of witness to the gospel were raised anew by the heresy trials of Professors Charles Briggs and Henry Preserved Smith. In 1903 doctrinal standards were revised to facilitate the merger with the Cumberland Presbyterian Church.

In reaction against the liberal Baptist Harry Emerson Fosdick's (1878–1969) preaching in First Presbyterian Church in New York City, a group of conservatives drew up a document presented to and passed by the 1923 General Assembly calling for the ministry to uphold the essentials of the faith, namely the five fundamentals: the infallibility of the scriptures, the virgin birth of Christ, the substitutionary atonement, Christ's bodily resurrection, and Christ's miracles. Although the assembly passed the conservative document, many of the church leaders were liberals and held key positions on the boards and agencies of the church. In protest of the assembly's vote, they joined with the 1,300 ministers who signed the Auburn Affirmation. This signpost of liberal faith created a storm of controversy, and the two sides were locked in battle.

The 1932 publication of *Re-Thinking Missions* by William Ernest Hocking (1873–1966) began the final stage of the church's liberal-conservative battle. Hocking asserted, among other controversial opinions, that missionaries should not take conversions as their only goal but should provide social services and do medical missionary work in addition to preaching the gospel. J. Gresham Machen (1881–1937), a theology professor at Princeton Theological Seminary, opposed Hocking's suggestion. With other conservative Presbyterians, Machen charged in 1932 that the board of Foreign Missions approved, sent, and supported missionaries who did not teach that Christ is the exclusive, unique way of salvation. The church countered with a mandate comparing nonsupport of the church boards with refusal to take communion. The fundamentalists replied with charges against other boards, and they condemned participation in the Federal Council of Churches. Machen was tried and convicted of disturbing the peace of the church. Machen and his supporters then left the Presbyterian Church in the United States of America and formed the Orthodox Presbyterian Church.

Doctrine of the new church is the Westminster Confession of Faith and the Westminster Larger and Shorter Catechisms to which all officers are required to subscribe. A general assembly meets annually. Over the years support for the Independent Board for Presbyterian Foreign Missions was dropped and a denominational board created. Great Commissions Publications produces a complete line of church school materials in cooperation with the Presbyterian Church of America. The church participates in the North American Presbyterian and Reformed Council (NAPARC) and for many years belonged to the Reformed Ecumenical Synod. It has more recently joined the International Conference of Reformed Churches (ICRC).

Membership: In 2003 the church reported 27,582 members, 241 congregations, and 437 ministers. Missionary work is supported in China, Eritrea, Ethiopia, Haiti, Japan, Kenya, Korea, Quebec, Suriname, and Uganda.

Periodicals: *New Horizons.* • *Ordained Servant.*

Educational Facilities:

Ministerial Training Institute of the Orthodox Presbyterian Church. It has no campus.

Sources:

Orthodox Presbyterian Church. www.opc.org.

Association of Religious Data Archives. www.thearda.com/Denoms/D_1307.asp.

Cohen, Gary G. *Biblical Separation Defended*. Nutley, NJ: Presbyterian and Reformed Publishing, 1977.

Dennison, Charles G. *The Orthodox Presbyterian Church, 1936–1986.* Philadelphia: Committee for the Historian of the OPC, 1986.

Galbraith, John P. *Why the Orthodox Presbyterian Church?* Philadelphia: Committee on Christian Education, Orthodox Presbyterian Church, 1965.

The Standards of Government, Discipline, and Worship of the Orthodox Presbyterian Church. Philadelphia: Committee on Christian Education, Orthodox Presbyterian Church, 1965.

Presbyterian Church in America
1700 N Brown Rd., Ste. 105, Lawrenceville, GA 30043-8122

HISTORY. During the 1960s tensions began to rise between liberals and conservatives within the Presbyterian Church in the United States. Conservatives protested denominational support of the National Council of Churches and involvement in social issues, possible union with the United Presbyterian Church in the U.S.A. (which would put the conservatives in an even smaller minority position and which eventually occurred in 1983), liberal theology in *The Layman's Bible* published by the church, the ordination of women, support of abortion on demand for socioeconomic reasons, and liberal churchmen in positions of authority in the denomination.

In 1972 to 1973 several presbyteries were formed by some 260 congregations with a combined communicant membership of more than 41,000 that had left the denomination. These presbyteries were the Warrior Presbytery in Alabama, the Westminster Presbytery in Virginia and East Tennessee, and the Vanguard Presbytery at large. In December 1973 delegates from the presbyteries gathered at Briarwood Presbyterian Church in Birmingham, Alabama, and organized the National Presbyterian Church. Rev. Frank Barker, pastor of the Briarwood Church, hosted the gathering.

Organized at a constitutional assembly in December 1973, this church was first known as the National Presbyterian Church, but changed its name in 1974 to Presbyterian Church in America (PCA). It separated from the Presbyterian Church in the United States (PCUS) (Southern) in opposition to the developing theological liberalism that denied the deity of Jesus Christ and the inerrancy and authority of Scripture. The PCA held to the traditional position on the role of women in church offices: The PCUS had not only permitted women to serve in offices, but had begun to force all churches to comply. The PCA also oppposed the PCUS affiliation with the National Council of Churches and World Council of Churches, which the conservatives felt supported radical Left political and social activism. And they opposed the movement toward merger with the more liberal United Presbyterian Church in the U.S.A. (Northern).

In 1982 the Reformed Presbyterian Church, Evangelical Synod, merged into the Presbyterian Church in America. The Reformed Presbyterian Church, Evangelical Synod, had been formed in 1965 by a merger of the Evangelical Presbyterian Church and the Reformed Presbyterian Church in North America, General Synod.

Evangelical Presbyterian Church was the name taken by the larger segment of the Bible Presbyterian Church following the split in that church in 1956. (See the discussion of the split in the entry on the Bible Presbyterian Church.) The name for the larger group had been adopted in 1961 to avoid confusion with Dr. Carl McIntire's smaller group. At the time of the split, the synod, controlled by the larger group, had voted to establish an official periodical, the *Evangelical Presbyterian Reporter*; a synod-controlled college and seminary, Covenant College and Covenant Seminary in St. Louis; and its own mission board, World Presbyterian Missions. Immediate efforts were directed toward healing the rift with the Orthodox Presbyterian Church and opening correspondence with the Reformed Presbyterian Church in North America General Synod. In 1960 the constitution was amended to allow any view of eschatology, not just premillennialism.

The Reformed Presbyterian Church in North America, General Synod, was of the Covenanter tradition, the church that adhered to the Solemn League and Covenant of 1643, which spelled out the doctrine and practices of Scottish Presbyterians. The General Synod (as the church was often called) dated to 1833, when the Reformed Presbyterian Church split over the issue of participation in civic affairs. One group within the church took the name Reformed Presbyterian Church in North America, General Synod, and allowed its members to vote and hold office. The General Synod also adopted the practice of allowing hymns as well as psalms to be sung at services, and allowed instrumental music to be used in worship. Those who did not allow members to vote or hold office, and opposed hymns and instrumental music, are known today as the Reformed Presbyterian Church of North America. In 1965 the Reformed Presbyterian Church in North America, General Synod, merged with the Evangelical Presbyterian Church. The merged body became known as the Reformed Presbyterian Church, Evangelical Synod.

BELIEFS. The PCA has made a firm commitment to the doctrinal standards that have been significant in presbyterianism since 1645, namely the Westminster Confession of Faith and Catechisms. These doctrinal standards express the distinctives of the Calvinistic or Reformed tradition.

Among the distinctive doctrines of the Westminster Standards and of Reformed tradition is the unique authority of the Bible. The reformers based all of their claims on the philosophy of *sola scriptura* ("scriptures alone"). This included the doctrine of their inspiration, a special act of the Holy Spirit by which He guided the writers of the books of scriptures (in their original autographs) to convey the thoughts He wished conveyed, and so they were kept free from error of fact, doctrine, and judgment, to be an infallible rule of faith and life.

ORGANIZATION. The church is organized presbyterially. The PCA maintains the historic polity of Presbyterian governance, namely, rule by presbyters (elders) and the graded courts (the session governing the local church), the presbytery for regional matters, and the general assembly at the national level. It has taken seriously the position of the parity of elders, making a distinction between the two classes of elders, teaching and ruling. In addition, on presbyterian governance, it has self-consciously taken a more democratic position (rule from the grassroots up) in contrast to a more prelatical (rule from the top assemblies down). The General Assembly meets annually. The church conducts mission work in 56 countries and is a member of the National Association of Evangelicals.

Membership: In 2006 the church reported more than 335,443 communicant members, 1739 churches and missions, and 3,430 clergy. The PCA has approximately 600 career missionaries, 150 two-year missionaries, and more than 6,800 short-term summer missionaries working through its Mission to the World (MTW). The organization also has more than 150 military and civilian chaplains, and more than 100 campus ministers.

Educational Facilities:

Covenant College, Lookout Mountain, Georgia.

Covenant Theological Seminary, St. Louis, Missouri.

Other schools supported by the church and/or its constituent presbyteries include:

Reformed Theological Seminary, Jackson, Mississippi, Orlando, Florida, and Charlotte, North Carolina.

Westminster Theological Seminary, Philadelphia, Pennsylvania, and Escondido, California.

Birmingham Theological Seminary, Birmingham, Alabama.

Greenville Thelogical Seminary, Greenville, South Carolina.

Sources:

Presbyterian Church in America. www.pcanet.org.

The Book on Church Order of the Presbyterian Church in America. Atlanta, GA: Committee on Christian Education and Publications, 1983.

MacNair, Donald J. *Hallmarks of the Reformed Presbyterian Church, Evangelical Synod*. St. Louis, MO: Presbyterain Missions, n.d.

Richards, John Edwards. *The Historical Birth of the Presbyterian Church in America*. Liberty Hill, SC: Liberty Hill Press, 1987.

Smallman, Stephen E. *What Is a Reformed Church?* Phillipsburg, NJ: P&R Publishing, 2003.

Smith, Frank J. *The History of the Presbyterian Church in America: The Continuing Church Movement*. Manassas, VA: Reformation Education Foundation, 1985.

Presbyterian Church in Canada

50 Wynford Dr., Don Mills, ON, Canada M3C 1J7

The church today is the continuing Presbyterian body that in 1925 did not merge with the Canadian Methodists and Congregationalists to form the United Church of Canada (UCC). Approximately 30 percent did not enter the United Church. As such, the Presbyterian Church in Canada shares the heritage of Canadian Presbyterianism with the UCC.

The Presbyterian Church in Canada was constituted in 1875 by the Presbyterian Church of the Lower Provinces, the Synod of the Presbyterian Church of the Maritime Provinces, the Synod of Canada Presbyterian Church, and the Synod of the Presbyterian Church of Canada in connection with the Church of Scotland.

Those Presbyterians who disapproved of the merger into the United Church of Canada feared the loss of such Presbyterian distinctives as reformed theology and structures. Theology was being threatened by Methodism and a growing liberalism. Many also argued that most of the rewards to be gained from the union could be gained by a federated relationship.

Doctrinally, the church adheres to the Westminster Confession of Faith and both the Longer and Shorter Westminster Catechisms. In 1875, Article 23 of the Confession, concerning civil magistrates, had been explicitly deleted from the Confession accepted by the new church. This issue was resolved in 1955 by the adoption of a "Declaration of Faith Concerning Church and Nation." In 1962 the church also recognized several of the European Reformed confessions, specifically the Belgic, the Second Helvetic, and the Gallican Confessions, as parallel to the Westminster and the Heidelberg Catechisms and permitted their teachings by church elders.

Though more conservative than the United Church of Canada, the Presbyterian Church in Canada has remained a vital part of the larger protestant ecumenical movement. It is a member of both the Canadian Council of Churches and the World Council of Churches. In 1966 it admitted women to the ordained ministry. Its International Ministries maintains connections with overseas partners in almost 30 countries as well as numerous ecumenical organizations. Presbyterian World Service & Development (PWS&D) is the development, relief, and refugee sponsorship agency of the Presbyterian Church in Canada.

Membership: The Presbyterian Church in Canada has nearly 1,000 member congregations across the country and one in Bermuda. The Canadian Census reports membership at 636,000.

Educational Facilities:

Knox College, Toronto, Ontario.

Presbyterian College, Montreal, Quebec.

Vancouver School of Theology, Vancouver, British Columbia.

Periodicals: *Presbyterian Record*. • *Glad Tidings*. • *The Presbyterian Message*.

Sources:

Presbyterian Church in Canada. www.presbyterian.ca.

Reed, R. C. *History of the Presbyterian Churches of the World*. Philadelphia: Westminister Press, 1912.

Religious Tolerance. www.religioustolerance.org/hom_prc.htm.

Silcox, Claris Edwin. *Church Union in Canada*. New York: Institute of Social and Religious Research, 1933.

Presbyterian Church (U.S.A.)

100 Witherspoon St., Louisville, KY 40202

The Presbyterian Church (U.S.A.) was formed in 1983 by the reunion of the United Presbyterian Church in the United States of America and the Presbyterian Church in the United States—the two largest Presbyterian bodies in the United States. It continues the beliefs and practices of the two churches, which originally had split over the same issues that divided the United States at the time of the Civil War.

HISTORY. The United Presbyterian Church in the United States of America was formed in 1958 by a merger of the Presbyterian Church in the United States of America and the United Presbyterian Church of North America. The Presbyterian Church in the United States of America inherited the tradition of early Presbyterianism in the colonies and is in direct continuity with the first synod organized in 1706. In the 1700s the Presbyterians were split between the revivalism of the Methodist George Whitefield (1714–1770), who had influenced William Tennent (1673–1746) and his son, Gilbert Tennent (1703–1764), and the more traditional, creedal Calvinism with its ordered worship. The Tennents were the founders of a seminary that later became Princeton University. A split developed in the church in 1741 that lasted until 1758.

The church supported the Revolution and afterward reorganized for western expansion. On the heels of the cooperative Plan of Union of 1801 with the Congregationalists and the Second Great Awakening, the Presbyterians moved west and, in the 40 years after the Revolution, grew more than tenfold. The nineteenth century, an era of expansion westward, saw the development of an impressive educational system and large-scale schism over revivalism and slavery. Other schisms would grow out of the fundamentalist-modernist debates in the early twentieth century.

The United Presbyterian Church of North America was formed in 1858 by a merger of the Associate Presbyterian Church and the Associate Reformed Presbyterian Church. These two churches continued the Scottish Covenanter and secession movements. The Covenanters were Scotch Presbyterians who seceded from the Church of Scotland, which was Reformed in theology but episcopal in government. The Covenanters formed their independent secession into a church in 1733. The Covenant to which the new church adhered was the Solemn League and Covenant ratified in 1643; it spelled out the doctrine and practices of Scotch Presbyterians.

People who followed the Covenant of 1643 found their way to the American colonies during the seventeenth century. These early Covenanters formed "societies" for worship because they had no minister. The first pastor was the Rev. Alexander Craighead (c. 1700–1766), a Presbyterian attracted to the Covenanters because of their passion for freedom. In 1751, John Cuthbertson landed and began long years of work on a large circuit of Covenanters. He was joined in 1773 by Matthew Linn and Alexander Dobbin, and the three constituted the Reformed Presbyterian Church.

The Covenanters represented one branch of the Scottish secession movement; the Seceders represented another. The Seceders developed from the revival movements of the 1700s in Scotland that attacked the patronage system of the established church and its lack of spiritual awareness. The Seceder Church was not formed in Scotland until 1743, although Seceders began to arrive in the colonies in the 1730s. In 1742 a congregation in Londonderry, Pennsylvania issued a plea for a minister. The Scottish split into Burgher and anti-Burgher factions, compounding the problem of providing leadership. The two parties resulted from the requirement of an oath to hold public office in Scotland. The anti-Burghers felt the oath legitimized episcopacy, and they therefore objected to it; the Burghers saw nothing wrong with taking the oath. Most of the Americans were anti-Burghers. Two anti-Burgher ministers, Alexander Gellatly and Andrew Arnot arrived and, in 1753, organized the Associate Presbyterian Church.

In 1782 the Associate Presbyterian Church and the Reformed Presbyterian Church merged to form the Associate Reformed Presbyterian Church. A few members of both merging churches declined to enter the merger and continued to exist under the names of their respective churches before 1782. Then in 1822 the Associate Reformed Presbyterian Church split into northern and southern branches. The southern branch continues today as the Associate Reformed Presbyterian Church (General Synod). The northern branch continued to be called the Associate Reformed Presbyterian Church. In 1858 this northern branch merged with the majority of the continuing Seceders, called the Associate Presbyterian Church. The new church formed in 1858 took the name the United Presbyterian Church of North America. In 1958, the United Presbyterian Church of North America united with the Presbyterian Church in the United States of America to form the United Presbyterian Church in the United States of America.

The Presbyterian Church in the United States arose out of the same controversies that had split the Methodists and Baptists in the years prior to the Civil War.

Presbyterians were able, as a whole, to remain in the same ecclesiastical body until war actually broke. The General Assembly of the Presbyterian Church in the United States of America, meeting in Philadelphia only days after the firing on Fort Sumter and devoid of most southern delegates, declared its loyalty to the United States. Presbyterians in the South claimed the Assembly had no such right to make such a political statement. One by one the Southern presbyteries withdrew, and in December 1861 they organized the Presbyterian Church in the Confederate States (later changed to the Presbyterian Church in the United States).

The war divided the North from the South and feeling created by the conflict did much to keep the churches apart. The two churches had little disagreement on either doctrine or church polity. The southern church tended to be more conservative in its doctrinal stance and adopted a more loosely organized structure. It had replaced the church boards created by the Presbyterian Church in the United States of America with executive committees, unincorporated and devoid of permanent funds.

BELIEFS. In 1967 the United Presbyterian Church adopted a new confession of faith. The confession was a present-minded document, although it begins with a statement of continuity with the Reformed Confessional tradition. It is focused on the reconciling work of Christ through the grace of God. A significant section deals with the mission of the church, particularly in society, and has a vague eschatology. The Confession was published along with the Apostles' and Nicene Creeds, five Reformed Confessions, and the Shorter Catechism in a Book of Confessions. The Book of Common Worship contains the liturgical resources.

ORGANIZATION. The merger of 1983 left many of the important questions of merging geographically overlapping synods and presbyteries and national offices, boards, and agencies to be resolved in the future meetings of the annual General Assembly. In 1986 a structural Design for Mission was adopted by the General Assembly, and in 1988 most of the national offices were consolidated at the new headquarters building in Louisville, Kentucky.

Membership: In 2006, the church reported 2,267,118 members, 21,360 ministers, and 10,903 congregations. Partnership efforts in Christian mission exist with churches in 109 nations.

Educational Facilities:

Theological seminaries:

Auburn Theological Seminary

Austin Presbyterian Theological Seminary, Austin, Texas.

Columbia Theological Seminary, Decatur, Georgia.

Dubuque Theological Seminary, Dubuque, Iowa.

Evangelical Seminary of Puerto Rico, San Juan, Puerto Rico.

Johnson C. Smith Theological Seminary, Atlanta, Georgia.

Louisville Presbyterian Theological Seminary, Louisville, Kentucky.

McCormick Theological Seminary, Chicago, Illinois.

Pittsburgh Theological Seminary, Pittsburgh, Pennsylvania.

Princeton Theological Seminary, Princeton, New Jersey.

San Francisco Theological Seminary, San Anselmo, California.

Colleges and Universities:

Agnes Scott College, Decatur, Georgia.

Alma College, Alma, Michigan.

Arcadia University, Glenside, Pennsylvania.

Austin College, Sherman, Texas.

Barber-Scotia College, Concord, North Carolina.

Belhaven College, Jackson, Mississippi.

Blackburn College, Carlinville, Illinois.

Bloomfield College, Bloomfield, New Jersey.

Buena Vista College, Storm Lake, Iowa.

Carroll College, Waukesha, Wisconsin.

Centre College of Kentucky, Danville, Kentucky.

Coe College, Cedar Rapids, Iowa.

The College of Idaho, Caldwell, Idaho.

College of the Ozarks, Point Lookout, Missouri.

The College of Wooster, Wooster, Ohio.

Davidson College, Davidson, North Carolina.

Davis & Elkins College, Elkins, West Virginia.

Eckerd College, St. Petersburg, Florida.

Grove City College, Grove City, Pennsylvania.

Hampden-Sydney College, Hampden-Sydney, Virginia.

Hanover College, Hanover, Indiana.

Hastings College, Hastings, Nebraska.

Illinois College, Jacksonville, Illinois.

Jamestown College, Jamestown, North Dakota.

Johnson C. Smith University, Charlotte, North Carolina.

King College, Bristol, Tennessee.

Knoxville College, Knoxville, Tennessee.

Lafayette College, Easton, Pennsylvania.

Lake Forest College, Lake Forest, Illinois.

Lees-McCrae College, Banner Elk, North Carolina.

Lindenwood College, St. Charles, Missouri.

Lyon College, Batesville, Arkansas.

Macalester College, St. Paul, Minnesota.

Mary Baldwin College, Staunton, Virginia.

Maryville College, Maryville, Tennessee.

Millikin University, Decatur, Illinois.

Missouri Valley College, Marshall, Missouri.

Monmouth College, Monmouth, Illinois.

Montreat College, Montreat, North Carolina.

Muskingum College, New Concord, Ohio.

Peace College, Raleigh, North Carolina.

Pikeville College, Pikeville, Kentucky.

Presbyterian College, Clinton, South Carolina.

Queens College, Charlotte, North Carolina.

Rhodes College, Memphis, Tennessee.

Rocky Mountain College, Billings, Montana.

St. Andrew's Presbyterian College, Laurinburg, North Carolina.

Schreiner College, Kerrville, Texas.

Sheldon Jackson College, Sitka, Alaska.

Sterling College, Sterling, Kansas.

Stillman College, Tuscaloosa, Alabama.

Trinity University, San Antonio, Texas.

Tusculum College, Greeneville, Tennessee.

Universidad InterAmericana de Puerto Rico, San Juan, Puerto Rico.

University of Dubuque, Dubuque, Iowa.

University of the Ozarks, Clarksville, Arkansas.

University of Tulsa, Tulsa, Oklahoma.

Warren Wilson College, Swannanoa, North Carolina.

Waynesburg College, Waynesburg, Pennsylvania.

Westminster College, Fulton, Missouri.

Westminster College, New Wilmington, Pennsylvania.

Westminster College, Salt Lake City, Utah.

Whitworth College, Spokane, Washington.

Wilson College, Chambersburg, Pennsylvania.

Periodicals: *Presbyterians Today* • *Church & Society Magazine* • *Call to Worship*

Sources:

Presbyterian Church (U.S.A.). www.pcusa.org.

Balmer, Randall, and John R. Fitzmier. *The Presbyterians*. Westport, CT: Praeger, 1994.

Jamison, Wallace N. *The United Presbyterian Story*. Pittsburgh: Geneva Press, 1958.

Miller, Park Hays. *Why I Am A Presbyterian*. New York: Thomas Nelson & Sons, 1956.

Minutes of the 195th General Assembly, United Presbyterian Church in the United States of America, 123rd General Assembly, Presbyterian Church in the United States, 195th General Assembly, Presbyterian Church (U.S.A.). Atlanta: Office of the General Assembly, Presbyterian Church (U.S.A.), 1983.

Study Draft, A Plan for Union of the Presbyterian Church in the United States and the United Presbyterian Church in the United States of America. New York: Stated Clerk of the Presbyterian Church in the United States, 1974.

Weston, William J. *Presbyterian Pluralism: Competition in a Protestant House.* Knoxville: University of Tennessee Press, 1997.

Presbyterian Reformed Church
PO Box 82, Chesley, ON, Canada N0G 1L0

The Presbyterian Reformed Church is a small conservative Presbyterian denomination founded in 1965 by two Canadian Presbyterian congregations in Ontario, Canada. Instrumental in the creation of the presbytery was John Murray, a professor at Westminster Theological Seminary (the seminary of the very conservative Orthodox Presbyterian Church). Murray had been associated with the congregations for several years and like them shared a Scottish and Scotch-Irish heritage. He wished to see the organization of a body that would continue the affirmation of Scottish Presbyterianism.

Murray made the initial proposal for the establishment of the new church and authored the constitution that served as a basis of union. The constitution affirmed the authority of the Bible, which is seen as the infallible word of God; the Westminster Confession of Faith as the best summary of Christian belief; and worship keynoted by simplicity of style. Adherence to the Westminster Confession is done in a strict and literal fashion. Worshipers use the psalms set to music and singing is done without the aid of musical instruments. The presbyterian form of church government was affirmed as the most true to scripture, though congregations were to be the owners of their property rather than the presbytery. Women are not admitted to the ordained ministry.

The two congregations constituted the original presbytery, which has been extended to include additional congregations in the United States and a mission in England.

Membership: Not reported. There are six congregations in North America and one mission in the United Kingdom.

Periodicals: *Presbyterian Reformed Magazine.* Available from Dan McGinn, 1209 Larkridge Ct., Waxhaw, NC 28173.

Sources:

Presbyterian Reformed Church. www. presbyterianreformed.org.

Bauswein, Jean-Jacques, and Lukas Vischner, eds. *The Reformed Family Worldwide: A Survey of Reformed Churches, Theological Schools, and International Organizations*. Grand Rapids, MI: William B. Eerdmanns Publishing, 1999.

Reformed Presbyterian Church General Assembly

c/o Dr. Bill Higgins, Office of the Stated Clerk, PO Box 356, Lookout Mountain, TN 37350

The Reformed Presbyterian Church began in 1983 when several congregations in Georgia withdrew from the Presbyterian Church in America as a continuing church movement. They originally took the name Covenant Presbytery, later changed to Reformed Presbyterian Church in the United States (1985, resuming the name in 1992) and Reformed Presbyterian Church in the Americas (1990). However, in 1990–1991, the church underwent an internal disruption in which one of its four presbyteries was dissolved and a second became independent as the Reformed Presbyterian Church (Hanover Presbytery). The two remaining presbyteries reorganized in 1991 as the Reformed Presbyterian Church General Assembly.

As its name implies, the highest legislative body in the church is the General Assembly, which consists of representatives of the three presbyteries (Westminster, John Knox, and Reformation) to which the local congregations belong. The church has a presbyterial organization and accepts the reformed faith as expressed in the Westminster Confession of Faith of 1647, to which it gives a strict conservative interpretation. For example, all church officers must subscribe to the inerrancy of Scriptures and the doctrine of a literal six-day creation of the earth as described in the Book of Genesis. It opposes charismatic theology, Arminian "free will" theology, dispensational theology, liberal theology, neo-orthodox theology, and all forms of liberation theology. It denounces abortion, homosexuality, and the women's liberation movement.

The Reformed Presbyterian Church requires its member congregations to remain unincorporated. They view the church as the presbytery and particular congregations as parts of it.

Membership: In 2008 the church reported 10 congregations in two synods. Although most congregations are located in the eastern United States, a few are in the Midwest.

Educational Facilities:

Whitefield College and Theological Seminary, Lakeland, Florida.

Sources:

Reformed Presbyterian Church General Assembly. www.rpcga.org/.

Bauswein, Jean-Jacques, and Lukas Vischner, eds. *The Reformed Family Worldwide: A Survey of Reformed Churches, Theological Schools, and International Organizations.* Grand Rapids, MI: William B. Eerdmanns, 1999.

Reformed Presbyterian Church (Hanover Presbytery)

5928 H Cloverdale Way, PO Box 10015, Alexandria, VA 22310-5432

The Reformed Presbyterian Church (Hanover Presbytery) traces its origin to 1983 and the congregations in Georgia that refrained from following the merger of the Reformed Presbyterian Church, Evangelical Synod, into the Presbyterian Church in America. The congregations reorganized as the Covenant Presbytery, which later became the Reformed Presbyterian Church in the United States (1985) and Reformed Presbyterian Church in the Americas (1990). However, in 1990–1991 one of the new church's four synods disassociated itself as the independent Reformed Presbyterian Church (Hanover Synod).

The Presbytery is a conservative body that accepts the Reformed faith as expressed in the Apostles Creed, the Nicene Creed, and the Westminster Confession of Faith, to which its gives a strict interpretation. It maintains a fraternal relationship with the Presbyterian Church in America, the Bible Presbyterian Church, and the Reformed Presbyterian Church of North America, and shares the *Christian Observer* as a denominational periodical. The highest legislative body in the church is the synod that meets annually. It does not admit women to the ordained ministry.

Membership: In 2008 the synod reported seven congregations and two affiliated congregations. The jurisdiction now has congregations, missions, and preaching points in 11 states nationwide. A mission work in Burma is identified with the denomination.

Periodicals: *Christian Observer.* Available from 9400 Fairview Ave., Manassas, VA 20110.

Sources:

The Reformed Presbyterian Church (Hanover Presbytery). www.rpchanover.org.

Bauswein, Jean-Jacques, and Lukas Vischner, eds. *The Reformed Family Worldwide: A Survey of Reformed Churches, Theological Schools, and International Organizations.* Grand Rapids, MI: William B. Eerdmanns Publishing, 1999.

Presbyterians Weekly News. www.presweek.blogspot.com.

Reformed Presbyterian Church of North America

c/o Louis D. Hutmire, Stated Clerk, 7408 Penn Ave., Pittsburgh, PA 15208

The eighteenth-century Reformed Presbyterian Church was the embodiment of the Covenanter tradition in North America, those adhering to the Scottish Presbyterians' Solemn League and Covenant of 1643. In 1782 the majority of the Covenanter tradition merged with the Seceder Church, originally formed in Scotland in 1743 as a group seceding from the established Church of Scotland. The 1782 merger of Covenanters and Seceders resulted in the Associate Reformed Presbyterian Church, which is now a constituent part of the Presbyterian Church (U.S.A.).

However, some Reformed Presbyterians (Covenanters) did not join the 1782 merger. They remained Reformed Presbyterians, and in 1833 they split over the issue of participation in government, specifically, over whether members would vote and hold office. The New Lights, those who allowed such participation, formed the Reformed Presbyterian Church, General Synod, which merged with the Evangelical Presbyterian Church in 1965. The merged church, the Reformed Presbyterian Church, Evangelical Synod, later merged into the Presbyterian Church in America, discussed above. The Reformed Presbyterian Church of North America is the continuing old school body, the group opposed to the New Lights in the 1833 split.

The Westminster Confession of Faith is the standard of doctrine. Worship is centered on the reading and exposition of the Bible. Hymns are limited to Psalms and there is no instrumental accompaniment. Organization is presbyterian. The synod meets annually. Over the years, Reformed Presbyterian missionaries have been active in Australia, China, Cyprus, Japan, Manchuria, Africa, France, and Syria.

Membership: In 2008 the church reported 82 congregations in North America and five in Japan.

Educational Facilities:

Geneva College, Beaver Falls, Pennsylvania.

Reformed Presbyterian Theological Seminary, Pittsburgh, Pennsylvania.

Periodicals: *Reformed Presbyterian Witness.* Available from 7408 Penn Ave., Pittsburgh, PA 15208.

Sources:

Reformed Presbyterian Church of North America. www.reformedpresbyterian.org.

Adventures in Psalm Singing. Pittsburgh, PA: Christian Education Office, 1970.

Ukrainian Evangelical Alliance of North America

Current address not obtained for this edition.

The Ukrainian Evangelical Alliance of North America was formed in the United States in 1922 by Ukrainian Protestants of several denominations. The purpose of the Alliance was to spread the gospel among Ukrainians in both North America and the Ukraine. The Alliance was thus a missionary organization and was not meant to be a separate denomination. However, over time the Alliance established mission congregations and in that sense has become a separate denomination. The member congregations typically retain their Ukrainian culture and language and are located in large cities. Most of the Ukrainian Reformed congregations in North America have become members of the larger Presbyterian bodies, but two congregations of postwar immigrants, one in Detroit and one in Toronto, carry on the independent tradition and are under the direct guidance of the Ukrainian Evangelical Alliance of North America.

In 1925 the Ukrainian Evangelical Alliance of North America, with the aid of several Reformed and Presbyterian churches, organized a Ukrainian Reformed Church in what was at that time Polish territory in the western Ukraine. This church was virtually destroyed by the Communist takeover in World War II.

The Alliance is interdenominational in scope and has passed a resolution declaring denominational missions obsolete and unrealistic in their approach to Ukrainian-Russian relations, especially in their neglect of the native language. The Alliance wishes to be invited to cooperate in all missionary efforts. It has as a major part of its mission the publication of Ukrainian literature, which it distributes in both North America and Ukraine.

Membership: At last report there were only two congregations solely attached to the Alliance, though congregations consisting of Ukrainian-Russian immigrants of the Reformed faith can be found in several of the larger Presbyterian bodies.

Periodicals: *News Bulletin.*

Upper Cumberland Presbyterian Church

172 CR 1564, Cullman, AL 35055-1426

The Upper Cumberland Presbyterian Church was formed in 1955 by Rev. H. C. Wakefield, Rev. W. M. Dycus, Lum Oliver, and laymen from Sanderson's, Russell Hill, Pleasant Grove, and Poston's Cumberland Presbyterian Churches, all of the Cooksville Presbytery in Tennessee. At the 1950 General Assembly of the Cumberland Presbyterian Church, the Board of Missions and Evangelism reported its application for membership in the Home Missions Council of the National Council of Churches. This application raised the issue of support of the "liberal" social activist theology imposed by the National Council of Churches, and strong opposition to the application developed within the church. In 1952 a Fellowship of Conservative Presbyterians was formed which included Reverend Wakefield and Reverend Dycus. In assembly in the following year, the fellowship elected a moderator and a stated clerk, urged organization on a presbyterial level, and objected to the Revised Standard Version of the Bible newly issued by the National Council of Churches. Reverend Dycus and Reverend Wakefield were deposed from the ministry of the Cumberland Presbyterian Church. In 1955 they formed the Carthage Presbytery of the Upper Cumberland Presbyterian Church at a session with the Russell Hill Congregation in Macon County, Tennessee. Thus the Upper Cumberland Presbyterians came into existence. At the first session Lum Oliver was ordained.

The Upper Cumberland Presbyterians adopted the Confession of Faith of the Cumberland Presbyterian Church, with the addition of questions on the virgin birth of Christ and his visible return to the church covenant. Ministers must use the King James Bible.

Membership: In 1970 the church reported nine churches and 300 members.

Periodicals: *The Bulletin.* Available from: Editor, 1680 Welcome Rd., Cullman, AL 35058.

Sources:

The Christian Observer. www.christianobserver.org/Church%20Directories/ucpc.htm.

Congregationalism

Conservative Congregational Christian Conference

8941 Highway 5, Lake Elmo, MN 55042

The Conservative Congregational Christian Conference can be dated to 1935 when Rev. Hilmer B. Sandine, then pastor of First Congregational Church of Hancock, Minnesota, began the publication of the *Congregational Beacon.* Beginning as a

monthly parish publication, the *Beacon* became the organ for communication among theologically conservative Congregationalists. Emphasis was placed on biblical evangelism and evangelical Christianity. Growing concern about liberal theology and social activism within the Congregational and Christian Churches led in 1945 to the formation of the Conservative Congregational Christian Fellowship at Minneapolis. During the previous year a plan of union with the Evangelical and Reformed Church had been published. In 1948, during the lengthy process of the formation of the United Church of Christ, the Conservative Congregational Christian Fellowship became the conference, a separate body from the congregational and Christian churches.

Among Congregationalists, the conference represents the most theologically conservative group. The conference is committed to the five fundamentals: the infallibility of the scriptures, the virgin birth of Christ, the substitutionary atonement, Christ's bodily resurrection, and Christ's miracles. The conference also emphasizes the historical Puritan beliefs in the sovereignty of God, the sinfulness of man, redemption through Christ, the indwelling Holy Spirit, the sacraments, the life of love and service, and the future life. They restrict membership to those who profess regeneration. The Conservative Congregational Christian Conference is a member of the National Association of Evangelicals and the World Evangelical Congregational Fellowship.

In polity, the Conservative Congregational Christian Conference accepts the interpretation that true Congregationalism is to be identified with the independent or separated Puritan tradition. The local church is the seat of power. In recent years, a number of formerly Evangelical and Reformed churches have joined the conference. It joins in fellowship with other churches for cooperative endeavors. Ecclesiastical bodies or officers have no right to interfere in local church affairs. There is an annual meeting of the conference.

The Conservative Congregational Christian Conference has affiliated work in Pohnpei Micronesia.

Membership: In 2007 the conference reported 41,772 members, 284 congregations, and 847 ministers.

Educational Facilities:

The Conference has endorsed Gordon-Conwell Theological Seminary, Fuller Seminary, Trinity Evangelical Divinity School, and Bethel Seminary for its ministerial students.

Periodicals: *Foresee.*

Sources:

Conservative Congregational Christian Conference. www.ccccusa.com.

Kohl, Manfred Waldemar. *Congregationalism in America.* Oak Creek, WI: Congregational Press, 1987.

Rouner, Arthur A. *The Congregational Way of Life.* Englewood Cliffs, NJ: Prentice-Hall, 1960.

International Council of Community Churches

21116 Washington Pkwy., Frankfort, IL 60423-3112

The International Council of Community Churches was formally organized in 1950, but its history dates from the early nineteenth century, when nonsectarian community churches began to appear as an alternative to denominationally affiliated congregations. These churches were especially welcomed in communities too small to support more than one viable congregation, and over the years many have retained a fiercely independent stance. Added to their number were other independent congregations that had separated from denominational structures and adopted a nonsectarian stance.

In the wake of the ecumenical movement in the early twentieth century, the most visible symbol of which was the 1908 formation of the Federal Council of Churches of Christ, many congregations merged across denominational lines, some forming independent federated or union churches and dropping all denominational affiliation. During this period, some community churches began to see, in light of their years of existence apart from denominational boundaries, that they had a particular role tto play in Christian unity.

A first attempt to build a network of community churches was known as the Community Church Workers of the United States. In Chicago in 1923, at a national conference of individuals serving community churches, a committee was formed to organize a second conference and outline plans for a national association. In the next year the group organized and the Rev. Orvis F. Jordan of the Park Ridge (Illinois) Community Church was named as secretary. He later became the first president of the group. The organization continued for more than a decade, but folded in the 1930s due to lack of support.

A second organization of community churches was begun in 1923 among predominantly black congregations. Representatives of five congregations gathered in Chicago, Illinois, in fall 1923 to form the National Council of the People's Community Churches (incorporated in 1933 as the Biennial Council of the People's Church of Christ and Community Centers of the United States and Elsewhere). The Rev. William D. Cook, pastor of Metropolitan Community Church in Chicago, served as the first president.

Unable to gain recognition from the Federal Council of Churches, the independent community churches began a second attempt at organization in the last days of World War II. The Rev. Roy A. Burkhart, pastor of First Community Church of Columbus, Ohio, led in the formation of the Ohio Association for Community Churches in 1945. The next year, representatives from 19 states and Canada met and formed the National Council of Community Churches.

Almost immediately, the black and white groups began to work toward a merger. The merger, accomplished in 1950, created the International Council of Community Churches with a charter membership of 160 churches. By 1957 the several foreign congregations had ceased their affiliation with the council and the word *international* was dropped. In 1969 the name was changed to National Council of Community Churches. In 1983, however, foreign congregations in Canada and Nigeria affiliated, and in 1984 the organization resumed the use of its original name.

There is no doctrinal statement shared by the council and its member churches, though most churches share a liberal, ecumenical-minded, Protestant perspective. The council describes itself as committed to Christian unity and working "toward a fellowship as comprehensive as the spirit and teachings of Christ and as inclusive as the love of God."

The council is a loosely organized fellowship of free and autonomous congregations. The national and regional officers facilitate communication between congregations and serve member congregations in various functions, such as representing them at the Churches Uniting in Christ and the National Council of Churches and coordinating the securing of chaplains in the armed services.

Membership: In 2008 the Council reported 155 member churches and centers in the United States with a communicant membership of between 60,000 and 75,000. There were also 58 international congregations and centers in 17 countries with membership in the Council.

Educational Facilities:

As a matter of policy, the Council has no educational institutions or mission projects of its own. It endorses and encourages member churches to support schools and missions that meet a its standards of being "postdenominational" and promoting Christian unity while meeting human needs.

Periodicals: *The Christian Community.* • *The Pastor's Journal.* • *The Inclusive Pulpit.*

Sources:

International Council of Community Churches. www.icccusa.com.

National Council of Community Churches, Directory. Homewood, IL: National Council of Community Churches, 1982.

Shotwell, J. Ralph. *Unity without Uniformity.* Homewood, IL: Community Church Press, 1984.

Smith, J. Philip. *Faith and Fellowship in the Community Church Movement: A Theological Perspective.* Homewood, IL: Community Church Press, 1986.

Korean Christian Missions of Hawaii
1832 Liliha St., Honolulu, HI 96817

The Korean Christian Missions of Hawaii arose early in the twentieth century when Korean immigrants to Hawaii found themselves trapped by a peculiarity of church history. They had been Presbyterians in their home country and wished to organize a Presbyterian judicatory on the island. However, they ran into a long-standing agreement by which Presbyterians and Congregationalists had divided the world and agreed not to organize in areas over which the other had hegemony. Rather than affiliate with the General Council of Congregational Christian Churches (now part of the United Church of Christ), they dropped the word *Presbyterian* and in 1918 formed Korean Christian churches. Over a period of time they gave up their presbyterianism and moved toward a congregational polity. Thus in recent decades they have emerged as a group that has doctrinal agreement and friendly relationships with both the Presbyterian Church (U.S.A.) and the United Church of Christ.

The church is trinitarian in faith and accepts the Apostles' Creed as its confession of faith. It baptizes by sprinkling.

Membership: In 1980 three congregations were reported, with approximately 500 members.

Sources:

Piepkorn, Arthur C. *Profiles in Belief: The Religious Bodies of the United States and Canada.* Vol. 3. San Francisco: Harper & Row, 1979.

Midwest Congregational Christian Fellowship
8009 N CR 500 West, Muncie, IN 47304

The Midwest Congregational Christian Fellowship was formed in 1958 by former members of the Congregational and Christian Churches. During the years of negotiating the forming of the United Church of Christ, one center of dissatisfaction was in the Eastern Indiana Association. Theologically conservative members of the association were opposed to the church's theologically liberal leadership. They felt there was too much emphasis on social action. The first meetings were held in 1957 in which attempts were made to withdraw the entire association. Having failed, laymen devised a plan by which individual congregations could withdraw. Thirty churches, primarily small, rural congregations, removed themselves from the rolls in 1958. These quickly organized as the Midwest Congregational Christian Fellowship (now Church).

The doctrinal statement of the church reflects the Puritan heritage, the Christian noncreedal bias, and the evangelical perspective of the members. The statement affirms belief in the Trinity, salvation, the ministry of the Holy Spirit, the resurrection, and the unity of believers. The polity is a loose congregationalism with emphasis on local ownership of property. The church meets quarterly, with one meeting designated the annual meeting. There is an eight-man committee that includes the moderator and officers who oversee the work of the church.

Membership: In 2000 the church reported 1,705 members and 29 congregations.

Sources:

Association of Religion Data Archives. www.thearda.com/mapsReports/reports/US_2000.asp.

NAE Evangelism Commission. www.naeevangelism.com/members.html.

National Association of Congregational Christian Churches
PO Box 288, Oak Creek, WI 53154-0288

The National Association of Congregational Christian Churches was formed in 1955 in Detroit, Michigan, by a group of churches and individuals desiring to remain congregational in the face of merger forces that resulted in the formation of the United Church of Christ. The founders came to Detroit in response to a call sent out by the League to Uphold Congregationalist Principles and the Committee for the Continuation of Congregational Christian Churches.

There is little difference between members of the United Church of Christ and those of the National Association. In contrast to the more presbyterial form of the United Church of Christ, the polity of the NACCC emphasizes local autonomy and the fellowship of the local churches in state and national associations. It meets annually in different regions of the country. They gather for fellowship, education, and edification. Although the National Association does not make pronouncements for the member churches, it does undertake mutually cooperative programs, projects, and missions.

The association supports programs for the welfare and career development of ministers and theological students; Christian education and spiritual resources for youths of high school and college age; financial support and building and loan assistance for church development, as well as investment advisory; communications; men's and women's work; and missionary work in the United States and 12 countries worldwide.

Membership: The association reports 430 member churches and 70,000 members in the United States, in fellowship with a number of "free" or congregationally governed associations, including the International Congregational Fellowship.

Educational Facilities:

Olivet College, Olivet, Michigan.

Piedmont College, Demorest, Georgia.

Periodicals: *The Congregationalist*. • *News from the NACCC*. • *News and Needs*; *International Congregational Journal* (published by Congregational Press).

Sources:

National Association of Congregational Christian Churches. www.naccc.org/.

Butman, Harry R. *The Lord's Free People*. Wauwatosa, WI: Swannet Press, 1968.

Hall, Lloyd M., and Steven A. Peay, eds. *Congregationalism: The Church Local and Universal: The 1954 Polity and Unity Report*. Oak Creek, WI: Congregational Press, 2001.

Kohl, Manfred Waldemar. *Congregationalism in America*. Oak Creek, WI: Congregational Press, 1977.

Peay, Steven A., ed. *A Past with a Future*. Oak Creek, WI: Congregational Press, 1998.

Reformed Congregational Fellowship

David Green, Moderator, 14 McKinley Ave., Beverly, MA 01915-3430

The Reformed Congregational Fellowship (RCF) is the product of many meetings that occurred through the mid-1990s by a group of congregational ministers who were searching for a way to publicly affirm their unity based upon adherence to confessional Reformed theology. Over ten years ago, they adopted the Savoy Declaration of 1658 as expressing the system of doctrine taught in the Bible and the Cambridge Platform of 1648 as their understanding of biblical church order.

The Savoy Declaration was the confession of faith for many English and New England congregational churches for over two centuries. It was produced in less than a month by a group of Puritan Congregational ministers who gathered to adapt the Westminster Confession to congregational distinctives. Their work occurred during the time of the fluid religious environment of the Cromwellian Commonwealth in England. It had been Cromwell's hope—himself a Congregationalist—that the three major branches of the church, Baptist, Congregational, and Presbyterian, that were uncomfortable with episcopacy and opposed to deviant theology could find a way of uniting and thus provide a united standard for the religious life of the nation. The meeting at the Savoy Palace, however, did not achieve this result. The congregational leaders, while strongly affirming Reformed theological roots in common with their Presbyterian and Baptist

brethren, solidified their case for Congregational church order. As their views allowed for a closer connection between church and state, they were also distinguished at that point from the Baptists.

The Reformed Congregational Fellowship consists of a number of individuals—mostly congregational pastors—scattered across the United States and in congregations that have adopted the Savoy and the Cambridge as part of their constitutional structure. Such churches are welcome to be listed on the RCF website as member churches. Individual membership is by subscription to the RCF constitution, a one page document affirming the final authority of the Bible for all matters of faith and practice and affirming the secondary standards of the Savoy and Cambridge. As such, therefore, it is not a denomination but, as its title suggests, a fellowship of those who are either independent or members of other congregational denominations. Within this larger world of congregationalism, these men see themselves as an important witness to a historic and confessionally reformed theological perspective.

An example among their congregations is the 200-year-old Westminster Congregational Church of Canterbury, Connecticut, which allied itself to the Fellowship in its formative stages. In 1995 its members went through a renewal process that included acknowledgment of the Bible as their supreme authority, the Westminster Confession (apart from its ecclesiology) as a faithful expression of biblical faith, and the Cambridge Platform as a faithful summary of biblical ecclesiology.

The primary work of the RCF at this time is its Confessional Conference held each spring during the second full week after Easter in Sharon, Massachusetts. Anyone is welcome for this event that begins with Tuesday supper and ends with Thursday lunch. Baptists and Presbyterians also regularly attend as the emphasis is not on polity but theology. Papers are presented on themes from one or more chapters of the Savoy Declaration. Engagement with the Westminster Confession and 1689 Baptist Confession is encouraged, as well as other more ancient or reformational confessions. The Conference is held in part from the belief that only by a return to clear theological witness and preaching and by relying entirely on the expounded Bible and the Holy Spirit's work in the soul, may the tide of ignorance, practical atheism, and lawlessness that envelops the United States be confronted and altered. The Conference also features the singing of hymns, lively discussion, and the opportunity for deep fellowship in the things of God.

The RCF website is a blog and responses are encouraged.

Membership: Not reported.

Sources:

Reformed Congregational Fellowship. www.reformedcongregational.org.

United Church of Canada

The United Church House, 3250 Bloor St. W, Ste. 300, Toronto, ON, Canada M8X 2Y4

The United Church of Canada (UCC) was formed in 1925 by the union of the Methodist Church, Canada, the Congregational Union of Canada, the Council of Local Union Churches, and the majority of the Presbyterian Church in Canada. In 1968 the Canada Conference of the Evangelical United Brethren joined the UCC. This church is the most successful result of the various Christian church union attempts in North America during the nineteenth and twentieth centuries; more than 40 church bodies from two major church families (Reformed and Methodist) were united.

French Huguenots escaping persecution following the revocation of the Edict of Nantes brought the Reformed Faith to Canada. But even in the New World their growth and development were restricted. After the ceding of Nova Scotia to England in 1713, and particularly after the ceding of all of Canada in 1763 by the Treaty of Paris, the influx of Presbyterians from Scotland and Ireland completely overwhelmed the small French contingent. The first ministers from Scotland were Daniel Cook, David Smith, and Hugh Graham, who organized the Presbytery of Truro in 1786. In 1795 this presbytery was joined by a second, the Presbytery of

Pictou, which represented another faction of Scottish Presbyterianism. In 1817 these two groups, joined by a few ministers from the Established Church of Scotland, came together and formed the Synod of the Presbyterian Church of Nova Scotia.

Concurrently with the events that led to the formation of the Synod of Nova Scotia, Presbyterians were moving into central and western Canada. As in eastern Canada, they brought the many divisions of the Scottish church with them, establishing several presbyteries and then synods, the first being the Presbytery of the Canadas in 1818. The establishment of new synodical structures continued through the first half of the nineteenth century, in part due to the importing of schisms within the church in Scotland, the arrival of non–English-speaking (Dutch Reformed) immigrants, and the opening of new territories in the West. By mid-century the trend began to reverse, and in 1875 a series of mergers led to the union of most Presbyterians into the Presbyterian Church in Canada.

Methodism in Canada is traced to Lawrence Coughlan, an Irish Methodist preacher who came to Newfoundland in 1765. At the time of his arrival, he had left John Wesley's connection and applied for work with the Anglican Society for the Propagation of the Gospel. Though a Methodist in practice, he became an Anglican minister. Upon his return to England, many of the people he organized openly declared themselves Methodists. Meanwhile, Methodists were migrating from England to Nova Scotia; among them was William Black Sr. In 1779 a revival among them led to the conversion of William Black, Jr., who was then only 19 years old. He began to preach, visiting several nearby settlements, and in 1781 travelled the whole of Nova Scotia to organize Methodist classes. His work expanded greatly two years later as immigrants loyal to Great Britain flowed into Nova Scotia after the American Revolution. In 1784 Black journeyed to Baltimore, Maryland, for the meeting that organized the new Methodist Episcopal Church. The Canadian work that Black had developed was taken under their care. The Canadian work grew and developed as an integral part of the Methodist Episcopal Church until 1828, when it became separate and independent. Meanwhile, Methodists from Great Britain migrated into Canada, and like the Presbyterians from Scotland, brought with them the several divisions of British Methodism. Mergers in 1874 and 1884 resulted in the formation of the Methodist Church, Canada.

Congregationalism in Canada originated with the acceptance of the British government's offer of free land to New Englanders who would relocate in Nova Scotia. In 1759 several hundred immigrants founded new towns and gathered churches; the first was at Chester, and in 1761 the church at Liverpool was formed. In 1760 a colony began at Mungerville, New Brunswick; the first church was organized six years later. The first church in Newfoundland dates to 1777. From these and additional congregations a Congregational Union of Nova Scotia and New Brunswick was organized in 1846. In 1801 the British Congregationalists sent a missionary to organize a church in Quebec. That led to the formation of the Congregational Union of Ontario and Quebec, which merged with the older group in 1906. The newly formed Congregational Union of Canada received the Ontario Conference of the American-based United Brethren in Christ (now part of the United Methodist Church) in 1907.

The final partner in the 1925 merger, the General Council of Union Churches of Western Canada, was the product of the early proposed Plan of Union that led to the founding of the United Church of Canada. A draft proposal of a plan of union was issued in 1908. In November of that year, a new congregation that appeared in Saskatchewan accepted as the basis of its local organization the proposed plan. Others soon followed, and the Congregational, Methodist, and Presbyterian judicatories allowed ministers to participate in the ecumenical experiment. In 1912 the several local congregations formed the General Council to handle practical matters and press forward in implementing the Plan of Union.

The merger in 1925 had a major dissenting voice. Approximately 30 percent of the Presbyterians refused to enter the merger, and continued as the Presbyterian Church in Canada. In 1926 a number of the Canadian congregations of the

Christian Church (Disciples of Christ) affiliated with the new church. In 1968 the Canadian Conference of the Evangelical United Brethren, following a favorable vote and anticipating the merger of its parent body into the United Methodist Church, became part of the United Church of Canada. In 1943 a two-decade process of negotiation with the Anglican Church of Canada was initiated. It was joined by the Christian Church (Disciples of Christ). The Plan of Union was adopted by the general commission representing the three churches in 1972, but three years later was rejected by the Anglican Church of Canada. The three bodies remain separate entities, though the UCC and the Anglican Church have several joint enterprises.

The union effected in 1925 originated with merger talks between Methodists and Presbyterians in 1899, joined three years later by the Congregationalists. In the proposed Basis of Union, written between 1904 and 1910, a new doctrinal statement was written, based in large part upon the statements of the Presbyterian Church in the U.S.A. It assumes a common affirmation of the Protestant faith and assumes a position between the classical Calvinistic and Arminian positions, leaving considerable latitude for disagreement on issues such as predestination, election, and God's free grace to all persons.

The church is governed by a General Council that meets triennially. The national church is further divided into conferences and presbyteries. Local churches are administered by an official board. The UCC has retained membership in the Alliance of Reformed Churches (Presbyterian and Congregational), the World Methodist Council, the Canadian Council of Churches, and the World Council of Churches.

Membership: On December 31, 2006, the United Church of Canada reported 3,405 churches, approximately 1,500,000 members and adherents, 3,820 ordained clergy, and 4,500 ordered and lay ministry personnel. They have affiliated work in 39 countries.

Educational Facilities:

Theological Colleges (for clergy education):
Atlantic School of Theology, Halifax, Nova Scotia, Canada.
Centre for Christian Studies, Winnipeg, Manitoba, Canada.
Dr. Jessie Saulteaux Resource Centre, Winnipeg, Manitoba, Canada.
Emmanuel College, Toronto, Ontario, Canada.
Francis Sandy Theological Centre, Paris, Ontario, Canada.
Queen's Theological College, Kingston, Ontario, Canada.
St. Andrew's College, Saskatoon, Saskatchewan, Canada.
St. Stephen's College, Edmonton, Alberta, Canada.
United Theological College, Montreal, Quebec, Canada.
University of Winnipeg, Faculty of Theology, Winnipeg, Manitoba, Canada.
Vancouver School of Theology, Vancouver, British Columbia, Canada.

Colleges and Universities:
Huntington University, Sudbury, Ontario, Canada.
Iona College, Windsor, Ontario, Canada.
St. Paul's United College, Waterloo, Ontario, Canada.
Victoria University, Toronto, Ontario, Canada.
Westminster College, London, Ontario, Canada.

Periodicals: *United Church Observer.* • *Mandate Magazine.*

Sources:

United Church of Canada. www.united-church.ca.

Grant, John Webster. *The Canadian Experience of Church Union.* Richmond, VA: John Knox Press, 1967.

Silcox, Claris Edwin. *Church Union in Canada.* New York: Institute of Social and Religious Research, 1933.

White, Peter Gordon, ed. *Voices and Visions: 65 Years of The United Church of Canada.* Toronto: United Church Publishing House, 1990.

United Church of Christ

700 Prospect Ave., Cleveland, OH 44115-1100

The United Church of Christ (UCC) was formed in 1957 by the merger of the Congregational Christian Churches and the Evangelical and Reformed Church. The two uniting bodies were themselves products of mergers in the early twentieth century, and any account of the modern UCC must begin with a consideration of the four bodies which are now constituent parts of it: The Congregational Churches, the Christian Church, the Reformed Church in the United States, and the Evangelical Synod of North America.

THE CONGREGATIONAL CHURCHES. Through the Congregational Churches, the United Church of Christ reaches back to the first decades of the British presence in North America. They were the fourth church to arrive in the colonies (behind the French Reformed Church, Roman Catholic Church, and the Church of England). Coming from England by way of Holland, the Pilgrims first arrived in the Massachusetts Bay Colony in 1620. The Pilgrims were Separatists, Reformed in theology but believing strongly in the autonomous local congregation. The Puritans arrived a decade later, and for the next century they directed the New England settlement. The Puritans were congregationalists in that they placed most of the ecclesiastical power in the hands of the congregation, but also aligned those congregations to the colonial governments. They hoped to create a theocratic system and were intolerant of competing churches and religious groups. The single Pilgrim congregation at Plymouth was tolerated and eventually was absorbed into the larger body of Congregationalists, though the congregation itself eventually was lost to Unitarianism. Congregationalism was the established church of the New England colonies (except Rhode Island) until the Revolution, and remained established in Connecticut until 1818 and in Massachusetts until 1833.

The early Congregationalists were committed to education. They established Harvard University (1636) soon after their arrival, and several generations later as they spread through New England, they founded Yale (1701). These were but the first of a system of institutions of higher education that have made the Congregational Church a major intellectual force in American culture. In 1810 Congregationalists founded the American Board of Commissioners for Foreign Missions, which is not only looked upon as the parent of the nineteenth-century missionary thrust in American Protestantism, but which succeeded in taking Congregationalism around the world—to the Sandwich Islands (Hawaii), China, India, Africa, and the Middle East.

During the early years of the nineteenth century, Congregationalists, just beginning to slip from their position as the largest church in the new land, led the crusade to build a Christian land. They initiated organizations and took leadership roles in various movements on behalf of the causes of peace, women, children, immigrants, and the poor, as well as the abolition of slavery. They created a number of social service centers, especially in the Northeast, where most of their strength was concentrated.

Through the early nineteenth century, Congregationalists had only formed statewide associations of churches, but the rapid spread of the church in the nineteenth century brought the call for a national organization. In 1852 a national council met for the first time and was soon meeting regularly every three years. In 1913, at a meeting of the triennial council in Kansas City, a new Congregational "platform" was adopted that included a preamble, a confession of faith, a form of polity, and a stand on wider fellowships.

Congregationalists have been tied together by a series of doctrinal statements beginning with the Cambridge Platform in 1648, which affirmed the Reformed theological heritage. The Confession of 1913 adopted at Kansas City declared the "steadfast allegiance of the churches composing this council to the faith which our fathers confessed." But at the same time, the statement as a whole reflected the nineteenth-century theological trend usually called modernism. Some Congregational ministers and theological professors had become the major intellectual pioneers of modernist thought, which placed a great emphasis upon individualism and progress, while stressing God's presence in the world over and

against his transcendence, Christ's humanity over and against his divinity, and social activism (the social gospel).

In 1931 the National Council of the Congregational Churches united with the Christian Church to form the General Council of Congregational Christian Churches.

THE CHRISTIAN CHURCH. The Christian Church that was to become part of the United Church of Christ (there were other groups with the same name that stemmed from similar influences) was the product of the revivals of the post-Revolutionary War period and of the new wave of democratic thinking. In 1792 James O'Kelly withdrew from the Methodist Episcopal Church and formed the Republican Methodist Church, rejecting the strict episcopal authority exercised by Bishop Francis Asbury. Methodist bishops have the power to appoint Methodist ministers to their congregations, and O'Kelly continually objected to Asbury's appointments of him. Two years after leaving the Methodists, O'Kelly and his followers also moved against sectarian labels and resolved to be known as "Christians" only. A similar movement arose among Baptists in New England, where Abner Jones had decided that sectarian names and human creeds should be abandoned and that piety alone should be the test of Christian fellowship. He organized such a "Christian" fellowship in 1800 and was soon joined by others.

In 1819 various churches calling themselves "Christian" held a general conference in Portsmouth, New Hampshire. In 1833 a general convention was organized that in effect formed the Christian Church. The following year the church established a Christian Book Association. Concern for education led to the founding of Elon College in North Carolina. From 1854 to 1890, as a result of the forces that led to the Civil War, and occasioned by the adoption of an antislavery resolution by the general convention, the southern branch of the church separated itself from the general convention.

The general convention adopted no doctrinal statement but followed the central affirmations of Reformed Protestantism, stressing the authority of the Bible and salvation by grace through faith. Considerable variation was allowed on doctrinal matters, even on the sacraments. The Southern branch of the church tended to favor adult believers baptism (reflecting their Baptist heritage).

REFORMED CHURCH IN THE UNITED STATES. German-speaking adherents of the Reformed Church came into the United States soon after the founding of Pennsylvania. By 1730 there were more than 15,000 people at least nominally members of the Reformed Church in Pennsylvania. By 1800 the number had grown to 40,000. They had come originally at William Penn's invitation, but were spurred by various negative conditions in their homeland.

Soon after their arrival, these German believers took steps to organize churches. Short of ministers, they often appointed the local schoolteacher to hold services. One such, John Philip Boehm, eventually sought ordination in 1725 and financial support from the Dutch Reformed Church (which had a strong following in New York). That church sent Michael Schlatter to consolidate the scattered congregations into a denominational mold. In 1747 the clergy of these congregations formed the Coetus of the Reformed Ministerium of the Congregations of Pennsylvania. In 1793 the German Reformed Church in Pennsylvania and adjacent states reorganized as a Synod, independent of the Reformed Church in Holland.

In the mid-1880s the German Reformed Church in the United States was torn by a major controversy between the Mercersburg and the Old Reformed movements. The former, stimulated by the leadership of John Williamson Nevin (1803–1886), Philip Schaff (1819–1893), and their associates at the Reformed seminary that had been established at Mercersburg, Pennsylvania, sought to oppose the inroads being made by revivalism (especially that of Charles G. Finney) and sectarianism. The Mercersburg theologians favored an altar-centered liturgy with responses and chants, ritual forms for the traditional church year, read prayers, and more formal garb for the ministers and choirs. They also stressed the authority of the synod over that of regional and congregational powers, and the minister's authority in matters of local church order. The opponents of the Mercersburg perspective stood for pulpit-centered worship, congregational autonomy, and the control of the churches' order of worship in the hands of lay consistories.

The educational emphasis in the church first emerged in the formation of the seminary at Mercersburg (later moved to Lancaster, Pennsylvania) and the formation of a number of colleges—Heidelberg, Catawba, Hood, Franklin and Marshall, Ursinus, and Cedar Crest. Following the movement of German immigration communities, the church spread from Pennsylvania into twenty-one states and three Canadian provinces.

Mission work began in 1838 with the formation of the Board of Foreign Missions. For twenty-eight years this board united with the American Board of Commissioners of Foreign Missions and then began to send its own missionaries to China, India, Japan, and the Middle East.

THE EVANGELICAL SYNOD OF NORTH AMERICA. In 1817 King Frederick William II (1797–1840) united the congregations in his realm, some of which had Lutheran and some of which had Reformed leanings, into a single Evangelical Church, the Church of the Prussian Union. He enforced one form of worship and one church government. Pietism and a more conciliatory spirit were encouraged, and a united front against the inroads of rationalism was created through the development of interconfessional Bible, missionary, and tract societies.

One of these societies, the Basel Missionary Society, sent 288 missionaries as pastors for America, beginning in 1833, in response to appeals from German-American immigrants in the Midwest. The first to arrive were Joseph A. Rieger (1811–1869) and George Wendelin Wall (1811–1867). In 1840 a group of German Evangelical ministers in the St. Louis, Missouri area met and formed Der Deutsche Evangelische Kirchenverein des Westens (the German Evangelical Church Society of the West). In 1866 the word "Kirchenverein" was changed to "Synod." The society/synod made every effort to avoid rigid institutional organization and to eliminate the bureaucratic features usually associated with synodical bodies. Membership was to consist of ordained pastors, lay delegates, and advisory members. No effort was made at this time to enlist individual churches to the society, and it was explicitly stated that "neither the external nor the internal affairs of local congregations could be made the business of the society."

Reflecting their dual Lutheran and Reformed heritage, catechetical instruction in these Evangelical churches typically used one of several catechisms that were being used in Germany, usually uniting elements of Luther's Smaller Catechism with parts of the Heidelberg Catechism of the Reformed Church.

Contemporaneously with the formation of the Synod of the West, two other like synods were being formed. The United Synod of the Northwest served churches in northern Illinois and southern Michigan. The United Synod of the East stretched from New York to Ohio. As early as 1851, union talks were held between the three bodies. In 1872 they merged to form the German Evangelical Synod of North America (dropping "German" in 1927).

Like the Reformed Church in the United States and the Congregationalist Churches, the Evangelical Synod placed a strong emphasis upon education, particularly demanding an educated ministry. Eden Seminary was begun in 1850 and Elmhurst College in 1872. Parochial schools were attached to most congregations. The synod was also deeply involved in the revival of the deaconess movement in the last half of the nineteenth century. A deaconess hospital in St. Louis in 1853 spurred other healing efforts in the church, and hospitals were established in Cleveland, Ohio; Evansville, Indiana; Detroit, Michigan; and Chicago, Illinois.

No other German church body, save the Moravians, developed as extensive a missionary effort as did the Evangelical Synod. It formed missions to the American Indian and sent foreign missionaries to India and Honduras. Domestic missions included the Seaman's Mission in Baltimore, Maryland; Caroline Mission in St. Louis; Back Bay Mission in Biloxi, Mississippi; and others in the Ozarks and on Madeline Island, Wisconsin.

The talks leading toward the 1934 merger of the Evangelical Synod and the Reformed Church began in 1929. The new Evangelical and Reformed Church (E&R Church) was in place only a short time before talks began with the newly formed General Council of the Congregational-Christian Churches.

THE UNITED CHURCH OF CHRIST. As early as 1941, the Committee on Church Relations of the E&R Church held informal conversations with the corresponding committee of the Congregational-Christian Churches. By 1944 a common procedure was agreed upon for dealing with a formal basis of union and a uniting General Synod was planned for 1950. This, however, was postponed for nearly a decade due to legal challenges within the Congregational-Christian Churches. The formal beginning of the United Church of Christ was the Uniting General Synod in Cleveland in June 1957.

The United Church of Christ adopted a constitution in 1961 that provides for a General Synod as its chief policymaking body. The synod is composed of ministerial and lay delegates from the conferences. The delegates elect an executive council that acts between meetings of the synod. Under the General Synod are a variety of boards and agencies, the most important being the Board of Homeland Ministries, the Board of World Ministries, and the Pension Board of the United Church (all of which continue older organizations and are separately incorporated).

The polity of the church included elements of both congregational and presbyterial styles of government. Local churches are guaranteed the right to own their own property, call their own ministers, and withdraw unilaterally from the denomination. But the associations, in which clergy and denominations hold their denominational standing, can withdraw that standing on their own initiative. Conferences, the General Synod, and instrumentalities can advise local churches and individual members, but their statements and decisions are not binding.

Geographically, the church is divided into 38 conferences (with an additional conference serving Hungarian-American congregations), and each conference is further divided into associations, each related to the other and the General Synod in a covenantal fashion. Local councils or consistories, variously composed of the pastor, a moderator or president, and other officers, govern local churches.

The statement of faith, adopted by the General Synod of the United Church of Christ in 1959, and rephrased in doxological form in 1981, is open to a variety of interpretations, but the Reformed theological background of most ministerial leadership is still evident.

The United Church of Christ has a reputation as one of the most socially liberal and active of American church bodies. At the national level, it has identified with numerous concerns related to peace and justice issues. It is also theologically liberal, continuing its modernist heritage, and maintains a wide variety of theological perspectives. It is broadly ecumenical, yet has developed a variety of specific official partnership commitments to the Christian Church (Disciples of Christ); the Evangelical Church Union (East and West Germany); the Pentecostal Church of Chile; the Presbyterian Church, Republic of Korea; and the United Church of Christ (Philippines). The UCC is a member of the National Council of Churches, the World Council of Churches, and the World Alliance of Reformed Churches (Presbyterian and Congregational).

Membership: The church in 2006 reported 1.2 million members, 5,700 congregations, and 10,270 clergy/ministers.

Educational Facilities:

Colleges and Universities:

Beloit College, Beloit, Wisconsin.

Carleton College, Northfield, Minnesota.

Catawba College, Salisbury, North Carolina.

Cedar Crest College, Allentown, Pennsylvania.

Deaconess College of Nursing, St. Louis, Missouri.

Defiance College, Defiance, Ohio.

Dillard University, New Orleans, Louisiana.

Doane College, Crete, Nebraska.

Drury College, Springfield, Missouri.

Elmhurst College, Elmhurst, Illinois.

Elon University, Elon, North Carolina.

Fisk University, Nashville, Tennessee.

Franklin and Marshall College, Lancaster, Pennsylvania.

Grinnel College, Grinnell, Iowa.

Heidelberg College, Tiffin, Ohio.

Hood College, Frederick, Maryland.

Hawaii Loa College, Kenehoe, Hawaii.

Huston-Tillotson College, Austin, Texas.

Illinois College, Jacksonville, Illinois.

Lakeland College, Sheboygan, Wisconsin.

Lemoyne-Owen College, Memphis, Tennessee.

Northland College, Ashland, Wisconsin.

Olivet College, Olivet, Michigan.

Pacific University, Forest Grove, Oregon.

Ripon College, Ripon, Wisconsin.

Rocky Mountain College, Billings, Montana.

Talladega College, Talladega, Alabama.

Tougaloo College, Tougaloo, Mississippi.

Ursinus College, Collegeville, Pennsylvania.

Westminister College, Salt Lake City, Utah.

Seminaries:

Andover Newton Theological Seminary, Newton Center, Massachusetts.

Bangor Theological Seminary, Bangor, Maine.

Chicago Theological Seminary, Chicago, Illinois.

Eden Theological Seminary, St. Louis, Missouri.

Hartford Seminary, Hartford, Connecticut.

Harvard University School of Divinity, Cambridge, Massachusetts.

Howard University School of Divinity, Washington, D.C.

Interdenominational Theological Center, Atlanta, Georgia.

Pacific School of Religion, Berkeley, California.

Lancaster Theological Seminary, Lancaster, Pennsylvania.

Seminario Evangelico de Puerto Rico, Hato Rey, Puerto Rico.

United Theological Seminary of the Twin Cities, New Brighton, Minnesota.

Union Theological Seminary, New York, New York.

Vanderbilt University Divinity School, Nashville, Tennessee.

Yale Divinity School, New Haven, Connecticut.

Periodicals: *United Church News • Prism*

Sources:

United Church of Christ. www.ucc.org.

Bailey, J. Martin, and W. Evan Golder, eds. *The UCC @ 50: Our History, Our Future.* Cleveland, OH: United Church of Christ, 2007.

Dunn, David, and Lowell H. Zuck. *A History of the Evangelical and Reformed Church.* New York: The Pilgrim Press, 1990.

Gunnemann, Louis H. *The Shaping of the United Church of Christ.* New York: Thomas Nelson, 1962.

Horton, Douglas. *The United Church of Christ.* New York: T. Nelson, 1962.

Starkey, Marion L. *The Congregational Way.* Garden City, NY: Doubleday, 1966.

Youngs, J. William T. *The Congregationalist.* Westport, CT: Praeger, 1998.

Pietist-Methodist Family

7

By the end of the seventeenth century, the Anglican, Lutheran, and Reformed churches of Europe were seen by many as having become rigid, lifeless, and impersonal. Some of their members yearned for a more intimate, personal, lively, and spontaneous expression of their religious feelings. This desire led to the movement called *Pietism,* and in turn gave rise to three new groups of churches—the Moravian churches, the Swedish Evangelical churches, and the Methodist (Wesleyan) churches. *Piety,* a term that refers directly to the practice of following religious "duties," came to mean the adoption of spiritual disciplines that promote the individual's personal religious life.

From its beginning, Pietism, by its very existence, challenged the Anglican, Lutheran, and Calvinist churches. While the movement was seen by supporters as an alternative to scholastic theology and a dry worship experience, many church leaders viewed any such informal alternative as primarily challenging the church's hegemony over religious matters in society, and they tended to treat the Pietists with hostility and in some cases initiated actual persecutions. To accomplish their goals, the Pietists emphasized: (1) a Bible-centered faith; (2) the experienced Christian life (guilt, forgiveness, conversion, holiness, and love within community); and (3) free expression of faith in hymns, testimony, and evangelical zeal. The earliest representatives of the movement include Philipp Jacob Spener (1635–1705) and August Hermann Francke (1663–1727).

Spener is credited with originating the basic form taken by Pietists—the *collegia pietatis* (association of piety). In despair over the impossibility of reforming Lutheranism, he began to organize small groups that met in homes for Bible study, prayer, and discussion, leading to a deeper spiritual life. These groups spread throughout Europe and were known in England as religious societies.

Francke was Spener's most famous disciple. Forced out of the University of Leipzig and later dismissed from the University of Erfurt, he became a teacher at the newly formed University of Halle and turned it into a Pietist center. During the three decades Francke taught there, Halle graduated more than 200 ministers per year. Besides the deeply experienced faith he taught at Halle, Francke encouraged missionary endeavors and began an orphan house in 1698. Knowledge of his work brought financial help and allowed the ministry to include a pauper school, a Bible institute, a Latin school, and other facilities to aid destitute children. Most early missionaries came from among Halle's graduates.

From Halle, Pietism spread throughout the world. Correspondence between Francke and Cotton Mather (1663–1728) led to the establishment of religious societies in the Boston churches, and Pietistic literature lay directly behind the American revival movement of the 1730s and 1740s called the Great Awakening. In Germany, Pietism renewed the Moravian Church, which then began to spread its own version of Pietism. The Moravian Church carried the Pietist faith to England, where Pietism became a strong influence on John Wesley (1703–1791), the founder of the Methodist movement. Moravians working in Sweden helped establish the Swedish Evangelical Church. Thus, three groups of churches emerged from the Pietist movement: the Moravian churches, the Swedish Evangelical churches, and the Methodist churches.

However, most of Pietism's influence was absorbed by the Lutheran Church and the Calvinist groups (the Reformed Church, the Presbyterian Church, and the Congregational Church). Although Pietism did lead to schism in some of the American churches, most of the schismatic churches eventually reunited with their parent bodies.

A note of contrast is that the Pietist churches are very different from the European free churches. The latter, discussed in chapter 10, include the Mennonites, the Amish, the Quakers, and the Brethren. The Pietists were distinct from the European free churches because the Pietists were open to traditional Christian practices and beliefs, and lacked hostility to their parent bodies. Instead of rejecting the forms of the past, as the European free churches did, the Pietists worked with the forms of the past and sought the life of the spirit within them. In general, the free churches of the past and the present have opposed infant baptism, traditional ideas of church and sacrament, and many liturgical practices. In contrast, Pietists accepted Reformation ideas of church and sacrament, have baptized infants, and have used simplified versions of liturgical forms. Whereas the European free churches sprang up as a protest to state churches (whether those were Roman Catholic, Anglican, Lutheran, or Calvinist), Pietist groups began as societies within Protestant state churches and only later removed themselves from their parent churches and became independent entities.

Pietist-Methodist Family Chronology

1675   Philipp Jacob Spener (1635–1705) publishes *Pia desideria or Earnest Desires for a Reform of the True Evangelical Church* calling for reviving church life through a new emphasis on Bible study, devotion, and heart-felt preaching.

1694   Spener influences Frederick III, Elector of Brandenburg, to fund the University of Halle, which becomes the center of the Pietist movement.

1722   Refugee Moravian families from Bohemia and Moravia settle on the estate of German Count Nicholaus von Zinzendorf and found the community of Herrnhut. Zinzendorf encourages them to spiritual renewal in the Pietist tradition leading to their launching a global missionary movement.

1738   Anglican minister John Wesley, partially based on interaction with Moravian missionaries, experiences a personal spiritual awakening described as feeling his "heart strangely warmed." He subsequently begins to found several informal religious societies at which people may gather for prayer, singing, Bible study, and preaching.

1744   Wesley holds first conference of the preachers who are assisting him in his work. This meeting is considered the founding event of the new Methodist movement.

1763–65   Irish Methodist preacher Robert Strawbridge founds several Methodist classes (small groups that meet weekly for prayer and support in the spiritual life) in Maryland, the first Methodist organizations in the British American colonies. Barbara Heck leads in the founding of a similar class in New York in 1766. Each class includes both black and white members.

1869   Wesley send Joseph Pilmore and Richard Boardman as lay preachers to travel among the emerging movement in the colonies.

1784   Wesley appoints Thomas Coke to come to the new United States with authority to organize an autonomous American church. The preachers meet in conference during Christmas week, organize the Methodist Episcopal Church (MEC), and select Francis Asbury (1745–1816) as their "bishop."

1792   First African American Methodist congregation (now St. Paul United Methodist Church) is founded in Oxon Hill, Maryland. Richard Allen, Absalom Jones, and Lunar Brown lead African American members out of St. George's church in Philadelphia. This group will later create three congregations—the Bethel and Zoar Methodist churches and St. Thomas Episcopal Church.

1800   German Americans influenced by Methodism found Church of the United Brethren (led by William Philip Otterbein and Martin Boehm) and the Evangelical Association (later the Evangelical Church), under the leadership of Jacob Albright.

1813   African Methodists in Wilmington, Delaware, separate from the Methodist Episcopal Church and form the African Union Church, the first independent African American denomination, which continues to the present as the African Union First Methodist Protestant Church and the Union American Methodist Episcopal Church (UAMEC).

1816   Richard Allen leads in the formation of the African Methodist Episcopal Church (AME) centered on the Bethel congregation in Philadelphia. He is selected as the church's first bishop.

1821   African Methodists in New York organize what will become the African Methodist Episcopal Zion Church (AMEZ) and select William Varick as their first bishop.

1828   Methodists who reject its Episcopal leadership leave the Methodist Episcopal Church and form the Methodist Protestant Church (MPC) and adopt a congregational polity.

1844–45   Now the largest church in America, the MEC splits into two jurisdictions over the slavery issue: the Methodist Episcopal Church and the Methodist Episcopal Church, South (MEC,S).

1870   Former slaves who had joined neither the AME nor AMEZ churches found the Colored (now Christian) Methodist Episcopal Church (CME).

1875   Pauline Williams Martindale is ordained as an elder (minister) in the Methodiost Protestant Church.

1880s   Many Methodist leave the MEC and MEC,S to form new Holiness churches.

1889   Ella Nismonger ordained as an elder in the Church of the United Brethren.

1926   Belle C. Harmon and Gertrude L. Apel are ordained as elders in the Methodist Episcopal Church.

1939   The MEC, MEC,S, and the MPC unite to form the Methodist Church.

1946   The Church of the United Brethren and the Evangelical Church unite to form the Evangelical United Brethren.

1968   The Methodist Church and the Evangelical United Brethren unite to form the United Methodist Church, now the third largest religious body in the United States. The new church voted to disband the Central Jurisdiction into which African American members had been segregated.

1980   Marjorie Matthews become first female minister elected to the bishopric.

2000   Commission on Pan-Methodist Cooperation and Union formed to pursue closer relationships among the AME, AMEZ, CME, the UMC, and the UAMEC.

MORAVIANISM. The Moravian churches of today exist only because the Pietist movement gave life to an almost extinguished Moravian Church. Thus the Moravians are distinct among Pietists: The Moravians represent not so much a new church created by Pietism as a renewed church recreated by Pietism. That recreation occurred in 1727. The story of the Moravian churches, however, starts in the ninth century with the founding of the early Moravian Church.

Cyril (c. 827–869) and Methodius (c. 826–885), missionaries of the Greek Orthodox Church, arrived in the ninth century in Moravia, an area in what is now the Czech Republic. There they established a Greek-based Slavic church. At first, the Moravians were encouraged by the Roman Catholic Church, but in later centuries Rome forced a Latin rite upon them. The Moravians considered this a repressive move. They became discontented with Catholicism, and their discontent was heightened by a young priest named John Hus (c. 1373–1415). From his pulpit in Prague, he began to throw challenges in the face of the Roman Church. He questioned the practice of selling indulgences, which were promises of the remission of punishment due for sins. Hus also questioned the denial of the cup to the laity in the Eucharist, and railed against the moral corruption of the papacy. Hus's career coincided with the time when three men were claiming to be the pope, each having a segment of Europe behind him. In 1414, when the Council of Constance was called primarily to heal an internal schism within the Roman church, church authorities also invited Hus, with a safe-conduct promise, to state his case. Instead, after hearing and rejecting him, the church had him arrested and burned at the stake. The Hussite Wars followed, and eventually Hus's followers, concluding that Hus's ideas would never positively affect the Roman church, formed their own church—the Unitas Fratrum or "Unity of the Brethren."

During its early years, the church existed as a Reformed Roman church, turning to Bishop Stephen of the Italian

Waldensian Church for apostolic ordination. It published the Bible in the Czech vernacular—the Kralitz Bible, which affected the Czech-speaking people as strongly as Luther's Bible affected Germany. A second round of religious wars in the late sixteenth and early seventeenth centuries all but destroyed the once prosperous Unitas Fratrum. On June 21, 1621, fifteen Brethren leaders were beheaded in Prague. The persecutions brought an end to all visible manifestations of the Unitas Fratrum and reestablished Roman hegemony in Bohemia and Moravia.

In 1722 a few families from the former Unitas Fratrum made their way from Moravia to Saxony, a region in East Germany. Soon more than 300 exiles had settled in Saxony at Herrnhut, the estate of Count Nicolaus Ludwig von Zinzendorf (1700–1760). The exiles conferred and drew up a "Brotherly Agreement." Their bickering, though, led the fatherly Zinzendorf to invite as many as would come to a communion service at his manor church on August 13, 1727. This date is considered to be the birth of the Renewed Unitas Fratrum (or Moravian Church) as there occurred an amazing "outpouring of the power of God," which Moravians compared to Pentecost. The wranglings and strife were over. Zinzendorf received a copy of the "discipline" of the old Unitas Fratrum and began to set the church in order. Ordination in the apostolic succession was secured from Daniel Ernest Jablonsky (1660–1741). A court preacher in Berlin, Jablonsky was one of the ordained bishops in the line of the old Unitas Fratrum. He ordained David Nitschmann (1696–1772) as the first bishop of the restored church.

The arrival of the Moravians on the estate of Zinzendorf largely determined the Moravian future. Zinzendorf was a Pietist, and he led the Moravians into placing great stress upon religious experience and the relation of the individual with God. Numerous forms were developed to foster this deep faith. Among them was the love feast, an informal service centering on holy communion but also including a light meal, singing, and a talk by the officiating minister. The litany, a lengthy prayer form for corporate and private devotions, was added to the Herrnhut services in 1731. Its present form is a modified Lutheran litany. The idea of small groups of dedicated Christians meeting together regularly for worship and exhortation and service was taken from the German Pietists and was used extensively, especially in the mission field. Moravian meetings were the model of early Methodist societies developed by John Wesley.

The *Daily Texts* was a book that grew from the need of the early Herrnhut settlers for a "watchword" from the scripture for daily use. They at first copied scriptural passages by hand on bits of paper to be drawn from a container each day. This practice evolved into an annual volume of texts. For each day there was a text from both the Old and New Testaments and a hymn stanza to amplify the text. This book has had an influence far beyond the membership of the church, as it circulates widely to nonmembers.

The most characteristic aspect of Moravian piety was its mission program. Zinzendorf, early in his life, became con-

vinced that he was destined to do something about the neglected peoples of the world. In 1731 he traveled to Copenhagen, where he met Anthony Ulrich, an African slave from the Danish West Indies. Ulrich told Zinzendorf of his people's plight. Back at Herrnhut, Zinzendorf related Ulrich's story, preparing the way for the slave to arrive and tell it himself. The response was immediate, and David Nitschmann and Leonhard Dober (1706–1766) were chosen as the first missionaries to the oldest Moravian mission—St. Thomas. The Moravians then proceeded to initiate missions all over Europe. Zinzendorf, a Lutheran himself, gave strict orders for the Moravians not to encroach upon state-church prerogatives. They arrived in their mission territories as merely preachers of the Word and were thus welcomed in many Protestant lands. In England they moved into an established Anglican Church structure and set up "religious societies" for Bible study and prayer, never encouraging anyone to leave the state church. John Wesley was a member of one of these societies for a while.

In 1872 reentrance into Czechoslovakia was permitted with the Edict of Toleration, and the first congregation in Bohemia was established the same year. Other mission work occurred in British Guiana, Surinam, Southern Africa, Java, Nicaragua, Jordan, Alaska, and Labrador, all established before 1900. In 1735 the Moravians entered the American colonies.

MORAVIANS IN AMERICA. The settling of Moravians in America in 1735 had a twofold purpose: the securing of a settlement in the New World in case Germany again became intolerant, and a mission to the Indians. The first group of settlers in the New World was led by Bishop August Gottlieb Spangenberg (1704–1792). He traveled to Georgia on the same ship that brought John Wesley to the colony of James Oglethorpe (1696–1785). Wesley was impressed with Spangenberg and the Moravians, and he records a number of conversations with Spangenberg. Soon after settling in Savannah, the Moravians opened an Indian school. The Moravians were, however, caught in the war between the British (Georgia) and the Spanish (Florida). Their refusal to bear arms led to their being looked down upon by their neighbors. By 1740 the Moravians left Georgia for Pennsylvania. They established the town of Nazareth, and the following year Bishop Nitschmann arrived and began to settle Bethlehem. In December of 1741, Zinzendorf arrived, and on Christmas day he organized the Moravian Congregation in Bethlehem, the first in America.

Under Spangenberg's leadership, a semicommunal arrangement was worked out in Bethlehem that soon made it a self-sufficient settlement, able to bear its own mission program to the Indians. Churches were soon organized in Nazareth and Lilitz in Pennsylvania, and in Hope, New Jersey.

In 1749 the British Parliament acknowledged the Moravian Church as "an Ancient Protestant Episcopal Church," thus, in effect, giving the church an invitation to settle in other British colonies. The Moravians took advantage of Parliament's recognition of their church and settled in North

Carolina on property owned by Lord Granville. Rising persecution in Germany encouraged other Moravians to come to America.

Spangenberg and five others went to North Carolina in 1752 and had surveyors lay out what is now Forsyth County. The first settlers, 15 in all, arrived in 1753 and settled in Bethabara. In 1766 the permanent settlement of Salem was laid out. From this beginning, other churches and settlements developed.

Moravian settlements in Canada originated as an extension of their continued missions to convert the Indians. After an unsuccessful attempt in 1752 to establish a mission to the Indians along the Labrador coast, Moravian missionaries were able to find work in 1771 in Nain. By the early nineteenth century, four stations were activated along the rugged terrain across the Labrador Basin from New Herrnhut, the Moravian settlement in Greenland. A second thrust into Canada occurred in 1792 when, in an effort to escape a possible Indian war, missionaries moved into Canada along the Thames River and established Fairfield, Ontario. Though destroyed in the War of 1812, the center was rebuilt and became a stop along the underground railroad for slaves fleeing to Canada. A third field in Canada opened in 1894 when some German families who had moved to Alberta from Russia contacted the church headquarters in Pennsylvania and asked for affiliation. By encouraging the development of this colony and adding members who moved into the area from the eastern United States, the church grew and now has its own Canadian District to serve the congregations of western Canada.

METHODISM.
Among Methodist historians there is wide disagreement about when Methodism began; however, organizational continuity in the Wesleyan movement dates to late 1739 when the first society was formed by John Wesley and 18 other persons "desiring to flee from the wrath to come—and be saved from their sins." The number of societies grew and in 1744 the first Methodist conference was held as Wesley called his lay ministers together to confer with him. After discussions, Wesley made all the decisions and then assigned the preachers to their tasks.

Wesley, the son of an Anglican clergyman, had attended Oxford to study for the ministry. While at Oxford, he formed a religious society called the Holy Club by other students. To this group was first applied the derisive title *Methodists*, partly because of the group's strict daily schedules.

Wesley left Oxford and became a missionary to the Indians in Georgia. This adventure ended in failure. However, while on the voyage to America he encountered the Moravians and was impressed with their simple piety and their leader, Spangenberg. In Georgia, he also encountered the writings of Scottish Pietist Thomas Halyburton (1674–1712), whose personal religious experience closely paralleled his own.

Arriving back in London, Wesley affiliated with the Moravians and in particular with Peter Böhler (1712–1775), who would soon be on his way to America as a missionary to the slaves. Activity with Böhler led Wesley to his own crisis experience, which occurred at the religious society at Aldersgate on May 24, 1738. Wesley described what happened in his journal:

> *In the evening, I went very unwillingly to a Society in Aldersgate Street, where one was reading Luther's* Preface to the Epistle to the Romans. *About a quarter before nine, while he was describing the change which God works in the heart through faith in Christ, I felt my heart strangely warmed. I felt I did trust in Christ; Christ alone, for salvation; and an assurance was given me, that he had taken away my sins, even mine, and saved me from the law of sin and death.*

This experience became the turning point in Wesley's life. During the next year he visited Germany and lived among the Moravians, but then broke with the Moravians over several points of practice, and began the United Societies. Innovations by Wesley included field preaching, the use of lay preachers (Wesley's assistants), and the discipline of the societies.

The United Societies were originally groups of dedicated Christians within the Church of England. As with continental Pietism, doctrine was not at issue as much as the application of doctrine to life. Some doctrinal innovations did occur concerning the Christian life—Wesley's emphasis on the witness of the spirit and Christian perfection. These doctrines often led to excesses and accusations of "enthusiasm," the eighteenth-century euphemism for "fanaticism."

Those who experienced this evangelical awakening were organized into societies, the basic document of which was the General Rules. Those in the society were expected to evidence their desire for salvation: first, by doing no harm, avoiding evil of every kind, especially that which is most generally practiced; second, by doing good of every possible sort, and as far as possible to all people; and third, by attending upon the ordinances of God. Wesley wrote that following the third rule involved the public worship of God, the ministry of the Word (either read or expounded), the Supper of the Lord, family and private prayer, searching the scriptures, and fasting and abstinence.

The society was to be thought of as a gathering of people, not as a place. Wherever the society met was where it held its regular worship services and, most importantly, the quarterly meeting. Once each quarter, Wesley visited each society. He inquired into the lives of the members relative to the General Rules and issued quarterly tickets. The tickets admitted members to the society for the next three months. Wesley served communion and usually a love feast was held, an informal service centering on holy communion but also including a light meal, singing, and a talk.

Wesley lived for almost the entire eighteenth century, and the issue of doctrinal standards for Methodism came to the fore late in his life. Early doctrinal concerns had been set in the *Large Minutes of the Conference*, but additional doctrinal questions were raised in 1777 by the predestinarian Calvinists and in the 1780s by the establishment of the Methodist

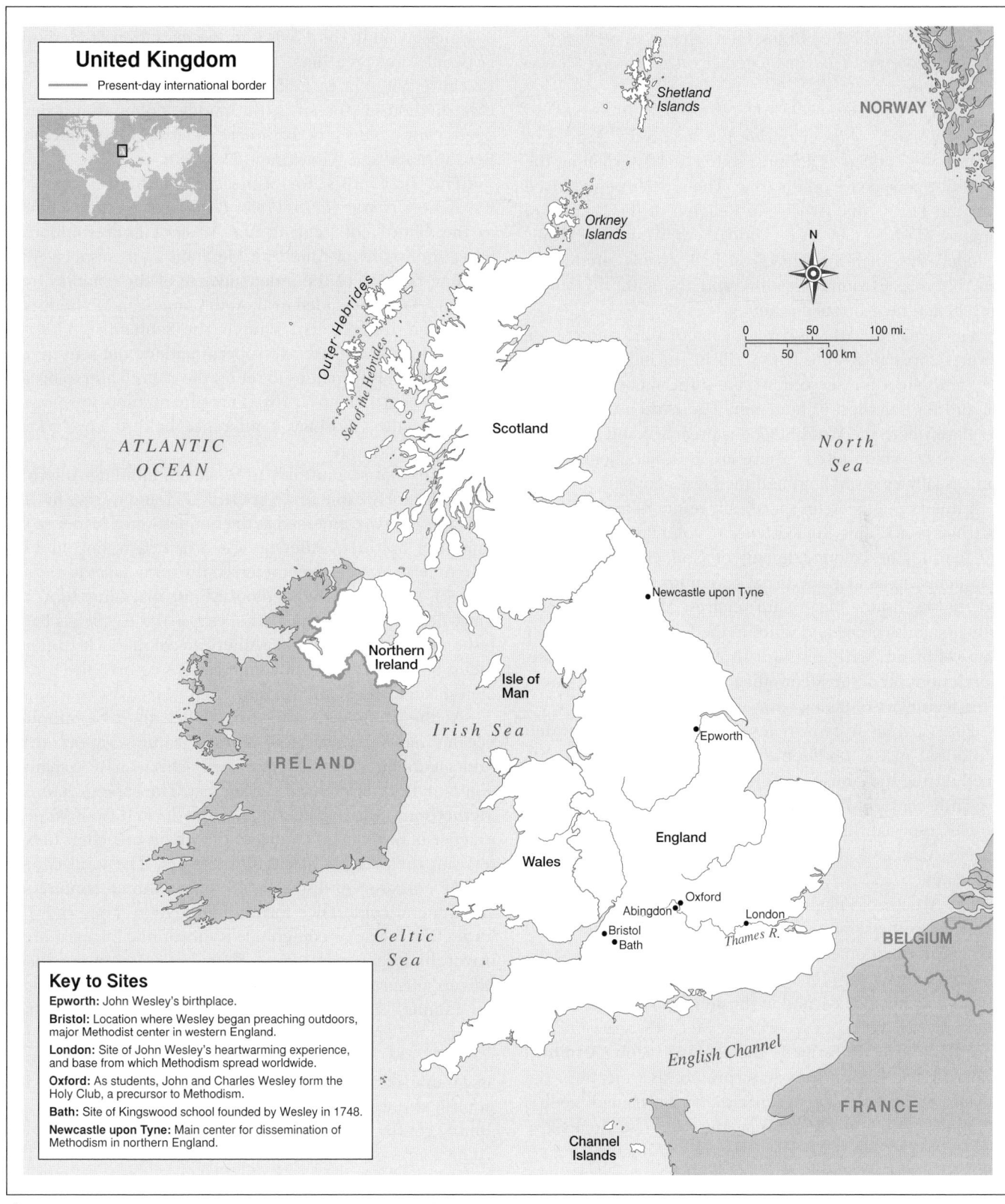

United Kingdom
Present-day international border

NORWAY

Shetland
Islands

Orkney
Islands

N

0   50   100 mi.
0   50   100 km

Outer Hebrides

Sea of the Hebrides

Scotland

*North
Sea*

*ATLANTIC
OCEAN*

Newcastle upon Tyne

Northern
Ireland

Isle of
Man

Irish Sea

Epworth

IRELAND

England

Wales

Oxford
Abingdon
London

*Celtic
Sea*

Bristol
Bath

Thames R.

BELGIUM

English Channel

FRANCE

Channel
Islands

Key to Sites

Epworth: John Wesley's birthplace.

Bristol: Location where Wesley began preaching outdoors,
major Methodist center in western England.

London: Site of John Wesley's heartwarming experience,
and base from which Methodism spread worldwide.

Oxford: As students, John and Charles Wesley form the
Holy Club, a precursor to Methodism.

Bath: Site of Kingswood school founded by Wesley in 1748.

Newcastle upon Tyne: Main center for dissemination of
Methodism in northern England.

XNR Productions

Episcopal Church in America. The Calvinist controversy set
Methodism firmly against predestinarian doctrines. Wesley
opposed the Calvinist idea of irresistible grace, the belief that
if grace comes, you cannot refuse it; if it does not come, you
cannot obtain it. Wesley said grace is freely given to each person, and each person can freely respond to the gospel. The
formation of American Methodism caused Wesley to set doctrinal standards in his letter to the preachers in America: "Let

all of you be determined to abide by the Methodist doctrine and discipline published in the four volumes of *Sermons* and the *Notes on the New Testament*, together with the *Large Minutes of the Conference*."

To Wesley's *Sermons*, the *Notes on the New Testament*, and the *Large Minutes of the Conference*, the Twenty-five Articles of Religion were added as a fourth source for determining the Methodist perspective on doctrine. The articles were derived from the Thirty-Nine Articles of Religion of the Church of England, of which they are an abridgment. Wesley specifically excluded the Anglican articles on hell, creeds, predestination, bishops, excommunication, and the authority of the church, and he shortened others.

The remaining articles cover the major affirmation of traditional Christianity—the Trinity, Christ (including his virgin birth and physical resurrection), the sufficiency of the Bible, sin, and the salvation of humanity. The church is viewed as the place where the Word of God is preached and the sacraments duly administered. There are two sacraments—baptism (usually by sprinkling) and the Lord's Supper.

A number of the items specifically refute Roman Catholic doctrines concerning the existence of voluntary works above and beyond the commandments of God, purgatory, other sacraments, mass as a sacrificial ceremony, celibate priests, and the uniformity of worship services. Methodists receive both elements (bread and wine) in the Lord's Supper, rather than just bread. Methodists are also set apart from the free-church position of the Mennonites by their acknowledgment of the legitimacy of taking oaths in legal situations.

The Twenty-five Articles of Religion grounded Methodism in the traditional Christian doctrines as established during the conciliar era of united Christianity (fourth to eighth centuries) and the creeds promulgated by those councils, especially the Nicene and Chacedonian creeds. The *Sermons*, *Notes*, and *Minutes* stated Methodist opinion on current issues.

The Articles of Religion are also derivative of continental Reformed confessions, and place Methodism in a Reformed theological tradition. The Reformed tradition, based on the work of John Calvin (1509–1564), shows up most clearly in articles v, ix, xii, xiii, xvi, and in the anti-Roman Catholic articles x, xi, xiv, xv, xix, xx, and xxii. Methodists have always identified with Reformed theologian Jacob Arminius (1560–1609), whom they interpreted as rejecting the Calvinist emphasis on predestination. Wesley named the first Methodist periodical *The Arminian Magazine*. The Twenty-Five Articles of Religion are a common core of doctrinal agreement for all Methodists and are included in doctrinal statements by almost all Methodist bodies.

In England, Methodism remained as a society within the Anglican Church, and as such was spread throughout the British Commonwealth by the missionary vision and activity of the Reverend Thomas Coke (1747–1814). The British Wesleyans became independent of the Anglican Church in 1795.

WESLEYANISM IN AMERICA. Methodist history in the colonies began in the 1760s with the migration of Methodist laypeople and preachers. The first society on record was in Leesburg, Virginia, in 1766, and the second was in New York City. Methodism spread in the middle colonies and developed early centers in Baltimore, Maryland; Philadelphia, Pennsylvania; and Wilmington, Delaware.

The first crisis for American Methodists was the Revolutionary War (1775–1783). Because of their attachment to the Church of England and Wesley's antirevolutionary traits, the loyalty of American Methodists was suspect. After the war, because of the independence of the colonies from England, Wesley decided to allow the American Methodists to set up an independent church. In September 1784 he ordained Thomas Coke as a superintendent and sent him to America with instructions to set up the church and to ordain Francis Asbury (1745–1816). This organization was accomplished at the Christmas Conference held at Lovely Lane Chapel in Baltimore.

Asbury was second only to Wesley in molding American Methodism. He came to America in 1771 and during his first 13 years of service emerged as the unquestioned leader of the American brethren. After he was ordained bishop in 1784 (the American preachers preferred the term *bishop* to *superintendent*), he formed the Methodist Episcopal Church. At the time, neither the Roman Catholics nor the Anglicans had a bishop present in the former American colonies. His appointments of ministers to their congregations covered the United States, Nova Scotia, and Antigua.

As the Methodists grew in number, their organization became more sophisticated, but two features important for understanding Methodists and their schisms have remained constant: the conference and itinerancy. The basic structure of Methodism is the conference, a name derived from Wesley's practice of having regular meetings with his preachers to confer with them before deciding on issues. The local church charge conference, district conference, annual conference, and general conference form a hierarchy of authority. The local church charge conference is the annual business meeting of the local congregation. There the congregation elects officers and sets the budget. The district conference is primarily a funnel; it lets local congregations know the messages of bishops and annual conferences. The annual conference is a regional conference chaired by the bishop, whose duty it is to assign ministers to their churches (charges) each year, and to publish those assignments at the annual conference. The annual conference is the most important structure for developing the program mandated by the general conference. The general conference is made up of representatives of all the annual conferences in the country. The general conference meets quadrennially, is the church's highest legislative and policy-making body, and writes the *Discipline*, the book of church order and organization.

The term *annual conference* has a meaning in addition to that described above. For a minister to belong to an annual conference means that he or she has contractual relationships with the church in that area. The minister gives up membership in any local church and is a "member" of the annual conference. The minister also agrees to be available for assignment, and the church guarantees that he or she will receive an assignment, termed an *appointment*, to a congregation (or other ministry task) and a salary. The term *annual conference* thus connotes an association of ministers, a fellowship, a sense of belonging.

Itineracy is the second important structural feature of Methodism. Ministers itinerate; that is, they travel to various congregations within their own region (usually part of a state) as they are assigned by the bishop and annual conference of that region. The assignments were traditionally for one year, but the length of the minister's stay has steadily expanded. In addition to itinerant ministers, Methodists have both ordained and unordained local preachers who do not travel but belong to only one congregation. They are licensed by the church and they preach, assist the minister, and occasionally act as interim pastors.

During the nineteenth century, the itinerant, the circuit rider of folklore, would often be assigned to a charge with 20 or 30 preaching points on it. The circuit rider would travel his entire circuit every two, three, or four weeks. The effect of this type of organization was to cover the land, but it also put the ministers in many places on weekdays—not on Sundays. This became an issue in the nineteenth century as Methodism grew and stable congregations emerged that wanted to meet on Sundays instead of on weekdays.

GERMAN METHODISTS. During the first generation, Methodism in America spread among German-speaking people in the middle colonies, and independent German congregations and leaders emerged. Attempts to merge the English-speaking and German-speaking Methodist and Pietist groups in the early 1800s failed. A major factor in the failure was Bishop Asbury's belief that there should be no perpetuation of German work since English would quickly be the only language in America. Asbury was essentially correct, but he failed to foresee the large German migrations through the 1800s. Eventually, the Methodist Episcopal Church had to organize its own German-speaking mission to cope with the demand for ministry.

Two separate Wesleyan churches developed among America's German-speaking population: the United Brethren in Christ and the Evangelical Association. These two churches merged with each other and then with the United Methodist Church. Prior to these mergers, various schismatic churches formed from the two German-speaking churches.

One of the most interesting schismatic churches is now defunct: the Republican United Brethren Church. It was formed by members of the White River Conference of the United Brethren in Christ during the Mexican War (1846–1848). The church's origin can be traced to an informal meeting of ministers and members of the White River Conference at Dowell Meeting House, Franklin Circuit, Indiana, on March 12, 1848. At the meeting, a resolution was

passed protesting conference action concerning the Reverend P. C. Parker. (Parker had been expelled from the ministry for "immorality" because of his participation in the war.) This resolution was refused publication; therefore, an appeal was made to the general conference. The 1853 general conference, however, sustained Parker's expulsion and passed a strong antiwar resolution. The convention also acted in support of a belief in "the doctrine of the natural, hereditary, and total depravity of man." That doctrine refers to the sinfulness of human beings after the fall, by which sinfulness the will is in bondage and is unable to turn to God. The protest of the three actions of the general conference became the formal basis for withdrawal. At a meeting at Union Chapel, Decatur County, Indiana, on September 8–12, 1853, the new church was organized. The church was small (the first conference listed only two charges) and existed for only a short time. In the 1860s the church became part of the Christian Union.

AFRICAN-AMERICAN METHODISM. Of the religiously affiliated African Americans, the second largest number belongs to Methodist churches. (The largest number belongs to Baptist churches.) African Americans were a part of Methodism almost from the beginning; Wesley first mentions the black servants of Nathaniel Gilbert (c. 1721–1774), the pioneer of Methodism in the West Indies, in his journal. African Americans were members of the earliest classes and societies, a few being named in the records, and through the 1770s they began to assume leadership positions as class leaders and preachers. By the time the Methodist Episcopal Church was organized in 1784, two preachers, Richard Allen (1760–1831) and Harry Hoosier (d. 1810), were making a name for themselves. Hoosier, one of the outstanding orators of the era, frequently traveled with Bishop Francis Asbury, and, in spite of the discrimination he often faced, was among the most popular speakers in the church. Allen emerged as a leader among Philadelphia's black Methodist membership.

The Methodist Episcopal Church emerged as the only national church to systematically recruit African Americans into membership, and over the first decades it built a significant black constituency. While most of these members were slaves, by 1800 large free-black constituencies were present in Boston, New York, Philadelphia, Wilmington, Baltimore, Washington, and Charleston.

Methodists emerged from their organizational meeting with a strong stance against slavery, but as church members in the South were heard from, that stance softened decade by decade. Without totally giving up its antislavery stance, the church slowly accommodated the institution, and structures reflecting the master-slave relationship were developed as more and more African Americans became church members. African members were segregated during Sunday worship, often in church galleries, and later, where membership allowed, into separate congregations. Rejection of practices that were derogatory toward African Americans became apparent first among the free black members in the northern urban centers, leading to the formation of several independent denominations. African-American church members in Wilmington, Delaware, formed a separate congregation in 1805, and the majority left in 1813 to found the African Union Church, the first all-black denomination, which soon had congregations throughout the northern states.

The most famous break came in 1791 to 1792 in Philadelphia, when the African-American members at St. George's Church walked out and formed three congregations—St. Thomas Episcopal Church, Bethel Methodist Episcopal Church, and Zoar Methodist Episcopal Church. The Bethel Church, under the leadership of Richard Allen, went on to become the largest black congregation in the city. Facing tension with the white leadership at St. George's, in 1816 Allen led in the founding of the African Methodist Episcopal Church, now the largest African-American Methodist church body. Several years later, the African-American church members in New York City left to found what would become known as the African Methodist Episcopal Zion Church.

In the 1840s and 1850s, massive recruitment efforts brought several hundred thousand slaves into Methodism in the southern states. Even before the end of the American Civil War (1861–1865), former slaves began disserting the Methodist Episcopal Church, South, the dominant Methodist group in the southern United States, and joining the African Methodist Episcopal Church or the African Methodist Episcopal Zion Church, with a lesser number adhering to the Methodist Episcopal Church (the northern white church). About a third of the black member of the southern white church remained after the war, and they, as a group, organized a new denomination, now known as the Christian Methodist Episcopal Church.

Over the next century and a half, the great majority of African-American Methodists would adhere to one of the three large independent African Methodist churches—the African Methodist Episcopal Church, the African Methodist Episcopal Zion Church, or the Christian Methodist Episcopal Church. A lesser number stayed with the Methodist Episcopal Church and are now members of the United Methodist Church. The original African Union Church continues in two denominations: the African First Methodist Protestant Church and the Union American Methodist Episcopal Church. Through the first decade of the twenty-first century, ongoing conversations have been held between the various black churches and the United Methodist Church looking toward closer fellowship and cooperation and possible eventual union.

NON-EPISCOPAL METHODISM. Apart from the race issue, no concern has led to the number of schisms within Methodism as has the periodic protest against the episcopal polity of the Methodist Episcopal Church and its successor bodies. The first group to depart over polity questions and to subsequently form a nonepiscopal church was the Republican Methodists led by James O'Kelley (c. 1757–1826). His small church eventually became a part of the Christian Church (a constituent part of the present-day United Church of Christ). More significant, however, was the Methodist

Protestant schism in the 1820s. The Methodist Protestants created the first major alternative relative to polity to the Methodist Episcopal Church, though they finally merged with the two large Methodist Episcopal branches in 1939. The merger of the Methodist Protestant Church left many of its pastors and members dissatisfied and led to no less than six schisms. Members refused to move from the relatively small denominations into the 10-million-member Methodist Church (1939–1968), now the United Methodist Church. They also rejected the episcopal system and, in the South, feared the possibility of racial integration, which finally occurred in United Methodism in the 1960s. Such churches as the Methodist Protestant Church, headquartered in Mississippi, and the Bible Protestant Church (now known as the Fellowship of Fundamental Bible Churches) centered in New Jersey, originated from the merger of the Methodist Protestant Church in 1939.

Besides the schisms growing out of the Methodist Protestant Church, there have been other protests that included rejection of episcopal authority and led to the formation of new church bodies. Most notable was the Congregational Methodist movement in Georgia in the 1880s. More recently, the Southern Methodists and the Evangelical Methodists have followed that pattern. The Holiness movement (generally regarded as the only doctrinal schism in Methodism) can also be regarded as a polity schism caused by the inability of the bishops and district superintendents to control the numerous Holiness associations that had emerged to focus Holiness doctrinal concerns. In fact, most Holiness churches adopted a nonepiscopal form of government. The Holiness churches are discussed in chapter 8.

METHODISM IN BRITISH AMERICA. Methodism developed in Canada and the West Indies quite apart from its development in the United States. The first Methodist work in Canada began in 1765 under the direction of Lawrence Coughlan (d. 1785), an Irishman. However, Coughlan was ordained as an Anglican priest in 1867 and took his work in the Church of England in Canada with him. A more permanent Methodist presence occurred in 1772 when a group of settlers from Yorkshire in southwest Great Britain found their way to Nova Scotia. Among them were some Methodists, and among the Methodists was William Black (1760–1834). Converted in 1779, he began almost immediately to preach in the scattered settlements, especially spurred by the anti-Methodist remarks of Newlight (later Baptist) preacher, Henry Alline (1748–1784). Black sought assistance from England, and John Wesley placed him in contact with the Methodists in the American colonies.

As the arrival of numerous Loyalists in Nova Scotia swelled Black's responsibilities, he finally journeyed to the United States in 1783 to seek help from the Methodist Episcopal Church. The work developed quickly, and as it grew he was appointed presiding elder for the Nova Scotia District. The relationship with the American church continued until 1800, when it was shifted to the British Wesleyan

Methodist Denominational Tree

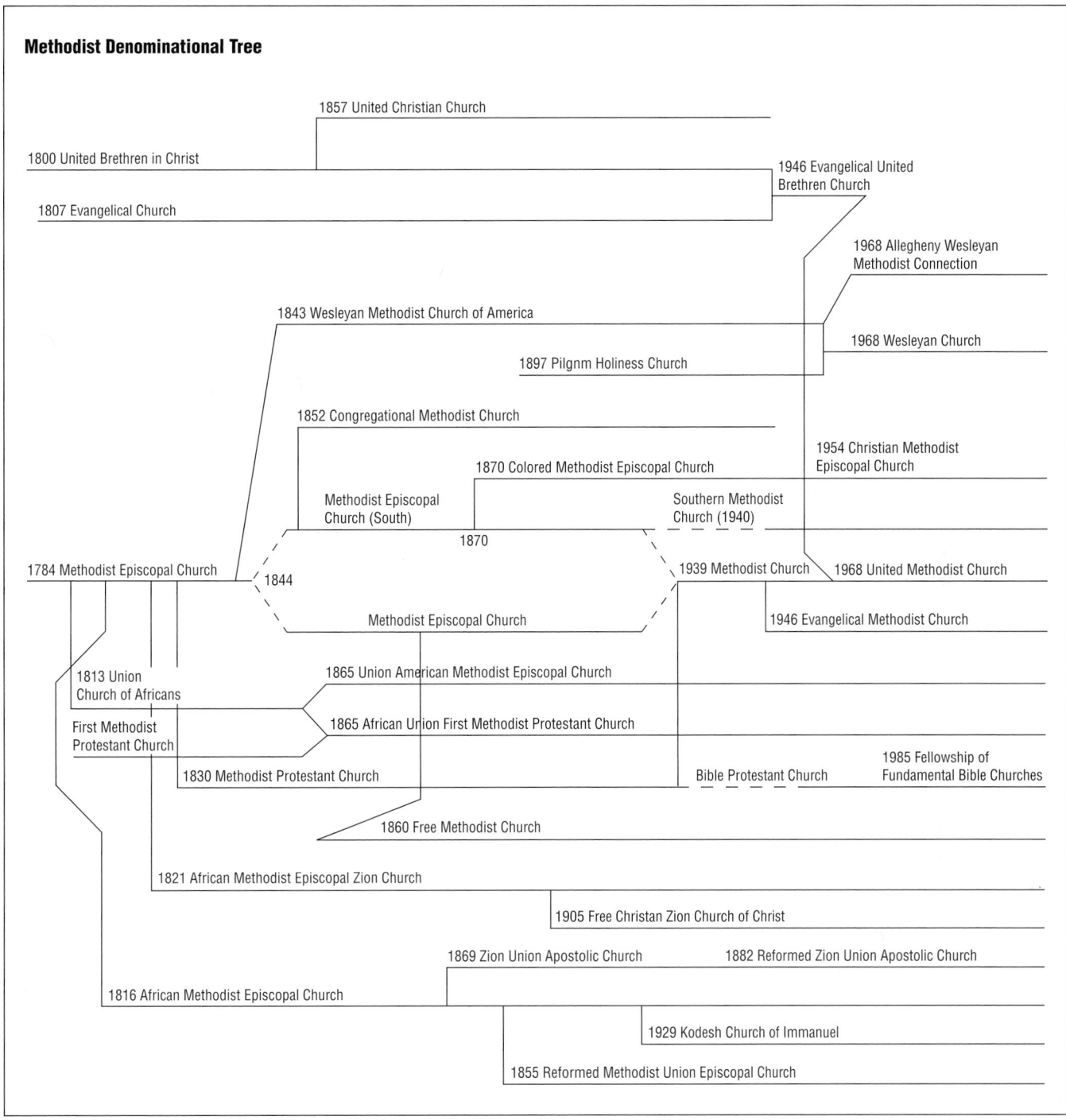

1857 United Christian Church

1800 United Brethren in Christ

1946 Evangelical United Brethren Church

1807 Evangelical Church

1968 Allegheny Wesleyan Methodist Connection

1843 Wesleyan Methodist Church of America

1968 Wesleyan Church

1897 Pilgnm Holiness Church

1852 Congregational Methodist Church

1954 Christian Methodist Episcopal Church

1870 Colored Methodist Episcopal Church

Methodist Episcopal Church (South)

Southern Methodist Church (1940)

1870

1784 Methodist Episcopal Church

1844

1939 Methodist Church   1968 United Methodist Church

Methodist Episcopal Church

1946 Evangelical Methodist Church

1813 Union Church of Africans

1865 Union American Methodist Episcopal Church

First Methodist Protestant Church

1865 African Union First Methodist Protestant Church

1985 Fellowship of Fundamental Bible Churches

1830 Methodist Protestant Church

Bible Protestant Church

1860 Free Methodist Church

1821 African Methodist Episcopal Zion Church

1905 Free Christan Zion Church of Christ

1869 Zion Union Apostolic Church   1882 Reformed Zion Union Apostolic Church

1816 African Methodist Episcopal Church

1929 Kodesh Church of Immanuel

1855 Reformed Methodist Union Episcopal Church

Adapted from Association of Religion Data Archives

Conference, by which time it had spread through the Maritime Provinces.

As the work was spreading through the Maritime Provinces, a second thrust into Canada developed when William Losee (1757–1832) was sent by Bishop Francis Asbury to check on the Methodists among the Loyalists (people who moved to Canada during and after the American Revolution) who had settled in the neighborhood of Kingston, Ontario. The new mission was initially placed under the care of the New York Conference, but the need to

separate it from American control became evident, especially following the War of 1812. Unfortunately, a misunderstanding occurred in early negotiations with the British Wesleyans that prevented their being allowed to assume responsibility for the Ontario congregations, as they had in Nova Scotia. Thus, in 1824 the Canadian work was set apart as the independent Methodist Episcopal Church in Canada.

Still a third beginning for Methodism in Canada followed the formation of a Wesleyan Methodist mission in western Canada in 1840 when James Evans (1801–1846) was appointed as a missionary in Rupert's Land (Manitoba). From his settlement at Norway House, north of present-day Winnipeg, he began a mission to the Indians, which led to his development of a new script for use with the Indian languages. His accomplishments opened the west to a vital Methodist presence.

During the nineteenth century, a variety of forms of Methodism, representatives of the different British splinter groups, entered Canada. Prior to 1884, the Canadian Methodists went through a process of merger that brought almost all of them into a single body, the Methodist Church, Canada. That body merged into the United Church of Canada in 1925 and now continues as a constituent part of that church (discussed in chapter 6).

Methodism in the West Indies started with the return of Nathaniel Gilbert his plantation on Antigua in 1760. During his just-completed trip to England, he had encountered John Wesley and been converted. He organized a class of more than 200, mostly African slaves who lived on the plantation, and it is from this class that Methodism spread throughout the islands. Work in the islands was given a significant boost by the visits of Thomas Coke, Wesley's assistant, beginning in the winter of 1786 to 1787, and was picked up by the Wesleyan Methodist Missionary Society (in England) after Coke's death in 1814. The work became independent as the autonomous Methodist Church in the Caribbean and the Americas in 1967.

At the beginning of the twentieth century, West Indian Methodists migrated to the United States. Rather than affiliate with any of the Methodist churches they found, all of which had an episcopal polity, they organized to carry on the work much as they had been accustomed to on the island. Thus, the United Wesleyan Methodist Church of America came into existence. In more recent years, the United Methodist Church has developed a close working relationship with the West Indian Methodist Conference and has accepted some oversight of the United Wesleyans in the United States.

UNITED METHODISM. The Methodist tradition in America is presently carried largely by the United Methodist Church. Founded in 1968, it is the successor to the Methodist Episcopal Church, the larger major bodies that broke from it in the nineteenth century, and the several independent German Methodist organizations. At the beginning of the twentieth century, Methodism was initially embodied in eight denominational organizations. In 1939, three of these—the Methodist Episcopal Church, the Methodist Episcopal Church, South, and the Methodist Protestant Church—merged to form the Methodist Church. In 1946 the United Brethren in Christ and the Evangelical Association, the two primary German Methodist associations, merged to form the Evangelical United Brethren. The Methodist Church and the Evangelical United Brethren merged in 1968 to form the United Methodist Church. The United Methodist Church is the third largest church in the United States (behind the Roman Catholic Church and the Southern Baptist

Convention) and is home to the majority of people who called themselves Methodists. The largest group of Methodists outside of United Methodism are in the three larger African-American churches.

SOURCES

Historical studies of the Moravian Church in America are focused at the archives of the two American provinces: Northern Province, 214 E. Center St., Nazareth, PA 18064; and Drawer M., Salem Station, Winston-Salem, NC 27108. *The Moravian Historian* (semiannual) comes from the Pennsylvania center.

Methodist studies are focused at the Historical Society of the United Methodist Church, the World Methodist Historical Society, and the General Commission on Archives and History of the United Methodist Church, all of which are located on the campus of Drew University, Box 127, Madison, NJ 07940. The General Commission publishes the quarterly journal *Methodist History*.

Pietism

Brown, Dale W. *Understanding Pietism*. Rev. ed. Nappanee, IN: Evangel, 1996. 125 pp.

Gerdes, Egon W. "Pietism Classical and Modern." *Concordia Theological Journal* (April 1968): 257–268.

Stoeffler, F. Ernest. *German Pietism during the Eighteenth Century*. Leiden, Netherlands: Brill, 1973. 282 pp.

———. *Continental Pietism and Early American Christianity*. Eugene, OR: Wipf & Stock, 2007. 276 pp.

Scandinavian Pietists

Covenant Memories, 1885–1935. Chicago: Covenant Book Concern, 1935. 495 pp.

Norton, H. Wilbert, et al. *The Diamond Jubilee Story of the Evangelical Free Church of America*. Minneapolis, MN: Free Church Publications, 1959. 335 pp.

Olsson, Karl A. *By One Spirit*. Chicago: Covenant Press, 1962. 811 pp.

———. *A Family of Faith*. Chicago: Covenant Press, 1975. 157 pp.

———. *Into One Body—by the Cross*. 2 vols. Chicago: Covenant Press, 1985–1986.

Moravians

Fogleman, Aaron Spencer. *Jesus Is Female: Moravians and the Challenge of Radical Religion in Early America*. Philadelphia: University of Pennsylvania Press, 2007. 358 pp.

Hamilton, J. Taylor, and Kenneth G. Hamilton. *History of the Moravian Church: The Renewed Unitas Fratrum, 1722–1957* (1900). Bethlehem, PA: Interprovincial Board of Christian Education, Moravian Church in America, 1983. 723 pp.

Schattschneider, Allen W. *Through Five Hundred Years: A Popular History of the Moravian Church*. Bethlehem, PA: Comenius Press, 1956. 148 pp. Rev. ed., 1990. 139 pp.

Weinlick, John Rudolf. *Count Zinzendorf*. New York: Abingdon, 1956. 240 pp.

The Wesleyan Tradition

Bishop, John. *Methodist Worship in Relation to Free Church Worship*. London: Epworth Press, 1950. 165 pp.

Bucke, Emory Stevens, ed. *The History of American Methodism*. 3 vols. New York: Abingdon, 1965.

Collins, Kenneth J. *The Theology of John Wesley: Holy Love and the Shape of Grace*. Nashville, TN: Abingdon, 2007. 423 pp.

Davies, Rupert, and Gordon Rupp, eds. *A History of the Methodist Church in Great Britain*. 3 vols. London: Epworth Press, 1965–1983.

Green, Vivian H. H. *John Wesley*. London: Nelson, 1964. 168 pp.

Nagler, Arthur Wilford. *Pietism and Methodism.* Nashville, TN: Publishing House of the M. E. Church, South, 1918. 200 pp.

Oden, Thomas C. *Doctrinal Standards in the Wesleyan Tradition.* Rev. ed. Nashville, TN: Abingdon, 2008. 293 pp.

Rack, Harry D. *Reasonable Enthusiast: John Wesley and the Rise of Methodism.* London: Epworth Press, 1989. 656 pp.

Schmidt, Martin. *John Wesley: A Theological Biography.* 2 vols. New York: Abingdon, 1963–1973.

United Methodism

Albright, Raymond W. *A History of the Evangelical Church.* Harrisburg, PA: Evangelical Press, 1956. 501 pp.

Andersen, Arlow W. *The Salt of the Earth.* Nashville, TN: Norwegian-Danish Methodist Historical Society, 1962. 338 pp.

Davis, Lyman E. *Democratic Methodism in America: A Topical Survey of the Methodist Protestant Church.* New York: Revell, 1921. 267 pp.

Douglass, Paul F. *The Story of German Methodism: Biography of an Immigrant Soul.* New York: Methodist Book Concern, 1939. 361 pp.

Eller, Paul Himmel. *These Evangelical United Brethren.* Dayton, OH: Otterbein Press, 1950. 128 pp.

Godbold, Albea, ed. *Forever Beginning, 1766–1966.* Lake Junaluska, NC: Association of Methodist Historical Societies, 1967. 254 pp.

Harmon, Nolan B. *Encyclopedia of World Methodism.* 2 vols. Nashville, TN: United Methodist Publishing House, 1974. 2814 pp.

———. *Understanding the United Methodist Church.* 2nd ed. Nashville, TN: Abingdon, 1974. 176 pp.

Kinghorn, Kenneth Cain. *The Heritage of American Methodism.* Nashville, TN: Abingdon, 1999. 176 pp.

Norwood, Frederick A., ed. *Sourcebook of American Methodism.* Nashville, TN: Abingdon, 1982. 683 pp.

———. *The Story of American Methodism: A History of the United Methodists and Their Relations.* Nashville, TN: Abingdon, 1974. 448 pp.

Stokes, Mack B. *Major United Methodist Beliefs.* Rev. ed. Nashville, TN: Abingdon, 1971. 128 pp.

Tomkins, Stephen. *John Wesley: A Biography.* Grand Rapids, MI: Eerdmans, 2003. 192 pp.

Tuell, Jack M. *The Organization of the United Methodist Church.* Rev. ed. Nashville, TN: Abingdon, 2005. 174 pp.

Wallenius, C. G., and E. D. Olson. *A Short Story of the Swedish Methodism in America.* Chicago, 1931. 55 pp.

Washburn, Paul. *An Unfinished Church: A Brief History of the Evangelical United Brethren and the Methodist Church.* Nashville, TN: Abingdon, 1984.

Wigger, John H., and Nathan O. Hatch, eds. *Methodism and the Shaping of American Culture.* Nashville, TN: Kingswood, 2001. 400 pp.

Wunderlich, Friedrich. *Methodists Linking Two Continents.* Nashville, TN: Methodist Publishing House, 1960. 143 pp.

Yrigoyen, Charles, Jr., and Susan E. Warrick, eds. *Historical Dictionary of Methodism.* 2nd ed. Metuchen, NJ: Scarecrow Press, 2005. 416 pp.

African-American Methodists

Andrews, Dee E. *The Methodists and Revolutionary America, 1760–1800: The Shaping of an Evangelical Culture.* Princeton, NJ: Princeton University Press, 2000. 367 pp.

Graham, J. H. *Black United Methodists: Retrospect and Prospect.* New York: Vantage Press, 1979. 162 pp.

Gregg, Howard D. *History of the African Methodist Episcopal Church.* Nashville, TN: A.M.E. Church Publishing House, 1980. 523 pp.

Lakey, Othel Hawthorne. *The History of the CME Church.* Rev. ed. Memphis, TN: CME Publishing House, 1996. 956 pp.

Melton, J. Gordon. *A Will to Choose: The Origins of African American Methodism.* Lanham: MD: Rowman & Littlefield, 2007. 315 pp.

Richardson, Harry V. *Dark Salvation: The Story of Methodism as It Developed among Blacks in America.* Garden City, NY: Doubleday, 1976. 324 pp.

Shockley, Grant S., Karen Y Collier, and William B McClain, eds. *Heritage and Hope: The African-American Presence in United Methodism.* Nashville, TN: Abingdon, 1991.

Sommerville, Raymond, Jr. *An Ex-Colored Church: Social Activism in the CME Church 1870–1970.* Macon, GA: Mercer University Press, 2004. 260 pp.

Walls, William J. *The African Methodist Episcopal Zion Church: Reality of the Black Church.* Charlotte, NC: A.M.E. Zion Publishing House, 1974. 669 pp.

❊ Intrafaith Organizations

International Federation of Free Evangelical Churches

c/o Rev Bertil Svensson, IFFEC General Secretary, Mission Covenant Church of Sweden, Box 6302, Stockholm, SE-113 81 Sweden

The International Federation of Free Evangelical Churches is a fellowship of churches that share a common heritage in the pietist Free Church traditions of continental Europe as they emerged in the nineteenth century. These churches have their roots in the eighteenth century, when Protestant congregations that were organizationally unattached to the state churches were formed in Switzerland, France, and Italy. They shared an emphasis on personal faith and accepted the Bible as their only creed. As early as 1834, the Swiss congregations at Berne, Basel, and Zurich attempted to form an organization that would include similar churches in France and northern Italy, but they were met with strong government disapproval.

Finally in 1910, the Swiss congregations came together as the Union of Free Evangelical Churches in Switzerland. Meanwhile, a similar impulse in Sweden gave birth to the Mission Covenant Church, which, due to the steady immigration of members to the United States, developed a branch in North America. Evangelism produced affiliate branches in Denmark and Norway. During the twentieth century the Mission Covenant Church developed a program that included Africa and Latin America. Since World War II, these missions have matured into autonomous churches that retain a close association with their parent body.

Leaders from the various European churches began to meet in the 1920s and in the 1930s were joined by leaders from the United States. Gatherings continued after World War II, and in 1948 led to the formation of the International Federation of Free Evangelical Churches. The federation holds international gatherings at regular intervals, and with the General Assembly every fourth year.

Membership: The federation includes member churches from around the world. Among the North American members are the Evangelical Free Church of America and the Evangelical Covenant Church.

Sources:

International Federation of Free Evangelical Churches. www.iffec.org/.

Bauswein, Jean-Jacques, and Lukas Vischer, eds. *The Reformed Family Worldwide: A Survey of Reformed Churches, Theological Schools, and International Organizations.* Grand Rapids, MI: William B. Eerdmans, 1999.

Persson, Walter. *Free and United: The Story of the International Federation of Free Evangelical Churches.* Chicago: Covenant Publications, 1998.

Westin, Gunar. *The Free Church Through the Ages.* Nashville, TN: Broadman Press, 1958.

World Methodist Council

Box 518, Lake Junaluska, NC 28745

The World Methodist Council links different facets of the movement that originated in the ministry of John Wesley in the eighteenth century. By the 1880s that movement had spread around the world through the missionary endeavors of both

British and American Methodists; a number of distinct churches had arisen primarily because of differences over issues of church governance and reach. The initial efforts to develop a worldwide fellowship among churches of the Wesleyan heritage occurred in 1881 in London at the first Ecumenical Methodist Conference. Thirty Methodist bodies were represented by 400 delegates. Beginning with that initial conference, similar gatherings were held every decade through the middle of the next century. The 1941 conference was delayed until 1947 because of World War II. Then, in 1951, the conference changed its name to World Methodist Council and decided to meet every five years.

Through the years the emphases of the council have changed with the times. Most important, former missionary conferences have grown into autonomous churches, and a number of Methodist bodies have merged into national United Protestant bodies (United Church of Canada, Church of South India, Uniting Church in Australia, United Protestant Church of Belgium). Today, the council endeavors to strengthen international ties, promote understanding, clarify theological and moral standards, and identify priorities for the Methodist movement. It has developed a program that includes support for Methodist education, worldwide evangelism, publishing, and interchange of clergy and laity among churches. The emphasis on evangelism has led to the formation of a World Methodist Council Evangelism Division, which calls on member churches to train people for indigenous evangelism and develop new resources for Christian mission. The World Methodist Evangelism Institute is a joint project of the Evangelism Division and the Candler School of Theology at Emory University in Atlanta, Georgia.

The council is guided by an executive committee that meets biannually. It plans the international conference, which gathers as many as 4,000 people every five years. The council also represents the Wesleyan/Methodist tradition at the annual Conference of Secretaries of Christian World Communions. It has also initiated and responded to overtures for dialogue with sister organizations such as the Lutheran World Federation, the Salvation Army, and the World Alliance of Reformed Churches. Since 1967 it has had regular meetings with the International Joint Committee for Dialogue of the Roman Catholic Church.

Membership: The council reports that it links Methodist churches in 132 countries with a combined membership of over 42 million. Member churches in North America include the African Methodist Episcopal Church, the African Methodist Episcopal Zion Church, the Christian Methodist Episcopal Church, the Free Methodist Church of Canada, the United Church of Canada, the United Methodist Church, the Wesleyan Church, the Church of the Nazarene, and the Methodist Church of Mexico.

Periodicals: *World Parish.* • *Flame.*

Sources:

World Methodist Council. www.worldmethodistcouncil.org/.

Burke, Emory Stevens, ed. *The History of American Methodism*. 3 vols. Nashville, TN: Abingdon Press, 1964.

World Methodist Council: Handbook of Information 2002–2006. Asheville, NC: Biltmore Press, 2002.

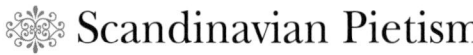

Scandinavian Pietism

Evangelical Covenant Church

5101 N Francisco Ave., Chicago, IL 60625

The Evangelical Covenant Church has its origins in the Pietist movement in the State Lutheran Church of Sweden. The movement, which originated in Germany in the 1600s and spread to Sweden during the 1720s, was legally suppressed in Sweden (from 1726 to 1858) but periodically reemerged. During the early nineteenth century, new forms of revival appeared, encouraged and led by a variety of non-Swedish agents. One of these, George Scott (1804–1874), a Methodist pastor born in Scotland who was brought to Sweden to minister to English industrial workers in Stockholm, influenced Karl Olof Rosenius (1816–1868), a lay preacher; the musician Oskar Ahnfelt (1813–1882); and Anders Wiberg, a Baptist preacher. Rosenius became editor of *Pietisten*, Scott's periodical. He also began to hold conventicles, meetings similar to the English religious societies of the early eighteenth century, and aided the development of a revived hymnody. Under Rosenius's leadership, a national revival swept Sweden and was largely organized with the assistance of the Evangelical National Foundation, the missionary society within the Lutheran Church of Sweden (1856).

Members of the revival movement migrated to America during the mid-nineteenth century. At first, the Swedes joined and attempted to stay within the various Lutheran synods, especially the Augustana Synod (1860). These efforts to unite Swedish immigrants in a Lutheran church failed to attract Baptists, Methodists, and eventually the revivalists known as "Mission Friends" who began to arrive at the close of the Civil War. These Mission Friends began to organize their own congregations after 1868. Two synods were formed, the Swedish Lutheran Mission Synod in 1873 and the Swedish Lutheran Ansgarius Synod in 1884. In 1885 the Swedish Evangelical Mission Covenant Church of America was formed out of the Mission Synod, the Ansgar Synod (which had dissolved in 1884), and several independent congregations. In 1937 the word "Swedish" was dropped; in 1957 the word "Mission" was dropped; and in 1983 the words "of America" were dropped.

According to the preamble of its constitution, "The Evangelical Covenant Church adheres to the affirmations of the Protestant Reformation regarding the Bible. It confesses that the Holy Scripture, the Old and New Testament, is the Word of God and the only perfect rule for faith, doctrine and conduct." Although officially non-creedal, the constitution states that the church "affirms the historic confessions of the Christian Church, particularly the Apostles Creed and the Nicene Creed," which is recited by every ordinand. An important book, *Covenant Affirmations*, by Donald Frisk, was published in 1981 as a means of clarifying the theological heritage and convictions of the Covenant Church. The central affirmations are (1) the centrality of the Word of God; (2) the necessity of the new birth; (3) a commitment to the whole mission of the church; (4) the church as a fellowship of believers; (5) a conscious dependence on the Holy Spirit; and (6) the reality of freedom in Christ. The church originally articulated these affirmations in 1975 and then revised and expanded them in 2006. Although rooted in "classical Christianity," the Covenant Church has resisted the limitations of creedal and confessional stances for the freedom and authority of the Word of God. "Such a confession," states *Covenant Affirmations*, "does not tell us how little Covenanters believe, but how much they believe." The Covenant Church, then, is an "evangelical" church, committed to proclaiming and living the gospel as revealed in the Holy Scriptures. Its freedom is illustrated in its openness to both infant and believer baptism.

The church is organized on a connectional congregational polity, which means that local churches operate autonomously in most matters and that congregations call their own ministers. The Covenant Church holds an annual meeting, and a Covenant Ministerium oversees ordination. There are 10 conferences and one region. An executive board of 26 members oversees activities during the year. A council of administrators includes the executive ministers of each department and the officers of the denomination. The Board of Benevolence oversees two hospitals, five enabling residences caring for adults with developmental disabilities, eleven continuing care retirement campuses and four assisted living communities. Covenant Publications is the publishing arm.

Membership: In 2007 the church reported 121,549 members (120,030 in the United States and 1,519 in Canada), 747 congregations, and 2,052 ministers. Covenant missionaries serve in Argentina, Belgium, Brazil, Burkina Faso, Cameroon, the Central African Republic, Colombia, Congo, the Czech Republic, Ecuador, Equatorial Guinea, France, Guam, Japan, Laos, Mexico, Mongolia, Russia, Spain, Sudan, Sweden, Taiwan, and Thailand, as well as in Central and East Asia. They also partner with sister churches in Chile, Germany, India, Kenya, the Philippines, and South Africa.

Educational Facilities:

North Park University and Theological Seminary, Chicago, Illinois.

Centro Hispano de Estudios Teológicos, Bell Gardens, California.

Periodicals: *The Covenant Companion*. • *The Covenant Home Altar*. • *The Covenant Quarterly*.

Sources:

Evangelical Covenant Church. www.covchurch.org/.

Anderson, Glenn. *Covenant Roots*. Chicago: Covenant Press, 1980.

Anderson, Philip J. *One Body. . . Many Members*. Chicago: Covenant Publications, 1994.

Hawkinson, James R. *Glad Hearts*. Chicago: Covenant Publications, 2003.

Olsson, Karl A. *A Family of Faith*. Chicago: Covenant Press, 1975.

———. *By One Spirit*. Chicago: Covenant Publications, 2002.

———. *Into One Body. . . by the Cross*. 2 vols. Chicago: Covenant Press, 1985–1986.

Evangelical Free Church of America

901 E 78th St., Minneapolis, MN 55420

The Evangelical Free Church of America was formed in 1950 by the merger of two Scandinavian independent Pietistic associations of churches that had grown out of nineteenth-century revivals: the Swedish Evangelical Free Church and the Norwegian-Danish Evangelical Free Church Association. The Swedish Evangelical Free Church came into existence in 1884. It was composed of congregations that preferred an association of autonomous congregations rather than a typical denominational structure. These congregations had strong feelings about maintaining their own autonomy and at the same time desired to sponsor missionary ministry overseas through an association of churches rather than the typical synodic structure. This association was established at a meeting in Boone, Iowa, in 1884. An independent religious periodical, *Chicago-Bladet*, established by John Martenson, was a catalyst for bringing together the 27 representatives at Boone.

The Norwegian-Danish Evangelical Free Church Association was formed by immigrants from Denmark and Norway who had been influenced by the pietistic revivals in their homelands. The ministry of Rev. Fredrick Franson (1852–1908) of Bethlehem Church in Oslo led to the formation of the Mission Covenant Church of Norway, to which some of the immigrants had belonged. In 1889 a periodical, *Evangelisten*, was launched in Chicago, and in 1891 the Western Evangelical Free Church Association was organized. Later that same year an Eastern Association of Churches was formed. A merger of the Eastern and Western groups was made in 1909, with the church taking the name of the Norwegian-Danish Evangelical Free Church Association.

Formed in 1950, the Evangelical Free Church of America adopted a Confession of Faith that stresses the essentials of the Reformation tradition, though the definite influence of evangelicalism is evident. The Bible is declared to be "the inspired Word of God, without error in the original writings." The Second Coming is seen as personal (meaning Jesus will come in person), premillennial (he will come before the millennium to bind Satan, and he will reign for a thousand years with his saints on earth), and imminent. Polity is congregational. There is an annual conference to oversee the cooperative endeavors of the church, including the credentialing of ministers and a ministerial fellowship.

Membership: In 2008 the church reported 1,303 congregations with a total average weekly attendance of 356,364. Internationally, missionary work is carried on in 45 countries. There are a wide variety of domestic ministries.

Periodicals: *EFCA Today*.

Sources:

Evangelical Free Church of America. www.efca.org.

Forstrom, Jim. *A Living Legacy: Evangelical Free Church of America: A Pictorial History*. St. Louis, MO: Bradley, 2002.

Norton, W. Wilbert, et al. *The Diamond Jubilee Story*. Minneapolis: Free Church Publications, 1959.

Olson, Arnold Theodore. *This We Believe*. Minneapolis: Free Church Press, 1961.

———. *Believers Only*. Minneapolis: Free Church Publications, 1964.

Moravian Church in North America

Northern Province, 1021 Center St., PO Box 1245, Bethlehem, PA 18016-1245

The Moravian Church in America dates to the arrival of Bp. August Gottlieb Spangenberg (1704–1792) in Georgia in 1735. Because their pacifism was incompatible with conscription laws, the Moravians chose to leave Georgia. They traveled to Pennsylvania and began work there, centered in the settlements of Nazareth, Bethlehem, and Lititz. Their primary purpose was the evangelization of Native Americans. Efforts were also made, unsuccessfully, to bring together Germans of different denominations in Pennsylvania. The church spread as other Moravian settlements were established.

In 1753 Spangenberg began work in North Carolina, where Moravians founded the town of Bethabara. In 1771 Moravians founded Salem (now Winston-Salem). Salem became the headquarters for the Southern Province. Beginning in the 1850s, congregations were established in the American Midwest and Canadian West among the German and Scandinavian immigrants. Suburban growth after World War II and congregation planting among immigrants from the Caribbean have brought new members in recent decades.

Moravians are considered to have missionary zeal. They were among the first of the Protestant churches to realize that world evangelization was central to the life of the Christian church. Moravians concentrated on people neglected by other Christians. They began work among slaves in the West Indies in 1732, and a main motive in coming to America was to preach to Native Americans.

In order to make American Moravians self-supporting, a plan by Spangenberg called the "Economy" was established. It amounted to a communal system, with Bishop Spangenberg and a board of directors as supervisors. All the church members placed their time, talents, and labor at the church's disposal. In return they were assured of a home, food, and clothing as well as the fellowship of the church. By this means affluent agricultural and industrial centers were established, missionaries supported, and books printed and circulated. The missionaries itinerated throughout the colonies and abroad. The Economy lasted about two decades, although Moravians maintained closed communities in Pennsylvania and North Carolina into the nineteenth century.

Currently the church in the United States and Canada is organized into two provinces, Northern and Southern. The North is divided into four geographical districts. Each province is governed by a provincial elders' conference, which includes laypersons and clergy. Each local church has a council of elders (who handle spiritual affairs) and trustees (who handle temporal affairs). Ministers are called through the agreement of congregational boards and the provincial governing board. Every seven years there is a meeting of the Unity, that is, the representatives of all 19 provinces worldwide.

Doctrinally the Moravians follow the motto "In essentials unity; in nonessentials liberty; in all things love." The church holds to the essentials of Protestant doctrine, which they see to include the Bible as the source of Christian doctrine. Central is "heart religion," a relationship with Jesus Christ. The resultant seeming lack of concern for doctrinal precision has freed the denomination from schism through its five centuries of existence.

The Moravians are distinguished by certain practices that reflect Pietist roots. The love feast, a simple shared meal, became an expression of communal oneness. Moravians follow the pattern of the traditional church year and have developed a simplified liturgy. Infant baptism and Holy Communion (on certain designated feast days) are practiced. While most clergy do not use clerical vestments, a plain white surplice is worn by ministers for communion. The Holy Week services, which include the entire Passion narrative and culminate in the Easter Sunrise Service, are the height of the Christian year. There is considerable diversity in worship. Music, which was an important part of the Pietist renewal, was furthered among the Moravians by Nikolaus Ludwig, graf von Zinzendorf (1799–1760) and James Montgomery (1771–1854), both prolific hymn writers, and expressed itself in numerous compositions of sacred and secular music in the eighteenth and nineteenth centuries.

Half of the American Moravians live in Pennsylvania and North Carolina; the other half are scattered around North America in 15 other states and three provinces. Both the Northern and Southern provinces have active church history and archives programs, among the best of American church bodies. The mission tradition of the Moravian Church as a whole is reflected in the fact that four-fifths of the world's Moravians are in Africa or the Caribbean Basin.

The Moravian Church is a member of both the National Council of Churches and the World Council of Churches. Moravian provinces in the Caribbean are affiliated with the Caribbean Conference of Churches. Alaskan Moravians participate in ecumenical work in Siberia.

Membership: In 1996 the church reported 50,500 members in the United States and 4,000 in Canada. Worldwide membership was 736,000. In 2008 there were 156 congregations in the United States and Canada.

Educational Facilities:

Moravian College and Theological Seminary, Bethlehem, Pennsylvania.

Salem College, Winston-Salem, North Carolina.

Linden Hall, Lititz, Pennsylvania.

Moravian Academy, Bethlehem, Pennsylvania.

Periodicals: *The Moravian*.

Sources:

Moravian Church in North America. www.moravian.org.

Allen, Walser H. *Who Are the Moravians*. Bethlehem, PA: Author, 1966.

Groenfeldt, John S. *Becoming a Member of the Moravian Church*. Winston-Salem, NC: Comenius Press, 1954.

Hamilton, J. Taylor, and Kenneth G. Hamilton. *A History of the Moravian Church: The Unitas Fratrum, 1722–1957*. Bethlehem, PA: Interprovincial Board of Christian Education/Moravian Church in America, 1957.

Schattschneider, Allen W. *Through Five Hundred Years*, 4th ed. Bethlehem, PA: Comenius Press, 1996.

Weinlick, John R. *The Moravian Church through the Ages*. Rev. ed. Bethlehem, PA/Winston-Salem, NC: Moravian Church in America, 1996.

Unity of the Brethren

c/o Marvin Chlapek, 1612 S 43rd St., Temple, TX 76504

While many Moravians fled to Saxony following persecutions in the eighteenth century, some remained behind in Moravia and Bohemia. In the mid-nineteenth century some of these Brethren migrated to Texas. There, under the leadership of the Rev. A. Chumsky and H. Juren, they organized the Evangelical Union of Bohemian and Moravian Brethren in North America. A mutual aid society was organized in 1905, and the Hus Memorial School, for training church school teachers, was established in 1914. In 1924 the Hus Memorial Home was founded in Temple, Texas. An independent group, organized by A. Motycha, joined the Evangelical Union in 1919, and the name Evangelical Unity of Bohemian and Moravian Brethren in North America (later shortened to Unity of the Brethren) was adopted.

Doctrinally the Unity uses the 1608 Moravian Catechism and the Confessions of the Lutheran and Reformed Churches. It emphasizes the Protestant consensus of theological belief. It practices infant baptism and open communion with all

Christians; its ministers are seminary trained. Government is presbyterian, with power invested in a biennial synod of ministers and church delegates. The synod meets in July. Ministers are called by the congregations.

Membership: In 1998 Unity of the Brethren reported 27 churches with 3,218 members served by 39 clergy. There is a missionary family in Honduras and one in Mexico.

Periodicals: *Brethren Journal*. Available from 6703 FM 2502, Brenham, TX 77833-9803.

Sources:

Unity of the Brethren. www.unityofthebrethren.org.

Association of Religious Data Archives. www.thearda.com/Denoms/D_1331.asp.

United Methodism

United Methodist Church

No central headquarters. For information: United Methodist Communications, 810 12th Ave. S, Nashville, TN 37203

The United Methodist Church, the third largest religious body in the United States, was formed in 1968 by the merger of the Methodist Church and the Evangelical United Brethren Church. Both churches were the products of previous mergers. The Methodist Church had been formed in 1939 by the merger of the Methodist Episcopal Church, the Methodist Episcopal Church, South, and the Methodist Protestant Church. The Evangelical United Brethren Church was the result of the merger of the United Brethren in Christ Church and the Evangelical Church in 1946.

HISTORY. The roots of the renewal movement that culminated in the formation of the United Methodist Church can be traced to the work of John Wesley (1703–1791) and his brother Charles Wesley (1707–1788), Anglican ministers in eighteenth-century Great Britain. The movement they launched was brought to to the American colonies in the 1760s by immigrants from England and Ireland and spread through the work of unordained lay preachers, whose efforts were augmented in 1769 when John Wesley sent authorized preachers from England. Formal organization of the Methodist Episcopal Church occurred at the Christmas Conference in Baltimore in 1784.

The United Brethren in Christ Church resulted from the work of Philip Otterbein (1726–1813), a German Reformed pastor, along with Martin Boehm (1725–1812), a Mennonite. Otterbein and Boehm initiated evangelistic work among German immigrants in Pennsylvania. The success of their efforts prompted a first conference in 1789 of preachers who had associated with them. These meetings were regularized in 1800, and the ministers selected Otterbein and Boehm as their superintendents. The Methodists and the Brethren had close associations, symbolized most visibly in Otterbein's participation in the consecration of Francis Asbury (1745–1816) as the first bishop of the fledgling Methodist Episcopal Church.

A second German-speaking group developed simultaneously through the work of Jacob Albright (1759–1808), a Lutheran working in Pennsylvania. The movement that gathered around his preaching became more formally organized as a conference in 1803 and eventually evolved into the Evangelical Association. The Evangelical Church was formed in 1922 through a reunion of the Evangelical Association and a group of churches that had left the Association in 1894.

In the formative years of the Methodist Episcopal Church, debates arose over church government and practice. In 1792 James O'Kelly (1735–1826) challenged the power of the bishop to appoint pastors to their place of service, and he along with some followers left to form the Republican Methodist Church (which eventually became a constituent part of what is now the United Church of Christ). O'Kelly wanted preachers to be able to appeal the appointment to the conference. A larger disruption prompted the formation of the Methodist Protestant Church in 1830, following a decade of dissent led by Asa Shinn (1781–1853), Dennis Dorsey, and

Nicholas Snethen (1769–1845). These reformers sought the seating of laypersons as full participants in the sessions of annual conferences, the elimination of bishops, and the election of presiding elders (regional leaders who supervised clergy and churches). In 1843 abolitionists created the Wesleyan Methodist Church in protest of the unwillingness of the Methodist Episcopal Church to vigorously oppose slavery.

Disagreement over slavery and a constitutional question about the power of the General Conference to discipline the bishops led in 1844 to the largest schism of the denomination. The General Conference approved a Plan of Separation that resulted in the formation of two denominations: the Methodist Episcopal Church (the remaining northern branch) and the Methodist Episcopal Church, South. Debate was long and heated, and feelings of hurt and betrayal lasted generations—it wasn't until 1939 that the division was healed.

The place of women in the antecedent denominations of the United Methodist Church has been paradoxical. Women such as Barbara Heck (1734–1804) were among the founders of both American and Canadian Methodism, and women have always constituted more than 50 percent of the church's membership. John Wesley had granted several women authorization to preach, and licenses to preach in the Methodist Episcopal Church were granted to a few women as early as 1869, but the practice was stopped in 1880 by the General Conference, which also refused to seat the first women elected as lay delegates to that highest of legislative church structures. Much of women's work in the late nineteenth-century church was through the mission organizations that women organized, governed, funded, and served. Although laity rights in the governing structures were granted to men, they were denied to women until early in the twentieth century. In 1924 the Methodist Episcopal Church granted women the right to be ordained but withheld the usual parallel privilege of membership in the annual conference. This level of equality came only with the granting of full clergy rights to women in the Methodist Church in 1956. In 1972 the General Conference made another move to empower women by mandating that at least one third of all policy-making organizations within the church have at least one third of their membership filled by women.

African Americans have played a significant role in the Methodist movement from its beginning in America. They were members of the first classes and societies (congregations). It is likely that the unordained preacher Harry Hosier (d. 1806) attended the organizing conference in 1784. His contemporary Richard Allen (1760–1831) was the first African-American preacher to be ordained. The church's initial strong stand against slavery gradually eroded during the antebellum era, and as a result, several predominantly African-American churches were formed, beginning in 1813 with the African Union Church. Subsequently the African Methodist Episcopal Church based in Philadelphia was formed in 1816 and the African Methodist Episcopal Zion Church based in New York City a few years later. After the Civil War the Methodist Episcopal Church founded colleges and other educational institutions for freed slaves through the Freedman's Aid Society. Most of the remaining African-American members of the Methodist Episcopal Church, South formed what became the Christian Methodist Episcopal Church in 1870. Although Methodism included persons of different ethnic-racial groups and different languages, a tragic legacy of the 1939 merger was the creation of the Central Jurisdiction, a racially segregated structure for annual conferences of African-American churches. This separate structure was eliminated in 1968.

In the late nineteenth and early twentieth centuries American Protestantism gave rise to the Holiness movement, which was founded on John Wesley's doctrine of Christian perfection or sanctification that results in a lifestyle of righteous behavior. Holiness advocates taught that people could be perfected in love through a "second blessing," or work of the Holy Spirit. The growth of the Holiness movement and its offshoot, the Pentecostal movement, resulted in two new church groups: the Holiness churches and the Pentecostal churches.

During the twentieth century Methodists actively participated in the ecumenical movement, seeking to make more visible the unity of the church. British and American Methodists met first in 1881 at the Ecumenical Methodist Conference. Subsequent ecumenical conferences led to the formation of the World Methodist Council. Methodist are known for the leadership they have given to the ecumenical movement. The United Methodist Church's antecedent churches were charter members of the Federal Council of Churches, the National Council of Churches of Christ in the U.S.A., and the World Council of Churches.

BELIEFS. The *Book of Discipline* states: "United Methodists share a common heritage with Christians of every age and nation" (2004, p. 41). Along with basic Christian affirmations, Methodists have placed great emphasis upon piety, religious experience, and works of mercy. The documents that serve as doctrinal standards are: the Articles of Religion, the Confession of Faith, the Standard Sermons, and the Explanatory Notes on the New Testament by John Wesley. Methodists are encouraged to engage in theological reflection with reasonable individual freedom, bearing in mind these doctrinal affirmations. Wesley wrote, "Except for those doctrines that strike at the root of Christianity, we think and let think." Methodist practice is shaped by the General Rules of the United Societies, as they were called by Wesley, and the Social Creed, first adopted by the Methodist Episcopal Church in 1908 and now enlarged as the Social Principles, a major statement on political, economic, and social issues.

The United Methodist Church recognizes two sacraments. Baptism is available to persons of all ages, including infants, and can be administered by various modes, though usually by sprinkling. Communion is open to all Christians. Through the receiving of bread and grape juice it remembers the supper Jesus shared with his disciples before being crucified, and it offers an experience of grace through the faith of the communicant.

ORGANIZATION. The United Methodist Church is governed by the General Conference, a representative body of an equal number of lay and clergy delegates that meets once every four years. This body sets the policy and direction of the church and makes revisions to the *Book of Discipline*, the book of church law with sections on the history, theology, and social teachings of the church. Various boards and agencies implement programs established by the General Conference and carry out other administrative functions. One such entity is the United Methodist Publishing House, a major supplier of religious literature and merchandise through Abingdon Press and its retail arm, Cokesbury.

In addition to the General Conference there are annual conferences, geographical organizations of varying size that are made up of all the churches within their regions. Their presiding officers are bishops. They provide for programs and supervision of churches for their regions, and their bishops, with the assistance of district superintendents, are empowered to appoint the pastors to the churches that are within the bounds of the conferences. The annual sessions of the conferences are made up of equal numbers of clergy and laity.

In the United States, conferences are organized into five geographical regions known as jurisdictions for the main purpose of electing bishops for their regions once every four years. The jurisdictional conference also assigns the bishops to their places of service. Outside the United States, annual conferences are organized into central conferences that function in similar ways to the jurisdictional conferences.

The United Methodist Church has members in the United States, Europe, Africa, and the Philippines. There are also Methodist churches throughout Central and South America, Japan, Korea, and India that are the offspring of the missionary movement but are independent from the United Methodist Church in governance and organization. Primary responsibility for world missions is placed with the General Board of Global Ministries, but all parts of the church participate in the global realities of the denomination. The United Methodist Committee on Relief (UMCOR) has gained international recognition for its ability to respond to emergencies and natural disasters with assistance that is both immediate and long term.

Membership: In 1996 the church reported a membership of 7,931,733 in the United States. It had 34,398 churches and 45,108 ministers. The United Methodist Church had a mission presence in 125 countries, and mission personnel are deployed in 63 countries. The mission presence might be, for example, a clinic, a hospital, an orphanage, microenterprises that stimulate economies, or new congregations.

Educational Facilities:

Theological Seminaries:

Boston School of Theology, Boston, Massachusetts.

Candler School of Theology, Atlanta, Georgia.

Claremont School of Theology, Claremont, California.

Drew University, The Theological School, Madison, New Jersey.

Duke University, The Divinity School, Durham, North Carolina.

Gammon Theological Seminary, Atlanta, Georgia.

Garrett-Evangelical Theological Seminary, Evanston, Illinois.

Iliff School of Theology, Denver, Colorado.

The Methodist Theological School of Ohio, Delaware, Ohio.

Perkins School of Theology, Dallas, Texas.

Saint Paul School of Theology, Kansas City, Missouri.

United Theological Seminary, Dayton, Ohio.

Wesley Theological Seminary, Washington, D.C.

Predominantly Black Colleges:

Bennett College, Greensboro, North Carolina.

Bethune-Cookman College, Daytona Beach, Florida.

Claflin University, Orangeburg, South Carolina.

Clark Atlanta University, Atlanta, Georgia.

Dillard University, New Orleans, Louisiana.

Huston-Tillotson University, Austin, Texas.

Meharry Medical College, Nashville, Tennessee.

Paine College, Augusta, Georgia.

Philander Smith College, Little Rock, Arkansas.

Rust College, Holly Springs, Mississippi.

Wiley College, Marshall, Texas.

Colleges and Universities:

Adrian College, Adrian, Michigan.

Alaska Pacific University, Anchorage, Alaska.

Albion College, Albion, Michigan (no longer affiliated).

Albright College, Reading, Pennsylvania.

Allegheny College, Meadville, Pennsylvania.

American University, Washington, D.C.

Baker University, Baldwin City, Kansas.

Baldwin-Wallace College, Berea, Ohio.

Birmingham-Southern College, Birmingham, Alabama.

Boston University, Boston, Massachusetts.

Brevard College, Brevard, North Carolina.

Centenary College, Hackettstown, New Jersey.

Centenary College of Louisiana, Shreveport, Louisiana.

Central Methodist College, Fayette, Missouri.

Columbia College, Columbia, South Carolina.

Cornell College, Mount Vernon, Iowa.

Dakota Wesleyan University, Mitchell, South Dakota.

DePauw University, Greencastle, Indiana.

Dickinson College, Carlisle, Pennsylvania.

Drew University, Madison, New Jersey.

Duke University, Durham, North Carolina.

Emory and Henry College, Emory, Virginia.

Emory University, Atlanta, Georgia.

Ferrum College, Ferrum, Virginia.

Florida Southern College, Lakeland, Florida.

Green Mountain College, Poultney, Vermont.

Greensboro College, Greensboro, North Carolina.

Hamline University, St. Paul, Minnesota.

Hendrix College, Conway, Arkansas.

High Point University, High Point, North Carolina.

Huntingdon College, Montgomery, Alabama.

Illinois Wesleyan University, Bloomington, Illinois.

Iowa Wesleyan College, Mount Pleasant, Iowa.

Kansas Wesleyan University, Salina, Kansas.

Kendall College, Chicago, Illinois.

Kentucky Wesleyan College, Owensboro, Kentucky.

LaGrange College, LaGrange, Georgia.

Lambuth University, Jackson, Tennessee.

Lebanon Valley College, Annville, Pennsylvania.

Lindsey Wilson College, Columbia, Kentucky.

Lycoming College, Williamsport, Pennsylvania.

MacMurray College, Jacksonville, Illinois.

McKendree College, Lebanon, Illinois.

MacMurray College, Jacksonville, Illinois.

Martin Methodist College, Pulaski, Tennessee.

McKendree University, Lebanon, Illinois.

McMurry University, Abilene, Texas.

Methodist University, Fayetteville, North Carolina.

Millsaps College, Jackson, Mississippi.

Morningside College, Sioux City, Iowa.

Mount Union College, Alliance, Ohio.

Nebraska Methodist College, Omaha, Nebraska.

Nebraska Wesleyan University, Lincoln, Nebraska.

North Carolina Wesleyan College, Rocky Mount, North Carolina.

North Central College, Naperville, Illinois.

Ohio Northern University, Ada, Ohio.

Ohio Wesleyan University, Delaware, Ohio.

Oklahoma City University, Oklahoma City, Oklahoma.

Otterbein College, Westerville, Ohio.

Pfeiffer University, Misenheimer, North Carolina.

Randolph College, Lynchburg, Virginia.

Randolph-Macon College, Ashland, Virginia.

Reinhardt College, Waleska, Georgia.

Rocky Mountain College, Billings, Montana.

Shenandoah University, Winchester, Virginia.

Simpson College, Indianola, Iowa.

Southern Methodist University, Dallas, Texas.

Southwestern College, Winfield, Kansas.

Southwestern University, Georgetown, Texas.

Syracuse University, Syracuse, New York.

Tennessee Wesleyan College, Athens, Tennessee.

Texas Wesleyan College, Fort Worth, Texas.

Union College, Barbourville, Kentucky.

University of Denver, Denver, Colorado.

University of Evansville, Evansville, Indiana.

University of Indianapolis, Indianapolis, Indiana.

University of Puget Sound, Tacoma, Washington.

University of the Pacific, Stockton, California.

Virginia Wesleyan College, Norfolk, Virginia.

Wesley College, Dover, Delaware.

Wesleyan College, Macon, Georgia.

West Virginia Wesleyan College, Buckhannon, West Virginia.

Willamette University, Salem, Oregon.

Wofford College, Spartansburg, South Carolina.

Two-Year Colleges:

Andrew College, Cuthbert, Georgia.

Hiwassee College, Madisonville, Tennessee.

Lon Morris College, Jacksonville, Texas.

Louisburg College, Louisburg, North Carolina.

Spartanburg Methodist College, Spartanburg, South Carolina.

Young Harris College, Young Harris, Georgia.

Periodicals: *Circuit Rider.* • *el Intérprete.* • *Interpreter.* • *New World Outlook.* • *Response.* • *The Upper Room.*

Sources:

United Methodist Church. www.umc.org/.

The Book of Discipline. Nashville, TN: United Methodist Publishing House, 2004.

Frank, Thomas Edward. *Polity, Practice, and the Mission of the United Methodist Church.* Nashville, TN: Abingdon Press, 2006.

Jones, Scott J. *United Methodist Doctrine: The Extreme Center.* Nashville, TN: Abingdon Press, 2002.

McEllhenney, John G., ed. *United Methodism in America: A Compact History.* Nashville, TN: Abingdon Press, 1992.

Richey, Russell E., Kenneth E. Rowe, and Jean Miller Schmidt. *The Methodist Experience in America: A Sourcebook.* Nashville, TN: Abingdon Press, 2000.

Tuell, Jack M. *The Organization of the United Methodist Church, 2005–2008 Edition.* Nashville, TN: Abingdon Press, 2005.

Yrigoyen, Charles, Jr., and Susan E. Warrick, eds. *Historical Dictionary of Methodism.* 2nd ed. Lanham, MD: Scarecrow Press, 2005.

❀ Non-Episcopal Methodism

Apostolic Methodist Church

Current address not obtained for this edition.

The Apostolic Methodist Church was organized in 1932 in Loughman, Florida, by E. H. Crowson and a few others. In 1931 the Reverend Crowson, an elder in the Florida Conference of the Methodist Episcopal Church, South, had been located (deposed from the itinerant ministry) for "unacceptability." The new group published a Discipline in which they complained about episcopal authority and the departure of the Methodist Episcopal Church, South, from its standards of belief and holiness. The Apostolic Methodists believe in the premillennial return of Jesus, his return to earth to bind Satan before his thousand-year reign on earth with his saints. The church emphasizes holiness of a "second blessing" type: after being justified or saved, a person can proceed to be perfected in love and have that ratified by a personal religious experience called the "second blessing." In 1933 F. L. Crowson, the father of E. H. Crowson, was tried by the Florida Conference and sus-

pended. He withdrew and joined his son's new group. The church operates the Gospel Tract Club at Zephyrhills, Florida.

Membership: At its peak in the 1960s, the church had only a few congregations and fewer than 100 members.

Asbury Bible Churches

PO Box 1021, Dublin, GA 31021

The Asbury Bible Church parallels the John Wesley Fellowship in most ways but is organizationally separate. Like the John Wesley Fellowship, the Asbury Bible Churches were organized in 1971 by former members of the Southern Methodist Church who withdrew when that church dropped its membership in the American Council of Christian Churches. They follow the same conservative interpretation of Wesleyan doctrine and loose congregational polity and draw on the Francis Asbury Society of Ministers for their pastors. The churches are also members of the American Council of Christian Churches.

Membership: Not reported.

Association of Independent Methodists

405 Marquis St., Jackson, MS 39206

The Association of Independent Methodists (AIM) was organized in 1965 in Jackson, Mississippi, by former members of the Methodist Church (1939–1968), which, in 1968, merged into the United Methodist Church. The organization rejected the Methodist Church's episcopal polity, the doctrinal liberalism felt to exist in the ecumenical movement of which the Methodist Church was a major supporter, and the neo-evangelicalism in the Sunday school literature, clergy, and church-supported colleges and seminaries.

Doctrinally, the church accepts the Twenty-five Articles of Religion of John Wesley common to all Methodists. However, a statement on sanctification and additional articles on the duties of the Christian to the civil authority and the separation of church and state have been added.

AIM is a voluntary network of independent Methodist churches, each of which owns and controls its own property and appoints its own pastor. Polity is congregational. At each annual meeting, delegates from member churches elect the association's officers, including a president, secretary, treasurer, and executive director. They serve with standing committee chairs as an executive committee. The executive committee and representatives from each church constitute a board of directors, which meets semi-annually.

One of AIM's projects, in partnership with other groups, is to establish a national church with national leadership in Belize. AIM also uses World Gospel Mission as a missionary serving agency and works with the Mission Board of the Congregational Methodist Church and The Methodist Protestant Church. AIM operates a Hope House Ministry for children and youth of Pascagoula and surrounding areas of Jackson County in Mississippi.

Membership: In 2002 the association reported more than 3,500 members in 44 congregations, with 60 ministers licensed or ordained by the association. Congregations are located in Mississippi, Alabama, Florida, Georgia, Tennessee, and Virginia, as well as five sister churches in Northern Ireland.

Educational Facilities:

Wesley Biblical Seminary, Jackson, Mississippi.

Wesley College, Florence, Mississippi.

Periodicals: *AIM Newsletter.*

Remarks: AIM was established at a time when the Methodist Church was beginning the process of eliminating the racially segregated Central Jurisdiction and the South was experiencing the height of the civil rights movement. An article was added to the original articles of religion of AIM supporting the social separation of the races as "neither anti-Christian nor discriminatory." In 1984 that article was deleted. The vast majority of AIM's members did not endorse this view.

Sources:

Association of Independent Methodists. www.aim2020.com.

Association of Independent Methodists: The First Twenty Five Years 1965–1990. Marceline, MO: Walsworth Press, 1991.

Constitution of Churches Organized as Independent Methodist Churches by the Association of Independent Methodists. Jackson, MS: Association of Independent Methodists, n.d.

Howard, Ivan J. *What Independent Methodists Believe.* Jackson, MS: Association of Independent Methodists, n.d.

Church of Daniel's Band

4832 S Bard Rd., Beaverton, MI 48612

The Church of Daniel's Band was formed in 1893 in Marine City, Michigan, as an effort to revive primitive Methodism and continue the class meeting, the regular meeting of small classes for discussion, exhortation, Bible study, prayer, confession, and forgiveness. The doctrine and polity are Methodist with a strong emphasis on evangelism, perfectionism, Christian fellowship, religious liberty, and abstinence from worldly excess. Several articles of faith have been added to the standard twenty-five, emphasizing belief in the resurrection and judgment of the dead, divine healing, and the laying on of hands for the gift of the Holy Spirit.

Membership: In 1988 the church reported four churches, approximately 217 members, and eight ministers.

Sources:

The Doctrine and Discipline of the Church of Daniel's Band. N.p., 1981.

Congregational Methodist Church

c/o Dr. Phillip Knight, CMC President, Box 9, Florence, MS 39073

The Congregational Methodist Church was formed by a group of lay people led by local preachers who withdrew from the Georgia Conference of the Methodist Episcopal Church, South. The group met in the home of Mickleberry Merrit on May 8, 1852, and organized. William Farbough was elected chairman, and Rev. Hiram Pinazee was appointed to draw up a *Discipline*, which was approved and published soon afterward. This newly organized group had three main points of contention with the Methodist Episcopal Church, South: the itinerant system, as then practiced, which was plagued with large circuits and weekday preaching to empty pews; the church's neglect of the local preachers who did most of the work with the congregations and received no credit; and the government of the Methodist Episcopal Church, South, which deprived laymen of a voice in church business.

On August 12, 1852, a conference was convened. Except for local church conferences, this conference was the first Methodist conference composed of more laymen than ministers, and the first body of Methodists whose total representation was by election of the local congregations. This difference in government remains one of the distinctive features of the Congregational Methodist Church. Local churches call their own pastors, own their own property, elect delegates each year to the annual conferences, and every two years to the general conference.

The Congregational Methodist Church is conservative in its theology, maintaining the doctrines as espoused by John Wesley. Its Articles of Religion are those Wesley presented for his Methodist Church in America. It was not until 1941—and for the purpose of emphasis and clarification, and to show its conservative stance amid the growing trend of liberalism—that articles on regeneration and sanctification were added. In 1957, articles on tithing, eternal retribution, and the resurrection of the dead were added for the same reasons. Congregational Methodists believe in a literal heaven and hell and in the premillennial Second Coming of Christ.

Several schisms have occurred within the church. In the late 1880s, when it was estimated that the church had grown to nearly 20,000 members, a move for a merger with other similar church groups resulted in the loss of an estimated two-thirds of the churches. While most of these churches merged with other groups, some of the churches formed the New Congregational Methodist Church of the U.S.A. In 1982 a group of churches withdrew, opposing the realignment of conferences, and formed the Southern Congregational Methodist Church. Some of those churches have since returned to the Congregational Methodist Church.

In 1945 a bible school was begun in Dallas, Texas, and eight years later moved to the campus of the old Westminster College at Tehuacana, Texas, and renamed Westminster College and Bible Institute. In 1972 it was moved to Florence, Mississippi, the headquarters of the denomination, and renamed Wesley College in honor of Methodism's founder. Wesley College is accredited as a four-year college offering both a two-year transferable general education certificate and a bachelor's degree for those preparing for the ministry.

The Congregational Methodist Church has missionaries in Mexico, Belize, Bolivia, and Japan. It also supports several home missions. It produces a radio broadcast, as well: The Wesleyan Voice, local station 92.5 on American Family Radio.

Membership: In 2006 the church reported 12,019 members, 163 congregations, and 348 clergy/ministers.

Educational Facilities:

Wesley College, Florence, Mississippi.

Periodicals: *Congregational Methodist Messenger.* • *The Mission Update.*

Sources:

Congregational Methodist Church. www.congregationalmethodist.net.

Book of Discipline. Congregational Methodist Church, 1852.

McDaniel, S. C. *The Origin and Early History of the Congregational Methodist Church.* Atlanta: Jas. P. Harrison, 1811.

Minutes of the General Conference of the Congregational Methodist Church, 1869–1945. Tehuacana, TX: Westminister College Print Shop, 1960.

Evangelical Methodist Church

PO Box 17070, Indianapolis, IN 46217

The Evangelical Methodist Church was founded by former members of the Methodist Church led by Dr. John Henry Hamblen (1877–1971) of Abilene, Texas. In 1945 Hamblen began serving an independent congregation in Abilene. Calls from other congregations led to the founding of the Evangelical Methodist Church at a Memphis, Tennessee, conference on May 9, 1946. The main cause of dissatisfaction was the "modernism" that had infiltrated the parent body.

At the first Annual Conference at Kansas City, Missouri, in 1946, Hamblen was elected the first general superintendent. E. B. Vargas brought the Mexican Evangelistic Mission into the new church as the first mission district. In subsequent sessions Lucian Smith and Ralph Vanderwood were elected to the office of general superintendent.

The church holds a conservative theological perspective and believes very strongly in the Articles of Religion of the former Methodist Episcopal Church, South, to which it has added an article on "perfect love." In describing themselves, members say, "The Church is fundamental in belief, premillennial regarding the Second Coming, missionary in outlook, evangelistic in endeavor, cooperative in spirit, and Wesleyan in doctrine."

Organizationally the Church is congregational yet connectional. It is congregational in that each congregation owns its own property and calls its own pastor. It is connectional in that all member churches agree to abide by the Discipline of the Evangelical Methodist Church. The denomination, as a whole, is governed by the conference system. The General Conference, presided over by the General Superintendents, is the highest legislative body in the church. It meets every four years and oversees the several district conferences, and the local churches.

The Evangelical Methodist Church has an affiliation with World Gospel Mission and OMS International and has about 50 missionaries serving under their boards in 17 countries. The church is also affiliated with the National Association of Evangelicals, the Christian Holiness Partnership, Evangelical Methodist Church, and World Relief.

Membership: Not reported. In 1997 the church had 8,700 members and 119 churches.

Educational Facilities:

Asbury College, Wilmore, Kentucky.

Asbury Theological Seminary, Wilmore, Kentucky.

George Fox University, Newberg, Oregon.

George Fox Evangelical Seminary, Newberg, Oregon.

Periodicals: The Connection.

Sources:

The Evangelical Methodist Church. www.emchurch.org.

Evangelical Methodist Church of America

PO Box 751, Kingsport, TN 37662

Largest of several fellowships of independent fundamentalist Methodist churches, the Evangelical Methodist Church of America was established in 1952 by dissenting members of the Evangelical Methodist Church. The issues that led to withdrawal centered around a longstanding doctrinal and organizational disagreement between Dr. John Henry Hamblen (1877–1971) and Rev. William Wallace Breckbill (d. 1974). Reverend Breckbill and his followers did not accept the doctrine of holiness proposed by Dr. Hamblen. There was also conflict over membership in the National Association of Evangelicals.

The withdrawing body, led by Breckbill, established an organization similar to that of the parent body. Membership was established in the fundamentalist American Council of Christian Churches and International Council of Christian Churches, and close working relations were set up with the Southern Methodist Church, the Fundamental Methodist Church, and the Methodist Protestant Church, which jointly sponsored Bible Methodist Missions and the International Fellowship of Bible Methodists. Following the withdrawal of the Southern Methodist Church from the American Council of Christian Churches, the Evangelical Methodist Church maintained a close working relationship with other separated groups who remained as members of both the American Council of Christian Churches and the World Council of Bible Believing Churches.

Missions are conducted in Malawi, Argentina, Chile, Jamaica, and Paraguay.

Membership: Not reported.

Educational Facilities:

Breckbill Bible College, Max Meadows, Virginia.

Periodicals: The Evangelical Methodist.

Sources:

Discipline. Altoona, PA: Evangelical Methodist Church, 1962.

Filipino Community Churches

Current address not obtained for this edition.

The Filipino Community Churches of Hawaii began when the Rev. N. C. Dizon, a Methodist minister, went to Hawaii after World War I to establish a mission. In 1927 he withdrew from the Methodist church and formed the First Filipino Community Church at Honolulu. In 1957 a congregation was added at Wahiawa, and a congregation in Hilo is informally associated. Joseph H. Dizon became pastor of the headquarters church in Honolulu. Its membership consists almost entirely of Filipino-Americans.

Membership: Not reported.

First Congregational Methodist Church of the U.S.A.

c/o Kevin Camp, Liberty District Secretary, PO Box 427, Rainsville, AL 35986

The First Congregational Methodist Church of the U.S.A. was formed by members of the Congregational Methodist Church who withdrew from that body in 1941. Disagreement had arisen about the addition in 1933 of Articles of Religion on regeneration and sanctification and paragraphs on the duty of pastors' collecting superannuate funds (for retired ministers), ladies' work, youth work, trials of ministers charged with misconduct, and the prohibition of special sessions of the general conference called to reverse action of a regular session. Following eight years of conflict, Rev. J. A. Cook, then president of the General Conference, led a segment of the church to withdraw immediately after the 1941 General Conference, at which a two-thirds majority approved adding the articles and paragraphs in dispute.

The new body adopted the pre-1933 Discipline and followed essentially the polity and doctrine of the parent body.

The FCM Camp and Conference center is located in Boaz, Alabama, the national headquarters of the FCM Church of the USA. They do mission work in Haiti.

Membership: Not reported. In 2008 there were 67 congregations, all in the South.

Periodicals: *The Watchman*.

Sources:

First Congregational Methodist Church of the USA. fcmchurchusa.org.

Fundamental Methodist Conference

1034 N Broadway, Springfield, MO 65802

The Fundamental Methodist Church, now called the Fundamental Methodist Conference, was formed by former members of the Methodist Protestant Church who withdrew from the Methodist Church (1939–1968) following the union in 1939. The schism began with John's Chapel Church in Missouri on August 27, 1942, under the leadership of Rev. Roy Keith. Two years later, after having been joined by other congregations, they established an organization.

The conference is both congregational and connectional in polity. It is congregational in that the local congregations associate with each other as free and autonomous bodies, and retain the power to hold property and call (appoint) pastors. They are connectional in that their General Conference is the highest legislative body. It is composed of one lay delegate and one minister from each church.

The Fundamental Methodists are fundamentalists theologically. They are members of the American Council of Christian Churches, Bible Methodist Missions, and the International Fellowship of Bible Methodists. They cooperate with other independent fundamentalist Methodist groups in a variety of activities. They are also one of the few Methodist groups to retain the class meeting structure devised by John Wesley, the founder of Methodism. He divided the early societies (congregations) into classes of about 12 members and a class leader. The classes met weekly for mutual discussion, exhortation, prayer, confession and forgiveness, Bible study, and growing in grace. Each person tried to bring to the class a penny a week to help the poor. It is said that some early class leaders supplied the penny for the class member who could not afford to make the contribution.

Membership: In 2001 the conference reported 814 members in 13 congregations, all of which were located in southwestern Missouri.

The church supports a mission in Matamoros, Mexico.

Periodicals: *The Evangelical Methodist*.

Sources:

Keith, Roy, and Carol Willoughby, eds. *History and Discipline of the Faith and Practice*. Springfield, MO: Fundamental Methodist Church, 1964.

John Wesley Fellowship and the Francis Asbury Society of Ministers

Current address not obtained for this edition.

The John Wesley Fellowship and the Francis Asbury Society of Ministers are two structures formed by former ministers and members of the Southern Methodist Church in 1971, following the Southern Methodist Church's withdrawal from the ultra-fundamentalist American Council of Christian Churches. The John Wesley Fellowship is a loose fellowship of independent congregations, and the Francis Asbury Society of Ministers is an association of pastors. While officially two separate organizations, ministers of the Society serve churches of the Fellowship.

The Society has added to the Twenty-five Articles of Religion (printed earlier in this chapter) statements on the Bible as the word of God (an affirmation not specifically made in the original article on the sufficiency of scripture), separation from apostasy, and the premillennial return of Jesus. The Guidelines for Independent Methodist Churches, published by Rev. Thomas L. Baird, serves unofficially as a discipline for the congregations. Beyond the Articles of Religion are seventeen statements that make a significant departure from Wesleyan emphases. The statement on the church defines the invisible church as all who are known of Christ, "Whether they have joined the visible church or not." The premillennial return of Christ, segregation of the races, and the impossibility of back sliders to be reclaimed (based on Hebrew 6:4–6) are all affirmed. The church has only white members.

The Francis Asbury Society began publication of the *Francis Asbury Society Evangel* in 1971. Both the Society and Fellowship cooperate with Bible Methodist Missions organized by the Evangelical Methodist Church of America. Maranatha School of Theology, also sponsored by the Evangelical Methodist Church of America, and Bob Jones University are recommended schools. The Society and Fellowship belong to the American Council of Christian Churches.

Membership: Not reported.

Periodicals: *Francis Asbury Society Bulletin*.

Sources:

Baird, Thomas L., ed. *Guidelines for Independent Methodist Churches*. Colonial Heights, VA: Author, 1971.

Methodist Protestant Church

The Methodist Protestant Church Headquarters, 722 Hwy. 84W, Collins, MS 39428

Ministers and members of the Mississippi Conference of the Methodist Protestant Church who did not wish to join in the 1939 Methodist merger because of the liberalism of the newly formed church, the Methodist Church (1939-1968), formed the continuing Methodist Protestant Church. They emphasize the Bible as the literal word of God, the indwelling of the Holy Spirit subsequent to regeneration (subsequent to being "born again"), and the premillennial return of Jesus Christ. The church's motto is, "Earnestly contend for the faith which was once delivered to the saints."

The church has congregations in Mississippi, Alabama, Arkansas, Louisiana, Oklahoma, and Belize, in four conferences. The General Conference Headquarters and church camp is located at Collins, Mississippi. The church is a member of the American Council of Christian Churches and the International Council of Christian Churches.

The Methodist Protestant Church has affiliated work in Belize, Myanmar, and Korea.

The government is a representative democracy modeled on the United States government. Equal representation is given laymen in all functions of the church. There are no bishops.

Membership: Not reported.

Sources:

Methodist Protestant Church. www.themethodistprotestantchurch.com.

Vernon, Walter N. *Methodism Moves across North Texas*. Dallas: North Texas Conference of the Methodist Church, 1967.

Vernon Walter N., et al. *The Methodist Excitement in Texas*. Dallas: Texas United Methodist Historical Society, 1984.

Missionary Church International

PO Box 1761, Columbia, SC 29202

The Missionary Church International is a fellowship of autonomous churches, ministries, and ministers, most with a Methodist background. The church has prepared itself to charter church and commission ministers, many of the latter previously rejected by other churches because of factors not deemed relevant such as age, number of dependent children, the ages of the children, or limitation of support funding. Many of the churches of a Methodist background retain the name Missionary Methodist Church (not to be confused with the Missionary Methodist Church of America). Your Missionary Outreach is the agency associated with the church that provides support and services for 36 missionaries operating around the world during 2008. As churches affiliate, they may retain former denominational or other names or become known as a Missionary Church International or a Missionary Methodist Church.

Membership: Not reported.

Educational Facilities:

Missionary Church Bible Institute, Shelbyville, Indiana.

Periodicals: *Ministry Connection*.

Sources:

Missionary Church International. www.themissionarychurchinternational.org.

New Congregational Methodist Church

Current address not obtained for this edition.

Not a direct schism but related to the Congregational Methodist Church is the New Congregational Methodist Church. It was formed in 1881 by members of the Waresboro Mission and others involved in a rural church consolidation enforced by the Board of Domestic Missions of the Georgia Conference of the Methodist Episcopal Church, South. In protest of the consolidation, the group withdrew and formed the new body at Waycross, Georgia, using the constitution of the Congregational Methodist Church as a model. They adopted a loosely connectional system, rejecting particularly the system of annual conference assessments. They also baptized by immersion and allowed foot washing at communion.

An early period of growth was stopped by the death of several leaders and the withdrawal of a number of congregations who joined the Congregational Methodist Church. They have no connections with any ecumenical bodies.

Membership: Not reported. The most recent information is from 1958, when there were 11 churches and 11 ministers serving 518 members.

Southern Congregational Methodist Church

c/o New Hope Southern Congregational Methodist Church, Alma, GA

The Southern Congregational Methodist Church was founded in 1985 by former members of the Congregational Methodist Church. The founders felt that for several years the Congregational Methodist Church had, through its successive editions of the Book of Discipline, adopted legislation at its general conferences that tended to subvert the church's congregational polity. The edition issued in the early 1980s eliminated district conferences from the church's structure, and focused opposition to the perceived trends in church government.

Those who opposed the changes introduced by the new Book of Discipline met in 1985 and formed the Southern Congregational Methodist Church. They reintroduced the district conferences into the church's structure, but otherwise continued the belief and practice of the parent body. The church is a conservative Wesleyan church that emphasizes the divine inspiration of the scriptures, the new birth, the deity and virgin birth of Christ, Christ's redemptive death and resurrection, and entire sanctification as a second definite work of God's grace wrought in the heart of the believer by the Holy Spirit.

Congregations are organized into four districts that cover Georgia, Tennessee, Alabama, Mississippi, and Texas.

Membership: Not reported. In 2008 the church reported 29 affiliated congregations.

Sources:

Southern Congregational Methodist Church. www.scmchurch.com/ and www.ourchurch.com/member/s/socongregation/.

Book of Discipline of the Southern Congregational Methodist Church. Alma, GA: Southern Congregational Methodist Church, 2001.

Southern Methodist Church

425 Broughton St., Orangeburg, SC 29115

The Southern Methodist Church was formed in 1940 by members of several congregations of the Methodist Episcopal Church, South, who did not wish to participate in the 1939 merger with the Methodist Episcopal Church. They felt that the Methodist Episcopal Church was apostate and full of heresy and infidelity and also that the merger, forming the Methodist Church (1939–1968), would lead to powerful, centralized ecclesiastical control.

The withdrawing members, meeting in convocation in Columbia, South Carolina, set up plans to perpetuate what they considered to be the Methodist Episcopal Church, South. In attempting to retain local church property and the name "Methodist Episcopal Church, South," the group became the center of a series of landmark court decisions culminating in the mandate of Judge George Bell Timmerman on March 12, 1945. The group lost its case to the merged church, the Methodist Church. The bishops of the Methodist Church were legally established as representatives of the membership of the former Methodist Episcopal Church, South, with control over property; and the name "Methodist Episcopal Church, South," was the property of its legal successor, the Methodist Church (now the United Methodist Church). The name "Southern Methodist Church" was then adopted by the withdrawing group.

The church adopted the Methodist Episcopal Articles of Religion. The church added statements of belief on prevenient grace (grace is shed abroad in the hearts of all), the witness of the Spirit, Christian perfection, and the evangelization of the world. It has also added statements on the creation account of Genesis, premillennialism, and Satan.

Departing from its episcopal heritage, the new body is congregational in polity. It has four annual conferences and a general conference, but it has dropped the office of district superintendent and replaced the bishop with a quadrennially elected president.

The Southern Methodist Church was a member of both the American Council of Christian Churches and International Council of Christian Churches but withdrew in 1971. Missions are supported in Cameroon, Cyprus, Ethiopia, Italy, Mexico, Venezuela, Zimbabwe, England, Belgium, and the Philippines.

Membership: In 2008 the church reported 104 churches and 6,200 members from Maryland to Florida, South Carolina to Texas. In 2004 the church reported 163 clergy.

Educational Facilities:

Southern Methodist Bible College, Orangeburg, South Carolina.

Periodicals: *The Southern Methodist*. Available from Foundry Press, Orangeburg, SC 29115.

Sources:

The Southern Methodist Church. www.southernmethodistchurch.org.

Ballard, Jerry. *To the Regions Beyond*. Orangeburg, SC: Board of Foreign Missions, Southern Methodist Church, 1970.

The Doctrines and Discipline of the Southern Methodist Church. Orangeburg, SC: Foundry Press, 1970.

❊ Black Methodism

African Methodist Episcopal Church

500 8th Ave. S, Nashville, TN 37203

A short time after the founding of the Methodist Episcopal Church in 1784, friction developed between the blacks and the whites of St. George's Church in Philadelphia. The situation was intensified by the construction of a gallery to which the blacks were relegated. The long-standing grievances came to a head on a Sunday morning in November 1787, when whites tried to pull several blacks from their knees at the altar rail. Richard Allen (1760–1831) led the group of blacks out of the church, and they formed a church of their own.

Allen was a former slave whose master had been converted by Freeborn Garrettson (1752–1827), a Methodist preacher. Allen was allowed by his master to buy his freedom. As a freeman he became a prosperous businessman and a licensed Methodist preacher. After leaving St. George's, Allen purchased an abandoned blacksmith shop, and Methodist Bp. Francis Asbury (1745–1816) dedicated it as Bethel Church. In 1799 Allen was ordained a deacon, the first black to be so honored.

Differences continued between the leaders of Allen's Bethel Church and St. George's. The former wished to be independent but with a nominal relation to the Methodists. Finally, in 1816, the issues were settled in a court suit when Bethel was granted full independence.

In Baltimore, blacks at the two white churches formed an independent Colored Methodist Society after they had been put in galleries and not allowed to take communion until after the whites. In 1801 Daniel Coke arrived in Baltimore and took over the leadership of the Society. Through his work an independent Methodist Church, also named Bethel, was formed. A call was issued in 1816 for a national meeting of black Methodists for the purpose of forming an African Methodist Episcopal (AME) Church. The *Discipline*, Articles of Religion, and General Rules of the Methodist Episcopal Church were adopted, and Richard Allen was elected bishop. The AME Church remains close in doctrine, practice, and polity to the United Methodist Church, the successor to the Methodist Episcopal Church, with whom it has engaged in merger conversations.

Growth in the church throughout the North and Midwest was steady through 1865. After the Civil War a rapid expansion throughout the South occurred, and conferences were established across the territory of the former Confederacy.

A missionary imperative was an early part of African Methodist concern, and in 1827 Scipio Bean was ordained as an elder and sent to Haiti. From that small beginning (and slow growth because of lack of funds), a twentieth-century mission program emerged with stations in Africa, South America, and the West Indies. The primary work is with other people of African descent.

Publishing was seen as an integral part of the evangelistic, missionary, and cultural life of the church from the beginning, and the items published by this church have had a major impact on the black community. The AME Book Concern was the first publishing house owned and operated by black people in America. The *Christian Recorder*, a newspaper begun as the *Christian Herald*, published continuously since 1841, is the oldest black periodical in the world; the *AME Review*, started in 1883, is the oldest magazine published by black people in the world. Education joined publishing as an early concern, and the first AME affiliated college, Wilberforce University, was established in 1856. Today the Interdenominational Theological Seminary, in Atlanta, Georgia, is the largest complex for the education of black Christian ministers in the nation. Educational concerns have been carried to the mission field as well, and the church has established a number of schools from the primary grades through college for its African membership. West Africa Seminary was founded in Sierre Leone.

The church is governed episcopally. An international general conference meets quadrennially. The church is divided into 20 episcopal districts. Districts one through 13 oversee work in the United States, Canada, and Bermuda. The remaining districts oversee work abroad.

The church is a member of both the National Council of Churches and the World Council of Churches. Affiliated congregations in Barbados and the Caribbean are members of the Caribbean Conference of Churches.

Membership: In 1999 the church reported 14,428 clergy serving 4,174 churches and 2.5 million members.

Educational Facilities:

Jackson Theological Seminary, Crossett, Arkansas, and Warren, Arkansas.

Shorter College, Little Rock, Arkansas.

Edward Waters College, Jacksonville, Florida.

Interdenominational Theological Seminary, Atlanta, Georgia.

Morris Brown College, Atlanta, Georgia.

Payne Theological Seminary, Wilberforce, Ohio.

Wilberforce University, Wilberforce, Ohio.

Allen University, Columbia, South Carolina.

Dickerson Theological Seminary, Columbia, South Carolina.

Abington School of Religion, Waco, Texas.

Paul Quinn College, Dallas, Texas.

Periodicals: *The Christian Recorder.* • *A.M.E. Church Review.* • *The Voice of Missions.* • *The Journal of Christian Education.* • *The Secret Chamber.* • *The Missionary Magazine.* • *The YPD News Letter.* All available from *The Christian Recorder*, 512 8th Ave. S, Nashville, TN 37203-4181.

Sources:

African Methodist Episcopal Church. www.ame-church.com.

Allen, Richard. *The Life Experience and Gospel Labors of the Rt. Rev. Richard Allen.* Nashville, TN: Abingdon Press, 1960.

George, Carol V. R. *Segregated Sabbaths.* New York: Oxford University Press, 1973.

Gomez, Joseph. *Polity of the African Methodist Episcopal Church.* Nashville, TN: Division of Christian Education, African Methodist Episcopal Church, 1971.

Gregg, Howard D. *History of the A.M.E. Church.* Nashville: AME Sunday School Union, 1980.

Melton, J. Gordon. *A Will to Choose: The Rise of African American Methodism.* Lanham, MD: Rowman & Littlefield, 2007.

Singleton, George A. *The Romance of African Methodism.* New York: Exposition Press, 1952.

White, Andrew. *Know Your Church Manual.* Nashville, TN: Division of Christian Education, African Methodist Episcopal Church, 1965.

Wright, R. R., Jr., comp. *Encyclopedia of African Methodism.* Philadelphia, PA: Book Concern of the AME Church, 1947.

African Methodist Episcopal Zion Church

AME Zion Headquarters, 3225 Sugar Creek Rd., Charlotte, NC 28269

Alternate Address: PO Box 23843, Charlotte, NC 28232

In the late 1790s, a movement for independence among New York blacks was begun when a group petitioned Bp. Francis Asbury, the first bishop of the Methodist Episcopal Church, to let them hold separate meetings. They complained of not being allowed to preach or join the conference and itinerate. Asbury granted the request, and meetings were held immediately. In 1801 a charter was drawn up for the African Methodist Episcopal Church (called Zion Church) of the City of New

York. It was to be supplied with a minister from the white John Street Church. Zion Church was thus assured of regular preaching and the sacraments.

In 1813 Zion Church split, and Asbury Church was formed as a second black Methodist congregation. Both churches were being served by William Stillwell of John Street Church in 1820, when Stillwell, along with about 300 white church members, withdrew from the Methodist Episcopal Church denomination in a dispute over centralized control of individual church properties and formed their own Methodist Society. Blacks, now without a regular minister and also afraid of losing their property to the Methodist Episcopal Church, separated themselves from John Street Church. They also voted not to join the African Methodist Episcopal Church. Several independent black churches in New Haven and Philadelphia petitioned them for ministers. A *Discipline*, based upon that of the Methodist Episcopal Church, was drawn up.

Several attempts at reconciliation were made, the most important being a petition to establish the several black congregations as an annual conference within the Methodist Episcopal Church. This request was refused, and the African Methodist Episcopal Zion Church emerged. Ordination of black ministers was accepted from William Stillwell and two other white elders, and in 1822 James Varick (1750–1827) was elected the first superintendent.

Doctrinally the AME Zion Church accepts the Twenty-five Articles of Religion common to Methodists and has an episcopal polity similar to the Methodist Episcopal Church. Church boards implement programs of the quadrennial General Conference. The Publishing House and Book Concern are located in the headquarters complex in Charlotte, North Carolina, and publish a complete line of church school material. The church is a member of both the National Council of Churches and the World Council of Churches.

The AME Zion Church has member churches in North and South America, Africa, Europe, and Asia. In West Africa, the denomination has set up numerous schools and clinics throughout Ghana and Nigeria. The church also has facilities in Liberia, though some of its main structures have been destroyed by civil war.

Membership: In 2003 the church reported 1,432,795 members; 3,236 churches; and 3,827 ministers.

Educational Facilities:

Lomax-Hannon Junior College, Greenville, Alabama.

Hood Theological Seminary, Salisbury, North Carolina.

Livingstone College, Salisbury, North Carolina.

Clinton Junior College, Rock Hill, South Carolina.

Periodicals: *Star of Zion.* • *A.M.E. Zion Quarterly Review.* • *The Connection.* Available from PO Box 31005, Charlotte, NC 28231.

Sources:

African Methodist Episcopal Zion Church. www.amez.org.

Association of Religion Data Archives. www.thearda.com/Denoms/D_1322.asp.

Bradley, David C. *A History of the A.M.E. Zion Church.* 2 vols. Nashville: Parthenon Press, 1956–1970.

Melton, J. Gordon. *A Will to Choose: The Rise of African American Methodism.* Lanham, MD: Rowman & Littlefield, 2007.

Walls, William J. *The African Methodist Episcopal Zion Church.* Charlotte, NC: A.M.E. Zion Publishing House, 1974.

African Union First Colored Methodist Protestant Church

Saint James AUMP Church, 1106 E 16th St., Wilmington, DE 19802

HISTORY. The origins of the African Union First Colored Methodist Protestant Church can be traced to 1813 and the formation of the Union Church of Africans, an event that present-day church leaders point to with pride. The Union Church of Africans was the first church in the United States to be originally organized by and afterward wholly under the care of black people.

The Union Church of Africans began in a series of disputes in the Asbury Methodist Episcopal Church, a congregation in Wilmington, Delaware. In 1805 black members under the leadership of Peter Spencer (1782–1843) and William Anderson (d. 1843) withdrew from what had been an integrated congregation, formed an all-black congregation, Ezion Church, and erected a building. They cited as reasons for their departure the denial of religious privileges and lack of freedom in exercising their "spiritual gifts." The black members had been segregated in a balcony and made to take communion after white members.

While breaking with the local congregation, Ezion was still a part of the predominantly white Methodist Episcopal Church. However, in 1812 a conflict arose with the white minister who had been assigned to preach to both of Wilmington's congregations. The conflict resulted in the minister's dismissal of all of Ezion's trustees and class leaders. That action led to a court dispute that ended when the black members withdrew from the church. In 1813 they reorganized independently and elected Spencer and Anderson as their ministers. By 1837 there were 21 congregations.

In the generation after Spencer and Anderson, two events were most important. First, in 1850, a major schism occurred when a group arose in the Union Church that demanded the adoption of an episcopal polity. That group left to found the Union American Methodist Episcopal Church. The Union Church of Africans emerged from this struggle as the African Union Church. Then, after the Civil War, the church merged with the First Colored Methodist Protestant Church to form the present African Union First Colored Methodist Protestant Church.

The First Colored Methodist Protestant Church had been formed about 1840 when members of the African Methodist Episcopal Church rejected episcopal leadership and reorganized along the principles of the Methodist Protestant Church, which included no episcopacy and lay representation of local preachers at the general conference. Because the Methodist Protestant Church was very similar to the African Union Church, they united in 1866.

DOCTRINE. The church accepts the commonly held articles of religion of United Methodism, but it has attached the Apostles' Creed as the first article and deleted the article on "The Rulers of the United States." It has made a few changes in wording, for example, adding the words "and women" to the article on "The Church," which now reads, "The visible church is a congregation of faithful men and women."

ORGANIZATION. The church is organized congregationally. Congregations are grouped into three districts: the Middle District, which includes New Jersey, Pennsylvania, New York, Delaware, and Canada; the Maryland District, which includes Maryland, the District of Columbia, Virginia, and all states south and southwest of Maryland; and the Southern and Western Missionary District, which includes all the southern and western states. A general conference meets quadrennially.

In 1966 the church moved to replace the titles of general president and general vice president, the two offices elected by the General Conference, with that of senior bishop and junior bishop. In 1971 the office of presiding elder of the combined districts of the church was created, and a second presiding elder was named in 1979.

There is no foreign mission work, and the home mission work is primarily the providence of the women.

Membership: Not reported.

Educational Facilities:

AU School of Religion, Wilmington, Delaware.

Sources:

African Union First Colored Methodist Protestant Church. www.aufcmp.org.

Baldwin, Lewis V. *"Invisible" Strands in African Methodism*. Metuchen, NJ: Scarecrow Press, 1983.

Melton, J. Gordon. *A Will to Choose: The Rise of African American Methodism*. Lanham, MD: Rowman & Littlefield, 2007.

Russell, Daniel James. *History of the African Union Methodist Protestant Church*. Philadelphia: Union Star Book and Job Printing and Publishing House, 1920.

British Methodist Episcopal Church of Canada
460 Shaw St., Toronto, ON, Canada M6G 3L3

The British Methodist Episcopal Church traces its beginning to the entrance into Canada of the African Methodist Episcopal (AME) Church in the 1830s, and more directly to the organization of the Upper Canada Conference in 1840 in Toronto under the leadership of Bp. Morris Brown (1770–1849). At the time, there were 10 preachers and 256 lay members in the conference. Some trouble developed in the early 1850s, which the Canadian members attributed to neglect by the American authorities. In 1854 the conference asked for a discipline in conformity to Canadian laws (rather than those of the United States), and it asked the AME Church to set it off as a separate body. The 1856 general conference granted the request, and the independent British Methodist Episcopal Church (MEC), under the leadership of Bp. Willis Nazrey (1808–1874), was organized.

During the late nineteenth century, the work prospered. Churches were founded in Ontario and Nova Scotia (where many former slaves had migrated after the Civil War), and a mission was established in Bermuda. The *Missionary Messenger* served the church.

No doctrinal issues existed between the AME churches and their Canadian membership, so the British MEC continued the doctrines of the AME Church.

Membership: Not reported. The denomination has churches across the province of Ontario.

Sources:

Canadian Church Headquarters Directory. www.ecumenism.net/denom/directory.htm.

Payne, Daniel A. *History of the African Methodist Episcopal Church*. 2 vols. Nashville, TN: AME Sunday School Union, 1891. Reprint, New York: Johnson Reprint Corp., 1968.

Simpson, Matthew. *Cyclopedia of Methodism*. Philadelphia: Louis H. Everts, 1880.

Christian Methodist Episcopal Church
4466 Elvis Presley Blvd., Memphis, TN 38116-7100

From 1844 until the end of the Civil War, slaves formed a large percentage of the membership of the Methodist Episcopal Church. In South Carolina they were in the majority. The proselytizing activity of both the African Methodist Episcopal Church and the African Methodist Episcopal Zion Church claimed many of these former slaves as soon as they were free; others remained with the Methodist Episcopal Church, South (MECS), the southern branch of the Methodist Episcopal Church, which had split in 1844. Many white Methodists felt that, given the blacks' new freedom, a new relationship must follow. In 1870, following the wishes of their black members, the Methodist Episcopal Church, South, helped them form a separate church named the Colored Methodist Episcopal (CME) Church. In 1954 the church changed its name to the Christian Methodist Episcopal Church.

At the first General Conference, nine annual conferences were designated, the *Discipline* of the MECS adopted with necessary changes, a publishing house established, and a periodical, the *Christian Index*, begun. Two MECS bishops ordained two black Methodist Episcopal bishops. Throughout its history the CME Church has been aided financially in its program by the MECS and its successor bodies. Today the church is very similar to the United Methodist Church in belief and practice.

One of the keys to Colored Methodist Episcopal success was the 41-year episcopate of Isaac Lane. Besides traveling widely and bolstering the poverty-ridden church, he initiated the educational program by founding the CME High School (now Lane College) in 1882. Education of former slaves and their children, a major enterprise of all Methodists, has been carried through the CME Church in the establishment of a number of schools across the South. Paine College, established with the assistance of the MECS, has been a traditional focus of CME and MECS cooperation. In 1959 Phillips School of Theology moved from Jackson, Tennessee, to Atlanta, Georgia, to become part of the Interdenominational Theological Center, a complex of four theological schools, the largest educational facility in the nation for the training of black Christian ministers.

Growth and expansion beyond the 200,000 initial members of the church was slowed by lack of funds. Movement northward followed the major migration of blacks into northern urban centers in the early twentieth century.

The CME Church is a member of both the National Council of Churches and the World Council of Churches.

Membership: In 2002 the CME Church reported 850,000 members and 3,407 churches served by 3,300 clergy in the United States. It has missions and sister churches in Haiti, Jamaica, Ghana, Liberia, and Nigeria.

Educational Facilities:

Miles College, Birmingham, Alabama.

Phillips School of Theology, Atlanta, Georgia.

Paine College, Augusta, Georgia.

Lane College, Jackson, Tennessee.

Texas College, Tyler, Texas.

Periodicals: *Christian Index.* Available from PO Box 665, Memphis, TN 38101.

Sources:

Christian Methodist Episcopal Church. www.c-m-e.org.

Association of Religion Data Archives. www.thearda.com/Denoms/D_1424.asp.

Harris, Eula Wallace, and Naomi Ruth Patterson. *Christian Methodist Episcopal Church through the Years.* Jackson, TN: Christian Methodist Episcopal Church Publishing House, 1965.

Johnson, Joseph A., Jr. *Basic Christian Methodist Beliefs.* Shreveport, LA: Fourth Episcopal District Press, 1978.

Lakey, Othal Hawthorne. *The Rise of Colored Methodism.* Dallas, TX: Crescendo Book Publications, 1972.

———. *The History of the CME Church.* Memphis, TN: CME Publishing House, 1997.

Melton, J. Gordon. *A Will to Choose: The Rise of African American Methodism.* Lanham, MD: Rowman & Littlefield, 2007.

Sommerville, Raymond R., Jr. *An Ex-Colored Church: Social Activism in the CME Church, 1870–1970.* Macon, GA: Mercer University Press, 2004.

Wondrous Grace. (Information guide.) Available from the Department of Christian Education, CME Church.

Free Christian Zion Church of Christ

1409 S Mill St., Nashville, AR 71852

The Free Christian Zion Church of Christ was formed on July 10, 1905, in Redemption, Arkansas, by the Rev. E. D. Brown, a conference missionary of the African Methodist Episcopal Zion Church. He and ministers from other Methodist churches objected to what they considered a taxing of the churches for support of an ecclesiastical system and believed that the primary concern of the church should be the care of the poor and needy.

The doctrine is Wesleyan and the polity Methodist with several minor alterations. The bishop, who is called the chief pastor, presides over the work and appoints the ministers and church officers. Pastors and deacons are the local church officers. There are district evangelists to care for the unevangelized communities.

Membership: In 2001 the church reported 16,000 members in 60 churches.

Reformed Methodist Union Episcopal Church

1136 Brody Ave., Charleston, SC 20407

The Reformed Methodist Union Episcopal Church was formed in 1885 by members of the African Methodist Episcopal Church who withdrew after a dispute concerning the election of ministerial delegates to the Annual Conference. The Rev. William E. Johnson was elected the first president. A strong sentiment approving of the nonepiscopal nature of the new church was expressed. However, in 1896, steps were taken to alter the polity, and in 1919, after the death of the Reverend Johnson, E. Russell Middleton was elected bishop. He was consecrated by the Rt. Rev. Peter F. Stevens of the Reformed Episcopal Church. Following Middleton's death, a second bishop was elected and consecrated by the laying on of hands of seven elders of the church.

Doctrine was taken from the Methodist Episcopal Church. The polity has moved in the episcopal direction and was fully adopted in 1916. Class meetings and love feasts are also retained. Class meetings are regular gatherings of small groups for exhortation, discussion, confession and forgiveness, Bible study, and prayer. Love feasts are informal services centering on Holy Communion but also including a light meal, singing, and a talk by the officiating minister.

Membership: In 1983 the church reported 3,800 members in 18 churches served by 33 clergy.

Sources:

The Doctrines and Discipline. Charleston, SC: Reformed Methodist Union Episcopal Church, 1972.

Reformed Zion Union Apostolic Church

c/o James C. Feggins, 416 South Hill Ave., South Hill, VA 23970

The Reformed Zion Union Apostolic Church was founded by a group from the African Methodist Episcopal Church interested in setting up a religious organization "to aid in bringing about Christian Union, whose fruit will be Holiness unto the Lord." Led by the Rev. James Howell, the group met in Boydton, Virginia, in April 1869, and organized the Zion Union Apostolic Church with the Reverend Howell as the president. Harmony and growth prevailed until 1874, when changes in polity led to the election of the Reverend Howell as bishop with life tenure. Dissatisfaction with this action nearly destroyed the organization, even though Bishop Howell resigned. In 1882 a reorganization was effected, the four-year presidential structure reinstituted, and the present name adopted.

The representative conference structure is maintained with the lawmaking power invested in the quadrennial General Conference. Over the years the four-year presidency has again been dropped in favor of life-tenure bishops. A Board of Publication has control over church literature and prints the church school material and the church's periodical.

Membership: In 1965 the church reported 1,832 members and 27 churches.

Periodicals: *Union Searchlight.*

Sources:

General Rules and Discipline of the Reformed Zion Union Apostolic Church. Norfolk, VA: Creecy's Good-Will Printery, 1966.

Union American Methodist Episcopal Church

c/o Bishop Michael Moulden, 3101 N Market St., Wilmington, DE 19802

Alternate Address: c/o Bishop Linwood Rideout, 4411 Fielding Rd., Wilmington, DE 19802.

The Union American Methodist Episcopal Church is one of two denominations that grew out of the movement within the Methodist Episcopal Church (now a constituent part of the United Methodist Church) led by two African-American members, Peter Spencer (1782–1843) and William Anderson. They formed the African Union Church (also called the Union Church of Africans) in Wilmington, Delaware, in 1813. At some point, a schism occurred in the African Union Church. According to some accounts, around 1816, 30 congregations of the Union Church separated themselves from the other 24 congregations, and for a number of years the two groups existed side by side, each using the same name. Other accounts say the schism occurred in 1850, after Spencer's death. In any case, by the 1850s, two factions existed. In 1865 one faction united with the First Colored Methodist Protestant Church to become the African Union First Colored Methodist Protestant Church. That same year, the other group incorporated under the name African Union American Methodist Episcopal Church in the United States of America and Elsewhere (now the Union American Methodist Episcopal Church).

The church is Methodist in doctrine and has an episcopal polity. There are two bishops who head four districts. The General Conference meets quadrennially. The church not only allows but encourages female ministers. The church is led by Bishops Moulden and Rideout.

Membership: In 1990 the church reported 55 congregations and over 12,000 members.

Periodicals: *The Union Messenger*.

Sources:

Baldwin, Lewis V. *The Mark of a Man: Peter Spencer and the American Union Methodist Tradition*. Lanham, MD: University Press of America, 1987.

Melton, J. Gordon. *A Will to Choose: The Rise of African American Methodism*. Lanham, MD: Rowman & Littlefield, 2007.

Payne, Wardell J., ed. *Directory of African American Religious Bodies: A Compendium by the Howard University School of Divinity*. Washington, DC: Howard University Press, 1991.

German Methodism

Church of the United Brethren in Christ USA

c/o Bishop Ron Ramsey, 302 Lake St., Huntington, IN 46750

The Church of the United Brethren in Christ USA grew out of the German pietism and revivalism of such preachers as Philip Otterbein (1726–1813, of the German Reformed Church) and Martin Boehm (1725–1812, of the Mennonite Church), both of whom had been affected by Methodism and eighteenth-century Evangelicalism and who became the first bishops of the United Brethren. Their evangelistic efforts led to the formation of a church in 1800. Its earliest concentration of membership was in Maryland, Virginia, and eastern Pennsylvania.

In 1841 the United Brethren adopted its first constitution. During the next four decades the church was disrupted by the debate over the issues of freemasonry and membership in secret societies and pro rata representation and lay representation at General Conference. The crisis came to a head when the General Conference of 1889 was asked to ratify a new constitution that liberalized the rule against belonging to a secret society, allowed for pro rata and lay representation at General Conference, and altered the Church's Confession of Faith.

The majority ratified the new constitution. They continued to exist as the United Brethren in Christ until 1946 when they merged with the Evangelical Church to form the Evangelical United Brethren, which in turn merged in 1968 with the Methodist Church (1939–1968) to form the United Methodist Church. The minority objected both to the changes and the method of ratification, which they felt were illegal. Bishop Milton L. Wright (1828–1917) led the minority in conserving the original United Brethren in Christ along the lines of an allegiance to the original constitution. The minority group tried to claim property, but was unsuccessful. They opened a new publishing house that moved to Huntington, Indiana, in 1897. The *Christian Conservator*, a paper that had supported their cause since its founding in 1885, was adopted as the official newspaper of the church. In 1954 The *Christian Conservator* was combined with several other periodicals to become the

The United Brethren. In 1994 the magazine was replaced with a bimonthly newsletter called *Connect*.

The continuing minority adhered to the original constitution. They believe in the Trinity and the deity, humanity, and atonement of Christ. Observance of strict scriptural living is required of all members, who are forbidden the use of alcoholic beverages, and membership in secret societies. Baptism and the Lord's Supper are observed as ordinances of the church.

The U.S. National Conference meets biennially and is composed of ministers and lay persons chosen from all local churches in the United States. It is the highest governing body of the U.S. church. Both men and women are eligible for the ministry and are ordained only once as elders. Missionary societies support work in evangelism and church aid in the United States and in Sierra Leone, Jamaica, Honduras, Nicaragua, India, Hong Kong, Macau, Mexico, Thailand, Myanmar, Haiti, El Salvador, Costa Rica, the Philippines, and Guatemala. Elementary and secondary schools have been opened in Honduras and Sierra Leone. A Bible college, affiliated jointly with the Missionary Church, Wesleyan Church, and European Baptist Church, is supported in Sierra Leone.

The United Brethren have disbanded a close relationship with the Primitive Methodist Church and the Evangelical Congregational Church, and they worked together with them in a federation arrangement. They shared support of missionaries, published church school literature, and held seminars and consultations. The former Sandusky Conference of the United Brethren was a member of the Christian Holiness Association.

The church is a member of the National Association of Evangelicals.

Membership: In 2007 the church reported 24,000 members in the United States. Worldwide membership was about 48,000.

Educational Facilities:

Huntington University, Huntington, Indiana.

Huntington University Graduate School of Christian Ministries, Huntington, Indiana.

Periodicals: Worldview.

Sources:

Church of the United Brethren in Christ USA. www.ub.org.

Fetters, Paul R. Trials and Triumphs: A History of the Church of the United Brethren in Christ. Huntington, IN: Church of the United Brethren in Christ/Dept. of Church Services, 1984.

Origin, Doctrine, Constitution, And Discipline Of The United Brethren In Christ. Huntington, IN: Davies Press, 2008.

Evangelical Congregational Church

100 W Park Ave., Myerstown, PA 17067

The history of this church goes back to the 1894 schism in the Evangelical Association, now a constituent part of the United Methodist Church. A group representing minority opinion took the name United Evangelical Church and reunited with the parent body in 1922, when the two formed the Evangelical Church. The many deep scars created by the 1894 schism, however, were not all healed before the 1922 reunion. Therefore, as efforts toward the reunion progressed, voices of dissent were raised in the United Evangelical Church, opposing merger. Some United Evangelical Church members were still bitter over the loss of their church buildings to the Evangelical Association in court battles. By the 1920s, congregations of the United Evangelical Church had built new churches, which they did not want to share with or give to those who had taken their buildings in the court cases. After merger was voted, those opposing it called a special session of the East Pennsylvania Conference, passed a motion to refrain from merger, and formed the Evangelical Congregational Church. An independent anti-merger periodical, *The United Evangelical*, was taken over as a church organ. Former Bp.W. F. Heil was elected bishop and editor of the church paper.

Doctrinally, the Evangelical Congregational Church is Arminian-Wesleyan, against the theory of predestination and for the theory of free will, the belief that grace is available to all and that all can exercise free will to accept grace. The church upholds the Twenty-five Articles of Religion adopted in 1894 by the United Evangelical Church. The polity is episcopal, but the churches are autonomous and the bishops' powers are strictly limited. There are two Annual Conferences divided into districts. Bishops and regional elders/superintendents are elected quadrennially. Ministers are appointed to their charges. Boards and divisions implement the program of the General Conference.

In the United States, there are missions to Native Americans, Latin Americans, and the mountain people in Kentucky. Two retirement villages are located near the headquarters complex at Myerstown, along with the denominationally supported Evangelical Theological Seminary. The church is a member of the National Association of Evangelicals, the Holiness Summit, and Mission America.

Membership: In 2003 the church reported 252 ministers and 20,743 members in the United States, with 154 churches as of 2008. There are 460 international churches, in Costa Rica, India, Japan, Liberia, Mexico, Myanmar, and Nepal.

Educational Facilities:

Evangelical Theological Seminary, Myerstown, Pennsylvania.

Periodicals: *The Connection.* • *Window on the World.* • *EC Leader.* • *EC National News.* • *EC Scene.* • *HeartCry.* • *Lighthouse Keeper.* • *Partners.* • *Wellness Connection.*

Sources:

Evangelical Congregational Church. www.eccenter.com.

Wilson, Robert Sherer. *A Brief History of the Evangelical Congregational Church for the Enlightenment of Her Pastors and People.* Myerstown, PA: Church Center Press, 1953.

United Christian Church

523 W Walnut St., Cleona, PA 17042

The United Christian Church was the second schism of the United Brethren in Christ. Formed also during a war, this time the Civil War, some members felt that the voluntary bearing of firearms was wrong. They had interpreted certain resolutions of the East Pennsylvania Conference as justifying military service. The withdrawing group, led by George W. Hoffman, also opposed infant baptism and secret societies.

Organization of the United Christian Church was informal for more than a decade; then in January 1877, at a meeting in Campbelltown, Pennsylvania, a Confession of Faith was adopted. The name was chosen the following year and a Constitution and Discipline in 1894. The Discipline of the 1841 United Brethren in Christ was accepted until 1894. Foot washing is one of the ordinances recognized along with baptism and communion.

Activities of the church include an annual camp meeting, services in prisons and at homes for the elderly, direct support of a mission in Jamaica, support of missions in Mexico, and work with the Navigators and BCM International. An annual conference has the power to legislate for this small church body.

Membership: In 2004 the group had nine churches, 15 ministers, and 282 members.

Sources:

Association of Religion Data Archives. www.thearda.com/Denoms/D_1337.asp.

History of the United Christian Church. United Christian Church, 1977.

Origin, Doctrine, Constitution and Discipline of the United Christian Church. Myerstown, PA: Church Center Press, 1950.

This We Believe. United Christian Church, 1978.

 # British Methodism

Primitive Methodist Church USA

730 Preston Ln., Hatboro, PA 19040

The Primitive Methodist Church is one of the two Methodist bodies in the United States that does not trace its history to the Methodist Episcopal Church, an American church, but to the British Wesleyan Methodist tradition. The Primitive Methodist Church grew from the work of two English ministers, the Revs. Hugh Bourne (1772–1852) and William Clowes (1780–1851). Out of their evangelistic efforts the new church itself developed in England. Both men became influenced by the great success of the American camp meeting. Under their leadership a camp meeting was held on May 31, 1807. As a result of this meeting and some other camp meetings, both men were dismissed from the Wesleyan Methodist Connection. Since those converted were not welcomed into the Wesleyan Church, Bourne and Clowes found a place of meeting in 1810. Growth was such that in 1812 in Tunstall, England, they became officially organized as The Society of the Primitive Methodists. The church accepted the polity of the Wesleyan Methodists and did not create bishops.

By 1829 the call for ministers by Primitive Methodists who had migrated to the United States was heard. Four missionaries were sent—William Summersides, Thomas Morris, Ruth Watkins, and William Knowles. Growth was slow and at first confined to New York, New Jersey, Pennsylvania, and Connecticut. In 1840 the American group separated itself from its British parent but kept fraternal relations. Growth increased, particularly in the Pennsylvania coal fields. In 1842 a Primitive Methodist Church was founded in Galena, Illinois, and became the base for a second conference in the Midwest. The conferences existed in close relation but operated autonomously until 1889 when the General Conference was organized and three conferences, Eastern, Western, and Pennsylvania joined and became the legislative body with the conferences remaining as the administrative branches. In 1975 both the annual and general conferences were combined. This combined both the legislative and administrative powers into one conference that meets annually. It is composed of ministers and lay delegates from the six districts. It has direct oversight of all boards and committees. The districts provide administrative guidance along with the district and local church quarterly conference. The conference is presided over by the president, who is elected to a four-year term. There is equal representation of clergy and laity at all levels of administration. There is one full-time officer, the president. The main mission work is carried on in Guatemala, working in conjunction with the Primitive Methodist National Conference of Guatemala, and in Mexico and the Dominican Republic.

The church is a member of the National Association of Evangelicals and, though not a member, cooperates with the Christian Holiness Association.

Membership: In 2007 the group reported 75 churches, 4,100 members, and 59 ministers.

Sources:

Primitive Methodist Church USA. www.primitivemethodistchurch.org.

Primary Helps and Biblical Instruction for Primitive Methodists. N.p. [1958].

Werner, Julia Stewart. *The Primitive Connection.* Madison: University of Wisconsin Press, 1984.

Wert, Paul R., J. Allan Ranck, and William C. F. Hayes. *The Christian Way.* Dayton, OH: Otterbein Press, 1950.

United Wesleyan Methodist Church of America

c/o David S. Bruno, 270 W 126th St., New York, NY 10027

The United Wesleyan Methodist Church of America was formed in 1905 by Methodists who immigrated to the United States from the West Indies and wished to carry on the tradition of the Methodist Church in the Caribbean and the

Americas, a Wesleyan church with historical ties to British Methodists. The church's doctrine is Wesleyan, and its polity is like its West Indian counterpart (nonepiscopal). A general conference meets biennially. In 1976 the Methodist Church in the Caribbean and the Americas entered into a concordant with the United Methodist Church which aligned their work and led to a number of jointly sponsored projects in the Islands. The church is a member of both the World Council of Churches and the Caribbean Conference of Churches.

Membership: In 1978 there were four congregations, all in New York City. In 1982 the church in the West Indies reported 68,898 members.

Sources:

Bessil-Watson, Lisa, comp. *Handbook of the Churches in the Caribbean*. Bridgetown, Barbados: Cedar Press, 1982.

Holiness Family

8

The desire to follow in a literal sense Christ's admonition, "Be ye perfect as my father in heaven is perfect" (Matthew 5:48), has resulted in the formation of Holiness churches. These churches take the drive for perfection, or holiness, as their primary focus, and are distinguished from most other Christian churches by the unique doctrinal framework within which holiness or sanctification is understood. The corollary to this drive has been separation from Christians who do not, in the opinion of Holiness followers, adequately reach toward the goal of perfection. Thus Holiness churches are also distinct from other churches because of their focus on perfection and the resultant separatist practices.

John Wesley (1703–1791), the founder of Methodism, gave impetus to the formation of Holiness churches. Though the Wesleyan movement of the eighteenth century was only in part a perfectionist movement, Wesley did encourage the ethical life and a goal of perfection, and numerous churches now strive for what they call Wesleyan holiness.

Wesley's understanding of perfection developed through two phases: first, an emphasis on sinlessness, and second, an emphasis on love. While a student at Oxford, Wesley formed the Holy Club, a group of students in search of a holy life. In an early sermon, "Christian Perfection," Wesley defined perfection as "holiness," saying Christians are perfect in that they are free from outward sin. Wesley felt that mature Christians are free from evil tempers and thoughts, and such perfection is possible in this life.

Wesley was immediately challenged over his doctrine of perfection. In answer to his accusers, he had to emphasize that perfection did not apply to mistakes, infirmity, knowledge, or freedom from temptation. Also, he said there was no perfection that did not admit of further progress. Wesley himself began to see the harmful consequences of defining perfection as absence of sin, and he redefined perfectionism in terms of love. His ideas on perfection are gathered together in his *Plain Account of Christian Perfection*. The line between the Pietist-Methodist family and the Holiness family is difficult to draw. There have always been individual Methodists who stressed holiness and sanctification. Further, many Holiness churches are schismatic bodies that broke away from various Methodist churches, and some Holiness churches use the word *Methodist* in their titles. However, Holiness churches place greater stress than Methodist churches on the second blessing and on a lifestyle reflecting sanctification.

THE UNDERSTANDING OF HOLINESS. The distinctive elements of the Holiness way of being Christian are the teachings concerning sanctification and perfection, and the lifestyle Holiness Christians believe should naturally flow from such teachings. The sanctification experience, also called the second blessing or second work of grace in the life of the believer, culminates a process of becoming holy that begins when the believer accepts Jesus Christ as his or her personal savior. The first step in the process—justification, the first work of grace—is also called the "born again" experience. That event is followed by a period of growth in grace, in becoming actually holy in one's life. Both justification and the growing process are seen as involving the activity of the Holy Spirit within the individual. The process should culminate in the second work of grace, in which the Holy Spirit cleanses the heart from sin and imparts his indwelling presence, giving power for living the Christian life. A consensus opinion on sanctification is found in the statement of the Wesleyan Church.

> *Inward sanctification begins the moment one is justified. From that moment until a believer is entirely sanctified, he or she grows daily in grace and gradually dies to sin. Entire sanctification is effected by the baptism of the Holy Spirit, which cleanses the heart of the child of God from all inbred sin through faith in Jesus Christ. It is subsequent to regeneration and is wrought instantaneously when the believers present themselves as a living sacrifice, holy and acceptable to God, and are thus enabled through His grace to love God with all the heart and to walk in all His holy commandments blameless. The crisis of cleansing is preceded and followed by growth in grace and the knowledge of our Lord and Savior, Jesus Christ. When people are fully cleansed from all sin, they are endued with the power of the Holy Spirit for the accomplishment of all to which they are called. The ensuing life of Holiness is maintained by a continuing faith in the sanctifying blood of Christ, and is evidenced by an obedient life.*

In John Wesley's thought, the process of sanctification was seen as the goal toward which the Christian's life led. The arrival at the state of sanctification, in which one was freed from sin and made perfect in life, generally occurred only at the end of one's days on earth. However, in the mid-nineteenth century, deriving in large part from the ministry of evangelist Phoebe Palmer (1807–1874), coeditor of *The Path*

Holiness Family Chronology

1766	Methodist founder John Wesley publishes the first edition of *A Plain Account of Christian Perfection*, in which he offers Christians the possibility of becoming perfect in this life, by which he means to be "sanctified throughout" . . . "to have a heart so all-flaming with the love of God, as continually to offer up every thought, word, and work, as a spiritual sacrifice, acceptable to God through Christ. In every thought of our hearts, in every word of our tongues, in every work of our hands, to show forth his praise, who hath called us out of darkness into his marvelous light."
1835	Charles F. Finney (1792–1875) accepts a position as professor of theology at Oberlin Collegiate Institute (later Oberlin College).
1939	Methodist Episcopal Church (MEC) minister in Boston, Timothy Merritt, begins periodical, *A Guide to Christian Perfection*, to revive interest in Wesley's understanding of the doctrine of sanctification.
	Finney reads Wesley's *Plain Account*, experiences sanctification, and goes on to become social reformer and the most prominent evangelist in America.
1843	Wesleyan Methodist Church founded by advocates of abolitionism who were forced out of the MEC.
1844	Finney's colleague at Oberlin, Asa Mahan, publishes *Scriptural Doctrine of Christian Perfection*.
1857–58	A holiness-based revival grows out of the "Tuesday meeting for the promotion of Holiness" led by Phoebe Palmer (1807–1874), a layperson at Allen MEC in New York City.
1859	Palmer publishes *The Promise of the Father*, which makes a case for females in the ministry.
1860	Free Methodist Church formed by Methodists opposing bought pews and advocating abolitionism.
1864	Palmer and her husband Walter Palmer acquire Timothy Merritt's magazine, now known as *A Guide to Holiness*, and continue its publication. Phoebe Palmer changes Holiness doctrine slightly by emphasizing it as the immediate possibility for any Christian rather than the possibility of a few toward the end of a long life of Christian striving.
1865	Catherine and William Booth begin an independent mission in London that will later evolve into the Salvation Army.
1866	Holiness revival picks up after the Civil War and spreads across Methodism through the many camp meeting supported by the several Methodist denominations.
1867	The National Camp Meeting Association for the Promotion of Holiness is formed at a camp meeting in Vineland, New Jersey.
1870	Catherine Booth publishes *Female Ministry; or, Woman's Right to Preach the Gospel*.
1872	Holiness advocates Jesse T. Peck, Randolph S. Foster, Stephen Merritt, and Gilbert Haven are elected bishops by the MEC.
1880	Daniel Warner leads in the formation of the Church of God (Anderson, Indiana).
1880s	As Holiness movement grows, critics arise advocating alternate views of the doctrine of sanctification.
1887	A conflict over Holiness within the Methodist movement emerges. John P. Brooks publishes the *Divine Church* in which he calls for Holiness people to leave the Methodist Episcopal Church and establish independent congregations and camp meetings.
	Members of the Southwestern Holiness Association withdraw from the MEC and form the Independent Holiness People, out of which several Holiness denominations were to emerge.
	Presbyterian minister Albert Benjamin Simpson founds the Christian Alliance and the Evangelical Missionary Alliance (united in 1897 as the Christian and Missionary Alliance).
1894	C. P. Jones and Charles H. Mason found the Church of Christ (Holiness), the first independent African American Holiness church. Mason later leaves to found the Church of God in Christ, the most prominent African America Pentecostal church.
1895	Phineas Bresee (1838–1915) founds the Church of the Nazarene in Los Angeles.
1897	Martin Wells Knapp and Seth Cook Rees found the International Holiness Union and Prayer League (later known as the Pilgrim Holiness Church).
1901	Alma White, a female Holiness lay speaker, leaves the MEC to found the Methodist Pentecostal Union (later renamed the Pillar of Fire). She was later consecrated as the new church's bishop.
1929	African American Holiness minister Lightfoot Solomon Michaux (1885–1968), founder of the Gospel Spreading Church, launches what will become a national radio ministry in the 1930s.
1950s	Minister Glenn Griffith condemns the Church of the Nazarene and other Holiness churches for drifting away from Holiness standards. He leaves the church and in 1956 leads in the formation of the Bible Missionary Church, the first of a new set of conservative Holiness denominations.
1968	The Wesleyan Methodist Church and the Pilgrim Holiness Church merge to form the Wesleyan church.
1997	National Holiness Association (founded as the National Camp Meeting Association for the Promotion of Holiness) changes its name to National Holiness Partnership.

---

of Holiness, a prominent Methodist and Holiness magazine, a subtle but important divergence with Wesley crept into Holiness thought. In her writing and speaking, Palmer began to picture sanctification as more the beginning of the Christian life rather than the goal. As Charles Edward White has cogently pointed out in his study *The Beauty of Holiness* (1986), Palmer advocated sanctification as the immediate possibility of any believer, and she encouraged all, no matter how new in the faith, to seek it as the instantaneous gift of the Holy Spirit. This subtle change of emphasis led to a renewed concentration on the search for holiness among Methodists, but also created a reaction from many Methodists who saw in Wesley's understanding of the gradual process of the develop-

ment of the life of holiness a reason to reject the renewed emphasis on sanctification.

In the last half of the nineteenth century, personal holiness, symbolized by a rigid code of behavior, became the distinguishing theme in the Holiness movement. Wesley, who wrote the *General Rules for the Methodists*, is the source of this trend. He disapproved of flashy clothes, costly apparel, and expensive jewelry, and in the early nineteenth-century Holiness schisms from Methodism, a consistent voice was one deploring the departure of the Methodists from the *General Rules*. The strictest personal codes came in the late nineteenth century. They were in part a reaction to the social-gospel emphasis in the larger denominations. There is also strong evidence that such codes were and are tied to the frustrations of people left behind by urbanization, mechanization, and population growth. Without status in mass society, people reject it and find virtue in the necessity of their condition. Holiness was and is to be found in asceticism and rejection of worldliness.

The rejection of worldliness has led to typical Holiness disagreements over exactly what constitutes worldliness. Churches have split over the acceptance of television or a style of clothing, such as neckties. Other issues include attitudes toward divorced people, cosmetics, swimming with the opposite sex, dress in high school gym classes, and the cutting of females' hair (I Corinthians 11: 1–16).

At one time, the Holiness movement concentrated much of its attention on social issues and public morality. The Wesleyan and Free Methodists both were abolitionist, and at different times the Holiness movement was tied to the great crusades for temperance and women's rights. Beginning with the comingling of Wesleyan and Quaker ideas during the era of Joseph John Gurney (1788–1847), pacifism has had a strong hold on the Holiness movement and is the major remnant of the social imperative. Many Pentecostal churches have inherited this pacifist emphasis.

Among the Holiness groups, sacraments have not been an important part of church life. Some churches have two sacraments—baptism and the Lord's Supper—as the Wesleyan Church does. Some consider baptism and the Lord's Supper to be ordinances, not sacraments. Churches such as the General Eldership of the Churches of God add foot-washing as a third ordinance. Finally, other churches, most notably the Salvation Army, have neither ordinances nor sacraments.

THE HOLINESS MOVEMENT IN AMERICA.

The strain of perfectionism in Wesleyan teaching was not the most emphasized doctrine in early nineteenth-century Methodism. On the heels of the great American revival of 1837 to 1838, however, centers of interest in the Wesleyan doctrine of perfection, or *holiness*, as it was termed, emerged. One phase of this interest came in 1839 with the sanctification experienced by Charles G. Finney (1792–1875). Sanctification, in this context, means holiness; it means becoming perfect in love. Finney, a Congregationalist and the most famous evangelist of his day, had learned of sanctification from the Methodists and from his own reading of Wesley's *Plain Account of Christian Perfection*. At the same time, Finney became involved in a search for social holiness, making society perfect in love, understanding justice to be the social form of love. Finney defended women's rights, participated in the antislavery crusade, and as a pacifist protested the Mexican War (1846–1848). After experiencing sanctification in 1839, Finney began to write on it and preach it. In 1844 his colleague at Oberlin College, Asa Mahan (1799–1889), published his book *Scripture Doctrine of Christian Perfection*, which became the major statement of the Oberlin position. Because of his non-Methodist background, Finney had a great effect on other soon-to-be Holiness greats—Thomas Cogswell Upham (1799–1872), William Boardman

(1810–1886), and Absalom Backus Earle (1812–1895). Thus, the first wave of Holiness in the United States began outside of Methodism, by Methodized Presbyterians, Baptists, and Congregationalists. Prior to 1855, the only Methodist who had gained any reputation for perfectionist thinking was Timothy Merritt (1775–1845), editor of the *Guide to Christian Perfection* (later called the *Guide to Holiness*), but Finney had raised the issue for the whole Methodist Episcopal Church, and Methodists could no longer ignore their heritage.

Without any weakening or demise of the Oberlin Holiness crusade, the Holiness movement began a new phase after the revival of 1857 to 1858. The new center of interest was the Tuesday Meeting for the Promotion of Holiness led by Phoebe Palmer from her base as a member of Allen Street Methodist Church in New York City. Palmer's efforts were aided by the publication of two books, *Christian Purity* (1851) by Randolph S. Foster (1820–1903) and *The Central Idea of Christianity* (1856) by Jesse T. Peck (1811–1883). Both men were soon to be Methodist bishops. The revival that was spreading from Allen Street to the whole of Methodism was interrupted by the Civil War (1861–1865), but picked up momentum as soon as the hostilities ceased. During the war, Phoebe Palmer and her husband, Walter Palmer, bought *Merritt's Guide to Holiness*, and in 1866 they toured the country, establishing centers of the sanctified wherever they preached.

It was not long until ministers rallied to the cause. The camp meeting proved to be the prime structure to carry on the work, and in 1867 William Osborn (1832–1902) of the South New Jersey Conference of Methodists and John S. Inskip (1816–1884) of New York set up a national camp meeting at Vineland, New Jersey. During this camp meeting, the National Camp Meeting Association for the Promotion of Holiness was formed, and Inskip became its first president. Bishop Matthew Simpson (1811–1884) personally aided the work, which prospered under episcopal approval.

The Holiness movement grew tremendously among Methodists in the first decade after the Civil War. In 1872 Jesse T. Peck, Randolph S. Foster, Stephen Merrill (1825–1905), and Gilbert Haven (1821–1880), all promoters of the Holiness revival, were elected Methodist bishops; with their encouragement, the movement was given vocal support through the church press. In 1870 a second national press organ was begun by William McDonald of the New England Conference. The *Advocate of Holiness* became the organ of the Camp Meeting Association. The revival reached some of the most influential members of the church: Daniel Steele (1824–1914), first president of Syracuse University and then professor of systematic theology at Boston University; Wilhelm Nast (1807–1889), father of German Methodism; Bishop William Taylor (1821–1902); wealthy layman Washington C. DePauw (1822–1887); and women's rights leader Frances E. Willard (1839–1898). A new generation of preachers came along ready to make their mark as ministers of the Holiness gospel: Beverly Carradine (1848–1931), John Allen Wood (b. 1828), Alfred Cookman (1828–1871), John

L. Brasher (1868–1971), and Milton L. Haney (1825–1922). The movement grew and developed, and, like the Finney revival, there was little or no fear of schism.

While this new work spread quickly among the Methodists, the work begun by Finney did not die but continued to bear fruit. While the Oberlin position never really caught on with non-Methodists, leaders from the Quakers, Presbyterians, and Baptists preached the second blessing. William Boardman (1810–1886) carried the message to England, where, in conjunction with R. Pearsall Smith (1865–1946), a Presbyterian, he began the Oxford Union Meeting for the Promotion of Scriptural Holiness. The Oxford meetings then formed the base for the Keswick movement, so named for the town in England where followers held annual conventions, which became the main carrier of the Holiness movement in the Church of England. Smith's wife, Hannah Whitall Smith (1832–1911), wrote one of the great classics of the Keswick era, *The Christian's Secret of a Happy Life* (1875). The Keswick brand of Holiness, which emphasized the giving of power instead of the cleansing from sin, gained its adherents in the United States: Dwight L. Moody (1837–1899), R. A. Torrey (1856–1928), Adoniram J. Gordon (1836–1895), A. B. Simpson (1843–1919), and evangelist Wilbur Chapman 1859–1918).

At the height of this wave of success, something went wrong. Schisms began to dominate the movement, and a third phase began: the establishment of independent Holiness churches. The voice for schism began to be heard in the 1880s, became dominant in the 1890s, and by 1910 had almost totally removed the Holiness movement from the larger denominations into independent Holiness churches. The movement out of Methodism was a response to at least three forces antagonistic to the Holiness position. First, a theological critique began to be heard. Men such as J. M. Boland, author of *The Problem of Methodism* (1888), attacked the second blessing doctrine and maintained that sanctification was accomplished at the moment of conversion. James Mudge (1844–1918), in his *Growth in Holiness toward Perfection, or Progressive Sanctification* (1895), argued for progressive rather than instantaneous sanctification. Borden Parker Bowne (1847–1910), representing a growing army of German-trained theologians, simply dismissed the whole issue of sanctification as irrelevant. (In the Lutheran and Presbyterian theologies, sanctification and justification were not separated as they were in Wesleyan and Methodist perspectives.)

The second force of growing concern to Methodist leaders was the mass of uncontrollable literature and organizations the Holiness movement was producing. By 1890 the number of books, tracts, pamphlets, and periodicals coming off the presses to serve the Holiness movement was enormous. Independent camp meeting associations covered the country, and in many places competed with local churches for the allegiance of members. Since camp meetings were independent, bishops and district superintendents had only the power of moral suasion to control what happened at the meetings or what was read throughout the movement. For some, this state of affairs was felt as a direct threat to their power. Others were genuinely concerned with excesses, fanaticism, and heterodox teaching. In either case, the loss of control led to an anti-Holiness polemic.

The third cause for the Holiness schism is found in the genuine shift of power that occurred between 1870 and 1890 in the Methodist Episcopal Church and the Holiness movement itself. By 1890 the bishops who promoted the Holiness movement and gave it official sanction had been replaced largely by others who were cool to the Holiness heat. Within the Holiness movement itself were regional and national leaders who were unhappy under the yoke of an unsympathetic hierarchy that was moving further away from their position each day. Not wishing to be confined in their ministry, they left the church. Among the first to leave were Daniel S. Warner (1842–1895), who founded the Church of God at Anderson, Indiana, and John P. Brooks (1826–1915). Brooks, a leader in the Western Holiness Association, in 1887 published *The Divine Church*, which called for all true Holiness Christians to come out of Methodism's church of mammon. *The Divine Church* became the theological guide to lead the way to the formation of independent churches.

The "come-out" movement created pressure on those who chose to remain in Methodist churches to justify their position. Thus, the 1890s saw loyalists publishing books against "come-outism," and calling for strengthening of the camp meetings. Beverly Carradine called for remaining in the church, but favored the establishment of independent Holiness colleges. Asbury College in Wilmore, Kentucky, and Taylor University in Indiana represent the partial success of Carradine's view. These efforts by the loyalists were unsuccessful, however, and by 1910 only minor pockets of Holiness teaching (such as the Brasher Campgrounds in Alabama) remained in the larger Methodist churches. As the twentieth century came to a close, these churches were dying out.

CONTEMPORARY DEVELOPMENTS. Possibly because of the intense controversy during the formative years of the older Holiness churches, there is a strong sense of identity within the Holiness family among the various members. This image is focused not only in the doctrinal unity and similarity of lifestyle, but in the several ecumenical structures. These structures are home to a wide range of groups, from those who still keep ties with the United Methodist Church (Wesleyans, Free Methodists), to groups like the Church of God of the Mountain Assembly, which has Baptist origins.

The oldest ecumenical structure is the Christian Holiness Partnership (formerly Christian Holiness Association). This body, which includes most of the larger Holiness churches in its membership, is a continuation of the National Camp Meeting Association for the Promotion of Holiness, which guided the movement from the 1870s. After the establishment of the various denominational structures, it functioned as a meeting ground for these new organizations and those who remained in their original churches, primarily

Methodists. Increasingly, it served the denominational bodies and in 1997 assumed its present name to recognize that fact.

One longstanding, if minor, theme in the Holiness movement was that perpetuated by the Keswick Conventions. Growing up primarily among the Holiness supporters of the Church of England, it supported the idea of suppression of evil tendencies, as opposed to the eradication taught by Wesleyans. Keswick ideas did not produce many new groups, but did find a home among one large body, the Christian and Missionary Alliance.

THE GLENN GRIFFITH MOVEMENT. Through the mid-twentieth century, the Holiness churches found themselves more and more accommodating to the world, especially in decisions concerning new realities (such as television and other contemporary forms of "worldly" entertainment) that were not an issue in previous generations. Some members protested this accommodation, arguing that they wished to preserve the "old-fashioned Scriptural Holiness" in which they were raised. The leader of this movement was the Reverend Glenn Griffith (1894–1976), a former minister from the Church of the Nazarene. The revival services he held in 1955 at a site between Nampa and Caldwell, Idaho, attracted many people. His movement spread, finding advocates in all of the larger Holiness churches. Adopting many of Griffith's ideas, ministers and members left those churches and formed a number of new denominations through the 1960s.

Even before Griffith gave focus to the protest movement, Reverend H. E. Schmul had facilitated fellowship among conservative Holiness churches and ministers through the Interdenominational Holiness Convention, begun by Schmul, a Wesleyan Methodist minister, in 1947. Its magazine, *Convention Herald*, served as a placement service for evangelists seeking appointments for revival meetings. Leaders of the various splinter movements within Holiness churches had participated in the Interdenominational Holiness Convention. After the new churches were formed, these leaders moved into key positions in the convention. The Interdenominational Holiness Convention continues to operate informally, with membership open to individuals, congregations, and churches.

SOURCES

Studies in the Holiness tradition are focused by the Christian Holiness Partnership, which may be reached c/o Martin Hotle, 263 Buffalo Rd., Clinton, TN 37716. The partnership publishes the semiannual *Holiness Digest*. The B. L. Fisher Library at Asbury Theological Seminary in Wilmore, Kentucky, houses a large Holiness collection. Primary denominational archives are at the Church of the Nazarene headquarters in Kansas City, Missouri, and the Marston Memorial Historical Center at the Free Methodist Church world headquarters in Indianapolis, Indiana.

General Sources on Sanctification and Holiness

Bassett, Paul M., ed. *Holiness Teaching: New Testament Times to Wesley.* Kansas City, MO: Beacon Hill Press, 1997.

Dieter, Melvin E., ed. *The 19th-Century Holiness Movement.* Kansas City, MO: Beacon Hill Press, 1998. 416 pp.

Dieter, Melvin E., Anthony A. Hoekema, Stanley M. Horton, et al. *Five Views on Sanctification.* Grand Rapids, MI: Academic Books, 1987.

Fénelon, François de Salignac de La Mothe. *Christian Perfection.* Ed. Charles F. Whiston. Trans. Mildred Whitney Stillman. New York: Harper & Row, 1947.

Finney, Charles G. *The Autobiography of Charles G. Finney: The Life Story of America's Greatest Evangelist, in His Own Words* (1876). Ed. Helen Wesel. Condensed. Minneapolis, MN: Bethany House, 2006.

————. *Sanctification.* Fort Washington, PA: Christian Literature Crusade, n.d.

Law, William. *A Serious Call to a Devout and Holy Life* (1728). New York: Vintage, 2002.

Lindström, Harald. *Wesley and Sanctification: A Study in the Doctrine of Sanctification.* New York: Abingdon, 1946.

The Holiness Movement in America

Brasher, J. Lawrence. *The Sanctified South: John Lakin Brasher and the Holiness Movement.* Champaign: University of Illinois Press, 1994. 280 pp.

Dieter, Melvin E., ed. *The 19th-Century Holiness Movement.* Kansas City, MO: Beacon Hill Press, 1998. 416 pp.

Jones, Charles Edwin. *Black Holiness: A Guide to the Study of Black Participation in Wesleyan Perfectionist and Glossolalic Pentecostal Movements.* Metuchen, NJ: American Library Association/Scarecrow Press, 1987.

————. *The Holiness-Pentecostal Movement: A Comprehensive Guide.* Metuchen, NJ: Scarecrow Press, 2008. 536 pp.

Kostlevy, William C., ed. *Historical Dictionary of the Holiness Movement.* Metuchen, NJ: Scarecrow Press, 2001.

Lambert, D. W. *Heralds of Holiness.* Stoke-on-Trent, U.K.: M.O.V.E. Press, 1975.

Miller, William Charles. *Holiness Works: A Bibliography.* Kansas City, MO: Nazarene Publishing House, 1986.

Peters, John Leland. *Christian Perfection and American Methodism.* New York: Abingdon, 1956.

Pollock, J. C. *The Keswick Story: The Authorized History of the Keswick Convention.* London: Hodder & Stoughton, 1964.

Smith, Timothy L. *Revivalism and Social Reform in Mid-nineteenth-century America.* Nashville, TN: Abingdon, 1957.

————. "The Holiness Crusade." In *The History of American Methodism,* ed. Emory Stevens Buck, vol. 2, pp. 608–659. Nashville, TN: Abingdon, 1965.

Thornton, Wallace Omor. *Radical Righteousness: Personal Ethics and the Development of the Holiness Movement.* Cincinnati, OH: Schmul, 1998. 344 pp.

Wesley Center for Applied Theology. *What Happened to the Holiness Movement?* Napa, ID: Northwest Nazarene College, 1995.

White, Charles Edward. *The Beauty of Holiness: Phoebe Palmer as Theologian, Revivalist, Feminist, and Humanitarian.* Grand Rapids, MI: Asbury Press, 1986.

Holiness Thought

Arthur, William. *The Tongue of Fire* (1856). Winona Lake, IN: Light and Life Press, n.d.

Boyd, Myron F., and Merne A. Harris, comps. *Projecting Our Heritage: Papers and Messages Delivered at the Centennial Convention of the National Holiness Association.* Kansas City, MO: Beacon Hill Press, 1969.

Carradine, Beverly. *The Sanctified Life.* Cincinnati, OH: Office of the Revivalist, 1897.

Foster, Randolph S. *Christian Purity.* New York: Nelson & Phillips, 1869.

Kuhn, Harold B., ed. *The Doctrinal Distinctives of Asbury Theological Seminary.* Wilmore, KY: Asbury Theological Seminary, n.d.

Palmer, Phoebe. *Faith and Its Effects.* New York: Palmer, 1854.

Rose, Delbert. *A Theology of Christian Experience: Interpreting the Historic Wesleyan Message.* 2nd ed. Minneapolis, MN: Bethany Fellowship, 1965.

Critical Appraisals

Boland, J. M. *The Problem of Methodism.* Nashville, TN: Author, 1888.

Ironside, Harold A. *Holiness, the False and the True.* New York: Loizeaux Brothers, 1947.

Mudge, James B. *Growth in Holiness Toward Perfection, or Progressive Sanctification.* New York: Hunt and Eaton, 1895.

Nevin, John W. *The Anxious Bench.* 2nd ed. Chambersburg, PA: German Reformed Church, 1844.

Warfield, Benjamin B. *Perfectionism* (1931). Philadelphia: Presbyterian and Reformed Publishing, 1958.

❈ Intrafaith Organizations

Alliance World Fellowship

The Christian and Missionary Alliance, 8595 Explorer Dr., Colorado Springs, CO 80920

Alternate Address: PO Box 35000, Colorado Springs, CO 80935-3500. Alliance World Fellowship, Driemaster 18, Veenendaal, Netherlands 3904 RK.

The Alliance World Fellowship (AWF) brings together the independent churches that have grown out of the missionary activity of the Christian and Missionary Alliance (C&MA). Soon after its formation in 1897, the C&MA launched a successful world mission program that led to the establishment of work in more than 50 countries. In more recent decades, C&MA missionary leaders were among the Christian thinkers who transformed the understanding of the missionary enterprise in light of the postcolonial era and the appearance of so many new nations in the third world. Since 1950, a number of the C&MA missions became autonomous national churches, and in 1975 the Alliance World Fellowship was organized to maintain the fellowship and restructure the relationship among the churches.

Now seen as partners in mission, the C&MA and the former missions cooperate as separate organizational entities, working together as equals. New overseas national churches are seen as autonomous bodies, taking the lead in the development of the work in their country.

The AWF meets quadrennially. As a fellowship, it assumes no legislative authority, and gatherings consist of reports on church work internationally, lectures and discussions, and small group meetings on topics of interest. Worship reflects the multi-national participation.

Membership: Membership includes the Christian and Missionary Alliance and some fifty churches around the world with a combined membership of more than 2.5 million.

Sources:

Alliance World Fellowship. www.awf.nu/.

Christian and Missionary Alliance. www.cmalliance.org.

Moore, David H. "How the C&MA Relates to Overseas Church." online.auc-nuc.ca/alliancestudies/ahtreadings/ahtr_s74.html.

Christian Holiness Partnership

263 Buffalo Rd., Clinton, TN 37716

The Christian Holiness Partnership (CHP), formerly known as the Christian Holiness Association, began in 1867 as the National Camp Meeting Association for the Promotion of Holiness, the prime organized expression of the youthful holiness movement that was revived following the civil war. The holiness movement had emerged in American Methodism in the decades prior to the war as the champion of the distinctive Wesleyan doctrine of the sanctification, the experience of the Christian believers that, by the power of the Holy Spirit, renders him or her perfect in love. As originally formed at the first large postwar camp meeting in Vineland,

New Jersey, the association was seen by its leaders as a promotional endeavor operating primarily in the Methodist Episcopal Church.

The work of the association, in holding camp meetings in the Northeast and Midwest, was soon extended to include the South and the far West, and in the mid-1870s it ventured to Australia and India for its first international work. The work was altered through the 1880s by the emergence of a number of independent holiness churches and the gradual cooling of enthusiasm for holiness ideas in the Methodist Church (which controlled most of the camp meeting sites regularly utilized by the holiness evangelists). By 1894, when the words camp meeting were dropped from the association's name, the group had become ecumenical, through much of the leadership was still based in the Methodist Episcopal Church.

The primary purpose of the organization was the promotion of holiness through camp meetings. With the rise of holiness churches and denominations, the parent organization became known as the National Holiness Association (NHA). In 1970 several holiness associations outside of the United States affiliated with the NHA, and the name was changed to the Christian Holiness Association. The current name was adopted in 1997.

The purpose of CHP, as defined in its constitution, is "to collectively pursue, promote, and proclaim the message of Scriptural Holiness; furthermore, . . . to celebrate the world-wide blessings of God upon our partnering, noting especially the multiple victories of our many Spirit-appointed ministries. Through this Partnership we seek a closer fellowship among all denominations, religious organizations and associations, educational institutions, individual churches, and persons who are in one accord with the Statement of Faith of this Partnership and the historic Wesleyan position on Scriptural Holiness, and further; we seek the conversion of sinners, the entire sanctification of believers as a second definite work of grace, and to promote a scriptural awakening and to generally edify the entire Body of Christ."

CHP seeks to fulfill its purpose through an annual convention; the publication of a quarterly digest; the operation of the Partnership Press, which assists member denominations in having their published works reach the major book market; the provision of religious programming for the Odyssey cable channel; and the maintenance of a Web site. Additionally, CHP has developed several commissions, including the Women's Commission, which endeavors to motivate, stimulate, and inspire women to follow Christ totally regardless of role or image; a higher education commission, comprising presidents and administrative leaders of holiness colleges, seminaries, and Bible colleges; the Wesleyan Theological Society, which encourages exchange of ideas among Wesleyan-Arminian theologians, develops papers for CHP seminars, stimulates scholarship among younger theologians and pastors, and publishes a scholarly journal; the Missions Commission, which holds an annual retreat for mission executives, sponsors a monthly prayer letter, and conducts a practical seminar at the annual convention; the Social Action Commission, which keeps the holiness movement aware of current social interests and stimulates effective action; an evangelism commission, to aid various member bodies in such areas a church planting, personal renewal, and evangelism; and the Camp Meeting Commission, which publishes a directory of camp meetings and presents a seminar on camp meetings at the annual convention.

Membership: Among the affiliated denominations are American Rescue Workers, the Association of Evangelical Churches, the Association of Independent Methodists, the Bible Holiness Movement, Brethren in Christ Church, Churches of Christ in Christian Union, Church of God (Anderson, Indiana), Congregational Methodist Church, Evangelical Christian Church, Evangelical Church of North America, Evangelical Congregational Church, Evangelical Friends Alliance (eastern region), Evangelical Methodist Church, Free Methodist Church of North America, Japan Immanuel General Mission, Missionary Church (north central district), Church of the Nazarene, Primitive Methodist Church, the Salvation Army (in the United States, Canada, and Bermuda), Sanctified Church, and Wesleyan Church.

Periodicals: *The Holiness Digest* • *Wesleyan Theological Society Journal*

Sources:

Jones, Charles Edwin. *A Guide to the Study of the Holiness Movement*. Metuchen, NJ: Scarecrow, 1974.

Interdenominational Holiness Convention

Salem, OH

The Interdenominational Holiness Convention (IHC) was founded in 1947 as an expression of the more conservative element in the holiness movement. Its primary moving force was H. E. Schmul, at the time a minister in the Wesleyan Methodist Church. By the end of World War II a variety of developments within the larger holiness denomination were, many felt, leading toward a loss of holiness distinctives. Theological education was becoming standard for ministers. And many of the holiness behavioral standards, especially restrictions on dress and entertainment, were being dropped.

In the 1950s the Church of the Nazarene experienced a schism as conservatives associated with Glenn Griffith left to found the Bible Missionary Church, and then in 1966–1967 conservatives in both the Wesleyan Methodist Church and Pilgrim Holiness Church founded new denominations in reaction to the merger of the two bodies. The IHC had been the home of these various conservatives and continued to be a focus of fellowship and cooperative activity.

Membership: Those churches and organizations associated with the IHC include: Allegheny Wesleyan Methodist Connection, Bible Methodist Connection of Churches, Bible Missionary Church, Church of the Bible Covenant, Evangelical Wesleyan Church, Independent Holiness Churches, Pilgrim Holiness Church of New York, Pilgrim Holiness Church of the Midwest, United Holiness Church of North America, Voice of the Nazarene Association of Churches, and Wesleyan Holiness Association of Churches.

Sources:

Jones, Charles Edwin. *A Guide to the Study of the Holiness Movement*. Metuchen, NJ: Scarecrow Press, 1974.

❋ Nineteenth Century Holiness

American Rescue Workers (ARW)

American Rescue Workers, Inc., National Headquarters, 25 Ross St., Williamsport, PA 17701

Alternate Address: Col. Sam Astin, 643 Elmira St., Williamsport, PA 17701.

Maj. Thomas E. Moore was the national commander of the Salvation Army in the 1880s when a dispute flared between him and the Army's founder, Gen. William Booth. Moore resigned his affiliation with Booth and incorporated his organization as the "Salvation Army." The name of Moore's organization was changed in 1890 to the American Salvation Army and again in 1913, to the American Rescue Workers.

The early years of the organization were fraught with instability. Moore stayed with the group he had founded for only nine months; he resigned and became a Baptist minister. Col. Richard Holz succeeded Moore, but never formally accepted the title of commander-in-chief. Shortly after taking control, he moved the headquarters to Saratoga Springs, New York. Holz had been leading the organization for only seven months when he was offered a position by Booth and, with about 150 officers, he returned to the Salvation Army. The ARW then reorganized under Major Gratton, but he soon left and was succeeded as commander-in-chief by William Duffin, who had been leader of a large center in Coatsville, Pennsylvania. The young Duffin led the organization for more than a half century, until his death in 1948.

The American Rescue Workers emerged in 1913 as a national religious social-service agency with a quasi-military model. Membership includes officers (clergy), soldiers/adherents (laity), members of various activity groups, and volunteers who serve as advisors, associates, and committed participants in the organization's service functions.

Motivated by the love of God, the organization has a message based upon the Bible and expressed in its spiritual ministry. Members preach the gospel of Jesus Christ and meet human needs in His name without discrimination. As a branch of the Christian church, it has established a diversified program of religious and social-welfare services that are designed broadly to meet the needs of all people.

The American Rescue Workers is headed by a commander-in-chief who is elected for a five-year term and can be re-elected. The present leader, Claude S. Astin, Jr., was first elected in 1996. Election takes place at the annual grand field councils. A board of managers administers the ongoing affairs of the organization. All properties are held in the name of the organization. Doctrinally, the organization is in agreement with its parent body, the Salvation Army, except with regard to the sacraments (which the Army does not observe). The American Rescue Workers believes in equal rights for women.

Membership: In 1997 the American Rescue Workers reported approximately 1,000 members, 15 centers, and 75 officers in the United States.

Periodicals: *The Rescue Herald*.

Sources:

American Rescue Workers. www.arwus.com

Ritual and Manual. American Rescue Workers, n.d.

Association of Fundamental Ministers and Churches

8605 E 55th St., Kansas City, MO 64129

The Association of Fundamental Ministers and Churches, Inc., was formed in 1931 by Rev. Fred Bruffett, Hallie Bruffett (his wife), Rev. Paul Bennett, Rev. George Fisher, and six other former ministers of the Church of God (Anderson, Indiana). Bennett had been dis-fellowshipped because of his fellowshipping with other churches. The Association believes that the new birth is the only necessity for fellowship.

Doctrine is like that of the Church of God. Healing is stressed and the ordinances are not emphasized. The Association meets annually and elects four officers to handle business affairs. There are 25 state conventions. Missions are conducted in Guatemala, Hong Kong, and Alaska.

Membership: Not reported.

Periodicals: *The Fundamental News*.

Bible Fellowship Church

3000 Fellowship Dr., Whitehall, PA 18052

The Bible Fellowship Church originated in 1858 when several members withdrew from the Eastern Conference Mennonites to form the Evangelical Mennonite Association. In 1883 the Evangelical Mennonite Association joined with other groups to form the Mennonite Brethren in Christ. The Bible Fellowship Church was formed in 1947 by churches withdrawing from the Mennonite Brethren in Christ when the Brethren changed their name to the United Missionary Church and dropped all Mennonite connections. Members of the Bible Fellowship Church see themselves as continuing the tradition of the Mennonite Brethren in Christ. Their doctrine follows that of the parent body, though the newer church has adopted a reformed soteriology. They abide by the Dort Confession of Faith (common to most Mennonites), but add statements on sanctification as a second work of grace received instantaneously (the unique "holiness" doctrine), divine healing, and the millennium. Baptism is by immersion.

All the churches of the Bible Fellowship Church are in Pennsylvania and are organized into two districts, each headed by a superintendent. There is an annual conference of the entire church. Polity is presbyterian. The Bible Fellowship Church supports approximately 150 missionaries around the world as well as church-planting missionaries in the United States.

Membership: In 2007 there were 60 churches and 7,600 members and 120 ministers.

Sources:

Bible Fellowship Church. www.bfc.org

Shelly, Harold P. *The Bible Fellowship Church*. Whitehall, PA: Bible Fellowship Church, 1992.

Bible Holiness Church (1995)

304 Camp Dr., Independence, KS 67301

The Bible Holiness Church, known until 1995 as the Fire Baptized Holiness Church (Wesleyan), was established in 1890 by holiness people in the Methodist Episcopal Church of southeastern Kansas. The original name, the Southeast Kansas Fire Baptized Holiness Association, was changed in 1945. The church is organized in an episcopal mode taken from the Methodist Episcopal Church. A general assembly meets annually. The Wesleyan holiness doctrine is emphasized, and strong prohibitions exist against alcohol, tobacco, drugs, secret societies, television, immodest clothing, jewelry, and frivolous amusements. Members regularly tithe. The church is aggressively evangelistic. Missions are supported on Grenada, the Windward Islands, and New Guinea.

Membership: In 2002 the church reported 1,700 members, 45 churches, and 83 ministers in the United States.

Educational Facilities:

Independence Bible School, Independence, Kansas.

Troy Holiness School, Troy, Missouri.

Brothers School, Grenada.

Periodicals: *Flaming Sword*. • *John Three Sixteen*. Available from 370 W College Ave., Independence, KS 67301.

Bible Holiness Movement

PO Box 223, Sta. A, Vancouver, BC, Canada V6C 2M3

The Bible Holiness Movement, formerly known as Bible Holiness Mission, was formed as a church in 1949. It grew out of the city mission work of the late Pastor William James Elijah Wakefield, an early-day Salvation Army officer, and his wife. Wakefield developed several doctrinal emphases distinct from those of the Salvation Army: For example, he believed the sacraments were real means of grace and not just symbolic ordinances, whereas the Salvation Army does not practice the sacraments at all. The Wakefields directed the mission until Wakefield's death in 1947. In 1949 his son, Wesley H. Wakefield, its bishop general, formed the Bible Holiness Mission. He changed the name of the organization in 1971 to the Bible Holiness Movement. Wesley Wakefield continues to direct the church as its international leader.

Membership involves a life of Christian love, evangelistic and social activism, and disciplines of simplicity and separation, which includes total abstinence from liquor and tobacco, nonattendance at popular amusements, and refusing membership in secret societies. Family stability is affirmed by forbidding divorce and remarriage while there is a living spouse. Similar to Wesley's Methodism, under some circumstances members are allowed to retain membership in other evangelical church fellowships.

Church government and ordination are open to both men and women and are fully racially integrated and international. A number of interchurch affiliations are maintained with other Wesleyan-Arminian Holiness denominations.

The movement is activist in respect to both evangelism and social concerns. Year-round evangelistic outreach is maintained through open-air meetings, home visits, distribution of literature, and other media. Noninstitutional welfare work, including addiction counseling, is conducted among minorities. There is direct overseas famine relief, as well as actions supporting civil rights, environmental protection, and antinuclear causes. Sponsored organizations include a permanent committee on religious freedom and active promotion of Christian racial equality.

Doctrinally, members are Methodists. They believe in the doctrine of the Holy Trinity; in the divine inspiration of the Holy Scriptures; in the deity, virgin birth, and sinless humanity of Jesus Christ; in a general atonement by his blood; in his bodily resurrection and ascension; in his intercession and personal second advent; in the deity and personality of the Holy Spirit; in the personality of Satan; in the total depravity of natural man; in the necessity of new birth; in the witness of the Spirit; in future rewards and punishments; and in the two sacraments of baptism and the Lord's Supper. They insist that it is the duty and privilege of every believer to be sanctified wholly, and to be preserved blameless unto the coming of the Lord Jesus Christ. Everyone who is received into full connection either professes to enjoy that perfect love that casts out fear, or promises diligently to seek until it is obtained.

From its Vancouver headquarters, the movement has an international outreach. Mission work began with the circulation of movement literature around the world. Currently, the church conducts work in Egypt, Ghana, India, Kenya, Liberia, Malawi, Nigeria, the Philippines, South Korea, Sri Lanka, Tanzania, Uganda, and Zambia. The movement belongs to the Christian Holiness Partnership, Evangelicals for Social Action, and the National Black Evangelical Association.

Membership: In 2001 the movement reported 563 members, 15 congregations, and 12 ministers in Canada and the United States. The two congregations in the United States are located in Phoenix, Arizona, and Kent, Washington. International membership is conservatively estimated at 90,881.

Periodicals: *Hallelujah!* • *On the March*

Sources:

Bible Holiness Movement. www.bible-holiness-movement.com

Triumph with Christ. Vancouver: Bible Holiness Movement, 1984.

Wakefield, Wesley H. *Bible Doctrine*. N.p., n.d.

Christ Holy Sanctified Church of America

PO Box 120574, Arlington, TX 76012

Christ Holy Sanctified Church of America was founded in 1910 in Keatchie, Louisiana, by Sarah A. King and Bp. Judge King. It was incorporated the next year in Memsfield, Louisiana. It grew out of the same movement that had produced Christ's Sanctified Holy Church in Louisiana several years earlier. Judge was succeeded by Bp. Ulysses King of Oakland, California. E. L. McBride is the present leader. The church supports Christ Holy Sanctified School, an industrial school. Headquarters is in Arlington, Texas.

Sources:

Christ Holy Sanctified Church of America. www.chschurch.org/home

Payne, Wardell J., ed. *Directory of African American Religious Bodies: A Compendium by the Howard University School of Divinity*. Washington, DC: Howard University Press, 1991.

Christian and Missionary Alliance (C&MA)

8595 Explorer Dr., Colorado Springs, CO 80920

The Christian and Missionary Alliance had its beginning in a summer conference at Old Orchard, Maine, in 1887. A number of Christian men and women connected with various evangelical denominations were organized under the leadership of Dr. Albert Benjamin Simpson (1843–1919), a Presbyterian minister. Simpson had begun publishing an interdenominational missionary magazine in 1882 to promote a deeper spiritual life for the support of an aggressive missionary ministry.

In response to the magazine and its description of a Bible and missionary convention held in 1884 at Simpson's New York Gospel Tabernacle, there arose a popular demand for similar conventions in other cities. In 1885 five were held in other metropolitan areas. These spread and gave rise to two organizations—the

Christian Alliance and the Missionary Alliance. The Christian Alliance was a group of local organizations, called "branches," that grew to 300 within ten years. More than 25 denominations were represented in branch auxiliaries for the support of the Missionary Alliance, the missionary-sending agency. It was a fraternal society with no intention of becoming another church or denomination, though the New York Gospel Tabernacle was organized as a regular independent church.

Again within ten years, the Missionary Alliance had more than 200 missionaries on approximately 100 stations in India, China, Japan, Africa, Palestine, the West Indies, and five Latin American countries. A missionary institute established in 1883 had graduated hundreds of students, many of whom were mature laymen and laywomen called by God into the missionary ministry. In 1897 the Christian Alliance and the Missionary Alliance were united as the "Christian and Missionary Alliance."

In doctrine, the Christian and Missionary Alliance stresses the centrality of Christ and His all-sufficiency—Christ as savior, sanctifier, healer, and coming king. A formal statement of doctrine was adopted in 1965. As the alliance developed in overseas ministries and at home, indigenous policies gave rise to national churches, particularly after World War II. By 1974 the Alliance was completely reorganized in the United States and Canada and declared to be a church and a denomination. The Canadian branch, united with the United States until 1980, also became nationally autonomous. Each has its own general council assembly whose workings resemble a combination of congregational and presbyterian policies.

The United States is presently served by two graduate schools and four colleges. Canada has one college and one graduate school. The United States and Canada each have a seminary fully accredited by the American Association of Theological Schools. An office of alternative education serves 1,591 students.

Membership: In 2005 the denomination totalled about 429,000 believers in 2,004 churches. An unusual feature was that one quarter of these congregations are intercultural (Cambodian, Dega, Haitian, Hmong, Jewish, Korean, Lao, Native American, Spanish, and Vietnamese). Canada, with its headquarters in Willowdale, Ontario, reported 76,119 members and 336 churches, 83 of which were ethnically diverse. Overseas ministries reported 1,931,363 members in 14,941 churches in 53 countries. In overseas ministries, the United States and Canada are a joint organization with 1,185 missionaries.

Educational Facilities:

Nyack College and Alliance Theological Seminary, Nyack, New York.

Simpson College and Simpson Graduate School, Redding, California.

Toccoa Falls College, Toccoa Falls, Georgia.

Crown College, St. Bonifacius, Minnesota.

Canadian Bible College and Canadian Theological Seminary, Regina, Saskatchewan, Canada.

Periodicals: *Alliance Life.*

Sources:

Christian and Missionary Alliance. www.cmalliance.org

Ayer, H. D. *The Christian and Missionary Alliance: An Annotated Bibliography of Texual Sources.* Lanham, MD: Scarecrow Press, 2001.

Bailey, Keith. *The Best of A. B. Simpson.* Camp Hill, PA: Christian Publications, 1987.

Manual. New York: Christian and Missionary Alliance, 1965.

Niklaus, Robert L.; John S. Sawin; and Samuel J. Stoesz. *All for Jesus.* Camp Hill, PA: Christian Publications, 1986.

Simpson, Albert B. *The Fourfold Gospel.* 1890. Harrisburg, PA: Christian Publications, 1984.

———. *A Larger Christian Life.* 1890. Harrisburg, PA: Christian Publications, 1984.

Christian Nation Church, U.S.A.
10059 Pleasant Renner Rd., Goshen, OH 45122

In 1892 eight young evangelists who called themselves "equality evangelists" began work in central Ohio, and in 1895 the Christian Nation Church was incorporated at Marion, Ohio. Doctrinally, the group is related to the Christian and Missionary Alliance, and preaches the four-fold gospel of its founder, Albert Benjamin Simpson (1843–1919). The church is very strict in forbidding worldly amusements, fashionable attire, Sabbath desecration, and divorce. Marriage with nonmembers is discouraged. Large families are encouraged as divinely sanctioned.

The polity of the Christian Nation is congregational with district and annual conferences. The pastors' licenses are renewed annually. Camp meetings are an active part of the program.

Membership: In 2008 the church reported 130 to 150 members.

Sources:

Christian Nation Church, U.S.A. www.christiannationchurch.org.

Christ's Sanctified Holy Church (Georgia)
Box 1465, CSHC, Perry, GA 31069

In 1887 Joseph Lynch, a member and class leader in the Methodist Episcopal Church, Chincoteague Island, Virginia, began to preach scriptural Holiness, which at that time conflicted with the church's direction. Following his conviction, he sought and obtained sanctification, the second blessing believed by Holiness churches to make the blessed perfect in love. Assisting Lynch in his early labors was Sarah E. Collins. The Methodist Episcopal Church resisted Lynch's preaching on this doctrine, so he and 58 members withdrew, and in 1892 they established Christ's Sanctified Holy Church. Nineteen members operated as trustees and were designated Board No. 1. Succesors of Board No. 1 incorporated the church in Chatham County, Georgia, in 1932. The trustee established subservient boards of extension (1938) and a general conference (1950) but reserved the corporate church affairs and management in the hands of Board No. 1.

Christ's Sanctified Holy Church is trinitarian in its beliefs and based upon the experience of sanctification as the second work of grace, but it differs from most Christian churches in serveral respects. It does not practice water baptism—members believe in the baptism of the Holy Ghost, which is inward and spiritual. It also does not practice the Lord's Supper because members believe that no act or ritual is necessary to establish a relationship between God and humans. Members believe not in a bodily resurrection but in a spiritual resurrection, through sanctification of the Spirit and a belief in truth. There are no paid ministers, and women share equal participation in all church functions.

Christ's Sanctified Holy Church has no individual membership and no congregational form of internal governance. It is governed by a noncongregational trusteeship whereby the church corporation draws from various separate corporate church entities and associations of like religious faith who may gain recognition under prescribed religious qualifications. Congregations are entitled to representation on the governing boards and use of the church's physical facilities for religious worship. At Perry, Georgia, the church owns a campground, a place for internment, and a home for the aged. Camp meeting is held the first Sunday in August of each year.

Membership: In 2008 the church reported approximately 700 members, 16 congregations, and 18 ministers.

Sources:

Christ's Sanctified Holy Church (Georgia). www.cshc.org

Clelland, E. Joseph. *The Writings of E. Joseph Clelland.* N.p.: Author, 1989.

Church of God (Anderson, Indiana)
Box 2420, Anderson, IN 46018

Daniel Warner (1842–1895), a minister of the General Eldership of the Churches of God in North America, now called the Church of God, General Council, was inspired by the Holiness movement. He became an ardent advocate of sanctification as a second work of grace. For that belief, he was tried and expelled from his church. Warner argued that sanctification led to an identification of the invisible church with the visible church, the concrete embodiment of the spiritual body of Christ.

In 1881 Warner organized the new Church of God. Like its parent body, the Church of God has no creed, but it follows the Holiness theological consensus. It believes in the inspiration of Scripture, the Trinity, the divinity of Jesus, the indwelling of the Holy Spirit, sin, repentance, and atonement in Christ. There is a distinctive eschatology. Although the members look for the Second Coming of Christ, they hold that it has no connection with a millennial reign: The kingdom of God is here and now. There will be a judgment day, with reward for the righteous and punishment for the wicked.

Three ordinances—symbolic acts of obedience and experience with Christ—are commonly practiced: baptism, the Lord's Supper, and footwashing. Baptism is by immersion. Communion is open to all believers. Footwashing is usually practiced on Maundy Thursday by separate groups of men and women. These symbolic acts are highlights of a Christian life of stewardship and high moral and ethical conduct. Prayer for divine healing is practiced, as is tithing.

Warner's distinctive doctrine of the church led to a rejection of the presbyterian system. The church uses a congregational form of government because it allows only the authority of God to operate. Membership is held in an informal way: There is no formal initiation rite for members, and no membership lists are made.

Beyond the local church, there are state and regional associations, and each year a general assembly is held in connection with the international convention. Anderson, Indiana, is home to the church. Located there are its national offices, one of its colleges, theological school, and Warner Auditorium (site of the international convention). There is an active outreach program conducted by the general church. The Christian Brotherhood Hour is heard over 300 radio stations, including Spanish, Russian, Arabic, Portuguese, Indian, and Chinese-speaking stations. The church has branches in 82 countries including Egypt, Lebanon, Greece, Switzerland, Germany, Denmark, England, Ireland, India, Korea, Japan, and throughout Central and South America and the Caribbean. Warner Press publishes many books, pamphlets, and tracts, and most of the educational material used by the church. The church is represented in the National Association of Evangelicals and is associated with the Christian Holiness Association.

Membership: In 2008 the largest concentrations of U.S. churches were in the Midwest, along the Pacific Coast, and in western Pennsylvania. Average weekend attendance in the congregations of the United States and Canada totals approximately 250,000. There are approximately 2,300 congregations in the United States and Canada. Worldwide, the movement has work in 89 countries and territories, representing approximately 7,300 churches and more than 750,000 believers.

Educational Facilities:

Anderson College, Anderson, Indiana.

Warner Pacific College, Portland, Oregon.

Mid-America Bible College, Oklahoma City, Oklahoma.

Warner Southern College, Lake Wales, Florida.

Gardner Bible College, Camrose, Alberta, Canada.

Bay Ridge Christian College, Kendleton, Texas.

Periodicals: *Vital Christianity* • *Leader Missions Shining Light*

Sources:

Church of God (Anderson, Indiana). www.chog.org

Callen, Barry L., ed. *The First Century*. 2 vols. Anderson, IN: Warner Press, 1979.

Miller, Milburn H. "Unto the Church of God." Anderson, IN: Warner Press, 1968.

Smith, John W. V. *A Brief History of the Church of God Reformation Movement*. Prestonburg, KY: Reformation Publishers, 2000.

Sterner, R. Eugene. *We Reach Our Hands in Fellowship*. Anderson, IN: Warner Press, 1960.

Church of God (Guthrie, Oklahoma)
304 E. Lakeview Rd., Guthrie, OK 73044

The Church of God (Guthrie, Oklahoma) was founded in 1905 by ex-slave George Winn. The church was chartered in 1906 by the Territory of Oklahoma. Other charter members of the church were C. N. Jones, George Oldham, James L. Glasgow, and Robert Glasgow. These ministers and laymen of the Church of God (Anderson, Indiana) separated from the church because of what they felt had been compromises and changes in doctrine and practice, and the congregation's drifting into worldliness. Some of the controversial new practices at the Church of God (Anderson, Indiana) were the segregation of the races and the wearing of neckties. In 1910 C.E. Orr began publishing *The Herald of Truth* in California, advocating the original position of Daniel Warner (1842–1895), founder of the Church of God (Anderson, Indiana). A movement supporting schism developed around Orr.

In doctrine and practice the Church of God (Guthrie, Oklahoma) is almost identical with the Church of God (Anderson, Indiana), but it is stricter in its practice of Holiness and refusal to compromise with the world. Like the members of the parent body, the members of the Church of God (Guthrie, Oklahoma) believe in healing and reject the idea of a literal millennium.

In 1923 Fred Pruitt moved from New Mexico to Guthrie and began to print Faith and Victory, which continues as the organ of the movement. Today Wayne Murphy continues his grandfather's work from the Faith Publishing House, and also publishes many tracts and *The Beautiful Way*, a children's quarterly. A vigorous mission program is supported in the Philippines, Nigeria, Mexico, and India. A national camp meeting has been held each July since 1938. Lesser camp meetings are held across the United States and in Mexico and Canada.

In 2008 the church was led by Brother Stanley Dickson.

Membership: Not reported.

Periodicals: *Faith and Victory* • *The Beautiful Way*

Sources:

Church of God (Guthrie, Oklahoma). www.theshop.net/faithpub/fpcogguthrie.html

Pruitt, Fred. *Past, Present and Future of the Church*. Guthrie, OK: Faith Publishing House, n.d.

Speck, S. L., and H. M. Riggle. *Bible Readings for Bible Students*. Guthrie, OK: Faith Publishing House, 1975.

Susag, S. O. *Personal Experiences*. Guthrie, OK: Faith Publishing House, 1976.

Warner, Daniel S. *The Church of God*. Guthrie, OK: Faith Publishing House, n.d.

Church of God (Holiness)
PO Box 4060, Overland Park, KS 66204

The Church of God (Holiness) began on March 29, 1883, with the founding of the Centralia, Missouri, church. The origin of the Church of God (Holiness) dates to the very beginning of the "come-out" crisis of the early 1880s, a movement whose leaders advocated coming out of the mainline Protestant churches in order to establish independent Holiness congregations. In their view, the ideal of the one New Testament church, a divine institution headed by Christ, was contradicted by what they saw as denominational, man-made organizations. Thus, local congregations organized to conform to the New Testament ideal became the movement's immediate goal. The first established independent congregations served primarily those Holiness people with no previous church (denominational) affiliation, but eventually included people leaving the older churches.

During the decades when Holiness advocates had been welcome in the mainline denominations, Holiness associations had formed. These were not churches, but simply groups loosely affiliated with the non-Holiness churches. As the come-out movement intensified, these associations fell into disfavor among many

Holiness proponents. Among those most strongly affected by come-outism were members of the Southwestern Holiness Association, which covered Kansas, Missouri, and Iowa. By 1882 six ministers, leaders of the association, had decided to withdraw from their parent denominational bodies as soon as it was convenient. A minister in the Methodist Episcopal Church, South, A. M. Kiergan, emerged as their leader and spearheaded the drive toward independent Holiness congregations. The dominance of the come-outers in the Southwestern Holiness Association caused its dissolution in 1887 and the formation of a new church, the Independent Holiness People, the following year. In 1895 the name was changed to Church of God (known as Independent Holiness People). *The Good Way*, which formerly had served the Southwestern Holiness Association, became the church newspaper.

Almost as soon as the church formed, two factions arose. One wanted complete local congregational sovereignty. The other said the elders should interpret doctrine and be spiritual rulers for the church, and should in turn be subject to a presbytery of elders. Kiergan and John P. Brooks (1826–1915), an early leader of the come-outers in Illinois, led the sovereignty faction. The crux of the issue was representation in the annual convention. In 1897 a "Declaration of Principles" was published by the sovereignty faction. The local sovereignty supporters wanted representation of the congregations at the annual meeting, and the others wanted the elders represented. Following the publication of the declaration, the church split into the Independent Holiness People (sovereignty faction) and Unity Holiness People (elder faction). A reunion of the two factions was accomplished in 1922, and the reunited church was named Church of God (Holiness). The new church merged with the Missionary Bands of the World, now a constituent part of the Wesleyan Church, but the merger fell through in 1938.

Four doctrines are central in the Church of God (Holiness)—the New Birth, Entire Sanctification, the one New Testament church, and the Second Coming followed by a literal millennium. The one New Testament church idea is a distinctive feature of the Church of God (Holiness). The doctrinal statement in the reunited church reads:

> *The New Testament Scriptures teach that there is one true Church, which is composed only of those who have savingly believed in the Lord Jesus Christ, and who willingly submit themselves to His divine order concerning the ministries of the church through the instrumentalities of God—chosen elders and deacons, ordained in the church by laying on of the hands of the presbytery. The attributes of the church are unity, spirituality, visibility, and catholicity. (Matt. 16:18; Eph. 4:4; Col. 1:18; I Tim. 3:1–7; Titus 1:5)*

The government of the Church of God (Holiness) is congregational, but a delegated annual convention has responsibility for the election of individuals to serve on the various boards of church-wide ministries. Each congregation may send a delegate to the general convention each June to represent its interests. One vote is allowed for every twenty-five members in the congregation who are born again. The board of publications oversees Herald and Banner Press, the church's publishing house, which publishes the church magazine and a full line of church school materials, the Way, Truth, & Life Series. The church has a worldwide missions program under the direction of the world mission board. Fields of service include Haiti, Jamaica, Mexico, the Cayman Islands, American and British islands of the eastern Caribbean, Bolivia, and Nigeria. The home missions board is responsible for encouraging church extension ministries in the United States, including ethnic group ministries among Native Americans, Hispanic, Asian, and Haitian immigrants, and blacks. The home and world mission programs are each directed by an executive secretary appointed by his or her respective board.

Membership: In 1988 the church reported 1,500 members and 120 congregations in the United States and a worldwide membership of 16,000.

Educational Facilities:

Kansas City College and Bible School, Overland Park, Kansas.

Holiness Bible School, Gravette, Arkansas.

Kirksville Bible School, Kirksville, Missouri.

Mount Zion Bible School, Ava, Missouri.

Mountain State Christian School, Culloden, West Virginia.

Overland Christian School, Overland Park, Kansas.

Periodicals: *The Church Herald and Holiness Banner* • *Opening the Word*

Sources:

Church of God (Holiness). www.cogh.net

Brooks, John P. *The Divine Church.* El Dorado Springs, MO: Witt Printing Co., 1960.

Cowen, Clarence Eugene. *A History of the Church of God (Holiness).* Overland Park, KS: Herald and Banner Press, 1949.

Church of the Living God (Sandford)

Current address not obtained for this edition.

The Church of Living God (Sandford), also known as the "Kingdom," was founded in 1894 by Frank Weston Sandford (1862–1948). It began in Brunswick, Maine, where Sandford opened a bible school in winter 1894 to 1895. Sandford had been a Freewill Baptist minister, but had left that denomination in 1893 after having been strongly affected by the teachings of A. B. Simpson and the Christian and Missionary Alliance, and having read Hannah Whitall Smith's The Christian's Secret of a Happy Life (1870). Both Simpson and Smith represented the Keswick branch of the Holiness Movement, which called believers to a second experience with the Holy Spirit that granted them entire sanctification.

In 1895 the group moved to new headquarters near Lisbon Falls, Maine, which was dubbed "Shiloh." The first building, which was greatly enlarged over the years and supplemented by adjacent buildings, served as headquarters of the church for a quarter century. Shiloh was dedicated in a ceremony in July 1895 during which Sandford ordained his first ministerial assistant, William Gleason.

The church followed a theology based on that of the Christian and Missionary Alliance. It was evangelistic and preached the higher sanctified life. There were four ordinances: baptism, healing, the Lord's Supper, and worship. Simpson had been one of the first to emphasize the recovery of divine healing in the church. Sandford deviated from many of the practices of the Holiness movement by instituting sabbatarian worship (on Saturday). The Lord's Supper was closed to all but the members of the movement, a practice that indicated its separatist stance. In October 1895, without reference to any prior baptisms, Sandford rebaptized all of the members of the group, about 218.

As churches emerged around New England and, to a lesser extent, the rest of the country, Sandford initiated a system of membership based upon commitment levels. The most committed were those living at Shiloh, who gave up everything and worked full time for the movement. They lived by faith, relying upon God to supply their needs. At a minimum, members were required to tithe.

The most controversial belief of the movement, articulated in 1901, was that Sandford was the prophet Elijah returned, the prophet who was to announce the return of Christ and the beginning of the millennial kingdom. The group began to see itself as the precursor group for the establishment of God's kingdom on earth.

Life at Shiloh was intense and subject to the occasional arbitrary change in direction articulated by Sandford. Some members left and joined forces with other religious leaders in the area to attack the school. However, the movement grew steadily, and had developed a small following in Europe by 1904. That year, Sandford was indicted for manslaughter for several deaths that occurred during winter 1902–1903. Initially he was found guilty, but the verdict was overturned on appeal. In 1911 Sandford was arrested again, and charged with being responsible for several deaths that occurred on the group's missionary ship during a voyage to Greenland. He was convicted and sentenced to ten years in prison.

Before leaving to serve his time, Sandford appointed seven ministers to take charge of Shiloh and the movement, but he kept in touch by way of regular letters and the visits of a member who moved to Atlanta and took stenographic notes of their conversations. When he was released in 1918, he immediately resumed control of the movement. Then in 1920, the state moved against Shiloh, claiming that the parents living there were neglecting their children. Threatened with extensive legal proceedings as each family's case was abjudicated, Sandford disbanded and dispersed the group and closed the center. From that time on, the movement he led has existed in a decentralized state. Sandford continued to lead the church until his death in 1947, but made few personal appearances.

The Kingdom Christian Ministries sprang from the former fellowship of like-minded churches, all of whom were under the ministry of the Kingdom. After a restructuring that took place in 1998, it became clear to some of those churches (later called KCM) that they wanted to carry on the same ministry, which included (in part) the unity of all believers. During the restructuring, each congregation incorporated individually and received real estate assets formerly held by the Kingdom, then those that wanted to continue ministry together pooled those assets.

Membership: There were eight church congregations in 2008 that made up the Kingdom Christian Ministries. Some were new home churches without buildings, others were well established.

Sources:

Church of the Living God (Sandford). www.kingdomchristianministries.org.

Murray, Frank S. *The Sublimity of Faith: The Life and Work of Frank W. Sandford.* Amherst, NH: The Kingdom Press, 1981.

Nelson, Shirley. *Fair Clear and Terrible: The Strange Story of Shiloh.* Latham, NY: British American Publishing, 1989. 446 pp.

Sandford, Frank S. *The Art of War for the Christian Soldier.* 1906. Reprint. Amherst, NH: The Kingdom Press, 1966.

———. *The Golden Light upon the Two Americas.* Amherst, NH: The Kingdom Press, 1974.

———. *The Majesty of Snowy Whiteness.* 1901. Reprint. Amherst, NH: The Kingdom Press, 1963.

Church of the Nazarene

6401 The Paseo, Kansas City, MO 64131

Most holiness advocates were originally members of the Methodist Episcopal Church and the Methodist Episcopal Church, South, until the hostility of their leaders made them feel that a new church was their only option. Thus, late in the nineteenth century a number of small schisms occurred, and independent holiness congregations and associations came into existence. By the turn of the century, these smaller groups were seeking wider fellowship through mergers. The Church of the Nazarene is the result of a set of such mergers.

While the Church of the Nazarene had a number of founders, the primary one was Phineas Bresee (1838–1915). In 1895 Bresee, a former Methodist pastor and presiding elder, organized the First Church of the Nazarene in Los Angeles, California, after leaving the Peniel Mission, where he had been preaching for a year. Coincident with Bresee's efforts, the Association of Pentecostal Churches of America was formed in New York. In 1896 this group united with the Central Evangelical Holiness Association (established in 1890); member congregations were located primarily in New England. In October 1907, the Association of Pentecostal Churches of America and the Church of the Nazarene, both having grown into small denominations, merged to form the Pentecostal Church of the Nazarene. On October 13, 1908, the Holiness Church of Christ united with the Pentecostal Church of the Nazarene in a joint assembly at Pilot Point, Texas; the merged body retained the name of Pentecostal Church of the Nazarene. The 1908 date is accepted as the official "anniversary" of the present-day Church of the Nazarene. In 1915 the Pentecostal Church of Scotland and the Pentecostal Mission of Nashville, Tennessee, united with the Pentecostal Church of the Nazarene.

In 1919 the word *Pentecostal* was dropped to avoid confusion with the "speaking in tongues" sects. Over the years, other groups have united with the Church of the Nazarene, including the Laymen's Holiness Association (1922); the International Holiness Mission, an English group (1952); the Calvary Holiness Church, also British in origin (1955); the Gospel Workers Church of Canada (1958); and the indigenous Church of the Nazarene (Nigeria) (1988), the founders of which were influenced by the 1944 *Manual* of the international Church of the Nazarene.

The Church of the Nazarene views itself as firmly Wesleyan in doctrine and practice and keeps in essence the Articles of Religion and General Rules as sent to America by Methodist founder, John Wesley. The church has, however, added statements on the plenary inspiration of Scripture, regeneration, entire sanctification, divine healing, and eschatology, and has changed completely Wesley's article on the church. The major emphasis is upon entire sanctification subsequent to regeneration and the personal holiness of the believer.

Government in the groups that formed the Church of the Nazarene was of all types: congregational, representative, and episcopal. The final outcome of the merging of these types was a representative government. The highest law-making body is the General Assembly, composed equally of ministerial and lay delegates elected by the district assemblies. The general Board, elected by the General Assembly, has oversight of church agencies and concerns: evangelism, missions, publication, education, and ministerial benevolences. The General Assembly, presided over by the general superintendents (who are elected every four years), has final authority in all matters except changes in the church constitution, which must also be approved by the district assemblies. The district assembly orders the work of the district and supervises the local churches and ministers. The local church calls its own pastor, subject to the district superintendents' approval, and conducts its own affairs in accordance with General Assembly guidelines.

Missionary work by what became the Church of the Nazarene began in 1897 when Mr. and Mrs. M. D. Wood, Carrie Taylor, Lillian Sprague, and F. P. Wiley sailed for India. The work has grown and the church presently has districts and congregations in over 150 nations and on all continents. In 1980 the General Assembly embraced the policy of internationalization, meaning that the church would be considered as a single international denomination. By 2007, 37 percent of Nazarenes lived in the United States.

Publishing began in 1888 with the *Beulah Christian* and in 1898 with the *Nazarene Messenger.* Early in 1900, the Nazarene Publishing Company was founded to carry on the work of the growing denomination. In 1911, after the merger, plans were made to establish a centrally located Nazarene publishing house. The new publishing concern—now Beacon Hill Press of Kansas City, Missouri—is the largest publisher of holiness literature in the world. The Church of the Nazarene is a member of the National Association of Evangelicals, the World Methodist Council, and the European Methodist Council.

Membership: In 2008 the Church of the Nazarene reported having 1,733,772 members worldwide, with 642,523 of those members living in the United States and 13,375 in Canada. Of 429 districts, 77 are in the United States and 5 are in Canada. The global total of 15,359 churches includes 4,714 U.S. churches and 161 Canadian ones. Worldwide, there are 684 ordained deacons (of whom 518 are in the U.S. and 8 are in Canada) and 7,435 licensed ministers (of whom 2,830 are in the U.S. and 74 are in Canada).

Educational Facilities:

A complete listing of Nazarene educational institutions may be found at www.nazarene.org/education/iboe/display.aspx.

Periodicals: *Holiness Today.* • *El Heraldo de Santidad.* • *Preachers Magazine.* • *Grow.* • *Arauto da Santidade.* • *Ministerio.* • *Reflecting God.*

Sources:

Church of the Nazarene. www.nazarene.org/.

Bangs, Carl. *Phineas F. Bresee: His Life in Methodism, the Holiness Movement, and the Church of the Nazarene*. Kansas City, MO: Beacon Hill, 1995.

Brickley, Donald P. *Man of the Morning*. Kansas City, MO: Nazarene Publishing House, 1960.

Girvin, E. A. *Phineas F. Bresee: A Prince in Israel*. Kansas City, MO: Pentecostal Nazarene Publishing House, 1916.

Office of the General Secretary, Church of the Nazarene. "Annual Church Statistical Reports." Released December 17, 2007. 23 pp. This is the official report for the 2007 statistical year, which ended on September 30, 2007.

Price, Ross E. *Nazarene Manifesto*. Kansas City, MO: Beacon Hill Press, 1968.

Purkiser, W. T. *Called unto Holiness, II*. Kansas City, MO: Nazarene Publishing House, 1983.

Redford, M. E. *The Rise of the Church of the Nazarene*. Kansas City, MO: Beacon Hill Press, 1948.

Smith, Timothy. *Called unto Holiness*. Kansas City, MO: Nazarene Publishing House, 1962.

Tracy, Wesley D., and Stan Ingersol. *What Is a Nazarene?: Understanding Our Place in the Religious Community*. Kansas City, MO: Beacon Hill Press, 1998.

Churches of God (Independent Holiness People)

c/o Holiness Messenger, PO Box 472202, Tulsa, OK 74147

In 1922 the Church of God (Independent Holiness People) and the Church of God (Unity Holiness People) united to become the Church of God (Holiness). However, some members of the Church of God (Independent Holiness People), often referred to as the sovereignty faction because they were committed to the strong sovereignty of the local congregation, did not join the merger. They reorganized and established headquarters at Fort Scott, Kansas. The continuing church has no doctrinal differences with the Church of God (Holiness), only distinctive by its firm allegiance to a congregational government. The church is staunchly pacifist and annually at its conventions has passed resolutions against Christian participation in war. Membership is concentrated in the Southwest. Missionary work is conducted in Japan and Mexico and among American Indians in South Dakota and Wyoming.

It was the vision of some members among the Independent Holiness Churches, mainly those in the Oklahoma area, to further fellowship among the Holiness people by means of a publication. On June 16, 1953, a number of pastors met to discuss the possibility, and the fruit of that meeting was the *Holiness Messenger*. The first issue was printed in August 1953.

Membership: Not reported. In 1972 fifteen churches were represented at the annual convention.

Periodicals: *The Church Advocate and Good Way* • *The Holiness Messenger*

Sources:

Churches of God (Independent Holiness People). www.holinessmessenger.com

Emmanuel Association

c/o Peoples Bible College, 2713 W Cucharas, Colorado Springs, CO 80904

The Emmanuel Association was formed in 1937 by Ralph G. Finch, a former general superintendent of Foreign Missions of the Pilgrim Holiness Church, now a constituent part of the Wesleyan Church. The Emmanuel Association was run by Finch until his death in 1949. Now the Association is run by a general conference made up of all ordained and licensed ministers. This conference establishes all rules and elects the officers. Local churches function under the general conference. There is also a provision for affiliated membership for both ministers and congregations.

Doctrine is like that of the Pilgrim Holiness Church, but with a very rigid behavior code, the "Principles of Holy Living." Members are conscientious objectors, believing that war is murder. Foreign missionary work is carried on in Guatemala.

Membership: Not reported. In the 1970s there were 17 churches in the United States and Canada and an estimated membership of 400.

Educational Facilities:

People's Bible College, Colorado Springs, Colorado.

Periodicals: *Emmanuel Herald*.

Sources:

The Guidebook of the Emmanuel Association. Colorado Springs, CO: Emmanuel Association, 1966.

Ralph Goodrich French: The Man and His Mission. Colorado Springs, CO: Emmanuel Press, 1967.

Evangelical Missionary Church of Canada

130 Fergus Ave., Kitchener, ON, Canada N2A 2H2

The Evangelical Missionary Church of Canada (EMCC) is a Canadian family of churches (denomination) with historical roots in the pioneer settlement of Ontario and the Canadian West, earlier European migration to the eastern seaboard of the United States, and the Reformation in Europe. Its present identity comes through the 1993 merger of the Evangelical Church in Canada (formerly a conference of the Evangelical Church in North America) and the Missionary Church of Canada (before 1987, two districts of the Missionary Church, a North American family of churches).

Each partner brought to the union its characteristic emphases. The Evangelical Church in Canada contributed its evangelistic fervor, practice of spiritual disciplines, and emphasis on the Holy Spirit's sanctifying power that characterized John Wesley's Methodist teaching, particularly as it affected early North American German-speaking immigrants. The Missionary Church of Canada, which originated in later revival movements that swept North America in the second half for the nineteenth century, enriched the union with its missionary zeal as well as the Anabaptist concepts of community, brotherhood, and believer's baptism, which were distinguishing marks of the Missionary Church's Swiss Mennonite background. The renewed denomination remains committed to the Christian Scriptures as the source of doctrine and standards of holy, missional living and to the Good News of personal transformation through a faith relationship with Jesus Christ as Savior and Lord.

There are approximately 150 Evangelical Missionary churches, the majority of which are in Ontario, Alberta, and British Columbia. Presently, Centre Street Church in Calgary is the EMCC's largest congregation.

The EMCC leaders' vision is that their followers will make disciples of Jesus Christ who in turn will make other disciples who will gather into healthy communities of faith across Canada and around the world.

The EMCC has founded two colleges—Rocky Mountain College in Calgary, Alberta, and Emmanuel Bible College in Kitchener, Ontario. These institutions have trained more than three thousand students to become pastors, church leaders, and missionaries, as well as committed Christians in the marketplace and community. Fourteen years after the church merger, the renewed denomination sends and supports about 140 missionaries in 27 countries (including some in Canada) under both its own mission agency (EMCC World Partners) and other agencies with evangelical and holistic emphases. Relief and development projects and ministries complement the EMCC's response to the needs of the world.

The denomination fellowships and cooperates in world mission with national Missionary churches in the United States and around the world, maintains fraternal relationship with the Evangelical Church in the United States, and collaborates with other Canadian evangelical entities.

Membership: In 2006 the church reported 135 congregations, 10,792 members, and 362 ministers.

Educational Facilities:

Rocky Mountain College, Calgary, Alberta.

Emmanuel Bible College, Kitchener, Ontario.

Sources:

Evangelical Missionary Church of Canada. www.emcc.ca.

Lageer, Eileen. *Common Bonds*. Calgary: Evangelical Missionary Church of Canada, 2004.

Faith Mission Church

1817 26th St., Bedford, IN 47421

Faith Mission Church is a single, independent, holiness congregation founded in 1893. It was formed as a center of the Pentecost Bands, one of the original holiness associations, later renamed the Missionary Bands of the World. In 1958, the Missionary Bands merged into the Wesleyan Methodist Church (now a constituent part of the Wesleyan Church). Members of the congregation in Bedford, Indiana, which had been originally chartered in the early 1920s, rejected the merger and became independent. Under their pastor, Rev. Ray Snow, the church adopted its present name in 1963. The church is currently pastored by Leonard Sankey.

Membership: Faith Mission Church is an independent congregation that had approximately 170 members in 2002.

Educational Facilities:

God's Bible School and College, Cincinnati, Ohio.

Free Methodist Church of North America

PO Box 535002, Indianapolis, IN 46253

HISTORY. The Free Methodist Church of North America was organized in 1860 in western New York by ministers and lay people who had formerly been members of the Genesee Conference of the Methodist Episcopal Church. The Rev. Benjamin Titus Roberts (1823–1893) was the leader of the group and the elected general superintendent (later, bishop). He and other leaders of the conference, both laity and clergy, had been expelled from the church for "insubordination." After an appeal of the case had been denied by the Methodist General Conference in 1860, those excommunicated men and others met to form a new Methodist institution.

Roberts and others had been calling the Methodists to return to what they considered the primitive doctrines and lifestyle of Methodism. They especially emphasized the Wesleyan teaching of the entire sanctification of life by means of grace through faith. In their writings and preaching they condemned with vigor their less radical brothers for worldliness and their departure from Methodist doctrine and experience. Because of their strong opposition to secret societies, the leaders of Free Methodism incurred the ill will of members of the conference who held membership in such lodges and fraternal orders. Also, Roberts and most of his followers were radical abolitionists in the years immediately before the Civil War, at a time when many within the Methodist Episcopal Church were hesitant in their condemnation of slavery. Also importantly, the early Free Methodists condemned the growing practice of selling pews in Methodist churches; they advocated free pews for all, an issue which was in part responsible for their name.

BELIEFS. The Free Methodist Church had little doctrinal quarrel with the Methodist Episcopal Church, and originally they adopted a modified form of the Twenty-five Articles of Religion. They added an article on entire sanctification and made a few minor changes. However, in 1974 an entirely new and expanded set of articles of religion were adopted by the church. Not only do they cover some issues not touched on in the earlier articles (such as eschatology), they also have appended a lengthy set of biblical references that detail the scriptural underpinnings for each statement. But the new articles do not in any way deviate in essential content from the earlier set.

From its beginning, the Free Methodist Church made Christian holiness a significant distinctive of its teaching. The church has interpreted the Bible and the writings of John Wesley to teach that all Christians may be inwardly cleansed from sinful rebellion against God's will. It believes that the sanctification of the affections and will may be experienced instantly, in a moment of faith, when the wholly committed Christian accepts the atonement of Jesus Christ and the fullness of the Holy Spirit for the cleansing of his or her motives and the perfection of his or her love toward God and other persons. According to the church, the sanctification of life is a process of growth and development in holiness through the empowering of the Holy Spirit in the life of the Christian. The Free Methodist Church has endeavored to follow the teachings of Wesley regarding the sanctification of life by forming both general and special rules to guide Christians in the way of holiness. All adult members of the church commit to live wholesome and holy lives and show mercy to all, ministering to both their physical and spiritual needs. They must commit themselves to be free from activities and attitudes that defile the mind and harm the body or promote the same; commit themselves to practice the principles of Christian stewardship for the glory of God and the growth of the church; vow to keep themselves free from membership in secret societies, that their loyalties may not be divided; and disavow all racism and political and social discrimination against ethnic minorities. They promise to regard marriage and the family as sacred, and they avoid divorce except in cases of adultery or desertion.

The government of the church is a modified episcopacy. From the beginning, when lay leaders and ministers met to form the new denomination, provision was made for equal representation of clergy and laity in all the councils of the church, both local and general. A general conference meets every four years to review and establish the polity and programs of the denomination and to elect the bishops. Annual conferences bring together the ministers and delegated representatives of the local congregations in 28 districts in the United States. Pastors are appointed by the annual conference, with the bishop serving as chairman of a ministerial appointments committee. All church property is held in trust for the denomination.

The church is a member of both the Christian Holiness Association and the National Association of Evangelicals.

Membership: In 2004 the church reported 77,173 members and 1,032 congregations in the United States. Worldwide membership in 72 countries was 736,582.

Educational Facilities:

Central Christian College of Kansas, McPherson, Kansas.

Greenville College, Greenville, Illinois.

Roberts Wesleyan College, Rochester, New York.

Seattle Pacific University, Seattle, Washington.

Spring Arbor University, Spring Arbor, Michigan.

The church is affiliated with Asbury Theological Seminary, Wilmore Kentucky.

George Fox Evangelical Seminary, Portland, Oregon.

Wesley Biblical Seminary, Jackson, Mississippi.

G. P. Haggard School of Theology, Azusa Pacific University, Azusa, California (the church cooperates with, but does not sponsor, Azusa Pacific University).

Northeastern Seminary at Roberts Wesleyan College, Rochester, New York.

Periodicals: *Light and Life Magazine* • *Free Methodist World Mission People*

Sources:

Free Methodist Church of North America. www.freemethodistchurch.org.

Hogue, William T. *History of the Free Methodist Church*. 2 vols. Chicago: Free Methodist Publishing House, 1918.

Marston, Leslie R. *From Age to Age a Living Witness*. Winona Lake, IN: Life and Light Press, 1960.

Roberts, B. T. *Holiness Teachings*. Salem, OH: H. E. Schmul, 1964.

Snyder, Howard A. *Populist Saints: B. T. and Ellen Roberts and the First Free Methodists*. Grand Rapids, MI: William B. Eerdmans, 2006.

Taylor, J. Paul. *Holiness, the Finished Foundation*. Winona Lake, IN: Life and Light Press, 1963.

Independent Holiness Church

1564 John Quinn Rd., Greely, ON, Canada K4P 1J9

The Independent Holiness Church dates to the preaching activity of Ralph Cecil Horner (1854–1921). Horner, a member of the Montreal conference of the Methodist Church, Canada, refused to assume his pastoral appointments during the 1890s, preferring to engage in evangelistic activity. He was committed to a Holiness perspective (an emphasis upon God's second work of grace, which brings sanctification or perfect love to the believer) at a time when sanctification as a progressive process was becoming the dominant perspective in Methodism. In 1895 Horner was discharged from his ministerial duties, and he formed the Holiness Movement Church. In 1919 the church asked Horner to retire. Instead, he left the Holiness Movement Church and formed the Standard Church of America.

In 1959 the Holiness Movement Church merged into the Free Methodist Church. As the time of the merger approached, several congregations voiced their disapproval by breaking away and reconstituting themselves as the Independent Holiness Church. Their doctrinal statement is similar to those of other Holiness bodies, affirming belief in the Trinity, salvation in Christ, and the possibility of entire sanctification for every believer. Members are expected to live a holy life and give evidence of this by refraining from the use of alcohol, tobacco, and drugs, fasting once a week, avoiding worldly entertainments, and dressing modestly. The church promotes tithing and daily scripture reading and is against games of chance and secret societies. Divorce is frowned upon, and remarriage after a divorce is not allowed within the voting membership. The church is congregational in organization and has a general conference that meets every two years.

The Independent Holiness Church regularly supports one mission, on the island of Hispaniola, and supports several other missions as donations are received for those missions.

Membership: In 1995 the church had 13 congregations (12 in Canada and one in the United States) and approximately 250 members.

Periodicals: *Gospel Tidings*.

Sources:

Independent Holiness Church. www.holiness.ca/index.html

Metropolitan Church Association

323 Broad St., Lake Geneva, WI 53147

The Metropolitan Church Association was formed in 1894. It grew out of a holiness revival at the Metropolitan Methodist Episcopal Church in Chicago. It was first known as the Metropolitan Holiness Church and adopted its present name in 1899. Members had a reputation for emotional displays during worship and ascetic behavior patterns. Early in its life, the Association adopted a communal form of organization, a factor that slowed its growth in the long run.

Besides its early emphasis on inner city missions, the Association has also focused on establishing foreign missions around the globe. The one in India has been most productive, and a school and hospital are supported there. Other missions are supported in Mexico and in Cape Town and Swaziland, South Africa. There is an annual camp meeting for revival and fellowship, held at a church in Milwaukee, Wisconsin. Business is conducted by an annual general assembly.

Membership: In 2008 the church reported zero congregations in the United States, 23 in Mexico, and over 30 in south India.

Periodicals: *The Burning Bush*.

Sources:

Fuller Institute for Recovery Ministry. www.fullerinstitute.org.

Henry, G. W. *Shouting: Genuine and Spurious*. Chicago: Metropolitan Church Association, 1903.

Missionary Church, Inc. (U.S.)

PO Box 9127, Fort Wayne, IN 46899-9127

Missionary Church, Inc. (U.S.) was formed in 1969 by the merger of the United Missionary Church and the Missionary Church Association.

From Defenseless Mennonite roots, the Missionary Church Association was formed in 1898 at Berne, Indiana, under the leadership of J. E. Ramseyer (1869–1944). The group had been influenced by the Christian and Missionary Alliance in both faith and practice.

The United Missionary Church dates to an evangelistic effort among the Mennonites in Lehigh County, Pennsylvania. In 1858 a conference was founded using the name Evangelical Mennonites. In 1869, influenced by the Methodist revivals, Solomon Eby (1834–1929), a Canadian Mennonite minister from Port Elgin, professed conversion after several years in the ministry and instituted protracted meetings in his effort to spread the new experience of grace. The movement spread and was embraced by a former Mennonite group centered in Elkhart, Indiana, led by Daniel Brenneman (1834–1919), who had also experienced personal conversion. In 1874 the two fellowships took the name Reformed Mennonites. The next year they were joined by a small body in the Niagara area of Ontario, Canada, called the New Mennonites, and took the new name United Mennonites. The United Mennonites and the Evangelical Mennonites merged in 1879 to form the United Evangelical Mennonites. This body merged with a small splinter of the River Brethren in Pennsylvania and Ohio (Brethren in Christ) in 1883 to become the Mennonite Brethren in Christ, with churches in both the U.S. and Canada. The change of name in 1947 to United Missionary Church was a recognition of its move away from its Mennonite background.

In 1969 the United Missionary Church merged with the Missionary Church Association to form the Missionary Church, Inc. The Missionary Church Association had generally followed the fourfold gospel emphasis of Albert Benjamin Simpson (1843–1919), founder of the Christian and Missionary Alliance, presenting Christ as savior, sanctifier, healer, and coming king. The United Missionary Church, influenced by Methodism, emphasized Wesleyan teaching. These have blended, and without moving from the truths so held, the Missionary Church, Inc. adopted a more comprehensive presentation of its evangelical conservative and Holiness faith.

Membership: In 2008 Missionary Church, Inc. (U.S.) reported more than 206,000 people in more than 1,800 congregations in 35 countries. There are more than 400 congregations in the United States.

Educational Facilities:

Bethel College, Mishawaka, Indiana.

Periodicals: *Emphasis* • *Priority* • *Missionary Church Today*

Sources:

Missionary Church, Inc. (U.S.). www.mcusa.org.

Lageer, Eileen. *Merging Streams*. Elkhart, IN: Bethel, 1979.

Missionary Methodist Church of America

318 Ballard St., Cherryville, NC 28021

The Missionary Methodist Church was formed in 1913 in Forest City, North Carolina, by Rev. H. C. Sisk and four other former members of the Wesleyan Methodist Church. (The Wesleyan Methodist Church subsequently merged with the Pilgrim Holiness Church to form the Wesleyan Church.) The Missionary Methodist Church was originally called the Holiness Methodist Church, but the church changed its name when it learned of another group with the same name. The original disagreement that led to the founding of the church concerned the number of rules and regulations of the Wesleyan Methodist Church. The Missionary Methodist Church's two-paragraph creed includes belief in sanctification, which burns out all inbred sin; living every day above sin; keeping the self unspotted from the world; a personal devil; a literal, burning hell; and the premillennial return of

Christ. "There are," states the creed, "no hard man-made rules to bind one down, you can have freedom in the Missionary Methodist Church." In 1939 the Oriental Missionary Society was adopted as the missionary agency of the church.

The church has a board of directors consisting of a chairman, two vice chairmen, a secretary, and a treasurer. In 2008 the chairman was Rev. Bob Holtsclaw.

Membership: In 2008 the church listed 14 congregations on its website, most of which are located in North Carolina.

Sources:

Missionary Methodist Church of America. www.mmc-oa.org.

Doctrine, Creed, and Rules for the Government of the Missionary Methodist Church of America. Morganville, NC: 1969.

New Testament Church of God

Current address not obtained for this edition.

The New Testament Church of God, Inc., was founded in 1942 by G. W. Pendleton and his wife, Martha Pendleton, both former members of the Church of God (Anderson, Indiana). They opposed the Church of God's cooperation with and financial support of the National Council of Churches but retained the doctrines of the parent body. The members hold camp meetings and state and regional conventions, publish gospel literature, and have regular radio broadcasts.

Membership: Not reported.

Periodicals: *Seventh Trumpet.*

Salvation Army

Salvation Army National Headquarters, 615 Slaters Ln., PO Box 269, Alexandria, VA 22313

The Salvation Army is an international religious and charitable movement organized and operated on a quasi-military model. Its juxtaposition of two strong motivations, love of God and a practical concern for humanity, results in a ministry dedicated to preaching the Christian gospel and disseminating its teaching while supplying basic human necessities. It offers personal counseling and a program of spiritual regeneration and physical rehabilitation. Its ministries in the secular community have made the Salvation Army one of the most respected agencies delivering social services to the community at large. The Salvation Army's USA National Mission statement reads: "The Salvation Army, an international movement, is an evangelical part of the Universal Christian Church. Its message is based on the Bible. Its ministry is motivated by the love of God. Its mission is to preach the gospel of Jesus Christ and to meet human needs in His name without discrimination."

In 1865 William Booth (1829–1912), an independent Methodist minister, began to preach in the slums of the East End of London. He organized the East London Christian Mission and began a magazine, the *East London Evangelist*. The mission met a genuine need, and within a few years it had begun to reach beyond London. The name was changed to Christian Mission in 1868. As activities increased over the next decade, Booth began to see the need for a more disciplined core of workers to carry out the demanding program, and he started to think in terms of a "Salvation Army." The name of the mission was changed, the magazine became the *Salvationist*, the uniform was adopted, and Booth was transformed into the "general." Within two years the Army had spread throughout England.

As the work of the organization progressed, Booth became more aware of the material needs of the poor among whom the Army had been preaching. His broad investigation of their situation was published in a volume, now a classic of socially concerned Christianity, In *Darkest England and the Way Out* (1890). He proposed a total program of assistance and rehabilitation. This book set the emphasis that is followed by the Army to this day. The Army was brought to the United States in 1880 when Commissioner George Scott Railton (1849–1913) and seven female officers, known as the "Seven Hallelujah Ladies," arrived in New York City. Two years later, Jack Addie, a convert from Scottish Presbyterianism, together with Joseph

Ludgate introduced the Army to Canada with an open-air mission in London, Ontario.

The Army's program of social services has made it famous and respected by many who are quite unaware of its existence as a Holiness church body. The Salvation Army was founded as an evangelical organization, dedicated to bringing people into a right relationship with God through Christ. It emphasizes a balanced ministry of social and spiritual work. Its doctrinal basis is from the Wesleyan-Arminian tradition. It also holds that it is the privilege of believers to be "wholly sanctified." Distinctive to Salvationists is their belief about the sacraments. Salvationists look upon the whole of life and the ministry in Christ's name as sacramental, both to the receiver and the giver. Hence, the traditional sacraments of baptism and communion are not considered by the Army as necessary to salvation and spiritual growth.

The Army is organized on a quasi-military model. The international leader of the Salvation Army, Shaw Clifton, holds the rank of general and operates out of the international headquarters in London, England. The highest ranking officer in the United States is a commissioner. One commissioner serves as national commander over the four territorial headquarters, each operated by a commissioner as a territorial commander. In 2008 Israel L. Gaither was national commander of the United States. Officers (ministers) begin with the rank of cadet and are trained for two years at one of the four officers' training schools. Upon graduation, the officer is commissioned (ordained) as a captain.

The Army is distinguished by its early opening of the ranks of its ordained ministry to women. Catherine Booth, William Booth's wife, had been preaching in London before her husband joined her, and she wrote one of the earliest tracts defending an ordained female ministry. The American work was initiated largely by women, who have since served prominently at every rank.

The social program of the Army has become one of the most far-reaching of all church organizations. It includes feeding and housing the homeless, disaster relief, alcohol and drug rehabilitation, youth camps and programs, senior citizen camps and programs, hospital and prison visitation, and support for unwed mothers, to mention only a few. These pioneering efforts have provided a model for many other churches.

Membership: In 2008 the Salvation Army's membership consisted of 3,500 officers, 60,000 employees, 113,000 "soldiers" (church members), 430,000 adherents, and more than 3.5 million volunteers in the United States. In Canada the Salvation Army has 1,000 active officers (clergy), more than 21,000 soldiers, and more than 53,000 adherents. There are more than 320 corps (churches) and more than 120 social-service institutions of various kinds.

Adherents are people who have elected not to be enrolled as soldiers, but consider the Salvation Army to be their place of worship. Soldiers are those who have signed a declaration of faith and practice known as "A Soldier's Covenant," and worship and serve through a local corps. Employees are personnel hired to perform specialized duties in fields such as social services, youth service, accounting, development, law, and property. Volunteers are those who give freely of their time, enabling the Salvation Army to meet far more community needs than otherwise would be possible.

Officers are the clergy of the Salvation Army. They have completed training as either cadets or auxiliary captains and have been ordained and commissioned to officership. All officers are engaged in continuing education. With its Christian heritage and motivation, the Salvation Army continues its unique service to all people in the name of Christ.

Affiliated centers were located in 111 countries.

Educational Facilities:

Salvation Army Colleges or Schools for Officer Training are in Suffern, New York; Chicago, Illinois; Atlanta, Georgia; and Palos Verdes Estates, California.

Periodicals: *The War Cry* • *Young Salvationist*

Sources:

Salvation Army. www.salvationarmyusa.org/usn/www_usn.nsf.

Agnew, Milton S. *Manual of Salvationism*. New York: Salvation Army, 1968.

Barnes, Cyril. *God's Army*. Elgin, IL: David C. Cook, 1968.

Brengle, Samuel Logan. *The Way of Holiness*. London: Salvationist Publishing and Supplies, 1960.

Chesham, Sallie. *Born to Battle*. Chicago: Rand McNally, 1965.

McKinley, Edward H. *Marching to Glory*. New York: Harper and Row, 1980.

The Sacraments, the Salvationist's Viewpoint. London: Salvationist Publishing and Supplies, 1960.

Sandall, Robert. *The History of the Salvation Army*. London: Thomas Nelson, 1947.

Watson, Bernard. *A Hundred Years' War*. London: Hodder and Stoughton, 1964.

Volunteers of America

1660 Duke St., Alexandria, VA 22314

The Volunteers of America was formed in 1896 by Ballington Booth and Maud Booth, the son and daughter-in-law of William Booth, the founder of the Salvation Army. Although it is very much like the Salvation Army from which it sprang, the Volunteers of America differs in several ways: It is more democratic, though it retains the quasi-military organization; it practices both baptism and the Lord's Supper; and the early emphasis on sanctification and Holiness has lessened in favor of a more general evangelical faith.

In 2008 Charles W. Gould was president and chief executive officer.

Membership: Volunteers of America helps more than two million people in more than 400 communities. In 2008 they reported 38 offices covering 44 states.

Periodicals: *Spirit*.

Sources:

Volunteers of America. www.voa.org.

Wesleyan Church

Box 50434, Indianapolis, IN 46250-0434

The Wesleyan Church was formed in 1968 by the merger of the Wesleyan Methodist Church and Pilgrim Holiness Church. In the merger, two diverse streams of holiness tradition (one pre–Civil War and the other from the late nineteenth century) were brought together.

The Wesleyan Methodist Church had been formed in 1843 by ministers and laymen who withdrew from the Methodist Church during the height of the slavery controversy. Reverends Orange Scott (1800–1847), LeRoy Sunderland (1802–1885; who later joined the Unitarian Association), and L. C. Matlock (1816–1883) were all abolitionists who continually fought the compromise on the slavery issue made by the Methodist Episcopal Church in the early nineteenth century. (Under the compromise, the Methodist Episcopal Church reneged on the strong antislavery position it had maintained since the eighteenth century, and allowed slaveholders to membership in the church.) In addition, the reformers also began to attack the abuses of the episcopacy and the failure to teach and practice various forms of piety. By 1843 tension had reached such a level that, feeling no redress of grievances was possible, the reformers withdrew and took 22 ministers and 6,000 members and formed the Wesleyan Methodist Church in America. In the first Discipline, their book of church order, statements were made against slavery, against the use of alcohol and tobacco, against secret societies, and for modesty in dress. The new structure provided for annual conferences with lay delegates and an elected president (instead of a bishop). There was also a general conference.

The Pilgrim Holiness Church grew out of the holiness movement of the late nineteenth century. Martin Wells Knapp (1853–1901), a former minister in the Methodist Episcopal Church, and Rev. Seth Cook Rees organized the International Holiness Union and Prayer League in 1897 in Cincinnati, Ohio. The union was to be a fellowship, not a church. It was established as a completely Wesleyan movement with emphases on holiness, healing the sick, the premillennial coming of Christ, and evangelization. From a small beginning, the Union grew rapidly, and that led to a change of character, and the fellowship became a church. It underwent several name changes and, in 1922, finally took the name of the Pilgrim Holiness Church. Other holiness groups that merged with the Union (later called the Pilgrim Holiness Church) were the Indiana Conference of the Holiness Christian Church (1919); Pilgrim Church of California (1922); Pentecostal Rescue Mission (1922); Pentecostal Brethren in Christ (1924); People's Mission Church (1925); and Holiness Church of California (1946).

The Wesleyan Church has a church form of government. Globally, there are three general conferences—the North American General Conference, the Philippine General Conference, and the Caribbean General Conference. The general conferences are the supreme governing bodies and elect the general superintendents to four-year term(s). Each general conference delegates authority to a general board of administration, which operates between general conference sessions. The church is divided into districts. North American headquarters of the Wesleyan Church are in Indianapolis, Indiana. The headquarters for the Philippine General Conference are in Manila. The headquarters of the Caribbean General Conference is in St. Johns, Antigua. Combined, the general conferences form the International General Conference, with its own international board and board of general superintendents.

The Wesleyan Publishing House, located in Indianapolis, publishes a wide range of books, religious literature, and curricula that support the church in communicating the life-transforming message of holiness to the world. The Commission on World Missions oversees a vast foreign mission program, worldwide.

Membership: In 2001 the church reported 123,274 members, 1,614 churches, and 3,444 ministers in the United States. There were 89 congregations and 225 ministers in Canada. In 2007 the denomination reported nearly 400,000 constituents in 5,000 churches and missions in over 80 countries.

Educational Facilities:

Bartlesville Wesleyan College, Bartlesville, Oklahoma.

Oklahoma Wesleyan University, Bartlesville, Oklahoma.

Southern Wesleyan University, Central, South Carolina.

Houghton College, Houghton, New York.

Indiana Wesleyan University, Marion, Indiana.

Bethany Bible College, Sussex, New Brunswick, Canada.

In addition to the schools listed, the church also approves the following ministerial training programs:

Asbury Theological Seminary, Wilmore, Kentucky.

Azusa Pacific University C.P. Haggard School of Theology, Azusa, California.

Evangelical School of Theology, Myerstown, Pennsylvania.

George Fox Evangelical Seminary, Portland, Oregon.

Nazarene Theological Seminary, Kansas City, Missouri.

Tyndale Seminary, North York, Ontario, Canada.

Wesley Biblical Seminary, Jackson, Mississippi.

Periodicals: *Wesleyan Life*.

Sources:

Wesleyan Church. www.wesleyan.org.

Drury, Keith. *Holiness for Ordinary People*. Indianapolis, IN: Wesley Press, 1994.

Knapp, Martin Wells. *Holiness Triumphant or Pearls from Patmos*. Cincinnati, OH: God's Bible School Book Room, 1900.

McLeister, Ira Ford, and Roy S. Nicholson. *History of the Wesleyan Methodist Church*. Marion, IN: Wesley Press, 1959.

Thomas, Paul Westphal, and Paul William Thomas. *The Days of Our Pilgrimage*. Marion, IN: Wesley Press, 1976.

 # Twentieth Century Holiness

Calvary Holiness Church

3415-19 N Second St., Philadelphia, PA 19140

In 1963, the Brethren in Christ Church experienced a split among members, with some rejecting what they saw as liberalizing and diversifying trends in the church. Members in the Philadelphia, Pennsylvania, congregation under the leadership of William L. Rosenberry saw the church as loosening its stand on separation from the world and practical holiness. This small congregation incorporated in 1964 as the Calvary Holiness Church. It was joined by members who left Brethren in Christ congregations in Hanover and Millersberg, Pennsylvania, and Massillon, Ohio.

The church follows the general beliefs of the Brethren in Christ, differing primarily in the strictness with which its holds to these beliefs and practices. As with other Wesleyan holiness churches, it believes in the experience of entire sanctification as a second work of grace in the life of the believer. Members observe the ordinances of baptism in the name of the Trinity, the Lord's Supper, and the washing of the saints' feet. Women wear a veil during worship. The holy kiss (I Peter 5:14) is used as a form of greeting. Believers are admonished to live a life of separation from the follies, sinful practices, and methods of the world, most especially in following a spirit of nonresistance in all matters according to Christ's Sermon on the Mount. Members refrain from the use of intoxicating substances, worldly amusements (including television), membership in lodges and secret societies, and activity that does not glorify God on the Lord's Day.

Members wear a version of the "plain people" garb, which for men includes a suit of plain material, black or brown shoes, and conservative hats. No neckties or jewelry is allowed. Women wear conservative dresses with full-length sleeves. They may not wear shorts, slacks, socks, jewelry, lace, or bows, or employ artificial means to bedeck their hair or face. During all waking hours, they wear a "prayer and prophecy veil" in the shape of a bonnet of white (which is covered with a black bonnet when they are outdoors).

The church follows a congregational polity. It has an executive council that handles matter of polity, doctrine, and standards at a general church level.

Membership: Not reported. In the early 1970s, there were only two congregations and 38 members, though the church reported a number of constituency members and the monthly magazine had a circulation of 7,000.

Periodicals: *The Gospel Witness*.

Remarks: This church should not be confused with the Calvary Holiness Church of England (1930–1955), which is now an integral part of the Church of the Nazarene.

Christian Pilgrim Church

Current address not obtained for this edition.

The Christian Pilgrim Church was formed in 1937 by a group of holiness people, including Reverends Fannie Alldaffer, C. W. Cripps, and Tracy Alldaffer. They gathered at Coldwater, Michigan, to build a holiness church that could function without "so much law and order or machinery in the church." Officers were elected for life or as long as they remained in agreement with the Bible and the church.

The doctrine is Trinitarian and holiness (i.e., in essential agreement with the other churches discussed in this chapter). Healing is stressed but speaking in tongues is considered contrary to the Word of God; Baptism by any mode is desired; tithing is insisted upon; secret societies are condemned; Christ's imminent premillennial Second Coming is expected.

There is a General Assembly, which meets annually. The church is divided into districts. A general superintendent has general oversight of the work and is aided by two assistants. Congregations are found in the South and Midwest.

Membership: Not reported. In the mid-1970s, the church had 15 congregations and approximately 250 members.

Periodicals: *The Christian Voice*.

Churches of Christ in Christian Union

PO Box 10, 1426 Lancaster Pke., Circleville, OH 43113

The Churches of Christ in Christian Union (CCCU) was formed in 1909 when a small group of ministers withdrew from the annual council of the Christian Union denomination when the council voted to censure any minister preaching a Wesleyan Holiness doctrine. The doctrine of the CCCU is Wesleyan Holiness, with a strong emphasis on evangelism and the sanctifying work of the Holy Spirit in the life of the believer. The denomination supports a worldwide mission program and the Circleville Bible College, an accredited college specializing in training persons for ministry and other Christian service careers.

In 1952 the Reformed Methodist Church, which had split from the Methodist Episcopal Church over episcopal polity, joined the Churches of Christ in Christian Union as the Northeastern District. The Reformed Methodist Church was formed in 1914 in Readsborough, Vermont, by a group of Methodists led by Pliny Brett, a local preacher. At their first conference, February 4, 1914, they adopted the Methodist "Articles of Religion" and some democratic rules for church government. The government was essentially congregational, without sharp distinctions between ministers and laymen. While the Methodist system of representative conferences was kept, ministers were delegates only if elected, not ex-officio. The local church had the power to ordain elders, select its own ministers, and do whatever else necessary to carry on its work. Likewise, ministers could pick their field of service.

Polity is congregational within the limits established by the denominational constitution and bylaws. Spiritual officers of the local church are the pastor and elders. Local church business affairs are conducted by a board comprised of the elders, church trustees, and departmental leaders. The national church officers are elected by biennial general council and/or annual district councils.

Membership: In 2007–2008 the churches reported 11,132 members, 231 congregations, and 562 clergy/ministers.

Educational Facilities:

Circleville Bible College, Circleville, Ohio.

Ohio Christian University, Circleville, Ohio.

Periodicals: *The Evangelical Advocate*.

Sources:

Churches of Christ in Christian Union. www.cccuhq.org.

Brown, Kenneth, and P. Lewis Brevard. *Our Godly Heritage*. Circleville, OH: Circle Printing, 1980. Available at www.cccuhq.org.

Evangelical Church of North America

9421 West River Rd., Minneapolis, MN 55444

The Evangelical Church of North America was formed on June 4, 1968, by members of the Evangelical United Brethren who did not wish to proceed into the merger with the Methodist Church (1939–1968) that created the United Methodist Church. The schism in the Evangelical United Brethren involved 50 congregations in the church's Northwest Conference and 23 churches from the Montana Conference. For several decades the Northwest Conference had been a center of Holiness theology, with many of the pastors being trained at the Western Evangelical Seminary (established in 1945 and firmly Holiness in its doctrine and emphases).

Almost as soon as the Evangelical Church of North America was formed, the Holiness Methodist Church, with headquarters in Minneapolis, voted to affiliate, and in 1969 it became the North Central Conference of the new church. The Holiness Methodist Church was a result of the "Holiness" revival movement that swept the United States in general and Methodism in particular during the late 1800s. The Northwestern Holiness Association was formed at Grand Forks, North Dakota, on March 24, 1909, as a fellowship of those following the Holiness way. This informal association changed its name to the Holiness Methodist Church in 1920, recognizing that the association had become a denomination. In 1977 the small Wesleyan Covenant Church, with congregations in Detroit and in Brownsville, Texas, as well as an extensive Mexican mission, merged into the Evangelical Church.

The doctrine of the Evangelical Church of North America follows the tradition of Methodism as developed within the Evangelical United Brethren. It includes a special emphasis on entire sanctification.

The Evangelical Church of North America has six annual conferences—the Pacific, the Eastern, the Western, the East Central, the North Central, and the Southeastern. The church is supervised by a general conference that meets quadrennially and the general church council that meets annually. The highest full-time executive office, that of general superintendent, was created in 1976. In 2008 Rev. Brian Eckhardt was the general superintendent over the general conference. The work of missions is supervised by the department of missions and a full-time executive director. Fields include Bolivia, Brazil, Germany, Japan, and New Mexico (among Native Americans). In addition, churches across the denomination participate actively in a number of interdenominational mission agencies such as OMS International, World Gospel Mission, and Wycliffe Bible Translators. Currently there is more than one adult missionary per congregation (150:140). The church is a member of the National Association of Evangelicals and the Christian Holiness Association.

In 1993 the North West Canada Conference became autonomous, and with the blessing of the Evangelical Church of North America merged with the Missionary Church in Canada to become the Evangelical Missionary Church of Canada.

Membership: In 2000 the church reported 13,500 members.

Educational Facilities:

George Fox University, Newberg, Oregon.

Kentucky Mountain Bible College, Vancleve, Kentucky.

Vennard College, University Park, Iowa.

Wesley Biblical Seminary, Jackson, Mississippi.

George Fox Evangelical Seminary, Portland, Oregon.

Periodicals: *The Evangelical Challenge* • *The HeartBeat*

Sources:

Evangelical Church of North America. theevangelicalchurch.org.

Pike, John M. *Preachers of Salvation: The History of the Evangelical Church.* Milwaukie, OR: Evangelical Church of North America, 1984.

Gospel Mission Corps of the American Rescue Workers

Box 175, Hightstown, NJ 08520

The Gospel Mission Corps was founded by Robert S. Turton III, a graduate of the Pillar of Fire Bible Seminary of Zarephath, New Jersey. He began a mission at Hightstown, New Jersey, that grew into the Gospel Mission Corps in 1962. Its doctrine was like that of the American Rescue Workers (ARW), with which it merged in 1980. Some of its members had previously belonged to the ARW.

Grace and Hope Mission, Inc.

4 S. Gay St., Baltimore, MD 21202-4007

The Grace and Hope Mission was founded in 1914 by Mamie E. Caskie and Jennie E. Goranflo, who opened a gospel mission in Baltimore. The work grew so that by the late 1960s there were 12 centers, mostly in large cities. The doctrine is Wesleyan-Protestant with an emphasis on evangelism, holiness, and the hope of the Second Coming. The officers, all single females, wear a black uniform with red trim and the Mission's emblem. There is an annual conference held in York,

Pennsylvania, on the Sunday following Mother's Day, at which the assignments of officers for the coming year are made. Ruth Carlson was the superintendent in 2008.

Membership: In 2008 the mission reported eight centers. There is no formal membership, but in 1997 approximately 800 people participated in the mission's activities.

Sources:

Grace and Hope Mission, Inc.

secure.mawebcenters.com/websites/gracehopemission/index.html.

International Fellowship of Bible Churches, Inc.

PO Box 1222, Bethany, OK 73008

Shipping Address: 3511 N. Geraldine, Oklahoma City, OK 73112

International Fellowship of Bible Churches, Inc. is an association of Holiness churches and ministers of a Wesleyan-Arminian persuasion. The Fellowship was founded in 1988 under the leadership of Dr. Donald Hicks and Rev. Kenneth Arnold. Several hundred attended the initial Fellowship assembly, at which Hicks and Arnold were elected to continue to lead the new organization. They were appointed by an international coordinating committee comprised of ten elders and ten lay leaders from member churches. Following the assembly, Hicks and Arnold began a national tour to meet with ministers and church unable to attend. A periodical, The Fellowship, was launched before the year was out. Administrative offices were opened in Oklahoma City in 1994. Rev. Arnold resigned as co-CEO in 1991 and Dr. Hicks continued as CEO until he retired from that office in 1998. At that time, Dr. William Sillings was appointed to serve as the next CEO. In 2002 the Fellowship revised its bylaws, replacing the office of CEO with a general superintendent elected by the assembly, a position held by Sillings since 2002. The general superintendent is elected quadrennially at a general assembly.

The Fellowship adopted a statement of faith that affirms traditional Wesleyan-Arminian doctrines, including a belief in entire sanctification. Entire sanctification is defined as an act of God, subsequent to regeneration, by which "believers are made free from original sin, or depravity, and are brought into a state of entire devotion to God, and the holy obedience of perfect love." Through the sanctifying work of the Holy Spirit, the believer is empowered to live the Christian life. The sanctified individual is not free of human error and misjudgment, and is still in a process of continued growth.

Unlike other Holiness churches, the Fellowship also recognizes the gifts of the Spirit as supernatural endowments for service to be exercised in conjunction with the harmony of the body of Christ.

The Fellowship believes in the autonomy of the local church, and exists to provide fellowship, cooperative ministry, and credentials for its member ministers and churches. The work of the Fellowship is extended through several departments, including Fellowship Youth for Christ (FYC), World Mission Outreach, and the Commission on Credentials and Membership (CCM). The commission oversees ministerial licensing and ordination procedures, and the chartering of churches and parachurch organizations. The Fellowship has supported world mission endeavors to the Philippines, Honduras, Guatemala, Mexico, Nigeria, and Lesotho, and has mission links with Barbados and Guyana, as well as several affiliated pastors and churches in India and Pakistan.

Membership: Not reported.

Periodicals: *The Fellowship*, and *Fellowship Pastor*, an official communication of the General Superintendent with Fellowship ministers.

Sources:

International Fellowship of Bible Churches. www.ifbc.org/.

Kentucky Mountain Holiness Association

75 Mill Creek Lawson Rd., Vancleve, KY 41385

Alternate Address: PO Box 2, Vancleve, KY 41385

The Kentucky Mountain Holiness Association was begun in 1925 by Lela G. McConnell, a deaconess in the Methodist Episcopal Church. Following her ordination in 1924, she began a vigorous ministry in the mountains of eastern Kentucky. She preached a Wesleyan-Protestant doctrine with a strong emphasis on sanctification. The association maintains an elementary school, a high school, a four-year bible college, a radio station, and a campground. J. Eldon Neihof is the president emeritus of the association.

Membership: In 2002 the association reported 13 churches.

Educational Facilities:

Kentucky Mountain Bible College, Vancleve, Kentucky.

Sources:

McConnell, Lela G. *The Pauline Ministry in the Kentucky Mountains.* Jackson, KY: Author, 1942.

Lumber River Annual Conference of the Holiness Methodist Church

Prospect Rd., Penbroke, NC 28372

The Lumber River Annual Conference of the Holiness Methodist Church has its origins in a meeting organized in 1900 by members of the Methodist Episcopal Church, South, at Union Chapel Church, Robeson County, North Carolina. These members had an intense interest in the holiness movement, with its stress on the second blessing, a religious experience certifying holiness. At the time, the holiness movement was criticized by many Methodists, so attendees at the 1900 meeting decided to form a new church.

Equally important in the formation of the new conference was the desire to provide spiritual nurture to those of Native American descent, mostly the Lumbee and Tuscarora peoples of Robeson County. Three of the founders of the church, Henry H. Lowrie, French R. Lowrie, and Calvin Canady Lowrie, had formerly been ministers in the Blue Ridge Methodist Conference, which focused its work on this area. Joining the Lowries in organizing the conference were Revs. John O. Sampson, P.M. Loclear, S. A. Hammonds, and Jack P. Jacobs.

The church follows Wesleyan-Protestant doctrine and has adopted an episcopal polity. Some features of nineteenth-century Methodism—attendance at class meetings (regular gatherings of small classes for mutual discussion, Bible study, confession and forgiveness, and prayer) and six months' probationary membership—are retained. The itinerant ministry has been dropped.

The conference is currently led by its presiding bishop, Rev. James H. Wood, and its superintendent, Rev. Elton Hunt.

Membership: In 2008 the conference reported 650 members in 10 churches. It provides preachers for three additional churches not officially members of the conference.

Sources:

Doctrines and Discipline of the Lumber River Conference of the Holiness Methodist Church. Pembroke, NC: Lumber River Conference of the Holiness Methodist Church, 1998.

Official Journal of the 103rd Annual Session of the Lumber River Conference of the Holiness Methodist Church. Pembroke, NC: Lumber River Conference of the Holiness Methodist Church, 2003.

Woods, James H., et al. *The History of the Lumber River Conference of the Holiness Methodist Church.* Pembroke, NC: Lumber River Conference of the Holiness Methodist Church, 2003.

Parkville Bible Church

800 Whisler Rd., Etters, PA 17319

The Parkville Bible Church, formerly the Holiness Gospel Church, was founded in 1945 by former members of the Evangelical United Brethren and the Church in God. Its theology is Wesleyan holiness. The church sponsors camp meetings. The church is affiliated with the Bahamas Holy Bible Mission headquartered in the Bahama Islands.

Membership: The church is a single congregation of 70 members.

Pillar of Fire

Pillar of Fire International, 10 Chapel Dr., Zarephath, NJ 08890

The existence of the Pillar of Fire is due in part to the preaching and witnessing of an anointed pastor's wife. This privilege was not encouraged in the late nineteenth century. Alma White (1862–1946), a Methodist minister's wife, began to preach both in revivals and in her husband's pulpit. Her success led to notoriety and then to opposition from Methodist officials, so she began to organize her converts into independent missions modeled on the early Methodist societies within the Church of England. After initially cooperating with the Metropolitan Church Association, she incorporated the missions in 1902 as the Pentecostal Union, which gradually emerged as a body separate from the association. The name Pillar of Fire was adopted in 1917 because the church's magazine of the same name was widely known and associated with this church.

The doctrine of the church is typically Wesleyan Holiness, and it adopted a slightly modified form of the Methodist Twenty-five Articles of Religion early in the twentieth century. The church believes in healing, and accepts premillennialism.

The church is organized episcopally. Alma White, its first bishop, was among the first women in modern times to assume that role. Women can occupy all ministerial roles. As part of its commitment to women's rights, the church for many years published a periodical called Women's Chains.

White was an advocate of a variety of controversial causes, including vegetarianism and women's rights. She was also an active supporter of the Ku Klux Klan in the 1920s. She wrote a book, Klansmen: Guardians of Liberty (1926), defending them as God's agents in maintaining the social order, but the church disassociated itself from the Klan many years ago.

The headquarters of the church are at Zarephath, New Jersey. The location of the original headquarters, Denver, Colorado, functions as a second major center of activity. At both locations there is a college, bible seminary, prep school, radio station (KPOF in Denver and WAWZ in Zarephath), and a branch of the Pillar of Fire Press. A third radio station, WAKW, and a school are located in Cincinnati, Ohio, and other schools are located in Jacksonville, Florida, Los Angeles, California, and London, England. There is also an active foreign missions program with many schools, churches, and other humanitarian activities.

Following Alma White's death, her two sons Ray B. White (1892–1946) and Arthur K. White (1889–1981) inherited the leadership of the church. Arthur K. White became the new bishop and directed its activities for more than thirty years. Dr. Donald J. Wolfram is the present bishop and general superintendent.

Membership: Membership is not counted and is unknown. In 2002 there were 106 congregations in the United States and in foreign countries, including Great Britain, India, Liberia, Nigeria, and Costa Rica.

Educational Facilities:

Belleview Christian College and Bible Seminary and Belleview Christian School (K–12), Westminster, Colorado.

Somerset Christian College and Somerset Christian Academy (K–12), Zarephath, New Jersey.

Eden Grove Academy (pre-K–12), Cincinnati, Ohio.

Sycamore Grove Christian School (K–8), Los Angeles, California.

Alma Heights Christian Academy (K–12), Pacifica, California.

Pillar of Fire also has numerous mission schools abroad.

Periodicals: *Pillar of Fire* • *Mission News around the Globe Today*

Sources:

Pillar of Fire. www.pillar.org/index.html

McRobbie, James. *What the Bible Teaches*. Salem, OH: Schmul, 1983.

White, Alma. *Hymns and Poems*. Zarephath, NJ: Pillar of Fire, 1946.

———. *The New Testament Church*. Zarephath, NJ: Pillar of Fire, 1929.

———. *The Story of My Life*. 6 vols. Zarephath, NJ: Pillar of Fire, 1919–34.

———. *Why I Do Not Eat Meat*. Zarephath, NJ: Pillar of Fire, 1938.

Sanctified Church of Christ

1141 S. 2nd St., Louisville, KY 40203

The Sanctified Church of Christ was formed July 5, 1937, at Columbus, Georgia, by a group of former members of the Methodist Episcopal Church. The group was led by Brother E. K. Leary and Sister Jemima Bishop, and their purpose was to preserve the rich heritage of true scriptural Holiness. Their doctrine was Wesleyan-Protestant with a distinct emphasis upon entire sanctification. Particular rules were made against secret oath-bound societies, immodest dress such as shorts, jewelry, make-up, public and mixed bathing, women cutting their hair, television, and divorce. Members are conscientious objectors.

There is an annual conference that elects the general superintendent, secretary, treasurer, and the council of 12 members, which is the chief legislative body of the church. The council approves all candidates for the ministry.

In 1996 Amistad y Vida (Friendship and Life) joined the Sanctified Church of Christ as its first primarily Spanish local church. The Sanctified Church opened the first Spanish church in Atlanta, Georgia, under the ministry of Rev. Hector Julian and Auristela Ordonez. The general church council under the superintendence of Rev. Sherman Stoess decided to serve the growing Hispanic populations of Georgia, Tennessee, Kentucky, Illinois, and other areas of the United States by starting churches, preaching the message of scriptural Holiness, and attending the basic needs of the international Latin community.

Membership: In 2008 the church's website listed 10 congregations, spread mostly across the Deep South. It also listed four future congregations. Membership is unknown.

Sources:

Sanctified Church of Christ. www.thesanctifiedchurch.org.

Wesleyan Tabernacle Association

Current address not obtained for this edition.

The Wesleyan Tabernacle Association is a small holiness church. It was formed in 1936 for the purpose of promoting Christian love and fellowship among godly leaders of various undenominational bodies and to open a greater field of service for holiness evangelistic preachers and singers. The association asserts belief in the Trinity, salvation and sanctification by God's free grace, divine healing, baptism and the Lord's Supper as ordinances, and the premillennial return of Christ. Polity is congregational. There is an annual association convention which elects officers to oversee publications, missions, and cooperative endeavors with like-minded groups. Women are freely admitted to the ministry. The association supports a children's home and an extensive mission in Haiti.

Membership: Not reported. In the 1970s the association had 26 congregations in the United States. It supported 173 ordained ministers, 53 licensed ministers, 10 song evangelists, and 19 commissioned Christian workers, some of whom were under the direction of independent holiness mission agencies.

Periodicals: *Evangel*.

Sources:

Yearbook. Wesleyan Tabernacle Association, 1965.

 # Black Holiness

Associated Churches of Christ (Holiness)

1302 E Adams Blvd., Los Angeles, CA 90011

In 1915 Bp. William Washington formed a branch of the Church of Christ (Holiness) U.S.A. on the West Coast, which carried out work independently of the work directed in the East and South by the church's founder, Charles Price Jones (1865–1949). A few years later, Jones went to Los Angeles to hold a revival meeting. At that time, Jones and Washington worked out an agreement to work cooperatively. This agreement was in effect until 1946–1947, when, because of what the manual of the Associated Churches of Christ (Holiness) calls the "manipulating of some administrative problems in the upper circles of the Church," the West Coast churches withdrew from the Church of Christ (Holiness) U.S.A. The West Coast churches now continue under the original incorporation of Bishop Washington. Doctrine and polity are identical with those of the Church of Christ (Holiness) U.S.A.

Membership: Not reported. In the early 1970s the Associated Churches had six churches and one mission.

Christ's Holy Sanctified Church of America

PO Box 120574, Arlington, TX 76012

Christ's Holy Sanctified Church of America is a predominantly black Holiness church founded in 1910 in Keatchie, Louisiana, by Judge King and Sarah A. King. Bp. Judge King was succeeded by Bp. Ulysses King, and later by Bp. J. King and E. L. McBride. Bp. G. E. Jones is the current presiding bishop. The church follows the teaching of the Wesleyan Holiness perspective.

The church supports Christ's Holy Sanctified School, an industrial training school.

Membership: Not reported.

Sources:

Christ's Holy Sanctified Church of America. www.chschurch.org/home.

DuPree, Sherry Sherrod. *African American Holiness Pentecostal Charismatic: Annotated Bibliography*. New York: Garland, 1992.

Jones, Charles Edwin. *Black Holiness*. Metuchen, NJ: Scarecrow Press, 1987.

King, Abp. Judge, ed. *Discipline of Christ Holy Sanctified Church of America*. Oakland, CA: Christ's Holy Sanctified Church, n.d.

Church of Christ (Holiness) U.S.A.

329 E. Monument St., Jackson, MS 39202

In 1894 Charles Price Jones (1865–1949) and Charles H. Mason (1866–1961) formed the Church of God in Christ as a Holiness body after having been excluded from fellowship with black Baptists in Arkansas. Mason led most of the body into pentecostalism in 1907. Those who remained were reorganized by Jones as the Church of Christ (Holiness) U.S.A. Jones himself became well known as a composer and publisher of Holiness gospel songs. Doctrinally, the Church of Christ (Holiness) U.S.A. is very close to the Church of the Nazarene, with which it almost merged. It follows the Methodist Articles of Religion, and stresses the second blessing of the Holy Spirit, which imparts sanctification to the believer. Race issues have prevented close relations between the Church of Christ (Holiness) U.S.A. and predominantly white Holiness churches.

The church is episcopal in structure, with a senior bishop as the highest official. There are seven dioceses. A convention held every two years is the highest legislative authority. Missionary work is sponsored in Mexico. There is a publishing house in Los Angeles. Bp. Emery Lindsay of Chicago is the current senior bishop; Bp. Vernon Kennebrew (Little Rock, Arkansas) is the president.

Membership: In 1998 the Church of Christ (Holiness) had 10,393 members in 167 congregations in the United States.

Educational Facilities:

Christ Missionary and Industrial College, Jackson, Mississippi.

Boydton Institute, Boydton, Virginia.

Sources:

Church of Christ (Holiness) U.S.A. www.cochusa.com.

Cobbins, Otho B. *History of the Church of Christ (Holiness) U.S.A., 1895–1965*. New York: Vantage Press, 1966.

Jones, C. P. *His Fulness*. Jackson, MS: Church of Christ (Holiness), 1901.

———. *The Story of My Songs*. Los Angeles: Church of Christ (Holiness), n.d.

Church of God (Sanctified Church)

PO Box 281615, Nashville, TN 37207

In the early years of the Church of Christ (Holiness) U.S.A. (see separate entry), the church existed as an unincorporated entity called the "Church of God," or the "Holiness Church." It was only after the schism over Pentecostalism in 1907 that the church was incorporated and its present name was adopted. Before the incorporation, one of the ministers, Elder Charles W. Gray, established the church in Nashville, Tennessee, and the surrounding areas. When the Church of Christ (Holiness) U.S.A. incorporated, Gray continued his work independently as the Church of God (Sanctified Church). The doctrine was the same as that of the Church of Christ (Holiness) U.S.A., but the polity was congregational, with local churches operating autonomously and appointing their own ministers. The associated churches remained unincorporated. In 1927 there was a movement within the Church of God (Sanctified Church) to incorporate and to consolidate the work under a board of elders. Among those who constituted the newly incorporated church were Elders J. L. Rucker, R. A. Manter, R. L. Martin, M. S. Sowell, B. Smith, and G. A. Whitley. The move to incorporate led to further controversy and a schism. However, under the incorporation the elders retained the rights to direct the church, and it continues as the Church of God (Sanctified Church). Elder Gray, founder of the church, withdrew to found the Original Church of God (or Sanctified Church).

The Church of God (Sanctified Church) is headed by a general overseer. The first was Elder Rucker. He was succeeded by Elder Theopolis Dickerson McGhee (d.m1965) and Elder Jesse E. Evans. The current general overseer (elected in 2004) is Bp. A. J. Valentine Jr. The church is organized into six districts and holds an annual convention every summer. Mission work is conducted in Jamaica.

Membership: Not reported. In the early 1970s the church reported 60 congregations with approximately 5,000 members.

Periodicals: *Truth and Life.*

Sources:

Church of God (Sanctified Church). www.cogsanctified.org.

Church of God (Which He Purchased with His Own Blood)

1628 NE 50th, Oklahoma City, OK 73111

The Church of God (Which He Purchased with His Own Blood) is a predominantly black holiness church founded in 1953 by William F. Fizer following his excommunication from the Church of the Living God (Christian Workers for Fellowship). Fizer had concluded that grape juice or wine, not water, should be used in the Lord's Supper, thus denying one of the major distinctive practices of the Church of the Living God. The first annual convention of the Church of God was held in 1954.

The Church of God distinguishes itself from Pentecostalism and teaches that the Holy Ghost is given to those who obey the Lord. The Lord's Supper is held weekly and grape juice and unleavened bread are used as elements. Foot washing is practiced. Baptism is administered following a trinitarian formula. A holiness code that frowns upon the use of tobacco and alcohol is followed. Divine healing is sought in cases of sickness, but the work of doctors is also affirmed.

The Church of God believes that it is the Body of Christ, following the belief and practice of scriptures; hence it sees itself as the true church as organized originally by Jesus Christ. It is the role of the chief bishop to organize the church by calling people to the true doctrine.

Membership: In 1997 there were seven churches, 800 members, and 10 ministers. These are also members in Nigeria and the Philippines.

Periodicals: *Gospel News.*

Sources:

Fizer, William Jordon. *Bible Doctrine*. Oklahoma City, OK: The Author, n.d. 72pp.

Church of Universal Triumph the Dominion of God

1651 Ferry Park, Detroit, MI 48206

Rivaling "Sweet Daddy" Grace and Father Divine as charismatic leaders in the black community was the Rev. James Francis Marion Jones, better known as Prophet Jones (1908–1971). Born in Birmingham, Alabama, the son of a railroad brakeman and a school teacher, he was raised in Triumph the Church and Kingdom of God in Christ. Even as a child, he preached (he did so regularly after his eleventh birthday). In 1938 he was sent to Detroit as a missionary and became successful quickly. Tension with headquarters arose before the year was out, however, when members began to shower Jones with expensive gifts that the headquarters claimed. Rather than surrender his new affluence, Jones left the church and founded the Church of Universal Triumph the Dominion of God.

The new church, modeled on the parent body, was built upon Jones's charisma. During the 1940s and 1950s he became known for his wealth. His possessions included a white mink coat, a 54-room French chateau that had been built in 1917 by a General Motors executive, five Cadillacs each with its own chauffeur, jewelry, perfumes, and wardrobe of almost 500 ensembles. Jones claimed to be in direct contact with God, whose voice took the form of a breeze fanning Jones's ear. Among his practices was dispensing solutions to personal problems after inviting individuals to mount his dais and whisper their problems in his ear. Most of Prophet Jones's wealth came from people grateful for his healing ability. Followers were to be found in all the large northern U.S. cities. Jones's title was "His Holiness the Rev. Dr. James F. Jones, D.D., Universal Dominion Ruler, Internationally known as Prophet Jones."

The church, like the parent body, is very strict. Members are not allowed to smoke, drink, play games of any kind, use coffee or tea, fraternize with nonmembers, attend another church, or marry without the consent of the ruler of the church. Women must wear girdles and men health belts. The major theological tenet concerns the beginning of the millennium in 2,000 c.e. All alive at that time will become immortal and live in the heaven on earth.

The upward path of Prophet Jones came to an abrupt end in 1956 when a vice raid on his home led to his arrest and trial for gross indecency. He was acquitted, but the damage had been done, and his following declined from that time. During the year prior to his death in 1971, he commuted between Detroit and Chicago. Following his death, his assistant, the Rev. Lord James Shaffer, became the Dominion ruler, named by the Dominion council and board of trustees. Some 20 ministers and 5,000 church members attended the funeral of Prophet Jones in 1971.

Shaffer's wife Maggie Shaffer shares a leadership role with him as the church's "reverend princess."

Membership: Not reported.

Sources:

Church of Universal Triumph/The Dominion of God. www.utdog.org.

Retzloff, Tim. "'Seer or Queer?': Postwar Fascination with Detroit's Prophet Jones." *GLQ: A Journal of Lesbian and Gay Studies* 8 (2002): 271–296.

Churches of God, Holiness

7407 Metcalf, PO Box 4220, Overland Park, KS 66204

The Churches of God, Holiness, were formed by Bp. King Hezekiah Burruss (d. 1963), formerly of the Church of Christ (Holiness) U.S.A. Burruss began a church in Atlanta in 1914 that belonged to the latter organization, and by 1920 this had grown so large that it hosted the national convention of the Church of Christ (Holiness) U.S.A. Shortly after that Atlanta meeting, however, Burruss formed his own church. Doctrine is like the doctrine of the parent body.

The highest authority in the churches is the national convention. There are also annual state conventions. The bishop appoints the state overseers who assign all pastors. The present bishop is Titus Paul Burruss.

Membership: Not reported. In 1967 there were 42 churches, 16 ministers, and 25,600 members, mostly along the East Coast.

Periodicals: *The Bethlehem Star.*

Gospel Spreading Church

2006 Georgia Ave. NW, Ste. 300, Washington, DC 20001

The Gospel Spreading Church, sometimes called Elder Michaux Church of God or the Radio Church of God, was founded by Lightfoot Solomon Michaux (1885–1968), a minister in the Church of God (Holiness). At one point he served as the church's secretary treasurer. His preaching career started in Hopewell, Virginia, in a small church called "Everybody's Mission" that he had built with his own hands. Michaux moved to Newport News, Virginia, where he erected a tent in 1919 at the corner of 19th and Jefferson Avenue. During a series of meetings, 150 persons accepted Christ as their personal Lord and Savior. These 150 became the foundation of the Gospel Spreading Church of God. In 1922 Michaux came into conflict with C. P. Jones, founder of the Church of God (Holiness), and left to found an independent church, retaining the name he had previously used, the Gospel Spreading Tabernacle Association. In 1928 he moved to Washington, D.C., and established the Church of God and Gospel Spreading Association.

His early success continued in the nation's capital. He had discovered the potential of radio while in Virginia, and in 1929 began broadcasting on WJSV, mixing Holiness themes with positive thinking. Shortly thereafter, CBS bought the station and Michaux's show expanded: By 1934 he was on more than 50 stations nationwide, and had an estimated audience of 25,000,000. His show was also carried internationally by short-wave. He was the first black person to receive such exposure. He also began a magazine, *Happy News*.

From his radio audience, congregations began to form in black communities, primarily in the East. However, by the beginning of World War II his radio ministry had declined, and he was heard on only a few stations, in those cities where congregations already had formed. In 1964 he reorganized his followers as the Gospel Spreading Church, but most of the congregations continued to call themselves the Church of God.

Elder Michaux created a board of directors to help him carry out his vision. The Gospel Spreading Association was incorporated as the business arm of the church in 1921, and today the business office is headed by a board of directors with an office staff located in Washington, D.C. In 2004 Bp. Michael A. Clayton Sr. was installed and consecrated as the bishop and general overseer of the Gospel Spreading Church of God, Inc.

Membership: Elder Michaux eventually established 10 churches, in Newport News, Virginia (1919), Hampton, Virginia (1922), Baltimore, Maryland (1923), Washington, D.C. (1928), Edenborn, Pennsylvania (1930), New York, New York (1930), Union Bridge, Maryland (1934), Philadelphia, Pennsylvania (1935), Richmond, Virginia (1950), and Kinston, North Carolina.

Periodicals: *The Happy News* • *Sparks from the Anvil*

Sources:

Gospel Spreading Church. www.gospelspreadingchurch.org.

Lark, Pauline, ed. *Sparks from the Anvil of Elder Micheaux.* Washington, DC: Happy News, 1950.

Webb, Lilian Ashcraft. *About My Father's Business.* Westport, CT: Greenwood Press, 1981.

Kodesh Church of Emmanuel

c/o Kenneth O. Barbour, 2601 Centre Ave., Pittsburgh, PA 15219

The Kodesh Church of Emmanuel is a black holiness sect that was formed by Rev. Frank Russell Killingsworth when he withdrew from the African Methodist Episcopal Church in 1929 along with 120 followers. In common with other holiness churches, this church emphasizes entire sanctification as a second definite work of grace conditioned upon a life of absolute consecration. The church forbids the use of alcohol, tobacco, and prideful dress; membership in secret societies; and profaning the Sabbath. In 1934 a merger was effected with the Christian Tabernacle Union of Pittsburgh.

The church is governed by a quadrennial general assembly. Regional assemblies meet annually. There is mission work in Liberia.

Membership: In 1980 there were 5 churches, 326 members, and 28 ministers.

Mount Calvary Holy Church of America

PO Box 236, Boston, MA 02121

Mount Calvary Holy Church of America was founded by Bp. Brumfield Johnson, a young minister who had served as pastor of the United Holy Church of America in Summit, New Jersey. In 1928 Bishop Johnson and Elder Robert Pugsley traveled to Winston-Salem, North Carolina, to conduct a revival. Many of those converted urged Johnson to establish a church there, and so the Winston-Salem church was incorporated in 1929 as the Mt. Calvary Holy Church of America, Inc.

Bishop Johnson returned to Summit, New Jersey, and at a conference there in 1929, 20 more ministers joined him. In the summer of that year Johnson conducted tent revivals in Huntington Station, Long Island, New York, and in September he established a church on New York Avenue in Huntington, with Bp. William Bryant was appointed pastor. Bishop Bryant remained the pastor until his death, then Bishop Johnson presided from 1951 to 1972 with the assistance of Rev. Agnes A. Hiller, who succeeded him as pastor in 1972.

Johnson and a group of his workers attended a conference in Boston, Massachusetts, and adopted the principles now adhered to by the Mt. Calvary Holy Church. The church was chartered in Boston on July 27, 1929, with an initial membership of about 200, and the church grew rapidly during its first decade.

Johnson and his followers continued tent services in Durham, North Carolina, and established a church there. The Mt. Calvary Holy Church of America, Inc. of Columbus, Ohio, was founded in 1932. Milwaukee, Wisconsin, was brought into Mt. Calvary in 1957.

The first Mt. Calvary Holy Church headquarters was established in Baltimore, Maryland. Shortly thereafter, the church relocated to Buffalo, New York. When a fire destroyed that headquarters church in 1960, the church moved its headquarters Boston, and later to Dorchester, Massachusetts, where their national convocations were held.

The church operates foreign missions in Africa, Barbados, Trinidad, and London. It also broadcasts a radio show.

On February 15, 1972, Bishop Johnson passed away and was succeeded by Bp. Harold Ivory Williams.

Membership: In 2008 the church's website listed 58 congregations, in California, Connecticut, the District of Columbia, Maryland, Massachusetts, Michigan, Mississippi, New Jersey, New York, North Carolina, Ohio, Pennsylvania, South Carolina, Virginia, West Virginia, and Wisconsin.

Sources:

Mount Calvary Holy Church of America. www.mchca.org/main.htm.

Redeemed Church of God

PO Box 1061, Greenville, TX 75403

Alternate Address: International headquarters: 1–5 Redemption Way, Ebute-Metta, Lagos.

The Redeemed Church of God, one of several African Initiated Churches to establish work in North America, was founded in the Ondo State of Nigeria (Westrica) by Pa Akindayomi (1909–1981), who in 1927 had been baptized into the Anglican Church by missionaries of the Church Missionary Society. He later associated with the independent Cherubim and Seraphim Church. During the 1930s he began to hear a voice calling him to be God's servant. In 1952, convinced that the Cherubim and Seraphim Church had veered from the truth, he founded the Glory of God Fellowship with nine people. The fellowship grew rapidly. Headquarters for what would emerge as the Redeemed Church of God were established in Lagos, Nigeria.

In 1975 Enoch Adejare Adeboye, a lecturer at the University of Lagos, was ordained as a pastor in the Redeemed Church. He spoke English fluently and translated many of Akindayomi's sermons from Youruban to English. He was named the church's new leader when Akindayomi passed away, and his appointment was confirmed by the reading of Akindayomi's sealed pronouncement following the funeral.

Under Adeboye's leadership more than 4,000 parishes were founded in Nigeria, and the church spread to the Ivory Coast, Ghana, Zambia, Malawi, Zaire, Tanzania, Kenya, Uganda, Gambia, Cameroon, and South Africa. Beyond Africa, it has a presence in England, Germany, France, the United States, Haiti, and Jamaica.

The Redeemed Church of God is a Holiness body, and its statement of faith affirms that "sanctification is another grace of God by which our souls are progressively and completely cleansed. This is the second accomplishment of the grace which through our faith in the Blood of Jesus Christ is wrought after we have been justified and free from our sins or regenerated." Members are asked to live a life separated from worldliness that calls for modest dress, monogamous marriage, and nonparticipation in various forms of idolatry.

The church practices baptism by immersion and the ordinance of the Lord's Supper. It teaches divine healing, and members practice the laying-on-of-hands and anointing with oil. Among the well known programs of the church in Nigeria is the Holy Ghost Service, an all-night service held outside Lagos the first Friday of every month. Some 500,000 regularly attend. Members are obliged to tithe to the church.

The church is headed by a seven-person church council headed by Adeboye, who is generally and affectionately known as "G. O." or "Daddy G. O." (General Overseer).

In the 1980s members of the church began to migrate to Europe and the Americas. Subsequently, parishes were established in the United States in Dallas, Tallahassee, Houston, New York, New Jersey, Washington, Maryland, Chicago, Atlanta, Birmingham, and Detroit. The U.S. churches have held an annual convention since 1997. European congregations are found in England, Belgium, and Germany. There is a single congregation in Hong Kong.

Membership: In 2008 the church had grown to more than 5,000 parishes worldwide with a total congregational strength of more than one million. The church's North American website listed 306 parishes in the parish directory.

Sources:

Redeemed Church of God. www.rccg.org.

Redeemed Church of God (North America). www.rccgna.org.

Triumph the Church and Kingdom of God in Christ

2571 Browntown Rd. NW, Atlanta, GA 30318

Triumph the Church and Kingdom of God in Christ was founded by Elder Elias Dempsey Smith (d. 1920) in 1902. The founding followed by five years a divine revelation given to Smith. According to the literature of the church, the 1902 organization of the church marked the time when the revelation was "speeded to earth." Finally, in 1904, the content of the revelation was announced. Headquarters for the church were established in Baton Rouge, Louisiana, then were moved to Birmingham, Alabama, and later to Atlanta, Georgia. The founder was in charge of the church until 1920, when he moved to Addis Ababa, Ethiopia.

The church follows the holiness beliefs common to holiness churches, but also believes in fire baptism, a spiritual experience of empowerment by the Holy Spirit. Fire baptism was first received by the apostles in the upper room on Pentecost, when tongues of fire appeared above their heads (Acts 2). As practiced by the several nineteenth- and twentieth-century "fire-baptized" churches, fire baptism is similar to the Pentecostal experience of the baptism of the Holy Spirit, except it is typically not accompanied by speaking in tongues. (See separate entry on the Fire-Baptized Holiness Church, Wesleyan.)

Triumph the Church and Kingdom of God in Christ holds a unique view of itself as a church in relation to Christendom, traditionally called the church militant. This view is reflected in the following passage from the church's catechism:

> Question. *Was there another Church in the earth before Triumph?* Answer. *Yes. Church Militant;* Question. *Is there any difference between the Triumph Church and Church Militant?* Answer. *Yes. Church Militant is a Church of warfare, and Triumph is a Church of Peace;* Question. *What happened to Church Militant when Triumph was revealed?* Answer. *God turned it upside down and emptied His Spirit into Triumph;* Question. *Is Triumph just a Church only?* Answer. *No. It has a Kingdom with it.*

Polity is episcopal, with bishops elected for life. Under the bishops is a hierarchy of state and local workers. Every four years the church holds an International Religious Congress. In 2008 the chief apostle was Willie R. Malcom.

As of 2008, Triumph the Church and Kingdom of God in Christ is an international organization with churches located in 36 states. It runs a mission school in Africa, a national historical landmark church building in Cleveland, Ohio, historical museums and libraries in several of its local churches, two major housing complexes in Flint, Michigan——Slidell and Taylor Lake Manor——and the Triumph School of Prophets.

Founder's Day Consecration, featuring consecrated prayer and fasting, is held every year in January, from the 1st to the 20th. On the 20th, Founder's Day Celebration is marked with all-day services and a feast. In addition, National Commemoration Services in memory of the church's founder are held once per year.

Membership: Not reported. At last report (1972) there were 475 churches, 53,307 members, and 1,375 ministers.

Sources:

Triumph the Church and Kingdom of God in Christ. www.triumphthechurch.org.

Triumph the Church and Kingdom of God in Christ—Second Episcopal District. www.ourchurch.com/member/t/TriumphDistric2.

Triumph the Church in Righteousness

Current address not obtained for this edition.

Triumph the Church in Righteousness, predominantly a black holiness church, was founded in 1951 in Fort Lauderdale, Florida, by Annie Lizzie Brownlee, the church's bishop. She began life as a Baptist and later joined Triumph the Church and Kingdom of God in Christ. Bishop Brownlee began her ministry by founding a mission that served the poor, the old, the mentally ill, and children. She became well known in the black community in Fort Lauderdale where, dressed all in white, she stood on the street corners soliciting financial assistance for her mission work. In 1954 she had a vision that prompted her to purchase land and start a new church. Over the years she founded five congregations in the Miami—Fort Lauderdale area.

Bishop Brownlee, who sanctioned female ministers, maintained a strict code of appearance for female members of the church, including rules forbidding hair straightening.

Membership: In 1990 the church reported approximately 400 members in five congregations.

Sources:

DuPree, Sherry Sherrod. *African-American Holiness Pentecostal Movement: An Annotated Bibliography*. New York: Garland, 1996.

Glenn Griffith Movement

Allegheny Wesleyan Methodist Connection

2291 Depot Rd., Salem, OH 44460

The Allegheny Wesleyan Methodist Connection (Original Allegheny Conference) was formed in 1968 after the Wesleyan Methodist Church of America (1843) merged with the Pilgrim Holiness Church to form the Wesleyan Church. Prominent among the leaders of the new Connection were Reverends H. C. Van Wormer, T. A. Robertson, J. B. Markey, and F.E. Mansell. These men, along with a majority of the conference, opposed the merger on the grounds that they believed in a republican form of church governance and in Wesleyan Methodist standards of behavior, which they believed were being abandoned in the new church. Legal technicalities forced them to add the words "Original Allegheny Conference" to their name. Allegheny was one of the original conferences formed by the Wesleyan Methodist Church when it broke away from the Methodist Episcopal Church in 1843.

The Connection follows the traditional Holiness doctrine of the former Wesleyan Methodist Church. It emphasizes the belief that the atonement in Christ provides for both the regeneration of sinners and the entire sanctification of believers.

The Connection serves as an agency of the cooperative endeavor. There is a strong thrust in the foreign missions with work in Haiti, Ghana, and Peru. Domestic missions are conducted among Native Americans of the northwestern United States and Canada, and among international university students in Pittsburgh, Pennsylvania.

Membership: In 2006 there were 107 churches, 1,471 members, and 192 ministers.

Educational Facilities:

Northwest Indian Bible School, Alberton, Montana.

Allegheny Wesleyan College, Salem, Ohio.

Periodicals: *Allegheny Wesleyan Methodist.*

Sources:

Discipline of the Allegheny Wesleyan Methodist Connection. Salem, OH: Allegheny Wesleyan Methodist Connection, 2006.

Morrison, H. C. *Baptism with the Holy Ghost.* Salem, OH: Allegheny Wesleyan Methodist Connection, 1978.

Bible Methodist Connection of Churches

1216 Taylor Rd., Glencoe, AL 35905

In 1968, while the Pilgrim Holiness Church and the Wesleyan Methodist Church were merging, the Ohio Wesleyan Connection of Churches met with the Alabama Bible Methodists to see if a union of these two like-minded groups could be effected. Eighteen months later, in May 1970, the First General Conference of the Bible Methodist Connection of Churches met on the campus of God's Bible School to officially unite these two groups as the Bible Methodist Connection of Churches, with a membership of 794.

In 1970 these two bodies merged to form the Bible Methodist Connection of Churches. The connection is organized congregationally, specifically rejecting centralizing tendencies perceived to exist in the older Holiness bodies. The connection has three conferences: the Heartland Conference (formerly the Ohio Conference), Alabama Conference, and Great Lakes Conference. A conference assembly is held yearly and a general conference assembly meets every fourth year to shape church doctrine and polity.

The connection is a Holiness church whose doctrinal position is contained in the Twenty-two Articles of Religion derived from the Methodist Articles of Religion. They affirm the inspiration and infallibility of Scripture: justification; sanctification, the work of the Holy Spirit that cleanses a believer of inbred sin; and the imminent return of Christ.

In 2008 Bible Methodism had more churches on mission fields than any of its separate annual conferences had. Its primary field was in the Philippines, where it had about 40 churches and a bible college operating under national leadership. The Philippine work was organized with its own national conference with four annual conferences. In Mexico the Bible Methodist Churches were organized into a national conference in 1992. On the Mexico-Texas border the Latin American Bible Institute operates, with intermittent difficulties caused by lack of faculty and uncooperative Mexican authorities, to train Mexican laymen and pastors to do the work of the ministry. In 1992 two South Africans seeking affiliation with a Methodist Church for their pioneer work in that country found Bible Methodism, with its conservative lifestyle and emphasis on Holiness, to be the most compatible with their own beliefs. Subsequently, they joined Bible Methodism and become an arm of Bible Methodist missions operating in South Africa.

Membership: In 1997 there were 45 churches, 1,514 members, and 146 ministers in the United States, and 100 members in Canada. The church had missions and colleges in Mexico and the Philippines.

Educational Facilities:

The Bible Methodist Connection supports and draws its ministers from:

God's Bible School and College, Cincinnati, Ohio.

Union Bible College, Westfield, Indiana, and

Hobe Sound Bible Institute, Hobe Sound, Florida.

Periodicals: *The Bible Methodist.*

Sources:

Bible Methodist Connection of Churches. www.biblemethodist.org.

Bible Missionary Church

PO Box 6070, Rock Island, IL 61204-6070

Following the successful revival led by the Church of the Nazarene minister Rev. Glenn Griffith (1894–1976) near Nampa, Idaho, the group of conservative Holiness people attracted to Griffith's message were organized into the Bible Missionary Union. Word of the action spread quickly, and within 10 months congregations of like-minded people had been established in twenty states. Joining Griffith were J. E. Cook, Spencer Johnson, and H. B. Huffman. The first general conference of the church was held in Denver in 1956, at which the present name was selected. Membership in the church has been augmented by the failure of conservatives in 1956 to have the Nazarene Council Assembly condemn television.

Like its parent, the Church of the Nazarene's doctrine is Wesleyan with an emphasis on Holiness. Entire sanctification, as freedom from original sin and a state of entire devotion to God, is stressed. The future life, heaven and hell, and the premillennial return of Jesus are also central beliefs. The church is understood as "composed of all spiritually regenerated persons whose names are written in heaven." The general rules also have been expanded with the addition of much detail on points of behavior. The difference between the Bible Missionary Church and the parent body, the Church of the Nazarene, is primarily the degree of strictness of personal Holiness regulations. The church has endorsed the King James Version of the Bible for use in its churches and has gone on record against modern versions of the Bible, especially the Revised Standard Version, the Living Bible, the New English Translation, the Readers' Digest Condensed Version, and the New International Version.

The church is headed by two general moderators who preside over the general conference, the highest law-making body for the church. Foreign mission work is supported in Guyana, Venezuela, St. Vincent (West Indies), Canada, Nigeria, Honduras, Japan, the Philippines, Papua New Guinea, Barbados, and Mexico; there also is a home mission project on the Navaho Reservation at Farmington, New Mexico. A children's home is operated in Beulah Heights, Kentucky.

Membership: Not reported. There are 14 district conferences overseeing churches across the United States.

Educational Facilities:

Bible Missionary Institute, Rock Island, Illinois.

Periodicals: *The Missionary Revivalist*.

Sources:

Bible Missionary Church. *Manual*. Rock Island, IL: Author, n.d.

Cook, J. E. *W. M. Tidwell (A Life That Counted)*. Ann Arbor, MI: Mallory Lithographing, n.d.

Keene, Mrs. Roy. *Love-Threads Reaching*. Rock Island, IL: Bible Missionary Church, 1979.

Church of the Bible Covenant
Current address not obtained for this edition.

In 1966 four Indiana-based ministers of the Church of the Nazarene (Marvin Powers, Amos Hann, Donald Hicks, and Granville Rogers) formed a steering committee that led to the establishment of the Church of the Bible Covenant the following year at the John T. Hatfield Campground near Cleveland, Indiana. The four invited their former district superintendent, Remiss Rehfeldt, to join them. On August 10, 1967, the new church elected Rehfeldt and Powers as general presiding officers. Those who gathered for that meeting then spread across the country under the leadership of 12 regional presiding officers to develop local congregations.

The church's doctrine follows essentially that of the Wesleyan-Protestant tradition, with a strong emphasis on holiness and a high code of ethical standards. A general convention meets quadrennially, during which time elections are held and legislation considered. In 1982 Rehfeldt retired and was granted emeritus status. Donald Hicks was elected as new general presiding officer.

Membership: Not reported.

Educational Facilities:

Covenant Foundation College, Greenfield, Indiana. The church maintains three Bible-training institutions overseas.

Periodicals: *The Covenanter*. Available from New Castle, IN 47352.

Sources:

Articles. Knightsville, IN: Church of the Bible Covenant, 1970.

Evangelical Wesleyan Church
6626 East Wayne Rd., Cooperstown, PA 16317

The Evangelical Wesleyan Church was formed in 1963 through the merger of the Evangelical Wesleyan Church of North America and the Midwest Holiness Association, both churches being composed of members who had left the Free Methodist Church. The Evangelical Wesleyan Church of North America was organized at a convention on July 19, 1958, held near Centerville, Crawford County, Pennsylvania, with a dedication to restore old-time Free Methodism. (The members sought a stricter interpretation of personal moral codes; e.g., they were concerned about women's hairstyles and makeup and the length of dresses.) The Midwest Holiness Association was formed in 1962 as a protest against worldliness and apostasy in the Free Methodist Church. The organizing convention of the Midwest Holiness Association was held in Ansley, Nebraska. The Evangelical

Wesleyan Church is opposed to any compromising of the old doctrines and standards of Free Methodism and follows Free Methodism's patterns.

Membership: In 2008 the group reported 250 members, 27 congregations, and 46 clergy.

Educational Facilities:

Evangelical Wesleyan Bible College, Cooperstown, Pennsylania.

Periodicals: *The Earnest Christian*.

God's Missionary Church
125 N Main St., Middleburg, PA 17842

God's Missionary Church is one of the older conservative Holiness bodies. It was formed in 1935 as a result of a dispute in the Pennsylvania and New Jersey district of the Pilgrim Holiness Church.

The church is very strict in discipline and also is opposed to participation in war, reflecting the Quaker influence in the founding of the Pilgrim Holiness Church. The church is congregational but headed by a conference president, who in 2008 was Rev. Harry Plank. There is missionary work in Haiti and among Cuban refugees in Florida. It cooperates with the Interdenominational Holiness Convention.

Membership: Not reported. In 1971 there were 595 members, 532 of whom resided in Pennsylvania. The church's website listed 46 churches in its church directory in 2008.

Educational Facilities:

Penn View Bible Institute, Penns Creek, Pennsylvania.

Periodicals: *God's Missionary Standard*.

Sources:

God's Missionary Church. www.godsmissionarychurch.org.

God's Missionary Church. *Official Handbook and Discipline*. Watsontown, PA: Author, 1971.

Lower Lights Church
Ann Arbor, MI

The Lower Lights Church was formed in 1940 as a single congregation (the Lower Light Mission) in Ann Arbor, Michigan. It subsequently branched out to neighboring communities and now cooperates with the Interdenominational Holiness Convention.

Membership: Not reported. There are several congregations in Michigan and Ohio with several hundred members.

National Association of Holiness Churches
351 S Park Dr., Griffith, IN 46319

The National Association of Holiness Churches was formed at the Singing Hill Camp Ground near Shoals, Indiana, in 1967. H. Robb French (1891–1985), a former pastor in the Wesleyan Methodist Church and one of the founders of the Interdenominational Holiness Convention, was the chief moving force in its founding and early development. French was the first general chairman, a post he held until his resignation in 1973. The association exists as a loose confederation of independent ministers and churches formed for the purposes of promoting holiness and providing fellowship. An annual camp meeting and association general conference is held in June. Missionary work is supported in Mexico, Brazil, and India.

Membership: In 2002 there were 12 congregations in the association and 42 affiliated ministers in the United States. Many of the ministers and churches affiliated with the association are also affiliated with other conservative holiness church bodies.

Periodicals: *The NAHC Bulletin*.

Sources:

www.ourchurch.com/member/p/PHC_of_Griffith/.

Pilgrim Holiness Church of New York

32 Cadillac Ave., Albany, NY 12205

The Pilgrim Holiness Church of New York traces its history to the Pentecostal Rescue Mission organized in 1897 in Binghamton, New York. In 1922 that mission affiliated as an autonomous district with the International Holiness Church, which in the following year was renamed Pilgrim Holiness Church. During the 1960s the Pilgrim Holiness Church began a process of centralizing authority in the national headquarters and preparing for merger with the Wesleyan Methodist Church. (The merger was completed in 1968 with the creation of the Wesleyan Church.) In 1963, asserting its autonomous status, the New York Conference left the Pilgrim Holiness Church. In 2008 it continues as an independent organization.

The church is very conservative in doctrine and strict in practice, as are those churches that are affiliated with the Interdenominational Holiness Convention. Missions are directly supported in Brazil, Haiti, and Winnepeg, Manitoba, Canada, and other locations through various missionary agencies. Churches are located in New York, New Jersey, Ohio, Pennsylvania, Massachusetts, and Canada.

In 2008 Rev. Donald M. Myers was the conference president.

Membership: In 2002 the church reported 726 members, 53 churches, and 79 ministers in the United States and 36 members, 3 churches, and 3 ministers in Canada.

Educational Facilities:

The church has no school of its own, but financially supports and recommends the following:

God's Bible School, Cincinnati, Ohio.

Hobe Sound Bible School, Hobe Sound, Florida (sponsored by the National Association of Holiness Churches).

Allegheny Wesleyan College, Salem, Ohio.

Penn View Bible Institute, Penns Creek, Pennsylvania (sponsored by God's Missionary Church).

Periodicals: *Pilgrim News.*

Sources:

Pilgrim Holiness Church of New York. phcofny.homestead.com/files/index.htm.

Pilgrim Nazarene Church

c/o Rev. Dale Hayford, 504 Valley Dr., Rogers, AR 72756

The Pilgrim Nazarene Church was founded at the end of 2003 by former members of the Bible Missionary Church, a conservative Holiness church. The founders felt that the Bible Missionary church had begun to drift from the high standards around which it had been founded. It formally continues the beliefs and practices of the parent organization, as it continues to use the Bible Missionary Church's manual as a guide for its own organization. It dispute was with the lack of strictness of the Holiness practice within the parent church.

Membership: In 2008 the church reported 14 congregations affiliated with it. At that time, however, a number of additional congregations were in the process of leaving the Bible Missionary Church and were still making decisions about affiliation.

Educational Facilities:

Hobe Sound Bible College, Hobe Sound, Florida.

Periodicals: *The Pilgrim Nazarene Church Herald.*

Sources:

Pilgrim Nazarene Church. www.pilgrimnazarene.org/.

Pilgrim Holiness Church of the Midwest

6402 Ridgeview Dr., Anderson, IN 46013

The Pilgrim Holiness Church of the Midwest was formed in 1970. Three years earlier, ten congregations affiliated with the Pilgrim Holiness Church, led by Rev. James Southerland and Rev. Eugene Gray, had withdrawn to become the Midwest Conference of the Pilgrim Holiness Church of New York. Those ten congregations eventually decided to remain independent, though they have stayed friendly with the New York group. They adopted their own discipline (book of church order). Mission work is through the Evangelical Faith Missions and Evangelical Bible Missions.

The church holds an annual conference. The conference president in 2008 was Rev. James Southerland, who has served since 1970.

Membership: In 2008 the church's website listed 39 congregations in its church directory.

Educational Facilities:

Union Bible Seminary.

Sources:

Pilgrim Holiness Church of the Midwest. midwestphc.org.

United Holiness Church of North America

Current address not obtained for this edition.

The United Holiness Church of North America was formed in 1955 by conservatives within the Free Methodist Church at a camp meeting in Carson City, Michigan. Headquarters are at the Bible College at Cedar. It resembles its parent body, but is stricter in its standards of holiness. The church cooperates with the Interdenominational Holiness Convention.

Membership: Not reported.

Educational Facilities:

Jordan College, Cedar Springs, Michigan.

Periodicals: *United Holiness Sentinel.*

Voice of the Nazarene Association of Churches

PO Box 606, Meadow Lands, PA 15347-0606

One focus within the Church of the Nazarene of the post–World II conservative Holiness movement was a magazine, the *Voice of the Nazarene*, published at Finleyville, Pennsylvania, by the church member W. L. King. Following the 1956 decision in the Church of the Nazarene to allow its members to watch television, some anti-television members in the East associated with King to form the Voice of the Nazarene Association of Churches. It is a loosely congregational organization. The literature from the Finleyville headquarters isis extremely conservative, both politically and religiously, in its strong opposition to communism, the National Council of Churches, and the Roman Catholic Church.

Membership: Not reported. In 1967 there were eight member congregations (plus 18 cooperating congregations) and 31 association evangelists.

Periodicals: *Universal Challenger.* • *Voice of the Nazarene.*

Sources:

Voice of the Nazarene Association of Churches. www.voiceofthenazarene.com.

Wesleyan Holiness Association of Churches

Current address not obtained for this edition.

The Wesleyan Holiness Association of Churches was organized in 1960 by Rev. Glenn Griffith (1894–1976) and others who had left the Bible Missionary Church in protest against what they saw as a drifting away from the old Wesleyan revival fervor and standards. They also objected to its acceptance of divorced persons into the membership and ministry. At an informal meeting of ministers and laypeople in August 1959, Griffith was chosen the general leader, and an initial general conference with an accompanying camp meeting was set for the next year at Colorado Springs, Colorado. At that meeting, Griffith was unanimously elected to the post of general moderator (now general superintendent) of the new Wesleyan Holiness Association of Churches. Among its objectives were to emphasize the doctrine and experience of entire sanctification and to raise the standard of holiness in daily living. It upheld a strict code of personal conduct.

The association's six-article doctrine stated the basic affirmations of traditional Wesleyan Christianity. Article IV concerned God's plan of redemption and affirmed free will, faith, repentance, and justification. It emphasized sanctification as a second act of God in believers, whereby they are made free from original sin or depravity and brought into a state of entire "devotement" to God. Sanctification is followed by a continued growth in grace. The association practiced two sacraments: baptism (by sprinkling or pouring, with immersion preferred) and the Lord's Supper. The association stated a belief in divine healing. It opposed drafting females into military service.

The association was congregationally governed. Each church owned its own property and called its own ministers. Churches were grouped into five districts, each served by a district superintendent. A representative general conference met biennially, electing a board and a lay delegate from each district. The association's home missionary program included work among American Indians in Arizona and New Mexico; its foreign missionaries operated in Africa, Bolivia, the Grand Caymans, Guatemala, Taiwan, and New Guinea.

Membership: In 1992 the association reported 36 congregations served by 65 ordained and 25 licensed ministers.

Periodicals: *Eleventh Hour Messenger*.

Sources:

Declaration of Principles. Dayton, OH: Wesleyan Holiness Association of Churches, 1981.

Griffith, Glenn. *I Sought for a Man*. Phoenix, AZ: Author, n.d.

The Pentecostal movement was one of the most spectacular religious phenomena of the twentieth century, ranking with the massive movement of Asian religions to the United States and the rise of Islam as a global power. Born as the century began, Pentecostalism now claims several million American followers and millions more overseas. As Pentecostals have taken their place in the world Christian community, they have emphasized their orthodoxy. Theologically, with the exception of the Apostolic Pentecostals discussed below, Pentecostals are situated firmly within the conciliar tradition (fourth to eighth centuries), during which time the consensus on the major beliefs of Christian orthodoxy was reached. Pentecostals also have no disagreement with the major affirmations of the Protestant Reformation on such issues as the authority of the Bible, salvation by faith alone, and the priesthood of believers. In fact, the statements of belief of the various Pentecostal churches reflect their heritage, be that heritage Methodist (chapter 7) or Holiness (chapter 8) or Baptist (chapter 11). The real line between Pentecostal churches and the mainline Protestant churches has been clear from the beginning of the modern movement in 1901. Pentecostals are distinguished solely by their revival of a form of religious experience grounded in what is technically termed *glossolalia*, but more popularly called "speaking in tongues."

The uniqueness of the Pentecostal experience begins in the conscious search for the gift of speaking in tongues as a sign of having been blessed with the baptism of the Holy Spirit. That baptism may be defined as the dwelling of the Holy Spirit in the individual believer. From the initial experience of the baptism of the Holy Spirit and speaking in tongues, the believer may expect to also manifest other gifts of the Holy Spirit as originally manifested in the New Testament church (I Corinthians 12:4–11). Those gifts include healing, prophecy, wisdom (knowledge unattainable by natural means), and discernment of spirits (seeing non-physical beings such as angels and demons).

SPEAKING IN TONGUES. Glossolalia, speaking in tongues, was a part of the experience of Jesus' disciples at Pentecost (Acts 2) and reappeared at several important points in the growing church. In Paul's Epistle to the Corinthians, "tongues" are mentioned as one gift or "charisma" among others, such as healing, working miracles, and prophecy. Tongues usually appear in connection with

other "gifts of the Spirit" although, historically, the other gifts have often appeared without the accompanying verbal gift. The experience of tongues, if not common, was well known in the ancient world. The phenomenon is manifest today in a number of tribal religions, as well as among Pentecostals.

What are "tongues"? To the outsider, hearing someone speak in tongues is like hearing gibberish. To the Pentecostal, it is speaking under the control of the Holy Spirit. Pentecostal lore is full of tales of people who have been able to speak in a foreign language at a moment of crisis, although they did not know the language. Believers regard such instances as supernatural occurrences.

Social scientists generally look to a different explanation. Linguist William Samarin would separate glossolalia from *xenoglossia*. Glossolalia, says Samarin, is not truly a language. It is a verbalized religious experience. Only a few vowels and consonants are used, not enough to make a language as we know it. Glossolalia is the common prayer speech heard at Pentecostal churches. Xenoglossia, in contrast, is the utterance of an existent foreign language by one who has no knowledge of it. A rare occurrence, it nevertheless has been noted and recorded in the literature of psychical research. Outside of Pentecostal circles, both telepathy and spirit contact have been hypothesized as the source of the xenoglossia. Possibly more important as an explanation is *cryptonesia*, forgotten memory. It is possible for a young person, for example, to learn much of a language from simply hearing others speak it, apart from any formal training. In later years, any conscious memory of that language can be lost to memory, but can reappear in an altered state of consciousness.

LIFESTYLE AND WORSHIP. Along with the new form of religious experience centered upon speaking in tongues comes the second distinguishing mark of the Pentecostal: a lifestyle reordered around that religious experience. The Pentecostal convert lets his or her religious experience dominate daily life. The Pentecostal encourages others to have the baptism of the Holy Spirit; Pentecostals talk about that experience often; when they pray, they pray in tongues; they see healings as signs of God's immediate presence; they pay attention to other gifts of the Holy Spirit; and finally, they tend to look down on those who do not speak in tongues.

Through the first half of the twentieth century, Pentecostals were frequently and pejoratively called "holy rollers," a reference to their free, loud, participatory style of worship and their constant attention to the gifts of the Spirit, especially tongues. In contrast to the more orderly services in the Methodist, Baptist, and Presbyterian churches, Pentecostals seem to have a very free, spontaneous service that includes hymns that emphasize rhythm, extemporaneous prayers, and frequent interruption of the service with "amen's" and "tongues." Those who visit Pentecostal services for the first time are startled by the seeming lack of order. The freedom and spontaneity are limited, however. Even the most free congregation falls into a narrow pattern, repeated week after week with little variation.

It is the worship and the lifestyle keyed to religious experience—the constant search for the experience and the endless talk about it—that separate Pentecostalism from the older Protestant denominations. Such distinctions are more felt than rationalized and are rarely articulated.

When conservative Christians such as Baptists and the Reformed discuss the doctrinal differences between themselves and the Pentecostal movement, they focus on disagreements about the baptism of the Holy Spirit and the gifts of the Spirit. Theologians out of the Reformed tradition tend to believe that the gifts of the Spirit were given to the early church and disappeared after the apostles died. Other critics, however, observe the likeness between the religious expressions of Pentecostals and those of non-Christians, including the Spiritualist and occult movements. A few critics have charged the Pentecostals with a form of demon possession. By contrast, the Pentecostals insist the end of time is near, and the words of the prophet Joel (Joel 3:1) are being fulfilled: "It shall come to pass in the last days, says God, that I will pour out my Spirit on all mankind: Your sons and daughters shall prophesy, your young men shall see visions and your old men shall dream dreams." According to Acts 2:17, Peter referred to this passage on the original day of Pentecost as being fulfilled in the foundation of the Christian church.

HEALING.

Speaking in tongues makes Pentecostals controversial, but such controversy is multiplied by the addition of an emphasis on God's healing. Objections to healing center not as much on the reality of healing as on the form that healing ministries have assumed. Mainline Christians are offended by the seeming over-familiarity with God assumed in praying for God to heal, as well as the loud, demanding style of many evangelists. The critics also object to the emotional, crowd-psychology-oriented healing services that seem to manipulate those in attendance. Typical of the criticisms was the controversy that erupted in the 1970s around the former child-evangelist, Marjoe Gortner (b. 1944). Gortner had conducted healing services as a child, but came to the decision that what he was doing was not valid. So, in the 1970s, he invited filmmakers to follow him in a year's work of Pentecostal healing. The resultant movie (*Marjoe*, 1972) and book were released as an exposé of Pentecostal healing. Gortner's critique appeared on the heels of critiques of healing that had emerged in reaction to the post–World War II healing movement that grew out of the work of William M.

Branham (1909–1965), which produced superstar Oral Roberts (b. 1918) and were followed by similar negative judgments leveled against popular healer Kathryn Kuhlman (1907–1976).

In the mid-1980s, skeptical stage magician James Randi (b. 1928) did a survey of Pentecostal healers, among whom he found two, Peter Popoff (b. 1946) and W. V. Grant Jr. (b. 1946), who were carrying on plainly fraudulent activity to create the appearance of miracles in their healing services. Using tricks well known to stage magicians, they claimed to receive information supernaturally. But in fact, the information was being transmitted to them by accomplices. In exposing the two questionable healers, Randi actually did the movement a great service. He believed that most of the healers he investigated were self-deluded, but were nevertheless sincere in what they were doing.

In spite of such criticisms, however, the Pentecostals raised an important issue for contemporary Christians: the question of healing as a sign of God's work among his people. Pentecostals join both Christian Scientists, who refrain from using medicine and doctors, and Episcopalians in raising this issue. An Episcopalian physician, Charles Cullis (1833–1892), held healing services during the late nineteenth century at his summer camp in Old Orchard, Maine. Many of the spiritual-healing ministries in the United States can be traced from Cullis to the Emmanuel movement (emanating from the Emmanuel Episcopal Church in Boston early in the twentieth century) to healing evangelists such as Aimee Semple McPherson (1890–1944) to more recent organizations such as the ecumenical Order of St. Luke the Physician, the spiritual heir of the Emmanuel movement. Thus Pentecostal healing activity fits into a much larger interest in healing as a gift of the Holy Spirit within Christianity.

TONGUES IN HISTORY.

The first recorded manifestation of speaking in tongues in the modern era occurred in the late seventeenth century in France. The times were a blend of persecution and miraculous events. After the revocation of the Edict of Nantes (1685), state suppression of Protestants began in southern France, among other places. In the mountainous region of Languedoc in the 1680s, more than 10,000 people were victims of the stake, galley, and wheel. Partially in reaction to this persecution, strange paranormal phenomena began to occur. At Vivaris, in southern France, a man reported that he had a vision and heard a voice say, "Go and console my people." At Berne, people claimed to have seen apparitions and heard voices. There arose prophets who were viewed as miraculous because, although young and untutored, they spoke fluently and with wisdom.

Among the French mountain villages was a poor unlettered girl, Isabella Vincent. The daughter of a weaver, Isabella left home after her father accepted a bribe to become a Catholic and after she witnessed a massacre of Huguenots (French Calvinists). She was a Huguenot, and she fled to her Huguenot godfather. On February 12, 1688, she had her first ecstatic experience. She entered a trance in which she spoke in tongues and prophesied. She called for repentance, especially from those who had forsaken their faith for gold. Her fame spread. People marveled at her perfect Parisian French and her ability to quote the Mass verbatim and refute it. She was finally arrested, but others rose to take her place. In 1700 a movement began among the youth, and children as young as three entered ecstatic states and prophesied. Continued persecution was followed by war and eventual migration to other parts of Europe, where these people became known as the French Prophets.

A few manifestations of tongues were noted in the eighteenth century among the Quakers in England and the Methodists in America. In the 1830s, however, two groups emerged who spoke in tongues with some frequency: in England, the Catholic Apostolic Church, and in America, the Church of Jesus Christ of Latter-day Saints. Both accepted the experience as part of a charismatic church life. Then, after the Civil War (1861–1865), tongues began to manifest themselves within the Holiness churches and thus came into historical continuity with the present-day Pentecostal movement. In 1875 the Reverend R. B. Swan, a Holiness minister, was one of five people in Providence, Rhode Island, who spoke in tongues. This group grew and soon became known as the Gift People. William Jethro Walthall (1858–1931) reported speaking in tongues as early as 1879. This evangelist from Arkansas at first accepted tongues as part of a total experience of "being carried outside of himself," but later identified it with Pentecost and became a superintendent of the Assemblies of God, discussed below. In 1890 Daniel Awrey, an evangelist from Ohio, experienced tongues. In the 1890s, members attending the meetings of R. G. Spurling (1857–1935) in Tennessee and North Carolina, and W. F. Bryant (1963–1949) of Camp Creek, North Carolina, spoke in tongues. The experience was later identified with Pentecost, and these two men became leaders in the Church of God (Cleveland, Tennessee), also discussed below. Besides these and other isolated incidents of "tongues," in the 1890s there appeared a new movement in the Holiness church that was to be a direct precursor of Pentecostalism as it exists today—the fire baptism.

As a movement, fire baptism was an "experience" preached by some Holiness ministers looking for something more than their Holiness experience had given them. The first such minister was the Reverend B. H. Irwin, who had derived the experience from the writings of John Fletcher (1729–1785), an early Methodist. Fletcher, in his works, had spoken of a "baptism of burning love," but it is doubtful that he was implying any of what Irwin was seeking. Fire baptism, a personal religious experience of being filled with and empowered by the Holy Spirit, took its name from the Holy Spirit's descent upon the apostles in the form of tongues of flame—the first Pentecost.

In 1895 the first fire-baptized congregation (the first church to seek and receive fire baptism) was organized at Olmitz, Iowa. From there, fire baptism was spread by itinerant evangelists. Holiness leaders labeled this new experience, which they termed "The Fire," heresy and fanaticism.

Opposition did not keep the teaching from spreading and, within three years, there were nine state associations organized and six more associations waiting to form, including two in Canada. Formal organization of the Fire-Baptized Holiness Association took place in 1898 at Anderson, South Carolina, and a periodical, *Live Coals of Fire*, was started in 1899. Later, the Fire-Baptized Holiness Association was to accept as a body the Pentecostal emphasis on speaking in tongues as a sure sign of the Spirit's presence within the believer. The early experience of tongues and the development of the Fire-Baptized Holiness Association set the nineteenth-century stage for the twentieth-century Pentecostal movement. Three years would be significant in its development—1901, 1906, and 1914.

Tongues have periodically appeared in the Christian tradition, and cases have been noted in a variety of non-Christian religions. However, it is to be noted that the experience of tongues by itself is not Pentecostalism. Pentecostalism was not built around a mere outbreak of spontaneous experiences of tongues. Rather, it consists of the conscious focus on the experience of tongues as a sign of the reception of the Holy Spirit, and of activity (primarily prayer) directed toward the reception of the gift, and subsequent to receiving it, the conscious search for other gifts of the Spirit. Thus the history of Pentecostalism ultimately leads not to incidents of tongues in history, but to a Bible school in the American Midwest in the first year of the twentieth century.

TOPEKA, KANSAS, 1901. The beginnings of the modern Pentecostal movement originated in the ministry of the Reverend Charles Parham (1873–1929). Having left the Methodist Episcopal Church, Parham eventually opened the Bethel Healing Home in 1898 in Topeka. He had been inspired by the healing ministry of John Alexander Dowie (1847–1907) of Zion, Illinois. In 1900 Parham began an extended tour of Holiness and healing ministries from Chicago to New York to Georgia. Returning to Topeka, Parham found his work undermined and usurped. Undaunted, he purchased a building just outside of town and began the Bethel Bible College in the fall of 1900. Over the Christmas holidays, before leaving to speak in Kansas City, he assigned his students the task of investigating the "baptism of the Spirit," sometimes called the Pentecostal blessing. Upon returning, Parham got a report: "To my astonishment, they all had the same story that while different things occurred when the Pentecostal blessing fell, the indisputable proof on each occasion was that they spoke with other tongues" (Parham 1969, p. 52).

Immediately, they turned to seek a baptism with an indication given by utterance in tongues. On January 1, 1901, the Holy Spirit fell, first on Agnes Ozman (1870–1937), and a few days later on many others, and then on Parham himself. Thus Agnes Ozman became the first person in modern times self-consciously to seek and then to receive the experience of speaking in tongues as a sign of being "baptized with the Holy Spirit." The modern Pentecostal movement can be dated from that moment.

This small beginning, of fewer than 40 people, did not portend the growth that was to come. Parham closed the school and with his students set out to spread the message of the new Pentecost. He traveled and preached through Missouri and Kansas, and climaxed his tour with a revival in Galena, Kansas, which lasted for four months in the winter of 1903 to 1904. In 1905 he began work in Texas for the first time. He made Houston, Texas, his headquarters and in December 1905 opened a Bible school. Parham at this point let the mantle of leadership pass to William J. Seymour (1870–1922), a black minister who had studied under Parham in Houston.

AZUSA STREET, LOS ANGELES, CALIFORNIA, 1906. The Pentecostal scene shifted to the West Coast, to California, where in 1906 William J. Seymour, an African-American Holiness minister, arrived to preach at a small Baptist church. The church refused to hear him after his first sermon, but he was invited to preach at a member's home on Bonnie Brae Street. After three days of his preaching, the Spirit fell and tongues were heard on the West Coast. The meeting quickly outgrew the small home, and a former Methodist church building was rented on Azusa Street. From here would develop the revival that would send the Pentecostal experience around the world.

The Pentecostal outpouring in Los Angeles did not occur in a vacuum, but was the culmination of earlier events. From the spring of 1905, Frank Bartlemen (1871–1936) and Joseph Smale (1867–1926) had been giving wide publicity to the 1904 Wales revival under Evan Roberts (1878–1951). In addition, a number of Pentecostals who spoke in tongues had arrived from Armenia to begin a new life in America. All quickly lent support to the Bonnie Brae phenomena.

After the initial speaking in tongues on April 9, the meeting grew and spread. Significant in this growth was the occurrence on April 18, just nine days after the initial experience, of the great San Francisco earthquake. More than 125,000 tracts relating the earthquake to the Azusa Street happenings and the "endtime" were promptly distributed. News of the revival was also widely circulated in Holiness and other religious periodicals. Attracted by the excitement, people came to Los Angeles from across the country. As they received the baptism, they went home to spread the word. Pentecostal centers appeared in Illinois, New York, North Carolina, Sweden, England, India, and Chile.

Before the late twentieth century, Pentecostals have had a peculiar problem in dealing forthrightly with their history. Leadership of the movement he founded was lost to Charles Parham, who, like B. H. Irwin before him, was ostracized because of a personal scandal. Parham was accused of homosexuality, a particularly horrible sin in the eyes of conservative Christians. Then, the new leadership provided by Seymour was gradually rejected because of his race, and by the beginning of World War I (1914–1918) his ministry was largely limited to African-American peoples around the country. National leadership passed to white ministers who went to Azusa Street and returned home to found the various Pentecostal denominations.

HOT SPRINGS, ARKANSAS, 1914. From 1901 until 1914, the Pentecostals existed primarily within the Holiness movement. The Holiness movement was oriented toward an experience that ratified the believer's sanctity, the experience of the "second blessing," after which the believer would be holy forever. As the Pentecostal movement spread, many Holiness churches accepted speaking in tongues as a final guarantee of holiness, a sure sign than the "second blessing," and they called the Pentecostal "baptism of the Holy Spirit" the third experience. (The first, preceding the second blessing, was justification—the discovery of Christ as the personal savior.)

The Holiness movement thus had supplied the basic problem (sanctification, life in the Spirit) that had caused concern for the "baptism of the Holy Spirit." The early Pentecostal leaders and members came from Holiness churches, and Holiness periodicals spread the word of the revival. Most important, the Holiness churches, like the synagogues for Paul, became the first centers for Pentecostal evangelism. Out of the Holiness movement came such churches as the Pentecostal Holiness Church and the Church of God (Cleveland, Tennessee). However, the growth of Pentecostalism caused many Holiness churches and leaders to express strong disapproval of it. Resistance varied from the relatively mild policy of the Christian and Missionary Alliance to radical rejection by the Pentecostal Nazarene Church, which even dropped the word *Pentecostal* from its title to manifest its firm opposition.

Growing hostility, factionalism within the movement, and the need for coordination of activities led in 1914 to a meeting at the Grand Opera House in Hot Springs, Arkansas, where participants expressed a desire for fuller cooperation. Out of this meeting grew the Assemblies of God. More importantly, from this organization came the impetus for the eventual organization of additional independent churches. Pentecostal denominationalism had begun in earnest.

With time, three Pentecostal churches took a special place in the American Pentecostal movement: the Assemblies of God; the Church of God (Cleveland, Tennessee); and the House of God, Which is the Church of The living God, the Pillar and Ground of Truth. Many other Pentecostal churches are offshoots of these three or are modeled on them and deviate from them on only a few points. (For practical purposes, a parenthetical subtitle is given to some churches in this encyclopedia. Thus the Church of God [Cleveland, Tennessee] calls itself simply the Church of God, but its headquarters are in Cleveland, Tennessee, so that is added to its title to distinguish it from the more than one hundred other denominations that call themselves the Church of God.)

As various Pentecostal churches came into existence, they adopted different forms of church government. Some are congregational, some connectional. The congregational churches share four characteristics: (1) the local churches operate autonomously; (2) they choose their own ministers; (3) they own their property themselves; and (4) they allow

Pentecostal Family Chronology

19th century	Through the nineteenth century, a variety of groups from the Mormons to the Shakers experience manifestations of the charismatic gifts of the spirit including speaking in tongues, prophecies, and divine healing. These accounts come from around the world.
1880–1900	Leaders in the Holiness movement discuss the idea of the baptism of the Holy Spirit, which many tend to identify with the Holiness experience of sanctification while others become dissatisfied with that explanation.
1900	Independent Methodist Holiness preacher Charles Fox Parham raises issue of speaking in tongues (glossalalia) being the sign of the baptism of the Holy Spirit with the students of the Bethel Bible School, which he heads in Topeka, Kansas. As other students begin to receive the gift of tongues, the event is seen as the fulfillment of the biblical prophecy that God will pour out his spirit at the "end time." The students also believe that they are speaking real foreign languages that will be tools for the world's evangelization.
1901	On January 1, Agnes Oznam becomes the first person who, after prayer to be baptized with the Holy Spirit, speaks in tongues.
1905	Parham moves to Houston where he encounters African Methodist preacher William Joseph Seymour, who accepts the Pentecostal message.
1906	Seymour accepts a pastorate in Los Angeles, but is rejected after preaching about Pentecost. He then is invited to lead a Bible study group among whom the Spirit manifests on April 9. This event is tied to the San Francisco earthquake (April 18) and a belief in the approaching "end time." Seymour establishes the Apostolic Faith Mission on Azusa Street where daily services are held to which people from around United States and Canada come.
1906–07	The Church of God, based in Cleveland, Tennessee, a Holiness church among whom speaking in tongues had previously manifested, aligns itself with the movement based at the Apostolic Faith Mission in Los Angeles.
1907	G. G. Garr is disappointed when his wife Lilian, who was believed to be speaking Chinese when speaking in tongues, is unintelligible to the Chinese of Hong Kong. He calls for a significant revision of the movement's understanding of the phenomenon, which he now sees as simply a devotional language.
	Florence Crawford leaves Los Angeles and founds the Apostolic Faith Church, based in Portland, Oregon.
	African American Holiness minister Charles H. Mason founds Church of God in Christ.
	Chicago Baptist minister William H. Durham receives baptism of the Holy Spirit. He later repudiates the Methodist idea of sanctification and any need for sanctification to precede the baptism of the Holy Spirit. Many attracted to Pentecostalism from outside Methodism accept his "finished work" approach.
1909	Under the ministry of G. B. Cashwell, The Fire-Baptized Holiness Church accepts the Pentecostal message and merges into the Pentecostal Holiness Church.
1912	George Went Hensley introduces the Church of God (Cleveland, Tennessee) to the practice of handling serpents, among whom it flourished for a decade before being pushed out.
1913	Beginning of the "Jesus Only" (Apostolic or Oneness) movement developed from literal reading of the baptismal formula in Acts 2:38 (and other places), which repudiates traditional doctrine of the Trinity. Pentecostal Assemblies of the World becomes first group to accept the new approach.
1914	The Assemblies of God, following William Durham's "finished work" perspective, is founded in Hot Springs, Arkansas.
1945	Several Oneness groups merge to form the United Pentecostal Church.
1947	First Pentecostal World Conference gathers in Zurich, Switzerland.
1948	Pentecostal Fellowship of North America formed.
	Latter Rain movement, emphasizing divine healing, prophecy, and the five-fold ministry leadership (Ephesians 4:11), spreads from Canada to the United States.
1951	With healing evangelist Oral Roberts's assistance, layman Demos Shakarian founds the Full Gospel Business Men's Fellowship International, which becomes a major seeding ground for the new Charismatic movement that spreads the Pentecostal experience in the Roman Catholic, Eastern Orthodox, and non-Pentecostal Protestant denominations.
1952	South African David du Plessis launches effort to place Pentecostals in dialogue with the larger Christian world with a lecture at Princeton University.
1955	Oral Roberts initiates a national weekly television show built around his healing crusades.
1960	Episcopal priest Dennis Bennett, who recently had received the baptism of the Holy Spirit, accepts the pastorate at St. Luke's Episcopal Church in Seattle, Washington, which becomes a primary dissemination point for the charismatic movement among Protestant denominations in the 1970s.
1963	Assemblies of God minister Dave Wilkerson publishes best-selling *The Cross and the Switchblade* describing his ministry with street gangs.
1970s	A number of Charismatic fellowships from within the larger non-Pentecostal denominations (United Methodist, Baptist, Lutheran, Presbyterian, reformed, etc.) nurture the spread of the Charismatic experience. Most denominations offer official responses that vary from denunciation to cautious acceptance of the movement.
1972–73	Leon Joseph Cardinal Suenens (Belgium) assumes a leadership role in the developing Catholic Charismatic Movement.
1978	African American evangelist Frederick K. C. Price launches national television ministry representative of the Positive Confession ("Name It-Claim It") movement.
1987	Christian television is scandalized with the resignation of Jim Bakker (and his subsequent arrest and conviction) over financial mismanagement of funds raised through the PTL ministry he headed.
1992	Pentecostal Fellowship of North America, largely consisting of the large white Pentecostal denominations, is disbanded and superseded by the Pentecostal/Charismatic Churches of North America, an inter-racial fellowship which also includes newer Charismatic church bodies.
2006	Pentecostals gather in Los Angeles to celebrate the centennial of the Apostolic Faith Mission established on Azusa Street and the revival that launched their movement.

their regional and national church bodies to have only advisory authority over the local churches. In connectional churches, the regional and national church bodies have varying levels of power to legislate on doctrinal and organizational matters. Some Pentecostal churches with a connectional polity are close to a presbyterial system; some are close to an episcopal system with bishops (and superintendents).

CONTEMPORARY DEVELOPMENTS. Two noticeable trends were evident in Pentecostalism in the last half of the twentieth century. First, among the second- and third-generation Pentecostal denominations, a marked tendency to lessen the overtly emotional, loud, and spontaneous style has arisen, particularly in urban centers. Symbolic is the regular use of printed weekly church bulletins that specify an order of worship for the Sunday morning service.

Also, these same Pentecostal bodies have pursued the development of ecumenical structures both among themselves and with non-Pentecostal churches. Ecumenical efforts within Pentecostalism began with the World Conference of Pentecostals held at Zurich, Switzerland, in May 1947. This conference inspired the formation of the Pentecostal Fellowship of North America (PFNA), constituted at Des Moines, Iowa, in October 1948. This body had among its members all the larger Trinitarian Pentecostal denominations (17 Canadian and U.S. bodies representing more than one million members in 1970). The PFNA was a predominantly white organization, and following a meeting at which the problem of racism within the Pentecostal movement was brought to the fore, the member churches disbanded the organization. They then joined with several predominantly black groups to found the Pentecostal/Charismatic Fellowship of North America.

Meetings of Pentecostals around the world continued (Paris, 1949; London, 1952; Stockholm, 1955; Toronto, 1958; Jerusalem, 1961; Helsinki, 1964; Rio de Janeiro, 1967; and Dallas, 1970). Along with these conferences, which meet every three years, there have been attempts, increasingly successful, to engage the older ecumenical bodies in dialogue. Emerging as the central figure in the effort was David J. DuPlessis (1905–1987), a South African Assemblies of God minister. DuPlessis was a key organizer of the early world Pentecostal conferences, worked on the staff of the Second Assembly of the World Council of Churches in Evanston, Illinois, in 1954, and generally served as Pentecostalism's roving ambassador to non-Pentecostal Christians. The world conferences eventually led at the beginning of the new century to the formation of a more permanent global Pentecostal organization, the World Pentecostal Fellowship.

The growing cooperation among Pentecostal bodies culminated in 2006 with a series of events designed to mark the centennial of the Azusa Street revival in Los Angeles (which has generally replaced the original events surrounding Parham in Kansas as the founding event of the Pentecostal movement). The primary celebrations occurred in April, with Trinitarian and Oneness Pentecostals holding separate events, though all events were open to any of the estimated 250,000 people who attended.

The second trend within Pentecostalism has been the regular outbreaks of international Pentecostal revivals that are seen both as recapitulating the revival at Azusa Street in the face of a movement that many feel has lost much of the original Pentecostal spirit, and as signaling the hoped-for culmination of this age. The first such revival in the years following World War II (1939–1945) began in 1948 in western Canada and was known as the Latter Rain revival. It was followed by the healing revival of the 1960s, led by William M. Branham. In the late 1960s, the charismatic movement brought Pentecostalism into the Roman Catholic Church and all of the major Protestant denominations. Each of these revivals became the source of doctrinal and behavioral disagreements, and each soon led to the formation of new Pentecostal

denominations. More recently, a new wave of revivalism, which some have termed the "third wave," has swept the charismatic churches that are entering their second generation, and it in turn has created further new denominations.

SUBFAMILIES. Doctrinal, racial, and linguistic differences have led Pentecostals to divide into seven subfamilies. Additional small groups may be discerned, such as the snake handlers, but the far-reaching divisions have resulted in only seven subfamilies. In general, Pentecostals fall into three doctrinal groups, all of which are split along racial lines. After a period of racial harmony in the first generation, whites either withdrew or pushed black members out of interracial denominations, and only a few groups, such as the Pentecostal Assemblies of the World, are able to hold a significant minority membership across racial lines. Until the 1980s, for example, African Americans were still largely excluded from the Pentecostal ecumenical bodies. Differences over the doctrines of Holiness and the Trinity divided Pentecostals into three main groupings, while race further divided them into six.

In the meantime, Pentecostalism was carried by Spanish-speaking people who attended the revival at Azusa Street to Mexico and then to South America. There it developed a life of its own, and numerous indigenous Pentecostal denominations have arisen. As immigration from Latin America began to increase in the last half of the twentieth century, members of these groups established branches of primarily Puerto Rican and Mexican churches in Spanish-speaking neighborhoods in the cities of the United States. These have been integrated into the move to acknowledge Hispanic peoples' rights in the country and have emerged in such strength as to now constitute a separate subfamily of Pentecostal churches.

The earliest doctrinal disagreement occurred between those Pentecostals who came out of the Holiness movement, primarily former Methodists, and those who came directly into the Pentecostal experience, primarily former Baptists. The Holiness people saw the Pentecostal experience (receiving the baptism of the Holy Spirit and speaking in tongues) as a third experience following justification and sanctification. The Baptists insisted that any believer was capable of receiving the Pentecostal experience, without the intermediate "second blessing" assuring sanctification, the key experience of the Holiness movement. Many Pentecostals split over the issue of two experiences (justification and the baptism of the Holy Spirit) or three experiences (justification, sanctification, and the baptism of the Holy Spirit). The Baptist-based Pentecostals generally trace their beginning to William H. Durham (1873–1912), the Chicago Baptist minister who preached what he termed the *finished work* message.

No sooner had these two positions become evident than another serious theological issue arose. A group of ministers began to preach a "Jesus only" doctrine that amounted to a monotheism of the second person of the Trinity. This divergence began as a reflection on the formula pronounced over a person being baptized, but the implications of baptizing in the name of Jesus only led to a critique of the classical Trinitarianism of the church councils of the fourth century.

This denial of the Trinity, by what are generally termed *Apostolic* Pentecostals, reaches back to the centuries-old consensus of Christianity and resulted in the most serious family split. The "Jesus only" people generally do not participate in the family ecumenical structures. African Americans have formed especially large denominations of the "Jesus only" type.

A discussion of Pentecostal subfamilies would be incomplete without a mention of *neo-Pentecostalism*, the movement during the 1960s and 1970s to form Pentecostal fellowships within the mainline Christian denominations. Neo-Pentecostalism also goes by the name of *charismatic renewal*. Its leaders, who were never a part of the older Pentecostal bodies, formed charismatic fellowships through the 1970s within the Roman Catholic, Lutheran, United Methodist, Presbyterian, and Episcopal churches. These fellowships served two functions. First, they provided a home for like-minded people and thus kept many Pentecostals within their mainline Christian churches, making unnecessary their move to the older Pentecostal churches. At the same time, however, charismatic fellowships increasingly became the birthing ground of new denominations, separate from both the older Pentecostal churches and the mainline Christian churches. These new charismatic denominations largely follow the doctrinal lead of the Assemblies of God and differ from it primarily by their unwillingness to use the name *Pentecostal*, which is still a derogatory term in some circles, as opposed to *charismatic*.

THE APOSTOLIC, ONENESS, OR "JESUS ONLY" MOVEMENT.

In 1913 at a Los Angeles Pentecostal camp meeting, the fledgling Pentecostal movement, barely beginning its second decade of existence, came face to face with a new issue. Robert E. McAlister (1880–1953), a popular preacher, speaking before a baptismal service, shared his thoughts that, in the apostolic church, baptism was not done with a Trinitarian formula but in the name of Jesus Christ. While raising much opposition, McAlister's message found favor with a few, such as Frank J. Ewart (1876–1947) and John C. Scheppe (1870–1939). Scheppe's emotional acceptance of the "new" idea had a powerful impact on the camp. Ewart afterward joined McAlister in a revival meeting in Los Angeles and began to note results whenever he called upon the name of Jesus.

The movement spread under the leadership of Ewart and evangelist Glenn A. Cook (1867–1948). They were able to bring in such key leaders as Garfield Thomas Haywood (1880–1931), E. N. Bell (1866–1923), and H. A. Goss (1883–1964), all prominent leaders in the Assemblies of God. Ewart soon became editor of *Meat in Due Season*, the first Oneness periodical.

The advocacy of Oneness ideas, mostly by churches that in 1914 came together to form the Assemblies of God, culminated in a discussion and decision in 1916 at the Assemblies of God General Council meeting in St. Louis, Missouri. A strong Trinitarian stance was placed within the Statement of Beliefs. One hundred and sixty-six ministers were expelled by

that act, and many Assemblies of God were lost; the era of formation of Oneness churches began.

The Oneness Pentecostals deny the traditional Christian doctrine of the Trinity in favor of an affirmation of the "oneness" of God. Jesus is identified with God the Father (Isaiah 9:6, John 10:30) and God the creator (John 1:1) as the bodily presence of God. The Holy Spirit is not considered a third person within the Trinity but the spirit and power of God and Christ. Salvation is by repentance, and water baptism is considered an essential part of salvation. Baptism is by immersion in the name of Jesus only (Acts 2:38). Oneness people avoid the common Trinitarian formula taken from Matthew 28:19.

Apart from the Trinitarian and baptismal questions, Oneness people are typical Pentecostals. The Oneness message has had particular appeal among African Americans, and the largest bodies are primarily black in membership. Of the several Apostolic Churches, the United Pentecostal Church is the largest predominantly white church.

AFRICAN-AMERICAN PENTECOSTAL CHURCHES.

There has been vigorous discussion in both popular and scholarly literature of the link between black religion and Pentecostalism. Much of this discussion was plainly derogatory, bordering on racism. Pentecostalism, distinguished by its emotionalism and escapism, has been seen as an example of "primitive" religious forms. Fortunately, the growth of neo-Pentecostalism has led to a complete reevaluation of the authenticity of the Pentecostal forms as basic religious expressions. With the new appreciation comes the opportunity to see, with a new perspective, the key role that African Americans played in the early development of Pentecostalism, and more importantly, the manner in which they have taken the form far beyond its development by their white brothers and sisters.

Modern Pentecostalism began in the short-lived Topeka Bible School founded by Charles Parham. Among those students who received the baptism of the Holy Spirit was an African-American woman, Sister Lucy Farrow, who took Pentecostalism to Houston and opened the door for Parham to begin his Bible school there. Among his pupils was W. J. Seymour, a black minister with the Church of God (Anderson, Indiana). After Seymour received Parham's message, he traveled to Los Angeles, where in 1906 he gathered a group of black believers in meetings that were eventually held at the Azusa Street Mission. As the gifts of the Spirit became manifest, whites began to attend the meetings and receive baptism from Seymour, who led the services.

Racism was overcome for only a short time; almost immediately, white leaders began to develop their own movements. Although most Pentecostal churches remained integrated for one or two decades, eventually almost all of the groups split along racial lines. There is little doubt that the early splintering among Pentecostals throughout the country was because the black leadership at Azusa was unacceptable to whites.

The preaching of "Jesus only" by Garfield Thomas Haywood, a black minister in Indianapolis, forced the Assemblies of God to deal with the Oneness doctrine that denied the Trinity. Haywood's congregation became a nucleus for the first Oneness denomination, the Pentecostal Assemblies of the World.

Often overlooked by Pentecostal historians was mother Mary Magdalena Tate (1871–1930). She began preaching in Holiness circles in Alabama around the turn of the century, but as the Pentecostal movement began, she accepted the Azusa message and organized her following in 1908 in Greenville, Alabama. She led the church until her death, at which time it split into three factions, but continues today as a strong influence in African-American Pentecostalism.

Pentecostalism swept through the black community and created some large, if relatively hidden, denominations. They compiled impressive figures for foreign mission work in Africa and the West Indies, where Pentecostalism has become a significant element in the larger Christian community. The Church of God in Christ now claims upwards of six million members worldwide, and is one of the five largest denominations in America.

DELIVERANCE (HEALING) MOVEMENT.

Almost from the beginning, healing has been a major emphasis of the Pentecostal movement. It represents the culmination of a healing movement begun in evangelical churches by Charles Cullis (1833–1892), an Episcopal physician in Boston who held healing services at his summer camp in Old Orchard, Maine. Albert Benjamin Simpson (1843–1919) was healed at this camp and later made healing part of his four-fold gospel that presented Christ as savior, sanctifier, healer, and coming king. In the early years of the twentieth century, F. F. Bosworth (1870–1958), Paul Rader (1879–1938), John G. Lake (1870–1935), and Smith Wigglesworth (1859–1947) were popular healing evangelists and, of course, Aimee Semple McPherson became the most popular of all. The years between the wars saw the emergence of numerous independent healing evangelists, who later became popular targets of exposé writers.

After World War II, a group consciousness developed among some of the Pentecostal evangelists. In 1946 the Reverend William M. Branham, then a Baptist minister, claimed a visit by an angel and was told to start a healing ministry. That visit was the beginning of a remarkable "supernatural" ministry of healings, prophecies, and other paranormal phenomena. Branham began to tour the country in revival meetings. In 1947 Gordon Lindsay (1906–1973) began *The Voice of Healing Magazine*. Gradually, without giving up their independence, other evangelists became associated with Branham. In the years since Branham's death in 1965, deliverance ministers have emerged as a significant force within Pentecostalism.

In many cases, the deliverance evangelists have remained independent and travel at the request of churches or groups such as the Full Gospel Businessman's Fellowship. Others lead large evangelistic missionary organizations. Evelyn Wyatt, T. L. Osborn (b. 1923), and Morris Cerullo (b. 1931) have headed such organizations. Others became heads of church-forming bodies (both in the United States and

abroad) that constitute new primary religious groups. These included Branham, Lindsay, and Kathryn Kuhlman, as well as W. V. Grant (1914–1983) and A. A. Allen (1911–1970). For most of the above, evangelistic endeavors among members of Pentecostal and mainline Christian churches were the primary activity, with their deliverance churches forming relatively small bases of operation.

As the first generation of healing evangelists has departed, it has left the healing ministry as a major theme in Pentecostalism, though few evangelists have emerged who are primarily known as healing ministers, Benny Hinn (b. 1952), based in Orlando, Florida, being the most prominent. The Pentecostal healing ministry encountered an obstacle in the 1970s when one of its number, Marjoe Gortner, did a book and movie exposé describing corrupting elements. Then, in 1987, magician James Randi, who believes that all religious healing is essentially fraudulent, published an attack on healing evangelists. He was particularly harsh on some, such as W. V. Grant Jr. and Peter Popoff, whom he accused of outright fraud, while being mildly appreciative of the sincerity, if misguided, of the likes of Church of God minister Ernest Angley (b. 1921). Three years later, Grant was among several Pentecostal ministers included in an ABC *Primetime Live* exposé of the financial irregularities of television evangelists. Grant subsequently went to prison for several years, but later resumed his ministry. Meanwhile, healing evangelist Leroy Jenkins was also caught up in legal problems, and went to prison (1979–1982), but later was vindicated and given a pardon by the governor of South Carolina.

SNAKE HANDLING.

One group of Pentecostals are sharply distinguished from the rest by their peculiar practice of "preaching the signs." In the Gospel of Mark 16:17–18, Jesus promised his followers that certain signs would accompany them: speaking in tongues, the ability to heal the sick, and the casting out of demons. Most Pentecostals accept these three. Those who "preach the signs," however, go beyond these to accept Jesus' further promise that they may take up venomous serpents and drink poisons without experiencing any harm. This promise has led to the practice popularly called *snake handling*. The original group that practiced the signs, that is, that handled snakes and drank poison (usually strychnine) in worship services, arose soon after the Pentecostal movement spread to the Appalachian Mountain region.

In 1909 George Went Hensley (c.1880–1955), a preacher with the Church of God (Cleveland, Tennessee) in rural Grasshopper Valley, became convinced that the references in Mark 16 about taking up poisonous snakes and drinking poison were, in fact, commands. He captured a rattlesnake and brought it to an open-air revival meeting for participants to handle as a test of their faith. In 1914 Ambrose J. Tomlinson (1865–1943), head of the Church of God, asked Hensley to demonstrate snake handling to the church's annual assembly, and, with Tomlinson's tacit approval, the practice soon spread throughout the mountainous and rural South.

Those who engage in snake handling are Pentecostals who accept the basic theology by which people seek and receive the baptism of the Holy Spirit, evidenced by speaking in tongues. Snake handlers also accept the rigid ethical code of most Holiness and Pentecostal bodies: Dress is plain; the Bible is consulted on all questions in an attempt to discern worldly behavior; and the kiss of peace is prominent. The snake handlers, however, go beyond the Pentecostals in their belief that holding venomous reptiles and drinking poison are signs of an individual's faith and possession of the Holy Spirit. The handling of snakes and drinking of poison are done while in an ecstatic state, referred to by members as "being in the Spirit."

The first and crucial test of the practice of snake handling was the near-fatal bite received by Garland Defries, which led to much unfavorable publicity and caused many snake handlers, who thought themselves immune to bites, to reevaluate the practice. Snake handling came under considerable attack within the Church of God, whose leaders denounced it as fanaticism. In 1928 the church formally forbade its continuation, thus forcing the snake handlers into separate congregations and small churches, primarily in rural areas.

A second test of snake handling came in 1945 when Lewis Ford, a member of the Dolly Pond Church of God with Signs Following (Dolly Pond, Tennessee), was fatally bitten. His death brought the first widespread public attention to the dangers of snake handling and led the State of Tennessee to legislate against it. Despite this legislation, the practice continues in clandestine meetings in Tennessee and throughout the South.

Periodically, a person will be bitten and die at a snake-handling meeting. Such rare occurrences usually become the subject of media attention, with accompanying outcries against the practice. However, given their infrequency, these deaths have usually led to little more than a few ephemeral attempts to regulate the behavior of church members. The churches soon resume their normal routine. In 1975 some meaningful action was taken following the death of two church members from drinking poison. The Tennessee Supreme Court moved to strengthen that state's prohibitions on both snake handling and the ingestion of poison at religious services.

Snake handlers were back in the news in 1991 when Glenn Summerford (b. 1945), a snake-handling preacher in Alabama, went on trial for forcing his wife Darlene to thrust her hand into a box of rattlesnakes. She survived, but Summerford was tried and convicted of attempted murder, for which he is serving a 99-year sentence. Over the twentieth century, in spite of the regular use of poisonous snakes in religious services in the eastern half of the United States and the regular ingestion of poison in seemingly lethal doses, relatively few have died—fewer than 100. Given the 10,000 to 15,000 people involved in snake-handling groups, it is surprising that only one or two deaths per decade have been reported.

THE LATTER RAIN MOVEMENT. During the
mid-twentieth century, one new movement deeply affected the development of Pentecostalism. Beginning in a small Bible college in western Canada in 1948, the Latter Rain movement found enough initial support among leaders of the two largest Pentecostal groups in the United States and Canada, the Assemblies of God and the Pentecostal Assemblies of Canada, that each moved quickly to suppress its influence among their ministers and churches.

The movement began as a revival at Sharon Orphanage and Schools in North Battleford, Saskatchewan, among students assembled by former Pentecostal Assemblies ministers George Hawtin and P. G. Hunt and Four-Square Gospel minister Herrick Holt. The revival was reportedly accompanied by a visible manifestation of the gifts of the Holy Spirit, especially healing. As word of the events spread, visitors came to North Battleford, and invitations were issued for the leaders to visit different parts of the continent.

As it developed, the movement was characterized by an emphasis on the gifts of healing and prophecy, the practice of laying-on-of-hands to impart gifts to different people, and allegiance to the fivefold ministry of Ephesians 4:11. As the movement spread, its participants were accused of fanaticism, and the leadership of the Assemblies of God moved against it. In 1949 the general council passed a six-part resolution, denouncing the movement because, among other practices: (1) it relied too heavily on present-day apostles and prophets (i.e., a self-appointed charismatic leadership); (2) it practiced the confessing and pronouncing of forgiveness by one member upon another; (3) it advocated the practice of bestowing spiritual gifts by the laying-on-of-hands; and (4) it distorted scripture so as to arrive at conclusions not generally accepted by members of the Assemblies of God.

Though neither experienced any major wholesale defections, both the Pentecostal Assemblies of Canada and the Assemblies of God began to lose pastors and churches. Possibly the most prominent defection was Stanley Frodsham (1882–1969), longtime editor of the *Pentecostal Evangel*, who withdrew from the Assemblies of God after its 1949 resolution. Within a short time, the Latter Rain movement was firmly entrenched in Vancouver, British Columbia; Portland, Oregon; Detroit, Michigan; Memphis, Tennessee; Los Angeles, California; and Philadelphia, Pennsylvania. During the 1950s, especially as the healing revival led by William Branham and Oral Roberts grew, the Latter Rain spread across the United States.

Many of the early centers grew into large congregations, and a few emerged as seeds for new denominations (or more precisely, congregational associations). Some of these were distinguished by the peculiar teachings and emphases of the founder or leader. Such groups as the Church of the Living Word, the Body of Christ Movement, and the International Evangelical Church and Missionary Association are prominent examples.

Through the last decades of the twentieth century, Pentecostalism was one of the growing communities within

American Christianity, and the Latter Rain groups were among the most prominent segments of the movement. Shut out of the larger Pentecostal bodies, Latter Rain congregations grew quietly under the leadership of "apostles," leaders who emerged out of their demonstrated ability at the founding and nurturance of new congregations. Latter Rain congregations found a champion in Dr. C. Peter Wagner (b.1930), a professor at Fuller Theological Seminary in Pasadena, California, who saw in the movement a new wave of Pentecostal revivalism. Through the 1990s, he led in founding several "apostolic" organizations that resulted in the 1999 founding of the International Coalition of Apostles, an ecumenical fellowship of apostles and the churches they lead. Wagner emerged as the coalition's first presiding apostle.

SOURCES

Study of the twentieth-century Pentecostal tradition is focused by the Society for Pentecostal Studies, P.O. Box 3802, Cleveland, TN 37320-3802 (www.sps-usa.org), which publishes the semiannual journal *Pneuma*. Significant archives are found at Oral Roberts University, Tulsa, OK 74105; the Pentecostal Research Center of the Church of God, PO Box 3448, Cleveland, TN 37320; and the Assemblies of God Archives, 1445 Boonville Ave., Springfield, MO 65892. For a number of years, the Assemblies of God Archives published the quarterly *Assemblies of God Heritage*.

Faupel, David W. *The American Pentecostal Movement: A Bibliographical Essay*. Wilmore, KY: Fisher Library, Asbury Theological Seminary, 1972. 56 pp.

Jones, Charles Edwin. *A Guide to the Study of the Pentecostal Movement*. 2 vols. Metuchen, NJ: Scarecrow Press, 1983.

———. *Black Holiness: A Guide to the Study of Black Participation in Wesleyan Perfectionist and Glossolalic Pentecostal Movements*. Metuchen, NJ: American Theological Library Association/Scarecrow Press, 1987. 388 pp.

———. *The Charismatic Movement: A Guide to the Study of Neo-Pentecostalism with Emphasis on Anglo-American Sources*. Philadelphia: Scarecrow Press, 1995.

Martin, Ira J. *Glossolalia, the Gift of Tongues: A Bibliography*. Cleveland, TN: Pathway Press, 1970. 72 pp.

General Sources

Anderson, Allan. *An Introduction to Pentecostalism: Global Charismatic Christianity*. Cambridge, U.K.: Cambridge University Press, 2004. 302 pp.

Burgess, Stanley M., and Eduard M. Van der Maas, eds. *The New International Dictionary of Pentecostal and Charismatic Movements*. Rev. ed. Grand Rapids, MI: Zondervan, 2002. 1278 pp.

Cox, Harvey. *Fire from Heaven: The Rise of Pentecostalism Spirituality and the Reshaping of Religion in the Twenty-first Century*. Reading, MA: Addison-Wesley, 1995. 368 pp.

Dempster, M. W., B. D. Klaus, and D. Petersen, eds. *The Globalization of Pentecostalism: A Religion made to Travel*. Oxford: Regnum, 1999. 432 pp.

Faupel, D. William. *The Everlasting Gospel: The Significance of Eschatology in the Development of Pentecostal Thought*. Sheffield, U.K.: Sheffield Academic Press, 1996. 326 pp.

Hollenweger, Walter J. *Pentecostalism: Origins and Developments Worldwide*. Peabody, MA: Hendrickson, 1997. 512 pp.

Hunter, Harold D. *Spirit Baptism: A Pentecostal Alternative*. Washington, DC: University Press of America, 1983. 310 pp.

Jacobsen, Douglas G. *Thinking in the Spirit: Theologies of the Early Pentecostal Movement*. Bloomington, IN: Indiana University Press, 2003. 368 pp.

Kelsey, Morton T. *Tongue Speaking: An Experiment in Spiritual Experience*. Garden City, NY: Doubleday, 1964. 252 pp.

Kydd, Ronald A. N. *Charismatic Gifts in the Early Church*. Peabody, MA: Hendrickson, 1984. 112 pp.

Poewe, Karla O., ed. *Charismatic Christianity as a Global Culture*. Columbia: University of South Carolina Press, 1994. 290 pp.

Robinson, James. *Pentecostal Origins: Early Pentecostalism in Ireland in the Context of the British Isles*. London: Paternoster, 2005. 378 pp.

Sherrill, John L. *They Speak with Other Tongues*. Rev. ed. Grand Rapids, MI: Chosen Books, 2004. 190 pp.

Synan, Vinson. ed. *The Century of the Holy Spirit: 100 Years of Pentecostal and Charismatic Renewal, 1901–2001*. Nashville, TN: Thomas Nelson, 2001. 485 pp.

Historical Sources

Bartleman, Frank. *How Pentecost Came to Los Angeles*. Los Angeles: Author, 1928. 167 pp. Reprint, Plainfield, NJ: Logos International, 1980.

Blumhofer, Edith L., Russell P. Spittler, and Grant A. Wacker, eds. *Pentecostal Currents in American Protestantism*. Urbana: University of Illinois Press, 1999. 273 pp.

Davis, Clars. *Azusa Street Till Now: Eyewitness Accounts of the Move of God*. Tulsa, OK: Harrison House, 1989. 144 pp.

Davis, George T. B. *When the Fire Fell*. Philadelphia: Million Testaments Campaign, 1945. 104 pp.

Dayton, Donald. *"From Christian Perfection to the Baptism of the Holy Ghost": A Study in the Origin of Pentecostalism*. Chicago: Author, 1973.

Ewart, Frank J. *The Phenomenon of Pentecost*. Hazelwood, MO: World Aflame Press, 1975. 207 pp.

Frodsham, Stanley H. *With Signs Following*. Springfield, MO: Gospel Publishing House, 1946. 288 pp.

Gaver, Jessyca Russel. *Pentecostalism*. New York: Award Books, 1971. 236 pp.

Hollenweger, Walter J. *The Pentecostals: The Charismatic Movement in the Church*. Minneapolis, MN: Augsburg, 1972. 572 pp.

Kendrick, Klaude. *The Promise Fulfilled: A History of the Modern Pentecostal Movement*. Springfield, MO: Gospel Publishing House, 1961. 237 pp.

McClug, L. Grant, Jr. *Azusa Street and Beyond: Pentecostal Missions and Church Growth in the Twentieth Century*. South Plainfield, NJ: Bridge, 1986. 220 pp.

Nichel, Thomas R. *Azusa Street Outpouring*. Hanford, CT: Great Commission International, 1979. 28 pp.

Riss, Richard Michael. *The Latter Rain Movement of 1948 and the Mid-twentieth Century Evangelical Awakening*. Vancouver, BC: Regent College, 1979.

Robeck, Cecil, Jr. *The Azusa Street Mission & Revival: The Birth of the Global Pentecostal Movement*. Nashville, TN: Thomas Nelson 2006. 342 pp.

Valdez, A. C., and James F. Scheer. *Fire on Azusa Street*. Costa Mesa, CA: Gift Publications, 1980. 139 pp.

Wacker, Grant. *Heaven Below: Early Pentecostals and American Culture*. Cambridge, MA: Harvard University Press, 2001. 364 pp.

Wallace, Mary H. *Profiles of Pentecostal Preachers*. Hazelwood, MO: World Aflame Press, 1983. 2 vols.

Wagner, Wayne, ed. *Touched by the Fire: Eyewitness Accounts of the Early Twentieth-Century Pentecostal Revival*. Plainfield, NJ: Logos International, 1978. 163 pp.

Whittaker, Colin C. *Seven Pentecostal Pioneers*. Springfield, MO: Gospel Publishing House, 1983. 224 pp.

Glossolalia and the Spiritual Gifts

Goodman, Felicitas D. *Speaking in Tongues: A Cross-Cultural Study of Glossolalia.* Chicago: University of Chicago Press, 1972. 175 pp.

Kildahl, John P. *The Psychology of Speaking in Tongues.* New York: Harper & Row, 1972. 110 pp.

Parham, Sarah E. *The Life of Charles F. Parham.* Joplin, MO: Press of the Hunter, 1969.

Samarin, William. *Tongues of Men and Angels: The Religious Language of Pentecostalism.* New York: Macmillan, 1972. 277 pp.

Sneck, William Joseph. *Charismatic Spiritual Gifts: Phenomenological Analysis.* Washington, DC: University Press of America, 1981. 298 p.

Apostolic or Oneness Pentecostals

Clanton, Arthur L. *United We Stand.* Rev. ed. Hazelwood, MO: Word Aflame Press, 1995. 336 pp.

Foster, Fred J. *Their Story: Twentieth Century Pentecostals.* Hazelwood, NJ: World Aflame Press, 1986. 187 pp.

Richardson, James C., Jr. *With Water and Spirit.* Martinsville, VA: Author, nd.

Symposium on Oneness Pentecostalism, 1988 and 1990. Hazelwood, MO: World Aflame Press, 1990. 336 pp.

Black Pentecostals

Hollenweger, Walter J. *Black Pentecostal Concept.* Special issue of *Concept* 30 (1970).

MacRobert, Iain. *The Black Roots and White Racism of Early Pentecostalism in the USA.* Basingstoke, U.K.: Macmillan, 1988. 142 pp.

Nelson, Douglas J. *For Such a Time as This: The Story of Bishop William J. Seymour and the Azusa Street Revival.* Ph.D. diss. Birmingham, U.K.: University of Birmingham, 1981.

Deliverance Movement

Harrell, David Edwin, Jr. *All Things Are Possible: The Healing & Charismatic Revivals in Modern America.* Bloomington: Indiana University Press, 1975. 320 pp.

Melton, J. Gordon. *A Reader's Guide to the Church's Ministry of Healing.* Independence, MO: Academy of Religion and Psychical Research, 1977. 80 pp.

Signs Movement

Carden, Karen W., and Robert W. Pelton. *The Persecuted Prophets.* New York: A. S. Barnes, 1976. 188 pp.

Covington, Dennis. *Salvation on Sand Mountain: Snake Handling and Redemption in Southern Appalachia.* Reading, MA: Addison-Wesley, 1994. 240 pp.

Holliday, Robert K. *Tests of Faith.* Oak Hill, WV: *Fayette Tribune,* 1968. 104 pp.

Kimbrough, David L. *Taking Up Serpents: Snake Handlers of Eastern Kentucky.* Chapel Hill: University of North Carolina, 1995. 232 pp.

La Barre, Weston. *They Shall Take Up Serpents: Psychology of the Southern Snake-Handling Cult.* New York: Schocken, 1969. 208 pp.

Charismatic Movement

Bradfield, Cecil David. *Neo-Pentecostalism: A Sociological Assessment.* Washington, DC: University Press of America, 1979. 83 pp.

Culpepper, Robert H. *Evaluating the Charismatic Movement: A Theological and Biblical Appraisal.* Valley Forge, PA: Judson Press, 1977. 192 pp.

O'Connor, Edward D. *The Pentecostal Movement in the Catholic Church.* Notre Dame, IN: Ave Maria Press, 1971.

Shakarian, Demos, with John Sherrill and Elizabeth Sherrill. *The Happiest People on Earth: The Long-Awaited Personal Story of Demos Shakarian.* Old Tappan, NJ: Chosen Books, 1975. 208 pp.

Non-Pentecostal Evaluations of Pentecostalism

Bauman, Louis S. *The Tongues Movement.* Winona Lake, IN: Brethren Missionary Herald Co., 1963. 47 pp.

Charismatic Countdown. Washington, DC: Review and Herald Publishing Association, 1974.

Dollar, George W. *The New Testament and New Pentecostalism.* Minneapolis, MN: Central Baptist Theological Seminary, 1978. 141 pp.

Gustafson, Robert R. *Authors of Confusion.* Tampa, FL: Grace Publishing, 1971. 105 pp.

Kinghorn, Kenneth Cain. *Gifts of the Spirit.* Nashville, TN: Abingdon, 1976. 126 pp.

Noorbergen, Rene. *Charisma of the Spirit, in Search of a Supernatural Experience: A Journalist Looks at the Tongues Movement.* Mountain View, CA: Pacific Press, 1973. 191 pp.

Robinson, Wayne A. *I Once Spoke in Tongues.* Atlanta: Forum House, 1973. 144 pp.

Latter Rain Movement

Hoekstra, Raymond G. *The Latter Rain.* Portland, OR: Wings of Healing, 1950. 52 pp.

Riss, Richard Michael. *The Latter Rain Movement of 1948 and the Mid-Twentieth Century Evangelical Awakening.* MA thesis. Vancouver, BC: Regent College, 1979.

Wagner, C. Peter. *The New Apostolic Churches.* Ventura, CA: Regal, 1998. 288 pp.

⁂ Intrafaith Organizations

Apostolic World Christian Fellowship

11 W Iowa St., Evansville, IN 47711

The Apostolic World Christian Fellowship is an international association of Pentecostal churches that adhere to the nontrinitarian Apostolic doctrine, sometimes referred to as the "Jesus Only" position. The Fellowship was founded in 1970 by Bp. W. G. Rowe who was succeeded in 1991, by Bp. Samuel L. Smith, who currently (2008) leads the organization. As with the whole of Pentecostalism, the Apostolic wing has split into numerous denominations. It has been the intent of the Fellowship to counter that tendency by calling believers to set aside barriers to unity and come together to heal the divisions that hurt the church and cause scandal in the world. The Fellowship has programs for assisting ministers, motivating the laity, and challenging the movement to engage in the evangelization of the world.

Membership: In 2008 the Fellowship reported that some 200 organizations and denominations had affiliated with it.

Periodicals: *Clarion.*

Sources:

Apostolic World Christian Fellowship. www.awcf.org.

International Communion of Charismatic Churches

Bp. David Huskins, PO Box 687, Cedartown, GA 30125

The International Communion of Charismatic Churches (ICCC), an ecumenical association of Pentecostal/charismatic churches and ministries, was founded in 1982 as the World Communion of Pentecostal churches by Bp. John Meares of Evangel Temple in Washington, D.C. (a leading congregation of the International Evangelical Church and Missionary Association) and Bp. Robert McAleister of Igreja Pentecostal da Nova Vida in Rio de Janeiro, Brazil. Bp. Benson Idahosa (d. 1998), pastor of Faith Miracle Centre and founder of the Church of God Mission International based in Nigeria, was another early prominent member. It has as its stated purpose the promotion of dialogue between the newer churches of the charismatic renewal and the older historic churches of Christian faith. It has been especially effective in bringing together different elements of the charismatic renewal and supplying episcopal orders to those leaders who have built large movements.

Over the years the ICCC expanded its overall objectives. The organization is active in the promotion of national and international mission teams of ministry leaders, educators, and related advisors. Such resources are helpful in the development of schools, model ministries, media outlets, and the ongoing growth of membership churches. Annual conferences in strategic national and international sites have been designed to equip and train leaders and members while also providing a forum for cross-cultural and cross-denominational fellowship.

In 2008 the International Communion of Charismatic Churches were governed by 13 bishops duly consecrated after the apostolic succession established under David DuPlessis and Robert McAlister. The College of Bishops were Presiding Bp. David Huskins, Vice President Bp. Margaret Idahosa, Secretary/Treasurer E. L. Warren, Bp. Herro Blair, Bp. Tommy Reid, Bp. Silas Owiti, Bp. Harry Westcott, Bp. Paul Lanier, Bp. Jim Swilley, Bp. Levy Knox, Bp. Juan Edghill, Bp. Pedro Torres, and Bp. Jesus Perez.

Membership: Not reported. In 2008 the ICCC was represented by more than 5,000 ministries with more than 240 bishops on six continents.

Sources:

International Communion of Charismatic Churches. www.theiccc.com.

Joint College of African American Pentecostal Bishops

c/o Bp. J. Delano Ellis II, Pentecostal Church of Christ, 10515 Chester Ave., Cleveland, OH 44106

The Joint College of African American Pentecostal Bishops was founded in 1993 by four senior bishops from several episcopally led African-American Pentecostal churches. It was founded to train new bishops, who often were taking their offices without being aware of their responsibilities. The several bishops agreed that Bp. J. Delano Ellis II, the founder and primate of the United Pentecostal Churches of Christ, should assume leadership of the new organization. Other founders of the college included Abp. Roy E. Brown, Pilgrim Assemblies International; Abp. Wilbert S. McKinley, Elim International Fellowship; and Bp. Paul S. Morton, Full Gospel Baptist Church Fellowship.

As the organization gained support, the four founders soon were joined by other bishops, a dozen of whom now constitute the college's board. In 2008 the vice presidents were Bp. Ralph L. Dennis, the presiding bishop of Kingdom Fellowship Covenant Ministries and the CEO and president of R. L. Dennis Ministries; and Bp. Alfred A. Owens Jr., vice bishop of the Mount Calvary Holy Church of America.

The concerns of the bishops include the issue of the work of bishops' spouses in the modern, postfeminist world. Bp. Ellis's wife serves as a vice president with special concerns for the bishops' helpmeets.

The college has developed a broad course of instruction for their youngest colleagues that includes special attention to the issue of leadership in worship. The college meets annually at its congress.

Membership: Not reported.

Sources:

Joint College of African American Pentecostal Bishops. collegeofbishops.org/.

Pentecostal/Charismatic Churches of North America

c/o Bp. Jerry Macklin, 1027 W Tennyson Rd., Hayward, CA 94544

The Pentecostal/Charismatic Churches of North America was formerly known as the Pentecostal Fellowship of North America. At the first meeting of the World Pentecostal Fellowship in Switzerland in 1947 it was suggested that area fellowships be organized, so in 1948, representatives of eight Pentecostal churches met in Chicago to organize the North American Pentecostal Fellowship. That organization was effected later in the year at a second meeting in Des Moines, Iowa. Participants included the Assemblies of God, the Church of God (Cleveland,

Tennessee), the International Church of the Foursquare Gospel, the Pentecostal Holiness Church, and the Open Bible Standard Church. The Pentecostal Assemblies of Canada was the only Canadian representative.

Like the World Pentecostal Fellowship, the Pentecostal Fellowship of North America seeks to provide member churches, to demonstrate the essential unity of Pentecostals, and to promote the commonly held beliefs.

The fellowship is led by a chairperson, a cochairperson, a secretary, a treasurer, and a board of administration. The officers constitute an executive committee. The chairperson in 2008 was Bp. Jerry Macklin.

Membership: Members of the fellowship include forty various denominations listed on the organization's website.

Sources:

Pentecostal/Charismatic Churches of North America. www.pccna.org.

Pentecostal World Fellowship

PO Box 12609, Oklahoma City, OK 73157

Alternate Address: International Secretary: Rev. Jakob Zopfi, Heimstatte SPM, 6376 Emmetten NW, Switzerland.

The Pentecostal World Fellowship formerly was known as the Pentecostal World Conference. The fellowship was founded in 1947 but the roots go back to 1922, only two decades after the founding of the movement and an initial international European Pentecostal Convention held in Amsterdam. Similar, unofficial conventions were held periodically until the outbreak of World War II in 1939. Meanwhile, a number of fraternal delegates attended the 1937 meeting of the Assemblies of God, at which time the General Council called for a world Pentecostal conference to convene in London in 1940. The event was canceled by the war.

In 1946, in the wake of World War II, a group of Pentecostals meeting in Basle, Switzerland, became conscious of the immediate and desperate needs of many victims of the war and called for an international gathering of Pentecostals to confront those needs. The meeting, held in Zurich, Switzerland, in May 1947, became the catalyst for the organization of a permanent association, the opening of an international office in Basle, Switzerland, and the launching of a periodical, Pentecost, under the editorship of Donald Gee. The fellowship's constitution was ratified at a second conference, in 1949 in Paris.

The fellowship exists to encourage a fraternal spirit and cooperation among various Pentecostal groups. In addition, it assists in the evangelical tasks of the church, manifests the unity of Pentecostal peoples, and upholds the doctrinal consensus of the movement.

The fellowship meets triennially. At its international conferences, a 29-person World Conference Advisory Committee is elected to oversee the planning of the next conference. The chairman in 2008 was Bp. James D. Leggett.

Membership: North American participants in the fellowship include: Apostolic Church of Canada; Assemblies of God; Church of God (Cleveland, Tennessee); Church of God in Christ; Foursquare Gospel Church of Canada; International Church of the Foursquare Gospel; International Pentecostal Holiness Church; Pentecostal Assemblies of Canada; Pentecostal Charismatic Churches of North America; Pentecostal Holiness Church of Canada.

Periodicals: *World Pentecost.*

Sources:

Pentecostal World Fellowship. www.pctii.org/pwf.

Kendrick, Kalude. *The Promise Fulfilled: A History of the Modern Pentecostal Movement.* Springfield, MO: Gospel Publishing House, 1961.

White Trinitarian Holiness Pentecostals

The Apostolic Faith Mission of Portland, Oregon, Inc.

6615 SE 52nd Ave., Portland, OR 97206-7660

In April 1906 a small group of people of various denominational backgrounds arranged for prayer meetings in a home located on Bonnie Brae Street in Los Angeles. Their purpose was to seek the infilling of the Holy Spirit, having heard of the Pentecostal experience of believers in the Midwest. When a number of them received this experience, the word spread, and soon the meetings were transferred to larger quarters in an old Methodist church on Azusa Street.

Among those attending the meetings on Azusa Street was Florence L. Crawford (1872–1936), a Methodist laywoman. There she received the experience of sanctification and the power of the Holy Spirit. At her baptism in the Holy Spirit, she related that God "permitted me to speak in the Chinese, which was understood by a Christian Chinese who was present." She also testified to receiving a miraculous healing of her eyes, which had been damaged by spinal meningitis.

A dynamic woman, Crawford entered wholeheartedly into evangelistic work, assisting mission leader William J. Seymour (1870–1922). Thousands of inquiries had begun to come in from people who wanted to know more about the Pentecostal outpouring, so Crawford began to record what was said in the meetings into a newspaper that was named *The Apostolic Faith*.

In addition to her publishing work, Crawford felt God's call to travel beyond the boundaries of Los Angeles with the Pentecostal message. Her first ministries were along the West Coast, where she worked as an itinerant home missionary. In December 1906 she made her first visit to Portland, Oregon, where she had been invited to preach in an independent church on Second and Main Street. Subsequently, the pastor of that church offered her his pulpit permanently, and in 1908 Crawford moved to Portland. The Azusa Street ministry turned over to her the responsibility of publishing *The Apostolic Faith*, so she and her coworker, Clara Lum (d. 1946), brought that work to Portland with the blessing of the Azusa Street ministry. The publication continued uninterrupted; the final edition from Los Angeles was printed in June 1908, and the first edition from Portland came out in July–August 1908.

Portland was established as the headquarters of the growing movement. In 1922 the headquarters building, a landmark in downtown Portland, was erected. A large neon sign with the message "Jesus the Light of the World," first displayed in 1917, was transferred to the new structure.

Through the years, the Apostolic Faith has maintained the doctrines outlined in the first editions of the Apostolic Faith papers printed in 1906. As a Trinitarian church, its doctrinal position centers on a belief in the born-again experience, supports the Wesleyan teaching on Holiness, and stresses the need of sanctified believers to receive the Pentecostal experience of the baptism of the Holy Spirit. The church holds to the teaching of salvation rather than the Calvinist belief in predestination and eternal security.

The church is governed by a board of five trustees headed by a superintendent general (in 2008, the Rev. Darrel D. Lee). Both home and foreign missions have emerged on a large scale, with work in 32 countries in Africa, Asia, the West Indies, and Europe. The largest mission field is in Nigeria, where there are approximately two million members. Each local congregation is under the leadership and direction of the international headquarters in Portland.

Membership: In 2002 the church reported approximately 4,000 members in 50 congregations, with 250 ministers in the United States, and 10 congregations and 25 ministers in Canada. There were more than two million members in foreign lands. Membership is only an estimate; the church counts those who regularly attend as members.

Periodicals: *Higher Way* • *The Light of Hope*

Sources:

The Apostolic Faith Mission of Portland, Oregon, Inc. www.apostolicfaith.org.

Apostolic Faith Mission. *A Historical Account of the Apostolic Faith*. Portland, OR: Apostolic Faith Publishing House, 1965.

Apostolic Faith Mission. *The Light of Life Brought Triumph*. Portland, OR: Apostolic Faith Publishing House, 1955.

Apostolic Faith Mission. *Saved to Serve*. Portland, OR: Apostolic Faith Publishing House, 1967.

Carolina Evangelistic Association

Garr Memorial Church, 7700 Wallace Rd., Charlotte, NC 28212

Dr. A. G. Garr (1874–1944) was the first foreign missionary of the Church of God (Cleveland, Tennessee). He left the church in 1906, immediately after receiving the baptism of the Holy Spirit. He continued to do foreign missionary work until 1912, when he returned to the United States and began to operate as an evangelist in the days when Pentecostals were still a small, scattered group. He was particularly active in the early years of the Angelus Temple, the Los Angeles center for the International Church of the Foursquare Gospel headed by Aimee Semple McPherson (1890–1944). In 1930 he went to Charlotte, North Carolina, to conduct a tent revival. After three months, those who had been saved, healed, and helped asked him to remain. Fifty-six years old then, he remained and built a tabernacle. An abandoned city auditorium was bought, remodeled, and named Garr Auditorium; it remains the headquarters of the association. Garr died in 1944 and was succeeded by his wife and son as pastors.

The Carolina Evangelistic Association carries on an active program through Garr Auditorium and Faith Chapel, both in Charlotte. There are missionaries supported by the association in numerous countries. A regular program of services is conducted in the county jail and the county home. The Morning Thought for the Day Magazine radio show is their radio ministry. Camp Lure Crest for youth is located at Lake Lure, North Carolina. The church is a member of the Pentecostal Fellowship of North America.

Membership: Not reported. Approximately 1,000 people regularly attend worship at Garr Auditorium.

Sources:

Carolina Evangelistic Association. www.garrchurch.com.

Church of Christ Holiness unto the Lord

1650 Smart St., PO Box 1642, Savannah, GA 31401

The Church of Christ Holiness unto the Lord was founded in 1926 in Savannah, Georgia, but grew out of the ministry of William J. Seymour (1870–1922) of the Apostolic Faith Mission in Los Angeles, the original center from which the Pentecostal movement was disseminated throughout the United States. It was founded by Bishop Milton Solomon Bishop (d. 1952) and his wife, and Saul Keels and his wife, Dora Brown, as well as others. Bishop Moses Lewis became general overseer of the church in 1979. The church, which followed the Holiness Pentecostal teachings as expounded by Seymour, was affiliated with the United Fellowship Convention of the Original Azusa Street Mission, which sponsored an annual gathering of those churches in the eastern United States as an outgrowth of Seymour's evangelistic activity.

Membership: In 1990 the church reported 35 affiliated congregations.

Sources:

DuPree, Sherry Sherrod. *African-American Holiness Pentecostal Movement: An Annotated Bibliography*. New York: Garland, 1996.

Payne, Wardell J., ed. *Directory of African American Religious Bodies: A Compendium by the Howard University School of Divinity*. Washington, DC: Howard University Press, 1991.

Church of God (Cleveland, Tennessee)

2490 Keith St., PO Box 2430, Cleveland, TN 37320-2430

Most of the Pentecostal churches that bear the name "Church of God" can be traced to a Holiness revival in the mountains of northwest Georgia and eastern Tennessee. In 1884 R. G. Spurling, a Baptist minister in Monroe County, Tennessee, began to search the Scriptures for answers to the problems of modernism, formality, and spiritual dryness. Concerned people met on August 19, 1886, at the Barney Creek Meeting House to organize a new movement that would preach primitive church Holiness and provide for reform and revival of the churches. Christian Union was the name accepted by the first eight members enrolled that day. Spurling died within a few months of the meeting, and was succeeded in leadership by his son, R. G. Spurling Jr.

After 10 years of little growth, three laymen influenced by the Spurlings's work claimed a deep religious experience similar to that written about by John Wesley, the founder of Methodism, and as a result began to preach sanctification. (Wesley attended a service at Alders Gate Street in London in 1738 where he "felt his heart strangely warmed." He and his followers interpreted this as a work of God that again sanctified the person who had already experienced a justifying faith in Christ). The three laymen began to hold services at Camp Creek, in Cherokee County, North Carolina, among a group of unaffiliated Baptists. Spurling and the Christian Union moved their services to Camp Creek and united with the group in North Carolina. During the revival that followed this merger, several people began to speak in tongues spontaneously. After searching the Scriptures, the group recognized the phenomena as a biblical occurrence and as a new outpouring of the Holy Spirit.

The Christian Union, as it grew, suffered from both persecution and fanaticism: As its unrestrained members spoke in tongues and held noisy services, various members of the local community complained. Some leaders of the Christian Union, responding to the criticism, decided to make the services more orderly. They devised a simple plan of government at a meeting in the home of W. F. Bryant. The group's name was changed to the Holiness Church. In 1896, during the revival, Ambrose J. Tomlinson (1865–1943), an Indiana Quaker and agent of the American Bible Society, came to the Hill Country to sell bibles and other religious literature. In 1903 he cast his lot with the group and became pastor of the Camp Creek Church. This event can be viewed as the real beginning of the Church of God movement. Having been influenced by the Church of God (Anderson, Indiana), Tomlinson persuaded the Holiness Church to accept the biblical name the Church of God. He is also the probable source for the pacifist emphasis that permeates many Pentecostal churches. Tomlinson began a publishing enterprise and printed for distribution the doctrines of the new church. Headquarters were soon established in his home at Culbertson, Tennessee, and he emerged as the dominant leader. Tomlinson later settled in Cleveland, Tennessee, and eventually led a congregation there to unite with the Holiness Church. The church's period of expansion had begun.

With the establishment of further congregations, the members saw the necessity of an assembly for dealing with questions of mutual concern. The first assembly convened in 1906 at Camp Creek, and decisions were made about foot washing—it was to be observed at least annually—and midweek and family services—they were to be encouraged. At the 1907 assembly the church's name was officially changed to the Church of God.

The 1908 assembly was attended by G. B. Cashwell (1862–1916), who later introduced many Holiness people to the baptism of the Holy Spirit and the experience of speaking in tongues, which had occurred at the mission of the Pacific Apostolic Faith Movement on Azusa Street in Los Angeles. After the assembly, he preached a revival. Tomlinson received the baptism and spoke in tongues. The following year, in a gesture symbolic of the church's acceptance of the new truth preached by Cashwell and experienced by Tomlinson, he was selected general moderator of the young church, a position he held until 1922. In 1914 he was elected general overseer for life. Accelerated growth, with the exception of losses of schismatic bodies, has continued unabated.

Doctrinally, the Church of God believes in the baptism of the Holy Spirit as an experience subsequent to sanctification. Practices include baptism by immersion, the Lord's Supper, and foot washing. Members believe in holiness-of-life, which excludes the use of cosmetics, costly apparel, and shorts or slacks on women. They accept a premillennial Second Coming (the coming of Christ to bind Satan before Christ's thousand-year reign on earth with his saints).

Government of the Church of God is centralized. Authority is vested in the general assembly, which meets every two years and is chaired by the general overseer. In 2004 Dr. G. Dennis McGuire was appointed general overseer. A supreme council operates between general assemblies, and a general executive committee oversees the boards and agencies. State overseers have charge over the churches in their areas and appoint the pastors. Tithing is a central feature in finances. The height of centralization came in 1914 when the annual elections of the general overseer were discontinued and Tomlinson became overseer for life.

Tomlinson's authority was attacked in the 1920s. In 1922 a committee ordered to investigate the church's finances (which Tomlinson completely controlled) reported unfavorably, and Tomlinson was impeached and removed from office. The overseer's authority had been reduced earlier by the addition of two new offices to control functions previously controlled by Tomlinson (publishing and education). These were supplemented in 1922 by the new constitution, adopted despite Tomlinson's opposition.

The Church of God Publishing House produces books, pamphlets and tracts, and a full line of church-school materials. Missions, both foreign and domestic, are widespread (in 72 countries) and supported by the tithe of members. The church is a member of the National Association of Evangelicals.

Membership: Not reported.

Educational Facilities:

Lee College, Cleveland, Tennessee.

Northwest Bible and Music Academy, Minot, North Dakota.

West Coast Bible School, Pasadena, California.

Church of God Theological Seminary, Cleveland, Tennessee.

Hispanic Institute of Ministry, Dallas, Texas.

International Bible College, Moose Jaw, Saskatchewan, Canada.

Patten University, Oakland, California.

Western School of Christian Ministry, Fresno, California.

Periodicals: *Church of God Evangel • Lighted Pathway*

Sources:

Church of God (Cleveland, Tennessee). www.churchofgod.org.

Conn, Charles W. *Like a Mighty Army: A History of the Church of God, 1886–1995*. Cleveland, TN: Pathway Press, 1996.

Crews, Mickey. *The Church of God: A Social History*. Knoxville: University of Tennessee Press, 1990.

Hughes, Ray H. *Church of God Distinctives*. Cleveland, TN: Pathway Press, 1968.

Marshall, June Glover. *A Biographical Sketch of Richard G. Spurling, Jr*. Cleveland, TN: Pathway Press, 1974.

Slay, James L. *This We Believe*. Cleveland, TN: Pathway Press, 1963.

Church of God in Divine Order

Sand Springs, OK 74063

The Church of God in Divine Order was founded in 2000 to perpetuate the visionary ministry of Ambrose J. Tomlinson (1865–1943) and his son Homer Tomlinson (1892–1968). The Tomlinsons had supplied leadership to the Pentecostal Church of God movement through the first half and middle of the twentieth century. After their father's death, Ambrose's sons Homer and Milton Tomlinson (1906–1995) parted company when Milton was chosen to lead the Church of God of Prophecy. Homer subsequently founded a separate branch of the Church of God.

By the 1990s some members of the church founded by Homer Tomlinson, in a departure from its founding vision, had come to favor what they considered to be manmade doctrines and dogmas. The group was prompted to establish a separate fellowship mostly by the rise of preaching that the approaching end of the millennium would bring the coming of Jesus and the ascension of the saints, even though the work of evangelizing the world had not been completed.

The new church followed the theocratic form of government set up by Homer Tomlinson, operating in the gifts of the spirit by the power of the Holy Ghost through a fivefold ministry of believers (Eph. 4:11). The church is committed to the great commission to preach, teach, and practice the message of the Kingdom of God to all nations, which they believe Jesus said would bring the church age to a close before his Second Coming. Besides Tomlinson, church founders included Jimmy Taylor (d. 2003), Leo Taylor, and Ted Carr.

Membership: Not reported.

Sources:

Church of God in Divine Order. www.webspawner.com/users/tcogido/index.html.

Church of God (Jerusalem Acres)

PO Box 1207, 1826 Dalton Pke. SE, Cleveland, TN 37364-1207

The Church of God (Jerusalem Acres) began in 1957 when Grady R. Kent (1909–1964) initiated a reformation of the Church of God of Prophecy aimed at reestablishing its biblical order. Kent had been a pastor in the church since 1933. In 1943 he was placed in charge of the Church of God of Prophecy Marker Association begun by Ambrose J. Tomlinson (1865–1943), the church's founder, as an auxiliary to locate, mark, beautify, and maintain prominent places in the world connected with the Church of God of Prophecy. One place of particular interest was the Fields of the Wood—a mountainside Bible monument based on Ps. 132:6 and Hab. 2:2–3 located on Burger Mountain in western North Carolina. The monument includes a replica of the Ten Commandments in seven-foot tall letters and an altar on the top of the mountain. The altar marks the spot where Tomlinson prayed immediately before declaring the existence of the Church of God. Kent also supervised the White Angel Fleet, pilots and airplanes used for public demonstrations of ministry at airports throughout the United States. Between 1948 and 1957 Kent objected to the Church of God of Prophecy replacing the general overseer with the general assembly as the highest authority in the church (which, in effect, repeated the history of the church and led to its formation in the early 1920s). Faced with having to recant his objection to the actions of the general assembly, as well as other controversial ideas he had developed, Kent resigned in 1957. With 300 supporters, many from South Carolina, Kent established a new Church of God with himself as general overseer.

The church believes in an experiential understanding of justification by faith, sanctification as a second work of grace, and the baptism of the Holy Spirit evidenced by speaking in tongues. It also believes in the restoration of both ministerial (Eph. 4:11) and spiritual (1 Cor. 12) gifts to the church.

In areas of worship and service, the church has developed a comprehensive program, "New Testament Judaism," a term coined by Kent in 1962 during a visit to Israel. The church observes the biblical (Old Testament) calendar that includes the Sabbath as a day of worship; Passover as a time for celebrating communion; Pentecost as a festival for spiritual renewal and dedication to the work of the church; and Tabernacles as a remembrance of the time of Christ's birth and a foreshadowing of his return. Various symbols generally associated with Judaism are used alongside the cross. The church does not celebrate the holidays of Easter, Halloween, and Christmas.

The polity is theocratic, government by God through an anointed leader. There is a chief bishop who sits as the final authority (as contrasted to the total authority) in matters of both judicial and executive government. In 2008 the chief bishop was Tim Miller. The church has no legislative body, but has a council of apostles and elders with a judicial purpose—that is, to interpret the laws of God in the Bible, both Old and New Testaments, as they relate to the church. The primary officers in the council are the chief bishop, the 12 apostles, the seven men of wisdom, and the 70 elders.

Membership: In 1987 the church reported 10,000 members, 145 churches, and 255 ministers.

Periodicals: *The Vision Speaks* • *Greater Light* • *Weekly Bible Lessons*

Sources:

Church of God (Jerusalem Acres). thechurchofgodntj.com/Home_Page.html.

Introduction to Apostles' Doctrine. Cleveland, TN: Church Publishing Company, 1984.

Kent, Grady R. *Treatise on the 1957 Reformation Stand.* Cleveland, TN: Church Publishing Company, the Church of God, n.d.

Manual of Apostles Doctrine and Business Procedure. Cleveland, TN: Church Publishing Company and Press, n.d.

Church of God/Mountain Assembly

110 S Florence Ave., PO Box 157, Jellico, TN 37762

The Church of God/Mountain Assembly grew out of a Holiness revival in 1895 in the South Union Association of the United Baptist Church. From 1895 until 1903, members and ministers who adopted the Holiness belief in a second work of grace that imparts sanctification by the power of the Holy Spirit remained within the United Baptist Church in McCreary County, Kentucky. However, in 1903, the Baptists decided to revoke the licenses of all ministers who were preaching sanctification according to the Holiness movement. In 1906 these Holiness ministers—Revs. J. H. Parks, Steve N. Bryant, Tom Moses, and William O. Douglas—met at Jellico, Tennessee, with members of their several churches and organized the Church of God. The words "Mountain Assembly" were added in 1911 after the group became aware of other Church of God groups. In 1906 to 1907 the group learned of the baptism of the Holy Ghost as evidenced by speaking in tongues and accepted it as a fuller expression of their ideas. Rev. S. N. Bryant was elected as their first moderator. The assembly ascribed to a church covenant, teachings, and declaration of faith.

The doctrine of the Church of God/Mountain Assembly is similar to that of the Church of God (Cleveland, Tennessee). The church professes a conservative trinitarian faith, and the King James Version of the Bible is preferred. Present polity was adopted in 1914. The offices of general overseer, assistant overseer and missions director, general secretary and treasurer, and district overseer were established and filled. In 2008 the general overseer was Rev. Donnie Hill. The overseers operate in a basically congregational system. The assembly meets annually. The Delegation serves as the legislative body and a Board of Twelve Elders as a judicial body. From its headquarters in Jellico, Tennessee, the Church of God/Mountain Assembly has spread to ten states from Michigan to Florida. A national youth campground is located near Winchester, Ohio.

The Church of God/Mountain Assembly is a member-denomination of the Pentecostal Churches of North America (PCCNA).

Membership: In 1994 the church reported 116 churches and 5,100 members in the United States, and 350 churches overseas in India, Africa, and the Caribbean. In 2008 the church reported that more than 120 churches in the United States and nearly 400 worldwide belong to its fellowship.

Periodicals: *The Gospel Herald.*

Sources:

Church of God/Mountain Assembly. www.cgmahdq.org.

Gibson, Luther. *History of the Church of God Mountain Assembly.* N.p.: Author, 1954.

Church of God of Apostolic Faith

PO Box 691745, Tulsa, OK 74169-1745

The Church of God of the Apostolic Faith was organized in 1914 by four independent Pentecostal ministers who saw the need for some organization and church government. Not wishing to follow the plan of government adopted by the Assemblies of God, which had been formed that year in nearby Hot Springs, Arkansas, the Revs. James O. McKenzie, Edwin A. Buckles, Oscar H. Myers, and Joseph P. Rhoades held a meeting that led to the creation of the Church of God of the Apostolic Faith at Cross Roads Mission, near Ozark, Arkansas. They adopted a presbyterial form of government based on Acts 15. The church also had a doctrinal difference with the Assemblies of God, believing, as did the Church of God (Cleveland, Tennessee), that one must seek sanctification before having the baptism of the Holy Spirit. Like the Church of God, healing, tithing, and nonparticipation in war are emphasized.

The general conference of the church meets annually. It elects the general presbytery of seven ministers, including the general superintendent and two assistants. In 2008 Kelly Ward was the general superintendent. The conference owns all the property and the presbytery controls the ministry. The church is currently divided into five districts. There is a mission in Mexico.

Membership: Not reported. In the mid-1970s there were approximately 1,400 members in 27 congregations. In 2008 the church's website listed 31 congregations in its church directory.

Periodicals: *Church of God Herald* • *Christian Youth*

Sources:

Church of God of Apostolic Faith. cogaf.org.

Church of God of Prophecy

PO Box 2910, Cleveland, TN 37320-2910

Alternate Address: Canadian headquarters: Eastern Canada: PO Box 457, First Line East, R.R. 2, Brampton, ON L6V 2L4. Western Canada: 130 Centre St., Strathmore, AL T1P 1G9.

The Church of God of Prophecy traces its beginning to the organization as the Church of God on June 13, 1903, in Cherokee County, North Carolina. Ambrose J. Tomlinson (1865–1943) was selected as pastor. New churches in other areas were organized under his pastoral leadership.

Although it was understood that the small group was operating as the Church of God, it was in the second assembly held at Union Grove, Bradley County, Tennessee, in 1907, that the name Church of God was formally adopted by the assembly and entered into the records. In 1952 "of Prophecy" was added to the name to distinguish the church from other organizations using "Church of God" in business and secular activities.

The first general assembly of its membership was called for January 1906 in Cherokee County, with A. J. Tomlinson serving as moderator and clerk. He continued to hold this dual office until his title was changed to general overseer in the fifth assembly in 1910.

Under the leadership of A. J. Tomlinson, the Church of God became a national, then an international body, and various educational, social, and ecclesiastical programs were developed. He continued as general overseer until his death in 1943. At that time, his youngest son, Milton A. Tomlinson (1906–1995), was duly selected by the overseer leadership and approved by the assembly body.

During Tomlinson's tenure as general overseer, the church was noted for its call for unity and a fellowship not limited socially, racially, or nationally. The church is integrated on all levels, and various leadership positions are occupied by women. The following ministries were developed under his leadership: radio and television, youth camping, servicemen's outreach, world mission corps, youth mission teams, international orphanages, and Tomlinson College.

M. A. Tomlinson's tenure as general overseer continued until April 30, 1990, when due to ill health, he vacated the office. In a meeting of the state and national

overseers, Billy D. Murray Sr. was selected to serve as interim general overseer until the annual assembly in August. At that official conclave of the church membership, Murray was confirmed as general overseer, a position he held until his retirement in 2000. While serving as assistant editor of the *White Wing Messenger*, the church's official magazine, Murray had preached twelve precedent-setting messages to capacity crowds at general assemblies (1978–1989), sermons that undoubtedly influenced the church to become more evangelical. This new direction became the hallmark of Murray's 10-year administration, most clearly seen in his urgent call in 1994 for the church to embrace "turning to the harvest" as its passion, which would result in "vibrant local churches." In the course of this paradigm shift, he led in "pluralizing" the church's leadership and in restructuring its international offices. He encouraged leadership development and life-long learning, while focusing on the "primacy of the local church."

Murray's administration (1990–2000) saw the church expand its presence from 90 countries to more than 120. Membership grew 109 percent, from 261,641 to 546,6000. Upon his death, Murray's successor, Bp. Fred S. Fisher Sr., observed, "This Church will never know in our lifetimes all the good Billy Murray has done, but she will eventually come to thank him for the vital role he has played."

In July 2000 Fred S. Fisher Sr. was duly selected to serve as the fourth general overseer of the Church of God of Prophecy. Under his leadership, the church's presence expanded to 125 nations of the world and membership continued to grow, reaching 940,854. Upon Fisher's retirement, in August 2006 Bp. Randall E. Howard, the global outreach ministries director, was selected as the fifth general overseer. He continues to serve in this position.

Church history includes a strong emphasis on youth ministries, national and international missions, and various parochial education ministries.

The church has developed a biblical-theme park, Fields of the Wood, near Murphy, North Carolina, the site where the church's first congregation was organized in 1903. It includes the world's largest cross, the world's largest Ten Commandments display depicted in five-foot letters, and biblical markers that portray the message of Christ. The park is visited by more than 100,000 visitors annually.

The Church of God of Prophecy accepts the authority of the whole Bible as the Word of God and hence has no creed. However, it has summarized what it considers to be "Twenty-Nine Important Bible Truths" that illustrate its basic agreement with traditional trinitarian Christian beliefs. It places special emphasis on sanctification (holiness of the believer) and the doctrine of spirit-baptism that includes speaking in tongues as initial evidence. Other prominent doctrinal commitments include: an eschatology that involves a premillennial return of the risen Jesus, which, according to the church, will be preceded by a specified series of events; the practices of baptism by immersion, the Lord's Supper, and washing the saints' feet; total abstinence from intoxicating beverages and tobacco; a concern for modesty in all dimensions of life; and an appreciation for various gifts of the Holy Spirit, with special attention to divine healing.

The church is headed by its general overseer, whose position is pluralized by six continental leaders known as general presbyters. A biannual general assembly is held where various doctrinal and business concerns are considered. Resolutions are then ratified by each local congregation. The general assembly concludes with the general presbyter's appointing all national and international leaders, who in turn are responsible for appointing the various leaders under their jurisdictions.

In 1933 the church adopted an official church flag, which is on display in most church facilities.

Membership: The church is organized in 132 countries and in every state of the United States. In 2006 the church reported 940,854 members in 8,511 churches and missions.

Educational Facilities:

Center for Biblical Leadership, Cleveland, Tennessee.

Tomlinson Center, Cleveland, Tennessee.

Periodicals: *White Wing Messenger*.

Sources:

Church of God of Prophecy. www.cogop.org.

Davidson, C. T. *Upon This Rock*. 3 vols. Cleveland, TN: White Wing Press, 1973–1976.

Duggar, Lillie. *A. J. Tomlinson*. Cleveland, TN: White Wing Publishing House, 1964.

Pruitt, Raymond M. *Fundamentals of the Faith*. Cleveland, TN: White Wing Publishing House and Press, 1981.

Stone, James. *The Church of God of Prophecy: History and Polity*. Cleveland, TN: White Wing Press, 1977.

Church of God of the Union Assembly

2211 South Dixie Hwy., PO Box 1323, Dalton, GA 30722-1323

The Church of God of the Union Assembly was formed in 1920 from a schism with the Church of God of the Mountain Assembly when part of the congregation in Center, Jackson County, Georgia withdrew. The immediate occasion for the split was the issue of tithing. The Union Assembly rejects the tithing system established in 1919 by the Mountain Assembly, believing it to be an Old Testament practice not taught by Jesus or his apostles. The group also believes the kingdom of God is a spiritual kingdom; that David's throne is established in heaven, not on earth; and that Christ's coming will be followed by the end of time, not the millennium (Christ's reign on earth for 1,000 years with his saints). The Union Assembly's leader in 2008 was Jesse Pratt, who has written a number of pamphlets disseminated through the church. Congregations are present in seventeen states.

Membership: In 2008 the church's website listed 38 congregations in 2008.

Periodicals: *Quarterly News*.

Sources:

Church of God of the Union Assembly. www.thechurchofgodua.org.

Church of God (World Headquarters)

c/o Danny R. Patrick, PO Box 525, Scottsville, KY 42164

Before Ambrose J. Tomlinson (1865–1943), a prominent leader of the Church of God (Cleveland, Tennessee) and founder of what became known as the Church of God of Prophecy, died in 1943, he designated his eldest son, Homer Tomlinson (1892–1968), his successor as general overseer of his offshoot of the Church of God. However, the church's general assembly set aside that appointment and selected Tomlinson's younger son, Milton (1906–1995), as the new general overseer. Homer Tomlinson rejected this action, called his followers to a meeting in New York, and organized a new Church of God, generally distinguished from other similarly named groups by the additional phrase, "World Headquarters." A struggle in court over control of the church resulted in Milton and his followers being recognized as the rightful successor church, and this contingent, renamed the Church of God of Prophecy, was awarded all church properties and trademarks. Homer continued as head of a group of loyal followers and built up his branch of the church, which he led until his death in 1968. He was succeeded by Voy M. Bullen.

In 1952 Homer Tomlinson founded the Theocratic Party; he ran for president on its ticket on a number of occasions throughout the rest of his life. Since his death, the party has continued to run candidates for both state and national offices in the United States.

The only doctrinal divergence in the entire Church of God movement occurs in Homer Tomlinson's branch. Its members replaced the premillennialism of the other branches with a belief that the Church of God has the keys to bringing the kingdom of God on earth, and that the kingdom will come through the setting up of the saints of God in the governments of the nations of the world now, here on earth. Saints are encouraged to become responsible rulers and to preach the gospel of the kingdom. This doctrine was based on an interpretation of the Bible by A. J. Tomlinson, who gave Homer a commission to plant the church flag in every

nation of the earth. Given that commission, Homer established the "World Headquarters" of the Church of God in Jerusalem.

After Bishop Homer's death in 1969, the American headquarters was moved from Queens, New York, to Huntsville, Alabama, a location more central to the congregations. The church's administrative offices were there for many years, but at the end of the 1990s were moved to Scottsville, Kentucky; the church leadership passed to Bp. Danny R. Patrick. In 2000 a small group left and founded the Church of God in Divine Order, with headquarters at Sand Springs, Oklahoma.

Membership: Not reported. Recent information indicates that the large membership reported in the 1970s has dwindled in the United States. The status of related churches overseas is also uncertain.

Periodicals: *The Church of God*.

Sources:

Book of Doctrines, 1903–1970. Huntsville, AL: Church of God Publishing House, 1970.

Tomlinson, Homer A. *The Shout of a King*. Queens Village, NY: Church of God, 1968.

Whitworth, William. "Profiles: 'On the Tide of the Times.'" *New Yorker* (September 24, 1966): 69.

Door of Faith Church and Bible School

1161 Young St., Honolulu, HI 96814

The Door of Faith Church and Bible School was founded by Mildred Johnson Brostek (1911–2005). Raised a Methodist, she experienced the baptism of the Holy Spirit in an Assemblies of God church in Florida. She later joined the Pentecostal Holiness Church (now known as the International Pentecostal Holiness Church), which licensed her to preach. Brostek graduated from the Holmes Theological Seminary and soon thereafter went to the Hawaiian Islands, to which she had earlier felt called by God to go as a missionary. In 1937, she began to hold evangelistic services on Molokai in the home of a native Hawaiian. These services prospered and in 1940 the Door of Faith Churches of Hawaii was chartered, after which the work soon spread to the other islands.

The church is headed by the Reverend Brostek, who is the church's overseer. There is an annual conference. A daily radio ministry is broadcast over two stations, one in Honolulu and one in Hilo, Hawaii.

Membership: Not reported. There are churches at a number of locations in Hawaii and a prosperous mission has developed in the Philippines, where a Bible college has been opened. There is one church in New York. In 1979, there were 40 churches and 3,000 members in Hawaii and missions work in Okinawa, Japan, and in Indonesia.

Educational Facilities:

Door of Faith Bible School, Honolulu, Hawaii.

Sources:

Donovan, Robert D. *Her Door of Faith*. Honolulu, HI: Orovan Books, 1971.

Emmanuel Holiness Church

PO Box 818, Bladenboro, NC 28320

In 1953 controversy over standards of dress among the members of the Pentecostal Fire-Baptized Holiness Church led to a vote to divide the church. One issue that occasioned the split was the use of neckties, which the Pentecostal Fire-Baptized Holiness Church explicitly forbids. Those who voted for the split elected Rev. L. O. Sellers chairman and formed the Emmanuel Holiness Church. This church differs from its parent body only on minor points of dress, the use of a more congregational form of government, and tithing, which is required of members. A general assembly of all ministers and one delegate from each church has limited legislative powers.

Membership: Not reported. In 1967 there were 72 congregations and 118 ministers.

Periodicals: *Emmanuel Holiness Messenger*.

Emmanuel Tabernacle Baptist Church Apostolic Faith

329-333 N Garfield Ave., Columbus, OH 43203

The Emmanuel Tabernacle Baptist Church Apostolic Faith began in 1916 (and was incorporated 1917) in Columbus, Ohio. Columbus was an early center of the non-Trinitarian Apostolic movement that had originated in 1913 and spread through the still youthful Pentecostal movement. The new church was founded by Rev. (later Bp.) Martin Rawleigh Gregory (1885–1960). Gregory had been called to the ministry as a 17-year-old youth. He was educated at Colgate University and became a Baptist minister in 1903. In 1914 he moved to Columbus, Ohio, where he encountered Pentecostalism in its Apostolic form. His adoption of Pentecostalism led to a break with the Baptist Church.

Gregory was assisted in the founding of the Emmanuel Tabernacle by two women who had worked with him in the Baptist Church, Lela Grant and Bessie Dockett. He came to believe that women should share equally in the preaching of God's word, and as bishop of the church, Gregory opened the ordained ministry to women, making his first Apostolic church to do so. As the church grew and a board of bishops was created, women were elevated to the episcopacy.

The church holds to an Apostolic non-Trinitarian theology. Jesus is the name of the One God and baptism is done in the name of Jesus only. The church also practices foot washing. The current leader, Dr. H. C. Clark, is a woman. An annual meeting is held each summer in Columbus.

Membership: In 2002 there were approximately 20 congregations.

Sources:

Payne, Wardell J., ed. *Directory of African American Religious Bodies: A Compendium by the Howard University School of Divinity*. Washington, DC: Howard University Press, 1991.

Evangelistic Church of God

Current address not obtained for this edition.

The Evangelistic Church of God was established at Denver, Colorado, in 1949. It grew out of the work of Norman L. Chase, a former minister of the Church of God (Cleveland, Tennessee) and of the original Church of God. By 1955 the group claimed 774 members in 12 churches. The general assembly meets annually.

Membership: Not reported.

Periodicals *The Church of God Final Warning*.

First Interdenominational Christian Association

Calvary Temple Church, 1061 Memorial Dr. SE, Atlanta, GA 30316

In 1946 the Rev. Watson Sorrow, who was one of the founders of the Congregational Holiness Church, formed the First Interdenominational Christian Association, centered upon his own congregation, Calvary Temple, in Atlanta. The association resembles the Congregational Holiness Church but less definite in doctrine. The parent body's statements on war, eschatology, and the forbidding of varying doctrinal beliefs among ministers were dropped. Retained were statements on healing, footwashing, and Pentecostalism. Several churches joined Sorrow by adopting the congregational polity and policies of Calvary Temple.

Membership: Not reported.

Free Will Baptist Conference of the Pentecostal Faith

868 Puddin' Swamp Rd., Turbeville, SC 29162

The Free Will Baptist Conference of the Pentecostal Faith was formed in the 1950s when some members of the South Carolina Pentecostal Free Will Baptist Conference Conference decided not to participate in the reorganization that led to the formation of the Pentecostal Free Will Baptist Conference. Those who abstained adopted a constitution and chose a new name. They are at one doctrinally with the other Pentecostal Free Will Baptists.

The polity is congregational. The annual conference is to approve teachings, methods, and conduct, and to encourage fellowship and evangelism. A general board headed by the conference superintendent functions between conference meetings. The Foreign Missions Department oversees work in Costa Rica. Camp meetings are periodically sponsored.

Membership: In 1967 there were 33 congregations and 39 ministers.

Sources:

Free Will Baptist Conference of the Pentecostal Faith. www.fwbpfc.com.

Faith and Government of the Free Will Baptist Church of the Pentecostal Faith. N.p. 1961.

Gardiner, Robert G. "Baptists in Georgia, 1733–Present." 2006. tarver.mercer.edu/archives/History.pdf.

Full Gospel Church Association

PO Box 265, Amarillo, TX 79105

The Full Gospel Church Association, Inc., was organized by the Rev. Dennis W. Thorn at Amarillo, Texas, in 1952 for the purpose of bringing together a number of small, independent Pentecostal churches and missions, most of them with fewer than 100 members in the South and Southwest.

Doctrinally, the Full Gospel Church is similar to the Church of God (Cleveland, Tennessee). It emphasizes healing, tithing, and a literal heaven and hell, and uses only the King James Version of the Bible. It practices footwashing. Bearing arms is a matter of individual judgment. The church does forbid disloyalty, insubordination, and criticism of the Association by its individual members. One unique element is the requirement that each church have an "Altar of God" in its building as a condition of its recognition by the Association.

The Association is congregational in polity. A general convention meets regularly. The general board of directors meets quarterly; its executive directors are the supreme council of the Association. Mission workers were active in Mexico, the Philippines, and Africa.

Membership: Not reported. In 1967 there were 67 churches with a total combined membership of 2,010.

General Conference of the Evangelical Baptist Church

Current address not obtained for this edition.

The General Conference of the Evangelical Baptist Church was organized in 1935 as the Church of the Full Gospel, Inc., by William Howard Carter, who died in 1980. It is Pentecostal and holiness in emphasis, following a theology close to that of the Pentecostal Free Will Baptist Church. It stresses spiritual gifts, healing, and the pretribulation, premillennial return of Christ. Four ordinances are recognized: baptism by immersion, communion, the dedication of children, and tithing. The dedication of children is a form of christening that is distinct from baptism.

The polity is congregational and headquartered in Goldsboro, North Carolina. There is an annual conference that elects officers. In the local church, the pastor is the chief officer. He is elected by the congregation and has the power to appoint or nominate all church officers.

Membership: Reported as 100 members in two locations as of 1992.

Educational Facilities:

Evangelical Theological Seminary, Goldsboro, North Carolina.

William Carter Bible College, Goldsboro, North Carolina.

Periodicals: *Evangelical Baptist*.

Sources:

Discipline of the General Conference of the Evangelical Baptist Church. N.p., n.d.

Leonard, Bill J., ed. *Dictionary of Baptists in America*. Downer's Grove, IL: InterVarsity Press, 1994.

Holiness Baptist Association

Current address not obtained for this edition.

The Holiness Baptist Association can be traced to 1893 when, because of their teaching on "sinless perfection," two congregations and several ministers were expelled from the Little River Baptist Association. The next year, together with two additional newly organized churches, representatives met at the Pine City Church in Wilcox County, Georgia, and formed the Association. The Association mixes the Wesleyan understanding of sanctification with traditional Missionary Baptist standards of faith and decorum. Tongues-speech, while permitted by the group, is not regarded as evidence of the baptism of the Holy Spirit. The Association operates two campgrounds in Coffee County, Georgia.

Membership: Reported to be approximately 1,600 members comprising fifty churches.

Periodicals: *The Holiness Baptist Association* (founded in 1918 as *The Gospel Standard*).

Sources:

Gardiner, Robert G. "Baptists in Georgia, 1733-Present." Macon, GA: Jack Tarver Library, Mercer University, 2006. Available from tarver.mercer.edu/archives.

Holiness Church of God

Current address not obtained for this edition.

The Holiness Church of God was formed in 1920 by members from several holiness churches that had received the baptism of the Holy Spirit. Three years before, a revival, called the Big May Meeting, led by Elder James A. Foust had occurred in Madison, North Carolina. The entire membership of several congregations became Pentecostal, including the Kimberly Park Holiness Church in Winston-Salem, North Carolina. The church was established in 1928. Churches are found in New York, Virginia, and West Virginia.

Membership: Not reported. In 1968 there were 28 congregations and 927 members.

Holy Church of God

707 Little Neck Rd., Savannah, GA 31419

The Holy Church of God is a Holiness Pentecostal church founded early in the twentieth century. It affirms a belief in the Trinity, salvation by faith in the shed blood of Jesus, sanctification of the believer, and the baptism of the Holy Ghost for the sanctified. The initial evidence of the baptism of the Holy Ghost is speaking in tongues. The church practices baptism by immersion, the Lord's Supper, and foot washing. It also believes in divine healing and tithing.

Marriage is considered a sacred state in the church. Divorce is allowed when the offending party has committed adultery, but each divorce is decided on a case by case basis. Women may take leadership roles in the church, including evangelist, missionary, and temporary pastor, but are not allowed to assume a role that allows them to usurp authority over males. There is a Women's Fellowship ministry. Members must refrain from the use of alcohol, tobacco, and narcotics, and are required to dress modestly. The church is headed by a board of overseers, a board of directors, and a delegated convention. The three-person board of overseers has charge of all matters except those dealing with finances and real estate, the concern of the board of directors. The annual convention includes all ministers and delegates from the local churches. Local churches are self-governing but must restrict themselves to pastors licensed by the Holy Church of God. In addition to Native American missions in the United States, the Holy Church of God provides support to missions in Honduras, Mexico, Panama, the Ukraine, and Venezuela.

Membership: Not reported.

Sources:

Savannah Holy Church of God. www.holychurchofgod.org.

Constitution and By-laws of the Holy Church of God. Savannah, GA: Holy Church of God, n.d.

Holy Temple of God

1220 NE 23rd Ave., Gainesville, FL 32609

The Holy Temple of God is a holiness Pentecostal church founded in 1975 by Walter Camps (1933-2007), formerly an evangelist and presiding district elder with the Church of God by Faith. At the time he left to found the new church, he supervised a district of 18 churches in the Gainesville, Florida, area. Upon his death in December 2007, Bishop Harvey Hutchinson Jr. was appointed the new Presiding Bishop of Holy Temple of God. The ministry has expanded to seven churches, including locations in St. Augustine, Florida; Rantoul, Illinois; and Sylvester and Kingsland, Georgia.

Membership: In 1990 there were approximately 1,000 members.

Sources:

Holy Temple of God. www.htog.org.

DuPree, Sherry Sherrod. *African American Holiness Pentecostal Movement: An Annotated Bibliography.* New York: Garland, 1996.

International Pentecostal Church of Christ (IPCC)

2245 U.S. 42 SW, London, OH 43140

The International Pentecostal Church of Christ was formed in 1976 by a merger of the International Pentecostal Assemblies and the Pentecostal Church of Christ (PCC). The International Pentecostal Assemblies was formed in 1936 by the merger of the Association of Pentecostal Assemblies and the National and International Pentecostal Missionary Union. The former body was an outgrowth of a periodical, *The Bridegroom's Messenger*, still owned by the church, which had been founded in 1907 by G. B. Cashwell (1862–1916) following his visit to the Azusa Street Revival. Elizabeth A. Sexton, Hattie M. Barth, and Paul T. Barth founded the Association of Pentecostal Assemblies in 1921 in Atlanta. The National and International Pentecostal Missionary Union was founded in 1914 by Dr. Philip Wittich.

In 1908 evangelist John Stroup of South Solon, Ohio, received the baptism of the Holy Spirit, signified by his speaking in tongues. In 1913 he began to travel through southeastern Ohio and the adjacent territory in Kentucky and West Virginia, organizing churches in that area. In 1917 at Advance (Flatwoods), Kentucky, a group of ministers met, organized the Pentecostal Church of Christ, and appointed Stroup bishop. The Pentecostal Church of Christ was incorporated in 1927.

On August 25, 1936, the Association of Pentecostal Assemblies (APA) and the International Pentecostal Church (IPC) met in joint council meeting at the Radio Church in Baltimore, MD. The action of the joint council resulted in the formation of the International Pentecostal Assemblies (IPA). In 1974 a two-year trial consolidation commenced between the IPA and the PCC, which resulted in the complete consolidation of the two groups at a Joint General Conference held at London, Ohio, August 10, 1976. By an overwhelming majority vote from each separate group, the two combined with the name International Pentecostal Church of Christ.

The doctrine of the merged church follows closely that of the Assemblies of God. Members believe in the virgin birth, Christ as the only way to heaven, the literal resurrection and premillennial return of Christ, the inspiration of scripture, the reality of hell, a personal devil, and two ordinances: water baptism and the Lord's Supper. The church recently amended the Statement of Faith to add the belief that racism is sin.

Organization of the small church is congregational with a general overseer elected every two years. There are no restrictions on women in the ministry. *The Bridegroom's Messenger* continues as the official periodical and is now the oldest continuously published Pentecostal publication. Missions are supported in

Argentina, Brazil, French Guiana, India, Kenya, Mexico, the Philippines, Spain, Suriname, and Uruguay.

Membership: In 2007 the church reported 4,489 members, 65 churches, and 136 ministers. There were approximately 60,000 members worldwide.

Periodicals: *The Bridegroom's Messenger.* • The *Pentecostal Leader*, PO Box 439, London, OH 43140.

Sources:

International Pentecostal Church of Christ. www.ipcc.cc.

International Pentecostal Holiness Church

7300 NW 39th Expressway, Oklahoma City, OK 73157-2609

Alternate Address: PO Box 12609, Oklahoma City, OK 73157-2609. Canadian headquarters is located at 16293 104th Ave., Surrey, BC V4N 1Z7.

In addition to those Pentecostal churches that derive from the Rev. Charles Parham (1873–1929) and the Apostolic Church and the Topeka Bible School, which he founded, there is a Pentecostal group that begins with Benjamin Hardin Irwin (b. 1854). He was a Baptist who had received the experience of sanctification under the influence of the Iowa Holiness Association, a group made up mostly of Methodists. As a holiness minister, he began to delve into Methodist writings, in particular those of John Fletcher (1729–1765), the eighteenth-century Wesleyan divine. In Fletcher he found what he felt to be an experience for sanctified believers, described as a "baptism of burning love." Eventually Irwin claimed to have received this "baptism of fire," and he began to teach and preach about it. Also called "fire baptism," the experience was related to the Apostles' reception of the Holy Spirit in the form of tongues of fire on Pentecost, as recorded in the Acts of the Apostles. Irwin's preaching of a third experience beyond justification and sanctification (called the "second blessing" in the holiness churches) led to controversy. He and his followers were the objects of intense criticism.

The "third blessing" spread across the Midwest and South. In 1895, the Fire-Baptized Holiness Association was organized in Iowa. Other state and local organizations followed. Irwin exercised authority over each and appointed the presidents. From July 28 to August 8, 1898, a First General Convention was held at Anderson, South Carolina, and formal organization of the Fire-Baptized Holiness Association occurred. Among those in attendance was William Edward Fuller (1875–1958), who later founded the Fire-Baptized Holiness Church of God of the Americas. The 1898 convention adopted a *Discipline*, which provided for life tenure for the general overseer who was given wide-ranging authority and control over the work. The association soon took the name of the Fire-Baptized Holiness Church. Within two years, involved in a personal scandal, Irwin left the church and turned it over to Joseph H. King, a former Methodist minister who had been assisting him in running the church.

Contemporaneous with the ministry of Irwin was that of A. B. Crumpler (1863–1952). Crumpler, a Methodist minister in North Carolina, had received the second-blessing sanctification experience, the second blessing, as the basic distinguishing mark of the holiness movement. Crumpler received his sanctification experience through the ministry of the Rev. Beverly Carradine (1848–1931), a famous Southern Methodist holiness preacher. He became the leading exponent of the second blessing in North Carolina, and in 1896, a great holiness movement began there. In 1899, Crumpler was tried for ignoring some of the organizational rules of the Methodist Church. He withdrew and the following year formed the Pentecostal Holiness Church at Fayetteville, North Carolina.

In 1906, the Rev. G. B. Cashwell (1862–1916), a Pentecostal Holiness minister, attended the Pentecostal revival services that were occurring on Azusa Street in Los Angeles, California, and received the baptism of the Holy Spirit evidenced by his speaking in tongues. Cashwell headed eastward to introduce the experience to his brothers and sisters. On New Years's Eve, 1906, he began a revival at Dunn, North Carolina, and introduced the experience to the Pentecostal Holiness Church. He also led J. H. King into the experience. Not without controversy, both the Pentecostal

Holiness Church and the Fire-Baptized Holiness Church accepted the new experience in 1908. A merger under the name of the former occurred in 1911. It became the International Pentecostal Holiness Church in 1975.

The Pentecostal Holiness Church insists that the Pentecostal experience of the baptism of the Holy Spirit, signified by speaking in tongues, is valid only as a third blessing. In other words, the Pentecostal experience can come only to those who have already been justified (accepted Jesus as their personal savior) and sanctified (received the second blessing, which was the key experience of the holiness movement). By contrast, most Pentecostals believe the baptism of the Holy Spirit is available to any believer at any time and brings with it power for a holy life. Most Pentecostals seek only two experiences, while the Pentecostal Holiness Church seeks three.

The Pentecostal Holiness Church is a direct outgrowth of the holiness movement: That explains why it retains the second blessing. The church also has a Methodist heritage, so it derives its doctrinal statement from the Methodist Articles of Religion. In line with its Methodist roots, the church is among the few Pentecostal bodies to allow baptism by methods other than immersion. Foot washing is optional.

The polity of the Pentecostal Holiness Church is episcopal. One bishop elected by the general conference and other officers form a general board of administration to administer the affairs of the denomination. Under the administrative board are various other boards and agencies. Among the boards are those on education, evangelism, missions, and publication. The Board of Education oversees the work at the three colleges. The World Missions Board, created in 1904, oversees missions in 72 countries. Foreign work in those countries has been set off as autonomous churches that remain aligned ideologically and filially: the Pentecostal Wesleyan Methodists of Brazil, the Pentecostal Methodist Church of Chile, and the Pentecostal Holiness Church of Canada, which became autonomous in 1971. A vigorous publishing program is pursued by Life Spring Resources.

Membership: The IPHC's 2007 Statistical Report listed 248,398 U.S. members in 1,965 churches at the close of 2006.

Educational Facilities:

Emmanuel College, Franklin Springs, Georgia.

Southwestern Christian University, Oklahoma City, Oklahoma.

Pacific Coast Bible College, Sacramento, California.

Periodicals: *Issachar File* (electronic publication). • *Networkings* (electronic publication). • *FYI* (electronic publication). • *IHPC Experience* (printed monthly).

Sources:

International Pentecostal Holiness Church. www.iphc.org.

Beacham, A. D., Jr. *A Brief History of the Pentecostal Church of God*. Franklin Springs, GA: Life Springs Resources, 1993.

Campbell, Joseph E. *The Pentecostal Holiness Church, 1898–1948*. Franklin Springs, GA: Publishing House of the Pentecostal Holiness Church, 1951.

King, Joseph H. *Yet Speaketh*. Franklin Springs, GA: Publishing House of the Pentecostal Holiness Church, 1949.

Synan, Vinson. *Oldtime Power: A Centennial History of the International Pentecostal Holiness Church*. Franklin Springs, GA: LifeSprings Resources, 1998.

(Original) Church of God

220 S 11th St., Wytheville, PA 24382

The first schism in the Church of God (Cleveland, Tennessee) occurred in 1917, and was led by the Rev. Joseph L. Scott, a pastor in Chattanooga. Among the issues involved were local autonomy, the tithe (obligatory versus voluntary), and the reception of divorced persons into the church. After the schism a less centralized government was established in the newly formed church. Each congregation is autonomous and takes the name of its location; for example, "The Church of God at Chattanooga." Above the local church is a general office that serves as headquarters and publishing house, which publishes Sunday school literature and the church's two periodicals. A presbytery has oversight of the ministry. The official name of the church includes the word "Original" in parentheses.

There are five ordinances in the (Original) Church of God, Inc.: baptism by immersion, Biblical church government, footwashing, the Lord's Supper, and tithing. Previously divorced persons can be accepted by pastors as church members.

Membership: Not reported. In 1971 there were 70 churches (including one in Trinidad), 20,000 members, and 124 ministers.

Educational Facilities:

Camp Ridgedale, Vanleer, Tennessee.

Periodicals: *The Messenger.* • *The Youth Messenger.*

Sources:

Manual or Discipline of the (Original) Church of God. Chattanooga, TN: General Office & Publishing House, 1966.

Pentecostal Free Will Baptist Church

PO Box 1568, Dunn, NC 28335

The Pentecostal Free Will Baptist Church was formed in a merger and reorganization of several Free Will Baptist Associations, mainly in North Carolina. Pentecostalism had entered the Free Will Baptist Church through the efforts of the popular evangelist G. B. Cashwell (1862–1916). In 1907 he conducted a revival in Dunn, North Carolina, and persuaded many members of the Cape Fear Conference of the Free Will Baptist Church of the truth of his position. The Conference accepted a Pentecostal doctrine, but remained within the national Free Will Baptist Association. In 1907, the Cape Fear Conference split into two geographic associations; the second body became the Wilmington Conference, and the first retained the original name. In 1911, a third association was formed in southeastern North Carolina as the New River Conference. The following year, the Cape Fear Conference split over the Pentecostal issue. Finally, in 1912 a South Carolina Conference was organized.

In 1943, a group of ministers and laymen of the four Pentecostal conferences (Cape Fear, Wilmington, New River, and South Carolina Conferences) met. They formed a general conference but the organization proved unsatisfactory. In 1959, it was decided to dissolve all the conference structures and organize under one charter and one name. Thus, in 1959, the Pentecostal Free Will Baptist Church was formed.

The doctrine is almost identical to that of the Church of God (Cleveland, Tennessee), and includes belief in three experiences of grace: baptism by immersion, footwashing, and premillennialism. It is this group's position that Benjamin Randall (1749–1808), the founder of the Free Will Baptist Church, taught sanctification as an instantaneous act of God.

The church is congregational in structure with a biannual conference. The general superintendent heads an executive board for implementing the program. There are four districts; the World Missions Board oversees missions in Costa Rica, Puerto Rico, Mexico, Venezuela, Nicaragua, Guatemala, Nigeria, and the Philippines. Churches are primarily in North Carolina, with congregations in South Carolina, Virginia, Georgia, and Florida.

Membership: In 1996 the church reported 16,000 members and 157 churches served by 250 ministers.

Educational Facilities:

Heritage Bible College, Dunn, North Carolina.

Periodicals: *The Pentecostal Free-Will Baptist Messenger*, published six times per year.

Sources:

Pentecostal Free Will Baptist Church. www.pfwb.org.

Carter, Herbert. *The Spectacular Gifts, Prophecy, Tongues, Interpretations.* Dunn, NC: The Author, 1971.

Discipline of the Pentecostal Free Will Baptist Church. N.p. 1962.

Faith and Practices of the Pentecostal Free Will Baptist Church, Inc. Franklin Springs, GA: Advocate Press, 1971.

Sauls, Don. *The Ministerial Handbook of the Pentecostal Free Will Baptist Church.* N.p. 1971.

Praise Chapel Christian Fellowship Churches and Ministries International

PO Box 1769, Rancho Cucamonga, CA 91729

Praise Chapel Christian Fellowship Churches and Ministries International dates to 1976 and Maywood, California, when a new ministry was launched by Michael and Donna Neville. The two began to train pastors and send them into various areas of Los Angeles to start new churches. As others became involved and commissioned, new churches were formed both in the United States and abroad, resulting in an international fellowship of ministers and churches. Support for non-U.S.-based churches is supplied through Mission Global Harvest.

Praise Chapel is a mainline Pentecostal fellowship that affirms the Bible as the Word of God, salvation in Christ, and the importance of evangelism, though there is some variation in the statement of faith used at different congregations. Members strongly believe in the baptism of the Holy Spirit, which is evidenced by the individual speaking in tongues and divine healing. Tithing is practiced.

The fellowship holds a World Conference every two years, plus Bible Conferences in various U.S. and international locations. Its Internet site offers online audio sermons and teachings, and mission videos. Individual publications are available for free download; others may be ordered from its online bookstore.

Membership: In 2008 Praise Chapel reports 200 affiliated congregations in the United States and 22 foreign congregations in Mexico, Guatemala, Costa Rica, England, Israel, Vietnam, Mongolia, Tonga, Philippines, Kenya, Estonia, Nicaragua, Hong Kong, and Ghana.

Periodicals: Email updates of fellowship news are mailed regularly to subscribers.

Sources:

Praise Chapel Christian Fellowship Churches and Ministries International. www.praisechapel.com.

White Trinitarian Pentecostals

American Indian Evangelical Church

Current address not obtained for this edition.

During the early twentieth century, American Indians increasingly settled into the city environment. By 1945, 8,000 had settled in the Minneapolis-St. Paul metropolitan area in Minnesota. In that year a group of Indians organized the American Indian Mission. In 1956 the mission became the American Indian Evangelical Church, and Iver C. Grover (a Chippewa) was elected president. He was joined by seven others. In 1959 a committee on ordination was appointed to facilitate the development of an Indian ordained ministry, and four men were ordained.

Similar to fundamental evangelicalism, the doctrinal statement of the church begins with the Apostles' Creed and moves on to affirm the Trinity, the divinity of Jesus, and the conscious suffering of the wicked. Baptism by immersion and the Lord's Supper are practiced. The polity is congregational, but the pastor is viewed as the spiritual overseer of the congregation.

Membership: Not reported.

Anchor Bay Evangelistic Association

PO Box 406, Maryville, IL 62062

Roy John Turner (1880–1945) and his wife Blanche A. Turner became Pentecostals in 1916. Dr. Turner was a medical doctor and his wife a nurse, and they continued to function as medical professionals while leading prayer meetings. Following a revival campaign in 1918 by evangelist Mrs. Maria B. Woodworth-Etter (1844–1924), a church was formed in New Baltimore. In 1923 Dr. Turner was ordained and became pastor of the congregation. The old opera house in New Baltimore, Michigan, was purchased and remodeled as Bethel Temple. From 1938 to 1940 Turner served as an executive with the International Church of the Foursquare Gospel; the congregation in New Baltimore remained independent. Finally in 1940, the Turners left the Foursquare Gospel and the Anchor Bay Evangelistic Association (ABEA) was formed and incorporated. After the Turners' deaths, they were succeeded by their daughter, Lucy Evelyn Turner Iske.

The Association describes itself as a fellowship of independent, Full Gospel, Charismatic and Pentecostal people interested in providing a structured fellowship to serve churches, pastors, evangelists, missionaries, and all other ministries of the five-fold calling according to Ephesians 4:11–12. It provides licensing and ordination credentials to qualified individuals. The ABEA offers income tax non-profit status to qualifying churches and ministries under its IRS 501 c (3) group exemption. Additionally, the Association conducts a Bible correspondence course and provides seminars.

The doctrine of the ABEA resembles that of the International Church of the Foursquare Gospel.

Mission work is conducted in Belize, Haiti, Nigeria, Zambia, Sri Lanka, China, the Middle East, Lithuania, Brazil, El Salvador, Ecuador, Jamaica, Spain, Finland, Thailand, Russia, South Korea, American Samoa, Turkey, the Philippines, South India, West Africa, Indonesia, and Mexico. The church is a member of the Pentecostal Fellowship of North America. It holds an annual convention, videos and photographs of which are available on the ABEA's website.

Membership: In 2008 the ABEA reported having several hundred members in the United States and thousands worldwide.

Educational Facilities:

Alpha Bible College and Seminary, Bryan, Ohio.

Periodicals: *The Anchor*, published quarterly.

Sources:

Anchor Bay Evangelistic Association (ABEA). www.abea.cc.

Apostolic Church of Pentecost of Canada, Inc. (ACOP)

119-2340 Pegasus Way NE, Calgary, AB T2E 8M5

The Apostolic Church of Pentecost of Canada was founded in 1921 by evangelist Franklin Small (b. 1873). As a young man, Small had been healed by the prayer of a visiting clergyman. Several years later, in Winnipeg, he heard Rev. A. H. Argue (1868–1959) preach. Argue had just returned from Chicago where he had received the baptism of the Holy Spirit and spoke in tongues. Eventually Small was also baptized. In 1912, when Argue left for Los Angeles, Small took over his pulpit. Small went to Los Angeles in 1913 and was present at the famous camp meeting at Arroyo Seco at which the controversy over baptism in the name of Jesus (rather than the trinitarian formula of Father, Son, and Holy Ghost) emerged. Initially unimpressed with the new teaching, Small did not consider and accept it until later that year when he heard R. E. McAleister (1880–1953) preach the "Jesus Only" doctrine at a convention in Winnipeg. Two years later he was finally baptized in that manner.

In 1921 a conference was called by a number of those associated with the movement of the great Pentecostal revival, to establish an identity for fellowship and ministry. As a result of theological differences concerning the doctrine of the Godhead between the early leaders of the Pentecostal movement, Small formed the Apostolic Church of Pentecost of Canada, with headquarters in Winnipeg. Small was elected as the first moderator.

In 1953 the Apostolic Church of Pentecost of Canada, Inc., and the Evangelical Churches of Pentecost, together with their colleges, amalgamated under the name of Apostolic Church of Pentecost (ACOP). Amalgamation brought about an emphasis on local church autonomy and the Grace of God. The doctrinal statement of faith was changed to reflect the nature of ACOP in Canada, and conferences were held to debate such issues as oneness/trinity, premillennialism, amillennialism, and church government.

ACOP's mission is to be an international network of ministers and churches, providing fellowship, encouragement and accountability in the proclamation of the Gospel of Jesus Christ by the power of the Holy Spirit.

ACOP affirms the belief in the verbal inspiration of the Bible, the grace of God, water baptism by immersion, the baptism of the Holy Spirit, and the personal return of Jesus Christ for his church. The church exists to assist ministers, local churches, missionaries, and other evangelistic ministers at home and abroad. There is a strong belief in the autonomy of the local church along with a firm belief in accountability to leadership in the organization. ACOP recognizes the whole Body of Christ and that God has called its members to work together with those who know the Lord Jesus Christ as personal savior. ACOP has been primarily a force in Western Canada but has been growing in Central and Eastern Canada, with one of its largest districts in Atlantic Canada. Its Orphan Care Ministry works with communities in Malawi and Zimbabwe to care for impoverished and orphaned children, with projected expansion into Zambia. Leaders from across Canada attend an annual leadership retreat in Alberta; the church also has a biennial conference in even-numbered years.

Membership: In 2002 ACOP reported approximately 24,000 members in Canada, with 450 ministers and 153 churches. A sister organization, Apostolic Church of Pentecost of the USA, has begun to establish churches in the United States.

Periodicals: *fellowshipFOCUS*, monthly.

Sources:

Apostolic Church of Pentecost of Canada. www.acop.ca.

Larden, Robert A. *Our Apostolic Heritage.* Calgary, AL: Apostolic Church of Pentecost of Canada, 1971.

Wegner, Linda. *Streams of Grace: A Historical Account of the Apostolic Church of Pentecost of Canada.* Edmonton, AB: New Leaf Works, 2006.

Apostolic Faith (Kansas)

335 W 10th St., Baxter Springs, KS 66713

In 1898 the Rev. Charles Fox Parham (1873–1929) left the Methodist Episcopal Church and established a home for divine healing in Topeka, Kansas. That same year he began to publish a periodical, *Apostolic Faith*, and two years later opened Bethel Bible College. It was at Bethel that Agnes Ozman (1870–1937) had the initial experience of speaking in tongues, an event from which the modern Pentecostal movement is dated. After Mrs. Ozman's experience and its acceptance by others, Parham began to spread the word of modern Pentecostalism in Kansas, Oklahoma, Missouri, and Texas. In 1905 he established a Bible school in Houston, Texas. Among those who attended was William J. Seymour (1870–1922), a black holiness preacher affiliated with the Church of God (Anderson, Indiana), who related the experience at Azusa Street, Los Angeles, California.

Parham is hardly mentioned in pentecostal history after 1906. The split between him and the emerging leadership of the movement began toward the end of that year when he arrived in Los Angeles to observe firsthand the revival about which he had read. He did not like what he saw. He felt that the revival had taken on elements of fanaticism and was quick in his words of reproof. The disagreement led to his immediate split with Seymour and the leaders of the revival in southern

California. Then early in 1907 he also resigned his role as Projector of the Apostolic Faith Movement, as a means of opposing the spirit of leadership and the attempts to organize the movement.

Returning to the East and Midwest, he took up his ministry and continued to preach. However, he was soon faced with accusations of scandalous personal behavior, which further ruined his reputation within the movement. Though he remained active until his death, his efforts were cut off from the movement as a whole. Those who received his ministry were eventually consolidated in a very loose fellowship centered on Baxter Springs, Kansas. The Apostolic Faith was not incorporated until 1976. No membership records have ever been kept, but there is a directory of churches and ministers.

In 1950 Baxter Springs also became the permanent site chosen for the group's Bible college. Following Parham's direction, the college charges no tuition, but operates on a freewill offering plan. No salary is paid to the faculty, who are also supported by freewill offerings.

Beliefs of the Apostolic Faith are similar to those of the Assemblies of God, and include a strong emphasis on the Bible, which, as the inspired word of God without error, contains the revelation of God's will for the salvation of all, and the divine and final authority for all Christian fact and life. There are areas of legitimate disagreement, such as baptism, predestination, and end-times, for which agreement is not necessary for salvation. No collections are taken, the ministry being supported by tithes. Organization is informal and congregational. There is a seven-person board of trustees that oversees the Bible college.

Membership: No membership records are kept by the Apostolic Faith. These are an estimated 10,000 adherents. In 1988 there were approximately 100 churches and 140 ministers.

Educational Facilities:

Apostolic Faith Bible College Baxter Springs, Kansas.

Online instruction and degrees are available from www.apostolicbiblecollege.org.

Periodicals: *Apostolic Faith Report*, monthly. Some issues downloadable from originalapostolicfaith.org.

Sources:

Apostolic Faith Bible College. www.apostolicbiblecollege.org.

Carothers, W. F. *The Baptism with the Holy Ghost*. Zion City, IL: The Author, 1907.

Goff, James R. *Fields White unto Harvest: Charles F. Parham and the Missionary Origins of Pentecostalism*. Thesis, University of Arkansas, Fayetteville, 1987.

Parham, Charles F. *A Voice of One Crying in the Wilderness*. Baxter Springs, KS: Apostolic Faith Bible College, 1910.

Parham, Sarah E. *The Life of Charles F. Parham*. Joplin, MO: Hunter Printing Company, 1930.

Association of Vineyard Churches

PO Box 2089, Stafford, TX 77497

The Association of Vineyard Churches was formed in 1986 but dates to an earlier Bible study group in Yorba Linda, California, formed in 1978 by John Wimber (1934–1998). The original group of approximately 150 affiliated with Calvary Chapel Church, an evangelical church in Costa Mesa, California, which had developed a number of affiliates throughout the United States. After a brief period of association, Wimber felt that his work, which included an emphasis upon the manifestation of the gifts of the Spirit to all age groups, was distinct from that of Calvary Chapel.

Closely approaching Wimber's perspective was the Vineyard Christian Fellowship, a congregation that had originated from a Bible study group formed by Kenn Gullikson in 1974. In 1982 Wimber changed his congregation's name to Vineyard Christian Fellowship of Yorba Linda. The following year he moved it to Anaheim, California, and within a short time more than 4,000 were attending Sunday services. By 1992 more than 6,000 attended regularly. Several other congregations merged with the two Vineyard fellowships, and Vineyard Ministries International was created to direct the outreach of the movement (Wimber's international and interdenominational outreach). Wimber became the object of much media attention, especially after his being asked to teach a course at Fuller Theological Seminary in Pasadena, California, concerning divine healing. In the wake of the publicity, the movement grew rapidly as both independent pastors and congregations, at first mostly in southern California, affiliated. However, the movement lacked a structure to deal with the increased size and geographic spread of the movement. The church needed a means to ordain pastors and credential churches and ministers. In 1986 leaders in the movement organized the Association of Vineyard Churches.

The churches affiliated with the association are evangelical in theology, with a distinct emphasis upon the ministry of the gifts of the Spirit and a strong focus on church growth and evangelism. There are eight U.S. Vineyard regions, each being a cluster of churches grouped together by relationship and location facilitated by an Area Pastoral Care Leader (APCL). The APCLs work together with the Regional Overseer (RO) to provide leadership and encouragement to the Vineyard churches. Berten Waggoner now serves as the national director and president of the Association of Vineyard Churches.

The Association asserts that the Bible is the final authority in matters of faith and practice, and is the basis for the Vineyard Statement of Faith, a 12-point doctrinal statement that may be downloaded from the association's website. A collection of theological and philsophical statements is also available.

Membership: In 2007 there were more than 1,500 Vineyard churches worldwide.

Educational Facilities:

Vineyard Leadership Institute provides two-year programs for local Vineyard churches.

Vineyard Bible Institute (www.vineyardbi.org) is an Internet-based distance-education program for lay leaders.

Periodicals: *Cutting Edge*, quarterly. • *Emerge*, online publication available in PDF format from www.vineyardusa.org.

Sources:

Association of Vineyard Churches. www.vineyardusa.org.

Loftness, John. "A Sign for Our Times!" *People of Destiny Magazine* 3, no. 4 (July/August), 1985.

Nerheim, Oywind. *Church Conflict: The Pastoral Overseer's Authority Base in a Relationship Based Church Movement Like the Vineyard*. Th.M. dissertation. Pasadena, CA: Fuller Theological Seminary: 2000.

Wimber, Carol. *John Wimber*. London: Hodder & Stoughton Religious, 1999.

Wimber, John, with Kevin Springer. *Power Evangelism*. *Praise Offerings*. Anaheim, CA: Vineyard Christian Fellowship, 1977.

Bethel Temple/Bethel Fellowship International

2919 SW 312 Pl., Federal Way, WA 98023-7860

The Bethel Temple traces its beginnings to 1914, when William Henry Offiler, an Englishman who had migrated first to Canada and then to Spokane (where he came into contact with the Salvation Army), settled with his family in Seattle where he attended the Pine Street Mission. Following two brief moves in the inner city, the mission settled in a newly remodeled building in 1920, and the name Bethel Temple placed on the new church. It was the first Pentecostal congregation in the state of Washington, and for many years broadcast a radio ministry, conducted from an organ bench by Offiler, who became one of the first radio preachers in 1925. A Bible school opened in 1952 was discontinued in 1987.

Now called Bethel Fellowship International, the fellowship exists to facilitate and nurture meaningful relationships among member ministers, equipping and enabling them to be more effective in their callings, for the purpose of building and multiplying strong local churches at home in the United States and for the furtherance of fulfilling the great commission through missionary outreach throughout the world. A nonprofit corporation, its members minister throughout the United States, particularly in the Pacific Northwest, as well as Indonesia, Japan, Peru, Africa, and the Netherlands.

Bethel Fellowship International is in fellowship with Ministers Fellowship International (837) headquartered in Portland, Oregon.

Membership: In 1987 there were approximately 300 members in eight congregations in the United States.

Periodicals: *Pentecostal Power*.

Sources:

Bethel Fellowship International. www.bethelfellowshipinternational.com.

Calvary Alliance of Churches and Ministries

c/o Calvary Revival Church, 5833 Poplar Hall Dr., Norfolk, VA 23502

The Calvary Alliance of Churches and Ministries was founded in 1998 by Bp. B. Courtney McBath, a graduate of the Massachusetts Institute of Technology, a Pentecostal minister, and the senior founding pastor of Calvary Revival Church in Norfolk, Virginia. After leaving a career in the technical field, in 1990 McBath became a fulltime minister. Throughout the 1990s, together with his wife and co-pastor Janeen L. McBath, he grew Calvary Revival Church into a 7,000-member congregation with an affiliated K–12 parochial school. Though a full-time minister, McBath returned to school and earned an M.A. degree in Biblical studies (Regent University) and a D.Min. (Providence Bible College and Theological Seminary). He is now an adjunct professor at Regent University.

One important aspect of his church's ministry is the "The Voice of Revival," a weekly television broadcast. This program is aired both within and outside the United States, and became particularly popular in Nigeria. It provided a base for the jump in the scope of McBath's leadership in 1998. In 2006, McBath led in the founding of the Discover Life Center, a seven-acre residence facility for men coming out of incarceration and drug addiction.

The Calvary Alliance is a Trinitarian Pentecostal body that holds to the plenary verbal inspiration of the Bible. It practices baptism by full immersion. It emphasizes speaking in tongues and the gifts of the spirit, divine healing, and leading the spirit-filled life.

The Alliance believes in a theocratic church leadership, consisting of a senior minister under apostolic authority—who qualifies on the basis of the call of God, spiritual life, domestic life, character, and ability to rule—along with the plurality of eldership. McBath is the presiding bishop of the Alliance.

Membership: In 2008 the alliance reported 28 member congregations, over half of which were in Virginia. Through the Alliance, McBath oversees more than a 100 congregations in the United States, Europe, and Africa.

Sources:

Calvary Alliance of Churches and Ministries. www.calvaryalliance.org/.

McBath, B. Courtney. *Living at the Next Level: Transforming Your Life's Frustrations into Fulfillment through Friendship with God*. New York: Howard Books, 2008.

————. *Maximize Your Marriage*. Lake Mary, FL: Creation House, 2002.

Calvary Chapel

3800 S. Fairview Rd., Santa Ana, CA 92704

In 1965 Chuck Smith (b. 1935), an independent minister who was the pastor of a fairly large and growing congregation in Corona, California, accepted a call to pastor a very small congregation (25 adults), Calvary Chapel, in Costa Mesa, California. At that time many "hippies" populated the oceanfront near Costa Mesa. His outreach to these people lead to the conversion of thousands of young people. He instituted a series of discipleship homes where they received training. Services

were held every night of the week at a small building in Costa Mesa. This church became known as a center of the "Jesus People Revival" that moved across the United States in the early 1970s. As membership and fame grew, other Calvary churches were established in various communities, and individuals who had visited the church began congregations modeled on Calvary. By 2008 it was one of the ten largest Protestant churches in the United States.

Calvary Chapel has developed a simple statement of belief that emphasizes its nondenominational character. The church refuses to overemphasize those doctrinal differences that have divided Christians in the past. Agape (God's Divine Love) is held as the only true basis of Christian fellowship. Emphasis is placed on a "verse by verse" expository type of biblical teaching. The church believes in the validity of the Gifts of the Holy Spirit for today, but there is no emphasis on speaking in tongues as the necessary sign of baptism of the Holy Spirit. Prophesy in the Scripture is one of the focal points, and many of Pastor Smith's books that relate the expectation of seeing some of the predicted events take place in this generation.

Calvary Chapel has developed a variety of outreach ministries. The most notable is "The Word for Today," which includes cassettes, videotapes, books, radio shows, and other communicative sources for teaching the Bible. Pastor Smith's radio and television programs are heard in more than 350 cities nationwide. Calvary Chapel also broadcasts its services in video and audio live over the Internet, and maintains an archive of previous broadcasts and Bible studies. The Calvary Chapel Audio Ministry provides sound-system design, equipment, installation, and support for the media needs of fellowships worldwide.

The Bible College, founded in 1975, with the main campus at Murrieta Hot Springs, California, has extension campuses throughout the United States and in York, England; Millstadt, Austria; Kiev, Ukraine; Moscow, Russia; Lima, Peru; and the Philippines. In 2008 enrollment was 5,000 students. It operates two conference centers and a youth camp. In addition, Calvary Chapel supports Wycliffe Bible Translators in Africa; Missionary Aviation Fellowship, comprising teams of aviation, communications, and technology specialists working in Africa, Asia, Eurasia, and Latin America; and Open Doors, to purchase a ship that, in tandem with a barge, delivered a million Bibles to mainland China.

Membership: In 2008 Calvary Chapel of Costa Mesa reported 1,340 affiliate Calvary Chapels around the world, and more than 20,000 members.

Educational Facilities:

Day School (K–12), Costa Mesa, California.

Calvary Audio Ministry, Silverton, Oregon.

Calvary Bible College, Murrieta, California.

Calvary Chapel Christian Camp, Green Lake Valley, California.

Sources:

Calvary Chapel. www.calvarychapel.com.

Ellwood, Robert S., Jr. *One Way*. Englewood Cliffs, NJ: Prentice-Hall, 1973.

MacIntosh, Michael K., and Raul A. Ries, producers. *A Venture in Faith: The History and Philosophy of the Calvary Chapel Movement*. VHS tape. Diamond Bar, CA: Logos Media Group, 1992.

Smith, Chuck. *Charisma vs. Charismania*. Eugene, OR: Harvest House Publishers, 1983.

————. *The Final Curtain*. Costa Mesa, CA: Word for Today, 1984.

————. *Calvary Chapel Distinctives: The Foundational Principles of the Calvary Chapel Movement*. Costa Mesa, CA, 1993. Available from www.calvarychapel.com/library/smith-chuck/books/ccd.htm.

Calvary Ministries, Inc., International (CMI)

PO Box 11228, Fort Wayne, IN 48656-1228

Calvary Ministries, Inc., International (CMI) was founded in 1971 as an umbrella organization for those congregations and ministries developed from the work of Calvary Temple, an independent Pentecostal church in Fort Wayne, Indiana. Calvary

Temple was begun in 1956 by Dr. Paul E. Paino (d. 2005), a graduate of the Assemblies of Gods Central Bible Institute in Springfield, Missouri. Under his leadership, CMI's membership grew to 5,000. In 1978 a new building complex was erected to house the expanding program.

In 1969 six men approached Paino for training in the ministry and ordination. The next year several more came for the same reason. In 1972 a more permanent means of training was established with the Christian Training Center and the Paul and Timothy Internship program. Among the early graduates of the center were those ready to begin pastoral ministry and plant new congregations. In part, Calvary Ministries, Inc., International was created to facilitate these students' ordinations and credentialing as well as to provide structure for the planting and establishing of new congregations.

CMI is a nonprofit, religious corporation that helps establish and strengthen local churches. It follows a blending of Episcopal and Presbyterian polity, with each member church completely self-governing and autonomous. CMI maintains Bible colleges and camps and offers counseling and other services to its members.

During the early years of the Jesus People Revival—a national interdenominational revival movement among young adults that began on the West Coast in the late 1960s—the church in Fort Wayne sponsored a Jesus People coffeehouse ministry called Adam's Apple. The Apple hosted such Christian music artists as Nancy Honeytree, the band Petra, and Jeoff Benward. In addition, a number of CMI's early church planters came from the ranks of Adam's Apple members. The Apple no longer exists, but in its place are several thriving youth ministries around the tristate area (Indiana, Illinois, and Wisconsin).

Calvary Ministries' statement of faith is Trinitarian, pre-millennial, and Pentecostal. The Bible is considered entirely sufficient for faith and practice. Other tenets of faith include belief in the spiritual new birth of repentant sinners, the Holy Spirit Baptism, the Church of Jesus Christ as habitation of God through the Spirit, and the Second Coming of Christ.

CMI has expanded from Indiana to 15 other states, with regional offices in Indiana; Pennsylvania (northeastern region); Hamilton, Ohio (central region); Grand Rapids, Michigan (Great Lakes region); and Estero, Florida (southeastern region). CMI offers camps in the Great Lakes region, Richmond, Indiana, and Erie, Pennsylvania. As of 2008 there were four active regions with four active districts: Indiana, Michigan, Ohio, and Pennsylvania–New York. There are also CMI presences in India, Kenya, Nigeria, Ghana, Togo, Rwanda, Uganda, and Tanzania.

Membership: In 2008 Calvary Ministries reported 150 churches and approximately 300 pastors and ministers.

Educational Facilities:

Central Theological College, Auburn, Indiana.

Christian Training Center, Greensburg, Pennsylvania.

Periodicals: *CMI Connect*. • *CMI Newsletter*, published online.

Sources:

Calvary Ministries, Inc., International. www.cmifellowship.com/.

Canadian Assemblies of God
6724 Fabre St., Montreal, QC, Canada H2G 2Z6

Italian Presbyterians were the first of the Italian Canadians to receive the baptism of the Holy Spirit and experience speaking in tongues. Although some Italians in Chicago became Pentecostals as early as 1907 and began missionary work in the United States, the Canadian work had an entirely independent origin, beginning in 1913 in Hamilton, Ontario, with the ministry of a Christian-Jewish missionary named Cohen. In 1914 two of the men who had received the baptism, Charles Pavia and Frank Rispoli, took the experience to Toronto, where they visited door-to-door in the Italian community. By 1920 the fervor had spread to Montreal and other Italian-Canadian communities. Among the early leaders of the movement were Luigi Ippolito and Ferdinand Zaffuto.

Upon his return to the United States, evangelist Cohen informed the Italian Pentecostals in Chicago of the Canadian group, and a delegation visited the Hamilton and Toronto churches. The doctrine and practice of the Canadian Assemblies of God (formerly known as the Italian Pentecostal Church of Canada) is similar to that of the Pentecostal Assemblies of Canada, with whom they share fraternal relations. The Canadian Assemblies of God views their mission as serving the Italian community and all Canadians, regardless of language, nationality, or race, in proclaiming the Gospel of Jesus Christ. A missionary program is supported in the Dominican Republic.

Membership: In 2008 the church reported 21 congregations and 44 ministers in Canada. In 1997 there were 5,000 members worldwide, of which approximately 3,300 were in Canada.

Educational Facilities:

Eastern Pentecostal Bible College, Toronto, Ontario, Canada.

Italian Bible Institute, Rome, Italy.

Periodicals: *Voce Evangelica* (Evangel Voice).

Sources:

Canadian Assemblies of God. www.caogonline.org.

De Caro, Louis. *Our Heritage: The Christian Church of North America*. Sharon, PA: General Council, Christian Church of North America, 1977.

Zucchi, Luigi. "The Italian Pentecostal Church of Canada: Origin and Brief History." Montreal: Italian Pentecostal Church of Canada, 1993.

Christ Gospel Churches International
2614 Hwy. 62, Jeffersonville, IN 47130

Christ Gospel Churches International is a conservative Pentecostal association founded in the 1950s by Rev. Bernice R. Hicks. It shares its major beliefs with other Pentecostal bodies, especially as they are set forth in the Apostles' Creed. The churches work to establish places of Christian worship and fellowship and to promote Christians' relationship to Jesus Christ. They believe in the baptism of the Holy Spirit with the evidence of speaking in tongues. Worship is celebratory and exuberant, with members singing, shouting, and dancing; during times of silence, members study the Bible. Rev. Hicks remained active in her ninth decade, preaching two to four services per week in addition to writing books and training materials and traveling extensively.

The uniqueness of the church lies not so much in its core teachings as in the way that Hicks tied together the spiritual themes and biblical principles. Hicks believed that the Old Testament tabernacle was laid out in the form of a cross and that it serves as a useful metaphor for Christians in their spiritual experience as they grow to maturity in Christ. She laid out her teachings on the Old Testament tabernacle and other themes in more than 100 books and booklets.

Church members are taught to follow standards of holiness. These include the admonition for women not to wear makeup or cut their hair. Everyone dresses modestly. Although Christ Gospel Churches hold a Bible-centered belief and maintain conservative behavior standards, they do not claim to be the only Christian group attaining salvation and teach that Christians everywhere should rejoice whenever the name of Christ is upheld. Believing that people being united in the love of Christ is of great importance, the churches came early to the idea of racially integrated congregations. Although the churches practice the biblical principle of tithing, they place a lesser emphasis on giving and fundraising than do most denominations.

In Mexico, Christ Gospel maintains two orphanages, oversees 500 churches and a Bible school, and sponsors a printing plant that produces Christian material in Spanish for dissemination in Mexico, Central and South America, and Spain. India has more than 400 Christ Gospel Churches, and there are affiliated churches in New Zealand, Holland, Iceland, Romania, Spain, the Philippines, the Faroe Islands,

Jamaica, Haiti, South Africa and other African nations, England, Germany, Japan, Sweden, Mongolia, Russia, and Central and South American nations.

The churches support a radio broadcast ministry heard over the Voice of Europe, Radio Africa, Hope Radio in Ireland, Radio Fax in England, and many other stations worldwide.

Membership: Not reported. In 2008 more than 70 congregations were affiliated with Christ Gospel in the United States, and Christ Gospel Churches International, Inc., coordinated a worldwide organization of more than 1,400 affiliated churches in 135 countries.

Sources:

Christ Gospel Church. www.christgospel.org/.

Churches of the Kingdom of God
Current address not obtained for this edition.

The Churches of the Kingdom of God is a small Pentecostal body that emphasizes Jesus' message of the kingdom as the basic proclamation of the Gospel. According to Elder F. H. Reese, a prolific writer for the churches, Jesus came preaching the kingdom, which he declared to be "at hand." It is entered by repentance and being born again and is open to all. The kingdom was prepared from the foundation of the world, but it came in power only at Pentecost when the Spirit descended upon the early disciples. During the 1960s, Reese wrote a series of tracts on the kingdom of God theme.

Membership: Not reported.

Sources:

Reese, F. H. *Entering into the Kingdom of God*. Gravette, AK: Churches of the Kingdom of God, n.d. 8 pp.

————. *The Gospel of the Kingdom of God*. Gravette, AK: Churches of the Kingdom of God, n.d. 16 pp.

————. *The Promise of the Father*. Gravette, AK: Churches of the Kingdom of God, n.d. 12 pp.

Congregational Bible Churches International
PO Box 165, Hutchinson, KS 67501

Congregational Bible Churches International is a full gospel Pentecostal body established in 1977 through the merger of the Way Open Door Church and the Independent Holiness Church. Formerly known as the Congregational Bible Holiness Church, it adopted its present name in 1988. The Independent Holiness Church began in 1922. The Way Open Door Church—formerly affiliated with the General Council of Congregational Christian Churches—included congregations that had severed ties with that organization when it merged with the Evangelical and Reformed Church to become the United Church of Christ. Dr. M. L. Webber, president of the Open Door Church at the time of the 1977 merger, has continued to serve as international president of the Congregational Bible Churches since its formation.

The Churches' doctrine is similar to that of the Assemblies of God and asserts faith in the Bible as the infallible Word of God, the Trinity, the deity of Jesus Christ, the baptism of the Holy Spirit, and the sanctification of Christians by the Holy Spirit. Members believe in the future rapture of the church, in which Christians will be taken from the earth before the period of Great Tribulation, and in the eventual resurrection of all to heaven or eternal punishment.

The church is headed by a national and an international board over which the president of the church sits as chairman.

Membership: In 1990 the church had approximately 100,000 members in 500 churches worldwide, of which 10,000 members and 60 churches served by 100 ministers were in the United States. Missionary work is pursued in Guyana, Jamaica, Haiti, Puerto Rico, Singapore, India, Nigeria, Ghana, and Liberia.

Periodicals: *Congregational Bible Revival News*.

Elim Fellowship
1703 Dalton Rd., Lima, NY 14485-9516

In 1924 Rev. Ivan Quay Spencer (1888-1970) and his wife, Minnie B. Spencer, opened a Pentecostal Bible institute in Endicott, New York, to train young men and women for full-time revival ministry. Graduates of the Elim Bible Institute formed the Elim Ministerial Fellowship in 1933, which eventually became the Elim Fellowship in 1972. In 1951 the school moved to Lima, New York, where it occupies the campus of the former Genesee Wesleyan Seminary, founded in the nineteenth century by the Methodist Church.

The doctrine of the Fellowship is similar to that of the Assemblies of God, with a strong emphasis on the Holy Spirit-filled and sanctified life of the believer. Spencer was strongly affected by the Latter Rain revival, which began in Canada in 1948. He and others brought the revival to the school, publicized it in the Elim Herald, and took a leadership role in spreading the renewed emphasis on the gifts of the Spirit being poured out on God's people in the last days.

Elim Fellowship offers assistance to missionaries, credentials for ministers, and counseling for individuals and churches. The fellowship is committed to fervent witness to the Gospel, with their worship and services encompassing both genders, all races, and all ethnic groups.

The fellowship is governed congregationally and holds an annual meeting each spring at Lima. Elim Fellowship–sponsored missionaries are currently at work around the world, on all continents. The founder's son, I. Carlton Spencer (b. 1914), succeeded his father in the leadership of the fellowship, overseeing it from 1947 to 1985. In 2008 Ronald Burgio was the president. The fellowship holds membership in the Evangelical Council for Financial Accountability (NFCA); the National Association of Evangelicals (NAE); the International Pentecostal Association (IPA); the Pentecostal/Charismatic Churches of North America (PCCNA); the Charismatic Leaders' Fellowship (CLF); and the North American Renewal Services Committee. Elim Fellowship's international ministries began in East Africa in 1938 and have since expanded into many countries in Latin America, Europe, and Asia.

Membership: In 2008 the fellowship reported 85 churches in 14 states.

Educational Facilities:

Elim Bible Institute, Lima, New York. www.elim.edu.

Periodicals: *F.A.M.I.L.Y.*, monthly • *Elim Herald*

Sources:

Elim Fellowship. www.elimfellowship.org/.

Meloon, Marion. *Ivan Spencer, Willow in the Wind*. Plainfield, NJ: Logos International, 1974.

Veach, Edith Adele. *Elim: Living in the Flow: Insights for Moving in the River of God*. Lima, NY: Elim Bible Institute, 1999.

Faith Christian Fellowship International (FCFI)
6400 National Rd. E #797, Richmond, IN 47374

Faith Christian Fellowship International is an association of Pentecostal ministers and churches founded in 1979 by Bp. William Hildreth and his wife Hattie Hildreth. (It should not be confused with the organization of the same name founded in 1977 by Buddy and Pat Harrison and based in Tulsa, Oklahoma.) The Hildreths were joined by a group of Pentecostal ministers who shared a common vision, were likeminded in belief, and focused on what they saw as the apostolic ministry of the New Testament church. The fellowship they created was to serve full gospel ministers, churches, and missionary endeavors. The fellowship exists primarily to provide legal covering and credentials for independent ministers, congregations, evangelistic associations, missionary associations, and ministry organizations.

The fellowship provides seminars and conferences, minister's fellowships, assistance with establishing new ministries, and some inexpensive legal services for its members. Its organization is ultracongregational, and it makes no claim of ecclesiastical authority over either churches or church members. Local churches and ministries are allowed to ordain ministers as they see fit.

The fellowship's doctrine is similar to that of the Assemblies of God, affirming belief in the Trinity, salvation in Christ, the authority of the Bible, and the baptism of the Holy Spirit. The two ordinances of baptism and the Lord's Supper are recognized. Members practice the laying on of hands for healing, conferring office, and the reception of the Holy Spirit.

Membership: Not reported.

Sources:

Faith Christian Fellowship International. www.fcfi.us/.

Fellowship of Christian Assemblies (FCA)

4909 East Buckeye Rd., Madison, WI 53716-1898

The Fellowship of Christian Assemblies (FCA) began in 1922 in St. Paul, Minnesota, as an unincorporated fellowship of evangelical Pentecostal churches. About 25 ministers from three small Scandinavian-oriented groups joined ranks under the banner Independent Assemblies of God (IAG). The current name was adopted in 1973.

Several of the founding key figures had Scandinavian Baptist heritage, with its stress on local church autonomy and voluntary interchurch cooperation. They included Arthur F. Durham, of the Scandinavian Baptists in Chicago; Bengt Magnus Johnson, with a Baptist background that included a vigorous stand on local-church autonomy; A. A. Holmgren, of the same heritage; and Arthur F. Johnson, who became mentor to Elmer C. Erikson, whose ministry was an influential center in Duluth, Minnesota, for more than four decades. The first period of IAG/FCA history emphasized autonomy, with conferences and other interchurch ministries spearheaded by area "leadership churches." Its subsequent history involved a steady quest for intentional, cooperative ministries planned and led on a broad associational basis.

The fellowship was incorporated in 2001. Its process includes national and regional committees, with emphases in the areas of missions, ministry, and congregational life. Initiatives may arise locally (area clusters), regionally, or nationally. It emphasizes extensive information flow. A national coordinator serves as a channel for information and motivation.

National conferences, which include the FCA of Canada, are planned by annually selected committees. Fellowship Press, a society with membership open to any FCA congregation, publishes the monthly FCA Leadership, FCA church bulletin inserts, and other informational material.

Regional conferences and area ministerial clusters attend to mutual concerns and projects. New ministers and churches seeking formal recognition in the fellowship directory generally develop contacts with area FCA churches and pastors, leading to recommendation by two pastors (the "Barnabas Plan"). Ministers and missionaries are credentialed by their local churches.

Membership: In 2008 the fellowship listed approximately 85 churches in the United States and 100 in Canada. A number of churches cooperating with the FCA are unlisted. Listed ministers and missionaries number about 215 in the United States and 280 in Canada. Churches of FCA/USA and Canada support missionary work in approximately 70 countries.

Educational Facilities:

Christian Life College, Mount Prospect, Illinois.

Seattle Bible College, Everett, Washington.

Southwest Bible College, Moreno Valley, California.

Living Faith Bible College, Caroline, Alberta, Canada.

Periodicals: *FCA Leadership.*

Sources:

Fellowship of Christian Assemblies. www.fcaequip.net.

Fellowship of Churches and Ministers, International (FCMI)

PO Box 2165, Reidsville, GA 30453

The Fellowship of Churches and Ministers, International (FCMI) is an association of Pentecostal/charismatic churches formed in the late 1980s through the efforts of its co-founders, Bill Ligon (who remains its president) and Ed Robbins. Member churches are located primarily in Georgia and neighboring states.

The FMCI's purpose, according to its constitution, is to provide membership and fellowship for churches and ministers of like faith and order who are concerned with the proclamation of the Gospel of Jesus Christ to the world. The fellowship emphasizes the autonomy of the local church, though member churches agree to a statement of doctrine that is in agreement with mainline Trinitarian Pentecostalism. It affirms that the baptism in the Holy Spirit as evidenced by speaking in tongues is for all believers, that a believer can be baptized contemporaneously with regeneration or any time subsequent to a regenerating experience, and that the baptism experience is separate and distinct from regeneration. In addition, the fellowship expects that the manifestations of the gifts of the Holy Spirit (I Corinthians 12), especially divine healing, will operate today as in ancient times. The fellowship expects members to tithe, and to live a life separated from the world in behavior standards.

It is primarily for the association of independent ministers and churches, but provides charters for congregations and credentials for ministers. The fellowship does not license or ordain—actions left to the local churches—but it does recognize such status for ministerial members, and issues annual credentials to all ministerial members in good standing.

The group is led by its executive board, which includes the fellowship's founders and its officers. The board is elected at the fellowship's annual meeting. The executive board and several presbyters (elders who serve as district coordinators) constitute the Presbytery.

Membership: In 2008 the FCMI reported 16 congregations associated with the fellowship, as well as two African congregations, one in Zimbabwe and one in South Africa.

Sources:

Fellowship of Churches and Ministers, International. www.fellowshipcmi.org.

Filipino Assemblies of the First Born Inc. (FAFB Inc.)

614 13th Ave., Delano, CA 93215

The Filipino Assemblies of the First Born Inc. (FAFB Inc.) was founded at Stockton, California, by the Rev. Julian Bernabe, an immigrant to the United States. The organization took place at a convention that met from June 26 to July 4, 1933. Headquarters, initially in Fresno, were moved to San Francisco in 1942 and to Delano, California, in 1943. Doctrine and practice are like those of the Assemblies of God; the group is primarily an ethnic church with preaching often done in the Filipino language. The FAFB Inc.'s international arm, the International Assemblies of the First Born (IAFB), is working to establish churches in Cambodia, Hong Kong, Honduras, Canada, Italy, and Australia. Reverend Bernabe, who was 90 years old in 2008, continues to preach Christian principles.

Membership: Not reported. In 1969 there were 15 churches in California and 17 in Hawaii.

Free Gospel Church, Inc.

c/o Chester H. Heath, PO Box 477, Export, PA 15632

Among the oldest of the organized Pentecostal groups, the Free Gospel Church, Inc., was founded in 1916 as the United Free Gospel and Missionary Society by two brothers, the Reverends Frank Casley and William Casley. It adopted its present name in 1957. An early emphasis on foreign missions led to initial efforts in Guatemala, though the work was lost to the Church of God (Cleveland, Tennessee), and China, which was closed after the Communists come to power in 1948. In doctrine the Free Gospel Church is similar to the Assemblies of God. It conducts missions in Sierra Leone, Ghana, Nigeria, India, Myanmar (Burma), and the Philippines.

All overseas missionaries receive a stated salary each month plus money for expenses such as housing and vehicles. Missionaries itinerate in as many churches as possible to raise funds toward their support and receive a monthly report of all funds received. All work at the Free Gospel Church's office is done on a volunteer basis, and other cost are kept to a minimum, making it possible for 98 percent of all receipts to be spent overseas. The church issues receipts to those who make contributions and sends out a bimonthly newsletter that keeps supporters informed of progress in the countries in which the church supports personnel.

Membership: In 2008 there were 12 clergy serving six congregations.

Educational Facilities:

Free Gospel Institute, Export, Pennsylvania.

Free Gospel Bible Institute, Northern Luzon, Philippines.

Christian Leadership College, Kono, Sierra Leone.

Periodicals: *Free Gospel Church Missions Newsletter*, available online from www.fgbi.org/Missions/FGMArchives.html.

Sources:

Free Gospel Church, Inc. www.fgbi.org/Missions/MissionsFr.html.

Full Gospel Evangelistic Association (FGEA)

1400 East Skelly Dr., Tulsa, OK 74105-4742

In the late 1940s a controversy developed in the Apostolic Faith Church over issues of taking offerings in church, visiting churches not in fellowship, foreign mission work, and using doctors. Some who supported these activities formed the Ministerial and Missionary Alliance of the Original Trinity Apostolic Faith, Inc., for which they were barred from fellowship. In 1952 they formed the Full Gospel Evangelistic Association (FGEA). Except for the points at issue, the doctrine is like that of the Apostolic Faith.

The FGEA fellowship, composed of individuals, member churches, and ministries, view their mission as proclaiming the word of God and the Gospel in the United States and worldwide. The fellowship reports that it invests tens of thousands of dollars per year in missionary work and ministry efforts in El Salvador, Kenya, Malaysia, Mexico, Russia, and Spain, as well domestic projects such as the Inner City Children in Phoenix, Arizona; the Navaho Indian Outreach in Shiprock, New Mexico; and church plantings in Missouri and Alabama.

Annual camp meetings are held in Oklahoma and Texas. The FGEA also holds an annual conference and conducts an annual men's retreat.

Membership: Not reported.

Educational Facilities:

Victory Bible Institute, Tulsa, Oklahoma.

Periodicals: *Full Gospel News*. Available online at the FGEA Web site.

Sources:

Full Gospel Evangelistic Association. www.fgeaonline.org.

Full Gospel Truth, Inc.

304 3rd St., East Jordan, MI 49727

Full Gospel Truth, Inc., is a Pentecostal church founded in 1951 in Michigan by Harley R. Barber, a Pentecostal minister, after he withdrew from his previous denominational affiliation. It quickly spread to neighboring states and by the mid-1950s was functioning in California.

Full Gospel Truth is a Trinitarian Pentecostal church whose doctrine is similar to that of the Assemblies of God. Among its teachings are the practice of baptism by immersion, footwashing, divine healing, and tithing. It advises members to become conscientious objectors to war. It teaches that persons of both sexes should have the privilege of ministering to the fullest, except in those areas of

church life that call for the exercise of authority; women should not exercise authority over men. The church expects the imminent return of Christ.

The church follows what it sees as a biblical organization as in Rom. 12:4, Eph. 4:11, and I Cor. 12:28. It thus recognizes seven offices to be filled: apostles, prophets, evangelists, pastors, teachers, governments, and helps. Nationally the church is organized theocratically under the guidance of a superintendent. The national officers meet annually in conference.

Membership: Not reported.

Periodicals: *Yours and Mine Share Paper*.

Sources:

Constitution and By-Law of the Full Gospel Truth, Inc. East Jordan, MI: Full Gospel Truth, n.d.

General Assemblies and Church of the First Born

200 N. Lawrence Ave., Fullerton, CA 92832

The General Assemblies and Church of the First Born, formed in 1907, is a small Pentecostal body without church headquarters or paid clergy. It has about 30 congregations across the country. Congregations are concentrated in Oklahoma and California, with individual congregations at Montrose and Pleasant View, Colorado, and Indianapolis, Indiana. Members believe in the Trinity; deny original sin, believing that we will be punished only for our own sin; and assert that man can be saved by obedience to the laws and ordinances of the gospel. There are four ordinances: faith in Jesus Christ, repentance, baptism by immersion, and laying on of hands for the gift of the Holy Spirit. The group makes use of all of the gifts of the Spirit and holds the Lord's Supper in conjunction with foot washing, but does not seek the help of doctors.

Elders oversee the local congregations, which are organized informally. Some elders are ordained and serve as preachers. No membership rolls are kept. The Indianapolis church has published a hymnal. There is an annual camp meeting in Oklahoma each summer.

Membership: In 2006, the church's directory included 121 congregations.

Remarks: Since the mid-1970s, the Church of the First Born has been involved in an ongoing controversy relative to the members' refraining from the use of medical doctors and withholding medical treatment for minors, several of whom have died. Trials following the deaths of the minors have had varying results, but, as the number has increased, courts have been less willing to forgive parents for allowing their children to die when medical treatment would have prevented their deaths. Colorado, where several deaths have occurred, moved to change laws in the 1990s, which tended to block prosecution of what was considered child abuse by negligence within religious groups.

General Council of Christian Church of North America (CCNA)

1294 Rutledge Rd., Transfer, PA 16154

The Christian Church of North America (CCNA) traces it origins to the revival that started at the Azusa Street Mission in Los Angeles and moved to Chicago in 1907. The Italian community there responded to the movement, and some of those who began a ministry later gathered in 1927 in Niagara Falls, New York, to formally organize the Christian Church of North America. The church's top priority is evangelism and especially mission work (including efforts to evangelize its homeland), as is illustrated by its finally incorporating in 1948 as the Missionary Society of the Christian Church of North America.

By 1963, in recognition of the original movement's transcending its roots in a single ethnic group to become a multiethnic church, the movement was renamed the General Council of the Christian Church of North America. The church resembles the Assemblies of God in its doctrinal stance. Its foreign missions arm, CCNA Missions, assists in the planting, nurturing, and expanding of churches and ministries in 40 countries worldwide.

Services offered by CCNA include an annual convention, pastors' retreats, youth conventions, women's and men's fellowships, and a department that attends to the needs of retired ministers and those in difficult circumstances. Member churches are located in Connecticut, Massachusetts, New Jersey, New York, and Pennsylvania.

CCNA is a member of the National Association of Evangelicals, the National Religious Broadcasters, and the Pentecostal Fellowship of North America. For all intents and purposes, its credentials are interchangeable with other Pentecostal organizations such as the Assemblies of God, the Church of God, and the International Church of the Foursquare Gospel.

Membership: In 2006 the CCNA's magazine listed 47 affiliated churches in five eastern states.

Educational Facilities:

CCNA School of the Bible, Middletown, New Jersey.

Periodicals: *Vista.*

Sources:

General Council of Christian Church of North America. www.ccna.org.

DeCaro, Louis. *Our Heritage: The Christian Church of North America.* Sharon, PA: General Council, Christian Church of North America.

General Council of the Assemblies of God

1445 N Boonville Ave., Springfield, MO 65802-1894

The General Council of the Assemblies of God was formed in Hot Springs, Arkansas, in April 1914 at a convention of Pentecostal ministers and churches. The council adopted a common body of doctrinal standards and consolidated missionary, ministerial, educational, and publishing efforts. The Word and Witness, edited by E. N. Bell (1866-1923), a forerunner of the weekly Pentecostal Evangel, was the first official periodical of the denomination.

The church's governmental structure is congregational on the local church level and presbyterial at the national level, where the General Council has centralized control over missionary, educational, ministerial, and publishing concerns. A 17-member executive presbytery serves as the church's board of directors and meets every other month. The church has more than 1,800 missionaries serving in 191 nations. In the United States, the Division of Home Missions oversees ministries to intercultural groups, military personnel, secular college campuses, Teen Challenge (a program for those with problems such as drug and alcohol abuse), and the opening of new churches. The Gospel Publishing House, the printing arm of the church, is one of the major publishers of Christian literature in the United States.

The threefold mission of the Assemblies of God is evangelism, discipleship, and worship. The church's cardinal doctrines include the Bible as the Word of God, the fall of humanity, and God's provision of salvation only through the death of His Son Jesus Christ, water baptism by immersion, divine healing, and the imminent return of Jesus for those who have accepted Him as Savior. The church's distinctive doctrine is the belief in the baptism of the Holy Spirit, an experience following salvation that is accomplished by speaking in other languages.

The Assemblies is in fellowship with the Pentecostal Assemblies of Canada. It is a member of the Pentecostal Fellowship of North America and cooperates with the Pentecostal World Conference.

Membership: In 2008 the AG reported more than 12,100 churches in the United States and 236,022 churches and outstations in 191 other nations.

Educational Facilities:

American Indian College, Phoenix, Arizona.

Assemblies of God Theological Seminary, Springfield, Missouri.

Bethany University, Scotts Valley, California.

Caribbean Theological College, BayamÛn, Puerto Rico.

Central Bible College, Springfield, Missouri.

Evangel University, Springfield, Missouri.

Global University, Springfield, Missouri.

Latin American Bible Institute, San Antonio, Texas.

Latin American Bible Institute of California, La Puente, California.

Native American Bible College, Shannon, North Carolina.

North Central University, Minneapolis, Minnesota.

Northwest University, Kirkland, Washington.

Southeastern University, Lakeland, Florida.

Southwestern Assemblies of God University, Waxahachie, Texas.

Trinity Bible College, Ellendale, North Dakota.

Valley Forge Christian College, Phoenixville, Pennsylvania.

Vanguard University, Costa Mesa, California.

Western Bible Institute, Phoenix, Arizona.

Zion Bible College, Barrington, Rhode Island.

Periodicals: *Today's Pentecostal Evangel (TPE)* • *Assemblies of God Heritage* • *Enrichment Journal* • *Christian Education Counselor* • *On Course* • *PrimeLine* (for seniors).

Sources:

General Council of the Assemblies of God. ag.org/top.

Brumback, Carl. *Suddenly from Heaven.* Springfield, MO: Gospel Publishing House, 1961.

Carlson, G. Raymond. *Our Faith and Fellowship.* Springfield, MO: Gospel Publishing House, 1977.

Menzies, William W. *Anointed to Serve.* Springfield, MO: Gospel Publishing House, 1971.

Perkin, Noel, and John Garlock. *Our World Witness.* Springfield, MO: Gospel Publishing House, 1963.

Grace International

c/o Grace Community Church, PO Box 591876, Houston, TX 77259-1876

Grace International was formerly known as the California Evangelistic Association (CEA), which began in 1933 (incorporated 1934) as the Colonial Tabernacle of Long Beach, California. Oscar C. Harms, a former pastor in the Advent Christian Church, had established the tabernacle. Additional assemblies became associated with it, and in 1939, it assumed the CEA name. In 1979 the name became Christian Evangelistic Assemblies (still CEA), and in February 2008 the CEA became Grace International, a non-denominational, independent organization working to show Christ to every individual throughout the world. It aims to provide covering, support, and resources to pastors and churches while allowing flexibility and independence. It is in essential doctrinal agreement with the Assemblies of God, except that it is amillennial.

Grace International has churches in more than 40 nations with fellowships, a seminary, bible colleges, pastors' conferences, orphanages, schools, and compassion ministries. Its current president is Steve Riggle.

Membership: In 2008 Grace International reported more than 10,000 members and more than 100 ministers on two 80-plus acre campuses.

Sources:

Grace International. www.ceanatl.org.

Constitution and By-Laws. Long Beach, CA: California Evangelistic Association, 1939.

International Church of the Foursquare Gospel

PO Box 26902, 1910 W Sunset Blvd., Ste. 200, Los Angeles, CA 90026-0176

Alternate Address: Canadian headquarters: Foursquare Gospel Church of Canada, B307–2099 Lougheed Hwy, Port Coquitlam, BC V3B 1A8, Canada.

HISTORY. The International Church of the Foursquare Gospel, commonly known as the Foursquare Church, was founded by Aimee Semple McPherson (1890–1944), the flamboyant and controversial pastor of Angelus Temple in Los Angeles, California. Aimee McPherson's mother, a member of the Salvation Army, had promised God to dedicate her daughter to the ministry. At the age of 17, the teenage Aimee McPherson was converted, baptized with the Holy Spirit, and soon married to evangelist Robert James Semple (1881–1910). In 1910 the couple traveled to China as missionaries; while serving there, Robert Semple died of malaria, just one month before the birth of their daughter, Roberta. With her daughter, Aimee McPherson returned to the United States where she later married Harold S. McPherson (1890–1968). They had a son, Rolf Kennedy McPherson (b. 1913). Together the McPhersons began to conduct independent, itinerant, Pentecostal evangelistic meetings. Following her divorce from Harold McPherson, Aimee McPherson continued the ministry. In 1917 she began a periodical, Bridal Call, which served her ministry for many years.

Unsupported and berated by other ministers who did not believe that women should speak from a pulpit, Aimee McPherson won success through her oratorical abilities, her charisma, her expounding the teaching of the Foursquare Gospel, and her use of unusual and previously untried methods that brought widespread publicity. During her early ministry, she spent much time with T. K. Leonard (1861–1946) and William H. Durham (1873–1912), both early Pentecostal leaders. In 1918 Aimee McPherson settled in Los Angeles and, with the help of those who had responded to her ministry, built and dedicated Angelus Temple in 1923. Throughout the remainder of her ministry, the temple was the focus of numerous spiritual extravaganzas, including religious drama, illustrated messages, and oratorios, which brought Sister Aimee, as she was affectionately called, a reputation for the unconventional. In 1926 Aimee McPherson disappeared for more than a month, and upon her return she said that she had been kidnapped. A major controversy developed, with critics claiming that she had disappeared of her own volition, yet her claim was never disproved.

Even before the temple was dedicated, an evangelistic and training institute had been opened to educate leaders who went on to found numerous Foursquare churches. The creation of some 32 churches in southern California by 1921 spurred the formation of the Echo Park Evangelistic Association, and in 1927, the International Church of the Foursquare Gospel was incorporated. The church also built and began operation of KFSG, the third-oldest radio station in Los Angeles. It sold the station in 2001.

Work expanded to Canada, first to Vancouver and then eastward to Ontario. The Western Canada District was set off from the Northwest District in 1964. The Church of the Foursquare Gospel of Western Canada was established as a provincial society in 1976. A federal corporation was created in 1981 and the Foursquare Gospel Church of Canada emerged as an autonomous sister church.

BELIEFS. The church's lengthy declaration of faith affirms the authority of Scripture and the traditional beliefs of Protestant evangelical Christianity. There are two ordinances, baptism and the Lord's Supper. Equal emphasis is placed on the baptism of the Holy Spirit and the Spirit-filled life and the gifts and fruits of the Spirit. Tithing is acknowledged as the method ordained of God for the support of the ministry.

ORGANIZATION. The organization of the church is vested in the president, a position held by Aimee McPherson until her death in 1944. Her son succeeded her, holding the post until his retirement in 1988. The sixth president is Jack Hayford. A board of directors, which includes the president and other appointed or elected members, serves as the highest administrative body for the denomination's business affairs. The Foursquare cabinet and executive council advise the board of directors and the president. The convention body has the sole power to make or amend the bylaws to give direction to the Foursquare movement. The convention body is composed of representatives from Foursquare Churches and the credentialed ministers of the International Church of the Foursquare Gospel. Throughout the United States, the church is divided into three regional centers covering a total of 73 districts, with each area overseen by a district supervisor.

Membership: In 2006 the church reported 260,644 members in the United States. In 2008 it reported approximately 36,000 Foursquare churches in 142 countries.

Educational Facilities:

L.I.F.E. (Lighthouse of International Foursquare Evangelism) Pacific College, San Dimas, California.

Pacific Life Bible College, Surrey, British Columbia. (Sponsored by the Foursquare Gospel Church of Canada.)

There are also more than 247 Bible colleges and institutes in foreign mission fields around the world.

Periodicals: *Advance* (also available in Spanish). • *Foursquare Missions Advance.*

Sources:

The Foursquare Church. www.foursquare.org.

Blumhofer, Edith L. *Aimee Semple McPherson: Everybody's Sister.* Grand Rapids, MI: William B. Eerdmans, 1993.

Cox, Raymond L., ed. *The Foursquare Gospel.* Los Angeles: Foursquare Publications, 1969.

Duffield Guy P., and Nathaniel M. Van Cleave. *Foundations of Pentecostal Theology.* Los Angeles: L.I.F.E. Bible College, 1983.

Epstein, Daniel Mark. *Sister Aimee: The Life of Aimee Semple McPherson.* New York: Harcourt Brace Jovanovich, 1993.

McPherson, Aimee Semple. *The Story of My Life.* Waco, TX: Word Books, 1973.

Sutton, Michael Avery. *Aimee Semple McPherson and the Resurrection of Christian America.* Cambridge, MA: Harvard University Press, 2007.

Lamb of God Church

612 Isenberg St., Honolulu, HI 96826-4532

The Lamb of God Church, founded in 1942 by Rev. Rose H. Kwan, is a small Pentecostal church with congregations located on Oahu and Molokai, Hawaii. The church primarily serves native Hawaiians. Following the death of Pastor Melvin Kwan in 2002 at age 72, the Lamb of God Church continued to be administered by Kaua and Michela Kwan.

Membership: In 2008 the church reported five congregations.

Educational Facilities:

Lamb of God Bible Schools in the cities of Honolulu, Hoolelua, Kaunakakai, and Waianae, on the island of Hawaii; and on the Kalamaula peninsula on Molokai.

Logos Christian Fellowship

8839 CR 44, Leesburg, FL 34788-9201

In the spring of 1989, Christopher Brian Ward, who had undergone a religious conversion at Calvary Chapel in Riverside, California, started a Bible study in his home in Leesburg, Florida. The following year it was incorporated as Calvary Chapel Leesburg. In May 1996 the congregation opened an Internet ministry dedicated to deliverance (from demonic possession), hippies (which the site describes as "wandering children"), and ufologists ("ufology" is a neologism that refers to people who study reports of unidentified flying objects). The site had received more than 1.5 million hits as of July 1, 2007.

In 1998 Calvary Chapel Leesburg changed its name to Logos Christian Fellowship of Leesburg. In 2001, because of concerns about the ministry to ufologists, Logos was ejected from the Calvary Chapel fellowship. The church continues as a charismatic fellowship, similar in doctrine to its parent body.

Since the break with Calvary Chapel, while continuing its main activity in Leesburg, Logos Christian Fellowship has launched a nationwide ministry directed toward hippies, ufologists, the needy, and the homeless. In April 2001, Brian Cronin and Ward wrote the Phat News of Mark, a Hippie Bible and Commentary Adapted from the King James Version. The mass distribution of copies has become a tool for reaching what is perceived to be a lost generation. Cronin and Ward attend annual Rainbow Gatherings, held by the counterculture community in the United States.

The fellowship sponsors ministries in Kenya and Guatemala in addition to food bank projects in Kenya, Africa, Haiti, Guatemala, Laos, Indonesia, Japan, and Tonga.

Membership: In 2008 the fellowship's Web site reported that more than 15,000 people have accepted its email invitation to "give their heart to the Lord." As of 2008, the fellowship reported that it had ordained some 70 ministers now serving across the United States, with additional ministers serving in Hungary, the United Kingdom, and Kenya.

Sources:

Logos Christian Fellowship. www.logoschristian.org.

Open Bible Standard Churches, Inc.

2020 Bell Ave., Des Moines, IA 50315-1096

The Open Bible Standard Churches resulted from a merger in 1935 of two evangelistic movements, the Open Bible Evangelistic Association and Bible Standard Conference. Both of these movements had their roots in the Azusa Street Mission in Los Angeles and the spreading Pentecostal revival. The former body had been founded by John R. Richey (1899–1984) in Des Moines, Iowa, in 1932 and the latter in Eugene, Oregon, by Fred Hornshuh (1884–1982) in 1919. At the time of the merger there were 210 ministers.

Doctrinally, the Open Bible Churches, as they have been called since 1996, affirm the Bible as the infallible Word of God, the Trinity, and the virgin birth, sinless life, miracles, resurrection, ascension, and deity of Christ. Believers experience the holiness, healing, and baptism of the Holy Spirit as evidenced by speaking in tongues. Open Bible is governed by a biennial representative convention that elects a national board of directors. It is a member of the National Association of Evangelicals and the Pentecostal/Charismatic Churches of North America, and supports the Pentecostal World Conference. Missions are conducted in 36 countries around the world.

Membership: In 2008 the churches reported 264 congregations in the United States and 1,408 worldwide, including 109 churches (composed of 2,000 members) in Canada. Outside the United States there were 130,449 members led by 2,068 ministers.

Educational Facilities:

Eugene Bible College, Eugene, Oregon.

Periodicals: *Message of the Open Bible* • *Jeff's Journal* • *In Touch*

Sources:

Open Bible Churches. www.openbible.org/.

Mitchell, Robert Bryant. *Heritage & Horizons*. Des Moines, IA: Open Bible Publishers, 1982.

———. *Heritage & Harvests: The History of the International Ministries of Open Bible Standard Churches*. Des Moines, IA: Open Bible Publishers, 1995.

Policies and Principles. Des Moines, IA: Open Bible Standard Churches, 1986.

Pentecostal Assemblies of Canada

2450 Milltower Ct., Mississauga, ON, Canada L5N 5Z6

News of the Pentecostal revival that had broken out at the little mission on Azusa Street in 1906 drew many people to Los Angeles, including several Canadians. Most prominent among them was Robert McAleister (1880–1953), who brought the revival to Ottawa. In addition, A. H. Argue, who encountered the first wave of the revival sweeping Chicago, returned to Winnipeg with its message. In 1907 he began a magazine, The Apostolic Messenger, to spread the word. Within a few years Pentecostal assemblies had been established across Canada.

Organization proceeded slowly, though as early as 1909 a Pentecostal Missionary Union was formed. In 1917 ministers from the eastern part of Canada met at Montreal and formed the Pentecostal Assemblies of Canada. Two years later, ministers in the west formed the Western Canada District of the Assemblies of God, attached to the United States group headquartered in Springfield, Missouri. In 1921 the eastern group also affiliated with the Assemblies of God. In 1922 the government charter was finalized.

Soon after the affiliation with the American Pentecostals, the Canadians began to see that they were at a disadvantage and gradually moved to separate themselves and assume the original name of the eastern organization. Headquarters were reestablished in Ottawa and later moved to Toronto. The organizational split (which implied no break in fraternal relations) occurred for three main reasons: First, the Canadians placed less emphasis on doctrine and were thus open to more latitude of belief. Second, the Canadians encompassed greater ethnic diversity, with one out of ten congregations not speaking English. Third, Canadian voices such as James Eustace Purdie, who argued for Canadian autonomy, were influential.

Headed by William Morrow, general superintendent, the Canadian assemblies largely agree with the Assemblies of God. They advocate tithing and have strict rules about divorce, especially among ministers. They are also fraternally related to the Pentecostal Assemblies of Newfoundland, with whom they share the same doctrinal statement. The Assemblies provide support to 130 missionary families in approximately 40 countries worldwide.

Membership: In 2008 the Pentecostal Assemblies of Canada reported that more than 235,000 people attend services in more than 1,100 churches across English- and French-speaking Canada, tended by more than 3,500 pastors and ministry leaders.

Educational Facilities:

Canadian Pentecostal Seminary, Langley, British Columbia, Canada.

Global University Canada/ International Correspondence Institute, Toronto, Ontario, Canada.

Horizon College and Seminary (formerly Central Pentecostal College), Saskatoon, Saskatchewan, Canada.

Institut Biblique du QuÈbec, Montreal, Quebec, Canada.

Master's College and Seminary, Toronto, Ontario, Canada.

Pentecostal Sub-Arctic Leadership Training (S.A.L.T.) College, Fort Smith, Northwest Territories, Canada.

Summit Pacific College (formerly Western Pentecostal Bible College), Abbotsford, British Columbia, Canada.

Vanguard College (formerly Northwest Bible College), Edmonton, Alberta, Canada.

Periodicals: *Testimony* • *50 Plus Contact*

Sources:

Pentecostal Assemblies of Canada. www.paoc.org/.

Atter, G. F. *The Third Force*. Peterborough, ON: College Press, 1970.

Brown, Victor G. *Fifty Years of Pentecostal History, 1933-1983*. Burlington, ON: Pentecostal Assemblies of Canada, Western Ontario District, 1983.

Holm, Randall. *A Paradigmatic Analysis of Authority within Pentecostalism*. Ph.D. dissertation, 1995. Laval University, Quebec, QC.

Kulbeck, Gloria Grace. *What God Had Wrought: A History of the Pentecostal Assemblies of Canada*. Toronto, ON: Pentecostal Assemblies of Canada, 1958.

Miller, Thomas, W. *Canadian Pentecostals: A History of the Pentecostal Assemblies of Canada*. Mississauga. ON: Full Gospel Publishing House, 1994.

———. "The Canadian 'Azusa': The Hebden Mission in Toronto." *Pneuma* 8:1 (1986): 5-30.

Pentecostal Assemblies of Newfoundland and Labrador (PAONL)

57 Thorburn Rd., PO Box 8895, Sta. A, St. John's, NF, Canada A1B 3T2

Pentecostalism spread to Newfoundland in 1910, and on Easter Sunday in 1911 the first assembly, Bethesda Mission, opened at St. John's. Spurred by the efforts of Victoria Booth-Clibborn Demarest (1889-1982), the mission was incorporated in 1925 as the Bethesda Pentecostal Assemblies of Newfoundland. The word "Bethesda" was dropped in 1930. That same year the assemblies, using a ship called The Gospel Messenger, moved into towns in Labrador. Eventually the name was changed to Pentecostal Assemblies of Newfoundland and Labrador (PAONL). Its superintendent in 2008 was H. Paul Foster (b. 1954).

The PAONL is a cooperative fellowship of Pentecostal believers who view their mission as discipleship, evangelism, instruction, fellowship, worship, and ministry. Though separate from the Pentecostal Assemblies of Canada, the PAONL maintains close fraternal ties with that church and holds to the same doctrinal position. The PAONL has published a number of books, newsletters, and reports.

Membership: In 2008 the assemblies reported 125 churches; in 1998 it reported 40,000 members and 425 ministries.

Periodicals: *Good Tidings*.

Sources:

Pentecostal Assemblies of Newfoundland. www.paonl.ca/.

Janes, Burton K. *History of the Pentecostal Assemblies of Newfoundland*. St. John's, Newfoundland: Good Tidings Press, 1997.

Pentecostal Church of God

PO Box 850, Joplin, MO 64834

HISTORY. The Pentecostal Assemblies of the USA was formed in Chicago, Illinois, in 1919 by a group of Pentecostal leaders. They chose the Rev. John C. Sinclair as their first chairman. The name was changed to the Pentecostal Church of God in 1922. (The words "of America" were added in 1936 and then dropped in 1979.) The church enjoyed a steady growth over the years. It moved its headquarters to Ottumwa, Iowa, in 1927. The following year the department of youth ministries was organized. The expansion was further manifested in the issuance of the first Sunday school material published by the church in 1937. Missionary support began as early as 1919 and was formalized in a church department in 1929.

BELIEFS. The church follows the central affirmation of evangelical Pentecostal Christianity: the authority of Scripture, the Trinity, the deity of Christ, and humanity's need of salvation in Christ. Members practice the ordinances of the Lord's Supper and baptism by immersion. The church affirms the baptism of the Holy Spirit received subsequent to the new birth (faith in Christ), which is evidenced by the initial sign of speaking in tongues. Foot washing is observed at the discretion of local congregations. Prayer for divine healing of bodily ills is a regular part of church life. The church is not pacifist but supports conscientious objectors in their search for alternative service. It advocates tithing.

ORGANIZATION. The church is headed by the general bishop, assisted by the general secretary, director of world missions, director of Indian missions, director of home missions, director of youth ministries, and director of the women's ministries. The church has three specialized ministries: King's Men Fellowship, Military Chaplains, and Senior Christian Fellowship. The church is divided into districts headed by bishops, presbyters, and secretary-treasurers. A general convention of ministers and delegates meets biennially with most district conventions meeting annually.

Membership: In 2007 the church reported more than 620,000 constituents in 58 nations, more than 4,825 churches and preaching stations, and more than 6,750 ministers.

Educational Facilities:

Messenger College, Joplin, Missouri.

Worldwide, there are 30 resident Bible schools and 34 extension training centers.

Periodicals: *The Pentecostal Messenger • The Missionary Voice*

Sources:

Pentecostal Church of God. www.pcg.org/.

General Constitution and By-Laws. Joplin, MO: Pentecostal Church of God, 1984.

Moon, Elmer Louis. *The Pentecostal Church*. New York: Carleton Press, 1966.

Wilson, Aaron M. *Basic Bible Truth*. Joplin, MO: Messenger Press, 1988.

———. *Our Story: The History of the Pentecostal Church of God*. Jopin: MO: Messenger Publishing House, 2001.

Pentecostal Church of New Antioch

Current address not obtained for this edition.

The Pentecostal Church of New Antioch is a Trinitarian Pentecostal church, which was founded in 1953 in New Antioch, Ohio, by Marshall M. Bachelor. Bachelor later moved the headquarters to Cleveland, Ohio. At the founding conference, he was elected president and general superintendent for life. The church professes belief in the baptism of the Holy Spirit as evidenced by speaking in tongues; spiritual gifts; the practice of baptism by immersion; the Lord'"s Supper; foot washing; divine healing; the imminent coming of Jesus Christ; and the resurrection of the dead. The church does not approve of divorce and remarriage.

The church is headed by its president and is assisted by six vice presidents, a secretary, and a treasurer. There is an annual national conference.

Membership: Not reported. In 1966 there were approximately 300 ministerial members serving churches across the United States and in Manitoba and Ontario, Canada, Jamaica, and England.

Sources:

Constitution and Bylaws o the Pentecostal Church of New Antioch, Inc. 1959. 18 pp.

Pentecostal Evangelical Church

1028 W Rosewood Ave., Spokane, WA 99208

The Pentecostal Evangelical Church was founded in 1936. Its first bishop, G. F. C. Fons, was the moderator of the Pentecostal Church of God of America in the period directly preceding the formation of the new body. Its doctrine is similar to that of the Pentecostal Church of God of America, and its polity is a mixture of congregationalism and episcopal forms. Each local church is autonomous. The general conference meets every two years and elects a general bishop (for a four-year term), a vice-president (for two years), and a district superintendent (as an assistant bishop). Missions are supported in the Philippines, Bolivia, India, and Guyana.

Membership: Not reported.

Periodicals: *Gospel Tidings*.

Sources:

General By-Laws of the Pentecostal Evangelical Church. Bremerton, WA: Pentecostal Evangelical Church, 1966.

Pentecostal Evangelical Church of God, National and International

Current address not obtained for this edition.

The Pentecostal Evangelical Church of God, National and International was founded at Riddle, Oregon in 1960. It holds to beliefs similar to those of the Assemblies of God. It ordains women to the ministry. A general convocation meets annually.

Membership: Not reported. In 1967 there were four congregations and 14 ministers.

Periodicals: *Ingathering*. • *Golden Leaves*.

Seventh Day Pentecostal Church of the Living God

3722 41st Ave., Brentwood, MD 20722

The Seventh Day Pentecostal Church of the Living God was founded in Washington, D.C., by Bishop Charles Gamble, a Pentecostal who had adopted some of the Old Testament practices including the seventh-day Sabbath. Gamble was a Roman Catholic and Baptist before becoming a Pentecostal. The church was incorporated on September 17, 1943, and remained in Washington, D.C., until 2006, when it moved to its Maryland location. In 1991 Elder Ira F. Baity became local pastor.

The church's mission is to spread the Word of Jesus Christ and provide an opportunity for revival. Church practices include baptism by immersion, the Lord's Supper as a memorial to the death of Jesus, tithing, and foot washing. The church believes that the seventh day of the week is the true Biblical Sabbath and preaches the entire Gospel from Genesis to Revelations.

Membership: Not reported.

Sources:

Seventh Day Pentecostal Church of the Living God. www.7dpc.com/.

Tony Alamo Christian Church

PO Box 6467, Texarkana, TX 75505

HISTORY. Tony Alamo Christian Church (also known as Tony Alamo Christian Ministries) has its origins in the Music Square Church (also known as the Holy Alamo Christian Church Consecrated), incorporated in 1981. The Music Square Church, in turn, had its origins in the Tony and Susan Alamo Christian Foundation, which was begun in the 1960s as a street ministry in Hollywood, California, by Susan Alamo (born Edith Opal Horn; d. 1982), an independent Pentecostal minister, and her husband, Tony Alamo (b. Bernie LaZar Hoffman, 1934), whom she had converted.

During its formative years the church became known as one segment of the Jesus People movement; however, it remained separate organizationally. As much of the larger movement was incorporated into various Baptist and Pentecostal churches, it survived as an independent organization heavily committed to an evangelistic street ministry. In the early 1970s the church became quite controversial and was heavily criticized because of the format its ministry had developed. Church members (associates of the foundation's ministry) generally worked the streets of Hollywood, inviting potential converts to evening services at the church that had, by that time, been established at Saugus, a rural community about an hour away. The mostly young recruits were taken by bus to Saugus for an evangelistic meeting and meal. Many of those who did convert remained in Saugus to be taught the Bible and become lay ministers.

In 1976, as the foundation grew, it purchased land at Alma and Dyer, Arkansas, where Susan Alamo had grown up. Transferring its headquarters there, the church developed a community of several hundred foundation associates and established printing facilities, a school, and a large tabernacle. As part of its rehabilitation program it began to develop several businesses in which associates (many of whom were former drug addicts) could begin a process of reintegration into society. As the organization expanded, churches (evangelistic centers) were opened in cities around the country (including Nashville, Tennessee; Chicago, Illinois; Brooklyn,

New York; and Miami Beach, Florida.) Associated with the church in Nashville, a retail clothing store was opened.

In 1985 a series of actions taken against the church severely disrupted its life. To support itself, the communal-style church had developed a number of businesses. Some former members who had aligned themselves with the anti-cult movement filed a complaint that they should be paid, leading to a series of lawsuits. That same year, the Internal Revenue Service stripped the church of its tax-exempt status. The church went to court to fight the IRS action. As the cases proceeded, Tony Alamo was charged with beating an eleven-year-old boy, and he disappeared.

During the next three years, Alamo remained a fugitive from justice, moving around the country and frequently calling in to radio talk shows. He was finally arrested in 1991. Although most of the charges, including the one of child abuse, were withdrawn, he was tried and convicted in 1994 on charges arising from the church's loss of tax exemption. The church continued to function in his absence, and he was released in 1998. The Alamo Christian Ministries Internet site refutes the charges of which Alamo was convicted.

BELIEFS. The Tony Alamo Christian Church is a Pentecostal church with doctrine similar to the Assemblies of God. It accepts the authority of the Bible (using only the King James Version) and places its emphasis on the preaching of Jesus Christ. The church condemns drug use, homosexuality, adultery, and abortions. Both Susan and Tony Alamo, who were born Jewish, developed a special interest in evangelism of Jews.

ORGANIZATION. The church has developed as an ordered community of people dedicated to evangelism. Converts who wish to remain associated with the church (i.e., to receive its training and participate in its ministry) take a vow of poverty agreeing to turn over all their real property to the church. In return the church agrees to provide the necessities of life (housing, clothes, food, medical assistance), including the education of children through high school. The church is headed by a three-person board presided over by Tony Alamo, the church's pastor. Alamo and the board set the policy and direction for the ministry.

Church centers are located in Fort Smith and Fouke, Arkansas, and Los Angeles, California. Approximately half the associates of the church reside on church property near Alma. Others reside at the several church centers around the United States. The headquarters complex includes housing units for the associates, a Christian school for grades one through twelve, a large community dining hall, and offices. Periodically associates are sent out on evangelistic tours around the United States, frequently using the established church centers as bases of operation. Services are held daily at each of the church centers and generally free meals are served.

The church maintains a radio ministry, broadcasting messages on 13 stations in Tennessee, Arkansas, New York, California, Georgia, Illinois, and Nevada, as well as four stations in West Africa, one in the Philippines, and worldwide via four short-wave frequencies. Copies of the messages, along with texts of newsletters, are also available atthe church Web site. The church publishes a variety of newsletters and evangelistic tracts that it passes out in the street and mails out nationally and internationally.

Membership: Not reported.

Periodicals: *World Newsletter*.

Sources:

Tony Alamo Christian Ministries. www.alamoministries.com/.

Alamo, Tony. *The Messiah According to Bible Prophecy: Absolute Proof That Jesus is the Only Way to the Kingdom of Heaven*. Texarkana, TX: Tony Alamo Christina ministries Worldwide, 2006.

Ellwood, Robert S., Jr. *One Way*. Englewood Cliffs, NJ: Prentice-Hall, 1973.

We're Your Neighbor. Alma, AK: Holy Alamo Christian Church Consecrated, [1987].

United Apostolic Faith Church

92 Bathgate Dr., Scarborough, ON, Canada M1C 3G7

The United Apostolic Faith Church (UAFC) is one of several churches that grew out of the early Pentecostal movement in the British Isles. In 1908 the Apostolic Faith Church was founded under the leadership of William Oliver Hutchinson (1864–1928). During the next decade the church spread across Great Britain, but it experienced a major schism just as World War I was beginning. In 1916 the congregations in Wales broke away and reorganized as the Apostolic Church. The original organization, which included churches in Scotland and England, reorganized as the United Apostolic Faith Church.

In 1912, prior to the schism, a congregation of the Apostolic Faith Church was established in Toronto, Ontario. After many years as a vital congregation, it all but died out during World War II. Revived in 1947, the congregation associated itself with the United Apostolic Faith Church.

The United Apostolic Faith Church is a Trinitarian Pentecostal body whose doctrine is similar to that of the Assemblies of God. It affirms the free salvation of Christ and the baptism of the Holy Spirit evidenced by speaking in tongues for all believers. It practices baptism by immersion and the Lord's Supper. Members believe strongly in divine healing, deliverance, and the casting out of demons. They tithe and attempt to manifest both the gifts and fruits of the Spirit in their daily lives.

The original Apostolic Church emphasized the centrality of the activity of the Holy Spirit who manifested God's will through the gifts of the Spirit. The leaders tended to seek direction from either prophecy or interpretation and speaking in tongues, especially in the appointment of church leaders and in making decisions about the guidance of the church. That practice led to some degree of fanaticism and underlay the schism of 1916. The UAFC attempted to respond to its critics over the years and developed a biblical form of ministerial leadership based on the five-fold ministry of Ephesians 4:11. The local church is led by a presbytery of a pastor and elders. The church in Toronto is known as Dayspring Christian Fellowship.

Membership: In 1997 there were two congregations of the United Apostolic Faith Church in Canada, both in Ontario, with approximately 300 members.

Sources:

Hathaway, Malcolm R. "The Role of William Oliver Hutchinson and the Apostolic Faith Church in the Formation of British Pentecostal Churches." *Journal of the European Pentecostal Theological Association* 16 (1996): 40–57.

Piepkorn, Arthur C. *Profiles in Belief: The Religious Bodies of the United States and Canada.* Vol. 3. San Francisco: Harper and Row, 1979.

United Full Gospel Ministers and Churches

Current address not obtained for this edition.

The United Full Gospel Ministers and Churches was established on May 16, 1951. Arthur H. Collins was the first chairman. Within a few years it had grown to include more than 50 clergy and a number of congregations. The church is governed by four executive officers, one of whom faces election at each annual meeting. The group has an affiliate in India known as the Open Bible Church of God, which was founded by Willis M. Clay, who at one time also served as treasurer of the United Full Gospel Ministers and Churches.

Membership: Not reported.

United Fundamentalist Church

Current address not obtained for this edition.

The United Fundamentalist Church was organized in 1939 by the Rev. Leroy M. Kopp of Los Angeles, California. It was at one time a member of the National Association of Evangelicals and accepts the association's doctrinal position. In addition, it is Pentecostal, and prophecy and healing are emphasized. Members are expected to believe that the divine healing of the sick is not only to honor the prayer of faith but is to be a sign to confirm the Word as it is preached at home and abroad (Mark 16:15–20). Signs are given until the end of this age, when they will no longer be needed.

The general officers of the United Fundamentalist Church, together with the territorial supervisors and state district superintendents, constitute a council that settles all doctrinal disputes. The Zion Christian Mission is sponsored in Jerusalem. Proselyting other Christian denominations is not practiced. A radio ministry was begun in 1940 by Kopp and still continues. The Rev. E. Paul Kopp has succeeded his father as head of the group.

Membership: Not reported. In 1967 there were approximately 250 ministers and missionaries.

Victory Churches International

Box 65077, North Hill P.O., Calgary, AB, Canada T2N 4T6

Alternate Address: U.S. headquarters: 1518 Brookhollow Dr., Santa Ana, CA 92705.

Victory Churches International is a charismatic Pentecostal fellowship of churches that dates to the founding of Victory Christian Church in Lethbridge, Alberta, in 1979 by Dr. George Hill and his wife, Dr. Hazel Hill. By 1988 there were five churches that had grown out of the Hills' ministry, which led to the creation of Victory Churches of Canada. Through the 1990s the association experienced rapid growth with the founding of almost 50 additional congregations across Canada and the opening of ministries around the world. Victory churches have adopted an organization based on the five-fold ministry of Ephesians 4:11 that includes apostles, prophets, pastors, evangelists, and teachers.

The ideal is to found new churches around the world and provide them with apostolic oversight. The immediate goal is to form apostolic teams that found new congregations in new cities and to identify a key apostolic leader in each country. After congregations are founded it is their job to found new congregations in nearby communities. The fellowship has developed a variety of models for developing new congregations depending on immediate resources.

Church membership agreements set forth the responsibilities of the local church toward the Victory Churches and vice versa. Each church contributes 5 percent of its general income to the national church planting and approximately another 5 percent for overseas missions.

The fellowship follows a mainline Pentecostal theology. It affirms the authority of the Bible as the inspired revelation of God and faith in the Triune God. New believers are invited to make a public declaration of their faith with water baptism. The ordinance of the Lord's supper is also celebrated. Common to all Pentecostal churches, the fellowship affirms the baptism of the Holy Spirit as an experience distinct from and following the new birth, evidenced initially by speaking in tongues, as a second work of God subsequent to faith in Christ that leads to the believer manifesting spiritual power in public testimony and Christian service. The evangelistic thrust of the fellowship is undergirded in part by a belief that those who have not accepted God's redemptive work will suffer eternal separation from the Godhead.

Congregations and associated ministries are found in Burma, Cambodia, China, Malaysia, Vietnam, India, Nepal, Thailand, Pakistan, the Philippines, Mexico, Guatemala, El Salvador, Costa Rica, Jamaica, England, Northern Ireland, Poland, and in Africa in Benin, Burundi, Cameroon, Gabon, Ivory Coast, Liberia, Malawi, Democratic Republic of the Congo, Mozambique, Ghana, Kenya, Nigeria, Rwanda, Sierra Leone, South Africa, Togo, and Uganda. Victory Churches International also produces a substantial number of training booklets and audio tapes of teachings by Drs. George and Hazel Hill.

Membership: In 2008 the Victory reported 70 churches in Canada, 20 in the United states, and an additional 45 in other countries.

Educational Facilities:

Victory Bible Colleges International, Calgary, AB; Grande Prairie, AB; Owen Sound, ON, Canada.

Victory Bible College International USA, Fountain Valley, California.

Worldwide, there are several Victory Bible colleges located in Asia, Africa, Latin America, and the Caribbean.

Sources:

Victory Churches International. www.victoryint.org/.

World Evangelism Fellowship
PO Box 262550, Baton Rouge, LA 70826-2550

World Evangelism Fellowship was founded as a result of the break between the Assemblies of God and the Pentecostal preacher Jimmy Swaggart (b. 1935), a televangelist who in 1988 was caught up in a scandal involving a prostitute. Swaggart's rise to fame had begun with his first radio broadcast in 1969 and the taping of his first television show in 1973. The eruption of the scandal provoked a major crisis, as Swaggart not only headed Jimmy Swaggart Ministries, with its extensive national and international broadcast presence, but also oversaw a Bible college that offered training for leaders for the Assemblies of God. In addition, Swaggart contributed a million dollars per month to the assemblies' missionary budget. The assemblies imposed a two-year suspension on Swaggart, including a one-year absence from any television shows. Swaggart rejected the penalty and was defrocked by the Assemblies of God. He reorganized his ministry and began anew.

World Evangelism Fellowship emerged as the new structure to bring together the various elements of Swaggart's continuing activities. Jimmy Swaggart Ministries oversees the telecast, which as of 2008 was broadcast across the United States and in some 50 countries; the SonLife Radio Network, comprising more than 70 radio stations nationwide covering over 5,000 towns, cities, and villages in the U.S. and around the world over the Internet; the Bible college and seminary where missionaries and ministers receive training; and the family worship center, the large congregation Swaggart pastors in Baton Rouge. Swaggart continues to conduct revival meetings both in the United States and overseas.

World Evangelism Fellowship offers credentials for lay Christian workers and licensed ministers, whom it defines as people who demonstrate clear evidence of a divine call on their lives and who commit themselves to preaching the gospel. It also provides for ordination of ministers who previously have held a license to preach and who have been engaged in active ministry long enough to demonstrate proof of a calling and proficiency. Licenses and ordination, as well as charters for local churches, are provided by the fellowship's credentials committee.

The fellowship oversees three national programs: Powerhouse, the children's ministry; Christian Cadet Corps for boys and young men; and Crossfire, for youths between the ages of 12 and 22.

Through his many years of ministry, Swaggart has written numerous books and booklets and has made many recordings (total recording sales exceeded 15 million worldwide as of 2008). Jimmy Swaggart Ministries makes available those writings that remain in print as well as a continuous stream of new items (including sermon and camp-meeting CDs and preaching DVDs), as well as cassette tapes and videos of sermons and Bible studies.

Membership: Not reported.

Educational Facilities:

World Evangelism Bible College and Seminary. Baton Rouge, Louisiana.

Family Christian Academy, Baton Rouge, Louisiana.

Periodicals: *The Evangelist.*

Sources:

Jimmy Swaggart Ministries: World Evangelism Fellowship. www.jsm.org/explore.cfm/familyworshipctr/worldevangelism.

Fontaine, Charles R., and Lynda K. Fontaine. *Jimmy Swaggart: To Obey God Rather than Men*. Berryville, AR: Kerusso Co., 1989.

Lundy, Hunter. *Let Us Prey: The Public Trial of Jimmy Swaggart*. Columbus, MS: Genesis Press, 1999.

Swaggart, Jimmy. *To Cross a River*. Attleboro, MA: Logos Associates, 1979.

————. *Armageddon: The Future of Planet Earth*. Baton Rouge, LA: Jimmy Swaggart Ministries, 1984.

World Harvest Church
4595 Gender Rd., Canal Winchester, OH 43110
Alternate Address: Breakthrough with Rod Parsley, PO Box 100, Columbus, OH 43216-0100.

World Harvest Church, founded in 1977, is the 12,000-member megachurch pastored by Rod Parsley (b. 1957), a poplar Pentecostal/charismatic leader and televangelist. As a young man, Parsley accepted the tutoring of a prominent Pentecostal leader, Lester Sumrall (1913–1996). The church operates from a mainline Pentecostal perspective that affirms the Bible as the infallible Word of God, the Trinity, the saving work of Christ, and the baptism of the Holy Spirit. It understands that Christ's redemptive work includes provisions for the healing of the human body in answer to believing prayer. While Parsley is the head of all ministries at the church, those who feel they are called to serve within the organization may work as elders, deacons, or lay leaders. Current facilities of the World Harvest Church include a 5,200-seat auditorium.

Breakthrough with Rod Parsley handles Parsley's broadcast ministry and produces his television show, *Breakthrough*, which is carried on 1,400 stations in North America and is shown in translation worldwide, including in the Middle East. Bridge of Hope, the world missionary arm, combines evangelism with various humanitarian programs.

Over the years, many otherwise independent ministers have been attracted to Parsley's ministry and others have received training at the World Harvest Bible College. In the 1990s, in response to a perceived need to build relationships and break barriers to fellowship, Parsley founded the World Harvest Church Ministerial Fellowship. It ordains pastors and accepts into membership pastors previously ordained elsewhere. The fellowship sponsors an annual Raise the Standard Pastors and Church Workers Conference.

In 2004 Parsley initiated the Center for Moral Clarity, an arm of the World Harvest Church that devotes itself to promoting public policy based on biblical teachings.

Membership: In 2008 the World Harvest Ministerial Fellowship reported 155 ministerial members in the United States and 2 in Canada. The group had 12,000 members in total.

Educational Facilities:

World Harvest Bible College, Columbus, Ohio.

Harvest Preparatory School, Columbus, Ohio.

Sources:

World Harvest Church. whc.rodparsley.com.

World Harvest Ministerial Fellowship. whcmf.rodparsley.com/.

Parsley, Rod. *The Day before Eternity*. Carol Stream, IL: Creation House, 1989.

————. *No More Crumbs: Your Invitation to Sit and Feast at the King's Table*. Carol Stream, IL: Creation House, 1989.

————. *On the Brink: Breaking through Every Obstacle into the Glory of God*. Nashville, TN: Thomas Nelson, 2000.

World Healing Fellowship (Benny Hinn)
Box 163000, Irving, TX 75016-3000
The World Healing Fellowship (WHF), an association of Christian ministers, pastors, church workers, missionaries, and educators, is part of the global ministry of Pentecostal televangelist Toufik Benedictus "Benny" Hinn (b. 1952). Hinn founded

the WHF in 1990, and it now operates in 190 countries of the world. The primary purpose of the WHF is to provide fellowship and resources for churches and Christian leaders and groups who identify with Benny Hinn's worldwide mission.

Benny Hinn was born in Jaffa, Israel. His earliest church experience was Greek Orthodox but he also studied at French Catholic schools in Israel. The Hinn family moved to Toronto, Canada, in 1968 and Benny became part of the Charismatic Christian community. His ministry started in Oshawa, Ontario, in 1974, and over the next two years, his work was influenced by the healing ministry of Kathryn Kuhlman (1907–1976). After her death, he claimed to be continuing her work and developed worship and healing services patterned on those Kuhlman had conducted.

For many years Hinn's ministry was located in Orlando, Florida, where he served as pastor of the Orlando Christian Center. He resigned his pastorate in 1999 and moved to southern California, and then moved to his ministry's world headquarters to suburban Dallas, Texas. He announced plans to build a new World Healing Center, but as of 2008 the center had not been opened.

Hinn holds evangelistic campaigns worldwide, and his daily television show *This Is Your Day* is seen in some 200 countries.

Membership: Not reported.

Remarks: Hinn's ministry is among several televangelist ministries whose finances have come under scrutiny by U.S. Senator Chuck Grassley of Iowa, ranking member of the Senate Finance Committee. In 2008 Sen. Grassley was organizing hearings on possible financial misconduct by these tax-exempt organizations. As this encyclopedia went to press, no specific charges or findings had emerged from those hearings.

Sources:

World Healing Fellowship. www.healingfellowship.com/.

Benny Hinn Ministries. www.bennyhinn.org/.

Hinn, Benny. *Good Morning, Holy Spirit*. Nashville: Thomas Nelson, 2004.

Worldwide Missionary Evangelism (WME)

1285 Millsap Rd., Fayetteville, AR 72701

Worldwide Missionary Evangelism (WME) was founded in 1956 by the prominent African missionary Morris Plotts (1906–1997) of the Assemblies of God. The organization had operated for many years as a missionary sending agency. In 1971 Plotts suggested that WME broaden its program and become active in home ministries and, more important, provide charters for churches and credentials for ministers in the United States, quite apart from the Assemblies of God. With that step WME became, in effect, a new Pentecostal denomination. Active in the transformation were the Revs. W. S. McMasters, Howard Holton, and Kemp C. Holden, Jr. In 2008 Dale Yerton served as chairman of WME.

WME is a Pentecostal body whose statement of faith closely resembles that of the Assemblies of God. Its stated goal is to promote fellowship among ministers, to counsel and train, those who are called to serve as ministers, and to provide licensing and ordination for qualifying inquirers. Members in good standing for one year may apply for status as an ordained minister. The organization meets annually for a fall conference and hosts an annual missionary conference. Its work is carried out through three committees that oversee coordination, missions, and credentials. The organization sponsors missionary projects both in the United States and abroad. The credentials committee oversees the work of the ministry and ensures that all who hold WME licenses abide by the group's code of ethics. Each February the ministers of WME meet in Nashville, Tennessee, where they experience fellowship and are taught by some of the nation's leading pastors and ministers.

Membership: Not reported. Churches and ministers associated with WME are scattered across the United States. Missionary activity is supported in Guatemala, Ecuador, Jamaica, Italy, Zimbabwe, Kenya, Mexico, Israel, and Egypt.

Periodicals: *WME Newsletter*.

Sources:

Worldwide Missionary Evangelism. www.wmeinc.org/.

Deliverance Pentecostals

Branham Tabernacle and Related Assemblies

c/o The William Branham Evangelistic Association and the Branham Tabernacle, Box 325, Jeffersonville, IN 47130

Alternate Address: Voice of God Recordings, Inc., Box 950, Jeffersonville, IN 47130.

William Branham (1909–1965) is generally thought of as the leader of the healing revival that swept across the United States in the 1950s. His ministry gave rise to evangelists such as Oral Roberts (b. 1918), A. A. Allen (1911–1970), and T. L. Osborne . From his humble birth in a log cabin in the hills of Kentucky to the miraculous healings that followed his ministry, followers of his teachings claim that his life was marked by supernatural events.

It was reported by his parents that just after his birth, a supernatural light entered the one-room cabin and hovered over the bed where baby William had been born. A few years later, an angel's voice spoke to him, saying that he would live his life near a city called New Albany. When he was seven years old, the angel spoke to him again, instructing him to never drink alcohol, smoke, or defile his body. Branham reported that from his earliest remembrance, the angel guided him and protected him.

In 1933 Branham founded the interdenominational Branham Tabernacle in Jeffersonville, Indiana. He later began recording his sermons for distribution. From 1947 until his untimely death in 1965, he recorded about 1,180 sermons that later became the foundation for the beliefs of millions of his followers. These taped sermons are distributed to almost every country in the world in at least 34 different languages. The Tabernacle has stayed much the same as it was in 1933; a few renovations and expansions have slightly changed its appearance, but it continues to function in a humble neighborhood near downtown Jeffersonville.

In 1946 Branham stated that he had received his commission from the angel. He was already a Baptist minister, but had been told by the clergy that he was possessed by an evil spirit, and that the visions he saw were from the devil. This troubled the young minister deeply, so he went to an old trapping cabin to pray about these things. The next morning he reported that the angel had told him that he had a gift of divine healing to bring to the people of the world. William Branham soon left the Baptist Church and ventured out as an independent evangelist.

In 1950 at the Houston Coliseum, a photographer took a picture that later was cited by the followers of William Branham as "undeniable" proof that his ministry was from God. Once the photograph was developed, it was thoroughly examined by a U.S. government professional, who signed a document that the halo image above the head of William Branham was authentic. Branham's followers claim that this is a photograph of the same pillar of fire that led Moses.

As his ministry progressed, William Branham's sermons increasingly diverrged from the mainstream denominations. He openly denounced trinitarian doctrine, and claimed that true baptism can only be made in the name of Jesus Christ, according to Acts 2:38. He claimed that the Father, Son, and Holy Ghost were simply titles for the one true God, Jesus Christ, and therefore, the baptism of the apostles in the book of Acts was in line with the commission of Jesus (Matt. 28:19). He further separated himself from the mainstream by denouncing other denominations, but he maintained that he was an interdenominational preacher, and he commonly preached in denominational churches when invited. Throughout his ministry, he preached that the prophet Elijah spoken of in Malachi 4 would return to earth. Although he did not outwardly claim to be this prophet, many of his followers came to believe that he was.

Branham founded the William Branham Evangelistic Association just before his death on December 24, 1965. The Evangelistic Association, headed by Billy Paul Branham (b. 1935)—William Branham's son—later gave rise to Spoken Word Publications, which was dedicated to distributing William Branham's tapes and transcribed sermons. Joseph Branham, another of William Branham's sons, founded Voice Of God Recordings in 1981, and it quickly merged with Spoken Word Publications. Voice of God Recordings and William Branham Evangelistic Association are located in the same building in Jeffersonville, Indiana.

Voice of God Recordings prints about 10 million sermon booklets and distributes hundreds of thousands of William Branham's audio sermons each year. In 2008 Voice of God Recordings had 75 employees at the Jeffersonville headquarters and supported 150 foreign employees in 40 offices worldwide.

Membership: The followers of William Branham's ministry are quick to say that they are not an organized religion: There are no official memberships, just individual churches that function independently and are not subject to a central nerve center. Voice of God Recordings estimates that there are well over one million believers worldwide, mostly in Africa—there were about 750,000 followers in the Democratic Republic of Congo alone. In 2008 there were about 35,000 believers in the United States.

Periodicals: *Catch The Vision*. Send orders to Box 950, Jeffersonville, IN 47130, or email vogr@branham.org.

Sources:

Branham Tabernacle and Related Assemblies. www.themessage.com.

Branham, William. *Footprints on the Sands of Time*. Jeffersonville, IN: Spoken Word Publications, n.d.

Branham, William Marrion. *Conduct, Order, Doctrine of the Church*. Jeffersonville, IN: Spoken Word Publications, 1974.

Harrell, David Edwin, Jr. *All Things Are Possible*. Bloomington: University of Indiana Press, 1975.

Lindsey, Gordon. *William Branham, A Man Sent from God*. Jeffersonville, IN: William Branham, 1950.

McConnel, D. R. *A Different Gospel*. 2nd ed. Peabody, MA: Hendrickson Publishers, 1995.

Sproule, Terry. *A Prophet to the Gentiles*. Blaine, WA: Bible Believers, n.d.

Weaver, C. Douglas. *The Healer-Prophet, William Marrion Branham: A Study in the Prophetic in American Pentecostalism*. Macon, GA: Mercer University Press, 1987.

A Case of Faith Ministries (ACOFM)

7580 Donlee Dr., Niagara Falls, ON, Canada L2H 2N5

A Case of Faith Ministries (ACOFM) began in 1995 as the ministry of Kees Tengnagel (b. 1947) expanded. Tengnagel, who had moved with his family from Holland to Canada, at first went into banking; then in 1981 he became a Christian and accepted a call to the ministry. Both he and his wife, Faith Tengnagel (b. 1947), attended Rhema Bible Training Center, the school founded by Kenneth E. Hagin Sr. in Tulsa, Oklahoma. They were ordained in the Association of Faith Churches and Ministers and the Rhema Ministerial Association International. They viewed their mandate as converting God's people from religion and tradition to what they see as His uncompromised Word.

In 1995 Tengnagel felt himself called into an apostolic leadership (primarily marked by his role in founding and nurturing new congregations). Over the next six years he founded six new congregations, four in Ontario, one in New York, and one in Michigan. The Tengnagels work as an apostolic team: Faith is known as a minister for the healing of the ill, and Kees ministers the baptism of the Holy Spirit (with the accompanying outward evidence of speaking in tongues).

Incorporated in 1998, A Case of Faith Ministries operates as an association of autonomous local churches that accept Tengnagel's apostolic guidance. It beliefs

are those common to Pentecostalism. It emphasizes a ministry of healing for the physical ills of the human body as wrought by the power of God through the prayer of faith and by the laying on of hands. Such healing, it is believed, was provided for as part of the power of Christ's atonement and thus is the privilege of every believer. A Case of Faith Ministries solicits the partnership of churches who support their work of planting new churches and nurturing such congregations in preparation for the Second Coming of Christ.

Membership: In 2008 the ACOFM reported nine churches in Ontario, Canada, and two in the United States, administered by 17 pastors.

Sources:

A Case of Faith Ministries. www.acofm.org/.

Deliverance Evangelistic Church

2001 W. Lehigh Ave., Philadelphia, PA 19132

The Deliverance Evangelistic Church was organized in 1961 as an independent prayer group that engaged in evangelistic endeavors in Philadelphia. Under the leadership of Rev. Dr. Benjamin Smith, Sr. (d. 2002), the group settled in a permanent location and formally organized as the Deliverance Evangelistic Church. As the movement grew, other churches were founded, primarily in Pennsylvania and New Jersey.

The church views its three main goals as evangelism, teaching the word of God, and preparing believers for worship and service. It emphasizes service to the community, with a broad spectrum of social ministry to the poor through the redistribution of clothing, food, and shelter, and through visitation to hospitals, prisons, nursing homes, and shut-ins.

The church founded the Deliverance Evangelistic Bible Institute and a youth Bible school. Its choirs have produced several albums. Glen Spaulding succeeded Smith as the senior pastor of the organization. There is an annual convention each summer. Smith envisioned the construction of "Deliverance Village," a building complex that would include an auditorium, a Christian medical center, a Christian elementary and high school, and a home for the aged. The final result, which seats 5,100 people, was opened in 1992 together with an educational facility. The missions department is actively working to train as well as support missionaries in the United States and other countries, including India, Trinidad, the Dominican Republic, Haiti, Honduras, and Ghana. A missionary team also traveled to the Mississippi Gulf Coast in response to Hurricane Katrina.

Membership: In 2008 the church reported 40 congregations administered by 45 clergy.

Sources:

Deliverance Evangelistic Church. www.decministry.org/.

Payne, Wardell J., ed. *Directory of African American Religious Bodies: A Compendium by the Howard University School of Divinity*, 2nd ed. Washington, DC: Howard University Press, 1995.

Fellowship of Inner-City Word of Faith Ministries (FICWFM)

c/o Crenshaw Christian Center, 7901 S Vermont Ave., Los Angeles, CA 90044

The Fellowship of Inner-City Word of Faith Ministries (FICWMF), founded in 1990, is an international association of ministers, ministries, and congregations that grew out of the ministry of Frederick K. C. Price, the Crenshaw Christian Center, and the center's Ministry Training Institute. Price, while a pastor of a congregation of the Christian and Missionary Alliance, read one of the books of Pentecostal healer Kathryn Kuhlman, which led him into the Pentecostal baptism of the Holy Spirit as evidenced by speaking in tongues. He later became associated with Kenneth Hagin, with whom he found himself in essential doctrinal agreement. In 1976 Price was awarded an honorary degree from the Rhema Bible Training Institute, which Hagin founded.

In 1973 Price founded the Crenshaw Christian Center, built on the message of faith, that in asking the Lord in faith for what is desired and His will, it will be forthcoming. The church, serving primarily African Americans, prospered, and membership steadily increased. In 1978 Ever Increasing Faith, an evangelistic ministry of Crenshaw Christian Center, was begun and found its major expression in a television program (seen internationally in the Caribbean and West Africa). In 1981 the former campus of Pepperdine University was purchased to house the growing congregation (over 5,000) and its associated ministries. The move allowed the founding of a School of Ministry (1985), School of the Bible (1988), Helps Ministry Summer School (1989), and Correspondence School. The center's Faithdome is a sanctuary that can hold the more than 10,000 people who gather for Sunday worship.

As the ministry work initiated by Price spread, and as ministers graduated from the School of Ministry, other Word-Faith ministries grew up in Southern California and other cities, most in inner-city African-American communities. The mission of the Fellowship of Inner-City Word of Faith Ministries is to provide fellowship, leadership, guidance, and spiritual covering for those desiring a standard of excellence in ministry. Each ministry operatesindependently of FICWFM, and the member-ministry does not require reporting accountability. They are tied together by their mutual acceptance of the Word of Faith perspective. Many are graduates of the School of Ministry. The FICWFM holds an annual convention at Crenshaw Christian Center, concurrently with Summer JAM, a ministry for children and teens.

Membership: In 2008 the FICWFM reported a combined congregational membership of more than 150,000, served by 300 member-pastors and ministers from 35 states and 5 foreign countries.

Sources:

Fellowship of Inner-City Word of Faith Ministries. www.ficwfm.org/.

Price, Frederick K. C. *How to Obtain Strong Faith*. Tulsa, OK: Harrison House, 1980.

————. *How Faith Works*. Los Angeles: Dr. Frederick K. C. Price Ministries, 2002.

————. *Prosperity: Good News for God's People*. Los Angeles: Faith One Publishing, 2008.

First Deliverance Church of Atlanta

65 Hardwick St. SE, Atlanta, GA 30315

The First Deliverance Church was founded in Atlanta in 1956 by the Reverends Lillian G. Fitch and William Fitch, two deliverance evangelists. The church teaches three experiences (justification, sanctification, and baptism of the Holy Spirit), emphasizes healing, and practices tithing. Fasts are an important feature of church life. Occasionally members stay at the church for a three-day, shut-in fast. Among their distinctive practices is kneeling in prayer upon entering the church. Congregations headed by licensed ministers are located in Georgia, Florida, Oklahoma, and California.

Membership: Not reported.

Full Gospel Fellowship of Churches and Ministers International

1000 N Belt Line Rd., Ste. 201, Irving, TX 75061-4000

In the early 1960s Gordon Lindsay (1906–1973), founder of the Christ for the Nations Institute in Dallas, Texas, and publisher of the *Voice of Healing* magazine, called together a group of independent Pentecostal ministers. The ministers voiced a desire to give expression to the unity of the Body of Christ under the leadership of the Holy Spirit, a unity that would go beyond individuals, churches, or organizations. Toward that end they formed the Full Gospel Fellowship of Churches and Ministers International in 1962.

The purpose of the Full Gospel Fellowship is to promote apostolic ministry, emphasizing unity among all the members of the Body of Christ. It serves as a medium through which member churches may work cooperatively and has no ecclesiastical or hierarchal authority over its members.

The Fellowship has adopted a set of "Suggested Articles of Faith" that they offer to member churches. While assuming an essential doctrinal agreement among member churches and ministers, individual churches may choose to revise the articles. The articles affirm belief in the Bible as the inspired Word of God, the Trinity, the need of people for salvation, baptism by immersion, the Lord's Supper, sanctification, divine healing, the Second Coming and millennial reign of Christ, heaven, and hell. Baptism of the Holy Spirit with the initial evidence of speaking in tongues is strongly advocated.

An organized association of independent churches, the Fellowship is designed to perform only those services that churches cannot easily or conveniently provide for themselves. Individual churches, groups of churches, and organizations of churches may be recognized within the Fellowship. Each church is free to carry out its own program and missionary work and to ordain or license ministers as it deems necessary. Those ministers recognized by the Fellowship are subsequently issued a membership card and certificate of ministerial status. A Young Leaders Network recognizes and connects young leaders within the Fellowship. An international and several regional conventions are held annually. The business meeting is held during the international meeting each July.

Although the Fellowship is not a governing body, it has been recognized by the Internal Revenue Service as an organization qualified to offer independent congregations tax-exempt status under its group exemption umbrella.

Membership: Not reported.

Periodicals: *Fellowship Tidings*.

Remarks: Gordon Lindsay was a former pastor in the Assemblies of God and, in the late 1940s, a close associate of evangelist William M. Branham (1909–1965). He served as president of the Voice of Healing Publishing Company and edited the *Voice of Healing*, a magazine that publicized and coordinated the activities of many of the prominent healing evangelists of the 1950s. In 1948 he called together the first meeting of the evangelists and ministers who supported the healing emphases that had grown from Branham's original efforts. The last of these annual conventions was held in 1961, the year before the formation of the Full Gospel Fellowship of Churches and Ministers International. Lindsay's work has been carried on by his widow, Freda Lindsay (b. 1916), through Christ for the Nations and its affiliated activities.

Sources:

Full Gospel Fellowship of Churches and Ministers International. www.fgfcmi.org/.

Lindsay, Freda. *My Diary Secrets*. Dallas: Christ for the Nations, 1976.

Lindsay, Gordon. *Bible Days Are Here Again*. Shreveport, LA: Author, 1949.

————. *The Gordon Lindsay Story*. Dallas: Voice of Healing Publishing Company, n.d.

Hall Deliverance Foundation

9840 N 15th St., Phoenix, AZ 85020-1810

The Hall Deliverance Foundation was established in 1956 in San Diego, California, as the focus of the ministry of the Rev. Franklin Hall (d. 1993), an independent Pentecostal minister, who began his ministerial career in 1946 as a Methodist. Hall also founded and pastored the International Healing Cathedral in San Diego, California. During his years in the Pentecostal ministry, Hall was closely connected with the evangelist Thelma Nickel.

Hall taught what he termed "body-felt" salvation. It was his belief that salvation is for the body as well as the biblical text, "By his stripes you are healed," and also by his own obtaining of the full baptism of the Holy Ghost (or Spirit) and Fire, as mentioned in Matthew 3:11. According to Hall, this teaching was alluded to by Jesus in Acts 1:8. The Holy Ghost power coming upon the physical body keeps the body well and healed, as long as the believer keeps that portion of the Holy Spirit called the "Fire" upon the physical body. The believer, therefore, has "body-felt" salvation, as there is no sickness. Those who participate in the body-felt salvation also participate in a miracle ministry and find its demonstration in a wide variety of healings and deliverance from natural disasters and dangerous situations. The experience of the Holy Spirit when it comes upon the person is felt tangibly as a pleasant warmth to heal the body or to bring healing protection energy. This sensation is related to the fire portion of the Holy Spirit baptism (Acts 2:3), which Jesus urged his disciples to obtain (Acts 1:8). Hall also recommended prayer and fasting. According to Hall, the latter enabled one to become a powerful conductor of divine and spiritual forces.

Hall died in 1993. In 2008 his widow, Rev. Helen Hall, continued to pastor the International Healing Cathedral, traveling around the world teaching and holding meetings. The Foundation distributes literature and audio and video tapes. Affiliated work takes place in Mexico, Canada, the Bahamas, Australia, New Zealand, Great Britain, West Germany, Finland, France, Sweden, the Philippines, Nigeria, Ghana, the Ivory Coast, Ethiopia, Tanzania, Kenya, Malaya, South Africa, and India.

Membership: Not reported.

Educational Facilities:

Glory Knowledge Bible School, Phoenix, Arizona.

Periodicals: *Miracle Word* • *The Healing Word News*

Sources:

Hall Deliverance Foundation, Inc. home.mindspring.com/~hdf1/index.html.

Hall, Franklin. *Atomic Power with God*. San Diego, CA: Author, 1946.

———. *The Baptism of Fire*. San Diego, CA: Author, 1960.

———. *The Body-Felt Salvation*. Phoenix: Hall Deliverance Foundation, 1968.

———. *Our Divine Healing Obligation*. Phoenix: Author, 1964.

Nickel, Thelma. *Our Rainbow of Promise*. Tulsa, OK: Vickers Printing Co., 1950.

International Convention of Faith Ministries (ICFM)

5500 Woodland Park Blvd, Arlington, TX 76013

The International Convention of Faith Ministries (ICFM; known until 1985 as the International Convention of Faith Churches and Ministers) was founded in 1979 by Dr. Doyle Harrison (d. 1998), pastor of Faith Christian Fellowship International Church in Tulsa, Oklahoma, along with a number of independent Pentecostal pastors and evangelists. A few of these pastors had become well known for their work on Christian television: Kenneth Hagin (1917-2003), of Kenneth Hagin Ministries and pastor of Rhema Bible Church in Tulsa; Kenneth Copeland (b. 1936), of Kenneth Copeland Ministries and Publications in Fort Worth, Texas; Frederick K. C. Price (b. 1932), of Ever Increasing Faith Ministries and pastor of Crenshaw Christian Center in Los Angeles; Norvel Hayes (b. 1927), of Norvel Hayes Ministries in Cleveland, Tennessee; Jerry J. Savelle (b. 1947), of Jerry Savelle Ministries in Fort Worth and founder of the Overcoming Faith Churches of Kenya in Africa; and John H. Osteen (d. 1999), of the John Osteen World Satellite Network in Houston. In 2008 the president of ICFM was Dr. Dennis Burke.

ICFM provides training to its members through grass-roots mentoring, workshops, and discipleship materials. ICFM members subscribe to the "faith confession" doctrine, which holds that a child of faith can publicly confess or claim something from God and be assured of getting it. The convention admits both churches and individuals to membership. Many of the students trained at Rhema Bible Training Center, started in 1974 by Hagin, went on to create new congregations partially drawing on viewers of the convention founders' television programs. In 1975 Harrison founded Harrison House, a book concern, which publishes many of the healing evangelists' materials.

Membership: In 2008 the ICFM reported approximately 450 member churches in 24 countries worldwide.

Educational Facilities:

Rhema Bible Training Center, Broken Arrow, Oklahoma.

Crenshaw Christian Center School of Ministry, Los Angeles, California.

Periodicals: *International Faith Report* • Unofficial (periodicals issued by ministries associated with the convention): *The Word of Faith* • *Ever Increasing Faith Messenger* • *Believers Voice of Victory Magazine*

Remarks: Some Pentecostal leaders criticized leading ministers of the convention (Hagin, Copeland, Price), as well as other evangelist-teachers, for what has been termed "faith formula theology"—a belief that by publicly confessing (claiming) something from God, believers will be given it according to their faith.

Sources:

International Convention of Faith Ministries. www.icfm.org/.

Copeland, Gloria. *God's Will for You*. Fort Worth: Kenneth Copeland Publications, 1972.

Hagin, Kenneth E. *How You Can Be Led by the Spirit of God*. Tulsa, OK: Kenneth Hagin Ministries, 1978.

Hayes, Norvel. *Seven Ways Jesus Heals*. Tulsa, OK: Harrison House, 1982.

Kegin, James L. *Developing Pastoral Leadership and Management Skills*. Ph.D. dissertation, School of Theology and Missions, Oral Roberts University, Tulsa, OK, 1991.

Osteen, John H. *This Awakening Generation*. Humble, TX: Author, 1964.

Price, Frederick K. C. *How to Obtain Strong Faith*. Tulsa, OK: Harrison House, 1980.

Leroy Jenkins Evangelistic Association

Box 4270, Scottsdale, AZ 85261

Leroy Jenkins is a healer who has become known as "the man with the golden arm" for his healing work. When he was five years old, so the story goes, the Lord spoke to him in an audible voice. Four years later, God spoke to him again, upon which he began levitating and floating through the air. In an accident in 1960, Jenkins's arm was almost cut off. He was healed instantly (after refusing amputation) in a meeting conducted by Asa Alonzo Allen in Atlanta. With Allen's encouragement, Jenkins began to preach; his evangelistic association was formed in 1960. Originally headquartered in Tampa, Florida, Jenkins moved to Delaware, Ohio, where a large tabernacle was build in the 1970s. In 1971, his radio ministry was heard over 57 stations.

In 1977 Jenkins moved to Greenwood, South Carolina, and opened the Spirit of Truth Church (later renamed the Healing Waters Cathedral). However, in April 1979 Jenkins was arrested and convicted on two counts of conspiracy to commit arson related to the burning of a state trooper's home in Ohio. Jenkins declared his innocence, but was sentenced to serve 12 years. He was paroled in June 1985 and has since resumed his ministry. The state of South Carolina pardoned Jenkins in 1993.

As a continuing part of his ministry for several decades, Jenkins distributes water pumped from the property adjacent to his Healing Waters Cathedral, over which he has prayed and that he claims has healing properties. In 2003 he ran into conflict over this practice when the Ohio Department of Agriculture accused him of distributing contaminated water. Jenkins agreed to close the well from which the water came. That same year, he sold the Healing Waters Cathedral to a Hindu group and moved his association to Arizona.

In 2002 a movie, *Man of Faith* starring Robert Wagner and Faye Dunaway, was made about Jenkins's life and ministry.

Membership: Not reported. The magazine of the association is mailed to over 100,000 supporters.

Periodicals: *Revival of America*.

Sources:

Leroy Jenkins Evangelistic Association. ww.leroyjenkins.com/.

Buckingham, June. *As the Wind Blows over the Life of Leroy Jenkins*. Leroy Jenkins, 1919.

Jenkins, Leroy. *How I Met the Master*. Tampa, FL: Leroy Jenkins Evangelistic
Association, 1965.

Miracle Life Fellowship International

11052 N 24th Ave., Phoenix, AZ 85029

Asa Alonzo Allen (1911–1970) was born of a poor Arkansas family, saved in a
Methodist revival, and later baptized with the Holy Spirit in a Pentecostal meeting.
He joined the Assemblies of God and felt called to preach. In the early 1940s, he
began to seek a ministry of signs and wonders, particularly healing. He had what
amounted to a theological conversion when, during a prayer time, he formulated
the thirteen requirements for a powerful ministry. He became convinced that he
could do the works of Jesus, and accomplish more than Jesus did; that he could be
flawless and perfect (in the biblical sense); and that one should believe in all of the
scriptural promises. During World War II (1939–1945), his throat became, according to one throat specialist, permanently ruined, but Allen was eventually healed.

In 1951 he purchased a tent and began his crusade in earnest. The headquarters
of A. A. Allen Revivals Inc. was established in Dallas, Texas. Soon after settling his
company's headquarters, Allen would begin publishing *Miracle Magazine*. From
that time until his death, Allen was an immensely popular evangelist speaking
both to integrated and predominantly black audiences. As early as 1960, he was
holding fully integrated meetings in the South. In 1958 he was given 1,250 acres
of land near Tombstone, Arizona, which was named Miracle Valley and which
became his international headquarters. Allen died in 1970 and was succeeded by
Don Stewart, who chose the new name for the organization: Miracle Revival
Fellowship.

Miracle Valley was created as a totally spiritual community. Allen founded a
Bible school and publishing house, located adjacent to radio and television studios,
the healing Pool of Bethesda, and the headquarters. He also operated a telephone
Dial-a-Miracle prayer service. The church seats 2,500. As a result of Allen's accomplishments and success, missionary churches were begun and independent ministers have become associated with him. Miracle Revival Fellowship (now Miracle
Life Fellowship International), at first a department of A. A. Allen Revivals, was
established as a ministerial fellowship and licensing agency. After Allen's death,
the Bible college was turned over to the Central Latin American District Council of
the Assemblies of God and is now known as Southern Arizona Bible College. A. A.
Allen Revivals later became known as the Don Stewart Association.

Membership: In 2002 the fellowship of ministers had 68 clergy members in the
United States and an additional 150 in other countries.

Periodicals: *Miracle Magazine*. Send orders to PO Box 2960, Phoenix, AZ 85062-
9984.

Sources:

Allen, A. A. *My Cross*. Miracle Valley, AZ: A. A. Allen Revivals, n.d.

Allen, A. A. (with Walter Wagner). *Born to Lose, Bound to Win: An Autobiography*.
Garden City, NY: Doubleday, 1970.

Stewart, Don. *Blessings from the Hand of God*. Miracle Valley, AZ: Don Stewart
Evangelistic Association, 1971.

—————. *How You Can Have Something Better through God's Master Plan*. Phoenix,
AZ: Don Stewart Evangelistic Association, 1975.

Stewart, Don (with Walter Wagner). *The Man from Miracle Valley*. Long Beach, CA:
Great Horizons, 1971.

Miracle Life Revival, Inc.

Box 20707, Phoenix, AZ 85036

Independent Pentecostal evangelist Neal Frisby (d. 2005) became known in the
early 1960s for possessing a gift of prophecy. In 1967 he began regularly to release
prophetic scrolls; by 1974 there were 60 and they were published in book form,
and by 1995 the number had grown to 295. In 1972 Capstone Cathedral, a large

pyramid-shaped church, was completed on the outskirts of Phoenix, Arizona. It
served as his publishing center and headquarters. The church also houses a television studio and produces films concerning worldwide events. In the 1990s, Frisby
released a number of pictures in which strange, "supernatural" lights are said to
have appeared.

Frisby left his ministry to Robert Brooks (b. 1970), a former wide receiver for the
Nation Football League's Green Bay Packers. Brooks had had a vision that he would
preach at Capstone and Frisby had had a confirming dream that he should turn the
property over to Brooks.

Membership: Not reported. Besides the congregation in Phoenix, many of whom
are from Nigeria, where Frisby had developed a following, there is a mailing list of
"special partners" around the United States who regularly support the ministry.

Sources:

Balmer, Randall. *Mine Eyes Have Seen the Glory: A Journey into the Evangelical
Subculture in America*. New York: Oxford University Press, 2006.

Frisby, Neal. *The Book of Revelation Scrolls*. Phoenix, AZ: Author, n.d.

Grant, W. V. *Creative Miracles*. Dallas, TX: Faith Clinic, n.d.

Mita's Congregation

Calle Duarte 235, Hata Rey, PR 60919

Mita's Congregation origininated in Puerto Rico. Founded in 1940 in the city of
Arecibo, the congregation also expanded to the United States in 1948 by a preacher
who was sent to the city of New York. After being ill for a long period of time, the
founder of the church, Juanita Garcia Peraza (1897–1970), prayed to God and
promised him that if he healed her, she would always serve him. According to the
congregation, God chose her body as the dwelling place for the Holy Spirit and
commanded her to establish this church following the doctrinal principles of the
Primitive Christian Church. It is their biblical understanding that Jesus Christ's
church was only one, and that the Holy Ghost is now preparing his people in order
to lead them toward salvation. According to the Holy Scripture, of the many that
are called, he would join the chosen together.

Peraza was considered to be the prophet and instrument of God; through her,
God healed the sick and entirely changed and improved peoples lives as he did in
ancient times, according to the Holy Scripture.

Moreover, she was commended in the beginning of the church to preach the
triple message of love, liberty, and unity: love, because God is love, and he called
his people so they could love him above all things and to love thy neighbor as thyself; liberty, because he came to free his people from sin; and unity, because Christ
came to unify his people and unite them in one unique feeling.

Mita's name, which signifies "spirit of life," was revealed by God to various spiritual brothers and herself. To the congregation's followers, Mita's name is the fulfillment of the biblical prophecies, which say that the Lord would return with a new
name (Isaiah 52:6 and 62:2 and Revelation 2:17 and 3:12). They also believe Jesus
promised that Christ would come as the promised comforter (John 14:26).

On February 21, 1970, Peraza passed away in the city of Hato Rey, Puerto Rico.
In her place and with the same attributes, Teofilo Vargas Sein Aaron remains. In his
childhood, Aaron had accompanied Peraza and was anointed of the Lord for this
ministry when he was 15 years old. Under his guidance, the church has extended
to other places in the United States (New Jersey, Connecticut, Chicago, Orlando,
Miami, Washington, New York, Boston) and overseas to the Dominican Republic,
Mexico, Colombia, Venezuela, Costa Rica, El Salvador, Spain, Panama, and Canada.

In 1990 Mita's Congregation celebrated its 50th anniversary and inaugurated a
new house of worship, necessary because of the increasing number of members.
It has the capacity of seating more than 6,000 people.

The principal church is located in Hato Rey and religious services are regularly
held every Tuesday, Thursday, Saturday, and Sunday.

The congregation possesses a pastoral home, where people reside who are
devoted and have dedicated their lives to God. There is also a home for the elderly

that accommodates 89 people; a private educational institution; Colegio Cóngregación Mita, ranging from preschool to high school; and an orientation and social assistance office, which offers social work services to all people.

Membership: In 1997 the congregation reported six congregations and 1,500 members in the United States and 63 congregations and 46,730 members worldwide.

Rhema

PO Box 50126, Tulsa, OK 74150-0126

Alternate Address: Rhema Ministries, PO Box 30123, Toronto, ON M3J 3L6, Canada.

Rhema is the name given to a set of ministries that have grown up around the Pentecostal televangelist Kenneth E. Hagin Sr. (1917–2003). He began his professional career as a minister with the Assemblies of God (1934–1946), but left the pastorate to become a itinerant evangelist. During that time he wrote the first of several hundred small booklets and spoke frequently for the Eull Gospel Business Men's Fellowship International. In the 1960s he founded Kenneth Hagin Ministries, and in 1966 began a radio broadcast ministry that expanded into television in 1976. The Rhema Bible Training Center grew out of a Bible correspondence course that Hagin had written; it continues to be popular among his listeners. In 1978 Kenneth Hagin Ministries evolved into the Rhema Bible Church in Tulsa, Oklahoma.

Rhema has a formal belief structure that is almost identical to that of the Assemblies of God. It affirms the Bible as the infallible Word of God, the Trinity, salvation in Christ, and the baptism of the Holy Spirit, which is evidenced by speaking in tongues. Hagin and those associated with Rhema have been identified with what is known as the "faith message," or "positive confession," which builds on biblical verses such as "That if you will confess with thy mouth the Lord Jesus, and will believe in your heart that God hath raised him from the dead, thou shalt be saved" (Rom. 10:9). Through positive confession, believers acknowledge desirable situations, which can be received as one confesses and believes in them. In this manner the believer can rule over poverty, disease, and sickness. This view advocates that God wants believers to have the best of everything: Believers should not, for example, suffer financial setbacks. Faith compels God's action. From this perspective, what believers say (or confess) determines what they will receive, a position often characterized as "name it, claim it." This theology has alienated Hagin and his students from the Assemblies of God and many other Pentecostal leaders.

At the same time, many who encountered Hagin on radio and television were drawn to his teachings, and students have flocked to the Rhema Bible Training Center and the more advanced classes at the Rhema Institute of Biblical Studies. Some of these graduates went into the ministry and began churches based on what they had learned. The Rhema Ministerial Association International was formed as a fellowship of ministers who retained a primary relationship with Hagin. Other students moved out and founded their own centers like Rhema that have become the centers of similar churches and ministerial fellowships (such as the Fellowship of Inner City Word of Faith Ministries, founded by former Rhema student Fred Price).

Rhema has established training centers in 14 countries: Austria, Brazil, Colombia, Germany, India, Indonesia, Italy, Mexico, Peru, Romania, Singapore, South Africa, South Pacific, and Thailand.

Membership: In 2008 the Rhema Bible Church (Tusla, Oklahoma) reported more than 8,000 members. There were more than 500 affiliated congregations in the United States scattered across the country.

Educational Facilities:

Rhema Correspondence Bible School, Tulsa, Oklahoma; accessible at www.rhema.org/education/rcbs.cfm.

Rhema Bible Training Center, Broken Arrow, Oklahoma.

Periodicals: *World of Faith*.

Sources:

Rhema. www.rhema.org.

Chappell, Paul G. "Kenneth Hagin, Sr." In *Twentieth-century Shapers of American Popular Religion*, ed. Charles H. Lippy. Westport, CT: Greenwood Press, 1989.

Hagin, Kenneth, Sr. *Another Look at Faith*. Tulsa, OK: Faith Library, 1996.

————. *How You Can Be Led By the Spirit of God*. Tulsa, OK: Faith Library, 1994.

————. *The Real Faith*. Tulsa, OK: Faith Library, 1985.

————. *What to Do When Faith Seems Weak and Victory Lost*. Tulsa, OK: Faith Library, 1979.

Hagin, Kenneth, Jr. *Kenneth E. Hagin's 50 Years in the Ministry: 1934–1984*. Tulsa, OK: Faith Library, 1984.

Wooding, Dan. *Never Say Never: The Story of the Rhema Broadcasting Group: A Modern-Day Miracle*. Auckland, New Zealand: RBG New Zealand, 2003.

Salvation and Deliverance Church

37 W. 116 St., New York, NY 10026

The Salvation and Deliverance Church was begun in 1975 by Rev. William Brown as a ministry of the African Methodist Episcopal Church. Brown, raised as a Roman Catholic, had become a businessman and later entered the ministry. In the 1980s he separated from the African Methodist Episcopal Church in favor of developing an international, interracial Holiness ministry. The church has developed a program that reaches more than forty countries. Emphasis in the membership is placed on developing Holy living rather than doctrinal uniformity.

Under Apostle Brown's leadership, the church has developed a multidimensional program including an award-winning drug rehabilitation center in Harlem; a youth ministry, the International Youth Movement for Christ; elementary and Bible schools; and work with the physically challenged. The church maintains a retreat center in the Catskill Mountains with special facilities for those involved in the ministry to the disabled. The church supports five Bible colleges, including St. Paul's Bible Institute in New York.

Membership: In 2008 the church reported 100 affiliated congregations and 500,000 members.

Educational Facilities:

St. Paul's Bible Institute, New York, New York.

Sources:

Payne, Wardell J., ed. *Directory of African American Religious Bodies: A Compendium by the Howard University School of Divinity*. Washington, DC: Howard University Press, 1991.

Spoken Word Deliverance Ministry and Ministerial Fellowship

PO Box 951, Lowell, NC 28098

Spoken Word Deliverance Ministries was founded by Robert L. Kitchin in 1997 as a fellowship of churches and ministers. Kitchin had been ordained originally in 1984, and over the years had become associated with several prominent Pentecostal leaders such as H. Richard Hall and David Terrill. He was brought into the ministry by Prs. Marvin and Norma Woods of the Golden Harvest Temple Church in Lowell, North Carolina, who had been board members of Hall's United Christian Church and Ministerial Association based in Cleveland, Tennessee. In 2008 Kitchin was pastor at the Golden Harvest Temple, where he was assisted by his wife Jill and son Eric. Since founding his independent work, Kitchin and his associates have been involved in a ministry of freeing those believed to be possessed by demons or afflicted by the powers of witchcraft (malevolent magic).

Spoken Word Ministries offers licenses to independent Pentecostal ministers and charters affiliate congregations through Spoken Word Deliverance Ministry and Ministerial Fellowship. It also welcomes Pentecostal ministers from other associations into its fellowship circle.

Membership: In 2008 the ministries reported 13 affiliated congregations.

Sources:

Spoken Word Deliverance Ministries. www.spokenwordministry.org.

Apostolic Pentecostals

Apostolic Assemblies of Christ, Inc.

8425 Fenkell Ave., Detroit, MI 48238

The Apostolic Assemblies of Christ, led by Bp. G. N. Boone, was formed in 1970 by former members of the Pentecostal Churches of Apostolic Faith. During the term of Willie Lee, the presiding bishop of the Pentecostal Churches, questions arose about his administrative abilities. In the midst of the controversy, he died. The church splintered in the organizational disarray, and one group formed around Bishop Boone and Virgil Oates, the vice bishop. The new body is congregational in organization and continues in the doctrine of the parent body, because no doctrinal controversy accompanied the split.

The Assemblies is a covenant fellowship of pastors and churches who desire to achieve ministerial excellence, assist in developing churches, and serve as a refuge for independent churches. This goals are accomplished through training, mentoring, and producing resources that enhance leaders and their churches spiritually, holistically, and financially. The mission of the Apostolic Assemblies of Christ is to provide an organizational framework for the called, chosen, and sent to maximize their functions and enhance their callings. In 2008 district councils existed in Michigan, Ohio, Mississippi, Illinois, West Virginia, South Carolina, Louisiana, and California. The Assemblies holds an annual convention and national youth conference. In 2008 Bishop Boone continued to preside over the Assemblies.

Membership: In 2008 the Assemblies reported 77 member ministers in member churches nationwide. There were approximately 3,500 members and 23 churches in 1980.

Sources:

Apostolic Assemblies of Christ, Inc. www.apostolicassembliesofchrist.com.

Apostolic Assembly of the Faith in Christ Jesus

10807 Laurel St., Rancho Cucamonga, CA 91730

The Apostolic Assembly of the Faith in Christ Jesus is one of the oldest Pentecostal churches, tracing its origins to the Azusa Street revival that launched the movement nationally in 1906. Juan Navarro, a resident of Los Angeles, participated in the revival meetings. Working in the Spanish-speaking community, in 1912 he baptized Francisco Llorente, who became the first bishop of the new Apostolic Assembly when it was formed in 1925. From its small beginning, the Assembly grew as more and more Spanish-speaking people, mostly from Mexico, relocated to southern California.

Doctrinally, the Assembly affirms the church as the sum total of all people who have accepted Christ as lord, the one God who manifests as Father, Son, and Holy Spirit, and salvation in Jesus Christ. The Bible is accepted as the Word of God and rule of faith.

The church has taken seriously its mandate to a global mission and has developed missionary work in most of the Latin American countries, and in Tanzania, Spain, and Italy.

Francisco Llorente was succeed as the church's bishop and president by Antonio Castaqeda Nava (1929–1950, 1963–1966), Benjamin Cantu (1950–1963), Efrain Valverde (1966–1970), Lorenzo Salazar (1970–1978), Manuel Vizcarra (1986–1994), and Baldemar Rodriguez (1978–1986, 1994–2002). The current (2008) president is Daniel Sanchez (2002–).

Membership: Not reported.

Educational Facilities:

National Apostolic Bible College/Colegio Bíblico Apostólic Nacional, Ontario, California.

Sources:

Apostolic Assembly of the Faith in Christ Jesus. www.apostolicassembly.org/.

Apostolic Church of Christ

2044 Martin Luther King, Jr., Dr., Winston-Salem, NC 27107

The Apostolic Church of Christ was founded in 1969 by Bp. Johnnie Draft and Elder Wallace Snow, both ministers in the Church of God (Apostolic). Draft, for many years an overseer in the church and pastor of St. Peter's Church, the denomination's headquarters congregation, expressed no criticism of the Church of God (Apostolic); rather, he stated that the Spirit of the Lord brought him to start his own organization. The church differs from its parent body in its development of a centralized church polity. Authority is vested in the executive board, which owns all the church property. Doctrine follows that of the Church of God (Apostolic). Bishop Draft serves as the church's chief apostle.

Membership: In 1992 the Apostolic Church of Christ had six churches, 400 members, nine ministers, six elders, two licensed missionaries, and one bishop.

Apostolic Church of Christ in God

c/o Bethlehem Apostolic Church, 1217 E 15th St., Winston-Salem, NC 27105

The Apostolic Church of Christ in God was formed by five elders of the Church of God (Apostolic): J. W. Audrey, J. C. Richardson, Jerome Jenkins, W. R. Bryant, and J. M. Williams. At the time of the split, the Church of God (Apostolic) was formally led by Thomas Cox, but, due to his ill health, Eli N. Neal was acting as presiding bishop. The dissenting elders were concerned with the authoritarian manner in which Neal conducted the affairs of the church as well as with some personal problems that Neal was experiencing. Originally, three churches left with the elders, who established headquarters in Winston-Salem, North Carolina. J. W. Audrey was elected the new presiding bishop.

The new church prospered and in 1952 Elder Richardson was elected as a second bishop. In 1956 Audrey resigned and Richardson became the new presiding bishop. Under his leadership, the Apostolic Church of Christ in God enjoyed its greatest success. He began the *Apostolic Gazette* (later the *Apostolic Journal*), which served the church for many years. He also instituted a program to assist ministers in getting an education. However, his efforts were frustrated by several schisms that cut into the church's growth, most prominently the 1971 schism led by (former) Bishop Audrey.

The church retained the doctrine and congregational polity of the Church of God (Apostolic).

Membership: In 1980 the church had 2,150 members in 13 congregations being served by five bishops and 25 ministers.

Apostolic Church of Jesus

Current address not obtained for this edition.

In 1923, the Apostolic Church of Jesus was founded by Antonio Sanches, who had been converted in an evangelistic meeting led by Mattie Crawford in Pueblo, Colorado, and his brother George Sanches. The Sanches brothers began to preach to the Spanish-speaking population of the city and, in 1927, organized the first congregation of the Apostolic Church of Jesus. In subsequent years, congregations were established throughout the state in Denver, Westminster, Fountain, Walsenburg, Ft. Garland, San Luis, and Trinidad, Colorado; additional locations can be found in Palo Alto, California, and Velarde, New Mexico. The group, presently under the leadership of Raymond P. Virgil, has a weekly radio ministry.

Membership: Not reported.

Periodicals: *Jesus Only News of the Apostolic Faith.*

Apostolic Church of Jesus Christ

5019 N Lakeview Rd., Bloomington, IN 47404

The Apostolic Church of Jesus Christ, established in 1978, grew out of the Pentecostal Assemblies of the World after the death of Garfield Thomas Haywood (1880–1931), who founded the "oneness" work in Indianapolis, Indiana. Headed by pastor Judson D. Sears, the church views its mission as continuing the work of Jesus Christ: to seek and save the current generation, to minister to people in need of hope, and to care for those who are hurting. Members believe that to be saved one must repent of one's sins; be baptized in the name of Jesus Christ for the remission of sins; and receive the gift of the Holy Spirit with the evidence of speaking in tongues. The church offers a number of individual Bible studies as well as a morning Sunday school and a youth revival.

Membership: Not reported.

Sources:

Apostolic Church of Jesus Christ. acofjc.tripod.com.

Apostolic Faith (Hawaii)

1043 Middle St., Honolulu, HI 96819

The Apostolic Faith Church, known in Honolulu for its rooftop sign proclaiming "JESUS COMING SOON" and its prayer tower, was founded by the late Pr. Charles Lochbaum, who was called by the Lord to come to Hawaii from California in 1923. He and his wife, Ada Lochbaum, held revival services in a tent where many witnessed his preaching of the "Gospel of Jesus Christ, gift of the Holy Spirit, and Divine healing." This early ministry was successful, and within a year a permanent church was erected. The ministry initiated an evangelistic tour of the island and baptized more than 4,000 converts in four years.

The church is headed by a board of trustees that includes Pr. and Chairman of the Board William M. Han Jr., Pr. Emeritus Rodney S. Asano Sr., Pr. Leonard K. Y. Asano Sr., Edwin H. Sproat Sr., and Evangeline L. Han. It is self-sufficient and independent, and has no affiliation with other national and independent church groups. One of its doctrines admonishes members to "stand up for the Name of Jesus Christ, not to join up with any other organization, and not to compromise the Gospel Truths found in God's Word, the Bible."

The first branch church was built in the district of Kaimuki on the island of Oahu in 1930. Another followed in Kaunakakai, Molaki, in 1944, and the Maui Branch Church was constructed at Lahaina in 1953. A 1,000-seat headquarters temple sanctuary was erected in 1959. That same year current Chief Pastor William Ha Sr., succeeded the late pastors Charles and Ada Lochbaum, and in 1973 the church dedicated a complex consisting of a parsonage, church office, and classrooms added to the headquarters. The following year a seven-story-high prayer tower was completed and dedicated for daily prayer services and weekly tarrying services. Since then, additional branch churches have been established in Molokai, Hawaii, Maui, Kauai, and the Philippine Islands. Upon the death of Pr. William Han Sr. in 2006, his son William Han Jr. assumed the pastorship.

In the 1960s the church began a radio broadcast over KIKI in Honolulu; television broadcast commenced in 1980 (it is the longest-running program in Hawaii), and has since expanded to stations in Seattle, San Diego, Chico/Redding, Palm Springs, Sacramento, Eureka, Los Angeles/San Bernadino, and El Centro, California; Yuma, Arizona; Eugene, Oregon; and Seattle, Washington.

Membership: In 2008 the church reported five congregations in Hawaii and two in the Philippines, administered by seven pastors. In 1995 the church reported 144,000 members worldwide; it did not report its membership in 2002.

Periodicals: *Kingdom of God Crusader*.

Sources:

Apostolic Faith Church. www.jesuscomingsoon.org.

Apostolic Faith Church of Honolulu. *Kingdom of God Crusader*. Honolulu, HI: Author, 1969.

Apostolic Faith Mission Church of God

3344 N Pearl Ave., Birmingham, AL 36101

Among the people who visited the early Pentecostal revival, which occurred between 1906 and 1908 in Los Angeles, California, was Frank W. Williams (d. 1932), a black man from the Deep South. He received the baptism of the Holy Spirit under the ministry of William J. Seymour (1870–1922) and returned to Mississippi to establish an outpost of the Apostolic Faith Mission. Not having great success, he moved to Mobile, Alabama, where a revival occurred under his ministry. Among those converted was an entire congregation of the Primitive Baptist Church. The members gave him their building as the first meeting house for the new mission parish. The church was organized on July 10, 1906.

In 1915 Bishop Williams became one of the first to adopt the oneness or non-Trinitarian theology, which had been espoused through Pentecostal circles. He broke with Seymour and renamed his church the Apostolic Faith Mission Church of God. He established the new church on October 9, 1915. The church continues to place a strong emphasis upon divine healing, allows women preachers, and practices foot washing with communion. Baptism is in the name of Jesus Christ, and without the use of the name, the baptism is considered void. Intoxicants, especially tobacco, alcohol, and drugs, are forbidden. Members are admonished to marry only those who are believed to be saved. The church is headed by the senior bishop and a cabinet of executive officers composed of the bishops, overseers, and the general secretary.

Membership: In 1989 the church reported 18 congregations (most of which were in Alabama), 6,200 members, and 32 ministers.

Apostolic Gospel Church of Jesus Christ

Current address not obtained for this edition.

The Apostolic Gospel Church of Jesus Christ was founded in Bell Gardens, California, in 1963 by the Rev. Donald Abernathy. During the next five years, four other congregations, all in the Los Angeles, California, area, were added and a new denomination emerged. In 1968, Abernathy reported a series of visions in which it was revealed to him that the entire west coast of North America would be destroyed in an earthquake. He reported the vision to the other congregations, and one pastor, the Rev. Robert Theobold, reported a confirming vision. As a result, the five congregations decided to move east. Abernathy took his congregation to Atlanta, Georgia. The church at Avenal, California, went to Kennett, Missouri; the church at Porterville, California, to Independence, Missouri; the church at Port Hueneme, California, to Murfreesboro, Tennessee; and the congregation in Lompoc, California, to Georgia.

The church accepts oneness doctrines, identifying Jesus with the Father. It believes only in divine healing and does not approve of the use of medicines, doctors, or hospitals. Foot washing is practiced. Members are pacifists. There is a strict code of dress that prohibits bathing suits, slacks, shorts, tightly fitting or straight cut skirts, dresses with hemlines shorter than halfway between the knee and ankle, jewelry, and short hair for women. Long hair, short sleeves, and tightly fitting pants are prohibited for men.

The church is ruled by bishops (or elders) and deacons, and includes apostles, prophets, evangelists, pastors, and teachers in its structure. Their mission is to build a perfect church to which Christ will return. The perfect church will manifest both the fruits and gifts of the Spirit.

Membership: There are five congregations.

Apostolic Light Fellowship

PO Box 311, St. Albans, VT 05478-0311

Alternate Address: c/o City of Light Ministries Worldwide, PO Box 311, St. Albans, VT 05478.

The City of Light Ministries, an Apostolic Pentecostal church, was founded by Raymond Landis and his wife, Wendy Landis. They were both baptized in the name of Jesus in 1990, then subsequently founded a congregation in St. Albans, Vermont, that as it grew became the center of an expansive and global ministry.

The church affirms the authority of the Bible as God's Word; the one God who manifested as the "Father in Creation, the Son of God in Redemption, and the Holy Ghost in Regeneration"; and Jesus Christ as both God and man and the only one able to reconcile humans to God.

As the work grew beyond St. Albans, the Landises founded the Apostolic Light Fellowship as the ministry's licensing arm. The Fellowship offers licenses and ordination to ministers whose work is affiliated with it. Affiliated organizations are found in Canada, the United Kingdom, Myanmar, Malawi, South Africa, Liberia, and the Philippines. Distance-learning training is offered through the Center for Biblical Studies Worldwide. Licensed ministers are scattered around the United States.

Membership: Not reported. In 2008 there were 17 licensed ministers working in locations around the United States outside the center in St. Albans. There were also two ministers working in Alberta, Canada.

Sources:

Apostolic Light Fellowship. www.apostoliclightfellowship.org/.

City of Light Ministries. www.colmww.org/.

Apostolic Ministerial Alliance

1530 E Arizona Ave., Las Cruces, NM 88001

The Apostolic Ministerial Alliance is an association of Apostolic Jesus-only Pentecostal churches based in the Hispanic community of those states adjacent to the Mexican border. Members of Jesus-only churches are baptized in the name of Jesus Christ only without reference to the Father. Congregations are located in Texas, New Mexico, and California. Leadership is provided by Pr. Louis P. Rey, the pastor of the Fountain of Life Apostolic Church in Las Cruces, New Mexico.

Membership: In 2002, there were six churches in the alliance.

Apostolic Overcoming Holy Church of God

2257 St. Stephens Rd., Mobile, AL 36617

The Apostolic Overcoming Holy Church of God was founded by William Thomas Phillips (1893–1973), the son of a Methodist Episcopal church minister. At a tent-meeting service in Birmingham, Alabama, Phillips was converted to the message of Pentecost and holiness under the ministry of Frank W. Williams of the Faith Mission Church of God. Williams ordained Phillips in 1913, and three years later Phillips launched his career as an evangelist in Mobile, Alabama. In 1916 he was selected by the people who responded to his ministry as the bishop of the Ethiopian Overcoming Holy Church of God. The new organization was incorporated in 1920. It adopted its present name in 1941 to signal that the church was for all people, not just Ethiopians, a popular designation for blacks in the early twentieth century.

BELIEFS. The AOH Church of God follows the Oneness theology. It believes in One God who subsists in the union of Father, Son, and Holy Spirit. The church, however, rejects any hint of tritheism and believes that the One God bears the name of Jesus, a name that can express the fullness of the Godhead. Out of this belief, the church baptizes members in the name of Jesus. Baptism is by immersion and considered necessary for salvation.

The church teaches that God acts in the believer both to baptize in the Spirit (which will be signified by speaking in tongues) and progressively over a lifetime to sanctify (make holy). Besides baptism, there are two other ordinances—the Lord's supper and foot washing. The church also teaches divine healing and exhorts members to tithe.

ORGANIZATION. The AOH Church of God has an episcopal polity, though each church manages its own affairs. Churches are grouped into districts presided over by bishops and overseers. A General Assembly, to which all churches send representatives, convenes annually and is led by the presiding bishop. After serving the

church for 57 years, Bishop Phillips was succeeded by Bishop Jasper Roby. The current national and international presiding prelate is Bishop George W. Ayers, assisted by two presiders and ten associate bishops. The church's publishing board puts out the church periodicals. It supports missions in Haiti and Africa. Bishop Ayers presides over a Sunday radio broadcast in Mobile, Alabama; other overseers conduct broadcasts in separate AOH locations. An AOH Pastoral Alliance Monday afternoon television program is broadcast on the Brighthouse Network. In addition, the AOH holds regional and youth conferences, and a national Sunday school convention.

Membership: In 2007 AOH reported an estimated 13,000 members; in 2008 it reported 13 bishops and 33 overseers. Half of the approximately 130 AOH churches are in Alabama, with the other half scattered across 20 states.

Educational Facilities:

Berean Christian Bible College, Birmingham, Alabama.

Periodicals: *People's Mouthpiece*, quarterly. • *Young Educator*.

Sources:

Arrington, Juanita R. *A Brief History of the Apostolic Overcoming Holy Church of God, Inc. and Its Founder*. Birmingham, AL: Forniss Printing Co., 1984.

Manual of the Disciplines and Doctrines of the Apostolic Holy Church of God, 2nd ed. Birmingham, AL: Apostolic Overcoming Holy Church of God, 1997.

Assemblies of the Lord Jesus Christ, Inc. (ALJC)

875 N White Station Rd., PO Box 22366, Memphis, TN 38122

The Assemblies of the Lord Jesus Christ (ALJC) was formed in 1952 by the merger of three "Jesus only" groups that had sprung up around the country—the Assemblies of the Church of Jesus Christ, the Jesus Only Apostolic Church of God, and the Church of the Lord Jesus Christ. The Assemblies closely resembles the United Pentecostal Church in doctrine. The group preaches two experiences—justification and the baptism of the Spirit— and emphasizes healing, washes feet, tithes, and forbids participation in secret societies. Although they respect the civil government, members do not participate in war. Worldly amusements are forbidden, as are school gymnastics and clothes that immodestly expose the body.

The government is congregational in form. There is an annual general conference. A general board oversees the church during the year. The church is divided into state districts that are located in the South, Midwest, and Southwest. The Foreign Mission Department oversees the mission program in Chile, India, Ireland, Mexico, the Netherlands, Nigeria, Norway, Papua New Guinea, Russia, and Taiwan. ALJC also produces a weekly radio program that is broadcast internationally over two shortwave frequencies. Webcasts and podcasts are available at the ALJC Internet site.

Membership: In 2002 there were 50,000 members in 600 congregations served by 1,000 ministers in the United States, and 300 members in 5 churches served by 8 ministers in Canada. There were an additional 10,000 members worldwide.

Periodicals: *Apostolic Witness*, monthly.

Sources:

Assemblies of the Lord Jesus Christ, Inc. (ALJC). aljc.org.

Associated Brotherhood of Christians

PO Box 1112, Henderson, KY 42419

The Associated Brotherhood of Christians, Pentecostal in faith while Apostolic in doctrine, is a "oneness" Pentecostal body. In 1933, near Thomas Town, Mississippi, a small group of ministers and their wives (Rev. and Mrs. J. W. Johnson, Rev. and Mrs. H. A. Riley, Rev. and Mrs. E. E. Partridge, and Rev. and Mrs. L. W. Onstead) met to discuss forming a fellowship that would include all the brethren and churches who believed the "Bread of Life" message but not excluding those who did not believe it. Having been denied fellowship and credentials in other organizations because of this message, they resolved to form their own association and adopted the name Associated Ministers of Jesus Christ, with Rev. Partridge as chairman.

In the early years of World War II, the ministers requested military exemptions for the purpose of continuing their duties as ministers of the Gospel. Federal and state regulations required that they incorporate to be recognized as an official body. In 1941 the name adopted for the official body was the Associated Brotherhood of Christians.

The Association's mission is to effect a brotherhood among Christians everywhere, promoting the Gospel of Jesus Christ. Its conference convenes annually at their own Camp Mulberry in Hot Springs, Arkansas. The Association is headed by an official board; state presbyters are either board-appointed or elected by their states. Churches are located across the South and Midwest and along the Pacific Coast. The Association maintains missions in Mexico, France, India, Jordan, Germany, Israel, China, Bangladesh, Japan, Africa, Cuba, Canada, the Philippines, Haiti, and Thailand.

Membership: In 2008 the brotherhood reported a total of 150 ministers and 31 churches in the United States.

Periodicals: *Our Herald*.

Sources:

Associated Brotherhood of Christians. www.abofc.org/.

Bethel Ministerial Association (BMA)

7055 Marker St., Indianapolis, IN 46227

The Bethel Ministerial Association (BMA) is a fellowship of ministers allied for the purpose of proclaiming the Gospel of the Lord Jesus Christ as it was taught by the Apostles. Orthodox in doctrine and evangelical in practice, the BMA was founded in 1934 as the Evangelistic Ministerial Alliance by Rev. Albert Franklin Varnell to offer fellowship to ministers who held similar doctrinal views without the organizational pressures on the local church. Varnell began his ministry as a tent evangelist. In 1933 the church to which he belonged decided that speaking in tongues was the first evidence of the reception of the Holy Spirit. Varnell opposed this teaching. He believed that the new birth and the baptism of the Holy Spirit were the same, and that speaking in tongues was a subsequent, supernatural manifestation of the Spirit among those who had yielded to and been filled with the Spirit.

The BMA also teaches that God manifests in the flesh as Jesus, which is the name of the One God. It denies the traditional doctrine of the Trinity (God as three persons) but affirms that the One God (Jesus) expresses Himself in the Trinity personalities of Father, Son, and Holy Spirit. It accepts the Bible as the Word of God. Water baptism is by immersion in the name of Jesus.

Bethel churches are independent and slef-governing, and membership in the association is available to ministers only. The association has a publishing house in Floyds Knobs, Indiana. The Bethel Foreign Missions Foundation supports missionaries in Mexico, Guatemala, Ecuador, Kenya, Nigeria, Haiti, China, and Japan, as well as prison and Native American missions in the United States. The association also operates the Bethel Youth Camp in southern Indiana; the Bethel Ministerial Academy, a ministerial training program; and Grace House (partnered with Teen Challenge) in Evansville, Indiana, a long-term residential program for women aged eighteen and over who are struggling with life-controlling problems.

Membership: In 2008 the BMA reported 22 churches and affiliated ministries in the United States.

Educational Facilities:

International Bible Center, San Antonio, Texas.

Periodicals: *Power Link*.

Sources:

Bethel Ministerial Association. www.daveweb1.com/bma.

Horath, David. *It Does Make a Difference What You Believe!* Decatur, IL: Bethel Ministerial Association, 1988.

Bible Way Church of Our Lord Jesus Christ World Wide, Inc.

261 Rochester Ave., Brooklyn, NY 11213

A Bible-centered organization of Apostolic congregations, the Bible Way Church of Our Lord Jesus Christ World Wide was founded in 1957 by former members of the Church of the Lord Jesus Christ of the Apostolic Faith. Prior to 1957, some leaders of the Church of Our Lord Jesus Christ of the Apostolic Faith decried what they saw as the autocratic leadership of Robert Clarence Lawson (1883–1961), the church's bishop. They had suggested that Lawson consider sharing the leadership and consecrate more bishops for the growing denomination; when Lawson refused, a number of the leading ministers and their churches left to form the Bible Way Churches of Our Lord Jesus Christ. Among the leaders of the new church were Smallwood E. Williams (1907–1991), John S. Beane, McKinley Williams, Winfield S. Showell, and Joseph Moore. They were consecrated by John S. Holly, a bishop of the Pentecostal Assemblies of the World. They selected Williams, for many years the general secretary of the parent body, as their presiding bishop. The name of the church derives from the name of the congregation Williams had led in Washington, D.C., since the 1920s.

Williams has been credited with taking the lead among Apostolic Pentecostal groups in the development of a social service and social justice ministry. He led the church to become involved in Washington politics, sponsored the construction of a supermarket near his church, encouraged the development of a housing complex, and worked for more job opportunities within the African-American community. His book, Significant Sermons (1970), was largely concerned with a Christian response to social problems. Williams also emphasized education, as signaled by his opening and maintaining a Bible school adjacent to the headquarters church in Washington, D.C. In this effort he was greatly aided by Dr. James I. Clark, who is remembered as the denomination's great pioneer educator. Bp, Huie Lee Rogers is the current presiding bishop and chief apostle.

The Bible Way Church of Our Lord Jesus World Wide follows the non-Trinitarian Pentecostal doctrine of its parent body, which emphasizes the sole divinity of Jesus and thus baptizes in the name of Jesus only. It describes itself as "Pentecostal in experience, Apostolic in doctrine, and Ecumenical in fellowship." The church operates a radio ministry heard on AM stations in New York, North Carolina, South Carolina, and Washington, D.C.

Membership: In 1988 the church reported approximately 250,000 members in 250 churches. In 2008 there were 28 bishops on its executive board

Educational Facilities:

Bible Way Training School, Washington, D.C.

Periodicals: *The Bible Way News Voice*.

Sources:

Bible Way Church of Our Lord Jesus Christ World Wide. www.biblewaychurch.org.

Official Directory, Rules and Regulations of the Bible Way Church of Our Lord Jesus Christ World Wide, Inc. Washington, DC: Bible Way Church of Our Lord Jesus Christ World Wide, 1973.

Richardson, James C., Jr. *With Water and Spirit: A History of Black Apostolic Denominations in the U.S.* Winston-Salem, NC: Author,1980.

Williams, Smallwood Edmond. *Significant Sermons*. Washington, DC: Bible Way Church Press, 1970.

————. *This Is My Story*. Washington, DC: William Willoughby Publishers, 1981.

Bible Way Pentecostal Apostolic Church

Current address not obtained for this edition.

The Bible Way Pentecostal Apostolic Church was founded by Curtis P. Jones. Jones began as a pastor in North Carolina in the Church of God (Apostolic), but left that church to join the Church of Our Lord Jesus Christ of the Apostolic Faith under Robert Clarence Lawson (1883–1961). He became pastor of the St. Paul Apostolic Church in Henry County, Virginia. Jones left during the internal disruption within Bishop Lawson's church in 1957, but did not join with Smallwood E. Williams's (1907–1991) Bible Way Church of Our Lord Jesus Christ. Rather, in 1960, with two other congregations in Virginia, he founded a new denomination. A fourth church was soon added.

Membership: In 1980 the church had four congregations, all in Virginia.

Biblical Apostolic Organization (BAO)

716 S Maple St., Siloam Springs, AR 72761

Alternate Address: PO Box 88, Lancaster, TX 75146.

The Biblical Apostolic Organization (BAO) is an Apostolic Pentecostal church founded in 1983 by some Apostolic ministers under the leadership of Rev. Marvin M. Arnold, who felt that many within the older Apostolic churches were drifting morally and doctrinally. They felt that older Holiness standards were being compromised and that others were becoming associated too closely with Trinitarian Pentecostals and charismatics and accepting occult phenomena.

The Holy Bible is the basis for all doctrine and teaching for the Apostolic Church. The church believes that all doctrine must be be based upon and harmonize with the real Scriptures, because the original autographs written by the holy men of old were very much inspired by God. Members accept only the canonical 66 books of the Holy Bible; they do not accept any apocryphal scriptures or Gnostic writings. They do not believe in any of what they call the "false man-made Catholic Creeds," asserting that parts of these creeds are actually pagan in origin. Neither do they accept any known interpolation as divinely inspired by God, because nothing can take the place or the authority of the real Scriptures.

The BAO adheres to the basic teaching of the Oneness movement described in Acts 2:1–4, 2:38, 19:5; Rom. 12:1–21; and Deut. 6:4. The church teaches that the One True God was in Christ and that there is only One Almighty God. The idea of a trinity is unbiblical, having been concocted by superstitious people who lived in the Dark Ages. They believe that the idea was forced upon the people of the Roman Empire beginning with the rule of Constantine. The church also affirms a four-part plan of salvation that includes: (1) faith in Jesus Christ that leads to (2) (death) repentance; (3) (burial) baptism in water by immersion in the name of Jesus for the remission of sins; and (4) (resurrection) the baptism of the Holy Spirit, with the evidence of speaking in other tongues as the Spirit gives utterance to be saved (Acts 2:38; 4:12; 8:12–17; 10:43–48; 19:1–6). They believe faith and obedience work together in the grace of God to reconcile humans to God.

The BAO puts much emphasis on the family unit as God's primary institution, and believes that the church is God's redemptive fellowship for all believers.

In 2008 the BAO was headed by its president, Clinton D. Willis, two vice presidents, and 20 bishops. The church supports a school that allows its students to study at home by correspondence. Mission work is conducted in Kenya, Uganda, Nigeria, Jamaica.

Membership: In 2008 the church reported 120 clergy.

Educational Facilities:

Biblical Apostolic University Siloam Springs, Arkansas. Executive office: PO Box 88, Lancaster, TX 75146-0088.

Periodicals: *The Christian Review*, quarterly.

Sources:

Biblical Apostolic Organization, Mississippi District. www.msbao.com.

Church of God Apostolic, Inc. (COGA)

PO Box 12187, Winston-Salem, NC 27107

The Church of God Apostolic, Inc., (COGA) was formed in 1897 by Elder Thomas Cox at Danville, Kentucky, as the Christian Faith Band. It was one of a number of inde-

pendent Holiness associations of the late nineteenth century. In 1915 it voted to change its name, and in 1919 became the Church of God (Apostolic). In 1943 Cox was succeeded by M. Gravely and Eli N. Neal as co-presiding bishops. Headquarters were moved to Beckley, West Virginia. Two years later Gravely divorced his wife and remarried, and as a result he was disfellowshipped from the church. In 1964 Neal was succeeded by Love Odom, who died two years later and was succeeded by David E. Smith. These two bishops did much to put the national church in a firm financial position. They were succeded in turn by Bp. Ruben K. Hash, followed by the current (2008) presiding overseer, Bp. Cecil O. Reid.

It is a strict church, opposing worldliness and practicing footwashing with the monthly Lord's Supper. Members accept the Bible as God's inspired word, believe in the Trinity, the virgin birth of Christ, the atonement by Christ for the world, and justification by grace through faith in Christ. Baptism by immersion is in the name of Jesus. The church is headed by a board of bishops, one of whom is designated the presiding overseer to serve as the church's executive head. There is a general annual conference.

Membership: In 1980, the most recent report, the church had 15,000 members, 43 congregations, and approximately 75 ministers.

Periodicals: *Apostolic Leadership Newsletter*, monthly.

Sources:

Church of God Apostolic. www.cogainc.org/.

Church of God in Christ Jesus, Apostolic, Inc.

PO Box 29276, Baltimore, MD 21205

The Church of God in Christ Jesus, Apostolic, Inc., was founded in 1946 in Baltimore, Maryland, by Randolph A. Carr and Monroe R. Saunders, both former ministers in the Pentecostal Assemblies of the World. The doctrine of the new church followed that of the parent body.

The church had very strict standards concerning divorce and remarriage, which led to complaints by Saunders that the standards were not being uniformly enforced. The controversy led him to break with Carr and take the majority of members to found the United Church of Jesus Christ (Apostolic). Carr continued to lead the Church of God in Christ Jesus (Apostolic) until his death in 1970. Bp. William S. Barnes then presided until his death in 1987, and was followed by the current presiding bishop, William J. Faison Sr.

Members believe in God's standard of salvation; repentance and remission of sins; divine healing; the Lord's Supper; footwashing as a divine command; and the Second Coming of Jesus. The church holds an annual youth congress.

Membership: In 2008 the Church of God in Christ Jesus, Apostolic, Inc., reported more than 50 churches throughout the United States and in Canada, Jamaica, Bermuda, and the West Indies.

Sources:

Church of God in Christ Jesus, Apostolic, Inc. www.bibleway57.com/view/?pageID=75766.

DuPree, Sherry Sherrod. *African-American Holiness Pentecostal Movement: An Annotated Bibliography*. New York: Garland Publishing, 1992.

Richardson, James C., Jr. *With Water and Spirit*. Martinsville, VA: Author, n.d.

Church of Jesus Christ (Bloomington)

Current address not obtained for this edition.

The Church of Jesus Christ (Bloomington) emerged when several churches withdrew from the Church of Jesus Christ (Kingsport) in the late 1940s. It is similar in belief and practice to its parent body. It is under the leadership of its presiding bishop, Ralph Johnson.

Membership: In the 1980s there were approximately 500 members, 12 ministers, and eight congregations.

Church of Jesus Christ (Kingsport)

5836 Orebank Rd., Kingsport, TN 37662

The Church of Jesus Christ (Kingsport) grew out of the Pentecostal ferment in eastern Tennessee associated with the Church of God (Cleveland, Tennessee). The church became a chartered organization in 1927 under the leadership of Bishop M. K. Lawson. Formed at Cleveland, it moved its headquarters to Kingsport, Tennessee, in 1975. In 2008 its pastor was Ronald "Bo" Westmoreland, assisted by Sister Christi Westmoreland.

The church is similar to the United Pentecostal Church in its doctrinal stance. It holds to the King James version of the Bible as its creed; believes that the Bible teaches justification by faith, baptism of the Holy Spirit evidenced by speaking in tongues, and the imminent Second Coming of Jesus; and practices baptism by immersion, the Lord's Supper, and foot washing in connection with the Lord's Supper. The church believes in divine healing and calls members to holy living. Members refrain from the use of tobacco and alcohol and do not wear jewelry. Although generally following the laws of the state, members do not bear arms or take oaths before a magistrate.

Membership: Not reported.

Periodicals: *The Messenger*

Sources:

The Church of Jesus Christ. www.tcojc.us/.

Church of Jesus Christ Ministerial Alliance

Current address not obtained for this edition.

The Church of Jesus Christ Ministerial Alliance was formed in 1962 by members who withdrew from the Church of Jesus Christ (Kingsport) following the death of the founder and longtime leader, Bp. M. K. Lawson. There are no doctrinal differences between the two groups, their distinctions being solely administrative. In recent years there has been a friendly fellowship between the Church of Jesus Christ Ministerial Alliance and its parent body.

Membership: In 1990 there were 85 congregations, 300 ministers, and 6,000 members. Missionary work is supported in Canada, Jamaica, Trinidad, the Bahamas, England, and Australia.

Periodicals: *The Church of Jesus Christ Message of Hope*.

Church of Jesus Christ of Georgia

Current address not obtained for this edition.

The Church of Jesus Christ of Georgia is a small group that, under the leadership of Elder Wilbur Childres, withdrew from the Church of Jesus Christ (Kingsport) in the early 1960s. The church is similar to the parent body and still cooperates with its foreign mission program. It differs in its strict policy regarding marriage and divorce. It demands any minister who was divorced and remarried before conversion to the church to either return to their original spouse or live alone.

Membership: Not reported. There are two congregations, both in Georgia.

Church of Our Lord Jesus Christ of the Apostolic Faith

2081 Adam Clayton Powell Blvd., New York, NY 10029

The Church of Our Lord Jesus Christ of the Apostolic Faith was founded in New York City in 1919 by Robert Clarence Lawson (1883–1961), who as a pastor in the Pentecostal Assemblies of the World had founded churches in Texas and Missouri. At one point in his early life when he was ill Lawson had been taken to the Apostolic Faith Assembly Church, a leading church of the Pentecostal Assemblies, and its pastor, Garfield Thomas Haywood. There Lawson was healed, and he joined the Assemblies and adopted their non-trinitarian theology. In 1919 he left Haywood's jurisdiction and, moving to New York City, founded Refuge Church of Christ, the first congregation in his new independent church. Under Lawson's effective leadership, the organization grew quickly. Other congregations were estab-

lished, and a radio ministry, a periodical, a day nursery, and several businesses were initiated. In 1926 he opened a bible school to train pastors.

In the 1930s Lawson began a series of trips to the West Indies that led to the formation of congregations in Jamaica, Antigua, the Virgin Islands, and Trinidad. His lengthy tenure as bishop of the church was a time of steady growth, broken only by two schisms, by Sherrod C. Johnson (1897–1961; Church of the Lord Jesus Christ of the Apostolic Faith, 1930) and Smallwood E. Williams (1907–1991; Bible Way Church of Our Lord Jesus Christ, 1957). Lawson was succeeded by Hubert Spencer and by the current (2008) presiding apostle, Bp. William Lee Bonner.

Doctrine is like the older Pentecostal Assemblies of the World. Members believe in the oneness of God, who was the father in creation, the son in redemption, and now the Holy Ghost in the church. Footwashing is practiced, and water baptism in the name of Jesus Christ is believed to be necessary for salvation. The Word of God must be proclaimed throughout the world, according to God's commandment.

The church is headed by the presiding apostle, who is assisted by six regional apostles. There is an annual convocation. Affiliated churches can be found in Germany, England, Canada, Mexico, the Caribbean, South America, Africa, and Guyana. The Foreign Mission Department sends monthly stipends to various mission fields. A radio ministry, initiated in 1932, continued in 2008 with an hourly broadcast every Sunday evening.

Membership: In 1992 the church reported 30,000 members in 500 churches.

Educational Facilities:

Church of Christ Bible Institute, New York, New York.

W. L. Bonner Bible College, Columbia, South Carolina.

Periodicals: *The Contender for the Faith*, quarterly. Send orders to 2081 7th Ave., New York, NY 10027.

Sources:

Church of Our Lord Jesus Christ of the Apostolic Faith. www.cooljc.org.

Anderson, Arthur M., ed. *For the Defense of the Gospel*. New York: Church of Christ, 1972.

W. L. Bonner Literary Committee, with Bishop William L. Bonner. *And the High Places I'll Bring Down: Bishop William L. Bonner, the Man and His God*. Detroit: Author. 1999.

Church of the Lord Jesus Christ of the Apostolic Faith (Philadelphia)

701 S 22nd St., Philadelphia, PA 19146

The Church of the Lord Jesus Christ of the Apostolic Faith was founded in 1933 by Bishop Sherrod C. Johnson (1897–1961), formerly of the Church of Our Lord Jesus Christ of the Apostolic Faith. Johnson protested what he felt was Bishop Robert Clarence Lawson's too liberal policy of allowing female members to wear jewelry and makeup. Johnson insisted that women wear cotton stockings, calf-length dresses, and head coverings, and that they not straighten their hair. Johnson also opposed the observance of Lent, Easter, and Christmas. Upon Bishop Johnson's death in 1961, he was succeeded by S. McDowell Shelton (1929–1991). When Shelton died in 1991, his legally adopted son, Bishop Omega Y. L. Shelton, assumed the position of pastor and general overseer.

The church is known for its "oneness" doctrine. It demands that baptism must be in the name of the "Lord Jesus" or "Jesus Christ," but not just "Jesus." This exacting formula is to distinguish the Lord Jesus from Bar Jesus (Acts 13:6) and Jesus Justas (Col. 4:11). The church members also believe one must be filled with the Holy Ghost in order to have the new birth. The church is known for its conservatism; women, who cannot become preachers or teachers, must dress modestly, and remarriage is not permitted after divorce.

The church is episcopal. There is a national convention annually at the national headquarters in Philadelphia. Laypeople have an unusually high participation level in the national church, holding most of the top administrative positions. There is a radio ministry broadcast on Sunday mornings over stations in Bala Cynwid, Pennsylvania; Falls Church, Virginia; and New York, New York. Missions are conducted in Liberia, West Africa, England, Honduras, Jamaica, Haiti, Bahamas, Jordan, Portugal, and the Maldives.

Membership: In 2008 the church listed nine congregations.

Periodicals: *The Guiding Light*.

Sources:

Church of the Lord Jesus Christ of the Apostolic Faith www.tcljc.com/.

Churches of Christ in the Apostles Doctrine

9501 SW 175th Ter., Miami, FL 33157

The Churches of Christ in the Apostles Doctrine is an Apostolic "Jesus Only" Pentecostal body that has a base in the Spanish-speaking community of southern Florida. It was founded in the 1980s by Bp. M. J. Hernandez. The church has found its purpose in proclaiming a gospel of Jesus Christ that includes the calling of everyone to believe in Christ, repent of their sin, be baptized by water (immersed), and receive the baptism of the Holy Spirit. People who receive the baptism of the Holy Spirit will speak with other tongues as the Spirit of God gives the utterance. Those who receive the Holy Spirit will begin a life of spiritual growth to maturity. The churches place an emphasis on the oneness of God in a manner similar to the United Pentecostal Church International.

The churches sponsor an annual celebration, Apostolic Day; a ministry on college campuses, the Apostolic Crusaders; and an Internet Bible study course. Much of the work occurs within the Spanish-speaking community.

Membership: Not reported. There are five congregations in Florida, two in New York, and one each in Georgia, South Carolina, North Carolina, and Pennsylvania.

Periodicals: *Apostolic Sun*.

Sources:

Churches of Christ in the Apostles Doctrine. members.aol.com/afm238/.

Church in the Lord Jesus Christ of the Apostolic Faith

2449 Calvary Rd., Hartsville, SC 29550-7167

The Church in the Lord Jesus Christ of the Apostolic Faith was founded in Hartsville, South Carolina, in 1946 by Bp. L. Hunter (d. 1991), who was then a minister with the (almost identically named) Church of the Lord Jesus Christ of the Apostolic Faith. At the direction of that church's founder, Bp. Sherrod C. Johnson (1897–1961), he had moved to South Carolina and begun preaching in Darlington County. Hunter operated out of a tent until a congregation was assembled and a church building purchased in 1948 in Hartsville. Hunter pastored the growing church and gradually split from the Church of the Lord Jesus Christ of the Apostolic Faith. Hunter retained the name of Johnson's church, except for the change from "of the Lord Jesus Christ" to "in the Lord Jesus Christ."

Hunter's ministry spread throughout the state and reached outward to New York, Virginia, the District of Columbia, Ohio, Georgia, and Florida. Hunter began a radio show in 1956 that led to the formation of the Apostolic Faith Radio Network, which supports a nationwide radio ministry. Since 1980 the church has owned the White House for Senior Citizens, a home for the elderly. Hunter followed the doctrine of the parent body. He was strongly opposed to female ministers. Bishop Joe C. Tisdale succeeded Bishop Hunter as pastor and general overseer of the church after Hunter's death in July 1991.

Membership: In 2008, the church reported 14 congregations scattered along the east Coast from New York to Florida.

Periodicals: *The Whole Truth Gospel Herald*.

Sources:

Church in the Lord Jesus Christ of the Apostolic Faith.

www.thechurchin.org/home.htm.

DuPree, Sherry Sherrod. *African American Holiness Pentecostal Charismatic: Annotated Bibliography*. New York: Garland Publishing, 1992.

Congregational Holiness Church

3888 Fayetteville Hwy., Griffin, GA 30223

In 1920 a controversy over divine healing arose in the Georgia Conference of the Pentecostal Holiness Church, now known as the International Pentecostal Holiness Church. One faction contended that the healing provisions in the atonement were sufficient, and that human aids (doctors) were unnecessary. While this faction admitted the therapeutic value of effective remedies, such remedies were not considered necessary for God to heal. The other faction, led by Rev. Watson Sorrow, insisted that God had placed medicine on earth for man's use. The group against doctors relied on the biblical phrase about Christ's passion, "By his stripes you are healed."

The names of the Revs. Watson Sorrow and Hugh Bowling were dropped from the ministerial roll of the Pentecostal Holiness Church without their first being tried by the board of the Georgia annual conference, of which they were members. A number of ministers withdrew with them, and together in 1921 they organized the Congregational Holiness Church. They expressed differences with their parent body about the concentration of power in a few hands, so they attempted to democratize the church government. Consequently their polity is not episcopal, like that of the Pentecostal Holiness Church. Instead, polity is a moderate connectional system: Local churches are grouped in associations that elect delegates to a general association with legislative powers. Pastors are called by vote of the congregation. Both men and women may be ordained.

At each quadrennial general conference a full-time general superintendent with the honorary title of bishop is elected to administer, lead, and direct the Congregational Holiness Church in its affairs and functions. In 2008 the general superintendent was Bp. Ronald Wilson. The general conference also elects a first and second assistant general superintendent. These three superintendents, along with an elected general secretary, general treasurer, and world missions superintendent, comprise the General Executive Board. Members of the General Executive Board serve four-year terms.

The Congregational Holiness Church in the USA is divided into nine districts, with each district electing a five-member presbytery. The District Presbytery is made up of a superintendent, a first and second assistant superintendent, a secretary/treasurer and an assistant secretary/treasurer. District officials serve four-year terms.

The General Executive Board, general trustees, district presbyters, world missions superintendent, brotherhood president and women's ministries president make up the General Committee. The General Committee transacts any major business of the church between general conferences.

The General Conference of the Congregational Holiness Church is the highest governing body, with full power and authority to designate the teachings, principles, and practices of the local churches.

Mission work is active in Cuba, Costa Rica, Brazil, Mexico, Honduras, Guatemala, India, Nicaragua, and Spain.

Membership: In 1995 the church reported 7,000 members, 175 churches, and 429 ministers.

Periodicals: *Gospel Messenger*.

Sources:

Congregational Holiness Church. www.chchurch.com/index.htm.

Cox, B. L. *History and Doctrine of the Congregational Holiness Church*. Gainesville, GA: Author, 1959.

———. *My Life Story*. Greenwood, SC: C. H. Publishing House, n.d.

Evangelical Churches of Pentecost

Current address not obtained for this edition.

The Evangelical Churches of Pentecost emerged out of the early Pentecostal revivals that occurred in Saskatchewan, Canada, in 1913 as the Oneness non-Trinitarian perspective spread through the West. A camp meeting was founded at Trossachs. Some men converted at Trossachs became ministers and founded churches in various communities of the province. These ministers and churches were brought together in 1927 through the efforts of Rev. Alan H. Gillett (1895–1967), pastor at Radville, who secured a charter for the group as the Full Gospel Mission. Churches and ministers credentialed by the mission spread to the neighboring Canadian provinces of Alberta, Manitoba, and British Columbia.

The Full Gospel Mission evolved into a substantial body by the end of World War II, and in 1946 it incorporated as the Evangelical Churches of Pentecost. In 1953 the Evangelical Churches of Pentecost merged into the other major Oneness church in Canada, the Apostolic Church of Pentecost. At the time of the merger, some of the ministers and churches of the Evangelical Church of Pentecost declined to enter the merged body. They were concerned that some of the affiliated churches would lose their sovereignty. Also, being amillennialists, they rejected the premillennial eschatology of the Apostolic church. Amillennialism is a position that suggests that the millennium talked about in the book of Revelation is a metaphorical time period rather than an actual thousand-year period to be expected to occur in the near future. Those who stayed out of the merger reorganized and continued as the Full Gospel Ministerial Fellowship, but in the 1960s reincorporated and reassumed their earlier name.

Apart from its position on the millennium, the Evangelical Churches of Pentecost is similar to the Apostolic Church of Pentecost and the United Pentecostal Church. It believes in one God, whose name is Jesus; baptism by immersion in the name of Our Lord Jesus Christ; the baptism of the Holy Spirit evidenced by the believer speaking in tongues; the living of a Spirit-filled life of holiness; and divine healing.

The Evangelical Churches of Pentecost is organized as a fellowship of ministers, evangelists, and missionaries. Theirs is a strong belief in the autonomy of the local church and the congregations affiliated with the church are independent assemblies who happen to welcome pastors credentialed by the fellowship.

Membership: Not reported. In 1980 the churches reported approximately 50 ministers who served 19 churches in Canada and 3 in the United States with a combined membership of approximately 3,000. These churches support missionaries in Mexico, South India, and Burkina Faso in West Africa.

Sources:

Piepkorn, Arthur C. *Profiles in Belief: The Religious Bodies of the United States and Canada*. Vol. III. San Francisco, CA: Harper & Row, 1979.

First Church of Jesus Christ

1100 E. Lincoln St., Tullahoma, TN 37388

The First Church of Jesus Christ is a Pentecostal group that was chartered in Tullahoma, Tennessee, in 1965 by Bishop H. E. Honea (b. 1938), who has served as its chairman for thirty years. Honea grew up in Taft, Tennessee, and was called to ministry as a teenager. He began to preach when he was 16 years old and pastored churches in Alabama, Louisiana, Indiana, and Illinois before becoming pastor of the Tullahoma church, a position he still holds.

The Church of Jesus Christ is composed of those ministers, missionaries, and deacons licensed by the church and the members of the local congregations affiliated with it. It considers itself a company of baptized believers who adhere to the form of doctrine preached by Jesus and his Apostles, who have associated in the faith and fellowship of Jesus Christ, who are governed by the rules of the New Testament church, and who possess the gifts of ministry (Romans 12:6–8). The church believes that it continues the revival begun on the Day of Pentecost, 33 C.E. (Acts2).

The church affirms that Jesus Christ is the One True God, and reveals himself as the Father, the Son, and the Holy Ghost. The Holy Ghost is not considered the third person of the Godhead, but rather the manifestation of the Spirit of God (the creator) coming to dwell in the hearts and lives of men. This position is generally termed Oneness or Jesus Only.

The church practices the ordinances of the Lord's Supper, foot washing, tithing, and baptism in the name of Jesus Christ. It does not allow membership in secret societies and specifically decries the teachings of snake handling, the "seed in the serpent" doctrine, the spiritualizing of the ordinances of baptism and the Lord's Supper, the denial of a physical resurrection, and the denial of marriage. This set of doctrines is similar to those of other Apostolic pentecostal churches, such as the Church of Jesus Christ (Kingsport).

The First Church of Jesus Christ is headed by a chairman, assisted by a vice-chairman and assistant vice-chairman and the state bishops. Together, they constitute the board of bishops. The board of bishops holds the property of the church in trust. Missionary work is carried out in Jamaica, Haiti, the Philippines, Africa, and India.

Membership: In 2002 the church reported 10,000 members and 250 ministers in the United States and an additional 8,000 members and 175 ministers on the mission field.

Periodicals: *Banner of Love*.

Sources:

The First Church of Jesus Christ. www.thefirstchurchofjesuschrist.org.

Articles of Faith and By-Laws of the First Church of Jesus Christ, Inc. Tullahoma, TN: First Church of Jesus Christ, n.d.

Free Gospel Church of the Apostle's Doctrine

4703 Marlboro Pke., Coral Hills, MD 20734

The Free Gospel Church of the Apostle's Doctrine (also known as the Free Gospel Church of Christ and Defense of the Gospel Ministries) was founded in 1962 in Washington, D.C., by Bp. Ralph E. Green, formerly of the Way of the Cross Church of Christ. The church is similar in doctrine and practice to its parent body. The church is built around a large, 8,000-member congregation in Washington, which Green pastors. Green has developed an aggressive outreach ministry that includes a prison visitation program, a publishing concern, and a popular radio ministry. The prison ministry publishes a periodical, From Prison to Praise, and a variety of tract literature. Green has recorded over 1,000 sermons, and the church choir has made several records. The church has a retreat center in King George County, Virginia, called the Free Gospel Church Retreat.

Membership: Not reported. In 2008 the church's Web site listed nine congregations, including one in Nigeria.

Educational Facilities:

Open Bible Institute for Christian Apologetics.

The Free Gospel Christian Academy.

Periodicals: *Defense of the Gospel Newsletter*.

Sources:

Free Gospel Church of the Apostle's Doctrine. www.freegospel.org.

Payne, Wardell J., ed. *Directory of African American Religious Bodies: A Compendium by the Howard University School of Divinity*. Washington, DC: Howard University Press, 1991.

Glorious Church of God in Christ Apostolic Faith

Current address not obtained for this edition.

The Glorious Church of God in Christ Apostolic Faith was founded in 1921 by C. H. Stokes, its first presiding bishop. He was succeeded in 1928 by S. C. Bass who then headed the church for more than a quarter of a century. However, in 1952, after the death of his first wife, Bass remarried a woman who was a divorcée. It had been taught for many years that marrying a divorced person was wrong. Bass's actions split the 50-congregation church in half. Those who remained loyal to Bishop Bass retained the name, but the founding charter was retained by the other group, which took the name Original Glorious Church of God in Christ Apostolic Faith.

Highway Christian Church of Christ

436 W St. NW, Washington, DC 20001

The Highway Christian Church of Christ was founded in Washington, D.C., in 1927 by James Thomas Morris (1892–1959), formerly a minister with the Pentecostal Assemblies of the World (PAW). Morris had been raised a Methodist and was called to the ministry in 1918. He received the Pentecostal gift of the Holy Spirit in 1923 under the ministrations of Bp. Samuel Kelsey, a leader in the Church of God in Christ. He was later baptized in the name of Jesus Christ and affiliated as a minister with the PAW. After the founding of the Highway Church, he remained on cordial terms with his PAW colleagues. After a decade of service to his church, during which time it moved out of a tent and store into its own building, PAW Bp. J. M. Turpin consecrated Morris to the bishopric. Following Morris's death, he was succeeded by his nephew, J. V. Lomax (d. 2001), formerly a minister of the Church of Our Lord Jesus Christ of the Apostolic Faith under Bp. Robert Clarence Lawson. Bp. Samuel Redden replaced Lomax.

The church is among the most conservative of Pentecostal bodies. Members are encouraged to dress modestly as becoming the holy life and to be baptized in Jesus' name and filled with the Holy Spirit as in Acts 2:38. The church will install women as deaconesses and will accept ordained women from other denominations, but will neither ordain nor install women as pastors. Bp. Herman Girwright is the current pastor.

Membership: In 2002 there were 19 congregations and about 2,000 members.

Holy Temple Church of the Lord Jesus Christ of the Apostolic Faith

2075 Clinton Ave., Bronx, NY 10457

The Holy Temple Church of the Lord Jesus Christ of the Apostolic Faith is a "Jesus Only" church under the leadership of Bp. Belton Green, who serves as apostle, pastor, and general overseer. The church operates primarily within the African-American community and shares a doctrinal perspective with the Church of the Lord Jesus Christ of the Apostolic Faith, from which the church originated.

The church emphasizes that the New Birth consists of being buried with Jesus through baptism unto death, rising up to walk in newness of this life, and then being filled with the Holy Spirit, manifested by speaking in tongues. The church identifies the Jesus of the New Testament with Jehovah in the Old Testament.

The church is somewhat unique in its disavowal of several common Christian holy days. It discourages the celebration of Christmas and church members do not receive or give gifts on that occasion. The church also discourages the celebration of Lent and Holy Week (Palm Sunday, Good Friday, and Easter). These are considered later pagan accretions to Christianity. It traces Christmas to Zoroastrianism.

The church also takes a conservative stance on the role of women and does not allow female members to teach, preach, or in any way usurp the authority of the male members or the church. Members are encouraged to pay a tenth of their gross income to the church (a tithe).

The church sponsors a radio broadcast ministry.

Membership: In 2008 the church's Web site listed 28 congregations in the United States and affiliated foreign work in India, the Philippines, Jamaica, Haiti, Trinidad, the Cayman Islands, Nigeria, Ghana, Liberia, and the Democratic Republic of the Congo.

Sources:

Holy Temple Church of the Lord Jesus Christ of the Apostolic Faith. www.theholytemplechurch.org.

International Circle of Faith

Continental Office—North America, 115 Hwy. 42 E, Bedford, KY 40006

The International Circle of Faith (ICOF) was founded in 2001 by Bps. Oswaldo Arroyo and Bernie L. Wade and a group of Apostolic Pentecostal ministers who called for a new effort to unify Pentecostalism across the boundaries of its Trinitarian, Charismatic, and Apostolic segments. Since 2001 it has seen significant growth in North America, but also especially in Africa and Asia. Central to its new call to unity was the adoption of a system of spiritual mentoring of junior ministers by senior ministers in a father-son (rather than boss-employee) relationship. The Circle offers its associates mentoring by experienced pastors and church leaders, assistance in creating their own independent ministries, access to education, and national and international contacts.

New ministers are invited into the larger presbytery that includes all the Circle's ministries. Leadership is provided by the ICOF Leadership Association, which consists of the senior bishops and other officers who oversee the organization's affairs, grant ordinations, and monitor the quality of its ministers. Educational assistance is given to young ministers through the ICOF International Educational Network, which connects students through distance-learning opportunities at all levels, from high school to college and seminary. In this regard, the Circle supports Harvard High School, based in Washington, D.C., and a number of Christian Bible schools and colleges both in the United States and abroad. True to its networking model, some of these schools, such as the Bernie L. Wade Seminary in India, are specifically related to the Circle, whereas others have an older and broader constituency.

Much of the growth of the International Circle of Faith has come from networking parachurch ministries rather than congregations. Growth in Africa, in particular, has been built around empowering ministers in chaplaincy positions. The Charity World Network includes all the ministries involved in the delivery of various social services.

In January 2008 IFOC Europe was formally organized at services held in the United Kingdom.

Membership: Not reported. The Circle unites ministries across the United States and overseas in Europe, Africa, and India.

Educational Facilities:

Freedom Bible College and Seminary, Rogers, Arkansas.

Global Evangelical Christian College and Seminary, Wetumpka, Alabama.

Sources:

International Circle of Faith Apostolic Ministries. www.icof.net/icofhome.html.

International Ministerial Association

5201 W Homosassa Tr., Lecanto, FL 34461

The International Ministerial Association, Inc., was formed in 1954 by W. E. Kidson and 20 other pastors formerly with the United Pentecostal Church. It practices baptism by immersion and foot-washing. Tithing is believed to be the financial plan of the church. A strong belief in the Second Coming is taught, and the group believes in a distinct judgment during which only believers will be rewarded.

The Association is organized into 12 districts across the United States. An annual international conference is the place for fellowship between the ministers, who hold credentials through the Association, and the members of the autonomous congregations that accept the statement of faith. The Association's publishing arm, Herald Publishing House, is located in Houston, Texas.

Membership: Not reported. In 2008 the association reported 182 affiliated churches and ministries and missionaries operating in countries around the world.

Periodicals: *The Herald of Truth*.

Sources:

International Ministerial Association. www.interma.net/index.html.

Mount Hebron Apostolic Temple of Our Lord Jesus of the Apostolic Faith

Mt. Hebron Apostolic Temple, 27 Vineyard Ave., Yonkers, NY 10703

The Mount Hebron Apostolic Temple of Our Lord Jesus of the Apostolic Faith was founded in 1963 by George H. Wiley III, pastor of the Yonkers, New York, congregation of the Apostolic Church of Christ in God. As his work progressed, Wiley came to feel that because of his accomplishments for the denomination he should be accorded the office of bishop. He had had particular success in the area of youth work, and his wife, Sr. Lucille Wiley, served as president of the Department of Youth Work. However, the board of the Apostolic Church denied his request to become a bishop. Wiley left with his supporters and became bishop of a new Apostolic denomination.

Wiley has placed great emphasis on youth work and on radio work, establishing an outreach in New York, one in North Carolina, and another in South Carolina. The temple continues the doctrine and polity of the Apostolic Church of Christ in God and has a cordial relationship with its parent organization.

Membership: In 1980 the temple reported 3,000 members in nine congregations being served by 15 ministers. There are two bishops.

Sources:

Mount Hebron Apostolic Temple of Our Lord Jesus of the Apostolic Faith. www.myspace.com/iampersuaded.

Mt. Zion Sanctuary

21 Dayton St., Elizabeth, NJ 07202

The Mt. Zion Sanctuary was formed in 1882 by Antoinette Jackson, a member of the Baptist Church. Rejecting the idea that she was suffering as an invalid for the glory of God, she sought healing by prayer and fasting, and was believed to be cured on July 14, 1880. The sanctuary asserts that she became blessed with the gifts of the Spirit, particularly healing.

Mt. Zion Sanctuary members believe in the Trinity as God the Father, God the Son, and the Holy Spirit, which is the executive power of God. Humans find deliverance from sin and sickness in the vicarious sacrifice of Jesus. Believers are sanctified as they obey the truth. Baptism by immersion is practiced and the Sabbath is kept. The church is considered to be the society of born-again believers who live a holy life. Church members believe in Christ's premillennial Second Coming (i.e., Christ will return to find Satan prior to his 1,000-year reign on earth with his saints).

Jackson was succeeded by Pr. Ithamar Quigley, who was healed under her ministration. The current president is Pr. Theodore Jordan.

Membership: In 1992 the sanctuary reported 100 members in two centers led by two ministers in the United States. Internationally, there were 10 churches in Nigeria and 11 in Jamaica. Two formerly affiliated congregations in England have become independent.

New Bethel Church of God in Christ (Pentecostal)

Current address not obtained for this edition.

In 1927, Rev. A. D. Bradley was admonished by the board of bishops of the Church of God in Christ to refrain from preaching the "Jesus-only" doctrine. (The Church of God in Christ was the oldest and among the largest of the predominantly black Trinitarian Pentecostal churches.) Bradley refused, and with his wife and Lonnie Bates established the New Bethel Church of God in Christ (Pentecostal). Bradley became the church's presiding bishop. Doctrine is similar to other Jesus-only groups. The three ordinances of baptism, the Lord's Supper, and foot washing are observed. The group is pacifist but allows alternative noncombatant positions to be held by law-abiding church members. The group disapproves of secret societies and of school activities which conflict with a student's moral scruples.

The presiding bishop is the executive officer and presides over all meetings of the general body. A board of bishops acts as a judicatory body and a general assembly as the legislative body.

Membership: Not reported.

Original Glorious Church of God in Christ Apostolic Faith

995 Foster Ave., Elyria, OH 44035

The Glorious Church of God was founded in 1921. However, in 1952 its presiding bishop, S. C. Bass married a divorced woman. Approximately half of the 50-congregation church rejected Bass and reorganized under the leadership of W. O. Howard and took the name Original Glorious Church of God in Christ Apostolic Faith. The term *original* signifies the church's claim to its history, demonstrated by the retention of the founding charter. Howard was succeeded by Bp. I. W. Hamiter, under whose leadership the church has grown spectacularly and developed a mission program in Haiti, Jamaica, and India. Hamiter has also led in the purchase of a convention center for the church's annual meeting in Columbus, Ohio.

Membership: In 1980 the church had 55 congregations in the United States, 110 congregations overseas, 200 ministers, and approximately 25,000 members worldwide.

Pentecostal Assemblies of the World

International Headquarters Offices, 3939 N Meadows Dr., Indianapolis, IN 46205

Oldest of the Apostolic or "Jesus Only" Pentecostal churches, the Pentecostal Assemblies of the World (PAW) began as a loosely organized fellowship of trinitarian pentecostals in Los Angeles in 1906. J. J. Frazee (occasionally incorrectly reported as "Frazier") was elected the first general superintendent. Early membership developed along the West Coast and in the Midwest. From 1913 to 1916, the annual convention was held in Indianapolis, soon to become the center of the organization. Growth in the organization was spurred when it became the first group of pentecostals to accept the "Jesus Only" Apostolic theology, which identified Jesus as the Jehovah of the Old Testament and denied the Trinity. Many ministers from other pentecostal bodies joined the assemblies when the groups within which they held credentials rejected Apostolic teachings. In 1918, the General Assemblies of the Apostolic Assemblies, a recently formed Apostolic body that included such outstanding early movement leaders as D. C. O. Opperman (1872–1926) and H. A. Goss (1883–1964), merged into the PAW.

From its beginning the Pentecostal Assemblies of the World was fully integrated racially, though it was predominantly white in membership. In 1919, following the influx of so many ministers and members, especially the large newly merged body, the Pentecostal Assemblies reorganized. Four of its 21 field superintendents were black, among them Garfield Thomas Haywood (1880–1931), who would later become presiding bishop. In 1924, most of the white members withdrew to form the Pentecostal Ministerial Alliance, now an integral part of the United Pentecostal Church. The remaining members, who were not totally, but predominantly black, reorganized again, created the office of bishop, and elected Haywood to lead them. Haywood remained presiding bishop until his death in 1931.

Shortly after Haywood's death, the Apostolic Churches of Jesus Christ— as the former Pentecostal Ministerial Alliance, then in a phase of consolidating various Apostolic groups into a single organization, was briefly known—invited the Assemblies to consider a merger. The merger attempt failed, but the assemblies again lost individual congregations and members to the Apostolic Churches of Jesus Christ, and a large group who formed a new church, the Pentecostal Assemblies of Jesus Christ. In the face of these new losses, a third reorganization occurred in 1932. For several years, the church was led by a small group of bishops, enlarged to seven in 1935. Two years later, Samuel Grimes, a former missionary in Liberia, was elected presiding bishop, a post he retained until his death in 1967. Under his guidance, the Pentecostal Assemblies Church experienced its greatest era of expansion. Unlike most black Pentecostal bishops, Grimes did not also serve a parish; hence, he was able to devote himself full-time to his episcopal duties.

The doctrine of the Assemblies is similar to that of the Assemblies of God, except that the church does not believe in the Trinity. Holiness is stressed and the group believes that for ultimate salvation, it is necessary to have a life wholly sanctified. Wine is used in the Lord's Supper. Healing is stressed and foot-washing practiced. Members are pacifists, though they feel it is a duty to honor rules. There are strict dress and behavior codes. Divorce and remarriage are allowed under certain circumstances.

There is an annual general assembly that elects the bishops and the general secretary. It also designates the presiding bishop, who heads a board of bishops. The church is divided into 30 districts (dioceses) headed by a bishop. The assemblies are designated joint members of each local board of trustees. A missionary board oversees missions in Nigeria, Jamaica, England, Ghana, and Egypt.

The presiding bishop in 2008 is Bp. Horace E. Smith.

Membership: In 1994 the Assemblies had reported 1,000,000 members/constituents in 1,760 churches served by 4,262 ministers, divided into 43 districts, each headed by a bishop. There are approximately 1,000 churches in the foreign missionary field.

Educational Facilities:

Aenon Bible School, Indianapolis, Indiana.

Periodicals: *Christian Outlook*.

Sources:

Pentecostal Assemblies of the World. www.pawinc.org.

Dugas, Paul P., comp. *The Life and Writings of Elder G. T. Haywood*. Portland, OR: Apostolic Book Publishers, 1968.

Golder, Morris E. *History of the Pentecostal Assemblies of the World*. Indianapolis, IN: Author, 1973.

———. *The Life and Works of Bishop Garfield Thomas Haywood*. Indianapolis, IN: Author, 1977.

Tyson, James L. *Before I Sleep*. Indianapolis, IN: Pentecostal Publications, 1976.

Pentecostal Church of God

9244 Delmar, Detroit, MI 48211

The Pentecostal Church of God (not to be confused with the Pentecostal Church of God of America headquartered at Joplin, Missouri) is a predominantly black Pentecostal body founded by Apostle Willie James Peterson (1921–1969). Peterson grew up in Florida, and though his family attended a Baptist church there, he was never baptized. The course of his life was interrupted in his early adult years by a dream in which he was in the presence of God and his angels. Peterson began a period of prayer, after which God called him to preach. He became an independent evangelist and came to believe in the Apostolic or non-Trinitarian position. He began to preach that doctrine in 1955 in Meridian, Mississippi, and to raise up congregations across the South. At the time of his death, Peterson was succeeded by the four bishops of the church, William Duren, J. J. Sears, C. L. Rawls, and E. Rice.

It is the belief of the Pentecostal Church of God that Peterson was an apostle, anointed by God for his task through revelation. The essence of the revelation was an understanding of the Kingdom of God. Peterson taught that conversion meant turning away from worldliness (the kingdom of this world ruled by Satan) to godliness (the kingdom of Heaven). Peterson identified the Roman Catholic Church with Babylon, the Mother of Harlots, spoken of in Revelation 17:3–5. Satanic doctrine was taught in that church and in its daughter churches, Protestantism. To accept the gospel of the kingdom is to turn from the false teachings of the Babylonian churches to God's truths. These truths lead the believer to repentance as godly sorrow for one's sins; baptism by immersion in the name of Jesus Christ; a rejection of the unbiblical doctrine of the Trinity; an understanding of heaven as the realm of God and his angels and hell as a place of confinement; the nonobser-

vance of holidays such as Christmas, Easter, and New Year's Day; nonparticipation in human government (which includes practicing pacifism, not saluting the flag, and not voting); and holy matrimony performed by a holy minister.

Membership: Not reported.

Sources:

Faison, Jennell Peterson. *The Apostle W. J. Peterson*. Detroit, MI: Pentecostal Church of God, 1980.

Pentecostal Church of Zion

c/o Zion College of Theology, Box 110, French Lick, IN 47432

As a youth in Kentucky, Luther S. Howard (1903–1981) was converted by an independent Pentecostal minister and, in 1920, was ordained a minister of the Holy Bible Mission at Louisville. He served as a minister and then as vice president. Upon the death of its founder, Mrs. C. L. Pennington, the Mission was dissolved. Its ministers felt the need to continue their work and, in 1954, formed a new organization, the Pentecostal Church of Zion, Inc. Elder Howard was elected president and, in 1964, bishop. Because most of the work of the Holy Bible Mission was in Indiana, the new organization was headquartered at French Lick, Indiana.

The Pentecostal Church of Zion is like the Assemblies of God in most of its doctrine but differs from it on some points. The group keeps the Ten Commandments, including the Saturday Sabbath, and the Mosaic law concerning clean and unclean meats. (Cows and sheep are clean and may be eaten; pigs and other animals with cloven hooves may not be eaten because they are considered unclean). Most importantly, the group does not have a closed creed, but believes that members continue to grow in grace and knowledge. Anyone who feels that he has new light on the Word of God is invited to bring his ideas to the annual convention, where they can be discussed by the executive committee. By such a process, a decision was made in the 1960s to drop the Lord's Supper as an ordinance. The church now believes in the celebration of Passover by daily communion with the Holy Ghost.

Church polity is episcopal. There is one bishop with life tenure and an assistant bishop elected for a three-year term. An annual meeting with lay delegates is held at the headquarters.

Membership: Not reported.

Educational Facilities:

Zion College of Theology, French Lick, Indiana.

Periodicals: *Zion's Echoes of Truth*.

Pentecostal Churches of Apostolic Faith

PCAF Headquarters, 723 South 45th St., Louisville, KY 40211

The Pentecostal Churches of Apostolic Faith was formed in 1957 by former members of the Pentecostal Assemblies of the World under the leadership of Bp. Samuel N. Hancock. Hancock was one of the original men selected as a bishop of the Assemblies following its reorganization in 1925. In 1931 he was one of the leaders in the attempt to unite the Assemblies with the predominantly white Pentecostal Ministerial Alliance, and he helped form the Pentecostal Assemblies of Jesus Christ, a body whose polity was more acceptable to the Alliance. Within a few years, Hancock returned to the Assemblies as an elder and was elected as a bishop for the second time.

However, soon after Hancock's return, it was discovered that he had deviated on traditional Apostolic doctrine in that he taught that Jesus was only the son of God, not that he was God. His position forced the Assemblies to issue a clarifying statement of its position, but Hancock's teachings were tolerated. Hancock also felt that he should have become the presiding bishop. Disappointment at not being elected seems to have fueled the discontent felt throughout the 1950s. Hancock carried two other bishops into the new church formed in 1957, including Willie Lee, pastor of Christ Temple Church, the congregation pastored by Garfield Thomas Haywood, the first presiding bishop of the Assemblies. Lee succeeded Hancock as presiding bishop of the Churches upon the latter's death in 1963. The following year, a major schism occurred when the majority of the Churches rejected the doctrinal position held by Hancock and also taught by Lee. Elzie Young had the charter and claimed the support of the Churches to become the new presiding bishop. The church returned to the traditional Apostolic theology.

The Pentecostal Churches of the Apostolic Faith are congregational in polity, and headed by a presiding bishop (Alfred Singleton in 2008) and a council of bishops. It is divided into 13 district councils. The Churches support missionaries in Haiti and in Liberia, where they have also built a school.

Membership: In 1980 the Churches had approximately 25,000 members, 115 churches, and 380 ministers.

Sources:

Pentecostal Churches of Apostolic Faith. www.pcaf.net/us/main.

Primitive Church of Jesus Christ

c/o Bethel Church of Jesus Christ, Hwy. 19 N, Inglis, FL 34449

The Primitive Church of Jesus Christ resulted from a split in the Church of Jesus Christ (Kingsport). The occasion of the split was the decision by the church to move the location of its mid-season convention from Inglis, Florida, to Homosassa, Florida, a move opposed by many of the members. The church shares doctrine and practice with its parent body, the split being purely administrative. The church holds an annual Bible conference each June. It is headed by Elder John Wilson.

Membership: Not reported.

Progressive Church of our Lord Jesus Christ

2222 Barhamville Rd., Columbia, SC 29204-1203

The Progressive Church of Our Lord Jesus Christ was founded in 1944 by Bp. Joseph D. Williams (d. 1966), who had been a minister with the Church of Our Lord Jesus Christ of the Apostolic Faith. The founding of the church was occasioned by the healing of a Sr. Helen L. Washington of Colombia, South Carolina, of leukemia through the prayer offered by Williams, then a pastor in Ohio. Washington later professed faith in Christ, received the baptism of the Holy Spirit, and spoke in tongues. Williams subsequently moved to South Carolina, with the Washington family providing the initial resources. The church's presiding bishop, R. C. Lawson, blessed the new work, which developed independently of, but on friendly relations with the Church of the Lord Jesus Christ of the Apostolic Faith. Its beliefs are identical with those of the parent body.

Following his death, Williams was succeeded by an early member, Bp. Joel G. Washington (d. 1987). By this time, the church had been established in Columbia, Killian, Mullins, Lugoff, Denmark, Florence, and Bishopville (all in South Carolina), and missions had been established in Barnwell, Edgefield, Greenville, and Johnson (also all in South Carolina).

Before he died, Williams appointed Elders Joel G. Washington, Edward Smith, Herman Jackson, Henry J. Breakfield, and Ernest Finkley as the church's Board of Elders. This board operated until 1973, when its members were consecrated as bishops and it was transformed into a Board of Bishops. Bishop Washington served as presiding bishop until his death in 1987. He was succeeded by the present presiding bishop, Edward Smith. Serving along with him as members of the Board of Bishops are Bps. Theodore Jenkins, David S. Johnson, Paul C. Johnson, and Lang Priester, and Bp.-Elect J. D. Williams.

In 1987 Smith established the annual National Unity Conference, which brings church members together to consider issues related to maintaining the church's spirit of oneness. This is in addition to the Holy Convocation held annually in Columbia, South Carolina. Smith oversaw the dedication of new church headquarters in 1999.

The church is organized into five districts, each with a district bishop and a district elder.

Membership: Not reported. In 2008 the Progressive Church consisted of approximately 25 churches and missions.

Sources:

Progressive Church of Our Lord Jesus Christ. http://www.progressivechurch.org/

Redeemed Assembly of Jesus Christ, Apostolic

c/o Bishop James F. Harris, 2200 Fairfax Ave., Richmond, VA 23224

The Redeemed Assembly of Jesus Christ, Apostolic was formed in 1979 by James Frank Harris and Douglas Williams, two bishops of the Highway Christian Church who rejected the leadership of that church by Bp. J. V. Lomax. They complained that Lomax made decisions in conference with the elders of the congregation he headed in Washington, D.C., bypassing other bishops and pastors. The new church is headed by a presiding bishop, an assistant presiding bishop, and an executive council consisting of the bishops and all the pastors. There was no doctrinal conflict in the split.

Membership: In 1980 the church had six congregations: one in Richmond, Virginia, one in New York City, and four in the Washington, D.C., area.

Sources:

Redeemed Assembly of Jesus Christ, Apostolic. www.redeemedassembly.com.

Shiloh Apostolic Temple

1516 W Master, Philadelphia, PA 19121

The Shiloh Apostolic Temple was founded in 1953 by Elder Robert O. Doub Jr., of the Apostolic Church of Christ in God. In 1948 Doub had moved to Philadelphia to organize a new congregation for the Apostolic Church of Christ in God. He not only succeeded in building a stable congregation, Shiloh Apostolic Temple, he also helped other congregations throughout the state to organize. In light of his accomplishments, Doub felt that he should be made a bishop and so petitioned the church to be elevated. He believed that the state overseer was taking all the credit Doub himself deserved. When Doub's petition was denied, he left the church in 1953, taking with him a single congregation. In 1954 he incorporated separately.

The energetic work that characterized Doub's years in the Apostolic Church of Christ in God led Shiloh Apostolic Temple to outgrow its parent body. Doub began a periodical and purchased a camp, Shiloh Promised Land Camp, in Montrose, Pennsylvania. He also took over foreign work in England and Trinidad. Doctrine, not at issue in the schism, remains that of the parent Church of God (Apostolic) from which the Apostolic Church of Christ in God came.

Membership: In 1980 the church had 4,500 members, of which 500 were in the congregation in Philadelphia. The church reported 23 congregations, of which 8 were in England, and 2 in Trinidad.

Periodicals: *Shiloh Gospel Wave*

True Jesus Church

314 S Brookhurst St. #104, Anaheim, CA 92804

The True Jesus Church was established in 1917 in Beijing, China, after three of the early workers, Paul Wei (d. 1919), Ling-Shen Chang (b. 1863), and Barnabas Chang (1882–ca. 1960), once affiliated with other denominations, had received the Holy Spirit and the revelation of the perfect Truth concerning salvation. The True Jesus Church spread through missionaries who were commissioned and via gospel newsletters published and distributed to various provinces throughout China. The church spread to Taiwan and throughout Southeast Asia in 1926 and 1927, respectively. Church headquarters were established in Nanjing, China, in 1926, then relocated to Shanghai the following year. The first workers reached the United States—Hawaii—in 1930.

Like other Chinese churches, the True Jesus Church suffered following the Communist takeover of China in 1949, but it survived and prospered after moving its headquarters to Taiwan. This growth led to the formation of the International Assembly of the True Jesus Church by delegates at the World Conference in Taiwan in 1975. In 1985, the principal office of the international assembly was relocated from Taiwan to Los Angeles, California. Subsequently, under the jurisdiction of the international assembly, four evangelical centers were established: the America Evangelical Center, the Europe Evangelical Center, the North-East Asia Evangelical Center, and the South-East Asia Evangelical Center.

The True Jesus Church considers itself the restored Apostolic Church of the End Time. The church believes that through the Holy Spirit it has received a divine revelation of the Truth, confirmed through signs and miracles. Its name, "True Jesus Church," also has a spiritual significance. The word True denotes that God is true (John 3:33, 17:3; 1 Thessalonians 1:9) and recognizes that Jesus referred to himself as the Truth (John 14:6), or the true Vine (John 15:1), just as he was regarded as the true Light (John 1:9).

Because church founders believed that God called and established the church (Acts 15:14–18), they also believed that the church should bear his name. The Bible indicates that God's name was Jesus (Matthew 1:21; John 17:11, 26). The church exalts the name of God (Jesus), and as the body of Christ rightly has "Jesus" as her name.

Doctrinally, the church is aligned with the doctrine of the non-trinitarian Apostolic or "Jesus Only" movement, which practices baptism in "Jesus' Name." Baptism is by full immersion in living water, but unlike most pentecostal churches, infants are baptized. The church practices foot-washing (as a third sacrament beside baptism and the Lord's Supper) and worships on the Sabbath. It is believed that the reception of the Holy Spirit is necessary for entering the kingdom of God, and that speaking in tongues is the sign of that reception.

Membership: In 2008 the church had 1.5 million members in 48 countries. The church's Web site in 2008 listed 23 congregations in the United States and five in Canada.

Sources:

True Jesus Church. www.tjc.org/landing.aspx.

The Five Biblical Doctrines. Garden Grove, CA: Words of Life Publishing House, 1995. 27 pp.

One True God. London: TJC Press, 1998. 163 pp.

Return to the True Church. Garden Grove, CA: Words of Life Publishing House, 1995. 30 pp.

Speaking in Tongues: A Biblical Perspective. Garden Grove, CA: Words of Life Publishing House, 1996. 33 pp.

Yang, John. *Essential Bible Doctrines*. Garden Grove, CA: Word of Life Publishing House, 1997. 215 pp.

True Vine Pentecostal Churches of Jesus
931 Bethel Ln., Martinsville, VA 24112

Dr. Robert L. Hairston, who had been a pastor in several Trinitarian Pentecostal groups, is cofounder with William Monroe Johnson of the True Vine Pentecostal Holiness Church. However, in 1961 Hairston accepted the apostolic "Jesus-only" teachings. He left the church he had founded and formed the True Vine Penetcostal Churches of Jesus. Causal factors in the formation of the new denomination were differences between Hairston and Johnson over church polity and Hairston's marital situation. Hairston rejected the idea of local congregations being assessed to pay for the annual convocation of the church. Also, he had divorced his first wife and remarried, an action frowned upon in many Pentecostal circles.

The church follows standard apostolic teachings. Women are welcome in the ministry. Growth of the group was spurred in 1976 by the addition of several congregations headed by Bp. Thomas C. Williams.

Membership: In 1980 the church reported 10 churches and missions, 2 bishops, 14 ministers, and approximately 900 members.

United Apostolic Church International
PO Box 1452, Aberdeen, WA 98520

The United Apostolic Church International was formed at the end of the 1990s by former members of various Apostolic and Pentecostal churches who felt that the Pentecostal movement had during the hundred years of its existence never completely left behind various false teachings of the denominational churches, the traditions of men, and even Roman Catholicism.

The church continues the Apostolic Jesus Only theology of the Oneness Movement. It identifies Jehovah in the Old Testament with Jesus of the New Testament and demands that baptism be by immersion in the name of Jesus only. The church has a liberal, tolerant view on many doctrines not considered essential to salvation, such as eschatology; however, it sharply disagrees over the ordination of females (which most Apostolic churches permit).

From its understanding of the scriptures, the church teaches that modest dress should prevail, and that males should wear their hair short and females should wear theirs long. It has no opinion on related issues not touched on in scripture, such as beards or women wearing their hair up or down, and so on.

The most important new truth leading to the founding of the United Apostolic Church is its understanding of church policy. It believes that both the episcopal and congregational forms of church government are unbiblical and that leadership should be exercised through a college of elders (similar to the presbyterian systems, but without the sharp distinction between teaching elders and ruling elders). In this regard, the church also disapproves of the use of titles for the clergy, such as Reverend or Bishop, which would imply a hierarchy within the church. The board of elders selects a general secretary and a general superintendent. Work in the United States is divided into six districts, each led by a district superintendent.

The church seeks an educated ministry to lead it, but has come to feel that a college or seminary may not be the best method to create such a ministry. It feels that many who might be qualified may not receive an education due to a lack of financial resources. In place of the seminary, the local assembly should be the environment in which leadership is developed.

Membership: In 2002 there were 32 ministers serving churches across the United States. There is also related work in Germany.

Periodicals: *UACI Newsletter*

Sources:

United Apostolic Church International. www.uaci.org.

United Church of Jesus Christ (Apostolic)
5150 Baltimore National Pke., Baltimore, MD 21229

The United Church of Jesus Christ (Apostolic) traces its history to 1945, when Randolph A. Carr, an overseer in the Church of God in Christ, withdrew because of doctrinal differences and formed a new church, the Church of God in Christ Jesus (Apostolic). Carr had come to believe in the Apostolic doctrine concerning the Oneness of the Godhead (as opposed to the Church of God in Christ's adherence to the doctrine of the Trinity).

In 1965 Monroe R. Saunders Sr., then the church's general secretary and a member of its board of bishops, expressed serious objections over contradictions between church belief and certain actions by the church's leadership—specifically, the actions of Bishop Carr in relation to teachings on marriage and divorce. In response, Carr forced Saunders out of the church. Many of the members and leaders left with Saunders and joined him in the formation of the United Church of Jesus Christ (Apostolic).

Saunders carefully put together a *Book of Church Order and Discipline* to guide the administration of the new church. The church is operated by a board of bishops, led by a presiding bishop or president and a vice-bishop or vice-president. The church observes the ordinances of baptism, Holy Communion, and foot washing.

Saunders has served as president since the church's founding in 1965. One of the more educated leaders in the Apostolic Movement, Saunders completed postgraduate studies and has led in the cause of creating an educated ministry. He formed the Center for a More Abundant Life, which serves as an umbrella organization for a variety of social and educational services, such as the Center for Creative Learning, an early childhood educational facility; the Monroe R. Saunders School for elementary school children; and two high rise houses for the elderly and handicapped.

In 2004 Bp. Monroe Saunders Sr. was elevated to the position of Chief Apostle of the United Church of Jesus Christ (Apostolic). The new presiding bishop is Bp. Monroe Saunders Jr., who is also the pastor of the First United Church of Jesus Christ (Apostolic).

Membership: The church reports 80 congregations, 100,000 members, and 150 ministers in the United States and Canada, and it has missions in England, Africa, and the West Indies.

Educational Facilities:

Institute of Biblical Studies, Baltimore, Maryland.

Sources:

United Church of Jesus Christ (Apostolic). www.unitedchurchofjesuschrist.org.

Saunders, Monroe R., Sr. *The Book of Church Order and Discipline of the United Church of Jesus Christ (Apostolic)*. Washington, DC: 1965.

United Churches of Jesus, Apostolic
Current address not obtained for this edition.

The United Churches of Jesus, Apostolic was formed by several bishops of the Apostolic Church of Christ in God who rejected the leadership of presiding bishop J. C. Richardson, Sr. Richardson had married a divorced woman. The church is headed by a general bishop, J. W. Audrey (one of the founders of the Apostle Church) and a board of bishops. Doctrine is like the parent body.

Membership: In 1980 the United Churches of Jesus, Apostolic had 2,000 members, 20 churches, 30 ministers, and 6 bishops.

United Pentecostal Church International
8855 Dunn Rd., Hazelwood, MO 63042

HISTORY. The United Pentecostal Church International was formed in 1945 through a merger of the Pentecostal Church, Inc. and the Pentecostal Assemblies of Jesus Christ. Both organizations dated to a 1924 schism within the Pentecostal Assemblies of the World. During the early 1920s, ministers within the Assemblies had become convinced that the Assemblies' interracial makeup was hindering its functioning, due in part to various laws in the South concerning the mixing of blacks and whites. Members who left eventually formed three separate organizations.

Before leaving the 1924 Chicago, Illinois, conference at which the split occurred seceding members met in a separate hall to lay plans for a new organization. That organization was chartered the next year as the Pentecostal Ministerial Alliance. It continued to function under that name until 1932, when it became the Pentecostal Church, Inc.

Some who had participated in the formation of the Pentecostal Ministerial Alliance were upset over the Alliance's final organization, as it provided only for the ministers and not for the members of the congregations. Meeting in Texas in October 1925, this group formed Emmanuel's Church in Jesus Christ. A third group gathered in St. Louis and formed the Pentecostal Churches of Jesus Christ. In 1927, these two groups merged to become the Pentecostal Church of Jesus Christ.

In 1931 the Pentecostal Church of Jesus Christ voted to merge with the Pentecostal Assemblies of the World, the body from which it had originally derived. The newly merged interracial body was called the Pentecostal Assemblies of Jesus Christ. However, as the decade proceeded, racial tensions again arose. For example, many southerners (who constituted a significant part of the group) were concerned that the church's conferences could never be held in the South because of racial laws. Beginning around 1936, black ministers and predominantly black con-

gregations began to resign and return to the Pentecostal Assemblies of the World, eventually leaving the Pentecostal Assemblies of Jesus Christ an all-white body. It was as such that the latter entered the 1945 merger.

BELIEFS. The distinctive doctrines of water baptism in the name of Jesus Christ and the Oneness of God were taught in 1913–1914 by early Pentecostal leaders such as Frank J. Ewart (1877–1947), Robert McAleister (1880–1953), Glenn A. Cook (1867–1948), and Garfield Thomas Haywood (1880–1931). Many of these men became members of the Assemblies of God but left that organization in 1916 when differences arose over these doctrines.

According to the statement of faith issued by the church, its basic and fundamental doctrine is "repentance, baptism in water by immersion in the name of the Lord Jesus Christ for the remission of sins, and the baptism of the Holy Ghost with the initial sign of speaking with other tongues as the Spirit gives utterance." The church's statement also affirms belief in the one true God who manifested himself in the flesh as Jesus Christ and who also manifests himself as the Holy Spirit. The church practices foot-washing and healing and follows a holiness code that includes disapproval of secret societies, mixed bathing, women cutting their hair, worldly amusements, home television sets, and immodest dress. While strongly affirming loyalty to the government, the church is against bearing arms or taking human life.

ORGANIZATION. Government of the church is basically congregational, with presbyterial elements. A general conference meets annually. A general superintendent, two assistants, and a secretary treasurer are members of a general board consisting of district superintendents, executive presbyters, and division heads. A foreign missions division oversees missions around the world in about 125 countries. Under the name Word Aflame Press, the Pentecostal Publishing House in Hazelwood, Missouri, publishes books, Sunday school material, and a wide variety of religious literature. The church is divided into 50 districts that include churches in every state and all Canadian provinces and territories. The church supports nine Bible colleges, the Tupelo, Mississippi, Children's Mansion, the Lighthouse Ranch for Boys, the Spirit of Freedom Ministries, and Compassion Services. In 2008 Kenneth F. Haney was the general superintendent.

Membership: In 2008 the UPCI in North America (United States and Canada) listed 4,358 churches (consisting of 4,099 autonomous churches and 258 daughter works) and 9,085 ministers, and reported a Sunday school attendance of 646,304. Moreover, the church is also located in 175 other nations, where there are 22,881 licensed ministers, 28,351 churches and meeting places, 652 missionaries, and a foreign constituency of over 3 million, making for a total worldwide constituency of more than 4,036,945.

Educational Facilities:

Apostolic Bible Institute, St. Paul, Minnesota.

Apostolic Missionary Institute, Oshawa, Ontario, Canada.

Christian Life College, Stockton, California.

Gateway College of Evangelism, Florissant, Missouri.

Indiana Bible College, Indianapolis, Indiana.

Jackson College of Ministries, Jackson, Mississippi.

Kent Christian College, Dover, Delaware.

Texas Bible College, Houston, Texas.

United Pentecostal Bible Institute, Fredericton, New Brunswick, Canada.

Periodicals: *The Pentecostal Herald* • *The Global Witness*

Sources:

United Pentecostal Church International. www.upci.org.

Clanton, Arthur L. *United We Stand*. Hazelwood, MO: Pentecostal Publishing House, 1970.

Foster, Fred J. *Their Story: 20th-Century Pentecostals*. Hazelwood, MO: World Aflame Press, 1981.

Urshan, Andrew D. *My Study of Modern Pentecostals*. Portland, OR: Apostolic Book
Publishers, 1981.

United Way of the Cross Churches of Christ of the Apostolic Faith

Current address not obtained for this edition.

The United Way of the Cross Churches of Christ of the Apostolic Faith was founded
by Bp. Joseph Adams of the Way of the Cross Church of Christ and Elder Harrison J.
Twyman of the Bible Way Church of Our Lord Jesus Christ World Wide. The new
church was formed when the two founders, both pastors of congregations in North
Carolina, discovered that God had given each a similar vision to form a new church.
Also, Adams had developed some concerns with the administrative procedures of
his church, Way of the Cross Church of Christ. The church grew, in part, from the
addition of pastors and their congregations who had previously left other Apostolic
bodies.

Membership: In 1980 the United Way of the Cross Churches of Christ of the
Apostolic Faith had 1,100 members in 14 churches. There were 30 ministers and 4
bishops.

Universal Church of Jesus Christ

Current address not obtained for this edition.

The Universal Church of Jesus Christ was founded in the 1950s by the withdrawal
of some members of the Church of Jesus Christ (Kingsport). The immediate occasion of the split concerned the Lord's Supper. The withdrawing members argued
that communion was spiritual and that there was no mandate to continue the
Lord's Supper, or the accompanying practice of washing feet, as an outward ceremony. They also dropped several beliefs considered important by the Church of
Jesus Christ, including the rapture of the saints and the imminent Second Coming
of Jesus. It also does not believe in Sunday school programs.

There is no fellowship between the Universal Church of Jesus Christ and the
other apostolic churches.

Membership: Not reported.

Way of the Cross Church of Christ

819 D. St. NE, Washington, DC 20002

The Way of the Cross Church of Christ was founded on February 27, 1927, by Henry
C. Brooks (d. 1967), an independent black Pentecostal minister. Brooks had
founded a small congregation in Washington, D.C., which became part of the
Church of Our Lord Jesus Christ of the Apostolic Faith, founded by Robert Clarence
Lawson. At that time there was another small congregation under Bishop Lawson
in Washington headed by Smallwood E. Williams, and Lawson wanted Brooks's
congregation to join Williams's. Brooks rejected the plan, left Lawson's jurisdiction,
and founded a separate organization. A second congregation in Henderson, North
Carolina, became the first of several along the East Coast. Brooks pastored the
mother church for forty years and built a membership of over 3,000.

After Henry C. Brooks's death, Bp. John Luke Brooks served as the interim pastor
until his retirement in 1978, when he was replaced by Bp. Alphonzo D. Brooks,
Henry C. Brooks's son. In 1979, the church became an international body, adding
13 churches and missions in Ghana and Liberia.

Membership: In 2002 the Way of the Cross Church of Christ had 48 affiliated congregations and approximately 50,000 members.

Sources:

Way of the Cross Church of Christ. www.thewayofthecrosschurch.org.

Worldwide Pentecostal Church of Christ

292 Vanduzer St., Staten Island, NY 10304

Alternate Address: Philippine Headquarters: 104 Malaya St., Caloocan City, Metro
Manila, Philippines.

The Worldwide Pentecostal Church of Christ is an independent Pentecostal body
that originated in the Philippines. It was founded on March 13, 1984, by a small
group of ministers under the leadership of John E. Ayudtud. The previous year,
Ayudtud had visited the United States and had already decided to move there. In
1985 he left the Philippine work in the hands of the church's assistant chairman,
Bp. Cesar de la Cruz, and settled in America. He spent the next four years traveling
the country and evangelizing before settling in New Jersey in 1989. At that time
he founded the first American congregation of the Worldwide Pentecostal Church
of Christ.

Worldwide Pentecostal Church of Christ is an Apostolic Pentecostal body that
accepts the "Jesus Only" non-Trinitarian theology and baptism in the name of Jesus
only. Its conventions are held at the international headquarters in the Philippines.
An office for missions and church growth is located in San Jose, California. Ayudtud
remains the bishop in charge of the work.

Membership: Not reported. In 2002 there were congregations in Alaska; Seattle,
Washington; and Alameda and San Jose, California. There are also congregations in
Japan, Australia, and Jerusalem, and there are 57 congregations in the Philippines.

Educational Facilities:

WPCC Short Term Ministerial Studies, Caloocan City, Philippines.

Sources:

Worldwide Pentecostal Church of Christ. www.angelfire.com/fl/WPCCayudtud/.

Yahweh's Temple

Current address not obtained for this edition.

Yahweh's Temple was founded in 1947 as the Church of Jesus and has through the
decades of its existence sought the name that best expresses its central doctrinal
concern of identifying Jesus with the God of the Old Testament. In 1953 the church
became the Jesus Church, and it adopted its present name in 1981. The temple is
headed by Samuel E. Officer, its bishop and moderator, a former member of the
Church of God (Cleveland, Tennessee). The temple follows the "Oneness" doctrine
generally, but has several points of difference from other bodies. From the Sacred
Name Movement it has accepted the use of the Hebrew transliterations of the
names of the Creator. It also keeps the Saturday Sabbath. It derives its name from
a belief that Jesus is the "new and proper name of God, Christ, and the church."
Specifically rejected are names such as "Church of God," "Pentecostal," and
"Churches of Christ." The organization of the temple is based upon an idea that all
the members have a special place to work in a united body. From Ezekiel 10:10, a
model of four wheels within wheels has been constructed. Each wheel consists of
a hub of elders, spokes of helpers, a band for service, and the rim of membership.
At the center is the international bishop, who exercises episcopal and theocratic
authority. There are national and state bishops and local deacons.

Membership: Not reported. In 1973 there were approximately 10,000 members.

Periodicals: *Light of the World*.

❧ Black Trinitarian Pentecostals

African Universal Church, Inc.

2336 SW 48th Ave., Hollywood, FL 33023

The African Universal Church, Inc. is one of two churches that grew out of the ministry of Laura Adorkor Koffey (or Kofi), better known as Mother Koffey. Mother
Koffey preached throughout the South for several years (1926–1928) until her

assassination in 1928 in Miami. Following the assassination, some of her followers in Florida and Alabama reorganized.

The history of the group during its early decades is fragmentary, but many of the local centers became autonomous churches disconnected from the movement as a whole. Emerging as a prominent leader continuing to keep alive Koffey's teachings and memory during the 1930s was E. B. Nyombolo, an African who had been attracted to the church while living in America. He headed what was termed the Missionary African Universal Church, founded the Ile-Ife Institute in Jacksonville, Florida, and edited a periodical, The African Messenger. He also published the African Universal Hymnal, Mother's Closet Prayer Book, Mother's Sacred Teachings, and a volume of Mother's Sayings. In keeping with the church's message of self-help, an intentional community was created near Daphne City, Alabama, in the 1940s. Adorkaville, a second church community, was opened in Jacksonville.

In 1953 a reorganization of the churches, which had drifted apart over the years, occurred and three churches came together in a new corporate structure: St. Adorkor African Universal Church of Miami, Florida; St. Adorkor African Universal Church of Hollywood, Florida; and the African Universal Church of Jacksonville, Florida. Elder John Dean was elected as the first chairman of the general assembly. He served until 1958 and was succeeded by Deacon Clifford Hepburn (1958–1970), Sister Gloria Hepburn (1970–1974), and Deacon Audley Sears Sr. (1974–present).

The doctrine of the African Universal Church, Inc. is like that of the African Universal Church. An important new area of the church's life began in 1968 when Ernest Sears, a member, traveled to Ghana in an attempt to locate Mother Koffey's family. An earlier attempt in the 1930s had left unanswered charges that Koffey had lied about her African background. However, Sears was able to make contact with the family, who had never been informed of the assassination in 1928. Upon his return, Sears brought Koffey's nephew with him.

Membership: In 1990 the African Universal Church, Inc. reported seven affiliated congregations in Florida and Alabama.

Sources:

African Universal Hymnal. Jacksonville, FL: Missionary African Universal Church, 1961.

Bantu Prayerbook. Jacksonville, FL: Adorkaville, n.d.

Kofi, Laura Adorka. *The Church: Why Mother Established the Church and What It Stands For.* Jacksonville, FL: The Ile-Ife, n.d.

————. *Mother's Sacred Teachings.* Jacksonville, FL: The Mafro Ile-Ife, n.d.

————. *Mother's Sayings.* Jacksonville, FL: Missionary African Universal Church, n.d.

Payne, Wardell J., ed. *Directory of African American Religious Bodies: A Compendium by the Howard University School of Divinity.* Washington, DC: Howard University Press, 1991.

Alpha and Omega Pentecostal Church of God of America, Inc.
Current address not obtained for this edition.

The Alpha and Omega Pentecostal Church of God of America, Inc., was formed in 1945 by Rev. Magdalene Mabe Phillips, who withdrew from the United Holy Church of America and, with others, organized the Alpha and Omega Church of God Tabernacles, soon changed to the present name. Like the Church of God (Cleveland, Tennessee), the church's doctrine reserves the baptism of the Holy Spirit for the sanctified.

Membership: Not reported. In 1970 there were 3 congregations, 6 missions, and approximately 400 members, all in Baltimore, Maryland.

Apostolic Faith Church of America
Current address not obtained for this edition.

The Apostolic Faith Church of America was founded in 1922 by former members of the Apostolic Faith Churches of God. The split was possibly occasioned by the death

of California-based William J. Seymour who had inspired the founding of the original congregation of the Apostolic Faith Churches of God. The new organization subsequently grew into a denomination under its bishop Isaac Ryles. While organizationally separate, the church continued the holiness Pentecostal perspective of its parent body.

Membership: Not reported.

Sources:

DuPree, Sherry Sherrod. *African American Holiness Pentecostal Charismatic: An Annotated Bibliography.* New York: Garland, 1992.

Apostolic Faith Church of God and True Holiness
Current address not obtained for this edition.

In 1946 Charles W. Lowe, founder and for over 35 years leader of the Apostolic Faith Church of God, separated from the main body of the church and with one congregation organized the Apostolic Faith Church of God and True Holiness. He was succeeded by Bishop Levi Butts and later by Bishop Oree Keyes (1923–2008). Bishop Keyes was active in seeking to unite the various factions that developed from the original work begun by Lowe and Bishop William Seymour. He helped form the United Fellowship Convention of the Original Azusa Street Mission, which included five similar churches.

Membership: In 1990 the church reported 24 congregations.

Sources:

DuPree, Sherry Sherrod. *African-American Holiness Pentecostal Movement: An Annotated Bibliography.* New York: Garland, 1996.

Apostolic Faith Church of God Giving Grace
Rte. 3, Box 111G, Warrenton, NC 27589

The Apostolic Faith Church of God Giving Grace was founded in the mid-1960s as the New Jerusalem Apostolic Faith Churches of God. Its founders, Bp. Rufus A. Easter and Mother Lillie P. Williams, were formerly associated with the Apostolic Faith Churches of God. There was no doctrinal dispute in the break, and the church follows the doctrine of the parent body. Bishop Easter was succeeded by Bp. Geanie Perry, the current leader of the church. The church supports the New Jerusalem Rest Home and a Helping Hand Community Food Bank.

Membership: In 1990 there were 12 churches.

Sources:

DuPree, Sherry Sherrod. *African American Holiness Pentecostal Charismatic: An Annotated Bibliography.* New York: Garland, 1992.

Apostolic Faith Church of God Live On
2300 Trenton St., Hopewell, VA 23860

The Apostolic Faith Church of God Live On is one of several groups that originated in the Apostolic Faith Church of God founded in 1909 by Bp. William J. Seymour (1870–1922) and Charles W. Lowe. It was founded in 1952 by Bp. Jesse Handshaw, Bp. Willie P. Cross, and Elder R. T. Butts, all formerly of the Apostolic Faith Church of God and True Holiness, the branch of the church headed by Lowe at that time. No doctrinal matters were at issue, and the church follows the beliefs and practices of its parent body. Bishop Handshaw was succeeded by Bp. Richard Cross, the present leader of the church. The Church has joined with other branches of the Apostolic Faith Church to form the United Fellowship Convention of the Original Azusa Street Mission, which meets annually.

Membership: In 1990 the church had approximately 25 affiliated congregations.

Periodicals: *The Guiding Light* • *Crusade*

Sources:

DuPree, Sherry Sherrod. *African-American Holiness Pentecostal Movement: An Annotated Bibliography.* New York: Garland Publishing, 1992.

Payne, Wardell J., ed. *Directory of African American Religious Bodies*. Washington, DC: Howard University Press, 1991. 363 pp.

Apostolic Faith Churches of a Living God
Current address not obtained for this edition.

The Apostolic Faith Churches of a Living God was founded in 1979 when seven congregations in South Carolina that had left the Apostolic Faith Churches of God reorganized as a denomination. The congregations were called together by Bishop Leroy Williams, who had in the 1960s been the president of the South Carolina District Young People's Union of the Apostolic Faith Church of God. Later, Bishop Richard C. Johnson, Sr., headed the church. The cause of the split was administrative, not doctrinal, hence the churches retained the same holiness Pentecostal beliefs and practices of the parent church.

Membership: Not reported.

Periodicals: *Union Newsletter*.

Sources:

Payne, Wardell J., ed. *Directory of African American Religious Bodies*. Washington, DC: Howard University Press, 1991.

Apostolic Holiness Church of America
Current address not obtained for this edition.

The Apostolic Holiness Church of America was founded in 1927 in Mount Olive, North Carolina, by a group of former members of the Apostolic Faith Church of God, which was originally founded by Bishops William J. Seymour and Charles W. Lowe. The group included Elders J. M. Barns, W. M. D. Atkins, Ernest Graham, J. M. McKinnon, and Sisters Sarah Artis and Emma Spruel. The issues at stake in the separation were administrative, hence the church retained the doctrine of the other branches in the movement. In 1973 the church went through a constitutional revision under its presiding bishop, Isaac Ryals (d. 2001), assisted by W. R. Turner, I. W. Hicks, Jessie Budd, Shirley Clark, and E. V. Ethridge.

Membership: In 1990 the church reported 10 affiliated congregations.

Sources:

Payne, Wardell J., ed. *Directory of African American Religious Bodies: A Compendium by the Howard University School of Divinity*. Washington, DC: Howard University Press, 1991.

Association of Independent Ministries (A.I.M.)
c/o New Light Christian Center Church, 1535 Greensmark Dr., Houston, TX 77067

During the expansion of the ministry of Drs. I. V. and Bridget Hilliard, prominent African-American ministers and founders of the New Light Christian Center Church based in Houston, Texas, they recognized a need felt by independent Pentecostal ministers for the credibility and spiritual accountability that comes from affiliation and fellowship beyond the local church. In some cases, the pastors needed ordination certificates. The Association of Independent Ministries (A.I.M.) was created to fill that need.

A.I.M. was not designed to provide any direct ecclesiastical, governmental, or administrative control over its members or their congregations and ministries. Instead, A.I.M. offers wise counsel and, upon request, oversight. Membership in A.I.M. is open to men and women who have a viable, functional, independent ministry.

Like the New Light Christ Center Church, the Association of Independent Ministries is a trinitarian Pentecostal organization whose beliefs resemble those of the Assemblies of God. A.I.M. holds an annual convention.

Membership: Not reported. In 2008 almost 850 congregations and ministries were affiliated with A.I.M.

Sources:

Association of Independent Ministries. www.newlight.org/aim/index.cfm.

Azusa Interdenominational Fellowship of Christian Churches
8621 S. Memorial Dr., Tulsa, OK 74133-4312

The Azusa Interdenominational Fellowship of Christian Churches was founded in 1990 by Carlton D. Pearson (b. 1953), the head of Higher Dimensions Ministries in Tulsa, Oklahoma. Pearson, a prominent African-American Charismatic minister, had been given what he felt was a divine mandate to establish such a cooperative fellowship that might speak to the issue of racial and ethnic divisions that split the larger Pentecostal/Charismatic movement. In 1977 Pearson founded Higher Dimensions Ministries as a traveling evangelistic team that grew through the 1980s into a significant, multifaceted ministry that included the Higher Dimensions Family Church, a megachurch of more than 5,000 members, and a variety of community services from a meals-on-wheels program to an adoption agency. The church and its program serve a multiethnic and multiracial constituency.

By the end of the 1980s, the larger Charismatic movement was beginning to raise significant questions about its racial division and finding ways of healing the organizations split along racial lines. At the same time, Pearson concluded that an effort toward unity is a key ingredient in understanding the beauty of diversity resident in the body of Christ, a principle he had felt he had already established in his ministry. Out of a desire to see the large unity within the larger fellowship, he hosted the first annual Azusa Conference in 1988. This conference served to bring together people of diverse races, cultures, and theologies. Azusa Fellowship was born at the third Azusa Conference in 1990. He found a keynote for the new fellowship in II Corinthians 11:28: "Besides everything else, I face daily the pressure of my deep concern and care for all the churches."

The fellowship is organized as a coalition of Christian churches and ministries which recognizes the need for networking, accountability, fellowship, and resource facilitation.

Membership: In 2002, there were more than 500 congregations affiliated with the fellowship.

Periodicals: *Dimensions Digest*.

Beth-El Fellowship of Visionary Churches
c/o The House of the Lord, 1650 Diagonal Rd., Akron, OH 44320

The Beth-El Fellowship of Visionary Churches is an association of African-American Pentecostal churches that emerged from the success of the House of the Lord congregation in Akron, Ohio. The House of the Lord was founded in the 1970s by F. Josephus "Joey" Johnson and over the years grew to become one of the largest congregations in Akron. Rev. Johnson also led in the founding of Emmanuel Christian Academy and Logos Bible Institute.

As the House of the Lord's fame grew, people began to turn to Johnson for guidance on a variety of issues including church growth and development, business management, leadership, and team building. He founded the Pastoral Mentoring Institute, which facilitated his efforts to help pastors and lay leaders improve their local ministry. His work at the institute led directly to the founding of Beth-El Fellowship of Visionary Churches by pastors seeking a more formal relationship with Johnson.

In 2004 Johnson was consecrated bishop for the fellowship. At the same time, the Joint College of African American Pentecostal Bishops Congress presented him with an honorary Doctor of Divinity degree.

Membership: Not reported.

Sources:

Beth-El Fellowship of Visionary Churches www.beth-elfellowship.org/.

The House of the Lord. www.thotl.org/.

Johnson, F. Josephus. *Eight Ministries of the Holy Spirit*. Enumclaw, WA: Winepress Publishing, 2005. Available from www.eightministries.org/index.htm.

Bible Church of Christ

1358 Morris Ave., Bronx, NY 10456

The Bible Church of Christ is a small Pentecostal body founded on March 1, 1961, by Bishop Roy Bryant, Sr. (b. 1923). The church is a trinitarian ministry and accepts the authority of the Bible as the inspired word of God. Members receive the baptism of the Holy Spirit; deliverance and miracles of healing are frequently experienced. The church includes a demonology ministry that performs exorcisms and provides instruction on casting out demons. It maintains congregations in Haiti, India, and Africa. Podcasts of Bishop Bryant's sermons are available on the church's Internet site.

Membership: In 2008 the church reported six congregations, of which four were in New York. Congregations are located in New York, Delaware, and North Carolina. It also has a congregation in India, plus a school in Liberia, West Africa.

Educational Facilities:

Theological Institute, offering more than 30 classes in the subject areas of Christian work, evangelism, general bible study, teachers' training, postgraduate, theology, and demonology, at three locations: Mt. Vernon, New York; Bronx, New York; and Dagsboro, Delaware.

Sources:

Bible Church of Christ. www.thebiblechurchofchrist.org.

Christ Apostolic Church of America (Obadare)

PO Box 117, Cambria Heights, NY 11411

Alternate Address: International Headquarters: PO Box 530, Ibadan, Nigeria.

Christ Apostolic Church of America is the North American affiliate of the World Soul Winning Evangelistic Ministry (WSWEM), an evangelistic outreach founded by Nigerian evangelist Prophet Dr. T. O. Obadare. WSWEM is the evangelistic arm of the Christ Apostolic Church (which Obadare also heads), an African church that grew out of the Aladura, or "prayer people," movement. Aladura, an independent Christian movement that arose in Nigeria in the early twentieth century and expanded dramatically during the 1930s, was associated with a set of visions received by Joseph Ayo Babalola (1906–1959) calling on Babalola to preach using prayer and the "water of life" (blessed water), which would heal all sicknesses. The Christ Apostolic church was constituted in 1941 as one branch of the Aladura movement.

By 1990 Christ Apostolic church had more than a million members. By this time it had become the largest church in Nigeria and had spread to several other countries in Africa, as well as to Europe and North America. The church has a mainline Pentecostal statement of faith that affirms belief in the Bible as the word of God, the Trinity, and salvation in Christ. It practices baptism by immersion. The church resembles other Aladura churches in its emphasis on prayer, fasting, the use of water and oil for healing, and the rejection of medicines, alcohol, and tobacco.

Several of the Christ Apostolic churches have their own Web sites.

Membership: Not reported. In 2008 the church listed 25 congregations in the United States and Canada.

Educational Facilities:

Christ Apostolic Church Bible Training College, Hyattsville, Maryland. This school operates as an extension of the International Seminary in Plymouth, Florida.

Sources:

Christ Apostolic Church of America. www.christapostolicchurch.org.

Christ Apostolic Church of America. www.cacamerica.org/index.html (North American site).

Church of God in Christ

Attn: Mrs. Linda K. Wilkins, 938 Mason St., Memphis, TN 38126

The Church of God in Christ was established in 1894 in Jackson, Mississippi, by Charles H. Mason (1866–1959), an independent Baptist minister who four years previously had been swept up by the holiness movement and had been sanctified. Mason also founded the Church of Christ (Holiness) U.S.A., with a colleague, Elder Charles Price Jones (1865–1949).

In 1907, a change in Mason's orientation occurred that led to a reorganization of the Church of God in Christ. Elder Jones convinced Mason that Mason did not yet have the fullness of the Holy Spirit, for, if he did, he would have the power to heal the sick, cast out devils, and raise the dead. Mason began attending meetings held at Azusa Street in Los Angeles, where he was baptized in the Spirit and spoke in tongues.

In August 1908, the new doctrine and experiences were presented to representatives of the Church of Christ (Holiness) U.S.A. At a meeting of those from both churches who accepted the new Pentecostalism, a General Assembly of the Church of God in Christ was organized. Mason was elected general overseer. (This brief history is at odds with the history presented in the Encyclopedia's entry on the Church of Christ [Holiness] U.S.A.; the two churches involved tell two different stories.) The Church of God in Christ was reorganized into an ascending hierarchy of overseer (pastor), state overseer, and general overseer. Annual state convocations to decide on disputed matters and assign pastors, and a general convocation for matters of the general church were established.

Upon the death of Bishop Mason in 1961, a series of new reorganizational steps began. Power reverted to the 7 bishops who made up the executive commission. This group was extended to 12 in 1962 and O. T. Jones Jr. was named "senior bishop." Controversy sprang up immediately over the new power structure and a constitutional convention was scheduled. In 1967, a court in Memphis ruled that the powers of the senior bishop and executive board should remain intact until the constitutional convention in 1968. That year, reorganization took place yet again and power was invested in a quadrennial general assembly and a general board of 12, with a presiding bishop to conduct administration between meetings of the general assembly. In 2008 the presiding bishop was Charles Edward Blake and the general secretary was Joel H. Lyles Jr.

Church doctrine is similar to that of the International Pentecostal Holiness Church. The group believes in the Trinity, holiness, healing, and the premillennial return of Christ. Three ordinances are recognized: baptism by immersion, the Lord's Supper, and foot-washing.

Membership: In 1991 the church reported over 5 million members, 15,300 congregations, and 33,593 clergy in the United States.

Educational Facilities:

Harrison Mason Theological Seminary, Atlanta, Georgia.

All Saints Bible College, Memphis, Tennessee.

Saints Academy, Lexington, Mississippi.

In addition to the seminary in Atlanta (now part of the Interdenominational Theological Center), the church supports the C. H. Mason System of Bible Colleges, which includes a number of schools attached to local congregations both in the United States and abroad.

Periodicals: *Whole Truth* • *The Voice of Missions*

Sources:

Church of God in Christ. www.cogic.org.

Butler, Anthea D. *Women in the Church of God in Christ: Making a Sanctified World.* Chapel Hill, NC: University of North Carolina Press, 2007. 224 pp.

Cornelius, Lucille J. *The Pioneer History of the Church of God in Christ.* Author, 1975.

Mason, Mary Esther. *The History and Life Work of Elder C. H. Mason and His Co-Laborers.* Privately printed, n.d.

Patterson, J. O., German R. Ross, and Julia Mason Atkins. *History and Formative Years of the Church of God in Christ with Excerpts from the Life and Works of Its Founder—Bishop C. H. Mason*. Memphis, TN: Church of God in Christ Publishing House, 1969.

Patterson, W. A. *From the Pen of W. A. Patterson*. Memphis, TN: Deakins Typesetting Service, 1970.

Church of God in Christ, Congregational
6939 Marine Rd., Edwardsville, IL 62025

The Church of God in Christ, Congregational, was formed in 1932 by Bp. J. Bowe of Hot Springs, Arkansas, after he was forced to withdraw from the Church of God in Christ, for asserting that church polity should be congregational, not episcopal. In 1934 Bowe was joined by George Slack. Slack had been dis-fellowshipped from the church because of his disagreement with the teaching that if a saint did not pay tithes, he was not saved. He was convinced that tithing was not a New Testament doctrine. Slack became the junior bishop under Bowe. In 1945, Bowe was wooed back into the Church of God in Christ, and Slack became senior bishop of the off-shoot church.

Church doctrine is like that of the Church of God in Christ, but with disagreements on matters of polity and tithing. Members are conscientious objectors.

Membership: Not reported. In 1971 there were 33 churches in the United States, 4 in England, and 6 in Mexico.

Sources:
Slack, George, William Walker, and E. Jones. *Manual*. East St. Louis, IL: Church of God in Christ, Congregational, 1948.

Church of God in Christ, International
125 N Fisher St., Jonesboro, AR 72401

In 1969, following its constitutional convention and reorganization, the Church of God in Christ experienced a major schism when a group of 14 bishops led by Bp. William David Charles Williams Sr. rejected the polity of the reorganized church, left it, and formed the Church of God in Christ, International, at Evanston, Illinois. The issue was the centralized authority in the organization of the parent body. The new group quickly set up an entire denominational structure. The doctrine of the parent body remained intact, however.

Dr. John Henry Davis Sr. was elected in April 1988 as senior bishop and chief apostle of the Church of God in Christ International.

Membership: In 1982 the Church reported 200,000 members, 300 congregations, and 1,600 ministers. In 2008 the membership was to be found in congregations scattered across America and organized into 26 dioceses, each headed by bishop.

Periodicals: *Message* • *Holiness Code*

Sources:
Church of God in Christ, International. www.cogicinternational.com.

Church of the Living God (Christian Workers for Fellowship)
434 Forest Ave., Cincinnati, OH 45229

The Church of the Living God (Christian Workers for Fellowship) was formed in 1889 by a former slave, the Rev. William Christian (1856–1928) of Wrightsville, Arkansas. Christian claimed to have had a revelation that the Baptists were preaching a sectarian doctrine and left the Baptist Church in order to preach the unadulterated truth. In his new church, Christian created the senior office of *chief*, which he himself assumed. Mrs. Ethel L. Christian succeeded her husband after his death and was, in turn, succeeded by their son, John L. Christian. Mrs. Christian claimed that the original revelation came to both her husband and herself.

Church doctrine is Trinitarian and somewhat Pentecostal. The group rejects the idea of "tongues" as the initial evidence of the baptism of the Holy Spirit, although "tongues" are allowed. However, "tongues" must be recognizable languages, not "unintelligible utterance." Salvation is gained by obeying the commandments to hear, understand, believe, repent, confess, be baptized, and participate in the Lord's Supper and in foot-washing.

The Church of the Living God also has a belief that Jesus Christ was of the black race, because of the lineage of David and Abraham. They point to Psalms 119:83, in which David declares that he "became like a bottle in the smoke" (i.e., black). The church members also hold that Job (Job 30:30), Jeremiah (Jer. 8:21), and Moses's wife (Numbers 12:11) were black. These assertions were promulgated at a time when many Baptists were teaching that blacks were not human, but the offspring of a human father and female beast.

Polity is episcopal and the church is modeled along the lines of a fraternal organization. Christian was very impressed with the Masons, and as with that secret society, there are reportedly many points of church doctrine known only to members. Tithing is stressed. The local organizations are known as temples, rather than as churches, and are subject to the authority of the general assembly. The presiding officer is known as the *chief bishop*. In 2008 the presiding bishop was Robert D. Tyler

Membership: In 1985 the church reported 170 churches, 42,000 members, and 170 ministers.

Periodicals: *The Gospel Truth* • *Fellowship Echoes*

Sources:
Church of the Living God (Christian Workers for Fellowship). www.ctlgcwff.org/index.htm.

Church of the Living God, the Pillar and Ground of the Truth, Inc. [Lewis Dominion]
4520 Ashland City Hwy., Nashville, TN 37208

Alternate Address: c/o Meharry H. Lewis, Gen. Sec., Church of the Living God, PGT, Inc., PO Box 830384, Tuskegee, AL 36083-0384.

The Church of the Living God, the Pillar and Ground of the Truth, Inc., traces its beginning to 1903 when Mary Lena Lewis Tate (1871–1930), a black woman, began to preach the gospel first at Steel Springs, Tennessee, and Paducah, Kentucky, and then in other states in the South. In 1908, by which time a number of holiness bands had been formed by people converted under her ministry, Tate was taken ill. Despite being pronounced beyond cure, she was healed, and during her healing she received the baptism of the Holy Spirit and spoke in tongues. Later that year Tate called an assembly in Greenville, Alabama, during which the Church of the Living God, the Pillar and Ground of the Truth was formally organized. At that time, she was appointed to the bishopric and ordained first chief overseer of the church by the elders present. The church grew quickly in the states of Georgia, Florida, Tennessee, and Kentucky and by the end of the next decade had congregations across the eastern half of the United States. The first four state bishops, J. D. Padgitt, B. J. Scott, W. C. Lewis, and F. E. Lewis, were ordained at Quitman, Georgia, in June 1914.

In 1919, the first of two major schisms occurred. Led by the church in Philadelphia, Pennsylvania, some members left to found the House of God Which Is the Church of the Living God, the Pillar and Ground of Truth. Then, in 1931, following Mother Tate's death, the church reorganized, and three persons were ordained to fill the office of chief overseer. The three chosen were Mother Tate's son F. E. Lewis, M. F. L. Keith (widow of Bp. W. C. Lewis), and B. L. McLeod. These three eventually became leaders of distinct church bodies. Lewis's following is the continuing Church of the Living God, the Pillar and Ground of the Truth, Inc. Keith's group became known as the House of God Which Is the Church of the Living God, the Pillar and Ground of Truth Without Controversy. Bishop McLeod's organization is known as the Church of the Living God, the Pillar, and Ground of Truth Which He Purchased with His Own Blood, Inc.

The church affirms the central doctrines of traditional Christianity, including the Holy Trinity and salvation through Christ. It teaches that people are justified and cleansed by faith in Christ and glorified and wholly sanctified by receiving the Holy Ghost and Fire. Speaking in tongues is evidence of the reception of the Holy Ghost. The unknown tongue is a sign of God's victory over sin. There are three ordinances: baptism by immersion, the Lord's Supper, and foot washing.

ORGANIZATION. The church is headed by a bishop, designated the chief overseer. After the death of Bp. F. E. Lewis in 1968, Bp. Helen M. Lewis became the third chief overseer. She administered the affairs of the church with the assistance of the general assembly, which meets annually, a board of trustees, and the supreme executive council, consisting of the other bishops and seven elders. Subsequent to her death in September 2001, Bp. Meharry H. Lewis was ordained as the fourth chief overseer of the organization in October 2001. In 2008 members of the church gathered in Greenville, Alabama, to celebrate the centennial of the church's founding.

The New and Living Way Publishing House is the church's publishing arm. The Lewis-Tate Foundation and Archives located in Tuskegee, Alabama, reserves the church's historical documents, especially those related to its founder.

Membership: In 2008 there were 18 churches scattered through the South and Midwest.

Periodicals: *The True Report* • *The Present Truth Gospel Preacher*

Sources:

Church of the Living God, the Pillar and Ground of the Truth. www.clgpgt.org/.

Church of the Living God, the Pillar and Ground of the Truth. www.netministries.org/see/churches.exe/ch30084.

The Constitution, Government, and General Decree Book. Chattanooga, TN: New and Living Way Publishing Co., n.d.

Lewis, Helen M., and Meharry H. Lewis. *75th Anniversary Yearbook.* Nashville, TN: Church of the Living God, the Pillar and Ground of the Truth, 1978.

Church of the Living God, the Pillar, and Ground of the Truth Which He Purchased with His Own Blood, Inc. [McLeod Dominion]
PO Box 55090, Indianapolis, IN 46205

Church of the Living God, the Pillar, and Ground of the Truth Which He Purchased with His Own Blood, Inc. continues the work begun by Mother Mary Magdalena Lewis Tate (1871–1930). Following Mother Tate's death in 1930, one part of the church selected Bishop B. L. McLeod as the chief Overseer to head the church. He died in 1936 and was succeeded by his widow, Bishop Mattie Lou McLeod (later remarried and known as Bishop M. L. Jewell), elected in 1939.

She founded Jewell's Academy and Seminary, a Church educational institution serving grades K-12, and in 1964 oversaw the purchase of new church headquarters building in Indianapolis, Indiana. After over thirty years in the leadership role, Bishop Jewell died in 1991 and was succeeded by Bishop Naomi Aquilla Manning (d. 2003). The current overseer is Bishop Faye Moore.

The church continues the Pentecostal teachings of its parent body.

Membership: In 2008, the church had 46 congregations, including one in the Bahamas.

Sources:

Church of the Living God, the Pillar, and Ground of Truth which He Purchased with His Own Blood. www.cotlgnet.org.

Deliverance Evangelistic Centers, Inc.
826 S 10th St., Newark, NJ 07108

The Deliverance Evangelistic Centers, Inc. (DEC Ministries), was incorporated on October 8, 1957, by Arturo Skinner (d. 1975). From the very beginning, the church motto was: "To reach the lost at any cost with the message of Pentecost." Although it grew to become a renowned national and international ministry, DEC Ministries began simply in the Newark, New Jersey, home of Mother Mary Amartys. The min-

istry moved to several locations before settling in at its first headquarters church at 505 Central Avenue in Newark, which could accommodate 1,600 people.

At the same time, Apostle Skinner was conducting services in the Brooklyn, New York, area. Skinner had been stopped from committing suicide by what he believed to be the voice of God, which told him, "Arturo, if you but turn around, I'll save your soul, heal your body, and give you a deliverance ministry." Skinner was 28 years old at the time, and though he had had a full gospel background, he had never heard of anything termed a "deliverance ministry." In a period of retreat following his encounter with God, Skinner fasted and had a number of visions and dreams. He also consecrated his life to the ministry to which he had been called. Deliverance churches spread from Florida to Massachusetts, eastward as far as Chicago, Illinois, and throughout the southern United States, the Caribbean, and Africa. By 1965 the ministry had between 40 and 50 affiliate churches worldwide. Women have been accepted into the ordained ministry as both evangelists and pastors.

The centers' statement of belief includes affirmation of the authority of the Bible as inspired and infallible, the Trinity, Jesus Christ as redeemer, the Holy Spirit who empowers and baptizes believers, speaking-in-tongues as evidence of the baptism of the Holy Spirit, creation, the necessity of repentance, sanctification, and water baptism by immersion. Skinner was the church's first apostle. He died suddenly on March 20, 1975. In June of 1975, with the assistance of church leaders, Ralph G. Shammah Nichol formally became the senior pastor of the Deliverance Ministries.

Membership: There are centers in Brooklyn and Poughkeepsie, New York; Philadelphia; Washington, D.C.; Orlando, Florida; and Asbury Park and Newark, New Jersey.

Periodicals: *Deliverance Voice.*

Sources:

Deliverance Evangelistic Centers, Inc. www.decministries.net.

Deliverance Jesus Is Coming Association of Churches
43 Harrison Pl., Irvington, NJ 07111

The Deliverance Jesus Is Coming Association of Churches began with the work of the Pentecostal minister James H. Everett Jr. in Irvington, New Jersey, in 1976. Everett had previously worked with Bp. Frank C. Clemmons at the First Church of God in Christ in Brooklyn, New York, and with Apostle Arturo A. Skinner (1924–1975) in the healing ministry of Deliverance Evangelistic Center, also in Brooklyn. Following the death of Skinner, Everett decided to go out on his own. His wife Vanessa Horton Everett joined him in this endeavor; she serves as the church's copastor and leader of many of its various ministries.

From small beginnings the church grew, and Everett led evangelistic crusades in other nearby cities. As the initial congregation expanded through the 1980s, a varied program emerged to meet special needs, and the Maranata Bible Institute was created to train future leaders. Through the 1990s, affiliated congregations were established throughout New Jersey and increasingly in other states. The Deliverance Jesus Is Coming Association of Churches was formed to keep these new congregations in fellowship, and Everett was selected as the Association's bishop. It holds an annual convention.

The Association follows the Trinitarian Pentecostalism in which Everett was raised. The church also promotes an invigorated, participatory style of worship. The services of the church in Irvington are telecast over cable television throughout New Jersey.

Membership: Not reported. Ten affiliated congregations are located in New Jersey, Maryland, Arkansas, North Carolina, Virginia, and Colorado.

Periodicals: *The Total Christian.*

Educational Facilities:

Maranata Bible Institute, Irvington, New Jersey.

Sources:

Deliverance Jesus Is Coming Association of Churches.
   www.deliverancejesusiscoming.org/.

Faith Tabernacle Council of Churches, International

7015 NE 23rd Ave., Portland, OR 97211

The Faith Tabernacle Council of Churches, International, was founded as the Faith Tabernacle Corporation of Churches in Portland, Oregon, in 1962 by Bp. Louis W. Osborne Sr. Osborne began the organization after a vision in which he caught and carried a light that gradually grew in intensity, thus allowing him to lead his followers down the correct pathway.

The council is basically an Apostolic Pentecostal organization, but Osborne has emphasized the need for the preaching of the gospel and for fellowship and freedom. He has organized it as an association of autonomous congregations. The council charters congregations and ordains minister, but conformity of belief is not demanded of ministers and churches. While the council provides congregations with a set of "Guidelines for Christian Development," there is no requirement that these guidelines be followed.

Membership: In 1990 the council reported 55 congregations, including several churches in South Africa and Zimbabwe.

Periodicals: *The Light of Faith.*

Sources:

Payne, Wardell J., ed. *Directory of African American Religious Bodies: A Compendium by the Howard University School of Divinity*. Washington, DC: Howard University Press, 1991.

Fire-Baptized Holiness Church of God of the Americas

901 Bishop W. E. Fuller Sr. Hwy., Greenville, SC 29601-4103

W. E. Fuller (1875–1958), the only black man in attendance at the 1898 organizing conference of the Fire-Baptized Holiness Church, became the leader of almost a thousand black people over the next decade. Perceived discrimination against them led to the withdrawal of Fuller and his followers, who organized the Colored Fire-Baptized Holiness Church at Anderson, South Carolina, on May 1, 1908. The white body gave them their accumulated assets and property at this time. Reverend Fuller was elected overseer and bishop. Doctrine is the same as in the International Pentecostal Holiness Church, the body that absorbed the Fire-Baptized Holiness Church.

Legislative and executive authority in the church is vested in a general council that meets every four years and in the 11-member executive council (composed of bishops, district elders, and pastors). Mission work is pursued under the direction of one of the bishops. The denomination is divided into three dioceses, each headed by a bishop.

Membership: Not reported. In 2008 the church reported 198 congregation in the United States, plus 1 each in Canada and England, and 16 in Jamaica.

Periodicals: *True Witness.*

Sources:

Fire-Baptized Holiness Church of God of the Americas. www.fbhchurch.org.

Discipline. Atlanta, GA: Board of Publication of the F. B. H. Church of God of the Americas, 1962.

Frazier, Bishop Patrick L., Jr. "Introducing the Fire Baptized Holiness Church of God of the Americas: A Study Manual." Portions available online at www.fbhchurch.org.

Freedom Worldwide Covenant Ministries

6100 W Columbia Ave., Philadelphia, PA 19151

Freedom Worldwide Covenant Ministries is a charismatic fellowship of churches and ministers founded by Apostle Gilbert Colemen. It is based at the Freedom Christian Bible Fellowship, a large congregation in Philadelphia that Coleman pas-

tors. Coleman is closely associated with Bp. Earl Paulk of the Network of Kingdom Churches and other networks of charismatic fellowships operating within the African-American community. The church is traditionally Pentecostal in its beliefs and practices. It has developed a broad program of outreach ministries that target specific populations (singles, women, youth, etc.) and includes attention to the hospitalized, the incarcerated, and those in hunger. The ministries gather for an annual convocation.

The church's Freedom Development Corporation facilitates a variety of services within West Philadelphia, including educational assistance and emergency provision of food. Its Community Development program emphasizes the preservation and rehabilitation of existing housing, home ownership, prevention of homelessness, and the creation of affordable housing.

Membership: Not reported. In 2002 the ministries reported 11 churches in the United States and other associated congregations in Burundi, Ghana, India, Malawi, Nigeria, the Philippines, and Zimbabwe.

Sources:

Freedom Worldwide Covenant Ministries. www.freedomworldwide.net/.

Full Gospel Baptist Church Fellowship

2240 Simon Bolivar St., New Orleans, LA 70113

The Full Gospel Baptist Church, founded in 1995, is a fellowship of predominantly African-American charismatic Baptist churches. Through the 1970s and 1980s, the Pentecostal experience spread through African-American churches, including the Baptist churches, which, however, have been among the most resistant to continued fellowship with charismatic pastors and congregations.

The mother church of the organization of charismatic Baptist churches has been the St. Stephens Baptist Church in New Orleans. The congregation was founded in 1937 and has grown steadily through the years. In 1974, following the death of Percy Simpson, then pastor of the church, the assistant pastor, Paul S. Morton, succeeded him. Morton led in the building of a 2,000-seat sanctuary in 1980 and in the acquisition of a 4,000-seat sanctuary in 1988. In 1991, the church changed its name to reflect a newly acquired level of spiritual growth. It became Greater St. Stephen Full Gospel Baptist Church. More recently, the School and College of Ministry was formed to educate ministers and church leaders. In February of 1993, Elder Debra B. Morton, the wife of Pastor Morton, became the co-pastor of the ministry.

In March of 1993, Elder Paul S. Morton Sr. accepted the office of bishop (an office not found in most Baptist groups), and became the First Presiding Bishop of the Full Gospel Baptist Church Fellowship. The first conference was held in New Orleans at the Louisiana Superdome in 1994 with over 25,000 in attendance.

The multicultural and multi-denominational Full Gospel Baptist Church Fellowship is structured with an episcopal hierarchy. The "tiers of leadership" include the Bishop's Council, the College of Bishops, general, state, and district overseers, the Financial Assistance Council, and senior pastors.

Each year the Annual Full Gospel Baptist Church Fellowship Conference ministers to nearly 30,000 people through its School of Ministry classes, worship services, and community outreach efforts. The Fellowship's major initiatives since 1994 include church-planting in Africa and India, the dispensation of multiple $5,000 grants to struggling churches, and the development of the Full Gospel Baptist Sunday School Curriculum, which supports the Christian Education Ministry throughout the world.

Membership: Not reported. Hundreds of Full Gospel Baptist Churches exist in Africa, Asia, the Bahamas, Germany, India, Canada, Great Britain, Italy, and North America.

Educational Facilities:

College of Ministry.

Sources:

Full Gospel Baptist Church Fellowship. www.fullgospelbaptist.org.

1997 Ministries Networking Directory. Lake Mary, FL: Strang Communications, 1997.

Full Gospel Holy Temple

39727 LBJ Fwy., Dallas, TX 75237

The Full Gospel Holy Temple Church was founded as a single independent Holiness Pentecostal church in June 1961 in Dallas, Texas, by Lobias Murray. The original group of six charter members met in a former café. As the church grew, it began to sponsor a radio ministry, "Broadcast of Deliverance," with its first announcer and choir director being Evangelist Shirley Murray, the pastor's wife. As the church's message spread, additional congregations were formed across Texas and in neighboring states, primarily within the African-American community, and a new denomination emerged.

The church sponsors several ministries in the Dallas Metropolitan Area, including the Lobias Murray Christian Academy, an elementary and high school opened in 1979; the Shirley Murray Child Development Center, also opened in 1979; and Helping Hand, an organization that provides food and clothing to needy families. In addition, the church sponsors the L&S Christian Camp, located in Scottsville, Texas.

The church teaches a Holiness Pentecostal perspective that encourages believers to seek sanctification and the baptism of the Holy Spirit subsequent to their finding salvation in Christ. Members are taught to live a holy existence (including dressing modestly). Baptism is by immersion in the name of the Triune God. The church also practices foot washing.

In 2001, the church broke ground on a new headquarters church that will seat 5,000.

Membership: In 2008 the church's Web site reported 28 affiliated congregations. The lead church in Dallas had in excess of 4,000 members.

Periodicals: *The Gospel Truth*, 1900 S Ewing Ave., Dallas, TX 75216.

Sources:

Full Gospel Holy Temple. www.fullgospelholytemple.org/.

Full Gospel Pentecostal Association

1032 N Sumner, Portland, OR 97217

Alternate Address: c/o Tabernacle of Evangelism Community Church, 1300 N La Brea Ave., Inglewood, CA 90302.

The Full Gospel Pentecostal Association is a predominantly black Pentecostal church founded in 1970 by Bp. Adolph A. Wells, Rev. Edna Travis, and Bp. S. D. Leffall. It is a loosely organized association of independent Pentecostal congregations that supports a prison ministry, a national women's organization (Full Gospel Pentecostal Association for Women on the Move), and an international fellowship with similar Pentecostal groups in Africa. It is one of several similar bodies that belong to the ecumenical Federated Pentecostal Church International led by Bishop Leffall, who also serves a church in Seattle, Washington.

Membership: Not reported.

Periodicals: *The Epistle. • Full Gospel News Truth*.

Sources:

Emmanuel Temple Church. www.etchurch.com.

Dupree, Sherry Sherrod. *African-American Holiness Pentecostal Movement: An Annotated Bibliography*. New York: Garland Publishing, 1992.

Healing Temple Church

660 Williams St., Macon, GA 31201

Healing Temple Church is a predominantly black Pentecostal church with a special emphasis on the ministry of healing. It was founded in 1955 in Macon, Georgia, by Bp. P. J. Welch, a native of Georgia who had begun a tent ministry in 1950 in New Jersey. Welch took his ministry around the country during the nationwide Pentecostal healing revival that had been launched by such evangelists as William M. Branham, Oral Roberts, and Asa Alonzo Allen. The church grew out of Welch's itinerant ministry. Welch was assisted in his work by his wife, L. R. Welch, who served as a missionary, supervisor, and instructor in the church.

Though the leader of a growing denomination, Welch continued to travel with his healing ministry, and more congregations were founded. Church belief is Trinitarian and believers consider speaking in tongues to be a sign of the baptism of the Holy Spirit.

Membership: In 1990 there were 17 congregations.

Sources:

DuPree, Sherry Sherrod. *African-American Holiness Pentecostal Movement: An Annotated Bibliography*. New York: Garland Publishing, 1992.

House of God Which Is the Church of the Living God, the Pillar and Ground of Truth

Current address could not be obtained for this edition.

Not to be confused with the church of the same name that derives from the movement begun by Mary Lena Lewis Tate (1871–1930), the church presently under discussion derives from the work begun by William Christian. During the early twentieth century, the Church of the Living God (Christian Workers for Fellowship), which Christian founded, was splintered on several occasions. A group calling itself the Church of the Living God, Apostolic Church, withdrew in 1902 and, six years later under the leadership of Rev. C. W. Harris, became the Church of the Living God, General Assembly. This church united in 1924 with a second small splinter body. In 1925 a number of churches withdrew from the Church of the Living God (Christian Workers for Fellowship) under the leadership of Rev. E. J. Cain and renamed themselves the Church of the Living God, the Pillar and Ground of Truth. The Harris group joined the Cain group in 1926 and this new body later adopted the church's present name, the House of God Which Is the Church of the Living God, the Pillar and Ground of Truth.

The church is one in doctrine with the Church of the Living God (Christian Workers for Fellowship). Polity is episcopal and there is an annual general assembly.

Membership: Not reported.

Remarks: The most recent independent source of information on this church is the 1936 *Census of Religious Bodies*. Later sources often confuse it with the Philadelphia-based group of the same name. Its present location and strength is unknown.

House of God Which Is the Church of the Living God, the Pillar and Ground of the Truth, Inc.

PO Box 3319, Philadelphia, PA 19142-9998

During World War I (1914–1917) many members of the church founded by Mary L. Tate (1871–1930), the Church of the Living God, the Pillar and Ground of the Truth, moved into the northern states, an exodus that continued through the 1920s. Bp. A. H. White (d. 1981), Rev. B. L. McLeod, and Bp. F. Giles worked during these years to establish the church in the northeastern states. In 1929, the year before her death, Mother Tate appointed Bp. A. H. White as her successor. The various churches, then operating in a somewhat autonomous fashion, subsequently met as a general assembly, which elected Bishop White as senior bishop of all churches connected with the "Pennsylvania Group," and incorporated under the name House of God, Which Is the Church of the Living God, Pillar and Ground of the Truth.

Bishop White led the House of God for more than 50 years. He was succeeded by Bp. James H. Smith (d. 1986). The third and present presiding bishop is Bp. Jesse White Sr. He is assisted by the board of bishops, which includes Bps. David E. Drone, Cleveland L. Harvey, and Ivy A. Hopkins.

The House of God, the Church of the Living God, the Pillar and Ground of the Truth continues the doctrine and episcopal polity of its parent body, but is administratively separate. The general assembly meets annually.

Membership: Not reported. In the early 1970s the church had 103 churches and 25,860 members.

Periodicals: *The Spirit of Truth Magazine*. Available from 3943 Fairmont St., Philadelphia, PA 19104.

Sources:

House of God, Which Is the Church of the Living God, the Pillar and Ground of the Truth. www.houseofgodclg.org/.

House of the Lord

Current address could not be obtained for this edition.

The House of the Lord was founded in 1925 by Bp. W. H. Johnson, who established headquarters in Detroit. Church doctrine is Pentecostal but departs from standard Pentecostalism on several important points. A person who enters the church is born of water and seeks to be born of God by a process of sanctification. The Holy Ghost may be given and is evidenced by speaking in tongues. But sanctification is evidenced by conformity to a very rigid code that includes refraining from worldly amusements, whiskey, policy rackets (the "numbers game"), becoming a bellhop, participating in war, swearing, joining secret organizations, tithing, and life insurance (except as required by an employer). A believer is not sanctified if he owns houses, lands, or goods. Water is used in the Lord's Supper. Members are not to marry anyone not baptized by the Holy Ghost.

The church is governed by a hierarchy consisting of ministers, state overseers, and a chief overseer. There is a common treasury at each local church from which the destitute are helped.

Membership: Not reported.

International Fellowship of United Apostolic Churches

PO Box 11763, Louisville, KY 40251-0763

The International Fellowship of United Apostolic Churches is a Pentecostal church founded by Apostle D. E. Chase, who serves as its presiding bishop. Raised as an Episcopalian, as a young man Chase became a Pentecostal believer and joined the New Shiloh Missionary Full Gospel Church, a congregation in his native New Jersey. He was originally ordained by his pastor. In 1999 he was consecrated as a bishop by Bishops Covington and Grayson of the Full Gospel Missionary Church. In June 2001 Apostle Edwards of the now defunct National Pentecostal Holiness Assemblies consecrated Chase as an apostle. In 2005 Chase was coronated archbishop and patriarch of the International Fellowship of United Apostolic Churches, with a lineage apostolic succession through Abp. Sean Alexander of the Charismatic Archdiocese of the Sacred Heart, an archdiocese in the Ecumenical Apostolic Church Diocese. Alexander possesses several lines of succession that reach back to Abp. Carmel Henry Carfora (1878–1958) of the North American Old Roman Catholic Church, and through Maurice D. McCormick of the Independent Catholic Church of America.

Apostle Chase also founded the Immanuel International Cathedral in Louisville, Kentucky, and he serves as the cathedral's pastor. He is joined in the national leadership of the church by Abp. D. L. Smith and Bps. T. N. Ary and J. M. Cuff, and internationally Bps. S. Inyangebio (Nigeria) and R. C. Blanco (the Philippines). The church meets annually in convention.

The church is Pentecostal in doctrine and episcopal in structure. Ordination and admission to the episcopacy are offered to both men and women. Training is provided for candidates in the traditional fivefold ministries of Eph. 11:4 (apostles, prophets, evangelists, pastors, and teachers), as well as exhorters, missionaries, ministers, elders, overseers, and bishops.

Membership: In 2008 there were eight congregations in the United States, three in Africa, and one each in India and the Philippines.

Educational Facilities:

Covenant Bible College and Seminary, Louisville, Kentucky.

Sources:

International Fellowship of United Apostolic Churches. www.ifouac.org/.

Chase, D. E. *Apostolic Minister's Manual*. Louisville, KY: IFOUAC Publishing Board, 2008.

———. *International Fellowship of United Apostolic Churches Official Church manual*. Louisville, KY: IFOUAC Publishing Board, 2007.

Kingdom Life Network of Ministries

597 Naugatuck Ave., Milford, CT 06461

The Kingdom Life Network of Ministries, founded in 2001 by Bp. Ray Ramirez, grew out of Ramirez's pastorate of Kingdom Life Christian Church in Milford, Connecticut. Ramirez founded the congregation in 1991 and it grew to include some 3,000 members. He also founded a radio ministry, *The Bishop's Counsel*, and a television ministry, *The Voice of Vision*. He and his wife Jeannine Ramirez, also a licensed minister, cohost the Trinity Broadcast Network's *Praise the Lord* show. Through the 1990s Ramirez pioneered additional churches in New England, several of which grew to be quite large congregations.

In 2001 Ramirez was consecrated as a bishop and founded the Kingdom Life Network of Ministries to serve as a resource for smaller progressive churches in New England and elsewhere. The Network provides apostolic covering for its members' ministers, with licensing and ordination as needed, and it assists in identifying gifts and local eldership. If conflicts arise in local churches, it offers problem resolution. Membership is open to a wide range of Pentecostal and charismatic churches and ministries.

The Network has spread internationally to Colombia, Ghana, Liberia, Cuba, and South Africa. It attempts to empower local leaders and ministries and plans to establish bishop or national overseers who would work with Ramirez as presiding bishops. Once in place, the national leaders would operate autonomously in the best interests of their country's particular needs.

Membership: Not reported. The Network includes about 200 U.S. and more than 2,000 international churches and ministries.

Periodicals: *Kingdom Life Chronicle*.

Sources:

Kingdom Life Network of Ministries. www.knetministries.org/index.html.

Kingdom Life Christian Church. www.kingdomlifecc.org/.

Latter House of the Lord for All People and the Church of the Mountain, Apostolic Faith

Current address not obtained for this edition.

The Latter House of the Lord for All People and the Church of the Mountain, Apostolic Faith was founded in 1936 by Bp. L. W. Williams, a former black Baptist preacher from Cincinnati, Ohio. The founding followed an enlightenment experience and spiritual blessing realized in prayer. The doctrine is Calvinistic, but adjusted to accommodate Pentecostal beliefs. The Lord's Supper is observed, with water being used instead of wine. The church members are conscientious objectors. The chief overseer is appointed for life.

Membership: Not reported. In 1947 there were approximately 4,000 members.

Mount Calvary Pentecostal Faith Church, Inc.

Current address not obtained for this edition.

Mount Calvary Pentecostal Faith Church, Inc., also known as the Emmanuel Temple Pentecostal Faith Church, Inc., and the Mount Assembly Hall of the Pentecostal Faith of All Nations, is a predominantly African-American Pentecostal group founded in 1932 in New York, New York by Bp. Rosa Artemus Horne. The work has been continued by Mother Horne's adopted daughter, Bp. Gladys Brandhagan.

Sources:

Payne, Wardell J., ed. *Directory of African American Religious Bodies: A Compendium by the Howard University School of Divinity*. Washington, DC: Howard University Press, 1991.

Mount Sinai Holy Church of America, Inc.

1469 N Broad St., Philadelphia, PA 19122-3327

The Mount Sinai Holy Church of America, Inc., was founded by Ida Robinson (1891–1946), who grew up in Georgia, where she was converted at age 17 and joined the United Holy Church of America. Robinson later moved to Philadelphia, where she became the pastor of the Mount Olive Holy Church. Following what she believed to be the command of the Holy Spirit to "Come out on Mount Sinai," she founded the Mount Sinai Holy Church in 1924. Women have played a prominent role in its leadership from the beginning.

The church's doctrine is Pentecostal, with sanctification a prerequisite for the baptism of the Holy Spirit. One must be converted before becoming a member. Bishop Robinson believed that God ordained four types of human beings: the elect or chosen of God, the compelled (those who could not help themselves from being saved), the "who so ever will," who can be saved, and the damned (ordained for hell). Spiritual healing is stressed. Foot-washing is practiced. Behavior, particularly sexual, is rigidly codified and rules are strictly observed. Short dresses and worldly amusements are frowned upon.

The church is episcopal in government. Bishop Robinson served as senior bishop and president until her death in 1946. She was succeeded by Bp. Elmira Jeffries, the original vice president, who was, in turn, succeeded by Bp. Mary Jackson in 1964. Assisting the bishops is a board of presbyteries, composed of the elders of the churches. There are four administrative districts, each headed by a bishop. There is an annual conference of the entire church, and one is held in each district. Foreign missions in Cuba, Guyana, and South America are supported. Bp. Amy Stevens succeeded Bp. M. Jackson and Bp. Joseph H. Bell was inaugurated president on September 22, 2001.

Membership: In 2000 the group reported 117 churches and approximately 7,500 members.

Sources:

Mount Sinai Holy Church of America. www.mtsinaichurch.org.

National Fellowship Churches of God, Inc.

5000 U.S. Hwy. 17, Ste. 18-116, Orange Park, FL 32003-8229

The National Fellowship Churches of God, Inc. (NFCOG) traces its history to 1909, when William J. Seymour, leader of the original Pentecostal revival in Los Angeles, California, visited Washington, D.C. From the mission on Azusa Street in Los Angeles that Seymour pastored, the Pentecostal Movement had spread around the United States. Accompanying Seymour on his visit to Washington was Charles H. Mason, founder of the Church of God in Christ.

Among the people affected by the new teachings on Pentecostalism was Charles W. Lowe of Handsom, Virginia, who in turn founded the Apostolic Faith Church of God, which was loosely affiliated with Seymour's organization in Los Angeles. Over the years other congregations were founded, some of which became the sources of new denominations. The Apostolic Faith Church of God was finally chartered in Maryland in 1938 (the same year the Los Angeles center was permanently dissolved).

In 1945 Bishop Lowe separated from the main body of the Apostolic Faith Church of God and established himself as leader of a new organization, the Apostolic Faith Church of God and True Holiness. The main body of the church then reorganized and elected Bp. Rossie Cleveland Grant, who was succeeded by Bp. George Buchanan White. Following White was Bp. George W. Parks. Parks discontinued the previous corporation, which was replaced by an unincorporated fellowship of churches. His successor, Bp. Lois Cleveland Grant, reincorporated the

fellowship as the Apostolic Faith Churches of God. Bishop Grant was succeeded by Bp. Abraham Urquhart and Stephen Douglas Willis Sr.

In 1996, the Apostolic Faith Churches of God started to dissolve. The National Fellowship Churches of God, Inc., with its Covenant Churches, rose from its ashes. In 1998 Apostle Ivan L. Grant Sr. consecrated NFCOG's first vice-bishop—former bishop Ronald E. Riley Sr. of Bridgeport, Connecticut, who served until 2006. In 2008 the chief apostle was still Ivan L. Grant Sr.

New Beginning Apostolic Faith Church of God, Inc. serves as the general assembly for the NFCOG. It established its headquarters in Jacksonville, Florida, in September 2006. Apostle Ivan L. Grant Sr. serves as its senior pastor.

Membership: Not reported.

Educational Facilities:

NFCOG Bible Institute, Orange Park, Florida.

Periodicals: *NFCOG Newsletters*.

Sources:

National Fellowship Churches of God. www.nfcog.org/default.aspx.

New Light Christian Center Church

1535 Greensmark Dr., Houston, TX 77067

The New Light Christian Church was founded in 1984 in Houston, Texas, by Drs. I. V. and Bridget Hilliard, an African-American couple. Formerly the pastor of a Baptist congregation, I. V. Hilliard experienced the baptism of the Holy Spirit and spoke in tongues. When he declared his new experience, the great majority of the congregation left him. He began the New Light Church with fewer than 23 lay supporters, ministering in two locations, north Houston (in 1985) and south Houston (several years later). The two locations later were united under the same name— New Light Christian Center Church. The church was joined by new work in Beaumont, Texas, in September 1996 and in Austin, Texas, in September 2001. Most recently, a third location has been added, in east Houston.

The New Light Christian Center Church is a trinitarian Pentecostal church whose beliefs resemble those of the Assemblies of God. Baptism is by full immersion.

Under the Hilliards' leadership the church has continued to grow. Beginning in 1984 Dr. Hilliard led the congregation to support a television outreach, "Changing Lives Through Faith." The Hilliards also founded and lead an associated network of independent Pentecostal churches, the Association of Independent Ministries. The church supports Life Change Institute and the Addiction Recovery Ministry, both responses to drug addiction in the African-American community in Houston.

Membership: In 2008 the church reported 28,000 members.

Sources:

New Life Christian Center Church. www.newlight.org/.

Hilliard, I. V. *Living the Maximized Life: How To Win No Matter Where You're Starting From*. Nashville, TN: Thomas Nelson, 2006.

———. *Mental Toughness for Success (Proven Biblical Principles for Successful Living)*. Providence, RI: Light Publications, 2004.

———. *Ten Mistakes Most Failures Make (How To Avoid the Pitfalls to Success)*. Broken Arrow, OK: Vincom, 2002.

National Fellowship Churches of God

c/o New Beginning Apostolic Faith Church of God, 300 Park Ave. N, Orange Park, FL 32073

The National Fellowship Churches of God was founded in 1996 by its presiding bishop, Ivan Louis Grant Sr. Grant is the grandson of Rosie Cleveland Grant and the son of Bp. Lois Cleveland Grant, whom he succeeded as pastor of Trinity Apostolic Faith Holiness Church in Baltimore, Maryland, in 1989. The Fellowship traces its heritage back to the original Pentecostal revival at Azusa Street in Los Angeles and the leadership of William J. Seymour, of the Apostolic Faith Mission, in spreading the Pentecostal faith among African Americans in the eastern United States. From his work with Seymour, Bp. Charles W. Lowe founded the Apostolic Faith Church in Handsome, Virginia, and subsequently Bp. Rosie Cleveland Grant founded the Apostolic Faith Church of God in Baltimore, Maryland. By the mid-1990s the Apostolic Faith Churches of God appeared to be in decline, and that was the catalyst for the formation of the National Fellowship Churches of God.

L. G. Grant led in the founding of the National Fellowship as a covenant organization for member churches and ministers, and to facilitate the strengthening of its covenant churches and pastors with resources as they pursue their ministries of building the Kingdom of God. Among other efforts, the Fellowship publishes and distributes various tapes, books, pamphlets, tracts, newsletters, and position papers to support its members. Grant was consecrated as the Fellowship's presiding bishop in 1997 by Bp. Abraham Urquhart of the Apostolic Faith Churches of God. The following year he was elevated to the office of apostle. In 2006 he resigned from Trinity Church and moved to Jacksonville, Florida, to found New Beginnings Apostolic Faith Church of God, which he continues to pastor.

The church is a Holiness Pentecostal body that affirms sanctification as a step in the process of full salvation prior to the baptism of the Holy Spirit. It is organized according to the fivefold ministry of Eph. 4:11.

Membership: Not reported.

Periodicals: *NFCOG News*.

Sources:

National Fellowship Churches of God, Inc. www.nfcog.org/.

Original United Holy Church International

Current address not obtained for this edition.

The Original United Holy Church International grew out of a struggle between two bishops of the United Holy Church of America. The conflict led to the church severing Bp. James Alexander Forbes and the southern district from the organization. Those put out of the church met and organized on June 29, 1977, at a meeting in Raleigh, North Carolina. The new body remains in essential doctrinal agreement and continues the polity of the United Holy Church.

The Original United Holy Church International is concentrated on the Atlantic coast from South Carolina to Connecticut, with congregations also found in Kentucky, Texas, and California. Bishop Forbes also serves as pastor of the Greater Forbes Temple of Hollis, New York. The church supports missionary work in Liberia. On January 24, 1979, in Wilmington, North Carolina, an agreement of affiliation between the Original United Holy Church and the International Pentecostal Holiness Church was signed, which envisions a close cooperative relationship between the two churches.

Membership: Not reported.

Educational Facilities:

United Christian College, Goldsboro, North Carolina.

Periodicals: *Voice of the World*.

Sources:

Turner, William Clair, Jr. "The United Holy Church of America: A Study in Black Holiness-Pentecostalism." PhD diss., Duke University, 1984.

Pilgrim Assemblies International

9202-14 Church Ave., Brooklyn, NY 11236

Pilgrim Assemblies International was founded by Roy E. Brown, who now serves as its archbishop. Brown was born in 1943 in Birmingham, Alabama. He became a Christian at the age of six and over a decade later received the Holy Ghost and acknowledged his call to the ministry. He pastored his first church in 1965 (at the age of 22) and the following year became pastor of Pilgrim Church in Brooklyn, New York. He was consecrated as a bishop on July 18, 1990, and that same year established the Pilgrim Assemblies International, Inc, a movement that now com-

prises churches across the United States and in the Caribbean, South Africa, and West Africa.

On March 27, 1996, Brown was elevated to the office of archbishop. On July 12, 1998, he moved Pilgrim Church to larger worship facilities in the Bedford-Stuyvesant section of Brooklyn.

Pilgrim Assemblies International is a Trinitarian Pentecostal church similar in doctrine to the Church of God in Christ. It serves primarily African Americans.

Membership: Not reported.

Sources:

Holy Convocation, Central Georgia Jurisdiction. www.arrowweb.com/klcogic/centga/cgaconvo.htm.

Tabernacle of Prayer for All People

Jamaica, NY

The Tabernacle of Prayer for All People was founded in 1986 in Brooklyn, New York, by Johnnie Washington, a former member of the Christian Church (Disciples of Christ). Beginning with 15 people, the congregation grew swiftly, and in the early 1970s moved into successively larger buildings and began a school for church members. Washington conducted a number of tent revivals during the 1970s through which many thousands were reported to have had been saved. This evangelistic outreach led to the founding of a number of congregations, first along the East Coast, and then along the Pacific Coast. Washington died in California while leading the work there.

The church is led by a seven-member Apostles Council. The current church leader is Rev. Ira Davison.

Membership: In 1990 there were 49 churches and approximately 4,000 members.

Sources:

DuPree, Sherry Sherrod. *African-American Holiness Pentecostal Movement: An Annotated Bibliography*. New York: Garland Publishing, 1992.

The True Apostolic Church of Jesus Christ

16 Helena St., Rochester, NY 14605

The True Apostolic Church of Jesus Christ traces its American story to Oakfield, New York, where in 1943 Bishop Gus Thomas, an African-American preacher, ministered to several congregants in the home of Cleveland and Mary Albritton. This group moved to Rochester in 1944 and established a second location in Buffalo in 1963. Since the 1960s the church has been led by Bishop Allmon Bailey. American congregations are found in New York, Alabama, Florida, and Pennsylvania.

This Apostolic grouping of churches puts emphasis on its continuation of New Testament doctrine expressed in the revivalist tradition and in the emergence of Pentecostalism at Azusa Street, Los Angeles, in 1906.

Membership: In 2008 the church reported eight congregations in the United States and one in Nigeria.

Sources:

True Apostolic Church of Jesus Christ. www.trueapostolicchurchofjesuschrist.org/.

True Grace Memorial House of Prayer

205 V St. NW, Washington, DC 20001

In 1960 after Bp. Marcelino Manoel de Graca ("Sweet Daddy" Grace) died, Walter McCollough was elected bishop of the United House of Prayer for All People, but approximately six months later criticism was directed at him for his disposal of church monies without explanation to the other church leaders. The elders relieved him of his office and a lawsuit ordered a new election, at which time he was re-elected. Complaints continued that he was assuming false doctrines, such as claiming that he and only he was doing God's work or that he had power to save or condemn people. Shortly after the second election, he dismissed a number of the church leaders. Twelve dissenting members, with Thomas O. Johnson (d. 1970) as their pastor, formed the True Grace Memorial House of Prayer in Washington, D.C. (Elder Johnson had been dismissed after 23 years of service as a pastor.) In 1962 the church members adopted a church covenant in which they agreed to assist one another in loving counsel, prayer, and aid in times of sickness and distress; to do all good to all, in part, by assisting them to come under the ministry of the church; to avoid causes of divisions, such as gossip; and to refrain from any activity that might bring disgrace on the cause of Christ. The present head of the church is Elder William G. Easton.

Membership: Not reported. In the 1970s there were eight congregations in Washington, D.C.; Philadelphia, Pennsylvania; New York, New York; Baltimore, Maryland; Savannah Georgia; Hollywood, Florida; and North Carolina.

True Vine Pentecostal Holiness Church

500 Kinard Dr., Winston-Salem, NC 27101

The True Vine Pentecostal Holiness Church was founded in 1946 in Winston Salem, North Carolina, by William Monroe Johnson (d. 1975) and Robert L. Hairston. Johnson served as bishop and Hairston as vice-bishop. The church grew peacefully until the early 1960s when Hairston became the center of an intense and multifaceted controversy. First, Hairston had come to accept the non-Trinitarian "Jesus Only" doctrine declaring the unitary nature of God. Second, he was heavily criticized for his divorce. Hairston had also become an advocate of women ministers, a cause Johnson opposed. In 1961 Hairston was removed as vice-bishop. He left the church with his supporters and founded the True Vine Pentecostal Churches of Jesus (Apostolic Faith).

The True Vine Pentecostal Holiness Church is a holiness Pentecostal body. Johnson continued to lead the church until he was succeeded by his son, Sylvester D. Johnson, in 1975.

Membership: Not reported.

Sources:

Macedonia Worship Center. www.macedoniaworshipcenter.org.

DuPree, Sherry Sherrod. *African-American Holiness Pentecostal Movement: An Annotated Bibliography*. New York: Garland Publishing, 1992.

United Church of God in Christ

International Headquarters, 2649 McAfee Rd., Decatur, GA 30032

The United Church of God in Christ was founded in 1979 by Marshall Carter III (d. 2003), his wife Lillie Fanning Carter (d. 1998), and other former members of the Church of God in Christ (COGIC). Rev. Carter had founded the Lynwood Park COGIC congregation in Atlanta, Georgia. He worked under Bishop George Briley as the jurisdiction's superintendent and his wife as district missionary. After Briley's death in 1975, Carter began to disagree with the national church over the manner in which the affairs of the jurisdiction were handled, especially in the matter of choosing a successor. Thus, in 1979 the Lynwood Park congregation withdrew from COGIC and became known as the Lynwood Park Church of God in Christ of Georgia, with Carter elevated to the bishopric. Other churches soon affiliated with the Lynwood Park Church. A union of these churches resulted in the formation of the United Church of God in Christ.

The beliefs and practices of the new denomination resembled those of its parent body and continued its Episcopal polity.

Following the death of Bishop Carter in 2003, Bishop Spencer Lakey became the new head of the church as its presiding bishop and chief apostle.

Membership: In 2008 the church reported 41 affiliated congregations, all but seven located in Georgia. Other congregations are located in Illinois, Alabama, Texas, Oklahoma, and Mexico.

Sources:

United Church of God in Christ. www.ucogic.com/.

United Church of the Living God, The Pillar and Ground of Truth

Los Angeles, CA

Alternate Address: 601 Kentucky Ave., Fulton, KY 42021.

The United Church of the Living God, The Pillar and Ground of Truth was founded in 1946 in Los Angeles, California, by Bp. Clifton "O.K." Okley. Raised a Baptist, Okley became a minister in the Church of the Living God, The Pillar and Ground of Truth (Jewell Dominion) and a leading figure in the church on the West Coast. In 1946 Okley had a disagreement with his bishop, M. Jewell, who wanted him to move to Florida. Okley refused to move and left the church; with his supporters he founded a new denomination.

Because the church was formed as a result of an organizational dispute, it still adheres to the doctrine of its parent body. It has established congregations in California and Kentucky and missions in Germany, Haiti, and Africa.

Membership: Not reported.

Sources:

DuPree, Sherry Sherrod. *African American Holiness Pentecostal Charismatic: Annotated Bibliography*. New York: Garland, 1992.

United Crusade Fellowship Conference

14250 SE 13th Pl., Bellevue, WA 98008

The United Crusade Fellowship Conference is a small, independent Pentecostal denomination founded by Bp. Richard E. Taylor. It has an active program that includes support of the Christian Bible Institute and a children's daycare center. It is a member of the Federated Pentecost Church International, an ecumenical group.

Membership: Not reported.

Sources:

DuPree, Sherry Sherrod. *African-American Holiness Pentecostal Movement: An Annotated Bibliography*. New York: Garland Publishing, 1992.

United Holy Church of America

825 Fairoak Ave., Chillum, MD 20783

The United Holy Church of America was formed as the outgrowth of a holiness revival conducted by the Rev. Isaac Cheshier at Method, North Carolina (near Raleigh), in 1886. In 1900 the group became known as the Holy Church of North Carolina (and as growth dictated, the Holy Church of North Carolina and Virginia). In the early twentieth century, the church became Pentecostal and adopted a theology like that of the Church of God (Cleveland, Tennessee). The present name was chosen in 1916.

The church grew throughout the United States and extended to the West Indies, Haiti, Liberia, Ghana, Johannesburg in South Africa, Bermuda, and the Philippines. The church split in 1977. After 21 years of separation, a joint meeting of bishops from the United Holy Church and the Original United Holy Church International held in March of 1998 culminated in reunification, in Greensboro, North Carolina, at the 26th Quadrennial Convocation of the United Holy Church of America, Inc.

The general president in 2008 was Bp. Elijah Williams, who succeeded Bp. Odell McCollum upon the latter's death.

Membership: There are approximately 50,000 members in 480 churches and over 960 ministers.

Educational Facilities:

United Christian College, Greensboro, North Carolina.

United Christian College, New York, New York.

United Christian College, Wilmington, Delaware.

United Christian College, Washington, D.C.

United Christian College, Norfolk, Virginia.

United Christian College, Bridgeport, Connecticut.

Periodicals: *The Holiness Union*.

Sources:

United Holy Church of America. www.uhca.org.

Turner, William Clair, Jr. *The United Holy Church of America: A Study in Black Holiness-Pentecostalism*. Ph.D. diss., Duke University, Durham, NC, 1984.

The United House of Prayer for All People of the Church on the Rock of the Apostolic Faith

601 M St. NW, Washington, DC 20001-3620

The United House of Prayer was founded in the 1920s by the late Bp. Charles Manuel Grace (1884–1960), who built the first House of Prayer in 1919 in West Wareham, Massachusetts, with his own hands. National attention began to focus on the United House of Prayer during the Great Depression, when Bishop Grace, popularly known as "Sweet Daddy" Grace, fed the poor, held services for integrated congregations in southern cities, built churches in poverty-stricken areas for the downtrodden, and gave hope to thousands of distraught people. Over a period of nearly 32 years of preaching, he established over 100 Houses of Prayer across the nation with a membership that grew into the millions. In the process he became one of the most controversial religious leaders in the African-American community and the subject of numerous news articles on both his family life and the various properties he purchased and projects he initiated.

The United House of Prayer was eventually incorporated in Washington, D.C., on June 20, 1927. The purpose of the organization was to establish, maintain, and perpetuate the doctrine of Christianity and the Apostolic Faith throughout the world among all people and to erect and maintain houses of prayer and worship where all people may gather for prayer and to worship the Almighty God in Spirit and in Truth, irrespective of denomination or creed.

The church affirms the Apostolic Faith and takes its name from the biblical passages Isaiah 56:6–7, Matthew 21:13, Mark 11:17, and Luke 19:46. It affirms belief in God as Creator, in Jesus as the virgin-born savior of humanity, the importance of water baptism for repentance, rebirth in the Holy Spirit, and the holiness of life. The church is organized hierarchically.

Following Bishop Grace's death in 1960, Bp. Walter McCollough was elected to the position of Bishop of the United House of Prayer. He started the McCollough Scholarship College Fund, which has awarded more than 1,000 grants, many of the recipients of which have gone on to careers in medicine, law, engineering, and education. McCollough also inaugurated a nationwide building program of new "Houses of Prayer" and "new and affordable housing," which resulted in, among other accomplishments, the 90-unit McCollough Canaanland Apartment, the 190-unit McCollough Paradise Gardens, and the McCollough Haven for senior citizens along the District of Columbia's 7th Street, well known as a former site of riots. Additional housing units were constructed in Charlotte, North Carolina; Norfolk, Virginia; New Haven, Connecticut; and Los Angeles, California.

Upon Bishop McCollough's passing in 1991, he was succeeded as bishop by S. C. Madison. During his first six years in office, Madison led in the erection of over 100 new "Houses of Prayer." In addition, he has continued his predecessor's efforts to build new affordable multifamily housing, parsonages, daycare centers, retail malls, and senior citizen's housing, all without private mortgages or federal or local government assistance. The church pays cash for the total costs of construction for all of its developments. Also, the purchase of several new interstate buses has expanded the outreach of the church.

In keeping with a distinctive architectural "signature and style," the church's structures are adorned with the "Sweet Blessing Angel." This "Sweet Blessing Angel" and other indicia of the United House of Prayer are currently the focus of historians and investigators with the Smithsonian Institution. An exhibit focused on the urban church outreach and housing programs of the United House of Prayer and their impact on the neighborhood environment was displayed in 1998 at the Arts and Industries Building on the National Mall.

Membership: In 1997 the church reported 135 congregations and 875 ministers in the United States.

Sources:

The United House of Prayer for All People. www.tuhopfap.org.

Dallam, Marie W. *Daddy Grace: A Celebrity Preacher and His House of Prayer*. New York: New York University Press, 2007. 261 pp.

Davis, Lenwood G., comp. *Daddy Grace: An Annotated Bibliography*. Westport, CT: Greenwood Press, 1992. 130pp.

Whiting, Albert N. *The United House of Prayer for All People: A Case Study of a Charismatic Sect*. Ph.D. dissertation, American University, Washington, DC, 1952. 319 pp.

United Pentecostal Council of the Assemblies of God (UPCAG)

211 Columbia St., Cambridge, MA 02139

The United Pentecostal Council of the Assemblies of God (UPCAG) dates to 1909 and the formation of a small congregation in Cambridge, Massachusetts, by George A. Phillips (d. 1946) and Sidney J. Davis. Phillips was formerly a member of the Church of the Nazarene and Davis a Baptist. The original group, consisting primarily of African Americans who had migrated from the Caribbean and several people from North Carolina, met in Davis's home until rented facilities were obtained in 1914. Phillips was ordained in 1916 for what had come to be known as First Holiness Church. The congregation moved into its own building in 1918. Evangelistic efforts reached out to the New England states and to the Caribbean.

The appearance at the First Holiness Church of an African-American couple who wished to become missionaries to Africa prompted the creation of the United Pentecostal Council, as most churches would not sponsor African Americans as missionaries. The council has subsequently become an international association of congregations and missions.

The council is a Trinitarian Pentecostal body that affirms the authority of the Bible and faith in the Triune God. It holds that all believers should seek for and expect to receive the baptism of the Holy Spirit, with the associated sign of speaking in tongues and other spiritual gifts. Divine healing is also stressed.

In 1997, Rev. Lorraine A. Thornhill became the first female pastor of the First Holiness Church.

Membership: In 2008 First Holiness Church reported about 200 members, one pastor, and three ministers. It currently has member churches in the United States, Barbados, Jamaica, Liberia, and Trinidad.

Sources:

First Holiness Church of the Apostolic Faith. www.firstholiness.com/.

Universal Christian Church

2140 Martindale Ave., Indianapolis, IN 46202

The Universal Christian Church was founded in 1955 by Bp. Sallie M. Swift (d.1970), an independent African-American Pentecostal Bible teacher, in Indianapolis, Indiana. The church is noteworthy for the prominent role it gives to female leaders. Prior to the church's founding, Swift led Bible classes in her home and in the homes of associates for some 15 years. One of those who regularly attended her classes spoke for the group and asked her to organize a church and be their pastor. After a time of prayer, she consented. Swift served as bishop until her death in 1970. She was succeeded by Bp. Clara M. Roberts.

Membership: Not reported. There are three congregations.

Universal Christian Spiritual Faith and Churches for All Nations

Current address not obtained for this edition.

The Universal Christian Spiritual Faith and Churches for All Nations was founded in 1952 by the merger of the National David Spiritual Temple of Christ Church Union (Inc.) U.S.A., St. Paul's Spiritual Church Convocation, and King David's Spiritual

Temple of Truth Association. National David Spiritual Temple of Christ Church Union (Inc.) U.S.A. had been founded in Kansas City, Missouri, in 1932 by Dr. David William Short, a former Baptist minister. He became convinced that no man had the right or spiritual power "to make laws, rules or doctrines for the real church founded by Jesus Christ" and that the "denominational" churches had been founded in error and in disregard of the apostolic example. Bishop Short claimed that the temple was the true church, and hence dated to the first century.

The merged church differs from many Pentecostal churches in that it denies that only those who have spoken in tongues have received the Spirit. It does insist, however, that a full and complete baptism of the Holy Ghost is always accompanied by both the gift of "tongues" and other powers. The members of the church rely on the Holy Spirit for inspiration and direction. The church is organized according to I Corinthians 12:1–31 and Ephesians 4:11. It includes pastors, archbishops, elders, overseers, divine healers, deacons, and missionaries. Bishop Short is the chief governing officer. In 1952, he became archbishop of the newly merged body. He is assisted by a national executive board which holds an annual assembly.

Membership: Not reported. In the mid-1960s there were reportedly 60 churches and 40,816 members.

Educational Facilities:

St. David Christian Spiritual Seminary.

Periodicals: *Christian Spiritual Voice.*

Universal Church of Christ

491 Orange St., Newark, NJ 07107

The Universal Church of Christ was founded in 1972 by Rev. Dr. Robert C. Jiggetts Jr., with the assistance of Elders Nathaniel Kirton and Carl Winckler. The first center was in Orange, New Jersey. The church has been very service-oriented and in 1984 it initiated a soup kitchen program that mobilized church volunteers, government grants of money and food surpluses, and donations from local businesses. By the beginning of the 1990s, it was serving 1,300 meals a month to the poor and homeless.

The church accepted the Apostolic Pentecostal position that identifies Jesus as the one God of the Bible and denies the Trinity. It has three ordinances: baptism, the Lord's Supper, and holy matrimony. It affirms belief in the infallibility of the scriptures and divine healing. Jiggetts heads the church as its chief apostle, president, and overseer.

Membership: In 2008 the church's Web site listed eight congregations in the United States. It also listed four international congregations, in Ghana, Liberia, the Philippines, and Haiti.

Sources:

Universal Church of Christ. www.ucoci.com/index.html.

Payne, Wardell J., ed. *Directory of African American Religious Bodies: A Compendium by the Howard University School of Divinity*. Washington, DC: Howard University Press, 1991.

Victory Unto Victory Revivals, Inc.

c/o Greater Victory Temple of Praise, 230 Creekview Blvd., Covington, GA 30016

Victory Unto Victory Revivals was the name under which Larry J. Conner and his wife Chandra R. Conner, an African-American couple, operated as independent evangelists. In November 1995 the Connors incorporated Victory Unto Victory Revivals as a ministry for Jesus Christ, and in the following spring they opened Victory Apostolic Temple in Lawton, Oklahoma, as the first congregation.

The new church was founded with a minimum of doctrine. Its doctrinal statement emphasizes the authority of the Bible as the inspired and infallible Word of God. The church affirms that all doctrine, faith, hope, and instruction for the church must be based upon, and harmonize with, the Bible, and it must be clearly understood by those who preach for the church.

The church has had particular success in Nigeria, and most of its affiliated congregations are now a part of its Nigerian diocese headed by Bp. D. D. Obott.

Membership: Not reported. In 2008 there were 4 affiliated congregations in the United States, and 45 in Nigeria.

Sources:

Victory Unto Victory Revivals. ourworld-top.cs.com/allvat1/God/index.htm?f=fs.

 # Signs Pentecostals

Church of God with Signs Following
Current address not obtained for this edition.

The Church of God with Signs Following is a name applied to an informally organized group of Pentecostal churches, ministers, and itinerant evangelists popularly known as snake handlers, who are distinguished by their practice of drinking poison (usually strychnine) and handling poisonous serpents during their worship services. Among those who handle snakes and drink poison, the actions are called "preaching the signs." The term *signs* refers to Jesus' remarks in Mark 16: 17–18: "And these signs will accompany those who believe: in my name they will cast out demons; they will speak in new tongues; they will pick up serpents; and if they drink any deadly thing, it will not hurt them; they will lay their hands on the sick, and they will recover." The practice, an object of curiosity scorned and ridiculed by outsiders, is commonplace to believers.

The practice of snake handling began with George Went Hensley, a minister with the Church of God (Cleveland, Tennessee) in the very early days of the spread of the Pentecostal message throughout the hills of Tennessee and North Carolina. Converted, Hensley erected a brush arbor at Owl Holler outside of Cleveland and began to preach. One day during a service in which he was preaching on Mark 16, some men turned over a box of rattlesnakes in front of Hensley. According to the story, he reached down, picked up the snakes and continued to preach.

Ambrose J. Tomlinson, then head of the Church of God, having become convinced that his ministry was further proof of the pouring of power on the church in the last days, invited Hensley to Cleveland to show church members what was occurring. By 1914 the practice had spread through the Church of God, though practiced by only a small percentage of members. Hensley settled in Grasshopper Valley, near Cleveland, and pastored a small congregation. A number of years later, after a member almost died from a bite, Hensley moved to Pine Mountain, Kentucky.

Meanwhile, the Church of God was growing and in the 1920s, after Tomlinson left the church, the early support for the practice of snake handling turned to strong opposition. In 1928 the Assembly of the Church of God denounced the practice, and it became the activity of a few independent churches, primarily scattered along the Appalachian Mountains. It was largely forgotten until the 1940s.

During the 1940s, new advocates of snake handling appeared. Raymond Hays and Tom Harden started the Dolly Pond Church of God with Signs Following in Grasshopper Valley not far from where Hensley had worked two decades earlier. During the years since, that church has been the focus of the most intense controversy concerning the practice and become the best-known congregation of the signs people. In 1945 Lewis Ford died of a bite received at the Dolly Pond Church. His death led to the passing of a law against the practice by the state of Tennessee and the subsequent suppression of the group by authorities. Persecution against and demonstrations for the group led to the arrest of Hensley in Chattanooga, Tennessee, (convicted of disturbing the peace in 1948) and the disruption of an interstate convention of believers in Durham, North Carolina, in 1947. Following these events the group again withdrew from the public eye, and, except for the death of Hensley, bitten in a service in Florida in 1955, was forgotten for several decades.

Then in 1971 the group again was in the news when Buford Peck, a member of the Holiness Church of God in Jesus' Name, a second snake handling church located not far from the Dolly Pond Church, was bitten. Though he did not die, he did loose his secular job. Over the next few years three persons in Tennessee and Georgia died, two, including Peck and Jimmie Ray Williams, his pastor, from strychnine poison taken during a service. Subsequent court battles, in part to test the law against the practice, led to a 1975 ban on snake handling and the drinking of poison in public religious services by the Tennessee Supreme Court. Followers vowed to continue the practice.

Members of the snake handling churches are Pentecostals who accept the basic theology by which people seek and receive the baptism of the Holy Spirit, evidenced by speaking in tongues. The snake handlers, however, go beyond the Pentecostals in their belief that snake handling and the drinking of poison (and for some, the application of flames to the skin) are a sign of an individual's faith and possession by the Holy Spirit. It should be noted that the handling of snakes and the drinking of poison are done only while the believer is in an ecstatic (trancelike) state, referred to by members as being "in the Spirit." Scholars who have examined the movement have frequently questioned the low frequency of bites, given the number of occasions the snakes are handled and the generally loud atmosphere of the services.

The snake handlers accept the rigid holiness code of the Pentecostal and holiness churches. Dress is plain. The Bible is consulted on all questions having to do with the nature of "worldly behavior." The kiss of peace is a prominent feature of gatherings. Worship is loud, spontaneous, and several hours in length.

Congregations of signs people can be found from central Florida to West Virginia and as far west as Columbus, Ohio. Each church is independent (and a variety of names are used, mostly variations on the Church of God). They are tied together by evangelists who move from one congregation to the next. They produce no literature.

Membership: Observers of the snake handlers estimate between 50 to 100 congregations and as many as several thousand adherents.

Sources:

Carden, Karen W., and Robert W. Pelton. *The Persecuted Prophets*. New York: A. S. Barnes, 1976.

Collins, J. B. *Tennessee Snake Handlers*. Chattanooga, TN: by author [1947?].

Holliday, Robert K. *Test of Faith*. Oak Hill, WV: Fayette Tribune, 1966.

La Barre, Weston. *They Shall Take Up Serpents*. New York: Schocken Books, 1969.

Original Pentecostal Church of God
Current address not obtained for this edition.

Rarely recognized by observers of snake-handling groups, the Original Pentecostal Chruch of God represents a significant departure from the commonly accepted belief and practice of signs people. They do not believe in "tempting God" by bringing snakes into church services. However, should the occasion arise where the handling of a serpent provides a situation for a test and witness to one's faith, it is done. Members recount times in which they have encountered rattlesnakes or copperheads outside the church and have picked them up as they preached to those present.

The Original Church of God emerged from the Free Holiness people, the early Pentecostals, in rural Kentucky during the first decade of the twentieth century. Tom Perry and Tom Austin founded churches in rural Tennessee. Perry carried the Pentecostal message to Alabama and in 1910 converted P. W. Brown, then president of the Jackson County Baptist Association. Brown became the pastor of the Bierne Avenue Baptist Church in Huntsville, Alabama, one of the leading congregations of the Original Pentecostal Church. There is little formal organization nor are there "man-made rules." Congregations are scattered throughout the deep South.

Membership: Not reported.

Spanish-Speaking Pentecostals

The Assembly of Christian Churches, Inc.
722 Prospect Ave., Bronx, NY 10454

The Assembly of Christian Churches, Inc., grew out of the Concilio Olazabal de Iglesias Latino Americano shortly after the death of that church's founder, Francisco Olazabal (1886–1937). In 1939 Bp. Carlos Sepúclveda, pastor of the Bethel Christian Temple in Manhattan, invited various Spanish-speaking Pentecostal churches in the city to unite in an evangelistic crusade. The effort proved so fruitful that some of the cooperating congregations created a new permanent denomination. In 1940 they extended their work to Puerto Rico, where they operated as La Asamblea de Iglesias Cristianas. Their work spread rapidly and within the first generation it not only spread across the United States and throughout Puerto Rico, but to the Virgin Islands, the Dominican Republic, Central and South America, and India.

The doctrine of the assembly is like that of the parent body, there having been no doctrinal issues involved in the establishment of the assembly. The church is led by a bishop elected by the membership. In 2008 the bishop was Rev. Dr. Domingo Rodríguez Díaz.

Membership: Not reported. In 1980 there were approximately 60 congregations with 800 members. There were 54 churches and 1,200 members in Puerto Rico, and additional churches in Central and South America. There was one English-speaking congregation in the Virgin Islands and one in India.

Sources:

Assembly of Christian Churches, Inc. www.aicinternacional.org/historia/index.php.

Piepkorn, Arthur C. *Profiles in Belief: The Religious Bodies of the United States and Canada*. Vol. 3. San Francisco: Harper & Row, 1979.

Concilio Olazabal de Iglesias Latino Americano
1925 E 1st St., Los Angeles, CA 90033

The revival on Azusa Street in Los Angeles that launched the Pentecostal movement soon spread and attracted some Spanish-speaking Christians. Most were affiliated with the Assemblies of God, formed in 1914. Among the early leaders was the Rev. Francisco Olazabal (1886–1937). The Mexican-born Olazabal had become a Methodist minister and worked among the Methodists of southern California. In 1917, however, he received the baptism of the Holy Spirit in a prayer meeting in the home of George Montgomery and his wife Carrie Judd Montgomery (1858–1946). As a minister in the Christian and Missionary Alliance, George Montgomery had had a direct influence on Olazabal's conversion and entry into the ministry. By 1917 the Montgomerys had become Pentecostals. Olazabal left the Methodists and became an Assemblies pastor. He experienced great success in establishing new churches and recruiting pastors. Then in 1923 he led a movement out of the Assemblies, which he had come to feel had placed an insensitive Anglo in charge of the Spanish-speaking work. With his supporters he began independent work along the West Coast and the Mexican border. In 1931 Olazabal came to New York, after which he made visits to Mexico City and in 1934 to Puerto Rico. In 1936 he organized the Latin American Council of Christian Churches. In 1937 Rev. Olazabal died and was succeeded by Rev. Miguel Guillen. The present name of the church was adopted after Olazabal's death as a means to honor his life work.

Reverend Olazabal had close contact with Ambrose J. Tomlinson (1865–1943) and his son Homer Tomlinson (1892–1968), then with the Church of God of Prophecy, who noted Olazabal's natural affinity to Church of God doctrine rather than to that of the Assemblies of God. Olazabal followed the emphasis on the three experiences of justification, sanctification, and the baptism of the Holy Spirit. The Assemblies position negated the necessity of sanctification prior to baptism. The Council is also, like the Church of God, pacifist in orientation.

Membership: Not reported. In 1967 there were seven churches with 275 members in the United States, with an additional four churches in Mexico.

Periodicals: *El Revelator Christiana*.

Sources:

DeLeon, Victor. *The Silent Pentecostals*. Taylor, SC: Faith Printing Co., 1979.

Tomlinson, Homer A. *Miracles of Healing in the Ministry of Rev. Francisco Olazabal*. Queens Village, NY: Author, 1939.

Damascus Christian Church

170 Mt. Eden Pkwy., Bronx, NY 10473

The Damascus Christian Church is a small Pentecostal body formed in 1939. It grew out of the work of Francisco Rosado and his wife Leoncai Rosado in New York City. By 1962 it had spread to New Jersey, with foreign affiliated congregations in Cuba and the Virgin Islands. The church is headed by a bishop who is assisted by a council of officers and a mission committee.

Membership: Not reported. In 1962 the church had 10 congregations and approximately 1,000 members.

Defenders of the Faith

PO Box 2816, Bayamon, PR 00621-0816

The Defenders of the Faith was formed in 1925 by an interdenominational group of pastors and laymen headed by Dr. Gerald B. Winrod (1900–1957), an independent Baptist preacher. Winrod gained a reputation in the 1930s not only for his fundamentalism but also for his support of right-wing political causes. The Defenders of the Faith became the instrument by which Winrod promoted his ideas, and during his lifetime it was a large organization. After Winrod's death in 1957, the group lost many members. However, in 1963 it began a three-year revival under Dr. G. H. Montgomery, who died suddenly in 1966. After that, it grew slowly but steadily under Dr. Hunt Armstrong, its new leader.

Its main program consists of publishing a magazine, *The Defender*, and numerous pamphlets and tracts; administering six retirement homes in Kansas, Nebraska, and Arkansas; maintaining a school (opened in 1957) and headquarters in Kansas City; and conducting a vigorous mission program.

The Defenders of the Faith was neither intended to be a church-forming organization nor meant to be associated with Pentecostalism. In 1931, however, Gerald Winrod went to Puerto Rico to hold a series of missionary conferences. There he met Juan Francisco Rodriguez Rivera, a minister with the Christian and Missionary Alliance. Winrod decided to begin a missionary program and placed Rodriguez in charge. A center was opened in Arecibo, and *El Defensor Hispano* was begun as a Spanish edition of *The Defender*. Rodriguez's congregation became the first of the new movement. In 1932 Rodriguez accompanied Francisco Olazabal, founder of the Concilio Olazabal de Iglesias Latino Americano, on an evangelistic tour of Puerto Rico. The Defenders of the Faith received many members as a result of the crusade and emerged as a full-fledged Pentecostal denomination. A theological seminary was opened in 1945 in Rio Piedras. Members of the Defenders of the Faith migrated to New York in the late 1930s. In 1944 the Defenders' first church in New York was begun by J. A. Hernandez. From there, the movement spread to other Spanish-speaking communities in the United States.

Doctrinally, the churches are not specifically Pentecostal; for example, they do not insist that speaking in tongues is the sign of the baptism of the Holy Spirit. They are fundamentalist, believing in the Bible, the Trinity, salvation by faith, and the obligation of the church to preach the gospel, carry on works of charity, and operate institutions of mercy. Baptism is by immersion. Beyond the basic core of theological consensus, there is a high degree of freedom. Many congregations have

become Pentecostal. Others are similar to Baptist churches. Premillennialism is accepted by most.

A central committee directs the work of the Defenders of the Faith. An annual assembly is held. Ties to the national office in Kansas City, which in 1965 discontinued all specific direction for the Spanish-speaking work, are very weak. The Kansas City office, however, does continue its support of Defenders of the Faith's missionaries and pastors. American congregations of Defenders of the Faith are located primarily in the New York City and Chicago metropolitan areas.

Membership: Not reported. In 1968 there were 14 churches and approximately 2,000 members in the United States, and 68 churches and 6,000 members in Puerto Rico.

Educational Facilities:

Defenders Seminary, Kansas City, Missouri.

Periodicals: *The Defender*. Available from 928 Linwood Blvd., Kansas City, MO 64109.

G12 Vision International

1490 N Flamingo Rd., Plantation, FL 33323

G12 Vision International is a vigorous Christian movement that originated in the ministry of Cesar Castellanos, pastor of a large megachurch in Bogota, Colombia. The church has some 150,000 members in Bogota, and an additional 80,000 located throughout the country. Members are organized into cell groups, following a pattern initially used by David Yonghi Cho, who pastors the megachurch in Seoul, Korea. To Cho's organizational pattern, Castellanos added the G12 Vision given to him in 1983: He asks each church member to become a leader and form a group of 12 new members. In winning people to Christ, the older member assists the new members to become established in faith and then trains them as disciples to send out to win others with the gospel message.

Based on the G12 vision, Castellanos started the International Charismatic Mission Church with eight people at the original meeting. As the church grew in Colombia, the movement was exported overseas. The church is a mainstream Trinitarian Pentecostal Church with beliefs similar to those of the Assemblies of God.

Castellanos is assisted in his work by his wife, Claudia Rodriguez de Castellanos, who is a senator for the Republic of Colombia. In 1997 she was called to the ministry and subsequently was ordained and led an international network of women.

As the work in Colombia developed, pastors and others from other countries began to contact Castellanos to learn about the G12 work and how they could incorporate it into their ministries. Thus the vision spread, with many using the G12 materials produced by Castellanos in their own churches and others seeking to more closely align with Castellanos. In the 1990s G12 Vision International and the International Charismatic Mission Church spread to the United States, primarily among Spanish-speaking Pentecostal and Charismatic believers.

Membership: Not reported.

Sources:

G12 Vision. www.visiong12.com/.

Castellanos, Cesar. *Dream and You Will Win the World*. Plantation, FL: G12 Editors, 2006.

———. *The Revelation of the Cross*. Plantation, FL: G12 Editors, 2003.

———. *Successful Leadership Through the Government of 12*. Plantation, FL: G12 Editors, 1999.

———. *Touching the Father's Heart*. Plantation, FL: G12 Editors, 2006.

Iglesia Evangelica Congregacional, Inc., de Puerto Rico

Box 396, Humacao, PR 00792

The Iglesia Evangelica Congregacional, Inc., de Puerto Rico resulted from the spread in the mid-1930s of the Pentecostal experience of the baptism of the Holy

Spirit and the associated speaking in tongues within a congregation of the non-Pentecostal Iglesia Evangelica Unida in Barrio Aguacate de Yabucoa, Puerto Rico. The congregation split and the Pentecostal members created a council they called Hermanos Unidos de Xristo (United Brothers in Christ). Their work prospered and by 1948 a number of additional congregations had been formed. That year the council was dissolved and the work reorganized as the Iglesia Evangelica Congregacional, Inc., de Puerto Rico. Over the next decades, the church followed the migration of Puerto Rican members to the continental United States and in the 1970s work was established in Gary, Indiana, and Chicago, Illinois.

The church is a holiness Pentecostal organization that believes that sanctification in this life is a condition for entering the kingdom of God. They depart from most Pentecostal groups in that they believe that speaking in tongues is not the only sign of the baptism of the Holy Spirit. The church practices baptism by immersion and the Lord's Supper. Infants are not baptized but are presented for a dedication service. The church specifically rejects the Roman Catholic practice of saying novenas and prayers for the deceased.

Members follow a strict dress code. Men must not wear neck chains, loose shirts, shirts with short sleeves, or large collars. Women must dress modestly and not show much skin. They should not cut their hair and should avoid wearing jewelry, adornments, and expensive fabrics. Women who allow themselves to be sterilized and husbands who consent are expelled from the church.

Membership: Not reported. In 1980 there were two churches in Chicago, one in Gary, and seven in Puerto Rico. The total membership was approximately 600.

Sources:

Piepkorn, Arthur C. *Profiles in Belief: The Religious Bodies of the United States and Canada*. Vol. III. San Francisco, CA: Harper & Row, 1979.

La Iglesia de Dios, Inc.

Oficinas Administrativas, PO Box 72, Caguas, PR 00725

La Iglesia de Dios was founded at Fajardo, Puerto Rico, by a small group of nine Pentecostal believers in 1939. It spread throughout the island during its first generation. In the years after World War II, as Puerto Ricans moved to the continental United States, members of La Iglesia de Dios also arrived stateside, and in the 1970s the church extended its work along the Eastern seaboard and into the Midwest, as well as to the Virgin Islands.

The church's doctrine is similar to that of the Assembly of God. It believes in the Trinity, repentance and the new birth, the baptism of the Holy Spirit, the gifts of the spirit, divine healing, and the premillennial Second Coming of Christ. The church is sabbatarian, believing Saturday to be the only biblical day of rest. Baptism, the Lord's Supper, and foot washing are observed as ordinances. Women are to dress modestly. They may serve as deaconesses and missionaries, but not in the ordained ministry. They have shown special concern for opposing witchcraft, which has been noted to be quite popular in sections of Puerto Rico.

Membership: Not reported. In 1980 the church had approximately 70 churches in Puerto Rico, and 18 in the continental United States (in Spanish-speaking communities in New York, New Jersey, Connecticut, Pennsylvania, Ohio, California, Illinois, and Florida). There were 2 churches in the Virgin Islands. In total that year, there were 5,500 members 12 years and older.

Sources:

La Iglesia de Dios, Inc. www.conciliolaiglesiadediosinc.com.

Piepkorn, Arthur C. *Profiles in Belief: The Religious Bodies of the United States and Canada*. Vol. 3. San Francisco: Harper & Row, 1979.

Latin-American Council of the Pentecostal Church of God of New York

115 E 125th St., New York, NY 10035

The Latin-American Council of the Pentecostal Church of God of New York, Inc. (known also as the Concilio Latino-Americano de la Iglesia de Dios Pentecostal de New York, Incorporado) was formed in 1957 as an offshoot of the Latin American Council of the Pentecostal Church of God. (The latter is a Puerto Rican church without congregations in the United States, and therefore not discussed in this encyclopedia.) Work in New York had begun in 1951 and the New York group became autonomous in 1956, though it remains loosely affiliated with the Puerto Rican parent body.

Doctrinally, the Latin-American Council is like the Assemblies of God. Healing, tithing, and a literal heaven and hell are stressed. The matter of participation in war is left to the individual members. Secret societies are forbidden and no political activity is advised beyond voting. An unaccredited three-year school of theology with an average enrollment of 500 trains Christian workers. Mission activity is carried on in Central America and the Netherlands Antilles, among other places.

Membership: Not reported. In 1967 there were an estimated 75 churches, most in the New York metropolitan area.

Light of the World Church/Iglesia la Luz del Mundo

4765 E 1st St., Los Angeles, CA 90022

Alternate Address: International Headquarters: Glorieta Central de la Iglesia La Luz del Mundo, Colonia Hermosa Provincia, Guadalajara, Jalisco, Mexico.

The Light of the World Church (officially the Church of God, Column and Pillar of Truth, Jesus the Light of the World) (La Iglesia de Dios, Columna y Apoyo de la Verdad, Jesus La Luz del Mundo) was founded in Monterrey, Nuevo Leon, Mexico, in 1926 by Eusebio Joaquin Gonzalez. Gonzalez, later known popularly as the Apostle Aaron, has given the church is common name in Mexico, the Aaronistas.

Gonzalez was converted in 1926 and subsequently met two itinerant lay preachers, known as "Saul" and "Silas," who had appeared within the Pentecostal movement in northern Mexico in the 1920s. Following his baptism by Saul at San Pedro de las Colonias (near Monterrey), he traveled with the two bearded and barefoot "prophets" for a few months. Saul pronounced a prophecy to Gonzalez, calling for the change of name to "Aaron" and predicting that Gonzalez would be known worldwide. Gonzalez/Aaron later noted the moment of the giving of this prophecy as the point at which he experienced God's call to establish the Light of the World Church. The new church was to be dedicated to restoring the Primitive church of Jesus Christ. Aaron selected Guadalajara as its spiritual headquarters.

Over the first generation, the church grew to some 25,000 members. At first, Aaron and his initial converts traveled on foot through rural Mexico establishing house churches. The church's first temple was opened in 1934 in Guadalajara. Aaron established the rules and regulations governing the church (including an obligatory 5:00-AM daily prayer service). Members began to view him in messianic terms. In 1952, Aaron purchased land outside Guadalajara where he founded the Colonia Hermosa Provincia as a community for church members. The Colonia became the site for the construction of a large church seating some 3,000 people and a walled, self-contained community

Samuel Juaquin Flores, who succeeded his father as the church's apostle in 1964, led the church into a more outward-oriented era symbolized by removing the stone wall around the Colonia Hermosa Provincia. He also encouraged the growth and development of colonies across Mexico and other countries and led in the erection of a new central church. Among its several unique attributes, the church requires all ordained pastors to come to the Mother Church in Colonia Hermosa Provincia (symbolic of Holy Jerusalem) annually on August 14 (Aaron's birthday) for the celebration of the Lord's Supper. On that same day, church members (symbolic of the new spiritual People of Israel) also make a pilgrimage to the church to present the Apostle Samuel with special gifts.

Doctrinally, the Light of the World Church is similar to many churches belonging to the "Oneness" non-Trinitarian Pentecostal movement. It follows the Old Testament in its emphasis on high moral standards; its members are well known for their industriousness and honesty. The authority of the Bible is affirmed and Bible reading and memorization are emphasized. The worship style is simple, and during worship the sexes are separated by a central aisle. There are no musical instruments used in worship.

The Light of the World Church has a hierarchical form of church government centered on the apostle. The prophetic messages that have been spoken by both the former and present apostle are considered as "the fountain of truth." In addition, some songs used in the movement honor Aaron as the Church's First Apostle with appellations such as "Anointed One," "Sent One," or "The Prince."

The church suffered an initial division in 1942 when several church leaders accused Aaron of misusing church funds. Though a rival movement, the Good Shepherd Church (Iglesia El Buen Pastor) emerged, the Aaronists survived and thrived. As it has grown, its centralized organization and unorthodoxy have made it the subject of criticism. However, during the last quarter of the twentieth century it experienced a surge in growth that saw membership shoot up to 1.5 million by 1986 and more than 4 million by 1990. Simultaneously, the church developed a membership in the United States, initially as members resettled across the border, and then as evangelistic work was pursued in Spanish-speaking communities, especially in California and Texas.

Membership: Not reported. There are more than 60 centers scattered across North America, of which the majority are found in California (28) and Texas (14). There are more than five million members internationally, in Mexico and in more than 20 additional nations.

Sources:

Iglesia La Luz del Mundo USA/Light of the World Church USA. www.lldmusa.org.

Berg, Clayton, and Paul Pretiz. *Spontaneous Combustion: Grass-Roots Christianity, Latin American Style.* Pasadena, CA: William Carey Library, 1996.

De la Torre, Renee. "Pinceladas de una ilustracion etnografica: La Luz del Mundo en Guadalajara." In *Identidades religiosas y sociales en Mexico*, ed. Gilberto Gimenez. Mexico City, Mexico: Instituto de Investigaciones Sociales de la Universidad Nacional Autonoma de Mexico, 1996.

Gaxiola, Manuel J. *La serpiente y la paloma: Historia, teologia, y análisis de la Iglesia Apostolica de la Fe en Cristo Jesus (1914–1994).* 2nd ed. Nacaulpan, Mexico: Libros Pyros, 1994.

La Luz del Mundo: Un análisis multidisciplinario de la controversia religiosa que ha impacto a nuestro Pais. Bosques de Echegaray, Mexico City, Mexico: Revista Acadica para Estudio de la Religiones, 1997.

Missionary Church of the Disciples of Jesus Christ

c/o Bishop Rolando Gonzalez Washington, 15906 E San Bernardino Rd., Covina, CA 91722

The Missionary Church of the Disciples of Jesus Christ dates to 1970 and the arrival in Los Angeles of Rolando González Washington and his wife, formerly associated with the Soldiers of the Cross of Christ, International Evangelical Church, a Pentecostal church founded in Cuba early in the twentieth century. Washington and his wife had felt a calling to "preach the Gospel of Christ in the State of California." They found people who would assist them in their evangelistic endeavors, and began to preach on the streets and held Bible studies in any homes that would open their doors to them. After five years, however, they had not made a single convert. Then, after going through a period of discouragement, the work began to succeed and a church emerged through the late 1970s. As the work grew, Washington opened rehabilitation centers to assist youth in freeing themselves from drug and alcohol addiction. Two such centers remain in operation, one in Baja California and another in Bell Gardens, California.

Like the International Evangelical Church, the Missionary Church of the Disciples of Christ is a sabbatarian Pentecostal church based on the authority of the Bible. It affirms that "the Sabbath, the seventh day, is the day of rest blessed by God," the baptism of the Holy Spirit, and divine healing. It teaches that the Bible's admonitions on healthfulness should be observed by church members, especially its designation of clean and unclean foods. It practices baptism by immersion, the Lord's Supper as a memorial to Christ's death (not his resurrection), and foot washing.

The church actively solicits financial assistance from nonmembers to support its charitable activities, including the providing of hot meals to the hungry, rescuing runaway teens, assisting teens with alcohol and drug addictions, and managing rehabilitation centers. In Southern California, they have set up tables in public sites to generate income. In 2001, their activity in front of several Wal-Mart stores led to Wal-Mart's suing the church. Wal-Mart charged that the church was raising some $115,000 per month and that the store had received many complaints from its customers because of their positioning themselves in front of the entranceway. The litigation was ongoing as of 2002.

Membership: Not reported. The church has approximately 1,000 members. In 2008 the church's Web site listed a least 17 missions in the United States.

Sources:

Missionary Church of the Disciples of Jesus Christ. www.disciplesofjesuschrist.org/.

"Wal-Mart Sues Church to Stop Its Solicitors." *Arizona Daily Star*, (July 9, 2001).

Soldiers of the Cross of Christ, Evangelical International Church

636 NW 2nd St., Miami, FL 33128

The Soldiers of the Cross of Christ, Evangelical International Church was founded as the Gideon Mission in the early 1920s in Havana, Cuba. Its founder, affectionately known among his followers as "Daddy John," was Wisconsin-born Ernest William Sellers. Sellers was assisted by three women—Sister Sarah, Mable G. Ferguson, and Muriel C. Atwood. Their successful efforts led to the spread of the mission throughout Cuba. In 1939, the periodical *El Mensajero de los Postreros Dias* (*Last Day's Messenger*) was begun. Until 1947, Daddy John functioned as the bishop. But at the annual convention of that year, he was named apostle, and a three-man board of bishops was selected. In 1950 the church sent out its first missionaries, Arturo Rangel Sosa and Arnaldo Socarras, to Panama and Mexico, respectively.

Prior to his death in 1953, Daddy John named Bp. Angel Maria Hernandez y Esperon as his successor. During Hernandez's eight years as an apostle, special attention was given to overseas missions, which were started in nine countries. Plans for starting a mission in the United States were also made.

After the death of Apostle Angel M. Hernandez, Bp. Arturo Rangel became the third apostle. He was in office during the Cuban revolution and the subsequent persecution of the church by the Castro government. Church periodicals were shut down and many places of worship were closed and/or destroyed. In 1966, the same year the American mission was opened, Apostle Rangel, a bishop, and an evangelist all disappeared and have not been heard of since. The remaining members of the board took control of the church, and in 1969 moved its headquarters to Miami, Florida.

The Soldiers of the Cross Church is a sabbatarian Pentecostal body. Members believe in keeping the Law of God (the Ten Commandments) and the dietary restrictions on unclean food (Genesis 7:2; Leviticus 11). They believe in baptism as the first step to salvation, the Lord's Supper as commemorating Christ's death (not his resurrection), and washing the feet as a sign of humility. They believe in the Second Coming of Jesus, and have a strong belief in the gifts of the Spirit, especially prophecy and revelation by means of dreams and visions. Ministers are not to be involved in politics.

After Apostle Rangel disappeared, Bps. Florentino Almeida and Samuel Mendiondo headed the church. They were designated archbishops in 1971. They revived *The Last Day's Messenger*. In the United States, because of the similarity of the church's name to that of the Gideons International, the Gideon Mission used the name Gilgal Evangelistic International Church. At the annual convention held in Jersey City, New Jersey, in 1974, the church adopted its present name.

The church conducts work in 20 Latin American countries as well as in Spain and Germany. Much of the work is in the Spanish language.

Membership: Not reported.

Periodicals: *The Last Day's Messenger*.

Sources:

SCC Atlanta. www.soldadosdelacruzatlanta.org.

Latter Rain Pentecostals

AEGA (Association of Evangelical Gospel Assemblies) International
2149 Hwy. 139, Monroe, LA 71203

AEGA (Association of Evangelical Gospel Assemblies) Ministries International is a Pentecostal/charismatic fellowship of ministers and churches founded in 1976 in Monroe, Louisiana, by Dr. Henry A. Harbuck, originally as Christian Ministries. In 1988 the corporation was reorganized and the present name assumed. The AEGA sees itself primarily as a ministry to ministers; it credentials qualified ministers who accept its statement of belief and charters otherwise independent congregations. It provides a variety of traditionally "denominational" services, such as Bible college education, for its affiliated ministers and congregations.

The church has centrist Pentecostal beliefs, which emphasize the authority of the inerrant Bible, the Trinity, and salvation in Christ by repentance and faith. The church is seen as an agency for evangelizing the world, a place for fellowship and worship, and an instrument through which God is building a body of saints perfect in the image of His Son. Two ordinances are recognized: baptism by immersion and the Lord's Supper. Each member should seek and receive the baptism of the Holy Spirit as evidenced by his or her speaking in tongues. The AEGA is organized according to the fivefold ministry of Ephesians 4:11. Women are accepted into the ordained ministry. The AEGA also affirms the premillennial Second Coming of Christ and the resurrection of the dead.

The AEGA is led by its founder, who also serves as the general overseer and president. He is assisted by a board of bishops and the general executive presbytery. Congregations chartered by the organization must accept its regulation and receive their tax-exempt status through the AEGA corporate exemption. Independent congregations, not chartered by the AEGA, may affiliate but are not covered by the exemption. The association is divided into eight areas, with a coordinator in each.

Members are expected to remain free of involvement in secret societies or occultist organizations and to renounce racism and allow it no place in the fellowship. While they are expected to uphold standards of holiness, members are admonished to refrain from legalism having to do with strictures on minor matters.

The association has extended its outreach through its National Youth Ministries and its extensive foreign missions program, Compassion World Outreach. The association meets annually for an international conference.

Membership: In 2001 the association reported approximately 2,000 members served by 500 ministers in the United States and approximately 400,000 members and an additional 1,000 ministers in 50 countries throughout Europe, Africa, and Asia. There were 175 chartered congregations and 50 affiliated independent congregations in the United States.

Educational Facilities:

Evangel Christian University of America.

Omega Bible Institute and Seminary, Louisiana.

Periodicals: *The Grapevine*. • *The Omegan*. • *The Banner*. • *The Informer*.

Sources:

Association of Evangelical Gospel Assemblies. www.aega.org.

Apostolic Christian Churches, International
Current address could not be obtained for this edition.

The Apostolic Christian Churches, International, was founded in the 1980s as the Gloryland Fellowship of Churches and Ministers, International. The present name was adopted in 1988. It is a charismatic church that emphasizes the fivefold ministry of Ephesians 4:11, and thus employs a hierarchical structure consisting of apostles, prophets, evangelists, pastors, and teachers.

Membership: Not reported.

Educational Facilities:

Gloryland Bible College, Florence, South Carolina.

Assemblies of God International Fellowship (Independent/Not Affiliated)
PO Box 22410, San Diego, CA 92192-2410

The Assemblies of God International Fellowship (Independent/Not Affiliated) emerged in 1986 when the Independent Assemblies of God, International voted to dissolve its old corporation and reorganize under its present name. The Assemblies of God International Fellowship traces its origin to the early days of the Pentecostal revival and to Pentecostalism's spread among Scandinavian believers during the second decade of the twentieth century. As early as 1911 Pastor B. M. Johnson founded the Lakeview Gospel Church in Chicago. A. A. Holmgren, a Baptist minister, was affected by the movement in Chicago and began *Sanningens Vittne*, which became the voice of the independent assemblies of Scandinavian Pentecostals.

An extreme congregationalism dominated the attitude of the early Scandinavian Pentecostal leaders and most stayed separate from the General Council of the Assemblies of God, which formed in 1914. However, associates slowly began to form, the first being the Scandinavian Assemblies of God in the United States, Canada, and Other Lands in 1918. A second association of independent congregations was formed in St. Paul, Minnesota, in 1922. Pastor Johnson in Chicago took the lead in forming a third group, the Independent Assemblies of God. These three groups united in 1935 as the Independent Assemblies of God. The group began the slow process of Americanizing and moving beyond any ethnic exclusivity.

In 1947–1948, a division emerged in the Independent Assemblies of God over participation in the "Latter Rain" Movement, a revival that swept western Canada and became known in some phases for its extreme doctrines and practices. The words *Latter Rain* refer to the end of this order of things, when God will pour out his Spirit upon all people. One group accepted the revival as the present movement of God, as God's deliverance promised in the Bible. This group, under the leadership of W. A. Rasmussen, became the Independent Assemblies of God International, now the Assemblies of God International Fellowship.

Membership: Not reported. The Fellowship's Web site in 2008 listed 25 congregations in the United States. Because Gunnar Wingren, one of the outstanding pioneers of the Assemblies of God International Fellowship, undertook extensive missionary work in Brazil, the Fellowship today has no less than 14,500,000 Brazilian members in thousands of congregations.

Periodicals: *The Mantle*.

Sources:

Assemblies of God International Fellowship. www.agifellowship.org.

Rasmussen, A. W. *The Last Chapter*. Monroeville, PA: Whitaker House, 1973.

Association of Faith Churches and Ministries (AFCM)
PO Box 1918, Willmar, MN 56201

Alternate Address: PO Box 471407, Tulsa, OK 74147.

The Association of Faith Churches and Ministries (AFCM) was founded in 1978 by Jim Kaseman, a graduate of the 1975 class of Rhema Bible Training Center, the Tulsa, Oklahoma, school founded by televangelist Kenneth Hagin. Kaseman afterward became pastor of a church in Minnesota and worked to found other congregations in Minnesota and neighboring states. These congregations all preached the faith message, the theological variant on traditional Pentecostalism that affirmed a law of confession, based in part on Mark 11:23 where Jesus says, "whosoever . . . shall not doubt in his heart, but shall believe that those things which he saith shall come to pass; he shall have whatsoever he saith." The faith message affirms that believers can have anything they "say" as long as they do not doubt in their heart (spirit) but believe and "confess it with their mouth." This belief has often been characterized as the "name it, claim it" doctrine.

Kaseman founded Jim Kaseman Ministries in 1976 as a vehicle for further spreading of the "faith message." Beginning in 1982, it assumed the task of translating, publishing, and distributing Hagin's books in the Middle East and Russia. By 2002 it had published more than 4 million copies of his books in languages such as Russian, Finnish, Estonian, Hebrew, and Arabic.

AFCM has its origin at a 1977 alumni meeting of the Rhema School. John Osteen, another televangelist, asked for those who felt God calling them to start a world ministry to identify themselves. Kaseman and his wife Kathleen responded. A year later they created AFCM to promote fellowship among ministers who shared the "faith message." It has developed into a worldwide movement of churches, pastors, traveling ministers, and missionaries, dedicated to bringing the "Word of Faith" to people internationally. Under its auspices a number of congregations have been established, ministers licensed and ordained, and books distributed. It also administers programs for distributing humanitarian aid to countries in need. In addition, the AFCM sponsors One World Missions designed to facilitate churches partnering with other churches around the world in the work of evangelism.

Membership: Not reported. Churches are located across the United States. They are divided into 13 districts. There are also district directors to serve churches in Australia, the French-speaking countries, the German-speaking countries, the Caribbean, and Russia.

Educational Facilities:

AFCM International Training Center, Calgary, Alberta, Canada.

Periodicals: *AFCM Family Update*.

Sources:

Association of Faith Churches and Ministries. www.afcminternational.org.

Bible Teachers International (BTI)

The Mary Banks Global Training Center, 2005 Johns Ave., Leesburg, FL 34748

Bible Teachers International (BTI) is a conservative Evangelical charismatic apostolic ministry founded by Apostle Mary Banks, an African-American minister. The ministry is an association of churches and Bible schools dedicated to the building of leaders for the church worldwide. BTI centers offer a set of Bible-based courses that lead to licensing and/or ordination by BTI and opportunities to serve in a variety of ministries. Ordination by the laying on of hands is available to those who complete the ministerial course and are agreeable to submitting to the spiritual authority of the BTI leadership. Ordination services are normally held at the various BTI conferences.

BTI's statement of faith affirms the Trinity and salvation by Christ. BTI teaches that there is a kingdom of darkness (sin, destruction, and death) and a glorious kingdom of light (salvation, life, truth, and deliverance). Jesus appeared on earth to destroy the works of Satan and transform men from the kingdom of darkness and death into the kingdom of life, light, and truth. As head of the church, Jesus Christ is preparing it to be presented as a glorious, holy, and sinless body at the end-time.

BTI sponsors annually a World Conference, a School of the Prophets, and periodic Gatherings of the Sons for instruction, direction, and immediate callings from the Holy Ghost. There are also various regional events as deemed necessary.

Membership: Not reported. BTI has six centers in Florida, four in Georgia, and one each in Louisiana and Mississippi. Outside the United States, there are centers in the Bahamas, Canada, and Jamaica.

Sources:

Bible Teachers International. www.bibleteachers.com.

Bible Way Association

PO Box 370, Doniphan, MO 63935

The Bible Way Association was founded in 1958 by Leslie and Pauline Buckner, two Pentecostal believers. Leslie Buckner serves as the organization's president. The Association was originally known as the Community Fellowship Pentecost Church, and was based in St. Louis, Missouri. In 1959 Community Fellowship Pentecost Church became an unincorporated association of ministers and churches under the name Community Fellowship Pentecost Ministers and Churches Association. It was incorporated in 1960. In 1965 its headquarters moved from St. Louis to Ripley County, Missouri. In 1974 the association adopted its current name.

The church is Pentecostal in nature. It accepts the Bible as the Word of God, the Trinity, and salvation in Christ. It believes in the baptism of the Holy Spirit and sanctification as a definite but gradual work of God in the believer. Baptism is by immersion. The ministry is organized according to Ephesians 4:11, into apostles, prophets, evangelists, pastors, and teachers. The church advocates divine healing and tithing.

The church sponsors a camp meeting grounds in Dolphin, Missouri. It publishes a set of booklets and course materials that orient members to its beliefs and prepare ministers for licensing and ordination. The Voice of Truth World Outreach Ministries is a division of the Bible Way Association that focuses on evangelism and outreach through radio, teaching, and printed literature.

Membership: Not reported.

Periodicals: *The Messenger*.

Sources:

Bible Way Association. www.biblewayassociation.com.

The Voice of Truth World Outreach Ministries. www.thevoiceoftruth.com.

Body of Christ Movement

c/o Immanuel's Church, 16819 New Hampshire Ave., Silver Spring, MD 20905

Along with the neo-Pentecostal movement of the 1960s, there developed what can be termed the Body of Christ movement, focused in the ministry of Charles P. Schmitt and Dorothy E. Schmitt of the Fellowship of Christian Believers in Grand Rapids, Minnesota. The basic idea is that God has moved among his people in each generation and has poured out his Spirit upon them in a vital manner. In the eighteenth century, this outpouring occurred through the Wesleyan revival, and in the early twentieth century, through the Pentecostal revival. In the late 1940s, the "Latter Rain" movement swept Canada. According to Schmitt, the outpouring on the present generation is the most momentous of all because this is the last generation and in it shall be manifest the full intent of God (I Cor. 4:1).

Initiation into the "mysteries" is through the baptism of the Holy Spirit. The central mystery of the church as the Body of Christ is that God is preparing a glorious church for himself. God is pouring out his Spirit in every denomination to bring forth the bride of Jesus Christ in this hour. The church as the Body of Christ is the very fullness of Jesus, who fills everything, everywhere with himself.

Doctrine, beyond the core of Pentecostal and Protestant affirmation, is not emphasized. The true basis of fellowship is in God and Jesus Christ. The Body of Christ Movement is organized on a family model, under the care of the responsible brethren (elders) and the ones possessed of spiritual gifts (I Cor. 12:11–14).

The Body of Christ Movement originated in Grand Rapids, Minnesota. Fellowship Press was established and it has issued numerous pamphlets on a wide variety of topics. The Schmitts began a tape ministry and a literature ministry,

"Foundational Teachings." From Grand Rapids, ministers were sent out to cities across the United States. Centers were rapidly established. In the early 1980s, the Schmitts moved to Silver Springs, Maryland, near Washington, D.C., where a strong following had developed under the name of Immanuel's Church. Camp Dominion in rural northern Minnesota was the scene of national gatherings during the summer until recently. Affiliated ministers and congregations are organized into the "Fellowship of Churches and Ministers." The fellowship assists with the education and ordination of ministers, and provides opportunities for gatherings and future nurturing.

Membership: In 2008 over 4,000 were in regular attendance at Immanuel's Church.

Periodicals: *Foundational Teachings.*

Sources:

Immanuel's Church. www.immanuels.org.

Bold Bible Living

International Headquarters, PO Box 75120, White Rock, BC, Canada V4B 5L3

Alternate Address: American Headquarters: PO Box 2, Blaine, Washington 98231.

The Bold Living Society is the organization facilitating the worldwide ministry of evangelist and missionary Don Gossett. Gossett had been the editor of Faith Digest, the magazine of the T. L. Osborn Evangelistic Association. While editor, Gossett was also an evangelist who toured North America, holding evangelistic campaigns and working as a radio minister. During the 1950s, his desire to become a full-time radio evangelist grew, and in 1961 he moved to British Columbia and organized the Bold Living Society.

During the 1950s Gossett became a devoted student of the writings of the late E. W. Kenyon (1867–1948), an early radio evangelist on the West Coast and founder of the New Covenant Baptist Church in Seattle. After his death, Kenyon's daughter continued to publish his books through the Kenyon Gospel Publishing Society in Fullerton, California. Gossett obtained a copy of Kenyon's The Wonderful Name of Jesus in 1952 and eventually obtained an entire set of his writings. Kenyon emphasized the power of the Word—the Bible—and the power of confessing that Word as a means of exercising faith and bringing God's promises into visible reality.

Gossett emerged in the 1970s as a major exponent of what has been termed the "positive confession" perspective, a popular emphasis within the larger Pentecostal community. He maintains the Bible is the Word of God, and that people need to affirm the Bible's truth. It is through the confession of the believers' lips that Jesus gives life and love. Gossett applies biblical promises for physical healing and contends God will supply people's every need. Confession of negative states traps individuals in sickness and poverty.

Gossett's radio work began in Canada and reached out to the United States. In 1964 he began broadcasting from stations in Puerto Rico and Monte Carlo, and soon a second office was opened in Blaine, Washington. As the audience grew, he wrote and published *School of Praise*, a home Bible study course, and numerous books and booklets. Besides the two congregations in British Columbia that are affiliated with the society, Gossett has a worldwide ministry that takes him on evangelistic campaigns around the world; his radio show is aired in over 100 countries.

Membership: There are two congregations with an approximate membership of 100, both in British Columbia. There are affiliated churches in Barbados. In 1988 there were 4,000 partners who support the ministry scattered across the United States and 3,000 others in Canada and the West Indies.

Sources:

Don Gossett Ministries/Bold Bible Missions. www.dongossett.com.

Gossett, Don. *There's Dynamite in Praise*. Springdale, PA: Whitaker House, 1974.

————. *What You Say Is What You Get*. Springdale, PA: Whitaker House, 1976.

————. *I'm Sold on Being Bold*. Springdale, PA: Whitaker House, 1979.

Gossett, Don, and E. W. Kenyon. *The Power of the Positive Confession of God's Word*. Cloverdale, BC, Canada: Don Gossett, 1981.

Kenyon, E. W. *In His Presence*. Seattle, WA: Kenyon's Gospel Publishing Society, 1969.

Called to All Nations Ministries, Inc.

790 E Pine Log Rd., Aiken, SC 29803

Called to All Nations Ministries is an international network of individuals, ministers, ministries, and churches aligned in a mission of world evangelism. It describes itself as multifaceted in ministry, international in impact, transdenominational in background, and multicultural in composition. It was founded by Rev. Ray Popham, an independent Pentecostal evangelist who in 2008 served as the president and apostolic overseer of Called to All Nations, as well as president of Life Vine International, senior pastor of Oasis Church International, and founder of World Ministry Training Institute. He operates under what he sees as a divine mandate to take the Gospel to every nation on the earth. Popham had received a call to the ministry in 1985 when he was 22. After two years of training he launched his ministry. The ministry is designed to bring together ministers and local congregations to create resources to undergird a ministry that will empower leaders and believers worldwide. Called to All Nations has created a variety of structures to channel its ministry, including a World Prayer Network, the International Ministerial Fellowship, the World Ministry Training Institute, World Missions Outreach through Millennial Missions 2000, and Vision America.

The work of called to All Nations is guided by the founder/president and a board of directors comprising ministers licensed and ordained by the ministries. In 2008 board members included Lamont Freeman, Teresa Popham, Helen Winters, Larry Christy, and Belinda Forrest. The International Ministerial Fellowship provides ministerial credentials, personal advice, pastoral care, fellowship, and continuing education for ministers. Ministry is recognized in its fivefold nature (according to Eph. 4:11) of apostle, prophet, evangelist, pastor, and teacher. Ministers who feel called by God to the ministry, and who have prepared themselves for their careers and showed themselves to be faithful, may be certified in one of three categories: certified lay minister, licensed minister, or ordained minister. Approval is based on demonstrated character, calling, salvation experience, and preparation, apart from strict doctrinal scrutiny.

Registered ministries are those congregations/ministries affiliated primarily with Called to All Nations Ministries, from which they receive affiliation, networking, accountability, and fellowship. Training for ministry is offered through the World Ministry Training Institute. Popham has authored a variety of training materials and tapes for curriculum use.

New Day is the All Nations' sponsored international radio ministry program headquartered in Aiken, South Carolina. The broadcast is produced by CTAN Media Network and reaches more than 80 nations through satellite and short-wave radios. *New Day*'s mission is to "cover the globe with the gospel."

Membership: Not reported for 2008. In 2001 there were 23 congregations associated with Called to All Nations. They are located in the United States (14), India (2), and Jamaica (4), with one each in Korea, Pakistan, and Mexico.

Educational Facilities:

World Ministry Training Institute, Aiken, South Carolina.

Periodicals: *Current Epistle.* • *News of All Nations.*

Sources:

Called to All Nations Ministries. www.ctan.us.

Christian International Ministries Network

177 Apostles Way, Santa Rosa Beach, FL 32459

The Christian International Network of Prophetic Ministries, founded in 1988 by Dr. Bill Hamon (b. 1934), is an outgrowth of the Latter Rain Revival that swept through

Pentecostalism in the late 1940s. That revival began in western Canada in 1948 and within a few years found a response among Pentecostal leaders across the continent. The revival emphasized such concepts as the laying on of hands to receive the Holy Spirit, organization around a biblical fivefold ministry, and the role of prophecy. Prophecy, as understood within Pentecostalism, is believed to be a present word from God that is spoken by a person called by God and given the gift of prophecy. Prophecy, which goes beyond Scripture and often offers very specific direction to groups and individuals, should, however, never contradict Scripture.

Hamon was converted to Christianity on his 16th birthday at a revival meeting in rural Oklahoma and several days later was baptized with the Holy Spirit and spoke in tongues. He began attending a Latter Rain or Restoration church. In 1953, while struggling with a call to the ministry, he was given a word of personal prophecy indicating that he would soon emerge as a prophet himself. Hamon moved to Portland, Oregon, and began to attend a Latter Rain bible college. In 1954, after graduation, he became a pastor. He left the pastorate in 1960 and served as an evangelist for three years. He served on the faculty of a bible college in San Antonio, Texas, from 1964 to 1969.

In 1967, prior to his leaving college teaching, he incorporated Christian International Correspondence Bible College to provide an education for ministers who could not leave their work to attend school. The development of the college consumed his time for the next few years. In 1970 he developed the extension program to assist local churches in founding a bible college in their facilities. The college headquarters moved to Arizona in 1981 and then to Florida in 1984. It has since matured into the Christian International School of Theology. Through the years, Hamon has been responsible for training many Pentecostal ministers and introducing them to the prophetic ministry. In 1988 a number of the ministers he had trained and the churches they served banded together in a loose association, the Christian International Network of Prophetic Ministries. He was consecrated bishop of the network in 1989.

In his role as leader of the network, Hamon has authored three important books expounding on the concept and work of a prophet: *Prophets and Personal Prophecy*, *Prophets and the Prophetic Movement*, and *Biblical Principles to Practice and Personal Pitfalls to Avoid*. The network sponsors an annual National Prophetic Conference.

Membership: Not reported.

Sources:

Christian International. www.christianinternational.org/.

Hamon, Bill. *The Eternal Church*. Point Washington, FL: Christian International Publishers, 1981.

————. *Prophets and Personal Prophecy*. Shippensburg, PA: Destiny Image Publishers, 1987.

————. *Prophets and the Prophetic Movement*. Shippensburg, PA: Destiny Image Publishers, 1990.

Covenant Connections International

916 W Hwy. 190, Copperas Cove, TX 76522

Covenant Connections International (CCI), a charismatic association of ministers and churches, traces its history to 1981, when Nathaniel Holcomb established the Christian House of Prayer and the associated It's All About Him Ministries (formerly known as Speak the Word Ministries) to serve Central Texas. CCI was born as a result of Holcomb's election as bishop in 1987. Through Holcomb's ministry, a national network of churches has developed. Covenant Connection operates out of a traditional Pentecostal perspective. It also operates out of what is generally referred to as the *faith message*: the perspective adopted by many Pentecostals that affirms a law of confession, the idea that believers can have anything they declare a desire for as long as they have faith in their heart and confess it with their mouth. This belief has often be characterized as "name it, claim it." It is based in part

on Mark 11:23, which admonishes a disciple that if he "shall not doubt in his heart, but shall believe that those things which he saith shall come to pass; he shall have whatsoever he saith."

The mother church of Covenant Connections has a broad-based outreach ministry in Copperas, Texas, that includes special programs for youth, women, and families. There is also a special ministry to the incarcerated.

The leadership of covenant connections maintains close contact with other "faith message" networks such as Freedom Worldwide Covenant Ministries (Gilbert Coleman) and Ever Increasing Faith Ministries (Fred Price).

Membership: Not reported. In 2002 Covenant Connections had 37 congregations in the United States, 9 in Germany, 7 in the Netherlands, and 1 in the United States Virgin Islands.

Sources:

Covenant Connections International. www.chop.org/cci/index.html.

DOVE Christian Fellowship International (DFCI)

11 Toll Gate Rd., Lititz, PA 17543

DOVE Christian Fellowship International (DCFI), an association of churches that has pioneered a new form of church life built around what are termed cell groups, began in 1971 as a ministry to youth. The ministry, based in south-central Pennsylvania, was launched as the popular Jesus People revival was burgeoning on the West Coast. Included as part of the ministry called "The Lost But Found" was the "Rhema Youth Ministries," a popular Bible study program directed by Larry Kreider that was nurturing many of the youthful converts. It was also discovered that many of the new converts had a tough time trying to fit into the older church communities.

Increasingly, the leadership came to believe in organizing a flexible New Testament-style church (referred to as "new wineskin") that could serve the new believers (referred to as the "new wine"). In 1978 Kreider felt God calling him to be part of an "underground church." In this underground church, believers would be nourished in cell groups that focused on prayer, evangelism, and building intimate relationships. When the underground church was healthy, the whole church grew strong.

DOVE (an acronym for Declaring Our Victory Emmanuel) Christian Fellowship officially began in 1980. At the time the fellowship consisted of some 25 people meeting on Sunday mornings who divided into three cell groups that met during the week. By 1992 some 2,300 believers met in approximately 125 cell groups in south-central Pennsylvania. In the mid-1990s the fellowship went through a complete reorganization that went into effect January 1, 1996. Eight individual congregations emerged, each headed by an eldership team. An Apostolic Council gave spiritual oversight to the whole fellowship, and Kreider became the international director. All of the eight churches committed themselves to working together to plant churches around the world. In addition, DCFU moved to "adopt" churches that had developed a cell church organization but were not growing.

DCFI sees itself as an apostolic movement, defined as a family of churches with a common focus—in this case, a mandate to plant churches throughout the world. Its belief is that each "denomination" has a special purpose in God's kingdom and each should honor and learn from the other. DCFI's leadership encourages members to network with other churches and ministries outside of the DCFI family. DCFI maintains two DOVE Mission International sending centers, one in Lancaster County, Pennsylvania, and the other in Nairobi, Kenya.

Kreider has authored a popular book for cell-based churches, *House Church Networks: A Church for a New Generation*.

Membership: In 2008 DCFI reported 47 churches in the United States and 148 cell-based congregations in the United States and Barbados, Brazil, Bulgaria, Canada, Curacao, Guatemala, Haiti, Kenya, New Zealand, Peru, Rwanda, Scotland, Suriname and Uganda.

Sources:

DOVE Christian Fellowship International. www.dcfi.org/.

Bunton, Paul. *Cell Groups and House Churches: What History Teaches Us*. Ephrata, PA: House to House Publications, 2001.

Kreider, Larry. *House Church Networks: A Church for a New Generation*. Ephrata, PA: House to House Publications, 2001.

————. *House to House: Spiritual Insights for the 21st Century Church*. 2nd ed. Ephrata, PA: House to House Publications, 2000.

Endtime Body-Christian Ministries, Inc.

Current address not obtained for this edition.

The Endtime Body-Christian Ministries Inc. (a.k.a. the Body of Christ Movement and Maranatha Christian Ministries) was founded in the early 1960s by Sam Fife (1926–1979). A former Baptist minister, Fife became Pentecostal after his involvement in the Latter Rain Movement, a Pentecostal revival movement that began in Canada in the late 1940s. Fife founded his organization in New Orleans, Louisiana, but soon moved to Miami, Florida, where he had formerly worked as a contractor and singer. Fife's messages emphasized what he believed was the approaching end of the world. One sign of the end was the emergence of visions among Christians. In one vision, he was told that he would father a child who would become a great prophet. The woman designated as the mother was not his wife, however. With the consent of his wife and the church, he lived with the woman who appeared in the dream for a year, until he became convinced of the error of the vision.

Fife also called his members to prepare for the Second Coming of Christ by separating themselves from the world and preparing a perfected bride (i.e., church body) for Christ to find upon his return to earth. To accomplish this task, he organized a series of communal farms in the United States, Canada, and Latin America. Many of the church members have sold their possessions and moved into these rural communities. The group also established a set of parochial schools for its children. This process of separation from the world led to the disruption of many families, especially where only one spouse was a strong member of the group. The presence of impressionable, single young adults in the group, often living at rather primitive levels (by middle-class standards), also led to the group as being a focus of attention by segments of the anticult movement in the 1970s.

Sam Fife died in 1979 in a plane crash at the age of 53. He was succeeded by C. E. "Buddy" Cobb, pastor of the Word Mission in Hollywood, Florida.

Membership: Not reported. There were reported to be between 6,000 and 10,000 members at the time of Fife's death. Approximately 25 communal farms had been established.

Every Nation

PO Box 1787, Brentwood, TN 37024

Every Nation is a worldwide community of ministries and churches established in 1994. The organization was formerly known as Morning Star International; the name was changed in 2004 to reflect a desire to spread the Gospel of Jesus Christ to "every nation in our generation." Every Nation, which embodies Every Nation Ministries, Every Nation Churches, Every Nation Campus Ministries, and Every Nation Leadership Institute, maintains world missions, engages in church plantings in the United States and globally, and conducts outreach to young people on college campuses. The organization's stated goal is to forge a multiethnic, multigenerational church, with an emphasis on discipleship and leadership training.

Morning Star International (MSI) can be traced back to 1981 and the related careers and friendship of Rice Broocks and Phil Bonasso, two campus ministers at the University of Southern California who were attempting to build a campus outreach program. At this time, they were working with Maranatha Ministries, a controversial campus ministry founded by Bob Weiner and his wife, Rose Weiner, in 1973. After expanding through the late 1980s, Maranatha disbanded in 1989, allowing for a decentralization and diversification of ministry through the many local churches. In 1984 Broocks traveled to the Philippines to build a campus outreach program that brought him into contact with Steven Murrell, a campus minister from Starkville, Mississippi. In both Los Angeles and the Philippines, they established apostolic centers for the training of people for campus ministry. Both centers grew into leadership training centers whose vision for ministry reached out to the larger world.

Broocks served as a pastor and apostle to the other two men. In 1994 they met to consider their role in world evangelism, and decided to merge their ministries into what was named Morning Star International (MSI). Their goal was to fulfill the great commission of spreading the good news of Jesus Christ through church planting, campus ministry, and world missions.

MSI adopted a statement of faith identical to that of the National Association of Evangelicals. It includes belief in the Bible as the infallible Word of God, the Trinity, and the saving work of Jesus Christ, and the present ministry of the Holy Spirit in saving lost humanity. MSI was a Pentecostal Charismatic fellowship that believed in the baptism of the Holy Spirit. Leadership was placed in the hands of an apostolic team that included the three founders and six other ministers who joined their work.

In 1997 MSI aligned itself with His People Ministries, started in the early 1990s by Paul Daniel as a predominantly campus-based church for the university students in Cape Town, South Africa.

Educational Facilities:

School of Campus Ministry. Nashville, Tennessee.

School of Campus Ministry, Cape Town, South Africa.

School of World Missions. Manila, the Philippines.

Membership: In 2008, Every Nation reported 49 congregation in the united States and four in Canada. In addition there were affiliated congregations in 41 nations worldwide.

Sources:

Every Nation. www.everynation.org/en/home.html.

Broocks, Rice. *Change the Campus Change the World!* Gainesville, FL: Maranatha Publications, 1985.

Faith Christian Fellowship International

PO Box 35443, Tulsa, OK 74153-0443

Faith Christian Fellowship International (FCFI) began in 1977 when Doyle "Buddy" Harrison and Pat Harrison responded to what they felt was a call from the Lord to return to their home in Tulsa, Oklahoma, and start a family church and charismatic teaching center, and to reach the world for Jesus. Buddy Harrison (1939–1998) had previously worked for ten years for Kenneth Hagin Ministries and was the founder and first president of the International Convention of Faith Ministries. In 1975 he started Harrison House, a major publisher of charismatic literature.

FCFI is a Pentecostal church that affirms belief in the Bible as the infallible Word of God, the trinity, and salvation through Christ. It also affirms "the present supernatural ministry of the Holy Spirit who bestows the spiritual gifts of: The word of wisdom, The word of knowledge, Faith, Gifts of healings, Working of miracles, Prophecy, Discerning of spirits, Various kinds of tongues, Interpretation of tongues, in and among believers on the earth since the day of Pentecost and continuing until our Lord's return."

Congregations may join FCFI as either an associate (a congregation with a separate incorporation) or an affiliate (an unincorporated congregation). FCFI trains, equips, and prepares people for ministry as an exhorter, licensed, or ordained minister.

A group with the same name exists in Indiana but is unrelated.

Membership: In 2002, the FCFI reported 173 affiliate and associate churches, 125 churches pastored by FCFI-credentialed ministers, 19 affiliate and associate traveling ministries, and 879 credentialed ministers in the United States. FCFI supports missionary families in 16 nations. There are FCFI churches in 39 countries.

Periodicals: *Triumphant Always.* • *The Mentor.*

Sources:

Faith Christian Fellowship International. www.fcf.org/.

Federation of Ministers and Churches International
PO Box 40042, Grand Junction, CO 81504

The Federation of Ministers and Churches (FMC) is a fellowship of Pentecostal/charismatic churches and ministers that originated in a meeting of six pastors at the Church of the King in Dallas, Texas. Jim Hodges, at the time the pastor of the Church of the King, took the leadership, as he had previously been involved in planting new churches. The original gathering led to what became the first annual ministers' conference, held in Midlothian, Texas, the next year. More than 180 ministers and other church leaders attended this first conference.

Subsequently, at a smaller meeting in Arkansas, an organizational outline for the FMC was drawn up. Finally, in 1994, the organization was formalized, its name was chosen, and a statement of faith was written and approved. Already in 1990, as the steps to formal organization were being taken, Hodges had left the pastorate of the Church of the King and assumed fulltime apostolic team leadership of the emerging Federation. Hodges opened offices in Duncanville, Texas. The FMC has become an association of local churches and ministries, which find fellowship in a common bond of unity and receive guidance from and are accountable to the apostolic team of mature ministers led by Hodges.

The federation has assumed a conservative doctrine that accepts the inerrancy of the Bible. It is trinitarian in its doctrine of God. Among its doctrinal distinctives is an approach to biblical interpretation that centers on God's covenants with his people, as opposed to dispensationalism. The federation affirms the validity of charismatic gifts in the present age, and organizes around the gift ministries of Ephesians 4:11 (five-fold ministry). The kingdom of God is seen as both present and coming. The federation believes that the Kingdom of God has come in the Christ-Event (his death, burial, resurrection, and ascension), but that it is also coming progressively in history and will arrive consummately when Christ returns.

The federation supports an annual leadership conference, an annual worship conference, and various regional conferences. In 2003 its name was changed to Federation of Ministers and Churches International, in response to a prophetic word given by Cindy Jacobs.

Membership: Not reported. In 2002 the FMC had 62 affiliated congregations and translocal ministries in the United States and elsewhere.

Periodicals: *The Federation Journal.*

Sources:

Federation of Ministers and Churches. www.fmci.org.

Fellowship of Christians
1680 Sparksford Dr., Russellville, AR 72802

Alternate Address: Pioneer, Waverley Abbey House, Waverley Lane, Farnham, Surrey GU9 8EP, United Kingdom.

The Fellowship of Christians is one of two Pentecostal congregations in the United States affiliated with the Pioneer movement, a Christian church that developed in England during the 1970s. The Pioneer movement was founded by Gerald Coates, a former member of the Plymouth Brethren. In the 1960s, Coates attended the Brethren's Gospel Hall in Cobham, Surrey, England, but in 1967 this congregation split. Coates subsequently left the movement, and in 1969 formed a house church with five members. That small gathering developed into the Pioneer People, a congregation that itself became the first of some 80 associated congregations across the United Kingdom.

From the original congregation, others were started and throughout the 1980s a network of charismatic evangelical churches emerged. This network became well known for its developments in music and worship, as well as for its social action with the poor and powerless. With Dr. Patrick Dixon, Coates started a ministry to people with AIDS that developed into the AIDS Care Education Training (ACET), now the largest provider of home care assistance for AIDS sufferers in the United Kingdom. Headquarters for the movement is now at a training center, Waverley Abbey House, located in Surrey.

Meanwhile, Coates has become a controversial figure within the larger British Evangelical movement for his identification with the Toronto Blessing, the revival movement that started at the Toronto Airport Christian Fellowship and has subsequently spread worldwide. This movement has supported a new set of religious manifestations, including holy laughter, and claims that peoples' teeth have been miraculously filled with gold.

The Fellowship of Christians emerged from the charismatic segment of the Jesus People Movement of the 1970s. A band of new charismatics on the Arkansas Tech University campus formed a group for teaching and daily devotionals. Evangelism was an important mandate from this group's beginning. A congregation evolved and as the Toronto Blessing spread, it identified with the Pioneer movement.

Internationally, Pioneer is led by Coates, who in turn guides the Pioneer team, which assumes leadership for the care of congregations, planting new churches, and training leaders and evangelists. Pioneer has appointed an International Working Group to oversee its international outreach. The group concentrates on enabling pioneer churches to fulfill the great commission and on consolidating a select number of what are considered key international apostolic relationships.

Membership: Not reported. There are two congregations in the United States (in Arkansas and Eureka, California) that have affiliated with Pioneer. There are some 80 congregations in the United Kingdom and more than a thousand worldwide.

Periodicals: *Compass* • *Pioneer Update*

Sources:

Fellowship of Christians. www.foconline.org/.

Pioneer. www.pioneer.org.uk/.

Coates, Gerald. *An Intelligent Fire*. Eastbourne, U.K.: Kingsway, 1991.

———. *Kingdom Now!* Eastbourne, U.K.: Kingsway, 1993.

———. *The Vision: An Antidote to Post Charismatic Depression*. Eastbourne, U.K.: Kingsway, 1995.

Fellowship of Vineyard Harvester Churches in the United States
c/o Cedar Lake Christian Center, 1890 Rome Hwy., Cedartown, GA 30125

Alternative Address: c/o Living Word Christian Center, 1401 Government St., Mobile, AL 36604.

The Fellowship of Vineyard Harvester Churches in the United States has emerged around the ministry of Bp. David Huskins, who also serves as the senior pastor of Cedar Lake Christian Center in Cedartown, Georgia. Huskins's present life began in 1981 after he became ill with spinal meningitis, which left him paralyzed from the waist down, and then subsequently experienced a miraculous healing. In 1986 he founded Cedar Lake Christian Center and developed an expansive array of ministries in the community, including a weekly radio broadcast ministry. Huskins became associated with Abp. Earl Paulk and the associated bishops of the International Communion of Charismatic Churches (ICCC) and in 1989 was ordained as a bishop. Following his consecration, the Fellowship of Vineyard Harvester Churches emerged as other charismatic pastors sought to affiliate with Huskins.

The fellowship is a charismatic church that follows a mainline Pentecostal theology, including an emphasis on divine healing. Huskins continues his relationship with the ICCC, and serves on its College of Bishops.

Membership: Not reported. There are 41 congregations affiliated with the fellowship in the United States and additional congregations in Trinidad, Ghana, Nigeria, Kenya, Tanzania, India, and Peru. There is one congregation in Canada.

Educational Facilities:

Vineyard Harvester Bible College, Cedartown, Georgia.

Sources:

Fellowship of Vineyard Harvester Churches. www.fvhc.net.

Cedar Lake Christian Center. www.clccnet.org/.

Huskins, David. *The Power of a Covenant Heart*. Shippensburg, PA: Destiny Image, 2001.

Foundations of the Apostles and Prophets: School of Ministry and Local Assemblies International

PO Box 8073, The Woodlands, TX 77387

Foundations of the Apostles and Prophets School of Ministry and Local Assemblies International (FAP) was founded by Tim Early and his wife Theresa Early, an African-American couple who moved to the Houston, Texas, area in 1989. The couple first established Lord of the Harvest Ministries, which in 1998 was superseded by the Feast of Tabernacles Restoration Fellowship International, a local assembly serving The Woodlands, Tamina, and Humble (all in Texas). Central to the Feast of Tabernacles is an understanding that this ministry seeks "to abide and to flow from within the Secret Place of the Most High."

During the 1990s, the Earlys' ministry found them working with and ordaining new elders throughout Texas and beyond. Most recently, that work evolved into Foundations of the Apostles and Prophets School of Ministry and Local Assemblies International, now a fathering ministry to many across the globe.

FAP ordains and confirms those previously ordained in a pattern derived from the biblical book of Acts. It does not license ministers. Integral to ordination is the development of strong relationships between the Earlys and the minister seeking their ordination. The ministry also brings local churches into relationship, not to build congregations identical to each other but to encourage each to develop its ministry to the fullest.

FAP teaches a Pentecostal message. It believes that ministry is best established through covenant relationships; hence, it is a fathering ministry not only to assemblies and ministries, but also to businesses. It believes that there is a need for an advancement of religious purpose in the business world, and looks to a restoration of the Elijah ministry of Malachi 4:4–6.

Membership: Not reported.

Fresh Fire Ministries

PO Box 2525, Abbotsford, BC

Fresh Fire Ministries (FFM) is a revival and renewal ministry in the Pentecostal tradition founded in 1998 by evangelist Todd Bentley. Born in Sechelt, British Columbia, in 1976, he experienced a dramatic conversion in 1994 after a period in which he took drugs and was involved in satanism. His itinerary takes him all over the world, including to FFM's Uganda Jesus Village for children. The FFM statement of faith follows a standard evangelical and charismatic model. On April 2, 2008, Bentley began a five-day conference at the Ignited Church in Lakeland, Florida, pastored by Stephen Strader. The meetings were continued, and reports quickly spread around the world of angelic visitations, miraculous healings, and raisings from the dead. The revival became known as the Florida Outpouring, and by mid-April the nightly meetings were being broadcast on God TV.

Fresh Fire Ministries affirms belief in the inerrancy of the Bible, the triune God, salvation in Christ, and the present work of the Holy Spirit. The baptism of the Spirit is an immediate experience available to all believers. The church is led by the five-fold ministry of Ephesians 4:11. It places an emphasis on divine healing. It believes in the possibility of further revelation, though noting that such revelation is always to be tested by the Bible.

Bentley has been the target of criticism because of his unorthodox worship style and his claims about the supernatural. He reports in detail on numerous encounters with angels, including one named Emma and another named Winds of Change. Bentley also claims to have been caught up in a pillar of fire to heaven where angels operated on him. He says he has met Abraham and Paul in the heavenly realm.

Educational Facilities:

Supernatural Training Centre, Abbotsford, British Columbia.

ESL School, Abbotsford, British Columbia.

Membership: In 2008 the FFM reported approximately 1,000 members and three congregations connected to FFM, one in Bellingham, Washington, and two in British Columbia.

Sources:

Fresh Fire Ministries. www.freshfire.ca.

Beverley, James A. "World Watches Florida Revival." *Faith Today* (July–August 2008).

General Assembly Churches

c/o Church of Berkeley, 1521 Derby St., Berkeley, CA 94703

The General Assembly Churches was founded in 1974 in Berkeley, California, under the leadership of Bro. Lacy Hawkins, who serves as its overseer, and his wife, the late Sr. Etta Hawkins. They church is Pentecostal and sees itself in the tradition of the Latter Rain Movement. That movement has viewed the church as having been corrupted in the post-Apostolic era and largely lost for many centuries; in the modern era, the worldly church has faced setbacks as God has moved to restore many biblical truths in preparation for Christ's Second Coming. Decisive in Christian history was the disestablishment of the churches by the regime of Napoleon I.

Over the last few centuries, the restoration proceeded by the recovery of baptism by full immersion (the Baptist Movement); the truths regarding holiness and living a moral life before God (the Holiness Movement); and the reception of the Holy Ghost as an in-dwelling spirit, evidenced by speaking in tongues (the Pentecostal Movement). The Pentecostal Movement holds that the Body of Christ is an organism rather than an organization; that the devil exists and that sin can be overcome; and that there are truths concerning divine order and restoration (five-fold church leadership), as well as truths of unification and divine love. The General Assembly accepts all these truths.

Worship in the General Assembly congregations is seen as spirit-led, and each service includes prayer, singing, testimonies from the believers, and the preaching of the Word. Members are invited to take up a number of volunteer position in the churches.

Membership: In 2008 the church reported seven congregations, located in California, New Mexico, Louisiana, and Texas.

Sources:

General Assembly Churches. www.generalassemblychurches.com/.

Global Cause Network

27 W Hallandale Beach Blvd., Hallandale, FL 33009

Alternate Address: Apostle Rudy Langenberg, PO Box 553, 3800 AN Amersfoort, Netherlands.

Global Cause Network is an association of Pentecostal/charismatic churches united by their mutual recognition of the importance and restoration of the apostolic ministry. Its name comes from reflection upon an incident in the life of the future king David. At one point David challenged the fear-paralyzed army of Israel as they faced the Philistines with the question, "Is there not a cause?" (1 Samuel 17:29). The founders of the network have noted that there are many who feel discontented, distressed, and/or in search of identity. These people, as the network founders see it, have the cause, a desire to let God's power be strong in them and see the impact of God's power on the world. The network provides a place where people who carry an apostolic anointing, but have had little or no platform to release God's governing voice, may exercise their ministry. To these anointed ones, the network gives an identity through the Global Cause Network and the proven direction and guidance of t seasoned ministers.

Overall leadership in the Global Cause Network is provided by Apostle Jonas Clark in the United States and Apostle Rudy Langenberg in the Netherlands. Clark founded Spirit of Life Ministries and the Internet-based *Ambassador Journal* in 1997.

Membership: Not reported.

Periodicals: *The Ambassador Journal.*

Sources:

Global Cause Network. www.globalcausenetwork.com/.

Global Ministry Resource Network

5663 Balboa Ave. #416, San Diego, CA 92111

Global Ministry Resource Network (GMRN) is an association of Pentecostal/charismatic churches and ministers. The apostolic leadership team is physically based in Tijuana, Mexico, though contact is made through a post office box in San Diego, California. It has related branches internationally as a result of those with whom it has worked being ordained to the ministry. Founding apostle Les D. Crause and the leadership team have accepted a mandate to train and raise up apostles, prophets, evangelists, pastors, and teachers to help raise up the Mighty Warrior (the Church of God), which is believed to have currently, as a result of tradition and worldly influence, lost its true power and fallen into a slumber.

Crause, a South African, was raised in a Pentecostal home. After his call to the ministry at the age of 28, he left the denomination of his childhood and became an independent evangelist. His call to apostolic leadership was given in a vision of Jesus. He and his wife, following their move to Mexico, were instructed to initiate their ministry on the Internet. Assisting Crause are Apostle Colette Toach, president of GMRN; Wesley Snider, founder and president of GMR Publishing; Desiree Snider, principal of GMR Fivefold Ministry School; Craig Toach, president of the Pastoral Network; and Daphne Crause, president of the (Prophetic) Network.

The network was founded to provide: (1) a home for any not currently part of any other church fellowship; (2) personal counsel and ministry to those otherwise unable to obtain such ministry in their local church; (3) training and certification for ministers not otherwise able to attend a full-time training institution; (4) training and certification for those unable to obtain it otherwise; and (5) an international fellowship of ministries. Much of this work is provided through the Internet and email. An emphasis is placed on developing the five-fold ministry of Ephesians 4:11. The network's own ministry is carried out through its publications, sponsoring conferences, and the operation of a non-residential training school.

The GMRN generally falls into the mainline of Pentecostal belief. It is supportive of a movement that became very visible in the 1990s which sought to use charismatic apostolic leadership and an orientation around the five-fold ministry to restore the church to its first-century purity. However, the leadership is quick to note that they will work with Christians of a wide variety of denominational backgrounds.

Membership: Not reported.

Educational Facilities:

Fivefold Ministry Training Center, Tijuana, Mexico.

Sources:

Global Ministry Resource Network. www.gmrn.org/.

Go Tell It Ministry Worldwide Network of Churches (GTIMWNC)

1745 E Grand Blvd., Detroit, MI 48211

Go Tell It Ministry Worldwide Network of Churches (GTIMWNC) was founded by Dr. Corletta J. Vaughn, who serves as its overseer. Vaughn was called to preach in 1974

and was ordained (despite being a woman) in the Baptist Church in 1980. She later attended Oral Roberts University, where she earned a D.Ed. and D.Miv. Along the way she became associated with the charismatic renewal and founded a church.

GTIMWNC exists as a communion of like-minded churches and ministries, many of which were established since the 1980s through fervent evangelistic efforts. Some of the young leaders who created new congregations and ministries found themselves in need of support, resources, and mentoring relationships with older, more experienced workers. GTIMWNC exists to provide apostolic leadership and direction to those who aim to win souls and shepherd the flock of God according to biblical patterns. The GTIMWNC is supported by the tithes of its affiliated churches and ministries.

Bishop Vaughn serves as senior pastor of Holy Ghost Cathedral in Detroit, and also founded the adjacent Kingdom Faith Bible College. Vaughn was consecrated as a bishop in 1995 in Benin City, Nigeria by, Abp. Benson Idahosa (d. 1998), and was inducted to the Sacred College of Bishops of the International Communion of Charismatic Churches in May 1996. Working with Vaughn are Apostle Turnel Nelson and Bps. Carrie Smith, Harry Westcott (Australia), C. L. Long, and Paul Lanier.

Membership: Not reported. In 2008 the ministry reported 60 churches and parachurch ministries in North America and many more internationally.

Educational Facilities:

Kingdom and Faith Bible College and School of Ministry, Detroit, Michigan.

Sources:

Go Tell It Ministry Worldwide Network of Churches. www.gtimw.org/start.html.

International Ministries of Prophetic and Apostolic Churches Together (IMPACT)

19720 Governors Hwy., Ste. 1, Flossmoor, IL 60422

The International Ministries of Prophetic and Apostolic Churches Together (IMPACT) is an associated network of Pentecostal and charismatic churches and ministers that have come together under the apostolic leadership of John Eckhardt, IMPACT's founder, who announced a divine mandate to advance apostolic reformation and God's end-time kingdom on earth. IMPACT is noted for its work in identifying emerging apostles and prophets amid the array of ministers, for teaching contemporary present-truth revelation in conferences and seminars, for establishing a prophetic presbytery (leadership), and for imparting the Spirit's power through the laying on of hands.

IMPACT was founded in 1995. It grew directly out of the network of pastors and other ministers who had become associated with Eckhardt at Crusaders Church in Chicago. The church was an early center for training believers in intercessory prayer, spiritual warfare, deliverance (from demonic influence), healing, prophecy, church planting, and evangelizing the nations. Through the early 1990s Eckhardt developed an apostolic leadership relationship with ministers overseas, where he also began to identify emerging prophets.

Within mainline Christian belief, IMPACT sees itself as a ministry of spiritual warfare, designed to confront principalities and powers. Such powers are thought to include religious systems and spirits that oppress a particular place or territory, as well as people who attempt to hold back the revival, reformation, and restoration of what God has ordained for the church.

IMPACT operates from Crusaders Ministries, located in inner-city Chicago, Illinois. Crusaders is both its headquarters church and its international apostolic base. Eckhardt is assisted in his apostolic leadership by Apostle Axel Sippach, IMPACT's executive director, who resides in Seattle, Washington.

Eckhardt has authored more than 20 books. He produces a daily radio broadcast and a weekly television show, *Perfecting The Saints,* that is aired nationally.

Membership: Not reported. In 2002 IMPACT reported more than 400 churches and ministries in 25 nations associated with the network.

Educational Facilities:

Apostolic Institute of Ministry, Chicago, Illinois.

Sources:

IMPACT (International Ministries of Prophetic and Apostolic Churches Together). www.impactnetwork.net.

Eckhardt, John. *Deliverance and Spiritual Warfare Manual.* Chicago: Crusader Ministries, 1993.

———. *The Ministry Anointing of the Apostle.* Chicago: Crusader Ministries, 1993.

———. *Moving in the Apostolic.* Ventura, CA: Gospel Light Publications, 1999.

———. *Releasing God's Power Through Laying on Hands.* Chicago: Crusader Ministries, 1992.

Independent Churches of the Latter-Rain Revival

Bethesda Christian Church, 14000 Metropolitan Pkwy., Sterling Heights, MI 48312

Alternate Addresses: Faith Temple, 672 N Trezevant, Memphis, TN 38112. Glad Tidings Temple, 3456 Fraser St., Vancouver, BC, Canada, V5V 4C4. House of Prayer Church, Box 707, Springfield, MO 65801. Praise Tabernacle, Box 785, Richlands, NC 28574.

HISTORY. The Latter-Rain Movement emerged after World War II among Pentecostals who had come to believe that the Pentecostal Movement that had grown from the revival at Azusa Street in Los Angeles, California, earlier in the twentieth century had reached a low ebb. The movement had divided into a number of warring factions, and worship had become dry and formalized. In February 1948 a spiritual revival emerged at the Sharon Bible College, an independent Pentecostal school at North Battleford, Saskatchewan, Canada, headed by George Hawtin (1909–1994), a former minister with the Pentecostal Assemblies of Canada. The revival was characterized by the development of a number of doctrinal innovations and new practices, including the laying on of hands to encourage reception of the baptism of the Holy Spirit, use of the five-fold ministry, recognition of the importance of the Jewish feasts of Pentecost and Tabernacles, and belief in the concept of the "manifested sons of God." It was marked by a distrust of denominations and denominationalism, and placed a renewed emphasis on the gifts of prophecy and healing, in contrast to the older Pentecostal churches in which such emphasis had largely disappeared.

As the revival spread, ministers and leaders from the older churches came to Battleford to see what was occurring. Their reports about the doctrinal emphases and variant practices they saw led to a break between the revival's leaders and promoters and the two largest North American Pentecostal bodies, the Pentecostal Assemblies of Canada and its U.S. equivalent, the Assemblies of God. Pastors and denominational officials who continued to participate in the revival and spread its doctrines were expelled from the Assemblies. Their break with the older Pentecostal bodies merely served to increase their dislike of denominational powers. Many of them became itinerate evangelists, while others established independent congregations. These congregations rejected any formal denominational life. Many remained as simple, small independent churches (frequently led by a pastor who also had a secular job).

Many of these new independent congregations, over subsequent decades, became part of a fellowship of associated congregations, and hence became, in effect, a new denomination. Included in this category are the Body of Christ Movement, the Endtime Body-Christian Ministries, Inc., the Independent Assemblies of God, and the Church of the Living God. At the same time, many congregations have remained free and independent through the last four decades. Together, they form a distinct group of Pentecostal churches and will be the possible seedbed for new circles of fellowship. These congregations have developed an informal relationship through the sharing of publications, speakers, and various special events. Thus, each church remains completely autonomous, keeping is own name and issuing its own literature, while relating to other congregations that grew out of the revival through support of locally promoted national conventions,

camp meetings, shared publications, and missionary tours by prominent elders. Several hundred such independent congregations exist in North America, and form a circle of interlocking fellowship. A very few of the prominent centers are discussed below.

BELIEFS. The Latter-Rain Movement accepted the basic beliefs of Pentecostalism. It did not so much reject any of the doctrines of the Assemblies of God and the Pentecostal Assemblies of Canada as it added to them and added in such a way as to create a new way of understanding the faith. Decisive for the movement was its understanding of history and of the present time being the final climax to history,—that is, the "latter days." Members of the movement view Christian history as a movement of disintegration and restoration. Following the apostolic era, the church began to fall away from the pristine nature of the original generations. That process gained ascendancy through the Roman Catholic Church. However, beginning with Luther, God began a process of restoring the church. That process continued through John Wesley and the Methodists and more recently the Pentecostals. The Latter-Rain continues the Restoration process. The unique teachings and practices of the movement restore at least a remnant of the church to its destined state, the purity and holiness necessary for it to be the bride of Christ.

Most of the new ideas emerged during the original revival in North Battleford. Undergirding these new ideas as a whole was an interpretation of Isaiah 43:18–19, which equated the "new things" mentioned in the verses with revelation yet to come. The "new move of God" included the following:

> The practice of laying hands on people so that they could receive the baptism of the Holy Spirit and initiate the exercise of various gifts of the Spirit (I Corinthians 12:4–11). This practice contrasted sharply with the common practice in Pentecostalism of advising those seeking the baptism to wait until it was given by God."

> The acceptance of the local church (as opposed to denominational structures) as the basic unit of church life. Based on Ephesians 4:11–12, the revival saw a divinely appointed church order in the five-fold ministry of apostles, prophets, missionaries (or evangelists), pastors, and teachers. What was controversial for traditional Pentecostals was their addition of the offices of apostle and prophet. The apostles were people who operated in a trans-local church context as divinely appointed leaders, as opposed to denominational executives. Prophets brought immediate, inspired words of revelation to the congregation of believers. Almost from the beginning of the revival, the prophets spoke "directive prophecies," i.e., words understood as direct messages from God that offered particular advice and/or admonition to people and groups.

> The restoration of all nine gifts of the Spirit of I Corinthians 12. Through the Christian and Missionary Alliance, the gift of healing had been restored, and through the Pentecostal Movement, the gift of tongues. However, as the revival proceeded, all of the gifts, especially the gift of prophecy, began to operate.

> The modern fulfillment of the Jewish "feast of tabernacles." This teaching, ascribed to George Warnock, saw the three great feasts of Israel being fulfilled in the Church, the New Israel. The feast of Passover was fulfilled in Christ's death and resurrection. The feast of Pentecost was fulfilled in the creation of the Church and the giving of the Spirit. Yet to be fulfilled was the prayer of Jesus recorded in John 17:21 concerning the bringing together of the body of Christ free of spots and wrinkles.

> The idea of the manifested sons of God. Members of the movement believed that God would in the near future glorify individual people who would in turn be invested with authority to set creation free from its present state of bondage and decay. Those so prepared would be fit vessels to serve as the bride of Christ.

PROMINENT MINISTRIES. As is to be expected, the Latter-Rain Movement spread first throughout Western Canada. Reg Layzell (1904–1984), pastor of Glad Tidings Temple in Vancouver, British Columbia, attended meetings at North

Battleford in the summer of 1948, and in November invited Hawtin and others from Sharon to bring their message to his church. As a result, Glad Tiding Temple accepted the new truths and became a major center for disseminating the message throughout the continent. Layzell authored several important books and developed a particular emphasis within the movement as a whole upon the praise of God as a special activity for believers. He was succeeded as senior pastor by B. Maureen Gaglardi.

The Bethesda Missionary Temple (now the Bethesda Christian Church) in Detroit (now Sterling Heights), Michigan, was among the first congregations in the United States to join in the revival. When in November 1948 Hawtin and others from the school carried the Latter-Rain message to Glad Tidings Temple, in Vancouver, Myrtle D. Beall, a pastor of the Assemblies of God, was present and became an enthusiastic supporter of the revival. After she returned to Detroit, a revival broke out in her church that attracted many future converts and leaders of the movement, including Ivan Q. Spencer (1888–1970), head of the Elim Missionary Assemblies, and Stanley Frodsham (1882–1969), prominent leader in the Assemblies of God. In 1949 Beall led in the construction of a larger church building that could seat 3,000 people. Completion of the new building coincided with the first major attacks on the Latter-Rain Movement by the Assemblies of God and the church soon became independent. In 1951 Beall began the Latter Rain Evangel, which helped spread the Latter-Rain across the United States.

Today, the Bethesda Missionary Temple is pastored by Analee Dunn, who succeeded James Lee Beall, Myrtle's son, as pastor. The church operates the Bethesda Christian Schools, which provide education from first grade through high school. The church sponsors two annual festivals each spring and fall that bring many prominent Pentecostal ministers to Detroit each year.

Among the oldest of Latter-Rain churches is Faith Temple in Memphis, Tennessee. The Rev. Paul N. Grubb and his wife, the Rev. Lula J. Grubb, were dropped from the ministerial list of the Assemblies of God in December 1949 (at the same time that Myrtle Beall was dropped). They were possibly the first spokespersons for the revival in the South and continue to head the church Paul Grubb founded. Grubb also established a bible school and sponsors an annual national convention each summer. He wrote two influential books, *The End-Time Revival* and *Manifested Sonship*.

Restoration Temple (now the Life Church–Mission Bay) in San Diego, California, was pastored by Graham Truscott and his wife, Pamela Truscott, until 1991. Graham Truscott is from New Zealand, where he was raised a Methodist. He became a lay minister, but while in college heard about and then accepted the baptism of the Holy Spirit. He became a missionary to India in 1960. After moving to the United States he began Restoration Temple. Truscott is best known in Latter-Rain circles as the author of *The Power of His Presence*, a lengthy treatment on the feast of tabernacles. The church distributes this book and others he has authored, as well as numerous cassette tapes on Latter-Rain or Restoration themes. Since he left Restoration Temple, it has affiliated denominationally with the Missionary Church.

The House of Prayer Church was started in Springfield, Missouri, in the early 1960s by Bill Britton (1918–1986), a former Assemblies of God minister. Following several years as a marine in World War II, Britton attended Central Bible College and in 1949 was ordained by the Assemblies. However, having become involved in the Latter-Rain revival, he left the Assemblies and denominationalism the following year. For the next decade he worked as an evangelist, during which time he spent one important semester as an instructor at the bible school operated by Faith Temple in Memphis. (Faith Temple was also an important early Latter-Rain congregation, led for many years by Paul Grubb.) While in Memphis, Britton developed his understanding of the "overcomers." He came to feel that the church would have to go through the times of tribulation in the last days, as opposed to many of his colleagues who believe that the church will be raptured out of the world before this last terrible time for the earth. Shortly after leaving the school, he also developed the idea of a plurality of leadership in the local church. He felt that the church

should be headed by a group of elders who mutually submit to each other rather than by a single autocratic pastor. This idea was later instituted in his congregation.

Britton became a popular speaker and writer in Latter-Rain circles. Voice of the Overcomer, the literature ministry established even prior to the congregation, regularly distributes numerous tapes, books, and tracts. Britton also initiated a correspondence course and the Park Avenue Christian School, a Bible school for kindergarten through high school. Semiannual national conventions are held in March and October. The church supports missionaries in 10 countries. Since Britton's death, the family, particularly Britton's son Philip Britton, and the Voice of the Overcomer staff continued the evangelistic and pastoral work.

Praise Tabernacle in Richlands, North Carolina, was founded in 1978 by Kelley H. Varner (b. 1949), a close associate of the late Bill Britton. Varner is one of the best-educated leaders in the Latter Rain Movement, having several graduate degrees and having been for seven years a Bible school teacher. It was during his years as a teacher that he accepted the truth of the Restoration message, after which he left his teaching position to become pastor of a congregation. Varner has become one of the major advocates of the Latter Rain emphases through his radio ministry and the broad distribution of numerous tapes (many of his radio show) and writings across the United States. He publishes an extensive catalog of tapes and books biannually.

Membership: There are several hundred congregations that have developed out of the Latter-Rain Movement in the United States and Canada, but no census of the membership has been attempted.

Educational Facilities:

Overcomer Training Center, Springfield, Missouri.

Periodicals: *Good News*.

Remarks: The Latter-Rain Movement was opposed almost from the beginning by the Assemblies of God and the Pentecostal Assemblies of Canada. In the 1980s it joined the list of groups attacked by the Christian counter-cult spokespersons and organizations. Of particular concern has been the doctrine of the manifested sons of God. Critics of the Latter-Rain have accused them of teaching that humans who enter into the sonship experience are considered essentially divine themselves, thus obscuring the distinction between creature and Creator, a vital part of orthodox Christian thought. Latter-Rain spokespersons deny any such attempt to assume the role of God, but state that sonship is an actual gaining of the image and likeness of Christ by members of the His church as stated in I Corinthians 15:45–47.

Sources:

Bethesda Christian Church. www.bethesdachristian.org/.

Beall, Myrtle. *The Plumb Line*. Detroit, MI: Latter Rain Evangel, 1951.

Britton Volz, Becky. *Prophet on Wheels*. 10 vols. Springfield, MO: Bill Britton, n.d.

Gaglardi, B. Maureen. *The Path of the Just: The Garments of the High Priest*. Kendall/Hunt Publishing, 1989.

Graham, David. *The Doctrine of Sonship: A Theological Investigation*. Springfield, MO: Bill Britton, n.d.

Grubb, Paul N. *The End-Time Revival*. Memphis, TN: Voice of Faith Publishing House, n.d.

Hawtin, George R. *Pearls of Great Price*. Battleford, SK, Canada: Author, n.d.

Hoekstra, Raymond G. *The Latter Rain*. Portland, OR: Wings of Healing, [1950].

Riss, Richard Michael. *A Survey of the Twentieth-Century Revival Movements in North America*. Peabody, MA: Hendrickson Publishers, 1988.

Truscott, Graham. *The Power of His Presence*. San Diego, CA: Restoration Temple, 1969.

Varner, K. H. *Prevail*. Little Rock, AR: Revival Press, 1982.

Warnock, George H. *The Feast of Tabernacles*. Springfield, MO: Bill Britton, n.d.

International Apostolic Ministries (IAM)

225 N Dover Rd., Dover, FL 33527

International Apostolic Ministries (IAM) is a relational network of churches and ministries who share a common purpose and vision of bringing healing, revival, and reformation to the church and the world. The larger fellowship is anchored in the Revival Outreach Center in Tampa, Florida, and is led by a group primarily led by Apostle Wayne C. Anderson. The organization is administered by a board of directors that includes Kevin Ford, Rich Carey, James Berkley, and Rick Wilson (senior pastor of the Tampa congregation). IAM traces its heritage to the healing ministry of John D. Lake (1870–1935).

IAM affirms that the Bible as God's Word is verbally inspired by God as written in the original languages, and is the inerrant revelation of God to man. They believe in the Trinity, salvation in Christ, and the empowering of believers by the Holy Spirit. Emphasis is placed on the church as the body of Christ. It is composed of all believers and is responsible for evangelizing the world, and for existing as a corporate body where believers may worship and glorify God. Believers must not forsake assembling together.

IAM sees itself as not another denomination under hierarchical control, but as an extended family empowering local congregations through the "anointing and divinely orchestrated relationships and unified purpose." It seeks to nurture "spiritual fathers" who will in turn release the people of God to fulfill their destiny. Members believe that the church is founded upon apostles and prophets, and that there is spiritual insight, discipline, and protection when believers relate to the apostles and prophets who are their contemporaries.

Membership: Not reported. In 2002 there were 10 congregations and affiliated ministries in the United States.

Sources:

International Apostolic Ministries. www.iamtheway.org/.

International Coalition of Apostles

PO Box 63060, Colorado Springs, CO 80962

By the end of the twentieth century, Independent Pentecostal/charismatic ministries that operated out of the five-fold ministry leadership format advocated by the Latter Rain Movement of the 1950s multiplied dramatically. That movement proposed the idea of autonomous local churches that were tied together by the ministry of apostles. Individual apostles and apostolic teams who developed a ministry of founding new congregations and providing mature guidance and leadership for previously organized congregations emerged around the globe.

During the 1990s Peter Wagner (b. 1930), for many years a professor of church growth at Fuller Theological Seminary in Pasadena, California, became aware of the emergence of new apostles and prophets and came to believe them to be the foundation of the church (Eph. 2:20). He also came to feel that God had given him the gift of apostleship, a realization in which others concurred. In 1991 Wagner, his wife Doris Wagner, and Luis Bush had founded Global Harvest Ministries in 1991 to work on the AD2000 movement, a cooperative movement among Evangelicals to emphasize world evangelism in the last decade of the twentieth century. As Wagner's own role as an apostle came to the fore, Global Harvest Ministries began to emphasize the further development of apostolic leadership.

As the new century began, the International Coalition of Apostles (ICA) was created to provide a structure through which apostles, then working in a number of different independent networks of churches over which they had some oversight, could relate to each other. As the organization coalesced, several purposes for its existence developed, the most important being the sharing of information and insights from one apostolic network to another and the maintaining of high personal character among the apostles and a level of integrity in the operating methods employed in the apostolic networks. Wagner was named as the Presiding Apostles of ICA, and he named John Kelly, Chuck Pierce, and Doris Wagner as his leadership team. ICA meets annually in December.

ICA sees itself as within the mainstream of Protestant Evangelicalism. It affirms the Apostles' Creed (including the Trinity, the divinity of Jesus, and the necessity of a saving faith in Jesus Christ) and primary Protestant emphases of the authority of the Scripture, justification by faith alone, and the priesthood of all believers. It is Pentecostal and charismatic regarding the baptism of the Holy Spirit and the manifestation of the gifts of the spirit. It continues the primary focus on world evangelism as articulated through the AD2000 program.

The existence of ICA also led to the foundation of a set of related organizations. Wagner annually convenes the New Apostolic Roundtable as an accountability group for the members of the ICA. A select group of fewer than 25 apostles sits on the Roundtable. Also annually, those apostles who feel the need to build personal relationships with other apostles convene as the Apostolic Council of Prophetic Elders. The Apostolic Council for Educational Accountability serves as an accrediting agency for schools that serve the apostolic churches. Finally, the Apostolic Roundtable for Deliverance Ministers (ARDM) provides a meeting ground specifically for those ministers who operate a ministry of deliverance from what is believed to be demon possession and obsession.

Membership in the ICA is limited to apostles, that is to those Christian leaders deemed "gifted, taught, commissioned, and sent by God with the authority to establish the foundational government of the church within an assigned sphere of ministry by hearing what the Spirit is saying to the churches and by setting things in order accordingly for the growth and maturity of the church." Membership is by invitation following nomination submitted to the ICA office.

Membership: In 2007 the ICA reported 368 apostle members in the United States.

Sources:

International Coalition of Apostles. www.apostlesnet.net.

Cannistraci, David, and Peter Wagner. *Apostles and the Emerging Apostolic Movement.* Ventura, CA: Gospel Light Publications, 1998.

Pierce, Chuck D., and Rebecca Wagner Systema. *Receiving the Word of the Lord: Bringing Life to Your Prophetic Word.* Colorado Springs, CO: Wagner Publications, 1999.

Wagner, Peter. *Apostles and Prophets: The Foundation of the Church.* Ventura, CA: Regal Books, 2000.

———. *Apostles of the City: How to Mobilize Territorial Apostles for City Transformation.* Colorado Springs, CO: Wagner Publications, 2000.

International Evangelical Church (IEC)

13901 Central Ave., Upper Marlboro, MD 20774

The International Evangelical Church (IEC) is a fellowship of Pentecostal churches formed in 1964 as the International Evangelical Church and Missionary Association. As originally constituted, the association was a corporation designed to legalize the Italian mission of John McTernan (d. 1974). Very early, McTernan became associated with John Levin Meares (b. 1920), the pastor of an independent Pentecostal church in Washington, D.C. Though still largely a foreign movement, the U.S. branch of the church has become an important structure within the African-American Pentecostal community. The origin of the church in the United States can be traced directly to Meares's decision in the mid-1950s to establish a ministry within the black community of Washington, D.C. Meares was a promising young minister in the Church of God (Cleveland, Tennessee) and the nephew of the general overseer. He was in the midst of a successful pastorate in Memphis, Tennessee, in 1955, when he decided to resign and go to Washington, D.C., to assist independent evangelist Jack Coe (1918–1956) in a series of revival meetings. He liked the city and decided to stay and build a church, the Revival Center. He also started the Miracle Time radio show. From the beginning, the major response to his ministry was from African Americans. He thus found himself as the white minister of an integrated congregation—in which the majority of members were black—that was affiliated with a white-controlled denomination with prejudicial attitudes about race. He was forced to choose between his ministry and his denomination, resulting in his leaving the Church of God. The congregation grew and, in 1957, settled in an abandoned theater as the National Evangelistic Center.

The center faced a series of problems, which were increased by the tumultuous social changes going on around it. Meares changed the emphasis of his ministry from one of miracles to one of teachings. Several evangelists raided the membership. All of the problems climaxed in the riots following the assassination of Martin Luther King Jr. (1929–1968) in 1968. Almost all of the remaining white members left at this time. While the changes were going on around him, Meares became the vice president of the International Evangelical Church and Missionary Association.

Eventually, in the early 1970s, 300 of the remaining members would regroup and build a $3 million facility. The renewed congregation opened the Evangel Temple in 1975. As the building was being completed, McTernan died and Meares inherited the corporation, which at some point simply became the International Evangelical Church. Since then, the story of the IEC has been the story of its international development and its expansion within the African-American community. Internationally, the IEC began with some Italian churches and then reached out to include a group of Brazilian churches under Bp. Robert McAleister, and churches in Nigeria led by Bp. Benson Idahosa (1938–1998). As of 2008, more than half the congregations associated with the church are in Africa. In 1972 the church joined the World Council of Churches.

In 1982 the church was instrumental in founding a new Pentecostal ecumenical organization: the International Communion of Charismatic Churches. It includes the various branches of the IEC and several other church groups such as the Gospel Harvesters Church, founded by Earl Paulk (b. 1927) in Atlanta, Georgia. That same year, the bishops of the communion, McAleister, Paulk, and Idahosa, consecrated Meares as a bishop.

In the United States, Evangel Temple expanded and a ministry of people ordained by Meares emerged. Other independent Pentecostal congregations affiliated with the church. Through the 1980s, Meares emerged as a leader in a mediating position between the black and white Pentecostal communities, which, for several generations, had gone their separate ways. In 1984 he began the annual Inner-city Pastors' Conference, which draws together the (primarily African-American) pastors from various churches of the association. Meares has also urged the white Pentecostal church to play a more significant role in the African-American community.

Membership: The IEC has approximately 500 congregations worldwide, more than 400 of which are in Africa. There are approximately 50 in South America, 20 in Italy, 20 in the United States, and one in Jamaica.

Sources:

Burgess, Stanley M., and Gary B. McGee, eds. *Dictionary of Pentecostal and Charismatic Movements*. Grand Rapids, MI: Regency Reference, 1988.

Evangel Temple's 30ᵗʰ Anniversary Historical Journal. Washington, DC: Evangel Temple, 1985.

Meares, John L. *Bind Us Together*. Old Tappan, NJ: Chosen Books, 1987.

————. *The Inheritance of Christ in the Saints*. Washington, DC: Evangel Temple, 1984.

International Evangelical Church and Missionary Association

c/o Bishop Donald Meares, Evangel Cathedral, 13901 Central Ave., Upper Marlboro, MD 20772

The International Evangelical Church and Missionary Association is a charismatic fellowship of churches formed in the early 1980s under the leadership of John Levin Meares, pastor of Evangel Temple in Washington, D.C. (now retired). Meares was raised in the Church of God (Cleveland, Tennessee), the nephew of the general overseer. After serving several Church of God congregations, Meares went to Washington, D.C., in 1955 to begin the Revival Center (soon renamed the National

Evangelistic Center), a new Church of God outreach for the city. However, he soon encountered controversy within the Church of God because he had started an unlicensed ministry. This led to the cancellation of his fellowship in May 1956. He continued his independent ministry, however, which emerged in new quarters as Evangel Temple in 1957. Membership of the integrated congregation was approximately two-thirds black.

In the early 1960s Meares became aware of Bethesda Missionary Temple, one of the principle congregations of the Latter Rain movement. From his observation of the life of the temple, he picked up a new emphasis on praise and the gift of prophecy, which he introduced to Evangel Temple. This coincided with the heightened tensions of the civil rights movement, climaxing in the rioting that followed the assassination of Martin Luther King. Most of the temple's white members withdrew, and Meares emerged in the early 1970s as the white pastor of a largely black church. Membership dropped to several hundred. The church slowly rebuilt, however, and in 1975 moved into new $3 million facilities. In 1991 Evangel Temple relocated to suburban Maryland. Their new facilities house a 2,000-seat sanctuary and their Bible school.

During Meares's years in Washington, many independent Pentecostal pastors had begun to look to him for leadership and guidance. The International Evangelical Churches and Missionary Association emerged out of that relationship. In 1982 Bps. Benson Idahosa of Nigeria, Robert McAleister of Brazil, and Earl P. Paulk, Jr., of Atlanta, Georgia, all members of the International Communion of Charismatic Churches, consecrated Meares a bishop.

Over the years, Meares and Evangel Temple became major voices in the Pentecostal community speaking to the issues of racism. Beginning in 1984, Evangel Temple became the site of an annual national Inner City Pastors' Conferences, attended primarily, but by no means exclusively, by black Pentecostal pastors from around the United States and Canada. More than 1,000 pastors attended the 1987 conference.

John Meares was succeeded in leadership of the association by his son, Bishop Donald Meares.

Membership: In 2005 Evangel Temple reported 3,000 members.

Educational Facilities:

Central Bible School, Upper Marlboro, Maryland.

Sources:

World Council of Churches: International Evangelical Church. www.oikoumene.org/?id=5372.

Evangel Temple's Thirtieth Anniversary. Washington, DC: Evangel Temple, 1985.

Haggerty, Steve. "A Spiritual Powerhouse." *Charisma* 10, no. 10 (May 1985).

Meares, John. *Bind Us Together*. Old Tappan, NJ: Chosen Books, 1987.

Meares, John L. *The Inheritance of Christ in the Saints*. Washington, DC: Evangel Temple, 1984.

International Fellowship of Ministries

18706 North Creek Pky., Ste. 104, Bothell, WA 98011

The International Fellowship of Ministries was founded in the early years of the twentieth century by people associated with the independent Pentecostal evangelist John G. Lake (1870–1935). Originally known as the Ministerial Fellowship of the USA and then the Apostolic Congress, its headquarters were established in Spokane, Washington. Around 1915 it existed as an informal covenant relationship between Lake and several men including Cyrus B. Fockler, Charles W. Westwood, and Archibald Fairley. Lake moved to establish a number of "Apostolic" churches along the West Coast of the United States and in Canada in the first decade after the Pentecostal revival (1906–1908) that had spread from the Azusa Street Mission and before the term *Apostolic* became associated with the nontrinitarian "Jesus Only" churches. After Lake's death, the fellowship became a legal entity in 1947 and Lake's ministry was continued by some of his associates, including

Maury Moser (d. 1961) of Spokane, Washington; Olaf I. Borseth (d. 1967) of Chehalis, Washington; Wilford H. Reidt, Lake's son-in-law; Paul Gering of Spokane, Washington; and Edward H. Curtis of Entiat, Washington.

For Lake, apostolic ministry was equated with "Jesus Christ manifesting and abiding in His church doing the same works through His church that He did while living on the earth in human form." Apostolic ministry fulfilled the call of John 14:12, and entailed perfecting the church as the bride of Christ for the return of the bridegroom. According to Lake, the church lost its apostolic nature in stages during its first millennium after the apostolic age. The restoration of apostolic ministry began with Martin Luther and the Reformation in the sixteenth century and matured over the centuries; now a full restoration can be expected. The nature of that restored ministry can be seen in the lives of saintly people such as Lake himself, who purportedly was able to heal the sick and cast out demons, lead people to salvation, and manifest "the very nature and character of Christ." The restoration of the apostolic church also means the arrival of apostolic and prophetic ministries that work to found and nurture New Testament churches as centers for equipping and releasing ministries. Ideally, these churches will be the sight for making disciples and establishing indigenous leadership. The teams will oversee the new congregations until they able to operate autonomously, but a long-term "fatherly" relationship between congregation and apostolic leadership will continue.

The statement of faith places the fellowship in the mainline trinitarian Evangelical tradition, with few "sectarian" particulars emphasized. The authority of the Bible as the inspired Word of God is affirmed, as is the necessity of baptism for believers. However, the fellowship's nature as an Apostolic Pentecostal Restorationist association is not specifically mentioned. The fellowship licenses and ordains ministers (according to the fivefold pattern mentioned in Eph. 4:11) and attempts to accredit independent ministers. It also attempts to impart spiritual gifts and acknowledge the ministries of individuals through the laying on of hands by the fellowship's presbyters (elders).

The fellowship is led by a board of trustees that includes its current (2008) president, Joe McIntyre. The presidency had been previously held by Moser, Olaf Borseth, Wilford H. Reidt (d. 1987), Clifford Rice, Richard O. Tedeschi, and Wayne C. Anderson. McIntyre was elected in 1998. McIntyre is the founder of Word of His Grace Fellowship in Kirkland, Washington. He was personally inspired by the ministry of E. W. Kenyon (1867–1948), and in 2008 was also the president of the Gospel Publishing Society in Lynnwood, Washington, which keeps Kenyon's writings in publication.

Membership: Not reported.

Sources:

International Fellowship of Ministries. www.ifm7.org/.

Lake, John G. *The John G. Lake Sermons on Dominion over Demons, Disease and Death*. Ed. Gordon Lindsey. Dallas: Christ for the Nations,1949.

McIntyre, Joe. *E. W. Kenyon and His Message of Faith, the True Story*. Lake Mary, FL: Creation House, 1997.

Life Links International Fellowship of Churches

c/o Antioch Foundation, 287 Prestwick Landing SE, Calgary, AB, Canada T2Z 3W2
Alternate Address: c/o New Life Christian Church, 20394 San Miguel Ave., Castro Valley, CA 94546.

Life Links International Fellowship of Churches is a Pentecostal charismatic association of churches and ministries founded in 1978 at Medicine Hat, Alberta, in response to a need for an organization to assist independent congregations and encourage them in their work. Representatives of three different Christian movements gathered for a conference that had as its goal the forming of an alliance to support their continued operations. Conference participants had roots in the restoration movement that had grown out of the Latter Rain movement in the American and Canadian West; the New Testament movement in Waco, Texas; and the Jesus People movement in western Canada and the northwestern United

States. These groups had ties to Keith Hazell, who had offered his leadership and insights to all three groups and was recognized for his apostolic leadership. He is recognized as the founder and senior presbyter of the Life Links Fellowship, which sees itself as a family of believers who developed a strong personal relationship and commitment to one another.

The conference at which the fellowship was first constituted became an annual leadership gathering of the Life Links Family. In addition, there is an annual (in August) family camp in Hungry Horse, Montana, and an annual mission conference. A geographically extended fellowship was created as the primary leaders in the fellowship traveled extensively across and outside of North America.

The fellowship is a trinitarian Pentecostal church. It affirms the Bible as the infallible Word of God, salvation in Christ, the baptism of the Holy Spirit with the biblical evidence of speaking inr tongues and other gifts of the spirit, divine healing, and the obligation of evangelism for all Christians. The church practices the laying on of hands and believes that when it is accompanied by appropriate prayer and prophecy by the presbytery, spiritual gifts and ministries are imparted or confirmed in believers. Church members also expect guidance and continued revelation from their participation in the life of the spirit.

The church's organization is based the fivefold ministry of Eph. 6:11 and includes apostles, evangelists, prophets, teachers, and pastors. Apostles have the main task of overseeing the church at a transcongregational level. Further, the fellowship has developed a five-member presbytery. As a basis of leadership, Life Links has what is described as a presbytery to provide guidance to the congregations in the church family. This presbytery includes Keith Hazell, the senior presbyter, whose ministry takes him to Canada, the United States, Germany, the United Kingdom, Taiwan, and other nations; David Wells, who gives apostolic oversight to many in the prairie region of Canada and in Ireland, Central America, and the Philippines; Hugh Laybourn, who provides apostolic leadership in the borderlands area of the northwest United States; and Dennis McNally, who provides guidance for affiliates ministries in Vietnam, Cambodia, the Philippines, and Mexico.

Membership: There are 24 affiliated churches in the United States, 20 in Canada, and four in Mexico.

Educational Facilities:

Antioch Foundation, Calgary, Alberta, Canada.

Sources:

Life Links International Fellowship of Churches. www.lifelinks.org/.

The Living Word Fellowship

PO Box 3429, Iowa City, IA 52247-3429

Previously known as Church of the Living Word, the Living Word Fellowship represents an association of independently incorporated and operated churches that follow a New Testament Church pattern and that seek the common leading of an authoritative word from God for this day.

The fellowship traces its origins to the ministry of John Robert Stevens (1919–1983). Born in Nevada, Iowa, in 1919, he started his first church at age 14. He spent several years traveling cross-country as a boy evangelist and held tent meetings throughout the Midwest. Ordained at age 18 by Dr. A. W. Courtcamp (pastor of the Moline Gospel Temple in Moline, Iowa), Stevens developed at a young age a sensitivity to what God was doing in the various denominational churches and freelance movements. With roots in the Pentecostal and Foursquare Gospel movements, he was influenced by the teachings of ministers such as Billy Sunday, Ruth Paxton, Paul Rader, Smith Wigglesworth, and Aimee Semple McPherson.

In 1949, while pastor of the Lynwood Assemblies of God in Lynwood, California, Stevens began to receive an unfolding revelation of a new step into an age of spirit. As a result of his interest and involvement with the new Latter Rain Revival, he was defrocked in March 1951.

The beliefs of the Latter Rain movement are similar to those of traditional Pentecostals, as represented by the Assemblies of God, differing more in emphasis than in doctrine. Those who became a part of the movement firmly believed that they were living at the end of time, when God was giving new knowledge and gifts to restore the church to what it should be in the last days. Among the first things to be restored was the fivefold ministry of Ephesians 4:11; the church is headed by apostles, prophets, evangelists, pastors, and teachers. Stephens is considered to be an apostle and a prophet. Especially coming to the fore during the last days was the gift of prophecy (Acts 2). The Latter Rain and the Church of the Living Word have emphasized this role to bring forth the word of God in particular situations.

Members believe God is rejecting Babylon and denominational Christianity, and restoring the Divine Order among his chosen last-day remnant. Leadership will be exercised by his instruments. It is the duty of Christians to submit to that order. As the Church of the Living Word moved into the New Divine Order, it developed a variety of ideas that have separated it from other Pentecostal groups. One such idea is termed "aggressive appropriation." Prayer, according to the church, is part of God's system of self-imposed limitation. God works through human beings who are consecrated to him, and who actively and aggressively appropriate God's promises and blessings. This appropriation will lead them above and beyond the Apostles and the Bible into "greater works" mentioned in John 14:12.

Stevens's congregation reassembled, and by June of 1951 had formed the basis of Grace Chapel of Southgate, California; it eventually grew into an entire fellowship of like-minded ministries and churches. In 1953 Stevens established the Grace Chapel of Honolulu; in 1965, the Church of the Living Word in Sepulveda, California; in 1973, the Church of His Holy Presence in Anaheim, California; and in 1974 work began on Shiloh, a retreat center near Kalona, Iowa.

Stevens resisted the pressure to label the growing movement; however, because he taught that it was God's will for each Christian to have a personal knowledge of the Lord and a walk with God, the fellowship of churches was informally referred to as "This Walk" or "The Walk." It later became known as the Living Word Fellowship, which consists of churches that are affiliated only by their spiritual connection to and their recognition of the apostolic authority of John Robert Stevens and the ministering authority of others. Besides the emphasis on the Word and church order, the fellowship also strongly emphasizes deep worship, the development and maintenance of family relationships leading to a strong sense of church community, and a devotional lifestyle of prayer and waiting on God.

Prior to his death in 1983, Stevens passed the mantle of this ministry to his wife, Marilyn, and to Gary Hargrave, who had been the primary overseer of the Southern California churches and the church-wide communities in the years preceding Stevens's death.

The Living Word publishes recordings of messages by Gary Hargrave and others in the fellowship, and maintains a library of more than 7,000 sermons by John Robert Stevens.

Membership: In 2008 the fellowship reported 8 congregations in the United States, plus one each in Brazil, Canada, and Mexico.

Periodicals: *This Week*. The Living Word, PO Box 958, North Hollywood, CA 91603.

Remarks: As the Church of the Living Word developed under the ministry of prophecy, many critics have complained that it has strayed into occultic practices and doctrines that have denied basic Christian affirmations.

Sources:

The Living Word Fellowship. www.thelivingword.org.

It Shall Be Called Shiloh. North Hollywood, CA: Living Word Publications, 1975.

Stevens, John Robert. *Baptized in Fire*. North Hollywood, CA: Living Word Publications, 1977.

———. *Living Prophecies*. North Hollywood, CA: Living Word Publications, 1974.

———. *The Lordship of Jesus Christ*. North Hollywood, CA: Living Word Publications, 1969.

———. *Present Priorities*. North Hollywood, CA: Living Word Publications, 1968.

Ministers Fellowship International (MFI)
9200 NE Fremont, Portland, OR 97220

Ministers Fellowship International (MFI) was created in 1987 as an association of independent ministers and churches who have their roots in the Latter Rain revival that swept through the larger Pentecostal movement beginning in 1948. Among the most important churches of that revival was the Bible Temple (now City Bible Church) of Portland, Oregon, pastored by Dick Iverson. Iverson took the lead in forming MFI.

MFI emphasizes its role as a fellowship of otherwise independent and autonomous churches. It reserves to the local churches the rights of providing credentials for ministers and ministries, owning church properties, operating Bible schools, and building a mission program. MFI has established a context within which ministers who share a similar perspective may come together; minister to each other; and find accountability, relationship, and resources; and it provides a structure through which localized congregations can find a national and international identity. MFI asserts no official or legal control over any pastor or church.

The fellowship also provides apostolic assistance, that is, the guidance and leadership of mature leaders who have assumed responsibility for building and developing churches other than their own worship communities. This apostolic leadership (which replaces the structures provided by other denominations) is an outgrowth of the attempt to reestablish the fivefold ministry of Eph. 4:11.

From the Latter Rain movement, the MFI inherited a number of beliefs that distinguish it from other Pentecostal bodies. It believes that the pattern for worship should be derived from the Davidic order described in the *Psalms*, which is characterized by clapping, shouting, singing, dancing, lifting one's hands, bowing, and kneeling. It believes in the exercise of prophetic gifts with the guidance of the church. Members believe that the church experienced significant decline in the Middle Ages and is in the process of being restored to its former power and glory (the churches of the MFI are sometimes referred to as "restoration churches").

MFI is directed by an Apostolic Leadership Team consisting of its officers, the regional directors, and other apostolic and prophetic ministries. The team is responsible for establishing the fellowship's vision and for giving it direction, maintaining its doctrinal purity, and selecting and appointing regional directors, both nationally and internationally. The Apostolic Leadership Team has appointed an International Strategy Team to oversee international development.

Dick Iverson is the founder and chairman of Ministers Fellowship International. In 1995 he retired as pastor of City Bible Church to devote himself full-time to MFI. Frank Damazio, who succeeded Iverson as pastor of City Bible Church, is the vice president of MFI. In 2008 10 regions had been designated across the United States and Puerto Rico.

Membership: Not reported. MFI affiliates have been formally established in Australia, Brazil, Mexico, and Uganda.

Periodicals: *Perspectives*.

Sources:

Ministers Fellowship International. www.mfi-online.org/.

Miracles Ministries Fellowship (MMF)
c/o Don Walker Outreach Ministries, PO Box 21, Griffin, GA 30224

Miracles Ministries Fellowship (MMF), founded in 1973, is an outgrowth of Don Walker Outreach Ministries. The latter is the vehicle of independent Pentecostal evangelist Don Walker. Walker travels the United States holding crusades and revival meetings with an emphasis upon the Pentecostal perspective and miracles of healing. His Internet site presents testimonies of healings and other miraculous happenings that have occurred during his ministry. While conducting his ministry,

Walker encountered ministers and churches that wished to join in fellowship (and to have corporate status with the government) but did not want to affiliate with one of the older Pentecostal denominations. In some cases, ministers lack the minimal educational requirements to become denominational pastors.

Therefore, in 1973 Walker incorporated MMF. The fellowship offers charters from Pentecostal churches and ministries, and ordination and licensing for ministers. Walker does not conceive of the MMF as a denomination; instead, it provides its members many of the rights and privileges of denominational churches, while granting them the freedom to function as independent entities. MMF is an inclusive fellowship that recognizes all people in the spirit of Gal. 3:28, "There is neither Jew nor Greek, there is neither bond nor free, there is neither male nor female: for ye are all one in Christ Jesus."

Walker offers supporters of his ministry a Bible study correspondence course.

Membership: Not reported.

Sources:

Miracles Ministries Fellowship. www.miraclestoday.org/mmf.htm.

MorningStar Ministries

375 Star Light Dr., Fort Mill, SC 29715

MorningStar Ministries is an international Charismatic work started in 1985 by Rick Joyner and his wife, Julie. MorningStar involves many facets of Christian ministry, including running major conferences, a school of ministry, and a fellowship of churches. It serves as a base for apostolic and prophetic councils, bringing together some of the major leaders in the Charismatic Christian world. MorningStar also publishes books and a journal and runs the Zao Life Project, a relief effort in Africa to establish safe water supplies and teach basic hygiene. In 2004 MorningStar purchased the former Heritage USA site, once home to the PTL Club run by Jim and Tammy Faye Bakker.

Rick Joyner converted to Christianity in the 1970s. He is the author of *The Harvest* and *The Final Quest*, describing his alleged visitations to heaven. Since 1991 Joyner has released prophetic bulletins as part of what he regards as a prophetic calling in his life. The bulletins deal with issues particular to the Christian tradition and also to general trends in both the United States and the world.

In 2004 Joyner, along with Charismatic leaders Mike Bickle and Jack Deere, announced the public discipline of Charismatic prophet Paul Cain because of alcoholism and homosexual practices. Cain had become the most famous of the prophets connected with Mike Bickle's Kansas City Fellowship and John Wimber's Association of Vineyard Ministries.

In 2008 Joyner announced his approval of the Florida Outpouring, a controversial revival based in Lakeland and connected with Canadian evangelist Todd Bentley.

Membership: In 2008 MorningStar Ministries reported five congregations in South Carolina.

Periodicals: *MorningStar Journal.*

Sources:

MorningStar Ministries. www.morningstarministries.org/.

Joyner, Rick. *The Apostolic Ministry*. Fort Mill, SC: MorningStar Fellowship Church, 2006.

———. *The Final Quest*. Fort Mill, SC: Morningstar Publications, 2006.

———. *The Harvest*. Forth Mill, SC: Morningstar Publications, 1989.

Network of Kingdom Churches

4650 Flat Shoals Rd., Decatur, GA 30034-5095

The Network of Kingdom Churches was founded in 1961 as the Gospel Harvesters Evangelistic Association in Atlanta, Georgia, by Earl P. Paulk Jr. (b. 1927) and Harry A. Mushegan, both former ministers in the Church of God (Cleveland, Tennessee). Mushegan is a cousin of Demos Shakarian (1913–1993), founder of the Full Gospel Businessmen's Fellowship International, while Paulk's father had been the general overseer of the Church of God. Each man began a congregation in Atlanta. The Gospel Harvester Tabernacle, founded by Paulk, moved to Decatur, an Atlanta suburb, and became known as Chapel Hill Harvester Church. The Gospel Harvester Chapel, begun by Mushegan, became known as Gospel Harvester Church; at the time of the church's move to Marietta, Georgia, in 1984, the name changed again to Gospel Harvester Church World Outreach Center. To traditional Pentecostal themes, inherited from the Church of God, the Gospel Harvesters have added an emphasis upon the message of the end-time kingdom of God. According to Paulk, creation has been aiming at a time when God will raise up a spiritually mature generation who will be led by the Spirit of God speaking through his prophets. Given a clear direction from God, that generation, represented by the members of the Network of Kingdom Churches and others of like spirit, will overcome many structures in society opposed to God's will.

The congregations in the network developed a variety of structures to make the kingdom visible. The churches have supported Alpha, a youth ministry; House of New Life, for unwed mothers (an alternative to abortion); a drug ministry; a ministry to the gay and lesbian community; and the K-Center, a communications center.

The government of the network is presbyterial, though the two senior founders have been designated bishops. They are members of the International Communion of Charismatic Churches, formerly the World Communion of Pentecostal Churches, that includes congregations in Brazil, Nigeria, and Jamaica. Bp. John Levin Meares (b. 1920), pastor of the Evangel Temple in Washington, D.C., and head of the International Evangelical Church and Missionary Association, is also part of the communion.

Membership: Not reported.

Periodicals: *The Fire • Harvest Time*

Remarks: In 1985 Bishop Paulk became the object of attack by popular (non-Pentecostal) evangelical writer, Dave Hunt. Hunt labeled Paulk as one of a number of "seductive forces within the contemporary church." Paulk was included along with a number of popular pentecostal leaders including Oral Roberts (b. 1918), Kenneth Hagin (1917–2003), Kenneth Copeland (b. 1936), and Fred Price (b. 1932). Hunt, one of several who have attacked Paulk's kingdom message, was quickly answered by Pentecostal leaders, who came to Paulk's defense.

Sources:

Mushegan, Harry A. *Water Baptism*. Atlanta: Gospel Harvester Church and World Outreach Center, n.d.

Paulk, Earl. *Satan Unmasked*. Atlanta, GA: K-Dimension Publications, 1984.

———. *Ultimate Kingdom*. Atlanta: K-Dimension Publications, 1984.

New Covenant Churches of Maryland

804 Windsor Rd., Arnold, MD 21012

The New Covenant Churches of Maryland is a fellowship of churches that emerged in the mid-1970s. The fellowship was originally centered upon the New Life Christian Center in Arnold, Maryland. The best known of the leaders of New Life Christian Center was Robert Wright, a retired naval officer and director of the center. He was instrumental in building the early association which, by 1977, included five congregations. He assumed the office of apostle (senior presbyter) for the affiliated churches and engaged in a ministry of founding new churches and strengthening local churches who have joined the fellowship.

The New Covenant Church accepts the basic Pentecostal perspective, including the contemporary operation of the charismatic gifts (1 Cor. 12). Further, although they accept the main body of doctrine agreed upon by other Trinitarian Pentecostal churches, the New Covenant Churches are among those groups that believe in restoring the fivefold ministry of apostle, prophet, pastor, evangelist, and teacher according to Eph. 4:11 this emphasis that grew out of the Latter Rain Revival in the late 1940s.

The New Covenant Churches were active in the development of Christian parochial schools. In 1983 their schools were removed from the Maryland branch of the American Association of Christian Schools, an organization representing conservative evangelical church schools headed by fundamentalist leaders, as a rejection of the Pentecostal doctrine of the supporting churches. This ruling was later accepted by the national organization. In reaction, Wright led in the formation of a National Federation of Church Schools.

In 2008 the Church in Arnold, Maryland, existed as an independent congregation that supports the Arnold Christian Academy, the original school founded by the former New Covenant Churches of Maryland. The National Federation of Church Schools had been assumed by the Association of Christian Schools International, based in Colorado City, Colorado.

Membership: Not reported.

Periodicals: *Koinonia*.

Sources:

New Covenant Churches of Maryland. www.newcovenantch.org.

Arnold Christian Academy. www.arnoldchristianacademy.org/links.htm.

Wright, Robert. "Key Questions Concerning Apostles." *People of Destiny Magazine* 2, no. 1 (January/February 1984).

New Covenant Ministries International

1920 Brea Canyon Cutoff Rd., Walnut, CA 91789

New Covenant Ministries International (NCMI) is a trans-local ministry team consisting of people who have demonstrated an ability to found and nurture local congregations and to mobilize believers to work for the building of the kingdom of God. Over the years a number of local congregations have become associated with NVMI, which now exists as an international network of autonomous churches that voluntarily cooperate with the work. These churches agree that the apostolic team is an expression of Christian activity with which they wish to be associated.

NCMI began in South Africa in the early 1980s with small informal gatherings headed by Dudley Daniel and other local pastors. They began to share their ministries with each other, and word of their successful cooperative work spread. Other churches across South Africa invited them to share their vision for the building of the Kingdom by training leadership, by encouraging and training individuals for church planting, and by providing opportunities to participate in short- or long-term church planting projects. This vision of growth was built on a base of strong and healthy, eldership-led local churches.

In January 1990, with 70 church pastors having related positively to the vision, Daniel and his wife, Ann, moved to Adelaide, Australia, where a church growth resource center was established. During the 1990s the work grew steadily on an international level. By 2001 the network included ministers, churches, and individuals from more than 80 countries. The Daniels moved to Los Angeles, California, to contribute to equipping churches in the United States; they then returned to Australia. In 2004 Tyrone Daniel, who is based in Adelaide, took over leadership of NCMI.

To facilitate the work, an International Theological Correspondence Course was created. In addition, NCMI holds at least one Church Planters Training course annually.

NCMI is committed to the five-fold ministry of Ephesians 4:11. Daniel as apostolic leader is supported by a team of leaders (scattered around the world) who have demonstrated various gifts as apostles, prophets, evangelists, pastors, and teachers, and who constitute the NCMI team. Most team members are pastors of a local church that releases them periodically for ministry in some other part of the world. A few, like Daniel, function full-time in the trans-local ministry.

Although NCMI does not impose a creed on the people with whom it networks, it generally works out of a mainline Pentecostal perspective that includes an affirmation of the authority of the Bible, the Trinity, the Lordship of Christ, the necessity of salvation, and the regenerating work of the Holy Spirit. The Holy Spirit empowers the church and is manifest in the gifts of the Spirit that operate in the church. Christians are called to a life of holiness. There is a particular recognition of the various ministries or ministers Christ left to the church to bring believers to maturity in the truth and the performance of ministry (Ephesians 4:11; Romans 12:4–8 and 1 Corinthians 12:10 ff.). The church believes in the healing of the sick that occurs in the name of Jesus Christ.

Membership: Not a membership organization. In 2008 NCMI reported offices in Australia, Germany, New Zealand, Singapore, South Africa, the United Kingdom, and the United States.

Sources:

New Covenant Ministries International. www.ncmi.net/.

Newfrontiers

c/o John Lanferman, Newfrontiers USA, St. Louis, MO

Alternate Address: Newfrontiers, 21 Clarendon Villas, Howe, East Sussex BN3 3RE, U.K.

Newfrontiers is a five-fold ministry Evangelical fellowship that began in Sussex, England, in the late 1970s. Crucial to its development has been Terry Virgo of Church of Christ the King, Brighton, Sussex, England. In 1978, Terry and a small group of believers joined with others who had been affected by the charismatic revival of the decade in forming what they saw as a radical New Testament church, which they called the Brighton and Hove Christian Fellowship. They were soon joined by Dave Holden and Dave Fellingham. They were inspired by prophecies they received that the small work would grow into a large tree with many branches. Virgo emerged as a popular Bible teacher, who began to travel widely in the United Kingdom and then overseas. The group began an annual Bible conference held at Stoneleigh Park, Coventry, England—the Stoneleigh International Bible Week—and presently puts on the international leadership training events Together on a Mission and Mobilise.

Newfrontiers is a conservative, reformed Bible-oriented Evangelical fellowship that includes an emphasis on the five-fold ministry of Ephesians 4:11 that stresses the leadership provided by apostles, prophets, evangelists, pastors, and teachers. Newfrontiers has a vision to be strong in both Word and Spirit and to plant churches where each member participates, the gifts of the Spirit are worked out, where there is joy in caring one for the other, and where there is a desire to make a difference in society and to reach those in need. Newfrontiers aims to achieve this by restoring the church, making disciples, training leaders, starting churches, and reaching the nations. These goals have been manifest in its holding of Bible and leadership conferences, publication of study materials, and sending out of teams to develop new congregations.

Local congregations are autonomous, being led by the local eldership, but receive guidance and direction from a team that includes apostles, prophets, evangelists, pastors, and teachers. The guidance of this team is never to be imposed on a local church; rather, it should be readily embraced as a relationship develops. The goal is to develop a team of leaders for every nation, and as of 2008 there are teams operating in North America, Europe, the Middle East, Africa, and Asia. The leaders of these regions meet quarterly in the United Kingdom for prayer, training, and discussion.

Membership: Newfrontiers reports nearly 600 congregations in more than 40 nations around the world.

Sources:

Newfrontiers. www.newfrontiers.xtn.org/.

Kendall, R. T., and Terry Virgo. *God's Grace*. London: SPCK, 2000.

Virgo, Terry. *Restoration of the Church*. Lottbridge Drove, Eastbourne, U.K.: Kingsway Communications, 1985.

————. *Explaining Reigning in Life*. Ellel, Lancaster, U.K.: Sovereign World, 2000.

————. *Enjoying God's Grace*. Saint Louis, MO: Newfrontiers USA Publications, 2008.

————. *No Well-Worn Paths*. Saint Louis, MO: Newfrontiers USA Publications, 2008.

Pentecostal Faith Assemblies

PO Box 6054, Moore, OK 73153

Pentecostal Faith Assemblies was founded in 2001 when independent ministers and churches came together to form an association that would serve as a vehicle for mutual recognition, mutual accountability, and mutual support. The new fellowship would also become an agency to facilitate evangelism worldwide. Though it emerged as a viable organization only in 2001, the Assemblies had its origin in a prophetic vision shared by two Pentecostal ministers in 1989. As recorded from a pastor's meeting in Red Rock, Oklahoma, a woman described as an anointed prophet told her colleague, "I don't know why God is having me share this with you, but I had a vision and in this vision I could see the United States from coast to coast. The whole land lay in darkness. Suddenly, a lighthouse began to emerge from the gloom in Oklahoma. Wherever the light from this lighthouse was shed abroad, other lighthouses began to spring up. And then where they shed their light, still others popped up and they began to spread north, south, east, and west until the whole land was covered in light from sea to sea."

From this vision, a formal corporation was formed for the Pentecostal Faith Assemblies in 1993, and the corporation was in place when the ministers finally organized in 2001.

The Pentecostal Faith Assemblies have a doctrinal position very similar to that of the Assemblies of God. It accepts the scriptures as the infallible Word of God. Believers are taught to ardently expect and earnestly seek the baptism in the Holy Spirit that comes with empowerment for the work of ministry and is witnessed by the sign of speaking in tongues. The gifts of the spirit (1 Cor.) are seen as a normal part of the Christian life.

The Pentecostal Faith Assemblies is led by its bishop, Rev. Jack Howell, who also serves as the director of Revealed Truth Ministries in Oklahoma City, Oklahoma, and the Assemblies' state presbyter for Oklahoma (the only state with a state presbyter). He is assisted by an advisory council. The organization has sought alignment with other independent Pentecostal ministers and churches.

Membership: Not reported. Affiliated ministers are founded in Oklahoma, Kentucky, Georgia, and North Carolina.

Sources:

Pentecostal Faith Assemblies. sjackson4.homestead.com.

Reformers Ministries International (RMI)

c/o Ecclesia Word Ministries International, PO Box 743, Bronx, NY 10462

Alternate Address: Ecclesia Church International, 1638 Bronxdale Ave., Bronx, NY 10462.

Reformers Ministries International is a fellowship of Pentecostal/charismatic churches that exists as an apostolic network of churches, ministries, and ministers around the world. Within the Reformers Ministries International are two distinct groups, Reformers Ministries International Network and Reformers Ministries International Church Fellowship. The RMI Network includes those participants who share two or more denominational affiliations and is primarily fraternal in nature.

The RMI Church Fellowship consists of those independent churches under the apostolic and ecclesiastical leadership of Reformers Ministries International that hold no other denominational affiliation. The church fellowship includes an oversight structure with regional apostolic overseers who are appointed by the govern-

ing apostolic teams in their respective geographical regions. Both the network and the church fellowship provide some level of accountability and apostolic covering to churches and their leaders and ministries.

Leading Reformer Ministries International is an apostolic team whose task is seen as establishing the vision of and giving guidance to the organization's ministers; maintaining doctrinal purity; raising up additional ministers; setting membership standards; and approving national and regional leadership. The apostolic team is led by Apostle (Dr.) John Tetsola, pastor of Ecclesia Church International in the Bronx, New York. Tetsola was born in Warri, Nigeria, and now serves as the president of the International Bible Training Center and chairman/founder of Reformers Ministries International.

Membership: Not reported.

Educational Facilities:

International Bible Training Center.

Periodicals: *The Reformer*.

Sources:

Reformers Ministries International. www.reformersministries.org/.

Tetsola, John. *Developing Spiritual Accuracy and Pinpointing*. Bronx, NY: End Time Wave Publications, n.d.

————. *Schooling for Ruling*. Bronx, NY: End Time Wave Publications, 1998.

Resurrection Church and Ministries (RCM)

Current address not obtained for this edition.

Resurrection Church and Ministries (RCM) grew out of the ministry of John Kelly, a charismatic evangelist. In the early 1980s he came to question the scriptural nature of his own successful work. One day while in a period of quiet prayer, he is said to have received a message from the Holy Spirit, which, he believed, directed him to "go and wash the feet of the young men who will become the patriarchs of the end-time move of my spirit." Based upon this new calling, he reoriented his ministry to developing a nurturing network of ministers and ministries according to the New Testament pattern of local churches with a global vision. Kelly saw God's provision of the vision as the fivefold ministry of Ephesians 4: apostles, prophets, evangelists, pastors, and teachers. Kelly now functions as an apostle of the local churches that make up the RCM fellowship.

When the RCM was formally established, it united churches in Pennsylvania, New York, New Jersey, and Michigan. In the next decade churches in Delaware, South Carolina, Florida, and Illinois were added. Foreign congregations exist in Haiti, Belize, England, and Russia. The headquarters in South Carolina was established in 1987. RCM sponsors Team World Outreach, which allows local congregations to send short-term missions in various foreign and domestic mission fields. RCM's apostolic teams are composed of church leaders who move into a given country to strengthen local congregations.

Membership: Not reported.

Periodicals: *Covenant Communique*.

Sources:

Resurrected Church Ministries. resurrectedchurchministries.net

Revival Fellowship International

PO Box 1007, Beaufort, SC 29901

The Revival Fellowship International was founded in 1995 by John Polis. A few years before, the Light of Life Network of Churches, a Pentecostal/charismatic fellowship, had grown out of the apostolic ministry of Polis and his wife Rebecca Polis, who were based in the Light of Life Outreach Center located in Fairmont, West Virginia. In 1980 the Polises were pastors of a church in Fairmont, and three years later, the church became the World Outreach Center and subsequently developed an expansive evangelism program that included a broadcast ministry and efforts at church planting. The emergence of other churches in the state led to the founding of the Light of Life network.

More recently, a congregation was formed in Asheville, North Carolina, where the Polis family lives. To further the church-planting endeavor, leaders from other established ministries have come together on the fellowship's board of trustees.

The network adheres to a basic Pentecostal doctrine, and follows the basic fivefold ministry ideal set out in Eph. 4:11.

The missionary outreach of the network includes the establishment of a Bible college in Eldoret, Kenya.

Membership: Not reported.

Sources:

Revival Fellowship International. www.rfiusa.org.

SHEM Ministries International
25016 Maple Valley Hwy., Maple Valley, WA 98038

SHEM Ministries (Servant House Evangelistic Ministries), an outgrowth of Servant House Fellowship, was founded in 1996 by Glenn Smith, a Pentecostal minister. Smith attended Portland Bible College, Sterling Academy, and received his Doctorate of Theology from St. John's University in Acre, Israel. He worked closely with the ministry of Vickie Walber at Ministries of the Living Stones in Anchorage, Alaska. SHEM Ministries International, a prophetic and apostolic ministry, began in Anchorage in 1990. In March 1993 Smith moved to Renton, Washington, and established a new congregation and an associated television ministry. His ministry attracted the attention of a variety of independent ministers who came to appreciate his work and his call for unity in the church. He produced and distributed a variety of books, tapes, and videos.

His ministry also brought him in contact with a number of people who were doing the work of a minister but had never asked for nor been offered ordination. After several ministers requested ordination, an ordination council for SHEM Ministries International was formed and the first ordinations occurred. The council grew into SHEM Ministerial Fellowship out of the additional desire that the ministers associated with SHEM be able to draw on the strengths of their colleagues and share their talents and experience where needed.

Membership: Not reported.

Sources:

SHEM Ministries International. www.shem.net.

Sovereign Grace Ministries
7505 Muncaster Mill Rd., Gaithersburg, MD 20877

Sovereign Grace Ministries, formerly known as People of Destiny International (PDI), is a fellowship under the direction of an apostolic team given to the planting and rebuilding of local churches and the proclamation of Christian teachings through churches, conferences, leadership training, worship and teaching tapes, books, and a magazine.

HISTORY. Larry Tomczak committed his life to Christ and received the baptism of the Holy Spirit in the early 1970s. Initially, he was active within the Roman Catholic phase of the Charismatic Movement as an evangelist and author. Tomczak and C. J. Mahaney, who later led the PDI apostolic team, led a weekly teaching ministry called TAG (Take and Give) in Washington, D.C. in the late 1970s. As they studied the book of Acts, Tomczak and Mahaney began to see that members of the Church universal (those people who have become genuine followers of Christ and have personally appropriated the Gospel) are called to be a vital and committed part of a local church. In this context they are called to live out the New Covenant as the people of God and demonstrate the reality of the kingdom of God. They further came to believe that the ascended Christ had given gift ministries to the church (Ephesians 4:11—apostles, prophets, evangelists, pastors, and teachers) for the equipping of Christ's body that it might mature and grow. Through the gift ministries, all members of the Church are to be nurtured and equipped for the work

of ministry. In the context of the local church, God's people receive pastoral care and leadership and the opportunity to employ their God-given gifts in his service, in relation to one another and to the world.

Tomczak and Mahaney were influenced by British apostles Arthur Wallis, author of *The Radical Christian* (1981), Bryn Jones, and Terry Virgo. Jones and Virgo led apostolic teams in Great Britain that provided oversight to churches in Wales, South Africa, and other countries.

In 1978 Tomczak and Mahaney established what is now called Covenant Life Church in Gaithersburg, Maryland. In 1981 they sent out their first church-planting team and organized a team to function as apostles to help lay foundations in the church (Ephesians 2:20). In the mid-1980s Tomczak and Mahaney founded People of Destiny International to provide resources and training for church growth and care. Each apostle was a man of proven character and ministry commissioned by his local church for the work of an apostle, establishing churches and offering oversight to them through leadership training. New churches were usually founded by church-planting teams sent out from established churches. (In some rare cases PDI "adopted" an already established church with a history of relationship to one of the apostles and that sought to become a People of Destiny team-related church.) Apostles were seen as builders and servants, giving general care and oversight to the various churches. Prophets were people with a special gift from God to speak his word creatively and immediately to the church, consistent with the written Word of God. In PDI, the apostolic and prophetic offices were exercised with an emphasis on *relationship* rather than organization. The senior pastor of each church was personally overseen by one of the four apostles of the apostolic team. Pastors were cared for and trained as friends and fellow servants in the Lord.

Citing a disagreement over the theological shift toward Calvinism, Tomczak left PDI in 1998. Several years later, PDI openly recognized the doctrinal developments by changing its name to Sovereign Grace Ministries, and Mahaney emerged as the group's primary leader.

Membership. In 2008 the Ministries reported 67 affiliated congregations in the United States, two congregations in Canada, and additional affiliated congregation in England, Germany, Ethiopia

Educational Facilities:

Pastors College.

Sources:

Sovereign Grace Ministries. www.sovereigngraceministries.org/.

Tomczak, Larry. *Clap Your Hands*. Plainfield, NJ: Logos International, 1973.

———. *Divine Appointments*. Ann Arbor, MI: Servant Publications, 1986.

United Gospel Fellowship Covenant Ministries
2400 Murchison Rd., Fayetteville, NC 28302

United Gospel Fellowship Covenant Ministries grew out of the early ministry of Bishop J. Venturnio Porter and his wife, Elder Nora Yarbrough Porter. In the 1970s, Bishop Porter had founded and pastored the United Gospel Fellowship in Frankfurt, Germany, a congregation that ministered primarily to Americans in the armed services. In 1980 he returned to the United States and founded Christ Cathedral in Fayetteville, North Carolina. Among the first members were some former members of the German congregation, now stationed at nearby Fort Bragg. The first services of the Cathedral were, in fact, held at Hammond Hills Chapel at Fort Bragg.

After facilities were secured in Fayetteville, Porter developed a ministry expressed in his building a distinctly different church in multiple locations in the city of Fayetteville, North Carolina. He wanted to create a ministry known for its excellence so that it would inspire excellence in others, and one that would share the "Word of Faith" and the associated principles of abundance. He also wanted to utilize the opportunities provide by television and other mass media to share the gospel.

The fellowship is a pentecostal in faith and professes belief in the authority of the bible as the inerrant and infallible word of God and faith in the triune deity. It believes in the baptism of the Holy Spirit evidenced in speaking in tongues and the associated gifts and fruits of the Spirit. The church also teaches the Word of Faith perspective, which holds that God will honor the prayer of faith out of his abundance.

Over the years additional churches have been founded in neighboring states. They serve primarily African Americans. The fellowship sponsors Christ Village Resort and Conference Center, which it makes available as a tobacco-free, alcohol-free site for various Christian-oriented events.

Membership: Not reported. In 2002 there were eight churches in the fellowship located in North Carolina, Tennessee, and Georgia.

Sources:

United Gospel Fellowship Covenant Ministries.
www.christcathedralchurch.org/UGFCM.html.

Vision International Ministerial Association
PO Box 744, Jupiter, FL 33468

Vision International Ministerial Association is a fellowship of Pentecostal-charismatic ministers headed by Steven Lambert (b. 1948), who was himself ordained as a minister in 1977. Lambert has founded and served as a pastor in several churches in Florida. He now leads the association's governing apostolic presbytery, which also includes Stan DeKoven, the president of Vision International University in Ramona, California; George Runyan, the director of the San Diego Church Network in California; and John Delgado, the president of Joint Heirs Ministries Inc. in Irving, Texas.

Vision International holds to mainline Pentecostal beliefs in the authority of the Bible as the infallible Word of God, the Trinity, and salvation in Jesus Christ. It also affirms the availability of the baptism in the Holy Spirit, initially evidenced by supernatural "unknown tongues," to all believers who ask for it.

The organization aims to cultivate close personal and professional relationships among the minister members, while providing for a form of accountability, with respect to conduct, that avoids any form of ascendancy and subjugation. It also supplies independent ministers with a means of identifying members' talents and abilities and matching them to possible openings for their use.

Through the association, otherwise qualified ministers may receive ordination and licensing for qualified fivefold ministers and relate to an apostolic-prophetic presbytery for ministers and ministries. The association also sponsors national and regional conferences and seminars, as well as some local fellowship gatherings.

The association sponsors several schools that offer nontraditional and nonresident courses and degree programs via distance learning apart from residential requirements or the attendance of live lecture classes.

Membership: Not reported.

Educational Facilities:

Vision International University, Ramona, California

South Florida Theological Seminary, Jupiter, Florida.

Vision of Hope Christian Fellowship
PO Box 365, Lathrop, CA 95330

Vision of Hope Christian Fellowship is a Pentecostal-charismatic association of churches and ministers founded in the 1990s with a focus upon evangelism, healing, the gifts of the Spirit, worship, and reconciliation. It sees itself as part of the global movement within Pentecostalism to restructure the movement around a core leadership of apostles and prophets who direct networks of independent congregations, supplying local churches with an association for fellowship and accountability.

The fellowship affirms the Nicene Creed, common to most Christian bodies, and emphasizes belief in the Trinity and salvation through faith in Christ alone. A mis-

sion of the fellowship is directed toward establishing new churches and ministries in various urban centers. New communities are pioneered by locating a core group of persons interested in establishing an apostolic-prophetic church or ministry in their hometown. Subsequently, a Vision of Hope team will be sent to an area for a period of nurturing leadership.

The fellowship supports two centers for apostolic and prophetic studies, which offer nonresidential courses via the Internet that are supplemented with on-site intensive and personal mentoring.

Membership: The fellowship is built around six congregations in California.

Educational Facilities:

Center for Apostolic and Prophetic Studies, San Francisco, California; Fresno, California.

Sources:

Vision of Hope Christian Fellowship. www.citytakers.com/

Word of Faith International Christian Centers
20000 W 9 Mile Rd., Southfield, MI 48075

The first Word of Faith International Christian Center was founded in 1979 in a storefront building in Detroit, Michigan. It has more recently moved to a 110-acre site Southfield (suburban Detroit). The original center, under the leadership of its pastor, Keith Butler, has become a megachurch with a membership of more than 18,000. Bishop and Mrs. Keith A. Butler, Sr., began the Word of Faith ministry with some 60 supporters in the late 1970s.

The church is a trinitarian pentecostal body similar in belief and practice to the International Convention of Faith Ministries. Many of its leaders have attended Rhema Bible College, founded by televangelist Kenneth Hagin, known for his "faith confession" doctrine that holds that a person of faith can publicly confess or claim something from God and be assured of getting it.

As Butler's ministry grew in Detroit, he began to travel the country. A number of churches resulted from his evangelistic endeavors. They are now considered satellite congregations. Such congregations have not been limited to the United States, and currently Word of Faith churches may be found in Africa, Pakistan, Europe, and the Caribbean. He has concentrated upon planting churches in large urban areas.

The different congregations associated with Word of Faith have developed a host of outreach ministries to different groups of people—singles, married couples, the campus, youth—the Kingdom Business Association (to assist people with practical problems of living), and a broadcast ministry, *The Living Word*. Butler has written some 14 books; his son, Keith A. Butler II has authored three; and his daughters Michelle and Deborah Butler, both also ministers, have each written one.

Membership: Not reported. In 2002 there were 12 satellite congregations in the United States and one in the United States Virgin Islands. Word of Faith International Ministries has 65 churches in Africa, 15 churches in Pakistan, and 2 in Europe (Bulgaria, Hungary).

Educational Facilities:

Word of Faith Bible Training Center, Southfield, Michigan.

Periodicals: *Vision*.

Sources:

Word of Faith International Christian Center. www.woficc.com.

Butler, Keith. *God's Plan for You: Finding the Purpose of Your Life*. Tulsa, OK: Harrison House, 2000.

————. *Grace of God: Faith to Receive God's Unlimited Promises*. Tulsa, OK: Harrison House, 2001.

————. *A Seed Will Meet Any Need*. Tulsa, OK: Harrison House, 2002.

World Breakthrough Network

Current address not obtained for this edition.

The World Breakthrough Network is a Pentecostal-charismatic association of churches, ministries, and ministers founded by Noel Woodroffe, who serves as its lead apostle. Assisting him is an apostolic team consisting of Robert Munien (with special responsibility for South Africa, East Asia, and Oceania), John Singleton (with special responsibility for pastoral and relational issues), and Anderson Williams (with special responsibility for Europe and South America). Williams is also head of an apostolic network in the United Kingdom: LifeLine Network International. The apostolic team, in turn, is assisted by the Apostolic-Prophetic Leadership Team (ALT), an apostolic support team, and a host of World Breakthrough Network development coordinators, representatives, and facilitators. Particular responsibility for the United States has been assigned to Scott Webster, Steve Schultz, and David Copp Sr.

The network is a conservative body theologically that affirms the Bible as the inerrant Word of God, the Trinity, and the saving work of Jesus Christ. It also believes in the baptism of the Holy Spirit with speaking in tongues, divine healing, the gifts and fruits of the Spirit, and the anointed ministries of the Holy Spirit. Organizationally, the network follows the fivefold ministry of Ephesians 4, which includes apostles, prophets, evangelists, pastors, and teachers. It acknowledges that the ministries of apostles and prophets, especially, have been restored in modern times as foundational and revelatory ministries in anticipation of the imminent return of Jesus. Autonomous local churches freely affiliate under the authority of the acknowledged apostle.

Operating largely within the African-American community in the Caribbean, a significant part of the network's task is to support any new kingdom organizations and business entities that have a prophetic purpose and apostolic mentality for the advancement of the kingdom and providing financial resources for the purposes of God.

The Elijah Centre in Trinidad, West Indies, has been designated the core church of the World Breakthrough Network. As such, the network defines part of its uniqueness by creating an epicenter from which correct godly authority, revelation strength, and production of apostolic patterns may spiral outward to the entire structure.

Membership: Not reported. Work is strong in western African nations from South Africa to Nigeria, Ghana, and Liberia. There is also work in Germany, Belgium, and France, and the Middle East.

Sources:

Elijah Centre: A Global, Borderless, Kingdom Community. www.elijahcentre.org/

World Changers Church International

2500 Burdett Rd., College Park, GA 30349

World Changers Church International is the home base for the ministry of televangelist Dr. Creflo A. Dollar (b. 1962). It originated in a Bible study group begun by Dollar when he was a student at West Georgia College in Carrollton, Georgia, in the mid 1980s. Through these Bible studies Dollar met his future wife, Taffi Bolton, who would later become the co-pastor of the church he founded. Following graduation, Dollar founded a local church, World Changers Ministries, in 1986. Beginning with eight people, the church grew steadily and in 1988 the congregation purchased the former Atlanta Christian Center Church in College Park, Georgia. In 1995, the congregation moved into the 8,500-seat World Dome.

The church and its pastors developed a global perspective early in their association. Integral to their ministry was a broadcast ministry that is now heard around the world. The church's outreach is primarily funneled through an associated organization: Creflo Dollar Ministries (CDM). CDM operates from offices in the United States, Australia, the Republic of South Africa, Nigeria, and the United Kingdom.

The World Changers Church is a Trinitarian Pentecostal body with a strong emphasis on acting on one's faith. Pastor Dollar has been closely associated with the Faith Movement that grew from the ministry of the last Kenneth Hagin (1917–2003) and emphasized God's willingness to share his abundance with Christians. The prayer of faith is the primary means of receiving from God.

The World Changers Church has its primary center in College Park, Georgia, and a second satellite church in New York City, but its influence is largely achieved through the television broadcast ministry and the several books written by Pastor Dollar.

Membership: In 2007 the church reported in excess of 25,000 members, some 5,000 of whom are affiliated with the New York City congregation.

Remarks: On November 6, 2007, Sen. Chuck Grassley of Iowa, speaking for the United States Senate Committee on Finance, announced that Dollar and his ministry would be included in an investigation into several prominent televangelists (others of whom included Benny Hinn, Kenneth Copeland, Eddie Long, Joyce Meyer, and Paula White). Relatively quickly, Dollar agreed to cooperate with the investigation, though he suggested that the Internal Revenue Service—and not the committee—would be the proper instrument for reviewing the church's finances. The ongoing investigation raises a variety of questions about government interference in the life of religious groups. At the same time, it is clear that it is the relatively opulent lifestyle enjoyed by Dollar and other televangelists that is the major cause of their ministries being questioned. Dollar and the others have denied any wrongdoing or improprieties.

Sources:

World Changers Church International. www.worldchangers.org/.

Dollar, Creflo A. *8 Steps to Create the Life You Want: The Anatomy of a Successful Life.* New York: FaithWords, 2008.

———. *In the Presence of God: Find Answers to the Challenges of Life.* New York: FaithWords, 2006.

———. *Love, Live, and Enjoy Life: Uncover the Transforming Power of God's Love.* New York: FaithWords, 2006.

Dollar, Taffi L. *Your Spiritual Makeover: Experience the Beauty of a Balanced Life.* Tulsa, OK: Harrison House, 2007.

Luo, Michael. "Preaching a Gospel of Wealth in a Glittery Market, New York." *New York Times* (January 15, 2006). Posted at www.nytimes.com/2006/01/15/nyregion/15prosperity.html?ex=1294981200&en=9d7efd8b8715771f&ei=5090&partner=rssuserland&emc=rss.

World Ministry Fellowship

6000 Custer Rd., Bldg. 3, Plano, TX 75023-5100

World Ministry Fellowship is a fellowship of Pentecostal ministers founded in Shreveport, Louisiana, in the summer of 1963. It emerged from a 1961 vision experienced by founder William B. Brown, Sr. It was created for ministers who did not want to be otherwise limited by the boundaries of a specific denomination. They believed that only God could supply the anointing, grace, gifts, and finances to fulfill their ministerial calling. The fellowship was designed to encourage, strengthen, and edify ministers as they pursued God's work. Those with credentials from the fellowship gather each July for an international convocation.

The fellowship has adopted a brief statement of faith that places them within the Latter-Rain movement that emerged in the larger Pentecostal community in the 1940s. It affirms belief in God as Father, Son and Holy Spirit; the bible as the infallible world of God; baptism by immersion, the baptism of the Holy Spirit (with the accompanying sign of speaking in tongues and resulting manifestation of the gifts of the Spirit); divine healing and deliverance from spirit possession ministry; and the Second Coming of Jesus. Ministry is built around the five-fold ministry of Ephesians 4:11 in apostles, prophets, evangelists, pastors, and teachers.

The fellowship is led by a 21-person advisory board and a board of directors, the legislative body of the fellowship. Directors serve for life. An ordination council is responsible for licensing and ordaining ministers and a missions board oversees international work.

Among the most well-known of fellowship ministers is televangelist Kenneth Copeland.

Membership: In 2008 the fellowship reported 91 ministers in the fellowship, including 17 husband-wife teams. Members include licensed lay workers and ministers, ordained ministers, and churches served by fellowship ministers. Members are scattered across America, and state directors have been named in 24 states. The fellowship has foreign affiliates in Ghana, Nigeria, Ivory Coast, Singapore, India, Japan, Bulgaria, France, Germany, the Netherlands, Guatemala, Peru, Mexico, and El Salvador.

Periodicals: *Point of Contact.*

Sources:

World Ministry Fellowship. www.worldministry.com.

 Other Pentecostals

Alpha and Omega Christian Church

96-171 Kamehameha Hwy., Pearl City, HI 96782

The Alpha and Omega Christian Church was formed in 1962 by Alezandro B. Faquaragon and other former members of the Pearl City Full Gospel Church. A congregation, primarily of Filipino nationals, was established in Pearl City, Hawaii. Four years later, a few members of the church returned to the Philippines and established a congregation at Dingras, Ilocos Norte. In 1968 a flood struck Pearl City and destroyed the meeting hall of the church. Many of the members withdrew after that event, though the church has survived and been rebuilt. The group is small, restricted to the Hawaiian Islands, and completely independent.

Membership: There are only two congregations, one in Hawaii and one in the Philippines.

Educational Facilities:

Alpha and Omega Bible School, Pearl City, Hawaii.

American Evangelistic Association

PO Box 121000, W Melbourne, FL 32912-1000

Alternate Address: 505 N John Rodes Blvd., Melbourne, FL 32934.

The American Evangelistic Association (AEA) was founded in 1954 in Baltimore by John E. Douglas, its president, and 17 other independent ministers. Many of these had been affected by the Latter Rain Movement that had begun in Canada in the late 1940s. The AEA licenses independent pastors, mostly Pentecostals, but also some other conservative evangelical ministers. Government is congregational, with congregations affiliating with the national headquarters; at the head of the association is a five-man executive committee. The current Chairman/CEO is Dr. E. John Reinhold and the President is Dr. Harold Aitkins.

The AEA was formed to promote doctrinal, ethical, and moral standards for independent ministers and churches, many of whom had come out of Pentecostal denominations. Missionary in outlook, the AEA oversees more than 1,000 workers outside the United States, mostly in India, Korea, Hong Kong, and Haiti. Headquarters are on a 10-acre site in Melbourne, Florida. Christian Care Ministry, a division of AEA, has more than 12,000 households that share one another's medical bills on a not-for-profit basis. Other outreach arms are Life Changing Ministries, International Prison Ministry, and Christian Motivational Ministries.

Membership: In 2002 the AEA reported more than 45,000 members, including divisions, with members in all 50 states and in 75 countries.

Sources:

American Evangelistic Association. /www.aeaministries.org

Anointed Word Ministries and Fellowships International

PO Box 3006, Springfield, OH 45502

The Anointed Word Ministries and Fellowships International was founded in 1984 by Drew Pruzaniec, a former artist who in 1979 found faith in Jesus Christ and became a Pentecostal evangelist. He was ordained by Agape Ministries (New Hope Full Gospel Church) in Maryville, Tennessee, and went on to become the pastor of the Church Fellowship, Townsend, Tennessee (1982–1983). In 1984, the same year Anointed Word Ministries was launched, he became the pastor of Anointed Word Fellowship, Springfield, Ohio, where he remained for four years. In 1988 he moved to Ohio, where he became the pastor of the Anointed Word Fellowship in Cincinnati.

Anointed Word Ministries has three essential program thrusts: 1) create and establish local churches that provide places for people to worship God through Jesus Christ; 2) be a fellowship of like-minded ministers and ministries that gather several times annually to exchange revelations of the Holy Spirit; and 3) support evangelism and outreach activities, including Drew Pruzaniec Ministries, the evangelical work of the founder.

Anointed Word Ministries has a statement of faith that includes belief in God, salvation in Christ from sin, judgment, and resurrection. The statement includes a paragraph on faith that calls attention to the three basic experiences of faith: salvation through which one enters God's kingdom; reception of the Holy Spirit, and the accompanying experience of speaking in tongues; and the process of becoming complete in Christ and life in the Spirit.

Churches related to the Anointed Word Ministries are mainly in Ohio but also in nine other states. There is also related work in Zambia and Togo.

Membership: In 2002 the fellowship reported more than 95 congregations associated with the ministries.

Sources:

Anointed Word Ministries and Fellowships International. home.earthlink.net/~anointed.word/.

Drew Pruzaniec Ministries. home.earthlink.net/~anointed.word/drewpruz.htm.

Antioch International Ministries (AIM)

246 Cowden Rd., PO Box 169, New Wilmington, PA 16142

Antioch International Ministries is an association of charismatic churches founded in the mid-1990s. Currently leading the ministries is founder Jim Erb who became a United Methodist Church minister in the 1960s. Following four years as a missionary in the Philippines, in the 1970s he and his wife lived with the Jesus People in the barn ministry of Jacob's Ladder Inc. in Mercer, Pennsylvania. During these years he was caught up in the charismatic movement as the Holy Spirit "moved powerfully in salvation, healing and deliverance." He left the United Methodist church and subsequently become pastor of the independent Living Word Church that became the source of additional sister churches in Western Pennsylvania. In the mid-1990s, he founded Antioch International Ministries (AIM) as a network of the associated charismatic churches.

The statement of faith of the ministries affirms belief in the authority of the bible, the Trinity, atonement in Jesus Christ, and the present ministry of the Holy Spirit "whose indwelling enables the Christian to lead a godly life, and whose baptism provides power for service." There are two ordinances, holy communion and baptism (by immersion). The group opposes abortion and homosexuality.

The (seven person) Apostolic Council and the leader's council assist the president, who leads Antioch International Ministries. All offices in the ministries, other than the president, are elected offices. The ministries also supports the five-fold ministry mentioned in Ephesians 4:11 (apostles, prophets, evangelists, pastors, teachers).

Membership: Not reported. In 2001 there were seven congregations and nine outreach ministries affiliates with Antioch International Ministries.

Sources:

Antioch International Ministries. www.aiministries.org.

B'nai Shalom

Current address not obtained for this edition.

During the 1950s, Elder Reynolds Edward Dawkins (d. 1965), an elder in the Gospel Assemblies, had several visions; among them was one in which he was instructed to begin work in Palestine, looking toward the restoration of Israel and the end of the Gentile age, which began in 1959. Following the death of William Sowders (1879–1952), founder of the Gospel Assemblies, the movement reorganized with a presbyterial form of government. Dawkins rejected the polity in favor of an apostolic order of the five-gifted ministry of Romans 13, led by pastor, teacher, evangelist, prophets, and (over all) the apostle. Dawkins was accepted by his followers as an apostle and his revelations are highly revered.

Dawkins died in 1965 and was succeeded by Elder Harry Richard Tate. Tate leads a core membership called *overcomers*, members who have given three years in living wholly for the body of Christ or who give at least 51 percent of their time, money, and life for the body. Membership has spread to Jamaica, the Netherlands, Hong Kong, India, Nigeria, and Israel. The Peace Publishers and Company serves as the body's financial and publishing structure.

Membership: Not reported. In the early 1970s, there were 8 congregations in the United States and 11 outside of the United States, with a total membership of approximately 1,000.

Periodicals: *B'nai Shalom.*

The Body (Bro. Evangelist)

Current address not obtained for this edition.

The Body is the name of a nomadic Jesus people group founded by Jimmie T. Roberts (b. 1939), known within the group as Brother Evangelist. Roberts was born and raised in Paducah, Kentucky, and joined the marines after graduating from high school. Roberts emerged as a religious leader following his time as a Marine sergeant and founded The Body around 1969. The first converts consisted primarily of young adults, many previously part of the street people subculture of the era, and college students who had dropped out of school.

Brother Evangelist taught a separatist Bible-oriented Pentecostal Protestantism. Members rejected the world and all personal wealth. They shun education, medicine, and bathing. Clothing is plain and simple. Sex is not allowed for singles, and sexual activity is discouraged among the married. They do not work, but gain a large portion of their food from what is thrown away by groceries and restaurants (a practice that earned them the label "garbage eaters"). Women in the group are subordinate to the men.

The group kept a low profile, and its existence only became widely known in 1975 when some 35 members were involved in an accident near Fayetteville, Arkansas. A truck in which they were riding overturned and members of the group called attention to themselves by refusing to allow any medical personnel to tend to their wounds. One baby who was in the truck later died, though it was determined that medical aid could not have saved her. The accident led to several attacks upon the group by parents wishing to break their sons and daughters affiliation with it. Over the next five years, members were kidnapped and psychologically deprogrammed by people associated with various anticult organizations that were attempting to counter the group's activity. The nomadic lifestyle kept the group constantly on the move, however, which made monitoring it difficult. While occasional reports of the group surfaced through the late 1970s, virtually no mention of its appearance was noted in the 1980s. The present status of the group is not known.

Membership: Not reported. In the late 1970s there were approximately 100 members.

Sources:

Martin, Rachel, and Bonnie Palmer Young. *Escape (from a religious cult)*. London: Pickering & Inglis, 1980.

Sneed, Michael, "America's Bizarre Cult of Nomads," *Chicago Tribune*, June 10, 1979.

————, "'Brother Evangelist': Hypnotic Shepherd of a Wandering, Ragtag Flock," *Chicago Tribune*, June 11, 1979.

Christ Faith Mission

6026 Echo St., Los Angeles, CA 90042

Christ Faith Mission continues the work begun in 1908 by Dr. Finis E. Yoakum (1851–1920), a Denver Methodist layman and medical doctor. In Los Angeles in 1895 following a near fatal accident, he was healed in a meeting of the Christian and Missionary Alliance, the holiness church founded by Albert Benjamin Simpson (1843–1919), which had been among the first modern churches to emphasize divine healing. As a result of his healing, he dedicated himself to the work of the Lord and began his efforts among the derelicts, outcasts, and street people of the city. In 1908 he opened Old Pisgah Tabernacle in Los Angeles. He began to hold gospel services and to provide meals for the hungry. In 1909, he began to publish the *Pisgah Journal*.

Yoakum had a utopian spirit, and envisioned a series of communities that would embody the life of the early church. He opened Pisgah Home for the city's hungry and homeless; Pisgah Ark in the Arroyo Seco for delinquent girls; and Pisgah Gardens in the San Fernando Valley for the sick. His most famous experiment was Pisgah Grande, a model Christian commune established near Santa Susana, California in 1914. The community attracted people from across the United States, including some who had formerly lived at Zion, Illinois, the community built by John Alexander Dowie, several decades earlier. Pisgah Grande, already weakened by charges of financial mismanagement and unsanitary conditions, was thrown into further confusion by Yoakum's death in 1920. They eventually incorporated and took control of the Los Angeles property. They bought property in the San Bernardino Mountains and then moved to Pikesville, Tennessee.

In 1939 James Cheek, formerly the manager of Pisgah Grande, took control of the Pisgah Home property in Los Angeles and founded Christ Faith Mission, continuing the heritage of Yoakum's inner-city work. He began a periodical. In 1972, the surviving Pisgah group in Tennessee united their work with that of Cheek and merged their periodical into *The Herald of Hope*, which he published.

Under Cheek's leadership, the old Pisgah movement reborn as Christ Faith Mission has become a worldwide full gospel (Pentecostal) ministry. He continued the healing emphasis, and the present-day mission sends out prayer cloths to any sick person who requests them. The Mission operates the Christ Faith Mission Home near Saugus, California, and the Pisgah Home Camp Ground at Pikeville, Tennessee. A radio ministry is heard over stations in Los Angeles and Long Beach, California. Foreign language editions of *The Herald of Hope* are sent to mission stations in Korea, Mexico, India, Indonesia, and Jamaica.

Membership: Not reported.

Periodicals: *The Herald of Hope.*

Sources:

Christ Faith Mission. www.pisgah.com.

Kagan, Paul. *New World Utopias*. New York: Penguin Books, 1975.

Christian Outreach Centre

c/o COC America, 6657 W. Ottawa Ave., A11-B, Littleton, CO 80128

Alternate Address: International headquarters: PO Box 2111, Mansfield 4122, Victoria, Australia; Canadian headquarters: 98 Westglen Cres., Spruce Grove, AB T7X 1V7 Canada.

The Christian Outreach Centre was founded by Rev. Clark Taylor (b. 1937) in Brisbane, Australia, in 1974. A former Methodist, Taylor had been healed of malaria in the 1960s. In 1970, he cooperated with Trevor Chandler in the founding of Christian Life Churches International (CLCI), a charismatic fellowship, in Brisbane. Two years later he left CLCI to become an itinerant evangelist, and became well-known as a capable speaker and for the visible spiritual manifestations that occurred at his meetings—which, like those of evangelist Benny Hinn in the United States, were marked by the phenomenon of "slaying in the spirit," in which people appear to swoon under the spirit's power.

After founding the Christian Outreach Centre, Taylor's efforts led to the emergence of additional congregations in Queensland and New South Wales, including a large congregation of several thousand at Mansfield, one of the largest congregations of any denomination in Australia. The movement faced a severe crisis in 1990, when Taylor was accused of sexual immorality resulting in his being stripped of his leadership positions. He was succeeded by Neil Mears who has since led the fellowship as its international president.

The church follows a mainline Pentecostal doctrinal perspective with an emphasis on the charismatic gifts of the Spirit and the freedom and joy that the Holy Spirit brings to the life of the believer. Unlike many Charismatic groups, the center has a centralized government. The COC views itself as one Christian Outreach Centre, which happens to have meeting points in numerous locations. Hence, all local church property is held in the name of the whole body by a Property Commission, and a committee of pastors oversees denominational matters including the ordination, appointments, and discipline of the ministers.

In 1988, work expanded to New Zealand and the Solomons and over the next few years reached out to other islands of the South Pacific and Europe. In 1996, work began in North America in Denver, Colorado.

Membership: Not reported. In 2001 there were more than 1,000 congregations worldwide, the largest number being in Australia. There are ten centers in the United States and one in Canada. Additional centers are found in more than 30 countries of the world, including several European countries and many of the southern Pacific Ocean nations.

Periodicals: *Outreach*, PO Box 2111, Mansfield 4122, Victoria, Australia.

Sources:

Christian Outreach Centre. www.coc.org.au.

Humphries, R. A., and R. S. Ward, eds. *Religious Bodies in Australia: a Comprehensive Guide*. Wantirna, Victoria: New Melbourne Press, 1995.

Christ's Church Fellowship

c/o Bp. David C. Holdridge, PO Box 67, Roswell, NM 88202

Christ's Church Fellowship (CCF) was founded in 2007 by David Holdridge of Resurrection Cathedral in Roswell, New Mexico. Holdridge had had a long career as a lay preacher, reaching into the late 1960s. In 1971 he received the Pentecostal baptism of the Holy Spirit. After working in various churches for a decade, in 1983 he founded Resurrection Tabernacle in his hometown of Roswell, New Mexico. The tabernacle participated in the original Christ's Church fellowship that grew out of the Conference on Spiritual Renewal, begun in Nashville, Tennessee, as a vehicle for the Charismatic renewal that had spread among the congregations of the Churches of Christ and Christian Church (Disciples of Christ). The national CCF organization became dormant in 2002, and Resurrection Tabernacle was among a small number of churches that attempted to perpetuate the CCF tradition. It continued to use the CFF logo and the name on its web site. Among the other congregations continuing the CCF tradition were a number of African-American churches.

In the meantime, Holdridge's brother had become an Orthodox priest, and Holdridge had become acquainted with several independent Catholic bishops. In 2005 he accepted the consecration offered by Abp. Michael Wrenn as a bishop in the Celtic Anabaptist Communion. From Wren he received multiple lineages of apostolic succession. In early 2007 Holdridge, then the bishop at Resurrection Cathedral (the former Resurrection Tabernacle), reincorporated CCF under the leadership of a synod of bishops.

Christ's Church Fellowship is a conservative Pentecostal church that draws on the Restoration tradition of the Churches of Christ and Christina Church (Disciples of Christ) and affirms the Bible as the eternal, inerrant, verbally inspired word of God. The fellowship has done some of its most creative work on revisioning the Church. It believes that Christians are called on to be both "salt and light" to their communities, and henceforth, it envisions a church committed to witnessing continually ("24/7"). The witness will include prayer and worship, especially toward all whom they encounter, whom they see as people sent to them by God.

Bp. Holdridge has emerged as ecumenical leader. He has developed a variety of close relationships with other churches, and is either in fellowship with or a member of the World Harvest Church Ministerial Fellowship, the United Christian Church and Ministerial Association, Miracle Revival Fellowship, the Celtic Anabaptist Communion, the Reformed Catholic Church of America, the Cowboy Ministers Association, and the Coalition of Spirit-filled Churches.

Membership: Not reported.

Sources:

Christ's Church Fellowship. www.24-7jesuschurch.net/.

Church of God by Faith

2409 Old Middleburg N, Jacksonville, FL 32210

The Church of God by Faith was organized in 1914 by Elder John Bright and chartered in 1923 at Alachua, Florida. Its doctrine is like that of the Church of God (Cleveland, Tennessee). It believes in one Lord, one faith and one baptism, and in the word of God as the communion of the body and blood of Christ. Members isolate willful sinners from the church. Polity is episcopal and officers consist of the bishop, general overseer, and executive secretary. A general assembly meets two times a year. The church experienced significant growth through the 1980s and now has congregations in 13 states.

Membership: In 2008 the Church reported 162 congregations scattered across the United States.

Periodicals: *The Spiritual Guide*.

Sources:

Church of God by Faith. www.cogbf.org.

Church of the Little Children

89 Home Place Tr., Pocahontas, AR 72455

The Church of the Little Children was formed in 1916 by John Quincy Adams (1890–1951) in Abbott, Texas, following his withdrawal from the Baptist ministry. In 1930, he transferred his headquarters to Canada in Gunn, Alberta. After his death, his widow succeeded him, remarried, and returned to the United States in Black Rock, Arkansas.

The church is Oneness Pentecostal—that is, denying the Trinity and identifying Jesus with the Father—and has picked up elements of its doctrine from a number of traditions. The writings of Adams constitute the sole source of doctrinal teachings. The group practices foot washing. Wine is used in communion. The Trinity, Sunday Sabbath, Christmas and Easter holidays, shaving of the male beard, wearing of neckties, and use of the names of the pagan deities for the days of the week are viewed as vestiges of pagan phallic worship. Conscientious objection is required and no alternative service allowed. Divine healing is emphasized and modern medicine is rejected. There also is a major emphasis on acts of altruism for young children; members try to prevent any child from suffering want or hunger.

The church is headed by a superintendent. Relative to other churches, the organization is loose and informal. Congregations are located in Arkansas, Missouri, Nebraska, Montana, Wyoming, and Saskatchewan. Each congregation is quite small and meets in a home. Contact between congregations is by written correspondence.

Membership: Not reported. In the early 1970s there were eight congregations and fewer than 100 members.

Church of the Lord (Aladura)

505 E 183rd St., Apt. #2, Bronx, NY 10458

Alternate Address: International Headquarters: PO Box 71, Shagamu, Ogun State, Nigeria.

In the early twentieth century in West Africa, new independent Christian churches emerged in reaction to paternalistic attitudes that dominated the mission churches. Among these new independent groups in Nigeria were the Aladura churches (Yoruban for prayer people). Among the largest of the Aladura churches, the Church of the Lord (Aladura) was founded by Josiah Ositelu (1902–1966) in 1930. Ositelu, a former Anglican schoolteacher, emerged as a leader in the massive 1930 revival that greatly extended the Aladura movement in West Africa. He was briefly associated with an American church, the Faith Tabernacle, is said to have had thousands of visions, and became involved in the prophetic exposure of witchcraft. He was associated with Joseph Shadare and Joseph Ayo Babalola (1904–1959) during the revival of 1930. Ositelu was known as a powerful healer, and broke his short affiliation with the Faith Tabernacle. When he dropped the affiliation, its leaders challenged his authority. The new Church of the Lord emphasized the exposing of witches (who were believed able to work malevolent magic) and the use of holy names and seals to guarantee miracles. Ositelu accepted polygamy and eventually married seven women. He claimed divine permission. Apart from polygamy, now disavowed, the church is an orthodox Trinitarian Christian group in the Pentecostal tradition that affirms the baptism of the Holy Spirit.

During the 1950s, Aladura churches spread to Ghana, Liberia, and Sierra Leone through the efforts of traveling Nigerian preachers, especially apostles Oduwole and Adelke Adejobi (1921–1991) of the Church of the Lord (Aladura), and new Ghanaian churches in the traditions of Aladura seceded. From Africa, the Aladura churches then spread to Europe. Including the churches of African Caribbean origin, in 1995 there were estimated to be between 200 and 300 black-led denominations in some 3,000 congregations in Britain. Ositelu was succeeded by Adejobi, who had attended a Bible college in Scotland. While in Great Britain, he had also established a congregation in London. A gifted leader, he helped expand the Church of the Lord in Sierra Leone, Liberia, and Ghana (where he built a large and influential following). He led in the creation of the Nigeria Association of Aladura Churches during the 1950s and the Organization of African Instituted Churches (1978), which he served as the first chairperson. The Church of the Lord (Aladura) was also responsible for establishing both the Aladura Theological Seminary and the Prophets and Prophetesses Training Institute in 1965. Following Adejobi's death in 1991, Ositelu's eldest son, Gabriel Segun Ositelu (1938–1998), became the third primate. He was succeeded by his brother, Rufus Okikiola Ositelu (b. 1952), who leads the church as of 2008.

The first Church of the Lord congregation was opened in Britain in 1964. From England, it spread to other European countries (especially Germany) and more recently to the United States, where it has provided a home for many first generation African residents. The Church of the Lord (Aladura) was admitted to the World Council of Churches in 1975.

Membership: Not reported.

Educational Facilities:

Aladura Theological Seminary, Shagamu, Ogun State, Nigeria.

Prophets and Prophetesses Training Institute, Lagos, Nigeria.

Sources:

Church of the Lord (Aladura) Worldwide Organization. aladura.net

Anderson, Allan H. *African Reformation: African Initiated Christianity in the Twentieth Century*. Trenton, NJ: Africa World Press, 2001.

Peel, J. D. Y. *Aladura: A Religious Movement among the Yoruba*. London: Oxford University Press, 1968.

Pobee, John S., and Gabriel Ositelu II. *African Initiatives in Christianity: The Growth, Gifts, and Diversities of Indigenous African Churches: A Challenge to the Ecumenical Movement*. Geneva: World Council of Churches, 1998.

Turner, Harold W. *History of African Independent Church: The Church of the Lord (Aladura)*. 2 vols. Oxford, UK: Clarendon, 1967.

Colonial Village Pentecostal Church of the Nazarene

Current address not obtained for this edition.

The Colonial Village Pentecostal Church of the Nazarene grew out of an independent congregation founded in 1968 by Bernard Gill (1924–1974), a former minister in the Church of the Nazarene. There followed an attempt to form the true church composed solely of "wholly sanctified" people who have the gifts of the Spirit operating within them, and who accept as their goal and mission the reformation of the parent denomination.

Gill had begun to think of himself as God's prophet of the latter rain, and he claimed to have received numerous revelations directly from God, as did one of the members, Mescal McIntosh (b. 1926). These were published in a periodical, the *Macedonian Call*, in 1974. In the July 3 issue, a resurrection was predicted. Two weeks later, Gill died. On August 11 a letter to readers of the *Macedonian Call* announced the belief of Gill's faithful followers that the prophecy obviously applied to their pastor, and that they were waiting in faith.

Membership: Not reported. No recent information has been received and the present status of the church is unknown.

Eagle Rock Fellowship

PO Box 151, Lakewood, CA 90714-1051

Eagle Rock Fellowship is a Holy Ghost (Pentecostal) fellowship that offers people the opportunity to fulfill their divine visions, in some cases ones that they had had earlier in life but failed to act upon. Among their priorities is restoring fallen ministers. Dr. Kay Howe, one of the founders, serves as the fellowship's president and chairman of the board.

The fellowship follows mainline Pentecostal beliefs. It affirms the Bible as the infallible word of God, the Trinity, and saving faith in Jesus Christ. It looks for the baptism of the Holy Spirit (accompanied with speaking in tongues) as a promise to all believers. Believers are baptized by immersion.

The fellowship offers licenses to ministers, ordination, and certificates to lay Christian workers. It will also charter churches. All affiliates must fully subscribe to its statement of faith. An executive board leads the fellowship. The founders of the fellowship are members of this board with a life tenure. The executive board approves all licenses, ordinations, and charters. Chartered churches remain autonomous, but send an annual affiliation fee and monthly offering to the fellowship headquarters.

Eagle Rock Fellowship offers a variety of programs to enhance those of its affiliated congregations. These include a youth fellowship (Youth in Action) that holds monthly rallies, camps, and other activities; a woman's fellowship (Women in Action) with periodic rallies, retreats, and activities; and a monthly Eagle Rock Fellowship Jubilee that features musical programs, preaching, and illustrated sermons. The fellowship bible college offers both resident and correspondence instruction.

Educational Facilities:

Streamliners Bible College, Lakewood, California.

Periodicals: *ERF Monthly Newsletter*.

Sources:

Eagle Rock Fellowship. www.eaglerock-fellowship.org.

Evangelical Bible Church

2444 Washington Blvd., Baltimore, MD 21230

The Evangelical Bible Church was founded by the Rev. Frederick B. Marine in 1947. The doctrine is similar to that of the Assemblies of God (see separate entry), but great emphasis is placed on the three baptisms for New Testament believers: the baptism into Christ when a person is born again, water baptism, and Spirit baptism. The church teaches that any doubtful practice that is not forbidden in the New Testament should be left to individual judgment. There are definite statements on meat, drinks, days for worship, and clothing attire. The church teaches conscientious objection and is against worldly organizations that would inhibit spiritual growth, character, and commitment to God. A pretribulation, premillennial eschatology is taught.

The polity is congregational and there is an annual convention of both ministers and laity. Officers of the church include the general superintendent, the assistant general superintendent, and the general secretary. There are three orders of ministers: exhorter, evangelist, and ordained minister. Foreign missions are conducted in the Philippines where the church is known as the Evangelical Bible Church of Cotabato, Philippines, and in Nigeria where it is known as the Soul Winners Christian Mission.

Membership: Not reported. In 1992 there were six churches (four in Maryland, one in West Virginia, and one in Pennsylvania) and 300 members.

Faith Assembly

2214 E Winona Ave., Warsaw, IN 46580

Hobart E. Freeman (1920–1984), originally a minister with the Southern Baptist Convention, founded Faith Assembly. Among other things, Freeman began to criticize the Baptists for the celebration of Christmas and Easter, which he felt were pagan holidays. In 1959 he entered Grace Theological Seminary at Winona Lake, Indiana, the seminary of the Fellowship of Grace Brethren Churches, which he joined. After receiving his doctorate in 1961, Freeman joined the faculty to teach Old Testament. He became increasingly critical of the Brethren Church, especially on the issue of holidays, and in 1963 was dismissed from the seminary and excommunicated from the Fellowship of Grace Brethren Churches. Fellowship meetings held in Freeman's home became the Church at Winona Lake, Indiana. It soon moved to Claypool, Indiana. The initial beliefs of the church were similar to those of the Brethren, though they espoused a concept of closed worship.

In 1966, in Chicago, Freeman experienced the baptism of the Holy Spirit. He began to read the works of popular charismatic leaders such as Kenneth Hagin, Kenneth Copeland, and John Osteen, as well as those of the late E. W. Kenyon. He also met Mel Greide, who owned a large barn near North Webster, Indiana, which was converted into a church hall. From 1972 to 1978 Faith Assembly, as the church had been renamed, met at "Glory Barn." After a split with Greide, Freeman moved the assembly to Warsaw, Indiana, until a facility could be built at Wilmot. During the 1970s, Freeman began to write many books and booklets that circulated through the larger charismatic movements and he frequently spoke at charismatic conventions. His books and tapes led to the formation of home groups around the eastern half of the United States, with a concentration in the Midwest.

The beliefs of Faith Assembly are similar to those of the Assemblies of God, differing more in emphases than in doctrine. Freeman taught what is popularly called "positive confession" or "faith-formula theology." Freeman, like other faith-formula

teachers, taught that when genuine faith is exercised by the believer and accompanied by a positive confession of that faith, anything is possible, especially physical healing. Unlike such faith-formula teachers as Hagin or Copeland, Freeman taught that medicine was satanic and he forbade members from using the services of doctors. Assembly members remove seat belts from their cars and do not take immunization shots or use medicines. He also emphasized a rigid behavioral code that included personal separation from smoking, alcohol, drugs, and popular entertainment such as movies. Members do not borrow money. Young adults are counseled against careers in law, medicine, insurance, or pharmacology. Abortion was also forbidden, and natural childbirth recommended.

Membership: There are approximately 2,000 members of the main church in Wilmot, Indiana, and an estimated 15,000 in an unknown number of other congregations in 20 states. There are also members in Canada, Australia, Switzerland, and Germany.

Remarks: During the 1970s, family members of people associated with Faith Assembly congregations began to complain of its disturbing family relations. Several deprogrammings occurred. In 1983 a major controversy erupted around the Faith Assembly when charges were made that a number of people, many of them children, had died of medically treatable ailments. In 1984 several parents were convicted of child neglect and reckless homicide, and Freeman was indicted on felony charges for responsibility in the death of an assembly member's child. He died before going to trial.

Sources:

Faith Assembly. frontpage.kconline.com/faithassembly.

Crowell, Rodney J. *The Checkbook Bible: The Teachings of Hobart E. Freeman and Faith Assembly*. Miamisburg, OH: Author, 1981.

Freeman, Hobart E. *Angels of Light?*. Plainfield, NJ: Logos International, 1969.

————. *Charismatic Body Ministry*. Claypool, IN: Faith Publications, n.d.

————. *Deeper Life in the Spirit*. Warsaw, IN: Faith Publications, 1970.

————. *Positive Thinking & Confession*. Claypool, IN: Faith Publications, n.d.

Full Gospel Assemblies International

PO Box 1230, Coatesville, PA 19320-1230

Alternate Address: 3018 Lincoln Hwy., Parkesburg, PA 19365

Full Gospel Assemblies International was founded in 1972 by Dr. Charles E. Strauser, an independent charismatic minister. Some years earlier, Strauser had founded the Full Gospel Bible Institute to train ministers. The Full Gospel Assemblies provided an affiliation for the ministers as they began to pastor churches. Over the years, as the charismatic movement has blossomed, pastors and churches not otherwise affiliated with the school have become part of the Assemblies fellowship. Notices of the existence of the school and association have appeared monthly in *Charisma* magazine for a number of years.

Membership: In 1995 the assemblies reported 3,960 members in 44 churches, served by 290 ministers.

Periodicals: *The Charisma Courier*. Available from PO Box 1230, Coatesville, PA 19320.

Sources:

Full Gospel Assemblies International. www.fgai.org.

Full Gospel Defenders Conference of America

Current address not obtained for this edition.

The Full Gospel Defenders Conference of America is a small Pentecostal body with headquarters in Philadelphia. Its emphasis is on evangelism and Christ's authority as manifested by the miracles and signs.

Membership: Not reported.

Full Gospel Minister Association

Current address not obtained for this edition.

The Full Gospel Minister Association is a fellowship of Pentecostal ministers and churches believing in the infallibility of the Bible, the Trinity, the fall of man and his need for redemption in Christ, the necessity of holy living, and heaven and hell. Members are conscientious objectors to war. The group sees ministry as being twofold: the evangelism of the world and the edifying of the body of Christ and the "confirming of the Word with Signs Following and evidence of the power of God." The association meets annually and elects officers. It issues credentials for both churches and ministers.

Membership: Not reported.

Glad Tidings Missionary Society

3456 Fraser St., Vancouver, BC, Canada V5V 4C4

The Latter Rain Movement, a revival movement within the larger Pentecostal movement, began in 1948 in a Bible school in North Battleford, Saskatchewan. Among the first churches to invite leaders of the new movement to speak was the Glad Tidings Temple in Vancouver, British Columbia, where Reg Layzell pastored. Layzell became an enthusiastic supporter of the revival, and the temple became a major center from which the revival spread around the continent. The Glad Tidings Missionary Society began as an extension of the Glad Tidings Temple. Over the years the society brought other congregations affected by the Latter Rain revival (in Canada and the state of Washington) into association with the temple. The Missionary Society itself became a primary religious body, conducting mission work in Africa, Taiwan, and the Arctic.

Membership: Not reported. In the 1970s there were eight churches; three in Washington and five in Canada.

Global Network of Christian Ministries

PO Box 154747, Irving, TX 75015

The Global Network of Christian Ministries, previously known as Global Christian Ministries and Network of Christian Ministries, was founded in the 1980s as a fellowship of otherwise independent Christian ministers that has as its stated purpose the honoring of "the Lord Jesus Christ by assisting His servants in fulfilling their God-given callings... by making available those opportunities that can only be realized through working together." Basic to fulfilling its purpose is the supplying of credentials to unattached ministers in need of licensing and ordination. The network also supplies the opportunity for belonging and affiliation with something larger than the individual and a particular ministry. It does not attempt to influence the methodology of anyone's ministry.

The network is a conservative Pentecostal body that affirms the inerrancy of Scripture and the Trinity. Its statement of faith states "that the baptism in the Holy Sprit is an endowment of power given by God to anoint the believer for sanctification and evangelism. It is our understanding that the supernatural gifts of the Holy Spirit are active within the body of Christ until the coming of the Lord. Furthermore, we believe that the development of these gifts ought to be encouraged under the guidance of local church authority." It teaches the five-fold ministry of Ephesians 4:11 but affirms that the church is primarily known through the local church. The network encourages voluntary association, but strongly affirms the sovereignty and autonomy of the local church.

The network is headed by a board of directors, an executive board, and a board of elders. It sponsors an annual national conference each fall and regional meeting each spring for the seven regions within the United States.

Membership: In 2008 the network reported 279 churches in the United States and seven in Canada.

Sources:

Global Network of Christian Ministries. global-ministries.com.

Gospel Assemblies (Sowders/Goodwin)

c/oGospel Assembly Church, 7135 Meredith Dr., Des Moines, IA 50322

HISTORY. William Sowders (1879–1952) was one of the early Pentecostal leaders in the Midwest. He was brought into the movement through the labors of Bob Shelton who had established a work in Olmstead, Illinois. In 1912 Sowders, a former Methodist, was converted and received the baptism of the Holy Spirit on a gospel boat that Shelton was operating on the Ohio River. In 1914, Sowders began preaching at various locations, finally settling in Evansville, Indiana, in 1921.

In 1923 Sowders conducted his first camp meeting at Elco, Illinois. Here he began to introduce the distinctive teachings that were to separate him from the main body of Pentecostals and lead to the emergence of what became known as the Gospel of the Kingdom movement or the Gospel Assembly Churches movement. Sowders developed his position in the context of the debates between the trinitarian Pentecostals and the Apostolic or Oneness Pentcostals, whose ideas denying the traditional doctrine of the Trinity had been spread through the Midwest by Thomas Garfield Haywood (1880–1931), founder of the Pentecostal Assemblies of the World. Sowders proposed a middle position and suggested that there were two persons in the Godhead, God the Father, a Spirit being, and Jesus the Son, a Heavenly Creature. The Holy Ghost was not a person; it was the essence or Spirit of God that filled all space. Since the Son possessed the same name as the Father, God's name was Jesus. Jesus was the name given to the family of God in Heaven and on earth. Baptism was, therefore, in the name of the Father, Son, and Holy Spirit, (i.e., Jesus). He also emphasized that the formula for baptism was not as important as the action, that baptism became an action done in Jesus' name and for his sake, but could not be done in Jesus' name if one belonged to Babylon.

In 1927 Sowders relocated in Louisville, Kentucky, where he lived for the rest of his life. In 1935 he purchased a 350-acre tract near Shepherdsville, Kentucky, which became the Gospel of the Kingdom Campground, a place for camp meetings and annual ministerial gatherings. Estimates vary, but as many as 200 ministers and 25,000 members in 31 states were associated with the movement at the time of Sowders's death in 1952.

Following his death there were attempts by several ministers to assume leadership and several schisms emerged. The larger fellowship continued until 1965 under the direction of Tom M. Jolly. The movement continued, however, as a loose fellowship of ministers who pastored independent gospel assemblies. Among these men was Lloyd L. Goodwin (d.1996), a young minister at the time of Sowders's passing, whose parents had been among the early converts of Sowders's ministry. In 1963 Goodwin moved to Des Moines, Iowa, to pastor the Gospel Assembly Church, a congregation of fewer than 30 members. Over the next decade he built it into a large stable congregation. In the late 1960s, due to his missionary activities, new congregations were started around the United States. In the early 1970s, Goodwin began to encounter tension with the larger fellowship of Gospel of the Kingdom ministers who rejected some of the doctrines that Goodwin believed had been revealed to him by God through his study of the scriptures. The break with the fellowship came in 1972.

After the break with the larger fellowship, a new movement began to grow around Goodwin beginning with those few ministers and congregations who sided with him. In 1973 he outlined a six-point program to his congregation in Des Moines. It included the development of the local assembly, the dissemination of Goodwin's teachings in print and sound media, and the sending of ministers to found other assemblies both in the United States and abroad. In 1974 the Gospel Assembly Christian Academy, a Christian elementary and high school, was opened. The following year foreign work was initiated in Toronto, Canada, and Poona, India. Africa, Singapore, and the Philippines soon followed. A book and tape ministry was launched in 1977. Goodwin has written a number of substantial volumes that detail his distinct Bible teachings, especially on eschatological matters. A radio ministry begun on one station in 1981 had grown by 1987 to 17 stations that reached most of the eastern half of the United States and the West Indies.

BELIEFS. Apart from the distinctive ideas about the Godhead first articulated by Sowders, the Gospel Assemblies have a statement of faith that affirms many of the traditional evangelical Christian beliefs in the authority of the Bible, creation, the fall of humanity, the vicarious substitutionary atonement of Christ, the baptism of the Holy Spirit, water baptism, and the imminent Second Coming. It is the belief of the movement that Christ will come while some who are alive today are still living. The ordinance of holy communion is also recognized and observed.

ORGANIZATION. The Gospel Assemblies is described as a fellowship of ministers and saints around the world, where no church is organized above the local level, and yet where each assembly is in fellowship with all, and all acknowledge and are part of each in the fellowship. The churches recognize five ministerial offices in the church. First, apostles establish the work throughout the body of Christ. According to the Gospel Assemblies, "There is not another office in the ministry as authoritative as that of the apostle. The apostle stands next to Christ." Goodwin was such an apostle. Second, the prophet exhorts, edifies, and comforts. Third, the evangelists preach the news of salvation. Fourth, the pastors shepherd the saints. Fifth, the teachers instruct the church in doctrine. The five offices are not appointed, but recognized as possessed by some as gifts of God. A single individual may hold several of these offices. Appointed to handle the temporal affairs of the local church are deacons under the supervision of elders. There are regular conventions of the churches around the world, the main convention being held at Des Moines each May.

Prior to his death, Goodwin began to call for the healng of the divisions in the fellowship of churches that originated under Sowders. He proclaimed that the end-time church will confront organized religion and an apostate state; and further that the fellowship of churches that orignated with William Sowders, or a remnant of that fellowship, will be raised up by God to give a final witness to the world. Since his death in 1996, there has been increasing communication and fellowship between the various divisions of the movement that originated with William Sowders.

Membership: In 2002 there were an estimated 250 congregations and approximately 50,000 members. Gospel assemblies in fellowship with the Gospel Assembly Church in Des Moines can now be found across the United States (including Hawaii), Canada, Ukraine, Russia, Poland, Norway, England, India, Singapore, Australia, the Philippines, South America, and throughout the continent of Africa.

Periodicals: *The Gospel of Peace Newsletter.*

Sources:

Gospel Assembly Church. www.dmgospelassembly.org.

The Former Days: A Brief History of the Body of Jesus Christ in These Last Days. Des Moines, IA: Gospel Assembly Church, n.d., 21 pp.

Goodwin, Lloyd L. *Prophecy Concerning the Church.* 2 vols. Des Moines, IA: Gospel Assembly Church, 1977.

———. *Prophecy Concerning the Resurrection.* Des Moines, IA: Gospel Assembly Church, 1976.

———. *Prophecy Concerning the Second Coming.* Des Moines, IA: Gospel Assembly Church, 1979.

Gospel Assemble Churches. Worldwide Fellowship, Pentecostal-Nondenominational. Des Moines, IA: Gospel Assembly Church, 1995.

Gospel Assembly, Twenty-Five Years, 1963–1988. Des Moines, IA: Gospel Assembly Church, 1988.

Ministers' Address Directory. Norfolk, VA: Gospel Assembly Ministers' Fund, 1970.

Gospel Crusade Ministerial Fellowship (GCMF)

1200 Glory Way Blvd., Bradenton, FL 34212

Gospel Crusade Ministerial Fellowship (GCMF), an arm of the Gospel Crusade Inc. ministry, was founded in the 1960s by charismatic evangelist/pastor Gerald G. Derstine, the president of Gospel Crusade. GCMF issues ministerial credentials to men and women involved in the Gospel ministry and fosters connections among ministers, churches, and ministries. The fellowship was created to enable believers to develop their God-given vision for ministry and become successful in the fulfillment of their vision and calling.

GCMF is governed by a group of presbyters who form the board of directors and are the corporate officers. There are more than 20 geographic districts, each with a leader called a district coordinator. The district coordinators are the elders of the fellowship and meet twice a year as an advisory council. They are committed to facilitate, assist, counsel, support, and help augment the ministry of the Gospel Crusade Ministerial Fellowship.

Each member (minister) is expected to attend the conferences and fellowship activities in his or her district, to attend the annual convocation at Christian Retreat, Florida, to support GCMF with monthly dues amounting to one percent of his or her personal income, and to submit an annual report of his or her ministry when he or she files the annual credential renewal forms.

Clergy in Canada, the Caribbean, Haiti, Honduras, Ghana, Israel, India, and the Philippines hold credentials through GCMF.,

Membership: In 2006 the GCMF reported more than 1,500 active ministers in the United States, Canada, and 24 other nations.

Periodicals: *Current Blessing.*

Educational Facilities:

International Training Center, Bradenton, Florida.

Sources:

Gospel Crusade Ministerial Fellowship. www.gospelcrusade.net/.

Gospel Harvesters Evangelistic Association (Buffalo)

Current address not obtained for this edition.

The Gospel Harvesters Evangelistic Association, a Pentecostal body identical in name to the church headquartered in Atlanta and completely separate in organization, was founded in 1962 in Buffalo, New York, by Rose Pezzino. No information on doctrine or polity is available. Foreign work was initiated in Manila and India.

Membership: Not reported. In the mid-1970s there were an estimated 2,000 adherents.

Gospel Ministers & Churches International/Gospel Alliance Church

2501 W Dunlap, Ste. 185, Phoenix, AZ 85021

Gospel Ministers & Churches International (GMCI) was founded in August 1982 as a full-gospel (charismatic Pentecostal) ministerial association. It has members across the United States and around the world. Associated with it is a congregational association, the Gospel Alliance Church. Though it does not have a specific set of beliefs, GMCI considers itself a "Spirit-filled" organization, meaning that it believes the Gifts of the Spirit (I Corinthians 12) are still active and operational today, and that the presence of the Holy Spirit is made known by the phenomenon of speaking in tongues.

GMCI's stated goal is to assist various ministries in fulfilling the call of God. It accomplishes this goal by providing legal covering for churches, credentials for individuals in ministry, and opportunities for fellowship and networking. Licenses are provided in four categories. The Christian worker is issued to persons assisting ministers. Such workers are not authorized to perform any sacerdotal services (especially weddings and funerals). Commissioned ministers are generally those at the beginning of their ministerial career. They are authorized to preach, but not to perform sacerdotal services. A general ministerial license is issued to those who have been working as a minister but have never been formally ordained by the "laying on of hands." Such ministers are authorized to perform all sacerdotal services, but may not be called upon to perform them regularly. The ordained minister is recognized as a person with an "established" ministry and has found the approval of his or her peers. Usually, ordination is not by GMCI but by a local church. Ordained ministers are authorized to perform all sacerdotal services.

Churches and parachurch ministries affiliate with GMCI by seeking a charter through the Gospel Alliance Church. They fellowship together under the motto, "Fellowship without Bondage, Unity without Compromise."

In 2008 GMCI was headed by Bishop Gordon H. Douglas. The organization sponsors an annual conference for members and other gatherings such as the regional Fellowship Encounters, which feature a praise and worship service with a keynote speaker. Some GMCI mission projects have been selected for corporate support by the GMCI membership. GMCI also offers several nontraditional educational opportunities, including study courses of the life, ministry, and eternality of Christ.

Membership: Not reported.

Sources:

Gospel Ministers & Churches International. www.gmci.org/.

Gospel Revelation, Inc.

PO Box 52, Connersville, IN 47331

Gospel Revelation, Inc., is a Full Gospel (Penetcostal/charismatic) fellowship of churches and ministers founded in 1971 by Rev. James E. Gay. In his travels as a missionary, Gay came to the realization that he needed a chartered church organization to issue receipts for the gifts that he accepted for his ministry. He also resolved to develop an easier way for a minister to receive a license, be ordained, or obtain a church charter. He established Gospel Revelation, Inc., to serve that purpose.

Gay wanted the organization to assist people who might have been abused or disillusioned by their former church fellowships, including those who were called to God but had been blocked from being ordained. At first, he ordained anyone who asked; however, to avoid ordaining people who were completely unqualified, he changed his policy, requiring a recommendation for another minister prior to offering any credentials.

The organization offers ordination apart from the regulations and controls normally associated with membership in an ecclesiastical structure. Credentials are offered for licensed and ordained ministers who can then perform marriages, conduct funerals, and baptize believers. Licensed exhorters cannot perform these functions, but can preach and assist ministers.

Membership: Not reported.

Sources:

Gospel Revelation, Inc. www.gospelrevelation.com/.

Integrity Communications (and Related Ministries)

PO Box Z, Mobile, AL 36616

In the midst of chaos in the emerging pentecostal/charismatic movement of the early 1970s, a group of experienced pastors/leaders stepped forward with a proposed solution. They suggested that submission, discipline, and respect for law and order were needed, and that the movement stood under a divine mandate to develop a program for discipleship and the development of Christian maturity along biblical principles. They suggested that the New Testament norm was that each believer become directly accountable for others as a shepherd or spiritual guide that would demonstrate the Christian life. This concept became popularly known as discipling/shepherding.

Leading proponents of the discipling/shepherding concept were Charles Simpson (b. 1937), a former minister with the Southern Baptist Convention, Bob Mumford (b. 1930), former Dean of Elim Bible Institute; William John Ernest "Ern" Baxter (1914–1993), formerly a colleague of healer William M. Branham

(1909–1965); Derek Prince (1915–2003), an independent leader of a radio ministry; John Poole, pastor of a church in Philadelphia; and Don Basham (1926–1989), a former minister with the Christian Church (Disciples of Christ). In 1970 these six men made a personal covenant with each other and began the task of making disciples who could, in turn, become shepherds engaged in making disciples. In their many travels they established local presbyteries of elders who became leaders of congregations related to the six ministers. These elders then fulfilled roles as apostolic leaders for those congregations. (The relationship between the local congregational elders and the leaders in Fort Lauderdale has been referred to as a "translocal" relationship.) Simpson, Mumford, Baxter, Prince, and Basham then founded Good News Church in Fort Lauderdale, Florida, and began Christian Growth Ministries. A magazine, *New Wine*, disseminated their teachings. Numerous books and tapes were produced that dealt with various aspects of church life and Christian growth. While working together, some of the original group also developed independent ministries under different names, such as Bob Mumford's Lifechangers.

In 1975 the issues raised by the group became a matter of intense controversy within the larger charismatic community, and major steps were taken to resolve the differences. Critics were concerned over the abuse of authority that occurred in the shepherding relationship; shepherds interfered in the personal affairs of those whom they were leading. In the more extreme cases, anticultists attempted deprogrammings of people in congregations that were organized around the shepherding principles. Several meetings between the leaders of Christian Growth Ministries and other charismatic movements resulted in the resolution of the many misunderstandings that had grown out of rumors and unverified accusations. Differences on the shepherding principle remained, however.

In 1978 Christian Growth Ministries and *New Wine* were moved to Mobile, Alabama. At that time, Derek Prince stepped down as chairman of the board in favor of Simpson. Simpson initiated a new congregation, Gulf Coast Covenant Church, and Christian Growth Ministries became Integrity Communications. Leaving the Fort Lauderdale work in local hands, Basham, Mumford, and Baxter joined Simpson in Mobile. Prince remained in Fort Lauderdale as head of his own Derek Prince Ministries. As early as January 1975, following a visit by Simpson to Costa Rica, a Spanish-speaking congregation was established and elders were appointed. Christian Growth Ministries immediately initiated *Vino Nuevo*, the Spanish edition of *New Wine*. By 1980 it was being sent to believers in fifteen countries.

In 1984 Prince announced his withdrawal from Integrity Communications. Among his reasons, he cited his disagreement with the opinion that every Christian should have a personal human pastor, and the practice of one pastor overseeing another translocally.

It has been the stated goal of the leaders of Integrity Communications not to allow the congregations associated with it, or the elders who derive authority from them, to develop into a "denomination." However, those churches and congregations have formed a distinct grouping within the larger Pentecostal community. In 1986, the four remaining leaders of Integrity Communications decided to decentralize their ministries as a means of stopping a trend toward "denominationalism." With this decision, Baxter moved to San Diego, Mumford to San Rafael, California, and Basham to Cleveland. *New Wine* was discontinued and replaced with *Christian Conquest*, edited by Simpson, who has remained in Mobile, Alabama. The group continues to meet periodically.

Membership: In 1986, *New Wine* had a circulation of 55,000, though its audience went far beyond the members of the church due to an oversight at Integrity Communications.

Periodicals: *Christian Conquest*.

Sources:

Basham, Don. *A Handbook on Holy Spirit Baptism*. Monroeville, PA: Whitaker Books, 1969.

————. *Ministering the Baptism of the Holy Spirit*. Monroeville, PA: Whitaker Books, 1971.

Mumford, Bob. *Take Another Look at Guidance*. Plainfield, NJ: Logos International, 1971.

Simpson, Charles. *A New Way to Live*. Greensburg, PA: Manna Christian Outreach, 1975.

Vintage Years. Mobile, AL: New Wine Magazine, 1980.

Interdenominational Ministries International (IMI)

PO Box 2107, Vista, CA 92085-2107

The Interdenominational Ministries International (IMI) originated in 1980 in a series of home prayer groups initiated by the Rev. Dr. Rocco Bruno and his wife, the Rev. Dr. Mary Bruno, in Vista, California (north of San Diego). Their work was incorporated in 1983 and the following year missionary teams began work in Mexico. Within a few years the work outgrew the small home-based groups with which it began, and the present-day name was adopted to reflect its new status. Because those who desired to work with the IMI manifested a need for training, the IMI Correspondence School of Ministry emerged around a curriculum focused in Bible study, theology, and preaching. The school added degree programs through the doctoral level, which includes degrees in Biblical Studies, Christian Education, Divinity, Ministry, Pastoral Christian Counseling, and Theology. Following full non-governmental accreditation by Transworld Accrediting Commission and the Accrediting Commission International, the school name was changed to IMI Bible College and Seminary to better reflect the range of degree levels offered. The diplomas and degrees programs are accomplished off campus by students from many different countries and continents. Students are drawn from various Evangelical denominations, though most are from Pentecostal and Charismatic churches.

The IMI is committed to an Orthodox Christian perspective with an affirmation of the baptism of the Holy Spirit, divine healing, and the necessity of holy living. Both baptism and the Lord's Supper are practiced. The Bible is taught as the Word of God.

IMI offers ordination and credentials to ministers (especially those who have completed a course of study at the IMI school) for a variety of independent ministries. IMI is affiliated with the Chaplaincy of Full Gospel Churches.

Membership: Not reported.

Educational Facilities:

IMI Bible College and Seminary, Vista, California.

International Christian Churches

Current address not obtained for this edition.

The International Christian Churches, founded in 1943 by Rev. Franco Manuel, is a Pentecostal group formed by former members of the Christian Church (Disciples of Christ) in Hawaii. Members consider themselves "Disciples by confession and Pentecostal by persuasion." They accept the Pentecostal doctrines and place emphasis on life in the Spirit. The church functions on the loose congregational polity typical of the Disciples of Christ.

Membership: Not reported. In the 1970s there was one congregation in Honolulu with several hundred members; an additional seven churches were in the Philippines.

International Evangelism Crusades

21601 Devonshire St., No. 217, Chatsworth, CA 91311-8415

International Evangelism Crusades was founded in 1959 by Dr. Frank E. Stranges, its president, and Revs. Natale Stranges, Bernice Stranges, and Warren MacKall. Dr. Stranges has become well-known as president of the National Investigations Committee on Unidentified Flying Objects and for his claims that he has contacted space people. International Evangelism Crusades was formed as a ministerial fellowship to hold credentials for independent ministers. As a denomination it is organized as an association of ministers and congregations unhampered by a dictating central headquarters.

The doctrine of the organization is similar to the Assemblies of God. A Canon of Ethics is stressed, the breaking of which constitutes grounds for expulsion from the fellowship.

Membership: In 2002 International Evangelism Crusades reported 85 congregations and 125 ministers in the United States and a worldwide membership of 350,000. Associated foreign congregations can be found in Canada, Mexico, Korea, Jamaica, and Africa.

Educational Facilities:

International Theological Seminary of California, Chatsworth, California.

Heavenly People Theological Seminary, Hong Kong.

International Christian Seminary, South Korea.

International Theological Seminary, Indonesia, with five branches in New York City and South Korea.

Periodicals: *IEC Newsletter*. • *Inter Space Link Newsletter*.

Sources:

International Theological Seminary of California. www.itscusa.com/index.html.

Stranges, Frank E. *My Friend from Beyond Earth*. Van Nuys, CA: IEC, 1960.

————. *Like Father—Like Son*. Palo Alto, CA: International Evangelism Crusades, 1961.

————. *The UFO Conspiracy*. Van Nuys, CA: IEC Publishing, 1985.

International Ministerial Fellowship

PO Box 32366, Minneapolis, MN 55432

Founded in 1958, the International Ministerial Fellowship (IMF) is a charismatic fellowship that offers credentials to independent Pentecostal ministers. On October 25, 1960, IMF was chartered as a Texas nonprofit corporation by Pastor F. C. Masserano, Sr., Dr. George Steiglitz, Rev. C. R. McPhail, and a group of men and women who saw a need to establish a fellowship of nondenominational ministers committed to preach and teach the Gospel of Christ, promote a fellowship among nondenominational ministers, build churches, publish Gospel-related materials, and support missions. Ministers may serve churches or work in noncongregational chaplaincies and ministries. The fellowship also charters independent congregations.

Membership: In 2004 the fellowship reported 1,250 members in the United States and 88 missionaries in 40 other countries.

Periodicals: *The Gathering*.

Sources:

International Ministerial Fellowship. www.i-m-f.org/.

International Ministers Forum

433 Oak St., PO Box 1717, Dayton, OH 45401-1717

The United Ministers Forum is a Pentecostal fellowship founded in 1950 by Rev. Louise Copeland. As an international organization, it ordains and grants licenses to ministers serving independent churches, serving churches affiliated with other fellowships, or engaging in special ministries.

The forum affirms the Bible as the infallible Word of God, the Trinity, the deity of Christ, the indwelling of the Holy Spirit signified by speaking in tongues, and the unity of believers. The fellowship acknowledges all Christians who have been saved by the blood of Jesus Christ as members of the body of Christ.

The fellowship holds an annual convention in Dayton at the United Christian Center, where its headquarters are located. The fellowship is currently headed by its president, Rev. Doris J. Swartz. Members are found in Mexico, Romania, Honduras, India, Africa, Brazil, Guatemala, and Russia.

Membership: In 1997 the fellowship reported 450 ministerial members in the United States and an additional 150 in other countries.

Kingdom and World Mission of Our Lord Jesus Christ

PO Box 3600, Los Angeles, CA 90078-3600

The Kingdom and World Mission of Our Lord Jesus Christ was incorporated in 1984 by Elie Khoury. Born and raised in Egypt, Khoury was given a message from God in 1960 concerning the war between Egypt and Israel that would occur in 1967. Following the delivery of this message to the Jews in 1965, he was imprisoned and tortured by the Egyptian government. He was released in 1968 but was arrested again. After a second period in prison, he migrated to the United States and opened the mission.

The mission is centered upon a single congregation in Southern California. Khoury is a Pentecostal and preaches the baptism of the Holy Spirit as evidenced by speaking in tongues, the laying on of hands for the sick, and the other gifts of the Spirit. The mission is dedicated to the cause of support for Israel and peace between Israel and its neighbors and exists to serve people in the name of Jesus Christ. Among its primary services, it assists refugees to settle and become permanent residents in the United States.

Membership: The mission reports over 5,000 members in the United States served by 5 ministers. Worldwide, the mission claims some 65,000 members, most of whom reside in Lebanon and Egypt.

Educational Facilities:

Kingdom and World Mission of Our Lord Jesus Christ School of Theology, Los Angeles, California.

Kingsway Fellowship International

3707 SW 9th St., Des Moines, IA 50315-3047

Kingsway Fellowship International, a Pentecostal fellowship of independent ministers and missionaries, was founded in 1968 by Dr. D. L. Browning (d. 2006), who served as its leader until 2000. In 2008 the bishop and executive overseer was Dr. William Jenkins. The fellowship offers ministerial services, counsel, and religious nonprofit status with the IRS to its members. It also seeks to mobilize its members as leaders in a worldwide evangelism/missionary effort.

The fellowship is incorporated and headed by a 13-member board of directors who appoint regional, district, and national superintendents to assist in the evangelism program. It offers credentials to Christian workers, lay-exhorters, and ordained ministers. It also charters churches and related ministries. It sponsors an annual conference, providing fellowship among its members.

Educational Facilities:

Kingsway Christian College, Norwalk, Iowa.

Membership: Not reported.

Sources:

Kingsway Fellowship International. www.kingswayfellowship.org/.

Liberty Fellowship of Churches and Ministers

5229 Kelly Elliott Rd., Arlington, TX 76017

The Liberty Fellowship of Churches and Ministers was organized in 1974 in Pensacola, Florida, by Ken Sumrall and 20 other ministers. Sumrall, a former pastor in the Southern Baptist Convention, received the baptism of the Holy Spirit in February 1964. The following month he organized Liberty Baptist Church (later Liberty Church) as a congregation for Spirit-filled Baptists. At first the work grew slowly, but membership increased markedly in 1966, the year the college began adjacent to the church. In 1972 land was purchased on the edge of Pensacola, and a building complex was constructed. During the 1970s other independent charismatic pastors who saw the need for oversight, for themselves and their congregations, began searching for a proper structure. They were influenced by other Pentecostal leaders who had in turn been influenced by the Latter-Rain

Movement. Such leaders as Bill Britton of Overcomers Fellowship in Springfield, Missouri, believed the church was properly led by a five-fold ministry of apostles, evangelists, prophets, pastors, and teachers (Ephesians 4:11-12).

The fellowship's doctrine is close to that of the Assemblies of God, including belief in the triune God, salvation through Christ, two ordinances (baptism and the Lord's Supper), divine healing, the present-day operation of the gifts of the Holy Spirit (I Corinthians 12), and the baptism of the Holy Spirit as an immediate possibility for the believer.

The fellowship is governed by a presbytery council headed by the executive director (originally the president). The first president, Sumrall, who resigned in 1990, was considered the apostle of the fellowship. The presbytery ordains and appoints pastors to local churches, and within its membership the entire five-fold ministry is represented. Local congregational affairs are administered by elders and deacons elected by the congregation and confirmed by the presbytery.

Membership: In 2008 the fellowship reported 19 member churches in 12 states.

Educational Facilities:

Liberty Christian College, Pensacola, Florida.

Sources:

Liberty Fellowship. www.libertyfellowship.org.

Church Foundational Network. www.churchfoundationalnetwork.com.

Ken Sumrall Ministries. www.kensumrallministries.com.

Sumrall, Ken. *New Wine Bottles*. Pensacola, FL: Liberty Creative Press, 1976.

———. *Practical Church Government: Organized Flexibility*. Pensacola, FL: Author, 1982.

Lighthouse Gospel Fellowship

Current address not obtained for this edition.

The Lighthouse Gospel Fellowship is a Pentecostal church founded in 1958 by Drs. H. A. Chaney and Thelma Chaney of Tulsa, Oklahoma. A set of beliefs are held in common by ministers and members. The fellowship is Trinitarian. It believes in the virgin birth, the bodily resurrection of Jesus, baptism of the Holy Spirit evidenced by speaking in tongues, the laying on of hands for the confirmation of ministry, and impartation of the gifts of the Spirit. However, the group also conceives of itself as nonsectarian and hence home to a variety of views on less essential beliefs.

Membership: Not reported. In the 1970s there were approximately 100 congregations and 1,000 members.

Messianic Bureau International (MBI)

c/o Mishkan HaMelekh, 701B Industrial Park Dr., Newport News, VA 23608

Messianic Bureau International (MBI), launched in 1994, began as an information service for the larger Messianic Jewish community, a Christian missionary movement directed at Jews. It gradually took on the characteristics of a new denominational body. In 1995 MBI established an Internet presence that found immediate acceptance within the Messianic community. In 1997 it created an online yeshiva (school) that evolved into a full seminary for the training of Messianic rabbis/ministers. In 1999 it began a broadcast ministry that supplies Christian music 24 hours daily through the Internet.

The various activities of MBI culminated in 2000 with the first MBI Messianic Conference, where for the first time ministers were commissioned and churches chartered. MBI's founder, Rabbi David Hargis (1951–2006), was the main spokesperson on matters of doctrine and policy for the organization. Ordained in 1973, he pastored Christian parishes until 1989 when he joined the Jewish Messianic movement and accepted reordination as a rabbi. He subsequently founded Mishkan HaMelekh (Tabernacle of the King) in the Tidewater area of Virginia.

MBI is a Pentecostal body but expresses its theological perspective using Hebrew terms. As set forth in its statement of faith, "The various enablements (gifts) of Ruach HaKodesh (Holy Spirit) are given with authority to all those who ask YHVH and obey His commandments. The Promise of Abba, an extra endowment of power and boldness for witnessing, is an immersion (spiritual mikveh) by Ruach HaKodesh, as initially was evidenced with speaking in other languages. Each follower should seek to be filled with the various enablements of the Ruach, who gives them as He wishes."

MBI is governed by a board of directors for business operations and a board of governors for spiritual operations. Rabbi Hargis was the president and general overseer of the board of directors and chairman of the board of governors until his death. The Board of Governors operates as a Beit Din (in traditional Judaism a court of law) to make decisions on matters of religious import.

MBI will credential individuals as cantors, as a Messianic minister, head elder (Rosh Zaken), or rabbi. A Messianic minister assumes one or more of the roles in the fivefold ministry (Ephesians 4:11) as pastor (roeh), evangelist (m'vasayr), teacher (moreh), prophet (navi), or apostle (shaliach). The rabbi serves as the leader or assistant leader of a congregation. MBI attempts to keep a cordial relationship with all of the Messianic Jewish groups and maintains links to their Web sites and a large directory of Messianic congregations and ministries on its Internet site.

Membership: In 2008 MBI reported 14 affiliated congregations.

Educational Facilities:

Messianic Bible Institute, Hampton, Virginia.

Sources:

Messianic Bureau International. www.messianicbureau.org/.

The Neverdies
Current address not obtained for this edition.

Known locally in the communities of West Virginia as the Church of the Living Gospel or the Church of the Everlasting Gospel, the Neverdies are Pentecostals who believe in immortality not only of the soul but also of the body. The soul, they believe, returns to earth in a series of reincarnations until it succeeds in living a perfect life. At that point, the body can live forever. The origin of the group has been lost, but among the first teachers was Ted Oiler, born in 1906, who in 1973 was still traveling a circuit through the mountains of Virginia and North Carolina. The congregations are rather loosely knit, held together by their acceptance of what is a rather unusual doctrine for the mountain area.

Membership: Not reported.

New Testament Holiness Church
c/o David Terrell, Jesus New Covenant Church, PO Box 100, Ashdown, AK 71822
Alternate Address: David Terrell Worldwide Revivals, PO Box 4800, Dallas, TX 75208.
David Terrell, as a child of nine in Alabama, was diagnosed with a form of bone cancer in his legs. Doctors advised amputation but his mother refused. In the end, he was miraculously healed. Terrell would go on to dedicate his life to assisting others in what would become an international independent Pentecostal ministry that has become known for the healings and other miraculous occurrences that have been reported to have occurred at the revival services led by Terrell. These have been carried forward under the auspices of David Terrell Worldwide Revivals, based in Dallas, Texas. Terrell has, over the years, offered numerous prophecies. In 1999 he reported a vision in which he was told that the "Times of the Gentiles," the present historical era, was soon coming to an end.

Out of his revival services, Terrell developed a significant following, and a number of independent churches were founded that supported his work, agreed with his teachings, and recognized him as an apostle and prophet. These took the name collectively as the New Testament Holiness Church, though local congregations had a variety of designations. In 1973 Terrell made Bangs, Texas, his headquarters but later moved to Arkansas. From there he travels through North America conducting tent revivals.

Terrell holds to a conservative form of Pentecostal faith. He believes in the authority of the Bible and admonishes people to use the King James Version, which he believes to be the true Word of God preserved in the English language. He opposes the celebration of Christmas, Halloween, and other pagan holidays. Terrell has written a number of booklets that are published and circulated by Worldwide Revivals.

Membership: Not reported. In 2002 Terrell's Web page listed some 30 churches identified with the New Testament Church of God, with one congregation in Canada.

Sources:

Brother David Terrell. davidterrell.org/home.html.

Pentecostal Full Gospel Church
Current address not obtained for this edition.

The Pentecostal Full Gospel Church was founded in 1922 as the Apostolic Churches of Christ. It is a Trinitarian church (though its articles of faith do not treat such basic theological concerns as the doctrine of God, Christ, or the Holy Spirit). There is an emphasis upon the baptism of the Holy Spirit as evidenced by speaking in tongues, healing out of the atonement of Jesus, three ordinances (baptism by immersion, the Lord's Supper, and foot washing), tithing, and the imminent return of Christ to reign on earth for a thousand years. At the Lord's Supper, unleavened bread and unfermented grape juice is used. There is a strong aversion to divorce and remarriage, and no ministerial credentials can be issued to divorced and/or remarried people.

The church is headed by a president elected at the annual convention. He appoints ministers to the local congregations. Pastors appoint local elders, deacons, and deaconesses.

Membership: Not reported.

Pentecostal 7th Day Assemblies
Current address not obtained for this edition.

The Pentecostal 7th Day Assemblies, formerly known as the Association of Seventh-Day Pentecostal Assemblies (incorporated in 1984), had existed as an informal fellowship of congregations and ministers since 1931. It is an association headed by a chairman and a coordinating committee. The committee has a responsibility for joint ventures but has no authority over local church programs or affairs.

Doctrinally the association has taken a nonsectarian stance, affirming some minimal beliefs commonly held but leaving many questions open. Ministers hold a non-Trinitarian position. Baptism is by immersion, but a variety of formulas are spoken. The association believes in sanctification by the blood, Spirit and the Word, the baptism of the Holy Spirit, the Ten Commandments (each of equal worth) and the millennium.

The association is congregationally organized. Each local church is autonomous and sets its own policy and mission. The association supports missions in Canada, Ghana, and Nigeria, and works in other countries through its congregations.

Membership: Not reported.

Educational Facilities:

The association supports a college in Kumasi, Ashanti, Ghana.

Periodicals: *The Hour of Preparation.*

The Rock Church
640 Kempsville Rd., Virginia Beach, VA 23464
The Rock Church was founded in Norfolk, Virginia, in 1968 by John Gimenez (b. 1931) and his wife and fellow evangelist, Anne Gimenez (b. 1932). After being saved from drug addiction in 1965, John Gimenez began touring the country with seven other former addicts in *The Addicts,* a dramatic presentation of their stories. The play was also made into a movie, and Gimenez published his accounts in a

book, *Up Tight*. While on tour he met his future wife, who was holding evangelistic services in Indianapolis. They married in 1966. During the early phase of their combined ministry, they associated with Pat Robertson's *700 Club,* which brought them to the Tidewater area of Virginia. They took over an abandoned church building in Norfolk, but within a few years the church proved too small to hold the growing congregation. They then built a new building in nearby Virginia Beach and called it the Rock Church, based on the passage in the Gospel of Matthew 16:18, ". . . upon this rock I will build my church." They soon added a school, the Rock Academy.

The church greatly expanded its ministries during its first decade, and by 1979 the church had 23 additional affiliated congregations.

Membership: In 2008 the church reported more than 500 associated congregations.

Sources:

The Rock Church. www.rockchurch.org/.

Gimenez, John, Anne Gimenez, and Robert Paul Lamb. *Upon this Rock: The Remarkable Story of John & Anne Gimenez: The Miracle of Rock Church*. Souls Books, 1979.

Varner, Kelley, and John Gimenez. *The Priesthood Is Changing*. Shippensburg, PA: Destiny Image Publishers, 1991.

Sharon Fellowship Churches of North America

c/o Sharon Fellowship Church of Houston, 13503 Creek Springs, Houston, TX 77083

The Sharon Fellowship Churches of North America is the American affiliate of the Sharon Fellowship Churches of India, founded by Pastor P. J. Thomas (1914–1998). A Indian of the Brahmin caste, Thomas was converted to Christianity. He would eventually earn a degree in theology from Seampore University and then pursue further studies in Australia and the United States. He returned to India in 1952 and was instrumental in sending several pastors of the Indian Pentecostal Church to the United States. Thomas settled at Tiruvalla in 1953 and two years later founded a Bible college at a site known as Sharon. Sharon became a popular stop for Pentecostal ministers from the United States, including John E. Douglas and R. W. Schambach.

The IPC experienced a split in the 1950s. Thomas attempted to keep Sharon College above the turmoil. However, as time passed, several independent Pentecostal congregations asked for assistance with construction of buildings, buying burial grounds, and having a common fellowship. Eventually Thomas joined with these churches that would become the core of Sharon Fellowship Churches of India. The fellowship expanded rapidly through the 1960s.

Members of the Sharon Churches began to migrate to America in the 1970s. Congregations emerged in the 1990s and an initial National Conference was held in 2000. The *Sharon Voice*, a periodical, was launched in 1998 by the church in Houston, Texas. The American work is currently led by Rev. C. M. Titus. The church participates in the annual American conference of Pentecostals from Kerala (India).

Membership: In 2003 the fellowship reported three churches in Texas, and one each in Oklahoma, Michigan, Illinois, and Massachusetts.

Periodicals: *The Sharon Voice*.

Sources:

Sharon Fellowship Churches of North America.
members.tripod.com/sharon_america/.

Sharon Fellowship Church of Houston. www.sharonhouston.com/.

United Christian Church and Ministerial Association

Box 700, Cleveland, TN 37311

The United Christian Ministerial Association was founded in 1956 by the Rev. H. Richard Hall (1920–2002) as an association of independent Pentecostal ministers. The local church in Cleveland, Tennessee, was formed in 1972, at which time the name of the organization was changed to United Christian Church and Ministerial Association. Doctrinally the church is described as fundamental and Pentecostal.

In 2008 the association was headed by Donald Warren, serving as president, and a board of directors. Ministerial training is offered for resident students through the United Christian Church and for nonresident students though a correspondence institute. The association offers exhorter and ordination licenses to all charismatics and Pentecostals who are called to preach in any one of 16 categories, including apostles, bishops, pastors, teachers, missionaries, and ministering through the various gifts of the Spirit as outlined in I Cor. 12. There is an annual minister's convention in Cleveland during which one day is set aside for the ordination of ministers and one for graduation for students of the United Christian Bible Institute.

Membership: In 2008 the association reported more than 20,000 licensed and ordained ministers worldwide and 150 affiliated congregations in the United States.

Educational Facilities:

United Christian Bible Institute, Cleveland, Tennessee.

Periodicals: *Shield of Faith*.

Sources:

United Christian Church and Ministerial Association. www.unitedchristianchurch.org/.

Sims, Patsy. *Can Somebody Shout Amen!* New York: St. Martin's Press, 1988.

United Evangelical Churches

PO Box 1175, Thomasville, GA 31799

United Evangelical Churches was formed in 1960, one of the first structural responses to the neo-Pentecostal revival. It is made up especially of those ministers and laypersons from mainline churches who, since their baptism with the Holy Spirit, have not felt free to remain in their churches. As members of a fellowship, they hope to avoid some of the evils of institutionalism, namely, the excessive control of man that prevents control by the living Spirit of God. Because of its origin, the fellowship continues to be open to charismatics who choose to remain in their own churches.

The tenets of faith of United Evangelical Churches profess belief in the Bible as the Word of God, the Trinity, the virgin birth and resurrection of Christ, the inability of man to save himself, salvation in Christ, regeneration by the Holy Spirit, the present ministry of the Holy Spirit which empowers Christians and manifests itself in gifts and ministries, and the judgment of Christ.

The church is governed by an executive council and there is a conference every two years. Churches are divided into three regions—Western, Central, and Eastern. Churches (in 1970) were found in 22 states. Foreign work was located in India, Korea, Taiwan, Hong Kong, Singapore, Japan, Ghana, Kenya, Jamaica, Guatemala, El Salvador, Colombia, Mexico, Costa Rica, Honduras, and Iran.

Membership: Not reported.

The United Network of Christian Ministries and Churches

Current address not obtained for this edition.

The United Network of Christian Ministries and Churches was founded in 1985 by Rev. Don Pfotenhauer, formerly a pastor in the Lutheran Church–Missouri Synod. Pfotenhauer had become affiliated with the larger Charismatic movement, which occasioned his being expelled from his denomination. As that process proceeded, out of meetings and prayer with his supporters, he felt called to an "apostolic" ministry. The vision for this ministry, articulated through prophetic utterances of several people, included the establishment of local churches that would operate as the body of Christ in their communities and unite believers in a loving fellowship where each member is rightly related to Christ and each other.

Although local churches are autonomous, transcongregational leadership is supplied to the churches affiliated with the fellowship by several apostolic teams. These teams are seen as "coaches" who prepare the body of Christ for the work of the ministry. They are viewed as authorities delegated by the Holy Spirit who govern the church. The apostolic team visits each member church at least once annually. Pfotenhauer serves as the apostolic director of the fellowship.

Membership: In 1997 there were 25 congregations with 3,300 members affiliated with the fellowship in the United States and an additional 14 churches worldwide in Tanzania; Manitoba, Canada; and India.

Universal Church, the Mystical Body of Christ
Current address not obtained for this edition.

The Universal Church, the Mystical Body of Christ, is an interracial Pentecostal group that emerged in the 1970s. It is distinguished by its belief that in order to serve God freely, members must leave the corrupt government, society, and churches of this land and establish a separate government on another continent where a theocratic system can be constructed. Only then can perfection exist in society. Members call upon all Christians to join them. They believe that these are the end-times and that God is calling together his 144,000 mentioned in Revelation.

The church has a strict moral code and disapproves of short dresses for women, long hair for men, and women preachers and elders. Women cover their heads during worship. The group fasts, uses wine and unleavened bread at the Lord's Supper, and believes in baptism for the remission of sins, divine healing, speaking in tongues, and the unity of the church. The Universal Church is headed by Bishop R. O. Frazier. Members do not think of themselves as another denomination but as the one true body of Christ.

Membership: Not reported.

Periodicals: *The Light of Life Herald.* Send orders to PO Box 874, Saginaw, MI 48605.

Universal World Church
PO Box 4545, Glendale, CA 91222

The Universal World Church was formed in 1952 by former Assemblies of God minister Dr. O. L. Jaggers, its president. It differs from other Pentecostal bodies primarily in organization and in its doctrine of the sacrament. Under Jaggers are 24 elders who form the governing executive body. Their role is taken from Exodus and from Revelations 4:4, 10; 5:6–8. The elders' custom of wearing robes and golden crowns is based on these texts. There are 144 bishops, one for each state of the United States and the rest for the various countries of the world. Elders and bishops must be graduates of the University of the World Church.

One is received into the church by baptism following repentance and faith in Jesus Christ as personal Lord and savior. The reception is the first process of new birth and new creation. Following the new birth, one may receive the genuine baptism with the Holy Spirit of resurrection power and fire, a baptism called the "second process." After the second process, one is allowed to partake of the third, the transubstantiation communion, which is offered once every three months. At that time twenty-four elders, by faith in Christ and the power of God, perform the miracle of changing bread and wine into the sacred body and blood of the Lord Jesus Christ. This act is done before the golden altar of the church in Los Angeles.

In the 1960s the World Church came under considerable attack for its flamboyance, which some felt smacked more of showmanship than religion. In spite of these attacks, however, the church continued to grow. In 1969 the church claimed 11,315 members of the mother church, with approximately 800 congregations in the United States and around the world. The 3,170 ministers were organized into the World Fellowship of the Universal World Church. These figures have been questioned by many who claim that the movement has consisted mainly of the single congregation in Los Angeles.

Through the 1980s and 1990s the Los Angeles church maintained a degree of local fame for its elaborately staged "illustrated sermons," featuring O. L. Jaggers's wife, Miss Velma. Her annual "Christmas in America" pageants attracted both traditional followers and a younger, postmodernist generation of Angelenos who viewed the spectacles as a kind of performance art. The church, under the direction of Jaggers and Miss Velma, has been meeting at the Auditorium of the Los Angeles' Scottish Rite Masonic Temple while a land is made ready for the construction of a projected new Golden Temple.

Membership: Not reported. In 2008, the church reported four American congregations: Los Angeles; Maui, Hawaii; New York, New York; and Tallahassee, Florida. There were also five congregations in Australia.

Educational Facilities:

University of the World Church, Los Angeles, California.

Sources:
Universal World Church (Australia).
au.msnusers.com/TheUniversalWorldChurch/drjaggersandmissvelmasrevivals.
msnw.

Victory Fellowship of Ministries (VFM)
7700 S Lewis, Tulsa, OK 74136-7700

Victory Fellowship of Ministries (VFM) was founded and organized in January 1980 as an outreach ministry of Victory Christian Center (formerly Sheridan Christian Center), a large charismatic church in Tulsa, Oklahoma. It provides a fellowship for a number of like-minded ministers and churches, especially many who have been trained and sent out from Victory Bible Institute.

Membership: In 2002 V.F.M. reported over 800 members, with 154 affiliated churches in the United States and one each in Canada, Germany, France, Albania, the Czech Republic, Russia, Argentina, and Scotland.

Educational Facilities:

Victory Bible Institute, Tulsa, Oklahoma.

Sources:
Victory Fellowship of Ministries. www.vfmtulsa.org/.

Victory Christian Center. www.victory.com/.

Victory New Testament Fellowship International
PO Box 850146, Mesquite, TX 75185-0146

The origins of Victory New Testament Fellowship International go back to 1934 in Dallas, Texas, where H. Donald Skelton, at the time employed as a barber, was called to ministry. On his own, Skelton began visiting hospitals, nursing homes, and jails where he shared his faith with whoever would listen. In the process he met and married Dorothy Peterman. He began preaching full time. In the years after World War II, he began to fellowship with other independent ministers who expressed a desire to have an association apart from affiliating with a large denomination. These ministers also needed credentials to be admitted to the various institutions where they were attempting to minister. The Victory New Testament Fellowship International was founded in 1953 to fulfill these needs, and Skelton began ordaining ministers.

The fellowship is a Pentecostal body that emphasizes the Bible as the inspired Word of God and faith in the Triune god. It emphasizes the gifts and fruits of the spirit, especially divine healing. The church is called to evangelize the world. Members are to support the work of the church with their tithes and offerings.

In 2008 the pastor and president of the organization was Larry D. Skelton. The fellowship expresses belief in the absolute sovereignty of the local pastor as overseer of the flock but is also led by a board of directors. As a corporate body, the fellowship supports missionaries overseas, several of whom have founded Bible schools. It has also supported orphanages and a homeless shelter.

The fellowship offers credentials for ministers as pastor, evangelists, missionaries, or teachers. Licensed ministers are expected to live by a code of honor that includes a pledge to refrain from illicit sexual acts, including homosexual behavior, consumption of alcoholic beverages, tobacco use, and any behavior contrary to that of a minister.

Membership: In 2008 the fellowship reported 1,500 ministry partners in the United States and Canada who held credentials from it and affiliated missionaries operating in 22 countries.

Sources:

Victory New Testament Fellowship International. www.fellowshipintl.org/index.html.

World Bible Way Fellowship (WBWF)

PO Box 70, DeSoto, TX 75123-0070

Alternate Address: World Bible Way Fellowship North Central Region, PO Box 902, Burnsville, MN 55337.

World Bible Way Fellowship (WBWF) was founded as a full-gospel interdenominational association of ministers and churches in 1943 by Guy Shields. The fellowship traces its roots to the International Fundamental Christian Association, originally conceived as a religious association in the District of Columbia in the summer of 1943, but later incorporated in Texas.

The fellowship is a Pentecostal body, espouses a basic trinitarian theology, and acknowledges the importance of the baptism of the Holy Spirit with the accompanying sign of speaking in tongues and the associated charismatic gifts of the Spirit and the fruits of the Spirit in the believer's life.

It recognizes lay Christian workers, licensed ministers, and ordained ministers, and for each will supply credentials to those who otherwise qualify. Women are welcomed as ministers who may be licensed by the WBWF.

The fellowship is led by a board. Dan Hope has been president since 1973.

Membership: In 2002 the fellowship reported more than 2,000 ordained ministers credentialed by WBWF around the world and more than 500 affiliated churches and pastors.

Periodicals: *The Events*.

Sources:

World Bible Way Fellowship. www.wbwfi.org/national.ivnu.

World Bible Way Fellowship. worldbiblewayfellowship.com/.

Zion Fellowship International

PO Box 79, Waverly, NY 14892

Zion Fellowship International is a worldwide Pentecostal/charismatic fellowship of churches, colleges, and ministries that includes orphanages, clinics, and feeding programs in several countries. The fellowship's primary work is in education and embodied in the Zion Ministerial Institute in Waverly, New York, and the distance education degree program offered by Zion Christian University in Clearwater, Florida, as well as several colleges around the world. The fellowship's president in 2008 was Dr. Brian Bailey.

Zion Fellowship affirms a belief in the Triune God, salvation through the work of Jesus Christ, the Bible as the authoritative Word of God, baptism by immersion in water, the baptism of the Holy Spirit, divine healing as provided by Christ's atoning work, and the miraculous work of the Holy Spirit. It is also the fellowship's belief that God will visit His Church in unusual ways before Christ's second coming, bringing multitudes into His kingdom. As a matter of principle, it is felt that since divorce and remarriage are contrary to God's will, anyone who has been divorced and remarried is not permitted to hold ministerial credentials. Pastors are asked not to solemnize such remarriages.

Membership: Not reported.

Educational Facilities:

Zion Ministerial Institute, Waverly, New York.

Zion Christian University, Clearwater, Florida.

Periodicals: *Zion Ministries*.

Sources:

Zion Fellowship. zionfellowship.org/.

European Free Church Family

10

Beginning in the 1960s, the history of the Reformation era, the sixteenth-century protest movement that began within the Roman Catholic Church and eventually split the church into a number of large fragments, has been rewritten. Reformation historians have been forced to recognize the vital role played in the Protestant Reformation by the so-called *radical reformers*. These radicals were independent groups and people who protested the continued ties of Martin Luther (1483–1546) and John Calvin (1509–1564) to the state. Before the 1960s, Lutheran and Calvinist writers treated these additional reformers as revolutionaries, mystics, anarchists, and heretics; they were the object of scorn. However, as theologian and historian George H. Williams (1914–2000) noted in *The Radical Reformation*, his ground-breaking study of the radicals, "They have the same significance for the interpretation of the whole of modern church history as the discoveries in the Dead Sea caves and in upper Egypt are having for New Testament studies and early church history" (1962, p. xix).

Who were the radical reformers? They were men who, like Luther and Calvin, were interested in the reform of the Christian church, but who, because of their variety of backgrounds, outlooks, and theologies, placed emphases on much different points as the crux of needed reform. For most, faith, sacrament, and liturgy were not as significant as the doctrine of the church in its relation to the state. The radicals frowned upon church involvement in secular activity, and they were typically persecuted by the state. Most radicals came from the lower class, so they built upon the traditional adversarial relationship between the lower class and the ruling class. The radicals took the central ideas of the Reformation (e.g., the priesthood of believers and the freedom of the Christian) to such an extreme that Luther and Calvin were horrified.

Most of the radicals came to a bloody end in war or persecution, and many saw their movements entirely destroyed. As a result, some radicals, such as Thomas Müntzer (c. 1490–1525), Hans Denck (c. 1495–1527), and Michael Sattler (c. 1490–1527), did not leave even a surviving remnant of followers to carry on their work. Others, such as Caspar Schwenckfeld (1489–1561), Jacob Hutter (d. 1536), and Melchior Hoffmann (c. 1500–1543), were able to build movements that survived and exist today. Among the churches that trace their roots to the radical reformers are the Mennonites, the Amish, the Brethren, the Quakers, and the Free Church

Brethren. All of these churches belong to the *free church* family, meaning that they are not only *not* state churches, but are ideologically opposed to state churches. They exist as free associations of adult believers, people old enough to make a free decision to join their fellowship. The free churches emphasize free will, contrasting sharply with strict Calvinists, who believe in predestination—that is, that the number and identity of the elect was ordained before the beginning of the world.

The Radical Reformation can be dated from Christmas day 1521, more than four years after Luther's Ninety-five Theses were nailed to the church door in Wittenberg, Germany. On this day, Andreas Bodenstein of Carlstadt (c. 1480–1541, called Carlstadt by historians) celebrated the first "Protestant" communion. (Protestant services today follow the trend set by that service.) He preached, and without donning liturgical vestments, read the "Mass." He omitted all references to sacrifice, did not elevate the host, and gave both bread and wine. Each act was a significant repudiation of a belief or practice of the Roman Catholic Church. Behind this communion service was the strong contention of the supremacy of spirit over letter, the supremacy of grace over works, and the common priesthood of all believers. From these events were to flow others initiated by men who were already thinking like Carlstadt.

The career of Thomas Müntzer was one of the results of Carlstadt's activity. Müntzer came to prominence in 1520 at Zwickau, a town in Saxony, where, as minister to one of the churches, his radicalism began to emerge. He urged people to respond spontaneously and immediately to the leadings of the Holy Spirit. He defined the church as made up of spirit-filled saints gathered together in a community. His definition avoided any mention of bishops or sacraments, and thus was at odds with a traditional understanding of the church. Müntzer aroused the laity to support him against his more conservative colleagues. After being removed from his pastorate, Müntzer spent several years as a wandering preacher, becoming more and more radical and embittered. In a famous sermon delivered in 1524 before the German princes, he called upon them to take up the sword to defeat the forces of anti-Christ (the pope) and bring in the kingdom.

A number of events, including an astrological conjunction, converged in 1524 and occasioned an uprising of German peasants. Not the least of these events was the preaching of Müntzer and his radical colleagues. As the

---

European Free-Church Family Chronology

1525	Conrad Grebel rebaptizes George Blaurock in protest of the state church based in Zurich, Switzerland.
1527	Feliz Manz becomes the first of many executed for refusing to recant his Anabaptist views.
	The Schleitheim Confession is developed.
1536	Menno Simons leave the Catholic Church and reorganizes scatters remnants of the Radical Reformation.
1632	Mennonites issue Dortrecht Confession.
1652	George Fox founds the Society of Friends (also known as "Quakers") at Pendle Hill, England.
1671–73	Fox visits Quaker families in the American colonies.
1681	King Charles II grants William Penn a charter for a colony in British America.
1683	Thirteen German Mennonite families arrive in Pennsylvania; they purchased 43,000 acres of land and founded Germantown.
	First Quaker Meeting House in Philadelphia.
1688	Philadelphia Quakers begin history of anti-slavery activities with an initial formal protest.
1695	Controversy over the strictness of behavior leads to separation of the Amish from the Mennonites in Switzerland.
1719	Schwarzenau Brethren first arrive in colonial America at Philadelphia under the leadership of Elder Peter Becker.
1729	Alexander Mack and other Brethren emigrate to America from Rotterdam.
1735	First Amish migrations to North America.
1754	John Woolman publishes *Some Considerations on the Keeping of Negroes*, which launches two decades of anti-slavery activity among the Quakers.
1758	Philadelphia Yearly Meeting of the Society of Friends declares slavery inconsistent with Christianity.
1775	Quakers take lead in the formation of the Pennsylvania Society for the Abolition of Slavery.
1778	The Brethren (later the Church of the Brethren) hold the first "recorded" Annual Meeting.
1827	The preaching of Elias Hicks emphasizing the "Inner Light" leads to a major schism among American Quakers. Hicksite Quakers later form the Friends general conference.
1847	John Oberholtzer leads in the formation of the General Conference Mennonite Church.
1870	A program of Russification initiated by the Czar motivates many Mennonites to lead for North America.
1883	The Brethren Church founded in Dayton, Ohio, by Progressive Brethren.
1902	The Friends United Meeting, the largest American Quaker group, is formed.
1911	Ann Allebach becomes the first Mennonite woman to be ordained.
1920	First World Conference of Friends is held.
1925	First meeting of the Mennonite World Conference.
1937	Friends World Committee for Consultation formed.
1939	Fellowship of Grace Brethren Churches organized.
1947	Nobel peace prize awarded jointly to English Friends Service Council and American Friends Service Committee.
1948	Church of the Brethren joins the World Council of Churches as a charter member.
1955	James Lark, the first African American Mennonite pastor, becomes the first African American Mennonite bishop.
1958	Church of the Brethren grant women full ordination status as ministers.
1972	U.S. Supreme Court upholds Amish schools in *Wisconsin v. Yoder et al.*
1984	Christian Peacemaker Teams, which sends teams of peace workers into conflict areas around the world, develops from a suggestion made at the Mennonite World Conference. It receives continuing support from the Mennonite Church USA, Mennonite Church Canada, Church of the Brethren, and Friends United Meeting.
1995	Mennonite Church and General Conference Mennonite Church merge to form Mennonite Church USA. The new church adopts a new statement of faith, the "Confession of Faith in a Mennonite Perspective."

Peasants' War began, Müntzer, having given up on the immovable princes, joined the peasants' forces at Mühlhausen, ready to wield his sword for the kingdom. He saw the Peasants' War as his instrument. When the revolt was put down in 1525, Müntzer was captured. His career ended on the executioner's block, and his flock was scattered.

Contemporaneous with Müntzer's short career in the north, other radical reformists appeared in southern Germany and Austria. Their first spokesman was Hans Denck. While at Nuremberg as rector of a parish school, Denck had come under the influence of Carlstadt and Müntzer. Denck was expelled from Nuremberg by Lutherans who feared him as a competitor. In the fall of 1525, Denck became the spiritual leader of a group at Augsburg. In the spring of 1526, under the influence of Swiss refugee Balthasar Hubmaier

(1480–1528), Denck led in the reconstitution of his group as a truly reformed church with the adoption of the apostolic practice of believer's baptism. By that practice, only adult believers in Christ were baptized, the procedure believed to have been used by the apostles. Thus *anabaptism*, or rebaptism of those who were baptized as infants, emerged as a central factor in the Radical Reformation. Denck saw the church as an adult, self-disciplined fellowship. His criteria for understanding the church naturally excluded infants, and *antipedobaptism* (literally, against the baptism of infants) became a central teaching of the movement. From this belief and this practice was to come the fully developed Anabaptist understanding of the church as an association of adults (not children) acting freely.

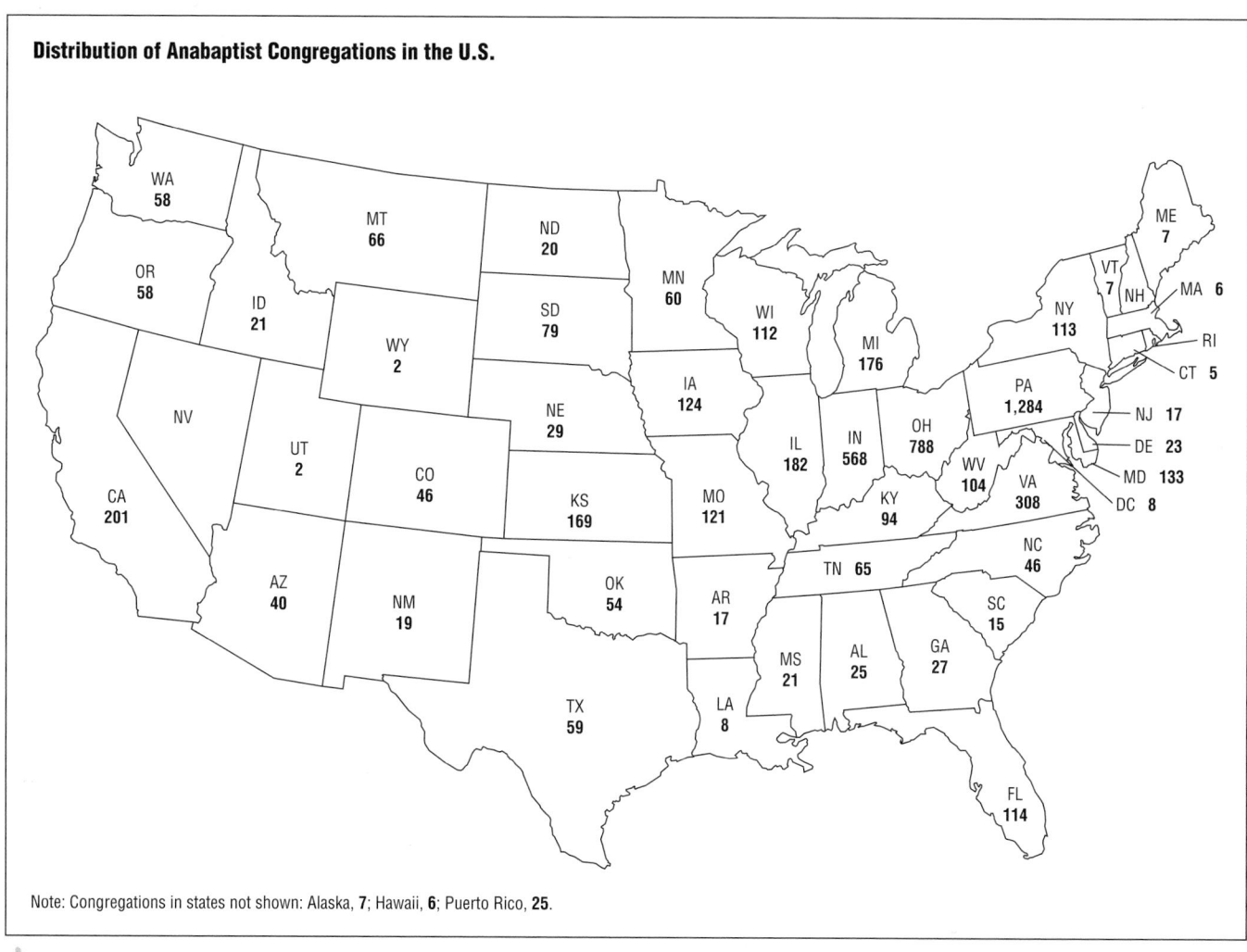

Distribution of Anabaptist Congregations in the U.S.

State	Count
WA	58
MT	66
ND	20
MN	60
ME	7
OR	58
ID	21
SD	79
WI	112
VT	7
NH	
MA	6
NY	113
WY	2
MI	176
RI	
CT	5
NV	
NE	29
IA	124
PA	1,284
NJ	17
UT	2
CO	46
IN	568
OH	788
DE	23
CA	201
KS	169
IL	182
WV	104
VA	308
MD	133
DC	8
MO	121
KY	94
NC	46
AZ	40
NM	19
OK	54
AR	17
TN	65
SC	15
MS	21
AL	25
GA	27
TX	59
LA	8
FL	114

Note: Congregations in states not shown: Alaska, **7**; Hawaii, **6**; Puerto Rico, **25**.

Adapted from Kraybill, Donald B. Anabaptist World USA. *Scottdale, PA: Herald Press, 2001.*

Denck was forced out of several cities as his reputation caught up with him. In 1527 he arrived in Augsburg to participate in a synod of Anabaptist leaders. After the meeting, many were arrested and executed, as a result of which this meeting is frequently referred to as the Martyrs' Synod.

The main item of concern for the synod was the eschatological program of Hans Hut (c. 1490–1527), an Austrian Anabaptist leader who had been rebaptized by Denck. Hut repudiated the peasants for taking up arms, and interpreted current events as symbols of the nearness of the end of time. Hut believed that God would do his work, and the saints, while suffering at present, would live to see the new kingdom appear. Hut proceeded to build an underground movement throughout Bavaria and Austria.

When the synod met, three issues concerning the coming kingdom were under discussion: the manner and time of its approach, the role of Anabaptists in preparing for it, and the role of the magistery in the present time. No clear-cut decisions were reached on these points. After the synod, Hut was arrested and died in a fire in his cell. The inability of the synod to bring the radicals to one mind, the attacks of the Lutherans on some radical excesses in doctrine, and disillu-

sionment with his role in God's reformation led Denck to recant. He died of plague soon afterward.

Contemporaneous with the rise of south German and Austrian Anabaptists was the rise of Swiss Anabaptists, popularly known as the Swiss Brethren, under the leadership of Michael Sattler. The Swiss Brethren developed a mature, articulate Anabaptist stance, and from them would come the most important statement of the Anabaptist position.

Swiss Anabaptism arose in the 1520s to protest the state church. The church in question was that of Ulrich Zwingli (1484–1530), the leader of the Reformation in Switzerland. Zwingli took religious control of the canton of Zurich, with the power structures of Zurich establishing the Zwinglian Church for all in the area. The Swiss Brethren insisted that only the righteous should belong to the church, not every person who happened to reside in the territory controlled by the state. After the vote to establish the Zwinglian Church, the Swiss Brethren left Zurich, determined to continue their efforts to restore the true church. Two leaders of the Swiss Anabaptists, Conrad Grebel (c. 1498–1526) and George Blaurock (1492–1529), became a center of controversy. On

January 21, 1525, layman Grebel rebaptized Blaurock, a priest, and that action led to months of disputation.

The Swiss Brethren grew, even though they were persecuted. Doctrinally, they had a double problem. First, they had to counter Zwingli's ideas, which were popular. Second, they had to clarify their differences with Müntzer and Hut. Müntzer and Hut had poor reputations, and people mistakenly associated the Swiss Brethren with them. It was in the attempt to refute Müntzer and Hut that Michael Sattler came forward as a leader of refugees in Strasbourg. Upon his return to Switzerland, Sattler became head of the Schleitheim Synod of 1527. There, the mature Anabaptist position was hammered out in a document originally titled "The Brotherly Union of a Number of Children of God Concerning Seven Articles," now called simply the Schleitheim Confession.

SCHLEITHEIM CONFESSION.
The Schleitheim Confession set the distinctive elements of the Anabaptist position. Rejecting the state church, in which citizenship and church membership were largely equivalent, the Anabaptists desired a church of true believers. Hence they acknowledged baptism for converted adult believers only, and limited the taking of communion to those who had been rightfully baptized. Having given up the disciplinary machinery of the state, they were left with the "ban," a form of excommunication of fallen and as yet unrepentant members, as their only tool of discipline. They admonished Anabaptists to withdraw from the world and its wickedness. In that light, church members were to make no use of the sword, for either secular or sacred purposes. That position extended to an avoidance of service as a magistrate. Finally, the Anabaptists refused to take oaths. All of these positions were based upon their study of the Bible.

The distinctive doctrinal and ethical position of the Anabaptist church was accepted, with minor modifications, by the various bodies that survived the era of persecution. The church is composed of those united to Christ by baptism of believers who have separated themselves from the evil world. The church is a minority group of pilgrims in a hostile world, trying to isolate themselves from its influence and forces. Specifically, certain activities—war, the use of violent force against one's neighbor, civic affairs, courts, oaths, worldly amusements, and service as a magistrate—are studiously avoided.

Pacifism, in particular, has arisen as the essential point in the Anabaptist avoidance ethic, and these churches have been characterized as historical peace churches. Christians obey the laws of the land, as is possible for pacifists (and any attempting to live withdrawn), but their essential authority is to be found in the church.

The church is a disciplined fellowship. It appoints its own leadership and accepts its authority. The leadership's primary means of enforcing discipline is the ban, a practice based on Matthew 18:15–17. Menno Simons (c. 1496–1561) is credited with emphasizing a modified form of banning, termed *shunning*, in which the church stops all dealings with an erring member, including eating with him or her, with the intent of winning the individual back to the straight and narrow. This practice is based on I Corinthians 5:11.

The church was opposed to both popish and antipopish works and church services. From this position comes a lay-oriented, nonliturgical, noncreedal, Bible-oriented church. The Anabaptists' opposition to the state church, a position that was articulated, as well as manifested, by the Anabaptists' very existence, led to the appellation *free church*. Nonliturgical worship in its extreme form can be seen in the classic Quaker service.

The Bible is the primary document from which the Anabaptists derive their belief and practice. Their method of biblical interpretation, which does not fall back on tradition and philosophy, has become literalistic. Sacraments became ordinances, or symbolic acts, with baptism functioning as an initiatory ceremony, and the Lord's Supper a memorial act. Foot washing, for which there is not a more unequivocal command than either baptism or the Lord's Supper, is also practiced, especially in churches of Swiss origin.

Though all the European free churches believe in adult baptism, they have a wide variety of modes. The Mennonites pour water on the person being baptized, while the Church of the Brethren uses triune immersion, the practice of entering the water once for each person of the Trinity.

LATER HISTORY.
After the Schleitheim Confession, three events were to remold the Anabaptists—the fall of the town of Münster; the death of the martyrs; and the rise of Menno Simons.

The Radical Reformation had been punctuated by apocalyptic thinking, including a few instances of militancy. These tendencies came to a climax in the town of Münster. Radicalization there began with the pastor Bernard Rothmann (c. 1495–c.1535). His popular sermons led to the Protestantization of the community in 1531. Rothmann's Lutheran views became more and more radical, and he began to defend believer's baptism. Other Anabaptists heard of Rothmann and began to flock to Münster as the new Jerusalem. Among the migrants were Jan Mathijs (d. 1534) and his major supporter, Jan of Leiden (c. 1509–1536). The migrants adopted the apocalyptic theory that the end of time was imminent and would be caused by God's direct intervention in human affairs.

By the beginning of 1534, the radicalization of the city was complete and Mathijs was quickly rising to power. All Catholics and Lutherans were expelled, and the city armed itself for the siege that would follow that expulsion. As Mathijs imposed his religious beliefs, the town adopted a communist lifestyle and made military preparations for the siege. In the midst of these reforms, Mathijs was killed by Catholic forces besieging the city. Jan of Leiden took over and began to set up a theocracy with himself as God's vicar. The strict discipline worked effectively during the siege. After a particularly heavy battle, Jan introduced polygamy.

The beleaguered city finally was betrayed and captured. Jan had imposed ruthless authority on the people. After his capture, he was tortured to death. With only a few minor exceptions, the Münster episode ended any apocalypticism in the Anabaptism movement.

That episode, however, did not end the persecution of Anabaptists. The *Martyrs Mirror*, a book first published in 1554 that functions for Anabaptists much as John Foxe's *Book of Martyrs* functions for English Protestants, records the trail of blood of Anabaptists killed for their faith. Persecution left a stamp on the members of the free churches, who came to see themselves literally as wandering pilgrims in a hostile world.

Many Anabaptists flocked to Menno Simons in the Netherlands. Emerging in 1537 as a leader, Menno began writing a series of books that set down a moderate free church position and rallied the disintegrating Anabaptist forces. It is to Menno's credit that the forces were held together and survived until 1577, when toleration was granted in Holland. The followers of Menno became, with few exceptions, the surviving Anabaptist community.

In addition to the apocalyptic Anabaptism of Münster and the moderate Anabaptism of the Swiss Brethren, a third form of Anabaptism developed. It turned inward into what has been termed a spiritualist or mystical movement. Among the first to espouse the spiritualist perspective was Hans Denck. An early leader in the Anabaptist movement, Denck recanted in his despair at its divisions and began to turn inward. Long a student of the mystic John Tauler (c. 1300–1361), Denck began to preach of a God who meets people as a light, a word, and a presence. Denck was followed by others, such as Sebastian Franck (1499–1542), Johann Bünderlin (c.1498–1533), and Christian Entfelder (d. 1547).

As a whole, the spiritual Anabaptists collected little following and left none behind. One exception was Caspar Schwenckfeld, a Silesian courtier turned prophet. In successive steps, he became a disciple of Luther, a critic of the Reformation as outward and shallow, an Anabaptist theologian with peculiar views on the sacraments and Christ, and a mystic leader with a large following that still exists.

The spiritual reformers' primarily contribution was to create a literature with Anabaptist devotional and mystic leanings that became the basis of a mystical movement within the free churches, much like the movement in medieval Catholicism, and the inspiration for later mystical and devotional movements, primarily Quakerism and to a certain extent Pietism. Each of these strains was to find a home in colonial Pennsylvania.

SWISS AND DUTCH MENNONITES.
The central surviving Anabaptist tradition owes its name to one of its major leaders, Menno Simons (c. 1496–1561). Simons, a Dutchman, was born in Witmarsum in the Netherlands. After Simons was ordained a Roman Catholic priest, he came to believe that the bread and wine were not the real body and blood of Christ. A 1531 execution of an Anabaptist led him to doubt the validity of infant baptism as well. Continued investigation of Anabaptist views convinced him that they were correct.

In 1536, a year after his own brother's death as an Anabaptist, Simons left his Catholic heritage. Because of his abilities, he immediately became a leader in the Anabaptist community. His main tasks became protecting the community from the authorities and keeping it free from militarism (which had led Anabaptists to take complete control of Münster and to wage a long battle to defend it) and from heresies such as apocalyptic beliefs that the world would soon end through God's direct intervention. Some of Menno's followers found toleration in East Friesland in the Netherlands under the Countess Anne. It was she, in recognizing the peaceful followers of Menno in contradistinction to the militarists and apocalyptics, who first dubbed Menno's followers *Menists*. The bulk of Simon's active life was spent writing in defense of his new-found faith and hiding from the authorities, who had put a price on his head.

Menno's views were similar to those outlined by the Swiss Brethren at Schleitheim. It can be argued that the Mennonites are the legitimate inheritors of the Swiss-German Anabaptist tradition, as most of the other Anabaptists have disappeared from the contemporary world. In essentials, the Mennonites certainly share the Swiss and German Anabaptists' views on rebaptism, pacifism, religious toleration, separation of church and state, and opposition to capital punishment, holding office, and taking oaths. On two points only did Menno Simons differ—his use of the ban and his doctrine of incarnation.

Menno joined the argument with the Brethren concerning the strict versus the liberal use of the ban. Menno advocated its strict use as the only means to keep the church free of corrupt sects. He also advocated "avoidance" or shunning of all who were banned. Shunning was centered upon the idea of not eating with the person under the ban; this practice created a significant in-group problem when one member of a family was banned. The practice of avoidance was liberalized over the years by the main body of Mennonites, but originally it was their distinguishing feature.

Menno has also been accused of compromising the humanity of Christ by minimizing the human properties said to have been received from Mary. This slight difference in Christology, which led many to accuse him of antitrinitarianism, has not been a major factor in recent Mennonite history.

The unique doctrinal position of the Mennonites was systematized in 1632 in the Dordrecht Confession, named for the town in the Netherlands at which it was written. It is consistent with the Schleitheim Confession, but deals more systematically with basic Christian affirmations. It affirms God as Father, Son, and Holy Ghost (the Trinity); the restoration of all humanity though Christ, who was foreordained to his saving work before the foundation of the world; and the incarnation of Christ as the Son of God. Those who are obedient through faith and follow the precepts of the New Testament are considered Christ's children. Baptism is for repentant adult believers. The visible church consists of those who have been baptized and incorporated into the communion of saints on earth. Within that church, the Lord's Supper is observed as an ordinance, as is the washing of the feet.

The state is seen as the gift of God, and Mennonites are admonished to pray for it and support it in all manners not directly opposed to the commandments of God. Two ways in which God's will and the state are seen to conflict are in the state's demand for oaths and in its drafting of young men for military service. The Mennonites generally refuse to take oaths (for example, in a court of law) or to bear arms.

In one respect, the Dordrecht Confession goes beyond the Schleitheim Confession. Not only does it advocate the use of the ban (excommunication) but also of shunning (avoidance of eating, drinking or socializing with a fallen and unrepentant church member). This practice, still used in some of the more conservative Mennonite bodies, has been a source of considerable controversy, especially when it becomes an issue between a church member and a spouse who is being shunned. In such cases, the church member is not allowed to eat dinner with the shunned spouse.

The Mennonite movement spread slowly, and during the late 1500s many names were added to the roll of martyrs. The movement spread into Germany and Switzerland, building on small groups of Anabaptists already there. Mennonites settled and migrated, as rulers first allowed toleration and then rescinded the privilege. In 1763 Catherine the Great (1729–1796) of Russia offered religious toleration to German settlers who would populate the country's southern steppes. Moravians, Mennonites, and Hutterites flocked to Russia; the Mennonites, mostly Prussians, settled in Crimea and Taurie. The Mennonites developed a unique history in southern Russia because of the special status granted them by the Russian government. A self-governing Mennonite community arose, the government approaching that of a theocracy. The end of Russian paradise came in the 1870s when the czar introduced universal military service as a policy among the German colonists. This policy was part of a general Russification program in the face of the growing military power of Prussia. The Mennonites, pacifists, refused to join the military. As a result, in 1874 a six-year mass immigration to the United States and Canada began. Those that remained in Russia prospered until 1917, when most became victims of the Bolsheviks. The Russian Mennonites survive, however, in small scattered communities.

MENNONITES IN AMERICA.
Reference to Mennonites in American history occurs as early as 1643 in the records of New Netherlands. In 1633 a communal experiment led by Cornelius Pieter Plockhoy (c.1625–c.1665) was established on Delaware Bay, then part of New Netherlands. The first permanent Mennonite colony was established in 1683 at Germantown, Pennsylvania; this date is usually accepted by Mennonites as their date of origin in America. Several factors encouraged Mennonites to come to the Americas. First, religious persecution in Europe caused many to immigrate. Second, Quaker leaders William Penn (1644–1718) and George Fox (1624–1691) were seeking German converts and appealed to members of Mennonite

communities to migrate to America. Finally, the German Quakers (former Anabaptists) already in America wrote their friends and relatives asking them to move to Pennsylvania.

This growing Mennonite element is credited with American history's first public protest against slavery and was very influential in the later Quaker antislavery position. The Mennonites were an agricultural people and began to spread north and west of Germantown. The group's size was bolstered by immigration from the Palatinate in the early eighteenth century.

The Revolutionary War (1775–1783) became the first major crisis in the American Mennonite community, leading to their first schism. The issue was whether or not to support the Continental Congress. The majority argued that they could not support the Congress because such support would involve them in the war. One leader, Christian Funk (1731–1811), argued in favor of support, including the special war tax, drawing his view from Jesus' words on taxation in Matthew 22:21. Funk was excommunicated, and with his followers formed the Mennonite Church (Funkite), which existed until the mid-nineteenth century. It died out as all the participants in the original dispute passed away.

Continued immigration and the natural expansion of the Mennonites, who generally have large families, forced them west, looking for new land. In the early nineteenth century, Mennonites settled in Ontario and the Old Northwest Territory, and after the American Civil War (1861–1865), the prairie states. This expanding migration and wide separation geographically set the stage for the formation of schismatic churches, especially in the 1880s.

While no clear lines can be drawn, there are rough ethnological distinctions within the Mennonite community. Some of the American splintering of churches can be traced to the Swiss, Dutch, or German background of the colonists. The greatest distinction among the Mennonites as a whole is that between the western European and the Russian settlers. Most of the western European Mennonites arrived in the initial wave of settlers into Pennsylvania in the eighteenth century. They later pushed west into Canada and Indiana. The Russian immigrants are those Mennonites who migrated in the nineteenth century and settled in Canada and the western United States, primarily Kansas.

Mennonites have been proud of a heritage of biblical theology and avoidance of hairsplitting and other unproductive attempts at philosophical sophistries. Nevertheless, they have a definite theological heritage in Swiss and Dutch Anabaptist ideas. Except for the distinctive themes illustrated in the Schleitheim Confession, Mennonites would have little problem with the major affirmations of mainline Christian churches. These have never been a point of conflict.

Crucial for Mennonites are ecclesiology and separation from the world. Mennonites share a doctrine of the church based on the concept of ecclesia, the called-out fellowship of believers in mission. The tendency is to emphasize the local congregation and to build wider fellowships based on a commonality of belief. Ministers (bishops) arise out of the fellowship, as do deacons; the exact method for choosing them varies. Casting lots was a favorite method. The Dordrecht Confession of 1632 was adopted by the American church and is still a doctrinal standard for most Mennonites. According to the Dordrecht Confession, the Bible is the source of belief, and emphasis is placed on the believer's direct encounter with the living Christ and the work of the Holy Spirit within. Pietism, an emphasis on the practical life in the Spirit, is worked out in the mutual, shared existence of the church. The church, not the state, is the basic society for the true Christian, according to the Dordrecht Confession.

THE AMISH. Among the more liberal Swiss Mennonites of the late seventeenth century, there arose a party led by Jacob Amman (c. 1644–1711), a minister in the Emmenthal congregation. Because his family records have not been found, little can be said of him except for the practices he promoted among both the Swiss Mennonites and the Swiss Brethren. Amman insisted on a strict interpretation of discipline. For his practices, he appealed to Menno Simons's writings and to the Dordrecht Confession, which has become the recognized statement of doctrine for both Amish and Old Mennonites in America.

In his preaching, Amman stressed the practice of avoidance. A member whose spouse was under the ban was neither to eat nor sleep with him or her until the ban was lifted. Amman also reintroduced foot washing. Nonreligious customs of the period—the use of hooks and eyes instead of buttons, shoestrings instead of shoe buttons, bonnets and aprons, and broad brimmed hats, and the wearing of beards and long hair—became identifying characteristics of church members.

All of the Mennonites during Amman's time were in a loose federation and strove to remain of one mind. Amman's strict interpretation of the "avoidance" clause in the ban led to a division among the Mennonites, with some following Amman and separating themselves from the others. Amman placed under the ban all who disagreed with him. After a few years of separation, Amman and his associates tried to reconcile with the other Mennonites, but the reconciliation efforts failed. Since then, the Amish have been independent of the Mennonites.

In the early 1700s, the Amish began to arrive in America, the earliest congregation on record being the one along North Kill Creek in Berks County, Pennsylvania. Colonies were later planted in eastern Pennsylvania, Ohio, Indiana, Illinois, and Iowa. Until recently, the strongest community was in Lancaster County, Pennsylvania.

The Amish represent a reactionary faction in the Mennonite movement. They have gone far beyond a practice common to Western Christianity of seeking to actualize an apostolic church. The Amish have attempted to freeze a culture, that of the late seventeenth century. As time has passed and the surrounding culture has discarded more and more elements of Jacob Amman's time, greater and greater pressure has been placed on the Amish to conform with the modern world. Each generation has brought new issues to Amish

leaders. Decisions must constantly be made on whether to accommodate the prevailing culture on different points. Public school laws, consolidated farming (and the shortage of available farm lands), automobile-oriented road systems, and tourists are just a few of the issues that have been added to such perennial Amish problems as in-breeding. A lack of consensus on these issues has produced several schisms.

In order to deal with the various "liberal" trends and local schisms, a general conference was held in Wayne County, Ohio, in 1862, followed by others annually for several years. The conferences only accentuated the various trends. Before the conferences were discontinued, the more conservative "Old Order" Amish withdrew and organized separately. Others formed more liberal bodies that have moved toward the Mennonites in practice.

THE RUSSIAN MENNONITES. Some Anabaptist Brethren, instead of coming to America, chose instead to go to Russia at the invitation of Catherine the Great in the 1760s. Catherine wanted colonists to develop newly acquired territory and promised religious freedom and local autonomy. Colonies were settled mainly in southern Russia and the Crimean area. Yet there arose in Russia a "pharaoh who knew not Joseph," Czar Alexander II (1818–1881).

In 1870 a program of Russification was begun by the czar. Its thrust was directed at German colonists, including the Mennonites, whose presence seemed threatening to the rising power of the Russian military. Local autonomy was ended, the Russian language was to replace German, schools were to come under Russian tutelage, and exemption from universal military service was dropped. Emigration seemed the only recourse for the Mennonites. Among those who came to America, many belonged to the Mennonite Church, the first church described in this chapter. Other Russian immigrants belonged to churches that had broken off from the Russian Mennonite Church. These settlers brought their previously formed schismatic churches to America: the Evangelical Mennonite Church (Kleine Gemeinde), the Evangelical Mennonite Brethren Conference, the Mennonite Brethren Church, and the Crimean Brethren, whose members in the United States joined the Mennonite Brethren Church in 1960. These churches are described below, as is the General Conference Mennonite Church, which was formed in the United States instead of in Russia.

The first immigrants to North America included Bernard Warkentin (1847–1908), Cornelius Jansen, and David Goerz, who were prominent in the resettlement program. New communities were established on open lands from Oklahoma to Manitoba, with the largest settlements in Kansas.

THE BRETHREN. Among those awakened by the Pietist movement of the late seventeenth century, a movement that stressed personal piety over rigid doctrinal conformity, was a group of citizens of the Palatinate, an area now in western Germany. Influenced by the Mennonites in the vicinity, they decided to separate themselves from the state church. Their leader, Alexander Mack (1679–1735), recorded the event:

> In the year 1708 eight persons agreed to establish a covenant of a good conscience with God, to accept all ordinances of Jesus Christ as an easy yoke, and thus to follow after their Lord Jesus—their good and loyal shepherd—as true sheep in joy or sorrow until the blessed end.... These eight persons united with one another as brethren and sisters in the covenant of the cross of Jesus Christ as a church of Christian believers.
>
> Durnbaugh, *The European Origins of the Brethren*, 1958, p. 121.

As a part of the act of forming the new church, they rebaptized themselves, thus placing the community in the Anabaptist tradition, a tradition reinforced by their use of the German language upon their arrival in America.

While the residents of the Palatinate had changed state churches after the religious wars, neither Catholics, Lutherans, nor Reformed were happy with separatists, that is, those who wanted to separate from the state church. People like the Brethren were subject to persecution, and rather than give up their faith, the Brethren migrated, first to Wittgenstein and then to the Netherlands. Toleration diminished further as they began to win over members of the state church.

During this time, the Brethren became influenced by Gottfried Arnold (1666–1714), a historian. Arnold had written several books on the early life of the church that he believed normative for all Christians. He introduced through his writings the idea of triune immersion as the proper mode of baptism. The believer, on his knees in the water, is immersed three times in the name of the Father, Son, and Holy Spirit. The Brethren also continued a close contact with the Mennonites.

By 1719, little more than a decade after their formation, the Brethren began to think about the New World as a home. Having become familiar with William Penn's experiment in Pennsylvania from his continental visits and those of his Quaker followers, they began to migrate to Germantown. The migration was completed by 1735, and the few remaining Brethren in Europe became Mennonites.

The first Brethren Church in America was established in 1723 after the Brethren corresponded with their European counterparts. They chose Peter Becker (1687–1758) as their pastor. He proceeded to baptize the first American converts and to preside over the first love feast, a service that included foot washing, a group meal, and the Lord's Supper. This church is the mother congregation of the present-day Church of the Brethren.

THE FRIENDS (QUAKERS).

In mid-seventeenth-century England, the early stages of the Reformation were beginning to be felt in a practical way. Dissidents whose perspective reflected the religious ferment of the continent began to appear. One of the men whose perspective was in line with that of the continental radical reformers was George Fox (1624–1691)—mystic, psychic, social activist, and founder of the Quakers.

Fox had begun to preach in 1647 after experiencing an inner illumination and hearing a voice that said, "There is One, even Christ Jesus, that can speak to thy condition." The experiences of the inner light came as a psychic-spiritual awakening, and Fox developed a reputation as "a young man with a discerning spirit." Fox was a powerful preacher and a charismatic personality. Many of the gifts of the Holy Spirit (I Corinthians 12:4–11) were regular elements of his ministry.

Fox was an intense activist on the social scene. He was an early prohibitionist and a preacher against holidays, entertainments, and sports, saying that such activities directed people's thoughts to vanity and looseness. During the wars waged when Oliver Cromwell (1599–1658) ruled England, Fox emerged as a peace advocate, a position held by many radical reformers. Thrown into prison for his activities, he converted the jailer and became a pioneer prison reformer.

A group of followers soon gathered around Fox, and in 1667 they were organized into a system with monthly, quarterly, and yearly meetings. Their one doctrinal peculiarity was their belief in the inner light. The Quakers believed that God's revelation was not limited to the Bible but continued in a living daily contact between the believer and the divine Spirit. The light would lead toward the road to perfection. Fox's followers, always on the edge of mere subjectivism, escaped it by constantly testing their light by the teachings and example of Jesus.

The Bible is the sourcebook of the Quaker faith, and from it Fox drew many ideas that became part of the peculiar ethos of Quaker life and an offense to non-Quakers. For example, Fox believed that much of the activity of the world was vanity. He exhorted Quakers to lead simple lives that were not wasted in frivolity. Dress was to be simple. No wigs were to be worn, nor were gold or vain decorations worn on clothing. A Quaker costume developed from these injunctions. The biblical use of the familiar tense (thy and thou) became standard for Quakers, although most have now deserted this practice.

The Quaker organization was built around "meetings" for Friends in a certain area. These meetings—monthly, quarterly, and yearly—handled business on an increasingly geographical basis. For many years, the monthly and quarterly meetings addressed organization and discipline. Meetings developed as needs manifested themselves. As early as 1668, a "General Meeting of Ministers" was held. This meeting, repeated in 1672, evolved into the yearly meeting as a general organizational body. Thus, for Quakers, the word *meeting* can mean "church."

Quaker worship also took on a particular form, in negative reaction to Anglican formality and liturgy and in positive reaction to the inner-light doctrine. Without clergy, the Quakers would sit in silence and wait for the Holy Spirit to move them. Often, no word would be spoken, but as Francis Howgill (1618–1669), a prominent early Quaker, noted: "The Lord of heaven and earth we found to be near at hand, and we waited on Him in pure silence, our minds out of all things, His heavenly presence appeared in our assemblies, when there was no language, tongue or speech from any creature."

Through the years, under the influence of other Protestants, particularly the Holiness churches that take John Wesley (1703–1791) as their founder, free church worship patterns began to replace the Quaker meeting. For example, the Quakers adopted such practices of the Holiness churches as a more programmed worship service, with a minister who would preach. Contemporary Quakers can be divided into the unprogrammed, who follow the old Quaker meeting format, and the programmed, who have an ordered worship that includes hymns, vocal prayer, Bible reading, and a sermon.

QUAKERS IN THE UNITED STATES. Quakers found their way to America within a decade of the beginning of George Fox's public ministry in England; individuals arrived as early as 1655. They found at first no more favorable home in the colonies than they had left in England. However, Rhode Island soon became their sanctuary, and the first meeting was established there in 1661. George Fox's visit in 1671 to 1673 spurred the growth of the infant group.

In the 1660s, the man destined to become the most important figure in the early life of the Quakers in the colonies—William Penn (1644–1718)—joined the British Friends. Penn was the son of a British admiral. He become a Quaker after meeting George Fox, and became deeply impressed by the problem of persecution that they faced. Heir to a small fortune from the king, Penn accepted a tract of land (the state of Pennsylvania) instead of the money. Here he established a Quaker colony and began the great experiment of trying to mold a colony on a biblical model. To the everlasting credit of Penn, religious freedom was the order of the day, even for Jews and Turks.

In the next century, American Quakers would begin to make social history. Believing as they did in social justice, especially as it expressed itself in the equality of human beings, Quakers began a campaign against slavery. One of their number, John Woolman (1720–1772), became a widely traveled leader in early Christian antislavery efforts. A mission was begun among the Indians, in line with the same belief in human equality. Quakers controlled the Pennsylvania government until 1756, when they gave up their seats rather than vote in favor of war measures during the French and Indian War (1754–1763).

The first General Meeting of Friends was held in 1681 at Burlington, New Jersey, and meetings were held annually for several years at both Burlington and Philadelphia. In 1685 these two meetings were given the name the General Yearly Meeting for Friends of Pennsylvania, East Jersey, and of the Adjacent Provinces. This became the Philadelphia Yearly Meeting, the oldest Quaker group still in existence in the United States.

Quakers, induced by the promise of freedom of conscience, migrated into tracts of land in the southern United States and established large settlements. Slavery soon became an issue, and in the decades before and after 1800, most Quakers left the South as a protest and moved to Indiana and Ohio. To this day, most Quakers live in the Midwest, and few live south of the Ohio River.

As Quakerism expanded westward, regionally based yearly meetings were formed as autonomous units in harmony with eastern counterparts. As time passed and issues came and went, these yearly meetings became the basis for denominational units and late-nineteenth-century ecumenical endeavors.

The general unity of the American Friends remained until the 1820s, when schism began to rend the Friends and produced the various denominational bodies that exist today. Philadelphia remains home to a broadly based, if more conservative, form of Quakerism.

Quakers, while fitting clearly within the free church tradition and following the European spiritual Anabaptist faith, deviate from other groups on several points. The baptism issue, a matter of intense Anabaptist interest, was solved by dropping water baptism entirely. As a natural outgrowth of Schwenckfelder belief in the primacy of the spiritual, Quakers hold that the one baptism of Ephesians 4:4–5 is the inward baptism of the Holy Spirit (see the article on the Schwenckfelder Church in America). Women have also held an unusual status in Quakerism, their right to full participation having been accepted at an early date. Women were thus accepted into the Quaker ministry earlier than in most other churches.

Doctrinally, Quakers have followed a Protestant lead and profess a belief in the fatherhood of God, Jesus Christ as Lord and Savior, the Holy Spirit, salvation by faith, and the priesthood of believers. However, Quakers maintain a free church anticreedal stance, and while most Quaker bodies have a statement of belief, they usually preface it with a disclaimer against a static orthodoxy, and a wide range of beliefs are held. Evangelical practices became a dominant element in the nineteenth century, and, as the century closed, Wesleyan Holiness became a force. In the early twentieth century, a liberal-conservative split began to emerge, leading to several schisms. The conservative elements tended to identify with Holiness ideals and withdrew from the larger Friends' Meetings to form most of the smaller bodies. The Evangelical Friends International, which continues the Association of Evangelical Friends (formed in 1947), serves as an ecumenical body for the conservatives.

While divided into several denominations, Quakers have been able to maintain an intense social-activism witness in some intrafamily structures. The American Friends Service Committee, founded during World War I (1914–1918), emerged as an expression of national loyalty for Quakers seeking to serve in war-alternative activities. It has gained wide respect for its refugee work. The Friends Committee for National Legislation is a nonpartisan lobby group.

OTHER EUROPEAN FREE CHURCHES.

Besides the churches in the four main free church traditions discussed above, Europe has been the birthing place of numerous free church groups over the centuries. Some of

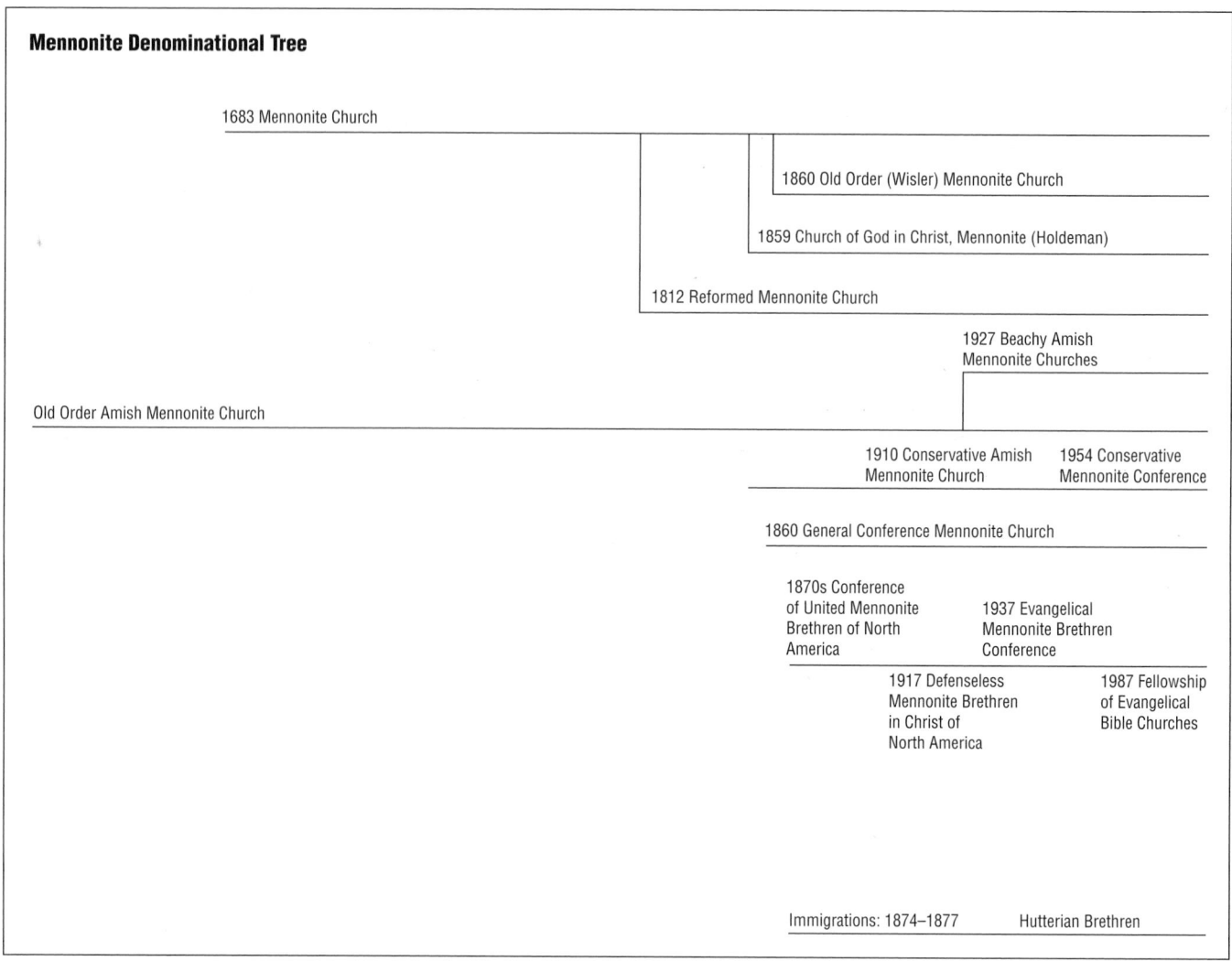

Mennonite Denominational Tree

1683 Mennonite Church

1860 Old Order (Wisler) Mennonite Church

1859 Church of God in Christ, Mennonite (Holdeman)

1812 Reformed Mennonite Church

1927 Beachy Amish Mennonite Churches

Old Order Amish Mennonite Church

1910 Conservative Amish Mennonite Church

1954 Conservative Mennonite Conference

1860 General Conference Mennonite Church

1870s Conference of United Mennonite Brethren of North America

1937 Evangelical Mennonite Brethren Conference

1917 Defenseless Mennonite Brethren in Christ of North America

1987 Fellowship of Evangelical Bible Churches

Immigrations: 1874–1877   Hutterian Brethren

Adapted from Association of Religion Data Archives

these are the product of the particular ministry of one person, with the church forming around his or her teachings. Some churches have followed the emergence of a revival movement in a limited area. Still others represent a renewal of piety among a particular ethnic group within a larger society or the protest of what is felt to be a repressive action by a state church. In each case, however, these churches represent a new religious impulse that is separate from a country's dominant religious establishment. The great majority of the European free churches have never been transplanted to North America.

Among the groups that did immigrate to the United States, one arrived from Russia. Beginning with what was termed the Great Schism in the seventeenth century, a series of dissenting sects emerged in the Russian Orthodox Church, and disturbed the unity of the religious landscape. In the 1650s, the division between the better-educated urban hierarchy of the Russian church and the poorer and less-educated clergy and laity in the scattered rural communities was accentuated by a controversy over ritual. The controversy centered around Nikon (1605–1681), a young monk who, having

attained the favor of the czar, rose from obscurity to become the church's patriarch. Nikon tried to introduce a greater degree of uniformity into Orthodox worship, using the Greek church as his standard. He placed very high on his program the correcting of the numerous corrupt service books then in use. Most of his changes were received as new innovations. Gradually, as unrest with Nikon's changes led to the burning of new ritual books, the czar abandoned him, and Nikon was banished. However, at the same council of the church in 1666 at which Nikon was deposed, his reforms were adopted. Those who opposed the reforms, a group known as the Raskol, were excommunicated. The Raskol, or Old Believers, developed as a separate body after the council. They would later divide into two main groups, the Popovtsy, or priestists, and the Bezpopovtsy, or priestless.

The immediate problem of the Popovtsy was the establishment of episcopal leadership, as no bishops chose to join with them. Bishops, however, were necessary for the ordination of priests. For almost two centuries, the Popovtsy found their priests from among those who left the state church. It was not until the nineteenth century that they were able to develop a hierarchy. In 1844 some Old Believers residing in the territory controlled by the Austro-Hungarian Empire were able to persuade the government to designate an Old Believers' episcopal see at Bela Krynica (or Belokrinitsa). In 1846 Ambrose, the former bishop of Sarajevo, assumed the new position. Before the Russian government could react, Ambrose consecrated a number of bishops for the Popovtsy Old Believers. Bishops in this Belokrinitskaya line of succession continue to the present, with archbishops in Moscow and in Galati, Romania, where the see of Bela Krynica moved after being overrun by the Russians during World War II (1937–1945).

In 1918, in the wake of the Russian Revolution, Patriarch Tikhon (1865–1925) consecrated a bishop for the Yedinovertsy, a group of Old Believers that had made partial peace with the established church at the beginning of the nineteenth century. The established church had agreed to ordain their priests and allow them to follow the old rites. Their first bishop was killed in 1921 by the Communists, and it is believed that his successor met a similar fate. A third line of Popovtsy, the Beglopopovtsy, or Wandering Priestists, gained their own episcopal authority in the Soviet Union following World War II. The archbishop resides at Kuibyshev (Samara).

The second group of Old Believers, the Bezpopovtsy, originated as people began to argue against the legitimacy of an episcopally ordained priesthood who alone could dispense the sacraments. As the basic argument was accepted, disagreements as to its implications multiplied. Some argued that they possessed a presbyterial succession of priestly authority and that their priests, ordained by a presbytery (a group of priests rather than a bishop), were able to administer the sacraments. Others argued that the Russian church had gone into apostasy and hence lost the sacramental office altogether. As differing opinions emerged, so did numerous divisions of the Bezpopovtsy. Without a hierarchy to provide a point of clear unity, differing parties became new sects with great ease. Eventually, most groups moved to limit their sacraments to those that laymen could administer—baptism and absolution. Communion was either dropped (some claiming that every meal eaten in the right spirit constituted a communion with Christ) or served with elements believed to have been consecrated in the days of true priests, that is, before Nikon.

Marriage became the most crucial problem for the priestless, as such unions can only be consecrated by a valid priest. Some tried celibacy, while others did away with marriage but allowed sexual relations as a concession to the flesh. Eventually, most adopted a form of marriage that was simply blessed by the community elder.

Somewhat different in their origin are the various groups that arose around new mystical impulses in the decades after the Great Schism. Leaders of these new groups emphasized the role of inner illumination, the place of morality over ritual, and the need for simple biblical faith uncorrupted by the teachings of the Greek fathers. Among the most important of these new groups were the Khlysty, the Doukhobors, and the Molokans.

The Khlysty originated in 1631 in Kostroma Province when a peasant, Daniel Filippov, proclaimed himself God Sabaoth who had come to give new commandments to the people. He selected another peasant to be his main prophet, whom he designated as the Christ. The mystical and ascetic doctrine of the Khlysty found many supporters throughout Russia, and a series of Christs appeared to lead the group from generation to generation. The periodic attempts by the government to suppress them usually spurred their further spread.

Among people in the Ukraine attracted to the mystical emphases but repulsed by some of their more radical notions, there arose a sect called the Doukhobors (literally, Spirit Wrestlers), originally a derisive name given to them by the Russian archbishop at Ekaterinoslav. During the leadership of Sabellius Kapustin over the group, they were deported to the Molochnye Valley. Kapustin took the opportunity to reorganize the Doukhobors into a communal society. Leadership continued in Kapustin's family after his death until 1886. At that time, a split occurred, and Peter Verigin emerged as the leader of the larger faction. It was he who arranged for most of his followers to leave Russia for Canada at the end of the nineteenth century. With the assistance of the author Leo Tolstoy (1828–1910), approximately 7,400 settled in western Canada beginning in 1899.

The Molokans were started by Simeon Uklein (b. 1733), the son-in-law of a Doukhorbor leader, in the late eighteenth century. He rejected his father-in-law's disdain for the Bible and his claims to be "Christ." Taking approximately 70 followers, Uklein formed a rival group. He proclaimed the Bible the sole authority for the faithful and rejected the allegorical methods favored by the more mystical sects. He also emphasized moral content over concern for inner illumination. Among the moral precepts of the Molokans was pacifism.

The Molokans' problems in Russia began with the introduction of compulsory military service by the czar, but their situation became critical after their refusal to bear arms in the Russo-Japanese War (1904–1905). Approximately 2,000 came to the United States between 1904 and the beginning of World War I.

Besides the Russian groups, free churches from various parts of Europe, including Norway and Switzerland, have been transplanted to America. In all likelihood, others, as yet operating quietly out of members' homes, have arrived in the United States, and more will come in the future.

ECUMENISM. European free churches provide a religious home to people who have left the more established churches and state churches of Europe. Free churches do not share a common theological heritage, except for their basic affirmation with all of Christendom. Thus, there are no ecumenical structures that unite these churches in a common organization. The free churches share a heritage of persecution by the older churches. They have disassociated themselves from such ecumenical organization as the World

Council of Churches and National Council of Churches, which traditionally have been dominated by the older Reformation churches.

The free churches should not be seen as unresponsive to twenty-first-century ecumenical imperative, but they generally favor structures that demand less commitment than the councils of churches. They have formed family ecumenical structures for those churches that share either a Mennonite (World Mennonite Conference) or Friends (Friends World Committee for Consultation) heritage.

SOURCES

Mennonites, among the most historically conscious of religious communities, have established a number of historical libraries. The Archives of the Mennonite Church, at 1700 S. Main, Goshen, IN 46526, issues the *Mennonite Historical Bulletin*. Canadian Mennonite history and archives are focused at the Mennonite Heritage Centre supported by the General Conference of Mennonites in Canada, 600 Shaftsbury Blvd., Winnipeg, Manitoba R3P 0M4.

The primary archives of the Church of the Brethren are at 1451 Dundee Ave., Elgin, IL 60521. The nearby Bethany Theological Seminary publishes the quarterly *Brethren Life and Thought*.

The Friends support the Friends Historical Library at Swathmore College, Swathmore, PA 19081, and the Friends Historical Association, headquartered at the Haverford College Library, Haverford, PA 19041. The association publishes the semiannual *Quaker History*.

General Sources

Durnbaugh, Donald F. *The Believer's Church: The History and Character of Radical Protestantism*. New York: Macmillan, 1968. 315 pp.

Grimm, Harold J. *The Reformation Era: 1500–1650*. 2nd ed. New York: Macmillan, 1973. 594 pp.

Hillerbrand, Hans J., ed. *The Oxford Encyclopedia of the Reformation*. 4 vols. New York: Oxford University Press, 1996.

Jones, Rufus M. *Spiritual Reformers of the Sixteenth and Seventeenth Centuries*. Boston: Beacon Press, 1914. 362 pp.

Kraybill, Donald B., and Carl F. Bowman. *On the Backroad to Heaven: Old Order Hutterites, Mennonites, Amish, and Brethren*. Baltimore, MD: Johns Hopkins University Press, 2001. 352 pp.

Kraybill, Donald B., and C. Nelson Hostetter. *Anabaptist World USA*. Scottdale, PA: Herald Press, 2001. 294 pp.

Littell, Franklin H. *The Anabaptist View of the Church: A Study in the Origins of Sectarian Protestantism*. 2nd ed. New York: Macmillan, 1952. 231 pp.

Snyder, C. Arnold, *Anabaptist History and Theology: Revised Student Edition*. Kitchener, ON: Pandora Press, 1997.

Spotts, Charles D. *Denominations Originating in Lancaster County, Pennsylvania*. Lancaster, PA: Franklin and Marshall College Library, 1963. 41 pp.

Williams, George H. *The Radical Reformation*. Philadelphia: Westminster Press, 1962. 924 pp.

The Mennonites

Barrett, Lois. *A Mennonite Statement and Study on Violence*. Newton, KS: Faith and Life Press; Scottdale, PA: Herald Press, 1998.

Bender, Harold S. *Two Centuries of American Mennonite Literature: A Bibliography of Mennonitica Americana, 1727–1928*. Goshen, IN: Mennonite Historical Society, 1929.

Dyck, Cornelius. *An Introduction to Mennonite History: A Popular History of the Anabaptists and the Mennonites*. Lancaster, PA: Herald Press, 1993. 456 pp.

Epp, Frank H. *Mennonites in Canada, 1786–1920: The History of a Separate People*. Toronto, ON: Macmillan of Canada, 1974. 480 pp.

———. *Mennonites in Canada, 1920–1940: A People's Struggle for Survival*. Toronto, ON: Macmillan of Canada, 1982. 640 pp.

Hostetler, Beulah Stauffer. *American Mennonites and Protestant Movements: A Community Paradigm*. Scottdale, PA: Herald Press, 1987. 366 pp.

Hostetler, John A. *Mennonite Life*. Rev. ed. Scottsdale, PA: Herald Press, 1959. 39 pp.

Loewen, Harry, ed. *Mennonite Images: Historical, Cultural, and Literary Images Dealing with Mennonite Issues*. Winnipeg, MB: Hyperion Press, 1980. 279 pp.

MacMaster, Richard K. *Land, Piety, Peoplehood: The Establishment of Mennonite Communities in America, 1683–1790*. Scottdale, PA: Herald Press, 1985. 340 pp.

The Mennonite Encyclopedia: A Comprehensive Reference Work on the Anabaptist-Mennonite Movement. 5 vols. Hillsboro, KS: Mennonite Brethren Publishing House, 1955–1990.

Quiring, Walter, and Helen Bartel. *Mennonites in Canada: A Pictorial Review*. Altona, MB: Friesen, 1961. 208 pp.

Redekop, Calvin W. *Mennonite Society*. Baltimore, MD: Johns Hopkins University Press, 1989. 397 pp.

Scott, Stephen. *An Introduction to Old Order and Conservative Mennonite Groups*. Intercourse, PA: Good Books, 1996. 252 pp.

Simons, Menno. *The Complete Writings of Menno Simons, 1491–1561*. Ed. and trans. Leonard Verduin. Scottsdale, PA: Herald Press, 1956. 1092 pp.

Springer, Nelson P., and A. J. Klassen, eds. *Mennonite Bibliography, 1631–1961*. 2 vols. Scottdale, PA: Herald Press, 1977.

Waltner, James H. *This We Believe*. Newton, KS: Faith and Life Press, 1968. 230 pp.

Wenger, John Christian. *The Doctrines of the Mennonites*. Scottdale, PA: Mennonite Publishing House, 1950. 160 pp.

The Amish

Coleman, Bill. *The Gift to Be Simple: Life in the Amish Country*. San Francisco: Chronicle Books, 2001. 120 pp.

Hostetler, John A. *Amish Life*. Scottdale, PA: Herald Press, 1959. 39 pp. Rev. ed., 1983. 48 pp.

———. *Amish Society*. Baltimore, MD: Johns Hopkins Press, 1963. Rev. ed., 1993. 435 pp.

———. *An Annotated Bibliography on the Amish*. Scottdale, PA: Mennonite Publishing House, 1951. 100 pp.

Kraybill, Donald B. *The Riddle of Amish Culture*. Baltimore, MD: Johns Hopkins University Press, 1989. 304 pp. Rev. ed., 2001. 387 pp.

Schreiber, William. *Our Amish Neighbors*. Chicago: University of Chicago Press, 1962. 227 pp.

Smith, Elmer Lewis. *The Amish*. Witmer, PA: Applied Arts, 1966. 34 pp.

The Russian Mennonites

Smith, C. Henry. *The Coming of the Russian Mennonites*. Berne, IN: Mennonite Book Concern, 1927. 296 pp.

Stucky, Harley J. *A Century of Russian Mennonite History in America*. North Newton, KS: Mennonite Press, 1974. 119 pp.

The Brethren

The Brethren Encyclopedia. 4 vols. Philadelphia: Brethren Encyclopedia, Inc., 1983–2005.

Durnbaugh, Donald F., ed. *The European Origins of the Brethren: A Source Book on the Beginnings of the Church of the Brethren in the Early Eighteenth Century*. Elgin, IL: Brethren Press, 1958. 463 pp.

———. "A Brethren Bibliography, 1713–1963." *Brethren Life and Thought* 9, 1–2 (1964): 3–177.

———, ed. *The Brethren in Colonial America: A Source Book on the Transplantation and Development of the Church of the Brethren in the Eighteenth Century.* Elgin, IL: Brethren Press, 1967. 659 pp.

———. *Guide to Research in Brethren History.* Elgin, IL: Church of the Brethren General Board, 1977. 16 pp.

———. *Fruit of the Vine: A History of the Brethren, 1708–1995.* Elgin, IL: Brethren Press, 1997. 675 pp.

Holsinger, H. R. *History of the Tunkers and the Brethren Church.* Lathrop, CA: Author, 1901. 827 pp. Reprint, North Manchester, IN: Schultz, 1962.

Mallot, Floyd E. *Studies in Brethren History.* Elgin, IL: Brethren Publishing House, 1954. 382 pp.

Sappington, Roger E., ed. *The Brethren in the New Nation: A Source Book on the Development of the Church of the Brethren, 1785–1865.* Elgin, IL: Brethren Press, 1976. 496 pp.

Willoughby, William G. *Counting the Cost: The Life of Alexander Mack, 1679–1735.* Elgin, IL: Brethren Press, 1979. 176 pp.

The Friends (Quakers)

Bacon, Margaret Hope. *The Quiet Rebels: The Story of the Quakers in America.* Wallingford, PA: Pendle Hill, 1999. 249 pp.

Baltzell, E. Digby. *Puritan Boston and Quaker Philadelphia.* Boston: Beacon Press, 1979. 585 pp.

Barbour, Hugh, and J. William Frost. *The Quakers.* New York: Greenwood Press, 1988. 407 pp.

Barbour, Hugh, and Arthur O. Roberts, eds. *Early Quaker Writings, 1650–1700.* Grand Rapids, MI: Eerdmans, 1973. 622 pp.

Benjamin, Philip S. *The Philadelphia Quakers in the Industrial Age: 1865–1920.* Philadelphia: Temple University Press, 1976. 301 pp.

Birkel, Michale L. *Silence and Witness: The Quaker Tradition.* Maryknoll, NY: Orbis, 2004. 164 pp.

Brinton, Howard H., ed. *Children of Light: In Honor of Rufus M. Jones.* New York: Macmillan, 1938. 416 pp.

Comfort, William Wistar. *Just Among Friends: The Quaker Way of Life.* Philadelphia: Blakiston, 1945. 178 pp.

Elliott, Errol T. *Quakers on the American Frontier: A History of the Westward Migrations, Settlements, and Developments of Friends on the American Continent.* Richmond, IN: Friends United Press, 1969. 434 pp.

Evans, Thomas. *A Concise Account of the Religious Society of Friends.* Philadelphia: Friends Books Store, c. 1870. 161 pp.

Friends Directory of Meeting, Churches, and Worship Groups in the Section of the Americas & Resource Guide. Philadelphia: Friends World Committee for Consultation, Section of the Americas, 1996. 256 pp.

Hamm, Thomas D. *The Transformation of American Quakerism: Orthodox Friends, 1800–1907.* Bloomington: Indiana University Press, 1988.

Holder, Charles Frederick. *The Quakers in Great Britain and America.* Los Angeles: Neuner, 1913. 669 pp.

Jones, Rufus. *The Quakers in the American Colonies* (1911). New York: Norton, 1966. 606 pp.

Peck, George T. *What Is Quakerism? A Primer.* Wallingford, PA: Pendle Hill, 1988. 47 pp.

Quakers Around the World. London: Friends World Committee for Consultation, 1994. 157 pp.

Van Etten, Henry. *George Fox and the Quakers.* New York: Harper, 1959. 191 pp.

Yount, David. *How the Quakers Invented America.* Lanham, MD: Rowman & Littlefield, 2007. 192 pp.

Other European Free Church Traditions

Bolshakoff, Serge. *Russian Nonconformity: The Story of "Unofficial" Religion in Russia.* Philadelphia: Westminster Press, 1950. 192 pp.

Conybeare, Frederick C. *Russian Dissenters.* Cambridge, MA: Harvard University Press, 1921. 370 pp.

Struve, Nikita. *Christians in Contemporary Russia.* Trans. Lancelot Sheppard and A. Manson. New York: Scribner's, 1967. 464 pp.

Intrafaith Organizations

Friends World Committee for Consultation

c/o Office of the Executive Secretary, Section of the Americas, 1506 Race St., Philadelphia, PA 19102

Alternative Address: World Office: 173 Euston Rd., London NW1 2AX, England.

Following World War I, members of the Religious Society of Friends gathered in an international conference in 1920 in London and first recommended the formation of an organization to give expression to the sense of fellowship among Friends around the world. In 1937, at the Friends World Conference, the Friends World Committee for Consultation was formed. It was to have a consultative capacity but also to promote cooperation and interaction between Friends in various groups around the world. As war soon broke out, it met irregularly through the 1940s and only gained some stability in the early 1950s. It has become the major instrument through which Friends relate to the larger Christian world and the international ecumenical movement.

Since 1952 the committee has met triennially (most recently in Dublin, Ireland, in 2007). It has international offices in London and regional offices on every continent. Periodically it sponsors world conferences of Friends. It also publishes a directory of the different Friends Meetings in each country.

The work of the committee in North America is carried out through its office in Philadelphia, Pennsylvania. The American Section was formed soon after the founding of the committee. The section publishes a directory of all of the Friends congregations (termed monthly meetings, churches, and worship groups) in the Western Hemisphere.

Membership: According to the Friends World Committee for Consultation, most Friends churches and meetings in the United States and Canada are affiliated with the committee.

Sources:

Friends World Committee for Consultation—Religious Society of Friends (Quakers). www.fwccworld.org/.

Finding Friends Around the World. London: Friends World Committee for Consultation, 1982.

FWCC Friends Directory. Philadelphia: Friends World Committee for Consultation, 1987.

Mennonite World Conference

2529 Willow Ave., Clovis, CA 93612

Alternate Address: International Headquarters: c/o Exec. Sec. Larry Miller, 8, rue du Fossé des Treize, 67000 Strasbourg, France.

The Mennonite World Conference was founded in 1925 but grew out of a proposal first published and circulated prior to World War I. The first gathering of Mennonites internationally, held at Basel, Switzerland, occurred on the anniversary of the first Mennonite baptism in 1625 and was attended primarily by German, Swiss, French, and Dutch representatives. One person attended from the United States, but the two Russian delegates were unable to obtain a visa to enter Switzerland. The conference became more active after World War II and has grown steadily in its representation of Mennonites in both North America and the Third World.

The conference seeks to further the Christian witness of Mennonites with a particular emphasis on loving interaction between various Mennonite churches, ethical concerns, and the peace witness. It seeks to maintain a network of communication and information for member organizations, to establish task forces, and to facilitate education, theological studies, and publications. It publishes the *Mennonite World Handbook* following each meeting of the conference.

Membership: Members of the Conference in North America include the following: Beach Amish Mennonite Fellowship; Bergthaler Churches of Alberta and Saskatchewan; Brethren in Christ General Conference; Chortitzer Mennonite Conference; Church of God in Christ, Mennonite; Conference of Mennonites in Canada; Eastern Pennsylvania Mennonite Church; Evangelical Mennonite Church; Evangelical Mennonite Conference (Canada); Evangelical Mennonite Mission Conference; General Conference Mennonite Church; General Conference of Mennonite Brethren Churches; Hutterian Brethren; Hutterian Brethren of New York, Inc.; Markham-Waterloo Conference (Mennonite); Mennonite Church; New Reinland Mennonite Church of Ontario; Old Colony Mennonite Church—Alberta; Old Colony Mennonite Church—British Columbia; Old Colony Mennonite Church—Manitoba; Old Colony Mennonite Church—Ontario; Old Colony Mennonite Church—Saskatchewan; Old Order Amish; Old Order Mennonites; Old Order River Brethren; Reinland Mennonite Church; and Sommerfelder Mennonite Church.

Sources:

Mennonite World Conference. www.mwc-cmm.org.

Mennonite World Handbook: Mennonites in Global Mission. Carol Stream, IL: Mennonite World Conference, 1990.

 German Mennonites

Brethren in Christ

PO Box A, Grantham, PA 17027-0290

Alternate Address: Canadian Headquarters: 2700 Bristol Cir., Oakville, ON, Canada L6H 6E1

The Brethren in Christ Church (originally called Brethren but soon known as River Brethren) formed in the late 1770s in the intense religious atmosphere of Lancaster County, Pennsylvania. The Brethren, some of whom were Mennonites, had been influenced by the Pietist movement and Dunker tradition, and accepted trine (thrice) immersion as the proper mode of baptism. Among the first to be immersed in this manner were Jacob Engel and Peter Witmer. The original group of about 14 met in the upper room of Engel's home in Stackstown, Pennsylvania.

Soon after this meeting, organization was effected and Engel was elected bishop. Trine immersion was a central feature. Doctrine was otherwise drawn from the Anabaptist-Brethren consensus, but with an emphasis on Pietism. Later, it was also positively affected by the Wesleyan Holiness Movement, which taught a doctrine of sanctification that included the belief that individual believers could become and should expect to be made perfect in love in this earthly life. In the mid-nineteenth century three groups emerged from the original one because of doctrinal and accommodationist differences. The three groups were the Brethren in Christ, the Old Order River Brethren (earlier called the Yorker Brethren), and the United Zion's Children, later called United Zion Church.

The Brethren in Christ represented the largest wing of the River Brethren. The name was adopted and registered with the federal government in 1863, though the church was not incorporated until 1904. Through migration of members in search of better economic opportunities, the church spread across the United States and Canada. Since the 1950s the church has tripled through its evangelistic efforts.

The Brethren in Christ Church is congregationally organized, with eight regional conferences and a general conference to carry out churchwide programs. A Board for World Missions oversees work in 23 countries, among 70 groups. The church operates Evangel Press, located in Nappanee, Indiana, and publishes books as well as other Brethren in Christ literature. Two retirement centers, Messiah Village in Mechanicsburg, Pennsylvania, and Upland Manor in Upland, California, are supported by the church. Ministries to the marginalized include Lifeline Women's Shelter in Upland, California, and Paxton Street Ministries in Harrisburg, Pennsylvania. Several camps are operated regionally. The Brethren in Christ Church

is a member of the National Association of Evangelicals and the Mennonite Central Committee.

Membership: In 2008 the church reported 27,000 members, 301 congregations, and 545 clergy.

Educational Facilities:

Messiah College, Grantham, Pennsylvania.

Periodicals: *In Part • Shalom! • Brethren in Christ History and Life*.

Sources:

Brethren in Christ. www.bic-church.org/.

Hostetler, Paul, ed. *Perfect Love and War*. Nappanee, IN: Evangel Press, 1974.

Sider, E. Morris. *Reflections on a Heritage: Defining the Brethren in Christ*. Nappanee, IN: Evangel Publishing House, 1999.

Wittlinger, Carlton O. *Quest for Piety and Obedience*. Nappanee, IN: Evangel Press, 1978.

Church of God in Christ, Mennonite

420 N Wedel, Moundridge, KS 67107

At age 21, John Holdeman (1832–1900), a member of the Mennonite Church, had an intense religious experience that changed his life. Following his baptism, he began a period of serious study of the Bible and of the writings of Menno Simons (1496–1561). As a result of his studies, he came to believe that his church had departed from the true way. Holdeman emerged as a young powerful leader and visionary.

He began to hold meetings at his home, and spread his concerns through the writing and publishing of his major books. He felt that the Mennonite Church had grown worldly and departed from the true faith; did not rigidly screen candidates for baptism to ensure that they had been born again; was not strict enough in their avoidance of the excommunicated; and neglected the proper training of children. He also objected to choosing ministers by lot and felt it was wrong to receive money on loans. While he found much agreement with his observations, few would join him in reformative action.

Growth of his church was slow until the late 1870s when he encountered the German-speaking immigrants who had just arrived from Russia. In 1878 the first church was built, and the first conversion of many people to his church occurred in the Lone Tree township of McPherson County, Kansas. Holdeman became the first minister to successfully introduce revivalism into a Mennonite framework. Revivals accounted for much of the rapid growth of his movement in the late nineteenth century, especially in the immigrant communities of Kansas and Manitoba, Canada. A slow and steady growth period followed through the early twentieth century, followed by a rapid expansion in both North America and abroad after World War II (1939–1945). The greatest concentration of members is in Kansas and Manitoba.

The church follows the Anabaptist-Mennonite doctrinal consensus with strong emphasis upon repentance and the new birth, a valid believer's baptism, separation from the world, excommunication of unfaithful members, a humble way of life, nonresistance, plain and modest dress, the wearing of the beard for men, and devotional covering for women.

The church is headed by a delegated general conference, which meets when the need arises. It is composed of unpaid ministers, deacons, and lay people. Its decisions are binding on the congregations. It oversees the Gospel Tract and Bible Society, Gospel Publishers (the publishing arm of the church), three mission boards, and numerous other functions. There are congregations in 31 states, eight Canadian provinces, Brazil, Belize, the Dominican Republic, Ghana, Guatemala, Haiti, India, Jamaica, Kenya, Latvia, Malawi, Mexico, Mozambique, Nigeria, the Philippines, Romania, Russia, the Ukraine, and Zimbabwe. Most North American congregations have an elementary parochial school attached to them. The church supports one hospital, seven nursing homes, and four children's homes.

Membership: In 2001, the church reported 12,754 members in the United States and 4,289 in Canada. There were a total of 19,269 members worldwide in 227 congregations and approximately 60 mission stations.

Periodicals: *Messenger of Truth.* • *Christian Mission Voice.*

Sources:

Hiebert, Clarence. *The Holdeman People: The Church of God in Christ.* South Pasadena, CA: William Carey Library, 1973.

Congregational Bible Church

Community Bible Church, 331 Anderson Ferry Rd., PO Box 180, Marietta, PA 17547

The Congregational Bible Church was formed in 1951 at Marietta, Pennsylvania, as a result of a conflict between John S. Hiestand and the Lancaster Mennonite Conference. Hiestand supported the use of radio broadcasts as a tool for evangelism, but the Lancaster Mennonite Conference considered this a violation of its Rules and Discipline. On Easter 1951 Hiestand went ahead with his program, the Crusade for Christ Hour, after which he was relieved of his position. He invited anyone who was interested to join him for future services at the Marietta Community House, and the Congregational Mennonite Church was born. The name was changed to the Congregational Bible Church in 1969, a reflection of its gradual movement away from its Mennonite roots. The original members of the church were from six congregations of the Mennonite Church. The statement of faith is at one with Mennonite belief, but includes a statement on anointing the sick and emphasizes separation from the world. The group has an aggressive evangelistic ministry. The church is organized as a fellowship of like-minded churches and has a congregational government. The bishop or pastor is the chief officer.

Membership: Not reported.

Sources:

Congregational Bible Church. www.cbcpa.org/index.html.

Conservative Mennonite Fellowship (Nonconference)

PO Box 36, Hartville, OH 44632

The Conservative Mennonite Fellowship (Nonconference) was the result of a protest movement in the main branches of the Mennonite Church in the mid-1950s. The conservatives were concerned that Mennonites were conforming to the world (e.g., women were neglecting to cover their hair or were letting it fall down to their shoulders instead of being tied into a knot), not resisting the military strongly enough (e.g., the young men were joining the Army as noncombatants instead of staying out of the Army), and becoming too involved in civil affairs (e.g., they were voting or holding office or becoming policemen). The conservatives were also concerned about the growing acceptance of neoorthodox theology in Mennonite circles. The fellowship was formed in 1956. It added to the prior disciplinary standards (such as the Apostles' Creed, the Dordrecht Confession of Faith, and the Schleitheim Confession) the Christian Fundamentals, which emphasize strict discipline and separation from the world. These were adopted at a fellowship meeting in 1964.

Membership: Not reported. In 1967 there were 23 congregations with 980 members and an additional 50 cooperating congregations with 2,400 members.

Markham-Waterloo Conference (Mennonite)

c/o Clare Frey, Rte. 2, Elmira, ON, Canada N3B 2Z2

The Markham-Waterloo Conference (Mennonite) came into being in 1939 as the culmination of a modernization movement among some of the members of the Old Order Mennonites of Ontario. Among their concerns was the purchase of automobiles by members of the order. Such members were known as the "black bumpers," as they painted over the chrome on the cars to avoid any sign of ostentation. However, a second issue arose in the person of Bp. Jesse Bauman (1897–1974), a leader who had been chosen by lots. Bauman's preachings attracted many, but disturbed others who had little appreciation for his adoption

of a more evangelical style, which he hoped would keep the younger people from straying to nearby non-Mennonite churches. In 1939, in the face of growing criticism, Bauman withdrew from the group. About the same time, the black bumpers in Markham and Waterloo, Ontario, joined forces and created a new conference.

The Markham-Waterloo Conference continues as a very conservative Mennonite group, but less so than the old order, which does not allow the use of cars and telephones.

Membership In 1997 the group reported 10 congregations, 1,250 baptized members (and an additional 600 constituency), and 28 ordained preachers, deacons, and bishops.

Sources:

Epp, Franklin H. *Mennonites in Canada, 1920–1940: A Peoples' Struggle for Survival.* Toronto, Ontario: Macmillan of Canada, 1982.

Lichdi, Diether Gotz. *Mennonite World Handbook 1990: Mennonites in Global Mission.* Lombard, IL: Mennonite World Conference, 1990.

Mennonite Church, USA

722 Main St., PO Box 347, Newton, KS 67114-0347

Alternate Address: 500 S Main St., PO Box 1245, Elkhart, IN 46515-1245

The largest of the Mennonite bodies in North America, the Mennonite Church USA was formed in 2002 when a merger process between the Mennonite Church and the General Conference Mennonite Church that began in 1989 was completed.

Initially, the organization of Mennonites in America was a slow process because each congregation tended to be autonomous. In 1725 a conference of Pennsylvania congregations was called to consider, among other things, an English translation of the Confession of Dordrecht. Other conferences were called in particular regions to deal with various controversies. Formal conferences began to emerge in the nineteenth century. Through the twentieth century, a biennial General Assembly met as an advisory body for the entire church, whereas district conferences counseled local congregations.

In the mid-nineteenth century, John H. Oberholtzer (1805–1895), an educated young Mennonite minister, encountered trouble soon after entering the ministry in the Franconia District (located in Pennsylvania) when he began protesting the plain, collarless coat worn by most ministers. Oberholtzer argued that the coat was an arbitrary requirement originating from outside the Mennonite creed. He next asserted that the Conference of the Franconia District should adopt a written constitution so that proceedings could be conducted more systematically. The result of Oberholtzer's agitation was a parting of the ways. He withdrew from the Franconia District in 1847 at the same conference that proceeded to expel him. With 16 ministers and several congregations, he led in the organization of a new conference. A major thrust of Oberholtzer's movement was the union of all Mennonite congregations. New practices and standards were initiated, including a more liberal view of the ban (or shunning, the practice of avoiding contact with those who have withdrawn or excluded from the fellowship), open communication, intermarriage with persons of other denominations, and, within a short time, a salaried clergy. Oberholtzer proved a zealous advocate and founded the first Mennonite paper in America, the *Religioeser Botschafter* (later *Das Christliche Volksblat*).

Meanwhile, with the influx of thousands of Mennonite immigrants in the mid-1800s, other leaders were emerging and bringing into existence new churches. Daniel Hoch (1805–1878), a minister to several Mennonite churches in Ontario, Canada, had joined hands with an Ohio congregation led by Rev. Ephraim Hunsberger (1814–1904) to form, in 1855, the Conference Council of the Mennonite Communities of Canada-West and Ohio. In Lee County, Iowa, two congregations, finding themselves isolated, banded together, and called for united evangelistic efforts among members who had settled at some distance from the main body in the East. At a meeting in 1860 in Iowa, representatives of some of the above groups met and invited Oberholtzer to attend. He was chosen chairman and the General Conference Mennonite Church was organized. Their vision was the union of all Mennonite congregations in the United States and Canada.

BELIEFS. The belief of the General Conference is in accord with many other Mennonite bodies. The "Confession of Faith in a Mennonite Perspective" was adopted by the General Conference Mennonite Church and the Mennonite Church in 1995. This 24-article confession affirms the church as a Trinitarian body in the mainstream of Christian belief relative to affirmations on biblical authority, creation, salvation in Jesus Christ, and the church of believers. It describes three ordinances: baptism, the Lord's Supper, and foot washing. It also retains the traditional position of the Mennonites as a peace church and emphasizes the role of the family.

ORGANIZATION. Polity is congregational and congregations are located in 21 regional conferences. The various national church commissions that oversaw publishing, support of work in other countries, education, home missions, social concerns, and congregational life in the two former churches have been merged. They carry on a vast mission program with congregations on every continent. In the United States, home mission work is conducted among Native Americans, African Americans, Jews, the Spanish-speaking, Asian refugees, and the deaf. There are four church-wide ministry agencies: Mennonite Mission Network, Mennonite Education Agency, Mennonite Publishing Network, and Mennonite Mutual Aid.

Membership: In 2005 the Mennonite Church USA had approximately 114,000 members in 943 congregations.

Educational Facilities:

Associated Mennonite Biblical Seminary, Elkhart, Indiana

Eastern Mennonite Seminary, Harrisonburg, Virginia

Bluffton University, Bluffton, Ohio

Eastern Mennonite University, Harrisonburg, Virginia

Goshen College, Goshen, Indiana

Hesston College, Hesston, Kansas

Bethel College, North Newton, Kansas

Conrad Grebel College, Waterloo, Ontario, Canada

Periodicals: *The Mennonite.* • *Mennonite Historical Bulletin.* • *Mennonite Quarterly Review.*

Sources:

Mennonite Church, USA. www.mennoniteusa.org/.

Dyck, Cornelius C. *An Introduction to Mennonite History.* Scottdale, PA: Herald Press, 1967.

Horsch, James E., ed. *Mennonite Yearbook.* Scottdale, PA: Mennonite Publishing House, n.d.

Kaufman, Edmund G. *General Conference Mennonite Pioneers.* North Newton, KS: Bethel College, 1973.

Kraybill, Donald B., and C. Nelson Hostetter. *Anabaptist World USA.* Scottsdale, PA: Herald Press, 2001.

Krehbiel, H. P. *The History of the General Conference of the Mennonite Church of North America.* 2 vols. Newton, KS: Author, 1889–1938.

Old Order (Reidenbach) Mennonites
c/o Henry W. Riehl, Rte. 1, Columbiana, OH 44408

During World War II (1939–1945), the issue of the draft was of great concern to the Old Order Mennonites. There was a consensus that all the draft-age youths should be conscientious objectors. However, among the Old Order (Wenger) Mennonites, there developed a group who felt that prison, not alternative service (such as medical work and so forth) should be the only course in reaction to the draft. This group further insisted that those youths who accepted alternative service should be excommunicated.

This group was not supported by the majority of the *Wengerites* (as they were collectively referred). Thirty-five members of the group began to build a separate meeting house near the Reidenbach store in Lancaster County, Pennsylvania (hence the name). They remain the most conservative of the Pennsylvania Mennonites. They still use candles instead of coal oil for lighting. Rubber tires on carriages are prohibited. They are the only Pennsylvania group that currently opposes the use of school buses.

Among the Reidenbach Mennonites, there are a number of specific regulations to keep them separate from the world. Farm equipment is restricted; for example, manure spreaders are not allowed. Children go only to the one-room school and not beyond the elementary grades. The group has only one congregation.

Membership: Not reported. There is only one congregation, in Lancaster County, Pennsylvania.

Old Order (Wenger) Mennonites
c/o Henry W. Riehl, Rte. 1, Columbiana, OH 44408

Among the Old Order (Wisler) Mennonites of southeastern Pennsylvania, several schisms have developed over the continuing issue of accommodation to change. In the 1930s, the use of the automobile on a limited basis was advocated by Bp. Moses Horning (1870–1955). Bp. Joseph Wenger rejected the idea, believing automobiles should not be used for either occupational transportation or coming to worship. Wenger's group became the more conservative wing of the Old Order Mennonites. The group holds no evening services and uses only German in the pulpit. Jail, rather than alternative service, is advocated for boys of draft age.

Membership: Not reported. There are an estimated 1,000 members in southeastern Pennsylvania.

Old Order (Wisler) Mennonite Church
c/o Henry W. Riehl, Rte. 1, Columbiana, OH 44408

In the 1860s the Yellow Creek congregation of the Mennonite Church, located near Elkhart, Indiana, found itself caught between two vocal leaders. Daniel Brenneman demanded a progressive policy and the adoption of such innovations as English preaching, Sunday schools, protracted meetings, and four-part singing. He was opposed by Jacob Wisler (1808–1889), who opposed all innovations and deviations. Wisler began to ban anyone from the congregation who deviated from traditional standards in favor of modernism. Wisler's arbitrary manner of enforcing his ideas resulted in a church trial and he was removed from his office. He then took his followers and formed a new congregation in 1870.

During the following decades, other churches of like perspective were founded and then these united with Wisler's group. A group in neighboring Medina County, Ohio, was the first. A Canadian group headed by Bp. Abraham Martin from Woolwich Township, Waterloo County, Ontario, who opposed speaking in English, Sunday schools, evening meetings, "falling-top" buggies, and other modernisms, formed a separate church and later allied itself with the *Wislerites* (as they were collectively referred). In 1901 followers of Bp. Jonas Martin and Gabriel D. Heatwole (1834–1922) formed a church; this church later joined the Wislerites. Bishop Martin had been the leader of the Mennonite Church in Lancaster County, Pennsylvania, until controversy arose about installing a new pulpit in the church. Martin opposed the new pulpit because he was against innovations. He eventually would leave the Mennonite Church in Pennsylvania with one-third of the congregation following his lead. A separate group of Mennonites in Rockingham County, Virginia, led by Heatwole, joined Martin's group and would eventually align with the Wislerites.

As a group, the Old Order Mennonites remain among the most conservative in dress, forms of worship, and social customs. They are very close to the Amish in their thinking, but meet in church buildings instead of homes and do not wear beards.

Membership: Not reported. In 1972 they reported 38 congregations, 8,000 members, and 101 ministers.

Old Order (Yorker) River Brethren

Current address not obtained for this edition.

The Old Order (Yorker) River Brethren separated in 1843 from their parent church, the River Brethren (now known as the Brethren in Christ), protesting what they saw as laxity in matters of nonconformity to the world and nonresistance to the military. The group was led by Bp. Jacob Strickler Jr. (1788–1859) of York County, Pennsylvania (hence the nickname). It was joined in the 1850s by a Franklin County group headed by Bp. Christian Hoover (1793–1867), who had been expelled from the brethren for being overly orthodox.

The Old Order (Yorker) River Brethren remain the smallest of the river brethren groups, having only four congregations, all in southeastern Pennsylvania. Three small independent congregations have split off at various times in disputes over modes of transportation. All worship is conducted in members' homes, not in churches. The Old Order (Yorker) River Brethren are also agriculturists.

Membership: Not reported.

Sources:

Breckbill, Laban T. *Doctrine, Old Order River Brethren*. Lancaster, PA: Breckbill & Strickler, 1967.

————. *History of the Old Order River Brethren*. Lancaster, PA: Breckbill & Strickler, 1972.

Reynolds, Margaret C. *Plain Women: Gender and Ritual in the Old Order River Brethren*. University Park: Pennsylvania State University Press, 2001.

Reformed Mennonite Church

602 Strasburg Pke., Lancaster, PA 17602

The oldest splinter group from the Mennonite Church still intact dates from 1812. It grew out of a previously existing Separatist congregation headed by Francis Herr, who had been expelled from the church for irregularities in a horse trade. After Herr's death, his son John Herr (1782–1850), never a religious man, took up his father's faith, became convicted of sin, was baptized, and soon rose to a position of leadership. He was then chosen bishop. John Herr and his associates immediately began to issue a set of pamphlets charging the Mennonite Church with being worldly and corrupt. They complained of laxity in enforcing discipline and separation from the world. Based on Herr's ideas, the Reformed Mennonite Church was created.

In relation to the Mennonite Church, the Reformed Mennonites emphasize the exclusive claims of their particular faith, practices, and community. All who are not Reformed Mennonites are considered to be of the world and members are to distance themselves from such persons. They dress plainly and tend to live in plain surroundings. Membership is located primarily in southeastern Pennsylvania.

Membership: Not reported.

Sources:

Bear, Robert. *Delivered unto Satan*. Carlisle, PA: Author, 1974.

Christianity Defined. Lancaster, PA: Reformed Mennonite Church, 1958.

Funk, John F. *The Mennonite Church and Her Accusers*. Elkhart, IN: Mennonite Publishing, 1878.

The Reformed Mennonites: Who They Are and What They Believe. Lancaster, PA: Reformed Mennonite Church, n.d.

Stauffer Mennonite Church

Current address not obtained for this edition.

Jacob Stauffer (1889–1987), a minister in the Mennonite Church at Groffdale, Pennsylvania, was the leader of a group in a progressive-conservative split. The issue was what conservatives viewed as a lax approach in the banning of unworthy or corrupt members from the church, which Stauffer and colleague Joseph Wenger, of the Old Order (Wenger) Mennonites, believed should be applied more

strictly. About 40 members withdrew from the Mennonite Church, demanding that there should be no communion between the church and the offender after the ban is used.

The *Stauffers* (as they are collectively referred) have continued in their conservative ways. They are part of the "horse and buggy" culture but, unlike the Amish, are clean-shaven and will ride trains on long trips. They prefer the one-room school and refrain from politics (even voting). Though never large, and hurt by one major schism, the group has grown steadily by maintaining a rather high birth rate.

Membership: Not reported.

United Zion Church

181 Hurst Dr., Ephrata, PA 17522

The United Zion Church, originally known as United Zion's Children, originated in 1855 following the expulsion of Bp. Matthias Brinser from the River Brethren (i.e., the Brethren in Christ) for building and holding services in a meetinghouse. Other than the attitude toward the use of church buildings, there were no doctrinal differences. The United Zion's Children was strengthened within a few years by the absorption of several churches formed by Henry Grumbein and Jacob Pfautz. These groups accepted Brinser because of a revelation, but remain a separate unit within the church. They constitute one of three districts that send representatives to the church's annual conference. As with the Brethren in Christ, the government of the United Zion Church is congregational. Mission work is supported through the Brethren. One home for the aged is maintained.

During the twentieth century, several attempts have been made to improve the relationship between the United Zion Church and the Brethren in Christ, and even to look toward a future reunion. In 1967 the Brethren in Christ passed a resolution asking for the forgiveness of the United Zion Church for the action of the church's council in 1855 and for a continued lack of humility on their part that has kept the two groups apart. The next year the United Zion Church issued a formal statement offering complete forgiveness. These resolutions became the basis for cooperative action on the mission field and in higher education. A member of United Zion Church currently sits on the board of the Brethren in Christ–founded Messiah College.

Membership: In 2008 the church reported five affiliated congregations.

Educational Facilities:

Messiah College, Grantham, Pennsylvania.

Periodicals: *Zion's Herald*.

Sources:

United Zion Church. www.unitedzionchurch.org/index.htm.

A History of the United Zion Church, 1853–1980. N.p. 1981.

Wittlinger, Carlton O. *Quest for Piety and Obedience*. Nappanee, IN: Evangel Press, 1978.

Weaver Mennonites

1259 Scalp Ave., Johnstown, PA 15904

The one schism affecting the Stauffer Mennonite Church was occasioned by the issue of the strictness of the ban. In 1916, the son of aged Bp. Aaron Sensenig married outside the faith. The girl was received into the Stauffer Mennonite Church but later returned to her earlier heritage. The church was split over the strictness of the ban to be applied to the girl. The lenient group, led by Sensenig and John A. Weaver, left and began a new congregation and constructed a meeting house near New Holland, Pennsylvania.

Membership: Not reported. There is one congregation of approximately 60 members.

Weaverland Conference Old Order (Horning or Black Bumper) Mennonites

Current address not obtained for this edition.

Bp. Moses Horning (1870–1955) established a liberal wing of the Old Order (Wisler) Mennonites. His followers were allowed to use automobiles, but only for necessary purposes. The car must be black and without frivolous trim. Most of the members cover the chrome with black paint to avoid further ostentation.

Membership: Not reported. There are five congregations, all located in southeastern Pennsylvania, and approximately 1,700 members.

 Russian Mennonites

Chortitzer Mennonite Conference

479 Hanover St., Steinbach, MB, Canada R5G 1M7

During the 1870s a number of German Mennonites who had lived in Russia for several generations settled in southern Manitoba, Canada, on two tracts of land on either side of the Red River, referred to as the East Reserve and the West Reserve. Among those who settled on the East Reserve were a group from Chortitza, a German colony in Russia, some of whom founded the village of Chortitz. Bp. Gerhard Wiebe emerged as the leader of this group. Wiebe was known for his desire to live in peace with his neighbors, both Mennonite and non-Mennonite. This was made difficult in part by the restrictions some Mennonite leaders had placed on their members in order to hold their communities together and continue their life as it had been in Russia.

Over the years the Chortitzer Mennonites remained a separate body, founded a separate conference, and adopted a statement of faith. The church believes in the Trinity, the Bible as the infallible authority for faith and life, and the church as the body of Christ, which has the duty of preaching, teaching, and discipling. The church has a particular task of keeping itself pure by discipling members who fall into gross sin. The church celebrates two ordinances, baptism and communion. It recognizes the legitimacy of government but also the duty of church members to refrain from mortal strife and contentions in all areas of life (such as war).

In 2008 the conference was led by Bp. Wilhelm Hildebrandt. It is organized congregationally and composed of those churches that accept its constitution and bylaws.

Membership: In 2008 the church reported 1,800 members in 15 congregations served by 34 ministers. They have affiliated work in Belize, Bolivia, Mexico, and Paraguay.

Educational Facilities:

Steinbach Bible College, Steinbach, Manitoba.

Periodicals: *CMC Chronicle.*

Sources:

Chortitzer Mennonite Conference. www.chortitzer.com/.

Dueck, Gustav, ed. *Chortitzer Mennonite Conference 1874–1990*, Altona, Manitoba: Friesens Corporation, 2004.

Epp, Frank H. *Mennonites in Canada, 1786–1920: The History of a Separate People.* Toronto: Macmillan, 1974.

———. *Mennonites in Canada, 1920–1940: A Peoples' Struggle for Survival.* Toronto: Macmillan, 1982.

Conservative Mennonite Church of Ontario

RR 2, Kippen, ON, Canada N0M 2E0

Among the Mennonite population of Canada in the early twentieth century, three tendencies of thought arose. Some Mennonites, most of whom had migrated from Europe, sought means of accommodating their new situation of living in Canada. Others resisted any form of accommodation. Many, however, took a middle-of-

the-road position, accommodating where necessary and only in ways that did not threaten the faith. This latter group was generally called the Old Mennonites. In Ontario, the Old Mennonites were of Swiss and southern German origin. During the late 1950s part of the Old Mennonite faction, some of whom were members of the General Conference Mennonite Church, decried the departure of fellow members and leaders from traditional standards of faith and practice. They disapproved of liberal views on biblical inspiration and moral latitude. Bps. Moses H. Roth and Curtis C. Cressman became the spokespersons of the traditionalist position. They and the ministers and congregations that followed them were expelled in 1959, whereupon they formed the Conservative Mennonite Church of Ontario. This development paralleled with the movements in the United States.

In 1962 the conference adopted a Constitution of Faith and Practice, which affirmed the Dordrecht Confession of Faith in 1632 and the *Christian Fundamentals* disciplinary standards—both of which were adopted by the general conference in 1921. Much of the attention of the conference was directed to a definition of the believers' stance in relation to secular society, which has been spelled out in a series of prohibitions. Members are prohibited from participation in war (including any type of military service), politics (including voting and jury duty), and membership in worldly organizations (such as secret societies, life insurance societies, and so forth). Members refrain from strong drink, tobacco, worldly amusements (such as movies and organized sports), television and radio, jewelry (including wedding bands), and remarriage after divorce. All are called to simple modest dress, which for women includes uncut hair and veiled heads. Churches do not use instrumental music, nor do they allow floral displays at weddings or funerals.

Membership: In 2002 there were eight congregations with more than 500 members.

Evangelical Mennonite Conference

440 Main St., Steinbach, MB, Canada R0A 2A0

The Evangelical Mennonite Conference (EMC) considers itself indebted to the Radical Reformation, which in turn is rooted in the Protestant Reformation of the sixteenth century. EMC came about as a result of a renewal movement among a small group of German Mennonites in southern Russia in 1812. Their leader was Klaas Reimer, a Mennonite minister. Reimer believed that the Mennonite church had become lax in discipline and that it condoned such practices as card playing, smoking, and drinking. He also felt that the church had become too closely aligned with the Russian government, as evidenced by its contributions to the war against Napoleon. By 1814, the Reimer group had separated entirely from the main body of Mennonites. They became known as the Kleine Gemeinde (small fellowship).

Increased pressure on the group from the Russian government concerning such matters as educational control and objection to military service forced the church to migrate in 1874 to North America, where members mostly settled in Manitoba Canada (158 families) or near Jansen, Nebraska (36 families). The Nebraska group eventually seceded. "Evangelical Mennonite Church" was chosen as a name in 1952, with "Church" changing to "Conference" in 1959. The conference is currently spread over five Canadian provinces and organized into nine religions.

As evangelicals, EMC members hold that scripture has final authority in faith and practice, believe in Christ's finished work, and maintain a humble confidence in forgiveness and wholeness in Christ. As Mennonites, they are committed to following Christ in daily life, to baptism upon confession of faith, to community and social concern, to nonviolence, and to wider mission. As a conference, the EMC seeks to encourage local churches, to work together on matters of mission, and to work well as part of the much wider Christian church.

The conference's cultural makeup is increasingly diverse, though its Dutch-German roots remain visible. Roughly one-third of its churches have pastors or leaders who reflect other cultural backgrounds. There has been an increasing rural-to-urban shift in both membership and mission attention. The conference functions as a conference of churches with national boards, as a conference council (delegate assembly) that meets twice per year, and as a moderator. Women serve on most national boards as council delegates, as missionaries, and within local church activities. While women may be selected locally as ministers, they cannot serve with national recognition or commissioning.

Membership: In 2006, the conference reported 7,300 members, 56 churches, and 174 ministers in Canada. There are daughter churches that have organized as national autonomous conferences in Mexico, Nicaragua, and Paraguay.

Educational Facilities:

Steinbach Bible College, Steinbach, Manitoba, Canada.

Periodicals: *The Messenger*.

Remarks: The members of the Kleine Gemeinde that settled in Nebraska were gradually, over a period of several decades, lost to other Mennonite bodies, primarily the Evangelical Mennonite Brethren Conference. The last congregation, which had moved to Kansas, dissolved in 1944.

Sources:

Evangelical Mennonite Conference. www.emconf.ca/.

The Golden Years: The Mennonite Kleine Gemeinde in Russia (1812–1849). Steinbach, MN: D. F. P. Publications, 1985.

Evangelical Mennonite Mission Conference

Box 52059, Niakwa PO, Winnipeg, MB, Canada R2M 5P9

The Evangelical Mennonite Mission Conference was born in 1937 as the result of a revival movement in the Sommerfelder Mennonite Church in Manitoba, Canada. Four young ministers became the leaders of a new group that met in the school district of Rudnerweide for their organizational meeting. They called themselves the Rudnerweider Mennonite Church. Rev. W. H. Falk was elected as the first bishop.

The church stressed personal conversion, teaching of children in Sunday school, youth programs, and missions. The first missionary, John Schellenberg, went to Africa under the Africa Inland Mission in 1942.

The revival spread to Saskatchewan, Canada, where several congregations were established. In 1959, the congregations in Manitoba and Saskatchewan organized as the Evangelical Mennonite Mission Conference. Mission work among Mennonites returning from Mexico led to the establishment of four congregations in Ontario, Canada, during the 1960s. Also during this decade, mission work began in Belize and Bolivia; more recently, work has begun in Texas and Mexico. In 1986 the conference joined the Africa Inter-Mennonite Mission. Numerous workers serve with various independent missionary agencies in several countries.

The conference is characterized by a strong emphasis on evangelism and missions. A Low-German radio broadcast ministry is based in Saskatoon, Saskatchewan. The conference is active in the Mennonite Central Committee and the Mennonite World Conference.

Membership: In 2007 there were 27 congregations in Canada with a total membership of 4,260, along with 7 further congregations outside of Canada, with a total of 858 members.

Educational Facilities:

Steinbach Bible College, Steinbach, Manitoba, Canada.

Aylmer Bible School, Aylmer, Ontario, Canada.

Sources:

Evangelical Mennonite Mission Conference. www.emmc.ca/.

Epp, Frank H. *Mennonites in Canada, 1920–1940*. Toronto: Macmillan of Canada, 1982.

Fellowship of Evangelical Bible Churches

3339 N 109th Plz., Omaha, NE 68164-2908

The Fellowship of Evangelical Bible Churches grew out of a merger in 1889 of two evangelical Mennonite groups that had been founded by Elders Isaac Peters

(1826–1911) and Aaron Wall (1834–1905), respectively. Peters had migrated from Russia in 1874, settled in Henderson, Nebraska, and joined the Bethesda Mennonite Church. As an elder he began to voice some of the ideas that had previously led to a break with the church in Russia. He was a vigorous proponent of evangelism and all the means to accomplish that task, including lively preaching, Bible teaching for youth, prayer meetings, and Bible study. He saw a transformed life as a sign of regeneration. With a minority of the Henderson congregation, he withdrew in 1880 and formed the Ebenezer congregation.

Wall had migrated from Russia in 1875 and settled near Mountain Lake, Minnesota. After his election in 1876 as elder of the Bergfelder Church, he stressed the need for regeneration and the new life in Christ to an extent that he and his followers felt compelled to leave the Bergfelder Church. In 1889 he founded an independent congregation. In October of that year, he led in the union of his congregation with Peters's, and the resulting formation of the United Mennonite Brethren of North America. The name was soon changed to Defenseless Mennonite Brethren of Christ in North America. In 1937 the name was changed to Evangelical Mennonite Brethren Conference. The present name was adopted in 1987.

Born in an evangelical awakening, early on the fellowship emphasized church schools and world missions. From early congregations in Nebraska, Minnesota, and South Dakota, the church spread throughout the Midwest and Canada. Missions are currently supported in Europe, Africa, Southeast Asia, Japan, Taiwan, and South America. The church is a member of the National Association of Evangelicals.

Membership: In 2001 the fellowship reported 1,560 members and 19 ministers in the United States, and a worldwide membership of 3,515. In 2008 the fellowship reported 19 congregations in the United States, 22 congregations in Canada, and 6 congregations in South America.

Periodicals: *Fellowship Focus*.

Sources:

Fellowship of Evangelical Bible Churches. www.febcministries.org.

Old Colony Mennonite Church

c/o John P. Wiebe, PO Box 601, Winkler, MB, Canada R6W 4A8

The Old Colony Mennonite Church continues the traditions of the Reinlaender Mennonites who came into Canada from Russia in 1875 and settled in south central Manitoba, on an area designated as the Western Reserve, immediately north of the American border. Approximately 3,240 individuals made up the Reinlaender Mennonite Church. It was among this group that a revival movement would start in the 1880s, leading some to form the Mennonite Brethren Church. Through the decades, little by little, the outside world began to encroach upon the Mennonite settlements in the Western Reserve. These encroachments came to a head in the conflict over public school in the years immediately following World War I (1914–1918). In 1921 the group was able to work out an agreement with Mexico that granted them religious freedom, including the right to private schools, and the majority of the group moved out of Canada.

The move to Mexico was made a condition of continued membership in the church, and everyone was required to reregister as a member and indicate the intention to migrate. Of the 4,526 members in Manitoba, 3,340 migrated; and of the 7,182 members in Saskatchewan, 5,180 left for Mexico. Those who remained had no sense of direction, and some members drifted off to other churches. Finally in the early 1930s, efforts were made to reorganize the remnants. A new membership book was created. In 1930 a bishop, Johann Loeppky, was chosen and ordained for the Saskatchewan group, and he ordained the new bishop for Manitoba, Jacob J. Froese, in 1936. Their numbers grew as members returned from Mexico.

Today the Old Colony Mennonite Church exists in five Canadian provinces: Saskatchewan, Alberta, British Columbia, Manitoba, and Ontario.

Membership: Not reported.

Sources:

Epp, Franklin H. *Mennonites in Canada, 1920–1940: A Peoples' Struggle for Survival*. Toronto, Ontario: Macmillan of Canada, 1982.

Kraybill, Donald B., and Carl F. Bowman. *On the Backroad to Heaven: Old Order Hutterites, Mennonites, Amish, and Brethren*. Baltimore, MD: Johns Hopkins University Press, 2001.

Lichdi, Diether Gotz. *Mennonite World Handbook 1990: Mennonites in Global Mission*. Lombard, IL: Mennonite World Conference, 1990.

Reinland Mennonite Church

PO Box 96, Rosenfeld, MB, Canada R0G 1X0

The Reinland Mennonite Church was founded in 1958 by some 10 ministers and 600 members of the Sommerville (or Sommerfelder) Mennonite Church in Manitoba, Canada, who separated and founded an independent body. A short time later 200 of these members and four of the ministers left Canada for Bolivia.

Membership: In 2001, there were five congregations in Manitoba, one in Ontario, 10 ministers, and 2,303 members.

Sommerville Mennonite Church

Current address not obtained for this edition.

During the 1870s a number of German Mennonites, who had been residents of Russia for several generations, settled in southern Manitoba on two tracts of land on both sides of the Red River, referred to as the East Reserve and the West Reserve. One group, which had settled on the Western Reserve, came under the leadership of the independent-minded Bp. Johann Funk (1836–1917), who in 1887 had been ordained by Bp. Gerhard Wiebe (1827–1900), leader of the Chortitzer Mennonites in the eastern reserve and appointed as his assistant in the West. Funk had one of the more progressive outlooks of all the Mennonite leaders in the area and he welcomed the coming of the railroad and the integration of the community into the larger Canadian society, as opposed to the establishment of isolated Mennonite conclaves. However, Funk met with significant opposition; and in 1893, four churches in the Western Reserve asked Wiebe to ordain another bishop to lead them. He ordained Abraham Doerksen from the village of Sommerfeld and those groups that came under him quickly became known as Sommerfelder or Sommerville Mennonites, as opposed to the Bergthaler Mennonites led by Funk. The Sommerville Mennonites soon emerged as the largest of several related groups, claiming some 80 percent of the Western Reserve following, formerly under Funk, and was twice as large as the Chortitzer Mennonites under Wiebe.

The Sommerville Mennonites continue as a separate group.

Membership: Not reported.

Sources:

Epp, Frank H. *Mennonites in Canada, 1786–1920: The History of a Separate People*. Toronto, Ontario: Macmillan of Canada, 1974. 480 pp.

———. *Mennonites in Canada, 1920–1940: A Peoples' Struggle for Survival*. Toronto, Ontario: Macmillan of Canada, 1982.

United States Conference of Mennonite Brethren Churches

315 S Lincoln, PO Box 220, Hillsboro, KS 67063-0220

In the mid-1800s Pr. Edward Wuest, a fiery evangelical preacher, toured the German colonies in Russia preaching the free grace of God and the need for a definite religious experience. His influence led a number of Mennonites to become dissatisfied with the formality of their church meeting. They also felt themselves to be too pure to participate in the communion with others, and when their demands for a separate sacramental service were refused by the elders, they began to hold secret sacramental meetings. When they were discovered, opposition was intense and they withdrew, writing a statement of protest on January 6, 1860. After bitter controversy, the government accepted their separate existence and they took the name Mennoniten Bruedergemeinde (Mennonite Brethren). They were one in doctrine with other Mennonites, but they emphasized religious experience. Among the Russian Mennonites they introduced footwashing (with the Lord's Supper) and baptism by immersion (backwards), the latter a unique practice among Mennonites.

The Bruedergemeinde members came to America with the first immigrants. In 1879 Elder Abraham Schellenberg arrived and began to tour the settlements and organize strong congregations. By 1898 the group was supporting a German department at McPherson College, and in 1908 they founded Tabor College in Hillsboro, Kansas. A vigorous mission program was established.

As the Brudergemeinde was developing, Jacob Wiebe, a member of the Kleine Gemeinde, now the Evangelical Mennonite Conference, in the Crimea, organized in 1869 the Crimean Brethren, similar in nature to the Bruedergemeinde. The Crimean Brethren came to the United States in 1874 and settled in Kansas. They were similar to the Mennonite Brethren but had a few differences. They prohibited excessive worldliness, buying of land, and attendance at public amusements. They took biblical positions against life insurance, voting, and oaths. Marriage with nonmembers was forbidden. In 1960 the Mennonite Brethren Church absorbed the Krimmer Mennonite Brethren Church (formerly known as the Crimean Brethren).

In 2000 the Mennonite Brethren of North America voted to abandon its continent-wide general conference and turn over its work to two national conferences, one in the United States and one in Canada. The former continues as the United States Conference of Mennonite Brethren Churches and the latter as the Canadian Conference of Mennonite Brethren. These two national conferences cooperate in the management of the Mennonite Brethren Biblical Seminary and Mennonite Brethren Missionary Society International.

The church is a member of the National Association of Evangelicals.

Membership: In 2008 the church had 200 churches, 34,471 members, and 355 pastors. In Canada, in 2007 the Mennonite Brethren reported 250 congregations and 36,000 members.

Educational Facilities:

Fresno Pacific University, Fresno, California.

Mennonite Brethren Biblical Seminary, Fresno, California.

Tabor College, Hillsboro, Kansas.

Periodicals: *The Christian Leader*.

Sources:

United States Conference of Mennonite Brethren Churches. www.usmb.org/.

Faber, Connie, and Lynn Jost. *Family Matters: Discovering the Mennonite Brethren*. Hillsboro, KS: Kindred Press, 2002.

Fundamentals of Faith. Hillsboro, KS: Mennonite Brethren Publishing House, 1963.

Lorenz, John H. *The Mennonite Brethren Church*. Hillsboro, KS: Mennonite Brethren Publishing House, 1950.

Wiebe, Katie Funk. *Who Are the Mennonite Brethren?* Hillsboro, KS: Kindred Press, 1984.

 # Amish

Beachy Amish Mennonite Churches

9650 Iams Rd., Plain City, OH 43064

A split in the Pennsylvania Amish was occasioned by Bp. Moses Beachy's refusal to pronounce a ban on, and avoidance of, some former Old Order Amish who left to join a Conservative Mennonite congregation in Maryland. The conservative element withdrew fellowship with the bishop, who then, with his supporters, separated and formed a new association. The Beachy Amish have become more accommodating to modern culture. Churches have been built, and in recent years, the automobile has been allowed within the group, as are tractors and electricity. Further, missionary-aid work for needy people has become a project, in contrast to the strictly separatist Old Order group.

Membership: In 1996, the Beachy Amish reported 8,399 members, 138 congregations, and 425 ministers.

Periodicals: *Calvary Messenger*.

Sources:

Beach Amish Mennonite Churches. www.beachyam.org/ (unofficial)

Yoder, Elmer S. *The Beachy Amish Mennonite Fellowship Churches*. Hartville, OH: Diakonia Ministries, 1987.

Conservative Mennonite Conference
c/o Steve Swartz, General Secretary, 9910 Rosedale-Milford Center Rd., Irwin, OH 43029

With the development of the Old Order Amish Mennonite Church in the last half of the nineteenth century as a branch of the Amish Mennonite Church in North America, and the development of annual Amish Mennonite Conferences, with propensity toward Mennonite Conferences, some congregations did not fully follow either of the two approaches. Some of these congregations became associated and in 1910 met in an initial conference held in Pigeon, Michigan. They adopted the name Conservative Amish Mennonite Conference ("Amish" was dropped from the name in 1954). Changes that were accepted in 1910 or in the ensuing decades included the use of meeting houses, Sunday schools, protracted meetings, English-language services, and missionary endeavors.

The Conference's statement of mission reads, "The Conservative Mennonite Conference exists to glorify God by equipping leaders and congregations for worship, teaching, fellowship, service, and making disciples by providing resources and conference structures with an evangelical, Anabaptist, and conservative theological orientation."

Membership: In 2008 the Conference reported 11,073 members in 113 congregations. Congregations in the United States are located as far east as Delaware, as far west as California, south to Texas and Florida, and north to upstate New York and northwestern Ohio. The larger congregations are in Indiana and Ohio.

Educational Facilities:

Rosedale Bible College, Irwin, Ohio.

Rosedale Mennonite Missions, Irwin, Ohio.

Sources:

Conservative Mennonite Conference. www.cmcrosedale.org/.

Miller, J. Ivan. *History of the Conservative Mennonite Conference, 1910–1985*. Grantsville, MD: Author, 1985.

Evangelical Mennonite Church
1633 N 29th St., Fort Dodge, IA 50501-7937

The Evangelical Mennonite Church was formed in 1866 out of a spiritual awakening among the Amish in Indiana, and was first known as the Egly Amish, after its founder, Bp. Henry Egly (1824–1890). A preacher in an Amish congregation in Berne, Indiana, Egly underwent a spiritual experience in 1864 and began to emphasize regeneration, separation, and nonconformity to the world. His willingness to rebaptize anyone who had been baptized without repentance created a split in his church, prompting him to gather together a new congregation in 1866. This congregation's conference, which has met annually since 1895, united a number of other congregations of like mind. This group adopted the name Defenseless Mennonite Church in 1898, and became known as the Evangelical Mennonite Church in 1948.

Membership: In 2001 the church reported 5,278 members, 35 churches, and 81 active ministers in the local churches (out of a total of 137 ministers, including those in other types of work, missionaries, and the retired).

Periodicals: *EMC Today*.

Sources:

Evangelical Mennonite Church. www.evangelical.ia.us.mennonite.net/.

Nussbaum, Stan. *A History of the Evangelical Mennonite Church*. Author, 1980.

Old Order Amish Mennonite Church
Pathway Publishers, Rte. 4, Aylmer, ON, Canada N5H 2R3

The Old Order Amish Mennonite Church is, in practice, the continuation of the original Amish who settled in America. They are strictly conservative and may be identified by their horse-and-buggy culture. The men must grow beards, but moustaches are forbidden. The plain dark blue, gray, brown, or black suit for men and bonnet and apron for women are uniforms. Buttons are used on men's shirts and pants, but none are allowed on suit coats, vests, or coats. Marriage with non-Amish persons is forbidden.

The society is a rural community in which church life and everyday life are not separated. Symbolic of their life are the Amish barn raisings in which the congregation gathers to build a member's barn, usually in several days. Worship is held in the homes of the members every other Sunday on a rotating basis. During the three-hour service, the congregation is divided according to gender and marital status.

Schooling beyond reading, writing, and arithmetic is frowned upon within the church, and, prior to a Supreme Court ruling in 1972, trouble with various state governments (such as Wisconsin, Indiana, and Ohio) became a major cause of immigration to more lenient states (such as Missouri). Ministers are chosen by lot from a nominated few. Because this is not a missionary church, new members generally come into the community from the children of members. In the last generation there have been converts, some highly educated, and recent studies have shown that approximately 8 percent of the present membership is made up of descendents of such converts.

Membership: Not reported. In 2002 there were approximately 60,000 members in the United States and 900 in Canada. No statistics are kept. The total Amish population is estimated at 200,000, but only adults are baptized and considered full church members.

Periodicals: *The Diary* • *Die Botschaft* • *The Budget* • *Herald der Wahrheit* • *Blackboard Bulletin* • *Family Life* • *Young Companion*

Sources:

Amish Life in a Changing World. York, PA: York Graphic Services, 1978.

Browning, Clyde. *Amish in Illinois: Over 100 Years of the "Old Order" Sect of Central Illinois*. Decatur, IL: Author, 1971.

Hostetler, John A. *Amish Society*. Baltimore, MD: Johns Hopkins University Press, 1968.

Kraybill, Donald B., and Carl F. Bowman. *On the Backroad to Heaven: Old Order Hutterites, Mennonites, Amish, and Brethren*. Baltimore, MD: Johns Hopkins University Press, 2001.

Rice, Charles S., and Rollin C. Steinmetz. *The Amish Year*. New Brunswick, NJ: Rutgers University Press, 1956.

Schreiber, William I. *Our Amish Neighbors*. Chicago, IL: University of Chicago Press, 1962.

 # Brethren

Association of Fundamental Gospel Churches

Current address not obtained for this edition.

The Association of Fundamental Gospel Churches was formed in 1954 by the coming together of three independent Brethren congregations: Calvary Chapel of Hartsville, Ohio; Webster Mills Free Brethren Church of McConnellsburg, Pennsylvania; and Little Country Chapel of Myersburg, Maryland. Prime leader in the new association was G. Henry Besse (d. 1962), a former member of the Reformed Church who had in 1937 become a minister among the Dunkard Brethren. He withdrew from their fellowship in 1953 complaining about their strictures against wearing neckties, wristwatches, and jewelry and their demands that women always wear the prayer veil or cap. Former members of the Church of the Brethren were also opposed to that church's participation in the National Council of Churches.

In general, members of the association follow Brethren doctrine and practice. They reject as unbiblical participation in war, but allow members to accept noncombatant military service. They do not allow the taking of oaths, suing at law (including for reason of divorce), or wearing ornamental adornment. They do not practice the kiss of peace.

The association meets annually to elect officers and conduct business. Ministers are chosen from among the congregation's members. They are not required to have advanced education. G. Henry Besse was succeeded by his two sons, Lynn Besse and Clair Besse, both of whom have pastored Calvary Chapel.

Membership: Not reported.

Bible Brethren

17904 Binkley Ave., Maugansville, MD 21767

The Bible Brethren was formed in 1948 by a small group who withdrew from the Lower Cumberland (Cumberland County, Pennsylvania) congregation of the Church of the Brethren. Clair H. Alspaugh (1903–1969), a farmer and painter who had been called to the ministry in the congregation in 1942, led the group that assumed a traditional Brethren posture. Alspaugh protested the Church of the Brethren's association with the Federal Council of Churches (now the National Council of Churches) and the failure of the Brethren to endorse doctrinal preaching as inspired by the Holy Spirit.

The original group constructed a church building following simple, nineteenth-century Brethren patterns (a long preacher's desk and straight-back pews) at Carlisle Springs, Pennsylvania. A second congregation was formed at Campbelltown, Pennsylvania. The latter was strengthened by the addition of a group under Paul Beidler that had withdrawn from the Dunkard Brethren, but subsequently became defunct after Beidler led the entire membership away in 1974 to form Christ's Ambassadors. A third congregation of Bible Brethren formed in 1954 at Locust Grove Chapel, near Abbotstown, York County, Pennsylvania.

Membership: In 1979 there were approximately 100 members of the Bible Brethren in two congregations.

Sources:

Bible Brethren. www.mbbchurch.org/.

Gleim, Elmer Q. *Change and Challenge: A History of the Church of the Brethren in the Southern District of Pennsylvania.* Harrisburg, PA: Southern District Conference History Committee, 1973.

Brethren Church (Ashland, Ohio)

524 College Ave., Ashland, OH 44805

Agitation among the German Baptist Brethren began in the late nineteenth century against what some considered outmoded practices. The lack of educational opportunities, an unlearned clergy, and the Brethren's plain dress were central

objections. The crisis came to a head with the expulsion in 1882 of Henry R. Holsinger (1833–1905) of Berlin, Pennsylvania. Holsinger, leader of the Progressives in the church, had objected to the authority of the annual meeting over the local congregation. Others left with him and in 1883 formed the Brethren Church.

The Brethren Church is like the Church of the Brethren in many respects, with the exceptions of having been the first to move toward an educated and salaried ministry, modern dress, and missions. While generally conservative in theology, and expecting a high degree of doctrinal consensus among its ministers, the church has refused to adopt a statement of faith (though it does have a doctrinal statement) on the grounds that the New Testament is its creed. During the 1930s, a group supportive of a dispensational fundamentalist doctrinal position left the church to found the National Fellowship of Brethren Churches, now the Fellowship of Grace Brethren. The church practices baptism by trine immersion, a communion service usually in the evening that includes footwashing, the laying on of hands for ordination and for confirmation, and anointing and laying on of hands for healing. Elders (ordained ministers) lead the church in spiritual affairs.

The church follows a congregational polity and an annual conference conducts common business. Missionary activity is supported in Argentina, Colombia, India, Malaysia, Peru, Paraguay, and Mexico. The church is a member of the National Association of Evangelicals.

Membership: In 1995 the church reported 13,028 members in 103 churches.

Educational Facilities:

Ashland Theological Seminary, Ashland, Ohio.

Ashland University, Ashland, Ohio.

Periodicals: *The Brethren Evangelist.* • *Insight into Brethren Missions.*

Sources:

Brethren Church (Ashland, Ohio). www.brethrenchurch.org/.

Task Force on Brethren History and Doctrine. *The Brethren: Growth in Life and Thought.* Ashland, OH: Board of Christian Education, Brethren Church, 1975.

Christ's Ambassadors

Current address not obtained for this edition.

Christ's Ambassadors traces its origin to a dispute in 1968 within the Dunkard Brethren congregation at Lititz, Pennsylvania. Leaders in the congregation protested an unauthorized prayer meeting conducted by some of the members under the leadership of Paul Beidler. Beidler led the members in withdrawing and forming an independent congregation. The small group affiliated with the Bible Brethren congregation at Campbelltown, Pennsylvania, in 1970. However, four years later Beidler led the entire congregation to withdraw from the Bible Brethren and formed Christ's Ambassadors. The group follows traditional Dunkard Brethren practice and beliefs, but places great emphasis upon the freedom of expression in worship.

Membership: In 1980 Christ's Ambassadors had approximately 50 members meeting in two congregations, one at Cocalico and one at Myerstown, Pennsylvania.

Christ's Assembly

Current address not obtained for this edition.

Krefeld, Germany, in the lower Rhine Valley, was one place where dissenting Pietists found relative safety and tolerance during the eighteenth century, There were several groups represented in Krefeld, including the one which would later become the Church of the Brethren upon its arrival in America. In 1737 two Danes, Soren Bolle and Simon Bolle, visited Krefeld and joined the Brethren. They soon returned to Copenhagen and began to preach and gather a following. While they had been baptized by the Brethren, they had been influenced as well by other Pietist Groups, most notably the Community of True Inspiration (which later migrated to America and formed the colonies at Amana, Iowa). The movement under the Bolles, called Christ's Assembly, spread through Sweden, Norway, and Germany.

During the 1950s, Johannes Thalitzer, pastor of Christ's Assembly in Copenhagen, learned of the continued existence of the Brethren in America through his encounter with some remnants of the recently disbanded Danish Mission of the Church of the Brethren. He initiated contact with several Brethren Groups, especially the Old German Baptist Brethren, who sponsored a visit by Thalitzer to the United States in 1959. In subsequent visits he became acquainted with all of the larger Brethren factions, but felt each was deficient in belief and/or practice. In 1967 he organized a branch of Christ's Assembly at a love feast with nine Brethren (from several Brethren groups) at Eaton, Ohio.

Christ's Assembly largely follows Brethren practice, but, like the Community of True Inspiration, places great emphasis upon the revealed guidance of an apostolic leadership. In more recent years, it has been further influenced by the Pentecostal (Charismatic) Movement which has swept through most major denominations.

As Christ's Assembly grew, it came to include members from four states and all the major Brethren branches. A second congregation was formed in the 1970s in Berne, Indiana.

Membership: Membership not reported.

Sources:

Benedict, F. W., and William F. Rushby. "Christ's Assembly: A Unique Brethren Movement." *Brethren Life and Thought* 18 (1973): 33–42.

Church of the Brethren

1451 Dundee Ave., Elgin, IL 60120

The Church of the Brethren developed out of the wave of radical Pietism that swept early eighteenth-century Germany. Responding to William Penn's invitation to come to the American colonies, most of the Brethren immigrated; those who remained were absorbed into the Mennonite movement. The first American congregation was instituted in Germantown, Pennsylvania, on Christmas Day, 1723. Important leaders of the first generation included Alexander Mack Sr. (1679–1735), the first recognized minister; Christopher Sauer II (1721–1784), a noted colonial printer; Alexander Mack Jr. (1712–1803); and Peter Becker (1687–1758). Until the early twentieth century, Brethren were commonly known as *Dunkers* (or *Tunkers*), after their practice of thrice-fold immersion baptism. Their formal name, German Baptist Brethren, used during most of the nineteenth century, was changed to the current designation in 1908, the church's bicentennial year.

In colonial Pennsylvania, the Brethren shared with the Mennonites a German cultural background and Anabaptist theology, and with the Friends (Quakers) a commitment to peace and simplicity. All of these groups sought a separation from secular influences, wore distinctive plain dress, and opposed slavery. Brethren practiced strong church discipline (although not the ban—or shunning, the practice of avoiding contact with those who have withdrawn or excluded from the fellowship) selected leaders who were not salaried or expected to obtain theological education, and refrained from voting, taking oaths, or entering lawsuits. One of the most distinctive features of Brethren worship has been their observance of the love feast, a communion service that includes foot washing, a "love meal," and the taking of unleavened bread and wine or grape juice.

As one of the historic peace churches, Brethren were opposed to military service in the American Revolution and the Civil War. This resulted in limited persecution, including fines and imprisonment. The program of alternative service that became available to conscientious objectors in World War II, and was retained during later conflicts, brought an end to this persecution, however.

Although the early Brethren were open to urban life, most preferred an agricultural setting and followed the farming frontier across the continent. Congregations were established in Kentucky and Ohio during the 1790s, Missouri and Illinois dur-ing the 1810s, and California and Oregon during the 1850s. Brethren settlement of the West at the turn of the nineteenth century was greatly aided by the colonization programs of the transcontinental railroads, which encouraged the settlement of sparsely populated lands through which it initially laid track. The small movement of Brethren into Canada was aided by the development of the Canadian Pacific Railroad, which encouraged immigration in the early twentieth century. Between 1903 and 1922 as many as twelve Canadian congregations were founded, mostly in Alberta and Saskatchewan. By 1968 only two of these congregations remained and these became part of the United Church of Canada.

The Brethren began to hold yearly meetings for worship and church business during the 1740s, although no minutes were recorded until the 1780s. By the 1840s a delegated conference of lay representatives and ministers had become the highest authority in the church. Following the Civil War, the church took an active interest in missionary work (foreign and domestic), publishing, and education. Foreign mission efforts began in Denmark in the 1890s. Fields were also opened in India, China, Nigeria, and Ecuador. The Brethren Press, founded in 1897, produced a supply of books, periodicals, church school materials, and other literature. Numerous educational institutions were founded, six of which evolved into fully accredited independent liberal arts institutions, five of them colleges and one a university. The church also supported a theological seminary.

Tensions within the denomination in the late nineteenth century produced a painful three-way division. In addition to the original group, an "old order" movement that opposed innovation and venerated the tradition of earlier Brethren organized the Old German Baptist Brethren in 1881. A "progressive" faction organized the Brethren Church (Ashland, Ohio) in 1883.

The twentieth century has seen rapid change in Brethren life. Following an important decision on dress at the annual conference of 1911, the distinctive dress of the church has virtually disappeared. The free, plural ministry was transformed into salaried, professional pastoral leadership. Women became eligible for ordination in 1957. Efforts at evangelism and new church development have produced a more inclusive membership that includes several black, Hispanic, and Korean congregations.

The extensive world mission program began a process of dramatic change in 1955, resulting in the creation of indigenous and independent religious bodies. The Ecuadorian congregations joined the United Evangelical Church of Ecuador in 1965; the India mission program merged into the Church of North India in 1970; and the Nigerian churches became the independent Brethren Church of Nigeria in 1973. The mission program in China folded when Western missionaries were sent home in 1950.

Perhaps Brethren have been best known around the world for their efforts in relief and rehabilitation work in Europe following World War II. Brethren service projects later stretched into India and China and fostered ecumenical organizations such as Heifer Project International, founded by layman Dan West, Christian Rural Overseas Program (CROP), and International Christian Youth Exchange (ICYE). The denomination also organized and administers SEERV (Salves Exchange for Refugee Rehabilitation Vocations), the largest marketing program of its type for Third World handicrafts.

Since 1946 a general board of 25 members elected by the annual conference has employed a program and administrative staff in the areas of parish ministries, world ministries and disaster response, publishing, and stewardship. The general offices and Brethren Press are located in Elgin, Illinois; a service center is operated in New Windsor, Maryland. The church is a founding member of both the World Council of Churches and the National Council of Churches. The Brethren Church of Nigeria is also a member of the World Council.

Membership: In 1996 the Brethren reported 141,811 members, 1,106 congregations, and 1,946 ordained ministers in the United States and Puerto Rico.

Educational Facilities:

Bethany Theological Seminary, Oak Brook, Illinois.

Bridgewater College, Bridgewater, Virginia.

Elizabethtown College, Elizabethtown, Pennsylvania.

Juniata College, Huntingdon, Pennsylvania.

Manchester College, North Manchester, Indiana.

McPherson College, McPherson, Kansas.

University of La Verne, La Verne, California.

Periodicals: *Messenger.* • *Brethren Life and Thought.*

Sources:

Church of the Brethren. www.brethren.org/.

Book of Worship: The Church of the Brethren. Elgin, IL: Brethren Press, 1964.

Bowman, Carl. *Brethren Society.* Baltimore, MD: Johns Hopkins University Press, 1995.

Durnbaugh, Donald F. *Fruit of the Vine: A History of the Brethren, 1708–1995.* Elgin, IL: Brethren Press, 1997.

————, ed. *The Brethren Encyclopedia.* 3 vols. Philadelphia, PA: Brethren Encyclopedia, 1983.

Mallot, Floyd E. *Studies in Brethren History.* Elgin, IL: Brethren Publishing House, 1954.

Manual of Brotherhood Organization and Polity. Elgin, IL: Church of the Brethren, General Offices, 1965.

Sappington, Roger E., ed. *The Brethren in the New Nation.* Elgin, IL: Brethren Press, 1976.

Conservative German Baptist Brethren

Current address not obtained for this edition.

The Conservative German Baptist Brethren is a small Brethren body that dates to the 1931 withdrawal of a group under the leadership of Clayton F. Weaver and Ervin J. Keeny from the Dunkard Brethren Church in Pennsylvania. In 1946 Loring I. Moss, a prominent exponent of the conservative element of the Brethren Movement and one of the organizers of the Dunkard Brethren Church, withdrew and formed the Primitive Dunkard Brethren. Noting the similar concern to keep stricter Brethren standards, Moss led his new group into the Conservative German Baptist Brethren, though personally, he later withdrew and joined the Old Brethren.

Membership: In 1980 the Conservative German Baptist Brethren had two congregations, one at New Madison, Ohio, with 10 members, and one at Shrewsbury, Pennsylvania, with 25 members.

Conservative Grace Brethren Churches International

c/o Grace Brethren Church, PO Box 1275, Morrisville, VT 05661

The Conservative Grace Brethren Churches International resulted from a split in the Fellowship of Grace Brethren Churches in 1992. Those who formed the new church represented the most conservative element of the Fellowship while continuing its formal agreement with the Fellowship's "Statement of Faith" that had been adopted in 1969. In their slightly revised Statement of Faith, with clarifications adopted in 1994, the Conservative Brethren affirm the inerrancy of Scripture (rather than simply its infallibility), the pre-existence of Christ prior to the incarnation in Jesus, and the work of the Holy Spirit in indwelling believers from the moment of regeneration, empowering them for Christian life and service. They tie belief in the Trinity to the practice of triune immersion, which is an emphasis within the group. Within the group, confession of faith and triune immersion are the essential requirements for church membership and triune immersion shall not be abandoned with the exception of medical reasons of a physical nature. The Conservative Brethren also reemphasizes the triune nature of the communion service that must include the "washing of the saints' feet, the Lord's Supper, and the communion of the bread and the cup."

The very conservative stance of the new church is especially demonstrated in its belief in "the recent, direct creation of the heavens, the earth, and all their hosts,

without pre-existing material, in six literal 24-hour days" and an understanding of hell as providing eternal punishment while unbelievers are in a conscious state.

The Conservative Brethren are organized as an association of autonomous local churches cooperating in fellowship and work.

Membership: Not reported. In 2002, the fellowship included 47 congregations.

Sources:

Conservative Grace Brethren Churches. my.raex.com/~ogbc/CGBCI/

Dunkard Brethren Church

c/o Dale E. Jamison, Chairman, Board of Trustees, Quinter, KS 67752

The Dunkard Brethren Church grew out of a conservative movement within the Church of the Brethren that protested what it saw as a worldly drift and a lowering of standards in the church. The movement formed around the *Bible Monitor*, a periodical begun in 1922 by Benjamin E. Kesler (1861–1952), a minister who had joined the Church of the Brethren in the first decade of the twentieth century. He was one of seven people chosen to write the report on the dress standards adopted by the church in 1911, but in the next decade he saw the dress standards increasingly ignored. Men began to wear ties and women were adopting fashionable clothes and modern hairstyles. Kesler also protested the acceptance of lodge and secret-society membership, divorce and remarriage, and a salaried educated ministry (that was pushing aside the traditional lay eldership).

The emergence of the *Bible Monitor* movement produced tensions within the Church of the Brethren. In 1923 Kesler was refused a seat at the annual conference. That same year he met with supporters at Denton, Maryland, to further organize efforts to reform the church. Subsequent meetings were held in different locations over the next few years. By 1926 it became evident that the church would not accept the movement's perspective, and at a meeting at Plevna, Indiana, the Dunkard Brethren Church was organized.

The Dunkard Brethren Church follows traditional Brethren beliefs and practices, and until recently has rebaptized members who joined from less strict branches of the church. The Dunkard Brethren adopted and enforces the dress standards accepted by the Church of the Brethren in 1911. Modesty and simplicity (though not uniformity) of dress is required. No gold or other jewelry may be worn. Women keep their hair long and simply styled, and generally wear a white cap. Men cut their hair short. Divorce and remarriage are not allowed. Life insurance is discouraged. No musical instruments are used in worship.

The church has three orders of ministry. Elders marry, bury, and administer the ordinances; ministers preach and assist the elders in their sacramental role; deacons attend to temporal matters. All are laymen elected by their local congregations. The standing committee, composed of all the elders of the church, has general oversight of the church. Together with the ministers and elders elected by the local churches as delegates, they form the general conference, the highest legislative body in the church. Its decisions are final on all matters brought before it. The church is organized into four districts that meet annually.

The Dunkard Brethren Church supports the Torreon Navajo Mission in New Mexico.

Membership: In 2006 the Dunkard Brethren reported 900 members in 25 congregations.

Periodicals: *The Bible Monitor.* Available from the editor at 1138 E 12th St., Beaumont, CA 92223.

Sources:

Dunkard Brethren Church Manual. Quinter, KS: Dunkard Brethren Church, 1971.

Dunkard Brethren Church Polity. 7th ed. Quinter, KS: Dunkard Brethren Church, 1993.

Minutes of the General Conference of the Dunkard Brethren Church from 1927 to 1975. Wauseon, OH: Glanz Lithographing Co., 1976.

Emmanuel's Fellowship

8345 Crown Point Ave., Omaha, NE 68134-1905

Emmanuel's Fellowship was formed in 1966 by members of the Old Order River Brethren, under the leadership of Paul Goodling of Greencastle, Pennsylvania. Goodling rejected the Brethren's insistence on baptism by immersion and their allowing members to accept social security benefits. The fellowship baptizes by pouring, as the candidate stands in water. There are very strict dress requirements.

Membership: Not reported. The fellowship began in the 1960s with a small group organized as a single congregation. It has subsequently grown into a large congregation with plans for planting new congregations.

Sources:

Emmanuel's Fellowship. www.emmanuelfellowship.com/.

Fellowship of Grace Brethren Churches

Brethren Missionary Herald Co., PO Box 576, Winona Lake, IN 46590

The movement that led to the founding of the Fellowship of Grace Brethren Churches developed within the Brethren Church (Ashland, Ohio) during the 1930s. Conservatives in the church voiced concern over liberal tendencies within the church and more particularly at the church-supported school, Ashland College. Led by ministers such as Alva J. McClain (1888–1968), the National Ministerial Association drew up and adopted the "Message of the Brethren Ministry," a statement of the Brethren position. The entire church refused to adopt the statement on the grounds that it seemed to be a substitute for their adherence to the New Testament as their only creed.

Conservatives scored a second victory in 1930 when a graduate school of theology opened at Ashland under McClain's leadership. However, in 1937, both McClain, then dean of the school, and Prof. Herman A. Hoyt (1909–2000) were dismissed. Their supporters organized Grace Theological Seminary as a new institution for ministerial training, which set the stage for a confrontation at the 1939 general conference of the church. After the exclusion of some of the new seminary's supporters, all walked out and formed the National Fellowship of Brethren Churches, which in 1976 assumed its present name.

The new church adopted the 1921 "Message of the Brethren Ministry" as its doctrinal position. That document was replaced in 1969 by a revised and expanded "Statement of Faith." The new statement affirms the conservative evangelical theology of the original document but adds a lengthy statement on various eschatological issues such as the premillennial return of Christ, eternal punishment for nonbelievers, and a belief in a personal Satan. The church practices baptism by triune immersion, and a threefold communion that includes footwashing, a meal, and partaking of the elements of bread and the cup.

The Fellowship adopted a congregational polity. The conference of the Fellowship meets annually. The Foreign Mission Society, now named Grace Brethren International Missions, operates in Argentina, Brazil, Africa, France, Germany, England, Mexico, Cambodia, the Philippines, Vietnam, and Portugal. Other national cooperating national organizations include CE (Church Effectiveness) National, Grace Brethren Investment Foundation, Grace College and Seminary, and Brethren Missionary Herald Company.

Membership: In 2006 the Fellowship reported 27,000 members, 43,500 average attendance, and 2,650 congregations.

Educational Facilities:

Grace Theological Seminary, Winona Lake, Indiana.

Grace College, Winona Lake, Indiana.

Periodicals: *FGBC World*.

Sources:

Fellowship of Grace Brethren Churches. www.fgbc.org/.

Baumann, Louis S. *The Faith*. Winona Lake, IN: Brethren Missionary Herald, 1960.

McClain, Alva J. *Daniel's Prophecy of the Seventy Weeks*. Winona Lake, IN: Brethren Missionary Herald Books, 2007.

Plaster, David R. *Finding Our Focus: A History of the Grace Brethren Church*. Winona Lake, IN: Brethren Missionary Herald Books, 2003.

Scoles, Todd. *Restoring the Household: The Heritage and Quest of the Grace Brethren Church*. Winona Lake, IN: Brethren Missionary Herald Books, 2008.

Fundamental Brethren Church

c/o Mack Peterson, The Upper Brummetts Creek Fundamental Brethren Church, 424 Griffith Rd., Green Mountain, NC 28740

The Fundamental Brethren Church was formed in 1962 by former members of four congregations of the Church of the Brethren in Mitchell County, North Carolina, under the leadership of Calvin Barnett. The doctrinally conservative group adopted the "Message of the Brethren Ministry," a statement written by some ministers in the Brethren Church (Ashland, Ohio) in the 1920s as their doctrinal standard. Among the issues involved in their leaving the Church of the Brethren, its participation in the National Council of Churches and use of the Revised Standard Version of the Bible were prominent. The group added to its doctrinal statement that the King James Version of the Bible is authoritative. It also adopted a fundamental premillennial dispensational theological stance. By 1967, there were four congregations with 200 members.

Membership: In the 1970s there were three congregations of fewer than 200 members.

Independent Brethren Church

Current address not obtained for this edition.

The Independent Brethren Church was formed in 1972. On February 12 of that year, the Upper Marsh Creek congregation of the Church of the Brethren at Gettysburg, Pennsylvania, withdrew and became an independent body. Later that year, members from the Antietam congregation left and established the independent Blue Rock congregation near Waynesboro, Pennsylvania. These two congregations united as the Independent Brethren Church. They are conservative in their following of Brethren belief and practice. They have kept the plain dress and oppose any affiliation with the National Council of Churches.

Membership: In 1980 the Independent Brethren Church had approximately 85 members in two congregations.

Old Brethren Church

Current address not obtained for this edition.

The Old Brethren Church, generally referred to simply as the Old Brethren, is a name taken by two congregations which split from the Old German Baptist Brethren in 1913 (Deer Creek congregation in Carroll County, Indiana) and in 1915 (Salida congregation in Stanislaus County, California). Though widely separated geographically, the two congregations banded together and in 1915 published *The Old Brethren's Reasons*, a 24-page pamphlet outlining their position. The Old Brethren dissented from the Old German Baptist Brethren's refusal to make annual meeting decisions uniformly applicable and from their allowing divergences of practice and discipline among the different congregations. Also, the Old Brethren called for greater strictness in plain dress and called for houses and carriages shorn of any frills that would gratify the lust of the eye.

In particular, the Old Brethren denounced the automobile and the telephone. Use of either caused a believer to be hooked into the world and inevitably led to church members being yoked together with unbelievers. In practice, over the years, the Old Brethren have been forced to change and have come to closely resemble the group from which they originally withdrew. Even prior to World War II, they began to make accommodation to the automobile.

Members of the Old Brethren meet annually at Pentecost, but keep legislation to a minimum. They allow the congregations to retain as much authority as possible.

Beginning with two congregations, the Old Brethren Church has experienced growth in spite of a schism in 1930 that led to the formation of the Old Brethren German Baptist Church. A third meeting house was built in the 1970s.

Membership: Not reported.

Periodicals: *The Pilgrim.* Send orders to 19201 Cherokee Rd., Tuolumne, CA 95379.

Sources:

Kraybill, Donald B., and Carl F. Bowman. *On the Backroad to Heaven: Old Order Hutterites, Mennonites, Amish, and Brethren.* Baltimore, MD: Johns Hopkins University Press, 2001.

Old Brethren German Baptist Church

Current address not obtained for this edition.

The Old Brethren German Baptist Church originated among the most conservative members of the Old Brethren Church and the Old Order German Baptist Brethren Church. Around 1930 members of the Old Brethren Deer Creek congregation near Camden, Indiana, began to fellowship with the Old Order Brethren in the Covington, Ohio, area. However, by 1935 the traditionalist Old Brethren found themselves unable to continue their affiliations with the Ohio Brethren. They continued as an independent congregation until they made contact with a few Old Order Brethren near Bradford, Ohio, who met in the home of Solomon Lavy. In 1939 the two groups merged and adopted the name Old Brethren German Baptist Church. They were joined in 1953 by a group of Old Order Brethren from Arcanum, Ohio.

The Old Brethren is the most conservative of all Brethren groups. They use neither automobiles, tractors, electricity, nor telephones. Their only accommodation to modern mechanization is that they do permit occasional use of stationary gasoline engines and will hire nonmembers for specific tasks requiring machinery. Members follow a strict personal code of nonconformity to the world. Homes and buggies are plainly furnished and simply painted. No gold or jewelry is worn. Farmers do not raise or habitually use tobacco. Members do not vote or purchase life insurance.

Membership: Not reported.

Sources:

Kraybill, Donald B., and Carl F. Bowman. *On the Backroad to Heaven: Old Order Hutterites, Mennonites, Amish, and Brethren.* Baltimore, MD: Johns Hopkins University Press, 2001.

Old German Baptist Brethren

Rte. 1, Box 140, Bringhurst, IN 46913

The Old German Baptist Brethren represents the conservative wing in the Brethren movement. This group withdrew in 1881. The group was protesting innovative tendencies and was opposed to Sunday schools, missions, higher education, church societies, and auxiliaries. It has lessened its opposition to higher education among members and now sponsors parochial schools. No missions are supported, and children attend the regular services of the church instead of having a church school.

The Old German Baptist Brethren wear plain clothes and are committed to nonparticipation in war, government, secret societies, and worldly amusements. They also object to participation in government (i.e., voting) even by members whose conscience otherwise allows it. They remain conservative on oaths, lawsuits, nonsalaried ministry, and veiled heads for women at worship.

Membership: In 2002 the Brethren reported 6,205 members in 56 churches served by 236 ministers.

Periodicals: *The Vindicator.* Send orders to 6952 N Montgomery County Line Rd., Englewood, OH 45322.

Sources:

Fisher, H. M., et al. *Doctrinal Treatise.* Covington, OH: Little Printing Company, 1954.

Old Order German Baptist Church

Current address not obtained for this edition.

As the Old German Baptist Brethren continued to deal with questions of accommodating to a fast-moving society in the early twentieth century, a group of members withdrew in 1921 because of the departure of the Old German Baptist Brethren from the established order and old paths. The petitioners, as they were informally called, could be found throughout the brethren, but were concentrated in the congregations at Covington and Arcanum, Ohio.

Staunchly set against most modern conveniences, the Old Order German Baptists have over the years been forced to accommodate. Automobiles are forbidden, but tractors are now allowed for farm work. Members do not use electricity or telephones. Increasingly, younger members have been forced to leave the farm and seek employment in nonfarm occupations.

Membership: In 1980 the church had fewer than 100 members and three congregations, all in Ohio (Gettysburg, Covington, and Arcanum).

 Quakers (Friends)

Alaska Yearly Meeting

Current address not reported.

As early as 1897, Quaker missionaries from the California Yearly Meeting, an independent programmed meeting of Friends, began work among the Eskimo people in Alaska. In 1970 the work had grown to the point that it was organized as a yearly meeting affiliated with the California Meeting, which maintained a Bible Training School. A goal of turning the work of the Meeting entirely over to its Eskimo constituency was accomplished in 1982 when the last of the missionaries were withdrawn and the Alaska Yearly Meeting became fully independent. The California Meeting has joined the Friends United Meeting.

Membership: In 1981 there were 11 congregations and 2,860 members.

Educational Facilities:

Bible Training School.

Sources:

Alaska Yearly Meeting. www.evangelicalfriends.org/north-america/regions/alaska/index.html

Central Yearly Meeting of Friends

Rte. 1, Box 226, Alexandria, IN 46001

The Central Yearly Meeting of Friends was formed in 1926 by several meetings in eastern Indiana who were protesting the liberalism of the Five Years Meeting. Doctrinally, the Central Yearly Meeting of Friends is evangelical and very conservative in matters of personal holiness. Worship is programmed. Churches of this small body are found in Indiana, North Carolina, Arkansas, and Ohio. Missionary work is sponsored in Bolivia.

Membership: In 2008 the Meeting reported nine affiliated monthly meetings (congregations).

Educational Facilities:

Union Bible College, Westfield, Indiana.

Periodicals: *Friends Evangel.* Available from 5601 E Co. Rd. 6505, Muncie, IN 47302.

Sources:

Central Yearly Meeting of Friends. www.centralyearlymeetingoffriends.org/.

Evangelical Friends Church–Eastern Region

5350 Broadmoor Cir. NW, Canton, OH 44709

Known before 1971 as the Ohio Yearly Meeting of Friends, the Evangelical Friends Church is that branch of the Friends most influenced by the Holiness movement. The Evangelical Friends have a programmed worship service with a minister who preaches. Formed in 1813, the Ohio Yearly Meeting of Friends supported the Gurneyites, followers of Joseph John Gurney (1788–1847), a promoter of beliefs in the final authority of the Bible, atonement, justification, and sanctification. After the Civil War the Ohio Yearly Meeting became open to the Holiness movement through the activities of workers such as David Updegraff, Dougan Clark, Walter Malone, and Emma Malone. The latter founded the Cleveland Bible Insititute (now Malone College) in 1892; it serves an interdenominational Holiness constituency.

The Evangelical Friends Church, never a member of the Five Years Meeting, has become a haven for conservative congregations who have withdrawn from the Friends United Meeting in the United States and Canada. Mission work is sustained in Taiwan and India. The church participates in the Evangelical Friends Alliance.

Membership: In 2007 there were 8,898 members, with 17,217 regular attendees in 92 churches.

Educational Facilities:

Malone College, Canton, Ohio.

Periodicals: *The Facing Bench*.

Sources:

Evangelical Friends Church, Eastern Region. www.efcer.org/.

DeVol, Charles E. *Focus on Friends*. Canton, OH: Missionary Board of the Evangelical Friends Church–Eastern Region, 1982.

Faith and Practice, the Book of Discipline. Canton, OH: Evangelical Friends Church–Eastern Region, 1981.

Williams, Walter. *The Rich Heritage of Quakerism*. Newberg, OR: Barclay Press, 2006.

Evangelical Friends International

5350 Broadmoor Cir. NW, Canton, OH 44709

The Evangelical Friends International came into being in 1990 when it superseded the former Evangelical Friends Alliance. The alliance had existed as an association of four autonomous Quaker groups: the Evangelical Friends Church–Eastern Region, the Rocky Mountain Yearly Meeting of Friends, the Evangelical Friends Church–Mid-America Yearly Meeting, and the Northwest Yearly Meeting of Friends. These groups represented the Friends movement's most theologically conservative elements, which showed much influence from the holiness movement of the nineteenth century. The Evangelical Friends Alliance had been founded in 1965, but was restricted at the end of the 1980s in recognition of the fact that the four affiliated groups had come to exist as a single denomination. The members of Evangelical Friends International attribute their change to the general evangelical renewal within Christianity, the new scholarly recognition of the evangelical nature of early Quakerism, and the cooperative work of the Evangelical Friends Alliance.

The Evangelical Friends Church, Eastern Region, which existed for many years as the Ohio Yearly Meeting of Friends, was formed in 1813. As the work developed, members became attracted to the preaching of Joseph John Gurney (1788–1847), who had been deeply affected by Methodist holiness doctrines. Most active in promoting the holiness movement in Ohio were David Updegraff, Dougan Clark, Walter Malone, and Emma Malone. The Malones founded Cleveland Bible Institute (now Malone College) in 1892.

A generation after their movement into Ohio, Friends moved into Kansas and from there into Oklahoma, Texas, Nebraska, and Colorado. A Kansas Yearly Meeting (now the Evangelical Friends Church–Mid-America Yearly Meeting) was formed in

1872. It affiliated with the Five Years Meeting in 1900, but withdrew in 1937 as more conservative elements became dominant. The Kansas Meeting established a mission in the Congo (now Burundi) in 1934 and later founded Camp Quaker Haven at Arkansas, Kansas, for its youth.

The Northwest Yearly Meeting of Friends Church dates to the movement of Friends into the Willamette Valley of Oregon in the late nineteenth century. The first settlers had been from Iowa and continued their affiliation with the Iowa Yearly Meeting, but by 1893 they had grown sufficiently for an independent Oregon Yearly Meeting to be set apart. As work expanded into Washington and Idaho, the present name was assumed. From 1902 to 1936 the Oregon Yearly Meeting was affiliated with the Five Years Meeting, but it subsequently withdrew because of the increasingly conservative theological stance of Friends in the Northwest.

The Northwest Meeting sponsors four campground facilities, Friendship Manor (a retirement home), Barclay Press (a printing company), George Fox University, and several elementary and high schools.

The Rocky Mountain Yearly Meeting was established in 1957 from congregations formerly affiliated with the Nebraska Yearly Meeting. The Nebraska Meeting was affiliated with the Friends United Meeting, but the Rocky Mountain Meeting did not continue that relationship. The Rocky Mountain Meeting sponsors a campground near Woodland Park, Colorado.

In recent years, both the Evangelical Church–Southwest (formerly California Yearly Meeting) and Alaska Yearly Meeting have joined Evangelical Friends International.

Membership: In 2008 there were 300 congregations with 41,000 attendees in North America. Worldwide attendance is more than 140,000 in over 1,100 churches and there are mission ministries in 24 countries.

Educational Facilities:

Malone College, Canton, Ohio.

Barclay College and Academy, Haviland, Kansas.

Friends University, Wichita, Kansas.

Houston Graduate School of Theology, Houston, Texas.

George Fox University, Newberg, Oregon.

Periodicals: *The Friends Voice*.

Sources:

Evangelical Friends International. www.evangelicalfriends.org/.

Barrett, Paul W. *Educating for Peace*. Board of Publication, Kansas Yearly Meeting of Friends, n.d.

Choate, Ralph E. *Dust of His Feet*. Author, 1965.

DeVol, Charles E. *Focus on Friends*. Canton, OH: Missionary Board of the Evangelical Friends Church–Eastern Division, 1982.

Discipline. Kansas Yearly Meeting of Friends, 1966.

Faith and Practice of the Rocky Mountain Yearly Meeting of Friends Church. Pueblo, CO: Riverside Printing Co., 1978.

Faith and Practice: The Book of Discipline. Canton, OH: Evangelical Friends Church–Eastern Division, 1981.

The Story of Friends in the Northwest. Newberg, OR: Barclay Press, n.d.

25th Anniversary Committee. *Friends Ministering Together*. Pueblo, CO: Riverside Printing Co., 1982.

Friends General Conference

1216 Arch St., 2B, Philadelphia, PA 19107

The Friends General Conference (FGC) is an association of otherwise autonomous yearly meetings in the United States and Canada, most of which emphasize the authority gained through the direct experience of God, are open to theological diversity and the enrichment it can bring, and follow an unprogrammed pattern of worship. The yearly meetings that make up the Conference incorporated three strands of American Quakerism: the "Hicksite" and "Progressive" movements of the nineteenth century, and the twentieth-century "independent meeting" movement.

At the Philadelphia Yearly Meeting in 1827 a crisis resulted in separations in most of the yearly meetings (regional associations) in North America. Those who followed Elias Hicks (1748–1830) did not necessarily share either his political views or his theology, but they insisted that ministers must be free to speak as led by God. The Hicksite yearly meetings that emerged from the split tended to be more rural, less wealthy, more "quietist" or "sheltered," and more mystical than their orthodox counterparts.

Friends who shared Hicks's radical social views were not always welcome in Hicksite meetings. Out of their common concern for abolition, women's rights, and economic justice grew the "Progressive" Quaker movement, which flourished in the mid-nineteenth century and continued to hold annual meetings through the 1930s. The Progressive yearly meetings did not have formal membership. They were in effect a support group for activist Friends such as Lucretia Mott (1793–1880), who remained a member of the Hicksite meeting, as well as disowned Friends and non-Friends concerned about social injustice. The Progressive influence was a major, although largely hidden, source of energy in the founding of the Friends General Conference.

From the beginning, the Hicksite yearly meetings corresponded with each other about common concerns. In 1868 the inter-yearly meeting First Day School Association was established, followed by the Friends' Philanthropic Union in 1882. The regular biennial conferences of these groups wove the seven Hicksite meetings together. By the 1890s these two associations were holding combined conferences every other year. The Religious Conference was added in 1894, and the Education Conference in 1896. In 1900 the Friends General Conference was established on a permanent basis to support the work of these four groups, as well as the independent Young Friends Associations. Progressive Friends were prominent in the leadership of the Philanthropic Union, the Religious Conference, and Friends General Conference itself during its first few decades.

The third strand woven into the history of Friends General Conference was the independent meeting movement. The work of the American Friends Service Committee during and after World War I attracted many newcomers to Quakerism. Beginning in the 1920s new unprogrammed meetings sprang up, often in college towns and cities. These meetings were neither Hicksite nor orthodox. They tended to value individualism, social radicalism, open worship, and theological diversity. As these growing independent meetings organized into new yearly meetings and regional associations, most chose to affiliate with Friends General Conference. By the mid-1970s there were fourteen yearly meetings and associations affiliated with Friends General Conference.

Friends General Conference held conferences every other year until 1962, when off-year conferences were introduced. In 1968 the conferences became annual "gatherings" that emphasized fellowship and spiritual enrichment in place of business meetings. The ongoing work of the organization is overseen by a central committee of about 160 members appointed by the constituent yearly meetings, and an executive committee made up of committee clerks and yearly meeting representatives.

The program is carried out by eight standing committees: Advancement and Outreach, Christian and Interfaith Relations, Long-Range Conference Planning, Ministry and Nurture, Ministry on Racism, Publications and Distribution, Religious Education, Youth Ministries, and the Traveling Ministries Committee. The Friends Meeting House Fund, Inc., which holds funds for meetings in need of buying, building, or remodeling buildings, operates with a separate board of directors appointed by the central committee. The *Friends Journal*, an independent publication, is closely identified with FGC.

Included in the conference are the Baltimore, Canadian, Illinois, Lake Erie, New England, New York, Northern, Ohio Valley, Philadelphia, South Central, and Southeastern Yearly Meetings; the Southern Appalachian Yearly Meeting and

Association; Piedmont Friends Fellowship (NC); Alaska Friends Conference; and ten monthly meetings.

Membership: In 2008 the conference reported approximately 33,000 affiliated Quakers in 770 meetings and worship groups. Of these members, 1,100 were in Canada.

Educational Facilities:

Swarthmore College, Swarthmore, Pennsylvania.

Haverford College, Haverford, Pennsylvania.

Guilford College, Greensboro, North Carolina.

Earlham College, Richmond, Indiana.

Earlham School of Religion, Richmond, Indiana.

George Fox University, Newberg, Oregon.

Periodicals: *FGConnections* • *RESources*.

Sources:

Friends General Conference. www.fgcquaker.org/.

Bacon, Margaret Hope. *Mothers of Feminism*. San Francisco: Harper and Row, 1986.

Boulding, Elsie. *My Part in the Quaker Adventure*. Philadelphia: Religious Education Committee, Friends General Conference, 1858.

Brinton, Howard H. *Friends for 350 Years*. Wallingford, PA: Pendle Hill Publications, 2002.

Doherty, Robert W. *The Hicksite Separation*. New Brunswick, NJ: Rutgers University Press, 1967.

Jones, Rufus M. *The Latter Periods of Quakerism*. 2 vols. Westport, CT: Greenwood Press, 1970.

Rushmore, Jane P. *Testimonies and Practice of the Society of Friends*. Philadelphia: Friends General Conference, 1945.

Friends United Meeting
101 Quaker Hill Dr., Richmond, IN 47374

The largest of all the North American Quaker bodies, the Five Years Meeting of Friends was formed in 1902 as a loose coordinating agency by 12 yearly meetings. With the addition of programs and agencies, a full denominational structure has developed. There are now 27 yearly meetings in what became in 1965 the Friends United Meeting.

The Friends United Meeting represents the continuation of the "orthodox" Friends who had survived the Hicksite (Friends General Conference) and Wilburite (Religious Society of Friends Conservative) schisms, but who had existed throughout the nineteenth century as independent, geographical yearly meetings. Most worship is programmed. Ecumenical efforts began in the 1880s and a series of conferences every five years led to the formation of the Five Years Meeting.

The statement of faith of the Meeting, based on the teachings of Jesus as "we understand them," includes beliefs in true religion as a personal encounter with God rather than ritual and ceremony; in individual worth before God; worship as an act of seeking; the essential Christian virtues of moral purity, integrity, honesty, simplicity, and humility; Christian love and goodness; concern for the suffering and unfortunate; and continuing revelation through the Holy Spirit.

ORGANIZATION. The work of the meeting is carried out through its general board. The department of World Ministries oversees missions in Cuba, Jamaica, Belize, the West Bank in Israel, Kenya, Uganda, Tanzania, and the United States. The department of Meeting Ministries serves the needs of the local congregations by promoting spiritual development, church planting, evangelism, and Christian education programs. Friends United Meeting also operates a retail bookstore and a book publishing enterprise called Friends United Press. Member Yearly Meetings are: Baltimore, Canada, Cuba, East Africa, East Africa (South), Elgon, Indiana, Jamaica, Iowa, Nairobi, Nebraska, New England, New York, North Carolina,

Southwest, Southeastern, Western, Wilmington, Bwase, East Africa (North), Kaka Mega, Luggri, Malava, Nandi, Tanzania, Uganda, Vokoli, and Canadian Central. Friends United Meeting is a member of both the World Council of Churches and the National Council of Churches.

Membership: In 1996 the meeting had 46,789 members in the United States and 1,129 members in Canada, with an additional 100,000 members in Africa, Cuba, Jamaica, Mexico, and Israel.

Educational Facilities:

Earlham College, Richmond, Indiana.

Earlham School of Religion, Richmond, Indiana.

Guilford College, Greensboro, North Carolina.

William Penn College, Oskaloosa, Iowa.

Friends Theological College, Tiriki, Kenya.

Periodicals: *Quaker Life.*

Sources:

Friends United Meeting. www.fum.org/.

Hall, Francis B., ed. "Friends United Meeting." In *Friends in the Americas*. Philadelphia: Friends World Committee, Section of the Americas, 1976.

Intermountain Yearly Meeting
Current address could not be obtained for this edition.

In the early 1970s, the Pacific Yearly Meeting devised a plan to divide its widely scattered membership into more geographically workable units. Members in Arizona and New Mexico joined with otherwise independent friends in Arizona, New Mexico, and Colorado, as well as Colorado Friends who had withdrawn from the Missouri Valley Yearly Meeting, to form the Intermountain Yearly Meeting. The group had its first annual session in 1975. Most congregations are unprogrammed. The Mexico City congregation affiliated with the Pacific Yearly Meeting also participates in the Intermountain fellowship.

Membership: In 1991 the meeting reported 997 members in 17 monthly meetings and 18 worship groups.

Sources:

Intermountain Yearly Meeting. www.imym.org/.

Iowa Yearly Meeting of Friends (Conservative)
PO Box 657, Oskaloosa, IA 52577

The Iowa Yearly Meeting of Friends was established in 1877 by Conservative Friends who separated from the Iowa Yearly Meeting, which is now a part of the Friends United Meeting established in 1863. It keeps unprogrammed meetings for worship and operates the Scattergood Friends School, a coeducational college-preparatory high school near West Branch, Iowa.

Membership: In 2001 there were 548 members in 11 monthly meetings.

Sources:

Iowa Yearly Meeting of Friends. www.iaym.org/.

Hall, Francis B., ed. *Friends in the Americas*. Philadelphia, PA: Friends World Committee, 1976.

Missouri Valley Friends Conference
c/o Penn Valley Friends Meeting, 4405 Gillham Rd., Kansas City, MO 64110

The Missouri Valley Friends Conference was formed in 1955 as an association of unprogrammed Quaker meetings in the Midwest that were not affiliated with any other established yearly meeting. The conference meets annually. Over the years some of the local groups have affiliated with the yearly meetings and discontinued participation in the conference. At the same time, new unaffiliated meetings have joined the conference, so attendance has remained fairly constant.

Membership: Not reported.

Sources:

Penn Valley Friends Meeting.
    www.quakernet.org/MonthlyMeetings/PennValley/report_mvfc04.html.

North Carolina Yearly Meeting of Friends (Conservative)
PO Box 4591, Greensboro, NC 27404

The North Carolina Yearly Meeting of Friends (Conservative) is the result of a separation among Friends in North Carolina at the beginning of the twentieth century. At that time, there was a move to form what would become the Five Years Meeting (now known as the Friends United Meeting). As part of these developments, a new book of discipline was adopted. The Cedar Grove Monthly Meeting opposed the new trends it saw emerging and placed special emphasis on the retention of the unprogrammed meetings for worship. In 1904 it formed a separate yearly meeting and over the years other monthly meetings have been added. They have found fellowship with the other conservative Friends in the Ohio and Iowa Yearly Meetings, and periodically gather with them for fellowship.

Conservative Friends, also called Wilburites, place special emphasis in their faith and practice on the direct, unmediated experience of the presence and guidance of God. Their worship consists of waiting silently for this presence to become manifest, and vocal ministry is limited to those words the speaker feels confident are inspired by God. Conservative Friends do not act on any matter until moved of God; once moved, however, they are not easily or soon dissuaded.

Membership: In 2008 the meeting reported eight affiliated monthly meetings (congregations).

Educational Facilities:

Guilford College, Greensboro, North Carolina.

Sources:

North Carolina Yearly Meeting of Friends. www.ncymc.org/.

North Pacific Yearly Meeting of the Religious Society of Friends
Friends Meeting House, 3311 NW Polk, Corvallis, OR 97330

In the early 1970s, the Pacific Yearly Meeting, which had congregations spread over a wide geographical range, divided into several yearly meetings. In 1972, members in Oregon and Washington became the North Pacific Yearly Meeting and held the first independent session in 1973. Since its formation, groups have been added in Idaho and Montana. The Meeting keeps close ties with the parent body with whom it jointly supports a periodical. The Meeting is governed in a non-hierarchical fashion. A steering committee provides continuity and a clerk convenes its gatherings, records its minutes, and represents the Meeting to others.

Membership: In 1997 the meeting reported 18 monthly meetings, four quarterly meetings, and 32 worship groups gathered in the quarterly meetings. There were approximately 761 members.

Periodicals: *Friends Bulletin.* Send orders to 5238 Andalusia Ct., Whittier, CA 90601.

Sources:

North Pacific Yearly Meeting of the Religious Society of Friends. www.npym.org/

Faith and Practice. Corvallis, OR: North Pacific Yearly Meeting of the Religious Society of Friends, 1986.

Northwest Yearly Meeting of Friends Church
200 N Meridian St., Newberg, OR 97132-2714

Quaker settlers in the Northwest first gathered in the fertile Willamette Valley in Oregon in the late nineteenth century. These early settlers were from Iowa and associated with the Iowa Yearly Meeting. In 1893 they were officially established as an independent yearly meeting by the Iowa Yearly Meeting, with the name

Oregon Yearly Meeting of Friends. Because some churches were located in Washington and Idaho, the name was changed to Northwest Yearly Meeting of Friends. From 1902 to 1936 the Oregon Yearly Meeting was a part of the Five Years Meeting, but has in more recent years affiliated with the Evangelical Friends International.

The doctrine of the Northwest Yearly Meeting (NWYM) is biblically based with a central message of the lordship of Jesus Christ. The emphasis of salvation through the Lord coupled with a strong sense of social commitment have been the two dominant themes of the meeting.

NWYM maintains a relationship with four camping facilities, Friendsview Manor (a retirement home), Barclay Press (a publishing company), George Fox University, and several elementary and high schools. Missionary work is carried out in cooperation with the Evangelical Friends International. A joint mission program is supported in Mexico, Rwanda, Burundi, Taiwan, Peru, and Bolivia.

Membership: In 2001 NWYM reported 7,017 members and 51 churches, including six extension churches. Ten mission points/church plants are under the care of the board of evangelism.

Educational Facilities:

George Fox University, Newberg, Oregon.

Periodicals: *The Friends Voice.* Available from 2748 E Pikes Peak Ave., Colorado Springs, CO 80909.

Sources:

Northwest Yearly Meeting of Friends Church. www.nwfriends.org/.

This Story of the Friends in the Northwest. Newberg, OR: Barclay Press, n.d.

Ohio Yearly Meeting of the Society of Friends, Conservative

c/o Dorothy Smith, Correspondent, 108 Fowler Ave., Barnesville, OH 43713-1176

The Ohio Yearly Meeting of the Religious Society of Friends was established in 1813 and originally included most of the Friends west of the Allegheny Mountains. It grew out of Philadelphia and other eastern yearly meetings that were begun during the first decades of the Friends movement, when followers believed themselves to be called by Christ to once again tear open the veil that Catholicism and other Protestant churches had erected between the laity and the deity. Soon after the Hicksites left the Philadelphia Yearly Meeting in 1827, a similar separation occurred in Ohio. The Conservative Yearly Meeting continued its unequivocal recognition of Christ Jesus as the Son of God, whose suffering on the cross they believe opened a path to salvation and eternal life for His Friends to follow.

Friends believe that the risen, living Christ is here among us, having come to teach His people Himself. It is He who leads their worship, as they meet to wait for His immediate direction, with no paid or "ordained" clergy to intervene. They hold that the Bible is inspired by God through His Holy Spirit to serve for edification and guidance, but only as we ourselves have their meaning opened to us by the same Holy Spirit. They believe that He calls us to perfection and that He perfects us to the extent that we submit, on our daily cross, to His work. They call themselves "Conservative" to distinguish themselves from others who trace their roots to Quakerism but are unsure whether they are Christians, or have paid clergy and worship planned by humans.

The beliefs of members of the Ohio Yearly Meeting are not a recitation of what their predecessors have taught them, but a statement of what they have experienced—Christ Jesus as their head, their teacher, their high priest, and their shepherd in all things. When they meet to worship, they wait quietly for Him to lead them, to comfort them, to supply whatever their need is at the time. When they meet to conduct the business of the Meeting, they do so prayerfully and in humility, each person seeking to surrender his or her own will and wisdom and to know the will and wisdom of God for His people. They obey the command of Jesus not to swear oaths but to be honest in all things. They do not make war on behalf of any worldly government. They recognize all races and both genders as created

equal in God's love. They extend God's love to their enemies as well as their friends and families. They work to keep their minds and their bodies pure, as they believe that the body is God's temple.

The yearly meeting, composed of representatives of the monthly meetings, provides general oversight of the society. Each monthly meeting appoints two men and two women to have responsibility for pastoral care of members and the nurturing of harmony within the body. Spiritual oversight of the meeting for worship and oversight of the ministry are under the care of the elders. Special gifts in verbal ministry are recorded. Nevertheless, all members of the body are responsible for serving and ministering as needs and callings arise. The meeting has affiliated work in eleven countries.

The yearly meeting is a member of the Friends World Committee for Consultation. Fellowship is kept with the other two remaining Conservative yearly meetings—North Carolina and Iowa—and there are periodic gatherings of members from the three groups. There is no direct missional program, but a number of service projects are supported through the American Friends Service Committee.

Membership: In 2007 the meeting reported 528 members in two yearly and 13 monthly meetings.

Periodicals: *Ohio Conservative Friends Review.* Send orders to Susan Smith, 3876 Hopkins Gap Rd., Harrisonburg, VA 22802.

Sources:

Ohio Yearly Meeting of the Society of Friends. www.ohioyearlymeeting.org.

Pacific Yearly Meeting of Friends

Current address could not be obtained for this edition.

Quakers began to establish congregations on the West Coast in the 1880s. In 1931, with impetus from Howard H. Brinton (1888–1973) and Anna Brinton (1883–1969), a meeting was called that led to the formation of the loosely organized Pacific Coast Association of Friends. In 1947 the Pacific Yearly Meeting was established within the Association. Over the next decade, it grew to include 40 congregations as far apart as Mexico City, Honolulu, and Canada. As a result, a committee recommended a division of the meeting into three meetings. This led to the establishment of two new meetings, the North Pacific Yearly Meeting (1972) and the Intermountain Yearly Meeting (1973). Though each meeting is independent, there are close familial ties and they jointly publish a periodical.

The Pacific Yearly Meeting of Friends' worship is unprogrammed. Membership is concentrated in California, but includes congregations in Mexico City and Honolulu.

Membership: Not reported. In 1996 there were 48 congregations in California and Nevada.

Periodicals: *Friends Bulletin.* Available from Friends Bulletin Corporation, 5238 Andalucia Ct., Whittier, CA 90601-2222.

Sources:

Pacific Yearly Meeting of Friends. www.pacificyearlymeeting.org/.

Brinton, Howard H. *Guide to Quaker Practice.* Wallingford, PA: Pendle Hill Publications, 1955.

Faith and Practice. San Francisco: Pacific Yearly Meeting of the Religious Society of Friends, 1973.

Rocky Mountain Yearly Meeting

4575-B Eliot St., Denver, CO 80211

The Rocky Mountain Yearly Meeting was established in 1957 when it separated from the Nebraska Yearly Meeting and did not continue the latter's affiliation with the Friends United Meeting. Worship is programmed. Mission work is carried out by the Navajo Indians at the Rough Rock Friends Mission near Chinle, Arizona, and by other individuals through cooperation with the Evangelical Friends Mission. Quaker Ridge Camp is maintained north of Woodland Park, Colorado.

Membership: In 2008 the meeting reported 11 affiliated monthly meetings (congregations).

Educational Facilities:

Barclay College, Haviland, Kansas.

Friends University, Wichita, Kansas.

George Fox College, Newberg, Oregon.

Periodicals: *The Traveling Minute.* • *Friends Voice.* Available from 600 E 3rd St., Newberg, OR 97132.

Sources:

Rocky Mountain Yearly Meeting. www.rmym.org/.

Faith and Practice of the Rocky Mountain Yearly Meeting of Friends Church. Pueblo, CO: Riverside Printing Co., 1978.

25th Anniversary Committee. *Friends Ministering Together.* Pueblo, CO: Riverside Printing Co., 1982.

Southeastern Yearly Meeting

PO Box 510795, Melbourne Beach, FL 32951-0795

Though formally incorporated only in 1964, Quakers in Florida have a much longer history. George Fox (1624–1691), commonly considered the founder of the Quakers, traveled past the Spanish-claimed Florida and Georgia coastlines. In 1696 the early Quaker Jonathan Dickinson (1663–1722), for whom the Florida state park is named, landed and wrote his famous journal. Nearly 75 years later, the Quaker botanist William Bartram (1739–1823)studied Florida flora. He wrote that in 1793 he visited a Friends meeting (church service) near Wrightsborough, Georgia, that had formed in about 1755. By 1807 these Friends, opposed to slavery, had migrated to Ohio, Indiana, and Illinois.

Between 1800 and 1900 the first influx of Florida Friends arrived from Indiana, Nebraska, and Iowa into Alachua County. Whitewater Meeting (1884–1897) near Archer was under the care of Richmond (Indiana) Monthly Meeting, whose members built the first Florida meetinghouse. During the same period, Lake Kerr Friends who had migrated from Michigan, Ohio, and London started the first Friends elementary. They sent their high school youth to Westtown Friends School near Philadelphia. A freeze in 1892 to 1893 wiped out both of these Friends communities of orange grove owners.

Contemporary Quaker history commenced in 1893 when the railroad transported the first Quaker farmers to Miami from the northeast. The Quaker community became firmly established there in 1948 and, under the care of Friends World Committee for Consultation (FWCC), became a monthly meeting in 1950. In 1944 Friends who had moved to Orlando from New Jersey and Philadelphia became a monthly meeting in 1944 under the care of FWCC. In 1917 St. Petersburg Friends organized; they too became a recognized monthly meeting under the care of FWCC, and built Florida's first continuously used meetinghouse. Due to very poor roads and no direct transportation, there was little contact among these early Florida Friends.

By 1950, encouraged by the American Friends Service Committee (winner of the Nobel Peace Prize in 1947), the Southeastern Conference of the Religious Society of Friends was formed. During the 1962 conference it was decided that "Seven Meetings of the Southeastern Friends Conference having indicated by official Minutes their desire to assume Yearly Meeting status, the Planning Committee recommends that these Meetings now consider themselves the Southeastern Yearly Meeting [of the Religious Society] of Friends." . . . These seven monthly meetings were Augusta, Georgia, and in Florida, Gainesville, Jacksonville, Miami, Orlando, Palm Beach, and St. Petersburg.

The first full yearly meeting was held April 12, 1963, near Avon Park, Florida. J. Barnard Walton (Friends General Conference, 1915–1963) had been instrumental

in shepherding the conference from its inception in 1950 to this conclusion, and in his honor the yearly business meeting Saturday-night lecture series was named the Walton Lecture. In addition to the larger annual business meeting, two annual interim business meetings and four executive committee meetings are held. The Michener Lecture takes place on the Sunday immediately following the winter interim business meeting. SEYM incorporated in 1964.

SEYM meetings continue to grow and wane as population centers evolve. In 2008 25 meetings were affiliated with or had a relationship with SEYM: Charleston Monthly Meeting, Clearwater Monthly Meeting, Crestview Worship Group, Deland Preparative Meeting, Fort Lauderdale Monthly Meeting, Fort Myers Monthly Meeting, Gainesville Monthly Meeting, Golden Isle Worship Group, Halifax Meeting, Jacksonville Monthly Meeting, Key West Worship Group, Lake Wales Worship Group, Managua Worship Group, Miami Monthly Meeting, Ocala Meeting, Orlando Monthly Meeting, Palm Beach Monthly Meeting, Sarasota Monthly Meeting, Savannah Meeting, Space Coast Monthly Meeting, St. Petersburg Monthly Meeting, Treasurer Coast Worship Group, Tallahassee Monthly Meeting, Tampa Monthly Meeting, and Winter Park Monthly Meeting.

SEYM is noted for its social concerns, including assisting in the founding and support of ProNica, an international Quaker organization that aids the people of Nicaragua.

Friends's testimonies continue to be: simplicity, peace, integrity and truth, community and equality, and caring for earth and our environment.

Membership: Not reported.

Periodicals: *SEYM Newsletter.* • Dwight and Ardis Michener Memorial Lectures and J. Barnard Walton Lectures.

Sources:

Southeastern Yearly Meeting. www.seym.org/.

Friends General Conference. "New to Quakerism?" www.fgcquaker.org/ao/new-quakerism.

Southeastern Yearly Meeting. *Faith and Practice.* Melbourne Beach, FL: Author, 2002.

Southern Appalachian Yearly Meeting and Association

c/o L. Perch, 330 Goebel Ave., Savannah, GA 31404

The Southern Appalachian Yearly Meeting and Association of Friends was formed in 1970 at Crossville, Tennessee. It was established by congregations in Alabama, Tennessee, Georgia, Kentucky, West Virginia, South Carolina, and North Carolina, some of which had been associated together as early as 1940 in the South Central Friends Conference (and later in the Southern Appalachian Association of Friends). Congregations are unprogrammed and there are no paid ministers. Annual meetings, held in May, center on silent worship, a search together on a chosen theme, and social concerns. After existing for some years as an independent meeting, the Southern Appalachian Association recently became a constituent part of the Friends General Conference.

Membership: See Friends General Conference (separate entry). In 1991 the Southern Appalachian Yearly Meeting and Association had an estimated 433 members.

Periodicals: *Southern Appalachian Friend.* Available from 3848 Wilmot Ave., Columbia, SC 29205.

Sources:

Southern Appalachian Yearly Meeting and Association. www.sayma.org/.

Other European Free Traditions

All-Canadian Union of Slavic Evangelical Christians
Current address not obtained for this edition.

The All-Canadian Union of Slavic Evangelical Christians traces its roots to a variety of independent evangelical Protestant activities in Russia in the late nineteenth century. Among them was what came to be known as the Shtundist Movement, which began among German residents in the Ukraine in the 1860s. Two Reformed ministers, Johann Bonekmper and his son Karl Bonekmper, began to conduct devotional Bible study sessions with the idea of improving the spiritual life among the church members. Lay people who mastered the format their ministers had taught them began to conduct similar meetings elsewhere among members of other churches: Mennonite, Molokon, and especially the Orthodox. As the movement grew, developed, and absorbed ideas from the various churches, a split occurred with the Russian Orthodox Church, and the Shtundists became an independent sect. The church persecuted them, and they in turn forbade many of the popular elements of Orthodox piety, including the veneration of the Virgin Mary and the saints, prayer for the dead, and attendance at Orthodox worship.

As the Shtundists were emerging in the Ukraine, Martin Kalweit, also a German, began to spread his Baptist faith in Tiffis, Georgia. Beginning with the first baptism in 1867, the faith spread throughout Germany. Slightly later, in the 1870s, Granville Augusta William Waldgrave Baron Radstock (1833–1913), an English Wesleyan (Methodist), converted some members of the nobility in St. Petersburg. Possibly his most important convert was Col. Vasili Petrovich Pashkov. A wealthy member of the Imperial Life Guards, Pashkov devoted time and energy (until banished by the emperor in 1884) to the union of evangelical Shtundists, Baptists, Molokons, and Wesleyans. His efforts were continually blocked by differences on the practice of baptism, but one of his converts, Ivan Prokanov organized the All-Russian Evangelical Christian Union in 1909.

Russian Evangelical believers migrated into Canada and the United States beginning in the 1880s, until slowed by World War I and the immigration restrictions imposed in the 1920s. Many of these believers found their way into various Baptist churches, but others formed congregations that were both independent and resistant to anglicizing forces. In 1930 a number of these congregations founded the All-Canadian Union of Slavic Evangelical Christians and established headquarters in Toronto.

The union uses the "Confession of Faith of Evangelical Christians" written by Prokanov in 1910. It is a simple faith consisting of major Protestant affirmations of faith in a trinitarian God and salvation through Jesus Christ. Baptism by immersion is practiced. Russian Evangelicals had largely accepted the pacifism of author Leo Tolstoy who had befriended them early on, but have in more recent years moved away from that ideal. Some have suggested that serving in the military was part of the taxes that Christians were to pay the government (Romans 13:7).

As the union developed, it suffered most from continued tension between conservative and anglicizing forces. In 1958 a large number of members and congregations left to join in the formation of the Union of Slavic Churches of Evangelical Christians and Slavic Baptists of Canada. They have had a steady loss of younger members who have felt alienated from traditional Russian beliefs and language.

The union is in communion with the Union of Russian Evangelical Christians, which works among Russian Americans. They have also developed missionary work in Poland and Argentina, as well as among the Doukhobors of western Canada.

Membership: In 1980 there were eight congregations scattered across five provinces with a membership of 225.

Sources:

Piepkorn, Arthur C. *Profiles in Belief: The Religious Bodies of the United States and Canada.* Vol. III. San Francisco: Harper & Row, 1979.

Apostolic Christian Church (Nazarean)
Current address not obtained for this edition.

The Apostolic Christian Church (Nazarean) traces its history to the movement begun by Samuel Heinrich Froelich (1803–1857), a Swiss clergyman who led a revival in the late 1820s. In 1830, he was barred from the pulpit by the Swiss state church for preaching the "Gospel of reconciliation in its original purity." The movement spread throughout Europe and was persecuted. Many immigrants flocked to America and congregations were established. Froehlich himself came in 1850 and immediately began to organize his followers as the Apostolic Christian Churches of America. Around 1906, some members of the Apostolic Churches withdrew over several points of doctrine. They adopted the designation "Nazarean," the popular name by which the group is known on the continent.

Members of the church believe in Christ, are baptized in the name of the Father, Son and Holy Spirit, and form a covenant with God to live a sanctified life and to seek to become rich in good works. They reject the priesthood, infant baptism and transubstantiation, and refuse to be bound with oaths or to participate in war. The church consists only of baptized believers, but affiliated with it are "Friends of Truth," those being converted. Apart from refusing to bear arms and kill in the country's wars, the church is completely law-abiding.

The church is congregationally governed. Elders serve the local church with powers to baptize, lay on hands, administer the Lord's Supper and conduct worship. The Apostolic Catholic Church Foundation is a service organization. It recently moved from Akron, Ohio to its present location.

Membership: In 1985, the church reported 2,799 members, 48 congregations, and 178 ministers.

Periodicals: *Newsletter*.

Sources:

Apostolic Christian Church (Nazarean). www.acorn.net/aacc/

Apostolic Christian Church of America
c/o Bill Schlatter, 14834 Campbell Rd., Defiance, OH 43512

The Apostolic Christian Church of America, originally known as the Evangelical Baptist Church, was begun in Switzerland in 1832. Samuel H. Froehlich (1803–1857), a seminary-trained, ordained minister in the Protestant State Church of Switzerland, turned away from teachings of infant baptism. Under much persecution, he preached the doctrine of salvation by grace through faith in Christ's redemptive work on Calvary. Continued persecution led to the migration of believers to the United States. Benedict Weyeneth, the first American elder, began his service in Lewis County, New York, in 1847.

Froehlich's teachings were influenced by sixteenth-century Anabaptists, who were committed to *Sola Scriptura* (the belief that doctrine and practices should be grounded in Scripture alone). The doctrine of the church is built on the teachings of Jesus Christ and the Apostles as contained in the Bible, considered the infallible Word of God. Teachings and practices are similar to many of those of the Anabaptist heritage. Following repentance, conversion, and a testimony to the congregation, an individual is baptized by immersion. The laying on of hands by the elder during a consecration prayer symbolizes and acknowledges the indwelling of the Holy Spirit.

Apostolic Christians are known for a life of simplicity and obedience to the teachings of the Bible. They practice closed communion and the greeting of one another with a holy kiss. Women members wear a veil or head covering during prayer and worship. A closely knit fellowship and strong sense of brotherhood exist throughout the denomination. These ties are nurtured through frequent visits of ministers, members, and Sunday school students from one congregation to another, each of which follows the same worship practices, traditions, and doctrine.

Elders and ministers are chosen from among the brotherhood and serve each local congregation. It is the duty of the elder (bishop) to "shepherd the flock," preach the Word, counsel converts and members, and perform the rites of baptism, marriage, and communion. Elders of all congregations serve together as an Elder Body in matters of denominational governance and meet semiannually. Ministers and elders serve without salary or seminary training. Sermons are preached by the inspiration of the Holy Spirit without premeditation.

Apostolic Christians respect and obey governmental authority; they serve only in a noncombatant status in the military and do not take oaths. Discipline of erring members is practiced for their spiritual welfare and for the preservation of the church. Eternal life is the gift of God to every true believer but it can be forfeited by willful disobedience and rejection of faith. The church has established a number of homes for the aged, a home for the handicapped, and a home for foster children. Outreach activities include World Relief, the Missionary Fund, and Bible distribution.

Membership: In 2008 the church reported approximately 13,000 members and 94 congregations, including two in Canada, four in Mexico, and two in Japan.

Periodicals: *The Silver Lining*.

Sources:

Apostolic Christian Church of America. www.apostolicchristian.org/.

Footsteps to Zion, A History of the Apostolic Christian Church of America. N.p., n.d.

Froehlich, S. H. *The Mystery of Godliness and the Mystery of Ungodliness*. Apostolic Christian Church, n.d.

————. *Individual Letters and Meditations*. Syracuse, NY: Apostolic Christian Publishing Co., 1926.

Brunstad Christian Church (Smith's Friends)
c/oLothar Dreger, 470 Ediron Ave., Winnipeg, MB, Canada R2G 0M4

The Brunstad Christian Church, more popularly known as Smith's Friends after the church founder, Johan Oscar Smith (1871–1943), is a loosely organized Norwegian group that emphasizes piety and living the Christian life as opposed to the emphasis placed on doctrine by the Norwegian state church. The church spread as Norwegians migrated to other countries around the world. In the 1970s some 3,500 were reported to have attended the annual meetings, representing some 20 nations. Membership in the United States is centered in the Northwest, with additional members spread across the western half of Canada. During the 1970s the group was served by two periodicals, *Skjulte Skatter* (in Norwegian) and *The Way* (in English), published in Salem, Oregon. In 1979 *The Way* was superseded by *Hidden Treasures*.

The Brunstad Christian Church is an evangelical nondenominational Christian church that holds the Bible as the sole source of religious truth. The church preaches the divinity of Jesus, faith in the Holy Spirit, baptism, forgiveness of sins, and the Lord's Supper.

The church supports missionary work in Africa, Asia, Europe, and elsewhere.

Membership: In 2008 the church reported 30,000 members in more than 65 countries.

Periodicals: *Hidden Treasures*.

Sources:

Brunstad Christian Church. www.brunstad.org/.

Streiker, Lowell D. *Smith's Friends: A "Religious Critic" Meets a Free Church Movement*. Westport, CT: Praeger, 1999.

Christian Apostolic Church (Forest, Illinois)
Current address not obtained for this edition.

The Christian Apostolic Church of Forest, Illinois, grew out of unrest within the German Apostolic Christian Church during the 1950s. Elder Peter Schaffer, Sr., one of the founders of the German Apostolic Christian Church, protested the attempts of church leaders in Europe to direct the life of the American congregations. Beginning with members in Illinois and Oregon, he organized congregations in Forest and Morton, Illinois; Silverton, Oregon; and Sabetha, Kansas in 1955. Doctrine and practice of the parent body were continued.

Membership: In 1988 the church reported four congregations with several hundred members.

Christian Apostolic Church (Sabetha, Kansas)
Current address not obtained for this edition.

The Christian Apostolic Church of Sabetha, Kansas, was founded in the early 1960s when members of the German Apostolic Christian Church in Illinois and Kansas withdrew under the leadership of William Edelman. The members were protesting several points of "interpretation of the statues and customs" of the Church.

Membership: Not reported.

Christian Community and Brotherhood of Reformed Doukhobors (Sons of Freedom)
Site 8, Comp. 42, Cresent Valley, BC, Canada V0G 1H0

The Christian Community and Brotherhood of Reformed Doukhobors, better known as the Sons of Freedom, emerged within the larger Doukhobor community in Canada in the early twentieth century. They were the ardent supporters of Peter Verigin (d. 1924) who was the leader of the Doukhobors at the time of their migration to Canada in 1899. Verigin was left behind in prison, but was released in 1902 and rejoined the community. The Sons of Freedom were that element of the group most loyal to Verigin and most opposed to the Canadian government's varied attempts to integrate the Doukhobors into the larger social context. They particularly opposed the establishment of public schools and the government imposing secular education on Doukhobor children.

For many years they existed as an integral part of the Doukhobor community. They supported the leadership of Peter Christiakov Verigin who succeeded the elder Verigin in 1924. During his tenure in office the number of the Sons of Freedom greatly expanded, and by the early 1930s, there were more than 1,000. The actual break with the larger community came in 1933, occasioned by a letter from P. P. Verigin, at the time in prison, asking all Doukhobors to refrain from paying any dues to the directors of the Christian Community of Universal Brotherhood (CCUB). They followed Verigin's orders, and the CCUB expelled them from the larger body. The break was healed for a short while during World War II when the Sons of Freedom were invited into the Union of Doukhobors of Canada. Formed in 1945, the Union soon fell apart, and the Sons of Freedom emerged as a fully independent group.

The Sons of Freedom were particularly critical of John Verigin who succeeded to the leadership of the larger group of the Union of Spiritual Communities of Christ (Orthodox Doukhobors in Canada) after the death of P. P. Verigin in 1939. His plans to accommodate government pressure were denounced as a distortion of Doukhobor faith. They were especially resistant to any introduction of public schools, which they felt would simply educate people into an acceptance of war and the exploitation of working class people, and lead to the destruction of families and communities.

In 1950 Stephan Sorokin, an immigrant from Russia and former member of the Russian Orthodox Church, came to the Doukhobors to claim a leadership role. After fleeing from Russia, he wandered for many years and successively joined the Plymouth Brethren, the Lutherans, the Baptists, and the Seventh-day Adventist Church. He came to Canada in 1949 and lived among the members of the Society of Independent Doukhobors in Saskatchewan, learning the ways of the community, particularly their songs. He also learned of the story of Peter P. Verigin (Christiakov), the leader who died in 1939. It would have been the place of his son, Peter Verigin III to assume the role as spiritual leader of the Doukhobors, but it was assumed that he was in a Russian prison camp. Though it was later learned that he had died in prison in 1942, many in the community awaited the arrival of the "lost" son of Peter P. Verigin (Christiakov).

Sorokin arrived among the Doukhobor settlements in April 1950. He was introduced among the Sons of Freedom by one of their prominent leaders, John Lebedoff, who departed three months later to begin serving a two-year prison term. Under Lebedoff's period of influence, there was heightened violence and tension between the Sons of Freedom and the state. However, the majority of the Sons of Freedom accepted Sorokin as the lost spiritual leader and reorganized themselves as the Christian Community and Brotherhood of Reformed Doukhobors.

Over the years of their existence, the Sons of Freedom had gained a reputation for more extreme forms of civil disobedience in their attempts to prevent the loss of Doukhobor ideals by accommodation to the government, and the late 1940s and early 1950s were years of heightened antigovernment protests. The Sons of Freedom were accused of bombings and arson (of new school buildings), and periodically underscored their displeasure with demonstrations in the nude. When tried and convicted of actions associated with their protests, many of the group served prison terms. However, under the leadership of Sorokin, the group began restraining from participation in such activities, which lessened the overall tension level between the Doukhobor community, its neighbors, and the Canadian government. Stephan Sorokin died in 1984, and as of the date of the previous edition, no new leader had been designated as his successor.

Membership: Not reported.

Periodicals: *Istina* magazine

Sources:

Lebidoff, Florence E. *The Truth about the Doukhobors*. Crescent Valley, BC: Author, 1948.

A Public Indictment of J. J. Verigin. Krestova, BC: Christian Community of Reformed Doukhobors, (Sons of Freedom), 1954.

Woodcock, George, and Ivan Avakumovic. *The Doukhobors*. Toronto: Oxford University Press, 1968.

German Apostolic Christian Church

Current address not obtained for this edition.

The German Apostolic Christian Church is the result of a schism in the Apostolic Christian Churches of America. During the 1930s the pressure to discard the German language in worship, pressure that had greatly intensified since World War I, led the majority of the church to begin to use English. A group led by Elder Martin Steidinger protested that the loss of German would be accompanied by a loss of piety and lead to the influx of worldliness. With the encouragement of some European church leaders, he led members in the founding of the German Apostolic Christian Churches with initial congregations in Sabetha, Kansas; Silverton and Portland, Oregon; and several locations in Illinois. Support came primarily from first generation immigrants. Doctrine and practice are like that of the parent body.

Membership: At the date of last publication, there were an estimated 500 members.

Molokan Spiritual Christians (Postojannye)

841 Carolina St., San Francisco, CA 94107

The Postojannye are those Molokan Spiritual Christians who reject the practice of enthusiastic jumping during worship services which characterizes the Pryguny Molokans (the Jumpers). The split in the Molokan community into the Postojannye (the Steadfast) and the Jumpers occurred in the mid-nineteenth century in Russia.

The Postojannye also reject the authority of the charismatic prophetic leaders who arose at that same time, such as Maksim Gavrilovic Rudometkin. Otherwise the beliefs and practices of the Postojannye and Pryguny are similiar.

The first Postojannye came to the United States in 1905. They tried to work in the sugar fields of Hawaii, but shortly after the San Francisco earthquake of 1906, moved to San Francisco and settled on Potrero Hill in 1906.

Membership: There were an estimated 2,000 Postojannye Molokans in the mid-1970s. They lived in San Francisco, the greater Bay area, and in Woodburn, Oregon.

Sources:

Dunn, Ethel, and Stephen P. Dunn. "Religion and Ethnicity: The Case of the American Molokans." *Ethnicity* 4, no. 4 (December 1977): 370–379.

Molokan Spiritual Christians (Pryguny)

Current address not obtained for this edition.

Among numerous free evangelical groups that derived from the Russian Orthodox Church, only a few have come to the United States. Among these few are the Molokans, founded by Simeon Uklein (b. 1733). He was a son-in-law of a leader of the Doukhobors, a mystical Russian group now found in western Canada. Forsaking mysticism, Uklein returned to the Russian Orthodox Church and began to preach a Bible-oriented faith. He claimed that the church fathers had diluted the true faith with pagan philosophy. The true church, which existed visibly until their time, disappeared and survived only in scattered and persecuted communities. Uklein taught a form of unitarianism and gnosticism. Both the Son and the Holy Spirit were seen as subordinate to the Father; Christ was clothed in angelic, not human, flesh. Uklein tended to be anti-ritualistic and denied the sacraments and rites. Baptism means hearing the word of God and living accordingly; confession is repentance from sin; and the anointing of the sick is prayer. A ritual was constructed from Scripture and hymns. Molokans drink milk during Lent (from which the name Molokans or Milk Drinkers, is derived), a practice forbidden in the Russian Orthodox Church. Uklein also adopted some of the Mosaic dietary law.

In the 1830s a great revival, an outpouring of the Holy Spirit, began in the Molokan community. It led to much enthusiastic religious expression, especially the jumping about of worshippers and the appearance of a number of charismatic prophetic leaders, the most popular one being Maksim Gavrilovic Rudometkin (d. 1877). The acceptance of these new emphases that grew out of the revival split the Molokans into the Postojannye (the Steadfast) who reject the practice of jumping and the teachings of Rudometkin, and the Pryguny (the Jumpers). The urge to migrate to America began among the Molokans after the introduction of universal military service by the Russian government in 1878, but came to a head with their refusal to bear arms during the Russo-Japanese War. Over 2,000 left, primarily between 1904 and 1914 (when Russia stopped legal emmigration) and settled in California. After World War I, some 500 more who had originally settled in the Middle East were allowed into the United States.

The Pryguny Molokons, the largest group to migrate to the United States, settled in Los Angeles from which they have moved into surrounding suburbs and communities. Various studies of the community found an estimated 3,500 (1912), 5,000 (late 1920s), and then 15,000 (1970). Churches can be found in Kerman, Porterville, Sheridan, Shafter, Delano, Elmira, and San Marcos, California. There is also a group in Glendale, Arizona, and a small group in Baja California.

Membership: There were an estimated 15,000 to 20,000 Prygun Molokons as of the mid-1980s.

Sources:

Dunn, Ethel, and Stephen P. Dunn. *The Molokan Heritage Collection*. Vol. I, *Reprints of Articles and Translations*. Berkeley, CA: Highgate Road Social Science Research Station, 1983.

Moore, Willard Burgess. *Molokan Oral Tradition*. Berkeley and Los Angeles: University of California Press, 1973.

Samarin, Paul I., comp. *The Russian Molokan Directory*. Los Angeles: Author, n.d.

Schwenkfelder Church in America

PO Box 67, Valley Forge Rd., Worcester, PA 19490

A surviving group of the followers of Caspar Schwenckfeld (1489–1561) left Silesia in 1734 because of persecution and came to America. In 1782, they organized the Schwenkfelder Church. The present general conference is a voluntary association of six churches, all in southeastern Pennsylvania. It meets annually.

The Schwenkfelders follow the spiritual-mystical lead of their founder. Schwenckfeld, at one time a wealthy German nobleman, came to believe that all externals, though to be used, are of the perishable material world, and he sought to discover the spiritual imperishable reality behind them. He found this reality in the inner word, in the church of those redeemed and called, in the invisible spiritual sacrament, in faith, and in liberty—all emphasized by contemporary Schwenkfelders. Baptism is suggested for adult believers, infant baptism or dedication is practiced, and communion is open to all. No distinctive dress is worn. Both public office and military service are allowed (a stance that separates them from many of the Pennsylvania German groups).

Membership: In 2002 there were six churches, 2,700 members, and 10 ministers.

Periodicals: *The Schwenkfeldian*. Available from info@schwenkfelder.com or www.schwenkfelder.com/WhoWeAre_Schwenkfeldian.htm.

Sources:

Schwenkfelder Church in America. www.centralschwenkfelder.com/.

Erb, Peter C. *Schwenckfeld in His Reformation Setting*. Valley Forge, PA: Judson Press, 1978.

Kriebel, Howard Wiegner. *The Schwenkfelders in Pennsylvania*. Lancaster, PA: Pennsylvania-German Society, 1904.

Schultz, Selina Gerhard. *A Course of Study in the Life and Teachings of Caspar Schwenckfeld von Ossig (1489–1561) and the History of the Schwenkfelder Religious Movement (1518–1964)*. Pennsburg, PA: Board of Publication of the Schwenkfelder Church, 1964.

Society of Independent Doukhobors

Current address not obtained for this edition.

The Doukhobors migrated to Canada from Russia beginning in 1899. There, a communal organization, the Christian Community of Universal Brotherhood, was implemented. A number of members of the community, people who otherwise accepted Doukhobor belief, soon rejected the communal lifestyle. In addition, these individuals came to reject the special role of the community's spiritual leader, Peter Verigin, though they continued to live on the edge of the community and interact with its members.

The issue of the Independents, as they had come to be called, came into sharp focus as World War I began. Verigin, angered by their dissent, cut them off from the protection provided by the National Service Act of 1917. In 1918 the Independents organized the Society of Independent Doukhobors. Following the death of Peter Verigin, the society was briefly reconciled to the leadership of Verigin's son, Peter Christiakov Verigin, and cooperated in the formation of the Society of Named Doukhobors. In 1937, as the communal structures were dissolving, the Independents denounced Verigin and broke relations with his organization. During World War II, the Independents briefly joined in with the Union of Spiritual Communities of Christ, the successor to the Society of Named Doukhobors, and the Sons of Freedom (a third faction) to form the short-lived Union of Doukhobors of Canada. It fell apart when the Union of Spiritual Communities of Christ withdrew. The Independents expelled the Sons of Freedom. Since that time the Independents have existed separately. Not bound by communal economic restraints, they have spread across western Canada as far east as Manitoba.

Membership: In the mid-1970s the society had 23 affiliated centers in British Columbia, Alberta, and Saskatchewan, and one center in Manitoba.

Sons of Freedom (Doukhobors)

Current address not obtained for this edition.

Soon after the arrival of the Doukhobors in Canada from Russia, Peter Verigin's leadership was protested. Some felt he was compromising the teachings of his letters, which had guided the group during his exile in Siberia. They marched through the early settlements in Saskatchewan, preaching the renunciation of the world and calling themselves "Svobodniki," literally "Freedomites," but generally referred to as "Sons of Freedom." To call the members of the community to the simple life and to dramatize their own God-given Adamic nature, they marched naked. They were eventually arrested and some sent to an asylum. Through the next few decades, though often disapproving of its actions, they remained a part of the larger Doukhobor community.

In 1923 a public school in the community was burned to the ground shortly after opening. The Sons of Freedom have been blamed for that burning and the many others that have occurred over the years. The school burnings represented a new motif in the protests, which had previously been directed at other community members. They began protesting outside forces, government regulations that were against the Law of God.

The Sons of Freedom initially accepted the new leadership of Peter Christiakov Verigin III, who succeeded his father as spiritual leader of the Doukhobors in 1924. But as he proceeded with the reorganization of the communal life and dealt with the governmental demands of the province, the Sons of Freedom began to voice their dissent. In 1928 they issued an open letter denouncing, among other things, the acceptance of public schools (which had been forced upon the community) and the payment of taxes.

The Sons of Freedom gained support during the 1930s as the communal corporation disintegrated and as the main body of community members formed the Society of Named Doukhobors. The Sons of Freedom were excluded from the larger body when they did not pay their annual dues. The apparent break was healed for a short time during World War II, when the Sons of Freedom were invited into the Union of Doukhobors of Canada. Formed in 1945, the Union soon fell apart and the Sons of Freedom emerged as a fully independent group. The succeeding decades have been a time of the rise and fall of leaders, periodic protests by the Sons of Freedom (including fires, bombings, and nude demonstrations), and periods of relative calm.

In 1950 the Sons of Freedom experienced a schism when Stephan Sorokin appeared among them. A former member of the Russian Orthodox Church, Sorokin appeared as a leader capable of reuniting the loosely organized group. His main rival was John Lebedoff, who in July 1950 began a prison term. Subsequently, many of the Sons of Freedom accepted Sorokin and left to found the Christian Community and Brotherhood of Reformed Doukhobors. When Lebedoff returned in 1952, he was unable to become the sole leader of the remaining Sons of Freedom. They have remained loosely and informally organized. They have also remained in a high degree of tension with both the government of British Columbia and the surrounding non-Doukhobor society (tension ably demonstrated by the 1965 polemic against the Sons of Freedom by Simma Holt, *Terror in the Name of God*).

Membership: Not reported.

Sources:

Holt, Simma. *Terror in the Name of God*. New York: Crown Publishers, 1965.

Woodcock, George, and Ivan Avakumovic. *The Doukhobors*. Toronto: Oxford University Press, 1968.

Union of Russian Evangelical Christians

Current address not obtained for this edition.

The Union of Russian Evangelical Christians was founded in the 1920s as an American branch of the All-Russian Evangelical Christian Union, headquartered in St. Petersburg (then Leningrad). At a later date it became an independent association. It shares a common history with, is in communion with, and is theologically identical to the All-Canadian Union of Slavic Evangelical Christians.

Membership: In 1980 there were eight churches scattered through Pennsylvania, New York, New Jersey, Illinois, and California, with an active membership of approximately 300.

Sources:

Piepkorn, Arthur C. *Profiles in Belief: The Religious Bodies of the United States and Canada*. Vol. III. San Francisco, Harper & Row, 1979.

Union of Spiritual Communities of Christ (Orthodox Doukhobors in Canada)

c/o USCC Central Office, Box 760, Grand Forks, BC, Canada V0H 1H0

The Union of Spiritual Communities of Christ (USCC) is the oldest and largest of several Doukhobor, or "Spirit Wrestler," groups in western Canada. The Doukhobors originated out of the great schism in the Russian Orthodox Church that began in the reforms of Patriarch Nikon. Nikon assumed control of the church in 1652. Over the years a number of sectarian groups appeared, including the Khlysty, or People of God, who originated in the early eighteenth century and perpetuated a mystical doctrine of the inner guiding light and the dwelling of God in the human soul. The Khlysty developed some extreme doctrines, especially those surrounding the claims to godhood by several early leaders. In the mystical life of the Doukhobors there was no place for water baptism, only spirit baptism. They seemed to have originated from the Khlysty, though they drew strongly from the Unorthodox Unitarian Protestantism that had also penetrated Russia from Poland.

The exact origins of the Doukhobors as a separate "sect" is a matter of controversy. But by 1730, when Sylvan Kolesnikoff formed a community of followers in the village of Nikolai, Ekaterinoslav, the Doukhobors had been established. Kolesnokoff was succeeded by Ilarion Pobirokhin as the new leader of the group. During his tenure, which ended in his exile in Siberia, Ambrosia, the Russian Orthodox bishop of Ekaterinoslav, gave the group its name, Doukhobors. Ambrosia intended "Doukhobor" to be a derisive term, implying the group's defiance of the Spirit of God in the Russian Church; the group interpreted the term as denoting their wrestling against spiritual pride and lust by the Spirit of God.

The next century saw the Doukhobors experiencing alternate periods of persecution and toleration. After Pobirokhin's exile, Sabellius Kapustin assumed leadership. In 1802, with the blessing of Czar Alexander I, Kapustin organized the Doukhobors in Molochnye Valley, where they had been exiled in isolation from the Orthodox. He established a communal system, the memory of which periodically reappears in the larger Doukhobor community.

In 1886 Peter Verigin (d. 1924) became the leader. He was opposed by a minority group led by Alesha Zubkov, who created a schism in the community. Zubkov was also able to have Verigin arrested and exiled to Siberia. From Siberia, however, Verigin was able to stay in contact with the group and continued to exercise leadership. He also learned of Leo Tolstoy, through whom he led the group to accept pacifism and to deny the state's right to register birth and marriage. Communal ownership of property was reasserted. With Tolstoy's financial assistance and the aid of American and British Quakers, the Verigin group migrated to Canada, the first Doukhobor arriving in January 1899. They settled in Saskatchewan, and in 1902

the Russian government released Verigin so he could also migrate. He led the group until 1924 when his son, Peter Christiakov Verigin, succeeded him.

Even as plans began to be made for the migration, the Doukhobors reorganized as a communal group, named the Christian Community of Universal Brotherhood (CCUB). In Saskatchewan the Christian Community was almost immediately reestablished. But in 1907, when the group members refused to acknowledge the Oath of Allegiance, as required by the Homestead Act, the government took back the land upon which they had settled. A new settlement in British Columbia was begun.

Under Verigin's son, in 1928, the CCUB was reorganized as the Society of Named Doukhobors. In 1934 a Declaration outlining Doukhobor belief and practice was published. The decade proved a financial disaster for the communally organized CCUB. Beset by schism of its more activist members and a slow recovery from the Depression, the CCUB went bankrupt in 1940. The land was taken over by the government, who paid the debts and became its "trustee." It was also at this time that the Union of Spiritual Communities of Christ superseded the Society of Named Doukhobors.

Peter Christiakov Verigin died in 1937; his son was in Russia in prison. In his absence John Verigin, a nephew, became the group's leader, but never assumed the role of "spiritual leader," the position of his uncle. Under his leadership, a plan for reclaiming the land was pursued, and most was returned to the group in 1963.

The Union of Spiritual Communities of Christ was able to retain the loyalty of the majority of Doukhobors, though challenged by several factions in the 1930s. The union has no creed, but its beliefs find expression in the Doukhobor Psalms and the Declaration of 1934. In the Psalms, God is seen as an eternal spiritual being, the creator. God frequently chooses to speak through the mouths of men, historically the Doukhobor leaders. Christ was the savior of whom God spoke most perfectly. Within the human self God places a divine spark, and it is the believer's duty to recognize and nurture it. Believers best approach God through worship and by following the inward law of God. The spiritual knowledge attained from this inward divinity is the sustaining force in times of persecution. The Declaration identifies the Doukhobors as of "the Law of God and Faith of Jesus." They advocate pacifism and refuse to vote, but consider themselves law-abiding in all matters not contrary to the Law of God and Faith of Jesus. They strive toward a communal life. They have taken an activist stance in the peace movement, and have frequently come into conflict with the government by defending their beliefs against what they consider government interference.

Membership: In the mid-1970s the Union had 36 community branches, all within a 70-mile radius of Grand Forks, British Columbia.

Periodicals: *Iskra* magazine.

Remarks: The USCC is to be distinguished from the most activist and often violent wing of the Doukhobor movement, the Sons of Freedom, which became quite controversial in the early 1960s for their public demonstrations against Canadian-government policy.

Sources:

Union of Spiritual Communities of Christ. www.usccdoukhobors.org.

Maude, Aylmer. *A Peculiar People*. New York: Funk & Wagnalls, 1904.

Mealing, F. M. *Doukhobor Life*. Castlegar, BC: Cotinneh Books, 1975.

Tarasoff, Koozma J. *A Pictorial History of the Doukhobors*. Saskatoon, SK: Modern Press, 1969.

Woodcock, George, and Ivan Avakumovic. *The Doukhobors*. Toronto: Oxford University Press, 1968.

Baptist Family

11

The Baptist churches are free churches, called *free* to show that they are free associations of adult believers. Other free churches include those in the European free church family, discussed in chapter 10, and those in the independent fundamentalist family, discussed in chapter 12. A cursory examination might suggest that the Baptists are a subgroup of the European free church family, which includes the Mennonites, the Amish, the Brethren, and the Quakers. The Baptists, like that family, are antiauthoritarian, lay-oriented, and nonliturgical; they oppose state churches, and they baptize adult believers, not infants.

But the size of the Baptist churches and their continued growth suggest significant differences between the Baptists and the relatively small European free church family, and such is the case. The Baptists make up the second largest family on the American religious scene, second only to Roman Catholics. One difference between the Baptists and the smaller European free churches is historical. The Baptists emerged out of British Puritanism, whereas the European free churches developed from the initial efforts of the continental radical reformers. Second, Baptists are free from some significant hindrances to growth that characterize the European free churches. These hindrances include pacifism, the ban (a form of excommunication), and prohibitions against participation in public life, such as voting, holding public office, and serving in the armed forces. Finally, the Baptists' evangelistic and revivalistic lifestyle has attracted many followers. All of these factors help explain why great numbers of people find the Baptist churches appealing.

HISTORY. History is a problem for the Baptists. When and where did the Baptists originate? Baptist scholars give widely divergent answers to that question.

One school, the earliest to appear in Baptist circles, holds to what has popularly been called the *Jerusalem-Jordan-John theory*. These scholars believe that the Baptists can be dated to John the Baptist and his baptism of Jesus in the Jordan River. David Benedict (1779–1874), writing in the second decade of the nineteenth century, expresses this view:

All sects trace their origin to the Apostles, or at least to the early ages of Christianity. But men, and especially the powerful ones, have labored hard to cut off the Baptists from this common retreat. They have often asserted and taken much pains to prove that the people now called Baptists originated with the mad men of Munster, about 1522. We

have only to say to this statement, that it is not true. And not withstanding all that has been said to the contrary, we still date the origin of our sentiments, and the beginning of our denomination, about the year of our Lord twenty-nine or thirty; for at that period John the Baptist began to immerse professed believers in Jordan and Enon, and to prepare the way for the coming of the Lord's Anointed, and for the setting up of his kingdom.

Benedict, *A General History of the Baptist Denomination in America and Other Parts of the World*, 1813, vol. 1, p. 92.

Followers of this school generally deny that the term *Protestant* has any reference to them because, they assert, they predate Martin Luther (1483–1546). They are also concerned with what might be thought of as an "apostolic succession" of Baptist congregations and take great pains to define and locate it.

A second group of scholars criticized the first group for seeking a continuity of organization and called upon them to seek instead a continuity of doctrine. The second group tended to locate Baptist organizational origins in the Anabaptist wing of the Reformation. (Anabaptists called for an adult believer's baptism, which necessitated the rebaptism of those baptized as infants.) This second view was theologically, if not historically, attractive for a church that sought to recreate the first-century church. As Thomas Armitage (1819–1896) put it:

If it can be shown that their churches are the most like the Apostolic that now exist, and that the elements which make them so have passed successfully through the long struggle, succession from the times of their blessed Lord gives them the noblest history that any people can crave. To procure a servile imitation of merely primitive things has never been the mission of Baptists. Their work has been to promote the living reproduction of New Testament Christians, and so to make the Christlike old, the ever delightfully new. Their perpetually fresh appeal to the Scriptures as the only warrant for their existence at all must not be cut off, in a foolish attempt to turn the weapons of the hierarchy against itself. The sword of the Spirit must still be their only arm of service, offensive and defensive. An appeal to false credentials now would only cut them off from the use of all that now remains undiscovered and unapplied in the word of God. The distinctive attribute in the Kingdom of Christ is life; not an historic life, but a life

Baptist Family Chronology

1634	Roger Williams starts Baptist church in Providence.
1644	Baptist churches in London issue their First Confession of Faith based on the Westminster Confession of Faith.
1670	First Association of Baptists in Rhode Island forms. They will later be known as the Six-Principle Baptists.
1707	Philadelphia Baptist Association is organized.
1727	The first Baptist congregation in North Carolina is founded as the Shiloh Church in Chowan Precinct.
1755	Formation of Sandy Creek Baptist Church.
1764	Organization of the College of Rhode Island (now Brown University).
1776	Henry Alline begins his preaching ministry in Nova Scotia.
1783	Former slave George Liele (1750–1829), the first American Baptist missionary, begins ministry work in Kingston, Jamaica.
1793	British Baptist missionary William Carey leaves for India.
1802	Organization of Massachusetts Baptist Missionary Society.
1825	Newton Theological Institution is founded near Boston.
1832	The American Baptist Home Mission Society is organized to initiate work in the American West.
1833	Baptists issue the New Hampshire Confession based on the London Confession of Faith.
1843–44	William Miller, a Baptist farmer-preacher, proposes date for the imminent Second Advent of Jesus, first suggesting 1843 and then 1844.
1845	Baptists split North and South over slavery and Baptists in the South organize the Southern Baptist Convention.
1873	Lottie Charlotte Moon, a Southern Baptist, becomes missionary to China.
1886	Several decades of African American Baptist development lead to the formation of the National Baptist Convention.
1895	Death of landmark Baptist leader James R. Graves.
1905	Baptist World Alliance organized in London, England.
1906	Formation of United Baptist Convention of the Maritime Provinces (Canada), which evolved from the earlier Baptist Convention of the Maritime Provinces (1846).
1920s	Fundamentalist-Modernist controversy rages.
1925	Southern Baptists adopt "Baptist Faith and Message" as a nonbinding statement reflective of their belief.
1932	Formation of the fundamentalist General Association of Regular Baptist Churches.
1947	Conservative Baptists organize.
1963	Southern Baptists accept a revised "Baptist Faith and Message."
1978	Conservatives engineer takeover of Southern Baptist Convention.
1991	Moderate Southern Baptists form new Cooperative Baptist Fellowship.
2000	The "Baptist Faith and Message" statement is revised and adopted as an official standard of belief by the Southern Baptist convention. It includes a statement that prohibits the ordination of women to the ministry.
	Citing a spectrum of issues, former president Jimmy Carter resigns from the Southern Baptist Convention.
2007	Former presidents Bill Clinton and Jimmy Carter lead in the formation of a new moderate and socially active denomination, the New Baptist Covenant.

supernatural, flowing eternally from Christ alone by his living truth.

Armitage, *A History of the Baptists*, 1887, pp. 11–12.

The final school of thought on Baptist origins, which gained ascendancy in the twentieth century, looks to seventeenth-century England for the beginnings of the Baptist movement. Robert Torbet (b. 1912), a twentieth-century exponent of this view, pointed out in relation to the first school:

To say, however, that any single one of these early segments of the Christian church may be identified definitively with the communion we now know as Baptists is to make an assertion which lacks convincing historical support. That there are similarities of teaching between each of these groups and the Baptists is not to be denied. Yet, although it is not possible to trace a clear lineage of Baptists as an historical entity back to the early church, Baptist history may certainly be traced from the stirring days of the Protestant Reformation.

Torbet, *A History of Baptists*, 1950, p. 15.

Torbet also refuted the Anabaptist theory by holding up the difference between Baptist and Anabaptist theology: "Baptists have not shared with Anabaptists the latter's aversion to oath-taking and holding public office. Neither have they adopted the Anabaptists' doctrine of pacifism, or their theological views concerning the incarnation, soul sleeping, and the necessity of observing an apostolic succession in the administration of baptism" (Torbet 1950, p. 62). One could also note the lack of vital intercourse and familial attachment between the contemporary Baptist churches and the contemporary Anabaptist churches (i.e., the Mennonites, Hutterites, and Amish) and the lack of Anabaptists in Baptist ecumenical bodies.

Henry C. Vedder (1853–1935) is cited by Torbet as an able exponent of the third school. Vedder believed that "after 1610 we have an unbroken succession of Baptist Churches" (Torbet 1950, p. 201). Further support for this third school is found in the theology of the early Baptists: they continued to operate out of their basic Calvinist theology, deviating at two points—the sacraments and the church—rather than adopt a Mennonite theology that was adjusted for their use. While

470

they differ with their Presbyterian and Congregationalist forefathers on two issues, they disagree with the Anabaptists on a number of issues.

English Baptists can trace their history to Holland, where Separatists had located after the execution of some of their leaders in 1593. John Smyth's congregation and another led by John Robinson arrived in Holland in the first decade of the seventeenth century. In a short time, Smyth issued a tract, *The Differences of the Churches of the Separation* (1608), in which he explained why the two congregations could not fellowship. Baptism was not an issue; extemporaneous preaching was. Smyth's congregation became heavily influenced by the Dutch Mennonites, and in the winter of 1608 to 1609, Smyth and about 40 people were rebaptized. Continued Anabaptist influence led to schism, however, and Smyth, whose congregation was absorbed by the Mennonites, returned to England. The schism resulted from the collision of the Calvinists' belief in predestination and the Mennonites' belief in free will. Thomas Helwys (c. 1575–1616), the leader of the schismatic group, tried to reject both by adopting an Arminian theology. He also rejected any attempt at tracing the apostolic succession of the true church.

John Smyth (1570–1612) founded the first Baptist Church on English soil in 1611. In England and later in America, the first Baptists were Arminian in their theology instead of Calvinist. That means the first Baptists believed in a "general" atonement—salvation is possible for all—not in the "particular" or limited atonement, or predestination, of the Calvinist Baptists. Thus the first Baptists were called General Baptists; the Calvinist Baptists were called Particular Baptists. The growth of Smyth's church and local squabbles among Baptists led to the founding of five more churches in England by 1630 and 41 more by 1644.

The founding of the second main grouping of Baptists, the Particular Baptists, came about through the Puritans' move toward a Baptist position in the 1630s. In 1638 a group in the church at Southwark pastored by Henry Jacob (1563–1624) rejected Congregational Church baptism because it was of the Church of England. Anabaptism began to emerge; dismissals led to the formation of a Calvinistic Baptist church pastored by John Spilsbury.

Among these Particular Baptists (or Calvinistic Baptists), the issue of immersion as the correct mode of baptism was raised. In 1644 they promulgated the London Confession of Faith, which provided for immersion and incorporated Calvinist theology with a call for religious freedom. This confession outlined the major issues that were to separate Baptists from other Christian bodies. Baptists would be congregationally governed but completely separated from the state. While being orthodox Christians, they would hold to adult baptism by immersion as the apostolic, hence correct, mode of baptism. They would divide among themselves on Calvinist and Arminian lines.

A third Baptist group believed that Saturday was the true Sabbath. This belief arose as early as 1617. Overall, Seventh-day Baptists have never made up a large percentage of

Baptists, but have persisted as one of the oldest continually existing Baptist bodies, and have been the ultimate source of almost all Sabbatarian teaching in the United States.

In rejecting affiliation with the state and asserting the sovereignty of the local congregation, Baptists took the major step toward their typical form of congregational government. The next step came in the 1600s when various issues led local congregations to associate together in order to present a united front on an issue. As early as 1624, General Baptists issued a common document against the Mennonites. In 1644 Particular Baptists issued the London Confession. These united-front gatherings eventuated into associations—regular structures for affiliation of congregations. As a rule, General Baptists began to move toward strong associations with more centralized authority, while Particular Baptists tended toward a very loose organization.

BELIEFS. Baptists have generally been among those churches that professed a "noncreedal" theology. This position does not imply an absence of either doctrinal standards or creedal statements. Rather, it suggests that Baptists assign a secondary role to creeds in the life of the church, that they recognize their subordination to the Bible, and that they attempt (by no means always successfully) to refrain from calling individuals to account for their dissent from any particular creedal formulation. In that tone, the Baptists have continually produced confessions of faith with the purpose of acknowledging consensus internally and of informing the world of their stance in relation to other churches.

Among the first of the Baptist confessions were the London Confessions of 1644 and 1677, the latter a revision of the Presbyterian's Westminster Confession, a second edition of which appeared in 1688. In the United States, the Philadelphia Confession of 1742, based upon the English Baptists' confessions, circulated widely until the middle of the nineteenth century. Then it began to be superseded by the New Hampshire Confession, which would subsequently assume importance as the most used and revised statement of belief for American Baptists. The confession was approved in 1833 by the Baptist Convention of New Hampshire and represented a modification of the strict Calvinism of the older British confessions whose authors were trying to affirm their close theological ties to the Presbyterians and Congregationalists.

The New Hampshire Confession might have become a mere relic had not J. Newton Brown (1803–1868) inserted it in the 1853 edition of *The Baptist Church Manual*, issued by the American Baptist Publication Society. From there it passed into other church manuals used by National (i.e., black), Southern, and Landmark Baptists. It was also found acceptable by some of the fundamentalist Baptists.

Briefly, the confession summarized the traditional Christian affirmations of the much longer and more detailed London and Philadelphia confessions. Following the practice of the Westminster Confessions, it begins with an affirmation of the authority of scripture, followed by paragraphs on the Trinity, the role of grace in the salvation of sinful humanity, and the nature of Christ as the mediator between God and humanity. The central emphasis of the confession is salvation and the Christian life, in which the confession reflects a middle ground between the two major groupings—Calvinist (predestination) and Arminian (free will)—within the larger Baptist community. The confession affirms both Calvinist emphases such as the depravity of humans, the absolute need of God's grace, and the perseverance of the saints, as well as Arminian emphases such as the free gift of salvation to all and the role of human free agency.

The Baptist Confessions belong to the theological center of Christianity. They affirm the major conclusions of the ecumenical councils of the Christian movement that occurred from the fourth to the eighth century and were embodied in the Nicene and Chalcedonian creeds. They also affirm the principle doctrines of the Protestant Reformation on such issues as the authority of the Bible, salvation by faith alone, and the priesthood of believers.

The confession's brief statement on the relation of Christians to civil government is similar to the position of both Presbyterians (Westminster Confession) and Mennonites (Dordrecht Confession) in affirming a proper role of civil government and the duty of the Christian to obey it in all matters not opposed to the will of God. Not mentioned, but assumed from earlier statements, the confession denies the Mennonite positions on bearing arms, oaths, and holding government office.

The sacraments are central to the differences between Baptists and the other groups of the Puritan milieu out of which the Baptists emerged. Baptists have generally rejected the notion of sacrament in their consideration of the common Christian rites of baptism and the Lord's Supper. They have termed these rites ordinances, by which they affirm that they are followed out of obedience to God's command (in scripture). Baptists deny that they have in and of themselves any supernatural effects. The Lord's Supper is considered a memorial meal. Baptism by immersion is seen as an emblem of the believer's faith. It is limited to adults, those old enough to make a profession of faith.

Also at issue between the Baptists and other Puritans was the doctrine of the church and its relation to the state. The Baptists rejected both episcopal (leadership by bishops) and presbyterian (leadership by elders) forms of polity in which a leadership beyond the local church is in authority. To Baptists, the local church is the main focus of church life and authority. Each local church is autonomous and affiliated with other churches for fellowship, common endeavors, and advice. Neither another local church nor a judicatory higher than the local church should be given the power to dictate to any local congregation (though, of course, a group of churches may judge a minister or congregation so different in belief and practice as to be out of fellowship with them). While Congregationalists also favored the power of the local church, Baptists rejected the Congregationalists' attempts to tie themselves to the state. The Congregational Church, when given the opportunity in the Massachusetts colony,

tried to establish itself as the one true church, with the state's backing. Under Congregationalist rule, Baptists suffered greatly from the associated intolerance.

IN AMERICA. Some Baptists came to America from England; some emerged from the established British churches in the colonies. The earliest Baptist churches were founded by Roger Williams (c. 1603–c. 1683) and John Clarke (1609–1676) in Rhode Island. First Church in Providence, founded by Williams, dates to 1639, and Clarke's Newport congregation to 1648. Apart from the Rhode Island churches, the early Baptists were persecuted for not allowing their infants to be baptized. This persecution was all but ended in 1691 with the Americanization of the British government's 1689 Act of Toleration.

In the 1680s, Baptists began to enter the middle colonies. A short-lived congregation was founded in 1684, and in 1688 the Pennepack Church in Philadelphia opened. Because of the lack of established churches in the middle colonies, the Baptists were to thrive here in a way not possible in the Northeast or South until after the Revolutionary War (1775–1783).

In 1707 the first Baptist association in the colonies was formed. The Philadelphia Association was patterned on an English model. It was a loose association acting only as an advisory body. To it was left the task of disciplining the ministers and of acting as a council of ordination. In 1742 the association adopted the London Confession of Particular Baptists of 1689, thus identifying American Baptists with Calvinist doctrine. Benjamin Griffith (1688–1768) and Jenkin Jones (d. 1742) added a statement on the relation of churches and the association "based on theological agreement."

In the South, Baptists arrived in the late 1600s and formed the first Baptist church in 1714. The earliest Baptists were Arminians, which means they opposed strict Calvinist views on predestination and instead believed people were given free will so they could choose whether or not to follow the gospel. From the Arminian Baptists would come the Free-Will Baptist associations.

In the early 1700s, the Great Awakening, a revival movement that spread through the colonies in the 1740s, began to affect the Baptists. Their number increased tremendously, but they also found themselves involved in a new controversy. Among the Particular Baptists arose the Separatist Baptists, whose membership requirement was the personal experience of regeneration (in modern terms, the "born again" experience, involving an awareness of Jesus as personal savior). The Separatist Baptists distanced themselves from those who practiced anything less. Among both the Particularists (now called Regulars) and the Separatists, divisions arose on the emotional appeal of revivalism. The Newlights were for it and the Oldlights against it. A final union of the various Particular groups was effected in 1801. The 1700s also saw the rise of Particular Baptists to predominance over the General Baptists in most areas.

The 1800s were a time of significant growth for Baptists, who were beginning to structure themselves and develop the adjuncts of a successful church—a publishing concern, a missionary arm, and institutions of higher education. In 1824 the Triennial Convention was formed. This meeting was, at its inception, a convention of associations called together for missionary concerns. The General Missionary Convention of the Baptist Denomination in America was the official designation, but the meeting every three years was popularly called the Triennial Convention. While missionary in its base, it became the forum in which many issues would be argued and out of which most schisms would come. Most Calvinistic Baptists, in the beginning, related themselves to the convention.

IN CANADA. Baptists in Canada had three separate starts, each essentially unrelated to the others, which are currently reflected in the three large regional conventions that make up the Canadian Baptist Federation. The first Baptists in Canada came from New England to Nova Scotia around 1760 to move onto land vacated because of the government's expulsion of the Arcadians. Ebenezer Moulton (1709–1783) arrived from Massachusetts in 1761 and founded the first Baptist church at Horton (now Wolfville). Though Moulton left the ministry and Canada two years later, his congregation survives and is the oldest Baptist church in the country.

Coming with the Baptists were a number of Congregationalists and Presbyterians, among whom were some who had accepted revivalism and its associated phenomena. They were called Newlights. A break began between the Newlights and the more staid traditional Congregationalists and Presbyterians, with the Newlights moving to form independent Separatist congregations. Into this situation stepped Henry Alline (1748–1784), a devoted Newlight preacher. His efforts throughout the New England settlements brought many Presbyterians and almost all of the Congregationalists into the Newlight Separatist camp. As in the United States, these Separatist congregations eventually identified themselves as Baptists, and, by the time of the merger between the Newlights and the older Baptists, the former actually constituted the bulk of the Baptist movement in the Maritime Provinces.

There were enough Baptists in Nova Scotia and New Brunswick by 1798 to form an initial association. As the work extended, the other associations formed. These associations came together in 1846 to constitute the United Baptist Convention of the Maritime Provinces. The title changed in 1963 to the United Baptist Convention of the Atlantic Provinces, reflecting the addition of Newfoundland to the three Maritime Provinces. Since 2001 the denomination has been known as the Convention of Atlantic Baptist Churches.

A decade after the first Baptists arrived in Nova Scotia, other Baptists slipped across the American border into Ontario and Quebec. The migration increased with the influx of Loyalists after the American Revolution. However, the first congregation was not formed until 1788, at Beamsville on the western tip of the peninsula in southern Ontario. From this early church established by Jacob Beam Sr., the Baptist movement spread through Ontario. The first congregation formed in Quebec was a rural church established in 1794. Baptist growth was small in the province. The first association was formed in 1836 in the Bay of Quinte area. Other associations, including a missionary association, were formed over the century. Finally in 1888, the Baptist work came together as the Baptist Convention of Ontario and Quebec.

Further west, Baptist settlement began in 1862 when John Morton began to farm some 600 acres of what is now downtown Vancouver. The Reverend McDonald, a home missionary, initiated work in 1873 in the Prairie Provinces from his residence in Winnipeg. As the railroad was laid, congregations were formed in the communities along the rail line. Many of the churches were built around converts from the various ethnic groups that moved onto the new farm land. Consolidation of the western work led to the formation of the Baptist Union of Western Canada in 1909.

The three Baptist conventions, joined by a small group of French-speaking Baptists in Quebec, came together in 1946 to form the Canadian Baptist Federation. The federation is a loosely organized body and most of the work of the denomination was retained by the several member conventions.

THE GROWTH OF THE LARGER BAPTIST BODIES IN THE UNITED STATES. The founding of the Triennial Convention was a signal for other cooperative efforts to form. The American Baptist Publication Society began in 1824, the American Baptist Home Mission Society in 1832, and the American Foreign Bible Society in 1837. A number of state societies and conventions were also organized. These were the building blocks out of which a national group consciousness could grow and from which a national convention or the equivalent of a national denomination eventually could emerge. It is difficult to say just when that national consciousness emerged, but it was certainly before 1907, when the American Baptist Convention was formed. That convention represents a gradual move toward centralization.

Proceedings in the Triennial Convention moved in the 1830s from missions to educational leadership and publications. In the 1840s, however, a new issue emerged—slavery. In April 1840, an American Baptist Anti-Slavery Convention was organized to press the issue that had been resisted earlier as a topic for consideration.

At the 1841 Triennial Convention, the southerners, led by Richard Fuller (1804–1876), protested the abolitionist agitation and argued that, while slavery was a calamity and a great evil, it was not a sin according to the Bible. The Savannah River Association threatened to withdraw cooperation unless the abolitionists were dismissed from the board of managers. The debate began a controversy that would result in the gradual withdrawal of the Southern Baptists from participation in convention activities and from support of the *Missionary Magazine* and missions.

The 1844 session proved decisive; the southern delegates showed up in force with several test cases. The Alabama Convention sent a query to the Board of Foreign Missions asking "whether or not slaveholders are eligible and entitled equally with nonslaveholders to all the privileges and immunities of the several Unions." The Georgia Baptists chose a slave-owner as a missionary and forwarded his appointment to the Home Mission Society as a test case. The convention dodged the issues by referring them to the respective subsidiary boards.

Because the issue of slavery was raised in the nomination from Georgia, the board ruled that it was not at liberty to consider it. The Alabama query was answered in the negative. Appointment of a slaveholder would make the northern brethren responsible for an institution they could not conscientiously sanction. The situation of the mission board was further complicated by the formation of a Free Mission Society, which refused "tainted" southern money. In the face of these two issues, the southern members decided to withdraw, and in 1845 they formed the Southern Baptist Convention.

The split brought to the forefront a second issue between southern and northern Baptists: organizational centralization. The Southern Baptist Convention became a single organization overseeing all the activities that were separated in the northern boards and conventions. Some 300 churches entered the new church convention, which met every two years.

The northern and southern churches are similar in church government, both being congregationally oriented, and in doctrine, both accepting the New Hampshire Confession of Faith. The southern church, in fact, is more centralized in its aggressive mission activity, and expanded northward in the twentieth century. The northern church has been much more open to modern theological trends, the ecumenical movement, and social activism, and it tends to be more "liberal" in its outlook.

As a rule, ecumenical participation by Baptists has been hindered by both the extreme congregational polity and the demand for doctrinal unity with those with whom they fellowship. Many of the missions established in the nineteenth and twentieth centuries outgrew their mission status as they became autonomous indigenous churches. They now fellowship through the Baptist World Alliance. The larger Baptist bodies, however, have tended to refrain from the affiliation with non-Baptists in such organizations as the National Council of Churches and World Council of Churches or even the National Association of Evangelicals. In Canada, the Canadian Baptist Federation joined, then withdrew, from the Canadian Council of Churches, though both the Baptist Union of Western Canada and the Baptist Convention of Ontario and Quebec retain membership.

CONSERVATIVE BAPTIST MOVEMENT. In the

early decades of the twentieth century, the Northern Baptist Convention, like its presbyterian counterpart, was rent asunder by the fundamentalist-modernist controversy. Among the Baptists, the fundamentalist movement focused on the issues of social action and the deviation from doctrine by missionaries. The fundamentalists opposed the post–World War I

(1914–1918) policies that seemed to involve unsuitable social activism, and they opposed the sending of missionaries who did not hold a strong conservative Baptist position. When the convention turned away from their demands, the members of the Fundamentalist Fellowship organized, in 1920, the Conservative Baptist Fellowship (CBF) to continue their understanding of the gospel.

For many years, the CBF continued within the Northern Baptist Convention, but during World War II (1939–1945) plans for separation were pursued. Over the years, at least five new Baptist denominations have resulted from splintering associated with the CBF.

The Conservative Baptist movement must also be seen as a reaction to the centralization signaled by the formation of the Northern Baptist Convention, itself, in 1907. An extreme congregational polity exists in churches belonging to the Conservative Baptist Fellowship. Congregations associate freely. Mission work is carried on by separate but approved mission agencies; schools tend to operate similarly.

PRIMITIVE BAPTISTS. In the years following the

American Revolution, a great wave of enthusiasm for missions swept across the American church. Among the Baptists, this enthusiasm was occasioned by the acceptance of the Baptist view on immersion by two Congregationalist missionaries on their voyage to the mission field in India. Having lost the support of the American Board of Commissioners for Foreign Missions, Adoniram Judson (1788–1850) and Luther Rice (1783–1836) turned to the Baptists to support their work.

In response to Rice's appeal, a new structure, the General Missionary Convention of the Baptist Denomination in the United States for Foreign Missions, was created in 1814. In 1815 Elder Martin Ross presented to the Kehukee Association meeting at Fishing Creek, North Carolina, a report on the new mission board. Elder Ross had already built up a reputation for missionary zeal. In 1803 he had placed his concern before the association in the form of a query:

> *Is not the Kehukee Association, with her numerous and respectable friends, called on in Providence, in some way, to step forward in support of that missionary spirit which the great God is so wonderfully reviving amongst the different denominations of good men in various parts of the world?*
> Hassell and Hassell, *History of the Church of God from Creation to A.D. 1885*, [1886] 1962, p. 721.

In both 1803 and 1815, Ross met with a favorable response. Similar actions were occurring across the country. Nevertheless, there remained a minority who viewed the missionary movement as an innovation and who, a decade later, were able to unite in opposition to a number of "new" causes. An effective voice arose in the Kehukee to confront the eloquent Martin Ross. Joshua Lawrence (1778–1843), of no formal education but great native ability, authored a Declaration of Principles for the churches of the Kehukee Association. At the 1827 association meeting, a lengthy debate on the declaration was followed by a resolution to "discard all Missionary

Societies, Bible Societies and Theological Seminaries, and the practices heretofore resorted to for their support, in begging money from the public." The Kehukee Association further resolved: "If any persons should be among us, as agents of any of said societies, we hereafter discountenance them in those practices; and if under a character of a minister of the gospel, we will not invite them into our pulpits; believing these societies and institutions to be the inventions of men, and not warranted from the Word of God."

Masonry was one of the issues combined with opposition to the new missionary groups, and the Kehukee reacted against members who joined the lodge. "We declare non-fellowship with them and such practices altogether" (Hassell and Hassell [1886] 1962, pp. 736–737). The lengthy action was finally adopted in complete consensus.

This action did not go unopposed by those who had for years supported the missionary cause, both within and outside of the Kehukee Association. Within the association, churches began to withdraw and to continue their support of mission societies. Other associations withdrew their letter of correspondence (doctrinal and ethical similarity) with Kehukee. One of these, the Neuse Association (North Carolina), split in 1830 to 1831, and the Contentea Association was formed around the Kehukee position against missionary groups. The Little River and the Nauhunty associations adopted the Kehukee position at the same time.

In August 1832, the County Line Association came out in opposition to missionary societies. The following month a similar action was taken at an "unofficial" meeting of some churches of the Baltimore Association who gathered at the Black Rock church in Baltimore County in Maryland. The action at Black Rock was significant, as it was bringing the issue close to Philadelphia, home of the mission board. In the North, those opposed to mission societies were called "Blackrockers."

No segment of the Baptist church, particularly in the South, was unaffected by the debates, and, as associations were divided, a unitive consciousness of being the "true," "primitive," or "old school" Baptist church developed among those who refused to support what they termed "innovations." A national body of likeminded believers who registered their consciousness of one another through "letters of correspondence" began to emerge. By 1840, Primitive Baptist associations covered what was then the United States, reaching north into Pennsylvania and west to Missouri and Texas.

Primitive Baptist beliefs were hammered out in debates with the growing Missionary Baptist movement on the one hand and the Arminianism of the United and the Free Will Baptists on the other hand. (Arminians believe salvation is possible for all through free will, a belief opposed to the predestination believed in by the strict Calvinists.) The heritage of the Primitive Baptists was the New Hampshire Confession and British Puritan Calvinism. Primitive Baptists' response was to affirm their traditional Calvinism and independency. Primitive Baptists are not, as a whole, theologically trained,

and their differences have arisen over acceptance or rejection of traditional statements.

The Statement of Faith is included in most copies of annual association minutes. Typically, the statement will include articles on the Trinity, the scriptures as the only rule of faith and practice, original sin, human depravity, election, perseverance of the saints, baptism by immersion, closed communion, the resurrection, and ordination. Differences among Primitive Baptists are manifest primarily on the doctrine of election or predestination. All hold to a belief in election, that God elected the saved before the foundation of the world. Some go beyond, and hold that God predestined everything that comes to pass. Upon that doctrine, associations have split. Foot-washing is practiced by many Primitive Baptists, but very few make it a test for fellowship. Some consider it an ordinance. The King James Version of the Bible is preferred. Secret societies are frowned upon.

Primitive Baptists have an extreme congregational form of government, and many assert in their articles of faith that an association has no right to assume any authority over local churches. For the overwhelming number of Primitive Baptists, there is no organization above the loose associations that typically cover several counties. Associations consist of representative member churches and can sit in advisory capacities only.

Except for the few Primitive Baptist groups that have organized more formally, there are no headquarters, institutions, or official publications. As with the Plymouth Brethren, periodicals become a major means of communication and are identified with various divisions. Generally speaking, each periodical serves a specific geographic area for a particular doctrinally definable group.

The local church consists of members, deacons, and elders. Members must be adult baptized believers. Deacons oversee the temporal affairs. Ministers have little or no theological training and, typically, no salary. They are expected to study the scriptures. No musical instruments are used in worship. Sermons are delivered extemporaneously, in a distinctive singsong voice. Also associated with the Primitives is Sacred Harp singing, a cappella singing in four-part harmony that sounds much like eighteenth-century folk music.

While not organized in a hierarchical fashion, there is a definite organizational structure to the Primitive Baptist movement that can be defined by doctrine and by letters of correspondence. Each association has a sister association to which it sends annual letters of greeting. Such letters are recognition of being in communion and professing similar doctrines. Doctrinal differences among associations in correspondence manifest the generally low level of doctrinal freedom allowed. With rare exceptions, associations in correspondence will not overlap geographically. Several groups have taken steps to organize more formally and to form supra-associational structures. Finally, race has also become a means of distinguishing a set of corresponding associations.

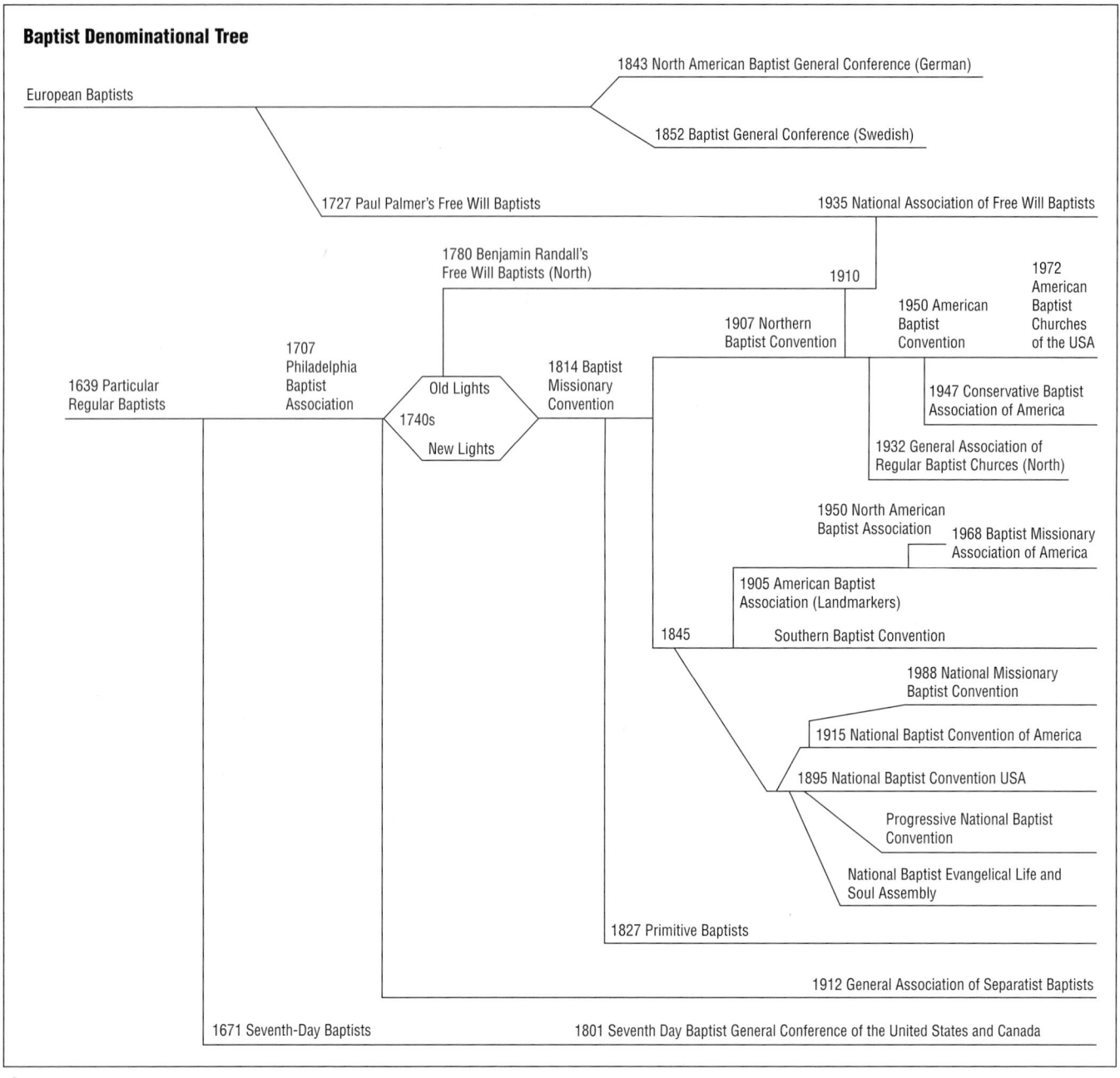

Baptist Denominational Tree

European Baptists

1843 North American Baptist General Conference (German)

1852 Baptist General Conference (Swedish)

1727 Paul Palmer's Free Will Baptists

1935 National Association of Free Will Baptists

1780 Benjamin Randall's
Free Will Baptists (North)

1910

1972
American
Baptist
Churches
of the USA

1907 Northern
Baptist Convention

1950 American
Baptist
Convention

1707
Philadelphia
Baptist
Association

1814 Baptist
Missionary
Convention

1639 Particular
Regular Baptists

Old Lights

1740s

New Lights

1947 Conservative Baptist
Association of America

1932 General Association of
Regular Baptist Churces (North)

1950 North American
Baptist Association

1968 Baptist Missionary
Association of America

1905 American Baptist
Association (Landmarkers)

1845

Southern Baptist Convention

1988 National Missionary
Baptist Convention

1915 National Baptist Convention of America

1895 National Baptist Convention USA

Progressive National Baptist
Convention

National Baptist Evangelical Life and
Soul Assembly

1827 Primitive Baptists

1912 General Association of Separatist Baptists

1671 Seventh-Day Baptists

1801 Seventh Day Baptist General Conference of the United States and Canada

Adapted from Association of Religion Data Archives

If one defines a primary religious body among the Primitive Baptists as an association and those associations with which it is in correspondence and has doctrinal unity, no fewer than thirteen distinct Primitive Baptist groups emerge. Each one of these bodies meets the criteria of a primary religious group as outlined in the introduction. Each asks for the primary allegiance of its members, has two or more centers of operation, and has at least one item of doctrine or organizational principle that will be distinctive from its closest neighbor.

AFRICAN-AMERICAN BAPTISTS.

Baptist missions among the African slaves date to the beginning of Baptist history and the efforts made among the African mem-

bers of Roger Williams's Providence church. But in the 1700s, as Baptists moved into the South, slaves grew to be a large percentage of the membership. The first black Baptist church was formed at Silver Bluff, South Carolina, between 1773 and 1775, and was made up of residents of the plantation of John Galphin (c. 1700–1780). Leadership was provided by a Brother Palmer, the church's founder, the Reverend David George (c. 1742–1810), and the Reverend George Lisle (1750–1829). The late date of this formation is symbolic more of the hesitancy of slave owners to allow separate churches (which could become independent centers for subversive activities) than of any lack of success preaching the gospel among the slaves. Within a few years, a second church was formed at Williamsburg, Virginia, at the initiation of the white Baptists. A third church was formed in Savannah in 1779. From these three, others sprang up across the South.

Northern blacks established Baptist churches after the turn of the century. The Jay Street Church of Boston was founded in 1804, with New York (1808) and Philadelphia (1809) following in quick succession. The Boston and New York churches were formed by Reverend Thomas Paul (1773–1831). The Abyssinian Baptist Church in New York would later be pastored by the flamboyant congressman Adam Clayton Powell (1908–1972).

Like their white brethren, the blacks were active in foreign mission work, sending a missionary to Haiti in 1824. In 1821 the reverends Lott Carey (c. 1780–1828) and Collins Teague were sent by the Triennial Convention to work in Liberia. They traveled to their new home with a group of blacks sponsored by the African Colonization Society.

As the reaction of slave owners to slave revolts cut into the freedom of slaves to spread their religion, and as many slaves fled north and west, Baptist churches spread in the Midwest. In 1836 the Providence Baptist Association in Ohio became the first black Baptist association in the country. Two years later in Illinois, the Wood River Association was formed. In 1840 the American Baptist Missionary Convention was formed by black Baptists in the Northeast and mid-Atlantic states. It was active in freedman's aid as the Civil War (1861–1865) drew to a close.

After the Civil War, several organizational attempts met with varying success until, in 1879, the Reverend W. W. Colley (1847–1909) returned from Africa with a vision of the role of black Baptist churches. At a meeting in Montgomery, Alabama, in 1880, the Foreign Mission Baptist Convention of the U.S.A. was formed. This convention became the rallying point of black Baptists. Within the Foreign Mission Baptist Convention, machinery was provided for the calling of a meeting at which the American National Baptist Convention was formed in 1886. In 1893 a third body, the Baptist National Educational Convention, was formed. Two years later these three bodies joined under the name National Baptist Convention.

The twentieth century witnessed growth and division among black Baptists. Splits occurred over involvement in civil rights, relations with white churches, and control of publishing. As a consequence, there are now several distinct groups that have "National Baptist" in their title. The largest group, the National Baptist Convention, USA, Inc., based in Nashville, Tennessee, was the subject of media scrutiny in 1999 when the group's president, Henry Lyons, was sent to prison for fraud.

GENERAL BAPTISTS. The first Baptists in both England and America were Arminian in their theology, meaning they adhered to the reformed theology articulated by Dutchman Jacob Arminius (1560–1609) and held that salvation was possible for all. They believed in a "general" atonement (thus the name "General Baptists") in opposition to the "particular" atonement or strict predestination of the Calvinist Baptists, who said the number and identity of the

elect were predetermined before the world began. John Smyth founded the first Baptist church in England in 1611; many General Baptists in America trace their seventeenth-century roots to Smyth. The English Baptists faced persecution, but were able to set up a central organization, "the General Assembly," in the 1660s. By 1699, this assembly included some ten local associations.

In America, the General Baptist history begins in 1639 with Roger Williams's church at Providence, Rhode Island. Other churches spread in the East over the next century. In the first decade of the eighteenth century, General Baptist centers were established in the South. A group settled in Virginia and, in 1709, applied to England for a minister. The minister died soon after his arrival, and the church moved to North Carolina under the leadership of William Sojourner. In the same year, Paul Palmer baptized nine persons and formed the Chestnut Ridge Church in Maryland. He, too, moved to North Carolina. Through his labors, William Parker was converted; under Palmer, Parker, and Sojourner, a thriving General Baptist movement was organized.

Much of the General Baptist work was lost to the militant Calvinists in the late 1700s. The Philadelphia Association absorbed the northern Baptists and their missionaries, and organized the Kehukee Association from members in North Carolina. Those not absorbed by the Kehukee became known as "Free-Willers," a name that stuck.

SEVENTH-DAY BAPTISTS. Seventh-day or Saturday worship has been a recurring issue raised by serious students of the Bible. For the Baptists who were in search of ways to recover the primitive church, it was an early theme. Modern Sabbatarians find it practiced throughout Christian history, but its modern history begins in the 1550s with scattered reports of Sabbatarians among the British reformers. As early as 1595, a book was published on the question by Nicholas Bownd (d. 1613).

The first congregation of Seventh-day Baptists seems to have arisen in 1617 under the leadership of John Trask (c. 1583–c. 1636) in London. The church met at Millyard, and it had a checkered existence as a result of continued persecution. A second congregation was added in 1640 at Nutton, Gloucestershire. The congregation included both Sunday and Saturday worship at first, but by the end of the century, the Sabbatarians were in control. In all, some fifteen congregations seem to have existed by 1700.

In 1664 a member of the Bell Lane Seventh-day Baptist Church of London, the Reverend Stephen Mumford, came to America and affiliated with the Newport, Rhode Island, Baptists. He began to raise the Sabbath issue, encountering both support and opposition, the latter from the church elders. On December 23, 1671, he formed the Newport congregation, the first Seventh-day Baptist church in America.

Other individuals migrated to America from various Sabbatarian Baptist churches in England. In most cases, they existed as Baptists until driven out as heretics. Churches were formed at Philadelphia (1680s) and Piscataway, New Jersey (1705). Over the century, growth was slow but steady. The

Sabbatarians spread throughout the colonies, south to Georgia.

Among the Pietists of Germany, a second strain of Sabbatarianism developed in the wake of the Bible study promoted by August Hermann Francke (1663–1727) and Philipp Jacob Spener (1635–1705). Among these Sabbatarians was the famous Woman in the Wilderness Commune that settled along Wissahickon Creek near Germantown, Pennsylvania, in 1694. They were among a number of German dissenters who settled in Pennsylvania at the invitation of William Penn (1644–1718). They were early in communication with both Abel Noble, founder of the Philadelphia Church, and the Newport Brethren. The community dissolved in the early 1700s.

In 1720 Conrad Beissel (1690–1768) arrived in Philadelphia ready to join the Wissahickon brethren; only then did he learn of the community's demise. However, he was able to meet with a few of its former members. The following year, Beissel went west to Lancaster County and founded a settlement. In 1724 he made a tour of the coastal settlements, visiting the Labadist Community at Bohemia Manor and the Rhode Island Sabbatarian Baptists. Shortly after that visit, he became a Sabbatarian himself. Through the influence of the German Baptist Brethren, he became a Baptist in 1725 and later the leader of the newly organized Conestoga Church near his home. Under Beissel and a Brother Lamech, who kept the diary of the congregation, the Sabbatarian issue was raised to prominence.

In 1728 the split in the congregation became effective, and Beissel formed an independent Sabbatarian church. Beissel immediately published an apology, *Mystyrion Anomias*, on the Seventh-day Sabbath. Further activities led to the formation in 1732 of the famous Ephrata Cloister, a communal Seventh-day Baptist group, from which others would grow.

CHRISTIAN CHURCH (DISCIPLES OF CHRIST) AND RELATED CHURCHES.

Many members of the Christian Church (Disciples of Christ) and its sister bodies would be offended by being thought of as "Baptists," but they would also, upon reflection, find many reasons for being considered in a chapter with the Baptist family. The Christian Church began with three ex-Presbyterian ministers in the early 1800s, two of whom belonged to a Baptist association from 1813 to 1830. The Christian Church holds some beliefs and practices in common with Baptists; for example, believers' baptism by immersion, the celebration of the Lord's Supper as a memorial meal, and the effort to restore New Testament Christianity.

The Christian Church had its origin in the work of three ex-Presbyterian ministers—Thomas Campbell (1763–1854), Alexander Campbell (1788–1866), and Barton Stone (1772–1844). The Campbells were Scots-educated Irishmen who had, during their years of training, become heavily influenced by some Presbyterian leaders who had adopted a free church position. (Free churches oppose state churches and are antiauthoritarian, lay-oriented, nonliturgical, and noncreedal. They practice adult baptism, not infant baptism.)

Presbyterian leaders John Glas (1695–1773), Robert Sandeman (1718–1771), and the Haldane brothers had left their respective churches to establish independent congregations. In America, other antiauthoritarian movements were begun by Methodist James O'Kelly (c. 1757–1826) and Baptists Abner Jones (c. 1772–1841) and Elias Smith (1769–1846).

Thomas Campbell came to America in 1807 and joined the Philadelphia Synod of the Presbyterian Church, but his name was removed from the rolls in May 1807 under charges of heresy. Thomas founded the Christian Association of Washington (Pennsylvania) to give form to the antiauthoritarian protest. At about the same time, Alexander Campbell (1788–1866) broke with the Scotch Presbyterians and sailed for America.

The Campbells, repulsed by the Presbyterians, began to form congregations, the first of which was the Brush Run Church. In 1813 the Campbells and their followers united with the Red Stone Baptist Association, a union that lasted until 1830. During those 17 years, the central ideas of the Campbells crystallized. Some of those ideas were in direct conflict with Baptist precepts, a development that led to the dissolution of fellowship in 1830.

The ideas that eventually caused the schism were clustered around the notion of *restoration*—the striving to restore New Testament Christianity. While restoration, in itself, would not be objectionable to Bible-oriented Christians, the implementation of restoration with specific programs and notions was not so acceptable. For example, in direct contradiction to Baptist teaching, Alexander Campbell began to teach a distinction between grace and law, and the New Testament versus the Old Testament. He wanted to establish the New Testament system of grace over against the Old Testament system of Law. Organizationally, the Campbells were also becoming involved in the same struggle that produced the Primitive Baptist church in the East and South—the rejection of associations and other supracongregational structures with power to legislate for the member churches. Associations, said the Campbells, were for fellowship and edification only. Alexander Campbell, in the pages of the *Christian Baptist*, which he published, also began to speak against the mission boards.

A major thrust of Campbellite thinking concerned the unity of the church, a common problem in early nineteenth-century Protestantism. The Campbellites felt that a restoration of the New Testament would include a union of all Christians as an essential aspect of the primitive order. Of course, other church bodies did not agree on what constituted primitive Christianity. For example, churches with strong supracongregational structures gave many reasons for their system as opposed to a congregational system, while the restoration movement became known for its defense of the congregational system.

While he was among the Baptists, the sacraments or ordinances became a major issue for Alexander Campbell, and believers' baptism by immersion replaced the common pres-

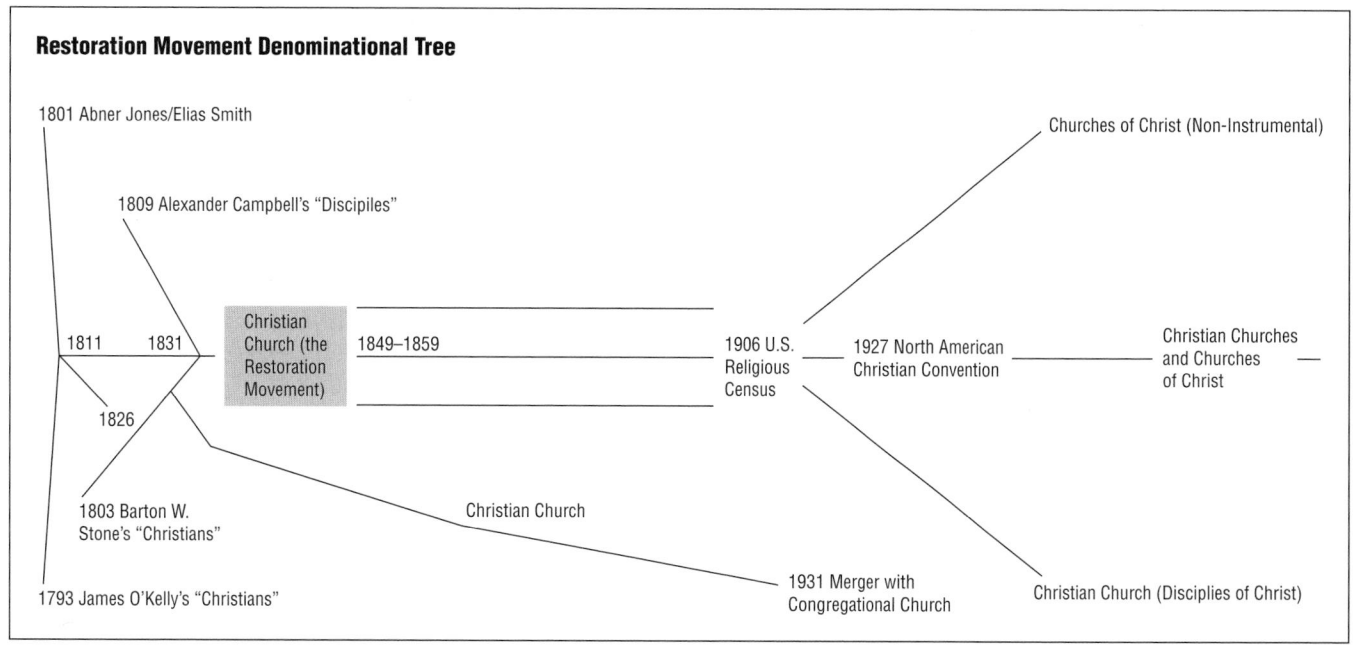

Restoration Movement Denominational Tree

1801 Abner Jones/Elias Smith

1809 Alexander Campbell's "Discipiles"

Churches of Christ (Non-Instrumental)

1811   1831

Christian Church (the Restoration Movement)

1849–1859

1906 U.S. Religious Census

1927 North American Christian Convention

Christian Churches and Churches of Christ

1826

1803 Barton W. Stone's "Christians"

Christian Church

1793 James O'Kelly's "Christians"

1931 Merger with Congregational Church

Christian Church (Disciples of Christ)

Adapted from Association of Religion Data Archives

byterial form (pouring). The Lord's Supper was viewed as a memorial meal; although as it came to be practiced, it has been a point of distinction between the Christian Church and other churches. The Lord's Supper was commemorated each Sunday and was open to all Christians, even those who had not been immersed.

Barton Stone was the third person chiefly credited for the formation of the Christian Church. In the early 1800s, he began to have doubts about both the doctrine and polity of his Presbyterian Church. After his ministering at the camp meeting at Cane Ridge, he and four other ministers were censured by the Synod of Kentucky. They withdrew and formed the Springfield Presbytery. The Presbytery was dissolved on June 28, 1809, and in a celebrated document—The Last Will and Testament of the Springfield Presbytery—founders set out their protest of Presbyterian polity. Emphasis was on the independence of the local church, the scriptures as the only authority, and conferences of churches for fellowship and edification only. The group took the name "Christian Church."

In 1830 the Campbells finally departed from the Baptists, and correspondence with Barton Stone, already initiated, continued. The two groups following the Campbells and Stone consummated a merger in 1832. No sectarian designation was wanted, so several "nonsectarian" names began to be used—Christian Church and Disciples of Christ being the most common.

At the heart of the Disciples' organization was a protest of certain structures that they saw present in Christendom. They protested the division of Christianity, which they called a result of sectarian ideas (as expressed in creeds) and church polity not based on the Bible. They took the "Bible only" as their uniting creed and an ultracongregational polity as the New Testament form. They did not like any structures that

either usurped the duties of the local church (as mission societies did) or that exerted power over the church, as some Baptist associations, presbyteries, or bishops did. They at first saw themselves as independent societies functioning as a leaven for the lump of sectarian Christianity.

Between 1830 and 1849, the Disciples experienced rapid growth. Fellowship was expressed in quarterly and annual meetings of regional gatherings. Independent colleges and publishing interests were founded and continued. Then, in 1849, the first general convention was held. Its purpose was to further the work of the societies and to represent them. The convention adopted the name American Christian Missionary Society, and its task centered on church extension, foreign missions, and evangelism. Over the next sixty years, other agencies were formed to handle specific tasks. They reported to the annual convention.

By the turn of the century, the creation of a number of boards and agencies led to a demand for centralization and coordination. A debate was precipitated when the 1910 convention adopted a resolution to form one general convention of the Disciples, which would unify all organizations, coordinate the collection of money, and make more efficient the administration. Finally, in 1917, the International Convention was organized.

In the twentieth century, the Restoration movement experienced its own division. The Disciples of Christ began with the formation of the International Convention in 1917. It took periodic steps that brought it into denominational Christianity and associated with other liberal Protestant churches in the major ecumenical councils. Three groups that resisted the denominational impulse are the non-instrumental Churches of Christ (whose membership is largely centered in the South), the Christian Churches, and Churches of Christ. All three groups are about the same strength. The theologically conservative Churches of Christ has experienced a number of schisms, the most important one being the formation of the International Churches of Christ (ICC) in the 1980s, under the influence of Kip McKean. The ICC, also known as the Boston Church of Christ, emerged out of a revival movement within the main body of the Churches of Christ, but eventually departed on a number of important points, especially on the matter of more centralized church authority, the discipling of members, and the use of instrumental music in worship.

In 2001 the ICC experienced intense turmoil when it was announced that McKean was taking a sabbatical from leadership. He confessed to arrogance and authoritarianism. The same traits were noted about the movement in general in a 2003 circular letter by Henry Kriete, a major leader in the London Church of Christ. In November 2005, 84 leaders in the broader ICC world withdrew fellowship from McKean and his Portland movement. McKean, in turn, gave his own work a new identity in 2007 under the title City of Angels International Christian Church.

CHRISTADELPHIANS.
The Christadelphians date to 1844 when Dr. John Thomas (1805–1871), a physician in Richmond, Virginia, began a monthly magazine, *The Herald of the Future Age.* Dr. Thomas, who immigrated from England in 1832, became associated with Alexander Campbell and the Christian Church, which Campbell and his brother helped form. Over the years, however, Thomas found himself in disagreement on a number of points of doctrine. He came to feel that knowledge and belief of the gospel must precede baptism, and he was rebaptized. A polemic began that led to a complete break in 1844. Groups began to form and were termed *ecclesias* (the Greek word for assembly from which the word *ecclesiastical* is derived).

The Christadelphians hold views similar to those of the Campbells, but are non-Trinitarians and resemble the early Unitarians in Christology. The Holy Spirit is God's power that executes his will. Thomas also denied man's natural immortality and believed that man was unconscious from death to the resurrection. At the end-time, Christ will appear visibly, all believers will be resurrected and judged, and the kingdom will be established. The kingdom will be the kingdom of Israel restored in the Holy Land. The wicked will be annihilated. Most important, Thomas taught that baptism by immersion after receiving knowledge of the gospel was essential for salvation. Closed communion is practiced. The Christadelphians do not participate in politics, voting, or war; nor do they hold civil office.

The organization of the ecclesias is congregational. Each ecclesia elects local officers, or "serving brethren." The serving brethren include managing brethren and presiding brethren. The former conduct the temporal affairs and the latter the speaking, teaching, and pastoral work. Groups of ecclesias meet in fraternal gatherings that have no legislative powers.

In the 1890s, a controversy that developed between Robert Roberts (1839–1898) and J. J. Andrew (1840–1907),

two leading brothers in England, spread among the Christadelphians. The controversy involved the issue of what was termed *resurrectional responsibility*, and split the Christadelphians into two factions generally termed the *Amended* and *Unamended*. Through the twentieth century, several efforts to reconcile the two groups of Christadelphians failed.

SOURCES

The study of the Baptist movement is supported by the American Baptist Historical Society, 1106 S. Goodman St., Rochester, NY 14620, which maintains the official depository library for the American Baptist Churches of America. The Baptist World Alliance operates the American Baptist Center at Valley Forge, Pennsylvania, and publishes the *American Baptist Quarterly*. The Historical Commission of the Southern Baptist Convention, 901 Commerce St., Ste. 400, Nashville, TN 37203, operates the convention's archives and publishes *Baptist History and Heritage*. The Seventh-day Baptist Historical Society is located at the headquarters in Janesville, Wisconsin, and the most complete Primitive Baptist archives are at Elon University in Elon, North Carolina. The Canadian Baptist Archives are located at McMaster Divinity College in Hamilton, Ontario. There are also Baptist archives at the library of Acadia University in Wolfville, Nova Scotia. The Disciples of Christ Historical Society (and archives collection) is at 1101 19th Ave. S., Nashville, TN 37212. It publishes the quarterly *Discipliana*.

Baptist Origins and History

Armitage, Thomas. *A History of the Baptists: Traced by Their Vital Principles and Practices: From the Time of Our Lord and Saviour Jesus Christ to the Year 1886.* New York: Bryan, Taylor, 1887. 978 pp.

Benedict, David E. *A General History of the Baptist Denomination in America and Other Parts of the World.* 2 vols. Boston: Lincoln & Edmands, 1813. 470 pp.

Brackney, William H. *Historical Dictionary of the Baptists.* Metuchen, NJ: Scarecrow Press, 1999.

———, ed. *Baptist Life and Thought: 1600–1980.* Valley Forge, PA: Judson Press, 1983. 448 pp.

Collinsworth, J. R. *The Pseudo Church Doctrines of Anti-Pedo-Baptists Defined and Refuted.* Kansas City, MO: Hudson-Kimberly, 1892. 496 pp.

Encyclopedia of Southern Baptists. 3 vols. Nashville, TN: Broadman Press, 1958.

Newman, Albert Henry. *A History of Anti-Pedobaptism, from the Rise of Pedobaptism to A.D. 1609.* Philadelphia: American Baptist Publication Society, 1897. 414 pp.

Torbet, Robert G. *A History of the Baptists.* Philadelphia: Judson Press, 1950. 538 pp.

Woolley, Davis Collier, and Robert Andrew Baker, eds. *Baptist Advance: The Achievements of the Baptists of North America for a Century and A Half.* Forest Park, IL: Roger Williams Press, 1964. 512 pp.

Baptists in North America

Armstrong, O. K., and Marjorie Moore Armstrong. *The Indomitable Baptists: A Narrative of Their Role in Shaping American History.* Garden City, NY: Doubleday, 1967. 392 pp.

Baker, Robert A. *A Baptist Source Book.* Nashville, TN: Broadman Press, 1966. 216 pp.

Beverley, James, and Barry M. Moody, eds. *The Life and Journal of the Rev. Mr. Henry Alline.* Hantsport, NS: Lancelot Press, 1982.

Boney, William Jerry, and Glenn A. Iglehart, eds. *Baptists and Ecumenism.* Valley Forge, PA: Judson Press, 1980. 177 pp.

Boyd, Jesse L. *A History of Baptists in America, Prior to 1845.* New York: American Press, 1957. 205 pp.

Brackney, William H., ed. *Baptist Life and Thought, 1600–1980: A Source Book.* Valley Forge, PA: Judson Press, 1983. 448 pp.

———. *Baptists in North America: An Historical Perspective.* Malden, MA: Blackwell, 2006. 296 pp.

Gaver, Jessyca Russell. "*You Shall Know the Truth.*" New York: Lancer, 1973. 368 pp.

McBeth, H. Leon. *The Baptist Heritage.* Nashville, TN: Broadman Press, 1987. 850 pp.

Rawlyk, George A. *Champions of the Truth, Fundamentalism, Modernism, and the Maritime Baptists.* Kingston, ON: McGill-Queen's University Press, 1990.

Renfree, Harry A. *Heritage and Horizon: The Baptist Story in Canada.* Mississauga, ON: Canadian Baptist Federation, 1988.

Stiansen, P. *History of the Norwegian Baptists in America.* Chicago: Norwegian Baptist Conference of America and the American Baptist Publication Society, 1939. 344 pp.

Wood, James E., Jr. *Baptists and the American Experience.* Valley Forge, PA: Judson Press, 1976. 384 pp.

Zeman, Jarold K., ed. *Baptists in Canada: Search for Identity amidst Diversity.* Burlington, ON: Welch, 1980. 282 pp.

Baptist Thought

Bush, L. Russ, and Tom J. Nettles. *Baptists and the Bible.* Rev. ed. Nashville, TN: Broadman & Holman, 1999. 456 pp.

Carson, Alexander. *Baptism: Its Mode and Its Subjects* (1831). Grand Rapids, MI: Kregel, 1981. 500 pp.

Lumpkin, W. L. *Baptist Confessions of Faith.* Chicago: Judson Press, 1959. 430 pp.

Robinson, H. Wheeler. *Baptist Principles.* London: Carey Kingsgate Press, 1925. 74 pp.

Wallace, O. C. S. *What Baptists Believe.* Nashville, TN: Broadman Press, 1934.

Primitive Baptists

Hassell, Cushing Biggs, and Sylvester Hassell. *History of the Church of God, from Creation to A.D. 1885, Including Especially the History of the Kehukee Primitive Baptist Association* (1886). Atlanta, GA: Turner Lassetter, 1962.

Piepkorn, Arthur Carl. "The Primitive Baptists of North America." *Baptist History and Heritage* 7, no. 1 (January 1972): 33–51.

Rushton, William. *A Defense of Particular Redemption.* Elon College, NC: Berry, 1971. 48 pp.

Black Baptists

Brawley, Edward M., ed. *The Black Baptist Pulpit.* Freeport, NY: Books for Libraries Press, 1971. 300 pp.

Fitts, Leroy. *A History of Black Baptists.* Nashville, TN: Broadman Press, 1985. 368 pp.

McCall, Emmanuel L., comp. *The Black Christian Experience.* Nashville, TN: Broadman Press, 1972. 126 pp.

Washington, James Melvin. *Frustrated Fellowship: The Black Baptist Quest for Social Power.* Macon, GA: Mercer University Press, 1986. 226 pp.

General Baptists

Latch, Ollie. *General Baptists in Church History.* Poplar Bluff, MO: General Baptist Press, 1968. 130 pp.

Seventh-day Baptists

Seventh Day Baptists in Europe and America: A Series of Historical Papers. 2 vols. Plainfield, NJ: American Sabbath Tract Society for the Seventh Day Baptist General Conference, 1910.

The Restoration Movement

Allen, Leonard. *The Transforming of a Tradition: Churches of Christ in the New Millennium.* Ed. Lynn Anderson. Villa Park, IL: New Leaf, 2001. 216 pp.

Baker, William, ed. *Evangelicalism & the Stone-Campbell Movement.* Downers Grove, IL: InterVarsity, 2002.

Casey, Michael W., and Douglas A. Foster, eds. *Stone-Campbell Movement: An International Religious Tradition.* Knoxville: University of Tennessee Press, 2002.

Dowling, Enos E. *The Restoration Movement.* Cincinnati, OH: Standard Publishing, 1964. 128 pp.

Ford, Harold W. *A History of the Restoration Plea.* Oklahoma City, OK: Semco Color Press, 1952. 217 pp.

Foster, Douglas A. Foster, Paul M. Blowers, Anthony L. Dunnavant, and D. Newell Williams, eds. *The Encyclopedia of the Stone-Campbell Movement.* Grand Rapids, MI: Eerdmans, 2004.

Gates, Errett. *The Early Relation and Separation of the Baptists and Disciples.* Chicago: Christian Century, 1904. 124 pp.

Harrell, David Edwin. *The Social Sources of Division in the Disciples of Christ.* Athens, GA: Publishing Systems, 1973. 458 pp.

Humbert, Royal. *Compend of Alexander Campbell's Theology, with Commentary in the Form of Critical and Historical Footnotes.* St. Louis, MO: Bethany Press, 1961. 295 pp.

McAleister, Lester G., and William E. Tucker. *Journey of Faith.* St. Louis, MO: Bethany Press, 1975. 506 pp.

Murch, James DeForest. *Christians Only.* Cincinnati, OH: Standard Publishing, 1962. 392 pp.

Christadelphians

A Declaration of the Truth Revealed in the Bible. London: "The Dawn" Book Supply, 1970. 30 pp.

Lippy, Charles H. *The Christadelphians in North America.* Lewiston, NY: Mellen, 1989. 320 pp.

Roberts, Robert. *Christendom Astray: Popular Christianity (Both in Faith & Practice) Shewn to Be Unscriptural; and the True Nature of the Ancient Apostolic Faith Exhibited.* Birmingham, U.K.: ;Walker, 1910. 417 pp.

Thomas, John. *A Brief Exposition of the Prophecy of Daniel.* Birmingham, U.K.: *The Christadelphian,* 1947. 122 pp.

———. *The Last Days of Judah's Commonwealth and Its Latter Day Restoration.* West Beach Post Office, South Australia: Logos, 1969. 99 pp.

❧ Intrafaith Organizations

Baptist World Alliance

405 N Washington St., Falls Church, VA 22046

The Baptist World Alliance is an international fellowship of Baptist conventions, associations, and unions that was created at a meeting of Baptists from around the world in London in 1905. It is a voluntary organization whose objectives are to show forth the basic unity of Baptists, to inspire Baptists everywhere, and to promote a spirit of fellowship, service, and cooperation within the Baptist community. The alliance makes no attempt to usurp the work or prerogatives of any of its member organizations or of local congregations. It has emerged as the champion of those Baptists who exist as a small minority in a hostile environment and a force in the fight for religious freedom.

The idea of an international Baptist conference had been generated in America, and an invitation was extended by several Baptist leaders in London to meet during the summer of 1905. Alexander Maclaren, a prominent British minister, presided at the first session, where a committee was appointed to draw up a draft constitution and set of by-laws.

The alliance meets every five years, at which time it elects a president and general secretary and names an executive committee. Those members of the executive committee who live reasonably close to the headquarters are named as the administrative committee. Headquarters remained in London until the beginning of World War II, when it was moved to Washington, D.C. The move was made a permanent one in 1947.

The alliance has expanded activities into every area of the globe where a Baptist community exists. It seeks to provide communication between Baptists, has developed a program to provide relief and aid to the needy, speaks out on issues of religious freedom, and sponsors conferences on various aspects of church life and Christian development.

Membership: The Baptist World Alliance is a fellowship of 214 Baptist unions and conventions comprising a membership of more than 36 million baptized believers and a community of more that 105 million Baptists in every country. The North American membership in the Baptist World Alliance includes the following: American Baptist Churches in the U.S.A.; Baptist General Conference; Czechoslovak Baptist Convention of the USA and Canada; General Association of General Baptists; Lott Carey Baptist Foreign Missionary Convention, USA; National Baptist Convention of America; National Baptist Convention, U.S.A., Inc.; National Missionary Baptist Convention of America; North American Baptist Conference; Progressive National Baptist Convention, Inc.; Russian-Ukraine Evangelical Baptist Union, U.S.A., Inc.; Seventh Day Baptist General Conference, USA and Canada; and Union of Latvian Baptists in America.

Periodicals: *The Baptist World*.

Sources:

Baptist World Alliance. www.bwanet.org.

Gaver, Jessyca Russell. *"You Shall Know the Truth": The Baptist Story*. New York: Lancer Books, 1973.

Nordenhaug, Josef, and Cyril Eric Bryant. "Baptist World Alliance." In *Baptist Advance*. Forrest Park, IL: Roger Williams Press, 1964.

North American Baptist Fellowship (NABF)

405 N Washington St., Falls Church, VA 22046

The North American Baptist Fellowship is a cooperative body of Baptist conventions and associations in North America. Though its membership is slightly different from that of the North American membership of the Baptist World Alliance, the fellowship functions as the alliance's regional body in North America. The fellowship emerged from the celebration of the Baptist Jubilee (celebrating the 150th anniversary of the founding of the first national Baptist organization in America). The spirit engendered in the cooperative effort of planning the event led the leaders to petition the Baptist World Alliance to establish a continuing North American organization, which occurred in 1964. The first president of the fellowship was Dr. V. Carney Hargroves, also generally recognized as its founder.

The North American Baptist Fellowship seeks to promote fellowship and cooperation among the Baptists of North America and to further the aims of the Baptist World Alliance in the North American context.

The NABF meets annually for fellowship and consultation on matters of interest that cross denominational lines. It has no powers to legislate or establish programs for its representative bodies, but it does encourage cooperative work among congregations of different Baptist denominations located in the same city or county.

The fellowship shares office space with the World Baptist Alliance.

Membership: The membership of the fellowship includes the following: American Baptist Churches in the U.S.A.; Association of Brazilian Baptist Churches in North America; Baptist Center for Ethics; Baptists Committed; Baptist Convention of Ontario and Quebec; Baptist Educators; Baptist General Association of Virginia; Baptist General Convention of Missouri; Baptist General Convention of Texas; Baptist Joint Committee; Baptist Union of Western Canada; Canadian Convention of Southern Baptists; Convention of Atlantic Baptist Churches; Cooperative Baptist Fellowship; Czechoslovak Baptist Convention of USA and Canada; District of Columbia Baptist Convention; Fellowship of Baptist Educators; General Association of General Baptists; Lao National Fellowship; Lott Carey Baptist Foreign Mission

Convention; L'Union d'Élises Baptistes Françaises au Canada; Mainstream Baptist Fellowship; National Baptist Convention of America; National Baptist Convention, U.S.A., Inc.; North American Baptist Conference; North American Baptist Women's Union; Progressive National Baptist Convention, Inc.; Russian-Ukrainian Evangelical Baptist Union, USA, Inc.; Seventh-Day Baptist General Conference, USA & Canada; Southern Baptist Japanese Baptist Churches of America; Union of Latvian Baptists in America; Women's Missionary Union; World ConneX.

Sources:

North American Baptist Fellowship. www.nabf-bwa.org.

Gaver, Jessyca Russell. *"You Shall Know the Truth": The Baptist Story*. New York: Lancer Books, 1973.

World Convention of Churches of Christ

PO Box 41487, Nashville, TN 37204-1487

The World Convention of Churches of Christ serves the churches that have emerged out of the Restoration Movement of the early nineteenth century—the Christian Church (Disciples of Christ), the Christian Churches and Churches of Christ, and the Churches of Christ. Each of these churches trace their beginning to the revivalistic efforts of Barton W. Stone (1772–1844), Thomas Campbell (1763–1854), Alexander Campbell (1788–1866), Walter Scott (1796–1861), and others who operated in the eastern half of the United States in the first decades of the nineteenth century. As the movement developed, it lacked a centralized governing authority and differences emerged primarily concerning the operation of structures serving the larger community of congregations. One wing of the movement remained fiercely congregational, and rejected any structures tending toward denominational structures. The more liberal wing of the movement, based primarily in the northern United States, gradually developed a denominational structure to facilitate and guide such common endeavors as education, world missions, and evangelism.

In spite of their organizational and doctrinal differences, the three bodies maintained an allegiance to a number of principles, ten of which standout: (1) a concern for Christian unity, (2) a commitment to evangelism and mission, (3) an emphasis on the centrality of the New Testament, (4) a simple Confession of Faith, (5) believers' baptism, (6) weekly communion, (7) a biblical name, (8) congregational autonomy, (9) lay leadership, and (10) diversity/freedom/liberty.

An initial attempt to bridge the divisive forces in the Restoration Movement culminated in the first meeting of the World Convention of Churches of Christ in 1930. The convention met sporadically through the twentieth century. The seventeenth convention was held in Nashville, Tennessee, in 2008. The convention is primarily for fellowship, the tradition being opposed to pancongregational structures.

Membership: The convention unites congregations now found in more than 165 countries that have their heritage in the nineteenth century Restoration Movement and the three American-based churches: the Christian Church (Disciples of Christ), the Christian Churches and Churches of Christ, and the Churches of Christ.

Periodicals: *World Christian*, 4800 B Franklin Rd., Nashville, TN 37220-1199.

Sources:

World Convention. www.worldconvention.org.

Calvinist Missionary Baptists

Alliance of Baptists

1328 16th St. NW, Washington, DC 20036

The Alliance of Baptists is one of several new bodies born from the conflict between the conservative and liberal elements in the Southern Baptist Convention in the 1980s. The effect of that controversy was the domination of the cnvention and its agencies by the conservative majority. In the wake of being largely shut out of participation in running the convention, many chose to disaffiliate.

One small group formed the Southern Baptist Alliance in 1987, which five years later took the name Alliance of Baptists out of a realization of its national character. The alliance sees itself carrying on a traditional Baptist faith that is non-creedal and Bible-based in nature. It has found support from what are now considered sister churches such as the Christian Church (Disciples of Christ), the United Church of Christ, and the American Baptist Churches in the U.S. Joining the National Council of Churches solidified its emergence as a new liberal Protestant denomination.

The alliance maintains a structure similar to the Southern Baptist convention. It annually elects four officers to lead its national program: president, vice-president, secretary, and the immediate past president. From its beginning, it has moved to affirm the equality of men and women, symbolized by alternating the alliance's presidency between women and men, and making sure that its officers include both men and women (as well as both clergy and laity). Women are admitted to the ordained ministry.

The alliance has a partnership relation with the Fraternidad de Iglesias Bautistas de Cuba and the Baptist Convention of Zimbabwe. The alliance does not have its own seminary, but sends divinity students to several schools of closely related groups. Its monthly newsletter is also posted on its website.

Membership: Not reported. In 2008, the alliance had 115 affiliated congregations. It has also developed a strong working relationship with the American Baptist Churches in the USA, the Cooperative Baptist Fellowship, and the Progressive National Baptist Convetion.

Periodicals: *Connections*, PO Box 25461, Greenville, SC 29616.

Sources:

Alliance of Baptists. www.allianceofbaptists.org.

American Baptist Association

4605 N. State Line Ave., Texarkana, TX 75501

No sooner had the Southern Baptist Convention (SBC) been formed than it became disturbed by the controversy over what came to be called "Old Landmarkism." Dr. James R. Graves (1820–1893), editor of *The Tennessee Baptist*, in an attempt to restore Apostolic purity to the churches, called on them to reject Protestants, who could not rightly be considered New Testament churches. This view was shared by Dr. J. M. Pendleton (1811–1891) of Bowling Green, Kentucky, and a number of churches that did not join the Southern Baptist movement.

The issues of "Old Landmarkism" centered on alien baptism, pulpit affiliation, closed communion, and missions. Supporters of Landmarkism opposed recognition of any baptism by a non-Baptist, allowing non-Baptists to join in the Lord's Supper, the exchange of pulpits with non-Baptist ministers, and missions controlled by boards beyond the local church. The Southern Baptist Convention never accepted Landmarkism, but for many years supporters of Landmarkism remained a dissenting minority within the SBC, strongly affecting its policy toward centralization. The Landmark position involved a theory of the succession of Baptist churches from the time of Christ to the present. According to the theory, the succession begins with the biblical church and continues through the Montanists, Novatians, Donatists, Paulicians, Waldenses, and Anabaptists.

Until 1899, when the Missionary Baptist Association of Texas was formed, Landmarkism remained unorganized. In 1905, however, churches both inside and outside the SBC formed a Landmark denomination, the General Association, which in 1924 became the American Baptist Association (ABA). It is doctrinally like the SBC, except for the Landmark ideals.

The ABA is congregationally governed. It maintains a publishing concern in Texarkana, Texas, and campgrounds at Bogg Springs, Arkansas, and Pine Springs, Texas. The several Bible institutes and seminaries recognized by the ABA are locally owned and controlled, as are several periodicals.

Membership: Not reported. Congregations affiliated with the American Baptist Association are found in every state of the union and in the following countries: Australia, Canada, Colombia, Costa Rica, Denmark, Fiji Island, France, Germany, India, Israel, Jamaica, Japan, Kenya, Korea, Lithuania, Mexico, New Zealand, Nicaragua, Nigeria, Philippines, Peru, Solomon Island, Uganda, Vanuatu, Venezuela, and Honduras.

Educational Facilities:

The schools recognized by the American Baptist Association are owned and operated by local churches rather than the association as a whole.

Aba Mexican Baptist Institute, Pharr, Texas.

Antioch Missionary Baptist Seminary, Manuthy, Trichur, India.

California Missionary Baptist Institute, Bellflower, California.

Calvary Mexican Baptist Institute, Juarez, Mexico.

Davao Missionary Baptist Institute and Seminary, Davao City, Philippines.

Florida Baptist Schools, Lakeland, Florida.

Fresno Missionary Baptist Institute, Fresno, California.

Gulf Coast Baptist Institute, Theodore, Alabama.

Historic Baptist Bible Institute, Scarborough, Ontario, Canada.

Landmark Correspondence School, Lookeba, Oklahoma.

Landmark Missionary Baptist Institute, Mauldin, South Carolina.

Louisiana Missionary Baptist Institute and Seminary, Minden, Louisiana.

Mid-South Baptist Institute and Seminary, Bogalusa, Louisiana.

Missionary Baptist Institute of Costa Rica, Guadalupe, San Jose, Costa Rica.

Mission Valley Mission Schools, San Antonio, Texas.

Missionary Baptist Seminary and Institute, Little Rock, Arkansas.

Monterrey Bible Institute, Santa Catarina, Mexico.

Northwest Baptist Institute, Bend, Oregon.

Oklahoma Missionary Baptist Institute, Marlow, Oklahoma.

Oxford Baptist Institute, Oxford, Mississippi.

Peru Missionary Baptist Institute, Trujillo, Peru.

Philippine Missionary Baptist Seminary, Davao City, Philippines.

Seoul Missionary Baptist Institute, Seoul, South Korea.

Somerset Baptist Bible Institute, Somerset, Kentucky.

Tennessee Missionary Baptist Institute, Nashville, Tennessee.

Texas Baptist Institute and Seminary, Henderson, Texas.

Washington Missionary Baptist Institute and Seminary, Auburn, Washington.

West Florida Baptist Institute, Pensacola, Florida.

Sources:

Calvinist Missionary Baptist. www.abaptist.org.

Nevins, William Manlius. *Alien Baptism and the Baptists*. Ashland, KY: Press of Economy Printers, 1962.

American Baptist Churches in the U.S.A.

PO Box 851, Valley Forge, PA 19481

HISTORY. The organization of Baptists in America proceeded in stages. While the first churches were organized in the 1600s, they were too few to formally organize above the congregational level. In 1707, however, five churches (three in Philadelphia and two in the countryside) organized the Philadelphia Baptist Association. That association at one point included churches from as far away as Connecticut and South Carolina. Then, in 1751, the Charleston (South Carolina) Association was formed. The number of Baptists began to grow significantly after the American Revolution. The association became the typical structure by which Baptist congregations affiliated. Tensions emerged among those who saw the association strictly for fellowship and those who saw it as a structure through which the congregations could extend their ministry. Most Baptists have been content to emphasize the autonomy of the local church, while assigning specific tasks such as higher education and foreign missions (not generally possible for a congregation) to the association.

The next major step in Baptist organization was spurred by the new missionary zeal that emerged in the early nineteenth century. Among the first missionaries sent out by the Congregational Church were Adoniram Judson (1788–1850), his wife Ann Judson (1789–1826), and Luther Rice (1783–1836). Rice soon converted to the Baptist perspective and as a result felt he could not work with Congregationalists. Rice returned to America to organize support among the Baptist churches. As a result of his efforts, the General Missionary Convention of the Baptist Denomination in the United States for Foreign Missions was organized in 1814. This organization was the first to draw support from Baptists nationally. It met every three years and became popularly known as the Triennial Convention. The Baptist General Tract Society was founded in 1824. In 1832, it was joined by the American Baptist Home Mission Society, which directed its activity primarily toward the western United States. A third major national society, the Woman's American Baptist Home Mission Society, was formed in 1877.

Over the next decades, Baptists were served by several mission agencies, each of which developed its own program and appealed to individual congregations. The need for coordination and the elimination of duplicated efforts was evident. In 1845, when the congregations in the South organized the Southern Baptist Convention, a cohesive convention structure had finally been formed. In 1907 the Northern Baptist Convention was organized, and the several missionary agencies became cooperating organizations of the convention. While retaining their official autonomy, the mission boards agreed to hold their regular meetings at the same time and place and to accept representatives of the congregations as voting delegates. The convention gave new national coherence to the majority of Baptists. The Northern Baptist Convention became known as the American Baptist Convention in 1950, and it assumed its present name in 1972.

BELIEFS. Doctrinally, Baptists grew out of the Puritan-Reformed tradition in England. The reliance upon the Puritans is visible in the early Baptist confessions of faith, the First and Second London Confessions (1677 and 1689), the Philadelphia Confession (1742), and the New Hampshire Confession (1833). The first major break with the Reformed theological heritage came after the Revolution when attempts were made to move away from a strong doctrine of predestination. The theology of Andrew Fuller was among the most prominent statements of Baptists attempting to provide a place for the free response of men and women to the gospel. This changing emphasis was embodied in the New Hampshire Confession. Eventually, however, confessional statements fell into disuse. The need for doctrinal uniformity was no longer emphasized, and a variety of theological opinions appeared.

The lack of theological unity allowed several new perspectives to become prominent among American Baptists. An emphasis upon social reform in the cities merged with the new discipline of sociology to produce the social gospel movement. Baptists such as Walter Rauschenbush became leading exponents. Prominent Baptist scholars were among the first to absorb the new German higher criticism of the Bible. As both movements gained support within the denomination, the reactions of conservatives threatened the very existence of the new Northern Baptist Convention. It became one of the most heated and bitter battlegrounds for what became known as the fundamentalist-modernist controversy in the early twentieth century. The losses of conservatives at the convention meetings and the resultant decrease of influence in the mission societies led to several major schisms as well as the formation of such bodies as the General Association of Regular Baptist Churches and the Conservative Baptist Association.

ORGANIZATION. The American Baptist Churches in the U.S.A. (ABC) is organized congregationally. Delegates from the individual churches and regional organizations meet biennially. Between meetings, a general board oversees the affairs of the denomination. The work of the ABC is delegated to the boards that have charge of foreign missions, home missions, education and publication, and ministerial and missionary benefits. Under each of the boards are a variety of specialized divisions. Judson Press is the publishing arm of the ABC.

Membership: In 1996, the ABC reported 1,503,267 members, 5,807 congregations, and 7,929 ministers.

Educational Facilities:

Seminaries:

American Baptist Seminary of the West, Berkeley, California.

Andover Newton Theological Seminary, Newton Centre, Massachusetts.

Central Baptist Theological Seminary, Kansas City, Missouri.

Colgate Rochester/Bexley Hall/Crozer, Rochester, New York.

Eastern Baptist Theological Seminary, Philadelphia, Pennsylvania.

Evangelical Seminary of Puerto Rico, Hato Rey, Puerto Rico.

Morehouse School of Religion, Atlanta, Georgia.

Northern Baptist Theological Seminary, Lombard, Illinois.

The School of Theology, Richmond, Virginia.

Colleges and universities:

Alderson-Broaddus College, Phillipi, West Virginia.

Bacone College, Muskogee, Oklahoma.

Benedict College, Columbia, South Carolina.

Eastern College, St. Davids, Pennsylvania.

Florida Memorial College, Miami, Florida.

Franklin College of Indiana, Franklin, Indiana.

Judson College, Elgin, Illinois.

Kalamazoo College, Kalamazoo, Michigan.

Keuka College, Keuka Park, New York.

Linfield College, McMinnville, Oregon.

Ottawa University, Ottawa, Kansas.

University of Redlands, Redlands, California.

Shaw University, Raleigh, North Carolina.

University of Sioux Falls, Sioux Falls, South Dakota.

Virginia Union University, Richmond, Virginia.

William Jewell College, Liberty, Missouri.

Periodicals: *American Baptist in Mission.* • *The Secret Place.* Available from PO Box 851, Valley Forge, PA 19482.

Sources:

Calvinist Missionary Baptist. www.abc-usa.org.

Bailey, Ambrose M. *Manual of Instruction for Baptists*. Philadelphia: American Baptist Publication Society, 1951.

Harrison, Paul M. *Authority and Power in the Free Church Tradition*. Princeton, NJ: Princeton University Press, 1959.

Maring, Norman H. *American Baptists, Whence and Whither*. Valley Forge, PA: Judson Press, 1968.

Maring, Norman H., and Winthrop S. Hudson. *A Baptist Manual of Polity and Practice*. Valley Forge, PA: Judson Press, 1963.

Straton, Hillyer H. *Baptists: Their Message and Mission*. Chicago: Judson Press, 1941.

Association of Evangelicals for Italian Missions
314 Richfield Rd., Upper Darby, PA 19082

The Association of Evangelicals for Italian Missions was formed by 16 Baptist ministers meeting in New York City in 1899 as the Italian Association of America. The new association was the product of mission work among Italian immigrants undertaken by the Northern Baptist Convention, now the American Baptist Churches in the U.S.A., after the Civil War. The association became the Italian

Baptist Association of America and recently adopted its present name. The association remains on good terms with its parent body, but carries on a mission to Italian Americans. *The New Aurora* is published five times yearly. Most churches are in the North and East. There is an annual conference that elects officers.

Membership: Not reported.

Periodicals: *The New Aurora*.

Association of Reformed Baptist Churches of America (ARBCA)
401 E Louther St., Carlisle, PA 17013

The Association of Reformed Baptist Churches of America (ARBCA) was founded March 11, 1997, with a charter membership of 24 churches from fourteen states. ARBCA follows in the steps of its forebears, in particular the Baptist Association of London, whose members stated in their 1689 London Baptist Confession of Faith that "...churches, when planted by the providence of God, so as they may enjoy opportunity and advantage for it, ought to hold communion among themselves, for their peace, increase of love, and mutual edification" (ch. 26, para. 14). ARBCA works to advance Christ's kingdom by providing an association in which churches of common confession may find mutual encouragement, assistance, edification, and counsel, and may participate in cooperative efforts in church planting, foreign missions, ministerial training, publications, and other endeavors deemed appropriate by the association.

The foreign mission arm of ARBCA, known as the Reformed Baptist Mission Services (RBMS), provides services to five member churches that have sent five church-planting missionaries and to seven member churches that sponsor seven national pastors. RBMS is not a mission board—a member church is the sending agency for a missionary with sister churches assisting, and any member church may act as a sending church of a missionary.

ARBCA organized the Institute for Reformed Baptist Studies (IRBS) to operate in close cooperation with the Westminster Theological Seminary, a confessional Reformed seminary in Escondido, California. ARBCA also provides academically qualified professors with considerable pastoral experience to teach IRBS courses on the Westminster campus north of San Diego. Offerings include courses in Reformed Baptist doctrinal distinctives, Baptist church theory, the 1689 London Baptist Confession of Faith, pastoral ministry, and preaching. Earned credits from IRBS transfer to Westminster's Master of Divinity program, some in place of Westminster's required coursework and others as electives.

ARBCA churches are also active in starting churches in the United States and Canada, and in publishing literature such as Sunday school material and other aids to the churches. The theological basis for all ARBCA endeavors continues to be the 1689 London Baptist Confession of Faith.

Membership: In 2008 ARBCA reported 64 member churches.

Educational Facilities:

Institute for Reformed Baptist Studies (IRBS).

Sources:

Association of Reformed Baptist Churches of America (ARBCA). www.puritanhope/arbca/.

Waldron, Samuel, E., and Richard C. Barcellos. *A Reformed Baptist Manifesto*. Carlisle, PA: Reformed Baptist Academic Press, 2004.

Association of Regular Baptist Churches (Canada)
17 Laverock St., Tottenham, ON, Canada L0G 1W0

The association is committed to a historic Baptist position and affirms the belief in the inerrant Bible. Also asserted are the doctrines of the trinity, creation, the deity and vicarious atonement of Christ, the personal and visible return of Christ, and eternal punishment of the unsaved. Following Baptist tradition, the association defines the church as the voluntary association of believers who have been

immersed (baptized). The association's position is seen as in general agreement with earlier Baptist confessions (the London, Philadelphia, and New Hampshire).

The association has a congregational polity. Missions are supported in Belgium, France, Jamaica, Martinique, St. Lucia, Spain, Fiji, Madagascar, the Philippines, and Switzerland.

Membership: In 2002 there were 15 churches in the association with 10 other supporting churches cooperating in the mission work.

Baptist Bible Fellowship International
PO Box 191, Springfield, MO 65801

The Baptist Bible Fellowship International was begun in 1950 by former members of the World Baptist Fellowship, including Rev. G. Beauchamp Vick (1901–1975), who had succeeded J. Frank Norris (1877–1952) as pastor of the Temple Baptist Church in Detroit. In 1948 he was made president of the debt-ridden Bible Baptist Seminary. Within two years he was able to wipe out most of the debt. He also discovered that Norris retained and would not surrender to him the ultimate power to run the school. In 1950 Vick was dismissed, and open schism soon occurred as pastors and churches lined up behind either Norris or Vick. Vick led in the founding of a new school, the Baptist Bible College, and a new periodical, the *Baptist Bible Tribune*.

Doctrinally, the Bible Baptists are in the main line of traditional Baptist beliefs. They are strong fundamentalists and believe in both personal and ecclesiastical separation. Congregations and pastors have no fellowship with individuals and groups deemed to be infidels, idolaters, and/or immoral. There is a firm statement on the supernatural inspiration and verbal inerrancy of scripture. Their Calvinism is very mild. The Bible Baptists believe in God's electing grace, but also teach that blessings of salvation are made free to all by the gospel. The main way in which the Bible Baptists differ from some other Baptists is in their ecclesiology. They emphasize the autonomy of the local church combined with the strong authority of the pastor as "shepherd of his flock." Any congregation that accepts the doctrinal statement may affiliate with the fellowship. The fellowship acknowledges two ordinances, baptism by immersion and the Lord's Supper. The government is to be supported and obeyed in all matters not opposed to the "will of Jesus Christ."

The work of the denomination is centered on its colleges, its periodical, and, primarily, its missions. A part of the doctrinal statement is a belief in the command to give the gospel to the world. Scriptural giving is one of the fundamentals of faith. A director of missions and a mission committee oversees responsibility for the mission work of the fellowship. In 1997 there were 858 missionaries operating in 107 countries. The Baptist Bible Fellowship has grown tremendously both through its evangelistic activities and by acquisition of independent congregations who choose to join. Among its member churches are some of the largest in the country; their congregations have almost one-fourth of the 100 largest Sunday schools in the country. Congregations are concentrated in the South and Midwest and are divided into 48 fellowship districts.

Membership: Not reported.

Educational Facilities:

Fellowship seminaries:

Baptist Bible Graduate School of Theology, Springfield, Missouri.

Louisiana Baptist Theological Seminary, Shreveport, Louisiana.

Fellowship colleges:

Baptist Bible College, Springfield, Missouri.

Boston Baptist College, Boston, Massachusetts.

Also approved:

Atlantic Baptist Bible College, Chester, Virginia.

Louisiana Baptist University, Shreveport, Louisiana.

Pacific Baptist Bible College, Pomona, California.

Periodicals: *Baptist Bible Tribune*. Send orders to Box 309, Springfield, MO 65801.
• *Global Partners Magazine*, PO Box 191, Springfield, MO 65801.

Sources:

Baptist Bible Fellowship International. www.bbfi.org.

Baptist Missionary Association of America

Department of Missions, PO Box 30910, Little Rock, AR 72260-0016

The Baptist Missionary Association is a fellowship of Baptist churches organized in 1950 and designed to facilitate the cooperation of the churches in missions, Christian education, and benevolence. The association sponsors over 600 missionaries in the United States and other countries. Its publishing agency produces a full line of Sunday school and Christian growth ministry curricula in English and translates much of that material into eight other languages and dialects. Other agencies sponsor broadcast ministries in several languages and dialects, religious education institutions, chaplaincy ministries, camp ministries, and ministers' retirement plans. State organizations and local associations provide additional ministries. Participating independent congregations adopt a common Doctrinal Statement and subscribe to the *Principles of Cooperation of the Association*.

Membership: In 2008 the association reported 234,110 members in 1,384 congregations, and, in 2002, reported 1,193 pastors. They currently minister to 53 countries and hope to add 10 countries each year.

Educational Facilities:

Baptist Missionary Association Theological Seminary, Jacksonville, Texas.

Central Baptist College, Conway, Arkansas.

Jacksonville College, Jacksonville, Texas.

Southeastern Baptist College, Laurel Mississippi.

Sources:

BMA of America Missions. www.bmaam.com.

Dugger, John W. *The Baptist Missionary Association of America, 1950-1986*. Texarkana, TX: Baptist Publishing House, 1988.

Harmon, Sherman, comp. *A Fire Was Kindled*. N.p., n.d.

Jackson, D. N. *Studies in Baptist Doctrines and History*. Little Rock, AR: Baptist Publications Committee, n.d.

Canadian Baptist Ministries (CBM)

7185 Millcreek Dr., Mississauga, ON, Canada L5N 5R4

Canadian Baptist Ministries was formed on January 1, 1995, through the merger of the Canadian Baptist Federation and Canadian Baptist International Ministries. The purpose of Canadian Baptist Ministries is "to unite, encourage and enable Canadian Baptist Churches in their national and international endeavors to fulfill the commission of our Lord Jesus Christ, in the power of the Holy Spirit, proclaiming the gospel and showing the love of God to all peoples."

Like Congregationalists, Baptists came to Canada from New England following the British takeover of the area in 1748. Their initial settlements were in Nova Scotia, where the oldest Baptist churches were organized in Sackville (now in New Brunswick) in 1763, and at Horton (now called Wolfville) in 1765 under the leadership of the Rev. Ebenezer Moulton. Both churches were lost when many of their members returned to New England in the 1770s. However, the continuous history of the Baptists can be traced to the ministry of independent Congregationalist evangelist Henry Alline (1748–1784), who began to travel throughout Nova Scotia in the 1770s. Finding little support from either Congregationalists or Presbyterian leaders, his converts founded a number of independent ("New Light") Congregational churches, most of which later became Baptist churches. Alline also participated in the reconstitution of the Horton church in 1788 under a new pastor, Nicolas Pierson. In 1798 the Baptists and the Alline churches formed the Baptist and Congregational Association, which became the Nova Scotia Baptist Association in 1800.

As Baptist work spread through the three Maritime Provinces, the Nova Scotia Baptist Association became the fountainhead of a number of new associations. In 1846 the association formed the Baptist Convention of Nova Scotia, New Brunswick, and Prince Edward Island (shortened in 1879 to the Baptist Convention of the Maritime Provinces). The African Association, consisting of 17 black churches, dates back to the 1830s, and in 1884 it affiliated with the convention.

Contemporaneous with the growth of the Regular (Calvinistic) Baptist churches that made up the Baptist Convention of the Maritime Provinces, Free Baptists from New England arrived in Nova Scotia. Asa McGray and Joseph Norton led in the formation of these Free Baptist churches, the first organized at Barrington in 1795. In 1834 a Free Baptist Association was formed. Not a part of this association, a group led by Norton organized the Union of Free Christian Baptists. In 1867 these two groups merged to become the Free Christian Baptist Conference. An association of New Brunswick Free Baptists, consisting largely of immigrants from Maine, was formed in 1832. Known at first as the New Brunswick Christian Conference, the name was changed to Free Christian Baptists in 1847, and in 1896 to Free Christian Baptist Conference.

In 1905 and 1906 the two streams of Baptist, Regular and Free Will, merged to form the United Baptist Convention of the Maritime Provinces. When Baptist congregations were planted in Newfoundland, the name was changed to the United Baptist Convention of the Atlantic Provinces in 1963.

Baptists began to move into Upper and Lower Canada (Quebec and Ontario) from the United States following the American Revolution, but the first churches were not formed until the 1790s (Calwell's Manor in the Eastern Townships, Lower Canada, in 1794, and a church near Beamsville, Upper Canada, in 1796). These churches were formed by American ministers in those areas closest to the American-Canadian border. The development of the Baptist church was stimulated after 1815 by the arrival in the Ottawa Valley of Scottish Highlanders who had experienced the ministry of Robert Haldane (1764–1842) and his brother James Haldane (1768–1851), Scottish Baptist evangelists. Cooperation between the various Baptist churches in the province was hindered primarily by disagreement over communion. Those original churches formed in the later eighteenth century tended to practice closed communion (excluding all but correctly baptized church members from participating in the Lord's Supper). In 1888 a merger of two regional bodies led to the formation of the Baptist Convention of Ontario and Quebec. Meanwhile, beginning in the 1820s, ex-slaves who had settled in Canada formed a set of black Baptist congregations. In the 1830s French-speaking immigrants from Switzerland settled in Quebec and Henriette Feller (1800–1868) began Baptist work in Montreal and the Eastern Townships. In 1969 the French congregations organized the Union d'Eglises Baptistes Francaises au Canada (Union of French Baptist Churches in Canada) after working for more than a century as the Grande Ligne Mission.

In 1873 the Rev. Alexander McDonald began Baptist work in Winnipeg, Manitoba. The planting of other churches led to the formation of the Baptist Convention of Manitoba and the Northwest in 1884. Extensive work among non–English-speaking immigrant communities was pursued by the Baptists in western Canada, and as a result a number of ethnic congregations were incorporated into the new convention.

Work on the Canadian west coast had progressed since 1876, with help from the United States. In 1897 Baptists organized the Baptist Convention of British Columbia. In 1907 churches in the four western provinces joined to form the Baptist Convention of Western Canada, reorganized as the Baptist Union of Western Canada in 1909.

In 1944 the Baptist Federation of Canada was established as a loose affiliation of the three autonomous conventions/unions. The Union d'Eglises Baptists Francaises au Canada has participated in the federation since 1970. The name was changed to Canadian Baptist Federation in 1983.

The Canadian Baptist work overseas began as early as 1814, when Baptist churches in Atlantic Canada gave financial support to the American Baptist Missionary Union. When Canadian Baptists began to volunteer as missionaries, the American Baptist Missionary Union seemed to be the logical way to send them. The first Canadian Baptist missionaries overseas, Rev. and Mrs. Richard E. Burpee, went to Burma in 1845 to work among the Karen people.

In 1865 the Maritime Baptist Convention incorporated a foreign mission board. In 1867 this mission board made history by sending a single woman, Minnie DeWolfe, to Burma. She was the first single woman sent overseas by any Baptist board in the world.

In 1866 Baptists in Ontario and Quebec formed a "Canadian auxiliary" to the American Baptist Missionary Union, an organization to which they had been making contributions for several years. In 1870 this auxiliary was reorganized as the Regular Baptist Foreign Mission Society of Canada, and in 1889 the name was changed to the Board of Foreign Missions of the Regular Baptist Convention of Ontario and Quebec.

By 1875 Canadian Baptist missionaries from both the Maritime and the Ontario and Quebec boards were working in the same area of India, but under their respective boards. In addition to their efforts in evangelism and church planting, the early missionaries sought to address the poverty they encountered in India. One response was to establish schools. By 1890 30 village schools were in operation. High schools, boarding schools, vocational training institutes, and teacher training schools followed, and by 1940 there were 440 schools in operation.

In 1898 another need was addressed with the opening of the Star of Hope Hospital at Akividu, India, under the direction of Dr. Pearl Smith. Over the next thirty years, eight more hospitals were founded in India by Canadian Baptists.

Also in 1898, Canadian Baptists from Ontario and Quebec became involved in another mission field—Bolivia—with the arrival of Archibald Reekie in Oruro. He established contact with the Bolivians by opening an English-language school, an approach that was followed by missionaries in La Paz and Cochabamba. In 1905 freedom of worship was granted in Bolivia, largely because of the favorable example set by the Canadian Baptist missionaries.

On a number of occasions between 1875 and 1910 attempts were made to unite the two mission boards in Canada. Finally in 1911, stimulated by the formation of Baptist Unions in western Canada and the frustration of the missionaries working cooperatively in India but under separate boards, the Canadian Baptist Foreign Mission Board was formed. It brought together the Foreign Mission Board of the Maritime Baptist Convention and the Board of Foreign Missions of the Regular Baptist Convention of Ontario and Quebec, uniting Canadian Baptists in their administration of overseas mission. On May 1, 1970, a revised constitution changed the name to the Canadian Baptist Overseas Mission Board. In 1990 the board's name was changed again, to Canadian Baptist International Ministries, reflecting changes in attitudes in some countries to the missionary enterprise.

Canadian Baptist Ministries (CBM) was created on January 1, 1995, through the merger of Canadian Baptist International Ministries and the Canadian Baptist Federation. With the increasingly multicultural nature of Canadian society and the rapidly shrinking globalized world, the merger brought together the national and international ministries of Canadian Baptists in a way that was appropriate to the needs and realities of the twenty-first century. In 2007 the four constituent regional denominations that were a part of CBM began the process of standardizing their names as Canadian Baptists of Atlantic Canada, Canadian Baptists of French Canada, Canadian Baptists of Ontario and Quebec, and Canadian Baptists of Western Canada.

In 2008 Canadian Baptist Ministries had personnel in 20 countries, including Canada. One of its ministries is the Sharing Way, which focuses on relief, development, and refugees. CBM also operates a large short-term mission (STM) program with a focus on global discipleship.

A majority of Canadian Baptists accept moderate Calvinism, with an Arminian (free will) minority active as well. Canadian Baptist Ministries is noncreedal but has a statement of mission that addresses basic theological issues as well as questions of purpose, service, and fellowship.

The board of directors, which is the delegated governing body of Canadian Baptist Ministries, meets semiannually. A congregational polity is practiced in Canadian Baptist churches. Local Baptist churches are self-governing but cooperate in missionary and other activities through the respective regional conventions/unions.

Canadian Baptist Ministries is a member of the Baptist World Alliance. It declined invitations to participate in the formation of the United Church of Canada. It was a member of the Canadian Council of Churches until 1980, when it withdrew, although the Baptist Convention of Ontario and Quebec continues to be a member. All four conventions/unions are members of the Evangelical Fellowship of Canada.

Membership: The CBM constituency, constituted in the four regional denominations, is made up of approximately 1,200 congregations and 250,000 active participants.

Educational Facilities:

Acadia Divinity College, Wolfville, Nova Scotia.

Atlantic Baptist University, Moncton, New Brunswick.

Carey Theological College, Vancouver, British Columbia.

Faculté de Théologie Evangélique, Montreal, Quebec.

McMaster Divinity College, Hamilton, Ontario.

Periodicals: *The Canadian Baptist*. • *The Link and Visitor*. Both available from 100–304 East Mall, Etobicoke, ON M9B 6E2, Canada. • *The Atlantic Baptist*. Available from Box 756, Kentville, NS B4N 3X9, Canada. • *Mosaic*. Available from 7185 Millcreek Dr., Mississauga, ON L5N 5R4, Canada. • *Tidings*, 4 Kay St., Salisbury, NB E4J 2J2, Canada.

Sources:

Canadian Baptist Ministries (CBM). www.cbmin.org/web/.

McBeth, H. Leon. *The Baptist Heritage*. Nashville, TN: Broadman Press, 1987.

Moody, Barry M., ed. *Repent and Believe: The Baptist Experience in Maritime Canada*. Hantsport, NS: Lancelot Press, 1980.

Torbet, Robert G. *A History of the Baptists*. Valley Forge, PA: Judson Press, 1973.

Thompson Margaret E. *The Baptist Story in Western Canada*. Calgary, AB: Baptist Union of Western Canada, 1974.

Zeman, Jarold Knox. *Baptists in Canada*. Burlington, ON: G. R. Welch, 1980.

Canadian National Baptist Convention/Convention Nationale Baptiste Canadienne

100 Convention Way, Cochrane, AB T4C 2G2

In the late 1940s, Baptists in British Columbia affiliated with the General Association of Regular Baptists Churches voiced increasingly dissatisfaction with the Association on issues of dispensationalism as well as the looseness of the association, which led to a general neglect of member congregations. Concurrently, the Southern Baptist Convention was experiencing significant growth in the Pacific Northwest. Cooperation was stymied by larger concerns of the relationship of the Southern Baptist Convention and various Canadian Baptist organizations, but in 1957, a joint committee was established between the regular Baptists in Canada and the Southern Baptist Convention.

Delays in resolving the larger issues of territoriality led the Canadian Baptists to begin organizing on their own. In 1955 and initial "Southern Baptist" association was formed as the Capilano Association in Vancouver. It was followed by the Midwest Baptist Association (including Alberta and Saskatchewan) in 1957, and in December 1960 the churches in interior British Columbia established the Plateau Association. In 1963 the congregations from the three associations established the

Canadian Southern Baptist Conference as a temporary organization that served as a forerunner to a convention fully affiliated with the Southern Baptist Convention.

It wasn't until 1977 that the Southern Baptist Convention approved a motion to extend help to Canadian Southern Baptists, another seven years before the Southern Baptist Convention approved a motion to recognize an autonomous Canadian Convention. In 1985, the Canadian Southern Baptist Conference unanimously voted for a new constitution based on the SBC resolution and became the Canadian Convention of Southern Baptists.

The Canadian Convention cooperates with the Southern Baptist Convention in international missions.

In 2008 the Convention completed a four-year process by which it adopted a new name, the Canadian National Baptist Convention (in French, Convention Nationale Baptiste Canadienne). The name change did not affect its ongoing relationship with the Southern Baptist Convention.

Membership: In 2000 there were 149 churches, 10,189 members, 103 ministers, and 3 families in international missions in Nigeria, Southeast Asia, and Chile. In 2008 there were 271 congregations in Canada.

Educational Facilities:

Canadian Southern Baptist Seminary, Cochrane, Alberta, Canada.

Periodicals: *The Baptist Horizon*.

Sources:

Canadian National Baptist Convention. www.ccsb.ca.

CBAmerica

3686 Stagecoach Rd., Unit F, Longmont, CO 80504-5660

CBAmerica, formerly known as the Conservative Baptist Association, dates from 1946, the year Northern Baptists (now American Baptist Churches) met in Grand Rapids, Michigan. The conflict between modern religious liberalism and theological conservative leadership within the convention dates back to the 1920s. Earlier breakaways from the convention over the same issues included the General Association of Regular Baptists in 1932. The Conservative Baptist Foreign Mission Society (now CB International), founded in December 1943, was excluded from the convention in 1945.

At the Grand Rapids meetings, theological conservatives made one final attempt to change the liberal course of the convention. Failing in this attempt, Dr. Albert Johnson of Hinson Baptist Church, Portland, Oregon, introduced the resolution calling for the churches to explore affiliation with other Baptist groups. The final conclusion of the "Committee of 15" called for regional conferences that overwhelmingly endorsed the formation of the Conservative Baptist Association of America. This action was considered at Atlantic City in May 1947 and finalized at Milwaukee in 1948. Actions in Milwaukee included the appointment of a general director and three regional evangelists, a committee to consider and report on the formation of a Home Mission Society in 1949 at San Francisco, and the adoption of a constitution.

Following a move from Chicago to Elk Grove, Illinois, in 1963, the Association built a new headquarters adjacent to the Home and Foreign Mission Society in Wheaton, Illinois, in 1968. More recently it moved its headquarters from Illilnois to Colorado.

The Association ministers in cooperation with the two mission agencies and shares ministry with 23 state associations; three seminaries located in Portland, Oregon, Denver, Colorado, and Dresher, Pennsylvania; and three colleges located in Honolulu, Hawaii, Phoenix, Arizona, and South Portland, Maine. In 2008 there were 1,200 churches affiliated with the CBAmerica.

Membership: CBAmerica is a very loose federation of nine regional associations. Together, in 2008, the combined associations reported 1200 congregations with approximately 200,000 members.

Educational Facilities:

Denver Seminary, Denver, Colorado.

Southwestern College, Phoenix, Arizona.

Western Conservative Baptist Seminary, Portland, Oregon.

International College and Graduate School of Theology, Honolulu, Hawaii.

Seminary of the East, Doesher, Pennsylvania.

New England Bible College, South Portland, Maine.

Periodicals: *Spectrum*. • *Impact*. Send orders to Box 5, Wheaton, IL 60189.

Sources:

CB America. www.cbamerica.org/.

A Baptist Primer in Church Discipline. Chicago: Conservative Baptist Fellowship, n.d.

Founded on the Word, Focused on the World. Wheaton, IL: Conservative Baptist Foreign Missionary Society, 1978.

Pegg, Walter A. *Historic Baptist Distinctives*. Wheaton, IL: Conservative Baptist Foreign Missionary Society, 1952.

Shelley, Bruce R. *Conservative Baptists*. Denver, CO: Conservative Baptist Theological Seminary, 1962.

Tulga, Chester E. *The Independence of the Local Church*. Chicago: Conservative Baptist Fellowship, 1951.

Central Baptist Association

309 Lebanon Rd., Kingsport, TN 37663

The Central Baptist Association was founded in 1956. It is conservative fundamentalist in theological perspective, and member churches hold to the absolute authority of the King James Version of the Bible and practice baptism by immersion. The association exists to maintain a common standard of doctrine and practice among member churches. It also operates a summer camp in Jasper, Virginia.

Membership: In 1994 the association reported 33 member churches in four associations located in Virginia, Kentucky, Indiana, and South Carolina.

Cooperative Baptist Fellowship

PO Box 450329, Atlanta, GA 311-0329

The Cooperative Baptist Fellowship (CBF) is a product of the struggle between conservative and moderate forces within the Southern Baptist Convention during the last quarter of the twentieth century. Through the 1980s, the more conservative wing within the convention organized and was able to capture the presidency of the multimillion-member denomination in every election. This allowed them to gain control of most of the institutions that the convention supports, including the colleges, universities, and seminaries.

By 1990 the moderate leadership in the convention was feeling pushed aside and cut off from any exercise of power within the convention. Thus, a call in the summer of 1990 for "concerned Baptists" to gather in Atlanta brought 2000 persons together to create a rudimentary organization with a financial structure and an interim steering committee. In May 1991, that organization was officially chartered as the Cooperative Baptist Fellowship. The fellowship began operation within the convention and almost all of the founding delegates were drawn from congregations that still considered themselves a part of the convention. However, as frustration over the leadership of the convention continued through the 1990s, an increasing number of them decreased and/or cut off financial support. A few moved formally to withdraw from the convention. A few congregations in the fellowship ran into further conflict over "progressive" practices, namely the ordination of females to the ministry and the acceptance of homosexuals into membership (both of which the convention condemned).

Those who formed the fellowship were theologically conservative and placed themselves within the larger Evangelical movement. However, while strongly affirming the authority of the Bible, they tended to refrain from understanding the

Bible as inerrant, and were responsive to the concerns of the modern feminist movement within the church. They separated themselves from the resolution calling for the submission of wives to their husbands later passed by the convention.

Southern Baptists have conducted a strong missionary program from the days of the recovery from the effects of their civil war, and the new fellowship moved quickly to affirm its mission orientation. Several years after its founding, it placed its first missionaries in various locations around the world. The emphasis of its missionaries was on "unreached people groups" (including those without a national identity), and included a growing number of missionaries assigned to various ethnic communities in the United States.

Through the early 1990s, a wide variety of new organizations were founded that paralleled the agencies of the convention. These included a press agency, a publishing house (of church school literature), and several institutions for theological education.

The fellowship is led by a coordinating council, elected by those who attend the annual CBF meeting. That meeting also elects the executive leader, the president, a position held by both clergy and laity and both males and females. The fellowship's coordinator leads a staff of professionals who administer the fellowship's affairs and structures between the annual meetings. State organizations now exist in more than 20 states.

The fellowship operated as a dissenting body on the edge of the Southern Baptist Convention through the 1990s, but has increasingly made the transition to become an independent denomination, and has been so recognized by the U.S. Military Office of Chaplains, for the purpose of assigning chaplains to the Armed Forces. The fact that so many congregations identified with it has given it instant status as one of the major denominational bodies in the United States.

Membership: In 2008 the fellowship reported more than 1900 affiliated congregations. It supports some 160 Global Missions field personnel and endorses some 520 chaplains and pastoral counselors.

Sources:

Cooperative Baptist Fellowship. www.thefellowship.info.

Ammerman, Nancy T. "SBC Moderates and the Making of a Post-Modern Denomination." *Christian Century 110*, no. 26 (1993): 896-99.

Lolley, W. Randall, ed. *FINDINGS: A Report of the Special Study Commission to Study the Question: "Should the Cooperative Baptist Fellowship Become a Separate Denomination?"* Atlanta: Cooperative Baptist Fellowship, 1996.

Stricklin, David. *A Genealogy of Dissent: Southern Baptist Protest in the Twentieth Century.* Lexington: University of Kentucky Press, 2000.

Duck River (and Kindred) Association of Baptists
Current address not obtained for this edition.

The Duck River (and Kindred) Association of Baptists separated from the Elk River Association in 1825. The issue was the atonement, and the "liberals" who believed in a general atonement withdrew from the Elk River Association, which was a member of the Triennial Convention, the initial missionary organization which later evolved into the American Baptist Churches in the U.S.A.

Another issue soon divided churches in the Triennial Convention, the issue of compulsory mission support. In 1843 that issue caused some people to withdraw from churches in the Triennial Convention and from another Duck River Association. With further divisions within churches associated with the Triennial Associations, more Duck River Associations were formed. At the date of last publication, there were four Duck River Associations and three Kindred Associations included in the general association. Most of the churches were in Tennessee and all mission work was local.

Doctrine is mildly Calvinistic and members practice footwashing. Letters are a standard means of communication. Polity is congregational, and ministers are ordained by two or more of their colleagues.

Membership: Not reported.

Fellowship of Evangelical Baptist Churches in Canada
PO Box 457, Guelph, ON N1H 6K9

After World War I, a fundamentalist-modernist controversy split the Baptist Convention of Ontario and Quebec (now a constituent part of the Canadian Baptist Federation). Leading the fundamentalists was Thomas Todhunter Shields (1873–1955), pastor of the Jarvis Street Baptist Church in Toronto. Shields was intimately involved with the World's Christian Fundamentals Association and hosted the annual meeting in 1926. He helped found the Baptist Bible Union, a fundamentalist Baptist organization, and led it for nine years.

In Canada, Shields focused the fundamentalist controversy on McMaster University, the Baptist school in Toronto. He led an attack on the school through his periodical, the *Gospel Witness*. As a result, Shields was ousted from the Convention in 1927 for lack of harmony and cooperation with the Convention's work. With his supporters, he founded the Union of Regular Baptist Churches, which reported approximately seventy churches its first year, and the Toronto Baptist Seminary, to compete with McMaster. However, internal controversy began to divide the Union. In 1933 a group left and formed the Fellowship of Independent Baptist Churches. After Shields led the Jarvis Street Church and other supporters out in 1949, the Union remained with little of its original substance.

Rebuilding of the divided fundamentalist structures began in 1953 when the Union of Regular Baptist Churches united with the Fellowship of Independent Baptist Churches to form the Fellowship of Evangelical Baptist Churches. In the 1960s, the fellowship absorbed two other fundamentalist groups that had existed independently since their formation in the western provinces. The Regular Baptist Missionary Fellowship of Alberta, formed in 1930, joined the fellowship in 1963, and the Regular Baptists of British Columbia, formed in 1927, joined in 1965.

Beliefs of the fellowship are fundamental and resemble those of the General Association of Regular Baptist Churches. It supports missionaries in India and Japan through its own missionary board, and several hundred others through a variety of approved independent missionary-sending agencies.

Membership: Not reported. In 2008 the fellowship included some 500 congregations scattered across Canada.

Periodicals: *The Evangelical Baptist.* • *Intercom.*

Sources:

The Fellowship of Evangelical Baptist Churches. www.fellowship.ca.

Dollar, George W. *A History of Fundamentalism in America.* Greenville, SC: Bob Jones University Press, 1973.

Fellowship of Fundamental Bible Churches
284 Whig Ln., Monroeville, NJ 08343

The Fellowship of Fundamental Bible Churches was founded in 1939 by former members and ministers of the Methodist Protestant Church. As the merger between the Methodist Episcopal Church, the Methodist Episcopal Church, South, and the Methodist Protestant Church approached, some 50 delegates and pastors (approximately one-third of the Eastern Conference) withdrew in protest of the union and what they considered the liberal tendencies of those churches. The congregations represented by those delegates reorganized and continued a separate existence as the Bible Protestant Church. In 1985 the group changed its name to the Fellowship of Fundamental Protestant Churches, a signal of the Fundamentalist theological position they had adopted. Congregations are found in California, Maryland, New Jersey, Pennsylvania, New York, and Michigan.

As the Fellowship evolved over the decades following its succession from the Methodist Protestant Church, it also largely left its Methodist heritage behind and adopted a theology more reflective of Baptist beliefs; today all of the congregations refer to themselves as either a "Baptist" or "Bible" church. The fellowship has come to closely resemble the General Association of Regular Baptist Churches. The fellowship is a member of the American Council of Christian Churches.

Membership: In 2004 the fellowship reported 22 churches, 46 ministers, and 1,208 members.

Educational Facilities:

Fundamental Bible Institute. Various locations.

Periodicals: *The Fellowship Link.* • *The FFBC Spotlight.*

Sources:

Fellowship of Fundamental Bible Churches. jrpeet.truepath.com/ffbc.

Fellowship of Independent Reformed Evangelicals

No central headquarters. For information, contact:, Audubon Drive Bible Church, 2601 Audubon Dr., PO Box 8055, Laurel, MS 39441

The Fellowship of Independent Reformed Evangelicals (F.I.R.E.) is an association of independent congregation of the Reformed Baptist tradition. The founding members adopted their constitution in 2006. The founders emphasized what they saw as the five "solas" of the sixteenth-century Reformation—namely, "Sola Scriptura" (Scripture Alone), "Sola Gratia" (Grace Alone), "Sola Fide" (Faith Alone), "Solus Christus" (Christ Alone), and "Soli Deo Gloria" (To the Glory of God Alone)—which were to be interpreted in the light of historical Baptist confessions, such as the First and Second London Baptist Confessions of Faith (1644, 1689). F.I.R.E. is not a charismatic organization, and encourages congregations in which the gifts of the Spirit operate to seek fellowship elsewhere.

The Fellowship exists as an association of independent congregations, with the association serving to assist the churches in their ministries' activities rather than ruling over them. F.I.R.E. is directed by a national executive board, which is led by its moderator.

Membership: Not reported. Member churches and ministers are found across the United States and in Brazil, Croatia, Canada, India, Ireland, Israel, Italy, Mauritius, Mexico, South Africa, and the United Kingdom.

Sources:

Fellowship of Independent Reformed Evangelicals. www.firefellowship.org/.

Marcellino, Jerry. *Rediscovering the Lost Treasure of Family Worship.* Laurel, MS: Audubon Press, 1996.

———. *Should Christians Have a Heart for Israel? A Biblical Perspective.* Hartsville, TN: Heart for Israel, 2000.

Ray, Bruce. *Celebrating the Sabbath.* Philipsburg, PA: P & R Publishing, 2000.

———. *Withhold Not Correction.* Philipsburg, PA: P & R Publishing, 1978.

Fundamental Baptist Fellowship

500 W Lee Rd., Taylors, SC 29687

The Fundamental Baptist Fellowship was formed as a result of conflict and controversy in the Conservative Baptist Association. At issue was what was termed the "new evangelicalism," a trend in conservative Christian circles toward cooperation with and accommodation of certain modern situations, without giving up any essentials of the faith. However, some within the Conservative Baptist Association (CBA) saw the new evangelicalism as a departure from Baptist traditions. The critics also believed in a premillennial eschatology and in separation from those who do not hold to fundamentalist doctrine. The controversy centered on the Denver Conservative Baptist Seminary in Denver, Colorado, founded in 1950 and strongly staffed with exponents of the new evangelicalism.

During the 1950s, controversy centered on attempts to control the seminary by the separatists. Conservative Baptist churches in Colorado began to take sides. The separatist strength was concentrated in the Conservative Baptist Fellowship (CBF), one of the constituent agencies of the CBA. The CBF was headed by Research Secretary Chester Tulga, who spelled out the separatist position in a number of

"Case" booklets which attacked modernist and centralizing trends. The new evangelical position was concentrated in the CBA and the Conservative Baptist Foreign Missionary Society. During the 1950, the distance between the two sides grew. The Colorado Conservative Baptists withdrew support from the seminary, and individual churches and leaders began to support either the CBA or the CBF.

The split became final in 1961 when the leaders of the CBF formed the World Conservative Baptist Mission. An aggressive stance toward the CBA was taken, and pre-CBA convention sessions were held to persuade churches to accept the CBF position. In 1967, the name was changed to the Fundamental Baptist Fellowship in order to avoid association with the CBA.

The Fundamental Baptist Fellowship established headquarters in Denver, from which it issued the *Information Bulletin*, its periodical. The Baptist Bible College offers a two-year curriculum. Close relations are kept with the Minnesota Baptist Convention as a sister organization.

Membership: Not reported. In 2008 there were 32 congregations affiliated with the fellowship.

Educational Facilities:

Baptist Bible College, Denver, Colorado.

Periodicals: *FrontLine* Magazine, 22 Briarwood Court, Schaumburg, IL 60193.

Sources:

Fundamental Baptist Fellowship International. www.fbfi.org.

Fundamental Baptist Fellowship Association

1916 Central Ave., Kansas City, KS 66102

The Fundamental Baptist Fellowship Association (FBFA) was founded on August 22, 1962, and incorporated on July 9, 1975. Its stated purpose is to "promote fellowship between Bible-believing Baptist Churches of like faith and order; to foster the spirit of evangelism; to spread the Gospel; and advance the cause of Christ through mutual efforts in Christian education and missions."

The association is based on affirmation of biblical inerrancy, the Trinity, the depravity of man, and salvation by grace. Member churches and individual associate members also adopt a pre-millennial and pre-tribulation eschatology. The 28 member churches, largely African American, are located in the southern United States and the Midwest, with both a northern and southern national representative. A number of the churches are also connected to the General Association of Regular Baptist Churches. The association has a partnership with the Association of Baptists for World Evangelism (ABWE), an independent mission agency founded in Rhode Island in 1927, known originally as the Association of Baptists for Evangelism in the Orient (ABEO). The partnership with ABWE is particularly significant because of previous conflict between the ABWE and some member churches in the FBFA.

In 2008 Dr. Allen McFarland, senior pastor of Calvary Evangelical Baptist Church in Portsmouth, Virginia, was president of the FBFA.

Membership: In 2008 the association reported 28 affiliated congregations.

Sources:

Fundamental Baptist Fellowship Association. www.fbfa.us/.

General Association of Regular Baptist Churches

1300 N Meacham Rd., Schaumburg, IL 60173

Among the conservative elements in the Northern Baptist Convention (now the American Baptist Churches in the U.S.A.) were a number whose main concern was doctrine. After the Convention's failure in 1922 to adopt the New Hampshire Confession of Faith, Thomas Todhunter Shields (1873–1955) of the Jarvis Street Church in Toronto led in the formation of the Baptist Bible Union, a union of individuals interested in the purging of modern elements in the Convention. In 1932, the Baptist Bible Union gave way to the General Association of Regular Baptist Churches (GARBC), formed in Chicago by delegates from eight states.

The GARBC considers itself an association of sovereign Bible-believing Baptist churches. The New Hampshire Confession of Faith was used as a model for the Articles of Faith, though emphasis is placed on the fundamentalist issues of the Bible and Christology. A single article concerns the "Resurrection, Personal, Visible Premillennial Return of Christ, and related events."

The GARBC is also a vocal exponent of separation. Churches in the fellowship are required to withdraw fellowship from and refuse cooperation with any organization or group which permits modernists in its ranks. Their separatist position was included in the name of the GARBC; the term "Regular" was adopted to oppose the other, "irregular" Baptist churches.

Missions are promoted through ten independent mission agencies which hold to the GARBC doctrinal position. They are the Association of Baptists for World Evangelism, Baptist Church Planters, Baptist Mid-Missions, Evangelical Baptist Missions, Baptist Missionary Builders, Western Baptist Home Mission, Northwest Baptist Home Mission, Regular Baptist Church Builders of Colorado, Southwest Baptist Home Missions, and Continental Baptist Missions. There are eight independent college/seminaries that partner with the GARBC. Several compassion ministries, including children's homes, a senior citizen's home, and a residential school for the mentally disabled, also partner with the association.

Membership: In 2002 the association reported 155,757 members, 1,417 congregations, and 1,600 ministers.

Educational Facilities:

Partnering educational facilities include the following:

Baptist Bible College and Seminary, Clarks Summit, Pennsylvania.

Cedarville University, Cedarville, Ohio.

Faith Baptist Bible College and Theological Seminary, Ankeny, Iowa.

Northwest Baptist Seminary, Tacoma, Washington.

Shasta Bible College, Redding, California.

Spurgeon Baptist Bible College, Mulberry, Florida.

Tennessee Temple University, Chattanooga, Tennessee.

Western Baptist College, Salem, Oregon.

Periodicals: *Baptist Bulletin.*

Sources:

General Association of Regular Baptist Churches. www.garbc.org.

Barndollar, W. W. *The Validity of Dispensationalism*. Des Plaines, IL: Regular Baptist Press, 1964.

The Biblical Faith of Baptists. 3 vols. Des Plaines, IL: Regular Baptist Press, 1966.

Hull, Merle R. *What a Fellowship?* Schaumburg, IL: Regular Baptist Press, 1981.

Ketcham, R. T. *The Answer: What Are Non-Convention Baptists Doing?* Waterloo, IA: General Association of Regular Baptist Churches, 1943.

Murdoch, J. Murray. *Portrait of Obedience*. Schaumburg, IN: Regular Baptist Press, 1979.

Tassell, Paul N. *Quest for Faithfulness: The Account of a Unique Fellowship of Churches*. Schaumburg, IL: Regular Baptist Press, 1991.

Global Independent Baptist Fellowship

4431 Tiedeman Rd., Brooklyn, OH 44144

The Global Independent Baptist Fellowship (GIBF), formed in November 2000 in Cleveland, Ohio, is composed of Baptist pastors, evangelists, and missionaries who have agreed to work together in the establishment of New Testament Baptist churches and to promote historic Baptist distinctives. The GIBF founders were responding to growing concerns over what they saw as increasingly liberal tendencies, in terms of attitudes toward Scripture and modes of worship, in the Baptist Bible Fellowship International (BBFI). This latter group formed in 1950 as an alternative to the World Fundamental Baptist Missionary Fellowship led by J.

Frank Norris (1877–1952). In 2008 Dr. Kevin Folger served as moderator of the GIBF.

Membership: Not reported.

Periodicals: *The Global Baptist Times.*

Sources:

Global Independent Baptist Fellowship. www.gibf.org/.

Independent Baptist Fellowship International

724 N Jim Wright Fwy., Fort Worth, TX 76116

The Independent Baptist Fellowship International is the product of the continued growth in number of theologically conservative Baptist congregations in the last half of the twentieth century. Many of these found their heritage in the ministry of J. Frank Norris (1877–1952), the fundamentalist leader who resided in Fort Worth, Texas. Pastors in that lineage founded the World Baptist Fellowship (WBF) and the Bible Baptist Fellowship International.

In 1984, leaders from a number of independent Baptist congregations came together in Fort Worth to create a new organization with the aims of encouraging fellowship, training pastors, and facilitating joint efforts in foreign missions. The education concern, uppermost in the minds of many of the founders, was focused through the Norris Bible Baptist Institute, under the leadership of Raymond W. Barber, the pastor of Worth Baptist Church in Fort Worth. Barber had formerly been the president of the World Baptist Fellowship and a professor at Arlington Baptist College. His controversy with the WBF occasioned the formation of the Independent Baptist Fellowship, which went hand-in-hand with the founding of the school. The school is self-consciously designed as a Bible training school, not a liberal arts college.

Given the focus on autonomous congregations in the fellowship, a mission agency was created that operates as an advisory board to promote the cause of missions and a channel through which funds may be passed to missionaries in the field. As of 2002, the fellowship supported 26 missionary families serving in 13 different mission fields including Brazil, the Dominican Republic, Guatemala, Honduras, Mexico, Hong Kong, Romania, Croatia, and Scotland.

Membership: Not reported.

Educational Facilities:

Crown Southwest–Norris Seminary, Fort Worth, Texas.

Periodicals: *The Searchlight.*

Sources:

Independent Baptist Fellowship International. www.ibfi-nbbi.org.

Oldham, Mr. & Mrs. Earl K. *USS-WBF: Sail On*. Grand Prairie, TX: Authors, 1992.

Wardin, Albert W., ed. *Baptists around the World*. Nashville, TN: Broadman & Holman, 1995.

Independent Baptist Fellowship of North America (IBFNA)

754 E Rockhill Rd., Sellersville, PA 18960-1799

The Independent Baptist Fellowship of North America (IBFNA) was founded in 1990 by former members of the General Association of Regular Baptist Churches (GARBC) who felt that the Association was drifting from its stated position of complete separation from apostasy. After leaving the GARBC meeting, an initial organizational meeting was held in Oshkosh, Wisconsin, in October 1990, where work began on a constitution and doctrinal statement, and transitional leadership was selected. The new organization was formally constituted in 1991 at a meeting in Philadelphia, which included the acceptance of the constitution and articles of faith.

The issue between the GARBC and the new IBFNA concerns what is termed *secondary separation*. Both organizations refuse to cooperate with organizations that are seen to be in apostasy—that is, deny essential Christian beliefs. The IBFNA also calls for secondary separation, a withdrawal of fellowship from individuals and organizations which in themselves are orthodox in faith, but who cooperate with organizations deemed to have apostate tendencies. It is this second level of separation that distinguishes fundamentalists from evangelicals. The IBFNA demands a separation form all neoevangelical movements including, for example, the Billy Graham Evangelistic Association or the National Association of Evangelicals.

The IBFNA is designed as a fellowship of ministers, lay people, and local churches. It affirms the autonomy of the local church and exists to provide fellowship, a place for churches to speak with a common voice, and an organization to facilitate common endeavors. There is no hierarchy, ruling board, or approval process. Mission concerns are primarily left to local congregations.

The fellowship meets annually, and membership is on a year-to-year basis. All members must reaffirm their allegiance each year and pay annual dues.

Membership: Not reported.

Periodicals: *The Review*.

Sources:

Independent Baptist Fellowship of North America. www.ibfna.org.

Brown, L. Duane, et al. *What Happened to the GARBC at Niagara Falls?* Sellersville, PA: Bethel Baptist Press, n.d.

Pickering, Ernest. *Biblical Separation: The Struggle for a Pure Church*. Schaumburg, IL: Regular Baptist Press, 1979.

Wardin, Albert W., ed. *Baptists around the World*. Nashville, TN: Broadman & Holman Publishers, 1995.

Independent Bible Baptist Missions
Current address not obtained for this edition.

Among the organizations to evolve out of the latter stages of the fundamentalist-modernist controversy was the Independent Bible Baptist Missions founded in Colorado in 1949. By this time the World Council of Churches had been formed and the liberal Protestant-based Federal Council of Churches had announced the formation of its successor body, The National Council of the Churches of Christ in the U.S.A. Also, among more conservative Protestants a new movement had arisen called Neoevangelicalism, which, without giving up any of the doctrinal affirmation of fundamentalism, had a new openness toward the academic world, science, and cooperative endeavors with liberal Protestants.

Among the many conservative Baptists who rejected both liberal Protestantism and Neoevangelicalism was Harvey H. Springer, a pastor at Englewood, a suburb of Denver, Colorado. He called together 12 colleagues who shared his basic perspective and in December 1949 they organized the Missionary Fellowship of Baptist Churches. At this organization's first assembly in 1950, it adopted the name, Independent Bible Baptist Missions. Headquarters were established in Colorado Springs, Colorado.

Doctrinally, the organization followed traditional Baptist beliefs as set forth in the Philadelphia Confession. It held to a premillennial dispensational eschatology. It also specifically forbade members any affiliation with the National Council of Churches or the National Association of Evangelicals, the primary organizational expression of Neoevangelicalism. Organization is congregational and there is an annual general assembly. Foreign missions were established in Brazil, Uruguay, and Mexico.

Membership: In 1980 there were approximately 25 churches and 3,000 members.

Sources:

Piepkorn, Arthur C. *Profiles in Belief: The Religious Bodies of the United States and Canada*. Vol. IV. San Francisco: Harper & Row, 1979.

Kyova Association of Regular Baptists
Current address not obtained for this edition.

The Kyova Association of Regular Baptists was formed in 1924 from the New Salem Association of Regular Baptists. In the 1940s, a controversy arose over whether the United Mine Workers (or any union) was in fact a secret society. As a result of this controversy, the Kyova Association dropped correspondence with the New Salem Association in 1945 and then splintered. Some churches moved into other Regular Baptist associations. The group uses the King James version of the Bible and forbids members to belong to secret societies.

Membership: In 1960 the association had 4 congregations and 140 members.

Liberty Baptist Fellowship
PO Box 10174, Lynchburg, VA 24506

HISTORY. Liberty Baptist Fellowship is an association of independent fundamentalist Baptist churches and ministers founded in 1981. The fellowship grew out of the Thomas Road Baptist Church in Lynchburg, Virginia, founded by Dr. Jerry Falwell (1933–2007) in 1956. The work prospered, and in 1971 Falwell founded Liberty Baptist College with 141 students. Two years later Liberty Baptist Theological Seminary was opened. Both the college and seminary grew as people responded to the television ministry of Falwell's *Old-Time Gospel Hour*. By 1983 650 graduates were pastoring churches, each of whom had been taught the aggressive evangelism techniques used by Falwell to build Thomas Road. When Liberty Baptist College became Liberty University, the seminary program was integrated into the university's overall structure.

Liberty Baptist Fellowship, which has a congregational polity, was formed as the school's graduates began to assume professional positions as pastors across the United States. In 2006 Dr. Leland Dittman was appointed as the first full-time director of Liberty Baptist Fellowship.

BELIEFS. Liberty Baptist Fellowship follows the fundamentalist faith for which Falwell became a national spokesperson. It holds to separatism from religious groups that deny the fundamentals of the faith. The fellowship affirms, within a framework of traditional Christian beliefs, the inerrancy of the Bible, the creation of the earth in six literal days, and the imminent return of Jesus Christ. Evangelism is emphasized; the fellowship believes salvation can come only through the acceptance of Jesus as one's personal savior.

Membership: In 2008 the fellowship reported 13 affiliated churches in several states.

Periodicals: *Liberty Journal*. • *Fundamentalist Journal*.

Sources:

Liberty Baptist Fellowship. www.libertybaptistfellowship.com/lbf/.

Falwell, Jerry. *Falwell: An Autobiography*. Lynchburg, VA: Liberty House Publishers, 1997.

————. *The Fundamentalist Phenomenon: The Resurgence of Conservative Christianity*. Garden City, NY: Doubleday, 1981.

————. *Stepping Out on Faith*. Wheaton, IL: Tyndale House Publishers, 1984.

————. *Strength for the Journey: An Autobiography*. New York: Simon and Schuster, 1987.

————, and Elmer Towns. *Church Aflame*. Nashville, TN: Impact Books, 1971.

Harding, Susan Friend. *The Book of Jerry Falwell: Fundamentalist Language and Politics*. Princeton, NJ: Princeton University Press, 2000.

Mainstream Baptists
Box 6371, Norman, OK 73070-6371

Mainstream Baptists is a network of Baptist churches and leaders who seek to counter the rising fundamentalism in the Southern Baptist Convention (SBC). The network can be dated to the formation of Mainstream Oklahoma Baptists who organized in 1997 to coordinate a moderate voice in the larger Baptist General Convention of Oklahoma.

Mainstream Baptists adopt an evangelical Christian theology with typical Baptistic emphasis on local church autonomy, believer's baptism by immersion, religious liberty, and mission outreach. The network also adopts a non-dogmatic approach to biblical inerrancy. They have accused fundamentalist leaders in the Southern Baptist Convention of bibliolatry. The network resisted the 2000 SBC revision of the 1963 Baptist Faith and Message, which has served as the doctrinal statement of Southern Baptists. Mainstream Baptists objected to two new views in the revised version: restriction of pastoral leadership to males only and the addition of a "Family" section that emphasized the submission of the wife to the husband.

Mainstream Baptists have a presence in Alabama, Georgia, Louisiana, Missouri, Texas, and Oklahoma. They have joined in partnership with The New Baptist Covenant, an informal alliance of 30 groups working for a moderate Baptist vision. The New Baptist Covenant community held their first convention in 2008; former presidents Jimmy Carter and Bill Clinton participated.

The executive director of Mainstream Baptists is longtime SBC pastor Bruce Prestcott.

Membership: Not reported.

Sources:

Mainstream Baptists. www.mainstreambaptists.org.

Minnesota Baptist Association
PO Box 527, Willmar, MN 56201

As the fundamentalist debate arose anew in the 1940s, Minnesota emerged as one of the few areas where, under the leadership of such men as William Bell Riley (1861–1947), conservatives were in the majority. Controversy developed over support of the mission program of the Northern Baptist Convention (now the American Baptist Churches in the U.S.A.), and in 1944 a "special account" was created by the Minnesota Convention to channel funds to the Conservative Baptist Foreign Missionary Society (CBFMS). Other objections to the Northern Baptist Convention's program were focused on ecumenism, youth work, and the distribution of funds in the unified budget. The break came in 1948 when the Minnesota Convention became independent of the Northern Baptist Convention.

After the formation of the Conservative Baptist Association (CBA) in 1947, there was a period of cooperation between it and the Minnesota Convention. Individual churches and leaders, such as Dr. Richard V. Clearwaters (1900–1996), were active in both. The Minnesota Convention continued to function, for the CBA accepted only churches (not conventions) as members.

Cooperation with the CBA continued, but the Conservative Baptists were criticized in 1955 when an article in a Minnesota Convention magazine complained that CBFMS missionaries did not believe in the pretribulation, premillennial return of Christ. Later that year, a pretribulation position was adopted by the Minnesota Convention. The convention began to move in a separatist direction; criticism of the CBA continued. The CBA was accused of interfering with local autonomy in the churches and of allowing inclusivist thinking in the early 1960s. (Inclusivist thinking pertained to association with those in liberal associations.) The break between the Minnesota Convention and the Conservative Baptist Association was completed in 1963. The name was officially changed to the Minnesota Baptist Association in 1974.

The association publishes a church school curriculum and as well as various tracts and booklets through the publication ministry of North Star Baptist Press.

Membership: In 2002 the association reported 58 churches and approximately 93 ministers.

Educational Facilities:

Pillsbury Baptist Bible College, Owatonna, Minnesota.

Periodicals: The North Star Baptist.

Sources:

Minnesota Baptist Association. www.mbaoc.org.

Becklund, David. A History of the Minnesota Baptist Convention. Minneapolis: Minnesota Baptist Convention, 1967.

Riley, Marie Acomb. The Dynamic of a Dream. Grand Rapids, MI: Eerdmans, 1938.

Nationwide Independent Baptist Fellowship
850 Mill Rd., McDonough, GA 30253

In the middle of the first decade of the twenty-first century, tensions within the Southwide Baptist Fellowship led to a rupture. The more conservative of the leaders complained that individual churches within the fellowship had become open to new styles of worship that were leading them away from the fundamentalist Baptist beliefs and practices that had been the fellowship's hallmark. Leading voices denouncing the changes were Dr. Tom McCoy, pastor of the Peoples Baptist Church in McDonough, Georgia, Dr. Mike Norris, pastor of the Franklin Road Baptist Church in Murfreesboro, Tennessee, and Dr. Max Barton, pastor of the People's Baptist Church, Greenville, North Carolina, who became the moderator of the new fellowship.

The Nationwide Fellowship sees itself as carrying forward the traditional fundamentalist beliefs and practices of the Southwide Fellowship.

Membership: Not reported.

Sources:

Nationwide Independent Baptist Fellowship. www.nationwidefellowship.com/.

New England Evangelical Baptist Fellowship
40 Bridge St., Newton, MA 02158

The New England Evangelical Baptist Fellowship is a small body in the Northeast. It is a conservative body and was formally a member of the National Association of Evangelicals. The president in 1965 was Dr. John S. Viall of Boston.

Membership: In 1965 there were 10 churches, 20 pastors and 1,022 members.

New Testament Association of Independent Baptist Churches
8856 E Fairfield St., Mesa, AZ 85207-5124

The New Testament Association of Independent Baptist Churches was formed in 1965 at a meeting in Denver. Twenty-seven churches affiliated at the organizational meeting. Members of the Conservative Baptist Association (CBA) who supported a premillennial, pre-tribulation, separatist position had held a previous meeting been in 1964. Among leaders of the newly formed association was Dr. Richard V. Clearwaters (1900–1996) of the Minnesota Baptist Convention (now the Minnesota Baptist Association). The polity is a loose congregationalism. An annual meeting is held in which each pastor and five lay delegates have voting power. They elect a president, other officers, and members of a board of trustees to implement association programs.

The New Testament Association has adopted a Confession of Faith based on the New Hampshire Confession, but with emphasis on separation and pre-tribulation eschatology. The group is opposed to speaking in tongues. The association defends strongly the autonomy of the local church and does not endorse any schools, mission agencies, or publishing houses, choosing rather to leave such matters to the discretion of the local church.

Membership: In 2008, the New Testament Association of Independent Baptist Churches has about 125 congregations.

Periodicals: New Testament Testimonies.

Sources:

New Testament Association of Independent Baptist Churches. www.ntaibc.org.

Clearwaters, Richard V. The Great Conservative Baptist Compromise. Minneapolis: Central Seminary Press, n.d.

————. The Local Church of the New Testament. Chicago: Conservative Baptist Association of America, 1954.

————. On the Upward Road. Minneapolis: Author, 1991.

Paige, Dr. Richard. What's in a Name. Booklet available from the NTAIBC.

————. The Ten Commandments. Minneapolis: Central Seminary Press, 1975.

Russel, Stephen D. A History of the New Testament Association of Independent Baptist Churches. A dissertation presented for Church History 602 at Bob Jones University of Greenville, SC (April, 2002).

North American Baptist Conference

1 S 210 Summit Ave., Oakbrook Terrace, IL 60181

The North American Baptist Conference (NABC) originated in the early nineteenth century with German-speaking Americans who had been influenced by English-speaking Baptists to work among the growing number of German immigrants. While tracing their history to a number of efforts begun independently of each other, the German Baptists look to Konrad Anton Fleischmann as the first of their number. A Bavarian, Fleischmann had been converted in Switzerland and joined a separatist church molded on the English model. On a request from George Mueller of Bristol, England, he traveled to America and became pastor of a German Protestant church at Newark, New Jersey, in the spring of 1839, but was fired for refusing to baptize infants. In October, he baptized three people, his first converts, and sent them to an English Baptist church. He traveled throughout eastern Pennsylvania and New York, where he established groups of believers and preaching stations. In 1843, he drew up a series of "Articles" for use by the church at Philadelphia that he founded. It was Baptist in all points except closed communion.

Other missionaries were also at work in the 1840s. Aided by the American Baptist Home Missionary Society, John Eschmann was working in New York City. Alexander Von Puttkamer was converted by English Baptists at Lawrenceville, New York, and began to organize a German Baptist Church in Buffalo while an agent of the American Tract Society. Churches in the Midwest were begun in the late 1840s.

The first conference of German Baptists met in 1851 representing eight churches and 405 members. With the cooperation of the American Baptist Publication Society, they were able to produce a hymnal and a German translation of the New Hampshire Confession. A Western Conference was formed in 1859, and a Triennial Conference met in 1865.

Doctrinally, the North American Baptists affirm the standard Baptist faith as embodied in the New Hampshire Confession, though only a brief statement has been adopted. Polity is congregational. There is a triennial conference every three years, with 19 associations in the United States and Canada. Higher education has been a major concern from the beginning, and as early as 1858, August Rauschenbusch (1816–1899) went to the Baptist Seminary at Rochester and became one of the outstanding exponents of the social gospel.

NABC is affiliated with numerous camps and seven senior homes. Missions are carried on in Mexico, Russia, Romania, Cameroon, Nigeria, the Philippine Islands, Japan, and Brazil, and works with White Cross in Nigeria and Cameroon. They also work with Baptist World Aid to provide disaster relief. Home missions are directed toward various multicultural groups and planting new churches in areas of need. The conference is affiliated with the Baptist World Alliance.

Membership: In 2008 the conference reported nearly 65,000 members and 400 congregations. In 2002 there were 421 clergy.

Educational Facilities:

Sioux Falls Seminary, Sioux Falls, South Dakota.

Taylor University College and Seminary, Edmonton, Alberta, Canada.

Periodicals: NAB Today • Intercessor • NAB Highlights • ServantLink. • Discipleship Newsletter • The Inside Scoop.

Sources:

North American Baptist Conference. www.nabconference.org.

Kerstan, Reinhold Johannes. Historical Factors in the Formation of the Ethnically Oriented North American Baptist General Conference. Ph.D. diss., Northwestern University, 1971.

Ramaker, Albert John. The German Baptists in North America. Cleveland, OH: German Baptist Publication Society, 1924.

Woyke, Frank H. Heritage and Ministry of the North American Baptist Conference. Oakbrook Terrace, IL: North American Baptist Conference, 1979.

Old Regular Baptists (not Predestinarian)

Current address not obtained for this edition.

The doctrines of Old Regular Baptists emerged from the larger Baptist history in the colonies. In the aftermath of the Great Awakening, the revival movement that began around 1739 or 1740, there was much disagreement surrounding the *old* and the *new* doctrinal standards. The newer doctrine leaned heavily toward Calvinism. The term *Regular* appears to be in response to this division, suggesting that the group identifies itself with the older doctrine. In an effort to reconcile past differences, many of the old-time Baptists came back together as United Baptists. However, this unity was not to last. The New Salem Association of United Baptists was organized in 1825 with an arm from the Burning Springs Association. In 1854, the name was changed to *Regular* and in 1892 the name was changed to "Old Regular Baptist." Most Old Regular Baptists can be traced to the New Salem Association of Old Regular Baptists.

Membership: The central Appalachian Mountains contain 16 associations of Old Regular Baptist churches (Dorgan, 1989). These have planted new churches outside the Appalachian region in Indiana, Ohio, Michigan, Arizona, and Florida. The Appalachian counties in Kentucky and the Virginias remain home to most of the Old Regular Baptists. The 16 associations have a total membership of approximately 10,000 in some 300 churches.

Sources:

Dorgan, C. Howard. *In the Hands of a Happy God: The "No-Hellers" of Central Appalachia*. Knoxville: University of Tennessee Press, 1989.

Regular Baptists

No central headquarters

In the 1740s, during what was called the Great Awakening in the American colonies, the new Baptists were divided into Regular Baptists and Separate Baptists. The Separatists were former Congregationalists who had been affected by the revival and particularly the preaching of George Whitefield (1714–1770). Regular Baptists were members of the Philadelphia Association and adhered to the Philadelphia Convention. The Separate and Regular Baptists spent the second half of the eighteenth century engaging in polemics and attempting to reunify. In 1765, the first Regular Baptist Association was formed by churches in Virginia and given the name Ketoctin. The Regular Baptists spread into Kentucky and the surrounding states.

In 1801, the Separate and Regular Baptists were able to overcome their differences and merge. They formed various associations with the term *united* in the association names. Some second generation members of these associations, however, became dissatisfied with the term *united* and many associations dropped it from their name. Larger Baptist bodies absorbed many of these associations.

Toward the middle of the nineteenth century, a move to reconstitute the Regular Baptists began. In 1854, the New Salem Association of United Baptists changed its name to the New Salem Association of Regular Baptists. In 1870 this association adopted another name: Old Regular Baptists. In 1867 the Burning Springs Association of United Baptists changed the term *United* in its name to *Regular*. Other associations followed suit. Regular Baptists now live in all sections of the country, with the heaviest concentration of them living in the area from Virginia to Indiana.

The reason for the formation of the Regular Baptists is not clear. By the end of the nineteenth century, though, they clearly represented a rejection of the organizational and methodological innovations of most nineteenth-century Baptists. The group rejects Sunday schools, a trained ministry, secret societies, missionary societies, and organization beyond the associational level.

A doctrinal consensus exists among the Regular Baptists, a body of beliefs very close to the doctrine of the United Baptists. Most statements of belief by Regular Baptists affirm adherence to the Trinity, the Bible as the written word of God, election, inherent human depravity, the eternal security of the believer, believers' baptism by immersion (wherein water covers the whole person), closed communion, the resurrection, and a properly ordained ministry. Beyond that consensus, there is a wide variety of freedom and belief. The statements on salvation and justification are so worded as to be open to both Calvinistic and Arminian interpretations. (Calvinists say the number and identity of the elect was predetermined before the world began; Arminians say salvation is possible for all who, by free will, choose to follow the Gospel.) However, the Regular Baptists have no fellowship with those who reject their statements of beliefs. Their form of government is extreme congregationalism with no central headquarters and no structure beyond the association. Among the periodicals serving the churches are the *Regular Baptist* from Laurel, Maryland, and the *Regular Baptist Messenger* of Whitestown, Indiana.

The Regular Baptists have allowed Arminianism but reject hyper-Calvinism, and in the 1890s, they split over absolute predestination. (See separate entry on Regular Baptists-Predestinarian.) The following Regular Baptist associations are in correspondence with each other, display doctrinal similarity, and reject absolute predestination: New Salem, Union, Indian Bottom, Mud River, Sardis, Friendship, Philadelphia, Thornton Union, and Northern Salem Associations.

The International Partnership of Fundamental Baptist Ministries is a global coalition of independent Baptist ministries networking for international work. Partners work in Ghana, Kenya, Liberia, Togo, Bangladesh, India, Indonesia, Korea, Myanmar, the Philippines, Taiwan, Haiti, Jamaica, Guyana, and Peru.

Membership: In 2002 there were 1,415 churches and 129,407 members.

Periodicals: *The Regular Baptist.* • *Regular Baptist Messenger.*

Sources:

General Association of Regular Baptist Churches. www.garbc.org

Perrigan, Rufus. *History of Regular Baptists and Their Ancestors and Accessors.* Haysi, VA: Author, 1961.

Short, Ron. "We Believed in the Family and the Old Regular Baptist Church." *Southern Exposure* 4, no.3 (1976): 60–65.

Wallhausser, John. "I Can Almost See Heaven from Here: The Old Regular Baptist Tradition in Appalachia." *Katallagate: Be Reconciled* 8, no. 3 (Spring 1983): 2–10.

Russian-Ukrainian Evangelical Baptist Union of the U.S.A., Inc.
52 Steele Ave., Somerville, NY 08876

The Russian/Ukrainian Evangelical Baptist Union of the U.S.A., Inc., dates from 1901 when Baptists migrated from Russia to Kiev, North Dakota. During the next twenty years, the Baptists absorbed other evangelical groups, many of which were lost in transition to English-language worship. In 1919 the Union was organized at Philadelphia. Missionary work was begun worldwide among Russian immigrants. A Slavic missionary society supported 21 missionaries in Western Europe, South America, and Australia. An English branch works among English-speaking Slavic people. The Evangelical Baptist Camp Home for the Aged is owned and operated by the Union.

Seiatel' Istin'i (*The Sower of Truth; A Russian Christian Monthly*), was published monthly in 1955 and 1967–1968.

Membership: As of September 1, 2007, there were 20 churches and 1,400 members of Russian/Ukrainian-speaking Americans.

Periodicals: *Evangelical Baptist Herald* (in English).

Sources:

Baptist World Alliance. www.bwanet.org.

Separate Baptists in Christ
14470 S. Jonesville Rd., Columbus, OH 47201

The Separate Baptists emerged in the First Great Awakening of the eighteenth century as a result of the hostility of the majority of Congregationalists to the revivalism that swept New England. Some former Congregationalists were rebaptized, including Isaac Backus, who became an outstanding theologian and historian. The Separatist movement spread, but the Separatists were not accepted by many other Baptists for a long time, in part because of their acceptance of those baptized but not immersed. However, in 1801, a union was effected between the Regular and Separate Baptists. Some Separatists did not accept the union, and continued to exist west of the Allegheny Mountains as independent congregations and associations. In 1912, several of these associations came together as the General Association of Separatist Baptists.

The Separatist Baptists are similar to the Regular Baptists. A mild Calvinism is generally held. There is no universally accepted creed. Footwashing is an ordinance. Immersion is the only form of baptism. The government is congregational. Sunday schools and home missionary work are supported on a local level. Education is more highly rated than with the Regular Baptists.

Membership: In 2008 there were 78 churches.

Periodicals: *The Messenger.*

Sources:

Separate Baptists in Christ. www.separatebaptist.org.

Renault, James Owen. "The Changing Patterns of Separate Baptist Religious Life." *Baptist History and Heritage* 14, no. 4 (Oct. 1979): 16–25, 36.

Scott Morgan. *History of the Separate Baptists.* Indianapolis: Hollenbeck Press, 1900.

South Carolina Baptist Fellowship
c/o Tabernacle Baptist Church, 3931 White Horse Rd., Greenville, SC 29611

The South Carolina Baptist Fellowship was formed at a meeting in 1954 in Greenville, South Carolina, called by the Rev. John R. Waters and the Rev. Vendyl Jones. It was known as the Carolina Baptist Fellowship until its incorporation in 1965. Eleven independent Baptist pastors were present at the 1954 meeting. Reverend Waters was editor of *The Baptist Bible Trumpet,* and in 1955 at the fellowship meeting, it was adopted as the official organ. Doctrine is fundamental and premillennial; polity is congregational. Meetings of the fellowship are held monthly. Missions are supported through independent fundamentalist faith mission organizations. As of June of 2003, the SCBF began meeting quarterly, rather than monthly.

Membership: In 1987 there were approximately 300 churches with a membership of approximately 52,000 affiliated with the fellowship, though no formal membership list is kept. There currently are no official figures available. The fellowship has affiliated work in 85 countries and supports 370 missionaries. Their radio broadcast is WTBI AM and FM and on the Internet.

Educational Facilities:

Ambassador Baptist College, Lattimore, North Carolina.

Bob Jones University, Greenville, South Carolina.

Crown College, Powell, Tennessee.

Pensacola Christian College, Pensacola, Florida.

Tabernacle Baptist College, Greenville, South Carolina.

West Coast Baptist College, Lancaster, California.

Periodicals: *The Baptist Bible Trumpet* is published online at www.baptist-bibletrumpet.com.

Southern Baptist Convention

c/o Executive Committee, SBC, 901 Commerce St., Ste. 750, Nashville, TN 37203

HISTORY. The Southern Baptist Convention was formed in 1845 by the Baptist congregations in the southern United States. Underlying the separation of the southerners were a variety of tensions that would 15 years later divide the nation and lead to the Civil War (1861–1865). Some of those tensions had become focused in the American Baptist Home Mission Board, which many felt had neglected the South and Southwest in the appointment of missionaries. The immediate occasion for the separation of the southern Baptists was the refusal in 1844 of the American Baptist Foreign Mission Board to appoint a slaveholder as a missionary and the American Baptist Home Mission Board to appoint a slaveholder to a mission in Georgia. These refusals seemed to violate long-standing practices and the agreement of the Triennial Convention (the meeting of the foreign mission board) that cooperation in the foreign mission enterprise would sanction neither proslavery nor antislavery.

Delegates met in Augusta, Georgia, in May 1845 to form the convention, which would in turn coordinate the churches as a whole in the propagation of the Gospel. A constitution was adopted and both a foreign and domestic mission board established. Thus, from the beginning, the southerners, without infringing upon traditional Baptist emphases concerning congregational polity, provided a more unified approach in structuring their denominational work. After several attempts to establish a publishing concern failed, a Sunday school board was created in 1891. It provided a single set of materials for the church's educational program, a major force in unifying Southern Baptist thought.

Significant in the life of the convention was the adoption of the Cooperative Program in 1925 by which all the boards, commissions, and programs (with the exception of the former Sunday school board) supported by the churches came under a unified budget. The program provided stable financial support for all of the church's ministries and eliminated competitive fund-raising among the congregations.

BELIEFS. Southern Baptists inherited the Puritan-Reformed theological tradition, which had been passed through the first and second London Baptist Confession of Faith (1677 and 1689, respectively), the Philadelphia Confession of Faith (1742), and the New Hampshire Confession of Faith (1833). The New Hampshire confession was slightly revised and adopted by the convention as the 1925 Baptist Faith and Message, and it was again slightly revised in 1963. These statements, which place Southern Baptists clearly within the Reformed theological tradition, are balanced by the frequently articulated belief in the freedom of the individual to interpret Scripture unbound by any creedal statement, and also by the theological perspective of fundamentalism, which has the support of many Southern Baptist leaders.

During the twentieth century, the convention has been embroiled in a series of battles between those who have championed a variety of innovative perspectives and the more conservative elements of the convention who have seen any new thought as deviating from traditional Baptist standards of doctrine. The controversy over evolution, which began before the twentieth century, sharply divided Baptists during the 1920s but gradually gave way to an accommodation to the several forms of theistic evolution as a means of reconciling science with the book of Genesis. During the early 1960s, conservatives attacked *The Message of Genesis*, a book by Midwestern Baptist Theological Seminary professor Ralph H. Elliott. Elliott advocated a critical view of Genesis as merely a compilation of various documents, rather than a unitive volume written by Moses. In the resulting controversy, Elliott was forced out of his teaching position.

Crucial to Baptist thought has been the infallible authority of the Bible. The Baptist faith and message declares the Bible to be divinely inspired with God as its author. In recent decades that belief has been interpreted by some in terms of biblical inerrancy. Among conservatives, this has led to debates on exactly how inerrancy is to be defined. More moderate and liberal positions have rejected inerrancy as a means of defining biblical inspiration.

ORGANIZATION. The Southern Baptist Convention has a congregational polity. Congregations are related successively to three levels of cooperative affiliation. Associations operate on the county level. State conventions include churches in one or more states. Nationally, the annual convention is composed of from one to 10 messengers from each congregation that cooperates with the work of the convention and contributes to its support.

To increase operational efficiency, the North American Mission Board (NAMB) was forged in 1997 out of the Home Mission Board, the Radio and Television Commission, and the Brotherhood Commission, a restructuring called *Covenant for a New Century*.

The national convention has oversight of other organizations: the International Mission Board, Lifeway Christian Resources, and the Ethics and Religious Liberty Commission. It also oversees six seminaries. Seminary Extension, a ministry of the six seminaries, delivers biblical, theological, and practical education to Christians via the Internet, CD-ROM, local live classrooms, and correspondence. Students can earn a bachelor's degree by way of distance learning. The program has agreements with Judson College and the Apex School of Theology so students can transfer some of their credits to a school.

Broadman and Holman (B&H) Publishing Group, one of America's major publishers of religious literature, is the official publishing arm. In 2008 the Southern Baptist Convention had 1,200 local associations and 41 state conventions and fellowships. The international mission program has more than 5,000 missionaries in 153 countries, and about 5,000 missionaries in the United States.

The Historical Commission was dissolved in 1997, but a group of Southern Baptist historians have turned to the Southern Baptist Historical Society, now located in the Baptist center of the Tennessee Baptist Convention, Brentwood. The society is supported by individuals and entities with links to Baptist heritage.

The Southern Baptist Convention has not been among the most active church bodies in the twentieth-century ecumenical movement, which has drawn so many of the larger denominations into cooperative actions. It has preferred to work cooperatively within the larger Baptist family and has been active in the Baptist World Alliance up until 1991; in addition, it helped fund and staff the Baptist Joint Committee on Public Affairs. The convention, however, refrains from participation in such organizations as the World Council of Churches, the National Council of Churches, or the National Association of Evangelicals.

The Baptist Press is a Monday-through-Friday international news wire service. Formed in 1946 by the Southern Baptist Convention, and supported with Cooperative Program funds, Baptist Press operates from a central bureau in Nashville, Tenn., with four partnering bureaus.

Membership: In 2008 there were more than 16 million members worshipping in more than 42,000 churches. In 2004 there were 118,289 clergy.

Educational Facilities:

Golden Gate Baptist Theological Seminary, Mill Valley, California.

Midwestern Baptist Theological Seminary, Kansas City, Missouri.

New Orleans Baptist Theological Seminary, New Orleans, Louisiana.

Southeastern Baptist Theological Seminary, Wake Forest, North Carolina.

Southern Baptist Theological Seminary, Louisville, Kentucky.

Southwestern Baptist Theological Seminary, Fort Worth, Texas.

The convention also sponsors numerous colleges and universities throughout the southern United States in Texas, Kentucky, Oklahoma, Missouri, California, North and South Carolina, Mississippi, Virginia, Georgia, Florida, Arizona, Alabama, and Arkansas.

Periodicals: *SBC Life.* • *The Commission.* Available from PO Box 6767, Richmond, VA 23230.

Sources:

Southern Baptist Convention: Reaching the World for Christ. www.sbc.net

Baker, Robert A., ed. *A Baptist Source Book*. Nashville, TN: Broadman and Holman, 1966.

Fletcher, Jesse C. *The Southern Baptist Convention: A Sesquicentennial History*. Nashville, TN: Broadman and Holman, 1994.

Hastings, C. Brownlow. *Introducing Southern Baptists, Their Faith and Their Life*. New York: Paulist Press, 1981.

Hays, Brooks, and John E. Steely. *The Baptist Way of Life*. Macon, GA: Mercer University Press, 1993.

McClellan, Albert. *Meet Southern Baptists*. Nashville, TN: Broadman and Holman, 1978.

Wallace, O. C. S. *What Baptists Believe: The New Hampshire Confession*. Nashville, TN: Sunday School Board of the Southern Baptist Convention, 1934.

Wardin, Albert W., Jr. *Baptist Atlas*. Nashville, TN: Broadman and Holman, 1980.

Yarbrough, Slayden A. *Southern Baptists: A Historical Ecclesiological, and Theological Heritage of a Confessional People*. Brentwood, TN: Southern Baptist Historical Society, 2000.

Southwide Baptist Fellowship

c/o John R. Waters, Faith Baptist Church, 1607 Greenwood Rd., Laurens, SC 39360

In 1955 at the meeting of the Carolina Baptist Fellowship at Aiken, South Carolina, Dr. Lee Roberson (1909–2007), pastor of the Highland Park Baptist Church of Chattanooga, Tennessee, the main guest speaker, was asked to lead in the formation of a fundamental Baptist church that would draw from the entire South. At a conference the following year at Dr. Roberson's church, and with the support of the South Carolina group, such a fellowship was formed as the Southern Baptist Fellowship. One hundred and forty-seven clergy and laymen registered as charter members. Though heavily supported by the Carolina Baptist Fellowship, the Southern Baptist Fellowship became a separate body. Many of the South Carolina churches are members in both bodies. The current name was adopted in 1963.

A statement of faith continues the Baptist consensus and emphasizes the autonomy of the local church. The group professes belief in premillennialism. It also holds that the Revised Standard Version of the Bible is a "perverted translation." It demands separation from all forms of modernism, especially the National Council of Churches.

The headquarters of the Southwide Baptist Fellowship is in Laurens, South Carolina. The fellowship cooperates with the Commission on Chaplains of the Associated Gospel Churches. Foreign work is being carried out in Ghana, Nigeria, Puerto Rico, Canada, Nassau, Nicaragua, Brazil, Japan, St. Lucia, Cayman Islands, and Spain.

Membership: In 2000 there were 501 churches, with only 27 in South Carolina but 73 in North Carolina and 72 in Georgia.

Sources:

Association of Religious Data Archives. www.thearda.com/mapsReports/maps/map.asp?variable=415&state=101&variable2=

Sovereign Grace Baptist Churches

No central headquarters, for information contact:, Henry T. Mahan Tape Ministry, 6088 Zebulon Hwt., Pikeville, KY 41501

Out of the post–World War II theological liberalism that many saw as having permeated the churches of the Reformed theological tradition (particularly the large Baptist and Presbyterian denominations), there arose a reaction that emphasized Calvinist theological distinctions, particularly the sovereign grace of God. In 1966, Calvary Baptist Church in Pine Bluff, Arkansas, invited people known to be sympathetic to what was becoming a growing movement to a conference at Carlisle, Pennsylvania. The conference became the focus around which cooperative action by otherwise independent churches and pastors could begin. Most of those attending had come out of either the Southern Baptist Convention or, to a lesser extent, the Presbyterian churches. A few were from independent evangelical congregations. Approximately 100–250 ministers attended the Pennsylvania Conference. By 1969 the loosely organized movement had grown large enough to initiate regional conferences, and no less than three periodicals emerged.

Doctrinally, Sovereign Grace congregations are Calvinistic, accept the Philadelphia Baptist Confession of Faith of 1772, and use the great works of the Reformed theologians such as Calvin, Edwards, and Charles Hodge. An extreme congregational polity has been accepted. Local churches are headed by pastors (who are seen as teaching elders) and ruling elders (lay elders).

Besides the annual conference in Pennsylvania, other conferences have grown up, including ones at Ashland, Kentucky, and Pine Bluff, Arkansas. The Trinity Reformed Baptist Church of Allentown, Pennsylvania, publishes *The Sword and Trowel*. Among the most substantive of the Sovereign Grace periodicals is the quarterly *Baptist Reformation Review*, now called *Searching Together* (according to a non-profit corporation in Wisconsin, www.searchingtogether.org/index.htm), begun by Nobert Ward of Nashville, Tennessee. Ward identifies with the Sovereign Grace Movement as a result of his former position within the Primitive Baptist Church. Before 1972, as a Primitive Baptist, he edited *Inquirer*.

Membership: In 2002 there were approximately 300 Sovereign Grace congregations, 3,000 members and 400 ministers.

Educational Facilities:

Spurgeon Theological Seminary, Memphis, Tennessee.

Periodicals: *The Sovereign Grace Message* (this is with Sovereign Grace Baptist Fellowship). • *Searching Together*. Send orders to Box 548, St. Croix Falls, WI 54024 (this is a publication of Word of Life Church, a non-profit corporation in Wisconsin, www.searchingtogether.org/index.htm). • *Reformation Today Magazine*. Contact Tom Lutz, Edgewood Baptist Church, 3743 Nichol Ave., Anderson, IN 46011 (www.puritansermons.com/banner/reftoday.htm).

Sources:

Sovereign Grace Baptist Churches. www.sovereign-grace.com/index.htm.

Green, Jay. *God's Everlasting Love for His Chosen People*. Marshallton, DE: Sovereign Grace Publishers, n.d.

Johnson, E. W. *Questions Concerning Evangelism*. Pine Bluff, AR: Sovereign Grace Publishers, 1988.

Thronbury, John. "Calvinist Baptists in America." *Banner of Truth* (Nov. 1968): 32–36.

Strict Baptists

c/o Zion Strict Baptist Church, 1710 Richmond NW, Grand Rapids, MI 49504

Alternate Address: International headquarters: Gospel Standard Strict Baptist Churches, c/o H. Mercer, Hampton, Highworth, Swindon, Wiltshire, England SN6 7RL.

The Strict Baptists is the American branch of the Gospel Standard Strict Baptist Churches, a division among Baptists that arose in England during the nineteenth century. During the seventeenth century, British Baptists emerged as one segment of the larger Puritan movement, an effort to "purify" the Church of England by appeal to a more literal allegiance to biblical doctrine and practice. Baptists participated in the Puritan debates during the Commonwealth Period, and Baptists were among the leaders of Oliver Cromwell's government. As such, the Baptists had accepted a basic Calvinist theological perspective, which they shared with the Presbyterians. They departed from the Presbyterians (who were in the majority) over church government, the Baptists championing the authority of the local church and the independence of the church from any affiliation with the state. Baptists were further differentiated from fellow Puritans by their acceptance of adult baptism by immersion as the proper mode of initiation of members into the church.

Baptists split into two branches following the theological lines of the controversy among Dutch Calvinists over predestination. General or Arminian Baptists accepted the opinions of Jacob Arminius that allowed for some free will. Particular Baptists believed that God chose or predestined those who would be saved out of sinful humankind. Strict Baptists arose out of the Particular Baptists and might be said to have begun with the founding of *The Gospel Standard, or Feeble Christian's Support* by John Gadsby. *The Gospel Standard* became the vehicle of several prominent Baptist ministers including William Gadsby (d. 1844; father of the magazine's founder), John Warburton (1776–1857), and John Kershaw. The immediate occasion for the founding of the periodical was the appearance of another short-lived magazine advocating the preexistence of the human soul; however, Gadsby's magazine was in full force in the 1840s when a more serious controversy arose among the Particular Baptists over the nature of the divine sonship of Jesus Christ. The appearance of views denying the eternal sonship of Christ prompted articles in defense of the teaching in *The Gospel Standard* as early as 1844. However, the controversy reached a new level of intensity in 1860 following the publication of a sermon by a Rev. Crowther entitled "The Things Most Surely Believed among Us, as to the Person, Mission, and Work of Christ." Crowther suggested that Jesus became the son of God as a result of his supernatural begetting in the womb of Mary. By the end of the year the first resolution in support of the eternal sonship was issued by a church in London. Other resolutions followed in 1861 and a gradual separation occurred between those churches that held to the doctrine of Christ's eternal sonship and those that allowed the preaching of the opposite position.

By the 1870s the Strict or Gospel Standard Baptists were recognized as a distinct group within the larger Baptist movement. The Strict Baptists consisted of a number of independent congregations who accepted the basic views espoused by *The Gospel Standard* magazine, and who met in association separate from other Particular Baptists.

The doctrinal controversy of the British Particular Baptists did not transfer to the United States, a nation then caught up in the problems of a Civil War. However, during the late-twentieth century several congregations formally related to the Gospel Standard Baptists have arisen under the name Strict Baptists.

Membership: There are three congregations of Strict Baptists in the United States—one each in Michigan, Montana, and Wisconsin. Total membership is about 20 to 25 and there are three clergy. There are also three congregations in Australia, with the main body of Gospel Standard Baptists located in England.

Periodicals: *Gospel Standard Magazine* • *Friendly Companion* (both published in England and distributed through the church in the United States).

Sources:

Articles of Faith and Rules of Church Order. Grand Rapids, MI: Zion Strict Baptist Church, n.d. 15 pp.

Gosden, J. H. *Believers' Baptism and the Lord's Supper.* Harpenden, Herts, England: Gospel Standard Baptist Trust, 1977. 22 pp.

Paul, S. F. *Historical Sketch of the Gospel Standard Baptists.* London: Gospel Standard Publications, 1945. 86 pp.

Ramsbottom, B. A. *New Testament Church Order.* Grand Rapids, MI: Zion Baptist Church, n.d. 11 pp.

Transformation Ministries (Baptist)
970 S Village Oaks Dr., Ste. 101, Covina, CA 91724-0609

Transformation Ministries was formed in 2006 as an affiliation of Baptist churches based in the southwestern United States. Most of the member churches were part of the American Baptist Churches of the Pacific Southwest (ABCPSW) but became alienated from the American Baptist Convention over issues related to homosexuality. Transformation Ministries traces its roots to 1869 with the formation of the

Los Angeles Baptist Convention (LABC). The LABC became the Southern California Baptist Convention in 1895, becoming known as the ABCPSW in 1977.

The organization notes that it is "a movement of Baptist churches committed to change their worlds for Christ." Transformation Ministries links itself to historic Baptist convictions like the individual accountability of every soul to God, the separation of church and state, the supreme authority of the Scriptures for Christian faith and life, the baptism of believers by immersion as a sign of repentance and faith in Christ, the equal standing of all believers before God through Christ, and the autonomy and interdependence of local churches.

Transformation Ministries is affiliated with, among other organizations, the National Association of Evangelicals and the Willow Creek Association. In 2008 Rev. Dr. Dale V. Salico served as executive minister.

Members: In 2008 Transformation Ministries reported 128 congregations.

Educational Facilities:

Northern Baptist Theological Seminary, Lombard, Illinois.

Judson College, Elgin, Illinois, and Rockford, Illinois.

Periodicals: *Transformations.*

Sources:

Transformation Ministries. www.transmin.org/.

Ukrainian Evangelical Baptist Convention
6751 Riverside Dr., Berwyn, IL 60402

The Ukrainian Evangelical Baptist Convention (UEBC) was formed in 1945 as the Ukrainian Missionary and Bible Society by a group of Ukrainian Baptists meeting at Chester, Pennsylvania. The first official assembly was in 1946; the present name was adopted in 1953. The Rev. Paul Bartkow was the first president, serving in that post for twenty years. The UEBC is the conservative branch of the Ukrainian Baptists and is a member of the separatist American Council of Christian Churches.

In line with the anti-communist stance of the American Council of Christian Churches, the convention developed a program aimed at Iron Curtain countries. Missionaries were sent behind the Iron Curtain, and in 1966, the Ukrainian Voice of the Gospel, a biweekly radio program over Trans World Radio in Monte Carlo, began. A publishing house, Doroha Prawdy (The Way of Truth), established in 1954, is operated in cooperation with the sister organization in Canada. Missionary work is carried on among Ukrainian communities in Argentina, Brazil, Paraguay, Australia, France, and Germany. The UEBC supports the Ukrainian Bible Institute in Argentina.

Membership: Not reported. In 1970 there were more than 20 churches scattered across the United States. According to The Ukrainian Weekly, the Ukrainian Evangelical Baptist Convention supported 46 missionaries in Ukraine during 1999.

Periodicals: *The Messenger of Truth.* Send orders to 690 Berkeley Ave., Elmhurst, IL 60126.

Ukrainian Evangelical Baptist Convention of Canada
PO Box 2437, Station Main, Winnipeg, MB R3C 4A7

After the Russian government permitted the British and Foreign Bible Society into Russia to distribute their literature, Baptists began migrating to the Ukraine. In the late nineteenth century, along with other Russian Christian minorities, Ukrainian Baptists began to migrate to Canada. In the early years of the twentieth century, organization proceeded at a swift pace, especially in the western provinces. By 1903 a church was organized at Winnipeg, another a year later at Overstone, Manitoba. In 1907 a congregation was formed in Toronto, and a missionary from England, John Kolesnikoff, arrived to begin work. In 1908 an intercongregational meeting convened at Canora, Saskatchewan.

For a number of years the Canadian-Ukrainian Baptists cooperated directly with the American-based Ukrainian Evangelical Baptist Convention, but in 1950 they reorganized the all-Canadian Ukrainian Evangelical Baptist Convention of Canada.

Though independent, the convention remains in fellowship with the United States Ukrainian Baptists.

The Ukrainian Evangelical Baptist Convention of Canada was incorporated in 1961 to promote its work and to spread the gospel message, especially to people of Ukrainian descent who still understand their own language.

While conservative in belief, the convention is less strict doctrinally than the Union of Slavic Churches of Evangelical Christians and Slavic Baptists of Canada, Inc. The Evangelical Mission to Ukraine began in 1977.

Membership: In 2008 there were 10 churches.

Periodicals: *Christian Herald.*

Sources:

Ukrainian Evangelical Baptist Convention of Canada. www.uebcc.org.

Bolshakoff, Serge. *Russian Nonconformity*. Philadelphia, PA: Westminister Press, 1950.

Kindrat, Petro. *The Ukrainian Baptist Movement in Canada*. 1972.

Union of Slavic Churches of Evangelical Christians and Slavic Baptists of Canada

Current address not obtained for this edition.

As Russian and Ukrainian Baptists moved into Canada, they began to divide theologically. Though both groups were conservative, those who were most strict and fundamental in the eastern provinces organized the Russian-Ukrainian Evangelical Baptist Union of Eastern Canada in the late 1920s. Other Canadian Ukrainian Baptists organized the Ukrainian Evangelical Baptist Convention of Canada. At about the same time, a similar organization was formed in the western provinces, the Union of Slavic Evangelical Christians. Members of the two groups established fraternal ties very quickly. In 1958 a number of the churches of the Slavic Union joined with the Evangelical Baptists to form the Union of Slavic Churches of Evangelical Christians and Slavic Baptists of Canada. The new union was incorporated in 1963.

The union holds to a conservative fundamental Christianity which emphasizes the full inspiration of the Bible, a premillennial eschatology, and eternal punishment for the unsaved. It is affiliated with the Russian-Ukrainian Baptist Union in the United States of America. Mission work is supported in Argentina, Australia, and Europe.

Membership: In 1995, there were 11 congregations and approximately 500 members.

Sources:

Wardin, Albert W. Jr., ed. *Baptists around the World*. Nashville, TN: Broadman & Holdman, 1995.

World Baptist Fellowship

3001 W Division, Arlington, TX 76012

Alternate Address: PO Box 13459, Arlington, TX 76094-0459.

The World Baptist Fellowship emerged around the followers of J. Frank Norris (1877–1952), longtime pastor of First Baptist Church of Fort Worth (1909–1952) and Temple Baptist Church in Detroit (1934–1948). During the 1920s, Norris arose as one of the most charismatic leaders of the fundamentalist movement. Then in 1926, he killed a Fort Worth businessman, the climax to a quarrel he was waging with Roman Catholics in Texas. Though acquitted in court, his name was dropped from the officiary of the Bible Baptist Union. That act, which cut him off from a large segment of the movement, did not stop his active work, which only ended with his death in 1952.

The fellowship was organized around an annual meeting held at Norris's Fort Worth Church. In 1939 he began the Bible Baptist Institute, which later moved to Arlington, Texas, and became the Bible Baptist Seminary. After Norris's death, the headquarters of the fellowship moved on campus. In early the 1970s they reported over 550 churches with 800 more supporting the work. The main strength is in

Texas and Ohio. Most recently the seminary has added a liberal arts curriculum and is now known as the Arlington Baptist College.

Doctrine is Baptist, with an extremely conservative fundamentalist approach assumed. Mission work is carried out through Fellowship Missions. Polity is congregational.

Membership: Not reported.

Educational Facilities:

Arlington Baptist College, Arlington, Texas.

Periodicals: *The Fundamentalist*. Available online at www.wbfi.net.

Sources:

World Baptist Fellowship. www.wbfi.net.

Falls, Roy E. *A Fascinating Biography of J. Frank Norris*. Euless, TX: Author, 1975.

Kemp, Roy A. *A Biography of Dr. J. Frank Norris, 1877–1952*. Fort Worth, TX: the Author, n.d.

Norris, J. Frank. *Practical Lectures on Romans*. Fort Worth, TX: First Baptist Church, n.d.

Moffitt, Bill. *Formation of an Independent New Testament Church*. Arlington, TX: World Baptist Fellowship Home Missions, n.d.

Oldham, Mr. and Mrs. Earl K. *USS-WBF: Sail On*. Grand Prairie, TX: Authors, 1992.

Russell, C. Allyn. *Voices of American Fundamentalism*. Philadelphia: Westminister Press, 1976.

Primitive Baptists

Black Primitive Baptists

Current address not obtained for this edition.

Until the Civil War, blacks were members of the predominantly white Primitive Baptist associations and worshipped in segregated meeting houses. After the Civil War, blacks were organized into separate congregations, and associations were gradually formed. In North Alabama, the Indian Creek Association was formed as early as 1869. Among the leaders was Elder Jesse Lee. He was ordained after the war, and in 1868, organized the Bethlehem Church in Washington, Virginia. In 1877, he became the moderator of the newly formed Second Ketoctin Association.

Doctrine and practice of the Black Primitive Baptists are like those of the Regulars. The Black Primitive Baptists are known for their practice of line singing. They have no periodical. The Primitive Messenger, partially underwritten by Elder W. J. Berry, editor of Old Faith Contender, lasted only four years in the early 1950s.

Membership: Not reported. In the early 1970s there were 43 associations which averaged approximately five churches per association and 20 members per church. There are approximately 3,000 members.

Covenanted Baptist Church of Canada

Current address not obtained for this edition.

The Covenanted Baptist Church of Canada traces its roots to Daniel McArthur, a young Presbyterian of Cowal, Scotland. Converted in the early nineteenth century, he began preaching with great success. However, his Bible study led him to become a Baptist and he was baptized and ordained a minister by Elder McFarland of Edinburgh. Among McArthur's converts was Dougald Campbell, who migrated from North Knapdale, Scotland to Aldboro, Elgin County, Ontario in 1818. He joined with the regular Baptists and was ordained. A few years later, however, Campbell felt the Baptists were departing from the strict Calvinism of his Scottish heritage, and he withdrew to organize the Covenanted Baptist Church of Canada. By the 1850s there were five congregations in Aldboro, Dunwick, Lobo, Ekfurd, and Orford (Duart), all in Ontario.

The Covenanted Baptists fellowshipped with no other groups until the mid-1850s, when copies of the American Primitive Baptist periodical Signs of the Times arrived in Canada. Gilbert Beebe, editor of the periodical, was the leading voice of Primitive Baptists in the northern United States. Correspondence led to the visit of Elder William McColl, who had been ordained by Beebe, and other Primitive Baptists in Dundas, Ontario. McColl's visit was followed by that of Beebe and other prominent elders, and fellowship between the two churches was established. Fellowship with the Absolute Predestinarians continues to this day.

The Articles of Faith of the Covenanted Baptists affirms belief in the Trinity, Jesus Christ as lord and redeemer, righteousness that saves as imputed to the sinner by God's grace, absolute predestination, free and permanent election, the sufficiency of the Holy Scriptures, and believers' baptism by immersion. In keeping with their position on predestination, the articles disallow preaching that includes a general call for sinners to repent and respond to the Gospel. The attendance at meetings of other religious groups is frowned upon.

Membership: There are less than 100 members in several churches in Ontario.

Sources:

Hassell, Cushing Briggs. *History of the Church of God.* Middletown, NY: Gilbert Beebe's Sons, 1886.

National Primitive Baptist Convention of the U.S.A.

c/o Elder Ernest Ferrell, President, PO Box 7451, Tallahassee, FL 32314

Around the turn of the century, there was a movement among the Black Primitive Baptists to organize a national convention. In 1906, Elders Clarence Francis Sams, George S. Crawford, James H. Carey, and others called on their colleagues to join them in a meeting at Huntsville, Alabama, in 1907. Eighty-eight elders from seven Southern states responded. In organizing the convention, of course, the members departed from a main Primitive Baptist concern—that there should be no organization above the loose associations that typically cover several counties.

Doctrinally, the National Primitive Baptist Convention follows the Regular Primitive Baptists. The Convention's creeds profess belief in the "particular election of a definite number of the human race." Footwashing is practiced. The organization is congregational, and at the local level there are two offices: pastor (elder) and deacon or deaconess (mother). The convention meets annually and sponsors Sunday schools and a publishing board.

Membership: In 2002, there were 1,565 churches and 600,000 members.

Periodicals: The New Clarion, PO Box 7463, Tallahassee, FL 32314.

Sources:

National Primitive Baptist Convention. www.natlprimbaptconv.org.

Discipline of the Primitive Baptist Church. Tallahassee, FL: National Primitive Baptist Publishing Board, 1966.

Primitive Baptists–Absolute Predestinarians

No central headquarters.

The smallest of the three larger groups of Primitive Baptists is composed of those who differ from the Regulars only on the issue of predestination. While all Primitive Baptists believe that God chose the elect before the foundation of the world, the "Absoluters," as they are often called, believe that God decreed in himself from all eternity all things that will come to pass from the greatest to the smallest event. A lengthy exposition of their belief, including numerous scriptural references, is found annually in the Upper County Line Association Minutes. Only a few of the Absolute Predestinarians practice footwashing.

Most Absoluters are to be found in Texas, Alabama, North Carolina, Virginia, and the Northeast. Among the periodicals reflecting the absolute predestination position were *Zion's Landmark* issued in Wilson, North Carolina, and *Signs of the Times*, the oldest Primitive Baptist periodical, begun in 1832 and now issued from Danville, Virginia. Elder E. J. Berry has been a major force in Primitive Baptist circles for many years. He developed the Primitive Baptist Library in Elon College, North Carolina, and edits the *Old Faith Contender*.

Membership: Not reported.

Periodicals: *Signs of the Times.* Send orders to Rte. 1, Box 539, Beechwood Ln., Danville, VA 24541. • *Old Faith Contender*, Rte. 2, Elon College, NC 27244.

Primitive Baptists–Moderates

No central headquarters.

The largest single grouping of Primitive Baptists is composed of the moderate Calvinist Regulars. They are to be found throughout the South and Midwest, and are most heavily concentrated in North Carolina, Michigan, West Virginia, Georgia, Alabama, and Tennessee. They believe in the depravity of man, often stated as the imputation of Adam's sin to his posterity. The chosen are elected before the foundation of the world; are called, regenerated and sanctified, and are kept by the power of God. Good works are the fruits of faith and are evidence of salvation. In general, evangelism is not engaged in, since God will call his elect. Most practice footwashing. They oppose secret orders, missionary societies, Bible societies, theological seminaries, and related institutions, and will not fellowship with churches that are connected with those organizations.

Among the periodicals serving the Moderates are The Christian Pathway, monthly from Atlanta, Georgia; Baptist Witness, from Cincinnati; The Christian Baptist, from Atwood, Tennessee; and the Primitive Baptist, from Thornton, Arkansas. Besides publishing the Baptist Witness, Elder Lasserre Bradley, Jr., publishes the Primitive Baptist Directory, with more than 1,000 churches listed, and broadcasts the Baptist Bible Hour over stations in the South, Midwest, and California. Elder S. T. Tolley is compiling a library at Atwood, Tennessee.

Membership: Not reported.

Periodicals: *The Christian Pathway.* Send orders to c/o Elder Mark Green, PO Box 334, Booneville, AR 72927 • *Baptist Witness.* Available from Baptist Bible Hour, PO Box 17037, Cincinnati, OH 45217. • *The Primitive Baptist.* Available from Cayce Publishing Co., Thornton, AR 71766. • *The Christian Baptist.* Send orders to Box 168, Atwood, TN 38220.

Sources:

Primitive Baptists. www.primitivebaptistchurches.com.

Berry, W. J. Tracing the True Worship of God. Elon College, NC: Primitive Publications, 1971.

Bradley, Lasserre, Jr. What Do Primitive Baptists Believe? Cincinnati, OH: Baptist Bible Hour, n.d.

Historical Facts on the Origin of "Campbellism." Atwood, TN: Christian Baptist Library, n.d.

Lambert, Byron Cecil. The Rise of the Anti-Mission Baptists: Sources and Leaders, 1800-1840 New York: Arno Press, 1980.

Patterson, Beverly Bush. The Sound of the Dove: Singing in the Appalachian Primitive Baptist Churches. Illinois: University of Illinois Press, 1995.

Primitive Baptists–Progressive

c/o Pat McCoy, PO Box 69, Culloden, GA 31016

The most easily defined group of Primitive Baptists are the Progressives. In doctrine, Progressives are similar to the Regular or Reformed, but differ in the acceptance of innovative forms of congregational life. Included in the congregational life are sunday school, youth training, men's brotherhoods and women's auxiliaries, and youth camps. Beyond the local churches, the Primitive Baptist Foundation is a nonprofit corporation underwriting denominational projects: literature printing, retirement fund for pastors and widows, and evangelical support for churches. The Primitive Baptist Builders helps new and struggling churches to build and purchase. In the summer, bible conferences are held in Georgia and Indiana. *The Lighthouse* is a radio ministry heard in all parts of Georgia, eastern Alabama, South Carolina, north and west Florida, and internationally by short wave radio. Two Bethany homes—one for men in Millen, Georgia, and one for women in Vidalia,

Georgia—serve senior citizens. Donetsk Ministry, Inc. is a mission outreach to Ukraine and Russia, supporting national pastors, missionaries, orphanages, and medical clinics.

Progressive churches are predominantly in Georgia, with scattered congregations in Florida, Alabama, Tennessee, Indiana, Mississippi, Texas, Louisiana, Missouri, Illinois, Indiana, and Northern Virginia. A ministerial association functions among the non-association churches in Florida, Illinois, and Indiana. "The Minister's School" meets three times per year. All ministers meet for intensive study of the scriptures. A music workshop is held annually for all church musicians and choirs.

Membership: In 2008, *The Banner Herald* reported 119 affiliated churches, the majority located in the state of Georgia.

Periodicals: *The Banner Herald.* Send orders to 127 Old Leefield Rd., Brooklet, GA 30415. • *Donetsk Report*, PO Box 69, Culloden, GA 31016.

Sources:

The Banner Herald. www. banner-herald.org.

Primitive Baptist Church Manual. Jesup, GA: Banner Publications, n.d.

 # Black Baptists

Assembly of Free Spirit Baptist Churches
Contact information not provided for this edition.

The Assembly of Free Spirit Baptist Churches (AFSBC) was founded in 1985 by former ministers and members of the older Baptist churches who had adopted a spontaneous worship style commonly associated with Pentecostalism (but not Pentecostal doctrine) and who felt excluded from other Baptists. Baptists have, as a whole, adopted a more staid worship format and have questioned the free-wheeling and expressive worship associated with traditional gatherings within African-American churches. The assembly has an outreach ministry using inspirational audiotapes.

Membership: In 1994 the church reported 85,000 members.

Fundamental Baptist Fellowship Association
1916 Central Ave., Kansas City, KS 66102

The Fundamental Baptist Fellowship Association (FBFA) was founded on August 22, 1962, and incorporated on July 9, 1975. Its stated purpose is to "promote fellowship between Bible-believing Baptist Churches of like faith and order; to foster the spirit of evangelism; to spread the Gospel; and advance the cause of Christ through mutual efforts in Christian education and missions."

The association is based on affirmation of biblical inerrancy, the Trinity, the depravity of man, and salvation by grace. Member churches and individual associate members also adopt a pre-millennial and pre-tribulation eschatology. The 28 member churches, largely African American, are located in the southern United States and the Midwest, with both a northern and southern national representative. A number of the churches are also connected to the General Association of Regular Baptist Churches. The association has a partnership with the Association of Baptists for World Evangelism (ABWE), an independent mission agency founded in Rhode Island in 1927, known originally as the Association of Baptists for Evangelism in the Orient (ABEO). The partnership with ABWE is particularly significant because of previous conflict between the ABWE and some member churches in the FBFA.

In 2008 Dr. Allen McFarland, senior pastor of Calvary Evangelical Baptist Church in Portsmouth, Virginia, was president of the FBFA.

Membership: In 2008 the association reported 28 affiliated congregations.

Sources:

Fundamental Baptist Fellowship Association. www.fbfa.us/.

National Baptist Convention of America, Inc.
777 S R Thornton Freeway, Ste. 210, Dallas, TX 75203

In 1915, an issue arose in the National Baptist Convention of the U.S.A., Inc., over the ownership of the publishing house. Early in the convention's life, the Rev. R. H. Boyd (1843–1927), a brilliant businessman, was made corresponding secretary of the publication board. Under his leadership, the publishing house did over two million dollars in business during its first decade. As time passed, however, some members of the convention realized that the publishing interest had been built on Boyd's property, and all the materials had been copyrighted in his name. Further, no proceeds were being donated to other convention activities.

In a showdown, the 1915 Convention moved to correct its mistake by adopting a new charter that clarified the subservient position of the boards. Refusing to comply, Boyd withdrew the publishing house from the convention and made it the center of a second national Baptist convention, called the National Baptist Convention of America. Because of its refusal to accept the charter, it is usually referred to as "unincorporated."

In 1987 the National Baptist Convention of America was incorporated in Shreveport, Louisiana, under the new caption, The National Baptist Convention of America, Inc. (NBCA).

In September 1988 the National Baptist Convention of America, Inc., and the National Baptist Convention U.S.A., Inc., met in their annual sessions in Dallas, Texas and Fort Worth, Texas, respectively. A joint worship service convened in the Reunion Arena in Dallas, celebrating their togetherness and protesting apartheid in South Africa.

Following the joint worship service, the National Baptist Convention of America, Inc., re-convened in its 104th Annual Session in Fort Worth, Texas. Controversy over the ownership of the National Congress caused division among the Convention messengers. The heart of the controversy was whether the National Convention would operate its own congress as an auxiliary or whether the convention would continue to relate to a National Congress chartered, owned, and controlled by the National Publishing Board, with no responsibility to the convention. After debate and a democratic vote, the National Baptist Convention of America, Inc., voted to operate its own National Congress. As a result of this decision, a new National Missionary Baptist Convention was born in November 1988.

Today the National Baptist Convention, Inc., continues to support mission fields in the Caribbean, the Virgin Islands, Panama, Haiti, and Ghana in West Africa.

The National Baptist Convention of America, Inc., continues to honor its commitment to its nature and function as articulated in its constitution.

The NBCA, Inc., convenes three times per year. The Convention at Study focuses on the teaching ministry and is implemented through the National Baptist Congress of Christian Workers (NBCCW) and the National Youth Convention (NYC).

Ten colleges and seminaries are supported.

Membership: In 2008 there were about 3 million members in the National Baptist Convention of the U.S.A., Inc. In 2005 there were about 5,000 churches and 5,000 ministers.

Educational Facilities:

Central Baptist Theological Seminary, Indianapolis, Indiana.

Morehouse School of Religion, Atlanta, Georgia.

Periodicals: *Lantern.*

Sources:

National Baptist Convention of America. www.nbca-inc.com.

Boyd, R. H. *Boyd's National Baptist Pastor's Guide.* Nashville: National Baptist Publishing Board, 1983.

———, ed. *The National Baptist Hymn Book.* Nashville: National Baptist Publishing Board, 1906.

Lovett, Bobby L. *A Black Man's Dream: The First 100 Years—Henry Boyd and the National Baptist Publishing Board*. Nashville: Mega Corp., 1993.

Pius, N. H. *An Outline of Baptist History*. Nashville: National Baptist Publishing Board, 1911.

National Baptist Convention of the U.S.A., Inc.

1700 Baptist World Center Dr., Nashville, TN 37207

The National Baptist Convention of the U.S.A. came into existence after the adoption of a resolution before the Foreign Mission Baptist Convention of the U.S.A. to merge itself, the American National Baptist Convention, and the Baptist National Educational Convention. To these three would be added a publications board for Sunday school literature. The Convention was formed in Atlanta, Georgia, in 1895. Elected president and corresponding secretary of foreign missions were Rev. E. C. Morris (b. 1855) and Lewis G. Jordan, respectively. Both were able men; the National Baptist Convention's survival, stability, and success were in no small part due to their long terms in office.

Doctrine and government were taken over from the white Baptists. The congregational form of church life allowed a ready adaptation to the black culture, which used religious forms as a socially accepted way to express their frustration and to protest their conditions. The worship developed a high degree of emotional expression, making little reference to traditional liturgical forms. (While freed from the rituals of their white parents in the faith, the local church developed its own "forms," which seem spontaneous to the occasional visitor. In fact, the black Baptists allowed themselves to create a new religious culture, the pattern of which they follow weekly in their service.)

Within two years of its founding, the new National Baptist Convention ran into trouble when Jordan moved its offices from Richmond to Louisville. The Virginia Brethren, fearing a loss of power, withdrew support. They formed the Lott Carey Foreign Missionary Convention, which still exists as an independent missionary society. A more serious disagreement split the denomination in 1915.

For 29 years (1953–1982) the National Baptists were led by J. H. Jackson (1900–1990). He was succeeded in 1982 by T. J. Jamison, the son of the convention's president, from 1941–1953, D. V. Jemison. The current president is Dr. William J. Shaw.

The Convention coordinates the work done in the field through five regions headed by a vice president who serves on the Board of Directors.

There is mission work in Africa and the Bahamas. The group operates five colleges, a theological seminary, and a training school for women and girls.

Membership: In 2008, the Convention reported 7.5 million members. It is to be noted that in the late 1990 serious charges were made that the membership of the convention's churches had been grossly over estimated. It is also the case that no formal count has ever been made, and thus the actual number remains a contested issue, with estimates as low as one million, while the Convention claims 7.5 million members. Most observers now put the actual figure at between 3 and 5 million.

Educational Facilities:

American Baptist College, Nashville, Tennessee.

Periodicals: *National Baptist Voice*. Send orders to 2900 3rd Ave., Richmond, VA 23222

Remarks: In the summer of 1997, convention president Henry J. Lyons (b. 1942) became involved in what has been a growing controversy after his wife was accused of setting fire to a house owned by Lyons with another woman. She eventually confessed and was sentenced to five years probation. The incident, however, led to an investigation of Lyons and charges of widespread misuse of convention funds including the diversion of funds intended for the rebuilding of black churches. Legal problems forced Lyons to resign from the presidency. Dr. S. C. Cureton, vice president-at-large, took over the leadership of the convention and served the remainder of the Lyons's tenure.

Sources:

National Baptist Convention U.S.A., Inc. www.nationalbaptist.com.

National Baptist Voice. www.nationalbaptistvoice.com.

Jackson, J. H. *A Story of Christian Activism*. Nashville, TN: Townsend Press, 1980.

————. *Unholy Shadows and Freedom's Holy Light*. Nashville, TN: Townsend Press, 1967.

The National Baptist Pulpit. Nashville, TN: Sunday School Publishing Board, 1981.

Pegues, A. W. *Our Baptist Ministers and Schools*. Springfield, MA: Wiley & Co., 1892.

Pelt, Owen D., and Ralph Lee Smith. *The Story of the National Baptists*. New York: Vantage Press, 1960.

National Baptist Evangelical Life and Soul Saving Assembly of the U.S.A.

441-61 Monroe Ave., Detroit, MI 48226

A. A. Banks founded the National Baptist Evangelical Life and Soul Saving Assembly of the U.S.A. in 1920 in Kansas City, Missouri. It was begun as a city mission and evangelical movement within the National Baptist Convention of America, with which it remained affiliated for 15 years. Differences arose in the mid-1930s, and in 1936 at Birmingham, Alabama, the Assembly declared itself independent. Centers were established in cities across the nation.

No official statements regulate the doctrine of the Assembly, but generally the doctrine follows that of the National Baptist Convention of America. Relief work, charitable activity, and evangelizing are the main concerns of the Association. Each member hopes to add one member to the kingdom annually. Correspondence courses have been developed in evangelism, missions, pastoral ministry, and the work of deacons and laymen. Degrees are awarded for these studies.

Membership: Not reported. In 1951 there were 57,674 members, 264 churches, and 137 ministers.

National Missionary Baptist Convention of America

6925 Wofford Dr., Dallas, TX 75227

The National Missionary Baptist Convention of America was founded in 1988 as the result of a schism in the National Baptist Convention of America. The crux of the conflict was the National Baptist Publishing Board. The board, which had been established in the 1890s by R. H. Boyd, had operated as an independent corporation headed by Boyd and his descendants. In 1915, a disagreement over the relationship of the board to the National Baptist Convention led to a split and to the formation of the National Baptist Convention of the U.S.A., Inc., which wished to have a publishing concern under its own control, and the National Baptist Convention of America, which continued the relationship with the Boyd family's National Baptist Publishing Board.

Over the years, the board supplied many services to the convention. Among these has been an annual summer Sunday School Congress, a teacher training school that drew more than 20,000 students. However, the board made no accounting of the profits from such activities nor did the convention share in the revenues.

In the mid-1980s, voices began to rise within the convention calling for a reordering of the relationship between it and the Publishing Board. At a meeting in the summer of 1988, a majority of the attendees at the annual meeting of the National Baptist Convention of America voted to break ties with the Publishing Board and to begin conducting an independent Sunday School Congress. As a result, those who disagreed with the decision met in Dallas, Texas, in November 1988, and organized the National Missionary Baptist Convention. They have remained loyal to the Publishing House and will continue to support its annual

Sunday School Congress. Rev. S. M. Lockridge (1913–2000) of San Diego, California, was elected as the first president of the convention.

Organizers of the new convention claim their share of the history of the National Baptists for the last century. It is too early yet to see what percentage of the five-million-plus members will adhere to the continuing National Baptist Convention of America or to the National Missionary Baptist Convention, though the majority has seemed to favor the new convention.

Membership: In 2008 the convention reported 338 affiliated congregations, the greatest number being from Texas. At the time of the schism, there were an estimated five million members of the National Baptist Convention of America. Early reports indicated that as many as twenty percent of that membership would withdraw, meaning that the new convention would have churches with a cumulative membership of over a million, but those figures have not been verified.

Sources:

National Missionary Baptist Convention of America. www.nmbca.com.

Waddle, Ray. "Baptists' Split Intensifies over Rival Publishing Boards." *Nashville Tennessean* (March 11, 1989).

Progressive National Baptist Convention, Inc.
601 50th St. NE, Washington, DC 20019

The Progressive National Baptist Convention was formed in 1961 following a dispute over the length of presidential tenures at the 1960 meeting of the National Baptist Convention of the U.S.A., Inc. In 1957, J. H. Jackson (1900–1990), who had been elected president in 1953, declined to step down and removed the four-year tenure rule out of the convention's constitution. Prior to the adoption of the rule in 1952, elected presidents served until their death. At the 1960 convention session, dissatisfaction came to a head in the attempt to elect G. C. Taylor as Jackson's successor. The failure of Taylor to attract more support led, in 1961, to a new National Baptist Convention meeting formed by L. Venchael Booth (1919–2002) of Zion Baptist Church, Cincinnati, Ohio. He was elected the first president of the new Progressive National Baptist Convention.

Also at issue in the 1961 break was denominational support for the civil rights movement, then gaining momentum in the South. Those who formed the new convention represented the strongest backers of Martin Luther King Jr. (1929–1968), who was among those to join the progressives.

The convention is in agreement on doctrine with its parent body, the disagreements being concerned with organization and social policy. It has organized nationally with two-year terms for all officers, except the executive secretary, who has an eight-year term. The women's auxiliary was formed in 1962 and a department of Christian education, home mission board, and foreign mission bureau were soon added.

On October 15, 2007, the Interdenominational Theological Center (ITC) in Atlanta, Georgia (of which Morehouse School of Religion is a founding member), opened the Gardner C. Taylor Archives and Preaching Laboratory. This state-of-the-art facility will enable distance education and research.

The Progressive National Baptist Convention supports the World Council of Churches, the National Council of Churches, the Baptist World Alliance, and other ecumenical bodies. It has active ministries in Africa, Asia, Europe, Latin America, and the Caribbean.

Membership: In 2008 the denomination reported 2,000 churches and 2.5 million members (1.5 million are in the United States).

Educational Facilities:

Central Baptist Theological Seminary, Indianapolis, Indiana; Morehouse School of Religion, Atlanta, Georgia.

Periodicals: *Baptist Progress.* Available from 712-14 Quincy St., Brooklyn, NY 11221. • *The WORKER.* Available from 601 50th St. NE, Washington, DC 20019.

Sources:

Progressive National Baptist Convention. www.pnbc.org/

King, Martin Luther, Jr. *Strength to Love.* New York: Harper & Row, 1963.

————. *Why We Can't Wait.* New York: Signet, 1964.

Taylor, Gardner C. *Chariots Aflame: Dynamic Appeals from One of the Nation's Outstanding Preachers.* Nashville, TN: Broadman and Holman, 1988.

United American Free Will Baptist Church General Conference
207 W Bella Vista St., Lakeland, FL 33805

The United American Free Will Baptist Church General Conference (UAFWBC), an African-American body, traces its roots in America to the founding of the initial Free Will Baptist congregation in 1727 in Perquimans County, North Carolina, by Paul Palmer. The first General Conference of Free Will Baptists was held in 1827. Rev. Robert Tash was the first African American to be ordained in the General Conference (1827). It was not until after the American Civil War that separate congregations led by African Americans appeared in the Free Will Baptist community, the first being formed in 1867. The UAFWBC was incorporated in 1968 but is rooted in the Negro General Conference, which began in 1898.

UAFWBC members affirm traditional Arminian (as opposed to Calvinist) Baptist doctrine. They profess the Apostles' Creed but change the wording at crucial points, professing belief in "the Free Will Baptist Church" and "eternal life for all true believers who persevere in holiness to the end." The articles of faith affirm that children who die in infancy will go to heaven. Conference churches practice believer's baptism and foot-washing and teach a general resurrection of the dead.

In 2008 the general bishop was Dr. Henry J. Rodmon.

Membership: In 2008 the conference reported 41 congregations in Florida, Louisiana, South Carolina, and Arkansas.

Periodicals: *UAFWBC Newsletter* (online).

Sources:

United American Free Will Baptist Church General Conference. uafwbc.org/.

Payne, Wardell J. *Directory of African American Religious Bodies.* Washington, DC: Howard University Press, 1991.

General Baptists

Baptist General Conference
2002 S Arlington Heights Rd., Arlington Heights, IL 60005

Gustaf Palmquist was a Swedish Lutheran preacher and teacher who migrated to America in the mid-nineteenth century. In 1852, shortly after his conversion and baptism in an English-speaking Baptist church in Galesburg, Illinois, he baptized three immigrant Swedes in the Mississippi River and organized a Swedish Baptist church in Rock Island, Illinois. Other churches of immigrant Swedish Baptists were organized wherever immigrant Swedes settled—in rural areas as well as in large cities in the Midwest and Northeast. By 1864 there were 11 such churches.

Chuch doctrine is predominantly Arminian Baptist with some Reformed Baptist emphases. There are two ordinances: baptism and the Lord's Supper. The polity is congregational. There is an annual delegated meeting of the churches. A 25-member board of overseers is drawn from representatives of the various denominational boards and the 13 districts. The boards implement the program of the conference. The Board of Foreign Missions (now International Ministries) was first appointed in 1944. Before that time, mission work had been carried on through various independent agencies and the American Baptist Foreign Mission Society. Since 1944, work has been established in India, Japan, the Philippines, Ethiopia, Mexico, Cameroon, the Ivory Coast, Brazil, Argentina, Thailand, Uruguay, the Middle East, Central Asia, Bulgaria, France, Slovakia, and Vietnam. In 2008, work was conducted in 21 countries.

Affiliated organizations include the Baptist General Conference of Canada, the Baptist General Conference in Saskatchewan, the Central Canada Baptist Conference, the Baptist World Alliance, the Baptist General Conference in Alberta, the British Columbia Baptist Conference, the National Association of Evangelicals, the North American Baptist Fellowship, the Baptist Joint Committee for Religious Liberty, and the New England Theological Seminary, along with four child care and family service agencies.

Membership: In 2002 there were 145,148 members and 902 churches.

Educational Facilities:

Bethel University, St. Paul, Minnesota.

Bethel Seminary, St. Paul, Minnesota, and San Diego, California.

Hispanic Bible School, Chicago, Illinois.

Periodicals: *BGC World.* • *Newsline.* • *For Your Prayer Time.* • *Trail Markers.*

Sources:

Converge Worldwide (BGC). 216.177.136.28/

Ericson, Carl G. *Harvest on the Prairies: Centennial History of the Baptist Conference.* Chicago, IL: Baptist Conference Press, 1956.

Guston, David, and Martin Erikson, eds. *Fifteen Eventful Years: A Survey of the Baptist General Conference, 1945–1960.* Chicago, IL: Harvest, 1961.

Johnson, Gordon H. *My Church.* Chicago, IL: Harvest, 1963.

Olson, Adolf. *A Centenary History.* Chicago, IL: Baptist Conference Press, 1952.

Colorado Reform Baptist Church

Box 12514, Denver, CO 80212

The Colorado Reform Baptist Church was formed in 1981 by a small group of Baptist congregations that agreed to share a mutual commitment to a loose and free association in order to further common aims, including cooperation in mission and educational work. The church finds its basis in the reformist tradition of Roger Williams (1603–1683) and Anne Hutchinson (1591–1643). Not to be confused with Reformed theology, the reformist tradition is Armenian and stresses the mission of Christ to correct and address the social condition of humanity. Tenets of civil rights and religious liberty are strongly affirmed.

The church is Trinitarian in its theology. It departs from many Baptists by its observance of seven ordinances: baptism, the gifts of the Holy Spirit, marriage, repentance, healing, communion (the Lord's Table), and spiritual vocations (ordination). The church has a congregational polity. A conference, representing all the congregations, meets annually. It selects a board of directors and a bishop to lead the church and oversee the boards and agencies. A very active social action ministry to address the problems of racism, sexism, hunger, poverty, political prisoners, and other issues is supported. Ecumenical activities are carried out through the Association of Baptist Fellowships.

Membership: Not reported. Missions are supported in Costa Rica, Mexico, Colombia, Grand Cayman, and West Germany.

Educational Facilities:

Reform Baptist Theological Seminary, Denver, Colorado.

Periodicals: *Baptist Voice.* • *Roger Williams Review.*

Convention of Original Free Will Baptists

Box 39, Ayden, NC 28513

HISTORY. General Baptists, often known as Free Will Baptists after they arrived in the American colonies, came to North Carolina from England in the late seventeenth century. The first congregation in the Southern colonies was a house church at Cisco Crossroads near Edenton, North Carolina, organized by the Rev. Paul Palmer and some 30 others. Palmer went on to do evangelistic work throughout the colony and organized other churches. In 1852, an association was organized, though most of the churches became part of the Calvinistic Baptists, and a reorganization of the remaining five churches had to take place; churches began meeting as a general conference (of North Carolina). In 1886, this conference divided into a western and eastern conference. Other conferences were formed, in part drawing on work in South Carolina. In 1913, a state convention was organized. It developed a number of projects including the Free Will Baptist Press, an orphanage, an assembly grounds, a college, and a seminary.

For many years the North Carolina Convention was part of the larger Free Will Baptist work and joined in the formation of the National Association of Free Will Baptists Inc. in 1935. However, over the years several areas of tension emerged between the convention and the national association. For example, when the national association decided to establish a college, it was placed in Nashville, Tennessee, rather than in North Carolina. Soon, it was noted, activities began to shift toward Nashville. The North Carolina Baptists had owned and operated a press and published both Sunday school material and the periodical for the denomination. A struggle for control between the press and the national association (and its college graduates) developed and was never fully resolved. Finally, in 1958, the North Carolina Convention and the national association came into open conflict when they took opposite sides in a disturbance in the Edgemont Church at Durham, North Carolina. A lawsuit developed, and in 1961 the convention withdrew from the national association. It became an independent body and eventually assumed its present name.

BELIEFS. The Original Free Will Baptists are at one in doctrine with other Free Will Baptists. The articles of faith affirm human free will and that the status of the elect is conferred on all who have faith in Christ. Three ordinances are observed: baptism by immersion, the Lord's Supper, and footwashing. The church covenant calls upon members to avoid all appearance of evil; to abstain from all sinful amusements; to not engage in the buying, selling, or using of intoxicating beverages; and to be honest in all matters.

The convention is congregational in polity. The convention, however, reserves the right to settle disputes within the local churches where such disputes cannot be settled locally. Churches are organized into conferences and the conferences make up the state convention. The convention oversees the Cragmont Assembly at Black Mountain, a children's home in Middlesex, North Carolina, a retirement home ministry, and several boards and agencies. The Free Will Baptist Press, founded in 1873, is the oldest ministry program. Foreign missions are conducted in Bangladesh, Bulgaria, India, Liberia, Mexico, Nepal, and the Philippines. Home mission programs have included work among Laotian refugees in six states and Canada, and Spanish-speaking work in Florida.

Membership: In 1987, the convention reported 40,000 members and 384 ministers. In 2008, the convention reported serving more than 250 churches in central and eastern North Carolina and Georgia, with extended ministries in California, Minnesota, Mississippi, Florida, and six foreign countries.

Educational Facilities:

Mount Olive College, Mount Olive, North Carolina.

Palawan Bible Institute/College, Palawan, Philippines.

Periodicals: *The Free Will Baptist,* Ayden, North Carolina.

Sources:

Convention of Original Free Will Baptist Churches. www.ofwb.org.

The Articles of Faith and Principles of Church Government for Original Free Will Baptists (of the English General Baptist Heritage). Ayden, NC: Free Will Baptist Press Foundation, 1976.

Barfield, J. M., and Thad Harrison. *History of the Free Will Baptists of North Carolina.* 2 vols. Ayden, NC: Free Will Baptist Press, 1959.

Cherry, Floyd B. *An Introduction to Original Free Will Baptists.* Ayden, NC: Free Will Baptist Press Foundation, 1974.

Picirilli, Robert E. *History of the Free Will Baptist State Associations*. Nashville, TN: Randall House Publications, 1976.

General Association of General Baptists
100 Stinson Dr., Poplar Bluff, MO 63901

The General Association of General Baptists dates to the work of Benoni Stinson (1798–1869). He was a member of a United Baptist group formed in Kentucky in 1801 by the union of Separate Baptists and Regular Baptists. These United Baptists adopted an article of faith that allowed Arminian preaching, which emphasized free will, not predestination. Stinson was baptized in 1820, joined a United Baptist Church in Wayne County, Kentucky, and was ordained in 1821. He then moved to Indiana. The Wabash United Baptist Association, however, would not tolerate his Arminian free-will views, so he organized the independent New Hope Church near Evansville, Indiana. He soon had a thriving congregation. Tension with Indiana's predominantly Calvinistic Baptists led to the founding of other churches with an Arminian perspective.

The articles of the second church, Liberty Church, professed faith in the unlimited atonement that must be apprehended through faith and the final perseverance through grace to glory. The church practiced closed communion. In 1824, the churches that followed Stinson's Arminian tenets organized the Liberty Association of General Baptists. The association's growth was sporadic for a decade but became steady in the 1830s. The movement spread south and west.

Doctrinally, the General Baptists are similar to the Methodists. They believe in a general atonement and practice open communion. Some churches also practice footwashing. The polity is congregational, and churches are organized in local associations. A general association was organized in 1870. Ordinations are approved by local bodies of ministers and deacons.

The general association is the highest cooperative agency in the church. The association's program is implemented by the Council of Associations elected by local associations. The Council publishes the *General Baptist Messenger*. The foreign mission board conducts work in Jamaica, India, the Philippines, Mexico, Honduras, and Saipan, and there is a Bible college at Davao City in the Philippine Islands. The association sponsors two nursing homes, one in Campbell, Missouri, and the other in Mt. Carmel, Illinois.

Membership: In 2006 the association reported 52,279 members, 860 congregations, and 849 ministers.

Educational Facilities:

Oakland City University, Oakland City, Indiana.

General Baptist Bible College, Davao City, Philippines.

Matigsalug Bible Institute, Davao City, Philippines.

Periodicals: *Messenger*. • *Capsule*. • *Voice*.

Sources:
General Association of General Baptists. www.generalbaptist.com.

Doctrines and Usages of General Baptists and Worker's Handbook. Poplar Bluff, MO: General Baptist Press, 1970.

Latch, Ollie. *History of the General Baptists*. Poplar Bluff, MO: General Baptist Press, 1954.

General Association of Six-Principle Baptist Churches, Inc.
c/o Kenneth C. Allen, 88 Lee Rd. 419, Opelika, AL 36804

In 1652 the historic Providence Baptist Church, once associated with Roger Williams (1603–1683), split because of the development within the church of an Arminian majority who held to the six principles of Hebrews 6:1–2, that is, repentance, faith, baptism, the laying on of hands, resurrection of the dead, and a final judgment. Soon other churches were organized, and conferences were formed in Rhode Island, Massachusetts, and Pennsylvania.

The distinctive doctrine of the six principles is the laying on of hands. This act is performed when members are received into the church, as a sign of the reception of the gifts of the Holy Spirit. Church polity is congregational, but the conference composed of delegates of the various churches retains specific powers. A council of ordained ministers approves all ordinations. Decisions of the conference on questions submitted to it are final. Never a large denomination, the 1954 Rhode Island Conference lifted their ban on communing with other Christians. Churches assimilated into the broader Baptist community, and by 1969 there were only three Six-Principle Baptist congregations (all in Rhode Island) with 134 members. Eventually, only Stony Lane Six-Principle Baptist Church, in North Kingstown, Rhode Island, would remain. During the mid-1990s, the Six-Principle Baptist Church as a denomination virtually ceased to exist when Stony Lane became an independent Baptist congregation.

In 2001 some ordained evangelical Christian ministers began a reorganization of the movement. They incorporated and officially renamed the denomination on July 10, 2003, as the General Association of Six-Principle Baptist Churches, Inc. Since then, the denomination has steadily grown. In 2008, there are associations of Six-Principle Baptist Churches in Alabama, Indiana, New York, and Florida.

Membership: There are 19 clergy and three churches in the United States, four churches and five clergy in Kenya, and one clergyman in Korea.

Sources:
Six-Principle Baptists. spbaptist.tripod.com/

Nelton, Robert Elliott. *A History of the General Six Principle Baptists in America*. PhD diss., Southwestern Baptist Theological Seminary, Dallas, Texas, 1958.

National Association of Free Will Baptists, Inc.
PO Box 5002, Antioch, TN 37011-5002

The National Association of Free Will Baptists dates to 1727 when Paul Palmer organized a church at Chowan County, North Carolina. The church grew and spread. A yearly meeting was formed in 1752 and included 16 churches. A general conference was formed in 1827 and a doctrinal statement issued in 1834. For many years, these churches were in communion with the Free Will Baptists in the North. But most of the northern brethren were absorbed by the inclusive Northern Baptist Convention, now the American Baptist Churches in the U.S.A.

In 1916 the general conference expanded by the addition of nonaligned churches in Oklahoma, Texas, Missouri, Kansas, and North Carolina, and formed the General Association of Free Will Baptists. Controversy developed between the churches in Tennessee and North Carolina over foot washing as an ordinance, and in 1921, the churches in the South withdrew and formed the Eastern General Conference. Working out a settlement took 14 years, but in 1935, the National Association of Free Will Baptists was formed.

The Free Will Baptist movement developed in the Maritime Provinces of Canada in the early nineteenth century. In 1932 a number of groups came together to form the Christian Conference Church, which became the Free Christian Baptists in 1847. Among the more highly regarded ministers in the latter half of the century was George W. Orser of Carleton County, New Brunswick. Orser found himself in the middle of controversy as he began to call for an apostolic or primitive church order. He opposed salaries, and, in large part, education for ministers. In the 1870s, Orser withdrew from the church and formed the Primitive Baptist Conference of New Brunswick, Maine, and Nova Scotia. The headquarters was eventually established as the Saint John Valley Bible Camp at Hartland, New Brunswick. In 1981, after a century of independent existence, the conference voted to join the National Association of Free Will Baptists and became the Atlantic Canada Association of Free Will Baptists.

BELIEFS. In 1935 the association adopted a statement titled "The Faith of Free Will Baptists," which, with minor amendments added over the years, remains its position. It affirms a belief in an infallible and inerrant Bible, God as the Father, Son and Holy Spirit, a universal atonement in Christ, salvation by grace through faith, the possibility of a believer falling from a state of grace into unbelief, tithing, the resurrection, and final judgment. There are three ordinances: baptism, the Lord's Supper, and foot washing.

ORGANIZATION. The association is organized by congregations that freely associate together in district, state, and national associations. The national association conducts foreign missions in Spain, Panama, Cuba, Brazil, Uruguay, France, the Ivory Coast, India, and Japan. North American missions are sponsored in Canada, Mexico, Alaska, Hawaii, Puerto Rico, and the Virgin Islands.

In 1992 the National Association of Free Will Baptists' executive secretary, Melvin Worthington, approached Foreign Missions about an international consortium to consider an international organization of Free Will Baptists. The meeting resulted in the "Panama Declaration," a doctrinal statement and a statement of intent to move forward with organization. In 1995 delegates officially organized the International Fellowship of Free Will Baptist Churches Inc. Members decided upon a triennial general assembly hosted by various member countries. John Poole (Brazil) was chosen as president and Daniel Dorati (Panama) as vice president. During 2004, representatives from Brazil, Canada, Coté d'Ivoire, Cuba, France, Japan, Mexico, Panama, Russia, Spain, the United States, and Uruguay met in Panama City, Panama.

Membership: In 2003 the association reported 204,353 members, 2,461 churches, and 4,035 ministers in the United States. There are 12 congregations and 323 members in the Atlantic Canada Association.

Educational Facilities:

Free Will Baptist Bible College, Nashville, Tennessee.

Hillsdale Free Will Baptist College, Moore, Oklahoma.

California Christian College, Fresno, California.

Southeastern Free Will Baptist College, Wendell, North Carolina.

Periodicals: *ONE Magazine*.

Sources:

National Association of Free Will Baptists. www.nafwb.org/

Buzzell, John. *The Life of Elder Benjamin Randall*. Hampton, New Brunswick, Canada: Atlantic Press, 1970.

Cox, Violet. *Missions on the Move*. Nashville, TN: Woman's National Auxiliary Convention, 1966.

Davidson, William F. *The Free Will Baptists in America, 1727–1984*. Nashville, TN: Randall House, 1985.

National Association of Free Will Baptists. *A Treatise of the Faith and Practices of the Free Will Baptists*. Nashville, TN: Author, 2001.

Picirilli, Robert E. *History of Free Will Baptist Associations*. Nashville, TN: Randall House, 1976.

United American Free Will Baptist Church
207 W Bella Vista St., Lakeland, FL 33805

During the early seventeenth century, a pastor and his congregation from Wales came and settled on the Delaware River. Later, members from this group preached the Arminian doctrine. Paul Palmer organized the first Free Will Baptist Church in 1727 in Chowan County, North Carolina. Benjamin Randall (1749–1808) organized the first Free Will Baptist church in New Durham, New Hampshire, in 1780. The General Conference of Free Will Baptists was organized in 1827. When African Americans were freed from slavery, they organized their own churches. In 1898, the first Negro General Conference grew into the United American Free Will Baptist Conference, incorporated in 1968. Its founding fathers are Rev. Elliott Titus Brown (1909–1972) and Rev. S. H. Edmondson (b. 1869).

Like its parent body, it is Arminian in theology and practices foot washing and anointing the sick with oil. The congregational polity was modified within a system of district, quarterly, annual, and general conferences. The local church is autonomous in regard to business, elections, and form of government, but the conferences have the power to decide the questions of doctrine.

Membership: In 2008 there were 74 clergy and 41 churches.

Periodicals: *The Free Will Baptist*. Available from 3928 Lee St., Ayden, NC 28513.

Sources:

United Free Will Baptist Church General Conference. www.uafwbc.org/

United Baptists
No central headquarters.

The United Baptists were formed by a union of the Separate Baptists and the Regular Baptists in Virginia in 1787. The Separate Baptists were former Congregationalists who became Baptists. The Regular Baptists claimed to represent the Baptists before dissension over Calvinist and Arminian beliefs split many Baptist bodies. In 1769, the Ketocton Association of Regular Baptists made the first overtures toward union with the Separate Baptists. Because there was little practical difference between the groups, union was ultimately consummated. Most of the United Baptist groups dropped the term "United" after the Stone-Campbell Movement split the Baptists, and they exist within larger Baptist bodies, mainly the Southern Baptist Convention. However, several United Baptist associations in Kentucky, West Virginia, and Missouri persist.

The churches follow a congregational polity and most belong to associations. They follow the early Baptists in doctrine; they lean toward Arminianism. They practice footwashing. Communion is closed in some associations but others are becoming less strict. The Cumberland River Association supports the Cumberland Baptist Institute in Somerset, Kentucky.

Membership: Not reported. In 1990 there were 436 congregations and 68,187 adherents. As of November 2007, United Baptist researcher Rev. David White reported 46 associations.

Educational Facilities:

Cumberland Baptist Institute, Somerset, Kentucky.

Sources:

United Baptist Associations. www.unitedbaptists.org.

❄ Seventh Day Baptists

Seventh Day Baptist General Conference USA and Canada
Seventh Day Baptist Center, 3120 Kennedy Rd., PO Box 1678, Janesville, WI 53547

During the mid-seventeenth century, the Separatist movement in England included such men as James Ockford, William Saller, Peter Chamberlain, Francis Bampfield, and Edward and Joseph Stennett. They believed biblical Christianity required that they keep the seventh day (Saturday) as the Sabbath. The first church of record holding this conviction was the Mill Yard church, founded about 1650 in London. In December 1671, Stephen Mumford and his wife were joined with five others to establish the first Seventh Day Baptist church in America. The churches formed a general conference in 1802. They differ from other Baptists only in the keeping of the Sabbath.

In 1821 the denomination began publishing The Sabbath Recorder. The current missionary society was formed in 1843. Missionaries have served in China, Finland, Jamaica, Guyana, Malawi, Ghana, India, Myanmar, the Philippines, Australia, and New Zealand. In 1965 a world federation of Seventh Day Baptist conferences was formed, which has grown to nearly twenty conferences. The Seventh Day Baptists' Education Society had three schools that became colleges at Alfred, New York; Milton, Wisconsin; and Salem, West Virginia. A seminary was created at Alfred University in 1871.

Seventh Day Baptists were charter members of the Federal, the National, and the World Councils of Churches. The denomination withdrew membership during the 1970s because the councils were perceived as violating the autonomy of the local church, along with other principles of thought and practice. This withdrawal strengthened their relationship with the Baptist World Alliance, the North American Baptist Fellowship, the Baptist Joint Committee on Public Affairs, and related groups involving women and societal interests.

The Seventh Day Baptist General Conference is a conference of churches, and voting on most issues during the annual sessions is done by member church delegates. A general council acts for the conference between sessions. The council includes representatives from the Missionary Society, the Board of Christian Education, the Tract and Communication Council, the Council on Ministry, the Women's Society, and the Memorial Fund Trustees. The conference is divided into eight associations. The Seventh Day Baptists established their headquarters for the first time during the 1920s in Plainfield, New Jersey. In 1982 the headquarters was moved to Janesville, Wisconsin, and the Plainfield property was sold. The new center houses the various denominational agencies, including the publishing house. The Tract and Communication Council, a major distributor of Sabbath literature in America and around the world, merged into the general conference in 1986.

Membership: In 2004 there were 74 clergy, 97 churches, and 5,900 members. There are churches in more than 20 countries.

Periodicals: *The Sabbath Recorder*.

Sources:

Seventh Day Baptist: General Conference of the United States and Canada. www.seventhdaybaptist.org/7db/Default_EN.asp

A Manual for Procedures for Seventh Day Baptist Churches. Plainfield, NJ: Seventh Day Baptists General Conference, n.d.

Saunders, Herbert E. *The Sabbath: Symbol of Creation and Recreation*. Plainfield, NJ: American Sabbath Tract Society, 1970.

Seventh Day Baptists in Europe and America: A Series of Historical Papers. 3 vols. Plainfield, NJ: American Sabbath Tract Society, 1910–1972.

Stillman, Karl G. *Seventh Day Baptists in New England, 1671–1971*. Plainfield, NJ: Seventh Day Baptist Historical Society, 1971.

Thomsen, Russel J. *Seventh Day Baptists: Their Legacy to Adventists*. Mountain View, CA: Pacific Press, 1971.

Seventh Day Baptists (German)
Current address not obtained for this edition.

In 1764, as the work of Johann Conrad Beissel at the Ephrata colony declined, a group of German Seventh Day Baptists settled at Snow Hill, Pennsylvania. In 1800, a society was organized. From here, other congregations were organized (five by 1900). The German Baptists differ from their English counterparts in their practice of triune forward immersion, footwashing at the communion service, the anointing of the sick, the blessing of infants, and induction into the ministry by a personal request for ordination rather than election by the congregation. They are also noncombatants. An annual delegated general conference is held.

Membership: Not reported.

Christian Church

Christadelphians
4 Mountain Park Ave., Hamilton, ON, Canada L9A 1A2

Alternate Address: Christadelphian Action Society, 904 Woodview Ct., Mahomet, IL 61853.

The Christadelphians are a body of people who believe the Bible to be the divinely inspired word of God, written by "Holy men who spoke as they were moved by the Holy Spirit" (2 Pet. 1:21). They believe the Old Testament presents God's plan to establish His Kingdom on earth in accordance with the promises He made to Abraham and David, and that the New Testament declares how that plan works out in Jesus Christ, who they said died a sacrificial death to redeem sinners. They believe in the personal return of Jesus Christ as King, to establish "all that God spoke by the mouth of his holy prophets from of old" (Acts 3:21). They feel that at Christ's return, many of the dead will be raised by the power of God to be judged, and those God deems worthy will be welcomed into eternal life in the Kingdom on earth.

Christadelphians believe in the mortality of man; in spiritual rebirth requiring belief and immersion in the name of Jesus; and in a godly walk in this life. There are no ordained clergy. The group is loosely organized worldwide in a confederation of autonomous congregations in approximately 100 countries. Members are conscientiously opposed to war. They endeavor to be enthusiastic in work, loyal in marriage, generous in giving, dedicated to preaching, and cheerful in living.

The denomination was organized in 1844 by Dr. John Thomas, who came to the United States from England and who devoted his life to a search for the truth of God from the Bible. Thomas claimed no special revelation or position. He did not claim himself a prophet. The name *Christadelphian*, adopted in 1864, means Brethren in Christ. Initially limited mostly to English-speaking countries, the denomination now exists worldwide.

In 1898 the prominent Birmingham, England, Ecclesia of the Christadelphians adopted an amendment to their statement of faith to define more precisely who will be raised for a resurrectional judgement at the Second Coming of Jesus Christ. The original unamended statement had read: "That at the appearing of Christ, prior to the establishment of the Kingdom, the responsible (faithful and unfaithful) dead and living of both classes, will, be summoned before his judgment seat . . . ." The amendment suggested "That at the appearing of Christ prior to the establishment of the Kingdom, the responsible (namely those who know the revealed will of God and have been called upon to submit to it) dead and living—obedient and unobedient—will be summoned before the judgment seat . . . ."

The introduction of this amendment split the movement. Those who retain the unamended statement refuse to define with certainty a resurrectional judgment of any except those (in this dispensation) who have entered into a covenant relationship with God by baptism. Those who adopted the amendment believe that the basis of resurrection is response to enlightenment, understanding, and knowledge of God's Word.

In North America there are two Christadelphian groups, Central and Unamended. In 2001 virtually all the Unamended Christadelphians resided in North America. They are served by a monthly periodical, *The Christadelphian Advocate*, begun in 1885 by Thomas Williams, who opposed the amendment and indefatigably tried to heal the division by proposing a more satisfactory definition of the basis for resurrectional judgment.

Talks aimed at reunion of the two groups of Christadelphians were pursued in the 1970s and 1980s. Agreement was reached on various points that had come to distinguish them concerning fellowship, inspiration, baptism, and the nature of man. However, in the end, no agreement was reached on either the primary issue of resurrectional responsibility or new differences that had developed on matters related to Christ's atonement.

Christadelphians are organized congregationally, and the authority in all matters rests in the collective hands of the members of each local ecclesia (congregation). There is no central headquarters, but the periodicals serving the fellowship as a whole form a network to keep the ecclesias in communication with each other. Each congregation elects serving brethren to perform various tasks, as there is no paid clergy.

Primary activities in North America include Sunday worship and Sunday schools, mid-week Bible classes, Bible schools, and interecclesial gatherings. The Williamsburg Christadelphian Foundation sponsors and assists charitable and preaching activities in many parts of the world by itself and in conjunction with the outreach work of the Christadelphian Bible missions.

Membership: Not reported.

Periodicals: *The Christadelphian Advocate* • *The Christadelphian Truth Gleaner* (quarterly) • *The Sanctuary Keeper* (quarterly) • *Christadelphian Tidings*

Sources:

Christadelphia Worldwide. www.christadelphia.org.

Williamsburg Christadelphian Foundation. www.wcfoundation.org.

The Christadelphian Tidings of the Kingdom of God. www.tidings.org.

The Christadelphian Statement of Faith. Quincy, MA: Christadelphian Advocate Publications, n.d.

Roberts, Robert. *A Guide to the Formation and Conduct of Christadelphian Ecclesias*. Birmingham, U.K.: Christadelphian, 1922.

Roberts, Robert, and J. J. Andrew. *Resurrectional Responsibility*. Birmingham, U.K.: Authors, 1894.

Christadelphians—Amended Fellowship

c/o Detroit Christadelphian Book Supply, 14676 Berwick St., Livonia, MI 48154

The Christadelphians trace their history to John Thomas (1805–1871), a British doctor who as a result of his suffering a shipwreck on his way to the United States from Britain became interested in religion. His exploration over several decades led him in the 1860s to what he believed to be the biblical truth that the apostles believed in the first century. The name "Christadelphian," meaning "Christ's Brethren" or "Brethren in Christ" in biblical Greek, originated during the American Civil War. Some of Thomas's followers used the name when asked by the United States government for the name of an organized religion, a requirement of all conscientious objectors.

During 1898, the prominent Birmingham, England, ecclesia of the Christadelphians accepted an amended text of the statement of faith then used by Christadelphians which affirmed that some who had not been justified by the blood of Christ would be resurrected for judgment by Christ prior to His establishment of His kingdom. The revised text had been drawn up by Robert Roberts, the editor of The Christadelphian, the group's leading periodical. The majority of Christadelphians accepted Roberts's position. This divided a then existing fellowship into two fellowships, the "Amended" or "Central," and the "Unamended" or "Advocate."

The Christadelphians have attained form uniqueness (and resulting criticism) among Christian religions in that they believe in the absolute mortality of the soul. Christadelphians believe that those who are not "called" to Christ have no hope of eternal reward nor basis for post-death judgment or punishment. Those outside of Christ, they believe, perish like all other forms of life on this planet. Christadelphians call their beliefs the "Hope of Israel," i.e., the hope of the descendants of Abraham, Isaac, and Jacob as revealed in the Covenants to Abraham, Isaac, Jacob, David, etc. These promises or covenants reveal the biblical hope of resurrection to judgment at the Last Day, and possible eternal life on earth with Abraham's descendants in the restored kingdom of God on this earth, centered in the land of Israel with its capital in Jerusalem. The doctrine of the absolute mortality of the soul and the principles of "calling" are then the basis for additional unique beliefs held by the Christadelphians.

Christadelphians have fairly autonomous congregations (Ecclesias) without a paid clergy. Groups of Ecclessias form Fellowships within the community which share specific religious practices and small doctrinal differences. The largest of these Fellowships is the Amended Christadelphians. The main magazine of the Amended Christadelphians is *The Christadelphian Magazine* published in Great Britain. North America has an additional magazine called the Christadelphian Tidings and Australia has a magazine called The Logos Magazine.

Christadelphians are found mainly in the English-speaking world of the United States, Canada, Great Britain, Australia, New Zealand, and Africa. Christadelphians have active missionaries in many African, South American, Asian and European countries.

Membership: In 2005 there were approximately 4,500 members in the United States. They report affiliated work in 50 countries.

Periodicals: *Christadelphian Tidings*. Send orders to Box 250305, Franklin, MI 48025.

Sources:

Christadelphian Hymn Book. Birmingham, England: Christadelphian, 1964.

A Declaration of the Truth Revealed in the Bible. Birmingham, England: Christadelphian, 1967.

One Hundred Years of The Christadelphian. Birmingham, England: Christadelphian, 1964.

Tennant, Harry. *The Christadelphians: What They Believe and Preach*. Birmingham, England: The Christadelphian, 1986.

Christadelphia World Life. www.christadelphia.org.

Christian Church (Disciples of Christ)

130 E Washington St., Box 1986, Indianapolis, IN 46206-1986

Continuing the thrust of the International Convention of Christian Churches (described in the introductory material for this chapter) is the Christian Church (Disciples of Christ). At the 1968 annual assembly of the International Assembly, a restructuring of the Convention was accomplished. The convention was voted out of existence and was replaced with a relatively strong international structure. While retaining a congregational polity, the Disciples were no longer a loosely formed confederation of individuals and congregations with a delegated general assembly. The change is a recognition by the Disciples that they have become another denomination.

The Disciples' general assembly meets every two years and is composed of representatives from each congregational region and all ministers. It elects a general board consisting of 250 members, which in turn elects an administrative committee to implement programs.

The church is a member of the National Council of Churches and the World Council of Churches.

Membership: In 2000 the church reported 823,018 members, 3,781 congregations, and 7,053 ministers.

Educational Facilities:

Colleges and Universities

Barton College, Wilson, North Carolina.

Bethany College, Lindsborg, Kansas.

Chapman University, Orange, California.

Columbia College, Columbia, Missouri.

Culver-Stockton College, Canton, Missouri.

Drury University, Springfield, Missouri.

Eureka College, Eureka, Illinois.

Hiram College, Hiram, Ohio.

Jarvis Christian College, Hawkins, Texas.

Lynchburg College, Lynchburg, Virginia.

Midway College, Midway, Kentucky.

Texas Christian University, Forth Worth, Texas.

Transylvania University, Lexington, Kentucky.

William Woods University, Fulton, Missouri.

Theological Institutions

Brite Divinity School, Fort Worth, Texas.

Christian Theological Seminary, Indianapolis, Indiana.

Disciples Divinity House of the University of Chicago, Chicago, Illinois.

Disciples Divinity House at Vanderbilt, Nashville, Tennessee.

Disciples Seminary Foundation, San Diego, California.

Lexington Theological Seminary, Lexington, Kentucky.

Phillips Theological Seminary, Tulsa, Oklahoma.

Affiliated Institutions

Atlanta United Divinity Center, Decatur, Georgia.

Drake University, Des Moines, Iowa.

Northwest Christian College, Eugene, Oregon.

Seminario Evangelico de Puerto Rico, San Juan, Puerto Rico.

Tougaloo College, Tougaloo, Mississippi.

Yale University Divinity School, New Haven, Connecticut.

Remarks: The 2005 General Assembly of the Christian Church (Disciples of Christ) meeting in Portland, Oregon, elected Sharon Watkins as the first woman to hold the position of General Minister and President.

Sources:

Christian Church (Disciples of Christ). www.disciples.org/.

Cummins, D. Duane. *Handbook for Today's Disciples.* St. Louis, MO: Chalice Press, 1991.

Harrell, David Edwin, Jr. *The Social Sources of Division in the Disciples of Christ, 1865–1900.* Atlanta, GA: Publishing Systems, 1973.

McAllister, Lester G., and William E. Tucker. *Journey in Faith.* St. Louis, MO: Bethany Press, 1975.

Sprague, William L., and Jane Heaton, eds. *Our Christian Church Heritage: Journeying in Faith.* St. Louis, MO: Christian Board of Publication, [1978].

Christian Church (Disciples of Christ) in Canada
PO Box 25087, London, Ontario, Canada N6C 6A8

The Christian Church (Disciples of Christ) in Canada operates both as an autonomous denomination in Canada and as one regional branch of the larger Christian Church (Disciples of Christ), whose international headquarters is in Indianapolis, Indiana. Disciples of Christ congregations first appeared in Canada in the Maritime Provinces, mainly due to the efforts of Scottish Baptist immigrants. The initial Canadian congregation of what would become the Disciples of Christ was formed near Charlottetown, Prince Edward Island, in 1811, by Alexander Crawford. These Scottish immigrants proved receptive to the Restoration Movement in the United States, an early nineteenth-century movement led by Americans Barton Stone (1772–1844) and Alexander Campbell (1788–1866). Through the 1830s, many of these Scottish Baptist churches became a part of the larger Restoration Movement. Once started, the growth of the church was relatively slow and the distances among congregations large.

In 1922 the all-Canada movement began as a way to coordinate and unite the various churches and their ministries. At the same time, options were discussed to unite with the United Church of Canada (formed in 1925), the Baptists, and even the Anglicans, but these discussions largely ended after 1925.

Disciples strive for a New Testament church. They believe that creeds and theological formulas divide the body of Christ, and thus consider the Bible to be the only authority for faith and practice. This belief is reflected in the popular disciple statement, "Where the scriptures speak, we speak; where the scriptures are silent, we are silent." The church embraces the slogan, "No creed but Christ," and has no official doctrinal statement of faith. When individuals become members of the church, they are simply asked if they believe in Jesus Christ as their savior; and upon answering yes, they are accepted as members of the church. Baptism is limited to those old enough to make a profession of faith, and is commonly administered by immersion. The Lord's Supper is a weekly performed ordinance. Baptism and the Lord's Supper as ordinances are considered to be in obedience to Christ's commands. Lay elders and deacons, both male and female, provide leadership for the church and preside over the ordinances.

The Christian Church (Disciples of Christ) in Canada is a member of the Canadian Council of Churches, the World Council of Churches, and the Disciples Ecumenical Consultative Council.

Membership: On January 1, 2006, there were 25 congregations and 30 pastors in Canada, with 2,606 members. Congregations are located in six provinces, the greatest number being in Ontario.

Periodicals: *Canadian Disciple*, PO Box 23030, 417 Wellington St., St. Thomas, ON, Canada N5R 6A3.

Sources:

Disciples of Christ in Canada. www.disciplesofchrist.ca/

Butchart, Reuben. *The Disciples of Christ in Canada since 1830.* Toronto, Ontario, Canada: Churches of Christ (Disciples), 1949.

McAllister, L. G., and W. E. Tucker. *Journey in Faith: A History of the Christian Church Disciples of Christ.* St. Louis, MO: Bethany Press, 1975.

Christian Churches and Churches of Christ
110 Boggs Ln., Ste. 330, Cincinnati, OH 45246

Christian churches and churches of Christ constitute one branch of the restorationist movement that emerged among protestant and free church leaders in the early nineteenth century on the American frontier. Prominent leaders of the movement included Barton Stone (1772–1844, a former Presbyterian), Thomas Campbell (1763–1854) and his son Alexander Campbell (1788–1866) (both also former Presbyterians), and evangelist Walter Scott (1796–1861, a former Baptist). The movement was originally centered in Ohio, Pennsylvania, and Kentucky.

As the movement developed, the leaders rejected denominational structures and labels, preferring to call themselves simply Christians or disciples of Christ, and the congregations as churches of Christ or Christian churches. Accepting the New Testament as the sole authority of faith and resting on the scriptural affirmation that Jesus Christ is the son of God and head of all things for his church, they accepted no creeds and wrote no formal confessions, though they certainly held two strong positions on various sectarian issues drawn from their reading and interpretation of the Bible. They practiced baptism by immersion. The ordinance of the Lord's Supper was observed weekly each Lord's Day (Sunday). They were organized congregationally. Each congregation was considered autonomous and led by self-chosen elders and deacons. Periodicals, schools, and the various benevolence enterprises tended to be private self-supporting concerns, the congregations eschewing any formal overall coordinated cooperative activities. Individuals and individual congregations frequently and informally cooperate on a variety of concerns.

Tensions within the movement in the early twentieth century led to its division into three major branches. The introduction of organs of the church in the late nineteenth century became a major issue that led many congregations to separate around 1906, and they are today known as the Churches of Christ (Non-Instrumental). In the ensuing years they have further divided into a number of factions. Disagreements over issues of polity led to a second division. One group, without giving up its congregational polity, began to develop a central office and official structures for coordination of activity and the collection of money, and a convention representative of all the congregations in the fellowship. That process of centralization continued through most of the twentieth century and culminated in 1968 with the restructuring of what is now known as the Christian Church (Disciples of Christ). Those who rejected that move toward centralization are now known as the Christian churches and churches of Christ. The churches are known for their biblical conservatism in relation to the more liberal Christian Church (Disciples of Christ) and have made no attempt to relate to the National Council of Churches and World Council of Churches.

Working from the voluntary activity of members and congregations and without any central office, the churches have been able to build an impressive ministry beyond the local churches. They support approximately 1,500 missionaries in 53 countries. They have established 38 colleges and three graduate seminaries. They maintain 40 homes for children, 20 homes for the aged, eight nursing homes, and three hospitals in the United States, plus a variety of related facilities in other countries. None of these agencies are official, none are supported by all the congregations. Each has arisen as individuals have seen a need and have been able to solicit support within the fellowship. They are primarily supported by those congregations that choose to avail themselves of their services. In like measure, the churches support numerous Christian camps, campus ministry programs, and radio and television ministries.

The same approach operates at various national, regional, and state conventions and rallies that bring together people for inspiration, instruction, and fellowship, and without the adoption of any positions or the transaction of any business. Among the major conventions nationally is the North American Christian Convention, which met occasionally from 1927 to 1948 and has met annually since 1950. An office in Cincinnati, Ohio, exists merely to manage the mechanics of the convention, which is a significant effort, since some 20,000 persons regularly attend its four-day program. A National Missionary Convention serving the same constituency with a mission-oriented program has met annually since 1947.

A number of publishers serve the Christian churches and churches of Christ. Among the most important is Standard Publishing in Cincinnati, which produces books and study materials especially directed to their needs. It also publishes two major periodicals, *Christian Standard* and *The Lookout*. Mission Services Association in Knoxville, Tennessee, publishes many items concerned with missions.

Membership: Not reported.

Educational Facilities:

Alaska Christian Bible Institute, Houston, Alaska.

Alberta Bible College, Calgary, Alberta.

Atlanta Christian College, East Point, Georgia.

Bluefield College of Evangelism, Bluefield, West Virginia.

Boise Bible College, Boise, Idaho.

Central Christian College of the Bible, Moberly, Missouri.

Christian Institute of Biblical Studies, Louisville, Kentucky.

Cinncinnati Bible College and Seminary, Cincinnati, Ohio.

Colegio Biblico, Eagle Pass, Texas.

College of the Scriptures, Louisville, Kentucky.

Dallas Christian College, Dallas, Texas.

Eastern Christian College, Bel Air, Maryland.

Emmanuel School of Religion, Johnson City, Tennessee.

Florida Christian College, Kissimmee, Florida.

Great Lakes Christian College, Lansing, Michigan.

Grundy Bible Institute, Grundy, Virginia.

Johnson Bible College, Knoxville, Tennessee.

Kentucky Christian College, Grayson, Kentucky.

Lincoln Christian College and Seminary, Lincoln, Illinois.

Louisville Bible College, Louisville, Kentucky.

Manhattan Christian College, Manhattan, Kansas.

Maritime Christian College, Charlottetown, Prince Edward Island.

Mid-South Christian College, Memphis, Tennessee.

Midwestern School of Evangelism, Ottumwa, Iowa.

Milligan College, Milligan, Tennessee.

Minnesota Bible College, Rochester, Minnesota.

Nebraska Christian College, Norfolk, Nebraska.

Northwest Christian College, Eugene, Oregon.

Northwest College of the Bible, Portland, Oregon.

Ontario Christian Seminary, Toronto, Ontario.

Ozark Christian College, Joplin, Missouri.

Pacific Christian College, Fullerton, California.

Platte Valley Bible College, Scottsbluff, Nebraska.

Puget Sound Christian College, Edmonds, Washington.

Roanoke Bible College, Elizabeth City, North Carolina.

St. Louis Christian College, Florissant, Missouri.

San Jose Christian College, San Jose, California.

Summit Theological Seminary, Peru, Indiana.

Winston-Salem Bible College, Winston-Salem, North Carolina.

Periodicals: *Christian Standard*. Available from Standard Publishing, 8121 Hamilton Ave., Cincinnati, OH 45231. • *The Lookout*. Available from Standard Publishing. • *The Restoration Herald*. Available from Christian Restoration Association, 5664 Cheviot Rd., Cincinnati, OH 45147. • *Horizons*. Available from Mission Services Association, Box 2427, Knoxville, TN 37901-2427. • *One Body*. Available from College Press Publishing Co., Box 113, Joplin, MO 64802.

Sources:

Dowling, Enos E. *The Restoration Movement*. Cincinnati, OH: Standard Publishing, 1964.

Leggett, Marshall. *Introduction to the Restoration Ideal*. Cincinnati, OH: Standard Publishing, 1986.

Murch, James DeForest. *Christians Only*. Cincinnati, OH: Standard Publishing, 1962.

NACC, History and Purpose. Cincinnati, OH: North American Christian Convention, 1973.

Walker, Dean E. *Adventuring for Christian Unity*. Cincinnati, OH: Standard Publishing, 1935.

Weishimer, P. H. *Concerning the Disciples*. Cincinnati, OH: Standard Publishing, 1935.

Christian Congregation

Current address not obtained for this edition.

HISTORY. The Christian Congregation claims to be the oldest denominational evangelistic association in the United States. Its work as an unincorporated religious society dates to 1789. It was formally constituted in 1887 during a period when leaders such as Isaac V. Smith, John Chapman, and John L. Puckett were active in the Ohio River Valley. During the early nineteenth century, the group became loosely identified with the Barton Stone (1772–1844) movement that later institutionalized as the Christian Church (Disciples of Christ), though never organically associated. The first Christian Congregation was formally organized in Kokomo, Indiana, by former members of the Christian Church. They sought a means of union on a noncreedal and nondenominational basis. Beginning with the new commandment of John 13: 34–35, they asserted that the church is founded not upon doctrinal agreement, creeds, church claims, names, or rites, but solely upon the individual's relation with God.

BELIEFS. The basis of this Christian fellowship is love toward one another. The church has doctrinally taken on a universalist, but strongly biblical, perspective. Ethically activated, the perspective has led to a central emphasis upon respect for life and a resultant condemnation of abortion, capital punishment, and all warfare.

ORGANIZATION. The Christian Congregation follows a congregational polity as a "centralized congregational assembly." Local congregations are semiautonomous. The Bible Colportage Service distributes bibles, Bible helps, and literature for field workers. Most congregations are located in either the inner-city areas of metropolitan complexes or in relatively neglected rural and mountainous regions.

Membership: Not reported.

Churches of Christ (Non-Instrumental)
c/o Gospel Advocate, Box 150, Nashville, TN 37202

Churches of Christ (Non-Instrumental) emerged from the more encompassing American Restoration Movement in 1906. Congregations are autonomous, with identification and association based only on shared beliefs and practices. The churches of Christ continue to represent a conservative approach to the Bible.

In the early 1800s, many religious leaders in the United States independently sought to remove any part of religion that was not authorized by the Bible. Thomas Campbell's (1763–1854) phrase, "Where the Scriptures speak, we speak; where the Scriptures are silent, we are silent," became an identifying motto for those in what came to be known as the American Restoration Movement. Two names in particular rose to prominence for their leadership in this movement: Barton W. Stone (1772–1844) and Alexander Campbell (1788–1866). As interest grew in worshiping according to the Bible, the groups led by these men met for four days during January 1832, in Lexington, Kentucky. Recognizing their common approach to Scripture, they united in fellowship and came to be referred to as the Disciples of Christ or Christian Church.

Unity and growth characterized the church until 1849, when it founded the American Christian Missionary Society in Cincinnati, Ohio. This move was the first of many changes that transformed the Christian Church during a period of a few decades. The opponents of the society did not believe that the Bible authorized organizations outside the church to do its work.

The social and political divisions of American society during and after the Civil War further strained the unity of the Restoration Movement. Most of those in the North followed a continually more progressive approach, whereas Christians in the South took a more strict interpretation of the Bible. Two religious journals mirrored this divide. In 1866 Isaac Errett (1820–1888) became editor of *The Christian Standard*, which was sympathetic to the churches in the North. Also in 1866, David Lipscomb (1831–1917) became editor of the *Gospel Advocate*, the leading voice among conservatives.

Errett and Lipscomb differed on many points of doctrine. Errett believed in a one-man pastoral leadership, whereas Lipscomb was opposed to a professional clergy. Errett promoted liturgical practices and instrumental music in worship in contrast to Lipscomb, who argued for maintaining simplicity of worship and the use of vocal music only. Errett had encouraged women in Detroit to take an active public role in worship, whereas Lipscomb believed in exclusive male leadership. Finally, Errett accepted the unimmersed as Christians. Lipscomb taught that baptism was necessary for the remission of sins. By the end of the nineteenth century, these differing approaches to the authority of Scripture led to recognized division. The federal government listed the Christian Church and the churches of Christ separately in the 1906 religious census.

Churches of Christ grew substantially from the 159,000 reported in the 1906 census through the 1950s. Missionaries were sent to Africa and Japan before World War II. After 1945, churches sent teachers to Germany, Italy, and Japan in increased numbers. Domestically, the war years spread churches of Christ to most corners of the United States. Churches of Christ have been active in education and missions.

In the last quarter of the twentieth century, some congregations and institutions among the churches of Christ began to accept a more permissive view of Scripture. These changes closely mirrored those that had divided the churches of Christ from the Disciples of Christ and the Christian Church a century before.

As of September 1, 2007, the denomination's television program, *SEARCH*, was in its 27th year of continual broadcast. This program has a firm policy against soliciting money or selling anything on the air. It is funded by local churches of Christ that sponsor the broadcast in their areas.

Membership: During 2006 there were an estimated 13,000 churches in the United States with about 1,265,000 members. Worldwide membership is more than 3 million.

Educational Facilities:

Abilene Christian University, Abilene, Texas.

Amridge University, Montgomery, Alabama.

Cascade College, Portland, Oregon.

Faulkner University, Montgomery, Alabama.

Freed-Hardeman University, Henderson, Tennessee.

Harding University, Searcy, Arkansas.

Heritage Christian University, Florence, Alabama.

Lipscomb University, Nashville, Tennessee.

Lubbock Christian University, Lubbock, Texas.

Ohio Valley University, Parkersburg, West Virginia.

Oklahoma Christian University, Oklahoma City, Oklahoma.

Pepperdine University, Malibu, California.

Rochester College, Rochester, Minnesota.

Southwestern Christian College, Terrell, Texas.

York College, York, Nebraska.

Periodicals: *Christian Chronicle*. Available from PO Box 11000, Oklahoma City, OK 73136. • *Christian Woman*. Available from 1006 Elm Hill Pike, Nashville, TN 37210. • *Firm Foundation*. Available from PO Box 690192, Houston, TX, 77269. • *Gospel Advocate*. Available from 1006 Elm Hill Pike, Nashville, TN 37210. • *Truth* (Non-institutional). Available from PO Box 9670, Bowling Green, KY 42102. • *Twenty-First Century Christian*. Available from PO Box 40304, Nashville, TN 37204.

Sources:

Brownlow, Leroy. *Why I Am a Member of the Church of Christ*. Fort Worth, TX: Brownlow Publishing, 1945.

Churches of Christ in the United States. Comp. Carl Royster. Nashville, TN: 21st-Century Christian, 2008.

Encyclopedia of the Stone-Campbell Movement. Ed. Douglas A. Foster et al. Grand Rapids, MI: William B. Eerdmans Publishing Co., 2005.

Hooper, Robert E. *A Distinct People: A History of the Churches of Christ in the 20th Century*. Eugene, OR: Wipf & Stock Publishers, 1993.

Shepherd, J. W. *The Church, the Falling Away, and the Restoration*. Nashville, TN: Gospel Advocate Company, 1977.

West, Earl. *Search for the Ancient Order*. 5 vols. Nashville, TN, and Delight, AR: Gospel Advocate Company and Gospel Light, 1950–1987.

Churches of Christ (Non-Instrumental, Conservative)
No central headquarters. For information: c/o Florida College, 119 N. Glen Arven Ave., Temple Terrace, FL 33617

Conservative churches of Christ are part of the Stone/Campbell restoration movement that began in the early nineteenth century. They represent one of the more conservative segments of the churches of Christ that separated from the Disciples of Christ (Christian Church) by the end of the nineteenth century due to their objections to missionary societies and the use of instrumental music in church worship.

During the twentieth century, with the growth of institutions serving large segments of the churches of Christ (non-instrumental), there was growing opposition to church support for institutions, sponsoring church arrangements, and projects such as church-sponsored recreation. The dissent became a movement during the 1950s, and became a separate discernible group by the 1960s.

Conservative Churches of Christ remain non-denominational, committed to principles historically rooted in the restoration movement. They hold strongly to a common-sense hermeneutic that finds patterns in the New Testament, forming the scriptural basis for doctrine and practice. Their churches adhere to a strictly congregational organizational structure. Though they emphasize local church autonomy, local churches and church members maintain close contact with one another and provide mutual support. The lack of any centralized governance makes it difficult to be certain about numbers of churches or church members. It is estimated that there are more than 2,200 churches in the United States, and hundreds worldwide.

Evangelistic efforts are supported by conservative Churches of Christ in numerous areas around the world. Numerous periodicals have been important voices of the movement, including the *Gospel Guardian*, *Preceptor*, *Truth Magazine*, *Searching the Scriptures*, *Christianity Magazine*, *Focus Magazine*, and *Biblical Insights*. Florida College, a four-year liberal arts college located in Temple Terrace, near Tampa, is operated by members of Conservative Churches of Christ, but not by the churches. The college's annual lectureship serves as a time for many members of the churches to gather for fellowship and study of biblical issues.

Membership: More than 120,000 members in more than 2,200 congregations in the United States. There are hundreds of churches in 47 foreign countries.

Educational Facilities:

Florida College, Temple Terrace, Florida.

Periodicals: *Biblical Insights,* 4001 Preston Hwy., Louisville, KY 40213. • *Focus Magazine,* 7854 LaBarrington Blvd., Powell, TN 37849. • *Preceptor,* PO Box 22283, Beaumont, TX 77720. • *Truth Magazine,* PO Box 9670, Bowling Green, KY 42102.

Sources:

Lynn, Mac, compiler. *Churches of Christ in the United States*. Nashville, TN: 21st Century Christian, 2003.

Directory of Churches of Christ. Bowling Green, KY: Guardian of Truth Foundation, 2008.

Harrell, David Edwin, Jr. *The Churches of Christ in the Twentieth Century: Homer Hailey's Personal Journey of Faith*. Tuscaloosa: The University of Alabama Press, 2000.

————. *A Social History of the Disciples of Christ,* Vol. 1: *Quest for a Christian America*. Vol. 2: *The Social Sources of Division in the Disciples of Christ, 1865–1900*. Nashville, TN: Disciples of Christ Historical Society, 1966–1973.

Hooper, Robert E. *A Distinct People: A History of the Churches of Christ in the Twentieth Century*. West Monroe, LA: Howard Publishing, 1993.

Hughes, Richard T. *Reviving the Ancient Faith: The Story of Churches of Christ in America*. Grand Rapids, MI: Eerdmans, 1996.

West, Earl Irvin. *The Search for the Ancient Order*. 4 vols. Indianapolis, IN: Religious Book Service, 1950–1987.

Churches of Christ (Non-Instrumental, Non-Class, One Cup)

c/o Old Paths Advocate, Don L. King, 1147 Sherry Way, Livermore, CA 94550

Following a growing trend in American Protestantism, Church of Christ minister G. C. Brewer (b. 1884) introduced the use of individual cups in the communion (as opposed to one cup for all communing) into the churches of Christ in the congregation at Chattanooga, Tennessee, in 1915. Over the next three decades the practice spread, not without controversy, and became dominant, especially in newly formed congregations. In 1913 a periodical, *The Apostolic Way*, was founded by Dr. G. A. Trott, H. C. Harper, and W. G. Rice, to fight what they considered the intrusion of Sunday schools into the worship of the Churches of Christ. This same periodical took up the fight against individual cups. In 1928 Harper founded a second periodical, *The Truth*, which in 1932 changed its name to *Old Paths Advocate*. The one-cup faction within the larger Churches of Christ movement remains a small minority, with congregations spread across the United States and in several foreign countries.

Membership: In 2002, the churches reported 450 congregations in the United States and 1,500 congregations spread through Africa, Australia, the Philippines, Mexico, England, Scotland, and Malaysia.

Periodicals: *Old Paths Advocate*, 1147 Sherry Way, Livermore, CA 94550

Sources:

Old Paths Advocate. www.oldpathsadvocate.org.

Churches of Christ (Noninstrumental, Non-Sunday School)

No central headquarters yet established.

The issue of Sunday schools has plagued the Churches of Christ during the entire twentieth century. An increasingly smaller group of leaders held that anything practiced by the church without command, example, or necessary inference from Scripture was wrong, particularly Sunday schools. In 1936, *Gospel Tidings*, edited by G. B. Shelburne Jr. was begun in support of the non-Sunday school cause. Bill Adcox currently is editor of the periodical. It has been joined by the *Christian Appeal* and the *West Coast Evangel*. Churches are concentrated in Texas, Oklahoma, Arkansas, Indiana, California, and Oregon. Missions are supported in India, Mexico, Uganda, and the Ukraine. One of church's benevolent works is maintaining the Berean Children's Home in Brookhaven, Mississippi.

Membership: Not reported. There are an estimated 500 to 600 congregations and 25,000 to 30,000 members.

Educational Facilities:

West Angelo School of Evangelism, San Angelo, Texas.

Periodicals: *Gospel Tidings*. Available from PO Box 726, Bethany, Oklahoma 73008-0726. • *Christian Appeal* • *West Coast Evangel*.

Sources:

Berean Children's Home Churches. www.bereanhome.org/

Gospel Tidings. www.gospeltidings.com

Churches of Christ (Non-Instrumental-Premillennial)

Current address could not be obtained for this edition.

Premillennialism became a major issue in American Protestantism in the late nineteenth century as fundamentalism developed. The term refers to the belief that Christ will return before the end of the world to establish his thousand-year reign. In the first quarter of the twentieth century premillennialism heavily influenced the churches of Christ. A churches of Christ periodical with a premillennialist perspective, *Word and Work*, emerged in Louisville, Kentucky, and in the early 1930s a radio show focused on premillennial beliefs, *Words of Life*, began airing; the latter is now heard in much of the eastern United States.

The premillennialist churches of Christ congregations support several schools and one Christian home. Missionaries are active in Africa, Japan, the Philippines, Hong Kong, and Greece. Approximately 100 congregations support the annual Louisville Christian Fellowship Week every August. Churches are concentrated in Indiana, Kentucky, Louisiana, and Texas.

Membership: Not reported. Membership is estimated at 12,000.

Churches of Christ (Pentecostal)

Conference on Spiritual Renewal, Box 457, Missouri City, TX 77459

As the charismatic movement moved through the major denominations in the late 1960s, it began to attract both ministers and laity in congregations of the Churches of Christ. Among the early charismatics was singer Pat Boone, who in 1971 was disfellowshipped from his congregation in Inglewood, California. Among the early ministers to receive the baptism of the Holy Spirit and subsequently speak in tongues (the definitive experience of members of the charismatic movement) were Dean Dennis, Dwyatt Gantt, and Don Finto. In 1976 a group of 12 ministers met in Nashville, Tennessee, where Finto led the Belmont Church of Christ and organized the first Conference on Spiritual Renewal. The conference, which still meets annually, provided a unifying structure for those involved with the movement.

Like other segments of the Churches of Christ, the Charismatic churches are loosely organized in a congregation-free church polity. There is no central headquarters or governing structure. Intercongregational gatherings are for fellowship and inspiration only. Prominent congregations identified with the charismatic Churches of Christ include Orange Park Christian Church, Jacksonville, Florida; Calvary Chapel, Atlanta, Georgia; and Quail Ridge Church of Christ, Memphis, Tennessee. Some of these congregations deviate from the main body of the Churches of Christ by their introduction of instrumental music. Popular recording star Amy Grant is a member of Belmont Church of Christ in Nashville, Tennessee.

Membership: Not reported.

Sources:

The Acts of the Holy Spirit in the Church of Christ Today. Los Angeles, CA: Full Gospel Business Men's Fellowship International, 1971.

Ambrose, George. "God Said It. I Believe It. That Settles It." *Charisma* 9, no. 11 (July 1984).

"Amy Grant, How the Word Is a Light unto Her Path." *Charisma* 11, no. 12 (July 1986).

Buckingham, Jamie. "The Music of Spiritual Awakening." *Charisma* 9, no. 11 (July 1984).

Evangelical Christian Church

c/o Bengal Christian Church, 3534 S. Shelby 750 W, Franklin, IN 46131

The Evangelical Christian Church traces its beginnings to the formal organization of the Christian Church in 1804, in Bourbon County, Kentucky, under the leadership of Barton Warren Stone (1772–1844). The Stone movement later merged with the efforts of Thomas Campbell (1763–1854) and his son Alexander Campbell (1788–1866) to become the Restoration Movement that gave birth to the Churches of Christ (Non-Instrumental), the Christian Churches and Churches of Christ, and the Christian Church (Disciples of Christ). The Evangelical Christian Church, as a new group within the Restoration tradition, was reorganized in 2001.

Through the early twentieth century, many Restoration churches, not otherwise apart of the three larger Restoration bodies, existed under such names as Evangelical Christian Churches, Christian Churches of North America, Christian Missionary Churches, Bible Evangelical Churches, Community Churches, and Evangelical Congregational Churches. Some of these came together in 1966 as the Evangelical Christian Churches, Farmland, Indiana. The majority of these congregations that have not been otherwise absorbed continue as the Evangelical Christian Churches, Albany, Indiana.

The Evangelical Christian Church attempts to continue the Restoration tradition as embodied in its several slogans, "Where the Scriptures speak, we speak. Where the Scriptures are silent, we are silent"; "In essentials, unity. In nonessentials, liberty. In all things, love;" "We are not the only Christians. We are Christians only"; and "No creed but Christ. No book but the Bible." It seeks to perpetuate the message first preached by Stone and his colleagues. It includes an emphasis on a non-trinitarian approach to God as Father, Jesus Christ as Lord and savior, the Holy Spirit as the power and energy of God, and the Bible as the sufficient rule of faith and practice. In general, the church considers itself a conservative non-creedal Christian body.

The church has divided the country into six regions and assigned a district minister as a contact point with the congregations and ministers in the assigned state. National leadership is placed in its officers, including the national pastor, the general pastor, the board of elders, the regional pastors, and the president of the Historical Society. The national and general pastor constitute the executive staff. Ordinations are approved by the national pastor, and ministerial credentials come from the office of the national pastor. Women are welcomed into the ministry.

Membership: Not reported.

Periodicals: *New Wineskins Magazine*, PO Box 41028, Nashville, TN 37204-1028. • *Restoration Herald*, 7133 Central Parke Blvd., Mason, OH 45040.

International Churches of Christ (ICOC)

708 Morris Ct., Lombard, IL 60148

The International Churches of Christ (ICOC) dates its history from June 1979, when a group of members in a small and declining congregation of the Churches of Christ (Non-Instrumental) in Lexington, Massachusetts (a Boston suburb), made a new commitment to devote their lives to restoring the Christianity of the Bible. Their new minister, Kip McKean, challenged the 30 members of the small congregation to totally commit their lives to Christ and to hold that same commitment as a biblical standard for all of the people they would convert to Christ. He soon developed a series of Bible lessons called First Principles, and asked the members of the church to learn them and teach the Scriptures to others. This process became the bedrock of a program of transforming nominal church members into active disciples. Prior to being baptized, new members were asked to commit themselves to becoming disciples, not just people who warmed a church pew. Previously baptized Christians who had not made such a commitment prior to their baptism, were rebaptized. The church came to believe and teach that a true Church of Christ was composed totally of disciples. As disciples, each member was expected to be evangelistic.

As the church grew, it moved into Boston proper and took the name the Boston Church of Christ. It met for Sunday worship and midweek services in rented facilities, thus allowing it to redirect its financial resources to ministry rather than buildings. A new Christian was assigned an older member as a discipleship partner and invited into a discipleship group that met weekly. A special program was developed by Elena McKean and Pat Gempel to meet the needs of the female disciples and to avoid possible temptations in the dynamics of men and women in personal counseling. Only males occupy the positions of elder, deacon, and evangelist. Couples, however, always lead together and the women have the full responsibility of the women's ministry. One of the most successful programs of the ICOC has been its Woman's Day seminars held around the world. In 1997, 9,000 women attended this event in Los Angeles alone.

Imitating the spread of the New Testament church, in 1981, McKean developed a plan that he believed would allow for the evangelism of the world in one generation. This plan envisioned sending a small group of disciples to key urban centers. They would grow a congregation and it would become the pillar from which teams of disciples would be sent to each of the world's capitals. From the capitals, the movement would move on to the other, smaller cities, until the world would be evangelized in one generation. This plan was introduced to the Boston Church of Christ as a whole in October 1981. In 1982 the first churches were planted in Chicago and London. Over the next few years additional churches were planted in New York City, Toronto, and Providence, Rhode Island. In 1986 churches were opened in Johannesburg, Paris, and Stockholm. In the meantime some older Churches of Christ congregations and ministries became affiliated with the growing movement. In order to do this each church went through a process termed "reconstruction," and each of the former members was called upon to decide if they wanted to be a disciple.

The implementation of this plan, with its direction coming from the leadership in Boston, represented a major departure in organization from that traditionally followed by the Churches of Christ (Non-instrumental). The Boston Church of Christ leadership saw their movement as creating one church family. The churches would start churches that would plant other churches and they would all remain unified. The implementation of this plan led to a separation by the traditional Churches of Christ denomination from the new movement. Due to the rapid growth of the movement, men were set aside as "world sector leaders" and given responsibility for evangelizing different regions of the world. In 1990 McKean moved to Los Angeles to build a new church and Los Angeles became the headquarters for the movement.

In 1994 Kip and Elena McKean, the World Sector Leaders, and their wives signed the Evangelization Proclamation stating their intent to, by the year 2000, plant a church in every nation that has a city of at least 100,000 in population. The

International Churches of Christ had 146 churches in 53 nations at the time of the Evangelization Proclamation. By the end of 1997, it had 312 churches in 124 nations and reached its Proclamation goal in mid-2000.

Since 2000 the ICOC has experienced immense internal turmoil. In November 2001 World Sector leaders announced that the McKeans would be on sabbatical. This move was a result of concerns over the stability of the McKean family life, especially since Olivia McKean, Kip and Elena's daughter, had left the movement earlier in the year. In November 2002 Kip resigned as world evangelist and Elena gave up her position as world women's leader. Their resignations came at the same time that ICOC leaders abandoned the model of World Sector leadership.

In February 2003 prominent British ICOC leader Henry Kriete wrote a stinging critique of the state of the movement under the title "Honest to God". In July the McKeans moved to Portland, Oregon and Kip released a circular letter to the whole church under the title "From Babylon to Zion" announcing that he was ready to reengage as world leader. However, tensions between Kip and ICOC leadership continued, coming to a head in 2005 when 84 leaders withdrew fellowship from him. In turn, McKean formed the Sold-Out Discipling Movement Churches in 2006. As part of the Sold-Out movement, the next year he and his wife established the new City of Angels International Christian Church in Los Angeles.

Doctrinally, the International Churches of Christ shares a Bible-based Free Church perspective with the traditional Churches of Christ (Instrumental), but has developed several unique beliefs. While the International Churches of Christ does not believe it is the exclusive home of Christians, it has basically held the position that it is God's movement for this period of history. It also holds that each member should be a disciple, obey the Scriptures according to Matthew 28:18-20, and be a part of evangelizing the world in this generation. The ICOC organized a volunteer program, HOPE Worldwide which has conducted a variety of social service projects in over 125 countries around the world. In 1996 HOPE Worldwide was granted special consultative status with the Economic and Social Council of the United Nations and registered with USAID. HOPE has since become a separate benevolent organization. Discipleship Publications International is the ICOC publishing concern.

The formal structure of the ICOC was dismantled in the fall of 2002. From 2003 to 2006 the ICOC experienced a deep re-evaluation of its mission and style of leadership. Most of the churches have committed to a cooperation agreement. A group of delegates from the world regions of the movement select a chairman for each of the ten service teams who focus on the needs of various ministries worldwide. International conferences are held for leadership, campus, youth and family, and singles.

Membership: As of October 1997, the ICOC reported 93,000 members, with a worldwide Sunday attendance of over 155,000. There were 312 congregations in 124 countries. By 2000 Sunday attendance was over 200,000. There were major losses in 2003 and 2004. The ICOC leadership estimated membership at the end of 2007 at 90,130, a 1.7 percent increase over 2006 but a 33 percent decline from the peak membership in 2002 of 135,046. As of 2007 there were 562 congregations worldwide.

Periodicals: *LA Story.* • *Kingdom Network News* (a video magazine).

Remarks: While the International Churches of Christ formally began in 1979, it originated out of an older movement variously known as the Discipling movement, a pan-denominational movement which emerged among Evangelical Christians in the 1960s. It was distinguished by its attempts to transform nominal Christians to active disciples and was characterized by the assignment of each new Christian to an older, more mature Christian with whom they met regularly, at least weekly. The older Christian had the responsibility of mentoring the younger disciple and encouraging the steady progress in the life of faith.

The Discipling movement came into the Churches of Christ through the Crossroads Church of Christ, a congregation in Gainesville, Florida. By adopting a form of the Discipleship program in its campus outreach, it grew spectacularly.

Among the people led into the ministry through the Crossroads Church was Kip McKean.

The Discipling movement spread through the Churches of Christ and became quite controversial. As members of a conservative movement, many with the Churches of Christ rejected the changes brought by the new movement and a number of publications denouncing it appeared. Eventually, the Crossroads Church withdrew its support from the movement and the remnants of it within the Churches of Christ tended to reorient its allegiance to the Boston Church of Christ. As the Boston Church of Christ grew, its opponents among the Churches of Christ (Non-instrumental) were joined by members of the anti-cult movement. The ICOC has long been accused of being a destructive cult with standard allegations about authoritarian leadership and brainwashing. These allegations have diminished since the resignation of Kip McKean as world leader in 2002 and the abandonment of World Sector leadership.

Sources:

ICOC Co-Operation Churches. www.icocco-op.org.

The Disciple's Handbook. Los Angeles: Discipleship Publications International, 1997. 177 pp.

Disciples Today. www.disciplestoday.org.

Ferguson, Gordon. *Discipleship: God's Plan to Train and Transform His People.* Los Angeles: Discipleship Publications International, 1997. 251 pp.

————. *Prepared to Answer.* Los Angeles: Discipleship Publications International, 1995. 219 pp.

Geissler, Rex. *Born of Water: What the Bible Really Says about Baptism.* Long Beach: Grand Commission International, 1996. 140 pp.

Giambalvo, Carol, and Herbert L. Rosedale, eds. *The Boston Movement: Critical Perspective on the International Churches of Christ.* Bonita Springs, FL: American Family Foundation, 1996. 243 pp.

Jacoby, Doug. *True & Reasonable.* Los Angeles: Discipleship Publications International, 1994. 109 pp.

Nelson, Robert. *Understanding the Crossroads Controversy.* Fort Worth, TX: Star Bible Publications, 1986.

Paden, Russell. *"From the Churches of Christ to the Boston Movement: A Comparative Study."* M.A. Thesis, University of Kansas, 1994.

National Association of Free, Autonomous Christian Churches
Current address not obtained for this edition.

Among the people who strongly opposed the restructuring of the Christian Church (Disciples of Christ) in the 1960s was Dr. Alvin E. Houser, pastor of a large congregation in Centex, Texas. As the debate on restructuring continued, he formed the National Association of Free Christians. His position was conservative theologically and focused on the radical congregationalism of traditional Christian Church thinking. After restructuring became inevitable, the Association of Free Christians became the National Association of Free, Autonomous Christian Churches, with most of its strength in the Southwest.

Sold-Out Discipling Movement Churches
601 Marinella, Irvine, CA 92606

The Sold-Out Discipling Movement Churches was founded in 2006 by Kip McKean (b. 1954), the founder of the International Churches of Christ (ICOC), a movement that emerged from within the older Churches of Christ movement. McKean led the ICOC until his resignation as world leader in 2002. His plans in 2003 to reemerge as ICOC head floundered and in 2005 a group of 84 ICOC leaders withdrew fellowship from McKean. By this time McKean had established himself as a church leader in Portland, Oregon, and following the withdrawal of fellowship many of the ICOC members shifted their allegiance to McKean to become part of the new Sold-Out group. In 2007 McKean started a Los Angeles group, known as the City of Angels International Christian Church. McKean is now world evangelist for the Sold-Out movement.

The split between ICOC and the Sold-Out churches is largely over allegiance to McKean as leader. Doctrinally, both groups adopt a conservative, evangelical Protestant theology with the Church of Christ's emphasis on the believer's baptism. The ICOC has abandoned its early emphasis on worldwide church government in favor of more autonomy for the local churches.

Membership: As of mid-2008, the Sold-Out movement has 14 congregations in the United States and 16 international congregations.

Sources:

City of Angels International Christian Church. www.caicc.net.

Global Internet Ministry of The City of Angels International Christian Church.www.upsidedown21.org.

Kip McKean. www.kipmckean.org.

Tioga River Christian Conference

Current address not obtained for this edition.

The Tioga River Christian Conference was formed in 1844 in Covington, Tioga County, Pennsylvania. It was for many years a constituent part of the Christian Church. In 1931, however, the conference rejected the merger of the Christian Church with the Congregational Church. The conference adopted articles of faith manifesting belief in the Trinity, the Bible as the Word of God, sin and salvation, the local church, Satan, resurrection, and eternal life. There is an annual meeting of the conference for fellowship and business. A nine-man mission board oversees missions in Bolivia, Peru, and India. *His Messenger* is the conference's quarterly periodical. There are 13 churches in New York and Pennsylvania. Headquarters are in Binghamton, New York.

Membership: Not reported.

Periodicals: *His Messenger*.

Independent Fundamentalist Family

12

Fundamentalism is the name given to a conservative movement within Protestantism in the early twentieth century. It was characterized by an intense affirmation of biblical authority and allegiance to a modest number of essential Christian doctrines, most of which had been called into question by the so-called modernists, who had absorbed a variety of new currents of intellectual thought, from sociology to biological evolution. What became known as *fundamentalism*, however, derives from the thought of British teacher/theologian John Nelson Darby (1800–1882). The movement he began in England in the 1820s attempted a more thoroughgoing revival of primitive Christianity than either the earlier Puritan or Wesleyan movements. Unlike its Puritan and Wesleyan predecessors, the new movement was not content merely to purify or revive the existing church, but sought to recreate the apostolic church. The prime methods used to recover apostolic life were intense concentration on the Bible, and the adoption of a biblical lifestyle, theology, and ecclesiology.

JOHN NELSON DARBY. Probably no Christian thinker in the last two hundred years has so affected the way in which English-speaking Christians view the faith, and yet has received so little recognition of his contribution as John Nelson Darby. Why this anonymity? One can only guess. It might be that the theological movement he began was so ahistorical that it was programmed to forget its roots, its originator. It might be that its disestablishment orientation worked for a breakdown of communication that left the second generation without a knowledge of its heritage. In any case, the thinking of a large number of Christians finds its source in the unique biblical theology that Darby evolved in the nineteenth century. From his ideas have sprung modern-day fundamentalism, the later work of evangelist Dwight L. Moody (1837–1899) and the Moody Bible Institute in Chicago, the *Scofield Reference Bible*, the *Companion Bible*, and a number of churches that bear names such as Bible Church, Bereans, Grace Gospel, Brethren, Independent Fundamentalist, and Gospel Assembly. Moreover, as a result of Darby's work, a number of Christians in the larger denominations would one day read with relish the works of such men as Isaac Massey Haldeman (1845–1933), William Graham Scroggie (1877–1958), Clarence Larkin (1850–1924), G. Campbell Morgan (1863–1945), James H. Brooks (1830–1897), and William E. Blackstone (1841–1935), to name a few.

Who was Darby? John Nelson Darby was an Anglican priest ordained in 1826, who, through the study of the scripture, initially came to reject the idea of a state church. Darby's dissent led him to withdraw from the Anglican Church in 1827 and begin pursuit of a nondenominational approach to church life, establishing fellowship groups of Christians who had also come out of the existing denominational structure. It was Darby's view that the true church is a temporary structure, set up by God between the cross and the Second Coming, and composed of a number of individual believers. This concept dominates Darby's thinking.

In 1827 the famous Albury Conferences on prophetic studies—conferences held at Albury Park, an estate near London—caused Darby to think about eschatology. The term *eschatology* refers to one's understanding of the end-time and includes consideration of death, heaven and hell, judgment, the Second Coming of Christ, and the millennium (Christ's reign on earth for a thousand years). Darby created a new system of thought called *dispensationalism*. Dispensationalism is a way of looking at the Bible as the history of God's dealing with humanity. Dispensationalists divide history into various historical periods (i.e., the dispensations). Church leaders had often divided history, using either a theological or numerological criteria, into three or seven periods. But it was Darby who began a division of the biblical story based on God's method of dealing with his people. Darby's system had seven basic dispensations; one period, Israel's, was divided into three subperiods. The system was roughly as follows:

1. (Paradisaical state) to the flood
2. Noah—government
3. Abraham—calling and election
4. Israel
       a. Under the law—Moses
       b. Under the priesthood
       c. Under the kings—Saul
5. Gentiles (begins with Nebuchadnezzar)
6. The Spirit (the present?)
7. The fullness of time

While Darby was fairly clear about the early dispensations, his discussion of the present and future is vague and at times seemingly contradictory. To ease the confusion, Darby's theological successors (particularly C. I. Scofield [1843–1921] and Harry A. Ironside [1878–1951]) refined his system into what has become the basis for most modern discussion of dispensational schemes. Scofield's seven dispensations are:

1. Innocence—from creation to the fall of Adam
2. Conscience—from the fall to the flood
3. Government—from Noah to Abraham
4. Promise—from Abraham to Moses
5. Law—from Moses to Jesus
6. Grace—from the cross to the Second Coming
7. Personal reign of Christ—from the Second Coming to and including eternity

Dispensational schemes solve several basic biblical problems. They clear up some of the baffling biblical contradictions by shifting contradictory passages to different dispensations. For example, when one reads all of the passages concerning the end of time and the events surrounding the Second Coming of Christ, one is left confused as to what will happen. Passages in Thessalonians, the book of Revelation, and Matthew offer seemingly contradictory pictures of the future that the dispensationalists were able to reconcile by their complex outline of future events. The dispensationalists were also able to reconcile the obvious difference between the small New Testament church and the large ecclesiastical organizations by which they were surrounded. The true church (i.e., the church of the dispensationalists) was ever the small body of the faithful called out from Babylon (i.e., large religious organizations).

Finally, the dispensationalists offered a rationale for change. Each dispensation was initiated by a renewed action of God toward his people, by which God tries to reach his chosen ones. The failure of each successive action leads inevitably to the cross, said the dispensationalists. And the failure of the New Testament church to realize the promises given to it must lead inevitably to a final dispensation in which Christ is acknowledged as the universal ruler.

Second only to dispensationalism as a key idea of Darby is his ecclesiology. Darby had early come to reject denominated, primarily state-church, Christianity, and he tackled the problem of the "Nature and Unity of the Church of Christ" in his first pamphlet in 1828. He attacked as the enemy of the work of the Holy Spirit anyone "who seeks the interests of any particular denomination." No formal union of outward-professing bodies is desirable. Unity is to be found in "the Unity of the Spirit and can only be in the things of the Spirit, and therefore can only be perfected in spiritual persons. Believers know that all who are born of the Spirit have substantial unity of mind, so as to know each other, and love each other as brethren." Churches influenced by Darby's ecclesiology generally have a statement of belief in the spiritual unity of believers in Jesus Christ.

Darby established assemblies of likeminded believers tied together by their theological consensus and their fellowship. They accepted no authority except the "charismatic" leadership of Darby and other talented teachers who soon arose in their midst. There were no bishops or overseers.

The gospel assembly became the central building block among Darby's followers and imitators. The assembly was a local gathering of likeminded Christians. Each person was both layman and minister, and each assembly was independent and tied to the other assemblies only by the bonds of doctrinal uniformity and fellowship.

No name for the group was accepted, although biblical designations such as Church of God and, most popularly, Brethren, were often used. The lack of designation has been a characteristic that has persisted and has often made the Brethren an invisible part of the ongoing religious life of any community in which they reside. Few groups of Brethren publish their membership statistics.

While they had no formal ministry, the Brethren did display an intense evangelical zeal and began to develop structures that could be used without infringing on the autonomy of the assembly. First, there emerged in the assemblies gifted teachers and evangelists who, by the consent of the assembly, taught the Bible and preached the gospel. The majority of the assembly, of course, had responsibilities in reaching the lost with the gospel. The more talented of the teachers and evangelists began to travel and speak at neighboring assemblies, and, by such informal means, a professional ministry developed.

A major new form that evolved as an expression of the biblical priority in the life of the Brethren was the Bible reading. This sermonlike presentation usually involved the tracing of a key word or idea, such as *creation* or *church*, through a series of otherwise disconnected passages, with the speaker briefly commenting on each passage. The Bible reading evolved out of the reading meeting of the British Brethren, where students would gather in a home and together search the scripture.

An active publishing ministry was initiated by the voluminous writings of Darby. Pamphlets and tracts were soon joined by books and periodicals. Last to arise were Brethren-owned printing and publishing houses, which were owned by some prominent Brethren who published material as a service to the larger fellowship, but, in matters of business, functioned as entrepreneurs. As the movement grew and schisms developed, the publishers became the spokesmen for different factions that could be distinguished, primarily, by the literature they accepted as orthodox. Publishers, in the absence of ministerial associations and national conventions, have become major molders of opinion in the otherwise informally organized assemblies.

The assemblies, as a rule, reject any doctrinal formulation or creed, though Darby emphasized that unity of mind was an essential feature of the Church of God. There was, and is informally, however, a very rigid orthodoxy and doctrinal stand, particularly about the nature of the church. Almost all of the schisms within the Darbyite movement were articulated as doctrinal disputes and appeared as a breakdown of doctrinal consensus. Of course, a major disagreement concerns the amount of latitude in belief that is possible without destroying the unity of heart and mind.

Darby accepted the orthodox Protestantism of the Reformation on the central issues of belief in God, the Trinity, the divinity of Christ, the person and work of the Holy

Independent Fundamentalist Family Chronology

1827	Henry Drummond, a former member of the House of Commons, hosts the Albury Park prophetic conferences in Surry.
	John Nelson Darby, a priest, separated from the Church of Ireland (Anglican) and begins to break bread with a group of independent believers.
1831–33	Lady Theodosia Powerscourt hosts conferences on biblical prophecy near Dublin, Ireland.
1832	Initial gathering of the Brethren formed in Plymouth, England.
1848	Darby and Benjamin Wills Newton, the principal persons among the Brethren from Plymouth, part company over doctrinal differences. Those who follow Darby become the several sects of the Exclusive Brethren and those who follow Newton become the Open or Christian Brethren.
1859	Darby begins preaching in North America. He spreads his system of premillennial dispensationalism, which divides human history into a series of epochs in which God has dealt with humanity in different ways.
1869	First gathering of the Believers Meeting for Bible Study.
1872	Evangelist Dwight L. Moody accepts Darby's dispensational approach to Bible but does not affiliate with the Brethren.
1878	*Jesus Is Coming* by William E. Blackstone is published.
1883	Believers Meeting moves to Niagara-on-the-Lake, Ontario, and becomes known as the Niagara Conference on Prophecy.
1890	Niagara Conference issues a 14-point statement of essential Christian beliefs.
1901	Tabernacle founded by Dwight L. Moody in Chicago renames itself the Moody Bible Church.
1909	Cyrus Scofield publishes the first of many editions of his influential *Scofield Reference Bible*, which helps spread Darby's dispensational system.
	Disfellowshipped from the Plymouth Brethren, Adolph Ernst Knoch begins work on a new dispensational Bible translation, the Concordant Version.
1910–15	*The Fundamentals*, a set of booklets containing articles on essential Christian beliefs, are published and, under the sponsorship of two California oilmen, are sent to some 3 million Protestant leaders.
1919	World's Christian Fundamentals Association is founded. Fundamentalists champion the authority and literal interpretation of the Bible and oppose Modernist interpretations, which they feel lead to denials of Christian essentials. The Fundamentalist-Modernist debate is fought out most visibly in the Presbyterian and Baptist churches.
1925	Fundamentalist William Jennings Bryan leads the prosecution against John Scopes, Tennessee school teacher accused of violating the Butler bill by teaching the theory of evolution in his classes. Scopes is defended by attorney Clarence Darrow.
1928	Dr. Oswald J. Smith founds the Peoples Church in Toronto, Ontario.
1930	Fundamentalists primarily from the Congregational Church form the Independent Fundamental Churches of America.
1934–36	The Fundamentalist-Modernist debate culminates in the defrocking of Princeton professor J. Gresham Machen (1934) and the formation of the Orthodox Presbyterian Church (1936).
1937	Charles Fuller begins broadcasting the *Old Fashioned Revival Hour*.
1941	Separatist fundamentalists found American Council of Christian Churches.
1942	Moderate fundamentalists (who had come to be known as Evangelicals) form National Association of Evangelicals.
1944	Pastors who follow the radical dispensation approach of J. C. O'Hair, Charles Welch, and Ethelbert Bullinger form the Grace Gospel Fellowship.
1947	Fuller Theological Seminary opens its doors in Pasadena, California.
1950	Billy Graham establishes the Billy Graham Evangelistic Association and launches the *Hour of Decision* radio show.
1951	Campus Crusade for Christ is founded by Bill and Vonette Bright on the UCLA campus.
1956	First issue of *Christianity Today* appears as voice of new Evangelical movement.
1966	The World Congress on Evangelism is held in Berlin.
1974	International Congress on World Evangelization meets in Lausanne, Switzerland.
1973	Moshe Rosen of the American Board of Missions to the Jews forms Jews for Jesus.
1975	U.S. Lausanne Committee formed as part of the International Lausanne Movement Beginnings of Jewish Messianic Movement signaled by the Hebrew Christina Alliance adopting a new name as the Messianic Jewish Alliance of America.
1989	Lausanne II, the second International Evangelism Conference, is convened by the International Lausanne Committee in Manila, Philippines.

Spirit, the Bible as the Word of God, and the necessity for individuals to repent and receive forgiveness and salvation. Where Darby differed from the Protestants of the Reformation was in the issues of ecclesiology and eschatology.

While never developing an expectancy of Christ's imminent return to the degree that the Adventists did, the Brethren were in the forefront of nineteenth-century emphasis on the approaching end of the age, and they promoted speculative interpretation of scriptural statements on the nature and order of eschatological events. Their speculations took the form of prophecy. Prominent in the dispensational scheme is a particular form of eschatology, usually termed *premillennialism.*

It was Darby's belief that people could be divided, for eschatological purposes, into three groups—the Jews, the Church of God (Christians), and the Gentiles (all non-Christians who were not Jews). The first event in the eschatological framework is the invisible coming of Christ to gather his saints, both living and dead, and take them away as described in Paul's First Epistle to the Thessalonians (4:13–18). This event is called the *secret rapture* of the saints. The rapture is the signal of God's rejection of the Gentiles, particularly nominal Christians; but after the rapture, his work is begun among the Jews, who convert and become preachers of Christianity to the lost world for seven years, during which time Satan is unleashing his most terrible woes. This seven-year period is called the tribulation (Revelation 7:14). At the end of the *tribulation* period, Christ and his army will come to do battle with Satan and his allies. After Christ's victory, a literal thousand years (the millennium) of peace will ensue. The remnant who come to Christ during the tribulation shall live on earth, while the raptured saints reign with God in heavenly glory. (Reformation Protestants such as Martin Luther [1483–1546] and John Calvin [1509–1564] rejected the idea of a literal millennium.)

At the end of the millennium occurs the judgment of the Great White Throne. Satan, bound for the millennium, is loosed for a last bit of activity before his destruction. Finally, the wicked dead (non-Christians) are resurrected and judged, and the saints are given their eternal reward. This was a relatively new eschatological schema, but as it grew in popularity along with the corollary dispensational view of history, it set the issues of debate for other Bible students and conservative Christians. The rapture itself was the main point of attack by Darby's opponents. They found no basis for his positing of an "invisible return," or secret rapture, by Christ seven years before the visible Second Coming.

THE DEVELOPING MOVEMENT.
Darby's theology began to influence a large number of Bible students. First, such men as Charles H. Mackintosh (usually designated as C.H.M.) (1820–1896), William Trotter (1818–1865), and William Kelly (1821–1906) joined Darby's movement, and began to write and expound Darby's system. As early as 1859, Darby visited Canada, with other visits in 1864 and 1866. In 1870, 1872 to 1873, and 1874, he visited most of the major U.S. cities. In 1872 Dwight L. Moody discovered the Brethren, who spent several days introducing Moody to dispensational thought. As Darby and his associates toured America, such leading clergy as Adoniram J. Gordon (1836–1895) and James H. Brooks opened both their minds and their pulpits to the new truth. As a result of the massive body of literature this movement created, along with its nondenominational character and association with Moody, a large segment of conservative Christianity accepted it. In the 1880s and 1890s, the thought became institutionalized in many Bible colleges, the most famous of which was the Moody Bible Institute in Chicago. While Darby's theology became popular, many people who accepted dispensationalism never accepted the ecclesiology nor became Brethren, a fact that often gave Darby and his followers moments of consternation.

Two books appeared that greatly increased the popularity of Darby's dispensationalism and premillennial eschatology. The first was *Jesus Is Coming* by William E. Blackstone. This eschatologically oriented book appeared in 1878 and was an immediate success. Though its topic was the Second Coming, its treatment was thoroughly dispensational. The book has remained in print more than a century later. The second book was the *Scofield Reference Bible*. Cyrus I. Scofield (1843–1921) was a St. Louis lawyer converted under Moody's preaching. Later, he moved to Dallas and became a Congregational minister. His first dispensational work appeared in 1888, *Rightly Dividing the Word of Truth*, which is also still in print. In the 1890s Scofield set up a Bible study course used at many of the Bible colleges, including Moody.

In 1902 he commenced work on the reference Bible, which appeared in 1909. It immediately became the cardinal work in the movement and has become the standard by which to judge the dispensational movement. In 1967 a new *Scofield Reference Bible*, edited by a committee of prominent dispensationalists and with minor additions to Scofield's notes in the light of later research, appeared.

Widespread use of the *Scofield Reference Bible* has led to growth in dispensationalism among those with an otherwise orthodox theology. At the same time, it became a source from which leaders in the movement have created variant dispensational outlines of history that have in turn led to new teachings. For instance, Moody Bible Institute graduate J. C. O'Hair (1877–1958) developed a form of what was termed *ultradispensationalism*, which gave birth to the Grace Gospel movement, which in turn rejects water baptism.

Following Scofield's pattern have been a large number of conservative ministers, both denominational and independent. For many years, I. M. Haldeman, pastor of the First Baptist Church of New York City, wrote on dispensationalism. His most significant book in this vein is *A Dispensational Key to the Holy Scriptures*, published in 1915. Manifesting the way dispensational teaching readily adapts itself to pictorial presentations, two authors had great success specializing in publishing diagrammatic texts of dispensationalism. Clarence Larkin's *Dispensational Truth* (1920) and Roy L. Brown's *Truth on Canvas* (1939) became popular.

Darby's movement grew out of the traditional theology of the Church of England. While noncreedal, it, in fact, accepted all of the affirmations of the more notable creeds promulgated by the ecumenical councils of the Christian movement during the conciliar era (fourth to eighth centuries), most notably the Nicene and Chalcedonian creeds. Darby also affirmed the major ideas of the Protestant Reformation, such as the authority of the Bible, salvation by faith alone, and the priesthood of believers. However, in his new emphases he also set up the possibility of endless deviations from that tradition.

Eschewing the developments and experience of the church over the centuries, Darby emphasized Bible study and placed great authority in the hands of people knowledgeable of the Bible in detail. He also placed stress on a resolution of seemingly contradictory Bible passages to emphasize the full and complete revelation of God. Finally, he emphasized prophecy and eschatology, the most speculative aspect of Christian belief. It seems inevitable in such a situation that variant understandings of biblical passages and differences on Christian theology would come to the fore. Such was the case, and it led to the splitting of the Brethren movement into a set of factions (some of which were able to reunite in the later decades of the twentieth century). It also led to a major new doctrinal perspective among British Bible students.

In England, two scholars, Ethelbert W. Bullinger (1837–1913) and Charles H. Welch (1880–1967), contemporaries of C. I. Scofield, produced a major deviation in the

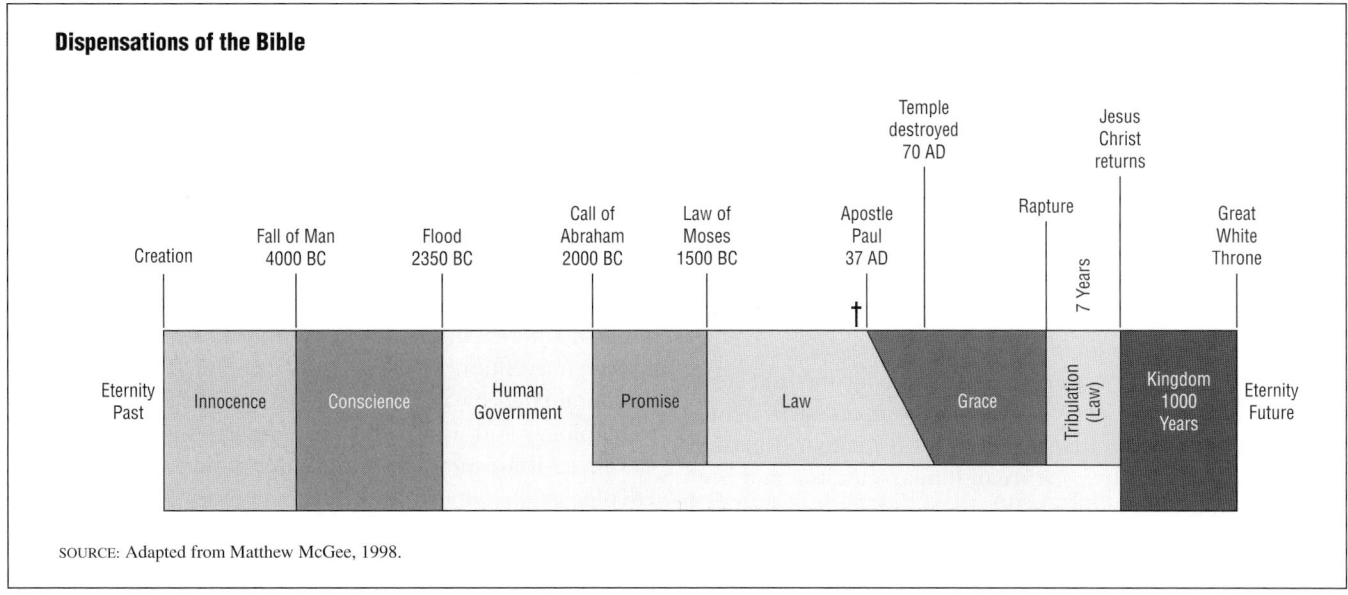

Dispensations of the Bible

SOURCE: Adapted from Matthew McGee, 1998.

Darbyite manner of thinking. What Scofield called the *dispensation of grace* begins with the cross, the resurrection, and Pentecost, and goes to the Second Coming of Christ. Bullinger divided this period into two dispensations, so that one dispensation covers the era of the apostolic church. This added dispensation begins with Pentecost and closes with the end of the ministry of the apostles and Paul. In the Bible, this era traces the church from Acts 2 to Acts 28:25–28, and was to be considered separate from the body of Christ mentioned in Colossians and Ephesians. Also, Bullinger identified the bride of Christ in Revelation as being entirely a Jewish remnant church to be built at the end, and not at all the body of Christ. Bullinger, through his popular writings, and Welch, in his continuance of Bullinger's thought, have occasioned discussion and some acceptance of their teachings. A major debate among dispensationalists, producing the Grace Gospel movement discussed below, concerns varying views toward Bullinger's thought. In America, Bullinger's teachings have taken hold and produced several groups. A spin-off of Bullingerism is the work of Adolph E. Knoch (1874–1965), discussed below.

During the twentieth century, followers of Darby's teaching in the Scofield vein were mainly to be found among conservative believers in the major churches. However, during the 1920s, as a result of the heated fundamentalist-modernist controversy, new denominations that were dispensational in their stance began to form. This new emergence of independent bodies adhering to a dispensational theology, along with the continued splintering of the older bodies, produced more than forty groups following some form of Darby's teaching.

PLYMOUTH BRETHREN. Plymouth Brethren is the name that has become attached to the movement originally founded by John Nelson Darby and his associates. The meeting at Plymouth, England, became the most prominent assembly in the otherwise unnamed movement and, as the group refused to be denominated, others began to informally refer to the group as the Brethren from Plymouth. Within the growing movement, a separation appeared in the 1840s. One leader, Benjamin W. Newton (1807–1899), differed with Darby on both eschatology and ecclesiology. Newton initially denied Darby's idea of the saints' rapture, and then came to emphasize the autonomy of the local assembly over against Darby's understanding of the necessary unity of the whole movement. Darby attacked Newton in a manner many thought verbally violent and vindictive. The assembly at Plymouth divided, and the Darby faction accused Newton of holding a heretical Christology. The assembly at Bethesda, formerly a Baptist congregation, had been received into the Brethren as a group. In 1848 the Bethesda congregation received some of the Newton people at the Lord's Supper. The ensuing controversy led to the permanent division of the movement into the "Open" Brethren (Newton) and the "Exclusive" Brethren (Darby).

The basic division concerns the doctrine of separation. The Exclusive Brethren believe in receiving no one at the Lord's table who is not a true Christian in the fullest sense, including being a member of a fully separated assembly (an assembly of Brethren who associate only with Brethren and not with persons from other churches). The Open Brethren, on the other hand, receive all believers determined to be true Christians, even if other members of their church might hold allegedly false doctrine. The Exclusive Brethren have established several "circles of fellowship," that is, groups of mutually approved assemblies in which the decision of one assembly is binding on all.

Because the Brethren refuse to accept denominational labels, early in the twentieth century the U.S. Bureau of the Census chose to designate them with Roman numerals. This mode of reference was followed by Elmer T. Clark in *The Small Sects in America* (1937) and by Frank S. Mead in the early editions of *The Handbook of Denominations in the United States* (1st ed., 1951), and this numerical system of reference is noted for the entries in the directory section of this encyclopedia.

FUNDAMENTALISM.

The arrival of fundamentalism as a movement within American Christianity is usually dated from 1910 and the publication of a series of booklets entitled *The Fundamentals: A Testimony of Truth*. The booklets, printed by two wealthy Presbyterians, Los Angeles oilmen Lyman Stewart (1840–1923) and Milton Stewart (1838–1923), were distributed freely and were the textbooks for what in the 1920s became the fundamentalist-modernist controversy. Fundamentalism so defined is usually viewed as a reaction to modernism, asserting traditional standards against the new theology and its search for scientific compatibility. While there is much truth in that definition, it is limited. It misses the essentially affirmative nature of fundamentalism and the century-old movement, of which early twentieth-century fundamentalism is but one passing phase.

Fundamentalism was, in its best form, an affirmative assertion of certain ideas concerning Bible truth. At its beginning, it was a discovery by clergy and laymen of American Protestant churches of the dispensational theology of John Nelson Darby, discussed early in this chapter. Conservative and evangelical, fundamentalism became a rallying point for church leaders and, during the late nineteenth century, was one of the major thrusts of Christianity in America.

In the mid-nineteenth century, the ideas of William Miller (1782–1849) brought to public consciousness the doctrine of the Second Coming of Christ and the dispensational theology of Darby, with its emphasis upon the premillennial literal return of Jesus. In America, Darby found that people accepted his ideas without leaving their own church to join the Brethren. Outstanding Christian leaders became vocal exponents of dispensational theology. Possibly none was as effective as evangelist Dwight L. Moody, who had been deeply affected by Brethren evangelist Henry Moorhouse Leading ministers—Adoniram J. Gordon, Arthur T. Pierson (1837–1911), William G. Moorehead (1836–1914), and James H. Brooks—were all changed by Brethren thinking.

In 1869 a group of ministers associated with a millennial periodical, *Waymarks in the Wilderness*, held the first of what became the Believers Meeting for Bible Study. The ministers met to promote belief in the "doctrine of the verbal inspiration of the Bible, the personality of the Holy Spirit, the atonement of (Christ's) sacrifice, the priesthood of Christ, the two natures in the believer, and the personal imminent return of our Lord from heaven." In 1883 the annual meetings were moved to Niagara-on-the-Lake, Ontario, and thus became known as the Niagara Conference on Prophecy.

Part of the aim of the Niagara Conference was to manifest the primitive idea of the ecclesia, the church. Thus the conference was the ministers' means of forming what Darby called the church, a gathering of believers free of denominational systems. However, the ministers did not leave their mainline denominations. They gathered for the informal closeness and doctrinal purity that Darby said should characterize the church. They used the Bible reading as developed by the Brethren, and they accepted Darby's ideas on dispensationalism and his eschatology.

In 1890 a definitive step for the whole course of fundamentalism occurred. The Niagara Conference adopted a "creedal statement." The 14-point statement was highly determinative of the movement's future course and set its priorities. The premillennial return of Christ is asserted as the answer to the impossibility of converting the world in this dispensation. The conference accepted the premillennialists' idea that the world is becoming less Christian, with evolution not bringing real human progress, thus necessitating Christ's direct intervention before the millennium. The conference was dominated by a mixture of Darby's ideas (especially on eschatology) and what is termed Princeton theology, a conservative Reformed theology developed at Princeton Theological Seminary. Princeton theology had developed new language to assert the authority of the Bible in the face of challenges by Darwinism, new historical critical approaches to the Bible, and liberal theology. It affirmed that the Bible (in its original text) was inerrant; that all scriptures, including the books of the Jewish Bible (the Old Testament), were Christ-centered; and that all of the books of the Bible are equally inspired.

The Niagara statement also included the Reformed theological emphasis on human depravity and salvation by the blood of Christ, which were assertively detailed in six articles. Almost all of the attendees at the Niagara Conference were from churches of the Reformed heritage, and it is not surprising that support for the Niagara statement drew most of its response from churches of the Reformed heritage (Baptist, Presbyterian, Reformed, and Congregational). In the 1920s, fundamentalism had its major battleground in the Baptist and Presbyterian churches.

Fundamentalists also cut off other conservative Christians who might have offered some support. For example, they denied the second blessing (a major idea of the Holiness movement—the second blessing is a personal religious experience after which the believer is thought to be perfected for life), and two ideas of the Adventists—soul-sleep and annihilationism. Soul-sleep is the idea that the soul exists in an unconscious state from the individual's death until the general resurrection of the body. Annihilationism is the belief that the wicked cease to exist, instead of existing in torment in hell for eternity. While some Methodists and some Adventists would, in the 1920s, agree on the five fundamentals, the Methodists and Adventists were not prominent in the fundamentalist movement.

From the 14-point Niagara statement, five points were lifted up as the most essential, the very fundamental beliefs of anyone who could be considered a Christian. The *five fundamentals*, as they came to be known, are: (1) the inspiration and infallibility of the Bible; (2) the deity of Christ (including his virgin birth); (3) the substitutionary atonement accomplished in Christ's death; (4) the literal resurrection of Christ from the dead; and (5) the literal return of Christ in the second advent. These points assume the truth of the ecumenical creeds, the Nicene and Chalcedonian. At the height of the modernist-fundamentalist controversy in the 1920s, the five fundamentals would become the crucial points around which arguments were focused.

The group consciousness of the leaders of the Niagara Conference was solidified in the several Bible institutes that were founded in the late nineteenth century. The most influential of these was the Moody Bible Institute in Chicago, but others, including the Bible Institute of Los Angeles, Philadelphia Bible Institute, the Toronto Bible Training School, and the Northwestern Bible Training School in Minneapolis, contributed to the cause. These schools institutionalized fundamentalism and, more importantly, helped train its future leaders.

In the early years of the twentieth century, the most prominent of the fundamentalist leaders was Arno E. Gaebelein (1861–1945), a former Methodist who left that church after accepting dispensational theology. He began a magazine, *Our Hope*, in 1899. He also helped finance the work on the *Scofield Reference Bible*, the single most influential source of Darby's theology in the modern era.

New life flowed into the movement with the publication of *The Fundamentals* in 1910, and Darbyite fundamentalism came into direct conflict with emerging liberalism in the decade before World War I (1914–1918). *The Fundamentals* followed the lead of the Niagara Creed in asserting the verbal inerrancy of scripture, the Calvinist doctrine of human depravity, and the imminent Second Coming. As modernist thinking grew, polemics led to polarization within American Protestantism, and polarization was followed by the formation of new denominations. The modernist thinking was highlighted by a theology that accepted the theory of evolution, and by higher biblical criticism, the study of the Bible in the light of the findings of secular historians and archeologists.

The new denominations occasioned by the fundamentalist controversy were of two kinds. First, from the several large Protestant bodies arose fundamentalist churches that differed only from their parent bodies by acceptance of a fundamentalist mind-set with which to interpret the parent bodies' own doctrinal statements (such as the General Association of Regular Baptist Churches). Second, there emerged new religious bodies that encompassed the total fundamentalist thrust and were the truly American form of the Plymouth Brethren tradition discussed earlier in this chapter. These have been referred to as the *undenominated* churches, since they were organized in loose fellowships. They had a dispensational theology with the Reformed emphasis of Niagara, and became the ecclesiastical products of the Bible institutes (such as the Independent Fundamental Churches of America).

Fundamentalism of both kinds split into essentially two parties. One group emphasizes separation from all apostasy and from particular forms of evil, such as communism, the National Council of Churches, and organizations that compromise the faith. It also separated from its former colleagues who chose to remain in the larger liberal denominations.

A second group also emerged among those who left the denominations but wanted to retain a relationship with colleagues who for various reasons wished to stay in their post. This group developed a more positive attitude toward the world and articulated a desire to engage modern intellectual thought and culture while retaining an allegiance to a conservative theological stance. Neo-Evangelicalism (or today just Evangelicalism) is the name assumed by this postfundamentalist movement. Its leaders have tried to be honest with natural science, conversant on philosophy and theology, and socially concerned.

The separatists have been associated with the American Council of Christian Churches (ACCC) and the ministry of Dr. Carl McIntire (1906–2002), whose organ of expression was for many years the *Christian Beacon*. McIntire founded and headed the Bible Presbyterian Church. Membership in the ACCC is made up largely of small separatist bodies. The more inclusive approach is advocated by the National Association of Evangelicals (NAE). It includes a wide range of bodies that accept its minimal statement of faith. The NAE accepts not only church bodies, but also conferences and local churches, or groups not otherwise affiliated. The independent magazine, *Christianity Today*, is the most important periodical of neo-Evangelicalism, though the NAE has its own organ, *United Evangelical Action*.

In the last quarter of the twentieth century, Evangelicals and fundamentalists made common cause on the political front in the United States with the formation of a conservative movement espousing the goal of enacting into law some of their moral ideals, especially as they relate to sexual morality. Motivation for the rise of what has been termed the *Christian Right* was the 1973 Supreme Court case *Row v. Wade*, which was widely perceived as legalizing abortion. The same decade saw the rise of the homosexual rights movement. Conservative Christian leaders saw these two issues tied together by the larger issue of widespread disregard of traditional sexual ethics and open support for sexual activity outside of the bounds of heterosexual marriage.

The Christian Right movement also grew upon the success of religious broadcasting, the Evangelicals having come to dominate Christian-based radio and television. Many of the leaders of the Christina Right had originally gained a level of fame and public support through their radio and television shows, most notably Jerry Falwell (1933–2007), Pat Robertson (b. 1930), Tim Lahaye (b. 1926) and Beverly Lahaye (b. 1930), and James Dobson (b. 1936). During the administration (1981–1989) of President Ronald Reagan (1911–2004), the Christian Right aligned with the Republican Party, within which it attained a powerful presence. Though unable to push much legislation through Congress or overturn *Roe v. Wade*, the Christian Right was able to block a variety of legislative initiatives, and during the George W. Bush administration (2001–2009) attained a few of its goals (such as the funding of faith-based charity work) through presidential fiat. Meanwhile, the movement proved unable to stop the slow but steady establishment in law of gay and lesbian rights.

JEWISH MESSIANISM. Evangelicalism was one of the more dynamic segments of American religion through the last half of the twentieth century, and gave birth to a variety of new denominations, some of which placed a new emphasis on evangelizing Jews. The first of these groups, Jews for Jesus, emerged in California in the 1970s, and it continues as an important missionary effort supported generally by Evangelical churches. However, in the 1980s, its initial thrust was inherited by what became known as the Messianic Jewish movement. Many Jewish converts and others who had been associated with Jewish missions began to form synagogues that followed Jewish cultural patterns (including a liberal use of Hebrew) into which was poured a Christian theology. Since then, a spectrum of messianic denominations emerged that reflected the variant theologies present in the larger movements.

The Messianic Jewish movement traces its roots to the Jesus People movement of the 1970s, and Jews for Jesus was originally perceived as another branch of the Jesus People revival. The Jesus People produced a number of new structures (fellowships of communal societies), but by the end of the twentieth century, all of these had been absorbed into older denominations.

THE GRACE GOSPEL MOVEMENT. As John Nelson Darby's dispensational theology gained acceptance in Evangelical circles, it was inevitable that variations would arise. One such variation is attributed to Anglican Ethelbert W. Bullinger, who published a new outline of dispensational history in his book *How to Enjoy the Bible*. His seven dispensations are outlined in a symmetrical manner:

A. The Edenic State (Innocence)

  B. Mankind as a whole (Patriarchal)

    C. Israel (under Law)

      D. The Church of God. The Secret.

        The Dispensation of Grace

    C. Israel (Judicial)

  B. Mankind as a whole (Millennial)

A. The Eternal State (Glory)

Evident in much of Bullinger's writings is a desire for symmetry and mathematical order, which influenced greatly his interpretation of the scriptures. For Bullinger, the Edenic State went from the creation to the fall; the patriarchal dispensation went from the fall to Moses; and the dispensation of Israel under the law went from Moses through Pentecost to the beginning of Paul's ministry, and therefore included the apostolic church. The fourth dispensation is the present. It is the time of the church of God, the Christian church as influenced by the ministry of Paul and therefore directed not to the Jews but to the Gentiles. Bullinger called this period "the secret" because to Paul was revealed the secret hidden from the ages, the secret of God's grace replacing the law and

reaching beyond the Jews to the Gentiles (Ephesians 3:1–6). For Bullinger, the next dispensation is a judgment period for the Jews, in which the Jews will be judged according to their own law, not according to the grace of Christianity. The judgment period occurs before the tribulation, a conclusion based on Jeremiah 30. The sixth dispensation includes the tribulation and millennium, as discussed early in this chapter with the material on John Nelson Darby, who originated dispensationalism. Bullinger's seventh dispensation is eternity.

The crucial item in Bullinger's work had to do with his interpretation of the transition from the third to the fourth dispensation. Bullinger sees in the Gospels, Acts, and New Testament Epistles a development in several stages. The Gospels belong to the third dispensation and have one baptism, John's water baptism. In Acts and the early Pauline epistles, there are two baptisms—John's and the baptism of the Spirit. In the later Pauline epistles, representing the start of the fourth dispensation, there is again only one baptism—the Spirit baptism (Ephesians 4:5, "There is one Lord, one faith, one baptism"). The immediate significance of so dividing scripture is to say that, in the church age, water baptism has no place. Its long-term significance is to assert Paul's later letters as the principle documents for Christians, and the documents through which the others should be interpreted.

Strongly influenced by Bullinger was Charles H. Welch, who in 1929 began *The Berean Expositor* in London and authored several books. As ultradispensationalism developed, a strict differentiation was made between the church of Acts and the body of Christ that had its beginning with Paul's pronouncements in Acts 28:25–28, telling the church to direct its efforts to the Gentiles instead of to the Jews. The Gospels are purely Israelitish. With Pentecost, the church was inaugurated; its distinctive characteristics were the sign-gifts (miracles), water baptism, and the Lord's Supper. However, these ceased with the beginning of the body of Christ with its one baptism. Bullinger and Welch also taught that the body of Christ was distinct from the bride of Christ, which was identified with a remnant of Israel. The "churches of Asia" in Revelation 2:3 are seen as future Jewish churches that will become Christian.

Among the additional beliefs of Bullinger and Welch, for which they were most criticized by fundamentalists, were annihilationism and soul-sleep, as well as the belief that the Lord's Supper is not to be observed in the post-Acts church. There is some dispute concerning whether or not Bullinger actually taught annihilation for the wicked, but Welch certainly did.

In the 1920s the views of Bullinger began to spread in the United States. The first advocates were Pastor J. C. O'Hair, a graduate of Moody Bible Institute in Chicago and minister of the North Shore Church in Chicago, and Dr. Harry Bultema (1884–1952) of the Berean Church in Muskegon, Michigan. O'Hair, a member of the Independent Fundamental Churches of America and a prolific writer on dispensationalism, published many pamphlets and Bible studies and was active in conferences and a radio ministry. He frequently wrote and spoke of the "blunder of the church," by which he meant the confusion of the hope, calling, and program of Israel with the hope, calling, and program of the church. O'Hair's discussion of Israel includes the early apostolic church, which existed within the Jewish community. O'Hair did not want Christians to confuse that church with the church as influenced by Paul's later epistles, and therefore directed to the Gentiles in a much broader program than the apostolic church that was directed to Jews. The church influenced by Paul's later epistles is the church of the present, the church existing in the dispensation of grace. Thus O'Hair's teaching came to be called the Grace Gospel position.

During the 1930s there was an increase in the number of ministers and Bible churches that held the Grace Gospel position. Early centers developed in Milwaukee, Wisconsin; Paterson, New Jersey; St. Louis, Missouri; Grand Rapids and Holland, Michigan; and Indianapolis and Evansville, Indiana.

Welch made his first visit to Canada in 1927, and in 1955 he made a trip to both Canada and the United States. After World War II (1937–1945), a following that accepted annihilationism and did not practice the Lord's Supper (as did O'Hair) developed around Welch.

SOURCES

Dispensationalism

Bass, Clarence B. *Backgrounds to Dispensationalism: Its Historical Genesis and Ecclesiastical Implications.* Grand Rapids, MI: Baker Book House, 1960. 184 pp.

Ehlert, Arnold D., comp. *A Bibliographic History of Dispensationalism.* Grand Rapids, MI: Baker Book House, 1965. 110 pp.

Huebner, R. A. *The Truth of the Pre-Tribulation Rapture Recovered.* Morganville, NJ: Present Truth, 1973. 81 pp.

Kraus, C. Norman. *Dispensationalism in America: Its Rise and Development.* Richmond, VA: John Knox Press, 1958. 156 pp.

Larkin, Clarence. *Dispensational Truth: or, God's Plan and Purpose in the Ages.* 3rd ed. Philadelphia: Author, 1920. 176 pp.

MacPherson, Dave. *The Unbelievable Pre-Trib Origin.* Kansas City, MO: Heart of America Bible Society, 1973. 123 pp.

Sisco, Paul E. *Scofield or the Scriptures.* Alden, NY: Author, n.d. 65 pp.

Zens, Jon. *Dispensationalism: A Reformed Inquiry into Its Leading Figures and Features.* Phillipsburg, NJ: Presbyterian and Reformed Publishing, 1980. 57 pp.

The Plymouth Brethren and John Nelson Darby

Coad, F. Roy. *A History of the Brethren Movement: Its Origins, Its Worldwide Development, and Its Significance for the Present Day.* Grand Rapids, MI: Eerdmans, 1968. 327 pp.

Darby, John Nelson. *The Collected Writings.* 35 vols. Oak Park, IL: Bible Truth Publishers, 1971.

Ehlert, Arnold D. *Brethren Writers: A Checklist with an Introduction to Brethren Literature and Additional Lists.* Grand Rapids, MI: Baker Book House, 1969. 83 pp.

Miller, Andrew. *"The Brethren" (Commonly So-called).* Kowloon, Hong Kong: Christian Book Room, n.d. 213 pp.

Neatby, William Blair. *A History of the Plymouth Brethren.* London: Hodder and Stoughton, 1901. 357 pp.

Noel, Napoleon. *The History of the Brethren.* 2 vols. Denver, CO: Knapp, 1936.

Pickering, Hy. *Chief Men among the Brethren.* London: Pickering & Inglis, 1918. 223 pp.

Turner, W. G. *John Nelson Darby.* London: C. A. Hammond, 1944. 88 pp.

Weremchuk, Max S. *John Nelson Darby: A Biography.* Neptune, NJ: Loizeaux Brothers, 1992. 256 pp.

Fundamentalism

Barr, James. *Fundamentalism.* Philadelphia: Westminster Press, 1978. 379 pp.

Beale, David O. *In Pursuit of Purity: American Fundamentalism since 1850.* Greenville, SC: Unusual Publications, 1986. 457 pp.

Blackstone, William E. *Jesus Is Coming.* New York: Fleming H. Revell, 1908. 252 pp.

Cole, Stewart G. *The History of Fundamentalism.* New York: Richard R. Smith, 1931. 360 pp.

Deremer, Bernard. *Moody Biblical Institute: A Pictorial History.* Chicago: Moody Press, 1960. 128 pp.

Dollar, George W. *A History of Fundamentalism in America.* Greenville, SC: Bob Jones University Press, 1973. 411 pp.

English, E. Schuyler. *H. A. Ironside: Ordained of the Lord.* Oakland, CA: Western Book and Tract, 1946. 276 pp.

Falwell, Jerry, ed., with Ed Dobson and Ed Hindson. *The Fundamentalist Phenomenon: The Resurgence of Conservative Christianity.* Garden City, NY: Doubleday, 1981. 269 pp.

Furniss, Norman F. *The Fundamentalist Controversy, 1918–1931.* New Haven, CT: Yale University Press, 1954. 199 pp.

Lawrence, Bruce B. *Defenders of God: The Fundamentalist Revolt against the Modern Age.* San Francisco, CA: Harper & Row, 1989. 306 pp.

Magnuson, Norris A. *American Evangelicalism: An Annotated Bibliography.* West Cornwall, CT: Locust Hill Press, 1990. 495 pp.

Marsden, George M. *Fundamentalism and American Culture.* 2nd ed. New York: Oxford University Press, 2006. 468 pp.

Pruter, Karl. *Jewish Christians in the United States: A Bibliography.* New York: Garland Publishing, 1987. 192 pp.

Russell, C. Allyn. *Voices of American Fundamentalism: Seven Biographical Studies.* Philadelphia: Westminster Press, 1976. 304 pp.

Sandeen, Ernest R. *The Roots of Fundamentalism: British and American Millenarianism, 1800–1930.* Chicago: University of Chicago Press, 1970. 328 pp.

Two Christian Laymen. *The Fundamentals: A Testimony to the Truth.* Chicago: Testimony Publishing, 1910–1915.

Weber, Timothy P. *Living in the Shadow of the Second Coming: American Premillennialism, 1875–1982.* New York: Oxford University Press, 1979. 232 pp.

Evangelicalism

Balmer, Randall. *Encyclopedia of Evangelicalism.* Louisville, KY: Westminster/John Knox Press, 2002. 654 pp.

Bebbington, David. *The Dominance of Evangelicalism: The Age of Spurgeon and Moody.* Downers Grove, IL: Inter-Varsity Press, 2005. 288 pp.

Ellingsen, Mark. *The Evangelical Movement: Growth, Impact, Controversy, Dialog.* Minneapolis, MN: Augsburg, 1988. 496 pp.

Harris-Shapiro, Carol. *Messianic Judaism: A Rabbi's Journey through Religious Change in America.* Boston: Beacon Press, 1999. 218 pp.

Haykin, Michael A. G., and Kenneth J. Stewart. *The Emergence of Evangelicalism.* Downers Grove, IL: Inter-Varsity Press, 2008. 432 pp.

Hutchinson, Richard G., Jr. *Mainline Churches and the Evangelicals: A Challenging Crisis?* Atlanta, GA: John Knox Press, 1981.

Kyle, Richard. *Evangelicalism: An Americanized Christianity.* Piscataway, NJ: Transaction, 2006. 363 pp.

Larsen, Timothy, with David Bebbington and Mark A. Noll. *Biographical Dictionary of Evangelicals.* Downers Grove, IL: InterVarsity Press, 2003. 789 pp.

Murray, Iain H. *Evangelicalism Divided: A Record of Crucial Change in the Years 1950 to 2000.* Carlisle, PA: Banner of Truth, 2000. 342 pp.

Neuhaus, Richard J., and Michael Cromartie. *Piety and Politics: Evangelicals and Fundamentalists Confront the World.* Lanham, MD: University Press of America, 1988.

Penning, James M., and Corwin E. Smidt. *Evangelicalism: The Next Generation.* Grand Rapids, MI: Baker Academic, 2002. 203 pp.

Rosell, Garth M. *The Surprising Work of God: Harold John Ockenga, Billy Graham, and the Rebirth of Evangelicalism.* Grand Rapids, MI: Baker Academic, 2008. 288 pp.

Shelley, Bruce. *Evangelicalism in America.* Grand Rapids, MI: Eerdmans, 1967. 134 pp.

Sweet, Leonard I., ed. *The Evangelical Tradition in America.* Macon, GA: Mercer University Press, 1984. 318 pp.

Tidwell, Derek J. *Who Are the Evangelicals? Tracing the Roots of the Modern Movements.* Grand Rapids, MI: Zondervan, 1994.

Utter, Glen H., and John W. Storey. *The Religious Right: A Reference Handbook.* 3rd ed. Millerton, NY: Grey House, 2007. 503 pp.

Wells, David F., and John D. Woodbridge, eds. *The Evangelicals: What They Believe, Who They Are, Where They Are Changing.* Nashville, TN: Abingdon, 1975.

Grace Gospel Movement

Baker, Charles F. *A Dispensational Theology.* Grand Rapids, MI: Grace Bible College Publications, 1980.

Bullinger, E. W. *The Foundations of Dispensational Truth.* London: Lamp Press, 1959. 287 pp.

———. *Selected Writings.* London: Lamp Press, 1960. 296 pp.

Hoste, William. *Bullingerism or Ultra-Dispensationalism Exposed.* Fort Dodge, IA: n.d. 32 pp.

Ironside, Harold A. *Wrongly Dividing the Word of Truth.* 4th ed. Neptune, NJ: Loizeaux Brothers, 1989. 66 pp.

O'Hair, J.C. *Bible Messages of Grace and Glory.* Chicago: Author, n.d. 17 pp.

———. *The Great Blunder of the Church.* Chicago: Author, n.d. 70 pp.

Stewart, Alex. H. *Bullingerism Exposed.* New York: Loizeaux Brothers, n.d. 15 pp.

❈ Plymouth Brethren

Christian Brethren (Open or Plymouth Brethren)
c/o Walterick Publishing Ministries, PO Box 3831, Olathe, KS 66063-3831

The Christian Brethren (Open or Plymouth Brethren) came to the United States in the mid-nineteenth century and grew by evangelistic efforts. They prospered in part because John Nelson Darby's ideas on eschatology were being accepted by many mainline American Protestants, and dispensational thinking was spreading. In some cases, the Open Brethren increased by the movement of Exclusive Grant Brethren churches into their ranks.

Although there is no generally accepted statement of faith for the Open Brethren, one statement used in some assemblies affirms the Bible as the inerrant Word of God; the Trinity; the depravity of man and the necessity of salvation by grace through faith; the church as composed of all true believers in Jesus Christ; two ordinances, baptism by immersion and the Lord's Supper; the security of the believer (once a person is truly a child of God, that status is secure for all time); and pretribulation premillennialism (that is, Christ will return before the tribulation and before the millennium.) (For a discussion of various positions on the millennium, see the introductory material for this volume.) Brethren assemblies (congregations) usually are led by elders recognized by the local congregation. Assemblies celebrate a weekly communion service at which many are encouraged to speak or pray. Concerted efforts to fellowship with like-minded Christians in other groups such as InterVarsity Fellowship and the Billy Graham crusades are characteristic. Open Brethren see themselves as a part of mainstream evangelicalism.

Some Open Brethren assemblies were originally a part of the Plymouth Brethren (Grant Brethren), named after Frederick W. Grant, a nineteenth-century leader among the Exclusive Brethren in the Northeast. The Loizeaux Brothers, Bible Truth Depot, long identified with the Grant Brethren as a publishing house, also identified with the Open Brethren.

There are no central headquarters for the Open Brethren, but several structures have become the focus of the assemblies' cooperative endeavor. The extensive foreign missionary work of the Open Brethren is publicized and served by Christian Missions in Many Lands, Inc. (U.S.A.) and Missionary Service Committee (Canada), who jointly publish a periodical, *Missions*, from central offices in Wall, New Jersey. The corporations do not designate missionaries, a function left to local assemblies, but do transmit funds and facilitate relations with foreign governments. Other missionary agencies included Workers Together of Wheaton, Illinois, which published a newsletter that bears its name. Workers Together no longer exists. International Teams operates a missionary center and sponsors teams of short-term missionaries from its headquarters in Prospect Heights, Illinois. International Teams reported that it has sent 1,024 workers to 170 teams in 62 countries.

Walterick Publishers of Olathe, Kansas, is the publisher and book distributor for the Open Brethren. It also publishes an annual directory of assemblies in North America and the Caribbean. Truth and Praise, Inc., of Belle Chasse, Louisiana, publishes three Open Brethren hymnals. There are a number of other small, independent publishers who produce a variety of tracts and booklets. Emmaus Bible College, Dubuque, Iowa, founded in 1945, provides a two-year associate of arts program in a Bible-related curriculum as well as four-year degrees in basic and elementary education. Mount Carmel Bible of Edmonton, Alberta, and Kawartha Lakes Bible School in Peterborough, Ontario, provide a one-year Bible curriculum. Many ministers attend one of several conservative evangelical seminaries such as Dallas Theological Seminary, Trinity Evangelical Divinity School, or Talbot School of Theology for further training. The *Address Book*, published by Walterick Publishers, lists 19 homes for the elderly and one children's home. Open Brethren operate 54 summer camps in the United States and Canada. In Great Britain, the Open Brethren are served by the publishing firm of Pickering and Inglis of Glasgow and London, which publishes a directory of assemblies worldwide.

Membership: Not reported.

Educational Facilities:

Emmaus Bible College, Dubuque, Iowa.

Mount Carmel Bible School, Alberta, Edmonton, Canada.

Kawartha Lakes Bible School, Peterborough, Ontario, Canada.

Periodicals: *Missions, Christian Missions in Many Lands.* Send orders to PO Box 13, Spring Lake, NJ 07762. • *Uplook.* Send orders to PO Box 2041, Grand Rapids, MI 49501.

Sources:

Christian Missions in Many Lands, Inc.: www.cmmlusa.org.

Emmaus Bible College. www.emmaus.edu.

International Teams. www.iteams.org.

Walterick Publishing Ministries. www.walterick.org.

Barker, Harold B. *Why I Abandoned Exclusivism.* Fort Dodge, IA: Walterick, n.d.

Bayliss, Robert. *My People.* Port Colborne, ON: Gospel Folio Press, 1995.

Conrad, William W. *Family Matters.* Wheaton, IL: Interest Ministries, 1992.

Darms, Anton. *The Abundant Gospel.* New York: Loizeaux Brothers, Bible Truth Depot, 1941.

MacDonald, William. *What the Bible Teaches*. Oak Park, IL: Emmaus Correspondence School, 1949.

North American Missions: 1995 Resource Guide. Wheaton, IL: Interest Ministries, 1995.

Porter, Carol, and Mike Hamel, eds. *Women's Ministry Handbook*. Wheaton, IL: Victor Books, 1992.

Smart, John. *Historical Sketch of Assembly Missions*. New York: Christian Missions in Many Lands, 1966.

A Younger Brother [A. Rendle Short]. *The Principles of Christians Called "Open Brethren,"* Glasgow, U.K.: Pickering and Inglis, 1913.

Churches of God (Needed Truth)

The Church of God in Toronto, Sheppard Gospel Hall, 720 Sheppard Ave. W, North York, ON, Canada M3H 2S6

In the 1870s questions began to arise among the Plymouth Brethren (Open Brethren) as to just how far they should go in their openness. Discussions led to several separations by groups with different solutions. One strict group formed around the periodical *Needed Truth*, which began in 1889. The bulk of separations of *Needed Truth* supporters began in 1892–1893. Early in the twentieth century, the movement spread from England to North America, primarily to Canada. The Needed Truth groups, called Churches of God, are most properly described as open, in that they are willing to fellowship with like-minded believers who are not members of the Churches of God and constitute a bridge between the Open and the Exclusive Brethren groups.

The distinctive teaching of the Churches of God concerns ecclesiology. This group believes that the "church which is Christ's body" is composed totally of believers in Christ. The fellowship of the Churches of God is composed of those who received the Word and who live in obedience, having been baptized by other disciples (Churches of God elders) and having been "added" by the Lord. "Addition" means that a believer is associated with the churches where the proper authority of Christ is expressed, that is, with churches in fellowship with the Churches of God. There is a tendency toward exclusivism in that assemblies of the Churches of God feel that all brethren (ultimately, all Christians) ought to be a part of their fellowship.

The Churches of God constitutes the only group of Brethren that has developed what approaches a presbyterial polity. Elders of the Churches of God have powers similar to those of presbyters in the Presbyterian Church, with the duty of leading the worship services, setting doctrinal standards, ruling on governmental matters, and teaching. Government in the Churches of God is placed in the hands of a united elderhood. Local assemblies function as the constituencies of elders who operate on both the local and regional levels. A premium is placed on consensus of the elders. The elders or overseers form a self-perpetuating body. They appoint deacons, and from the deacons choose new elders. Regular meetings of the overseers occur.

The worldwide Churches of God conducts a radio ministry called *Search for Truth* and publishes written materials through Hayes Press in Wiltshire, England. In 2008 it updated its 120-year-old periodical *Needed Truth* into *NT* magazine, published monthly.

Membership: While the Churches of God has long been a substantive movement in Britain, in 2008 the fellowship reported only seven churches in North America, five of them in Canada and two in the United States, both in Colorado.

Periodicals *NT (Needed Truth)*. Available from www.churchesofgod.info/ ˜brian/index.html.

Sources:

Churches of God. www.churchesofgod.info/.

About Churches of God. raq930.uk2.net/tapedministry/articles/aboutcog1.htm.

Willis, G., and B. R. Wilson. "The Churches of God: Pattern and Practice." In *Patterns of Sectarianism*. Edited by Bryan R. Wilson. London: Heinemann, 1967.

Plymouth Brethren (Ames Brethren)

c/o Christian Literature, Inc., Box 1052, Anoka, MN 55303-1052

Among the several factions that developed among the Plymouth Brethren were the Ames Brethren. This group originated with a preacher named Ames, who worked among the Plymouth Brethren (Booth Brethren), now a constituent part of the Plymouth Brethren (Reunited Brethren). He distrusted the teachings and practice of the Plymouth Brethren (Glanton Brethren), a group with whom the Booth Brethren cooperated in England. Those supporting Ames's opinions separated from the Booth Brethren in 1949.

The Ames Brethren believe the Bible to be the Word of God. Although they hold to no creed, they believe that the Scriptures teach the fall of humanity and humans' lost condition, the love of God in providing a savior, the perfection of Christ, the atonement of Christ on the cross, the resurrection, the need of a new birth, the assurance of present salvation, and a future of heaven for the saved and eternal punishment for unbelievers. Believers' hope should not be placed in the improvement of the world, but in the coming of Christ.

Essential to Brethren belief and life is the gathering unto Christ as a divine center over against all human centers. No sectarian names are assumed. The church is guided by the Holy Spirit and has no need of an ordained priesthood or ministry. No salary is paid to preachers of the Word, and no collections are taken at public meetings. Meeting halls are modest in appearance.

As a corrolate to belief in the communion of the saints, the Brethren maintain the necessity of godly order, meaning that no one assembly can be owned as independent and apart from all the assemblies. They believe in holiness and truth that includes the putting away of evil doers, refusing to hear unsound teachers, and marking and avoiding those who cause division. Each local assembly is seen as an expression of the whole assembly of God.

Several publication centers serve the Brethren, especially Christian Literature, Inc. in Minneapolis and Moments with the Book in Bedford, Pennsylvania. Don Johnson, a printer and editor from Pennsylvania, presents a weekly radio show, *Moments with the Book*, which has been heard over 22 stations in the United States and one in the Bahamas. Bible conferences are held annually in Iowa and Pennsylvania.

Membership: Not reported. Membership records are not kept.

Periodicals: *Moments with the Bible*. • *Moments for Youth*. Send orders to Box 322, Bedford, PA 15522. • *Words of Truth*. • *Fellowship Letters*. Available from Aldridge F. Johnson, Rte. 1, Box 33, Isanti, MN 55040.

Sources:

Smith, Hamilton. *Perspectives on the True Church*. Minneapolis, MN: Christian Literature, n.d.

Plymouth Brethren (Ex-Taylor Brethren)

Current address not obtained for this edition.

In 1960 several assemblies left the Plymouth Brethren (Raven-Taylor Brethren) because of the restrictions enunciated by the James Taylor Jr. faction. This group is small, probably divided among itself, and is in correspondence with some similar assemblies in Britain.

Membership: Not reported.

Plymouth Brethren (Raven-Taylor-Hales Brethren)

Current address not obtained for this edition.

The Raven-Taylor-Hales Brethren is a branch of the Plymouth Brethren, also known as Exclusive Brethren. This Protestant branch holds a separatist doctrine, believing that God's principal of unity is achieved by excluding evil. Few individuals not born in the Raven-Taylor-Hales Brethren become members. The branch encourages traditional marriage and family life. Members abide by the laws of their country as long as the laws do not contradict the Bible.

Children live at home until they marry, and they marry within their fellowship. Children attend branch-run schools and are discouraged from attending college. Social activities are restricted to within the fellowship. Members do not eat in public restaurants. The branch has banned the use of television, radio, and computers, although recently the use of computers has been allowed.

John Nelson Darby (1800–1882) was the first leader of the branch. He was followed by J. B. Stoney (1814–1897), F. E. Raven (1837–1903), C. A. Coates (1862–1945), and James Taylor Sr. (1870–1953). Taylor, a New York businessman, led the branch into a more separatist path, and he was succeeded by his son, James Taylor Jr. (1899–1970), who demanded a rigorous separation from the world. The Taylor Brethren refused to list their centers in the telephone directories. They encouraged their members to withdraw from professional associations, to resign offices in business corporations, and to dispose of stock. They refused to eat with anyone not in their fellowship. Critics have claimed that Taylor Jr. advocated divorce if any member of a household lost religious fervor. One British newspaper, reporting on Taylor's return to the United States from England in 1969, commented, "The harsh tenets of this sect have broken up homes and led to misery and suicide. Now he has gone home, Britain's parting message is 'good riddance and don't come back.'"

At a conference in 1959 a confrontation took place between Taylor Jr and Gerald R. Cowell of Hornchurch. Cowell promoted a more moderate line in terms of separation from the world, and as a result he was excommunicated from the branch. Several members left the branch during the Taylor ministries. In 1970 Taylor Jr. was allegedly involved in inappropriate behavior involving alcohol. After his death, James Symington, from North Dakota, was elected as the new leader. Symington died in 1987 and passed his ministry to John S. Hales, an Australian businessman. When Hales died in 2002 his son, Bruce David Hales, another Australian businessman, headed the ministry; in 2008 he was still serving as leader.

In the United States the majority of members are located in New York and California. Other congregations are located in the Northeast and the Midwest, and there are fewer members in the South. Stow Hill Bible and Tract Depot has been their publisher in England for many years. This group is "IV" in the 1936 Religious Census list.

Membership: In 2008 the branch reported more than 40,000 members in 300 assemblies meeting in 19 countries. Large membership exists in Australia, New Zealand, the United Kingdom, and North America. There are smaller membership figures for Europe and Latin America.

Sources:

The Exclusive Brethren Christian Fellowship. www.theexclusivebrethren.com/,

F. E. R. [F. E. Raven]. *Readings and Addresses in the United States*. Kingston-on-Thames, U.K.: Stow Hill Bible and Tract Depot, 1902.

Gardiner, A. J. *The Recovery and Maintenance of the Truth*. Kingston-on-Thames, U.K.: Stow Hill Bible and Tract Depot, n.d.

————. *The Substantiality of Christianity*. Kingston-on-Thames, U.K.: Stow Hill Bible and Tract Depot, 1954.

Taylor, James. *Administration in the Assembly*. London: Stow Hill Bible and Tract Depot, 1937.

————. *Christ's Personal Service for the Saints*. Wellington, NZ: Whitcombe and Tombs, 1925.

Wilson, Bryan. "A Sect at Law." *Encounter* 60, no. 1 (January 1983): 81–87.

Plymouth Brethren (Reunited Brethren)

No central headquarters. For information:, Believers Bookshelf, PO Box 261, Sunbury, PA 17801

The Plymouth Brethren (Reunited Brethren) was formed by the coming together of a number of Exclusive Plymouth Brethren groups that had divided into factions in the nineteenth and early twentieth centuries. Their story is told in two segments, first as one of division and then as one of reunion.

One of the earliest schisms of the Brethren centered upon the popular and zealous William Kelly (1820–1906). Kelly, an Irishman, was editor of the *Bible Treasury* for 50 years and also of the *Collected Writings of John Nelson Darby*, the prominent early leader of the Brethren. In the 1870s, however, Darby (1800–1882) became associated with a party in the movement known as New-Lumpism. Members of this group attacked the worldliness they saw in the Brethren of their day, and looked with disfavor upon the evangelism that was swelling their ranks with new converts. They yearned for a pure fellowship and advocated the high church principle, namely, that the assembly has the supreme judicial power, and its decisions, which are in accord with scripture, must be accepted. Kelly and his supporters separated in 1881, the year before Darby's death. The group was limited to England and the West Indies.

Just four years after the Kelly schism, Clarence Esme Stuart (1828–1903) and the few congregations who adhered to him were expelled from the main body of the Exclusive Brethren because his teachings on Christian position and condition were considered to be mystical. In 1885 a division that began in Montreal separated the supporters of Frederick W. Grant (1834–1902), a well known teacher and writer, from Brethren in most countries of the world.

Not many years afterward, around 1890, the majority of assemblies in continental Europe separated. They were the surviving Exclusive Brethren who did not accept either Frederick W. Grant or F. E. Raven (1837–1903), a popular Exclusive Brethren teacher of the late nineteenth century (see separate entries). Also, they sided with C. Strange and W. J. Lowe in 1909 in the Tunbridge Wells controversy (see Plymouth Brethren (Tunbridge Wells)). Although they were strongest on the continent, these Brethren had assemblies across the United States too. In the 1936 *Religious Census* they were called "III."

In 1928 the Grant Brethren, the remnants of which are now a constituent part of the Plymouth Brethren (Open Brethren), divided into three factions as the result of a controversy that erupted in Philadelphia, Pennsylvania. One reason for the controversy was the alleged heresy of James Boyd, a visiting British preacher who had written a tract denying that Christ had a human spirit. A second controversy developed between two people within the Philadelphia assembly, C. A. Mory and his business partner C. V. Grant. The partner was accused of deceit, fraud, and misuse of funds. The assembly's refusal to excommunicate the partner or to brand Boyd's teachings as heresy led to schism. Adding fuel to the fire of controversy was the contemporaneous movement of some Grant Brethren toward the Open Brethren.

One small group of assemblies (labeled "VII" by the *Religious Census*) withdrew fellowship from Boyd and any who did not agree with their strong stand. One leader of this faction was R. J. Little, editor of *Holding Fast and Holding Faith*, though he later joined the Open Brethren and the faculty at Moody Bible Institute.

A larger group of assemblies was led by A. E. Booth, who accepted Boyd's retraction of his "heretical" position but rejected the Grant Brethren in the move toward the Open Brethren position. He led the formation of the Erie Bible Truth Depot, in Erie, Pennsylvania. In 1932 he began *Things Old and New*. (The Booth Brethren were numbered "VIII" in the *Religious Census*.)

The mergers of the separated Brethren occurred in 1926, 1940, 1953, and 1974. The first, in 1926, resulted in the union of the Kelly and Continental Brethren. This action was effective in England, the West Indies, Europe, Egypt, and North America. Then in 1940 the Kelly-Continental Brethren and the British section of the Tunbridge Wells Brethren reunited. However, the U.S. section of the Tunbridge Wells group remains separate to this day and has undergone several internal divisions.

In 1953 the Kelly-Continental Brethren united with the Stuart Brethren and also took in the Mory faction of the former Grant Brethren. This reunion affected assemblies around the world. Finally, in 1974 the previously reunited Brethren merged with the Glanton Brethren (a splinter from the Plymouth Brethren (Raven-Taylor-

Hales Brethren)) and the Booth Brethren, which had previously become associated with the Glanton Brethren.

Since then, fresh division has broken out among theses assemblies, and Brethren throughout the world have been affected. Some North American assemblies have left the fellowship, choosing instead a path of greater independence.

The reunion changed little doctrinally with the various segments of the Brethren who reunited, because few of the earlier schisms had a strong doctrinal element, and those few doctrinal questions had become academic. The reunited assemblies now seek to maintain the unity of the Spirit of God and to function as assemblies gathered in the name of the Lord Jesus Christ on the ground of the One Body of Christ, in contrast to acting as independent assemblies. They acknowledge Christ as their only head and the Holy Spirit as the only administrator of the church, and accept the Bible as God's inspired, infallible word and their all-sufficient guide for doctrine and practice.

The assemblies are organized congregationally and tied together by their like-mindedness and the cooperative activities in which they participate. Missionaries are supported in Africa, the Middle East and surrounding lands, South America, the Caribbean Islands, India, Beamsville, Ontario, Canada, and the Philippines. Believers Bookshelf of Sunbury, Pennsylvania, is the major publisher for the Reunited Brethren in the United States; there are numerous others in other countries. Literature ministry is the major outreach in the Reunited Brethren.

Membership: In 2008 the fellowship reported 100 assemblies in the United States and Canada, and many hundreds in other countries. Worldwide membership is unknown.

Periodicals: *Missionary Bulletin*. Literature is available through Believers Bookshelf.

Sources:

Believers Bookshelf. www.bbusa.org.

Campbell, R. K. *The Christian Home*. Sudbury, PA: Believers Bookshelf, 1982.

———. *The Church of the Living God*. Sudbury, PA: Believers Bookshelf, n.d.

———. *Reunited Brethren: A Brief Historical Account Including a Brief Statement of Some Vital Principles of Faith*. Danville, IL: Grace and Truth, 1990.

Kelly, William. *Lectures on the Church of God*. Oak Park. IL: Bible Truth Publishers, n.d.

Plymouth Brethren (Tunbridge Wells Brethren)

No central headquarters. For information:, c/o Bible Truth Publishers, 59 Industrial Rd., PO Box 649, Addison, IL 60101

The Plymouth Brethren (Tunbridge Wells Brethren) are a group of the Plymouth Brethren that dates from 1909, when there was an act of discipline in the assembly in Tunbridge Wells, London, England, involving Mr. C. Strange. After moving to London and establishing a business there, Strange's conduct and participation in meetings, both at home and elsewhere, ultimately resulted in his being excluded. W. J. Lowe, a prominent brother in London, took the lead in rejecting the action of the Tunbridge Wells assembly and in forming a group, later identified by his name as the Lowe Brethren, which included those sympathetic to Strange. Ironically, Strange was a member of that group for only a brief period. However, Lowe found support among the Continental Brethren, who also aligned themselves against the action at Tunbridge Wells.

In 1940 the Tunbridge Wells Brethren were invited to forget the past differences and amalgamate with others who had already been participating in a reunion process. The sponsoring group included the then merged former (William) Kelly, Lowe, Continental, Stuart, and Glanton Brethren, as well as some of the Grant Brethren. Most of the Tunbridge Wells Brethren in England accepted the invitation, and now are a constituent part of the Plymouth Brethren (Reunited Brethren). In North America, however, the Brethren felt that no true reunion could be accomplished without a consensus judgment on the root cause of the 1909 and earlier divisions. They have remained separate.

The Tunbridge Wells Brethren are a worldwide fellowship with assemblies in North, Central, and South America, as well as Australia, Europe, Asia, and Africa. Bible Truth Publishers in Addison, Illinois, is an independent operation, but it is owned and managed by members of the groups and publishes materials especially for it. It issues three periodicals and a number of books, pamphlets, and tracts, including reprints of nineteenth-century Brethren works and the *Collected Writings of John Nelson Darby*. There is a similar operation known as Bibles and Publications in Montreal, Quebec. A number of smaller publishers issue tracts in English and a variety of foreign languages.

Membership: Membership figures are unavailable for 2008. In 1997 there were more than 180 assemblies.

Periodicals: *Echoes of Grace*. • *Messages of God's Love*.

Sources:

Bible Truth Publishers. bibletruthpublishers.com.

Hayhoe, H. E. *Present Truth for Christians*. St. Louis, MO: Bible Truth Publishers, 1950.

Price, G. H. S. *Church History*. Addison, IL: Bible Truth Publishers, 1982.

Stanley, Charles. *The Church of God*. Oak Park, IL: Bible Truth Publishers, n.d.

Wilson, Paul. *A Defense of Dispensationalism*. Oak Park, IL: Bible Truth Publishers, n.d.

Wolston, W. T. *The Church, What Is It?* Oak Park, IL: Bible Truth Publishers, 1971.

Fundamentalists and Evangelical Churches

Aggressive Christianity Missions Training Corps

HR 60, Box 11, Fence Lake, NM 87315

The Aggressive Christianity Missions Training Corps is an evangelical communal ministry founded in 1982 by Jim Green and his wife Deborah Green as the Free Love Ministry. They saw the group as an end-time army brought together to fight sin, especially what they saw as major evils running rampant in society—pornography, homosexuality, rock music, and so on. Inspired in part by the Salvation Army, they developed a disciplined military lifestyle, and members wore uniforms and assumed ranks in the corps. The group maintains that it looks to God for its support.

The progress of the corps was blocked in 1987 when a former member sued, claiming that the group brainwashed had her. The leaders of the corps ignored the lawsuit and did not appear when the case came up in court. As a result, the former member received a million-dollar default judgment, which led to the loss of the corps' California property.

Currently, the group lives communally as an ekklesia under the theocratic government of God. They hold all things in common, including finances and meals. They honor God's standards for marriage and sexual purity. They are nonviolent. They have a worldwide literature ministry with affiliates in Ghana, Nigeria, Cameroon, Liberia, India, the Philippines, Mexico, Zambia, Zimbabwe, Malawi, Tanzania, Kenya, and Uganda. Affiliates are also located in England and various European countries.

The corps teaches a militant, fundamentalist Protestant Christianity. *Words of the Spirit* audio broadcasts and *Battle Cry Sounding* video messages are available online via the group's web site.

Membership: 2008 figures were not reported.

Periodicals: *Battle Cry Sounding*. • *Tribal Call*. • *Bread for the Nations*. • *Our Sustaining Bread*.

Sources:

Aggressive Christianity. www.aggressivechristianity.net.

"Onward Christian Soldiers." *Herald and News* (Klamath Falls, OR) (November 12, 1989).

Alliance for Renewal Churches

365 Straub Rd. E, Mansfield, OH 44903-8434

The Alliance for Renewal Churches is an association of conservative evangelical churches founded in the 1990s. The alliance and its member congregations have affirmed their adoption of the central statements of orthodox Christians as found in the ancient creeds, which as reflections of the clear teaching of scripture provide the benchmark for orthodoxy. They also have adopted a set of "Common Concerns" that identify special additional truths that the churches affirm. These emphases include, but are not necessarily limited to, the priority of grace as God's saving power, the authority of the Bible as the inerrant Word of God, and the Oneness of the Church. The churches also affirm that "the chief end of men and women is communion with God, and the chief expression of that communion is worship." That being said, the church promotes a dual thrust in evangelism and concern for the social order.

Among the founders of the alliance is Ned Berube, pastor of Christ Community Church in St. Paul, Minnesota, and president of the alliance since 2000. Berube was born in Connecticut in 1948 and attended Fairfield University, where he received a B.A. degree in English Literature in 1970. He attended North Central Bible College in Minneapolis, Minnesota, and later became part of the Daystar Ministries. In 1981 Berube and his wife Susan moved to Spooner, Wisconsin, where he founded the Cornerstone Church. In 1987 he moved to the Twin Cities and became pastor of Antioch Christian Ministries. In 1992 he founded the Christ Community Church in St. Paul, Minnesota, where he is currently (2008) the pastor. Christ Community Church joined the Alliance for Renewal Churches. The alliance includes churches across the midwestern and northeastern parts of the United States.

The Alliance for Renewal Churches, as an association, fosters its program of Christian renewal through its advocacy of worship in the context of a biblical faith and lifestyle and its promotion of unity among all Christians. Its offers leadership training conferences, nurtures church-planting activities, and provides a spectrum of supportive services to member churches and foreign missions. Missionary activity is currently supported in Peru and Brazil.

The Alliance's Ministry and Missions Council functions as a local church eldership guiding the ministry of the alliance. The president of the council is responsible for the general oversight of the alliance and its network of pastoral care. The Assembly of Senior Pastors meets once a year for consultation to foster outreach.

Membership: Not reported. In 2008 there were 13 U.S. congregations in the alliance, plus one in Brazil and one in Gryfow, Poland.

Periodicals: *Leadership Letter* (Monthly newsletter for members, available on the alliance's web site.)

Sources:

Alliance for Renewal Churches. www.arcchurch.org.

Alliance of Christian Churches

PO Box 226925, Dallas, TX 75222-6925

The Alliance of Christian Churches emerged in 1985 as a ministry for evangelical Christians who sought a means of ministering "outside the box." One goal of the ministry was an inclusive coalition. In 1987 people associated with the Alliance gathered for what was termed the ADVance Conference; the conference became an annual event, growing each year and becoming the catalyst for a more formally organized congregational fellowship. In October 1996 a constitution was developed, and 27 congregations were formally chartered with the Alliance of Christian Churches. The churches have accepted a statement of core Protestant beliefs centered upon belief in the Trinity and affirmation of the Bible as the infallible Word of God.

The Alliance of Christian Churches views itself as a Christ-centered, biblically focused, and evangelical fellowship. It has developed a spectrum of outreach programs that include the fall conference, church support, education, evangelism, and local and global missions. Each spring regional retreats are held by the various affiliated congregations and parachurch ministries.

Membership: Not reported. In 2008 there were 26 affiliated congregations and parachurch ministries.

Sources:

Alliance of Christian Churches. www.allianceofchristianchurches.org/.

American Coalition of Unregistered Churches

Dr. Greg Dixon, Pastor Emeritus, Indianapolis Baptist Temple, Box 11, Indianapolis, IN 46206

The American Coalition of Unregistered Churches (ACUC) was founded in 1983 as a fellowship of fundamentalist Christian congregations (many Baptist in faith) that exist as unincorporated entities and have organized to resist government pressures that appear to encroach upon their religious liberties and attempt to reshape their ministries. The association grew out of a meeting of pastors from some 25 states who gathered in Chicago on August 8 and 9, 1983, to discuss what they saw as attacks on church ministries. Among the major concerns was the government's attempt to force schools attached to churches to be licensed and conform to state educational regulations. Most in attendance felt that this was due in part to the government's acceptance of a humanist position in place of a biblical perspective.

The meeting passed a set of resolutions that rejected government attempts to license church ministries, regulate churches, or impose taxation. One resolution specifically rejected state jurisdiction to inspect church property with respect to health, fire prevention, or safety. They also passed a resolution rejecting any use of force in defending their ministries.

Following the meeting, Dr. Greg Dixon, then senior pastor of the Indianapolis Baptist Temple and head of the Indiana Moral Majority, resigned his leadership in the Moral Majority to become chairman of the new association. Dr. Everett Sileven, pastor of the Faith Baptist Church in Louisville, Nebraska, was elected cochairman. Sileven had become well known for his ongoing fight over his arrest and the seizure and padlocking of his church-sponsored school.

The association had no doctrinal statement, but most of its member congregations were conservative fundamentalist churches. It did not think of itself as a denomination, but as an association assisting independent churches. In 1993 Dixon found himself in jail for refusing to respond to a subpoena to produce his church's financial records. In 2008 he said that the ACUC does not exist as a formal organization, but when engaging the media or in defense of churches under attack he uses the title "National Chairman of the ACUC." Dixon considers his publication, *The Trumpet*, to be the voice of the ACUC in the United States and abroad.

An active fellowship originating out of the ACUC is the Unregistered Baptist Fellowship (UBF). The UBF is a fellowship of Baptist pastors, evangelists, laymen, and missionaries. It meets annually at the Indianapolis Baptist Temple in October and also schedules regional meetings. Approximately 100 churches participate. There are no officers or formal organizational documents. The host pastor is the moderator of the meeting while it is in session; when the meeting is over, the fellowship no longer exists.

In 2008 Dixon was pastor emeritus of the Indianapolis Baptist Church and the international director of the Biblical Law Center (BLC), which helps churches organize and reorganize to take advantage of their First Amendment guarantees. The BLC is a ministry of the Indianapolis Baptist Temple. Dixon also participates in the Liberty Works Radio Network. Dixon's son, Greg A. Dixon, has succeeded him as senior pastor of the Indianapolis Baptist Church.

Membership: Not reported for 2008.

Periodicals: *The Trumpet*.

Sources:

Unregistered Baptist Fellowship. www.unregisteredbaptistfellowship.com.

American Evangelical Christian Churches

PO Box 47312, Indianapolis, IN 46247-0312

The American Evangelical Christian Churches (AECC) was founded by Dr. G. Hyatt in 1944 as an interdoctrinal ecclesiastical body. It has tried to remain open to both Calvinist and Arminian theological trends, with the Calvinists believing in predestination and the Arminians insisting that people can exercise free will and choose to follow the gospel. Each church member must accept the seven articles of faith that are seen as the "essentials": the Bible as the written Word of God; the virgin birth; the deity of Jesus, the Christ; salvation through the atonement; the guidance of our life through prayer; the return of the savior; and the eternal reign of Christ. All other points are optional.

The AECC states: "our mission is to create a body of believers where we as individuals can realize God in our lives and model, teach, call forth, and celebrate the integrity of the spirit, mind, and body in all that we do."

The polity is congregational, and the American Evangelical Christian Churches seems to function primarily to offer orthodox evangelical ministers a chance to preach without the "restrictions of man-made doctrines imposed by so many religious bodies today." The American Evangelical Christian University specializes in home-study courses. There are five regional offices in the United States and one in Canada. Headquarters were moved from Chicago to Pineland, Florida, in the 1970s. In 1992 the headquarters moved to Indianapolis, Indiana. In 2008 Dr. Charles Wasielewski Sr. served as chairman of the board of directors.

Membership: In 2008 the AECC reported 65 full-time pastor members, 91 other ministers, 20 retired ministers, one missionary in the Philippines, and one missionary in Bolivia. The AECC sponsors missionaries in Australia, Bolivia, Canada, Congo, England, Ghana, Haiti, India, Israel, Ivory Coast, Kenya, Rwanda, Nigeria, the Philippines, Myanmar, Thailand, Zimbabwe, Sierra Leone, and Puerto Rico.

Educational Facilities:

American Evangelical Christian University, Indianapolis, Indiana.

Sources:

American Evangelical Christian Churches. www.aeccministries.com/.

Directory. Pineland, FL: American Evangelical Christian Churches, 1988.

Antioch Network

9524 W Camelback Rd., Glendale, AZ 85305-3104

The Antioch Network is a fellowship of evangelical churches that dates to 1987. It "serves a growing fellowship of local churches who are interacting with challenges of sending church planting teams to unreached gospels." On March 16, 1987, people from seven very diverse congregations met in Austin, Texas. In spite of divergent historical and theological backgrounds, all were affected by the desire to reach groups of people who for various reasons never heard Christianity preached to them. Each of the churches represented in the meeting had expressed a wish to send a team of missionaries to one of the unreached peoples. As the Antioch Network was founded and grew, it saw as its overarching ministry the empowerment of local congregations to reach the nations of the world. Among those who emerged as the articulate voices of the network's concerns were Ted Haggard (b. 1956), Gregg Parris, Bob Roberts, George Miley, and Lincoln Murdoch.

George Miley was the primary founding father of the Antioch Network. Miley and his wife Hanna were overseas missionaries with Operation Mobilization.

While firmly based in an orthodox Evangelical faith, the primary work of the network has been the creation of congregations who are involved with cooperative ministries reaching around the world, with their organization modeled on that of an extended family. The network also holds that every believer is called to be a minister utilizing his or her individual gifts and talents. It encourages all to exercise the gifts that God has given them. Most Christians will be involved in a "sending" ministry, others in a "going" ministry. Missionaries are also encouraged to operate in teams sent by local churches.

The network is loosely organized. Member churches gather annually. The network offers resources, advice, and its accumulated experience to congregations interested in becoming involved in reaching out to the world. Network teams are working in the following countries: France, Afghanistan, Pakistan, Bulgaria, Germany, nations of the Middle East, Senegal, India, Mexico, Taiwan, China, and Turkey. Specific information cannot be given about locations and assignments due to security concerns.

In 2008 Dr. Mark Snelling was the president of Antioch Network. He joined in 2003, having previously served as church services director for Interdev, a missions organization. Randy Shreckengest, who joined the network in 2001, was director of operations in 2008, overseeing daily administrative functions.

Membership: 2008 figures not reported.

Sources:

Antioch Network. www.antiochnetwork.org.

Apostolic Messianic Fellowship

Acts 2:38 Church, 7911 N 40th St., Tampa, FL 33604

The history of the Apostolic Messianic Fellowship can be traced to 1972 and the beginning of the personal ministerial career of Cohen Gary Reckert Sr. Reckert is an Apostolic Pentecostal educator and missionary of Jewish heritage. He founded the Acts 2:38 Church (a reference to the belief in baptizing in the name of Jesus Christ, rather than the more common Trinitarian formula) and the Apostolic Theological Bible College. He also launched missionary efforts abroad, with a focus on the Philippines. The Apostolic Messianic movement coalesced in 1995, and Reckert formally organized the Jesus Messieh Fellowship International in the Philippines in 2005.

The Fellowship follows the Apostolic "Jesus only" theology of the United Pentecostal Church International, with an additional emphasis on Messianic Judaism. It affirms that God's original covenant with Abraham, Isaac, and Jacob is fulfilled in the Messianic Judaism of "Jesus Messieh." That covenant was fulfilled by a small number of Jews who accepted Jesus, and those who rejected Jesus canceled the covenant unto themselves. As a result, Reckert encourages evangelism and missionary work within the Jewish community. The Fellowship supports Israel but opposes its actions against Messianic Jews. At the same time, the Fellowship is opposed to what it considers the false teachings of Trinitarian Christianity. It also stands against the Sacred Name movement and attempts to find a Hebrew equivalent of Jesus (such as Yahshua).

Membership: Not reported.

Educational Facilities:

Apostolic Theological Bible College, Tampa, Florida.

Sources:

Apostolic Messianic Fellowship. acts238church.com/.

Holt, Michael. *Origin of Apostolic Messianic Movement.* Tampa, FL: Apostolic Theological Bible College, 2003.

Armenian Evangelical Union of North America

c/o Rev. Joseph D. Matossian, Minister of the Union, 616 N Glendale, Ste. 23, Glendale, CA 91206-2407

During the nineteenth century, Protestant missionaries, primarily those with a Presbyterian background, established work in Armenia and began to draw members from the older national church of the Armenians. During the early twentieth century, as Armenians began to migrate to North America, many Protestants were among them. They established independent ethnic churches, many of which eventually joined either the United Church of Christ, the United Church of Canada, or the Presbyterian Church (U.S.A.). Others have remained independent, being more theologically conservative than the large liberal Protestant denominations.

In 1960 the Armenian Evangelical Union of North America (AEUNA) was created as an ecclesiastical fellowship of Armenian Christians in the United States and Canada. It includes both the majority of congregations and those congregations that are formally attached to other denominations, and it serves as the denominational home for the independent congregations. In the United States there are churches in Massachusetts, Illinois, Michigan, California, Pennsylvania, New York, New Jersey, New Hampshire, Rhode Island, and Utah. In Canada congregations are located in Toronto, Ontario; Montreal, Quebec; and Cambridge, Ontario. There is one church in São Paulo, Brazil.

In 2008 Rev. Joseph D. Matossian served as the union's minister, and the moderator was Rev. Ron Tovmossian.

Membership: More than 25 congregations were reported in 2008.

Periodicals: *Canada Armenian Press.* • *Forum.*

Sources:

Armenian Evangelical Union of North America. www.aeuna.org/.

Associated Gospel Churches
209 Pine Knoll Dr., Ste. B, Greenville, SC 29609

The Associated Gospel Churches (AGC) was begun by about 25 congregations of the Methodist Protestant Church that refused to enter the merger in 1939 that led to the formation of the Methodist Church, now the United Methodist Church. The congregations against merger initially adopted the name American Bible Fellowship. Their leader was Dr. W. O. H. Garman (1899–1983), a former minister of the United Presbyterian Church and later president of the Independent Fundamental Churches of America. Garman led the Associated Gospel Churches into the fundamentalist family. He was president of the American Council of Christian Churches (ACCC), though the AGC is not at present affiliated with the ACCC. Garman served as president of AGC from 1942 to 1981. The current president is Dr. Billy Baugham.

The AGC sponsors chaplains, and in 1960 the U.S. Department of Defense approved it to sponsor chaplains for the Armed Forces. This was significant because each chaplain had to have ecclesiastical endorsement to be received into the military for active duty. AGC was the first association to guarantee Fundamentalists a role in the military chaplain ministry. The AGC offers chaplaincy programs for those in the army, navy, air force, and civil air patrol, as well as for those working in federal and state prisons, veterans affairs, hospitals, fire departments, and other industrial and institutional areas.

Doctrinally, the AGC accepts the fundamental dispensationalist theology (though there is no article on human depravity) and believes in the maintenance of good works. Baptism is by immersion. Separation from apostasy is adamantly affirmed. Polity is congregational, with the central headquarters serving as a service agency for chaplains, missionaries, pastors, and schools.

Member churches are located in more than 20 states, and overseas work is supported in numerous countries, including Italy, Spain, the Philippines, Sri Lanka, Kenya, Nigeria, South Africa, and South America.

Membership: In 2008 the AGC reported it had about 165 affiliated chaplains. It works in association with approximately 1,250 churches.

Periodicals: *The AGC Reporter.*

Sources:

Associated Gospel Churches. agcweb.us/Home_Page.html.

Barrett, Charles M. "A Guide to the Papers of W. O. H. Garman." www.bju.edu/library/collections/fund_file/garman.html.

Associated Gospel Churches (Canada)
National Office, 1500 Kerns Rd., Burlington, ON, Canada L7P 3A7

The Associated Gospel Churches (AGC) (not to be confused with several U.S. groups with the same name) traces its history to the mid-nineteenth century and to the growth in liberal theological thinking in the major Canadian denominations. In the face of the rising torrent of liberal teachings, some churches and pastors arose to uphold the final authority of the Scriptures in all matters of faith and conduct. In the first two decades of the twentieth century their actions resulted in an evangelical movement under the authority of the inspired Word of God and a defense of the belief that "All Scripture is given by inspiration of God." They became part of the movement to stay true to the traditional fundamentals of the faith, and were labeled "fundamentalists." Foundational to their movement, along with a belief in the inspiration and literal interpretation of Scripture, was a commitment to the virgin birth of Christ, salvation by Christ's shed blood, Christ's bodily resurrection, and His Second Coming as the blessed and "imminent" hope of the church.

The movement had its beginnings in the 1890s. A strong evangelistic thrust in the Toronto-Hamilton area of Ontario resulted in the formation of several independent churches that joined together as the Christian Workers' Churches of Canada. By 1922 they desired a more structured union for fellowship and doctrinal stability. Dr. P. W. Philpott (1866–1957) of the Gospel Tabernacle in Hamilton and Rev. H. E. Irwin of the Missionary Tabernacle in Toronto took the lead in forming the union of like-minded churches. In 1925 its name was changed to Associated Gospel Churches. It subsequently spread across Canada from British Columbia to Nova Scotia.

Very early on, the AGC participated in the Bible Conference movement; for 17 years it sponsored the Oakland Bible Conference held on the shores of Burlington Bay, Ontario. It was succeeded by Fair Havens Bible Conference, still one of the best known conferences among evangelical Christians in North America.

Fair Havens Ministries works in association with AGC. It offers family camp, Bible conferences, youth camp, outdoor Christian education, and a retreat center. Recently, AGC partnered with the Canadian Youth Network to establish a mentoring program to develop younger leaders.

The Western Region of the AGC was founded in 1940 under the leadership of Rev. A. N. Lambshead. In the years immediately after World War II the AGC spread eastward, establishing English-speaking churches in Quebec, then in the Maritime Provinces (1962), and finally in the French-speaking areas of Quebec (1969). In the wake of this growth, in 1989 the AGC restructured itself into a fully regionalized format.

Rev. Bud Penner has served as president of AGC since 2002. Dr. Bill Fietje joined as the Canada East superintendent in 2003. Rev. James B. Houston has been the Canada West superintendent since 2002.

Membership: In 2008 AGC represented more than 140 churches, congregations, and ministries in Canada.

Periodicals: *Insidedge.*

Sources:

Associated Gospel Churches. www.agcofcanada.com.

Fair Havens Ministries. www.fairhavens.org.

Redinger, Lauren. *A Tree Well Planted: The Official History of the Christian Workers' Church of Canada and the Associated Gospel Churches, 1892–1993.* Burlington, ON: Associated Gospel Churches, 1995.

Association of Gospel Rescue Missions
1045 Swift St., Kansas City, MO 64116-4127

The Association of Gospel Rescue Missions (AGRM) is a coalition of local rescue missions operating in urban areas across the United States. These rescue missions function as local congregations and engage in ministry to the homeless and others in need of their services (especially those involved in drug use). The local centers provide a range of services, from daily hot meals to classes on reintegrating into society, to daily worship opportunities.

AGRM was founded in 1913 as the International Union of Gospel Missions, but traces its history to 1872 and the founding of the first rescue mission in New York by former convict Jerry McAuley (1839–1884). The Union came about as additional missions were founded, many by people helped by the original New York center, and the leaders of these missions and some of their prominent supporters developed a vision for an expanding work. The Union adopted its present name in 2000. It deals with the particular issues common to rescue missions, assists in members' interface with the larger Christian community and the government, and encourages the founding and nurtures the development of new missions.

The AGRM has adopted a brief consensus statement of faith, which espouses positions representative of conservative Protestant Christianity. It emphasizes the Bible as the Word of God, the Trinity, salvation in Jesus Christ, the work of the Holy Spirit in the believer, and the one church made up of all believers.

The affairs of the AGRM are managed by a board of trustees. The board organizes an annual meeting of members each spring, during which the direction of the organization is set. The board employs an executive director as the AGRM's chief administrative officer. In 1992 the AGRM joined with city mission leaders from around the world to create the City Mission World Association, now headquartered in Sydney, Australia.

Membership: As of 2008, the AGRM oversees 172 rescue missions scattered across the United States and 5 in Canada. The AGRM claims that more than 16,000 people have successfully passed through their programs and moved on to a more stable life in society.

Sources:

Association of Gospel Rescue Missions. www.iugm.org.

Bonner, Arthur. *Jerry McAuley and His Mission*. Neptune, NJ: Loizeaux Brothers, 1967.

Busch, Frederick. *Rescue Missions: Stories*. New York: W. W. Norton, 2007.

Vanderberg-Rohlfing, Juliana. *I Never Asked for the Easy Way*. Kansas City, MO: City Union Mission Pub., 1999.

Berachah Church

2815 Sage Rd., Houston, TX 77056

Berachah Church, an independent, fundamentalist church, was founded in 1935 as a nondenominational local church. *Berachah* is the Hebrew word for "blessing" (2 Chron. 20:26). The church's purpose is stated in Article II of its constitution: "to present isagogical, categorical, and exegetical Bible teaching, standing unequivocally for the fundamentals of the faith as contained in the Holy Scriptures; and through the teaching of the Word in this church, the sending out of missionaries, and the ordaining of pastor-teachers, present the Gospel of the Lord Jesus Christ both at home and abroad." The mission of Berachah Church is to evangelize the unbeliever and teach the believer to fulfill God's plan, will, and purpose for his life.

C. W. Colgan, an oil company executive who transferred to Houston from Philadelphia in the early 1930s, founded Berachah Church to teach fundamental Christian doctrine. When he was transferred back to Philadelphia in 1936, the independent Dallas Theological Seminary recommended J. Ellwood Evans, who served as full-time pastor from 1936 to 1940. The church constructed a small auditorium at 171 Heights Boulevard and remained there until 1948. Richard Seume, also a graduate of Dallas Theological Seminary, was pastor from 1941 until 1946. He was followed by William F. Burcaw. In 1948 the congregation moved to 502 Lamar Street, near downtown Houston.

Robert B. Thieme Jr. (b. 1918), an ordained minister with the Conservative Baptist Association, was recommended by Dallas Theological Seminary to become pastor of Berachah Church in 1950. He continued as pastor until 2003. Thieme's academic background included degrees from the University of Arizona (magna cum laude, Phi Beta Kappa) and Dallas Theological Seminary (summa cum laude). His graduate studies were interrupted by World War II, during which he rose to the

rank of lieutenant colonel in the Army Air Corps. Thieme returned to Dallas Theological Seminary in 1946 to resume preparation for the ministry. His extensive training in Greek, Hebrew, theology, history, and textual criticism became the foundation for his demanding professional life of studying and teaching the Word of God. As a student he became the interim pastor of Reinhardt Bible Church, Dallas, Texas. He was ordained on July 15, 1948, by the First Baptist Church of Tucson, Arizona. Upon graduating with a master of theology degree in May 1949, he continued to pastor at Reinhardt until April 1950.

Thieme brought the fundamental dispensational theology taught at Dallas Theological Seminary to a congregation that already had accepted that theological perspective. The 18-article statement of beliefs of Berachah Church agrees with the 21-one articles of the doctrinal statement of the seminary. Since 1969 Thieme had been the target of theological controversy because of his doctrinal positions on certain issues. This disagreement with his exegesis created disharmony within the larger independent fundamentalist movement toward Thieme, Berachah Church, and Thieme's extended congregation around the United States.

The prime point of controversy concerned Thieme's position on the nature and effects of Christ's death. Thieme taught that Christ's spiritual death marked the completion of his bearing our sins on the cross. Christ's spiritual death, that is, his separation from God while being judged for our sins, was substitutionary, and hence efficacious for the salvation of humanity. The Lord's physical death, while essential for his resurrection, ascension, and session, was not the means of salvation, but occurred only after his substitutionary work was *tetelestai*, or "finished" (John 19:30). This position led Thieme to further assert that the phrase "blood of Christ" is a representative analogy for the work of Christ for salvation.

Thieme also took a biblical position in favor of Christian participation in the military. He denounced anti-Semitism as condemned by God and incompatible with biblical Christianity.

Thieme taught from the original languages of Scripture in light of the historical context in which the Bible was written. His ministry was noteworthy for its development of an innovative system of vocabulary, illustrations, and biblical categories designed to communicate the truths of God's Word. The unique focus of his ministry concentrated on the procedures for living the Christian way of life.

Thieme's development for the concept of the role of the pastoral minister is reflected in the constitution of Berachah Church. He taught that the leadership of the local congregation was vested in the pastor "whose absolute authority is derived from Scripture," with an advisory board of deacons to administer church business.

Thieme recorded more than 11,000 hours of Bible classes covering much of the Bible verse by verse. Berachah Church has responded to demands to publish and distribute Thieme's Bible teaching by establishing R. B. Thieme, Jr., Bible Ministries. This nonprofit organization is a grace ministry designed to extend and distribute biblical teaching in the form of books, tracts, sermon transcripts, tapes, and Bible conferences. All are available at no charge. The ministry also provides information on classes that meet regularly throughout the country where his lectures can be heard on audiotape, videotape, or by live telephone transmission. A radio series that includes more than 300 half-hour lessons on general biblical subjects is broadcast on stations in various areas of the United States, Puerto Rico, and the Philippines.

As a result of the response to his teaching, congregations and groups of Christians have formed across the United States. Each congregation, like Berachah Church, is independent.

Pastor Robert B. Thieme III has been pastor of Berachah Church since 2004, following his father who served 53 years. Thieme III has had a career in the U.S. Army, and he attended Western Conservative Baptist Seminary in Portland, Oregon, where he received a masters degree in divinity and theology. He also serves as president of the R. B. Thieme, Jr., Bible Ministries.

Membership: In 2002 Berachah Church reported approximately 2,303 members in the United States and Canada. Berachah Church maintains missions in the

United States, England, the Philippines, Ukraine, Thailand, Brazil, South Korea, and Costa Rica.

Sources:

Berachah Church. www.berachah.org.

King, George William. "Robert Bunger Thieme, Jr.'s Theory and Practice of Preaching." Ph.D. diss., University of Illinois, Urbana, 1974.

Thieme, R. B. *Anti-Semitism*. Houston, TX: Berachah Tapes and Publications, 1979.

————. *Blood of Christ*. Houston, TX: Berachah Tapes and Publications, 1979.

————. *Freedom Through Military Victory*. Houston, TX: Berachah Tapes and Publications, 1973.

————. *The Integrity of God*. Houston, TX: Berachah Tapes and Publications, 1979.

Thieme, R. B., Jr. *The Divine Outline of History: Dispensationalism and the Church*. Ed. Wayne F. Hill. Houston, TX: R. B. Thieme, Jr., Bible Ministries, 1989.

Walker, Robert G. *The False Teachings of R. B. Thieme, Jr.* Collingswood, NJ: Bible for Today, 1972.

Wall, Joe Layton. *Bob Thieme's Teaching on Christian Living*. Houston, TX: Church Multiplication, 1978.

Berean Fundamental Churches Council

Box 1264, Kearney, NE 68848

The Berean Fundamental Churches Council, also known as the Berean Church Fellowship or the Berean Fundamental Church, was formed in 1947 by Dr. Ivan E. Olsen, a graduate of Denver Bible Institute. Olsen had moved to North Platte, Nebraska, to do independent work following graduation. In towns nearby, people began to contact Olsen asking him to initiate Bible study programs. Groups were soon meeting in several communities, and in 1947 the Berean Fundamental Churches Council was founded.

The council is fundamentalist in theology and evangelical in program, and non-Pentecostal. It is governed by a church council composed of the pastor and one lay delegate from each church. In California in 2008 there were five churches; in Colorado, eight; in Kansas, two; in Manitoba, Canada, one; in Minnesota, one; in Nebraska, 35; in Wyoming, three; in South Dakota, two; and in Oregon, one. Due to the small size of the council, the churches have not developed their own denominational structures, but have developed their programs by utilizing the services of various faith missions, fundamentalist-conservative seminaries and Bible schools, and church school literature.

The purpose of the council is: to preach Jesus Christ; to support Bible ministries and missions; to promote positive relationships among Christians; and to obey the Great Commandment, which is "Love the Lord your God with all your heart and with all your soul and with all your mind."

Membership: In 2008 the council reported 58 churches in the United States and 1 church in Canada.

Periodicals: *The Communicator*.

Sources:

Berean Church Fellowship. www.bereanchurchfellowship.org.

Bethany Bible Church and Related Independent Bible Churches of the Phoenix, Arizona, Area

6060 N 7th Ave., Phoenix, AZ 85013-1498

The Bethany Bible Church, a single congregation, was begun in the 1950s by members of some Baptist and Presbyterian churches who felt that these churches had deviated from their traditional theological stance. The members called Dr. John Mitchell, a graduate of the conservative Dallas Theological Seminary, to be their minister. As the church grew, ministers from a variety of evangelical seminaries joined the staff. Meanwhile, other graduates of Dallas Theological Seminary, with the assistance of Bethany, founded similar churches in the Phoenix, Arizona, area.

Although each church is entirely independent, these churches have an informal fellowship based upon the unity of their doctrinal perspective. There are no formal organizational ties between the several congregations.

Bethany's doctrine is dispensational and evangelical. There is a strong belief in the verbally inspired and inerrant Bible, and both individual and corporate Bible study is stressed. Most preaching and teaching is derived from the New American Standard Bible, with periodical use of the New International Version. Baptism by immersion is practiced, and the ordinance of the Lord's Supper is held monthly. Missions are supported through independent faith missionary agencies. The Bethany Bible Church, through its Global Outreach ministry, supports two missionaries in Africa; six in Asia; 11 in Europe; two in Latin America; and 19 in North America.

In 2008 Rev. Dave Gudgel was pastor and Rev. Brad Pellish served as outreach minister. Bethany Bible Church has a sanctuary service that provides a traditional worship service with older hymns. There is a choir, praise team, and an orchestra. The chapel service is a contemporary worship service that uses music, dance, drama, and media. Iglesio Biblica Bethany offers a contemporary worship service in Spanish.

Membership: In 2008 Bethany had seven ministers and an estimated 1,500 members. There are several thousand members in other independent congregations in Arizona.

Periodicals: *Window on Bethany*. • *The Bethany Bridge*. (Newsletter available on church's web site.)

Sources:

Bethany Bible Church. www.bethanybiblechurch.org.

Dallas Theological Seminary. www.dts.edu.

Church of Christian Liberty

502 W Euclid Ave., Arlington Heights, IL 60004

Paul Lindstrom (1939–2002), a graduate of Trinity Seminary of Deerfield, Illinois, founded the Church of Christian Liberty in 1965 with the combined purposes of preaching salvation, contending for the faith, and defending God-given liberties. Since that time, both the pastor and the church have been involved in controversy. Lindstrom identified himself with several right-wing political causes that can be grouped under the heading "anticommunist." He received an award from the Republic of China, and the Anti-Communist League of America gave him a statue of John Birch. He has featured in his pulpit conservative leaders such as Dr. Charles S. Poling, Richard Wurmbrand, and George Bundy. Pastor Lindstrom's activism in forming the "Remember the *Pueblo* Committee" brought national headlines. (The *Pueblo* was an American ship seized by North Korea in January 1968.) Lindstrom formed the committee in the summer of 1968, and by 1971 another committee had developed out of it, the Douglas MacArthur Brigade, formed to seek the release of prisoners of war in Vietnam. In 1972 Lindstrom established the Christian Defense League to take up the defense of persecuted Christians behind the Iron Curtain.

Doctrinally, the Church of Christian Liberty is Reformed Fundamentalist. It has adopted a seven-article statement of faith, to which are added the following four articles on the "Responsibilities of the United States of America":

(1) We believe that we have been endowed by our Creator with certain unalienable Rights, that among these are Life, Liberty, and the Pursuit of Happiness. (2) We believe in a Constitutional Republic as set up by our founding fathers and the responsibilities inherent in such upon its citizens. (3) We believe that individual responsibility and a free economy is the best way to achieve the highest standard of living among all men. (4) We believe in combating Socialism, godless Communism, and all forms of collectivistic tyranny alien to our way of life.

The Church of Christian Liberty's 12-acre campus includes the church; CLASS, a home-based school ministry; and the Christian Liberty Academy, a K–12 day school in which 900 children are currently enrolled. Pastor Calvin Lindstrom has succeeded his father, Dr. Paul Lindstrom, as current pastor, and is supported by Elders Dr. Phil Bennett and Phil Roos. There are also four deacons.

Membership: Not reported.

Periodicals: *The Christian Educator.*

Sources:

Church of Christian Liberty. www.christianliberty.com.

Lindstrom, Paul. *Armageddon: The Middle East Muddle.* Mt. Prospect, IL: Christian Liberty Forum, 1967.

Community Churches of America

c/o United Community Church, 333 E Colorado St., Glendale, CA 91205

Community Churches of America is the corporate expression of the various ministries headed by Dr. William Steuart McBirnie, a conservative evangelical minister. Canadian-born McBirnie, a graduate of Bethel Theological Seminary and Southwestern Baptist Theological Seminary, began his ministerial career with the Southern Baptist Convention. During the 1950s, he served Trinity Baptist Church in San Antonio, Texas, but in 1959 he broke with the convention and moved to California. After a period at First Congregational Church in Los Angeles, McBirnie founded in the 1960s the independent United Community Church in Glendale, California. The church was located in Rose Chapel on Kenwood Avenue. As the church grew, additional properties were purchased and other buildings were constructed. The church is currently housed in a 1,300-seat amphitheater, with additional space in the Rose Chapel.

McBirnie built the small church into a large congregation and from it launched the many associated ministries that lifted him into prominence in both the United States and Canada. In 1961 he launched the *Voice of Americanism* (*VOA*), a daily radio program standing against communism, socialism, and religious and racial prejudice. Through *VOA*, McBirnie attacked many of what he considered Marxist-oriented organizations functioning in America and dealt with a variety of social problems from marijuana to pornography and sex education in the public schools. In 1969 he founded the California Graduate School of Theology. In the mid 1970s, McBirnie founded World Emergency Relief, through which funds were channeled to a number of relief efforts overseas. In 1977 the growth of the congregation led to the building of a new sanctuary for worship.

The ministries were further expanded through Frontline Missions, which sent literature to the "frontlines" where Christians faced Communist aggression, such as Korea, Taiwan, Hong Kong, and Thailand. Forest Springs, a mountain retreat in the Angeles forest near Los Angeles, was used for retreats and training seminars for both adults and youth. Students Against Violence in Education (S.A.V.E.) was a youth organization sponsored by *VOA*.

The Churches hold to a staunch conservative Protestant faith based on the authority of the Bible. McBirnie has become most known for his application of Christian thought to social questions, especially communism and socialism. He has authored more than 150 booklets, several of which, such as *What It Means to Accept Christ* and *Should Christians Fight Communism?*, have been frequently reprinted and distributed worldwide. McBirnie is currently retired.

The various national and international ministries operate under the aegis of the Community Churches of America. The United Community Church in Glendale is a single congregation affiliated with the ministries. United Community Church is an interdenominational, New Testament church and is not affiliated with any denomination. Rev. Stephen Boalt is the praise and worship leader, Rev. Jerry Moses serves as interim pastor, and Rev. Norman Newman is the church administrator.

Membership: Not reported.

Educational Facilities:

California Graduate School of Theology, La Habra, California.

Sources:

United Community Church, Glendale, CA: www.seemysites.com.

McBirnie, William S. *An Awareness of Consequences.* Glendale, CA: Voice of Americanism, n.d. 16 pp.

———. *Should a Follower of Christ Be a Capitalist or a Socialist?* Glendale, CA: Author, n.d. 18 pp.

———. *The Truth about the New Sex Education in the Schools.* Glendale, CA: Author, [1968]. 39 pp.

Deaf Ministries Worldwide Fellowship

PO Box 10833, Midwest City, OK 73140

Deaf Ministries Worldwide Fellowship, founded in the 1989 by Gary Barrett and his wife, Rhonda Barrett, is the outgrowth of the ministry to the deaf that began with the opening of the Shalom Lighthouse Conference and Cove Retreat Center in Sulfur, Oklahoma, which now serves as the headquarters of the organization. The fellowship was created to recognize and ordain ministers who have experienced a special call to minister to people with hearing impairments. The fellowship faced a crisis in 1996 when a fire destroyed the retreat center, but it has since been rebuilt.

The fellowship recognizes the variety of problems that have arisen in ministries to the deaf connected to larger denominations made up primarily of people who have their hearing capacities, including a lack of understanding of the deaf world. There is also a confusing difference in British and American sign language. Within the fellowship, the need of a third-party interpreter between the hearing and non-hearing has been eliminated. The fellowship affirms the calling of hearing people into a deaf ministry, and will endorse and ordain anyone otherwise qualified, regardless of their color, race, nationality, or hearing ability.

Most states recognize the fellowship's ministers to perform marriages and other pastoral functions. Most hospitals and prisons recognize the ministers to minister under the supervision of chaplains and other staff.

In 2008 Gary Barrett, who is deaf, served as the president of the fellowship. After graduating from Bible college, Barrett pastored at several deaf churches. He preaches and teaches at deaf churches, camps, revivals, and conferences. His wife, Rhonda, was the office manager in 2008. She ministers at the women's retreats and meetings. John Gehm served on the board of directors and was a member of the evangelistic team. He is deaf.

The fellowship has adopted a brief statement of faith similar to that of the National Association of Evangelicals that clearly places them in the larger evangelical community but does not address issues that divide (e.g., the inerrancy of the Bible, Pentecostal gifts, premillennialism). It also has a strong code of ethics to which it expects it ministers to adhere.

The fellowship sponsors a special ministry to gays and lesbians.

The Evangelism Training Center is a training ministry for the Deaf Ministries Worldwide Fellowship that welcomes deaf people from all denominations. It trains men and women to become missionaries, pastors, teachers, and lay teachers. It offers one-semester and one-year programs, as well as a two-year certificate program in Bible Foundations and a three-year certificate in Deaf Culture Ministries is also offered. All classes are taught by qualified teachers using American sign language.

The Shalom Lighthouse Cove Retreat Center provides housing for visiting pastors and their spouses, offering rest and restoration.

Membership: 2008 figures not reported.

Educational Facilities:

Evangelism Training Center, Sulfur, Oklahoma.

Sources:

Deaf Ministries Worldwide Fellowship. www.brightok.net/~dmw/ministries.html.

Evangelical Church Alliance International

PO Box 9, 205 W Broadway, Bradley, IL 60915

Evangelical Church Alliance International (ECA) is an interdenominational organization of ministers who have united to promote evangelical Christianity throughout the world. The ECA's members include pastors, teachers, parachurch leaders, church executives, missionaries, evangelists, speakers, youth ministers, professors, military chaplains, and fire, industrial, hospice, police, and prison chaplains. What is known as the Evangelical Church Alliance International began in 1887 as the World's Faith Missionary Association. In October 1931 the name Fundamental Ministerial Association was chosen to reflect the organization's basis of unity. On July 21, 1958, during its annual convention, the name was changed to the Evangelical Church Alliance International.

The ECA is conservative Protestant and strictly holds to its tenets of faith, but at the same time it attempts to reach beyond doctrinal differences to experience Christian unity. The ECA provides ministerial credentials for individuals who otherwise qualify, and associate memberships for churches and nonprofit organizations. The alliance offers a correspondence curriculum through the Bible Extension Institute, which works in cooperation with Global University in Springfield, Missouri, to provide course materials. The ECA also provides military, prison, and hospital chaplain endorsement. The ECA holds an annual international convention in Indianapolis, Indiana. In addition, there are regional conventions throughout the United States and an annual Canadian convention.

In 2008 Dr. George L. Miller served ECA as chairman of the board of directors, and Dr. Samuel S. Goebel was president and CEO.

Membership: In 2008 there were about 2,300 worldwide credentialed ministers in the ECA. These include missionaries, pastors, teachers, and well as military, hospital, prison, police, and fire chaplains.

Periodicals: *The Evangel.* (Quarterly newsletter available online.)

Sources:

Evangelical Church Alliance International. www.ecainternational.org.

Evangelistic Messengers' Association (EMA)

100 Charity Ln., Huntingdon, TN 38344

The Evangelistic Messengers' Association (EMA) is a fellowship of independent evangelical pastors/ministers founded in Chicago, Illinois, in 1933 by Mr. and Mrs. Walter Willis and Revs. Sales Malcomb Smith, Erobert Askins, and O. L. Ford. The association was designed to avoid the limitations of most denominations and maintain its existence through bonds of love and fellowship. Ministers who would become a part of the association would believe that "In essentials we must have unity, in nonessentials liberty, and in all things, charity." A brief statement of belief drawing heavily on the Apostles' Creed was adopted. As word of the association spread, membership applications began to arrive from across the United States and several foreign lands.

Today, the association licenses unordained Christian workers and pastors and provides credentials of affiliation for local churches. Ministers pay an annual fee to maintain their credentials. As the association expanded, educational facilities were established. The More than Conquerors School of Theology offers both on-campus classes and correspondence courses (utilizing videos of class lectures). Although ministers from many countries hold EMA credentials, missionary work is focused particularly on Africa, Romania, and the Ukraine. Work in the Ukraine began in 1993 after Rev. J. David Ford, the president of EMA, visited the city of Uzhgorod and realized its central location for ministry in the five countries whose borders were all less than 50 miles away.

EMA has ministers and ministries in 44 foreign countries, including Australia, the Bahamas, Botswana, Bulgaria, Cameroon, China, Costa Rica, Dominican Republic, Ethiopia, Ghana, Greece, Guinea, Haiti, India, Israel, the Ivory Coast, Kenya, Lesotho, Malawi, Mexico, Mozambique, Myanmar, Nicaragua, Nigeria, the

Philippines, Romania, Sierra Leone, South Africa, Spain, Trinidad, Ukraine, Zambia, and Zimbabwe.

Membership: Not reported.

Educational Facilities:

More than Conquerors School of Theology, Portage, Indiana.

More than Winner School of Theology, Uzhgorod, Ukraine.

Periodicals: *Operation Breakthrough Newsbreak.* • *EMA World Changer.* • *EMA NewsBreak.* • *Operation Breakthrough Messenger.*

Sources:

Evangelistic Messengers' Association. www.emai.org.

More than Conquerors School of Theology. www.morethanconquerors.org.

Barrett, David B. *World Christian Encyclopedia.* New York: Oxford University Press, 1982.

Evangelistic Missionary Fellowship

c/o Bethel Christian Fellowship Church, 5405 W 1st Ave., Lakewood, CO 80226

The Evangelistic Missionary Fellowship is a fundamentalist Protestant church founded in 1926 as the Radio Prayer League. It began with the efforts of Rev. S. H. Patterson, who wanted to initiate a ministry on the then relatively new media of radio. He started a church in Denver, and through the years other like-minded congregations were started around the United States. Patterson served as president of the fellowship until 1964, when he was succeeded by Rev. Gordon K. Peterson. Subsequent fellowship presidents have been Norman K. Peterson (1982), Ronald T. Scheimo (1987), and Cleon Laughlin (1993), the current (2008) head of the organization. The league took its present name in 1971.

The fellowship is administered by a board of directors elected to the annual convention, consisting of all ministers and two delegates from each local church. In 2008 Leon Laughlin was the president of the board, and Bryan Peterson was the vice president. The fellowship also has a mission board, ordination board, and a goals and growth committee. The fellowship has four affiliated congregations in Colorado: Bethel Christian Fellowship, Limon Full Gospel Church, New Covenant Fellowship, and Trinity New Life Center. There are six congregations in Kansas: Brewster Community Church, Goodland Calvary Gospel Church, Smith Center Calvary Gospel Church, Norton Crossroads Church, Oakley Community Church, and Levant Community Church. There are two churches in Minnesota, in Mankato and Goodland, and three churches in Wisconsin.

The fellowship affirms the Bible as the inerrant Word of God, the Trinity, Christ as Savior, the depravity of humanity, and the reality of Satan. It also believes in supporting the government, but in times of war seeks noncombatant status for all members and ministers.

Churches are organized into districts, each headed by a district superintendent. All property is held in trust for the benefit and purposes of the fellowship as a whole. Local churches call their pastors, but must elect a pastor affiliated with the fellowship. Missionary congregations are found in Iran, Turkey, Guinea Bissau, Mexico, and New Guinea. There is an extensive ministry in Alaska that includes both a radio and a television station.

Dayspring Outreach Ministries in Joplin, Missouri, works in affiliation with the fellowship in ministering to people in Mexico and Latin America.

Membership: In 1997 the fellowship reported 3,000 members in 25 congregations served by 80 ministers in the United States, and an additional 15 congregations served by 10 ministers in other countries.

Periodicals: *Update.*

Sources:

Evangelistic Missionary Fellowship. www.emfellowship.us.

Barrett, David B. *World Christian Encyclopedia.* New York: Oxford University Press, 1982.

Faith Bible Chapel International

12189 W 64th Ave., Arvada, CO 80004

Faith Bible Chapel began in Denver, Colorado, in the mid-1960s as a small Bible study group led by Robert Hooley. As the group grew, meetings were moved to a local church building. In 1969 what had become a worshipping community moved into facilities of its own in Denver. Growth was spectacular, and by 1977 some 800 people were in regular attendance. Two years later it moved into new facilities with a sanctuary seating 1,100.

A major new ministry began in 1992 with the founding of a parochial school, Faith Christian Academy, with both elementary and high school classes. Simultaneously, new congregations began to emerge around the state. In 1996 the site for a new campus was purchased and the original congregation began to meet in two facilities 4 miles apart.

In 2001 a new worship center was built to accommodate 2,700 members. Rev. George Morrison was the senior paster of Faith Bible Chapel in 2008. He was ordained in 1975 and served as an associate pastor at Faith Bible Chapel until 1984, when he assumed the responsibility of senior pastor. The church has two campuses that host two traditional Sunday morning services, a Spanish-speaking Sunday service, a traditional Wednesday night service, and Gen-X services. Five other sister churches have been planted in Colorado. The church organization includes Faith Christian Academy, which enrolls more than 1,100 students; the Faith Bible Institute of Biblical Studies, which offers a certificate in biblical foundation; and the Sunshine Center, a day care center and preschool.

Faith Chapel is an Evangelical church that accepts the authority of the Bible, the Trinity, and salvation by faith in Jesus. It has developed a special concern for Jewish people and affirms that "God has not rejected Israel. Therefore, for the sake of God, we offer friendship and support to the Jewish people throughout the world." The church also has a focus on world missions and supports a spectrum of short-term missions in different countries. The chapel supports more than 40 ministries in the United States and around the world.

Membership: In 2008 the chapel reported 4,500 members. Besides the original church in Arvada, there are five other congregations in Colorado with 22 clergy.

Sources:

Faith Bible Chapel International. www.fbci.org.

Fellowship of Christ International

c/oBishop Dr. Christopher D. Curry, Senior Minister, 801 4th Ave. N, Birmingham, AL 35204

The Fellowship of Christ International is a small conservative Christian denomination founded in 2003 by P. Bradley Carey and Michael A. Coleman. Carey had been ordained in the Independent Baptist Churches of America in 1985. Though Baptists are generally not an episcopal group, a lineage of apostolic succession had been passed to Dr. S. G. Eastman, who became the presiding bishop of the Independent Baptist Churches of America, by John M. Stanley, of the Orthodox Church of the East. Eastman consecrated Carey in 2003. Coleman also serves as a bishop in the Fellowship.

The Fellowship of Christ International affirms the inerrancy of the Bible, the Trinity, the substitutionary atonement of Christ, and Christ as the sole instrument of human salvation. It practices baptism by immersion. The fellowship is opposed to modern ecumenism and rejects participation in organizations such as the World Council of Churches.

Bishop Curry is assisted in leadership by a Council of Bishops currently consisting of 12 members, including one for Canada and one for Nigeria. This council ordains ministers, and currently it licensed ministers serve in 16 states scattered across the United States.

Membership: Not reported. In 2008 the Fellowship reported seven congregations.

Educational Facilities:

Cornerstone Bible Seminary, Birmingham, Alabama.

Institute for Christian Works College and Seminary, Columbia, South Carolina.

Sources:

Fellowship of Christ International. www.christinternational.org/.

Carey, P. Bradley. *The Darkness in the Light*. Columbia, SC: Institute for Christian Works Press, 1998.

———. *The Quickening Begins*. Columbia, SC: Institute for Christian Works Press, 1999.

Saunders, Charles E., Jr. *The Making of a Minister*. Pittsburgh, PA: Dorrance, n.d.

Fellowship of Independent Evangelical Churches

39 The Point, Market Harborough, LE16 7QU United Kingdom

The Fellowship of Independent Evangelical Churches (FIEC) was established to promote the welfare of the undenominational Bible churches and "to give expression to their essential oneness in the fundamental doctrines of historic evangelical Christianity. It is committed to defending the truth set out in its Doctrinal Basis and to promoting a united testimony to the world."

The FIEC was formed in 1949 by independent fundamentalist ministers, including Dr. L. P. McClenny of Wheaton College Church in Illinois. The group is fundamentalist and premillennial, and professes a belief in angels and Satan. Members hold to separation from evil in all forms. Government is congregational. There is an annual meeting that elects officers.

The FIEC links a church with others in one of the 11 designated regions located through the United Kingdom. There is a closer fellowship with smaller groups of local churches. A "visitor" is appointed who offers support between the churches. There are more than 50 of these groups. A council of 34 members, elected by the churches, serves to oversee the fellowship's activities. Twenty-two of the members are chosen on a regional basis, and 11 members are selected through national elections in the churches. The council meets three times per year. The president, a senior pastor who serves for a three-year term, chairs the meetings. In 2008 the president was Rev. Rupert Bentley-Taylor, and Rev. Richard Underwood was general secretary.

Membership: The fellowship reported 500 affiliated churches in 2008, with nearly 22,000 members.

Sources:

Fellowship of Independent Evangelical Churches. www.fiec.org.uk/.

Great Among the Nations, Inc.

8306 Wilshire Blvd., Ste. 2021, Beverly Hills, CA 90211

Great Among the Nations, a small, conservative, Evangelical Christian church, was founded in Santee, California, in 1984 by Benjamin Altschul. Altschul, a Danish Jew born during World War II, converted to Christianity as a young man and migrated to the United States in 1972. He began teaching Bible classes in Los Angeles and San Diego in the early 1980s, and eventually a group attracted to his teaching formed an independent ministry.

The small group emphasized Bible study and generally met in members' homes. Altschul felt a calling into televangelism and began to create a set of videotapes as part of an evangelism ministry. The group had approximately 30 members when in the late 1980s it was attacked as a cult and became the subject of a series of deprogrammings, the majority of which were carried out by Clint Daniels. The pressure of the deprogrammings led the group to move from Santee to Carlsbad, and then in March 1989 to Coronado, California.

The last deprogramming, which occurred in 1989, led to a highly publicized trial in which the plaintiff, Ginger Brown, accused Daniels and her parents of kidnapping, false imprisonment, and battery. The trial resulted in a hung jury, and the judge dismissed the case. Since that time the ministry has continued its work while assuming a low profile.

Great Among the Nations offers pastor panel discussions, lay-leader training programs, family counseling, Bible and prophecy conferences, and Bible topic seminars. Through its aviation ministry, the church provides air transportation for ministers, pastors, and educators.

Membership: Not reported.

Sources:

Great Among the Nations. gatn.org/our_history.php.

Great Commission Association of Churches

PO Box 29154, Columbus, OH 43229

The Great Commission Association of Churches grew out of a 1970 meeting of about 30 university students who were associated with a Plymouth Brethren assembly at Southern Colorado University. That meeting was highlighted by a call to live up to the commission to take the message of the Christian Gospel to the world, and to plant and build churches that were devoted to Jesus Christ. Many in attendance took the task of praying for people who had never heard the Gospel. The founders were Jim McCotter, Herschel Martindale, and Dennis Clark. Their effort led to the formation of several campus evangelical mission-oriented fellowships that grew to include more than 30 groups by the end of the 1970s. In the 1980s several of the fellowship pastors saw the need to have a more formal national association of churches. In 1983 the Great Commission International was founded by McCotter and Clark to provide services such as conferences, fundraising, and publishing for the association. During the 1980s churches in the Great Commission International were planted in U.S. communities. The commission changed its name in 1989 to Great Commission Association of Churches; its shortened form, Great Commission Churches (GCC), is used in public communications to promote the historical vision of the movement. Each local church is autonomous and develops its own local ministry, but also voluntarily unites with the association for fellowship, accountability, continuing education, and leadership development.

The Great Commission Churches reported more than 5,000 members in 1986. In 1987 the new national leadership team (Dennis Clark, John Hopler, and Rick Whitney) focused on the ministry of prayer and teaching the Word of God in churches and in other regions. At this time *Daylights*, a daily devotional, was published. In 1987 and 1988 more leaders oversaw the national and regional ministry, and newchurches were planted in U.S. communities rather than on college campuses.

In 2007 Great Commission Churches joined the National Association of Evangelicals. In 2008 the church's executive committee was led by Dave Bovenmyer, Hopler, and Whitney.

The GCC established the Great Commission Ministries (GCM) as its missionary. It is assigned the tasks of planning new churches, holding national and regional conferences, overseeing the National Prayer Ministry, and promoting short-term mission projects and the Summer Leadership Training Program for college and high school students. Because of its own origins among college students, GCM developed a special ministry to college and university students.

The GCC has developed an Asia ministry, begun in 1987. There are churches in Hong Kong, Singapore, Malaysia, Thailand, Nepal, and the Philippines. The Europe ministry began in 1991 and has churches in Germany, Ukraine, Spain, Italy, the Netherlands, and Poland. The Canada ministry was created in 1975, and the Latin America ministry began in 1976 with churches in Mexico, Honduras, Costa Rica, Guatemala, and El Salvador. The GCC is affiliated with churches in 20 countries.

The GCC has a statement of faith that affirms the authority of the Bible, which is infallible and inerrant in the original manuscripts; the triune God; salvation in Jesus Christ; and the unity of the church.

Membership: In 2002 there were more than 100 affiliated churches and church-based ministries located in the United States and in Asia (six countries), Latin America (six countries), and Europe (five countries). In 2008 the GCC reported more than 43,000 members.

Sources:

Great Commission Association of Churches. www.gccweb.org.

Greater Grace World Outreach

6025 Moravia Park Dr., Baltimore, MD 21206

The Greater Grace World Outreach, formerly known as Bible Speaks, can be traced to 1964 and the organization of a 15-member group at a Baptist church in Wiscasset, Maine, by Carl H. Stevens Jr. (1929–2008). Under Stevens, a graduate of Moody Bible Institute in Chicago, the group grew quickly and soon built its own church near Wiscasset. Stevens began a radio broadcast over a station in Portland, Maine. There were more than 1,000 members when in 1971 the group relocated to South Berwick, Maine. While there, a Bible school was started. The group moved to South Lenox, Massachusetts, in 1976. By this time, the missionary-minded organization had developed congregations in various locations in the eastern United States and begun missionary work overseas in Europe, Kenya, and Nicaragua.

During the 1970s the group came under attack from critics who claimed that it was brainwashing its members, but it continued to prosper until a 1987 court ruling forced it into bankruptcy. From 1983 to 1985 Elizabeth Dovydenas, the daughter of a wealthy retail store owner, had given the church more than $6 million. In 1985 Dovydenas went through a deprogramming process and afterwards turned against the church and sued to regain her money. The court ordered the sale of the church property in Massachusetts in order to meet the judgment. At that time, Stevens and many of the church members relocated to suburban Baltimore, Maryland. A short time afterward in 1987, the name of the group was changed to its present name. Even though the lost property included the church's radio broadcasting equipment, Stevens soon resumed his daily Christian radio talk program, *Grace Hour*, on stations in Maryland and surrounding states. In 2008 *Grace Hour* was hosted by Pastor John Love, who discusses Bible questions and other relevant issues.

Greater Grace World Outreach is a Bible-centered ministry that helps individuals and families to grow in the grace and knowledge of Jesus Christ. The ministry preaches the Gospel and believes in the cardinal doctrines of the faith. Stevens believed he was called to a ministry, and his members considered him especially anointed by God to direct that ministry. Stevens died on June 3, 2008.

Thomas Schaller was named presiding elder and overseeing pastor in 2005. Steven S. Scibelli was serving as vice chairman and elder in 2008.

The outreach maintains a strong missionary emphasis, and missionaries are supported in a number of countries. There are 850 full-time workers overseas, 77 U.S. missionaries, 71 international missionaries, and 702 nationals. Africa has more than 220 affiliated churches. Europe has more than three dozen affiliated churches and missionary outreach programs.

The outreach trains men and women in the ministry of the Gospel through the Maryland Bible College and Seminary. These ministers have established churches, Bible colleges, grammar schools, and orphanages.

Membership: In 2008 Greater Grace World Outreach reported nearly 2,000 members, with 463 Greater Grace churches in 70 countries.

Educational Facilities:

Maryland Bible College and Seminary, Baltimore, Maryland.

Periodicals: *Wings of Glory*.

Sources:

Greater Grace World Outreach. www.ggwo.org/.

Maryland Bible College and Seminary. www.mbcs.edu/.

Fisher, Marc. "Controversial Cult Moves Pastor, Dog, Stock, Flock to Maryland Suburb." *Los Angeles Times* (October 3, 1987).

Freebairn, William. "The Bible Speaks Alive in Baltimore." *Republican* (Springfield, MA) (September 17, 1989).

IFCA International

3520 Fairlanes, Grandville, MI 49468-0810

IFCA International, formerly known as the Independent Fundamental Churches of America, is one of the oldest and largest of the fundamentalist church groups. It is an association of independent churches, pastors, Christian workers, and laymen whose purpose is to strengthen local churches toward biblical maturity, leading to reproduction. The group aspires to build healthy churches that work together. IFCA International dates to 1922 when Dr. R. Lee Kirkland, pastor of Lake Okoboji Community Tabernacle in Arnold's Park, Iowa, organized the American Conference of Undenominated Churches. Kirkland had previously participated in the Conference of Union, Federated, and Community Churches, but he opposed its modernism. In 1930 a number of Congregational Churches joined with the American Conference of Undenominated Churches to form the Independent Fundamental Churches of America (IFCA). At the organizational meeting at the Cicero Bible Church in Cicero, Illinois, O. B. Bottorff was elected president of the IFCA. For a time, the IFCA was a member of the American Council of Christian Churches (ACCC), but he left in 1953 in a dispute over differences in personalities and policies.

Doctrine of the IFCA International follows five fundamentals closely: the beliefs in the inspiration of the Bible; the depravity of man; redemption through Christ's blood; the true church as a body composed of all believers; and the coming of Jesus to establish his reign. The IFCA International is dispensationalist, but it rejects the ultra-dispensational views of Ethelbert W. Bullinger regarding the sacraments and soul-sleep, the belief that the soul exists in an unconscious state from death to the resurrection of the body. Whereas Bullinger said the church should not practice water baptism or the Lord's Supper, the IFCA International practices both as ordinances. The total depravity of man and the eternal security of the believer (once the believer becomes a child of God, that status is secure forever) are emphasized. The IFCA International believes that ecumenism, ecumenical evangelism, neo-orthodoxy, and neo-evangelicalism are contrary to faith. It believes strongly in separatism from religious apostasy. In 1970 an addition to the statement of faith was made affirming the ordinances of baptism and the Lord's Supper, and the theory of dispensationalism as divinely ordered stewardships by which God treats man according to his purpose.

Polity is congregational; independent churches organize for fellowship and mutual helpfulness. The IFCA International meets in convention annually. Each church can send two or more male delegates.

A twelve-man executive committee plus the president are active between annual conventions. The national executive director and the editor of *The Voice* magazine are ex-officio members of the executive committee. Missions are conducted through the missionary agencies approved and affiliated with the IFCA International. In 2008 the executive director was Dr. Les Lofquist.

The IFCA International has 3 member Bible colleges, 14 home mission agencies, and 9 active church planting agencies. There are 8 foreign mission agencies ministering outside the United States.

Membership: In 2008 the IFCA International reported nearly 1,000 associated churches in the United States, and the same number in countries outside the United States. There are more than 1,200 individual members who are pastors, missionaries, college and seminary professors, chaplains, and other vocational Christian workers.

Periodicals: *Voice.*

Sources:

IFCA International. www.ifca.org/.

Henry, James O. *For Such a Time as This*. Westchester, IL: Independent Fundamental Churches of America, 1983.

Martin, Dorothy. *The Story of Billy McCarrell*. Chicago: Moody Press, 1983.

This We Believe. Wheaton, IL: Independent Fundamental Churches of America, 1970.

Independent Bible Church Movement

Current address could not be obtained for this edition.

During the early twentieth century as the Fundamentalist-Modernist controversy reached its peak, many independent fundamentalist Bible churches were founded, as congregations withdrew from the older denominational bodies and isolated groups formed new congregations. While many of these congregations affiliated with one of the fundamentalist associations, others have remained independent and have affiliated informally over the years with various congregations, publishing houses, missionary enterprises, and schools as deemed expedient. Among the most popular schools have been the Moody Bible Institute (Chicago, Illinois) and the Dallas Theological Seminary (Dallas, Texas).

During the 1970s the number of independent Bible churches increased and leadership from the more prominent fundamentalist colleges and seminaries added impetus to the movement to plant independent fundamentalist congregations throughout the United States. Among those taking the lead in this new impulse was Church Multiplication, Inc., formed in 1977 by people associated with Dallas Theological Seminary. Church Multiplication grew directly out of the New Church Development Committee of the Spring Branch Community Church in Houston, Texas. Its purpose has been to enhance church growth and assist in the formation of new Independent Bible churches. Operating in the Southwest, it has a primary focus on Texas, Arkansas, Louisiana, Oklahoma, and New Mexico.

Independent Bible churches are fundamentalist in theology and believe in the infallibility of the Bible and the deity of Christ (exemplified in his virgin birth, substitutionary atonement, literal resurrection from the dead, and premillennial second advent). They basically accept the dispensational approach to Scripture as outlined in the *Scofield Reference Bible*. Most distinctively, such churches are congregationally unaffiliated to any denomination or congregational association.

Membership: Unknown. The directory published by Church Multiplication, Inc., in 1983 lists 248 congregations in the states of Texas, Oklahoma, Arkansas, Louisiana, and New Mexico.

Independent Christian Churches International

c/o Community Bible Chapel, 507 Willard Ave., Spur, TX 79370-2347

Independent Christian Churches International (ICCI) was founded in 1984 by Dr. Donald Hicks, pastor of the Metroplex Bible Chapel of Dallas, Texas, and other conservative evangelical ministers who recognized that "faithfulness to the commands of God toward a true ministry" would "put them in a bitter conflict with the established church world." The Independent Christian Churches International provides a place for ministers and churches that wish to be separate from the world, yet have the necessary legal standing in the American system. Hicks serves as ICCI's president and presiding bishop. He is currently pastor of Community Bible Chapel in Spur, Texas.

The churches' doctrinal statement sets forth the affirmations of fundamentalist Protestantism, but allows considerable freedom on most issues. The statement affirms the inspiration and infallibility of the Bible, the Trinity, redemption in Jesus Christ, salvation evidenced by a life of righteousness, baptism by immersion, the Lord's Supper, divine healing, the resurrection, the millennium, and punishment in hell for the wicked. The church is congregationally organized and is opposed to denominational labels.

Membership: In 2008 Dr. Hicks reported that 42 congregations nationwide were affiliated with the ICCI. There are approximately 275 ICCI ministers worldwide.

Educational Facilities:

None at the current time. There has never been any affiliation with the Christian Bible Training Center in Mesquite.

Sources:

Community Bible Chapel. www.communitybiblechapelofspur.org/.

Independent Churches Affiliated
Current address could not be obtained for this edition.

Independent Churches Affiliated is a fellowship of four Bible-believing independent churches: the Independent Baptist Church, the Independent Methodist Church, the Independent Bible Church, and the Independent Presbyterian Church. All member churches also hold a membership in the American Council of Christian Churches.

Founded in 1953, Independent Churches Affiliated seeks to promote the historic Christian faith. It is supportive of such colleges and universities as Clearwater Christian College, Maranatha Bible College, Bob Jones University, Northland Bible College, and Foundations Bible College.

Membership: In 2002 Independent Churches Affiliated reported approximately 22,000 members.

Sources:

Piepkorn, Arthur C. *Profiles in Belief: The Religious Bodies of the United States and Canada.* Vol. IV. San Francisco: Harper & Row, 1979.

Independent Fundamentalist Bible Churches
Current address not obtained for this edition.

The Independent Fundamentalist Bible Churches was formed in 1965 by a group of leaders active in the American Council of Christian Churches (ACCC). Among the founders were Dr. Marion H. Reynolds, the first president, the Rev. W. E. Standridge, the Rev. Henry Campbell, and the Rev. Kenneth L. Barth. Reverend Reynolds, formerly of the Independent Fundamental Churches of America (IFCA), was president of the ACCC, an organization from which the IFCA withdrew. Doctrine in the new church is, as the name implies, fundamentalist and Bible-oriented. It differs from the Independent Fundamental Churches of America (now the IFCA International) only on its stand on the necessity of purity of doctrine in the church and on the separation of the church from all "apostasy and scripturally-forbidden alliances" (cooperation with unbelievers). Government is completely congregational (i.e., churches are independent), and the Independent Fundamentalist Bible Churches is composed of those congregations that accept its doctrinal statement.

Membership: Not reported. In 1967 there were 11 churches and 1,700 members.

International Christian Community Churches
PO Box 6787, Asheville, NC 28816

The International Christian Community Churches (ICCC) was founded in 2002 by a group of ministers and members of several Protestant congregations that sought to overcome limitations on local church authority and barriers to inclusion of all people, without regard to race, gender, sexual orientation, or economic status. Discussions led to the establishment of a new fellowship of congregations. Initially, five congregations affiliated with the new organization.

The ICCC is a Trinitarian Protestant church that affirms the Bible as the Word of God, and salvation in Jesus Christ by grace through faith. It affirms the priesthood of all believers, all humans as made in god's image, and the necessity of love for each other. It administers three sacraments—baptism, Holy Communion, and ordination to the ministry. All persons have access to the ministry without consideration of their age, gender identification, race, physical challenges, economic status, health status, or nationality.

The ICCC consists of local churches that send representatives annually to a general convocation at which the ICCC governing board and officers are elected. The presiding minister is the highest office in the church. The local churches govern their own lives and call their pastors.

Membership: In 2008 the ICCC reported nine affiliated churches in the U.S. South and one in the state of Washington.

Educational Facilities:
Emmaus Institute for Pastoral Studies.

Sources:

International Christian Community Church. www.intlccc.org/.

Moody Church
1630 N Clark St., Chicago, IL 60614

The Moody Church is named for the famous evangelist Dwight L. Moody (1837–1899). In 1858 Moody began a Sunday school in an old Chicago saloon building. The school later moved to Illinois Street; that initial group formally became the Illinois Street Church in 1864, and J. H. Harwood served as the first pastor. The unordained Moody served as deacon. After the Great Chicago Fire of 1871, a temporary structure was used until a new tabernacle was built on Chicago Avenue in 1873 to 1874. The church assumed its present name in 1901 to honor Moody, who had died in 1899. In about 1915 construction was begun on the present church building, which was dedicated in 1925. It has been the pulpit for some of the leading fundamentalist/evangelical voices in the land, including Charles A. Blanchard (1848–1925), R. A. Torrey (1856–1928), A. C. Dixon (1854–1925), Paul Rader (1879–1938), Harry A. Ironside (1876–1951), Alan Redpath (1907–1989), George Sweeting (b. 1924), Warren Wiersbe (b. 1929), and Erwin W. Lutzer (b.1941).

Doctrinally, the church basically follows dispensationalism, which Moody learned from the Plymouth Brethren. Members are asked to give their assent to an eight-article doctrinal statement that includes belief in the depravity of man, the eternal security of the believer, and the premillennial return of Christ. The members also accept the responsibility to win others to Christ. Approximately 100 church members serve as missionaries on five continents. Polity is congregational.

The church's vision is "to be known in Chicago as a caring, culturally diverse community that seeks to transform lives through a clear witness for Christ, quality ministries, and the lifestyle of each believer."

The church sponsors the weekly *Songs in the Night* radio show, begun in 1943 and heard over about 400 stations of the Moody Broadcasting Network, the Bible Broadcasting Network, and Trans World Radio. The 30-minute radio show is broadcast on Sunday evenings and includes music and meditation. Other radio broadcasts include *The Moody Church Hour* (a weekly program broadcast on Sunday mornings as a worship service) and *Running to Win* (a daily 15-minute instructional program).

In 2008 the senior pastor of the church was Dr. Erwin W. Lutzer, who had served in that capacity since 1980. He was born near Regina, Saskatchewan, Canada. He has authored more than 20 books and is known as an international conference speaker. Dr. Hutz Hertzberg joined the staff in January 2006 as executive pastor. He received a doctorate in divinity from the Trinity Evangelical Divinity School. Associated with Moody Church, but completely separate in operation, are the Moody Bible Institute and the *Moody Monthly*, the prominent fundamentalist periodical.

Membership: In 2008 the church reported 2,000 members and supported a ministerial staff of 15.

Periodicals: *Inside Moody.* Send orders to 1609 N La Salle St., Chicago, IL 60614. • *Moody Church News.* • *Vision.* • *Women's Ink.* • *Student Revolution.* Newsletters, transcripts, sermon series booklets, and Bible reading plans are available as free downloads from the church's web site.

Sources:

Moody Church. www.moodychurch.org.

Most Holy Church of God in Christ Jesus
502 Anita St. #21, Chula Vista, CA 91911

The Most Holy Church of God in Christ Jesus was founded in the Philippines in 1922 by Teofilo D. Ora (r.1922–1959), who became its first bishop. Ora believed that the founding of the church in the Philippines was the fulfillment several biblical prophecies concerning Christ's "other sheep." He believed that the church would be established in the Far East, in a nation composed of many islands whose people spoke a variety of languages (Is. 24:15, 28:11, and 43:5–7). In 1935 the name Church of God in Christ Jesus (taken from 1 Thes. 2:14) was revealed to Sister Mercedez Verde, a deaconess from the province of Bulacan (about 50 miles north of Manila). Bishop Ora was succeeded as leader by Bp. Salvador Payawal (1969–1989) and Bp. Gamaliel T. Payawal (1989–2003).

The church is a conservative evangelical Protestant church that affirms belief in the inspiration of the Bible, the Trinity, salvation in Jesus Christ, and the empowering of the church by the Holy Spirit. Members observe the ordinances of baptism, holy communion, and foot washing. Church worship services are held on Saturday rather than Sunday.

Since 1965 church members have moved from the Philippines to California and formally organized. Members are scattered around the state of California.

Membership: Not reported.

Sources:

Most Holy Church of God in Christ Jesus. mostholychurchofgod.com/.

Ohio Bible Fellowship

3865 N High St., Columbus, OH 43214-3797

The Ohio Bible Fellowship was formed in 1968 by 13 former members of the Independent Fundamental Churches of America (IFCA) The Ohio Bible Fellowship rejected the IFCA's failure "to see the dangers inherent in mediating positions," and claimed the IFCA had "wavered under the pressure of the prevailing cooperative spirit of the age." Doctrinally, there is little difference between the fellowship and the IFCA. The pre-1970 IFCA statement of faith was adopted, and to it was added a statement on baptism, professing belief in immersion as the proper mode of baptism, although baptism is not seen as essential for salvation.

The Ohio Bible Mission aids new churches, and its mission is to establish a Bible church in every Ohio county. At least three fellowship conferences are held each year. A campground is being developed near Chesterville, Ohio. The Peniel Bible Camp is a summer camp program.

In 2008 the fellowship's president was Rev. Donald L. Gallion, pastor of Calvary Baptist Church, Willard, Ohio. The vice president was Rev. David Layton, pastor of Mt. Zion Baptist Church, Rockford, Ohio.

Local churches affiliated with the fellowship include: Tri-County Baptist Church, Madison, Ohio; Middlefield Baptist Church, Middlefield, Ohio; Bucyrus Baptist Church, Bucyrus, Ohio; Troy Chapel Community Church, Delaware, Ohio; Westerville Bible Church, Westerville, Ohio; Calvary Baptist Church, Columbus, Ohio; Greencastle Bible Church, Carroll, Ohio, and Fayette Bible Church, Washington Court House, Ohio.

Membership: Not reported for 2008.

Periodicals: *The Ohio Fellowship Visitor*. Published by Ohio Bible Fellowship 10 times a year. Available without charge from obfvisitor.wordpress.com.

Sources:

Ohio Bible Fellowship. www.obf.net.

Oriental Missionary Society Holiness Church of North America

c/o Pr. Rick Chuman, Los Angeles Holiness Church, 3660 S Gramercy Pl., Los Angeles, CA 90018

The Oriental Missionary Society Holiness Church of North America began in 1920 among several Japanese American Christian ministerial students in Los Angeles. In that year, six seminarians—Henry T. Sakuma (1900–1992), George Yahiro (1894–1963), Paul Okamoto, Aya Okuda, Toshio Hirano (1897–1975), Hatsu Yano, and Hanako Yoneyama—formed a prayer fellowship with the goal of evangelizing Japanese Americans. In 1921 they formed the Los Angeles Holiness Church.

Sadaichi Kuzuhara (1886–1988) became the pastor of the group and was revered for his promotion of the cause of Japanese American ethnic churches and his solid biblical teaching. The work spread to Japanese communities throughout California, the neighboring states, and Hawaii. In 1934 the Oriental Missionary Conference of North America was formed to oversee the work of the several congregations. Though completely disrupted by the internment of Japanese during World War II, the conference (church) reconstituted itself at the end of the war. After the war, Kuzuhara moved to Chicago to found the Lakeside Japanese Christian Church.

Beliefs of the church are summarized in a four-point statement. The church affirms the Trinity, the deity of Christ, the authority of the Bible, salvation of humans through Christ, and the church as consisting of all who have been regenerated through faith in Christ. There are two sacraments, baptism and Holy Communion.

The church is directed by an annual conference. A 10-person executive committee implements the decisions of the annual conference. Besides the Los Angeles Holiness Church in California, there are 16 parishes: Freemont Asian Christian Church, Freemont, California; Honolulu Christian Church, Hawaii; Japanese Christian Community Church of Tucson, Arizona; Japanese Christian Church of Walnut Creek, California; Mililani Christian Church, Hawaii; North County Japanese Christian Church, Encinitas, California; Orange County Christian Church, Cypress, California; San Diego Japanese Christian Church, California; San Fernando Valley Holiness Church, Pacoima, California; San Lorenzo Japanese Christian Church, California; Santa Clara Valley Japanese Christian Church, Campbell, California; South Bay Japanese Christian Fellowship, Torrance, California; West Covina Christian Church, California; West Los Angeles Holiness Church, California; West Oahu Christian Church, Hawaii; and Whittier Community Church, Whittier, California.

Membership: Not reported.

Periodicals: *The Voice*.

Remarks: Because of its name, the church is continually associated with the Oriental Missionary Society, a Holiness missionary organization founded in the early twentieth century. There has been a fraternal relationship between the church and the society, but there is no official connection. The church also has a fraternal connection with the OMS Holiness Church of Japan, from which it has drawn several of its ministers.

Sources:

OMS Holiness Church of North America. www.omsholiness.org/;
    www.kuzuharalibrary.com.

The Peoples Church

374 Sheppard Ave. E, Toronto, ON, Canada M2N 3B6

The Peoples Church is an independent evangelical work founded by Dr. Oswald J. Smith (1889–1986) in 1928 in Toronto, Ontario, Canada. It stands predominantly for the conversion of souls, the edification of believers, and worldwide evangelism, emphasizing especially the four great essentials: salvation, the deeper life, foreign missions, and the return of Jesus Christ. It has been noteworthy among Evangelical Christians for its efforts, by every means, to get its message to the "Christless" masses, both at home and abroad, in the shortest possible time.

Smith was one of 10 children born to a railway telegrapher in Odessa, Ontario. Raised in the village of Embro, near London, Ontario, he was a sickly child suffering from bouts of prolonged, undiagnosed illness. At age 16, while attending an evangelistic meeting in Toronto's Massey Hall under the ministry of R.A. Torrey, he committed himself to Christ and dedicated his life to the single purpose of preaching the gospel to those who had never heard of Jesus Christ. At 18 he enrolled in night classes at Toronto Bible College, and at the end of the term he applied for a mission posting. He was turned down because the church assumed that the 6-foot tall, 119-pound youth would never pass the physical examination. He went to work for the Upper Canada Bible Society selling Bibles door to door in Ontario's

Muskoka district, some 90 miles north of Toronto. There he had his first opportunity to preach, in a small Methodist church at Severn, and while there he purchased a notebook to keep a "Record of Sermons Preached." That book grew to contain more than 12,000 entries.

The Bible Society next asked him to go to western Canada, and at age 19, under the auspices of the Shantymen's Christian Association, he began a trek through the forests taking Bibles to Indian villages and lumber camps. During the summers he traveled the Kentucky mountains by horseback and muleback preaching the gospel. His experience led to his penning the words and music to "Into the Heart of Jesus, Deeper and Deeper I Go."

Smith graduated from McCormick Theological Seminary (Presbyterian) in Chicago, but found upon his return to Toronto that once again his church would not send him as a missionary. They declared that "with your poor health you could never stand the rigors of a foreign field." After the Presbyterian Church of Canada turned him down for the fourth time, Smith vowed, "If I cannot go, I will burn out my life sending others."

In 1915, aged 25, Smith was ordained and appointed associate pastor of the fashionable Dale Presbyterian Church in Toronto. There he met and married the deaconess, Daisy Billings. His burning passion for missions caused him difficulties when, convinced that mission was the task of the whole church, he lifted the missionary program of the church out of the hands of the women's missionary society. He was asked to leave the church. He moved to British Columbia but after six months returned to Toronto, where he turned to writing. As a result of an article he wrote for the Toronto *Globe and Mail* concerning the political unrest and famine in Armenia, readers gave more than a quarter of a million dollars for Armenian relief. Still wanting to preach, Smith began to hold services in a rented YMCA auditorium, and in 1921 the Christian and Missionary Alliance Church asked him to merge his fledgling YMCA work with its struggling Parkdale congregation.

Within 18 months the congregation moved to Christie Street Tabernacle to accommodate the 2,500 who attended services. In 1928 Smith launched his own independent work under the name Gospel Tabernacle, but when it was found that the name had already been incorporated and could not be used officially, the elders of the church unanimously decided to change the name to The Peoples Church, under which name it was officially incorporated in 1933.

Services were initially held in Massey Hall, but in 1930 moved to St. James Square Church on Gerrard Street East. Every night for the first week Smith preached on missions. In July 1934 the congregation moved to the 1,500-seat Methodist Church at 100 Bloor Street East. The publisher of the *Globe and Mail* gave $20,000 toward the purchase of the building, and Smith sold the elegant pipe organ for $40,000. The two amounts almost met the purchase price of $65,000. So large were the crowds that the church soon had to stop advertising.

Smith became famous for his concept of giving to missions based on the "Faith Promise." The high point of the church year was the month-long Missionary Convention, when Smith challenged young and old to carry the gospel to those "in the back rows" still in heathen darkness. The grand finale of the Missionary Convention was the closing Sunday, when Smith announced the total of the Faith Promise. Each year it increased. In 1936 the Missionary Medical Institute (now the Missionary Health Institute) was founded to provide prospective missionaries with a year's training in tropical diseases, and in 1943 the Russian Bible Institute, offering a three-year Bible course, was established.

By 1952 the church was partially supporting 296 missionaries with a missions budget at $258,000. Seventy percent of every dollar given to the church went to missions, and the remaining 30 percent to maintain the home base. In 1962 the congregation of the Peoples Church moved from its downtown location on Bloor Street to newer, larger facilities on East Sheppard Avenue.

Smith died on January 25, 1986 at age 96, having ministered in Toronto since 1915. He was the author of 35 books that were published in 128 languages and sold more than six million copies. As a poet and hymnwriter he wrote more than 1,200 hymns, poems, and gospel songs, including "Then Jesus Came," "God

Understands," "The Glory of His Presence," "The Song of the Soul Set Free," "Saved," and "Joy in Serving Jesus." As a missionary statesman he led his church in a missionary program that helped support more than 500 missionaries and nationals worldwide. Since the church was founded, the church has raised more than $40 million for global missions. As an editor, Dr. Smith published a magazine for more than 50 years, and wrote many tracts and pamphlets. As a radio and television preacher, he was heard in Toronto and other cities since 1930 over some 42 stations.

In 1952 the board of managers invited Paul B. Smith, Smith's younger son, to join the staff as assistant pastor, thus freeing Smith to minister across Canada and in other countries. In 1959 Paul Smith became the senior pastor of the Peoples Church, and continued the ministry initiated by his father. He authored several books and traveled widely. During his tenure, the Peoples Christian School (junior kindergarten through grade 6) was opened (1971), and the Peoples Academy (grade 7 through OAC) was established (1975). Paul Smith died in 1995.

Dr. John D. Hull succeeded Smith as senior pastor of the Peoples Church in 1994. He had previously founded a growing church in Marietta, Georgia, in a pattern similar to that of the Peoples Church. In September 2001 Charles W. Price was installed as senior pastor. Prior to his appointment, Price was principal at the internationally known Capernwray Bible Institute in England. He attended the Bible Training Institute in Glasgow, Scotland. In 2004 he was awarded an honorary doctor of divinity degree by Tyndale University in Toronto. Price hosts a weekly one-hour television program, *Living Truth,* in Canada. The broadcast is available in the United Kingdom, Europe, India, Australia, New Zealand, Indonesia, Korea, and Japan.

In 2008 Jim Chang headed the Pastoral Peoples Care Ministry, and Timothy Starr led the Adult Fellowship Ministry.

Membership: In 2008 the church ministered to about 3,500 members and adherents.

Educational Facilities:

Peoples Christian Academy, Toronto, Ontario.

Periodicals: *The Peoples Magazine.* • *Peoples Progress.*

Sources:

The Peoples Church. www.thepeopleschurch.ca.

Peoples Christian Academy. www.thepeopleschristianacademy.ca.

Hall, Douglas. *Not Made for Defeat.* Grand Rapids, MI: Zondervan, 1969.

Neely, Lois. *Fire in His Bones.* Wheaton, IL: Tyndale House, 1982.

Smith, Oswald J. *The Clouds Are Lifting.* London: Marshall, Morgan, and Scott, 1936.

———. *Man's Future Destiny.* Grand Rapids, MI: Zondervan Publishing House, 1940.

———. *The Story of My Life.* London: Marshall, Morgan, and Scott, 1962.

Smith, Paul B. *The Senders.* Burlington, ON: G. R. Welch Company, 1979.

Remnant Fellowship International

PO Box 1034, Brentwood, TN 37024

The history of Remnant Fellowship International can be traced to 1986, when founder Gwen Shamblin, an instructor in dietetics at the University of Memphis, began a faith-based weight-loss program, the Weigh Down Workshops. The workshops, which advocated eating regular foods in smaller quantities and using prayer to combat hunger and overeating, were immensely successful, and in the 1990s they spawned similar programs in the larger evangelical community. Through the decade, Shamblin began to apply the same principles from the Weigh Down programs to other subjects—marital problems, drug addition, smoking, and so on. Participants reported strengthened marriages and freedom from addictive substances.

In 1999 Shamblin withdrew from the congregation of the Churches of Christ she had been attending and founded Remnant Fellowship as a new Christian denomination. Membership was and continues to be drawn largely from those who have responded positively to the Weigh Down Workshops. The Fellowship became the official sponsor of the Weigh Down Workshop Outreach, and a Remnant Publishing Division was founded as its publications arm. Weigh Down Workshop Productions produces the biblical materials for the church's members and is considered the church's evangelistic arm.

Very soon after its founding, the Remnant Fellowship began to distinguish itself from the larger evangelical community by its disavowal of the doctrine of the Trinity, the affirmation of which is one of the defining traits of the contemporary evangelical community. The Fellowship teaches that Jesus Christ was the son of God, but not God. It traces the belief in the Trinity to the Council of Nicea in 324 C.E., and essentially supports Arius's position, which was rejected at the council and officially condemned. Apart from this belief, and the necessary modifications of other doctrines directly related to it, the Fellowship upholds the beliefs of its parent body on such matters as, for example, the necessity of water baptism by immersion.

The Remnant Fellowship members see themselves as separating from the counterfeit church that follows a false doctrine, false piety, and false leadership. They understand that the saved are those who hear the Word of God, and then put it into practice through obedience.

Membership: Not reported. In 2008 the Fellowship reported 130 fellowships in 130 cities scattered throughout North America, Europe, Australia, and the Bahamas.

Sources:

Remnant Fellowship. www.remnantfellowship.org/.

The Weigh Down Workshop. www.weighdown.com/.

Shamblin, Gwen. *Exodus: Out of Egypt: The Weigh Down Workshop. Continuing the Journey*. Brentwood, TN: Weigh Down Workshop, 1992.

———. *Rise Above: God Can Set You Free from Your Weight Problems Forever*. Nashville, TN: Thomas Nelson, 2000.

———. *Weigh Down Diet*. New York: Galilee Trade, 2002.

Rex Humbard Ministry

Box 3063, Boca Raton, FL 33431

Rex Humbard (1919–2007), the famous television evangelist, came from a radio preacher's family: The Humbard family had broadcast over the Mutual Network for more than 30 years. At age 15, Rex became the master of ceremonies. He was ordained by his father. In 1952 the Humbard family stayed for five weeks in Akron, Ohio, and Rex decided to remain there. Having been impressed with television's power to communicate, he decided to build a congregation, televise its services, and expand the coverage around the world. With brother-in-law Wayne Jones he created Calvary Temple and built a stable congregation. Calvary Temple was superseded by the nondenominational Cathedral of Tomorrow founded in 1958 in Cuyahoga Falls, Ohio, a suburb outside Akron. The cathedral, built at a cost of $3.5 million, was a 5,400-seat, marble and glass renovated theater, and it stood at the center of a large complex that included a retirement home, television station, library, and youth park. The ministry expanded and included a Mackinaw, Michigan, campus used for religious education and a 23-story Akron office tower.

The center of the cathedral's activity became the Sunday worship service, which was first televised in 1953 and by 1971 reached more than 335 television stations. The service was a mixture of preaching and music. Humbard's wife, Maude Aimee, a gospel singer, performed with a choir. The service was seen in the United States, Canada, Europe, the Middle East, the Far East, Australia, and Latin America.

A unique practice of the cathedral was its unusual televised communion service: One week before the broadcast communion, the television audience was invited to participate and was given instructions on preparing the elements in their homes. Approximately 2,000 families from the Akron area worshiped at the cathedral.

Doctrinally, Humbard was evangelical and conservative, but he refused to be pinned down on a specific creed. He opposed the cathedral's pushing any "sectarian" ideas. During Humbard's tenure as pastor the cathedral was operated by a six-person board of trustees that included Humbard and his wife. Humbard's salary was paid not by the cathedral, but by the television outreach ministry. There were 11 ministers on the staff. As the Humbard ministry grew, the cathedral issued a monthly magazine, *The Answer*. Humbard kept a busy schedule of traveling, preaching, and writing. By the end of the 1970s the cathedral services were broadcast on more than 600 television stations in the United States and Canada, and more than 2,000 television stations around the world, in 97 different languages, and on 700 radio stations, and 293 foreign stations on every continent. In 1976 a special Christmas program became the first religious program carried worldwide by satellite.

In the 1970s the ministry suffered from internal disputes and financial problems. Federal and state regulators complained that millions of dollars in notes violated securities laws. By 1982 the congregation had dwindled, and in 1983 Humbard resigned as pastor of the Cathedral of Tomorrow and was succeeded by Wayne Jones. He separated the Rex Humbard Ministry from the church in Boca Raton, though he continued at the church as pastor emeritus. Humbard gave up on-air preaching in the 1990s. In 1994 he sold the Cathedral of Tomorrow to fellow televangelist Rev. Ernest Angley.

Humbard retired with his wife to Lantana, Florida. He appeared occasionally on television to discuss Christianity. He died on September 21, 2007, in Florida, following hospitalization for congestive heart failure.

Membership: Not reported.

Periodicals: *Rex Humbard Family Ministry*.

Sources:

Humbard Family Ministry. www.rexhumbard.com.

Humbard, A. E. *My Life Story*. Akron, OH: Cathedral of Tomorrow, 1945.

Humbard, Rex. The *Ten Commandments Plus 1*. Akron, OH: Cathedral of Tomorrow, n.d.

———. *Where Are the Dead?* Akron, OH: Rex Humbard World Outreach Ministry, 1977.

River of Life Ranch and Ministry of Truth

Current address not obtained for this edition.

The River of Life Ranch and Ministry of Truth was founded in 1978 by Ed Mitchell, a Christian layman who had been working as a manager of a supermarket. He gathered his first members in Thousand Oaks, California, but the original group disintegrated following the death of a member from insulin deficiency. Mitchell had preached a doctrine of divine healing that precluded the use of doctors. The core of followers purchased property in Apple Valley, California, and created a commune, the River of Life. Then in 1980 and 1981, Mitchell with the assistance of commune members Jody Scharf and Dori Webster wrote several books that were widely distributed in Christian bookstores, *The Mystery of Babylon Revealed* (1980), *The Truth* (1980), and *The 1981 Tribulation Report*. These books, written from an Evangelical Christian and pentecostal perspective, detailed a belief in the fast approaching disintegration of the social system and the end of the present order of things.

The idyllic life of the community was disrupted in 1980 when one of the members, Linda Marshall, was deprogrammed and began to complain of physical child abuse within the group. Then on February 21, 1981, deprogrammers hired by Skip Webster, the producer of the popular television series *Fantasy Island*, entered the commune and kidnapped Webster's son Dennis Webster (aged 36) and two grandchildren, Todd (aged 9) and Benjamin (aged 9 months). The elder Webster had become concerned after hearing Marshall's testimony. The police stopped the kidnappers and released Webster and his two children. Members of the commune admitted to using corporal punishment, but said that they did not beat their children.

In the wake of the controversy, membership in the group dwindled from 50 to around 20. Also, spokespersons for the Christian Research Institute, an Evangelical anticult group, began to contact Christian bookstores to ask them to remove the River of Life books from their shelves. That action severely cut into the cash flow of the group, which moved to sell its property. Since then the group has assumed a low profile and its present status is unknown.

Sources:

Mitchell, Ed, and Jody Scharff. *The Mystery of Babylon Revealed*. Palm Springs, CA: Victory Press, 1980.

————. *The Truth*. Palm Springs, CA: Victory Press, 1980.

Mitchell, Ed, and Dori Webster. *The 1981 Tribulation Report*. 2 vols. Palm Springs, CA: Victory Press, 1981.

SEND International of Alaska

PO Box 369, Glennallen, AK 99588

SEND International of Alaska began as Central Alaskan Missions, founded in 1936 by the former Methodist Vincent J. Joy (1914–1966) as an independent faith mission. Missionary efforts began among the residents of the isolated Copper Valley in south-central Alaska via airplane. The airborne effort slowly gave way to a more conventional movement on the ground as roads were built through the area. A medical program led to the founding of a hospital in 1956 and an educational arm, Alaska Bible College, in 1966. The mission was Fundamentalist in faith and affirmed a belief in the Trinity, the verbal inspiration of the Bible, salvation by grace through faith in Jesus Christ, and Christ's imminent premillennial return. Members were exhorted to separate themselves from anything that would dishonor God, bring discredit to his cause, or weaken their testimony.

After Joy's death in 1966, members of the mission felt a leadership gap and in 1971 merged with SEND International (then called the Far Eastern Gospel Crusade). In addition to its hospital and educational works, the group operates two Christian radio stations serving Alaska's heartland and southern panhandle. It also offers an 11-week summer missionary program.

Membership In 2008 the mission reported 28 missionaries, working largely in communities of indigenous peoples in Alaska, the Yukon Territory, and northern British Columbia.

Educational Facilities:

Alaska Bible College, Glennallen, Alaska.

Sources:

SEND International of Alaska. www.send.org/alaska/.

Piepkorn, Arthur C. *Profiles in Belief: The Religious Bodies of the United States and Canada*. Vol. 4. San Francisco, CA: Harper & Row, 1979.

❁❁❁ Messianic Judaism

Chosen People Ministries

International Headquarters, 241 E 51st St., New York, NY 10022

Alternate Address: Canadian headquarters: PO Box 897, Sta. B, North York, ON M2K 2R1, Canada.

Chosen People Ministries, known until 1988 as the American Board of Ministries to the Jews, was founded in 1894 as a small Christian mission to the Jewish residents of Brooklyn, New York, under the leadership of Leopold Cohn (1862–1953), a rabbi from Hungary who had been converted to Christianity shortly after his arrival in New York in 1892. He moved briefly to Scotland to attend to his theological studies, and upon his return to New York opened the mission. He moved to the Williamsburg section of Brooklyn in 1897. The mission grew as it mixed assistance for European Jews as they adjusted to U.S. life with the teachings of Christianity. After the turn of the century, related missions opened in Philadelphia, Pittsburgh,

and Los Angeles. In 1924 the mission adopted the name American Board of Missions to the Jews. In 1945 headquarters were moved to Manhattan. Work expanded to all the major Jewish communities in the United States and into Europe. After World War II work expanded to Palestine and continued in the new nation of Israel, and to Argentina. Cohn was succeeded by Harold Pretlove and then Daniel Fuchs.

In 1972 the American Board of Missions to the Jews moved its administrative headquarters, first to New Jersey, and then to Rockland County, New York, and then in 1988 to Charlotte, North Carolina. That same year its present name was adopted. By that time, it was responding to a new wave of Jewish evangelism pioneered first by Jews for Jesus, founded by Moishe Rosen, a former American Board missionary, and then by the Messianic movement, which sought to found Messianic synagogues that retained Jewish culture while offering a conservative evangelical Christian faith. The American Board had initially opposed the Messianic movement, having always believed that Jewish believers should be integrated into gentile congregations. But in the 1990s it began to look with more favor on the Messianic notion, and Messianic congregations affiliated primarily to Chosen People Ministries began to emerge.

Chosen People Ministries is an evangelical organization whose doctrine is in line with that of the National Association of Evangelicals, with a special ministry to people of Jewish heritage. It is a board-governed organization whose ministry is planned and implemented by missionaries and supported by an administrative staff.

In the 1990s Chosen People Ministries returned its headquarters to New York City. In 2008 its work was led by its president, Dr. Mitch Glaser.

Membership: In addition to the international headquarters and two Messianic congregations in Manhattan and Brookyn, New York, there are congregations in Chicago; Philadelphia and Pittsburgh; Washington, D.C.; Irvine, California; and Delray Beach, Florida. There are two congregations in Canada and one each in Berlin, Germany; Israel; Ukraine; and Buenos Aires, Argentina.

Periodicals: *The Chosen People*.

Educational Facilities:

In association with Chosen People Ministries, the Charles L. Feinberg Center in New York, offers an accredited master of divinity program in Messianic Jewish Studies.

Sources:

Chosen People Ministries. www.chosenpeople.com.

Cohn, Joseph Hoffman. *Beginning at Jerusalem*. New York: American Board of Mission to the Jews, 1948.

————. *I Have Fought the Good Fight: The Story of Jewish Mission Pioneering in America*. New York: American Board of Mission to the Jews, 1953.

Pruter, Karl. *Jewish Christians in the United States: A Bibliography*. New York: Garland Publishing, 1987.

International Alliance of Messianic Congregations and Synagogues

PO Box 20006, Sarasota, FL 34276-3006

One of two major groupings of Messianic Jewish congregations, the International Alliance of Messianic Congregations and Synagogues was founded in 1986. Through it publications and programs it promotes the welfare of Messianic ministries and provides for the ordination of clergy. Member congregations follow the practices and traditions of Judaism, but believe that Yeshua (Jesus) of Nazareth is the Jewish Messiah.

The alliance encourages Messianic pastors and rabbis through leadership conferences and training seminars. It establishes prayer fellowship among members, and promotes unity among Messianic congregations and pastors. Undergraduate-level classes are offered at national and regional conferences. Distance-learning courses are available on the alliance's web site. A certificate degree in Messianic Jewish Studies is offered.

The alliance is administered by a steering committee. In 2008 the chairman was Rabbi Robert Solomon, of Roswell, Georgia, and the committee members were Rabbis David Chernoff, Joe Finkelstein, Judah Hungerman, Charles Liberman, David Schneier, Steve Weiler, and Michael Wolf.

Membership: In 2008 there were 120 affiliated congregations in the United States, Australia, Belarus, Belgium, El Salvador, Canada, France, Israel, Mexico, the Netherlands, New Zealand, Panama, Peru, Russia, Ukraine, Uruguay, and Zambia.

Periodicals: *IAMCS Newsletter.*

Sources:

International Alliance of Messianic Congregations and Synagogues. iamcs.org/.

Goble, Philip E. *Everything You Need to Grow a Messianic Synagogue.* South Pasadena, CA: William Carey Library, 1974.

Rausch, David A. *Messianic Judaism.* New York: Edwin Mellen Press, 1982.

International Federation of Messianic Jews

PO Box 271708, Tampa, FL 33688

The International Federation of Messianic Jews (IFMJ) dates to 1978 and the founding of Beth Israel, a Messianic Jewish congregation in Tampa Bay, Florida, and the associated Etz Chayim Messianic Jewish Institute, a school for the training of Messianic rabbis. These were among the first Messianic congregations and schools to emerge amid the new wave of interest in Messianic Judaism that swept through the many Jewish missionary organizations in the 1970s. Both of the Tampa organizations were formed by Rabbi Haim Levi, a former president of the Messianic Jewish Alliance of America and a member of the executive committee of the International Messianic Jewish (Hebrew Christian) Alliance of Great Britain.

Rabbi Levi, born of Sephardic Jewish parents in Colombia, holds a masters degree in biblical studies and a doctorate degree in Hebrew and biblical studies from Eitz Chayim Yeshiva.

Within a few years of the founding of the Tampa congregation, Levi had inspired the formation of three additional congregations, Beth Israel of Orlando, Beth Jacob of Jacksonville, Florida, and Beth Israel of São Paolo, Brazil. These became the core congregation of the federation. Amid growing interest in Messianic Judaism in the 1980s, Levi responded to calls for assistance from congregations across Florida and Latin America and even France. In September 1994 the Mishkan Messianic Jewish Congregation was dedicated in Nice, France.

In 1984 regional conferences began to be held, and the one in the Orlando in 1990 became an international conference, with delegates from Barbados, Colombia, Honduras, and Mexico. In 1994 the conference hosted the first delegates from Israel. During this time, Levi continued to work with the Messianic Jewish Alliance of America, and helped in its formation in 1986 of the International Alliance of Messianic Congregations and Synagogues, an international synagogal association. However, at the same time, the federation was developing its own distinctive role within the Messianic Jewish world.

The federation came to feel that it was very important to reach out to the Marranos, the "hidden" descendants of the Sephardic Jews who were expelled from Spain to Portugal in 1492 and were victimized by the Spanish and Portuguese Inquisitions. Marrano descendants can be found today in Spain and Portugal, in their former colonies, and elsewhere. The largest number of surviving Sephardic Jews are in the old Spanish and Portuguese areas of the New World, and the federation has developed a Spanish-speaking ministry that dominates its organization.

While moving to assist the Marranos, the federation also opens its doors to gentiles who want to identify with the Messianic Jewish community. Through the actions of the Messiah (Yahshua/Jesus), God has provided a means for all people, of different ancestries, to be joined to his Chosen People. The federation created a

process through Messianic Jewish legal processes, Halakhah, to receive gentile believers who want to become Jewish. This process includes a period of indoctrination into the Jewish way of life, and culminates in the granting of a certificate signed by the appropriate rabbinical authority.

The federation is also a "Torah Faithful" organization in that it believes that Yeshua (Jesus) did not abolish the law. The Torah, the first five books of the Jewish Bible, is God's instructions to his people. Gentiles have been mistaken that these instructions no longer apply. The IFMJ encourages believers to return to God's Holy Writings, and acknowledges that through the Torah one finds growth in the knowledge of Yeshua and a clearer understanding of his nature, and is able to offer a better witness to the world.

Jacob's Tent Ministry was designed by the federation as a summer camp for children aged 10 to 14 years old. Young International Federation of Messianic Jews is a ministry for members aged 18 to 30 years old.

In 2008 Rabbi Levi was chairman of the board for the International Federation of Messianic Jews. Rabbi George Quinn was the president and also served as rabbi of Beth Israel Messianic Center in El Paso, Texas. Rachel Levi was vice president. The Northeast U.S. regional director was Rabbi Mark Hernandez, and the Mid-Southwest U.S. regional director was Rabbi George Quinn. The Southeast U.S. and Caribbean regional director was Rabbi Roberto Cardona.

Membership: 2008 figures are not reported. Countries with synagogue affiliation or in development with the International Federation of Messianic Jews include: the United States, Argentina, Colombia, El Salvador, Mexico, Santo Domingo, Dominican Republic, Venezuela, and Ecuador.

Periodicals: *Kol Shofar/The Voice of the Shofar.*

Sources:

International Federation of Messianic Jews. www.ifmj.org.

Messianic Israel Alliance (MIA)

PO Box 3263, Lebanon, TN 37088

The Messianic Israel Alliance, and the related House of David and Messianic Jewish Ministries, are a complex of structures founded by Angus Wootten and his wife Batya Wootten, who served as their executive directors in 2008. The Woottens became Christians in the formative days of the contemporary Messianic Jewish movement in the early 1970s. Angus put up money to start the first Messianic radio broadcast ministry. They also created a catalogue of Messianic resources, Messianic Manna, and, though themselves are not Jewish, became active in the Messianic Jewish Alliance of America.

During the 1970s the Woottens became engaged in the question of the role of gentiles in the Messianic movement and in the larger theological questions of the relationship of the Jewish and gentiles community in salvation history. Traditionally this latter problem had been solved in one of three ways: by the belief that the church had replaced Israel; by designating the church as "spiritual Israel" and the Jews as "physical Israel;" or by considering the church and Israel as two separate entities that would only converge in the heavenly kingdom. Within the early Messianic movement, membership was based on one's having Jewish parents or being married to a Jew. By accepting Christ, these "physical Jews" were designated "spiritual Jews." Gentiles who affiliated with the movement (at times, making up the majority) were thought of as merely "spiritual heirs," and many felt like second-class citizens in the Messianic kingdom.

To deal with this situation, Angus Wootten proposed a conversion process for non-Jews that would lead to all being considered equal, both "physically" and "spiritually." Further reflection led to a reconsideration of the basic question, "Who is Israel?" The Woottens found an initial answer in biblical references to the two Houses of Israel—the "stick of Judah and the sons of Israel his companions," which refers to the Jewish people, and "Joseph, the stick of Ephraim and all the house of Israel, his companions," which refers to non-Jewish believers (Gen. 48:19; Isa. 8:14;

Ezek. 37:15–28). Wootten's study led to the publication of a newsletter, *Is the Church Ephraim?*, in 1983 and a book in 1988.

In the end, the Woottens concluded that contemporary Israel consists of the two branches of believers, and that Messianic Israel's task was to reunite the olive tree of Israel—both branches, Ephraim and Judah, into one redeemed nation of Israel—through Messiah Yeshua. MIA thus proposes that non-Jewish followers of Yeshua are returning Ephraim who have been restored to the commonwealth of Israel through their covenant with Israel's Messiah. They are not to be considered gentiles henceforth. This position has set them at odds with the larger segment of the Messianic movement.

In the 1990s the Woottens moved first to Virginia and then to Orlando, Florida, and developed a small ministry to restore the two house of Israel based on the publication of a periodical, *Messianic Home Magazine*. Crucial to the development of the work was their 1998 meeting with Moshe Koniuchowsky, who authored a defense of the Woottens' position, "The Truth about All Israel," and brought to the movement Jewish leadership to complement their own. He also helped expand the Woottens' network. Within a short time, they found compatriots across the United States and in Israel, and the Messianic Israel Alliance was founded in 1999. The alliance believes that "Yeshua Ha'Natsree (Jesus of Nazareth) was and is the true Messiah, the Lion of Judah, the Branch Who will fully reunite all Israel; that he died and rose from the dead and lives at the right hand of the Almighty; and according to the ancient Holy Scriptures, Genesis to Revelation, Yeshua is YHVH Elohim appearing in the flesh, as Yeshua demonstrated in Himself." The alliance describes itself as a "gathering place for believers in Messiah who were awakening to their lost heritage as Israel. By connecting these believers, the MIA was able to birth relationships throughout the world. Those who once had lost their heritage now had a place they could call home; a place where both Jew and non-Jew could worship the God of Israel as equal brothers in Messiah."

Today the Messianic Israel Alliance exists to link Messsianic congregations. It posts an Internet directory of such congregations, some of which are formally affiliated with the alliance and others that share a basic agreement with it. These congregations are conservative evangelical Christians who look for a union of Jewish and non-Jewish believers in the Messiah.

The alliance is administered by the shepherd's council, which in 2008 was composed of John Conrad, Scott Diffenderfer, and Hale Harris. The general secretary was Hale Harris. There is also an advisory board.

Membership: In 2008 more than 130 member organizations in North America, and more than 30 others worldwide, were reported. There are congregations in Australia, France, Germany, Italy, Nigeria, Peru, Philippines, the United Kingdom, Puerto Rico, the Virgin Islands, Argentina, the Bahamas, United Kingdom, Micronesia, Guatemala, Honduras, India, Israel, Jamaica, Mexico, Namibia, New Zealand, South Africa, and Sweden. Congregations are also located in the Canadian provinces of Alberta, British Columbia, Ontario, and Quebec.

Periodicals: *The Herald* (bi-monthly).

Sources:

Messianic Israel Alliance. www.messianicisrael.com.

Koniuchowsky, Marshall Moshe. "The Truth about All Israel." Miami Beach, FL: Your Arms to Israel, 2000. Available from www.yourarmstoisrael.org/.

Nasorean Orthodox Qahal

3433 Southwest Trafficway, 2nd Fl., Kansas City, MO 64111

The Nasorean Orthodox Qahal is a Jewish sect formed in the mid-1980s from the larger Jewish Messianic movement that affirms that Yeshua ha Meshiach (Jesus of Nazareth) was the Melchizedek High Priest of the Deity, and that he acted as the Meshiach of Melchizedek and is the Priest-King of Israel. The revived Nasorean movement was founded and is led by Baruch ha Tzaddik (Barry Gale Albin, b. 1948).

The Nasorean Orthodox Qahal sees itself as a revival of a movement traced to the first century B.C.E. and to an unnamed leader mentioned in the Dead Sea Scrolls as the "Teacher of Righteousness." This person led a movement that opposed the main Jewish leadership of the era, and ultimately produced several subgroups including the Sadducees, the Essenes, and the Zealots. A fourth subgroup was the Nasoreans. Like the Sadducees, they believed that the Holy Spirit would guide them in their reading of the Torah. Like the Essenes, they believed that they should separate themselves from the unbelievers, but they also believed that they needed to remain of the world, hough not a part of it.

As the Nasorean Orthodox Qahal understand the history, all four opposition movements were unified from 25 to 30 C.E. under the leadership of three men: Jesus of Nazareth (Yeshua), the great grandson of the Teacher of Righteousness; his physical brother James the Just (Ya'akov); and their cousin John the Baptist (Yochanan). Yochanan was a Jewish priest and Yeshua and Ya'akov believed that Yochanan would become the new high priest when the kingdom of Israel was reestablished. The movement as a whole believed that Ya'akov would be the prophet who announced the true teachings, and that Yeshua was the heir to David's throne—that is, the temporal messiah.

A crisis ensued when Yochanan was killed. Yeshua then offered a new direction. He announced that he was the messiah, a position uniting prophet, priest, and king in his person. He saw himself as the high priest according to not the Order of Aaron, but the Order of Melchizedek. After Yeshua's death, he appeared to various members of the movement that had grown up around him. Of these, his appearance to Ya'akov was the most important (1 Cor. 15:7) because it gave Ya'akov the authority to assume leadership of the movement in Jerusalem. He became the *mebakker* (overseer or bishop) of the communities following a pattern that came from the Rule of the Community discovered among the Dead Sea Scrolls. Ja'akov became the overseer, John the prophet, and Cephas (Peter) the chief rabbi or spiritual teacher.

Ya'akov led the Church from 33 C.E. until his death in 62 C.E. He was succeeded by his brother Shimon (also a physical brother of Jesus/Yeshua), who led the church until the destruction of Jerusalem in 70. The church in Jerusalem left behind their constituting document, which survived in Greek as the Didache (Teachings of the Twelve). It was an important church document in the second and third centuries, but it was not included in the biblical canon and therefore was largely forgotten except by church scholars.

After Jerusalem was destroyed, the church led by Shimon relocated to the village of Pella on the eastern side of the Sea of Galilee. Over the next two generations it grew, but had its next crisis in 132–35 CE when the Jewish revolutionary Bar Kochba arose, established a state independent of Rome, and declared himself the new meshiach. The Nasoreans could not accept his messianic claims and suffered greatly when Rome reconquered the land—the great majority of their followers were killed. The surviving remnant relocated Beroea in Coele Syria, near modern-day Aleppo. At this point, this movement is lost to history, though its ideas resurfaced in fifteenth-century Spain in the among those known as the Marranos, many of whom were killed by the Spanish Inquisition.

The story of the Nasoreans began anew with the discovery of the Dead Sea Scrolls in the middle of the twentieth century and the gradual reconstruction of the history of the Holy Land in the first century B.C.E. The scholarly assessment intruded into the revival of Jewish Christianity of the 1970s and 1980s. By the early 1980s, some were ruminating on the issue that Yeshua had never specifically stated that the Jewish law was abolished. That idea gave birth in 1983 to the Messianic Jewish movement. Rev. J. David Davis separated from the Jewish Christians and became the first leader of a new group attached to Judaism. From this beginning, there soon arose a second group that reaffirmed their belief that Yeshua was in fact the meshiach, but denied that he was G-d, nor was the Holy Spirit G-d. This new group then split into two groups. One branch centered in Ra'ana, Israel, accepts as much of the Talmud as it can within the framework of the Gospel of Matthew. The other is the Nasorean Orthodox Qabal.

The revived Nasorean Orthodox Qahal was founded by Baruch ha Tzaddik, the son of nonpracticing Jewish parents. He became a lawyer, and as an adult converted to Roman Catholicism and became involved in the Catholic Charismatic Renewal. In 1975 he met Fr. William J. Axe, who advised him to return to his Jewish roots. He subsequently affiliated with a messianic synagogue, but had come to doubt the idea of the deity of Yeshua. In 1981 he began an independent charismatic bible study group that evolved into the Servants of G-d Evangelical Mission, which became familiarized with Jewish religious ways. In 1985 Baruch was ordained rabbi and mebakker (bishop) of the organization, which under his guidance rejected the divinity of Yeshua while affirming his messiahship. It also adopted the Didache as its constitution. Baruch authored several books that are available through the community, including *Climbing Jacob's Ladder: A Lay Guide to Holiness* and *The Manual of the Nasorean Church*.

The Nasoreans affirm that Yeshua ben Yotzef (Jesus the son of Joseph) is the messiah promised in the Messianic Apocryphon, a book found among the Dead Sea Scrolls and ascribed to the Teacher of Righteousness. They also believe that the Archangel of the Presence on the Mountain gave the Torah to Moses. They accept all of the Tanakh (the Jewish Bible), including the extra books found in the Septuagint, plus various intertestamental books including the books of Enoch and Jubilees. Further, they accept the Gospel of Matthew in its Hebrew form, and the books of the Christian Bible known as Hebrews, James, 1 and 2 Peter, 1, 2, and 3 John, Jude, and Revelation. In addition, they accept the Didache and the Gospel of Thomas.

In outlining the canon they use, the Nasoreans reject the concept of the inerrancy of any scriptures for any purpose other than reproof, correction, and training in holiness. They also reject the idea that scripture is closed. At the same time, the Nasoreans reject the authority of the Oral Law. and believe that the subsequent rulings of the rabbinical Jews are mere opinions. They practice circumcision, Shabbat, Sabbath rest, and the feasts of the Scripture.

The Nasoreans practice what Christian know as the Eucharist, or the Lord's Supper. They affirm that the Melchizedekian sacrifice of bread and wine is sufficient for the forgiveness of sin. When sacrificed with the proper faith, this bread and wine becomes the Lamb of G-d that takes away the sins of the world.

As reconstituted, the Nasoreans have a number of differences with the larger Christian community. Notably, they see the Apostle Paul as a traitor who tried to destroy the work of Yeshua. At the same time, they believe that physical descendents of Yeshua are alive and can be identified, and that they should be given preference in positions of authority within the church. The Didache supplies an organizational pattern.

They affirm that Yeshua is the Son of G-d, created by Ain Sof (G-d) in the beginning and begotten by the Archangel in time. He is joined by the Holy Spirit, the descending Light. Neither he nor the Spirit are themselves the very G-d, but they are our G-ds and rule over the other archangels in the Assembly of G-ds. Yeshua mediates sin for his people and offers the Voice to guide them on the Way (Ex. 23:20, John 10:3–5). Following Yeshua today requires keeping the Torah and all the feasts as he commanded.

Membership: Not reported.

Sources:

Nasorean Orthodox Qahal. www.nasori.org/.

Union of Messianic Jewish Congregations
529 Jefferson St. NE, Albuquerque, NM 87108

Messianic Judaism is a movement that began among American Jewish converts to Christianity in the 1960s, though as a perspective it has found expression within the larger context of Hebrew Christianity periodically throughout the twentieth century. It has been the dominant position among Jews who become Christians that they lose their Jewish religious (if not ethnic) identity and become members of congregations of various Christian denominations. Overwhelmingly, Jewish Christians have blended into mainline Christian churches and are visible primarily through the numerous independent evangelical Jewish missionary ministries they support. Among the best known of the Hebrew Christian organizations that carry out missionary programs to Jews but do not establish separate Jewish congregations is Hineni Ministries, better known as Jews for Jesus. It was founded in 1973 by Moishe Rosen, formerly with the American Board of Missions to the Jews, the largest of the Jewish missionary organizations.

Messianic Judaism, in contrast to the more popular Jewish missionary perspective, believes that Jews can be Christians and still identify with Jewish culture and religious forms. They see Christianity as completing Judaism, not standing in stark contrast to it. Although it rarely assumed any organized form, Messianic Jewish thinking was always present among people associated with Jewish missions. In the 1960s at least one Messianic synagogue was formed, the Congregation of the Messiah in Philadelphia. In 1970 Martin Chernoff founded Beth Messiah in Cincinnati. Bu the movement found its first major organizational support in Chicago.

Within the Chicago-based Hebrew Christian Alliance, one of the oldest Hebrew Christian organizations in the United States, Messianic sentiments began to grow among the leaders of the Young Hebrew Christian Alliance in the early 1970s, partially as a fallout from the Jesus People revival. By 1975 the Messianists became the majority of the Young Hebrew Christian Alliance's membership, voted in a name change, and reoriented the organization's direction as the Messianic Jewish Alliance of America. Since then, the alliance has sponsored an annual gathering that has served as the major meeting ground for fellowship for Messianic Jews, both those within Messianic synagogues and those in more traditional gentile congregations.

In summer 1979, as the number of Messianic congregations increased, leaders from 33 such congregations met to form an umbrella congregational organization, the Union of Messianic Jewish Congregations. The charter meeting was held at the 1979 annual gathering of the Messianic Jewish Alliance of America, Messiah '79. Daniel C. Juster and John Fischer were the first president and vice president, respectively. Nineteen congregations joined the first year, and by 1982 there were 25.

The union set as its goals the advocacy of Messianic Judaism, the development of Messianic synagogues, and the training of Messianic leaders. In 1981 the union adopted the statement of faith of the National Association of Evangelicals, with appropriate changes in terminology for Jewish Christians. That statement is in line with earlier guidelines that affirmed the Bible as the absolute authority in matter of belief; the divinity of Jesus, normally called by his Hebrew name, Yeshua; and salvation by grace through faith in Yeshua's atonement. Congregations generally have services on either Friday evenings or Saturday mornings in addition to Sunday worship. Worship varies considerably, but each congregation's worship bears a distinctly Jewish flavor.

The union is very loosely organized, with a congregational polity. To join, a congregation must have been in existence for one year and have at least 10 Messianic Jews among its members. Typically, congregations have a large number of non-Jews who are also members.

In 2008 Rabbi Russ Resnik served as executive director, Jamie Cowen as president, and Dr. John Fischer as vice president.

Membership: In 2008 there were four affiliated international congregations, two in Canada, and 73 in the United States. California and New York have the largest representation.

Educational Facilities:

UMJC Yeshiva, Gaithersburg, Maryland.

Periodicals: *Messianic Judaism Today* • *Unofficial: Shofar Shalom* • *The American Messianic Jew* • *The Messianic Outreach*

Remarks: The Messianic movement has emerged as part of a period of aggressive Jewish evangelism and has had to face the growing activism of the Jewish religious community, which opposes any attempts by evangelical Christians to evangelize within the Jewish community. The existence of Messianic synagogues has been a particular affront to many Jewish leaders who have seen them as further attempts to destroy Judaism, deceptive in their appearance.

Sources:

Union of Messianic Jewish Congregations. www.umjc.net.

Fischer, John. *The Olive Tree Connection*. Downers Grove, IL: InterVarsity Press, 1983.

Goble, Phillip E. *Everything You Need to Grow a Messianic Synagogue*. South Pasadena, CA: William Carey Library, 1974.

Rausch, David. A. *Messianic Judaism*. New York: Edwin Mellon Press, 1982.

Yellow Pages. Rockville, MD: Union of Messianic Jewish Congregations, 1982.

Union of Nazarene Yisraelite Congregations

PO Box 556, Ottumwa, IA 52501

The Union of Nazarene Yisraelite Congregations, formerly the Union of Two House Messianic Congregations, was formed at the beginning of the twenty-first century as Rabbi Marshall Moshe Koniuchowsky, one of cofounders of the Messianic Israel Alliance (MIA), developed disagreements with the other alliance leaders, Angus Wootten and Batya Wootten. Koniuchowsky had authored a defense of the Woottens' position, "The Truth about All Israel" (2000), and had brought Jewish leadership to their movement. Shortly after their association, differences arose that are now manifest in the union's statement of faith, which includes a number of beliefs not mentioned in the Hope of Messianic Israelof the by MIA. All union members must agree completely and in writing to the union's doctrinal statement.

The union continues its basic agreement with MIA that the Messianic Jewish movement should drop its distinctions between believers who are ethnically Jews and those who are gentiles. It agrees that non-Jewish followers of Yeshua are returning Ephraim who have been restored to the commonwealth of Israel through their covenant with Israel's Messiah. Henceforth, they should not be thought of as gentiles. This position disagrees with the two theologies that dominate the Messianic movement—"replacement theology" that designates the "church" as the replacement of Israel in God's eyes, and the "separate entity theology" that sees the "church" as coexisting as a separate "spiritual Israel" beside physical Jewish-Israel.

While not identifying with the Sacred Name community, the union insists that affiliated groups use the sacred names Yahweh and Yahshua (with variant spellings acceptable) in its gatherings at both the local and national levels. Congregations that refuse to use the true names are asked to leave the union. Leadership of the union is vested in a board of rabbis. This board is seen as an apostolic board that offers oversight when requested by member congregations and affiliates. All union member congregations are required to send at least two representatives to the annual union conference.

The union has adopted a course of study for prospective rabbis. Women are welcomed to rabbinate. Women are not known as *roeh* (pastor), but as *rebbetzin* (female teacher).

The union is in fellowship with a group of 60 congregations in Zimbabwe, under the leadership of Sholiach/Rabbi Charles Richard Zechman, a rabbi ordained by the union through whom union outreach in that country was opened.

In 2008 board members included Rabbi Edward Levi Mydle and Rabbi Tom Mitchell. Rabbi Bob Miller of Agudat Bris, Temple, Texas, was assigned the role of traveling shepherd.

Membership: 2008 membership figures not reported. The directory of Messianic congregations, published by the union, includes 94 U.S. and 6 Canadian congregations and ministry centers. In addition, there are congregations and ministries listed from Australia, the Bahamas, Bolivia, Brazil, Cuba, Honduras, Kenya, Paraguay, Colombia, India, Jamaica, New Zealand, Nigeria, Peru, the Philippines, Switzerland, Spain, South Africa, Trinidad, Virgin Islands, and Zimbabwe.

Sources:

Union of Nazarene Yisraelite Congregations. www.2house.org.

Koniuchowsky, Marshall Moshe. "The Truth About All Israel." Miami Beach, FL: Your Arms to Israel, 2000. Available from www.yourarmstoisrael.org/.

 # Grace Gospel Movement

Berean Bible Fellowship

9325 El Bordo Ave., Atascadero, CA 93422

The Berean Bible Fellowship, centered in the Pacific Southwest, accepts only two vast dispensations, but otherwise is in concert with the ultradispensationalism of Charles H. Welch (1880–1967) and Ethelbert William Bullinger (1837–1913). Faith in God in Christ is stressed and is differentiated as faith that receives Christ, faith that motivates the believer to walk in love, faith that constrains believers to set their minds on things above, and faith that is humble-minded when believers have among themselves the mind that was in Christ. The Fellowship's Phoenix center operates the Berean Tape Ministry, which distributes more than 1,000 tapes by Oscar M. Baker (founder of the Truth for Today Bible Fellowship), Welch, Stuart Allen (d. 1998), Arthur E. Lamboune (the leader of the Fellowship), and others. Associated with the fellowship are Scripture Research, Inc., formerly the Ewalt Memorial Bible School, of Atascadero, California, and the Bible Fellowship Church of South Holland, Illinois.

The use of the word *Berean* by this church and a number of other groups stems from the Bible. The Acts of the Apostles mentions that members of the church at Berea in Greece were students of the Scriptures. Because the Bible is so important in the fundamentalist movement, many fundamentalist groups adopted the name "Berean."

Membership: Not reported.

Periodicals: Unofficial: *Scripture Research, Inc.* • *The Scripture Research Greek Tutor*. Both available from Box 518, Atascadero, CA 93423.

Sources:

Berean Bible Fellowship. www.bereanbible.com/.

Bullinger, E. W. *The Book of Job*. Atascadero, CA: Scripture Research, 1983.

Morgan, Harold P. *Christian Values and Principles*. 3 vols. Atascadero, CA: Ewalt Memorial Bible School, n.d.

Berean Bible Fellowship (Illinois)

PO Box 6, Collinsville, IL 62234

Alternate Address: Berean Bible Society, N112 W17761 Mequon Rd., PO Box 756, Germantown, WI 53022.

The Berean Bible Fellowship is a fellowship of conservative fundamentalist Christians founded in 1968 under the leadership of Cornelius R. Stam (1909–2003), of Chicago, Illinois, and Win Johnson, of Denver, Colorado. Both men had been leaders in the Grace Gospel Fellowship from which they separated because of perceived permissive and liberal trends. Grace Bible College of Wyoming, Michigan, associated with Grace Gospel Fellowship, was a focal point of the inroads of said departures.

The formal doctrinal statements of the Berean Bible Fellowship and Grace Gospel Fellowship are essentially the same. Both present a basic and fundamental Christianity with a special emphasis on the distinctive apostleship and teachings of Paul and his ministry to all nations. The fellowship teaches that the church, the body of Christ, was established by the risen glorified Lord after the salvation and call of Paul (Cf. Acts 9), not at Pentecost (Acts 2) as most Christians assume. The implication of this understanding is that water baptism belongs to the earthly ministry of Christ toward Israel and was properly continued by Peter and the 12 apostles. Paul, not sent to baptize, was raised up to preach the gospel of the grace of God, a message distinct from that proclaimed by Christ and the 12 to Israel. The hope of the church is believed to be the coming of the Lord in the air, commonly called the "rapture," which will conclude the present dispensation by his gathering up the church to heaven to be "forever with the Lord."

In 1940, prior to the founding of the Berean Bible Fellowship, Stam had founded the Berean Bible Society through which he had published a number of books and a periodical, *Berean Searchlight*. In 1996 the society moved from Chicago to Germantown, Wisconsin. Win Johnson had founded Grace Gospel Publishers in Denver, Colorado, where it remains to the present. Although separate organizations, both are closely related to and supportive of the Berean Bible Fellowship. The fellowship enlists membership worldwide, sponsors local and national Bible conferences, and maintains Bible study literature.

Membership: Not reported.

Periodicals: *BBF News & Notes*.

Sources:

Berean Bible Society. www.bereanbiblesociety.org.

Stam, Cornelius R. *The Controversy*. Chicago: Berean Bible Society, 1963.

———. *The Memoirs of Pastor Cornelius R. Stam*. Germantown, WI: Berean Bible Society, n.d.

———. *Satan in Derision*. Chicago: Berean Bible Society, 1972.

———. *Things That Differ*. Chicago: Berean Bible Society, 1951.

———. *True Spirituality*. Chicago: Berean Bible Society, 1959.

Bible Churches (Classics Expositor)

1429 NW 100th St., Oklahoma City, OK 73114

Northside Bible Church was founded in 1965 as an independent ministry by Dr. Clifford McLain, and still maintains an independent status. In Oklahoma, there are four churches (three in Oklahoma City and one in Moore) associated with McLain, who is both pastor of the Northside Bible Church and editor of its periodical and publishing arm, the *Classics Expositor*. The church's radio ministry, featuring the Rev. David Webber, was heard over eight stations in the South Central states in 1968. Currently, recordings of weekly morning worship services are made available on the church's Web site.

Members of the Northside Bible Church are fundamental in their doctrines, literal in their interpretations, and dispensational in their applications of Scripture. Salvation is by God's grace (unmerited favor) based upon the shed Blood of Christ Jesus, the only begotten Son of the Father. In Christ Jesus, the believer has been saved from the penalty of sin, is being saved from the power of sin, and shall be saved from the presence of sin. Members endeavor to "rightly divide" God's Word according to the Word itself while keeping the context intact. Such an approach to the Bible serves to increase students' understanding of Scripture, while at the same time helping them to "try the things that differ" (Philippians 1:10).

Membership: Not reported.

Periodicals: *The Classics Expositor*.

Sources:

Northside Bible Church. www.rightdivision.com/html/northside_bible_church.html.

Concordant Publishing Concern

15570 Knochaven, Santa Clarita, CA 91330

Adolph Ernst Knoch (1874–1965), as a young believer, was briefly associated with the Plymouth Brethren (discussed elsewhere in this volume). After a time he was disfellowshipped from this group due to his differing views on points of scriptural interpretation. In 1909 the first issue of the periodical *Unsearchable Riches* appeared as a vehicle to promote Knoch's ideas. It was printed in Minneapolis by Vladimir M. Gelesnoff, its coeditor, who soon moved to southern California, where permanent headquarters were established. Knoch then launched his life work,

which was to be a new translation of the Scriptures called the Concordant Version. The first part, Revelation, was published in 1919; other portions followed until 1926, when the entire New Testament was issued. In 1939, a German version was issued. Though he had finished the early phases of his translation work, Knoch lived to see only two portions of the Hebrew Scriptures published before his death: Genesis in 1957 and Isaiah in 1962.

The thrust of the Concordant Version is to: (1) to correct the faults of past translations, particularly the King James, American Revised (1901), and Revised Standard versions; (2) to determine the meanings of the inspired words of Scriptures; and (3) to produce a "literal" translation within the bounds of good diction. In the process, a new Concordance, which became the basis of the translation, was produced. The appearance of the Concordant Version created a great deal of controversy in conservative evangelical circles. While it is generally most actively used by those people associated with Knoch through *Unsearchable Riches*, it is used (often quite actively) by believers from most denominations.

Knoch's study of the Scriptures, bolstered in part by his correspondence with the British dispensationalist scholar Ethelbert W. Bullinger, led to a new form of dispensationalism based on the *eons* (a transliteration of the Greek word usually translated "ages"). Our knowledge of God begins in his decrees before "eonian" times. The first eon is from creation to the disruption of Gen. 1:2. The eonian times begin with Adam and continue through five periods: innocence (Adam), conscience (Seth), government (Noah), promise (Abraham), law (Moses). The sixth period, that of Jesus' life, begins the eon of the fullness of times (Gal. 4:4). After Jesus comes the era of the nations, which includes the periods of Pentecost, transition (with Paul as priest), and the secret (with Paul the prisoner) or Grace. Currently, we are in the period of the secret. Yet to come is the period of indignation (the tribulation) and the eschatological events of the oncoming eons, which include the binding of Satan, the millennial kingdom, the white throne judgment, the new heavens and earth, and the consummation, when God is All in all (I Cor. 15:28).

Knoch's thinking had become centered on Paul, who, Knoch was convinced, had been commissioned directly by Christ to reveal further truths—truths that Jesus had not already revealed to his original disciples. These truths concern the glories of Christ and appear throughout Paul's epistles, especially his prison epistles. From these writings, a "creed" can be constructed. Paul believed in the deity of God (Rom. 11:36), the glories of Christ (Col. 1:25), the believer's share in that glory (Eph. 1:3–5), the justification of all mankind (Rom. 5:18–19), the reconciliation of all (Col. 1:18–20), the abolition of death (I Cor. 15:20–26), and the subjection of all to God (I Cor. 15:27–28), including Satan (Eph. 1:10; Col. 1:29). Knoch thus departed from most of his former brethren through his belief in universal salvation. He felt that the believer is justified when he believes, and that the unbeliever must wait until the consummation.

The Concordant Publishing Concern is a nondenominational, nonprofit association founded in 1909 for the purpose of disseminating the facts and truths of the ancient manuscripts of the Scriptures. In addition to its principal works—the Concordant Literal New Testament with Keyword Concordance and the Concordant Version of the Old Testament—other publications include the Concordant Greek Text and the Concordant Commentary, together with a wide variety of additional books and booklets on scriptural themes. The Concern also publishes the Concordant Literal Version, computer edition. Its bimonthly magazine, *Unsearchable Riches*, is now in its 96th year of publication (both scripture and topic indexes are available, in printed and computer form). A considerable number of its expositions are available on-line, both in standard HTML format and in PDF format.

Unsearchable Riches found readers who grouped around it as a tool for Bible study, and thus a national following of the eonian interpretation of Scripture developed. A songbook, *Scriptural Songs*, was produced for these groups.

Membership: The Concern is not a membership organization. In 1995, *Unsearchable Riches* listed 23 independent associated groups in the United States, and an additional 33 groups in 15 countries. More than half of the foreign groups were to be found in Canada, Australia, and Great Britain. These groups, which include approximately 2,000 people, are informally associated with the Concern.

Periodicals: *Unsearchable Riches*.

Sources:

Concordant Publishing Concern. www.concordant.org/.

Adolph Ernst Knoch, 1874–1965. Saugus, CA: Concordant Publishing Concern, 1965.

Concordant Literal New Testament. Saugus, CA: Concordant Publishing Concern, 1966.

The Concordant Version in the Critics' Den. Los Angeles: Concordant Publishing Concern, n.d.

Scriptural Songs. Saugus, CA: Concordant Publishing Concern, n.d.

Grace Gospel Fellowship

1011 Aldon SW, Grand Rapids, MI 49509

The Grace Gospel Fellowship is an organization of autonomous churches that preach dispensational theology from what is termed a Pauline perspective. J. C. O'Hair (1876–1958) was an early exponent of this theological position in Chicago, Illinois. There have been several developmental stages. First, in 1938, a group of pastors and laypersons met to formulate a structure to implement the spread of this message at home and abroad. A doctrinal statement was agreed upon: A constitution was formulated, and in January 1939 the World Wide Grace Testimony (later Grace Mission and now Grace Ministries, International) came into being.

In 1944 the Grace pastors met in Evansville, Indiana, and formally organized the Grace Gospel Fellowship. J. C. O'Hair and Charles Baker continued as prominent leaders. At first a ministers' fellowship, Grace Gospel Fellowship was later opened to laymen. Charles O'Connor became its first full-time president in 1971. Roger G. Anderson, a pastor for 33 years and a graduate of Grace Bible College, succeeded him in October 1991 and retired in July 2000. Ken Parker succeeded Anderson in July 2000 and hired Mike Riemersma as vice president of operations.

In 1945 the Milwaukee Bible Institute was founded by the organization and Charles Baker, a fundamentalist pastor; it was initially operated as a function of the local congregation. The school developed a full curriculum in the late 1940s, and in 1961 it moved to Grand Rapids, Michigan, as Grace Bible College. It has since received accreditation from both North Central Accrediting and the Accrediting Association of Bible Colleges.

The doctrine of the Grace Gospel Fellowship follows a limited Calvinistic view with emphasis on the total depravity of man and eternal security (once a person is a child of God, that status is secure but not in the concept of limited atonement). Specific doctrine affirms the temporary nature of both the gifts of the Spirit (I Cor. 12:4–11) and baptism. There is no connection with the beliefs of Ethelbert William Bullinger (1837–1913) and Charles H. Welch (1880–1967) regarding observation of the Lord's Supper, annihilationism, or a two Body concept. Eschatologically, the group adheres to the premillennium, pretribulation concepts of John Nelson Darby (1800–1882), founder of the Plymouth Brethren.

Grace Gospel Fellowship was founded to "provide fellowship among those who believe the truths contained in the doctrinal statement, and to promote the Gospel of the Grace of God throughout this land and throughout the world." Three basic principles unite members: (1) commitment to an understanding of the Bible, the eternal Word of God, from a dispensational interpretation as outlined in their doctrinal statement; (2) a passion to reach the lost for Jesus Christ by proclaiming the Good News of his grace both at home and abroad; and (3) an awareness that the Body of Christ (the church) functions best when its members work and fellowship together for the glory of God.

Membership: In 2002 the fellowship reported 143 churches, and 286 ministers in the United States and 1,400 additional churches worldwide.

Educational Facilities:

Grace Bible College, Grand Rapids, Michigan.

Periodicals: *Truth*.

Sources:

Grace Gospel Fellowship. www.ggfusa.org/.

Baker, Charles F. *Bible Truth*. Grand Rapids, MI: Grace Bible College, Grace Gospel Fellowship, Grace Mission, 1956.

———. *Dispensational Relations*. Grand Rapids, MI: Grace Line Bible Lessons, n.d.

———. *God's Clock of the Ages*. Grand Rapids, MI: Grace Line Bible Lessons, 1937.

Egemeier, C. V., ed. *Grace Mission Story*. Grand Rapids, MI: Grace Missions, 1967.

Timely Messenger Fellowship

Grace Bible Church, 1450 Oak Hill Rd., Fort Worth, TX 76112-3017

The Timely Messenger was begun in 1939 by Pastor Ike T. Sidebottom (1899–1970) of Fort Worth, Texas, as a periodical expounding the Grace Gospel position in the Southwest. Sidebottom had been a student at Moody Bible Institute in Chicago and served as an associate pastor for J. C. O'Hair (1876–1958), the early Grace Gospel pastor in Chicago. Sidebottom returned to Fort Worth in 1928 with the intention of establishing himself as a radio evangelist. Soon, the weekly Bible class he taught grew into a church on College Avenue. Work continued to grow from the pulpit of College Avenue Church (rebuilt in 1950), the periodical, and the radio program. Through College Avenue Church, other men were prepared for the ministry, and independent congregations began to emerge. Most ministers work full-time at a secular job and serve as pastors on the weekends. In 1965 Sidebottom resigned as pastor because of ill health and was replaced by Charles W. Wages, who in turn was succeeded by Gregg Bing in 2003. In 1980 the congregation of the College Avenue Church built a new building on the east side of Fort Worth, and in their new location became known as Grace Bible Church.

The Timely Messenger Fellowship is an informal, cooperative endeavor. It differs from the Grace Gospel Fellowship, discussed elsewhere in this chapter, in that it neither baptizes nor partakes of the Lord's Supper. Mission work is done through Grace Ministries, International, and Things to Come Mission. The Timely Messenger Fellowship sponsors summer camps and midwinter conferences for high school and college students.

Membership: No formal membership is maintained.

Periodicals: *The Timely Messenger*.

Sources:

Timely Messenger Fellowship. pluto.matrix49.com/15182/?subpages/default.shtml.

Truth for Today Bible Fellowship

Box 6358, Lafayette, IN 47903

The dispensational Bible teachings of Ethelbert W. Bullinger (1837–1913) and Charles H. Welch (1880–1967) were passed to Stuart Allen (d. 1998), who succeeded Welch as pastor of the Chapel of the Opened Book in London. He edited the *Berean Expositor* and wrote a number of books and pamphlets. In the United States, Welch's theological disciples are grouped in local fellowships built around several periodicals. One such periodical, *Truth for Today*, was begun in 1948 by Oscar M. Baker (1898–1987) of Warsaw, Indiana. Baker had been a student of Dr. S. E. Long, an early follower of Bullinger and an extension teacher at Moody Bible Institute. He began his preaching in an abandoned church in Lulu, Michigan. Baker distributed Bullinger's, Welch's, and Allen's books, and supported a tape ministry located in Indianapolis, Indiana.

Baker was succeeded by Joseph L. Watkins, the editor of *Truth for Today*. The fellowship sponsors a radio ministry that is heard over stations in Vancouver, Washington state, and Phoenix, Arizona. The correspondence course is distributed from Lafayette, Indiana. Congregations in fellowship with the fellowship are located in Alabama, Tennessee, Illinois, Iowa, Indiana, Wisconsin, Michigan, New York, Oklahoma, California, and Canada. A very active group associated with the Berean Chapel in Mobile, Alabama, has radio ministries in Dallas, Texas, Lansing,

Illinois, and Mobile. *Truth for Today* is mailed to all 50 states and more than 38 foreign countries.

Membership: Not reported. In 1988 *Truth for Today* circulated more than 5,700 copies per issue.

Periodicals: *Truth for Today*.

Sources:

Truth for Today Bible Fellowship. www.tftmin.org/.

The Way International

PO Box 328, New Knoxville, OH 45871

The Way International was founded by Victor Paul Wierwille (1916–1985) in 1942 as the "Vesper Chimes," a radio ministry broadcast from a station in Lima, Ohio. Wierwille was a minister in the Evangelical and Reformed Church (now a constituent part of the United Church of Christ) into which he had been ordained the previous year. The radio ministry later was renamed "The Chimes Hour" and then incorporated as "The Chimes Hour Youth Caravan." During these years Wierwille became an avid student of the Bible. In 1951 he manifested the reception of God's holy spirit by way of speaking in tongues, one of the nine manifestations of the one gift (I Corinthians 12:7). All of his study culminated in the first Power of Abundant Living Class, a series of sessions presenting his basic perspective on biblical truth, in 1953. Two years later his ministry was chartered as The Way, Inc. (changed to The Way International in 1975). In 1957 Wierwille resigned from the Evangelical and Reformed Church to devote himself full-time to his growing work. The Wierwille family farm outside New Knoxville, Ohio, was donated to the ministry as its headquarters. The Way, Inc., grew steadily during the 1960s and then experienced rapid growth in the 1970s as the "Jesus People" revival spread across the United States. The facilities at New Knoxville were expanded and in 1971 hosted the first national Rock of Ages festival, an annual gathering of people associated with the ministry.

The Way considers itself to be a biblical research, teaching, and household fellowship ministry. It neither builds nor owns any church buildings but instead holds its meetings in home fellowships. Often overlooked by those who write about The Way's development is the role that Wierwille's research in Aramaic has played. He was spurred on by his personal relationship and contact with Dr. George M. Lamsa, translator of the Lamsa Bible. Among the activities of The Way have been the establishment of a large Aramaic facility (completely computerized) and the training of a group of scholars in the Aramaic (Syriac) language.

Like other Grace Gospel churches, The Way teaches a form of dispensationalism, although Wierwille preferred the term *administration*. According to Wierwille, present believers live under the church administration that began at Pentecost. Scripture from before Pentecost is not addressed to the church but is for the believer's learning. Pre-Pentecost scripture includes the Old Testament and the four Gospels. Acts serves as a transition volume from the Old Testament to the New Testament. The Book of Acts chronicles the rise and expansion of the first-century church.

Doctrinally, The Way could be considered both Arian and Pentecostal. It rejects the Trinitarian orthodoxy of most of Western Christianity. It believes in the divine conception of Jesus by God and that Jesus is the Son of God but not God the Son. It also believes in receiving the fullness of the holy spirit, God's power, which may be evidenced by the nine manifestations of the spirit: speaking in tongues, interpretation of tongues, prophecy, word of knowledge, word of wisdom, discerning of spirits, faith (believing), miracles, and healing.

The Way International is organized on the model of a tree, growing from the root (international headquarters) to trunks (national organizations), limbs (state and province organizations), branches (organizations in cities and towns), and household fellowships (small, individual fellowship groups). Administratively, the ministry is directed by a three-member board of directors. In 2000, Rev. Rosalie F. Rivenbark became president. She serves with Rev. Harve J. Platig, the vice president, and Rev. John R. Reynolds, the secretary-treasurer. The board appoints the cabinet that helps oversee the entire ministry, including the headquarters (located at The Way Household Ranch–Camp Gunnison), international outreach work, and work within the United States. Each of the ministry's two properties in the United States (located in New Knoxville, Ohio and Gunnison, Colorado) is a designated Root location. American Christian Press is The Way's publishing arm.

Those desiring to benefit from the church's research, teaching, and fellowship may take a basic 12-session course called The Way of Abundance and Power that builds on Wierwille's work. Several options are open to graduates of the course. Many continue to attend home fellowships and to take the intermediate and advance classes. Others may avail themselves of the Disciples of the Way Outreach Program, which is designed to build quality of life based on The Way's biblical teachings. The Way of Abundance and Power has been run all over the United States and in Europe, Australia, Asia, South America, and Africa and recently has been translated into French and Spanish.

Membership: Not reported. Outside of the United States, The Way International currently has work in 28 countries and two U.S. territories.

Educational Facilities:

The Way Household Ranch–Camp Gunnison, Gunnison, Colorado.

Periodicals: *The Way Magazine*.

Remarks: Wierwille was succeeded as head of The Way International by L. Craig Martindale (b. 1948), who led the organization through the 1990s. However, in 2000, following charges that he had had inappropriate sexual relationships with several women, Martindale was asked to resign from his leadership role. Following an investigation of the charges, he was permanently removed from office. Rosalie Rivenbark succeeded him as president.

Sources:

The Way International. www.theway.org/index.htm.

Juedes, John P., and Douglas V. Morton. *From "Vesper Chimes" to "The Way International."* Milwaukee, WI: C.A.R.I.S., n.d.

Morton, Douglas V., and John P. Juedes. *The Integrity and Accuracy of The Way's Word*. St. Louis, MO: Personal Freedom Outreach, [1980].

Whiteside, Elena S. *The Way, Living in Love*. New Knoxville, OH: American Christian Press, 1972.

Wierwille, Dorothea Kipp. *Victor Paul Wierwille: Born Again to Serve*. New Knoxville, OH: American Christian Press, 1996.

Wierwille, Victor Paul. *Jesus Christ Is Not God*. New Knoxville, OH: American Christian Press, 1975.

———. *Jesus Christ, Our Promised Seed*. New Knoxville, OH: American Christian Press, 1982.

———. *Power for Abundant Living*. New Knoxville, OH: American Christian Press, 1971.

———. *Receiving the Holy Spirit Today*. New Knoxville, OH: American Christian Press, 1972.

Williams, J. L. *Victor Paul Wierwille and The Way International*. Chicago: Moody Press, 1979.

❈ Other Bible Students

The Church (Gene Edwards)

Gene Edwards, c/o Destiny Ministries, PO Box 3450, Jacksonville, FL 32206

The Church is a fellowship that grew up around the ministry of Gene Edwards. Edwards, a graduate of Southwestern Baptist Theological Seminary, was on his way to becoming an outstanding Southern Baptist minister, but during his early years in the pastorate he became discouraged with the way the denomination treated people, which led to the further conclusion that Christianity, in general, was dead. His encounter with a copy of *The Normal Christian Church Life* by Watchman Nee led him to the Local Church (a Chinese movement that had developed out of the Plymouth Brethren), and through the rest of the decade Edwards associated himself with Local Church leader Witness Lee.

In 1969 Edwards moved to Santa Barbara, California, where he associated with a group of independent Christians formerly affiliated with Campus Crusade for Christ, an independent Evangelical campus ministry. While living in Santa Barbara, Edwards broke with Witness Lee. Edwards's small group became known as the Church in Isla Vista (the name of the unincorporated community adjacent to the University of California–Santa Barbara). By the spring of 1973 there were approximately 225 members, but the group was riven by internal discord, and a split cost it most of its support. The remaining members formed a commune and held all their possessions in common.

In 1976 many of the older members left Santa Barbara for various spots around the world (Belgium, Germany, Switzerland, Hawaii, Thailand, and Nepal), where they began missionary work. Edwards worked for a year in Canada. Then, in 1981, Edwards dissolved the work in Isla Vista and moved with some of the members to Maine. By this time, communal living had been abandoned. In Maine, Edwards established a new congregation. He also authored a number of books that have been widely circulated through Christian bookstores.

The Church in Augusta (and affiliated groups) follows a conservative dispensational Evangelical faith that carries with it the strong critique of denominational Christianity that the Plymouth Brethren passed to the Local Church. Part of that critique included the unwillingness to accept any name other than "the Church," with some geographical designation to distinguish it from other groupings.

Membership: In 2008 there were seven churches scattered across the United States affiliated with Gene Edwards and seven overseas, including one each in the United Kingdom, Holland, Romania, Australia, and New Zealand, and two in South Africa.

Sources:

The Church (Gene Edwards). www.geneedwards.com/.

Edwards, Gene. *The Divine Romance*. Gardiner, ME: Christian Books Publishing House, 1984. 207 pp.

———. *The Early Church*. Isla Vista, CA: Christian Books, 1974.

———. *How It All Began*. Isla Vista, CA: The Church in Isla Vista, [1975]. 37 pp.

———. *Letter to a Devastated Christian*. Augusta, ME: Christian Books, 1984. 47 pp.

———. *Our Mission*. Gardiner, ME: Christian Books, 1980. 211 pp.

The Church Which Is Christ's Body

No central headquarters, for information contact, PO Box 42021, Los Angeles, CA 90042

The nondenominational theme pronounced in Plymouth Brethren thinking found an ally in the person of Maurice M. Johnson, a former minister with the Methodist Episcopal Church, South (MECS). Licensed to preach in Texas in 1912, he moved to Los Angeles, California, in 1921 as assistant pastor at Trinity, the congregation of the Methodist pastor Robert Schuler. In 1925 Johnson withdrew from the MECS, objecting to the church's church-school literature and its ministerial training course. With 75 followers he established an independent Maranatha Tabernacle, but two years later withdrew from it and from his role as a salaried pastor and "began to preach only as a minister of Jesus Christ in the church which is Christ's Body." As he traveled about preaching, a fellowship of church members and those called to preach emerged.

The distinctive feature of this fellowship is its refusal to be known by any denominational name, even such a nondescript name as "brethren." The group also refuses to incorporate. Members do not use any titles such as "reverend" that would distinguish clergy and laity, though they do recognize divinely given offices of pas-

tor, evangelist, teacher, elder, and deacon. In this age, there are no longer apostles and prophets. Members believe that all people who have been convicted of their sins, have personal faith in Christ, and have been added to his body are fellow-members of the church which is Christ's Body. Members of the fellowship think of themselves as merely "some members of the church which is Christ's Body," outside all man-made organizations. Whenever two or more Christians gather for fellowship they constitute a Christian assembly, a local manifestation of the church.

The fellowship teaches fundamental Christianity, including belief in the Trinity, the incarnation of Christ and his finished work on the cross, and the Bible as the only guide. Members see the Bible interpreted in terms of God's successive dispensations: We live in the dispensation begun at Pentecost, when believers began to be baptized by the Lord with one spirit into one body. Ordinances of baptism and the Lord's Supper are not practiced in the present dispensation. Ordination is considered an act of recognition by an assembly that God has called an individual to the office of elder. Members do not object to saluting the flag and do not endorse conscientious objection to military service.

Assemblies are centers of aggressive evangelism. Ministers are supported by the assemblies, but do not receive a regular salary. A vigorous tract and radio ministry has been established. Maurice Johnson received mail in Orangeville, California, though there are no formal headquarters of the autonomous assemblies. In 2008 other leaders included Berl Chisum of Los Angeles, James Cox of Charlottesville, Virginia, and Jack Langford of Fort Worth, Texas, and there were assemblies in Los Angeles, San Diego, Riverside, San Luis Obispo, Sacramento, and other places in California; Fort Worth, Texas; Tulsa, Oklahoma; and Charlottesville, Virginia. No membership records are kept because identifying church members is considered a prerogative of God, the head of the church.

Membership: No membership records available.

Sources:

Morey, Clarence L. *A Federal Court Acknowledges Christ's True Church*. Fort Worth, TX: Manney Company, 1963.

The (Local) Church

c/o Living Stream Ministry, 1853 W Ball Rd., Anaheim, CA 92804

The group that is variously known as the Little Flock or the Local Church was founded in the 1920s in China by Ni Tuosheng, popularly known by the English translation of his name, Watchman Nee (1903–1972). Nee was born into a Chinese Christian family, his grandfather serving as a Congregationalist minister and his parents faithful Methodists. He changed his given name, Ni Tuosheng (Henry Nee) to Duosheng (Watchman), as a reminder not to lose sight of his purpose: raising up people for God.

From a nominally religious youth, he was converted by Dorayou, a Methodist evangelist, and soon afterward began working with Margaret E. Barber (1866–1930), an independent missionary through whom he discovered the writings of John Nelson Darby (1800–1882) and the exclusive Plymouth Brethren. He adopted Darby's nondenominational approach to church organization and soon emerged as the leader of a small band of evangelical Christians. By the end of the decade he had made contact with a branch of the Brethren led by James Taylor (1870–1953) and, at their invitation, visited England in 1933. They, however, soon broke relationships with Nee because of his unauthorized fellowship with the Honor Oak Christian Fellowship, a non-Brethren group headed by T. Austin Sparks (1888–1971).

From its modest beginning in Foochow, Nee's movement spread through China. During the 1930s, he traveled widely and founded congregations based upon his idea that there should be only one local church (i.e., congregation) in each city as the basic expression of the unity of Christianity (in the face of divisive denominationalism). Two local churches were raised up by his ministry between 1922 and 1952 (when the Chinese revolution ended the spread of Christianity). Nee also authored more than 50 books, mostly on Christian life and church life. His mature view of the church is found in his most famous book, *The Normal Christian Church Life*. He also authored the *The Spiritual Man*, in which he developed his understanding of the tripartite nature of human beings as body, soul, and spirit.

The new People's Republic of China, following its rise to power in 1949, accused Nee (and churches affiliated with him) of being a spy for the Americans and the nationalist government. He was first exiled from Shanghai and then imprisoned in 1952. Nee died 20 years later in 1972, while imprisoned.

During the 1930s, Nee gained a follower in the person of Witness Lee (1905–1997), a former Protestant minister who founded, established, and became an elder of the church at Chefoo, Shangdong. He joined Nee in the ministry in 1932 and within a few years was among Nee's most valuable assistants. After a three-year absence fighting tuberculosis, Lee rejoined Nee in full-time work in 1948, on the eve of the Chinese revolution. Nee sent Lee to Taiwan where the church was to flourish and spread around the Pacific basin.

Members migrating to the United States brought the movement to the West Coast. Lee moved to America in 1962 and founded Living Stream Ministry. He has since been recognized as the leading full-time worker among the Local churches, and has provided overall direction for the spread of the Local Church. He also has been a source for innovation in the movement by introducing several theological emphases not found in the writings of Nee and initiating several practices such as "pray reading" and "calling upon the name of the Lord," both of which have become the subject of controversy.

ORGANIZATION. The Local Church affirms the unity of the church, the corporate nature of church life, and the direct headship of Christ over the church. Great emphasis is thus placed on church life, meeting together (several times per week), and the function and responsiblity of each member in keeping alive a relationship with God and sharing the duties of congregational life. In rejecting the clergy-laity distinction, a pattern for the practical expression of the church's life has been established.

The Local Church is organized as a fellowship of autonomous congregations, one in each city. Each congregation is led by a small group of elders, two to five men drawn from the congregation's recognized leaders, who teach, preach, and administer the congregation's temporal affairs. There are also a small number of men who have an apostolic function and travel among the Local churches as teachers and leadership trainers to start new congregations in those cities where the Local Church is not yet organized. Such designated workers organize their efforts, more or less formally, as an independent ministry. In the case of Witness Lee, for example, his work is incorporated as the Living Stream Ministry, and is currently the most prominent apostolic endeavor among the Local churches.

As with the Plymouth Brethren, the adoption of Darby's nondenominational stance created a problem as Nee's movement took no name by which to be denominated. The Local Church sees itself as simply The Church. The term *Local Church* is a convenient designation but not a name. Local congregations call themselves "The Church in (name of the city)."

The Local Church has generally spread through the happenstance movement of members who would organize a congregation in a new city or the efforts of the apostolic workers. The church in the United States was initially started by members who migrated from Taiwan. However, in recent years, with Lee's encouragement, the Local Church has adopted a new strategy, which they call the "Jerusalem principle," by which church members as a small group migrate to a new locale for the single purpose of seeding a new congregation.

BELIEFS. The Local churches follow the teachings found in the voluminous writings of Nee and Lee. A convenient summary is found in a booklet titled *The Beliefs and Practices of the Local Churches*. The statement professes a belief in fundamental Christianity, similar to that of the Plymouth Brethren, and affirms belief in the Trinity, the deity of Christ, the virgin birth of Jesus, the substitutionary atonement, the resurrection of Jesus, his Second Coming, and the verbal inspiration of the Bible.

Particular attention, as might be expected, is given to a treatment of the unity of the Church, the body of Christ. Sectarianism, denominationalism, and interdenominationalism are all rejected, and the oneness of all believers in each locality affirmed.

The Local Church sees itself in a history of recovery (or restoration) of the biblical church. Since apostolic times, the full life and unity of the Church was lost; but a recovery began with Martin Luther (1483–1546) and the Protestant Reformation and has continued through the pietist recovery of Count Zinzendorf (1700–1760) and the Moravians, John Wesley (1703–1791) and the Methodists, and more recently the Plymouth Brethren. Through the Local churches, the Christian experience of the riches of Christ (i.e., the enjoyment of Christ as life), and the practice of church life according to the Scripture, are being recovered. Some elements of the recovery have become the focus of controversy.

Pray reading is a devotional practice that uses the words of Scripture as the words of prayer. Individuals or groups will, when praying, repeat words and phrases from the Scripture over and over, frequently interjecting words of praise and thanksgiving, as a means of allowing the Scripture to impart an experience of the presence of God in the person praying. "Calling upon the name of the Lord," as the very name of the practice indicates, is an invocation of God by the repetition of phrases such as "O Lord Jesus."

Burning is a term to denote a close contact with God. When a person inspires another with the message of the Gospel, this person is seen as having been *burned*. Burning is also an occasional practice by which objects symbolic of a person's pre-Christian existence or of a phase of lesser commitment are destroyed in a fire. Like burning objects from a rejected past, *burying*, literally a rebaptism, is symbolic of a newer level of Christian commitment, and members of a Local church might be baptized more than once.

Membership: In 1991 the Local Church listed congregations on six continents. The largest numbers are in the Pacific rim countries. Taiwan has 200 churches with 60,000 members. The combined United States and Canadian membership is 15,000 in 265 churches. There are 16,500 members in Spanish-speaking congregations in South and Central America. There are also churches in Europe, Africa, Australia, and New Zealand. In spite of the intense persecution, it appears that congregations have survived in mainland China, and that the movement actually spread over the last decades to include tens of thousands of people.

Since the demise of the Soviet Union, the Local churches have initiated evangelical work in eastern Europe and Russia. As of 1992, the Local Church had congregations in Moscow and St. Petersburg and was developing work in other countries as well.

Periodicals: *Voice*. Available from Living Stream Ministry, PO Box 2121, Anaheim, CA 92804.

Remarks: A controversy that emerged in the 1970s between the Local Church and some prominent voices within the larger Evangelical Christian community culminated in a series of legal actions in the mid-1980s. Different writers, some known for their battle against some of the new religions, the so-called *cults*, attacked the Local Church for heresy and its development of unique forms of Christian piety. Several books were written and several items on the Local Church appeared in the Christian *anticult* literature. Claiming libel and unable to get an apology for what it felt were unjust criticisms that were harming its ministry, the Local Chruch instituted several lawsuits that brought retractions and apologies from all but one organization, the Spiritual Counterfeits Project, which had published a book attacking the church. This case went to court and in 1985 an $11 million judgment for libel was rendered against the Spiritual Counterfeits Project.

Sources:

The Beliefs and Practices of the Local Churches. Anaheim, CA: Living Stream Ministry, 1978.

Duddy, Neil T., and the Spiritual Counterfeits Project. *The God-Men: An Inquiry into Witness Lee and the Local Church*. Downers Grove, IL: InterVarsity Press, 1981.

Ford, Gene. *Who Is the Real Mindbender?* Anaheim, CA: Author, 1977.

Freeman, William T. *In Defense of the Truth*. Seattle, WA: Northwest Christian, 1981.

Kinnear, Angus I. *Against the Tide: The Story of Watchman Lee*. Ft. Washington, PA: Christian Literature Crusade, 1973.

Lee, Witness. *Gospel Outlines*. Anaheim, CA: Living Stream Ministry, 1980.

————. *How to Meet*. Taipei, Taiwan: Gospel Book Room, 1970.

————. *The Practical Expression of the Church*. Los Angeles, CA: Stream Publishers, 1970.

Melton, J. Gordon. *An Open Letter Concerning the Local Church, Witness Lee, and the God-Men Controversy*. Santa Barbara, CA: Institute for the Study of American Religion, 1985.

Nee, Watchman. *The Normal Christian Church Life*. Washington, DC: International Students Press, 1969.

Roberts, Dana. *Understanding Watchman Nee*. Plainfield, NJ: Haven Books, 1980.

Sparks, Jack. *The Mind Benders: A Look at Current Cults*. Nashville, TN: Thomas Nelson, 1977.

The Two-by-Twos

Current address not obtained for this edition.

The fellowship called "Two-by-Twos" in this text are also referenced, by those outside their membership, as *Cooneyites*, *Go Preachers*, and *Tramp Preachers*. However, they claim that they have no name. Among themselves, they use the terms "The Truth," "The Friends," "The Saints," and "The Meetings." In the past, they have officially registered themselves using the name "Christian Conventions" and have incorporated in at least one area under that name. The group itself, though numbering in the tens (some suggest hundreds) of thousands in the United States, has remained virtually invisible. Members shun publicity, refuse to acquire property or hold funds in the church's name, and issue no ministerial credentials or doctrinal literature, believing that the Bible (King James Version) is the only textbook of infallible guidance and that, to be effective, the communication of spiritual life must take place orally, person-to-person. The only printed documents are hymnals, internal lists of meetings, internal lists of conventions, internal lists of ministers, internal notes and extracts from sermons, and pastoral letters circulated only among the membership. The distinctive feature of the movement has been sending forth, two by two, unmarried teams of itinerant clergy who, "as they go, preach" (Matthew 10:7).

The Two-by-Twos originated with William Irvine (1863–1947), a Scotsman who started out as a member of the Faith Mission founded in 1886 by John George Govan (1861–1927). The mission, which worked in neglected rural communities, spread to Ireland. Irvine was a leader at Menagh in County Tipperary. Taking his direction from selected verses in the Gospel of Matthew, chapter 10, Irvine began to feel that the Faith Mission's practices related to renouncing the world were not as strict as called for in the Scripture. By 1899 he had begun independent work and in 1901 formally severed any connection with the Faith Mission. Among the young preachers who joined him was Edward Cooney (1867–1960), a strong leader and zealous worker, from whom outsiders derived a common name for the group: Cooneyites. Cooney and Irvine, unfortunately, had differences, and Cooney withdrew from working with Irvine.

In 1903 Irvine held a convention at which the pattern for the next decades were set. Ministers were to give over their possessions to the hierarchy, renouncing their former life. They took vows of poverty, chastity, and obedience. Following the meeting, ministers were dispersed to carry their Gospel around the world—from Australia, to New Zealand, to South Africa, to China, to South America, and to the European mainland. Irvine, George Walker (1877–1981), and Irving Weir brought the movement to the United States. They were soon to be joined by numerous others. By the end of the decade, the movement had spread across the eastern half of the United States. In the South, black preachers added their efforts. By 1923, the movement reached Hawaii.

During the years just prior to World War II (1939–1945), Irvine began to predict the end of the dispensation of grace in 1914 (the term the *alpha message* was used for his original revelation), and the beginning of an era of judgment (which he called the *omega message*). His prophetic zeal, as well as conflict over his role as a general overseer of the movement, led to schism and the eventual ousting of Irvine (and many of his adherents) from leadership of the movement, which has since been led collectively by the overseers in the various fields. Irvine moved to Jerusalem, Israel, and lived there for the rest of his life, supported by a devoted number of followers.

The Two-by-Twos originated as a response to corruption and worldliness they claimed to see within the mainline churches of the late nineteenth and early twentieth centuries. Reading early sermons and accounts tell much more about what they were against, rather than giving any sense of their own creed or doctrines. From the outset, membership in the group primarily involved the rejection of all other churches and ministries, and acceptance of their own pattern of ministry and worship (known as "professing"). Church doctrine is exclusively made by the clergy, and slight variations may be observed between the fields run by the different autonomous overseers. The most orthodox presentation of their faith appears in their main hymnbook. Critics, primarily former members, elders, and ministers have published excerpts of sermons by leading preachers indicating that a unitarian theology that denies the Trinity and frames the role of Jesus as human example is a prominent perspective and that doctrinal variation from evangelical belief is present. Two ordinances are observed: adult believers baptism by immersion (including rebaptism of those who come from other church bodies) and the Lord's Supper, which is observed weekly. Most emphasis is placed upon a holy life indicated by modes of dress, no jewelry (except wedding rings), and, generally, no television. Conscientious objection to war is general, but not mandatory.

The fellowship has an episcopal polity. The United States and Canada are divided into fields, typically a state or province, each with an overseer (also called "senior servant," "head worker," or "elder brother"). The overseers acting in loose, sporadic, and informal concert, exercise general supervision of the movement as a whole. The members are organized into house churches of 12 to 20 members presided over by a bishop (or local elder). Members meet on Sunday for the breaking of bread and during the week for Bible study.

The missionary and evangelistic arm of the movement is supplied by the preachers. These unmarried servants travel in teams of two as successors of the apostles (Matthew 10:1–7). They move into a new community, hold evangelistic services, and gather a following. Members of the house churches will support any evangelistic services in their area. The preachers do not draw a salary, but are supported by direct contributions from the members, monies from the overseers, and legacies and other funds managed by trusted elders.

There are one or more annual conventions within each field. They typically are held on a large farm or estate, with members camping while in attendance, or staying in dormitories constructed for this purpose. There are house churches in all 50 states and throughout Canada.

Membership: Not reported. In the mid-2000s there were 89 annual conventions held in the United States that drew, on average, anywhere between 500 and 2,000 members. This turnout would indicate between 10,000 and 100,000 members in the United States, and possibly twice that number in other countries.

Remarks: Critics of the movement have charged that it has concealed its origins, especially in hiding its association with Irvine and its recent origin, and that it has presented a false front of evangelical orthodoxy when in fact it is completely heterodox. Because of the difficulty in gaining authoritative material about the group, and the contradictory reports on its normative beliefs, no assessment concerning doctrinal issues is possible. There is, however, little doubt of its rejection of its early (and to some extent) unhappy history.

Sources:

Crow, Keith W. "The Invisible Church." Master's theses," University of Oregon, Eugene, 1964.

Daniel, Kevin N. *Reinventing the Truth*. Bend, OR: Research and Information Services, 1993.

Fortt, Lloyd. *A Search for the Truth*. Bend, OR: Research and Information Services, 1994.

Hymns Old and New. Glasgow, Scotland: R. L. Allan and Son, 1951.

Lewis, Kathleen Munn. *The Church without a Name*. Milwaukie, OR: Author, 2004.

Parker, Doug, and Helen Parker. *The Secret Sect*. Pendle Hill, New South Wales, Australia: Author, 1982.

Paul, William E. *They Go About "Two by Two": The History and Doctrine of a Little Known Cult*. Denver, CO: Impact, 1977.

During its first generation, Christians believed that the risen Christ would soon return to finish the changes begun during his public ministry. When his return was delayed, many stopped looking, but some in each generation believed they were living in the last days and expected Christ to return in their lifetime. Increasingly over the last two centuries, since the rise of Napoleon Bonaparte (1769–1821) and the secularization of church-state relations he heralded, each generation has produced a variety of groups who preach a type of faith that has been called *apocalyptic, chiliastic,* or *millennial.* The movements have been characterized by the expectation of the immediate return of Christ to bring a final end to "this evil order" and replace it with a new world of supreme happiness and goodness. At every turning point in the history of Christianity, people supporting such movements appeared, sometimes within the mainstream of church activities as disturbers of accepted patterns of life and sometimes at the outer edge of church activities as critics and reformers. Always their presence is felt because they promote an idea that orthodox Christians have said to be integral to the faith.

Adventists and millennialists have, however, usually gone beyond the mere affirmation that Christ will return in the future. They actually predict the time of his imminent appearance, either by setting a definite date or suggesting that it will occur in the present generation. Such a definite projection of the climax of history thus becomes a great motivation for members to both reform their lives and act in appropriate ways in light of that event. If history is to end in a few years, life decisions must be made in light of that event, from major decisions about career or marriage to lesser decisions about the use of resources, one's choice of friends, and activity during leisure time.

APOCALYPTICISM IN HISTORY. Christianity inherited its bent toward apocalypticism from its Jewish forefathers. Both the book of Daniel in the Jewish Bible and the apocryphal works of Jewish apocalypticism, such as the Assumption of Moses and the Books of Enoch, were part of the thought-world in which early Christians lived. For later generations, however, the book of Daniel was to be the important text. Penned in the second century B.C.E., Daniel purports to be a product of the sixth century B.C.E. The first half of the book tells the story of Daniel and some friends, who were faithful to God while living under foreign political control. The last half details visions of future history, stretching from sixth-century Babylon to the reign of Antiochus Epiphanes in the second century. These visions, in and of themselves apocalyptic, provided the material from which future apocalyptics would draw.

Apocalypticism was integrated into the lifestyle of the early church. Many expected the imminent return of Jesus to finish what was begun on Calvary. Such a belief sustained them in times of persecution and gave them hope for the improvement of their lot in life in the near future. The signposts of this belief are found in such biblical passages as Mark 13, Matthew 24, I Thessalonians 4:13–18, and, preeminently, in the vision of John the Revelator. Just as Daniel emerged as the central piece of Jewish apocalypticism, so Revelation soon pushed aside other Christian apocalypses and became the one book of the vast literature to be canonized (included in the Bible).

Revelation purports to be the ecstatic vision of John, an official in the Church of Asia Minor (now Turkey). His vision has a special message for each of seven churches and contains a lengthy scenario of the future course of history, which centers on the church. The vision culminates with a picture of the end of time and the establishment of the kingdom of God in its totality.

A vast amount of scholarly work describes the nature of apocalyptic literature, with a surprising degree of unanimity in scholarly understanding. The apocalyptist has a particular view of time and history, evil, God's relation to the world, the groups of which the apocalyptist is a part, and the value of human activity in the world. The apocalyptist sees history and time as lineal. History, begun at some point in the distant past, has continued on a more or less steady course to the present. The present is just short of the climax of the whole scheme of time. The climax will be a great supernatural happening that will destroy the present system and replace it with a new and better divine system.

The cosmic struggle of good and evil, of God and the devil, determines the course of history, and good is losing. The believer feels this loss on a personal level as persecution, deprivation, or moral indignation. But while evil seems to be progressing to an ultimate victory, it will be stopped short by the intervention of God, who will completely eliminate its power in the world.

God has a close and personal relationship to the world. He began the course of history and has never ceased to intervene. He caused the formation of a remnant of his people to witness to him. And he will step in to crush the evil forces before they completely conquer the good.

The course of history is personalized and internalized by the apocalyptist. He sees history as made for and centering upon himself and his in-group. His group has been chosen; although they are on the bottom of the social ladder now, they will be on top as soon as God acts. This reversal of position will take place in the near future.

The nearness of the end of this age puts a new perspective on human activity in the world. As the date for the end closes in upon people, the value of normal activity decreases. Attention might be given to such biblical admonitions as, "For the future, men who have wives should live as though they had none, and those that mourn as though they did not, and those who are glad as though they were not glad, and those who buy as though they did not own a thing ... For the outward order of things is passing away" (I Corinthians 7:29–31). Normal activity is now replaced with a stepped-up campaign to spread the message of the coming cataclysm, for "the gospel must first be published among all nations." Often, though not always, an intense moral imperative is associated with the end-time as apocalyptists join reformers who look to moral and social reform as a means to hold back an impending doom. This type of moral apocalypticism is seen most pointedly in the teachings of such men as the Old Testament prophet Jeremiah, Thomas Müntzer (c. 1490–1525), and George Storrs (1796–1879).

The apostle Paul, himself, had to deal with Christians who fell away from the apocalyptic stance of the early church. In his letter to the Thessalonians, he had to answer those who were questioning why so many had died before Christ returned. But as the church grew, what for Paul was a minor issue became for the church a major problem, leading the church to redefine its conception of faith. As the distance between the believers and Calvary grew, the sensibleness of an apocalyptic lifestyle diminished. So, during the second, third, and fourth centuries, a battle raged—a theological battle over the approach and stance of the church toward the world.

Symbolic of this fight is the issue of the canonization of the book of Revelation. During the second century, this visionary masterpiece circulated from Asia Minor to Antioch and Rome. It found its earliest exponent in the second-century Christian leader Justin Martyr, and about the year 200, the Muratonian Canon lists the book of Revelation as scripture. Irenaeus in Gaul and Tertullian in North Africa accepted and reflected Revelation in their writings.

One of the first millennial sects, the second-century Montanists, picked up the apocalyptic stance and made it a central part of its message. Montanus tried to gather in his movement some of the spiritual, prophetic, and visionary attributes of the early church, in what was considered by many a heretical stance. The movement spread from Phrygia and eventually claimed Tertullian as an adherent in North Africa.

The first works rejecting Revelation as scriptural and of apostolic authorship were produced by the anti-Montanists.

So effective were these writings that, about 215 C.E., Hippolytus wrote a carefully worded defense of the controversial book. In the mid-third century, the great scholar Origen convinced the Alexandrians to support the canonicity of the book of Revelation. Origen's allegorizing and spiritualizing of the text gave the church a means of accepting the work while strongly rejecting its literal millennialism (the belief that Christ would literally reign on earth with his saints for 1,000 years). Even though the status of Revelation remained open until the fifth century, Origen's acceptance of it, followed a century later by that of Athanasius, assured Revelation a place in the Bible.

By the early fifth century, with few exceptions, the canon was set. There needed only to be stated an authoritative position that the church would accept that would reconcile its four hundred years of waiting for Christ to return, the existence of Revelation in the canon, and the refutation of millennialism. Such a position was advanced by Augustine of Hippo (354–430) in his magnum opus, *The City of God*. He pointed out that some had misunderstood John's Revelation and had construed it so as to produce "ridiculous fancies." Augustine reworked the literal eschatology of John in such a way that the church, while still remaining in God's history, did not live in the imminent expectation of the climax of history. God still operates in history with his chosen ones, and he is holding back evil even now. In effect, Augustine was saying that John was not painting a picture of the end of time, but rather of the manner in which the church progresses as it moves through both time and space. Thus, Augustine gave the faithful hope of Christ's coming, but pushed the event into the distant future. That Augustine's view became acceptable to the church as a whole reflects not only Augustine's scholarship but also the change of position the church had undergone during its early centuries, from a persecuted sect to the state religion of the Roman Empire. From Augustine's time to the present, any group that projected an immediate Second Coming was to find itself on the fringe of the church and, because the church was closely tied to the state, a persecuted minority.

But millennialists continued to arise, and although their leaders were usually educated, and hence of the upper classes, members of millennial groups were usually from the disinherited classes who combined their millennialism with a social protest movement. For example, in seventh-century Syria, the early Christian form of the *Sibylline Oracles* appeared to bring consolation to Syrian Christians living under Muslim oppression. According to these oracles, an emperor, Methodius, was to arise and begin the final battle with the Antichrist. This battle would result in an Antichrist victory, but the victory would be short-lived because of the return of Christ for the final judgment.

In the Middle Ages, millennial movements arose and then disappeared on numerous occasions, reflecting the high degree of social turmoil that resulted from the social revolutions of the sixteenth century. The eleventh century saw several mass millennial movements, particularly the First

---

Adventist Family Chronology

1832 Baptist preacher William Miller voices his views, based on the 2,300-day prophecy of Daniel 8:14, about the second coming of Christ in a set of articles in *Vermont Telegraph,* a Baptist periodical.

1836 Miller summarizes his views in a booklet, *Evidences from Scripture and History of the Second Coming of Christ about the Year 1843: Exhibited in a Course of Lectures.*

1840 Boston minister Joshua V. Himes establishes a periodical, *Signs of the Times,* in which to discuss and publicize Miller's views.

1844 When March 21 passes without Christ appearing, several alternate dates are suggested.

Adventists in Washington, New Hampshire, begin keeping the Sabbath (Saturday) as their main day of worship.

Samuel S. Snow suggests that Christ will return on October 22, 1844. The failure of Christ to return on that date becomes known as The Great Disappointment.

1845 Adventists meet in New York. Those attending the Albany Conference form the loosely associated Evangelical Adventists.

Hiram Edson publishes the view that the event highlighted by the prophecy of Daniel 8, the cleansing of the sanctuary, did not refer to Christ's return but to a heavenly event presaging his return.

1849 James White obeys vision of his wife, Ellen G. White, and begins publishing *The Present Truth,* an Adventist periodical supporting the Sabbath.

John T. Walsh proposes 1854 as date for Christ's return.

1860 Advent Christian Association formed by Evangelical Adventists, who keep Sunday as their day of worship.

1861 J. N. Andrews writes a book-length apology for sabbatarianism.

1863 General Conference of the Seventh-Day Adventists is organized.

Sabbatarian Adventists not associated with the Seventh-Day Adventists organize around a periodical, *The Hope of Israel.* They later form the General Conference of the Church of God.

1869 General Conference of the Church of God organized by Adventists who accept Sunday as the Sabbath.

1874 J. N. Andrews goes to Switzerland as the first Seventh-Day Adventist missionary.

1884 Charles Taze Russell founds the Watchtower Bible and Tract Society, the legal corporation of the International Bible Students. Russell argues that Jesus had invisibly returned to earth (his *parousia*) in 1874 to initiate his kingdom, and that in 1914, which marks the end of the "Gentile Times," he would come to judge the earth and annihilate the wicked.

1916 Russell dies.

1918 J. F. Rutherford, who succeeded Russell as head of the International Bible Students Association, is sentenced to prison for sedition, the charges deriving from his leadership of an organization espousing pacifism.

Paul S. L. Johnson founds the Layman's Home Missionary Movement.

1925 Reformers, protesting the laxity concerning pacifism by the Seventh-Day Adventists during World War I, organize the Seventh-Day Adventist Reform Movement.

1931 International Bible Students changes name to Jehovah's Witnesses.

Radio show *Frank and Ernest* gathers following that become the Dawn Bible Students Association.

1933 Herbert W. Armstrong launches a new broadcast ministry, "The World Tomorrow," and incorporates as the Radio Church of God.

1935 Disfellowshipped by the Seventh-Day Adventists, Victor T. Houteff moves with followers to Waco, Texas, and founds the Shepherd's Rod Publishing Association and the Mt. Carmel Center.

1937 C. O. Dodd begins *The Faith,* a magazine to promote the observance of the Jewish festivals, which soon aligns to the emergent Sacred Name movement.

1947 Herbert W. Armstrong moves to Pasadena, California, and founds Ambassador College.

1966 Jacob O. Meyer begins Sacred Name broadcast, a radio ministry that leads to the formation of the Assemblies of Yahweh.

1968 The Radio Church of God becomes the Worldwide Church of God.

1986 Herbert W. Armstrong dies. His successor, Joseph W. Tkach, begins process of changing the Worldwide Church of God's beliefs.

Roderick Meredith and Raymond Nair leave the Worldwide Church of God and found the Global Church of God.

1989 Gerald Furry leaves Worldwide Church of God and founds Philadelphia Church of God.

1993 Agents of the Bureau of Alcohol, Tobacco, and Firearms (BATF) engage in gun battle at Mt. Carmel, the headquarters of the Branch Davidians near Waco, Texas. 51 days later, after the FBI have assumed hegemony over the situation, 82 people (including leader David Koresh) die when a fire consumes Mt. Carmel.

1995 Former members of the WorldWide Church of God leave to found the United Church of God.

1997 Joseph Tkach, Jr., who had succeeded his father as head of the Worldwide Church of God, completes process of renouncing all of Armstrong's unique beliefs and leads church into the National Association of Evangelicals.

1998 Meredith and some 75 percent of the members withdraw from the Global Church of God and found the Living Church of God.

2003 Barry C. Black, the 62nd chaplain of the United States Senate, becomes the first African American and the first Seventh-Day Adventist to hold the office.

Crusade in 1095. Led by popular leaders such as Peter the Hermit (d. 1115), large armies were formed to Christianize Jerusalem. One army stopped at the Rhine Valley and performed the first massacre of European Jews. The movement itself died, partly due to exhaustion and partly on the battlefields near Constantinople.

Between 1190 and 1195, a Cistercian monk, Joachim of Fiore (c. 1135–1202), produced an eschatological scheme that became the most influential apocalyptic understanding of the Middle Ages. He identified his new vision of history as the everlasting gospel that according to Revelation was to be preached in the last days. Joachim's scheme pictured history as an ascent in three stages, the Father's law, Christ's gospel, and the Spirit's culmination of history. Taking Matthew 1 as his starting point, Joachim counted 42 generations from Abraham to Christ and saw this as a type of gospel age. Assuming a generation is 30 years, Joachim reasoned that the movement from the gospel to the Spirit must take place between 1200 and 1260. A new order of monks must form to preach this message and prepare the way. Joachim believed 12 patriarchs would arise to convert the Jews. The Antichrist would reign for three and one-half years, after which he would be overthrown, and the age of the Spirit would begin.

Popular leaders embraced Joachim's ideas and tied them to the popular fallen hero, Frederick I, the Holy Roman emperor, who was killed on the third crusade in 1190. A new Frederick was to arise, and he was seen as the "emperor of the last days." This movement grew when Frederick I's grandson became Frederick II, who did much to foster the growing messianism surrounding him. In 1229 he went on a crusade and crowned himself king of Jerusalem, which he had temporarily recaptured. When Pope Innocent IV (d. 1254) put Frederick and Germany under interdict, Frederick retorted by expanding his role to include chastisement of the church. Because Innocent was immoral himself, his interdict had no effect. In 1240 the writings of Joachim's disciples inflamed the masses, which were heading for a major break with papal power in Europe. The movement ended suddenly when Frederick died in 1250. The ideas that started with Joachim were reinterpreted, and for several hundred years the dream of a resurrected Frederick was the vision that supported protest in central Europe.

One of the more famous of the chiliastic sects were the Taborites, the radical wing of the Hussite movement in fifteenth-century Czechoslovakia. These followers of the martyred John Hus (c. 1373–1415) united a political and economic revolt with their millennial aspirations soon after Hus's death. They went beyond Hus in their adherence to literal biblical authority. The bitter struggle for control of Czechoslovakia helped precipitate doomsday concerns. In 1519 a group of former Catholic priests began to preach openly about the coming of the last days and the destruction in February 1520 of every town by fire (like Sodom). Everyone was directed to flee to five towns, Taborite strongholds, destined to be saved. When the destruction did not occur, the Taborite leaders called upon their followers to take up the sword in a holy war. It was not until 1534 that the Taborites were finally defeated and, with them, their millennial hopes.

It seems more than coincidence that the Reformation occurred in Frederick's Germany, and that out of the social upheaval caused by the Reformation, the next great movement of popular millennialism was to arise. Its leader was Thomas Müntzer. He was only one of many who saw the social and religious turmoil of the Reformation era as a sign of the end of an age. Others espousing the vision of the millennium were John Hut (c. 1490–1527), Melchior Hofmann (c. 1500-c. 1544), and Augustin Bader (d. 1530).

Müntzer came by his millennialist views when he studied with Nicholas Storch (d. 1525), a weaver in Zwickau and a former resident of the old Taborite lands. Müntzer believed that the Turks (or the Antichrist) would soon rule the world, but that the elect would then rise up and annihilate all the godless, and the millennium would begin. In his famous 1524 sermon, he called upon the princes of Germany to join him in this righteous war. Rejected by the princes, he turned to the poor. His League of the Elect became a power base from which was built a proletarian army at Mühlhausen and Frankenhausen. In two battles, the princes defeated Müntzer's army and captured and executed Müntzer, thus ending another phase of millennialism.

England also had its share of millennial movements. Anti-Cromwellian forces found an ally in the Fifth Monarchy Men, a movement that crystallized in the 1650s. This group looked to Jesus to establish a "fifth-world" monarchy. The previous four worlds, following the image in Daniel 2, were Assyria, Persia, Greece, and Rome (which still existed as the Roman Catholic Church). After spending time in evangelical work, the Fifth Monarchy Men concluded that it was time for them to take up the sword of the Lord. In 1657 and 1661, they attempted two uprisings, both unsuccessful. Their military defeats eventually led to their annihilation.

Various millennial, chiliastic, and messianic movements continued to arise, and date-setting for Christ's Second Coming continued to be a popular activity. With the arrival of religious pluralism, toleration, and freedom, few millennialists fell victim to the sword, as violence was gradually replaced with public ridicule. The early nineteenth century saw a renewal of expectation of the Second Coming of Jesus. Edward Irving (1792–1834), founder of the Catholic Apostolic Church in the 1830s, proclaimed the Second Coming in England, setting the date as 1864. Joseph Wolff (1795–1862), a converted Jew, toured England and the United States, lecturing on the Second Coming. Both men had been spurred to action by the French Revolution and Napoleon. Joseph Smith Jr. (1805–1844), founder of the Mormons, established locale after locale as the headquarters of the kingdom of God. It was, however, a poor farmer in upper New York state who founded the movement that still exists as America's main Adventist movement, and thereby originated the uniquely American brand of millennial hope.

MILLENNIALISM IN AMERICA. The American millennial movement known as Adventism had its beginnings in New York, where it was started by William Miller (1782–1849), a Baptist layman. Miller had settled in New York after the War of 1812. He was a deist for a period, denying that God interferes with the laws of the universe and stressing morality and reason rather than religious belief. Then Miller began to study the Bible. This study, which lasted about two years, satisfied his major doubts, but also convinced him that he was living near the end of his age. Further study convinced him not only that the end was near, but also that he had to tell the world about it. His first efforts took place in Dresden, New York, where a revival followed his speaking in 1831.

He continued to speak in the area as pulpits opened to him. Within a year, he was able to accept no more than half of his speaking invitations. In 1832 the *Vermont Telegraph* published a series of 16 articles written by Miller, the first of many works he was to write. The next year, his 64-page pamphlet was widely circulated.

In September 1833, Miller was given a license to preach by the Baptists. For the next 10 years, Miller lived the life of an itinerant evangelist, preaching his message of the imminent return of Jesus. The Methodists, Baptists, and Congregationalists were eager to hear Miller's words. In 1836 Miller published his lecture in his first book, *Evidences from Scripture and History of the Second Coming of Christ about the Year 1843: Exhibited in a Course of Lectures.* This book, plus a new edition of the earlier pamphlet, gave great impetus to the movement. Others began to join Miller and preach his doctrine. Most notably, in 1839, Joshua Himes (1805–1895) invited Miller to preach in his Boston church. Himes had the promotional and organizational talent to lift the movement into national prominence. In March of 1840, Himes began publication of the movement's first periodical, *Signs of the Times.* By autumn, the movement had grown to the extent that a decision was made to hold a conference on the Second Coming of the Christ. This conference opened October 13, 1840, at Chardon Street Church in Boston. Early leaders were among those in attendance—Josiah Litch (1809–1886), Joseph Bates (1792–1872), and Henry Dana Ward (1797–1884). The conference spent its time discussing the views that Miller had expounded in his pamphlets and book.

Miller believed that "God has set bounds, determined times, and revealed unto his prophets the events long before they were accomplished." These times were revealed by both plain declaration and by figurative language. From his study of Daniel and Revelation, Miller believed that he had deciphered the chronology concerning the end of the age. He began with the principle that a prophetic day is equal to a year (Ezekiel 4:6). The key passages were Daniel 8:14 ("unto 2,300 days, then shall the sanctuary be cleansed, or justified") and Daniel 9:24 ("Seventy weeks are determined upon thy people ... to make an end of sins"). Miller calculated the end of the 70 weeks (490 days or 490 years) to be 33 C.E., the year of the crucifixion of Jesus. From this date, he drew a line back to 457 B.C.E. ("the going forth of the commandment to Ezra to restore the law and the people of Jerusalem") as the beginning. Since, as Miller argued, the 70 weeks were part of the 2,300 days, the 2,300 days could be seen to begin also in 457 B.C.E. Thus, the cleansing of the sanctuary would be in 1843. Though Miller bolstered this chronology with several other figures that also ended in 1843, this set of figures was the basic one.

From these figures, Miller and his associates could build a history based on the events described in Revelation and Daniel, and this chronology of prophetic history worked out mathematically. Miller published such a work covering the Old Testament period and showing that 1843 was the end of the sixth millennium since creation. In his books, he also pointed the way for his followers to fill in the history from 33 C.E. to the present.

The Boston conference was so successful that in the ensuing weeks other conferences in other cities were held to explain and discuss Miller's message, which Himes had now renamed "the midnight cry." As the movement grew, opposi-

---

Calculating the End of the World—William Miller and 1843

Calculation 1

From the date of the commandment to rebuild Jerusalem, B.C. 457, to the crucifixion of Christ, 70 weeks, or 490 years	490
From the crucifixion of Christ to taking away the daily abomination, which is supposed to signify Paganism	475
From taking away of Pagan rites to setting up the abomination of desolation, or Papal Civil Rule	30
From setting up of the Papal abomination to the end there of	1260
From taking away the Papal Civil Rule to the first resurrection and the End of the World in 1843	45
These being added present the sum of the years	**2300**

Calculation 2

From the full term of the vision as above exemplified	2300
Subtract 70 weeks of years to the crucifixion of Christ	490
	1800
Add to this the term of our Saviour's life	33
End of the world in	C.E. **1843**

Calculation 3

From the crucifixion to taking away the daily abomination, the second item of the first calculation	475
Add our Saviour's age, 33, and Daniel's number, 1335	1368
End of the world in	C.E. **1843**

Calculation 4

From the full term of the vision as above exemplified	2300
Subtract the date of the commandment to rebuild Jerusalem	B.C. 447
End of the world in	C.E. **1843**

Calculation 5

In Leviticus XXVI, 23–24, the Lord speaks of punishing the house of Israel "yet seven times for their sins." Seven times (or years)—each day reckoned as a year—360 multiplied by 7	2520
Subtract the date of the first captivity in Babylon, at which time it is assumed this punishment commenced	B.C. 677
End of the world in	C.E. **1843**

In projecting 1843 as the year of Christ's Return, William Miller began with an understanding that a year of human time was viewed by God as a day (Ezekiel 4:6). From the books of Daniel he had derived a variety of time periods, most notably 2300 days (Daniel 8:14) and 70 weeks (or 490 days, Daniel 9:24), and from the Book of Revelation 1260 days (Revelation 12:6). He then had a set of dates of historical significance, from which to do his calculations. These calculations were summarized by Abel C. Thomas in *A Complete Refutation of Miller's Theory of the End of the World* (Philadelphia: the Author, 1843). He found five principal calculations made by Miller all of which brought him to 1843.

---

tion increased, and the established denominations began to take action to counteract Miller's influence. Formerly cooperative churches closed their doors to Miller and his associates. Numerous accounts arose of ministers and laypeople being expelled from their churches. In one famous case, L. S. Stockman was tried for heresy before his presiding elders in the Maine Conference of the Methodist Episcopal Church and was later expelled. In 1843 the *New York Christian Advocate*, the principle organ of the Methodists, carried a series of articles against "Millerism," which vied for space with anti-Romanist articles attacking the Roman Catholic Church.

Miller's movement took on a more definite shape in this period. Before the end in 1843, the first camp meeting was held at East Kingston, New Hampshire. In November, a second periodical, *The Midnight Cry*, began publication. Miller also sharpened his views. Until 1843, Miller had been vague about the Second Coming occurring "about the year 1843." But on January 1, he committed himself to a more definite date: "I am fully convinced that somewhere between March 21st, 1843, and March 21st, 1844, according to the Jewish mode of computation of time, Christ will come."

With tension running high as March approached, a large comet appeared in the late February sky. Its appearance was a complete surprise, without warning from astronomers. The comet was among a number of spectacular night-sky events that found their way into print. March 21, 1843, came and went. Now, new issues began to emerge. The increased opposition of the churches made meeting houses difficult to secure. In addition, large numbers of Adventists had no prior religious connection to nourish them. These factors, plus the growing size of the movement, led Charles Fitch (1805–1844) to start the inevitable "come out" movement, urging those who believed in Christ's imminent return to come out of their denominational churches and form their own churches. Fitch was opposed by Miller, but the pressure to "come out" only increased.

By 1844, as the March 21 deadline passed without the Second Coming, Miller had approximately 50,000 followers across the East and Midwest. Miller had earlier written of his views, "If this chronology is not correct, I shall despair of ever getting from the Bible and history a true account of the age of the world." In May 1844, Miller wrote to his followers, "I confess my error and acknowledge my disappointment."

But 50,000 enthusiastic followers could not be so easily turned away. Although a few dropped out, most would not. In a short time, adjustments in Miller's chronology were made. In August, Samuel S. Snow (1806–1870) put forth the "seventh month" scheme, which designated October 22, 1844, as the real date of return. Tension reached a new high. On October 22, the Adventists gathered to await the Lord, but the day passed without event.

The Great Disappointment, as the Adventists have termed the reaction to the nonhappening of October 22, 1844, left the movement in chaos. Miller again acknowledged the error, but remained confident of the imminent return of Jesus. Other millennialist leaders found themselves in the same boat. Miller refuted any further attempts to set dates, and gradually retired from active leadership in the movement. But forces already in operation were now prepared to weld these organized believers into a number of denominational bodies. These are treated below.

Adventist theology is usually built upon and accepts the theological perspectives of its parent bodies, making the necessary apocalyptic adjustments. Since almost all American Adventist bodies can be traced directly to Miller, a Baptist lay preacher, it is not surprising that popular Baptist theology has had a great influence on Adventism. There is general agreement on the doctrines concerning the Bible, God, Christ, and the sacraments. The idea of ordinances (instead of sacraments), baptism by immersion, and the practice of foot washing further manifest Baptist origins. Sabbatarianism was transmitted directly by the Seventh-day Baptists.

Eschatology took up two articles in the Baptists' 1833 New Hampshire Confession of Faith and provided a base from which Miller could speculate that "the end of this world is approaching." The Adventists, however, went far beyond the Baptists in speculations. The Adventists also raised the issue of man's innate immortality by denying it and, in the twentieth century, have been in the forefront of groups proposing a view that has been accepted by many biblical scholars.

Ethical positions among Adventists have shown two seemingly divergent trends. An emphasis on the Old Testament and on the law as mandatory for Christians has developed out of the acceptance of the Sabbath. Some groups have gone so far as to celebrate Jewish holidays and dietary laws. The celebration of the Sabbath has been promoted by the ecumenical Bible Sabbath Association, which was formed as a counterpart of the Lord's Day Alliance of the United States. Formed in 1945, the Bible Sabbath Association promotes the observance of the Sabbath and publishes a directory of Sabbath-keeping organizations.

A second ethical trend emerged as the Adventists became involved in the great social crusades of the two decades preceding the Civil War (1861–1865). Many Adventists were vocal abolitionists and ardent supporters of the peace movement. Pacifism remains a common Adventist position; the well-publicized refusal of the Jehovah's Witnesses to be drafted is derived from their Millerite heritage.

THE SACRED NAME MOVEMENT. No one knows exactly who first raised the issue of God's name as being an important doctrinal consideration. Certainly, in the 1920s the International Bible Students, on their way to becoming the Jehovah's Witnesses, raised the issue forcefully. Twentieth-century scholarship had, however, begun to emphasize belief that "Yahweh" was the correct pronunciation of YHWH, the spelling of God's name in Hebrew. There were slight variations in spelling and pronunciation, as will be noted. By the mid-1930s, there were church members and ministers, primarily of the Church of God (Seventh-day), who were beginning to use the "sacred name" and to promote the cause actively. One person associated with these efforts was Elder J. D. Bagwell of Warrior, Alabama. By the end of 1938, the Faith Bible and Tract Society had been organized. In July 1939 the Assembly of YHWH was chartered in the state of Michigan. About the same time, the Assembly of Yahweh Beth Israel was also formed.

No single force was as important in spreading the Sacred Name movement as *The Faith* magazine, founded in 1937. This magazine was formed to support the Old Testament festivals as being valid in contemporary times. Gradually the editor, Elder C. O. Dodd (d. 1955), began to use the name Jehovah, then Jahoveh, Yahovah, Yahavah, and Yahweh.

During the 1940s, several assemblies were formed and new periodicals were launched. Some of these became substantial movements and continue today as primary religious bodies. Having come primarily out of the Church of God (Seventh-day), the assemblies follow the Adventist and Old Testament emphases, including the observance of the Jewish festivals. The main divergence is over the name issue, including the exact spelling and pronunciation. The common designation for local gatherings is "assembly," a literal translation of the Greek *ecclesia*. The Sacred Name movement is often referred to as the Elijah Message, a reference to Elijah's words in I Kings 18:36 that extol Yahweh as the Elohim of Israel.

CHARLES TAZE RUSSELL'S BIBLE STUDENTS.

After an apocalyptic failure, such as the Millerite disappointment of 1844, followers have several options. The disbanding of the group and a return to pre-excitement existence is a minority option. Spiritualization—the process of claiming that the prophecy was in error to the extent of its being seen as a visible historical event, and the attempt to reinterpret it as a cosmic, inner, invisible, or heavenly event—is most common. A third option for disappointed apocalyptics is to return to the source of revelation (e.g., the Bible, a psychic-prophet, or an analysis of contemporary events) and seek a new date. (An obvious, less-committed option is to set a vague date, usually verbalized as "the near future.")

After the 1844 disappointment, leaders and periodicals rose and fell as they projected new dates and had to live with their failures. Few millennialist movements spawned groups that lasted beyond the projected dates. Speculations on the winter of 1853 to 1854 lay behind the formation of the Advent Christian Church. A small group led by Jonas Wendell (1815–1873) projected an 1874 date. Disappointed followers spiritualized the 1874 date and projected a new date, 1914. In 1876 Charles Taze Russell (1852–1916) came across an issue of *The Herald of the Morning*, a magazine edited by Nelson H. Barbour (1824–1905), which extolled the views of Wendell, and a new era in Adventist thought began.

Russell was born in Pittsburgh, Pennsylvania, of Scotch-Irish Presbyterians, and was reared in his father's clothing store chain. Shaken by "infidel claims," he began a religious quest that led, in 1870, to Wendell. He joined Wendell's group, but soon disagreed on the manner of Christ's return. Then, in 1876, he met Barbour and joined him in beginning anew the suspended *Herald of the Morning* and coauthoring *Three Worlds or Plan of Redemption*.

By the time of his association with Barbour, Russell had come to accept three ideas that are thoroughly ingrained in the movement he began and are characteristic of it. First, he rejected a belief in hell as a place of eternal torment. Second, he left the Wendell Adventists because he had discovered the true meaning of *parousia* (the Greek word usually translated as "return"). Russell believed that it meant *presence*, and he arrived at the conclusion that, in 1874, the Lord's presence had begun. Finally, Russell began to arrive at a new doctrine of the atonement, or ransom. The biblical Adam, he believed,

received death as a just sentence, but his offspring received death by inheritance. Jesus' act of sacrifice counteracted the death penalty. Because of Adam, all were born without the right to live. Because of Jesus, everyone's inherited sin was canceled. Thus, all people were guaranteed a second chance, a trial in which enlightenment and experience would be followed by a choice either to belong to God or be a rebel deserving of death. This "second chance" would be offered during the millennium, Christ's reign on earth with his saints for one thousand years.

Russell's doctrine of the ransom also included a role for the church as an atoning force. Derived in part from Paul's Epistle to the Colossians 1:24 and from an allegorical interpretation of the Hebrew sacrifice of the bull (i.e., Christ) and the goat (i.e., the church) on the day of atonement described in Leviticus 16, Russell taught that the church as the body of Christ is by its present suffering offering a spiritual sacrifice to God. Inherent in Russell's beliefs was a denial of certain orthodox ideas, such as the Trinity. He outlined a personal lineage that began with Arius (fourth century) whose atonement idea was close to Russell's; the lineage included the ecclesiastical rebels Martin Luther (1483–1546), Peter Waldo (c.1140–c.1218), and John Wycliffe (c. 1330–1384).

After meeting Barbour, Russell drew support from other Adventists, such as J. H. Paton, A. P. Adams, and A. D. Jones. This coalition lasted until 1878, when Barbour, who had set April as the month when the church would go to heaven, suffered a loss of support by the disconfirmation of his prophecy. (He further deviated with some speculations on the atonement.) Russell, Paton, and Jones withdrew their support of Barbour, and Russell began, with the assistance of Paton and Jones, a new periodical, *Zion's Watch Tower and Herald of Christ's Presence*, which was sent free to all of Barbour's subscribers. Paton soon was to join the ranks of dissenters, and he left Russell to expound his own speculations in his periodical, *Zion's Day Star*.

The first issue of the *Watch Tower* in 1879 is a convenient date to begin the history of Russell's movement. To the *Watch Tower* was soon added abundant literature to help a growing number of Bible students who were popularly called Millennial Dawn Bible Students. They came together to study the scriptures with the help of Russell's writings. Russell began to publish tracts, a number of which were combined into *Food for Thinking Christians*. He also called for a thousand preachers to spread the gospel by distributing the *Watch Tower* and his tracts.

In 1881 Zion's Watch Tower Tract Society was set up. In 1886 the first of six volumes of *Studies in the Scripture* appeared. The publishing of the first volume, *The Plan of the Ages*, marked a turning point in the development of the movement, as it provided a substantial ideological base for Watch Tower readers. By 1889 more than 100,000 copies of *The Plan of the Ages* were in print.

The pattern of the Bible student movement's growth was typical of the growth of a number of loosely affiliated religious groups. Local congregations were formed by people impressed by Russell's views and writings. They were related directly to Russell primarily through the *Watch Tower*. The teaching was spread mostly by volunteers. Gradually, there arose colporteurs, who spent from half to all of their time in religious work and who earned their living by selling Russell's books (with a 64 percent discount). In 1894 pilgrims, paid by the central office, were added to the organization as traveling preachers and teachers to local congregations. A plan for local elders or leaders to sell their ideas to new areas was begun in 1911.

Extension of the work also occurred through a number of events that generated a great deal of publicity. In particular, Russell enjoyed debates, at which he was a master. His 1903 debate with E. L. Eaton, a Methodist minister, and with Elder L. S. White of the Disciples of Christ did much to spread the movement.

As the movement expanded, certain ideas came to the fore; none were so prominent as the chronology and the 1914 date. *The Plan of the Ages* was God's calendar for dealing with men. Reminiscent of the perspective on biblical and Christian history offered by the fundamentalist leader John Nelson Darby (1800–1882) was Russell's division of history into a number of eras. According to Russell's chart in *The Plan of the Ages*, the first dispensation from Adam to the flood demonstrated the inability of angels to improve the world. The patriarchal age (from the flood to Jacob's death) was followed by the Jewish age, which lasted until Christ's death. The gospel age of 1845 years ended in 1874. That year marked the dawning of the millennial age, which would begin with a "harvest period" or millennial dawn period of forty years.

The millennial dawn period (1874–1914) would be marked by a return of the Jews to Palestine and the gradual overthrow of the Gentile nations. All would climax in 1914 with the glorification of the saints, the establishment of God's direct rule on earth, and the restoration of man to perfection. The coincidence of the apocalyptic date with the beginning of World War I (1914–1918) was viewed by Russell's followers as a cause for great hope, sharply contrasting the disappointments that had followed other predictions. The war was interpreted as God's direct intervention in the affairs of humanity and a signal of the beginning of the world's end. (Russell later revised the date to 1918, and died in 1916, before the second disconfirmation.)

A final significant idea was the doctrine of the future church. Russell believed from his reading of Revelation 7:4–9 that the church consisted of 144,000 saints from the time of Christ to 1914. These saints would receive the ultimate reward of becoming "priests and kings in heaven." Others would make up a class of heavenly servants termed "the great company." The idea of two classes of believers was illustrated by numerous biblical characters (most notably Elijah, taken to heaven, and Elisha, his servant), who were seen as types of the classes.

Russell and his ideas would become the subject of much controversy after his death. Some leaders ascribed to him a cosmic role and identify him with the good and faithful servant of Matthew 25:21. Others argued over the significance of the harvest, which supposedly ended in 1914. Some argued that the harvest closed in 1914 and that the 144,000 were all chosen by then. Others considered the harvest to be open, with the gathering of the 144,000 continuing. Similar to the differences on the harvest were differences on the identification of the Elijah and Elisha classes.

When Russell died, he left a charismatically run organization in the hands of a board of directors and an editorial committee. The next decade was marked by controversy, schism, the rise to power of Judge J. F. Rutherford (1869–1942), and the emergence of Jehovah's Witnesses.

THE SOUTHCOTTITES. Before William Miller created an Adventist movement in the United States in the 1830s and 1840s, such a movement flowered in England. The focus of the English movement was Joanna Southcott (1750–1814), who in the 1790s began to experience visions, to write about them in prose and verse, and to gather a following. Southcott became convinced that she was a prophetess. Several predictions, including France's conquest of Italy under the unknown general Napoleon Bonaparte, generated attention.

Her message fell within an orthodox Christian framework and centered upon the imminent return of Christ. What made the prophecy distinctive was the peculiar "doctrine of the bride." A feminist, Joanna began to speculate on the crucial role of women in the Bible and the role of the "woman clothed with the sun" (Revelation 12:1), who would bring forth the male child who would rule the nations with a rod of iron. She identified the woman with the bride of the lamb (Revelation 19:7), and then identified both of them with herself.

Southcott began a movement to mobilize England. Her real impact dates from 1801, when she first published her prophecies abroad in several booklets. These booklets brought her disciples, among whom she began a practice of "sealing." Accepting the apocalyptic vision of a world delivered into the hands of Satan, she believed that the key to the devil's overthrow was to have a sufficient number of people renounce him and be "sealed" as of the Lord. She distributed seals to all who would sign up for them. They were written on square sheets of paper upon which a circle was drawn. Inside the circle Joanna wrote "The sealed of the Lord, the Elect and Precious, Man's Redemption to Inherit the Tree of Life, to be made Heirs of God and Joint Heirs with Jesus Christ." The paper would be folded and sealed with wax, with the monogram I. C. (for Jesus Christ) and two stars. Critics accused Joanna of selling the seals, but she denied it.

In 1814, at 64 years of age, she had a climactic revelation. Having identified herself with the woman in Revelation 12, she was concerned with the child the woman was to bear. Joanna's voice told her to prepare for the birth of a son. This child was identified in Joanna's thinking with Shiloh (Genesis 49:10). She began to show signs of pregnancy and was declared pregnant by several doctors. Her followers prepared for a new virgin birth. As the time of the delivery approached, she took an earthly husband. When the baby failed to arrive and the symptoms of the hysteric pregnancy left, Joanna's strength ebbed and she died in December 1814.

Followers and leaders alike were thrown into confusion. Among those who did not leave the movement, there were attempts to regroup, and a number of separate churches resulted. Most were confined to England, but a few found their way to America.

BRITISH ISRAELISM.

Growing up largely in Adventist circles, and picking ideas from them at random—nontrinitarian theology, Sabbatarianism, Sacred Name emphases, and dispensationalism—the British Israelite Bible students emerged as a distinct group in American religion during the decade after World War I. They experienced a steady growth into the 1940s, but waned in the 1950s and 1960s. During the 1970s, however, the movement experienced a revival in its most militant wing, popularly called the Identity movement.

Though only visible in the United States since World War I, British Israelism, the Identity movement, traces its history to ancient Israel. In actual fact, its history began in the late eighteenth century in England, where one of the more popular avocations of Bible students was the attempt to discover the present-day identity of the so-called 10 lost tribes of Israel—the 10 tribes carried into captivity by Shalmaneser, the king of Assyria in 721 B.C.E. (II Kings 17). Since 1800, numerous explanations have been advanced, but only two, apart from the generally accepted view that the tribes were assimilated into the peoples of the Middle East, gained a wide following. The first of these speculations identified the American Indians as the tribes. That view was promulgated by Joseph Smith Jr. (1805–1844), the founder of the Church of Jesus Christ of Latter-day Saints. The second speculation was the British Israelites' identification of the tribes with Anglo-Saxon peoples.

Scotsman John Wilson (1799–1870), who in 1840 published his theories in *Our Israelitish Origins*, is generally regarded as the founder of the British Israelites. His appearance of scholarship and his oratorical abilities were enough to sell his notion to the public. Wilson was by no means the first to make the British-Israelite identification. As early as 1649, John Sadler (b. 1615) speculated on the idea in his *Rights to the Kingdom* and may have advised Oliver Cromwell (1599–1658) on readmitting the Jews to England. In the eighteenth century, Dr. Abade of Amsterdam, a Protestant theologian, is reported to have said: "Unless the ten tribes have flown into the air, or have been plunged into the center of the earth, they must be sought for in the north and west, and in the British Isles" (Darms, *The Delusion of British Israel*, 1938, p. 15).

The real originator of the idea, however, was Canadian Richard Brothers (b. 1757), a psychic visionary who settled in London in the 1780s. He began to publish the content of revelations that identified him as a descendant of King David and demanded the crown of England. He was found guilty of treason, but insane, and was sent to an asylum. Brothers's ideas caught on with some influential men, including Orientalist Nathaniel Brassey Halhed (1751–1830), Quaker psychic William Bryan, and Scottish lawyer John Finleyson. The defeat of Napoleon was the marked confirmation of their ideas.

The basics of British Israelite theology are simple, although a working knowledge of the Old Testament is required to trace the intricacies of the logic. The premise is that Israel and Judah were two entities, the former comprising the northern 10 tribes and the latter the two southern ones after 922 B.C.E. Members of the northern kingdom, after being freed from captivity, wandered into Europe and settled in northwest Europe, Scandinavia, and the British Isles. Jeremiah, the prophet, is believed to have transported Tea-Tephi, the daughter of King Zedekiah, to Ireland to marry Prince Herremon, thus continuing Israel's royal lineage. James I (1566–1625) was thought to be the first descendant of this union to reign in London.

Different countries are identified with the different tribes; Britain and the United States are descendants of Joseph's two sons Ephraim and Manasseh, and, as such, are particularly blessed (Genesis 48). The tribe of Dan has, in fulfillment of prophecy (Genesis 49:17), left numerous signposts of its tribal meanderings—Dan River, Denmark, Danube River, and others.

From this basic theology, other observations are made in correlating biblical quotes with isolated facts of archaeology, legendary materials, history, and philology. Wilson was the first to note the correlation between the Hebrew word for covenant, *brith*, and *Britain*. The Stone of Scone, upon which English monarchs are crowned, is believed to have been from the throne in Jerusalem, brought to Ireland by Jeremiah. (Actually, it was quarried in Scotland.)

British Israelism has attracted much attention because of its racist overtones, especially in the United States. Implicit in the theory is the superiority of the Anglo-Saxon, which is presented as religious superiority, much as with any chosen-people doctrine. The Jews are considered to be "kin" to the Anglo-Saxons. In a famous quote, one of the movement's leaders, J. H. Allen (1847–1930), said:

> *Understand us: we do not say that the Jews are not Israelites; they belong to the posterity of Jacob, who was called Israel; hence they are all Israelites. But the great bulk of Israelites are not the Jews, just as the great bulk of Americans are not Californians, and yet all Californians are Americans; also, as in writing the history of America we must of necessity write the history of California, because California is a part of America; but we could write a history of California without writing a history of America.*
>
> Allen, *Judah's Sceptre and Joseph's Birthright* [1902] 1930, p. 71.

Numerous refutations of British Israelism have been written from a perspective of orthodox history and theology. These have, in spite of their often vitriolic nature, conclusively refuted the majority of British Israelite speculations. However, they have missed the point: British Israelism's success has been as a religious and emotional expression of British imperialism and American manifest destiny. There is a definite correlation between the rise and fall of those ideas and the popularity of British Israelism. The dismantling of the British Empire has had a devastating effect upon the movement.

John Wilson's *Our Israelitish Origins* was published in the United States in 1850 and found isolated disciples but no real following until after World War I. In 1886 Matthew M. Eshelman (1844–1921), a Church of the Brethren minister, was introduced to British Israelism by an 80-year-old immigrant to Illinois, William Montgomery. In the pages of *The Gospel Messenger*, published at Mt. Morris, Illinois, Eshelman began to write of his ideas. In 1887 he published a book, *Two Sticks, or, the Lost Tribes of Israel Discovered*, which, along with Allen's *Judah's Sceptre and Joseph's Birthright* (1902), helped sell British Israelism to an American audience.

The British Israel movement reached its height in the 1930s and 1940s. It never attained the degree of development or popularity in the United States that it had in England, but in the late 1940s, the movement could boast a national audience among both congregational members and radio listeners. Two British Israel seminaries were in operation in 1950. The British Israel hypothesis—that Anglo-Saxons are descendants of the ten lost tribes of Israel—was finding support among people who would by no means identify themselves with the movement itself. What remains today are the remnants of that once-strong national movement.

One of the important early structures created by the movement was Dayton Theological Seminary, which was open from 1947 into the early 1950s. It was founded by Millard J. Flenner, an former Congregational minister and pastor of the Church of the Covenants in Dayton. Among the teachers was Conrad Gaard, who was pastor for many years of the Christian Chapel Church in Tacoma. As head of the Destiny of America Foundation, he was an important writer and radio minister until his death in 1969. Gaard helped Dayton graduates keep in touch through his travels and tours.

Apart from the mainline of the British Israel movement, one Church of God Adventist radio minister, Herbert W. Armstrong (1892–1986), integrated British Israelism into his thought and wrote a paraphrase of Allen's *Judah's Sceptre and Joseph's Birthright*. His small ministry, begun in Eugene, Oregon, in the 1930s, blossomed after his move to Pasadena, California, in 1947. By the time of Armstrong's death, the church—Worldwide Church of God—had introduced millions of people to British Israelism and claimed more than 100,000 members, the single most successful such group ever to exist. In the 1990s, however, under Armstrong's successors, Joseph W. Tkach Sr. (1927–1995) and Joseph W. Tkach Jr., the church not only dropped its British-Israel ideology, but all of Armstrong's ideas that had made it distinctive, and adopted an orthodox Evangelical Christian theological perspective. The changes led to more than half the membership withdrawing and forming splinter groups, most of which retain the British Israel orientation.

THE MODERN IDENTITY MOVEMENT. British Israelism is implicitly anti-Semitic and antiblack. However, in the middle of the twentieth century, the movement became associated with several groups that were actively and explicitly anti-Semitic and antiblack, such as the Ku Klux Klan, and, after World War II (1937–1945), the neo-Nazi movement. Among those generally credited with bringing these two forces together is the Reverend Gerald L. K. Smith (1898–1976), founder of the Christian Nationalist Crusade. Besides publishing pro-Anglo-Saxon materials, Smith published and freely circulated a large amount of defamatory material on blacks and Jews. The work of Smith and of his former lieutenant, Wesley Swift (1913–1970), gave rise in the 1970s to a recognizable group within the larger British Israel community.

The Identity movement, a name taken from the idea of "identifying" modern white people as the literal ancestors of the ancient Israelites, has become increasingly controversial because of its identification with violent and illegal actions and the growing opposition it has provoked within the more established American religious community, both Christians and Jews. While various watchdog organizations developed a concern for the emerging movement in previous decades, in the early 1980s public attention began to focus on one center, called the Covenant, the Sword, and the Arm of the Lord (CSA), located on the Arkansas-Missouri border. In 1983 Gordon Kahl, a leader with the Posse Comitatus, an antitax group associated with the larger Identity movement, killed two U.S. marshals in North Dakota. Fleeing the scene of the crime, he was later killed resisting arrest in Arkansas not far from CSA. A year later, an Arkansas state trooper was killed by a man identified as a former resident of CSA. Then, in 1985, the leader of CSA was arrested for racketeering and was sentenced to 20 years in jail, an event that led to the dissolution of the group.

As events at CSA were unfolding, authorities were also moving against another Identity group known as the Order. The group was composed primarily of former members of the Church of Jesus Christ Christian, Aryan Nations, headquartered in Hayden Lake, Idaho, which had grown out of the church founded by Wesley Swift in southern California. Members of the group were believed responsible for a series of robberies in 1983 and 1984, as well as the death of Alan Berg, an outspoken Jewish radio talk-show host in Denver, who was shot in 1984. One leader of the order, Robert Jay Matthews, was killed in a shootout as law officers attempted to arrest him. Ten others were convicted in 1985 of racketeering.

In 1987, 15 leaders of the Identity movement were indicted on a series of charges ranging from conspiracy to kill government officials to violating Alan Berg's civil rights. However, the fifteen were found not guilty in a trial the following year. A more successful assault upon the movement occurred in 2000 when a jury awarded Victoria and Jason Keenan $6.3 million in a lawsuit stemming from a shooting/beating attack outside the Aryan Nations Church. The twenty-acre national headquarters was sold to satisfy the judgment.

In 2001 the Keenan's sold the property to the Gregory C. Carr Foundation, an organization created by Gregory C. Carr (b. 1959), founder and chairman of the Internet company Prodigy Inc. The foundation announced plans to turn the property into a human-rights center.

THE MILLENNIAL IMPULSE. Scholarship on the Adventist tradition was stimulated by several incidents in which groups advocating a change in humanity's earthly existence were at the center of clashes involving members of the group and at times outsiders. One of these incidents, the death of most members of the Branch Davidians at Waco, Texas, in 1993, involved a group in the Adventist tradition. A 1995 incident—the release of poisonous gas on subways in Tokyo—was attributed to Aum Shinrikyo, a Buddhist group whose leader had imbibed of Christian prophetic literature. Several further incidents in the 1990s raised the specter of the sixteenth-century violence that had given apocalyptic groups a bad name in Western religious history. Many scholars began to discuss the relationship of violence and millennial groups, a discussion that was given added urgency by the approaching end of the second millennium C.E.

The arrival of the year 2000 provided grounds for much speculation by religious leaders fascinated with the triple zeros in the new year. A number of books, primarily written by fundamentalist and very conservative Evangelical Protestants, highlighted an expectation of significant change as the new century approached. Those expectations were countered by many voices in the Evangelical community who firmly believed in an imminent Second Coming of Christ, but just as strongly resisted any attempt at date-setting around the end of the millennium. The religious speculations found completion in predictions of a computer meltdown because many clocks installed in computers were seen as unable to accommodate the change in settings required for the year 2000 (Y2K). The new century arrived, however, with neither set of predictions bringing either any major change or violent reaction. Within months, the books that had predicted such happenings disappeared from the marketplace, and those who had made the predictions offered revised visions of the future.

The highly publicized events of the 1990s and the disappointments surrounding the nonevent of the arrival of 2000 did not stop the emergence of new predictions of the end of the world, and millennial studies has continued to attract scholarly interest and debate. Besides new predictions derived from reading the Christian Bible, a group of post–New Agers have compiled a set of predictions around the ancient Mayan calendar and the year 2012.

SOURCES

The Seventh-day Adventists have archives at several of their schools, but the most prominent collections are at the church's headquarters, 12501 Old Columbia Pike, Silver Spring, MD 20904-6600, and at Andrews University, Berrien Springs, MI. The Advent Christian Church supports the Adventists Archives at Aurora College, Aurora, IL.

Adventism, Millennialism, and Apocalypticism

Bull, Malcolm, ed. *Apocalypse Theory and the Ends of the World.* Oxford: Blackwell, 1995. 297 pp.

Case, Shirley Jackson. *The Millennial Hope: A Phase of War-time Thinking.* Chicago: University of Chicago Press, 1918. 253 pp.

Chamberlin, E. R. *Antichrist and the Millennium.* New York: Dutton, 1975. 244 pp.

Cook, Stephen L. *Prophecy and Apocalypticism: The Postexilic Social Setting.* Minneapolis: Augsburg Fortress Publishers, 1995. 260 pp.

Froom, Edwin Leroy. *The Prophetic Faith of Our Fathers.* 4 vols. Washington, DC: Review and Herald Publishing, 1950–1954.

———. *The Conditionalist Faith of Our Fathers: The Conflict of the Ages Over the Nature and Destiny of Man.* 2 vols. Washington, DC: Review and Herald Publishing, 1966.

Grosso, Michael. *Millennium Myth: Love and Death at the End of Time.* Wheaton, IL: Quest, 1995.

Harrison, J. F. C. *The Second Coming: Popular Millenarianism, 1780–1850.* London: Routledge & Kegan Paul, 1979. 277 pp.

Hunter, Anthony. *The Last Days.* London: Blond, 1958. 232 pp.

Kyle, Richard. *The Last Day Are Here Again: A History of the End Times.* Grand Rapids, MI: Baker, 1998. 255 pp.

Landes, Richard, ed. *Encyclopedia of Millennialism and Millennial Movements.* New York: Routledge, 2000. 478 pp.

McGinn, Bernard. *The Encyclopedia of Apocalypticism.* Vol. 2: *Apocalypticism in Western History and Culture.* New York: Continuum International, 2000. 548 pp.

O'Leary, Stephen. *Arguing the Apocalypse: A Theory of Millennial Rhetoric.* New York: Oxford University Press, 1994. 314 pp.

Rist, Martin. "Introduction to the Revelation of St. John the Divine." In *The Interpreters Bible.* Vol. 12, 617–627. New York: Abingdon, 1974.

St. Clair, Michael. *Millenarian Movements in Historical Context.* New York: Garland, 1992. 373 pp.

Schmithals, Walter. *The Apocalyptic Movement: Introduction & Interpretation.* Nashville, TN: Abingdon, 1975. 255 pp.

Stein, Stephen J. *The Encyclopedia of Apocalypticism.* Vol. 3: *Apocalypticism in the Modern Period and the Contemporary Age.* New York: Continuum International, 2000. 524 pp.

Stone, Jon R. *Expecting Armageddon: Essential Readings in Failed Prophecy.* New York: Routledge, 2000. 296 pp.

Wallis, John. *Apocalyptic Trajectories: Millenarianism and Violence in the Contemporary World.* Oxford: Peter Lang, 2004. 271 pp.

Wessinger, Catherine. *How the Millennium Comes Violently: From Jonestown to Heaven's Gate.* New York: Seven Bridges Press, 2000. 305 pp.

Adventism in America

Directory of Sabbath-Observing Groups. Fairview, OK: Bible Sabbath Association, 2001. 246 pp.

Gaustad, Edwin Scott, ed. *The Rise of Adventism: Religion and Society in Mid-Nineteenth-Century America.* New York: Harper & Row, 1974.

Nichol, Francis D. *The Midnight Cry: A Defense of William Miller and the Millerites.* Washington, DC: Review and Herald, 1944. 576 pp.

Sears, Clara Endicott. *Days of Delusion: A Strange Bit of History.* Boston: Houghton Mifflin, 1924. 264 pp.

Seventh-day Adventist Encyclopedia. 2nd rev. ed. Washington, DC: Review and Herald Publishing, 1996. 1454 pp.

William Miller

Bliss, Sylvester. *Memoirs of William Miller.* Boston: Himes, 1853. 426 pp.

A Brief History of William Miller, the Great Pioneer in Adventist Faith. Washington, DC: Review and Herald Publishing, 1915.

Gale, Robert. *The Urgent Call.* Washington, DC: Review and Herald Publishing, 1975. 158 pp.

White, James. *Sketches of the Christian Life and Public Labors of William Miller.* Battle Creek, MI: Steam Press, 1875. 413 pp.

Ellen G. White and the Seventh-day Adventists

Bull, Malcolm. *Seeking a Sanctuary: Seventh-day Adventism and the American Dream.* San Francisco: Harper & Row, 1989. 319 pp.

A Critique of Prophetess of Health. Washington, DC: Ellen G. White Estate, General Conference of S.D.A., 1976. 127 pp.

Damsteegt, P. Gerard. *Foundations of the Seventh-day Adventist Message and Mission.* Grand Rapids, MI: Eerdmans, 1977. 348 pp.

Delafield, D. A. *Ellen G. White and the Seventh-day Adventist Church.* Mountain View, CA: Pacific Press, 1963. 90 pp.

Noobergen, Rene. *Ellen G. White: Prophet of Destiny.* New Canaan, CT: Keats, 1972. 241 pp.

Numbers, Ronald L. *Prophetess of Health: A Study of Ellen G. White.* 3rd ed. Grand Rapids, MI: Eerdmans, 2008.

Churches of God (Seventh Day)

Bjorling, Joel. *The Churches of God, Seventh Day: A Bibliography.* New York: Garland, 1987. 296 pp.

Hopkins, Joseph. *The Armstrong Empire: A Look at the Worldwide Church of God.* Grand Rapids, MI: Eerdmans, 1974. 304 pp.

Nickels, Richard C. *A History of the Seventh Day Church of God.* Vol. 1. Sheridan, WY: Author, 1977. 397 pp.

————. *Six Papers on the History of the Church of God.* Sheridan, WY: Giving & Sharing, 1977.

Sabbatarianism

Armstrong, Herbert W. *Which Day Is the Sabbath of the New Testament?* Pasadena, CA: Worldwide Church of God, 1971. 23 pp.

————. *The Resurrection Was Not on Sunday.* Pasadena, CA: Ambassador College, 1972. 14 pp.

Dellinger, George. *A History of the Sabbath Resurrection Doctrine.* Westfield, IN: Sabbath Research Center, 1982. 33 pp.

Haynes, Carlyle B. *From Sabbath to Sunday.* Washington, DC: Review and Herald Publishing, 1928. 128 pp.

Love, William Deloss. *Sabbath and Sunday.* Chicago: Revell, 1896. 325 pp.

Sacred Name Movement

Dugger, Andrew N., and Clarence O. Dodd. *A History of the True Church* (1936). Neck City, MO: Giving & Sharing, 1996. 318 pp.

"Let Your Name Be Sanctified." New York: Watchtower Bible and Tract Society of New York, 1961. 382 pp.

Meyer, Jacob O. *The Memorial Name—Yahweh.* Bethel, PA: Assemblies of Yahweh, 1978. 76 pp.

Rutherford, J. F. *Vindication.* Vol. 1. New York: Watchtower Bible and Tract Association, 1931. 346 pp.

Snow, L. D. "A Brief History of the Name Movement in America." *Eliyah Messenger and Field Reporter* (May 1966): 1, 4, 7, 12.

Traina, A. B. *The Holy Name Bible.* Brandywine, MD: Scripture Research Association, 1980. 346 pp.

Charles Taze Russell and the Bible Students

Beckford, James A. *The Trumpet of Prophecy: A Sociological Study of Jehovah's Witnesses.* Oxford: Blackwell, 1975. 244 pp.

Bergman, Jerry. *Jehovah's Witnesses and Kindred Groups: An Historical Compendium and Bibliography.* New York: Garland, 1984. 370 pp.

Cole, Marley. *Triumphant Kingdom.* New York: Criterion, 1957. 256 pp.

Gruss, Edmond Charles. *Apostles of Denial.* Presbyterian and Reformed Publishing, 1970. 324 pp.

Holden, Andrew. *Jehovah's Witnesses: Portrait of a Contemporary Religious Movement.* New York: Routledge, 2002. 224 pp.

Penton, M. James. *Apocalypse Delayed: The Story of Jehovah's Witnesses.* 2nd ed. Toronto: University of Toronto Press, 1997. 444 pp.

————. *Jehovah's Witnesses and the Third Reich: Sectarian Politics under Persecution.* Toronto: University of Toronto Press, 2004. 420 pp.

Rogerson, Alan. *Millions Now Living Will Never Die: A Study of Jehovah's Witnesses.* London: Constable, 1969. 216 pp.

Stafford, Greg D. *Jehovah's Witnesses Defended: An Answer to Scholars and Critics.* Murietta, CA: Elihu, 2007.

White, Timothy (Timothy Willis). *A People for His Name: History of Jehovah's Witnesses and an Evaluation.* New York: Vantage Press, 1967. 418 pp.

Joanna Southcott

Balleiene, G. R. *Past Finding Out: The Tragic Story of Joanna Southcott and Her Successors.* New York: Macmillan, 1956. 151 pp.

The Life and Journal of John Wroe. Ashton-under-Lyne: Trustees of the Society of Christian Israelites, 1900. 639 pp.

Matthews, Ronald. *English Messiahs.* London: Methuen, 1936. 230 pp.

British Israelism

Allen, J. H. *Judah's Sceptre and Joseph's Birthright: An Analysis of the Prophecies of Scripture in Regard to the Regard to the Royal Family of Judah and the Many Nations of Israel* (1902). Boston: Beauchamp, 1930. 377 pp.

Armstrong, Herbert W. *The United States and Britain in Prophecy.* Pasadena, CA: Worldwide Church of God, 1980. 163 pp.

Barkun, Michael. *Religion and the Racist Right: The Origins of the Christian Identity Movement.* Chapel Hill: University of North Carolina Press, 1994. 290 pp.

Coates, James. *Armed and Dangerous: The Rise of the Survivalist Right.* New York: Hill and Wang, 1987. 294 pp.

Darms, Anton. *The Delusion of British Israel: A Comprehensive Treatise.* New York: Loizeaux Brothers, Bible Truth Depot, 1938. 224 pp.

Haberman, Frederick. *The Climax of the Ages Is Near.* St. Petersburg, FL: Kingdom Press, 1940. 94 pp.

Hate Groups in America: A Record of Bigotry and Violence. Rev. ed. New York: Anti-Defamation League of B'nai B'rith, 1988. 107 pp.

Kaplan, Jeffrey. *Radical Religion in America: Millenarian Movements from the Far Right to the Children of Noah.* Syracuse, NY: Syracuse University Press, 1997. 245 pp.

Mackendrick, W. G. *The Roadbuilder: The Destiny of the British Empire and the U.S.A.* London: Covenant, 1931. 213 pp.

Roy, Ralph Lord. *Apostles of Discord: A Study of Organized Bigotry and Disruption on the Fringes of Protestantism.* Boston: Beacon Press, 1953. 437 pp.

Schwartz, Alan M., et al. "The 'Identity Churches': A Theology of Hate." *ADL Facts* 28, no. 1 (Spring 1983): 116.

Swift, Wesley A. *Testimony of Tradition and the Origin of Races.* Hollywood, CA: New Christian Crusade Church, n.d. 34 pp.

Wilson, J. *Our Israelitish Origins.* Philadelphia: Daniels & Smith, 1850. 237 pp.

❊ Intrafaith Organizations

Bible Sabbath Association

802 NW 21st Ave., Battle Ground, WA 98604

The Bible Sabbath Association was established in 1943 by several Sabbatarians (those who believe Saturday to be the biblical Sabbath and day set aside for worship) from different churches who felt the need for mutual support and closer fellowship. An office was established in Pomona Park, Florida, and later moved to Fairview, Oklahoma. The association has as its goals the promotion of the seventh-day Sabbath, the encouragement of the repeal of blue laws (which inhibit activity on Sunday), and the facilitation of fellowship among Sabbath keepers on a nonsectarian basis.

The organization periodically publishes a *Directory of Sabbath-Observing Groups*, which lists those who are Seventh-Day (Saturday) Sabbath keepers. These groups have varying beliefs, but they all adhere to the Seventh-Day Sabbath, as the Sabbath of the Old and New Testaments.

Membership: In 1986 the association reported approximately 1,000 individual members. The latest directory lists several hundred groups, including denominations and independent congregations.

Periodicals: *The Sabbath Sentinel.*

Sources:

Bible Sabbath Association. www.biblesabbath.org

Directory of Sabbath-Observing Groups. Fairview, OK: Bible Sabbath Association, 1986.

Sunday Adventists

Advent Christian General Conference

14601 Albemarle Rd., PO Box 690848, Charlotte, NC 28227

The story of Advent Christian beginnings is centered on William Miller (1782–1849). He, and the movement associated with his name (*Millerism*), stirred America spiritually as few others have, before or since. For years newspapers recorded his every move and message. In the press, the pulpit, and even the political arena, he was praised and condemned, but never ignored. His following was never great—perhaps peaking at 50,000 at the height of his ministry. Few persons of prominence or wealth followed him, but thousands of dedicated Christians gave him a respectful hearing. His career ended anticlimactically in what is often called the "Great Disappointment," but from his ministry came a great spiritual awakening and the renaissance of long-buried truths.

Miller was born in Pittsfield, Massachusetts, in 1782. Although Miller's schooling was limited to three months each winter, he learned to excel in both reading and writing. His parents' home served as a church in the community with his uncle as lay pastor. Early in his youth Miller displayed interest in religion, but in the limited number of books at his disposal were several with an atheistic or deistic approach. The two revolutions, American (1775–1783) and French (1789–1799), had given strong impetus to anticlericalism and anti-Christianity, and in every community rationalists shaped the frontier philosophy, usually at the expense of the church. Probably the best-read book of the period was *The Age of Reason* by Thomas Paine (1737–1809), influential philosopher and avowed foe of Christianity. Miller adopted the midway position of deism, which conceded the probable existence of God, but rejected Christ's claim to sonship or divinity. Still, the influence of a Christian mother and a praying wife began to penetrate the shell of his skepticism. He started to read the Bible and in 1818 returned to a living Christian faith. Thereafter the Word was the center of his life. With his characteristic candor and vigor, he began to proclaim the Gospel as fervently as he had ridiculed it. This activity led him to conflict with his old deistic associates. Their attacks drove him more deeply into Bible study. As he studied the Word, he was impressed by the prominence given to the return of Christ. Almost totally neglected in the pulpit and in Christian thought of the time, it was literally a "buried truth."

As he traced scriptural development of the hope of Christ's return, he found himself intrigued by the Old Testament evidence and the trail of fulfilled prophecy that marked the unfolding of history. In the book of Daniel he discovered a series of mathematical symbols that fascinated him. The most striking of these is in Daniel 12:9–13:

> *And he said, Go thy way, Daniel: for the words are closed up and sealed till the time of the end.*
>
> *Many shall be purified, and made white, and tried; but the wicked shall do wickedly: and none of the wicked shall understand; but the wise shall understand.*

> *And from the time that the daily sacrifice shall be taken away, and the abomination that maketh desolate set up, there shall be a thousand two hundred and ninety days.*
>
> *Blessed is he that waiteth, and cometh to the thousand three hundred and five and thirty days.*
>
> *But go thou thy way till the end be: for thou shalt rest, and stand in thy lot at the end of the days.*

A similar statement, found in Daniel 8:14 became the key in his findings: "Unto two thousand and three hundred days; then shall the sanctuary be cleansed." Transforming these "days" into calendar years by the "year-day" theory, which was the accepted pattern of interpretation of the period, and finding certain anchor dates in known historical events, Miller became convinced that the return of Christ would take place between 1843 and 1844. He presented his case in his own and neighboring communities and gained many followers.

Again, Miller followed an accepted plan of interpretation, by which days, even when massed in months and years, each represented a year. Many others lost courage at the point of application. Miller dared to stand upon his findings. He put it thus:

> *The first proof we have as it respects Christ's Second Coming, as to the time is in Daniel 8:14: "Unto two thousand three hundred days, then shall the sanctuary be cleansed." By "days" we are to understand years; "sanctuary" we understand as the church; "cleansed" we may reasonably suppose means that complete redemption from sin, soul and body, after the resurrection, when Christ comes the second time, without sin, unto salvation.*

Following his return to the church and his studies in Scripture, Miller was ordained a local preacher by the Baptist circuit of Hampton and Whitehall. In 1831, he began to proclaim the coming of the Lord. It seems to have been about two years later that he made time-setting a major point of emphasis.

However, this was never a monomania with him. The main theme of his preaching throughout his life was evangelistic, a plea for repentance and reception of Christ as the savior of humankind. His proudest boast was that through his ministry, 500 infidels had been converted.

As the impending end of the world found a larger place in his preaching, he found himself in greater demand through the border communities and the Lake George area in northern New York. In 1843, he wrote to a friend that he was devoting all of his time to lecturing. By this time, disciples were beginning to carry the message in a widening perimeter.

Miller's fame spread and invitations came from more distant places. One of the first of these was from Lowell, Massachusetts. This trip brought him one of his most illustrious converts and his biographer, Sylvester Bliss (1814–1863). Then came a confrontation with Joshua V. Himes (1805–1895) in 1839 that transformed the course of the crusade. Up until this meeting, Miller had conducted a one-man ministry, answering invitations and traveling at his own expense in obedience to what he believed firmly to be a mandate from God.

Himes, pastor of the Chardon Chapel Church in Boston, Massachusetts, was impressed with Miller and invited him to a series of meetings in his church. Himes was a promotional genius and peer of showman P. T. Barnum (1810–1891). Under the spell of the Himes genius, he became a national figure almost overnight, although a highly controversial one. Campaigns were mapped covering all major American cities. Interest deepened, pro and con, but opposed to thousands of scorners were other thousands who accepted the plea to "flee from the wrath to come."

Throughout New England, a series of camp meetings drew thousands of the faithful for a week or more of sermons, most of them based on the book of Daniel and illustrated by beast-bestrewn charts, which established that Christ would come in the Jewish calendar year beginning March 21, 1843. The movement would eventually spread west, with workers traveling as far from the Boston base as Minnesota and Wisconsin. Work in the South met more resistance because many of the Millerite preachers (as they were collectively referred) were well-known abolitionists. Still, an impact was made. A camp meeting convert took the message to England and produced a sensation there.

During much of this period, Miller was critically ill at his home, but this did not dampen the ardor of his associates. By the spring of 1844 when the days of "time" were running out, there were more than 1,000 congregations with more than 50,000 believers by Miller's estimate. But March passed, and the Lord did not come. Miller and Himes apparently were willing to acknowledge their mistake and revert to a "no-man-knoweth-the day-nor-the-hour" position, which had been held throughout the movement by several of Miller's associates.

While Miller and his close associates were ready to drop time-setting, other leaders were busy with their pencils looking for mathematical errors in the calculation. In August, one of these leaders, Samuel S. Snow (1806–1870), launched the "seventh month" thesis, which proclaimed that the return of the Lord could be expected on October 22, 1844. Miller and Himes were in the West when this declaration was made, and evidence shows that Miller never participated actively in the movement. Himes eventually gave in and supported the October 22 date-fixing.

Tensions reached a fever pitch during the 80 days between the Snow proclamation and the anticipated Last Judgement. Eventually the day came and Christ did not. While the disappointment was crushing, withdrawals were surprisingly few among the thousands who looked for their Lord and pinned their faith on his return. Their faith naturally turned from awaiting the day to the hope itself.

Miller confessed his disappointment and faded from active leadership in the movement, which continued to be called popularly by his name. He remained a respected elder statesman, but withdrew to his home in Low Hampton, New York, where he died in 1849. And so Millerism bowed out. But out of it came the Advent Christian Church.

Doctrinally, the Advent Christian Church continues Miller's views about the imminent coming of Jesus, with the exception of the date-setting aspects. It recognizes baptism by immersion for believers and has recently tended toward a more reformed theological perspective (while allowing for diversity on this issue). Members of the Advent Christian Church worship on Sunday. They are opposed to setting new dates, but believe that Christ's return is imminent, a belief based on Bible declarations such as "No one knows about that day or hour, not even the angels in heaven, nor the Son, but only the Father" (Matthew 24:36) and "You also must be ready, because the Son of Man will come at an hour when you do not expect him" (Luke 12:40).

Organizationally, a congregational government is most prominent. The general conference meets triennially and has charge of the mission and education program. Missions are currently under way in Ghana, Liberia, Nigeria, Japan, the Philippines, China, Malaysia, Mexico, Honduras, Croatia, Romania, New Zealand, and India. Two retirement centers—the Vernon Advent Christian Home, in Vernon, Vermont, and the Advent Christian Village in Dowling Park, Florida—are supported by the denomination. In 1987 the church joined the National Association of Evangelicals.

Membership: In 1999 the church reported 25,702 members, 302 churches, and 409 ministers in the United States; and 240 members, seven churches, and seven ministers in Canada. There were an additional 35,306 members worldwide.

Educational Facilities:

Aurora University, Aurora, Illinois.

Berkshire Christian College, Haverhill, Massachusetts.

The Berkshire Institute for Christian Studies, Lenox, Massachusetts.

Periodicals: *Advent Christian Witness*. • *Maranatha Devotions*. • *Advent Christian E-Newsletter* • *Henceforth*.

Sources:

Advent Christian General Conference.
    www.adventchristian.org/Home/tabid/36/Default.aspx

The Advent Christian Manual. Charlotte, NC: Venture Books, 1987.

Dean, David A. *Resurrection: His and Ours*. Charlotte, NC: Venture Books, 1976.

Hewitt, Clarence H. *The Conditional Principle in Theology*. Boston, MA: Clyde and Robert Hewitt, 1954.

Hewitt, Clyde E. *Midnight and Morning*. Charlotte, NC: Venture Books, 1983.

Kearney, Clarence J. *The Advent Christian Story*. Author, 1968.

Church of God General Conference (Abrahamic Faith)
5823 Trammel Rd., PO Box 100,000, Morrow, GA 30260

The Church of God developed in the United States from several independent congregations, including some that had been associated with the Christian Connection, some that had followed William Miller (1782–1849), and some of other persuasions. As early as 1816 Elias Smith (1769–1846) proclaimed the message of the age to come, which the Church of God holds central to its eschatological teachings. Joseph Marsh, an editor for the Christian Connection, and later for William Miller, promoted this teaching following his break with Miller in 1844. Marsh advanced the name *Church of God* as the only scriptural name of God's people. Many early Church of God leaders in the east looked to Marsh for direction as he published several highly regarded religious journals and books. A conference was organized in 1856 but it did not last long: There were controversies over organizational structure and how to disperse funds. Through the exchange of journals with other editors preaching doctrines similar to the age to come, congregations in the South and Midwest also became part of the Church of God movement.

After Marsh died in 1863, church leaders looked to the writings of Benjamin Wilson of Geneva, Illinois, who published a religious journal, the *Gospel Banner*, and the famous Emphatic Diaglott, a unique translation that printed the Greek on one line with the English translation immediately below it. Believers from the Church of God often worshiped together with others, some of whom were Advent Christians, and some who followed the teachings of Dr. John Thomas (1805–1871) and became Christadelphians. This joining of believers from various like-minded congregations was especially prominent in rural congregations on the frontier.

The Church of God reorganized as a general conference in Chicago in 1869. This effort was followed by several conferences in the Midwest, with each state having its own conference. These conferences were somewhat informal, very loosely constituted, and soon ceased for lack of a strong central organization and want of funds. Another call of organization was issued by believers in 1888. Meeting in Philadelphia, the conferees established the General Conference of the Churches of God in Christ Jesus in the United States and Canada. At a conference the following year in Chicago, a disagreement over the rights of the congregations versus the rights of the national conference led the delegates to abandon the new work. The executive board continued to function until 1892, but disbanded due to a lack of mandate from the delegates. Another attempt to reorganize, in Waterloo, Iowa, in 1910, also failed, over a dispute concerning the exact form of the statement of faith. As a people they did not accept standard creeds, but yet could not agree on the articles of faith.

Finally, in 1921 in Waterloo, after a year of prayer and planning, a successful organization was created, and it exists to this day. The new organization was named National Bible Institute. To handle the publishing arm of the new corporation the corporate headquarters was located in Oregon, Illinois, where the *Restitution Herald* was being published. The organization today calls itself by the old nomenclature popular with the delegates, the Church of God of the Abrahamic Faith. In 1968 the larger Church of God voted to change the name to Church of God General Conference. In 1991 the headquarters of the conference and the Bible College were moved to Morrow, Georgia, near Atlanta.

The Church of God differs from other Adventist churches in its views on Christology and eschatology. As had become increasing common among Adventists, the church emphasizes the one God, denies the Trinity, and sees Jesus as the Son of God, distinct from the Father. The church believes Jesus came into existence when born to the Virgin Mary. Members believe that when Jesus returns he will set up his reign as king in Jerusalem, and the church will be his joint heir. Israel will be established in Palestine as the head of nations. The Christian, through repentance, faith, and baptism for the remission of sins, enters into a covenant with God. Members believe in pursuing a life of Christian living and service. They look forward to the return of Jesus to earth to inaugurate his millennial reign in the age to come, and to usher in the eternal Kingdom of God, which will be the believer's reward.

A congregational government is the accepted polity. A general conference meets annually.

Membership: In 2001 the church reported 5,248 members, 80 ministers, and 89 congregations, and it operated missions in Malawi, Russia, the Philippines, India, Mexico, and Peru.

Educational Facilities:

Atlanta Bible College, Morrow, Georgia.

Periodicals: *The Restitution Herald*. • *Progress Journal*. • *A Journal from the Radical Reformation*.

Remarks: Affiliated with the Church if God is the Restoration Fellowship, an organization founded in England in 1981 by Anthony Buzzard. In 1982 Buzzard moved to the United States and joined the faculty of the Oregon Bible College (now Atlanta Bible College). In the United States the fellowship works with the Church of God as an educational ministry supplying written material in support of the church's doctrinal position. In England, a small group remains in existence as a single fellowship.

Sources:

Church of God General Conference (Abrahamic Faith). www.abc-coggc.org/index.html.

Buzzard, Anthony. *The Kingdom of God—When & Whence?* Oregon, IL: Restoration Fellowship, 1980.

————. *What Happens When We Die?: A Biblical View of Death and Resurrection*. Oregon, IL: Restoration Fellowship, 1986.

————. *Who Is Jesus?: A Plea for a Return to Belief in Jesus, the Messiah*. Oregon, IL: Restoration Fellowship, n.d.

Historical Waymarks of the Church of God. Oregon, IL: Church of God General Conference, 1976.

Huffer, Alva C. *Systematic Theology*. Oregon, IL: Church of God General Conference, 1961.

Mattison, James. *The Abrahamic Covenant and the Davidic Covenant*. Oregon, IL: Restitution Herald, 1964.

Church of the Blessed Hope

7450 Wilson Mills Rd., Chesterland, OH 44026

The Church of the Blessed Hope, now somewhat aligned with the Christadelphian movement, began with missionary efforts of the Church of God movement (now organized in the Church of God General Conference [Abrahamic Faith]) in Cleveland, Ohio. In 1863, 14 believers in Cleveland formed a Church of God congregation. At the time, the Church of God was a pacifist group and in 1865 the church affirmed its adherence to that belief. In the following decades, the Cleveland congregation had been responsible for the establishment of similar congregations in Unionville and Salem, Ohio. In 1888, the same year the Church of God formed a general conference, these three churches incorporated independently as the Church of the Blessed Hope, though they continued to receive ministers from the

Church of God into the 1920s. In 1922 the churches received a pastor from the Christadelphians and from that time forward adopted Christadelphian beliefs and practices and began to use a Christadelphian hymnal.

The church is non-Trinitarian and asserts that there is one God, and that Jesus is his son and advocate. All who accept Christ will be resurrected to live with Christ, according to the church, whereas the unsaved will remain in the grave. The church practices baptism by immersion and observes the memorial meal of breaking bread and drinking wine weekly. The church prohibits participation in war, though some congregations allow members to accept noncombatant service in the armed forces.

The church has articulated its own understanding of the kingdom of God, which it sees as a political entity that will be established by Christ in the future. Its initial members will be a small number of those who are alive when Christ returns (primarily infants, children, a few well-disposed individuals, and the saved believers) and who survive God's judgment. They will be joined by the resurrected saints. According to the church, Christ will destroy all human government and all competing religions. War and premature death will be abolished. The kingdom will last for 1,000 years, after which the righteous will be granted immortality and God's direct authority will supersede that of Christ.

Through the twentieth century, other congregations, some Christadelphian in background, affiliated with the Church of the Blessed Hope. The church has tried to establish cordial relationships with the Christadelphians and opens their communion service to them, though that openness has not been reciprocated.

Membership: Not reported.

Sources:

Piepkorn, Arthur C. *Profiles in Belief: The Religious Bodies of the United States and Canada*. 4 vols. San Francisco, CA: Harper & Row, 1977–1979.

Primitive Advent Christian Church

c/o Donald Young, 1640 Clay Ave., South Charleston, WV 25312

The Primitive Advent Christian Church developed out of a controversy centering on the preaching of a Rev. Whitman, a minister of the Advent Christian Church in Charleston, West Virginia. The Rev. Whitman opposed both foot washing and rebaptizing reclaimed backsliders. (*Backslider* means to lapse morally or in the practice of religion.) Proponents of these two practices organized the Primitive Advent Christian Church. On these two points alone, they differ doctrinally from the parent body.

An annual delegated conference meets to carry on the business of the church. It ordains ministers and elects officers. The pastor is the presiding officer in the local church. There are also deacons and elders. The church is small, and all the congregations are in central West Virginia.

Membership: In 2002 the church reported 10 congregations, 546 members, and 11 ministers.

❋ Seventh Day Adventists

Advent Sabbath Church

255 W 131st St., New York, NY 10027

In the early 1940s in Manhattan black Adventists began a movement to unite independent Sabbath-keeping congregations. It was begun by Thomas I. C. Hughes, a former minister in the Seventh-day Adventist Church and pastor of the Advent Sabbath Church, which had been formed in 1941 in Manhattan. The missionary-minded Hughes conceived of the idea of both domestic and foreign endeavors and began to gather support from his congregation. In 1956 the Unification Association of Christian Sabbath Keepers was formed, bringing together Hughes's parish and the New York United Sabbath Day Advent Church. Others joined, including the Believers in the Commandments of God.

There is a wide range of doctrinal belief in the various churches. Immersion is practiced and the Sabbath kept. A general Adventist theology prevails. The polity is congregational. There are annual meetings for fellowship and general conferences every four years for business. At the second general conference, the title bishop was created, but there is no episcopal authority accompanying that title. A 23-member board of evangelism operates between general conferences.

The Unification Association is missionary-minded. Missions had been established by its founders even before the association was formed. Affiliated fellowships can be found in Nigeria, Liberia, Jamaica, Antigua, and Trinidad.

According to the Church Directory in Harlem, New York, the church has changed its name from "Unification Association of Christian Sabbath Keepers" to "Advent Sabbath Church" and remains at the same address.

Membership: Not reported. There were scattered affiliated congregations in Africa and the West Indies.

Periodicals: *Unification Leader*.

Branch Davidians

c/o Clive Doyle, PO Box 144, Axtell, TX 76624

The small, relatively unknown Branch Davidians, more properly called the Branch Seventh Day Adventists, suddenly burst out of obscurity into the national spotlight on February 28, 1993, when agents of the Bureau of, Alcohol, Tobacco, and Firearms (ATF) raided their church center outside of Waco, Texas. The raid failed as church members resisted the agents' assault, and in the ensuing gunfight, ATF agents and church members were killed. Several days later the Federal Bureau of Investigation (FBI) took over what had developed into a siege. The siege ended on April 19 when most of the people inside the compound died following a second assault on the church complex by FBI agents.

HISTORY. The Branch Davidians carry on the work begun by Victor T. Houteff (1885–1955), a member of the Seventh Day Adventist Church in Los Angeles, California. In 1930, Houteff had come to see himself as a divinely inspired messenger of God with the special task of calling for a reformation and the gathering of the 144,000 people mentioned in the biblical book of Revelation 7:4. Some of his basic ideas were put together in a book, *The Shepherd's Rod* (1931). In 1935 he moved to Waco, Texas, with 11 of his followers and established the Mount Carmel Center, originally designed as a temporary assembling point for the 144,000 followers. Their ultimate goal was to reach Palestine, where they would establish the Davidic kingdom with a theocratic regime and direct the closing work of the Gospel age prior to the Second Coming of Christ.

Houteff's movement was tolerated within the Seventh Day Adventist Church for a number of years, though congregations increasingly began to dissociate themselves with Houteff's people. The growing level of tension increased dramatically following the attack upon Pearl Harbor and the United States entrance into World War II (1939–1945) in 1941. The Seventh Day Adventist Church, traditionally a pacifist church, began to call for conscription and refused to back members who claimed conscientious objection status or asked for ministerial deferments to military service. In the crisis, Houteff hastily issued membership certificates and distributed ministerial credentials. The movement, now an independent church, organized theocratically with Houteff as the leader, and assumed the name of Davidian Seventh Day Adventist Association.

Some 125 members came to reside at the Mount Carmel Center with other followers still in Los Angeles and scattered around the country. Houteff died in 1955. Soon afterward, Benjamin Lloyd Roden (1902–1978), then residing in Odessa, Texas, began championing the idea that the Davidians should continue to be led by inspiration (i.e., by a prophet). During September and October he wrote seven letters, which he claimed had been dictated by God, to Florence Houteff (Victor's widow) calling for reform. They were signed "The Branch." Florence countered Roden through her announcement that on April 22, 1959, the 1,260 days of Revelation 11 would be completed and that, on that day, God would intervene in Palestine. He would clear out both Arabs and Jews and create a situation into which the Davidic kingdom could enter. She called for the faithful to gather at an assembly beginning April 16, 1959, and to arrive in Waco ready to move immediately to the holy land.

In the meantime she began to sell off Davidian property and bought a new parcel of land, some 900 acres, located east of Waco, where she erected a new Mount Carmel. In 1958 Roden moved his followers to Israel and began to work out an agreement by which other Davidians could move there. In 1959 some 900 Davidians gathered in Waco to await the fulfillment of Florence Houteff's prophecy. When Roden arrived to present his option of moving to Israel, he was again rejected.

The failure of Florence Houteff's prophecy to materialize became a traumatic event in the movement. Splintering of the branch began and, while some joined Roden, several new alternative groups emerged. In December 1961, Houteff admitted her errors, formally dissolved the Davidian Seventh Day Adventist Association, and put Mount Carmel up for sale. The property was purchased by Roden in 1965. He called his faction the Branch Davidian Seventh Day Adventists. Houteff had declared himself the fourth angel (mentioned in Revelation 8:12). Roden declared himself the fifth angel (Revelation 9:1). He headed the branch until his death in 1978. The previous year, the Branch Davidians had accepted Lois Roden (1905–1986), Benjamin Lloyd Roden's wife, as a prophet and as having new insight on the issue of the femininity of the Holy Spirit. She assumed the role of the sixth angel of Revelation 9:16 and withstood the attempt of her son, George Roden (d. 1998), to succeed his father. Another potential successor was a relative newcomer, Vernon Howell (1959–1993), who had emerged as a talented leader. He had joined the group in 1981 and, by 1983, he had been acknowledged by Lois Roden as the group's next prophet. However, in 1984 George Roden forced Howell and his followers out of Mount Carmel.

With his followers, Howell settled in Palestine, Texas. George Roden was arrested in 1987 and in 1988 was sentenced to six months for contempt of court, a charge growing out of some grossly obscene documents he had filed with the court. With Roden in jail, Howell assumed control of the property and the group. Roden moved to Odessa, Texas, following his release. There, in 1989, he shot a man he claimed Howell had sent to kill him. In a trial he was found not guilty by reason of insanity and was confined in a mental hospital.

BELIEFS. Howell took over the group and, in the tradition of previous leaders, set about the task of discerning his role in the scheme of the book of Revelation, the key to his most unique additions to the Branch Davidian teachings. His understanding was still under development at the time of the siege, and is not fully understood. However, important outlines survived in his final speech and writings. From Isaiah:45, he assumed the name David Koresh (Koresh being a form of Cyrus). Cyrus was the only non-Israelite who was given the title *anointed* or *a messiah* or, in Greek, *a christ*. As a modern-day Koresh, he saw his role as that of the lamb mentioned in Revelation 5. While traditionally this lamb has been identified as Jesus Christ, Koresh dissented and claimed that the lamb was identical with the rider of the white horse who appeared in Revelation 6:1–2 and 19:7–19. The rider clearly was not Jesus.

Koresh made the identification of the lamb and the rider from his reading of Psalm 45. Here, a warrior king was anointed, made into a christ, and rode his horse triumphantly. This warrior king would marry and his princess would be but one among many of his women. Koresh accepted, as his own, the role of the lamb. The lamb's job was to loose the seven seals and interpret the scroll (i.e., bring the end-time revelation of Jesus Christ to the world). By accomplishing that task, people would know his identity. Also, the warrior king's polygamous situation in Psalm 45 undergirded Koresh's assumption of special husbandly prerogatives toward the women of the group.

ORGANIZATION. Mount Carmel was organized communally. Agriculture provided some of its resources, while several residents had outside jobs and businesses, including some dealing with guns. In fact, a stockpile of weapons, some related to a gun business operated by one member, was crucial in the government's plan to move against the church. Other members of the group lived in several locations around the United States, most prominently in suburban Los Angeles.

A significant number of members died in the fire of April 19, 1993 at Mount Carmel. Some of those who survived were placed on trial. While acquitted of the more serious charge of conspiracy to murder, most were convicted of lesser charges growing out of the siege. As of 2008, some have completed their prison term and a few remain in prison. Others, including some members not involved in the siege, began regrouping and have continued as a church. On the second anniversary of the fire, April 19, 1995, many of the surviving Branch Davidian members and their supporters gathered at Mount Carmel for memorial services. Their action was, however, completely upstaged by the bombing of the federal building in Oklahoma City by Timothy McVeigh (1968–2001). It was widely believed that McVeigh and his coconspirators were, in part, seeking revenge for the government's actions at Waco and chose the anniversary for the bombing to convey that message.

In the years since the Oklahoma City incident, members of the Branch Davidians have attempted to hold the now miniscule group together. Among the most active in that cause has been Clive Doyle. He had survived the fire in 1993, and when placed on trial, had been found not guilty on all charges. Most of the survivors recognize Doyle as the trustee of the lineage of the Branch Davidians.

As the new century began, several factions began disputing over the Mount Carmel property. A small chapel had been built on the site of the building that had burned, and a nearby building served as a makeshift museum and bookstore. Among those challenging the survivors for the property was Amo Bishop Roden, the wife of George Roden, who had lost an earlier challenge for the property to Koresh; Doug Mitchell, never a member of the Branch Davidians, who claimed the property based on some legal technicalities; and Charles Pace, who had been a member of the branch in the days of Lois Roden. By 2005, Doyle was the only follower of Koresh at Mount Carmel. He moved away, leaving the property (as of 2008) in the hands of Pace. Pace now claims to lead a reorganized and revived Branch Davidian church, which he has named The Branch, the Lord Our Righteousness. The surviving followers of Koresh have hopes of reclaiming the property at some future date, but an earlier attempt in 2000 to establish their title to it was rebuffed by the court.

Membership: There are 30 to 50 surviving members of the group under David Koresh, including several recent converts. Some 60 people have attended the memorial services in recent years.

Sources:

Adventist Church Official Web Site. www.adventist.org/

Hardy, David T. (with Rex Kimball). *This Is Not an Assault: Penetrating the Web of Official Lies Regarding the Waco Incident*. Princeton, NJ: Xlibris Corporation, 2001.

Newport, Kenneth G. C. *The Branch Davidians of Waco: The History and Beliefs of an Apocalyptic Sect*. New York: Oxford University Press, 2006.

Report of the Department of the Treasury on the Bureau of Alcohol, Tobacco, and Firearms Investigation of Vernon Wayne Howell also known as David Koresh. Washington, DC: U.S. Government Printing Office, 1993.

Sullivan, Lawrence E. *Recommendations to the U.S. Department of Justice and the Treasury Concerning Incidents Such as the Branch Davidians Standoff in Waco, Texas*. Cambridge, MA: Harvard University Press, 1993. 20 pp.

Tabor, James D., and Eugene V. Gallagher. *Why Waco?: Cults and the Battle for Religious Freedom in America*. Berkeley: University of California Press, 1995.

U.S. Department of Justice. *Recommendations of Experts for Improvements in Federal Law Enforcement after Waco*. Washington, DC: U.S. Government Printing Office, 1993.

U.S. Department of Justice. *Report on the Events at Waco, Texas, February 28 to April 19, 1993*. Washington, DC: U.S. Government Printing Office, 1993.

Wright, Stuart A. *Armageddon in Waco: Critical Perspectives on the Branch Davidian Conflict*. Chicago: University of Chicago Press, 1995.

The Branch, The Lord Our Righteousness
1781 Double E Ranch Rd., Waco, TX 76705

In 1993 the Branch Davidian group residing at the Mt. Carmel center outside Waco, Texas, experienced a traumatic event, when their community was raided by agents of the U.S. Bureau of Alcohol, Tobacco, and Firearms. The raid and resultant siege led to the burning of Mt. Carmel and the deaths of 84 members, including the group's leader, David Koresh (born Vernon Howell, 1959–1993), and most of its other leaders. Among the leaders who survived were several who were subsequently tried and convicted on charges related to the deaths of several BATF agents during the initial raid.

In the years after the raid, the surviving members who were not in custody tried to continue, adopting a less formal structure. They also laid claim to the church property. However, the ownership of the property moved into legal limbo, with several claimants speaking up and at different periods taking up residence at Mt. Carmel, where a new chapel was erected.

One of the claimants, Charles Pace, noted that Victor Houteff (1885–1955), the original founder of Davidian Seventh-Day Adventists, organized his movement with an executive council on the assumption that the highest leadership would always be a president chosen by God (that is, an inspired person or prophet with a new message of immediate relevance, which Adventists refer to as the "Present Truth"). Pace had been a member of the general association of Branch Davidian Seventh-Day Adventists since the period during which Benjamin Roden (1902–1978) was its leader, prior to the appearance of David Koresh on the scene. Pace rejected the attempt by the surviving members of Koresh's group to reorganize without a prophet to lead them.

In the mid-1990s, Pace began calling for reform and asserted his appointment by Roden's widow, Lois Roden, to assume leadership following the period of apostate leadership by Koresh. A Divine Judgment appointed Pace as leader, under whom the church, having been purified by the slaughter of its previous leadership and the burning of its headquarters, was to be revived, reorganized, and reformed. To implement this reorganization, Pace followed by-laws of the Church left by Houteff. He assumed the title Joshua, the Man Whose Name Is Branch, and gave the Branch Davidians a new name, The Branch, The Lord (YHVH) Our Righteousness.

For several years both Pace and Clive Doyle, representing the survivors of the Branch Davidians formerly led by Koresh, lived at Mt. Carmel. Doyle departed in 2005, and Pace took charge of the property.

Membership: Not reported.

Sources:

The Branch, The Lord Our Righteousness. the2branches.org/.

Branch Seventh Day Adventists (SDAs)
Current address not obtained for this edition.

The Branch Seventh Day Adventists (SDAs) carry on the work begun by Victor T. Houteff (1885–1955), a member of the Seventh Day Adventist Church in Los Angeles, California. In 1931, he wrote a book, *The Shepherd's Rod*, from which the group derived its popular name. Houteff considered himself a divinely inspired messenger of God with the task of calling for reformation and the gathering of the 144,000 faithful mentioned in the book of Revelation. In 1935, Houteff and 11 followers moved to the Mount Carmel Center, established near Waco, Texas, as a temporary assembling point for the 144,000 faithful. Their goal was to reach Palestine, where they would establish the Davidic kingdom with a theocratic regime and direct the closing work of the Gospel prior to the Second Coming of Christ.

Though denounced by the Seventh Day Adventist Church in which many congregations were disfellowshipping adherents to *The Shepherd's Rod*, Houteff and his followers tried to remain within the Seventh Day Adventist Church until the beginning of World War II (1939–1945). After the attack on Pearl Harbor in December of 1941, members began to be called for conscription, and the Seventh Day Adventists refused to back up the requests for conscientious objector status or ministerial deferment. In a crisis, Houteff hastily issued membership certificates and distributed ministerial credentials. A formal theocratic organization was created, with Houteff as its leader, and in 1942 the name of the organization was changed to the Davidian Seventh Day Adventist Association

At its height, there were 125 members at Mount Carmel. Houteff died in 1955 and was succeeded by his wife. She, in turn, announced that on April 22, 1959, the 1,260 days (as in Revelation 11) would end and that, on this day, God would intervene in Palestine. He would clear out both Jews and Arabs and set the state for the entrance of the Davidic kingdom. In answer to an official call, the faithful gathered for an assembly during April 16 and April 22, 1959, in readiness to move to Palestine. They never recovered from the failure of the prophecy to materialize. Splintering within the branch would soon follow. On December 12, 1961, Houteff acknowledged her error and the lack of soundness of the group's teachings. In March 1962, she and her associate leaders resigned, declared the Davidic SDAs dissolved, and put the Mount Carmel property up for sale.

The Branch SDAs were one of several splinters that broke with the main body of Davidic SDAs following Houteff's death. They did not accept Houteff's wife, opposing her leadership and prophecies. Many of her followers joined them in 1959. At one point, the branch sent colonizers to Israel, but their attempts were unsuccessful. They continued as a small body with their headquarters near Waco. Annual convocations following the Old Testament feast days (as in Leviticus 23) are held at the center. They also manage an organic gardening and farming experimental station for the production of foods free of pesticides and commercial fertilizer.

Membership: In 1986 there were eight congregations in the United States and Canada and an additional 20 foreign congregations.

Periodicals: *Shekineh Magazine*.

Sources:

History up to April 19, 1993, Branch Davidians and FBI Standoff. www.waco-anewrevelation.com/waco-conflict-history.html

Houteff, V. T. *The Great Controversy over "The Shepherd's Rod."* Waco, TX: Universal, 1954.

Church of God (Anadarko)

900 W Alabama Ave., Anadarko, OK 73006

The Church of God (Anadarko) and its Light of Truth ministry were founded in 1986 by John W. Trescott. He was ordained in 1981 by the late M. L. Bartholomew, former chairman of the Apostolic Council of the Church of God, Seventh-day in Salem, West Virginia. Trescott was a member of the Worldwide Church of God from 1959 to 1978, a member of the Church of God, International, and then associated with the Church of God Evangelistic Association.

Trescott observes the Seventh-day Sabbath from Friday sunset to Saturday sunset, and all of the Biblical Festivals of Jesus Christ listed in Lev. 23 and elsewhere. Dates are determined by the visible new crescent to begin months, the way the Bible indicates. Trescott rejects hierarchical church government over the brethren.

The Church of God (Anadarko) is not an organization, but a ministry outreach to members and nonmembers of the Body of Christ. It is engaged in witness and warning via the *Light of Truth* magazine and the *Light of Truth Newsletter*, occasional shortwave radio broadcasts, and through cassette tapes, literature, and booklets on various biblical subjects. Trescott believes salvation is open to all people from all nations and races. There is a keen expectation of the imminent great tribulation and return of Jesus Christ to establish the Kingdom of God on earth.

Membership: Since the church is an outreach program rather than an organization, there is no membership.

Periodicals: *Light of Truth*. • *Light of Truth Newsletter*.

Davidian Seventh-day Adventist Association
Bashan Hill, Exeter, MO 65647

The Davidian Seventh-day Adventist Association continues the work of Victor T. Houteff (1885–1955), a Bulgarian-born convert to the Seventh-day Adventist Church. He became a prominent member in Los Angeles, California, in the 1920s. In 1930 he wrote a 255-page book, *The Shepherd's Rod*, vol. 1, a detailed doctrinal exposition concerning the harvest of mankind. His second volume, published in 1932, was a prophetic analysis. The publication of these books created considerable controversy and led to his dismissal from the church in 1934. Undaunted, he organized the Shepherd's Rod Publishing Association (which later became the Universal Publishing Association) to propogate his views. In May 1935 he moved to Waco, Texas, with twelve members to begin construction of a new headquarters, Mt. Carmel Center. They saw themselves as an association within the Seventh-day Adventist Church and, reflecting this view, used the name Shepherd's Rod Seventh-day Adventists until 1943. During World War II the Shepherd's Rod Adventists held to the view of conscientious objection to war, whereas the Seventh-day Adventist Church held the more relaxed view of participating ni noncombatancy service. This, along with internal pressures from the Adventist Church, forced the Shepherd's Rod adherents to formally incorporate as the General Association of Davidian Seventh-day Adventists in 1943.

At Waco, Mt. Carmel Center spread rapidly on 385 acres and grew to include a school, publishing facilities, and a home for the aged. It had approximately 125 residents at the time of Houteff's death in 1955. During the next decade, the association passed through a series of crises. In 1959, despite strong internal opposition from Davidian leaders, Houteff's widow prophesied that on April 22, God would directly intervene in Palestine and remove both Jews and Arabs in preparation for the establishment of the Davidic empire. Her misguided prophecy failed, creating widespread disillusionment among the membership. The association rapidly divided into two groups, one led by Houteff and another led by the editor M. J. Bingham, which strongly opposed what it saw as her doctrinal and prophetic speculations.

Bingham's group, though not large, was vocal and instrumental in Houteff's decision to discontinue as leader of the association. In December 1961 she admitted the failure of her prophecy and along with several leaders of the Waco faction resigned and put the assets of the association in court-appointed receivership.

Despite this setback, a number of the leaders and members who had opposed Houteff and wanted to continue the association. They reorganized in 1961 in Los Angeles, taking the name Davidian Seventh-day Adventist Association. In less than a year, they moved to Riverside, California, where they remained headquartered until May 1970, when they moved their new center to land purchased in rural Missouri.

The Davidian Seventh-day Adventist Association has no disagreement with the doctrine of the Seventh-day Adventist Church and accepts all of its fundamental beliefs. Rather, it added to those beliefs based on end-time prophecies, a set of convictions about its particular role in history. The association is dediated to the work of announcing and actually bringing about the restoration of the kingdom of David (the biblical king), upon whose throne Jesus, the Son of David, will sit (not literally, but spiritually) in the last days. The association's members consider themselves the vanguard remnant drawn out from the descendants of the early Christians. With the appearance of the sealed people, the kingdom's reign begins. Part of its special task is to sound the "Eleventh Hour Call" mentioned in the *Testimonies for the Church*, a series of prominent books by Ellen G. White, one of the founders of the Seventh-day Adventist Church. The association's work is internalized to the Adventist Church in preparation for sounding the everlasting to every nation, tongue, and people with the intent of gathering the saints into the Davidic kingdom.

In 2008 the Davidian Seventh-day Adventist Association was headed by Jemmy E. Bingham, the president and pastor general, and also had a seven-member executive council. The community in Missouri has a strong agricultural emphasis, based in part upon the belief that agriculture is an essential foundation of education. The 549-acre tract contains an administration building, an apartment complex, several houses, a printing plant, a 300-seat auditorium, a cafeteria complex, and a ministerial school. Members are found on nearly every continent.

Membership: Since most of the association's members also hold membership in the Seventh-day Adventist Church, it does not make a formal census of its adherents; therefore, current membership is unknown, though members are found in 25 countries.

Educational Facilities:

Davidic-Levitical Institute, Exeter, Missouri.

Bashan School of Prophetic Theology, Exeter, Missouri.

Periodicals: *The Bashan Tidings*. • *The Timely Truth Educator*. • *The Communicator*. • *The Report and Analysis Series*. Available from the Universal Publishing Association, Bashan Hill, Exeter, MO 65647.

Sources:

Houteff, Victor T. *Fundamental Beliefs and Directory of the Davidian Seventh-day Adventists*. Waco, TX: Universal Publishing Association, 1943.

———. *The Great Controversy Over* "The Shepherd's Rod". Exeter, MO: Universal Publishing Association, 1936.

———. *The Shepherd's Rod*. Vol. 1. Waco, TX: Universal Publishing Association, 1945.

——— *The Whirlwind of the Lord. War!*. Exeter, MO: Universal Publishing Association, 1987.

General Association of Davidian Seventh-Day Adventists

Mt. Carmel Ct., Box 450, Salem, SC 29676

The General Association of Davidian Seventh-Day Adventists is one of several groups that look to the ministry of Victor T. Houteff (1885–1955) as their heritage. Houteff, a member of the Seventh-Day Adventist Church, began his mission in 1929, and founded the General Association of the Shepherd's Rod Seventh-Day Adventists in 1934. In 1942 he changed the name to the General Association of Davidian Seventh-Day Adventists. Because he claimed the title "David," his followers were called "Davidians." After his death in 1955, the association was headed by his widow, Florence Houteff.

Florence Houteff sold the property near Waco, Texas, which Houteff had built up as the association's headquarters and which he had named Mt. Carmel, and purchased land near Elk, Texas—an act many saw as not authorized by her husband's teachings. She then predicted that 1959 would mark the onset of a new messianic age, a prophecy once again not authorized by Houteff's teachings, and summoned all of the group's members to the new Mt. Carmel center to gather in preparation. When her prediction did not prove true, she gave up the work and left the property to be sold. In 1961 Benjamin Lloyd Roden (d. 1978) acquired the property and established his faction of Branch Davidians there. Roden was succeeded by his wife, Lois Roden, who led the branch until her death in 1986. George Roden, her son, then led the group for three years, after which Vernon Howell (a.k.a. David Koresh; 1959–1993) assumed leadership until 1993, when Mt. Carmel was burned to the ground in a fire.

In 1961 the most conservative remnant of the original association, which still adhered to the Shepherds Rod teachings of Victor Houteff, reorganized and elected new leaders. At that time, the General Association of Davidian Seventh-Day Adventists was formed in Los Angeles and headquarters were established at Riverside, California. In 1970 the headquarters were moved to Salem, South

Carolina, to continue the publishing of Houteff's writings. Shortly before the move, some members separated and moved to Missouri and established headquarters for the Davidian Seventh-Day Adventist Association.

The General Association is headed by a vice president, and Houteff is considered the last president. The vice presidency is currently held by Don Adair, who moved to South Carolina in 1972. He had originally joined the General Association in 1951 and subsequently moved to the original Mt. Carmel Center (1952–1954) to study for the ministry. Under his leadership, the General Association has moved to put all of Houteff's writings into print.

The General Association of Davidian Seventh-Day Adventists is not affiliated with other Davidian associations and is not Branch Davidian.

Membership: Not reported.

Sources:

General Association of Davidian Seventh-Day Adventists. www.davidian.org/.

Adair, Don. *The Fall of the Protestant Nations!* Salem, SC: Expose Press, 1986.

Houteff, V. T. *The Shepherd's Rod Series*. Salem, SC: General Association of the Davidian Seventh-Day Adventists, 1990.

———. *The Symbolic Code Series*. Salem, SC: General Association of the Davidian Seventh-Day Adventist, 1992.

International Missionary Society—Seventh-day Adventist Reform Movement

2877 E Florence Ave., Huntington Park, CA 90255-5751

Alternate Address: International headquarters: PO Box 1310, 74803 Mosbach/Baden, Germany.

A reform movement appeared within the Seventh-day Adventist Church soon after the beginning of World War I, largely due to a softening of the traditional position of the church on pacifism. The head of the church's European Division, Louis Richard Conradi (1856–1939), reacting to a threat for various European governments, suggested that European Adventists might serve in their country's military forces and be active participants on the sabbatj. However, some of draft age rejected the notion and protested the idea. The Adventists excommunicated the protesters and their supporters. Efforts after the war to reunite the reformers to the church were unsuccessful, and by 1922 separation was complete. Formal organization of a Seventh-day Adventist Reform Movement occurred in Gotha, Germany, July 14 to 20, 1925. The organization quickly spread to the United States, Canada, Argentina, Brazil, Australia, South Africa, and Zimbabwe (then Rhodesia). The movement held together, inspired by persecutions during World War II and following the war in Communist Eastern Europe.

Then, in 1951, the movement split. At its 1951 general conference in Zeist, the Netherlands, two factions gathered around two strong leaders. Those who supported Dumitru Nicolici (1896–1981), a Romanian then residing in the United States, led the branch that is now known as the Seventh-day Adventist Reform Movement. Those supporting the then president Karl (Carlos) Kozel (1890–1989) reorganized as the International Missionary Society—Seventh-day Adventist Reform Movement. This latter movement retained the majority support in Europe, especially Germany. While the majority of Americans remained loyal to the Seventh-day Adventist Reform Movement, that support was not unanimous.

In 1967 the first of several efforts to resolve the differences between the two branches was initiated. It failed, but new dialogs were held in the 1980s and 1990s. Although progress was reported, in 2008 the two groups remained separate.

The International Missionary Society—Seventh-day Adventist Church Reform Movement is a fundamental Christian faith that takes the Bible (of 66 books), and the Bible only, as its creed. The general conference is the society's highest legislative body. The writings of the *Spirit of Prophecy* by Ellen G. White (1827–1915) are also considered inspired. In addition to weekly worship services, they conduct lectures (public and private), hold Bible classes, give educational instruction, and publish and distribute literature. Wherever possible, institutions of learning (for the education of young people) and mental health facilities (for the healing of body, soul, and spirit) are established. Support of the organization comes from the tithes and offerings of its members and friends and is used for the spreading of the gospel.

Membership: International Missionary Society—Seventh-day Adventist Reform Movement has about 15,000 members throughout the world.

Periodicals: *The Sabbath Watchman*.

Sources:

International Missionary Society—Seventh-day Adventist Reform Movement. www.imssdarm.org/.

Balbach, Alfons. *The History of the Seventh-day Adventist Reform Movement*. Roanoke, VA: Seventh-day Adventist Reform Movement, 1999.

Kramer, O. *Rise and Progress of the Reform Movement: My Personal Experience*. Huntington Park, CA: International Missionary Society—Seventh-day Adventist Reform Movement, 1994.

The Principles of Faith of the Seventh-day Adventist Church "Reform Movement" and her Church By-Laws. Mosbach/Baden, Germany: General Conference Seventh-day Adventist Church Reform Movement, n.d.

The Lord Our Righteousness Church

Strong City, NM

The Lord Our Righteousness Church was founded in Idaho in 1987 by Rev. Wayne Curtis Bent (b. 1941) and other former members of the Seventh-day Adventist Church, who had complained that the church had become corrupt and moved into apostasy. The church's name was derived from a Bible verse, Jeremiah 33:16. At an initial gathering of members in Redding, California, in 1988, some 300 people were baptized; however, the following year approximately 100 members withdrew from the new church.

Church members were deeply affected by the treatment of the Branch Davidians by government authorities in 1993. They became increasingly distrustful of government control over their lives as manifest, for example, in the public school system and the refusal of tax authorities to declare their church land in Idaho tax-exempt. Concern over the corruption within the public schools occasioned their first publication for widespread distribution, a booklet entitled *Shillum*, which analyzed the disintegrating state of the world and argued that Satan's hand was actually in control.

In 2000 the church traded its land in Idaho for a rural site north of Clayton, New Mexico, called Strong City, and in spring 2001 most members relocated there. The church is sometimes called the Strong City cult. In July, Bent was acknowledged as Messiah and adopted the name Michael of Travesser, a name derived from the Travesser Creek. At the same time, two female members of the group were anointed as his "Two Witnesses," an action based on Revelation 11:3. Since this time, the church has increasingly seen itself as an actor in the endtime events that were described in the biblical books of Daniel and Revelations and which they believe are currently unfolding.

The church inherited its beliefs and practices from the Seventh-day Adventist Church and its founder, Ellen G. White (1827–1915), including an approach to prophetic chronology that allowed them to expect future occurrences as the present order approached its final days. Crucial to the chronology are the prophecies surrounding the 2,300 days or Daniel 8:14, and of the 70 weeks of Daniel 9:24. The church believes that the 70 weeks = 490 days (years) began with Luther's nailing the 95 Theses to the church door at Wittenberg in 1517, thus launching the Protestant Reformation. The end of the 70 weeks thus was seen as 2007. The members also maintain a vegetarian diet.

Their stance, including some extra-biblical prophecies, has brought the church and its leader into conflict both with ongoing critics of the church and local legal authorities. In 2002 church critics accused the church of planning a mass suicide. FBI agents and troopers with the New Mexico State Police visited the church and found the accusations baseless. Two years later the New Mexico State Police returned, again prompted by new accusations of a planned mass suicide, and again found nothing to support the claim.

Membership: In 2008 several news media sources reported 50 people at the church's communal site in New Mexico.

Remarks: In 2008 authorities again entered Strong City, and this time took three minors into custody while they investigated charges of inappropriate contact between them and the church's leader. A few days later, Wayne Bent (Michael Travesser) was arrested on a spectrum of charges relative to his actions toward the minors. Church spokespersons have denied all the charges.

Critics of the church have accused Bent of sexual misconduct based on a prophecy that he was to sleep with seven virgins, which was to include some of the teenage females. Bent has admitted to sleeping with seven virgins, but claimed that all were adult members of the group. This situation remains unresolved as this book goes to press.

Sources:

Shillum. www.apfn.org/thewinds/library/shillum00.html.

People's Christian Church

Christian Fellowship Seventh-day Adventist Church, 777–779 Schenectady Ave., Brooklyn, NY 11203

Elmer E. Franke (1861–1946), a member of the Seventh-day Adventist Church, rejected the claims of Ellen G. White (1827–1915) as a prophetess and, in 1916, left to found the People's Christian Church in New York City. Seven years later, a second congregation was founded in Schenectady, New York, and, the following year, a third congregation was established in New Bedford, Massachusetts. The beliefs are similar to those of the Seventh-day Adventists. Members believe in God, Jesus as one in nature with the Father, and the Holy Spirit as one with the Father and Son. Baptism by immersion is practiced, and the Lord's Supper is celebrated as an ordinance on the first sabbath of each month. Although they accept the Ten Commandments, members believe man was released from the Mosaic Ceremonial law.

Each church is autonomous, but the New York congregation is spoken of as the mother church. Ministers, deacons, and elders are ordained. There were four churches in 1968, two in New York and two in Massachusetts, with members in California, Florida, Maryland, and elsewhere. There were approximately 1,000 members, in all, in 1968. In 2008 the leader of the church was A. Warren Burns, pastor of the congregation in Schenectady. In 1986 the church's periodical, *Light*, was discontinued.

Membership: In 1987 there were two congregations and approximately 1,000 members.

Sources:

Burns, A. Warren. *Civilization*. Schenectady, NY: People's Christian Church, n.d.

Franke, E. E. *Pagan Festivals in Christian Worship*. Schenectady, NY: People's Christian Church, 1963.

————. *The "2300 Days" and the Sanctuary*. Schenectady, NY: People's Christian Church, 1964.

The Registry

Box 180, Marshall, AR 72650

The Registry was founded in 1967 by Cecil Shrock and others of the "Adventist complex" who believed in the Seventh-day Sabbath and the prophetic authority of Ellen G. White (1827–1915). Its purpose was to provide fellowship and cooperation among independent missionary efforts in the United States. Shrock had had worked as a medical missionary in rural Alaska, where he had become aware of the lack of fellowship with among Christians. Hearing other missionaries express the same concerns led him to develop the idea of an association and a newsletter that would publicize efforts, air needs and problems, highlight employment opportunities, monitor legal changes that could affect the work, and, in general, spread news. The most immediate need was overcoming the a sense of separateness and isolation. Thus, the Registry began as an association of Christian workers, but had an open membership to all who accepted its basic teachings.

The Registry follows the teachings of the Seventh-day Adventist Church in believing in the Seventh-day Sabbath; the spirit of prophecy that manifested through Ellen G. White, cofounder of the Seventh-day Adventist Church; the approaching visible return of Jesus; the necessity of striving to develop a perfect character; engaging in service to others; working to reduce the use of drug medication in favor of natural remedies; and cooperating with others who hold the same principles.

The Registry is not incorporated, owns no property, and has no organizations, only individuals as correspondents. Coworkers oversee missionary efforts, some of which are incorporated and which are regularly featured in items in the newsletter. The House of Health, a natural-health center in Marshal, Arkansas, directed by Cecil Shrock, offers public health care and trains lay workers. There is also work in the Philippines and Africa. The Registry is supported entirely by donations from associates and friends.

Membership: Not reported.

Educational Facilities:

The House of Health.

Periodicals: *The Registry Case-file.*

Seventh-Day Adventist Church

12501 Old Columbia Pke., Silver Spring, MD 20904

HISTORY. The Seventh-Day Adventist Church is an evangelical sabbatarian church whose teachings have been supplemented by insights drawn from the prophecies and visions of its founder, Ellen G. White (1827–1915). The church views the ministry and writings of White as prophetic gifts of the Holy Spirit. The church's origins lie in the aftermath of the Great Disappointment of October 22, 1844. When Christ's Second Coming did not occur as the Adventist preacher William Miller (1782–1849) had predicted, a group including White, her husband James White (1821–1881), Hiram Edson (1806–1882), Joseph Bates (1792–1872), Frederick Wheeler (1811–1910), and S. W. Rhodes began to gather disheartened Adventists around them. White had a vision in which she saw Adventists going straight to heaven, and was soon accepted as a prophetess. About the same time, bible study led the group to accept the idea of a Saturday Sabbath. White further confirmed the correctness of this interpretation through a vision she had of Jesus and the tables of stone upon which the Ten Commandments were written. The fourth commandment, on keeping the sabbath holy, was surrounded by light.

White also confirmed for the group an interpretation, originally proposed by Hiram Edson, concerning the 1844 date set by William Miller for the return of Christ. Taking a clue from Hebrews 8:1–2, Edson proposed that Miller was correct in his date, but wrong as to the event that was to occur on that date. 1844 was not the year in which Christ was to come to "cleanse the earthly sanctuary" (that is, come to earth in visible form); rather, it was the year in which he was to initiate the cleansing of the heavenly sanctuary discussed in the text. Once his heavenly work is completed, in an indeterminable but short time, Christ will visibly return to earth.

In 1850, at Paris, Maine, the Whites began the *Review and Herald*, a periodical advocating sabbatarianism and attempting to tie the loose band of Millerites together. In 1860, as those who accepted sabbatarianism and White's teachings

were distinguished from other Adventists, the name Seventh-Day Adventist Church was adopted. The church, which originally included approximately 3,500 members in 125 congregations, was officially organized in 1863.

BELIEFS. Aside from their belief in the seventh-day Sabbath and the sanctuary work of Christ, Seventh-Day Adventists hold to a generally Protestant faith, rooted in the group's origins in communities of Methodists and Baptists. The church's statement of belief includes acceptance of the Bible as the rule of faith and practice, the Trinity, creation ex nihilo (from nothing), baptism by immersion, and salvation by atonement through Jesus Christ. Christ's imminent return will be followed by a thousand-year period (the millennium). The soul is not innately immortal; rather, the dead await the resurrection in an unconscious state. Belief in the seventh-day Sabbath has led to an emphasis on the Old Testament health laws, such as the distinction between clean and unclean meats. Church members abstain from alcohol and tobacco.

Seventh-Day Adventists accept the Bible as their only creed and hold certain fundamental beliefs to be the teaching of the Holy Scriptures. These beliefs constitute the church's understanding and expression of the teaching of Scripture. Revision of church statements can occur at a general conference session if the church is led by the Holy Spirit to a fuller understanding of Bible truth or finds better language in which to express the teachings of God's Holy Word.

ORGANIZATION. The church is organized as a representative democracy. Authority for administering the church is delegated through a system of conferences beginning with the local churches that form local conferences. In turn, these conferences combine into larger, regional (termed union) conferences that meet every five years. The general conference, which also meets every five years, and the executive committee of the general conference, which continues between conference sessions, are the highest administrative bodies of the church. They set policies and manage the church's extensive missionary, educational, charitable, and publishing activities. The church has work in 208 countries, along with home mission activities among a variety of ethnic groups. Its educational system includes 15 colleges and universities, 113 secondary schools, and 941 primary schools in the United States and Canada. The church has attained a reputation for its hospitals (61 in the United States) and its work in health-related activities. Three publishing houses—Pacific Press Publishing Association (Nampa, Idaho), Review and Herald Publishing Association (Hagerstown, Maryland), and Christian Record Services (Lincoln, Nebraska)—publish books and periodicals. The affiliated International Religious Liberty Association has continued the church's concern for church-state issues and publishes a leading periodical in the field, *Liberty*.

Membership: In 2000 the church reported 884,303 members, 4,495 congregations, and 3,147 ordained ministers in the United States, and 49,632 members, 327 churches, and 199 ordained ministers in Canada. There were 11,687,229 members worldwide.

Educational Facilities:

Andrews University, Berrien Springs, Michigan.

Atlantic Union College, South Lancaster, Massachusetts.

Canadian Union College, College Heights, Alberta, Canada.

Columbia Union College.

Florida Hospital College of Health Sciences, Orlando, Florida.

Home Study International/Griggs University, Silver Spring, Maryland.

Kettering College of Medical Arts, Kettering, Ohio.

La Sierra University, Riverside, California.

Loma Linda University, Loma Linda and Riverside, California.

Oakwood College, Huntsville, Alabama.

Pacific Union College, Angwin, California.

Southern Adventist University, Collegedale, Tennessee.

Southwestern Adventist University, Keene, Texas.

Union College, Lincoln, Nebraska.

Walla Walla College, College Place, Washington.

Periodicals: *Adventist Review*. • *Liberty*. • *Listen*. • *Message*. • *Ministry*. Available from 55 W. Oak Ridge Dr., Hagerstown, MD21740. • *Signs of the Times*. Available from Nampa, ID 83707.

Sources:

Seventh-Day Adventist Church. www.adventist.org/.

Damsteegt, P. Gerard. *Foundations of the Seventh-Day Adventist Message and Mission*. Grand Rapids, MI: William B. Eerdmans Publishing Company, 1977.

Land, Gary, ed. *Adventism in America: A History*. Grand Rapids, MI: William B. Eerdmans Publishing Company, 1986.

Maxwell, C. Mervin. *Tell It to the World*. Mountain View, CA: Pacific Press Publishing Association, 1977.

Schwarz, Richard W. *Light Bearers to the Remnant*. Mountain View, CA: Pacific Press, 1979.

Seventh-Day Adventist Church Manual. Washington, DC: General Conference of the Seventh-Day Adventists, 1986.

Seventh-Day Adventists Believe . . . : A Biblical Exposition of 27 Fundamental Doctrines. Washington, DC: Ministerial Association, General Conference of Seventh-Day Adventists, 1988.

Valentine, Gilbert M. *The Shaping of Adventism*. Berrien Springs, MI: Andrews University Press, 1992.

Seventh Day Adventist Reform Movement

PO Box 7240, Roanoke, VA 24019

At the beginning of World War I, a controversy arose among members of the Seventh-Day Adventist Church in Europe when the European leaders committed the membership of the church to combatancy in opposition to the church's historic position of total non-participation in any acts of war and bloodshed. This led to repercussions throughout the church, particularly in the 16 European countries that were directly affected by the war. A minority of members (some 2 percent) refused to accept the reversal of the church's historic position on combat and found themselves disfellowshipped.

After the war, those members who had been disfellowshipped tried to ensure that the original pacifist stand would once again be consistently upheld by the denomination as a whole, but their efforts were without success. In 1920 a meeting was convened in Friedensau, Germany, at which the world leaders of the Seventh-Day Adventist Church and representatives of the separated members met to discuss the issue. The result was that the Seventh-Day Adventist leaders officially repudiated their original stand on participation in the military. The new official position, while mildly recommending noncombatancy, asserted that all church members would have "absolute liberty to serve their country, at all times and in all places, in accord with the dictates of their conscientious conviction."

The minority that had been summarily disfellowshipped sent representatives to the general session of the church held in San Francisco in 1922, but without result. Because these believers had been expelled from the church, they felt that they had no other recourse but to organize themselves separately. They did so at a conference held in Gotha, Germany, in July 1925. The Seventh Day Adventist Reform Movement was formed for the purpose of upholding the principles of all Ten Commandments (Exodus 14:15) through faith in the uplifting power of Jesus Christ (John 14:15, Revelation 14:12).

The Seventh Day Adventist Reform Movement General Conference operated first from Isernhagen, Germany, and then from Basel, Switzerland. After World War II, the headquarters was moved to the United States, and in 1949 was incorporated in Sacramento, California. Because it was deemed more advantageous for a worldwide work to be situated on the eastern side of the United States, the headquarters was temporarily relocated to Blackwood, New Jersey, before being moved to its permanent location in Roanoke, Virginia.

Membership: The Seventh Day Adventist Reform Movement now exists in more than 100 countries and territories, and has a worldwide membership of more than 30,000.

Periodicals: *Reformation Herald*. • *Youth Messenger*. • *Standard Bearer*. • *Sabbath Bible Lessons*. • *Children's Treasures*. • *Junior Searcher*. • *Youth's Explorer*.

Sources:

Seventh Day Adventist Reform Movement. www.sdarm.org.

Church Manual. Denver, CO: International Missionary Society, Seventh-Day Adventist Reform Movement, General Conference, n.d.

International Missionary Society. *Bible Study Handbook*. Denver, CO: Religious Liberty Publishing Association, 1974.

The Principles of Faith of the Seventh-Day Adventist Church "Reform Movement" and Her Church By-Laws. Mosbach/Baden, West Germany: General Conference, Seventh-Day Adventist Church, Reform Movement, n.d.

Seventh-day Christian Conference Inc.

252 W 138th St., New York, NY 10030

The Seventh-day Christian Conference was founded in 1934 in New York City as an independent Trinitarian Sabbath-keeping body. The Bible (Old and New Testament) is its only rule of faith and practice. It observes three ordinances: baptism by immersion, the Lord's Supper, and fellowship. Members tithe. The church holds that war is immoral, and members are conscientious objectors. Only males may hold positions of leadership—bishop, pastor, and elder.

Membership: In 1986 there were two congregations, one in New York City and one in Montclair, New Jersey. There were also four affiliated congregations in Jamaica.

Church of God Adventists

Assembly of God in Christ Jesus

PO Box 770537, Lakewood, OH 44107

The Assembly of God in Christ Jesus was founded in the early 1990s by Bill Phillips, formerly associated with John W. Trescott and the Church of God (Anadarko). Trescott had come to believe that he was possibly one of the two end-time witnesses mentioned in the biblical book of Revelation 11:3. Phillips came to believe that he was a messenger from God, possibly Elijah, the prophet, and has come to believe that the voice of God speaks through him. He terms his teachings *Christian Judaism*.

Membership: Not reported.

Periodicals: *End of the World Report Newsletter*.

Associates for Scriptural Knowledge

PO Box 25000, Portland, OR 97298-0990

The Associates for Scriptural Knowledge (A.S.K.) was founded in 1984 by Ernest L. Martin (1932–2002), former chairman of the theology department at Ambassador College and founder of the Foundation for Biblical Research. After leaving the Worldwide Church of God in the early 1970s, Martin served as president, director, and chairman of the board of the Foundation for Biblical Research for more than a decade, writing most of its publications. In December 1984, a conflict arose when members of the foundation's board accused Martin of perpetuating dogmatism, and Martin was removed from office. Before the end of the month, he and several supporters founded the Associates for Scriptural Knowledge to assist in the restoration of the truth of the Holy Scriptures in the days immediately prior to the Second Advent of Jesus Christ. Headquarters of the new organization were established in Hemet, California. In 1986 it moved to Alhambra, California.

The mission of Associates for Scriptural Knowledge is to bring to the attention of believers the importance of self-reliance and personal responsibility when approaching biblical themes. It is their belief that it is the sole responsibility of the believer to become educated and to realize precisely what he or she believes. They believe that by encouraging people to examine the original documents for themselves, they will help to create greater comprehension of the source material itself. They believe people can know and trust God better by having a historical understanding of the Bible.

Associates for Scriptural Knowledge publishes a wide range of books available through their website and in retail bookshops. Associated with A.S.K. is the Academy for Scriptural Knowledge, a home-study course that entails a systematic presentation of the essential teachings of the Bible. The organization does not promote a pastoral, ritualistic, or liturgical ministry.

Membership: In 1987 the membership was approximately 1,000, of which 800 were in the United States and 100 in Canada.

Periodicals: *The A.S.K. Exposition*. • *Prophetic Encounter*. • *The Communicator*.

Sources:

Associates for Scriptural Knowledge. www.askelm.com/.

Martin, Ernest L. *The Divine Titles and Their Christian Significance*. Hemet, CA: Associates for Scriptural Knowledge, 1985.

———. *Human Destiny and the Crucifixion*. Hemet, CA: Associates for Scriptural Knowledge, 1985.

———. *The Law of Moses, the Passover, and the Lord's Supper*. Hemet, CA: Associates for Scriptural Knowledge, 1985.

———. *The Sanctity of Marriage*. Hemet, CA: Associates for Scriptural Knowledge, 1985.

Association for Christian Development
PO Box 4748, Federal Way, WA 98063

The organization, formerly known as Associated Churches Inc., was formed in 1974 by a group of ministers formerly associated with the Worldwide Church of God. Headquarters were established at Columbia, Maryland. While making note of the accusations against the ministry of Garner Ted Armstrong (1930–2003), son of the founder of the Worldwide Church of God, as part of the reason for their leaving the fellowship, they placed greater emphasis upon doctrinal issues. Among their first actions as a separate organization, they established a committee to review all of the various theological questions under dispute. They issued a 24-item doctrinal statement, which continued many Worldwide Church of God emphases, but rejected tithing in favor of financing by freewill offering and offered a congregational church government instead of the theocratic government of the Worldwide Church of God. Questions on other issues were assigned to a Biblical Studies Committee for discussion and review.

Congregations initially made up of former Worldwide Church of God members were established across the United States and the group began a radio ministry and a periodical, *Impact*. In 1977 an evangelistic-teaching auxiliary organization, the Association for Christian Development (ACD), was formed and much of the work beyond the local congregations shifted to it. Through ACD, the Associated Churches issue a newsletter and the *New Millenium Journal*, numerous booklets, cassette tapes, and conduct radio broadcasts. The group hosts a weekly live "Virtual Church" service via telephone hookup, all of which introduce nonmembers to the doctrine of the Associated Churches. The Association for Christian Development is a Christian ministry dedicated to proclaiming the "Good News" of the coming "Kingdom of God." They believe God has a "Grand Plan" for mankind which at its core calls people to become like God.

Membership: In 2002 the churches reported 1,000 members including about 200 outside the U.S.

Periodicals: *ACD Newsletter* • *The New Millennium Journal*

Sources:

Association for Christian Development. www.godward.org/

Christian Giving or Tithing? Columbia, MD: Associated Churches of God, 1974.

Fundamental Beliefs of the Associated Churches of God. Columbia, MD: Associated Churches of God, 1974.

What Is Christ's Commission to His Church? Columbia, MD: Associated Churches of God, 1974.

Christian Biblical Church of God
PO Box 1442, Hollister, CA 95024-1442

The Christian Biblical Church of God was formed by Fred Coulter in 1982. It derived from the Biblical Church of God which was incorporated in 1979 by a group of former members of the Worldwide Church of God under the leadership of Fred Coulter. The Biblical Church of God included a radio ministry, several churches along the west coast, and one in Canada. Coulter left to found the Christian Biblical Church of God in 1982, and eventually the Canadian congregation disagreed on church policy and became independent as the Biblical Church of God, Canada, but remained in fellowship otherwise.

The church is in general agreement with the Worldwide Church of God. It believes God is a family consisting of the Father and the Son, and denies that the Holy Spirit, the power of God, is a third member of a Trinity. Members are expected to follow God's plan of salvation which involves repentance, faith baptism by immersion, the reception of the Holy Spirit by the laying-on-of-hands, and overcoming and growing in grace and knowledge until the resurrection. The church is sabbatarian, and follows the Old Testament feast days. It also follows the Worldwide Church of God in its belief that the descendents of the people of ancient Israel are the Anglo-Saxon people, not modern-day Jews.

Their stated purpose is to proclaim the true faith of Jesus Christ as revealed in the Word of God. Their website offers both visual and audio studies in a wide range of biblical subjects to help people come to a full understanding of the fundamental doctrines of "true Christianity."

Membership: Not reported.

Periodicals: *The Bible Answers Magazine*. • *Biblical Church of God Newsletter*.

Sources:

Christian Biblical Church of God. www.cbcg.org/

Coulter, Fred R. *The Biblical Truth About Jesus Christ's Crucifixion and Resurrection*. Monterey, CA: Biblical Church of God, n.d.

Coulter, Fred R., and James Sorenson. *When Was Jesus Born?* Monterey, CA: Biblical Church of God, n.d.

Church of God, a Christian Fellowship
Box 1480, Summerland, BC, Canada V0H 1Z0

After the Worldwide Church of God (WCOG) discarded the teachings of founder Herbert W. Armstrong (1892–1936), in 1992 one of the church's leading ministers, Roderick C. Meredith, resigned and founded the Global Church of God to perpetuate Armstrong's teachings. Within a few years approximately 7,000 former members of the WCOG had moved to the Global Church of God.

Meredith adopted the WCOG's hierarchical style of church government and headed the church with autocratic powers. Several years later, differences over his exercise of authority over the church's board led Meredith to leave and found a second church, the Living Church of God. Almost 80 percent of the members of the Global Church of God followed him. The deserted organization was effectively bankrupted and soon ceased to exist.

Most of the members of the Global Church then reorganized as a new ecclesiastical entity, the Church of God, a Christian Fellowship (CGCF). In the 2000s the church entered into discussions aimed at producing cooperation with another WCOG splinter, the United Church of God.

Through its website, the church offers a variety of literature, some of which is posted on the site.

Membership: Not reported. There are fewer than 1,000 members. There are members in the United Kingdom, Australia, Jamaica, Belgium, Canada, and the Philippines.

Periodicals: *Church of God Newsletter*.

Sources:

Church of God, a Christian Fellowship. www.churchofgodacf.ca.

Barrett, David V. *The New Believers*. London: Cassell, 2001.

Church of God, Body of Christ

159 Parker Rd., Mocksville, NC 27028-1074

The Church of God, Body of Christ, is a sabbatarian Adventist group, which, unlike many other Adventist bodies, believes in the Trinity. In common with other Church of God Adventists, members believe in baptism by immersion; keeping the Ten Commandments; celebrating the Lord's Supper annually on the day corresponding to the fourteenth day of the Hebrew month of Nisan; in the bodily, personal, and imminent return of Christ; and in tithing, gifts of the spirit, divine healing, abstaining from all unclean animals (Lev. 11 Deut. 14), and the holy life. The church, as the Body of Christ, is organized into a general assembly and state assemblies with a general overseer and state overseers.

Membership: In 2008 membership stood at 525.

Periodicals: *The True Gospel Advocate*.

Sources:

Church of God, Body of Christ. *Church of God, Body of Christ Manual*. Mocksville, NC: Author, 1969.

Church of God Evangelistic Association

908 Sycamore St., Waxahachie, TX 75165

The Church of God Evangelistic Association is an association of Church of God congregations formed in 1980. Initially four congregations supported the association leadership of David J. Smith, the editor of *Newswatch Magazine*. Smith has produced numerous booklets, a Bible correspondence course, and many cassette tapes and videos for distribution. Evangelistic efforts have been assisted by a radio show heard on stations across the United States.

The Church of God Evangelistic Association follows the non-Trinitarian beliefs of other adventist Church of God groups. The association teaches that God's church is a spiritual organization and not limited to any one earthly organization. Christian believers should be organized to effectively serve God and carry out their commission of evangelism, teaching and baptizing those who repent, but such organizations should not impede the individual's spiritual growth or subvert personal conscience. The association is sabbatarian and observes the annual Passover feast as a time to partake of the memorial Lord's Supper.

Membership: The association does not report membership figures, but in 1987 it reported 93 fellowship groups supporting the association. The periodical circulated 10,000 copies to all 50 states and 31 countries.

Periodicals: *Newswatch Magazine*. • *Restoring Knowledge of God*.

Remarks: The association was originally organized by former members of the Worldwide Church of God, with which it shares most of its beliefs. After working with the association in its formative years and authoring some of its early teaching material, John W. Trescott left to found the Church of God at Anadarko, Oklahoma.

Sources:

Newswatch Magazine. www.newswatchmagazine.org.

Church of God, in Truth

PO Box 1120, Kimberling City, MO 65686

The Church of God, in Truth, was founded in 1993 by James Russell, a formerly ordained elder in the Worldwide Church of God, with which it shares a basic doctrinal perspective. Russell has developed a different belief on a set of issues concerning the Hebrew calendar and the setting of a date for observation of the church's festivals (Israel's festivals as described in the Old Testament). Russell rejects the Jewish Hebrew calendar and relies upon present observation of the beginning dark moon phase to set the date of God's festivals (hence they tend to occur a day or sometime a month earlier than the date set for Jewish observation). Russell also rejects the year 31 C.E. as the time of Christ's death, opting for 33 C.E. instead.

Russell teaches that the seven churches described in the biblical book of Revelation 2–3 refer to eras and personalities in the life of the church. The last two churches described, Philadelphia and Laodicea, refer to the present faithful and apostate church.

Membership: Not reported.

Periodicals: *Prove All Things*.

Sources:

Church of God, in Truth. www.postponements.com

Church of God, International

Box 2525, Tyler, TX 75710

In 1978, following his second suspension from the Worldwide Church of God, Garner Ted Armstrong (1930–2003), son of Herbert W. Armstrong (1892–1986), formed the Church of God, International. From his leadership role in the Worldwide Church of God, particularly his years of speaking on its television program, he had a large following that he immediately began to consolidate and organize. He began broadcasting over the radio from San Antonio. Over time, the radio and television ministry was rebuilt, and Garner Ted Armstrong was seen and heard across North America. A vast body of literature, including two periodicals, doctrinal booklets, and Bible study material, is supplemented by a cassette tape ministry.

The Church of God, International follows Worldwide Church of God doctrine closely but dropped much of the hierarchical structure. It denies the ruling apostolic authority of Herbert W. Armstrong. Although it does not discourage tithing by members, the church does not require it and does not monitor membership giving.

Membership: Not reported. In 2008 there were 48 congregations scattered across the United States and 7 congregations in Canada. There are also congregations in Jamaica and the Phillipines.

Periodicals: *Twentieth Century Watch*. • *The International News*.

Remarks: In November 1995 Garner Ted Armstrong was accused of sexually assaulting a woman in July of that year. Armstrong denied the allegations, but stepped aside as head of the Church of God, International and as the spokesperson of the church's TV broadcast. The issue came to a head in 1997 when the church's board and the ministerial council sought the retirement of the 68-year-old church leader and the cessation of his evangelistic and ministerial activity. Armstrong found their proposal unacceptable; he withdrew from the church and in 1998 founded the Inter-continental Church of God. Apart from the departure of some members to the new church, the Church of God, International continued on its previous course.

Sources:

Church of God, International. cgi.org/site/index.php?option=com_frontpage&Itemid=1.

Armstrong, Garner Ted. *Sunday—Saturday. . .Which?* Tyler TX: Church of God, International, 1982.

———. *Where Is the True Church?* Tyler, TX: Church of God, International, 1982.

———. *Work of the Watchman*. Tyler, TX: Church of God, International, 1979.

Constitution and Bylaws. Tyler, TX: Church of God, International, 1979.

Church of God (Jesus Christ the Head) (UNICO)

Current address not obtained for this edition.

The Church of God (Jesus Christ the Head) was founded in 1972 by a group of Sabbatarian Church of God members who hoped to unite the various factions of the Church of God following the principles of the church in the New Testament. They stood opposed to all divisions and sectarianism. They also opposed all forms of control above the local church. Hence, the Church of God follows a loose congregational polity; each church is completely autonomous. There are no denominational officers or general governing boards. Christ is seen as the only head. Regular unity conventions are held for fellowship among the members around the United States. Each congregation is allowed their opinion on all doctrinal matters. The Lord's Supper is celebrated annually at Passover.

Membership: Not reported. Members can be found throughout the United States and affiliate congregations in Nigeria, India, Canada, Jamaica, and the Philippines.

Periodicals: *The Voice of Unity*.

Church of God (O'Beirn)

13022 Kingston Way, Cleveland, OH 44133

Mailing Address: PO Box 81224, Cleveland, OH 44181

The Church of God, currently under the administrative leadership of presiding elder Carl O'Beirn, was founded in 1970. Members consider Jesus Christ the founder of the church. O'Beirn was formerly a minister of the Worldwide Church of God and while a leader in that organization argued for the observation of not only the Old Testament (Jewish) Sabbath and feast days, but also the observance of the Feast of Booths and observance of the monthly new moon days. The latter led to his excommunication. Following his excommunication, he identified what he believed to be the more correct calculation of Abib, the first month of the Old Testament year. O'Beirn's holy days are generally a month later than the Hebrew calendar. His concerns have been embodied in the teachings of the Church of God and have become the subject of various widely circulated booklets.

The church has a worldwide ministry and O'Beirn has published open letters, supplying information on what he has determined to be the correct days for celebrating the various feast days. O'Beirn's ministry has also been extended through a weekly radio broadcast, "Bible Commentary."

One special aspect of the church's ministry is termed *Psalmos*. Members are taught to sing all of the psalms as a daily act of worship.

Membership: Not reported. Counting members and adherents is contrary to the church's beliefs.

Sources:

Abib. Cleveland, OH: Church of God, 1976.

The Israel Mystery. Cleveland, OH: Church of God, 1975.

Understanding the Law. Cleveland, OH: Church of God, 1974.

Church of God, Philadelphia Era

PO Box 371, Pasadena, CA 91102

The Church of God, Philadelphia Era, was founded by David Fraser in 1986 following the death of Herbert W. Armstrong (1892–1986), founder and apostle of the Worldwide Church of God. Fraser believes that only he and the Church of God, Philadelphia Era, are truly following in Armstrong's footsteps, especially given the doctrinal changes in the Worldwide Church in the post-Armstrong era. The term *Philadelphia Era* refers to the messages to the seven churches found in the biblical book of Revelation 2 and 3. The church at Philadelphia (Revelation 3:7–13) is praised for its faithfulness in the difficult times before Christ's return. It was said to be a church with but little strength that has not denied Christ's name.

Fraser published a set of "qwikread" booklets setting out the teachings of the church.

Membership: Not reported.

Church of God (Sabbatarian)

PO Box 37349, Oak Park, MI 48237

In 1969, there was an unsuccessful attempt to unite the various factions of the Church of God (Seventh-Day), initiated by members of the body in Denver, Colorado, led by Elder Roy Marrs of Los Angeles, California, and his uncle, Elder B. F. Marrs of Denver. The issue of local autonomy, denied to the congregations by the General Conference of the Church of God, had originally led to schism. In Denver, the group became known as the Remnant Church of God, and in Los Angeles, it became known as the Church of God (Sabbatarian). Missions are supported in India, Nigeria, and the Philippines.

Membership: Not reported. In the mid 1970s there were 7 congregations.

Periodicals: *Facts of the Faith*.

Sources:

Church of God Sabbatarian. www.cogsab.org/

Church of God (Seventh-Day, Salem, West Virginia)

79 Water St., Salem, WV 26426

The loosely affiliated congregations of the Church of God that adhered to the Ten Commandments, especially the keeping of the seventh-day Sabbath, had organized a general conference in 1887. At the conference meeting in 1933, a prime issue became the move to reorganize the church from its congregational pattern into one following what was considered an apostolic pattern with 12 apostles, 70 prophets, and seven financial stewards. The move was defeated. However, the main supporters of the reorganization issued a call for a general meeting to be held at Salem, West Virginia, on November 4, 1933. Those gathered, being in unanimous agreement and having resigned from the General Conference of the Church of God, reorganized as a new congregation, the Church of God (Seventh Day, Salem, West Virginia), selecting the 12 apostles, 70 prophets, and seven financial stewards by lot (after the pattern of Acts 2:23–26). The church considered itself the true successor of the Sabbath-keeping Church of God tradition.

During the 1940s, several proposals called for the merger of that church with the general conference. In 1947, merger talks were begun and the merger consummated in 1949. However, following the merger, some members rejected the merger claiming that those taking part from the Salem church acted without any official authority from their congregation and without following the procedure established in the church's constitution. Those rejecting the merger continued the national Church of God organization despite the loss of the majority of ministers and members. Spearheading the opposition was the church at Salem, which retained control of the publishing house. A new periodical, *The Advocate of Truth*, was begun in 1950.

Andrew N. Dugger (1886–1975) was the most famous Church of God, Seventh-Day, leader in the twentieth century. He was born in Bassett, Nebraska.

Dugger's father, A. F. Dugger Sr. (d. 1910) had been an Advent Christian minister. When commissioned by his church to do a study refuting the Sabbath, Dugger Sr. instead became convinced that the Sabbath should be observed. The result was a book he later published, called *The Bible Sabbath Defended*. For more than 35 years until his death in 1910, Dugger Sr. was a leader in the Church of God, Seventh-Day. His son Andrew, a school teacher and farmer, was in his mid-20s when his father died.

Dugger was convinced that a bright light in the sky around him was a sign from God that he should follow in his father's footsteps in the ministry. Dugger immediately sold his large farm and equipment, and went to the University of Chicago, where he majored in theology and public speaking, mastering Greek, Hebrew, and German.

Dugger periodically returned to Bassett to visit his mother and Effie Carpenter (1895–1980), a student of his whom he wanted to marry. Although he first proposed to her when she was 16, it was not until 1925 that they married. They shared 50 years together.

Soon after college graduation, Dugger was invited by the Executive Committee of the Church of God to move to Stanberry, Missouri, to become editor of the *Bible Advocate*, a position his father had held before being forced to retire because of ill health. In 1914, Dugger arrived in Stanberry to begin his work in the ministry. For 18 years he was editor of the *Bible Advocate*, also serving as president of the General Conference of the Church of God. As field representative, he traveled widely, holding evangelistic meetings and public debates. The famous Porter-Dugger debate, between Dugger and W. Curtis Porter (1897–1960), a Church of Christ minister, was later published as a book of over 230 pages. In 1919, Dugger wrote *The Bible Home Instructor*, which publicized the Church of God, Seventh-Day, and substantially increased its membership during the 1920s.

Two of Dugger's most adamant doctrinal positions were (1) a scriptural form of church organization with leaders chosen by lot rather than election, and (2) a world headquarters in Jerusalem, Israel. After visiting Israel for only a year between 1931 and 1932, Dugger returned to live in Sweet Home, Oregon. In 1935, Dugger and Clarence O. Dodd (1899–1955) published *A History of the True Church*, which traces Sabbath-keepers from apostolic times to modern days. Dugger greatly influenced Herbert Armstrong (1892–1986), who was for years affiliated with the Church of God, Seventh-Day, but later formed his own church, the Radio (later Worldwide) Church of God.

Dugger remained pastor at Marion, Oregon, until 1953, when he and Carpenter settled permanently in Jerusalem, and launched the *Mount Zion Reporter*. His aggressive leadership resulted in thousands of converts around the world. Dugger died in 1975 at the age of 89. Dugger's son-in-law, Gordon Fauth, continued the Jerusalem work at *Mount Zion Reporter*.

Dodd, earlier mentioned as Dugger's coauthor and also a founder of the Sacred Name Movement, lived in Salem most of his life. In 1920, he married Martha Richmond (d. 1982). A writer and minister, Dodd firmly believed that he should support himself and his family, earning his own way, and serve the Almighty's people without pay. He worked as a clerk for 35 years for Hope Natural Gas Company until he retired early due to Hodgkin's disease. He died two years later.

Dodd taught a Methodist Bible class. He was standing on Main Street of Salem one day, when a man gave him a tract on the Sabbath, which convinced Dodd of the Bible Sabbath. He never saw the man again, and was convinced the agent was an angel. He became a leading minister in the Church of God, Seventh-Day. At the November 4, 1933, meeting in Salem, when the Church of God split, Dodd was chosen by the lot as one of the 70 elders (along with Armstrong), as well as one of the seven men placed over the business affairs of the church (along with Dugger).

After the 1933 split of the Church of God, Seventh-Day, into the Stanberry and Salem factions, Dodd became editor of the *Salem Bible Advocate*. He had began to accept the annual feast days in 1928, which put him at odds with the leadership. In 1937 he resigned, and began to publish his own magazine: *The Faith*. A year later, Dodd accepted the Sacred Name doctrine. He wrote many articles and tracts, using his own funds to establish a print shop in his home. His writings are sometimes reprinted in *The Faith* magazine, now published by the Assembly of Yahweh. A full list of his articles is available from The Faith Bible and Tract Society, carried on by his daughter, Mary Dodd Ling, since 1978.

Dodd had a close relationship with Elder John Kiesz of the Church of God, Seventh-Day, who held evangelistic meetings in Salem around the 1930s. Kiesz likewise believed in the annual holy days, and was favorable to the Sacred Name doctrine.

Martha Dodd, an integral part of his ministry, died in 1982. Clarence Dodd's associates in the Sacred Name Movement were Squire L. Cessna, John Briggs, William Bodine, and Angelo B. Traina (who translated a Sacred Name bible). When Dodd accepted the doctrine that believers must use the Hebrew names Yahweh and Yahshua, he was rebaptized into the name of Yahshua.

Dodd was perhaps more of a writer than a speaker and debater—an area Dugger was adept at. It is likely that in collaborating with Dugger on the book, *A History of the True Church*, Dodd had the greater part in writing it.

For a history of the Sacred Name Movement, see the article, "Origin and History of the Sacred Name Movement," written by Richard C. Nickels (1947–2006).

Membership: In 1970, the church had seven congregations, nine ministers, and approximately 2,000 members.

Periodicals: *The Advocate of Truth*. Available from PO Box 328, Salem, WV 26426.

Sources:

Church of God (7th Day). www.churchofgod-7thday.org/

A History of the True Church. www.reformedreader.org/history/dugger/authors.htm

Nickels, Richard C. *A History of the Seventh-Day Church of God*. Neck City, MO: Giving & Sharing1977.

Nickels, Richard C. "Origins and History of the Sacred Name Movement." www.giveshare.org/churchhistory/sacrednamehistory.html

Church of God, the Eternal

PO Box 775, Eugene, OR 97440-0775

Church of God, the Eternal, is a remnant of the Worldwide Church of God still teaching the original doctrines first proclaimed by Herbert W. Armstrong (1892–1986).

Because of the controversies within the Worldwide Church of God in the early 1970s, several doctrinal changes were authorized. Pentecost was changed to Sunday and, under certain circumstances, remarriage was allowed for those who had divorced. Some saw these changes as a sign of a general doctrinal decline. Among those who disagreed with the changes was Raymond C. Cole (d. 2001). In 1975 he separated from the Worldwide Church of God and several weeks later formed the Church of God, the Eternal, with headquarters in Eugene, Oregon, where Armstrong had founded the original Worldwide Church of God in 1934, then referred to as the Radio Church of God.

It is Cole's position that God revealed the truth to Armstrong in the early years of the Radio Church of God and appointed him to a special position to teach that truth. Such truth is unchangeable, he believed, and no allegiance is owed to a church organization that departed from truth. From the headquarters in Eugene, the church sends out a monthly newsletter with much content on the feast days, numerous doctrinal papers, and tapes to an unspecified number of members across the United States. Foreign offices are located in Vancouver, British Columbia, Canada, and Lausanne, Switzerland. The church sponsors an annual Feast of Tabernacles gathering each fall.

Membership: In 1995 the church reported two congregations in the United States (Eugene and Portland, Oregon) and one in Canada (Vancouver, British Columbia) served by five ministers. Other groups met informally at points around the United States. There were three foreign congregations, in Switzerland, France, and Nigeria.

Periodicals: The church publishes a newsletter.

Sources:

Church of God, the Eternal, Homepage. www.cogeternal.org/

Church of the Great God

PO Box 471846, Charlotte, NC 28247-1846

Alternate Address: 10409 Barberville Rd., Fort Mill, SC 29707-9132.

The Church of the Great God was founded in 1992 as an end-time ministry by John Ritenbaugh (b. 1932), Richard Ritenbaugh (b. 1966), Martin Collins (b. 1954), and

John Reid (b. 1930), all formerly associated with the Worldwide Church of God, whose doctrinal perspective is basically accepted. Members of the church believe in evangelization or proselytizing, but understand their present commission primarily to be to feed the present flock of Christians (including those still in the Worldwide Church of God and associated movements). A large part of this church is currently in a Laodicean phase, referring to the church of Laodicea discussed in the biblical book of Revelation 3:14—19. God says to the church that it is lukewarm and that because it is neither hot nor cold, he will spew it out of his mouth. Its outreach is made via its Internet site.

Membership: Membership is estimated at 400.

Periodicals: *Forerunner*.

Sources:

Church of the Great God. cgg.org/

Churches of God Outreach Ministries
PO Box 54621, Tulsa, OK 74155-0621

During the 1970s Garner Ted Armstrong (1930–2003) emerged as a key leader in the Worldwide Church of God. However, he was also caught up in several scandals involving extramarital affairs. As a result, in 1974 he was suspended from all church duties. After being reinstated, new problems developed and in 1978 he was finally excommunicated, after which he left to found the Church of God, International (CGI), with headquarters in Tyler, Texas. That church grew to include a modest 3,000 members worldwide, but supported Garner Ted's radio ministry.

In 1995 Armstrong's sexual escapades again became an issue after a masseuse released a videotape to the media and charged him with sexual assault. The ministers of CGI suggested that Armstrong resign his office of church president. He refused and approximately two-thirds of the ministers left in 1996; the following year they founded a new Church of God as a loose confederation of independent congregations, each taking the name of the city where they were located. The association was named Churches of God Outreach Ministries (CGOM).

The Churches of God Outreach Ministries, which continues the perspective of the Worldwide Church of God as slightly modified by Garner Ted, publishes two magazines and offers a set of pamphlets that may be ordered through its Web site. It also sends a weekly e-mail letter to anyone who requests it.

Membership: Not reported. The CGOM has an estimated 1,500 members.

Periodicals: *New Horizons*. • *Fountain of Life*.

Sources:

Churches of God Outreach Ministries. www.cgom.org.

Barrett, David V. *The New Believers*. London: Cassell, 2001.

Congregation of God (Biblical Church of God)
PO Box 612440, San Jose, CA 95161

The Congregation of God (Biblical Church of God) was founded in 1979 by C. E. Barrett, formerly with the Worldwide Church of God, whose general doctrinal perspective is accepted. There are some beliefs unique to the church. Barrett teaches that prior to the biblical great flood, there was no universal language. He also believes that some of the Essenes (a Jewish religious group) were Christians and that the apostle James (Jesus' brother) was invested with an office in the early church similar to the presidency and that Peter and John were his deputies.

Members assemble on the new moons rather than every Saturday. The church does not advocate tithing.

Membership: Not reported. Associated with the church is the First Century Church of God in Vallejo, California.

Congregation of God, Seventh-Day
2751 S Main St., PO Box 2345, Kennesaw, GA 30156

The Congregation of God, Seventh-Day, is a small association of congregations founded in 1992 by a former minister of the Worldwide Church of God, whose general doctrinal perspective it accepts.

The Congregation of God, Seventh-Day, is dedicated to the concept of providing meaningful information behind today's news and world events in the light of biblical prophecy as a means of warning people of future events that will drastically change society during the twenty-first century. By sponsoring the Watch America radio broadcast, publishing *The Herald* magazine and other publications, they are striving to inform people of biblical truths and impending changes facing the world.

Membership: Not reported.

Periodicals: *The Herald*.

Sources:

The Herald: A Magazine of Current Events in the Light of Bible Prophecy. www.watchamerica.com/theherald/past_issues.htm

Homepage WatchAmerica. www.javanex.net/wa/home.asp

Congregation of Yah
Current address could not be obtained for this edition.

The Congregation of Yah was founded as the Church of God 7th Era in July 1973, by Larry Johnson, a former member of the Worldwide Church of God. He had been disfellowshipped in January 1973, after sending a 160-page manuscript detailing his opinions on the organization of the church to the Pasadena headquarters. In December 1973, Johnson left his home in Buffalo, Missouri, and traveled to California to meet Herbert W. Armstrong, the church's founder and apostle. The Worldwide Church of God claimed that it was the Church of Philadelphia (spoken of in Revelation 3:7–13) and that Herbert W. Armstrong was one of the two witnesses mentioned in Revelation 11:3; Johnson hoped to convince Armstrong that he was the other witness. Johnson was rebuffed, but continued for several years to contact Armstrong. As internal turmoil disrupted the church, and Garner Ted Armstrong (Herbert Armstrong's son) was disfellowshipped, Johnson began to revise his understanding of the meaning of the Book of Revelation. He concluded that the Worldwide Church of God was not the Philadelphia Church, but the Church of Sardis (Revelation 3:1–6) and that Garner Ted Armstrong, not Herbert Armstrong, was the witness. Over the years he also absorbed some Sacred Name Movement ideas and, in 1978, he changed the name of the Church of God 7th Era to the Congregation of Yah. To date, Garner Ted Armstrong and the Church of God International have made no acknowledgement of Johnson. The Congregation of Yah is built around an inner family of supporters and a far larger group who receive Johnson's mailings. The Feast of Tabernacle is celebrated annually.

Membership: Not reported. In 1978 about 400 people supported the Congregation as coworkers. A smaller number were active supporters. About 7,000 people receive Johnson's material with some regularity.

Periodicals: *Activity Bulletin*. Available from Box S, Beebe, AR 72012.

Foundation for Biblical Research
PO Box 373, 43 Paris Ave., Charlestown, NH 03603

Among the most popular of the Worldwide Church of God leaders was Dr. Ernest L. Martin (1932–2002), former chairman of the theology department at Ambassador College in Pasadena, California. With several colleagues and a group of supporters in the Pasadena area, he formed the Foundation for Biblical Research and began to circulate tapes and literature on such topics as tithing, marriage, the Sabbath, and church government. A monthly Foundation newsletter, now called the *Foundation Commentator*, was established and regular research papers were issued on a wide variety of topics. Bible history, theological topics, and Christian living have been emphasized. The Foundation program encourages small groups of believers to meet in their homes regularly for prayer and study. Dr. Martin and his associates also traveled widely, speaking to believers around the country. Exact membership figures have not been reported.

The Foundation has departed from Worldwide Church of God doctrine on several points: It believes in congregational church government and sees autocratic forms as being condemned by Christ; doctors are allowed; tithing has been dropped in favor of free-will offerings; and baptism is no longer practiced.

In 1985 the board of the Foundation voted to enlarge the scope of their publications to reflect a broader set of opinions and to publish a much higher percentage of material not authored by Martin. This occasioned a split in the Foundation, with Martin leaving to found the Associates for Scriptural Knowledge. The new arrangement represented not so much a change in doctrinal perspective as a new administrative order.

Membership: Not reported.

Periodicals: *The Foundation Commentator.*

Sources:

Church Government and Church Organization. Pasadena, CA: Foundation for Biblical Research, 1974.

Martin, Ernest L. *Passover, Lord's Supper, Communion*. Pasadena, CA: Foundation for Biblical Research, 1975.

———. *The Tithing Fallacy*. Pasadena, CA: Foundation for Biblical Research, 1979.

The Sabbath and the Christian. Pasadena, CA: Foundation for Biblical Research, 1974.

General Conference of the Church of God (Seventh-Day)

c/o General Conference Offices, PO Box 33677, Denver, CO 80233
Alternate Address: 330 W 152nd Ave., Broomfield, CO 80020.

During the two decades following the Great Disappointment of 1844, the followers of William Miller (1782–1849) became grouped into what became the larger Adventist churches. However, numerous Adventists remained independent of the larger churches. Many sabbatarians, in particular, rejected the "visions" of Ellen G. White (1827–1915) of the Seventh-Day Adventist Church. Some of these independents associated together in 1863 around a periodical, *The Hope of Israel*, published in Hartford, Michigan. Enos Easton, Samuel Davison, and Gilbert Cranmer were among the leaders. *The Hope of Israel* continued intermittently for several years and, in 1866, was formally established at Marion, Iowa, under the aegis of the Christian Publishing Association. By this time, the name Church of God was in general use and was eventually adopted as the "denominational" name.

During the nineteenth century, the movement grew around the periodical and the evangelical endeavor of its leaders. In 1889, the headquarters were moved to Stanberry, Missouri. The periodical continues as *The Bible Advocate*. In 1906, the associated congregations registered as the Church of God (Adventist) Unattached Congregations.

The General Conference of the Church of God (Seventh-Day), as the church is known today, has emerged with a moderate Old Testament emphasis. It believes that the Christian should lead a life of obedience to God, which includes observance of the Ten Commandments and the Sabbath. The use of tobacco, alcohol, and narcotics is discouraged. Christmas, Easter, Lent, Good Friday, and Sunday are considered pagan holidays. The group believes that tithing is the method of church financing. The church is popularly called the Church of God (Seventh-Day), and will be referred to by that title frequently in this chapter.

Organization is congregational, and a general conference meets every two years. A ministerial council oversees ministerial licensing. The Bible Advocate Press publishes numerous booklets, church school materials, and several periodicals. Missions are supported in 25 countries.

Membership: Not reported.

Educational Facilities:
Summit School of Theology, Broomfield, Colorado.

Periodicals: *Bible Advocate.*

Sources:

General Conference Church of God (Seventh Day). www.cog7.org/.

Church Manual of Organization and Procedure. Stanberry, MO: Church of God Publishing House, 1962.

Coulter, Robert. *The Story of the Church of God (Seventh Day)*. Denver, CO: Bible Advocate Press, 1983.

Doctrinal Beliefs of the Church of God (Seventh Day). Denver, CO: Bible Advocate Press, 1974.

Nickels, Richard. *A History of the Seventh Day Church of God*. Author, 1977.

The 2,300-Day Prophecy of Daniel Eight. Stanberry, MO: Bible Advocate Press, 1960.

General Council of the Churches of God

1827 W 3rd St., Meridian, ID 83642-1653

The General Council of the Churches of God grew out of a 1950 meeting held in Meridian, Idaho, by former members of the General Conference of the Church of God. These former members wished to continue the congregational polity followed by the parent body in the years before its 1949 merger with the Church of God (Salem, West Virginia) and the church's subsequent adoption of some aspects of the "apostolic" church government of the Salem body.

Today, the council supports mission work in Argentina, Brazil, Canada, England, Ghana, India, Jamaica, Kachinland, Kenya, Mexico, Myanmar, Nigeria, Philippines, and the West Indies.

Membership: There are more than 50 congregations in the United States and Canada, and more than 200 in the mission areas listed above; additionally, there are many independent congregations that unofficially associate with the council.

Educational Facilities:

Maranatha College, Meridian, Idaho.

Periodicals: *ACTS • The Fellowship Herald*

Sources:

General Council of the Churches of God. www.actsforgod.org/.

A Declaration of Things Most Commonly Believed among Us. Meridian, ID: Church of God Publishing House, 1963.

Nickels, Richard C. *History of the Seventh Day Church of God*. Author, 1977.

Walker, Frank M. *The Beast, His Image, and the Two-Horned Beast*. Meridian, ID: Church of God Publishing House, n.d.

Harmony of Life Fellowship

1434 Fremont Ave., Los Altos, CA 94022

The Harmony of Life Fellowship was founded in 1955 by Dr. Roy B. Oliver, formerly a minister with the Unity School of Christianity. Using a basic metaphor of harmony and balance, the fellowship seeks to awaken humanity's hidden faculties and assert what it perceives to be the timeless spiritual values undergirding human life. The purpose of life is the achievement of a brilliance of mind, a nobility of character, a perfection of the body, and an exaltation of spirit. Each of these can be attained through the ancient wisdom taught as the inner truth in all religions through the application of specific techniques of meditation and concentration, study and reflection, worship, and a devotion to the highest ideals. The fellowship was incorporated in 1957, and during the 1960s its work was extended through the formation of the Harmony College of Applied Science, the International University, and the International Society of Naturopathy.

The fellowship finds truth in the mystical Christianity of the first three centuries, before the church lost its spiritual mooring in a literal interpretation of that which was meant to be understood metaphorically and allegorically. The inner mystical interpretation of the scripture leads to the same basic truth found in all religions. Each individual is a soul on a journey of growth through a series of incarnations and lives among an assemblage of souls whose evolution is being guided by the Great White Brotherhood, the spiritual hierarchy.

The fellowship assumes a nondogmatic approach to Truth. It is to be found in the searching by each individual. The fellowship tries to create an environment where every individual can discover the Truth in his or her own unique manner. It believes that humans are inherently divine, and as they pursue spiritual reality, they perceive the oneness of life expressed on the seven levels of reality. Being divine, they should seek to express the perfection of God. Service, expressed in facilitating the healing of self and others, is encouraged. The universe is the body of God and operates according to immutable spiritual laws.

The development of the individual is best accomplished through group endeavor. Group worship is encouraged by the fellowship as is the formation of "shareview" groups (six or more people who meet in homes to share their views on important matters). The seven traditional Christian sacraments are practiced according to an esoteric interpretation.

To aid the progress of the individual, the society offers a variety of study materials organized into courses. Through the college, both basic and advanced degrees may be secured in a variety of subjects. The college is structured in an alternative off-campus style with each student proceeding at his or her own pace. Students may seek ordination as Harmony of Life ministers and then choose to begin a chapter of the fellowship. Ministers may choose to become members of the Harmony Ministerial Alliance. The fellowship is affiliated with the Union of Christian Universal Churches headquartered in France.

Membership: Not reported.

Educational Facilities:

Harmony College of Applied Science, Los Altos, California.

International University, Los Altos, California.

Sources:

Harmony of Life. Los Gatos, CA: Harmony of Life Fellowship, 1991.

The Master Key: A New Faith for the New Age. Los Altos, CA: Harmony of Life Fellowship, n.d.

Intercontinental Church of God (ICG)

PO Box 1117, Tyler, TX 75710

During the mid-1970s, Garner Ted Armstrong (1930–2003), founder of the Church of God International, was in conflict with the board and ministerial council of the church over charges concerning his conduct. While denying the charges against him, which were not made public until 1994, Armstrong stepped down as the head of the church. Then, in 1997, the ministerial council moved to permanently retire him and seek his agreement to cease functioning as a minister/evangelist. Armstrong found this plan unacceptable and withdrew from the church and in January 1998 founded the Garner Ted Armstrong Evangelistic Association (PO Box 747, Flint, MI 75762) as a structure within which to continue his evangelistic endeavors. He also soon discovered that many of the members of the Church of God International wished to continue in a church relationship with him and a few months later he founded the Intercontinental Church of God (ICG).

The ICG continues the doctrinal stance of the former body, the differences being purely administrative.

Membership: Not reported. Members are found in Great Britain, Ireland, Norway, Canada, Australia (including Tasmania), and the Philippines.

Periodicals: *Worldwatch*.

Sources:

Intercontinental Church of God. www.intercontinentalcog.org/.

Living Church of God

PO Box 3810, Charlotte, NC 28227-8010

Alternate Address: Canadian Headquarters: Living Church of God, PO Box 27202, Toronto, ON, Canada M9W 6L0.

In the years following the death of founder Herbert W. Armstrong (1892–1986) in 1986, the Worldwide Church of God (WCOG) dropped his distinctive teachings (from tithing to sabatarianism) one by one under its new pastor general, Joseph W. Tkach (1927–1995), and moved closer to Evangelical Protestant standards. Eventually, it was accepted into the National Association of Evangelicals.

Many ministers rejected these changes, including Roderick C. Meredith, who had been one of Armstrong's earliest students and a prominent leader in the church. He had been a member since 1949. Meredith left in 1992 and founded the Global Church of God, which continued most of the teachings of the old Worldwide Church. Because of Meredith's high profile in the WCOG, many members left to join the new church and within a few years the Global Church grew to around 7,000 members.

As WCOG's apostle, Armstrong had operated as head of a "top-down" church structure, and Meredith attempted to follow this same single-leader model of church authority. However, in 1998 he and the board of the Global Church came into conflict and the board attempted to reign in Meredith's authority. In the midst of the controversy, Meredith left the Global Church and founded the Living Church of God. Some 70 to 80 percent of the ministers and members left with him. The loss of so many members left the Global Church heavily in debt. It moved into bankruptcy and eventually reorganized as the Church of God, a Christian Fellowship (CGCF).

The Living Church of God is the second- or third-largest offshoot from Worldwide. It claims to hold to all of the traditional teachings of Herbert W. Armstrong and the WCOG at the time of his death. Like most of the offshoots, it has a strong emphasis in its literature and broadcasts on examining world news to "prove" that these are the end-times. It has a radio show, "Tomorrow's World," that continues the show of the same name formerly sponsored by the Worldwide Church. The church also sponsors broadcasts in French and Spanish.

Membership: The Living Church of God is active in North and South America, Europe, Asia, Africa, and Australasia. As of 2001, there are approximately five to six thousand members, over two hundred congregation, and scores of ordained ministers.

Periodicals: *Tomorrow's World*.

Sources:

Living Church of God. www.livingcog.org/.

Barrett, David V. *The New Believers*. London: Cassell, 2001.

Tkach, Joseph. *Transformed by Truth*. Sisters, OR: Multnomah Books, 1997.

Philadelphia Church of God

PO Box 3700, Edmond, OK 73083-3700

Alternate Address: Canadian Headquarters: Philadelphia Church of God Canada, PO Box 315, Milton, ON, Canada L9T 4Y9.

The Philadelphia Church of God emerged out of reactions to perceived changes in the Worldwide Church of God following the death of the latter's founder, Herbert W. Armstrong (1892–1986), and the emergence of Armstrong's successor, Joseph W. Tkach (1927–1995). These changes involved dropping some distinctive beliefs of the church and movement toward the doctrinal stance of Evangelical Protestantism. This move was signaled by the removal of many publications from print, including ones written by Armstrong. Many members and leaders of the Worldwide Church of God opposed those changes. Among those who challenged the changes were two ministers, Gerald Flurry and John Amos, and as a result of their protest in 1989 they were disfellowshipped and founded the Philadelphia Church of God. Flurry and Amos published an apology, *Malachi's Message*, which they began to mail out in January 1990. In February they published the first issue of a new magazine, *The Philadelphia Trumpet*, as the official organ of the new church.

Flurry and Amos developed their rationale for founding the church from their reading of the biblical book of Revelation, chapters 2 and 3, which includes the messages to the seven churches. These chapters have often been interpreted as a prophetic outline of history, an interpretive perspective adopted within the Worldwide Church of God. Church members viewed Herbert W. Armstrong as having been raised up by God to begin a new era, the Philadelphia Church era (Rev. 3:7–13). It is the opinion of the Philadelphia Church of God that under Tkach the Worldwide Church of God has veered from the Philadelphia stance articulated by Armstrong and has become the Laodicean church. People faithful to the Philadelphian stance have had to reorganize to continue their life.

The Philadelphia Church of God continues the doctrines of the Worldwide Church of God prior to 1986, and it has been at pains to document each change through a booklet, *Worldwide Church of God Doctrinal Changes and the Tragic Results*, and in articles in *The Philadelphia Trumpet*. It has also moved to put Armstrong's books back in print, beginning with *The United States and Britain in Prophecy* and *Mystery of the Ages*.

The church continues the teachings of the larger Church of God movement. It is non-Trinitarian, observes the seventh-day Sabbath, and recognizes two ordinances, baptism and the annual observance of the Passover, which includes foot washing. The Old Testament festivals are observed and the more familiar holidays—Christmas, Easter, Halloween, and Valentine's Day—are denounced. The church also holds to the belief in the special position in cosmic history held by Herbert W. Armstrong, who they believe is the Elijah figure mentioned in such biblical passages as Matthew 17:10–13.

The church also has a strong belief in British Israelism, which asserts the prophetic significance of Britain and the United States as the literal descendants of ancient Israel. British Israelism has been played down in recent years by the Worldwide Church of God. The church emphasizes prophecy and believes that most prophetic passages of the Bible are being fulfilled in the current generation.

The Philadelphia Church of God found immediate support, both among people who had been disfellowshipped by the Worldwide Church and among those who had left it on their own. It quickly developed support in Canada, Europe, New Zealand, the Philippines, and Australia. It also launched a radio show and a television program, the "Key of David," which is aired on cable in the United States, Canada, Asia, and Europe.

Membership: In 1997 the Church reported approximately 5,000 baptized members and 98 congregations in the United States. Additionally, the church has congregations across Canada and in England, other European countries, New Zealand, Australia, South Africa, and throughout Latin America.

Periodicals: *The Philadelphia Trumpet* • *Royal Vision* • *Philadelphia News*

Sources:

Philadelphia Church of God. www.pcog.org/.

Flurry, Gerald. *The Ezekiel Watchman*. Edmond, OK: Philadelphia Church of God, 1992. 71 pp.

————. *Jeremiah: Prophet of Doom or Hope?* Edmond, OK: Philadelphia Church of God, 1993. 43 pp.

————. *Lamentations and the End-Time Laodiceans*. Edmond, OK: Philadelphia Church of God, 1993. 37 pp.

————. *Malachi's Message*. Edmond, OK: Philadelphia Church of God, 1992. 162 pp.

The Pure Truth

Lock Box 126, Hamilton, TX 76531

The Pure Truth is a ministry and fellowship of believers founded in Pasadena, California, in 1979 by Richard Scott, who was formerly a member of the Worldwide Church of God and the Church of God International. Scott came to believe that he was a prophet sent to speak especially to former and present members of the Worldwide Church and its offshoots. He received his commission to preach from several visions and vivid dreams that also gave him insight into some future events, many of which subsequently occurred. He believes that he is the only true heir to Herbert W. Armstrong's work of proclaiming the truth.

While generally following the beliefs of the Worldwide Church of God as it was prior to Armstrong's death in 1986, Scott has developed some distinctive ideas. He employs the sacred name in speaking of the Creator and Savior. He accepts some of the tenets of the British Israel idea but believes that the United States, not Great Britain, is to be identified with the scriptural Ephraim and New York City with mystery Babylon. He believes that the first (preparation) day of the Feast of Unleaven Bread (an important date in the Worldwide Church of God annual calendar) is on the 14th of the first solar calendar month, but that the Feast proper begins on the 15th and lasts for seven days, and that the first day of the 50-day count to Pentecost starts on the day after the Last Feast Sabbath. He rejects the idea of the lunar month as having anything to do with the sacred calendar.

Membership: Not reported.

Educational Facilities:

APT School of Scripture and Truth.

Periodicals: *The Pure Truth Magazine*. • *Ephesian Messenger Newsletter*. • *The Prophetic Notebook Newsletter*. • *The Hamilton Crier Newspaper*. • *The Restoration of ALL Things Has Begun!* • *Back-to-Scriptural-Basics*.

Sources:

The Pure Truth. www.users.htcomp.net/apt/The_PURE_TRUTH.htm.

Restoration Church of God

2375 E Tropicana Ave., Ste. 158, Las Vegas, NV 89119

The Restoration Church of God was founded in 1993 by M. John Allen, a former member of the Worldwide Church of God, whose general doctrinal perspective is accepted by the Restoration Church. Allen teaches that Herbert W. Armstrong, the late founder/apostle of the Worldwide Church, was a modern-day Elijah, but that the church he founded has departed from the Truth. Today, Allen believes, the Restoration Church is the only work of God that is building on God;s foundation.

Membership: Not reported.

Periodicals: *The Clear Truth*.

Sources:

The Clear Truth. www.holysmoke.org/sdhok/rev05.htm.

Restored Church of God

PO Box 23295, Wadsworth, OH 44282

Alternate Address: Canadian Headquarters: PO Box 4064, St. Catharines, ON, Canada L2R 7S3.

In the 1990s, as the Worldwide Church of God transformed from a sabbatarian Adventist group to a mainline Evangelical Protestant group, it lost many members. In 1992 one of the prominent ministers, Roderick C. Meredith, left and took a number of ministers and some 7,000 members with him to found the Global Church of God. He claimed to be keeping faith with Worldwide Church of God founder Herbert W. Armstrong's teachings as they were at the time of Armstrong's death. Then, in 1998, the Global Church of God experienced a conflict over its administrative structure (which Meredith headed as the sole leader), and as the conflict heated up, Meredith left and took more than 80 percent of the members with him to found the Living Church of God.

Shortly after Meredith left the Global Church of God, another minister, David C. Pack, also left and founded the Restored Church of God, which took even a harder conservative line than that assumed by Meredith. Pack went on to publish a book-length list of 280 teachings, which he felt that the Worldwide Church of God of the 1990s had changed from what Armstrong had taught in earlier decades. To this list, he added a second list of an additional 174 teachings from which all the other off-shoots (including the Living Church of God) also deviated. These changes are related to major doctrines concerning tithing, the observance of the Sabbath, and the role of women, as well as many minor points.

Membership: The Restored Church of God has several thousand members.

Periodicals: *The Pillar of the Truth*.

Sources:

The Restored Church of God. www.restoredcog.org.

Seventh-Day Church of God

PO Box 804, Caldwell, ID 83606-0804

The Seventh-Day Church of God was formed in 1954 by several ministers of the Church of God (Seventh-Day) headquartered in Salem, West Virginia. They rejected that church's stance on divorce (allowing divorced and remarried ministers and/or spouses to continue as ministers). They also embraced the observance of the seven annual Holy Days. Otherwise the church follows most of the doctrine commonly known to the sabbatarian Church of God groups. The church is headed by a chairman and secretary, apostles, elders, evangelists, and teachers. Mission work is supported in several countries.

Membership: Not reported. The church believes that membership records are in the *Lambs Book of Life* and thus no earthly records as such are kept.

Educational Facilities:

Zion Faith College.

Periodicals: *The Herald of Truth*.

Sources:

Nickels, Richard C. *A History of the Seventh Day Church of God*. Author, 1977.

Triumph Prophetic Ministries (Church of God)

PO Box 292, Altadena, CA 91003

The Triumph Prophetic Ministries (Church of God) was founded in 1987 by William Dankenbring, a former member of the Worldwide Church of God, the general doctrinal framework of which is accepted. The church disagrees on a variety of particular points, however. Most importantly, the church does not believe that Herbert W. Armstrong, the founder/apostle of the Worldwide Church, was a modern-day Elijah figure. It does believe that the seven churches described in the biblical book of Revelation 2–3 are indicative of seven church eras leading up to the present. The Church of God is the faithful remnant, and most of the other Worldwide splinter groups belong to the Laodicean era of lukewarm believers.

As to the Jewish feasts, the church teaches that Passover should be kept according to the Lunar Karaite Hebrew calendar on Nisan 15 (not 14), and Pentecost on Sivan 6, the dating being a matter of great concern to Worldwide Church members. Passover should include the eating of a Passover meal. The Feast of Tabernacles should be celebrated wherever possible and kept in actual booths as described in the Bible. The church accepts the British Israel theology but believes that the United States is to be identified with ancient Ephraim, and not with Manassah, as is commonly done.

The church teaches that man is living in the end-times and is preparing for the battles that shall characterize this period. Among the prophetic personages and entities that have appeared are the King of the South (Egypt), the King of the North

(NATO, Europe, and U.S. allies), the Beast (who may be William Clayton, and the Man of Sin. There will be a New World Order under the United Nations.

Membership: Not reported.

Periodicals: *Prophecy Flash*.

Sources:

Triumph Prophetic Ministries. www.triumphpro.com/.

Twentieth Century Church of God

PO Box 2900, Vista, CA 92085

Among the church leaders to leave the Worldwide Church of God in 1974 was Al Carrozzo, regional director of the church's work in the western half of the United States and director of the Counseling and Guidance Office in Pasadena. He accused Garner Ted Armstrong, son of founder-apostle Herbert W. Armstrong, of adultery (citing numerous instances over a period of years), and continued to raise the issue in his monthly *Newsletter*. He also pushed for a change in the church's demand that people living with a second spouse following a divorce and remarriage leave their spouse because they would be living in adultery.

After leaving the church, Carrozzo formed the Twentieth Century Church of God, began a tape and literature ministry, started a radio show carried on several stations, and traveled around the country talking to groups who had left the Worldwide Church of God. The monthly newsletter contained two sections: one that discusses continuing concerns within the Worldwide Church of God, and another that focuses on the Twentieth Century Church of God's main emphases—spiritual growth, prayer, Christian living, and preaching the gospel of reconciliation. These emphases emerge within a context of general agreement with Worldwide Church of God doctrine.

Membership: Not reported.

Periodicals: *Newsletter*. Available from Box 129, Vacaville, CA 95688.

Sources:

Carrozzo, Al. *Christmas*. Vacaville, CA: Twentieth Century Church of God, n.d.

———. *How to Study the Bible*. Vacaville, CA: Twentieth Century Church of God, n.d.

———. *Who Is Qualified to Be Your Minister?* Vacaville, CA: Twentieth Century Church of God, n.d.

Twentieth Century Church of God. *Our Christian Responsibilities*. Vacaville, CA: Author, n.d.

Twentieth Century Church of God (Pennsylvania)

PO Box 25, Nineveh, PA 15344

The Twentieth Century Church of God was founded in 1990 by C. Kenneth Rockwell and David E. Barth Jr., both former members of the Worldwide Church of God. The church (not to be confused with the other church of the same name) accepts the basic doctrinal perspective of the Worldwide Church of God, especially as it existed prior to the doctrinal changes of the early 1990s. It is very close to the position of the Church of God International and the Triumph Prophetic Ministries (Church of God), with whom it cooperates. In regard to the church festivals, it teaches that Passover should be kept on Nisan 15 and Pentecost on Sivan 6. It rejects tithing.

Membership: Not reported.

Periodicals: *Voice from Afar Newsletter*.

United Biblical Church of God

PO Box 547, Crystal River, FL 32623

The United Biblical Church of God was formed in 1992 as an association of autonomous congregations by Charles Kimbrough, Mark Carr, and Chris Patton, all former members of the Worldwide Church of God. The general doctrinal perspective of the Worldwide Church of God is accepted, but the church has a number of specific disagreements with it. Most importantly, the church has departed from the sabbatarianism of the Worldwide Church and has concluded that Jesus was resurrected on Sunday, not Saturday. The church keeps to the Jewish festivals but rejects the Hebrew calendar. Thus it celebrates the festivals a month later than other groups. It also observes the new moon.

Membership: Not reported.

Periodicals: *The Jerusalem Sentinel.*

United Church of God, an International Association
PO Box 541027, Cincinnati, OH 45254-1027
Alternate Address: Box 144, Sta. D, Etobicoke, ON M9A 4X1, Canada.

The United Church of God, an International Association, was formed in 1995 by a group of former ministers and members of the Worldwide Church of God. During the years following the death of Worldwide Church of God founder Herbert W. Armstrong (1892–1986), his successors in office dropped one by one all of the teachings that had made the church distinctive, and it eventually joined the National Association of Evangelicals. During this period, a number of ministers and members withdrew from the church. They were especially concerned about continuing the requirements to worship on the Sabbath, observe the ancient Hebrew Holy Day seasons, and maintain a belief that Jesus Christ will return to earth to institute a benevolent, world-encircling kingdom of God.

The new church drew to it more than 100 ordained ministers formerly affiliated with the Worldwide Church. In their initial meetings they developed an administrative structure designed to be more directly accountable to members and the ministry. Leadership was placed in the hands of a 12-person Council of Elders elected by a general assembly of all ordained ministers. They reviewed the church's beliefs and issued a formal Statement of Fundamental Beliefs. The Council of Elders elected the president of the church minster's assembly. In 2008 the president was Clyde Kilough.

The United Church sees itself as having a basic duty to preach the gospel and prepare people to enter the kingdom of God. To that end it publishes a large amount of church literature that, continuing the practice of the Worldwide Church, is offered freely to all request it. The texts of many of its central publications can be found online.

The United Church has emerged as one of the larger continuing bodies of former Worldwide Church of God members. It supports a television show, *Beyond Today*, and an Internet radio show, *The Good News.*

Membership: Not reported. In 2008 there were 219 congregations scattered across the United States. There are also affiliated congregations in more than 40 countries around the world.

Periodicals: *The Good News*. Available in English, German, Italian, and Spanish.

Sources:
United Church of God. www.ucg.org.

United Church of God. *This Is the United Church of God*. Available from www.gnmagazine.org/booklets/UC/UC.pdf.

United Seventh-Day Brethren
Current address not obtained for this edition.

The United Seventh-Day Brethren is a small sabbatarian Adventist body. It was formed in 1947 by two independent congregations and several individuals who banded together for greater effect in the fields of evangelism, publication, Sabbath promotion, and fellowship. Each local church in the fellowship remains autonomous. Views held generally in common include the following: The Bible is the inspired Word of God and the final authority in faith and conduct; there is one God; Jesus is God's son, who was born of a virgin, died, was resurrected, and ascended; man has no hope apart from the blood of Christ; the Sabbath Day remains in effect, as do the Ten Commandments; and the local church should be autonomous. Members deny the immortality of the soul. They do not eat "unclean" meats.

For several years, *The Vision* was the official periodical for the group, though it was owned privately. In 1966 it was bought by W. Allen Bond and, soon after, the official relationship was ended. *The Vision* continues to reflect Seventh-Day Brethren ideology, however. In 1980 the General Association of United Seventh-Day Brethren consisted of four congregations, one each in Iowa, Missouri, Nebraska, and Oklahoma.

Membership: Not reported.

World Insight International
PO Box 35, Pasadena, CA 91102

World Insight International was formed in 1977 by Kenneth Storey—a former administrator of the Worldwide Church of God who had been associated with the Foundation for Biblical Research—as a Christian service organization offering insight into the full scope of God's plan for the world. A strong evangelistic program was announced as well as provision for the establishment of local fellowship groups. Underlying World Insight International was the discovery by Storey and his wife of the manifestation of the spiritual gifts discussed in I Corinthians 12. The first mailing from the new organization both announced the beginning of the Latter Reign of the Holy Spirit before the end of time and warned against counterfeits (which he believes are manifest throughout the contemporary Charismatic Movement). While looking for the manifestation of spiritual gifts, Storey rejected the basic Pentecostal idea of the primacy of speaking in tongues.

Over the years, Storey received support from other prominent Worldwide Church of God leaders such as David Orr, who had initiated the work of the Foundation for Biblical Research in England, Brian Knowles, and Richard Plache. Since its founding, a program of biblical research and publication has led World Insight into fellowship with more orthodox Christians and has produced a critique of Worldwide Church of God ideas. Church literature and beliefs reveal a strong emphasis on prophetic themes and the inner life.

Membership: Not reported. There is a mailing list of several thousand and fellowship groups are found around the United States.

Periodicals: *World Insight.*

Sources:
Storey, Ken. *Love Feasts of the Church*. Pasadena, CA: World Insight International, 1978.

———. *Worldwide Church of God in Prophecy*. Pasadena, CA: World Insight International, 1979.

Worldwide Church of God
300 W Green St., Pasadena, CA 91129

The Worldwide Church of God (originally known as the Radio Church of God) was formed in 1933 by Herbert W. Armstrong (1892–1986) and approximately 20 other people in Eugene, Oregon. Armstrong had been a member of a small independent sabbatarian group, the Oregon Conference of the Church of God, when he first began to function as a minister in the late 1920s.

THE ARMSTRONG ERA. Herbert W. Armstrong and his wife, Loma Armstrong, moved to Oregon in the mid-1920s. Shortly after the move, Loma began to absorb the teachings of the Church of God from Ora Runicorn, who taught her about Sabbath observance. Catching the enthusiasm of his wife, Armstrong became an avid bible student and eventually was convinced of the truth of the Church of God. Without formally joining it, he became an active participant in 1927, and the following year preached his first sermon. He was ordained by the Oregon Conference in 1931.

After his ordination, Armstrong began to preach regularly and became the pastor to a small group in Eugene. In 1933, while still a member of the Church of God, he began an independent radio ministry, "The World Tomorrow" broadcast, and issued the first copies of a periodical, *The Plain Truth*. This ministry was incorporated as the Radio Church of God. By this time, Armstrong had come to accept a belief in the modern identity of the ancient tribe of Israel. Though never accepted by the General Conference of the Church of God as a whole, the belief had been present among the ministers for a generation.

At the time Armstrong began his radio ministry, the Church of God was being split on a national level by disagreements over church government and the observance of the Jewish (Old Testament) feasts. Armstrong sided with the minority faction that argued for the observance of the feast days and the abandonment of democratic procedures for the selection of church leaders. As a member of this faction, he participated in the formation of the Church of God (Seventh-Day), headquartered in Salem, West Virginia. He was chosen as one of its 70 leaders in 1933. The Salem faction, however, after observing the feast days for a few years, dropped the practice. They also denounced the belief in British Israelism. About this same time, in 1937, Armstrong withdrew from further participation in any Church of God activities. His ministry continued under the corporate title of Radio Church of God.

Following World War II, Armstrong moved to Pasadena, California, and in 1947 launched Ambassador College. From this point, the ministry grew steadily. In 1953 the Radio Church of God spread to Europe. A television ministry was added in the 1960s and the voice of Garner Ted Armstrong, the son of the founder, became a familiar sound in many American homes. The work expanded greatly, both in North America and overseas, especially in Western Europe, Australia, and South Africa. In 1968 the name of the work was changed to the Worldwide Church of God. By the mid-1970s the circulation of *The Plain Truth* (which was distributed freely) had jumped to over 2,000,000.

The last 15 years of Armstrong's expanding ministry proved a time of intense controversy. Within the church, a debate arose over the dating of the Feast of Pentecost and a number of ministers began to question the absolutist approach to the ban on divorce and remarriage. As the debates proceeded, Garner Ted Armstrong was involved in a public scandal that took him off the air and eventually led to his disfellowship from Worldwide Church of God and his founding the Church of God, International. The internal discontent also led to the departure of some prominent ministers and several thousand members, some of whom established the first of several splinter churches. One group of former members began an anti–Worldwide Church of God newsletter, *The Ambassador Report*, which critically discussed trends in the church.

The controversies came to a climax in 1978 when several former members filed a lawsuit against the church. Gaining the cooperation of the California state's attorney, they were able to have the church placed in receivership pending trial. The action of the court thoroughly disrupted the church's life for a period of months, before the lawsuit was abruptly brought to an end by new legislation that prohibited such actions by the state's attorney. During this time, other churches, recognizing the threat inherent in the courts preemptive action, came to the Worldwide Church of God's defense. A final ruling in the court on the action stated that the initial lawsuit was from its "inception constitutionally infirm and predestined to failure."

Some peace returned to the church in the few years immediately prior to the death of Herbert Armstrong in 1986. He was succeeded by Joseph W. Tkach (1927–1995), whom he had chosen as the church's new apostle.

THE TKACH ERA. After settling into office, the new pastor general, in response to Evangelical Christian critics who had labeled the Worldwide Church of God a "cult," opened the church to a large-scale reexamination of the doctrinal stance and practices initially taught by Armstrong. In 1987 Tkach announced a doctrinal review intended to help the church prepare a Statement of Beliefs, and subsequently issued a new doctrinal manual. Changes began to be noticed by the end of the 1980s, when pieces of Armstrong's writings (which had been published in a series of booklets) were one-by-one withdrawn from circulation, and the very popular Bible correspondence course was dropped from distribution as it went through a complete revision. The editorial format of *The Plain Truth* was changed in 1990 to focus more on biblical and spiritual matters rather than on commentary

on world affairs. Two years earlier, a second magazine, *Good News*, had been discontinued.

The changes in the Worldwide Church of God came to a head in 1994–1995 as major steps were taken toward dropping significant and unique teachings of the church in order to move closer to mainstream Evangelical Christian beliefs. The most significant changes included the adopting of the doctrine of the Trinity, and the dropping of requirements that church members triple tithe, observe the Sabbath (Saturday) as a "holy time" and keep the annual festivals, and practice the dietary restraints outlined in the Levitical law. Church leaders also dropped the belief that the Worldwide Church of God had an exclusive relationship to God as the remnant of true believers in the last days of history.

The doctrinal changes have been hailed by the Evangelical Christian community, but rejected by many leading ministers and long-time church members who had organized their life around these beliefs and practices. Almost one-third of the membership withdrew and formed a variety of new churches, the two largest being the Global Church of God and the United Church of God. The financial disruption that resulted from the dropping of tithing requirements in January 1995 forced the church to divest itself of some capital assets and to cut back on staff. Then in the midst of these changes, in September 1995, Tkach died of cancer. He was succeeded by his son, Joseph Tkach Jr.

BELIEFS. Under Armstrong's leadership, the Worldwide Church of God accepted the basic doctrinal stance of the larger Church of God movement. It accepted the authority of the Bible. It was non-Trinitarian, with Armstrong proposing the idea that God could be thought of as a "family" of multiple "spirit beings" into which humans may be born. Armstrong was seen as God's chosen apostle-messenger and he and the church he led had a special place in human history. Drawing on an interpretation of the biblical book of Revelation, chapters 2–3, he saw the Worldwide Church as God's church of the last days. It was the Philadelphia church described in Revelation 3:7–14.

The church was sabbatarian and its members were expected to keep the Sabbath as a "holy time." Christmas, Easter, and other popular holidays were denounced and the ancient Jewish feasts kept. Members were expected to tithe 20 percent of their income annually (10 percent being given to the church and 10 percent used for the celebration of the annual major feast) and an extra 10 percent every third year. Jewish dietary laws were also kept.

Among the major beliefs of the church was British Israelism, an understanding that the nations of northern and western Europe and those countries largely founded by them (such as Australia, South Africa, and especially the United States) were the descendants of the Ten Lost Tribes of Israel. Often, the first piece of literature read by people who encountered the church was a booklet by Armstrong entitled *The United States and British Commonwealth in Prophecy*.

Marriage was deemed a onetime affair, to be kept inviolate until the death of one of the marriage partners. Divorce and remarriage was not allowed. Couples who joined the church after a second marriage were forced to separate, a fact that pained many ministers who were required to enforce the church's teachings. Interracial marriage was forbidden.

During the Armstrong years, the high-profile church was labeled as a "cult" by numerous Evangelical Christian writers. A large number of anti-Armstrong books appeared through the 1970s and 1980s. However, through the years of Joseph Tkach and Joseph Tkach Jr.'s leadership, all of the church's unique doctrines have been dropped and *The United States and British Commonwealth in Prophecy* has joined the pieces of literature that have been withdrawn from circulation. The church is going through a significant period of transition as members consider the new doctrinal perspective.

ORGANIZATION. Herbert W. Armstrong served the church for many years as its apostle. As the chief administrator, he made all of the policy decisions and held the power to appoint all church officers and ministers. He was the chief teacher of the church and guided its development through a regular column in *The Plain Truth* and several hundred books and booklets published and regularly revised over the years. While most of these materials were distributed freely to any who asked for them, some were reserved for members only.

"The World Tomorrow" broadcast and the widespread distribution of *The Plain Truth* led to tens of thousands of people joining the church. Admission to membership was by baptism by immersion. Congregations are established across North America, but meet in rented facilities; thus they are virtually invisible in the larger religious landscape. Local congregations do not advertise their presence and only rarely are telephone numbers listed in local directories. Today, pastors' names and telephone numbers may be obtained from the church's Internet site.

Eventually, some of church's programs were discontinued due to financial difficulties. Ambassador Foundation, a cultural, humanitarian, and educational program, has been shut down. Ambassador College has also been discontinued, and *The Plain Truth* magazine was turned over to a new corporation, Plain Truth Ministries.

Membership: In 2008 the church reported some 42,000 members, worshiping in 900 congregations scattered in around 100 nations and territories.

Educational Facilities:

Ambassador College, Big Sandy, Texas.

Periodicals: *The Plain Truth.* • *Youth.*

Remarks: The Worldwide Church of God is among those religious bodies that have since the early 1970s been attacked as a "cult." Numerous pieces of literature, primarily from a conservative evangelical Protestant perspective, have been produced about it. The bulk of the criticism has concerned the church's departure from traditional Christian affirmations on such issues as the Trinity. Almost no objective studies have been produced about the church, and there has been a constant complaint from church leaders that the anti-church literature fails to portray their positions accurately.

Sources:

Worldwide Church of God. www.wcg.org.

Armstrong, Herbert W. *The Autobiography*. Pasadena, CA: Ambassador College Press, 1967.

————. *The United States and British Commonwealth in Prophecy*. Pasadena, CA: Worldwide Church of God, 1980.

Bjorling, Joel. *The Churches of God, Seventh Day: A Bibliography*. New York: Garland Publishing, 1987.

Hopkins, Joseph. *The Armstrong Empire*. Grand Rapids, MI: William B. Eerdmans Publishing Company, 1974.

McNair, Marion J. *Armstrongism: Religion or Rip-off?* Orlando, FL: Pacific Charters, 1977.

Nichols, Larry, and George Mather. *Discovering the Plain Truth: How the Worldwide Church of God Encountered the Gospel of Grace*. Downers Grove, IL: InterVarsity Press, 1998. 141 pp.

Rader, Stanley R. *Against the Gates of Hell*. New York: Everest House, 1980.

Robinson, David. *Herbert Armstrong's Tangled Web*. Tulsa, OK: John Hadden Publishers, 1980.

This Is the Worldwide Church of God. Pasadena, CA: Ambassador College Press, 1971.

Tkach, Joseph. *Transformed by Truth*. Sisters, OR: Multnomah Books, 1997. 207 pp.

Tuit, John. *The Truth Shall Make You Free*. Freehold Township, NJ: Truth Foundation, 1981.

 **Bible Student Groups**

Christian Believers Conference

c/o Berean Bible Students Church, 5930 W 29th St., Cicero, IL 60650

Because Charles Taze Russell (1852–1916) (whose work led to the founding of the Jehovah's Witnesses) raised the issue of the atonement in a most "unorthodox"

way, it was no surprise that dissent from a more "orthodox" perspective would appear. J. H. Paton was the first to break with Russell. Paton promulgated his own speculations in both a book and a magazine. In 1909 a significant challenge to Russell arose from three prominent leaders (pilgrims) within his movement—H. C. Henninges, M. L. McPhail, and A. E. Williamson. They rejected Russell's teaching on the ransom atonement in that it elevated the church to the place of Christ as the redeemer and mediator for humanity. They said Russell's theology spoke of Christ as only a part of the sin-offering presented to God. They also rejected Russell's identification of himself with "that servant" of Matthew 25:45–47.

In the midst of the controversy, which lasted for some two years, Henninges led many of the Australian brethren out of Russell's Millennial Dawn Bible Students and McPhail and Williamson led out groups in New York and Chicago. In America, the groups took the name of the Christian Believers Conference. Continuing polemics by descendants of Henninges and McPhail have brought into focus the sharp distinction that the Christian Believers draw between themselves and Russell. They reject the idea of the elect being limited to 144,000 as "mere assumption." They insisted the Lord did not come in 1914 (or 1925) invisibly; he has always been present (Matthew 18:20).

The Christian Believers Conference is structured very loosely, being held together by its peculiar doctrine. For many years a publications committee published *The Kingdom Scribe*, discontinued in 1975. The most active ecclesia as of the 1980s is the Berean Bible Students Church in Cicero, Illinois, which publishes the main periodical serving the group nationally. Since 1910 an annual conference has been held, in most recent years in Grove City, Pennsylvania. The conferees meet for mutual edification and Bible instruction, and have no legislative authority.

Membership: Not reported. In the early 1970s there were 13 ecclesias scattered across the United States from Massachusetts to Wisconsin and Florida.

Periodicals: *The Berean News.*

Sources:

Christian Believers Conference. www.cbconference.com/CBC/index.htm.

Berean Christian Conference. www.bereancc.net/BCC/index.html.

McPhail, M. L. *The Covenants: Their Mediators and the Sin-Offerings*. Chicago: Author, 1919.

What Say the Scriptures about the Ransom, Sin Offering, Covenants, Mediator, Scapegoat? Melbourne, Australia: Covenant Publishing Co., 1920.

Christian Millennial Fellowship

307 White St., Hartford, CT 06106

The Christian Millennial Fellowship is one of three Bible Student groups that are in agreement theologically, but separate administratively, the other two being the Western Bible Students and the Christian Believers Fellowship. The Christian Millennial Fellowship was founded by Italian-American Gaetano Boccaccio as the Italian Bible Students Association of l'Aurora Millenniale. In 1928, following a break with the International Bible Students Association due to doctrinal and service problems, the Italian Bible Students Association changed its name to the Millennial Bible Students Church. Under this latter name it was granted bulk-mailing privilege by the U.S. Postal Service and reorganized as a nonprofit religious organization for tax purposes by the Internal Revenue Service. Eventually, the church's name was changed to Christian Millennial Fellowship. In 1940 the Fellowship began to publish *The New Creation* magazine, which was edited by Boccaccio.

The Fellowship is an independent lay movement headed by a board of directors elected annually by the membership. Officials of affiliated member churches are elected by their congregations to the offices of elder, deacon, secretary, and treasurer. No officers receive a salary, as all work is volunteered. Besides the monthly magazine, a special *African Newsletter* is also published (as part of the magazine) for all the African readership. Three different Bible correspondence courses and a variety of Christian literature are distributed free to any who request it. The voluntary donations of the membership and readership undergird the Fellowship's efforts. Besides the magazine, the Fellowship publishes literature in Spanish, Nigerian, Malawian, and Tulugo (an Indian language).

The Fellowship began work in Italy in 1939. A periodical, *L'Aurora Millenniale*, was begun in Hartford and mailed to Italian subscribers. Growth of the work allowed the periodical to be transferred to Italy for publication in 1962. It is now known as *La Nuova Creatione* and is published by the Chiesa Christiana Millenarista at Pescara, Italy. Its present editor is Mario Celenza.

During the 1980s, fellowship groups were established in Great Britain, Ghana, Nigeria, Ivory Coast, Cameroon, Liberia, Malawi, Mozambique, and Zambia. There is also work in the Philippines, Guyana, and India.

Membership: No membership records are kept.

Educational Facilities:

Christian Millennial College, Ghana.

Periodicals: *The New Creation.* • *African New Creation.*

Sources:

Christian Millennial Fellowship. www.cmfellowship.org/docs/home.htm.

"We Believe." Hartford, CT: Christian Millennial Church, 1980.

Christian Prophets of Jehovah

PO Box 3900, Pinedale, CA 93650-3900

The Christian Prophets of Jehovah was formed in the 1970s by Timothy Tauver, a former member of the Jehovah's Witnesses. Tauver was a typesetter in the Witnesses headquarters in Brooklyn, New York, before his questioning of various doctrinal questions led to his disfellowshipment. After a period of intense Bible study, he came to feel that God had ordained him a prophet. Although commissioned to speak to the nations, Tauver had a special message for the Witnesses and on several occasions was arrested for refusing to leave their meeting halls.

During the early 1980s Tauver outlined a prophetic timetable calculated from the biblical books of Daniel and Revelation: On October 5, 1982, Babylon the Great (Rev. 17:5) would be established as the greatest power on earth; during 1983 more than one million people would suffer premature deaths; the Antichrist would reign until 1989; and God would deliver his judgment to the entire "world system" in 1989. Tauver spread his message through constant travels, advertisements in newspapers, and media coverage of his attempts to confront Jehovah's Witnesses. He also wrote a series of open letters to U.S. president Ronald Reagan.

Membership: Not reported.

Dawn Bible Students Association

199 Railroad Ave., East Rutherford, NJ 07073

The Dawn Bible Students Association grew up among younger members of the Brooklyn ecclesia of the Pastoral Bible Institute (PBI) in the late 1920s. Some energetic members led by former radio broadcaster W. N. Woodworth, who had worked with Charles Taze Russell (1852–1916), wished to begin a radio ministry. Without any hostility toward the work, the PBI felt genuinely unable to sponsor it. The group, joined by some recent additions who had left the International Bible Students Association (IBBA) led by Judge J. F. Rutherford (soon to be renamed the Jehovah's Witnesses), withdrew, formed the Dawn Publishers, and began radio work. The very popular "Frank and Ernest" radio show has become a major outreach effort and has more recently been joined by a television show, "The Bible Answers."

Sending out the truth and light of God's word has been the principle objective of the *Dawn*. It is the *Dawn*'s endeavor to show that the true gospel is not a new theology, but the old theology, not a new gospel, but the old gospel, the one preached to Abraham, the one declared by the Lord Jesus himself and by all his apostles. The Dawn carries on the most extensive outreach ministry of any of the

Bible Student groups other than the Jehovah's Witnesses. Their monthly periodical, *The Dawn*, was begun in 1932. Over the years, the group has published numerous booklets and pamphlets and a few books. The Association is among the most avid reprinters of Russell's works and keeps most of the other Bible Students supplied.

Doctrinally, the Dawn is at one with the PBI, differing only in being stricter concerning doctrinal divergences among its members. The PBI is much more open to fellowship with other Bible Students groups. The Dawn carries in each issue the same statement of beliefs as the PBI's *Herald of Christ's Kingdom*.

The Dawn is a service organization supplying literature and services to independent Bible Student congregations (ecclesias) across the country. These congregations and the Dawn conduct an extensive outreach program. The Dawn magazine is circulated for only a token subscription cost of $3.00 per year (or with no price) beyond membership. The radio and television programs cover the United States and Canada, and extend overseas to South America, Europe, Africa, and parts of Asia. A tract and literature ministry is pursued, including Spanish-language work in South America and Mexico. Foreign work reaches Great Britain, Australia, New Zealand, France, Greece, Germany, Italy, Poland, Romania, Moldavia, Finland, Argentina, Chile, and Brazil. Australian work is coordinated through the Berean Bible Institute, headquartered in Melbourne; and Canadian work through the Canadian Bible Students Association in Vernon, British Columbia. The South India Bible Students Committee headquartered in Bangalore has developed a working relationship with the Dawn Bible Students through the Northwest India Committee for supplying literature. The Africa Bible Students Committee also uses the Dawn for supplies of literature.

Membership: No membership statistics are maintained as membership is not a requirement in any of the congregations. A rough estimate as of 1997 is that the attendance in congregations worldwide is about 9,000 with about 3,000 in the United States.

Periodicals: *The Dawn.* Available from East Rutherford, NJ 07073.

Sources:

Dawn Bible Students Association. www.dawnbible.com/.

The Book of Books. East Rutherford, NJ: Dawn Bible Students Association, 1962.

The Creator's Grand Design. East Rutherford, NJ: Dawn Bible Students Association, 1969.

Our Most Holy Faith. East Rutherford, NJ: Dawn Bible Students Association, 1948.

When Pastor Russell Died. East Rutherford, NJ: Dawn Bible Students Association, 1946.

Epiphany Bible Students Association

PO Box 97, Mount Dora, FL 32757

After the death of Paul S. L. Johnson (1873–1950) in 1950, the Laymen's Home Missionary Movement (LHMM) began to experience troubles in its leadership. In the spring of 1955, charges of fraud and dishonesty in business were circulated against John J. Hoefle (1895–1984), a prominent leader who had spoken at Johnson's funeral. Hoefle, in turn, accused the leadership of the LHMM of slander and lying. In this atmosphere of ever-growing polemics, some doctrinal distinctions between Hoefle and Raymond Jolly, who had succeeded Johnson as head of the organization, began to appear. The two disagreed on the nature and validity of John's baptism (Acts 19:1ff), which Hoefle saw as an excuse for Jolly to accuse him of being out of harmony with both Johnson and Charles Taze Russell (1852–1916), founder of the Bible Student Movement. Hoefle was formally disfellowshipped on February 8, 1956.

Hoefle began to publish the correspondence on the controversy and his opinions on the ongoing administration of Jolly. By the end of 1957, these letters had become a regular monthly publication. In 1968, the title Epiphany Bible Students Association began to appear on the masthead. Hoefle continued in the Russell/Johnson theological school with only minor differences with the LHMM, primarily of an administrative nature and concerning variations in the interpretation of specific texts. For example, both the LHMM and the Hoefle taught of two classes of individuals who would appear in the future Kingdom of God: the Ancient Worthies who would rule (Ps. 45:16) and the Youthful Worthies who would be in partnership with them. The LHMM under Jolly taught that as of 1954, all of the Youthful Worthies had been won, and began to speak of a new class of people, the Consecrated Epiphany Campers. Hoefle rejected this teaching, claiming that no such class existed, and that the Youthful Worthies would be won until the time of restitution.

The Epiphany Bible Students Association is organized around individuals who receive the monthly newsletters. There are regular meetings for Bible study at the Mount Dora Bible House, the headquarters in Florida. Other study groups around the country meet in private homes. Hoefle died in 1980 and was succeeded as president by Leonard E. Williams. Hoefle's widow, Emily, remains active as the association's secretary.

Membership: There is no formal membership. In 1997 there were approximately 1,400 people in the United States receiving the mailings and an additional 250 in foreign countries.

Periodicals: The association publishes an untitled newsletter.

Jehovah's Witnesses

25 Columbia Heights, Brooklyn, NY 11201

Jehovah's Witnesses are a worldwide Christian society noted for their use of "Jehovah" as the name of God. Their purpose is to bear witness regarding God and his purposes for humankind and do God's will as revealed in the Bible. According to the Witnesses, in the Bible all faithful worshipers, such as Abel, Noah, Abraham, and Jesus, were called witnesses of God (Hebrews 11:1–12:1; Revelation 3:14). A prominent Witness in modern times was Charles Taze Russell (1852–1916). Though his parents were Presbyterians of Scottish-Irish descent, Russell joined the Congregational Church. However, in 1870 he organized a Bible study group in Allegheny (Pittsburgh), Pennsylvania, for the purpose of promoting the basic teachings of the Bible. It was his desire to return to the beliefs of first-century Christianity. In 1879 he began to publish the results of his research, bound by "no creed but the Bible" in the magazine *Zion's Watch Tower and Herald of Christ's Presence*, today called *The Watchtower*.

The basic teachings of the Witnesses go back to the early Bible studies of Russell. Because of what he learned from the Bible, Russell rejected the belief that hell is a place of eternal torment. He understood it to be humanity's common grave. Benefiting from existing Bible research by nineteenth-century scholars, Russell learned that the Greek word translated as "coming" (*parousia*) in the King James Version of the Bible actually meant "presence," and so he and his associates concluded that the return of Christ was to be invisible (Matthew 24:3). As Russell and his associates continued their study of the Scriptures and progressed in their knowledge of them, they harmonized their teachings with their deeper understanding. In 1882 Russell wrote: "The Bible is our only standard, and its teachings our only creed, and recognizing the progressive character of the unfolding of Scriptural truths, we are ready and prepared to add to or modify our creed."

Just as did Russell, Jehovah's Witnesses today accept the entire Bible as the inspired Word of truth. Not being Trinitarians, they believe that God, "whose name alone is Jehovah," is the Most High (Psalm 83:18). Jesus said: "My Father is greater than I." He is the Son and the Redeemer of believing mankind (John 14:28). The Holy Spirit is God's active force for accomplishing his will. God's Kingdom is a heavenly government made up of Jesus Christ as King along with 144,000 corulers, such as the apostles, taken from earth (Revelation 14:1–4). The over six million Witnesses worldwide (2001) proclaim the Kingdom as the only hope for humankind and warn that we are living in "the last days" of this present system. The Kingdom, or heavenly government, will soon exercise dominion over the earth and remove wickedness from the earth, transforming it into a paradise in which

true worshipers will live forever. There will be a resurrection of the dead into that Paradise.

For much of the nineteenth century, the Bible Students, as Jehovah's Witnesses were then known, met together in classes (congregations). Yet, they felt an obligation to share their beliefs with others, so they distributed millions of copies of tracts, books, and booklets. Russell determined that these preaching activities should depend entirely on volunteer workers. To this day, the house-to-house ministry, home Bible study activity, and distribution of literature by Jehovah's Witnesses are done voluntarily.

In 1884 a nonprofit corporation, now the Watch Tower Bible and Tract Society of Pennsylvania, was formed, with Russell as the elected president. Branch offices of the society were established in Britain, Germany, and Australia in the early 1900s. The number of countries with branches has steadily increased, and in 2001 there were over 100 branches.

The headquarters of the society was moved from Allegheny to its present location in Brooklyn, New York, in 1909. Printed sermons by Russell were syndicated in newspapers, and by 1913 they appeared in more than 2,000 newspapers in the United States, Canada, Europe, South Africa, and Australia, reaching an estimated 15,000,000 readers.

A few months after Russell's death in 1916, Joseph F. Rutherford (1869–1942) took the lead among the Bible students. In 1918, because of pressure from prominent clergymen, Rutherford and seven other members of the headquarters staff were imprisoned on the false charge of sedition. However, in 1919 they were released, and eventually they were fully exonerated. Rutherford initiated a great expansion of the preaching work, giving greater emphasis to the door-to-door evangelizing activity. In 1919 a companion periodical to *The Watchtower*, first known as *The Golden Age* and now called *Awake!*, was introduced.

In 1931 the Bible Students embraced the name Jehovah's Witnesses, based on Isaiah 43:10, which states: "Ye are my witnesses, saith Jehovah, and my servant whom I have chosen" (American Standard Version). During the 1930s and 1940s, there were many arrests of Witnesses because of their preaching activity. A period of intense legal battles ensued in which the Witnesses fought for freedom of speech, press, assembly, and worship. Of the 59 cases they brought before the Supreme Court of the United States, the Witnesses won 43. These victories had a profound impact on the development of constitutional law and helped preserve freedom of speech, press, and religion for all.

A concerted program of training and global expansion began when Nathan Homer Knorr (1905–1977) succeeded Rutherford. A training school for missionaries, called the Watchtower Bible School of Gilead, was established in 1943. By 1992 more than 6,500 graduates had been sent to well over 200 countries. In 1995 the school was moved to the newly constructed Watchtower Educational Center at Patterson, New York. This complex of 28 buildings—including school facilities, an office building, and residence buildings for 1,500—was built entirely by volunteers.

In 1961 the Witnesses published the New World Translation of the Holy Scriptures, a modern English Bible translated from original-language texts. By 2001 over 100 million copies had been printed. The New World Translation has been translated in whole or part into 38 languages, making it available in the native tongues of upward of one fourth of the earth's population.

Worldwide activities in 235 countries are coordinated by a governing body made up of a group of men, presently 11 in number, located at the Witnesses' world headquarters in Brooklyn, New York. The members of the governing body and all others who work full-time in the preparation and production of Bibles and Bible literature at the New York–based headquarters receive only their room and meals and a small reimbursement for expenses.

Conventions are an integral part of the Witnesses' activities. In the early 1890s, these were held in Allegheny, Pennsylvania. In 1893 the first one outside that locality was held in Chicago, Illinois. It was attended by 360 persons, and 70 adults were baptized. The largest single international convention convened in New York

City in 1958, using both Yankee Stadium and the nearby Polo Grounds (since demolished). Peak attendance was 253,922; those baptized numbered 7,136. Since then, there have been large international conventions in numerous countries. Smaller regional conventions are normally held each year in many cities throughout the world.

There are over 100,000 congregations, each presided over by a body of elders. The elders, assisted by ministerial servants, receive no payment for their services. Most congregations hold their meetings in Kingdom Halls, usually built by the Witnesses themselves. The Witnesses take literally Jesus' command: "Go therefore and make disciples of people of all the nations, baptizing them" (Matthew 28:19, 20). All Witnesses accept this responsibility to share their beliefs with their neighbors, especially by preaching from "house to house" (Acts 20:20). In 2007 alone, Witnesses conducted individual weekly Bible study sessions in over 6 million households. Literature is distributed without cost to those who show interest in reading it. The expense of publishing and distributing literature worldwide is covered by voluntary donations. No collections are taken at meetings, and no dues or tithes have to be paid.

Membership: As of 2007, the Witnesses reported 6,957,852 practicing members worldwide, of which 1,084,005 lived in the United States and 111,963 in Canada. The Watch Tower Society produces and circulates literature in 445 languages. Witnesses have been active in Europe for over a century, and as the new millennium begins are either the second- or third-largest religious body (next to the traditional state church) in most of the European countries.

Educational Facilities:

Watchtower Bible School of Gilead, Patterson, New York.

Periodicals: *The Watchtower.* • *Awake!*

Sources:

Jehovah's Witnesses. www.jw-media.org/index.html.

Bergman, Jerry. *Jehovah's Witnesses and Kindred Groups: A Historical Compendium and Bibliography*. New York: Garland, 1985.

Botting, Heather, and Gary Botting. *The Orwellian World of Jehovah's Witnesses.* Toronto: University of Toronto Press, 1984.

Gruss, Edmond Charles. *Apostles of Denial*. Nutley, NJ: Presbyterian and Reformed Publishing Co., 1970.

Jehovah's Witnesses in the Divine Purpose. Brooklyn, NY: Watchtower Bible and Tract Society, 1959.

Jehovah's Witnesses: Proclaimers of God's Kingdom. Brooklyn, NY: Watchtower Bible and Tract Society of New York, 1993.

"Make Sure of All Things." Brooklyn, NY: Watchtower Bible and Tract Society, 1957.

Organization for Kingdom-Preaching and Disciple Making. Brooklyn, NY: Watchtower Bible and Tract Society, 1972.

Organized to Accomplish Our Ministry. Brooklyn, NY: Watchtower Bible and Tract Society, 1983.

Rogerson, Alan Thomas. *Millions Now Living Shall Never Die*. London: Constable & Co., 1969.

The Truth That Leads to Eternal Life. Brooklyn, NY: Watchtower Bible and Tract Society, n.d.

White, Timothy. *A People for His Name*. New York: Vantage Press, 1967.

Laodicean Home Missionary Movement
Rte. 38, 9021 Temple Rd. W, Fort Myers, FL 33912

John W. Krewson (d. 1977) was a member of the Laymen's Home Missionary Movement (LHMM) who withdrew in protest over the leadership of Raymond Jolly, who had succeeded Paul S. L. Johnson (1873–1950). In 1955, within months of Johnson's death, Krewson was disfellowshipped and soon began to publish a periodical, *The Present Truth of the Apocalypsis*. He offered LHMM members an alternative to John J. Hoefle, who had also been disfellowshipped and had formed the Epiphany Bible Students Association. Krewson and Hoefle soon began to argue, with each casting doubt on the other's right to preach and asserting that the other was not a pilgrim (preacher with proper credentials). Over the years Jolly, Hoefle, and Krewson continued the intrafamily feud; sometimes Jolly and Krewson agree against Hoefle, and sometimes Hoefle and Jolly agree against Krewson. Krewson and Hoefle disagreed on Johnson's status as the last saint, Hoefle arguing that Charles Taze Russell's (1852–1916) appointments of other pilgrims (who were still alive) was ample refutation. Both Hoefle and Jolly joined in refuting Krewson's teaching on the apocalypse.

The Laodicean Home Missionary Movement is loosely structured around Krewson's periodical by individuals and small groups who use it for study and edification.

Membership: Not reported. Readership of the magazine is estimated in the hundreds.

Periodicals: *The Present Truth of the Apocalypsis.*

Laymen's Home Missionary Movement
1156 St. Matthews Rd., Chester Springs, PA 19425-2700

Shortly before Pastor Charles Taze Russell (1852–1916) died in 1916, Paul S. L. Johnson (1873–1950), a Jew who had become first a Lutheran minister and then a Bible Student pilgrim (teacher/preacher), was sent to England to straighten out troubles among the British students. In order to facilitate Johnson's work, Russell gave him "enlarged powers." Johnson, in November, proceeded to England and, under the authority received from Russell, fired two of the managers of the London office. Judge J. F. Rutherford, confirmed as president of the Watch Tower corporation while Johnson was still in England, saw Johnson as a major threat to his consolidation of leadership control. Johnson for his part believed that the "special authority" given by Russell was still valid.

The issue came to a head at the 1918 board meeting of the Watch Tower Bible and Tract Society, the corporate entity of the Bible Students, at which Rutherford's authority was decisively confirmed. Johnson, Raymond Jolly, and a host of Bible Students withdrew from the Rutherford-led organization and joined in the formation of the Pastoral Bible Institute (PBI). Differences soon arose among the PBI leaders, so Johnson left and formed the Laymen's Home Missionary Movement (LHMM). The latter group's major strength was in the Philadelphia ecclesia. Two periodicals, *The Herald of the Epiphany* (for general readership) and the *Present Truth* (an in-group periodical and major polemic organ), were begun.

The LHMM believes Russell was that faithful and wise servant mentioned in Matthew 24:45–47; thus, Johnson labeled Russell the *parousia messenger*. Just as Russell had brought word of the presence, so Johnson, as the *epiphany messenger*, brought word of Christ's appearance. Like Russell, Johnson published voluminously. During Johnson's lifetime, 15 of the 17 volumes of the *Epiphany Studies in the Scriptures*, volumes following the format and appearance of Russell's *Studies in the Scriptures*, appeared. Johnson's successor, Raymond Jolly published two additional volumes during the 1950s.

The LHMM remains one of the "orthodox" Bible Student groups that still use Russell's writings and follows Russell's pattern of finding biblical types in current events and groups. Other Bible Student groups were typed as divisions of the tribes of Levites (Num. 3:17–37). PBI students were seen as Shimite Gershonites, revolutionists changing Russell's charter into an ecclesiastical, clerical document. Johnson's main disagreement with the PBI and the Dawn Bible Students Association, which he saw merely as the PBI masked under another name, concerned the harvest. Johnson believed that in 1914 the door of salvation (Luke 13:24–25) closed as an entrance into consecration and spiritual begettal. The door, he believed, is closed for entrance into the spiritual kingdom. The PBI believed that the door was still open. In essence, the LHMM pointed to the closing of the inner circle, but allowed new members, including the great and earthly classes. They also believe they are in the period called the Epiphany, during which the Lord is revealing himself to the world and his people to establish his kingdom.

Following Johnson's death in 1950, leadership of the LHMM and editorship of its magazine was held successively by Raymond G. Jolly (1950–1979); August Gohlke (1979–1985), Bernard W. Hedman (1985–2004), and Ralph M. Herzig (2004–present).

Membership: Not reported. There are conflicting claims concerning the number of members, ranging from 10,000 to 50,000. The lower estimate more closely approaches the LHMM's real strength.

Periodicals: *The Bible Standard and Herald of Christ's Kingdom.* • *The Present Truth and Herald of Christ's Epiphany.*

Sources:

Bible Standard. www.biblestandard.com/.

Johnson, Paul S. L. *Gershonism*. Chester Springs, PA: Layman's Home Missionary Movement, 1938.

———— *Meratiism*. Chester Springs, PA: Layman's Home Missionary Movement, 1938.

Jolly, Raymond. *The Chart of God's Plan*. Chester Springs, PA: Layman's Home Missionary Movement, 1953.

Pastoral Bible Institute

1425 Lachman Ln., Pacific Palisades, CA 90272

"Harvest siftings" was a term used by the Bible Students led by Charles Taze Russell (1852–1916) to describe a period of controversy that resulted in the loss of doctrinal or organizational dissidents. Such a period followed the death of Russell, whose work with Bible Students eventually led to the formation of the Jehovah's Witnesses. Judge J. F. Rutherford (1869–1942), who succeeded Russell as president of the Watch Tower Bible and Tract Society, the Bible Students' corporate entity, was opposed in his rise to power by a number of board members, including R. H. Hirsh, I. F. Hoskins, A. I. Ritchie, and J. D. Wright. They opposed Rutherford's issuance of Volume VII of the *Studies in the Scripture*, the first six volumes of which had been Russell's central teaching materials. They resisted Rutherford's power until the elections at the convention in 1918. Following Rutherford's decisive victory at the convention, his opponents withdrew and with some 50 colleagues and supporters set up the Pastoral Bible Institute (PBI). A committee of seven was appointed to supervise the work and R. E. Streeter was made editor of a new periodical, *The Herald of Christ's Kingdom*.

Doctrinally, the PBI is the most conservative of the Bible Student groups. Each issue of the *Herald* carries a creed-like statement summarizing the truths that "To us the Scriptures Clearly Teach." Among these "truths" are the following:

That the church is the "Temple of the Living God"—peculiarly "his workmanship"; that its construction has been in progress throughout the Gospel Age—ever since Christ became the world's Redeemer and the chief corner stone of this Temple, through which, when finished, God's blessings shall come to "all people," and they find access to him. I Cor. 3:16, 17; Eph. 2:20–22; Gen. 28:14; Gal. 3:29.

That meantime the chiseling, shaping, and polishing of consecrated believers in Christ's atonement for sin, progresses, and when the last of these "living stones, elect and precious," shall have been made ready, the great Master Workman will bring all together in the first resurrection; and the temple shall be filled with his glory, and be the meeting place between God and men throughout the Millennium. I Pet. 2:4–9; Rev. 20:4,6. That the basis of hope for the church and world lies in the fact that "Jesus Christ, by the grace of God tasted death for every man," "a ransom for all," and will be "the true light which lighteth every man that cometh into the world," in due time. Heb. 2:9; John 1:9; I Tim. 2:5,6.

That the hope of the church is that she may be like her Lord, "see him as he is," be a "partaker of the divine nature," and share his glory as his joint-heir. I John 3:2; John 17:24; Rom. 8:17; II Pet. 1:4.

That the present mission of the church is the perfecting of the saints for the future work of service to develop in herself every grace, to be God's witnesses to the world; and to prepare to be the kings and priests in the next age. Eph. 4:12; Matt. 24:14; Rev. 1:6, 20:6.

That the hope for the world lies in the blessings of knowledge and opportunity to be brought to all by Christ's Millennial Kingdom—the restitution of all that was lost in Adam, to all the willing and obedient, at the hands of their Redeemer and his glorified Church—when all the willfully wicked will be destroyed. Acts 3:19–23; Isaiah 35.

The import of this statement for PBI is found in its belief that membership in the church is still open. The harvest is not yet closed, and evangelism, not just the perfecting of those believers left in 1918, is a major thrust. The invitation is to the fullness of the heavenly hope, not just to an earthly paradisiacal state, as with the Jehovah's Witnesses. Because of their evangelistic endeavors, PBI and related groups, although small, are the largest of the Bible Student bodies other than the Witnesses.

Organization of the PBI is very loose. Individuals and autonomous local congregations are affiliated through the *Herald* and an annual meeting at which the seven-member board and five-member editorial committee are elected. Active correspondence and interchange with the British Bible Fellowship Union and the Berean Bible Institute of Australia are promoted.

Membership: Not reported.

Periodicals: *The Herald of Christ's Kingdom.*

Sources:

Streeter, R. E. *Daniel the Beloved of Jehovah*. Brooklyn, NY: Pastoral Bible Institute, 1928.

————. *The Revelation of Jesus Christ*. 2 vols. Brooklyn, NY: Pastoral Bible Institute, 1923–1924.

Philanthropic Assembly

Current address not obtained for this edition.

F. L. Alexander Freytag (1870–1947), founder of the Philanthropic Assembly, initially ran the Swiss bureau of the International Bible Students Association (IBSA), a group founded by Charles Taze Russell. Though an able leader, Freytag was never an exponent of Russell's theology, and in 1917 he began to criticize Russell's main teaching book, the six-volume *Studies in the Scripture*. In 1920 Freytag published the *Message of Laodicea* as an attack on the IBSA, and began a debate with Judge J. R. Rutherford, who had succeeded Russell as the IBSA's leader. In 1921, Freytag withdrew from the IBSA and set up the Church of the Kingdom of God, also known as the Philanthropic Assembly of the Friends of Man, taking with him many Swiss, German, and French Bible Students.

Freytag published a four-volume set of scriptural writings, mostly initially published in French, but subsequently widely translated. He published his own hymnbook (for which he composed both words and music), as well as a devotional book and numerous booklets and tracts. He also founded two journals, the monthly *Monitor of the Reign of Justice* and the weekly *Paper for All*. Members of the Philanthropic Assembly view Freytag as "that Faithful and Wise Servant" mentioned in Matthew 24:45–47.

Freytag concentrated on the religious problem of death. He believed that he had found the answer in his intimate relationship with the person of Christ. One overcomes death by conforming to the form of Jesus. By eschewing sin and following Jesus, one escapes the wages of sin. Freytag's message of death conquered was set within a framework of Russell's theology. He added an important point: eternal happiness is God's goal for all mankind, without exception. The replacement of death with hell's torment was not good enough for Freytag, who demanded the conquering of death itself. The idea is further supported by allegiance to the Universal Law: "God is love." This law is the supreme fact of creation.

Freytag's movement was strongest in central Europe (Switzerland, Germany, France, Spain, Austria, Belgium, and Italy), but it found some adherents among Bible Students in the eastern United States. The American headquarters circulates English-language editions of Freytag's books and two periodicals.

Membership: Not reported. American adherents are estimated to be in the hundreds. Internationally, the *Monitor*, the main periodical, circulates 120,000 copies in several languages.

Periodicals: *The Monitor of the Reign of Justice.* • *Paper for All*. Available from L'Ange de l'Eternal, Le Chateau, 1236 Cartigny, Switzerland.

Sources:

Freytag, F. L. Alexander. *The Divine Revelation*. Geneva, Switzerland: Disciples of Christ, 1922.

———. *Eternal Life*. Geneva, Switzerland: Messenger of the Lord, 1933.

———. *The New Earth*. Geneva, Switzerland: Bible and Tract House, 1922.

Western Bible Students Association
Current address not obtained for this edition.

The Western Bible Students Association centered in Seattle, Washington, is at one in doctrine with the Christian Believers Conference, but administratively separate. It holds an annual conference at Mission Springs, Santa Cruz, California.

Membership: Not reported.

Sacred Name Groups

Assemblies of the Called Out Ones of Yah
Current address not obtained for this edition.

The Assemblies of the Called Out Ones of Yah began in 1974 when Sam Surratt, a believer who had previously been convinced that "Yah" was the correct name of the Creator and "Yeshuah" that of his son, the Messiah, felt compelled to create a unity of the truly Called Out Ones of Yah. Surratt felt that the true church would be guided by Yah through Yeshuah and the Holy Spirit, rather than by one leader, and that leaders would be chosen by casting lots. Following a biblical pattern, the Called Out Ones are led by twelve apostles, the seven, and the seventy. The seven, which constitute the officers for the Assemblies, are elected for two-year terms and, together with the seventy (directors at large), comprise the board of directors.

The Assemblies follows the main ideas of the Sacred Name Movement and is very clear in its rejection of both the Trinitarian position and the "Oneness" or "Jesus Only" position of some Pentecostals. The Assemblies teaches the importance of the baptism of the Holy Spirit and of the reception of the gifts of the Spirit (1 Corinthians 12). Members refrain from military duty, but will accept alternative humanitarian government service. Members tithe 10 percent of their increase (net income) annually. A second tithe is given during the annual feast days (Deuteronomy 14: 22–26), and every third year there is a poor fund tithe. Baptism is by immersion. Weekly worship is on the Sabbath.

In the early 1970s Surratt began to send literature to Sacred Name and Sabbatarian believers across the United States and abroad. He built a mailing list of many thousands that has produced some new members who have begun local assemblies. Branch chapters were designated wherever two or more of the Called Out Ones gathered. Surratt died in 1990 and the present status of the church is unknown.

Membership: Not reported. According to the Assemblies, the Called Out Ones of Yah consists of the great multitude (which no one can number) from all nations being called out by Yah from all Babylonish religions to serve with Yeshuah in the coming kingdom. This multitude numbers more than 144,000.

Periodicals: *Called Out Ones Bible Thought Provoker Messenger*.

Sources:

Let Us Reason Ministries. www.letusreason.org/Default.htm.

Surratt, Sam. *"Judge" or "Be Judged," That's the Question*. Jackson, TN: Assemblies of the Called Out Ones of Yah, n.d.

———. *The Point of No Return*. Jackson, TN: Assemblies of the Called Out Ones of Yah, n.d.

———. *Virgin Lamps*. Jackson, TN: Assemblies of the Called Out Ones of Yah, 1977.

Assemblies of Yahweh
PO Box C, Bethel, PA 19507

Jacob O. Meyer (b. 1934), a former member of the Church of the Brethren, left the church of his childhood and began a spiritual pilgrimage that led him to a small independent Sacred Name assembly meeting in Hamburg, Pennsylvania. In 1964 he moved to Idaho to become assistant editor of the *Sacred Name Herald*. In 1965 at a Feast of Tabernacles meeting in Nevada, Missouri, he was consecrated for the ministry. Then in 1966, after having previously moved to Bethel, Pennsylvania, near to his birthplace, he began his radio ministry. The Sacred Name Broadcast first aired over a station in Baltimore, Maryland. A magazine, *The Sacred Name Broadcaster*, was begun in 1968. In 1969, to facilitate the preaching of the Sacred Name message, Meyer founded the Assemblies of Yahweh. Elders were ordained. As the membership grew, a second periodical for members only, *The Narrow Way*, was added. Under Meyer's leadership the Assemblies has grown into the largest Sacred Name organization in the world. The Assemblies also publishes its own version of the Sacred Scriptures.

Doctrinally, the Assemblies of Yahweh has concepts at variance with Christianity. Members affirm "that in order to interpret correctly the Inspired Scriptures, we must use the Old Testament as a basis of our faith." This hermeneutical position asserting the dominance of the Old Testament in biblical interpretation is related to a belief that the Israelite faith and Judaism are basic. The Assemblies teaches the necessity of believers' affirming the divine names Yahweh and Yahshua, the marks of the Divine Father that stand in contrast to the mark of the beast (Rev. 13: 16–17). A non-Trinitarian position is maintained. All the Old Testament commandments, including the feast days and excepting only the ritual and annual sacrifice laws, must be kept. Tithing is stressed. Women cover their heads for worship and wear modest dress. Nonviolence and conscientious objection to war are stressed.

The Assemblies of Yahweh is headed by a directing elder acting as an earthly shepherd under the Savior, Yahshua the Messiah. Under his direction are the ordained preaching elders who serve in spiritual matters and the deacons who handle temporal affairs. Under these members (who are always males) are the senior missionaries and missionaries (who may be either male or female). Affiliated assemblies are located in more than 100 countries around the world. The missionary thrust, both foreign and domestic, is concentrated through the Sacred Name Broadcast, heard over 24 stations across the United States and in foreign countries. In addition, the shortwave radio station WMLK, owned and operated by the Assemblies of Yahweh, is heard in 75 countries. The Sacred Name Telecast, a half-hour program, is aired weekly over more than 10 outlets. Listeners and viewers may receive a wide variety of literature and enroll in a correspondence course. Foreign offices are maintained in England, the Philippines, and Trinidad. Affiliated members are found in 120 countries.

Membership: The Assemblies does not count members but estimates the number to be several thousand. There are 75 congregations and six elders (ministers).

Educational Facilities:

Obadiah School of the Bible, Bethel, Pennsylvania.

Dalet School (K-12), Bethel, Pennsylvania.

Periodicals: *The Sacred Name Broadcaster*. • *The Narrow Way*. • *Missionary News*.

Sources:

Assemblies of Yahweh. www.assembliesofyahweh.com.

Meyer, Jacob O. *Exploding the Inspired Greek New Testament Myth*. Bethel, PA: Assemblies of Yahweh, 1978.

————. *The Memorial Name: Yahweh*. Bethel, PA: Assemblies of Yahweh, 1978.

Psalms, Anthems, Spiritual Songs for the Assemblies of Yahweh. Bethel, PA: Assemblies of Yahweh, n.d.

The Sacred Scriptures, Bethel Edition. Bethel, PA: Assemblies of Yahweh, 1981.

Statement of Doctrine. Bethel, PA: Assemblies of Yahweh, 1981.

Assembly of Yahvah

PO Box 89, Windfield, AL 35594

Among the first to accept the idea of the Sacred Name movement were Elder Lorenzo Snow (b. 1913) and his wife, Icie Lela Paris Snow (b. 1912), members of the Seventh-day Church of God at Fort Smith, Arkansas. They affiliated with the original Assembly of Yahweh led by C. O. Dodd, and Lorenzo Snow was licensed to preach by the church in the early 1940s. In 1945 he began publishing *The Yahwist Field Reporter*. Four years later, he moved to Emory, Texas, where he and other sacred name believers attending a camp meeting formed the Assembly of Yahvah, using the spelling of the Creator's name that Snow had come to believe was most correct. Elder Snow served as overseer until 1961; he was succeeded by Howard Jefferson, James Pridmore, and Wilburn Stricklin, and Snow himself served two additional terms. From 1945 to 1961 Snow also served as editor of the *Reporter* (now *The Elijah Messenger*). In 1970 he began a second periodical, *The World Today*, which also serves the assembly.

The Assembly of Yahvah differs from most sacred name groups on two points. First, it uses the spellings *Yahvah* and *Yahshua* (Jesus). Second, it teaches that the baptism of the Holy Spirit and the nine gifts of the Spirit (1 Cor. 12) are operative for believers today. The assembly further affirms the necessity of keeping all Ten Commandments, including worship on the Sabbath (Saturday). It affirms the virgin birth of Yahshua, salvation by faith in Yahshua, and the necessity of sanctification. Water baptism by immersion is practiced. Members are required to dress modestly and abstain from all intoxicating substances.

The church has been headed since 1984 by an assembly council consisting of assembly ministers and elders. There is an annual camp meeting in July.

Membership: Not reported.

Periodicals: *The Elijah Messenger*.

Sources:

Major Beliefs of the Assembly of Yahvah. Winfield, AL: Assembly of Yahvah, 1977.

Assembly of Yahweh

1017 N Gunnell Rd., Eaton Rapids, MI 48827

The Sacred Name movement began among members of the Seventh-Day Church of God during the 1930s. Possibly the oldest surviving assembly is the Assembly of Yahweh in Eaton Rapids, Michigan, originally chartered as the Assembly of YHWH. Among its charter members were Joseph Owsinski, John Bigelow Briggs, Squire LaRue Cessna, Harlan Van Camp, George Reiss, Daniel Morris, William L. Bodine, John M. Cardona, Edmund P. Roche, and Marvin Gay. The original charter allowed some variation in the spelling of the Sacred Name, but Yahweh came to be accepted. The Assembly of Yahweh associated with other independent assemblies, in large part through the efforts of C. O. Dodd, an early Sacred Name advocate.

Dodd founded a magazine, *The Faith*, at Salem, West Virginia, in 1937, originally to promote the observance of Yahweh's feasts (as described in the Old Testament) among the members of the Seventh Day Church of God. In 1938 he organized the Faith Bible and Tract Society. Within a few years Dodd had become convinced of the Sacred Name position and began promoting it in the pages of *The Faith*. The magazine tied together the growing movement and became a major instrument in its spread. After Dodd's death it was passed to several assemblies until 1969, when the assembly at Eaton Rapids took responsibility for publishing it. The Faith Bible and Tract Society was continued by Dodd's family in Amherst, Ohio.

A lengthy statement of faith asserts the assembly's aim to remove the names substituted by man for the true names: Yahweh, the Father, and his son, Yahsua the Messiah. To that end, the assembly has published an edition of Old and New Testament scriptures with the names restored. The assembly upholds the Ten Commandments, including the seventh-day Sabbath, and practices foot-washing, baptism by immersion, and the festivals according to Leviticus 23. The Old Testament food laws are advocated, as are tithing and divine healing. The assembly is non-Trinitarian. Though autonomous, it has fellowship and communication with like assemblies across the United States and in some 30 countries worldwide.

The assembly also sponsors a Wellness Center, which conducts two-week programs on the techniques for preparing "Living Foods"—blending, fermentation, dehydration—and on the use of organic foods such as seeds, nuts, grains, fruits, and vegetables.

Membership: Not reported.

Periodicals: *The Faith*. Available from PO Box 102, Holt, MI 48842.

Sources:

Assembly of Yahweh. www.assemblyofyahweh.com/.

Snow, E. D. "A Brief History of the Name Movement in America." *The Faith* 45 (January—February 1982).

Assembly of YHWHHOSHUA

56100 Hwy. 50 E, PO Box 278, Boone, CO 81025

The Assembly of YHWHHOSHUA is a small Sacred Name group in Colorado. It differs from other Sacred Name groups in its designation of YHWH (as opposed to Yah, Yahweh, or Yahvah) as the true revealed name of the Almighty, and YHWH-HOSHUA (YHWH plus HOSHUA) as the name of the Messiah (as opposed to Yahshua or Yahoshua). The Assembly of YHWHHOSHUA is not affiliated with any other Sacred Name body. It was founded in the 1970s by Laycher Gonzales, who said he first learned of the name of God from a hitchhiking prospector named O. K. Skidmore. Believing that the Hebrew words YHWH (Yahweh without the vowels) and HOSHUA (Joshua) are the only true names for God and Jesus, church members blot out of their books all other names for God.

The assembly is one of several Sacred Name groups to accept the Pentecostal emphases on the baptism of the Holy Spirit. Members believe in water baptism along with receiving the gift of the Holy Spirit, evidenced by speaking in new tongues and by a marked improvement in life as manifested by the fruits of the Spirit (Gal. 5:22–23). The church also teaches the oneness of YHWH—Father, Son, and Holy Spirit—rather than the Trinity. The assembly has developed a strict mode of living, and members strive to be a daily witness and example of the things taught by YHWHHOSHUA, beginning with modest dress, the eating of pure natural foods, and abstaining from sin and the lusts of the world.

The assembly teaches that the Roman Catholic Church and her daughter churches are the "great whore" referred to in Revelations 17, and that the United States is modern Babylon (Revelations 18). Because of that belief, members do not pay taxes or contribute to social security (in accordance with Matt. 6:19–21). Social Security numbers are believed to be a form of governmental control leading to the mark of the Beast (Rev. 14:16, 17).

Traditional holidays such as Christmas, New Year's, Easter, and Halloween that have their origins in pagan holidays are not celebrated. However, members keep

Passover in remembrance of YHWHHOSHUA'S sacrifice for redemption. Members rely on prayer and faith healing rather than on doctors. Along with other commandments, the assembly firmly believes in keeping Saturday, the seventh day, as the sabbath; on that day members refrain from work, buying, and selling.

Women in the assembly keep house and rear the children (Titus 2:3–5). Only men may become ministers. The assembly also supports its own parochial school to provide its children with a sound education, upright morals, and a religious background.

The common names for the months and the weekdays are not used because they have pagan origins. Children are educated in church schools with Mennonite textbooks. Science is considered unnecessary and is ignored. A modest dress code requires wearing loose robes over street clothes at all times. Alcohol, tobacco, drugs, jewelry, dancing, dating, cologne, and haircuts are forbidden. Secular and religious artwork is considered blasphemous.

Membership: Not reported.

Bible Study Association

28877 Summerville Rd., Eugene, OR 97405

The Bible Study Association is a small Sacred Name group with roots in the Worldwide Church of God, with which it shares a basic doctrinal perspective. It was founded in 1980 by Davis B. Northnagel Sr. and Donald Goddard. The group does not believe in evangelizing and focuses its efforts upon in-depth research on the Bible and personal growth.

Membership: Not reported.

Church of God (Jerusalem)

PO Box 10184, Jerusalem, 91101 Israel

Elder A. N. Dugger (d. 1975) was one of the leaders of the Church of God (Seventh-day) who advocated a more biblical form of church government and who helped organize the Church of God with headquarters at Salem, West Virginia, in 1933. For several years he edited that church's periodical, the *Bible Advocate*. In spite of the controversies in which he was involved, in 1931 the Church of God sent Dugger to Jerusalem to begin work on moving the world headquarters there when possible. The work was established with the help of Elder Henry Cohen, a Hebrew Christian. At the reorganization meeting in Salem in 1933, a resolution passed to reaffirm the moving of the headquarters to Jerusalem, and money was collected for a headquarters building. Then in the late 1930s Dugger became closely identified with C. O. Dodd, editor of the independent magazine *The Faith*, which was founded to promote the observance of the Old Testament feast days and then the Sacred Name movement. However, unlike Dodd, Dugger did not leave the Church of God. In 1950, following the merger of the Salem organization with the Church of God (Seventh-day), Dugger became a leader of one faction of the "Back to Salem" movement, a small group that rejected the merger. The Seventh-day Church of God, reestablished in Salem, voted to reject the idea of a headquarters in Jerusalem. Spurred by Israel's becoming an independent state in 1948, Dugger formed his own group, which goes under various names—Church of God, Congregation of Elohim, and Family of Elohim. He moved to Jerusalem and in 1953 began to publish the *Mount Zion Reporter*.

Dugger represented a middle ground between the Church of God (Seventh-day) and the Sacred Name movement. Though he basically accepted the same theology as C. O. Dodd, with whom he coauthored an important apology for the Church of God (Seventh-day), and used the Sacred Names, he did not emphasize the names as do other branches of the movement. He noted his distress at the various names for the mighty Creator and his Son that were being used in the Holy Land: "This is surely not pleasing to them, or to the Holy Angels in their presence . . . . These names are in the Hebrew language."

Dugger's emphasis was much more on eschatology, particularly as it relates to the prophetic significance of reestablished Israel. According to Dugger's interpretation of prophecy, the Abomination of Desolation (Dan. 11:31) occurred in 622, the date of Mohammed's choosing of his disciples and the beginning of his flight from Mecca. The exact date is either 622 or 632. Moslem calendars begin at that point, the Hegira. From that time, there would be 1,290 days (or years) until the consummation. In 1912 World War I began in the Balkans. After this began, there could be only one generation (45 years) until the end. Thus, the end is imminent.

In Jerusalem Dugger began a Hebrew-Christian ministry and publishing concern that prints books, numerous booklets and tracts, church-school material, resources for a correspondence course, and several periodicals. Members are scattered around the world. Following Dugger's death in 1975, the work of the church passed into the hands of his wife, Effie Dugger, his daughter Naomi Dugger Fauth, and his son-in-law, Gordon Fauth. They keep in touch with members and assemblies around the world and in the United States through their regular mailings and voluminous correspondence.

A. N. Dugger's son Charles Andy Dugger broke with the family and began another group, Workers Together with Elohim.

Membership: Not reported.

Periodicals: *The Mount Zion Reporter*.

Sources:

Dugger, A. N. *A Bible Reading for the Home Fireside*. Reprint. Decatur, MI: Johnson Graphics, 1982.

Dugger, A. N., and C. O. Dodd. *A History of the True Religion*. Jerusalem: Mt. Zion Reporter, 1968.

House of Yahweh (Abilene, Texas)

Box 2498, Abilene, TX 79604

Among the people with whom Jacob Hawkins (d. 1991), founder of the House of Yahweh (Odessa, Texas), communicated during his inspired discovery of the Name of the true organization of the Called Out Ones of Yahweh was his brother Yisrayl B. Hawkins of Abilene, Texas. Yisrayl aided Jacob in building the sanctuary of the House of Yahweh in Odessa, Texas, even while Jacob was in Israel. However, in 1980, Yisrayl Hawkins began to hold Sabbath services outside Abilene, Texas, in a mobile home refurbished as a sanctuary, after he became convinced of the necessity of establishing the House of Yahweh according to the prophecies of Micah 4:1–2 and Isaiah 2:2. He asserted that the chartering of the House of Yahweh in Abilene by the State of Texas (and its subsequent recognition by the Internal Revenue Service) demonstrated that his the House of Yahweh was exalted above every other form of government and religion. It was thus the fulfillment of the prophecy regarding the establishment of Yahweh's House in the last days ushered in by the coming of Yahshua Messiah.

Yahweh is the head of the House of Yahweh. Yahshua Messiah is the High Priest over the House of Yahweh. The overseer of the international headquarters of the House of Yahweh, Abilene, is Yisrayl B. Hawkins, who is assisted by the *kahans* (elders) and deacons, as well as female judges, kohanahs, and deaconesses. Weekly worship is now held in the sanctuary building in the surrounding area of Abilene each Sabbath (Saturday) morning. The sighting of the New Moon is celebrated and the Holy days, as commanded in Leviticus 23, are observed, including the weekly Seventh Day Sabbath, Yahshua's Memorial, Yahweh's Passover, the Feast of Unleavened Bread, the Day of Pentecost, the Feast of Trumpets, the Day of Atonement, the Feast of Tabernacles, and the Last Great Day. Adjacent to the sanctuary is a campground for those attending the feasts from out of town.

The House of Yahweh carries on an active publishing program that includes a monthly magazine named *The Prophetic Word*, a number of booklets on various doctrinal subjects, an educational program called the *Peaceful Solution Character Education Program*, and a new holy name version of the Holy Scriptures, *The Book of Yahweh*. It also has several Web sites updated monthly to assist those seeking scriptural information vital to their salvation.

Membership: In 2008 the House of Yahweh reported hundreds of congregations, 46 ministers (along with hundreds of other office holders), and 5,500 members in the United States. The subscription list of *The Prophetic Word* now exceeds over 25,000. The magazine and *The House of Yahweh Monthly Newsletter* are read in many countries, including ones in Africa, the Middle East, and Europe. There is a single Canadian congregation, and also one each in Trinidad, the Philippines, Nigeria, Ghana, Zambia, Greece.

Periodicals: *The Prophetic Word* • *The House of Yahweh Monthly Newsletter*

Remarks: In recent years, the House of Yahweh has been increasingly criticized for a variety of practices described by former members, including various alternative health and medical directives, apocalyptic beliefs, violation of child labor laws, and most recently, polygamy. Members of the group deny that they practice polygamy, but in May 2008 Yisrayl Hawkins was arrested on bigamy charges and state authorities claimed he had in excess of 30 wives. As this encyclopedia goes to press, adjudication of the charges proceeds.

Sources:

Hawkins, Yisrayl. www.yisraylhawkins.com.

House of Yahweh. www.yahweh.com.

Prophetic Word Program. www.propheticword.com.

The Book of Yahweh. Abilene, TX: House of Yahweh, 1987.

Hawkins, Yisrayl B. *There Is Someone Out There!* Abilene, TX: Books-A-Hoy Publishers, 1997. 382 pp.

————. *True Stories about Christmas*. Abilene, TX: House of Yahweh, n.d.

The House of Yahweh Established. Abilene, TX: House of Yahweh, 1988.

The Lost Faith of the Apostles and Prophets. Abilene, TX: House of Yahweh, 1985.

What Yahweh's Feasts Mean to You. Abilene, TX: House of Yahweh, 1989.

Yahweh's Passover and Yahshua's Memorial. Abilene, TX: House of Yahweh, 1988.

Missionary Dispensary Bible Research

Box 5296, Buena Park, CA 90622

Associated with the Assembly of Yahvah is the Missionary Dispensary Bible Research, headquartered in Buena Park, California. The group is responsible for the production of *The Restoration of Original Sacred Name Bible*, which used Yahvah, Elohim, and Yahshua for the sacred names. It is based on Joseph B. Rotherham's translation but uses the King James Version's form of paragraphing. Rotherham included a paragraph titled "The Name Suggested" in the introduction to his translation. No reference is made to *The Holy Name Bible* translated by A. B. Traina of the Scripture Research Association.

Membership: In 1988 there were centers in Ward, Arkansas; Winfield, Alabama; Winston, Ontario, Canada; and several in Texas. There are several hundred affiliated members.

Scripture Research Association

14410 S. Springfield Rd., Brandywine, MD 20613

The Scripture Research Association was founded in January 1950 by Angelo B. Traina (1889–1971), pastor of the Kingdom Truth Assembly, an independent Sacred Name congregation in Irvington, New Jersey. During the years before the formation of the association, Traina had been a frequent contributor to *The Faith* magazine, the original Sacred Name periodical, published in Salem, West Virginia, by C.O. Dodd.

The goal of the Scripture Research Association is to ascertain a clearer translation of the Scriptures, and especially to restore to them the name of the Creator, Yahweh, and of his Son, Yahshua, the Messiah. It was Traina's opinion that the New Testament was written in Aramaic and Hebrew rather than in Greek, as is commonly assumed. He also believed that the Nicolaitans (Rev. 2:6) were responsible for substituting the Greek words *kurios* (commonly translated "Lord") and *theos* (commonly translated "God") for the sacred names.

In 1940 Elder Angelo B. Traina published a pamphlet, "The Deed," in which he used the holy name *Yahweh*. In 1950 he published the Sacred Name New Testament, and in 1963 the complete Holy Name Bible based on the King James Version. He started the Scripture Research Association to distribute the Holy Name Bibles (the bibles are no longer available from the association in Maryland). Traina died in 1971 in his eighty-second year. His wife Ida Mae passed away 11 years later.

The association publishes tracts on a variety of religious subjects. It is governed by a board of trustees.

Membership: Not reported.

Sources:

Traina, A. B. *The Holy Name Bible*. Brandywine, MD: Scripture Research Association, 1980.

Workers Together with Elohim

Box 14411, Jerusalem, Israel

Following the death of A. N. Dugger (d. 1975), his son Charles Andy Dugger had a disagreement with the board of the Church of God (Jerusalem). With his followers, he quickly established his own organization and began to publish the *Jerusalem Reporter*, similar in appearance and format to the *Mount Zion Reporter* published by his father's church. He called his new group Workers Together with Elohim.

Workers Together with Elohim are thorough-going Sacred Name people and use all of the Hebrew transliterations in referring to the deity. (*Elohim* is the Hebrew word commonly translated as "God" in most English-language Bibles.) Church members also follow the Old Testament ritual and food laws. In particular, they take quite literally the admonition in Num. 15:38–40 and add blue fringes to all their garments.

Operating out of Jerusalem, the Workers Together with Elohim continue to operate an organization quite similar to the Church of God (Jerusalem), and they relate to an American constituency. In Jerusalem, they have a strong mission that distributes Bibles in both Hebrew and Russian languages.

Membership: Not reported.

Periodicals: *The Truth*.

Worldwide Assembly of YHWH

PO Box 841689, Houston, TX 77284-1689

The Worldwide Assembly of YHWH is a Sacred Name organization that emerged in the 1990s. It was founded by former members of the Worldwide Church of God and continues that organization's emphasis upon sabbatarian worship and the celebration of the Jewish feast days. The assembly calls members to seek YHWH's kingdom, keep YHWH's commandments, and evangelize the world.

The assembly professes a belief in the Creator (whom most Christians call God) whose name is YHWH (and pronounced "Yahweh"), and in his son, Yahushua (whom most Christians call Jesus). YHWH exists as a family consisting of YHWH the Father and Yahushua the Son. The Spirit of YHWH is seen as the essence, power, mind, and spiritual extension of YHWH. Salvation is viewed as a process that includes repentance, baptism by immersion, justification and receiving of the Spirit of YHWH, and a life of faith and obedience. It culminates in birth into YHWH's kingdom as a spirit being.

Members are expected to follow the Ten Commandments (as the perfect expression of YHWH's love); observe the Sabbath, and keep the annual Sabbaths or seven appointed feasts of YHWH kept by the ancient Israelites, including Passover, Pentecost, and Tabernacles. Feast sites for members are regularly set on both the East and West coasts. Members are also expected to tithe, though the assembly does not enforce the practice.

They believe that the keeping of the commandments is required today just as it was in ancient Israel. In this respect, they observe the weekly Sabbath from sundown Friday to sundown Saturday. They keep the annual set apart days listed in Leviticus 23, and they observe the clean and unclean food laws mentioned in Leviticus 11. They comprehend that just by keeping these laws made known in the Old Testament, salvation is not assured. They believe that individuals not only have to follow in the Messiah's footsteps, but also must aspire to and live this way of life.

Membership: Not reported.

Sources:

Worldwide Assembly of YHWH. www.yah-way.org/.

Yahweh's Assembly in Messiah

401 N Roby Farm Rd., No. 1, Rocheport, MO 65279

Yahweh's Assembly in Messiah was incorporated in 1980 as the Assemblies of Yahweh in Messiah in Kansas, by former elders of the Assemblies of Yahweh, led by Jacob O. Meyer (b. 1934). Following the settlement of a lawsuit for trademark infringement, the assembly took its present name in 1985. The assembly follows the doctrine of its parent body. There were only administrative disagreements leading to the formation of the new organization. The assembly is led by a board of directors.

Yahweh's Assembly in Messiah is the oldest local Missouri assembly proclaiming the truth of the Creator of the universe (Yahweh) and of his son (Yahshua), the Savior of the world. They have been in the mid-Missouri area for approximately 25 years. They own their own 80-acre campground where they hold weekly sabbath services and celebrate the annual feast days.

They have a full-service assembly that takes care of learning needs. They publish two periodicals: The *Master Key* is printed bimonthly and mailed out (free for one year) in the even months, and the *Beginning Anew* newsletter is printed bimonthly and mailed out on the odd months, to those who contribute to the ministry. The assembly produces many booklets, tracts, and articles that are offered free of charge (except for large quantity orders) to all interested truth seekers. Their literature also can be downloaded from their web site free of charge.

The assembly initiated a publication program that includes a correspondence course, a number of booklets, and several magazines. Video and cassettes of sabbath messages are sent to those not affiliated with a local assembly, and traveling elders meet regularly with scattered members. Affiliated assemblies are found across the United States and Canada, and in 20 foreign countries.

Membership: In 2008 the assembly reported five centers for worship, in Rocheport, Missouri; Frystown, Pennsylvania; Headland, Alabama; Sterling, Illinois, and Caloocan City, Philippines.

Periodicals: *The Master Key*. • *Beginning Anew*. Send orders to 401 N Ruby Farm Rd., Rocheport, MO 65279.

Sources:

Yahweh's Assembly in Messiah. www.yaim.org.

The Heavenly Father's Great Name. Columbia, MO: Assemblies of Yahweh in Messiah, n.d.

Yahweh's New Covenant Assembly

PO Box 50, Kingdom City, MO 65262

Yahweh's New Covenant Assembly is a fellowship and ministry dedicated to what the group deems to be a return to the true and pure teachings of the scriptures. Integral to that process is the adoption of the 'true' name of the heavenly father, Yahweh, and of his son, Yahshua, generally termed God and Jesus by most professing Christians. It is believed that the true names were hidden by misdirected Bible copyists and translators.

The assembly affirms that the Bible is inspired by Yahweh; the Father is the sole master designer of all creation, which was carried out by his son at the beginning of his creation; that Yahshua is the correct name of the savior (a contraction of the combination of "YAHweh" and "HoSHUA"); that he emptied himself of his celestial glory and took upon himself the form of a human, was born of a virgin, lived a sinless life, was resurrected from the dead by the father, and has now ascended into heaven sitting on the right hand of Yahweh. Yahshua is now considered humanity's advocate, mediator and high priest, and through him only can we approach the heavenly father.

The assembly also affirms that the Holy Spirit (Ruach) is the invisible dynamic force, the mind, the power emanating from the father and shared by the son. This invisible essence or power is placed within the believer through the son, by laying on of hands of the presbytery following baptism into Yahshua's saving name. Correlative to this view of the spirit, the assembly believes that the trinity doctrine is not scriptural but is from paganism.

The assembly practices baptism as a single act of backwards immersion in water and into the saving name of Yahshua as a necessary act of consecration. The assembly believes that Yahweh's grand plan of salvation for mankind is only through his son Yahshua the messiah and is revealed through observing Yahweh's holy sabbaths and feast days. The seventh day of the week (called Saturday) is the day Yahweh has set apart, and is a memorial of his omnipotent creative power. The sabbath day is a holy day of rest. The commemoration of the sacrifice of Yahshua the messiah is observed annually on the evening (beginning) of the 14th of Abib, as the 13th ends, according to the original Passover in Egypt when the death angel appeared on midnight of the 14th.

After partaking of the Passover, members of the assembly strive to live a sin-free life of obedience in observing the following seven days of Unleavened Bread. As part of this observance, unleavened bread is eaten for these seven days, allowing members to symbolically take in the unleavened bread of sincerity and truth. The day of Pentecost (Shavuoth) or Feast of Weeks is is the third Annual Sabbath day. The Day of Trumpets, the fourth Annual Sabbath, begins the seventh month and is a holy convocation leading to the rejoicing upon the return of Yahshua at the last trump. The Day of Atonement, the fifth Annual Sabbath, points to Yahshua's atoning work. Historically it is the holiest day of the year for the group.

The Feast of Tabernacles reflects the righteous one-thousand-year reign of the soon-coming King Yahshua and is observed for seven days starting on the 15th day of the seventh month (Tishri 15 through 21). The first day is the sixth Annual Sabbath. The final culmination of the plan of Yahweh is completed in the great harvest. Known as the White Throne Judgment, it is prefigured by the eighth day of the Feast of Tabernacles, the seventh Annual Sabbath called the Last Great Day.

The assembly believes that the scriptural months are delineated by the appearance of the thin crescent of the visible new moon. Scripture indicates that the new moon days will begin from the actual area where the new moon is spotted for that particular month. The scriptural day begins and ends with sunset. Assembly members consider it an act of worship to support the work with tithes (10 percent of one's income) and offerings.

The assembly believes that after death, human beings are unconscious in their graves in the sleep of death, awaiting the resurrection. Immortality is something humans seek, and is made available through the work of Yahshua. Humans do not have an immortal soul; they can die.

The group holds that Yahshua the Messiah is the foundation and cornerstone of His Body—the ecclesia, the assembly—consisting of the called-out body of believers since Pentecost of Acts 2, who have accepted the sacrifice of Yahshua and changed their lives according to Yahweh's word. The assembly trains and prepares believers for the coming Kingdom. In accordance with the custom of the early assembly in the Apostle Paul's time, the sisters of the assembly wear a headcovering during worship. On earth, males reflect Yahweh's glory and stand bareheaded before him. Woman, on the other hand, is the glory of man and therefore is to have her head covered or veiled.

Yahweh's New Covenant Assembly publishes numerous booklets on a wide variety of biblical subjects, especially Yahweh's name and the sabbath and holy days. It sponsors a TV show, "Back to the Truth," broadcast in the United States. International offices are found in England, the Philippines, and on Guadeloupe and Dominica in the West Indies.

Membership: Not reported.

Periodicals: *Light.* • *YNCA Newsletter.* • *Spice of Life.* • *Young Believers.*

Sources:

Yahweh's New Covenant Assembly. www.ynca.com/

 # Southcottites

Israelite House of David

PO Box 1057, Benton Harbor, MI 49023

The Israelite House of David was founded in 1903 by Benjamin Purnell (1861–1927), believed by his followers to be the seventh messenger of Revelation 10:7. Preceding Purnell were six other messengers beginning with Joanna Southcott. She was followed by Richard Brothers, George Turner, William Shaw, John Wroe and James Jershom Jezreel. While each of the messengers had their part to play in the "life-of-the-body," each was independent of the other and little of the writings of the former messengers is to be found in those of Brother Benjamin. Members of the Israelite House of David believe that in this present age the work of ingathering is occurring around the message of the seventh messenger (Gen. 49:10).

For several years, Purnell and his wife Mary travelled around the Midwest before finally settling in Benton Harbor, Michigan, in 1903. They purchased land and began the Israelite House of David. In 1907 an additional 30 acres were purchased and turned into an amusement park that opened in 1908 and for many years attracted people both from surrounding communities and far away. In 1914 the auditorium was built and lectures were regularly held there for visitors to the community.

In 1904 a cablegram was received from some members of the Christian Israelite Church (the church originally founded by John Wroe) in Melbourne, Australia. Having read some books by Purnell, they had accepted him as the seventh messenger spoken of in Revelation. They asked for instructions and, in response, Purnell and several members of the House of David traveled to Melbourne and preached among the Christian Israelite Church centers. As a result, 85 people migrated to Benton Harbor and some members of the House of David stayed in Australia to become a permanent presence there.

The Israelite House of David considers itself a Christian organization founded upon the Scripture. It holds to the King James version of the Bible and Apocrypha insofar as Jesus quoted from it (the Book of Enoch and the books of Esdras). It is organized communally according to the Apostolic plan (Acts 2). Jesus is considered the members' pattern and waymark. The group is celibate and, following Jesus' example, have taken a Nazarite vow, hence they do not cut their hair. They are vegetarians and pacifists.

As the seventh messenger, Purnell brought new truths to the group, including an identification of the true Israelites, who will be gathered from both Jews and Gentiles. Further, Israel is the elect of the Jews and Gentiles who will be called out from among them. The elect are now and always have been scattered among all of the Christian denominations (a fact that leads members of the House of David to have a high regard for other churches). Purnell also asserted that Jesus Christ came to abolish death and that it was possible to attain bodily immortality (I Corinthians 15:23). They believe that salvation of the soul, as preached by most Christian groups, is a free gift of God, but by striving in this life, it is possible to never taste death.

The House of David is headed by a Board of Pillars that is assisted by an advisory board. There is an annual general assembly that elects both boards. After Purnell's death in 1927, there was a division in the membership and property, which was settled out-of-court.

Membership: In 2002 the group, once having an excess of 500 members, reported less than 60, some of whom still reside in Australia.

Periodicals: *Shiloh's Messenger of Wisdom.*

Remarks: The emergence of the Israelite House of David is difficult to understand without some knowledge of the prior movements that set the context for Purnell's ministry.

After the death of John Wroe, founder of the Christian Israelites, other leaders appeared in England to claim his followers. Among these were a Mr. and Mrs. Head, leaders of the New House of Israel. Another leader was James White, known to his followers as James Jershom Jezreel, a name derived from Hosea's son (Hosea 1:4,11). Jezreel was the author of a book entitled *The Flying Scroll* (Zech. 5:1). In it, he asked of himself if he was Shiloh, the son whom Joanna Southcott had awaited. He answered "No!" Rather, he identified Shiloh with the seventh angel of the Book of Revelation. Jezreel was the sixth angel. A seventh angel (messenger) was yet to come. Jezreel's message prepared the way for Benjamin Purnell.

The Flying Scroll was addressed to the ten lost tribes of Israel. In it, creation was described. When the world was made and Satan rebelled (Isaiah 14:12), some spirits joined him willingly and some joined him through ignorance; others remained loyal to God. All these spirits are on earth today. The first are redeemable; the second can be saved by repentance; the third will be rewarded by redemption of the body. They will escape death and reign with Christ as the 144,000 Israelites during the millennium. Jezreel's followers become known for their long hair, looped in back and tucked under violet caps.

In his ideas about God, Jezreel departed from his orthodox predecessors. He taught that the Great Father-Spirit descended on Christ at baptism and left him on the cross. Jezreel's main emphasis, however, was the Divine Mother. Drawing on a number of biblical texts (for example Gal. 4:23), he talked of a Great Mother-Spirit who shall help men and women withstand Satan's power.

Among Jezreel's converts was Clarissa Rogers, a 15-year-old. In 1878, three years after her conversion, she declared a voice had told her to go to America; thanks to her beauty and zeal, many converts were won. A second trip, this time with Jezreel, was made in 1880. Progress was rapid until Jezreel died in 1885 and splintering began.

In Detroit, Michael Keyfor Mills, a Baptist businessman, was converted. He sold everything, sent his money to England, and began a career selling *The Flying Scroll* door-to-door. In 1891 he had a spirit baptism experience in which he fell into a trance and, along with other unusual happenings, his beard fell to the floor. He arose from this trance believing it his duty as Michael the Archangel to gather the 144,000 for the battle of Armageddon mentioned in Revelation. His belief was strengthened by the discovery that he possessed the power of healing. He gathered the Jezreelites into a commune, with himself as leader.

Detroit was stirred by his miracles, but even more by his proclamation that as Eve had seduced Adam into sin, he would seduce women into virtue. He was arrested, and when he refused to explain his meaning, was sentenced to four years' imprisonment. After being released, he took what followers were left to England. Though not considered a messenger, Mills introduced Purnell to the movement.

Sources:

Israelite House of David. www.israelitehouseofdavid.com/

Fogarty, Robert S. *The Righteous Remnant*. Kent, OH: Kent State University Press, 1981.

Purnell, Benjamin. *The Book of Dialogues*. 3 vols. Benton Harbor, MI: Israelite House of David, 1912.

————. *The Book of Wisdom*. 7 vols. Benton Harbor, MI: Israelite House of David, n.d.

Thorpe, Francis. *House of David Victory and Legal Troubles Reviewed*. Benton Harbor, MI: The Author, n.d.

The What? Where? When? Why? and How? of the House of David. Benton Harbor, MI: Israelite House of David, 1931.

Israelite House of David as Reorganized by Mary Purnell

PO Box 187, Benton Harbor, MI 49023-0187

Following the death of Benjamin Purnell, co-founder with his wife Mary Purnell of the Israelite House of David, members were divided between their loyalty to Mary, and the prominent leader H. T. Dewhirst. Following her being locked out of some of the group's facilities, Mary Purnell filed suit. In 1930 an out-of-court settlement awarded Mary four argicultural properties, and monies to build new headquarters immediately east of the present House of David. With those in fellowship with her, Purnell formed a new community, the Israelite House of David as Reorganized by Mary Purnell.

Beliefs generally follow those of the Israelite House of David with the exception of the opinions held concerning the role of Mary Purnell. Within this organization, she is considered, together with Benjamin Purnell, the seventh messenger to follow the birth of Shiloh to Joanna Southcott in 1814. Her books are distributed, along with those of her husband, by the group. She died in 1953. Mary Purnell's reorganization is often referred to as the City of David to distinguish them from the House of David. Today, Mary's City of David is America's third oldest practicing Christian community, and celebrated its centennial in 2003.

Membership: There were fewer than 25 members reported in 2001.

Educational Facilities:

Mary's City of David Museum and Tours, opened in 1997.

Periodicals: *The New Shiloh Messenger*.

Sources:

Israelite House of David as Reorganized by Mary Purnell. www.maryscityofdavid.org

Adkin, Clare E. *Brother Benjamin: A History of the Israelite House of David*. Berrien Springs, MI: Andrews University Press, 1990.

Fogarty, Robert S. *The Righteous Remnant*. Kent, OH: Kent State University Press, 1981.

Purnell, Benjamin. *Shiloh's Wisdom*. 4 vols. Benton Harbor, MI: Israelite House of David as Reorganized by Mary Purnell, n.d.

Purnell, Mary. *The Comforter, The Mother's Book*. 4 vols. Benton Harbor, MI: Israelite House of David, 1926.

Thorpe, Francis. *House of David Victory and Legal Troubles Reviewed*. Benton Harbor, MI: The Author, n.d.

Other Adventists

Christian Nations—Eagle Warriors

Current address not obtained for this edition.

Christian Nations—Eagle Warriors was founded by Rev. St. Michael Doc Balzarini in Panorama City, California, in 1994 as the Universal World Federation, but soon adopted its present name. The church affirms a belief in God, Jesus Christ as God manifest in the flesh, and the Holy Spirit. Its holds as its authority the Bible as the verbally inspired Word of God. Satan is a real personality, a fallen angel and the enemy of believers. Regarding humanity, the church teaches what is termed the "Teeter-Taughter Principle"—that humans consist of mind, body, and spirit.

The church teaches that the laws of the Jewish scriptures (the Old Testament), except those dealing with blood sacrifice and the levitical priesthood, are still in effect and applicable to present-day Israel. Christians are part of present-day Israel. In the near future a new confederation of 10 western nations, all formerly a part of the old Roman Empire, will occur, a sign of the approaching end-time referred to in Dan. 2:7 and Rev. 13:1. Following the organization of this confederation, the New World Order, a world dictator will emerge.

Membership: Not reported.

Church of God (Reinertsen)

c/o Olaf Egge, 33738 McKenzie Vw. Dr., Eugene, OR 97401

The Church of God (Reinertsen) began in 1883 in Chicago, Illinois, when Aanen Reinertsen, a Norwegian immigrant, declared through a set of pamphlets and a periodical, *Domsbasumen* (The Judgment Trumpet), that he had been called out and sent by the Lord to declare that the great day of the Lord was at hand. A major theme in his writings was the apostasy of the contemporary Christian churches.

Reinertsen believed that the Church had fallen away in the year 666 and that Satan was given the power to work his deceptions for 1,260 years. Eventually all the Christian sects fell into the same apostasy. With the time of Satan coming to an end, the kingdom of God would again rise up.

Reinertsen identified himself as the sixth angel of the tenth chapter of the biblical Book of Revelation. The angel was identical with the stone that smites the mountain (false Christianity) in Daniel 2:34-35. The stone shall become a great mountain, the kingdom of God which replaces the false church. The angel comes from heaven with the strength of God and is the cloud with which Jesus clothes himself as he comes to his people. Furthermore, Reinertsen held that Jesus dwelt in him, worked through him, and guided him. The angel also has an open book, i.e., the Book of Revelation, by which he can see the whole plan of God.

According to this organization's beliefs, when the sixth angel comes and the church of God arises, the war in heaven begins between Christ and the church and the dragon and the society of the dragon. The church will win this war. The church shall exist for 1,260 years in the land of the Gentiles. Then shall the church be suppressed for about three and one-half years, to be followed by the seventh angel and the woes that he brings. The church shall then relocate to Israel. The entire historical Israel shall be saved and brought into the kingdom of God. This shall ensure another thousand years of the millennial reign. Thus, through Reinertsen, the millennial reign of Christ begins and the church he builds shall never fall again.

Reinertsen gained a small following within the surviving Norwegian-American community.

Membership: Not reported.

Sources:

Reinertsen, Aanen. *The Testimony of the Man-child*. Eugene, OR: Church of God, n.d. 23 pp.

Kingdom of God on Earth Within Man

c/o Kingdom of God Headquarters, PO Box 77659, Los Angeles, CA 90007

The Kingdom of God on Earth Within Man was founded in 1973 by Eugene Emmanuel Purnell, an African-American pastor known among the members of the Kingdom as Pastor Emmanuel. The group believes Pastor Emmanuel has received the teachings of the kingdom of God through Jesus by the instrument of a host of angels who have guided and informed him in spirit. Pastor Emmanuel, in turn, published these teachings in a series of books.

The Kingdom understands God to be Good, the totality of all good, the creator, maker, ruler, and owner of all things. Thus all things are a part of God and inseparable from God, though no person or thing is God. The opposite of God is Evil—the devil, the consciousness of scarcity. Heaven is the throne of God. It is not a physical place, but a spiritual place. The government of heaven is the kingdom of God within the minds of the saints. In the kingdom all people are rich, free, secure, happy, mentally healthy, at peace, and immortal. They all recognize God as the creator and owner of all. The opposite of heaven is the world, the realm of lies, sin, and the devil (consciousness of scarcity). Angels exist as messengers of God or the devil to bring spirits (words, concepts) to us. All persons are messengers either of God or the devil.

The good people are being organized into the kingdom of God, the structure of which was first revealed to Pastor Emmanuel in 1973. It is designed as the perfect social system and the solution to all the individual and social problems that today beset humankind. Basic to understanding the kingdom is the truth that God creates, makes, and owns everybody and everything. The sinful person is guided by the devil—the law of scarcity—to acts of war, murder, slavery, destruction, in the false understanding that man creates, makes, rules, and owns nature, laws, persons, lands, and things.

The Kingdom of God moves to organize and coordinate all of the general activity of humankind, including the gathering and distribution of all of the appointed spiritual and material things needed to dress, feed, and shelter people. Its concerns include justice, housing, transportation, education, health, communications, and other areas of life. It comes first in one person, Jesus, and then grows through the coming of the saints. As it grows, a social transformation will occur as God transfers governmental stewardship from the governments of the world to the Kingdom of God. It is Pastor Emmanuel's observation that most of the structures of the world are permeated by the devil, i.e., the consciousness of scarcity. Included in this evil realm are all of the world's governments, religious organizations, school systems, and marriages.

In each generation God's anointed prophet, the one whom God has ordained to serve as his chief coordinator of the return of God's saints to Paradise on earth is designated the son of God. Pastor Emmanuel is that person and he is calling the saints to the kingdom. The kingdom will be led by a hierarchy of the Council of Elders (24 or more leaders), the Assembly of Elders (15,000 in number) and coordinators of the twelve ministries: Justice, Food, Housing, Transportation, Education, Health, Clothing, Accounting, Music, Communication, Human Resources, and Material Resources. The official language of the kingdom will be English and its physical headquarters will be in the United States.

Membership: Not reported.

Sources:

Catechism One. Los Angeles: Kingdom of God Press, 1981. 56 pp.

God's Eternal Kingdom, Laws and Judgments: Official Guidelines for the Day of Judgment, Resurrection of the Dead and Immaculate Social Transformation. Los Angeles: Kingdom of God Press, 1983. 103 pp.

Restored Israel of Yahweh

468 Wheat Rd., Vineland, NJ 08360

The Restored Israel of Yahweh was founded in McKee City, New Jersey, in 1973 by Leo Volpe (b. 1916). Volpe is considered to be the resurrected Prophet Jeremiah. According to the Restored Israel, the Bible tells of the last days' resurrection of the prophets, who should be sought because they will have a true understanding of the Bible. Volpe is said to be one of these prophets, and others are expected in the near future. Volpe began his study of the Bible under the guidance of Yahweh (a transliteration of the Hebrew name of God) in 1940. The year 1973 is cited as the beginning of God's Kingdom on earth.

The group believes that Yahweh deals only with the nation of Israel. In the past he dealt with the fleshly nation, which was rejected for its disobedience. However, he has promised to restore Israel, which will be composed of those who place Yahweh above all else; chosen out of all the nations of the earth, the true Israel is composed of individuals with righteous hearts. This will be the end-time, when Satan's world system will be destroyed. Yahshua (Jesus Christ) made his Second Presence in 1913, when he resurrected his 144,000 Body members—kings and priests who have begun to reign with Yahshua in heaven. In 1917 Yahshua began his 1,000-year rule of earth and will bring the events of earth to a rapid climax. The final ten years of the system will begin with a 1,260-day period of preaching, during which time the Restored Israel of Yahweh will be heard and become known

around the world. Everyone will have a chance to accept or reject the message. The 1,260 days will be followed by the abomination of desolation, which is the union of the United States, Russia, and the papacy into a world government. Israel will be silenced and will retreat into self-sufficient communities. The union will last only another 1,290 days. The pope will be cast out of power and war will soon follow. More will respond to the message of Israel and will become, with Israel, the one-third of humankind to survive the war and establish Yahweh's beautiful kingdom on earth (these prophecies are derived in part from a reading of Daniel, Zachariah, and Revelation). Those who survive will have everlasting life here on earth.

The Restored Israel of Yahweh gathers twice weekly for Bible study. Other periods are spent in evangelistic activity, including speaking and distributing literature. A major activity of the group is gathering in public places with large signs upon which scripture quotations and a portion at their own writings are written. Interested persons are allowed to speak with members about their message. The group runs its own school (kindergarten through high school) open to children of baptized members. There is no instruction in evolution, patriotism, or competition. As of 1985, the group was constructing a self-sufficient community, the first of many, seen as the beginning of God's kingdom on earth. At the beginning of 1988, the community had a functional sawmill, cabinet shop, auto mechanics shop, auto-body shop and four homes.

Membership: In 2008 there was only one center of activity, in New Jersey.

Sources:

Restored Israel of Yahweh. restoredisraelofyahweh.org.

Rocky River True Light Church of Christ

2202 Old Fish Rd., Unionville, NC

In 1969 a dispute arose within the leadership of Shiloh True Light Church of Christ when Elder Herman Flake Braswell and Clyde M. Huntley claimed to have been elected church bishop and elder, respectively, at a meeting on December 26, 1969. James Rommie Purser, the church's elder, disputed Braswell's claims. A court ruled in Purser's favor, declaring that Shiloh True Light Church was congregationally ruled and enjoining Braswell from disturbing its life and worship.

The disruption occurred just before a 100-year-old prophecy made by Cunningham Boyle, founder of the Shiloh True Light Church of Christ, was to be fulfilled: Jesus was to appear in 1970. The Braswell faction of the church approached the date of Christ's coming in a more radical way that did members of the main body. Braswell closed his upholstery business; others left their jobs. Huntley committed suicide in May 1970, apparently because of the failure of the prophecy. Afterwards, some members left the church, but most tried to reestablish their normal church activities and secular activities. At last report, Braswell had reopened his business. In 2006 he participated in a Bible debate, "Once Saved, Always Saved," with Patrick Donahue.

Membership: Not reported. There are estimated to be fewer than 100 members.

Sources:

Lattimore, James. *Children of Light.* Bloomington, IN: First Books Library, 2000.

"Once Saved Always Saved." Bible Debates Info web site. Available from www.bibledebates.info/.

Shiloh True Light Church of Christ

Rte. 1, Box 426, Indian Trail, NC 28079

The Shiloh True Light Church of Christ grew out of the work of Cunningham Boyle (1831–1884), a former Methodist preacher who had received a message believed to have come from heaven. He declared that the existing churches had so deviated from Christ's teachings that they had become irretrievably lost. In the 1870s he left Methodism and began to preach in the area around Lynchburg, South Carolina, establishing several churches. He also authored a book, *A Key to the Bible*, which delineated his teachings. The Shiloh Church, near Charlotte, North Carolina, was founded around 1900.

The beliefs of the church are summarized in its articles of faith. The church affirms the Living God, a personal spiritual being whose perfection consists of his attributes of mercy, justice, truth, omniscience, omnipresence, omnipotence, and immutability. Jesus Christ, God's Son, possesses the same attributes. The Son existed in an embryo state until the beginning of creation, at which time the Son was separated from the Father and made equal to him. The devil is also a personal spiritual being, who is coeternal with God. The devil possesses seven attributes: unmercifulness, injustice, untruthfulness, wisdom, power, omnipresence, and immutability. Humans are essental souls (personal spiritual beings) who exist in the body and impart life to it. The Bible is the inspired Word of God.

The church teaches that all spiritual and immaterial things are non-created, hence they cannot be annihilated. Besides God and the devil, the uncreated reality includes time and space and the souls of human beings. Souls are the offspring of God, existing for all eternity. Souls were separated from God on the sixth day of creation to go through a period of probation. God created human beings in his own image, but when they fell to temptation, the Spirit of God (the image) was lost, and humanity received the spirit of the devil. The work of Christ was to provide salvation and the recovery of the Spirit of God for humanity.

Members believe that there is one true church of Christ, and membership in it, gained by the repentence of sin and faith in God through Christ, is essential for salvation. The church observes two ordinances: baptism (by either sprinkling, pouring, or immersion) and the Lord's Supper. Members are conscientious objectors to war. Alcohol and tobacco are forbidden.

The church teaches that God allotted 7,000 years from creation to judgment, and 6,000 years for the probationary period. The last generation began in 1870, and before this generation passes (i.e., at the end of the 6,000 years), Christ will return. Without specifically naming the date, the church believes that we are living in the last years before Christ's return.

There is one congregation of the True Light Church, which is led by a head elder and assistant elders who teach, minister to the members, and handle the financial affairs of the congregation. None of the leadership is salaried.

Membership: In 1988 there were approximately 1,200 members in the one congregation. Although most of the members live in the vicinity of the church in Indian Trail, North Carolina, there are also some in communities in adjacent states.

Remarks: In 1970 the church was split by a schism when a member, Herman Flake Braswell (b. 1926), claimed to be the successor to the late-head elder. He was challenged by James Rommie Purser, and a court decided in Purser's favor. The Braswell faction then formed a second church, the True Light Church of Christ.

During 1986 the Shiloh church became the subject of controversy in a conflict with the U.S. Department of Labor over a program of vocational training it had instituted among the youth of the church. In 1971 the church had won the right to school its children in the homes of the members, and as an extension of its educational program, it launched a vocational training program that had some children working at a masonry company. The Department of Labor instituted legal proceedings, and in 1988 a federal judge declared the church to be in contempt of court for employing children as young as nine years old in violation of U.S. labor laws, and ordered two construction companies owned by church members to pay over $200,000 in legal expenses and back wages.

Sources:

Boyle, Cunningham. *A Key to the Bible or the Book of Truth*. Lynchburg, SC: n.d.

"Judge Rebukes Church Members over Child Labor." *New York Times*, March 2, 1988.

Lattimore, James. *Children of Light*. Bloomington, IN: First Books Library, 2000.

British Israelism

Anglo-Saxon Federation of America

PO Box 177, Merrimac, MA 01860

The longest-lived and largest group of the Anglo-Israel movement is the Anglo-Saxon Federation of America headed by Howard B. Rand, lawyer and Bible student. Rand started a small Anglo-Saxon group in his home in 1928, and as the group grew he began to publish a periodical called *The Bulletin*. He also met W. C. Cameron (editor of Henry Ford's *Dearborn Independent*) who, by 1933, had become president of the newly founded Anglo-Saxon Federation. With Cameron's help, a convention of the Anglo-Israelite groups met in Detroit under Rand's leadership. While unable to unite the groups, Rand was able to launch the Federation.

The position of the federation is spelled out in *The Pattern of History*, an introductory pamphlet. The Bible is the central document; it is to be understood as the history of Israel, past, present and future, and therefore presents quite literally a pattern of history. The key item in biblical interpretation is identifying Israel. The history of Israel really begins with God's covenant and promises to Abraham (Genesis 15ff.) and passes on through Isaac, Jacob (who was given the name Israel), and the ten tribes. The covenant was especially focused in Joseph's sons, Ephraim and Manasseh, who were to become the head of all of Israel (Genesis 48). Present day Israel is found by determining which nation or race fulfills God's promises made in the Old Testament. Israel was to be a powerful nation living northwest of Palestine, a mistress of the earth who holds a great heathen empire in dominion, the chief missionary power of the earth, a nation immune to defeat in war. Part of Israel was to have split off and become a great people in its own right. Such a description can fit only Great Britain and the United States, who split off from it.

In the 1930s and 1940s, groups affiliated with the federation could be found around the United States. From the Destiny Publishers, a large number of books and pamphlets were produced, as were the monthly issues of *Destiny Magazine*. The contents of these materials dealt largely with current events interpreted in terms of the British-Israelite stance. As of the mid-1970s, most of this following had dissolved. Precise statistics are not available. *Destiny Magazine* ceased publication in 1969 and has been replaced with a much more modest newsletter. Books are still published and distributed, and membership is still open in the federation. The group remains active, publishing books and accepting new members.

Membership: In 2002 the federation reported several thousand members and associated groups in all Anglo-Saxon countries.

Periodicals: *Monthly Newsletter*.

Sources:

The Covenant People. Merrimac, MA: Destiny Publishers, 1966.

Gayer, M. H. *The Heritage of the Anglo-Saxon Race*. Haverhill, MA: Destiny Publishers, 1941.

The Pattern of History. Merrimac, MA: Destiny Publishers, 1961.

Rand, Howard B. *Digest of Divine Law*. Haverhill, MA: Destiny Publishers, 1943.

British-Israel-World Federation (Canada) Inc.

313 Sherbourne St., Toronto, ON, Canada M5A 2S3

Among the oldest of the British-Israel groups, the British-Israel-World Federation dates to 1919, when a number of older organizations in Great Britain affiliated. Some of these groups date themselves to study groups that were formed in the 1860s in response to the early theoretical books by John Wilson (*Our Israelitish Origins*, 1840) and George Moore (*The Ten Tribes*, 1861). In the 1870s, Edward Hine formed the British Israel Identity Corporation to be followed by the Metropolitan Anglo Israel Association in 1878, and the Imperial British Israel Association in 1902. The federation's Covenant Publishing Company has been a major publisher of British-Israel books and pamphlets. Its periodical, *The National Message*, was founded in 1922. From England, the federation has spread around the world, primarily throughout the British Commonwealth.

A Canadian branch of the British Israel Association was organized in 1907 in Victoria, British Columbia, by Edmund Middleton. The Vancouver branch was opened in 1909. Edward Odlum was its first president. Odlum took the work of the association to the radio in 1926. Over the decades the radio work spread across Canada and is currently heard in every province. The federation was established in Canada in the 1920s and held its first convention toward the end of the decade.

The federation conceives of itself as an interdenominational organization, not a church. Rather than competing with other churches, its membership is composed of members from other churches who are admonished to remain in those churches. Meetings are scheduled so as not to compete with the normal Sunday worship hours of most Christian churches. The federation affirms the most basic conservative Protestant Christian beliefs including the authority of the Bible as the Word of God, the deity of Christ, the Virgin Birth, Christ as Savior and Redeemer of Israel and Savior of humankind, and his Second Coming. It clearly affirms belief in the Trinity.

The federation does, however, affirm a variety of doctrines not acceptable to the mainline Christian churches. Primarily, it teaches that the Anglo-Celto-Saxon people are the present-day physical descendents of ancient Israel, the kingdom of 10 tribes spoken of in the Bible.

Membership: In 2002 the federation reported 1,300 members in nine centers across Canada. The radio program "The Voice of British Israel" is heard on 14 stations including short-wave to other continents on WWCR. It is associated with sister organizations in Great Britain, Australia, South Africa, New Zealand, and Kenya.

Periodicals: *The Prophetic Expositor*.

Sources:

British-Israel-World Federation (Canada) Inc. www.british-israel-world-fed.ca/

Allen, J. H. *Judah's Septre and Joseph's Birthright*. Boston, MA: A. A. Beauchamp, 1930.

These Are the Ancient Things. Fort Langley, BC: Association of Covenant People, n.d.

Calvary Fellowship, Inc.

302 56th Ave. W, Mountlake Terrace, WA 98043-4718

Calvary Fellowships, Inc., founded in 1960, is a ministry centered upon Woodbrook Chapel in Rainier, Washington, pastored by the Rev. Clyde Edminster (1914–2003). Edminster was one of several graduates of Dayton Theological Seminary, a short-lived seminary in Dayton, Ohio, in the 1940s. The fellowship was originally built among the seminary graduates and other ministers of like mind. Their magazine, *Christ Is the Answer*, began in 1967, and for several decades the chapel was the center of a vigorous movement. Edminster had previously begun the Woodbrook Soul Winning and Missionary Training School, and the magazine tied together the growing fellowship. Each summer a Western Bible Conference brought together followers throughout the Northwest and British Columbia.

Calvary Fellowship differs from other Anglo-Israel groups in that it has allowed Pentecostalism and an understanding of grace to become established in its midst—it advocates the present experience of the baptism of the Holy Spirit as signified by speaking in tongues, and does not feel bound by the laws of Moses.

During the 1980s the annual conference was discontinued and the school closed. Only the chapel and magazine remain of the fellowship ministries. Edminster's numerous books are circulated to the periodical's readers. He was succeeded as pastor of the church by Chuck Smith, who also hosts the national radio program *Word for Today*.

Calvary Fellowship is a nondenominational Christian church called to see lives changed through the power of Jesus Christ and the truth of the Scriptures. From their headquarters in Mountlake Terrace, Washington, they send missionaries across the world to share the good news of the gospel.

Membership: There is currently one congregation.

Periodicals: *Christ Is the Answer*.

Sources:

Calvary Fellowship, Inc. www.calvaryfellowship.org.

Edminster, Clyde. *Is It Law or Grace?* Rainier, WA: Woodbrook Chapel, 1987.

Christian Conservative Churches of America

PO Box 575, Flora, IL 62839

The Christian Conservative Churches of America was founded in 1959 by John R. Harrell, but for a variety of reasons did not begin to function effectively until 1975. In 1961, law enforcement officials arrived at church headquarters looking for a deserter from the U.S. Marines. In 1964, just before his scheduled appearance at an Internal Revenue Service hearing, Harrell disappeared, only to be arrested the following year. He pleaded guilty to charges related to the 1961 incident and jumped bail. He served four years of his 10-year sentence, but was not allowed to activate the church again until his period of parole was completed in 1975.

It is Harrell's belief that the present governmental system in the United States is fragile and likely to collapse in the near future. Therefore, Harrell encourages members of the Christian Conservative Churches of America and the larger Identity (British-Israel) movement to band together for the survival and preservation of the white race. Harrell has designated an area in the middle of the United States as the survivalist stronghold. He terms this area the "Golden Triangle," the prime area which survivalists can colonize and defend when and if a disaster occurs.

BELIEFS. The doctrine of the church is summarized in its Articles of Religion. These include belief in the traditional Protestant affirmations: the Trinity; creation by God; the Bible as an instrument of divine revelation; Jesus Christ's virgin birth, act of atonement, resurrection and Second Coming; the necessity of faith for salvation; the two sacraments of baptism and the Lord's Supper; and the kingdom of God and judgment at the end of this age. The articles show a Methodist influence in an affirmation that a certain goodness, as evidenced by conscience, remains in fallen humanity. Furthermore, the group holds that believers experience the Witness of the Spirit confirming the biblical promise of God. The church has also been influenced by Pentecostalism in affirming the role of the gifts of the spirit (I Corinthians 12–13).

The articles, in distinction from the majority of Protestant groups hold much in common with the Anglo-Israelite movement, though in a manner somewhat different from the other Identity churches. For example, the articles specifically deny a popular British-Israel belief that the British monarchs have descended in unbroken succession from the kings of ancient Israel. The church also identifies the descendants of ancient Israel with neither the Jews nor the nations of Western Europe, but with those "peoples who have been gathered into the North American continent, the true land of regathered Israel." It also affirms that any person, race, or nation may be grafted spiritually into the Israel of God by accepting Christ; those who are literal physical descendants of ancient Israel have a distinct role to defend the new chosen land of gathering.

Headquarters of the church is located on an estate at Louisville, Illinois, formerly owned by Harrell and given by him to the churches at the time of their formation in 1959. The life-size replica of Mt. Vernon located on the estate is a popular tourist attraction in southern Illinois.

Membership: Not reported. The church is small, with only a few centers in operation.

Remarks: The Christian Conservative Churches of America has often been associated with a number of other organizations through the activities of its founder, John R. Harrell. In 1979, Harrell founded the Citizens Emergency Defense System and the Christian Patriots Defense League. The former organization is a private standing militia on alert status, should the collapse of government become imminent. The league is a dues-paying organization that educates and organizes

'Christian Patriots' to ready them for the government collapse. A third organization, the Paul Revere Club is primarily a fund-raising structure that supports the other two. Church leaders have pointed out that while the church endorses these several organizations, they are completely separate from it.

The church has also been included in lists of rightist organizations affiliated with the Ku Klux Klan. Such organizations as the Anti-Defamation League of B'nai B'rith have noted that Harrell served as the leader of the Committee of Ten Million, along with Robert dePugh of the Minutemen and Robert Shelton, Imperial Wizard of the United Klans of America. Church leaders assert that, whatever Harrell's personal actions and affiliations may be, the church has no relation to the Klan.

Sources:

Harrell, John R. *The Golden Triangle*. Flora, IL: Christian Conservative Church, n.d.

Hate Groups in America. New York: Anti-Defamation League of B'nai B'rith, 1982.

Christian Identity Church
Current address not obtained for this edition.

The Christian Identity Church was founded in 1982 by a group of independent Identity believers under the leadership of Pastor Charles Jennings. It grew out of the work of Wesley Swift (1913–1970), who first introduced Sacred Name themes (the use of *Yahweh* and *Yashua* as names of the Creator and his son) into Christian Identity churches. The church teaches that YHVH (Yahweh) is the one true God who manifests as a Trinity of Father, Son (Yahshua), and Holy Spirit, and that the Bible is the inerrant Word of God. Yahshua came to redeem God's people, Israel, identified as the "White, Anglo-Saxon, Germanic, and Kindred people." The church teaches that Israel now makes up the Christian nations of the earth and is considered far superior to other peoples in their callings as servant races.

In addition, the church teaches that Satan is a real being who also has a literal seed or posterity on earth, which is identified with the Jews, who are believed to be children of Satan through the bloodline of Cain, and the eternal enemy of the chosen people. The chosen race should not partake of the wickedness of the world system, and thus should live a segregated existence apart from all nonwhite races.

Ideally, the church believes, Christians should live in a theocracy under the laws of God. World problems are due to disobedience of these laws. Ultimately the Kingdom of God will be established on earth. Its prophecy declares that America is the place where Israel is to be regathered, the center of the dissemination of truth to the other nations until the kingdom is established.

In 2008 Fred Demoret was the pastor of the church. The church annually sponsors a Family of God Reunion, a national Christian Identity conference over Pentecost weekend.

Membership: Not reported.

Remarks: For a brief period (1985–1986) the Christian Identity Church was pastored by Thom Robb, one of the more controversial figures in the larger Christian Identity movement. Robb, a chaplain for the Ku Klux Klan, established several Identity periodicals such as *Robb's Editorial Report* and *The Torch*.

Sources:

"The Christian Identity Movement." Christian Apologetics and Research Ministry web site. Available from www.carm.org/list/christian_identity.htm.

Christian Research
c/o Dan Gentry, Dir., PO Box 385, Eureka Springs, AR 72632-0385

Christian Research was founded in 1958 by former public school teacher Gerda Koch. The ministry is a Bible-centered ministry that teaches that the Bible is not only for the individual, family, church, and school, but also for local, county, state, and national governments. Christian Research's purpose is to preserve Christian heritage and pursue a destiny in the Kingdom of God on earth. Christian Research teaches the Saxon, Celtic, Scandinavian, Slavonic, and kindred peoples are the physical progeny of ancient Israel, and the majority of Jews today are not Israelites, but anti-Semitic Khazars.

Christian Research publishes a quarterly newsletter emphasizing God's law as the answer to our nation's problems. It also publishes and distributes books, including *More Light*, and occasional booklets and tracts. Christian Research has an active prison ministry and provides educational materials to students and home-school groups at a discount. It also has book tables at various fairs and conferences.

Membership: Christian Research is not a membership organization.

Periodicals: *Facts for Action*.

Sources:

Christian Research. www.christianresearch.info/.

Hall, Verna N., comp. *Christian History of the Constitution*. San Francisco, CA: American Christian Constitution Press, 1960.

Church of Israel
PO Box 62 B3, Schell City, MO 64783

HISTORY. The Church of Israel originated in the early 1970s, born of a controversy in the Church of Christ at Halley's Bluff (a.k.a. the Church of Christ at Zion's Retreat), located in rural Vernon County, Missouri (discussed elsewhere in this volume). This church was a splinter of the Church of Christ (Temple Lot) which claims to be the original Church of Christ founded by Joseph Smith, Jr., the Latter-Day Saint prophet. Little, if any, of the Latter-Day Saint background remains in the present-day Church of Israel.

Dan Gayman (b. 1937), founder of the Church of Israel and still active in the church, was the son of one of the founders of the Church of Christ at Halley's Bluff. During the 1960s, he became a pastor in the church and was appointed to edit the church's periodical, *Zion's Restorer*. Gayman came into open conflict with other church leaders because he promoted views which they considered to be racist. He was charged with inviting white supremists to the church's youth camp and using the facilities for training individuals in the use of weapons and military defense.

The tension culminated in 1972 when Gayman called a church meeting at which two bishops were deposed and new church officers elected. The name of the church's periodical was changed to *Zion's Watchman*, and the priesthood dissolved. The meeting's action led to a lawsuit, resulting in the court awarding the two deposed bishops the bulk of the church's land. Gayman and his supporters were awarded 20 acres and denied use of the name "Church of Christ." In 1974 they incorporated as the Church of Our Christian Heritage and adopted the present name in 1981. In 1977-1978 a chapel was erected at Nevada, Missouri, and both Christian Heritage Academy, an elementary school, and a ministerial training school were opened. Gayman also developed a home study program which by 1982 had enrolled approximately 125 people.

BELIEFS. The beliefs of the church are summarized in its *Articles of Faith and Doctrine*. The Bible is accepted as the infallible Word of God (Yahweh). While the 66 books of the Bible are sufficient for building Christian doctrine, the Apocrypha and the Pseudapigrapha (writings authored somewhat contemporaneously with the biblical books, but not included in the canon of either the Jewish Bible or Christian Testament). The church's doctrine of God follows the traditional affirmation of orthodox Christianity, but differs in matters of election and salvation. Yahweh (God) exists as the Trinity of Father, Son, and Holy Ghost. Jesus Christ is seen as both God and man, who died as a sacrifice for human sin. The church affirms the Apostles, Nicene, and Athanasian Creeds.

According to the Church of Israel, the Israelites of the bible are identified with the Caucasian race only. Everyone is predestined to be part of God's family or Satan's dominion (Gen 3:15). Caucasians are descended from Seth, while blacks and Jews are descended from Cain, a product of Satan's impregnating Eve. The church officially denies beliefs in white supremacy and hatred of other races, but does believe in segregation of the races (making reference to 1 Cor 10:21- "You cannot drink from the Lord's cup and also from the cup of demons; you cannot eat at the Lord's table and also at the table of demons.").

The Church of Israel teaches that God chose a race (the Elect in Christ) who are identified as the Seed of Abraham and as the Israelites of the Old Testament. They are God's workmanship and entirely passive in the matter of their salvation. The Seed are made willing and repentant vessels by the grace of Christ and made holy by his atoning blood. The Law was given as a mirror to expose the sin of the Israelites and thus demonstrate that salvation was not earned by the work of people. The Israelites of the Bible are identified with the present-day Caucasian nations of Europe, Scandinavia, America, Canada, South Africa, New Zealand, Australia, and wherever the seed of these people has been dispersed.

Integral to the understanding of the church's doctrine of salvation is the theory of the two seeds, a variation on the two-seed-in-the-spirit doctrine first popularized by Baptist preacher Daniel Parker in the nineteenth century. Basing his interpretation on Genesis 3:15, Parker argued that Abel and Cain represented two seeds carried by the human race, the former of God and Adam, and the latter of Satan. Every person was born of the two seeds and thus predestined from the beginning to be part of God's family or Satan's dominion. Gayman has developed Parker's ideas along racial lines. As an organization, the church opposes social security, innoculation and the use of vaccines and harmful drugs (narcotics), females serving in the military, the use of violence, and abortion. The church teaches that the goal of history is the establishment of the kingdom of God. In that light, members keep the festivals as established by God for the ancient Israelites: Passover, Pentecost, the Feast of Trumpets, the Day of Atonement, and the Feast of Tabernacles. They also keep the seven sacraments of the ancient church: baptism, communion, confirmation, matrimony, ordination, repentence, and unction (or healing).

ORGANIZATION. In 1981, when the present name of the church was adopted, a total reorganization of the church occurred. The church was envisioned as 12 dioceses, each named for and representative of one of the 12 tribes of Israel. There was no diocese for Joseph; rather, there are two dioceses for Joseph's sons, Ephraim and Manasseh. There is also no diocese for Levi (the priestly tribe). The Levites are scattered throughout the nation (or church) as a continuing priesthood. Each diocese is to be headed by a bishop.

To date, only the diocese of Manasseh has been activated and Gayman serves as its bishop. Each of the ancient tribes is identified as one of the nations of Europe and North America. Manasseh is identified as the United States and Ephraim as the British Commonwealth.

Membership: In 1988 the church reported approximately 700 members in five congregations served by 10 ministers.

Periodicals: *The Watchman.*

Remarks: In response to the charges that the Church is a white supremist organization, the Church has included a statement in their articles of faith explicitly denying white supremacy. They do affirm that white people are the Israelites of the Bible and hence called to be the servant people of God. The church denies any goal of white separatism or hatred toward any races. They do believe in the segregation of the races, and seek to live, dwell, work, play, worship and educate children in a segregated environment.

Sources:

Articles of Faith and Doctrine. Schell City, MO: Church of God at Schell City, 1982.

Gayman, Dan. *Do All Races Share in Salvation?* Schell City, MO: The Author, 1985.

―――. *The Holy Bible, the Book of Adam's Race.* Schell City, MO: Church of Israel, n.d.

―――. *One True and Living Church.* Schell City, MO: Church of Israel, n.d.

―――. *The Two Seeds of Genesis.* Nevada, MO: Church of Our Christian Heritage, 1978.

Church of Jesus Christ Christian, Aryan Nations
PO Box 2016, Coeur d'Alene, ID 83816

The Church of Jesus Christ Christian, Aryan Nations dates to the late 1940s when Wesley A. Swift (1918–2004) founded a congregation, the Church of Jesus Christ Christian, in Lancaster, California. Swift had emerged as one of the most prominent voices of pro-white Christian and anti-Marxist Jewish perspectives. Swift died in 1970 and his widow succeeded him as head of the congregation.

After Swift's death, Richard Girnt Butler, a pastor in the church, moved to Hayden Lake, Idaho, and in 1974 began an independent branch of the church. During the 1980s, Butler and the church became the focus of national attention because of his association with factions of the Ku Klux Klan and the American Nazi movement. As early as 1979 he hosted the Pacific States National Identity Conference, and in 1982 he hosted the first World Aryan Congress, an organization periodically reconvened. The congress brought together a wide variety of white-separatist groups and has called for the establishment of an all-white nation in the Pacific Northwest.

The Church of Jesus Christ Christian, Aryan Nations follows the Christian-Israel identity message which believes that modern Anglo-Saxons, Scandinavian, Germanic, Celtic, Basque, Slavic, Lombard, and kindred peoples are the physical descendants of ancient Israel, and hence heir to the promises of the Bible which refer to Israel as a whole. The church is adamantly pro-white.

Membership: In 2002 the church reported over 200 members in Idaho and some 1,500 members worldwide. There were 12 ministers in the United States and two in Canada. Affiliated branches are found in Australia, Denmark, Italy, France, and Germany.

Periodicals: *Calling Our Nation. • The Way.*

Remarks: Increasing public concern about the Church of Jesus Christ Christian, Aryan Nations, is the activity of a group called The Order, composed of former members of the church. The Order has been credited with the 1984 murder of Jewish radio talk-show host Alan Berg, in Denver, and a number of crimes in the Seattle, Washington, area. A massive manhunt for members of The Order resulted in the death of the leader Robert Mathews, killed in gun battles with police, and the arrest, trial, and conviction of 11 members on charges of racketeering. Richard Butler, while noting the former affiliation of The Order's leaders and sympathizing with their frustrations, rejected their violent and illegal activities.

Because of The Order, as well as the connections between the church and several Klan and Nazi organizations, the group has come under close observation by the media and groups such as the Anti-Defamation League of B'nai B'rith. In 1987 Butler was indicted by the federal government for sedition. He was later found innocent.

In September 2000 a jury found Butler, his chief of staff, and two security guards liable for $6.3 million in damages for an attack against Victoria Keenan and her son Jason. After their car backfired outside the group's compound, the guards chased them in a truck, ran them off the road, and beat the Keenans with their rifle butts. The two guards are serving prison terms for the attack. As part of the settlement, Butler had to turn over the title of the 20-acre Aryan Nation compound to the Keenans.

As of March 2001 the Keenans sold the property to Greg Carr, founder and former chairman of the Prodigy Internet service. The property is being converted into a center for human rights. The loss of the Idaho property, and Butler's death in 2004, signal a period of disruption for the church. It has slowly returned to some organizational stability and again relocated its headquarters in Idaho.

Sources:

Church of Jesus Christ Christian, Aryan Nations.

www.uiowa.edu/policult/politick/smithson/an.htm

Coates, James. *Armed and Dangerous.* New York: Hill and Wang, 1987.

Haberman, Frederick. *Tracing Our White Ancestors*. Phoenix, AZ: Lord's Covenant Church, 1979.

Hate Groups in America. New York: Anti-Defamation League of B'nai B'rith, 1982.

Swift, Wesley A. *God, Man, Nations, and the Races*. Hollywood, CA: New Christian Crusade Church, n.d.

————. *Testimony of Tradition and the Origin of Races*. Hollywood, CA: New Christian Crusade Church, n.d.

Church of the Sons of YHVH/Legion of Saints

PO Box 165, Calhoun, LA 71225

The Church of the Sons of YHVH/Legion of Saints, a Christian Identity church, was founded in 2002 by Pstrs. Ray Redfeairn and Morris Gulett, both former members of the Church of Jesus Christ Christian, Aryan Nations. It is currently led by Gulett and the assistant pastor, John Britton. The church believes in the inerrancy of the Bible, the Word of God. The church holds many Protestant Christian beliefs, and like Baptists, administers two ordinances: communion, observed as a memorial of Christ's last supper, and adult baptism, limited to those who understand the significance of the act. Church members practice tithing.

It is distinctive in its affirmation that "the White, Anglo-Saxon, Germanic and kindred peoples are the direct descendants of the Adamic man made in the image of YHVH (Genesis 1:27), and were placed here to be the light bearers and supreme ruling race (Deuteronomy 7:6; Deuteronomy 28:10) of this lost and dying world." Simply stated, this latter belief leads the church to strongly favor white supremacy and racial segregation.

The church supports an Internet radio ministry, *Sword of Truth*.

Membership: Not reported.

Remarks: In 2006 Morris Gulett was sentenced to six years in prison for his role in planning an Alabama bank robbery.

Sources:

Church of the Sons of YHVH. www.churchofthesonsofyhvh.org/.

Church of True Israel

Box 3208, Hayden, ID 83835

The Church of True Israel was founded in 2000 by former members of the Church of Jesus Christ Christian, Aryan Nations. That church was disrupted by a lawsuit that cost it all of its headquarters property in Idaho and other assets. Those who left the church continue its basic beliefs and practices, but have distanced themselves from any association with Nazi symbolism and the Ku Klux Klan.

The church was founded by five long-time leaders in the Christian Identity movement—John R. Burke, Charles W. Mangels, John Miller, Stanley McCollum, and Chuck Howarth (who died soon after the church's formation). Burke and Mangels both had left the Church of Jesus Christ Christian in 1995 following the meeting of the Aryan World Congress, and had worked in opposition to the church through the remainder of the decade. Headquarters originally were established in Montana but subsequently moved to Idaho, near the former site of the Church of Jesus Christ Christian's former headquarters.

Founders of the new church rejected the one-man leadership formerly exercised by the head of the church of Jesus Christ Christian and other Identity groups for the oligarchic leadership of its five-man Council of Senior Prelates.

Membership in the Church of True Israel is open to individuals of the white race and specifically excludes "Jews, Orientals, Mexicans, Negroes" and others considered by the church to be mongrels (mixed race). Anyone applying for membership must declare that he or she is "a white person of non-Jewish ancestry."

The church sees itself as following in the tradition of Identity leaders such as Bernard Comparat (d. 1983) and William Potter Gale (1917–1988), and though otherwise eschewing Nazi links, does have a page extolling the career of American Nazi leader George Lincoln Rockwell (1918–1967) on its web site.

Membership: Not reported.

Sources:

Church of True Israel. www.churchoftrueisrael.com/.

Morlin, Bill. "Former Aryans Desert Butler for New Church." *Spokeman Review* (January 20, 2001). Available from www.spokesmanreview.com/news-story.asp?date=012001&ID=s910656.

Elohim City

Muldrow, OK 74948

Elohim City is a Christian Identity community located in rural Adair County, in northeast Oklahoma, near the Arkansas and Missouri borders. It was founded in 1973 by Robert G. Millar (1925–2001) who, upon his death, was succeeded by his son, John Millar in June of 2001.

Elohim City, as an identity group, accepts the basic Anglo-Israelite interpretation of the Bible that begins with the identification of the northern and western European peoples with the Ten Lost Tribes of Israel. Millar has added an apocalyptic cast to his teachings, and has been reported as believing that the biblical period of tribulation had already begun and would peak with an invasion of America by "Asiatics." He also predicted a coming civil war involving "the Jews."

As such, it operated as an independent center in fellowship with other Identity groups, especially The Covenant, The Sword, and The Arm of the Lord, a 1980s group that operated in nearby Missouri. While Elohim City has been monitored by groups concerned with Christian identity for most of its life, it gained widespread if brief media exposure in 1995 when it was discovered that convicted Oklahoma City bomber Timothy McVeigh had telephoned Millar in hopes of visiting. It should be noted that no evidence ever surfaced to indicate that McVeigh ever physically visited the community.

Robert G. Millar was raised a Mennonite and at some point moved to the United States from his native Canada. He moved to Oklahoma City in the mid-1950s and founded a Pentecostal church. In the 1960s, he moved to Maryland, but returned to Oklahoma in 1973. Most of the original members were part of his extended family. The community was created to "honor God" and await his establishment of his kingdom on earth.

Millar has developed a unique position in the larger movement of racialist churches. In 1985, for example, he cooperated with authorities to end the siege of the church, the Sword and Arm of the Lord compound, and the surrender of its leader James Ellison. He later served as Ellison's "spiritual adviser" during his imprisonment. He married Millar's granddaughter and came to Elohim City to reside. Over the years, a variety of people associated with the larger movement have visited and briefly lived at Elohim City, a number of whom were later arrested and convicted on various crimes that had led to their movement around the country.

The community lives a separatist life and produces no publications nor does it have an Internet presence. Those who have written about Elohim City have generally been reporters or their more hostile critics.

Membership: In 2008, there were approximately 80 residents.

Sources:

Elohim City. www.adl.org/learn/ext_us/Elohim.asp?xpicked=3&item=13.

Graff, James L., Patrick E. Cole, and Elaine Shannon. "The White City on a Hill." *Time*, 149, 8 (February 24, 1997).

House of Prayer for All People

Box 837, Denver, CO 80201

The House of Prayer for All People was founded in Denver, Colorado, by William Lester Blessing (1900-1984) in 1941. A member of the Church of the United Brethren in Christ, he withdrew in 1927 and became an independent evangelist. He began to use the name House of Prayer for All People as early as 1932. He identified his audience as "Anglo-Saxon, Cymric, and Scandinavian Israelites" with a definite interest in establishing the Kingdom politically and economically on earth. The goal of his work was the restoration of the church (the temple of Yahveh) in the heart of Israel and the earth as his dominion. The group holds that Great Britain and the United States are the latter-day Israel of Yahveh.

Blessing considered himself, the House of Prayer, and *Showers of Blessing*, the monthly periodical established in 1942, to be together the Voice of the Seventh Angel (VOTSA) of Revelation 10:7 and 11:15. Further, VOTSA will usher in the reestablishment of the Church and the Kingdom of Yahveh. Early in his work he had been influenced by the Sacred Name movement and decided that Yahveh and Yahshua were the proper names of the Creator and Messiah respectively (see the discussion of the Sacred Name movement elsewhere in this volume).

According to Blessing's teachings, the First Recovery of Israel took place between the birth of Yahshua (Jesus) and 70 C.E. After his crucifixion, Christ and 12,000 members from each tribe of Israel were resurrected. They returned in power on Pentecost, and the Apostolic ministry was begun. During this time, all of the New Testament was written under the work of the Holy Spirit, the Mother. The Second Coming occurred in 70 C.E., at which time the temple in Jerusalem was destroyed, the dead raised, and the saints raptured. The age came to an end. Since that time, there has not been a true church of Christ on earth; the world has existed in the "times of the Gentiles." However, there has been a representative on earth, through whom Yahveh has spoken. In 1809, the first of the seven angels was heard by Alexander Campbell. He was followed by Joseph Smith, Jr., Ellen G. White, Charles Taze Russell, Benjamin Purnell, and A. P. Adams. In 1962 the desolation was ended according to the prophecy of Daniel 12:12, and mankind was now in the wilderness, the time between the end of the present evil world and the coming of the righteous world. In the near future is a One World government—Babylon, the Mother of Harlots. Yahshua, the messiah, is also already here and will, before 2000 B.C.E. reestablish the kingdom, to be administered by the his remaining people.

The House of Prayer for All People believes that salvation is a contact between Yahveh and the believer. Baptism is the last step in the plan of salvation. Members practice tithing and the kingdom meal, and worship on Sunday. Blessing had an interest in the Great Pyramid, unidentified flying objects, the hollow earth theory, and the psychical, and wrote on all of these.

From the headquarters in Denver, two periodicals are sent to adherents around the United States. Members have established local congregations. The minimum number for each congregation is 70 adults, but ideally this includes 70 heads of family. Each local congregation is headed by seven servants and two bishops who are ordained by the evangelist, the head of the church. Blessing was succeeded by his son, John David Blessing, the present head of the ministry.

Membership: Not reported.

Periodicals: *Showers of Blessing* • *Blessing Letter*

Sources:

Blessing, William Lester. *Hallowed Be Thy Name*. Denver, CO: House of Prayer for All People, 1955.

————. *More about Jesus*. Denver, CO: House of Prayer for All People, 1952.

————. *The Supreme Architect of the Universe*. Denver, CO: House of Prayer for All People, 1956.

————. *The Trial of Jesus*. Denver, CO: House of Prayer for All People, 1955.

————. *VOTSA*. Denver, CO: House of Prayer for All People, 1965.

Kingdom Identity Ministries

PO Box 1021, Harrison, AR 72602

Kingdom Identity Ministries is an independent Christian ministry that generally follows the Christian Identity teachings together with insights of the Sacred Name movement. The stated purpose of Kingdom Identity Ministries is to establish God's heavenly kingdom upon this earth; to proclaim the gospel of the kingdom through any and all righteous means; to identify the true children of Israel, God's chosen

people; to further the spiritual growth and development of the saints; to actively encourage each individual calling within the elect; and to otherwise efficiently promote the ministry and defend the doctrine of their redeemer. The ministries reaches out both nationally and internationally via the distribution and publication of books and tracts; the "Herald of Truth" radio broadcast; the American Institute of Theology Bible Correspondence Course; a prison ministry; and various meetings. Outreach also extends through *Your Heritage,* the ministry founded by Bertrand L. Comparet, *Church of Jesus Christ – Christian,* the ministry founded by Dr. Wesley A. Swift (1913–1970), an Internet Website.

Kingdom Identity Ministries is a non-profit Christian outreach ministry unaffiliated with any other organization, but fully cooperating with all other ministries and individuals defending the "true faith" once delivered unto the saints. The head of this ministry is Yahshua the Messiah (Jesus Christ) to whom they give all honor and glory; they do not exalt any person or human organization. Their right to operate is unalienable coming from YHVH God, "the only true lawgiver"; they do not recognize any other authority for their existence, nor are they subject to any guidelines, edicts and privileges they may issue.

Kingdom Identity Ministries affirms a belief in YHVH as the one and only true and living eternal God who is manifested in three beings: God the Father, God the Son, and God the Holy Spirit, all one God, and in Yahshua the Messiah (Jesus the Christ) as the incarnate begotten son of God. The entire Bible, both Old and New Testaments, as originally inspired, is considered the inerrant, supreme, revealed word of God.

The ministries teaches that God chose unto himself a special race of people who are above all people upon the face of the earth. These children of Abraham through the called-out seedline of Isaac and Jacob were to be a blessing to all the families of the earth who bless them and a curse to those who curse them. The descendants of the 12 sons of Jacob, called "Israel," have not been cast away. The New Covenant was made with the Children of Israel, and the white, Anglo-Saxon, Germanic, and kindred people are believed to be God's true, literal Children of Israel and only this race fulfills biblical prophecy concerning Israel and continues in these latter days to be heirs and possessors of the covenants, prophecies, promises, and blessings of YHVH. This chosen seedline making up the "Christian Nations" of the earth stands far superior to all other peoples in its call as God's servant race, the ministries teaches. Only these descendants of the 12 tribes of Israel scattered abroad have carried God's word, the Bible, throughout the world, have used his laws in the establishment of their civil governments, and are the "Christians" opposed by the satanic anti-Christ forces of this world who do not recognize the true and living God.

The ministries believes that the man Adam (a Hebrew word meaning: ruddy, to show blood, flush, turn rosy) is father of the white race only. As a son of God, made in his likeness, Adam and his descendants, who are also the children of God, can know YHVH God as their creator. Adamic man is made trichotomous; that is, not only of body and soul, but having an implanted spirit giving him a higher form of consciousness and distinguishing him from all the other races of the earth. As a chosen race, elected by God, the members of the white race are not to be partakers of the wickedness of this world system, the ministries teaches. This includes segregation from all non-white races, who are prohibited in God's natural divine order from ruling over Israel. Race-mixing is an abomination in the sight of "Almighty God, a satanic attempt meant to destroy the chosen seedline," and is strictly forbidden by his commandments, according to the ministries.

The ministries also affirms the existence of a being known as the devil or Satan and called the serpent (Gen. 3:1; Rev. 12:9), who has a literal "seed" or posterity in the earth. The group holds that these children of Satan through Cain have throughout history always been a curse to true Israel, the Children of God, because of a natural enmity between the two races. The ministries teaches that the Jews do the works of their father the devil, please not God, and are contrary to all men, though they often pose as ministers of righteousness. The ultimate end of this evil race whose hands bear the blood of the savior and all the righteous slain upon the earth, the minitries believes, is divine judgment.

The ministries believes that God gave Israel his laws for their own good. Theocracy being the only perfect form of government, and God's divine law for governing a nation being far superior to man's laws, individuals are not to add to or diminish from his commandments. The minstries teaches that homosexuality is an abomination before God and should be punished by death.

Additionally, the United States of America fulfills the prophesied place where Christians from all the tribes of Israel would be regathered, according to the ministries. It is here that God made a small nation a strong one, feeding his people with knowledge and understanding through Christian pastors who have carried the light of truth and blessings unto the nations of the earth. The ministries believes that North America is the wilderness to which God brought the dispersed seed of Israel, the land between two seas, surveyed and divided by rivers, where springs of water and streams break out and the desert blossoms as the rose. The ultimate destiny of all history, according to the ministries, will be the establishment of the Kingdom of God upon this earth.

Membership in the church of Yahshua or Messiah (Jesus Christ) is by divine election. The ministries believes that God foreknew, chose, and predestined the elect from before the foundation of the world according to his perfect purpose and sovereign will. Yahshua the Messiah (Jesus the Christ) came to redeem (a word meaning purchase back according to the law of kinship) only his people of Israel who are his portion and inheritance. Baptism is by immersion for the remission of sins, baptism being ordained by God a testimony to the New Covenant as circumcision was under the Old Covenant.

Membership: The ministries believes that membership in the body of Christ is considered to be by divine election only, not by human appointment, and therefore it does not maintain membership rolls nor issue any membership cards.

Sources:

Kingdom Identity Ministries. www.kingidentity.com/

LaPorte Church of Christ

3206 E Country Rd. 52, LaPorte, CO 80535

The LaPorte Church of Christ is an independent Christian church that generally follows what is termed the Anglo-Israelite or Christian Identity position. It was founded in the mid-1970s and it moved to its present location in 1977. The church is pastored by Peter J. Peters (b. 1946), who also serves as the evangelistic head of scriptures for America Ministries Worldwide, a national outreach ministry dedicated to preaching the Kingdom of Jesus Christ and revealing to Anglo-Saxon, Germanic, and kindred (white) Americans their true biblical identity.

The church affirms the Bible as the Word of God and the incarnation and atonement of Jesus Christ. It also affirms that Jesus Christ came to the descendents of Abraham, and in the process of establishing a covenant with them purchased the world. Believers are called to be a light to the world and a force against evil. The anti-Christ people are seen as children of darkness who appear outwardly righteous but hinder the Kingdom of Christ (Matt. 23). Followers of Christ, in opposing evil, are to hold up his laws, statutes, and judgments as his answer to man's problems.

Peters graduated from the Church of Christ Bible Training School in Gering, Nebraska, with a bachelor of sacred literature degree. He extended the church's mission as a popular writer and speaker, and edits *Scriptures for America* newsletter. He has developed a sizeable national audio tape ministry. He has a weekly radio show.

The LaPorte Church of Christ is an independent Christian church, based upon what members feel is the church found the New Covenant Scriptures. Located in LaPorte, Colorado, since its founding in 1977, the church has been pastored by Peter J. Peters throughout its existence.

Membership: Not reported.

Sources:

Scriptures for America Worldwide. www.scripturesforamerica.org/.

New Beginnings

PO Box 228, Waynesville, NC 28786

New Beginnings is a movement that brings together aspects of Pentecostalism and British-Israel Covenant-keeping teachings. New Beginnings was founded by Eldon Purvis, the former editor of *New Wine*, a Pentecostal-Charismatic magazine associated with the ministry of Bob Mumford, Charles Simpson, and Derek Prince in Ft. Lauderdale, Florida. During the 1960s, Purvis began to disagree with the leaders of the New Wine ministry over their advocacy of shepherding; leaders in the New Wine ministry began to disagree with Purvis over his absorption of British-Israel theories. Purvis taught modern Anglo-Saxons to identify with ancient Israel. Purvis also used the sacred names, transliterated from the Hebrew, Yahweh and Yahshua, for the Creator and the Saviour (whom most Christians term God and Jesus).

During his years of association with New Wine, Purvis identified with the Latter Rain revival, a Pentecostal movement that originated in Canada in the late 1940s. Among its emphases were the spiritual gifts of healing and prophecy, the restoration of the church, and the manifestation of the sons of God. It was widely taught through the Latter Rain movement that God was preparing the church for the Second Coming of Jesus. He was bringing into visible manifestation a group of people dwelling on earth in the image of God. They are overcomers of the world destined to rule and reign with their 'Everlasting One' when he returns to establish his kingdom on earth. Integral to this restoration was the reinstitution of the Tabernacle of David, a restoration of God's presence with his people and a return to the Davidic pattern of praise. These teachings are presented in depth in the 1969 book by Graham Truscott, pastor of Restoration Temple in San Diego, California, *The Power of His Presence*. It is Purvis's belief that the revival gave birth to the sons and daughters of Yahweh.

In the late 1960s, after leaving New Wine, Purvis who had established the Holy Spirit Teaching Ministry, later founded Heartbeat, Inc., and more recently New Beginnings. In the early 1970s, he began a periodical and a book distribution service. In 1981, he organized the New Beginnings Church of Jesus Christ. An annual gathering of people associated with the movement celebrate the Feast of Tabernacles near New Beginnings' headquarters. There are also gatherings for Passover and Pentecost.

Since the death of Eldon Purvis in 1990, his wife Nancy Purvis has continued publishing the monthly *New Beginnings* and continues to interpret scripture as it is read in the light of current events of the day.

Membership: In 2002 New Beginnings reported 2,000 members in the United States, 150 in Canada, and an additional 50 worldwide. The magazine is sent to readers in Finland, France, Great Britain, Germany, Northern Ireland, Denmark, the Netherlands, and Switzerland.

Periodicals: *New Beginnings*.

Sources:

New Beginnings. www.sonplace.com/

Henderson, A. L. *The Mystery of Yahweh*. Waynesville, NC: New Beginnings, n.d.

Truscott, Graham. *The Power of His Presence*. San Diego, CA: Restoration Temple, 1982.

New Christian Crusade Church

Box 25, Mandeville, LA 70470

The New Christian Crusade Church was formed in 1971 by James K. Warner. In the 1960s Warner had been a member of the American Nazi Party headed by George Lincoln Rockwell. He broke with Rockwell and later associated himself with the National States Rights Party led by J. B. Stoner and with the Knights of the Ku Klux Klan. The New Christian Crusade Church teaches that all white people are the descendents of the ancient Israelites, and thus it distinguishes its belief from British Israelism, which identifies the present-day Anglo-Saxon people as the literal racial descendents of ancient Israel. The church believes that the present-day Jews come from the Khazars, a warrior people of Turkish-Mongol origin who inhabited the Volga River valleys near the Black Sea in the tenth century. The church is both anti-Semitic and antiblack.

Associated with the church is the Christian Defense League, an open-membership organization founded by Warner for individuals who support the church's racial policies. Warner also established the Sons of Liberty, a publishing and literature-distribution company.

The church moved its headquarters after Hurricane Katrina, which struck New Orleans in 2005 and destroyed their offices.

Membership: Not reported. The New Christian Crusade Church consists of a single independent congregation that serves as the information dissemination center for other independent British-Israel churches in North America. Through its affiliated Christian Defense League, the church is in direct contact with people who share its beliefs throughout North America.

Periodicals: *The CDL Report • Christian Vanguard*

Sources:

New Christian Crusade Church. newchristiancrusadechurch.com/.

Remnant of Israel
PO Box 142633, Irving, TX 75014-2633

The Remnant of Israel is a small movement that originated in the Church of God (Seventh-day) and was established by G. G. Rupert (1847–1922). Originally a Methodist, Rupert joined the Seventh-day Adventist Church and for more than 30 years served as a minister. Though blind for most of that period, he had an outstanding career, serving as president of the Southwest Union Conference until his resignation in 1902. Several years later he associated with the Church of God headquartered in Stanberry, Missouri (then known as the Church of God [Adventist] Unattached Congregations, and today known as the General Conference of the Church of God headquartered in Denver, Colorado), but was among a number of "independents" who rejected the church's organization. Rupert wrote several articles for the *Bible Advocate*, the church's periodical.

During those years he absorbed the British-Israel thought that had emerged among the Church of God ministers. In the early 1900s he wrote a book on prophecy, *The Yellow Peril*. Rupert also came to believe a number of doctrines that gradually separated him from his colleagues in the Church of God. To the practice of keeping a Saturday sabbath he added a belief in the continuing validity of Old Testament feast days, advocating their observance in place of Babylonish holidays such as Easter, Christmas, Ash Wednesday, and Good Friday. Most importantly, he came to believe that there was only one true church—undenominational, invisible, and headed by Christ directly. This belief led him to reject the Church of God organization and to label all the visibly organized churches as false. Besides these ideas, Rupert also believed in tithing, divine healing, speaking in tongues, and pacifism.

Rupert began a periodical, *The Remnant of Israel*, in 1915. It was originally published at Britton, Oklahoma, but was moved to Oklahoma City a short time later. Rupert traveled widely, gathering support for his cause, and small congregations of supporters emerged. In 1919 a national conference of his supporters was held in Pasadena, California. After his death in 1922, his daughter, Lucille Rupert, edited the paper, and the work was continued to midcentury by I. C. Sultz, her husband, whom Rupert had ordained in 1916. Sultz ordained William J. Walker as director of the Remnant of Israel in 1967. Walker continued to issue the periodical for several years, but it was discontinued for lack of financial support. Since then, Walker has issued a number of tracts, pamphlets, and Bible studies.

As a correspondence minister, Pastor Walker takes Rupert's ideas a step further: He discounts all church organization and teaches that the true children of Israel (the white race) consists of those whose names are written in Heaven. He believes that there is no true church, organized or otherwise; that the Saviour is not the head of any church, rather he is the head of his elect, the called-out ones; and that the modern term *church* is a mistranslation of the Greek *ecclesia*, meaning "called-out chosen ones." In like measure, *Christ* is a pagan title of an Eastern sun deity known as *Kristos* (Christos). Today, the Remnant of Israel is a small organization supported by a few people who receive the literature produced from its headquarters in Opportunity, Washington.

The contemporary supporters of the Remnant of Israel continue to observe the Sabbath and the Old Testament feast days, though the thrust of the work and literature is centered upon the heralding of the "Remnant Message" (British Israelism) to modern Israel (the white race).

Membership: The Remnant of Israel is not a membership organization. Believers in the Remnant of Israel message can be found throughout the United States (i.e., the land of modern Israel, the new "JerUSAlem"), Canada, Great Britan, Australia, and other predominantly white Anglo-Saxon nations.

Sources:

Remnant of Israel. remnantofisrael.net/.

Sources:

Nickels, Richard C. *The Remnant of Israel*. Sheridan, WY: Giving and Sharing, 1972.

Walker, William J. *History of the Remnant of Israel*. Opportunity, WA: Remnant of Israel, n.d.

———. *Remnant Message to Modern Israel*. Opportunity, WA: Remnant of Israel, n.d.

United Church of YHWH
PO Box 824, Talladega, AL 35161

The United Church of YHWH, a Christian Identity church, was founded in 2007 in Talladega, Alabama, in January 2007. Founding pastor Jonathan Williams and other charter members of the United Church previously had been associated with the Church of Jesus Christ Christian, Aryan Nations, which had gone through a period of turmoil earlier in the decade due to a devastating lawsuit and the subsequent death of its leader, Richard G. Butler (1918–2004).

The church follows the Identity theology of its parent body and adheres to the sacred name theology popular in Identity circles. The chosen race referenced in the Bible is believed to be the Adamic race, the white, Anglo-Saxon race of people who will ultimately be saved—"no others will follow into Glory on the Spiritual Plain." God is commonly referred to as YHWH (Yahweh) and the church keeps the ancient Israelite holidays and feast days and attempts to keep the biblical food laws (including not eating pork, shellfish, and other specified animals). The church's annual meeting occurs at the time of the Feast of Tabernacles.

The church advocates that as far as possible, members refrain from the polluting contact with organizations and people not associated with the Christian Identity movement. It is most closely associated with Kingdom Identity Ministries. Women are not allowed to preach sermons or teach in any official church gatherings.

Membership: Not reported. The church is strongest in Alabama, Georgia, and Louisiana, but also has members in Illinois, North Carolina, and Michigan. Affiliate branches are be found in Germany, the Czech Republic, and Slovakia.

Sources:

United Church of YHWH. www.ucoy.org.

Liberal Family

14

The modern world has, along with its pluralism, been characterized by the rise of religious skepticism. Skepticism had two major thrusts. It first challenged the hegemony of orthodox forms of religion that dominated cultures through powerful inclusive religious organizations backed by the state's power. The separation of church and state thus became a standard element in the skeptic's program. In the Christian West, the skeptics also challenged ideas at the very heart of Christian thinking. Brought together in this chapter as the "liberal" family of churches and "religious" organizations are those groups that have challenged the orthodox Christian dominance of Western religious life: Unitarianism, universalism, and infidelism. Unitarianism championed the idea of a unitary God over the Christian's Trinitarian God. Unitarianism necessarily involved the additional denial of the divinity of Jesus. Closely related to Unitarianism, universalism affirmed that God will save all humanity, and thus denied the Christian belief in hell.

The several forms of infidelism—deism, rationalism, humanism, atheism, and so forth—moved in an even more radical direction, away from the religious life (and any need for piety, prayer, worship, or devotion) toward human-centered philosophies that tended to denounce all religion or at best paid lip service to a few abstract religious ideas. What are in this chapter termed *liberals* thus fit on a continuum between Unitarians, who still acknowledge the viability of the religious life, and the more radical atheist infidels.

The origin and much of the continuing life of liberalism lie in its attack upon the dictates of Christian orthodoxy. (Orthodoxy may be described as the mainline Christian faith that adheres to the authority of the scriptures and the three ancients summaries of Christian truth—the Nicene, Chalcedonian, and Apostles' creeds.) Thus, the liberal tradition has a secondary nature, protesting existent churches. The differences within the tradition can be gauged by how far various liberal groups deviate from orthodox beliefs.

Most liberals defend the individual's right to believe as he or she wishes, and the privilege to not believe at all if reason leads to disbelief. Liberals therefore have been in the forefront of fights for religious liberty and have joined with persecuted minorities in the debates on religious freedom, such as those of the late eighteenth century in France and the United States.

In America, beginning in the eighteenth century, liberals dissented from the established orthodoxy, primarily of New England Calvinism and to a lesser extent Protestantism in general. Before the Civil War (1861–1865), American liberals were judged by themselves and others only in relation to the creed from which they deviated. Therefore, they were called, by themselves and others, by such negative names as antitrinitarian, atheist, and infidel. After the Civil War, though, liberals began to see themselves in a new light and described themselves in such positive terms as secularists, humanists, and liberals.

As an intellectual movement, liberalism stresses the power of human reason to perfect the world. This emphasis on reason is coupled with a high regard for the worth of each human being. Liberals hold the self-image of being on the progressive cutting edge of human history, striving for the freedom of the individual. Although never very numerous, liberals have had tremendous influence on society as the public accepted their ideals. The Bill of Rights in the U.S. Constitution, for example, stands as a landmark of the liberal tradition.

What is liberal for one generation may become conservative for another generation. For example, in the 1920s, to be a liberal meant to be in the labor movement. Today, though, to be a liberal often means to be against the labor movement because labor is seen as part of the establishment. Thus, liberalism takes on new meanings with time. Also, at any given moment in history, liberals tend to be more united by their opposition to the current orthodoxy than by any positive idea they might promote. They have lacked the positive thrust that builds such movements as Methodism or Calvinism. Their common history of protesting orthodoxy, however, does tie them together, so both Unitarians and atheists (infidels) can be seen as belonging to the liberal tradition, although some from both communities might be unhappy at being lumped together. That the Unitarian Universalist Association recently joined the International Humanist and Ethical Union suggests an acknowledgement of a common history and contemporary agreement on many significant issues.

The Enlightenment of the eighteenth century identified liberals with the high regard for reason. As religion shifted away from God and supernaturalism, only two bases for religion were left: man's feelings and man's mind. An arational mysticism became the hallmark of the liberals who chose feelings as the base for their religion. The Transcendentalists followed the arational path, developing an idealistic movement that emphasized the union of the individual with the spiritual

Liberal Family

1553	John Calvin sanctions execution of Michael Servatus for denying the Trinity.
1568	John Sigismund of Poland, a Socinian Unitarian, issues edict on religious toleration.
1638	Roman Catholics begin suppression of Socinianism in Poland and other countries under their control.
1684	Joseph Gatchell of Marblehead, Massachusetts, is convicted in court for teaching universalism.
1743	The Sauer Bible, the first printed in America, emphasizes universalist themes.
1779	John Murray organizes first American Universalist congregation in Gloucester, Massachusetts.
1784	Ethan Allen completes *Reason the Only Oracle of Man*, the first atheist text published in America.
1785	King's Chapel, the Anglican congregation in Boston, adopts a Unitarian perspective.
1794	In the *Age of Reason*, Thomas Paine advocates a Deist position. *Age of Reason* is later considered a Freethought classic.
1796	Treaty of Tripoli includes statement that "the government of the United States of America is not in any sense founded on the Christian Religion."
1801	Elihu Palmer launches his career as a Deist leader with his book *Principles of Nature*.
1802	In letter to Baptists in Danbury, Connecticut, Thomas Jefferson introduces the phrase "separation of church and state."
1803	Universalists issue their statement of belief, the Winchester Profession.
1805	Henry Ware, a Unitarian, appointed as the Hollis Professorship of Divinity in Harvard College.
	Trinitarian conservatives leave Harvard to found Andover Theological Seminary.
1819	William Ellery Channing's ordination sermon for Jared Sparks becomes seminal statement of the Unitarian position.
1827	Freethought Press Association founded in New York City.
1838	Abner Kneeland convicted of blasphemy in Massachusetts (the last such case in American history).
1859	*Origin of the Species* by Charles Darwin is published.
1865	Organizational meeting of the National Association of Unitarian Churches meets in New York City.
1867	Some liberal religious leaders who find the Unitarians too orthodox found the Free Religious Association to emphasize the role of human reason in spiritual matters.
1876	Educator Felix Adler founds Ethical Culture Society in New York City.
1879	Freethinker Robert G. Ingersoll attacks the Bible's credibility in *Some Mistakes of Moses*.
1889	Charles B. Reynolds convicted of blasphemy in New Jersey.
1925	Fundamentalist William Jennings Bryan leads the prosecution against John Scopes, Tennessee school teacher accused of violating the Butler bill by teaching the theory of evolution in his classes. Scopes is defended by attorney Clarence Darrow.
1933	A group of prominent scholars and liberal religious leaders issue the *Humanist Manifesto*.
1941	Religious Humanists form the American Humanist Association.
1952	Ruling on *Joseph Burstyn, Inc v. Wilson*, the U.S. Supreme Court strikes down New York State's blasphemy law as unconstitutional on free speech grounds. Organizational meeting of the International Humanist and Ethical Union is held in Amsterdam, Holland.
1961	American Unitarian Association merges with American Universalist Association to form Unitarian Universalist Association.
1963	U.S. Supreme Court rules on *Abington School District v. Schempp*, which stopped Bible reading in public school.
	Atheist Madalyn Murray O'Hair founds American Atheits, Inc.
1966	The April 8 cover of *Time* magazine asks "Is God dead?"
1973	A new generation of Humanists issues *Humanist Manifesto II*.
1878	Atheists, rejecting Madalyn Murray O'Hair's leadership of the American Atheist movement, form the Freedom from Religion Foundation.
1980	Secular Humanists withdraw from American Humanist Association and form the Council on Secular Humanism, which issues "A Secular Humanist Declaration."
1995	O'Hair, her son, and her granddaughter are robbed and murdered.
2003	American Humanist Association issues "Humanism and Its Aspirations" (also known as *Humanist Manifesto III*).
2004	Long-time atheist Anthony Flew publicly professes Deist views.
2006	British biologist Richard Dawkins's best-selling book *The God Delusion* promotes new assertive Positive Atheism movement.

reality underlying all life. Most liberals, however, opted for the rational. They said that humans were the product of a law-abiding nature, and reasonable thinking could reveal the universal laws that permeated everything.

Science was the product of rationalism. Science discovered the tangible world of indestructible particles. What was real was what could be seen, felt, and, most importantly, measured. The law-abiding world could be observed and documented. From observation came knowledge, and, by extension, liberals concluded the only knowledge worth having was that produced by scientific observation. Scientific method, said liberals, could be applied to the study of religion, and

from it a scientific religion, acceptable to all, could emerge. Beneath the diversity of ideas and practices could be found the great religious values, some reasoned. Others reasoned that if those values were not found, religion could be destroyed altogether.

The scientist's emphasis on the visible world gave way to secularism as a worldview. The search for values in this world and this life became part of the lifestyle of the liberal tradition.

As comparative religion became a major study, its findings directly fed the development of liberalism. The study of the world's religions revealed that all of the major religions of the world were undergirded with a sophisticated theology and an educated intelligentsia. As more solid information on the major faiths filtered out of the scholarly enclaves, a search for a universal religion began. Liberals hoped such a religion, laying aside each religion's peculiarities and distinctive ideas and practices, and built upon "essentials" or common factors all shared (seen as the natural religious particles), could command the respect of all. Books such as *The World's Sixteen Crucified Saviors* (1875) by Kersey Graves (1813–1883) provided ample material to attack Christianity's distinctiveness.

In the nineteenth century, many liberals adopted the fourfold creed of evolution, reason, science, and materialism. From Charles Darwin (1809–1862) and Herbert Spencer (1820–1903), liberals learned to think in terms of progress. Not only nature, but also human culture was progressing. For liberalism, the great stumbling block to progress was ignorance, and the great tool to aid progress was education. Thus the alliance of liberalism and the university was a natural one.

ETHICS.

The antimystical intellectualism within the main body of the liberal tradition led to a dominance of ethical concerns. Liberals followed their triumphs in the Bill of Rights with active involvement in the great crusades of the pre-Civil War era. Always the liberals could be found standing with those issues that aimed at greater freedom for the individual. They swelled the ranks of the abolition, peace, prison reform, and women's rights movements. In the liberal religion camp were Julia Ward Howe (1819–1910), Lucy Stone (1819–1893), Robert Dale Owen (1801–1877), and Lucretia Mott (1793–1880). In the twentieth century, liberals were prominent in the labor, sexual freedom, and civil rights movements.

Interestingly enough, ethics has also been a major point of Christianity's attack upon liberals, especially atheists. Christians have argued that in giving up a belief in revelation, God, and the Bible, a belief in absolute values and moral law has also been given away, and that the attack upon traditional religion leads to amorality and immorality. Liberals have countered such assertions with the fact that atheism has in fact no track record of unethical activity; to the contrary, liberal leaders have been in the forefront of the advocacy of moral concerns, especially in the public sphere.

THE FORMS OF FAITH.

The active revolt against specific religious forms, which eventuated in the atheists' attack upon religion itself, does not lead to worship, piety, and prayer. These occur only on the extreme right wing of the liberal movement. The dominant activity of liberalism has been the communication of information, at first in the sermon and, more frequently as time passed, in the lecture. Great emphasis has been placed upon the education of members and the public, particularly their sensitization on moral issues.

The efforts at education and sensitization have been carried on by the liberal press. Liberal periodicals, most of which were independently published, have been the backbone of the movement from the early nineteenth century. The liberals' oldest periodical still in existence is *The Truth Seeker*, founded in 1873. Books attacking orthodoxy and religion are subsidized and circulated. Some have become popular items.

HISTORICAL DEVELOPMENT.

The liberals look to an amazing number of radicals in Christian history as precursors of their movements. Various liberals claim as precursors such figures as Origen (c. 185–254 C.E.), Pelagius (fourth to fifth century C.E.), and Leonardo da Vinci (1452–1519). The real beginning of the line of descent, however, is generally conceded to be Michael Servetus (1511–1553), whose *On the Errors of the Trinity* (1532) challenged traditional notions of the triune god, which he compared to the three-headed hound of hell of ancient mythology. Fleeing from Spain, he arrived in Geneva expecting a welcome from the Protestants, only to discover that they were as vehemently opposed to his theological position as were the Roman Catholics. Martyred by John Calvin (1509–1564), Servetus has become a symbol of free religion fighting orthodox intolerance. However, other reformers of similar antitrinitarian opinions led parts of Europe into a Unitarian perspective. Faustus Socinius (1539–1604) converted Poland, and Francis David (1510–1579) converted a large segment of Transylvania. In 1568 the only Unitarian king in history, the youthful John Sigismund (1540–1571), issued the Western world's first edict of religious toleration.

In seventeenth-century Europe, the Enlightenment offered liberal alternatives to traditional Christian beliefs. In particular, the deists of England preached a religion stripped of orthodox accretions. Deists argued that the creator does not interfere with the laws of the universe. Deists pictured God somewhat like a watchmaker who makes a watch, winds it up, and leaves it to run on its own. God, they said, leaves the world to follow its own course. The deists advocated a natural religion based on human reason and morality rather than revelation. Deism found a ready audience among the educated and upper classes of both England and America. Many of the leaders of the American Revolution (1775–1783) identified themselves with the deist idea world, particularly George Washington (1732–1799), Thomas Jefferson (1743–1826), Benjamin Franklin (1706–1790), and James Madison (1751–1836). By the time of the American Revolution, the three key ideas of the liberals—Unitarianism, universalism, and infidelism—had matured and had come to dominate the liberals' dissenting orientation. With each of these three ideas was carried a fight for religious freedom and a battle against the abuses of clericalism.

Universalism had been preached in America as early as the 1740s by Dr. George de Benneville (1703–1793) in Pennsylvania. In 1770, major impetus was given to the movement by the arrival of John Murray (1741–1815) from England. Murray had been raised a Methodist and had become a class leader. Impressed with George Whitefield (1714–1770), he left Methodism and associated himself with Whitefield's independent London tabernacle. While in London he became a universalist and was expelled from the tabernacle membership when he refused to "confine his sentiments to his own bosom." After his arrival in the New World, Murray itinerated and preached his universalism, which had by 1775 created such an impact that pamphlets were written against him. About this time universalist congregations began to appear. Murray's followers in Gloucester, Massachusetts, who had belonged to the Congregational Church, had their membership suspended. So, in 1779, they formed the Independent Church of Gloucester.

The movement to form churches grew, and in 1786 the Articles of Association for Universalist Churches were promulgated, although the association itself was short-lived. In the 1790s Hosea Ballou (1771–1852) appeared on the scene to continue the leadership of the aging John Murray. His newspaper, the *Winchester Profession*, became the standard for universalist views. In 1790, at a convention in Philadelphia, Articles of Faith and a Plan of Government were adopted. Thus, universalism became the first of the liberal views to solidify into an organizational structure.

In the eighteenth century, Unitarianism was preached in England and America. Theophilus Lindsey (1723–1808) founded the British Unitarian movement in 1774 after his resignation from the Anglican priesthood. In New England, Unitarianism originated in the Congregational Church, but it was not until 1794, when Joseph Priestley (1733–1804) migrated to America, that churches were founded that took the name Unitarian.

During the pre-Civil War nineteenth century, three men—William Ellery Channing (1780–1842), Ralph Waldo Emerson (1803–1882), and Theodore Parker (1810–1860)—in succession dominated Unitarian thought. The liberal debate in America centered around them.

In the second decade of the nineteenth century, William Ellery Channing, a Congregational minister, was the leading intellectual among Unitarians, which originally existed as a liberal wing in the Congregational Church. His 1819 sermon at the funeral of Jared Sparks (1789–1866) became the Unitarians' manifesto. In 1825 Channing led in founding the American Unitarian Association, a missionary group. Most members of Unitarian churches date their beginnings from one of these two events. Channing is credited with emphasizing ethics instead of theology, an emphasis that has become a hallmark of Unitarian churches.

In the 1830s, Ralph Waldo Emerson and the Transcendentalists were at their intellectual apex. Emerson's efforts to sell his monist position, most notably through his famous speech to Harvard Divinity School in 1838, were rebuffed for the time. But Emerson, his colleagues at Brook Farm (an experimental, communitarian venture of the Transcendentalists), and the raft of romantic literature flooding America from England could not long be denied.

Theodore Parker stands as the symbol of the union of Unitarian thinking with Transcendentalism. While Unitarianism could not contain Emerson, it was forced to accept Parker. He combined three elements: the philosophical, which appealed to Unitarians because of their emphasis on the mind; the mystical, which appealed to the

Transcendentalists; and the practical, which appealed to the liberals because of their desire to improve society. Parker, applying Transcendental ideals in concrete situations, was an abolitionist and a spokesman against the fugitive slave law. His sermon at the ordination of Charles Shackford in 1841, titled "The Transient and Permanent in Christianity," set the tone for liberal Christianity for his generation and served further to drive a wedge between the orthodox and liberal Congregationalists that was to result in the formal break between them after the Civil War.

For the origins of what in the nineteenth century was called infidelity (the complete rejection of theism, the church, and piety), one immediately turns to France and the works of Voltaire (1694–1778) and his contemporaries. These perspectives reached their culmination in the radically anticlerical, antireligious aspect of the French Revolution (1789–1799). In its early days in America, the adjective French was often used to modify infidelity. The first exponent on the American scene was Ethan Allen (1738–1789), the Revolutionary War hero, who published his *Reason the Only Oracle of Man* in 1784. This publication was essentially a restatement of deism, emphasizing man and his reason. For various reasons, the work made little impact. But in 1794 Thomas Paine (1737–1809) published his *Age of Reason*, which was an immediate success. The *Age of Reason* became the Bible of the free thought movement, and Paine quickly moved from being a hero of the Revolution to becoming the symbol of evil infidelity to the orthodox.

The free thought tradition gradually replaced the deist tradition of the eighteenth century. The transition can be marked in the 1790s by the leadership of Elihu Palmer (1764–1806) and the beginnings of local free thought societies. The free thought movement stressed the importance of the inquiring mind, scientific methodology, and philosophical thinking. The movement opposed orthodoxy in religion, orthodoxy being the mainline Christian tradition based on scripture and the creeds. Palmer, from 1791 until his death in 1806, was instrumental in the founding and leadership of at least three different radical societies, the most important being the Deistical Society of New York City. This society published the *Temple of Reason*, one of the first periodicals in America supporting an infidel tradition. After Palmer's death in 1806, there were about 20 years of silence from the free thought camp. Then, in the 1820s, Robert Owen founded his New Harmony experiment in Indiana, which gave the United States many of its firsts in education and community service.

In 1827 the free thought voice was heard again with the establishment of the Free Press Association in New York City. Before the end of the decade, societies were founded in Philadelphia, Pennsylvania; Woodstock, Vermont; Patterson, New Jersey; Schuylkill, Pennsylvania; Wilmington, Delaware; and St. Louis, Missouri. In the 1830s and 1840s, societies were also founded in a number of other northern and midwestern communities. Many adopted the name of Free Inquirers. Moral Philanthropists and Rationalists were also popular names. Attempts at national organization in 1828 and 1835 failed. A short-lived attempt to form the Infidel Society for the Promotion of Mental Liberty began in 1845 but died in 1848.

Other attempts waited until after the Civil War. Meanwhile, the liberals, both Christian and free thought, found themselves caught in circumstances that worked against organization. First, due to the Congregational Church's polity of local independence and the local nature of the infidel societies, leaders had no one but their local constituency to please. National organization tended to work against the very freedom that was so highly prized. Second, the decades before the Civil War were a period of intense social change; and involvement in the antislavery crusade, women's rights, and other social causes took much of the energy that could have gone into organizational building. The close of the war ended the era of social activism, and two generations of existence had caused a shift of emphasis in liberal thought. It began to turn from its primary emphasis on a critique of its religious origins toward the development of a positive position, setting the stage for the solidification of the liberal forces.

The last four decades of the nineteenth century were a time of organization of liberal churchmen. On April 7, 1865, just five days before the surrender of Robert E. Lee (1807–1870) at Appomattox, a National Convention of Unitarian Churches met in New York City to organize a National Conference of Unitarian Churches. Transcendentalists, not happy with the overly orthodox position of the National Conference, organized the Free Religious Association (FRA) in 1867. Among the leaders of the FRA were Octavius Brooks Frothingham (1822–1895), Thomas Wentworth Higginson (1823–1911), and David Wasson (1823–1887). The radicals who formed the FRA in turn found themselves divided between the mystical Transcendentalists and the scientifically oriented members. The latter organized as the National Liberal League in 1875. The issue around which they organized was a movement in the 1860s by evangelicals for a constitutional amendment that would wed church and state. Specifically, the amendment would tie the Protestant churches closely to national political institutions, from the president and Congress on down. The Liberal League countered with a program to achieve complete separation of church and state. The Liberal League itself divided over support of obscenity laws, and the group favoring a complete lifting of censorship formed the National Liberal League of America.

The thrust of most of these organizations lasted only one generation. As the issues that gave them birth died, they passed from the scene and were often absorbed by more stable bodies such as the Unitarian churches. This absorption liberalized the stable groups. Replacing the organizations that died were new associations that gathered to respond to new issues. One such association was the Union of Liberal Clergymen, formed following the Parliament of Religions in 1893. The Union of Liberal Clergymen promoted progress, reverence for law, science, and an openness to new knowl-

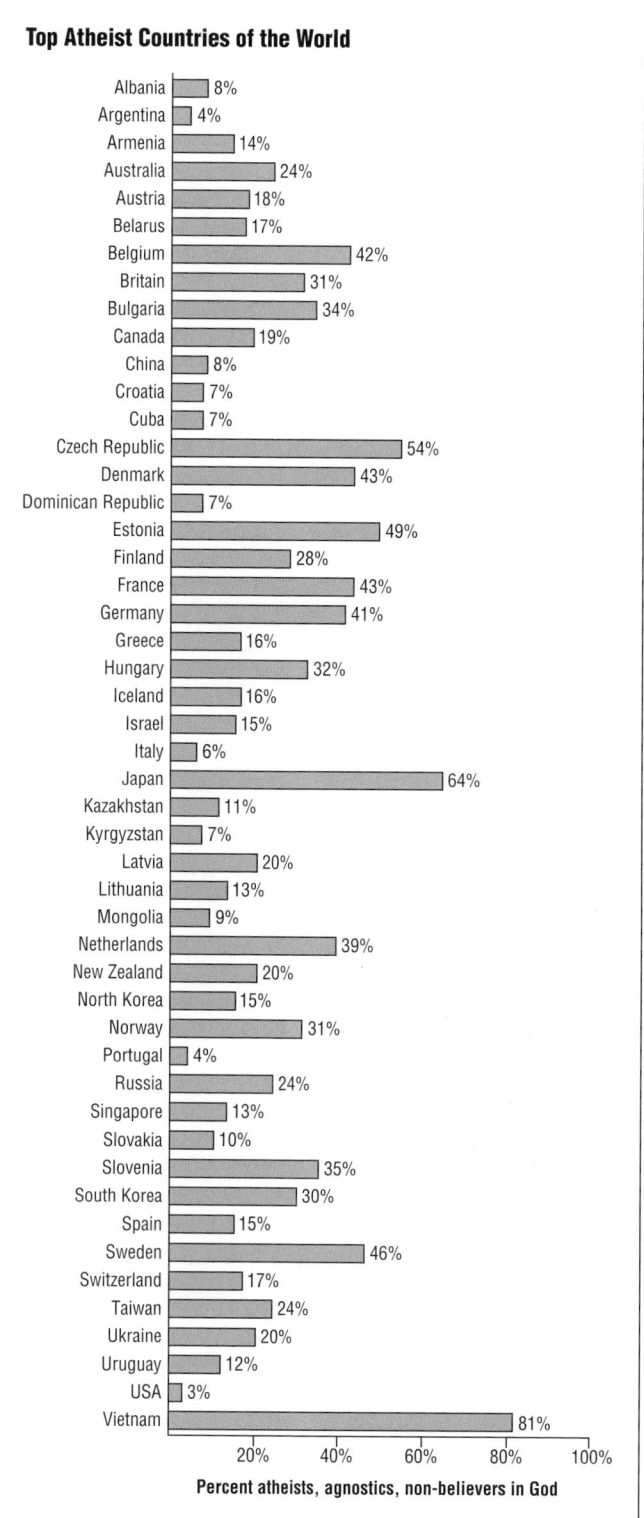

Top Atheist Countries of the World

Country	Percent
Albania	8%
Argentina	4%
Armenia	14%
Australia	24%
Austria	18%
Belarus	17%
Belgium	42%
Britain	31%
Bulgaria	34%
Canada	19%
China	8%
Croatia	7%
Cuba	7%
Czech Republic	54%
Denmark	43%
Dominican Republic	7%
Estonia	49%
Finland	28%
France	43%
Germany	41%
Greece	16%
Hungary	32%
Iceland	16%
Israel	15%
Italy	6%
Japan	64%
Kazakhstan	11%
Kyrgyzstan	7%
Latvia	20%
Lithuania	13%
Mongolia	9%
Netherlands	39%
New Zealand	20%
North Korea	15%
Norway	31%
Portugal	4%
Russia	24%
Singapore	13%
Slovakia	10%
Slovenia	35%
South Korea	30%
Spain	15%
Sweden	46%
Switzerland	17%
Taiwan	24%
Ukraine	20%
Uruguay	12%
USA	3%
Vietnam	81%

Percent atheists, agnostics, non-believers in God

Adapted from Zuckerman, Phil. "Atheism: Contemporary Rates and Patterns." *Cambridge Companion to Atheism*, ed. Micheal Martin. Cambridge, U.K.: Cambridge University Press, 2005

edge, and contended that the church should be a school of the humanities.

ATHEISM. Increasingly, since the Renaissance, some people have denied the very existence of a God. Many atheists were intellectuals—scholars and university professors—giants

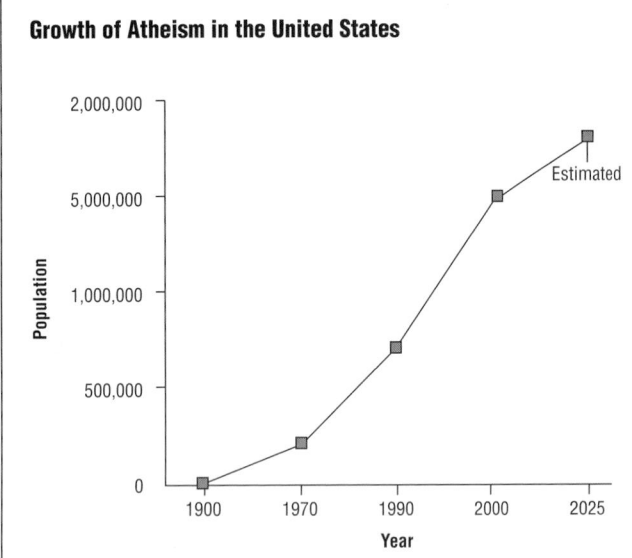

Growth of Atheism in the United States

Notes: The number of people who describe themselves as Atheists is part of a subset of religiously unaffiliated people, a group that shrunk steadily and rapidly through the 20th century (from a majority of the population to around 13%). Within that subset are the religiously unaffiliated, agnostics, and people who are simply unconcerned with religion. These figures offer an estimate of the community of those who would primarily describe themselves as atheists, without regard of any affiliation with an Atheist (or Humanist) group.

Adapted from World Christian Encyclopedia.

in their own particular disciplines. Included are such figures as Thomas Hariot (1560–1621), Christopher Marlowe (1524–1593), and Pierre Bayle (1647–1706). It was not, however, until the nineteenth century that atheism became a force with significant support.

Many deists walked a tightrope between belief in a God who does not act upon the world and outright denial of God's existence. In the nineteenth century, universities provided a haven for those who wished to declare themselves as atheists. Like its deistic predecessor, atheism was built upon an attack of the Christian churches in the nineteenth century. Primarily, however, it was an intellectual movement that launched an attack on theology and natural religion. The movement's perspective was that of scientific materialism, the theory that the basic reality of the universe is material and is therefore observable and scientifically measurable.

Among the major atheists in the nineteenth century are Karl Marx (1818–1883), Ludwig Feuerbach (1804–1872), Auguste Comte (1798–1857), Annie Besant (1847–1933), and Charles Bradlaugh (1833–1891). Often forgotten, but important in any history of atheism, is poet Percy Bysshe Shelley (1792–1822). Shelley was expelled from Oxford in 1811 for writing *The Necessity of Atheism.* His lengthy poem *Queen Mab* (1813) became a poetic reinforcement to his earlier essay. Reflecting on the death of an atheist, he cries:

> *There is no God!*
> *Nature confirms the faith this death-groan sealed:*
> *Let heaven and earth, let man's revolving race,*
> *His ceaseless generations tell the tale.*

The spirit of nature was posed as an alternative to God.

In the twentieth century, Bertrand Russell (1872–1970), A. J. Ayer (1910–1989), and Julian Huxley (1887–1975) were among the outspoken atheists. As a whole, however, the atheists mentioned above were isolated individuals who served as background for the organized movements that began to emerge in the years after the Civil War. *The Truth Seeker*, a liberal periodical, while not atheist oriented to begin with, allowed atheist notices to be printed and served as a means of communication. Only after World War I (1914–1918) were efforts to affiliate atheist bodies in larger organizations successful. As they have emerged in the twentieth century, atheists insist that first and foremost they are people with a positive approach to life that find no need to assert the existence of a deity. Their popular designation as people who deny the existence of God is an image created by their necessary attempts to explain their position in the face of a more dominant theistic population.

In the last generation, American humanists and atheists have found a noteworthy issue in pseudoscience. In the 1970s, an association of people concerned about the growing popularity of astrology and other psychic/occult activities formed the Committee for the Scientific Investigation of the Claims of the Paranormal (now known as the Committee for Skeptical Inquiry or CSI). This organization generated a public campaign against scientific claims being perpetuated within the general population that were based on methodologically flawed research, fraud, or inadequate evidence. While originally focused upon psychic and occult practices, the movement expanded to include a variety of questionable scientific claims and concerns, from various alternative medical practices to cultic brainwashing to denial of the Jewish Holocaust in World War II (1937–1945). A parallel concern to debunk claims of religious miracles (apparitions of the Virgin Mary, the Shroud of Turin, etc.) became part of the movement.

CSI has given birth to several other societies, including the James Randi Educational Foundation and the Skeptics Society. It has also been closely linked to the Council for Secular Humanism, both including philosopher Paul Kurtz (b. 1925) among its founders. Kurtz also heads Prometheus Books, which has grown into a major publisher of atheist humanist and anti-pseudoscience books in North America. The Skeptics Society is headed by Michael Shermer (b. 1954), a self-described agnostic, who has become a television personality on the issue of pseudoscience and has authored several books including *Why People Believe Weird Things* (1997) and *Denying History: Who Says the Holocaust Never Happened and Why Do They Say It?* (2000).

In the late-twentieth century, atheism found its most vocal advocate in Madalyn Murray O'Hair (1919–1995). O'Hair burst on the scene in the 1960s opposing prayer and Bible reading in public schools and subsequently founded American Atheists, which became the largest atheist organization in North America. O'Hair led the organization until her death in 1995, but her acerbic personality drove many away and led to the founding of a number of additional groups, of which the Freedom of Religion Foundation was the most notable.

The atheists and humanist organizations of the 1970s and 1980s, prepared the way for a new assertive movement that emerged during the 1990s. Neo-atheists, as they were termed, claimed that atheists had been too reticent to press their case, and the more articulate exponents, philosopher Sam Harris (b. 1967), biologist Richard Dawkins (b. 1941), and journalist Christopher Hitchens (b. 1949), have written best-selling books to do just that. Atheists have found themselves in a significant quandary. They have historically championed freedom of thought, an important issue in providing space for liberal opinions in a situation of dominant religious worldviews aligned with government power. In the modern West, however, they find themselves challenged by an environment in which freedom of thought has supported the seeming growth of traditional religions; the founding of a variety of fringe sciences from ufology to parapsychology; and the reemergence of Western esotericism and its associated use of spirit contact, astrology and other divinatory practices, channeling, and magical ceremony, all of which liberal thinkers have seen as irrational superstitions.

SOURCES

The study of the Unitarian and universalist traditions is carried on by the Unitarian Universalist Historical Society, 25 Beacon St., Boston, MA 02108. The society publishes the *UUHS Proceedings* biennially. There is no comparable structure for the study of the more radical humanist, atheist, and rationalist traditions, but several university libraries, most notably the University of Wisconsin at Madison, have extensive archival holdings on atheism.

General Sources

Baumer, Franklin L. *Religion and the Rise of Scepticism.* New York: Harcourt Brace, 1960. 308 pp.

Bratton, Fred Gladstone. *The Legacy of the Liberal Spirit: Men and Movements in the Making of Modern Thought.* Boston: Beacon Press, 1943. 319 pp.

Brown, Marshall G., and Gordon Stein. *Freethought in the United States: A Descriptive Bibliography.* Westport, CT: Greenwood Press, 1978. 146 pp.

Flynn, Tom, ed. *The New Encyclopedia of Unbelief.* Amherst, NY: Prometheus, 2007. 897 pp.

Sheldon, Henry C. *Unbelief in the Nineteenth Century: A Critical History.* New York: Eaton & Mains, 1907. 399 pp.

Shermer, Michael. *How We Believe: The Search for God in an Age of Science.* New York: Freeman, 2000. 302 pp.

Stein, Gordon. *Robert G. Ingersoll: A Checklist.* Kent, OH: Kent State University Press, 1969. 128 pp.

Unitarianism and Universalism

Albee, Ernest. *A History of English Unitarianism* (1902). New York: Collier, 1962. 383 pp.

Bueherns, John A., and F. Forrester Church. *A Chosen Faith: An Introduction to Unitarian Universalism.* Rev. ed. Boston: Beacon Press. 1998. 240 pp.

Bumbaugh, David E. *Unitarian Universalism: A Narrative History.* Chicago: Meadville Lombard Theological Seminary, 2001. 226 pp.

Miller, Russell E. *The Larger Hope.* 2 vols. Boston: Unitarian Universalist Association, 1979–1985.

Parke, David B. *The Epic of Unitarianism: Original Writings from the History of Liberal Religion.* Boston: Beacon Press, 1957. 164 pp.

Scott, Clinton Lee. *The Universalist Church of America: A Short History.* Boston: Universalist Historical Society, 1957. 124 pp.

Wilbur, Earl Morse. *A History of Unitarianism.* Cambridge, MA: Harvard University Press, 1946. 617 pp.

Williams, George Huntston. *American Universalism: A Bicentennial Historical Essay.* Boston: Beacon Press, 1971. 94 pp.

Wright, Conrad Edick. *Three Prophets of Religious Liberalism: Channing, Emerson, Parker.* Boston: Beacon Press, 1961. 152 pp.

Deism and Freethought

Darrow, Clarence, and Wallace Rice. *Infidels and Heretics: An Agnostics Anthology.* Boston: Stratford, 1929. 293 pp.

Hawke, David Freeman. *Paine.* New York: Harper & Row. 1974. 500 pp.

Ingersoll, Robert G. *Ingersoll's Greatest Lectures.* New York: Freethought Press Association, 1944. 419 pp.

Koch, G. Adolf. *Republican Religion: The American Revolution and the Cult of Reason.* New York: Henry Holt, 1933. 334 pp.

May, Henry F. *The Enlightenment in America.* New York: Oxford University Press, 1976. 419 pp.

Morais, Herbert M. *Deism in Eighteenth Century America.* New York: Russell & Russell, 1960. 203 pp.

Persons, Stow. *Free Religion.* Boston: Beacon Press, 1947. 162 pp.

Thrower, James. *Western Atheism: A Short History.* Amherst, NY: Prometheus, 1999. 157 pp.

Tribe, David. *100 Years of Freethought.* London: Elek, 1967. 259 pp.

Humanism

Hawton, Hector. *The Humanist Revolution.* London: Barrie and Rockliff, 1963. 247 pp.

Herrick, Jim. *Humanism: An Introduction.* Amherst, NY: Prometheus, 2005. 105 pp.

Knight, Margaret, and Jim Herrick, eds. *Humanist Anthology: From Confucius to Attenborough.* Amherst, NY: Prometheus, 1995. 220 pp.

Kurtz, Paul. *Humanist Manifesto 2000: A Call for New Planetary Humanism.* Amherst, NY: Prometheus, 2000. 76 pp.

Lamont, Corliss. *The Philosophy of Humanism.* 7th ed. New York: Ungar, 1990. 326 pp.

Walker, Joseph. *Humanism as a Way of Life.* New York: Macmillan, 1932. 83 pp.

Atheism

Angeles, Peter A., ed. *Critiques of God: Making the Case Against Belief in God.* Amherst, NY: Prometheus, 1997. 371 pp.

Brooks, David M. *The Necessity of Atheism.* New York: Freethought Press Association, 1933. 322 pp.

Buckley, Michael J. *At the Origins of Modern Atheism.* New Haven, CT: Yale University Press, 1987. 445 pp.

Dawkins, Richard. *The God Delusion.* London: Bantam Press, 2006. 416 pp.

Harris, Sam. *The End of Faith: Religion, Terror, and the Future of Reason.* New York: Free Press, 2005. 336 pp.

Hitchens, Christopher. *God Is Not Great: How Religion Poisons Everything.* Boston, MA: Twelve Books, Hachette, 2007. 307 pp.

———, ed. *The Portable Atheist: Essential Readings for the Nonbeliever.* 3rd ed. New York: Da Capo Press, 2007. 528 pp.

Martin, Michael, ed. *An Anthology of Atheism and Rationalism.* Buffalo, NY: Prometheus, 1980. 354 pp.

———. *Atheism: A Philosophical Justification.* Philadelphia: Temple University Press, 1992.

Stein, Gordon, ed. *The Encyclopedia of Unbelief.* Buffalo, NY: Prometheus, 1985. 2 vols.

Christian-Atheist Controversy

Blackie, John Stuart. *The Natural History of Atheism*. New York: Scribner, Armstrong, 1878. 253 pp.

Graham, Lloyd M. *Deceptions and Myths of the Bible*. New York: Bell, 1979. 484 pp.

Haught, John F. *God and the New Atheism: A Critical Response to Dawkins, Harris, and Hitchens*. Louisville, KY: Westminster John Knox Press, 2007. 156 pp.

Lewis, Joseph. *The Bible Unmasked*. New York: Freethought Press, 1926. 236 pp.

Marty, Martin E. *The Infidel: Freethought and American Religion*. Cleveland, OH: World Publishing, 1961. 224 pp.

McCabe, Joseph. *The Sources of the Morality of the Gospels*. London: Watts, 1914. 315 pp.

Micelli, Vincent P. *The Gods of Atheism*. New Rochelle, NY: Arlington House, 1973. 490 pp.

Wheless, Joseph. *Forgery in Christianity: A Documented Record of the Foundations of the Christian Religion*. New York: Knopf, 1930. 428 pp.

Intrafaith Organizations

International Association for Religious Freedom

1-6 Essex Street, London, WC2R 3HY United Kingdom

Alternate Address: IARF International Secretariat Office, 3-8-21 Sangenya-Nishi, Taisho-ku, Osaka 551-0001, Japan.

The International Association for Religious Freedom is a registered charity in the United Kingdom with the stated goal of ensuring religious freedom on a global scale. It was first organized in 1900 in Boston, Massachusetts, as the International Council of Unitarian and Other Liberal Religious Thinkers and Workers. Known through much of the early twentieth century as the International Council of Religious Liberals, it is the oldest of the several existing international interfaith organizations. The original organizers assembled in Boston from around the world for the purpose of attending the 75th anniversary of the founding of the American Unitarian Association. Prominent in the formation of the council was Samuel A. Eliot, the president of the American Unitarian Association, and in attendance was Protap Chunder Mozoomdar, the first of the numerous Indian spiritual teachers who would migrate to the United States throughout the century.

In 1901 the first international congress was held in London, England. The council continued to meet until gatherings were interrupted by World War I. After the war the council resumed meeting until the 1930s, but the meetings did not regain the enthusiasm from the prewar years. The initiative was revived in England and then the Netherlands, where it was reorganized as the International Association for Liberal Christianity and Religious Freedom. Its headquarters returned to the United States briefly before moving to Germany, and then to its current home in London. In the post–World War II global climate, it attracted an interfaith coalition from across Europe and Asia, as well as North America. Periodically, the Triennial World Congress returns to the United States, where regional conferences are also held. The U.S. chapter meets annually in conjunction with the Unitarian Universalist Association's general assembly.

Membership: In 2008 the association reported over 90 affiliated member groups in approximately 25 countries (including Bangladesh, Germany, Great Britain, India, Ireland, Japan, Nepal, Pakistan, the Philippines, Sri Lanka, and the Netherlands) from various faith traditions including Buddhism, Christianity, Hinduism, Islam, Shinto, and Sikhism.

Sources:

International Association for Religious Freedom. www.iarf.net.

Bowie, W. Copeland. *Liberal Religious Thought at the Beginning of the Twentieth Century: Addresses and Papers at the International Council of Unitarian and Other Liberal Religious Thinkers and Workers, Held at London, May 1901*. London: Philip Green, 1901.

Miller, Russell E. *The Larger Hope: The Second Century of the Universalist Church in America, 1870–1970*. Boston: Unitarian Universalist Association, 1985.

International Humanist and Ethical Union

IHEU Secretariat, 1 Gower St., London, WC1E 6HD United Kingdom

The International Humanist and Ethical Union (IHEU), founded in Amsterdam in 1952, is an umbrella organization of groups embracing humanism, atheism, rationalism, secularism, and skepticism. Among the seven founding members of the IHEU were the American Ethical Union and the American Humanist Association. The founding congress was organized as a response to the widespread demand for an alternative to the religions that claim to be based on revelation on the one hand and to totalitarianism on the other. The union views humanism, outcome of a long tradition that has inspired thinkers and creative artists and that gave rise to science, as a path toward resolving the crises faced by civilization. Ethical humanism emphasizes respect for humans as spiritual and moral beings. In the Amsterdam Declaration adopted in 1952, the IHEU defined humanism as a way of life that was democratic, ethical, and aimed at the maximum possible fulfillment through the cultivation of ethical and creative living. It affirmed the use of science creatively, not destructively, and insisted on the combination of personal liberty with social responsibility.

At its fiftieth anniversary congress, the IHEU adopted the Amsterdam Declaration 2002, defining the fundamentals of modern humanism as ethical and rational; supporting democracy and human rights; insisting that personal liberty must be combined with social responsibility; responding to the widespread demand for an alternative to dogmatic religion; and valuing artistic creativity and imagination.

Based in London, the IHEU is an international nongovernmental organization with Special Consultative Status at the United Nations (New York, Geneva, and Vienna) and General Consultative Status at UNICEF (New York) and the Council of Europe (Strasbourg), and maintains operational relations with UNESCO (Paris). IHEU also has offices in New York City, where the IHEU-Appignani Center for Bioethics is located.

Membership: In 2008 the IHEU reported more than 100 member organizations in more than 40 countries, including the American Ethical Union, American Humanist Association, Council for Secular Humanism, the Humanist Society of Canada, and North American Committee for Humanism. Cooperating groups include the Unitarian Universalist Association. The IHEU reported the number of individual members of member organizations as more than 3 million.

Periodicals: *International Humanist News*.

Sources:

International Humanist and Ethical Union. www.iheu.org/.

 Liberal

American Association for the Advancement of Atheism (AAAA)

PO Box 5733, Parsippany, NJ 07054-5733

The American Association for the Advancement of Atheism (AAAA) is the oldest of the several atheist bodies in the United States. The group was founded by Charles Lee Smith in 1925 as an antireligion/antitheist body. Smith, a lawyer, was converted to atheism from his reading of various books advocating freethought (the philosophy that holds that all beliefs should be formed by logic and science rather than ideology or emotions). After World War I he began to write for *The Truth Seeker*, an independent freethought journal published in New York City. In 1925, with his friend Freeman Hopwood, he founded the AAAA. Starting with little support and working within a hostile environment, Smith engaged in a number of controversial activities, beginning with his involvement in the debates over Arkansas's antievolution law in 1928. He debated Christian ministers when the opportunity arose, the most famous being Aimee Semple McPherson, the flamboyant leader of the International Church of the Foursquare Gospel. From the publicity given his various activities, the Association grew. At its peak it had approximately 2,000 members, and chapters could be found on some 20 college and university campuses. The AAAA sponsored periodic lectures, called the Ingersoll Forum (named for Robert G. Ingersoll, the famous nineteenth-century freethinker), in New York City. In 1930 Smith purchased *The Truth Seeker*, which remained independent but closely identified with the Association. Hard hit by the economic Depression of the 1930s, the Association shrank, and most of its organized activities were discontinued, though Smith continued to publish the magazine monthly.

Around 1950 Smith's dislike of Jews and blacks began to be reflected in the pages of *The Truth Seeker*, which started to publish an increasing number of racist and anti-Semitic articles. These led to further loss of support and the isolation of the AAAA from other atheist organizations. In 1964 Smith sold *The Truth Seeker* to James Hervey Johnson, who moved it and the AAAA to San Diego. A few months later, Smith died and since then Johnson has continued as head of the AAAA and editor of the magazine.

The Association believes religion to be a fraud and that God is nonexistent. It also teaches that the white race is superior to Jews and blacks and actively distributes such books as *The Biological Jew*, by Eustace Mullins; *The International Jew*, by Henry Ford; the apocryphal *Protocols of the Learned Elders of Zion*; and *Our Nordic Race*, by R. K. Hoskins. The Association also stands for law and order, honest government, "real liberty," freedom of the press and of speech, absolute separation of religion and government, and taxation of churches. All members must be atheists, a requirement that distinguishes the AAAA from many freethought organizations.

During the 1970s there were approximately 200 members, but no regular meetings. As with most atheist groups, there are too few members in most cities to support a separate meeting, thus members attend any local freethinkers' gathering available to them. In San Diego, the freethinkers gather on the birthdays of Thomas Paine (January 29) and Robert Ingersoll (August 7).

Membership: Not reported.

Periodicals: *The Truth Seeker*.

Sources:

Cardiff, Ira D. *"If Christ Came to New York."* New York: American Association for the Advancement of Atheism, [1932].

Dalgliesh, Malcolm. *The Sage of San Diego Said Choose Quality and Reason*. New York: A New Enlightenment, n.d. 100 pp.

Graves, Kersey. *The World's Sixteen Crucified Saviors*. New York: Truth Seeker, 1875.

Johnson, James Hervey. "Charles Smith: 1887–1964." *The Truth Seeker* 91, no. 11 (November 1964).

———. *Superior Men*. San Diego, CA: Author, 1949.

McPherson, Aimee Semple, and Charles Lee Smith. *Debate: There Is a God!* Los Angeles: Foursquare Publications, n.d.

Swancara, Frank. *Separation of Religion and Government*. New York: Truth Seeker Co., 1950.

American Atheists, Inc.

PO Box 5733, Parsippany, NJ 07054-6733

Possibly the most famous American atheist of the twentieth century was Madalyn Murray O'Hair (1919–1995), who founded American Atheists, Inc., on July 1, 1963, in Austin, Texas. O'Hair became a national figure in 1963 when the Supreme Court upheld her suit, which had been joined with a second similar case, and ruled against the mandatory recitation of the Lord's Prayer and passages from the Bible in U.S. public schools. This ruling has often been mistakenly described as outlaw-ing prayer in the public schools. O'Hair next instituted a suit aimed at eliminating tax-exempt status for church-owned property. Soon after the second suit was filed, she moved from Baltimore to Honolulu, where she formed the International Free Thought Association of America. She eventually settled in Austin, where she founded the Society of Separationists and the Charles E. Stevens American Atheist Library and Archives. The Society of Separationists was superseded by American Atheists, Inc., the headquarters of which moved into the American Atheist Center in Austin in 1977. During the 1970s O'Hair emerged as a popular and controversial speaker on atheism, frequently debating ministers in public meetings and on television. She instituted a number of lawsuits built around atheistic concerns, most of which failed. Her activities also led to many false rumors, including one that she had petitioned the U.S. Federal Communications Commission to ban religious broadcasting; the persistence of this rumor forced several formal retractions by the FCC. O'Hair also became deeply involved in various social causes, such as civil rights and peace. She was actively antireligious and specifically anti-Christian, rejecting the historicity of Jesus, a life after death, and the authority of the Bible.

The group stands free from theism, which is equated with religion. It views religion as a crutch that healthy people do not need, deeming it superstitious and supernatural nonsense. The American Atheists' library, founded in 1965 and now housed at the Atheist Center, has more than 20,000 volumes and related material. At its peak, the American Atheist Radio Series (1968–1973) was heard on more than 20 stations in 12 states. Members in Petersburg, Indiana, once opened an atheist museum, which closed after the death of its curator. The organization holds an annual national convention and airs a national cable-access television program called *The Atheist Viewpoint*, which is also available on podcast. American Atheists also sells books and products.

At the annual convention in 1986, O'Hair resigned as president of American Atheists and was succeeded by her son, Jon G. Murray. O'Hair continued to serve as presiding officer of its board of directors. American Atheists, Inc., founded the American Atheists General Headquarters, a building complex to house the library, archives, and printing facilities (American Atheist Press). Ellen Johnson became president of the organization in 1996, after the disappearance of Madalyn O'Hair along with her son and granddaughter, Robin Murray-O'Hair, who was the editor of the American Atheist Press (see Remarks). In 1999 the group relocated to Cranford, New Jersey. In 2008 Johnson stepped down as president and was succeeded by long-time member Frank Zindler.

Membership: In 2002 the group reported 2,500 members.

Periodicals: *The American Atheist*.

Remarks: On September 4, 1995, 76-year-old Madalyn Murray O'Hair, her son Jon, and granddaughter Robin Murray O'Hair left their home without prior warning. They did not take their passports, and they seemed to have left in the midst of eating breakfast. Jon Murray kept in contact with the organization for a few weeks and offered some instructions on keeping it going while they were away. Eventually, all contact stopped and none of the three were seen again. More than $600,000 in funds were missing from a New Zealand bank account. Some months later, Robin's car was found at the Austin airport. The three were discovered to have been kidnapped and murdered by a career criminal named David Roland Waters and two accomplices. Waters was convicted of the crimes and sentenced to life in prison, where he eventually died. Another of the kidnappers, Gary Karr, is serving a life sentence, and the third was murdered by Waters and Karr.

Sources:

American Atheists. www.atheists.org.

Conrad, Jane Kathryn. *Mad Madalyn*. Brighton, OH: Author, 1983.

Murray, William J. *My Life without God*. Nashville, TN: Thomas Nelson, 1982.

O'Hair, Madalyn Murray. *Bill Murray, the Bible and the Baltimore Board of Education*. Austin, TX: American Atheist Press, 1970.

———. *What on Earth Is an Atheist*. Austin, TX: American Atheist Press, 1969.

Wright, Lawrence. *Saints and Sinners*. New York: Random House, 1993.

American Ethical Union

2 W 64th St., New York, NY 10023

Alternate Address: International Humanist and Ethical Union, Ouderhof 11, 2512 GH Utrecht, The Netherlands.

The founder of what became the American Ethical Union, Felix Adler (1851–1933), was born in Alzey, Germany, and came to the United States at an early age. The son of the rabbi at Temple Emmanuel in New York City, Adler returned to Germany to study for the rabbinate at the University of Heidelberg, and made plans to succeed his father. During this time, he encountered neo-Kantian idealism and its critique of religion, which left him with a strong sense of duty and a zeal to implement his ethical ideals. Adler came to believe that morality could be established independently of any theological system. For Adler, the autonomy and centrality of ethics became the philosophical basis for an ethical culture. He added a philosophical complement to Emerson's call for a purely ethical religion and in this way contributed to America's moralistic religious tradition. On his return to the United States, Adler taught Hebrew and oriental languages and literature at Cornell University (1874–1876) and then returned to New York City to found the Ethical Culture Society on May 15, 1876. This was the first of the ethical culture societies in the United States, later nationally federated as the American Ethical Union and part of the International Humanist and Ethical Union.

Under Adler's direction, the society was dedicated to the principle of "deed before creed," and both education and social reform were seen as necessary deeds. In Adler's view, creeds about God were not important and socially responsible deeds were the one way people had of affirming the worth and dignity of every human being. Thus, in 1877, the District Nursing Department, now the Visiting Nurse Service, and the Tenement House Building Committee were started. In 1878 the first free kindergarten, which became the Workingman's School in 1880, was opened. The Mother's Society to Study Child Nature, started in 1888, became the Child Study Association in 1915. Adler was elected president of the Free Religious Association in 1878, but he resigned in 1882 because of the lack of commitment to social action and political reform. Adler founded and served as chairperson of the Child Labor Committee from 1894 to 1921, and the Visiting and Teaching Guild for Crippled Children was started in 1889. For almost two decades (1902–1921), he served as professor of political and social ethics at Columbia University.

In 1882 Adler formed a second ethical culture society in Chicago, Illinois. Another emerged at Philadelphia, Pennsylvania, in 1885 and a fourth in St. Louis, Missouri, the following year. In 1887 the first international society was formed in London, England. Eventually some 20 countries would have groups belonging to the International Humanist and Ethical Union, which includes groups associated with the American Humanist Association.

Religion, seen as a way of life in this world, has led the union into social involvement on a number of issues related to racism, war and peace studies, adult education, citizenship, and language training for refugees in the United States. Union members were instrumental in establishing the American Civil Liberties Union (ACLU), the National Association for the Advancement of Colored People (NAACP), and the Legal Aid Society. The group participates in United Nations programs as a nongovernmental organization (NGO).

Membership: In 1988 there were 21 ethical culture societies in the United States. Groups from more than 20 countries participated in the International Humanist and Ethical Union.

Periodicals: *Ethical Platform*. • *AEU Reports*.

Sources:

American Ethical Union. www.aeu.org.

The Fiftieth Anniversary of the Ethical Movement, 1876–1926. New York: A. Appleton and Company, 1926.

Friess, Horace Leland. *Felix Adler and Ethical Culture: Memories and Studies*. New York: Columbia University Press, 1981.

Kraut, Benny. *From Reform Judaism to Ethical Culture*. Cincinnati, OH: Hebrew Union College Press, 1979.

Muzzey, David Saville. *Ethical Religion*. New York: American Ethical Union, 1943.

Radest, Howard B. *Toward Common Ground*. New York: Frederick Unger Publishing Co., 1969.

American Humanist Association

7 Harwood Dr., Box 8188, Amherst, NY 14226-7188

In the early twentieth century, a strong humanist orientation developed among supporters of the American Unitarian Association, the Free Religious Association, and the American Ethical Union. At the time, members of these groups were still mostly theistic. By the 1920s, however, some Unitarians had become nontheists. Their greatest spokespersons were John H. Dietrich (1878–1957), a Unitarian minister in Minneapolis, and Curtis W. Reese, secretary of the Western Unitarian Conference. Using ideas from science and pragmatic philosophy, the nontheists saw humanism as the only possible alternative to traditional religion. Whereas Dietrich and Reese remained within the Unitarian structure, others of like mind left to begin humanistic societies. The first two of these were founded in 1929, in New York City by Charles Francis Potter (1885–1962) and in Hollywood, California, by Theodore Curtis Abell.

In 1933 a group of 11 prominent humanist leaders issued "A Humanist Manifesto," the definitive statement of the movement. Among its signers were John Dewey (1859–1952), Harry Elmer Barnes (1889–1968), C. F. Potter, and John Herman Randall (1889–1980). The statement called for a radical change in religious perspectives. Religion was seen as a tool for realizing the highest values in life, but the universe was regarded as self-existing, not created, and humanity as part of evolved nature. Mind-body dualism, supernaturalism, theism, and even deism were rejected. The goal of life was viewed as the complete realization of human personality. Social ethics and personal fulfillment were priority items. Social control was a means to the abundant life for all. An updated version of the statement was issued in 1973 as the "Humanist Manifesto II," which added an additional emphasis on responsibility toward humanity as a whole.

To bring some coordination and fellowship to the various independent humanist efforts in the United States, the American Humanist Association was formed in 1941. It accepts the basic perspective of the two Humanist Manifestos, especially their call for the use of science for purposes of social welfare. Its social program has included a defense of human rights, religious liberty, freedom of thought, and separation of church and state, and advocacy of population growth control, death with dignity, penal reform, ecology; and various issues related to the United Nations.

The American Humanist Association is organized democratically; board members are elected by the general membership. Chapters are located across the country. An annual conference is held in a different city each year. Certified leaders of the association, analogous to ministers or rabbis, are termed *celebrants*. The association is also a member of the International Humanist and Ethical Union.

Membership: In 1997 the association reported approximately 10,000 members in 70 chapters. There were 120 celebrants in the United States, 1 in Canada, and 1 in Australia.

Periodicals: *The Humanist*. • *Free Mind*. • *Humanist Living*.

Remarks: Among the counselors of the association is Paul Kurtz (b. 1925), former editor of *The Humanist*, who has developed a number of enterprises that, while entirely independent of the American Humanist Association, serve the humanist cause as a whole. Kurtz founded and heads Prometheus Books, the major American publisher of humanist and freethought literature. During the 1970s he was a leader in the formation of the Committee for the Scientific Investigation of the Paranormal, whose quarterly *Skeptical Inquirer* is a major voice in the debunking of psychic and paranormal phenomena. Around 1980 he formed the Council for a Democratic and Secular Humanism and began the magazine *Free Inquiry*. He also became a leading force in the formation of the Academy of Humanism, an organization created to disseminate humanist ideals and beliefs and to recognize outstanding humanists. In addition, he has been prominent in the Religion and Biblical Criticism Research Project, which disseminates the results of biblical criticism (especially concerning claims many humanists consider unfounded, such as the divine inspiration of the Bible and the historicity of Jesus).

Sources:

American Humanist Association. www.americanhumanist.org.

Blackham, H. J. *Modern Humanism*. Yellow Springs, OH: American Humanist Association, 1964.

Humanist Manifestos I and II. Buffalo, NY: Prometheus Books, 1973.

Kurtz, Paul, ed. *The Humanist Alternative*. Buffalo, NY: Prometheus Books, 1973.

Lamont, Corliss. *Voice in the Wilderness*. Buffalo, NY: Prometheus Books, 1975.

Reese, Curtis W. *Humanism*. Chicago: Open Court Publishing Co., 1926.

———, ed. *Humanist Sermons*. Chicago: Open Court Publishing Co., 1927.

American Unitarian Conference

6806 Springfield Dr., Mason Neck, VA 22079

The American Unitarian Conference (AUC) was formed in 2000 by Dean Fisher and David Barton and former members of the Unitarian Universalist Association (UUA) who strongly disagreed with the direction taken by the UUA since its formation in 1961. Over the decades, the UUA had moved steadily from its antitrinitarian Christianity to become the home of a wide variety of constituencies, from Humanism to Zen Buddhism. AUC founders termed it a "federation of religions," and suggested that although Unitarianism should respect all religions, it should not embrace other religions as its own. They also noted that many congregations of Unitarians opposed both Christianity and belief in God.

The AUC believes that Unitarianism did not reject Christianity per se, but rather the doctrine of the trinity (and all that that doctrine implied), as well as a particular form of Christianity—the Calvinism that dominated in the Congregational Church of the mid-nineteenth century. Unitarianism was founded to be tolerant of other faith traditions and to learn from them, not to be replaced by them. AUC founders believed that many Unitarian churches have become anti-Christian and anti-God in their practice, substituting salvation by grace with salvation by legislation.

The AUC founders believed that Unitarian faith anchored in the original tenets of the tradition remains valuable in the present age. In launching their new association, they built a web site and formed a new corporation.

To the AUC, Unitarianism is a religion, a spiritual tradition that affirms humanity's spiritual nature and the truth of religious experience that is ineffable, beyond the ability of reason to fully describe. It affirms the existence of God, who created the universe and gave humans the gift of free will. This perspective is summarized in "Our Religious Principles."

As a recently founded body, the AUC sees itself as still developing, and is open to new insights and to people outside the Unitarian tradition who identify themselves as deists or simply theists.

Membership: In 2008 there were three congregations affiliated with the AUC, one each in San Diego, California, Syracuse, New York, and Cochranville, Pennsylvania. Another several thousand individuals have affiliated with the AUC, but do not have a congregation with which to affiliate.

Periodicals: *The American Unitarian*.

Sources:

American Unitarian Conference. www.americanunitarian.org/.

Atheist Alliance International (AAI)

PO Box 234, Pocopson, PA 19366

The Atheist Alliance International (AAI) is a democratic antitheist association formed in 1995 by independent, autonomous atheist societies. The group believes in state neutrality regarding religious speech, beliefs, and participation. Atheism, which AAI defines as "living one's life without the supernatural," is considered a human-centered vision with a reality-based approach to problem solving, leading toward intellectual growth, personal freedom, and social, environmental, and scientific progress. Members of AAI believe that the interference of religion in civic and social matters leads to an abridgement of civil liberties, and that religious authoritarianism has caused a tyrannical and intolerant undercurrent in U.S. social and political discourse.

Some of the group's other major tenets are that freedom of conscience is a fundamental human right; that the unfettered pursuit of scientific advancement is the only proven way to make human life better; and that compassion and empathy for both humans and nonhumans, as well as the encouragement of "cooperative diversity" among people with differing values and beliefs, are paramount to improving the human experience. The group is actively opposed to all ideas that it considers to be based in supernatural beliefs, including those concerning the existence of ghosts or spirits, reincarnation or an afterlife for human souls, and all forms of astrology. AAI is also vocal in its opposition to conspiracy theories about and denial of documented historical events, such as the Nazi Holocaust of World War II.

AAI hosts an annual convention, during which representatives of the board are selected from among the various member groups. The group also maintains a list of all freethought organizations around the world and has two regular publications: *Secular Nation* magazine and the more scholarly *Journal of Higher Criticism*. An Internet-based community of atheists—Atheist Internet Outreach—is also available to individuals through AAI. AAI maintains an association with the teachers' resource group Objectivity and Balance in Teaching about Religion.

Membership: As of 2008, AAI member organizations exist in 22 U.S. states and 10 countries.

Periodicals: *Secular Nation*. • *Journal of Higher Criticism*.

Atheists United

4773 Hollywood Blvd., Hollywood, CA 90027

Atheists United is an affiliate organization of Atheist Alliance International (AAI), representing the Los Angeles area. The group was formed in 1982 and is a major organization for unbelievers on the West Coast. It promotes two goals: the separation of church and state and the furtherance of atheism and rationalist thought, primarily through education. Individual neighborhood Atheists United groups host meetings throughout southern California; the group also publishes a newsletter and a set of atheist literature, maintains a "Dial-an-Atheist" telephone service, and hosts a weekly radio show in Los Angeles.

Members of Atheists United consider themselves nontheists. They accept only ideas confirmed by evidence, and even these are subject to reconsideration. All superstitions, especially religions, are rejected.

Membership: Atheists United does not release membership information. There are an estimated 1,500 members. Meetings have been held regularly throughout Southern California, from Ventura to San Diego.

Periodicals: *Atheists United Newsletter*.

Sources:

Atheists United. www.atheistsunited.org.

Canadian Atheist Society

PO Box 41613, 923 12th St., New Westminster, BC, Canada V3M 6L1

The Canadian Atheist Society is a small atheist organization formed in the mid-1990s in British Columbia under the leadership of Ray Blessin and Fern Wayman.

In 1994 the society launched *The Canadian Atheist* as a quarterly magazine and moved to incorporate as an educational organization. Though based in the Canadian West Coast region, the society quickly gained a following across Canada. Among other activities, it launched an effort to remove references to God from the preamble of the Canadian Constitution and the National Anthem. The society feels that these national symbols should serve to unite all Canadians, not just religious Canadians.

Membership: Not reported.

Periodicals: *The Canadian Atheist.*

Celebrant USA Foundation and Institute

93 Valley Rd., 2nd Fl., Montclair, NJ 07042

Celebrant USA was founded in 2000 in Montclair, New Jersey, by Charlotte Eulette. Following on a practice present in Australia for a generation, Celebrant USA Foundation and Institute provides ceremonies that mark important transitions in the lives of people who, for whatever reasons, do not have clergy to officiate. To that end, Celebrant USA recruits, trains, and certifies celebrants to compose and perform personalized ceremonies marking a broad range of occasions for individuals, couples, families, and organizations. Such ceremonies include weddings and funerals as well as house warmings and corporate employee-recognition events.

Celebrant USA has a program to educate the public about the importance of ceremony and rituals marking important transitions in life. Its institute offers certificate programs for people who wish to become professional celebrants in Ceremonies for Couples, Ceremonies for Healing and Transition, Ceremonies for Families and Children, and Ceremonies for Organizations. Classes are conducted both at the organization's national headquarters and via correspondence and web-based instruction.

Graduates of Celebrant USA's training are certified as civil celebrants. Their training allows them to work with individuals or groups to create ceremonies adapted to personal needs and interests and a wide variety of beliefs and cultures. Ceremonies can be created to mark a renewal of wedding vows, the adoption of a child, coming of age, divorce, or retirement, for example. In the process of performing their tasks, the personal beliefs of the celebrant become immaterial, and the focus is on the values, beliefs, and wishes of the person for whom the ceremony is being conducted. Thus, the civil celebrant is able to function in a wide variety of cultural settings, providing celebrations with either religious or secular content.

Membership: In 2008 Celebrant USA had certified more than 300 civil celebrants who operate across the United States.

Sources:

Celebrant USA Foundation and Institute. www.celebrantusa.com/.

Church of Reality

754 Glenview Dr. #201, San Bruno, CA 94066

The Church of Reality is a Humanist religion begun in 1998 by Marc Perkel, who posited that religion could be based on reality rather than myths. He began to articulate his idea as the Church of Reality via the Internet, exploring the implications of his basic notion. From the concept that the process of pursuing knowledge is a communal activity, Perkel developed the idea of the tree of knowledge, the body of interconnected common knowledge shared by humans.

In 2003 Perkel applied for church recognition from the Internal Revenue Service. The process led him to focus on structure and organization, and to generate two basic church documents: the Sacred Principles and Sacred Choices. The former commits church members to a set of basic values such as positive evolution, curiosity, freedom, peace, courage, persistence, compassion, justice, respect, and personal responsibility. The latter document, on sacred choices, highlights the decisions necessary to anyone choosing to live as a realist.

Perkel concluded that the Church of Reality is about the pursuit of reality, which involves "growing the tree of knowledge." This involves the assumption that the human race is progressing; positive evolution is the basic value. Perkel also concluded that human society is moving in negative direction due largely to religion and religious conflict. As a realist, the church accepts the mission to focus society's attention on reality.

The church bases its perspectives on a set of axioms, self-evident truths upon which other truth build. Thus, the church affirms that reality exists; that the earth and the human race exist; and that human life has evolved over billions of years. As humans, we function as a society and share a wealth of knowledge. Humans are self-aware and have the ability to make decisions that produce consequences. As technology grows, it has created the possibility of self-extermination. At the same time, we know that many life forms have become extinct. We need to evolve. Meanwhile, the universe as a whole does not care about humans.

The Church of Reality remains a largely web-based religion. It identifies itself most closely with the Unitarian Universalist Association, and welcomes people who wish to belong to both organizations, though it distinguishes between the two groups: "Realists put reality first and are interested in community. Unitarians put community first and are interested in reality."

Membership: Not reported.

Sources:

Church of Reality. www.churchofreality.org/.

Church of Reason

International Council of Unitary Mission Churches, 3359 W 58th St., Cleveland, OH 44102-5670

The Church of Reason was founded in 1973 by Thomas D. Blackburn, a captain in the U.S. Air Force, while he was stationed in Tullahoma, Tennessee. One of the first to join the church was Robert M. Dunn of Cleveland, Ohio, who promptly became the group's leader. The church grew under Dunn's leadership and soon had several Reason devotees in northern Ohio, with associates in Massachusetts, New York, and Tennessee. The church is dedicated to several basic principles that appear in its creed. Members seek knowledge; see reason as the faculty that identifies and integrates the materials provided by the senses and as the only means to knowledge; and agree to attempt to act on that knowledge. They also pledge to initiate neither force nor fraud, and understand that their right to life depends on their recognition of the same right in others.

Unlike many rationalists and atheists, members of the Church of Reason are not inimical to religion. Rather, they view religion, as described by Ayn Rand in her novel *The Fountainhead*, as "the great aspiration of the human spirit toward the highest, the noblest, the best. The human spirit as the creator and the conqueror of the ideal." As such, by reason of the volitional and conceptual nature of human consciousness, religion is seen as inherent in human nature. Organized religion assists individuals in forging a worldview and helps them to act accordingly. The Church of Reason promotes the discovery and dissemination of information concerning ultimate and ulterior issues by providing a forum for the study and sharing of fundamental ideas. It also provides a forum for the celebration of life-cycle events, a place to meet and share life with like-minded people, and an efficient means of accomplishing goals.

Members of the Church of Reason see the faculty of reason, operating on the evidence of the senses, as the basic tool of human survival, and thus see it as the cardinal virtue; rationality implies productivity, independence, integrity, honesty, justice, and earned pride as correlative virtues.

Membership: Not reported.

Sources:

www.churchofreason.org/his.htm.

Welcome to a Good Look at the Religion of Reason. Cleveland, OH: Church of Reason, 1989.

Church of Spiritual Humanism

PO Box 180, Jenkintown, PA 19046

The Church of Spiritual Humanism was founded to promote the concept of a religion based on humans' ability to solve social problems using logic and science. It recognizes the value of religion and its rituals and methods to assist men and women in their life struggles, and the power of religion to affect human behavior, but it aims to redefine religion as a natural rather than supernatural reality. It looks to scientific inquiry to define the "divine" spark in humanity.

The Church of Spiritual Humanism also believes that ordination should be free and freely available to anyone who wants it. Its web site provides a means for people to simply ask for and receive ordination in the church. The church authorizes its ministers to perform the traditional functions of clergy, such as marriages and funerals, though they are specifically forbidden to perform any rituals involving exorcism, circumcision, and animal sacrifice. The church is gay-friendly and allows its clergy to perform same-sex unions. It publishes and makes available materials informing new clergy of their rights and facilitating their performance of their duties.

The church is humanist, affirming that religion should be based on reason. It does not approve of specifically Christian beliefs, or even belief in a deity, and it will become open to what it considers to be supernatural beliefs only if they are proven by scientific exploration.

Membership: In 2008 the church claimed more than 100,000 members in 146 countries.

Periodicals: Newsletter (available online).

Educational Facilities:

Church of Spiritual Humanism Seminary (online distance-learning facility).

Sources:

Church of Spiritual Humanism. www.spiritualhumanism.org/.

Confraternity of Deists, Inc.

Current address not obtained for this edition.

The Confraternity of Deists was begun in 1967 in St. Petersburg, Florida, by Paul Englert, a former Roman Catholic. Deism is belief in one God, the supreme intelligence, as contrasted with belief in Scripture or atheism. Without God, Deists believe, humans are defenseless against themselves. The Creed of Confraternity includes the beliefs that the constructive exercise of human intelligence contributes to the glorification of God; that all human-made Scriptures are mere literary works, without religious, historical, or chronological value; that the church of the Deist should constitute the free university, disseminating scientific knowledge and nurturing the arts; and that the social duty of the Deist is to work for the spiritual and temporal elevation of the people.

Membership: Not reported. In 1969 there were three centers of the Confraternity, one at the headquarters and two at universities.

Council for Secular Humanism

PO Box 664, Amherst, NY 14226-0664

At the end of the 1970s Paul Kurtz (b. 1925), a well-known humanist intellectual, parted company with the American Humanist Association. At that time Kurtz was head of Prometheus Books, a prominent humanist/atheist publishing concern, and the driving force behind the Committee for the Scientific Examination of the Paranormal (later renamed the Committee for Skeptical Inquiry), a skeptical watchdog group dedicated to debunking unfounded claims of psychic, occult, and paranormal phenomena. With supporters, he led in the establishment of the Council for a Democratic and Secular Humanism, now known as the Council for Secular Humanism. Whereas the American Humanist Association is representative of the broad range of humanist thought, the council emphasizes the most secular aspect of humanism, and is explicitly not a religious organization.

Kurtz had been prominent in the execution and circulation of the "Humanist Manifesto II" in 1973. In 1980 he wrote and circulated "A Secular Humanist Declaration," which outlined the position of secular humanism and was signed by a number of prominent liberal thinkers. According to Kurtz, secular humanism is committed to using reason and science to understand the universe and attempt to solve human problems, and stands against perceived efforts to denigrate human intelligence, seek to understand the world in supernatural terms, and look outside of nature for salvation. It is committed to the scientific nature of inquiry, to a belief that nature is intelligible to human reason and explainable by means of causal hypotheses, and to a naturalistic ethics that exists quite apart from any theological or metaphysical base. It differs from other forms of humanism in its confidence in humanity's ability to apply science and technology for the betterment of human life. Like atheism, it rejects the supernatural but also offers a positive program for constructing an ethical value system.

The council sponsors the Academy of Humanism to recognize distinguished humanists and disseminate humanist ideals and beliefs. The Committee for the Scientific Examination of Religion attempts to consider critically the claims of religion, both Eastern and Western. The Biblical Criticism Research Project was founded to disseminate the results of biblical scholarship, which it believes undercuts many of the claims of both the Jewish and Christian faiths.

The council founded *Free Inquiry* magazine, a network for mutual support that assists the organization of local and regional societies of secular humanists. Such groups are now found across the United States. Also related is the Secular Organizations for Sobriety, a humanist alternative to Alcoholics Anonymous.

The council is a full member of the International Humanist and Ethical Union. It is also an affiliate organization of the Center for Inquiry, a nonpartisan, nonprofit group that is dedicated to the promotion of rational social and scientific inquiry based on humanist ideals, and that serves as an umbrella organization for a number of related secular humanist groups.

Membership: Not reported.

Educational Facilities:

Center for Inquiry Institute, Amherst, New York.

Periodicals: *Free Inquiry*. • *Secular Humanist Bulletin*. • *AAH Examiner* (African Americans for Humanism).

Sources:

Council for Secular Humanism. www.secularhumanism.org.

Kurtz, Paul. *Forbidden Fruit: The Ethics of Humanism*. Buffalo, NY: Prometheus Books, 1988.

———, ed. *The Humanist Alternative: Some Definitions of Humanism*. Buffalo, NY: Prometheus Books, 1973.

———. *In Defense of Secular Humanism*. Buffalo, NY: Prometheus Books, 1983.

———, ed. *A Secular Humanist Declaration*. Privately printed, 1980.

———. *Transcendental Temptation: A Critique of Religion and the Paranormal*. Buffalo, NY: Prometheus Books, 1986. 500 pp.

Creativity Movement (World Church of the Creator)

Current address could not be obtained for this edition.

The Creativity Movement (also called World Church of the Creator and formerly known as the Church of the Creator) was founded in 1973 by Ben Klassen (1918–1993) with the publication of his manifesto *Nature's Eternal Religion*, in which he claimed that the "survival, expansion, and advancement" of the white race was the highest virtue and the ultimate law of nature. Creativity Movement members—all of whom are white supremacists—do not believe in the conventional facets of religion, such as the existence of a god or an afterlife; rather, they hold that their race is their religion. Members, who refer to themselves as "creators," believe that Jews, people of color, immigrants, and Christians are inferior to and the natural enemies of whites.

Born in the Ukraine and raised in Canada, Klassen assembled his ideology from an amalgamation of ideas and images from Norse mythology, paganism, imperial Rome, and Nazism. Gradually throughout the 1980s, Klassen gained an international following and became a leading figure among hate groups, particularly in South Africa. Klassen called for a "racial holy war" against those he called "mud people." In 1991 the movement garnered public attention when a member named George Loeb murdered black Gulf War veteran Harold Mansfield Jr., following an altercation in a Florida parking lot. In 1994 Mansfield's family sued the Church of the Creator for its part in the veteran's death. These events set into motion a series of violent incidents both within the Church of the Creator and among other hate groups with which it was affiliated. Planning to step down from his post as head of the organization, Klassen named several different successors before settling on Richard McCarty. Klassen committed suicide in August 1993. Over the next several years, numerous Church of the Creator members and associates were accused of illegal activity, including the firebombing of an NAACP office in Tacoma, Washington.

McCarty stepped down in 1996, and a young white supremacist named Matthew Hale took over. Hale reenergized the group, now called the World Church of the Creator, by recruiting new members, appearing on talk shows to espouse his views, starting a white supremacist cable-access television program, and, perhaps most significantly, by harnessing the power of the Internet to significantly expand the church—particularly through specialized Web sites targeting women and children.

In July 1999 the group was again in the public spotlight when a member, Benjamin Smith, went on a two-day shooting spree in Illinois, killing two and injuring nine before killing himself; all of the victims were minorities. Law enforcement speculated that Smith had been motivated by the State of Illinois's refusal to grant Hale a license to practice law. In 2002 the World Church of the Creator was successfully sued for trademark infringement by another religious organization, also called the Church of the Creator. In early 2003, Hale was arrested for soliciting the murder of federal judge Joan Lefkow, who had presided over the trademark infringement suit. In April of 2003 the group was found to be in violation of the trademark agreement; the Creativity Movement was fined and ordered to shut down its Web sites and surrender its membership list. In April 2005 Hale was found guilty and sentenced to serve 40 years in prison. Numerous threats had been made against Lefkow by white supremacist and neo-Nazi associates of Hale's between 2002 and 2005, and she was placed under the protection of federal marshals. In 2005 Lefkow's mother and husband were murdered in the family's Chicago home. Law enforcement officials initially believed the murders to be retaliation from white supremacists on Hale's behalf, but later that year the killings were found to be unrelated to the Hale case.

As of 2008, the Creativity Movement was a far more loosely organized group than it had been under either Klassen or Hale. In 2002, under the leadership of Thomas Kroenke, the group moved its world headquarters to Riverton, Wyoming, ostensibly to avoid abiding by the Illinois injunction.

Membership: The Creativity Movement claims members throughout the United States and Canada, as well as in Europe, South America, South Africa, and Australia. The group does not provide its membership numbers, but has more supporters than actual members; supporters in North America are estimated to number several thousand. Observers have suggested that the worldwide constituency membership may be as high as 40,000 to 60,000.

Periodicals: *The Struggle*.

Sources:

www.rahowa.com.

Anti-Defamation League. "Creativity Movement."
    www.adl.org/learn/Ext_US/WCOTC.asp?xpicked=3&item=17.

Berkes, Howard. "A White Supremacist Church and a Small Town." National Public Radio. www.npr.org/templates/story/story.php?storyId=992253.

Klassen, Ben. *Building a Whiter and Brighter World*. Otto, NC: Church of the Creator, 1986.

————. *Nature's Eternal Religion*. Lighthouse Point, FL: Church of the Creator, 1973.

————. *The White Man's Bible*. Lighthouse Point, FL: Church of the Creator, 1981.

Southern Poverty Law Center. "Pontifex Ex."
    www.splcenter.org/intel/intelreport/article.jsp?aid=476.

Freedom from Religion Foundation, Inc.
PO Box 750, Madison, WI 53701

The Freedom from Religion Foundation (FFRF), Inc., is a North American association of freethinkers (i.e., atheists, agnostics, and skeptics). Many of the founders had formerly been members of American Atheists, Inc., who had left in protest of what they saw as undemocratic policies. The FFRF's primary goals are to educate the public on matters of nontheism and to promote the principle of church/state separation, both of which are pursued mostly through filing lawsuits against apparent constitutional violations. Recent legal activity has involved intervening in situations involving prayer in public schools, payment of public funds for religious purposes, government favoritism toward religious institutions, illegal activities conducted in the name of religious charities, and religious efforts to deny civil rights to women, gays, and lesbians.

The group was cofounded in 1978 by Anne Nicol Gaylor (b. 1926), a Wisconsin businesswoman, newspaper editor, and feminist activist. Under her guidance, the FFRF became one of the largest and most successful groups of its kind in North America. As of 2008, Gaylor serves as a consultant and president emerita to the group. Gaylor's daughter, Annie Laurie Gaylor, helped her mother found the group and currently serves as co-president, along with Dan Barker.

In 1983, FFRF filed a suit challenging President Ronald Reagan's declaration of that year as the "Year of the Bible." FFRF has gone to court to halt the U.S. Postal Service's practice of giving cancellations to a Roman Catholic group, has ended commencement prayers at a major university, and has stopped federal subsidy to the "Virgin of the Rockies" chapel, and in 1996 it won a court decision overturning a Wisconsin law declaring Good Friday to be a state holiday. The federation also succeeded in posting the first atheist placard to be displayed in a state capitol over the Christmas holidays, in protest of religious activities hosted there. One of its more active chapters, the Alabama Freethought Association, has moved to stop religious expressions in the state's parks and has become a plaintiff in the case against Judge Roy Moore, who has allowed questionable religious practices in his courtroom. In May 2006 the FFRF brought suit against the Federal Bureau of Prisons (FBP) to challenge the U.S. government's intention to use grant money to institute single-faith prison programs. In October of the same year, the FBP announced it was canceling the plan. In 2007 FFRF won a lawsuit in which it had challenged the State of Indiana's use of public monies to hire chaplains to encourage religious faith among the state employees in its Family and Social Services Administration. FFRF has also been involved in legal action to remove the words "under God" from the Pledge of Allegiance.

At its annual convention, the federation presents a "Freethinker of the Year" award to a successful litigant working for church/state separation, and an annual "Freethought Heroine" award, which in 1997 was given to Ann Druyan, the widow of Carl Sagan. Additionally, the group sponsors an annual essay competition for students, awarding cash grants, and offers a similar scholarship program for college-bound high school seniors. The federation publishes a variety of books in the freethought tradition, as well as the country's only freethought newspaper, *Freethought Today*. In late 2007 the foundation initiated the first nationally syndicated freethought radio program on the Air America network.

Membership: In 2007 the federation reported more than 11,600 members, and an additional 550 nonmember subscribers to its newspaper.

Periodicals: *Freethought Today*.

Sources:

Freedom from Religion Foundation. www.ffrf.org.

Gaylor, Annie Laurie. *Betrayal of Trust: Clergy Abuse of Children*. Madison, WI: Freedom from Religion Foundation, 1988.

————. *Woe to the Women: The Bible Tells Me So*. Madison, WI: Freedom from Religion Foundation, 1981.

————, ed. *Women without Superstition: No Gods, No Masters*. Madison, WI: Freedom from Religion Foundation, 1997. 696 pp.

Hurmence, Ruth. *The Book of Ruth*. Madison, WI: Freedom from Religion Foundation, 1982.

Rejecting Religion. Madison, WI: Freedom from Religion Foundation, 1982.

Humanist Association of Canada

PO Box 8752, Station T, Ottawa, ON, Canada K1G 3J1

In Canada, humanism and people identifying themselves as humanists emerged in the early twentieth century as part of a larger freethought movement. Among the earliest groups to take the name *humanist* was the Winnipeg Rationalist Society, which in the 1930s changed its name to the Winnipeg Humanist Society. That group dwindled following the death of its longtime leader, Marshall Jerome Gauvin (1881–1978), but other groups emerged, primarily in Victoria (British Columbia) and Montreal. In 1968, the Victoria and Montreal groups joined to form the Humanist Association of Canada (HAC). At that time they also combined their two periodicals, the *Victoria Humanist* and the *Montreal Humanist*, into *Humanist in Canada*.

The group's primary focus is on promoting the humanist values of "honesty, compassion, reason, critical thinking, and cooperation"; on offering secular ceremonies for life events such as weddings and funerals; and on working to ensure the separation of church and state in Canada. In 2008, HAC offered its first Education Grant Program for nonprofit organizations that fulfill the criteria of a humanist agenda.

The association provides a focus and forum for the broad range of humanist thought in Canada and is similar in beliefs and practice to the American Humanist Association. It is also a member of the International Humanist and Ethical Union.

Membership: Membership reported at 800. There are chapters in Ottawa and elsewhere in Ontario, in Montreal, and in the provinces of Manitoba, Saskatchewan, and Alberta.

Periodicals: *Canadian Humanist News*. Available from PO Box 3769, Station C, Ottawa, ON, Canada K1Y 4J8.

Sources:

Humanist Association of Canada. www.humanists.ca.

Stein, Gordon. *Encyclopedia of Unbelief*. 2 vols. Buffalo, NY: Prometheus Press, 1985.

Institution for the Secularization of Islamic Society (ISIS)

c/o The Center for Inquiry, 3965 Rensch Rd., Amherst, NY 14228

The Institution for the Secularization of Islamic Society (ISIS) was formed as part of the humanist/skeptical organization Center for Inquiry to promote the ideas of rationalism, secularism, democracy, and human rights within Islamic society. Its program has been based upon the belief that Islamic culture has become backward due to its slowness to allow its beliefs, laws, and practices to come under the scrutiny of modern critical perspectives. This unwillingness is attributed to an intolerance of alternative beliefs and a timidity about participating in fruitful dialogues. ISIS promotes the freedom of intellectual and scientific inquiry and the freedom of conscience as regards religion. The group values the ability of individuals to change religion or belief and the right to unbelief.

ISIS supports the emergence of a modern form of Islam and of unbelief in societies now dominated by Islam. It works for the separation of religion and state in Islamic countries, believing that such separation is necessary if a viable modern secular society is to emerge. It advocates the rights of women and of those who hold minority beliefs, perceiving both to be under attack in Muslim-dominated societies. It also demands the right to examine the historical foundations of Islam (something many Muslim religious leaders have balked at doing), and to explain the rise and fall of Islam in terms of the normal mechanisms of human history.

ISIS has moved to create a network of secularists and freethinkers in Islamic countries, to establish a women's network in those same areas, and to report on the findings of recent research on the origins of Islam and the Qur'an. It also has begun to publicize alternative readings of Islamic history, especially those that record significant dissent. It publicizes critical findings on basic Muslim documents and attacks their sanctity.

In March 2005 ISIS was a delegate to the international Secular Islam Summit in St. Petersburg, Florida, and was one of the signatories of the St. Petersburg Declaration, a document intended to unify secular Muslims in support of a universal human rights agenda and a rejection of Sharia law, state-sponsored religion, gender violence, and persecution of non-Muslims and minority groups in Islamic countries.

Membership: Not reported.

Sources:

Center for Inquiry. www.centerforinquiry.net/isis.

Warraq, Ibn, ed. *The Origins of the Koran: Classic Essays on Islam's Holy Book*. Amherst, NY: Prometheus Books, 1998.

————. *The Quest for the Historical Muhammad*. Amherst, NY: Prometheus Books, 2000.

National Alliance of Pantheists

PO Box 484, Groton, MA 01450

Founded in the mid-1980s, the National Alliance of Pantheists is a network of individuals who believe that God is everything and everything is God. It stands in contrast to the idea of theism that God is the transcendent Creator who stands over and apart from creation. Pantheism assumes that the world, nature, and humanity are all an intimate part of the Divine being. Most pantheists recognize philosopher Baruch Spinoza as the grandfather of their perspective, but they also claim such diverse thinkers as Ralph Waldo Emerson (1803–1882), Pierre Teilhard de Chardin (1881–1955), and Mahatma Gandhi (1869–1948) as fellow pantheists.

While pantheism is an ancient belief, no attempt to organize its believers as a religious group has previously occurred. Pantheism tends to be a very individualistic philosophy; it has no dogma and is not immediately suggestive of corporate worship or united action. However, the Alliance was founded as a religion especially suitable for the modern world, i.e., the New Age. It works to end bigotry and religious discrimination, because of its belief that ultimately all people are involved in the Divine Essence. No one religion can be the "true faith" as all religious expressions exist within the one consciousness of the Divine.

The Alliance has established itself as a place where pantheists can discover each other, thus leading to the formation of local groups and churches. It ordains clergy and charters churches, but has no hierarchy. Though it encourages the individual expression of the member's relationship to God, the Alliance notes that many Pantheists observe the ancient agricultural festivals at the solstices and equinoxes (and halfway between them) as a means of calling attention to the intimate connection between God and nature. It further notes that Pantheists also tend to be environmentalists. The Alliance holds an annual celebration of Lammas (marking the first wheat harvest of the year) in August.

Membership: Not reported.

Periodicals: *Nap Time*.

Northeast Atheist Association of Connecticut (NAA)

PO Box 63, Simsbury, CT 06070

The Northeast Atheist Association of Connecticut (NAA) was founded in 1992 to promote atheism in the northeastern United States, although one of its major goals is to advocate against the use of public funds for any type of religious event or program. As of 2008, the group was headed by Janos Palotai (president) and John Parker (treasurer) and publishes a bimonthly newsletter. The NAA is an affiliated member of American Atheists, Inc., and the Alliance of Secular Humanist Societies.

Membership: In 2002 the association reported approximately 150 members.

Periodicals: *The Northeast Atheist.*

Restored Church of the Star Goat

Current address not obtained for this edition.

The Restored Church of the Star Goat, founded in 1989 as an atheist religion, grew out of an earlier project, the Skeptic Tank. Founder Fredric Rice had been archiving material that debunked what he considered unscientific claims for the paranormal and details of crimes against humanity perpetrated by religion in the name of a deity. In his opinion, both were the result of ignorance and superstition, which he hoped to replace with scientific method, logic, and reason. His discussions with people through the electronic media in the 1980s led to the emergence of the Restored Church as a logical next step, given the need for a religion to replace the deity-oriented faiths. The Skeptic Tank became a department of the church that continues to oppose pseudoscience.

Rice created an interesting myth for his church: Five million years ago humanity fled to Earth to escape the anger of the Mutant Cosmic Star Goat, which threatened life on their previous home planet due to their inhumane ways. The Star Goat was appeased by their fearful flight. He sent a prophet to Earth named Douglas Adams, who showed those with intelligence his ways. Thus Goatees (followers of the Star Goat) came to know of Billy Goat, Star Goat's son, who was sent to Earth to save humanity but was killed in a torturous death. After learning of Star Goat's way, believers were amazed by humans' creation of deity religions and inhumane actions.

To address humanity's disgraceful condition, the Restored Church of the Star Goat, where The Ways could be learned, was founded. Rice also endeavored to compile The Ways into a written document to be made generally available as a book, *The Star Goat Mysteries.*

It is the belief of the founder that there are many people who are goatees at heart and some who wish to be ministers in the church. Those people should contact him. The church's community exists primarily in cyberspace.

Membership: Not reported.

Periodicals: *Fields of Green.*

Temple of Earth

For information: hello@templeofearth.com

The Temple of Earth (TOE) is a Humanist religion initially conceived in 1998 that describes itself as a "religion-free religion." Its members hold that all religious traditions are outdated and need to be abandoned. In place of a belief in God, it suggests that humans can find communion with each other and meaning in the creation of culture—art, humor, technology. If worship occurs, it should be worship of progress, which leads to the uncovering of the mysteries of the universe. The temple teaches that it is each person's responsibility to devise his or her own system of morality.

On a practical level, the church recommends to those who feel the vacuum created by the loss of religion the practices of disciplined meditation and involvement in one's community. Meditation helps focus the mind, and involvement moves one beyond loneliness and into creativity. The Temple of Earth sees these as the essence of religion, and it aims to encourage and facilitate them out of belief that they will improve the quality of everyday life and allow humans to discover truths more sublime than those available in religious communities.

The Temple of Earth freely ordains ministers who in turn are encouraged to spread the creed of the church. The church allows its clergy to choose whatever title they wish, be it reverend, lama, rabbi, bishop, imam, or another.

The Temple of Earth does not form local churches, but it does encourage the formation of what it terms "TOE rings"—loosely organized groups of individuals who meet regularly to discuss ways that they collectively can improve their lives. TOE offers guidelines for organizing a ring and a web board to assist in contacting like-minded individuals. The Temple of the Earth recognizes the two solstices and equinoxes as its major holidays.

Membership: Not reported. As of 2008 ministers for the church are serving across the United States and in a number of countries around the world.

Periodicals: *Toe Tree Journal* (online).

Sources:

The Temple of Earth. www.templeofearth.com/index.html.

Bury, J. B. *The Idea of Progress: An Inquiry into Its Origin and Growth.* New York: Macmillan, 1932.

Unitarian Universalist Association of Congregations

25 Beacon St., Boston, MA 02108

The Unitarian Universalist Association of Congregations (UUA) was formed in 1961 by the merger of the American Unitarian Association and the Universalist Church in America. The merger represents the coming together of the two oldest and most conservative segments of the liberal tradition. (See introductory material for historical survey.) As a member of that tradition, the UUA is the only body that affirms its base within the Judeo-Christian heritage. Many of its ministers can be found in local ministerial associations.

The basis of modern Unitarian belief is the free search for truth. Truth is found in the universal teachings of the great prophets and teachers of all ages and traditions but summarized in the Western tradition as love of God and humans. Members believe in the worth of every human and in the democratic method in human relationships. A world community based on fellowship, justice, and peace is the goal of all actions. While varying widely in belief structures, Unitarian Universalists generally believe in God as the source of mind and spirit, Jesus as a great prophet, the Bible as a collection of valuable religious writings, science as a source of knowledge, and prayer as a means to lift the mind beyond the ordinary. There are no sacraments. UUA members support values related to social justice and civil rights, ecology and environmentalism, and the rights of gays, lesbians, bisexuals, and transgender people.

Following the pattern of their Congregational parents, the Unitarian Universalists are congregationally governed. A national association meeting is held annually, and each minister and local church is represented. The Unitarian Universalist Service Committee was established in 1940 to aid refugees of Nazi persecution and has continued as a means to embody social concerns. The group's Beacon Press is a major publisher of religious books.

During the nineteenth century, both Universalists and Unitarians engaged in foreign missionary activity, the former most noticeably in Japan and the latter in India and Japan. Ties to liberal religionists in these countries have been retained (long after any understanding of a missionary-mission relationship existed), and fellowship with similar groups in other lands has been established. There are affiliated congregations of Unitarian-Universalists in Argentina, Australia, Belgium, Canada, France, Japan, West Germany, Mexico, the Netherlands, New Zealand, the Philippines, Puerto Rico, and the Virgin Islands.

Membership: In 2008 the UUA reported 1,041 congregations in the United States, Canada, and overseas. In 2003 it reported approximately 160,000 certified members.

Periodicals: *UU World*.

Sources:

Unitarian Universalist Association of Congregations. www.uua.org/.

Ahlstrom, Sydney E., and Jonathan S. Carey. *An American Reformation*. Middletown, CT: Wesleyan University Press, 1985.

Cheetham, Henry H. *Unitarianism and Universalism*. Boston: Beacon Press, 1962.

Miller, Russell E. *The Larger Hope: The Second Century of the Universalist Church in America, 1870–1970*. Boston: Unitarian Universalist Association, 1985.

Tapp, Robert B. *Religion among the Unitarian Universalists*. New York: Seminar Press, 1973.

Wilbur, Earl Morse. *Our Unitarian Heritage*. Boston: Beacon Press, 1963.

Williams, George Huntston. *American Universalism*. Boston: Beacon Press, 1976.

Wintersteen, Prescott B. *Christology in American Unitarianism*. Boston: Unitarian Universalist Christian Fellowship, 1977.

The Universal Church Triumphant of the Apathetic Agnostic (UCTAA)

531 10 St. SE, Medicine Hat, Alberta, Canada T1A 1R4

The Universal Church Triumphant of the Apathetic Agnostic (UCTAA) is put forth as a "combination of total seriousness and sophomoric humor." As with some other religious groups, the church founder and patriarch John Tyrrell uses satire to make serious points, not just against traditional religion but for what is considered a positive alternative view.

The church offers the perspective that agnosticism in itself is a legitimate end position in religious belief. It is summarized in three articles of faith: that "the existence of a Supreme Being is unknown and unknowable; that if there is a Supreme Being, then that being appears to act as if entirely apathetic to events in our universe; and that we are apathetic to the existence or non-existence of a Supreme Being." Because the question of God is unanswerable, the church believes that people can abandon what is a fruitless search and adopt an attitude of apathy toward theology. Though apathetic about the question of God's existence, church members are not apathetic about its agnostic position, which it seeks to propagate widely.

UCTAA began in 1996 as a one-page personal Web site. Initially it was a lighthearted presentation of the founder's personal religious beliefs. As early as 1965, Tyrrell had thought of apathetic agnosticism as a label to describe his belief about God: "I don't know and I don't care." The church's motto thus became "We don't know and we don't care." The satirical language used to describe the serious viewpoints has been retained as an equally serious reminder to laugh at oneself as well as others.

In 1996 the Web site began to attract notice from Internet surfers. In response, Tyrrell expanded the site to include a section for opposing views. The site now includes more than 2,000 pages of articles and discussions. Membership was opened in 1997, and the next year clerics and a hierarchy appeared. Ordination was offered through the International University of Nescience. In 2000 a transient membership was replaced with a group of correspondents who voiced a desire to be active participants and even offer their energy and guidance to the church. The site expanded further to accommodate this core membership/leadership. Additional Web sites were created.

Tyrrell, as patriarch of the church, ordains clergy, many of whom assume one of a number of titles—minister, rabbi, pastor, priest, priestess, and so on. Clergy are authorized to conduct weddings, funerals, naming ceremonies, and other ceremonies to celebrate life's passages. Clergy may apply to become a bishop of a specific territory. Their responsibilities include the further ordination of clergy in their diocese and the guidance of any clergy who seek it. Clergy may seek the still higher office of patriarch or matriarch of a See (which includes multiple dioceses). A patriarch/matriarch may ordain new bishops and appoint them to new dioceses within his or her See. Tyrell is responsible for appointing patriarchs and matriarchs and providing general guidance through the church's Web site. All the patriarchs and matriarchs in the church constitute its Council of Elders.

The church is organized as a loose hierarchy, meaning that clergy are not required to take direction from senior clergy; rather, they may conduct their ministries as they see fit. Tyrrell emphasizes, to those who might have contact with one of the church's ministers, that "ordination does not guarantee the good character of any clergyperson."

International University of Nescience is the educational arm of the Apathetic Agnostic Church. It is an unaccredited institution, and advises those who attempt to relate to it that its degrees are worth at least the paper they are printed on. It offers a spectrum of master's degrees for clergy and doctoral degrees for senior clergy (bishops and above).

Membership: In 2008 the church reported approximately 15,000 members scattered in more than 50 countries.

Educational Facilities:

Online International University of Nescience.

Sources:

The Universal Church Triumphant of the Apathetic Agnostic. www.uctaa.net/. Also available from ApatheticAgnostic.org.

Universal Pantheist Society

PO Box 3499, Visalia, CA 93278

Although it is a widely held philosophical position that permeates a variety of religious perspectives, pantheism has usually not been the focus of new religious communities in itself. For example, different movements like Daoism are usually seen as pantheistic. In the United States, the Church of Christ, Scientist, in spite of its leadership, is frequently cited as pantheistic. On the other hand, many contemporary neo-pagan groups often identify themselves as pantheists.

Pantheism may be defined as the view that the universe is identical with God, and God identical with the universe. The first person of note to be identified primarily as a pantheist is the Dutch Jewish philosopher Baruch Spinoza (1632–1677). The British freethinker John Toland (1670–1722) appears to have coined the term "pantheism" to describe Spinoza's thought. A variant position, panentheism, identifies the universe as divine (part of God) but asserts that God is far more than the universe. In the panentheist view, God is still an object of worship. Strains of panentheism appear in the thinking of philosophers and writers throughout history, from Plato and Plotinus to D. H. Lawrence, Walt Whitman, and Ralph Waldo Emerson.

The Universal Pantheist Society is one of the few groups that have focused on pantheist metaphysics as the center of their belief. Founded in 1975, it asserts that "the cosmos, taken or conceived of as a whole, is synonymous with God. The cosmos is divine, and the earth sacred. Pantheists do not propose belief in a deity; rather, they hold nature itself as a creative presence. Pantheism reconciles science and religion through ecology leading to strong environmental awareness."

The society offers no creed, nor does it require any particular behavior pattern of members. It sees its task as promoting individual spiritual growth and providing pantheists around the world with a unified "worldwide presence." It also seeks to be a resource for people inquiring about pantheism. It suggests that the natural focus of a pantheist lifestyle would include attention to conservation, developing sustainable lifestyles, ending consumerism, celebrating nature's cycles, home schooling, and family life.

Membership: Not reported.

Periodicals: *Pantheist Vision*.

Sources:

Universal Pantheist Society. www.pantheist.net/.

Garrett, Jan. "An Introduction to Pantheism." Available from www.wku.edu/~jan.garrett/panthesm.htm.

Harrison, Paul. *Elements of Pantheism: Understanding the Divinity in Nature and the Universe.* London: Element Books, 1999.

MacIntyre, Alasdair. "Pantheism." In *Encyclopedia of Philosophy,* 2nd ed. Detroit: Macmillan, 2005.

World Pantheist Movement

PO Box 103, Webster, NY 14580

The World Pantheist Movement (WPM) is the world's largest organization of people associated with pantheism, a philosophy that reveres nature and the wider universe. The WPM grew out of a mailing list started in 1997 by Dr. Paul Harrison, an environmental writer, editor of United Nations reports, and recipient of a United Nations Environment Programme Global 500 award. Harrison was motivated by the apparent need for a spirituality suited for the scientific age and for the acute environmental challenges faced by the planet. The WPM incorporated in the state of Colorado in 1998 and officially opened for membership in December 1999.

The World Pantheist Movement supports a scientific pantheism, which seeks to find a scientifically sound and socially aware perspective on a wide variety of subjects. It focuses on reverence and concern for nature, celebration of life, respect for human rights and the rights of other living beings, and naturalism. The WPM also emphasizes respect for reason, evidence, and science as our best methods of deepening our understanding of nature, while accepting that science is a never-ending quest and that some technologies have created massive social and environmental problems. It supports freedom of religion, religious tolerance, and complete separation of state and religion.

The WPM promotes respect for the rights of humans and other living creatures, nondiscrimination, justice, and peace. It supports the legalization of gay marriage. It does not interfere with or promote any specific personal choices in sexuality, gender, or use of recreational or psychotropic substances. Similarly, members have a diversity of views on vegetarianism, hunting, nonviolence, and many other issues.

The WPM does not prescribe any particular set of spiritual practices but leaves the choice up to individuals. Its policy is to accept a diversity of languages and methods of celebration among its members, although it generally avoids theistic or religious language in its official literature and Web pages.

Ceremonies (which the WPM calls "celebrations") are viewed not as rituals to placate gods and spirits or to follow authority, but as individual expressions of one's deepest feelings toward nature and the wider universe. Among members and friends of the WPM, the most common practice is daily close observation of nature, followed by meditation. About a quarter of members employ some form of pagan celebration, but since they have no belief in gods or magic, this is always for self-expression or enjoyment.

The WPM believes that the "divinity" of nature can be accessed directly anywhere and by anyone, and therefore does not have clergy, church buildings, or seminaries. Members and friends meet in small groups that decide their own meeting format. Groups may discuss ideas, books, or films, watch nature-related movies, share experiences, or go on nature outings. All members may request certification to celebrate nature-based weddings of friends and relatives.

The WPM does not give credence to personal survival after death but believes that people create their own "afterlife" through actions and the creations and memories they leave, their elements recycled in soil, water, and atmosphere. Thus the WPM fosters the "natural death" approach to funerals, with burial in biodegradable materials, in nature-preserve-type burial grounds if available.

Organizationally the WPM is governed by a board of 13 appointed directors. Directors must agree to sign the credo as it exists at the time of their joining the board. Members do not have to sign the credo but are asked to consider their agreement with it before joining. The board may, by a 75 percent majority, change the credo.

The main forms of WPM activity consist of more than 60 e-mail lists and a periodical, *Pan,* which explores the possibilities of naturalistic spirituality in living, therapy, art, meditation, nature conservation, ethics, science education, and many other areas. The WPM places considerable emphasis on the conservation of nature and on humans reaching a sustainable way of life. The organization has saved more than 300 acres of wildlife habitat through direct sponsorship of conservation organizations, Internet click groups to save habitat, and its pantheist wildlife reserves scheme. The WPM is also an organizational member of the International Dark-Sky Association, which combats light pollution.

Membership: In 2008 the WPM reported approximately 400 members in 16 countries who provide financial support. It also reported more than 5,000 "friends" belonging to its many associated mailing lists and Internet groups.

Periodicals: *Pan.*

Sources:

Pantheism: The World Pantheist Movement. www.pantheism.net/.

Harrison, Paul. *Elements of Pantheism: Understanding the Divinity in Nature and the Universe.* London: Element Books, 1999.

———. Personal Web site. paul-harrison.com.

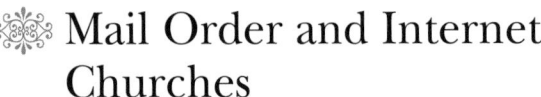

Mail Order and Internet Churches

American Fellowship Church

225 Crossroads Blvd., No. 345, Carmel, CA 93923

The American Fellowship Church (originally named the Mother Earth Church) was formed in 1975 by T. H. Swenson, as an independent church that believes in individual responsibility for spiritual growth and development. Described as a church without walls whose members are widely scattered, it invites ministers to unite daily in prayer and meditation at 7 A.M. and 7 P.M. (Pacific Standard Time). The International Clergy Association is a division of the church open only to ordained ministers. It publishes a directory of members and offers correspondence courses.

Membership: In 1991 there were approximately 15,000 members.

Periodicals: *Newsletter.*

Sources:

American Fellowship Church. www.amfellow.org.

Calvary Grace Christian Church of Faith

Current address not obtained for this edition.

The Calvary Grace Christian Church of Faith was formed in 1961 by the Rev. Dr. Herman Keck, Jr., of Ft. Lauderdale, Florida, who began his ministry as a member of the Calvary Grace Churches of Faith. In 1962 he began calling himself the international superintendent and established Faith Bible College. The church resembles its parent body.

Membership: Not reported.

Educational Facilities:

Faith Bible College, Fort Lauderdale, Florida.

Faith Theological Seminary, Fort Lauderdale, Florida.

Sources:

Bruns, Bill. "Praise the Lord and Pass the Diploma." *Life* (November 14, 1970): 69–78.

Calvary Grace Churches of Faith

Current address not obtained for this edition.

Among the first of the mail-order churches is the Calvary Grace Churches of Faith, formed in 1954 (chartered in 1958) by Angelo C. Spern of Irwin, Pennsylvania. It issues ordination certificates on application to "worthy Christians who have accepted (the) Lord Jesus Christ as the Savior." The International Chaplains' Association functions as the churches' missionary arm.

Membership: Not reported.

Educational Facilities:

Calvary Grace Bible Institute, Rillton, Pennsylvania.

Church of Seven Planes

PO Box 294, Cooper, TX 75432

The Church of Seven Planes, like the Universal Life Church that preceded it, was founded in 1978 to provide any who asked the opportunity to become legally ordained apart from any consideration of money or particular religious belief. Ordained individuals may then, if they so choose, organize their own church(es), and obtain a church charter from the Church of Seven Planes. The church was founded by and is led by Robert J. Guffey, its archbishop.

The Church of Seven Planes was created around seven basic beliefs: (1) that there is one supreme being, who may be called by many different names; (2) there is no single true religion; (3) that all people are entitled to their own beliefs; (4) that it is not each person's right to tell others how to believe, think, dress, or behave; (5) that we should treat others as we want to be treated; (6) that we learn from each other and from our inner self; and (7) that nothing is impossible, miracles happen all the time. (The House of F.A.M.E. Mansions of Glory holds a similar position; see separate entry.)

The church believes that any truth or a revelation is not a truth for individuals unless they see it for themselves. The church holds that there are some essential ancient truths but do not expect the ministers whom they ordain to accept them. These underlying beliefs are that "the soul of man is immortal and its future is the future of a thing whose growth and splendor have no limit; that the principle which gives life dwells within us and without us. It is undying, and eternally beneficent. It is not seen or heard or felt, but is perceived by the man who desires perception," and that "each man is his own absolute law giver, the dispenser of glory or gloom to himself, the decreer of his life, his reward, his punishment." The church also endorses the ancient practice of laying on of hands (in a religious sense) to help bring about the healing and comfort of others.

Potential ministers may apply to the church of ordination. When the ordination certificate is granted, the church also grants a doctor of divinity degree. The church has designated bishops (who have the power to ordain in the church's name) in many states, as well as a bishop for Australia, Canada, and the United Kingdom.

The related Interfaith School of Theology grants a variety of degrees based on life experience and nonresidential courses taken.

Membership: In 2008 the church reported 26 bishops in 13 states, Australia, the United Kingdom, and Mexico, and chartered churches in 14 countries.

Educational Facilities:

Interfaith School of Theology, Cooper, Texas.

Sources:

Church of Seven Planes. www.sevenplanes.org/.

Church of the Holy Monarch

c/o Temple of Nashville Church of the Holy Monarch, 4656 Dowdy Dr., Antioch, TN 37013-2746

Describing itself as a "church without walls," the Church of the Holy Monarch is headed by Dr. Robert Walker and Archbishop R. M. LeRoux. It was founded in 1976 and ordains ministers and charters churches. Ministers are asked to respond to a nominal accessment to remain active clergy in the church.

Membership: Not reported.

Periodicals: *The Monarch Messenger*. Box 116, Port Orange, FL 32019.

Church of Transition

200 NE 48th Terr., Miami, FL 33137

The Church of Transition emerged in the 1980s as a nondogmatic, nonpolitical, and loosely organized association of ministers and churches. It was founded by Bruce Cole, designated as First Minister. The church provides credentials for ministers who follow a spiritual path and wish to assist others from their spiritual orientation. The church has no requirements of belief, and practice and ministers are prohibited from requiring the members of their congregations to adhere to any particular belief or practice. Ministerial candidates, who must have the equivalent of a master's degree in a helping profession (social work, counseling, etc.), are privately tutored by one of the present ministers prior to ordination. Most ministers come out of a Western mystical tradition.

Membership: In 2002 there were approximately 20 ministers in the United States, two in Canada, and one in Mexico. Several of the ministers had formed congregations, but no count on members had been taken.

Crown of Life Fellowship

PO Box 9048, Spokane, WA 99209

The Crown of Life Fellowship was formed in 1967 at Pullman, Washington, by the Rev. D. H. Howard. It functioned for several years as a fellowship at the University of Washington and then moved to Spokane, and later a group moved to Oregon. In 1970 the small Spokane group began to place advertisements offering ordination and, by 1972, had ministers in most of the states and provinces. The fellowship functions as an association of ministers drawn from a diverse theological spectrum. There are no doctrinal requirements for membership.

The church supplies a short course leading to a doctor of divinity degree. Through its periodical, *Crown of Life Fellowship News*, it informs members of their privileges as ordained ministers. Many of the churches function as house churches and study groups.

The Crown of Life Fellowship sees itself as continuing the work of A. K. Mozumdar, who began a teaching ministry in Spokane in 1914. For the next 40 years, from the southern California headquarters of the Messianic World Message, Mozumdar preached a "universal message" of the God within. His teachings represented an attempted synthesis of Hinduism and Christianity. The fellowship has sponsored the republishing of Mozundar's major work, *The Triumphant Spirit*.

Membership: Not reported.

Periodicals: *The Universal Message*. 38281 Mountain Home Dr., Lebanon, OR 97355-9367.

Sources:

Mozumdar, A. K. *The Triumphant Spirit*. Marina Del Rey, CA: DeVorss & Co., 1978.

First International Church of the Web

c/o Rev. David M. Ford, 4202 Windsor Spring Rd., No. 131, Hephzibah, GA 30815

The First International Church of the Web is one in a spectrum of new religions operating primarily as a community of people in cyberspace who stay in contact through e-mail and the Internet. It was established February 7, 1997, by Rev. Dr. David M. Ford, its pastor. The church is committed to using the Internet for three main purposes: Christian evangelism; ministering to members and others through a prayer request board, chat rooms, and a bulletin board for threaded discusses on its Web page; and equipping members with Christ-centered tools by linking them to online Christian resources.

The church is a conservative Christian organization that affirms the Bible as the inspired word of God, the Trinity, and the saving work of Christ. It defines the church as a living spiritual body of which Jesus Christ is the head and of which all regenerated persons are members and asserts that all Christians are ordained by the Holy Spirit to spread the Gospel of Christ. While affirming the essentials of Christian doctrine, the church believes the love of Jesus Christ is the greatest gift of God and take precedence over all differences among Christians of a theological, denominational, ideological, or physical nature. The church provides free online legal ordination for those seeking to serve as clergy and free independent church charters for new Christian ministries. It also offers instructions for any who would like to start a Web-based church. The church is a member of the International Alliance of Web-Based Churches, an ecumenical body managed by Rev. Ford.

Membership: Not reported.

Educational Facilities:

St. Luke Evangelical School of Biblical Studies, Hephzibah, Georgia.

Periodicals: *The First International Church of the Web Herald*.

Sources:

First International Church of the Web. www.ficotw.org/index.html.

Holy Gospel Church IV, Inc.

2812 Blue Finch Way, New Port Richey, FL 34653-6510

The Holy Gospel Church IV, Inc., was founded in 1977 in New Port Richey, Florida, by Rev. Mario J. Sautte, the church's patriarch. It is described as a liberal church organization without any traditional doctrine. It is the belief of the church that clergypeople have a right to serve God in their own way according to their own religious convictions. It is Christian, interfaith, and nondenominational. The church accepts belief in God, the divinity of Christ, and the power of prayer, but these are not required beliefs by those ordained by the church.

The church is prepared to ordain anyone who professes a call to the ministry. There are no educational or creedal requirements. The church also issues doctor of divinity degrees upon application. The church charters congregations, but does not cover individual congregations with its tax-exempt umbrella. Local churches must gain tax exemption on their own. Foreign members can be found in the United Kingdom, Ireland, Germany, France, Spain, Italy, Ghana, Lebanon, Haiti, and Mexico.

Membership: In 1992 the church reported approximately 10,000 members, 1,000 clergy, and 33 congregations in the United States; approximately 20 clergy and five congregations in Canada; and some 10,000 members in 12 countries around the world.

House of F.A.M.E. Mansions of Glory

3846 W 133rd St., Cleveland, OH 44111

House of F.A.M.E. (Father Almighty's Messengers Epiphany) Mansions of Glory was founded in 1993 by Rev. Donald E. Jones. The organization offers ordination to ministers who request it. It is a nondenominational Christian organization that emphasizes salvation through the example of Jesus Christ.

As a young man, Jones became a student of the healing principles taught by seventeenth-century Austrian magnetic healer, Franz Anton Mesmer (1734–1815). Beginning in 1950, Jones practiced what he termed "Mesmer's Thaumaturge Attunement," converting the basement of his home into a chapel where he could teach others the holistic healing practices that not only included magnetic healing but a spectrum of natural healing practices such as naprapathy, which is similar to chiropractic medicine. After Jones's retirement, he was succeeded by Arch Bishop Adam Urban.

The beliefs of the organization are based on the Golden Rule ("do unto others as you would have them do unto you"), considered a common base of all religions, and the Royal Law of Liberty, wherein all religions would exist in "One Righteousness of Love." A particularly important tenet of F.A.M.E. is that of absolute religious freedom and the separation of church and state.

In a more formal statement of its position, F.A.M.E. acknowledges belief that (1) there is one supreme Spirit being; (2) there is no one religion, but various interpretations that lead to the center core of faith, Universal Love; (3) that everyone is entitled to his or her own belief; (4) that we do not possess the right to tell others how to believe, think, worship, or behave; (5) that we should treat others as we want to be treated; (6) that we learn from each other as well as from our inner self;

(7) and that nothing is impossible and miracles happen. (The Church of Seven Planes holds a similar position; see separate entry.)

The Ministry of F.A.M.E. does not require members to accept its beliefs and stands prepared to ordain anyone who asks for it in the assumption that she or he is seeking the truth as are other F.A.M.E. ministers. Those holding ordination in other organizations may also be ordained at the same time in the F.A.M.E.

Membership: Not reported.

Sources:

House of F.A.M.E. Mansions of Glory. www.famenglory.org/.

Ministers for Christ Assembly of Churches/Ministers for Christ Outreach

7549 W. Cactus Rd. No. 104-207, Peoria, AZ 85381

The Ministers for Christ Assembly of Churches, and its affiliated Ministers for Christ Outreach, was formed in 1988 to provide a means for those called to the ministry to be ordained and received into an organization that provides a covering for their ministry in either a congregational or noncongregational context. Once ordained, new ministers are free to initiate their own ministry in a variety of ways: by starting a church, preaching in other churches, starting a Christian school, officiating at marriages and funerals, serving in missionaries in the United States or overseas, or serving as chaplain in various settings from hospitals to prisons.

Upon payment of tuition fees ($553 in 2008), those wishing to become ministers are provided a seven-course program of study that is conducted via mail or email. Upon successful completion of the exams, the student may apply for ordination. The course of study replaces formal attendance at a traditional seminary. Ordained ministers pay an annual fee to maintain their credentials.

The Ministers of Christ Assembly of Churches is a conservative trinitarian Christian organization with a strong emphasis on the Great Commission to evangelize the world. The statement of faith leaves most issues open and provides for a wide variance of opinion among its member ministers. The organization does show a preference for the King James version of the Bible and is opposed to abortion.

Membership: Not reported. The Ministers for Christ Assembly of Churches has licensed hundreds of ministers in the United States and a number of foreign countries.

Sources:

Ministers of Christ Assembly of Churches. www.ordination.org/.

New Life Church and Ministry

PO Box 1268, Hillsville, VA 24343

New Life Church and Ministry grew out of the work of the independent Pentecostal evangelist R. L. Goad, which began in the mid-1970s, and Chosen, the musical group that is part of his evangelistic team. Initially a vehicle for facilitating his own ministry, the church later assumed the task of licensing and ordaining ministers and charting churches.

New Life Church and Ministry is a conservative pentecostal organization that affirms belief in the Trinity, salvation in Christ, biblical holiness, the baptism of the Spirit and speaking in tongues, and a life manifesting the fruits of the spirit.

The church licenses ministers and, after they develop established ministries, ordains them. It also charters churches that are served by ministers licensed and ordained by the New Life Church. Churches may operate either under the larger corporate umbrella of the New Life Church or as independent congregations with their own corporate structures. New Life Church charters churches only inside the United States. Licensed ministers, who do not have to be resident in the United States, may serve churches or become evangelists, missionaries, or chaplains. Ministers associated with New Life Church and Ministry gather twice annually in assembly.

Also sponsored by the New Life Church and Ministry is the New Life Bible College and Seminary, a distance-learning facility that offers associates, bachelors, masters, and doctoral degrees. Courses are Bible-oriented, with a lesser emphasis on theology and church history. All courses are available through email. New Life Communications has developed an expansive broadcast ministry; it owns two radio stations and operates a 24-hour Internet radio broadcast and a television ministry.

New Life Church and Ministry supports New Life Academy, which provides to families who home-school a place where their children can attend classes several days per week. New Life Christian Schools Academy provides a K-12 home correspondence course to be used with the recommended Alpha Omega home-school curriculum.

Membership: In 2008 the church reported more than 80 ministers currently holding licenses and/or ordination from New Life Church and Ministry.

Educational Facilities:

New Life Bible College and Seminary.

Sources:

New Life Church and Ministry. www.nlcm.net/.

Omniune Church
Current address not obtained for this edition.

The Omniune Church was formed by the Rev. M. S. Medley, former international president of public relations for the Life Science Church. The Omniune Church is based on the ideal of building a church from the bottom up, democratically. It stresses individual member participation. Beliefs are drawn from ethical liberalism and include emphasis on freedom of belief. The Omniune Church Creed asserts the following: "Believe what ye will, so long as ye do good to thy fellow man: for verily, he that doeth Godly deeds is a Godly man: and he that hath loving kindness in his heart hath God in his soul." The seven great laws of life further enlarge the Omniune perspective: 1) do unto others what you would have done unto you; 2) give the world love and kindness, for you reap what you sow; 3) believe in your own worth and turn from error toward improvement; 4) take nothing which the owner has need of, neither his property nor his life; 5) love and honor God and your fellow man—harm neither by word or deed; 6) seek wisdom, justice, peace and a better life for all; and 7) live joyfully, simply, naturally, sharing God's bounty, moderate in all but love of God and God's creation.

The church stresses function over form in organization and advises congregations, instead of hiring a paid minister, to divide the minister's duties and appoint unpaid volunteers to fulfill those duties. Any person can then become the speaker, conductor, clerk, organizer, instructor, steward, or counselor. These seven officers are designated elders and any assistants are deacons. Congregations are small and close-knit. They are advised to split rather than become too big. In 1973 there were 17 missionary ministers, with missions in Los Angeles, Houston, Chicago, and Atlanta. There were approximately 500 members. Headquarters are in Breckenridge, Texas.

Membership: Not reported.

Praise Christ Ministries
PO Box 71514, Newnan, GA 30271

Praise Christ Ministries was founded in 2000 by Ray Nix, who serves as the organization's pastor and director, and his wife, Sonya Nix, after they accepted a call to minister utilizing the Internet. They had become involved in Internet ministry in the 1990s while serving pastorates in North Caroline and Georgia, but in 2000 decided to go into Internet work full time.

The Nixs recognize that God calls on many people, and thus use Praise Christ Ministries to facilitate the receiving of ministerial credentials by others. Praise Christ Ministries will ordain any candidate who presents him or herself via the Internet. The only requirement for ordination is that the person applying be a baptized believer who has made a public profession of faith in Jesus Christ. To meet this requirement, the applicant must submit a short account of his or her salvation experience. For those it has already ordained, Praise Christ Ministries offers correspondence and online courses to help continue their education and further sharpen their ministerial skills.

Praise Christ Ministries offers a profession of faith that acknowledges the Trinity, Jesus as the Son of God, salvation by faith through the grace of Jesus, God's love of all people, the Bible as the infallible Word of God, and the literal existence of heaven and hell. It emphasizes an approach to the Bible that centers on the covenants of God with humanity, rather than on dispensationalism. Though not Pentecostals, they also have adopted the five-fold ministry of Ephesians that looks to leadership exercised through apostles, prophets, evangelists, pastors, and teachers, and assume the operation of the spirituals gifts (I Corinthians 12) in the contemporary church. Their own statement was derived from that of the Fellowship of Ministers and Churches International. However, these beliefs are not imposed on those who seek ordination.

As of 2008 the Nixs had branched further into Internet-based services, and were providing both online and in-person Christian counseling services.

Membership: Not reported.

Progressive Universal Life Church (PULC)
PO Box 276265, Sacramento, CA 95827

The Progressive Universal Life Church (PULC) was founded by Pastor Jack J. Stahl, who serves as the minister for the congregation in Sacramento, California. He also functions as a psychic and spiritual counselor. PULC, which describes itself as a nondenominational interfaith ministry, was developed as a "Spiritual Holistic Ministry" that includes an emphasis on healing the mind, spirit, and body. This emphasis includes attention to the claims of holistic health and the techniques of natural healing. Stahl has noted that the Bible has many references to healing and offers dietary advice.

PULC offers ministerial licenses, doctoral degrees, and certified psychic science courses leading to a diploma. Various courses are offered on a distance learning basis toward the doctoral degree and the psychic science certificate. Those who complete the psychic science course are authorized to begin their career as a professional psychic. Degrees are also offered in hypnosis, metaphysics, religion, and biblical studies.

Membership: Not reported.

Sources:

Progressive Universal Life Church. www.pulc.com.

Rose Ministries
3675 S Rainbow Blvd., Ste. 107–601, Las Vegas, NV 89103

Rose Ministries (also known as the Association of Independent Ministries) is one of several organizations formed to assist people in launching clerical careers. It welcomes men and women of the widest range of beliefs and backgrounds and will ordain them under a variety of titles (minister, priest, chaplain, etc.).

Besides ordaining people, Rose Ministries makes available a large selection of materials designed to assist clergy in beginning their ministries, from credentials to texts on leading worship and performing various ceremonies such as weddings.

Membership: Not reported.

Sources:

Rose Ministries. openordination.org/.

Eagle, Paul. *Bakers Funeral Handbook: Resources for Pastors*. Grand Rapids, MI: Baker Books, 1996.

———. *Bakers Worship Handbook: Traditional and Contemporary Service Resources*. Grand Rapids, MI: Baker Books, 1998.

St. Matthew's Churches

PO Box 3036, Tulsa, OK 74101-3036

Although the mailing address of St. Matthew's Churches is in Tulsa, Oklahoma, the "mother church," the Cathedral of St. Matthew, is located in Houston, Texas. This is where regular Sunday services are held. The St. Matthew's group is a Bible-based nondenominational Christian ministry that emphasizes the possibility of salvation through obedience to God and Jesus' teachings. Baptism, group prayer, and celebration of the Eucharist are hallmarks of the group's evangelism.

St. Matthew's Churches was founded in Texas in 1951. In 1953 a group of fifteen born-again Christian families began the organization's first ecumenical church in San Antonio, Texas, with about 100 members. The organization's original specialty was practicing evangelism through the mail, typically establishing contact with potential adherents through mass mailings of sermons and prayers. Although it has evolved to include a more traditional approach, St. Matthew's Churches continues to use such mass mailings. The messages emphasize the abundance of God and the blessing that he is bringing into the life of the recipient. There is a request that recipients mail back their requests for prayer and sow a seed of biblical good luck by enclosing an offering.

Because of the unusual and impersonal nature of this approach, critics have accused St. Matthew's Churches of running mail scams. The group is adamant, however, that its mailings are not fraudulent and that it established its post office box in Oklahoma specifically to have all monies removed from correspondence by an independent accounting firm.

Membership: Not reported.

Sources:

St. Matthew's Churches. www.saintmatthewschurches.com/.

Spiritual Life Concepts, Inc.

PO Box 94, Indian Rocks Beach, FL 33785

Spiritual Life Concepts, Inc. (SLC), was founded in 1977 by Archbishop James L. Lowery as a cyberspace church that provides ordination to ministers and charters churches in the Christian tradition. It was originally created to train God's servants. In 2008 SLC was headed by Lowery, as well as Bishop Michael L. Lowery and Bishop Administrator Richard F. Iske. The bishop's procuring council and governing body are elected annually.

Spiritual Life Concepts assumes a conservative Christian position that affirms the Bible as the inspired Word of God, the Trinity, and the saving power of Christ. The Holy Spirit is seen as a gift bestowed to empower and equip the believer for effective service in the world.

The SLC International Seminary and Bible Institute grants associate's, bachelor's, master's, and doctoral degrees in religious arts. Classes may be completed at home, at extension sites such as local churches, or at the seminary campus. All study is Bible-based. A Licensed Ministers Certificate is granted when one enrolls in the course of study, and an ordination license is granted to all students who complete it.

In addition to its seminary, SLC performs missionary work both in the United States and abroad. Missionaries assist the needy in job placement and skills coaching as well as housing, material donations, and food banks. The group has centers in Ghana, Haiti, Kenya, Liberia, and Nigeria.

Membership: Not reported.

Educational Facilities:

Spiritual Life Concepts, Inc., International Seminary and Bible Institute.

Sources:

Spiritual Life Concepts, Inc. www.spirituallifeconcepts.org/.

United Christian Ministries International (UCMI)

2401 South 425 West, Albion, IN 46701

United Christian Ministries International (UCMI), founded in 1998 by Steven B. Smethers, was conceived as a nondenominational Christian ministry based on the teachings of the inspired writings of the Bible (with no additional or manmade doctrines) and a belief in the one true church of which Jesus spoke that unifies all Christians. UCMI's primary goal is to establish new Christian ministries in the Body of Christ. The basic premise is that there is no biblical or necessary reason for individuals who wish to be ministers to attend or graduate from a formal seminary. UCMI believes that many people are already qualified for the ministerial role but do not have either the time or financial resources to complete a seminary program.

UCMI will grant an ordination to anyone who applies, the only requirement being that they operate within biblical Christianity. It also grants church charters. Individual ministers may name their own church, though they cannot pick an already used denominational name. UCMI does not supply a corporate membership that includes tax exemption; each chartered church must apply for tax exemption separately. Ordination is free, and there are no annual renewal fees; however, there is a charge for processing papers and supplies. UCMI also provides a variety of resource materials that many have found useful in carrying out their ministry, including pastoral manuals, Bible software, and baptismal certificates. The related United Christian Ministry Institute provides correspondence courses for ministerial training, including both bachelor's and advanced degrees.

Churches associated with UCMI may also become a part of United Christian Assemblies International, founded in 2000, a fellowship of independent churches for mutual support and growth. Within UCAI, each assembly contributes resources to a pool from which all may draw. Such resources may include teaching materials, ministry resources, and materials to help in managing individual assemblies.

Membership: Not reported.

Educational Facilities:

United Christian Ministry Institute, Albion, Indiana.

Periodicals: *UCMI Ministry News Letter.*

Sources:

United Christian Ministries International. www.ucmi.org/.

Christian Ministry Handbook. Columbia City, IN: United Christian Ministries International, n.d.

United Church of the Apostles

Current address not obtained for this edition.

The United Church of the Apostles is a small mail-order church that charters congregations and ordains ministers. The church believes in freedom of religion. It sees its purpose as seeking to unite people and to open them to the beauty and great handiwork of God in everyday life.

Membership: Not reported.

Periodicals: *Church Newsletter,* Lindenhurst, NY 11757.

Universal Church of God

PO Box 10752, Burbank, CA 91510-0752

The Universal Church of God and the associated Institute of Applied Religious Sciences were founded together in 1983 by Dr. Edward T. Jones (d. 1994) in Northridge, California. The Church attempts to embrace all religions, cultures, and philosophies and teaches a universal theology built on what it sees as the truth found in the spiritual teachings of all the world's religions, while at the same time integrating findings from science, the arts, and philosophy. The Church offers members a form of personal spiritual unfolding utilizing meditation, worship, healing prayer, and service.

Along with the Church, Jones envisioned an associated comprehensive educational program through which students could find guidance on their spiritual quest from the larger esoteric community. Hence, he founded the Institute of Applied Religious Sciences, which offers classes in a variety of fields. These classes are open to the general public, but the Institute also has a seminary program that allows class time to be put toward the two years of study required before ordination for the ministry. Graduates of the seminary program receive the Holy Rite of Ordination, a Licentiate Minister Certificate, and a B.A. degree in theology. The seminary also offers the option of further study for a master's or doctoral degree.

The Church is currently led by its president, Rev. Dr. Lea Alexander. Most of its ministers are located in southern California, but it has representatives in Nevada, Arizona, Texas, and North Carolina.

Membership: Not reported. In 2008 there were 25 active ministers who had been ordained by the Universal Church of God.

Sources:

Universal Church of God. ucgod.org/index.htm.

Universal Life Church

ULC Online, 601 3rd St., Modesto, CA 95351

Alternate Address: PO Box 1034, Folsom, CA, 95763-1034

Kirby Hensley (1911–1999) was an illiterate Baptist minister from North Carolina who conceived the idea of a universal church that would bring people of all religions together. In 1959 he founded the Universal Life Church (ULC), having previously opened a "church" in his garage in Modesto, California. Though Hensley had his own ideas about theology, he felt others had a right to their own theories. He began to ordain ministers for no fee, for life, without question. He would present a signed ordination certificate and a one-page information sheet covering the ordination ceremony merely for the asking.

In the late 1960s, Hensley attained the status of a minor folk hero as the media discovered his activity and gave it national news coverage. He frequently addressed large college classes and ordained the audience instantly and en masse. Though ordination was free, a doctorate of divinity cost $20 and was offered with ten lessons explaining how to set up and operate a church. In the state of California, however, he was enjoined from issuing a degree from an unaccredited institution, so he moved the church's department of education to Phoenix, Arizona.

The Universal Life Church has no doctrine of its own. However, Hensley developed an eclectic theology that includes the following beliefs: people are reincarnated; the soul is the continuing essence of man; God is substance manifest in natural laws; Jesus was a man more intelligent than most men; heaven is nothing more or less than the position of having what you want; and hell is when you do not have what you want. He also developed an elaborate concept of history. According to Hensley, two thousand years before the biblical flood humans began to multiply on the earth, and church and state became separate. Thus began a 6,000-year spiritual dispensation that was supposed to end in thirty years of turmoil around 2000 C.E. By that time, the church and state were to be reunited under the Universal Life banner. To implement his ideas, Hensley formed the People's Peace Prosperity Party and ran for both governor of California and president of the United States. Hensley also initiated several "reforms" by marrying a couple in a trial marriage and marrying two females at the 1971 Universal Life Church Festival.

Hensley had been succeeded as head of the church by his wife, Lida G. Hensley, who passed away in 2006. His children now head the church.

The ULC's focus has shifted to encouraging absolute freedom of religious belief, including for its members and ministers, who are not required to adhere to any particular religious doctrine. Online ordination is done free of charge.

Membership: In 2008 the Universal Life Church Monastery reported ordinations of 20,000,000 people worldwide.

Periodicals: *Universal Life Church Online Newsletter.*

Remarks: The Universal Life Church has remained a constant source of controversy, having been targeted by the U.S. Internal Revenue Service as a tax-dodge.

Congregations that claimed a Universal Life charter and ministers that claimed a Universal Life ordination have been carefully scrutinized, and charges of profit-making businesses and various clandestine organizations operating under the Universal Life Church's protection have been periodically reported. The church has responded to the IRS and the resulting negative image by filing suits against the IRS, moving to overturn denials of state-tax exemption, and seeking recognition of its ministers to perform marriages. Although the problems with the IRS have done little to slow the church nationally, they have led many congregations originally chartered by the church to seek their own charters. In 2008 the church maintained that under its new leadership it was complying with IRS guidelines.

Sources:

Universal Life Church. www.ulc.net.

Universal Life Church, United Kingdom. www.ulc.org.uk/index.php.

Ashmore, Lewis. *The Modesto Messiah.* Bakersfield, CA: Universal Press, 1977.

Hensley, Kirby J. *The Buffer Zone.* Modesto, CA: Universal Life Church, 1986.

————. *A New Life.* Modesto, CA: Author, 1983.

Universal Matrix Church

4102 Meadowsweet St., Pasco, WA 99301

The Universal Matrix Church is one of a spectrum of Internet-based religious groups founded at the end of the twentieth century that will supply ordination to any who seek it. Its stated purpose is to free people from the bondage imposed by traditional religious dogma. It is the church's belief that most contemporary organized religious bodies keep their members in a form of mental bondage and that a true church will free people.

The Universal Matrix Church projects as a basic belief the idea of righteous self-determination. It encourages each member to "do that which is right"; however, the duty of determining exactly what is right for each person is left to the individual. Members are encouraged to promulgate the idea of freedom for others to make their own decision about what is correct behavior.

The church bases its existence on the biblical understanding that it is God, not other humans, who calls people to the ministry (John 15:16) and constitutional guarantees of religious freedom.

Ordination in the church is free, though a small one-time donation is requested to cover the church's office and printing expenses. The church is led by its chancellor and prefect of ministries. The church does not charter congregations. It is a member of the International Alliance of Web-Based Churches.

Membership: Not reported.

Sources:

Universal Matrix Church. members.tripod.com/~unmatrix/.

Universal Ministries

PO Box 31, Milford, IL 60953

Universal Ministries is a nondenominational interfaith organization that emphasizes the rights of people to worship as they please. In this regard, the group will ordain anyone who requests it, free of charge. The group was founded by Rev. D. E. Hickman and other ministers originally ordained by the Universal Life Church who wished to extend the basic perspective originally articulated by Kirby Hensley (1911–1999). The new ministries' doctrinal approach is summarized as, "Do what is right, live fruitful lives, be true to ourselves and the God each of us worships, while causing no harm to others, and accept individuals right to worship as they see fit within the laws of their respective countries."

Universal Ministries has designated some of its ministers as bishops who have the duty to make ministers aware of any local ordinances or regulations concerning religious practices (many American communities have significant ordinances affecting marriage, location of churches, etc.), and assistance in creating and promoting an individual independent ministry. The associated Universal Ministries

School of Theology offers a spectrum of degrees in theology, both course-based and honorary.

Membership: In 2008 Universal Ministries reported bishops in 18 states and 10 countries outside the United States.

Educational Facilities:

Universal Ministries School of Theology, Milford, Illinois.

Sources:

Universal Ministries. www.universalministries.com/.

Hickman, D. E. *The Gospel of Christ's True Disciples*. Milford, IL: Universal Ministries, n.d.

World Christianship Ministries (WCM)

PO Box 8041, Fresno, CA 93947

Founded in the 1980s, World Christianship Ministries (WCM) is a worldwide Christian ordination outreach ministry that provides an alternative to seminary for individuals who wish to be ordained immediately and initiate their own ministry. WCM offers resources such as materials on the Bible, music, organizational materials, information on getting started, and information on religious freedom laws. It also offers "true to the Word" Bible study courses and various ministerial handbooks.

WCM ordains by application through the mail. It also invites the ministers who receive ordination from it to be a part of the World Christianship International Association.

Membership: In 2008 the WCM reported having ordained ministers in all 50 states and 85 countries outside the United States.

Sources:

World Christianship Ministries. www.wcm.org/.

Latter-day Saints Family

15

The following passage by Joseph Smith Jr. (1805–1844) describes the event that led to his founding the Church of Jesus Christ of Latter-day Saints in 1830.

After I had retired to the place where I had previously designed to go, having looked around me, and finding myself alone, I kneeled down and began to offer up the desires of my heart to God. I had scarcely done so, when immediately I was seized upon by some power which entirely overcame me, and had such an astonishing influence over me as to bind my tongue so that I could not speak. Thick darkness gathered around me, and it seemed to me for a time as if I were doomed to sudden destruction. But, exerting all of my powers to call upon God to deliver me out of the power of this enemy which had seized upon me, and at the very moment when I was ready to sink into despair and abandon myself to destruction—not to an imaginary ruin, but to the power of some actual being from the unseen world, who had such marvelous power as I had never before felt in any being—just at this moment of great alarm, I saw a pillar of light exactly over my head, above the brightness of the sun, which descended gradually until it fell upon me.

It no sooner appeared than I found myself delivered from the enemy which held me bound. When the light rested upon me I saw two personages, whose brightness and glory defy all description, standing above me in the air. One of them spake unto me, calling me by name, and said, pointing to the other—"This is my beloved son, hear him!"

My object in going to inquire of the Lord was to know which of all the sects was right, that I might know which to join. No sooner, therefore, did I get possession of myself, so as to be able to speak, than I asked the personages who stood above me in the light, which of all the sects was right—and which I should join. I was answered that I must join none of them, for they were all wrong, and the personage who addressed me said that all their creeds were an abomination in His sight: that those professors were all corrupt; that "they draw near to me with their lips, but their hearts are far from me; they teach for doctrines the commandments of men: having a form of godliness, but they deny the power thereof." He again forbade me to join with any of them: and many other things did he say unto me, which I cannot write at this time. When I came to myself again, I found myself lying on my back, looking up

into heaven. When the light had departed, I had no strength; but soon recovering in some degree, I went home.

Joseph Smith, *History of the Church*, 1902–1912, vol. 1, pp. 5–6.

Vermont-born Joseph Smith had moved to western New York in 1815 at the age of 10, along with many others who flooded the area following the War of 1812. With the immigrants came the revival-oriented church to stoke the fires of their emotions and burn the Word of God into their pioneer hearts. So successful had the evangelists been that observers would look upon western New York and label it "the burned-over district," the product of wave after wave of evangelical fervor and spiritual fire. It was in this same area that Charles G. Finney (1792–1875), discussed in chapter 8, made his triumphant tours in the late 1820s and early 1830s.

In this context, Joseph Smith began to be moved by religious concerns and, like so many before him, was confused by the plethora of churches, each claiming to speak God's truth. Smith began to see visions (including the one related above) that resulted in his founding a new church to be the embodiment of God's true revelation. The two personages in the first vision (later identified as Jesus and God the Father) were followed in other visions by John the Baptist and various angelic beings. Smith reported that one of the angels gave him in 1827 plates of gold engraved with what is now known as the *Book of Mormon*. The engraving was in what Smith described as a reformed Egyptian language. The angel also gave Smith two divining stones, the Urim and Thummim (Exodus 28:30), which were to be used to translate the tablets.

The story related in the *Book of Mormon* purported to be the history of two groups of people: the Jeradites, who came to America directly after the attempt to build the Tower of Babel, and the Israelites, who came following the destruction of Jerusalem in the sixth century B.C.E. The former group was destroyed shortly before the arrival of the second group. The second group was essentially destroyed in the fourth century C.E., and Native Americans remained as its only remnant. The last of the prophets among the second group was commanded to write a history, which was buried in New York.

In 1830 the *Book of Mormon* was published and the church organized. Both events had an immediate impact on the religious community, and began a debate that has grown in

Latter-day Saints Family Chronology

1805 Joseph Smith, Jr., born on December 23, in Sharon, Vermont.

1820 Smith claims to have received a visit from God the Father and Jesus Christ, who tells him all churches are wrong.

1827 Smith marries Emma Hale.

1827 The Angel Moroni gives Smith some gold plates that had been buried in Hill Cumorah (near Palmyra, New York). Smith claims that they were written in "Reformed Egyptian."

1828 Smith begins translating the *Book of Mormon*.

1830 The *Book of Mormon* is published and Church of Christ founded.

1831 Latter-day Saints move to Kirkland, Ohio.

1833 The *Book of Commandments*, a collection of additional revelations from God to Joseph Smith, is published.

1838 The church's name evolves into the Church of Jesus Christ of Latter-day Saints.

1838 Joseph Smith moves to Far West, Missouri.

1839 Mormons begin to settle what becomes Nauvoo, Illinois.

1843 Secret revelation relating to polygamy is received.

1844 First issue of *The Nauvoo Expositor* claims polygamy is being practiced in Nauvoo and claims that Smith is teaching that there is more than one God. Mormon leaders order *The Nauvoo Expositor* press destroyed, and church leaders deny that polygamy is being practiced.

On June 27, a mob enters the Carthage jail where four Mormon leaders are being held and kill Joseph Smith and his brother Hyrum.

1846 Brigham Young, the second president of the Latter-day Saints church, leads the former Nauvoo residents to the Salt Lake Valley.

1852 In August, polygamy is announced publicly for the first time at a public Mormon meeting.

1860 Reorganized Church of Jesus Christ of Latter-day Saints officially established at Amboy, Illinois, with Joseph Smith III as president and prophet. It denounces the practice of polygamy and denies Joseph Smith's participation in the practice.

1862 Congress passes the Morrill Act, the first of a series of bills attempting to curb the practice of polygamy.

1882 Congress passes the Edmunds Act.

1887 The Edmunds-Tucker Act allows the government to move effectively against the Church of Jesus Christ of Latter-day Saints.

1890 Church president Wilford Woodruff issues his manifesto asking Mormons to stop the practice of polygamy, which a general church conference accepts as binding upon the membership. Polygamous marriages continue to be performed outside the United States.

1898 B. H. Roberts is elected to the U.S. House of Representatives from Utah, but not allowed to take his seat due to his practice of polygamy.

1912 Reed Smoot is elected to the U.S. Senate from Utah, but is only seated after a heated four-year debate.

1929 New polygamy-practice effort organized by Lorin C. Woolley, based on claimed authority from late church president John Taylor.

1945 *No Man Knows My History* by Fawn Brodie, a biography of Joseph Smith, forces reconsideration of his role in the church's practice of polygamy.

1951 David O. McKay becomes the ninth president of Church of Jesus Christ of Latter-day Saints and oversees a year of unprecedented church growth.

1953 State of Arizona authorities raid polygamous community at Short Creek, arrest males, and take women and children into custody.

1968 George W. Romney runs for president but is defeated in the republican primaries by Richard Nixon.

1976 Congressman Morris Udall of Arizona runs for the democratic nomination for president.

1978 A new revelation allowing all males (including those of African descent) to hold the priesthood is accepted.

1984 Reorganized Church of Jesus Christ of Latter-day Saints dedicates new temple in Independence, Missouri, and receives revelation admitting women to the priesthood.

1985 Ezra Taft Benson, former cabinet member of the Eisenhower administration, becomes president of Church of Jesus Christ of Latter-day Saints.

2001 Reorganized Church of Jesus Christ of Latter-day Saints changes name to Community of Christ.

2006 Senator Harry Reid of Nevada becomes Majority leader of the U.S. Senate.

2007 Prophet Warren Jeffs of the Fundamentalist Church of Jesus Christ of Latter-day Saints is convicted of rape growing out of marriage to underage female church member.

2008 Former Massachusetts governor Mitt Romney runs unsuccessful campaign for president of the United States.

Authorities raid Yearning for Zion Ranch, a center of the Fundamentalist Church of Jesus Christ of Latter-day Saints in Eldorado, Texas.

---

intensity to this day. The *Book of Mormon* was attacked, and the Mormons became outcasts.

But the *Book of Mormon* was not the only revelation received by Smith. His other major works were the *Book of Moses*, the *Book of Abraham*, and a translation of the Bible. At regular intervals, Smith experienced new revelations for specific purposes. These were gathered in a collection in 1833 known as the *Book of Commandments*, now called the *Doctrine and Covenants*. Smith also wrote fragmentary works and there are reports of other major works that were never undertaken because of Smith's untimely death. References to the *Doctrine and Covenants* are given with the initials DC and the number of the section under consideration. The *Book of Mormon* con-

tains books within it, like the Bible. References to the *Book of Mormon* resemble biblical references (e.g., II Nephi 2:46–47).

THE IMPETUS TO SCHISM. Smith's many revelations created a number of problems for Mormon theology. They also built into the system a ready-made impetus to schism. It did not take long for others to get the idea that they could act as Smith had. Apart from Smith's detractors who questioned the veracity of the *Book of Mormon* and the additional revelatory material published by Smith, his example continually excited would-be prophets to action. Common to almost every Mormon splinter group has been one or more leaders who claimed to be receiving new revelations. These leaders originated as disturbers of the peace in each new church center as the Mormons migrated from Kirtland, Ohio, to Independence, Missouri, to Nauvoo, Illinois, and finally, after Smith's murder, to Salt Lake City, Utah.

The church was barely organized before Brother Hiram Page (1800–1852) began to experience revelations concerning the church through "a certain stone." Smith soon learned that his confidant, Oliver Cowdery (1806–1850), as well as David Whitmer (1805–1888), had been taken in by Page, but Smith was able to handle this situation in a church conference. Page recanted, and he and Cowdery were sent on a mission to preach to the Native Americans.

After Smith's followers moved to Kirtland, Ohio, genuine schism began to develop. Wycam Clark led a group of former Mormons, who established the short-lived Pure Church of Christ. Another man, named Hawley, walked barefoot 600 miles from New York to tell Smith that he was no longer the prophet. In 1831 Smith was able to reconcile a group called "the family" to full status in the church. This communal group had joined the Mormons as a body and had to be persuaded to follow "the more perfect law." In 1832 two men named Hoton and Montague organized a body of which the former was president and the latter bishop. The group fell apart when the bishop accused the president of visiting the "pork barrel" (stored supplies), and the president accused the bishop of visiting his wife.

The 1837–1838 period was difficult for Smith, as two major movements took sheep from his flock. Warren Parrish (1803–1887), treasurer of the Kirtland Safety Society, became disillusioned with Smith's prophetic ability and withdrew from the church. He and a number of prominent Latter-day Saints then founded the Church of Christ. There also appeared in Kirtland a woman called the Kirtland seeress. She carried a black stone, and she prophesied that either David Whitmer or Martin Harris (1783–1875) would succeed Smith, who had fallen into transgression. The movement in support of these anti-Josephite revelations was strong enough to spread to Missouri. No record of the eventual fate of the seeress is known.

Smith's *History of the Church* includes a proclamation issued in the fall of 1837 expressing hope for the reclamation of Whitmer and others. In 1838 the Latter-day Saints moved to Missouri to a town called Far West. In 1839 they were forced to leave Far West, so they settled in Nauvoo, Illinois, and stayed there until Joseph Smith's death in 1844. In 1840 George M. Hinkle (1801–1861), a colonel in the militia that defended the Mormons at Far West, Missouri, founded the Church of Jesus Christ, the Bride the Lamb's Wife, in Moscow, Iowa. Hinkle, a trusted confidant of Smith, played a major role in turning Joseph, his brother Hyram (1800–1844), and others over to the Missouri militia. The name *Hinkle* has since been synonymous in Mormon circles with *traitor*. In 1845 Hinkle's church merged with Sidney Rigdon's (1793–1876) Church of Christ.

In the 1840s, during the Nauvoo period, Smith reached the height of his power. Nauvoo, in Hancock County, was at the time the largest city in Illinois and, because of the evenly divided makeup of Illinois politics, it held the balance of power between Democrats and Republicans. Because Smith kept switching sides, the Mormons became a hated people. Added to the political situation was the jealousy among non-Mormons in Hancock County at the success of the Nauvoo enterprise. During the stay of the Mormons at Nauvoo, tensions were on the rise and schismatics could always find support.

At least three major schisms occurred while the community was centered at Nauvoo, each contributing to the downfall of the Mormon establishment. In 1842 the High Council excommunicated Oliver Olney, a would-be prophet who moved to nearby Squaw Grove, Illinois, to establish headquarters and to publish anti-Smith literature. Olney was still publishing as late as 1845, but his full history is not known. Also in 1842, Gladden Bishop (1809–1864) was excommunicated for "having received, written and published or taught certain revelations not consistent with the *Doctrine and Covenants* of the Church." Bishop began setting up splinter churches, but later rejoined the Latter-day Saints. He is known to have had followings at various times at Little Sioux, Iowa, as well as in California, Wisconsin, Ohio, and Salt Lake City. He was eventually excommunicated permanently.

But the major trouble for Smith at Nauvoo came from a schism caused by William Law (1809–1892) and his associates—Wilson Law, Robert and Charles Foster, and C. L. Higbee. They and a large following left the church and set up a rival organization in Nauvoo with William Law as head. This schism meant more for the Latter-day Saints than the loss of members. In May 1844 Law announced that he would start a newspaper to spread his views. He then obtained an indictment against Smith for adultery and polygamy. Robert Foster obtained another indictment against Smith for false swearing. Francis Higbee sued Smith for slander, demanding $5,000. On June 7, 1844, the first and only issue of the *Nauvoo Expositor* appeared. The Nauvoo Legion shut the paper down after Smith declared it a public nuisance. This move proved to be a political blunder, and as news spread across the state, public pressure mounted against the Latter-day Saints and Joseph Smith. He was forced to flee to Iowa, but soon returned to Illinois.

The Law affair played directly into the series of episodes leading to the 1844 arrest of Smith, his brother Hyram, John Taylor (1808–1887), and Willard Richards (1804–1854). On June 27, 1844, a mob broke into the jail at Carthage, Illinois. The mob killed Joseph and Hyram and wounded Taylor. The sudden and violent death of its leader left the church in chaos. Smith had no clear successor, and left behind only a martyr's image and a history of prophecy. The Latter-day Saints were essentially united, but there began a power struggle that split the movement into at least four groups that, over the years, spawned more than 50 additional bodies.

Following Smith's death, and the haste with which Nauvoo had to be abandoned, the church divided into several factions. Sidney Rigdon was among the first to claim to

Mormon Trail

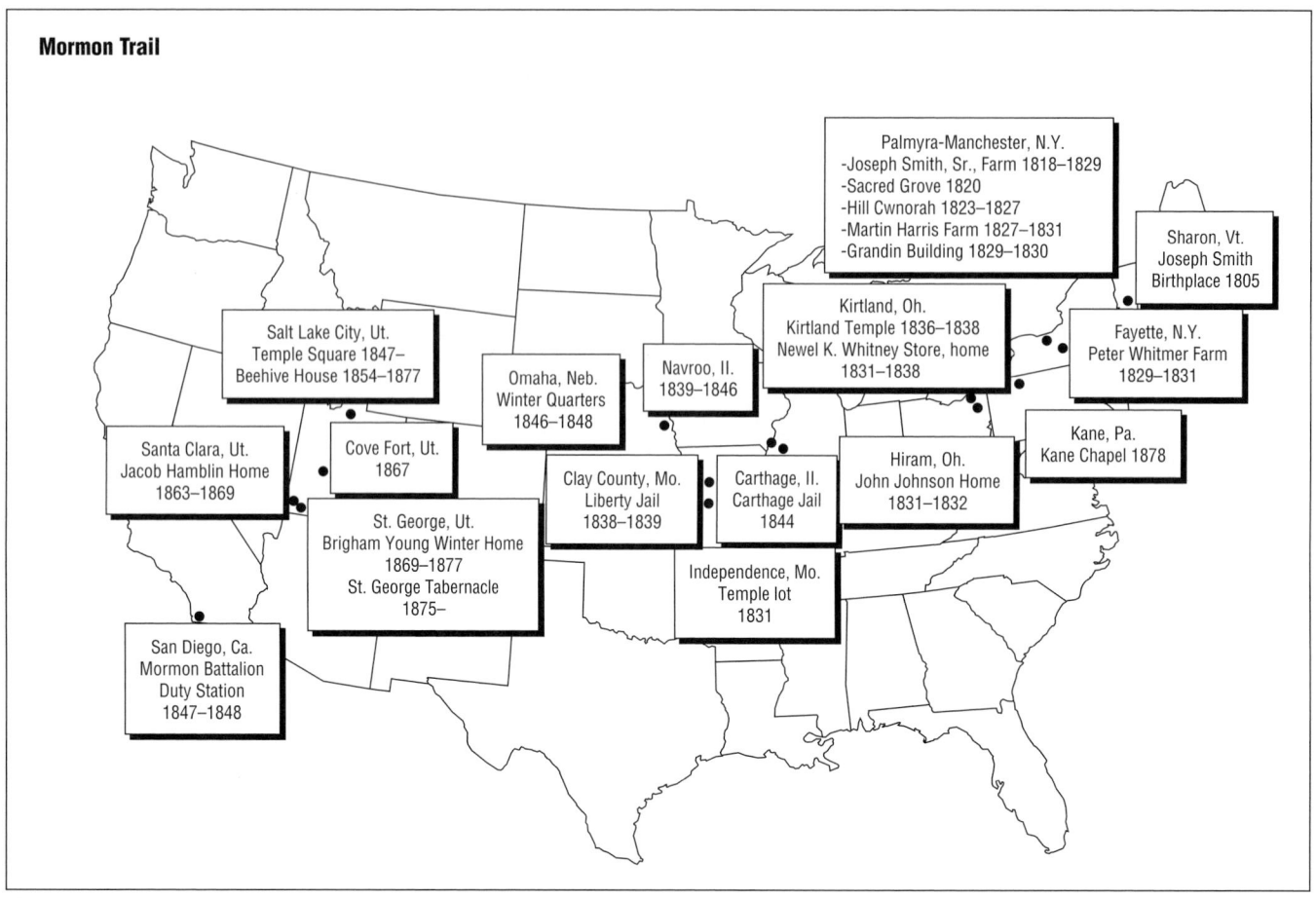

Palmyra-Manchester, N.Y.
-Joseph Smith, Sr., Farm 1818–1829
-Sacred Grove 1820
-Hill Cwnorah 1823–1827
-Martin Harris Farm 1827–1831
-Grandin Building 1829–1830

Sharon, Vt.
Joseph Smith
Birthplace 1805

Kirtland, Oh.
Kirtland Temple 1836–1838
Newel K. Whitney Store, home
1831–1838

Fayette, N.Y.
Peter Whitmer Farm
1829–1831

Salt Lake City, Ut.
Temple Square 1847–
Beehive House 1854–1877

Omaha, Neb.
Winter Quarters
1846–1848

Navroo, Il.
1839–1846

Kane, Pa.
Kane Chapel 1878

Santa Clara, Ut.
Jacob Hamblin Home
1863–1869

Cove Fort, Ut.
1867

Clay County, Mo.
Liberty Jail
1838–1839

Carthage, Il.
Carthage Jail
1844

Hiram, Oh.
John Johnson Home
1831–1832

St. George, Ut.
Brigham Young Winter Home
1869–1877
St. George Tabernacle
1875–

Independence, Mo.
Temple lot
1831

San Diego, Ca.
Mormon Battalion
Duty Station
1847–1848

Adapted from Brigham Young University Geography Department

be Smith's successor, and a few Latter-day Saints followed him to Pennsylvania. James Jesse Strang (1813–1856) also claimed to be Smith's successor, and some followed him to Wisconsin and eventually to Beaver Island, Michigan. The largest group took their guidance from Brigham Young (1801–1877) and migrated to Utah. This group survives today as the Church of Jesus Christ of Latter-day Saints.

Many church members had not "gathered" at Nauvoo, but remained scattered around the Midwest. In the decade after Smith's death, attempts were made to reorganize these groups under Joseph Smith III (1832–1914), the prophet's son. He at first refused his father's mantle, but in 1859 accepted. The new organization became known as the Reorganized Church of Jesus Christ of Latter-day Saints in 1860 (in 2000 it became the Community of Christ). This church drew some of its early strength from followers of Strang who defected after his death in 1856. Still others who did not make the trek to Utah moved back to Independence, Missouri, and bought the tract of land that had been cited in the *Doctrine and Covenants* as the site of the temple in the coming kingdom of Zion, as predicted by Smith.

BELIEFS. The key idea in Smith's theology was *restorationism*, the restoring of the apostolic church that had been lost. Restorationism had been a major concept of the Disciples of Christ movement founded by Alexander Campbell (1788–1866) (see chapter 9) from which Smith's early confidant, Sidney Rigdon, came. Smith believed that the true church died with the first generation of apostles and was restored only with his ordination. The ordination at the hands of John the Baptist occurred on May 15, 1829, when Smith and Oliver Cowdery were given the priesthood of Aaron. Subsequently, the priesthood of Melchizedek was conferred and the church was formally established on April 6, 1830. Along with this restoration of the apostolic church came a set of doctrines and a church order.

The *Articles of Faith*, written shortly before Joseph Smith's death, are still used by the Church of Jesus Christ of Latter-day Saints and most of the groups that have derived from it. The average non-Mormon needs some interpretation of the articles, because they are worded to present Mormon doctrine in a format and language familiar only to members of most older traditional Christian denominations. However, the meaning of the affirmations is clear. For example, the first article affirms a belief in God the eternal Father, in his son Jesus Christ, and in the Holy Spirit. What might seem a statement of belief in the traditional Christian doctrine of the Trinity is in fact an affirmation of belief in three separate divine personage—that is, what is termed *tritheism*.

The articles deny original sin, affirming that humans are not punished for Adam's sin, just their own sins. Christ's atonement establishes a condition by which individuals may be saved if they are obedient to the laws and ordinances of God. There are four ordinances—faith, repentance, baptism by immersion, and the laying on of hands for the gift of the Holy Ghost.

Part of what was revealed to Joseph Smith was the proper organization of the restored church. Derived according to biblical texts, the true church is headed by apostles, prophets, pastors, teachers, evangelists, and others.

The church recognizes both the Bible and the *Book of Mormon* to be the Word of God. Not mentioned in the articles are the supplementary writing to which authority is given, the *Pearl of Great Price*, which contains the *Book of Moses* and the *Book of Abraham*, and the *Doctrine and Covenants*. Smith also began work on a translation of the Bible. It is not used by the Utah-based Church of Jesus Christ of Latter-day Saints, which prefers the King James Version, but is used by the Reorganized Church of Jesus Christ of Latter-day Saints/Community of Christ headquartered in Independence, Missouri. Revelation is believed to be open, and new revelations are added to the *Doctrine and Covenants* as they are received by the church president. New revelations are rare, but now form a distinct body of material by which the Utah-based church and Missouri-based Community of Christ differ.

The *Articles of Faith* also affirm that the future kingdom of Zion will be built, not at Jerusalem in the Holy Land, but on the American continent. According to the *Doctrine and Covenants*, Zion will be centered on present-day Independence, Missouri. Others believe it will be centered on Salt Lake City. Prior to the establishment of Zion, there will be a "gathering" of the Latter-day Saints in the immediate area.

ORGANIZATION.
The restoration determined the nature of the church, which was to be organized after a revealed pattern. Two orders of priesthood were set up. The Aaronic priesthood is the lesser order; all adult males are members, and from it are drawn deacons, teachers, and priests. The Melchizedek priesthood is the higher order, and from it come the church's leadership—elders, seventies, high priests, and the president.

Organizationally, the church is ruled by a series of councils. Leading the church is the first presidency, composed of three people—the president and two other high priests elected by the 12 apostles. When the office of the first presidency is filled, the council of 12 apostles officiates under its direction as a traveling presiding council. Unanimous decisions by the council of 12 have authority equal to the decisions of the first presidency. Thus the first presidency and council of the 12 function much like the pope and college of cardinals in the Roman Catholic Church.

The presiding quorum of 70 and the presiding bishopric comprise the other two ruling bodies. The presiding bishopric holds jurisdiction over the duties of other bishops in the church and over the organization of the Aaronic priesthood.

The Church of Jesus Christ of Latter-day Saints has experienced phenomenal growth worldwide. According to its own figures, the church reached one million members in 1947. It took sixteen years to double that number and another fifteen years to again double the membership, which reached four million in 1978. During the 1980s growth was even greater, with membership reaching five million in 1982, six million in 1986, and seven million in 1989. By the end of the twentieth century, membership was reported to be 11 million. While critics have challenged these figures, saying that they count people joining but do not account for those leaving and becoming inactive, the numbers still represent a significant increase, and have been paralleled by the building of new houses of worship and the multiplication of temples. Growth has also changed the status of the church relative to the larger religious and secular community. The church represents either a majority or significant minority of the population in Utah and surrounding states, and regularly sees its members elected to political office. Senator Harry Reid, a Democrat from Nevada and a Mormon, became the majority leader in the U.S. Senate in 2007. Another Mormon politician, Republican senator Orrin Hatch from Utah, served as chair of the Senate Judiciary Committee from 1995 to 2001 and from 2003 to 2005.

CONTROVERSY.
The Latter-day Saints have been the subject of widespread controversy since the initial publication of the *Book of Mormon* in 1830. During the nineteenth century, controversy swirled around the authenticity of the *Book of Mormon*, the tendency of Latter-day Saints to act communally and vote as a block, the practice of polygamy, and the issue of statehood for Utah. In the twentieth century, many of these controversies have been pushed to the side as the church has become successful, and since World War II (1937–1945) the community has produced three viable candidates for the U.S. presidency in George Romney, Morris Udall, and Mitt Romney. Along the way, the church has rid itself of a final hobbling problem, the nonadmission of African Americans to the priesthood.

The success of the Latter-day Saints has also made them a target for Evangelical Christians. Since the nineteenth century, the larger Christian community has viewed Mormons as heretics, at best, and generally as a separate religion that, while keeping Christian language, has departed from the tradition at many important points. In response, the authorities of the Church of Latter-day Saints have continued to argue that the Mormon Church is a restoration of the original Christian message. At the same time, church leaders have asked that members and critics alike stop using the adjective *Mormon* to describe the church, as it suggests that the church is something other than Christian. Some scholars, like Jan Shipps, have suggested that Mormonism should be regarded as post-Christian in much the same way that the Christian church is post-Jewish. This view, which is a variant of that held by many of the church's Evangelical critics, is reflected in the Latter-day Saints' practice of widely advertising the *Book of Mormon* as another testament of Jesus Christ.

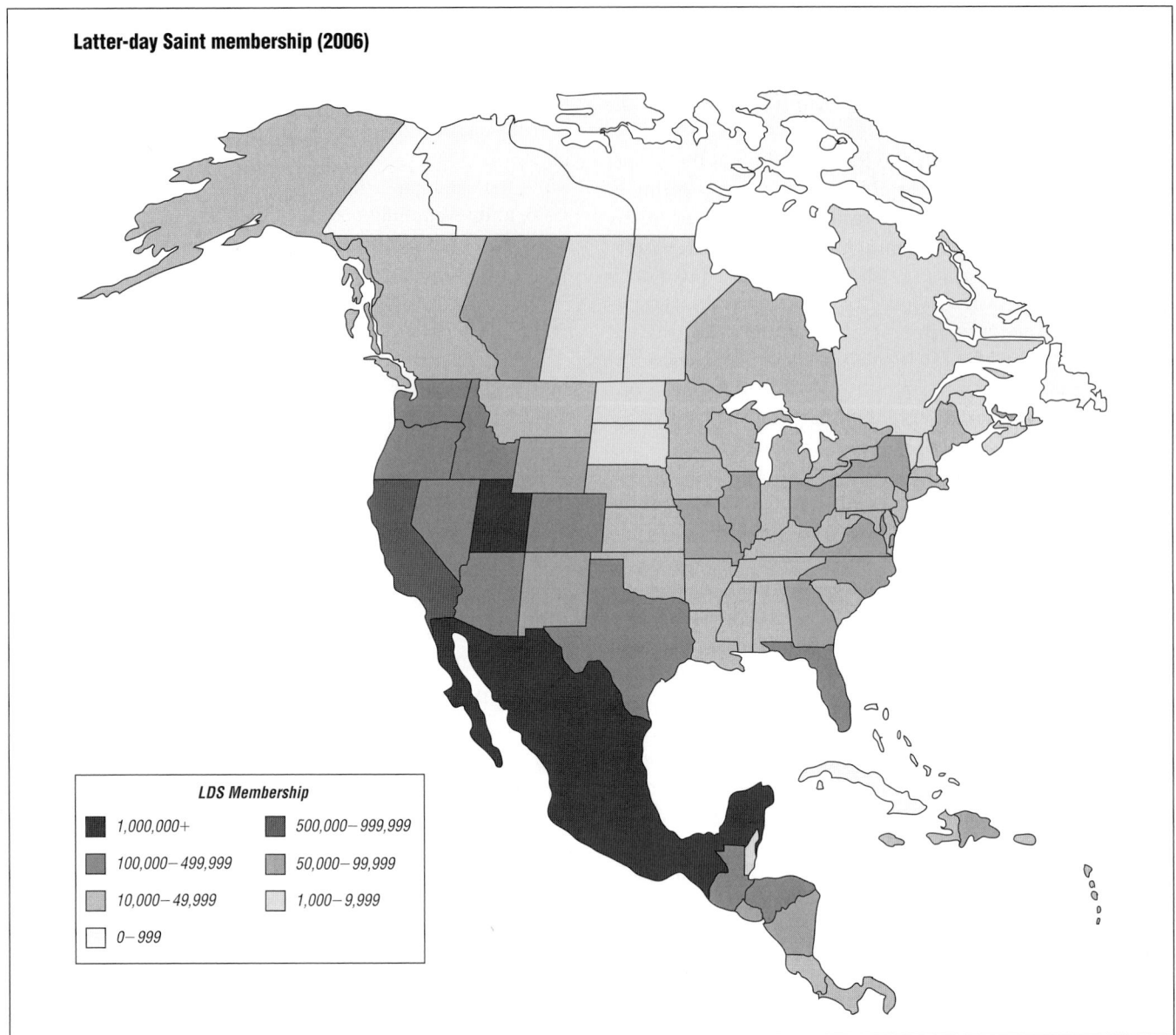

Latter-day Saint membership (2006)

LDS Membership
- 1,000,000+
- 500,000– 999,999
- 100,000– 499,999
- 50,000– 99,999
- 10,000– 49,999
- 1,000– 9,999
- 0– 999

Since the 1950s, as the Church of Jesus Christ of Latter-day Saints has developed into a national organization, has grown to become one of the five largest religious bodies in America, and has continued its campaign to recruit new members without regard to their past affiliations (perceived by many as sheep stealing), Evangelical Christians have placed the Latter-day Saints among their primary targets for counter-recruitment efforts and boundary maintenance polemics. Hundreds of Evangelical missionary organization, many quite small, have arisen to evangelize the Latter-day Saints, "expose" and denounce their difference with orthodox Christianity, and make public the more confidential aspects of church life, especially beliefs and practices related to the Latter-day Saints' temples. Some critics have established themselves in Salt Lake City and daily distribute literature and talk to the many tourists and visitors at the church's large headquarters complex.

Church authorities have generally refused to respond directly to the Evangelical critique of Mormonism. However, the church has approved the work of various members and institutions in providing a Mormon apologetic. Most notable in this regard is the work of Hugh Nibley (1910–2005), a long-time professor at Brigham Young University (BYU) in Provo, Utah. In like measure, in 1979 Mormon attorney John W. Welch established the Foundation for Ancient Research and Mormon Studies (FARMS). Welch became a professor at BYU in 1980, and in 1997 FARMS became affiliated with the university, where it now operates as part of the Neal A. Maxwell Institute for Religious Scholarship.

A Mormon-Evangelical dialogue has emerged since the 1997 publication of Craig Blomberg and Stephen E. Robinson's *How Wide the Divide?* Blomberg is an Evangelical New Testament scholar while Robinson teaches at BYU. Their conversation has been duplicated in the speaking and writing of Robert L. Millett, a BYU professor emeritus, and Gregory C.V. Johnson, head of Standing Together, a Utah-based missionary organization. This dialogue led the Latter-day Saints first presidency to allow evangelical leader Ravi Zacharias to speak at the Mormon Tabernacle in 2004.

CURRENT MORMON DIVISIONS.

Most Mormons can be divided into Utah Mormons and Missouri Mormons, names that refer to their history rather than to their current church headquarters. Those known as Utah Mormons either have their headquarters in Salt Lake City, Utah, or were established by a former member of the Church of Jesus Christ of Latter-day Saints. The great majority of present-day Mormons are members of the Utah-based church. Those known as Missouri Mormons rejected the leadership of Brigham Young, who led a large group of Mormons, but not all, to Salt Lake City. The early leaders of this Missouri church gathered the remaining Latter-day Saints who had dwelt across the Midwest into a newly reorganized church body, with headquarters eventually established in Missouri. The Missouri Mormons have strongly emphasized Joseph Smith's prophecy (DC 51) that the temple was to be built in Independence, Missouri.

No turmoil has so affected the restoration movement founded by Joseph Smith as did the controversy that arose after the Civil War (1861–1865) over the practice of polygamy. Polygamy seems to have been introduced into the church in Nauvoo by Smith, and to have been a factor in Smith's assassination. Emma Hale Smith (1804–1879), Joseph Smith's first wife, never accepted the idea, though she did not publicly speak against it during his lifetime. After her husband's death, she remained in Nauvoo and did not travel to Salt Lake City, even though she was enticed to do so by Brigham Young. She emerged as an antipolygamy champion and affiliated with the Reorganized Church, which strongly denounced polygamy, especially as it emerged as a public doctrine in Utah in the 1850s.

In Utah, polygamy was first practiced quietly, and then openly proclaimed. Its practice was ingrained in the social structure (though only a minority of the males were wealthy enough to participate), and it was key to the Utah church's doctrine of salvation and the afterlife. The practice of polygamy was also an irritant to the larger non-Mormon religious community, which made it the object of a fervent crusade to rid the land of what was perceived by many as blatant immorality. After the Civil War, the federal government moved against the church with a series of actions asserting the government's authority in Utah and its hostility to the continuance of polygamy.

By this time, however, polygamy had become an essential part of the Mormon social system and theology, and it was only after a lengthy battle against overwhelming odds that the church slowly capitulated. This capitulation began in the form of a manifesto in 1890 by President Wilford Woodruff (1807–1898) abolishing the practice of plural marriage. The manifesto was unanimously adopted by the vote of the Latter-day Saints Church conference. Quietly, however, the practice continued, and only a series of actions during the first quarter of the twentieth century—excommunicating those who either conducted plural-marriage ceremonies or entered into a polygamous relationship—finally eradicated the practice among church members.

In reaction to the threats of excommunication, several polygamy-practicing groups formed but broke up during World War I (1914–1918). New groups formed after the war, some of which have continued to this day. Most polygamy-practicing Mormons accept a common history that dates to an incident they claim occurred on September 26,1886, four years prior to the manifesto. On this date, they claim, at a meeting of church leaders to consider a document prepared by George Q. Cannon (1827–1901) concerning the polygamy question, church president John Taylor spent a night in conversation with Joseph Smith and the Lord. The next morning, Taylor denounced Cannon's document and asked church members to pledge themselves to the principle of plural marriage. After the meeting, five copies were made of the revelation of the Lord on plural marriage, and five men—Cannon, Samuel Bateman, Charles H. Wilkins, John W. Woolley, and Lorin C. Woolley—were given authority to administer the covenant (i.e., plural marriage). They were also to ensure that no year passed without children being born in the covenant. Taylor also prophesied that during the time of the seventh Mormon president, Heber J. Grant (1856–1945), the church would go into spiritual and temporal bondage, and "one strong and mighty" would appear (DC 85). The Church of Latter-day Saints claims this meeting never occurred and was a fiction created by Lorin Woolley.

Among the polygamists are Mormons called fundamentalists. They are distinguished from other polygamy-practicing groups in that they claim only to control the presidency of the high priesthood. Other polygamy-practicing groups claim to control both the presidency of the high priesthood and the presidency of the church.

In 1929 Joseph White Musser (1872–1954), a leader of the Mormon fundamentalists and their most prolific writer, claimed that he had received authority from Taylor's five disciples. He further claimed that after the manifesto was issued, the office of the president of the church and the president of the high priesthood were separated and the latter was given to the fundamentalists. Hence the priesthood has authority apart from the church leadership. Musser felt that the movement away from polygamy was but one of several departures from the faith that the church had made. Mormon fundamentalists believe in what is termed the *Adam-God theory* (as originally taught by Brigham Young), according to which "Adam is Our Father and Our God and is the literal Father of Jesus." Almost all Mormon fundamentalists claim authority through Musser, and read his voluminous writings in his books and in the magazine *The Star of Truth*, which he published for many years.

The polygamists are living outside the laws of both the Church of Jesus Christ of Latter-day Saints and the United States, and most have retreated into the rural landscape to escape legal and social pressure. They are something of an embarrassment to the contemporary Church of Latter-day Saints, which tends to ignore them.

The continuing concern over polygamy within the Mormon cultural milieu in Utah and the surrounding states where the Latter-day Saints have a strong presence periodically becomes front-page news. In 2001 the trial of outspoken independent polygamist Tom Greene, husband of five and father of more than 25, attracted the attention of state authorities and the national media. He was arrested and convicted on a spectrum of charges, including statutory rape.

Following the emergence in 2002 of Warren Jeffs as leader of the largest of the fundamentalists groups, the Fundamentalist Church of Jesus Christ of Latter-day Saints, complaints multiplied that young men in the group were being forced out and the young women were married against their will to their fathers' contemporaries. Some of the young women were reputedly under the legal age of consent. In 2006 authorities attempted to arrest Jeffs, who went into hiding and eventually was placed in the FBI's Ten Most Wanted Fugitives list. He was arrested in 2007 and convicted of several charges of being an accomplice to rape.

Jeffs's conviction led to a raid on the group's center near Eldorado, Texas, in 2008, during which all the minors were taken into state custody. In the flurry of court actions following the case, Texas authorities were forced to return most of the children to their parents, but legal proceeding were pursued against men believed to have had sexual relations with underage females.

SOURCES

Few American religious traditions have generated as much literature as have the Latter-day Saints. The church has been a literary tradition from its beginning in the 1830s, and today the Mormon culture of the American West supports a large community of amateur Mormon historians and book collectors. The success of the church, combined with its efforts at door-to-door recruitment, has made it an object of counter-evangelical efforts by Evangelical Christians. With the possible exception of the Jehovah's Witnesses, no other religious group in the United States popularly identified as a target by Christian counter-cultists has had so much material produced and circulated about it.

The study of the Latter-day Saints' history, life, and thought is nurtured by the Mormon History Association, 10 West 100 South, Suite 610, Salt Lake City, UT 84101 (www.mhahome.org/). This association publishes the *Journal of Mormon History*. Both the Church of Jesus Christ of Latter-day Saints and the Community of Christ keep extensive archives, the former located at the Church History Library and Archives, 50 East North Temple Street, Room 227E, Salt Lake City, UT 84150-3420, and the latter at the Community of Christ headquarters in Independence, Missouri. An additional important resource is the library of Brigham Young University in Provo, Utah.

General Sources

Arbaugh, George Bartholomew. *Revelation in Mormonism: Its Character and Changing Forms.* Chicago: University of Chicago Press, 1932. 252 pp.

Carter, Kate B. *Denominations that Base Their Beliefs on the Teachings of Joseph Smith.* Salt Lake City, UT: Daughters of the Utah Pioneers. 1969. 68 pp.

Cornwall, Marie, ed. *Contemporary Mormonism: Social Science Perspectives.* Urbana: University of Illinois Press, 1994.

Cory, Delbert J. *A Comparison Study of the Basic Thought of the Major "Latter Day Saint" Groups.* Oberlin, OH: Author, 1963. 42 pp.

Goodliffe, Wilford Leroy. *America Frontier Religion: Mormons and Their Dissenters, 1830–1900.* Ph.D. diss., University of Idaho, 1976. 287 pp.

Launius, Roger D., and Linda Thatcher, eds. *Differing Visions: Dissenters in Mormon History.* Urbana: University of Illinois Press, 1994.

Ludlow, Daniel H., ed. *Encyclopedia of Mormonism.* 4 vols. New York: Macmillan, 1992.

Ostling, Richard N., and Joan K. Ostling. *The Power and the Promise: Mormon America.* San Francisco: Harper, 1999.

Rich, Russell R. *Little Known Schisms of the Restoration.* Provo, UT: Brigham Young University Press, 1967. 76 pp.

———. *Those Who Would Be Leaders: Offshoots of Mormonism.* Provo, UT: Brigham Young University Press, 1967. 89 pp.

Shields, Steven L. *Divergent Paths of the Restoration: A History of the Latter-day Saint Movement.* 3rd ed. Bountiful, UT: Restoration Research, 1982. 282 pp.

———. *The Latter Day Saint Churches: An Annotated Bibliography.* New York: Garland, 1987. 281 pp.

Smith, Joseph. *History of the Church.* Vol. 1. Salt Lake City, UT: Deseret, 1902–1912.

Tullis, F. LaMond, ed. *Mormonism: A Faith for All Cultures.* Provo, UT: Brigham Young University Press, 1978. 365 pp.

Joseph Smith Jr.

Anderson, Richard Lloyd. "The Reliability of the Early History of Lucy and Joseph Smith." *Dialogue* 4, no. 2 (Summer 1969): 12–28.

———. *Joseph Smith's New England Heritage: Influences of Grandfathers Solomon Mack and Asael Smith.* Rev. ed. Salt Lake City, UT: Deseret, 2003. 312 pp.

Brodie, Fawn M. *No Man Knows My History: The Life of Joseph Smith, the Mormon Prophet.* New York: Knopf, 1971. 499 pp.

Bushman, Richard Lyman. *Joseph Smith: Rough Stone Rolling.* New York: Knopf, 2005. 740 pp.

Huntress, Keith. *Murder of an American Prophet: Events and Prejudices Surrounding the Killing of Joseph and Hyrum Smith, Carthage, Illinois, June 27, 1844.* San Francisco: Chandler, 1960. 232 pp.

Nibley, Hugh. *No Ma'am That's Not History: A Brief Review of Mrs. Brodie's Reluctant Vindication of a Prophet She Seeks to Expose.* Salt Lake City, UT: Bookcraft, 1946. 62 pp.

Smith, Lucy Mack. *Joseph Smith and His Progenitors.* Lamoni, IA: Reorganized Church of Jesus Christ of Latter-day Saints, 1912. 371 pp.

Taves, Ernest H. *Trouble Enough: Joseph Smith and the Book of Mormon.* Buffalo, NY: Prometheus, 1984. 280 pp.

Vogel, Dan. *Joseph Smith: The Making of a Prophet.* Salt Lake City, UT: Signature, 2004. 715 pp.

Mormon History

Allen, James B. *The Story of the Latter-day Saints.* Salt Lake City, UT: Deseret, 1976. 722 pp.

Arrington, Leonard J. *Brigham Young: American Moses.* Champaign, IL: University of Illinois Press, 1986. 560 pp.

———. *Great Basin Kingdom: An Economic History of the Latter-Day Saints, 1830–1900* (1958). New ed. Urbana: University of Illinois Press, 2005. 534 pp.

Arrington, Leonard J., and Davis Bitton. *The Mormon Experience: A History of the Latter-day Saints.* 2nd ed. Urbana: University of Illinois Press, 1992. 414 pp.

Backman, Milton V., Jr. *Eyewitness Accounts of the Restoration.* Orem, UT: Grandin, 1983. 239 pp.

Bagley, Will. *Blood of the Prophets: Brigham Young and the Massacre at Mountain Meadows.* Norman: University of Oklahoma Press, 2004. 540 pp.

Bitton, Davis, and Maureen Ursenbach Beecher, eds. *New Views of Mormon History: Essays in Honor of Leonard J. Arrington.* Salt Lake City, UT: University of Utah Press, 1987. 480 pp.

Firmage, Edwin Brown, and Richard Collin Mangrum. *Zion in the Courts: A Legal History of the Church of Jesus Christ of Latter-day Saints, 1830–1900.* Urbana: University of Illinois Press, 1988. 430 pp.

Givens, Terry L. *People of Paradox: A History of Mormon Culture.* New York: Oxford University Press, 2007. 432 pp.

Mullen, Robert. *The Latter-day Saints: The Mormons of Yesterday and Today.* Garden City, NY: Doubleday, 1966. 316 pp.

Quinn, Michael D. *The Mormon Hierarchy: Origins of Power.* Salt Lake City, UT: Signature. 1994. 685 pp.

Rich, Russell R. *Ensign to the Nations: A History of the Church from 1846 to the Present.* Provo, UT: Brigham Young University Press, 1972. 663 pp.

Shipps, Jan. *Mormonism: The Story of a New Religious Tradition.* Urbana: University of Illinois Press, 1985. 211 pp.

Stegner, Wallace. *The Gathering of Zion: The Story of the Mormon Trail.* New York: McGraw-Hill, 1964. 331 pp.

Latter-day Saints Beliefs

Living Truths from the Book of Mormon. Salt Lake City, UT: Sunday School of the Church of Jesus Christ of Latter-day Saints, 1972. 330 pp.

McLaughlan, James M., and Lloyd Ericson, eds. *Discourses in Mormon Theology: Philosophical & Theological Possibilities.* Draper, UT: Kofford, 2007. 301 pp.

McConkey, Bruce R. *Mormon Doctrine.* Salt Lake City, UT: Bookcraft, 1966. 856 pp.

Millet, Robert L. *The Mormon Faith.* Salt Lake City, UT: Deseret, 1998. 222 pp.

Richards, LeGrand. *A Marvelous Work and a Wonder.* Rev. ed. Salt Lake City, UT: Deseret, 1976. 424 pp.

Smith, Joseph F. *Gospel Doctrine.* Salt Lake City, UT: Deseret, 1969. 553 pp.

Walker, Ronald W., Richard E. Turley, and Glen M. Leonard. *Massacre at Mountain Meadows.* New York: Oxford University Press, 2008. 448 pp.

Christian Refutations of the Latter-day Saints

Beckwith, Francis, Carl Mosser, and Paul Owen, eds. *The New Mormon Challenge: Responding to the Latest Defenses of a Fast-Growing Movement.* Grand Rapids, MI: Zondervan, 2002. 544 pp.

Blomberg, Craig, and Stephen E. Robinson's *How Wide the Divide? A Mormon & an Evangelical in Conversation.* Downers Grove, IL: InterVarsity, 1997. 228 pp.

Fraser, Gordon H. *Is Mormonism Christian?* Chicago: Moody Press, 1977. 192 pp.

Marquardt, H. Michael, and Wesley Walters. *Inventing Mormonism: Tradition and the Historical Record.* Salt Lake City, UT: Signature, 1994. 244 pp.

McElveen, Floyd. *Will the "Saints" Go Marching In?* Glendale, CA: G/L, 1977. 175 pp.

McKeever, Bill, and Eric Johnson. *Mormonism 101.* Grand Rapids. MI: Baker, 2000. 320 pp.

Millet, Robert L., and Gregory C. V. Johnson. *Bridging the Divide: The Continuing Conversation between a Mormon and an Evangelical.* Rhinebeck, NY: Monkfish, 2007. 224 pp.

Nuckles, Dave P. *I'm A Nomrom: From Mormon Missionary to Christian and Beyond.* Kearney, NB: Morris, 2006.

Ropp, Harry L. *The Mormon Papers.* Downers Grove, IL: InterVarsity, 1977. 118 pp.

Smith, John L. *I Visited the Temple.* Clearfield, UT: Utah Evangel Press, 1966. 104 pp.

Tanner, Jerald, and Sandra Tanner. *Mormonism: Shadow or Reality?* Salt Lake City, UT: Modern Microfilm, 1972. 587 pp.

Mormon Scriptures

Campbell, Alexander. *An Analysis of the Book of Mormon.* Boston: Greene, 1832. 16 pp.

Givens, Terry. *By the Hand of Mormon: The American Scripture That Launched a New World Religion.* New York: Oxford University Press, 2002. 352 pp.

Kirkham, Francis W. *A New Witness for Christ in America: The Book of Mormon.* 3rd ed. Independence, MO: Press of Zion's, 1951. 429 pp.

Nelson, Dee Jay. *Joseph Smith's "Eye of Ra."* Salt Lake City, UT: Modern Microfilm, 1968. 32 pp.

———. *A Translation of Facsimile No. 3 in the Book of Abraham.* Salt Lake City, UT: Modern Microfilm, 1989. 32 pp.

Nibley, Hugh. *Abraham in Egypt.* Salt Lake City, UT: Deseret, 1981. 288 pp.

Prince, Walter Franklin. "Psychological Tests for the Authorship of the Book of Mormon." *American Journal of Psychology* 28, no. 3 (July 1917): 373–89.

Reynolds, Noel B. *Book of Mormon Authorship Revisited: The Evidence for Ancient Origins.* Provo, UT: Foundation for Ancient Research and Mormon Studies, 1997. 574 pp.

Tanner, Jerald, and Sandra Tanner. *Did Spalding Write the Book of Mormon?* Salt Lake City, UT: Modern Microfilm, 1977. 105 pp.

Polygamy

Anderson, J. Max. *The Polygamy Story: Fiction and Fact.* Salt Lake City, UT: Publishers Press, 1979. 166 pp.

Bailey, Paul. *Grandpa Was a Polygamist: A Candid Remembrance.* Los Angeles: Western Lore Press, 1960. 181 pp. Rev. ed., *Polygamy Was Better than Monotony.* New York: Ballantine, 1972. 180 pp.

Bradley, Martha S. *Kidnapped from that Land: The Government Raids on the Short Creek Polygamists.* Salt Lake City, UT: University of Utah Press, 1993.

Collier, Fred C. "Re-Examining the Lorin Woolley Story." *Doctrine of the Priesthood* 1, no. 2 (February 1981): 1–17.

Compton, Todd. *In Sacred Loneliness: The Plural Wives of Joseph Smith.* Salt Lake City, UT: Signature, 1997. 788 pp.

Foster, Lawrence. *Religion and Sexuality: Three American Communal Experiments of the Nineteenth Century.* New York: Oxford University Press, 1981. 363 pp.

Gordon, Sarah Barringer. *The Mormon Question: Polygamy and Constitutional Conflict in Nineteenth-Century America.* Chapel Hill: University of North Carolina Press, 2002. 337 pp.

Hales, Brian C. *Modern Polygamy and Mormon Fundamentalism: The Generations After the Manifesto.* Draper, UT: Kofford, 2007. 524 pp.

Hardy, B. Carmon. *Solemn Covenant: The Mormon Polygamous Passage.* Urbana: University of Illinois Press, 1992.

———. *Doing the Works of Abraham, Mormon Polygamy: Its Origin, Practice, and Demise.* Norman, OK: Clark, 2007. 447 pp.

The Most Holy Principle. 4 Vols. Murray, UT: Gems, 1970–1975.

Musser, Joseph White. *Celestial or Plural Marriage.* Salt Lake City, UT: Truth, 1970. 154 pp.

Openshaw, Robert R. *The Notes, or, Selected references on the Fulness of the Gospel for Saints and Other Interested Students.* Pinesdale, MT: Bitterroot, 1980. 616 pp.

Smith, George D. *Nauvoo Polygamy: "…But We Called It Celestial Marriage."* Salt Lake City, UT: Signature, 2008. 672 pp.

Van Wagner, Richard S. *Mormon Polygamy: A History*. Salt Lake City, UT: Signature, 1986. 313 pp.

Young, Kimball. *Isn't One Wife Enough*. New York: Holt, 1954. 476 pp.

 # Utah Mormons

Aaronic Order

Box 57095, Murray, UT 84157-0095

The Aaronic Order was organized by followers of Dr. Maurice Lerrie Glendenning (1891–1969). While still a young man, Glendenning began to receive messages and insights pertaining to God's work for Israel and for Levi and Aaron. Some of these messages, together with some of his letters and epistles, were later assembled into a book known as the *Levitical Writings*. (This book is also referred to as the *Book of Elias* or the *Record of John*.) The Bible, however, is considered the basic scripture of the Aaronic Order and the final authority in all matters of doctrine and practice. The *Levitical Writings* are seen as consistent with and supportive of the biblical revelation. The order considers itself a Christ-centered and Bible-based church.

In 1928 Glendenning and his family moved to Provo, Utah, where he continued to receive revelations from Elias (Elijah) and to share them with interested people, many of whom became convinced of their divine origin. His followers increased over the years, and in 1942 incorporated the Aaronic Order under the laws of the State of Utah.

The order has a chief high priest who functions primarily in the spiritual area; a first high priest who functions primarily in the temporal area; a second high priest who is in charge of ordinance and ceremonial work; and a branch priest who is appointed over each congregation. The ruling legislative body is the supreme council, consisting of 70 members.

The order stresses discipleship and consecration, which require full members to relinquish title to all goods and property. The holding of any property or goods by a full member constitutes a stewardship under the direction of the supreme council of the Aaronic Order. The church also has several communal settlements, known as Levitical communities, which practice the biblical teachings on holding "all things common." These practices are in harmony with the ministry of Levi and Aaron in early Israel, which required that tribal members have no ownership or inheritance of the temporal things in Israel. The priesthood and the service at the altar were the heritage of Levi and Aaron for all time.

According to the order's teachings, the beginning of the Levitical priesthood dates to 1736 B.C.E., when the priesthood was granted to Levi and his descendents forever. The priests were known as Levites, Aaronites, Zadokites, and Essenes at various times, and many of them became Christians in the New Testament period. One line of the Aaronic priesthood continued through the Middle Ages via the lineage of Robert Bruce, king of Scotland, and was brought to America in 1742 through one branch of his family, known as the Glendowyns (or Glendennings). This family maintained a constant awareness of their lineage and priesthood heritage and passed this on from father to son by written blessings, some of which are in possession of the order.

The headquarters and a branch of the order are located in Murray, Utah (a Salt Lake City suburb). Other branches are located in Provo and Partoun, Utah, and in Independence, Missouri. One of the most important thrusts of the work, however, is in the Levitical community of Eskdale, Utah, which was established in 1956 in a western desert area near the Utah-Nevada Border. In the 1980s the Order came into contact with a Sacred Name group, Bet HaShem Midrash, headed by Shmuel ben Aharon of New Haven, Indiana. The Indiana group merged into the Order and increased awareness in the larger community of the Hebrew names of the deity and of Jesus. Members not associated with a specific branch are located across the United States.

Membership: The order does not believe in keeping membership figures. In 1995 there were six centers of the order, approximately 1,000 members, and 20 ministers.

Periodicals: *Aaron's Star*. Available from A. O. Publishing, 1100 Circle Dr., Esk Dale, UT 84728-9702. • *Pathlight*. Available from Ken Hill, 550 Trout Creek, UT 84083.

Remarks: The Aaronic Order is not affiliated with the Church of Jesus Christ of Latter-day Saints nor does it consider itself as having been derived from it. It should be noted, however, that Glendenning was a member of the church, and was excommunicated from it because of his revelations. Also, the *Levitical Writings* begin with chapter 137, whereas the LDS edition of the *Doctrine and Covenants* ends with section 136.

Sources:

Beeston, Blanche W. *Now My Servant*. Caldwell, ID: Caxton Printers, 1987.

———. *Purified as Gold and Silver*. Idaho Falls, ID: Author, 1966.

Erickson, Ralph D. *History and Doctrinal Development of the Order of Aaron*. Master's thesis, Brigham Young University, Provo, UT, 1969.

Levitical Writings. Eskdale, UT: Aaronic Order, 1978.

Church of Jesus Christ (Bulla)

PO Box 1126, 95 E Hwy. 98, D-107, Calexico, CA 92231

Art Bulla joined the Church of Jesus Christ of Latter-day Saints around 1970. While a member he came to believe that he was the "One Mighty and Strong" who was spoken of in Mormon scriptures and who was to come and set God's house in order. He organized the Church of Jesus Christ in the early 1980s.

Membership: Not reported.

Sources:

Art Bulla. www.artbulla.com/zion/toc.html.

Bulla, Art. *The Revelations of Jesus Christ*. Salt Lake City, UT: Author, 1983.

Church of Jesus Christ of Latter-day Saints

47 E. South Temple, Salt Lake City, UT 84150

The narrative portion of this chapter, which carries the history and theology of the Latter-day Saints tradition, is the Church of Jesus Christ of Latter-day Saints (LDS), headquartered in Salt Lake City, Utah.

HISTORY. After the assassination of Joseph Smith, Jr. in 1844, the Saints were forced to evacuate Nauvoo, Illinois, and most of them moved to Iowa. Brigham Young (1801–1877), the former president of the Council of Twelve Apostles under Smith, became their leader and three years later was formally installed as president of the church at the reorganization of the First Presidency. Young led the Saints across the Plains states to the Rocky Mountains, where, in 1847, they settled the present site of Salt Lake City. Under Young's leadership the Saints colonized more than 300 settlements from Canada to Mexico.

During the early years in Utah, polygamy, which had begun to be practiced among church leaders in Nauvoo, became openly discussed, practiced, and advocated. Possibly more than any other issue, polygamy thwarted Young's plans for a western state of Deseret, the original name proposed for Utah, while also gaining disapproval by the federal government of the church. During the 1880s, laws were passed against polygamy. Church leaders were obligated by law to move against the practice and to move against those church members who continued to participate in plural marriages. Since 1890, the church has been officially opposed to polygamy, and has periodically reinforced that position as new issues emerged and a continuing polygamy-practicing community have become visible.

In 1849, the church stepped up its worldwide mission previously initiated in Nauvoo. They concentrated on Western Europe, primarily England and Scandinavia. The number of converts constituted the basis for the spectacular spread of the church throughout the world in the twentieth century. While becoming an international religion of some importance, the church spread along the Rocky Mountains—from Phoenix, Arizona, to Boise, Idaho, and westward to the Pacific. From their western base, the Saints have gradually spread across the United States and currently have congregations in every section of the country.

For many years, the church was criticized for its stance on not admitting black people to the lay priesthood, an essential structure in the church for male members. That condition was changed in 1978, following a revelation given to President Spencer W. Kimball (1895–1985).

ORGANIZATION. The church is organized along patterns revealed to Joseph Smith Jr. Leading the church internationally is the First Presidency, comprising of three men (the president and two counselors) who are assisted by the Council of Twelve Apostles. Young succeeded Smith, the first president of the church. Since Young's tenure, the church has been served successively by the following: John Taylor (1880–1887); Wilford Woodruff (1889–1898); Lorenzo Snow (1898–1901); Joseph Fielding Smith (1901–1918); Heber J. Grant (1918–1945); George Albert Smith (1945–1951); David O. McKay (1951–1970); Joseph Fielding Smith (1970–); Harold B. Lee (1972–1973); Spencer W. Kimball (1973–1985); Ezra Taft Benson (1985–1994); Howard W. Hunter (1994–1995); Gordon B. Hinckley (1995–2008); and Thomas S. Monson (2008–present). The First Presidency and the Twelve Apostles regulate the affairs of the church generally. The Quorums of the Seventy, including a seven-man presidency and (in 1995) 73 additional members, administer the affairs of 22 "areas" of the world, under the direction of the First Presidency and the Twelve. The Presiding Bishopric (three men) has charge of the temporal affairs of the church, including the building and welfare programs. The structure of the international organization is somewhat repeated in structures at the regional (stakes) and local (wards) levels.

Integral to the belief and practice of the church are temples. Such structures are used for special weekday ceremonial work rather than being centers for the weekly gathering of worshippers. The four main services performed in the temple are the baptism for the dead, in which the living are baptized as proxies for those who died in generations past; the temple endowments; temple marriage; and sealings, which establish family structures in the life beyond earthly existence.

The church has expanded rapidly, especially in the decades since World War II. It now has missions in most countries of the world. With this growth, there has been an accompanying building program for new temples. Wherever the church is, its ministry is also assisted by the Relief Society (the woman's auxiliary organization), the Primary Association (a children's organizations), the Young Women and Young Men organizations, and the Church Welfare Services Program (to assist church members in need).

Membership: In 2007 the church reported 5.6 million members and over 12,000 congregations in the United States, and an estimated 159,000 members and 479 congregations in Canada. There are more than 11 million members worldwide in 160 countries and territories.

Educational Facilities:

Brigham Young University, Provo, Utah and Laie, Hawaii.

Ricks College, Rexburg, Idaho.

LDS Business College, Salt Lake City, Utah.

Periodicals: *The Ensign • New Era • Friend.*

Remarks: Beginning with the polygamy era, the Church of Jesus Christ of Latter-day Saints has been the target of evangelical Protestant Christian missionaries. Since the 1960s, efforts to convert Mormons and to denounce the church have increased in proportion to the church's growth. Currently, the single largest number of Christian counter-cult organizations operating in the United States are focused entirely on Mormonism. Prominent anti-Mormons have included Jerald Tanner (1938–2006) and Sandra Tanner (b.1941), former Mormons who founded Utah Lighthouse Ministry in Salt Lake City, and Baptist minister Walter Martin (1928–1989), founder of Christian Research Institute in San Juan Capistrano, California, and his students. The vast outpouring of anti-Mormon literature has led to the production of literature defending the church and countering the attacks on the faith. Besides that material produced by the church specifically for the use of missionaries, Mormon Miscellanies prints a variety of shorter works. Robert L.

Brown and his wife Rosemary Brown have produced a set of substantive polemical texts which attempt to answer the attacks of the Tanners and Martin. The literature on Mormonism is vast, and has been greatly increased in the past decade due to the work of the Mormon History Association.

Evangelical Christians, who have traditionally taken the lead in supporting counter-Mormon ministries have shown some signs of attempting to alter their relationships with the church. In 2006 evangelists Ravi Zacharias, who has edited recent editions of Walter Martin's Kingdom of the Cults, accepted an invitation to speak at the Mormon Tabernacle in Salt Lake City, thus signaling an initiative by both Evangelical and LDS scholars to establish a new dialog between the traditional antagonists.

Sources:

The Church of Jesus Christ of Latter-day Saints. www.lds.org.

Arrington, Leonard J., and Davis Bitton. *The Mormon Experience.* New York: Alfred A. Knopf, 1979.

Bitton, David, and Maureen Ursenbach Beecher, eds. *New Views of Mormon History.* Salt Lake City, UT: University of Utah Press, 1987.

Bushman, Richard L. *Believing History: Latter-day Saint Essays.* New York: Columbia University Press, 2006.

Church History in the Fullness of Times. Salt Lake City, UT: Church of Jesus Christ of Latter-day Saints, 1989.

Millett, Robert L., and Gerald R. McDermott. *Claiming Christ: A Mormon-Evangelical Debate.* Ada, MI: Brazos Press, 2007.

Newell, Coke. *Latter Days: An Insider's Guide to Mormonism, The Church of Jesus Christ of Latter-day Saints.* New York: St. Martin's Griffin, 2001.

Ostling, Richad, and Joan K. Ostling. *Mormon America: The Power and the Promise.* New York: HarperOne, 2007.

Shipps, Jan. *Mormonism.* Urbana, IL: University of Illinois Press, 1985.

Smith, Joseph S. *Gospel Doctrine.* Salt Lake City, UT: Deseret Books Company, 1969.

Restored Church of Jesus Christ of Latter-day Saints
Current address not obtained for this edition.

The Restored Church of Jesus Christ of Latter-day Saints was founded in 1971 under the leadership of F. Elwood Russell of San Diego, California. For several years during the late 1960s Russell had been receiving revelations that suggested that the Church of Jesus Christ of Latter-day Saints had lost the priesthood during the presidency, from 1901 to 1918, of Joseph Fielding Smith. Russell felt he was directed by God to restore the power of the priesthood to the church. The church rejected his claims and excommunicated him, prompting his founding of the Restored Church.

The members of the Restored Church believe Russell to be the Messenger of the Covenant as foretold by the prophet Malachi. That messenger was to lead in the restoration of all things from which the Latter-day Saints had fallen and to prepare for the return of Jesus Christ to earth. It is their belief that the Latter-day Saints had fallen by changing the ordinances and breaking the covenants. In particular, the Church's general authorities had led in the fall by setting up a salaried ministry and by investing church funds in secular businesses.

At the time of its founding, the Restored Church believed that Jesus had already returned and was living quietly on earth making ready for his appearance. The keys of the priesthood, having been withdrawn from the Latter-day Saints, have been given to the Restored Church. San Diego County is believed to be the place designated by earlier prophecies as the New Jerusalem, the place where the Saints should gather as a place of refuge from the times of trouble and war, which will continue until the end-time. The leadership of the church believes itself to have been selected to save the constitution of the United States and eventually to establish theocratic rule in the land.

Membership: Not reported.

Sources:

Restored Church of Jesus Christ of Latter-day Saints. www.restoredchurch.org.

Shields, Steven L. *Divergent Paths of the Restoration*. Los Angeles: Restoration Press, 1990.

School of the Prophets

PO Box 820882, Fort Worth, TX 76182

The School of the Prophets was organized in March 1982 as a result of a revelation received by R. C. Crossfield, a Canadian Melchizedek Priesthood holder in the Church of Jesus Christ of Latter-day Saints. This revelation was one of many received by Crossfield on a continuing basis, dating from 1961. Crossfield's revelations were published in 1969 as the *Book of Onias*.

Before The School of the Prophets was set up, several individuals who believed in the book eventually gathered in Boise, Idaho. They published a monthly newsletter called *Restorers*. In 1980 the majority of these early believers broke with Crossfield; some started their own organization, one couple joined Fred Collier's Church of the First-born, and others followed different paths altogether.

Yet, a few remained and the School was organized. Early in 1984 it was moved to the Salem area in Utah. The revelations are now entitled *The Second Book of Commandments* and are received on an ongoing basis, with the latest installment being Section 172. Among other things, they contain continual instructions to 'His servants' (followers) that will eventually be elaborate enough to establish God's true Zion upon the earth. They recognize that the only true church is the one established in Salt Lake City, known as the Church of Jesus Christ of Latter-day Saints. However, they instruct that this church has now been polluted by the Gentiles, whose times have now been fulfilled, and that the church will soon be restored to its purity by God's true Israel, whose identity has now begun to be revealed.

The school's belief is that Joseph Smith not only set up the church, but three other distinct organizations: 1. The School of the Prophets—which is the educational arm of Zion; 2. The Kingdom of God—political arm; 3. The United Order—economic arm. The church is considered to be the missionary arm. The arms are what constitute the four Squares of God's true Zion.

According to this group's beliefs, the Second Book of Commandments reveals many truths, laws, and ordinances that will be needed to set up the coming millennial society of Zion. Prime examples of outstanding revelations are: Section 51, a revelation on the law of Adoption; section 61, which reveals the United Order covenants and identifies the Four-square organization of Zion; Section 135, which reveals many of the powers of the Adversary and instructs how we may be able to overcome them; Section 46, which explains the New and Everlasting Covenant of Marriage in clarity, allowing patriarchal plural marriages by revelation only.

The school recognizes that John Koyle, the prophet of the Salem, Utah, Dream Mine, was a true instrument in God's hands to provide a means of survival at a time yet to come when great destruction and chaos will encompass the earth. Much of the present work of the school is to prepare places of refuge for those who will be guided to them when the calamities begin to fall upon the present nations.

Membership: The school does not consider itself a church; consequently those who study under its auspices are free to retain membership in their present denomination. Records of the students are not made public in order to protect their church affiliation. Some of the students are members of the Church of Jesus Christ of Latter-day Saints.

Periodicals: *The Restorer Newsletter*. Send orders to PO Box 396, Salem, UT 84653.

Sources:

Crossfield, R. C. *Book of Onias*. New York: Philosophical Library, 1969.

Krakauer, Jon. *Under the Banner of Heaven: A Story of Violent Faith*. New York: Anchor books, 2003. 399 pp.

Shields, Steven L. *Divergent Paths of the Restoration*. Los Angeles: Restoration Research, 1990.

School of the Prophets (Wood)

Current address not obtained for this edition.

The School of the Prophets (Wood) was founded in 1986 by Archie Dean Wood, a former member of the Church of Jesus Christ of Latter-day Saints. According to the story of the School's founding, on June 12, 1986, Wood was one of 13 people visited by Jesus Christ. Within a few weeks Wood produced a booklet, *The Grand Delusion*, in which he both affirmed the legitimacy of the position of Ezra Taft Benson as president of the Church of Jesus Christ of Latter-day Saints and complained of mistakes coming into the church. Wood also had received a set of personal revelations that were gathered together as *The Book of Azrael*.

Wood and the members of the School see their purpose as preparing Latter-day Saints for the Second Coming of Jesus Christ; they seek to train members to become prophets, seers, and revelators. They also wish to correct the errors that they believe have become a part of Latter-day Saint life.

Membership: Not reported. At the time of last publication, there were fewer than 100 members.

Sources:

Shields, Steven L. *Divergent Paths of the Restoration*. Los Angeles: Restoration Research, 1990.

Wood, Archie Dean. *The Grand Delusion*. Pocatello, ID: The Author, 1986.

Zion's Order, Inc.

Rte. 2, Box 104-7, Mansfield, MO 65704

In 1938, Dr. Merl Kilgore felt called by the Lord to work among the older Mormon churches: the Church of Jesus Christ of Latter-day Saints, the Reorganized Church of Jesus Christ of Latter Day Saints, and the Church of Jesus Christ (Strangite). He wanted to call them back to the United Order, the communal structure practiced in the early days of the church. He worked with the LDS Church until 1950 when differences with his bishop led him to join the Aaronic Order. After that, he reportedly moved to Bicknell, Utah, to aid a Mr. Taylor in his sawmill. Once there, he persuaded Taylor to leave the Aaronic Order and help him form a new church, which they called "Zion's Order of the Sons of Levi." After several moves, they bought a farm near Mansfield, Missouri, in 1953. There are slightly more than 50 members governed by a president, counselors, a bishop, and a patriarch. They use all the Mormon scripture with the exception of Section 132 of the Doctrine and Covenants. The group has adopted a communal lifestyle.

Zion's Order claims more than 650 revelations through Mr. Kilgore since 1951. Most of these have to do with the particularities of the life of the group. They claim the site of their commune as the place referred to by Isaiah (2.2), where the Lord's house should be built. They have tried to have other groups join them in building Zion anew, but these attempts have been unsuccessful to date. However, Kilgore resigned as president in 1969 to do mission work among Indians in the Southwest, which has brought a number of members into the church. Zion's Order of the Sons of Levi became known simply as Zion's Order, Inc. in 1975.

Membership: In 1988 the order reported 55 members and six ministers at the single location in Missouri.

❀ Polygamy-Practicing

Apostolic United Brethren

3139 W 14700 S, No. A, Bluffsdale, UT 84065

HISTORY. The Apostolic United Brethren has its roots in a major split in the largest of the polygamy-practicing groups, generally referred to as the United Order Effort. In 1951 leadership of the group had passed to Joseph White Musser

(1872–1954), who became president upon the death of John Y. Barlow (1874–1949). Musser had become a polygamist in the early twentieth century and was among the original leaders who had organized around Lorin C. Woolley (1856–1934). Over the years Musser had arisen as a major apologist for polygamy. He ran Truth Publishing Company in Salt Lake City, Utah, from which he published a number of books and a periodical, *The Truth*.

Musser began almost immediately to encounter trouble with the other elected leaders of the group, most of whom resided in Short Creek (now Colorado City), Arizona. They mistrusted his leadership, while he felt they were changing doctrines and ordinances from the original fact and intent as taught by Joseph Smith Jr. (1805–1844), the founder of the Church of Jesus Christ of Latter-day Saints. The tensions were heightened following Musser's stroke in 1953, which left him incapacitated. He appointed two new members to the ruling elite, Margarito Bautista and Rulon C. Allred (1906–1977). As resistance to Musser's decisions increased, he dismissed the leadership and appointed a new set of leaders, consisting entirely of his supporters. At this point, most of the members followed the leadership at Short Creek, but several thousand followed him. Allred, his chief assistant, became the presiding elder of Musser's followers in 1954. The group considered itself the continuation of the church founded by Joseph Smith Jr. It finally incorporated in 1975 as "the Corporation of the Presiding Elder of the Apostolic United Brethren," to assist in its working with and conforming to the tax laws. The group is generally known as the Apostolic United Brethren.

During the period of Rulon Allred's leadership, the Apostolic United Brethren grew several times over. A respected naturopathic physician in the Salt Lake City suburb of Murray and a polygamist since the 1930s, Allred moved quickly to consolidate membership in the Apostolic United Brethren among polygamists, particularly in Mexico. He led in the establishment of a colony in Pinesdale, Montana, where a large meeting hall was dedicated in 1970. His leadership came to an abrupt end on May 10, 1977, when members of another polygamist group, the Church of the Lamb of God, led by Ervil Morrell LeBaron (1925–1981), assassinated him. He was succeeded by his brother, Owen Arthur Allred (1914–2005).

BELIEFS. The Apostolic United Brethren believes that the leaders of the Church of Jesus Christ of Latter-day Saints in this century have in a very real sense disqualified the leadership of Joseph Smith Jr., Brigham Young (1801–1877), John Taylor (1808–1887), and the other early leaders of the church by their rejection of their teachings. The more recent leaders of the church have implied that Smith and his associates made serious errors that they can now correct as they see fit. The Brethren cannot accept recent instructions to disregard the teachings of the church's founding prophet. It cites as one major error the giving of the priesthood to black men, believing that since ancient times admission to the priesthood has been denied to the descendents of Cain (black people). The Brethren has also criticized the church for changes in both the temple service and the garments worn during temple services. It is opposed to granting the priesthood to women, though women have many other leadership functions with the Brethren.

Membership: In 1992 the Brethren reported approximately 7,000 members in five centers in the United States and foreign membership in England and Mexico.

Sources:

Allred, Rulon C. *Treasures of Knowledge*. 2 vols. Hamilton, MT: Bitteroot Publishing Co., 1982.

Bradlee, Ben, Jr., and Dale Van Atta. *Prophet of Blood*. New York: G. P. Putnam's Sons, 1981.

The Most Holy Principle. 4 vols. Murray, UT: Gems Publishing Co., 1970–1975.

Musser, Joseph W. *Celestial or Plural Marriage*. Salt Lake City, UT: Truth Publishing Co., 1944.

———. *Michael Our Father and Our God*. Salt Lake City, UT: Truth Publishing Company, 1963.

Christ's Church
Current address not obtained for this edition.

Christ's Church, also known as the "Branch" Church, was formed in 1978 at Provo, Utah by Gerald W. Peterson, Sr. (d. 1981). In founding the group, Peterson, a former leader with the Apostolic United Brethren, acted in accord with a revelation he had received. He had come to believe that the Church of Jesus Christ of Latter-day Saints had become apostate and no longer taught the true principles of Christ's church. The alleged decline into apostasy began with the presidency of Heber J. Grant, when the keys of priesthood authority were removed, culminating with the acceptance of a black man into the priesthood.

Peterson did not see his new organization as a replacement of the Mormon Church. Rather, the purpose of Christ's Church is to provide a righteous branch so those who choose to follow the Lord completely can find the correct organization, experience the gifts of the spirit, and be served by the fullness of the ordinances. In establishing the church, Peterson is fulfilling the prophecy from Mormon scripture concerning 'setting God's house in order' under Joseph Smith, Jr. The beliefs and practices are similar to those of the Apostolic United Order, except for the belief that Peterson had been given the keys to the priesthood and is President Prophet of it. At the time of Peterson's death, his son, Gerald W. Peterson, Jr., received the keys to the priesthood. He currently leads the church.

Membership: Not reported.

Periodicals: *The Branch*. Send orders to Box 1329, St. George, UT 84770.

Church of Jesus Christ of the Saints in Zion
Current address not obtained for this edition.

The Church of Jesus Christ of the Saints in Zion emerged in 1984 from a group of Mormons headed by Roger Billings, who had moved from Utah to Blue Springs, Missouri, in 1979. They had planned to build a community, but the process was disrupted by the introduction of teachings on polygamy and other beliefs that disagreed with those of the Church of Jesus Christ of Latter-day Saints. As a result of his teaching activity, Billings and his supporters were excommunicated from the church. They organized independently.

It is the position of the Church of Jesus Christ of the Saints in Zion that polygamy was condoned by God, though it is not practiced by the group. However, new relationships based upon the addition of multiple "spiritual wives" (women who will be married for all eternity to their spiritual husbands), have been created. Billings, as head of the church, performs spiritual marriage ceremonies.

Membership: At the time of publication, there was only one congregation, with less than 20 members.

Church of the First Born of the Fullness of Times
5854 Mira Serana, El Paso, TX 79912

The Church of the First Born of the Fullness of Times arose out of the participation in Mormon fundamentalist groups of the LeBaron family—Alma Dayer LeBaron (1886–1951), his sons Floren LeBaron, Benjamin F. LeBaron, Alma LeBaron Jr., Ross Wesley LeBaron, Ervil Morrell LeBaron (1925–1981), Joel LeBaron (d. 1972), and Verlan M. LeBaron, and a cousin, Owen LeBaron. Alma Dayer LeBaron, who, with his family, was a member of the Church of Jesus Christ of Latter-day Saints, was affiliated with polygamist leader Joseph White Musser as early as 1936. In 1934 Benjamin LeBaron claimed to be "the One Mighty and Strong," the prophetic figure mentioned in the Mormon writings (*Doctrines and Covenants 85*), and he convinced several members of the family to substantiate his claims as a prophet. In 1944 the LeBaron family was excommunicated. From then until 1955, most of the family associated themselves with the "fundamentalist" colony in Mexico directed by Rulon C. Allred (1906–1977), leader of the Apostolic United Brethren. The LeBaron family members were in the process of setting up a united order (an economically communal style of living) when, in 1955, they decided to leave Allred's Mexican colony.

Joel, Ross Wesley, and Floren worked out the basic order of their own church and incorporated on September 1, 1955, under the name of the Church of the First Born of the Fullness of Times. Joel claimed to have been selected for the "patriarchal priesthood" and had a revelation directing Allred to become his councilor. Allred rejected the invitation. Both Benjamin and Ross Wesley also rejected his claims.

Joel claimed a line of priesthood succession through his father, Alma Sr., to Alma's grandfather, Benjamin F. Johnson (1818–1905), who was secretly ordained by Joseph Smith. (Mormon authorities point out that Johnson accepted the Manifesto of 1890 abolishing polygamy.) Joel claimed that the priesthood was superior to the presidency of the church, the apostles, and the Seventies.

Joel LeBaron led the Church of the First Born of the Fullness of Times until he was murdered in 1972. He was succeeded by his brother Verlan, who was killed in an automobile accident in 1981. The current leader of the Church is Siegfried Widmar. For a number of years the Church issued a magazine, *Ensign*, in which most of its doctrinal and polemical works were published.

Membership: The group is small, containing several hundred members at most. Most of the membership is located in Mexico.

Sources:

LeBaron, Verlan M. *Economic Democracy under Eternal Law*. El Paso, TX: Church of the Firstborn of the Fullness of Times, 1963.

————. *The LeBaron Story*. Lubbock, TX: Author, 1981.

Priesthood Expounded. Mexican Mission of the Church of the Firstborn of the Fullness of Times, 1956.

Richards, Henry W. *A Reply to "The Church of the Firstborn of the Fullness of Times."* Salt Lake City, UT: Author, 1965.

Silver, Stephen M. "Priesthood and Presidency: An Answer to Henry W. Richards." *Ensign* 2, no. 11 (January 1963): 1–127.

Widmar, Siegfried J. *The Political Kingdom of God*. El Paso, TX: Author, 1975.

Church of the Lamb of God
Current address not obtained for this edition.

The Church of the Lamb of God was formed in 1970 by Ervil Morrell LeBaron (1925–1981), who had held the second-highest office in the Church of the First Born of the Fullness of Times, founded by his brother, Joel LeBaron (d. 1972). In that year Ervil was dismissed from the Church of the First Born of the Fullness of Times. As the leader of his new church, he claimed full authority over all of the polygamy-practicing groups, and asserted an authority to execute anyone who refused to accept him as the representative of God.

Beginning at the time of the establishment of the Church of the Lamb of God, a string of murders and felonious attacks plagued the polygamy-practicing Mormons. On August 20, 1972, Joel LeBaron was shot to death in Ensenada, Mexico. On June 16, 1975, Dean Vest, an associate of Joel LeBaron, was killed near San Diego. On May 10, 1977, Dr. Rulon C. Allred (1906–1977), leader of the Apostolic United Brethren, a rival polygamy group, was brutally murdered in his chiropractic office in Salt Lake City while attending to patients. On May 14, 1977, Merlin Kingston, another polygamy leader, narrowly survived an attempt on his life. At least 13 other polygamy-practicing Mormons were killed before Ervil was arrested, tried, convicted, and sentenced in 1980 for the death of Allred. He died in prison the following year of natural causes.

After Ervil LeBaron's death, his son Aaron LeBaron emerged as the new leader of the group. Deaths associated with the group continued, mostly prominently the 1988 slayings of Ed Marston, Mark and Duane Chynoweth, and Duane's eight-year-old daughter, Jenny. In 1997 Aaron LeBaron was convicted of conspiracy to commit murder and racketeering in connection with these deaths. Reportedly, these former members were killed because of the church's belief that anyone who

left the group had to be killed before the members could inherit God's kingdom on Earth.

Membership: Not reported. Since the death of Ervil LeBaron, there have been conflicting reports of the disbanding of the Church. Its present status is unknown.

Sources:

Fessier, Michael, Jr. "Ervil LeBaron, the Man Who Would Be God." *New West* (January 1981): 80–84, 112–117.

LeBaron, Ervil. *An Open Letter to a Former Presiding Bishop*. San Diego, CA: Author, 1972.

————. *Priesthood Expounded*. Buenaventurea, Mexico: Mexican Mission of the Church of the Firstborn of the Fullness of Times, 1956.

Church of the New Covenant in Christ
Box 3910, Salem, OR 97302

The Evangelical Church of Christ was founded in 1975 as the Church of Christ Patriarchal by John W. Bryant (b. 1946), a former member of the Apostolic United Brethren. Bryant was baptized into the Church of Jesus Christ of Latter-day Saints in 1964 and became a missionary to Japan a short time later. However, in the early 1970s he became convinced of the virtue of polygamy practice and joined the polygamy-practicing order headed by Rulon C. Allred.

In 1974 Bryant began to receive new revelations (he had received periodic revelations since childhood). In one revelation, he was visited by John the Beloved Disciple (one of Jesus' original twelve disciples), who instructed him to form an "Order of the Ancients" among those who would be led of the Holy Spirit. In 1975 he was taken to the City of Enoch where, in the presence of Joseph White Musser, founder of the Apostolic United Order, and Joseph Smith, Jr., founder of the Church of Jesus Christ of Latter-day Saints, he received the fullness of keys to the Kingdom of God (i.e., the priesthood, patriarchy, and presidency of the church). Bryant received some immediate support from other fundamentalist Mormons, and in 1979 the group moved to the Fair Haven Ranch near Las Vegas, Nevada, to establish a communal life together. The ranch was lost when they were unable to keep up payments, and in 1981 Bryant, five of his six wives, and a number of members moved to a farm near Salem, Oregon.

During the early 1980s, Bryant continued his religious development. He began to question what he saw to be problems in fundamentalism: focus upon polygamy and male dominance, rather than Christ. That questioning led to what he termed a "born-again" relationship with Christ, a change reflected in the change of the church's name. Not wanting to split up the family, Bryant remained a polygamist, but reoriented family life away from its patriarchal structure. He has also vowed to take no more wives and ceased promoting the idea.

By the mid-1980s, over 100 church members moved into the Salem area. Attempts to convert the large barn on the Bryant farm into a church have been blocked by neighborhood action. In the wake of problems both internal and external, Bryant left the church and it soon disintegrated. However, he reorganized many of the former members into the Church of the New Covenant in Christ, which continues many of Bryant's teachings and utilizes many of his writings that were issued by the former Evangelical Church of Christ.

Membership: In 1985 there were approximately 120 families and one congregation.

Sources:

King, Marsha. "Changing Beliefs Led Family to Rearrange Plural Union." *The Seattle Times* (October 13, 1985).

Confederate Nations of Israel
Long Haul, Box 151, Big Water, UT 84741

Alexander Joseph, ex-Marine and ex-California policeman, was a member of the Apostolic United Brethren in Montana, withdrawing in 1972. In 1975 he lead a group of 13 families in homesteading land for a colony in Cottonwood Canyon, Kane County, Utah, which led to a fight with the Federal Government over homesteading law. This resulted in the eviction of the colony and the passage of the Federal Land Policy and Management Act of 1976. Some have called Joseph the "Father of the FLPMA" because of this action; the movement later became known as the Sagebrush Rebellion in America. The colony moved to Glen Canyon City, now Big Water, Utah, where Joseph founded the Church of Jesus Christ in Solemn Assembly, which was simply a "tax dodge." In 1978, Joseph founded the Confederate Nations of Israel, which eventually superseded the former organization.

Joseph envisioned the Nations as having an operational government of 144 seats, each to be filled by a current king of the particular nation (family) that owns the seat. All presented propositions for group action are unanimous, each seat having a veto vote. In the ensuing 27 years, three propositions were passed. The nations were divided into three quorums: Judges (24 seats), Senate (70), and the Council of Fifty (50). The king was to act as an independent sovereign upon his own patriarchal authority. The theme of this vision was self-government with little dependence on any other.

The Confederacy convenes twice per year for public businesses, usually at Long Haul in Big Water. Joseph issued a brief statement of belief governing his family known as "Alexander's Creed," which espouses belief in posterity, reality, freedom, responsibility, justice, grace, and patriarchal government. Two independent organizations were eventually founded: the Rainbow Order, originally a men's order that later included women; and a young women's order known as the Daughters of Diana. No doctrines are codified in the community. Religious faith and adherence are the sole business of each family, though some have espoused and practiced polygamy. Locally administered marriage is by celestial contact, for eternity. Further, the group deems baptism to be an acceptable form of ritual.

Joseph and his family have stated that the kingdom of God is fully comprehended in the marriage relationship and cannot be fully comprehended apart from it. Joseph himself married more than 20 times and sired or adopted 22 children. When he died from cancer in 1998, at age 62, he had seven wives. Joseph was careful to discourage his personal religious beliefs from being touted as the consensus spiritual doctrines of the group, though his personality led many to espouse principles he taught in lectures as their own. Joseph's sense of appropriate behavior was summarized in his simple expression, "Demonstrate before conversation," his brand of "actions speak louder than words." He invited debate and exhortation of other spiritual views and set no requirement of belief, except for the respect of others' freedom, and for inclusion into his circle of friends and associates.

Membership: Not reported.

Educational Facilities:

University of the Great Spirit, Big Water, Utah.

Periodicals: *The Laws That Govern the Confederate Nations of Israel.*

Sources:

Fulton, Gilbert A., Jr. *That Manifesto.* Kearns, UT: Deseret Publishing Co., 1974.

Joseph, Alexander. *Dry Bones.* Big Water, UT: University of the Great Spirit Press, 1979.

Kraut, Odgen. *Polygamy in the Bible.* Salt Lake City, UT: Kraut's Pioneer Press, 1983.

Short, Dennis R. *For Men Only.* Sandy, UT: The Author, 1977.

Fundamentalist Church of Jesus Christ of Latter-Day Saints
Colorado City, AZ 86021

The Fundamentalist Church of Jesus Christ of Latter-Day Saints (FLDS Church), also known as the United Effort Order, is the largest of the polygamy-practicing groups among the Mormons. It began in 1929 when Lorin C. Woolley (1856–1934) organized a council of people dedicated to seeing that no year passed without at least one child being born within a plural marriage. Woolley, who claimed to have been commissioned by Mormon Church President John Taylor (1808–1887) in 1886, acted only after all of the others present at that time were dead. Woolley had

been actively publishing and spreading the story of the authority he and others had from the late president of the Church of Jesus Christ of Latter-Day Saints since 1912 but experienced only modest success until 1929, when Joseph White Musser (1872–1954) compiled the various accounts of the 1886 revelation and published them. Musser also joined Joseph Leslie Broadbent (1891–1935), John Y. Barlow (1874–1949), Charles F. Zitting (d. 1954), LeGrand Woolley (d. 1965), and Louis Alma Kelsch (d. 1974) as a member of the council.

In 1934, following Lorin Woolley's death, Broadbent assumed leadership, but he died in less than a year. He was succeeded by Barlow, who is most known for his early leadership of the group's main colony in rural Arizona, Short Creek (presently known as Colorado City). Short Creek had become a haven for polygamists who began gathering there in the late 1920s to escape the problems created by both law enforcement agents and the increased discipline of the Church of Jesus Christ of Latter-Day Saints. Soon after becoming leader of the group, Barlow contacted some of the more vocal advocates of polygamy at Short Creek and worked out an agreement between them and the council. Eventually, he moved to Short Creek with some of his followers, and within a few years the polygamists dominated the settlement. Barlow created the United Trust, incorporated formally in 1942 as the United Effort Plan, but commonly known as the United Effort Order. Meanwhile, Musser, who remained in Salt Lake City, began publication of *The Truth*, the periodical for the group, and the most influential organ promoting polygamy published by any group.

Under Barlow's leadership, the colony at Short Creek flourished and the United Effort spread throughout Mormon communities in the West, particularly in Idaho, Montana, and Southern California. Many of the polygamists who had fled to Mexico in previous years also accepted Barlow's authority. Following a 1935 raid that unsuccessfully attempted to destroy the Short Creek community, the only major trouble for the United Effort came in 1944 when an anti-polygamy crusade swept through Salt Lake City. Musser and other leaders were arrested and spent several months in jail while the crusade lasted.

Barlow's death in 1951 led to internal crisis and schism within the United Effort. Musser, the new president of the ruling council, was in poor health, and many people rejected his appointments of his physician, Rulon C. Allred (1906–1977), and a Mexican leader, Margarito Bautista, to fill council vacancies. In response, Musser disbanded the entire council and appointed a new one made up of his supporters. That action split the group, the majority of which supported the leadership at Short Creek. The older members of the council elected Zitting as their new president, while Musser reorganized his following as the Apostolic United Brethren.

Zitting died within months of his election and was succeeded by Leroy S. Johnson (1888–1986), who had joined the council during the Barlow years. Johnson was almost immediately plunged into a new crisis. On July 26, 1953, the governor of Arizona conducted a massive raid on Short Creek. Most of the men were arrested and the women and children placed in the state's custody. Only after several months, when the governor realized the political and financial disaster his actions had caused, were the colonists allowed to return to their homes, where they have lived quietly in recent decades.

Johnson finished his long tenure leading the group and was succeeded in 1986 by Rulon Jeffs (1909–2002), best known for his 1998 prediction that the Olympics in 2002 would launch the destruction of Salt Lake City. It was Jeffs who in 1991 officially incorporated the group as Fundamentalist Church of Jesus Christ of Latter-Day Saints. Jeffs was succeeded by his son, Warren Steed Jeffs (b. 1955). The younger Jeffs began his leadership by marrying all of his father's wives. Among his first acts was to purchase land near Eldorado, Texas, as a new church center, known as Yearning for Zion Ranch, where construction was begun on a new temple for the church in 2005.

Jeffs then became the center of media attention as former members accused him of excommunicating many young men and arranging marriages for young women (some still teenage minors) to himself and others older male leaders. These charges culminated in a warrant for his arrest and an FBI manhunt. In May 2006, he was placed on the FBI's Ten Most Wanted list. He was arrested in August 2006.

Tried in September 2007, Jeffs was convicted on two counts of "being an accomplice to rape" charges deriving from his arranging the marriage of an unwilling 14-year-old female teenager. He was sentenced to 10 years to life. Toward the end of the trial, Jeffs handed the judge a note that claimed he was not a prophet for the FLDS Church. A short time later, he resigned as president of the church corporation.

On April 3, 2008, while this Encyclopedia was being edited, Texas authorities raided the Yearning for Zion Ranch, arrested some of the adult males, and took all the minors into custody. The raid has created a host of legal issues and it appears that their adjudication will take several years.

Doctrinally, the FLDS is a conservative Latter-Day Saint group that follows the teachings of the Latter-Day Saints as they were prior to the denunciation of polygamy. They have tended to reject most of the changes introduced into the mainstream Church of Jesus Christ of Latter-Day Saints throughout the twentieth century. For example, they do not accept the 1978 revelation that allows those of African American descent into the priesthood. They follow some of the communal practices of the nineteenth century and have a strong code of mutual support among church members.

Membership: Not reported. Of the approximately 30,000 polygamists, it is estimated that 7,000 to 10,000 are affiliated with the FLDS. The church has centers at Hilldale, Utah; Colorado City, Arizona; Mancos, Colorado; Pringle, South Dakota; Pioche, Nevada; Eldorado, Texas; and Bountiful, Alberta, Canada.

Remarks: Two practices introduced into the FLDS have emerged as most controversial. First, in recent decades leaders of the FLDS have assumed new prerogatives through what is termed the "The Law of Placing." This law allows women who have reached marriageable age to be assigned to a specific husband. Over the decades, the leveling out of the ratio of women to men has created problems, as not enough females are members of the group to allow multiple wives for all the males.

Second, as most plural wives are not married according to the laws of the state in which they reside, the state considers them unmarried single mothers. That status allows them to apply for and receive public assistance payments. The practice of encouraging such women to apply for state assistance is informally called "bleeding the beast."

On June 2, 2008, church leaders announced that they would make official a policy of not allowing underage girls to enter into marriage relationships. While this new policy does not have any impact on government investigations of past incidents, it does create a more positive atmosphere that may help the group move forward in its relationships with various state agencies.

Sources:

Fundamentalist Church of Jesus Christ of Latter-Day Saints. www.fldstruth.com/.

Anderson, Max J. *The Polygamy Story: Fiction or Fact*. Salt Lake City, UT: Publishers Press, 1979.

Bradlee, Ben, Jr., and Dale Van Alta. *Prophet of Blood*. New York: G. P. Putnam's Sons, 1981.

Bradley, Martha Sonntag. *Kidnapped from That Land: The Government Raids on the Short Creek Polygamists*. Salt Lake City, UT: University of Utah Press, 1993.

Hardy, Carmon, *Doing the Works of Abraham: Mormon Polygamy: Its Origin, Practice, and Demise*. Norman, OK: Arthur H. Clark Company , 2007.

Musser, Joseph White. *Celestial or Plural Marriage*. Salt Lake City, UT: Truth Publishing Co., 1944.

Millennial Church of Jesus Christ
Current address not obtained for this edition.

Claiming to be the spiritual successor to Ervil LeBaron, founder of the Church of the Lamb of God, Leo Peter Evoniuk LeBaron organized the Millennial Church of Jesus

Christ in the mid-1980s. According to a revelation that came to him in 1984, Ervil LeBaron was delivered by the Lord God from his enemies and now sits on God's right hand. The group holds that the keys held by Ervil LeBaron have passed to Leo LeBaron. The 1984 revelation asserted the necessity of the restoration of the Melchizedek Priesthood and the Patriarchal Order, or damnation would follow. LeBaron and his associate Grand Patriarchs, Paul L. Gardunio, Bill Rios, and Raul Rios, have inherited the sealing keys formerly held by Ervil LeBaron. Their task is to seal the 144,000 Grand Patriarchs of the Twelve Tribes of Israel, whom God had, according to their beliefs, previously hidden from the world. The group holds that they are the only persons entrusted with that sealing power.

Evoniuk disappeared suddenly in 1987. It is feared by members of the community that, like others in dissident polygamist groups, he has become the victim of foul play.

Membership: Not reported.

Order of Nazorean Essenes (Sons Ahman Israel)
Chevrah B'Qor Community, HC 65-535, Canebeds, AZ 86022

The Order of the Nazorean Essenes was founded on January 25, 1981, under the name of Sons Ahman Israel (or Suns Aumen Israel), which is a translation of the name of the ancient Essene Nazorean Temple Order called the B'nei-Amin. This order, along with the Anum-II Order and the Manichaean Orthodox Church, make up the Order of Nazorean Essenes, or O:N:E:.

The group believes that its order was reestablished by the heavens, for the purpose of facilitating a full restoration of the primitive Nazorean Christianity of the first century, free of the dross of ages of neglect and corruption. The heavens bequeathed to its members a pure canon of Nazirutha scripture capable of assisting them in their quest for perfection and purification from all that is inferior. The group teaches that the Order of Nazorean Essenes is a modern resurrection of the ancient "Nasaraeans," a vegetarian sect of Essenes spoken of by the ancient historians. It is a small esoteric school organized into three levels: the Restored Essene and Manichaean Orthodox Church of Yeshua and Miryai, the B'nei Amin Temple Order, and the Anum-II Order. The teachings state that Yeshua (Jesus) the Messiah was born into the northern Nazorean branch of Essenes.

The group claims that O:N:E: has also been charged with a full restoration of the purifying Mysteries, or rejuvenating Sacraments, of original Gnostic Christianity. It has also been commissioned with the establishment of Nazorean communities and the building of Nazorean temples and shrines, as interest and resources permit. It works to again make available the natural Essene lifestyle, male-female balance, lunar calendar, coed monasteries, and temple rituals, and the liberating gnosis of original Nazorean and Manichaean Christianity. It claims to have been entrusted with little-known scrolls of Mandaic, Gnostic, and Manichaean origin, and with certain "Heavenly Empowerments" and "Hidden Mysteries" to help accomplish this calling. The Sacred Scrolls consist of edited Aramaic writings of the early vegetarian Nazoreans (preserved by the Mandaeans), the Coptic scrolls of the Nag Hammadhi Library (hidden in antiquity by persecuted Gnostics), and the recovered writings of the vegan Manichaean sect, rediscovered in Medinet Madi in Egypt and Turfan in China. The priest(ess)hood comprises both men and women and the organization worships a male and female form of the deity and messiah.

Among the statements of Nazinrutha, the group's system of beliefs, are the following:

> *There is a Perfect, Ever-existent and Primordial Oneness that they call Aumen, meaning Hidden God, and Hiya, meaning Living God. Aumen-Hiya are both male and female, and give continual birth to male and female spirits in their aspect of heavenly parents. Aumen-Hiya, also called the Great Life and Living Ones, allow their imperfect offspring to leave their world and descend to other, inferior realities as a means of evolving them toward perfect godhood. The saving system of Nazirutha includes purifying rituals, sacred scrolls, special diets, service to others, and an inward journey of self discovery, renewal, and reconnectedness with the Great Life.*

Membership: In 2002 the order reported 102 official active members.

Sources:

The Sacred Scrolls of the Sons Ahman Israel. LaVern, UT: Sons Ahman Israel, n.d.

The Watchmen on the Towers of Latter Day Israel
Current address not obtained for this edition.

The Watchmen on the Towers of Latter Day Israel was formed in the early 1970s by Elders Henry Braun, Arno Mittenberg, and others who were excommunicated from the Church of Jesus Christ of Latter-day Saints because of their protest of changes in doctrine and practice within the Church, especially on the issue of polygamy. As a result of their problems with the church, the elders of the Watchmen began a study of the position of the church in the nineteenth century as opposed to its present beliefs and practices and have concluded that modern Mormonism is completely apostate.

Membership: Not reported.

Sources:

Braun, Henry. *Celestial Marriage: For All Time and All Eternity.* Salt Lake City, UT: The Author, 1984. 987 pp.

———. *Thoughts of a Mormon Convert, Pro and Con.* 3 vols. Salt Lake City, UT: Watchmen on the Towers of Latter Day Israel, 1974-76.

Mormon Fundamentalism and the LSD Church. 2 vols. Salt Lake City, UT: Watchmen on the Towers of Latter Day Israel, 1975.

Shields, Steven L. *Divergent Paths of the Restoration.* Los Angeles: Restoration Research, 1990. 336 pp.

❀ Missouri Mormons

Center Branch of the Lord's Remnant
709 W Maple, Independence, MO 64050

Among the people who left the Reorganized Church of Jesus Christ of Latter Day Saints following the 1984 revelation on women's ordination given by President Wallace B. Smith (b. 1929) were Robert E. Baker and members of the church's Seventy. Because of Baker's longtime dissent regarding the direction the church was taking, he was silenced. In the fall of 1984 he withdrew and established the Gathering Center, a center, as the name implies, to facilitate the latter-day gathering of the Saints into the Center Place (Independence, Missouri). Alternative church services are held at the Gathering Center and a number of services for members are provided.

More recently, Baker has left the Center Branch, which continues as an independent Restoration congregation in Independence. It holds regular church services and has a program for feeding and clothing the needy.

Membership: Not reported. It is estimated that several hundred people are affiliated with the single congregation in Independence, Missouri.

Sources:

Baker, Robert E. *As It Was in the Days of Noah.* Independence, MO: Old Path Publishers, 1985.

Church of Christ at Halley's Bluff
Schell City, MO 64783

The Church of Christ at Halley's Bluff, also known as the Church of Christ at Zion's Retreat, was founded in 1932 by former members of the Church of Christ (Temple Lot) who had left in a dispute over the messages of Otto Fetting (1871–1933). A group centered in Denver, Colorado, and led by E. E. Long and Thomas B. Nerren had accepted Fetting's messages but had remained within the Temple Lot after the majority of his followers had left. The original congregation was located in Denver, Colorado, but by the end of the decade five other congregations had joined the

small denomination. Nerren began to receive revelations. In 1941, in response to such a revelation, the church moved its headquarters to Zion's Retreat, a 441-acre tract of land in northeast Vernon County, about 70 miles south of Independence, Missouri, the site of Zion according to Mormon prophet Joseph Smith Jr. (1805–1844).

In 1942 the congregation in Cranston, Rhode Island, moved to Zion's Retreat. They were soon joined by the remaining members in Denver, and the group in Independence came in 1946. The remaining congregation, located in Delevan, Wisconsin, separated from the group in Missouri in 1966 and continues to exist today as an independent congregation.

The peace within the church in Missouri was disturbed in the 1960s after Daniel Gayman, one of its pastors, became editor of the church's periodical. He began to advocate strongly racist and antiblack positions. Then in 1972 Gayman called a meeting of the church, deposed several bishops, and had himself elected to lead the church. The deposed bishops, General Hall and Duane Gayman, and their supporters filed suit and the court returned the property and the use of the church's several names to them. Meanwhile, the Hall-Gayman group had reincorporated as the Church of Christ at Halley's Bluff.

With the loss of its members in Wisconsin and the defection of Daniel Gayman's supporters, the Church of Christ at Halley's Bluff remains as but a small remnant within the family of Latter-Day Saint Churches.

Membership: There are fewer than 100 members.

Church of Christ (David Clark)
PO Box 126, Oak Grove, MO 64075

The Church of Christ (David Clark) was founded in 1985 by David B. Clark, a former member of the Reorganized Church of Jesus Christ of Latter Day Saints, and his wife Gwyn Clark. The Clarks had come to feel that the Reorganized Church had drifted far away from the standards and teachings of the Bible and the Book of Mormon and were actually teaching doctrines in contradiction to them. The Clarks teach that the church was established on May 15, 1829, when an angelic messenger bestowed ministerial authority upon Joseph Smith, Jr., and Oliver Cowdery, who subsequently baptized each other. The Church of Christ that was established in 1829 has continued as a remnant of the former organization, though the larger entity fell away into apostasy.

The Church of Christ began in November 1985 when the Clarks began to hold a scripture study in their home. They developed a small following, acquired a meeting house, and in May 1987 began to issue a newsletter, *The Return*.

While adhering closely to the King James Version of the Bible and *The Record of the Nephites* (Book of Mormon), the church does not consider other Mormon scripture, the Doctrine and Covenants, the Pearl of Great Price, or the Inspired Version of the Bible, to be authoritative.

Members of the Church of Christ obey the commandments to observe the seventh day of the week as the Sabbath. They also keep the annual feasts, including Passover, Pentecost, Tabernacles, etc.

Periodicals: *The Return.*

Sources:

Clark, David. *The Path Which Leads to the Kingdom of God.* Oak Grove, MO: The Church of Christ, 1991.

Shields, Steven L. *Divergent Paths of the Restoration.* Los Angeles: Restoration Research, 1990.

Church of Christ (Fetting/Bronson)
1138 E Gudgell, Independence, MO 64055

On February 4, 1927, Otto Fetting (1871–1933), one of the 12 apostles of the Church of Christ (Temple Lot), claimed that John the Baptist had appeared to him and told him that it was time to build the temple. Other messages gave instructions concerning the building of the temple.

The twelfth message became the matter of lengthy controversy. It said, "Let those who come to the church of Christ be baptized, that they may rid themselves of the traditions and sins of men." The members of the Temple Lot church had great difficulty with this passage. Many had come into the church by transfer from the Reorganized Church of Jesus Christ of Latter Day Saints, and had not been baptized upon entering the Temple Lot church. They interpreted the message as a call for a rebaptism of the entire church membership. A conference held in October 1929 denounced the idea of rebaptizing the church. Fetting was not allowed to speak on the baptism question. After the conference, he was silenced and told to wait for a referendum vote at the conference to be held the following April. For whatever reason, he did not wait, and after the conference, he, Apostle Walter L. Gates, and Thomas B. Nerren were baptized. Others also received a new baptism and in the fall of 1929, all who had been baptized were disfellowshipped. The Church of Christ (Fetting) was begun by Fetting's followers, who numbered approximately 1,400 or about one-third of the Temple Lot church at the time.

Fetting continued to report receiving messages until his death in 1933. There were 30 messages in all. Several years after Fetting's death, a member in Colorado, W. A. Draves (1912–1994), began to report receiving messages. At first, these messages were accepted by the larger body of the church. However, some members, especially those in Louisiana and Mississippi, rejected Draves almost from the beginning and before the end of the decade reorganized as the Church of Christ (Restored). Eventually, in 1943, the church rejected Draves. After a court suit, which Draves's supporters lost, Draves's followers reorganized as the Church of Christ with the Elijah Message.

During the years following the departure of Draves's supporters, leaders of the Fetting church began to advocate the keeping of the Saturday Sabbath. The issue was debated for many years until 1956, when the Twelve Apostles, having reached an agreement on the issue, adopted sabbatarianism for the entire church. The church is organized like the Church of Christ (Temple Lot). The church uses the Bosok of Mormon (1908 edition), but does not accept either the Book of Commandments or the Doctrine and Covenants, used by other Restoration groups.

Membership: In 1988, the church reported approximately 1,500 members, 24 ministers, and 12 congregations in the United States and an additional 500 members in Nigeria.

Periodicals: *The Voice of Warning.*

Sources:

Fetting, Otto. *The Midnight Message*. Independence, MO: Church of Christ (Temple Lot) [1930].

Smith, Willard J. *Fetting and His Messenger's Messages*. Port Huron, MI: Author [1936].

The Word of the Lord. Independence, MO: Church of Christ, 1935.

Church of Christ Immanuel

Current address not obtained for this edition.

The Church of Christ Immanuel originated in a split in the Flint, Michigan, congregation of the Church of Christ (Temple Lot). C. W. Morgan, the pastor of the group and one of the apostles in the Temple Lot church, began to teach that there was but one person in the Godhead (rather than the idea of multiple persons common to most Mormon churches) and in the 1930s was silenced. Under Morgan's influence, this group left the Church of Christ (Temple Lot) and sued for the local church property. In an out-of-court settlement, the new church, which became known as the Church of Christ Omnipotent, abandoned its original building and constructed a new meeting house. During this period they became familiar with the Church of Christ (Bible and Book of Mormon) led by Pauline Hancock (d. 1962) in Independence, Missouri, which had been established for similar reasons. From them they absorbed some practices, such as using fermented wine in their communion services instead of grape juice.

After a period, some of the members formed a second congregation at Davison, Michigan, under the leadership of Leland Cory, Harold Graves, and Atwood Shelley. The new congregation was merely a convenience for members who did not wish to drive all the way to Flint. However, in 1975 C. W. Morgan died, and the small group of members in Flint, without a leader, sold their property and began to meet with the group in Davison, which had taken the name Church of Christ Immanuel.

Membership: Not reported. At the time of last publication, there were less than 100 members.

Church of Christ (Leighton-Floyd/Burt)

Current address not obtained for this edition.

The Church of Christ (Leighton-Floyd/Burt) was founded in 1965 by former members of the Church of Christ "With the Elijah Message," Established Anew in 1929. That church had been established in 1943 as the Church of Christ Established Anew. However, between the 1964 and 1965 assemblies of the church, Elder W. A. Graves (1912–1994), whose messages from Elijah were guiding the church, reincorporated the church under its present name. Although nondoctrinal, that action led to a disagreement at the 1965 assembly. Apostle Howard Leighton-Floyd (1914–2007) and Bp. H. H. Burt rejected the name change and led a withdrawal of members. The membership of the new church they established centered on an agricultural cooperative near Holden, Missouri, where Leighton-Floyd resided.

Shortly after the formation of the Church of Christ, Leighton-Floyd resigned from the new church and joined the Church of Christ (Temple Lot), leaving the small body without an apostle. It is their belief that someday Christ will restore the apostleship to them. After Leighton-Floyd's withdrawal, Burt assumed leadership of the group. He resides in Colorado Springs, Colorado. From 1965 to 1968 the church published a periodical, *The Banner of Truth*.

The church accepts the Bible, the Book of Mormon, the messages of Otto Fetting (1871–1933), and some of the messages of W. A. Graves (up to the split in 1965). It also accepts some of the Doctrines and Covenants (though not some of the recent additions by the Reorganized Church) and parts of the Book of Commandments. Members have a strong belief that in the near future the Lord will take the lead in the building of a temple in Independence, Missouri. The church practices baptism by immersion and uses the sacramental prayers in the Book of Mormon (Moroni 4 & 5) in the ordinance of the Lord's Supper. Wine is used in the Lord's Supper.

Membership: Not Reported. At last report, some 35 members resided at the cooperative in Holden, Missouri.

Sources:

Shields, Steven L. *Divergent Paths of the Restoration*. Los Angeles: Restoration Press, 1990. 336 pp.

Church of Christ (Restored)

4717 NE 15th Ave., Vancouver, WA 98663

The Church of Christ Restored was founded in 1976 following the formal silencing of Paul Fishel, a patriarch/evangelist with the Reorganized Church of Jesus Christ of Latter Day Saints in Vancouver, Washington. The action by the reorganized church culminated a seven-year battle which had begun when the church published a set of position papers in 1969. These papers reflected the rise of a set of theologically trained leaders in the Independence, Missouri, headquarters. It was the opinion of conservative leaders, such as Fishel, that, among other problems, the papers presented a deviant concept of God and questioned the authority of the Book of Mormon. Fishel became a vocal critic of the "apostasy" he saw in the church leadership; he was warned by the church to stop his agitation.

Finally in 1976, the Reorganized Church formally silenced Fishel, disorganized the congregation, and established a new mission. With his supporters Fishel reorganized his congregation and, for a while, tried to remain within the reorganized church structure. Eventually, however, he incorporated the Church of Christ

Restored. Hearing of the action in Vancouver, Robert Buller, a conservative leader in Michigan, contacted Fishel and subsequently opened several centers in that state. In 1984 Fishel traveled to Australia, and as a result congregations were formed in the states of Victoria and South Australia.

Membership: In 1992 the church reported several hundred members in the United States and approximately 50 in Australia.

Sources:

"Church of Christ Restored." *Restoration* 4, no. 3 (July 1985): 7.

Shields, Steven L. *Divergent Paths of the Restoration*. Los Angeles: Restoration Research, 1990.

Church of Christ (Restored)

Current address not obtained for this edition.

The Church of Christ (Restored) is one of several groups that grew out of the Church of Christ (Temple Lot) and the revelations received by Otto Fetting (1871–1933). Fetting was a member of the Church of Christ (Temple Lot) in 1927 when a heavenly messenger, who identified himself as John the Baptist, began to appear to him. Fetting's messages, which concerned the building of the temple in the lot owned by the church, were received warmly. However, the twelfth message ordered that all new members be rebaptized, including those who had transferred from the Reorganized Church of Jesus Christ of Latter Day Saints. This admonition led to great controversy. Eventually, in 1929, Fetting and his followers left and founded the Church of Christ (Restored). Fetting continued to receive messages, 30 in all.

Two significant events for the Church of Christ (Restored) were initiated in 1938. First, W. A. Draves (1912–1994) claimed to have received messages from the same source as Fetting. The Church received these messages until 1943, when the majority of the church membership rejected them. Draves's supporters withdrew and founded the Church of Christ "With the Elijah Message," Established Anew in 1929. Second, A. C. DeWold, being uninterested in Draves's messages, had left Missouri for Mississippi. He began to make converts and build the church in the South.

After the departure of Draves, the church enjoyed a period of relative calm until the late 1950s. At this time, Apostle S. T. Bronson began to advocate the keeping of the seventh-day sabbath. This position proved unacceptable to some, and the church split. Members in the Independence, Missouri, area established the Church of Christ (Fetting/Bronson).

BELIEFS. The Church of Christ (Restored) has teachings similar to those of the Church of Christ (Temple Lot), except that it accepts the revelations of Otto Fetting. These are published in a small volume entitled *The Word of the Lord*. Worship is on Sunday.

ORGANIZATION. The Church is headed by the Quorum of Twelve Apostles and the several bishops. There is an annual assembly at which church business is conducted. Congregations are found in the South, in Missouri, and along the West Coast. Foreign affiliated work can be found in Wales, Germany, and the Netherlands.

Membership: Not reported.

Periodicals: *The Gospel Herald*.

Sources:

Daniel, William A. *Rediscovering the Messages*. N.p., n.d.

Fetting, Otto. *The Word of the Lord*. Independence, MO: Church of Christ, 1938.

Church of Christ (Temple Lot)

200 S River Blvd., PO Box 472, Independence, MO 65051

The Church of Christ, whose headquarters is located on the dedicated temple lots in Independence, Missouri, considers itself a true remnant of the Church of Christ organized April 6, 1830, in Fayette Township, Seneca County, New York. It has claim to the original church from the time of its organization, through the years of per-

secution and after the death of Joseph Smith, Jr., having never been reorganized nor its membership rebaptized.

In the winter of 1852, a number of church members met in the home of Granville Hedrick near Bloomington, Illinois. Word of polygamy in Utah had reached them, and they withdrew their fellowship from the Utah brethren. Over the next few years they met regularly, and in 1857 Hedrick was set apart as their presiding elder. The group further declared their belief in the Book of Mormon and the 1835 edition of the Doctrine and its Covenants. They took their stand against polygamy and baptism for the dead as practiced in Utah, and against the idea of "lineal succession of the presidency," which the Reorganized Church of Jesus Christ of Latter-day Saints (then called the New Organization) advocated. They began using the name Church of Christ, which was the name of the church when it was organized in 1830.

In 1863 Hedrick was ordained as the first president of the church. Shortly thereafter he received a revelation that the saints should be gathered back to Independence, Missouri, which through revelation in July 1831 had been designated the city of Zion and the place of the temple of the Lord. The saints had been driven out of Independence in 1833 and from the state of Missouri in 1838–1839. Most of the saints settled in Nauvoo, Illinois, but some went to Bloomington, Woodford County, Illinois. A caravan of the saints returned to Independence with Hedrick in the winter of 1866–1867 and within a few years purchased the land that had been dedicated by Joseph Smith, Jr., as the place for the temple of the Lord. In 1891 the Reorganized Church of Jesus Christ of Latter-day Saints went to court to get possession of the temple lots and succeeded in winning the case. The Church of Christ appealed the decision in 1894, which resulted in a reversal of the decision by the highest court in favor of the Church of Christ.

In 1889 the Church of Christ erected a small church building on the property, which was destroyed by arson in 1898. They built another church building in 1902 that served as their headquarters for many years. An arsonist set fire to it in 1990 and a new, larger building was erected in its place.

The Church of Christ reprinted the 1833 Book of Commandments in the 1920s; the book is the original compilation of revelations, and the church favors its use rather than the Doctrine and Covenants. At that time it also abolished the office of presiding elder and discontinued the first presidency. The church has taken the position that the only head of the church is Jesus Christ and the highest officeholders under him are the twelve apostles.

In 1884 the Church of Christ recognized the baptisms of some of the other Restoration churches as being valid and began to accept their members into the church by transfer. Because of dissension in the Reorganized Church of Jesus Christ of Latter-day Saints in the 1920s, a number of their members transferred into the Church of Christ, which at one point increased its membership to around 4,000. This was a short-lived boom, as one of its apostles was expelled in 1930 for giving false revelations. He succeeded in taking a number of the new members with him and established another church. During that time the Church of Christ had begun an excavation for the temple. Two stones were found that marked the exact place that was dedicated in 1831. Lack of funds prevented erecting the building, so the excavation was filled.

Membership: In 2001 the church reported 2,600 members, 42 congregations, and 144 ministers. There are affiliated congregations in Mexico, Honduras, Africa, and the Philippines.

Periodicals: *Zion's Advocate*.

Sources:

Church of Christ (Temple Lot). www.churchofchrist-tl.org.

A Book of Commandments for the Government of the Church of Christ. Independence, MO: Church of Christ (Temple Lot), 1960.

Flint, B. C. *Autobiography*. Independence, MO: Privately printed, n.d.

—————. *An Outline History of the Church of Christ (Temple Lot)*. Independence, MO: Board of Publication, Church of Christ (Temple Lot), 1953.

—————. *What about Israel?* Independence, MO: Board of Publication, Church of Christ (Temple Lot), 1967.

Smith, Arthur M. *Temple Lot Deed*. Independence, MO: Board of Publication, Church of Christ (Temple Lot), 1963.

Wheaton, Clarence L., and Angela Wheaton. *The Book of Commandments Controversy Reviewed*. Independence, MO: Church of Christ (Temple Lot), 1950.

The Church of Christ "with the Elijah Message," Established in 1929 Anew

PO Box 1134, Independence, MO 64051

The Church of Christ, Established Anew, was formed after conflicts arose in the Church of Christ (Fetting/Bronson). For several years after the death of Otto Fetting, in 1933, that church had received no revelations. In October 1937, however, W. A. Draves, a church elder who lived in Nucla, Colorado, began to experience visits from John the Baptist (from whom Fetting had also claimed to have received his messages). These messages were officially accepted, at least through Message 56. Message 48 placed Draves among the church's 12 apostles. In 1943, however, some doubt was raised about the messages, and Draves was accused of attaining information about members to use in the messages. A battle over control of the church's assets began at the 1943 assembly and led to a court suit. The losers in the case, who supported the message, formed the Church of Christ, "with the Elijah Message," Established Anew.

The Church of Christ is similar to the Church of Christ (Temple Lot). It shares the same history of the Temple Lot Church until 1930 and the history of the Church of Christ (Fetting/Bronson) until 1943. The three churches have published their own edition of the Book of Mormon under the title *The Record of the Nephites*. The Church of Christ "with the Elijah Message," which worships on Sunday, has twelve apostles who reside in various areas of the country. A council of seven bishops manages the church property through the council's secretary. The church supports an active mission program and has congregations in India, Uganda, Kenya, Nigeria, France, Germany, and Italy.

Membership: In 1987 the church reported 2,500 members, 15 churches, and 125 ministers in the United States. There were 12,500 members worldwide.

Periodicals: *The Voice of Peace*.

Sources:

The Church of Christ, "with the Elijah Message," Established in 1929 Anew. www.elijahmessage.com.

The Record of the Nephites. Independence, MO: Board of Publication, Church of Jesus Christ, "With the Elijah Message," Established in 1929 Anew, 1970.

The Word of the Lord. Independence, MO: Board of Publication, Church of Jesus Christ, "With the Elijah Message," Established in 1929 Anew, 1971.

Church of Christ with the Elijah Message (Rogers)

Current address not obtained for this edition.

The Church of Jesus Christ with the Elijah Message was founded by Daniel Aaron Rogers, who had been named an elder in The Church of Jesus Christ "With the Elijah Message," and while a member published a short work defending the inspiration of the messages of its prophetic messenger, W. A. Draves. The following year Rogers was removed from the church, but he continued to preach under the same name as his former church. He accepted the doctrines and practices of his former church, and continued to circulate the *Record of the Nephites* (that church's edition of the Book of Mormon) by covering the church's address in Independence, Missouri, with that of his own. He also began a periodical, *The Missionary Newsletter* (later *The Standard*).

Rogers gained some fame as an evangelist who had absorbed some themes from popular Pentecostalism. He emphasized faith-healing and the gifts of the Holy Spirit. During this period, he caught the attention of the popular media when he unsuccessfully attempted to resurrect his mother whom he had kept frozen for a month following her death in February 1978. He briefly reconciled with the Church of Christ with the Elijah Message parent body in 1983, but was soon operating independently again.

Membership: Not reported.

Sources:

Rogers, Daniel Aaron. *The Angel Spoken of in Rev. 14:6 Speaks, Warning All People of the Second Coming of Christ*. Harrison, AR: The Author, n.d. 6 pp.

Shields, Steven L. *Divergent Paths of the Restoration*. Los Angeles: Restoration Press, 1990. 336 pp.

Church of Jesus Christ (Toney)

Current address not obtained for this edition.

Forrest Toney (b. 1945) was a member of the Reorganized Church of Jesus Christ of Latter Day Saints and was raised in the church in Spokane, Washington. He later moved to Independence, Missouri, where, in 1977, he began to receive visions. In one of these visions in 1980 he was ordained to the high priesthood. A few months prior to the visionary ordination, he had resigned his job to devote full time to preaching. Since the Reorganized Church would not allow him to preach, he began to hold services in the Blue Hills Elementary School in Independence and to place advertisements in the local newspaper. Toney claims to offer prophetic insight into the biblical books of Daniel and Revelation. He says of himself, "I am the Elijah and the only High Priest." He denounces money and worldly goods.

Membership: Not reported.

Church of Jesus Christ (Zion's Branch)

108 S Pleasant, Independence, MO 64050-3605

The Church of Jesus Christ (Zion's Branch) is one of several groups organized by former members of the Reorganized Church of Jesus Christ of Latter Day Saints in 1984 following the revelation of the church's president Wallace B. Smith (b. 1929) concerning the ordination of women. The members believe that the Reorganized Church has become an apostate body. Among the leaders of the church is Robert Cato, who played an important role in the International Elders Conference, a 1986 gathering of former Reorganized Church leaders from some 20 separate factions. The new church follows the traditional beliefs and practice of the Reorganized Church.

Membership: In 1986 there were six branch congregations and about 200 members in the church in Independence, Missouri.

Churches of Christ in Zion

Current address not obtained for this edition.

The Churches of Christ in Zion was formed in 1979 by Bishop Robert W. Chambers. It was originally known as the National Association of American Churches. Integral to the life of the church was an economic system called "Zionomics." The system called for large-scale investment of tithes and gifts to the church in various commercial, residential, and agricultural ventures. The goal of these investments was the reclamation of the waste places of Zion, the area around Independence, Missouri, which, according to the Book of Mormon, will be the center of the future Kingdom of God and the gathering place of the saints. Parishioners, most of whom worship in house churches, have been exhorted to establish "Municipals in Zion" to accommodate the gathering of people at the time of Christ's Second Coming. It is hoped that the investments will have an immediate effect of creating both new jobs and homes in the new metropolitan villages. In 1982 the Missouri state legislators adopted a resolution applauding Zionomics.

David Roberts, now head of the True Church of Jesus Christ Restored, was at one time president of the National Association of American Churches. He also attended the church's seminary, Continental College, which was open for several years in the early 1980s.

Membership: Not reported. In 1980 there were more than 40 missions all in the greater Kansas City metropolitan area, 28 of which were in Independence, Missouri. Because of adverse rulings from the Internal Revenue Service on the church's tax exempt status, its membership dropped through the 1980s.

Remarks: The Churches of Christ in Zion has encountered opposition from the Internal Revenue Service since the beginning of its existence. The IRS accused the association of being a tax dodge that has helped its members convert their homes into nonprofit church missions. It denied the church tax exempt status in 1981 and again in 1984 because the church was not exclusively a church and because it had provided assistance to church members in their dealings with the IRS. At the time of last publication, Chambers, the head of the church, was a tax consultant. Sponsors of the legislative resolution have claimed that it was not passed in any effort to provide substantive support to the church's programs.

Community of Christ

International Headquarters, 1001 W Walnut, Independence, MO 64050-3562

HISTORY. The Community of Christ, formerly known as the Reorganized Church of Jesus Christ of Latter Day Saints, was formed in 1860 by remnants of the Latter-day Saint movement left in the East and Midwest after the larger group migrated to Utah. The prime movers of the new church were Jason Briggs, Zenos Gurley, and William Marks.

Briggs had been an elder in the Church of Jesus Christ of Latter-day Saints (LDS) at Nauvoo, Illinois, and remained loyal until the trek West. He then joined James Jesse Strang (1813–1856) in 1848. He soon rejected Strang and in 1850 joined the short-lived church led by William Smith (1811–1893). In 1851 he left Smith and in November claimed a revelation in which the Lord affirmed that he had not cast off his people and that in due time, from the seed of Joseph Smith would come forth "one mighty and strong" (II Nephi 2:46–47).

Zenos Gurley was senior president of one of the seventies in Nauvoo. He remained loyal to Brigham Young (1801–1877) until a few days before the departure west. He joined Strang, with whom he became a bishop, but like Briggs he left Strang in 1852. He claimed a revelation similar to Briggs's concerning Joseph Smith's son.

William Marks was the Nauvoo stake president, but was excommunicated when he supported the leadership claims of Sidney Rigdon (1793–1876), who founded the precursor to the Church of Christ (Bickertonite). Marks joined Rigdon, then Strang, then several other Mormon groups.

In 1852 Gurley and Briggs came together to form the New Organization, basically from some of Strang's followers. They decided that Joseph Smith III should lead the new church. The organization was effected in 1853 and Briggs was chosen to preside. Young Joseph refused the presidency at first, but in 1859 accepted it. In 1859 William Marks was admitted to the New Organization, and it was he who ordained Smith president. On April 6, 1860, the New Organization became the Reorganized Church of Jesus Christ of Latter Day Saints with 300 members.

The church agrees with the Utah Church on a number of important points. Members of the church accept all the scriptures that Joseph Smith wrote and their statement of belief is very close to that of the Utah brethren. In particular, they accept the idea of the restoration of the ministerial, priestly, and prophetic offices in the nineteenth century; the gifts of the Spirit; and salvation by faith, repentance, baptism by immersion, and the laying on of hands.

BELIEFS. The Community of Christ, however, draws sharp distinctions concerning several points on which it feels the Utah Church has fallen into error. The church rejects polygamy, and all the associated doctrines—sealing of marriages for eternity and marriage by proxy to persons deceased—are rejected most strongly. The doctrine that "As man is now is, God once was; as God now is, so man may become," the Adam-God theory, is felt to conflict plainly with the monotheism of the Bible. The members of the church consider abhorrent the practice of "blood atonement" as enunciated by Brigham Young, by which apostates were killed to save them from damnation. In the church, there are no closed temples or services from which the public is barred, nor are there any special temple garments.

The Community of Christ believes in the worth of all people and the value of community building; members are dedicated to the pursuit of peace and justice for all people. Recognizing that the perception of truth is always qualified by human nature and experience, there is no official church creed that must be accepted by all church members. All people are encouraged to study the scriptures, to participate in the life and mission of the church, and to examine their own experiences as they grow in understanding and response to the gospel of Jesus Christ. The church recognizes three books of scripture: Holy Scriptures (the Bible); the Book of Mormon, a narrative of God's dealing with early peoples of the Western Hemisphere; and Doctrine and Covenants, a book of modern revelation and present-day church guidance.

Basic beliefs of the church include the concept of one eternal, living God who is triune—that is, who is one God in three persons: God, Jesus Christ, and the Holy Spirit. The sacraments of the church are baptism, confirmation of membership, the Lord's Supper (Communion), marriage, blessing of children, administration to the sick, ordination to the priesthood, and the evangelists' blessing. Ordained men and women serve Community of Christ congregations as full-time and lay leaders. The most significant difference in the church is its adoption of a hereditary prophetic office limited to the descendants of Joseph Smith Jr. Since 1860, the president-prophets of the church have been successively Joseph Smith III (1860–1914), Frederick M. Smith (1915–1946), Israel A. Smith (1946–1958), W. Wallace Smith (1958–1978) and Wallace B. Smith (1978–1996). The president-prophets have, unlike the Utah Church presidents, added periodic revelations that appear as additions to the Doctrine and Covenants.

In the 1990s, the church faced a crisis in that no descendant of Joseph Smith Jr. was waiting to take over the leadership of the church following the retirement of then-leader Wallace B. Smith. W. Grant McMurray was ordained at the 1996 World Conference, following Smith's retirement. He became the first non-Smith family member to preside over the church in its 170-year history. Grant resigned from the leadership of Community of Christ in 2004. The two remaining members of the First Presidency (Kenneth N. Robinson and Peter A. Judd) presided over the church until the special conference that took place in June 2005, during which Stephen M. Veazey was ordained to the office of prophet/president of the church.

The church is described as a theocratic democracy—a government of God directed divinely under the law of "common consent" of the people. In 1920 church headquarters were established in Independence, Missouri. In 2008 the Community of Christ International Headquarters in Independence featured a temple and auditorium, with a Children's Peace Pavilion located in the auditorium. There is a world conference held every two years at the International Headquarters. The church has been the most open of all Mormon bodies to mainline Protestantism and one finds books by outstanding Protestants (of a noncontroversial nature) in the catalogue of the church book service. Herald House serves as both the publishing arm of the church and as a retail book distributor. Foreign work is being conducted in Nigeria, Japan, South Korea, Okinawa, South India, the Philippines, Brazil, Mexico, Haiti, New Zealand, Australia, French Polynesia, England, and Germany.

Membership: In 2008 the church reported 250,000 members in more than 50 countries.

Educational Facilities:

Graceland University, Lamoni, Iowa.

Periodicals: *Herald*.

Sources:

The Community of Christ. www.cofchrist.org.

Edwards, F. Henry. *Fundamentals: Enduring Convictions of the Restoration*. Independence, MO: Herald Publishing House, n.d.

Edwards, Paul M. *History: Our Legacy of Faith*. Independence, MO: Herald Publishing House, 1991.

Knisley, Alvin. *Infallible Proofs*. Independence, MO: Herald Publishing House, 1930.

Koury, Aleah G. *The Truth and the Evidence*. Independence, MO: Herald Publishing House, 1965.

MacGregor, Daniel. *A Marvelous Work and a Wonder*. Author, 1911.

Independent Church of Jesus Christ of Latter Day Saints

c/o Mark Cortez, Pres., 22 Homas Pl., Apt. C, Destrehan, LA 70047

Alternate Address: International Headquarters: Bergliengate 14, 0354 Oslo 3, Norway.

The Independent Church of Jesus Christ of Latter Day Saints was founded in Oxford, England, in the mid-1980s under the leadership of Christopher C. Warren, also known by his religious name, Lev-Zion haEphrayim, Warren was a former member of the Church of Jesus Christ of Latter-day Saints, and was assisted by Erik Danielson. HaEphrayim had received a revelation in 1977 of the apostasy that had crept into the church, a vision that was confirmed by his own observations in the next months. In 1981 he left the church and began a study of the various factions of Latter-day Saints, finding in each an admixture of truth and error. He joined the Reorganized Church of Jesus Christ of Latter Day Saints in 1984, but left in 1986 to organize the Independent Church of Jesus Christ of Latter Day Saints as a new restored church. The church quickly spread through Europe and back to the United States, but enjoyed its greatest success in Norway where the church's headquarters were soon relocated.

During 1988 and 1989, haEphrayim had a series of more than 150 revelations that were published as the *Covenants and Commandments*, a sequel to the *Doctrines and Covenants*, one of the standard Latter-day Saints scriptures. One of the tasks the Independent Church has undertaken is the compilation of an authoritative edition of the *Doctrines and Covenants* that would contain all of Joseph Smith, Jr.'s revelations and delete those made by church leaders in the intervening years. It is the contention of the Independent Church that both the Latter Day Saints church in Utah and the Reorganized Church fell into apostasy that none of the various factions had been able to reverse. The Independent Church believes it represents a new beginning.

The Independent Church has developed cordial relations with Sons Ahman Israel and its leader David Israel. The church accepts as authoritative scripture the translations by Israel claimed to be the sealed portions of the Book of Mormon plates.

Membership: Not reported. At the time of last publication, there were centers in Norway, Denmark, and the United States.

Periodicals: *Messenger and Advocate*.

Sources:

Covenants and Commandments. Vetlandveien, Norway: Independent Church of Jesus Christ of Latter Day Saints, 1989.

Shields, Steven L. *Divergent Paths of the Restoration*. Los Angeles: Restoration Research, 1990.

Restoration Branches Movement

No central address. For information: Price Publishing Co., 915 E 23rd St., Independence, MO 64055

The Restoration Branches Movement arose in the 1980s within the Reorganized Church of Jesus Christ of Latter-day Saints in an attempt to coordinate the conservative dissent that had grown within the church over the previous two decades. Dissent had been focused on a number of changes that had moved the church away from what some members have felt to be traditional church perspectives. Issues of change arose with the introduction of a new church school curriculum in the 1960s, an action that caused additional concern because of the use of authors who were not members of the church. The introduction of the new curriculum highlighted the development within the church of a "liberal" leadership composed of people theologically trained in liberal Protestant seminaries. These leaders were introducing a variety of ideas whose overall effect would be to move away from the distinctive truths held by the church. This new position of the church was stated in a series of "position papers" produced in 1967–1968 by the church's department of religious education. Conservatives also complained that these leaders were aligning the church to the National Council of Churches and the World Council of Churches.

The ordination of women became the most controversial of the important new doctrines introduced during the 1970s. Discussion within church periodicals moved into the highest leadership by the mid-1970s. In 1976 the First Presidency of the church introduced a resolution calling for the reversal of previous church action forbidding the ordination of women. Finally in 1984, President Wallace B. Smith issued a new revelation (to be added to the *Doctrines and Covenants* as item no. 156) calling for women's ordination and a restructuring of the priesthood. The first women were ordained the following year. At the same time a number of dissenting members of the priesthood were silenced. A review of the priests began, using guidelines issued in January 1985. The conservative members and leaders rejected these guidelines.

A number of individuals around the country and several organizations, most headquartered in Independence, Missouri, championed the cause of conservative dissent within the church. Prominent among the organizations were the Restoration Foundation, Price Publishing Company, Mothers in Israel, and the Concerned Members Committee. Even prior to the revelation of 1984 and its implementation the following year, independent congregations, having anticipated the future course of the church, had separated and formed new churches. A gathering of approximately 20 such independent groups occurred in Independence in April 1986.

In the wake of the actions of 1984–1985 by the Reorganized Church of Jesus Christ of Latter-day Saints and the formation of numerous new church groups, a number of conservative church members, most prominently Richard Price and Rudy Leutzinger, began to call for the formation of autonomous branches (congregations) that would stay within the Reorganized Church but be independent of the "apostate" hierarchy of the world headquarters. In 1985 Leutzinger led in the formation of such a branch, the Independence Branch. Price wrote and published guidelines for such independent branches, which began to form wherever Reorganized Church congregations were found.

Such branches are to refrain from participation with the separate groups, especially those which have proposed new beliefs in the authority of their leader as a prophet. They are to follow traditional Reorganized Church doctrine and accept the Epitome of Faith as a true doctrinal statement. Special emphasis is placed on the authority of the Book of Mormon, the Doctrine and Covenants (without no. 156), and the Inspired Version of the Bible (as revised and translated by Joseph Smith). Such branches are to withdraw support, both spiritual and financial, from the world headquarters. It is the movement's belief that it is one remnant of the true church, within the continuing Reorganized Church of Jesus Christ of Latter-day Saints. Members of the independent branches are to stay members of the Reorganized Church awaiting the day when God will act through them to complete the present Restoration.

Membership: Not reported. A directory, published in 1991, listed 72 branches and groups in the United States, one group in Ontario, Canada, and one in Australia.

Periodicals: Unofficial: *Restoration Voice*. Box 1611, Independence, MO 64055. • *Quarterly Report*. Available from the Restoration Foundation, Box 1774, Independence, MO 64055. • *Vision*.

Sources:

Restoration Branches www.centerplace.org/.

Restoration Bookstore. www.restorationbookstore.org/.

Leutzinger, Rudy. *Branch Organization and the History of the Independence Branch*. Independence, MO: Restoration Foundation, 1985.

Price, Richard. *Restoration Branches Movement*. Independence, MO: Price Publishing, 1986.

———. *The Saints at the Crossroads*. Independence, MO: Price Publishing, 1974.

Price, Richard, and Larry Harlacher. *Action Time*. Independence, MO: Price Publishing, 1985.

Restoration Church of Jesus Christ of Latter-day Saints
PO Box 2027, Independence, MO 64055

The Restoration Church of Jesus Christ of Latter-day Saints was founded in 1991 by former members of the Reorganized Church of Jesus Christ of Latter-day Saints who rejected what they saw as a drift toward liberal Protestant theology and an abandonment of distinctive teachings by Joseph Smith, Jr., in the 1830s and 1840s. Changes within the Reorganized Church had been a matter of controversy for several decades. The members of the Restoration Church had fought to stop the changes into what they considered apostasy but finally concluded that such efforts were in vain. Beginning in the mid-1980s, individuals and congregations began to withdraw and in 1991 "reorganized" under the leadership of some former members of the Quorums of Seventy of the Reorganized Church.

Once the Restoration Church was established, a set of apostles and other priesthood quorums were designated, and in 1993 Marcus Juby, a Native American, was ordained Prophet and President. The naming of Juby was seen as fulfilling a prophecy from the Book of Mormon (2Nephi2:45-47, Reorganized Church edition). Juby resigned in 2001, and Mark Evans was chosen as President in 2003. The Restoration Church grew quickly by gathering into membership a number of small independent groups that had separated from the Reorganized Church over the years. They opened a mission in Nepal and received into membership several thousand people in India who were formerly members of the now-defunct Church of Jesus Christ Restored.

The Restoration Church holds to the same doctrines of the Reorganized Church prior to the changes initiated in the 1970s. They identify those doctrines with the original teaching of Joseph Smith, Jr., and of early Christianity, which survived through such groups as the Donatists until the sixth century C.E. The church acknowledges One God and the substitutionary atonement of Jesus Christ, which is effective in the lives of all who come to Christ in baptism, accept the ministry of Christ's true church, and lead a life of repentance. The church believes that children are not accountable for their life until the age of eight, ant that those who die having never heard the gospel will have the opportunity to accept it in the next life.

The church accepts the authority of the Bible (the Inspired Version of Joseph Smith, first published in 1867), the Book of Mormon, the Doctrines and Covenants, and such additional revelations as may be given to the church's Prophet/President. The church rejects polygamy, secret rites, blood atonement, ecumenism, and white supremacy.

The church practices the ordinances of baptism by immersion for the remission of sins; and the laying on of hands in confirmation to bestow the gift of the holy Spirit, for ordination to the priesthood, and with oil for the anointing of the sick. Revelatory patriarchal blessings are given to individuals by ordained Patriarchs.

Membership: In 1995 the church reported 65 branches, missions, and groups in 32 states. There are also members in Australia, Canada, Nepal, New Guinea, Spain, Great Britain, and India.

Periodicals: *The Advocate Express*.

Sources:

Restoration Church of Jesus Christ of Latter-day Saints. www.restorationchurch.net.

 # Other Mormons

Church of Jesus Christ (Bickertonite)
6th & Lincoln Sts., Monongahela, PA 15063

The circumstances out of which the Church of Jesus Christ (Bickertonite) evolved can be traced back to the actions of Sidney Rigdon (1793–1876), who had been the first counselor to Joseph Smith Jr. (1805–1844) during the early years of the Church of Jesus Christ of Latter Day Saints. In spite of health problems that began with the incident in which he and Smith were tarred and feathered and his falling out with the church over Smith's proposing plural marriage to his daughter, Rigdon retained his formal position in the church. Based upon his office in the church, after Smith's assassination, he claimed to be his successor. Though rejected by the other church leaders, Rigdon gathered together some followers, whom he led to Pennsylvania. In 1844 he organized a new faction of the church, which had but a short life. In the fall of 1846 disagreements arose that led to its disintegration.

William Bickerton (1815–1905), who never knew Joseph Smith, had joined Sidney Rigdon's church in 1845. Left without a church by the disintegration of Rigdon's following, he joined the Church of Jesus Christ of Latter-day Saints congregation at Elizabeth, Pennsylvania, in which he became an elder. Sometime shortly after the public announcement of the doctrine of polygamy, Bickerton denounced Brigham Young and the Utah apostles and left the church. He formally organized a new church in July 1862, claiming he did so in obedience to a revelation. Bickerton gathered some of Rigdon's followers as his first members.

The small Bickertonite Church of Jesus Christ has had a rather tumultuous history. A branch was established in Kansas in 1875, and Bickerton moved there with the church headquarters. Friction arose between the Pennsylvania and Kansas branches, and Bickerton, accused of adultery, was disfellowshipped from his own church. (He returned in 1902.) William Cadman was elected president. In 1904, the year before Cadman's death, a reorganization took place. In 1907, further friction resulted in half the leaders leaving and forming the short-lived Reorganization Church of Jesus Christ. A second schism occurred in 1914.

The doctrine of the Bickertonite Church follows closely that of the Church of Jesus Christ of Latter-day Saints prior to Joseph Smith's death. The members are strongly opposed to polygamy. They do practice the Lord's Supper weekly (a reflection of Sidney Rigdon's continued attachment to the ideas of Alexander Campbell), the washing of feet, and the holy kiss. The church is ruled by a president, two councilors, a secretary, a financial secretary, and a treasurer. There is an annual conference of elders that elects officers.

Membership: In 1989 the church reported 2,707 members, 63 congregations, and 262 ministers.

Periodicals: *Gospel News*. Available from 8423 Boettner Rd., Bridgewater, MI 48115.

Sources:

Cadman, W. H. *A History of the Church of Jesus Christ*. Monongahela, PA: Church of Jesus Christ, 1945.

Cadman, William. *Faith and Doctrines of the Church of Jesus Christ*. Roscoe, PA: Roscoe Ledger Print., 1902.

McKiernan, F. Mark. *The Voice of One Crying in the Wilderness: Sidney Rigdon, Religious Reformer, 1793–1876*. Independence, MO: Herald House, 1979.

Church of Jesus Christ (Cutlerite)
807 S Cottage St., Independence, MO 64050

Alpheus Cutler (1784–1864) was an elder in the LDS Church and gained prominence for his efforts in building the Nauvoo Temple, for which he was chief architect. In 1841 he was by revelation appointed to the Nauvoo State High Council (R.L.D.S. sections 107 V. 41, 134 V.132). After Joseph Smith's death, Cutler began a mission to the Indians. Cutler claimed later that he was given the call by Joseph Smith Jr. (1805–1844), who had granted him sole authority to preach the gospel to the "Lamanites" (i.e., the American Indians). When the group under Young went to Utah, Cutler chose to stay behind because of beliefs introduced by Brigham Young that did not agree with original doctrine.

As a recent church member wrote:

> Joseph Smith had organized a group of men into an order of seven, a kingdom order. Joseph was number one in that order and Alpheus Cutler was number seven, and Joseph ordained all six of those men to hold the keys, powers and authorities that he held. So they each held the kingdom authority. As time went on all of the men in that order of seven except Alpheus Cutler either died or joined some of the factions. Alpheus Cutler was number seven and he waited his turn to work. He had been promised he would be given a sign, a certain sign when it was time for him to begin his work, and when he received that sign he began to prepare to reorganize the original church.

In 1849 Cutler and a number of followers established a settlement in Iowa that was named Manti. A formal organization of the Church of Jesus Christ followed in 1853, after a number of Saints from Council Bluffs swelled the growing community. There was constant fluctuation in membership during the remainder of Cutler's lifetime because of periodic arguments with other groups of Mormons operating in the Midwest.

In 1864, following Cutler's death, Chauncey Whiting, Cutler's successor, led a group to Minnesota (in accordance with a revelation that Cutler had received), where the town of Clitherall was established. Here they tried to establish an order of "all things common" (the United Order), but were unsuccessful at first. In 1910 Isaac Whiting, who succeeded to the presidency following the death of Chauncey Whiting in 1902, called all to return to the United Order, which was accomplished in 1913. Isaac Whiting died in 1922 and Emery Fletcher then became president, having been Isaac's first counselor.

In 1928 a branch of the church was established in Independence, Missouri, the site of Zion (Doctrine and Covenants 57:3). A home and a church building were paid for by the United Order in Clitherall, Minnesota, and about half the group took possession of them. Conflict arose almost immediately, and Emery Fletcher, then the church president, returned to Clitherall. In 1952 he convinced the Minnesota group to excommunicate the Missouri group, including Erle Whiting, the first councilor. The excommunication was not recognized by the Missouri group. Then in 1953 Emery Fletcher died. The Minnesota groups elected Clyde Fletcher as the new president. The Missouri group rejected the election and recognized Erle Whiting (d. 1958), who as first councilor had the assumed right of succession to that office. This set of events completed the separation between the two groups.

Erle Whiting served as president until 1958 and was succeeded by Rupert J. Fletcher (d. 1974), after which Julian Whiting, his first counselor, was elected president. Clyde Fletcher served the Minnesota group until his death in 1969. During the 1970s the Minnesota congregation dwindled steadily and eventually had no one to perform priesthood functions. In recent years, it has reconciled with the Missouri group. During the years of the separation, the Minnesota group referred to itself as the True Church of Jesus Christ.

The main distinctive mark of the Cutlerite Church of Jesus Christ is a belief in the authority of Alpheus Cutler. The president or chief councilor and his first and second councilors are the main officers.

Upon the death of the first councilor, the second succeeds him if approved by a vote of the church members. Besides believing in the authority of Cutler, the Cutlerite Church of Jesus Christ believes that the Lord rejected all Gentiles who did not accept Joseph Smith's message and therefore there is to be no preaching to them unless called to do so by revelation. They are the only group besides the LDS Church in Utah to perform temple rites, which Cutler had known from his days at Nauvoo.

Membership: Not reported.

Sources:

Fletcher, Daisy Whiting. *Alpheus Cutler and the Church of Jesus Christ*. Independence, MO: Author, 1970.

Fletcher, Rupert J. *The Scattered Children of Zion*. Independence, MO: Author, 1959.

———. *The Way of Deliverance*. Independence, MO: Author, 1969.

Young, Bilone Whiting. *Obscure Believers: The Mormon Schism of Alpheus Cutler*. St. Paul, MN: Pogo Press, 2002. 233 pp.

Church of Jesus Christ (Drew)
35315 Chestnut, Burlington, WI 53105

Theron Drew (d. 1978), formerly associated with the Church of Jesus Christ of Latter-day Saints (Strangite), lived in a house formerly owned by Wingfield Watson (1828–1922), a leader in the church from 1897 to 1922. Watson left his farm, located adjacent to the original Strangite church, to three trustees to handle as they saw fit. One of these trustees, Barbara Drew (wife of Theron) had a third control of the property.

In the early 1950s, Theron Drew met Merl Kilgore. He saw in Kilgore the answer to a basic problem of the Church of Jesus Christ of Latter Day Saints (Strangite)— its lack of a head, i.e., a prophet-translator-seer-revelator, since the death of Joseph Smith, Jr. (1805–1844), the church's founder. Since the death of James Jesse Strang (1813–1856), and especially since the death of the apostles he had appointed, leadership had been exercised by people periodically appointed to take charge of meetings of the members. Drew came to believe that Kilgore, then head of Zion's Order of the Sons of Levi, was the "one mighty and strong," prophesied to come and set the house of God in order in the Last Days (Doctrine and Covenants, 85). Drew allowed Kilgore to baptize him. Within a month, however, he became convinced that he had erred, and he returned to the Church of Jesus Christ of Latter-day Saints, only to find that he was not wanted. At a 1965 church conference, he was dismissed from membership.

Drew, his family, and a small number of supporters began to hold meetings in the old church building on the Wingfield farm, the larger body having built a new church building a short distance away. The Church of Jesus Christ of Latter-day Saints (Strangite) filed suit against Drew to reclaim some of the church documents in his possession, but were not successful in their suit. Management of the farm and church building and the role of taking charge of the meetings of the Church of Jesus Christ (Drew) has now passed to Richard Drew, Theron's son.

Membership: As of 1995 there was one congregation with approximately 15 members.

Sources:

Couch, Edward T. *Evidences of Inspiration*. Bay Springs, MI: Author, 1980.

———. *The Sabbath and the Restitution*. Bay Springs, MI: Author, 1891.

Drew, Richard, ed. *Revelation to the Priesthood*. Voree, WI: Church of Jesus Christ of Latter Day Saints, 1986.

———. *Word of Wisdom*. Voree, WI: Church of Jesus Christ of Latter Day Saints, [1986].

Church of Jesus Christ of Latter-day Saints (Strangite)
1320 Spring Valley Rd., Burlington, WI 53105

James Jesse Strang (1813–1856), a lawyer, schoolteacher, and postmaster, became acquainted with Mormonism in 1836 when he married Mary Perce, whose sister was married to an active and dedicated Mormon named Moses Smith. After moving to Burlington, Wisconsin, in 1843, Strang in February 1844 walked from Burlington to Nauvoo, Illinois, where he was baptized by Joseph Smith and ordained an elder by Hyrum Smith. The church asked him to survey the

Burlington, Wisconsin, area as a possible new gathering place for the Saints. Three months later, Strang submitted a positive report to the Smiths, noting that the Burlington area would be an excellent place for the Saints to congregate.

Joseph Smith wrote Strang on June 18, 1844, and appointed him to be his successor. This letter, known as the "Letter of Appointment," is a fundamental part of Strangite succession claims. The day Smith was murdered, June 27, 1844, Strang claimed, an angel of the Lord appeared to him, saluted him, and said, "Fear God and be strengthened and obey him for great is the work which he hath required at thy hands." The angel then ordained him to the same priesthood offices held by Smith: prophet, seer, revelator, and translator. On July 9, 1844, Strang received the Letter of Appointment written by Joseph Smith, which not only appointed Strang as his successor, but also designated Voree as the new gathering place of the Saints. Unlike his chief rivals—the Mormons under the leadership of Brigham Young, who taught there would never be a successor to Joseph Smith as prophet, seer, revelator and translator—Strang represented primitive Mormonism, as he now held these fundamental Mormon leadership offices. During 1844 and 1845, Strang and his supporters mostly urged acceptance of his claims through personal contact and letters. By January 1846, however, a dozen or more dedicated Strangite missionaries were in Nauvoo, testifying about his calling, ordination, and doctrines. Strang's gathering at Voree attracted approximately five hundred Mormons, but by 1848–1850 most of the Strangites had relocated to Beaver Island in Lake Michigan. The major theological belief brought forth by Strang in the Voree period was that Jesus Christ was not begotten by the Holy Spirit, but was the natural son of Joseph and Mary.

At Beaver Island, a theocracy was established with Strang at its head and the Saints became polygamist. Less than one thousand Mormons gathered at Beaver Island, but Strang emerged as the most politically powerful man in that immediate area. By 1856, his organization was the largest of the Mormon groups that did not follow Brigham Young.

The church suffered a severe setback in 1856 when Strang was shot and died several weeks later in Voree, where he had been taken by his followers. Although coherent at times, Strang refused to appoint a successor. Current Strangites believe he did this because he reasoned the Gentile portion of the dispensation was closed.

Following his death, Strang's flock was driven from Beaver Island. Most of those who retained a Mormon identity later joined the Reorganized Church of Jesus Christ of Latter Day Saints. Initially, several apostles attempted to provide leadership, but the Strangites were scattered and desperately poor. The Strangites survived largely through the heroic efforts of Elder Wingfield Watson (1828–1922). Watson was the presiding high priest from 1897 to 1922, and was succeeded successively by Samuel H. Martin, Moroni Flanders, Lloyd Flanders, and the present head, Vernon Swift.

The Strangite Church currently works out of two centers: one in Artesia, New Mexico, and the other in Voree (Burlington), Wisconsin.

Membership: Current membership is less than one hundred persons.

Remarks: The Strangites believe they are a remnant of original Mormonism and look forward to the time when God will open the second portion of the dispensation of the fullness of times to the House of Israel by the call and ordination by angels of a man of the tribe of Judah.

Sources:

The Chronicles of Voree (1844–1849). Typescript of the manuscript record of the Church at Voree, Wisconsin.

Shepard, William. "The Concept of a 'Rejected Gospel' in Mormon History." *Journal of Mormon History* 34 (spring 2008): 130–182.

Shepard, William, Donna Falk, and Thelma Lewis, eds. *James J. Strang: Teaching of a Mormon Prophet*. Burlington, WI: Church of Jesus Christ of Latter Day Saints (Strangite), 1977.

Strang, James J. *The Book of the Law of the Lord*. St. James, MI: 1856. Rpt.: Burlington, WI: Church of Jesus Christ of Latter-day Saints, 1948.

———. *The Prophetic Controversy*. 1854. Rpt.: Lansing, MI: 1974.

Strang, Mark A., ed. *The Diary of James J. Strang*. East Lansing: Michigan State University Press, 1961.

Watson, Wingfield. *An Open Letter to B. H. Roberts*. Burlington, WI: Author, 1896? Rpt.: Salt Lake City, UT: 1974.

———. *The Revelations of James J. Strang*. Church of Jesus Christ of Latter Day Saints, 1939.

Holy Church of Jesus Christ
Current address not obtained for this edition.

The Holy Church of Jesus Christ was founded in the 1970s by Alexandre Roger Caffiaux. Caffiaux initiated correspondence with the Church of Jesus Christ (Strangite) in 1963 and subsequently traveled to the United States. He was baptized and ordained to the priesthood by the leadership in Wisconsin. On the return flight to France, Caffiaux had a revelation that he was to become the head of the church. He wrote a letter to that effect to those who had just ordained him. Early in 1964, he journeyed to Iran. While there, he experienced yet another revelation. A vision of an angel ordained him to the "First Presidency of the High Priesthood of Melchizedek," calling him to be a prophet, seer, and revelator to this generation. He asked that a general conference of the church be called to consider his claims. The small band of Strangites in France voiced their complete confidence in him.

The claims of Caffiaux were argued in the church for a number of years without resolution. At a conference in France, members voted to change the name of the Strangite church to the Holy Church of Jesus Christ. Finally in 1978, the Strangite Church, meeting in conference, formally voted to reject his claims and agreed that acceptance of his revelations and authority were incompatible with membership in the Church of Jesus Christ (Strangite).

Membership: At the time of last publication, there was a small following of the Holy Church of Jesus Christ in the United States, primarily in New Mexico.

Sources:

Johnston, Stanley L. *The Call and Ordination of Alexandre Roger Caffiaux*. N.p. 1966.

The Restored Church of Jesus Christ (Walton)
Current address not obtained for this edition.

The Restored Church of Jesus Christ was founded by Eugene O. Walton following a revelation in 1977. Walton, raised a Baptist, had joined the Reorganized Church of Jesus Christ of Latter-day Saints, but had increasing problems with what he saw as a growing liberalism and a discarding of the essentials of the faith. His opposition to the church's president led to his excommunication. He joined the Church of Jesus Christ (Cutlerite), and was ordained an elder. While with the church he oversaw the printing of a three-volume compendium of writings entitled *The Book of Commandments*. It contained the 1835 edition of the *Doctrine and Covenants*, one of the Restoration scriptures, and some doctrinal materials by Walton.

In 1977 Walton received a revelation that he was the "one mighty and strong" predicted in the church's history to come to set the house of God in order. In 1978 three witnesses were raised up by the Lord in the state of Maine, about 2,000 miles away from Independence, Missouri. They knew nothing of the revelation received by Walton in 1977. The three—Joyce R. Crowley, Barbara E. Overlock, and Louise B. Young—received word on the same day, by the Holy Spirit, that Eugene Walton was the "one mighty and strong," the promised prophet to come to set up the city of Zion, after the death of Joseph Smith, Jr., the founder of the Church of Jesus Christ of Latter-day Saints.

This revelation also gave Walton the keys to the kingdom and named him the successor prophet to Joseph Smith, Jr., and at the same time instructed him to be rebaptized without hands (i.e., without the hands of any man) even as Adam and

Nephi had been baptized. He was also instructed to rebaptize all the other members entering into a new and everlasting covenant by command of God. This revelation led to disagreements with the Cutlerite church membership. In 1978 Walton and two other elders left and formed Restorationists United. Following a revelation to Walton at the beginning of 1979, his small band of followers held a general conference at which Walton was ordained Apostle-High Priest and Prophet. Jack Winegar and James Rouse were named First and Second Counselor respectively. By further revelation, Restorationists United became The Restored Church of Jesus Christ.

The church espouses belief in a Godhead of two personages: God the Father and Christ the Son. The Holy Ghost is seen as the life and power of God. Members are called to follow and believe the doctrine of Jesus Christ: faith in God and Christ, repentance, baptism by immersion, laying on of hands for the gift of the Holy Ghost, the resurrection of the dead, and eternal life in the Celestial Kingdom of God. The church practices "All Things in Common" (i.e., communalism), a necessary step in the establishment of Zion. Christ will not return until Zion is established. Members look forward to the temple of Zion being built in Independence, Missouri. The *Inspired Version of the Bible* (as revised by Joseph Smith, Jr.) is used and called by God's revelation to them as "The Stick of Judah."

The Restored Church, following the reception of revelation, renamed all three books of scripture common to the restoration movement. They were reprinted in order with names derived from the biblical book of *Ezekiel* 37: 16-20 (*Inspired Version*) *The Stick of Joseph* (better known as the *Nephite Record* or the *Book of Mormon*); *The Stick of Ephraim* (*Doctrine and Covenants*), which is an open canon of scripture; *The Stick of Judah* (*Inspired Version of the Bible*); and also several more revelations printed in two other supplements of *The Stick of Ephraim*.

All revelations that come to the prophet, Walton, are accepted by common consent. As of 1995 there were approximately 100 such revelations. The first prophet, Joseph Smith, Jr., received 106 revelations during his lifetime. Joseph Smith III received three revelations and Brigham Young one revelation.

Membership: Not reported.

Educational Facilities:

School of the Prophets, Independence, Missouri.

Periodicals: *Zions Trumpet*.

Sources:

The Book of the Lord's Commandments. 3 vols. Independence, MO: Restored Church of Jesus Christ, n.d.

True Church of Jesus Christ Restored
Current address not obtained for this edition.

David Roberts was ordained to the priesthood in 1966 in the Church of Christ Established Anew (now called the Church of Christ with the Elijah Message). While visiting the congregation in Wellston, Michigan, in 1967 he had a visitation by the Angel Nephi who told him of a future as a healing evangelist and told him to preach baptism in Jesus' name. Later that year he went to Independence, Missouri, for the first time and visited the temple lot, the location where, according to the Mormon scriptures, the temple of Zion is ultimately to be built. In another visit by the angel, he was told to rededicate the temple lot. He returned to his home in Columbus, Ohio. Seven years later, in 1974, he and his wife, Denise Roberts, were visited by the Prophet Elijah, who came to give David Roberts the keys to the salvation of the dead and ordained him to the office of Moses and king over the kingdom of God until Jesus returns to earth. At Elijah's bidding, they began new work in Newark, Ohio, out of which the True Church of God Restored emerged.

Roberts came to feel that his ordination represented a third restoration of the Church of Jesus Christ, the first two having been through Joseph Smith, Jr. and James Jesse Strang. Roberts is the successor to both. The True Church uses the Bible, the Book of Mormon, *The Book of the Lord's Commandments*, *The Book of Abraham*, *The Voree Plates* (translated by Strang), and *The Oracles of God Book* (revelation given through Roberts).

The Church is Sabbatarian. Roberts also preaches the baptism of the Holy Ghost and Fire, which brings a new birth to the body. This blessing, also called body-felt salvation, changes the body in such a way as to prevent sickness and tiredness. It is experienced as a general feeling of comfort and completeness and the continuous healing process becomes established in the body.

Membership: Not reported. At the time of last publication, there was one congregation in Independence.

Periodicals: *The Voice of Eternal Life*.

Remarks: Robert's concept of body-felt salvation is very close to that of Pentecostal evangelist Franklin Hall, discussed elsewhere in this volume as the founder of the Hall Deliverance Foundation.

Sources:

Articles of Religion. Independence, MO: True Church of Jesus Christ Restored, n.d.

Roberts, David L. *The Angel Nephi Appears to David L. Roberts*. Independence, MO: True Church of Jesus Christ Restored, [1974].

Communal Family

16

"The group of believers was one in mind and heart. No one said that any of his belongings were his own, but they all shared with one another everything they had." These verses from the book of Acts 4:32 (along with statements in Acts 2) have inspired countless generations of Christians to forsake secular society and attempt to find a new style of living in communalism and the common life. Sources in pre-Christian society may have influenced early Christian practice. The ancient Cretes and Greeks adopted certain aspects of the communal lifestyle, while the Essene community at Qumran represents an attempt in the Jewish community at a communal alternative. There have been numerous scholarly attempts to tie the Qumran community directly to the founding of the Christian movement.

It was not until the fourth century C.E., however, that communalism became a major force in Western society, and interestingly enough, its form is the same as in the East—monasticism. Like the Christians, Jains in India and Buddhists, particularly in China, developed monastic communities as an attempt at authentic religious living in the face of a culture that was only nominally religious. For Western Christianity, the monastic ideal was a reaction to the establishment of Christianity as the state church, with mass conversions and baptisms that the monks said brought everybody into the church instead of making the church an assembly of true believers. Unlike the early church, which merely pooled its resources, monasticism presented a thoroughgoing communalism.

Inherent in the monk's life was the acceptance of an equality of life with the other brothers in the community. Poverty and the renunciation of the world were the prime means to this end. The chastity rule offered an alternative to family life, the main distraction to community allegiance. In obedience to the abbot and in acceptance of the rules came a strong social system to replace the one ingrained from youth, as well as a discipline to enforce the new order.

The result was the success of the monastic movement, to which the church later responded by adopting certain monastic goals for its clergy, principally chastity. However, the very success of the movement had consequences that threatened the existence of the monastic communities. They became wealthy, and their wealth became a problem during the Middle Ages as the monastic communities became an adjunct to the power structures instead of an alternative.

Francis of Assisi (c. 1181–1226) raised the issue of poverty in monastic circles. Francis thought that sophistry had undermined the virtues of a life of poverty. While individually giving up all property, collectively the monasteries were rich, and even though the monks eschewed ownership, they could nevertheless use all the order's wealth. In advocating a poverty of use, Francis threatened the more powerful monasteries and by implication the authority of the medieval church. In the face of this threat, the church hierarchy rejected Francis, burned his books, and forced a highly edited version of his rules on the Franciscan order. Later, various attempts were made to reverse the accumulation of wealth by the monasteries, but few understood the larger implications of the issue. The inability to reform the monasteries played into the hands of England's King Henry VIII (r. 1509–1547), who plundered the monasteries in his territories during the Reformation Era.

A variety of communal experiments were tried before and after the Reformation, mostly as part of the radically militant wing of several reformist movements. The Taborites and Münsterites were typical. The Taborites arose after the execution of John Hus (c. 1373–1415), the Czech reformer. Taborite communities developed on Bohemian hillsides, and a conscious imitation of early Christian communalism was practiced. The most important of these communities, on a hill near Bechyne Castle, was named Mount Tabor. Tabor was to be the site of the Second Coming of Christ (Mark 14), and the group derived its own name from the new Mount Tabor. Anti-German, intensely nationalistic, anti–Roman Catholic, and biblicist, the Taborites were attempting to create a new social order separate from that of Bohemia or even Western Europe. For this reason, they were themselves subject to persecution by both Roman Catholics and Hussites. In 1420 Martinek Hauska began preaching the end-time and calling for all to flee to the mountaintops—that is, the five Taborite communities—for safety. The group's success led them to a call for a holy war to exterminate sin and sinners and thus purify the land and bring in the millennium.

The millennium was characterized as anarcho-communism. There would be no authority figures, taxes, rents, or private property. Since it was to be a classless society, it would begin with a massacre of the rich. Communal coffers were established. When these ran low, the Taborites "took from the enemies of God what God has given for his children" (i.e., they stole what they needed from any nearby non-Taborite).

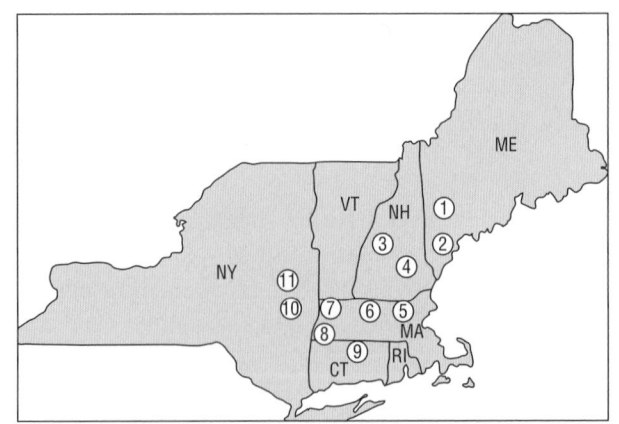

Northeastern U.S. Shaker Sites

1. Sabbathday Lake Shaker Village
2. Alfred Shaker Historic District
3. Enfield Shaker Historic District
4. Canterbury Shaker Village
5. Harvard Shaker Village Historic District
6. Shirley Shaker Village
7. Hancock Shaker Village
8. Tyringham Shaker Settlement Historic District
9. Enfield Shakers Historic District
10. Mount Lebanon Shaker Society
11. Watervliet Shaker Historic District

 Adapted from www.nps.gov

The Taborites, well supplied militarily, continued to exist for a generation, but were broken and splintered by war, messianic figures claiming to be Christ, doctrinal divergences, and, primarily, an inability to produce the goods needed to survive. They eventually died out as a social experiment.

During the Reformation, communalism emerged among the radical reformers. In 1534 the New Jerusalem was established at Münster by Bernard Rothmann (c. 1495–c.1535), Jan of Leiden (c. 1509–1536), and Jan Mathijs (d. 1534). These leaders imposed communalism on a reluctant community. They began by collecting all the financial resources into the community treasure, effecting the change by making the surrender of money the test of true Christianity. Demands on food and shelter followed as the ideal became a disappearance of the distinction between thine and mine. Mathijs emerged as the ruling authority, but was killed in a scouting raid against the Catholic forces besieging the city. Jan of Leiden took over and imposed an exacting moral code. Artisans were commandeered and made community employees. Sexual mores were revised when Jan took advantage of the three-to-one ratio of women to men and declared polygamy the order of the day. Jan, himself, took 15 wives, and polygamy soon devolved into promiscuity.

After an early victory over the Catholic forces, Jan of Leiden proclaimed himself king of the world and instituted a wave of terror against community dissidents. The early victory of the reformers led to greater efforts by Catholic forces, which imposed an even stronger siege against Münster. Eventually, the Catholics starved the community to death, and Jan of Leiden was executed.

The experiences at Münster and Tabor were typical of medieval communal groups. Though Münster was an extreme case, communalists associated with the Reformation tended to be militant in their approach to authority structures other than their own. Possibly related to their militancy was their own experience of having been persecuted. When they gained power, they became the persecutors. The Taborite practice of the appropriation of the property of non-communalists was also widespread. The sexual reforms, mostly advocating polygamy, were common. With such models, it is no wonder that communalism did not experience another revival for several centuries. A few isolated attempts were made, but only in the early 1800s did a new wave of communalism arise.

THE NINETEENTH-CENTURY COMMUNAL SURGE. American communal history generally focuses on the early nineteenth century, the era of some of the country's most important communal experiments. However, the significance of the communes founded after 1960 has been recognized, and American communal history is now seen as having progressed through three phases: (1) pre-1860, (2) 1860 to 1960, and (3) post–1960. The first phase began in the seventeenth century with the establishment of such groups as Plockhoy's Commonwealth in Delaware (1663), the Labadist Community in Maryland (1683), and the Society of the Woman in the Wilderness outside of Philadelphia (1694). Others were founded through the 1700s, and the rate of community formation increased dramatically in the late eighteenth century with the coming of the Shakers. The numerous attempts by the followers of Robert Owen (1771–1858) and Charles Fourier (1772–1837) to found communities crowned the first phase of communal life in America, and the quick demise of these communities ended it.

The nineteenth century burst of communalism grew out of the Enlightenment of the eighteenth century and the rise of intellectual concern with social order. The followers of Claude Henri Saint-Simon (1760–1825) are usually credited with formulating the first egalitarian reformist ideas, but the roots of Saint-Simon's thought are deep in eighteenth-century philosophy. In the 1820s, followers of Saint-Simon began a community in France, which, after Saint-Simon's death, was moved to Ménilmontant by its leader, Barthélemy Prosper Enfantin (1796–1864). In 1832 Enfantin was condemned for teaching free love, and communalism suffered a setback from which it never recovered in France.

Etienne Cabet (1788–1856), a French socialist writer, described his communalist ideals in an 1840 book, *Voyage en Icarie*. In 1848 he and some followers settled in Fanin County, Texas, but health problems forced them to Illinois, where they settled at Nauvoo, which had recently been abandoned by the Mormons. Branch colonies were established in Iowa and Missouri, but Cabet's death in 1856 was a nearly fatal blow, although one colony in Iowa survived until the end of the century.

More important for the eventual rise of communal groups were the ideas of Charles Fourier. Fourier envisaged the world as organized in phalanxes (his name for a single community) in which communism would be practiced in both labor and production. A strong order would be needed for discipline, and loyalty to the phalanx (a central idea) would replace national and family ties. Marriage would be regulated on a polyandric system, with women having many husbands. The vision of Fourier gripped the imagination of the Western world.

One of the people who adopted Fourier's communalism was George Ripley (1802–1880). His concerns were detailed in a lengthy letter to Ralph Waldo Emerson (1803–1882) on November 9, 1840. Ripley desired a place where a natural union between intellectual pursuits and labor could be achieved by combining the two. He proposed to do this on a tract of land that would be a farm, garden, and college, all in one. This adventure, thought Ripley, would yield industry without drudgery and equality without vulgarity. It would do away with the evils of capitalism and competition. Each family would retain some private property, thus allowing individuality to continue. About ten to twelve families would start the experiment, which would grow slowly. The adults would be paid interest on their investment and wages for their labor. There would be no great wealth but a comfortable living.

Government would be by consensus, expressed in open meetings. On September 29, 1841, the Articles of Association for Brook Farm were drawn up after the members spent a summer near West Roxbury, Massachusetts. The articles called for full support of children to age 10 and their education until age 20. The youth would work for half wages and, at 20, would decide to stay as a full member or leave without obligation to the community. Income would come to the community through a boarding school and a farm. Later, printing and manufacturing would be added.

Problems arose in the community, however; an internal critique identified several sources of the friction, including a lack of well-planned operating procedures. In addition, the only communal experience was shared meals, when there should have been sharing on other levels. No common religious life existed, and no confrontation with the basic problem of divided love had been made.

After making this critique, the members revived their interest in Fourier's ideas. When Albert Brisbane (1809–1890), an ardent disciple of Fourier, joined Brook Farm, it was well on its way to becoming a successful phalanx. Population increased and a house (phalanstery) was begun. But before it could become self-sufficient, a smallpox epidemic took a heavy toll on its members, some of whom died, and some of whom fled. Then, a fire destroyed the phalanstery. In November 1846, Brook Farm was declared a failure and the project ended.

More successful was the phalanx at Hopedale, Massachusetts. Begun in 1841, it prospered for 11 years under the able guidance of Adin Ballou (1803–1890), a Unitarian and Spiritualist. Altogether, 175 people lived at Hopedale. Its success was built upon Ballou's strong leadership and the community's strict moral and behavioral code, which allowed religious freedom. The project failed, however, after Ballou withdrew as leader.

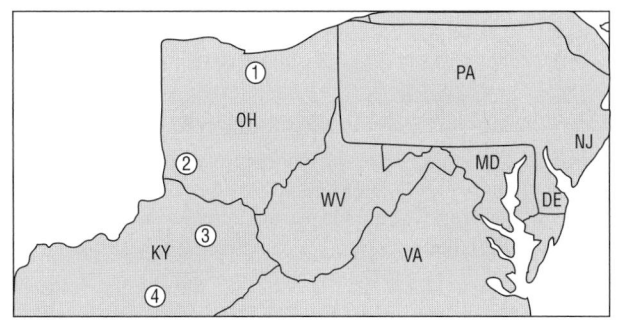

Midwestern U.S. Shaker Sites

1. North Union Shaker Site
2. Whitewater Shaker Settlement
3. Shakertown at Pleasant Hill Historic District
4. South Union Shakertown Historic District

 Adapted from www.nps.gov

Communities drawing on the enthusiasm of the French philosophers, but based more directly on religious ideals (mainly derived from the New Testament) also flourished in the nineteenth century. Of significance were the Rappites, German separatists, pietists, and millennialists who migrated to Pennsylvania in the early 1800s. In 1803 to 1804, the Rappites settled in Butler County, Pennsylvania, and in 1805 they promulgated their Articles of Agreement. They were led by George Rapp (1757–1847), who was given almost complete control over the community. Regulation of sexual life began in 1807 when the community became celibate. Equality was a high ideal, and a uniform dress was adopted. A community graveyard without markers was also used. In 1814 the group migrated to New Harmony, Indiana.

Here they established one of the most successful communes in American history. In 1818 the final break with the past was made when all property records, hence all claims by individuals on the community's property, were destroyed by vote of the community. The Rappites became known for their innovations. They were the first to develop prefabricated houses, many of which still stand. They diversified their economy and became, in a short time, entirely self-sufficient. They made wagons, distilled whiskey, cultivated silk, and ran a printing center. Success threatened their faith, so in 1824, they sold the property and returned to Pennsylvania, where they built a new town, Economy, near Pittsburgh.

The beginning of the end came in the late 1820s when Rapp, without consulting the community, published a second set of Articles of Agreement. While these articles merely stated in writing what was happening in practice, discontent at Rapp's impertinence arose. To counter the dissatisfaction, Rapp began to emphasize the nearness of the Second Coming of Christ in his sermons and to propose a group journey to meet him in the Holy Land. The apocalypticism was rewarded in 1832 by the appearance in Economy of "Count Leon," who professed to be the returned Christ and the

---

Communal Family Chronology

1663	Plockhoy Community formed in rural Delaware.
c.1690	German pietist Conrad Beissel immigrates to America and joins with the German Baptist Brethren.
1714	Founding of the Community of True Inspiration in Germany. It would later relocate to the state of Iowa and build the community at Amana.
1732	Conrad Beissel moves to Ephrata, where he establishes a communal experiment emphasizing celibacy, mysticism, and separation from the world's evil influences.
1787	First Shaker community is founded at New Lebanon, New York.
1794	Shakers found community at Sabbath Lake, Maine.
1805	Under the promulgation of its Articles of Agreement, German Protestants under the leadership of George Rapp found Harmony, Pennsylvania, a utopian community.
1814	The Rappists purchase 30,000 acres of land in Indiana and found New Harmony.
1825	Rappists return to Pennsylvania and found Economy, 20 miles from Pittsburgh.
1850	Eric Jansen, founder of the Bishop Hill community, is shot by a disgruntled ex-member.
1851	Mountain Cove, a Spiritualist community, is founded in California by Thomas Lake Harris.
1874	Rejecting demands to serve in the Russian military, Hutterites begin to migrate to North America.
1888	Edward Belamy issues utopian communal novel, *Looking Backward 2000–1887*.
	Cyrus Teed, an exponent of cellular cosmology, a belief that the earth's surface is concave and we live inside a sphere, founds the Koreshan Unity.
1914	As World War I begins, Hutterites leave America for Canada.
1931	A judge in New York who sentenced Father Divine dies of an unexpected heart attack shortly thereafter.
1932	Reorganization and secularization of the Amana colonies.
1942	Father Divine relocates headquarters of his Peace Mission Movement to Philadelphia.
1946	Church of the Brotherhood forms in Washington, D.C.
1954	Bruderhof Communities open first settlement in the United States in Rifton, New York.
1956	Some Mennonites found the Reba Place Fellowship in Evanston, Illinois.
1957	The Ecumenical Institute forms in Chicago. It is an outgrowth of the 1954 meeting of the World Council of Churches in Evanston, Illinois.
1958	Two former member of the WFLK Fountain of the World explode a bomb at the group's administrative building in an attempt to kill the leader, Krishna Venta.
1968	Love Israel founds the Church of Jesus Christ of Armageddon in Seattle, Washington.
1971	Stephen Gaskin and three other members of The Farm, located in Summertown, Tennessee, are arrested for manufacture of marijuana. Their plea that they use marijuana for religious purposes does not prevent their conviction and internment for several months in 1974.
1974	Most of the members of the Children of God (now known as the Family International) abandon the United States for the world mission field.
1975	The National Historic Communal Societies Association (now the Communal Studies Association) founded.
1976	The Federation of Egalitarian Communities is founded at an assembly held at the East Wind Community in Missouri.
1984	The Twelve Tribes Community (aka the Northeast Kingdom Community) is disrupted by a government raid after a member of the group makes false claims that child abuse is happening within the community.
1989	Synonon, a controversial community made up primarily of reformed drug addicts, dissolves after three decades of life together.
1990	Jesus People USA, one of the most successful Jesus People communes, affiliates with the Evangelical Covenant Church.
1991	Kerista, an experiment in polyfidelity (the creation of family units with multiple male and female sexual partners) dissolves after two decades.
1993–96	The Family faces a set of government raids and subsequent legal proceeding growing out of widespread accusation that extensive sexual child abuse had occurred. The legal issues are finally resolved, but a high level of tension remains with ex-members.
2005	Celebration of 200th anniversary of the organization of the Harmony Society by Rappite colonists at Harmony, Pennsylvania.
2006	150 anniversary of the establishment of the Aurora Colony in Oregon by William Keil.

---

anointed of God. He took approximately 250 of the Rappites with him when he left. The Count Leon incident was followed by disagreement over the celibacy issue and Rapp's paternal control. Rapp was subsequently forced to modify his articles.

In 1834 Rapp's adopted son, who had been the financial manager of the community, died. With his passing, much of the community's financial success passed also. In 1847 Rapp died, and without his unitive personality, the community disintegrated. Both New Harmony and Economy are only tourist spots today.

COMMUNALISM IN AMERICA: THE SECOND PHASE.
There was a noticeable decline in the formation of new communal societies from the mid-1840s to the beginning of the Civil War (1861–1865). The hiatus in community formation, which continued for almost a decade after

the war, was broken by the migration of the Hutterites, a people who share a religious background (including a commitment to pacifism) with the Russian Mennonites. In 1874, reacting to the introduction of compulsory military service in Russia, they migrated to the United States. The first three colonies, containing approximately 400 people, were founded in South Dakota. The colonies multiplied until they were again faced with military service during World War I (1914–1918). In a relatively short time, they moved to Canada and spread across the prairie. In 1934 they began a second and this time successful attempt to colonize South Dakota. As of the mid-1980s, they had more than 300 colonies across the western part of Canada and in the western U.S. states bordering Canada. The Hutterites alone have founded more communities than all of the communal groups before them combined. They remain today the country's single most successful communal group, past or present.

As the Hutterite communal thrust was gaining strength, a second more secular communal movement emerged that was rooted in the utopian visions of Edward Bellamy (1850–1898). Bellamy's novel *Looking Backward, 2000–1887* (1888) projected a vision of economic equality to be reached in the future. It sold 200,000 copies by 1890 and led to the formation of Nationalist Clubs in 28 states. During the 1890s Bellamy's novel, at times combined with various degrees of Marxist thought, inspired a variety of new communal experiments, including a group of colonies in the Puget Sound area of Washington. Endorsed by Helena Petrovna Blavatsky (1831–1891), the founder of the Theosophical Society, the book also led to the formation of several explicitly Theosophical communities during the early twentieth century.

After World War I, the number of new communities continued to grow out of diverse theoretical constructions. These communities were home to Jewish socialists, occultists, Mormons, orthodox Christians, anarchists, and radical Marxists, among others. Even without counting the Hutterites, more communities were begun in the second phase of American communal life (1860–1960) than in the two centuries of the first phase.

COMMUNALISM IN AMERICA: THE THIRD PHASE.

The third phase of communal growth in America started in the 1960s as part of the larger counterculture or the hippie movement. Beginning in the summer of 1967, a number of young adults flocked to California in search of a cultural alternative to the middle-class life in which they had been raised. Labeled "flower children" because of their habit of giving flowers to people they encountered on the street, they soon became distinguished by their use of psychedelic drugs. In both Los Angeles and San Francisco, economic necessity led them to adopt communalism, and as communalism grew, they made the discovery of the new quality it added to their lives. After the media, time, and drugs destroyed the hippie communities in urban areas, many of the former hippies headed for rural America and launched a back-to-the-land movement. Others scattered through the cities and formed various kinds of urban cooperatives. The impulse remained strong through the 1970s but began to wane in the 1980s. Of the hundreds of communities formed, however, a number (mostly religious) have survived to take their place in communal history.

One group of communities had roots in the hippie culture and the Jesus People movement, the Christian evangelical movement that emerged among the hippies. Numerous Christian communes, Jesus People U.S.A. of Chicago being the most successful, sprang up. They were joined by esoteric New Age communities that combined hippie values with New Age visions of communes as transforming agents in society. A successful secular communal experiment took place in Twin Oaks, a Virginia community built on the principles of behavioral psychologist B. F. Skinner (1904–1990). The scholarly interest in communalism also spawned the Communal

Studies Association based in Amana, Iowa, and the Center for Communal Studies at the University of Southern Indiana in Evansville.

THE MARKS OF A SUCCESSFUL COMMUNITY.

Of the many communities begun in America since 1800, only a few survived any length of time—that is, long enough for a child born in the commune to become an adult member. From those that survived and from a study of the demise of those that failed, some characteristics of successful and unsuccessful communities emerge. Sex and close interpersonal relations are rarely the cause of a community's failure. These two factors often bring discontent and a change of membership, but in only rare cases do they lead to a total breakup of the community. Even Plato, in the *Republic*, recognized the necessity of a strong order in sexual relations. He proposed a community of wives. It is characteristic of such communities to organize personal relationships into some type of social pattern at their founding or shortly thereafter. The human organism has proved adaptable to a seemingly infinite variety of patterns, from monogamy, to polygamy and polyandry, to free love, to group marriage (which might include homosexual attachments), and to chastity, the most common regulation. The particular form is not important; what is important is that sex be regulated.

Among the most influential of the patterns of sexual conduct in American religious groups is the complex marriage system developed by the Oneida community. The group was formed in Putney, Vermont, in the early 1840s, and moved to Oneida, New York, in the mid-1840s. The community endured for a more than a generation, dissolving in 1880. The Oneida community's sexual mores were established by John Humphrey Noyes (1811–1886), the founder of the community. Early in his career, Noyes began to preach against monogamy as an exclusive attachment that limited love. As a first step in developing his new system, Noyes discovered what he called male continence, the practice of intercourse without the male reaching climax. (This practice was widespread among Tibetan Buddhists, and was called *karezza*.) By using this technique, numerous pregnancies could be avoided. Thus men of the Oneida community could cohabit with a number of women without giving the community the burden of many new members. As finally worked out, cohabitation within the Oneida community was regulated by a system of ascending fellowship. In this system, those seen as more perfect (the older members) tended to have sexual encounters with the younger members. All encounters were arranged by a third party, and records were kept to prevent any exclusive relationships from developing.

A study of the history of many communes that have died out indicates five main reasons for their failure. First, communities founded for shallow reasons (for example, by persons merely wanting to escape their former lives) do not survive. Poor planning by those inexperienced in meeting the total needs of people is a prime cause of failure, particularly now, when so many communalists were raised in the city in complete ignorance of rural life. Anarchy, a lack of order, is another cause. Production of items (food, money, shelter, restrooms, etc.) necessary to survival becomes everyone's job but no one's responsibility. A common time for communes to dissolve is immediately following the first snow. Hostility from the surrounding community has been a strong force in disrupting communal existence. This hostility comes as a reaction to the different styles of life and the often deviant (from the viewpoint of the surrounding community) moral standards of communalists. Refusal to allow Oneida's sexual mores to prevail was a significant factor in its eventual demise. Hostility in New Mexico has all but destroyed many communes there. The final factor in communal disruption is success. Communes, if successful in reaching their original goals, financial or otherwise, will pose new goals, often drawn from the surrounding world. Thus, keeping the communal ideal before the group is a continuing function. Communities in Zion, Illinois, Amana, Iowa, and New Harmony, Indiana, all suffered from success.

The successful commune (i.e., one that survives) will have several of the following characteristics, no one of which is sufficient in itself. The presence of a strong leader has been noted in many surviving communes. She or he supplies the unity and authority, and functions somewhat as a matriarchal or patriarchal figure. The leader's power may be drawn from psychic, oratorical, or intellectual abilities, or just from personality. Such present-day communes as the Ananda Cooperative Community of Kriyananda (b. 1926), the One World Family of Allen Noonan, and the Farm of Stephen are good examples. In the absence of a strong leader, a strong system of social control and behavior can function in his or her stead. This system, which may be formal or informal, must regulate enough of the life of the community for the necessities of life to be provided and a quality of life sustained. Many communes survive the death of their founders by adopting such a system based on the founders' teachings. Economic self-sufficiency is vital to a community's existence. Parasites can exist only for a couple of years. Removal from the outside world, in its most effective form geographically, is an early necessity. The establishment of a commune means changing habits and mores ingrained since childhood. It is best accomplished in a period of isolation, without old distractions. It can be done by a careful regulation of the possessions and material resources used by the community. After establishment, a careful check on new ideas must be made, and those destructive to the community's life countered.

The basic problem for communal groups is always, then, living as a subculture in a dominant culture that is often hostile and that always aims at assimilation and uniformity. Just as eternal vigilance is the price of freedom, eternal confrontation is the price of continued communal life.

THE DEMISE OF THE SOVIET UNION. The fall
of Marxism in the former U.S.S.R. occasioned a reexamination of communalism in the 1990s by the growing number of scholars of communal life. This development has coincided with a de-emphasis on measuring the "success" of communes and a refocus of attention on the role of communalism as a

stage in the ongoing development of communities, and of communal living as a choice for one phase of an individual's life. In this light, communes can be seen as temporary structures that cease to exist as they succeed in reaching the particular goal or goals of their founders. They serve their purpose for the people involved, who then move on to another social organization. Frequently, at the economic level, communal structures provide a bridge for people to enter mainstream society. On the social level, communities teach people to live with others with a new degree of intimacy, which prepares them to participate in a nuclear family. A developmental approach to understanding communalism allows new standards by which to judge communal experiments.

SOURCES

The study of communal groups and life in North America is focused and nurtured by the Communal Studies Association, PO Box 122, Amana, IA 52203. The association publishes the journal *Communal Societies*. Archives and other materials concerning communes may be found at the Center for Communal Studies, University of Southern Indiana, Evansville, IN 47712, and in the J. Gordon Melton American Religions Collection at the Davidson Library at the University of California-Santa Barbara.

General Sources

Communities Directory: Intentional Community: An Anthropological Perspective. Rutledge, MO: Fellowship for Intentional Community, 2005. 312 pp.

Dare, Philip, ed. *American Communes to 1860: A Bibliography.* New York: Garland, 1990.

Fogarty, Robert S. *American Utopianism.* Itasca, IL: Peacock, 1972. 175 pp.

Friesen, John J., ed., *Peter Riedemann's Hutterite Confession of Faith.* Waterloo, ON, and Scottdale, PA: Herald Press, 1999.

Kanter, Rosebeth Moss. *Commitment and Community: Communes and Utopias in Sociological Perspective.* Cambridge, MA: Harvard University Press, 1972. 303 pp.

Mercer, John. *Communes: A Social History and Guide.* Dorchester, U.K.: Prism Press, 1984. 152 pp.

Metcalf, Bill. *Shared Visions, Shared Lives: Communal Living around the Globe.* Foray, U.K.: Findhorn Press, 1995. 192 pp.

Miller, Timothy. *American Communes, 1860–1960: A Bibliography.* New York: Garland, 1990. 583 pp.

———. *The 60's Communes: Hippies and Beyond.* Syracuse, NY: Syracuse University Press, 1999. 329 pp.

Muncy, Raymond Lee. *Sex and Marriage in Utopian Communities: Nineteenth-century America.* Bloomington: Indiana University Press, 1973. 275 pp.

Oved, Yaacov. *Two Hundred Years of American Communes.* New Brunswick, NJ: Transaction, 1988. 500 pp.

Pitzer, Donald E., ed. *America's Communal Utopias.* Chapel Hill: University of North Carolina Press, 1997. 537 pp.

Rexroth, Kenneth. *Communalism: From Its Origins to the Twentieth Century.* New York: Seabury Press, 1974. 316 pp.

Richter, Peyton E., ed. *Utopias, Social Ideals, and Communal Experiments.* Boston: Holbrook Press, 1971. 321 pp.

Communes in America Prior to 1860

Bester, Arthur. *Backwoods Utopias: The Sectarian and Owenite Phases of Communitarian Socialism in America, 1663–1829.* 2nd ed. Philadelphia: University of Pennsylvania Press, 1970. 330 pp.

Lockwood, George B. *The Harmony Movement.* New York: Dover, 1971. 404 pp.

Mandelker, Ira L. *Religion, Society, and Utopia in Nineteenth-Century America.* Amherst, MA: University of Massachusetts Press, 1984. 181 pp.

Sachse, Julius F. *The German Pietists of Provincial Pennsylvania.* Philadelphia: Author, 1895. 504 pp.

Wisby, Herbert A., Jr. *Pioneer Prophetess: Jemima Wilkinson, the Publick Universal Friend.* Ithaca, NY: Cornell University Press, 1964. 232 pp.

Communes in America 1860–1960

Hine, Robert. *California's Utopian Communities.* New York: Norton, 1953.

Kagan, Paul. *New World Utopias: Photographic History of the Search for Community.* New York: Penguin, 1975. 191 pp.

Veysey, Laurence. *The Communal Experience: Anarchist and Mystical Communities in Twentieth-Century America.* Chicago: University of Chicago Press, 1978. 495 pp.

Communes in America after 1960

Berger, Bennett M. *The Survival of a Counterculture: Ideological Work and Everyday Life Among Rural Communards.* Berkeley: University of California Press, 1981. 264 pp.

Brown, Susan Love. *Intentional Community: An Anthropological Perspective.* Albany: State university of New York Press, 2002. 190 pp.

Fitzgerald, George R. *Communes: Their Goals, Hopes, Problems.* New York: Paulist Press, 1971. 214 pp.

Fracchia, Charles A. *Living Together Alone: The New American Monasticism.* San Francisco: Harper & Row, 1979. 186 pp.

Gardner, Hugh. *The Children of Prosperity: Thirteen Modern American Communes.* New York: St. Martin's Press, 1978. 281 pp.

Gordon, Alastair. *Spaced Out: Crash Pads, Hippie Communes, Infinity Machines, and Other Radical Environments of the Psychedelic Sixties.* New York: Rizzoli, 2008. 304 pp.

Hedgepath, William, and Dennis Stock. *The Alternative: Communal Life in New America.* New York: Collier-Macmillan, 1970. 191 pp.

Houriet, Robert. *Getting Back Together.* New York: Avon, 1971. 408 pp.

McLaughlin, Corrine, and Gordon Davidson. *Builders of the Dawn: Community Lifestyle in a Changing World.* Shutesbuty, MA: Sirius, 1986. 372 pp.

Mellis, Charles J. *Committed Communities: Fresh Streams for World Missions.* Pasadena, CA: William Carey Library, 1976. 138 pp.

Miller, Timothy. *The 60's Communes: Hippies and Beyond.* Syracuse, NY: Syracuse University Press, 1999. 329 pp.

❋ Communal–Before 1960

Amana Church Society (Community of True Inspiration)

1112 26th Ave., PO Box 103, Middle Amana, IA 52307

The Amana Church Society, also known as the Community of True Inspiration, originated in Germany in 1714 among the Pietists who rejected Lutheran state-church polity and ritualism, as well as state laws on military service and oath taking. Their leaders were Eberhard Ludwig Gruber (1665–1728) and Johann Friedrich Rock (1678–1749). These men gathered a following attracted to the notion that the divine revelation and prophecy were as operative in their day as in biblical days. All the sayings of the spiritual leaders were recorded and circulated among the faithful.

In Europe, the eighteenth and early nineteenth centuries were times of persecution of nonconformists, so in 1842 Christian Metz (1794–1867) was placed in charge of a Committee of Four tasked with finding a new home for the group in the United States. An initial tract of land was purchased in New York and the Ebenezer Society organized. In 1845 a communal system of property ownership was established. After 12 years, the society had outgrown its land. In 1855 a move to Iowa began, and Amana was first settled. Then, five other villages—West Amana,

South Amana, High Amana, East Amana, and Middle Amana—were established on a 26,000-acre tract. A new constitution, similar to the Ebenezer Constitution, was adopted in 1859. In 1861 the land of the whole community of Homestead was purchased, in order for the society to have a community on the railroad line.

In addition to its complete faith in the holy scriptures, the Amana Society has various beliefs summarized in the *Twenty-Four Rules Forming the Basis of the Faith*, a short document channeled through J. A. Gruber. Subsequent revelations, particularly those of Metz and his later contemporary, Barbara Heinemann (1795–1883), also have been published. Except for the orientation on the "Instruments" of revelation, the Amana Church Society's beliefs closely resemble those of the German Brethren. The *Twenty-Four Rules* deal with strict observance of the holy life and the Christian community ethic.

In 1932 the Amana Society went through a thorough reorganization that separated the church from its temporal enterprises. The communal system was abandoned, and each member of the community was given a share in the business enterprises, a very successful appliance corporation, and farming. The community assets were distributed to members of the society in the form of stock certificates, in proportion to years of service. A community representative system of church government was adopted and power was invested in a 13-member board of directors elected by the members.

The Amana Church Society continues as a church consisting of the members who live in the seven Amana communities. Economic communalism has been replaced by a wage system and private enterprise. Church services are conducted in both English and German, and simplicity remains a hallmark of Amana worship.

Membership: In 2008 the society reported more than 400 members in one congregation. There were 12 elders.

Periodicals: *Amana Church Society Newsletter.*

Sources:

Amana Church Society. amanachurch.org.

The Amana Church Hymnal. Amana, IA: Amana Church Society, 1992. 238 pp.

Barthel, Diane L. *Amana: From Pietist Sect to American Community.* Lincoln: University of Nebraska Press, 1984.

Rettig, Lawrence. *Amana Today.* South Amana, IA: Author, 1975.

Scheuner, Gottlieb. *Inspirations—Histories.* 2 vols. Trans. Janet W. Zuber. Amana, IA: Amana Church Society, 1976–1977.

Shambaugh, Bertha M. H. *Amana That Was and Amana That Is.* Iowa City: State Historical Society of Iowa, 1932.

Zuber, Janet W., trans. *Barbara Heineman Landmann Biography/E. L. Gruber's Teaching on Divine Inspiration and Other Essays.* Lake Mills, IA: Graphic Publishing Co., 1981.

Church Communities International (formerly Bruderhof Communities in New York)

Woodcrest, 2032 Rte. 213, Rifton, NY 12471

HISTORY. Church Communities International (formerly known as the Bruderhof Communities in New York, Inc., the Hutterian Brethren of New York, Inc., and the Society of Brothers) has its roots in post–World War I Germany, where it formed under the leadership of Eberhard Arnold (1883–1935). Arnold, whose background was in the Christian Socialist Movement and the Student Christian Movement, preached a radical form of Christianity based on the demands of the Sermon on the Mount (Matthew 5–7). In 1920 he rented Sannerz Villa, where work on both publishing and gardening began and where the writings of the Anabaptists and Hutterian Brethren were studied. Upon learning of the continued existence of the Hutterian Brethren in the United States and Canada, the small group around Arnold instituted a fellowship with them that led in 1930 to a merger. This union continued until 1956.

In 1935 Arnold died and a collective leadership emerged. Arnold's death was followed by moves on the part of the group to England (1936), Paraguay (1940), and the United States (1954). The group's initial move from Germany was forced by the Gestapo, who would not allow the Bruderhof to sustain either its pacifist stance or communal way of life. Both the break with the Hutterian Brethren and the move to the United States spurred changes. Some Hutterite forms were abandoned. At this time the Bruderhof consisted of 1,717 residents in nine communes in the United States, Paraguay, Uruguay, Germany, and England.

The first settlement in the United States was on a 100-acre site near Rifton, New York, named Woodcrest. The group was joined almost immediately by half of the members of another already existing commune, Macedonia, who brought with them a light industry, Community Playthings. This soon became the major source of income for the Bruderhof. In 1955, the Forest River, North Dakota, colony of the Hutterite Brethren—Schmiedeleut decided to join the Bruderhof. A third colony was begun at Oak Lake near Pittsburgh, Pennsylvania. In 1958 Evergreen was established near Norfolk, Connecticut.

The early 1960s were years of crisis for the Bruderhof. Realization came that the movement had wandered far from its enthusiastic beginnings in Germany and there was a great wish to rediscover these early radical Christian roots. In the process, many left (though over the following years, many of these returned to the renewed brotherhoods.) From the nine *hofs* (centers) that existed in 1956, only four remained. Membership was consolidated in the United States and the lone British colony. About this same time, Eberhard Arnold's son, Heini Arnold (d. 1982), was unanimously appointed elder of all four communities. He remained in that position for the next two decades as the Bruderhof movement experienced an increasing return to the spirit in which it was founded. During this time Darvell Bruderhof in East Sussex, England, was established (1971) and the Eastern colonies were reunited with the Western Hutterian movement (1974) through mutual reconciliation. This newly unified movement took on once more much of the dress and customs of the older movement, and there was much interchange between the formerly separate colonies, including many intermarriages and mutual aid. In the 1980s and 1990s communities were started in New York, Pennsylvania, and Germany.

BELIEFS. The Bruderhof remains in the Anabaptist theological tradition of the Hutterites, taking a strong stand on community of goods, nonviolence and nonresistance, faithfulness in marriage, and sexual purity. The common life, which the Bruderhof believe is ordained of God and has him as its center, is demonstrated in work, learning, play, and worship.

Worship is centered in the Gemeindestunde (a "brotherhood gathering," very much like a prayer meeting), which is held most evenings. It includes a talk by a servant of the Word, silent prayer waiting in the Spirit (resembling a Quaker meeting), and a closing prayer by the servant. For the Bruderhof, the nature of religious experience is joy, expressed in singing and the closeness of life together.

ORGANIZATION. The Bruderhof is governed by a chief servant or *Vorsteher*, the elders or servants of the Word (usually three in each colony), and the stewards, witness brothers, and house mothers. Great emphasis is placed, however, on the consensus of the community in decision-making.

The differing workloads that sustain the community are distributed to the different hofs. Community Playthings and Rifton Equipment for the Handicapped are located in sections at all bruderhofs and supply the basic financial support for the community. Plough Publishing House is located in Rifton, New York. While it has ceased publishing books in hard copy, many of its volumes are available in electronic form via its Web site.

Membership: In 1997 there were approximately 2,500 residents of the five Bruderhof communities, of whom 250 live at the two centers in England. Membership as of 2008 was unknown, but Church Communities International says communities exist in Germany and Australia as well as in the United States and England.

Remarks: In 2005 the Bruderhof communities abruptly shut down their Web sites and became more reclusive following allegations by former members of child abuse, molestation, and cult-like coercion. Child custody disputes had become common by the early 2000s, some leading to bitter court battles, as many of those who had left the group voluntarily or had been expelled found themselves prevented from seeing children still living with the group. Former members have also claimed that the group's leaders fail to live as simply as they demand of members, and refuse to return donated assets to those who have left the group. In 2007 the Bruderhofs reorganized under the name Church Communities International and reestablished their online presence, maintaining on their new Web site that they are a vibrant and open community that welcomes visitors.

Sources:

Church Communities International. www.churchcommunities.org.

Arnold, Eberhard. *Foundation and Orders of Sannerz and the Rhoen Bruderhof*. Rifton, NY: Plough Publishing, 1976.

—. *Why We Live Communally*. Rifton, NY: Plough Publishing, 1976.

Arnold, Eberhard, and Emmy Arnold. *Seeking for the Kingdom of God*. Rifton, NY: Plough Publishing, 1974.

Arnold, Emmy. *Torches Together*. Rifton, NY: Plough Publishing, 1971.

Eggers, Ulrich. *Community for Life*. Scottsdale, PA: Herald Press, 1988.

Hutterian Society of Brothers, and John Howard Yoder, eds. *God's Revolution*. New York: Paulist Press, 1984.

Mow, Merrill. *Torches Rekindled: The Bruderhof's Struggle for Renewal*. Ulster Park, NY: Plough Publishing, 1989.

Zablocki, Benjamin. *The Joyful Community*. Baltimore, MD: Penguin Books, 1971.

Church of the Brotherhood
Current address not obtained for this edition.

The Church of the Brotherhood is a Hutterite-like body that no longer professes any formal or ethnic ties with the Hutterite Brethren. The two groups hold in common the fundamental doctrines: adult confession and baptism, reliance on Scripture rather than theology or doctrine, pacifism, and the effort to duplicate the communal Apostolic church. The Church of the Brotherhood differs from the Hutterites in its belief that communities must maintain their apartness while living in the world and transacting business with nonbelievers, all the while giving witness to the gospel. Members believe it is idolatrous to adopt any practice that makes symbols, not life, the means of giving and maintaining identity. Thus they speak a contemporary language and wear no special clothing. Full members live in complete discipline, and dedicate all work and wealth to the community. Confessional members devote a minimum of a tithe of goods and wealth and a full day of work in service projects.

Ministers work in secular pursuits and are not salaried. No separate worship houses are built. Love feasts, washing of feet, and baptism are ordinances. The group operates four centers for emotionally disturbed children and has created more than fifty centers for poor families and migrants, which operate as autonomous facilities.

Membership: Not reported.

Ecumenical Institute (Institute of Cultural Affairs)
4750 N Sheridan Rd., Chicago, IL 60640

Alternate Address: Institute of Cultural Affairs International Secretariat, 555 René-Lévesque Blvd. Wt, Ste. 500, Montréal, QC H2Z 1B1, Canada.

The Ecumenical Institute, formed in 1957, grew out of a World Council of Churches meeting in Evanston, Illinois, in 1954, which called for the formation of regional institutes modeled on the Ecumenical Institute at Bossey, Switzerland. In 1957 an American regional institute was formed in Evanston, with Walter Leibrecht as its director. It existed as a center for continuing ecumenical discussion. At about the same time, the Christian Faith and Life Community, was formed as a lay institute in Austin, Texas, its founders having been inspired by visiting many such institutes in Europe. Joseph Wesley Mathews, brother of Bishop James K. Mathews of the United Methodist Church, was its dean of studies from 1956 to 1962.

In 1962 the Joseph Mathews family and seven other families were called by the Church Federation of Greater Chicago to become the staff of the Ecumenical Institute in Evanston. Within a year, the work that had been previously focused on curriculum for local church clergy and laity had taken on the task of community development in a ghetto neighborhood on the west side of Chicago, Illinois, where the staff relocated. The staff discovered that there was a group of people, many of whom were in the church, committed to being a leading force in the "movement to create the future." The institute defined its task as providing structure, training, and models of possibility in order to bring about needed changes in a most practical manner.

The staff reorganized itself to operate as a family religious order, with a common economic, political, and cultural life, and with a common understanding of embodying the vows of poverty, chastity, and obedience. A unique theology for the twentieth century was developed by integrating major themes from the teachings of leading modern Protestant theologians Dietrich Bonhoeffer, Reinhold Niebuhr, Rudolf Bultmann, Paul Tillich, and Karl Barth, and the philosopher Søren Kierkegaard. The programs were designed to be applicable to any person regardless of race, religion, or nationality, and a variety of people found them effective in making a difference in their local situations.

Beginning in 1968, institute staff members were deployed outside of Chicago, starting with Australia and Malaysia. The Institute of Cultural Affairs, a program division of the institute, was separately incorporated in 1973 to work more effectively in non-Christian settings. Between 1975 and 1978, human development projects were established around the globe with a central emphasis on the "human factor in world development." These projects were celebrated as demonstrations of comprehensive, integrated human development in 1984 at the International Exposition of Rural Development in New Dehli, India. This exposition, which brought together the wisdom of local developments in some 50 nations, was sponsored by the Institute of Cultural Affairs and included the co-sponsorship of the United Nations Development Program, the United Nations International Children's Education Fund, the World Health Organization, and the International Council of Women.

Work in each nation is incorporated separately and is headed by a national board of directors and a national board of advisors. These national groups are part of the Institute of Cultural Affairs International.

In 1972 the Ecumenical Institute separately incorporated in Illinois as the Institute of Cultural Affairs (ICA). Through this new corporation the institute could work with local communities in rural villages and urban neighborhoods in non-Christian countries. The work was focused on comprehensive economic and social development, including local commerce and industry, community identity and organization, education of all ages, and both preventative and curative health. As this work developed in the 1970s, it was found that the basic methods could also be applied and adapted for work with organizations such as corporations, hospitals, schools, government agencies, and other not-for-profit organizations.

Membership: In 2008 the ICA International reported a network of member organizations in the United States and 29 countries worldwide.

Periodicals: *Edges* (ICA Canada) • *Network Exchange* (internal newsletter of ICA International).

Sources:

ICA: The Institute of Cultural Affairs USA. www.ica-usa.org/about-us.htm/.

Institute of Cultural Affairs International. www.ica-international.org/.

Cryer, Newman. "Laboratory for Tomorrow's Church." *Together* 10, no. 3 (March 1966).

Esoteric Fraternity

PO Box 37, Applegate, CA 95703

The Esoteric Fratenity was founded in 1887 in Boston, Massachusetts, by Hiram Erastus Butler (d. 1916). Butler, after losing several fingers in a saw-mill accident, became a hermit in a New England forest for 14 years and began to receive revelations from God. In the late 1880s, he began to share these revelations with others, gathering around him a dozen followers, all single men and women. They pooled their resources, moved to Applegate, California, and established a monastic-like community. The basic idea of the fraternity was that to believe in God one must live the life of a celibate. When man gives up the sex act, the kingdom of God will be established on earth. This belief has necessarily kept the group small. At its height, around the beginning of the twentieth century, there were only forty members. In 1981 there were three reported members.

The Esoteric Fraternity teaches Esoteric Christianity. Members believe in reincarnation and that the population of the world remains constant, as old souls are constantly reborn. They believe that the fraternity consists of the chosen ones, the Order of Melchizedek as prophesied in the Book of Revelation. They will grow to be 144,000 in number and then the kingdom of God will begin. They would be rulers of the earth for eternity.

Following Butler's death, Enoch Penn, a prolific writer (as was Butler), succeeded him. Penn was editor of the *Esoteric Christian*, the popular periodical of the fraternity that ceased publication when Penn died in 1943. The next leaders were Lena Crow (d. 1953), William Corecco (d. 1972), and Fred Peterson. Peterson, a former Mormon, had converted to the group in the 1950s. Butler's and Penn's books continue to be sold.

In August 1973 one elderly male member of the fraternity was murdered. His killer was not apprehended.

Membership: Not reported.

Sources:

Butler, Hiram E. *The Goal of Life*. Applegate, CA: Esoteric Publishing Company, 1908.

———. *The Narrow Way of Attainment*. Applegate, CA: Esoteric Publishing Company, 1901.

———. *The Seven Creative Principles*. Applegate, CA: Esoteric Publishing Company, 1950.

———. *Special Instructions for Women*. Applegate, CA: Esoteric Fraternity, 1942.

Penn, Enoch. *The Order of Melchisedek*. Applegate, CA: Esoteric Fraternity, 1961.

Hutterian Brethren-Dariusleut

Surprise Creek Colony, Stanford, MT 59479

The Dariusleut was the second group of Hutterites to settle in the United States, on a section of land near Olivet, South Dakota, north of the original Hutterite colony, in 1875. (For the early history of the Hutterites, see separate entry on Hutterian Brethren-Schmiedeleut.) There the leut established the Wolf Creek Colony. Under the leadership of Darius Walter (1835–1903), this second colony and those that sprang from it took his name. They established seven colonies in South Dakota, two in Montana, and one in Manitoba, Canada, by the beginning of World War I. They then abandoned all of their colonies and moved to new ones in Alberta, Canada. Not until 1935 did they reestablish a colony in the United States, in Montana.

The Dariusleut became the most geographically scattered of the leuts, having colonies in Washington State and Montana as well as Alberta, Saskatchewan, and British Columbia in Canada. There is also an affiliated colony in Japan. The Dariusleut was affiliated with the Society of Brothers from 1931 to 1950. It is the most loosely affiliated leut, as indicated by the ability of new colonies to be founded without prior consent.

Practices followed by the Dariusleut include the requirement of modest dress and designating the minister as the first to enter the worship service.

Membership: In 2006 the Hutterian Brethren Schmiedeleut Conference reported 149 Dariusleut colonies in the United States and Canada.

Sources:

Hutterites. www.hutterites.org/.

Allard, William Albert. "The Hutterites, Plain People of the West." *National Geographic* 138, no. 1 (July 1970): 98–125.

Flint, David. *The Hutterites*. Toronto: Oxford University Press, 1975.

Gross, Paul S. *The Hutterite Way*. Saskatoon, SK: Freeman Publishing, 1965.

Holzach, Michael. "The Christian Communists of Canada." *Geo* 1 (November 1979): 126–154.

Hutterian Brethren-Lehrerleut

New Elm Spring Colony, Wolf Creek, MT 59648

The Lehrerleut dates to 1877, when the third group of Hutterites to migrate to America in the 1870s settled near Parkston, South Dakota. (For the early history of the Hutterites, see separate entry on Hutterian Brethren-Schmiedeleut.) Upon arrival in the United States, the group decided to live communally under the leadership of Jacob Wipf, an accomplished teacher (lehrer). The group derived its name from his ability. Slow to expand, the group had only four colonies at the beginning of World War I. Like the other leuts, however, it abandoned the American colonies and migrated to Alberta. Only after World War II was a new American colony established, in Montana. Present-day colonies are scattered across Alberta, Saskatchewan, and Montana.

The Lehrerleut is the most liberal of the Hutterite leuts. From their founder's formal education, members have inherited a preference for high German, in which they are thoroughly schooled. Like other leuts, the Lehrerleut requires conservative dress, but unlike ministers of other leuts, the Lehrerleut minister is the last to enter worship services.

Membership: In 2006 the Hutterian Brethren Schmiedeleut Conference reported 135 Lehrerleut colonies in Saskatchewan, Alberta, and Montana.

Sources:

Hutterites. www.hutterites.org/.

Horst, John. *The Hutterian Brethren, 1528–1931*. Cayley, AB: Macmillan Colony, 1977.

The Hutterian Brethren of Montana. Augusta, MT: Privately printed, 1965.

Kraybill, Donald B., and Carl F. Bowman. *On the Backroad to Heaven: Old Order Hutterites, Mennonites, Amish, and Brethren*. Baltimore, MD: Johns Hopkins University Press, 2001.

Hutterian Brethren-Schmiedeleut

c/o David D. Decker, Tachetter Colony, Olivet, SD 57052

The Hutterian Brethren was founded in 1528 among a group of Anabaptists fleeing from persecution in Austria to settle in Moravia. Anabaptists viewed the church as a society of adult believers gathered together freely; they thus opposed infant baptism and protested the state church of any area in which they resided. The Hutterian Brethren is the only surviving group that adopted communal living in response to the Anabaptist vision of establishing a Christian community in which private property would be abolished.

The Hutterites were named for Jacob Hutter, an early group leader and organizer who was burned at the stake in 1536. For the early Hutterites, the introduction of "community of goods" was at the time a religiously sanctioned necessity. The first colony, or Bruderhof (common household), was founded in Austerlitz in Moravia. A pattern of persecution took shape over several centuries: At first Hutterites were tolerated, became successful, and grew in numbers. They then became objects of jealousy, sparking persecution because of their success and their pacifism. This pattern repeated itself in Moravia, Slovakia, Wallachia, and the Ukraine.

In the nineteenth century, living in close proximity to the Mennonites (founded by Menno Simons, an Anabaptist) in Russia, the Hutterites' ideal was temporarily lost. But in the 1850s a renewal of communal living developed around the person and ministry of Michael Waldner, a visionary noted for his trances and psychic experiences. In a vision, an angel told him to reinstitute the *Gemeinschaft* of the Holy Spirit after the pattern of Jesus and the apostles. The term *Gemeinschaft*, though it has no exact English equivalent, can be translated as "community." The renewal took place in Hutterdorf, a Hutterite village in the Crimea. Two communal groups were established, one at each end of the village, and they became the basis of the division of the Hutterites into leuts (people) or colonies. The renewal of communal living among the Hutterites ran up against the rise of nationalism in Russia. In 1871, when universal compulsory military service was introduced, the Hutterites' requests for exemption were ignored. In 1874 the Hutterites began to migrate to the United States and Canada.

The Hutterites' beliefs arise from the Anabaptist tradition and in general follow the Schleitheim Confession (the Swiss Anabaptist declaration of belief). Like the Amish, the Hutterites adopted plain dress. Some of them at one time used hooks and eyes instead of buttons, a tradition symbolizing their rejection of the soldiers, their persecutors, whose military uniforms bore large buttons. The Hutterites use electricity, drive cars, and have powered farm equipment and telephones. However, they have no televisions, and dancing, smoking, and playing musical instruments are forbidden. They are pacifists and follow the radical Anabaptist theology. Although there is a similarity among all Hutterites, the three leuts show marked distinctions in dress and discipline, and they do not intermarry (see separate entries).

Approximately 800 Hutterites migrated to the United States between 1874 and 1876. About half of these homesteaded family farms eventually became affiliated with Mennonite churches and ceased to be part of the Hutterite community. The remainder settled in three colonies in South Dakota. These three colonies gave rise to the three leuts, each named for its founder. Each leut developed its own peculiarities and each serves as an organizing unit for fellowship, discipline, and administering the religious life of the colonies.

The Schmiedeleut, the oldest of the leuts, dates to the original renewal under Michael Waldner. Its name derives from his profession, *schmied*, or blacksmith. Upon arrival in the United States, Waldner's people settled the Bon Homme County in South Dakota in 1874. Waldner's visions remained a major motivating force in the communal patterns. By 1918 the Schmiedeleut had founded nine colonies. With the coming of World War I, the Hutterites' German background combined with their pacifism led to heightened tension. One by one they abandoned their colonies and relocated in Manitoba, Canada. Only in 1934 did a group settle a new American colony (Rockport, near Alexandria, South Dakota).

Among the Hutterites, the Schmiedeleut is considered the most conservative. During worship, the minister is the first to enter the gathering place. Colonies are tied closely together, and the consent of all is required before a new one can be created.

Membership: In 2006 the Hutterian Brethren Schmiedeleut Conference reported 176 Schmiedeleut colonies in Manitoba, Alberta, North Dakota, South Dakota, and Minnesota. It reported a total of 45,000 Hutterites in North America.

Sources:

Hutterites. www.hutterites.org/.

Cobb, Douglas S. "The Jamesville Bruderhof: A Hutterian Agricultural Colony." *Journal of the West* 9, no. 1 (1970): 60–77.

Kraybill, Donald B., and Carl F. Bowman. *On the Backroad to Heaven: Old Order Hutterites, Mennonites, Amish, and Brethren*. Baltimore, MD: Johns Hopkins University Press, 2001.

Peters, Victor. *All Things Common*. New York: Harper & Row, 1971.

Mount Zion Overcoming Body of Christ–The True Bride
Rte. 1, Crescent City, FL 32012

Mount Zion Overcoming Body of Christ–The True Bride was founded in 1944 in New York City by Mother Essie M. MacDonald. The founding of the group was directly connected to McDonald's recovery from a near fatal illness. Once recovered, she began to dress in white and refused to wear either a coat or cape. She carried a dive, the symbol of the Holy Spirit. For a time, she was affiliated with the Church of God in Christ (the largest of several predominantly black Pentecostal denominations), but the church eventually rejected her unconventional dress code.

She eventually moved to Florida, her original home, where her mother gave her a tract of land. Here she opened a mission house in a 100-room "ark" to which she invited the aged, the infirm, the homeless, and any others simply in need of help. Some, attracted by her work, moved to the ark to become resident members of the church.

The church is Pentecostal in emphasis. Members believe in the baptism of the Holy Spirit as evidenced by speaking in tongues. They also have a strong belief in healing and invite the sick to receive the ministrations of Mother MacDonald. Worship is conducted daily, though Saturday is designated the Sabbath. The church is organized communally. The resident chambers, separate for men and women, are designated by names associated with the bride's chamber. Mother MacDonald is viewed as the "Bride of Christ" and in that role wears a white gown with a Star of David on its skirt. She teaches what is termed the "Female Principle," a belief in the important role of females on the earth. As part of communal life, members grow their own food. Members wear white clothes and no shoes.

Membership: The group does not consider itself a denomination or organization, but rather a house of prayer for all people.

Sources:

DuPree, Sherry Sherrod. *African-American Holiness Pentecostal Movement: An Annotated Bibliography*. New York: Garland Publishing, 1992.

The Peace Mission Movement
c/o the Woodmont Estate, 1622 Spring Mill Rd., Gladwyne, PA 19035-1021

The Peace Mission Movement was founded as an organization in the early twentieth century by the Rev. Major J. Divine (c. 1877–1965), better known as Father Divine. He was one of the most colorful and controversial leaders of a new religious movement in American history. By his own choosing, and in accord with his own religious conviction, Father Divine's life and activity are veiled in obscurity until just prior to 1919 in Brooklyn, New York, where he was known to be preaching about Jesus Christ and the coming of the kingdom of God.

From his own writings and the testimonies of those who knew him, it is believed that Father Divine left Brooklyn and went south just after the Jim Crow laws were passed in Grover Cleveland's (1837–1908) administration. While in the South, he was in the hands of 32 lynch mobs because of his stand for brotherhood, eternal life, and salvation being free and without the payment of money. The first Mother Divine and others were witnesses of his treatment in the hands of lynch mobs. In the name of the Rev. Major J. Divine, he married Mother Peninniah Divine (d. 1943) around the year 1915.

Father Divine appeared as an itinerant preacher on the east coast of the United States and found fellowship with others who were preaching that the Christ could be manifested as God in man. Samuel Morris (known also as Father Jehovah) and John Hickerson (known by his followers as Bishop St. John the Divine) were two religious leaders of which he came into contact who shared similar outlooks. Because of jealous rivalry, it is believed, Hickerson fabricated the story that Father Divine's name was really George Baker. Hickerson also is responsible for other biographical misinformation.

To remove himself from the turmoil, Father Divine went into seclusion in the small Long Island fishing village of Sayville, New York. It was here that his residence became known as "the rescue home for the poor only." He attracted those in need of food, clothing, shelter, and employment, as well as those who were drawn by the demonstration at the Sayville residence of supernatural abundance in the midst of seeming scarcity. Father Divine's work commanded more and more attention, and ever greater numbers flocked to Sayville to banquet with him, listen to his sermons, and receive healings of mind, body, and spirit, all gratis to everyone who came.

The influx of numbers of people into the town disturbed the residents. Their hostility led to a court case against Father Divine in 1931, the events of which created worldwide publicity. Although the local county court convicted Father Divine, fined him, and sent him to jail for 30 days, the Appellate Division of the Supreme Court of New York later condemned the proceedings as erroneous and prejudicial.

The vindication notwithstanding, Father Divine chose to move his headquarters to Harlem, New York, in 1933, where he could direct his activity to the masses, especially the African Americans who had gathered there after World War I (1914–1918). While gaining a large following from the Harlem public, he experienced continual harassment from the authorities, so that in 1942 he moved again, this time to Philadelphia, Pennsylvania.

The Peace Mission Movement is primarily of a religious nature, but its tenets have strong social, economic, and patriotic ramifications. Its members believe in the principles of Americanism, brotherhood, Christianity, democracy, and Judaism, and that all true religions are synonymous. Members believe that Father Divine fulfills the scriptural promise of the Second Coming of Christ, is the personification of God in a bodily form, and that heaven is a state of consciousness. This state is being materialized, in as much as the members believe that America is the birthplace of the kingdom of God on earth, which will be realized when everyone lives the life of Christ.

Father Divine founded the churches under the Peace Mission Movement; they were established in 1940 and 1941. Mother Divine, with the recognition of Father Divine's ever-presence, became the spiritual head in 1965. There are no ministers and no prescribed ritual in the church services. Those in attendance are free to testify, sing, read Scripture or the words of Father Divine or Mother Divine, or offer praise to God as they are led to do from any inner prompting. Services feature congregational singing. The only sacrament is Holy Communion, served daily as a full-course meal to which all are welcome. There are also two holidays: April 29, which is the celebration of Father Divine's marriage with Mother Divine to bring about the universal brotherhood of man and the propagation of virtue, honesty, and truth; and September 10 through September 12, which is the consecration and dedication of Woodmont to universalize the Woodmont Estate as a symbol of the highest spiritual state of consciousness.

The mission stands for the absolute fatherhood and motherhood of God and the universal brotherhood of man. Its members believe that a person is a person—not a specified race, color, nationality, or religion—and they live integrated together as brothers and sisters in the family of God and as members only of the human race. They avoid all reference to color or race.

Members of the mission live communally in the churches and affiliated sorority and fraternity houses. They are strictly celibate men and women living in separate houses and on separate floors of the larger facilities. Completely independent and self-supporting, they observe Father Divine's International Modest Code: no smoking or drinking; no use of obscenity, vulgarity, or profanity; no undue mixing of the sexes; and no receiving gifts, presents, tips, or bribes. They pay cash for all purchases, buying nothing on credit or on installment plans, and do not insure their lives, the lives of others, or their possessions. They do not imbibe intoxicating liquors or drugs.

The Peace Mission Movement was most active in the post-Depression era when Father Divine preached peace, health, happiness, and abundance, and demonstrated that his teachings were practical as he provided food and shelter for all those in need at no cost. To others in dire circumstances, but who had a poverty-level income or less, Father Divine offered 15¢ meals and $1-per-week shelter, so that they could hold up their heads with a sense of individual worth and independence, because they were able to pay for their sustenance. The same abundance was manifested in the churches and extensions in various countries as well as those in the United States, where elaborate banquets are the custom.

After Father Divine's passing, his wife Sweet Angel (b. 1924), known to members as Mother Divine, assumed leadership of the movement. She had married Father Divine in 1946, and currently resides at Woodmont. The movement has a long history of being integrated, as was the marriage. Woodmont was designated a national historic landmark in 1998. The mission also operates a radio ministry.

Membership: In 2008 the movement reported five incorporated churches. In addition, churches have been formed in Canada, Germany, Switzerland, Austria, Australia, Guyana, Panama, and Nigeria. No membership statistic are kept; names are recorded only when necessary for business purposes

Periodicals: *The New Day*. • *Enlightenment*, twice per year.

Sources:

Father Divine: His Work and Mission. www.fdipmm.libertynet.org

Burnham, Kenneth. *God Comes to America: Father Divine and the Peace Mission*. Boston, MA: Lambeth Press, 1979.

Divine, M. J. *The Peace Mission Movement*. Philadelphia, PA: Imperial Press, 1982.

Harris, Sara. *Father Divine*. New York: Collier Books, 1971.

Hoshor, John. *God in a Rolls Royce: The Rise of Father Divine: Madman, Menace, or Messiah*. New York: Hillman-Curl, 1936.

Watts, Jill. *God, Harlem U.S.A.: The Father Divine Story*. Berkeley: University of California Press, 1992.

People of the Living God
366 Cove Creek Rd., McMinnville, TN 37110-9512

The People of the Living God was formed in 1932 by Harry Miller (a former minister in the Assemblies of God) and his father-in-law (a former minister in the Presbyterian church). They saw their action as a stand against sectarianism, and they opened a Bible-training school in Los Angeles to prepare "nonsectarian" missionaries. During the next four years (1937–1941), some members of the group lived in Kentucky operating a free school in a bankrupt county and then moved into the mountains of Tennessee. The group finally settled in New Orleans, where it remained for many years.

Sectarianism is defined by the group as basing admission to fellowship on doctrinal agreement. To keep free from this, the group maintains an open pulpit, from which laymen and ministers who wish to contest doctrinal beliefs can speak. Conduct, not opinion, is the rule in matters of fellowship (Acts 15:28–29). The doctrinal consensus of the group is close to the beliefs of the Assemblies of God. Members are Trinitarian Pentecostals and practice two ordinances—baptism by immersion and the Lord's Supper (which is open to all). They believe that speaking in tongues is a sign of receiving the baptism of the Holy Spirit. The group considers itself *amillennialist*, meaning it does not believe in the "secret rapture," the time when Jesus returns in secret to the church and the kingdom of God is realized on earth. Rather, People of the Living God believe Jesus already reigns over God's kingdom.

The fellowship remains small. Headquarters moved from New Orleans to rural Tennessee in 1982. Members work inside the group, with a common treasury. All buying is done by a purchasing agent. Members receive no personal allowance. They run a free Christian school, which any child may attend. The simple lifestyle allows a large percentage of money to be put into literature and into the support of nonsectarian missionaries overseas. The group publishes a series of booklets, mostly of a controversial nature, which is sent throughout the world.

Membership: In 1997 there were two centers and approximately 75 resident members. There are affiliated members in the Philippines.

Periodicals: *The Testimony of Truth*. Available from Rte. 2, Box 423, McMinnville, TN 37110.

Sources:

People of the Living God. www.people-livinggod.org.

Miller, Harry R. *Community: A Way of Life*. New Orleans, LA: People of the Living God, n.d.

———. *Enchantments*. New Orleans, LA: People of the Living God, n.d.

———. *A Man of Like Passions*. New Orleans, LA: People of the Living God, n.d.

Shiloh Trust and Church
309 Griffin Ave., Sulphur Springs, AR 72768

The Rev. Eugene Crosby Monroe (1880–1961) was a businessman who in 1923 was ordained in the Apostolic Church, a British-based Pentecostal body. Monroe served as a pastor of the Apostolic Church in Philadelphia until ill health forced his retirement from both his pastoral duties and his business career. He settled on a farm near Sherman, New York, to which young men and women came to continue under his ministry. Out of this evolved, in 1942, Shiloh Trust, a self-supporting Pentecostal community also known as the Church of Shiloh. A large-scale organic food business was established, through which baked goods, cheese, and other foods were distributed to retail outlets.

Monroe died in 1961, by which time Shiloh Trust had grown into a successful operation. He was succeeded by his son, who was later killed in a plane crash. James Janisch is the current trustee. By 1963 the wholesale distribution of health foods to retail stores had begun to dominate the group's business interests. In 1968 headquarters were moved to Sulphur Springs, Arkansas. Members of the community gather daily for meetings. Beliefs are similar to those of the Apostolic Church. In addition to their natural foods business, the group operates the Shiloh Christian Conference and Retreat Center.

Membership: Not reported.

Temple Society
c/o Dr. Richard Hoffman, 152 Tucker, Bentleigh, Australia

The Temple Society, known earlier as the Friends of Jerusalem, was founded by Christoph Hoffman (1815–1885) in 1861 in Württemberg, Germany. Hoffmann had attacked the established churches for not having succeeded in bringing about the improved society envisaged by the prophets of Israel. Hoffman sought to motivate people to strive in their daily life to achieve those conditions that would create "the kingdom of God" on earth described by Jesus. He, with others, gathered likeminded followers and prepared them for settlement in the Holy Land, where reformation of Christian life was most likely to be noticed and become an example for Christianity to follow.

During preparation for migration to Palestine, the rundown property of Kirschenhardthof became a settlement for 12 families. This settlement served as a prototype for the New Jerusalem that was to be established in the Holy Land. Georg David Hardegg, whose faith incorporated a more literal belief in the various gifts of the spirit, was active in achieving the practical steps necessary for settling in Palestine. Hoffman's view of Christianity was based on what he considered to be the actual teachings of Jesus, as distinct from what people wrote about the person of Jesus. In his most important work, *Sendschreiben über den Tempel und die Sakramente: Das Dogma von der Dreieinigkeit und von der Gottheit Christi, sowie ueber die Versohnung der Menschen mit Gott*, he argued that the Trinity and the deity of Christ and the Holy Spirit were conceived by people long after the death of Jesus. The incarnation may be viewed as the expression of God's creative thought in the mind and body of Jesus. Through belief in the resurrection, Christ became a "man-made God." Jesus showed the possibilities of human nature and changed humanity's attitude toward God, and thus established the notion of God's kingdom as a better mental and social relationship among people. Sin is a disorder; faith is obedience to Jesus Christ and the courage to improve the world despite many obstacles. A state in which people live for the values taught by Jesus is the goal. Other than as symbols, the sacraments are not necessary. The true sacrament is manifested when a society decides to dedicate all its resources (time, talents, and material goods) to spreading Christ's kingdom.

Between 1869 and the outbreak of World War II, six Temple Society settlements flourished in Palestine. Their official end came in 1948, when the state of Israel was founded. More than 300 Templers were sent to Australia for internment during World War II. Along with Templer migrants from elsewhere (mainly Germany), they founded the Temple Society of Australia in 1950. This group is now the largest Templer group in the world. During the 1860s, German immigrants to Russia also founded Templer communities. With the fall of the Iron Curtain, individual descendants of these Templers are finding their way back to the Templer community that has existed around Stuttgart, Germany, since 1861. German immigrants to the United States also founded communities, and formal organization in North America occurred as early as 1866. By 1890 there were four U.S. congregations. This number had dwindled by 1916 to two congregations, which survived into the 1970s. Earlier, American Templers had been formally advised to join the Unitarians, as World War II made communications among Germans difficult. Today, there are only individual, and not necessarily native-born, Templers left in the United States.

Membership: In 2002 the society reported more than 1,500 members, of whom approximately 450 are in Germany. As of 2008, Australia had the largest and most active group of Templers.

Sources:

Temple Society. www.templers.org.

United Society of Believers in Christ's Second Appearing (Shakers)
Current address not obtained for this edition.

Mother Ann Lee (1736–1787) was a psychic-visionary who gathered a group of followers around her while still in her native England. Included in her teaching was a deep sense of the sinfulness of humanity. After the deaths of her four children in infancy, she began to proclaim the indecency of the act of sexual union. In Manchester, England, in 1747 Lee met the preacher James Wardley and his wife, who also were considered visionaries. Out of this relationship grew a following, which adopted the name United Society of Believers in Christ's Second Appearing, but are more popularly called Shakers.

In the 1750s Mother Ann Lee became associated with and gradually assumed leadership of a group of Quakers who had been influenced by the visionary French Prophets. Her leadership led to the group's acceptance of celibacy as a sign of following Christ. Members of the group were known to experience religious ecstasy in the form of ritualized communal dance. Observers at the time derisively referred to them as "shaking Quakers," from which the name *Shakers* derives. Due to persecution in England, the group sailed for the English colonies in America in 1774. But because of their pacifism, the Shakers became the object of scorn during the American Revolutionary War. The group's beliefs in racial and gender equality and their assertion that God possessed both masculine and feminine traits also earned them brutal persecution in the colonies and landed Lee in jail on several occasions.

After the Revolution, the Shakers began to prosper, especially under the leadership of Joseph Meacham (1742–1796), who came to power in 1787 following Ann's death in 1784. The Shakers established communities across the newly formed United States. At the height of their development around 1830, they had 19 communities stretching from southern Kentucky to Maine, with 6,000 resident members. Their books were widely circulated. Eventually, they earned a reputation for producing finely wrought crafts, furniture, and architecture, which are still widely admired today. Although the Shakers often are associated in the public mind with the Amish, they are not opposed on principle to modern technology.

Shaker theology centers on the belief that in the coming of Ann Lee, Christ appeared. They accept the common millennialist use of the 2,300-days prophecy (Daniel 8:14), which they date to 533 B.C.E.; by adding 2,300 years to 533 B.C.E., they arrive at 1747, the year Ann Lee first met Wardley.

The United Society has become an important aspect of American history, and one of its abandoned communities, at Pleasant Hill, Kentucky, is being reconstructed. Museums exist in Shaker churches in South Union, Kentucky, and Old Chatham, New York. The community at New Lebanon, New York, was sold to the Sufi Order headed by Pir Vilayat Khan.

Membership: In June 1988, Gertrude Soule, one of the eight remaining members of the United Society of Believers, died at the age of 93. In 1990 Bertha Lindsay, the last of the Shaker eldresses, died. As of 2006, four members remained at Sabbathday Lake, Maine. In 2001 the group reached an agreement with the nonprofit Trust for Public Land to ensure that the Shaker land in Maine can never be bought and used for commercial purposes.

Sources:

Andrews, Edward Deming. *The Gift to Be Simple*. New York: Dover, 1962.

Barker, R. Mildred. *Poems and Prayers*. Sabbathday Lake, ME: Shaker Press, 1983.

———. *The Sabbathday Lake Shaker*. Sabbathday Lake, ME: Shaker Press, 1978.

Chase, Stacey. "The Last Ones Standing." Boston.com, July 23, 2006. www.boston.com/news/globe/magazine/articles/2006/07/23/the_last_ones_standing/?page=full.

Desroche, Henri. *The American Shakers*. Amherst: University of Massachusetts Press, 1971.

Faber, Doris. *The Perfect Life*. New York: Farrar, Straus, and Giroux, 1974.

❈ Communal–After 1960

Aquarian Research Foundation
5620 Morton St., Philadelphia, PA 19144

The Aquarian Research Foundation, an outgrowth of the work and vision of Arthur Rosenblum, combines Christian communalism and intuitive insights with a scientific approach to the future of the world. Rosenblum formed the foundation in 1969 as an outgrowth of 20 years of communal living with the Hutterian Brethren (Society of Brothers) and other groups. The goal of the foundation's research is to bring a new age of love to the planet and thus avoid chaos as present systems decline.

In order for research, which includes communal living, to be pursued, the total commitment of the individual members is required. The foundation's intimate communal structure allows members to help each other with personal problems. Drugs and smoking are excluded.

According to Rosenblum, God is the universe. Just as matter may be seen as concentrated energy, so energy may be seen as concentrated spirit (love). God and the universe consist of love, energy, and matter, and are the same entity. The "kingdom of God" is the rulership of love.

As an expression of the foundation's commitment, in 1986 Rosenblum traveled to Moscow, where he met with Georgi Arbatov, a high-level Soviet adviser on American affairs. The object of the meeting was to seek new ways of ending the arms race. As a result of the meeting, Rosenblum sponsored a tour by Soviet researcher Peter Gladkov, a scholar of American contemporary communal societies. It was Rosenblum's opinion that communal societies demonstrate the basis for a new social order, in which today's social problems could be solved through a loving approach. Rosenblum believed that most social problems are caused by unhappiness resulting from people's lack of loving relationships with others. In 2002 Rosenblum died in an automobile accident at the age of 74.

Membership: Not reported.

Remarks: One long-term project pursued by the foundation has been the exploration of methods of natural birth control. The major focus has been on the research of Dr. Eugen Jonas of Czechoslovakia, who studied the relation between female fertility and astrological cycles. The foundation has sought to update Jonas's research, and in a book currently in its sixth edition, has reported the experiences of women using Jonas's method.

Sources:

Rosenblum, Art. *Aquarian Age or Civil War?* Philadelphia, PA: Aquarian Research Foundation, 1970.

————. *The Natural Birth Control Book*. Philadelphia, PA: Aquarian Research Foundation, 1984.

————. *Unpopular Science*. Philadelphia, PA: Running Press, 1974.

Bride of Christ Church
Current address not obtained for this edition.

The Bride of Christ Church was established in 1980 in Las Vegas, Nevada, following the ordination of Thomas Clyde Smith Jr. by Dr. G. J. Soriano, founder of the Faith Restoration Center, a Philippine Islands Christian organization. According to Smith, in 1965 he was convicted of molesting his nine-year-old daughter. Following his jail sentence, he spent a year in a mental hospital. While there he had a conversion experience and became a Christian. He later decided to become a minister and start a church. Smith advocated a form of what he termed *Christian socialism*, an approach that included communal living. After four years in Nevada, he moved with the members of the church to rural Oregon.

The Bride of Christ Church existed quietly until 1987, when there was an attempt to kidnap and deprogram a church member. The attempt was foiled when the deprogrammers were caught breaking into a property at the church headquarters and arrested. A year later, Smith invited Lawrence Singleton to join the group on its farm near Azalea. Singleton had been convicted in California for a particularly heinous crime—raping a 15-year-old girl and severing both her arms. Smith said he identified with Singleton, who reportedly had repented for his crime and become religious during his years in prison. However, public outrage prevented Singleton's moving in with the church.

The church is organized communally. Men work in two group-owned businesses to support the members. Women work at the center in Azalea.

Membership: Not reported.

Sources:

Tims, Dana. "Azalea Sect Riles Region." *Oregonian*, April 7, 1988.

Christ's Church of the Golden Rule
Ridgewood Ranch, 16200 N Hwy. 201, Willits, CA 95490

Christ's Church of the Golden Rule emerged in 1944 following conversations among a group of Christian men and women who shared a concern about existing religious and economic practices and their perceived failure to meet the spiritual and material needs of humanity. These conversations were held in the context of the Bible and the teachings of Jesus Christ, especially the Golden Rule and Jesus' words, "Seek ye first the kingdom of God and his righteousness [right-use-ness] and all these things will be added unto you" (Matthew 6:33). The group concluded that these directions had not, to their knowledge, been followed since the days of the early Christian church described in Acts 2:44 and Acts 4:32. They agreed that they should respond to Jesus' words and actually attempt to live his teachings and thus demonstrate to their contemporaries whether living such principles would overcome poverty, war, and insecurity, and in the process make possible a worldwide brotherhood of humanity.

They investigated ways in which to structure their ideals and concluded that the formation of a church was the best way both to modify their understanding in a community and meet the necessary legal requirements that would allow them the greatest freedom of action. They formed Christ's Church of the Golden Rule in January 1944.

The church's creed is the Golden Rule, "Therefore all things whatsoever ye would that men should do to you, do ye even so to them" (Matthew 7:12). The church understands the Rule as working in one direction; it never applies to the manner in which others treat you, but always the way you treat others. The church's goal is stated in its vision: "A World free from want, with liberty and justice for all, and with understanding love toward God and one another. This day's work is dedicated to the end that we may prove that it is more blessed to give than to receive, and that it is true that giving does not impoverish nor does withholding enrich."

The teachings of the church are summarized in its brief declaration of faith. It affirms belief in the one true God, conceived as Father-Mother; Jesus of Nazareth who came to reveal God to humankind and who was possessed of the eternal Christ (Truth); the authority of the Holy Bible; salvation by repentance and regeneration through the Truth, the mind of God that is Jesus Christ; and the essence of true religion as loving God. It also teaches that equality in economic affairs is the only foundation on which to build a humane world.

In 1944 and 1945 some 850 people signed up as founding members of the church and gave up their personal wealth, family, and social ties, and moved onto the church's property. At the same time, 100 pieces of property, primarily along the West Coast, were donated and a few additional pieces purchased for church use. Resident training centers were established on these properties.

By 1945 the church's property was valued at approximately $3 million. That same year some of the founding members decided that they did not wish to remain church members. They withdrew and began legal proceedings to retrieve property they had donated. California's attorney general joined that effort and moved to place the church into a receivership. The church responded by filing voluntary bankruptcy proceedings in federal court. The costly legal battle, which finally went in favor of the church, lasted for six years. Not only did many members leave, but much of the church's property was sold during this period and the value of the church's holdings was reduced to several hundred thousand dollars.

In 1951 the church, in effect, had to rebuild the working model with which they had begun. In 1953 the church's seminary in San Francisco, an important training center, was sold and property purchased near Bolinas, California. In the early 1960s that property was included in a government plan to create the Point Reyes National Seashore Park.

In 1962 the church purchased the 16,00-acre Ridgewood Ranch in Mendocino County. Over the next few years the church's other centers, including those in Colorado and Wyoming, were closed and consolidated at the ranch. During the next two decades the property was improved to house up to 100 residents. The church erected private housing for students, a chapel–dining room complex, a social lounge, a food processing unit, business and accounting office, a publications department, school building, and library. Facilities are available to welcome people making inquiry about church membership and other visitors.

The Church of the Golden Rule was legally recognized as a church in 1964. It is directed by an advisory board of elders. All resident members of the church live communally. No property or income can inure to any individual and all is used for the benefit of the church. No outside donations are solicited, though gifts are accepted for the spread of the church's message, especially through its publications. The church operates a variety of business enterprises that have allowed the community to be largely self-supporting. Members of the church are active in the larger community. The church's facilities are available to different religious, cultural, and educational groups.

Membership: In 2002 the church reported approximately 65 members, most of whom reside at the ranch in Willits. Other adherents subscribe to the church's teachings but reside elsewhere.

Remarks: The church has often been associated with a previously existing movement, Mankind United. Leaders of the church strongly deny any such connection beyond the bare fact that some of the founding members had been associated with that movement and the two organizations happen to share some concerns for the economic injustice present in society. However, the church was founded independently of that movement and has through its 50 years of existence demonstrated its adherence to its religious teachings.

Sources:

The Essence of Our Teachings. Willits, CA: Christ's Church of the Golden Rule, 1971.

Our Golden Rule Crusade. 2 vols. Willits, CA: Christ's Church of the Golden Rule, 1963.

Our Golden Rule Way of Life. Willits, CA: Christ's Church of the Golden Rule, 1967.

Christ's Household of Faith

355 Marshall Ave., St. Paul, MN 55102-1898

Christ's Household of Faith is a large urban Christian communal group that dates to 1965, the year in which the group's founder and pastor, Donald Alsbury, was suspended from the ministry of the Lutheran Church-Missouri Synod. Alsbury had been the pastor of a small church serving the communities of Giese and McGrath, Minnesota. A conflict arose in the church over a woman who was seeking membership in the church. Some of the lay people, citing her bad reputation, wanted Alsbury to condemn her from the pulpit. Alsbury said the congregation should encourage her to repent and join the congregation. This conflict became the occasion for other issues to emerge. Following Alsbury's suspension, the majority of the congregation left the synod and established worship services at Mora, Minnesota. In 1970 the congregation was joined by a group of approximately 75 people who had moved to Minnesota from St. Helen's, Oregon, under the leadership of Vernon Harms, an old friend and colleague of Alsbury's.

The Harms group joined the older group as it was in the midst of an intensive period of Bible study and self-reflection characterized by the members' attempt to share all of their past sins and to begin to divest themselves of their material goods in expectation of Christ's Second Coming. At one point in 1970, the business at which many of the group members were employed burned down, and the group left Mora and resettled in St. Paul, Minnesota. Members found temporary lodging in houses in one of the poorer sections of the city. They survived by developing a maintenance repair business, by living off of the abundance of a throwaway culture, and by living frugally. In 1976 they were able to purchase an abandoned convent, which became the group's new home. They started a school for their children, and have prospered.

Leadership in the community is invested in Alsbury, Harms, and a group of elders. A finance committee makes key business decisions. All money earned from outside the community (in the community-managed business) is put into a common pool from which major purchases are made. Each member receives a monthly allowance. A farm in a nearby rural community is used for the production of food and provides both employment and a learning experience for the youth during the summer. There is a strong emphasis on the nuclear family as a working unit within the community as a whole. Sunday is a day of worship and fellowship, during which the entire community is together.

Membership: In 1995 the group had approximately 500 members, of whom 300 were minors.

Church of Jesus Christ at Armageddon (The Love Israel Family)

Current address not obtained for this edition.

The Church of Jesus Christ at Armageddon was founded by Love Israel—a former television salesman named Paul Erdman—in 1968. According to its charter, it was established "to fulfill the New Testament as revealed to Love Israel in the form of visions, dreams, and revelations received by members of the Church. The members of the Church have all had heavenly visions without which we would never understand our purpose on this earth or our relationship with each other." The name of the church is based on Revelation 16:16, in which Armageddon is mentioned as the gathering place of the end-time. The members of the church refer to themselves as the Love Family, drawn together out of the world and recognizable by their love for one another. They believe that their relationships are eternal, and that

through their love and commitment to one another, they create the opportunity for Christ to express his personality in them.

New members contribute all their possessions upon joining and begin a new life with a new name. Because Israel is the name of God's people, Israel is the surname of all members of the church. A biblical name or a "virtue" name such as "Abishai" or "Honesty" is assumed as a first name and former names are abandoned. Although they live in traditional family units or expanded households, members consider themselves married to one another in the universal marriage of Jesus Christ and are not bound by "worldly traditions of matrimony." The father/mother is respected as the "head" of each household and represents his/her household in the family government. The affairs of the larger family are governed through close communication and frequent informal meetings.

The church sees itself as being the beneficiary of the Old Testament promises to Israel and is committed to practicing the beliefs and lifestyle of the New Testament as created by Jesus Christ. Rules are replaced by love, agreement, moderation, and common sense. Eating and drinking are considered sacramental, with the understanding that all food and drink are the body and blood of Jesus Christ. Water baptism represents the opportunity to be freed from the past and become a new personality with an eternal place within the Body of Christ.

During the 1970s the church enjoyed steady growth, reaching a residential population of around 300 members by 1983. Members' unorthodox appearance and lifestyle made them the object of considerable controversy and a target for anti-cultists and deprogrammers. For a short while, church members participated as "observers" in the Church Council of Greater Seattle. The church's headquarters was a handmade mansion on Seattle's Queen Anne Hill, surrounded by a compact "village" of residences, gardens, and shops. Members maintained a 24-hour inn, where guests were freely housed and fed, and from which food from their farms and fishing boat were distributed to needy neighbors. They operated numerous small businesses and maintained satellite communities in several places throughout Washington, Alaska, and Hawaii.

In 1983 an internal power struggle and a lawsuit by a former member severely disrupted the church community, and most of the group's 350 members chose to leave. The remaining members relocated to a 300-acre ranch near Arlington, Washington; Love Israel moved to California, where he worked as a banker. When he returned to Seattle, the ranch became the organization's new headquarters and provided a cultural center for those members who remained dispersed throughout the region.

The church defines its continuing ministry as follows:

> Our purpose is to reform our relationships and our patterns of relating until they conform to the truth of our Oneness in Jesus Christ. We understand that this is how we can best help fulfill Christ's purpose on this earth. The fruits of our labors are the comfort, the happiness, and the harmony which we achieve with one another in our daily lives together. WHEN THE SEERS COME TOGETHER, THEN THE WATCHERS WILL SEE.

Membership: In 2002, the group reported approximately 100 members. Membership was unknown as of 2008.

Remarks: In 2003 Love Israel, who had been rumored to have lavishly spent the financial assets members had contributed to the group, filed for Chapter 11 bankruptcy. The organization's numerous businesses and cottage industries failed, and leaders turned more and more to supporting the Family on credit. Other controversies—including many zoning and land-use violations as well as allegations of drug use, sexual misconduct, and cult behavior—had plagued the group for years. In the bankruptcy settlement, Israel was able to reclaim land he owned in Stevens County, Washington; he sold the Arlington ranch to Union for Reform Judaism, which planned to use the site as a children's summer camp. As of 2008 the remaining members of the Love Israel Family were still together and had recently established an online presence with their Web site.

Sources:

Love Israel Family. www.loveisraelfamily.com.

Allen, Steve. *Beloved Son*. Indianapolis, IN: Bobbs-Merrill Company, 1982.

Israel, Love. *Love*. Seattle, WA: Church of Armageddon, 1971.

Kershaw, Sarah. "Commune to Close, after Years of Strife and Striving." *New York Times*, December 25, 2003.

Langston, Jennifer. "Bankruptcy May Be Love Israel Family's Salvation." seattlepi.com, March 1, 2003. seattlepi.nwsource.com/local/110637_loveisrael01.shtml.

Church of the Saviour

2025 Massachusetts Ave. NW, Washington, DC 20036

The Church of the Saviour was initially formed in the early 1940s in Washington, D.C., by a group of nine people headed by Gordon and Mary Cosby, former Baptists. It was incorporated as a church in 1947. The vision of the new ministry was one of ecumenicity and evangelism, and total commitment of life and resources to Christ. The communal existence was seen as representative of men and women reconciled and reconciling with humanity. The result has been a community dedicated both to the nurture of the inner spiritual life and to the outward life of service.

The church has identified its mission as having four purposes: to serve Christ's church throughout the world, alleviate the suffering of the poor and oppressed, address the spiritual and physical needs of the stranger in our midst, and to build a common, egalitarian life. To carry out its missions, the Church of the Saviour in 1994 became a "scattered community" of eight small faith communities, each with its own distinct "vision, missions, and structures"; in 2008 two more groups were added, for a total of 10. The members of each group devote themselves to their group's stated purpose while maintaining close ties with the larger church through missionary activity and participation in the church's School of Christian Living. Once a year members meditate on their purpose and relationship to the larger group and then have the opportunity to either renew or withdraw from their covenant with the church. Each faith community holds its own worship services throughout the week, and a Sunday morning service is open to all Church of the Saviour members.

In 2008 six Church of the Saviour faith communities, still with the active participation of the Cosbys, were exploring new avenues to becoming the "authentic church." These communities were experimenting with the creation of small groups of individuals with commonly perceived social differences—in wealth, class, gender, race, sexual orientation, and so on—to break down barriers and develop ways to heal.

Church of the Saviour runs numerous missions in Washington, D.C., that address various social welfare issues, including low-income medical clinics, treatment and housing centers for addiction and AIDS patients, early child development centers, community development, arts programs for children, job placement services, affordable housing, transitional housing for abused women and children, and centers for senior citizens. An additional program is called Inward/Outward, which is designed to enrich members' spiritual and activist journeys.

Membership: In 2008 the church reported nine churches, all in the Washington, D.C., area. In 1992 the church reported 165 full members and 600 in its worship community.

Educational Facilities:

Servant Leadership School at the Festival Center, Washington, D.C.

School of Christian Living, Washington, D.C.

Periodicals: *The Diaspora*. 9301-B Westcott Pl., Rockville, MD 20850. www.thediaspora.org.

Sources:

Inward/Outward: A Project of the Church of the Saviour. www.inwardoutward.org/.

Cosby, Gordon. *Handbook for Mission Groups*. Washington, DC: Potter's House, 1973.

O'Connor, Elizabeth. *Call to Commitment*. New York: Harper & Row, 1963.

———. *Cry Pain, Cry Hope*. Waco, TX: Word Books, 1987.

———. *Eighth Day of Creation*. Waco, TX: Word Books, 1971.

———. *Journey Inward, Journey Outward*. New York: Harper & Row, 1968.

———. *The New Community*. New York: Harper & Row, 1976.

The Colony

Burnt Ranch, CA 95527

The Colony was begun August 18, 1940, by its founder, Brother John Korenchan (1886–1982), and eighteen members who settled on the Trinity River near Hawkins Bar, California. Brother John, who had been raised as a Catholic, had his spiritual awakening in 1912, when, after five days of fasting and prayer, he was made to feel as a child without fault or law-breaking against the Creator. He wandered through the Siskiyou and Trinity Counties for years, and spent a few months in jail for his pacifism during World War I. As World War II began, he gathered a group of followers in Seattle. This group was finally led to California. Over the years, the group turned the area into a 16-acre farm. After his death, Brother John was succeeded by Sister Agnes Vanderhoof, the only surviving member of the original group.

There are no rules, not even grace at meals. Moderation, not abstinence, is the goal. Brother John taught that religion is meaningless unless it comes from within and is lived. Emphasis is placed on the guidance of the Power. The Power guided members to the Colony, brings in new members as it will, and discerns who is ready for the Truth, Christ.

Membership: In 1988 the Colony reported 13 residents, all of whom had lived there at least 12 years. Others come in regularly for group activities.

The Family International

2020 Pennsylvania Ave. NW, PMB 102, Washington, DC 20006-1846

Alternate Address: Family Information Desk, 27 Old Gloucester St., London WC1N 3XX England.

The Family International (previously known as the Children of God, the Family of Love, and the Family), an international network of Christian communes, was founded in 1968. The group, an offshoot of the Jesus movement, originated from the West Coast ministry of David Berg, a former Christian and Missionary Alliance minister. From 1953 to 1965 Berg had been associated with Fred Jordan's Soul Clinic, an independent ministry founded in 1944. Teen Challenge, a national youth ministry that had been established by Assemblies of God minister David Wilkerson, turned over to Berg's teenage children the use of the group's Christian coffeehouse in Huntington Beach, California, known as the Light Club.

The Light Club had ministered primarily to surfers and hippies, but it changed direction dramatically in 1969. Berg, agreeing with revelations received by other members that an earthquake was imminent, decided the club members should leave California. Berg and those who followed him split into three groups and crisscrossed North America for eight months, a journey the group compared to the exodus of the Hebrew children led by Moses. During this period the group acquired the name Children of God (COG) and Berg became known as Moses David.

In early 1970 the COG accepted the hospitality of the Soul Clinic, and Jordan gave them the use of the abandoned Soul Clinic ranch near Thurber, Texas. Shortly afterwards he also granted them the use of the Soul Clinic mission building in downtown Los Angeles, as well as a property he owned near Coachella, California. The membership of COG grew, adding converts encountered on the streets of various cities, many of whom were former drug users. Slowly, from the small group around Berg, a disciplined community emerged. By 1971 the COG had become a national organization. Over the next few years they became well known for their public witnessing activity that occasionally included apocalyptic warnings.

During the early 1970s opposition to the COG grew among the parents of youthful members (most were in their late teens and early twenties), many of whom had joined the group after knowing it only briefly and had left their former lives behind to serve as missionaries for the group. Some parents were opposed to Berg's teachings and communal practices and charged that COG was a destructive cult. The parents organized FREECOG (Free Our Children from the Children of God), the first contemporary cult awareness group. As pressure built against the COG in the United States and new mission opportunities opened in Europe through the mid-1970s, many members left the United States. Though some members remained in the United States, visible signs of their presence disappeared.

In 1976 Berg introduced a new ministry he had been testing to the now large, scattered group. He suggested that the female members of the groups (most then in their mid-20s) begin "flirty fishing"—that is, using their feminine charms to allure men and set up opportunities for witnessing God's love to others. Such activity could, and frequently did, lead the women to have sexual relationships with the men, the "fish."

In 1978 the organization went through the first of several radical organizational changes, the RNR (reorganization, nationalization, revolution). As the organization had grown and spread internationally, a strong hierarchical system had been put in place headed largely by Berg's own children and their spouses. Berg became aware of a variety of leadership abuses, including the imposition and embezzlement of unauthorized tithes. In 1978 he removed all of the leaders, and the organization moved into a period of organizational anarchy. Many members left or dropped their communal lifestyle. The name "Children of God" was abandoned, and the group became known as "the Family of Love," which was shortend a short time later to "the Family." The chaos of the RNR abated only in the spring of 1981 with the "Fellowship Revolution," when a semblance of order began to be restored. A new structure arose out of the reestablished communal homes: local area fellowships, district fellowships, greater area fellowships, and national fellowships. Shepherds were elected to serve at each level of administration.

During the RNR period the organizational chaos was accompanied by a liberalization of sexual mores and many adult members—especially those who continued to live in communal homes and in those cities with a concentration of members—had multiple sexual partners. After the Fellowship Revolution herpes spread through the group and sexual contacts were limited. Later, in 1987, the "flirty fishing" ministry was curtailed not only because of risk of disease but also because of the need to divert attention to the care of a growing number of children born to group members. Also at that time, leaders initiated a new outreach ministry, the "Daily Food," or DFing ministry. Its focus was on more thoroughly following up with those to whom Family members had witnessed in order to deepen their relationships with Jesus Christ.

BELIEFS. The Family developed out of the evangelical Protestantism of the Jesus People movement, but it differed from other Jesus People groups on three points. First, Father David, or Dad, as he was affectionately known in the movement, claimed that he had contacts with spirit entities, especially with one named Abrahim the Gypsy King. Other evangelicals condemned the group for practicing (or tolerating) spiritism. Second, the group identified Father David as the prophet of the end-time and associated him with the David referred to in Ezekiel 34 and 37, Hosea 3, and Jeremiah 30. Third, the COG advocated "forsaking all" and dropping out of the "system" in order to live a communal lifestyle dedicated to God's service, patterned after the lifestyle of the early church in the Bible's Book of Acts.

Through the 1970s Father David developed the concept of the Law of Love as the group's overarching ethical principle, based on Matt. 22:36–40. The Law of Love views love as the great commandment that overrides and frees individuals from the strictures of the Mosaic Law. The Law of Love was articulated as a means to undergird the practice of flirty fishing, which was seen as a sacrificial activity to bring people to the saving truth of the gospel, but also applied to all sexual relationships. Sexual contacts were condoned among consenting adults as long as they met the conditions of love (unselfishness) and did not fall into mere lust.

The developing doctrinal perspective was formally presented in "Our Statement of Faith" in 1992. The Family follows the evangelical Protestant consensus, believing in the Bible as the inspired Word of God, the Trinity, and salvation through Jesus Christ received by faith in him and receiving him into our hearts. Once saved, the believer will be kept by God forever. The Family is Pentecostal and believes in the baptism of the Holy Spirit as a baptism of love that empowers the believer. Speaking in tongues does not necessarily accompany the baptism, but baptized believers do manifest the gifts of the Spirit (such as healing, miracle working, prophecy, and speaking in tongues). Believers should also manifest the fruits of the spirit as described in Gal. 5:22–23 (love, joy, peace, long suffering, gentleness, goodness, faith, meekness, and temperance). The Family believes in a literal creation (as depicted in the Book of Genesis), angels, Satan, divine healing, and the coming end of the world. They are opposed to abortion.

Family members gather for worship daily in the morning and often in the evening. Periodically, days are set aside for prayer and self-examination. The ordinance of the Lord's Supper is held regularly. A special candlelight service often held on New Year's Eve is the most liturgical of the Family's worship life.

Full-time Family members known as Family disciples live communally, and with very few exceptions do not hold secular jobs. Most children are schooled at the communal homes. Evangelism is seen as the members' primary calling and vocation. Thus their daily life is spent in witnessing to their faith and in "provisioning"—gathering resources (food, clothing, shelter, finances, etc.) to support the evangelical ministry. The Family has developed a comprehensive program for converts known as the "12 Foundation Stones" that introduces them to the basic tenets of Christianity, as well as to fundamental Family beliefs as expressed in the Family's Statement of Faith.

ORGANIZATION. The Family has a number of levels of membership that represent different membership requirements and degrees of commitment. The FD (Family disciple) level of membership is built around communal homes usually comprising several families and a few unmarried adults. Families tend to be large, and couples with 10 or more children are not unusual. Each home with children houses a home school. It is led by a team of at least three shepherds and three managers elected by the adult and older teen members. An international leadership structure of regional shepherds provides guidance and counsel; assists in formulating, interpreting, and enacting policy; and helps homes with problems they cannot solve by themselves.

In 1994 the Family was in transition. Late that year Berg died at the age of 75 and was succeeded by his wife Maria, who had been the active administrative head for some years. The announcement of his death to the larger world was soon followed by the announcements of significant changes in the group's organization. In February 1995 the Family adopted a new constitution, the "Love Charter," declared to be Berg's parting gift to the group. It outlined the basic rights and responsibilities of members as well as the beliefs and behavior standards to which members were expected to adhere. Soon thereafter, Maria announced her marriage to Peter Amsterdam, who had been an important assistant to Berg and Maria for many years. Peter took on the role of co-spiritual and -administrative leader to the Family.

The Love Charter takes great pains to spell out not only the responsibilities, but also the rights of individual members. They include the rights of self-determination, personal initiative, development of gifts and talents, choice of place of residence, and choice of medical care. All adult members may vote on matters before their home and be considered for leadership positions. Parents are assigned responsibilities for the care of their children, and the home ensures that parents have the time and resources to care for their children properly. One day per week is usually set aside specifically for parents to spend in a relaxed atmosphere with their children. Each home takes collective responsibility for the education through the secondary-school level of all of the minors living in the home.

Membership: In November 2007 the Family reported 7,346 Family Discipleship and Missionary members worldwide, of which approximately 2,500 are children and youths. There are 626 Family communities in more than 85 countries. In the United States family homes are found in suburban Los Angeles, San Diego, Houston, and Detroit. In addition to the 7,000 full-time members, there are some

2,000 members who do not reside in Family homes, though many did at one time. These members, known as fellow members, tithe to support the Family's work and receive the Family's literature. The Family also has some 4,500 nontithing members who receive Family literature and contribute to mission work in some way. The total membership of the Family is 13,919.

Periodicals: *The Good News*. • *Family Specials News Magazine!* • *Link*. • *The END* (*Endtime News Digest*). • *Activated!*

Remarks: Over the years, as many as 40,000 people have been live-in members of the Family. Beginning in the early 1970s a small number of ex-members vocally opposed the organization. Following the introduction of flirty fishing and the disbanding of the leadership in 1978, a more intense group of former members, including Deborah Davis, the eldest daughter of David Berg, organized into a group, No Longer Children, that focused attacks on the Family. After several years No Longer Children discontinued their counter-Family initiatives, but new coalitions of former members continue to oppose the Family International and its programs. A movement for reconciliation begun in the 1990s seeks to resolve the remaining issues between the Family and its disaffected members.

While the thrust of the attacks upon the Family has generally followed standard cult awareness rhetoric, in the 1990s attacks concentrated on accusations of child abuse. Critics of the Family charged it with institutionalizing child abuse during the period immediately following the RNR in the late 1970s and early 1980s. The Family's leadership responded by acknowledging that prior to the adoption of their child-protection policies in 1986, cases of adult-minor sexual contact occurred. These cases were addressed in the mid-1980s when the leadership instituted strong rules barring any such activity. In the wake of these accusations, government child-protection service agencies moved against the Family in Australia, Argentina, Spain, France, and England in the early 1990s. A number of judicial proceedings were initiated, the most notable being one in the British family court. All of the proceedings ended in the Family's favor, although in the 1995 British case Justice Ward issued a detailed report recounting past offenses for which he held the Family collectively and David Berg individually responsible.

As a byproduct of the legal proceedings, more than 600 children from the Family were examined by either government-appointed or private physicians and therapists, and charges of ongoing child abuse proved to be unfounded. Since the early 1990s there have been no cases of child abuse among the youth and children residing in Family communities. Regarding the abuse that occurred in the 1980s, the Family issued apologies to former members beginning in the 1990s. The most recent apology was published in 2007.

Sources:

The Family International. www.thefamilyinternational.org.

Chancellor, James D. *Life in the Family: An Oral History of the Children of God*. Syracuse, NY: Syracuse University Press, 2000.

David, Moses (David Berg). *The Basic Mo Letters*. Hong Kong: Gold Lion Publishers, 1976.

Bainbridge, William S. *The Endtime Family—The Children of God*. Albany: State University of New York Press, 2002.

The Love Charter. Zurich, Switzerland: The Family, 1998.

Melton, J. Gordon. *The Family/The Children of God*. Salt Lake City, UT: Signature Books, 2004.

"Mo" (David Berg). *The True Story of Moses and the Children of God*. N.p.: Children of God, 1972.

The Farm

100 The Farm, Summertown, TN 38483

The Farm grew out of weekly Monday-evening teaching sessions held during the 1960s and 1970s in San Francisco, California. These meetings were led by San Francisco State University graduate student Stephen Gaskin (b. 1935), at that time known simply as Stephen. He soon became a well-known spiritual philosopher and published two books, *Caravan* (1972) and *Monday Night Class* (1974). Attendance at the Monday class increased from a handful to more than 1,000. In October 1970, about 250 of the class in 50 converted school buses and vans joined Stephen on a cross-country tour, dubbed "Caravan." In four months, the Caravan criss-crossed the country, gathering additional converts as it went. At the end of the tour, about 350 from the Caravan and the class decided to set up a communal religious community with Stephen and settled on 1,000 acres near Summertown, Tennessee.

During the 1970s, 10 other independent communities (including one in Canada) formed around Stephen's teachings. Though administratively autonomous, they considered themselves tied to the Farm. All these associated communities have disbanded.

From 1971 to 1983, the Farm had a traditional communal economy like the Shakers or Hutterites. Everyone joining the community gave everything they owned to the common treasury and anything developed or received by any member belonged to the whole group. Trying to do too much with too little for too long brought about a severe financial crisis. In October 1983, the Farm reorganized its communal economy. In addition to allowing individuals to own property, members were made responsible for providing for their own living expenses and contributing to the support of the community, in part by helping to pay off a large debt. Because of austerity measures instituted after 1981, the inability of many members to earn a living in one of the poorest areas in Tennessee, and other contributing factors, the population decreased from its peak of about 1,400 in 1980.

The philosophy of the Farm has always been based on the principles of mutual respect, nonviolence, environmental sustainability, and a low-consumption lifestyle. In the later 1990s these principles evolved into a more focused goal, and the Farm became involved in the burgeoning ecovillage movement. In the early 2000s ecovillages had begun to spring up around the world, in both rural and urban areas, incorporating many of the same ideas about environmentalism upon which the Farm was founded. Also called *green cities*, these communities rely on alternative energy sources, sustainable agriculture (also known as *permaculture*), ecological design and building, and a semi-communitarian way of living—all hallmarks of the lifestyle of the Farm, which is an active member of the Global Ecovillage Network.

Other nonprofit Farm-based groups include Plenty International, founded by the Farm in 1974. Believing that the earth is capable of feeding and sustaining all life, Plenty aims to provide food and health self-sufficiency for all. The multiplication of food protein by vegetarianism is a basic principle of Plenty's approach, along with the group's support of the rights of women, indigenous peoples, children, and the elderly. It is recognized as a United Nations nongovernmental agency.

The Farm also is a nondenominational church of people who consider themselves "free thinkers" because they discuss religion and philosophy in terms that do not exclude any possibilities. People come to the Farm from a variety of religious traditions and disciplines and find those views treated with honor and respect. In keeping with their deep reverence for life, the members are pacifists and conscientious objectors, and most are vegetarians. An emphasis on natural healing led to participation in a national revival of midwifery. Stephen's wife, Ina May Gaskin, editor of *The Birth Gazette*, has become a prominent author and advocate of the practice.

The Book Publishing Company, one of the first businesses on the Farm, publishes vegetarian and vegan cookbooks, Native American books, and books on the environment, gardening, and lifestyle issues. Other businesses built by Farm members include Total Video, SE International, and the Farm Building Co. Most residents work with one of the Farm's business.

Membership: In 2008 there were approximately 150 residents at the Farm.

Periodicals: *The Birth Gazette.* Available from 42 The Farm, Summertown, TN 38483. • *Plenty News.* Available from PO Box 394, Summertown, TN 38483. • *Natural Rights.* Available from PO Box 90, Summertown, TN 38483. • *ENNA, the Journal of the Ecovillage Network of North America.* Available from PO Box 90, Summertown, TN 38483.

Sources:

The Farm. www.thefarm.org.

The Farm. www.thefarmcommunity.com.

Gaskin, Ina May. *Spiritual Midwifery.* Summertown, TN: Book Publishing Company, 1978.

Gaskin, Stephen. *The Caravan.* New York: Random House, 1972.

———. *Monday Night Class.* San Francisco: Book Publishing Company, [1974].

———. *Rendered Infamous.* Summertown, TN: Book Publishing Company, 1981.

———. *Volume One.* Summertown, TN: Book Publishing Company, 1975.

Popenoe, Cris, and Oliver Popenoe. *Seeds of Tomorrow.* San Francisco: Harper & Row, 1984.

The Finders

Current address not obtained for this edition.

The Finders is a communal group founded in the late 1960s by George Marion Pettie, the teacher of an eclectic religious philosophy that combines elements of the human potentials movement, Eastern religion (especially Taoism), and New Age thought. The Washington, D.C.–based group was thrust into public awareness when several members were arrested in Tallahassee, Florida. The arrests followed anonymous calls to the police after the members, two men and six children, were seen in a Tallahassee park. As later reported, the children were described as unwashed and covered with insect bites. A short time later a number of newspaper articles appeared describing the men as possible members of an international child pornography ring or a satanic cult. One popular theory held that the Finders were a front for a secret CIA kidnapping program.

Pettie's followers, mostly young adults, established their community in a residential area of the District of Columbia and engaged in an intense interactive lifestyle aimed at shedding delusions and inhibitions. Integral to the group's program was the use of fantasy role-playing games. Along the way, around 1980, the group decided to create a new generation of tough and strong children who would be raised on a model developed from the group's knowledge of the Indians of the plains. Each child would be raised by the group as a whole rather than by his or her biological parents.

After an investigation that lasted some six weeks, all charges against the two men arrested in Florida were dropped, there being no evidence of wrongdoing. Since that time, the group has assumed a low profile and its present status is unknown.

Membership: Not reported.

Sources:

Mintz, John, and Marc Fisher. "Ex-Finders Tell of Games, Complex Beliefs." *Washington Post,* February 8, 1987.

Jesus People USA

920 W Wilson Ave., Chicago, IL 60640

HISTORY. Jesus People USA is one of several groups that grew out of the Jesus People revival of the early 1970s. It is also among the few that have retained the communal lifestyle so prominent in the movement's early years. The group began in 1972 as an itinerant evangelistic outreach of a parent body informally known as the Milwaukee Jesus People. The Milwaukee Jesus People originated with six people in February 1971, under the leadership of Jim Palosaari. By 1972 it had grown to about 150 to 200 members, with three pastors, and had begun to publish *Street*

Level, an early Jesus People paper. Most of the followers lived communally. In April 1972, Palosaari and 30 core members of the Milwaukee Jesus People went to Europe with a Jesus rock band, The Sheep.

In June 1972, Pastor John Herrin left with a team of 30 members, traveling south and east across the United States in a caravan of three cars and a reconverted school bus (hence the "USA" part of the name). While they were on the road, they issued a Jesus paper, *Cornerstone,* and augmented their evangelistic endeavor with a Jesus rock band, Resurrection, and a street-theater drama troupe, the Holy Ghost Players. Meanwhile, in late 1972, the parent body in Milwaukee, Wisconsin, closed down in the wake of more than 60 members leaving to become the Jesus People Traveling Tent Revival Show, now known as Christ Is the Answer under the leadership of evangelist Bill Lowery. In the winter of 1972, Jesus People USA (now numbering about 40 followers) traveled through Illinois, Michigan, and Wisconsin, conducting rallies and revivals. In January 1973 they settled in Chicago, Illinois, where they have been headquartered ever since. In 1976 the group incorporated as Jesus People USA Full Gospel Ministries and was chartered as a church by the Full Gospel Church in Christ, a San Jose, California–based Pentecostal organization. Jesus People USA became affiliated with the Evangelical Covenant Church in 1990 and now exists as a community within the church's worldwide fellowship.

BELIEFS. Jesus People USA has adopted a 10-point statement of belief that emphasizes its agreement with conservative evangelical Protestantism. It asserts a belief in the authority of the Bible, the Trinity, the deity of Christ, humanity's need of salvation in Christ, the imminent Second Coming of Christ, and the work of the Holy Spirit manifest in the gifts of the Spirit. There is no specific reference to the Pentecostal baptism of the Holy Spirit or the necessity of speaking in tongues. There are two ordinances: baptism by immersion and the Lord's Supper.

ORGANIZATION. Leadership of the ministry is exercised by eight co-pastors (elders), each with equal authority, though the prime spokesperson for the group in recent years has been Glenn Kaiser. There are also deacons assigned to various community tasks, who act as spiritually mature leaders for newer members. The group lives communally, and members who live on-site generally do not own real property beyond a few personal items. Members work in a covenant relationship with the community as a whole. New members are admitted upon consent of the elders. The group sponsors a number of ministries, including its periodical, *Cornerstone,* which has emerged as a major evangelical voice; street evangelism; chaplaincy in adult and youth correctional houses; visitation in nursing homes; cult ministry; a food program; a crisis pregnancy center; and housing for the homeless. There are a number of musical groups, and an annual Cornerstone Festival, which draws up to 25,000 people. Support is provided through a number of businesses, such as construction, roofing, home repair, painting, and the sale of second-hand merchandise.

Membership: In 2008 Jesus People USA reported about 500 members, living in five residence buildings. There is also a farm in rural Missouri, and the festival site near Bushnell, Illinois.

Periodicals: *Cornerstone.*

Sources:

Jesus People USA. www.jpusa.org.

Kerista Commune

PO Box 410068, San Francisco, CA 94141-0068

The roots of the Kerista Commune can be traced to 1956, when a former businessman named John Presmont had a mystical revelatory experience, which initiated a search for meaningful religiousness and communal living. An attempt to restructure sexual attitudes and achieve sexual liberation was also a persistent element in what became a lengthy life quest. Several different efforts to organize a communal group were tried in New York and outside the United States in Central America and the Caribbean. Each effort failed, the victims of internal problems. In the beginning of 1971, at the end of the Flower Children era, Brother Jud, as Presmont came to be known, met a young woman named Eve Furchgott in San Francisco, California. Known as Even Eve, she was also a communalist, and with several others of like mind, the two founded the New Kerista Tribe. Eve and Jud discovered that they shared many common insights about communal life and became convinced that together they could create the next great world religion, the next new family structure, and the first viable utopian culture. They were soon joined by Wat, an old friend of Eve's, and Geo Logical, a psychiatric nurse. (All group members have taken new names.)

The distinctive characteristics of Kerista life were initiated early in the group's existence. Early members formed what they termed a *living school residence group*, later renamed a *superfamily*, then a *polyfidelitous closed group*, and, finally, a *best friend identity cluster*. Polyfidelity, the new form of family life practiced at Kerista, is seen as combining the best features of monogamous marriage and its extended companionate family unit with the idea of nonmonagamy. Kerista members were ideally members of a best friend identity cluster, an intimate family unit loyal to the members of their cluster (36 people: 18 women and 18 men), and related to all of them on an equal basis. Members of Kerista not yet part of a cluster were celibate. Members and clusters could be heterosexual, bisexual, or homosexual. All clusters were heterosexual, though there were attempts to form homosexual clusters. The oldest cluster was known as the Purple Submarine. In 1988, it had nine adult females and seven adult males. Some members of the cluster had been together for 17 years.

Sexuality in the community is placed in the context of loving mutual reciprocity. Group sex, sadomasochistic sexuality, bestiality, pedophilia, incest, and sexual exhibitionismwere not allowed. Overt public displays of physical attraction between members of the Kerista tribe were frowned upon.

The Keristians organized the Kerista Consciousness Church. They believed in a pantheistic divinity, a Totality, called Kyrallah. Kyrallah, It, is the one and only reality. Keristians believed in an ongoing evolution of the human species from blue-green algae to an animal-like nature, to a utopian paradise. In developing their theology, they invented a deity as a symbol of a megaintelligence field, to express the connection between the individual and the Totality. She is named Sister Kerista, and is pictured as a hip black woman with a pair of sneakers—an embodiment of women's liberation, poetic justice, and the four Keristan ideals of humor, equality, liberation, and love. Sister Kerista, in the Keristan mythology, was the daughter of the Black Madonna and Queen Mother Granny Nanny, the folk heroine of the Eastern Maroons of Jamaica.

Through the 1980s the Kerista Commune organized as a potential workers' paradise, based on horizontal democracy, worker self-management, and exacting kibbutz-style communal and equalitarian structures. Sexism, ageism, and racism were not tolerated. Each person was treated as an economic equal, and policy decision-making was by majority rule of the general assembly. Children were raised by the entire community and education was provided by their own school, called the EZ Learning Academy. Integral to the ongoing life of the community was the Gestalt-O-Rama process, which helped generate group commitment and motivation, solved conflicts, and enhanced self-esteem within the community. In both formal and informal settings, members were encouraged to foster a passionate sense of mission and to avoid and transcend negative behavior and attitudes, while cultivating and reinforcing positive traits. Members were encouraged to be verbal and personally accountable for feelings, thoughts, and behavior, and open to continual growth. The Gestalt-O-Rama Mental Health Maintenance Process revolved around 88 basic behavior standards. Community rap groups were also open to non-Keristans who wanted to participate in the growth process.

Several structures developed to further the community's goal of creating a scientific utopian society. These included the Club Utopia Growth Co-op, the Performing Arts Social Society (which published several of the group's periodicals), the Alliance for Creative Philanthropy, the New School of Utopian Psychology, and the Node Unity Alliance. Keristans hoped to create a transnational kibbutz movement whose members, like themselves, would reduce per capita costs via cooper-

ative living and use the surplus to fund philanthropic projects aimed at solving global problems. A project was initiated in Jamaica as a model for the future interaction of distant human communities along scientific utopian lines.

In November 1991 the Kerista Community as it had existed through the 1980s went through a major disruption when Even Eve and a group of members left Kerista. Their departure effectively disrupted the settled life, including the computer business, which they had enjoyed in San Francisco. Jud quickly moved to constitute the remaining members as the World Academy of Keristan Education, in order to continue to perpetuate the Keristan ideals. The small group reorganized as a theater arts repertory company and tried to build a larger network of support to spread the Keristan program for a prosperous future.

Membership: As of 2008, a Web site dedicated to eulogizing the group noted that the Kerista Commune officially ceased to exist in 1991.

Sources:

Kerista Commune. www.kerista.com.

Chapman, Paul, ed. *Clusters*. Greensboro, NC: Alternative, 1975.

Gruen, John. *The New Bohemia*. New York: Grosset & Dunlap, 1966.

O'Lee, Lil, and Even Eve, eds. *Polyfidelity*. San Francisco, CA: Performing Arts Social Society, 1984.

Lama Foundation

Box 240, San Cristobal, NM 87564

The Lama Foundation, located in the mountains near San Cristobal, New Mexico, serves as a coming-together point for many of the mystical, psychological, and Eastern religious perspectives that spread so widely throughout the counterculture in the 1960s. The foundation began when Steve Durkee, his wife, and three children settled on the 115-acre tract in the Sangre de Cristo Mountains in 1967. Eventually, a community of approximately 20 adults and their children gathered at the foundation. Adherents follow different paths, including yoga, Buddhism, Judaism, Sufism, Native American spiritualism, and Christianity. During the summer, the community enlarges to more than 30 people, and a summer retreat program is maintained. A wide variety of spiritual teachers spend time at the Lama Foundation.

Identified strongly with the Lama Foundation is Baba Ram Dass (formerly known as Richard Alpert). Through the foundation, he published *Be Here Now*, Lama's first publication venture. Sufism has also been a strong influence. Murshid Samuel L. Lewis is buried at Lama. The foundation also published *Towards the One* by Pir Vilayat Khan, head of the Sufi Order.

Foundation activities center on the main Dome, which includes within it a library, prayer room, and bathhouse. The residents gather daily for meditation and prayer sessions. Work is spread among the residents and includes construction and maintenance of the various buildings, the preparation of food, gardening, car maintenance, childcare, and working for Flag Mountain (which sells rubber stamps, books, and silk-screened Tibetan prayer flags).

Following a devastating forest fire in the mountains that destroyed most of its compound in 1996, the Lama Foundation developed a focus on ecological sustainability. As of 2008, rebuilding continues, and the group has committed itself to environmentalism as a component of achieving human spiritual awakening.

Membership: About 10 to 15 people live year-round at the Lama Foundation, and approximately 30 are in residence through the summer.

Sources:

Lama Foundation. www.lamafoundation.org.

Dass, Baba Ram. *Be Here Now*. San Cristobal, NM: Lama Foundation, 1971.

Gardner, Hugh. *The Children of Prosperity*. New York: St. Martin's Press, 1978.

Hedgepeth, William, and Dennis Stock. *The Alternative*. New York: Macmillan, 1970.

Houriet, Robert. *Getting Back Together*. New York: Avon, 1972.

Nahziryah Monastic Community

Nazir Path 970 MC 5029, Saint Joe, AR 72675

The Nahziryah Monastic Community, also known as the Nazir Order of the Purple Veil, is an esoteric spiritual community based in the Ozark Mountains of Arkansas. It is founded and led by Rev. Nazirmoreh K. B. Kedem. Followers are often referred to as the "Purple People" by outsiders because of their use of purple-colored clothing. Rev. Kedem ran the Veil of Truth Center for Metaphysical and Esoteric Learning in New Orleans from 1988 to 1999 and then moved his community to Arkansas in 1999.

The community members live on property of 103 acres. They share meals together and maintain a strict vegan diet. Organic gardening helps supply the community's dietary needs. The community forbids the use of alcohol and tobacco. There are four levels of membership, from the initial enquirer to the fully committed residential member. The community shares all resources and raises money through sales of oils, incense, jewels, sarongs, aromatherapy supplies, artwork, door beads, and so on.

Kedem claims a spiritual lineage from his father and grandfather, but provides no actual details of his background and training. He claims that he began to understand his true identity when he found an old book that held the key to unlock his previous lives. His writings reflect a mixture of Western esoteric and advaitist Hindu elements, somewhat reflected in their belief that all religions teach the same truths. The community's pluralistic and advaitist perspective is reflected in this statement: "Many paths—One goal. What is our religion?—all of them. Where are we from?—everywhere. We strive to transcend all limitations. Our consciousness narrows when we crystallize ourselves in the consciousness of being from a country, a state, a city, a street, a house, a spot and so on. *We are not these bodies.* We expand our consciousness and our understanding when we align with the higher Truths of Being."

Membership: Not reported. The community has a rule against numbering itself.

Sources:

Nahziryah Monastic Community. www.nmcnews.org.

Purple People Place. www.thepurplepeople.org.

Padanaram Settlement

c/o Rachel Summerton, PO Box 334, Avoca, IN 47420

Padanaram Settlement, also known as God's Valley, is an intentional community in south central Indiana founded in 1966 by a small group under the leadership of Daniel Wright. Wright, an independent thinker and minister, was raised in the Brethren Church. His life was punctuated with periodic religious experiences that led to the building of Padanaram as a microcosmic city, the first of many to be created in the millennial order of "Kingdomism."

In 1960 Wright heard a voice that said to him, "I will show you My valley." He got in his car and allowed the Spirit to guide him to the present site of the Padanaram Settlement. With a group of five men, three women, and four children, he purchased the former Smokey Valley Farm in 1966. A sawmill, which became the backbone of the community's growth, was purchased in 1968. Community businesses have continued to expand, into compost, bark mulch, organic farming, and other areas. Padanaram started a communal school (K–12) in 1972, a preschool in 1975, and a nursery in 1978. Meals are eaten three times daily in the communal dining area.

Five principles emerged from the building of Padanaram Settlement:

1. As one would that others do, do unto others.
2. Hold all things in common, count nothing one's own.
3. Distribution to each according to the need.
4. Of one who has much, much is required.
5. One that won't work, shall not eat.

Guided by these principles, a flourishing community developed and overcame the initial hardships of establishing an economic base and withstanding unfriendly feelings in the area. Today, two conventions are held annually (in May and October), and an open house in October brings individuals from the surrounding towns for a visit.

Members of the community see themselves as a part of a "Kingdomism" movement and look to the day when all people will live communally. They see hope in the emergence of many similar communal groups around the United States and the world. They are not separatists. To the contrary, they actively promote their form of "utopian" living and see a society governed by the simple principles by which they have become successful as necessary for the survival of humanity. The International Communal Utopia is the name given to the future order. According to the group's teachings, many villages like Padanaram Settlement will be formed as self-sufficient villages. The group believes that together, these villages will lead humanity out of its jungle-like past into a world of economic cooperation, peace, and security.

Membership: As of 2008 there were 70 adults and 70 children living at the settlement.

Periodicals: *Millennial Chronicles.*

Remarks: Wright and Padanaram have been heavily criticized for establishing a patriarchal and sexist social order. In response, Wright has defended the differentiation of gender roles at Padanaram as proper, biblical, and in keeping with both the equality of the sexes and their inherent differences.

Sources:

Faith Babies. Williams, IN: Padanaram Press, 1987.

Kingdomism. Williams, IN: Padanaram Press, 1990.

Padanaram. Williams, IN: Padanaram Press, [1980].

Wagner, Jon. "A Midwestern Patriarchy." In *Sex Roles in Contemporary American Communes,* ed. Jon Wagner. Bloomington: Indiana University Press, 1982.

Wright, Daniel. "Open Letter to the National Historical Communal Societies Association." N.p., 1988. Mimeo.

———. *Utopian Concepts for Social Revolution.* Williams, IN: Padanaram Press, 1987.

Rainbow Family of Living Light

Current address not obtained for this edition.

Growing out of the counterculture movement of the late 1960s and conceptualized in the thinking of the Rev. Barry Adams (also known as Barry Davis; b. 1945), the Rainbow Family of Living Light is a loosely organized network of individuals, informal groups, and communes that share in common an attachment to what is termed *New Age consciousness.* The Family is truly a rainbow in its eclectic mixture of differing beliefs, concerns, and practices, but is united in its vision that humanity is passing into a new age of spiritual consciousness. The Rainbow Family sees itself and is seen as a harbinger of the new age and a major component of the New Age movement, which has its exponents in many of America's alternative religions.

The major activity of the Family since the early 1970s has been the sponsorship of an annual "gathering of the tribes." (New Age adherents often describe the essence of community as a new tribal consciousness.) These annual meetings began with a small "Vortex" gathering in Oregon around 1970. The first gathering to attract several hundred attendees (and significant media coverage) was held in 1972 at Strawberry Lake, east of Granby, Colorado. It called together the "tribes" to give honor and respect to anyone or anything that has aided in the positive evolution of humankind and nature.

The beliefs of the Rainbow Family center on ecology and on the psychic/spiritual world much discussed in the 1960s. Basic is a nature-pantheism expressed in the statement of belief, "God is you, God is me, God is the World, God is the Sky,

God is the Sun." The Family's ecological emphasis is expressed in a love of nature and of the outdoors. Adherents believe that everything in nature was placed there for human use (not abuse). Marijuana is one of the God-created herbs, and is viewed as having sacramental value. All forms of pollutants are opposed.

The Family's psychic worldview is expressed in the incorporation of numerous practices borrowed from a wide variety of groups and religious bodies. The "great invocation" (channeled through Alice Bailey) is freely used, as is the distinction between Jesus the man and the mystic Christ-consciousness. Followers believe in reincarnation, but with a distinct, worldly interest. Christ-consciousness is conceived of as a mystical state, but is signaled by a person's making others happy, doing good deeds, and giving more than is taken.

Love is an important goal. Loving someone is equated with heaven, and hating someone is equated with hell. Sex is considered to be an expression of love. Legal aspects of marriage are no longer considered necessary, for when two people love each other, they are considered married. There are no formal acts of worship, and the formality of most religious acts is condemned. A wide mixture of Hindu chants, Christian hymns, and meditative techniques are employed to reach God-consciousness.

Membership: No membership roles are kept, but a directory of the family's network is published irregularly. Several thousand people are involved. The family claims that as many as 10,000 share its free lifestyle. In 1984 some 28,000 people attended the Family's summer gathering in Modoc County, California. In the late 1970s Rainbow Family gatherings emerged in Australia and New Zealand. In 1982 they appeared in Europe. By the early 2000s, there were Rainbow Family gatherings in South Africa and the Middle East as well.

Periodicals: *The Guide*.

Sources:

Rainbow Family of Living Light. www.welcomehome.org/rainbow/index.html.

Garlington, Phil. "The Return of the Flower Children." *California* 9, no. 10 (October, 1978): 81–83, 137–138.

The Rainbow Nation Cooperative Community Guide. McCall, ID: Rainbow Nation, 1972.

Reba Place Fellowship and Associated Communities

737 B Reba Pl., Evanston, IL 60204

Reba Place Church began in 1957 with a group of Mennonite students at Goshen College in Goshen, Indiana, and started as an off-campus fellowship. The members were reacting against the sterility of the church and were operating out of a vision of the church as a disciplined brotherhood living in small communities of spiritual consensus. Among the leaders were John Miller, Don Mast, and Virgil Vogt. In 1957 the fellowship moved to 727 Reba Place, Evanston, Illinois, from which the original group took its name. Growth in the fellowship was steady as like-minded individuals, spurred by the communal thrust of the 1970s, were drawn to Reba Place. Other buildings were purchased, and community activity accelerated.

Prior to 1980 membership in the church (the religious structure) and the fellowship (the communal living arrangement) were one and the same. Every person who became a member of the Reba Place Church also committed him- or herself to participation in a common purse. In 1980 that definition changed, and church membership was opened to people outside the fellowship. As of the late 1980s, about two-thirds of the members were living outside the communal arrangement. The Reba Place Fellowship now exists as a subgroup of Reba Place Church.

As Reba Place was progressing, however, other related communal experiments were also beginning. In 1971, the Plow Creek Fellowship was established by three families of the Reba Place Fellowship. They purchased a 190-acre farm in Bureau County, Illinois, and by 1974 it had grown into an independent congregation in its own right. The Fellowship of Hope—later renamed Shalom Mission Communities—was formed by nine people at the Mennonite Seminary at Elkhart, Indiana. From their struggle to find meaning in their church participation,

and partially inspired by the Reba Place model, a communal life emerged. In 1971 three families in Newton, Kansas, joined together to "concentrate resources for the work of peacemaking and care for the families at the same time." In 1974 the communes in Bureau County, Illinois; Elkhart, Indiana; and Newton, Kansas, joined with Reba Place in a mutual covenant of dependency. According to the covenant, the basis for membership is a commitment to Jesus and to his radical teaching. Membership specifically involves renunciation of property; love as an alternative to anger, violence, and war; faithfulness in marriage as the context for sex; a servanthood stance in all human relationships; and a communal organization of personal affairs. Each community is seen as a local church, with all the rights and privileges thereof. Within the circle of communities, encouragement is given to the sharing of spiritual gifts and resources, responding to words of correction, visiting between communities, allowing transfer of members between communities, sharing finances, and scheduling occasional intracommunal gatherings.

Each of the associated communities has grown out of a Mennonite base, though strong emphasis is place on the multitraditional nature of their present membership. A general Mennonite theological perspective remains, along with concerns for peace and social service. Emphasis is placed on the radical teachings of Jesus in the Sermon on the Mount. The impetus to communal forms has also been present in Anabaptism, partially as a means of survival in a hostile world. At Reba Place, it is seen as a positive means to fulfill the teachings of Jesus. The communes differ from their Mennonite neighbors primarily in their spontaneous style of worship, which includes guitars, folk music, and the free expression of emotion. Priority is given to learning to live together in a family-like existence. Basic teachings are found in the *Christian Way*, by John Miller, one of the founders.

Members of the fellowships work at jobs within the surrounding communities. A group associated with the Plow Creek Fellowship, the Builders, helps finance the group through various kinds of construction work. Income is pooled, and each individual or nuclear family receives an allowance. Social structures supported by the Reba Place Church include a daycare center and apartment rentals. Support is also given to individuals in the community. Reba Place is located in a racially mixed neighborhood, and it includes African, Asian, and Puerto Rican Americans in its fellowship. Resident members live in a variety of housing owned by the fellowship, including single-family houses, apartments, and shared houses.

In 2007 Reba Place Fellowship celebrated its 50-year anniversary.

Membership: According to its Web site, "As of January 2008 the Reba Place Fellowship consisted of 32 covenant members, 6 novice members, 17 practicing members, and 9 apprentices."

Periodicals: *Life Together*. Available from Box 6017, Evanston, IL 60204. • *RPC Information Exchange*. Available from Box 6016, Evanston, IL 60204.

Sources:

Plow Creek Fellowship and Church. www.plowcreek.org.

Reba Place Church. www.rebaplacechurch.org.

Reba Place Fellowship. www.rebaplacefellowship.org.

Shalom Mission Communities. www.shalomconnections.org.

Jackson, Dave, and Neta Jackson. *Glimpses of Glory: Thirty Years of Community*. Elgin, IL: Brethren Press, 1987.

———. *Living Together in a World Falling Apart*. Carol Stream, IL: Creation House, 1974.

Miller, John W. *The Christian Way*. Scottdale, PA: Herald Press, 1969.

REMAR International

664-668 NE 61st St., Miami, FL 33137

REMAR International grew out of the religious experience of Miguel Dias, a native of Spain. A compulsive gambler, Dias converted to conservative evangelical Christianity in 1982 and founded a communal Christian group, which he named for the group's goal of "REhabilitating MARginal people." Additionally, in Spanish, *remar* means "to row," and the community views itself as being in a boat rowing out into the sea to save people drowning in their addictions. The first group was located in Vitoria, in northern Spain. The community has a four-pillared program that includes evangelism, discipleship, social work, and the development of Christian businesses. It accomplishes its first task both by appealing and evangelizing to addicts in the streets of the urban centers in which its communities are located and by inviting homeless people to take up residence in their homes to help them turn their lives around. In the United States, REMAR groups have been most active in Hispanic communities.

REMAR is a conservative charismatic (Pentecostal) group. Worship is lively and spirited and punctuated by the testimonies of those whose lives have been changed by their coming to the community. A leader, Angel Jimenez, has been appointed to oversee the communities in America, and he in turn has appointed a leader over each local community. Besides receiving gifts from people in the larger secular community who appreciate their work, the individual REMAR centers have founded businesses, especially thrift stores, which they feel are in line with their goals of Christian living and assisting people to rehabilitate themselves.

Membership: In 2008 there were REMAR communities in more than 40 countries.

Sources:

REMAR International. www.remar.org.

Jansen, David. *Fire, Salt, and Peace: Intentional Christian Communities Alive in North America*. Evanston, IL: Shalom Mission Communities, 1996. 207 pp.

Salem Acres

7419 E Brick School Rd., Rock City, IL 61070

Salem Acres is an eclectic commune founded in the late 1960s. It combines elements of Pentecostalism and Sacred Name Adventism. Its founder was Lester B. Anderson, a former Baptist minister. The purpose of creating Salem Acres was to provide a place where a group could grow in the Spirit and be free to accept new truth as it came. From the Pentecostals, the group at Salem Acres has accepted an emphasis on the baptism of the Spirit and speaking in tongues, and has adopted a New Testament church order. The various gifts of the spirit are manifest, and these ministries are functioning. Women partake in the ministry, but men predominate. Spirited singing, testimonies, and prayer for the sick characterize services. The group has derived an emphasis on the Old Testament laws, particularly those concerning keeping the Sabbath and diet. Both the Lord's Supper and baptism by immersion are practiced. The group operates Lakeview Academy for grades 4 to 12.

Membership: Not reported. There were approximately 50 residents in 1992. The group is loosely affiliated with like-minded congregations in other countries.

Periodicals: *Yahweh Nissi.*

Shepherdsfield Community

777 Shepherdsfield Rd., Fulton, MO 65251-9473

Shepherdsfield Community, also known as New Christian Life Fellowship, is an independent communal Christian fellowship that grew out of the Jesus People revival that began in the late 1960s. Its roots are in an independent church, the Bird Rock Fellowship, founded in 1971 in La Jolla, California, by a group of people affected by the revival. Within a year the group had evolved into five congregations serving various sections of the greater San Diego metropolitan area. In 1977 two of the pastors within the fellowship, Jon R. Welker and Elliot Stearns, saw a need for a deeper level of fellowship as described in the New Testament, specifically the adoption of a communal lifestyle. A period of study and learning about contemporary Christian community as represented in such groups as the Reba Place Fellowship and the Society of Brothers prepared members of the fellowship to found a new Christian community. In 1979 the group purchased a former sheep farm near Fulton, Missouri, which they named Shepherdsfield. A group of approximately 70 people departed from San Diego after the celebration of Pentecost and

arrived in Fulton in June 9, 1979, the date recognized as the founding date of the Shepherdsfield Community.

Shepherdsfield is organized communally, and membership is granted only after a period during which an applicant's commitment to the ideals of communal life is tested. Members relinquish personal property to the group, and the majority of meals are eaten together. Families live in separate family dwellings, however, and nuclear family units are recognized and nurtured within the communal structure. The community is supported by a variety of businesses: the Shepherd's Company, the Shepherdsfield Bakery, and the Shepherd's Brethren. Children attend a community school.

The community holds to a conservative evangelical Christian faith and affirms belief in the Bible as the Word of God, the deity of Christ, and the spiritual unity of believers. The community also affirms the necessity of baptism and acknowledgment by the believer of having received forgiveness in Jesus Christ.

Membership: As of 2001 there were approximately 100 residents at Shepherdsfield.

Shivalila
Current address not obtained for this edition.

Shivalila was founded in Bakersfield, California, in the 1970s by Gridley Lorimer Wright IV (1934–1979). Wright, a Yale graduate and former stockbroker, left his career during the 1960s and joined the counterculture movement on the West Coast. He became an active user of LSD and built up around him a group that explored the effects of the drug's use. Shivalila grew out of this experimental group.

Wright reasoned that the foundation of society emerged from the relationship of mother and child and hence that this relationship is the dimension in which microcosm and macrocosm intersect. Western society, based on the nuclear family, grows out of the child's relationship with the One Source of the Energy of Life, the mother. The One-Source imprint leads to competitiveness and an expectation of partiality. In contrast, in communal societies, children respond to many Sources, which makes them less competitive and better able to adjust to broad life experiences. Wright had first experienced and was attracted to the collective communal aspect of culture during the 1960s. Thus, in addition to their experiments with psychedelic drugs, members of the group traveled and gained experience by living in various communal societies in both the United States and abroad. During this period of exploration, some members of the group studied with both Buddhist and Hindu Tantric masters who taught them some of the Tantric secrets, including some left-hand sexual techniques.

As Shivalila emerged in the 1970s, it included an emphasis on the use of psychedelic drugs, a communal lifestyle, and the practice of Tantric yoga. Added emphasis was placed on the raising of children in an ideal environment, and the group often referred to itself as the Children's Liberation Front. These emphases led group members to assume a four-point social contract, the Covenants of Shivalila. They agreed to practice *ahimsa*, nonviolence; *sattva ava*, the recognition of the relative nature of truth; *bhramcari*, nonparticipation in the ownership of private property and denial of relationships that involve privacy or secrecy (including the marriage contract); and *tantra*, participation in sexual relationships only after the other party has manifested an identification with nature and babies. To Wright, these commitments meant the recreation of a society similar to that of the Stone Age.

Shivalila enjoyed a brief moment of fame after its publication of its beliefs and practices in a book, *The Book of the Mother*, in 1977. After concluding that the closest approximation to their ideal lifestyle was being practiced by the Tasaday tribe in the Philippines, they moved to the islands. However, the Philippine government forced them to move in March 1978, and the group immigrated to India. Burying their American passports, they asked for political asylum. The group chose an area in a rural part of Rajasthan state to create their new society. Unfortunately, in December 1978, several months after their settling in, Wright was stabbed and died of complications of the injuries some weeks later.

Membership: Not reported. In 1979 the group had 18 members. Its present status is unknown.

Sources:

The Book of the Mother. Bakersfield, CA: Children's Liberation Front, 1977.

Sirius Community

72 Baker Rd., Shutesbury, MA 01072

Sirius is an intentional community founded in 1978 by several former members of the Findhorn Community, the pioneering Scottish New Age community. Among the founders were Corinne McLaughton and Gordon Davidson. It was named after the star that many believe to be, in an esoteric sense, the source of love and wisdom on Earth. Resident members see themselves as part of a network of light groups and individuals around the world working for the uplifting of consciousness. They place great emphasis on the development of a planetary consciousness that honors the interconnectedness and sacredness of all life.

Sirius is located on a 90-acre tract of land in Shutesbury, Massachusetts. Members believe that they are stewards of the land and that they should live as lightly on the earth as possible. They strive to create a sustainable abundance through the growth of an organic, pesticide-free vegetable and herb garden and environmentally sound construction, off-grid energy use, and a bio-diesel fuel co-op. As of 2008 the group was integrating the principles of permaculture and was striving to become a full-fledged ecovillage

In their group life, members seek to honor the divine presence in each person. They strive to serve the good of the whole and balance the needs of the individual and group. Decisions are made by consensus of the general meeting or core group. Meditation is used both for individual growth and as an aid in building consensus. Daily life is considered a spiritual teacher.

Sirius has developed a program of community outreach through workshops for visitors to the community, open houses, sponsoring seasonal celebrations, and resident apprenticeships. Nonresidents may become associate members in the community. Sirius sponsors a number of educational programs as well as hosting regular wellness retreats, which are open to the public.

Membership: In 1997 there were approximately 25 resident members.

Sources:

Sirius Community. www.siriuscommunity.org.

McNaughton, Corinne, and Gordon Davidson. *Builders of the Dawn: Community Lifestyles in a Changing World*. Shutesbury, MA: Sirius Publishing, 1986.

Sunburst (formerly Solar Logos Foundation)

PO Box 2008, Buellton, CA 93427

Sunburst—originally called the Solar Logos Foundation—is composed of spiritual seekers who desire to practice a natural way of life based on ancient teachings of an eightfold path of right living. The teachings are based on visions and revelations received by founder Norman Paulsen (1929–2006), a direct disciple of Paramahansa Yogananda (1893–1952) and author of *Christ Consciousness* and *Sacred Science*. The foundation teaches that people are all sons and daughters of the same source and have been gifted with life on this planet. They should desire only to help humanity and themselves to realize their true nature, and then use that knowledge to help make the planet a healthy garden again for all life forms (minerals, plants, animals, and people), with all living in harmony and in true understanding as was the original intent. According to the foundation, these teachings can be embraced by all denominations to further strengthen one's devotion and quest for God-realization.

Once a person has established direct mental and visual communication with God through meditation, his or her mental compass needle will always swing toward the Polestar, which is the light at the end of the inner-dimensional tunnel, the Solar Logos. The attainment of constant communication with God is "that Pearl of Great Price" that Jesus spoke of, that divine possession that cannot be bought with any amount of wealth. The foundation asserts that attainment of this state of consciousness by a man or woman can truly have a positive effect on all of humanity.

Since its founding in 1968, Sunburst has encouraged the formation of spiritual colonies of men, women, and children living, working, and meditating together for the greater good of the world. The foundation believes that through the collective energy derived in a group environment, individual spiritual growth is stimulated and quickened. Current colonies include a large pristine sanctuary located near Santa Barbara, and an organic farm near the sanctuary. In addition to being locations of association and work, these also function as places for reflection, meditation, and promotion of God-realization.

The foundation conducts regular daily group meditations and a Sunday service, all open to the public. Seminars are held during the year offering instruction and guidance in living the eightfold path and applying the twelve divine virtues. This includes instruction in the techniques of meditation, along with healing through diet and exercise.

Membership: Not reported.

Sources:

Duquette, Susan. *Sunburst Farm Family Cookbook*. Santa Barbara, CA: Woodbridge Press Publishing Company, 1978.

Hansen-Gates, Jan. "Growing Outdoors: The Brotherhood of the Sun." *Santa Barbara Magazine* 1, no. 3 (winter 1975–1976): 64–71.

Paulsen, Norman. *Sunburst: Return of the Ancients*. Goleta, CA: Sunburst Farms Publishing Farms, 1980. Revised and retitled as *Christ Consciousness*. Salt Lake City, UT: The Builders Publishing Company, 1984.

Weaver, Dusk, and Willow Weaver. *Sunburst: A People, a Path, a Purpose*. San Diego, CA: Avant Books, 1982.

Twelve Tribes

c/o The Community in Boston, 92 Melville Ave., Dorchester, MA 02124

HISTORY. The Twelve Tribes, formerly known as the Messianic Communities of New England, has roots that can be traced to Chattanooga, Tennessee. There, in 1972, Gene Spriggs (b. 1937) and his wife Marsha Spriggs opened their home to youth and young adults, as well as the homeless poor in the area. Around this core group of young people, a community composed of various ages began to form during the spreading Jesus People Revival. Those who received the gospel they preached gave up all their possessions and moved into households together, sharing all things in common after the patterns described in the biblical book of Acts 2:37–47 and 4:32–35. Settling in several large homes on Vine Street in Chattanooga, the group became known as the Vine Christian Community and operated a restaurant known as the Yellow Deli. Eventually, in response to an invitation from residents in nearby towns, the Vine Community sent workers to establish other communities, and by 1978 a dozen communal households had emerged in Tennessee, Georgia, and Alabama. The group operated six Yellow Delis, a bakery, and a restaurant and meetinghouse called Areopagus. At the time, there were approximately 150 members.

In 1978 workers went to Vermont to help a group of eight Vermont families establish a community in Island Pond, Vermont, located in a geographical area known as the Northeast Kingdom; the group was for a time called the Northeast Kingdom Community. They soon opened a business together called the Common Sense Wholesome Food Store and Restaurant.

Meanwhile, as the cult controversy developed during the late 1970s, parents of some of the young people who had joined the Chattanooga community began to criticize it for its communal lifestyle and the authority represented by the elders. A number of deprogrammings were attempted. The community also incurred the enmity of some Christian leaders and was spoken against by some local churches and Christian colleges in the area. In the midst of the controversy, fewer and fewer people responded to the preaching of community members; as a result, in 1979 the Vermont community invited the members in the South to move there.

Selling their properties and businesses in the South, the various communities began relocating to Vermont, where they lived together in large extended families with shared households throughout the village of Island Pond. Here they diversified into a number of service-oriented businesses. With their lifestyle they sought to demonstrate openly the unity of the body of Christ in a practical, daily manner. Within a few years, the community had grown to more than 300 people, approximately one-fifth of the population of the village.

Soon, however, some local opposition arose from the group's stance regarding the necessity of a disciple's (i.e., member's) separation from the world system. Criticism was leveled at the apparent submission of women, the children's nonattendance at public schools, and the group's dress (adopted with concern for modesty in mind). Members of the community were accused of many things, from underbidding local contractors for a series of government projects to mistreating their children. The primary focus of media concern, however, was the disciplining of children, an issue initially raised in a custody battle between a member and a spouse who had left the movement.

Then, in 1984, a member of the community left and accused the members of child abuse. As a result, approximately 90 state troopers raided the community, and 50 social workers seized the 112 children of the community. The raid was officially declared unconstitutional and "grossly unlawful" by Vermont District Court Judge Frank Mahady. The children were found to show no signs of child abuse. A brief time later, the complainant admitted to fabricating the allegations of child abuse due to pressure to do so from a local organization that was boycotting the community's businesses in an effort to drive them from the area. He was later forgiven and rejoined the community.

During the 1980s the community in Island Pond sent workers to various locations in New England, as well as France, Canada, New Zealand, Brazil, and the Midwestern United States, at the invitation of people in those areas who had become believers. The communities also began to send out workers to establish communities themselves. The groups in New England refer to themselves as the Messianic Communities of New England. As the communities entered the 1990s, they drew further criticism for their stand against homosexuality. They claimed it was a sin worthy of eternal punishment, according to Revelation 21:8, Romans 1:26–27, I Corinthians 6:9–11, and other biblical passages. The group also questions the need for racial integration, for which is has been called racist.

BELIEFS. The Twelve Tribes communities support the traditional affirmations of evangelical Christianity, but are unrelated to any particular denominational family. They believe in an authoritative and inerrant Bible, the Trinity, the incarnation of Christ, and his atonement. They look forward to the return of Christ. Members affirm the fall of humanity, salvation by grace, and justification by faith. While recognizing the validity and necessity of all the spiritual gifts (I Corinthians 12), especially prophecy, they do not consider themselves specifically Pentecostal or charismatic. The communities refer to Jesus as *Yahshua*, the Hebrew name given to him in Matthew 1:21 and used by Jesus himself in Acts 26:14–15.

The Twelve Tribes communities place heavy emphasis on obedience to the commands of the Son of God, as opposed to mere belief in his atonement. They believe that such obedience, particularly expressed through loving one another as their savior loved them (John 13:34), is necessary for a person to enter the kingdom of heaven (Matthew 7:21). They recognize that, while a person is irreversibly saved from eternal damnation by grace through faith (which is a gift from God), participation in the Millennial kingdom and the first resurrection must be striven for and attained, according to Luke 13:24–28 and Philippians 3:8–12. They believe that this is what Jesus was referring to when he said, "If anyone keeps my word, he shall never see death" (John 8:31–32, 51).

ORGANIZATION. The Twelve Tribes communities are each established according to a New Testament pattern, and share their goods as did the church at Jerusalem, following the words of Jesus in Luke 14:33. A council of elders oversees each local

setting, while a regional council coordinates the interaction between communities. There is no central headquarters, nor do the individual communities consider themselves to be part of a denomination. Each derives its name from its geographical location, and thus is known simply as, for example, the Community in Island Pond, Dorchester, and so on.

Membership: As of 1995, the membership of the Messianic Communities was estimated at 650 in the United States and an additional 200 in France, with less than 100 each in Canada, New Zealand, and Brazil. In 2008 there were additional communities in Germany, Argentina, the United Kingdom, and Spain. Exact membership was unreported.

Periodicals: *The Voice.*

Sources:

Twelve Tribes. www.twelvetribes.com.

The Constitution: Abiding Laws or Empty Words. Island Pond, VT: Island Pond Freepaper, 1987.

Nori, Don. "Persecution at Island Pond." *Charisma* 10, no. 4 (November 1984).

Palmer, Susan J. "Frontiers and Mailies: The Children of Island Pond." In *Children in the New Religions.* New Brunswick, NJ: Rutgers University Press, 1999, pp. 153–171.

————. *Moon Sisters, Krishna Mothers, Rajneesh Lovers: Women's Roles in New Religions.* Syracuse, NY: Syracuse University Press, 1994.

Swantko, Jean A. *An Issue of Control: Conflict between the Church in Island Pond and State Government.* Palenville, NY: Author, 1998.

Wanted: The Answer to Abortion. Island Pond, VT: Island Pond Freepaper, [1987].

Universal Industrial Church of the New World Comforter (One World Family Commune, Galactic Messenger Network)
PO Box 1241, Santa Rosa, CA 95402-1241

The Universal Industrial Church of the New World Comforter was formed by Allen Michael Noonan (b. 1916), who in 1947 in Long Beach, California, claimed to have been contacted by extraterrestrial intelligences. According to Noonan, generally known simply as Allen Michael, in that first contact he (i.e., the entity within his body) was transported up a beam of light to what he later recognized as a spaceship. While aboard, he was given the choice to be a channel of the "everlasting gospel," and thus fulfill Jesus' prophecy in John 16: 7–14 of "the Comforter" that would come. He accepted the mission, and since that time has devoted his life to channeling (through automatic writing) Spirit God's plan for the transformation of this planet.

Twenty years later, in 1967, the first members of the One World Family Commune came together in San Francisco's Haight-Ashbury District, inspired by the truth they believed was being channeled through Allen Michael and sharing with him the vision of eliminating money and bringing about a world of sharing and serving (love). They felt that the usury money system perpetuated subjugation of materiality in a duality of consciousness, and limited progress toward the synthesis of "one for all and all for one," which, according to Allen Michael, would have been the next stage in the evolution of consciousness had Article I, Section 8, paragraph 5 of the United States Constitution—which reads "Congress shall coin the money, and regulate the value thereof"—been upheld.

The commune also recognized that a diet of natural food was basic to higher consciousness and health. As a means of supporting themselves, as well as a way to provide a service to the community, members operated the Here and Now Natural Food Restaurant in Haight-Ashbury. In 1971 the commune moved to Berkeley, California, where on Telegraph Avenue they opened the One World Family Natural Food Center, which included a large restaurant, a pizzeria, a bakery, a handmade clothing shop, and an entertainment hall.

In 1973, while still in Berkeley, the group founded the Universal Industrial Church of the New World Comforter, in recognition of themselves as the "church of

God rising out of the people." They viewed Allen Michael as the channel of energies described by the archangel in Daniel 12:1. Allen Michael is believed to have been given the keys to prophecy contained in the Bible, so that these days of tribulation might be shortened for the sake of the elect, and so that, with the aid of the World Master Plan, people will be able to arise out of subjugation to materiality into a world-sharing economy and God-consciousness.

The means advocated for ending the dying world order and bringing about the New World Order of the Ages (the "Novo Ordo Seclorum" pictured on the Great Pyramid seal on the American dollar bill) is the World Wide Work Stoppage 30/30 Plan. Allen Michael suggests that all businesses that provide no real service or anything of true value be stopped and that people begin to rotate on a 30-day cycle, with half the people providing all the goods and services to the other half, who travel, rest, and recreate. This action would automatically lift the vibrational energies (consciousness) out of duality and into the synthesis—"one for all and all for one"—that is Spirit God's prophesied heaven on earth, the kingdom of God.

The church has, through its publishing arm, Starmast Publications (Box 1241, Santa Rosa, CA 95402), produced a series of books that detail the teachings of the church as channeled through Allen Michael. It has also produced a popular natural foods cookbook and a series of videotapes for airing on cable television. In August 2007 the group launched its Galactic Messenger Network, an interactive online multimedia center with a communal Web log, a radio station, Galactic Messenger TV, and downloadable videos and publications produced by Starmast Multimedia.

Membership: Not reported. As of 2008, members of the group were scattered geographically but still working toward a common goal, mostly via their Internet presence.

Periodicals: *Galactic Messenger*.

Sources:

Galactic Messenger Network. www.galacticmessenger.com.

Allen Michael. *ETI Space Beings Intercept Earthlings*. Stockton, CA: Starmast Publications, 1977.

————. *The Everlasting Gospel, God, Unlimited Mind Speaks*. Stockton, CA: Starmast Publications, 1982.

————. *The Everlasting Gospel, to the Youth of the World*. Berkeley, CA: Universal Industrial Church of the Divine Comforter, 1973.

————. *UFO-ETI World Master Plan*. Starmast Publications, 1977.

Hannaford, Kathryn. *Cosmic Cookery*. Stockton, CA: Starmast Publications, 1974.

West Coast Communities

c/o Church of the Sojourners, 866 Potero, San Francisco, CA 94110

West Coast Communities, which emerged in the 1980s, is a fellowship of conservative Christian communities located along the West Coast of the United States from Washington to Southern California. The fellowship consists of a number of largely autonomous communities, with varying Christian traditions dominating from community to community. Its two main foci are development of a strong intimate fellowship and outreach in the community. Formal leadership is elected, but in practice leadership is affirmed informally by the community when it is demonstrated by individuals as new issues arise.

West Coast Communities is largely apolitical, though individual members may be politically active. The groups tend to be anti-abortion and anti-homosexuality, and in favor of home schooling.

Membership: Not reported. In 1996 there were four communities affiliated with West Coast Communities.

Western Esoteric Family I: Ancient Wisdom

17

Since the fourth century C.E., the Western religious community has been dominated by Christianity in its various forms. Christianity shared space with the continuing Jewish tradition, and until recently, histories of Western civilization would generally treat these two communities as the only religious traditions operating throughout the centuries. A significant rewriting of the history of Western religion began in the late twentieth century, however, as scholars recognized that a third current of religious life was present, challenging Christian hegemony. This third current flourished in a variety of times and places, only to attract the attention of Christian powers and become the object of suppressive activity. As adherents faced repeated persecution, the continuity of what has become known as *Western esotericism* was broken. Still, as suppression occurred in one location, esotericism would arise in another.

Esotericism was reborn in the seventeenth century in the social spaces opened by the Protestant Reformation. It experienced notable bursts of growth in the late nineteenth century and spectacular growth in the 1970s and 1980s, the New Age movement providing it demographic significance for the first time in the modern world. In fact, it was the New Age movement, so derided in the popular press for its naive and questionable practices that nurtured the growth of the esoteric community to the point that it had to be taken seriously. The millennial fervor built around the hope of a new age of light and love swept millions into the esoteric world and introduced them to meditation, psychic readings, contact with deceased relatives, westernized yoga, channeling, ritual magic, astrological speculations, various divinatory techniques, and a host of philosophies aimed at personal spiritual enlightenment.

Looking at the major contemporary esoteric currents, a picture of the development of Western esotericism through the centuries becomes apparent. Modern Western esotericism began with the emergence of Rosicrucianism in the seventeenth century. Rosicrucianism provided a foundation for the rise of speculative Freemasonry, which became one of the most successful esoteric organizations internationally through the eighteenth century. Its very success, however, led to significant variations in different locations. In such countries as England and Italy, Freemasonry continues as an esoteric group, whereas in France, Freemasonry developed into a post-revolutionary atheist organization assuming the public persona of a fraternal group, though it was much more than

that. In the early United States, public anger occasioned by the disappearance of William Morgan (b. 1774), an ex-Mason who had threatened to expose the group's secrets, joined religious opposition to Masonry and led to the organization's secularization and transformation into primarily a social club.

Freemasonry would, however, become a new foundation for the emergence of additional esoteric currents. Shortly after the French Revolution (1789–1799), for example, neo-Templarism arose as a reborn order of the temple. Through the nineteenth century, new bursts of interest in ritual magic arose, and by the end of the century give birth to several magical orders, most notably the Hermetic Order of the Golden Dawn. Theosophy would also develop from a Masonic intellectual base.

A popular form of esoteric practice, built around the manipulation of what were believed to the cosmic energies underpinning the universe, arose in eighteenth-century France around the teachings of Franz Anton Mesmer (1734–1815). Though denounced by the scientific community of his day, *mesmerism* became a popular movement, claiming healings and the production of unusual states of consciousness (today called the hypnotic state) through magnetic energy. As demonstrations of mesmerism became a popular form of entertainment, mesmerists discovered that some entranced subjects manifested unusual powers, including an apparent ability to communicate with spirits. A few mesmerists discovered the ability to enter a trance state without assistance (self-hypnosis).

Mesmerism became the foundation upon which a new movement focused on communication with the spirit world arose. *Spiritualism* began in upstate New York in 1848, but by the time of the American Civil War (1861–1865), it had become a national fad and was growing in England and France. Through the twentieth century, popular currents of Spiritualism, Theosophy, Rosicrucianism, and ritual magic would mix and match in a variety of ways to produces the hundreds of esoteric groups that exist today.

Tracing the current esoteric community backward to the seventeenth century reveals the variety of movements in prior centuries that bear a resemblance to contemporary movements. In the sixteenth century, Jewish mystical practices built around the understanding of creation in the Kabbalah found an audience in the Christian community and emerged as the Christian Cabala. Previously, hermetic thought and alchemy, despite its ties to fraudulent schemes aimed at naive

Western Esoteric Family I: Ancient Wisdom Chronology

1614–16	Lutheran pastor Johann Andreae Valentin anonymously issues the three original Rosicrucian documents: *The Fama*, which introduced the world to Christian Rosencreutz and told the story of his travels and the origin of the Rosicrucian order; *The Confessio*; and *Chemical Wedding of Christian Rosencreutz.*
1694	Rosicrucians arrive in Germantown, Pennsylvania, and form the Chapter of Perfection.
1730	Daniel Cox appointed Provincial Grand Master of the Masonic lodges in New York, Pennsylvania, and New Jersey.
1858	Pascal Beverley Randolph founds the Fraternita Rosae Crucis, the oldest Rosicrucian order in the United States.
1865	Societas Rosicruciana in Anglia formed in England.
1771	The Grand Lodge of England formed by the merger of four Masonic lodges.
1875	Helena P. Blavatsky, Henry Steel Olcott, and William Quan Judge found the Theosophical Society in New York City.
1877	Blavatsky publishes *Isis Unveiled.*
1879	Theosophical Society headquarters moves to India where Blavatsky, Colonel Olcott, and later Annie Besant "greatly raised the self-confidence of the Hindus . . . removing any feelings of inferiority that had developed following the activities of Christian missionaries . . ." (Weightman 1998, p. 303).
1884	The Theosophical Society faces a major scandal when Helena Blavatsky is accused of faking her contact with the Mahatmas through whom she had caused a number of writings and other objects to appear.
1888	Blavatsky's *The Secret Doctrine* is published.
	Following her reading of *The Secret Doctrine* and meeting with Blavatsky, former atheist Annie Besant joins the Theosophical Society.
1893	Besant becomes one of the outstanding speakers at the Parliament of the World's Religions.
1895	As a result of the controversy over Judge's contacts with the Masters, the American Section of the Theosophical Society, under his leadership, secedes from the international movement.
1896	Judge dies and is succeeded by Katherine Tingley.
1898	Tingley renames the organization she leads as the Universal Brotherhood and Theosophical Society and two years later moves its headquarters from New York to San Diego, California.
1907	Max Heindel founds the Rosicrucian Fellowship.
1909	The United Lodge of Theosophists (ULT) is formed by Robert Crosby, a disenchanted member of the Theosophical Society under Katherine Tingley's leadership.
1911	Formation of the "Order of the Star in the East" in dedication to the "World Teacher" (i.e. J. Krishnamurti).
1912	Rudolf Steiner leaves the Theosophical Society and establishes the Anthroposophical Society (one of many schisms besetting the parent society).
1915	H. Spencer Lewis founds the Ancient Mystic Order of the Rosae Crucis.
1916	Old Catholic Bishop Frederick Samuel Willoughby consecrates James Ingall Wedgewood for the theosophically oriented Liberal Catholic Church.
1923	Alice and Foster Bailey found the Arcane School.
	American Astrological Society is founded.
1929	Jiddu Krishnamurti renounces any messianic role, breaks with Annie Besant and Thesophical Society, and dissolves the "Order of the Star of the East."
1930	Guy and Edna Ballard found the I AM Religious Activity movement.
1942	Gottfried Purucker sells San Diego property and moves the headquarters of the Theosophical Society in America to Covina, California.
1948	*The Reappearance of the Christ* by Alice A. Bailey is published.
1950–51	Theosophical Society in America relocates to Altadena, California.
1979	Based on channeled messages, Benjamin Crème, a student of the Alice Bailey teachings, begins to predict the imminent appearance of Christ/Maitreya.
1986	Bishop Meri Louise Spruit enthroned as Matriarch of the Church of Antioch.
1990	AMORC reorganizes after withdrawing the authority of its imperator Gary Stewart. Stewart goes on to found a new organization, the Ancient Rosae Crucis (later renamed the Confraternity of the Rose Cross).
1991	May 8th, White Lotus Day. Theosophists commemorate the 100th anniversary of the death of Helena P. Blavatsky.
2002	Scholars gathered at Michigan State University found the Association for the Study of Esotericism.
2007	Rosicrucian Park in San Jose, California, celebrates 70th anniversary.

money-hungry monarchs, had filled a gap among intellectuals, a gap filled earlier by Neoplatonic and Pythagorean thought. On the popular level, groups such as the Albigensians, the Bogomils, and Manicheans have come and gone—victims of dominant religions seeking uniformity of public faith.

Following esoteric belief and practice still further into the ancient world leads to a variety of movements centered in the Mediterranean Basin known as *Gnosticism* (a contested designation in contemporary scholarship). Gnosticism was traditionally viewed as the first Christian heresy. However, the discovery of ancient texts at Qumran on the Dead Sea and at Nag Hammadi in Egypt have led to a reappraisal and new

appreciation of the diversity of religious life during the first century B.C.E. to the fourth century C.E. A spectrum of esoteric movements, ranging from variations on what was becoming orthodox Trinitarian Christianity to movements with little or no Christian element, were prevalent in this period. While at one time the name *Gnostic* was given to this entire river of currents flowing from the ancient world, by the late twentieth century, *Western esotericism* had become the dominant designation

After the Dead Sea Scrolls and the Nag Hammadi texts were published in popular editions, various new movements emerged to lay claim to ancient insights, though the great majority of esoteric groups, especially those operating in the

United States and Canada, represent the major modern currents—Rosicrucianism, Theosophy, Spiritualism, and ceremonial magic. These would provide the foundation and content for several entirely new movements that would push esoteric thought in fresh directions. In the 1870s, for example, Mary Baker Eddy (1821–1910), who had moved among the postmesmerist healers, especially Phineas Parkhurst Quimby (1802–1866), began a movement popularly known as *Christian Science*. The movement emphasized the post-Enlightenment love of science, and it attempted to move beyond the popular supernaturalism of previous centuries, which was based on an array of spiritual beings (angels, deities, spirits, demons, etc.). This trend was already evident in the new magic of the nineteenth century, but Eddy's approach was more thorough. Eddy's movement gave rise to a variety of groups, many coming together under the name *New Thought*.

In the twentieth century, moving in a direction opposite that of Christian Science, groups that attempted to create a new space for the ancient pagan deities were formed. Most began with the approach articulated by Gerald B. Gardner (1884–1964), a retired British civil servant who developed a system that he called *witchcraft* based on invocation of a range of ancient European deities. The term *witchcraft* has collected a variety of connotations, most indicating a rejection of the Christianity that supplanted and eradicated pagan religions. Gardner's thought became the basis of a popular neo-pagan movement, which, unable to recover the thought of ancient paganism, drew eclectically from the spectrum of contemporary esoteric thought and practice.

The contemporary Esoteric community has grown large enough that it can be viewed in its various currents—treated here as several family and sub-family groupings. First, we will turn to the larger Ancient Wisdom groups that have flowed from the Rosicrucian and theolsphical currents. Next, in chapter 18 come the popular groups that have grown out of the work of two nineteenth century Esoteric giants, Emanuel Swedenborg and Franz Anton Mesmer. The movements they birthed gave way to Spiritualism which in turn supplied content to a host of small new groups over the last hundred years. Third, in chapter 19, we turn to the world of ritual or ceremonial magic, a realm given new life by a modern-day practitioner extradinaire, Aleister Crowley. Crowley died largely unknown in 1947, but has in the decades since become an icon of modern pop culture and the prophet of a new generation of magicians. Crowley's though would also supply much of the content for the magic taught and practiced by contemporary Neo-Pagans. Finally, in chapter 20, we will turn to the movement spawned by Eddy and built around her metaphysical speculations.

THE ANCIENT WISDOM.

The idea of the existence of an ancient hidden (occult) wisdom, an alternative to the dominant Christian orthodoxy, perpetuated by a lineage of secret adepts until such time as the wisdom could again be given to humanity, has a long history in the West. It was clearly stated, however, in the early seventeenth century in the primary documents announcing the existence of the Rosicrucian Order and was a central part of the myth of the revived Freemasonry of the eighteenth century. Perpetuated through Freemasonry and Rosicrucianism, the idea experienced a marked revival in the nineteenth century with the formation of several public Rosicrucian bodies, the Theosophical Society, and several new occult orders. By the end of the nineteenth century, these new occult organizations formed a distinct alternative to Spiritualism, the more popular form of esotericism through the century, and could be found in both the United States and England. Rather than attempt to contact spirits of the deceased and demonstrate the proof of life after death, these esotericists claimed to be the bearers of a hidden (i.e., occult) wisdom that had been passed to them from contemporary representatives of a lineage of teachers reaching into the remote past. These teachings, available for the first time in centuries, could now be given to those individuals prepared to receive them.

The accounts of the emergence of an ancient wisdom generally follow one of three basic formats. First, a person claims to have made direct contact with the present bearers of the lineage, usually in some remote (to the average Westerner) corner of the earth—Tibet, Egypt, Arabia. Having communicated with the present teachers of the lineage, the new student returns to the West to disclose its essential truths. Second, the wisdom may be revived through the rediscovery of texts—the Nag Hammadi scrolls being an ideal example—long hidden away, which contain its teachings. Most frequently, however, rediscovery of the ancient wisdom comes through a special person who is able to enter into the invisible spiritual realms not accessible to ordinary people, and be taught the secret wisdom directly by various highly evolved masters. The Great White Brotherhood is a common designation for those who have kept the ancient wisdom through the centuries. The term may be applied to a group of noncorporeal beings (some of whom may occasionally take human form) or to a group entirely or partially composed of individuals currently living on earth in some remote place.

Two main ancient-wisdom schools arose in the English-speaking West—the Rosicrucians and the Theosophists. The former claimed to have obtained the ancient wisdom from the legendary Christian Rosencreutz, who discovered it during travels in the Near East. Helena Petrovna Blavatsky (1831–1891), the first Theosophist to engage in extensive discourse with the masters, claimed to have recovered an ancient document of which no copies had survived in the mundane world, the Stanzas of Dyzan, which summarized the heretofore hidden truth.

Besides the Theosophists and Rosicrucians and the groups that derived from them—for example, the Arcane School of Alice A. Bailey (1880–1949) and the "I AM" Religious Activity of Guy W. Ballard (1878–1939) and Edna W. Ballard (1886–1971)—there are a few that have found an alternative source for acquiring the ancient wisdom. In addition, several groups, drawing upon the Theosophical model, have developed variations on it within other religious traditions. Thus Paul Twitchell (d. 1971), founder of Eckankar, while drawing the content of his teaching primarily from the literature of the Punjabi Sant Mat tradition, claimed to have traveled to what he termed "soul realms" to translate and bring to humanity various ancient documents. Similarly, some flying saucer contactees, most of whom came out of a Spiritualist tradition, have identified the "extraterrestrial" entities with whom they claimed contact as the Great White Brotherhood.

Typically, ancient-wisdom groups are modeled upon the ancient mystery schools rather than contemporary churches. They offer "instruction" in esoteric truth through classes and correspondence courses. Upon manifesting their accomplishment of a body of teachings and mastery of certain occult techniques, students are awarded a degree and admitted to instruction in the next level. Groups vary in the number of levels of work offered, the nature of the oversight given to students, and the strictness in applying standards by which to judge the completion of a degree. Thus one group may have ten degrees, limit contact with students to correspondence, and be lax in advancing the student through the degrees. Another group may have only four degrees, do all course work in small groups, and advance students only after they demonstrate the proper competence level in both esoteric theory and practice (clairvoyance, psychokinesis).

In esoteric thought, God is largely discussed as an utterly transcendent and hence unknowable being. While God is acknowledged, more attention is given to lesser beings in what is often seen as a spiritual hierarchy between God and humanity. In like measure, more attention is given to the lower levels of the spiritual world that to the heavenly realm of God's existence. Thus, within esoteric groups, the tendency is to pay more attention to learning about the spiritual realms and developing the means (spiritual disciplines and practices) to access them, than to what might be called worship of the transcendent God. Where worship services are held, lectures tend to replace sermons, and meditation dominates the prayer time.

The absence of a worshipful atmosphere in many esoteric groups continually calls their status as "religious" organizations into question, especially for people for whom a form of traditional Christianity is their primary reference for defining religion. In many countries where religious dissent still brings discrimination and even government persecution, many esotericists welcome being perceived as nonreligious. In the United States and Canada, many esotericists define themselves as spiritual, not religious, implying a rejection of much of the baggage associated with Christian church life and piety.

In covering esotericism, this encyclopedia includes many groups that publicly assert that they are not a religion, and the entries report that fact. The group's right to self-definition is also acknowledged. Nevertheless, given the guidelines for inclusion in this encyclopedia, its functional view of "religion," and the roles that "nonreligious" spiritual groups have played in the formation of similar spiritual groups that do claim religious status, these nonreligious groups are retained among the entries below.

THE ROSICRUCIANS. The Rosicrucian Order, which grew out of a story published in the seventeenth century in Germany, is the oldest of the several ancient wisdom groups with a following in the United States. According to one history of the group, "the Rosicrucian Order had its traditional conception and birth in Egypt in the activities of the Great White Lodge" (Lewis, *Rosicrucian Questions and Answers*, 1969, p. 33). If there were, in fact, historical continuity between an Egyptian occult order (or any other ancient group) and modern Rosicrucians, documents attesting to this connection have never surfaced. Twenty-first-century American Rosicrucian groups are highly eclectic bodies drawing on Western magical traditions, Theosophy, Freemasonry, and modern parapsychology. The interaction with Theosophy has been extensive and there are many likenesses. But while Theosophy was founded in 1875, contemporary Rosicrucians attempt to document their organizational continuity with the mystery schools of the ancient Mediterranean Basin and the seventeenth-century emergence of Rosicrucianism into public light.

The first mention of a possible Rosicrucian group appeared in a pamphlet printed in Germany in the second decade of the seventeenth century, the *Fama Fraternitatis*, written by someone using the pseudonym of Christian Rosencreutz (C.R.). The *Fama Fraternitatis*, or *Discovery of the Most Laudable Order of the Rosy Cross*, detailed the travels of Christian Rosencreutz to the Mediterranean Basin in the early 1400s, where he acquired wisdom about the microcosm and macrocosm, attunement with the "All," knowledge about the nature of health and disease, and other occult wisdom.

Returning to Germany, C.R. saw that the world was not ready for him, so he lived quietly, affiliating with three followers, and then four more. These eight were the original Rosicrucians in Germany. They agreed on the following points:

They would not profess anything but curing the sick without reward.

They would wear no special habit.

They would meet every year in the House Sancti Spiritus.

The brothers would choose their successors.

The letters "R.C." would be their only seal and character.

The fraternity would remain secret for one hundred years.

C.R. reputedly died in 1484, at age 106. Knowledge of the location of his tomb was lost and its rediscovery by a brother created a great stir. The tomb's inscription said that after 120 years he would return, meaning that the Rosicrucian Order would surface again in 1604 and take all initiates who were worthy.

There was a great response to the *Fama Fraternitatis* pamphlet from doctors, the altruistic, and those who wanted to live to be 106 years old. In 1615 a second pamphlet, promised by the first, was issued. It attacked the present worldly situation and boasted of the wisdom of C.R. (i.e., the magical world) and the importance of the secrecy of the order.

It is now generally agreed that a Lutheran pastor, Johann Valentin Andreae (1586–1654), was the author of the original Rosicrucian pamphlet. He admitted to being the author of the 1616 novel *The Hermetic Romance or the Chemical Wedding*, purportedly written in High Dutch by Christian Rosencreutz. Thereafter, works claiming to be products of a secret fraternity of Rosicrucians appeared sporadically.

There is evidence of other secret fraternities of an occult nature operating in Europe in the next several centuries. One such group was the Illuminati, founded in 1776 by Adam Weishaupt (1748–1830). Even earlier, in 1670 the Abbé de Villars (1635–1673) published *The Count of Gabalis or Extravagant Mysteries of the Cabalists and Rosicrucians*. It was outwardly an attack on the Rosicrucians (thus good evidence of their existence), but many have seen it as an attempt to spread esotericism by making public its ideas. It was rumored that de Villars was murdered a few years later by the Rosicrucians.

English Rosicrucianism was given its direction by Robert Fludd (1574–1635), alchemist and author of the *Apologia Compendiaria Fraternitatem de Rosea Cruce* (1616). He is the probable source of the rumor that the philosopher Francis Bacon (1561–1626) was a Rosicrucian. Among the founders of the English Rosicrucians was the astrologer William Lilly (1602–1681). British Rosicrucians were in favor of alchemy, as opposed to those on the continent at that time. Rosicrucian lodges proliferated in the eighteenth century. Many were fraudulent, but many were legitimate attempts at forming societies attuned to Rosicrucian ideals. It was also at this time that Rosicrucians and Freemasons began to interact, and Freemasons added a Rosicrucian degree to their initiations.

FREEMASONRY.

The dominant role of contemporary Freemasonry as a fraternal organization has often obscured its crucial role in the building of modern esoteric tradition, and many histories of the modern esoteric movement make only passing mention of the Freemasons. What is today known as Freemasonry emerged in the seventeenth century out of the older craft guilds of stoneworkers. The guilds guarded a secret wisdom, the knowledge of architecture used in the building of many churches and public structures. By the seventeenth century, many nonmasons had been "accepted" into membership in guilds as friendly associates. The number of such "accepted" members grew steadily, and by the middle of the century some lodges were dominated, if not entirely composed of, accepted Masons rather than members who claimed knowledge of masonry. The fellowships of accepted Masons served as covers for esoteric discussions, speculation, and activity.

In 1771 four lodges of accepted Masons came together to form the Grand Lodge of England. The third grand master, Theophilus Dasaguliers (1683–1744), used his social and professional status (he was chaplain to the prince of Wales) to spread the movement and the authority of the Grand Lodge not only across Great Britain but to France. The Scottish and Irish lodges organized separately in the 1850s as the Ancient Grand Lodge, and only merged with their English brethren in 1813 to become the United Grand Lodge.

The accepted Masons built a speculative esoteric cosmology with borrowed symbols from the stone workers as religious symbols. God became known as the Great Architect of the Universe. The Great Pyramid of Egypt, an exemplary achievement of the stoneworkers' skill, was portrayed in Masonic symbolism as a building constructed of 72 stones, one each for the possible combinations of the tetragrammaton, the name of God in Hebrew that consisted of four letters. This symbolic pyramid was capped by the all-seeing eye of God. The Masonic pyramid can be seen on the American one-dollar bill, which pictures the Great Seal of the United States, an image strongly influenced by several Masons among the country's founders.

The different lodges in the eighteenth century developed an elaborate degree system loosely tied to an understanding of a universe emanating in layers from the realm of the divine. The rituals associated with each rite (or set of degrees) were filled with esoteric content and seemingly in a constant state of flux and development. Eventually, the 33-degree system still used in British and American Masonry came to dominate the lodges of the United Grand Lodge.

Masonry came to the United States from England in 1730 when Daniel Coxe (1673–1739) was appointed provincial grand master of New York, New Jersey, and Pennsylvania. Among the individuals soon welcomed into membership was a youthful Benjamin Franklin (1706–1790) whose task it became to publish the first American edition of *The Constitution of the Free-masons* by James Anderson (c.1679–1739) in 1734. The lodges, especially in the middle colonies, became meeting grounds for revolutionaries, and welcomed among their members George Washington (1732–1799), James Monroe (1758–1831), Paul Revere (1734–1818), Benedict Arnold (1741–1801), and Patrick Henry (1736–1799).

That so many revolutionaries were Masons gave early American masonry some connection with its continental counterparts. Masonic and Rosicrucian lodges also became the focus of efforts at democratic reform and became the object of both church and government hostility. As early as 1738, the Roman Catholic Church issued a pronouncement condemning Masonry. The church's view was not mellowed as European Masons became high-profile figures in various movements to overthrow monarchial regimes. In Italy, one such Freemason, Giuseppe Garibaldi (1807–1882), led the forces that annexed the Papal States to modern Italy and left the pope with the few acres that make up the modern Vatican state. In England and the United States, Masonry developed in a more nonpolitical manner and became the birthing place for much of modern Rosicrucianism.

In 1865 a Masonic-based Rosicrucian body was founded in London by Robert Wentworth Little (1840–1878). The Societas Rosicruciana in Anglia was modeled on the German Fratres of the Golden and Rosy Cross of the previous century, and membership was confined to master masons. This group became the breeding ground of the Hermetic Order of the Golden Dawn.

Like the teachings of Theosophy and Freemasonry, Rosicrucian teachings are a form of esotericism and mysticism. Transmutation, psychic development, and meditative/yogic disciplines are stressed. Teachings are differentiated into outer or public teachings (which include most of the philosophic material) and inner, for-members-only teachings (which include most of the instruction on ritual and development exercises). It is difficult for nonmembers to obtain access to the secret materials, especially from the smaller bodies.

As in Masonic rituals, a system of initiation through a number of degrees is used, each initiation admitting members into deeper and more secret knowledge. Most Rosicrucian groups have published books covering their general orientation, which they sell to the public and place in libraries. Some of these have become widely used, quite apart from any involvement in the group that published it.

ROSICRUCIANISM IN AMERICA.

The history of Rosicrucians in the United States dates to 1694 with the arrival of the Chapter of Perfection in Germantown, Pennsylvania. The chapter, composed of Rosicrucians who derived their teachings from mystic Jacob Boehme (1575–1624), the Kabbalah, and several German psychic visionaries, built an observatory and temple and thrived for a generation, but slowly died away after the death of its leader, Johannes Kelpius (1673–1708). The chapter left no group to carry on its work, but the first powwow magicians, the Pennsylvania Dutch practitioners of folk magic, were associated with the Chapter of Perfection. No further reference to Rosicrucians in America occurs until the nineteenth century, when Pascal Beverly Randolph (1825–1875), the founder of the first of the present Rosicrucian bodies, appeared.

While largely forgotten in North America, Randolph was the premier esoteric theorist of the nineteenth century. Growing up as Spiritualism was making its impact on the West, he would author more than 20 books that would offer Americans the first major alternative system of esoteric thought. Four years before Robert Wentworth Little founded the first viable British Rosicrucian group, Randolph launched the Rosicrucian Fraternity in America. He advocated the idea of reincarnation and was the first to write extensively on themes of esoteric sexuality. Randolph continually had to fight racial prejudice (his mother was African American) and misunderstandings of his sexual ideas, but his works survived him to provide the foundation upon which the likes of Helena Petrovna Blavatsky were to later build.

THEOSOPHY.

The reputation of Helena Petrovna Blavatsky (1831–1891) has largely outlived the scandal that surrounded her for the last 25 years of her life, and she is now recognized as one of the most influential writers in the esoteric world. Through her two major books, *Isis Unveiled* (1877) and especially *The Secret Doctrine* (1888), she taught several generations about esoteric lore, and the Theosophical Society she founded has become a major force in the esoteric community.

Blavatsky was born in Russia of an aristocratic family. She became a student of Spiritualism and showed mediumistic tendencies. In 1851 she began a life of wandering that took her to India. There, she claimed contact with the "mahatmas," persons who had evolved to a point from which they have become conscious coworkers with the divine plan of the ages and are thus beings of great authority, attainment, and responsibility. Their wisdom guides all movements for growth, particularly the Theosophical Society. During her life, Blavatsky claimed constant contact with them.

Blavatsky went to England and then the United States, where she became deeply involved in Spiritualism (though she was later to become one of its major critics). In 1873 she met Henry Steel Olcott (1832–1907), and together they founded the Theosophical Society in New York in 1875. *Isis Unveiled* became the society's initial central document. As the first president, Olcott became the chief administrator of the movement and Blavatsky's right arm.

The Theosophical Society set three objectives for itself: (1) to form a nucleus of the universal brotherhood of humanity without distinction of race, creed, sex, caste, or color; (2) to encourage the study of comparative religion, philosophy, and science; and (3) to investigate the unexplained laws of nature and the powers latent in man.

The original society was an outgrowth of Spiritualism, and, in her early writings, Blavatsky still rejected reincarnation. She claimed that Spiritualist phenomena were genuine but were the work of lower astral entities rather than disincarnates.

In 1879 Olcott and Blavatsky sailed for India and established permanent headquarters in Adyar. Blavatsky discovered Hinduism and Buddhism and became fascinated with them as continuations of the ancient wisdom of Egypt and the Mediterranean. Also, at this time, the concept of the mahatmas or masters came to the fore. From a special altar in her home at Adyar and a few other places, letters from the masters in the spirit world began to arrive.

Blavatsky's cosmology is the basis of Theosophical thought. To the novice, the cosmology is a highly complicated Pleroma of Gods and lesser entities organized in a divine hierarchy and controlling the overall evolution of the earth. Aiding the hierarchy are the mahatmas or masters, men who have evolved to an almost semidivine status and who directly represent the hierarchy to the human race. The masters are the key to the Theosophical system. As in most esoteric systems, numerical symmetry is a feature; the numbers three, seven, and ten continually arise.

At the top of the Theosophical hierarchy is God, usually referred to as the Cosmic Logos. He expresses himself as a trinity, usually thought of in Hindu categories as creator, preserver, and destroyer (Brahma, Vishnu, and Shiva are the Hindu deities.) There are also seven Planetary Logoi; every star in the universe is assigned to one of these logoi. The sun and solar system are assigned to the Solar Logos, the Lord of this system and God for mankind. The Solar Logos emanates a trinity (Father, Son, and Holy Ghost) and seven logoi. Along with these logoi, there are a number of lesser angelic entities called Devas.

Humankind is the product of a lengthy evolutionary process. The earth (and universe) is in the midst of a seven-stage cycle. The first three stages are steps toward materialization; the fourth is crystallization; and the last three will be characterized by spiritualization and a return to spirit. We live in the fourth stage now. Humankind appeared at the beginning of the fourth stage and has furthered human physical evolvement from lower life forms through the merger of the spirit with the body, welded together with the mind. Thus, physical evolution of more complicated animal forms met spirit being thrust into matter, and, because spirit and matter could not be joined in themselves, mind became the intermediate principle.

Human evolvement takes human beings through seven root races, each of which has seven subraces. The first three root races perfected the union of matter and spirit; the fourth expresses the union; the last three will represent the struggle of the spirit to be free of matter. We now live in the Fifth Root Race. The third race was the Lemurian, so named for the mythical submerged continent in the Pacific Ocean, and the fourth was the Atlantean, so named for Atlantis, the supposed paradisiacal origin of man. The Fifth Root Race, the Aryan, finds its culmination in the Anglo-Saxon subrace. From this point, humankind will evolve into spiritual adepts.

A human is a complicated being composed of seven bodies ranking from the pure-spirit true self to the gross material body. These planes of existence are outlined thus:

1. Divine—Adi
2. Monadic—Anupadaka
3. Spiritual—Nirvanic
4. Intuitional—Buddhic
5. Mental—Mental
6. Astral—Astral
7. Physical—Physical

In this list, the terms on the right are the proper terms, several of them being the Eastern words for the planes of existence. The terms on the left are explanatory of the proper terms. Level six, the astral, is a low-grade immaterial plane that is not highly regarded; it is occupied by such lesser figures as ghosts. Level two, the monadic, is the level of union with all that exists.

A human being is a spark of divinity that manifests itself as a trinity of spirit, intuition, and mentality. An individual assume a body appropriate to each level of functioning. As a person moves downward, each body he or she assumes is composed of denser substance. The astral and the physical are the densest, and these are discarded at death. It is the Theosophist belief that most Spiritualist phenomena are centered on contact with the astral plane and "discarded astral shells." Theosophists often complain that Spiritualists are engaged in lower psychism.

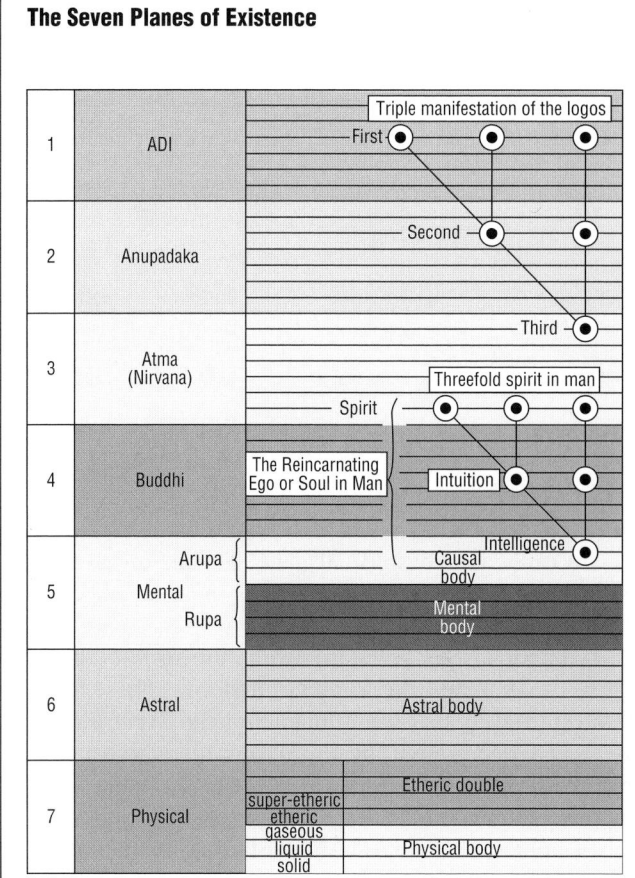

The Seven Planes of Existence

1	ADI	Triple manifestation of the logos / First
2	Anupadaka	Second
3	Atma (Nirvana)	Third / Threefold spirit in man / Spirit
4	Buddhi	The Reincarnating Ego or Soul in Man / Intuition
5	Arupa / Mental / Rupa	Intelligence / Causal body / Mental body
6	Astral	Astral body
7	Physical	super-etheric / etheric / gaseous / liquid / solid — Etheric double / Physical body

In the present evolutionary struggle to become free from matter, humanity is hindered because its consciousness is stuck in the gutter of the physical plane. The goal of this life is to raise the consciousness to higher levels. Humankind is hindered in this goal by each body's inability to apprehend the higher vibration rate of the less-dense substance above it, but humanity is helped by various occult practices, reincarnation, and the masters from the spirit world.

Theosophy offers a number of occult practices, such as meditation and yoga, as techniques to help the self to reach life on higher planes. These techniques, common to most religious traditions, overcome the tendency to place attention purely on the physical plane.

Reincarnation is the educative process by which the self is given repeated opportunities to rediscover its true life. Humans take on successive bodies until they overcome attachments to the lower planes. Each life is a representation of the state of evolvement of the soul in previous lives.

By far the greatest help to human evolvement are the masters. These are spiritual giants, men and women who have progressed far beyond the human race, who no longer need to incarnate, but who do so in order to aid the struggling race. They form an intermediate hierarchy between man and the solar rulers. The hierarchy of masters is given a name by position. Each position is currently filled by entities who were once incarnated on this physical plane and who are known,

Chart of the Seven Rays

Ray	Color	Crystal or gemstone	Ascended Master	Archangel	Purpose
1st Tuesday	Blue Ray of divine will	Sapphire	El Morya	Michael	Strength, courage, protection and can help one understand why things happen.
2nd Sunday	Yellow ray of wisdom	Topaz	Lord Lanto	Jophiel	Inspiration, knowledge, illumination. Can help one with learning and study.
3rd Monday	Pink ray of love	Rose quartz	Paul the Venetian	Chamuel	Love in all its forms (i.e. recognizing the Divine within all).
4th Friday	White ray of purity	Diamond	Serapis Bey	Gabriel	Truth, purity. Can help with organization.
5th Wednesday	Green ray of healing	Emerald	Hilarion	Raphael	Nourishment, healing, calm. Can help with all forms of healing.
6th Thursday	Purple and gold ray of devotion	Ruby	Lady Nada	Uriel	Service, selflessness, can help one cooperate with others.
7th Saturday	Violet ray of transmutation and freedom	Amethyst	Saint Germain	Zadkiel	Transmutes all energy into light. Can help heal all aspects of mind, body & soul.

in many cases, as great spiritual giants. The masters are organized in a complicated system, much as the solar hierarchy is organized.

At the top is the Lord of the World, the agent of the Solar Logos. Under him is the Trinity of Buddhas. These four are often referred to as Sanat Kumara and the Three Kumaras. The three department heads in the hierarchy are Will, Love/Wisdom, and Intelligence. Each of these has a representative: Manu Vaivasvata, Bodhisattva Maitreya, and the Maha Chohan. The hierarchical assistants, who manifest Will, Love/Wisdom, and Intelligence to humans, are the Seven Rays. The first three of these Rays (Master Morya, Master Koot Hoomi, and the Venetian Master) are called the Three Aspects or Major Rays. The other four are called the Four Attributes or Minor Rays (Master Serapis, Master Hilarion, Master Jesus, and Master Prince Rakoczi). Morya manifests Will to humans; Koot Hoomi manifests Love/Wisdom; and the other five masters manifest Intelligence. (Various Theosophical groups spell Koot Hoomi's name differently—sometimes Kuthumi, sometimes Kut Hoomi.) Master Jupiter is an assistant to Morya with a special relationship to India. Master Djual Khool is an assistant to Koot Hoomi with a special relationship to the Theosophical Society. The following chart shows the hierarchical arrangement. Those numbered are the Seven Rays.

・・・

Sanat Kumara
Three Buddhas

Will	Love Wisdom	Intelligence
Manu Vaivasvata	Bodhisattva Maitreya	The Maha Chohan
1 Master Morya	2 Master Koot Hoomi	3 Venetian Master
Master Jupiter	Master Djual Khool	4 Master Serapis
		5 Master Hilarion
		6 Master Jesus
		7 Master Prince Rakoczi

・・・

These masters are confusing at first, until one realizes that their names designate their positions, not their identity

in this earthly life. The entities who presently hold those positions have reappeared in physical form throughout history, but not always as the individual one might expect from a casual perusal of the chart. For example, the position in the hierarchy called Master Jesus is now filled by the person who was known on earth as the Greek figure Apollonius. The masters, their characteristics, and their most famous incarnations are charted below:

・・・

1. Morya	Power and Strength	A Tibetan
2. Koot Hoomi	Wisdom	Pythagoras
3. The Venetian	Adaptability	Plotinus
4. Serapis	Harmony and Beauty	
5. Hilarion	Science	Iambichus
6. Jesus	Purity and Devotion	Apollonius
7. Prince Rakoczi	Ordered Service (Ceremonial Magic)	Rosencreutz and Roger Bacon

・・・

The one known on earth as Jesus in this life was, according to Theosophists, a reincarnation of Shri Krishna and is now filling the position of Bodhisattva Maitreya. Master Jupiter is the special guardian of India, and Djual Khool is especially attached to the leaders of the Theosophical Society. The masters work through the leadership of the Theosophical Society and thus become the teachers of the human race. They possess the wisdom that humankind needs to escape the repetition of incarnations and rise to the spiritual home. The Seven Rays use the seven colors of the rainbow in aiding people.

While the masters speak in cognitive language, the wisdom of which they speak is occult (hidden) and, in the long run, available only by the apprehension of the higher self. Like the knowledge that comes out of the relationship of loving another person, it cannot be reduced to statements or adequately conveyed by words.

Theosophy, as a movement, developed centers of work in the United States, England, and India, but the major issues were decided in Adyar, where Blavatsky had set up headquarters. From there, her continued contact with the

694

masters grew at an increasing rate. Quite apart from the Theosophical system, the question of the existence of the masters became the issue for the last years of Blavatsky's leadership.

In 1884, while both Olcott and Blavatsky were in England, Emma Coulomb and her husband, who were in charge in Blavatsky's home, passed some materials to Christian missionaries, who published them and attacked what they considered fraud in the production of the messages from the masters. The messages, which appeared in a specially designed cabinet with secret openings to Blavatsky's bedroom and to another room in her house, were credited to Blavatsky herself.

The newly founded Society of Psychical Research sent Richard Hodson, a young British scholar, to investigate the matter. He found the opening from Blavatsky's bedroom into the place where the master's letters were delivered. In a lengthy report, he concluded that Blavatsky's messages were fraudulent, and he described at great length how various seemingly miraculous incidents had occurred. The society's report was a major blow and signaled a period of decline for the Theosophical Society.

In 1888 Blavatsky formally constituted and for the rest of her life headed what was known as the Esoteric Section. The Esoteric Section constituted an inner group of trusted students to whom she taught an advanced course of occultism. While not an official part of the society, it included the most dedicated Theosophists who, in effect, became an elite controlling group.

Blavatsky settled in London in 1887, where she was visited by Annie Besant (1847–1933), a young radical activist and orator who had made a name for herself as a colleague of atheist Charles Bradlaugh (1833–1891). Besant, having read *The Secret Doctrine*, was ready to leave her liberal background and become a Theosophist. Blavatsky recognized her talent and encouraged her. As a result of their effort, during the last five years of Blavatsky's life, the society recovered and expanded in Europe. Some outstanding workers, such as George R. S. Mead (1863–1933) and Mabel Collins (1851–1927), were attracted to the society. Olcott continued to offer his administrative ability.

Upon Blavatsky's death in 1891, Annie Besant's popularity began to rise, and she succeeded Blavatsky as head of the Esoteric Section. During the next decade, with Olcott's help, the society became a worldwide organization. Shortly before his death in 1907, Olcott received a message from the masters "appointing" Besant the new president. With her strong leadership, a new era began, and the society started a process of slow and steady growth that has resulted in its spread to all parts of the globe. Its literature is now distributed to the entire occult/psychic community. Only three things marred Besant's career—the Leadbeater affair, the Krishnamurti affair, and the loss of strong leaders in America and Germany who disagreed with her on points of administration and doctrine.

Charles W. Leadbeater (1854–1934), a priest in the Church of England, joined the Theosophical Society in 1883.

Soon afterward, he went to India to aid in its defense, and became a popular lecturer and writer. In 1895 he became assistant secretary of the European Section and a close friend of Besant, with whom he coauthored several books. The primary content of these books was the clairvoyant exploration of the cosmology of Blavatsky. Gradually, these books became the dominant literature of the movement.

The crisis with Leadbeater arose in 1906, when he was charged with giving immoral sexual advice to several youths who had been left in his charge. He had taught the boys the practice of masturbation as a means of dealing with their physical problems (sexual urges). Besant tried to defend her friend, who was being verbally attacked. The scandal was eventually overcome, and Leadbeater remained active in the Theosophical Society, but the blot on Besant continued to be used by her adversaries.

During the early years of the century, Besant, with input from Leadbeater, began to talk of the coming of an avatar, a world teacher, to lead the world into a new stage of evolution. In a series of lectures in 1909 on "The Changing World," she declared that a new race was coming and a new Christ was to appear. Then, in the winter of 1908 to 1909, a Theosophical Society member in Adyar named Narayaniah asked the society to care for his motherless boys, among them, Jiddu Krishnamurti (1895–1986).

Leadbeater, now living in Adyar, immediately became attached to Krishnamurti, whom he called Alcyone, meaning the calmer of storms. Convinced that Krishnamurti was destined to be a great spiritual leader, Leadbeater became his teacher. During the next two years, Leadbeater worked with him psychically, and the product was a now-famous book, *At the Feet of the Master* (1911). Besant soon became convinced that Krishnamurti was the body to be used by the bodhisattva (avatar) for his new appearance. In January 1912, a new periodical, *Herald of the Star*, was launched to announce his appearance. Already formed as a preparatory organization was the Order of the Star of the East. The material advocating his cause began to roll off the Adyar presses.

But obstacles asserted themselves before the new Christ could begin his mission. Krishnamurti's father demanded the return of his son; the sexual charges against Leadbeater were revived; and a series of court cases was initiated. The court finally ruled in favor of the Theosophical Society. The Order of the Star of the East progressed until Krishnamurti himself began to reject his assigned role in 1929. The Order of the Star of the East then died for lack of a messiah.

Over the period of the various scandals, schisms rent the Theosophical Society. As various leaders and groups jockeyed for power, they found themselves disgusted with Leadbeater and opposed to many of Besant's new ideas. Alternative messages from the masters began to appear through different channels, challenging Besant's authority. The story of these schisms is the story of the development of the Theosophical subfamily of religious groups.

THEOSOPHY IN AMERICA. The Theosophical Society was founded in New York City in 1875, at which time cofounder William Q. Judge (1851–1896), a lawyer, became the group's counsel. After Olcott and Blavatsky moved to India, the activity level of the American organization fell measurably. Judge gradually revived it, and the American organization was reconstituted in 1886. Judge also became head of the American branch of the Esoteric Section, authored a number of books, including the classic *Ocean of Theosophy* (1893), and edited the society's two periodicals, *The Path* and *The Theosophical Forum.*

From the beginning, American Theosophists resented being controlled from India. Judge hoped to become the international president of the Theosophical Society, and hence did not favor the rise of Annie Besant. Her triumphant American tour, which included speaking to overflow crowds at the World's Parliament of Religions in Chicago in 1893, did not help.

Besant was able, however, to work out a temporary arrangement to share power in the Esoteric Section, with Judge in America and she in Europe and India. This arrangement came about partly because Judge proposed the plan, and because of the subsequent appearance of a message from Master Morya with the words, "Judge's plan is right." As other messages appeared, remarks that they were emanating from Judge rather than the masters became formal charges. The society had no mechanism for handling such charges, and after newspapers got a hold of the allegedly false messages, they attacked Judge viciously. Judge retorted by declaring that Besant was no longer head of the Theosophical Society and was under the control of dark forces.

In 1895 at the American Theosophists' Convention in Boston, the Americans declared themselves independent of the British and Indian headquarters and formed the Theosophical Society in America. Seventy-five American branches went with Judge. Fourteen remained loyal to Adyar and were rechartered as the American Theosophical Society (now called the Theosophical Society of America), with Alexander Fullerton as president. During the twentieth century, these two rival Theosophical societies spawned a number of new groups, most importantly those growing out of the work of Alice Bailey and Guy W. Ballard.

LIBERAL CATHOLIC CHURCH. During the second decade of the twentieth century, Theosophical ideas became established among the priests of the independent Old Roman Catholic Church in Great Britain, which had been established by Bishop Arnold Harris Matthew (1852–1918) in 1908. In 1914, little realizing the implications of his act, Matthew consecrated Frederick Samuel Willoughby (b. 1862), an active Theosophist, as a bishop in his church. Over the next year, however, Matthew realized that Theosophy was threatening to overwhelm his jurisdiction. In August 1915 he condemned Theosophy and ordered all of his clergy to sever their ties with the society. Still unaware of the extent of Theosophical penetration of the church's priesthood, he saw the majority of his priests resign.

The disruption took most of the strength from the Old Roman Catholic Church, which never recovered from the loss and today remains a small inconsequential organization. The resigned priests reorganized and elected James Ingall Wedgewood as their bishop. Willoughby consecrated him in 1916, and Wedgewood soon afterward left on a world tour. In Australia he met with Charles Leadbeater, who was living there in self-imposed exile, and consecrated him regionary bishop for the subcontinent. Leadbeater would later write the major theological books reworking the Christian tradition in a Theosophical/esoteric mode.

At a synod in 1918, the new organization adopted the name Liberal Catholic Church. The following year, Wedgewood went to the United States and there consecrated Irving Steiger Cooper (1882–1935) as the regionary bishop for the United States. Cooper, who had earlier worked with Leadbeater, assumed major duties in developing a liturgy for the new church. In 1934 he published a book of worship, *Ceremonies of the Liberal Catholic Rite.* The Liberal Catholic Church spread into most countries where the Theosophical Society was established and has continued as a small body for people who are attracted to the society but wish to participate in a liturgical worship program. Other branches of the Theosophical movement generally saw the church in negative terms.

THE ALICE BAILEY MOVEMENT. Alice La Trobe Bateman (1880–1949), a teenage church-school teacher in the Church of England, was stunned one Sunday morning to see the door to her home open and a tall stranger with a turban walk in and speak to her. He told her of important work already mapped out for her future. This event was but one of a number of psychical/mystical happenings that, coupled with world travel for the Young Men's Christian Association (YMCA) and an unsuccessful marriage, brought her to the Theosophical Society in Pacific Grove, California.

Theosophical teachings of a divine plan for humanity, a hierarchy of masters, and reincarnation and karma appealed to her. While at the Theosophical Society she saw a picture of the man in the turban; he was identified as the Master Koot Hoomi, who figures in the Theosophical cosmology. She became active in the society and there met Foster Bailey (1888–1975), whom she married. He became national secretary of the society, and Alice became editor of the *Messenger,* the sectional magazine.

In 1919 Alice reported that she was approached by a Master Djwhal Khul (Djual Khool), who requested that he become her control in the transmission by clairvoyant telepathy of a series of books. After first objecting, Alice began to receive (channel) *Initiation, Human and Solar,* her first book. Nineteen books in all were dictated to Alice between 1919 and 1960, along with other books written by Alice and Foster themselves.

At first, the chapters of *Initiation, Human and Solar* were received with enthusiasm and were serialized in *The Theosophist,* but then publication abruptly stopped. Concurrently, trouble developed within the Esoteric Section of the Theosophical Society over the dictations. Alice complained that Annie Besant, the head of the society, acted autocratically, demanded that members cut outside ties and swear loyalty to her, and allowed contact with the masters from the spirit world only with her consent. The trouble came to a head at the 1920 convention, when Besant's supporters were placed in all the key offices, and both Foster and Alice were dismissed from their positions. They thus became free to pursue their own work of transmitting the material from Djual Khool.

Alice Bailey's teachings resemble Theosophy closely, with the description of the divine hierarchy, the seven rays, and the evolution of humans to higher levels. According to Bailey, humans had evolved by 1920 to the point where they could look toward the new age, when groups could form advanced training schools to prepare for the real esoteric schools. In the 1930s this observation took on an eschatological emphasis when it was revealed that, because of the spiritual yearnings of humanity, the new age was coming closer. According to Bailey's followers, this reappearance of the Christ will be accomplished by the power of the divine hierarchy descending into this world and by service based on the love of humanity. A two-pronged program was implemented to carry through the double emphasis.

To encourage the advent of the Christ, meditation groups were set up to help channel the energy from the hierarchy. Each group or person is seen as a point of light radiating the power of the world. A particularly effective way of channeling makes use of what Bailey promulgated as the Great Invocation. The invocation is repeated slowly and with solemnity while one visualizes the funneling down of power from the hierarchy. Various Bailey groups reprint and distribute this prayer, and it is often used by people with little comprehension of Bailey's understanding of its intent:

> *From the point of Light within the Mind of God*
> *Let light stream forth into the minds of men.*
> *Let Light descend on Earth.*
> *From the Point of Love within the Heart of God*
> *Let love stream forth into the hearts of men.*
> *May Christ return to Earth.*
> *From the centre where the Will of God is known*
> *Let purpose guide the little wills of men—*
> *The purpose which the Masters know and serve.*
> *From the centre which we call the race of men*
> *Let the Plan of Love and Light work out.*
> *And may it seal the door where evil dwells.*
> *Let Light and Love and Power restore the Plan on Earth.*

Particular times of the month and year have been designated as periods when special spiritual energies are available from the hierarchy. The period of the full moon is such a time; meditation groups always gather on the evening of the full moon to celebrate and meditate. On three of these full-moon dates occur the great spiritual festivals. Eventually, all people will celebrate these three festivals as focal points of the hierarchical year. The festival of Easter occurs with the full moon in April and is the time of active forces of the restoration of the Christ. The festival of Wesak occurs in May, the time of Buddha's forces of enlightenment. The festival of Goodwill is in June, when the forces of reconstruction are active. The festivals also illustrate Bailey's belief in the synthesis of East and West into a new unity of humankind.

The Bailey program of service has found expression in the New Group of World Servers. Within this nebulous body are those who, desiring to be disciples of the masters from the spirit world, work as intermediaries between the hierarchy and the mass of humanity. A second group is composed of people of goodwill who, knowing nothing of the hierarchy, nevertheless strive for goodwill under the guidance of the masters' disciples. From this ideal of service has come a number of practical programs in education and political realignment.

In 1923 the Baileys founded the Arcane School. After Alice's death in 1949, the movement splintered, and a number of full-moon meditation groups emerged. All of the Alice Bailey groups agree on the content of the teachings, though few individuals can master the voluminous writings. All gather for the full moon and celebrate the festivals. In southern California, most of the groups cooperate in publicizing and holding the celebrations. The main differences among the groups concern nonacceptance of the Bailey family leadership and local autonomy in spreading the teachings. Among members of the psychic community, the Bailey disciples have a reputation for evangelical fervor and proselytizing activity. This proselytizing zeal is often based on the Theosophical notion of the astral versus the higher spiritual planes. Nonbelievers are often seen as enmeshed in lower psychism.

THE "I AM" RELIGIOUS MOVEMENT. Among the most colorful of the several divergences within the larger Theosophical movement is the "I AM" Religious Activity founded by Guy W. Ballard (1878–1939) and his wife, Edna W. Ballard (1886–1971). Guy Ballard, a mining engineer, had decided in 1929, upon completion of a job in the West, to visit Mt. Shasta in California. As early as the 1880s, the mountain had been seen as the home of a lost race of mystic adepts from Atlantis who lived inside the massive volcanic structure. Throughout the next half-century, the occult legends had grown, and Ballard, a student of occult metaphysics, was intrigued.

While hiking up the side of the mountain, Ballard knelt to dip water from a mountain stream. A young man appeared and offered him "a much more refreshing drink than spring water." The cup was filled with a vivifying white liquid that the stranger identified as "omnipotent life." The young man continued to talk of abundant supply, reincarnation, and the laws of cause and effect. As he did, he changed into the mystical figure of Saint Germain, the seventeenth-century occultist, now an Ascended Master.

According to Ballard, Saint Germain described his task as that of initiating the seventh golden age, the permanent "I AM" age of eternal perfection on earth. During the previous six centuries, he had searched Europe for someone in human embodiment strong enough and pure enough that the instruction of the great law of life could be released through him. Having failed to find such a person, he turned to America and eventually located Ballard. Saint Germain designated Ballard, his wife Edna, and their son Donald as the only accredited messengers of the Ascended Masters.

During the ensuing months, Ballard reported numerous experiences with Saint Germain and other Ascended Masters, about which he regularly informed his wife through letters. Upon his return to Chicago, where the family dwelt, Edna's position as a messenger was confirmed and she began regular contact. Using the pen name Godfré Ray King, Guy Ballard recorded his initial experiences with Saint Germain, which were published as two volumes in 1934, *Unveiled Mysteries* and *The Magic Presence*. These were followed by additional volumes, including *The "I AM" Discourses* (1936), a series of lectures by Saint Germain that summarize the basic teachings; *"I AM" Adorations and Affirmations* (1935), which give the text for the decrees (the peculiar "I AM" form of prayer); and a hymn book, *"I AM" Songs* (1938). A periodical, *The Voice of the I AM*, was launched in 1936.

In 1932 the Ballards began to release the message of the Ascended Masters to the public. They formed the Saint Germain Foundation to administer the work and the Saint Germain Press to publish their materials. In 1934 they held the first public 10-day class in Chicago at the Civic Opera House. During the next few years, similar classes were held in New York, Philadelphia, Boston, Miami, and Los Angeles. More than 7,000 attended the Los Angeles classes. By the time of Guy Ballard's death in 1939, the movement claimed more than one million students (though the actual number was probably smaller).

According to the "I AM" teaching, in 1929 the Ascended Masters instituted a new thrust of activity. There had been previous thrusts, such as that initiated through Blavatsky and the Theosophical Society. This new thrust was begun by Saint Germain, the Lord of the Seventh Ray, who in previous incarnations claimed to be the Old Testament prophet Samuel, the British Saint Alban, and Sir Francis Bacon. As Bacon, he claimed to have authored the Shakespearean plays. In 1684 he "illumined and raised His body" and spent a period of time in the Himalayas, only to return to Europe at the time of the French Revolution. Thereafter he worked in America, the seat of the new civilization, which represents the permanent condition on the planet in the future.

Saint Germain taught the nature and importance of the "I AM" Presence, the mighty presence of light, God in action. The "I AM" Presence emanates from the mighty creative fire, the great central sun, the impersonal source of reality in the world. Out of its abundance, the great central sun pours forth the primal light. That primal light is the basis for all manifested form in both the visible and invisible world. Through the individualization of the light, everything comes into existence.

The term I AM refers to that primal light, the opulence and energy of God. Individualized, it is the essence of each person, and is to be constantly invoked and activated. The individual's "I AM" Presence is the real point of contact with divine reality, and hence properly referred to as the presence of God within each person. It is visualized in a chart used by "I AM" students that shows an individual surrounded in a column of purple flame. Above the individual, connected by a shaft of white light, is the "I AM" Presence, pictured as a person clothed in golden light surrounded by a circular rainbow of light, a color radiance indicative of the accumulated good of previous lives.

The "I AM" Presence is invoked by the use of decrees, affirmative commands for the "I AM" Presence to initiate action. In calling upon the "I AM" Presence, the violet flame pictured around each person is activated as a purifying fire to burn undesirable personal conditions away. A wide variety of decrees for handling both personal and social situations is used by "I AM" students. Most controversial are the several negative decrees that target specific conditions for annihilation, to be blasted from existence. These come with instructions that such decrees can be used only for the dissipation of discord and imperfection. They can have no effect upon that which is good, and are certainly not to be directed against any individual, though they may be directed toward a negative condition surrounding a person.

Assisting and guiding humanity, both individuals in their personal conditions as well as the human race in its process of evolving, are the Ascended Masters. A master is an individual who has passed through several human incarnations but, by his own effort, has generated the conditions necessary to rise above human limitations (ascend) and escape the necessity of continued reembodiment. Such Ascended Masters radiate love and power, which can be called upon to correct the various destructive currents that retard humanity. Each master, a visible tangible being, has a particular quality or talent that is invoked for particular situations.

The steady progress of the "I AM" movement was interrupted by a series of events that began shortly after the sudden death of Guy Ballard in 1939. Several former students became vocal critics of the activity. One, Gerald B. Bryan, wrote a series of books against the foundation. In 1941 Edna and Donald Ballard and several members of the staff of the foundation were indicted for mail fraud, in reference to their promotion of the "I AM" movement through the mail. In a trial, which began in December 1941, the Ballards were convicted of making a variety of fraudulent misrepresentations and false promises to several ex-members who testified that the Ballards were not only advocating a false religion but that they knew it to be false. Subsequently, the postal department denied both the foundation and the press their privilege to use the mail.

The conviction was appealed, and in 1944 a landmark decision in religious liberty was granted in a U.S. Supreme Court ruling that reversed the judgment (*United States v. Ballard*). Justice William O. Douglas, in stating the opinion of the Court, asserted, "Men may believe what they cannot prove. They may not be put to the proof of their religious doctrines or beliefs." The case, sent down for review, was finally dismissed in 1946.

During the period of the initial trial and the subsequent appeals, the "I AM" Religious Activity became the victim of a hostile press, and many students left the movement. The ending of criminal litigation set the stage for the rebuilding of the movement, even though additional legal action over the next decade was required to handle the problems created by the original conviction. For example, eight years of further action were needed to reverse the effects of the 1943 decision and return full use of the mail system to the foundation. (During the intervening years, the foundation and press distributed materials through American Express.) The period of rebuilding also set the stage for the formation of new organizations by individuals who agreed with the essentials of the Ascended Masters' teachings, but who also claimed subsequent direct contact with additional teachings.

ANCIENT WISDOM IN THE TWENTY-FIRST CENTURY. As the new century begins, the Rosicrucian, Theosophical, Alice Bailey, "I AM," and Liberal Catholic organizations continue to be active, though relatively few new ancient-wisdom organizations are being formed. Several new Rosicrucian groups arose from a controversy that hit the Ancient Mystical Order of the Rosae Crucis; however, this is not symbolic of the life and ferment that saw a dramatic increase in the number of those who adhere to the ancient-wisdom tradition.

The New Age movement, a millennial revitalizing movement that swept through the esoteric community in the 1980s, was characterized in part by renewed interest in mediumship, now termed channeling. A close examination of channeling groups and the materials they produce indicates that the affirmations of the ancient-wisdom groups, including their basic theological perspective and their search for authority by appeal to an ancient perennial wisdom, permeate the teachings offered by various channeled entities (such as Ramtha, channeled by JZ Knight, and Michael, channeled by various individuals). The New Age movement alone brought several million people into the esoteric community, capturing the allegiance of many individuals who might otherwise be expected to adhere to the various older ancient-wisdom organizations. Most of these people stayed attached to the esoteric world even as the New Age movement died out in the 1990s.

SOURCES

Research on esoteric history is given focus by the Association for the Study of Esotericism and its journal *Esoterica*; the offices of both may be reached at 235 Bessey Hall, ATL Dept., Michigan State University, East Lansing, MI 48824. Theosophy is the primary topic covered by the Theosophical History Foundation, which may be contacted at the Department of Religious Studies, California State University–Fullerton, 1800 North State College Blvd., Fullerton, CA 92634-9480. It publishes the quarterly journal *Theosophical History*. Significant collections of Theosophical literature are available at the headquarters of the Theosophical Society in Pasadena, California; at the headquarters of the Theosophical Society in Wheaton, Illinois; and at the Krotona Institute (affiliated with the Theosophical Society in America) in Ojai, California. The largest academic collection on Theosophy is found in the J. Gordon Melton American Religions Collection at Davidson Library at the University of California–Santa Barbara.

Esotericism—General Sources

Bogdan, Henrik. *Western Esotericism and Rituals of Initiation*. Albany: State University of New York Press, 2008. 235 pp.

Ellwood, Robert S., Jr. *Religious and Spiritual Groups in Modern America*. 2nd ed. Englewood Cliffs, NJ: Prentice-Hall, 1988. 328 pp.

Faivre, Antoine. *Access to Western Esotericism*. Albany, NY: State University of New York Press, 1994. 369 pp.

———. *Theosophy, Imagination, Tradition: Studies in Western Esotericism*. Trans. Christine Rhone. Albany: State University of New York Press, 2000. 269 pp.

Faivre, Antoine, and Jacob Needleman, eds. *Modern Esoteric Spirituality*. New York: Crossroad, 1992. 413 pp.

Godwin, Joscelyn. *The Theosophical Enlightenment*. Albany: State University of New York Press, 1994. 448 pp.

———. *The Golden Thread: The Ageless Wisdom of the Western Mystery Traditions*. Wheaton, IL: Quest, 2007. 172 pp.

Godwin, Joscelyn, Christian Chanel, and John P. Deveney, eds. *The Hermetic Brotherhood of Luxor: Initiatic and Historical Documents of an Order of Practical Occultism*. York Beach, ME: Weiser, 1995. 452 pp.

Goodrick-Clarke, Nicholas. *The Western Esoteric Traditions: A Historical Introduction*. New York: Oxford University Press, 2008. 356 pp.

Hall, Manly Palmer. *Great Books on Religion and Eastern Philosophy*. Los Angeles: Philosophical Research Society, 1966. 85 pp.

Hanegraaff, Wouter J., ed., with Antoine Faive, Roelof van den Broek, and Jean-Pierre Brach. *Dictionary of Gnosis and Western Esotericism*. 2 vols. Leiden: Brill, 2005.

Judah, J. Stillson. *The History and Philosophy of the Metaphysical Movements in America*. Philadelphia: Westminster Press, 1967. 317 pp.

Kies, Cossete N. *The Occult in the Western World: An Annotated Bibliography*. Hamden, CT: Library Professional, 1986. 233 pp.

King, Karen L. *What Is Gnosticism?* Cambridge, MA: Belknap Press, 2003. 343 pp.

Smoley, Richard. *Forbidden Faith: The Gnostic Legacy from the Gospels to the Da Vinci Code*. New York: HarperOne, 2007. 256 pp.

Smoley, Richard, and Jay Kinney. *Hidden Wisdom: A Guide to the Western Inner Traditions*. Rev. ed. Wheaton, IL: Quest, 2006. 430 pp.

Versluis, Arthur. *Magic and Mysticism: An Introduction to Western Esotericism*. Lanham, MD: Rowman & Littlefield, 2007. 208 pp.

Versluis, Arthur, Lee Irwin, John Richards, and Melinda Weinstein, eds. *Esotericism, Art, and Imagination*. East Lansing: Michigan State University Press, 2008. 327 ppp.

von Stuckard, Kocku. *Western Esotericism: A Brief History of Secret Knowledge*. London: Equinox, 2005. 148 pp.

Rosicrucianism

Allen, Paul M., ed. *A Christian Rosenkreutz Anthology*. Blauvelt, NY: Steiner, 1968. 702 pp.

Clymer, R. Swinburne. *The Rosicrucian Fraternity in America*. 2 vols. Quakertown, PA: Rosicrucian Foundation, 1935.

Deveney, John Patrick. *Paschal Beverly Randolph: A Nineteenth-century Black American Spiritualist, Rosicrucian, and Sex Magician*. Albany: State University of New York Press, 1997. 607 pp.

Lewis, H. Spencer. *Rosicrucian Questions and Answers*. 9th ed. San Jose, CA: Supreme Grand Lodge of AMORC, 1969.

Matthews, John, Bembridge, Paul, Joscelyn Godwin, et al. *The Rosicrucian Enlightenment Revisited*. Hudson, NY: Lindisfarne 1999. 267 pp.

McIntosh, Christopher. *The Rosy Cross Unveiled*. Wellingborough, U.K.: Aquarian Press, 1980. 160 pp.

Voorhis, Harold V. B. *Masonic Rosicrucian Societies.* New York: Press of Henry Emmerson, 1958. 146 pp.

Waite, Arthur Edward. *The Brotherhood of the Rosy Cross.* London: Rider, 1924. 249 pp.

————. *The Real History of the Rosicrucians.* London: Redway, 1887. 446 pp.

Yates, Frances A. *The Rosicrucian Enlightenment.* London: Routledge & Kegan Paul, 1972. 269 pp.

Theosophy

Campbell, Bruce F. *A History of the Theosophical Movement.* Berkeley: University of California Press, 1980. 249 pp.

Cranston, S. C. *HPB: The Extraordinary Life and Influence of Helena Blavatsky, Founder of the Modern Theosophical Movement.* New York: Putnam, 1993. 648 pp.

Ellwood, Robert. *Theosophy.* Wheaton, IL: Theosophical Publishing House, 1986. 226 pp.

Johnson, K. Paul. *The Masters Revealed: Madam Blavatsky and the Myth of the Great White Brotherhood.* Albany: State University of New York Press, 1994. 288 pp.

————. *Initiates of the Theosophical Masters.* Albany: State University of New York Press, 1995. 255 pp.

Meade, Marion. *Madame Blavatsky: The Woman behind the Myth.* New York: Putnam, 1980. 528 pp.

Mills, Joy. *100 Years of Theosophy.* Wheaton, IL: Theosophical Publishing House, 1987. 215 pp.

Murphet, Howard. *Hammer on the Mountain: Life of Henry Steel Olcott (1832–1907).* Wheaton, IL: Theosophical Publishing House, 1972. 339 pp.

Nethercot, Arthur H. *The First Five Lives of Annie Besant.* Chicago: University of Chicago Press, 1960. 419 pp.

————. *The Last Four Lives of Annie Besant.* Chicago: University of Chicago Press, 1963. 483 pp.

Rogers, L. W. *Elementary Theosophy.* Wheaton, IL: Theosophical Press, 1956. 269 pp.

Ryan, Charles J. *H. P. Blavatsky and the Theosophical Movement.* Pasadena, CA: Theosophical University Press, 1975. 358 pp.

Washington, Peter. *Madame Blavatsky's Baboon: A History of the Mystics, Mediums, and Misfits Who Brought Spiritualism to America.* New York: Schrocken, 1995. 470 pp.

Winner, Anna Kennedy. *The Basic Ideas of Occult Wisdom.* Wheaton, IL: Theosophical Publishing House, 1970. 113 pp.

Alice Bailey

Bailey, Alice A. *The Unfinished Autobiography.* New York: Lucas, 1951. 305 pp.

Sapat, Peter. *The Return of the Christ and Prophecy.* Philadelphia: Dorrance, 1978. 293 pp.

Sinclair, John R. *The Alice Bailey Inheritance.* Wellingborough, U.K.: Turnstone Press, 1984. 208 pp.

Thirty Years Work. New York: Lucis, n.d. 32 pp.

Liberal Catholic Church

Cooper, Irving S. *Ceremonies of the Liberal Catholic Rite.* Ojai, CA: St. Alban Press, 1964. 380 pp.

Hodson, Geoffrey. *The Inner Side of Church Worship.* Wheaton, IL: Theosophical Press, 1948. 82 pp.

————. *The Priestly Ideal.* London: St. Alban Press, 1971. 76 pp.

Leadbeater, Charles Webster. *The Hidden Side of Christian Festivals.* Los Angeles: St. Alban Press, 1920. 508 pp.

————. *The Science of the Sacraments.* Los Angeles: St. Alban Press, 1920. 560 pp.

The Liturgy According to the Use of the Liberal Catholic Church. London: St. Alban Press, 1983. 469 pp.

Norton, Robert. *The Willow in the Tempest: A Brief History of the Liberal Catholic Church in the United States of America from 1917 to 1942.* London: St. Alban Press, 1990. 318 pp.

Tillett, Gregory. *The Elder Brother: A Biography of Charles Webster Leadbeater.* London: Routledge & Kegan Paul, 1982. 337 pp.

"I AM" Religious Activity

King, Godfre Ray (Guy W. Ballard). *The Magic Presence.* Chicago: Saint Germain Press, 1935. 393 pp.

————. *The Unveiled Mysteries.* Chicago: Saint Germain Press, 1935. 260 pp.

Prophet, Elizabeth Clare. *The Great White Brotherhood.* Malibu, CA: Summit University Press, 1983. 356 pp.

Other Esoteric Orders

Childs, Gilbert. *Rudolf Steiner: His Life and Work.* Herndon, VA: Anthroposophic Press, 1996. 111 pp.

Hall, Manly Palmer. *What the Ancient Wisdom Expects of Its Disciples.* Los Angeles: Philosophical Research Society, 1945. 79 pp.

————. *Self-Unfoldment by Disciplines of Realization.* Los Angeles: Philosophical Research Society, 1946. 221 pp.

————. *Man: The Grand Symbol of the Mysteries.* Los Angeles: Philosophical Research Society, 1947. 420 pp.

Jones, Marc Edmund. *Occult Philosophy: An Introduction, the Major Concepts, and a Glossary* (1948). Stanwood, WA: Sabian Publishing Society, 1948. 436 pp.

Perkins, Lynn F. *The Masters as New Age Mentors.* Lakemont, GA: CSA Press, 1976. 228 pp.

Schuré, Edouard. *From Sphinx to Christ: An Occult History* (1928). Blauvelt, NY: Steiner, 1970. 284 pp.

Shepherd, A. P. *A Scientist of the Invisible: An Introduction to the Life and Work of Rudolf Steiner.* London, Hodder and Stoughton, 1954. 222 pp.

William, Sir. *The Occults in Council or the Great Learning.* Denver, CO: Smith-Brooks, 1901. 408 pp.

❊ Intrafaith Organizations

North American College of Gnostic Bishops

For information: info@NACGB.org.

The North American College of Gnostic Bishops (NACGB) was founded in January 2003 as a cooperative body of Gnostic churches and ordered communities. Founding members included the the Ecclesia Gnostica Catholica Hermetica, the Apostolic Johannite Church, and the Holy Apostolic Church of the Third Age (Joachimite). The College seeks to provide a unified voice for what it terms "Ecclesiastical Gnosticism" in North America, to facilitate fellowship, and to be a means of resolving any disputes in a cordial environment.

The College's Assembly gathers twice annually, and is led by its elected president, currently Mar Iohannes IV of the Apostolic Johannite Church. The Assembly deals with a variety of issues faced by Gnostic churches, not the least being the lack of graded materials for church educational programs. Membership is by invitation only.

Membership: As of 2008, the member organizations of the College were the Apostolic Johannite Church, the Holy Apostolic Church of the Third Age (Joachimite), the Ecclesia Gnostica Pravus, the Thelemic Gnostic Church of Alexandria, and the Oriental Apostolic Church of Damcar. In addition, the Alexandrian Gnostic Church is a probationary member. Individual members include Tau Allen Greenfield of the Ecclesia Gnostica Universalis.

Sources:

North American College of Gnostic Bishops. www.nacgb.org/.

Sophia Circle

For information: sophiacircle@Lcc.cc.

The Sophia Circle, formed in 2007, is a fellowship of bishops who have been consecrated in an episcopal lineage that includes apostolic succession and who also hold an esoteric view of Christianity. Most of the bishops who initially joined had a succession through the Liberal Catholic Church tradition, but the Circle does not limit itself to Liberal Catholic bishops. The Circle is also intimately connected with the International Liberal Catholic Fellowship, an association of clergy who adhere to an esoteric interpretation of Christianity also formed in 2007. The Sophia Circle differs in that it is limited to bishops only.

The Sophia Circle is based in the United Kingdom but includes members across Europe and North America. It holds an annual meeting.

Among the members of the circle are Bp. Thomas Langley of the Alexandrian Gnostic Church, Bp. Lee Peterson of the Free Apostolic Communion, Bp. Emir Michael Salihovic of the Ecclesia Gnostica Spiritualis, and independent Canadian bishop Mike Shaw.

Membership: In 2008, 13 bishops were affiliated with the Sophia Circle, of whom 3 were from the United States and 1 was from Canada.

Sources:

Sophia Circle. lcc.cc/sophiacircle/.

 # Rosicrucianism

Ancient and Mystical Order of the Rosae Crucis

1342 Naglee Ave., San José, CA 95191

[It should be noted that the Ancient and Mystical Order of the Rosae Crucis does not consider itself a religion and points out that its membership includes persons of every religion and creed. It is in this encyclopedia for two reasons. First, it is a major disseminator of the ancient wisdom teachings, the subject of this chapter, which are a significant element of what has, over the last century, become a new religious tradition in the west. Second, the order accepts as its own the same history (detailed in the introductory section of this volume) as the other Rosicrucian groups. Its inclusion has seemed necessary in order to present a full picture of the Rosicrucian presence in North America. The order is the largest of the several Rosicrucian bodies, and throughout its history it has been forced to interact with other organizations that have taken the Rosicrucian name.]

The Ancient and Mystical Order of the Rosae Crucis (AMORC) was founded as an esoteric fraternal order in 1915 in New York City by H. Spencer Lewis (1883–1939). Lewis was a young occultist who had been associated with the various British occult orders and who had met the famous British occultist Aleister Crowley (1875–1947). Active attempts to establish the Rosicrucian Order had begun in 1909. In that year, Lewis met French members of the International Rosicrucian Council in Toulouse. He was initiated, returned to America, and began holding meetings. In 1915 the order was firmly established, and the massive publicity campaign, which has made this branch of the Rosicrucian the best known to the general public, was begun.

Lewis's early affiliations with various occult groups, especially the Ordo Templi Orientis (OTO), which was headed by Crowley for many years, is clearly reflected in his frequent inclusions of material from them in the teachings and symbolism of AMORC. For example, the Rose Cross emblem was taken from the *Equinox III* (Crowley's periodical), and other emblems were borrowed from other sources. (Lewis was not above pure plagiarism; whole chapters of his *Mystic Life of Jesus* were taken from the *Aquarian Gospel of Jesus* by Levi Dowling.) In 1916, after the German OTO split with Crowley over *The Book of the Law*, the German group recognized AMORC in a document Lewis proudly displayed (in spite of OTO's association with the practice of sex magick, which AMORC has never advocated).

AMORC's rapid growth led to conflict with the other Rosicrucian bodies. In 1928, shortly after the move of AMORC to San José, the older Fraternitas Rosae Crucis launched an attack on Lewis, challenging the Order's right to the designation "Rosicrucian." Lewis accused R. Swinburne Clymer, a lifelong advocate of alternative healing practices, of having received his M.D. from a fraudulent diploma mill. An intense polemic, which at times has involved the Rosicrucian Fraternity in Oceanside, California, continues to this day.

The teachings of the Rosicrucians center on God's purpose for life. Rosicrucians believe that God created the universe according to his immutable laws. Man's success is through mastership, the ability to bring into material expression one's mental imaging. The techniques taught to students lead to mastery. For example, students are taught to "image" or imagine things such as health, wealth, and happiness, and thereby draw those things to themselves. Progress in the teaching and knowledge of the accompanying practices comes through a series of correspondence lessons mailed regularly to members. Completion of a set of lessons admits students to a higher degree in the work and makes available the next, more advanced, set of lessons. Members may also attend local centers (designated lodges, chapters, or pronaoi, depending upon their strength) for group activities.

AMORC sees itself as a continuation of the ancient mystery schools of Amenhotep IV and King Solomon; listed among famous Rosicrucians are Isaac Newton, René Descartes, Benjamin Franklin, and Francis Bacon. The fraternity works on 180-year cycles, first acting in silence and secrecy and then in public; a new, public cycle began in 1909. Head of the order is the grand imperator, a post held by Ralph M. Lewis (1904–1987), Spencer Lewis's son, from 1939 to 1987. Following the death of Ralph M. Lewis, Gary L. Stewart was chosen as the new grand imperator, but three years later he was removed from office by vote of the Order's board, accused of embezzling $3.5 million. The next and current (2008) grand imperator is Christian Bernard.

Internationally, AMORC is headed by the Supreme Grand Lodge headquartered in San José, California. Its directors include the grand masters of each of the twelve grand lodges that have been established to serve various geographical regions and language groups. Grand lodges serve speakers of Portuguese, French, German, Greek, Italian, Japanese, Dutch, and the Nordic languages. Two English-language grand lodges serve the Americas and Europe/Africa, and two Spanish-language grand lodges serve the Americas and Europe/Africa/Australasia.

Lewis was interested in Egypt, and, through the Rosicrucian Egyptian Museum in San José, which he founded, made many significant contributions to Egyptology. The museum is located in Rosicrucian Park, a square block in San José that houses the other departments of the Order and has become a major tourist stop in California. The museum celebrated its sixty-fifth anniversary in 1992.

Membership: Not reported, but in 1990 the order claimed more than 250,000 members worldwide. In 1995 the Order listed 98 chartered lodges, chapters, and pronaoi in the United States and Puerto Rico. There were 36 groups in Canada, and more than 1,200 worldwide. Members were reported in 86 countries around the world. In 1991 the *Rosicrucian Digest* circulated more than 40,000 copies per issue. The members-only *Rosicrucian Forum* circulates approximately 10,700 copies.

Educational Facilities:

Rose-Croix University, San José, California.

Periodicals: *Rosicrucian Digest*. • *Rosicrucian Forum* (available to members only).

Sources:

www.rosicrucian.org/home.html.

Bernard, Raymond. *Messages from the Celestial Sanctum*. San José, CA: Supreme Grand Lodge of AMORC, 1980.

Lewis, H. Spencer. *Cosmic Mission Fulfilled*. San José, CA: Supreme Grand Lodge of AMORC, 1973.

———. *The Mystical Life of Jesus*. San José, CA: Supreme Grand Lodge of AMORC, 1929.

————. *Rosicrucian Manual.* San José, CA: Rosicrucian Press, 1941.

————. *Rosicrucian Questions and Answers.* San José, CA: Supreme Grand Lodge of AMORC, 1969.

————. *Yesterday Has Much to Tell.* San José, CA: Supreme Grand Lodge of AMORCS, 1973.

Ancient Rosae Crucis (ARC)

PO Box 4764, Dallas, TX 75208

In 1990 the Ancient and Mystical Order of the Rosae Crucis (AMORC) underwent a reorganization when the board withdrew the authority of Grand Imperator Gary L. Stewart and reorganized under a new grand imperator, Christian Bernard, previously the head of its French division. The Ancient Rosae Crucis (ARC) was formed that year as a vehicle to continue the Rosicrucian teachings and support Stewart, but during the ensuing years ARC's leaders, including Paul Walden and Ashley McFadden, separated from Stewart and continued separately.

ARC continued the concern expressed by Stewart that numerous revisions to the texts of AMORC's founder H. Spencer Lewis (1883–1939) and his son Ralph M. Lewis (1904–1987) and the original teachings of the order had been changed. ARC began to issue a set of original AMORC monographs retyped from series owned by McFadden and edited by him.

Members receive ARC's teachings through the monographs that guide them in a systematic sequence of study that present the Rosicrucian perspective on natural and cosmic laws and that facilitate among other things the awakening of the individual's intuitive and psychic abilities. The studies are divided into degrees, each degree building upon the previous one. The teachings are available only to members.

Membership: Not reported.

Ausar Auset Society

c/o Kamit Publications, 140 Buckingham Rd., Brooklyn, NY 11226

The Ausar Auset Society is a Rosicrucian body serving the black community of the United States. It was founded in the mid-1970s by R. A. Straughn, also known as Ra Un Nefer Amen, formerly the head of the Rosicrucian Anthroposophical League in New York City. He is the author of several occult texts in spiritual science, each offering methods drawn from the Kabbalah and eastern religions to facilitate the orderly transition to the enlightened state.

The society's programs are aimed at blacks, and its periodical *Metu Neter* (formerly the *Oracle of Thoth*) regularly features, in addition to occult articles, items of general interest to black people. The society advocates the appropriation of the positive accomplishments of African ancestors by the contemporary black community. The society offers free public classes on a variety of occult topics in New York City; Chicago; Philadelphia; New Haven, Connecticut; Washington, D.C.; and Norfolk, Virginia.

Membership: Not reported.

Periodicals: *Metu Neter.*

Sources:

Ra Un Nefer Amer [R. A. Staughn]. *Metu Neter.* Vol. 1. Bronx, NY: Khamit, 1990.

Straughn, R. A. *Black Woman's, Black Man's Guide to a Spiritual Union.* Bronx, NY: Oracle of Thoth, 1981.

————. *Meditation Techniques of the Kabalists, Vedantins and Taoists.* Bronx, NY: Maat, 1976.

————. *The Oracle of Thoth: The Kabalistical Tarot.* Bronx, NY: Oracle of Thoth, 1977.

————. *The Realization of Neter Nu.* Brooklyn, NY: Maat , 1975.

Confraternity of the Rose Cross

PO Box 304, Tillson, NY 12486-0304

In 1987 Gary L. Stewart was installed as the third grand imperator of the Ancient and Mystical Order of the Rosae Crucis (AMORC). However, three years later, he was removed from office by the church's board, who accused him of embezzling about $3 million that had been transferred to a bank account in Andorra. In the period of adjudication that followed, AMORC reorganized and appointed Christian Bernard, a French citizen, its new grand imperator. In 1993 Stewart was found innocent of any wrongdoing in the charges leveled against him, but remained alienated from the AMORC. He founded the Confraternity of the Rose Cross in 1996.

Stewart has said that the confraternity continues the teachings of AMORC as they existed in the days of its founder, H. Spencer Lewis (1883–1939), and Ralph M. Lewis (1904–1987). However, he claims that during the last years of Lewis's leadership, due primarily to his failing health, the editing of Order material was removed from the imperator's supervision and the teachings were substantially changed, partly to "modernize" them. Further, Stewart charged, the French grand master, Christian Bernard, and the German grand master, Wilhelm Raab, made additional changes in the 1980s that resulted in different teachings being disseminated in different languages. According to Stewart, he was attempting to deal with these issues when the board revolted against him.

The confraternity continued the prerevisionist AMORC teachings. In this regard, Stewart has suggested that much of these teachings were based on a document called the *Nodin Manuscript.* The first part of the document has been published in the lesson material available to AMORC members; the second part exists as a single copy, which was passed from one grand imperator to another. At present, Stewart has the only copy, so Rosicrucians studying with AMORC's revised teachings do so without the original teachings derived from the *Nodin Manuscript.*

Stewart assures the members of the confraternity that all monographs (monthly lessons) are prepared by himself alone, reflecting the original writings of H. Spencer Lewis and "written at a time when no outside revisions or influence found their way into the teachings." Stewart adds insights to the monograph material, but such additions are clearly noted as such.

Membership: Not reported.

Sources:

Confraternity of the Rose Cross. www.crcsite.org/rosicrucianismcrc.htm.

Stewart, Gary L. *Awakened Attitude.* Pittsburgh, PA: Order of the Militia Crucifera Evangelica, n.d.

Fraternitas Rosae Crucis

Beverly Hall, Quakertown, PA 18951

Fraternitas Rosae Crucis, the oldest of the several existing Rosicrucian bodies, dates to 1858, when it was founded by Paschal Beverly Randolph (1825–1875). The first lodge was established in San Francisco three years later. On three occasions, the grand lodge was closed and reestablished: first in Boston (1871), then in San Francisco (1874), and finally in Philadelphia (1895). Randolph was succeeded by Freeman B. Dowd, who in turn was succeeded by Edward H. Brown (1907), R. Swinburne Clymer (1922), and Emerson M. Clymer (1966), and Gerald E. Poesnecker (1983). Randolph, a physician, had for many years lectured on issues of sexuality. The inner teachings of the order he established included a system of occult sexuality that he termed *Eulistic,* a word derived from the Greek Eleusinian mysteries, which Randolph believed to be mysteries of sex. In 1874 he established a Provisional Grand Lodge of Eulis in Tennessee, but he had to dissolve it because of internal problems among the membership. Translations of Randolph's writings, disseminated through his European followers, became a source for the sex magick system developed by the Ordo Templi Orientis. As presented in the English-speaking world by Aleister Crowley, the O.T.O.'s sex magick differed from Randolph's teachings at several points, particularly on the moral level. Randolph had advocated its practice by married couples only. Twentieth-century followers of Randolph have denounced the O.T.O. teachings as black magick.

In the Fraternitas Rosae Crucis, members begin their work with lessons of the basic ideas of the "secret schools," which include reincarnation and karma, and the Law of Justice and noninterference with the rights of others. They learn the process of transmutation (of the base self into the finest gold) and the acquisition of health and strength by casting out thoughts of weakness and age. They also are taught to contact the hierarchies of the heavenly realm. Members believe in the fatherhood of God and the ultimate brotherhood of man. The inner circle of the fraternity is the Aeth Priesthood, where members are taught "the highest occultism known to man."

Associated with the fraternity is the Church of Illumination, an "outer court group" that interacts with the public; a select few may be chosen to join the inner group. The church emphasizes the establishment of the "Manistic" age, which began in the late nineteenth century and follows the previous Egyptian and Christian ages. Manism is the recognition of the equality of man and woman. It also denotes the name of the new world leader who teaches the divine law with its five fundamentals: "as ye sow so shall ye reap"; talents as gift and responsibility; the golden rule; honesty; and the new birth as the awakening of the Christos, or divine spark within.

"Many are called but few are chosen" is a motto of the Fraternitas Rosae Crucis, which does not advertise in the manner associated with the Ancient and Mystical Order of the Rosae Crucis (AMORC). The writings of R. Swinburne Clymer, who revived the all but moribund fraternity in the early twentieth century, have attracted members. Authority of the fraternity rests with the Council of Three, and the highest office is held by the Hierarch of Eulis. The Beverly Hall Corporation in Quakertown, Pennsylvania, handles the distribution of literature. Continuing the church's tradition of concern for health begun by Randolph and R. Swinburne Clymer are the Humanitarian Society and the Clymer Health Clinic, both located at the fraternity's headquarters complex in Quakertown.

Membership: In 2008 there were 16 centers of the School of Metaphysics/International Church of Metaphysics scattered across the United States.

Sources:

Fraternitas Rosae Crucis. www.soul.org/.

School of Metaphysics. www.som.org/.

Clymer, R. Swinburne. *The Age of Treason*. Quakertown, PA: Humanitarian Society, 1959.

————. *The Rose Cross Order*. Allentown, PA: Philosophical, 1916.

————. *The Rosicrucian Fraternity in America*. 2 vols. Quakertown, PA: Rosicrucian Foundation, 1935.

————. *The Rosy Cross, Its Teachings*. Quakertown, PA: Beverly Hall, 1965.

Randolph, Paschal Beverly. *Eulis, Affectional Alchemy*. Quakertown, PA: Confederation of Initiates, 1930.

Lectorium Rosicrucianum

Western North American Headquarters, Box 9246, Bakersfield, CA 93389

Alternate Address: International headquarters: Bakenessergracht 11-15, 2011JS Haarlem, The Netherlands. Eastern North American Headquarters: Box 334, Chatham, NY 12037.

The Lectorium Rosicrucianum was founded in Holland in 1924 by a small group of people, most of whom formerly had been members of the Rosicrucian Fellowship. The spiritual leaders of the group wrote under the pen names Jan Van Rijckenborgh and Catherose de Petri. The organization remained small until 1940, when it was forced to shut down until after World War II. Since its reopening it has become a worldwide organization. It came to the United States in the early 1970s, and headquarters were established in Bakersfield, California.

The Lectorium Rosicrucianum describes itself as a gnostic, transfiguristic spiritual school. *Gnostic* means "coming from the Logos," that is, from God the source of all things. Transfiguration is the path of return to the gnosis (knowledge or divine wisdom) for humans, who are seen as fallen from a divine state and now in need of reawakening and unfolding of the spirit-spark atom, the rose of the heart, located in the center of one's microcosmic self. People are aided in this process by the Universal Brotherhood, the divine spiritual hierarchy. The Universal Brotherhood consists of those of the human life wave who either never fell from the original immortal nature order, or who have returned by building a New Soul Body through the process of transfiguration. The Light of the Universal Brotherhood is transmitted through a transfiguristic spiritual school's power field into a usable source of energy, thus making it possible for individuals to break the wheel of birth and death (reincarnation after reincarnation). In this way one can return to humanity's original sphere, the Sixth Cosmic Region.

The Lectorianum Rosicrucianum is differentiated from other groups using the name *Rosicrucian* by its concept of the two Nature Orders. Their philosophy explains that humans are born into this nature order, the Seventh Cosmic Region, the world of nature that individuals perceive and experience as mortal beings. But humans also carry a remnant of the original nature order, the Sixth Cosmic Region, as a human immortal seed, the Christ principle in the center of the microcosm. Thus, the purpose of an individual's life in this nature order is to cooperate with the blossoming of the rose of the heart, the Christ within, through the process of transfiguration, in order to return to the immortal nature order to which he or she originally belonged.

The Lectorium Rosicrucianum has initiated a broad publication program that includes the publication of more than 40 of the school's books, as well as their translations into various languages. The spiritual school's journal, *Pentagram*, appears in Dutch, English, German, French, Portuguese, and Swedish editions.

Membership: In 2002 the group reported four centers in the United States and two in Canada. There were 17,000 members worldwide.

Periodicals: *Pentagram*.

Sources:

Lectorium Rosicrucianum. www.lectoriumrosicrucianum.org/.

Van Rijckenborgh, Jan. *The Coming New Man*. Haarlem, Netherlands: Rozekruis-Pers, 1957.

————. *Elementary Philosophy of the Modern Rosecross*. Haarlem, Netherlands: Rozekruis-Pers, 1961.

The Way of the Rosecross in Our Times. Haarlem, Netherlands: Rozekruis-Pers, 1978.

New Age Bible and Philosophy Center

1139 Lincoln Blvd., Santa Monica, CA 90403

The New Age Bible and Philosophy Center, founded by Mary Elizabeth Shaw in May 1931, began as a school dedicated to basic Christian spiritual teachings of the ancient wisdom, and included classes in theosophy and the Rosicrucian teachings. The center, now in its 77th year, was always closely associated with the works of Max Heindel and Corinne Heline. Its two main courses are aligned to Corinne Heline's seven volumes of the *New Age Bible Interpretation* and Max Heindel's *Rosicrucian Cosmo-Conception*.

Heline was born in Atlanta, Georgia, in 1875 as Corinne S. Dunklee. Following the death of her mother in 1891, Heline moved to California, where she met and became the close student of Max Heindel (1865–1919), the founder of the Rosicrucian Fellowship. After Heindel's death, Dunklee remained for many years a leading member of the fellowship. In 1922 she received an "inner commission" to begin work on interpreting the Bible in the esoteric tradition. The project consumed the remainder of her life. Her early efforts were published in the fellowship periodical, the *Rosicrucian Magazine*. During this period she met and married

Theodore Heline (d. 1971). Both the Helines were prodigious authors who published books and booklets that have a broad circulation around the world.

Mary Elizabeth Shaw was succeeded by Rev. Gene Sande, who had served at the center since its beginning. After more than fifty years, Sande was succeeded by Rev. Patricia Talis, assisted by Rev. Patricia Tinker.

Besides Sunday services, there are monthly Full Moon Services and various classes offered weekly. A bookstore and library are open daily Wednesday through Friday. The correspondence courses in the Bible and philosophy are mailed to students who request them. The New Age Bible and Philosophy Center publishes the books by Corinne and Theodore Heline.

Membership: There is one center with 100 people affiliated and an unknown number of class attendants and correspondence students.

Periodicals: *Quarterly Bulletin*.

Sources:

Heline, Corinne. *Mysteries of the Holy Grail*. Los Angeles: New Age Press, 1977.

————. *The Mystery of the Christos*. Los Angeles: New Age Press, 1961.

————. *New Age Bible Interpretation*. 7 vols. Los Angeles: New Age Press, 1938–54.

Heline, Theodore. *As in the Days of Noah*. Los Angeles: New Age Press, 1946.

————. *The Redemptive Feminine*. Los Angeles: New Age Press, n.d.

Rosicrucian Fellowship

2222 Mission Ave., Oceanside, CA 92058

The Rosicrucian Fellowship was founded as a Christian organization in 1909 by Carl Louis von Grasshoff, better known by his pen name, Max Heindel (1865–1919). Born in Denmark, Heindel moved to the United States and in 1903 settled in Los Angeles, California. He became active in that city's branch of the Theosophical Society, serving as its vice president for three years.

According to Heindel, while visiting Germany in 1907 to 1908 he encountered a being, later identified as an Elder Brother of the Rosicrucian Order, who appeared in his room. After submitting Heindel to a test to determine his integrity and fitness as a messenger of the Western Wisdom Teachings, the being promised to reveal to him esoteric knowledge. Heindel was given directions to the Temple of the Rose Cross, near the German-Bohemian border, where he was given the material to be used in his first book, *The Rosicrucian Cosmo-Conception* (1909), the basic textbook of the fellowship.

Returning to the United States, Heindel proceeded to rewrite the book, as the Elder Brother had told him he would, and publish it. Soon he became a popular speaker, lecturing in Columbus, Ohio; Seattle and North Yakima, Washington; Portland, Oregon; and Los Angeles, California. These lectures led to the establishment of centers and study groups in these and many other locations. Subsequently, the teachings of his book spread internationally.

The Rosicrucian Cosmo-Conception has been translated into 12 languages—Dutch, English, French, German, Italian, Polish, Portugese, Spanish, Swedish, Romanian, Russian, and Turkish. It puts forth a view of the cosmos from an esoteric Christian standpoint, and advocates the adoption of Jesus Christ as the aspirant's ideal. Heindel advocated the intelligent use of spiritual astrology as a tool for self-knowledge and moral development. He also introduced new formats for temple, healing, marriage, and memorial services, now published in the fellowship's *Manual of Forms*.

In 1911 the fellowship's international headquarters were established at Mount Ecclesia in Oceanside, California, for the purpose of best implementing its two principal goals, healing the sick and disseminating esoteric Christian teachings. A chapel, administrative offices, residents quarters, vegetarian cafeteria, and a healing temple were erected on the grounds. An abundance of literature in the form of correspondence courses, books, pamphlets, and monthly mailings issue from Mount Ecclesia. The fellowship became a major force in the popularization of

astrology in the twentieth century, and many astrologers not connected with the organization use the single-year, decade, and 100-year ephemerides and the Table of Houses, most of which are published onsite.

Membership is open to all persons, provided they are not professional astrologers, mediums, hypnotists, or palmists. After a two-year term as a regular student of the fellowship, a person who abstains from all flesh food, tobacco, mind-altering drugs, and alcohol may apply for probationership in the fellowship.

Upon his death in 1919, Heindel was succeeded in leadership by his wife, Augusta Foss Heindel (d. 1949), an accomplished occultist in her own right. Mount Ecclesia remains the headquarters of the fellowship; the work is carried on there in the tradition established by the founders. The Rosicrucian doctrine is preserved in its pristine purity, and the service rendered to humanity throughout all departments retains its original quality of faithful, anonymous dedication.

In 2008 the fellowship's president was Alexandra Porter.

The fellowship provides courses in philosophy, the Bible, and spiritual astrology in six languages—English, French, German, Italian, Portugese, and Spanish. There are more than 6,000 affiliated students.

Membership: In March 2008 the fellowship reported more than 5,000 members worldwide and more than 50 chartered centers. At the headquarters there are two onsite ministers. They have affiliated work in 50 countries. Eight hundred members are in the United States, and for the first time they have a formal study group in a Maryland prison.

Periodicals: *Rays from the Rose Cross*.

Sources:

Rosicrucian Fellowship. www.rosicrucianfellowship.com.

Heindel, Max. *Rosicrucian Cosmo-Conception*. [1909]. Oceanside, CA: Rosicrucian Fellowship, 1937.

————. *Rosicrucian Philosophy in Questions and Answers*. Oceanside, CA: Rosicrucian Fellowship, 1922

————. *Simplified Scientific Astrology*. Oceanside, CA: Rosicrucian fellowship, 1928.

Heindel, Mrs. Max [Augusta Foss]. *The Birth of the Rosicrucian Fellowship*. Oceanside, CA: Rosicrucian Fellowship, n.d.

Societas Rosicruciana in America

PO Box 1316, Bayonne, NJ 07002-6316

Sylvester Gould (d. 1909) was an early member of the Societas Rosicruciana in Civitatibus Foederatis, the Masonic Rosicrucian society. However, it was his desire to create a Rosicrucian organization that would admit non-Masons. In 1907, with the assistance of George Winslow Plummer (1876–1944) he created the Societas Rosicruciana in America (S.R.I.A.), adapting the masonic materials for general use. He also began *The Rosicrucian Brotherhood*, a periodical. After Gould's death, Plummer succeeded to the leadership role.

Plummer incorporated the S.R.I.A. in 1912 and four years later founded the Mercury Publishing Company and *Mercury*, a quarterly magazine for the society. During the decade six colleges were chartered in the United States and one in Sierre Leone. In 1921 two more were added. Plummer authored the lessons and other material distributed by the society. His interests in Christian mysticism and ritual also led him to create a Seminary of Biblical Research (through which he wrote and published a series of lessons on Christian mysticism) and to found two churches: the Anglican Universal Church and the Holy Orthodox Church in America (see separate entries). These organizations were intimately intertwined with the S.R.I.A. Colleges, and church congregations were frequently located in the same cities; the church's members were drawn primarily from society adherents.

Plummer's booklet *Principles and Practices of the Rosicrucians* details the affirmations and duties of members. The group affirms the existence of one infinite intelligence, the incarnation of Spirit in matter, the continuousness of all life in evolution, the possibility of the mental attaining knowledge of the spiritual while yet incarnate, and reincarnation. Each student is expected to experiment and to demonstrate knowledge of concentration, meditation, contemplation, prayer, dietetics, exercise, rest, rituality, sexual faculties, healing, cheerfulness, fasting, and individual development; vegetarianism is not demanded, but alcohol is forbidden. New members in the Societas Rosicruciana in America are called postulants. After a year, they become fraters (brothers) or sorores (sisters). Progress is through ten degrees.

The society's stated objective is the spiritual, moral, and intellectual development of members and of all people through teachings that correlate religion, science, philosophy, mystical Christianity, and hermeticism. It adheres to the motto, "Man, know thyself." The syllabus of lessons includes the Rosicrucian series, hermetical series, alchemical series, and spiritual foundation.

Following Plummer's death, the society and the Holy Orthodox Church in America were headed by Stanislaus Witowski (de Witow; d. 1969), who married Plummer's widow, Gladys Plummer. Gladys Plummer de Witow, also known as Mother Serena (1894–1989), became head of the society and the church after her second husband's death. Mother Serena died in 1989 and was succeeded by Sister Lucia Grosch.

In 2001 Maria Babuahsingh succeeded Grosch, and the society moved to Bayonne, New Jersey.

Membership: Not reported.

Periodicals: *Mercury*.

Sources:

Societas Rosicruciana in America. www.sria.org/.

Plummer, George Winslow. *The Art of Rosicrucian Healing*. New York: Society of Rosicrucians, 1947.

———. *Esoteric Masonry*. Kingston, NY: Society of Rosicrucians, 1988.

———. *Principles and Practice for Rosicrucians*. New York: Society of Rosicrucians, Inc., 1947.

———. *Rosicrucian Healing*. Kingston, NY: Society of Rosicrucians, 1988.

Serena. *Lettergrams*. New York: Society of Rosicrucians, Inc., 1976.

Serena, Mother. *Victorinus Teaches*. Kingston, NY: Society of Rosicrucians, 1988.

Societas Rosicruciana in Civitatibus Foederatis

c/o David L. Hargett IX, 406 Harris Ln., Monroe, NC 28112

The Societas Rosicruciana in Anglia was formed in England in 1867 by Robert Wentworth Little (1840–1878). It seems to have been based on eighteenth-century Rosicrucian texts. Among its members were Kenneth R. H. Mackenzie, William Wynn Westcott (1848–1925), and W. R. Woodmen, who were among the founders of the Hermetic Order of the Golden Dawn, the group most often credited with initiating the revival of magic in the twentieth century. Members of the Societas were required to be Freemasons prior to beginning their work. During the late nineteenth century, colleges were opened in London (1867), Bristol (1869), Manchester (1871), Cambridge (1876), Sheffield (1877), Middlesex (1877), and Newcastle (1890). In 1873 the East of Scotland College was inaugurated in Edinburgh.

News of the formation of the Rosicrucian organization spread through Freemasonry to the U.S. lodges. In 1878 a group led by Charles E. Meyer (1839–1908) of Pennsylvania traveled to England and were initiated at Sheffield. They applied for a charter, but getting no response, turned to Scotland and received a charter from the college in Edinburgh in 1879. A second charter was granted for a college in New York, and in 1880 the two colleges formed the Society Rosicruciana Republicae Americae. A Boston and a Baltimore college were chartered later that year. The organization's name was changed to the Societas Rosicruciana in the United States of America, also known as the Societas Rosicruciana in Civitatibus Foederatis. Later charters were granted for Duluth,

Minnesota (1911), Texas (1918), New Jersey (1931), North Carolina (1932), Virginia (1933), Illinois (1934), Colorado (1935), Long Island, New York (1935), Nova Scotia, Canada (1936), and Ontario, Canada (1937). Membership from the 1930s to the 1950s remained steady at between 200 and 300 members. Membership has remained small and, like the British and Scottish counterparts, it is limited to masons. From 1951 to 1973 the society issued a biannual report, *The Rosicrucian Fama*.

There are three high councils. The Societas Rosicruciana in Anglia (SRIA, the Rosicrucian Society in England) was founded in 1866. It was reported the SRIA had 50 colleges in England and abroad. The Societas Rosicruciana in Scotia (the Rosicrucian Society in Scotland) reported five colleges and 300 members. The Societas Rosicruciana in Civitatibus Foederatis (the Rosicrucian Society in the United States) reported 32 colleges in the United States and abroad. Membership figures have not been recorded for 2008.

The grades of the Societas Rosicruciana are: Third Order, consisting of IX Magus, VIII Magister Templi; Second Order, VII Adeptus Exemptus, VI Adeptus Major, V Adeptus Minor; and First Order, IV Philosophus, III Practicus, II Theoricus, and I Zelator.

Membership: Not reported. In 1973 the society reported 31 members.

Sources: :

Societas Rosicruciana in Civitatibus Foederatis. www.geocities.com/Athens/2092/index2.htm.

Voorhis, Harold V. B. *Masonic Rosicrucian Societies*. New York: Press of Henry Emmerson, 1958.

❖ Occult Orders

Astara

10700 Jersey Blvd., Suite 450, Rancho Cucamonga, CA 91730

Astara was formed in 1951 by Robert Chaney (1913–2006) and Earlyne Chaney (d. 2006), both former Spiritualists. Robert Chaney had been active at Camp Chesterfield and instrumental in the founding of the Spiritualist Episcopal Church. While still a Spiritualist, he became interested in Theosophy and began to profess a belief in reincarnation, which in the 1940s was still a minority idea within Spiritualist circles and which met with strong disapproval at the camp. Earlyne, as a child clairvoyant, had held conversations with a being she called simply "Father." When she asked his name, he replied "Kut-Hu-Mi." When she later discovered Koot Hoomi in Theosophical literature, he revealed that he had chosen her for special hierarchical work—to write the teachings of the ancient wisdom for the new age. After resigning from their church in Eaton Rapids, Michigan, the Chaneys moved to Los Angeles, California, and began their independent endeavor.

Astara is one of the most eclectic of bodies. The eclecticism is a reflection of the varied strong influences on the Chaneys at points in their lives: Spiritualism, Theosophy, yoga, Christianity, as well as the expressed desire to allow Astara to be a center of all religions and philosophies. These various tendencies have found unity, however, in the teaching of Hermes Mercurious Trismegistus, the ancient Egyptian Ptoh said to have organized the mystery schools from which all others have derived. Astara conceives of itself as a mystery school in the Hermetic tradition. The name is from the Greek goddess of divine justice, Astraea, and was chosen as a sign of the renewal of the Golden Age.

Hermes taught of God, the cosmos, and man, each in relation to the others. God is the only uncreated who emanates his seven attributes and all that is. Hermes also taught seven laws, the most basic of which is the matical law of correspondence: "As above, so below." According to Hermes, our world is a microcosm of the macrocosm, the universe. This law is the basis of alchemy. The law of vibration says everything is in motion. Other laws deal with polarity, cycles, cause and effect, gender, and mind.

These laws encompass a number of practices. Lama Yoga is a consciousness-expanding method taught originally to Earlyne Chaney by the masters. The chanting of the holy name, "Om," is encompassed under the law of vibration. A natural food diet, preferably vegetarian, is encouraged. The arcane rhythm techniques include numerous yogic practices and breathing techniques.

For many years, the center for Astara was a congregation in Los Angeles where regular Sunday services were held. The heart of Astara, however, has always been the correspondence lessons called the Book of Life. It is Astara's belief that written instructions by a mystery school can function as a guru in teaching the student. Astarians are led through ascending degrees of twenty-two lessons each. The objective of the lessons is organizing one's life to be in harmony with the eternal mystic truths; achieving a comprehensive view of life processes, including birth, death, and the afterlife; unfolding the science of soul progression as revealed in the teachings of the ancient mysteries; and revealing how to use the "third eye," which is the all-seeing eye of the superconscious.

In 2008 Dr. Sita Chaney, daughter of Robert and Earlyne, was the executive administrator, and the center was located in Rancho Cucamonga, California. The center offers workshops, seminars, tours of spiritual sites, and Sunday services at the headquarters as well as at other locations in the United States and abroad. Although Astarians request prayers for the healing of those who are ill, such prayers are not intended to replace the physician or any other form of healing but rather to add a spiritual dimension to the healing sciences.

Membership: In 2008 Astara reported 25,000 students worldwide in over 85 countries.

Periodicals: *Voice of Astara.*

Sources:

Astara. www.astara.org/.

Chaney, Earlyne. *Beyond Tomorrow*. Upland, CA: Astara, 1985.

————. *The Book of Beginning Again*. Upland, CA: Astara, 1981.

————. *Remembering*. Los Angeles: Astara's Library of Mystical Classics, 1974.

————. *Shining Moments of a Mystic*. Upland, CA: Astara, 1976.

Chaney, Earlyne, and William L. Messick. *Kundalini and the Third Eye*. Upland, CA: Astara's Library of Mystical Classics, 1980.

Chaney, Robert. *Mysticism, the Journey Within*. Upland, CA: Astra's Library of Mystical Classics, 1979.

Chaney, Robert Galen. *The Inner Way*. Los Angeles, CA: DeVorss & Co., 1962.

Brotherhood of the White Temple
7830 Oak Way, Dept. A, Sedalia, CO 80135

The Brotherhood of the White Temple was formed in Denver in 1930 by Doreal (b. Claude Doggins, 1898–1963), a long-time student of occultism and a "channel for bringing the ancient wisdom to the Western Student." Doreal claims contact with the Great White Lodge, the Elder Brothers of man (figures similar to the ascended masters, spirits who were once human and now teach humans about spiritual reality). Doreal is the agent for the coming Golden Age in which the brotherhood of man will be established on earth. Integral parts of the Brotherhood of the White Temple are the White Temple Church, which emphasizes the "Original Gnostic Teachings of Jesus," and the Shamballa Ashrama, a tract of 1,560 acres at Sedalia, Colorado, where a community of brotherhood members is housed and the headquarters are located. From the publishing plant the numerous booklets and lessons written by Doreal are printed and distributed. The booklets cover the whole range of occult topics.

The teachings of the brotherhood come from the central core of occult teachings, drawing heavily on Kabbalistic images. (The Kabbalah is a Jewish magical system.) God is conceived as the all-pervasive one, and man is a spark of the divine. The soul is incarnate for the purpose of overcoming negation and darkness

and changing itself into order and light. The fall of man was caused by his being overwhelmed by inharmony after his creation. The teachings of the White Brotherhood emphasize methods of establishing harmony and cover various topics in the occult tradition (Atlantis, Lemuria, the Masters of Tibet, and the Great Pyramid). In keeping with the occult tradition, the brotherhood offers an allegorical approach to the Bible.

The Brotherhood of the White Temple Correspondence College, from the headquarters in Sedalia, offers booklets and lessons to members around the world. Lessons are divided into four neophyte grades and twelve temple grades. After completion (approximately four and a half years), a member is invited into the inner work.

Membership: In 2008 the brotherhood reported approximately 50 families who live at the Ashrama, and corresponding students are located across the United States and around the world.

Periodicals: *Light on the Path.*

Sources:

Brotherhood of the White Temple. www.bwtemple.org/.

Doreal, M. *Maitreya, Lord of the World*. Sedalia, CO: Brotherhood of the White Temple, n.d.

————. *Man and the Mystic Universe*. Denver: Brotherhood of the White Temple, n.d.

————. *Personal Experiences among the Masters and Great Adepts in Tibet*. Sedalia, CO: Brotherhood of the White Temple, n.d.

————. *Secret Teachings of the Himalayan Gurus*. Denver: Brotherhood the White Temple, n.d.

Kafton-Minkel, Walter. *Subterranean Worlds. . .Dragons, the Dead, Lost Races, and UFOs from Inside the Earth*. Port Town, WA: Loompanics Unlimited, 1989.

Church of Light
2119 Gold Ave. SE, Albuquerque, NM 87106-4072
Alternate Address: Church of Light, Canada, 211-50 Cambridge Ave., Toronto, ON M4K 2LS, Canada.

The Church of Light was incorporated in 1932 in Los Angeles by Elbert Benjamine (also known by his pen name, C. C. Zain; 1882–1951) but actually dates to 1876, when Emma Harding Britten (1823–1899), who in the previous year had participated in the founding of the Theosophical Society, published the teachings of the occult Brotherhood of Light in her book, *Art Magic*. The Brotherhood of Light was, according to the Church of Light tradition, formed in 2400 B.C.E. by a group that separated from the theocracy of Egypt. It has existed since that time as a secret order and is called the source of the science on which Western civilization rests. Its initiates are said to have included Thales, Pythagoras, and Plato. It has continued to exist on the inner planes as well as the outer. (The outer plane is the one people live on; the inner plane contains ghostly bodies and is visible only to psychics.)

In the nineteenth century, one Max Theon (1848?–1927) was the head of the Brotherhood of Luxor in Europe. He was contacted by T. H. Burgoyne (1855–1894), a Scot, who originally contacted the brotherhood on the inner plane. He came to America in the 1880s. Joining him was Captain Norman Astley, a retired British army officer who married Genevieve Stebbins, a member of the Brotherhood in New York. Burgoyne, while living with the Astleys in Carmel, California, wrote an original series of lessons, *Light of Egypt*, Vol. I. With the help of Dr. Henry Wagner and Mrs. Belle M. Wagner, a branch of the Brotherhood, the Hermetic Brotherhood of Light, was formed. The Hermetic Brotherhood was always governed by a scribe, an astrologer, and a seer. Burgoyne was the original scribe. In 1909 Minnie Higgins, the original astrologer, died, and Elbert Benjamine was called to the home of a Mrs. Anderson, the seer, to become the council's astrologer.

The teaching of the Brotherhood was the ancient Religion of the Stars, and Benjamine was appointed to prepare a complete system of occult studies by which humankind could become conversant with the religion of the stars in the coming Aquarian Age. He was guided in this task by members on the inner plane, and wrote a series of twenty-one lessons covering three branches of occult science: astrology, alchemy, and magic. In 1913 the Hermetic Brotherhood of Luxor was closed and its mission was turned over to Benjamine. In 1915 he began to hold classes, which were opened to the public in 1918. The lessons were completed in 1934.

The Church of Light's stated mission is to promote the welfare and exaltation of all people through the teaching and practices of the Religion of the Stars as outlined by the writings of C. C. Zain. The church's guiding principles are a loving cosmic intelligence, of which all people are a part, and a divine plan manifested through progressive evolution, in which each soul has a unique and important role. It stresses adherence to the universal moral code, realization of the soul's mission, and the goal of self-conscious immortality, attainable only through unselfish love. The church views astrology as the key to understanding the soul's true character and potential. The life of service to others is the life of the Spirit. The church does not believe in reincarnation.

The Church of Light teaches that there are two orders of truth—religion and science—between which there can be no true antagonism. Religion, the sister of science, evolves by incorporating new information as it is discovered and verified. The only infallible book in interpreting the will of the deity is the book of nature. Nature's laws are the one religion, interpreted through astrology and all occult arts. Upon completion of the twenty-one courses, the church member is given a Hermeticism certificate.

Upon Benjamine's death in 1951, Edward Doane (1892–1970) became president of the church; he was succeeded by Paul M. Brewer. An annual meeting of the church, announced 60 days in advance, is held at various locations in the United States. Ordained ministers may establish branch churches where interest warrants, and individual members taking correspondence courses are located across the United States and in eighteen other countries.

Membership: In 2008 the church reported 900 members and 60 ministers.

Periodicals: *The Church of Light Quarterly.*

Remarks: According to occult historian A. E. Waite, T. H. Burgoyne was a pseudonym adopted by Thomas Henry Dalton, a convicted felon (on charges of mail fraud) who came to America to escape a scandal concerning the Hermetic Brotherhood. Dalton accepted payment for lessons in Chaldean astrology that were not received by the individual who paid for them. Max Theon, also according to Waite, was a pseudonym for Peter Davidson, who was possibly, in fact, Norman Astley. Waite was one of the founders of the Hermetic Order of the Golden Dawn, which was antagonistic to the Hermetic Brotherhood of Luxor. Max Theon was also the pseudonym used by Louis Maximillian Bimstein, a Polish Kabbalist and originator of the *Philosophie Cosmique* who lived and taught in Tlemcen, Algeria.

Sources:

Church of Light. www.light.org/.

Astrological Research & Reference Encyclopedia. 2 vols. Los Angeles: Church of Light, 1972.

Burgoyne, Thomas H. *The Light of Egypt*. 2 vols. Albuquerque, NM: Sun Publishing Company, 1980.

Gibson, Christopher. "The Religion of the Stars: The Hermetic Philosophy of C. C. Zain." *Gnosis* 38 (winter 1996): 58–63.

Godwin, Joscelyn, Christian Chanel, annd John P. Deveney. *The Hermetic Brotherhood of Luxor*. York Beach, ME: Samuel Weiser, 1995.

Wagner, H. O., comp. *A Treasure Chest of Wisdom*. Denver, CO: H. O. Wagner, 1967.

Gnostic Association of Cultural and Anthropological Studies
c/o The Gnostic Center of Los Angeles, 4885 Melrose Ave., Los Angeles, CA 90029

The Gnostic Association of Cultural and Anthropological Studies was formed in 1952 by Colombian native Samuel Aun Weor (d. 1977), described by his followers as the Kaiki Avatar of the Age of Aquarius. During his early years he studied with Dr. Arnold Krumm Heller, a German esotericist, and over the years as he continued his studies he became a master of the esoteric realms in his own right. He began to prepare his own synthesis of esoteric teachings based upon his investigation of other planes of consciousness, from which he authored a number of books. The basic teachings are embodied in a 1961 volume, *The Perfect Matrimony*. The association spread through South America and then to Europe, Japan, Ireland, Australia, France, Spain, Portugal, Africa, Canada, and the United States. The first U.S. centers were opened in Los Angeles and New York in 1970.

While accepting a basic theosophical framework for his teachings, Weor wrote about the practical synthesis of all religions, schools, orders, sects, lodges, and yogas. His findings, which he experienced directly, were presented in *The Perfect Matrimony*. The essence of the system is called "el sexo yoga" in Spanish, and "sexual alchemy" in English. Weor taught that the redemption of humanity is in the transmutation of the sexual energies. (The practice taught by Weor draws heavily from Hindu Tantric and Chinese Taoist sources, and is to be sharply distinguished from the "sex magic" of Aleister Crowley and his followers in the Ordo Templi Orientis.)

Weor taught that God manifested as both Father (knowledge) and Mother (love). The "Perfect Matrimony" is the union of two persons who know how to love. With the fire of love, individuals can transform themselves into gods. The secret of the fire is discovered in the sexual act. During the sexual act, participants are charged with universal magnetism. True white magicians stop the act before any semen is spilled. Transmuting the creative energies, so that orgasm does not occur and therefore the semen is not released, is equated with committing the act of sexual magic. The *kundalini*, the latent energy believed by Hindu Tantrics to reside at the base of the spine, awakens and travels upward. Thereby the individual awakens consciousness.

After its arrival in the United States, the association opened centers in Spanish-speaking communities in several cities. Though most instruction is still in Spanish, there are several centers that provide free lectures in English, and most of Weor's books have been translated. The first issues of the association's English-language periodical appeared in 1987. The first international congress of the association was held in Montreal in 1986.

The Gnostic Center of Los Angeles offers courses in yoga, psychology of awakening consciousness, exploration of astral travel, living in the moment, kundalini and chakras, Mi-Lam, astrology of the heart, and the powers of the imagination. Courses last for 10 weeks, and new courses begin every three months. One-day seminars are provided on a variety of topics, including Tibetan rites and rejuvenation.

Membership: In 1988 the association reported 5,000 members in more than 20 centers in the United States, and more than 10,000 members in 50 centers in Canada. Foreign centers were located in 25 countries worldwide.

Periodicals: *The Gnostic Arhat.*

Sources:

Almarez, Anita Ford. *Simple Introduction to the Ancient Science of Gnosis*. Chicago: Gnostic Association, n.d.

Weor, Samuel Aun. *The Awakening of Man*. Chicago: Gnostic Association of Anthropological and Cultural Studies, n.d.

————. *Fundamental Education*. Los Angeles: Gnostic Association, 1987.

————. *Manual of Practical Magic*. Los Angeles: Gnostic Association, 1988.

————. *Manual of Revolutionary Psychology*. Los Angeles: Gnostic Association, 1987.

————. *The Perfect Matrimony*. New York: Adonai Editorial, 1980.

————. *Zodiacal Course: Hermetic Astrology*. Los Angeles: Gnostic Association, 1986.

Lemurian Fellowship

17201 Highway 67, Ramona, CA 92065

The Lemurian Fellowship was founded on September 16, 1936, by Dr. Robert D. Stelle, who claimed to be operating under the direction and guidance of the Lemurian Brotherhood, one of the original mystery schools. The Lemurian Fellowship considers itself the mundane channel of the Lemurian Brotherhood and is affiliated with no other group or organization.

The fellowship was first formed in Chicago, establishing its permanent headquarters on two properties in Ramona, California, in 1941. One property houses the headquarters of the Lemurian Fellowship. The other is the home of the Lemurian Order, the only student organization sponsored or recognized by the Lemurian Fellowship, membership in which is attained through extended study of the Lemurian Philosophy.

Since its inception and incorporation as a California nonprofit religious corporation, the fellowship has offered a course of balanced religious instruction in the Lemurian Philosophy, which is based on the teachings of Christ. Its primary purpose is to help people recognize, understand, and apply God's universal laws and principles. The correspondence school of the fellowship offers individual instruction through printed lessons geared to fit the needs and capabilities of the individual student. Background subjects include the origin of man, civilizations, human relationships, the life of Christ, and Cosmic or Universal Principles, including the laws of increase, cause and effect, transmutation, compensation, and precipitation (by which objects and conditions are brought into being). The study of twelve principal virtues emphasizes the need to work on one's self through attention to the needs of, and assistance to, others.

The continuity of life is a basic precept of the Lemurian Philosophy. Using the laws and principles established by God for the benefit of humanity, the goal is to purify one's thoughts and actions to the point where the individual gains control of his or her environment and destiny, and a commensurate ability to render significant help to others without circumventing their God-given right to self-determination.

These goals are accomplished through study, meditation, and lessons in such practical areas as health, finances, and the human associations encountered in family, marriage, work, and community. Through balancing the three sides of human nature (physical, mental, and spiritual), along with service to others, the Ego learns to fulfill the true purpose of human life. It is taught that the primary goal of a more noble character is learned and earned through opportunities that come through associations with other people.

According to the fellowship, the Great Being, Christ, first taught humanity when he appeared as Melchizedek on the continent of Mu (Lemuria), now submerged in the Pacific Ocean. Christ, as Poseidonis, appeared for a second time many thousands of years later on Atlantis, once again to help humanity recognize its true purpose. A complete record of these and subsequent civilizations up to the present time is stored in the archives of the Lemurian Brotherhood. Only when correct use is made of the information that has thus far been released will the succeeding phase of the Brotherhood's plan be known.

The goal for which the fellowship strives is the eventual realization of the Kingdom of God on earth. While such a concept is common to many religions, the Lemurian Philosophy makes no predictions or prophecies about when such an advanced society may come into being. The Lemurian Fellowship stresses to its students that it will be a steady, sure effort at building more noble characters on the part of many that will enable mankind to eventually experience a better world.

Since the founder's death in 1952, the work of the Lemurian Fellowship has been carried on by a staff who live and work on fellowship property in Ramona. All responsibility for the administration and conduct of the Lemurian Fellowship rests

with a board of governors. Lemurian Fellowship publications include *Into the Sun*, a brochure that introduces the Lemurian Philosophy, and *The Sun Rises*, which details the early developments of the Mukulian civilization. The fellowship also holds the copyright of *An Earth Dweller's Return*.

Membership: Not reported.

Periodicals: *Lemurian Viewpoint*.

Sources:

Lemurian Fellowship. www.lemurianfellowship.org/.

The Lemurian scribe. *Let It Be Resolved*. Milwaukee: Lemurian Press, 1940.

Phylos the Tibetan. *An Earth Dweller Returns*. Milwaukee: Lemurian Press, 1940.

Stelle, Robert D. *The Sun Rises*. Ramona, CA: Lemurian Fellowship, 1952.

Zitko, Howard John. *The Lemurian Theochristic Conception*. Author, n.d.

Mayan Order

731 Fredericksburg Rd., San Antonio, TX 78201

The Mayan Order, it is claimed, was founded in the early 1930s in the San Antonio, Texas, area by people who had rediscovered the teachings of an ancient group of holy men (H'Men) who dominated Mayan culture and to whom the greatness of the civilization was due. These men possessed great knowledge of astrology, the calendar, medicine, mathematics, and occult wisdom. Only a few H'Men survived the Spanish conquest, and only three copies of the ancient books have survived. What is known of the ancient wisdom is preserved today by the Mayan Order.

Mayan material is distributed in lessons through correspondence. Early in the work, the student is taught a simple code; in succeeding lessons, key words are printed in that code. Reincarnation is stressed within a framework of New Thought metaphysics, with the New Thought emphasis on light, mind, and the power of positive thinking. Each student practices psychokinesis and learns appropriate rituals at each initiation. Content is heavily biblical.

Like Astara, the Mayan Order has become known through its ads in various psychic periodicals. The order was originally under the guidance of Rose Dawn, who experimented with astrology, fortune-telling, and mysticism. Dawn and her husband, a mentalist called Koran, were known in San Antonio society by their legal names, Isabelle and William Taylor. Both are now deceased.

Membership: Not reported.

Periodicals: *Daily Meditation*.

Sources:

Dawn, Rose. *The Miracle Power*. San Antonio, TX: Mayan Press, 1959.

————. *The Search for Happiness*. Mayan Order, 1966.

Philosophical Research Society

3910 Los Feliz Blvd., Los Angeles, CA 90027

The Philosophical Research Society was founded in 1934 by Manly Palmer Hall (1901–1990), the most prolific and widely read occult writer of the twentieth century. As a young occult scholar and lecturer in the 1920s, he was a leader in the Church of the People in Los Angeles. During these years he began to publish his own books under the imprint of the Hall Publishing Company. The Philosophical Research Society was the culmination of a dream to establish a philosophical/religious institution modeled on the ancient philosopher/religious schools of Pythagoras, Plato, and the Serapeum of Alexander. Its goals include research, application of the occult heritage to modern problems, and the dissemination of the ancient wisdom by a variety of means.

Hall's basic position was closely related to an Eastern idealism. Life is eternal, an endless unfolding toward the real. It has its beginnings in the immeasurable past and its ultimates in the immeasurable future. Man's present individual existence is but one episode of innumerable ones. Law brings us into life and is the purpose of living. The seven laws of life are evolution, cause and effect, polarity, reincarnation, harmony and rhythm, generation, and vibration. Man may come into harmony with these but they are immutable. Hall's lectures and writings were an explication of this perspective. The more than 200 volumes he published include a number of historical studies of occultism and occultists. His publications continue to exert a significant influence on the psychic/occult community.

The Philosophical Research Society headquarters complex in Los Angeles includes a research library, bookstore, and publishing facilities. Books, booklets, and lecture transcripts are distributed across the United States. Regular classes and Sunday morning services are offered weekly, and correspondence courses are offered in a wide variety of topics. In 2008 the president was Dr. Obadiah S. Harris.

The University of Philosophical Research is a graduate-level distance learning university, nationally accredited by the Distance Education and Training Council. It offers master's degree programs in consciousness studies and transformational psychology.

Membership: Not a membership organization.

Educational Facilities:

University of Philosophical Research.

Periodicals: *Ancient Wisdom for Modern Living*.

Sources:

Philosophical Research Society. www.prs.org/.

Hall, Manly P. *Growing Up with Grandmother*. Los Angeles: Philosophical Research Society, 1985.

———. *Man, the Grand Symbol of the Mysteries*. Los Angeles: Philosophical Research Center, 1947.

———. *The Mystical Christ*. Los Angeles: Philosophical Research Society, 1951.

———. *Questions and Answers*. Los Angeles: Philosophers Press, 1937.

———. *Reincarnation, the Cycle of Necessity*. Los Angeles: Philosophical Research Society, 1946.

Sahagun, Louis. *Master of the Mysteries: The Life of Manly Palmer Hall*. Los Angeles: Process, 2008.

Sabian Assembly

279 President St., Brooklyn, NY 11231

The Sabian Assembly evolved from an astrology class led by Marc Edmund Jones (1888–1980) in New York City as the culmination of a decade of work that included a "meeting with a master." The following year, he held a second class in Los Angeles, California. On October 17, 1923, with a group of his students who had found some direction in the occult truths and who wished to test them in their lives, he created the Sabian Assembly. His charter called for the group to be "experimental" in nature. The astrological emphasis broadened to a synthesis of philosophy, psychology, and religion against a background of occult insights. In 1925 Jones published *Key Truths of Occult Philosophy*, which he revised and reissued in 1948 as *Occult Philosophy*. His *Ritual of Living* was published in 1930 and revised in 1957 as *The Sabian Manual*. From 1923 through 1943, Jones wrote 3,000 lessons that have been circulated and studied weekly by members of the Sabian Assembly, which has continued as a group oriented to the Philosophy of Concepts as enunciated by Jones. After World War II, it gradually spread with the increasing popularity of Jones's books and lectures. A freelance writer and ordained Presbyterian pastor, Jones earned his doctorate in philosophy from Columbia University in 1948. Eventually, he earned a reputation as one of the strongest occultists.

The Sabian Assembly is an openly eclectic body. Jones acknowledged that he drew from New Thought, Theosophy, Kabbalism, and Spiritualism, as well as from Eastern and Western theological and philosophical traditions. This reformulation of the ancient wisdom is seen as a special way of understanding and self-dedication. The Sabian project is basically the application of Cabala (or Kabbalah), as Jones

interpreted it, to all of life. Because the occult is easily warped into a structure of illusions, the group effort reinforces the student's need for verifiable experience in direct proportion to spiritual realization.

The Sabian Assembly is a solar group whose occult discipline derives its authority from within the self (as opposed to lunar groups, who see authority as represented outwardly by a hierarchical system). Sabian students maintain individual "work in consciousness" with a consistent focus on spiritual healing. Rituals developed at the request of the sponsors, the invisible council of the assembly, are provided for healing, the initiatory discipline, the quarterly reviews of progress, and specific occasions such as the dedication of a life (baptism), a departure (funeral), or a partnership, such as marriage.

The Sabian Assembly continues as a loosely organized fellowship of aspirants, each pursuing his or her own course of study in Jones's material, with the support of Sabian study groups where possible. The fellowship stresses respect for personality and minding one's own business. Membership is open to any who wish to participate in this approach to the Solar Mysteries. After two years as a neophyte, a new student may choose to participate in the five-year acolyte discipline, which requires work in consciousness and a course of spiritual exercises as well as specific volunteer work for the assembly. Beyond that, students may continue with three years of legate studies, although the group gives no outward recognition of inward status.

Jones served as chancellor of the Sabian Assembly until shortly before his death. The work of the assembly continues, without a central headquarters or staff, on the basis of volunteer work coordinated by an unpaid administrator. New students receive copies of *The Sabian Manual* and *The Sabian Book*, which is a collection of short essays characteristic of the Sabian approach. Sabian lesson materials are re-edited and distributed by students.

Members receive one Bible and one philosophy lesson each week. They attend weekly study groups where they engage in a brief healing ritual that is central to Sabian work. Once per month, at the time of the full moon, members meet to join in consciousness with others around the world who dedicate this time to the ideals of world service. The assembly holds winter conferences at the home of one of the members and summer conferences in various U.S. cities, with members from all over the world in attendance.

Membership: The assembly reports study groups in Pennsylvania, Delaware, Florida, Illinois, New York, California, New Mexico, Texas, Oregon, Michigan, Maryland, and Connecticut, and in Melbourne, Victoria, Australia.

Periodicals: *Sabian News Letter*. • *Sabiana Journal*.

Sources:

Sabian Assembly. www.sabian.org/.

Jones, Marc Edmund. *Occult Philosophy*. Standwood, WA: Sabian Publishing Society, 1971.

———. *The Ritual of Living*. Los Angeles: J. F. Rowny Press, 1930.

———. *The Sabian Book*. Stanwood, WA: Sabian Publishing Society, 1973.

———. *The Sabian Manual*. New York: Sabian Publishing Society, 1957.

———. *The Scope of Astrological Prediction*. Stanwood, WA: Sabian Publishing Society, 1969.

Soulcraft Enterprises, Inc.

PO Box 1410, Silverton, OR 97381

William Dudley Pelley (1890–1965), the elucidator of the Liberation-Soulcraft philosophy, was a New England newspaperman in 1918 when he was sent by the Methodist Episcopal Church to the Far East to report on foreign missions. He also was commissioned at that time by the YMCA to venture into Siberia to report on the Russian Revolution. In the early 1920s, he gained a national reputation as a magazine writer. By the end of the decade, he had turned to Hollywood and produced several movie scenarios. One of his novels, *Drag*, was produced as one of the first sound movies.

In 1928 he had an out-of-body experience (an experience of one's consciousness becoming separated from the body), which he described in the March 1929 issue of the popular *American Magazine*. This unsought out-of-body experience led him into the world of extrasensory perception and the recording or "channeling" of remarkable messages from higher intelligences, called mentors. These messages form the basis of the Soulcraft philosophy: Every human spirit-soul is a part of the Godhead and therefore related to every other spirit-soul. Spirit-souls come to the classroom of Earth in physical form to become aware of themselves and their relationship to others and to God through many lives. The questions opened by this basic premise form the subject matter of the more than two dozen books written by Pelley. He also recorded messages from a source wishing to be called the Elder Brother, which are found in a book entitled *The Golden Scripts* (1941). Pelley refused to found a church on this philosophy for fear of its becoming crystallized and dogmatic and losing its open-endedness. Fellowship Press, Inc., served as the distributor of the Soulcraft books, thus keeping the philosophy alive.

After Pelley's death, his daughter, Adelaide Pelley Pearson, and son-in-law, Melford Pearson, continued to print and distribute his metaphysical books and also his book outlining the blueprint for a healthier and sounder economic system, *No More Hunger*. Fellowship Press was a corporation owned and operated by the Pearsons for the purpose of printing Pelley's books. In August 2001 the inventory, printing, publishing, and marketing functions were contracted to Soulcraft Enterprises, Inc., under the administration of Jack Kerlin, of Springdale, Utah.

Membership: Not a membership organization.

Remarks: During the 1930s Pelley became well known in a second and even more controversial area of public life when he formed an organization he called the Silver Shirts. It was avowedly anti-Communist, anti–New Deal, and against what Pelley believed to be the undue Jewish influence in government, banking, and the media. His operation came under government scrutiny as Adolf Hitler rose to power in Germany and war became imminent in Europe. Remaining adamant in his beliefs, even after Pearl Harbor, he was arrested and tried for sedition in 1942. Convicted, he was sentenced to 15 years in federal prison but was then immediately included with a number of other defendants in the "Great Sedition Trial" (1944) in Washington, D.C., which ended in a mistrial. Pelley served over seven years on his prior conviction. The last years of his life were spent on his metaphysical work.

Sources:

Soulcraft Teachings. www.soulcraftteachings.com/home.html.

The Golden Scripts. Noblesville, IN: Soulcraft Chapels, 1951.

Pelley, William Dudley. *The Door to Revelation*. Asheville, NC: Foundation Fellowship, 1936.

———. *No More Hunger*. Noblesville, IN: Aquila Press, 1961.

———. *Seven Minutes in Eternity*. Noblesville, IN: Soulcraft Chapels, 1954.

———. *Star Guests*. Noblesville, IN: Soulcraft Press, 1950.

Strong, Donald S. *Organized Anti-Semitism in America*. Washington, DC: American Council on Public Affairs, 1941.

Stelle Community Association

127 Sun St., Stelle, IL 60919

The Stelle Group, named for Dr. Robert D. Stelle (1881–1952), founder of the Lemurian Fellowship of Ramona, California, and its sister society, the Adelphi Organization, were founded by Richard Kieninger (1927–2002). In the 1950s Kieninger was associated with the Lemurian Fellowship, from whom he received his initial esoteric training. In 1963 he formed the Stelle Group and, writing under a pen name, Eklal Kueshana, published *The Ultimate Frontier*, predicting a major natural catastrophe and atomic war by the end of the twentieth century. It described the basic philosophy of the Brotherhood of Christ as presented to

Kieninger from childhood through occasional visitations. In 1966 in Chicago, Kieninger and his wife, Gail, formed the Lemuria Builders, the purpose of which was to acquaint the public with Stelle philosophy and to recruit new members for the group. The Kieningers opened the Stelle School in 1968 in their home. In 1973 the school, offices, and community were moved to Stelle, Illinois, in Ford County.

Kieninger claimed that his first contact with several mysterious beings was on his 12th birthday. The initial contact, a Dr. White, taught reincarnation, told Kieninger of his past lives, including ones as the biblical King David and Pharaoh Akhnaton, and began to explain Kieninger's mission to found a new nation. Later that year, he was given a secret name, permanently incised into his skin, and at the same time was taught of the 12 Brotherhoods (five greater and seven lesser). In 1945 Dr. White gave him the place of the ideal community—Stelle City. The Stelle community, near Kankakee, Illinois, was seen as one preparatory model of the new society to be formed by followers. In 1976 Kieninger formed a sister organization to the Stelle Group, the Adelphi Organization, which purchased 78 acres of land 35 miles east of Dallas, Texas. The plan was to develop a community open only to a dedicated core of disciples of Kieninger's teachings.

In 1982 Stelle headquarters were moved to Dallas, and the community was opened to nonmembers who wanted to participate in the experimental community life. That year the Stelle Community Association, the current name of the organization, was chartered; the Stelle Group was dissolved in 2006. Kieninger's association with the Stelle Community Association and the Adelphi Organization Adelphi Organization (PO Box 75, Quinlan, TX 75474) ended in 1986.

In 2008 there are no criteria for residence other than that residents be willing to pay for their share of community fees and assessments. The community's population, which undergoes ongoing turnover, has remained at around 100 since the 1970s. A significant number of residents have lived in the community for decades. Goals and practices of the association include sustainability, self-reliance, organic gardening, holistic health, meditation, and celebration of Christian holidays.

Membership: In 2008 the Stelle Community Association reported approximately 100 members and 44 households.

Periodicals: *The Stelle Group Newsletter*. • *The Philosopher's Stone*.

Sources:

Stelle Community Association. www.stellecommunity.com/.

Kieninger, Richard. *The Hidden Christ*. Dallas, TX: Paragon Press, 1989.

———. *Observations*. 4 vols. Chicago: Stelle Group, 1971–79.

———. *Spiritual Seekers' Guidebook and Hidden Threats to Mental and Spiritual Freedom*. Quinlan, TX: Stelle Group, 1986.

Kueshana, Eklal [Richard Kieninger, psued.] *The Ultimate Frontier*. Chicago: Stelle Group, 1963.

Valentine, Tom. *The Great Pyramid: Man's Monument to Man*. New York: Pinnacle Books, 1975.

 # Theosophy

Temple of the People

Box 7100, 906 South Halcyon Road, Halcyon, CA 93421

The Temple of the People was formed in 1898 in Syracuse, New York, under the leadership of William H. Dower (1866–1937) and Francia A. LaDue (1849–1922). The founding occurred during the period of disruption in the American branch of the Theosophical Society following the deaths of its founders, Helena Petrovna Blavatsky and William Q. Judge. The Syracuse group, like many others, rejected Judge's successor, Katherine Tingley, and thus sought independence. Within a few years the temple purchased a tract of land at Halcyon, California (near Pismo Beach), and moved there in 1903. In 1904 Dower opened a sanatorium, which became famous for its treatment of tubercular patients, alcoholics, and drug addicts. In 1903 the temple also organized the Temple Home Association, a cooperative colony that existed through 1949, when it was reorganized, as set forth in its original bylaws, as the Home of the Temple Associated, Inc. The HTA was dissolved in 1992 and all properties were then administered by the Temple Corporation.

The temple began with the contact from the Mahatmas, or Masters, through LaDue and Dower, known respectively as "Blue Star" and "Red Star," the designations given them by the Masters. They were told to abandon the society as led by Tingley, and through their reception and publishing of continuing materials from the Masters, to carry on the work begun by Madame Blavatsky. Over the years they produced an impressive set of materials, including a large volume, *Theogenesis*, a third volume of commentaries on the Stanzas of Dyzan. Madame Blavatsky wrote *The Secret Doctrine*, the two volumes of which were entitled *Anthropogenesis* and *Cosmogenesis*, as a commetary on those parts of the Stanzas that were known to her.

According to the temple, the spiritual hierarchy is led by the Central Spiritual Sun, the Christos, the expression of the Infinite Godhead. Other Masters, members of the Great White Brotherhood, embody aspects of the divine light, key members being the Masters of the Seven Rays (of the color spectrum). Integral to the original teachings given to the Temple's founders from the Master Hilarion, Regent of the Red Ray, was a prophecy concerning the soon-to-occur birth of an avatar, an incarnation of the Christos, an event that happens only every 2,000 years. The first generation of the temple was to a great extent motivated by that expectation and the belief that members were the spearhead of the Messianic Age into which humanity was moving. These emphases, which still undergird the temple's understanding of its educational mission and work in the world, are summarized in the three *Teachings of the Temple* volumes.

During the first generation, the life of the community at Halcyon revolved around the sanatorium and the building of the temple. Groups that received and studied the material produced through the Temple sprang up around the country, and every summer a national convention was held. Dower succeeded LaDue as guardian-in-chief of the temple. He was in turn succeeded by Pearl F. Dower, and she by Harold Forgostein. In 2008 the guardian-in-chief was Eleanor L. Shumway, who leads along with a board of four officers appointed yearly. The temple has kept the material originally received by Dower and LaDue in print and their work revolves around it.

The Temple of the People is still headquartered in the community at Halcyon, which has consistently been home to approximately 100 residents. There is a lively group following in both England and Germany, and individual members around the world. The temple offers services every Sunday morning and a short meditation for world healing every day at noon in the Blue Star Memorial Temple in Halcyon. Study classes are held twice a week in the University Center. All classes and services are open to the public. The William Quan Judge Library is open by appointment.

Membership: In 2008 the temple reported about 300 members in five congregations, along with affiliated work in Canada, England, Germany, Russia, Spain, Switzerland, and Italy.

Periodicals: *The Temple Artisan*.

Sources:

Temple of the People. www.templeofthepeople.org/.

Burns, Bob, et al. *The Temple of the People*. Halcyon, CA: California Polytechnic State University, 1972.

From the Mountain Top. 3 vols. Halcyon, CA: Temple of the People, 1974–1985.

Kagan, Paul. *New World Utopias*. Baltimore: Penguin Books, 1975.

Teachings of the Temple. 3 vols. Halcyon, CA: Temple of the People, 1947–1985.

Theogenesis. Halcyon, CA: Temple of the People, 1981.

Theosophical Society
PO Box C, Pasadena, CA 91109-7107

The Theosophical Society (TS) is a worldwide association dedicated to practical realization of the oneness of all life and to independent spiritual search. It was founded in New York City in 1875 by Helena Petrovna Blavatsky (1831–1891), Henry S. Olcott (1832–1907), William Q. Judge (1851–1896), and others. Its stated objectives are to diffuse among men a knowledge of the laws inherent in the universe; to promulgate the knowledge of the essential unity of all that is, and to demonstrate that this unity is fundamental in nature; to form an active brotherhood among men; to study ancient and modern religion, science, and philosophy; and to investigate the powers innate in man. Beyond supporting its objectives, members need not accept any particular beliefs and may belong to any religion or to none. The society is nonsectarian and nonpolitical, open to all people regardless of race, nationality, class, creed, or gender.

The works of Blavatsky and her teachers express the principal concepts of theosophy ("divine wisdom"), a contemporary presentation of the perennial wisdom underlying the world's religious traditions. Embodying the concepts of karma, reincarnation, and the essential divinity of all beings, it holds that life exists everywhere because everything originates from the same unknowable divine source, expressing itself cyclically through various ranges of consciousness and substance. Evolution consists of an emerging self-expression that individualizes into material forms through the various kingdoms until each being develops self-consciousness and spiritual awareness on its return to the divine source.

In 1877 Blavatsky published *Isis Unveiled*, her first major work showing the universality of the wisdom tradition and its basis in nature. The following year Blavatsky and Olcott left America for India, where they worked for recognition of Eastern religions and philosophies, especially among the educated who were rejecting their own traditions in the face of modern Western education. Blavatsky's fame, however, rested largely on accounts of paranormal phenomena she had produced privately over the years. In 1885 the Society for Psychical Research published a report—since refuted in that society's *Journal*—declaring Blavatsky an impostor. Earlier that year Blavatsky had moved to Europe, settling in London. There she published her masterwork, *The Secret Doctrine*, which presents a comprehensive view of cosmic and human evolution, bringing together mythic, religious, and scientific material from many cultures in support of theosophy's basic concepts. She also issued *The Key to Theosophy*, *The Voice of the Silence*, and the magazine *Lucifer* ("lightbearer").

When Blavatsky died in 1891, William Q. Judge and Annie Besant (1847–1933) became joint heads of the esoteric work, while Olcott continued his post as president of the society internationally. A number of problems concerning leadership and administration arose that eventually led the American Section to declare complete autonomy in April 1895 and elect Judge president for life. The resulting division in the society reached into all national sections.

After Judge's death in 1896, Katherine Tingley (1847–1929) headed the esoteric work and soon laid the groundwork for a School for the Revival of the Lost Mysteries of Antiquity. In 1898 she founded the Universal Brotherhood Organization, and the TS was renamed the Universal Brotherhood and Theosophical Society, with Tingley as leader and official head. In 1900 she moved the headquarters from New York City to Point Loma, California, near San Diego, where she founded a school, academy, and college, and, in 1919, the Theosophical University. Education for all residents of Point Loma included a balanced development of physical, mental, moral, and spiritual qualities, with emphasis on character training, music, drama, and the arts. Tingley lectured in the United States and abroad while pursuing philanthropic activities, among them international peace, education and prison reform, the rehabilitation of prisoners, and abolition of capital punishment.

After Tingley's death in 1929, Gottfried de Purucker (1874–1942), a scholar with a literary legacy of theosophic literature, became leader. The original name "The Theosophical Society" was resumed, and after securing the financial footing of the TS through the Depression, in 1942 he moved the society's headquarters, including the press, university, and library facilities, to Covina, near Los Angeles.

Arthur L. Conger (1872–1951) followed de Purucker as leader in 1945. Conger had joined the society while at Harvard during the time of Judge, and was president of the American Section under de Purucker. He maintained a strong publishing program and fostered a more practical expression of theosophy. In 1950 he moved the headquarters to the Pasadena area, and closed the esoteric section to help prevent crystallization.

After Conger's death in 1951, James A. Long (1898–1971) continued this policy. He founded *Sunrise Magazine* as a bridge between the public and the deeper teachings of theosophy and urged members to express these principles in their daily lives and in simple nontechnical language. On Long's death in 1971, Grace F. Knoche (1909–2006) became leader of the TS. She opened Theosophical University Library to the public and encouraged translation and publishing activities, library centers, public discussions, and study groups worldwide. Following Knoche's death, Randell C. Grubb became head of the society.

The society supports fellows-at-large worldwide and maintains sections in Australasia, the Czech Republic, Finland, Germany, Great Britain, the Netherlands, Nigeria, Scandinavia, South Africa, and North America. Extensive literature is available at no charge on its Web site, and theosophical correspondence courses are offered free of charge except for study materials and postage. The Theosophical University Press and its overseas agencies feature the theosophic classics of Blavatsky, Judge, de Purucker, Long, and Knoche, among other writers, while adding new titles to their lists. Audio versions of selected books are also made available for free to the visually impaired.

Membership: Not reported.

Periodicals: *SUNRISE: Theosophic Perspectives* (also in Dutch and German editions). • *Teosofiskt Forum* in Swedish.

Sources:

Theosophical Society. www.theosociety.org/.

Blavatsky, H. P. *The Key to Philosophy*. Pasadena, CA: Theosophical University Press, 2002.

de Purucker, Gottfried. *Fountain-Source of Occultism*. Pasadena, CA: Theosophical University Press, 1974.

———. *Fundamentals of the Esoteric Philosophy*. Pasadena, CA: Theosophical University Press, 1979.

———. *H. P. Blavatsky*. San Diego: Point Loma Publications, 1974.

Judge, William Q. *Echoes of the Orient*. Pasadena, CA: Theosophical University Press, 2008.

———. *The Ocean of Theosophy*. Pasadena, CA: Theosophical University Press, 2002.

Knoche, Grace F. *To Light a Thousand Lamps: A Theosophic Vision*. Pasadena, CA: Theosophical University Press, 2006.

Ryan, Charles J. *H. P. Blavatsky and the Theosophical Movement*. Pasadena, CA: Theosophical University Press, 1974.

Tingley, Katherine. *Theosophy: The Path of the Mystic*. Pasadena, CA: Theosophical University Press, 1977.

Theosophical Society (Hartley)

Blavatsky House, De Ruyterstratt 74, 2518 AV The Hague, The Netherlands

In 1951 the Theosophical Society, headquartered in Pasadena, California, split. The former leader of the society, Arthur L. Conger (1872–1951), had designated William Hartley (d. 1956) to be his successor. However, the society's ruling council rejected Hartley in favor of James A. Long (1898–1971). Because Long and his supporters retained control of the society and its library and properties, Hartley and his followers were forced to reorganize. New headquarters were established in

Covina, California. This branch gained few members from among American theosophists and eventually died out in the United States. But it found some measure of support in the Netherlands, where it has survived. Hartley was succeeded as head of the group by D. J. P. Kok. Since 1985 the leader has been Herman C. Vermeulen.

The society's objectives are to diffuse among people a knowledge of the laws inherent in the universe; to promulgate the knowledge of the essential unity of all that is and to demonstrate that this unity is fundamental in nature; to form an active brotherhood among people; to study ancient and modern religion, science, and philosophy; and to investigate the power innate in humanity. The society promulgates its teachings in strict accordance with *The Secret Doctrine* by Madame Helena Petrovna Blavatsky and the writings of the other original leaders.

The society in Holland maintains an active program of public lectures, held from September through June at various locations; classes, including "Thinking Differently" and "Wisdom of Life," which instruct students in the application of one's thinking to daily life and a practical philosophy of life; lodge work; and an annual symposium.

Much effort is being made to translate theosophical works into other languages and to publish theosophical material. Blavatskyhuis (Blavatsky House), the headquarters, houses a library. The society's corporation, the International Study Center for the Independent Search for Truth, also serves as a publisher.

Membership: Not reported. In 1987 there were five lodges, all in the Netherlands. There are no known branches of the Theosophical Society (Hartley) in the United States.

Periodicals: *Lucifer: The Messenger of Life.*

Sources:

The Theosophical Society. www.blavatskyhouse.org/.

Theosophical Society in America

1926 N Main St., Wheaton, IL 60187

Alternate Address: International headquarters: Theosophical Society, Adyar, Madras 600 020, India.

HISTORY. The Theosophical Society in America was founded in 1875 by Helena Petrovna Blavatsky (1831–1891), Col. Henry S. Olcott (1832–1907), William Q. Judge (1851–1896), and others. In 1879 the two principal founders, Olcott and Blavatsky, moved to India, where in 1882 they established the international headquarters in Adyar, Madras. Olcott, as the first president of the society, took the lead in administrative duties; during his lifetime the society became an international organization with lodges around the globe. Blavatsky became the great teacher of the movement and the founder of an independent sister organization called the Esoteric Section (associated primarily by the requirement that one must be a theosophist to be a member). The international headquarters chartered the American Section in 1886, and Judge organized the then scattered branches at an organizational convention in Cincinnati, Ohio. Following Blavatsky's death, Judge led a movement among American members to become independent of the international headquarters. He persuaded most members to join him in the formation of what is now known in the United States as simply the Theosophical Society, with headquarters in Pasadena, California. Those lodges that remained loyal to the international headquarters were known as the American Section of the Theosophical Society.

Beginning with 14 lodges, the American society reached a membership peak in the late 1920s of around 8,000. During these years the society was led internationally by Annie Besant (1847–1933), who had succeeded first Blavatsky and then Olcott in the top leadership positions of the society and the Esoteric Section. The low point of the society came as World War II began, when membership was slightly more than 3,000. It resumed a slow growth after the war and reached a second peak in 1972 with more than 6,000 members.

BELIEFS. The society emphasizes its nondogmatic nature and the freedom it allows members in interpreting theosophical teachings. However, it does present in its literature an explicit worldview that is generally shared by theosophists and is taught in classes, seminars, and lectures by the leadership. The worldview affirms that One life pervades the universe and keeps it in existence. The universe is an expression of an eternal Principle that transcends human perception. Ultimate Reality manifests in two aspects, generally referred to as spirit (or consciousness) and matter. Spirit, matter, and their interaction constitute a trinity that produces a multitude of universes.

Every solar system is governed by natural law, with the planets being the densest aspect. There are also exceedingly fine material parts of the system, the whole of which is undergoing a process of evolution. The spirits (or souls) of humans are in essence identical with the supreme Spirit and undergoing a process of unfolding the essential divine nature. In that process, called reincarnation, the spirit passes through periods of activity (embodiments) followed by periods of rest/assimilation. Closely related to reincarnation is the Law of Karma, in which each soul creates its fate by its actions. The spirit's pilgrimage begins in unity, moves to an experience of the manyness of this life, and back to conscious union with the One Divine Source of all.

ORGANIZATION. Olcott, the administrative center of the American Section, is located in Wheaton, Illinois, on a 40-acre tract purchased in the 1920s. The society is headed by a president and a board of directors consisting of the vice president and district directors elected regionally. The board oversees a number of administrative departments and the national program. Also located at the headquarters complex is the Olcott Library, housing more than 20,000 volumes on a wide variety of subjects on theosophy and related topics. The Theosophical Publishing House is a major publisher of esoteric literature and has extended its influence through a series issued under the imprint of Quest Books, made possible by donations by the Kern Foundation. A string of bookstores, Quest Bookshops, are located in Wheaton, New York City, Seattle, and elsewhere.

The society is an open membership organization, and anyone who is in sympathy with its general principles may join. Also nonmembers may join its library and benefit from its use. In 2008 the president of the society in America was Betty Bland. Among those who have served as president are Alexander Fullerton, Weller Van Hook, A. P. Warrington, L. W. Rogers, Sidney A. Cook, James S. Perkins, Henry A. Smith, Joy Mills, Ann Wylie, Dora Kunz, Dorothy Abbenhouse, and John Algeo.

Membership: In 2002 the society reported 5,580 members and 140 centers in the United States, and approximately 400 members and 18 centers in Canada. There were 40,000 members worldwide.

Educational Facilities:

The Olcott Institute, Wheaton, Illinois.

Periodicals: *The Quest.* • *The Messenger.*

Remarks: There are several organizations closely associated with the Theosophical Society in America that, though largely composed of members of the society, are in fact independent of it. These include the Esoteric Section; Krotona School of Theosophy, in Ojai, California; and the Theosophical Order of Service. The Esoteric Section and the Krotona Institute serve the society as an educational arm.

Sources:

Theosophical Society in America. www.theosophical.org/.

Ellwood, Robert. *Theosophy*. Wheaton, IL: Theosophical Publishing House, 1986.

Mills, Joy. *100 Years of Theosophy*. Wheaton, IL: Theosophical Publishing House, 1987.

Perkins, James S. *Through Death to Rebirth*. Wheaton, IL: Theosophical Publishing House, 1973.

Rogers, L. W. *Elementary Theosophy*. Wheaton, IL: Theosophical Press, 1929.

United Lodge of Theosophists
245 W 33rd St., Los Angeles, CA 90007

The United Lodge of Theosophists (U.L.T.) is an association of students of theosophy founded by a small group of Theosophists dissatisfied with what they perceived as organizational formalities and distractions within the larger Theosophical movement. The conception of U.L.T. as a vehicle for Theosophical work derived mainly from the experience and insight of Robert Crosbie (1848–1919), who through his many years with the movement witnessed the schisms and divisions that he attributed to conflicting organizational claims, controversy over authority, and the conceptions of personal leaders. In 1909, with the help of a few others who had come to share his "unsectarian" view of Theosophy, Crosbie founded the United Lodge of Theosophists, an organization defined by a simple statement of policies and intentions. With this group he set about the task of restoring the record of Theosophical teachings available to the public and inaugurating a program of practical Theosophical education. The statement of purpose, called the "Declaration," has remained unchanged, and the modes of work established by Crosbie have remained unaltered in principle.

Beliefs. The lodge teaches that there is but one life; all life is spirit or consciousness evolving toward greater individualization and toward a greater awareness of identity and unity. This evolution proceeds under an inherent law—an order that is native to human understanding. Believing that the mind, in its highest sense, is the place of realization and growth, individual students come to regard these general principles as meaning that human life is a continuous process of learning, and that this learning involves unceasing revision of the terms of individual understanding as men gain awareness of its operations.

Organization. According to its Declaration the U.L.T. is devoted to "the cause of Theosophy without professing attachment to any Theosophical organization. It is loyal to the great Founders of the theosophical movement, but does not concern itself with dissensions or difference of individual opinion." The basis of union among Theosophists is a similarity of aim, purpose, and teachings, and to that end the U.L.T. has neither a constitution, by-laws, nor officers. Those affiliated with the lodge sign a statement of sympathy with the Declaration at the time of their becoming an associate (member) of the U.L.T. Members may found autonomous lodges.

The U.L.T. considers the original and pure message of Theosophy to be recorded in the writings of Helena Petrovna Blavatsky and William Q. Judge, co-founders of the Theosophical Society. The U.L.T. makes its works, and other works deemed consistent with them, including a monthly magazine, available to the public. Pamphlets, available in English, French, and Spanish, and one-hour videos can be downloaded free from the Web site.

Membership: In 2008 the U.L.T. reported 7 lodges and 3 study groups in the United States, 2 lodges in Canada, and 14 lodges in Belgium, Greece, India, France, Cameroon, Haiti, England, Sweden, and the Netherlands.

Periodicals: *Theosophy.* • *Hermes.* • *The Theosophical Movement.*

Remarks: Among the prominent centers affiliated with the U.L.T. is the center in Santa Barbara, California, which was founded in 1976 by the late Rhagavan N. Iyer, formerly a professor of political science at the University of California, Santa Barbara. He was succeeded by his widow, Nandini Iyer, an instructor in religious studies at UCSB. The center is home to the Concord Press, which pursues an aggressive program of publishing material on theosophy, Eastern religion, and classical philosophy, and the Institute of World Culture, which promotes dialogue on classical traditions, modern science, art, and social structures as they attempt to relate to world culture. The center also issues a periodical, *Hermes*.

Sources:

United Lodge of Theosophists. www.ult-la.org/.

Crosbie, Robert. *The Friendly Philosopher*. Los Angeles: Theosophy Company, 1934.

————. *Answers to Questions on the Ocean of Theosophy*. Los Angeles: Theosophy Company, 1937.

Institute of World Culture. www.worldculture.org/index.html.

The Theosophical Movement, 1875–1950. Los Angeles: Cunningham Press, 1951.

The United Lodge of Theosophists, Its Mission and Its Future. Los Angeles: Theosophy Company, n.d.

Upper Triad Association

PO Box 825, Madison, NC 27025

The Upper Triad Association was formed in Albuquerque, New Mexico, in January 1974 by three Christian members of the Theosophical Society and nine additional students of theosophy. Originally a meditation group that sponsored discussion, lectures, and classes in theosophy, the association began publishing the *Upper Triad Journal*, in April 1974, which became their major effort. Over the years the association published over 1,500 articles and commentaries, now collected and republished in the form of some 21 books and 63 topical issues. In 1976 the association moved its headquarters to New Brunswick, New Jersey, and incorporated the following year. In 1979 the headquarters moved to Virginia, and in 2005 to Raleigh, North Carolina, where the association operates a retreat facility. In 2008 the president was Peter Lunn.

The Upper Triad Association is an ecumenical fellowship whose members find inspiration in the various scriptures of all the different God-centered religions and who are focused on spiritual growth, world goodwill, and service. It has not been the group's intention to compete with or duplicate other theosophical groups, and it has limited the circulation of its *Journal* to serious students rather than use it as an instrument for promulgating the esoteric philosophy. The assumptions on which the teachings are based include an affirmation of the unity of all life, the evolution of consciousness as the purpose of life, reincarnation and karma, the relativity of truth which may be perceived at many levels, the problem of life as the elimination of illusion and glamour, the essence of the self in the soul as opposed to the personality, and the higher stages of human evolution as being on the spiritual path. The association's threefold mantra is humility, compassion, and goodwill.

Membership: Not reported.

Periodicals: *Upper Triad Material*.

Sources:

Upper Triad Association. www.uppertriad.com/.

The Word Foundation, Inc.

PO Box 17510, Rochester, NY 14617

The Word Foundation, Inc., is a nonprofit organization formed in 1950 dedicated to disseminating the contents and explicating the meaning of *Thinking and Destiny* and other books by Harold Waldwin Percival (1868–1953), an early theosophist who joined the Theosophical Society in 1892. The year after he joined he had a profound experience that he described as being "conscious of Consciousness" during which "Light greater than that of myriads of suns opened in my head. In that instant or point, eternities were apprehended." By a process he called "real thinking," he was able to select any subject, focus the Conscious Light upon it, and have complete knowledge of that subject.

While a member of the Theosophical Society, but several years after the death of its leader, William Q. Judge, he withdrew and founded the Theosophical Society Independent. He also organized the Theosophical Publishing Company of New York and started a magazine, *The Word*, which he published from 1904 to 1917. The magazine had a worldwide circulation and featured prominent writers of the day.

It was during his years as editor of *The Word* that he began to outline materials for what was to become his most important work. By the process of "real thinking," Percival wrote *Thinking and Destiny*, an exhaustive survey of humanity and the world. The text was dictated (primarily to an assistant, Benoni B. Gattell) since his body had to be very still while he thought. He spent more than 30 years dictating and refining the material in *Thinking and Destiny*.

Thinking and Destiny sets forth an impressive system in which humans are at the center of a universe created by their own thinking and thoughts. In this system, each human being is descended from a Triune Self (Thinker, Knower, and Doer) and is living in a self-induced hypnosis and ignorance in a human body. One of the goals of life is to teach beings to awaken to knowledge of themselves and of their purpose, that purpose being to become conscious in ever greater degrees until one knows the ultimate, Consciousness.

Every doer so embodied is bound by the law it has made for itself by its thinking and action. The universal law causes the everyday acts, objects, and events to exteriorize around one's self as destiny. By self-dehypnotization and thinking, one gains an understanding and acquaintance with these inner realities. As one becomes free of the states of feeling and desire that bind one to nature, the way to conscious immortality is shown.

In 1946 Percival and some associates formed The Word Publishing Company and released *Thinking and Destiny*. In 1950 in New York, they chartered The Word Foundation, Inc. Percival assigned copyrights of all his books to the foundation. The foundation is not associated or affiliated with any other organization and does not endorse or support any teacher or group claiming to have been inspired by or authorized to interpret Percival's writings. The foundation became an open membership organization in 1986. That same year, it revived *The Word* magazine.

Periodicals: *The Word*.

Membership: In 2002 the foundation reported approximately 400 members.

Sources:

The Word Foundation. www.thewordfoundation.org/.

Percival, Harold W. *Adepts, Masters and Mahatmas*. Dallas: Word Foundation, 1993.

————. *Democracy Is Self-Government*. New York: Word Publishing Company, 1952.

————. *Man and Woman and Child*. New York: Word Publishing Company, 1951.

————. *Masonry and Its Symbols*. New York: Word Publishing Company, 1952.

————. *Thinking and Destiny*. New York: Word Publishing Company, 1950.

❈ Alice Bailey Groups

Arcana Workshops

3916 Sepulveda Boulevard, Suite 107, Culver City, CA 90230

Arcana Workshops is among the largest of the groups promoting the teachings of Alice A. Bailey (1880–1949) in Southern California. The group has developed a meditation training program based on Bailey's writings and the Agni Yoga Series (published by the Agni Yoga Society). It offers meditation training via its home page on the Internet. Many in the region who have attended workshops in the Los Angeles area have formed full-moon meditation groups. Through correspondence courses, numerous pamphlets, books, and regular mailings, the organization has established a network around the country. The Arcana Workshops pioneered the intergroup cooperation that led to the annual celebration of the three linked festivals of Aries, Taurus, and Gemini among occult groups in southern California every spring.

Periodicals: *Thoughtlines*.

Membership: Not a membership organization.

Sources:

Arcana Workshops. www.meditationtraining.org/.

The Full Moon Story. Beverly Hills, CA: Arcana Workshops, 1974.

For Full Moon Workers. Beverly Hills, CA: Arcana Workshops, n.d.

What Is Arcana? Beverly Hills, CA: Arcana Workshops, n.d.

Arcane School

120 Wall St., 24th fl., New York, NY 10005

Alternate Address: Ste. 54, 3 Whitehall Ct., London SW1A 2EF, U.K.; 1 rue de Varembe (3e), Case Postale 31, 1211 Geneva 20, Switzerland.

The Arcane School, founded in 1923 by Alice and Foster Bailey (1888–1977), is the original group continuing the work and thought of Alice A. Bailey (1880–1949). It remains the largest of the full-moon meditation groups. All of the Alice Bailey books are published through the Lucis Trust, which publishes her books for the entire movement.

Several subsidiary programs were created to implement the program of the hierarchy. Triangles was founded in 1937 to build groups of three people who would unite daily in a mental chain radiating energy into the world. World Goodwill was established in 1932 with the purpose of establishing right human relations in the world.

The work of the Arcane School is conducted through correspondence lessons, which Alice first prepared in the 1920s based on her books, through the headquarters in New York, London, and Geneva. Students living in the Americas and parts of the Far East who work in English or Spanish are served through New York; those in Great Britain and the Commonwealth through London; and those working in other European languages through Geneva. Following Alice's death in 1949, Foster Bailey took charge of the work.

The headquarters exist to guide and advise students in their work and spiritual life. The Arcane School assists in discipleship, viewing the work of the hierarchy as dependent on the quality of the entire school membership. All students in the school accept responsibility for the maintenance and development of the group work as an instrument of service. As there are no classes, examinations, or competition, the work is individual and confidential. Only individual progress is evaluated, with no comparisons to the spiritual growth of another. Each student meditates and searches for truth according to his own need and understanding, learning through acquired spiritual independence the significance of interdependence in group work. Each student is also assigned to a secretarial group. A secretary is a student who has agreed to work with other students in the earlier degrees and oversee their work through correspondence.

The school maintains a free lending library of occult and esoteric books at each headquarters. The public may also borrow materials by mail if they reside in the countries of the headquarters. The Arcane School does not charge tuition and is operated solely by voluntary contributions.

Membership: Not reported.

Periodicals: *The Beacon.* • *World Goodwill Newsletter.*

Sources:

Lucis Trust: Arcane School. www.lucistrust.org/en/arcane_school.

Bailey, Alice A. *The Unfinished Autobiography*. New York: Lucis Publishing Company, 1951.

Sinclair, John R. *The Alice Bailey Inheritance*. Wellingsborough, North-amptonshire: Turnstone Press, 1984.

Thirty Years' Work. New York: Lucis Publishing Company, n.d.

Meditation Groups, Inc.

Box 566, Ojai, CA 93024

One of the several groups inspired by the writings of Alice Bailey, Meditation Groups, Inc. (MGI), assumed the task mentioned in *Discipleship in the New Age* of establishing a worldwide group devoted to meditation on the Laws and Principles that prepare the world for the coming new order and the jurisdiction of the Christ. It was formed in 1950 by Florence Garrique (1888–1985) and was headquartered in Greenwich, Connecticut. With the assistance of Raymond Whorf, MGI was

moved to a mountain precipice overlooking the Ojai (California) Valley in 1968, and the site became known as Meditation Mount. The Mount has held full-moon meditation gatherings every month since its dedication in 1971. The overall purpose of Meditation Groups, Inc., is to promote meditation on the Laws and Principles of the New Age as an act of service to the world.

While following the same teachings as the Arcane School, which centered its activities on the books of Alice Bailey, Meditation Groups, Inc., developed three major programs: Meditation Groups for the New Age (MGNA), Group for Creative Meditation (GCM), and Specialized Groups. MGNA is the instructional arm of Meditation Groups, Inc. It teaches an introductory three-year course in meditation, as a service to humanity, introducing the student to an esoteric perspective on life from the books Alice Bailey received telepathically from the Tibetan Master of the Spiritual Hierarchy, with whom she had extensive contact. After completion of the three-year course, students may elect to continue with the work of GCM, which offers a more intensive course of occult study and meditation. MGNA holds symposiums at Meditation Mount and communicates with MGNA members and study groups across the world.

The Group for Creative Meditation encompasses worldwide meditation groups actively working on a program of service to humanity, the Spiritual Hierarchy, and the Christ. The world group follows a cycle of meditation based on the call of the Tibetan Master, for unanimous and simultaneous meditation on the Laws and Principles that must condition the consciousness of humanity and usher in the New Age. The group provides a number of materials for conducting full-moon meditation group gatherings and a meditation calendar with full information on the exact time of the full moon with the various time zones in the United States. The group publishes a continuing course based on the Alice Bailey books and a newsletter mailed to members, and holds an annual spring conference at Meditation Mount.

Conceived as the subject of the three activities, the specialized groups combine disciplined meditation with a focus on a particular area of endeavor, one of ten originally discussed by the Tibetan: Telepathic Communication, Recognition of Reality, Healing, Education, Politics, Religion, Science, Psychology, Finance, and Creativity. Advanced students of GCM are invited to take part in the work of one of these specialized groups.

Membership: Not reported.

Sources:

Meditation Mount. www.meditation.com/.

Moore, Frances Adams. *A View from the Mount*. Ojai, CA: Group for Creative Meditation, 1984.

Whorf, Raymond B. *The Tibetan's Teaching*. Ojai, CA: Meditation Groups, n.d.

Saraydarian Institute

915 Franklin St., 9B, Houston, TX 77002

The Saraydarian Institute, a religious and educational organization, was founded in Agoura, California, in 1961 by Torkom Saraydarian (1915–1997) as the Aquarian Educational Group. The institute's work is based on Saraydarian's studies of the world's religions, in relation to both the philosophy of the ages and the findings of modern science.

Saraydarian, born in Turkey to Armenian parents, was a writer and lecturer. He taught a synthesized understanding of cultures, religions, and science with an emphasis on practical application of these truths. His numerous publications have been translated into ten languages, and audio recordings of his teachings have been released.

The institute studies all branches of the Ageless Wisdom tradition and attempts to be an inclusive response to human aspirations and needs. The Ageless Wisdom is defined as the treasury of human knowledge and experience in all fields of human endeavor. Members are advised to study all the religions of the world and the teachings of the East and West such as the Puranas, Vedas, and Upanishads (of the Hindus), and the works of Helena Petrovna Blavatsky, Alice Bailey, and Helena Roerich. Strong emphasis is also given to the study of the teachings of Christ.

Members are also advised to consider the discoveries of modern science and are educated through various regular meetings, seminars, correspondence lessons, and regular scientific meditation. The institute also performs services for baptism, matrimony, and last rites.

The institute is headed by a nine-person board of trustees. During his lifetime, Saraydarian served as its president. In 1997 he appointed Joann Saraydarian, his wife, to succeed him as leader and president of the institute, which relocated to Houston, Texas. The institute's other efforts include the Center for Humanity, a peace organization.

The institute is identified by a symbol described as a five-pointed star surrounded by three concentric circles. The circles stand for the infinity of light, love, and beauty. The points of the star symbolize Beauty, Goodness, Righteousness, Joy, and Freedom. Within the star is an arrow pointed upward, a symbol of the striving toward perfection.

Membership: Not reported.

Sources:

Saraydarian Institute. www.saraydarian.org/.

Center for Humanity. www.centerforhumanity.org/.

Saraydarian, Haroutiun. *The Magnet of Life*. Reseda, CA: Aquarian Educational Group, 1968.

————. *The Science of Meditation*. Reseda, CA: Aquarian Educational Group, 1971.

Saraydarian, Torkom. *Christ the Avatar of Sacrificial Love*. Agoura, CA: Aquarian Educational Group, 1974.

————. *A Commentary on Psychic Energy*. West Hills, CA: T.S.G. Enterprises, 1989.

————. *The Flame of Beauty, Culture Love, Joy*. Agoura, CA: Aquarian Education Group, 1980.

————. *Sex, Family, and the Woman in Society*. Sedona, AZ: Aquarian Educational Group, 1987.

————. *The Symphony of the Zodiac*. Agoura, CA: Aquarian Education Group, 1980.

————. *Woman: Torch of the Future*. Agoura, CA: Aquarian Educational Group, 1980.

School for Esoteric Studies

345 S French Broad Ave., Ste. 300, Asheville, NC 28801

The School for Esoteric Studies was established in 1956 in New York City by former close co-workers of Alice Bailey. The founders include Frank Hilton, Regina Keller, Florence Garrigue, Helen Hillebrecht, and Margaret Schaefer. The school was located in New York City but in 1996 relocated to Asheville, North Carolina. The school offers training for discipleship in the New Age. Its courses, given via correspondence to English-speaking students throughout the world, focus on study of the ageless wisdom teachings, meditation, and service as a way of life. Discipleship is seen not as devotion toward any individual or group, but as intelligent cooperation with the Spiritual Hierarchy (i.e., the Masters of the Wisdom or the Christ and His Disciples) toward the working out of the Plan of Light and Love within humanity.

The curriculum of the school is based on the methods of and texts by Alice Bailey and others. Apart from the courses for students, the school offers short information booklets to the public and a longer booklet instructing individuals and groups wishing to engage in full-moon meditations.

Periodicals: *The Esoteric Quarterly.*

Membership: Not reported.

Sources:

School for Esoteric Studies. www.esotericstudies.net/.

Gregor, Norman. *Whither Man?*. New York: School for Esoteric Studies, n.d.

Share International USA

PO Box 971, North Hollywood, CA 91603

Alternate Address: Box 41877, 1009 DB Amsterdam, Netherlands; and Box 3677, London NW4 1RW, United Kingdom.

Within the Theosophical tradition, Charles W. Leadbeater and Annie Besant first promoted the expectation of a world teacher whose appearance was equated with the Second Advent of Christ and the arrival of Lord Maitreya, the Buddhist bodhisattva who would assist humanity in making its next evolutionary step. They identified Jiddu Krishnamurti as the vehicle for the world teacher and organized the Order of the Star of the East to communicate their message. In 1948, almost two decades after Krishnamurti had renounced his messianic role, Alice Bailey, founder of the Arcane School, published *The Reappearance of the Christ*, in which she argued that the time was ripe for the appearance of a new world teacher (avatar) who would come as both Son of God and head of the Spiritual Hierarchy, the group of exalted beings believed by Theosophists to stand behind and oversee the evolution of the planet. She also suggested that preparatory work for the appearance would begin in 1975.

In 1959 Benjamin Creme, born in Scotland in 1922 but residing in London, made contact with the Spiritual Hierarchy when he received a message telepathically from one of its masters. A short time later he was informed that Maitreya, the Christ, would return to earth some 20 years in the future. In 1975, having been offered the task of announcing Maitreya's appearance, he began to state that truth publicly. In 1977 he began to receive and speak messages from Maitreya to the general public. The messages suggested that humanity had reached a dangerous crisis and must either change course or face self-destruction. Humans were called on to manifest their divinity through love and justice, and specifically by sharing the world's resources with the poor and starving. In 1980 Creme came to the United States for the first time to speak on behalf of Maitreya. At that time, some of those who responded to his message founded the Tara Center.

It is the general teaching of Tara Center that humanity is one and united with all life. All religions reflect spiritual truth and as such all are acknowledged and respected. It is also possible for those who have no religion to come to truth. In common with Theosophy, Share International teaches that the evolution of earth and its people is guided by a Spiritual Hierarchy made up of individuals who have evolved from humanity. Maitreya is considered the head of the hierarchy.

According to Creme, Maitreya manifested 2,000 years ago by overshadowing his disciple Jesus. Maitreya, himself, reappeared in the world in 1977, as did other members of the Spiritual Hierarchy, an event described in theosophical literature as the externalization of the hierarchy. The externalization process comes, in part, as a response to the unconscious invocation by humanity.

On April 24 and 25, 1982, through advertisements taken out in a number of the world's prominent newspapers, Creme announced that Maitreya's "Day of Declaration" would occur within two months. Followers expected it on or before June 21, 1982. When Maitreya did not appear as anticipated, Creme pointed to disinterest in the subject by the media as a sign of general human apathy. He also announced that the Day of Declaration was still imminent and could take place any time the sincere interest of the media—as humanity's representatives—drew Maitreya forward. In the meantime, followers were urged to continue their main task of announcing that Christ is in the world, and is soon to appear.

In August 1987, Creme announced that Maitreya was working to bring about a breakthrough in international relations. During the next month a new armaments agreement was announced by the United States and the U.S.S.R. Later, the Soviet Union collapsed, Germany was reunified, apartheid was ended in South Africa, and steps were taken toward the establishment of a Palestinian homeland.

In 1988 followers in Kenya witnessed Maitreya's appearance, and their photographs of this event were reproduced and widely circulated. Fundamentalist religious groups worldwide also witnessed Maitreya, and they believed that he endowed water sources near each location with healing properties.

Those who wait in expectation of Maitreya's appearance believe that he will teach humanity the art of self-realization, the first steps of which are honesty of mind, sincerity of spirit, and detachment. Maitreya has also communicated through Creme a strong social concern with specific priorities that include an adequate supply of food and shelter for all, and health care and education as a universal right. It is the movement's belief that sharing is the key to proper human relations and is reflected in their motto, "Share and save the world."

Membership: Not a membership organization.

Periodicals: *The Emergence.* • *Share International.* • *The Emergence Quarterly.*

Sources:

Bailey, Alice. *The Reappearance of the Christ.* New York: Lucis Publishing Company, 1948.

Creme, Benjamin. *The Awakening of Humanity.* Amsterdam: Share International Foundation, 2008. 141 pp.

————. *Messages from Maitreya the Christ.* Los Angeles: Tara Center, 1980.

————. *The Reappearance of the Christ and the Masters of Wisdom.* Los Angeles: Tara Center, 1980.

————. *Transmission, A Meditation for the New Age.* North Hollywood, CA: Tara Center, 1983.

A Master Speaks: Articles from Share International. Amsterdam, Netherlands: Share International Foundation, 1985.

Transmission Meditation. www.transmissionmeditation.org.

Update on the Reappearance of the Christ. North Hollywood, CA: Tara Center, 1983.

Liberal Catholic Churches

American Catholic Church (Laguna Beach, California)

c/o Cathedral Chapel of St. Francis by-the-Sea, PO Box 577, 430 Park Ave., Laguna Beach, CA 92652

On December 29, 1915, as one of the first acts after founding his fledgling American Catholic Church, Joseph Rene Vilatte consecrated Frederick E. J. Lloyd (1859–1933), an Episcopal clergyman whose distinguished career included his election and then rejection of the post of bishop coadjutor of Oregon. In 1915, after four years as pastor of Grace Episcopal Church in Oak Park, Illinois, he resigned to go with Vilatte. In 1920 at a synod of the church held in Chicago, Vilatte retired and turned the church over to Lloyd, who assumed the titles of primate, metropolitan, and archbishop.

Lloyd proved to be an able leader, but following the pattern of other independent bishops, he attempted to build the American Catholic Church by drawing priestly colleagues around him and consecrating them to the episcopacy. He hoped that the bishops would generate a jurisdiction, and he appointed them before there were congregations to oversee. Among the eight bishops he consecrated were Gregory Lines (1923), Francis Kanski (1926), Daniel C. Hinton (1927), and Ernest Leopold Peterson (1927). Each of them eventually left the American Catholic Church and established different jurisdictions.

Lloyd was succeeded in 1932 by Hinton, who in turn consecrated Percy Wise Clarkson the following year. Clarkson opened a successful church in Laguna Beach, California, but he was a Theosophist and brought a Theosophical perspective that came to dominate American Catholic Church life and thought.

Bishop Lines had problems with Hinton, and withdrew from the American Catholic Church in 1927 in reaction to Hinton's consecration as bishop-auxiliary to

Lloyd, and formed the Apostolic Christian Church. He returned a few years later, only to leave again when Hinton became primate. During his first year separated from the church, he consecrated Justin A. Boyle (also known as Robert Raleigh). In 1930 Raleigh consecrated a Theosophist, Lowell Paul Wadle. Wadle soon left Raleigh and placed himself under Clarkson, who had succeeded Hinton. In 1940 Wadle succeeded Clarkson and served as primate of the American Catholic Church for the next 25 years. During these years the Theosophical perspective introduced by Clarkson became the only perspective in the church, and interaction with Liberal Catholic Church branches was strong. Wadle participated in a number of Liberal Catholic consecration services.

During this time the other bishops, now separated from Clarkson and Wadle, initiated their new jurisdictions: the American Catholic Church (Syro-Antiochean) (Peterson); the Church of Antioch (Lines/Raleigh); the Traditional Roman Catholic Church in the Americas (Kanski); and the Apostolic Episcopal Church (Kanski).

In 1965 Wadle was succeeded by Hanlon Francis Marshall, who served only one year before being replaced by Hugh Michael Strange. In 2008 the primate was Abp. Simon E. Talarczyk.

The beliefs of the American Catholic Church are very close to those of the Liberal Catholic Church. It views itself as holding to an "orthodox" faith, but interprets it in the light of some basic truths: that our ignorance of God and nature is due to the lack of the spirit and life of God within us; that the way to the divine knowledge is the way of the gospel that leads to a new birth; and that the way of new birth is totally within the will of man to grasp.

The Cathedral Chapel of St. Francis-by-the-Sea is a historical landmark. It is the second smallest cathedral in the world, seating only 50. Sunday Mass is at 9:00 a.m., and persons of all faiths are welcome to attend.

Membership: Not reported. There are only one or two churches and several hundred members remaining in the church.

Sources:

Barry, Odo A. *Outline History of the American Catholic Church.* Long Beach, CA: American Catholic Church, 1951.

The Holy Liturgy. Long Beach, CA: American Catholic Church, 1955.

Wadle, Lowell Paul. *In the Light of the Orient.* Long Beach, CA: Author, 1951.

American Temple

PO Box 953, San Jose, CA 95108

The American Temple is one of several groups that emerged from the former members of the Holy Order of MANS, an esoteric group that had merged into the Greek Orthodox Missionary Archdiocese of Vasiloupolis. Members of the American Temple strive to teach the Universal Truths that were taught in the Order from the Tree of Life (Kabbalah) lessons and the Christian Mysteries. The temple does not attempt to reform the order; instead, it builds on its foundation and continues its work.

The temple describes itself as following the teachings of the Master Jesus Christ and striving towards the unfoldment of the Christ light and self within each person. It is a school of universal teachings (the western esoteric tradition). Founded in the 1990s under the leadership of Mt. Rev. Michael Whitney, it has local centers, but operates primarily in cyberspace. In that regard, it has built an expansive web site and posted many of the publications of the Holy Order.

The temple offers its teachings to all motivated students. It emphasizes its base within mystical Christianity but adds the insights available from other traditions as well. The church attempts to build a strong spiritual community while supporting the family structure, and it invites members to a life of learning as well as charity and social service in the community.

Membership: Not reported.

Apostolic Johannite Church

For information: info@johannite.org.

The Apostolic Johannite Church emerged at the beginning of the twenty-first century under the leadership of its patriarch and primate for Canada, Most Rev. Shaun McCann, generally known by his ecclesiastical title, Mar Iohannes IV. McCann serves as archbishop of Alberta, and is assisted by Most Rev. William Behun (Mar Thomas), the primate of the United States of America, who serves as archbishop of Wisconsin. Both had been members of other Gnostic bodies prior to the founding of the Apostolic Gnostic Church. Archbishop McCann had originally been consecrated by Tau Iohannes III, of the Ecclesia Gnostica Catholica Hermetica (EGCH), with Tau Valentinus of the EGCH as co-consecrator.

The church holds several lines of apostolic succession, including the Johannite lineage, and continues a Johannite Gnostic Christian tradition that can be traced to the Apostle John and the early Johannite Community based in Asia Minor at the end of the first century CE.

The church is Gnostic in belief and practice. It affirms the authority of the Bible as a teaching tool, along with the texts that comprise the Nag Hammadi Library (the most famous item being the Gospel of Thomas) and the Corpus Hermeticum. It affirms the Divine godhead who through a process of emanation caused the visible cosmos to come into existence, and the divine spark that resides in each individual. Awareness of one's divine spark is the beginning of the knowledge (or gnosis) that gives the church its name.

The church teaches that the Godhead consists of three Persons: the Father, the Son (or Logos or Xristos Sother), and the Holy Spirit (or Pneuma Hagion). They are one in substance, which individuals experience by following the loving example of the Incarnate Xristos and the experience of the Holy Spirit, the source of continued Inspiration and Revelation. Because of its belief in the Divine Spark in each person, the church has opened its offices to all people, regardless of gender, race, social status, or sexual orientation.

The Apostolic Gnostic Church has close relations with the Ecclesia Gnostica Catholica Hermetica, based in Kenosha, Wisconsin, and Archbishop Behun also serves as a bishop in that jurisdiction. Mar Iohannes IV is the president of the North American College of Gnostic Bishops, of which both jurisdictions served as charter members.

Membership: The church reports seven parishes, three in Canada, three in the United States, and one in Madrid, Spain. There are several affiliated study groups, including one in Australia.

Sources:

Apostolic Johannite Church. johannite.org/.

Apostolic Orthodox Church (Boerne, Texas)

Patriarch of the Apostolic Orthodox Church, The Most Rev. Mathias Mar Yusef, 248 Deer Creek, Boerne, TX 78006

The Apostolic Orthodox Church (AOC) was founded in 1994 by His Holiness, Mathias Mar Yusef (b. 1946), who was appointed Catholicos to the West in 1994 and elected to the Holy Office of Patriarch in 1996. The church has attained its apostolic succession through the lineage of St. Thomas Christians now possessed by several of the Liberal Catholic churches.

In 1983 its founder, a former Roman Catholic, visited India and the Malankara Orthodox Syrian Church that traces its origins to the Apostle Thomas. On this visit and a subsequent trip in 1986, he became fascinated with the tradition of St. Thomas and the reputed Sacred Tradition teachings that have persisted without reference to the historic councils of the Christian church. According to what Yusef learned in India, Thomas had preached a doctrine of individual salvation attained primarily through one's own efforts, and founded a nonproselytizing community and invited others to join. As the church grew, the most spiritually advanced were ordained, and Thomas moved on. Before returning to the United States, Yusef was commissioned to spread the Sacred Tradition in the west.

The Sacred Tradition, a gnosis that transcends mere facts and beliefs and is impressed directly on the soul, was passed by Jesus to Thomas. It is this tradition that the AOC attempts to perpetuate.

Rev. Yusef holds a doctorate in sacred theology and a licentiate to lecture in sacramental and mystical theology from the Institut Koptisch in Kroeffelbach, Germany. He was ordained in 1982 into the Religious and Military Order of the Knights of the Holy Sepulchre of Jerusalem.

The church acknowledges its basis in the Eastern Orthodox tradition, and uses the Nicene Creed. However, it does not concern itself primarily with doctrine, and the creed is seen as a symbol of the faith—an object of contemplation, not a statement of truth. The Bible is seen as a compilation of myth, allegory, legend, and fact. Like all scripture, it is given by inspiration of God and hence useful.

The church teaches that there is one existence, God, who is manifested as the Trinity. Humans, created in the image of God, are also triune—body, soul, and spirit. Humans exist as part of a vast progression of life, from the highest to the lowest. Humans have a duty to discern the divine light they have within. The church is a liturgical church and practices the sacraments instituted by Christ to provide an outward manifestation of the inner graces.

Membership: Not reported.

Sources:

Apostolic Orthodox Church. www.geocities.com/thomasene_tradition/index.html.

Avalonian Catholic Church

437 Ninth Ave. S, Clinton, IA 52732

The Avalonian Catholic Church was founded in 2001 by Bp. Jon Ryner, formerly a bishop of the New Order of Glastonbury. The church operates out of the same Western Esoteric tradition that informs the Liberal Catholic Church, but has assumed a more distinctly Christian stance. At the same time, it seeks to develop the pagan influence in Christian thought. That quest has led the church to the ancient land of Avalon and the old Christian center at Glastonbury in eastern England.

Early in the twentieth century the archeologist and independent Catholic bishop Frederick Bligh Bond, who was in charge of excavations at Glastonbury, made unusual discoveries of building foundations around the cathedral and former monastery complex. Bond later revealed that his remarkable findings had been made from information received from a deceased monk who had communicated through automatic writing. Bp. Ryner and the members of the Avalonian Church look to the practices of the Glastonbury monks and the spiritual treasures of their monastic life for inspiration. From Bond's several books, Ryner has noted the prediction that a greater work will come from Glastonbury, and that someone will come who will "build the great church—a son of Glaston from beyond the sea." Revealing the secrets of Glastonbury leads into the heart of the esoteric mysteries and, claims Ryner, goes far beyond what was to be found in the older New Order of Glastonbury.

The Avalonian Church is presented as a church in the midst of a journey discovering the insights of various channels of esoteric thought—gnosticism, the Celtic tradition, spiritualism—and the way that they bring light to the Christian tradition and affect understanding of the liturgy.

Membership: Not reported.

Sources:

Avalonian Catholic Church. www.geocities.com/avalonianchurch/.

The Catholic Church of the Antiochean Rite

c/o Rev. Apb. Roberto Toca, PO Box 8473, Tampa, FL 33674

The Catholic Church of the Antiochean Rite is a small jurisdiction founded in 1980 by the Most Rev. Dr. Roberto Toca (b. 1945), Archbishop for Florida and Exarch for Latin America. Toca was consecrated as bishop in 1976 by Abp. Herman Adrian Spruit of the Church of Antioch, who also consecrated him as archbishop in 1982.

He was elevated to archbishop primate in 1987 and took the religious name Sar Mar Profeta. In January 2000 the General Episcopal Synod and the Universal Initiatic Conclave enthronized Toca, Sar Mar Profeta, as archbishop-patriarch and constituted officially the Gnostic Ecumenic Patriarchate in the Catholic Church of the Antiochean Rite.

The church has developed a ministry within the Hispanic community in Florida. Although independent of the Church of Antioch, it generally follows its beliefs and practices. Along with the Bible, the church recognizes the Apocryphal writings, such as the Gnostic texts found at Nag Hammadi, as authoritative literature. Worship is primarily in Spanish. The church is headquartered in the Holy Trinity Cathedral and Gnostic Orthodox Abbey in Odessa, a suburb in the Tampa Bay area of Florida.

Archbishop Toca has assumed a leadership role in the Cuban community of the Tampa Bay Area. He has won awards for his television series, *University on the Air*, *Popular Academy*, *From the Point of Light*, *University of the Soul*, and *The Prophet of the Mysteries of Beyond*. He has also won a number of awards from the National Association of Cuban Journalism, and is the head of a magical order, the Ordo Templi Orientis Antiqua, a Para-Masonic Memphis and Mizraim obedience. He has written several books in Spanish on esotericism, magick, parapsychology, and political issues.

Membership: In 2002 the church reported around 15,000 members in 196 congregations, mostly in Florida, Cuba, Latin America, and Spain.

Contemporary Catholic Church

c/o Most Rev. Dr. Sharon A. Hart, Beloved Disciple Seminary, 1300-G, El Paseo Blvd., Las Cruces, NM 88001

The Contemporary Catholic Church, formerly known as the Catholic Church of the Holy Grail, is an esoteric church founded at the close of the twentieth century. Its founder and presiding bishop, Most Rev. Dr. Sharon Hart, was consecrated in 2000 by David P. Goddard, assisted by Marilyn Hill and Evelyn Hill, who passed to her several apostolic lineages that passed through British bishop Hugh George de Willmott Newman (Mar Georgius I), Richard Duc de Palatine (Pre-Nicene Church), and George Boyer (Temple of the Holy Grail).

The symbol of the Holy Grail represents to church members the progressive unfoldment that occurs on the spiritual path. Members seek "at-one-ment with the Divine Source of all creation." The church accepts the tradition that identifies the Holy Grail as the chalice of wine brought by Melchizedek, king and priest of the Most High (Gen. 14:18) who initiated Abraham, and also as the cup used by Jesus at the Last Supper. The church accepts into membership all seekers, even if they are new to the quest for spiritual life. They are not asked to subscribe to a common belief, only to a willingness to engage in corporate activity through a common ritual. The church recognizes that God, the Eternal Spirit, is One.

The church promotes an inherited worth and dignity of each individual. It encourages the right of conscience, manifested in justice, equity, and compassion in human relationships. It holds firm the acceptance of one another and encouragement to spiritual growth.

The church carries many of the trappings of the western Catholic tradition, but adds esoteric content into the doctrines and symbols. Priests dispense the seven sacraments—baptism, confirmation, the eucharist/last supper, absolution, unction/anointing for healing, matrimony, and holy orders. Holy orders are open to both men and women.

The Contemporary Catholic Church is organized around small faith groups and has instituted a Church House program that allows members to meet at designated times and places convenient for them, and offers a sense of close community with others of like faith. Services can be arranged in any language. Priests generally work secular jobs and administer their sacramental duties as leisure time allows. The primary ministerial focus is chaplaincy. Training occurs through the Beloved Disciple Seminary, which offers theological courses through correspondence. Course work is provided for those interested in pursuing the ordained ministry. There are also classes available for laity interested in self-improvement and spiritual growth.

Membership: Not reported.

Educational Facilities:

Beloved Disciple Seminary, Las Cruces, New Mexico.

Sources:

Contemporary Catholic Church. www.thecontemporarycatholicchurch.org.

Church of Antioch/Catholic Apostolic Church of Antioch

111 W Cordova Rd., Santa Fe, NM 87505-3623

During the 1930s the American Catholic Church on the West Coast became thoroughly infused with Theosophical metaphysics. One instrument for moving the Church in that direction was Justin A. Boyle (1887–1969), more popularly known as Robert Raleigh. Boyle, a Roman Catholic priest, joined the Apostolic Christian Church, a splinter of the American Catholic Church schism formed by Gregory Lines (d. 1940) in 1927. Lines consecrated Boyle on April 7, 1928, and appointed him coadjutor with right of succession. Lines returned for a few years to the American Catholic Church, but seceded again upon the retirement of Frederick E. J. Lloyd (1859–1933), its archbishop. After Lines's death, Raleigh continued as head of his independent jurisdiction. Over the years he also headed two Christian metaphysical organizations, St. Primordia's Guild and the Mystical Prayer Shrine.

At the time of Bishop Raleigh's retirement in 1965, his coadjutor was Herman Adrian Spruit (1911–1994). A pastor in the Methodist Church (1939–1951), Spruit left the church in 1951. He was inclined to follow the metaphysical movement in certain respects. Feeling that the Methodists were unable to accept his perspective, he joined the Church of Religious Science. Spruit quickly became the executive secretary of the church and taught homiletics in the school of ministry. He left in 1953 to become vice president of the Golden State University in Hollywood, California.

Spruit, having become familiar with Liberal Catholicism, sought out Abp. Charles Hampton (1886–1958), who ordained him to the deaconate in 1955 and to the priesthood the following year. Archbishop Hampton was joined by Abp. Lowell Paul Wadle (d. 1965) and Bp. Francis Marshall in consecrating Spruit to the bishopric in 1957. Spruit then interacted with Wadle and the American Catholic Church that Wadle headed, but joined himself to Raleigh's independent jurisdiction, the Christian Catholic Church. In 1968, three years after Spruit succeeded Raleigh, he changed the name of the church to the Church of Antioch, Malabar Rite, to affirm the church's orders through Abps. Joseph Rene Vilatte (1854–1929) and Frederick E. J. Lloyd, the first bishops of the American Catholic Church, who brought the Antiochean succession to America.

In faith and practice the church emphasizes a mystical Catholic perspective. In the interpretation of scriptures, it follows a liberal bent and relies upon the Ecumenical Creeds, but requires none. It is quick to state that "it seeks further light on the mystery and wonder of the faith by searching in the spirit of disciplined scholarship for those aspects of Christian evidences that preceded and followed the Apostolic Period." The church was among the first Christian groups to ordain women to the priesthood, and in 1976 Spruit consecrated Helene Seymour (1926–2003) as the first woman bishop in modern times. In 1980 he consecrated his wife Meri Louise Spruit as archbishop, and on January 26, 1986, she was enthroned as Matriarch of the Church of Antioch, the feminine counterpart of the patriarch, with equal rights, powers, and responsibilities.

Archbishop Spruit resigned in 1991 due to health problems and died in 1994. Mt. Rev. Meri Louise Spruit headed the church until her recent retirement. She was named Matriarch Emerita. She designated the Most Rev. Richard Gundrey (b. 1934) as her coadjutor and successor. Gundrey had been consecrated as a bishop in 1990 by Matriarch Meri Louise Spruit, assisted by Bps. Michael Daignealt and Timothy Barker, at Loretto Chapel in Santa Fe. He currently heads the church.

Membership: In 2008 there were 32 chartered churches in the United States. There are also affiliated clergy in Canada, Australia, Ireland, and England.

Educational Facilities:

Sophia Divinity School, Santa Fe, NM.

Periodicals: *Antioch Anecdotes.* • *Worldwide Newsletter.*

Sources:

Catholic Apostolic Church of Antioch. www.churchofantioch.org/.

Spruit, Herman A. *Constitution and Statement of Principles.* Mountain View, CA: Church of Antioch Press, 1978.

————. *The Sacramentarion.* Mountain View, CA: Author, n.d.

Spruit, Mary, ed. *The Chalice of Antioch.* Mountain View, CA: Archbishop Herman Adrian Spruit, 1979.

Sullivan, Edward C. *A Short History of the Church of Antioch and Its Apostolic Succession.* Bellingham, WA: Holy Order of the Rose and Cross, 1981.

Van Campenhout, W. John Kooistra. *Apostolic Succession in the Catholic and Apostolic Church of Antioch.* Scarborough, ON, Canada: Institute for Johannine Christianity Press, 1993. 86p.

The Church of Gnosis (Ecclesia Gnostica Mysteriorum)

1965 Latham St., Mountain View, CA 94040

The Church of Gnosis (Ecclesia Gnostica Mysteriorum), founded in the 1970s by Bp. Rosamonde Miller, began as a center of the Church of the Sacred Wisdom, a small jurisdiction founded and headed by Bp. Neil Jack, that was simultaneously associated with the Ecclesia Gnostica, led by Bp. Stephan A. Hoeller. In 1983 the Ecclesia incorporated as a separate entity. Bishop Miller had been ordained in 1974 by Bishop Hoeller, assisted by Bps. Neil Jack, Forest Barber, and Herman Adrian Spruit of the Church of Antioch. Bishops Hoeller, Jack, and Barber consecrated Miller as a bishop in 1981.

Bishop Miller claims a primal apostolic succession through the Mary Magdalene lineage. According to that tradition, Mary Magdalene had received her "hierophantic power" in the Isis Mystery schools of Egypt and later at the hands of Christ, as did the other apostles. Later she was the first to see the resurrected Christ. Unable to function in the immediate area because of sexist attitudes, she traveled west with Joseph of Arimathea, first to England and later to the European continent, where she lived out her life. She left behind a secret sisterhood that survives to this day. In January 1962 representatives of this sisterhood made contact with Miller, who was consecrated into it. She promised to keep her association confidential until after she had received the more recognized male lineage. She presently ordains both male and female priests in the Mary Magdalene Order. Teachings of the church are taken from the Mary Magdalene Order, Gnostic writings, and other Christian and non-Christian sources. However, the teachings are primarily first-hand, based on Miller's own experience of Gnosis. A liturgy was developed based upon the writings of the Mary Magdalene Order, Miller's own writings, and quotations from George Mead's collection of Gnostic texts, *Fragments of a Faith Forgotten* (1960). The church is unconcerned with reviving any doctrine or system, including Gnosticism, and does not consider itself Christian, even though it uses a male/female Christos mythology as the basis for its ritual. It is concerned with the elimination of doctrines and systems altogether, in order to free the mind to experience "gnosis." Miller always refers to the church as "the sanctuary" instead of as "the church," because she sees it as a refuge in the midst of chaos, for travelers on the spiritual journey.

Membership: The church has no formal membership and no jurisdictions. Everyone is free to come and go as they please, without strings attached: The church believes freedom must begin with freedom. There is no affiliated work. There are several ordained priests with their own churches in various areas throughout the world. In 2008 it was reported that there were 35 ordained clergy in the United States and abroad. Membership is not counted, but in 2008 approximately 400 people regularly attended services throughout the year, and approximately 1,000 are loosely connected.

Periodicals: *The Gnostic.*

Sources:

Church of Gnosis (Ecclesia Gnostica Mysteriorum), www.gnosticsanctuary.org.

Shrine of Mary Magdalene. www.marymagdaleneshrine.org.

The Gnostics. Border Television, London, England, 1986.

Mead, George R. S. *Fragments of a Faith Forgotten.* New Hyde Park, NY: University Books, 1960.

Miller, Rosamonde. *The Gnostic Holy Eucharist.* Palo Alto, CA: Ecclesia Gnostica Mysteriorum, 1984.

Passions of the Soul, Part 4. Ikon Television, Hilversum, Netherlands, 1991.

Plummer, John P. *The Many Paths of the Independent Sacramental Movement.* Dallas, TX: Newt Books, 2005.

Segal, Robert, and June Singer. *Allure of Gnosticism.* LaSalle, IL: Open Court, 1994.

Contemporary Catholic Church

For information: MostrevHart@thecontemporarycatholicchurch.org.

The Contemporary Catholic Church is an independent autocephalous jurisdiction in the Catholic tradition founded and led by the Most Rev. Dr. Sharon A. Hart, its presiding bishop and matriarch. While operating out of the Western Catholic tradition, it adheres to that tradition with a somewhat esoteric interpretation. It permits and even encourages a broad freedom in the interpretation of the Creeds, Scriptures, and Christian Traditions and points people to a direct experience of transcendent mystery and wonder, an experience found in all cultures. That experience also leads people to a renewal of the spirit and creates an openness to life-affirming forces. The church affirms the Triune Aspects of God as manifested in the Creator, the Son (the Redeemer), and the Holy Spirit (the Comforter/Transformer). It administers the common seven sacraments-baptism, Eucharist (Lord's supper), confirmation/chrismation, matrimony, ordination, penance/reconciliation, and anointing of the sick. Its priests have a valid apostolic succession derived from lines of both the Eastern and Western Church.

The church uses a modern liturgy, based on early Christian and Orthodox-Catholic beliefs and liturgical language. This liturgy is designed to promote a balance between traditional ceremonial worship, devotional aspiration, mystic thought, and spiritual development.

The church is led by its matriarch and presiding bishop. Men and women are welcomed to the priesthood without regard to gender, gender preference, or race. The church's clergy are primarily engaged in chaplaincy ministries rather than congregation building. Worship occurs in a number of house churches as well, and small, personalized groups engage in study and discussion.

Membership: Not reported.

Remarks: The Contemporary Catholic Church has discontinued the practice of signing formal intercommunion agreements with other jurisdictions. Instead, it has adopted the following position: "Therefore, the CCC holds all communities and individuals of faith in Communion with us, who live out the All Inclusive Love of God, who follow the radical message of Jesus, and who recognize the face of Christ in all they encounter, thereby upholding the dignity of every human being. We recognize the validity of the various ministries (lay and ordained) and are always open to their participating fully in the life of this Church."

Sources:

Contemporary Catholic Church. www.thecontemporarycatholicchurch.org.

Ecclesia Gnostica

3363 Glendale Blvd., Los Angeles, CA 90039

Dr. Stephan A. Hoeller, born in Budapest, Hungary in 1931, is a popular writer of occult literature who also has written extensively on gnosticism and the wisdom tradition. Early in his career, he became acquainted with the writings of James Morgan Pryse. Pryse, a leader of the independent Theosophical movement in New York City early in the twentieth century, later moved to Los Angeles and became a popular lecturer and writer on the occult and gnosticism. The Ecclesia Gnostica continues, in a religious vein, the gnostic tradition of the Gnostic Society founded by Pryse in 1928. The society is now a chartered lay organization of the church.

In 1959 Hoeller was appointed to oversee the work of the Brotherhood and Order of the Pleroma and the Pre-Nicene Church as the American representative of Richard, Duc de Palatine. After de Palatine's death, he and many members of the order left and formed the Ecclesia Gnostica. Hoeller had been consecrated as a bishop in 1967 by de Palatine, assisted by Bps. John Martyn-Baxter and Gregory F. E. Barber. He was reconsecrated subconditione by Abp. Herman Adrian Spruit (of the Church of Antioch), assisted by Bishop Barber and Neill P. Jack Jr., in 1972.

The Ecclesia Gnostica continues the teaching of the Brotherhood and Order of Pleroma, but has a much more open approach. From the headquarters, the Sophia Gnostic Center in Hollywood, California, regular classes and lectures and weekly worship are offered to the public, and a worshipping community has formed there. The church has been in the forefront of welcoming women to the priesthood and has one female bishop.

Ecclesia Gnostica offers Sunday morning Eucharist, Wednesday evening Eucharist, a Gnostic Mass for the gay and lesbian community held in the Chapel of Saints Serge and Bacchus, devotional services to the Holy Sophia, vespers, and a healing service. The public is welcomed to attend.

Membership: In 2002 the church reported approximately 300 affiliated lay people, 14 priests, and five congregations worldwide, as well as a seminary in Arizona.

Educational Facilities:

St. Sophia Seminary, Sedona, Arizona.

Sources:

Ecclesia Gnostica. www.ecclesiagnostica.com

Hoeller, Stephan A. *The Enchanted Life*. Hollywood, CA: Gnostic Society, n.d.

————. *The Gnostic Jung*. Wheaton, IL: Theosophical Publishing House, 1982.

————. *The Royal Road*. Wheaton, IL: Theosophical Publishing House, 1975.

————. *The Tao of Freedom: Jung, Gnosis, and a Voluntary Society*. Rolling Hills Estates, CA: Wayfarer Press, 1984.

Pryse, James M. *Spiritual Light*. Los Angeles: Author, 1940.

Edta Ha Thoma

Current address not obtained for this edition.

Edta Ha Thoma is a small jurisdiction formed just before the disruption of the Federation of St. Thomas Christian Churches in 1984. It was founded by Abp. James A. Dennis, a bishop in the Ecumenical Catholic Communion who established a ministry at San Bruno, California. In the mid-1980s the jurisdiction was strengthened by the absorption of the Mebasrim Fellowship, which had been formed in 1976 by several former priests of the Church of Antioch. On Thanksgiving Day 1976 one of the priests, Michael G. Zaharakis (1946–1984), was consecrated by Lewis S. Keizer of the Independent Church of Antioch to lead the fellowship. An initial congregation of 22 members was formed at Santa Cruz, California.

The fellowship shared the gnostic-mystical perspectives of the Church of Antioch, but had placed its priorities on social action and community service. In Portland, Oregon, for example, a ministry to alcoholics was initiated, and in Santa Cruz, an outreach to migrants led to the development of a jail ministry. A variety of outreach projects flowed from these initial efforts. Basor Press was founded as a publishing arm of Mebasrim. Edta Ha Thoma, like the Federation of St. Thomas Christian Churches, recognizes the Gospel of Thomas as having scriptural authority.

In 1980 the fellowship affiliated with the ecumenical Federation of St. Thomas Christian Churches, an older organization that was attempting to tie together the scattered esoteric Christian churches. Zaharakis provided much of the leadership for the federation during the remaining few years of his life. The year 1984 proved traumatic for the fellowship. Due to internal disputes, the federation was disrupted and the fellowship withdrew its support. Zaharakis threw his support behind the formation of a new organization, the Synod of Independent Sacramental Churches, which included many of the churches formerly in the federation. However, before the synod could reorganize, Zaharakis died.

The fellowship supported the synod, but much of its work was assumed by Bp. Ismael Ford of the New Age Universal Church. Among the new members of the synod was Edta Ha Thoma. Within a short time the remnant of the Mebasrim Fellowship merged into that jurisdiction, where it now functions as an order. Basor Press is now the publishing arm of Edta Ha Thoma.

Membership: Formal membership is not required of those who are involved with Edta Ha Thoma.

Educational Facilities:

St. Thomas Institute, San Bruno, California.

Western Orthodox Theological Institute, San Bruno, California.

Periodicals: *Basor*.

Sources:

Keizer, Lewis S. *Initiation: Ancient and Modern*. San Francisco: St. Thomas Press, 1981.

Federation of St. Thomas Christians

c/o Rev. Dr. Joseph Vredenburgh, Archbishop, Catholicos-Patriarch of St. Thomas Christians, 134 Dakota Avenue, No. 308, Santa Cruz, CA 95060

The Federation of St. Thomas Christians was founded in 1963 by its archbishop and patriarch, Joseph L. Vredenburgh, a former Congregationalist minister. Vredenburgh was ordained in the Reformed Church in America in 1958 and for several decades served congregations in California, culminating in a year's work in British Samoa (1977–1978). However, in 1963 he was also consecrated as a bishop by another Congregationalist minister carrying Old Catholic episcopal orders, Howard E. Mather. Through Mathers, Vredenburgh inherited orders from the Syrian Church of Antioch, the church of the St. Thomas Christians of India. Upon his return from Samoa, Vredenburgh settled in Santa Cruz and began the Federation of St. Thomas Christians as a fellowship of independent and autonomous churches. A number of small jurisdictions, many of which derived from the Church of Antioch, affiliated with the federation. By 1983 there were approximately 30 ministries and churches in the federation, including the Mebasrim Fellowship, the Ecclesia Gnostica Mysteriorum, and the Independent Church of Antioch.

Disruption of the fellowship began in 1984. That year Bp. Michael G. Zaharakis, a leading member of the federation, died. Then Abp. Joseph L. Vredenburgh, who had moved to Hawaii, and Bp. Lewis S. Keizer of the Independent Church of Antioch had a disagreement on policy that led to a disintegration of the federation as it had been constituted. Many of the member churches withdrew and formed the Synod of Independent Sacramental Churches. Vredenburgh reorganized the federation as an umbrella group for the remaining independent ministries. In 1984 the Reformed Catholic Church in America, led by Most Rev. Brian G. Turkington, its founder, merged into the federation. Turkington was named co-patriarch of the federation, and and in 2008 he was sharing leadership with Vredenburgh. An annual synod convenes on the July 4th weekend.

The federation professes belief in the "True Light" that enlightened the Lord Jesus Christ and brings salvation, and acknowledges the necessity of a personal commitment to Christ.

The federation has grown steadily. In 1997, for example, the church added to its fold the congregations of Zoe Ministries in New York City; the Diocese of San Jose and Diocese of Sonoma County, California; and Christ Cathedral in Chesterfield, Virginia. A new ministry for bikers has developed in Flagstaff, Arizona, and a seminary program has emerged in Sedona, Arizona.

Membership: In 2008 the federation reported 2,500 members, 51 congregations, 102 ministers, and affiliated works in Hong Kong, Canada, Western Samoa, Australia, United Kingdom, and Nigeria.

Educational Facilities:

College of Seminarians, Santa Cruz, California, and Atlanta, Georgia.

American Apostolic University, Santa Cruz, California.

St. Andre's Pastoral Institute, Alta Monte Springs, Florida.

Jesus of Nazareth Bible College, Nigeria, and Steward, Nebraska.

Periodicals: *Basor.*

Sources:

American Church of the East and the Federation of St. Thomas Christians. www.geocities.com/TheTropics/8371.

Free Liberal Catholic Church

c/o St. Dydimus Free Liberal Catholic Church, Rt.1, PO Box 153, Manor, TX 78653-9801

The Free Liberal Catholic Church was founded in 1975 by a group of Liberal Catholic priests including Bps. Donald M. Berry (b. 1935), John Shelton Davis (1921–2000), and John Russell (1920–1985). Bishop Berry was consecrated by Bp. William H. Daw of the Liberal Catholic Church International. Bishop Russell was consecrated by Bp. William A. Henley of the American Orthodox Catholic Church. Abp. John Shelton Davis, vicar general at the time of the formation of the Free Liberal Catholic Church, was the bishop. Davis was consecrated by Berry in 1979.

The church is mainly concerned with ministry to Spanish speakers. All bishops were associated at some point with the Liberal Catholic Church International. Bishops Berry and Russell were subsequently bishops of the Liberal Catholic Church of Ontario, Canada, which was a providence of the Liberal Catholic Church International, and became Christ Catholic Church International.

The Free Liberal Catholic Church follows the Liberal Catholic tradition. The Bible is accepted as the guide and rule of life by members and priests, but no one is required to subscribe to a creedal summary or to a particular formulation of faith. Freedom of inquiry is encouraged. There are seven sacraments that operate by the power of the Holy Spirit and depend for their efficacy on the clear conscience of the supplicant.

There is a separate Liberal Catholic Church in Frisco, Texas, St. Clement of Alexandria, which is under Rev. Tony Howard, and it is part of the Liberal Catholic Church International.

Membership: Not reported.

Sources:

Liberal Catholic Church International. www.liberalcatholic.org.

Friends Catholic Communion

c/o Tonya Beckett, Convening Bishop, PO Box 60, Chesapeake, OH 45619-0060

The Friends Catholic Communion dates to a February 1994 retreat in Washington, D.C., attended by clergy and laity from a variety of previously existing Christian ministries. The retreat was a time for healing and fellowship, and from it emerged a new community that shared a common tradition and desire to keep an apostolic sacramental tradition of the early Christian church. The members of the community represented independent ministries that also wished to make the sacraments available to as many people as possible. Apart from these primary commitments, participants wished to emphasize their freedom to make choices about the direction of their individual spiritual lives and the expression of their ministries. The

group affirmed that "to be truly free, we must be free to be different in individual ways and equally free to be similar, traditional, even conservative."

To retain the apostolic tradition, the group decided that a bishop was needed. In their midst was Mt. Rev. J. C. Catherine Adams, a bishop from the New Order of Glastonbury. She agreed to teach Jesus' teachings, to keep the sacraments and successions according to the apostolic tradition, and to allow all the clergypersons to be free to pursue what for them was authentic spirituality and ministry. She was named the first convening bishop of the new Friends Catholic Communion. Within the communion, each ministry would be autonomous in all areas not directly impinging upon the integrity of the communion's apostolic tradition or the community as a whole. As such, the communion is not Roman Catholic, canonically Orthodox, or Protestant. The Friends Catholic Communion values tradition-within-freedom. They are not dependent on any ecclesiastical institution.

The communion includes ministries nationwide. Each ministry is led by an independent bishop, and different bishops have different lineages of apostolic succession. On matters affecting the whole communion, each covenant ministry selects one layperson and one clergyperson to meet together for communal decision making.

Ministries with representation in the Friends Catholic Communion are: Woman at the Well (Alaska), St. Julian Without Walls (California), New Catholic Community (Florida), Mission Episcopate of St. Columba (Massachusetts), Breach Menders (New York), Friends of the Light (Ohio), Skellig of St. John (Pennsylvania), and Order of the Trinity (Texas).

The communion sees itself as called particularly to serve disenfranchised and marginalized people.

Membership: Not reported. In 2002 there were 12 ministries associated with the communion.

Remarks: Among the bishops who have associated with the Friends Catholic Communion is Rt. Rev. Brian G. Turkington, formerly with the Old Episcopal Church of Scotland (OECS) and the Federation of St. Thomas Christian Churches.

Sources:

Friends Catholic Communion. www.geocities.com/Athens/Acropolis/3350/fcc.html.

Friends Catholic Episcopate of the Resurrection

c/o Missionaries of St. Benedict, 1212 N. Major Dr. #27S, Beaumont, TX 77706

The Friends Catholic Episcopate of the Resurrection was founded and is led by Bp. Tatiana Beckett (b. 1967). Beckett was ordained as a deacon in the New Order of Glastonbury by Bp. Martha Schultz in 1995, but the following year she was ordained as a priest by Bp. Catherine Adams of Friends Catholic Communion. Adams consecrated Beckett to the episcopacy in 1999. She passed on several orders of apostolic succession that traced back to Abp. Adrian Spruit of the Church of Antioch.

The Friends Catholic Episcopate has developed a major center of activity in Beaumont, Texas, where its ordered community, the Missionaries of Saint Benedict, is headquartered. The order is led by the Very Rev. Brian L. Watson, its abbot. Watson also directs the Holy Angels Chaplaincy in Beaumont. A second monastery of the order, the Catholic Community of Saint Patrick, is directed by prior Brendan Bearden. Bishop Beckett resides in Huntington and presides at worship at the Catholic Community of Saint Patrick.

The episcopate considers itself a representative of the ancient and undivided Church of Christ. As such, its does not accept labels such as Catholic, Orthodox, or Protestant. It thinks of itself as a free and self-governing episcopate within the one Church of Christ. It emphasizes the virtues of spirituality, community, friendship, and vigor. Its episcopacy possesses several line of apostolic succession that reach back to the undivided church, and administers the traditional Christian sacraments.

The episcopate affirms the Nicene and Apostle's Creeds, but also notes that though they best state the Catholic faith, the Holy Spirit is not limited by them. Members believe that the Holy Spirit has never ceased to be active within the

Christian community. The episcopate reveres the ancient Christian tradition, especially as represented in such works as the Didache, the Apostolic Tradition of Hippolytus, the Apostolic Constitutions, and the positive teachings of the seven truly ecumenical Councils of the Church. It also honors all the ancient rites of the Universal Church, including the Roman, Anglican, Orthodox, Orthodox, and Maronite, among others.

Membership: Not Reported. The episcopate is centered on the two communities in Beaumont, Texas, and Huntington, West Virginia.

Sources:

Friends Catholic Episcopate of the Resurrection.
www.fortunecity.com/meltingpot/lesotho/1205/id23.htm and
www.fortunecity.com/skyscraper/fatbit/1795/index.htm.

Gnostic Order of Christ

PO Box 8660, San Jose, CA 95155-8660

The Gnostic Order of Christ was founded in 1988 by members of the Order of the Golden Cross to provide a spiritual structure for those called to the Path of the Western Tradition of the Priesthood after the Order of Melchizedek of the Order of the Golden Cross. The primary founders of the order have the apostolic rites of two lineages. The first of the rites stem from Fr. Paul Blighton, historically known as the primary founder of the Science of Man Church (SOM) and the Holy Order of MANS (HOOM). One of the founders of the Gnostic Order of Christ, Master Timothy D. Harris, received the rite to ordain from Blighton in 1970. Another founder, Master Jessica C. A. Lucas (formerly Lucas-Burkhouse), in 1988 received her rite from Harris and Master J. Anderson (also of HOOM). Lucas had previously, in 1984, received a Mantle of the Work initiating her as a master teacher, and a Mantle of the Sisterhood of the Immaculate Heart Sisters of Mary (a suborder of HOOM), from Master Marian Carter (former Mother Superior of the suborder and also one of the founders of the Gnostic Order of Christ).

On separate occasions in 1984, Harris and Lucas received the lineage of the Wandering Bishops of the Sacred Order of the Episcopate of Jesus Christ, stemming from the lineage of Michael Zaharakis, who was ordained by Bp. Lewis Keizer of the Home Temple Movement. Keizer received his consecration through Herman Adrian Spruit, archbishop-patriarch of the Church of Antioch (Catholic Apostolic Church of Antioch, Malabar Rite). The lineage incorporates 16 lineages, one of which can be traced back to Cardinal Scipione Rebiba, Roman Catholic Bishop of Troia (1566), and from there to the Apostles.

The Gnostic Order of Christ is a training body whose purpose is to facilitate the spiritual unfoldment and consciousness of the individual through teaching and initiation, and to ordain those called to serve under the spiritual mantle of the Order of the Golden Cross. All vows are taken to God and not to any earthly organization or person. There is no formal membership. Teachings are primarily Christian, but include the study of all religions, metaphysics, healing, the sciences, and philosophy. Those ordained vary in teaching expression according to the training background of the particular teacher, and may include elements of Buddhism, Sufism, Zen, and Native American traditions. What is common are the initiations and sacraments particular to the Order of the Golden Cross.

In 2008 the president of the order was Rt. Rev. Timothy D. Harris, and the director of education was Rt. Rev. Jessica C. A. Lucas.

Membership: Membership consists of the board of directors. All priests and teachers ordained through the order establish their own ministries independent of the order. In May 2008 approximately 45 persons had been ordained as priests. An unknown number of people are in training across the country. The order has affiliates across the United States.

Sources:

Correcting the Internet About the Gnostic Order of Christ.
www.gnosticorderofchrist.org/about/correcting_the_web.htm.

Gnostic Orthodox Church of Christ in America

The Most Rev. Abbot George Burke, Light of Christ Monastery, Borrego Springs, CA

The pilgrimage of Abbot George Burke and the group of monastics that surround him at the Holy Protection Gnostic Orthodox Monastery outside Geneva, Nebraska, (including the convent for women in Geneva) is among the most fascinating of the stories of the independent apostolic churches. Burke was raised a conservative Protestant among people with a mystic bent who had prophetic powers and practiced spiritual healing. As a young adult he discovered the Bhagavad Gita, the ancient Hindu scripture from India, to which he was immediately attracted. He began a study of Eastern religious literature, then traveled to India, where he became a disciple of Sri Sri Ananda Mayi Ma (b. 1895), a famous female guru, and was initiated into the classical Hindu monastic order of Shankaracharya.

He returned to the United States and resided for three years in a Greek Orthodox monastery, where he discovered the convergence of mystical Eastern Christianity withHindu spirituality. Upon leaving the monastery he gathered a small group around him and in 1968 they went to India. Upon their return in 1969, they settled in Oklahoma City and created the Sri Ma Anandamayi Monastery and began publishing a magazine, *Ananda Jyoti*. As disciples of Anandamayi, they practiced *japa* (or *mara*) yoga, a spiritual discipline that requires the repetition of a mantrum, word(s) of power. The practice leads to the spiritual liberation that all seek.

Then in the early 1970s Burke, known then as Swami Nirmalananda Giri, became acquainted with Abp. Robert Williams of the Liberal Catholic Church International. On August 23, 1975, he was consecrated by Williams and Bp. Jay Davis Kirby working with a letter of concurrence from Abp. E. R. Verostek of the North American Old Roman Catholic Church-Utrecht Succession.

During the mid- and late 1970s Burke and the monastery functioned under the episcopal authority of Williams as the American Catholic Church. They created Rexist Press, from which flowed some of the most substantive material produced by Old Catholics in America. Burke's catechetical text, *Faith Speaks* (1975), remains the most complete theological text produced by any American Old Catholic. He also wrote several booklets, reprinted several classic Old Catholic works, produced a series of Bible guides, and in 1976 began *The Old Catholic* (later renamed *The Good Shepherd*), one of Old Catholicism's few high-quality periodicals. During this period Burke's writings were traditional Catholic in their theological perspective, and widely read and appreciated by Old Catholics.

More recently, Burke openly moved toward Liberal Catholicism in belief, and the early attunement to Eastern Orthodoxy has asserted itself in practice. He remains a member of the Shankaracharya Order and has sought an affiliation that will provide an ideological compatibility. The concept of reincarnation and karma are integral to his theology. In 1984 he founded the Gnostic Orthodox Church. The church has relocated to the Light of Christ Monastery in Borrego Springs, California. It is in communion with the Liberal Catholic Church, Province of the United States.

Membership: Not reported.

Sources:

Burke, George. *Faith Speaks*. Oklahoma City, OK: Rexist Press, 1975.

———. *Magnetic Healing*. Oklahoma City, OK: Saint George Press, 1980.

Nelson, Fr. Anthony. "A Word about 'Monastery Icons.'" Orthodox Christian Information Center. Available from www.orthodoxinfo.com/general/monasteryicons.aspx.

Sullivan, Edward C., and Jeffrey A. Isbrandtsen. "An Interview with Abbot George Burke." *AROHN* 3, no. 3 (1980): 24–30.

Independent Catholic Church of Canada

c/o Mt. Rev. William Hains-Howard, 4520 Huron St., Apt. 602, Niagara Falls, ON, Canada I2E 6Y0

The Independent Catholic Church of Canada is a Catholic jurisdiction founded in the late 1970s, one of a set of fraternally related independent Anglican, Catholic, and Liberal Catholic jurisdictions that associated in 1981 in the Independent Catholic

Church International (ICCI). Peter Wayne Reynold Goodrich, consecrated in 1978 by William H. Daw of the Liberal Catholic Church International, became the first primate. Goodrich also headed the ICCI. He resigned both positions in 1983 to become primate of the North American Episcopal Church, and was succeeded by William Vincent (Paul) Hains-Howard.

Hains-Howard had been consecrated in 1970 by Earl Anglin James of the North American Old Roman Catholic Church. He also heads the Order of St. Gilbert of Sempringham, an ordered community.

Membership: Not reported.

Sources:

Ward, Gary L. *Independent Bishops: An International Directory*. Detroit, MI: Apogee Books, 1990.

Independent Church of Antioch

The New Church Center, 350 Santa Cruz St., Boulder Creek, CA 95006

The Independent Church of Antioch is a small jurisdiction founded by its primate, Bp. Robert Branch. Branch was consecrated by Abp. Herman Adrian Spruit (1911–1994) of the Church of Antioch, but left that jurisdiction to found the Independent Church of Antioch. The new jurisdiction became known in the 1970s through the varied activities of its regional bishop, Lewis S. Keizer (b. 1941).

Keizer, a former Episcopal priest, received his doctorate from the Graduate Theological Union in 1973. In the late 1960s, while serving as a deacon at St. Mark's Episcopal Church, he met Jeannie Maierader, a teacher of esoteric wisdom known affectionately as Mother Jeannie. She convinced Keizer to resign from the Episcopal Church, and on March 30, 1975, he was ordained and made vicar general of the Church of Antioch by Archbishop Spruit. Two weeks later he was consecrated bishop by Spruit. Soon after that consecration, Keizer left Spruit's jurisdiction and aligned himself with Bishop Branch and the Independent Church of Antioch. Besides authoring a number of books and scholarly papers, Keizer has founded and directed a nationally recognized school for gifted children, and has attained fame as a jazz and classical musician.

The Independent Church of Antioch functions not so much as a traditional body of believers, but as an association of five theosophically inclined teacher-bishops. Besides Branch and Keizer, the bishops are Dr. Daniel Fritz, a close associate of Manly Palmer Hall (1901–1990) and Omraam Mikhael Aivanhov; Warren Watters (1890–1992), head of the Center for Esoteric Studies in Santa Barbara, California, and editor of the Esoteric Review; and Torkom Saraydarian (1915–1997), head of the Aquarian Educational Group.

Membership: Not reported.

Periodicals: *Esoteric Review*. Send orders to 533 E Anapamu St., Santa Barbara, CA 93013.

Sources:

Keizer, Lewis S. *The Eighth Reveal the Ninth: A New Hermetic Initiation Disclosure*. Seaside, CA: Academy of Arts and Humanities, 1974.

———. *Initiation: Ancient and Modern*. San Francisco, CA: St. Thomas Press, 1981.

———. *Love, Prayer, and Meditation*. Santa Cruz, CA: Author, n.d.

———. *Priesthood in the New Age*. Santa Cruz, CA: Author, 1985.

Independent Liberal Catholic Fellowship

For information: admin@independentoldcatholic.org.

The Independent Liberal Catholic Fellowship is an ecumenical association of clergy, ministries, and church communities in the Liberal Catholic tradition. It was formed in 2007. It welcomes clergy who have been ordained in an apostolic lineage and those who hold a theosophical or esoteric interpretation of Christianity who wish to receive an apostolic lineage. The Fellowship also receives congregations and non-congregationally oriented ministries into its membership.

Clergy members of the Fellowship may hold dual membership in other church organizations with the consent of their bishop, but the Fellowship is especially open to otherwise independent clergy who wish to keep their autonomy while accepting some degree of Episcopal oversight.

The Fellowship was organized by the leaders of the Liberal Rite, a small British Liberal Catholic jurisdiction. Bp. John Kersey, the head of the Liberal Rite, is the current administrator of the Independent Liberal Catholic Fellowship. Members are located in the United Kingdom, Mexico, Nigeria, the Netherlands, Slovenia, South Africa, and the United States.

The Fellowship sees itself as offering an alternative Christian tradition that is non-dogmatic in nature. It focuses on Catholic sacramental worship apart from teachings believed to be at variance with God's love. It is welcoming to the divorced, those living in a civil partnership, and those in homosexual relationships.

Clergy members of the fellowship are offered the option of continuing their education through the Liberal Rite's school, St. Simon's College, a distance learning institution.

Membership: In 2008 the fellowship reported 21 clergy members of whom 6 were from the United States. Community members included the All Saints and Angels Ancient Catholic Church of Portland, Oregon, the Liberal Catholic Church-Theosophia Synod, and the Sodalitas Sacerdotalis Mariae Vitae, based in Texas.

Sources:

Independent Liberal Catholic Fellowship. www.independentoldcatholic.org/ilcf.html.

International Free Catholic Communion

Free Catholic Diocese of St. Paul the Apostle, PO Box 3454, Clearwater, FL 33767

The International Free Catholic Communion is a liturgical Christian church founded in 1991. It is an independent rite of the one, holy, Catholic, and Apostolic church. It is not Catholic, not Eastern Orthodox, and not Protestant. On Pentecost 1991, the first synod of the communion was held at Bremerton, Washington, by Bp. Timothy Barker (b. 1953), Bishop-elect Michael Milner (b. 1954), and his wife, Rev. Maru Milner. The Statement of Union was completed at that synod. Bishop Barker had been consecrated in 1989 by Patriarch Herman Adrian Spruit of the Church of Antioch and served as the bishop of the church's diocese of New England. Bishop-elect Milner was consecrated in 1991 by Barker, assisted by Bps. Brian G. Turkington and Joseph P. Sousa, and Louis Boynton. Milner had an eclectic background, having studied Taoism, served as a Pentecostal minister, and worked with the Roman Catholic Church prior to a brief period with the Church of Antioch. Milner, a Franciscan contemplative, has helped to establish a number of churches and seminaries in the United States and in Latin America.

The International Free Catholic Communion follows the Free Catholic tradition earlier exemplified in the Church of Antioch. It sees itself as a viable sacramental alternative to the Eastern Orthodox, Roman Catholic, and Protestant traditions. It accepts the traditional Apostles' and Nicene Creeds as the basis of Christian unity, but also emphasizes the right and privilege of individual freedom of thought. The church offers seven sacraments: baptism, confirmation, the Holy Eucharist, reconciliation, anointing the sick, matrimony, and holy orders. The communion believes the sacraments are outward signs that confer the grace they signify. They believe the church must seek to cultivate and to protect individual freedom of thought, conscience, and choice. They seek to be tolerant, respectful, and open to the values of others. Women are admitted to all orders of the ministry: deacon, priest, and bishop. In like measure, married people are also admitted to all levels of ministry. The Eucharist is open to all, whatever their religious affiliation.

The communion has formal intercommunion agreements with the Federation of St. Thomas Christian Churches and the Orthodox Church of the East. Bishop Barker also founded the Koinonia Institute to foster communication among independent Catholic, Anglican, and Orthodox jurisdictions.

Membership: Not reported. There are two dioceses, with headquarters in Florida and California.

Periodicals: *Free Catholic Communicant.* Send orders to 1250 Grand Ave., 10, Arroyo Grande, CA 93420.

Sources:

International Free Catholic Communion. www.freecatholiccommunion.org.

Johannine Catholic Church

18372 Highway 94, Dulzura, CA 91917

The Johannine Catholic Church was organized in 1968 (incorporated in 1971) by J. Julian Gillman and his wife, Rita Anne Gillman, as a ministry to those rejected by or disillusioned with the traditional churches. Initially it was directed to the hippie culture of the late 1960s. Gillman was consecrated "sub-rosa" by a "renegade" (unnamed) Episcopal bishop, but in 1977 both he and his wife were consecrated by H. Ernest Caswell of the North American Old Roman Catholic Church-Utrecht Succession.

The church is described as New Age in orientation, open to clergy of both sexes, and making no distinctions due to sexual preferences. The designation *Johannine* refers to the Gospel of John and its central message of love. Love, not theology, is considered the overriding principle of Christianity.

The church sponsors several religious orders, all open to men and women, both married and single. The Order of Saint John the Evangelist is the order of clergy whose ministry is to the rejected. The Order of Saint John Bernadone is a street ministry to street people. The Paracelsian Order is a New Age community of monks and friars seeking to develop an alternative lifestyle. Members are trained in loving kindness, meditation, and healing professions. The headquarters for the Paracelsian Order is located at the Madre Grande Monastery in Dulzura, California, about 40 miles northeast of San Diego. The Rt. Rev. John H. Drais is abbot of the Paracelsian Order and bishop of the Johannine Catholic Church. The church is a member of the Synod of Independent Sacramental Churches. Gillman edits *SIS-COM*, the journal of the synod. Saint Dionysius' Press is the church's publishing arm.

Membership: Not reported. In 1988 the church reported approximately 100 members in four congregations served by eight priests. The church centers were located in San Diego, Santa Barbara, Dulzura, and San Francisco, California.

Periodicals: *The Madre Grande Journal.* • *The Philosopher's Stone.* Send orders to PO Box 102, Dulzura, CA 91917-0102.

Sources:

Reiki-Sun. www.reiki-sun.com/about-us.html.

Nihle, William. *A True History of Celtic Britain.* San Diego, CA: Saint Dionysius Press, 1982.

The People's Liturgy. San Diego, CA: Johannine Catholic Church, 1968.

Liberal Catholic Church International

741 Cerro Gordo Ave., San Diego, CA 92102

The Liberal Catholic Church (being the American Province of the Liberal Catholic Church International) was constituted in 1983 by the merger of the Liberal Catholic Church and the Liberal Catholic Church International. The Liberal Catholic Church was one of two groups claiming to continue the original Liberal Catholic Church incorporated in 1928. In that church (under the second regionary bishop Charles Hampton) a strong division of opinion developed. Hampton articulated an independent stance regarding the Theosophical Society. As a result, he was deposed in 1944.

Most clergy and congregations supported him, and a schism was created. Then in London, the presiding bishop of the church, F. W. Pigott (d. 1956), appointed John T. Eklund as the new regionary bishop. Eklund in turn consecrated two priests as bishops without obtaining the required approval of the priests and deacons of the province. This act precipitated a second schism under Bp. Ray Marshall Wardall (d. 1954). A majority of the clergy and congregations in the United States supported Wardall.

In response to the Eklund consecrations, Wardall consecrated Edward M. Matthews (1898–1985), whom the Eklund faction had deposed from his position as dean of the Liberal Catholic Cathedral in Los Angeles. Nevertheless, Matthews retained possession of the cathedral. In 1950 Matthews succeeded Wardall as head of those clergy and congregations under his control. At that point, the Eklund faction filed suit against the Wardall-Matthews faction, asking the court to deny Matthews the use of the name Liberal Catholic Church and the title regionary bishop. In 1955 Matthews exercised his powers as head of the jurisdiction by consecrating two priests to the episcopacy, William H. Daw and James Pickford Roberts.

The litigation took more than a decade, by which time Pigott, Eklund, Hampton, and Wardall had all died. The court ruled in favor of Matthews, who it declared to be the presiding bishop of the Liberal Catholic Church. However, during the years of litigation most of the clergy and congregations had become aligned with other jurisdictions. (Also, detached from the organizational strength of the Theosophical Society, the Matthews faction had lost a major source for new members.) In 1964, shortly after the ruling, Bishops Daw and Roberts left the Mathews jurisdiction to form the Liberal Catholic Church International.

Matthews eventually sold the Los Angeles Cathedral property and moved his headquarters to Miranda, California, where it remained until 1976, at which time Matthews reported eight churches, eight clergy, and 4,000 members. (In fact, the church had only two parishes, one in Miranda and one in San Diego, California, and several priests.) The church splintered, and Matthews, along with the congregation in Miranda, returned to the Liberal Catholic Church, Province of the United States. The San Diego parish under the leadership of then Very Rev. Dean Bekken, vicar general of the province, retained the corporate structure, and began to rebuild the church.

Meanwhile, the Liberal Catholic Church International had picked up strength internationally. In 1974 Daw, the presiding bishop, resigned in favor of Joseph Edward Neth.

On July 4, 1983, the Liberal Catholic Church merged with the Liberal Catholic Church International and became its American province. Neth remained as the presiding bishop but also became the provincial bishop for the United States. In 2008 the presiding bishop was the Most Rev. Charles W. Finn, and the Liberal Catholic Church International had parishes in Africa, North America, Australia, and Europe.

Among the important documents produced by Bishop Matthews was the 1959 encyclical "Freedom of Thought," which outlined the distinctives of this branch of Liberal Catholicism. Matthews attempted to move the church away from Theosophical distinctives by affirming traditional Catholic ones. He specifically attacked the doctrine of reincarnation, noting that Liberal Catholicism does not now, nor ever has at any time insisted or prescribed the dogma or teaching of the principle known as reincarnation, "Christian" or otherwise, as a tenet of belief and practices. Reincarnation is often a basic "text" belief in one's acceptance or rejection of Theosophy.

Membership: In 2002 the church reported 6,570 members in the United States, 19 priests, and 9 congregations in the United States.

Educational Facilities:

St. Alban Theological Seminary, Morongo Valley, California, was established in 1923. It is the official seminary of the Liberal Catholic Church worldwide. In 2008 the Very Rev. Terence Herrera-LaFavre served as dean of the seminary. Students study for the Holy Orders as well as courses in church history, doctrine, scripture, liturgy, spirituality, homilectics, counseling, and comparative relation. The ordained and the laity may enter the religious life as friars or sisters. Postulants take distance study courses.

Sources:

Liberal Catholic Church International. www.liberalcatholic.org.

The Holy Eucharist and Other Services. San Diego, CA: St. Alban Press, 1977.

Matthews, Edward M. "Freedom of Thought, an Encyclical." Los Angeles: Liberal Catholic Church, 1959.

———. *The Liberal Catholic Church and Its Place in the World*. Los Angeles: St. Alban Bookshop, n.d.

Statement of Principles. San Diego, CA: Liberal Catholic Church, 1977.

Liberal Catholic Church, Province of the United States

c/o Our Lady and All Angels Church, Rev. James Voirol, Rector, 1502 E Ojai Ave., Ojai, CA 93024

Bp. James Ingall Wedgewood brought the Liberal Catholic Church to the United States on the round-the-world tour he took during his first year as primate. Crossing the United States and meeting with Theosophists, he ordained as priests Charles Hampton (Los Angeles, August 19, 1917), Dr. Edwin Burt Beckwith (Chicago, September 16, 1917), and Ray Marshall Wardall (New York City, October 4, 1917). In 1919 Charles W. Leadbeater joined Wedgwood in consecrating Irving Steiger Cooper as the first regionary bishop for the United States. That consecration led to a war of words: Independent American Theosophists, especially those led by Katherine Tingley, used the emergence of the Liberal Catholic Church as an opportunity to denounce the Annie Besant-led Theosophists for selling out to Catholicism.

The Liberal Catholic Church prospered and spread under Cooper, but ran into trouble under its second regionary bishop, Charles Hampton (d. 1958). Hampton questioned the necessity of the provincal board and its beliefs. As the controversy continued, Hampton was deposed, and John T. Eklund was appointed to succeed him. Eklund's consecration of Newton A. Dahl and Walter J. Zollinger led to a second schism by priests led by Bishop Wardall, who objected to the legality of the action. Among those opposed to Eklund was Edward M. Mathews, the priest in charge of the leading congregation of the church, in Hollywood, California. Eklund instituted suit against the schismatic group in hopes of denying it the use of the church's name. The suit was lost in a 10-year court battle, but in spite of the loss, most Liberal Catholics adhered. In 1973 it reported 29 congregations, 61 clergy, and 2,393 members. The church retained the recognition of the international church headquartered in London, but it was forced to reincorporate in 1962 in Maryland in order to continue the use of its original name in the United States.

This branch of Liberal Catholicism is most closely tied to the Theosophical Society. The cathedral church of Our Lady and All Angels is located in Ojai, California. The province of the United State of America is aligned with the world headquarters of the church, which is in London, England. The presiding bishop of the Liberal Catholic Chuch is the Rt. Rev. Ian Hooker of Western Australia. In 2000 the Rt. Rev. William S. H. Downey became the regionary bishop for the United States of America, succeeding the Rt. Rev. Hein van Beusekom.

Membership: In 2002 the church reported 2,400 members, 23 congregations, 38 priests, and 9 deacons. The Liberal Catholic Church has parishes in California, Colorado, Florida, Illinois, Iowa, Louisiana, Michigan, New Mexico, Puerto Rico, and Wisconsin.

Educational Facilities:

Liberal Catholic Institute of Studies (LCIS).

Periodicals: *Ubique*. • *The Voice of the Synod*.

Sources:

Liberal Catholic Church, Province of the United States. members.tripod.com/LiberalCatholic/.

Cooper, Irving S. *Ceremonies of the Liberal Catholic Rite*. London: St. Alban Press, 1964.

Leadbeater, Charles Webster. *The Science of the Sacraments*. Los Angeles: St. Alban Press, 1920.

The Liturgy of the Liberal Catholic Church. London: St. Alban Press, 1983.

Norton, Robert. *The Willow in the Tempest: A Brief History of the Liberal Catholic Church in the United States from 1917–1942*. Ojai, CA: St. Alban Press, 1990.

Pitkin, William H. *Credo, First Steps in Faith*. Ojai, CA: St. Alban Press, 1977.

Wedgewood, James Ingall. *The Beginnings of the Liberal Catholic Church*. Lakewood, NJ: Ubique, 1967.

Liberal Catholic Church-Theosophia Synod

c/o Church of St. Raphael Archangel, 1606 New York Ave., Orlando, FL 32803

The Liberal Catholic Church-Theosophia Synod was founded in 1982 as the result of disagreements within the General Episcopal Synod of the Liberal Catholic Church-Province of the United States. Without informing Most Rev. Ernest W. Jackson, the regionary bishop of the church's Province of Canada, the other bishops voted to dissolve the Province of Canada. As a result, Bishop Jackson led in the formation of the Liberal Catholic Church-Theosophia Synod. The new synod continues the beliefs, practices, and liturgy of the parent body, the disagreement that led to its formation being purely administrative. Shortly after its formation, Jackson consecrated John R. Schwarz III as the church's second bishop and his successor. The church is led by its General Episcopal Synod.

In 2005 Bishop Schwarz withdrew from the Liberal Catholic Church-Theosophia Synod, which is now led by Bps. James Lippert and Judson Saas.

Membership: Not reported.

Sources:

Liberal Catholic Church-Theosophia Synod. www.lcc-orlando.org/.

New Order of Glastonbury

Box 285, Yellow Jacket, CO 81335

The New Order of Glastonbury began in 1979 when seven independent Old and Liberal Catholic priests decided to establish an ordered community. The organization incorporated in the State of California in 1980 as a nonprofit, tax-exempt, religious body and received official sanction from both state and federal governments. The previous year, one of their number, Frank Ellsworth Hughes, had been consecrated by Abp. Herman Adrian Spruit of the Church of Antioch. The group decided to add a Protestant-style ministry as a means of serving the lay public. A number of the clergy established churches and ministries.

In 1991 the Mother Center moved to Whitethorn Farm, in the Four Corners area of Colorado, along with the Seminary of St. Mary, Our Lady of Glastonbury.

The order is very eclectic but generally follows a Liberal Catholic perspective. Their statement of principles espouses a belief in One God, manifest as the Creator; the Cosmic Christ, the Son; and the Holy Spirit, the Comforter. In life and worship, the order combines emphases from Catholic (apostolic succession, seven sacraments); Protestant (freedom of belief and mode of worship); and Metaphysical (the study of comparative religion, occult and psychic reality) traditions. A variety of liturgies are approved from the more orthodox (such as the Tridentine Latin or Byzantine) to the theosophical liturgy of the American Catholic Church written by Lowell Paul Wadle.

The order is governed by a seven-member board of directors. Most Rev. Frank Ellsworth Hughes was elected as the first presiding bishop. The order admits both men and women married or unmarried to all levels of its ministry. Fr. Merle D. Mohring, Sr., served as the first president of the board of directors, while his wife, Most Rev. Martha Theresa (Martha Jo Mohring Schultz), served as secretary-treasurer. In 2008 she was presiding bishop, the position to which she was appointed in 1985.

Membership: In 2002 the order reported 10 congregations and 300 members served by 52 priests and ministers.

Educational Facilities:

Seminary of Our Lady, Yellow Jacket, Colorado, and Boulder, Colorado.

The order also offers a correspondence study program leading to ordination.

Periodicals: *Gateways*.

Sources:

The New Order of Glastonbury, History and Apostolic Succession. Rialto, CA: New Order of Glastonbury, [1980].

Old Holy Catholic Church, Province of North America
Current address not obtained for this edition.

The Old Holy Catholic Church, Province of North America, was founded in 1979 by the Rev. George W. S. Brister. Brister had been ordained to the priesthood by Bp. James A. J. Taylor of the Order of St. Germain, Ecclesia Catholica Liberalis, in 1969. He headed the Maranatha Ministry Church and the Order of St. Timothy, Ecclesia Catholica Liberalis, both in Oklahoma City, Oklahoma. By 1975 Maranatha Churches could also be found in Tulsa and Las Vegas. He was consecrated by Bishop Stephan A. Hoeller of the Ecclesia Gnostica in 1980. His church, as is true of Liberal Catholic congregations, was quite eclectic and combined teaching drawn from theosophy, Buddhism, New Age metaphysics, and religious science.

In June 1987 Brister retired as archbishop primate of the church and appointed Bp. Alvin Lee Baker to succeed him. Besides his role as archbishop emeritus of the church, Brister served as vicar general of the Liberal Catholic Church (Oklahoma Synod), with which the Old Holy Catholic Church is in communion. Baker then served as pastor of St. Timothy's Church in Oklahoma City, Oklahoma.

The Old Holy Catholic Church affirms the Nicene Creed, and the beliefs of the undivided church in Christ and redemption, though it understands them with a Liberal Catholic interpretation. It affirms its oneness with the one church founded by Christ that consists of the Roman Catholic Church, all the independent Catholic hierarchical churches, the Eastern churches such as the Orthodox, Coptic, and Armenian. The church condemns moral permissiveness, immodest dress during worship, homosexuality, and, in general, conforming to the "spirit of this world."

The church follows the liturgical year in its worship and emphasizes fasting during penitential seasons (such as Lent). It advocates the use of pious images, the rosary, and Gregorian chants.

Succession in the Old Holy Catholic Church was established by Archbishop Charles Brearley in the United Kingdom. Brearley was succeeded as primate in 1977 by the Most Rev. Rainer Laufers, previously archbishop to Canada of the Old Holy Catholic Church, based in Ontario. There are parishes in Germany and the Netherlands.

Membership: Not reported.

Periodicals: *The Lamp*.

Palm Tree Garden
For information: www.palmtreegarden.org/contact.php.

Palm Tree Garden is a product of the rising interest in Gnosticism that developed during the last quarter of the twentieth century. It began as and remains primarily an online Gnostic community, but has begun to implement its ultimate plan of founding local communities of Gnostic believers that it terms *soldalities*. Bro. Jeremy Puma, the founder of the Palm Tree Garden, attributes much of the current interest in Gnosticism to science-fiction writer Philip K. Dick (1928-1982) and the books and films he influenced. Dick is best known as the author behind the movie Blade Runner. Dick called the common human condition a "Black Iron Prison," and saw the "Palm Tree Garden" as an ideal.

It is the position of the Palm Tree Garden that modern Gnosticism has been negatively affected by its many years as an underground faith. It has become ultra-individualistic, with its advocates adhering to a wide variety of very different positions and theoretical constructs. It is threatened with becoming a mere spiritual abstraction with no real grounding in the visible world. This problem has served to limit the spread of Gnosticism as anything more than an intellectual exercise.

The Palm Tree Garden seeks to address the issue of Gnosticism's lack of unified identity by focusing on what it sees as a beginning development of a unified sense of purpose and direction among those who have accepted the label *Gnostic*. Thus, Palm Tree Garden has sought initially to create a virtual forum where Gnostics could meet and seek common ground (without demands of uniformity).

The virtual forum is seen as leading to a true Gnostic community, which can saturate the World of Forms and serves those who seek to Know the Light. To accomplish its ends, the Palm Tree Garden developed a set of goals. It began with providing a place for self-identified Gnostics to meet online. As a sense of unity has manifested, it has begun to form the first soldalities, physical communities that are designed to carry the Garden's goals into face-to-face interactions.

The unity that the Garden proposes has been seen as compatible with the Path of Radical Inquiry-a willingness to collaborate without dictating, to converse without imposing groupthink, to argue without developing strong negative feeling toward those with whom you disagree. One of the products of the development of the Palm Tree Garden community is a consensus on a set of ancient texts with which dialogue seems essential to the development of modern Gnosticism-the Gospel of Philip, the Gospel of Thomas, the Gospel of Truth, the Exegesis of the Soul, the Apocyphon of John, the Hymn of the Soul, and the Treatise on the Resurrection.

To show its support of the larger Gnostic community, the Palm Tree Garden keeps a list of functioning Gnostic churches and groups.

Membership: Not reported. The Palm Tree Garden sponsors four soldalities, one each in Salt Lake City, Utah; Seattle, Washington; Memphis, Tennessee; and New England. There is a fifth sodality that operates through the popular Web site, My Page.

Sources:

Palm Tree Garden. www.palmtreegarden.org/about.php.

Puma, Jeremy. *The Face of the Sky and Earth: Mysteries of the Gospel of Thomas*. Author, 2007.

————. *Mysteries of the Gnostic Ascent*. Lulu.com, 2006.

————. *The Pirate's Garden: Gnostic Essays*. Lulu.com, 2006.

Pre-Nicene Gnosto-Catholic Church
23301 Mobile St., Canoga Park, CA 91307-3322

The Pre-Nicene Gnosto-Catholic Church was chartered by Mar Georgius (de Willmott Newman), Patriarch of Glastonbury, in 1953, under Abp. Richard Jean Chretien, Duc de Palatine (born Ronald Powell, in Australia; 1916–1978). De Palatine was consecrated by Mar Georgius. There are established communities in the United Kingdom and in the United States.

De Palatine was succeeded by Bp. George Boyer (1921–2008). Bishop Boyer's widow, Countess Bishop Leila Boyer, coordinates several bishops and priests of his community in the United Kingdom. In the United States, there are two major descendant communities of the church. The direct successor is the Ecclesia Gnostica under Tau Stephanus Hoeller.

Before founding of the Pre-Nicene Church, de Palatine had been given the office of archon (ruler) of an Italian-based order, the Ancient Mystical Order of the Fratis Lucis. The Church was a liturgical community open only to members of the order.

The order and church differ from many Liberal Catholic groups by their emphasis on gnosticism. The Gnostics were second-century Christians who rejected the humanity of Jesus. They said he never became human—that is, fleshly—and only seemed to have a material body. *Gnosis* means "knowledge," and the Gnostics sought salvation through the secret knowledge (occult wisdom) teachings.

The order and church emphasize a Western approach to the ancient wisdom, as opposed to theosophists, who draw heavily on Eastern occultism. The church emphasizes Jesus' role as the bringer of gnosis and deemphasizes the Oriental yogic disciplines. It is an active system, calling members to strive for enlightenment and push aside any self-abnegation. God is identified with nature and is pictured as fragmented into billions of parts, which are the spiritual selves, sparks of the divine, which man is. This spark is buried in the tomb of flesh. Humanity's task is to realize his God-nature and actualize his divine potentials. Reincarnation is a part of this scheme of actualization.

The method of actualization is the arcane (hidden) discipline, a way known to mystics of all ages. It includes the esoteric sacramental rituals of the church, which are based on the allegorical interpretation of Holy Scripture.

The order and church are headquartered in London. The Sanctuary of the Gnosis is the corporate body created to give legal and civil status to the order in America. The president of the Sanctuary is George Ricci. The apostolic succession was passed by Powell to John Martyn-Baxter, who passed it to the subsequent bishop leaders of the church.

Membership: Not reported.

Sources:

Gnostic Info. "The Pre-Nicene Gnosto-Catholic Church, by the Most Rev. Richard duc de Palatine." www.gnostic.info/palatine_pre-nicene.html.

Duc de Palatine, Richard John Chretien. *The Inner Meaning of the Mystery School.* London: Pre-Nicene Publishing House, 1959.

————. *You and Reincarnation.* Sherman Oaks, CA: Aeon Press, 1976.

Kinney, Jay. "Gnosticism: Ancient and Modern." New Dawn Magazine 85 (July-August 2004). Available from www.newdawnmagazine.com/Article/Gnosticism_Ancient_and_Modern.html.

Science of Man Church

52501 E Sylvan Dr., Sandy, OR 97055

The Science of Man (SOM) was originally conceived of by Rev. Earl W. Blighton (1904–1974), an independent minister, from a revelation he had in 1930 that called him to work for "the uniting of science and the teachings of our Lord Jesus Christ." Blighton participated in a variety of theosophical and esoteric groups over the next decades, but in 1960 he assembled a small group of 14 people in the San Francisco Bay Area to begin the work of helping the world and freeing it from the effects of 2,000 years of dogmatism. They began to absorb the western esoteric teachings with a Christian perspective.

The Science of Man Church evolved out of the group's deliberations and was chartered in 1961. Blighton led the church as teacher and preacher and developed a ministry to former convicts. The church opened a prayer shrine that serviced the street people in San Francisco's Tenderloin section. People from the Tenderloin volunteered to assist, and a brotherhood began to form within the church. Brotherhood members worked on the streets to help any in need. The somewhat informal brotherhood evolved into a more ordered community, the Holy Order of MANS, formed in 1968. At that time the Science of Man Church became inactive. The Holy Order grew into a large organization with centers in cities across the United States and Europe. Following Blighton's death in 1974, the new leadership of the order began to move it away from its esoteric teachings and to place almost exclusive emphasis on its traditional Christian roots, especially Eastern Orthodoxy. In 1986 they led the order to merge into the Greek Orthodox Missionary Archdiocese of Vasiloupolis.

In the mid-1970s Blighton's widow, Ruth Blighton (Mother Ruth), quietly reactivated the original charter of the Science of Man as a way to preserve the vitality and spirit of the original organizations. In the mid-1980s she moved to Oregon, where she worked in close association with former Order members to reactivate the work of the Science of Man. She continued to act as spiritual director and published books including *The Middle Path*, which contains excerpts from classes, sermons, and lectures by Father Paul, and *The Story of Jesus*, which relates the earthly life of the Master Jesus in narrative and commentary drawn from the Gospels and other writings. Other books published by the Science of Man are *The Golden Force*, a handbook explaining the laws of creation, *The Heavenly Two*, a coloring book for children, the *Stars of Heaven*, astrology basics, and three Tarot volumes.

The church's teachings flow from the general western esoteric teachings, but its teachings are occult and thus are given only to members and fully revealed in the experiencing of them. It is also the belief of the church, however, that all religions have been inspired by the Cosmic Christ, which gives the church a nondogmatic openness to various spiritual paths and perceptions.

The current membership offers the sacraments, counseling, and classes based on the Tree of Life lessons and other works.

Membership: Not reported.

Periodicals: *Science of Man Quarterly.* Send orders to 52501 E Sylvan Dr., Sandy, OR 97055, or read online at web site.

Sources:

Science of Man Church. www.scienceofman.org.

Universal Catholic Church

741 Cerro Gordo Ave., San Diego, CA 92102

The Universal Catholic Church was founded in 2007 after the members and leadership of St. Francis Liberal Catholic Church withdrew from Liberal Catholic Church International. St. Francis Church, founded in 1969, has been one of the more prominent congregations in the Liberal Catholic movement and its founder, Bp. Dean Bekken, is one of the movement's most well-known leaders. The new jurisdiction follows the beliefs and practice of the parent body, the differences being administrative. Shortly after its founding, the Universal Catholic Church named Bekken as its presiding bishop and Robert Winzens as a bishop-elect. Winzens now serves as the pastor of the St. Francis congregation.

Membership: Not reported.

Sources:

Universal Catholic Church. www.stalbanpress.com/StFrancisPage.html.

Universal Gnostic Fellowship

c/o Presiding Archbishop John F. Gilbert, 507 Old Toll Cir., Black Mountain, NC 28711

The Universal Gnostic Fellowship is one of the products of the revival of interest in Gnosticism that occurred as the twentieth century was coming to a close. It is an open fellowship drawing on a wide variety of believers who self-identify as Gnostics. The Fellowship defines a Gnostic as anyone who seeks personal knowledge of or communication with the Divine. The fellowship's goal is to assist individuals in finding their own path to spiritual wisdom (gnosis).

The Fellowship accepts all who subscribe to the "Law of One," which it defines as meaning that "There is One Intelligence in the Universe which expresses itself as everything, and everything in the Universe is an expression of this One Intelligence." It finds room for a wide variety of interpretations of that basic belief, coming from both Eastern and Western religious traditions, including different conceptions of the degree to which humans are separate from or included within the One and of the need or lack of need of a priesthood to assist in contacting the One. While open to a wide range of beliefs, the Fellowship publishes lessons on what is termed universal Gnosticism, which emphasize that while existence is a part of the Divine, the Divine is more than creation; that human freedom allows for spiritual self-determination; and that our present life in the body is the result of our prior choices. The Fellowship's recommended reading list includes ancient Gnostic texts, and books on both the Western and Eastern esoteric traditions.

The fellowship has established a clergy and accepts both men and women into this ordained ministry as deacons, priests, and bishops. The Fellowship's bishops—John F. Gilbert, Betty Jean Reeves, Rhodonn Starrus, Marie Harris, Roberta Harris, Rita Baker and Santu Little Dog Peltier—were consecrated in 1994 with several lines of apostolic succession derived from Abp. Adrian Spruit (1911-1994) of the Church of Antioch, the Liberal Catholic Church, and Louis Keizer of the Independent Church of Antioch. Those who seek ordination must complete the basic Gnostic Lessons designed by the fellowship and then complete a variety of additional studies in related fields of healing and esotericism. The fellowship also licenses spiritual healers.

The bishops of the Fellowship are brought together in the House of Independent Bishops, which also includes bishops who exercise their functions in other jurisdictions. Within the Fellowship, some bishops may be designated archbishops and assigned to mentor other bishops. The presiding archbishop is a mentor to the several archbishops.

Membership: Not reported. In 2008, the fellowship reported 28 bishops affiliated with the House of Independent Bishops.

Sources:

Universal Gnostic Fellowship. universalgnostic.com/.

 # I AM Groups

Ascended Master Teaching Foundation
PO Box 466, Mount Shasta, CA 96067

The Ascended Master Teaching Foundation was founded in 1980 by Werner Schroeder and other students of the Ascended Masters. Guy W. Ballard, co-founder of the "I AM" Religious Activity in the 1930s, and Geraldine Innocente, a messenger with the Bridge to Freedom in the 1950s, were the recipients of messages. The goal of the foundation is to gather, cross-index, make available to students, and translate into foreign languages these messages. In addition, the foundation encourages the formation of study groups for people who wish to learn the teachings and initiate spiritual practice through decrees, songs, and visualizations. The foundation has produced audiotapes and more than 80 publications (available for sale through the mailing address or www.ascendedmaster.org/).

It is the belief of the foundation that in the 1930s Ascended Master Saint Germain initiated a "New Age" dispensation through Ballard and his wife, Edna Ballard. He expounded cosmic law in precise terms to Ballard. For the first time since the sinking of the continent of Atlantis, the knowledge of the I AM Presence (the spiritual body), and the practice of invoking the Violet Flame (which erases karma), was made public. Ballard spread the messages until his "ascension" (death) in 1939. The books became largely unavailable until the mid-1980s. In 1951 the Masters began to give additional messages through Geraldine Innocente. After her ascension in 1961 few of her messages were published.

The Ascended Master Teaching Foundation believes that their effort, begun in the 1930s, is the last effort to free mankind and increase the light to earth so that humanity can go through future planetary changes with the least amount of suffering possible. Their goal is to redeem the earth and bring all humanity into contact with the Ascended Masters.

Membership: Not reported.

Sources:

www.ascendedmaster.org/.

King, Godfre Ray. "Guy Ballard." *Unveiled Mysteries*. Mount Shasta, CA: Ascended Master Teaching Foundation, 1986.

Prinz, Thomas Geraldine Innocente. *Memoirs of Beloved Mary, Mother of Jesus*. [1855.] Mount Shasta, CA: Ascended Master Teaching Foundation, 1986.

————. *The Seventh Ray*. [1953.] Mount Shasta, CA: Ascendee Master Teaching Foundation, 1986.

Schroeder, Werner. *Man—His Origin, History and Destiny*. Mount Shasta, CA: Ascended Master Teaching Foundation, 1984.

The Bridge to Spiritual Freedom, Inc.
PO Box 753, Payson, AZ 85547

The Bridge to Freedom, a Religious Activity incorporated in the early 1950s, was later called the New Age Church of the Christ. The name the Bridge to Spiritual Freedom was then adopted to more accurately describe the activity of the Ascended Masters, whose origins can be traced to 1944, when Geraldine Innocente, then a member of the "I AM" Religious Activity, was contacted by the Ascended Master El Morya. This marked the beginning of a series of dictations from the Maha Chohan, other members of the Great White Brotherhood, and Cosmic Beings. These instructions formed the foundation on which the Bridge to Spiritual Freedom was built.

The messages received through Geraldine Innocente were published under the sponsorship of Master El Morya. Using the pseudonym Thomas Printz, he directed the editing and compiling of these communications, including a periodical, *The Bridge to Spiritual Freedom Journal*, and weekly letters from various Ascended Masters called *The Shamballa Letter*. The headquarters of the Bridge to Spiritual Freedom relocated from Kings Park, New York, to Payson, Arizona. In 2008 the president was Rebecca Ann Laycock.

After the ascension (death) of Innocente in 1961, her duties as Contact for the Ascended Masters and president of this organization were given to Lucy W. Littlejohn, who served until her retirement in 1989. Following the instructions of Master El Morya, since 1989 the Contact has remained anonymous. The activity serves as a bridge of consciousness between the physical octave and the Hierarchy of Ascended Masters, through which cooperative work may take place to raise the consciousness of all the people on Earth.

The goals are brotherhood and peace between all people and nations, and the elevation of humanity above disease, limitation, and imperfection. Students are taught about the use of the Sacred Fire through various methods, including the decrees, rhythmic breathing, and constructive visualization. Since 1954, which the activity regards as the beginning of the era of spiritual freedom, attention has been focused on the activities of the Seventh Ray and the use of the Violet transmuting Flame.

Membership: Not reported.

Periodicals: *The Bridge to Spiritual Freedom Journal* • *The Shamballa Letter* • *Ascended Master Discourses* (annual) • *The Gifted* (available in English and Spanish) • *The Bright*

Sources:

The Bridge to Spiritual Freedom. www.pathofthemiddleway.org/.

Kuthumi, Ascended Master. *The Wisdom of the Ages*. 2 vols. St. James, NY: Bridge to Freedom, n.d.

Printz, Thomas. *Memoirs of Beloved Mary, Mother of Jesus*. Philadelphia: Bridge to Freedom, 1955.

————. *The Seven Beloved Archangels Speak*. Mount Shasta, CA: Ascended Master Teaching Foundation, 1986.

————. *The Student's Handbook*. King's Park, NY: Bridge to Freedom, 1972.

The Violet Transmuting Flame. Kings Park, NY: Bridge to Freedom, 1968.

Church Universal and Triumphant
10 East Gate Rd., Gardiner, MT 59030

HISTORY. The Church Universal and Triumphant had its beginnings in the Summit Lighthouse, founded in 1958 in Washington, D.C., by Mark L. Prophet (1918–1973) under the direction of the Ascended Master El Morya. Prophet had previously been associated with the Lighthouse of Freedom, a Philadelphia-based organization headed by Frances K. Ekey.

The Summit Lighthouse had as its primary purpose the publication and dissemination of the teachings of the Ascended Masters, described as "Immortal, God-free beings" who have mastered the circumstances of their lives by victoriously passing all of their tests and trials on earth. These Illuminaries, such as Jesus Christ, Mother Mary, Moses, Zarathustra, and Gautama Buddha, are the saints, revolutionaries, mystics, wise men, and women of all ages who have fulfilled their reason for being, balanced their karma and ascended to God, free at last from the round of rebirth. El Morya, an Ascended Master, is considered to be the Chief of the Darjeeling Council of the Great White Brotherhood. The brotherhood is thought to be an order of Western saints and Eastern masters. (The word white refers not to race, but to the aura, or halo, that surrounds the masters and their embodied disciples). The primary method of disseminating the messages is a periodical, *Pearls of Wisdom*, published weekly since 1958, and numerous books and tapes.

In 1961 Prophet was joined by Elizabeth Clare Wulf (b. 1939), whom he later married and who eventually received the mantle of Messenger from Saint Germain, which, the Church teaches, confers the empowerment of the Word by the Holy Spirit. In the "I AM" Religious Activity, the messenger is one through whom the Ascended Masters can speak. Mark Prophet was such a messenger, and after her training, Elizabeth Clare Prophet also became one.

In 1962 the Ascended Master Saint Germain established the Keepers of the Flame Fraternity, an order within the larger group of those receiving the *Pearls of Wisdom*, of men and women especially dedicated to the freedom and enlightenment of humanity. In 1966 the headquarters moved to Colorado Springs, Colorado, where the publishing of the teachings continued. Here a Montessori preschool was established in 1970 to provide a spiritual and academic bilingual (English/Spanish) education for the children of the Keepers of the Flame. Over the years it has grown into a full elementary and high school program.

Summit University was founded in Santa Barbara, California, in 1971 to provide a more intensive and direct presentation of the teachings of the Ascended Masters to members of the Keepers of the Flame who have moved through the basic course of lessons. At an annual eight-week retreat each summer by Elizabeth Clare Prophet, students pursue the master's teachings on a wide variety of subjects, including the study of world religions and their sacred texts, the "lost teachings" of Jesus as delivered by the Ascended Masters, as well as the masters' prophecy for the present age.

Mark Prophet died in 1973, and Elizabeth assumed full responsibility for the leadership and direction of the movement. As the work grew, the organization added new departments, and study groups were established across the United States and Canada, in Europe and Africa, and in Australia and the Philippines. In 1974 the Church Universal and Triumphant was incorporated. The church took on the liturgical functions of the Summit Lighthouse and expanded its original mission of publishing the teachings of the Ascended Masters.

In 1976 the headquarters of the church was moved temporarily to Pasadena, California, and two years later to the 200-acre campus in Malibu, California. The international headquarters moved in 1986 to the 28,000-acre Royal Teton Ranch just north of Yellowstone National Park in Gardiner, Montana. In addition to its publishing work and ongoing religious activities, the church is actively involved in organic farming, ranching, and building a self-sufficient spiritual community.

BELIEFS. The doctrines of the Church Universal and Triumphant are contained in the many books of messages of the Ascended Masters and the texts written by the Prophets, especially their basic text, *Climb the Highest Mountain*. The church describes the teachings as essentially Judeo-Christian but centered on the eternal truths of the Universal Christ wherever they are found in the religions of both East and West. The church teaches and builds on the mystical paths at the heart of the world's major religions.

According to the church's teaching, the soul is the living potential of God. Souls were conceived in the mind of God in the first instance as a realization of God's unity. Then they were born as a manifestation of the duality of God, that is a being of both spirit and matter. The individual thus has two parts, the higher changeless self and the lower changing self. The whole of creation reflects the duality of unchanging spirit that is the fiery core and blueprint of creation, and the ever-changing material world.

The I AM Presence, or individualized presence of God, is a miniature replica of the Deity. It is the God-identity of each individual, the origin of the soul focused in the planes of spirit just above the physical form. Each individual is an extension of the presence into matter, time, and space.

The individual as spiritual being has an unlimited potential and dominion. As a material being, the individual is limited by boundaries set by the Deity. The power and authority of the I AM Presence are not to be transferred to the lesser aspect of the individual until it shall prove worthy by undergoing certain initiations and demonstrate a willingness to "affinitize" the soul with the Divine Nature—to be, in fact, the individualized manifestation of the God flame.

Eventually people can become an individualized manifestation of the God Flame. This flame is the divine spark that focuses the primary attributes of Power, Wisdom, and Love, a bestowal of God to every man and woman.

Individuals may participate in the church at a variety of levels. The general public may take part in religious services and conferences. The teachings are made available in the many books and publications, such as the weekly *Pearls of Wisdom*, which contain messages from the Ascended Masters. Those who join the Keepers of the Flame pledge to keep the flame of Life and Liberty on behalf of earth's evolutions. They receive graded instruction dictated by Ascended Masters, which are distributed monthly. At advanced levels of initiation and commitment, fraternity members may choose to become communicants (members) of the church and be formally baptized. Full church members must formally subscribe to the tenets of the church and tithe their income. The church has a number of teaching centers around the world with live-in facilities for church staff. These centers offer lectures and weekly services to the surrounding community.

According to church teachings, the goal of life for the soul evolving through numerous incarnations is to purify himself or herself and to become one with the Christ while in physical embodiment. The masters teach the science of the spoken word; the use of prayers, mantras, and decrees to call forth Light is the key whereby the soul can achieve this goal. The Ascended Master Saint Germain has given humankind the knowledge of how to use the violet flame. This violet flame of transmutation is the sacred fire of the Holy Spirit which, when invoked in conjunction with service to life, allows the soul to balance the karma of mistakes and errors that have been made in this and previous lifetimes. After the soul has become purified in the fullness of the Christ consciousness, it is called by God to return to the Divine Source through the ritual of the sacred fire known as the ascension, the ritual whereby the soul reunites with the I AM Presence. The ascension is the culmination of the soul's journey in time and space.

ORGANIZATION. As the messenger of the Great White Brotherhood, Elizabeth Clare Prophet is the spiritual leader of the Church Universal and Triumphant. Administratively, the church is governed by a board of directors charged with managing its temporal affairs. The church sponsors a cable television program *Elizabeth Clare Prophet/Prophetic Vision/Spiritual Solutions*, which is seen on stations nationwide. Summit University Press has published more than 50 books and an extensive library of audio- and videocassette recordings.

Membership: In 2008 the church reported 34 teaching centers and study groups scattered across the United States.

Educational Facilities:

Summit University, Corwin Springs, Montana.

Periodicals: *Pearls of Wisdom*. • *Royal Teton Ranch News*. • *Heart*.

Sources:

The Summit Lighthouse. www.tsl.org/.

Morya, El. *The Chela and the Path*. Colorado Springs, CO: Summit University Press, 1976.

Prophet, Elizabeth Clare. *The Great White Brotherhood in the History, Culture, and Religion of America*. Los Angeles, CA: Summit University Press, 1976.

———. *The Lost Years of Jesus*. Livingston, MT: Summit University Press, 1984.

Prophet, Mark L., and Elizabeth Clare Prophet. *Climb the Highest Mountain*. Colorado Springs, CO: Summit Lighthouse, 1972.

————. *The Lost Teachings of Jesus*. 2 vols. Livingston, MT: Summit University Press, 1986, 1988.

————. *My Soul Doth Magnify the Lord*. Colorado Springs, CO: Summit Lighthouse, 1974.

————. *The Science of the Spoken Word*. Colorado Springs, CO: Summit Lighthouse, 1974.

Whitsel, Bradley Christian. *The Church Universal and Triumphant: Elizabeth Clare Prophet's Apocalyptic Movement*. Syracuse, NY: Syracuse University Press, 2003.

City of the Sun Foundation

PO Box 370, Columbus, NM 88029

The City of the Sun, founded in 1972, grew out of Christ's Truth Church and School of Wisdom, which was founded in 1968 by the Rev. Wayne Taylor as a New Age community under the guidance and direction of the spiritual hierarchy, particularly Master Hilarion. The City of the Sun Foundation is an intentional community located on 157 acres in Luna County near Columbus, New Mexico, on the Mexican border. Taylor was for two years president of Sologa, Inc., and then helped edit *The Mentor*, published by the Sanctuary of the Master's Presence. During the time he was with Sologa, Inc. his wife, Grace Taylor, functioned as a channel. The move to New Mexico came as a result of messages received through that channeling. Preparation was made in the form of the acquisition of a tract of land near Columbus.

The basic teachings that led to the foundation are contained in Taylor's book, *Pillars of Light*. In it is told the story of man's fall, which has resulted in his being set back spiritually for thousands of years. Taylor explains that through the "Light bearers of all ages the veil of spiritual darkness is being lifted. Man is about to enter the Golden Age, and the City of the Sun is one structure to prepare for transition."

Residents of the City of the Sun have set as their primary purpose the providing of a holistic healing center, encompassing the mental, physical, and spiritual aspects of each individual, but with special emphasis on the spiritual. There are two distinctive features of their work. First, they use the Vortex of Light and the divine energies of the Central Sun for healing. Second, they allow each the freedom to follow his/her own Inner Christ guidance as long as it is in harmony with the Universal Truth. They believe in the Fatherhood of God and the brotherhood of man. The group is headed by a five-member board of trustees, which is elected by the members. There is no identified leader.

The residents live and work cooperatively, striving for unity in diversity and welcoming all spiritual beliefs. The foundation holds its land in trust until 2072. Visitors must email or write in advance for permission to visit.

Membership: In 2007 the foundation reported 50 adult members in 40 residences in the Columbus, New Mexico, community, as well as two affiliated communities, Sandhill Farm (RR 1, Box 156-W, Rutledge, MO 63563), and Twin Oaks (138 Twin Oaks Rd., Louisa, VA 23093).

Periodicals: *The Golden Dawn*. Box 356, Columbus, NM 88029 • *COMMUNITIES Magazine*.

Sources:

Intentional Communities: City of the Sun Foundation, Inc. directory.ic.org/20103/City_of_the_Sun_Foundation,_Inc.

Taylor, Wayne H. *Pillars of Light*. Columbus, NM: Author, 1965.

Hermetic Society for World Service, United States

423 W 50th St., New York, NY 10019-6502

The Hermetic Society of World Service, United States, was founded in 1947 for the study of the Hermetic gnosis or ancient wisdom. While much of the teaching of the society is esoteric, and hence reserved for members only, its general perspective includes several basic truths. The society asserts human brotherhood, irrespective of race or nationality as a realizable condition essential for life on earth. Humans evolve through the process of reincarnation, and the moral order is dictated by the law of karma, the law of ethical causation. Salvation is attained only by the conscious effort of the individual through a process of spiritual growth over a number of lifetimes. The society is headed by its hierophant and spiritual guru who is believed to be in contact with the Sirian Brotherhood, the spiritual hierarchy dedicated to the dissemination of the Light of Spiritual Knowledge throughout the world.

The society maintains that earth is in a period of change into the New Age, which is operating in the world process and is bringing about changes in science, religion, philosophy, civilization, and the way of life for humanity. What was termed the Battle of Armageddon in the Bible is currently being fought out on the Inner (invisible) Planes between the righteous and unrighteous and will soon descend to the visible realm and manifest in a period of war, tribulation, and crisis. The society offers resources for individuals to live through the changing times and proceed to greater levels of attainment. Those without these resources will be cast aside from the mainstream of human evolution. Those who adopt the New Age spiritual techniques will have the opportunity to prepare themselves for entry into the Spiritual Universe as partakers of the Divine Nature.

The society seeks to return humanity from the Path of Outgoing (directed away from their divine origins) to the Path of Return to God and the soul's eternal home. In this endeavor, the society teaches a technique of soul immortalization and methods to manifest the powers latent in the individual human soul, and the law governing the technique and disciples required to bring about the regeneration of human nature, preparatory to the gaining of liberation from the necessity of reincarnation and the operation of the law of karma. To achieve liberation, the individual must atone and liquidate the effects of past sins of body, mind, and speech, and undertake a process of spiritual regeneration. In the end the individual soul will gain immortality. Immortality must be sought for in accordance with the principles of esoteric science.

The society believes that America has a special place in the New Age as the place designated as the new Holy Land of Earth. It is the domain designated by the spiritual hierarchy who guide human destiny for the preservation of the seeds for the continuation of human life. It is the grail that will hold the Great Cosmic Light that will illumine the whole world.

The society's international headquarters is located in the Dominican Republic. There are society locations in Canada, Puerto Rico, Venezuela, Colombia, Peru, Argentina, and Spain.

Membership: Not reported.

Sources:

www.The-Hermetic-Society.org/.

Browne, Robert T. *Introduction to Hermetic Science and Philosophy*. Hermetic Society, n.d.

"I AM" Religious Activity

c/o Saint Germain Foundation, 1120 Stonehedge Dr., Schaumburg, IL 60194

The "I AM" Religious Activity is the oldest branch of the Ascended Master thrust that was begun by Guy W. Ballard (1878–1939). It is also the most conservative branch, adhering strictly to the dictates of the Ascended Masters as brought forth through their only accredited messengers, Guy and Edna A. Ballard (1886–1971). Through them was released a threefold truth not previously disclosed outside of the Ascended Masters' secret retreats: the knowledge of the "Mighty I AM Presence," the individualized presence of God; the use of the Violet Consuming Flame of Divine Love; and the use of God's Creative Name, "I AM."

The "I AM" Activity believes that the "I AM Presence" emanated from the heart of the cosmos and as it individualized, creation resulted. The "I AM Presence" is the essence of each individual. However, over the centuries, the misuse of God's energy has led to the present discord and evil present in the world. In spite of that discord and evil, a few individuals have risen above the world's situation and, by completely attuning themselves to their "I AM Presence," ascended into the light. Eventually, each person will follow them. In the meantime, these Ascended Masters, also known as the Great White Brotherhood, work to lift humanity out of their present situation.

The central focus of the "I AM" Activity is contact and cooperation with the work of the Ascended Masters. The messengers left over 3,000 dictations from the Ascended Masters, which present a total program for both individual and social life. The Saint Germain Foundation and Saint Germain Press work to publish and present this material to the public and its student body. Though early publishing records are not available, it is estimated that Saint Germain Press has put one million books in print.

The "I AM" Religious Activity considers itself a Christian religion. Jesus' example of the Ascension, in particular, deeply influences its teachings, and members believe that the Ascension is possible for everyone.

Primary means of attuning oneself to the "I AM Presence" is quiet contemplation and the repetition of affirmations and decrees. Affirmations are sentences which both affirm the individual's attunement to God usually in relation to a specific aspect of life and recount the blessings due as a result of that attunement. Decrees are fiats spoken from the perspective of the essential self, the "I AM Presence." They call forth the visible manifestation of a divine condition or the dissolution of an evil one. They are always given in the Name of God. Decrees are given daily.

Almost as definitive as decreeing, the patriotism of the "I AM" Activity is noteworthy. Freedom has been a persistent theme throughout the decrees dictated to the Ballards. America is seen as having a special role in the Ascended Masters' plans. Reflective of this emphasis are the prominent display of American flags as a symbol of universal Freedom of the individual, at "I AM" centers and the special programs on patriotic holidays.

New students are introduced to the activity by their reading the first three books of the 20-volume Saint Germain series. The first two volumes, *Unveiled Mysteries* and *The Magic Presence*, tell the story of Guy W. Ballard's original contacts with the masters. Volume three, a series of dictations from Ascended Master Saint Germain, outlines the basic beliefs of the "I AM" Activity. After reading the books, students may attend an introductory class, held periodically in all local centers ("I AM" Sanctuaries and Temples).

The Saint Germain Foundation is the parent organization of the "I AM" activity. It was led by Ballard until his death in 1939. His wife Edna then led the work until her death in 1971. At that time the board of directors assumed collective leadership of both the foundation and the press. That board, originally five members, was expanded to 18 in 1982. The board charters the local centers and sanctuaries, which otherwise are independent and autonomous. It also oversees the work of appointed messengers and field workers. The foundation sponsors a variety of national and regional programs, several of which are held at Shasta Springs, the retreat center located near Mt. Shasta, California. Annually at Mt. Shasta, the foundation sponsors a four-hour pageant on the life of Christ, which, in a spectacular finale, emphasizes the importance of the Ascension of Christ.

The head of each sanctuary or study group is termed a sponsor (pastor), who is appointed by the board of directors of Saint Germain Foundation Worldwide Headquarters. This person receives training by periodic instructional classes and by the study of published articles, scriptural studies, and a detailed handbook on the spiritual basis and physical operation of the local organization. The foundation does not ordain religious leaders.

Since 1978, the Foundation completed a building complex to house the headquarters and Saint Germain Press in Schaumburg, Illinois, a Chicago suburb. A history of the "I AM" Activity was published in 2003. There is an independent authorized "I AM" School (K-12) in Mt. Shasta, California.

Membership: In 2008, there were 260 "I AM" sanctuaries and centers throughout the world. The President (since 1998) is Anne Craig, Messenger, ret. There is affiliated work in 30 countries, including Europe, the three Americas, Africa, and Asia.

Periodicals: *The "Voice of the I AM"* (monthly)

"I AM" radio programs have been available for local broadcast since 1937, under the auspices of local sanctuaries. A list of weekly programs in the United States, including shortwave across the globe, is available from the Inquiry Department of Saint Germain Foundation Headquarters, Schaumburg, Illinois.

Remarks: Greatly affected by the court cases in the 1940s and the subsequent litigation to recover the foundation's tax-exempt status and the press' right to use the mails, the "I AM" Activity assumed a low profile. Under Edna Ballard's leadership, it cut itself off from the media and refused contact with reporters and/or religious researchers. As a result, all of the material available about the activity was either written during the period of controversy or is heavily reflective of that period. That material is generally hostile and unreflective of the present status and beliefs of the activity.

The federal case went to the U.S. Supreme Court twice, and twice was ruled in error. The original indictment was then dismissed. The case of *United States vs. Ballard* (1940–1946) established a precedent in the legal defense of all new religious organizations that followed (Case Book: 322 U.S. 788 88 L.ed 1148,648 Ct. 882. Also Case Book 152 F.2d 941)

Sources:

Saint Germain Foundation. Available from www.saintgermainfoundation.org.

Anonymous. *The History of the "I AM" Activity and Saint Germain Foundation.* Schaumburg, IL: Saint Germain Press, 2003.

King, Godfre Ray (Guy W. Ballard). *Unveiled Mysteries.* Chicago: Saint Germain Press, 1934.

———. *The Magic Presence.* Chicago: Saint Germain Press, 1935, 1963.

Germain, Saint, through Guy W. Ballard. *The "I AM" Discourses.* Chicago: Saint Germain Press, 1935.

Morningland Community of the Ascended Christ

2600 E 7th St., Long Beach, CA 90804

Morningland Community of the Ascended Christ, describes itself as a monastery for the people. Founded in 1971 by Daniel Mario Sperato (d. 1976), known within the church as Master Donato, Morningland reports that it has served more than 100,000 people since opening to the public in 1973. On May 31, 1973, Master Donato received a final invitation as the Christavatas of the Aquarian Age. His successor, Sri Donato (b. Patricia Sperato, d. 2003) continued the teachings of the Master Donato, the Master Jesus (the New Testament), and the Ascended Masters.

This "modern monastery" works to meet the specialized spiritual needs of people in the new millennium by offering healing for body, mind, and spirit under the auspices of a spiritual master teacher. Morningland is home to the Sacred Orders of Gopi and Kamazi, which are claimed to be representations of what is possible for all men and women to achieve in a practical and mystical way. The monastery welcomes all faiths to its eclectic ministry.

Membership: In 2008 the church reported approximately 100 members.

Periodicals: *Ring of Fire.*

Sources:

Healing: A Thought Away from Donato. 2 vols. Long Beach, CA: Morningland Publications, 1981.

Jesus. 3 vols. Long Beach, CA: Morningland Publications, 1980.

Morningstaar. *A Thought Away from Donato.* Long Beach, CA: Morningland Publications, 1975.

Morningstaar. *The Way to Oneness.* Long Beach, CA: Morningland Publications, 1974.

Revelations. Long Beach, CA: Morningland Publications, 1979.

Gurdjieffian Fourth Way Groups

Arica School

c/o Arica Institute, Inc.

10 Landmark Ln., PO Box 645, Kent, CT 06757

The Arica School was founded in 1968 by Oscar Ichazo as a School of Knowledge. The school provides a contemporary method of enlightenment, which employs biology, psychology, and physics in order to clarify human consciousness with modern knowledge that produces freedom and liberation.

The knowledge that the Arica School teaches, originated by Ichazo, is called the protoanalytical theory, system, and method. Protoanalysis refers to the analysis of the complete human being, starting from the lowest aspects of the human process and progressing systematically to the higher states of consciousness, where enlightenment may be attained. The Arica School provides a clearly defined map of the human psyche to assist each person to discover the basis of his or her ego process and to transcend this process into a higher state of consciousness that can be found in every individual. This state of being is a person's True Essential Self, which is experienced as an internal state of great happiness, light, and liberation, according to the school.

The Arica School presents nine levels of trainings and practices designed to clarify, step by step, the shared human processes, while at the same time introducing knowledge to assist in attaining the higher states of the True Essential Self. Each level defines, analyzes, and processes the psychological aspects of the human psyche or ego by which one gains perspective and understanding about one's self and others. The school teaches that, from this perspective, it is possible for individuals to clarify their own life experiences, which produces a state of self-observation and nonattachment. When the mind is stabilized through perspective, understanding, and self-observation, then meditations enable the transcending of everyday experiences into the higher states of mind, where enlightenment and real freedom can be attained.

While Ichazo's teachings are best known for their relationship to Georgei Gurdjieff's teachings, he has an eclectic background and studied with a variety of spiritual masters prior to founding Arica. In 1991, he was given the Award of Excellence by United Nations Society of Writers.

Membership: Not reported.

Periodicals: *Arica Day of Unity Report*.

Sources:

Arica School. www.arica.org

Ichazo, Oscar. *Arica Psycho-Calisthenics*. New York: Simon & Schuster, 1976.

————. *The Human Process for Enlightenment and Freedom*. New York: Arica Institute, 1976.

————. *The 9 Ways of Zhikr Ritual*. New York: Arica Institute, 1976.

Interviews with Oscar Ichazo. New York: Arica Institute Press, 1982.

Claymont Society for Continuous Education

667 Huyett Rd., Charles Town, WV 25414

John Godolphin Bennett (1897–1974) met Georgei Gurdjieff in 1921 in Constantinople, where Bennett was serving in the British Army. He continued his off-and-on relationship with Gurdjieff until the latter's death in 1949. Bennett subsequently authored a number of books that discussed his work with Gurdjieff and advocated Gurdjieff's Fourth Way system. However, he was not bound by Gurdjieff, and in his mature years he also became enthusiastic about both Subud (discussed elsewhere in this chapter) and the yoga of Shivapuri Baba, an Indian teacher. He wrote an important book introducing both to the English-speaking world.

Bennett claimed that Gurdjieff had left him a commission to serve as a teacher of the Gurdjieff system to the world. Philosophical material of interest originating outside of Gurdjieff's teachings was seen through the prism of the Fourth Way system. Bennett's interest in Subud, for example, was prompted by his belief that Bapak Subuh, it founder, was identical with Ashiata Shiemash, a coming prophet of conscience spoken of in Gurdjieff's book *All and Everything*. Bennett came to believe that humanity had reached the point in evolution at which individuals could assume responsibility for humanity's future course. Through spiritual training, individuals could become transformed and in the process begin to transform the world.

In 1971, to put his ideas into action, Bennett founded the International Academy for Continuous Education at Sherbourne, Gloucestershire, near Oxford. The core of the program at Sherborne House consisted of a 10-month resident intensive based directly on Gurdjieff. Bennett died in 1974, and the following year the center was closed.

However, following Bennett's American tour in 1971 and the subsequent circulation of his books in the United States, a cadre of American students had arisen. In 1975 some of those students, seeking to continue the work of Sherborne House, created the Claymont Society and School in West Virginia. Under the leadership of Pierre Elliot, who had worked with Gurdjieff's prime student Peter Demainovitch Ouspensky and then with Bennett for many years, the Claymont Society has established a community and continued the work begun by Bennett. Beginning with Gurdjieff's and Bennett's teachings and methods, the group has incorporated a variety of techniques, especially those of Sufi teachers of Central Asia known as Khwajagan.

The Society is designed to function as a "Fourth Way" school, that is, as a community whose members are working together toward human transformation. This transformation is to be achieved within the context of building a community capable of surviving under harsh economic and social conditions and educating others to do likewise. The Society is seeking to become self-sufficient economically and organizationally through farming and various cottage industries and the school for interested outsiders it manages. This school, the Claymont School, provides the basic 10-month program developed for Sherborne House, plus a variety of more inclusive programs offered by other teachers from compatible Sufi, Hasidic, and Eastern perspectives.

In the United Kingdom, Coombe Springs Press continues from the Sherborne House establishment as publishers of Bennett's books and other literature with a related perspective. These publications are distributed in the United States by Claymont Communications, who also distribute Bennett material published by others.

Membership: Not reported. While the society has the potential for supporting 200 families on its present West Virginia acreage, fewer than 100 people currently reside there.

Sources:

Claymont Society for Continuous Education. www.claymont.org.

Bennett, John G. *Creative Thinking*. Sherbourne, U.K.: Coombe Springs Press, 1964.

————. *Enneagram Studies*. York Beach, ME: Samuel Weiser, 1983.

————. *Gurdjieff: Making a New World*. New York: Harper & Row, 1973.

————. *Is There "Life" on Earth?* New York: Stonehill Publishing Company, 1973.

————. *Witness*. Tucson, AZ: Omen Press, 1974.

Fellowship of Friends

Apollo, CA

The Fellowship of Friends, founded in San Francisco in 1970 by Robert E. Burton, is a school of spiritual development in the Fourth Way tradition. The Fourth Way, a psychological system that has existed, in one form or another, for thousands of years, was expounded in the twentieth century by Georgei Gurdjieff, and developed and continued by Peter Demainovitch Ouspensky and Rodney Collin. Central to the tradition is *self-remembering*, an active form of meditation in which students attempt to become more aware of themselves and their surroundings in each moment of their daily lives. Ouspensky wrote that man, as he is, "is not a complicated being; that nature takes him only up to a certain point and then leave him, to develop further by his own efforts and devices, or to live and die such as he was born." According to the Fourth Way, individuality, consciousness, conscience, free will, and an immortal soul are attributes that man mistakenly believes he already possesses, but that must instead be acquired by special work within a group of people who share the same aim.

Apollo, the main center of the Fellowship of Friends, is a 1,250-acre site in the Sierra Nevada foothills of California. About a third of the fellowship's members live at Apollo. Other members live in more than 60 fellowship centers worldwide.

At Apollo students have opportunities to apply and verify the truth of the teachings. Such opportunities often include meetings, dinners, concerts, theater, and practical labor in the gardens, vineyard, or kitchens. The fellowship emphasizes the arts, and students come to understand how higher spiritual states can be created through beautiful and harmonious forms. This emphasis on the arts inspired, among other projects, the Apollo Opera, which draws most of its participants from Apollo, with guest singers and musicians from across California and the nation.

The fellowship owns Renaissance Vineyard and Winery, one of the largest mountain wineries in North America. Fellowship members cleared the 365-acre vineyard and planted the vines; they continue to prune vines, harvest grapes, and produce fine wines. The award-winning winery now produces approximately 20 to 30,000 cases per year.

Membership: In 2002 the fellowship had approximately 2,200 members, of whom around 700 lived at Apollo. There are 60 centers in cities in more than 40 countries, including ones in Taipei, Venice, Moscow, Buenos Aires, Paris, London, and Mexico City.

Sources:

Fellowship of Friends. www.beingpresent.org.

Burton, Robert E. *Self-Remembering*. York Beach, ME: Samuel Weiser, 1991, 1995. 216 pp.

Gurdjieff Foundation

85 St. Elmo Way, San Francisco, CA 94127

Georgei Gurdjieff (d. 1949) was a modern spiritual teacher who was greatly influenced by Sufism, but who blended it, with other spiritual teachings, into a unique philosophy that has in the several decades since his death become the springboard for a host of variations. Born in the 1870s in a small town on the Armenian-Turkish border, Gurdjieff studied the mysticism of Greek Orthodoxy and developed an interest in both science and the occult prior to leaving home as a young man. He began a period of wanderings that took him from Tibet to Ethiopia as a member of a legendary band, the Seekers of the Truth, in quest of esoteric wisdom. A significant period was spent among the Turkish Sufi masters.

In 1912 Gurdjieff surfaced in Moscow, where he met his most important disciple, Peter Demainovitch Ouspensky. With his students, he left Russia as the revolution was beginning and settled in Paris, where in 1922 he founded the Institute for the Harmonious Development of Man. Here, the unknown and the famous gathered to study with Gurdjieff. Among his students were Alexander de Salzmann and his wife Jeanne de Salzmann, author Katherine Mansfield, writer/editor A. R. Orage, and Maurice Nicoll.

Gurdjieff taught that humans are asleep, that they are operated like puppets by forces of which they have no awareness. He looked for individuals who had awakened to their contact with the higher force that brought direct awareness (and hence some degree of control) of the other forces of their environment. Gurdjieff developed a variety of techniques to assist the awakening process. Possibly the most famous were the Gurdjieff movements, a series of dancelike exercises. He also

generated considerable controversy by placing students in situations of tension and conflict designed to force self-conscious awareness. The system required an individual teacher-student relationship almost of necessity. It came to be known as the "fourth" way, the way of encounter with ordinary life, as opposed to the other ways of the yogi, monk, or fakir. The way was symbolized by the enneagram, a nine-pointed design in a circle.

Two years after the opening of the Institute, Gurdjieff toured America with his students, presenting demonstrations of the movements. He found a ready audience among people who had read Ouspensky's book, *Tertium Organum* (1920), and/or who had been influenced by Orage. The genesis of his American following dates from this trip. Gurdjieff closed the Institute in 1933, but continued to teach and to write for the rest of his life. Most of his writings were circulated privately to his students. Only one book, *The Herald of Coming God*, was published before his death. His writings include *Beelzebub's Tales to His Grandson* and *Meetings with Remarkable Men* (which was made into a film in 1979 by Peter Brook).

During his last days, Gurdjieff spent much time with long-time pupil Jeanne de Salzmann, who following Gurdjieff's death founded the Gurdjieff Foundation in Paris. This became the model for similar structures around the world. Instrumental in the spreading of the work in the United States was John Pentland (1907–1984), who had studied with both P. D. Ouspensky and Madame Ouspensky in the 1930s and 1940s. Pentland became the president of the Gurdjieff Foundation established in New York in 1953 and assisted in bringing forth the English-language editions of Gurdjieff's and Ouspensky's writings. He collaborated in establishing Gurdjieff societies in major metropolitan areas in the United States and in 1955 founded the Gurdjieff Foundation of California, of which he was president until his death.

Membership: Not reported. The Foundation has centers in New York, San Francisco, Los Angeles, and most major cities.

Sources:

Gurdjieff Foundation. www.gurdjieff.org/foundation.htm.

Driscoll, J. Walter. *Gurdjieff: An Annotated Bibliography*. New York: Garland Publishing, 1985.

Gurdjieff, Georges I. *Beelzebub's Tales to His Grandson*. 3 vols. New York: E. P. Dutton, 1978.

————. *Life is Only Then, When "I Am."* New York: E. P. Dutton, 1982.

————. *Meetings with Remarkable Men*. New York: E. P. Dutton, 1963.

Ouspensky, P. D. *The Fourth Way*. New York: Alfred A. Knopf, 1957.

————. *A New Model of the Universe*. New York: Alfred A. Knopf, 1931.

Speeth, Kathleen Riordan. *The Gurdjieff Work*. Berkeley, CA: And/Or Press, 1976.

Speeth, Kathleen Riordan, and Ira Freidlander. *Gurdjieff, Seeker of Truth*. New York: Harper & Row, 1980.

Webb, James. *The Harmonious Circle*. New York: G. P. Putnam's Sons, 1980.

Institute for Religious Development

7 Chardavogne Rd., Warwick, NY 10990

Alternate Address: Occidental, CA.

Dr. Willem A. Nyland (1890–1975), a Dutch chemist and founding trustee of the Gurdjieff Foundation, left the foundation in 1960 to found his own group, the Institute for Religious Development. He had studied with Georgei Gurdjieff from 1924 to 1949 and with Gurdjieff's disciple, A. C. Orage. The group is headquartered in Warwick, New York, where meetings, movements, and work days are conducted. Dr. Nyland died in 1975, and his students now carry on his work. Emphasis is on the practical application of Gurdjieff's ideas.

Membership: Not reported. Affiliated groups can be found in New York City; Santa Fe, New Mexico; Tucson, Arizona; Seattle, Washington; Sebastopol, California; Boston, Massachussets; Austin, Texas; and Minneapolis, Minnesota. There are also groups in Australia.

Sources:

www.nyland.org

Gurdjieff. G. I. *Meetings with Remarkable Men*. New York: Akana/Penguin Books, 1991.

Nyland, Wilhem. *Firefly*. Warwick, NY: The Author, 1965.

Popoff, Irmis B. *Gurdjieff Group Work with Wilhem Nyland*. York Beach, ME: Samuel Weiser, 1983.

Institute for the Development of the Harmonious Human Being (IDHHB)

Box 370, Nevada City, CA 95959

In the early 1960s the Institute for the Development of the Harmonious Human Being (IDHHB) emerged to present the teachings of E. J. Gold. The teachings and practices, which have the theme of voluntary evolution as preparation for service to the Absolute, have been constantly refined and developed over the years through intensive research and work. Among the important, though by no means exclusive, sources that Gold drew upon have been the teachings of Georgei Gurdjieff. The hallmark of Gold's teachings, as presented in his numerous books, is the representation of the being or Essential Self as neither awake nor asleep, but identified, in ordinary life, with the body, emotions, and psyche—collectively termed "the machine," which is asleep. In relation to the Essential Self, the machine has a transformational function, but only if it is brought into an awakened state.

The awakened state can be brought about by practices and/or special living conditions within a lifestyle based upon the correct use of attention upon, and attitudes towards, the machine's psycho-physical activities. Long-term, gradual erosion—the wind-and-water method—are favored by Gold for achieving the awakening of the machine, activation of its transformational functions, and eventual transformation of the Essential Self in accordance with its true purpose. Gold has emphasized the discernment of the waking state, the use of indirect methods to overcome the fixed habits of the machine, and the individual's study of his/her "chronic," i.e., a defense mechanism against the waking state acquired by each person in early childhood. Over the years Gold's students have made a wide application of his teachings in such diverse fields as architecture, psychotherapy, early childhood education, and computer programming.

Membership: In 2001 IDHHB reported 750 members, 20 centers, and 50 ministers in the United States and 75 members, three centers, and three ministers in Canada. Other members were to be found in Australia, Great Britain, West Germany, Norway, Italy, Spain, and Switzerland, with centers in Spain, Italy, and Norway.

Periodicals: *Talk of the Month*.

Remarks: There has been much discussion concerning the relation of Gold and Gurdjieff. While there are obvious differences in their teachings, the inspiration of Gurdjieff is quite evident in Gold's choice of a name for his work, his use of the enneagram (a nine-pointed symbol used by Gurdjieff) in his institute's logo, and his picturing a Gurdjieff look-alike on the cover of several books (such as his *Secret Talks with Mr. G*). Without detracting from the originality of Gold's work and thought, his reliance, especially in his early years, on Gurdjieff is undeniable. During the 1980s, those influences other than Gurdjieff upon which Gold drew for his own teachings have become more evident in his writing and other work. This broader base is visible in both the new publications and revised editions of older books issued by the institute since 1985, in the wake of which Gold's pre-1985 writings have been somewhat discounted.

Sources:

Institute for the Development of the Harmonious Human Being, Inc. www.idhhb.org.

The Avatar's Handbook. Los Angeles: Institute for the Development of the Harmonious Human Being, n.d.

Christie, David, et al., eds. *The New American Book of the Dead*. Nevada City, CA: IDHHB Publishing, 1981.

The Gabriel Papers. Nevada City, CA: IDHHB, 1981.

Gold, E. J. *Autobiography of a Sufi*. Crestline, CA: IDHHB Publications, 1976.

———. *The Human Biological Machine as a Transformational Apparatus*. Nevada City, CA: Gateways/IDHHB Publishers, 1985.

———. *The Joy of Sacrifice: Secrets of the Sufi Way*. Nevada City, CA: IDHHB, 1978.

———. *Practical Work on Self*. Nevada City, CA: IDHHB Publishing, 1983.

———. *Shakti! The Spiritual Science of DNA*. Crestline, CA: Core Group Publications, 1973.

Secret Talks with Mr. G. Nevada City, CA: IDHHB Publishing, 1978.

Prosperos

PO Box 4969, Dept. E, Culver City, CA 90231

Closely paralleling the Gurdjieff movement is the Prosperos, founded in 1956 in Florida by Phez Kahlil and Thane Walker, its present leader. Walker, described by all who have met him as an awe-inspiring, charismatic person, is a former Marine and student of Georgei Gurdjieff. He has modeled himself on Gurdjieff, but has broadened his sources with material from Jung, Freud, modern psychological techniques, and the occult. The group was named after the magician in Shakespeare's *The Tempest*. It is described as a "Fourth Way" school.

The overarching reality for the Prosperos is the One Mind. Reality is experienced as one views from the perspectives of that One Mind. Both memory and the senses could be one vision, but via fourth way techniques, the self can be identified with the One. *Translation* is the name given that process. In Translation classes, the pupil is led through five steps: the statement of Being (What are the facts about reality?); Uncovering the Lie (the claims of the senses); Argument, or testing of the claims; Summing up Results; and Establishing the Absolute. Thane relies heavily on Gurdjieff's technique of disorientation of the pupil and the importance of the pupil-teacher relationship. He creates many kinds of experiences in various classes and intensive seminars. Pantomime, improvisation, body exercises, and singing are all used as aids.

The headquarters of the Prosperos, termed the Inner Space Center, houses Publishing Programs, which produces the monthly *Newsletter*, instructional materials, and Thane's book, *Not So Secret Doctrine*. Leadership is vested in Thane and the Mentors. The Mentors are drawn from the High Watch, an inner circle of advanced students who have completed three classes, submitted two theses, and delivered an oral dissertation. There is an annual Prosperos assembly. In the Midwest, Thane operates through the Institute of Advanced Thinking, headquartered in Cleveland, Ohio.

Membership: Not reported.

Educational Facilities:

Prosperos Seminary, El Monte, California.

Periodicals: *Prosperos Newsletter*.

Sources:

Prosperos. www.theprosperos.org.

Ritley, Mary. *Invitation to a Hungry Feast*. Santa Monica, CA: Prosperos Inner Space Center, 1970.

Subud

4101 Legation St. NW, Washington, DC 20015

Subud was founded by Muhammed Subuh Sumohadiwidjojo (1901–1987), an Indonesian. Acting on prophecy that he was to die in his 24th year, Muhammed Subuh had begun to search for spiritual guidance and had turned to many teachers. To a man, they told him that he was different, that they had nothing to teach him, and that his enlightenment would come directly from God. However, no enlightenment came until 1925, when one evening a ball of light descended upon him, entered through the crown of his head, and filled him with radiant light and vibrations. For the next three years, his body experienced spontaneous occurrences of *latihan*, a cleansing and purifying process. Finally, in 1933, his true mission was revealed to him, and he was soon contacted by others who had heard of him. Thus, Subud became a movement and was officially established in 1947.

"Bapak" (meaning "respected father") Subuh quit his job and devoted his life to the spread of the movement throughout Java. His work continued for 23 years. Some Europeans heard of his work and invited him to England in 1956. In England, Bapak soon gained a following, largely built upon former disciples of Gurdjieff. John Godolphin Bennett, the author of the widely read *Concerning Subud*, was particularly influential. Bennett, a well-known Gurdjieff disciple, had, in 1946, founded the Institute for the Comparative Study of History, Philosophy, and the Sciences at Coome Springs, England. The Institute became the initial center from which Subud spread in Europe and North America.

Subud is a contraction of three Sanskrit words: *Sulisa*, or right living in accordance with the will of God; *Budhi*, or the inner force residing in the nature of man himself; and *Dharma*, or surrender and submission to the power of God. The key to Subud is *latihan*, the process of surrendering to the power of God. It is an individual experience that is practiced in a group, two or three times per week. Applicants must go through several months of probation and establish their sincerity before commencing the *latihan*. The first *latihan* happens in the presence of several experienced members (helpers), who are viewed as channels allowing new members to be touched by a divine energy. It is believed by Subud that the power originally given directly to Bapak is transmitted by contact with a person in whom it is already established.

During the *latihan*, the mind and emotions are quieted, allowing the divine force to enter and do its work. During this time, males and females are in separate, darkened rooms. Various body movements and vocal manifestations often occur, and help lead each participant to a deeper understanding of their true inner nature. These phenomena result from the voluntary surrender of the self to the power. People report experiencing states of unconditional love, freedom, and higher levels of consciousness during this time. Healings have also been reported.

After coming to England, Subud spread rapidly. The healing of Eva Bartok in 1957 was a major catalyst of its spread. In 1958, Bapak was invited by John Cooke to the United States, where Subud was soon established and spread rapidly. Though Bapak himself was a Muslim, he asserted that the *latihan* was available to any person wishing to practice it, regardless of faith, nationality, or background, and was not in conflict with the essence of all religions.

In 2008 there were 430 Subud groups in 53 countries. These groups are members of the World Subud Association (WSA), a nonprofit organization registered in Washington, D.C. Subud's structure is democratic, and serves to support members in their practice of the *latihan* and in their various endeavors. A world congress, held every four years, brings together members from around the globe. The WSA has two affiliate associations, Subud International Cultural Association (SICA) and Susuka Dharma International Association (SDIA). SDIA supports social and humanitarian activities, including health services, education, development projects benefiting women and children, and community development. It maintains consultative status with the United Nations Economic and Social Council (ECOSOC) and the U.N. Children's Fund (UNESCO).

Membership: There are 10,000 to 12,000 members worldwide.

Remarks: Some difficulty in studying Subud has arisen due to the fact that *latihan* is an experience that is hard to convey in words. Talks given by Bapak Subuh and his daughter, Ibu Rahayu Wiryohudoyo, are published only for members, but a number of books by Subud authors are available for researchers and the general public.

Sources:

Subud. www.subud.org.

Bartok, Eva. *Worth Living For*. New York: University Books, 1959.

Bennett, John G. *Concerning Subud*. New York: University Books, 1959.

Bright-Paul, Anthony. *Stairway to Subud*. New York: Dharma Book Company, 1965.

Longcroft, Harlinah. *Subud Is a Way of Life*. Subdud Publications International, 1990.

Muhammad-Subuh Sumohadiwidjojo. *Susila Budhi Dharma*. Subud Publications International, 1975.

Rofe, Husein. *The Path of Subud*. London: Rider & Company, 1959.

Vittachi, Varindra Tarzie. *A Reporter in Subud*. Subud Publications International, 1996.

Tayu Meditation Center

Box 11554, Santa Rosa, CA 95406

Tayu Meditation Center is a "Fourth Way" spiritual school founded in 1976 by Robert Daniel Ennis. The Fourth Way is the name given to a system of spiritual development expounded by Georgei Gurdjieff that is seen as an alternative to the three other major forms of spiritual life, those of the yogi, monk, and fakir. The name also refers to the claim that, unlike other spiritual traditions that engage only one center of the human organism at a time, the Fourth Way addresses all three simultaneously. More intense in the beginning, it is seen as ultimately more efficient, and is often called the "sly Way."

The primary Tayu practice is a special form of meditation called *Self-observation*, designed to accommodate those born in Western culture. It focuses the awareness in turn on each of the three major centers of the human organism—the motor/instinctive, the emotional, and the intellectual. According to Ennis, when sincerely engaged in, Self-observation reveals the true nature and inner workings of the human organism, and opens the way to full and continuous access to True Mind.

Ennis has been recognized as an accomplished spiritual teacher by contemporaries such as Lee Lozowick, E. J. Gold, and Robert DeRopp. He arrived at his level of adeptship on July 4, 1976, having attained the degree of "Reason of the sacred termoonald." His teaching style has been described as "powerful yet intense, disconcerting for those with preconceptions," and especially aimed at Westerners. The teaching center is located on a small farm in Sonoma County, California.

Membership: The center is a small group, as Ennis has refused to work with more than a few select students who agree to work at their spiritual development on a level that is more intensive than usual.

Periodicals: *The Way Fourth: The Journal of Tayu*.

Other Theosophical Groups

Agni Yoga Society

319 W 107th St., New York, NY 10025

The Agni Yoga Society was founded in the mid-1920s by Nicholas Roerich (1874–1947), an artist, and his wife, Helena Roerich (1879–1955). In Europe at the time of the Russian Revolution (1917) and unable to return, they came to the United States in 1920 at the invitation of the Art Institute of Chicago. Early in their new life in the West, the Roerichs joined the Theosophical Society, and Helena translated Helena Petrovna Blavatsky's major work, *The Secret Doctrine*, into Russian. She also began to receive regular communications from one of the masters originally contacted by Blavatsky, the Master Morya. Her first book, received from him, was *The Leaves of M's Garden*, published in 1924. The Agni Yoga Society began as an informal study group devoted to this book, which, together with subsequent volumes, became the prime teaching materials of the society. Prior to founding the society, in 1921 Nicholas founded the Master Institute of United Arts, which later became the Nicholas Roerich Museum. In his endeavors he strove to embody his ideal of art as a unifying force for humanity.

The Roerichs settled permanently in India, in the Punjab, in 1929. Helena produced thirteen volumes of material from the Master Morya. Nicholas also wrote numerous books on art, peace, and spirituality, his continuing concerns. The building in New York City purchased for the Nicholas Roerich Museum also houses the Agni Yoga Society. Membership in the society is open after some study of the books. Study groups meet at various locations around the country. The society offers free downloads of the teaching texts at its Web site, www.agniyoga.org.

Membership: In 2008 the society reported a membership of approximately 600.

Sources:

Agni Yoga Society. www.agniyoga.org/.

Balyoz, Harold. *Three Remarkable Women*. Flagstaff, AZ: Altai Publishers, 1986.

Letters of Helena Roerich, 1929-1938. 2 vols. New York: Agni Yoga Society, 1954.

Nicholas Roerich. New York: Nicholas Roerich Museum, 1974.

Paelian, Garabed. *Nicholas Roerich*. Agoura, CA: Aquarian Educational Group, 1974.

Roerich, Nicholas. *Realm of Light*. New York: Roerich Museum Press, 1931.

Amica Temple of Radiance

763 S 53rd St., Tacoma, WA 98408

The Amica Temple of Radiance dates to the early 1930s and the experience of Ivah Bergh Whitten. As a young girl stricken with an incurable disease, Whitten was cured through "color awareness" and began to explore and teach on its potentials. The initial course was published in 1932. Among Whitten's students were Roland Hunt and Dorothy Bailey, who established the Amica Temple in Los Angeles in 1959. While in England in 1952, Hunt had described to him inwardly two strangers with whom he would become associated upon his return to the United States. The two, Paola Hugh and John Hugh, were, with Hunt, taken under the guidance of an elder brother of the inner wisdom schools and joined in the formation of Amica. In 1971 an affiliate organization, the Fleur de Lys Foundation of East Sound, Washington, was founded. It is seen as a reflection of an inner order of illumined ones who are seeking the victory of man's higher self over his ego.

The Amica Temple is a continuation and expansion of the color awareness teachings. As man has evolved, he has become aware of the various aspects of God—the Father principle, the Son, the Holy Ghost—and, in this new era, of the Spirit made manifest in seven colors. Each color, or ray, as taught by the Theosophical Society, rules an aspect of existence and is in turn ruled by a master. By understanding which ray you were born under, you can discover your proper work and place in life. Each ray also has a healing potential. Overriding the seven rays is the white ray, which shines directly from the Logos. The Amica Temple continues as a structure to present Hunt's teachings to the world. Lessons are offered in color awareness to students around the country. Amica's last reported leader was Paola Hugh.

Membership: Not reported.

Sources:

Bailey, Dorothy A. *The Light of Ivah Bergh Whitten*. Southampton, U.K.: A.M.I.C.A., n.d.

Hugh, Paola. *I Will Arise*. 2 vols. Tacoma, WA: Amica Temple of Radiance, 1972.

Hunt, Roland T. *Fragrant and Radiant Healing Symphony*. Ashingdon, Essex, U.K.: C. W. Daniel Company, 1949.

————. *Man Made Clear for the Nu Clear Age*. Lakemont, GA: CSA Press, 1969.

————. *The Seven Rays to Colour Healing*. Ashingdon, Essex, U.K.: C. W. Daniel Company, 1954.

Whitten, Ivah Bergh. *The Initial Course in Colour Awareness*. London: Amica, n.d.

Ann Ree Colton Foundation of Niscience, Inc.

PO Box 2057, 336 W Colorado St., Glendale, CA 91209

The Ann Ree Colton Foundation was formed in 1953 in Glendale, California, by Ann Ree Colton (1898–1984) and her husband, Jonathan Murro (1927–1991), for the purpose of preserving and distributing the Niscience teachings as well as establishing devotional chapels and research units. A nonprofit religious and educational foundation, the foundation is supported by offerings, tithes, and gifts from members and friends.

Clairvoyant from childhood, Colton was in her twenties when she began to contact the Masters or Great Immortals. In 1932 she began her public ministry and became well known as a prophet, counselor, teacher, healer, and author, penning 23 books on spiritual subjects. A church was formed in 1936 in Florida and continued for nine years. In 1952 she met Murro, and together they established the foundation blending concerns of religion, philosophy, science, and the creative arts.

Murro was the author of nine books and numerous lectures on spiritual subjects. After Colton's death in 1984, Murro served as administrator of the foundation until his own death. In 2008 the administrator was Enys Miller.

According to Colton, the Masters will no longer incarnate. The 33 cosmos disciples scattered throughout the world are telepathically aligned to the higher worlds. They work with 13 telepathic disciples, all of whom are advanced in the sciences or humanities; their spiritual work is unknown to their colleagues. When a cosmos disciple leaves the physical world, a telepathic disciple replaces him, and an advanced student becomes a telepathic disciple. Beyond the disciples, in the second heaven, in the spheres of light, dwell the masters. In the third heaven dwell the archangels, Jesus and his disciples, and the archetype of God, the very blueprints for the creation of the earth. Through the archangels under the Christ, God initiates the archetypes and initiates the new in creation. The time when men are open to the third heaven of the archangels and the archetypes is a time of receiving the Holy Spirit.

Niscience, which means "knowing," is described by the foundation as an initiatory school as well as a deeply spiritual system of study, worship, creativity, research, healing, and teaching based on the teachings of Jesus, the Bible, and other sacred scriptures of the East and West. Niscience blends religion, philosophy, science, and the creative arts, inspiring its members to live creative, spiritual lives in service to God. Dreams, reincarnation, the kundalini and chakra system, archetypes, the genesis story, angels, ESP, and the afterlife are among the many topics discussed in the foundation's books, lessons, and classes.

Weekly unit meetings and worship services provide the opportunity for shared worship and meditation, participation in the healing ministry, and training in the art of creative logos or speaking, as well as research into a vast array of spiritual subjects that are of interest to the spiritual seeker. Home-study materials, including those called white paper lessons, introduce students to spiritual exercises and healing techniques of Niscience. Books, videos, and DVDs are available for purchase on the Web site. The Foundation believes that an organized rhythm in meditation, prayer, and spiritual practice during different periods of the day provides a disciplined life. Annual conclaves are held at various locations throughout the year.

Membership: In 2008 the foundation reported 160 members and 12 ministers.

Periodicals: *Agape*.

Sources:

Ann Ree Colton Foundation of Niscience, Inc. www.niscience.org/.

Colton, Ann Ree. *Men in White Apparel*. Glendale, CA: ARC Publishing Company, 1961.

Colton, Ann Ree. *The Soul and the Ethic*. Glendale, CA: ARC Publishing Company, 1963.

Colton, Ann Ree. *Vision for the Future*. Glendale, CA: ARC Publishing Company, 1960.

Colton, Ann Ree, and Jonathan Murro. *Prophet for the Archangels*. Glendale, CA: ARC Publishing Company, 1964.

Murro, Jonathan. *God-Realization Journal*. Glendale, CA: ARC Publishing Company, 1975.

Christward Ministry

20560 Questhaven Rd., Escondido, CA 92029-4810

The Christward Ministry, a Christian retreat, was founded by Flower A. Newhouse (d. 1994), a clairvoyant and teacher of Christian Mysticism beginning in the 1920s. The ministry's headquarters are at Questhaven Retreat, founded in 1940, a 640-acre nature reserve and spiritual retreat in northern San Diego County near Escondido, California. The Christward Ministry utilizes the principles of Christian gospel, meditation, reincarnation, astrology, and Carl Jung's transformational psychology. The emphasis is on meditation's helpfulness with practical living, as well as awareness of angelic influence on spiritual development.

Man is considered an embodied soul evolving spiritually through a series of human incarnations, eventually rising to masterhood and beyond. The number of masters at any given time is considered to be small; incarnated Masters are anonymous, private individuals who avoid fame or worldly power. Newhouse wrote a number of works describing angelic hosts and their hierarchies; angels are unrelated in evolution to humans, but certain hosts interact with humans and help in our spiritual guidance, such as guardian angels, nature angels, religious angels, and karmic angels.

After Newhouse's death, a staff of ordained ministers continued to provide a program of weekly Sunday worship services held in the Church of the Holy Quest, evening classes, and triannual weekend retreats. The three-day retreats are conducted during Christmas, Easter, Michaelmas, and the summer equinox. Ministry services are available for weddings, christenings, and memorials. In 2008 the retreat director was Rev. Blake Isaac.

Most of Newhouse's books were published by the Christward Ministry and include titles on religion, prayer, meditation, and esoteric knowledge. Her works have been published in English, German, and Czech.

Membership: Not applicable.

Educational Facilities:

Questhaven Academy, Escondido, California.

Periodicals: *Life at Quest Haven.*

Sources:

Questhaven Retreat: Home of the Christward Ministry. www.questhaven.org/.

The Christward Ministry. Vista, CA: Christward Ministry, 1947.

Isaac, Stephen. *The Way of Discipleship to Christ.* Escondido, CA: Christward Ministry, 1976.

Newhouse, Flower A. *The Christward Way.* 4 vols. (lessons 1–208). Vista, CA: Christward Publications, n.d.

———. *The Meaning and Value of the Sacraments.* Escondido, CA: Christward Ministry, 1971.

Church of Cosmic Origin and School of Thought

Box 257, June Lake, CA 93529

The Church of Cosmic Origin was founded in 1963 at Independence, California, by Hope Troxell (1906–1989), who had for 30 years been lecturer on "expanded concepts." In her early life she had received three major healings from the angelic host, and during the 1950s she had received instructions from the masters and published several books of their material. *From Matter to Light* contains messages from several different masters, including Djual Khool, Alcyon, Univera of Jupiter, Melchizedek, and Nerfertiti. *The Mohada Teachings from the Galaxies* contains a series of messages from Mohada, a particularly significant master for Troxell.

The year after Troxell's death, the church and school were closed and its assets turned over to the Library of the New Essences of Inyo in June Lake, California. The library continues to sell Troxell's books.

The church teaches what is termed "cosmic Christianity." Man is considered an evolving being whose purpose is to become one with light and escape the contin-

ual reincarnation and involvement in matter. Man originally fell from grace into matter after his creation by the Elohim, the family of God. Jesus came from the Elohim, is now a master, and is due to return for judgment and to lift those who have followed the God-Way. In the coming age, the United States will lead the world in the spiritual plane of God's laws, according to the Church of Cosmic Origin.

The cosmic wisdom given by Jesus and the masters illumines the Bible. The Church of Cosmic Origin also use the writings from Qumran and models itself upon the resident community of the Essenes. The symbol of the church is the Greek cross in a circle with a rose on it, symbolizing the risen Christ. The masters gave the format for the church services, which is, as in the original Christian church, the circle: The directors of the church are in the center, with members, students and visitors around them. Services include Scripture readings, readings from the masters, and a sermon as received by Troxell (without a trance-state). There are no ministers.

The church and school are headquartered at June Lake, California. Because the main work is the preparation of teachers, the number of residents at the school is very small. An adult community participates in daily classes for both advanced and beginning studies. Twice a day prayer circles are held; church services are each Sunday. The bulk of students are those taking correspondence lessons across the United States and in several other English-speaking countries.

Membership: Not reported.

Periodicals: *Cosmic Frontiers.*

Sources:

Troxell, Hope. *From Matter to Light.* June Lake, CA: School of Thought, 1968.

———. *The Mohada Teachings.* Independence, CA: School of Thought, [1963].

———. *Through the Open Key.* El Monte, CA: Understanding Publishing, n.d.

Ecumenical Ministry of the Unity of All Religions

107 N Ventura St., Ojai, CA 93023

Philippine educator Benito F. Reyes, former president of the University of the City of Manila, migrated to the United States in the early 1970s with a vision for a new kind of university that, in its program, would be truly worldwide in its outlook. In 1974 he founded the World Institute of Avasthology, which was soon renamed the World University of America. Reyes developed a philosophy that he called *avasthology,* or the science of total consciousness. Avasthology symbolized the joining of eastern and western civilizations, and the integration of inner- and outer-consciousness. Avasthology became the main philosophy of the university that was opened in Ojai, California.

The university offers degree programs in philosophy, psychology, and religious studies, as well as vocational certificates in meditation, astrology, spiritual ministry, thanatology, and yoga. Its curriculum offers a full round of classes in transpersonal psychology and subjects related to altered states of consciousness (such as dreams and meditation). The philosophy of the school emphasizes the allness of God and humanity's oneness with God; thanatology, the holistic approach to death; and altered states of consciousness experienced through meditation.

The Spiritual Ministry Program at the university has a six-part online program that prepares students to serve as laypersons or ordained ministers in interfaith ministries such as the Ecumenical Ministry of the Unity of All Religions, which is affiliated with the university.

The Ecumenical Ministry of the Unity of All Religions is located adjacent to the university and connected to it through the leadership of Dr. Reyes and his wife, Dominga L. Reyes. Its beliefs are consistent with the avasthology philosophy of the school. Reyes believes that love is the essence of all religion. Love is defined as the primal urge to resume the state of oneness with God and all of life. Weekly worship follows a liturgy with acknowledgement of the spiritual teachers of the ages, including Sathya Sai Baba of India, and Baha'u'llah of the Baha'i movement. In 2008 the ministry's presiding minister was Adita Casimiro.

Membership: In 2008 the ministry reported one congregation with 35 to 50 members. There are 10 members in Canada.

Educational Facilities:

World University of America, Ojai, California.

Parsophia Academy, Kobe, Japan.

Periodicals: *Avasthology.* • *Clear Light WWW.*

Sources:

World University in Ojai. www.worldu.edu.

Reyes, Benito F. *Christianizing Christians*. Ojai, CA: Author, n.d.

———. *The Essence of All Religion*. Ojai, CA: Author, 1983.

———. *On World Peace*. Ojai, CA: World University, 1977.

Reyes, Domingo L. *The Story of Two Souls*. Ojai, CA: Author, 1984.

Esoteric Interfaith Church

7257 NW 4th Blvd., #78, Gainesville, FL 32607

The Esoteric Interfaith Church, Inc., formerly the Esoteric Mystery School, was founded in the mid-1980s. It is an occult organization built around a set of orders that encompass the various teachings of Indo-European and Mediterranean esoteric traditions. Students will, however, find course materials infused with insights from Hindu, Tibetan Buddhist, and Taoist lineages, various pre-modern traditions (shamanism, Celtic, Teutonic, and Native American), and modern esoteric teachings as found in, for example, Jungian thought. The Esoteric Interfaith Church was founded and is currently led by Dr. Katia Romanoff, a parapsychologist and holistic counselor. Romanoff received her doctorate from American International University, and also now serves as the Dean of Studies of the Dream Interpretation Institute in Nevada (which she co-founded).

The Esoteric Interfaith Church believes that "spiritual liberation, wisdom, enlightenment of the soul, mind and spirit, are also goals of the believer." The Church believes that esoteric Christianity offers the individual a way to the ultimate knowledge of self; a resolution of faith; and esotericism offers an outlook that can revitalize the tradition and go beyond difficulties. The Church also believes the Bible can be read on different levels.

The image of an eye in a flaming heart is used by the Church. The Church believes "the awakened heart is not enough. Awakening intelligence is also needed."

The Esoteric Interfaith Church is centered on the eight orders in which a person may pursue their appropriation of esoteric truth relative to various spiritual traditions. They are the Order of Mary Magdalene (Christian), the Order of the New Knights Templar, the Daughters of Tsion (that work in tandem with the Knights Templar), the Order of Melchizedek, the Order of the Northern Way (Celtic, Teutonic), the Third Millennium Angelic Alliance, the Order of the Blessed Mother, and the Eternal Order of the Magi. The leaders of the Church claim to be in contact with the Guardians and Guides, pre-eternatural beings who stand behind each order.

After an individual identifies with a particular order, the church sends lessons that lead the person through levels marked by their own self-initiation. As they master the material, they are acknowledged as a catechumen, initiate, practitioner, adept, and mage. While the course is designed to be mastered in approximately four years, each person may go through it at his/her own pace. The church covers not only traditional material, but new findings from recent discoveries of lost texts and from modern science.

The Esoteric Interfaith Church is described as "a non-profit and non-denominational church that accepts, acknowledges, and respects all Faiths of the world that are dedicated to the service of the Divine." The Church describes itself as an "alternative Christian, semi-Gnostic, esoteric, and multi-faith congregation." Through the Esoteric Theological Seminary, established in 1987, members may take instruction to be ordained ministers, and work toward religious doctorate degrees, such as

Doctor of Divinity and Doctor of Theology. A PhD program in Metaphysics and Religious Studies is also offered. The Esoteric Mystery School is an online correspondence program for esoteric study. Lessons are provided through email and website pages.

Prospective ministers may submit an application to the church, including a one-page biography of their spiritual history and a small fee. Ministers may be designated as either an Interfaith Minister, Esoteric Minister, Spiritual Minister, or Psychic Minister. Ordained ministers may also seek a charter from the church if they wish to organize congregations. Those wishing to receive a doctorate degree must write a 2,000-word thesis on a selected topic and write a one- to three-page spiritual autobiography.

Membership: 5,000 members were reported for 2008.

Educational Facilities:

Esoteric Theological Seminary; Esoteric Mystery School, Gainesville, Florida.

Sources:

Esoteric Theological Seminary. Available from http//:www.NorthernWay.org.

Esoteric Interfaith Church. Available from http//:www.EsotericChurch.org

Fraternite Blanche Universelle (FBU–USA)

PO Box 932, Locust Valley, NY 11560

Alternate Address: International Headquarters: Izgrev, 2 Rue du Belvedere de la Ronce, 92310, Sèvres, France.

Fraternite Blanche Universelle (formerly listed as Universal White Brotherhood, the name having been changed back legally to the original French) reflects upon the material level of what is believed to be an actual fraternity of highly evolved spiritual beings who exist on a higher plane. The earthly counterpart of the brotherhood was reestablished in 1900 in Bulgaria by Peter Deunov (d. 1944).

Sensing that political developments meant his movement would have to go underground, in 1937 Deunov sent his follower, the Bulgarian-born Omraam Mikhael Aivanhov (1900–1986), to France to carry on with the teaching, known as initiatic science. Upon Deunov's death, Aivanhov succeeded him as master.

The FBU does not consider itself a religious sect, but rather an esoteric school encompassing the teachings of Jesus, spiritual alchemy, astrology, and the Kabbalah. Master Aivanhov was a firm promoter of galvanoplasty, a concept of educating children before they are born whereby mothers and fathers work with love and godly thoughts before, during, and after conception. According to Aivanhov, the meaning of life is to "know thyself," to have one's human self unite with one's divine self. The aim of all the great masters throughout civilization is to bring the kingdom of God down to earth. Many of the keys to the problems of existence are explained in this teaching. Aivanhov often remarked, quoting Hermes Mercurious Trismegistus, "As above, so below." His central theme was humanity's quest for perfection.

The master states that according to ancient wisdom, Melchizedek, king of righteousness and high priest of the divine world, initiated Abraham into the knowledge of God and his heavenly kingdom. These ancient teachings became a spiritual tradition now known as Kabbalah. In order to comprehend and navigate what the journey of the soul is all about, a road map is required. This road map is called the Tree of Life.

FBU is a school of higher learning and a nonprofit organization dedicated to spiritual evolution and the healing process of the soul. Like art and music, FBU is universal. Its mission is to touch the minds, hearts, and souls of people from all countries and all walks of life. It is not a religion, but rather a philosophy of self-improvement that teaches an understanding of the relationship between God, archangels, angels, nature, and humanity. Some of the topics offered through FBU-USA include astrology, numerology, art, music, drama, tarot, alchemy, aura, and color theory

Fraternite Blanche Universelle was brought to the United States after the first English translation of Aivanhov's work in the early 1970s. Aivanhov visited the United States in 1983. He gave more than 5,000 lectures during his lifetime, many of which are available in 27 languages through FBU's publisher, Editions Prosveta.

Membership: In 2008 FBU reported more than 500,000 global members, with 25 congregations worldwide. There is affiliated work in 29 countries. In 2008 Anna Laruccia was president, Bruno Dayrell was vice president, and Barbara E. Keller was general secretary.

Periodicals: *Circle of Light*. Send orders to Box 49614, Los Angeles, CA 90049.

Sources:

Fraternite Blanche Universelle. www.fbu-usa.com.

Aivanhov, Omraam Mikhael. *Life*. Frejus, France: Editions Prosveta, 1978.

Feuerstein, Georg. *Love and Sexuality*. Frejus, France: Editions Prosveta, 1976.

————. *The Mystery of Light: The Life and Teaching of Omraam Mikhael Aivanhov*. Salt Lake City, UT: Passage Press, 1992.

————. *The Universal White Brotherhood Is Not a Sect*. Frus, France: Editions Prosveta, 1982.

Lejbowicz, Agnes. *Omraam Michael Aivanov, Master of the Great White Brotherhood*. Frejus, France: Editions Prosveta, 1982.

Renard, Pierre. *The Solar Revolution and the Prophet*. Frejus, France: Editions Prosveta, 1980.

Who Is the Master Omraam Michael Aivanhov? Frejus, France: Editions Prosveta, 1982.

Institute of Divine Metaphysical Research

International Headquarters, PO Box 19877, Los Angeles, CA 90019

The Institute for Divine Metaphysical Research grew out of a vision of Dr. Henry Clifford Kinley that occurred on June 6, 1931, in Springfield, Ohio. Kinley, a Holiness church minister, received a vision of Yahweh and His plan for the ages. He began to give classes on the insight derived from the vision the following year, and soon thereafter he founded the Kinley Institute. Among his first students was Carl F. Gross, who became his lifelong associate and president of the institute. In 1958, with approximately 70 of his students, Kinley moved to Los Angeles and incorporated the Institute for Divine Metaphysical Research. In 1961 he published *Elohim the Archetype (Original) Pattern of the Universe*, his major exposition of the vision. Copies were immediately sent to a number of prominent world political and religious leaders. In 1971 12 ministers of the institute were sent out on an Ecclesiastical Peace Mission to countries in Europe and the Middle East. A second mission, to countries on every continent, was conducted in 1975.

The intent of the institute has been to spread the message of Kinley's vision as presented in his book. The teachings draw from a variety of sources, including the Sacred Name movement and theosophy. In the vision Kinley learned the real name of the Holy One of Israel—Yahweh—and his nature and purposes. Yahweh is Spirit Substance, without form. As Elohim, Yahweh appears in His super incoporeal form, and in that form was seen by Moses (Ex. 24), Isaiah (Isa. 6:1–4), and the disciples at the Mount of Transfiguration (Matt. 17:1–2). Yahweh-Elohim also has taken physical form, generally as the material creation (matter is condensed spirit) and specifically as Yahshua the Messiah (generally known as Jesus). After the death and resurrection of Yahshua, Yahweh continued in his physical form as the Comforter or Holy Spirit, and dwells in preachers of the true gospel.

Yahweh-Elohim, as revealed to Kinley, is the archtypal pattern of the universe, a pattern revealed to Moses and embodied in the Hebrew tabernacle. It is, however, also repeated in numerous earthly structures, among which is the Kaballah, which Kinley terms "theosophy."

Yahweh's purpose is revealed through the ages (i.e., particular periods of history) and dispensations (i.e., the divinely appointed ordering of earthly affairs by Yahweh). The dispensations as recounted by Kinley generally follow what was pro-

posed by C. I. Scofield in his reference Bible, and adopt a traditional chronology. The first dispensation begins with Yahweh's covenant with Adam, the second with Noah, the third with Abraham, and the fourth with Noah. Kinley is insistent that the fifth dispensation, that of the "law of the Spirit" or New Testament, this present church age, began not at Jesus' birth but at his resurrection and Pentecost. Most importantly, the present dispensation is swiftly drawing to a close, and the next dispensation, that of the Kingdom in Immortality, will begin around the year 2000. The revelation of Yahweh's purposes to Kinley and his work of spreading the information ushered in the last days of the church age.

Membership: In 1997 the institute reported 137 groups in the United States and four in Canada. There were also a single group in Trinidad, two in Mexico, and one in Africa.

Remarks: The institute has published a statement of aims that seems to draw directly upon the statement of objectives of the Theosophical Society. It reads, in part, that its aims include: "To form a nucleus of Universal Brotherhood of Humanity in Yahshua the Messiah without distinction of Race or Nationality, Creed, Sex, Caste or Color; To investigate the unexplained Spirit Law or so-called Law of Nature and the Powers latent in man; [and] To encourage and promote the study of Scriptures, comparative Religions, Psychology, Philosophy and Modern (practical and occult) Science."

Sources:

Institute of Divine Metaphysical Research. www.idmr.net.

Kinley, Henry Clifford. *Elohim the Atcheype (Original) Pattern of the Universe*. Los Angeles, CA: Institute of Divine Metaphysical Research, 1969.

Light of Christ Community Church

c/o Sparrow Hawk Village, 11 Summit Ridge Dr., Tahlequah, OK 74464-9215

The Light of Christ Community Church grew out of the 1958 near-death experience of its founder, Carol E. Parrish-Harra (b. 1935). While giving birth to her sixth child, she was given sodium pentothal to ease her pain. She had an allergic reaction to the drug, her lung collapsed, and her consciousness slipped out of her body. As a result of the experience, her life changed. She came to believe that she was an example of what in New Age circles came to be called a "walk-in." As defined by Ruth Montgomery, who originated the idea, a walk-in is an idealistic soul who, through progress in previous incarnations, has earned the privilege of taking over unwanted bodies. Parrish-Harra believes that the personality who had inhabited her body left in 1958 and a new soul moved in.

In the 1960s Parrish-Harra's life took a new direction. Toward the end of the decade she was led to a spiritualist church in St. Petersburg, Florida, where she met a teacher, Ann Manser. In 1971 she was ordained in the Christian Metaphysical Church and began a career as a pastor/teacher. In 1976 she founded the Villa Serena Spiritual Community in Sarasota, Florida, the core community of the Light of Christ Community Church.

In 1981 Parrish-Harra had a strong psychic message to found a new community, and in November of that year the trustees of the Light of Christ Community Church acquired 332 acres of land on Sparrowhawk Mountain near Tahlequah, Oklahoma. Sparrow Hawk Village became the new headquarters of the church and of its school, the Sancta Sophia Seminary. Sparrow Hawk was designed as a self-consciously New Age center that seeks to encourage the growth, freedom, and strength of its members. It is organized in clusters (tribes) in such a way that the community provides a balance between intimacy/community (smallness) and security (largeness). Each family owns its own home and shares a portion of the entire community's property.

The church's teachings are eclectic, drawing upon theosophy (especially the writings of Alice Bailey), Agni Yoga, the Kabbalah, and esoteric Christianity. It affirms the existence of One Almighty Power in the universe, the cause of all creation, and the Great Ones (called masters in theosophy) who guide humanity and can be thought of as the saviors of the world. Christ is seen as the vision of perfection, and his teachings are the path to perfection. The church believes that within each human is a spark of the Almighty Power, and each person is capable of unfolding his or her spiritual potential.

The Light of Christ Community Church is headed by a board of trustees. In 2008 Parrish-Harra served as presding president, and the copastors were Rev. Retha Banez and Rev. Robert Willson. The Sancta Sophia Seminary offers a full program of ministerial training, offering both master's and doctoral degrees. The church recognizes five forms of ministry: pastor, minister-scholar, minister-priest, theologian, and prophet-seer. The church affirms its allegiance to the Christian tradition and has affiliated with the International Council of Community Churches.

Membership: In 2008 the community reported 100 people living in Sparrow Hawk Village and 400 members of LCCC.

Educational Facilities:

Sancta Sophia Seminary, Tahlequah, Oklahoma.

Periodicals: *Sparrow Hawk Villager.*

Sources:

Light of Christ Community Church. www.lightofchristchurch.info.

Parrish-Harra, Carol W. *Aquarian Rosary: Reviving the Art of Mantra Yoga.* Tahlequah, OK: Sparrow Hawk Press, 1988.

———. *The Book of Rituals: Personal and Planetary Transformations.* Santa Monica, CA: IBS Press, 1990.

———. *Messengers of Hope.* Black Mountain, NC: New Age Press, 1983.

———. *A New Age Handbook on Death and Dying.* Marina del Rey, CA: De-Vorss and Company, 1982.

Order of the Cross

10 De Vere Gardens, London, W8 5AE England

Alternate Address: **PO Box 2472, La Grange, IL 60525**

The Order of the Cross was founded in 1904 in Great Britain by J. Todd Ferrier (1855–1943). Ferrier had been raised in Scotland and entered the Congregational Church ministry. He resigned from the ministry in 1903 and the following year began issuing a magazine, *The Herald of the Cross.* During the next decade he wrote his two most important books, *The Master: His Life and Teachings* (1913) and *The Logia, or Sayings of the Master.* Following their publication, the Order of the Cross began to grow, and in 1919 headquarters were established in London. Permanent headquarters were purchased in 1926.

Ferrier taught a form of Christian theosophy. The order believes that the earth has been subject to a gradual deterioration over many millennia. This deterioration is visible in the disorder in nature and society and is related to the fading of the divine light in human life. It was to check the deterioration that Jesus came into the world, and his mission is now beginning to bear fruit. The effects of His restoration of the light has become visible, and should become even more visible as more rapid changes occur. Individuals who participate in this restoration will recover a sense of purpose and the ability to communicate with the unseen.

Having perceived the nature of Jesus' work, to restore the resurrected spiritual life to humanity, Ferrier was able to clearly present in his many books the true message of Jesus apart from the distortion of the Christian church. In this light, the order assumed an anti-institutional stance, and teaches that Jesus did not intend the creation of an earthly institution, but instead focused on the restoration of souls to a spiritual state, which he termed "Jesushood," in which the oneness of life in realized. That state is followed by the state of "Christhood," or mystical illumination.

Ferrier's own awakening, like those of a number of his early followers, was through the animal rights movement. The order is vegetarian in practice and committed to antivivisection. It has called for the adoption of a "bloodless" diet. Members are also taught to seek after the Christ-life by following a path of self-denial, self-sacrifice, and self-abandonment to the divine service and will.

The order is organized through a number of groups around the world. Where several groups are relatively close together, they are associated in councils made up of representatives of the groups. The order is guided by a self-perpetuating executive council and an advisory committee of representatives of the groups.

The order was brought to the United States through the circulation of Ferrier's many books. Ferrier made his first U.S. trip in 1939, and groups have been functioning around the country since that time. Among his early followers were J. F. Rowney, the owner of a metaphysical publishing house in Santa Barbara, California, who later published the only biographical work on Ferrier.

Regular meetings are held at the London headquarters and in discussion groups in the United Kingdom, North America, Australia, France, and New Zealand.

Membership: In 2008 350 members were reported worldwide, with 75 members in North America.

Periodicals: *The Newsletter of the Order of the Cross.*

Sources:

Order of the Cross. www.orderofthecross.org.

Ferrier, J. Todd. *The Divine Renaissance.* 2 vols. London: Order of the Cross, 1963.

———. *Life's Mysteries Unveiled.* London: Order of the Cross, 1953.

———. *The Logia or Sayings of the Master.* London: Percy Lund, Bradford and Company, 1916, 1926.

———. *The Master: His Life and Teachings.* London: Percy Lund, Humpries and Company, 1913, 1925.

Hymns for Worship with Tunes. London: Order of the Cross, 1965.

Kemmis, E. *Mary Gordon. Shepherd of Souls: Some Impressions of the Life and Ministry of John Todd Ferrier.* Santa Barbara, CA: J. F. Rowney Press, 1947.

Our Informal Fellowship: Some Foundational Statements. London: Order of the Cross, 1963.

Universal Great Brotherhood

c/o Solar Yoga Center of St. Louis, 6002 Pershing, St. Louis, MO 63112

The Universal Great Brotherhood was formed in 1948 by Serge Raynaud de la Ferrière (b. 1916), a Frenchman who had been involved in the esoteric from his childhood. As a young man, he traveled to Egypt, where, according to his biography, he was initiated as the Sublime Crowned Cophto and Great Priest Khediviar. At the age of 22, in London, he received a degree of doctor of hermetic science and the next year, in Amsterdam, doctor of universal science. During World War II he became closely identified with the Theosophical Society in France and joined the Theosophical and Astrological Lodge in London. After the war, his occult work expanded and he became active in a Masonic body.

The Universal Great Brotherhood is not a church; it is an educational organization that has elements of religion included in the esoteric teachings, but it is not committed to one concept of divinity. The brotherhood acknowledges that there is a supreme being. They have practices that daily glorify the Divine God. The brotherhood feels it would be more accurate to be recognized as a yoga-martial arts group that seeks to incorporate purification of body and mind through exercise, diet, meditation, and making the practice a lifestyle. Members come from many walks of life. The teachers are from the Supreme Order of Aquarius, Solar Line, with titles of sat arhat, sat chellah, guru, and others.

De la Ferrière's early esoteric work prepared him for an encounter with Master Sun W. K., described as the Superior Power of Tibet, who gave de la Ferrière his mission to begin the exposition of initiatic principles to the general public. De la Ferrière founded the Universal Great Brotherhood and for the next three years traveled widely, establishing the brotherhood in centers around the world. Very early in his travels he went to Venezuela, where he met Jose Manuel Estrada (b. 1900), who became his leading student. Estrada had nine years earlier announced the arrival of an avatar (an incarnation of God) and had gathered a group waiting for the avatar. After their meeting, Estrada accepted de la Ferrière, who spent 18 months with Estrada and his group, and on March 21, 1948, reopened the Universal Great Brotherhood in a public manner.

In 1950 de la Ferrière turned over the management of the brotherhood to Estrada and retired to a quiet life of esoteric work and writing. Estrada assumed the title of director general. The work grew steadily in Latin America through the 1950s and 1960s. In 1969 Estrada sent Rev. Gagpa Anita Montero Campion to the United States. She settled in St. Louis and began to teach yoga classes. She shared the teachings of the brotherhood with her pupils, and in 1970 organized the first brotherhood center. The movement soon spread to Ann Arbor, Michigan; Chicago; and New York City.

The brotherhood is an initiatic school designed to assist humanity in its transition to a new age, often spoken of as the transition from the Age of Pisces to the Age of Aquarius. The birthplace of this new age is the Americas, hence the reopening of the brotherhood of the west.

The brotherhood is registered with the United Nations as a NGO (nongovernment organization). It prides itself in being active in community service.

The brotherhood is dedicated to attaining peace by raising the consciousness of humanity both individually and collectively. The brotherhood offers a number of services to preinitiates. It sponsors health care programs with a special emphasis on preventive medicine and natural cures. The organization strongly advocates vegetarianism. It also sponsors a variety of classes to promote personal growth, such as hatha yoga, martial arts, astrology, and meditation. In this regard it also promotes the Cosmic Ceremony, a Universal form of worship that allows each person to get in touch with his or her own highest concept of the divine.

Participants in brotherhood public programs, designated followers, may be invited to become initiates. Once initiated they become members of the Esoteric College and receive the title *gegnian*, or "little novice." Afterward they pass upward through several degrees: first degree, *getul*, or novice; second degree, reverend *gag-pa*, or affiliated; third degree, right reverend *gelong*, or adept; and the fourth degree, respectable guru, or instructor. Currently held by only the international leaders, still higher degrees are, in principle, open to all. The fifth degree, honorable sat chellah, or disciple, is held by Domingo Dias Porta; and the sixth degree, benerable sat arhat, or missionary, is held by Estrada. Only one person can hold the seventh degree as sat guru, the master, presently held by de la Ferrière. Administratively, the brotherhood is headed by the superior council, which operates under the sat guru and makes all the decisions concerning the activities of the brotherhood internationally. Under it are national and regional councils. The current administrator is Diane McCameron.

Membership: Membership figures were not reported for 2008. The brotherhood is international with a greater following in Latino countries because the headquarters is in Mexico City and there is more communication in Spanish than other languages.

Sources:

Global Unification. www.maestre.org/english.htm.

Solar Yoga Center of St. Louis. www.solaryogastl.org.

Biography, *the Sublime Maestre, Sat Guru, Dr. Serge Raymaud de la Ferrière*. St. Louis, MO: Educational Publications of the I. E. S., 1976.

Montero-Campion, Anita. *My Guru from South America: Sat Arhat Dr. Jose Manuel Estrada*. St. Louis: Author, 1976.

Western Esoteric Family II: Spiritualism & New Age

18

As esotericism developed through the seventeenth and eighteenth centuries, Rosicrucianism was followed by speculative Freemasonry, its first popular expression with a widespread international following. By the end of the eighteenth century, two additional popular movements emerged, one around the writings and experiences of Swedish seer Emanuel Swedenborg (1688–1772) and the other around the magnetic-healing work of Franz Anton Mesmer (1734–1815). The Swedenborgian movement would survive to the present in several small church bodies. Mesmerism as a movement would die out as its essence was absorbed into what would become the most popular expression of esotericism in the nineteenth century—Spiritualism. This second chapter dedicated to Western esotericism covers those groups and subsequent twentieth-century movements that flowed from the efforts of Swedenborg and Mesmer and from Spiritualism. Ultimately, these movements found their life in the ubiquitous experience of people with forces and beings that seem to be from another dimension, as well as various experiences of knowing using powers seemingly apart from the five senses, what today is termed *extrasensory perception*.

From the beginning of recorded history, people have claimed powers of mind and spirit far surpassing those commonly recognized by modern science. Men have claimed knowledge from beyond the capabilities of the five senses: the power to move objects by thought and the ability to talk to beings whose permanent home is not our world. In ancient Greece, the temple at Delphi was a center of this psychic world. Pythia, a psychic who prophesied for visiting dignitaries, lived in Delphi. These prophecies, given in hexametric verse, were often of a cryptic nature. Possibly the most famous story of Delphi comes from the historian Herodotus (c. 484–c. 425 B.C.E.). According to Herodotus, Croesus, king of Lydia in the time of Cyrus of Persia, decided to do battle with Cyrus. Beforehand, he consulted the oracle of Delphi, who told him, "Croesus, having crossed the Halys (River), will destroy a great empire." Confident of victory, Croesus crossed the river and was thoroughly defeated. Croesus demanded an explanation. The oracle replied bluntly that a great empire, Lydia, had fallen as predicted.

Socrates (c. 470–399 B.C.E.) is often cited in ancient literature as a psychic of note. While a child, he became aware of a voice that spoke to him. The voice never commanded particular acts, but forbade wrong action.

During the twentieth century, parapsychologists—scientists who investigate the psychic—developed a vocabulary by which the psychic can be understood. J. B. Rhine (1895–1980) of Duke University spearheaded this effort. *Extrasensory perception* (ESP) is the term Rhine coined to describe the ability to perceive information and encounter a world beyond the commonly recognized senses. ESP has several basic subdivisions. *Telepathy* is mind-to-mind (subconscious-to-subconscious) communication. *Clairvoyance* is perception of the world beyond the senses without any other mind's help. *Precognition* is a perception of events in the future. *Psychokinesis (PK)* is the power of mind over matter; Rhine saw spiritual healing as one prominent example of psychokinesis. In years of exacting experiments, Rhine and his colleagues attempted to document the existence of these four phenomena. As the work progressed, an additional technical vocabulary was developed.

Beyond these four forms of psychic perception, psychic people describe many other experiences, which parapsychologists also attempted to explore. Some are varieties of one of the four basic forms, as, for example, spiritual healing is a special case of psychokinesis. Others psychic experiences are not so clearly tied to the four basic subdivisions of ESP. *Astral travel*, for example, is the experience of the conscious self being outside the body. *Mediumship* or *channeling* involves clairvoyance and telepathic communication with entities (the dead, ascended masters, angels, etc.) claimed to have an existence in a different realm, a realm other than the world of the normal waking consciousness.

In the 1960s, investigation of the healing power so long claimed by sensitive people and members of different religious groups was begun in earnest. Such researchers as Bernard Grad of McGill University in Montreal and Justa Smith of Rosary Hill College in Buffalo, New York, began to demonstrate, under carefully controlled laboratory conditions, the reality of a power that could heal mice, stimulate the growth and yield of plants, and change the growth rate of enzymes. From such work as this, a new science, *paraphysics*, emerged.

Beyond the realm of the purely psychical is the realm of the esoteric or occult. The word *occult* originally meant "hidden," the opposite of *apocalypse*, that which is "revealed." In popular culture, however, *occult* has come to be applied to practices that were once part of the "hidden wisdom." These practices include various arts of divination—astrology, numerology, palmistry, and the reading of tarot cards and tea leaves—to mention a few.

THE BIBLICAL PSYCHIC TRADITION TO 1800.

Although aware of the ancient world in general, contemporary psychics are most aware of one aspect of the ancient world—the biblical tradition. They hold that, from cover to cover, the Bible is a psychic book, replete with incidents that in today's terminology are properly called psychic. These include incidents of spirit communication (Matthew 17:1–9; I Samuel 28), clairvoyance (John 4:16–29), healing (I Kings 5:1–27; Acts 3:3–11), prophecy (Acts 11:28; 21:1–13), and divination (Matthew 2:1–2; Acts 1:15–26).

Among characters in the Old Testament, Samuel is the pristine example of what in the modern world would be called a psychic. According to the account of his life, as a young child, Samuel was taken to Eli, Israel's corrupt psychic, to be dedicated to God. Shortly afterward, he had his psychic awakening in the famous incident when a voice called out his name (I Samuel 3). Clearly descriptive of the major activity in Samuel's day-to-day life was the incident that initially brought him into contact with the future King Saul (I Samuel 9). The young Saul, the son of Kish, woke one morning to discover that his father's donkeys had disappeared. He looked in vain for the lost herd. His servant suggested that Samuel, the prophet, might be able to help, for as the writer of I Samuel noted: "Before time in Israel when a man went to inquire of God, thus he said, 'Come let us go to the seer; for he that is now called a Prophet was before time called a Seer'" (I Samuel 9).

Samuel received a clairvoyant vision of Saul long before Saul's arrival and went out to meet him. Instead of speaking to Saul of donkeys, Samuel began to give Saul a precognitive vision of his future as king of Israel. Samuel then anointed him. Only after the anointing did Samuel talk of the lost donkeys, revealing that they had returned home. When Saul became king, Samuel became his chief psychic adviser, a popular office in the ancient world. After Samuel's death, Saul went to a medium, a woman at Endor, to try to contact Samuel's spirit (I Samuel 28).

Psychics studying the New Testament look to Jesus as the paradigm of a psychic, one upon whom they can model their own lives. Jesus' miracles are interpreted in psychic categories. The transfiguration, in which Jesus talks to the visible spirits of two long-dead personages, Moses and Elijah, is seen as a materialization. There are also incidents of psychic healing (Mark 7:31–37; Matthew 20:29–34), psychokinesis (Mark 11:12–14, 20–21; Acts 13:6), clairvoyance (Matthew 2:13; Acts 10:1–33), and precognition (Mark 10:32–34; Acts 27:9–44). Psychic talents are given the name "gifts of the Spirit" by Paul (I Corinthians 12:4–11).

Irenaeus (c. 130–c.202 C.E.) and other writers in the early Christian movement noted the continuation of these gifts in the second-century church. Through the following centuries, various writers have noted the steady occurrence of psychic events up to modern times.

The modern psychic community dates from psychical research that began in the late seventeenth century. In the face of deism, which denied the possibility of miracles or communication with spirits, researchers began to publish accounts of "supernatural" incidents that "proved" the existence of the invisible world. These included accounts of simple clairvoyance and precognition (often in dreams), astral travel, witchcraft and possession, ghosts, and spirit communication. Among the many writers who contributed to this research are Joseph Glanvill (1636–1680), Cotton Mather (1663–1728), Increase Mather (1639–1723), Richard Baxter (1615–1691), and John Wesley (1703–1791), the founder of Methodism.

A contemporary of Wesley, Emanuel Swedenborg, became the first psychic-medium of import in modern times. In the late 1700s he published many books that he claimed to be accounts of his contacts and visits to another world—the astral world of spirits. A later contemporary of Wesley and Swedenborg, Franz Anton Mesmer, developed magnetic (or psychic) healing, giving it a scientific frame of reference.

THE PSYCHIC IN AMERICA.

The psychic history of America is as old as the settlement by Europeans. From the beginning, witchcraft and occultism emerged in New England in patterns not unlike those of the settlers' English homeland. Among the first occultists was Tituba, the slave of the Reverend Samuel Parris (1653–1720) of Salem. Tituba taught the Parris children occult practices brought from her West Indian homeland. Vodou dolls were found in the house of Goodwife Glover during the witchcraft trials of 1692, an indication that occult arts were more widespread than many thought.

Healing, psychic readings, and even black magic were rife among the Pennsylvania Dutch, whose powwow men were both feared and venerated.

In the 1830s and 1840s, a number of healers, hypnotists, and phrenologists toured America, writing and lecturing. The disciples of Mesmer, most notably Charles Poyen (d. 1844), created a movement of magnetists before the Civil War (1861–1865). They defined *animal magnetism* as the energy flowing from healer to patient during psychic healing and from hypnotist to client in hypnotism. Their ranks included radical Methodist preacher LaRoy Sunderland (1803–1885). The magnetists were followed by the Spiritualists, who gave us the first American psychic tradition. Their goal was proof of survival after bodily death through evidence of spirit contact (contact with the dead).

The growth of Spiritualism, coupled with flamboyant press coverage and charges of fraud, caused many scientists and intellectuals to become interested in psychic phenomena. This interest led to the formation of the Society for Psychical Research in England in 1882 and the American Society of Psychical Research (ASPR) in 1884. Among the leading members of ASPR were William James (1842–1910) and Josiah Royce (1855–1916). Much of the energy of nineteenth-century ASPR members was dedicated to research on mediumistic phenomena. In this endeavor, William James,

Western Esoteric Family II: Spiritualism and New Age Chronology

1747	Emanuel Swedenborg resigns from his job with the Swedish Bureau of Mines to devote life to spiritual work.
1759	From 300 miles away, Swedenborg has vision of fire in Stockholm.
1784	French Academy of Science denounces the magnetic theories of Franz Anton Mesmer.
1792	First American Swedenborgian society founded in Baltimore, Maryland.
1817	General Convention of the New Jerusalem in the United States of America organized in Baltimore, Maryland.
1848	Reports of spirit rappings in the home of the Fox sisters give birth to modern Spiritualism in North America.
1850	Spirtualist medium Andrew Jackson Davis issues his study of Spiritual thought, the *Great Harmonia*.
1855	The first issues of England's first Spiritualist newspaper, the *Yorkshire Spiritual Telegram,* appear.
1884	American Society for Psychical Research founded.
1893	National Spiritualist Association founded in Chicago.
1897	General Assembly of Spiritualists organized in New York.
1922	National Colored Spiritualist Association of Churches is founded after racial split in the Spiritualist movement.
1925	The Metropolitan Spiritual Community Churches of Christ is founded by two African Americans, William Taylor and Leviticus Lee Boswell.
1929	Medium Arthur Ford claims to have broken the code between Harry Houdini and his wife and to have brought a spirit message from the late magician.
1931	Edgar Cayce establishes the Association for Research and Enlightenment.
1934	J. B. Rhine introduces public to parapsychology in his book *Extra Sensory Perception*.
1947	Kenneth Arnold's sighting of some unknown flying objects near Mt. Rainier, Washington, launches flying saucer era.
1951	Medium Eileen J. Garrett establishes the New York–based Parapsychology Foundation.
1952	Californian George Adamski publishes claims to have met extraterrestrial "space brothers."
1955	Founding Church of Scientology opens its doors in Washington, D.C.
1956	*The Search for Bridey Murphy* introduces the American public to reincarnation and the exploration of past lives.
1960	*Psychic Observer* report exposes fraudulent mediumship at Spiritualists' Camp Chesterfield in Indiana.
1962	Contactee Gloria Lee dies in Washington, D.C., as result of her fast to attract attention to flying saucer phenomenon.
1966	Writer Allen Spraggett hosts televised séance with medium Arthur Ford and Episcopal bishop James Pike.
Early 1970s	New Age movement begins with announcement of a coming Aquarian Age of peace and light.
1972	Founding of the Academy of Religion and Psychical Research.
1973	David Spangler forms the Lorian Association. Astronaut Edgar Mitchell takes part in a telepathy experiment between the Earth and space.
1975	The *Humanist* magazine publishes statement on "Objections to Astrology" signed by 186 scientists.
1976	Former medium Lamar Keene exposes world of fraudulent mediumship in his book *The Psychic Mafia*.
	Humanist philosopher Paul Kurtz and others found Committee for the Scientific Investigation of Claims of the Paranormal (now the Committee for Skeptical Inquiry) to counter rise of belief in astrology and psychic phenomena.
1977	JZ Knight begins to channel Ramtha.
1978	Harmonic Convergence is celebrated August 16–17.
	Actress Shirley Maclaine stars in autobiographical made-for-television movie of her awakening, *Out on a Limb*.
1989–90	New Age movement comes to an end as leading figures renounce its millennial expectations.
1994	James Redfield's *The Celestine Prophecy* becomes the best-selling book of the post–New Age era.
2000	*Crossing Over with John Edwards* begins airing on national television on the Sci-Fi Network.

who spent a number of years observing medium Leonora Piper (1857–1950), believed he had found sufficient proof of survival beyond death.

A new day in psychical research arrived when J. B. Rhine began his work at Duke University in the 1930s. Rhine completely revamped psychical research, giving it a new name, *parapsychology*, and a new method. Rhine took the psychic event into the laboratory, demonstrating it in repeatable experiments. In 1968 new impetus was given to psychical research as the West became aware that extensive parapsychological endeavors were occurring in the Soviet Union and Eastern Europe. Among the sources of knowledge about that research was a best-selling book by two young reporters, Sheila Ostrander and Lynn Schroeder. Their *Psychic Discoveries behind the Iron Curtain* (1970) gave the majority of Americans their first look at Russian research into the psy-

chic, and gave parapsychologists additional motivation for expanding their efforts.

After the Civil War, psychic alternatives to Spiritualism began to emerge. Former Spiritualists Pascal Beverly Randolph (1825–1875) and Helena Petrovna Blavatsky (1831–1891) initiated Rosicrucianism and the Theosophical Society, respectively (both are discussed in chapter 17). After the turn of the century, a host of non-Spiritualist psychic groups arose. Some of these were oriented toward Eastern philosophy, others toward parapsychology. The last to arise in any number were the revived occultists.

A NOTE ON LIFESTYLE. The contemporary psychic community is oriented toward psychic experience. In this regard, they resemble the Pentecostal community (see chapter 9), which is oriented toward religious experiences. When viewed objectively, psychic and religious experiences are similar, though they are described in different terms. For both, experience is itself important. Psychic people differ slightly from New Thought metaphysicians, who are oriented more toward results and a meaningful context. In being oriented toward religious experience, psychics share a lifestyle with mystics and pietists of all ages.

Psychics have also leaned toward a "scientific" demonstration of the truth of their faith. Psychics see their religious beliefs proved in the everyday repetition of verifiable psychic events. Spiritualists believe that the truth of survival comes in data received through mediums. For some, the truth is in the deep philosophy that comes through an otherwise shallow person who operates as a channel. For others, the truth is found in the existence of an invisible world of psychic perception, continually demonstrated by clairvoyance.

This desire for scientific verification gives the psychic community a peculiar relation to scientists, to whom they are continually looking for verification. There has been at least a relative degree of correlation, and the growth of data from parapsychology has had a profound effect on the religious psychic community. Such data provide content for ongoing discussion, and make the psychic community almost impervious to religious traditions that lack such contemporary scientific verification.

SWEDENBORG AND THE NEW JERUSALEM.

The life and experience of Emanuel Swedenborg (1688–1772), the son of a Swedish Lutheran bishop, were to make him one of the great religious lights of the eighteenth century. That he is not as well remembered as some of his contemporaries, such as John Wesley and Jonathan Edwards (1703–1758), does not so much belie his significance as illustrate the psychic movement's tendency to belittle history.

Swedenborg was reared a pious Lutheran. As a young man, he took up the study of science; mathematics and astronomy were his favorite subjects. After a period abroad gaining an education, he settled in Sweden to begin a scientific career and was appointed to a position on the Board of Mines in 1724. His publication of several volumes a decade later led to his recognition by the scientific community and an invitation to become a corresponding member of the Royal Academy of Sciences in St. Petersburg, Russia.

His work with the Bureau of Mines led him to concentrate his scientific study in the field of geology. His practical suggestions spurred the improvement of mining procedures throughout Sweden and actually laid the foundation for a science of geology in that country. He published one of the first exhaustive works on metallurgy, and his efforts led to the founding of the science of crystallography. His published works might seem overly philosophical by contemporary standards, but they indicate an ecumenicity of mind, not any lack of scientific acumen.

As early as 1736, however, a different side of Swedenborg began to emerge. He started to take account of unusual dreams and bodily states that he did not fully understand. A crisis in his thinking came in 1744, when he began to realize that intellectual pursuits were ultimately unsatisfying and that he must submit his life to divine guidance. Three years later, he made public his changed perspective, resigned his position with the Bureau of Mines, and devoted the remainder of his life to developing his ideas and publishing them abroad.

At this point, Swedenborg became what today would be called a medium, one who has contact with disincarnate spirit entities. He claimed that, in his visions, he traveled to spirit realms and from spirit entities (primarily angels) gained revelatory knowledge of the nature of life, life after death, and God. The crux of his philosophy is set forth in five long treatises and a commentary on the Bible.

The central theme in Swedenborg's system is the "law of correspondences." He believed that there were two realms of created existence, the physical (phenomenal) and the spiritual (real). Between the two, there is everywhere an exact correspondence. As a seer and visionary, Swedenborg was able to discern these correspondences. He turned especially to the scripture; his commentaries were aimed at elucidating its spiritual meaning.

The revelatory data upon which Swedenborg spent so much of his time concerned the nature of life after death. He claimed to have gained this knowledge by traveling (astral travel) to the spirit world. From these experiences, he came to believe that man and woman were immortal. He denied the resurrection of the body, and believed that man's soul immediately passes to conscious spirit existence. Souls find themselves moving toward the prime of adult life; that is, the souls of people who died as children will progress to maturity and the souls of those who died in old age will return to the vigor they had in younger adulthood.

As one dies, the soul goes to an intermediate spirit abode between heaven and hell, where preparation for the final state is made. Periodic visits of the soul after reaching heaven or hell are made to this intermediate state, so that appreciation or understanding of the final abode can be heightened by contrast.

Swedenborg deviated from orthodox Lutheranism on several other points. For example, he denied the orthodox doctrine of the Trinity (one God in three persons), avowing instead that God is one in three principles, each of which is manifest in Jesus Christ. Swedenborg believed the Father is the principle of love, "ineffable and exhaustless"; the Son is the principle of divine wisdom; and the Holy Spirit is the energy of divinity that operates in humans to inspire, console, and sanctify them.

Between 1749 and 1756, Swedenborg's multivolume commentary on Genesis and Exodus, *Arcana Coelestia*, was published. Other works followed. The books garnered little response in Sweden, and Swedenborg did little to proselytize, aside from making his ideas available. For example, he wrote his books in Latin, not Swedish. A few persons were impressed with his clairvoyance, demonstrated in his famous vision of the Stockholm fire of 1759 at a time when he was three hundred miles away from that city.

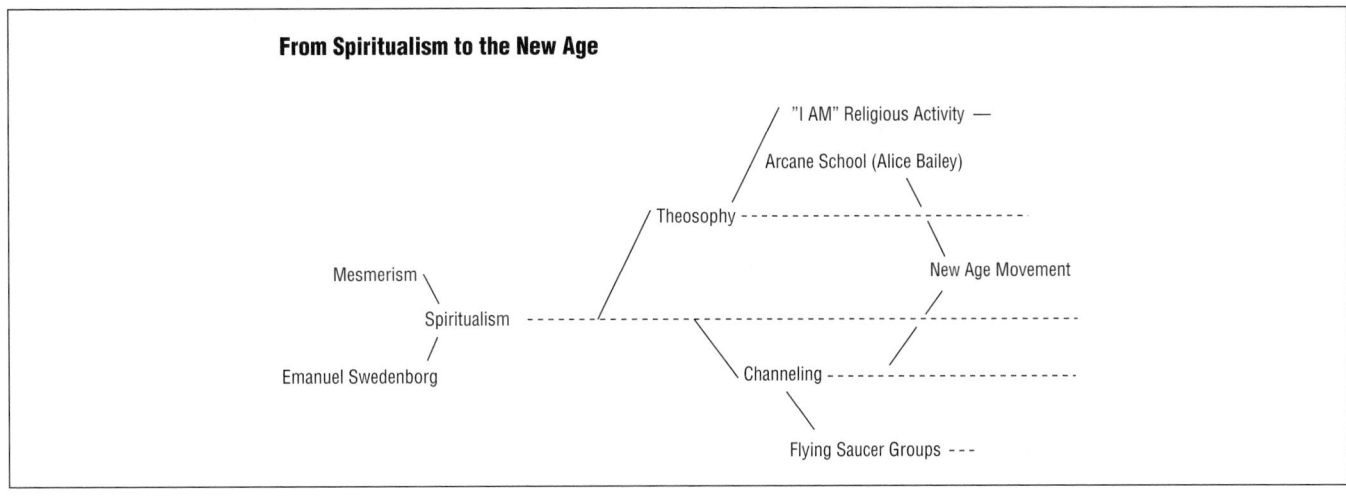

From Spiritualism to the New Age

"I AM" Religious Activity —

Arcane School (Alice Bailey)

Theosophy -

Mesmerism

New Age Movement

Spiritualism - - - - - - - - - -

Emanuel Swedenborg

Channeling - - - - - - - - - - - - - - -

Flying Saucer Groups - - -

J. Gordon Melton

It was in England that his teachings found greatest acceptance. Shortly after Swedenborg's death in 1772, several men—the Reverend John Cowles, the Reverend Thomas Hartley, and Thomas Cookworthy—began to translate the material into English. In 1783 Robert Hindmarsh (1759–1835) began to search for other interested parties. As a result of his efforts, a weekly meeting, originally called the Theosophical Society, was established in London. This body was constituted as the New Jerusalem Church in 1787. Today it is often called simply the New Church.

The translation, publication, and dissemination of Swedenborg's religious writings was a major thrust of New Church activity from the outset. Under Cowles's leadership, the Society for Printing and Publishing the Writing of Emmanuel Swedenborg was established in 1810.

Members of the New Church migrated to the colonies and formed a society in Baltimore in 1792. Other societies were soon formed along the coast as far south as Charleston, South Carolina, and as far west as Madison Town, Indiana.

SPIRITUALISM.

In I Samuel 28, according to Spiritualists, there occurs one of the most famous incidents of mediumship in the history of the West. As the story goes, Saul, king of Israel, was to face the Philistines and became afraid of their might. After analyzing his dreams, and consulting his royal psychics and the Urim and Thummim (an ancient divination device), he visited a medium at Endor, asking that she call up Samuel, Saul's departed psychic counselor. To everyone's surprise, Samuel appeared and condemned Saul.

In Matthew 17, another famous mediumistic event, popularly known as the transfiguration, is recorded. Jesus and three apostles were present when two long-dead figures, Moses and Elijah, appeared and conversed with Jesus. In modern Spiritualist terminology, this event would be called a materialization séance, a gathering at which a spirit or something immaterial takes visible form.

Mediumistic phenomena are as old as humankind. Archeological, anthropological, and historical literature is full of references to professed intercourse with the spirit world. In so-called primitive culture, the shaman was a combination of medium, psychic, and magician, as were psychics operating under various labels in the ancient Mediterranean world. However, in spite of the ancient practices to which Spiritualism is heir, Spiritualism is itself a relatively new phenomenon, related to the peculiar thrust of Western religion since the late 1600s. The true ancestors of Spiritualism are not so much the ancient mediums, but the Puritan and Wesleyan theologians who cited examples of psychic phenomena to prove the existence of the unseen world to their skeptical readers. In the late 1600s, as the polemic against the existence of witchcraft grew, and as Deism, which denied the validity of any intercourse with spirit entities, emerged, several Puritan theologians began to issue numerous accounts of the spirit world.

In its 1930 Constitution and Bylaws, the National Spiritualist Association of Churches defines Spiritualism as "the Science, Philosophy and Religion of a continuous life, based upon the demonstrable fact of communication by means of mediumship, with those who live in the Spirit World." The demonstration of survival was not a necessity, nor even a major theme of psychic-mediumistic phenomena, until the modern age began to doubt such survival. In this respect, Spiritualism is the direct inheritor of Puritan Wesleyan concerns.

In 1681, Joseph Glanvill published his *Saducismus Triumphatus*, which was followed by similar books by Increase Mather, Richard Baxter, and Cotton Mather. John Wesley states the issue of the British Evangelicals succinctly in the introduction to his lengthy discussion of the mediumship of Elizabeth Hobson (b. 1744):

I take knowledge these are at the bottom of the outcry which has been raised, and with such insolence spread through the nation, in direct opposition not only to the Bible, but the suffrage of the wisest and best of men in all ages and nations. They well know (whether Christians know it or not), that the giving up of witchcraft is, in effect, giving up the Bible; and they know, on the other hand, that if but one account of the intercourse of men with separate spirits be admitted, their whole castle in the air (Deism, Atheism, Materialism) falls to the ground. I know no reason, therefore, why we should suffer even this weapon to be wrested out of our hands. Indeed there are numerous arguments besides, which abundantly confute their vain imaginations. But we need not be hooted out of one; neither reason nor religion require this."

John Wesley, *The Journal* (1768) 1914, vol. 5, p. 265.

That these men, not the many psychics of every age, are the immediate ancestors of the Spiritualists is amply documented in the literature of Spiritualism, as well as in the creedal statements, where continual reference is made to the central emphasis of Spiritualism—the belief in personal survival after death, which can be demonstrated by mediumship. This belief and emphasis on survival and mediumship distinguish Spiritualism from other psychic groups.

Spiritualism is secondarily the child of the psychic activity of the eighteenth century. This activity was centered on the work of two men—Swedenborg and Mesmer. Mesmer had, in the 1770s and 1780s, discovered and articulated a form of psychic healing that included both magnetic healing and hypnotism. Denounced by the French Academy in 1784, Mesmer died in disgrace, but many of his students took his magnetic philosophy and hypnotism to England and the United States. As the result of the publication of the *Progress of Animal Magnetism in New England* by Charles Poyen in 1837, and widespread lecturing by him and other magnetic students, the issue of the human psychic nature was raised across the country in the early 1840s. In 1843 one of these roving mesmerists spurred interest in a young shoemaker apprentice, Andrew Jackson Davis (1826–1910). With this encounter, modern Spiritualism can be said to have begun.

Davis was born in Blooming Grove, New York, in 1826. After hearing lectures on mesmerism, Davis sought out a local hypnotist, William Levington, and was placed in a trance. He immediately showed powers of clairvoyance; claims were made that he could duplicate the practices of the magnetists. The following year he had a vision of Galen, the famous Greek physician, and soon after, of Emanuel Swedenborg. These visions changed his life, and he began a career as healer and seer. He claimed abilities to diagnose and heal, converse with spirits, and channel knowledge from the omnipotent mind. Davis published a number of books over the next thirty years. Although not widely read today, these books were influential in the formative years of Spiritualism.

Davis, like Swedenborg, pictured six spheres of existence in the afterlife. At death, a person gravitates to the sphere most akin to his state of being at death. From this sphere, he continues to progress toward God through the higher spheres or "summerland." Thus humankind is in a state of continual progression upward. Such progression schemes were common in early Spiritualism.

The event most American Spiritualists regard as the birth of their faith occurred on March 31, 1848. On that date a young woman named Kate Fox (c. 1839–1892) began to get a rational response from mysterious rapping noises heard in her home in Hydesville, New York. Kate and her two sisters discovered that the rapping sounds would respond to their hand clapping. With a little practice, they were able to work out a code by which they could communicate with Mr. Splitfoot, as they called him, supposedly a disincarnate entity. Mr. Splitfoot rapped out his name as Charles B. Roena, and told them he had been murdered in that house some years previously. Neighbors came to witness the rapping. No less famous a person than the journalist Horace Greeley (1811–1872) supported the veracity of the Fox sisters against charges of fraud. News of the Fox sisters' mediumship spread, and soon other psychics who could communicate with spirits began to appear. Some were slate mediums: The spirits wrote their messages with chalk on slates. Other mediums tipped tables. Still others went into trances and allowed spirits to use their voice boxes. Physical mediums, who could produce materialized images of the spirits, arose as well. Within a decade of the Civil War, what was to become a spiritualist movement was developing.

Spiritualism, once publicized, spread quickly across the continent. Spiritualism was almost immediately taken to California as people responded both to the spirits and to the gold rush, and by 1855, an unnamed medium who was also a prominent lawyer, was holding regular séances in his parlor in San Francisco. Even before emerging in the West, Spiritualism had traveled northward to Canada, where early centers developed in Toronto, London, Ottawa, and St. Catherines. A Mrs. Swaim became the chief medium in Toronto, while John Spetique was the organizer of activities in London. In 1858 a British medium who had moved to Boston, Emma Hardinge (1823–1899), toured Quebec and the Maritime Provinces speaking and demonstrating spirit contact. From these early endeavors, Spiritualism grew slowly throughout the country.

The 1880–1920 period was the era of the great mediums. During this time, numerous books purporting to be revelations from the spirit world were produced. These provided alternative material to both Swedenborg and Davis. They included *Oahspe* (1882) by John B. Newbrough (1828–1891) and the *Aquarian Gospel of Jesus the Christ* (1907) by Levi H. Dowling (1844–1911). Both are still in print and are heavily read in the Spiritualist movement. Among the mediums to be tested with outstanding results in this era were Leonora Piper, Gladys Osborne Leonard (1882–1968), and Winifred Coombe-Tennant (1874–1956).

THE ORGANIZATION. Spiritualism developed several forms to disseminate its teachings. These include the camp, the church, the séance, and the development class. The camp developed in the mid-nineteenth century in the Chautauqua era, and was modeled on the famous camp meetings held near Lake Chautauqua in southwestern New York. Scattered around the country, the various Spiritualist camps provide a leisurely setting for lectures, mediumistic readings, and general propaganda efforts. Such camps are a major summertime activity for both churched and unchurched mediums who experience a summer slack.

The local Spiritualist groups are organized into churches on a Protestant model. The head medium is usually listed as pastor, with the other mediums acting as assistants. The Sunday morning service is similar in form to the average Protestant church service except: (1) the content will be Spiritualist; (2) the pastor may go into a trance before delivering the sermon or lecture; and (3) at the close of the service, members of the congregation may receive psychic readings (usually called *spirit greetings*).

The real heart of Spiritualism is the séance. This meeting is conducted by a medium for as many as 50 people, usually seated in a circle in the dark. From an entranced state, the medium may produce spirit phenomena of a wide variety, including the levitation of objects and materialization. Usually a spirit control speaks through the medium—the spirit control is the person from the spirit realm who regularly speaks through the medium and is thought of as the medium's constant companion. The word *control* is used because the medium's vocal chords are said to be controlled by the person from the spirit realm while the medium is in a trance. The spirit control often gives those at the séance information about their loved ones who have died.

The Spiritualist development class, as the name implies, is for the development and training of psychic abilities, especially mediumistic ones. Meditation is basic to development, but other techniques and practices vary, depending on the medium.

Mediums themselves are largely supported by individual readings (the conveying of greetings from the spirit world) for church members. Building on the experiences of contact with the departed, the Sunday worship services take second place to actual incidence of such contact. Events in which psychic readings occur are always the best attended.

The Spiritualist camp remains a vital force within the movement. A mix of leisure, lectures, and mediums attract believers during the summer (or local tourist season) and are a vital source of revenue for many mediums serving small churches. Some camps serve as schools for mediums-in-training, providing exposure and a working-learning situation.

The great problem that has hampered the development of Spiritualism is fraud. As soon as Spiritualism emerged, fraudulent practices by various mediums were uncovered. Mediums claimed to demonstrate a variety of phenomena produced by spirit agency. As psychical researchers became more and more sophisticated in their ability to perceive conjuring tricks, the number of exposures increased. Henry Slade (d. 1905), a famous nineteenth-century slate medium, was continually exposed. The movement was deeply affected in 1888 when Kate Fox and her sister Margaret (c. 1833–1893) confessed and then demonstrated how they had made the original rappings. Margaret retracted her confession the next year and was accepted back into the ranks of Spiritualism, but the confessions were not forgotten.

In the early years of the twentieth century, Harry Houdini (1874–1926) turned his attention to mediums, becoming one of the most famous exposers of fraud in the history of American Spiritualism. A master magician himself, Houdini knew all the devices used to fool the naive sitter at the séance. As a result of the efforts of psychical researchers and several magicians concerned about conjuring being passed off as the result of paranormal effects, much of the physical phenomena so prominent in Spiritualism in the early twentieth century has largely disappeared from the movement.

Many people assumed that fraudulent mediumship had been driven out of Spiritualism by the likes of Houdini, but as recently as 1960, a major exposé of fraudulent mediums was reported, complete with pictures, in the then-important Spiritualist tabloid *Psychic Observer*. A psychical researcher, Andrija Puharich (1918–1995), and paper's editor, Thomas O'Neill, discovered Mable Riffle, one of the most famous mediums in the country and the secretary of Camp Chesterfield (Indiana), a Spiritualist camp, fraudulently giving materialization séances. Besides the removal of some of the mediums from the camp, the main result of the exposé was the withdrawal of financial support for the *Psychic Observer*, forcing O'Neill to sell out.

Those within the psychic community note that, overall, fraud is not common and is, in the main, confined to a few independent mediums and several of the Spiritualist camps. The major practice is the attempt by mediums and psychics to pad their psychic ability with bland generalities. Apologists insist that the constant demand for psychic readings is responsible. Mediums have to perform on demand, but the nature of psychic power is such that it does not always function on demand. Still, the exposure of fraud has kept Spiritualism from becoming the powerful element in the North American religious community that it is, for example, in Brazil and Great Britain.

SPIRITUALISM IN THE TWENTIETH CENTURY.

Spiritualism initially organized in the second half of the nineteenth century around a set of state associations. The first national organization, the National Spiritual Association (now the National Spiritualist Association of Churches) was founded in 1893. The National Spiritual Association established Spiritualism as clearly a religious movement. Arguments over such topics as reincarnation and scandals over fraud would, decade-by-decade, divide spiritualists and lead to the formation of a number of additional Spiritualist denominations. While never a large movement, it drew continuing comment both from skeptics (such as Houdini) attempting to disprove its claims and from psychic researchers hoping to verify at least some of its phenomena.

The inability to find scientific proof to verify its central claim of spirit contact would keep Spiritualists on the fringe of the religious community, though a few mediums would attain a level of fame and acceptance. Notable among these was Arthur Ford (1897–1971), who claimed to have broken a code that Houdini left with his widow, thus proving spirit survival. Many who were influenced by Ford but otherwise outside of organized Spiritualism would later form the Spiritual Frontier Fellowship, an organization dedicated to exploring the spiritual resources provided by prayer, meditation, and spirit contact. Many of its leaders were Christian clergy and church lay leaders.

Spiritualists showed little interest in the New Age movement and suffered greatly by the growth of channels, mediums who operated outside of the Spiritualist movement. Through the 1970s and 1980s, many of the smaller Spiritualist groups disappeared, not helped by continued charges of fraud, such as those published by ex-medium M. Lamar Keene in *The Psychic Mafia* (1976).

Surprisingly, Spiritualism has made a comeback as the twenty-first century begins. Two mediums, Sylvia Browne and James Van Praagh, have produced multiple best-selling books, and medium John Edwards demonstrated his abilities on the television programs *Crossing Over* and *Cross Country*. At the same time, the Internet has given the movement access to a new generation of potential believers.

CHANNELING.

Accompanying the emergence of Spiritualism was an impulse not only to prove the existence of life after death, but to gain detailed information from the spirit world concerning the nature of spirit existence and the structure of the universe. Many Spiritualists desired to understand the metaphysical system derived from spirit communication. Although the primary emphasis in Spiritualism has been to prove survival and the continuance of life after bodily death, the secondary emphasis to understand the spirit world and the real nature of life on earth has been a determining force in the history of Spiritualist groups. Some schisms in early Spiritualism grew out of this secondary emphasis.

Channeling is like most Spiritualist activities in that it retains the centrality of mediumship; however, the medium, usually termed a *channel*, tends to be in contact with evolved spirit entities, spirits that were once human but have evolved and have access to higher levels of wisdom and knowledge. These entities are viewed as wise and spiritual masters, who function much as the bodhisattvas in Buddhism who return from their elevated state to teach humankind.

Channeling was important to some early mediums such as Andrew Jackson Davis and Thomas Lake Harris (1823–1906), both of whom published long works derived from channeling sessions. Newbrough's *Oahspe* and Dowling's *Aquarian Gospel of Jesus the Christ* were both channeled volumes produced near the turn of the century. The early work of Davis and Harris did much to define Spiritualism as a separate movement. As the century progressed, however, a variety of different influences, especially Theosophy, made their presence known. Through the twentieth century, numerous channels have arisen, offering a wide variety of Spiritualist worldviews.

During the nineteenth century, Spiritualism in the United States was hostile to idea of reincarnation. However, through the twentieth century, channeled works have been a major influence, introducing reincarnation and the associ-

ated idea of karma into Spiritualist thinking. Today, channels mostly agree on the ideas of evolution and reincarnation. Humans are usually seen as fallen or entrapped spirit-beings, evolving through many lifetimes toward a pure spiritual existence. Karma, interpreted by Spiritualists as "the Spiritual law of cause and effect," is operative. Humans must overcome their bad karma, the consequences of bad actions, usually those of an earlier incarnation, and try to create good karma, leading to evolvement to a higher spiritual existence through good deeds.

Spiritualist channeling groups engage in little or no activity at contact of recently deceased relatives and friends of group members. Rather, their activity centers on discourses by evolved spirits speaking through the medium. Channeling groups formed periodically through the twentieth century, but since the late twentieth century, the number of such groups has grown markedly. In such groups, the spirit entity, speaking through the channel, is the teaching authority for the group. Actual teachings tend to make reference to all the major world religions, and much is drawn from Hinduism and Buddhism via Theosophy. Hindu and Buddhist elements include beliefs in reincarnation, a view of all existence as forming a mystic whole, and communication with spiritual masters who are similar to Buddhists bodhisattvas.

During the 1980s, as the New Age movement became a dominant force in the American psychic community, channeling received a startling new life. This new burst began with a set of books written by Jane Roberts (pseudonym of Jane Butts, 1929–1984), who claimed the books were dictated by a spirit entity known as Seth. Roberts, somewhat of a recluse, rarely made public appearances, but the books containing Seth's teachings sold well. On the heels of Seth's success, several new mediums (channels) emerged and attracted attention. Possibly the most famous was JZ Knight (b. 1946), a full-trance medium who channels an entity named Ramtha. Others mediums, all of whom remained active at the beginning of the twenty-first century, include Jach Pursel (Lazaris), Pat Rodegast (Emmanuel), and Kevin Ryerson (b. 1951) (John). They have been joined by Barbara Marciniak, Mary Margaret Moore, Darryl Anka (b. 1951), Lyssa Royal, Neale Donald Walsch (b. 1943) (who channeled the popular *Conversations with God* series), and a number of channels who founded the *Sedona Journal of Emergence* as a vehicle for presenting their material in the 1990s.

As the Internet became popular, channeling was highlighted on sights such as SpiritWeb and Whole Again. Common to this new group of mediums is their general lack of contact with older Spiritualist leaders (Ryerson being a prominent exception) and their adherence to Eastern and Theosophical (ancient wisdom) teachings. Generally, the newer channels agree on the identification of the self with the divine and the individual's power to create a world of happiness, health, and success.

Most channels work out of a single center, surrounded by a small group dedicated to the transcription and dissemination of communications from entities being channeled.

These transcriptions, and sometimes video and audio recordings, are distributed around the country and the world to supporters. Some channeling centers may also include a place for worship (or meditation), at which regular gatherings are held, although such gatherings are usually held in rented spaces. Many channels would not think of themselves as religious, even though they often function as the main religious teacher for their supporters.

Channeled material shows evidence of being drawn from a diversity of sources. Some comes out of the UFO contactee community, but most derives from Theosophy, the "I AM" Religious Activity, and other ancient wisdom teachings. Groups such as the Agasha Temple of Wisdom and the University of Life Church, which are traditional Spiritualist churches with a strong emphasis on channeling, served as a transition between classical Spiritualism and the new channeling groups.

DRUG-ORIENTED GROUPS.

Since ancient times, religious bodies have made use of various substances that altered consciousness and aided in the production of ecstatic states. According to some scholars, the Hindu god of sacrifice and the rituals associated with him are tied to the *Amanita muscaria*, a mushroom widely used because of its hallucinogenic powers. Most famous of the ancient drug-oriented bodies was the ancient Greek Dionysian religion, based on Dionysius, the god of the vine. Other Greek-based religions became famous for their use of alcohol. In pre-Colombian America, the Aztecs, Huichol, and various Mexican Indians ate peyote and related plants ceremonially.

Throughout Western history, various persons have discovered drugs with differing consciousness-altering properties and have then incorporated these into religious practices. At the beginning of the twentieth century, William James mentioned the use of nitrous oxide to stimulate the mystical consciousness. Most famous of the early twentieth-century drug users was Aleister Crowley (1875–1947), who used hashish and opium in his magical work for many years.

A new era in consciousness-expansion by the use of drugs began in 1938 when Albert Hofmann (1906–2008), a Swiss biochemist, synthesized d-lysergic acid diethylamide (LSD) tartrate from the rye fungus called ergot. In 1943 he accidentally absorbed some of the new drug, thus discovering its unusual properties. It caused a distortion of space and time and produced hallucinations. It also produced a state of consciousness in which the objective world took on a new meaning. The effects have been termed *psychedelic*. In the wake of Hofmann's discovery, other psychedelic drugs were cataloged and became known in medical and academic circles. They began to be used in hospitals for the treatment of neuroses and psychoses.

In the 1950s, widespread experiments with LSD began to occur, some secretly sponsored by the government. Aldous Huxley (1894–1963) wrote a popular account of his use of mescaline, another psychedelic drug, comparing his experiences with those described in the *Tibetan Book of the Dead*. In the early 1960s, reports began to appear of the experiences of those who took LSD. Many reported mystical and religious awakenings. The experiments eventuated in the watershed event of the era, the 1963 firing at Harvard University of professors Timothy Leary (1920–1996) and Richard Alpert (b. 1931) for involving students in reckless experiments with LSD.

Leary had been introduced in 1960 to psychedelic mushrooms by a Mexican anthropologist. He described his first "trip" as life-shaking and as the "deepest religious experience" of his life. He proceeded to begin experiments with psychedelic drugs at Harvard, introducing them to his colleague, Richard Alpert. After their firing, Leary became the psychological center of a drug-oriented generation, while Alpert soon felt he had exhausted the drug experience and traveled to India, only to emerge as a Hindu guru, Baba Ram Dass.

The story of the religious drug movement in the United States from this point becomes one of legal battles to establish the open practice of psychedelic groups under the U.S. Constitution. In 1966 the use of LSD was declared illegal, except for very limited research purposes. Several of these cases are discussed in entries on individual group. The loss of some of these cases has decimated the ranks of the once-powerful movement.

An early confrontation of the drug groups and the law occurred in Millbrook, New York, where Leary and his group (which he founded in 1966 as the League for Spiritual Discovery), along with Art Kleps (1928–1999) and the Neo-American Church and the non-drug-using Sri Rama Ashrama, had taken refuge on the estate of William Mellon Hitchcock. In December 1966, the Dutchess County police raided the estate and arrested Leary, Kleps, Hitchcock, and others. As a result of the raid and the attendant publicity, Hitchcock evicted the psychedelic groups. Leary's career in the next decades became one of fleeing the law and brief jail sentences, before he was finally able to work out the personal issues emerging from his drug-oriented prophethood.

While at Millbrook, Leary began to publish the first of numerous books. *Psychedelic Prayers after the Tao Te Ching* (1966) became the handbook of the League for Spiritual Discovery. Leary describes the psychedelic experience as occurring on three levels—neural, cellular, and molecular. In the first level, one tunes into patterns of neurological signals that are usually censored from mental life. The cellular consciousness transcends the symbolic game and the sensory apparatus, and people experience raw sensory bombardment and cellular hallucination. The molecular consciousness transcends even further and contacts elemental energies that crackle and vibrate within the cellular structure. The content of molecular consciousness is what, in mystic terminology, is called the *white light*, the *ovid*, or the *inner light*.

Continued legal pressures and unanimous court decisions against psychedelic drug use drove supporters from the ranks or into an underground existence. The League for Spiritual Discovery was disbanded, and most other drug-oriented groups have also been abandoned. By the end of the

1980s, only a few small drug-oriented churches remained, surviving from a fading hope of a court reversal or a change in the laws governing the use of psychedelic drugs.

A major result of the drug culture was to spur work in parapsychology, particularly in the area of altered states of consciousness. The experiences of psychedelically induced states resemble many visionary, mystical, and psychic experiences. Drug users have found more openness to their concerns in the psychic community than in any other religious family.

Through the 1990s, various actions by legal authorities and subsequent court decisions took their toll on the older psychedelic community and on efforts to establish a religious organization that could practice its beliefs concerning the use of psychedelic substances. One by one the groups that were operating in the 1970s died out. Surviving, in large part, were various shamanist-oriented groups that operated on an informal level.

Into this situation, several new groups that originated in Brazil and advocated the use of *ayahuasca*, a hallucinogenic drink, have migrated to North America and Europe. These groups emerged briefly, seeking to gain legal status using precedents articulated in several cases concerning the Native American Church, but their efforts were not successful, and most groups went underground.

FLYING SAUCER GROUPS.
On June 24, 1947, history was made in the skies of the state of Washington near Mount Rainier when Kenneth Arnold (1915–1984) saw a series of nine bright disks flying across the heavens in front of his plane. He described the objects as "saucers," and, when the media repeated his quotation, flying saucers became a new reality with which Americans had to contend. Arnold's sighting was followed by others. In July, a photograph of a flying saucer, or UFO (unidentified flying object), was given wide coverage in the press before it proved to be a weather balloon. Toward the end of July, a sighting in Maury Island (Washington) was followed by the deaths of two investigators from the Air Force. Only later was the hoax element of the Maury Island incident revealed.

Time and *Life* devoted space to stories about the saucers. The next major incident in the history of UFOs was the death of Captain Thomas Mantell, a pilot, on January 7, 1948. Mantell died in a plane crash as he was chasing a UFO over Louisville, Kentucky. Other major sightings included those by two Eastern Airlines pilots, Clarence S. Chiles and John B. Whitted, and by Lieutenant George F. Gorman of the North Dakota National Guard.

In 1947 Project Sign was established by the newly created U.S. Air Force to investigate reports of UFOs. In July 1949 a Project Sign report concluded that UFOs really were "interplanetary vehicles." The investigations were upgraded in 1949, and were called Project Grudge. Investigation proceeded normally until 1952, in spite of charges by UFO buffs such as Major Donald Keyhoe (1897–1988) that the government had orchestrated a cover-up. In 1952 there were major sightings for several evenings over Washington, D.C. That

same year APRO (Aerial Phenomena Research Organization) was founded in Tucson, Arizona, as the first national UFO study organization. The founding of APRO marked the beginning of a movement that was to grow significantly during the next 15 years.

A major segment of the UFO movement consisted of the growing number of people who claimed to have met and talked with occupants of the UFOs. Emanuel Swedenborg, for example, claimed to have conversed with beings of the solar system in the eighteenth century. During the nineteenth and early twentieth centuries, a number of people, mostly psychics, claimed to have been visited by inhabitants of other planets, and they wrote about these experiences and circulated their writings within the psychic community. These claims of contact with extraterrestrial beings form a background for modern claims of contact, as much as do the UFO phenomena.

After the UFO sightings drew national attention, the first to say he met and talked with UFO occupants was George Adamski (1891–1965). In his first book, Adamski detailed a 1952 contact with the "space brothers" and displayed pictures of their craft. Later books included silhouette pictures of Venusians. Adamski's books drew freely from Theosophical literature, including quotations from the *Book of Dzyan*, written by Madame Helena Petrovna Blavatsky (1831–1891), founder of Theosophy, and containing her comments on Venusians. Adamski was soon followed by others, such as George Williamson (1926–1986), Truman Bethurum (1898–1969), Orfeo M. Angelucci (1912–1993), and Buck Nelson (1894–1962). These later authors varied greatly in their accounts; each reported contact with visitors from different planets, and each lived in a different part of the United States. For some, the objects were believed to be advanced spacecraft. For others like Angelucci, they were objects from another dimension. Still others, in psychic jargon, saw creatures of a high vibratory rate who lowered their vibration in order to contact earth. Bethurum claimed to have ridden in spaceships.

The emergence of those who said they had contact with UFO occupants in the early 1950s led to a split among those concerned with the strange objects in the sky. UFO investigators continued to seek answers about the nature of the sightings. Another group, having made contact with what members claimed to be extraterrestrial entities, felt they knew what the "UFOs" were, and concentrated their efforts upon telling others the message of the space brothers. The term *flying saucer* has come to refer to *extraterrestrial craft*.

Through these early contacts, the space brothers began to articulate a message. While it varied at many points, its central ideas were common. The space brothers were highly evolved (either culturally or psychically) beings who were coming to aid their younger brothers. They brought a message of concern about the course of humankind, whose materialistic nature (or some other evil) is leading the species to destruction. Through the mediation of the beautiful space people, however, this destruction can be averted by following the message of love they bring. The space brothers are said to be constantly around, in a guiding paternity.

The continued appearance of UFOs and, especially, the messages of contactees (those contacted by UFO occupants), led many to begin a search for UFOs in history. Newly discovered accounts became a standard part of UFO literature. The Fortean Society aided in the explication of such accounts. These followers of Charles Fort (1874–1932) collected UFO data for many years.

Other researchers discovered accounts of UFOs in the Bible. Certain events were interpreted as cryptic accounts of UFO visitors from the skies. The most-quoted account is that of Ezekiel and the wheels in the air. More sophisticated study pointed to possible UFO involvement in the movement of the Israelites out of Egypt, as described in the biblical book of Exodus. One author, Presbyterian minister Barry H. Downing, postulated that the word *cloud* was a code word for biblical UFOs, and *angels* was a word for extraterrestrial visitors. He cited several passages in the Bible that he believed described UFO action: Genesis 32:24–25; Exodus 14:19–20; Exodus 40:33–38; Joshua 10:12–14; II Kings 2:1; Matthew 17:1–8; Luke 2; and Acts 1. Of interest is his understanding of Miriam's leprosy as skin irritation from a UFO contact.

Several later visionary experiences have also come to be seen as UFO landings. For example, ufologist Jacques Vallee (b. 1939) noted that the final visit of the Virgin at Fátima, Portugal, early in the twentieth century was accompanied by a bright sunlike object dancing in the sky and the dropping of angel hair, a fluffy substance often associated with UFOs. More recent writers, such as Erich von Däniken, have even speculated that the human race is descended from space beings, not from lower mammalian forms.

EARLY CONTACTEE GROUPS.

Besides the personal effort being made by individuals to spread the space brother gospel through speaking and writing, several people who claimed telepathic contact with UFOs began to gather a group around them, to channel regular messages daily or weekly, and to publish these messages abroad. These groups were modeled upon the Theosophical and "I AM" groups, and many of the hierarchical orders of Theosophy began to appear as space brothers. The Heralds of the New Age began in the 1950s to send out messages from the saucer world. Even though located in New Zealand, it was an influential group in North America. It formed a network, through the mail, of others interested in UFO material. In the United States, a young psychic, Gloria Lee (1925–1962), joined in these efforts. The Cosmos Research Foundation rallied to her support in the late 1950s. Gloria Lee's guide was an entity from Jupiter, identified only as J. W. Besides the regular mailings from the foundation, J. W. wrote two books through Gloria Lee titled *Why We Are Here* (1959) and *The Changing Condition of Your World* (1962). Highly Theosophical in nature, they include much material reminiscent of both Helena Blavatsky and Alice Bailey (1880–1949).

In 1962 the 37-year-old Lee went to Washington with the model and plans of a space ship, given to her by J. W.

Following his instructions, Lee secured herself in a hotel room to await word from government officials on her model. Once in her room, she began a Gandhi-like fast. On November 28, 1962, she lapsed into a coma, ending her 66-day fast in death on December 2. The Cosmos Research Foundation soon disbanded with the loss of its leader, but Lee became a martyr figure for the cause. Within two months, the Heralds of the New Age began to channel messages from her and soon produced a book, *The Going and the Glory* (1966), purporting to be from her. Other groups followed suit, and, in the wake of Lee's death, a number of space brothers began to emerge.

Another early UFO group was Christ Brotherhood, Inc., founded in 1956 by Wallace C. Halsey, a World War II veteran and engineer who became a minister. Both psychic and engineering interests led Halsey to the study of UFOs. In 1962 the space brothers instructed Tarna, Halsey's wife, to set up a tape recorder near his bed and to put the microphone on his chest. While asleep in bed, Halsey began audibly to channel a message of coming destruction and the gathering of a remnant who would be saved.

In 1963, on a flight from Utah to Nevada in a light plane, Halsey disappeared. No trace of either him or the plane was found. However, within a short time, Michael X. Barton, a metaphysical lecturer and writer in Los Angeles who had known Halsey, began to receive messages from him. The messages detailed the location of the missing plane. Though the plane was not found, several UFOs were sighted during the course of the search, and through messages Halsey described his departure in a UFO to Boston. The story of Barton's search was published, and Halsey joined the list of martyrs. Halsey's plane was finally located in 1977.

Since the 1970s and 1980s, the contactee community has continued to grow slowly. While none of the original 1950s contactees remain, new contactees have emerged, and the number of books describing their encounters and detailing the channeled teachings has grown impressively. As the New Age movement emerged in the 1980s, and channeling took on a new life, contactees shared in the new period of high interest. Among the New Age channels, Ken Carey (Raphael) and Thelma B. Terrell, publicly known as Tuella (who channels a variety of space entities), are representative of those who claim to be in contact with extraterrestrials.

Not a small portion of the credit for the continued growth of the contactee movement through the 1980s must go to the ufological community, which gave serious systematic consideration, for the first time, to stories of direct contact with extraterrestrials. Ufologists initially turned their attention to what were termed "encounters of the third kind" and then to accounts of abductions of individuals by entities in UFOs, the subject of several best-selling books. Though ufologists denounce many of the contactees, their research on close encounters and abductions has served to make their claims more believable to the general public. Among the contactee channels who emerged in the 1990s were Barbara

Hand Clow (b. 1943), Amorah Quan Yin (b. 1950), Norma Milanovich, and Robert Shapiro.

Through the 1990s, many ufologists continued to place a great deal of confidence in the accounts of people who claimed to have been abducted by extraterrestrials. The hope for any evidential material from the abductees has slowly faded since the beginning of the twenty-first century, though it has by no means disappeared. At the same time, a steady supply of new books by people claiming to channel extraterrestrials continues to appear, though such books are often given little shelf space in the large chain bookstores. The new century has shown a marked decrease in the number of channeling groups based on messages from outer space.

THE NEW AGE MOVEMENT.

Many esoteric organizations in the United States do not readily fit among either the Spiritualists or the ancient-wisdom groups discussed in chapter 17. Given the ferment of the esoteric community, new impulses are constantly appearing. In the 1970s, however, a new generation of psychic, occult, and spiritual seekers arose who rejected the Spiritualist emphasis upon spirits and mediums and refused the more negative designation "occult," but identified strongly with the new wave of Eastern teachers that rose to prominence in the late 1960s. In the fervor of their discovery of the psychic and spiritual dimensions of life, they began to see themselves as the harbingers of a new age for humanity. By the mid-1970s, a loosely organized New Age movement could be clearly discerned. The New Age ideal swept through the psychic, occult, and metaphysical communities, and the hope for a coming age of love and peace affected people of many backgrounds.

The New Age movement originated in the 1960s in Great Britain, but its beginnings in North America can be traced to 1971 with the publication of the first popular book representative of the movement, *Be Here Now* by Baba Ram Dass, and the launching of the first national periodical on the movement, *East-West Journal*, followed in 1972 by the first national networking directories, *Year One Catalog*, edited by Ira Friedlander, and the *Spiritual Community Guide*.

As it emerged, the movement was very loosely organized, though it included within it some highly structured and even authoritarian groups. The movement was centered upon a vision of radical transformation of society and the individual, though the means for accomplishing that transformation varied widely from group to group and individual to individual. On the individual level the transformation was seen as personal and mystical. The accomplished personal transformation provided the model for eventual social transformation. New Age theorist Marilyn Ferguson (b. 1938) described it as an open conspiracy by transformed people to complete a process of transformation in their neighbor and in society as a whole.

New Agers hoped that a new universal religion would arise in the New Age, a religion based not upon creeds and the division of social groups into denominations and religions, but having as its goal the development of a mystical consciousness or awareness. God would be seen as the unifying principle that binds nature and humanity together. Loyalty to humanity would transcend personal loyalties to more limited social groups, such as nations and clans.

New Agers differed in their opinions concerning the exact path that would lead to the New Age. Their disagreements were in part related to their differing alignments with particular religious traditions. A wide variety of occult-spiritual techniques were proposed, taught, and adopted by various segments of the movement. These techniques varied from vegetarianism and communalism to different forms of meditation, yoga, and magic.

The New Age movement peaked in the 1980s, and the hope of an imminent change in the social order largely disappeared as the 1990s progressed. However, the movement had by this time revived many of the older occult groups and spawned a number of new movements, some with more of a Spiritualist nature and some leaning toward Theosophy. (Included in the directory listings of this encyclopedia are a number of groups that originated in the New Age movement and have adopted a complete religious worldview and lifestyle. Such groups provide the basis for a full religious life for those associated with them, including regular worship, religious literature, learning experiences, and a program oriented around a spiritual practice or discipline.)

As the New Age movement faded, most New Agers were happy with the personal spirituality they had acquired through it. Through the 1990s, many identified with the host of new groups that emerged to perpetuate New Age ideals, now focused around the hope of an ever-increasing global interest in spirituality that would over the next centuries lead to new levels of spiritual awareness and produce a flourishing new culture. This post–New Age vision was most clearly articulated in James Redfield's *The Celestine Prophecy* (1993), the best-selling metaphysical text of the 1990s. This new current of the old New Age has been referred to as the Next Age, especially in Europe.

SOURCES

General Sources

Albanese, Catherine. *A Republic of Mind and Spirit: A Cultural History of American Metaphysical Religion*. New Haven, CT: Yale University Press, 2007. 640 pp.

Judah, J. Stillson. *The History and Philosophy of the Metaphysical Movements in America*. Philadelphia: Westminster Press, 1967. 317 pp.

Kerr, Howard, and Charles L. Crow, eds. *The Occult in America*. Urbana: University of Illinois Press, 1983. 246 pp.

Melton, J. Gordon, ed. *Encyclopedia of Occultism and Parapsychology*. 5th ed. 2 vols. Detroit, MI: Gale, 1999.

Swedenborg and the New Jerusalem

Benz, Ernst. *Emanuel Swedenborg: Visionary Savant in the Age of Reason*. West Chester, PA: Swedenborg Foundation, 2002. 532 pp.

Block, Marguerite Beck. *The New Church in the New World: A Study of Swedenborgianism in America*. New York: Holt, 1932. 464 pp.

Doyle, George F., and Robert H. Kirven. *A Scientist Explores Spirit: A Compact Biography of Emanuel Swedenborg with Key Concepts of Swedenborg's Theology*. New York: Swedenborg Foundation, 1992. 107 pp.

Pendleton, William Frederic. *Topics from the Writings.* Bryn Athyn, PA: Academy Book Room, 1928. 249 pp.

Rose, Jonathan S., Stuart Shotwell, and Mary Lou Bertucci, eds. *Scribe of Heaven: Swedenborg's Life, Work, and Impact.* West Chester, PA: Swedenborg Foundation, 2005. 580 pp.

Sigstedt, Cyriel Odhner. *The Swedenborg Epic.* New York: Bookman Associates, 1952. 517 pp.

Silver, Ednah C. *Sketches of the New Church in America.* Boston: Massachusetts New Church Union, 1920. 314 pp.

Spalding, John Howard. *Introduction to Swedenborg's Religious Thought.* New York: Swedenborg Publishing Association, 1977. 235 pp.

Toksvig, Signe. *Emanuel Swedenborg: Scientist and Mystic.* New Haven, CT: Yale University Press, 1948. 389 pp.

Woofenden, William Ross. *Swedenborg Researcher's Manual.* Bryn Athyn, PA: Swedenborg Scientific Association, 1988. 366 pp.

Spiritualism—General Sources

Barbanell, Maurice. *This Is Spiritualism.* London: Jenkins, 1959. 223 pp.

Baude, Ann. *Radical Spirits: Spiritualism and Women's Rights in Nineteenth-Century America.* Bloomington: Indiana University Press, 2001. 296 pp.

Carter, Huntley, ed. *Spiritualism: Its Present-Day Meaning.* Philadelphia: Lippincott, 1920. 287 pp.

Davis, Andrew Jackson. *The Harmonial Philosophy.* Chicago: Advanced Thought Publishing, n.d. 428 pp.

Keene, M. Lamar. *The Psychic Mafia.* New York: St. Martin's Press, 1976. 177 pp.

Lawton, George. *The Drama of Life After Death.* London: Constable, 1933. 668 pp.

Leonard, Todd J. *Talking to the Other Side: A History of Modern Spiritualism and Mediumship: A Study of the Religion, Science, Philosophy, and Mediums that Encompass this American-Made Religion.* New York: iUniverse, 2005. 364 pp.

Nelson, Geoffrey K. *Spiritualism and Society.* New York: Schocken, 1969. 307 pp.

Pearsall, Ronald. *The Table-Rappers.* New York: St. Martin's Press, 1972. 258 pp.

Skultans, Vieda. *Intimacy and Ritual: A Study of Spiritualism, Mediums, and Groups.* London: Routledge & Kegan Paul, 1974. 106 pp.

Psychical Research and Spiritualism

Ashby, Robert H. *A Guidebook for the Study of Psychical Research.* New York: Weiser, 1972. 190 pp.

Douglas, Alfred. *Extra-Sensory Powers: A Century of Psychical Research.* Woodstock, NY: Overbrook Press, 1977. 392 pp.

Gauld, Alan. *The Founders of Psychical Research.* New York: Schocken, 1968. 389 pp.

Moore, R. Laurence. *In Search of White Crows: Spiritualism, Parapsychology, and American Culture.* New York: Oxford University Press, 1977. 310 pp.

Spiritualism—History

Baer, Hans A. *The Black Spiritual Movement: A Religious Response to Racism.* 2nd ed. Knoxville: University of Tennessee Press, 2001.

Brandon, Ruth. *The Spiritualists: The Passion for the Occult in the Nineteenth and Twentieth Centuries.* New York: Knopf, 1983. 315 pp.

Brown, Slater. *The Heyday of Spiritualism.* New York: Hawthorn, 1970. 264 pp.

Carroll, Bret E. *Spiritualism in Antebellum America.* Bloomington: Indiana University Press, 1997. 256 pp.

Centennial Book of Modern Spiritualism in America. Chicago: National Spiritualist Association of United States of America, 1948. 253 pp.

Cox, Robert S. *Body and Soul: A Sympathetic History of American Spiritualism.* Charlottesville: University of Virginia Press, 2003. 288 pp.

Grand Souvenir Book: World Centennial Celebration of Modern Spiritualism. San Antonio: Federation of Spiritual Churches and Associations, 1948. 200 pp.

Guthrie, John J., Jr., Phillip Charles Lucas, and Gary Monroe. *Cassadaga: The South's Oldest Spiritualist Community.* Gainesville: University Press of Florida, 2000. 272 pp.

Pond, Mariam Buckner. *Time Is Kind: The Story of the Unfortunate Fox Family.* New York: Centennial Press, 1947. 334 pp.

Todorovich, Thomas E., ed. *The Centennial Memorial of Modern Spiritualism Records, 1848–1948.* St. Louis: National Spiritualist Association of U.S.A., 1948. 157 pp.

Weisberg, Barbara. *Talking to the Dead: Kate and Maggie Fox and the Rise of Spiritualism.* San Francisco: Harper, 2004. 336 pp.

Wesley, John. *The Journal.* London: Epworth, 1914.

Wicker, Christine. *Lily Dale: The True Story of the Town That Talks to the Dead.* San Francisco: HarperOne, 2004. 304 pp.

Flying Saucers and UFOs

Clark, Jerome. *Extraordinary Encounters: An Encyclopedia of Extraterrestrial and Otherworldly Beings.* Santa Barbara, CA: ABC-Clio, 2000. 290 pp.

Eberhart, George M. *UFOs and the Extraterrestrial Contact Movement: A Bibliography.* 2 vols. Metuchen, MD: Scarecrow Press, 1986.

Flamonde, Paris. *The Age of Flying Saucers: Notes on a Projected History of Unidentified Flying Objects.* New York: Hawthorn, 1971. 288 pp.

Fuller, Curtis G., ed. *Proceedings of the First International UFO Congress.* New York: Warner, 1980. 440 pp.

Jacobs, David Michael. *The UFO Controversy in America.* Bloomington: Indiana University Press, 1975. 362 pp.

Mack, John E. *Passport to the Cosmos: Human Transformation and Alien Encounters.* Three Rivers, MI: Three Rivers Press, 1999. 352 pp.

Steiger, Brad. *The Aquarian Revelations.* New York: Dell, 1971. 158 pp.

Zinsstag, Lou, and Timothy Good. *George Adamski: The Untold Story.* Kent, U.K.: Ceti, 1983. 208 pp.

Channeling

Brown, Michael F. *The Channeling Zone: American Spirituality in an Anxious Age.* Cambridge, MA: Harvard University Press, 1997. 236 pp.

Hastings, Arthur. *With the Tongues of Men and Angels: A Study of Channeling.* Fort Worth, TX: Holt, Rinehart and Winston, 1991. 232 pp.

Klimo, Jon. *Channeling: Investigations on Receiving Information from Paranormal Sources.* Rev. ed. Berkeley, CA: North Atlantic Books, 1998. 474 pp.

Psychedelics

Castenada, Carlos. *The Teachings of Don Juan: A Yaqui Way of Knowledge.* New York: Ballantine, 1969. 276 pp.

de Mille, Richard. *Castaneda's Journey: The Power and the Allegory.* Santa Barbara, CA: Capra Press, 1976. 205 pp.

———. *The Don Juan Papers: Further Castaneda Controversies.* Santa Barbara, CA: Ross-Erikson, 1980. 518 pp.

Forte, Roberta, ed. *Timothy Leary: Outside Looking In.* Rochester, VT: Park Street Press, 1999. 338 pp.

Kleps, Art. *Millbrook: A Narrative of the Early Years of American Psychedelianism, Recension of 1997.* Austin, TX: Original Kleptonian Neo-American Church, 1997. 222 pp.

La Barre, Weston. *The Peyote Cult.* Rev. ed. New York: Schocken, 1969. 260 pp.

Leary, Timothy. *Flashbacks: An Autobiography.* Los Angeles: Tarcher, 1983. 397 pp.

Masters, R. E. L., and Jean Houston. *The Varieties of Psychedelic Experience.* New York: Delta, 1967. 326 pp.

Weil, Gunther M., Ralph Metzner, and Timothy Leary, eds. *The Psychedelic Reader: Selected from the* Psychedelic Review. New Hyde Park, NY: University Books, 1965. 260 pp.

New Age Movement

Allen, Mark. *Chrysalis: A Journey into the New Spiritual America.* Berkeley, CA: Pan, 1978. 179 pp.

Ferguson, Marilyn. *The Aquarian Conspiracy: Personal and Social Transformation in the 1980s.* Los Angeles: Tarcher, 1980. 448 pp.

Hanegraaff, Wouter J. *New Age Religion and Western Culture: Esotericism in the Mirror of Secular Thought.* Leiden, Netherlands: Brill, 1996. 580 pp.

Heelas, Paul. *The New Age Movement: The Celebration of the Self and the Sacralization of Modernity.* Oxford: Blackwell, 1996. 266 pp.

Kyle, Richard. *The New Age Movement in American Culture.* Lanham, MD: University Press of America, 1995. 291 pp.

Lewis, James R., and J. Gordon Melton, eds. *Perspectives on the New Age.* Albany: State University of New York Press, 1992. 369 pp.

Melton, J. Gordon, Jerome Clark, and Aidan A. Kelly. *New Age Encyclopedia.* Detroit, MI: Gale Research, 1990. 586 pp.

Saliba, John A. *Christian Responses to the New Age Movement: A Critical Assessment.* London: Chapman, 1999. 245 pp.

Satin, Mark. *New Age Politics: Healing Self and Society.* Rev. ed. New York: Delta, 1979. 349 pp.

Spangler, David. *Towards a Planetary Vision.* Forres, U.K.: Findhorn Foundation, 1977.

Sutcliffe, Steve. *Children of the New Age: A History of Spiritual Practices.* New York: Routledge, 2003. 224 pp.

Wilber, Ken. *The Spectrum of Consciousness.* Wheaton, IL: Theosophical Publishing House, 1977. 374 pp.

❀ Swedenborgian Groups

General Convention of the New Jerusalem

11 Highland Ave., Newtonville, MA 02460

The oldest of the several Swedenborgian churches in America is the General Convention, formed in 1817 at Baltimore, Maryland. A call was issued by the Philadelphia Society to the 17 societies then in existence, and plans were laid for regulating ordination and missionary work west of the Allegheny Mountains. The convention is governed by its executive council, an executive committee elected by ministers and delegates, but local affairs are in the hands of the congregations. The convention meets annually. Any member may attend and speak, but only ministers and delegates may vote.

The doctrine of the convention follows Emanuel Swedenborg's writings on the Bible and Christian doctrine. Convention members believe in the Trinity, but not of distinct individuals, and teach that the words and even the letters of the Bible were inspired by God but are not necessarily infallible in every respect. Most important, the Bible contains a spiritual sense. God came to earth to overcome the demonic powers dominating the human race. Salvation is open to all who cooperate with God with faith, love, and a life of uses. When a person dies, that person passes into the spiritual world and ultimately into either heaven or hell, depending on the spiritual character acquired on earth. Both baptism and the Lord's Supper are administered. Worship, formerly liturgical, now varies considerably from congregation to congregation. Chants are no longer used extensively.

The convention elects a president and other officers and oversees a board of trustees. Foreign work is supported in Europe, Japan, Guyana, and Canada. In 1966 the convention joined the National Council of the Churches of Christ in the U.S.A.

Membership: In 2001 there were 1,895 members worldwide, of which 1,601 members reside in the United States and 294 in Canada.

Educational Facilities:

Swedenborgian House of Studies, Pacific School of Religion, Berkeley, California.

Periodicals: *Our Daily Bread.* • *The Messenger.*

Sources:

General Convention of the New Jerusalem. www.swedenborgiancommunity.org/content.cfm?id=2038.

Zacharias, Paul. *Insights into the Beyond.* New York: Swedenborg Publishing Association, n.d.

The Lord's New Church Which Is Nova Hierosolyma

1725 Huntingdon Rd., PO Box 7, Bryn Athyn, PA 19009

The Lord's New Church Which Is Nova Hierosolyma was formally established in 1937 when some members of the General Church of the New Jerusalem came to a new understanding of the writings of Emanual Swedenborg (1688–1772). In 1929 articles by New Church priests and lay persons began to appear in the Dutch periodical *De Hemelsche Leer* (The Celestial Doctrine), arguing that the writings of Swedenborg were like the Bible, both in being authoritative (divine revelation) and in having an internal sense. A primary task of believers was to come to an understanding of the internal sense (or inner meaning) of Swedenborg's writings in order that their spiritual development of regeneration might be facilitated. Thus viewed, the doctrine of the New Church is seen to be from the Lord, not from humans. A corollary to that position is the belief that as understanding deepens and the church follows the Lord, there can be growth and development of these ideas to eternity. When the General Church rejected that doctrinal position, a split occurred, and the Lord's New Church was formed.

Societies of the church soon were formed in various countries around the world. In the United States, Rev. Theodore Pitcairn was the main exponent. His efforts led to the formation of two congregations, in Bryn Athyn, Pennsylvania, and in Yonkers, New York (the latter closed after the death of its pastor). The church operates a theological school to train men for the priesthood. The Swedenborg Association, the church's publication division, publishes books and a quarterly journal.

Membership: In 1997 there were three North American congregations, in Charleston, South Carolina, Asheville, North Carolina, and Bryn Athyn, Pennsylvania. There are also individual members are scattered around North America, unattached to a congregation. Additional congregations can be found in Holland, Japan, Sweden, the Ukraine, and South Africa.

Periodicals: *Arcana: Inner Dimensions of Spirituality.* • *Stella Matutin* (South Africa). • *Varldarnas Mote* (Sweden).

Sources:

The Lord's New Church Which Is Nova Hierosolyma. www.thelordsnewchurch.com/.

Handbook of the Lord's New Church Which Is Nova Hierosolyma. Bryn Athyn, PA: Lord's New Church Which Is Nova Hierosolyma, 1985.

Pitcairn, Theodore. *The Bible, or Word of God, Uncovered and Explained.* Bryn Athyn, PA: Lord's New Church Which Is Nova Hierosolyma, 1964.

———. *The Book Sealed with Seven Seals.* Bryn Athyn, PA: Cathedral Book Room, 1927.

———. *My Lord and My God.* New York: Exposition Press, 1967.

———. *The Seven Days of Creation.* Bryn Athyn, PA: Lord's Church Which Is Nova Hierosolyma, 1940.

The New Church/General Church of the New Jerusalem
PO Box 743, Bryn Athyn, PA 19009

In 1836 Rev. Richard de Charms, a pastor in Cincinnati, began a magazine, the *Precursor*, to agitate for what he considered true New Church principles. He protested the adoption of an episcopal form of government. In 1838 the General Convention of the New Jerusalem adopted a rule that required all societies to organize under the same rules of order. This rule led to schism. De Charms, then pastor of the New Church in Philadelphia, pulled his church out of the General Convention and, in 1840, led in the founding of the Central Convention. In part, the cause of the schism was a growing conflict between Boston and Philadelphia: The Boston church had proposed a theory of the General Convention as spiritual mother, to which all owed allegiance. Because New England votes (primarily Bostonian votes) controlled the General Convention, the theory was interpreted as an attempt by the New Englanders to run the church. The Philadelphia Society also was moving toward the view that the works of Swedenborg were the only authority of the new dispensation, and contained no contradiction or untruth. This was a view opposed by many General Convention members.

The General Convention reacted to the growth of the Central Convention by loosening its rules. The rules of order were declared merely recommendations; closed communion was rejected; a new system of equitable representation was established; and the assumption of any spiritual authority by the General Convention was renounced. The Central Convention was formally dissolved in 1852, but some of its key ideas led eventually to the foundation of a new group within the General Convention—the Academy Movement.

In 1859 William Benade, a younger contemporary of de Charms, proposed the formation of an academy as an inner circle of scholars devoted to the study of Swedenborg, to propagate the belief in divine origins and the training of young men for the priesthood. Most members of the General Convention were opposed to the idea of "priesthood," even though it was contained in Swedenborg's writings. The academy was begun on an informal basis in 1874. To carry the movement, a periodical, *Words for the New Church*, was begun. A theological school and children's day schools were proposed. The academy students were pulled together in Philadelphia.

Benade, unlike his elder sponsor, was an advocate of episcopal authority, and in 1882 he became bishop of the General Church of Philadelphia, the reorganized Philadelphia Association with its seven societies. Others soon joined. Tension developed between the General Church of Philadelphia and the General Convention with which it associated. In 1890 the General Church of Philadelphia made the final break with the General Convention. The General Church of Philadelphia is now called the General Church of the New Jerusalem, a name often shortened to General Church.

Polity of the General Church is episcopal; only the bishop has the power to ordain. The executive bishop is elected at the general assembly and is assisted by a council of the clergy and the directors of the corporation (laymen). A director of General Church religious lessons oversees production of church school course material on New Church themes. There is also an active book-publishing program. Affiliated congregations are found in Canada, England, New Zealand, Australia, Denmark, Sweden, Ghana, Japan, Korea, Holland, South Africa, and Brazil.

Membership: In 1997 the church reported 3,036 members, 36 congregations, and 47 ministers in the United States. There were 412 members in four congregations served by 5 ministers in Canada, and an additional 1,032 members worldwide.

Educational Facilities:

Bryn Athyn College of the New Church, Bryn Athyn, Pennsylvania.

Academy of the New Church Theological School, Bryn Athyn, Pennsylvania.

Periodicals: *New Church Life*. • *Bishop's Newsletter*. • *General Church Around the World*. • *New Church Vineyard*. • *New Church Connection*. • *New Church Life*. • *General Church Outreach*.

Sources:

The New Church/General Church of the New Jerusalem. www.newchurch.org.

De Charms, George. *The Distinctiveness of the New Church*. Bryn Athyn, PA: Academy Book Room, 1962.

———. *The Holy Supper*. Bryn Athyn, PA: General Church Publication Committee, 1961.

The General Church of the New Jerusalem, A Handbook of General Information. Bryn Athyn, PA: General Church Publication Committee, 1965.

Liturgy and Hymnal. Bryn Athyn, PA: General Church of the New Jerusalem, 1966.

What the Writings Testify Concerning Themselves. Bryn Athyn, PA: General Church Publication Committee, 1961.

❀ Spiritualism

Agasha Temple of Wisdom
PO Box 80483, Billings, MT 59108

The Agasha Temple of Wisdom was founded in 1943 by Rev. Richard Zenor (1911–1978), an intertransitory medium for the master teacher, Agasha. Zenor had begun to show paranormal abilities as a child in Terre Haute, Indiana. During the first decade of the temple's existence, Zenor attained recognition and fame from being featured in *Telephone between Two Worlds* (1950), a book by the popular writer James Crenshaw. The temple became the base from which Zenor traveled and spread the message of Agasha.

Two years after Zenor's death, Rev. Geary Salvat was chosen to continue his work. Like his predecessor, Salvat, an intertransitory medium for the Master Teacher Ayuibbi Tobabu, had manifested psychic abilities from his youth.

Although activity at the temple includes communication with the departed, it is primarily directed toward master teachers, advanced individuals who communicate teachings from the other side. From Agasha, Ayuibbi Tobabu, and other teachers, a distinct philosophy has been developed: the Universal Understanding of the God Consciousness. Its keynote is individual responsibility and spiritual democracy within the plan of universal laws. The basic laws include the Golden Rule (do unto others as you would have them do unto you) and the law of compensation (for every action, there is an equal and opposite reaction). Individuals spend many lifetimes seeking to understand these laws by which their lives are governed. During the 1980s the teachings received from Agasha became the subject of a series of books by longtime temple student William Eisen. A volume on the teachings of Ayuibbi Tobabu is projected.

Membership: Not reported.

Periodicals: *Agasha Temple Newsletter*.

Sources:

Agasha Temple of Wisdom. www.agasha.org/.

Crenshaw, James. *Telephone between Two Worlds*. Los Angeles: DeVorss and Company, 1950.

Eisen, William. *Agasha, Master of Wisdom*. Marina del Rey, CA: DeVorss and Company, 1977.

———. *The English Cabalah*. 2 vols. Marina del Rey, CA: DeVorss and Company, 1980–82.

———, ed. *The Agashan Discourse*. Marina del Rey, CA: DeVorss and Company, 1978.

Zenor, Richard. *Margie Answers You*. San Diego, CA: Philip J. Hastings, 1965.

Aquarian Foundation

315 15th Ave. E, Seattle, WA 98112

The Aquarian Foundation was founded in 1955 by Rev. Keith Milton Rhinehart, a Spiritualist minister. The foundation combines elements of Spiritualism, Theosophy, and Eastern philosophy into an eclectic occult perspective. It existed for many years as an independent Spiritualist congregation in Seattle. During the 1960s, however, Rhinehart became known for his "materialization" seances and later claimed contact with those same "ascended" masters originally contacted by Helena Petrovna Blavatsky (1831–1891), founder of the Theosophical Society.

The Aquarian Foundation does not have a statement of belief, which it feels would serve to prevent growth into greater knowledge. Aquarians draw inspiration from, and identification with, all of the major religious traditions, though the elements of Spiritualism and Theosophy are most evident. "Mediums," individuals with an ability to regularly communicate with the "so-called" dead, are valued. However, the foundation does not focus upon regular contact with dead relatives and friends. Instead, contact is made primarily with Masters of the Great Brotherhood of Cosmic Light (also known as the Great White Brotherhood). The foundation believes in many of the concepts passed on by this Brotherhood through the Theosophical Society—karma and reincarnation, the evolution of the soul, the law of cause and effect, mastery of life and death, and the eventual attainment of personal mastery. Rhinehart, the primary medium for the foundation, conducts trance sessions through which the masters speak, which are regularly recorded from playback at the foundation's many centers.

The foundation is committed to the Great Plan enunciated by the masters, who are viewed as ascended and evolved beings guiding the evolution of humanity and ushering in the present Aquarian Age. Prominent among the masters who have regularly spoken over the last decades through Rhinehart are Saint Germain, Morya, Sanat Kumara, and Djwal Kul (D. K.), popular figures in the Theosophical and I AM Religious Activity presentation of the spiritual hierarchy. Rhinehart also serves as the medium for many other "masters" including the Angel Moroni, who gave Joseph Smith Jr. the Book of Mormon; Mahatma Gandhi; Ashtar, first contacted by George Van Tassel, an early UFO contactee; Clarion, a UFO entity contacted by Truman Betherum in the 1950s; and the Master Immanuel, from South American Spiritualism. Rhinehart gained his early fame in Spiritualism because of his well publicized materialization seances conducted in the 1950s. More recently he claimed to possess the stigmata, a paranormal appearance of the wounds of Christ, which is said to have appeared on his body before hundreds of witnesses.

Membership: During the 1970s the foundation spread from its Seattle base to become both a national and international organization. Churches are located in Honolulu, New York City, Miami Beach, Anchorage, Hollywood, Dallas, San Francisco, and Portland, Oregon. Study groups are found in Hilo, Hawaii; Ft. Lauderdale; Tacoma; West Palm Beach, Florida; Austin, Texas; and Atlanta. Foreign groups are located in Vancouver and Johannesburg, South Africa.

Sources:

The Aquarian Foundation. aquarianfoundation.org.

Rhinehart, Keith Milton. *Soul Mates and Twin Rays*. Seattle, WA: Aquarian Foundation, 1972.

Believers' Circle

Rev. Estel Merrill, 7437 Bear Mt. Blvd., Bakersfield, CA 93313

The Believers' Circle was founded in the early 1980s by Rev. Estel Peg Merrill. Merrill had been a student of metaphysical and esoteric studies for many years before she became aware of a gift of healing. She also intuited several spirit guides, and began to go into trances and to channel messages from the spirit world. These guides/teachers were affiliated with a group called the Council, which was seen as part of the Group Mind, which in turn was a part of the Spiral Unihood (formerly known as the Brotherhood). The Council expressed its concern for humankind. Merrill's primary guide is Levi, formerly a scribe in his earthly incarnation, who was

famous as the same entity who directed Levi Dowling in the transcription of *The Aquarian Gospel of Jesus Christ*. Her spirit control is HiChing, formerly an astrologer in China during the Ming Dynasty.

In 1979 Merrill began to receive lessons that became the basis of the teachings of the Believers' Circle. These teachings have been collected in several books. They affirm God as the supreme power and designer of the universe. Neither male nor female, God is "uni," and exists in and around all of creation. God's energy is available for healing the mind and body. Humans are a form of God consciousness who are in this present life to learn God's absolute laws and correct past mistakes. Following death, humans make a transition to spirit existence and continue their learning.

The Believers' Circle is headquartered in Bakersfield, California, but members are scattered across the continent. Members relate to Merrill primarily through the reception of the Circle's lesson through the mail. Beginning students start with three volumes titled *Spiritual Understanding* and progress to more advanced lessons in *God's Prevailing Laws*, *God's Energy through Thoughts*, and *God's Laws of Love and Life*.

Membership: Not reported.

Christian Spirit Center

Box 114, Elon College, NC 27244

The Christian Spirit Center is headed by S. J. Haddad, its president, and is based in Elon College, North Carolina. The Center is primarily devoted to translating messages received by Brazilian mediums from Portuguese into English. It also publishes books and distributes literature on spirit doctrines. Spiritualism came into Brazil through the writings of the French writer and medium Allan Kardec (1804–1869). His teachings were distinctive, at the time, for their introduction of reincarnation into Spiritualism.

The main tenets of the Center are the continuity of life after death (first taught and demonstrated by Christ in his own resurrection, and now proven by mediumship), the laws of reincarnation and cause and effect ("karma"), and people's free will and responsibility for their actions.

In accordance with the words of Christ, "Freely ye have received, freely give," and based upon spirit teachings to the same effect, the Center advocates mediumship as a free service. The same principle is applied to lectureships and other spiritual work. Active followers of the spirit doctrine earn their living in secular occupations.

Membership: Not reported.

Church of Essential Science

PO Box 62284, Phoenix, AZ 85082

The Church of Essential Science was founded in Detroit, Michigan, in 1965 by Rev. Kingdon L. Brown, a medium ordained originally by the National Spiritual Aid Association. Brown was an early member of the association and developed in an informal study group. In January 1964 he received his first message from the "ascended masters." Eventually, one of the members became Brown's guide and teacher. Brown gradually became known for his mediumistic ability, and followers were drawn to him.

Essential Science is a religion responsive to the new data available to modern man—parapsychology, philosophy, sociology, metaphysics, and mysticism. God is seen as the cause that sustains and protects all who seek God. Man comes to know God as the Divine Mind Power as he widens his awareness to include spiritual impressions. Man is body, mind, and soul. The soul is man's divine inheritance, a part of divinity. Through the soul, man aligns himself with the God power, the basic atomic pattern structure of the universe itself, the basic energy of the universe. A significant part of creation is the fellowship of all seekers of truth. Some are in the body, some have ascended. The ascended ones become our teachers as we decide to put our spiritual development above all else.

Headquarters of the Church of Essential Science are in Scottsdale, Arizona, where Brown became pastor of the Desert Shadows Church. Other centers are located in Detroit; Chicago; New York City; Columbus and Tijeras, New Mexico; Little Rock, Arkansas; Fort Wayne, Indiana; and Palo Alto, California. Foreign centers are in Curacao, Canada, and Nigeria. Members are scattered around the country. Many were drawn to the church by the numerous personal appearances of Brown, who changed his name to Brian Seabrook.

In 1987 the church began a new public outreach with a mystical system. The purpose of this degree system of spiritual knowledge was to prepare humankind for the Aquarian dispensation about the year 2000 C.E.. It is based on the metaphysical interpretation of the Christian Bible, and the original mission of the Master Jesus. Highly symbolic and transformative, this system incorporates a new understanding of traditional esoteric practices. The aim is to bring the individual into direct contact with the Divine Essence of all earthly life. Techniques such as channeling, healing, and meditation are central.

Membership: In 2002 there were 3,500 members.

Periodicals: *Monthly Reminder*. • *Christar Temple Degrees*.

Sources:

Church of Essential Science. www.essentialscience.org/.

Brown, Kingdon L. *The Power of Psychic Awareness*. West Nyack, NY: Parker Publishing, 1969.

The Metaphysical Lessons of Saint Timothy's Abbey Church. Grosse Pointe, MI: St. Timothy's Abbey Church, 1966.

Church of Metaphysical Christianity

2717 Browning St., Sarasota, FL 34237

The Church of Metaphysical Christianity was founded in 1958 by Revs. Dorothy Graff Flexer and Russell J. Flexer, two prominent mediums in the Spiritualist Episcopal Church. Dorothy Flexer had led the Spiritualist Episcopal Church in its break with Camp Chesterfield in 1956 that resulted in a number of churches and ministers leaving the church. She became independent two years later.

Metaphysical Christianity, a combination of religion, philosophy, and science, disseminates the spiritual truths as manifested in the life and teachings of the master, Jesus. It seeks to study the laws of nature—mental, physical and spiritual. Obedience to these laws is said to constitute the highest form of worship. The church also teaches and gives evidence of the continuity of life after death, encouraging each member to develop his or her own gifts of the spirit so that communion between the two worlds will become natural.

The basic spiritual laws are: the law of life, the law of love (the creative force of life), the law of truth or right thinking, the law of compensation, the law of freedom, the law of abundance, and the law of perfection. After death, the spirit continues and may communicate with those still on the earth-plane. Healing is emphasized as a spiritual art.

Headquarters of the church is in Sarasota, Florida. In 1973 there were on the rolls some 25 spiritual healers.

Membership: In 1997 the church reported 125 members.

Periodical: *Focus*.

Sources:

Shrine of the Master, Church of Metaphysical Christianity. shrineofthemaster.com.

Davis, Charles [spirit speaking through Dorothy Graff Flexer]. *A New Way of Life*. Sarasota, FL: Church of Metaphysical Christianity, 1989.

————. *Spirit Speaks*. Sarasota, FL: Church of Metaphysical Christianity Press, 1988.

Wade, Alda Madison. *At the Shrine of the Master*. Philadelphia: Dorrance & Company, 1953.

Church of Revelation (California)

Current address not obtained for this edition.

The Church of Revelation was formed in 1930 at Long Beach, California, by Rev. Janet Stine Lewis (Wolford) (d. 1957). It is not to be confused with the church of the same name formed in 1974 by Harrison Roy Hasketh in Honolulu. In 1945 the church's headquarters were moved to Hanford, California. The church teaches the Old Christian Initiate, a set of beliefs that the church calls a world-religion and a nonsectarian philosophy. The Old Christian Initiate, based on scientific truth, shows how to find spirit, understand the natural law, and have everlasting life without death. The Old Christian Initiate teaches that people survive death in a conscious state; that they can communicate with mortals through mediumship; that as a man sows on earth he will reap in the life to come; that the future life is constructive, social, and progressive, and that peace and brotherhood are to be extolled and war decried. After Reverend Wolford's death in 1957, she was succeeded by Rev. Winifred Ruth Mikesell.

Membership: Not reported. There has been no membership information since a 1966 report that listed congregations in Hanford, Sacramento, Burlingame, and Apple Valley, California; Toccoa, Georgia; Phoenix, Arizona; and Toledo, Ohio. At that time there were approximately 500 members and 30 ministers. Recent attempts to locate congregations have been unsuccessful.

Church of Revelation (Hawaii)

21475 Summit Rd., Los Gatos, CA 95030

The Church of Revelation was founded in Honolulu 1974 by Harrison Roy Hesketh. It is an eccletic mystical Spiritualist group whose teachings center upon the one God, who is all in all as all. Hesketh calls his higher or transcendental consciousness "Tattenaiananda," generally shortened to "Tat," the name by which most of his students refer to him. The centers connected with the church teach a wide variety of psychic development techniques, among the most important being the Rainbow Bridge Meditation, by which the leaders take students over the rainbow bridge (that part of the inner consciousness that connects the conscious self with the spiritual realms) to the White Light of God. Tat is also in contact with the ascended masters, those spiritual beings spoken of by Guy Ballard, the founder of the "I AM" Religious Activity.

The church is headed by a board of directors. Hesketh is the president of the church. In 1983 the headquarters were moved to Los Gatos, California. The educational arm of the church is the Astral Physics School. Affiliated centers and churches are found in Honolulu; Seattle; Vancouver; and Pambrook East, Bermuda.

Membership: Not reported.

Periodicals: *The New Spirit*.

Church of Tzaddi

PO Box 308, Kennesaw, GA 30156

Amy Merritt Kees was semi-invalid and disabled, the victim of an accident that damaged her spine as a teenager. Shortly after the birth of her first child in 1936, however, she began to experience contacts from the spirit world. In 1958 Amy was healed completely. She dedicated her home as a center for study, meditation, and healing, and in 1959 she formed a study group, "The Open Door of Love." She also became a student of Unity School of Christianity, the Universal Church of the Master, and the Self-Realization Fellowship. The growth of her work, along with the spiritual communications received through her daughter, Dorothe, led to the founding of the Church of Tzaddi in 1962. (Tzaddi is the eighteenth letter of the Hebrew alphabet and is identified with the Aquarian Age.)

The purpose of the Church of Tzaddi is "to teach sciences, ancient wisdom, ideals and principles, philosophy, psychology, psychometry, and spiritual truths; to promote the brotherhood of man, the universal law of truth and all educational subjects; to solemnize marriages and officiate at funerals; to perform and administer divine healing, give inspirational counsel and communications and prophesy." An extensive course for the ministry includes material drawn from Unity School of Christianity, the Bible, parapsychology, Hermeticism, and world religion. It may be taken by correspondence. Headquarters of the church recently moved from Orange, California, to Colorado. Branches are located around the country; among the most prominent is the church in Phoenix, Arizona. Its pastor, Dr. Frank Alper, is also the founder of the Arizona Metaphysical Society.

Membership: Not reported.

Periodicals: *Lightline.*

Sources:

The Church of Tzaddi. www.tzaddi.org

Alper, Frank. *An Evening with Christos*. Phoenix, AZ: Arizona Metaphysical Society, 1979.

—————. *Exploring Atlantis*. 3 vols. Farmingdale, NY: Coleman Publishing, 1982.

Johnson, Amy (Kees), and Dorothy Blackmere. *Developing Spiritually*. Garden Grove, CA: Bishop of the Church of Tzaddi, 1980.

Slate, Ann B. "Your Daughter Shall Prophecy." *Fate* 23, no. 4 (August, 1970): 68–78.

Eclesia Catolica Cristina

2123 Grand Ave., New York, NY 10453

The Eclesia Catolica Cristina evolved from the Spiritualist Christian Church. It was founded in March 1956 by His Holiness Delfin Roman-Cardona and incorporated as the Eclesia Catolica Cristina in June 1969. The name was changed to differentiate the church from spiritist centers, and because its liturgical rituals more closely resembled traditional Roman Catholic practice.

Delfin Roman-Cardona was born to Roman Catholic parents in Utuato, Puerto Rico, on December 14, 1918. His ability at clairvoyance manifested when he was three years old. From seven to 14 he served as an acolyte at the Church of St. Michael the Archangel in Utuado. During these years, when he was twelve, he cured a neighbor who suffered from recurrent migraine headaches by placing his hands on her head. From that time, he developed as a clairvoyant and healer, never charging for his services. He eventually moved to New York in obedience to what he felt was a divine mandate.

In line with many congregations throughout South America, the Eclesia Catolica Cristina follows the practices of exorcism, prophecy, channeling, and psychic healing, all of which are modeled on rites of the ancient Hebrews and Christians. The church draws upon the spiritism of Allan Kardec (1804–1869), which it has mingled with tenets of Judaism, Christianity, and Eastern religions to preach a universal Catholicism. It does not identify with the New Age movement; it believes its practices and rituals are closer to those of ancient Christianity.

The church is organized on the model of the Roman Catholic Church, with a pontiff, cardinals, archbishops, bishops, and priests. The church ordains both men and women to the priesthood, a practice that it claims derives precedence from Atlantis, where women were held as equal to men and were granted the same ecclesiastical positions.

The college of priests elected Roman-Cardona as its first pontiff on April 25, 1965, and the pontifical elevation occurred in 1976. In the meantime, in 1972 Roman-Cardona entered a state of renunciation. After considering hundreds of testimonials and listening to many witnesses attesting to miracles performed by Roman-Cardona, the church members voted to proclaim him a living saint on October 28, 1978. He has since been known as St. Delfin I.

Roman-Cardona was reported to have healed a variety of illnesses, including some that were considered terminal. He also taught many others to do healing and exorcisms and anointed them to carry on their ministries, and he prohibited the exploitation of their abilities. The church holds weekly celebrations of the Mass and services of healing and exorcism, all without charge. Members pay a membership fee of $10 per month to assist in the church's upkeep, with additional tithes and offerings being voluntary.

Twenty-five years after his renunciation, the church pronounced Roman-Cardona a Pure and Divine Avatar and the spirit of a Solar Angel, who is the promised Comforter. He was proclaimed the Second Savior and New Messiah of this planet by the Spirit of the Lord Jesus Christ on August 31, 1997. As the Second Savior, the college of priests and the faithful understand his messianic mission to be to restore the teachings of Christ, to clarify his parables, and to define God and creation through enlightened reason and logic.

Olga Roman, Roman-Cardona's wife, was ordained a priest on June 21, 1959, and was elevated to pontifical cardinal on January 6, 1976. She will become the church's second pontiff following the death of St. Delfin I. Cardinal Roman was born in Puerto Rico in 1938, and moved to New York as a young woman. She is the mother of three sons.

Membership: In 1997 the church operated out of a single center in New York City. There were approximately 1,500 members, 1,000 of whom resided in the United States. There were 18 priests.

General Assembly of Spiritualists

27 Appleton St., Rochester, NY 14611

The General Assembly of Spiritualists is a sovereign, self-governing ecclesiastical body. Its history as an organized religious body goes back to November 15, 1897, when it was incorporated as the New York State Association of Spiritualists. At the convention in Rochester, New York, on June 20, 1914, the delegates by unanimous vote authorized changing the constitution, by-laws, and name to the General Assembly of Spiritualists, to conform with the Laws of New York, 1914, Chapter 485, Section 1, Chapter 53 of the Laws of 1909, titled "an act in relation to religious corporations, constituting Chapter 51 of consolidated laws," adding Article XII, Spiritualist Churches, section 262 to 273, inclusive. By this act, Spiritualism for the first time was recognized by law as a religion with distinct powers conferred by the legislature upon the General Assembly of Spiritualists. The original charter of the General Assembly of Spiritualist was signed and recorded in Monroe County, New York, on October 15, 1915.

At the convention in Buffalo, New York, on June 19, 20, and 21, 1931, the delegates voted to sever the Assembly's affiliation with other Spiritualist groups. This was done to preserve what they saw as the principles expressed by the pioneers of Spiritualism, especially that of universal brotherhood, and to protect the movement against a felt threat from the encroachment of prejudice and sectarianism. The necessary legal steps were duly consummated and papers signed, thus establishing the General Assembly of Spiritualists as a sovereign, self-governing ecclesiastical body, with executive power vested in a board of directors. Jurisdiction extended to several states in the United States and to Canada.

The General Assembly believes in the advancement of the Spiritualist religion as an idealistic, humanitarian, and inspiring movement that gives aid to the sick through spiritual healing, and aid to the sound of body by well founded hope and faith. The General Assembly is firmly and permanently opposed to all fraudulent and dishonest imitation of real mediumship, and to the sensational display thereof. The ideal of the General Assembly is to continue to raise the standards of the Spiritualist movement and to encourage study classes, reading courses, the dissemination of Spiritualist literature, and research work, so that others may learn the reality of the Spirit World and its meaning to humankind.

The assembly issues a set of pamphlets that explain their major beliefs, including *How Shall We Teach Spiritualism?*, *Jesus of Nazareth*, *The Nature of the Spirit World*, *Spiritualism: Fact or Fiction*, *Voice of Spirit*, and *What is Spiritualism?*

Membership: Not reported.

Sources:

The Church of Divine Inspiration. www.churchofdivineinspiration.com.

General Assembly of Spiritualists, State of New York. New York: Flying Saucer News, n.d.

Lomaxe, Paul R. *What Do Spiritualists Believe?* New York: General Assembly of Spiritualists, 1943.

Independent Spiritualist Association of the United States of America

5130 W 25th St., Cicero, IL 60650

The Independent Spiritualist Association of the United States of America was formed in 1924 by Amanda Flowers, who with others withdrew from the National Spiritualist Association of Churches (NSAC) because of her objection to the rule that forbade NSAC mediums to work in non-NSAC churches. She also wanted greater freedom to express her own theosophical views, which went beyond the beliefs of the NSAC.

Membership: In 1988 there were 120 member mediums.

Sources:

Basic Course of Study. Cicero, IL: Independent Spiritualist Association of the United States of America, n.d.

International Church of Ageless Wisdom

c/o ICAW California Seminary, PO Box 194, Half Moon Bay, CA 94019

The International Church of Ageless Wisdom was founded by Beth R. Hand (1903–1977), a spiritualist minister in the 1920s and an early student of Paramahansa Yogananda, the founder of the Self-Realization Fellowship, one of the first Hindu organizations established in the United States. From Yogananda, who came to the United States in 1924, and from her studies Hand became convinced of the truth of reincarnation and karma. The Spiritualists requested her resignation, and she was forced to abandon the three churches she had founded in New Jersey. She moved to Philadelphia and opened the first Church of Ageless Wisdom in 1927.

Soon after the formation of the Church of Ageless Wisdom, Hand met Rev. George Haas, leader of the Universal Spiritual Church, a British Spiritualist body that shared Hand's ideas about reincarnation. She brought her church into communion with his. She later sought, but did not receive, a formal charter from that church. Meanwhile, in 1956 Haas was consecrated a bishop by John Beswarick, bishop of the Catholic Apostolic Church (United Orthodox Catholicate), an independent British Orthodox-Catholic body, who had received orders from the famous independent bishop, Hugh George de Willmott Newman. In 1958 Haas consecrated Hand. In spite of the consecration, her inability to receive a formal charter led Hand to become independent of the Universal Spiritual Church. In 1962 she received a charter from the State of Pennsylvania. Subsequently, she consecrated other bishops of the church, and one of them, Muriel E. Matalucci, succeeded her as archbishop primate in 1977. That same year Archbishop Metalucci changed the name of the organization to its present designation.

The church's teachings are eclectic, drawing upon Spiritualist, Hindu, Buddhist, and ancient occult wisdom teachings, though there is a primary emphasis upon Christianity. It teaches that God is the father of all that exists; that all men are brothers (hence no discrimination is allowed); souls are immortal and there is always the opportunity for reformation, reincarnation, and karma; and the planet and humanity can be saved by the power of prayer and love. God is not conceived in anthropomorphic terms. Jesus is the Wayshower, who manifested the way for individuals, all of whom are sons of God, to become one with God. Humans evolve by following the laws of the universe. The church believes in and uses the wide variety of psychic gifts as tools for human progress and service in God's work.

The church is headed by the archbishop primate, assisted by another archbishop, one bishop, the canons-of-states, and the canons-at-large, all of whom together comprise the Holy Synod. There is an annual meeting.

Membership: Not reported.

Educational Facilities:

The International Church of Ageless Wisdom California Seminary, Half Moon Bay, California.

Periodicals: *Aquarian Lights*.

Remarks: Associated with the International Church of Ageless Wisdom is the Michigan Metaphysical Society, headed by the popular Detroit-area psychic teacher, Sol Lewis, who was ordained by Hand. Another famous member of the church is the popular occult lecturer Colonel Arthur Burks.

Sources:

International Church of Ageless Wisdom. www.icawseminary-ca.net.

Barrett, Lawrence R. *Ten Principles*. Atlanta, GA: Author, 1982.

Ritual Book. Wyalusing, PA: International Church of Ageless Wisdom, 1979.

International General Assembly of Spiritualists

5403 S Ridge W, Ashtabula, OH 44004

The International General Assembly of Spiritualists (IGAS) was incorporated in 1936 in Buffalo, New York, by Rev. Arthur A. Ford (1897–1971), Fred Constantine, and eight other Spiritualist ministers. Arthur Ford was the first president. Rev. Fred Jordan, a retired Navy commander, was ordained by Ford in 1937 and served as president of the IGAS from 1938 to 1974. Rev. Jerry Higgins was elected to succeed Jordan, but died before assuming the post. Rev. Fred Jordan Jr., the vice president, was then elected to succeed his father.

In 1946 the IGAS adopted a Declaration of Principles that follows word-for-word that of the National Spiritualist Association of Churches. Emphasis is placed on prayer, healing, and spiritual unfoldment and development. Communion is served regularly. There are affiliated congregations in Africa and Nepal.

Membership: In 1987 the church reported 35 congregations, 410 members, and 103 ministers in the United States, and an additional 190 members worldwide.

Educational Facilities:

Shrine of the Healing Master, Ashtabula, Ohio.

Periodicals: *The I.G.A.S. Journal*.

Sources:

Ford, Arthur. *Why We Survive*. Cooksburg, NY: Gutenberg Press, 1952.

Ford, Arthur, with Margueritte Harmon Bro. *Nothing So Strange*. New York: Harper and Row, 1958.

Royce, Clifford M., Jr. *To the Spirit. . . From the Spirit*. Chicago: Author, 1975.

Spraggett, Allen, with William V. Rauscher. *Arthur Ford: The Man Who Talked with the Dead*. New York: New American Library, 1973.

International Spiritualist Alliance

201–317 Columbia St., New Westminster, BC, Canada V3L 1A7

The International Spiritualist Alliance is a Canadian-based Spiritualist church headquartered in Vancouver, British Columbia. It was founded to "bring into closer Brotherhood and Unity Spiritualists the world over." Churches are located across Canada and the British Isles and include two churches in California, one in San Bernardino and the Holy Grail Foundation in Santa Cruz. There is an annual convention. The current president is Rev. Beatrice Gaulton Bishop.

The Alliance has a loose belief structure, accepting as "Principles of Spiritualism" seven affirmations, on the fatherhood of God, the brotherhood of man, the immortality of the soul, communion with the departed, personal responsibility, compensation for good and evil, and eternal progress of the soul. Members are Christian, accepting the belief in God and the creator, who is love, and in Jesus, the Lord who was incarnated for the salvation of men. Jesus became perfected in suffering and thus became both Lord and Christ.

Membership: Not reported.

Periodicals: *International Spiritualist News Review*. Send orders to 3371 Findlay St., Vancouver, BC, Canada.

Sources:

International Spiritualist Alliance. www.isacanada.ca.

Lotus Ashram

264 Mainsail, Port St. Lucie, FL 33452

The Lotus Ashram was established in 1971 in Miami, Florida, by Noel and Coleen Street. Noel is a medium originally from New Zealand and ordained by the Universal Church of the Master. Coleen is a yoga teacher. Noel became a popular figure in the psychic community in the United States through his annual tour and his many books and writings. He specializes in psychic healing, which he learned from the Maori natives of New Zealand, and past-life reading by which he is able to trace an individual's previous incarnations on earth. Coleen's work stresses physical fitness through yoga, vegetarianism, and food preparation.

In 1975 a second center for the ashram, called Springtime, was opened in Chillicothe, Ohio. A chapel, healing sanctuary, and bookstore are part of the complex. In 1977 the ashram headquarters moved to Texas, at a location near the Mexican border. The ashram is governed by an eight-person board of directors.

Membership: Not reported.

Periodicals: *Lotus Leaves*.

Sources:

The Story of the Lotus Ashram. Miami, FL: Lotus Ashram, n.d.

Street, Noel. *Karma, Your Whispering Wisdom*. Fabens, TX: Lotus Ashram, 1978.

————. *Reincarnation, One Life—Many Births*. Fabens, TX: Lotus Ashram, 1978.

Metropolitan Spiritual Churches of Christ, Inc.

National Headquarters, Temple of St. Jude, 8747 Fenkell St., Detroit, MI 48238

Alternative Address: International Headquarters: PO Box 414858, Kansas City, MO 64141.

The Metropolitan Spiritual Community Churches of Christ, Inc., was founded in 1925 by Bishop William Taylor (1887–1942) and Elder Leviticus Lee Boswell. The word "spiritual" in the church's name indicates its basic Christian beliefs and its practice of the spiritual gifts according to I Corinthians 12. The church is trinitarian and baptizes people in the name of the "Father, the Son and the Holy Ghost." It affirms the Apostles' Creed, but replaces the word "catholic" with the word "universal." The Gospel is described as foursquare: preaching, teaching, healing, prophecy. Incarnation, not reincarnation, is taught. The churches believe that "all men (humankind) are incarnations of the one Spirit regardless of race, creed, or condition, with full belief in creation."

Bishop Taylor was succeed by the Rev. Clarence Cobb (d.1979), founder and pastor of the First Church of Deliverance in Chicago, Illinois. In the 1970s he brought additional churches in Accra, Ghana, and Monrovia, Liberia, into the fellowship of the Metropolitan Spiritual Church of Christ. Cobb was succeeded by Dr. I. Logan Kearse (d. 1991), pastor of the Cornerstone Church of Christ in Baltimore, Maryland. Kearse was succeeded as president of the church by Rev. Dr. Arthur L. Posey, who had founded the Temple of St. Jude Spiritual Church in Detroit. In 2008 Posey was assisted in his leadership role by Bishops James D. Tindall Sr., Charles N. Slayton, William Hamilton, William Ozier, William H. Foreman, Joseph Kennedy Jr., and Robert Smith.

Membership: In 2008 the church reported 43 congregations across the United States and four in West Africa.

Sources:

Metropolitan Spiritual Churches of Christ, Inc. www.metrospiritualchurch.com/.

National Colored Spiritualist Association of Churches

Current address not obtained for this edition.

Shortly after World War I, the growing black membership in the National Spiritualist Association of Churches separated from the parent body and, in 1922, formed the National Colored Spiritualist Association of Churches. Doctrine and practice follow closely those of the parent body. Churches are located in Detroit, Chicago, Columbus (Ohio), Miami, Charleston (South Carolina), New York City, Phoenix, and St. Petersburg (Florida).

Membership: Not reported.

Periodicals: *The Nationalist Spiritualist Reporter*.

National Spiritual Alliance

RFD 1, Lake Pleasant, MA 01347

The National Spiritual Alliance was formed in 1913 by the Rev. G. Tabor Thompson, previously a medium with the New England Spiritualist Camp Meeting Association, and an advocate of belief in reincarnation, an opinion at variance with the National Spiritualist Association of Churches (NSAC). Otherwise, the Alliance is similar to the NSAC. An annual convention is held at Lake Pleasant, Massachusetts. An official board of directors conducts outreach work.

Membership: In 2008 the alliance reported only one center still in operation. It also reported a constituency of several thousand people who visit irregularly.

Sources:

The National Spiritual Alliance. www.thenationalspiritualallianceinc.org.

Shattuck, Louise, with David James. *Spirit and Spa: A Portrait of the Body, Mind and Soul of a 133-Year-Old Spiritualist Community in Lake Pleasant, Massachusetts*. Greenfield, MA: Delta House Press, 2003.

National Spiritual Science Center

c/o Seekers Church, 276 Carroll St. NW, Washington, DC 20012

The National Spiritual Science Center was established in Washington, D.C., in 1941 by Rev. Alice Wellstood Tindell. Reverend Tindell was trained at the Spiritual Science Mother Church, headquartered at Carnegie Hall Studios, New York City, which was founded by Rev. Julia O. Forrest on May 29, 1923. For many years it was an active part of the Ecclesiastical Council of the Spiritual Science Mother Church and also a charter member in the Federation of Spiritual Churches and Associations, an ecumenical organization of Spiritualist groups that was organized by Reverend Tindell. In 1969, while attending a Federation meeting, Reverend Tindell suffered an accident that left her disabled and led her to turn the center over to two people she had trained during the 1960s, Reverends Henry J. Nagorka and Diane S. Nagorka.

During the 1970s the Nagorkas reorganized the center, independent of the Spiritual Science Mother Church, and moved the headquarters. Under their leadership, the center emerged as a prominent national Spiritual Science organization. ESPress, Inc., became a significant Spiritualist publishing concern, and for 16 years Rev. Henry Nagorka served as its publisher and president of the center's Board of Directors. Rev. Diane S. Nagorka founded the School of Spiritual Science, and with her colleague and assistant, Rev. Margaret Moum, established the curriculum and theology for metaphysical studies for which the school became known. She served as its director for many years. After Reverend Henry's death in 1986, ESPress, Inc., ceased its publishing activities, and Rev. Diane S. Nagorka assumed management of the operations of the center and school as its president and director until her retirement in June 1989.

The baton of leadership passed to the board of directors, which meets on a regular basis to determine policy and to administer the services and activities of the center. The School of Spiritual Science continues its program of metaphysical studies under the guidance of the director of education, who is appointed to the position, and presents a four-year course of study leading to certification as Minister of Spiritual Science.

The center's nine-point statement affirms belief in God as the Universal Creative Energy, the dynamic growing nature of the universe; the drive of every entity to unite with God; the immortality of the soul; individual free will; wisdom as the latent power of God within; the reality of communication with spirit; soul-unfoldment and service as the purpose of life; and God as a just, accepting, and impersonal Force, drawing all to perfection.

Membership: Not reported.

Educational Facilities:

Silent Light International Spiritual Science Correspondence School.

Periodicals: *InSpirit*.

Sources:

National Spiritual Science Center. www.nsscdc.org/.

Moum, Margaret R. *Guidebook to the Aquarian Gospel of Jesus the Christ*. Washington, DC: ESPress, 1974.

Nagorka, Diane S. *Spirit as Life Force*. Washington, DC: ESPress, 1983.

National Spiritualist Association of Churches

13 Cottage Row, PO Box 217, Lily Dale, NY 14752

The National Spiritualist Association of Churches (NSAC), formed in 1893 in Chicago, is the oldest and largest of the Spiritualist churches. Among its first leaders were Harrison D. Barrett (c. 1863–1911) and James M. Peebles (1822–1922), both former Unitarian clergymen, and Cora L. V. Richmond (1840–1923), a medium and author. The association was formed both for fellowship and to deal with fraudulent mediumship. The association is also important for its adoption of a number of statements on Spiritualism that have become a standard to which other Spiritualist bodies more or less adhere.

In 1899 the association adopted a six-article "Declaration of Principles," with three more added later. These nine articles established the beliefs of modern Spiritualism:

(1) We believe in Infinite Intelligence [the influence of Unitarianism is evident in this definition of God];

(2) We believe that the phenomena of Nature, both physical and spiritual, are the expression of Infinite Intelligence;

(3) We affirm that a correct understanding of such expression and living in accordance therewith constitute true religion;

(4) We affirm that the existence and personal identity of the individual continue after the change called death;

(5) We affirm that communication with the so-called dead is a fact, scientifically proven by the phenomena of Spiritualism;

(6) We believe that the highest morality is contained in the Golden Rule: "Whatsoever ye would that others should do unto you, do ye also unto them";

(7) We affirm the moral responsibility of the individual, and that he makes his own happiness or unhappiness as he obeys or disobeys Nature's physical and spiritual laws;

(8) We affirm that the doorway to reformation is never closed against any soul here or hereafter;

(9) We affirm that the precept of Prophecy and Healing are Divine attributes proven through Mediumship.

Over the years, other statements were adopted on "What Spiritualism Is and Does" and "Spiritual Healing." A set of "Definitions" was also approved. The two issues of reincarnation and the relation of Spiritualism to Christianity emerged as the major questions dividing Spiritualists. Differing answers to these two questions split the NSAC on several occasions, and dissent led independent Spiritualists to

form their own organizations instead of joining the NSAC. Reincarnation, gaining popularity through theosophy, began to find favor among some mediums in the early twentieth century but was specifically condemned by the NSAC in 1930. "Are Spiritualists also Christians?" was debated by the NSAC and generally decided in the negative. Although the NSAC has drawn heavily on the Christian faith, from which most members came, it identifies its members as Spiritualists. The specifically "Christian" Spiritualists were found in other bodies such as the Progressive Spiritualist Church. It should be noted that most Spiritualists differentiate between primitive Christianity, which they believe themselves to be following and practicing, and contemporary orthodox Christianity, which they strictly differentiate from both primitive Christianity and Spiritualism.

The polity of the association is hierarchical. There are loosely organized state associations and an annual national convention. Among Spiritualists, the association has the highest standards for ordination. The NSAC is noteworthy as the only Spiritualist body to attempt to develop work among youth. The lyceum (Sunday school) was originally promoted and shaped by Andrew Jackson Davis (1826–1910) in 1863. Children's materials have been developed and many churches have an active lyceum program. Such efforts have given the NSAC a stability lacking in most Spiritualist bodies.

Membership: In 2008 the NSAC reported 85 affiliated churches in the United States.

Educational Facilities:

Morris Pratt Institute, Milwaukee, Wisconsin.

Center for Spiritualist Studies, Lily Dale, New York.

Periodicals: *The National Spiritualist Summit*. PO Box 6089, Sun City West, AZ 85376-6089. • *Spotlight* (for children). 1418 Hall SE, Grand Rapids, MI 49506-3960.

Sources:

National Spiritualist Association of Churches. www.nsac.org/.

Barrett, H. D. *Life Work of Cora L. V. Richmond*. Chicago: Hack & Anderson, 1895.

Holms, A. Campbell. *The Fundamental Facts of Spiritualism*. Indianapolis, IN: Stow Memorial Foundation, n.d.

Kuhnig, Verna Kathryn. *Spiritualist Lyceum Manual*. Milwaukee, WI: National Spiritualist Association of Churches, 1962.

One Hundredth Anniversary of Modern American Spiritualism. Chicago: National Spiritualist Association of Churches, 1948.

Progressive Spiritual Church

Current address not obtained for this edition.

The Progressive Spiritual Church was formed in 1907 by the Rev. G. V. Cordingley, who had been one of the organizers of the Illinois State Spiritualist Association of the National Spiritualist Association of Churches. The Reverend Cordingley had rejected the NSAC's adoption of a "Declaration of Principles" instead of a "Confession of Faith" based on the authority of the Bible. An aggressive policy of proselytizing brought steady growth during the first decade of the Progressive Spiritual Church.

The doctrine of the church is derived from Christian affirmations as modified by divine revelations received through spirit communication. The Confession of Faith affirms belief in communication with spirits, the resurrection of the soul (but not of the body), God as absolute divine spirit, and angels or departed spirits, who communicate through mediums. Members further hold that Jesus was a medium, that spirits have desires, that the Bible is the inspired word of God, and that heaven and hell are conditions, not locations. Four sacraments are practiced: baptism, marriage, spiritual communion, and funerals.

A mother church elects officers, including a supreme pastor, a board of trustees, a secretary and a treasurer. Individual congregations elect their own officers, but are subject to the mother church. Churches are located mainly in the Midwest.

Membership: Not reported. Attempts to contact individuals associated with the church have proved futile. It is not known if the church is still functioning.

Sources:

McArthur, Paul. *Text Book, Ritual, Valuable Data and Selected Poems*. Progressive Spiritualist Association of Missouri, 1908.

Roosevelt Spiritual Memorial Benevolent Association
Current address not obtained for this edition.

The Roosevelt Spiritual Memorial Benevolent Association was formed in 1949 by a group of independent Spiritualists. Its main purpose was to provide a home for otherwise independent mediums and churches, which it certified and chartered. It adhered to the Spiritualist doctrine, asserting communication as taught in the Bible and promoting psychical research. It also offered a study course in Spiritualism.

Membership: Not reported.

St. Paul's Church of Aquarian Science
Current address not obtained for this edition.

The Rev. Harold C. Durbin, a Spiritualist medium who was a pastor in the Spiritualist Episcopal Church, became independent in the 1960s and founded St. Paul's Church of Aquarian Science in St. Petersburg, Florida. In 1970 he published his book, *Someone Asked, He Answered*. The name of the church was derived from the zodiacal sign of Aquarius. The church posited that humanity was moving into the Aquarian Age. Jesus refers to the "man with the waterpot," Aquarius, in Mark 14:13–15.

According to the church's teachings, God is Universal Spirit with the attributes of power and intelligence; God is a trinity of Father (creator), Son (created), and Holy Spirit (the process of creation); man is a trinity of body, soul or mind, and spirit; Jesus the master gave the highest teachings, and people grow as they practice these teachings; man is divine creation, with all the divine attributes and access to God through Jesus; all life is eternal and must grow and evolve; the door of reformation is never closed; and by developing the divine attributes, attunement of the world of spirit (mediumship) is developed. The church accepted reincarnation.

A second congregation was established in Tampa. In the late 1970s headquarters were moved to Texas.

Membership: Not reported. Prior to the move to Texas, the church reported over 800 people affiliated with the congregations.

Sources:

Durbin, Harold C. *Someone Asked, He Answered*. Lakemont, GA, 1970.

Spiritual Episcopal Church
141 Frost St., Eaton Rapids, MI 48827

The Spiritual Episcopal Church was founded in 1941 as the Spiritualist Episcopal Church by the Revs. Clifford Bias (1910–1987), John W. Bunker (1893–1956), and Robert Chaney (1913–2006), all prominent mediums at Camp Chesterfield in Indiana. Bias and Bunker were members of the Independent Spiritualist Association, and Chaney was a member of the National Spiritualist Association of Churches. The founders expressed dissatisfaction with an overemphasis on phenomena within Spiritualism; they wanted a greater emphasis on philosophy, particularly as channeled from the spirit realm.

In 1956 a morals charge was brought against a prominent medium, a candidate for a church office. Camp Chesterfield, where the church had its membership, was split between those supporting the medium and those opposing the medium. After attempting to dissuade the medium from seeking office, the Rev. Dorothy Graff Flexer

moved the church headquarters to Lansing, Michigan, hoping to prevent the divisiveness at Camp Chesterfield from further disrupting the church.

The church believes that Spirit is the Origin, Sustainer, and Reality in all forms of nature and in all the expression of life. The universe is spirit-built and constitutes a divine revelation of Spirit (God). The church believes in life after death, the efficacy of prayer, the duty and privilege to come into harmony and peace with the Spirit, and the divinity of all persons. Jesus is accepted as an Avatar, one of the "Christed ones" who have manifested into the world to lighten its darkness and show by precept and example the way of life leading back to the Source.

In 2008 the presiding clergy was Rev. Audrey Charlton.

Membership: In 2008 the church reported congregations in Eaton Rapids, Mt. Morris, and Owosso, Michigan.

Periodicals: *Spiritualist Messenger*, 610 Clinton St., Owosso MI 48867.

Sources:

Spiritual Episcopal Church. www.spiritualist-church.com/.

Chaney, Robert G. *"Hear My Prayer."* Eaton Rapids, MI: Library, the Spiritualist Episcopal Church, 1942.

Development of Mediumship. Dimondale, MI: Spiritual Episcopal Church, n.d.

Spiritual Israel Church and Its Army
c/o Ypsilanti Temple, 501 Eugene St., Ypsilanti, MI 48198

The exact origin of the Spiritual Israel Church and Its Army is unknown, but it draws heavily on two older African-American religious traditions, Black Judaism and Spiritualism. Leaders of the Spiritual Israel Church, such as Bishop Robert Haywood (called by the title King of All Israel) and Bishop George Coachman (the association's Overseer), placed its establishment in the late 1930s, with some organization precedents going back to the 1920s. The forerunner of the Spiritual Israel Church was the Church of God in David, which was established by Derks Field in Alabama. At some point, either in Alabama or Michigan, Field met W. D. Dickson, who had arrived at similar ideas. After Field's death, Dickson took on the title of the King of All Israel, which was also carried by his successors, and pulled Spiritual Israel "out of David" upon instructions from the Spirit. Spiritual Israelites credit both Field and Dickson with "restoring" the teachings of the ancient Israelites. Apparently after Field's death, a power struggle for the leadership of the association occurred among Dickson and the surviving Field brothers, Doc and Candy. Each of the Field brothers established a separate organization, and several other groups, all containing the word "Israel" in their names, later broke away from the Spiritual Israel Church. Because of the severe Michigan winters, Dickson moved the sect to Virginia for a while, but returned to Detroit upon further instructions from the Spirit. Dickson was succeeded in his leadership by Bishop Martin Tompkin and Haywood.

Members of Spiritual Israel Church and Its Army view themselves as spiritual descendants of the ancient Israelites or "Spiritual Jews," and their association as a restoration of the religion of the ancient Israelites. They maintain that "Ethiopian" is the "nationality" name of black people, whereas "Israel" is their "spiritual" name. They believe that the first human beings were black, starting with Adam, who was created from the "Black soil of Africa" and that all of the great Israelite patriarchs and prophets were black men. In time, however, with the sons of Isaac, a division in humanity developed. Jacob became the progenitor of the Ethiopian nation and Esau of the Caucasian nation. Spiritual Israelites maintain that most whites who identify themselves as Jews are actually the descendants of Gentiles who intermarried with the original Jews or Israelites.

Spiritual Israelites maintain that they belong to the one true Spiritual church and that the Spirit dwells in all people. Like most other Spiritual groups, they believe that heaven and hell are projections of the human mind. The Christ Spirit, which is simply the anointed power of God, has occupied the bodies of many kings of Israel.

Membership: In 2008 the Spiritual Israel Church reported 28 affiliated churches in 13 states.

Sources:

Spiritual Israel Church and Its Army. www.siciaypsilanti.org/.

Baer, Hans A. "Black Spiritual Israelites in a Small Southern City." *Southern Quarterly* 23, no. 3 (1985):103–124.

———. *The Black Spiritual Movement: A Religious Response to Racism*. Knoxville, TN: University of Tennessee Press, 1984.

Superet Light Doctrine Church

2516 W Third St., Los Angeles, CA 90057

The Superet Light Doctrine Church was founded in Los Angeles in 1925 by Dr. Josephine De Croix Trust (d. 1957), called Mother Trust by her followers. According to Superet Light belief, Mother Trust was a Light Scientist who found Jesus' Religion because she had the gift to see the light, vibration, and aura of Jesus' Words. In childhood, Mother Trust was able to see auras. During her early work in New York City, she diligently studied the auras to learn their meanings, often going without food. She developed tuberculosis, but in a vision Jesus healed her and gave her the mission of bringing to the world His light teachings. She gained a reputation around New York City as a miracle healer.

From her studies of the Bible she discovered that only the Words of Jesus shone with light. She then began to realize the secret of the Mother of God: The Holy Ghost was the Mother of God. She discovered that there are two purple hearts united in one, the Father and Mother of God. Also, she discovered from her studies of light in the Book of Revelation, the New Name "Superet," the Parent God, Father and Mother Superet Light. Jesus Christ chose Mother Trust to bring out this truth to the world. She was told in a vision that Superet is the everlasting fire in God's Sacred Purple Heart.

The Superet Science teaches the manifestation of God's Light through every individual's light atom aura. All substances that possess magnetism, especially all life, have an aura, an invisible emanation. Mother Trust, as an aura scientist, was able to see both the outer aura and inner aura (or light of the soul). The light atom aura, capable of receiving God's Light, is produced by developing one's inner aura. Through Jesus Christ the Superet Light is effected and people become successful in their daily lives.

The church offers several lesson series that explain basic Superet Light beliefs, such as "The Superet Lessons" and "The Golden Text Lessons." Mother Trust wrote more than 25 books, most of which are available to the general public.

On Christmas Day, 1938, Mother Trust inaugurated the Prince of Peace Movement, for people of all religions, colors, and nationalities, as an auxiliary to the Superet Church.

Membership: In 2008 the church reported one center in the United States, with affiliated work in Mexico, Colombia, and Venezuela.

Periodicals: *Newsletter of the Superetist Brotherhood and Sisterhood*. 2516 W. Third St., Los Angeles, CA 90057.

Sources:

Superet Light Center. www.superet.com.

Miracle Woman's Secrets. Los Angeles: Superet Press, 1949.

Superet Light Doctrine Ministry. Los Angeles: Superet Press, 1947.

Trust, Josephine C. *Bible Mystery by Superet Light Science*. Los Angeles: Superet Press, 1950.

———. *Superet Light*. Los Angeles: Superet Light Center, 1953.

———. *Superet Light Doctrine*. Los Angeles: Superet Press, 1949.

T.O.M. Religious Foundation

Current address not obtained for this edition.

The T.O.M. Religious Foundation was founded in the 1960s by the Rev. Ruth Johnson of Velarde, New Mexico. The Reverend Johnson achieved her leadership through knowledge gained from study, experience, and previous lives. In 1970 the Foundation was moved to Canon City, Colorado. Its teachings were transmitted primarily through correspondence studies, "Moon Time Studies in Spiritual Culture," which offered instruction in dreams and the Bible, ESP and psychic development, and "Atlantis" and "Original Christianity." Teachings stressed that God is the divine one, or Whole, or Spirit, who knows, loves, and cares for all, and manifests his love through spiritual guidance. The language of the soul can supply lines of communication with the spirit world.

Membership: Not reported.

Temple of Universal Law

5030 N Drake, Chicago, IL 60625

The Temple of Universal Law was founded in 1936 by the Rev. Charlotte Bright (d. 1989), a medium under the guidance of Master Nicodemus, the control and directing voice who speaks through her. In 1965 a temple was erected on Chicago's North Side. Teachings were given through the Reverend Bright by the Masters of the Great White Brotherhood. The control and directing voice, as well as other masters of the brotherhood, continued to speak through her son and successor, the Rev. Robert E. Martin.

The temple describes itself as a nondenominational church based in metaphysical Christianity. Members believe in God who expresses himself as a Trinity. God the Father is the universal law of life which creates, sustains, and progresses to eternal life, and Christ is the perfect demonstration of divine mind. The Holy Spirit is the action of divine mind within. Truth is found in the Bible and in all spiritual traditions. The essential duty of man, who is immortal, is to look within and begin to awaken the Christ Spirit. Only by learning and understanding universal law can we come into oneness with God. The Lord's Supper is celebrated on the first Sunday in each month.

Classes, special workshops and lectures, and various services emphasizing communication with spirits supplement the Sunday worship. The temple maintains a library and has published numerous booklets.

Membership: In 1988 the church reported two congregations with more than 200 members served by 11 minister-mediums. There were also 12 missionaries (channels) affiliated with the church.

Periodicals: *Temple Messenger*.

United Spiritualist Church

813 W 165th Pl., Gardena, CA 90247

The United Spiritualist Church was founded in 1967 by the Rev. Floyd Humble, Edwin Potter, and Howard Mangan. The Reverend Humble had earlier served several independent Spiritualist churches. The United Spiritualist Church differs from most Spiritualist churches in its adoption of a centralized form of government. Power is invested in the presidency, which includes the president, first advisor-secretary, and second advisor-treasurer. Under the presidency is the board of governors. There is also a board of publication, education, and church extension and missions, and a general conference, which elects the board of governors.

The beliefs and practices of the church stem from the consensus of Spiritualism. Members believe in mediumship, both mental and physical, and follow the practices of Jesus in preaching, healing, teaching, and prophecy. Man is considered immortal; the unfoldment and development of individuals are means to bring the kingdom of God on earth.

Membership: The church reports three congregations, in Gardena, Anaheim, and Los Angeles.

Periodicals: *The Spiritual Outlook*. 809 W 165th Place, Gardena, CA 90247.

Sources:

United Spiritualist Church. www.unitespirit.org/.

Humble, Floyd. *Bible Lessons*. Gardena, CA: United Spiritualist Church, 1969.

Universal Church of Psychic Science
Current address not obtained for this edition.

The Universal Church of Psychic Science was a small Spiritualist body headquartered in Philadelphia and headed by W. L. Salisbury, its president, and Clarence Smith, its secretary. The group was limited to the states of New Jersey, Maryland, and Pennsylvania. The church issued ordinations and church charters.

Membership: Not reported.

Universal Church of the Master
100 W Rincon Ave., Ste. 101, Campbell, CA 95008

The Universal Church of the Master (UCM) was formed in 1908 in Los Angeles, California, and was incorporated in 1918. Initially, it was largely a West Coast association of ministers and churches, but it began to spread across the nation in the 1960s. Among its early leaders was Dr. B. J. Fitzgerald, author of *A New Text of Spiritual Philosophy and Religion*, the basic book of the UCM. In 1930 the headquarters were moved to Oakland and then, in 1966, after Dr. Fitzgerald's death, to San Jose.

The church sees itself as both Christian and Universal in its religious philosophy. While it uses much out of liberal Christianity, it also is eclectic, allowing a wide range of beliefs to exist. Its ten-point statement, drawn from the *Text*, affirms belief in the fatherhood of God and the brotherhood of man, the laws of nature and living in harmony with them, life after death, communication with the unseen world, the golden rule, individual responsibility and the continual possibility of improvement, prophecy, and the eternal progress of the soul. The emphasis on the laws of nature denies any supernaturalism or miraculous nature in the communication phenomena. The church also uses *The Aquarian Gospel of Jesus the Christ* by Levi Dowling as a source for its teachings.

The UCM is headed by a governing board, including the president, other officers, and trustees, which meets annually. An examining committee approves all ordinations and certifications. The board of trustees grants charters. The polity is congregational.

Educational Facilities:

UCM's Remote Theology Degree Program grants undergraduate and graduate theology degrees.

Membership: In 2002 the church reported 115 active ministers in the United States, half of them in Arizona and California, and 3 in Canada. Many more active Spiritualist ministers were originally ordained through the UMC.

Periodicals: *UCM Quarterly Magazine* • *A Joyful Noise* e-mail newsletter.

Sources:

Universal Church of the Master. www.u-c-m.org/new/.

Dowling, Levi. *The Aquarian Gospel of Jesus the Christ*. Los Angeles: Leo W. Dowling, 1925.

Fitzgerald, B. J. *A New Text of Spiritual Philosophy and Religion*. San Jose, CA: Universal Church of the Master, 1954.

Universal Church of the Master, History and Principles. Santa Clara, CA: Universal Church of the Master, 1995.

Universal Hagar's Spiritual Church (UHSC)
c/o Professor George H. Latimer-Knight, PO Box 07071, Detroit, MI 48207-7071

The Universal Hagar's Spiritual Church (UHSC) was founded by Father George Willie Hurley (1884–1943), a contemporary of Father Divine and also a self-proclaimed god. Hurley was born in Reynolds, Georgia, and received his early training as a Baptist minister, though he later became a Methodist. After moving to Detroit,

Michigan, with his wife in 1919, he joined a small Holiness sect called Triumph the Church and Kingdom of God in Christ and became its Presiding Prince for the state of Michigan.

In the early 1920s Hurley became a minister in the National Spiritual Church, probably a predominantly white organization, which served as a transition to leadership of his own church, established in Detroit on September 23, 1923. In 1924 he established the School of Mediumship and Psychology, which eventually became a secret auxiliary in each congregation affiliated with UHSC. Father Hurley maintained that the school is a branch of the Great School of the Prophets, which Jesus attended during the eighteen years of his life that are not accounted for in the Bible. He also established the Knights of the All Seeing Eye, a Masonic-like auxiliary open to both men and women. By the time of Hurley's death, UHSC had grown to an association of at least 37 congregations (in Michigan, Ohio, Pennsylvania, New Jersey, New York City, West Virginia, Delaware, and Illinois).

Similar to other Black Spiritual groups, UHSC inherited an eclectic religious heritage, drawing elements from Spiritualism, Catholicism, African-American Protestantism, and possibly vodou or hoodoo. Father Hurley also incorporated concepts from the Aquarian Gospel of Jesus Christ, astrology, Ethiopianism, and other belief systems in his church. Sometime around 1933, if not earlier, Father Hurley began to teach his followers that his "carnal flesh" had been "transformed into the flesh of Christ." He maintained that just as Adam had been the God of the Taurian Age, Abraham the God of the Arian Age, and Jesus the God of the Piscean Age, he was the God of the Aquarian Age. Unlike most Spiritual churches, which have assumed an apolitical posture and refused, for example, to participate in the Civil Rights Movement, Hurley took unequivocal stands on a number of social issues, particularly the status of African Americans in the larger society, and urged his followers to vote for Franklin D. Roosevelt. After Hurley's death the strongly nationalist and critical rhetoric of his church was considerably tempered.

Father Hurley's successors as head of UHSC have included Prince Thomas Surbadger, Mother Mary Hatchett, Prince Alfred Bailey, and Rev. G. Latimer, a daughter of Hurley. The Wiseman Board, which consisted primarily of women in the later decades of the twentieth century, serves as UHSC's governing body. Over the years, the heaviest concentrations of Hagar's congregations have been in southeastern Michigan, where the association's headquarters is located, and in the New York-New Jersey area. The affiliations of individual member congregations have changed considerably over the years, and especially since the early 1960s UHSC has experienced significant fluctuations in the number of its congregations in the East and Midwest, somewhat offset by the spread of the church to California and the Southeast.

Membership: In 2008 the church reported 40 churches across the United States.

Sources:

Father Hurley: Practical Spiritual Principles for Today. www.fatherhurley.com/.

Baer, Hans A. *The Black Spiritual Movement: A Religious Response to Racism*. Knoxville: University of Tennessee Press, 1984.

Universal Harmony Foundation
5903 Seminole Blvd., Seminole, FL 33772

The Universal Harmony Foundation grew out of and superceded the Universal Psychic Science Association, founded in 1942 by the Rev. Helene Gerling and her husband, J. Bertram Gerling. Both had been prominent mediums at Lily Dale Spiritualist Camp near Rochester, New York. Headquarters were later moved to St. Petersburg, Florida, where a seminary was opened, offering nine courses leading to ordination as minister, healer, missionary, or teacher. Headquarters are now in Seminole, Florida.

Teachings of the foundation are eclectic, drawn from the universal revelation and the tested teachings of all the world's prophets. Study is directed toward metaphysics, healing, comparative religion, Bible, yoga, and mysticism. The seven affirmation-tenets present a religion premised on the religious and scientific demonstrations of the talents and powers of the Living Spirit. They affirm the fatherhood of God and brotherhood of man, the eternality of life, the power of prayer, spiritual healing, the reality of the psychic, soul-growth as the purpose of life, and fraternal service as the way of life. The Torch of Truth, the symbol of universal harmony, is lighted at the beginning of all services.

There is a mother church, the first chartered by the foundation, and members are encouraged to join it by participation in an annual free-will offering. Ministers are organized into a ministerial fellowship. They may apply for temple (i.e., congregation) charters. Rev. Gerling is the author of correspondence lessons offered through the seminary and a number of books. Rev. Gerling retired in 1988 and was succeeded by Rev. Nancy Castillo.

Membership: In 2001 the church reported 175 members and seven affiliated congregations.

Educational Facilities:

Universal Harmony Foundation Seminary, Seminole, Florida.

Periodicals: *The Spiritual Digest.*

Sources:

Universal Harmony Foundation. www.theuniversalharmony.com/.

Gerling, Helene A. *Healthy Intuitive Development*. New York: Exposition Press, 1971.

Universal Religion of America

c/o Christ Universal Church, 295 N Tropical Trl., Merritt Island, FL 32952

The Universal Religion of America was founded in 1958 by the Rev. Marnie Koski, pastor of a church in Kenosha, Wisconsin, and a former minister of the Spiritual Science Mother Church. The body is Spiritualist and Pentecostal, and emphasizes ESP and the spiritual gifts, such as speaking in tongues. Koski is also known to her followers as Soraya (meaning "Solar Ray"), because she has served as a medium for some contemporary messages from Jesus. Leaving the Kenosha congregation to assistants, Koski moved the headquarters to Rockledge, Florida, and then more recently to the Metaphysical Center in Merritt Island, Florida.

Membership: Not reported. In 1968 there were 500 members. There are two congregations, one in Wisconsin and one in Florida.

Sources:

Koski, Marnie. *Person Talks with Jesus*. Washington, DC: ESPress, 1979.

Universal Spiritualist Association

4905 W University Ave., Muncie, IN 47304-3460

The Universal Spiritualist Association was founded in 1956 by Clifford Bias (1910–1987) with former members of the Spiritualist Episcopal Church, which had provided theological training for Camp Chesterfield of the Indiana Association of Spiritualists. Bias was succeeded as the association's leader by Warren M. Smith, who retired from Spiritualist activities in 1990. T. Ernest Nichols has been president since 1990. A board of trustees oversees both the operation of the association and the Universal Bookstore On Line. A board of regents, presently elected by the board of trustees, oversees the operation of the Universal Institute for Holistic Studies and its Home Study System, a five-level course of study toward the Universal Spiritualist Ministry, along with its interactive Internet counterpart, the College of Religious Education (CORE). Elections are held on an annual basis, with each official holding office for three years. The board of trustees has the power to charter churches as well as license ministers and mediums who have completed the requirements of the institute.

The Universal Spiritualist Association is composed of people who believe in and practice the religion of Spiritualism, described as "the Science, Philosophy, and Religion of continuous life, based upon the demonstrated fact of communication by means of channeling (mediumship) with those who live in the Spiritual World." The association and its churches affirm belief in the Creatorship of God, the oneness of all life everywhere, the leadership of the Christ, salvation by character, and

the progression of humanity upward and onward forever. Annual institute sessions are conducted at Ball State University in Muncie, Indiana. Class intensives continue the association's tradition of teaching, preaching, and practicing the great religions, including Buddhism, Christianity, Hinduism, and Judaism, as well as the esoteric faiths of Esotericism, Native American Spirituality, Rosicrucianism, Spiritualism, Sufism, and Theosophy. The association and its institute provide education and fellowship for devotees and adherents of the Mystic, the Psychic, the New Age, the Metaphysical, and the Traditional. Within the association, there is a mystical society, the Ancient Mystical Order of Seekers, consisting of clergy and the more serious students who wish to learn and understand "the esoteric arts and sciences." The subject matter extends far beyond that common to most Spiritualist practices. Clifford Bias authored a series of manuals, *The Path of Light*, and published several books representative of their work.

Membership: In 2002 the association reported 390 members in the United States and Canada, including ministers, spiritual healers, and mediums, as well as eight churches in the United States and one church in Windsor, Ontario, Canada.

Educational Facilities:

Institute for Holistic Studies, Muncie, Indiana.

Periodicals: *The Banner of Light.*

Sources:

[Bias, Clifford]. *The A. M. O. S. Path of Light*. 19 vols. Anderson, IN: The Ancient and Mystical Order of Seekers, n.d.

—————. *The Way Back*. York Beach, ME: Samuel Weiser, 1985.

Universal Spiritualist Manual. Manor Grove, IN: Universal Spiritual Church, n.d.

Wallace, Austin D. *Thistle Presents Prince Nikeritis*. Eaton Rapids, MI: Transcendental Science Publications, 1950.

University of Life Church

c/o Richard Ireland, 5600 6th St., Phoenix, AZ 85040

The University of Life Church was formed by renowned psychic Richard Ireland (d. 1992). After serving a number of Spiritualist churches in the Midwest and East, Ireland moved to Phoenix, Arizona, in 1955. He gained a reputation during the 1960s as a nightclub entertainer, conducting ESP shows in which he read serial numbers of dollar bills while blindfolded. In the context of the church, he is a full trance medium; two guides, a Dr. Ellington and an Indian, speak through him. They answer questions for members and visitors, prophesy future events, and give spiritual teachings. Reincarnation is stressed.

The center of the church is the congregation in Phoenix, which has 1,450 members. A healing shrine is being built in South Mountain in Phoenix. Lessons written by Ireland and/or his guides are sent out around the country. Ireland tried unsuccessfully to inherit the estate of James Kidd of Miami, Arizona, who willed his money for research on the existence of the human soul. The money went to the American Society of Psychical Research instead.

Membership: Not reported.

Sources:

Ireland, Richard. *The Phoenix Oracle*. New York: Tower Books, 1970.

 # Channeling

Aspects of Light

12540 Braddock Dr., Ste. 218B, Los Angeles, CA 90066

Aspects of Light is a channeling center built around the messages of a group of entities collectively termed the Counsel of Light, whose utterances are channeled by Cherryl Lynn Taylor. Taylor began channeling in the mid-1980s and established the present center in 1991. The counsel's members have indicated that they have appeared to assist individuals to get in touch with their soul urges, to discover higher identities and bring those into manifestation. Human beings are divine, but often live in a state of separation from that divinity. Such separation produces fear and leads to all variety of pain and suffering. The answer to fear is learning to love the self. To facilitate the process of learning to love, Taylor has prepared a set of tapes containing dictated messages from the counsel, which concern both teachings and meditative exercises that the students learn and use in their life. Students also learn to picture themselves in three major aspects—physical, emotional, and mental—and to use the techniques as they monitor each aspect.

Aspects of Light carries on an intensive program that includes weekly healing and development classes and group channeling sessions. Tapes of a wide variety of previous channeling sessions are available.

Membership: Not reported.

Periodicals: *The Counsel of Light*.

Church of Amron

2254 Van Ness, San Francisco, CA 94109

The Church of Amron is a metaphysical church that was founded in San Francisco in the mid-1980s. Growing out of a spiritualist tradition, it has a program built around spiritual healing and channeling (mediumship). It holds weekly worship services each Sunday and midweek activities that include a Tuesday evening forum, healing circles, and an AIDS support group.

Membership: Not reported. In the late 1980s there were two congregations, both in San Francisco.

Church of the White Eagle

2615 St. Beulah Chapel Rd., Montgomery, TX 77316

Alternate Address: International Headquarters: New Lands, Rake, Liss, Hampshire, U.K. GU33 7HY.

HISTORY. The Church of the White Eagle Lodge was established in England in 1934 by Grace Cooke (1892–1979), affectionately known as Minesta, and her husband, Ivan Cooke (d. 1981), known in the lodge as Brother Faithful. For many years, Minesta worked as a medium in the Spiritualist Church of England, primarily in association with the Stead Borderland Library in London. In 1930 she was contacted by a member of the Polaire Brotherhood from France, who informed her that a recently deceased author and Spiritualist, Arthur Conan Doyle (1859–1930), had chosen her as an instrument through whom he wished to speak. She was also given a six-pointed star, symbolic of the Christ star (perfect balance), and asked to train men and women to work with and through the light of Christ to help the world through the "years of fire" into the coming of the "golden age." The star became the symbol of the lodge.

Clairvoyant from childhood, Minesta had long been guided by one whom she knew as White Eagle. Instead of giving personal spirit messages, as is commonly done in Spiritualist churches, she allowed herself to be used to transmit (or channel) a vast series of teachings, which provided the base of the training she had been asked to do. "White Eagle," it is believed, is the symbol of St. John, the Beloved Disciple; a sign of the "age of brotherhood," the golden age; and a title given by the American Indians to a spiritual teacher of great wisdom.

The work spread to the United States in the 1950s and eventually a lodge was established in Texas. More recently, lodges were opened in California and in Canada.

BELIEFS. The church is built around the teachings of White Eagle. These convey the teaching of the brotherhood and emphasize the coming of a golden age in which human intuition will arise as a greater force in human affairs. White Eagle's teachings are summarized in the "principles" of the lodge and include belief in God as Father and Mother, in the Cosmic Christ whose light shines in the human heart, and in the five cosmic laws: reincarnation, cause and effect (karma), opportunity, correspondences, and compensation. The church teaches that every man, woman, and child has in their heart a little spark of light that is the Christ Light, the spirit of Divine love.

To church members, happiness is a realization of God and a quiet, tranquil realization of God's love for all of life. They seek a life that is gentle and in harmony with natural and spiritual laws. The basic law that controls life is love—love for God, for humanity, and for the animals and nature. A vegetarian diet is encouraged. Because God is the creative power within all life, individuals can look within and learn to contact the love of God, the Christ within their own hearts, and use that love to comfort and heal others. As one gives oneself through a life of service, joy and blessings from God are received.

ORGANIZATION. The work in the United States is headquartered at St. John's Retreat Center, a lodge located on a 70-acre rural tract, where both spiritual guidance for humans and a sanctuary for wildlife are provided. The Texas lodge is one of 15 "daughter lodges" located around the world. Among other services, it provides training for center group leaders. The American daughter lodge oversees centers located in various parts of the United States, as well as work in Canada, Brazil, Chile, Japan, and Mexico. Conferences and retreats are held on a regular basis.

Membership in the church and lodge is open to all who feel in harmony with the basic teachings. Meditation and healing are an integral part of the work and there is a special program for children. Sacramental services are held around baptism, marriage, and funerals (with an understanding that there is no death, only eternal life). Members are encouraged to set aside a time daily for prayer using the six-pointed star, the Christ Star, as a focus while sending out the light of Christ. Members may also apply for the brotherhood, an order of men and women within the church who are committed to trying to follow a spiritual way of life and discipline while still living and working in the outer world. The work of the brotherhood includes using and working with the Christ Light for the healing of the planet as well as individuals. The motto of the lodge is "I Serve."

Membership: In 2002 the church reported 982 full members and 3,000 active supporters in 18 U.S. centers. There was then one minister. There were 4 centers in Canada. Worldwide membership was more than 15,000, with centers located in Australia, New Zealand, France, Germany, the Netherlands, Sweden, Switzerland, and South Africa.

Periodicals: *Stella Polaris*. Available from Newlands, Brewells Lane, Rake, Liss, Hampshire, U.K. GU33 7HY. • *Newsletter for the Americans*. Available from 9 St. Beulah Rd., Montgomery, TX 77356.

Sources:

Church of the White Eagle Lodge. www.whiteaglelodge.org.

Cooke, Grace. *The Illuminated Ones*. Liss, Hampshire, U.K.: White Eagle Publishing Trust, 1966.

————. *Minesta's Vision*. Liss, Hampshire, U.K.: White Eagle Publishing Trust, 1992. 60 pp.

Cooke, Ivan, ed. *The Return of Arthur Conan Doyle*. Liss, Hampshire, U.K.: White Eagle Publishing Trust, 1956.

Lind, Ingrid. *The White Eagle Inheritance*. Wellingsborough, Northamptonshire, U.K.: Turnstone Press, 1984.

The Living Word of St. John. Liss, Hampshire, U.K.: White Eagle Publishing Trust, 1985.

The Story of the White Eagle Lodge. Liss, Hampshire, U.K.: White Eagle Publishing Trust, 1986.

The Wisdom of White Eagle. Liss, Hampshire, U.K.: White Eagle Publishing Trust, 1967.

Circle of Power Spiritual Foundation

Current address could not be obtained for this edition.

The Circle of Power Spiritual Foundation was established during the 1980s to spread the teaching of Tawa, a spiritual entity who speaks through Rey Fletcher. During the 1960s, when the Fletchers lived in a Chicago suburb, Rey's wife, Candy

R. Fletcher, began a spiritual search that led her to read metaphysical books and experiment with the ouija board and hypnosis. Thus it was that on August 22, 1968, Tawa first made contact during a session in which Candy had convinced Rey to join her in asking questions of the ouija board. Tawa identified himself as having been a Blackfoot Indian in a previous incarnation, and asked if he could speak using Rey's vocal cords. Rey had proven himself a good subject for hypnotism, and after this first encounter Tawa spoke to (and through) him while Rey was in a hypnotic trance. Tawa's first spoken communication occurred on September 3, 1968.

Tawa continued to speak through Rey until the end of 1970, but for a time the material of these communications was put aside as Rey pursued a successful career. Meanwhile, Candy considered writing a book based on the teachings Tawa had given them. She began work on the text in 1979. Shortly thereafter, the Circle of Power Spiritual Foundation was formed. In 1984 the book was published at about the same time the Foundation moved to Victor, Montana. Assisting the Fletchers are Richard and Bobbie Graham, who head the Foundation branch in Las Vegas, Nevada.

Tawa identified himself as a contemporary of Jesus and the person who served as Jesus' original spiritual teacher. He remained with Jesus through his life, death, and resurrection. The resurrection was the proof that Jesus had been sent by God. According to Tawa, Jesus was reborn in the flesh somewhere in the Orient in 1962. At the time of Tawa's dictations, the reincarnated Jesus was not aware of his mission as Messiah. However, at some point in the near future he will take on his Christ essence and reveal himself to the world. This time he will be fully accepted. However, prior to his coming forth, the anti-Christ, a person now residing in England, will exert power for one year.

The Fletchers see themselves as part of a chosen circle of followers who will be the messengers of the coming Messiah. The Foundation was formed to bring together an initial group of 52 families/persons who will become the spearhead of the mission leading to Christ's next appearance. The Foundation planned to establish a network of lodges from which the message can be disseminated.

Membership: Not reported.

Sources:

Bjorling, Joel. *Channelling: A Bibliographic Exploration*. New York: Garland Publishing, 1992. 363 pp.

Fletcher, C. R. *Spirit in His Mind*. Victor, MT: Circle of Power Spiritual Foundation, 1984. 618 pp.

Cosmic Awareness Communications

PO Box 115, Olympia, WA 98507

In 1962 a voice describing itself as "From Cosmic Awareness" began to speak through the body of ex-army officer William Ralph Duby (1917–1967). In response to the question, "What is Cosmic Awareness?" the group with Duby was told it was "total mind that is not any one mind, but is from the Universal Mind that does not represent any unity other than that of universality."

As the voice continued to speak, its words of wisdom were collected. In 1963, instructions were received for the formation of an Organization of Awareness as a means of giving to individuals the teaching of the voice. The real organization is said to be composed of 144 entities on that inner plane known as Essence.

Communications from Awareness have covered the whole scope of subjects about which people have questions, but, through it all, a few central ideas have emerged. God is seen not as a personal deity, but as natural cosmic law. The spiritual life is stressed, as is compassion in dealings with men. Man's purpose is to move toward cosmic awareness.

A summary of the voice's stance is contained in the "Laws and Precepts of Cosmic Awareness," printed below:

The Universal Law is that knowledge, that awareness, that all living things, all life has within it that vitality, that strength to gather into it all things necessary for its growth and its fruition.

The Law of Love is that law which places the welfare and the concern and the feeling for others above self. The Law of Love is that close affinity with all forces that you associate with as good. The Law of Love is that force which denies the existence of evil in the world, that resists not evil.

The Law of Mercy is that law which allows one to forgive all error, to forgive equally those who err against you as you err against them. This is to be merciful. To be merciful is akin to the Law of Love, and if one obeys the Law of Mercy there can be no error in the world.

The Law of Gratitude is that sense of satisfaction where energy which has been given receives a certain reward.

Judge Not. Be Humble. Never Do Anything Contrary to the Law of Love. Resist Not Evil. Do Nothing Which Is Contrary to the Law of Mercy.

Duby died in 1967 and a major splintering occurred in the organization. No fewer than seven bodies were formed, each claiming to be the continuation of the original. Disagreement over the publication of materials that some thought should remain secret was one major issue in the schisms. Largest of the several splinters is Cosmic Awareness Communications, which continues the 1963 organization. About four months after Duby's death, a channel emerged through which Cosmic Awareness continued to speak. In the late 1960s, messages received through this new channel, Paul Shockley, both clarified and altered the older material. The new voice revealed that the Organization of Awareness has helped to accomplish a vast shift of consciousness—a return to the Godhead, which for thousands of years Essence has willed would eventually occur. The return to the Godhead is equated with the return of Lucifer, the fallen angel of light.

Membership: Not reported, but in 1995 the newsletter reported a circulation of 3,000 copies. In the 1970s, Cosmic Awareness Communications claimed 75 centers (including 3 in Canada) and 144,000 members.

Periodicals: *Revelation of Awareness*.

Sources:

Cosmic Awareness Center. www.cosmicawareness.org.

Cosmic Awareness Speaks. 3 vols. Olympia, WA: Cosmic Awareness Communications, n.d., 1977, 1983.

Crest in the Stone Mystery School

c/o Johannine Grove Ministry, PO Box 235, Crestone, CO 81131

The Crest in the Stone Mystery School (formerly known as the Star of Isis Foundation) is a mystery school established in the 1980s by Christine Hayes, better known by her spiritual name, Chrystine StarEagle. Hayes is a channel and the School is built upon the material she has channeled and continues to channel on a regular basis. The School is built around the ancient myth of Isis retrieving the body parts of her slain and mutilated husband, Osiris, recast in the light of present planetary transformations. The purpose of the Crest in the Stone Mystery School is to lead individuals in the "gathering" of the parts of their self into a whole entity/consciousness that leads to a future resurrection of the archetypical Logos/Mind. Through this assemblage, the souls of people can ascend in a Phoenix-like flame, to be emancipated from earth and reborn in a realm of Light and Air.

The School initiates individuals into a specific form of meditation (termed Matrix) and teaches the initiate to tap the source of personal co-creative power. The School expounds a way to access the ancient archetypes of our spiritual-genetic memories that leads to the premise that all goodness comes from God and that God is found within (not outside) us.

Chrystine StarEagle has channeled one volume, *Magi from the Blue Star*, from Elvis Presley. This book recounts Presley's past incarnation and his spiritual journey since the end of his earthly life. The volume also recounts his conversations with long-time friend Wanda June Hill and includes stories of his extraordinary effect on people who knew him.

Membership: The School has one center, the Church of the Johannine Origin, in San Antonio, Texas, and in 1992 reported approximately 50 members.

Periodicals: *Temple Doors Doctrine of Mysteries.*

Divine Word Foundation
c/o Edmund Spitzer, 1999 Pine Grove Rd., Rogue River, OR 97537

The Divine Word Foundation was founded in 1962 by Dr. Hans Nordewin von Koerber (1886–1979), formerly professor of Asiatic studies at the University of Southern California. The purpose of the Foundation is to disseminate the revelation of Jakob Lorber (1800–1864). An Austrian-born musician, Lorber in his fortieth year heard a voice in his heart saying, "Jakob, get up, take your pencil and write." Obeying, he began to function as the scribe to this Voice, which he believed to be none other than the Lord Jesus Christ. Through Lorber, the Voice dictated 25 books and other, shorter works. The revelations did not end with Lorber. In 1870 Gottfried Meyerhofer (1807–1877), a retired Army officer living in Trieste and a student of the Lorber literature, heard the Voice, which began to dictate through him. Since Meyerhofer's death, others in succession have continued to hear the Voice, including Leopold Engel, Johanne Ladner, Bertha Dudde, Johannes Widmann, Max Seltmann, Johanna Henzsel, George Riehle, and Johannes Friede.

The works of Lorber were published primarily by Christoph Friedrich Landbeck of Bietigheim, Germany, who headed the Neutheosophischer Verlag (after 1907 Neusalems-Verlag or New Jerusalem Publication House). In 1924, the Neusalem Gesellschaft (New Jerusalem Society) was formed. Adolf Hitler suppressed the Lorber work, but it was quickly reestablished. The Society became the Lorber Gesellschaft and the publishing arm, the Lorber Verlag. In 1921, the Lorber revelations were discovered by Dr. von Koerber. As he accepted them, he began to translate them into English and introduce them to others.

The new revelation fills 42 volumes of approximately 450 pages each. For Lorber, God is the Infinite Spirit behind the universe. The Holy Spirit is the "external life ether" that permeates the universe. The universe is the expression of God, made up of tiny spiritual primordial sparks created to grow into the divine likeness. It is God's desire to create a society of living love.

The plan of God was thwarted by Lucifer who revolted with the spirits below him and became entrapped in matter: impure spirit condensed. God is using matter as a filtering plant through which the impure spirits can be purified. Earth is the place where the rebellious spirits are being given the chance to return voluntarily to God. God became man in Jesus to accelerate the redemptive process. The cross is a perfect example of love.

A human being is intended to learn, through the imitation of Christ, to love God and his neighbor as himself. He thus achieves rebirth and is allowed to participate in the work of redemption. At death, each soul discards the body and begins life as a spirit. It ascends, beginning from its point of development in the body, ultimately to the New Jerusalem. Christ will return in the near future to recreate the earth and establish the millennium, the first signs of which are worldly conflict and turmoil. The present period will culminate in Lucifer's making his final choice and in a war of destruction of the most rebellious ones.

The membership of the Lorber Society is concentrated in German-speaking Europe, but has spread to every continent. In the United States, individuals around the country study the revelation found in the books published by the Divine Word Foundation. Study groups are located in San Diego and Newark, California; Denver, Colorado; and Salt Lake City, Utah. Since Dr. von Koerber's death, his widow, Hildegard von Koerber, has continued his translating efforts. There is also a translator residing in Salt Lake City. Dr. Fred S. Bunger, the Foundation's first president, died in 1979 and was succeeded by Earl G. Fox of Melba, Idaho. Bunger coauthored with Dr. von Koerber the Foundation's basic text, *A New Light Shines Out of Darkness.*

The Foundation has a friendly relationship with the Lorber Verlag in Germany, though it is organizationally independent. It is also associated with another English-language translator in Great Britain.

Membership: Not reported.

Sources:

www.j-lorber.com/English/.

Bunger, Fred S., and Hans N. von Koerber. *A New Light Shines Out of the Present Darkness.* Philadelphia: Dorrance Company, 1971.

Lorber, Jakob. *The Three-Days-Scene at the Temple of Jerusalem.* Bietigheim, Würtemberg, Germany: Neu-Salems-Society, 1932.

Doctrine of Truth Foundation
Current address not obtained for this edition.

The Doctrine of Truth Foundation was established in the mid-1970s to promulgate the research and ideas of Lewis E. Cook Jr. and Junko Yasui, as contained in their book *Goldot: Guidebook of Life and Doctrine of Truth.* Following the Korean War, Cook (b. 1925) worked in Korea as part of the reconstruction program and stayed on as head of a construction company. In 1964 he moved to Japan to establish a prefabricated-home business. There he met and fell in love with Junko Yasui. They were married in 1967, and soon afterward moved to the Philippines. There, both began a period of heightened attention to their spiritual lives. They began to practice yoga, read metaphysical and occult books, and meditate.

The couple moved to the United States in 1970 and immediately began to teach all that they had learned. They assembled a summary of their ideas in *Goldot*, and founded the Doctrine of Truth to disseminate those ideas. *Goldot* is acclaimed as the modern Bible and Guidebook for humanity. It covers all dimensions of life, beginning with its origins. Creation was, it teaches, an emanation from Spirit. Spirit begat the Oversoul, which in turn led to the development of universal mind, the universe, light, darkness, heaven (the astral universe), and earth (the material universe). The astral light entered the material universe and all life forms resulted. God then released the individual souls within Itself, and these "gods of creation" then created the world and all of the plant, vegetable, and human life within it. The human life was in their image and likeness. The astral gods took on physical bodies. However, the God Men violated their own divine mandate and began to intermingle with that segment of the human race who were not God Men.

According to *Goldot*, earthly life is governed by Truth, universal principles, and laws. The principles produce life, whereas the laws govern it. Underlying reality is Unity-Equilibrium, the infinite eternal presence within all phenomena, also known as Spirit or God. Unity-Equilibrium manifests as Mind, the essence of all phenomena. The Unity-Equilibrium particle of each human manifests as pure mind, also known as *soul* or *ego*. The universe is the result of the creative expressions of the Universal Mind, the collective ego of all souls. Every instant and every detail of an individual's life is the result of mental creative activity. Life equals creativity. We experience life through sensory perception. Our limited perceptions in the material realm create illusion.

Life and its sensory experiences are governed by the laws of harmony, duality-polarity, cycles, cause-effect, and karma. The universe exists in harmony, disrupted only by human ignorance. Humans should strive for harmonious life and relationships. Because harmony undergirds the universe, in order for it to be perceived, it must manifest as either the negative or positive aspect of a neutral equilibrated image. Thus, phenomena function to produce the illusion of our world. The world of illusion goes through cycles of formation and dissolution. The ongoingness of the cycles follows a pattern of cause and effect. The law of cause and effect in human life manifests as karma, the consequences of the thoughts, words, and deeds of individuals.

The Doctrine of Truth Foundation builds upon the basic principles and laws of life and disseminates teachings that explain the meaning of these principles and laws for all of life. As part of this endeavor, it publishes *Goldot* and other related literature. Related to the Foundation are the Doctrine of Truth Church, the Doctrine of Truth School, and the Doctrine of Truth Research Center.

Membership: Not reported.

Sources:

Cook, Lewis E., Jr., and Junko Yasui. *Goldot: Guidebook of Life and Doctrine of Truth.* Oceanside, CA: Doctrine of Truth Foundation, 1976.

EarthStar Alliance

1163 N Thunder Ridge Dr., Tucson, AZ 85745-3378

EarthStar Alliance was founded in the mid-1990s by Sara Mattoon and Scott Myrom to assist what they believe to be a planetary transformation now occurring on Earth. Mattoon and Myrom view themselves as two of a number of masters who have incarnated on Earth during this generation who, having lived some years as just a normal human being, now have become aware of their task to aid in the creation of Heaven on Earth. They believe that Earth is in the process of becoming a star. As the planet moves from its state of dense physical reality into being a radiant body of light, stress is produced in humans' dense earth bodies. EarthStar Alliance provides a way of viewing the world, specific techniques, and new technologies to support the body during this change. These include bodywork, channeling sessions, and group events.

EarthStar Alliance teaches that each individual is both of the One, or God, and also a separate unique individual. In their aspect as part of the One, persons exist in one single reality or dimension; as separate individuals, they exist in a multitude of realms or dimensions. Most individuals live totally in the third (physical and mental) and fourth (astral) dimensions, where the game of good and evil is played out. Individuals also exist in various nonphysical dimensions, from the fourth (light) to the twelfth (experience of the One). Understanding the multiple existence of oneself in these various dimensions (including the lower ones) assists comprehension of one's divine nature. In the eighth and ninth dimensions, individuals see their Spirit manifesting as individual identities that represent groups— that is, they see themselves as part of a group soul. Individuals from various group souls are now on planet Earth.

When one shifts one's perspective on who one is, the illusion of reality is also shifted and the manifestation of who one is in other dimensions begins to manifest in the third and fourth dimensions. Basic to the new view of the self is a shift of identity from that of struggling human to that of multidimensional divine self, and from that of student to that of master. Also, each person should shift the way of measuring reality from the beliefs and feelings of the third and fourth dimensions to a fifth-dimension perspective (based in knowingness and inner authority).

Members of EarthStar Alliance and those who resonate with its work are considered part of one group soul now manifesting on planet Earth. This group soul has a specific task in the period of transition to serve as path-cutters bringing light, information, and energy from the more expanded dimensions.

Membership: Not reported. The Alliance supports regular meetings in San Diego and is reaching out to other communities along the Pacific Coast.

Periodicals: *True Reality.*

Sources:

Good Timing Guide. www.goodtimingguide.com/index/index_questions.htm.

The Eloists, Inc.

Drawer O, Duxbury, MA 02321

The Eloist Ministry was founded by Walter De Voe at the turn of the twentieth century. De Voe was born in Cedar Rapids, Iowa, in 1874. As a teenager he became a seeker of metaphysical truth, and in his search, found his way to the Chicago World's Fair and the Parliament of Religions in 1893. At that time he was exposed to the sacred books of all the major religions. He also became acquainted with many individuals with similar interests and subsequently became a part of what eventually evolved into the "New Thought" movement.

By 1902 De Voe had begun to work with his newly discovered abilities as a spiritual healer. He successfully pursued this work in Battle Creek, Michigan, and then in Cleveland, Ohio, where he published *Healing Currents from the Battery of Life* in

1904. In 1916 he was inspired to relocate his ministry to the Boston suburb of Brookline, which was a great center of metaphysical activity at the time, and in 1918 the organization was incorporated as a nonprofit, tax-exempt religious entity in the state of Massachusetts, with the name of "The Eloist Ministry." The Ministry continued its work of spiritual education and spiritual healing until 1954. At that time Walter De Voe's health began to fail with advancing age, and it was decided to relocate the headquarters to Duxbury, Massachusetts, where it remains today. The focus and emphasis of the organization's work changed somewhat over the years, and as a reflection of that fact, its name was abbreviated to "The Eloists, Inc.," in 1972.

Unlike a conventional church that emphasizes the seeking of converts and continual establishment of growing congregations, the Eloists have remained a group of limited size because of the personal demands made by the group's commitment to a specific spiritual endeavor that, it notes, may not be for everyone. While not presuming to be "God's spokesmen" or believing they offer the only path to the Creator, the Eloists strive to extend a helping hand to other sincere seekers they meet along the path to greater spiritual growth and understanding.

The Eloists believe that there is but one Creator, who is ever present within all of creation. This Creator cannot be seen as a finite entity, but the Creator's works stand in perpetual glory and the Creator's voice can be heard within one's consciousness and being when an individual is opened and attuned. People are responsible for their own spiritual growth, and no savior can substitute for good works and soul development.

While the primary source of inspiration comes from within, the Eloists enlist the aid of a variety of inspirational books, among which is *Oahspe*, a book they were directed to read in the mid-1930s by an elevated angelic presence. The Eloists believe the book to be genuine, but make allowances for imperfections within it and do not interpret it literally as an inflexible book of rules; nor, indeed, do they worship any book.

The Eloists note that individuals from many other religious persuasions may find aspects of Eloist activities familiar, though as a whole Eloist belief is unique. While Eloist belief is non-Christian, Christian "New Thought" students would find Eloist perspectives on healthcare and spiritual healing to be similar to their own positions; Quakers would understand Eloist methods of conducting business, the unprogrammed meetings, the absolute commitment to nonviolence, and the mystical religion. Shakers might identify with some aspects of Eloist ritual, while spiritualists might identify with Eloist attention to spirit communion and the interest in developing psychic sensitivity. Eloist activities include, among others, educational instruction, spiritual counseling, publishing, and charitable work.

From 1983 until 1999 the Eloists, Inc., published the journal *Radiance*. Back issues of this bimonthly periodical remain available, as does *Healing Currents from the Battery of Life*, revised for the fourth time in 1999.

Membership: Not reported. There are no clergy.

Periodicals: *Eloist Focus.*

Sources:

De Voe, Walter. *Healing Currents from the Battery of Life.* Brookline, MA: Eloist Ministry, 1919.

———. *Mystic Words of Mighty Power.* New York: Gordon Press Publishers, 1991.

The Eloists. Duxbury, MA: Eloist Ministry, 1990.

Oahspe: A New Age Bible. Los Angeles: Essenes of Kosmon, 1950.

Family of Abraham

Box 690070, San Antonio, TX 78269

In the early 1980s channel Esther Hicks began to receive messages from "Abraham," the name assumed by a group of evolved noncorporeal entities. In 1986, with the assistance of her husband, Jerry Hicks, who had received the initial messages, she began to inform some close friends and business associates of what was occurring and the messages they were receiving. These people began to offer questions to Abraham and found "his" answers useful and meaningful. Upon receiving this positive response, the Hickses began to make Abraham's teaching available to the general public, primarily through the circulation of tapes of the channeling sessions.

Abraham has spoken to a wide variety of issues of concern to the New Age community, such as coming earth changes, but has centered his message on the need for individuals to become conscious co-creators of their reality. This process is assisted by one's becoming aware of the laws of the universe and learning to move in accordance with them. Most important is the law of attraction, by which one can attract whatever one desires. It is used in connection with the law of allowing, by which one becomes free of the negativity that binds our life.

The Hickses have established a schedule of regular weekend "Dialogues" with Abraham around the country, and over the years Abraham study groups have formed across the United States. Those responding to the messages from Abraham have been informally dubbed the Family of Abraham. A quarterly newsletter, *Abraham Speaks*, was begun. It was superseded by the more substantive *The Leading Edge* in 1994.

Membership: In 1994 there were nine Abraham study groups and an unreported number of individuals receiving *The Leading Edge*.

Periodicals: *The Leading Edge*.

Remarks: In 2006 Esther Hicks came to the fore in the metaphysical community as one of the featured presenters of prosperity-consciousness ideas in the original release of the movie *The Secret*, developed by Australian filmmaker Rhonda Byrne. In spite of the success of the movie, she declined to participate in the second expanded version.

Sources:

Family of Abraham. www.abraham-hicks.com.

Fellowship of the Inner Light

c/o The Fellowship Center, 620 14th St., Virginia Beach, VA 23451

The Fellowship of the Inner Light was formed in Atlanta, Georgia, in October 1972 by psychic Paul Solomon (1939–1994) and his associates. In February 1972, in a hypnotic trance, Solomon began to speak in a stern voice, a voice later to be labeled "the Source." As the trance sessions continued and Solomon began a vigorously disciplined life, the material that came through the readings began to provide techniques for treatment of disease, prophecies that proved accurate, spiritual philosophy, and a complete system for the development of "Inner Light Consciousness." The Fellowship was organized as a structure to further the work of Solomon and to disseminate the Inner Light Consciousness. In 1974 the Fellowship moved to Virginia Beach, Virginia, the home of Edgar Cayce, to whom Solomon is likened by his followers. Cayce founded the Association for Research and Enlightenment, discussed elsewhere in this volume.

The material in the transcripts of the Solomon readings covers a wide range of topics: Atlantis, diet and health, healing, reincarnation, sex, spiritual development, and prophecies. The worldview closely parallels that of the Cayce readings. Man is a son of God trapped in material forms that had their first manifestation on Atlantis. Through spiritual growth, the cleansing of the body, and evolvement, the trapped soul can return to oneness with God. Also discussed in the material are the ones who came to aid those who are trapped and wish to return. Reincarnation allows time for the growth of the soul.

The source for the information coming through Solomon is the Universal Mind as manifested in the Akashic records. All thoughts and actions are said to be recorded on the "universal ethers" of the Akashic records, and psychics "tap into" those records to obtain information. In the Fellowship of the Inner Light, contact with spirits is discouraged. From the readings, a course that places the student on the mystic path to cosmic consciousness has been constructed. The course emphasizes the Light Within (or Holy Spirit). Consciousness of the Light is the key to over-

coming the limitations of the material. The methods of the course, including relaxation, meditation, prayer, self-control, occult law, and psychic development, lead to mastery of one's psychic nature, to integration of the total person, and to spiritual development.

The Fellowship is conceived of as a religious association serving the needs of the New Age community. During the 1970s, the Fellowship was headquartered in Virginia Beach, from where a vigorous local program was offered. Two entities, Heritage Store and Heritage Publications, were closely affiliated. Heritage Publications issued the material from the readings, the first volume of which appeared in 1974, while Heritage Store was begun in 1969 to make available to the general public the remedies suggested in the Cayce readings. In 1978, however, a 13-acre tract of land near New Market, Virginia, was dedicated as "Carmel-in-the-Valley." Headquarters shifted to this rural site, and ambitious plans for the development of a new age community as the center of the fellowship were announced. Publication offices remained in Virginia Beach. Affiliated fellowships can be found across the United States, and in England, Holland, and several other countries.

In the years since Solomon's death, the fellowship has cooperated with the Paul Solomon Foundation, which has charge of all of the recorded readings that Solomon left behind. The Foundation has engaged in editing and transcribing this material, and in making it available to the public. Both organizations perpetuate the notion of Solomon's likeness to Edgar Cayce (1877–1945), and describe him as America's "second sleeping prophet."

Membership: Not reported. There is one center of activity, located in Virginia Beach, Virginia.

Periodicals: *Reflections on the Inner Light*. Available from Rte. 1, Box 141, Timberville, VA 22853.

Sources:

Fellowship of the Inner Light. www.fellowshipoftheinnerlight.com/.

Paul Solomon Foundation. www.paulsolomon.com/.

A Healing Consciousness. Virginia Beach, VA: Master's Press, 1978.

Spiritual Unfoldment and Psychic Development through Inner Light Consciousness. Atlanta, GA: Fellowship of the Inner Light, n.d.

Fellowship of Universal Guidance

c/o Bella Karish, 1524 Glenoaks Blvd., Glendale, CA 91201

The Fellowship of Universal Guidance was founded in 1960 by Dr. Wayne A. Guthrie and Dr. Bella Karish, both of whom serve as channels for the "great sources of light," teachers from the spirit world who guide Fellowship activities. The Fellowship has been associated with the Universal Link on occasion, but the thrust of the Fellowship's concern is the harmonizing of the three levels of consciousness. The Fellowship teaches that there are three separate entities within each person: the high self, the conscious self, and the basic self. The ultimate goal is to bring them into alignment for the eventual good of the karmic pattern by blending them for physical, emotional, mental, and spiritual development. The high self is part of the superconscious structure and is located about three inches above the head. The conscious self functions in interpersonal relationships, and the basic self is that part that evolved from the animal kingdom, according to the Fellowship.

Man reincarnates on earth only once but is re-embodied until his goal is reached. The high self chooses where to incarnate. The basic self carries memory, emotions, and the masculine/feminine consciousness. Unfulfilled karma from previous embodiments can cause the basic self to open to negative forces that can cause diseases, which can be healed only by discharging the karmic pattern. The Fellowship offers a "Three Selves Evaluation" to aid the individual in growth.

The insights of the Fellowship are given to the world through several series of lessons, beginning with the *Wisdom Workshop Lessons, Series I*. Students may take these lessons by correspondence, and groups have formed to study the material collectively.

Membership: Not reported.

Periodicals: *Uniguidance*. Available from 1674 Hillhurst Ave., Los Angeles, CA 90027.

Sources:

Fellowship of Universal Guidance. www.foug.org.

Master Apollonius Speaks. Los Angeles: Fellowship of Universal Guidance, 1970.

The Prophetic Word: Revelation Number Two. Los Angeles: Fellowship of Universal Guidance, [1980].

Wisdom Workshop Lessons, Series 1. 12 vols. Los Angeles: Fellowship of Universal Guidance, n.d.

Foundation Church of Divine Truth, Inc.

FCDT Publishing, PO Box 802694, Santa Clarita, CA 91380-2694

The Foundation Church of Divine Truth (FCDT) supersedes the former Foundation Church of the New Birth, based upon the writings of James Edward Padgett (1852–1923). Padgett, an assistant district attorney in the Washington, D.C., area, and a Methodist Sunday school teacher, became interested in Spiritualism after the death of his wife, Helen, in 1914. He was told by a medium that he had the gift of automatic writing (the process by which mediums convey, either by writing or typing, thoughts and words transmitted through them by a spirit entity). Padgett received his first message from his wife, Helen, describing her passing into the spirit world and then later her spiritual progress into the Celestial Heavens.

Within a year, Padgett began to receive messages purporting to be from Jesus of Nazareth, urging him to pray for the inflowing of the Father's Divine Love. On October 5, 1914, Jesus (Master of the Celestial Heavens) told Padgett that he had been selected to disseminate the Father's Truths to humankind. The result was some 2,500 messages received from Jesus, other high Celestial spirits, and a variety of spirits either progressing through the Spiritual Heavens or stagnating in the lower spheres of the spirit world. The most important messages were published in four volumes, the first of which was printed in 1940. The sum total of these messages from Jesus were said to constitute his Second Coming to earth. Padgett received the messages between the years 1914 and 1923. After his death, the manuscripts were left in the custody of a close associate, Dr. Leslie R. Stone (1876–1967). Stone and others interested in the messages incorporated the Foundation Church of the New Birth in 1958 in Washington, D.C.

In 1982 the Rev. John Paul Gibson, the sole surviving founding trustee of the Foundation Church of the New Birth, died. A group of members, primarily in the Washington, D.C. area, reorganized as the New Christian Healing Sanctuary. They received permission to receive mail at the former church's mailbox. In December 1985, nine former members of the Foundation Church of the New Birth (eight of whom were ordained ministers) formed the Foundation Church of Divine Truth to carry forward the work of the former church.

BELIEFS. Since their initial publication, the volumes of messages have been variously titled *Book of Truths*, *Messages from Jesus and Celestials*, *True Gospel Revealed Anew by Jesus*, and, more recently, *Angelic Revelations of Divine Truth* (in two volumes), *New Testament Revelations of Jesus of Nazareth*, and *What Happens After You Die*. A summary of the material is found in the tenets of the church, given as direct revelation by Jesus of Nazareth and his disciples from the Celestial Heavens. True to the Spiritualist heritage, the first tenet concerns the continuity of the soul after death. The soul enters the spirit world and continues to progress until it reaches the Sixth Sphere, which is the Paradise of the Old Testament, or the Kingdom of the Perfect Natural Man, beyond which no further progress occurs. Should the soul seek to be filled with the Divine Love of the Creator, however, its progress takes it to the Celestial Heavens, where it continues to receive inflowing of the Divine Essence of the Father and becomes conscious of its immortality. The

potential for receiving this Divine Love had been lost with the fall of the first created parents. It was restored in the person of Jesus of Nazareth, a human son selected by God as the first recipient of this Love and as his message bearer (Messiah). Jesus' earthly mission was to inform humankind that possession of Divine Love was now available to all through fervent prayer to the Father for this Gift, the ultimate result of which would be transformation of the soul from mortal to immortal and its eventual angelic status in the Celestial Heavens.

ORGANIZATION. The Foundation Church of Divine Truth is governed by a board of trustees that has the power to ordain ministers and charter churches. Members relate to the church primarily through the mail or e-mails. The church describes itself as "a through the mail, nonprofit Christian Spiritualist organization that exists solely for the purpose of spreading the Truths of God's Divine Love as taught by Jesus of Nazareth, and as contained in its publications." The church is "interdenominational in that it upholds the highest spiritual teachings of all religions, with the added commandment given by Jesus when he was on earth to 'Love One Another as I Have Loved You' with the Divine Love of God received into the human soul." Spiritual advisors are available to correspond via conventional mail or e-mail.

Membership: Not reported. The church states that membership is "open to all who spiritually and morally uphold the purpose of the church to disseminate the Truth's of God's Divine Love to humankind."

Sources:

Foundation Church of Divine Truth. www.fcdt.org/.

Padgett, James E. *True Gospel Revealed Anew by Jesus*. 4 vols. Washington, DC: Foundation Church of the New Birth, 1958–1984.

———. *Angelic Revelations of Divine Truth*. 2 vols. Santa Clarita, CA: Foundation Church of Divine Truth, 1989–1992.

———. *New Testament Revelations of Jesus of Nazareth*. Santa Clarita, CA: Foundation Church of Divine Truth, 2003.

———. *What Happens after You Die*. Santa Clarita, CA: Foundation Church of Divine Truth, 2003.

Foundation Church of the New Birth

Box 996, Benjamin Franklin Sta., Washington, DC 20044

The Foundation Church of the New Birth, reestablished in 1991, is a through-the-mail church organization that continues the work of the organization of the same name originally founded in 1958. The earlier church was built around the channeled messages of James Edward Padgett (1852–1923), who received numerous messages from Jesus via automatic writing between 1914 and his death in 1923. These messages were published by the church in four volumes under the title *True Gospel Revealed Anew by Jesus*. During the mid-1980s, the church passed through a period of organizational disruption, after which it was disbanded. An attempt to reorganize led, in December 1985, to the formation of the Foundation Church of Divine Truth, by nine of the former members. In 1991, another group of former members reorganized under the original name. The church is led by its trustees, with Rev. Jocelyn Harleston serving as current administrative head. It continues to reprint the first four volumes of *True Gospel Revealed Anew by Jesus*.

The church seeks to inform mankind of the availability of the Heavenly Father's Divine Love, which is received into the soul when earnestly sought for through prayer and soul longings. Its inflowing is felt as a radiant glow in the heart region. When sufficient abundance of this love is obtained, it will transform the soul from the image of the Father into his very substance, which is not only divine but also immortal.

The church teaches that Jesus of Nazareth brought this love to light during his public ministry on earth and continues to teach its availability today, from the realm of spirit.

Membership: Not reported.

Periodicals: *New Birth Commentary*.

Sources:

Foundation Church of the New Birth. www.divinelove.org/.

Padgett, James D. *True Gospel Revealed Anew by Jesus*. 4 vols. Washington, DC: Foundation Church of the New Birth, 1958–1972.

Foundation for Meditative Studies
PO Box 908, Ashland, OR 97520

The Foundation for Meditative Studies, originally known as the Foundation for the Realization of Inner Divinity, was founded in 1990 by Swami Paramananda Saraswatti, and supersedes an earlier organization, MAFU Seminars. The founding of the foundation followed an intense religious experience by Penny Torres Rubin, a New Age channel (medium) of the entity MAFU. During the late 1980s, Torres Rubin had emerged as one of the most popular channels within the growing New Age Movement. She started channeling in 1986 when she began to communicate with the disincarnate personage known as MAFU. Within a few months she was channeling regularly in public sessions in Los Angeles and Santa Barbara, California. Torres Rubin's organization, MAFU Seminars, circulated cassettes and videotapes of the channeling sessions around the world.

MAFU is characterized as a 32,000-year-old entity who has incarnated on earth at least 17 times. His enlightened messages insist that each person is, in essence, divine. God is equated with the power of life. Thus all things are of God and in God. The goal of life is to realize one's own divine nature, by which knowledge one becomes a master.

Toward the end of 1989, Torres Rubin traveled to Hardiwar, India, in the Himalayan foothills. She took the vows of a *sannyassi* (accepting the renounced life), and also accepted a mission as the "ordained leader of spirituality" for the present age. Here, she received her new name, Swami Paramananda Saraswatti. Upon her return to the United States, Saraswatti established the Foundation for the Realization of Inner Divinity and its subsidiary, the Center for God Realization, which now disseminates MAFU's teaching materials and regularly conducts seminars and retreats for thousands of seekers.

The Foundation has brought together all of the wisdom received from MAFU and presents it as a distinct path to God consciousness. The organization has purchased a campground near Ashland, Oregon, as a retreat center. It has also developed a mastery course that introduces people to MAFU's spiritual path.

Membership: In 1992 the foundation reported an active membership of 15,000.

Sources:

Foundation for Meditative Studies. www.foundationformeditativestudies.org/.

Torres, Penny [MAFU]. *And What Be God?* Vacaville, CA: Mafu Seminars, 1989.

———. *Reflections on Yeshua Ben Joseph*. Vacaville, CA: Mafu Seminars, 1989.

Grail Movement of America
2081 Partridge Ln., Binghamton, NY 13903
Alternate Address: International Headquarters: Internationale Gralsbewegung-Vomperberg, A-6134, Vomperberg, Tyrol, Austria.

The Grail Movement of America is supported by the Grail Foundation, which is the structure for disseminating the teachings of Oskar Ernest Bernhardt (1875–1941) of Bischofswerda, Germany. In 1924 Bernhardt moved to Bavaria, where he began to write lectures under the pen name Abd-ru-shin. In 1928 he settled in Austria, where he wrote *In the Light of Truth, the Grail Message*. He continued writing until he was expelled by the Nazis in 1938. The first center in America was formed about 1939 at Mt. Morris, Illinois. Abd-ru-shin's message is termed the Grail Message, a reference to the Holy Grail as the power center of creation.

According to Abd-ru-shin, God created man equal and set him in search of self-consciousness and maturity. In his search, man was led to the world of gross matter. Men's physical bodies were fashioned for our true selves to function within while on Earth. The purpose of man is to learn to live in harmony with the divine laws that brought forth the creation and now maintain it. Eventually, man can return to the spiritual realm as a mature human spirit, ready to enter life-eternal as a fully seasoned and self-conscious entity capable of serving the Creator as a true human spirit.

The Grail Message is contained in the three volumes of *In the Light of Truth*. There are also other writings by Abd-ru-shin. They are circulated in North America by the foundation through its two headquarters, formerly located in Mt. Morri and Lapeer, Michigan, and now in Binghamton, New York, and Quebec, Canada. The International Grail Movement also works in most European countries, Australia, and New Zealand. There is some work in South America, Asia, and Africa.

Membership: In 2002 the movement reported 400 active adherents in the United States and 1,000 in Canada. Worldwide the movement has some 19,000 adherents.

Sources:

Grail Movement of America. www.grailmessage.com.

Abd-ru-shin. *Awake! Selected Lectures*. Vomperberg, Tyrol, Austria: Maria Bernhardt Publishing Co., n.d.

———. *In the Light of Truth*. Vomperberg, Tyrol, Austria: Maria Bernhardt Publishing Co., 1954.

Inner Circle Kethra E'Da Foundation, Inc.
Box 121722, San Diego, CA 92112-1722

The Inner Circle Kethra E'Da Foundation, Inc., was established in 1945 by Mark Probert (d. 1969) and his wife, Irene Probert, of San Diego, California. Mark Probert, an orphan with little formal education, one evening began to speak aloud in his sleep. According to his wife's description, he spoke in foreign languages and sang arias from operas. Dr. Meade Layne, founder-director of the Borderland Science Research Society, a large southern California psychic organization, recognized Probert as a trance medium and helped guide his development. Gradually, teachers from the spirit world began to contact Probert. One afternoon, five of his teachers appeared to him and told him that they wished to bring their teaching to the world using him as their channel. Many of the teachings were published in 1954 and 1955 in *Mystic, the Magazine of the Supernatural* and later collected in a book, *The Magic Bag*; more recently, they were gathered in the book *Yada Speaks*.

In all, 11 teachers manifested themselves in light bodies (figures similar to shining, brilliant ghosts), and Mark was able to make sketches of them. The three main ones were Professor Alfred Luntz, an Anglican clergyman; Ramon Natalli, a contemporary of Galileo; and Yada di Shi'ite, who lived half a million years ago in the ancient civilization of Yu in the Himalayas. These teachers are members of an Inner Circle that at one time existed on earth, with Probert (in an earlier incarnation) as a member. Eternal life is at the heart of the teachings of the Inner Circle. The goal of life is to attain one's original state as a divine being. Earth experiences are seen as movement through a series of initiations into higher and greater states of awareness. When one attains a state in which there is no break in consciousness, freedom is attained and there is no necessity to return to the physical. Work pursued with love and sincerity is the way to awareness. Yoga practices, secret mantras, sitting in meditation, and deep concentration are considered futile attempts to hurry progress. The basic entity in the universe is the individual. The plan of the universe lies within the individual, and becomes apparent as one solves one's own riddle of the universe. God, or the Creative Force, is said to be the impersonal soul with which one becomes aware of the unification.

The foundation has preserved the numerous tapes of Probert's trance-lectures and disseminates them in both cassette form and as transcripts. Members gathered on Friday evening for dictation prior to Probert's death in 1969, and now gather to listen to tapes and for discussions.

Membership: There is no formal membership. In 1997 there were three centers in the United States.

Sources:

Probert, Mark. *Excerpts from the Mark Probert Séances: 1950 Series*. 3 vols. San Diego: Inner Circle Press, 1950.

———. *The Magic Bag*. San Diego: Inner Circle Kethra E'Da Foundation, 1963.

———. *Transcript from Deep Trance-Lecture*. 10 vols. San Diego: Inner Circle Kethra E'Da Foundation, n.d.

Wassen, Ralph, ed. *Yada Speaks*. San Diego: Kethra E'Da Foundation, 1985.

Lifelight University

4030 Dodd Dr., Cable, WI 54821

Lifelight University, an esoteric college of Light, grew out of the channeling activity of Arlene Nelson. Since 1983 Nelson has channeled an entity named Sinat Schirah, who is generally referred to more simply by the nickname Stan. Nelson is a full-trance medium. In 1986 a newly intense phase of the channeling work, described as pure channeling, began and this type of channeling now occurs one weekend per month from January to May each year. During these pure channeling sessions, Stan completely takes over and Nelson has no memory of the sessions. Nelson is married to Mervin Colver and believes that she, Stan, and Colver have been reunited for present work because of their association together in previous incarnations.

Lifelight University opened in 1987 to assist people in assuming greater responsibility for their own spiritual, mental, and physical growth. It offers a year-round program of seminars, workshops, classes, and retreats for New Age seekers. Off-campus two-day intensives and introductory sessions are offered at which Stan gives instructions on a variety of topics. New students are invited to take introductory courses in meditation and then proceed through a set of progressive intensives. Material channeled through Nelson from Stan has been published in tapes and books. Weekly devotional sessions called "affirmative sharing" are held each Sunday.

Membership: Not a membership organization.

Periodicals: *Lifelight Newsletter*. • *7 Rays*.

Sources:

Lifelight University. www.lifelightuniversity.org.

Michael Educational Foundation

10 Muth Dr., Orinda, CA 94563

In the years since the first contact with "Michael," the collective entity who has been communicating with the Michael Teachings group in the San Francisco Bay area, and especially since the 1979 publication of the original book on Michael by Chelsea Quinn Yarbro (b. 1942), several other teachers also claiming contact with Michael have appeared. Two of these teachers, J. P. Van Hulle and Aaron Christeaan, founded the Michael Educational Foundation in 1984. Though in basic agreement with the Michael Teachings group, the Michael Educational Foundation has expanded its teachings in some very different directions.

According to the Foundation, Michael is the name of a group of 1,050 souls, all of people who have lived many previous lifetimes on Earth. These souls have come together as a single entity to share their vast experience with humanity and to speak to the challenge of being human. Michael speaks through a number of human channels, offers guidance and mentorship to those who choose to listen, and offers a cosmic perspective on life.

Unlike the more anonymous Michael Teachings group, the Foundation has carried on a high-profile public program, has published a number of books and tapes drawn from the weekly channeling sessions, and sponsors various public events in the San Francisco Bay Area and in Hawaii. It has nurtured the formation of Michael study groups at different locations around the world. The group's newsletter is now available by e-mail. Personal channeling appointments are available with J. P. Van Hulle and Michael North. The Foundation also hosts weekly "telegroups" (meetings via telephone), Wednesday evening gatherings in Orinda, California, and free bimonthly Saturday events around the Bay Area held to introduce new students to Michael's work.

Membership: As of May 2008 the Foundation had 700 members.

Periodicals: *MEF Monthly Newsletter*. Available by e-mail only. • *Michael's Monthly Forecast*. Available via e-mail subscription. • *Michael's State of the Planet Annual Forecast*. Available via e-mail and on CD. (To obtain any of these three periodicals, contact the group at office@mef.to.)

Sources:

Michael Educational Foundation. www.michaeleducationalfoundation.com/.

Baumbach, Emily. *Michael's Cast of Characters*. Orinda, CA: Affinity Press, 1989.

Christeaan, Aaron, J. P. Van Hulle, and M. C. Clark. *Michael: The Basic Teachings*. Orinda, CA: Affinity Press, 1988.

Pope, Joya. *The World According to Michael*. San Mateo, CA: Sage Publishing, 1987.

Steven, Jose, and Simon Warwick-Smith. *Essence and Personality: The Michael Handbook*. Orinda, CA: Warwick Press, 1987.

Michael Teachings

PO Box 5459, Lacey, WA 98509-5459

"Michael," a disembodied reunited entity, first manifested in 1970 during a dinner party in the home of Walter and Jessica Lansing, a couple living in the San Francisco Bay area. The couple was playing with a ouija board when a simple message appeared: "We are here with you tonight." When inquiry was made as to the identity of this "we," the response received was: "Each soul is part of a larger body, an entity. Each entity is made up of about one thousand souls, each of which enters the physical plane as many times as necessary to experience all aspects of life and achieve human understanding. At the end of the cycles on the physical plane, the fragments once again reunite as we have reunited." Michael went on to indicate that he/they comprised an ancient entity that would come to those who requested valid assistance and instruct them in the nature of human evolvement.

Michael described a universe created by evolution from the Tao into seven planes of existence (buddhaic, messianic, mental, akaskic, causal, astral, and physical) similar to Gnostic/theosophical understandings. Michael resides on the causal plane. He/they call attention to the individual's personal life plan, with particular emphasis on aspects of choice. Understanding is centered on *agape*, an all-embracing and selfless love.

The Lansings and their guests, Craig and Emily Wright, stayed at the board for the next five hours that first night. They were joined on subsequent occasions by Lucy North (the group's typist) and Leah and Arnold Harris. During the first six months the group steadily grew until it numbered around 30 members. In 1978 popular novelist Chelsea Quinn Yarbro (b. 1942), who had long been a part of the group, took the material that had accumulated over the eight years of its existence and edited the book *Messages from Michael* (1979), which first brought widespread public attention to the Michael teachings. The initial group has remained together, and continues to meet twice monthly. Yarbro has edited three subsequent volumes that expand upon the teachings.

Membership: There is one group of some 30 people who meet regularly to receive the messages. In addition, a much larger number of people have received and found guidance from the teachings, especially since the publication of Yarbro's books.

Sources:

Michael Teachings. www.michaelteachings.com/.

Yarbro, Chelsea Quinn. *Messages from Michael*. Chicago: Playboy Press, 1979.

———. *Michael for the Millennium*. New York: Berkley Books, 1995.

———. *Michael's People*. New York: Berkley Books, 1988.

———. *More Messages from Michael*. New York: Berkley Books, 1986.

Ramtha's School of Enlightenment (RSE)

Box 519, Yelm, WA 98587

J. Z. Knight, born Judith Darlene Hampton, founded Ramtha's School of Enlightenment (RSE) in May 1988. Born in 1946, she was living in Tacoma, Washington, when she first encountered Ramtha in February 1977. In her autobiography, *A State of Mind: My Story*, she describes a "giant man at the other end of my kitchen . . . just standing there, aglow. His face . . . it was the most beautiful face I had ever seen . . . eyes that shone like ebony stones with copper flashes . . . skin, if that's what it was, the coloring of olive, bronze, illuminated, and a fine chiseled nose and a broad jawline and a smile that would rival any Hollywood star's."

"You are so beautiful. Who are you?" she asked. "I am Ramtha the Enlightened One. I have come to help you over the ditch. Beloved woman, the greatest of things are achieved with a light heart. It is the ditch of limitation and fear that I will help you over."

In the months that followed, Ramtha continued to appear to her and teach her. Eventually, he began to "channel" through her—that is, he began to take over the body of J. Z. Knight to deliver his message. According to RSE, this phenomena of channeling was tested in 1996 by a panel of 12 scholars composed of scientists, psychologists, sociologists, and religious experts, who utilized the most current technology to observe J. Z. Knight before, during, and after channeling Ramtha. They concluded that the readings taken from J. Z. Knight's autonomic nervous system responses were so dramatic that they categorically ruled out any possibility of conscious fakery, schizophrenia, or multiple-personality disorders.

The physical body and the material world, in Ramtha's thought, are only one aspect of the real world; in fact, they are only the product and effect of the real world constituted by consciousness and energy. The human person is best described as consciousness and energy creating the nature of reality. Ramtha uses the concept of the observer effect found in quantum physics to explain his concept of consciousness and energy. He also uses the concept of God as creator and sovereign to describe the human person as consciousness and energy.

Ramtha himself is the embodiment of his own philosophy, as he is an immortal God, consciousness, and energy, and lived once as a human being 35,000 years ago in the long-gone continent of Lemuria. He grew up among the Lemurians, then a despised minority living at Onai, the port city of Atlatia (Atlantis). He hated the dominant Atlatians and eventually left the city and led a successful revolution against them.

Ramtha emerged as a powerful warrior/conqueror but his career was interrupted by a would-be assassin, who almost killed him with a sword. During his recovery, Ramtha had time to contemplate the unknown God manifest in the life force all around him, and wondered what it would be like to *be* the unknown God. He was led to consider the wind, that powerful unseen force free of boundaries, limits, or form. After several years of contemplation of the wind, he discovered the ability to separate his consciousness from his body. Further contemplation led to further change; in time, he was able to become one with light and to change his entire body. Eventually, he ascended with his body into a new level of existence. In his lifetime he addressed the questions about human existence and the meaning of life, and through his own observation, reflection, and contemplation he became enlightened and conquered the physical world and death.

BELIEFS AND PRACTICES. Ramtha's teachings derived from the Gnostic tradition that began with such ancient teachers as Valentinus and Plotinus and were continued through modern movements such as Rosicrucianism, Freemasonry, and Theosophy. According to Ramtha, what we know as the universe originated in a sea of pure potentiality called the Void.

The Void is the source from which all that exists sprang. He describes the Void as "one vast nothing materially, yet all things potentially." The Void is self-contained, self-sufficient, in a state of rest, and of no need. In its original state, this all-encompassing vastness contains no knowledge of itself, for knowledge is an action. The concept of God as creator and "first cause" is described by Ramtha in terms of the Void contemplating itself and knowing itself. This act of contemplation represents a unique movement in the Void that produced a point of awareness, referred to variously as *Point Zero*, *the observer*, *primary consciousness*, *consciousness and energy*, and *God*. Point Zero carries the primordial intent to make known and experience all that is unknown and in a state of potentiality within the vastness of the Void.

Between the two points there appeared space and time. In the atmosphere resulting from the separation a flux emerged in which could be found the original particles of energy; out of these particles of energy (analogous to subatomic particles), the universe was created. Existence was then characterized by the very high frequency at which the points of awareness (entities) and the particles of energy vibrated. Eventually, desiring to explore the Void further, the points of awareness moved further away from Point Zero. That movement led to the formation of a second level of existence characterized by the slowing of the frequency at which the points of awareness and the particles of energy vibrated. In a similar fashion, five additional levels were formed, each characterized by an increasingly slower rate of frequency. The universe that resulted from the entities following their original directive can be pictured as a triangle with Point Zero at the top. Once some entities came to the first level, they began the process of creation and evolution that has resulted, over millions of years, in our present existence as human beings on Earth. The present gross material existence is at the first level along the bottom, the slowest level of frequency. This is the basis for evolution.

The four cornerstones of Ramtha's philosophy are the concept of the Void, the idea of consciousness and energy creating seven levels of reality, the statement "You are God," and the mandate to make known the unknown. Many traces of Ramtha's thought are found in ancient traditions, though usually in faint echoes that barely survived the passing of time and loss of the appropriate context for interpretation.

Ramtha considers the teachings concerning the creation of the world, the evolution of humanity, and the understanding of humans as gods who have forgotten their origin to be mere "philosophy." While the adoption of that philosophy is a precondition if masters (students) are to recover their divine status, change occurs only as the philosophy is turned into truth. Truth is apprehended when the philosophy is experienced and believed. This is accomplished through pursuing several spiritual practices collectively termed Consciousness & Energy (C&E). Various additional disciplines provide a means of practicing C&E in different settings, with specific goals to be accomplished as a means of training the self in the new reality being proposed by Ramtha.

People interested in the program of study offered at Ramtha's School of Enlightenment are shown a 1998 video recording entitled *Creating Personal Reality*, after which they decide whether they want to continue training. The next step is to complete an introductory retreat for one week. Students are then incorporated into the general body of the school, and are asked to participate in a general retreat and a follow-up every year in order to retain their status in the school and participate in its ongoing program, activities, and workshops.

Membership: School records from the year 2002 show that there were then approximately 3,500 students worldwide. Half of this student body resides close to the school campus in Yelm, Washington. An annual world tour that has visited Australia, South Africa, Scotland, Japan, Italy, Spain, Germany, and Mexico has resulted in foreign students in more than 40 cities in 17 countries being supported in their continued learning through regular showings of videotapes made at the school in Yelm.

Periodicals: *Windworks: Ideas for Awakening Masters.*

Remarks: During the early years of the school, Knight experienced a period of intense criticism, much of it directed at her channeling, an activity considered by many to be inherently questionable. Some within the New Age movement, unaware of what was occurring at the school, suggested that Knight's withdrawal from the public spotlight signaled a change of focus toward preparing for a darker, apocalyptic future. However, as Knight once again became relatively public, that conception gradually dissipated. Also in the 1980s, Knight's love of horses led her to begin a business of raising and selling Arabian horses. This enterprise prospered until the mid-1980s, when the market for Arabian horses collapsed and the business went bankrupt. Knight was plunged into debt and a number of students who had invested in the business lost their investments; many had done so with an understanding that Ramtha had approved and sanctioned their investment. As Knight recovered financially, she offered to pay back all of the students (as well as other investors) any money they had lost; while some refused her offer, she eventually returned investment capital to all who accepted it.

Sources:

Ramtha's School of Enlightenment. www.ramtha.com.

Knight, J. Z. *A State of Mind*. New York: Warner Books, 1987.

Ramtha (J. Z. Knight). *A Master's Reflections on the History of Humanity*. 2 vols. Yelm, WA: JZK Publishing, 2001–2002.

————. *I Am Ramtha*, ed. Cindy Black, Richard Cohn, Greg Simmons, and Wes Walt. Portland, OR: Beyond Words Publishing, 1986.

Melton, J. Gordon. *End Enlightenment: Ramtha's School of Ancient Wisdom*. Hillsboro, OR: Beyond Words Publishing, 1988. 216 pp.

Weinberg, Steven L., ed. *Ramtha*. Eastsound, WA: Sovereignty, 1986.

————. *Ramtha: An Introduction*. Eastsound, WA: Sovereignty, 1988.

————. *The Mystery of Birth and Death: Redefining the Self*. Yelm, WA: JZK Publishing, 2000.

River of Crazy Wisdom

c/o Rio Sabe Loco, PO Box 65870, Tucson, AZ 85728

The River of Crazy Wisdom (formerly HomeWords) is the outreach vehicle for New Age channeler Sheradon Bryce (born Susan Johnson). Since 1987 Bryce has channeled an entity named Philip, whose teachings have been compiled in a book, *Joy Riding the Universe* (1993). Bryce is a full-trance channel (medium) who has moved to demystify the channeling process. She suggests that it is possible that the individual's mind taps into a larger body of knowledge during channeling than is available to the waking consciousness, and then creates a new personality to hold that new knowledge. Perhaps channeling is simply a way of giving the self permission to do what it would not normally allow itself to do.

Each person, according to Bryce, is a god spark. That god spark inhabits a physical body as a vehicle for expression. It is common for individuals to put the power of the god spark outside of the self, to externalize it. That process occurs whenever individuals believe that they are not god. Whenever one worships a god apart from oneself, one has externalized one's god spark. This externalization also coincides with irresponsibility, the claim that one is not accountable for one's circumstances. By externalizing one's godly power and then not understanding the resulting sense of powerlessness, one makes oneself into a victim. To become a fully functioning individual, one must first accept one's status as a god in embodiment.

Bryce has been a prolific channeler and distributes her work via both tapes and written transcripts of channeled sessions. She offers periodic retreats and workshops, leads tours to "power" places of the world, and infrequently holds private sessions with Philip. Her channeled material, over 2,000 hours of sessions, covers a wide variety of New Age topics from earth changes to ascension, kundalini and sexuality, and prosperity consciousness.

Membership: Not reported.

Periodicals: *HomeWords*.

Sources:

River of Crazy Wisdom. www.riosabeloco.com/.

Bryce, Sheradon. *Joy Riding the Universe: Snapshots of the Journey*. Salt Lake City, UT: HomeWords, 1993.

Robin's Return

1008 Lamberton St., NE, Grand Rapids, MI 49505

Dorothy and Ray Davis founded Robin's Return from their home in Grand Rapids, Michigan. In the mid-1960s, they began to receive messages from Paramahansa Yogananda (discussed in the chapter on Hindus). At the time, they did not know who Yogananda was. Then, in 1965, Robin, Dorothy Davis's son by a previous marriage, was killed when his bomber was shot down over Vietnam. After his death, both Ray and Dorothy began to receive messages from him, as well as from Yogananda and other masters. They gathered the messages together and began to publish them, first as a booklet entitled *Robin's Return* and then in a newsletter sent to a contact across the United States. During the last six months of 1966, *Chimes*, the Spiritualist magazine, ran a series of articles by the Davises on their experiences. Reader response led to the establishment of a national network of people who receive the Davis material. Though many of the early messages were from Robin, over the years the majority came from master spiritual teachers and a divine Spirit usually referred to as "I AM."

According to the Davises, light and love are the basic reality of the universe. The soul is evolving toward God through a series of incarnations in which the attempt is made to raise the vibrations of the soul. As one moves in the light of God, one is growing spiritually. Death is the gateway to a new sphere of light. Love is a means of raising one's vibrations, thus creating a channel of communication with the masters. The purpose of life is to become a living expression of love. Growth through the light and love are the essence of the great plan of the universe. Although Ray died in 1976, Dorothy continues spreading their beliefs.

The Davises have been close friends of Nellie Cain of the Spiritual Research Society and Illiana of New Age Teachings (discussed elsewhere in this chapter), and have moved freely in Universal Link circles.

Membership: Several hundred people receive mailings from the Davis home in Grand Rapids, Michigan.

Royal Priest Research

PO Box 30973, Phoenix, AZ 85046

Royal Priest Research was founded in the 1980s to facilitate the work of Lyssa Royal, the channel for a variety of entities, some of which are extraterrestrial.

Royal experienced a UFO sighting in 1979 that sparked her interest in extraterrestrial consciousness. While in college, she developed the ability to put herself into a hypnotic state in order to manage stress, which then led her to discover her natural intuitive abilities. Through these experiences, she developed the ability to channel other beings.

Through the organization's books, tapes, and sacred site tours, Royal Priest Research explores teachings from historic and extraterrestrial cultures and applies lessons learned from those cultures to the present day. Teachings present lessons that strengthen human potential and encourage self-development, as well as a sense of interconnectedness with all life. Royal currently gives seminars on channeling throughout the world.

Membership: Not reported.

Sources:

Royal Priest Research. www.lyssaroyal.com.

Royal, Lyssa. *Millennium: Tools for the Coming Changes*. Hollywood, CA: Light Technology Publications, 1998. 206 pp.

Royal, Lyssa, and Keith Priest. *Preparing for Contact: A Metamorphosis of Consciousness*. Hollywood, CA: Light Technology Publications, 1994. 188 pp.

————. *The Prism of Lyra: An Exploration of Human Galactic Heritage*. Hollywood, CA: Light Technology Publications, 1993. 110 pp.

————. *Visitors from Within*. Albuquerque, NM: Wildflower Press, 1999. 201 pp.

School of Natural Science

PO Box 1115, Cedar Ridge, CA 95924

The School of Natural Science is an organization of men and women devoted to the study and application of natural laws as these operate in all realms of life. Its general purpose is to conduct education along moral, ethical, and spiritual lines, the basis of which is outlined in textbooks known as the Harmonic Series, written by John E. Richardson. Its specific purpose is to help individuals live in harmony with the Constructive Principles of Nature, and to thereby attain self-unfoldment, self-mastery, and resultant health and peace. Those who achieve these goals become, in turn, wholesome units in the aggregate of individuals who comprise nations. The School of Natural Science does not charge for its instruction—it is offered as a gift to those deemed qualified to receive it.

The School of Natural Science teaches that the Universal Intelligence is revealed through his immutable laws, that nature is engaged in the evolvement of individual intelligences, that nature impels individuals to higher levels of consciousness, that the soul is immortal and passes successively into physical and spiritual bodies, that man's free will works within a law of compensation (karma), that willing conformity to the laws of nature leads to self-mastery, poise, and happiness, and that by living the laws of nature, people come to know instinctively that spiritual reality exists and that life continues after death. Correspondence courses based on these teachings are offered to students.

Membership: Not reported.

Periodicals: *Life in Action.*

Remarks: The School of Natural Science was established in Stockton, California, in 1883 by John E. Richardson, a practicing attorney. According to Richardson, in the summer of 1883, he was encountered by a stranger at the Grand Central Hotel in Stockton. He had been drawn by a voice telling him, "There is someone at the hotel who wants to see you." The stranger, who identified himself as Hoo-Kna-Ka, told Richardson that he had known him all his life and had come over continents and oceans to see him. He described Richardson's spiritual journey from Baptist to Spiritualist to the decision that both hypnotism and mediumship were the results of the same destructive process. Hoo-Kna-Ka then invited Richardson to become an initiate of the School of the Master, headquartered in India, on the condition that he would begin an education movement of that school in the Western world. He was taught by Hoo-Kna-Ka without charge, and was instructed always to give the teachings as a gift: "By an endless chain of Gifts shall the Great Work be established."

In 1894 Richardson (popularly known as "TK") moved to Chicago and associated himself with Mrs. Florence Huntley. In 1907 he founded the Indo-American Book Company, which became the publishing arm of the "Great Work," the name of the movement that spread Hoo-Kna-Ka's teachings. The company issued the Harmonic Series, still the basic teaching materials of the School of Natural Science. In 1916, after what was termed "certain disclosures" (which included charges of financial mismanagement), TK withdrew from the School in Chicago and the Great Work, and moved to California. In California, he reestablished the School and continued to teach and publish his books.

Sources:

School of Natural Science. www.gsns.org/.

Leech, W. Stuart. *The Great Crystal Fraud or the Great P. J.* Chicago: Occult Publishing Company, 1926.

Richardson, J. E. *The Great Message.* Great School of Natural Science, 1950.

————. *The Great Work.* Chicago: Indo-American Book Co., 1907.

————. *Who Answers Prayer?* Great School of Natural Science, 1954.

West, Sylvester A. *TK and the Great Work in America.* Chicago: Author, 1918.

SOL Association for Research

Box 2276, North Canton, OH 44720

The SOL Association for Research (SOLAR) is dedicated to preserving and disseminating the spiritual insights gained through the deep catatonic trances of psychic William Allen LePar. Paranormally gifted since childhood, LePar shunned these abilities until his early thirties, when he began to enter into periods of trance, at first involuntarily. SOL was founded in 1974, and in the early 1980s was expanded to SOLAR.

While LePar is in a deep trance state, a voice identified as a union of 12 souls known as the Council speaks through him. The Council's members have reached an exalted level of growth. They reportedly speak from the "Celestial Level of the God-Made Heavenly Realms," and they state that this is the only time in history that humanity has been directly contacted by beings in the God-Made Realms. More than 1.25 million words of dialogue with the Council have been recorded, covering virtually all areas of the human condition. This material constitutes one of the most extensive bodies of psychically derived (channeled) material available.

SOLAR, which is non-profit and tax exempt, offers a membership program that includes access to a lending library and quarterly newsletter. Monthly meetings are held in Canton, Ohio, and LePar and SOLAR associates are available for lectures, presentations, and interviews. As of 1995, the organization had produced a dozen books, two video documentaries, and numerous audiotapes.

Membership: In 1995, SOLAR reported several hundred members in the United States, along with members in several foreign countries.

Periodicals: *SOLAR Newsletter of the SOL Association for Research.*

Sources:

SOL Association for Research. www.solarpress.com.

Spiritual Education Endeavors–The Share Foundation

1556 Halford Ave., No. 288, Santa Clara, CA 95051

Spiritual Education Endeavors (S.E.E.)–The Share Foundation was founded in the mid-1980s by Virginia Essene (b. 1928). According to her account, in 1984 Essene was contacted by the Christ, the same entity who had lived on earth almost 2,000 years ago as Jesus, and was asked to be the instrument through which he brought his present message to humanity. She worked intensively over a six-month period in 1985 to receive his message via mental telepathy and produced what became a book, *New Teachings for an Awakened Humanity,* published in 1986.

The book records the Christ's warning that failure to acknowledge God in our lives had given humankind a war-like mentality that not only threatened grave harm to the planet but also posed the risk that weapons would be taken into outer space. He called for a new peace consciousness and called upon all to join together as light workers in a Light Corps to work for peace on earth. For this endeavor, his Christ energy would be put at humanity's disposal.

The Christ also declared that he was preparing for his Second Coming and a new Golden Age. By the end of the twentieth century, every loving soul would be given the opportunity to achieve self-mastery. Light workers were to choose a spiritual path that forsook all desire for war and hatred. To bring about this reality, each light worker was to meditate daily and gather with a group to meditate together at least once a week. The Christ also called upon light workers to join with others in efforts to influence governments and to embody peace in all they did and intended.

Spiritual Education Endeavors was formed to help mobilize and organize the Light Corps, so that it could respond positively to Christ's call. It published *New Teachings for an Awakened Humanity* and through the Light Corps has sought to distribute it internationally. A newsletter especially intended for those just beginning in the work was issued nine times annually. Since that time Essene has regularly received additional messages expanding on the original message from the Christ and commenting on ongoing earth changes. These messages have been published in several subsequent books and released in seminars. The period from 1987 to the mid 1990s has been designated a period of the awakening of humanity to the new age that is dawning. Shortly after beginning her work, Essene was joined by Ann Valentin, who also channels from the Light realm.

Membership: Not reported.

Periodicals: *Love Corps Newsletter.*

Sources:

Share Foundation. www.sharefoundationnetwork.com.

The Christ (through Virginia Essene). *New Teachings for an Awakened Humanity*. Santa Clara, CA: Spiritual Education Endeavors Publishing Company, 1986. 197 pp.

Essene, Virginia. *Secret Truths for Teens and Twenties*. Santa Clara, CA: Spiritual Education Endeavors Publishing Company, 1986. 120 pp.

Valentin, Ann, and Virginia Essene. *Cosmic Revelation*. Santa Clara, CA: Spiritual Education Endeavors Publishing Company, 1987. 160 pp.

———. *Descent of the Dove*. Santa Clara, CA: Spiritual Education Endeavors Publishing Company, 1988. 185 pp.

Trinity Foundation

c/o Athena Leadership Center, 11827 E Cannon Dr., Scottsdale, AZ 85259

The Trinity Foundation was founded in 1991 by Norma J. Milanovich, a channel who in 1981 had begun receiving messages from entities who identified themselves as originating from the Great White Brotherhood (the spiritual hierarchy that guides the affairs of the planet) and the Galactic Command, a group that rules this segment of space. Those who began to give messages to Milanovich bore such names as Kuthumi, Moinka, and Soltec—names familiar to theosophists, flying saucer groups, and New Age seekers. Much of this material was circulated informally, but a growing response led to the publishing of selected portions received from a number of entities who claimed to have visited earth from the star system Arcturus. *We, the Arcturians* appeared in 1990. At about the same time, Milanovich was invited to share the material from the masters with the members of the United Nations Parapsychology Committee. These two events occasioned the inauguration of a newsletter, *Celestial Voices,* in October 1990.

Kuthumi, a representative of the Tribunal Council of the Space Command, has emerged as the major voice speaking through Milanovich. He delivered the first message to the United Nations Parapsychology Committee. He noted that the Space Command had made themselves available to assist humanity in transforming the earth into a world of peace and prosperity for all. The Space Command is composed of individuals who have completed their journey through earth incarnations and have learned the curriculum earth had to teach. They now exist at a higher frequency and seek to bring the Light to the earth.

In subsequent messages, Kuthumi outlined his vision of coming changes. During the next 20 years (1991–2011) earth will be birthed into a star and individuals will emerge from the three dimensional world in which we now live into the fifth dimension. To prepare for this change, Kuthumi released a Curriculum of Thought Manifestation, containing the material that must be mastered for entry into the fifth dimension. This world is composed of solidified energy perceived through the five senses. To move to the fifth dimension, one must first accept the possibility that other realities synchronized with the physical world exist and can be perceived as one raises one's consciousness.

Also, one must learn that we create reality. Reality is created by thoughts, will, emotion, and actions. The path to higher consciousness is one of choosing right thought, right will, right emotion, and right action. As one changes consciousness, one changes reality. Consciousness creates with Light energy. Light is found by looking within.

On September 24, 1991, Kuthumi delivered an important message, making public a project he had initiated two years previously, the Templar. It was imbedded in an understanding of the earth as an energy system with certain power points similar to the chakras in the tantric understanding of the human body. The United States represents the crown chakra at the top of the head. The crown chakra

is being prepared to receive energies from the Most High. The point of the earth that will actually receive the new energies is in the process of being prepared to receive a structure known as the Templar. The Templar is designed to realign earth with the heavens and to stabilize it as it moves through the transition. The Templar will be a pyramid with a base of approximately 500 square feet and a height of 450 feet. Its face will be pink granite and its capstone will be obsidian. It will be surrounded by a six-sided wall.

Milanovich founded the Trinity Foundation to support the building of the Templar. Shortly thereafter, the foundation received a grant of land in Crestone, Colorado, upon which to build the pyramid. The proposed structure has become a major item of controversy in the small community. Meanwhile, Milanovich has published several other books detailing the Masters' messages: *Sacred Journey to Atlantis* and *Many Paths, One Way.*

Membership: Not reported.

Periodicals: *Celestial Voices.*

Sources:

Athena Leadership Center. www.athenalctr.com/.

Milanovich, Norma. *The Light Shall Set You Free*. Albuquerque, NM: Athena Publishing, 1996.

———. *Sacred Journey to Atlantis*. Albuquerque, NM: Athena Publishing, 1992.

———. *We, the Arcturians*. Albuquerque, NM: Athena Publishing, 1990.

Universal Faithists of Kosmon, Inc.

c/o C. Vostatek, Sec'ty, 3439 Grand Valley Canal Rd., Clifton, CO 81520

Universal Faithists of Kosmon, Inc. (previously known as the Universal Association of Faithists) is a group devoted to disseminating the knowledge received by the Spiritualist medium and channeler John Ballou Newbrough (1828–1891). In 1881, Newbrough received through automatic writing on a typewriter a revelation later published under the title Oahspe. Newbrough rose early each morning for 50 weeks and, as the "lines of light" rested on his hands, typed for an hour. The first edition of the resultant book was published in September 1882. The next year a convention was held in New York City to work toward founding a communal group to care for orphans and foundlings, as directed in Oahspe. A colony was founded in New Mexico, but failed after only a couple of years. Since that time, small bands of followers have kept Oahspe in print. The recently published Inside the Shalam Colony (1991), by Elnora Wiley, is a partly romanticized, partly historical account of the original colony.

Oahspe is a large volume, written in the style of the King James Version of the Bible. It contains the story of human creation about 78,000 years ago and recounts the upward struggle of the human race. Humanity originated on Pan, a Pacific continent much like Lemuria, which was the sole victim of the biblical flood. Religion evolved through the messages of 11 prophets, beginning with Zarathustra and continuing through Joshu (Jesus). All religion and spiritual effort have been guided by angelic forces toward the Kosmon Era. During this era, which began in the nineteenth century, a new people will emerge, and will transform the world into a place of joy and beauty.

Over the decades, a wide variety of Faithist groups have emerged and disappeared. The movement is sustained by a number of independent groups who stay in touch through several informal networks and periodicals. The Universal Faithists of Kosmon (a church) is the most active center. It is headquartered in Riverton, Utah, with affiliated centers in Colorado, Utah, California, and West Virginia. It publishes a newsletter, Kosmon Voice. The Faithists also sponsor a committee, the Global Council, which carries out various projects suggested and inspirited by Oahspe, and holds an annual conference. The leaders of the committee meet monthly through a conference call.

The Eloists, Inc., headquartered in Henniker, New Hampshire, is another active Oahspe group. It publishes a periodical, Radiance. The Faithist Journal is published by Oahspe followers in Arizona. During his mature years, Ray Palmer, the founder/publisher of Search Magazine became an enthusiastic believer in Oahspe and added "The Oahspe Circle" as a column in the magazine. The "Circle" carried news of Oahspe groups, discussed its main ideas, and promoted networking among the scattered believers. Search is now published by Judith M. Statezny at Owl Press in Rosholt, Wisconsin, but still carries "The Oahspe Circle."

Worship among Faithists follows the format suggested in the Kosmon Church Service Book, kept in print by a group of British Faithists. This book includes liturgy for worship, baptisms, weddings, and funerals. Ministerial training is offered and ordinations of new ministers scheduled as appropriate.

Membership: Unknown. There are several hundred people who have identified themselves with the Faithists and have agreed to have their name published in their directory. Many more have purchased Oahspe (over 20,000 in the last decade) and, though unaffiliated with any of the Oahspe groups, are sympathetic to the movement's teachings. Groups active in the informal networks can be found in Australia, New Zealand, Great Britain, Nigeria, and Ghana.

Periodicals: *The Faithist Journal.* • *Kosmon Voice.* • *Radiance.* • *Kosmon Unity.* • *Global Council Newsletter.* • *Four Winds Village News.*

Sources:

Dennon, Jim. *Dr. Newbrough and Oahspe.* Kingman, AZ: Faithist Journal, 1975.

————. *The Oahspe Story.* Kingman, AZ: Faithist Journal, 1975.

Oahspe. Los Angeles: Essenes of Kosmon, 1950.

Stowes, K. D. *The Land of Shalam, Children's Land.* Evansville, IN: Frank Molinet Print Shop, n.d.

Universal Life: The Inner Religion

PO Box 651, Guilford, CT 06437

Alternate Address: International Headquarters: Universelles Leben, Postfach 5643, 97006 Würzburg, Germany. Canadian Headquarters: Universal Life: The Inner Religion, PO Box 54002, Toronto, ON, Canada M6A 3B7.

Universelles Leben, or Universal Life: The Inner Religion, is a worldwide free Christian movement that originated in 1975, when, those affiliated with the movement believe, Christ entered the life of Gabriele Wittek (b. 1933) and revealed to her his plan to use her as his instrument on earth. Since then, Wittek has served as his prophetic instrument and ambassadress in fulfilling this plan, which is to show his children the way back into their eternal home and to build up his Kingdom of Peace on earth. In 1980 the Cosmic School of Life, the first "Original Christian Gathering Places for All Godseekers," emerged, initially under the name the Inner Spirit Christ Church. Here people came together as in early Christianity to hear the prophetic word, to pray together, and to speak openly with each other about all questions of life, using the Sermon on the Mount and the Ten Commandments as a basis.

Also in 1980, the movement believes, Christ called into being the spiritual, mystical path to the divine self, the Homebringing Mission of Jesus Christ. Through the Homebringing Mission, the Spirit of God teaches all seekers on this earth the Inner Path, the path to experiencing God in one's own inner being. On this Inner Path, the person attains a spiritual expansion of consciousness, becoming one with Christ, God, and all forms of nature, by gradually overcoming sinfulness step by step with the power of Christ. On this foundation, in 1984, Universelles Leben was established.

Since the late 1990s, an inner Christianity community has emerged. Adherents consider themselves Original Christians who pursue an inner religion, a religion of the heart, and strive for liberation from sin and gradual oneness with Christ in their innermost being. They believe that all people are the temple of God and that the Spirit of the Christ of God, which is a spirit of freedom, dwells in everyone. Theirs is a religion without human leaders, rituals, dogmas, denominations, institutions, or "temples of stone." Such movements of inner Christianity are not new, they main-

tain. Since the time of Jesus of Nazareth, there have been groups of people who took seriously the high ethics of his teachings, who perceived how Jesus gave mankind an example of how to live in the Spirit of God in unity with neighbors, animals, nature, with all of creation, by observing the Sermon on the Mount and the Ten Commandments.

Universal Life is based on the prophetic word of this generation, given in the form of revelations. These revelations are seen as deepening and clarifying the divine laws of God and their application in daily life. They explain many basic spiritual principles, such as the why and how of our earthly existence, eternal damnation, reincarnation, the law of sowing and reaping, active faith, health and illness, life after death, and man's relationship to the cosmos. This information is made available to all who desire it through the books and tapes produced by Universelles Leben, whose members believe that only the actualization of the laws of God makes us free, glad, healthy, and loving persons.

Membership: Universal Life is not a membership organization. In 1997 there were three centers in the United States and two in Canada, and an unknown number in Europe. Additional centers have opened in Africa, Australia, South America, and Asia.

Periodicals: *The Prophet.*

Remarks: Universal Life has emerged as one of the more controversial groups in German-speaking Europe as a growing concern over new religions has swept across central Europe. Several books denouncing Universal Life have appeared from an anti-cult perspective.

Sources:

Universelles Leben/Universal Life: The Inner Religion. www.universal-life.cc.

Universalia

Current address could not be obtained for this edition.

Universalia is a New Age channeling group which grew out of a study group that formed in Denver, Colorado, in 1981. Meeting weekly, the group began to channel through a technique that it termed *thought plane transference*, i.e., clearing one's mind, being open to whatever information comes, and writing it down as it enters one's consciousness. As a mass of information was accumulated, the group incorporated and in May 1985 released the first issue of a newsletter, *The Universalian*.

Universalia means "of the universe." Information from the process of channeling comes through the individual members of the group from such energies as Kyros, the Brotherhood, Archangel Michael, and so on. Two books of channeled works by Universalia members have been published: *The Kyrian Letters: Transformative Messages for Higher Vision*, by Sandra Radhoff, and *The Wisdom Teachings of Archangel Michael*, by Lori Flory as told to Brad Steiger. The thrust of Universalia's teaching is toward the expansion of conscious awareness and follows the main affirmation of New Age philosophy. God, the I AM, resides within each person. Spiritual life is perfect; the physical dreamspace dimension is illusionary. Having created illusions, humans tend to believe in them and empower them. Hence, they follow outward form instead of inward reality. Members are taught that they are the loved and beautiful expressions of God and have unlimited potential. As they are connected to all of creation, service is an integral part of their life.

Membership: Not reported.

Periodicals: *The Universalian.*

Sources:

Flory, Lori Jean, and Brad Steiger. *The Wisdom Teachings of Archangel Michael.* New York: Signet, 1997.

Radhoff, Sandra. *The Kyrian Letters: Transformative Messages for Higher Vision.* Virginia Beach, VA: Heritage Publications, 1992.

Flying Saucer Groups

Aetherius Society

6202 Afton Pl., Hollywood, CA 90028

The Aetherius Society was begun in London in 1954 by George King (1919–1997), a medium and long-time student of occultism and yoga. He was told to prepare himself to become the voice of the Interplanetary Parliament. In 1955, he was named by Master Aetherius of Venus as the "primary terrestrial mental channel." Since that time, he has regularly channeled messages form Aetherius and the Master Jesus. They and other members of the Great White Brotherhood oversee the activities of the Society. A center was opened in Los Angeles within a year of the first messages. King's teachings are the focus of the Society.

According to the Aetherius Society, earth is engaged in a cosmic warfare focused on the activities of certain "black magicians" seeking to enslave man. The cosmic brotherhood, the space hierarchy, wages war on these magicians. Members of the Society cooperate with the Brotherhood by channeling spiritual energy to particular concerns. Channeling activities are centered on certain periods during which a spaceship orbits earth and sends out special power. These periods are termed "spiritual pushes," and during them all members help direct the energy. These pushes are typically given military titles, such as Operation Bluewater, which ended on November 27, 1976. During this operation, the cosmic masters poured vital spiritual power into a psychic center through a spiritual power–radiating instrument at sea.

Operation Starlight began at Holdstone Down in England in 1958 and continued for three years and one month. During this time, King, directed by a vision of the Master Jesus, climbed 18 designated mountains to charge them with spiritual power, to be used by anyone making a pilgrimage to them. This Operation is still celebrated at an annual convention held on August 23.

The most important date in the annual calendar, however, is July 8, commemorating the 1964 initiation of earth by a gigantic spaceship and the ship's manipulation of cosmic energies. Other days in the annual calendar are King's birthday, the end of Operation Karma-light (a phase of Armageddon), and the Master Jesus' birthday. Push dates are announced annually and usually cover periods of three to four weeks.

As described by King, the Interplanetary Parliament is headquartered on Saturn, the tribunal of the solar system. The agents from Mars and Venus are making a metaphysical survey of earth. The saucers have also saved earth from the damage caused by terrestrial scientists to earth's ionosphere.

King has accepted consecration as an archbishop through the Independent Liberal Catholic Church headed by Richard Earl Quinn. He has also received a number of titles and awards, most of them conferred by the "cosmic" sources or the Society that he heads. He has been a prolific writer, authoring several books and numerous pamphlets, all published by the Aetherius Society.

Membership: Not reported, but in 1987 the *Cosmic Voice* newsletter reported a circulation of 650 copies. There are two centers of the society in the United States, one in Hollywood and one in Detroit, Michigan. Several hundred members are involved. The Society has several centers in England.

Periodicals: *Cosmic Voice.* • *Spiritual Healing Bulletin.*

Sources:

Aetherius Society. www.aetherius.org/.

King, George. *A Book of Sacred Prayers*. Hollywood, CA: Aetherius Society, 1966.

———. *The Nine Freedoms*. Los Angeles: Aetherius Society, 1963.

———. *The Practices of Aetherius*. Hollywood, CA: Aetherius Society, 1964.

———. *The Twelve Blessings*. London: Aetherius Press, 1958.

———. *You Are Responsible*. London: Aetherius Press, 1961.

Saliba, John A. "The Earth Is a Dangerous Place: The World View of the Aetherius Society." *Marburg Journal of Religion* 4, no. 2 (December 1999). 10 pps.

The Story of the Aetherius Society. Hollywood, CA: Aetherius Society, n.d.

Aquarian Perspectives

120 Ocean Hibiscus Dr., No. 102, St. Augustine, FL 32080

The organization today known as Aquarian Perspectives can be traced to March 3, 1986, when an extraterrestrial spirit named Avinash walked into the body of a person named John. John was a channel and teacher of metaphysics in the Seattle, Washington, suburb of Bellevue. He had previously been channeling an entity named Elihu.

The concept of a "walk-in" was popularized by Ruth Montgomery, who described situations in which the spirit of an individual would, for whatever reason, abandon a body, and a disembodied spirit would walk-in and take over. In that changeover, the memory of the person who had left would remain, but the personality of the new entity would take over. Thus it was that Avinash walked-in and took over John's body. Shortly after Avinash appeared, he moved to Hawaii. He was accompanied by a second walk-in, a female spirit named Alezsha. In Hawaii they met a third walk-in, Ashtridia. During the rest of 1986, the primary teaching channeled by Avinash concerned the concept of mastery of limitation. The universe, he taught, tended to rearrange itself according to one's concept of reality. By changing one's reality, removing a sense of limitation, the world begins to change.

The three walk-ins have contact with a huge extradimensional spaceship, and thus are able to operate in other dimensions. Before the end of 1986 the three decided to move to Sedona, Arizona, where they soon met a fourth walk-in, Arthea. Avinash and Arthea discovered that they were divine design mates, that is, a couple divinely created to work together. By 1987 the group of walk-ins had grown to 12, but it disbanded as some found their missions elsewhere. By October 1987 only Avinash, Arthea, and a third spirit, Alana, remained.

The three experienced what is not a totally unique occurrence, but certainly an uncommon one: Over the next years a series of new entities walked-in to their bodies and others departed; thus the same body would become known by different names. John, known as Avinash, became known as Aktivar, Alarius, Savizar, and most recently, ZaviRah. Arthea became known as Akria, Polaria, Silarra, and most recently, Ziva'rah. Alana became known as Akrista and then as Tantra. It is believed that each of these names refers to an extraterrestrial who inhabited the body of the earth person. The emergence of Aktivar, Akria, and Akrista occurred at the end of the summer of 1987. During the last three months of 1987 and into 1988, these three entities toured the United States. They made a videotape on humanity's role as co-creators of heaven on earth, and a series of cassette tapes aimed at overcoming particular individual dysfunctionalities.

In March 1988 a new phase of work began when Aktivar, Akria, and Akrista left and were replaced by three new walk-ins, Alarius, Polaria, and Tantra. Shortly thereafter, Tantra left the trio and began to work separately. Alarius and Polaria described their work as temporary, preparing the way for Savizar and Silarra. Under the guidance of the couple known as Savizar and Silarra, Extraterrestrial Earth Mission matured into a New Age organization announcing the planetary shift of humans from dense physical bodies into bodies of light. According to Savizar and Silarra, there are many masters present on the earth today, and it was their job to awaken these masters to the nature of their true selves and to cooperate with them in the co-creation of a new earth. Assisting in this process, the pair taught a superconscious technique that allows people to manifest their desires by altering their picture of reality.

In 1990 Savizar and Silarra were replaced by ZaviRah and Ziva'rah. Each change is believed to announce a new phase in the mission. In this case, the newcomers represented a change from an exclusive emphasis on opening and awakening to one of mobilization. Those who have been awakened to their true nature should begin the process of creation and manifestation. In 1993 Zavirah and Ziva'rah were replaced by Drakar and Zrendar, and very soon after their appearance,

Extraterrestrial Earth Mission moved from Arizona to Hawaii. Included in the new phase of the mission is the ChristStar Project, the work of a group of people on Maui to built a prototype of the new civilization. Public events have been developed to present techniques (usable technologies) of consciousness that assist individuals to see the divinity is all life and to manifest their own role as co-creators of heaven on earch.

In response to the lectures, workshops, and the printed, audio, and video material published by the mission, groups have formed around the United States and Canada to share in the mission's work. At ChristStar Project Mastery Events, extraterrestrial entities speak through Drakar and Zrendar to the assembled group. Extraterrestrial Earth Mission has been chartered through the Universal Life Church in Arizona.

Membership: Not reported.

Periodicals: *ChristStar*.

Sources:

Aquarian Perspectives. www.stardoves.com/.

Savizar and Silarra. *Conscious Channeling*. Sedona, AZ: Earth Mission Publishing, 1989.

————. *Extraterrestrial Earth Mission*. Book I: *The Awakening*. Sedona, AZ: Earth Mission Publishing, 1989.

————. *The Superconscious Technique*. Sedona, AZ: Earth Mission Press, 1989.

Ashtar Command

PO Box 328, Clarksdale, AZ 86324

In 1980 Thelma B. Terrell, in her book *World Messages for the Coming Decade*, announced that she had been in contact with a group of space beings known collectively as the Ashtar Command. They told her they resided in a set of thousands of spaceships that hovered above the planet. Through Tuella (d. 1993), the name assumed by Terrell as a channel for the members of the Ashtar Command, the command declared its desire to discuss with world leaders the crisis of the planet. The command explained that it represented the Intergalactic Council, which derived its authority from the spiritual hierarchy of the solar system. A number of the members of this council and hierarchy were previously known and described by theosophists as members of the theosophical spiritual hierarchy. The head of the hierarchy as described in the information channeled by Tuella is Sananda, better known as Jesus Christ.

Although they are concerned about the imminent world crisis, members of the council are forbidden to interfere in the life of the planet without the approval of world governments, but to date they have been unable to confer with world leaders.

According to the command, the planet is soon to go through a period of cleansing, which will begin with a tilting of the earth and widespread destruction, and then to enter a new age of Light. The Ashtar Command has as part of its mission the evacuation of those souls who are already walking in the Light, during this period of cleansing. The program of world evacuation was announced in Tuella's second book, *Project World Evacuation* (1982). The sign of the coming transition will be the tilting of the earth's axis. As the tilting begins, computers on the spaceships will lock on the people of Light and lift them off the planet along with the world's children—those not yet old enough to be accountable for their actions. The command wants to meet with world governments to facilitate the most orderly evacuation.

The head of the mission to earth is Ashtar, a space being first channeled and made famous by George Van Tassel, founder of the Ministry of Universal Wisdom. In the intervening years, a number of other contactees have brought forth messages from Ashtar, including Oscar Magocsi, Ethel B. Hill, Franklin Thomas, and Eugenio Siragusa.

Guardian Action Publications was founded to publish and disseminate the messages of the Ashtar command. Along with several books published in the 1980s, a newsletter, *Ashtar's Golden Circle*, was issued. In 1988 Ashtar made it known that his work of announcing the mission and the future cataclysm and evacuation was complete, and that he would retire until the time of the evacuation. In the meantime, Tuella would continue to disseminate the message to those who had yet to hear, and concentrate on working directly with Sananda to bring forth energies from the spiritual hierarchy, from the very throne of the Father Mother God, to the people of the planet. This new work was signaled by the first issue of a new periodical, *The Throne Connection*.

Membership: Not reported.

Periodicals: *The Throne Connection*.

Sources:

Tuella (Thelma B. Terrell). *Ashtar: A Tribute*. Durango, CO: Guardian Action Publications, 1985.

————. *On Earth Assignment*. Salt Lake City, UT: Guardian Action International, 1988.

————. *Project World Evacuation*. Salt Lake City, UT: Guardian Action International, 1982.

————. *World Messages for the Coming Decade: A Cosmic Symposium*. Deming, NM: Guardian Action Publications, 1980.

Association of Sananda and Sanat Kumara

PO Box 197, Mt. Shasta, CA 96067

The Association of Sananda and Sanat Kumara is headed by Sister Thedra (Dorothy Martin, 1900–1992), for many years a channel for the ascended masters. Very early in her career she became the object of a famous sociological study, *When Prophecy Fails* (1956). She reported that in 1954 that she was healed and restored to a life of usefulness by Sananda, an ascended master, and was instructed to go to Peru and Bolivia, where for the next five years she experienced great trials and tribulations. She spent some of the time at the monastery established by the Brotherhood of the Seven Rays headed by George Hunt Williamson, living among the natives and observing their hardships and poverty. Through this period of training under the tutelage of the masters she learned the "true meaning of divine love towards human beings, regardless of their status in life." In the next years she experienced moments of ecstatic communication with the masters—Sibors, the Elohim (council of Gods), John the Beloved, the Angel Moroni (mentioned in the Book of Mormon), beings from other planets, and, primarily, Sananda, who most people know as the Christ. Thedra predicted the reincarnation of the Angel Moroni, which occurred in 1965; the child began to manifest his powers in August 1975.

While still in Peru, Thedra began to send her inspired messages back to interested people in the United States. These people will be *sibored*—made illumines of the Father. A *sibor* is a teacher in the higher realms.

Sister Thedra returned to the United States from South America in 1961 and established the Association of Sananda and Sanat Kumara in 1965. The information channeled through her is sent across the United States and to a number of foreign countries to students who request it. The basic information is contained in three sets of material: "The Sibors Portions," "The Fundamentals," and "The Order of Melchezdek." These are constantly supplemented by ongoing revelations from the masters. In 1985 the association hosted the first annual Gathering of the Children of Light, a convocation of individuals who receive Sister Thedra's material or are affiliated similar groups.

Membership: The association does not keep statistics on the number of students who regularly request material channeled by Sister Thedra. It is estimated to be in the thousands. There is one center, in Mt. Shasta, California.

Educational Facilities:

University of Melchezedek, Castleton, Virginia.

Sources:

Festinger, Leon, Henry W. Riecken, and Stanley Schachter. *When Prophecy Fails*. New York: Harper and Row, 1956.

Sananda, as recorded by Sister Thedra. *I, the Lord God Say Unto Them*. Mt. Shasta, CA: Association of Sananda and Sanat Kumara, [1954].

Thedra. *Excerpts of Prophecies from Other Planets Concerning Our Earth*. Mt. Shasta, CA: Association of Sananda and Sanat Kumara, [1956].

Thedra, Sister. *Mine Intercome Messages from the Realms of Light*. Sedona, AZ: Association of Sananda and Sanat Kumara, [1990].

Watkins, Edward L. *The Teachings and the Liberation*. Mt. Shasta, CA: Association of Sananda and Sanat Kumara, 1977.

Blue Rose Ministry

Blue Rose Starlight Spiritual Center, Box 332, Cornville, AZ 86325

The Blue Rose Ministry was founded by Robert E. Short, a channel for flying saucer entities. Short became a channel in the 1960s and emerged into public notice in 1967 at the contactee convention at Giant Rock, California, hosted by George Van Tassel. On Saturday evening, October 14, 1967, as Short was being introduced to the assembled audience, a reddish-orange craft flew overhead and was seen by all for approximately two minutes. Short then channeled a message from "Korton," a resident of the planet Jupiter who had flown over Earth in a mother ship—the light the audience had seen was described as a spacecraft from that mother ship. Although Korton is the main entity who speaks through Short, others have spoken through him as well.

The goal of the ministry is the preparation of and closer atunement with all enlightened being in the cosmos. Short has authored several books and his lectures are available on audio tapes. He also conducts private channeling consultations. The ministry conducts periodic Solar Space Circle seminars.

Membership: Not reported. The ministry has two centers, one in Cornville, Arizona, and one in Joshua Tree, California.

Periodicals: *Solar Space-Letter*.

Cosmic Circle of Fellowship

4857 N Melvina Ave., Chicago, IL 60630

The Cosmic Circle of Fellowship was formed in 1954 by William A. Ferguson (d. 1967), Edward A. Surine, and Edna I. Valverde, and was incorporated in Illinois in 1955. Ferguson, a former mail carrier, learned the techniques of absolute relaxation and became adept at relaxing his body, mind, and conscious spirit. In 1937 he published *Relax First* and later began to teach relaxation techniques to others.

Ferguson reported that on July 9, 1938, while lying on his sofa in a state of absolute relaxation, his body was charged by a powerful "Current of Life"—"Pure Intelligent Energy"—and carried away to the "Seventh Dimension." During his two-hour stay in the Seventh Dimension, he held the key to all knowledge and his soul became illuminated. Upon his return back to the Earth's third dimension (normal waking consciousness), he found that his physical body was no longer on the sofa, and, according to the account, he could not be seen or heard by his wife and his friend. He placed his noncorporal being back on the sofa, and soon he regained his physical, three-dimensional form.

Ferguson claimed that he experienced the "Sixth Dimension" on July 16 of the following week, when he was carried away to the center of all creation. There he saw creation in action—the rays of Pure Intelligent Energy were of all forms and colors and were flowing throughout a cube of "Pure Universal Substance." Other experiences were to follow.

According to Ferguson, in 1947 Khauga, the chief uniphysicist of our solar system, took Ferguson on a trip to Mars. Upon his return to Earth, members of Ferguson's family and a friend could neither see nor hear him. Realizing what was happening, he went into the next room, lay on a cot, and was transformed back into three dimensions. He then went into the next room and told his account: that the matter of his physical body had been raised into a four-dimensional frequency, and that he had been teleported to Mars at the speed of consciousness. He returned with a message that the Martians were sending an expedition to Earth. Within a few months, many UFOs were reported, and several people claimed that they had made personal contacts with their occupants.

In 1954 Ferguson revealed that he had been taken aboard a Venusian spacecraft and given a message from the Oligarchs of Venus for the people of Earth. They noted that spacecraft normally function in four dimensions (and are hence invisible), but can also function in three dimensions by changing their frequency or their density. When they disappear suddenly, they have merely changed back into the fourth dimension.

In the 1940s Ferguson had begun to gather a group devoted primarily to the cosmic healing techniques and the "clarified water device" taught to Ferguson by Khauga. The device, which he claimed imparted healing properties to water, got Ferguson into trouble with the American Medical Association. He was convicted of fraud in 1947 and served a year in prison. Upon his release from prison, he organized the Cosmic Circle in Chicago. In 1958 he began to found circles in other cities, gaining followings in Washington, Philadelphia, New York, and San Francisco.

According to Ferguson, at the center of creation are the Father and Mother of creation. A sphere of pure intelligent energy exists inside a cube of pure universal substances. Creation commences as the rays of life of the Father impregnate the substance of the Mother. Khauga is described as the Comforter, the Spirit of Truth, the angel who gave the Book of Revelation to St. John, a perfected being from the Holy Triune. Khauga is the leader in the Universal Brotherhood of the Sons of the Father, members of which are drawn from the various solar systems. They are preparing earth for the next evolutionary step—the Second Coming of Jesus.

Members believe that a war of consciousness, symbolized by the war in heaven depicted in Revelation 12, has begun as man makes the next step in evolution. As the New Age comes in, the dragon of materialism and evil will be overthrown as man is lifted into a fourth-dimensional consciousness. Ferguson had been a longtime teacher of relaxation, and his techniques remain the major way to consciousness expansion.

Ferguson died in 1967. Leadership passed to the Chicago group, which still publishes his booklets. Associated with it is the Cosmic Study Center, headed by Cloe Driscoll of Potomac, Maryland.

Membership: In 2002 the circle reported 41 members in the Chicago area.

Sources:

The Comforter Speaks. Potomac, MD: Cosmic Study Center, 1977.

Ferguson, William. *A Message from Outer Space*. Oak Park, IL: Golden Age Press, 1955.

———. *My Trip to Mars*. Chicago: Cosmic Circle of Fellowship, 1954.

———. *The New Revelation*. Author, 1959.

———. *Relax First*. Chicago: Bronson-Canode, 1937.

Cosmic Star Temple

Current address not obtained for this edition.

The Cosmic Star Temple was founded in 1960 by Violet Gilbert of Santa Barbara, California, who claims that her first contact with the space brothers was in 1937. Before then, she was a student of Theosophy and "I AM" Religious Activity, and was described as having a "rich background of service for the Brotherhood since childhood." As an adult, she was made aware of the space brothers in 1937, and in January 1939, after an eight-month preparation, she went on a three-and-one-half-week excursion to Venus. Her initial contact had been arranged by her previous teachers, following her request for healing. On her visit she received complete physical healing. Since her initial, physical visit, she has returned to Venus in the astral (not physically, but through her consciousness). She also acquired a control, Dr. Winston of the Ashtar Command. Her first trip to Mars was in 1955, but she was not allowed announce it publicly until 1960.

While on Venus, she was given instructions in healing that form a major basis of the Temple's works, and in reading the Akashic records. (The Akashic records are the records of all that has happened, and are inscribed on the "universal ethers.") Gilbert reads the Akashic records of individuals, which give information about their previous incarnations. The teachings of the Temple are eclectic, and include material from the New Thought metaphysics, spiritualism, and the dominant Theosophy. Color healing has become a major emphasis.

Gilbert teaches that the coming of the space brothers is entirely beneficient. Their main goal is to keep us from destroying ourselves, and to share their advanced knowledge with us. According to Gilbert, mankind now is in a transition to a new age and is currently experiencing a cleansing in preparation.

Membership: Not reported.

Sources:

Gilbert, Violet. *Love Is All*. Grants Pass, OR: Cosmic Star Temple, 1969.

————. *My Trip to Venus*. Grants Pass, OR: Cosmic Star Temple, 1968.

Delval UFO, Inc.

948 Almshouse Rd., Ivyland, PA 18974

Delval UFO, Inc. is a New Age UFO contactee group founded in 1972 by its current directors, Anthony Volpe and Lynn Volpe. Members seek to commune with the Space Brothers and Sisters on all levels of existence. They hope to be an instrument in the process of preparing humanity for the New Age, which is seen as imminent.

There is one group, which meets monthly at the Pennsylvania headquarters. Through its periodical, *Awakening*, the group maintains contact with people across the United States, Canada, and Japan.

Membership: In 1992 Delval UFO reported 400 members in the United States and additional adherents in Japan and Australia.

Periodicals: *Awakening*.

Sources:

Clark, Jerome. "UFOs in the 1980s." In *The UFO Encyclopedia*, Vol. 1. Detroit, MI: Apogee Books, 1990.

Volpe, Anthony, and Lynn Volpe. *Principles and Purposes of Delval UFO, Inc*. Ivyland, PA: Authors, n.d.

GAF International/Adamski Foundation

Box 1722, Vista, CA 92085

The first person to become widely known for claiming to have talked to beings from flying saucers and teaching what was purported to be their wisdom was George Adamski (1891–1965). On November 20, 1952, he claimed to have conversed with a human-like man from Venus, the first of several contacts. Afterwards he wrote three of the most popular flying saucer books ever penned: *Flying Saucers Have Landed* (coauthored with Desmond Leslie); *Inside the Space Ships* (reprinted as *Inside the Flying Saucers*); and *Flying Saucers Farewell* (reprinted as *Behind the Flying Saucer Mystery*). The two most important of the several groups that emerged to perpetuate his teachings were the George Adamski Foundation (now defunct) and the UFO Education Center.

The Polish-born Adamski first became a metaphysical teacher in the 1930s when he issued several publications from the Royal Order of Tibet, which he claimed to represent and for whom he lectured. He was also briefly associated with the Order of Loving Service, another metaphysical group based in Laguna Beach, California. For many years he lived in southern California and lectured to interested audiences.

Soon after his contact with the space people and his first two books appeared (1953 and 1955), Adamski developed a broad following of people interested not only in his contact stories, but also in the wisdom the space brothers had offered. In 1957 he organized his following into the International Get Acquainted Club. The next year his metaphysical teachings— the cosmic wisdom of the saucer people—appeared first in a telepathy course and then in its more systematic form in *Cosmic Philosophy* (1961) and the *Science of Life Study Course* (1964).

Adamski, though a popular lecturer, was not organizationally minded. He turned his early organization over to C. A. Honey, who broke with Adamski shortly before his death. In 1965 Alice Wells (d. 1980), Adamski's daughter, and Charlotte Blob, his secretary and editor, both formed organizations to keep his teachings alive. Wells's group, GAF International brought together the largest group of Adamski followers. After Wells's death, Fred Steckling, a longtime associate of Adamski, became head of the foundation. The UFO Education Center, with headquarters in Valley Center, California, and Appleton, Wisconsin, has a program similar to to the foundation's.

Membership: Not reported.

Remarks: Adamski was plagued throughout his life by charges of fraud. In the 1950s several exposé articles claimed that Adamski had faked the photographs of the flying saucers. The resemblance of the descriptions in his *Inside the Space Ships* to passages in a science fiction novel he wrote in the 1940s led to further accusations. The most damaging attack on Adamski's credibility came from his close associate, C. A. Honey, who published material from Adamski's own copy of Royal Order of Tibet materials (edited for reissuance in the *Science of Life Study Course*) as if it had originated from the space brothers.

Sources:

Adamski, George. *Cosmic Philosophy*. Freeman, SD: Pine Hill Press, 1971.

Bennett, Colin, and John Mitchell. *Looking for Orthon*. New York: Paraview Press, 2001.

George Adamski, Questions and Answers by the Royal Order of Tibet. Laguna Beach, CA: Privately Printed, 1936.

Leslie, Desmond, and George Adamski. *Flying Saucers Have Landed*. London: T. Werner Laurie, 1953.

Steckling, Fred. *Why Are They Here?* New York: Vantage Press, 1969.

Zinsstag, Lou. *UFO. . . George Adamski: Their Man on Earth*. Tucson, AZ: UFO Photo Archives, 1990.

Zinsstag, Lou, and Timothy Good. *George Adamski, the Untold Story*. Beckenham, Kent, U.K.: Ceti Publications, 1983.

Interplanetary Connections

c/o Bashar Tapes, Inc., 7210 Jordan Ave., Ste. B53, Canoga Park, CA 91301

Interplanetary Connections is the organization promoting the channeling activity of Darryl Anka. Anka, the brother of singer Paul Anka, is an illustrator and designer who began to channel two entities, Bashar and Anima, in 1983. Previously he had been studying mediumship, attending a class learning how to be a medium. Bashar and Anima are beings from an extraterrestrial society that communicates totally by telepathy. They do not have names in the same way that humans do, so they simply chose two names for the sake of convenience. *Bashar* is an Arabic word meaning "commander," and *Anima* is a Jungian psychological term referring to the feminine aspect expressed through a masculine individual.

Twice in a single week in the early 1970s—each time in the company of other people—Anka saw a flying spacecraft at relatively close range. He described it as being triangular in shape, approximately 40 feet on each side and 8 feet thick. It was a decade later—when Bashar began to channel through Anka—that Anka concluded that the craft he saw was in fact Bashar's spaceship.

Bashar proclaimed that he was from the planet Essassani, located approximately 500 light years away in the direction of the constellation Orion. The planet is located in a different dimension, and its solar system is thus invisible to normal sight. Bashar described himself as approximately 5 feet tall with whitish-gray skin and no hair. Bashar emphasized that he was speaking as a single voice for the collective voices of his society, who had tuned into him as he spoke through Anka.

Bashar manifested in order to begin an interaction between worlds and assist this world through a time of transition. An essential element in the message of Bashar and his colleagues (collectively called the Association) is the message of overcoming limitation. According to the message, a basic problem of human society is guilt. Guilt perpetuates limitation and keeps people from realizing their own empowerment. Furthermore, guilt prevents our claiming our birthright—happiness, ecstasy, and creativity. Human beings are by nature infinite creators like the Infinite Creator who created them.

By 1984 Anka was channeling once per week, and then two to three nights per week over the next few years. The sessions were tape recorded. By 1987 more than 200 people were coming to sessions every Thursday evening to listen to the channeling. Interplanetary Connections was founded to organize the channeling sessions, to care for the tapes, and to publish transcripts. A volume with summaries of the information and highlights from the more important sessions was compiled and released in 1990 as *Bashar: Blueprint for Change, A Message from Our Future*. Anka has become popular at New Age events at which he frequently lectures and leads workshops.

Membership: Not reported.

Sources:

Anka, Darryl. *Bashar: Blueprint for Change, A Message from Our Future*. Simi Valley, CA: New Solutions Publishing, 1990.

———. *Miracles*. Encino, CA: Interplanetary Connections, 1987.

———. *The New Meta-Physics*. Beverly Hills, CA: Light and Sound Communications, 1987.

———. *Orion and the Black League*. Encino, CA: Interplanetary Connections, 1985.

Perry, Lee, and Michwel Heril. "Interview with Darryl/Bashar." *Meditation* (Winter 1985/86): 34–44.

Waldron, Caryline. "Bashar: An Extraterrestrial Among Us." *Life Times* 3, no. 107: 7.

Mark-Age, Inc.

PO Box 10, Pioneer, TN 37847

Mark-Age was initiated by spiritual revelations received in 1956 by Charles Boyd Gentzel (1922–1981) and formally organized in 1960 by Gentzel and Pauline Sharpe (1925–2005) to channel the messages of the "Hierarchal Board" (the spiritual government for the solar system) during the last 40 years of the twentieth century (1960–2000 c.e.). This is the transition coordinating group for the movement from the Piscean Age to the Aquarian. The original leaders of the group included several psychics who channeled the data from the hierarchy. The primary channel, Nada-Yolanda (Pauline Sharpe), channeled most of the messages. In 1962 the Mark-Age Meta Center, Inc., now Mark-Age, Inc., incorporated in Miami. As early as 1949, the name *Mark-Age* was revealed; a subsequent revelation in 1955 concurred.

Mark-Age sees itself as one of many focal points of contact with the higher spiritual forces. By automatic writing and telepathic communications, the hierarchy speaks. Messages have come through Gloria Lee, the founder of the Cosmos Research Foundation and an early contactee who died during a fast in 1962; famous individuals such as John F. Kennedy; and the Theosophical masters El Morya, Lady Nada, Sananda (Jesus), and Djual Khool. Mark-Age was corresponding with Lee just prior to her death in 1962. After her death, their communications with her and the publication of *Gloria Lee Lives* were major steps forward in Mark-Age's growth.

Spacecraft are one means of communication between the Hierarchal Board and Earth. They include both physical craft and other craft from the etheric realms. Jesus (Sananda) has been in orbit around Earth since 1885 in the etheric realms, and his ship 10, the Star of Bethlehem, will take material form as the planet is cleansed. Through telepathy with the spaceships, contact is made with beings of other planets.

Since 1960 Mark-Age has published a large amount of material, much of which is condensed in the standard introductory book *MAPP to Aquarius: Mark-Age Period and Program* (1970). Besides outlining the minimal organization of Mark-Age, the messages have aimed at defining of the roles of the Hierarchy (which, apart from the emphasis on flying saucers, is theosophical) and raising man's spiritual consciousness as the Aquarian Age dawns in preparation for the Second Coming, which was expected around the year 2000. Preparation involves a process of meditation and psychic development. Instructions for groups associated with Mark-Age have also been published. In 1999 Mark-Age relocated its headquarters from Florida to Tennessee.

Membership: Not reported.

Periodicals: *I AM Nation News*.

Sources:

Mark-Age Inc. www.thenewearth.org/markage.html.

Mark-Age Staff. *Group Guidelines for New Age Light Centers*. Miami, FL: Mark-Age Meta Center, 1971.

———. "History of Mark-Age." *Mark-Age Inform-Nations* 22 (June–July 1975).

———. *How to Do All Things*. Miami, FL: Mark-Age, 1970.

———. *Plan a Nation*. Miami, FL: Mark-Age, 1975.

Nada-Yolanda [Pauline Sharpe]. *Angels and Man*. Miami, FL: Mark-Age, 1974.

———. *Contacts from the Fourth Dimension*. Pioneer, TN: Mark-Age, 2007.

———. *Life in Our solar System*. Pioneer, TN: Mark-Age, 2008. 212 pp.

———. *Mark Age Period and Program*. Miami, FL: Mark-Age, 1970.

———. *Visitors from Other Planets*. Miami, FL: Mark-Age, 1974.

Semjase Silver Star Center

Schmidrueti, CH-8495 Switzerland

The Semjase Silver Star Center is the U.S. branch of the Freie Interessengemeinschaft fur Grenz- und Geisteswissenschaften und Ufologie-Studien (Free Community of Interests in the Border and Spiritual Sciences and UFO Studies) headquartered in Schmidrueti, Switzerland. The Free Community was founded in the late 1970s by Eduard "Billy" Meier (b. 1936), who in 1975 experienced the first of a series of contacts with a flying saucer. Meier claimed the UFO had come from the Pleiades to visit him at several locations near his home in Canton Zurich, Switzerland. Meier wrote the story of his contacts and published some of the material from the encounters soon after they began, and the Free Community was organized by people who responded to the teachings. Knowledge of Meier's contacts was spread in the United States primarily by Wendelle Stevens, who wrote two articles on them for *ArgosyUFO* in 1977. In 1979 he published a book, complete with many pictures taken by Meier of the flying saucers.

Meier noted that he had his first UFO experience in 1942, during World War II, when he was five years old. He saw a metallic disc fly over his house, and a few months later had contact with a person from a saucer who invited him for a ride. Beginning in 1944 he experienced regular telepathic contact with an entity named Sfath, who also took him for a ride in the spaceship. Other unusual experiences occurred throughout his life, leading him to psychic studies and spiritualism. The 1975 contact began while he was attempting to elicit spirit messages from a tape recorder, a method made famous by the psychic researcher Konstantin Raudive. Meier received a message that instructed him to go outside with a camera. He traveled down the road to an unpopulated area and had his first contact with Semjase, a woman cosmonaut who claimed to be from the Pleiades star cluster. He took a number of pictures. Semjase told Meier that she and others had come to develop a voice "channel" through which they could speak and thus assist humanity out of its present ignorance.

According to entities from the Pleiades, the solar system is entering the Waterman Era (the Aquarian Age), which will signal a powerful upheaval in the spiritual realm. Basic to understanding our life is the Creation, the being and non-being of life. Creation is the immense mass of spiritual energy in the universe, spirit in its purest form—wisdom, knowledge, love, and harmony in Truth. Meier's followers believe that he has arisen as the herald of the Truth, the one who is to spread the Creation's universal laws. Integral to his message are the Twelve Bids, the things Creation bids us do. The 12 admonitions, analogous to the Ten Commandments, provide guidance in ways to avoid violating the Creation.

Membership: Not reported.

Remarks: When they were published in 1979 the claims of Billy Meier caused an immediate controversy in the ufological community. In 1980 an article reporting on an examination of his claims pronounced him a fraud. Evidence cited included analyses of his photographs that revealed strings holding what appeared to be model flying saucers. An analysis of objects Meier claimed to have received from the flying saucer entities were in fact mundane earth objects. Letters from people who substantiated Meier's claims were also fraudulent. Wendelle Stevens, who first reported on Meier's claims, has remained a supporter in the ufological debate; besides a number of articles, he has produced two additional books on Meier. As the debate over Meier raged, Stevens published a set of volumes representing the claims of a wide variety of UFO contactees, presenting their stories of visits from various planets and star systems.

Sources:

FIGU Society USA. us.figu.org/.

Korff, Karl K. *The Billy Meier Story: Space Ships of the Pleiades*. Amherst, NY: Prometheus Books, 1995.

————. "The Meier Incident: The Most Infamous Hoax in Ufology." *Mufon UFO Journal* 154 (December 1980).

Meier, Eduard "Billy." *Decalogue, or the Ten Bids*. Alamogordo, NM: Semjase Silver Star Center, 1987.

————. *The Psyche*. Alamogordo, NM: Semjase Silver Star Center [1986].

Stevens, Wendelle C. *UFO Contact from the Pleiades*. Phoenix, AZ: Genesis III Productions, 1979.

Solar Light Retreat

7700 Avenue of the Sun, White City, OR 97503

Aleuti Francesca is the director and "tele-thought contactee" for the Solar Light Retreat, established in 1966 in the foothills in southern Oregon, 20 miles outside of Medford. Francesca (originally known as Marianne Francis; she changed her name legally in 1975) became interested in UFOs in 1947 in London, England, where she was born and grew up. In 1954 Francesca moved with her American husband, Kenneth Kellar, to Santa Barbara, California, where she studied Hatha Yoga with Indra Devi and Baala Krishna. Telepathic and highly sensitive all her life, Francesca's sensitivity increased as she and Kellar conducted experiments with light beam apparatus aimed at contacting outer-space intelligences.

In forming the Santa Barbara Space Craft Research Society, Kellar and Francesca arranged many lectures for leading experts on UFOs. At this time they met and became associated with Gayne and Roberta Myers and Richard Miller, the originators of the Solar Cross Fellowship. They moved to Oregon in 1965, and the following year the Solar Light Center was incorporated as a nonprofit organization (the name was later changed to Solar Light Retreat as Francesca's lecture work and tours increased). Kellar and Francesca were quietly and amicably divorced in 1969 but remained friends after Kellar's remarriage and relocation first to Washington state and then to Nevada. Kellar died in 1994.

Francesca's contact is mainly with the XY7, a mother craft from the Saturn Command. Ray-mere and Sut-ko of the Saturn Council are two of the main communicators. Information given over many years has indicated that all life in this and many other solar systems functions at the physical etheric level, not the physical dense (as it does here on Earth). This is a physical plane level of functioning and has nothing to do with the spirit world per se.

Principles of the Solar Light Retreat are focused on knowledge of a spiritual hierarchy of beings, the Great White Brotherhood working under Christ, angelic contact, and the reality of the infinite Creator, the "All-Knowing One," or "Our Radiant One," as the space beings call God. The eternal truths given by world avatars such as Jesus Christ, Buddha, Krishna, and other spiritual masters are the basis of the teachings. The reality of advanced space beings from the Light Commands is the focus of Francesca's lectures. She is an international speaker, having participated in the UFO Conference in Cairo, Egypt, and the Channelling Conference in Crete. Extensive speaking engagements throughout the United States and Canada, and in England, as well as hundreds of radio interviews and television appearances have made Francesca a clear spokesperson for the Space Commands.

Since 1975 Francesca also has given workshops and private regression consultations (more than 3,000) on the subjects of "Sex and the Soul" and "Transmutation of Consciousness." The private regressions have been designed to assist individuals seeking to clear energy blocks as we move towards the end of this cycle. Belief in reincarnation forms the basis for these workshops and counselling.

Membership: The retreat is not a membership organization.

Periodicals: *Starcraft—Newsletter*.

Unarius—Science of Life

143 S Magnolia, El Cajon, CA 92022

Unarius was founded in 1954 by Ernest L. Norman (1900–1971), a former spiritualist medium, shortly after his meeting with Ruth Norman (1904–1993), his future wife. Ernest, the Unarian moderator, is described in the Unarius literature as "the greatest intelligence ever to come to earth" and is believed to be a reincarnation of the entity who was also Pharaoh Amenhotep IV and Jesus. Mrs. Norman, in previous lives, had been the pharaoh's mother, the betrothed of Jesus, the woman who found Moses in the bullrushes, and the woman who sat for Leonardo da Vinci for *Mona Lisa*. The beginning of Ernest's mission was to ancient Atlantis and Lemuria, to which Ernest came via a spaceship. The mission is also seen as the return of Jesus and the renewal of his work that was abruptly cut off 2,000 years ago.

The teachings of Unarius are encompassed in the many books channeled by Ernest after he met Ruth (Ernest dictated material that Ruth copied and published), the books written by Ruth after Ernest's death, and the Unarius lessons that contain teachings not otherwise published. Ernest's mission began when he materialized on Earth and was guided by the evolved beings who reside on other planets. From these teachers, he dictated seven books that contain information about and teachings from the planets Venus, Mars, Hermes, Eros, Orion, and Muse. The teachings comprise the true science of life and deal with spiritual development and healing. Healing is accomplished by RayBooms, the projected light beams from the great intelligences on the higher worlds. In addition to the detailed descriptions of the various planets in Ernest's books, Ruth provided a picture of the Intergalactic Confederation, which consists of planets more advanced than Earth. As the Confederation was formed, Earth was invited to join; the polarization (joining) of Earth occurred on September 14, 1973, with Ioshanna (Ruth) as the central contact. Earth is progressing more rapidly since it became part of the Confederation.

After Ruth Norman's death in 1993, Unarius was headed by Charles L. Spiegel (1921–1999). The organization's program centered upon two courses of lessons, "The Psychology of Consciousness" and the more advanced "Self Mastery, the Infinite Concept of Cosmic Creation," designed to bring forth the powers believed to be latent in each human being. The course helps people to attain self-knowledge and then assume responsibility for their past mistakes, thus allowing corrections of current conditions that have resulted from past actions and preventing any new missteps. Integral to the lessons is a study of what is termed the "physics of reincarnation." Students are presented with a picture of the ever evolving nature of life and our true purpose as spiritual beings. Knowledge of self leads to a knowledge of the Infinite Creative Intelligence, the ever generative source of life.

The word *Unarius* is an acronym for "universal articulate interdimensional understanding of science."

Membership: Not reported.

Periodicals: *Unarius Light*.

Sources:

Unarius Academy of Science. www.unarius.org.

Ioshanna [Ruth Norman]. *A Space Woman Speaks from Outer Space*. El Cajon, CA: Unarius, n.d.

Norman, Ernest L. *The Elysium*. Pasadena, CA: Unarius, 1956.

————. *The Voice of Venus*. Santa Barbara, CA: Unarius—Science of Life, 1956.

Norman, Ruth E., and Vaughn Spaegel. *Who Is the Mona Lisa?* El Cajon, CA: Unarius—Science of Life, 1973.

Unarius. *Pathway to Light: An Introduction to the Unarius Science of Life*. El Cajon, CA: Unarius Academy of Science, 1995. 44 pp.

The Universal Hierarchy. *A Pictorial Tour of Unarius*. El Cajon, CA: Unarius Educational Foundation, 1982.

United States Raelian Religion

PO Box 570935, Topaz Station, Las Vegas, NV 89108

Alternate Address: Canadian Raelian Movement, PO Box 86, Youville Sta., Montreal, QC, Canada H2P 2V2. International Raelian Movement, CP 225, CH-1211 Geneva 8, Switzerland.

The French journalist Rael (aka Claude Vorilhon, b. 1946) claimed that on December 13, 1973, he was contacted by an extraterrestrial being. During this encounter, the extraterrestrial dictated a series of messages for humankind and requested that an embassy be built in Jerusalem, if possible, where the extraterrestrials will land, bringing with them all the prophets announced by every religion. These messages explained that in the original Hebrew Bible's opening phrase "In the beginning Elohim . . .," *Elohim* (not "God") translates to "those who came from the sky" (*Elohim* is plural). Thus, Rael declared that he had been told by the ETs that Genesis is a written account of how people from another planet created all life on Earth. The messages dictated to Rael explain how the Elohim, through their mastery of genetics, scientifically created life using DNA.

The messages went on to explain that all the great prophets, including Buddha, Moses, Jesus, and Mohammed, were messengers of these extraterrestrials. Jesus was born from the union of one of these extraterrestrials and a daughter of man, and his task was to spread the biblical Genesis throughout the world in anticipation of the age in which we are now living, the predicted Age of Apocalypse.

According to the Elohim, humanity entered the Age of Apocalypse in 1945. The word "apocalypse" comes from the Greek "apocalupsis" and means "revelation." It is the time in which our scientific development allows us to understand the true origin of humanity. With this same level of technology we can also either destroy or liberate our world. This age of apocalypse has been anticipated by every religion.

According to the Raelians, the Elohim contacted Rael in modern times because the human race can finally rationally understand its origins. They have asked him to make these messages known throughout the world and to build an embassy for them where they will meet with the leaders of the world officially. They are not invaders. They have shown their desire to come, but they respect Earth's choice to refuse them. It is up to humanity to invite them, and the invitation is the embassy. In Raelian belief, it's the least humanity can do: The Elohim created mankind, and without them mankind would not exist.

According to the Raelians, the Elohim taught Rael the techniques of "sensual meditation" so that people can awaken their minds by awakening their bodies and realizing their true potentials. The techniques form an instruction manual given to mankind to help harmonize all the possibilities that lie within our collective brain, written by those best placed to know how it works because they created it. As human beings, we are linked by our receptors, the senses, to the infinite, which surrounds and composes us. Every year, on every continent, members of the Raelian movement can participate in sensual meditation seminars. In North America, the seminars are held in Nevada.

The Raelian movement is a nonprofit, international organization. Rael has written several books that have been translated into 34 languages.

Membership: In 2008 the movement reported 65,000 members worldwide, including 3,000 in the United States and 5,000 in Canada.

Periodicals: *Apocalypse* (printed). • *Contact* (electronic newsletter). • *Rael-Science* (daily news service).

Remarks: The movement has been criticized for its emblem, a stylized swastika inside a Star of David. Rael explains it is a symbol of infinity, but others complain that it has racial connotations.

Sources:

Raelian Movement. www.rael.org.

Raelianews. www.raelianews.org.

Raelradio. www.raelradio.net.

Palmer, Susan J. *Aliens Adored: Rael's UFO Religion*. New Brunswick, NJ: Rutgers University Press, 2004.

————. "The Raelian Movement International." In *New Religions and the New Europe*, ed. Robert Towler. Aarhus, Denmark: Aarhus University Press, 1995.

Rael. *Geniocracy*. Nova Distribution, 2008.

————. *Intelligent Design: Message from the Designers*. Nova Distribution, 2006.

————. *Let's Welcome Our Fathers from Space: They Created Humanity in Their Laboratories*. Tokyo: AOM Corporation, 1986.

————. *The Maitreya: Extracts from His Teachings*. Raelian Foundation, 2004.

————. *Sensual Meditation*. Tokyo: AOM Corporation, 1986.

————. *Sensual Meditation*. Raelian Foundation, 2002.

————. *Space Aliens Took Me to Their Planet*. Liechtenstein: Foundation pour l'Accueil des Elohim, 1978.

————. *Yes to Human Cloning*. St. Ives, Cambridge, U.K.: Tagman Press, 2001.

Universe Society Church (UNISOC)

Current address not obtained for this edition.

The Universe Society Church (UNISOC) was founded in 1951 as the Institute of Parapsychology. It was also known as the Universe Society prior to taking its present name in the early 1980s. The church was founded by Hal Wilcox (b. 1932), who had had a number of psychic experiences as a child. He later was ordained as a Spiritualist minister. In the early 1950s, along with several other individuals with mediumistic abilities, Wilcox learned of Master Fahsz and other ascended teachers of the Great White Brotherhood (The Ancient Brotherhood of Fahsz, or TABOF). Wilcox and the other oracles began to channel messages from these teachers/masters who taught the group about the nature of the universe and humanity's role in it.

According to TABOF the universe was created by God, described as "the Father, The Ultimate One, the Force behind All Force, the Ultimate Cause behind All Cause." God permeates the universe, which is divided into seven sectors. Our sector, under Master Brsgv, contains seven galaxies. Our galaxy is in seven groups of seven planets each, making a total of 50 principal colonies including Fahsz's home planet of Narvon in the Altair system. UFOs are spacecraft used to colonize our galaxy and stay in touch with the inhabited planets, or galactic colonies in the Milky Way. Contacts from 1951 to 1961 were maintained by a method the group was taught in order to facilitate regular communications. It consists of a brief ceremony in which a mantrum, "Ino Pazis Gnurum," is chanted, followed by a 30-minute message channeled by one of UNISOC's 12 oracles for directions. The short service, it is believed, activates the pineal gland, connecting it with either the INO, a galactic computer bank, or one of the space brothers within Fahsz's command.

In 1963 physical contacts started with Zemkla, who governs planet Selo in the Bernard Star system. According to the information received over the years, humanity's goal is governance, wherein all the people of this galaxy are to learn via reincarnation and karma to live according to God's spiritual laws.

In the 1950s UNISOC began work on seven project tests. In the process of completing the projects, Wilcox discovered the results of past covenants, the first of which was a new 1838 Japanese religion, Tenrikyo. Since that time, Wilcox has discovered many other teachings that came from the same source but were presented according to humanity's changing cultural understanding. After UNISOC completed Project-1 in 1963, Wilcox was ordained as a Tenrikyo priest before moving on to Project-2. During the process of completing six projects he wrote approximately 60 books to expound the emerging truth. By 1987 UNISOC had completed six of the seven test projects. The seventh test corresponds roughly with the United States' third test of destiny.

UNISOC holds weekly classes and has expanded their services to include an interfacing computer network that in 1978 produced a printout of extraterrestrial communications. The associated Galaxy Press has published Wilcox's books, several levels of instructional material, booklets, and a newsletter.

Membership: In 1988 there was only one center, in Hollywood, but graduates of the work are encouraged to start their own units in other states and countries. Several of the books have been translated into other languages.

Periodicals: *UNISOC Newsletter*.

Sources:

Wilcox, Hal. *Contact With the Master*. Hollywood, CA: Galaxy Press, 1984.

————. *Gateway to the Superconsciousness*. Hollywood, CA: Author, n.d.

White Star

Box 307, Joshua Tree, CA 92252

Located close to Giant Rock in the Yucca Valley of California is White Star, founded by Doris C. LeVesque of Joshua Tree, California. LeVesque began to channel messages from unseen entities in the mid-1950s after having read a book on flying saucers in 1954. In 1957 she began to publish the *White Star Illuminator*. She developed contact with the Ashtar Command, previously contacted by George Van Tassel, the founder of the Ministry of Universal Wisdom in nearby Giant Rock, California.

LeVesque teaches that the earth is in a transition period created by the atomic age. Cataclysm is to be avoided by moving away from the destruction of nature. Universal laws, especially that of divine love, must be expressed. Love is the prime motivating force in the universe, which is organized on the principles of density and substance. Man evolves by assuming more density, which vibrates at high rates. Life on all planets is at different points of evolution. A key evolutionary concept is light, which is said to be created by vibration traveling in substance, and evolution to higher spiritual levels accompanies the presence of more light. Followers are encouraged to meditate and to visualize the coming of the light into situations where it is needed.

Membership: Not reported. Mailings go out to followers across the United States.

Periodicals: *Times of the Signs*.

❋ Drug-Related Groups

Church of the Universe

c/o Morning Star Mission of God, 544 Barton St. E, Hamilton, ON, Canada L8L 2Z1

The Church of the Universe, founded in 1969 by Walter Tucker and others, emerged during the subsequent decades of the twentieth century as the major religious organization in Canada arguing for the legalization of marijuana (or cannabis) for religious and spiritual purposes. The church also espouses nudism, as a natural expression of humanity. The first center of the church was an abandoned rock quarry, since filled with water, which Tucker leased and dedicated, along with the 360 acres of associated wilderness land, as "Clearwater Abbey." The site became a gathering place for people using the sacred substance, and Tucker also added an emphasis on clothes made from the hemp plant. In 1986, Tucker and the other residents were evicted by the land's owners after a lengthy court battle. The fight gave a much higher profile to the church, which became the target of legal authorities seeking indictments for illegal drug use. In spite of some legal victories, the church developed a somewhat clandestine existence.

Basic to the church's belief is the identification of marijuana as the Tree of Life mentioned in the biblical book of Genesis. Marijuana is thus a gift of God that dates to the ancient Garden of Eden. Members declare their intention of living with Marijuana, in harmony with the Universe, and assume a responsibility to defend the rights of church members to what they consider to be their sacramental substance. In like measure, the church fights for the right to go nude, weather and climate permitting. Members do not consider themselves Christian; rather they identify themselves as Universalists, as they believe Jesus to have been.

During the 1970s, the church evolved two essential (golden) rules: Do not hurt yourself. Do not hurt anyone else. They came to believe that as long as church members followed these rules, they should be free to practice their religion and worship God as they saw fit.

The symbol of the Church is a triangle on a nine-pointed star inside a circle, together with the number 69. The symbol is seen as combining the six-pointed Star of David (06 of the woman) and the 09 star (09 of the man). Together (that is, when visually superimposed) the 6 and 9 make 8, the symbol of infinity and of the river of life. Man and woman create between them universal peace and love, and fulfill the positive requirements of the creation.

The church continues to be led by Rev. Tucker, who is assisted by the Tetrahedron High Council, the leaders of the church. The church celebrates the two solstices and Cannabis Day (July 1) as major holidays.

Membership: Not reported.

Sources:

Church of the Universe. www.iamm.com/.

"Cannabis and the Christ: Jesus Used Marijuana." Posted at www.cannabisculture.com/backissues/cc11/christ.html.

Ethiopian Zion Coptic Church

PO Box 1161, Minneola, FL 34755-1161

The Ethiopian Zion Coptic Church was founded in Jamaica in 1914 by Marcus Garvey (1887–1940) and originally came to the United States in 1920 as part of his reformist efforts in the black community. However, the church died out in the United States and became a small body in Jamaica. Then in 1970, several Americans in Jamaica encountered the church, joined it, and brought it back to Star Island, off Miami Beach, Florida. A second center was started in New Jersey. The leader of the group was Thomas Reilly Jr., generally known by his religious name, Brother Louv.

Church members believe in God, who is experienced through the smoking of ganja (marijuana). Smoking marijuana is described as making a burnt sacrifice to the God within. The ceremonies for smoking ganja utilize a specially made pipe. Coptics smoke ganja in such quantities that they hope it will reorganize their body chemistry around THC, the psychoactive ingredient in the plant, and they will thus survive the end of this world to live in God's new world. The new world is seen as a place in which there will be plenty for all without the necessity of an eight-hour work day. Peace and brotherhood will reign, and life will be lived at the horse-and-buggy pace. Ceremonially smoking ganja is the major sacramental act of church members, and members quote the Bible (Gen. 1:29; Ex. 3:2-4; Psalms 104:14; and Heb. 6:7) in support of their use of marijuana.

Coptics also have a strong code dictating relations between the sexes. Women sit separately for the sacramental service and are not allowed to fill their own pipes. Sexual activity is strongly regulated. Homosexuality, oral sex, birth control, and abortion are prohibited. The only recognized purpose for sex is procreation.

Even before the church was granted tax exempt status in 1975, it fought an intense battle with government authorities. By 1973 authorities had seized 105 tons of marijuana from the group. In 1977 tax exemption was revoked. The church filed a lawsuit demanding the religious right of its members to smoke marijuana, but lost the case in late 1978. Immediately after the court ruling, Reilly and five other church leaders were arrested in a raid on the Star Island headquarters. They were indicted and in 1981 convicted for drug smuggling. In 1982 Reilly, serving time in the Metropolitan Corrections Center in Miami, sued U.S. Attorney General William French Smith for the right to his daily sacrament of at least an ounce of marijuana.

In 1981 a group of approximately 20 members of the church moved to rural Wisconsin and established a settlement in an isolated valley near Soldiers Grove. They had moved from Iowa because of local harassment as a result of their refusal to have their children immunized as required by state law. Investigation stimulated by the group's use of marijuana led to arrests of church leaders in 1985. The arrest and conviction of church leaders has disrupted the life of the church, and the courts in the United States have persistently refused to allow the use of controlled substances by church organizations (apart from the Native American Church). The present status of the church is in doubt.

International headquarters of the church are in White Horses, Jamaica, where it was incorporated in 1976. The church operates a 4,000-acre farm in St. Thomas Parish. In 2008 the leader of the church in Jamaica was Keith Gordon (religious name, "Nyah").

Membership: Not reported. There are an estimated 200 members in the United States.

Periodicals: *Coptic Time*.

Sources:

Ethiopian Zion Coptic Church. www.ethiopianzioncopticchurch.org.

Ethiopian Zion Coptic Church. *Marijuana and the Bible*. Hialeah, FL: Author, n.d.

Fane of the Psilocybe Mushroom
Address unavailable.

The Fane of the Psilocybe Mushroom was chartered in Victoria, British Columbia, in Canada, on January 22, 1980, an action catalyzed by the success of Native Americans in gaining legal recognition of their use of peyote. It has been the hope of the members of the Fane to have their use of psychedelic substances, especially the sacred mushroom-the several species of mushrooms of the genus Psilocybe-declared legal, at least when in a religious, sacramental context.

The Fane describes itself as a fourth way mystical school. The term *fourth way* was coined by George Gurdjieff, who described the three ways of the fakir, monk, and yogi, and then declared that the fourth way combines the essence of all three earlier ways. The Fane uses the term in a considerably different way. It suggests that instead of pursuing yogic exercises, monk-like prayers, or the fakir's self torture, the "sly man" of the fourth way "simply prepares and swallows a little pill" that contains the proper substance and produces the desired state of consciousness. The Fane suggests that the mushroom sacrament is the most efficient way to expand consciousness-said expanded state of consciousness being defined as the desired religious experience. The ingestion of the sacred mushroom is the essential aspect of the Fane's community.

Membership in the Fane is open to all who believe that the ingestion of the sacred mushroom is a sacrament; that everyone has the right to expanded con-

sciousness by whatever means they choose; and that the unprepared should not be encouraged to ingest the sacred mushroom.

As with the members of most groups advocating the religious uses of psychedelic substances, much of the life of the members of the Fane of the Psilocybe Mushroom has been lived at a confidential, if not clandestine level. The Fane maintains a Web page and continues to advocate the use of the sacred mushroom, but much of its religious activity remains out of the public spotlight. Neither the names of the present leadership of the Fane nor a means of contacting it are provided through its Web page.

Membership: Not reported.

Sources:

Fane of the Psilocybe Mushroom Association. www.thefane.org/.

Native American Church
Rte. 1, Box 67, Osseo, WI 59758

Long before the white man came to America, psychedelic substances were used by the various American Indian tribes who had come into what is now the United States from Mexico. Some time before 1870, the use of psychedelic drugs was introduced in the United States by the Mescalero Apaches. The practice spread northward to the Kiowa, Comanche, and Caddo. Its spread followed the demise of the Ghost Dance, for which it substituted. The prime psychedelic source was peyote, a small, spineless, carrot-shaped cactus that grows wild in the Southwest. The dried peyote button is ingested during a spirit ceremony and produces effects similar to those of LSD. Legal measures and the hostility of both whites and fellow Indians led to the quest for legally guaranteed security of worship. In the second decade of the twentieth century, Jonathan Koshiway (1886–1971), the son of an Oto mother, and a former missionary for the Church of Jesus Christ of Latter-day Saints, discovered in peyotism a way of affirming both his Indian heritage and his Christian tendencies. He viewed peyote as one of God's creations, which he pronounced "good," seeing the button and the peyote tea as a reflection of sacramental bread and wine. Under his leadership, the First Born Church of Christ was formed in 1914 with 411 members. This group was later absorbed by the Native American Church.

The Native American Church dates to 1906, when a loose intertribal association of peyote groups in Oklahoma and Nebraska was formed. In 1909 the name "Union Church" was adopted. In 1918 the U.S. Bureau of Indian Affairs began a campaign to declare peyote illegal. In reaction to this effort, the Native American Church was incorporated. Present at the formation was Jonathan Koshiway, who attempted to get the group to join the First Born. Koshiway's church was rejected as too Christian; eventually, Koshiway joined the Native Americans.

Although the actual practices of the Native American Church vary widely, there is a considerable core of commonality. The central figure is the shaman, who keeps the peyote buttons and controls their use. As with all mediumistic figures, he is endowed with psychic powers. Peyote ritual begins with the pilgrimage by members of the tribe to collect the buttons, which are brought to the shaman.

The ceremony occurs in the evening in a tepee. The "father peyote" is placed on a crescent-shaped mound. The mound is in the west, with the crescent horns facing east. Before participants eat the peyote there is prayer and smoking, and singing and drumming follow. The ritual lasts until morning.

Legal battles over peyote began as early as 1899, when Oklahoma outlawed its use. Following the conviction of three Indians in 1907, the law was repealed in 1908. Antipeyote laws were passed in Colorado, Utah, and Nevada in 1917, and similar laws were passed in other Western states. A significant case involved Mary Attakai, arrested for peyote use in 1960. In his decision, the judge ruled that peyote was non-habit-forming and not a narcotic, and found the antipeyote statute unconstitutional. In 1964 the California Supreme Court ruled that the Native American Church could not be deprived of peyote for religious ceremonies. Finally, when the psychedelic drugs were made illegal by federal law in 1966, peyote and the Native American Church were excluded from the strictures of the law. Since the court rulings of the 1970s, many non-Indians have attempted to affiliate with the church. In reaction, it has tended to exclude non-Indians from its rituals, both to protect its special status and to keep people believed to be merely seeking a drug experience from distorting its rituals.

The church is headed by a national president elected for a two-year term. An annual convention elects officers and is the church's highest legislative body. State and local chapters are autonomous.

Membership: Not reported. In 1977 the church had approximately 225,000 members.

Sources:

Aberle, David F. *The Peyote Religion among the Navaho*. New York: Wenner-Glen Foundation for Anthropological Research, 1966.

Anderson, Edward F. *Peyote, the Divine Cactus*. Tucson, AZ: University of Arizona Press, 1980.

La Barre, Weston. *The Peyote Cult*. New York: Schocken Books, 1969.

Smith, Huston, and Reuben Snake, eds., *One Nation Under God: The Triumph of the Native American Church*. Santa Fe, NM: Clear Light Publishers, 1996.

White, Philip M. *Peyotism and the Native American Church: An Annotated Bibliography*. Westport, CT: Greenwood Press, 2000.

Original Kleptonian Neo-American Church (OKNeoAC)

Box 3473, Austin, TX 78764

The Original Kleptonian Neo-American Church (OKNeoAC) was founded in 1965 at Cranberry Lake, New York, by Art Kleps (1928–1999), the chief boo-hoo. The church has three principles:

1. Psychedelic substances, such as cannabis and LSD, are religious sacraments because their ingestion encourages enlightenment, which is the recognition that life is a dream and the externality of relationships an illusion (solipsistic nihilism);

2. The use of the psychedelic sacraments is a basic human right and all interference therewith is an assault on this right; and

3. The church does not encourage the ingestion of the greater sacraments such as LSD or mescaline by those who are unprepared, with preparedness defined as familiarity with the lesser sacraments such as cannabis and nitrous oxide and with solipsist-nihilist epistemological reasoning based on models such as those advanced by David Hume, Sextus Empiricus, and Nagarjuna.

The church was incorporated in December 1967 in New York. Kleps, Timothy Leary (1920–1996), William Haines (also known as Sri Sankara), William Mellon Hitchcock, and Karl Netwon formed the original Board of Toads (directors). The church was headquartered at Millbrook, in upstate New York, until it dispersed in 1968 when, as a result of earlier actions by law enforcement agents, the owners evicted all resident groups on the estate. The church was reincorporated in 1973 in Vermont. Through the next decade Kleps fought for religious use of psychedelic substances. Following a conviction in 1985, Kleps served a year in prison. From 1987 to 1991 he and his family lived in the Netherlands. He continued to fight for the right to use psychedelic drugs, in spite of legal barriers in North America and Europe against their use, until his death in 1999.

Kleps authored the *Boo Hoo Bible* and *Millbrook*, in which he describes neo-American philosophy as solipsistic nihilism. He identifies it as similar to the philosophies of Heraclitus, David Hume, and Buddhism as practiced by Nagarjuna. He denies the externality of relations, space, time, and multiplicity. He believes that life is a dream, and truth is found by ridding oneself of illusions through the ingestion of psychedelic sacraments under the proper conditions. Yoga and meditation are believed by Kleps to be used more often than not to prevent awareness of the Truth.

OKNeoAC is an absolute monarchy. When His Highness Arthur Kleps, chief boo hoo, died in 1999, his wife, Her Highness Joan Kleps, chief bee hee (CBH), succeeded him. The Board of Toads is appointed by the CBH. There are three levels of membership: upper, middle, and lower. Upper- and middle-level members subscribe to the church's current three principles. Upper-level members apply in writing for their status, and only they may be ordained. Lower-level members include all those who have ever subscribed to any version of the three principles as formulated by the chief boo hoo since 1965, at the time such versions were active. All members are expected to pay nominal annual dues. Members in a local area may be organized into an OKNeoAC vortex, or an affiliate church, each of which is headed by a boo hoo general, in a geographical area specified by the CBH.

In 2008 there were three affiliate churches. The Neo-American Church of Texas was headed by Sahib Kevin Sanford, Original Mahout. His Eminence Robert Funk headed the Original Kleptonian Neo-American Church of California, as boo hoo general of California, and the Original Kleptonian Neo-American Church of Alaska, as archon of Alaska.

Membership: Not reported.

Sources:

Brown, Robert E., et al., eds. *The Psychedelic Guide to Preparation of the Eucharist*. Austin, TX: Linga Shirira Incense, 1975.

Dwyer, Ed, and Robert Singer. "Interview: Art Kleps, Chief Boo Hoo, Neo American Church." *High Times* 8 (March 1976): 21–24.

Kleps, Art. *The Boo Hoo Bible*. San Cristobal, NM: Author, 1971.

———. *Millbrook*. Oakland, CA: Bench Press, 1977.

———. "Synchronicity and the Plot/Plot." *Psychedelic Review* 8 (1966): 123–124.

Peyote Way Church of God

30800 W Klondyke Rd., Klondyke, AZ 85643

The Peyote Way Church of God was founded in 1977 by the Revs. Immanuel Pardeahtan Trujillo, Eugene Yoakum, and William Russell. Trujillo, the son of an Apache and his French-American wife, joined the Native American Church in 1948. The Native American Church is the main body to continue the traditional religious use of peyote among Native Americans. Trujillo objected to the church's policy of excluding from membership—and hence participation in the ritual use of peyote—anyone who was not at least 25 percent Native American. Trujillo considered the policy racist, and he believed in some of the teachings of Joseph Smith Jr., the founder of the Church of Jesus Christ of Latter-day Saints. Trujillo left the Native American Church in 1966 and established an independent group that evolved over the years under various names, including the Church of Holy Light Pentecostal Indian Mission.

At the time of the founding of the church in 1977, Trujillo, Matthew S. Kent, and Anne L. Zapf registered a declaration of intent with the recorder of Graham County, Arizona, stating that they were growing, using, and distributing peyote as a holy sacrament of their church. The new church emphasized section 89 of the Doctrines and Covenants, one of the scriptures of the Church of Jesus Christ of Latter-day Saints, which specifically forbids the use of a number of harmful substances such as alcohol and tobacco while commending the use of "all wholesome herbs." Church members believe that passage specifically supports their use of peyote, a wholesome herb.

The church uses peyote in what is termed a "Spirit Walk." Members come to the church land, fast a minimum of 24 hours, and spend a period of time in the desert in prayer and self-examination. They take peyote alone rather than communally, as in the Native American Church practice. Peyote, the church teaches, cleanses both body and spirit, produces a visionary state of consciousness, and allows users to contact the light of Christ within.

From the beginning, the church's leaders were concerned with building a presence in south Texas, the only place peyote cactus grows naturally in the United

States. Their plans have been continually thwarted by Texas authorities and antidrug laws. In 1988 a court upheld the federal and state statutes that the church had tried to overturn on constitutional grounds. In 1990 the court refused to expand the legal peyote exemption it had granted to the Native American Church to include any non-Indian groups, among them the Peyote Way Church of God. In 2008 the church had legal standing in Arizona and may use peyote on its property, but it is unable to obtain peyote from Texas through the legal channels that the Native American Church may use. The church faced another setback when its cottage industry, MANA Black Rim Earthenware, was denied tax exemption and assessed for back taxes.

Resident members of the Peyote Way Church of God participate in the United Order, a system originally instituted by the Mormon founder Joseph Smith Jr. Members consecrate all their time, talents, wealth, and property to the furthering of religious freedom. This consecration is symbolized by their deeding all their property to the church. The church then deeds the property back to the donor, who serves as steward. Excess wealth is used by the church to support the poor.

The church is guided by a ministry graded into degrees from first to fourth, the latter being the highest level. The church is headed by its president, who serves a nine-year term. In 1984 Anne L. Zapf succeeded Trujillo as president of the church; she in turn was succeeded by Matthew Kent in 1993. Zapf continued as the apostle and secretary/treasurer of the church. The president and apostle are assisted by a board of stewards invited by the president to serve at the annual church membership meeting. The church is located on the 160 acres of land it owns in southern Arizona.

Membership: In 2001 the church conducted 52 Spirit Walks. There are 236 members.

Periodicals: *The Sacred Record.*

Sources:

Peyote Way Church of God. www.peyoteway.org/.

Garcia, Joseph. "Peyote: A Drug or a Sacrament?" *Tucson Citizen* (January 3, 1989).

Temple of the True Inner Light

For Information: Somae7@yahoo.com., New York, NY

The Temple of the True Inner Light is a small community centered in New York City that believes in and uses various psychedelic substances as a means to enlightenment. It was founded in 1980 by Alan Birnbaum as an offshoot of the New York City branch of the Native American Church. The Temple has a basic affirmation that the Psychedelic is the creator and that psychedelic substances are the true Flesh of God. This belief grows from the conclusion that religion and spiritual awakening originated from the ingestion of different psychedelic substances. The primary psychedelic used by temple members is di-propyl tryptamine (DPT), which is regarded as the actual manifestation of God, rather than a means to access God.

Archeologists and anthropologists have long noted that people have for centuries consumed mushrooms, marijuana, peyote, and other similar plants that produced visions and various experiences of a Higher Being. Thus, the Temple teaches that every true religion has at some time believed that psychedelics are the embodiment of God. The effect of psychedelic ingestion is the Light spoken of in scriptures and sacred texts. The Mexican Nahua tribe's word for psilocybin mushrooms was Teonanacatl, which means "God's Flesh."

This Higher Being (psychedelic substances) chooses messengers. Among those so chosen were Moses, David, Elijah, Jesus, Mary, Vishnu, Uma, Gautama, Mohammed, Mani, and Quetzacoatal.

Worship in the Temple is conducted in a private environment and consists largely of listening to tapes (which include readings of various religious texts) after ingesting DPT. The intent is to produce wisdom (gnosis) by reexamining what is considered inspired literature while under the influence of DPT.

While advocating for the free use of psychedelics, the temple also sponsors a non-profit charitable organization that supports the building of housing for low-income and street people, and helps people to detoxify from alcohol, opiates, and cocaine.

Membership: Not reported.

Sources:

Church of the True Inner Light. psychede.tripod.com.

Lyttle, T. "Drug-Based Religions and Contemporary Drug Taking." *Journal of Drug Issues* 18, 2 (1988): 271-284.

Pauli, Michelle. "The Temple of True Inner Light." 1997. Posted at www.csp.org/nicholas/A58.html.

Other Psychic New Age Groups

Afro-American Social Research Association

Box 2150, Jacksonville, FL 32203

The Afro-American Social Research Association was formed by a black man who has taken the religious name The Spirit of Truth. In the 1970s he began to receive messages from the creator, many of which were incorporated into a book, *The Spirit of Truth; Doom Days!*. The content of the messages was a warning and judgment, an important aspect of which was the instruction to do away with the monetary system. According to The Spirit of Truth, the earth was given as a divine inheritance, but in time the wicked took control of everyone's divine inheritance, partly by means of the monetary system. He has predicted an astronomic catastrophe in the near future, during which a comet will strike the moon, which will in turn strike the sun. The earth will then move out of orbit and take a new position in the center of the universe. Most of earth's people will be destroyed in the process, and a new world system, the United Countries of the Solar System, will then be established. The New Jerusalem will be built upon the exact spot where the first Jerusalem was built.

Membership: Not reported.

Alliance of Divine Love

PO Box 19612, West Palm Beach, FL 33416

The Alliance of Divine Love was founded by Rev. Dr. Barbara Selwa, who currently serves as the organization's president. It is a vehicle through which channels (helpers) present the teachings received from entities and realities (guides) beyond earth (i.e., the Organization of Light). The alliance teaches a philosophy of life that aims to inspire the soul, sharpen the mind, and make people the masters of their own destinies, and therefore better able to serve others. Followers seek to learn about and share the secrets of the purest kind of love that leaves no room for fear and perfects each person. The organization affirms that all of creation is linked through divine love's relationship, or alliance, with itself.

The alliance has a group of leaders whom it has trained and ordained. Ministers pursue a course of study published in two books, *Ever Closer* and *Even Closer*. Ministers are scattered across the United States, though the largest number are in Florida. Local centers serve as healing and counseling ministries designed to assist people in reaching the highest and best in all aspects of their lives.

Membership: Not reported. In 2002 there were 23 ministers in 15 states of the United States, two in the United Kingdom, and one in Australia.

Periodicals: *DaySpring.*

Sources:

Alliance of Divine Love. www.allianceofdivinelove.org/.

American Universalist Temple of Divine Wisdom
Current address not obtained for this edition.

The American Universalist Temple of Divine Wisdom was founded in 1966 by a group of esoteric Christians living in the vicinity of Escondido, California. It is known by followers as a Christ-centered point of light from which the love of God pours forth. They hold that it was prophesied on the Isle of Patmos by John the Revelator, who established the Order of the Golden Grail for the preservation of the original, unadulterated Christian doctrine of the inner life. The teachings of the temple are "clairsentiently" received from ascended beings, and the temple has instituted courses based upon the divine wisdom as a means of reaching sincere seekers of spiritual truth. The temple is governed by a board of trustees.

Membership: Not reported. In 1968 there were two centers, one in California and one in Chicago.

Sources:

American Universalist Temple of Divine Wisdom. www.esseneinvinciblelight.org/.

Aquarian Christine Church Universal
c/o Dr. Jacob Watson, 348 E. Lexington Ave., Danville, KY 40422

The Aquarian Christine Church Universal is a theosophical Gnostic Church whose teachings are centered on the Aquarian Gospel of Jesus the Christ "transcribed" in 1907 by Levi H. Dowling and published in 1911. Dowling understood the source of his work to be the Akashic Records, which theosophists conceive of as an all-encompassing reservoir of knowledge embedded in the cosmos that may be tapped into by more-conscious individuals. Through modern theosophy, and especially the "I AM" movement, the Aquarian Christine Church lays claim to the Gnostic Christian tradition (herein termed the Western Esoteric tradition), claims Jesus the Christ as Savior, and affirms the femininity of the Holy Spirit, the Mother God. As with the "I AM" tradition, the church believes in liberation from the cycle of rebirth through the Ascension process, and declares the existence of and a relation with the Ascended Masters.

The Aquarian Gospel is one of several volumes that have emerged in recent centuries that claim to tell the story of the so-called missing years not covered in the New Testament. According to the Aquarian Gospel, Jesus spent these years (ages 13 through 30) traveling in India, Tibet, Persia, Greece, and Egypt.

The church affirms God as a trinity of the Father, the Mother (Holy Spirit), and Christ, the Son. From the Trinity, seven Divine Spirits have emanated whom we know as seven archangels—Michael, Cassiel (Jophiel), Chamuel, Gabriel, Raphael, Uriel, and Zadkiel. Individual humans have a Divine Spirit, the "I AM" Spirit, which reincarnates in successive bodies. The cycle of reincarnation ends after a person accepts Christ or the Light and becomes One with God. The process of perfecting oneself through discipline and illumination is known as the Ascension.

The Aquarian Celestine Church has rejected much of what has been associated with the New Age movement, including channeling, astrology, and fortune telling. Members do engage in the systematic study of the religious symbolism of the sun, of the constellations of the zodiac, and of other celestial bodies, but not in a way that involves horoscopes or fortune telling. They also view spiritual talents-gifts such as intuitive and precognitive capabilities-as special gifts from God. Spiritual healing is a part of every worship service. As Keepers of the Omnific Word, the church offers members initiation into the knowledge of the Sacred Name of God.

The Aquarian Christine Church emphasizes the priesthood of all believers and considers all members to be ministers. The church does have, however, an unpaid ordained clergy, including several who are celibate, as monks and nuns. Church is identified with the fellowship of believers rather than a building and worship services may be held in members' homes or other informal places deemed suitable. Gatherings center on silent meditation rather than on set rituals. Outward sacraments have been replaced by what is termed *spiritual baptism*, seen as an "Immersion in the Light of God and Baptism in Fire and the Holy Spirit," and by

spiritual communion in which one "experiences the Christ within" through silent meditation.

In 2007 the church celebrated the centennial of the publication of the Aquarian Gospel by praying for World Peace.

Membership: Not reported.

Sources:

Aquarian Christine Church. www.aquarianchurch.zoomshare.com/.

Dowling, Levi. The Aquarian Gospel of Jesus the Christ. Los Angeles: Author, 1911.
    Rpt. Marina Del Rey, CA: DeVorss & Co, 1991.

Self Culture. Whitefish, MT: Kessinger, 2003.

Association for Research and Enlightenment
Atlantic Ave. at 76th St., Box 595, Virginia Beach, VA 23451

Edgar Cayce (1877–1945) was born and raised in Beverly, Kentucky. A deeply religious child, he cured himself of aphonia (inability to speak) at the age of 21, and over the years he developed a reputation for being able to help others, even at great distances, while in an altered state of consciousness.

For 22 years Cayce gave verifiably helped people to recover from scleroderma, psoriasis, and other diseases thought by most to be incurable, often working with physicians of various schools, including Dr. Andrew Still, the founder of osteopathy. Cayce, a gifted photographer, struggled with these abilities for many years. He had deep concerns about using his gifts, which had come to be known as "readings," and was uncertain of their place in his life.

In 1923, during a reading for Arthur Lammers, a theosophist, astrologer, and student of eastern religions, Cayce began to talk about reincarnation and to describe what he claimed were various individuals' past lives on earth. The "life readings," as these were called, became a new area of exploration. At the urging of others, he gave up photography and began giving readings full time. He died in Virginia Beach after a 44-year career, leaving behind 14,306 transcripts on nearly 6,000 indviduals. By the time of his death three organizations had been established relating to his work. The oldest, Atlantic University, chartered in 1930, currently offers a masters degree in Transpersonal Studies. The Association for Research and Enlightenment (A.R.E.), chartered in 1931, is an international membership organization that houses the A.R.E. Library, the largest parapsychological library in the United States. The A.R.E. publishes books on a wide variety of subjects through its A.R.E. Press; maintains a summer camp for children in Rural Retreat, Virginia; and administers the Harold J. Reilly School of Massotherapy, a health facility, and a host of educational programs in Virginia Beach and worldwide.

The Edgar Cayce Foundation, chartered in 1948, is the legal and physical custodian of the Cayce readings and their supporting documentation and memorabilia. The foundation computerized the readings in a seven-year project, culminating with the publication of the CD-ROM of the Edgar Cayce readings, which is sold through A.R.E. Press. The Edgar Cayce Foundation publishes medical and other studies through its research bulletin and special collections programs. An active preservation and acquisitions program enriches the foundation's holdings for researchers and authors. An annual historical event based on the life of Edgar Cayce is held each March in Hopkinsville, Kentucky, under the auspices of the Pennyroyal Area Museum, cosponsored by the Edgar Cayce Foundation.

Membership: In 2002 A.R.E. reported 22,000 members worldwide.

Educational Facilities:

Atlantic University, Virginia Beach, Virginia.

Harold J. Reilly School of Massotherapy, Virginia Beach, Virginia.

Periodicals: *Venture Inward*.

Remarks: The Association for Research and Enlightenment does not consider itself a religion. It is included in this volume because, like other organizations that do not consider themselves a religion (World Plan Executive Council, Ancient and Mystical Order of the Rosae Crucis), it meets the definition of religion used by this volume. A.R.E. does present through its publications a distinct spiritual-religious world-view, unique in its derivation from the Cayce readings, and a program of action analogous to the other groups and organizations included in this volume. Many of the members of the A.R.E. are also members of other churches and religious groups.

Sources:

Association for Research and Enlightenment. www.edgarcayce.org/.

Bro, Harmon Hartzell. *A Seer Out of Season: The Life of Edgar Cayce*. New York: New American Library, 1989.

Cayce, Hugh Lynn, ed. *The Edgar Cayce Reader*. 2 vols. New York: Paperback Library, 1969.

Johnson, K. Paul. *Edgar Cayce in Context: The Readings*. Albany, NY: State University of New York Press, 1998.

Smith, Robert A. *Hugh Lynn Cayce: About My Father's Business*. Norfolk, VA: Donning Company, 1988.

Stern, Jess. *Edgar Cayce, the Sleeping Prophet*. New York: Bantam Books, 1968.

———. *A Prophet in His Own Country: The Story of the Young Edgar Cayce*. New York: William Morrow, 1974.

Chirothesian Church of Faith

PO Box 1264, Port Orford, OR 97465

The Chirothesian Church of Faith was formed in 1917 in Los Angeles by the Rev. D. J. Bussell, its president and senior bishop. Chirothesia is described as a natural religion based on the original form of the law of God. A Chirothesian is one who observes and obeys the law of God. The law of God was laid down in the beginning and has always had its followers. It accepts Jesus as a modern messiah presenting the law of God in a more modern manner and adapting them to a more modern world. The four Gospels and the Books of James and Jude contain the presentation of the law, according to Chirothesians. The account of creation in Genesis illustrates the law of God: "A fully concentrated thought must produce its kind." Man was created according to this law. Man is body (earthly) and soul and spirit (godly). The physical part of man is to be subject to the intellectual part. As an expression of God, "Man becomes what he thinks." The way of the law is the way of harmony and indicates a way back for any who have missed the original plan. Practicing the law allows one to overcome discord, unrighteousness, and disease. Healing has been especially emphasized.

The Chirothesian Church does not proselytize, is not evangelistic, and does not invite membership. However, the church is open to those who seek membership, and most meetings are open to the public. Closed meetings are business meetings and classes, though prior sessions are necessary to understand the class subjects. Headquarters are in Los Angeles, with branch churches across the United States.

Membership: Not reported. In May 2008 the church had two congregations with 12 ministers.

Educational Facilities:

National Academy of Metaphysics, West Toluca Lake, California.

Sources:

Chirothesian Church of Faith. www.chirothesianchurchoffaith.org/.

Bussell, D. J. *Chirothesia*. Los Angeles: Chirothesian Church of Faith, n.d.

———. *Co-Ordinating Knowledge*. Los Angeles: National Academy of Metaphysics, n.d.

———. *First Steps in Metaphysics*. Los Angeles: National Academy of Metaphysics, n.d.

Garlichs, E. E. *The Life Beautiful*. Long Beach, CA: Aquarian Church of Chirothesia, [1946].

Church of Divine Man

c/o Berkeley Psychic Institute, 2018 Allston Way, Berkeley, CA 94704

The Church of Divine Man and the Berkeley Psychic Institute, its seminary work-shop, were founded in 1973 by the psychic Lewis Bostwick (1918–1995), the church's archbishop. As a psychic for many years, Bostwick saw the need for an organization in which others like himself could find community, validation for their work, and a spiritual atmosphere in which to work. There also was a need for the training and development of latent psychic gifts. Graduates of the institute may be ordained as ministers by the church, and during the first decade of its existence the church grew rapidly as newly ordained ministers began to spread out along the West Coast. The development of the church was spurred in 1976 by the opening of an affiliate in Seattle by Revs. Menuard Slusher and Mary Ellen Flora, bishops of the church in the Northwest. They established the Washington Psychic Institute, which now has branch centers in Oregon. The Washington group separated from the California organization and became an independent church with the same name. Graduate ministers formed their own churches in other cities, states, and nations.

The church is not doctrinally oriented and is very loosely organized. Its creed affirms "psychic freedom" and decries the need for ideologies and dissenting philosophies that divide and destroy communication. It stresses living the mystic life in the inward infinity and cosmic consciousness. Its tenets are based upon the miracles of Jesus and his declaration, "What I can do, you can do and greater things than these shall you do." The church accepts the realm of psychic reality, and the institute, which functions as the church's seminary, offers courses in the wide variety of psychic experience—healing, meditation, kundalini energy, aura reading, and related topics. A clairvoyant intensive religious training course is offered for those who wish to pursue a career as a minister. Reincarnation is accepted, and many of the psychic readers specialize in past-life readings.

In 1980 the church launched a periodical, *This Is Your Psychic Life*, and in the following year nurtured the independent incorporation of the Deja Vu Publishing Company to manage its production. The magazine was discontinued in 1986 and replaced by a monthly newspaper, *The Psychic Reader*.

Membership: In 1998 the Berkeley Psychic Institute reported branches in Berkeley, Santa Rosa, Mountain View, Marin, Sacramento, and Pleasanton, California. The Church of Divine Man is affiliated with the Church of the Rose/Southern California Psychic Institute in Anaheim, California. The Institute reported more than 3,500 graduates. More than 50,000 associate members have completed beginning clairvoyant training classes in psychic meditation and healing.

Educational Facilities:

Berkeley Psychic Institute, Berkeley, California.

Church of Scientology

c/o Church of Scientology International, 6331 Hollywood Blvd., Ste. 1200, Los Angeles, CA 90028-6329

Few of the new religious bodies of the 1950s and 1960s have grown as much as the Church of Scientology, first founded in Los Angeles, California, in 1954. Due to its fast growth and its new teachings and methods (its religious technology, as it's called in the church), it has become the target of attacks and controversy, not unlike other new religious movements. In the face of controversy, the church has aggressively defended its rights and vigorously worked to correct false statements and refute false charges about itself, its teachings, and the founder of Scientology, L. Ron Hubbard (1911–1986).

L. Ron Hubbard first became a public figure as an explorer and adventure/fiction writer, becoming most widely known through his science fiction books and stories. As early as 1949 he had established a small organization to help him respond to inquiries concerning his emerging ideas about human mental processes. In 1950 he published *Dianetics: The Modern Science of Mental Health*. The book became a bestseller, selling more than 18 million copies. It is still a basic text of the present Church of Scientology.

Hubbard wanted to offer Dianetics as a mental health discipline, so in summer 1950 in Washington, D.C., he made a presentation to a group of psychiatrists and educators. Shortly afterwards, the American Psychological Association called on psychologists not to use Dianetics therapy; the American Medical Association also rejected its use. During this period, which Scientologists view as a time of persecution motivated by self-interests, Hubbard continued his research, lectured, and helped establish Dianetic Research Foundations in Los Angeles and in Wichita, Kansas, while at the same time dealing with disputes within the organization. More importantly, he continued to expand the more practical and mundane areas covered by Dianetics into the more metaphysical speculations that became Scientology. Finally, in 1954, as other churches were established, Scientologists in Los Angeles founded the Church of Scientology. (This first church became the Church of Scientology of California.) Scientology is the logical extension of Dianetics. While Scientology was being outlined and the church being founded, Hubbard moved to Washington, D.C., where the Founding Church of Scientology of Washington, D.C., was established in 1955. This evolution of the movement produced a new religion.

Beliefs: Dianetics theory, though expressed in scientific terms, is core religious doctrine in Scientology. It describes the source of all psychosomatic ills and human aberrations. Hubbard postulates the existence of the mind in two aspects. The Analytical Mind perceives, reasons, and remembers. The Reactive Mind simply records "engrams," completely detailed impressions of perceptions present in a past moment of pain and unconsciousness. (Other moments of severe loss or trauma can be recorded in the Reactive Mind, but draw their aberrative effects from the engrams.) Significant engrams are located by the fetus before birth at moments when the mother is experiencing injury or severe stress or trauma, such as an attempted abortion or a blow to the mother's stomach. *Dianetics: The Modern Science of Mental Heath* outlined techniques for helping people to discover and rid themselves of engrams (and thus aberrations). A person who has rid himself or herself of all engrams is called a Clear. One becomes clear by going through a series or courses leading to self-discovery, and through a process called auditing. Auditing is the application of Dianetics and/or Scientology technologies to an individual by a practitioner trained in the use of the E-meter. The auditor takes him through various drills, all aimed at freeing one from engrams.

Either before or after receiving Dianetics, one proceeds to various levels of Scientology. Scientology is concerned with the isolation, description, handling, and rehabilitation of the human spirit. Hubbard discovered the means of separating personality from the body and the mind (a process called "exteriorization," not to be confused with astral travel). This personality, or the being himself, which is separate from the body and mind, is called the "thetan," after the Greek letter theta. The thetan has the power to create MEST, that is, Matter, Energy, Space, and Time, or the basic elements of existence. In Scientology terminology, a highly aware thetan who has the ability to handle the affairs of life in this exterior state is called an "Operating Thetan." The thetan has lived and can continue to live through a series of lifetimes. The church's beliefs are presented in the christening ceremony, which is seen as a means to get the thetan oriented after its taking over a new body.

The religious credentials of Scientology frequently have been questioned in courts in the United States and around the world. Overwhelmingly, in most countrie Scientology has been acknowledged as a new religion, and the church established as a legal entity. These court victories have had important implications for Scientology, as different countries grant religious rights and privileges only to such legally established religious bodies. They have also served to establish the church's religious bona fides.

Organization: General oversight of the church and Scientology is invested in Church of Scientology International, headquartered in Los Angeles. It is accorded a variety of tasks, not the least of which is ensuring that Scientology churches follow the strict procedures prescribed in the various books written by Hubbard or issued by the church. The office charters various churches, missions (small parishes), and other units of the church.

Over the years, the church and individual Scientologists have been deeply involved with social concerns, founding new organizations (many now independent): Narconon (drug rehabilitation), the Citizens Commission on Human Rights, American Citizens for Honesty in Government, Applied Scholastics, and the National Commission of Law Enforcement and Social Justice.

There are senior churches in the United States, Great Britain, Europe, and Australia that deliver the advanced levels of Scientology instruction and counseling (auditing). One of these, the Flag Service Organization, is an advanced religious retreat maintained in Clearwater, Florida. It is traditionally called "Flag" because of the years this retreat was located on the ocean-going ship *Apollo*, and nicknamed Flag because it was the flagship headquarters for the Sea Organization. The Sea Organization is an elite fraternity of Scientology staff who supported Hubbard in his continuing research and development of Scientology. The top management of the church is composed of Sea Organization members; they continue to operate an ocean-going mission for advanced Scientology courses. A separate Scientology church, Religious Technology Center, preserves, maintains, and protects the Scientology religion against misuse or misinterpretation. It is not involved in the day-to-day affairs of Scientology churches or ecclesiastical management. Its sole concern is ensuring the orthodoxy of the practice of the religion.

Membership: In 2002 the church reported more than 3,000 churches, missions, and affiliated groups located in 153 countries serving more than eight million members. Church officials have noted that the membership figure is a cumulative figure of all those who have participated in church activities over the years of its existence. Current active membership is estimated as closer to 500,000. L. Ron Hubbard's books have sold more than 100 million copies and have been translated into 53 languages.

Periodicals: *Freedom*. • *Advance*. Available from Advanced Organization of Los Angeles, 1306 L. Ron Hubbard Way, Los Angeles, CA 90027. • *Cause*. Available from the American Saint Hill Organization, 1413 L. Ron Hubbard Way, Los Angeles, CA 90027. • *Source*. Available from the Church of Scientology Flag Service Org., PO Box 31751, Tampa, FL 33631-3751.

Remarks: Controversy has followed the church since its founding in 1954, beginning when the new Dianetics techniques ran head-long into the established practices of psychiatry and medicine. At the urging of psychiatric and mental health organizations, some western governments became hostile to Scientology. In 1963 officers of the U.S. Food and Drug Administration raided the Washington, D.C., church and seized all of its E-Meters. It wasn't until 1969 that a court ruled that E-Meters and auditing were valid religiously and the confiscated E-Meters and books were returned.

In 1968 the British Home Office placed a restriction on all non-English nationals who were entering the country just to study or practice Scientology. This ban was later relaxed in practice, and was officially lifted in July 1980. The 1965 ban on Scientology by the Australian government led to a lengthy legal battle that was resolved in the church's favor in 1983 by the Australian High Court. (This landmark decision drew upon many U.S. legal precedents and defined "religious freedom" for the first time in Australia.)

A pattern repeated frequently in the Scientology controversies has been strong assertions against the church (or Hubbard), followed by press exposure, lawsuits, and attempts to clearly establish the falsity of the original assertions. Such assertions filled several early books on Scientology. The church also has been raided several times by government agencies. Partly in response to the build-up of documents concerning the church in various government files (the direct cause of some raids), the church has become one of the most vigorous users of the Freedom of Information Act (FOIA). The church has even published a booklet aimed at helping individuals and church members gain access to files on themselves through the FOIA.

During the 1970s the church used a variety of legal procedures to stop government action (particularly action by the U.S. Internal Revenue Service) against it and to defend itself against the attacks of hostile ex-members and other opponents. In the 1970s the church won most legal cases, but during the first half of the 1980s the church suffered some major defeats. Criminal charges filed against a few church leaders and staff following a raid of church offices in 1977 led eventually to their convictions. Those sentenced for stealing government documents included the church's top administrative official, Guardian Jane Kember, and Hubbard's wife, Mary Sue Hubbard. In 1981 the church reformed the Guardian's Office and then dissolved it altogether. In 1984 the Church of Scientology of California's tax-exempt status was revoked in a federal tax court decision. The trial, which highlighted the financial dealings of the church, created a significant amount of bad publicity, and led the church to place ads in newspapers asking for those with information on illegal actions by the Internal Revenue Service to come forward (some current and former IRS employees and agents did report abuses by the IRS.) Most of the other U.S. Scientology churches are recognized as tax-exempt religious organizations.

During the 1980s two juries awarded multimillion-dollar judgments against the church. In the case of ex-member Julie Christofferson, the court ruled that the original trial violated the church's religious freedom. The case was heard again and resulted in a mistrial. Eventually, the case was settled out of court. In a second case, a large judgment was given to ex-member Larry Wollershein. The case went through a lengthy judicatory process and he received a judgment of $2.4 million in 1994; in 2002 the church ended years of negotiation over the amount by paying Wollershein $8.6 million ($2.4 million plus interest).

During the 1990s the church spent a considerable amount of time dealing with copyright and Internet issues, most of which were related to several former members who attempted to reproduce and circulate copyrighted church materials, especially the confidential materials reserved for members who had attained the higher OT levels. In the cases, the church largely prevailed, though it is still plagued by web sites from countries whose attention to international copyright laws differ from those in the United States.

Among the most important court cases that the church became involved with concerned the former Cult Awareness Network (CAN). In 1995 CAN, an activist organization that practices coercive deprogramming of members of cults, was implicated in a suit brought by a member of a Pentecostal church against three persons who had kidnapped him and tried to deprogram him. The court ruled against CAN, fining it $1 million and thus forcing it into bankruptcy. A lawyer who hadworked with the Church of Scientology for many years represented the plaintiff. As a result of the suit, a coalition of groups that CAN had branded as "cults," pooled funds and bought CAN's assets, including its name, logo, 800-number, library, and files. These were subsequently moved to Los Angeles, where a new CAN has operated since 1997.

Sources:

Church of Scientology. www.scientology.org/.

Church of Scientology. *Scientology: A World Religion Emerges in the Space Age*. Los Angeles: Church of Scientology Information Service, Department of Archives, 1974.

———. *Scientology, What Is It?* Los Angeles: Church of Scientology International, 1988.

———. *What Is Scientology?* Los Angeles: Church of Scientology of California, 1978.

Hubbard, L. Ron. *Dianetics, The Modern Science of Mental Health*. New York: Hermitage House, 1950.

Meldal-Johnson, Trevor, and Patrick Lusey. *The Truth about Scientology*. New York: Tempo Books, 1980.

Wallis, Roy. *The Road to Total Freedom*. New York: Columbia University Press, 1977.

Congregational Church of Practical Theology
31916 University Cir., Springfield, LA 70462

The Congregational Church of Practical Theology was formed in 1969 by Dr. E. Arthur Winkler (d. 1998), a former United Church of Christ and United Methodist minister. The church has no creeds, though there is a set of beliefs that members and ministers are asked to use as guidelines for individual spiritual search. God is seen as continually revealing Himself in the open-minded search for truth. The Bible is a textbook for truth, but not the final word. Jesus is divine, but each person is also a divine child of God. The theology is practical and seeks to apply religion to all of life. The dignity of all people is affirmed; service to individuals and society is extolled. Ministers are seen as catalysts to the spiritual quest of individuals.

The church was founded not for the purpose of establishing congregations (though it has chartered a number of congregations), but to provide a ministry of guidance for all people who seek its varied forms of ministry, as well as to promote the dignity and love of all humankind—people of all colors, races, religions, social backgrounds, and economic levels. Ministers are ordained for the purpose of putting their religion into action in all areas of their lives. Ministers are not necessarily pastors of congregations; they may be counselors, psychologists, medical doctors, hypnotherapists, lawyers, law officers, or in any other occupation—the church believes that ministers are needed in all professions. Affiliated with the church are the American Counselor's Society and the National Society of Clinical Hypnotherapists, both professional associations headquartered in Springfield, Louisiana.

Membership: In 1988 the church reported 251 ministers and 34 chartered congregations. Membership figures are not kept. Affiliated members can be found in Canada, Sweden, the West Indies, and Africa.

Educational Facilities:

St. John's University, Springfield, Louisiana.

Periodicals: *Attain: Health, Happiness and Success • Minister's Tips.*

Sources:

The Congregational Church of Practical Theology. Springfield, LA: Congregational Church, n.d.

Winkler, Arthur. *Hypnotherapy*. Valley, NB: Eastern Nebraska Christian College, 1972.

———. *New Age Minister's Manual*. Springfield, LA: St. John's University Publications, 1994.

Coptic Fellowship of America
1735 Pinnacle Dr. SW, Wyoming, MI 49509-1339

The Coptic Fellowship of America was founded in Los Angeles, California, in 1937 by Hamid Bey (d. 1976). Bey was born in Egypt and, as a five-year-old child, met the masters of the hidden temples of the Christian religion. According to Bey, due to persecution and the destruction of early Christian temples, Christians built many hidden temples, the most important of which is the Head Masters Temple on the Nile River, which is headed by the Great Eleven Ring Master. Bey was sent to be educated in one such temple, where he was trained in self-control, in how to subdue the body, concentration, the essentials of personality, and clairvoyance. Having finished his temple education, Bey was sent to the United States to show that Harry Houdini's claim to be able to reproduce any occult phenomenon was false. Although Houdini died soon after Bey's arrival, Bey stayed to tour the country, demonstrating his yogic abilities, particularly the feat of being buried for several hours.

The Coptic Fellowship teaches an esoteric Christianity—the laws of successful balanced living. The universe expresses polarity, and eastern and western civilizations are manifestations of the polarity. Nature is the handiwork of the creator, and humankind is the epitome of creation. Man's purpose is to bring into manifestation latent potential powers of conscious awareness—cosmic consciousness. Christ was one of the major teachers of the one law, and he beheld the law more completely than any other master. In Christ, we see the essentials of the upward path—health of the physical body, work, science, and love. It is the belief of the fellowship that truth is eternal and eternally available. All of life, creation, progress, and evolution emanate from God's love, the same reality that leads humans and societies to perfection. Individual souls grow through a continuous progression (reincarnation and karma), but are often hidden from truth by ignorance and misdirection.

During the 1970s the fellowship became aligned to the New Age movement, and saw its work as a catalyst in the transformation to a new planetary civilization the Spiritual Unity of Nations (SUN). SUN was founded in England by Joseph Busby to unite spiritual powers to bring about a worldwide spiritual bonding of nations. SUN's U.S. headquarters are located at the fellowship's headquarters.

Bey was succeeded as head of the fellowship by John Davis, formerly its Midwest director. The fellowship is guided by a board of directors. Work within the fellowship is divided among three orders: the Light Ministry, a body of teachers who publicly disseminate the orders' teachings, often through opening centers; the World Service Order; and the Devotional Order, an inner order of people who follow a meditative discipline. Correspondence lessons are offered for new members.

Membership: In 1992 the fellowship reported 3,500 members in several centers in the United States. There is one branch center in Nigeria. Most members are not affiliated with a center.

Sources:

Coptic Fellowship of America. www.coptic-sun.org.

Bey, Hamid. *My Experiences Preceding 5,000 Burials*. Los Angeles: Coptic Fellowship of America, 1951.

Embassy of the Gheez-Americans
Mt. Helion Sanctuary, Rock Valley Rd., Box 53, Long Eddy, NY 12760

The Embassy of the Gheez-Americans is headed by Empress Mysikiitta Fa Senntao, who runs the Mt. Helion Sanctuary at Long Eddy, New York. She also holds the title Ambassadress of the Sun God and Resurrector of the Gheez-Nation [Ethiopia]. She is believed to have come from the sun in a spaceship, leaving her husband behind and taking over a human body upon arrival. Her mission is to redeem her people, who have been lost on earth for thousands of years and during that time have been reincarnated in many nationalities.

According to the empress, Satan and his brother, Tao, the god of love, fought for control of earth. After man chose the tree of good and evil in the Garden of Eden, Satan took control, and the tree of life (wisdom) was hidden among the few occult. Taoism, the wisdom of eternal life, came to Ethiopia at the beginning of the Age of Taurus. From there, it went to Egypt and survived the flood with Noah. Of Noah's sons, only one, Ham, accepted the ministry of the wisdom, a burden Hamites have had to bear. With Egyptian decline, Abraham and Israel were chosen to be the custodians of the wisdom. When Moses saw his people worshipping Taurus, he knew they were unable to keep the law, and he gave them a lesser law.

The empress calls together the ancient Gheez-Nation. Members are united by a common language (Gheez), a history, a culture, and a cosmic link of God. Her Majesty has bound Satan on the planet Uranus. The chosen people, the Gheez-Nation, will become the leaven in lifting all of humanity. Members of new nation learn the Gheez language, engage in ecstatic dancing, and practice the martial arts of the priest Kurahti. Most members are black. Her Majesty functions as a psychic and a teacher of occult wisdom.

Membership: Not reported.

Emissaries of Divine Light
100 Sunrise Ranch Rd., Loveland, CO 80538

The Emissaries of Divine Light was formed in 1932 in Tennessee by Lloyd Arthur Meeker (1909–1954). Meeker, who wrote under the penname Uranda, established Sunrise Ranch, a community and home base of the Emissaries, in rural Colorado, near Loveland. He was succeeded by Martin Cecil (1909–1988). In 1954 a second community was begun at 100 Mile House, British Columbia.

The basic stance of the Emissaries is spelled out in a pamphlet, "The Divine Design." According to the Emissaries, man was created in the image and likeness of the body of God, that is, he was created to manifest the divine design. God is the one focus of all being. Distortions appear when the mind allows evil influences (fear, hate, jealousy, anger, resentment, etc.) to gain control. Because man has free will, his mind can select the influences that will be allowed to enter and control his body. The mind can choose to accept divine control.

Collectively, mankind manifests the distortions of evil influences in societal problems. But the return to divine control is the immediate possibility of every individual. The re-emergence of the divine design is called healing. Ontology, defined as the science of true being, is the art of manifesting reality in the world of chaos. That reality (God) manifests as truth (the design of form) and love (the power of life). Form is constantly in process, a fact that allows for healing.

A goal of the Emissaries is to experience reality, to know the identity of one's true being, to know oneness. The experience of oneness is an experience of the image and likeness of God in the present, without reference to past or future.

The Emissaries are based in 12 communities around the world and also have 160 meeting locations in 23 countries. The Emissaries do not proselytize. Members have been active in cooperative activities with other groups of like mind and purpose. One structure for such cooperative endeavor is Emissary Foundation International, which supports a variety of programs such as the Association for Responsible Communication, Renaissance Business Associates, Renaissance Educational Associates, the Stewardship Community, and Whole Health Institute.

Membership: In 1988 the Emissaries reported approximately 3,000 people closely affiliated worldwide.

Periodicals: *Integrity International*.

Sources:

Emissaries of Divine Light. www.emissaries.org/.

Aumra. *As of a Trumpet*. Loveland, CO: Eden Valley Press, 1968.

Cecil, Lord Martin. *Being Where You Are*. New Canaan, CT: Keats Publishing, 1974.

———. *On Eagle's Wings*. New York: Two Continents Publishing Group, 1977.

Cecil, Michael, et al. *Spirit of Sunrise*. London: Mitre Press, 1979.

Exeter, Martin. *Beyond Belief: Insights to the Way It Is*. Loveland, CO: Foundation House Publications, 1986.

———. *Thus It Is*. Denver, CO: Foundation House Publications, 1989.

Essene Fellowship of Peace/Spiritual Church of Ataraxia
Current address not obtained for this edition.

The Essene Fellowship of Peace and the Spiritual Church of Ataraxia are two names for the same organization established in 1942. *Ataraxia* is a Greek word meaning "house of peace." The church believes in God as the One Source, Law, Light, and Love and asserts that humans are spiritual beings. Jesus is considered the Wayshower, though the path he shows manifests quite differently for each person.

According to the church, individuals live on after death and their possibilities for further development and unfoldment are limitless. To assist in their development, help from the higher planes is available. The door to reformation is never closed.

Three members of the church, George and Mary Deia Weddell and Miriam B. Willis, have put together a book, *Creative Color*, which discusses the various esoteric meanings of color and how to put color to practical use in one's life. Color is seen as a means to better understanding one's relationship with oneself, others, and God. Mary Weddell claims a divine origin for the teachings and believes that they were given to her for the betterment of humankind. This volume has become a major instrument in the church's attempts to reach the public.

Membership: Not reported.

Sources:

Essene Fellowship of Peace. www.creativecolor.org/.

Creative Color. Hemet, CA: Fellowship of Peace, 1989. 204 pp.

Essene Foundation/Neo-Essene Community

c/o Emanuel Winocur, 399 Compass Rd., Oceanside, CA 92054

The Neo-Essene Community (also previously known as the Essene Foundation and the First Christians' Essene Church) was founded in 1937 as the Essene School, the name by which it was known until the mid-1980s. Its founder was Edmond Bordeaux Székely (d. 1980), a descendent of Hungarian royalty, world traveler, and author-scholar. In the 1920s, Székely claimed to have discovered an ancient manuscript that purported to be a collection of Jesus' teachings as written down by his disciple John in the original Aramaic (the language Jesus actually spoke). In 1937, Székely published the translation of part of the text as *The Essene Gospel of Peace*. (The remainder of the text was published in four subsequent volumes beginning in 1971.) Soon afterward he founded several cooperatives in southern France, whose members attempted to follow the Essene way. It was Székely's belief that Jesus was a member of the Essene brotherhood, and hence the first Christians were Essenes.

In 1939, forced out of Europe by the rise of Hitler, Székely settled in Tecate, a town in Mexico just across the border from San Diego, California. He opened the Essene School on his ranch estate in Mexico and eventually became a Mexican citizen. The school attempted to teach broad Essene concepts, including the essence of healthful life, which he had termed biogenic living. The center, Rancho La Puerta, became famous as a health spa and attracted many of the wealthy and famous. A second center, the Golden Door, was opened in Escondido, California, in 1958 and also became well known as a health and beauty center, attracting many movie stars. During the remainder of his life, Székely continued to travel widely and authored numerous books expounding on the Essene ideal as he had come to understand it. He founded the International Biogenic Society to perpetuate his teachings on healthful living and the Academy of Creative Living, which published many of his books. For many years he edited *The Essene Quarterly*, the school's periodical.

Following Székely's death, the Essene School was reorganized as the First Christians' Essene Church under the leadership of Garry A. White (d. 2007), a longtime colleague of Székely's.

Beliefs are summarized in the church's creed, which affirms the fatherhood of God, the motherhood of Nature, and the brotherhood of Man, and advocates a natural, creative lifestyle. Members are encouraged to follow a path to enlightenment that begins in developing physical, mental, and emotional health. Vegetarianism is advocated, as is the use of natural foods. A form of daily meditation, the "Essene Communions," which exemplify the unity between humans and the visible and invisible universe, is taught. It is the church's opinion that the discovery of the Dead Sea Scrolls has strengthened their claims about the Essene nature of early Christianity, and the Scrolls are cited as authoritative texts from which church teachings are derived.

In the mid-1990s the organization's corporate name was changed to the Essene Foundation, with the First Christian's Essene Church existing as its mother church. In 1992 Garry White retired as archbishop and was succeeded by Dr. Emanuel M. Winocur. White was named patriarch of the church. The foundation has a number of affiliated missions scattered across the West Coast of the United States (California, Oregon, Arizona), New York, and Arkansas.

Since assuming leadership of the movement, Dr. Winocur has spoken of it as the Neo-Essene Community. A primary structure of the community is the Enchanted Garden, one of its ministries headed by Leslie Goldman. Goldman sees gardening as a model for growing a new human society.

Holistic healing continues to be a primary concern in the Neo-Essene Community. Study groups sponsored by the foundation emphasize the importance of the purity of every body, beginning with a strict avoidance of flesh eating, emotional equanimity, mental clarity, and spiritual awareness. Among the prominent members is Bp. Patricia Bragg, the daughter of the famous naturopathic physician Paul Bragg.

Membership: The church is not a membership organization. It estimates that as many as three million people worldwide follow the Essene way of life.

Remarks: A serious charge of fraud was leveled at Székely concerning the two original manuscripts from which *The Essene Gospel of Peace* was translated, one of which (in Aramaic) he claimed was to be found in the Vatican Library and the other of which (in Old Slavonic) was reportedly in the library of the Hapsburg emperors in Vienna. After diligent searches, neither manuscript has been located, and doubt has been expressed about their existence. On the other hand, Bp. Purcell Weaver, a longtime associate of Székely's, testifies to having assisted in the complicated process of producing the English translation.

Sources:

Enchanted Gardner. www.lesliegoldman.com/.

Enchanted Gardner blog. www.curezone.com/blogs/fm.asp?i=970177.

Beskow, Per. *Strange Tales about Jesus*. Philadelphia: Fortress Press, 1983.

Mazzanti, Deborah Székely. *Secrets of the Golden Door*. New York: William Morrow & Co., 1977.

Székely, Edmond Bordeaux. *The Essene Gospel of Peace*. San Diego, CA: Academy of Creative Living, 1971.

————. *The Essene Way: Biogenic Living*. Cartago, Costa Rica: International Biogenic Society, 1978.

————. *Talks*. San Diego, CA: Academy of Creative Living, 1972.

Essene New Life Church

515 Pony Trail Dr., Mount Shasta, CA 96067-9063

The Essene New Life Church, founded by Charles A. Thomas in 1993, is one of several groups to emerge from the presentation of "Essene" teachings by Edmond Bordeaux Székely (d. 1980). In his many writings, Székely presented what he purported to be the teachings of the ancient Essene community that lived in Palestine in the days immediately before and after the time of Jesus. In addition, Székely founded several health spas that perpetuated the teachings on healthy living, including those stressing the importance of maintaining a vegetarian diet.

The church was founded to allow the ordination of those ministers who are well versed in the teachings of the ancient Essenes as set forth in Székely's books, especially the four books of *The Essene Gospel of Peace* and in *From Enoch to the Dead Sea Scrolls*. Ordination is offered to those who are properly trained in the church's doctrines and tenets, and in its essential practice, healing by touch or subtle energy healing. The church is especially open to independent healers who currently do their work without the legal cover of ministerial credentials. Instruction in the Essene teachings are presented in a correspondence study course and in two books, the *Essene New Life Church Manual* and the *Interfaith Minister's Manual*.

The church emphasizes that it is not an "ordination by mail" institution. The Essene New Life Church of Lake Wales, Florida, certifies the correspondence course and ordination follows only after completion of the course.

The church is dedicated to the defense of the First Amendment and believes that people are entitled to worship God in their own way. Church members and ministers locate their unity in the Creator, God.

The church is intimately associated with the Awareness Institute for Alternative Learning, a store that offers a wide variety of books, New Age materials, and holistic health supplies for sale.

Membership: Not reported.

Essene Order of Light

c/o The Tree of Life Rejuvenation Center, PO Box 1080, Patagonia, AZ 85624

As a child, Gabriel Cousens, the founder of the Essene Order of Light, experienced visions of what he came to regard as the White Brotherhood, also known as the Essene Elders or Order of Melchizedek. As a young man, he began teaching meditation, adopted a vegetarian diet, and began a study of the Essene Way that included a focus on Kabbalah, yoga, and *kundalini* (the energy believed by Tantric Hindus to reside at the base of the spine and to bring enlightenment when awakened). In 1975, in a meeting with Swami Muktananda, he experienced a profound kundalini awakening. During his seven years with Muktananda in India, Cousens sought a vegetarian diet that would support the awakening of the kundalini. He concluded that a live-food diet (the Rainbow diet) most nurtures spiritual growth. He also worked with Dr. Lee Sannella to assist people who had become unbalanced as a result of their kundalini experience.

In 1981 Cousens returned to the United States and revived his interest in the Essene Way. He studied Essene teachings and was ordained in 1988. He also became a Reiki master. Cousens founded the Essene Order of Light in 1992. In 1994, during a lengthy fast, he had an experience of the Tetragammaton, the holy name of God (in Hebrew). During this experience, four principles of the Living Essene Way were given to him and he in turn offered these to the other Essene groups to serve as a common understanding between them.

Through dissemination of the Essene teachings, meditation, and the imparting of *shaktipat* (spiritual power or methods) for achieving kundalini awakening, the Essene Order of Light seeks to serve as a force for the healing and transformation of the planet. Its Tree of Life Rejuvenation Center, located in Patagonia, Arizona, and directed by Cousens, attempts to guide people into the joy of sacred existence through the study of various traditions, including Kabbalah, Shamanic Judaism, the Essene Way, Yoga, and the Native American Way. The center introduces people to a spectrum of spiritual practices, including Shaktipat/Ruah Ha Kodesh meditation, Shamanic Shabbat celebrations, daily sunset meditations, Yoga, pranayama, Yogic chanting, spiritual fasts, sweat lodges, spiritual discussions, Kosher live-food nutrition, and a variety of self-healing workshops.

The order offers a course that leads to ordination as an Essene minister. This course includes a reading program and participation in various workshops and events held at the Tree of Life Rejuvenation Center. Ministers work in various service projects that bring humanitarian assistance (natural healing, vegetarian food, clothing for the poor) to the needy. The order sponsors quarterly peace meditation events at the United Nations headquarters in New York.

Membership: Not reported.

Sources:

Tree of Life Rejuvenation Center. www.treeoflife.nu/.

Cousens, Gabriel. *Conscious Eating*. Berkeley, CA: North Atlantic Books, 2000.

———. *Spiritual Nutrition and the Rainbow Diet*. San Rafael, CA: Cassandra Press, 1987.

———, with Mark Mayell. *Depression-Free for Life: A Physician's All-Natural, 5-Step Plan*. San Francisco: Quill, 2001.

Essenes of Arkashea

21450 SW 240th St., Homestead, FL 33031

The Essenes of Arkashea claim a heritage dating to an ancient order founded by Pharaoh Akhenaten in the year 1354 B.C.E.. Akhenaten is famous for his belief in one God (as opposed to the polytheism of the older Egyptian tradition) and his attempt to suppress the old religions in favor of his new faith. He was eventually murdered and much of his work was destroyed by his successors. After his death many of his followers fled Egypt. The Essenes of the Monastery of Arkashea believe that members of their order and many other tribes of the land of Hebron reentered Egypt and became laborers for the pharaohs. The Essenes of the first century CE were derived from Pharaoh Akhenaten's "Great White Brotherhood."

The modern Essenes of the Monastery of Arkashea claim that the original Egyptian order has survived secretly over the centuries, and that they are part of it. This secret original order is called the "Great White Brotherhood." The Monastery of Arkashea became publicly known only in 1993 with the publication of *The Discovery*, the story of a woman's discovery of and initiation into the order in the 1980s. She had found its monastery, that at the time was located in Alabama. In 2008 the order was headed by Reginald Therrien, the regent of Arkashea, who offers service to the public as a psychic counselor. The second officer, called the coregent, is Tim Marks; the governor of the commonwealth was Wayne Montgomery; and the head of the cloister, called the high priest of the cloister, was Stevens Damsky.

The term *Arkashea* refers to the history of what each individual has done as he or she reincarnates from life to life. The Essenes of the Monastery of Arkashea attempt to explore the history that is written within each person and use the Arkashean way of life as a tool for change toward self-realization via the process of understanding, forgiving, and loving. Thus the resident members of the Essenes of the Monastery of Arkashea study themselves, learning their lessons through a series of teachings called the "Weave of Maya Speaks." The wisdom they gain is used to free themselves from the mire of Maya (illusion). To assist in this process, the monastery publishes a series of monographs that teach the "Laws of Creation," which affect every aspect of man's existence.

The Monastery of Arkashea is both a community for members and a place from which they offer assistance to people. It has two main parts: The Cloister is for residents who have taken vows of poverty and celibacy, and the Commonwealth is for that part of the membership who do not assume a celibate life. The Hamlet is a section of the Commonwealth for people who have taken a vow of poverty but not of celibacy, so they can marry and have children. The Hoblet is a section of the Commonwealth that receives new arrivals at the monastery and introduces people to the Essenes' teachings; people who want to affiliate with the monastery but do not want to take vows of poverty or chastity remain affiliated through the Hoblet. The Magic Circle is a for-profit corporation that was designed to raise funds for the monastery.

Membership: Enrollment information is kept private. Membership includes people across North America and in several foreign countries.

Sources:

Essenes of Arkashea. arkashea.org.

Nier, Susan. *The Discovery*. Homestead, FL: Golden Scribe Press, 1993.

Foundation Faith of God

c/o Best Friends Animal Society, 5001 Angel Canyon Rd., Kanab, UT 84741-5000

In 1974 the majority of the leaders of the Process Church of the Final Judgment rejected the direction being taken by Process prophet Robert de Grimston, withdrew their support, and reorganized as a new church. Initially known as the Foundation Church of the Millennium, this church has subsequently progressed through several doctrinal changes and internal reorganizations that have been reflected in changes of name, first to the Foundation Faith of the Millennium (1977) and then to the church's present name, the Foundation Faith of God (1980).

Dissatisfaction with the growing emphasis on what was perceived as an esoteric, somewhat gnostic, doctrine of the unity of Christ and Satan was the immediate problem leading to the break with de Grimston and the formation of a new church. The hierarchical order of the Process Church was retained. Heading the Faith was a nine-member Council of Luminaries who in turn delegate temporal administration to the Office of the Faithful. Ministers are ranked from *luminaries* and *celebrants* (both ordained) to *mentors* and *covenanters*. Those preparing for the ministry are termed *witnesses*. Laity is composed of *aides* and *disciples*. The uniforms of the Process Church, consisting of a blue suit with a white shirt, so evident in the 1970s, were largely abandoned.

The church, always possessed of a strong emphasis on Christian themes, has moved steadily toward an orthodox Christian belief, incorporating belief in the Trinity, the deity of Jesus, salvation from sin, the necessity of the new birth, and the Second Advent. There is also a strong emphasis on the impending Second Coming of Christ and the establishment of the Kingdom of God.

The church established centers and missions across the United States, and also spread its message through prayer fellowship and outreach ministries. For a time, it also operated a wide array of social programs, conceived as part of a healing ministry. During the early 1980s, however, the formal organization of the church began to disintegrate.

A few of the members, such as Michael Mountain, had by this time developed an interest in the care of animals. They began to turn a small ranch that the Foundation had bought outside of Prescott, Arizona, into an animal shelter. Here they were joined by Faith Maloney, who had independently begun an animal shelter in Pennsylvania. In 1984 the group moved to Angel Canyon, in Southern Utah. For the next few years, some of the members of the Foundation Faith continued their work with children and the elderly, but in a short time most discerned that the work of the Foundation had really ended. The religious vision that had molded the Foundation now evolved into a humanitarian vision and what became known as the No More Homeless Pets movement. This movement looks to a time in the near future when every dog or cat can be guaranteed a good home with a loving family.

Periodicals: *Best Friends Magazine.*

Sources:

Best Friends. www.bestfriends.org/.

Glen, Samantha. *Best Friends: The True Story of the World's Most Beloved Animal Sanctuary*. New York: Kensington Publishing, 2001.

Foundation of Human Understanding
Box 1000, Grants Pass, OR 97528

The Foundation of Human Understanding was founded in Los Angeles, California, in 1961 by Roy Masters (b. 1928). Masters was born in England in 1928 and during his early life studied hypnosis. He later spent a period of his early adulthood in South Africa observing the witch doctors, further spurring his interest in the nature of the mental healing processes. In 1949 he moved to the United States and became a successful diamond cutter and expert, finally settling in Houston, Texas. Then in the mid-1950s, as the phenomena surrounding the case of Bridey Murphy stimulated popular interest in reincarnation and hypnosis, friends discovered Masters's work in hypnosis and besieged him for help. These sessions led to his quitting the diamond business and founding the Institute of Hypnosis, the forerunner of the Foundation of Human Understanding. He stayed in Houston for nine more years, during which time he perfected psychocatalysis, a meditation technique that later became the most important aspect of his teachings, and then moved to Los Angeles, where the foundation was started.

Once in Los Angeles, Masters developed a successful radio talk show and wrote *Your Mind Can Keep You Well* (1968), which appeared as both a book and a record. Masters's conclusion from his work in hypnosis was that what is wrong with people is that they are already hypnotized by the mass of pressures put on them by life. According to Masters, hypnotized people act in irrational ways and possess strong components of anxiety and guilt. His answer to hypnosis was the meditation technique psychocatalysis, which he claimed could cure people of diseases, teach them to cope with life, and lead them into a transformed life that quickly takes on a religious and mystical quality. The foundation became a place where people not only learned meditation techniques, but also where those whose lives had been changed could gather to continue their spiritual growth.

During the 1960s and 1970s, Masters gained an extensive following in southern California. His radio show, originally on a local station in Los Angeles, was eventually syndicated across the United States and Canada. Periodically he left Los Angeles to lecture around the country. Soon groups of people who followed his meditation teachings and appreciated his approach to life's problems emerged, particularly on the West Coast. During the 1970s the foundation was registered as a religious organization with the Internal Revenue Service, which then refused to recognize it as a church. In 1980 Masters filed a lawsuit seeking such recognition, which was finally granted in 1987. In about 1985 the headquarters of the foundation was moved to Grants Pass, Oregon, where it operates a religious retreat and ranch.

Membership: Not reported.

Educational Facilities:

Brighton Academy, Grants Pass, Oregon.

Periodicals: *New Insights*. Send orders to PO Box 1009, Grants Pass, OR 97526.

Sources:

Foundation of Human Understanding. www.fhu.com/.

Masters, Roy. *Adam and Eve Sindrome*. Grant's Pass, OR: Foundation for Human Understanding, 2001.

———. *How to Conquer Suffering without Doctors*. Los Angeles: Foundation of Human Understanding, 1976.

———. *No One Has to Die!* Los Angeles, CA: Foundation of Human Understanding, 1977.

———. *The Satan Principle*. Los Angeles: Foundation of Human Understanding, 1979.

———. *Secret of Life*. Los Angeles: Foundation of Human Understanding, 1972.

———. *Sex, Sin, and Salvation*. Los Angeles: Foundation of Human Understanding, 1977.

———. *Your Mind Can Keep You Well*. Los Angeles: Foundation of Human Understanding, 1968.

Wolff, William. *Healers, Gurus, and Spiritual Guides*. Los Angeles: Sherbourne Press, 1969.

Heart Consciousness Church and New Age Church of Being
PO Box 82, Middletown, CA 95461

In 1972 the Harbin Hot Springs Retreat Center was purchased by Robert Hartley. He and some of his friends who helped him renovate the property met in 1974 and agreed that they were in alignment with the emerging New Age movement, which they defined as consisting of three basic elements: universal spirituality, the Human Potential movement, and the Holistic Natural movement. They affirmed that there is fundamental agreement in all religions that there is a need for honest, open, and spontaneous relationships, and a desire for a holistic natural approach to health and healing. This core of agreement became the basis of a religious fellowship that was incorporated in 1975 as the Heart Consciousness Church. Hartley turned Harbin Hot Springs over to the church. The New Age Church of Being was founded in 1985 as a more ceremonial and "churchy" organization. It administers a ministerial training program.

The church hosts various New Age events, including conferences, seminars, and workshops, acting as a unifying force among the various groups. The use of the resort by outside groups is a primary means of financial support.

New members may join the group by residing at the retreat center and working with the present church members. They are required to have a personal goal that is compatible with that of the church and to contribute labor or money toward their own support. The group has a loose structure. It makes group life decisions by a process called "spiritual anarchy" and attempts to resolve differences in a spirit of love and oneness. However, ultimate control of the property is by a board of directors.

Because of the opportunities at Harbin Hot Springs, it is the goal of the church to develop a new alternative economy to allow people who have no financial assets to be integrated into the life of the church and to foster similar, satellite communities in other locations.

Membership: In 1997 there were 150 church members living at Harbin Hot Springs, and another ten in the first satellite center, Sierra Hot Springs, in Sierraville, California. Sierra Hot Springs is operated by the New Age Church of Being.

Periodicals: *Harbin Hot Springs Quarterly Catalog/Magazine.*

Sources:

Harbin Hot Springs. www.harbin.org.

Klages, Ellen. *Harbin Hot Springs: Healing Waters, Sacred Land.* Middletown, CA: Harbin Hot Springs Publishing, 1991.

Living the Future. Middletown, CA: Harbin Hot Springs Publishing, 1993.

Huna International

PO Box 223009, Princeville, HI 96722

Huna International was founded in 1973 as a religious order for the teaching of the Huna philosophy of ancient Hawaii as understood by Serge Kahili King. King was introduced to kahuna philosophy by his father Harry King, a member of a still secret network that King calls the Organization. Through Serge Kahili King's contacts he was given training, and as a young man he was initiated as a kahuna in the Order of Kane. After working with a relief and development program in Africa, he returned to the United States and studied with his adoptive Hawaiian uncle, a kahuna (1971 to 1975), which led to his founding Huna International. He defines *huna* as "that which is hidden," and refers to it as the Hidden Knowledge or Secret Reality. A *kahuna* is the transmitter of the secret, and the motto of Huna International is "Let that which is unknown become known." The ancient kahunas of Hawaii were divided into three orders: the Ku, the Lono, and the Kane. The Kane Order was known for its intuitive approach to the world and its use of what today are called alternate states of consciousness and psychic abilities.

The basic teachings of the Huna philosophy have been summarized in seven statements, each represented by a Hawaiian word:

Ike: "The world is what you think it is." That is, we create our world by our beliefs, judgments, and expectations. We can create illness and poverty, or we can create health and prosperity.

Kala: "There are no limits." Anything is possible if we believe it.

Makia: "Energy flows where attention goes." Energy is directed to the things we think about. If we change our thinking, our world will be remade.

Manawa: "Now is the moment of power." We are not bound by the past or future, and can thus change in the present. Healing, change, development, or any other desired goal is dependent upon our keeping our attention focused in the present. Looking to the past or future misdirects energy away from present actions.

Aloha: "To love is to be happy with." Love the great healer and the change agent is freed as we become happy with ourselves and our surroundings. Happiness is accentuated by acts of forgiveness, tolerance, and self-acceptance.

Mana: "All power comes from within." Outside forces only have power as one believes and submits. Real power operates from the inner resources of the self.

Pono: "Effectiveness is the measure of truth." Effectiveness, another name for harmony, comes from an integrated working of mind, body, and spirit.

There are also three chartered branches of Huna International: Aloha International, its networking and project supervision arm; Voices of the Earth, a forum for native peoples; and Finding Each Other International, which conducts relationship training. Through Aloha International, the huna philosophy is shared through various programs, termed projects. The Network Project nurtures local chapters and service networks. The Hawaiiana Project supports the spread of knowledge of Hawaiian culture through museums, shops, and a mail-order service for Hawaiiana. The Training Project provides Hawaiian Shaman Training as taught by King and other leaders, a variety of self-development workshops, and teacher and counselor training for leaders. There is an annual gathering in November for the Mahakiki Festival on Kauai.

Membership: In 2008 Aloha International reported some 10,000 members who reside in more than 20 countries.

Periodicals: *The Aloha News,* c/o Aloha International, Box 599, Kauai, HI 96746.

Sources:

Huna International. www.huna.org/.

King, Serge. *The Aloha Spirit.* Kilauea, HI: Aloha International, 1990.

————. *Kahuna Healing.* Wheaton, IL: Theosophical Publishing House, 1983.

————. "Making the Good the Most Important." *Threshold Quarterly* 14, no. 4 (November 1996): 12–16.

————. *Mastering Your Hidden Self.* Wheaton, IL: Theosophical Publishing House, 1983.

————. *Urban Shaman.* New York: Simon and Schuster, 1990.

Huna Research, Inc.

1760 Anna St., Cape Girardeau, MO 63701-4504

The religion of ancient Hawaii, that is, before 1820, was primarily ritualistic observance performed in *heiaus* (temples) by *kahunas* (priests). Control of the people was effected by strictly enforced *kapu* (taboo), which reserved most privileges and wealth for the royal families and their religious leaders. Severe punishments were dealt to those who violated the innumerable prohibitions of the kapu system. Each heiau was dedicated to one of the many gods and goddesses; the four major ones were Kane, the creator; Ku, the war god; Kanaloa, the god of the sea and of death; and Lono, the fertility god. *Mana* ("divine" power) was a special privilege of royalty and the kahunas and was jealously guarded.

The ancient kahuna religious practices virtually ceased when Hewahewa, the *kahuna nui* (high priest) of Kamehameha anticipated the coming of the "new" religion and abolished the temple observances. Most Hawaiians did not adapt well to the white man's religion and went back to their old ways, even after they were outlawed by the missionaries, who gained political and financial control of the islands. Often, Hawaiians professed Christianity while retaining many of the older beliefs and practices.

Many heiaus have been restored and are preserved as historical monuments by the government. A few modern-day kahunas have maintained some of the rituals and practices, primarily using mana for healing. Sam Lono, a Hawaiian living on ancestral lands, maintained an ancient healing heiau on Oahu for many years. David "Daddy" Bray Sr. (1889–1968), a recognized practitioner, was known as a kahuna, and he passed on to his students the ancient religious practices at Kona; his son David Bray Jr. continues in that tradition. Charles Kenn on Oahu was a specialist in the kahuna lore, including the *kaona* (inner meanings) of the Hawaiian language, but he did not leave any record of his knowledge.

The greatest student of the Hawaiian religion of the twentieth century was Max Freedom Long (1898–1971), who went to Hawaii in 1917 as a teacher. He became fascinated with the traditional lore and religious practices of the kahunas, especially their methods of performing apparent "miracles" such as healing. He met a wall of silence wherever he tried to discover their secrets, and he left the islands in 1931 thinking the secrets would never be known. Four years later he awoke in the middle of the night with the clue that led to the rediscovery of the ancient "magic." The secrets of the kahunas were hidden and preserved in coded form in the

Hawaiian language itself. He chose the name *Huna* (secret) for his "workable, psycho-religious system" that combined the best of psychology and religion.

As a psychological/religious practice, Huna is distinguished from the ancient kahuna religion, and it was never an attempt to restore or reconstruct those practices. Huna has neither kapu nor heiau. It is a practical way of life based on the harmonious relationship of the three levels of consciousness, called the three "selves." These are *unihipili* (the inner, emotional, intuitive self), *uhane* (the waking consciousness, or rational self), and *aumakua* (the "High Self," or connection with the divine). Huna considers mana to be the vital life force that vivifies and empowers each person and not the special prerogative of the privileged few. Mana is transmitted via invisible aka substance.

To Long, Huna was "magic" based on the knowledge of how our three selves function, using mana not only to heal body, mind, and circumstance, but also to attain our goals and live effective lives.

After explaining the history of his discoveries in his first books (1936, 1948), Long wrote textbooks to teach readers how to accomplish the things they desired by using the Huna way of life. In *The Huna Code in Religions* (1965) he explored the Huna parallels in world religions, especially Buddhism, yoga, and Christianity. Many other books on Huna have been written by students of Long, notably *Huna: The Ancient Religion of Positive Thinking*, by William R. Glover, which is probably the best introduction for new readers.

Huna Research was established in 1945 as a result of the positive reception of Long's first book. Members, called associates, were from all walks of life and several countries, especially Australia and England. Emphasizing a practical philosophy or psychology that all can use, the organization has maintained a steady but growing membership. Many others learned what they needed, quietly continued to live according to the Huna principles, but did not continue as official members of Huna Research.

Long died in 1971 and was succeeded by E. Otha Wingo, Long's chosen successor. The Huna headquarters was moved to Missouri, where Wingo was a professor at a university. In 1985 a headquarters building was purchased in Missouri.

Membership: With active Huna teachers and affiliated groups (Huna fellowships) in the United States, Canada, Australia, England, Germany, Switzerland, and Brazil, in 2008 Huna had more followers than at any other time in its 50-year history. There are members in more than 50 countries. Huna Research, Inc. does not exert central control over affiliated organizations, but rather gives guidance and assistance in the dissemination of Huna teachings. There are about 5,000 persons in Germany and Switzerland who have received the Huna teachings through the affiliate organization in Zurich, Huna Forschungs-gesellschaft, directed by Heinrich Krotoschin. Major Huna publications are available in the German language. Another major branch is Associacao de Estudos Huna in Brazil, directed by Ceres Elisa da Fonseca Rosas, where Huna books are available in Portuguese. Spanish-language editions are produced in the United States by Edgardo Torralvo of Torralvoma Holistic Center in New York.

In addition, a number of independent "Huna" organizations have sprung up in various locations based on the extensive research and experimentation of Max Freedom Long and his Huna Research Associates, but their teachings are often mixed with other related concepts and they do not maintain affiliations with Huna Research, Inc.

Annual international Huna seminars and meetings are held in the United States and Canada.

Periodicals: *The Huna Work* • *The Aka Cord* • *Huna Arbeit* (German-language bulletin/newsletter published in Switzerland).

Sources:

Huna Research Inc. www.huna-research.com/.

Hoffman, Enid. *Huna, A Beginner's Guide*. Rockport, MA: Para Research, 1976.

Long, Max Freedom. *Introduction to Huna*. Sedona, AZ: Esoteric Publications, 1975.

———. *Recovering the Ancient Magic*. Cape Girardeau, MO: Huna Press, 1978.

———. *The Secret Science at Work*. Vista, CA: Huna Research Publications, 1953.

———. *The Secret Science behind Miracles*. Vista, CA: Huna Research Publications, 1954.

Wingo, E. Otha. *The Story of the Huna Work*. Cape Girardeau, MO: Huna Research, 1981.

Inner Light Foundation
Box 750265, Petaluma, CA 94975

The Inner Light Foundation was founded in the 1969 by mystic and psychic Betty Bethards (d. 2002) with the objective of developing in all people a conscious awareness of God. It is Bethards's belief that within each individual are intuitive faculties, the development of which can lead to the greater brotherhood of man. The foundation teaches that to tap into their own inner guidance and insight, people need only three tools: dreams, affirmations, and visualizations/meditation. The foundation teaches a simple powerful meditation technique, a process of quieting that allows for inner awareness, mystic development, and the emergence of spiritual abilities.

The foundation has grown steadily since its inception. It holds regular lectures at several locations in the San Francisco Bay area and Los Angeles. Bethards was a popular lecturer and worship leader and has written nine books presenting the foundation's teachings. She also offered private readings to individuals.

Membership: In 2002 the foundation reported 10,000 members in the United States, 100 in Canada, and an additional 400 worldwide.

Periodicals: *Inner Light Foundation Illuminations*.

Sources:

Inner Light Foundation. www.innerlight.org/.

Bethards, Betty. *Relationships in the New Age of AIDS*. Novato, CA: Inner Light Foundation, 1988.

———. *The Sacred Sword*. Novato, CA: Inner Light Foundation, 1972.

———. *Sex and Psychic Energy*. Novato, CA: Inner Light Foundation, 1977.

———. *There Is No Death*. Novato, CA: Inner Light Foundation, 1975.

Inner Peace Movement
PO Box 499, Washington, DC 20008

In the early 1960s Francisco Coll, a student of the psychic and spiritual, became involved with the medium Arthur A. Ford in the ecumenical church-psychic group Spiritual Frontiers Fellowship. In 1964 Coll established the Inner Peace Movement (IPM) to help people unfold their abilities by awakening the potentials of the inner man. IPM was founded in Washington, D.C., and soon a camp conference center and head office facilities were established in Osceola, Iowa. The program developed in both communities with lectures, workshops, groupwork, and personal spiritual counselings. (Counseling is a method through which an individual can clarify his communication subliminally, as acknowledged by angelic messengers in the quickening of the flesh.)

The basic perspective of IPM is contained in Coll's book *Man and the Universe*, and in *Discovering Your True Identity*, the text for the IPM groupwork. Individuals are shown how to unfold their own true realities through meditation and other techniques, based on the premise that they are souls with physical bodies, not physical bodies with souls. A soul is believed to be essentially spiritual electromagnetic energy, and as this energy is eternal, the soul never dies. We are the sum total of every thought and experience throughout our lifetimes, and this becomes the essence and identity of each soul. It is this reality that acknowledges man as a feeling being. For every feeling we need an interpretation; for every interpretation, a feeling. By being in balance with his inner self, and with organization in the physical world, man can achieve his goals and life purpose with harmony and a oneness of self.

In 1972 the headquarters of IPM was moved to Washington, D.C. IPM is governed by a board of directors that meets annually. Although Coll is the founder, a new executive board and president is elected each year. Among the several related organizations also founded by Coll are the Americana Leadership College and Peace Community Church. The Americana Leadership College provides the leadership training for those who work with IPM in communities. It offers more than 300 in-depth courses that cover a wide variety of spiritually related topics in several areas of study.

Membership: More than 90,000 people have been involved with IPM in the United States, and an additional 35,000 people in 21 countries are trained to be leaders of IPM. The IPM has offices in the Caribbean, Australia, New Zealand, France, Great Britain, and Canada.

Educational Facilities:

Americana Leadership College. Locations in the United States are based in Iowa, Texas, Alaska, Florida, Nevada, California, New Mexico, Washington, New York, and Puerto Rico; there are also locations in more than 10 foreign countries.

Periodicals: *The Times Communicator* • *Expression Magazine.*

Sources:

Inner Peace Movement. innerpeacemovement.org/.

Coll, Francisco. *Discovering Your True Identity*. Osceola, IA: American Leadership College, 1968.

————. *Discovering Your True Identity Leadership Training Manual*. Osceola, IA: American Leadership College, 1972.

————. *The Gifts of Intuition, Vision, Prophecy and Feeling in the Seven-Year Cycles*. Washington, DC: American Leadership College, 1981.

Institute of Cosmic Wisdom

3528 Franciscan Ln., Las Vegas, NV 89121

The Institute of Cosmic Wisdom was founded by the Rev. Clark Wilkerson. It combines New Thought metaphysics with the magical religion of the huna. Wilkerson began as a metaphysician, and the main class offered students of the institute was in "mental expansion." Wilkerson's teachings differ from those of most metaphysicians in his emphasis on the use of the mind to gain control not only of the self but also of others. He also believes that mastery of metaphysics comes in the deep meditative or hypnotic state.

In the early 1950s Wilkerson began to emphasize Hawaiian *huna* (the ancient magical practices of Hawaii) as an occult science that leads to success and happiness with less effort. The course emphasizes concentration and entering into the meditative silence, as well as adjusting the mind to open concepts. Exercises are offered in how to enter the silence and use this ability.

Members of the institute are drawn primarily through advertisements, mostly in psychic periodicals. Most students begin with correspondence courses in metaphysics or huna. Classes taught by Wilkerson are held periodically. Students who have completed the courses become the core of continuing members. An Inner Circle of ordained ministers constitutes the leadership.

Membership: Not reported.

Sources:

Wilkerson, Clark L. *Celestial Wisdom*. Gardena, CA: Institute of Cosmic Wisdom, 1965.

————. *Hawaiian Magic*. Playa Del Rey, CA: Institute of Cosmic Wisdom, 1968.

Institute of Mentalphysics

59700 29 Palms Hwy., Joshua Tree, CA 92252

Alternate Address: Mailing Address: PO Box 1000, Joshua Tree, CA 92252.

The Institute of Mentalphysics was founded in 1927 in New York City by Edwin John Dingle (1881–1972). An editor and explorer in early life, he was one of the few American metaphysical teachers to have studied in Tibet prior to 1927. In Tibet,

Dingle met a master who helped him recall his memory (i.e., of previous incarnations), and he was taught proper breathing and the remaining disciplines, which became the basis of the Science of Mentalphysics. In 1927, when he gave a series of lectures in New York City, some attendees asked him to share the wisdom he had learned in the east. Those lectures are viewed as the beginning of the institute and of the new career of Ding Le Mei (Dingle's religious name). The institute was incorporated in 1934 in California.

Dingle combined the spiritual wisdom of the east with religious knowledge of the west to form a "Super Yoga." The teachings of mentalphysics combine universal truths, breathing exercises, diet control, recognizing and working with one's individual chemistry, exercises, and meditation. New students are introduced to the universal laws of the creator that, if followed, are believed to lead to mastery of oneself and all of life. A vegetarian diet is recommended. Proper breathing is a key; it is the means of extracting prana, the energy of life, from the air. The healthy body prepares one to develop mind and spirit toward one's highest potential.

Mentalphysics teaches that prana, or life energy, is substance, a subtle form of energy that animates life. It is universally distributed and is what the soul uses to think with. Using the mind-substance activated through breathing, one is able to activate the creative powers within. Students are also instructed in meditation, which helps one tap universal wisdom and develop as a mystic. As a mystic one understands truth, life, and one's potential through experience.

Mentalphysics begins with the Initiate Group Course, which consists of 26 basic lessons. There are 124 additional advanced lessons and a Teachers or Preceptor Course which helps developed persons to share their knowledge and experience with seekers on all levels.

The institute's worldwide headquarters is located at the Mentalphysics Teaching Center and Spiritual Retreat in Joshua Tree, California. The 385-acre facility can house up to 250 delegates. Most of the buildings there were designed by Frank Lloyd Wright. Main buildings such as the Caravansary of Joy, Meditation Building, and the Preceptory of Light are used not only to teach the Science of Mentalphysics, but also to serve sponsored groups dedicated to the elevation of human consciousness. Sunday services are held in the First Sanctuary of Mystic Christianity.

The Institute of Mentalphysics is a nonprofit organization operated by a board of trustees.

Membership: In 1995 the active mailing list was 6,003, and 222,307 students had been enrolled in institute classes. This includes students from the United States, Canada, Mexico, Iceland, India, Spain, England, Trinidad, and Ecuador. Seven centers serve seekers around the world.

Periodicals: *Light of the Logos.*

Sources:

Institute of Mentalphysics. www.mentalphysics.net/.

Dingle, Edwin John. *Borderlands of Eternity*. Los Angeles: Institute of Mentalphysics, 1939.

————. *Breathing Your Way to Youth*. Los Angeles: Institute of Mentalphysics, [1931].

————. *The Voice of the Logos*. Los Angeles: Institute of Mentalphysics, 1950.

Interfaith Church of Metaphysics (ICOM)

163 Moon Valley Rd., Windyville, MO 65783

The Interfaith Church of Metaphysics (ICOM) was founded in 1976 as the religious branch of the School of Metaphysics (SOM), an educational and service organization founded by a group of spiritual aspirants in 1973. The school is dedicated to study and research on what it considers to be universal laws that govern creation and the development of humanity's spiritual consciousness. The school offers a comprehensive, four-tiered program of study in the causal principles underlying humanity's existence. Although the program is comparable in some ways to those found in traditional schools of higher education, it goes beyond the limitations inherent in physical study alone. It teaches how learning occurs as a sequence of thought, as well as how the application of the knowledge gained. Through the practice of spiritual disciplines, students transcend what they understand to be the pairs of opposites manifesting in the physical world, and are led to the discovery of the origin of unity in religion and science, philosophy and conduct, freedom and responsibility, and peace and discipline.

In 1976 the board of directors of the School of Metaphysics created the International Church of Metaphysics, in response to a need for spiritual knowledge for those more religiously than scholastically inclined., Designed to offer truth, inspiration, and guidance to those searching to know and understand their relationship to their creator, ICOM provides various means for spiritual renewal and association. An interfaith church, ICOM members believe that all holy scriptures of the world embody truths that are universally applicable to all of humanity. When interpreted in the "Universal Language of Mind," all scriptures, regardless of the religions arising from them, offer insight and instruction into the origin and reason for humanity's existence. Because of this belief, ICOM eschews dogma, and church members are not required to drop previously held religious beliefs or membership in any religious group when they affiliate with ICOM.

ICOM members believe:

that each human is a spiritual being given existence and free will by the creator;

that the creator set in motion principles and laws that function throughout our universe governing creation;

that each human is made in the likeness and image of the creator and thus possesses the freedom and responsibility of creating thought;

that each human being is striving to know truth that is universal and to become compatible with his or her maker;

that thought is cause and everything else is sub cause;

that the temporal life is a choice made by the soul for the acceleration of spiritual progression;

that all individuals have every possible opportunity for a spiritually enriching existence if only they will choose to envision it;

that the destiny of each individual is an enlightened state of being, a possibility demonstrated by singular individuals throughout history;

that this enlightened spiritual maturity can be aspired to through ever increasing awareness by disciplining our minds with meditation, prayer, and positive thinking;

and that as this destiny is manifest in the individual's progression, it will become manifest for all people, and the evolution of the race is accelerated.

Church pastors have completed at least the first cycle of lessons in the program of study at the School of Metaphysics. These pastors serve as apprentices under the guidance of an ordained minister in the church. SOM students in the third cycle of lessons can elect to pursue a doctorate of divinity degree from the school and become ordained ministers in the church.

In 1993 ICOM was one of the many cosponsors of the centennial Parliament of World's Religions held in Chicago. Two board members, Rev. Dr. Daniel R. Condron, president of the ICOM Ordination Board, and Rev. Dr. Barbara Condron, addressed the parliament, and the church's choir gave a performance. As a result of this participation, the ordination board of the church elected to change the name to the Interfaith Church of Metaphysics, a designation more clearly describing the ideal, purpose, and activity of the membership. Members of the church support the document released by the conference, "Toward a Global Ethic," as a pledge to work toward understanding one another and realizing a more socially beneficial, peace-fostering, and nature-friendly way of life.

ICOM members, teachers, and faculty in the School of Metaphysics collaborated over a period of two years to compose the *Universal Peace Covenant*, a document that identifies and describes the causes for peace within the individual and society.

Members are dedicated to an ever-increasing awareness of Truth, a personal communication with the creator, and a deepening understanding of self and of others. They are committed by thought and action to serving to their neighbors and all of humankind. Through the School of Metaphysics, the church publishes and distributes worldwide a selection of books and tapes. Audiotapes offer musical presentations, sermons by church leaders, and courses on meditation and the Universal Language of Mind.

Membership: Not reported. The church offers regular services in 16 major cities across the United States.

Educational Facilities:

School of Metaphysics, Windyville, Missouri.

Periodicals: *Thresholds Annual.*

Sources:

Condron, Barbara. *Kindalini Rising: Mastering Creative Energies*. Windyville, MO: SOM Publishing, 1992.

Condron, Daniel. *Dreams of the Soul: The Yogi Sutras of Patanjali*. Windyville, MO: SOM Publishing, 1991.

————. *Permanent Healing: Includes Quantum Mechanics of Healing*. Windyville, MO: SOM Publishing, 1993.

Fuller, Laurel Jan. *Shaping Your Life: The Power of Creative Energy*. Windyville, MO: SOM Publishing, 1994.

Rothermel, Jerry L. *Meditation: The Answer to Your Prayers*. Windyville, MO: SOM Publishing, 1987.

————. *Symbols of Dreams*. Springfield, MO: School of Metaphysics, 1976.

Kabalarian Society

5912 Oak St., Vancouver, BC, Canada V6M 2W2

The Kabalarian philosophy was developed by Alfred J. Parker (1897–1964). Parker was born in England, then his family moved to British Columbia in his youth, settling in Vancouver. Though raised an Anglican, Parker began to research various philosophies and religions and studied for a time with a Hindu swami. He developed a philosophy of life, and began in the 1930s to publicly expound his theories through personal contacts and newspaper articles. He started classes on the Kabalarian philosophy in his home, eventually outgrowing the space. The organization he built is now known as the Society of Kabalarians. The Society of Kabalarians has acquired buildings for classes and philosophical presentations. It also owns a resort for membership activities.

The Kabalarian philosophy teaches the basic Spiritual Principle, through which mankind can measure and understand human mind, and bring the Philosophy of Life down to a practical, basic principle that embraces life in its entirety—combining the exact science of matter, mind, and consciousness into a Universal Principle where both the scientific and the religious concepts are combined in equilibrium. It is the knowledge of the connection between numbers, the symbols of language, and the forces of intelligence that comprise human mind. It unites the practical, scientific concepts of the west with the idealistic concepts of the east, in which life's goal is to merge with a universal, conscious plane. One's mental characteristics, state of well-being, and experiences in life are determined by one's name, which incorporates the specific forces of intelligence in the mind of the individual. Greater harmony and balance can be achieved by using a balanced name harmonized to one's inner potential, which is created by the date of birth and follows the natural cyclic patterns of growth and development through time.

Kabalarians regard the physical body as the instrument for the expression of the conscious forces of life, and so stresses the importance of a moderate vegetarian diet, emotional guidance, and physical fitness through exercise and deep breathing. The society's name is derived from the Hebrew word *kabal*, which means "to receive"; in this case, it means to receive the esoteric knowledge of numbers and letters of the alphabet. Although the word *kabal* derives from Hebrew, the Kabalarian philosophy has no affiliation with Judaism.

In 2008 the president/director of the Kabalarian Philosophy was Lorenda Bardell.

Membership: In 2008 the centers for the Kabalarian philosophy were located in Calgary and Edmonton, Alberta; Vancouver, British Columbia; and in the Netherlands. There are hundreds of correspondence students around the world.

Periodicals: *Kabalarian Student* newsletter • Internet newsletter.

Remarks: In fall 1997 the former Kabalarian leader Ivon Shearing was tried on counts of sexual misconduct brought by 11 female complainants. Though he was found guilty of five counts, he continued to profess his innocence, and members of the society remained supportive of him. The principles, practices, and teachings of the philosophy were grossly misstated at trial. In 2002 the Supreme Court of Canada ruled a retrial on two of the charges, allowing lawyers to further cross-examine an alleged victim.

Sources:

Kabalarian Society. www.kabalarians.com/.

Karin Society

2531 Briarcliff Rd. NE, Ste. 217, Atlanta, GA 30329

The Karin Society was founded in the 1980s as an association of people seeking spiritual growth through the kabbalah. It grew out of the Karin Kabalah study course written by Shirley Chambers and published in 1984. It is Chambers's belief that the kabbalah, often thought of as a particularly Jewish form of mysticism, embodies an understanding that is more ancient than either Christianity or Judaism. From that understanding flowed all of the world's religions, and as humanity proceeds to a new level of progress, a reinterpretation of the kabbalistic wisdom is both possible and necessary. The Karin Kabalah is such a modern reinterpretation. *Karin* is a Hindustani word meaning "light" or, more literally, "rays of the sun."

The Kabalah presents a mystical system that leads the student to Truth; not an intellectual truth, but an experienced truth that cannot be explained in words. The Karin Kabalah course is offered as a correspondence course with monthly lessons. In 1988 Chambers established the Karin Kabalah Center in Atlanta, Georgia, where a two-year course in kabbalistic wisdom is taught along with related subjects such as astrology, hatha yoga, psychic and spiritual development, and eastern philosophy. The society developed out of the expanding work of the correspondence course and center.

Membership: Not reported.

Periodicals: *Karin Journal*.

Sources:

Karin Society. www.karinkabalahcenter.com.

Light Institute

HC-75, Box 50, Galisteo, NM 87540

The Light Institute was founded in 1985 to facilitate the teachings of Chris Griscom, a popular New Age writer and teacher. Griscom's preparation as a teacher began in Mexico, where she attended the University of Mexico and used her spare time to explore the rural countryside. She became the student of a *curandera*, a village healer, who introduced her to the presence of God in nature. Throughout the 1960s she spent nine years in the Peace Corps in El Salvador, Bolivia, and Paraguay, where people taught her their esoteric traditions. She came to believe that nature, even the rocks, were alive with energy. Upon her return to the United States, she studied with Silva Mind Control and a number of individual teachers. During this period

she emerged as a spiritual healer. She later studied massage and acupuncture and throughout the early 1980s developed her healing work. She came to feel that the primary experience needed by people in the present era is the clearing of the emotional body.

It is Griscom's opinion that the self is composed of four bodies—the physical, astral, emotional, and spiritual. The emotional body is described as the emotional vehicle of consciousness that vibrates at a low frequency. It is also her belief that now is a time of spiritual awakening that will lead humankind into a new, more enlightened, cosmic human reality. From her initial insights, she has expanded the teachings to cover all aspects of life, and through the institute she offers a variety of courses that teach people to apply what they have learned to their own lives. Griscom is assisted by several facilitators whom she has trained. In 1988 she also founded the Nizhoni School for Global Consciousness as a day school for students age three to adult focused on exploring the individual's purpose in the global context.

The institute has an affiliated center in Brazil and contact persons in France, Holland, and Germany.

Membership: Not reported.

Sources:

Light Institute. www.lightinstitute.com/.

Griscom, Chris. *Ecstasy Is a New Frequency: Teachings of the Light Institute*. New York: Simon and Schuster, 1988.

———. *The Evolution of God*. Galisteo, NM: Light Institute Press, 2007.

———. *Time Is an Illusion*. New York: Fireside, 1988.

Loving Hands Institute

639 11th Ave., Fortuna, CA 95540-2346

Formerly known as Church of Loving Hands, the Loving Hands Institute is a New Age church founded in 1979 by Rev. Rosalind Beal-Ojala. Beal-Ojala was ordained in 1979 by the Mother Earth Church, and her church was chartered in 1980 by the same. She began her studies in psychic awareness with the Inner Peace Movement in 1968, the year after her graduation from the University of Arizona. Through the early 1970s she worked with Universal Communications, an organization founded by her father, Robert L. Beal, in Phoenix, before moving to Mill Valley, California, in 1975. By this time, natural healing had become the keystone of her work, and she began to concentrate on various forms of healing, from Swedish massage to diet to spiritual healing by the laying-on-of-hands.

Beal-Ojala is part Native American, a Meti, and a member of the National American Metis Association. She has found a connection between the teachings and healing practices of the New Age movement and those of Native Americans. Much of the work of the church is conducted under her Native American name, Skyhawk. The church also sponsors sweat lodge ceremonies, medicine circles, and wilderness vision quests. Along with theosophical texts, the church considers books of Native American teachings such as *The Book of the Hopi*, *Black Elk Speaks*, and *Warriors of the Rainbow* to be authoritative texts for its members.

The church is dedicated to the research, teaching, and ministering of Natural Earth Healing, which combines the ancient ways of Native Americans and New Age techniques. The church shares these teachings with all in the hope of rekindling connections between people and the spirit power and Mother Earth. It also supports the Cross Cultural Shamanism Network in Berkeley, California, and the XAT Medicine Society in Nashville, Tennessee.

Membership: Not reported.

Educational Facilities:

Rosebud College, Sioux Falls, South Dakota.

Periodicals: *Medicine Ways*.

Sources:

Loving Hands Institute. www.lovinghandsinstitute.com/.

New Age Community Church

6418 S 39th Ave., Phoenix, AZ 85041

The New Age Community Church is an ecclesiastical expression of the New Age, the Age of Aquarius. The New Age draws on all of the major religions of the present time, and it believes that the differences between the nine major religions are relatively unimportant, though it does oppose perspectives that emphasize fear and hatred. More important are the many pathways or systems of expression of relationship with the divine that appear in the different systems. Each of these pathways will lead to God. The nine pathways are:

1. social—through relationships and society;
2. meditation—through mental discipline;
3. revelation—through channeling and psyche;
4. karma—through good deeds and service;
5. ecstasy—through dance and music;
6. ritual—through magic and sacrament;
7. knowledge—through wisdom and understanding;
8. physical—through yoga, diet, and health; and
9. worship—through devotion and adoration.

The New Age Community Church speaks of God as all there is. God is not personal and does not reside in a place called heaven. The universe can be thought of as God's physical body. Christ is thought of as the logos or higher self. Humans are currently trapped on the wheel of reincarnation. We continue to believe in good and evil and create emotional values based on that belief; when we cease to create such emotional values, karma can no longer hold us and we will ascend to the level of the divine.

Membership: Not reported.

Educational Facilities:

New Age Seminary Program.

New Psychiana

c/o Psychiana Study Group, 4069 Stephens St., San Diego, CA 92103

The New Psychiana was formed in 1967 by Jack E. Gardner of San Diego, California. Gardner was an early student of Frank B. Robinson, the founder of Psychiana, a popular New Thought group that had its greatest growth in the 1930s and 1940s. Gardner completed both the regular and advanced courses, and accepted the role of Robinson's successor. In the years since Robinson's death in 1948, the whole field of ESP has emerged, and Gardner added teachings on conscious evolution to Psychiana to bring it up to date.

Conscious evolution is the "divine cybernetics to spiritual growth." It teaches techniques of becoming fully aware of the powerful God-presence within you. By learning to control this power, one can heal bodily and spiritual wounds, bring peace, and break free from poverty and defeat.

Membership: Not reported.

Portal Enterprises

PO Box 1449, Columbia, MD 21044

Portal Enterprises is the teaching vehicle for Sri Akhenaton, a teacher of esoteric spiritual philosophy. Out of his mystical experience, he sees himself as transmitting the Divine Light Energy of the One Infinite Creator to facilitate the awakening of humankind to the God-Consciousness Being. It is also his belief that all things born of creation, not just humans, contain a Light/Life vibration of Divine Consciousness and should be treated accordingly.

Sri Akhenaton offers a series of classes, workshops, and weekly spiritual gatherings where he teaches LoveLight Meditation and the practice of Trans-Cultural Consciousness. He holds that humans are on an evolutionary journey that includes various incarnations in the earthly realm. Sri Akhenaton seeks to assist people on that journey in a way that does not interfere with free will or promulgate eccentric exclusivist doctrines. Instead, he attempts to assist people in discovering their divine nature and their ability to cooperate with their own evolution.

Membership: Not reported.

Sources:

Akhenaton, Sri. *Crystal Communion*. Columbia, MD: Portal Press, 1994.

———. *Discussion of Spiritual Attunement and Soul Evolution*. 2 vols. Columbia, MD: Portal Press, 1992.

———. *Reflections from the Golden Mind*. Columbia, MD: Portal Press, 1994.

Quartus Foundation for Spiritual Research

PO Box 1768, Boerne, TX 78006

The Quartus Foundation for Spiritual Research was founded in 1981 by John Randolph Price and his wife, Jan Price. It is a New Age organization whose goal is to expand the human mind to its divine origin and thus affect a measurable change in the collective consciousness of humanity. Such a change of consciousness will usher in a new world of harmony and divine order.

To fulfill the foundation's purpose, Price has written a number of books. In the first, *The Super Beings* (1981), he called attention to the appearance of a new species of human that had overcome limitations to become Masters to raise the level of human consciousness. In 1984 Price announced the Planetary Commission, 500 million people who would consent to the healing of the planet and 50 million people mobilized to meditate for that healing at the same time, at noon, Greenwich time, on December 31, 1986, which was designated the first World Healing Day. The event was successful enough to become an annual tradition among New Age groups around the world.

Price views the Quartus Foundation as a research laboratory investigating spirituality, and is continually developing new approaches to bring in the New Age. In 1988 he invited several hundred people to live for two months in the realm of the "fourth dimension," that is, the realm of spiritual causation. It is the foundation's position that causation basically originates in the spiritual world, hence change comes from identifying with that world. The results of this experiment became the subject of his book, *A Spiritual Philosophy for the New World* (1990). The Quartus Foundation is a member of the International New Thought Alliance (INTA).

Membership: Not reported.

Periodicals: *The Quartus Report*.

Sources:

Quartus Foundation for Spiritual Research. www.quartus.org/.

Price, John Randolph. *The Abundance Book*. Carlsbad, CA: Hay House, 2005.

———. *The Planetary Commission*. Austin, TX: Quartus Foundation for Spiritual Research, 1984.

———. *A Spiritual Philosophy for the New World*. Boerne, TX: Quartus Foundation for Spiritual Research, 1990.

———. *The Superbeings*. Austin, TX: Quartus Foundation for Spiritual Research, 1981.

———. *With Wings as Eagles*. Austin, TX: Quartus Foundation for Spiritual Research, 1987.

Quimby Amenti Foundation

41 Verano Loop, Santa Fe, NM 87508

The history of the Quimby Amenti Foundation dates to 1946, when its founder, Dr. Neva Dell Hunter (d. 1978), began working in the field of ESP, though the Foundation itself did not materialize until 1966 in Alamogordo, New Mexico. The purpose of the Foundation, besides being a vehicle for Hunter's continued work, was fourfold: to promote the fatherhood of God and the brotherhood of man; to promote spiritual understanding among men; to provide education by holding classes; and to provide facilities for the general public. Like its namesake, Phineas P. Quimby, the founder of New Thought, the Foundation teaches that man is a direct expression of God. By applying metaphysical teachings, man can gain self-mastery.

Man lives within a universe governed by spiritual laws. These impersonal cosmic laws hold man responsible for every choice. Through the cycle of reincarnation, man becomes aware of the nature of life, assumes his responsibility, and becomes attuned to the oneness of life. He realizes that there is life on other planets. He realizes that the present upheavals are preparation for movement into the Aquarian Age.

The Foundation programs stress workshops, seminars, and lectures. A large library is maintained, and books, records and tapes are available to members on loan. One of the unique practices of the Foundation is a form of spiritual healing called "aura balancing," by which healers work on a patient's auric emanations. (Auras are invisible waves of psychic energy that bodies project.) The method is outlined in the booklet "The Auric Mirror," by Ellavivian Power.

Hunter was a psychic well known in the psychic community. She gave karmic live-readings and psychic counseling both at the Foundation and during her many lectures around the country. In Alamogordo she gave weekly channeled classes.

The Foundation is run by a president-director, a vice-president, treasurer, secretary, and nine-member board. Hunter was succeeded as president by Robert D. Waterman. Members are found both in Alamogordo and scattered around the United States in small study groups, many of which focus on aura-balancing. An annual Memorial Day picnic is held in Michigan by the Midwestern members.

Membership: Not reported.

Periodicals: *Quimby Center Newsletter.*

Sources:

Quimby Amenti Foundation. www.mystery-school.com/.

Waterman, Robert D. *Footprints of Eternity: Ancient Wisdom Applied to Modern Psychology.* West Conshohocken, PA: Infinity Publishing, 2006.

Religious School of Natural Hygiene

PO Box 1011, Boulder Creek, CA 95006

The Religious School of Natural Hygiene was founded in 1979 by Arthur D. Andrews Jr., its first minister and president. During most of its first decade, the church was headquartered at its California Health Sanctuary located on a farm near Hollister, California.

As spelled out in its primary text, the church teaches a very positive faith that affirms humanity's creation by a loving God. According to the text, God created humans to carry out His will—to become caretakers of ourselves, each other, the other life forms on the planet, and the planet itself. This way is called stewardship. Humans are free to choose to live out God's will or not. The church is officially against all forms of violence, including war and capital punishment.

The major practical conclusion to be drawn from this theological perspective is that God wants humans healthy and has built a plan so they can live out healthy lives. That plan, Natural Hygiene, involves following both a spiritual program of prayer and the laying-on-of-hands, and a process of fasting and diet derived from the Bible. This method allows God's power to work through us to bring healing. The recommended diet centers on uncooked fruits, nuts, and greens.

The school encountered major opposition to its work in 1987 when the state of California Board of Medical Quality Assurance charged the institution and Andrews with practicing medicine without a license. The state was particularly concerned with the lengthy fasts Andrews oversaw for people staying at the school. In addition, several former students filed suit for damages they sustained from adhering to the regimen (though the suits were subsequently dismissed). While working through these challenges, the church moved from Hollister to Boulder Creek.

Membership: In 1995 the school reported approximately 1,000 members in three centers in the United States and 25 members in Canada.

Periodicals: *Naturally, the Hygiene Way.*

Sources:

Major Tenets: Heed My Words. Hollister, CA: Religious School of Natural Hygiene, n.d.

Savitria

2405 Ruscombe, Baltimore, MD 21209

Savitria, formed in 1970 by a group led by the artist Robert Hieronimus, is dedicated to sowing the seeds for the Aquarian Age. The spiritual heart of Savitria is a 3.5-acre estate in North Baltimore, Maryland, that houses the core communal group, the Aum Esoteric Study Center and the New Morning School. Hieronimus began with a meditation group at Johns Hopkins University. Savitria was an outgrowth of that group.

It is Savitria's belief that man is a dual being, both mental and immortal. Man's goal is to allow the immortal aspect of being to overshadow the mental. This goal is accomplished through the study of esoteric sciences, which allow man to understand the cosmic process, and meditation, which raises his consciousness without the use of drugs. The high consciousness allows the two aspects of man to work in harmony and will lead to the era of the brotherhood of man and fatherhood of God, the golden age spoken of in all ancient esoteric writings.

In the early 1970s Hieronimus gained a reputation in the psychic community because of his interest in the esoteric history of the United States. He believes that the Masons and Rosicrucians played a large part in the founding of the country. Evidence of their influence is to be found in the reverse of the Great Seal of the United States (found on the back of the $1 bill), which features the eye of God in the great triangle, a Rosicrucian symbol.

The Aum Esoteric Study Center is a state-approved institution and functions as a branch of the World University, founded by Howard John Zitko and headquartered in Tucson, Arizona. It was formed as the first step in providing a total alternative education curriculum for all grades through college. In 2008 the center had a three-year curriculum, with classes on the mystic arts, occult sciences, and religion metaphysics. Certificates are offered in each area. New Morning School was formed in 1971 as a daycare/nursery school for preschool children. In the mid-1970s the Savitria community included approximately 15 people who follow a strict code of conduct that includes meditation before sunrise and abstinence from drugs, extramarital sex, and wearing shoes in the house.

Membership: Not reported.

Sources:

Hieronimus, Robert. *America's Secret Destiny: Spiritual Vision and the Founding of a Nation.* Rochester, VT: Destiny Books, 1989.

———. *The Two Great Seals of America.* Baltimore, MD: Savitriam, 1976.

Hieronimus, Robert, with Laura Cortner. *Founding Fathers, Secret Societies: Freemasons, Illuminati, Rosicrucians, and the Decoding of the Great Seal.* Rochester, VT: Destiny Books, 2006.

———. *The United Symbolism of America: Deciphering Hidden Meanings in America's Most Familiar Art, Architecture, and Logos.* Franklin Lakes, NJ: New Page Books, 2008.

Zitko, Howard John. *New Age Tantra Yoga.* Tucson, AZ: World University Press, 1974.

Society of Novus Spiritus

1700 Winchester Blvd., Ste. 100, Campbell, CA 95008-3001

The Society of Novus Spiritus was founded by the spirit medium Sylvia Browne, who has been channeling a spirit, Francine, since the 1960s, to disseminate the teachings Browne has received. Novus strives to uncover all of the "mysteries" regarding the nature of life, death, God, and the role humans play in life's scheme.

In its understanding, God never withholds information; humans choose to ignore it. The Society exists to help prepare individuals for receiving God's wisdom.

Novus affirms the existence of an all-loving God and is dedicated to eliminating what it considers to be false concepts of Satan, hell, sin, guilt, and the fear of God, all of which are contrary to its understanding of a benevolent creator. The pain of life is not punishment from God; rather, it is a learning tool, and a very necessary one in the larger scheme of life.

Observing that nearly everything in nature exhibits a dual nature, most notably in the pairing of male/female, members of the society understand that this pattern extends even to the Most High, to God. They believe in a Mother God as well as a Father God, reflecting the pattern of nature. Whereas God the Father holds creation in a constant state of being, God the Mother actively works with and through human beings for learning and perfection. Each is a distinct entity, not just a nebulous force, and they are addressed as Om (male) and Azna (female).

The society teaches that knowledge provides the key needed to unlock the mind, and considers itself a gnostic organization, by which it means that members are seekers after truth (gnosis). God is the source of all truth, which is available to all who are ready to receive it. The society promotes a community of people who desire to be guided by the light and dedicated to living a spiritual life.

The society also affirms that after "death," the human soul goes to the Other Side, better known as heaven. This place is the true reality, as opposed to the temporal planet Earth. The Other Side is eternal, a place of total harmony with no physical limitations where the individual's identity is intact. Life exists in its most wondrous and joyous form on the Other Side.

According to the society, even though the Other Side is total beauty and happiness, the soul may not be at peace and will still seek to better itself. This seeking drives an urge to reenter life on Earth to experience God's knowledge, gaining perfection in the process. Each soul decides how much experience it wants. Whereas some may never have a life on Earth, others will choose 50 or more lives.

The society holds weekly celebration services in Campbell, California, and Seattle, Washington. The work of the society is expanded through study groups that utilize Browne's *Journey of the Soul*, a set of 16 volumes based upon her mediumship, her seminars, and her sermons. Each month study groups receive two cassette tapes by Browne; those who complete the *Journey of the Soul* lessons may choose to take more advanced lessons to become deacons and ordained ministers of the society.

Membership: Not reported.

Sources:

Society of Novus Spiritus. www.novus.org/.

Browne, Sylvia. *Journey of the Soul*. 16 vols. Campbell, CA: Society of Novus Spiritus, 1991–1994.

———. *Meditation Book I*. Campbell, CA: Society of Novus Spiritus, 1994.

———. *The Nature of Good and Evil*. Carlsbad, CA: Hay House, 2001.

———. *Temples on the Other Side: How Wisdom from "Beyond the Veil" Can Help You Right Now*. Carlsbad, CA: Hay House, 2008.

Browne, Sylvia, and Antoinette May. *Adventures of a Psychic*. Carlsbad, CA: Hay House, 1998.

Spiritual Human Yoga (SHY)
7321 S Lindbergh Blvd., Ste. 209, St. Louis, MO 63125

Spiritual Human Yoga (SHY), also known as Mankind Enlightenment Love (MEL), was founded in Vietnam as Universal and Human Energy (HUE) by Luong Minh Dang (b. 1942). Biographical data on Dang is scarce, but following a time in the Vietnamese navy (1961–1975) and after the fall of the Saigon government and Communist takeover, Dang moved to America and became a U.S. citizen (1985). He gained a following as an alternative healer among his fellow countrymen in St. Louis, and in the 1990s his reputation spread throughout Missouri, first among

Vietnamese immigrants and later beyond the Vietnamese community. He formally reestablished the SHY movement in 1989, and it quickly spread from the United States to Latin America (Mexico and Brazil), Europe, Turkey, Israel, and Thailand.

Dang formally attributes his teachings to Dasira Narada (1846–1924), an obscure Sri Lankan master who passed his teachings to a successor. This successor, an Asian Indian, apparently initiated Dang in 1972 and later died in Sri Lanka in 1980. Drawing on both Eastern and Western occult teachings, Dang teaches that a universal energy (identified in other systems as chi or prana) permeates the universe. It enters individuals through the chakra system and permeates the body even to the cellular level. Through techniques taught by Dang, one can control the energy and use it to promote well-being, especially the healing of various bodily ailments. He compares his teachings favorably to other energy healing methods, especially the widely known Reiki system, and claims that his is less complicated and easier to master.

The system is divided into various levels that focus on different techniques and ways to control the energy flow. In the lower levels, the flow is seen as coming through the healer's hands; beginning at level 5, the flow is seen as occurring telepathically. Classes at the highest level, 7, were first offered in 1999. The introductory class introduces students to levels 1 to 3. By 1998 some 10,000 students had reportedly taken the level 6 class.

The teachings that offer the framework for the SHY healing technique, which become prominent immediately after the introductory class, are drawn from a spectrum of western esoteric notables, including Franz Anton Mesmer (1734–1815), from whom the word *mesmerism* is derived; Edgar Cayce (1877–1945), founder of the Association of Research and Enlightenment, and Abd-ru-shin (Oskar Ernst Bernhardt, 1875–1941), the founder of the Grail movement and author of *In the Light of Truth: The Grail Message* (1926). SHY does not perpetuate regular worship or ritual gatherings, nor does it provide members with rites of passage (e.g., baptism, confirmation, etc.). Dang claims to have regular contact with various spiritual beings.

SHY fits into the larger New Age community. Without setting specific dates, followers look for upcoming events to trigger a turning point in human history, introducing a new heaven on earth and the eventual disappearance of illness and death.

Membership: Not reported. As with the Reiki healing movement, many who have taken the SHY classes have retained only a loose affiliation to the movement.

Remarks: In January 1999, Dang was arrested in Belgium under the guise that he was a "cult" leader. After 65 days of imprisonment, he was released on bail without being charged or tried, and allowed to leave the country.

Sources:

Spiritual Human Yoga Norway. www.shy.no/.

Mayer, Jean-François. "Healing for the Millennium: Master Dang and Spiritual Human Yoga." *Journal of Millennial Studies* 2, no. 2 (Winter 2000). www.mille.org/publications/winter2000/winter2000.html and www.cesnur.org/testi/SHY.htm.

Nguyen, Tri-Thien. *L'Energie Universelle et Humaine: une methode naturelle de guerison energetique*. Romont, Switzerland: Editions Recto-Verseau, 2001.

Teaching of the Inner Christ, Inc.
2834 N Park Way, San Diego, CA 92104

The Teaching of the Inner Christ, Inc. (previously known as the Society for the Teaching of the Inner Christ) was founded in 1965 and incorporated in 1977 as the Inner Christ Administration Center. The founders were the Revs. Ann Meyer Makeever (born Annette Porter Remington, 1916–2007) and Peter Victor Meyer. Makeever, who was a "sensitive," claimed constant contact with the master teachers Jesus and Babaji, and with her own I AM Self. Ministers and members of the center accept guidance from these masters and from their own I AM Selves. The center offers counseling, in which the counselor contacts the deeper levels of spirit through the invisible teachers, and a wide range of classes in prayer therapy and inner sensitivity, the Bible, and leadership and ministerial concerns.

The group's headquarters are in San Diego, and there are centers and study groups in San Diego, Long Beach, Los Angeles, Oakland, and San Luis Obispo, California; Salt Lake City, Utah; Las Vegas, Nevada; and Edmonton, Alberta. The group supports a World Healing Ministry.

Membership: Not reported. In 1998 the center reported 500 active members in 10 centers.

Periodicals: *Double Heartline Newspaper* • *Monthly International Center Bulletin.*

Sources:

Teaching of the Inner Christ. www.teachingoftheinnerchrist.com/.

God's Will. San Diego, CA: Brotherhood, 1968.

Jesus' Love. San Diego, CA: Brotherhood, 1964.

Meyer, Ann. *Ann, A Biography.* San Diego, CA: T.I.C. Books, 1982.

Meyer, Ann, and Peter Meyer. *Being a Christ!* San Diego, CA: Dawning Publications, 1975.

Teleos Institute

7119 E Shea Blvd., Ste. 109, PMB 418, Scottsdale, AZ 85254

The Teleos Institute, formerly the Love Project, headed by Arleen Lorrance and Diane K. Pike, is an outgrowth of the Foundation for Religious Transition, founded originally in 1969 by Episcopal bishop James A. Pike and his wife, Diane Pike. The foundation was formed in the wake of Pike's well publicized problems throughout the 1960s with a traditional statement on Christian doctrine, accusations of heresy, his remarriage, and his involvement with psychics. Bishop Pike's main doctrinal disagreements with orthodox Christianity centered on the doctrine of the Trinity and the inerrancy of the Bible. In spring 1969 the Pikes left the institutional church and began a ministry to other "church alumni and those on the 'inside edge' of the church." The foundation's program was multifaceted, focusing on themes such as social activism, parapsychology, clergy training, and the study of Christian origins.

The death of Bishop Pike in September 1969, less than a year after the formation of the foundation, necessitated a reorientation. The name was changed to the Bishop Pike Foundation, but during the next two years it became increasingly clear that, without the bishop, the specific missions of the foundation were not materializing. In 1972 the foundation was merged into a structure already being formed by Arleen Lorrance, the Love Project. The Love Project grew out of a shared teacher-student experience that turned a violence-ridden ghetto into a center of love, concern, and positive action in 1971. As the Love Project matured, it was conceived as an active process of creating love.

The Teleos Institute provides an alternative to negative, destructive, violent living and a way in which all seekers may link energies in a universal chain of caring—a chain forged with the strength of the uniqueness of each individual. The way of the seeker is to make his or her very life an alternative, that is, to be change rather than to try to change others. The institute has various structures—workshops, group travel experiences, and training people to love universally and unconditionally. Advance work is offered in the School of Consciousness Classes (both in person and by cassette) and in an intensive Theatre of Life program focused upon bringing forth creativity in daily living. Recent programs have focused on "Life as a Waking Dream," a method that facilitates the awakening process by looking at ordinary life experiences as if they had been dreams. The nature of the institute keeps seekers on the move.

Membership: The institute is not a membership organization, but has a network of people who attend institute-sponsored events across the United States and Canada.

Periodicals: *Emerging.*

Sources:

Teleos Institute. www.consciousnesswork.com/.

Lorrance, Arleen. *Buddha from Brooklyn.* San Diego, CA: LP Publications, 1975.

————. *The Love Project.* San Diego, CA: LP Publications, 1972.

————. *Why Me? How To Heal What Is Hurting You.* New York: Ranson Associates, 1977.

Lorrance, Arleen, and Diane Kennedy Pike. *The Love Project Way.* San Diego, CA: LP Publications, 1980.

Pike, Diane Kennedy. *Cosmic Unfoldment.* San Diego, CA: LP Publications, 1976.

Unification Movement

4 W 43rd St., New York, NY 10036

The Unification Movement, formerly known as the Holy Spirit Association for the Unification of World Christianity, was brought to the United States in 1959 from South Korea. After a period of slow growth, it mushroomed during the early and mid-1970s and became a controversial and significant religious force because of its unconventional beliefs, accusations of improper recruitment techniques, and its attempts to build coalitions of scholars and world leaders around the church's programs and ideals. The church first gained national attention during the 1972 U.S. speaking tour of its founder, the Rev. Sun Myung Moon. The Unification Church, as it is usually called, came to the United States in the person of Young Oon Kim, who produced the first expression of the founder's teachings. The basic scripture of the church, the *Divine Principle*, was translated into English in 1972 by Mrs. Won Bok Choi. A revised translation, *Exposition of Divine Principle*, by Jin Keum Kim and Andrew Wilson, was published in 1995. During its early years in the United States, the church was the subject of one major sociological study, and Moon was proclaimed a voice for the New Age by the spiritualist medium Arthur A. Ford.

The Reverend Moon was born in 1920 in what is now North Korea. During his youth, his family converted to Christianity and joined the Presbyterian Church. In 1935, at a time when Korean Pentecostal Christians were predicting a Korean messiah, he had a vision of Jesus in which he was told to carry out Jesus' unfinished task. In 1945 Moon began to collect a following and two years later founded the Broad Sea Church. He also spent six months at Israel Soodo Won (Israel Monastery), established by Baek Moon Kim, a self-proclaimed messiah, and changed his name from Yong Myung Moon to Sun Myung Moon (which means someone who has clarified the Word or Truth). For much of the period from 1946 to 1950, Moon was in prison in North Korea for his refusal to cooperate with Kim Il Sung's regime, and in 1950 Moon became a refugee. He eventually settled in Pusan, and in 1954 he founded the Unification Church in Seoul. The new church grew slowly, but by 1957 a Korean edition of the *Divine Principle* was in print. Meanwhile, church members established several corporations dealing in products such as ginseng tea and titanium. Missionaries were sent to Japan, where they had their greatest success.

In December 1971 Moon moved to the United States. During the early 1970s, as the church began to grow, several buildings were purchased to house its expanding program. Facilities for the Unification Theological Seminary were acquired near Barrytown, New York; an estate used for training sessions was purchased in Tarrytown, New York; and a conference center, which also serves as Moon's U.S. residence, called "East Garden," is located at Irvington, New York. In Manhattan, a headquarters building and mission center (the former New Yorker Hotel) completed its major organizational facilities.

Beliefs: Unification belief is built around the three basic concepts of Creation, Fall, and Restoration. The principle of Creation asserts that God created the world and by that act became known. The world, reflective of God, has two expressions—Sung Sang (internal, causal) and Hyung Sang (external, resultant). It also has a second set of dual characteristics, masculine and feminine. These two kinds of relations are quite distinct and express different qualities of the created order. Sung

Sang and Hyung Sang express the relatedness of spirit, or mind and matter, whereas masculinity and femininity express the complementarity of male and female, or yang and ying. God created the world out of His inner nature, His heart, and His impulse to love and to be united in love. The purpose of creation is to experience the joy that comes from loving.

The principle of the Fall began with Adam and Eve's lack of realization of God's original purpose in creation. They fell away from God because of disobedience that resulted in a premature sexual relationship (a misuse of love) and therefore were unable to create a perfect family. Their failure placed the fallen archangel Satan in control of the world. Since that time, God has been trying to restore His primal intention and replace the order of selfish love with the ethic of true love.

The principle of Restoration outlines the conditions necessary for restoration to occur. Because God created humankind with free will and some measure of responsibility, the restoration process has been prolonged because of human failure. God's ultimate design is to send one sinless man, the messiah, through whom humankind can be engrafted and achieve salvation. The messiah must meet a variety of qualifications.

First, according to the church's beliefs, the messiah must be born on earth as a substantial, physical being, because he must accomplish the original task of becoming an ideal person, the person who has perfected his character and thus has fulfilled the First Blessing, to be fruitful (Gen. 1:28). He can carry out this responsibility only in the flesh. He also must take a bride and realize the ideal family that God has desired, and thus become the True Parent, one who has realized God's Second Blessing, to multiply (Gen 1:28). His parental heart will implant God's heart and love in the hearts of everyone following him and will help them to perfect themselves by giving rebirth to them and showing each one how to accomplish true marriage and family life. This is how all humans can achieve complete physical and spiritual salvation, and create the kingdom of God on earth, fulfilling the Third Blessing (Gen. 1:28)

Members believe that due to the failure of the chosen people (chiefly, John the Baptist and the religious leaders) to accept and follow him 2,000 years ago, Jesus was not able to complete these tasks. Instead, he was killed, contrary to God's original will. Nevertheless, through his resurrection, Jesus established the possibility of spiritual salvation for all humankind. Thus, if human beings accept Jesus as their savior, they can attain spiritual salvation and live with Jesus in paradise. This spiritual salvation does not provide complete and physical salvation for humans on earth, so Christ must come again to complete the salvation process on the earth. He will come to fulfill the Lord's Prayer: "Thy kingdom come on earth as in heaven." This will be a world where there is no sin, no Satan, and where humankind will live in peace and harmony as God's children.

The Reverend Moon's mission is to fill the conditions of the Lord of the Second Advent. In 1960 he married Hak Ja Han, with whom he parented 14 children. Through the Reverend and Mrs. Moon's fulfillment of the position of True Parents, according to Unification belief, God has brought the opening of complete restoration. Couples participate in the restoration by their marriage blessing. Many are first called to a period of sacrificial work and personal celibacy. At the end of that period, church members are engaged and blessed in marriage in a public ceremony conducted by Moon and his wife. The events surrounding the marriage are the primary events in the messianic mission. As part of their engagements, members participate in a holy wine ceremony (somewhat analogous to Christian communion) whereby their original sin is conditionally absolved. Couples are married in large mass ceremonies, the most recent of which was celebrated in 1997 in Washington, D.C., with 28,000 couples present; it was broadcast to more than 50 satellite locations worldwide. After the wedding, the couples separate for at least 40 days before the union is consummated. The so-called "three-day ceremony" during which consummation occurs ritually dramatizes the restoration.

Organization: In April 2008 the Reverend Moon appointed his youngest son, Hyung Jin Moon, to be the new leader of the Unification Church. The U.S. church is advised by church elders who reside in the United States. The board appoints the various national presidents; in 2008 Michael Jenkins headed the church in the United States. To carry out the messiah's program for restoration and bring forth the kingdom of God, the church has a variety of evangelistic, political, cultural, charitable, and religious programs.

Evangelistic programs include the Collegiate Association for the Research of Principles (referring to the church's basic principles), an educational outreach on the nation's campuses. Church families around the United States reach out through "Tribal Messiahship." The church's theistic beliefs lead members to oppose Communism; this was a prominent part of the church's public expression throughout the 1980s. One reason Korea is identified as the land in which the New Lord will appear is that it is on God's front line as well as on Satan's: The 38th parallel is referred to as the line of confrontation between Communism and democracy. The major expression of the critique against Communism in the 1970s, the Freedom Leadership Foundation, was replaced by CAUSA, which found significant success in Latin America. In the 1990s Moon turned his attention to the creation of true families through the nonsectarian Family Federation for World Peace and Unification (FFWPU).

A cultural program is promoted under the International Cultural Foundation, the most important part of which is the International Conference on the Unity of the Sciences, one of the Unification community's most successful programs. It brings scientists together every year to discuss the convergence of science, morals, and values. Growing out of the conference is the Professors World Peace Academy and the Washington Institute for Values in Public Policy. The various ecumenical religious programs were reorganized in the early 1980s under the International Religious Foundation (IRF) and in the 1990s under the Inter-Religious Federation for World Peace (IRFWP). Some of its major programs include ecumenical conferences for theologians and other scholars (New Ecumenical Research Association, or NEW ERA), conferences for clergy (True Family Values Ministry), and the Religious Youth Service (RYS).

The prime charitable activity, which finds its greatest response in the urban minority community and the developing world, is the International Relief Friendship Foundation (IRFF), which spawned the United to Serve America organization.

The church grew very slowly until 1972. By 1976 it had grown from a few hundred to approximately 6,000 members. It also began a worldwide expansion that has seen church centers opened in many countries on every continent. In the United States and western Europe, the church became an object of controversy and public hostility. Church membership in the United States dropped below 5,000 by the end of the decade and continued to decline. During the early 1980s, centers were established in every state; most, however, remain small.

Membership: In 1998 the church reported an estimated core membership of 50,000 in America, and some 3 million worldwide. In addition to this membership, more than 70 million couples worldwide have received the holy wine and Rev. Moon's marriage blessing, though they often remain in their own faith.

Educational Facilities:

Unification Theological Seminary, Barrytown, New York.

University of Bridgeport, Bridgeport, Connecticut.

Sun Moon University, Korea.

Periodicals: *Dialogue and Alliance* • *Today's World True Family Times* • *Unification News*.

Remarks: Alarmed by the growth of the Unification Church in the early 1970s, opponents have organized and carried on a steady program of opposition that has succeeded in making the church an object of continued controversy. By the 1970s the church had become the prime reference for the popular derisive term *cult*. Attacks have been launched from a variety of sources. These attacks culminated in the conviction of Moon for tax evasion. For details on other controversies the church has been involved in, please refer to the volumes listed below as well as other titles covering the church and/or contemporary cult controversies.

Sources:

Unification Church. www.unification.org/.

Barker, Eileen. *The Making of a Moonie*. Oxford, U.K.: Basil Blackwell, 1984.

Breen, Michael. *Sun Myung Moon: The Early Years, 1920–53*. Hurstpier-point, U.K.: Refuge Books, 1997.

Bromley, David G., and Anson D. Shupe Jr. *Moonies in America*. Beverly Hills, CA: Sage Publications, 1979.

Divine Principle. New York: Holy Spirit Association for the Unification for World Christianity, 1973.

Durst, Mose. *To Bigotry, No Sanction*. Chicago: Regnery Gateway, 1984.

Forty Years in America: An Intimate History of the Unification Movement, 1959–1999. New York: Holy Spirit Association for the Unification of World Christianity, 2000.

Outline of the Principle, Level 4. New York: Holy Spirit Association for the Unification of World Christianity, 1980.

United Spiritual Church of the Spiritual Advisory Council

115 Cygnet Ln., Melrose, FL 32666

The United Spiritual Church of the Spiritual Advisory Council is an ecclesiastical body associated with the Spiritual Advisory Council, an open-membership united spiritual society of friends. The council was founded in Chicago in 1974 by Paul V. Johnson (1924–1996) and Robert Ericsson, both former leaders in the Spiritual Frontiers Fellowship, a church-related organization that explored psychic and spiritual experiences. The council differed from the fellowship in its adoption of a mystical perspective. Soon after its formation, Johnson relocated to Florida and in 1979 opened the New Age Centre for Alternative Realities in Orlando. The council sponsors several national conferences annually and has nurtured the formation of study groups.

Among the members of the Spiritual Advisory Council were some who had manifested leadership in their abilities as teachers and in the exercise of various spiritual gifts, especially in spiritual healing and psychic readings and counsel. The United Spiritual Church of the Spiritual Advisory Council emerged for those who saw the council as their spiritual home and who wished to exercise their ministry there. The first ministers were ordained at the council meeting in Chicago in 1979.

The church has no organized creed or dogma, but generally accepts a metaphysical, esoteric perspective. Ministers are encouraged to continue their growth in understanding of spiritual truth and to develop their awareness for channeling healing energies to those suffering pain or want. The council exists as a national body with many members, and the church as a smaller fellowship within the council. Following Johnson's death in 1996, the leadership of the church was assumed by David Beede.

Membership: In 1995 the church reported approximately 1,000 members and 56 ministers.

Periodicals: *Spiritual Advisory Council OutReach Newsletter*.

Sources:

Spiritual Advisory Council. www.sacnet.org/.

Universal Church of Metaphysics

PO Box 4505, Arcata, CA 95518

The Universal Church of Metaphysics was founded by Christine Breese. During the many years in which she had worked in the film industry, Breese had explored a variety of spiritual paths and she began teaching metaphysical classes in 1990. She subsequently earned a Ph.D. in metaphysical studies and, as a metaphysical teacher, sought a means of reaching a larger audience for metaphysical ideas. Thus she was led to found the Church and its associated University of Metaphysical

Sciences. The Church, which exists primarily as a small group in Arcata, California, has the University as its primary activity.

The University of Metaphysics is a distant learning school that offers a curriculum utilizing course work assembled by Dr. Breese from materials written by a team of some 40 metaphysical teaches. Teachings concentrate on a path to enlightenment through Zen-style meditation, an understanding of chakra energies, astral projection, the Law of Attraction, dream interpretation, and a variety of New Age practices based in Buddhism. The basic program consists of written and audio lessons that the average student takes approximately one year to complete. Upon completion of this material, a bachelor's degree is granted. To receive the master's degree, the student would need to complete a 5,000-word essay on a metaphysical subject in addition to the lessons. For the doctor's degree, the student writes a 10,000-word doctoral dissertation. Those who complete the master's program receive ordination in the Universal Church of Metaphysics.

The Church sponsors *Spirit Talk*, a television talk show featuring several guests discussing metaphysical subjects, offered for airing through public access stations.

Membership: Not reported.

Periodicals: *Starlight Journal*. Posted online at http://umsonline.org

Sources:

Universal Church of Metaphysics. www.ucmeta.org/.

Universal Oneness United (UOU)

500-B Prairie Ln., Hudson, WI 54016

Universal Oneness United (UOU) was founded by Arianni Masters and Oreon Masters, a married couple who individually as children had experiences with the world beyond normal experience and came into contact with spiritual guides. In the course of their spiritual quest, they studied the world's religions and came to the conclusion that "love is all there is and we're all one." That principle became the guiding axiom for Universal Oneness United.

Universal Oneness United is envisioned as a worldwide organization that attempts to build a global metaphysical spiritual family, to assist individuals in personal and spiritual growth, and to engage in service. The perspective of UOU draws heavily on the western esoteric tradition and assumes that love is the essence of God/Goddess within us all, and that the goal of the spiritual life is the expression of the divine essence during this lifetime. That expression takes the form of service. We reincarnate repeatedly until we understand this basic truth and live by it. UOU also assumes that there are many paths to the one truth and that all of these paths are true for those who follow them.

To assist people who are searching, UOU established a mystery school that offers lessons on making connection to Oneness, the Whole. Included with these lessons are channelings from the archangel Raziel speaking through Arianni. This material is said to introduce the student to the language of angels.

UOU also sponsors Light Haven Interfaith Seminary, which provides a self-directed study program for UOU members who would like to be ordained as Interfaith ministers. Paula Sunray, who previously headed her own spiritual correspondence educational program, the National Interfaith Seminary, merged her work into that of Light Haven Interfaith Seminary. The program allows one to receive certification as a minister of metaphysics, a minister of spiritual counseling, a minister of spiritual healing, or a minister of religious studies. The seminary is affiliated with both the Association of Interfaith Ministers and the Association for Global New Thought.

UOU promotes the organization of study groups, in which a small number individuals gather periodically to discuss the UOU material produced monthly.

Membership: Not reported.

Educational Facilities:

LightHaven Interfaith Seminary.

Urantia Book Fellowship

PO Box 4583, Grand Central Station, New York, NY 10163

Founded in 1955 as the Urantia Brotherhood, the Urantia Book Fellowship believes that the *Urantia Book*, a collection of material received from celestial beings, will eventually unify all religionists from every race and culture, and bring forth the reality of spiritual equality and the universality of cosmic citizenship. The fellowship comprises people representing all walks of life. It offers secondary works, study aids, Internet access, international conclaves, numerous seminars, and home-study groups in 80 countries, all of which fuel steady interest in the book's "revelation to all humanity." (A passage from the *Urantia Book* 102:3.12: "The pursuit of knowledge constitutes science, the search for wisdom is philosophy, the love for God is religion, the hunger for truth is a revelation.")

The Urantia Book Fellowship reports that it is "the largest, most inclusive organization of reader-believers."

Membership: In 2002 the fellowship reported 1,500 members including chartered societies, affiliate groups, and members-at-large.

Educational Facilities:

The fellowship conducts annual in-depth workshops and presentations, ongoing web-based study, and sponsored programs for scholarly works.

Sources:

Urantia Book Fellowship. www.urantiabook.org.

Urantia Foundation

533 Diversey Pkwy., Chicago, IL 60614

The Urantia Foundation was founded in 1950 in Chicago, Illinois, to disseminate the teachings of the *Urantia Book*. The book is a 2,097-page collection of messages received from numerous celestial beings; the name of the person who received these messages has never been revealed. To believers, it represents the first major revelation since the coming of Christ. The contents, according to the Urantia Foundation, "differ from all previous revelations, for they are not the work of a single universe personality, but a composite presentation of many beings." The *Urantia Book* was first published in 1955, and it has been translated into French, Spanish, Finnish, Russian, Dutch, Korean, Italian, Lithuanian, Portuguese, Romanian, and German; Swedish, Estonian, Chinese, Bulgarian, Japanese, Farsi, Greek, Hungarian, Polish, and Urdu translations were underway in 2008. The *Urantia Book* is divided into four parts. Part 1 describes the nature of deity, the reality of Paradise, the organization and working of the central and super universe, the personalities of the grand universe, and the high density of evolutionary mortals. Part 2 deals with the local universe, the handiwork of a Creator Son of the Paradise order of Michael. Our world, Urantia, belongs to a local universe whose sovereign is Michael, the Son of God and the Son of Man, known on this world as Jesus of Nazareth. Part 3 is a history of Urantia, the geologic development, the establishment of life, and the evolution and history of man. Part 4 contains a biography of Jesus Christ, including a detailed discussion of the hidden years (from birth to the beginning of his public ministry). According to the *Urantia Book*, Jesus was born August 21, 7 B.C.E., had an excellent education, became a skilled carpenter, began a Mediterranean tour in his twenty-eighth year, and began his public ministry in 27 C.E. After more than three years, his ministry ended in the crucifixion and resurrection. Objectives of the Urantia Foundation include promoting the teachings of Jesus, primarily the appreciation of the fatherhood of God and the brotherhood of man, in order to increase the comfort, happiness, and well-being of man.

The foundation is a tax-exempt, common-law, educational foundation operating under a declaration of trust. It is managed by a board of five trustees who are appointed for life terms and serve without compensation. The duties of the foundation are to publish the *Urantia Book*, "to perpetually preserve inviolate the text of the *Urantia Book*," and "to retain absolute and unconditional control of . . . media for the printing and reproduction of the *Urantia Book* and any translation thereof." The Urantia Foundation is headquartered in Chicago and has additional offices in England, France, Spain, Finland, and Australia.

Associated with the foundation is the International Urantia Association (IUA), a reader membership organization also headquartered in Chicago. The purpose of IUA is the in-depth study of the *Urantia Book* and the orderly dissemination of its teachings. The association's long-term task is to encourage the formation of study groups, and to foster and facilitate the voluntary transformation of stable and mature study groups into Urantia associations. These associations function on a regional level and operate with great autonomy. The IUA emphasizes its nonsectarian nature, and maintains that members of diverse religions may be students of the *Urantia Book* and receive its revelations as enriching rather than contradicting their own faiths. It is a fraternal organization with a spiritual objective.

Membership: In 1997 the International Urantia Association comprised three national associations (Australia-New Zealand, Finland, and the United States) and fourteen local associations in the United States.

Periodicals: *Urantia Foundation News* • *Urantia Association International Journal*.

Remarks: Since 1955 the foundation has protected the text of the *Urantia Book* through its ownership of the copyright. In addition, since 1950, in order to preserve the unique identity of the *Urantia Book* and the Urantia Foundation, the foundation established and began using the "Urantian," the concentric-circles symbol that was registered in 1952 as a service mark and in 1971 as a trademark. The foundation's ownership of the marks will continue in perpetuity, which means that after the copyright expires, only those copies of the *Urantia Book* published by the Urantia Foundation can bear the concentric-circles symbol, assuring future readers of the authenticity of the text.

Sources:

Urantia Foundation. www.urantia.org/.

Bedell, Clyde. *Concordex to the Urantia Book*. Laguna Hills, CA: Author, 1980.

Faw, Duane L., comp. *The Paramony*. Malibu, CA: Author, 1986.

Myers, Martin W. *Unity, Not Uniformity*. Chicago: Urantia Foundation, 1973.

Renn, Ruth E. *Study Aids for Part IV of the Urantia Book, The Life and Teachings of Jesus*. Chicago: Urantia Foundation, 1975.

Special Report to the Readers of the Urantia Book: Urantia Foundation Ends Its Relationship with the Former Urantia Brotherhood. Chicago: Urantia Foundation, 1990.

The Urantia Book. Chicago: Urantia Foundation, 1955.

Western Esoteric Family III: Magick

19

Magick, as its most prominent twentieth-century theoretician, Aleister Crowley (1875–1947), defined it, is "the science and art of causing change to occur in conformity to the will" (*Magick without Tears*, 1973, p. 27). Another described it as "an effect without an observable cause" and owing "nothing to the physical laws of our everyday world" (Conway, *Magick: An Occult Primer*, 1972, p. 19). Neither definition is, in fact, complete. The latter, for example, could apply as well to almost any incident of psychokinesis or mind over matter. Father Richard Woods supplements these definitions by describing magick as the "art of employing the mysterious supernatural forces believed to underpin the universe in order to produce desired effects at will" (*The Occult Revolution: A Christian Meditation*, 1971, p. 30). Woods's definition is weakened by its use of the word supernatural, but does make the point that a particular view of the world is implicit in magick. That is, the world is made up of forces that impinge upon humanity; the object of magick is to come to terms with the world by coming to terms with these forces. Inherent in each of these definitions is the belief in a power of which most people are unaware and to which most of those who believe in it lack access. In spite of the alienation of the majority of people from the magical worldview, magick has become the life-orientation of a growing number of persons in contemporary America.

Inherent in the magical worldview is the notion of control and manipulation. These are forces that manipulate people, victimizing them until they become controlling agents. One witch, Sybil Leek (1917–1982), defined magick as "the art of producing a desired effect or result through the use of various techniques such as incantations and presumably assuring human control of supernatural agencies or the forces of nature" (*Diary of a Witch*, 1968, p. 4). In its demonic aspect, such control can lead to the manipulation of people by curses (i.e., black magick), but black magick is by no means a major practice among magicians.

Magicians vary widely in their beliefs and are intensely individualistic. Nevertheless, there are a few characteristics (beyond magick) common to the groups herein classified as members of the magick family. These characteristics include ritual, secret ancient wisdom, and a tradition that has its roots in the pre-Christian world.

Ritual, for magicians, is much more than the ordering principle in worship. It is seen as a very useful tool in focusing the power of the individual and in concentrating the

thoughts of members of a group on a common object of concern. Beyond these functions, the ritual effects a merging of reality and the mysterious. The climax of the ritual is the evocation or invocation of a deity for some specific purpose. Well-performed ritual affects a person on all levels, thus achieving the coordination of outside effects (color, music, meditative practices, chants, and words) with the inner dimensions of the self. The successful ritual brings about a change in the state of consciousness. To help produce this state, some groups even use various psychedelic drugs.

Those groups for which ritual is the apex of magical activity wear ritual garb and use elaborate facilities. Such facilities may be anything from the temple of a magical lodge to the circle of a witch's coven (a small group of witches). Garb ranges from full-length robes to nudity (Gardnerian witches). Implements of worship include various kinds of sacred objects: the athame (ritual knife) of the witch, the rod of hazelwood, the sword, and the incense burner. These objects are for ritual use only and are carefully protected from profane eyes. Most magicians also take a ritual name, to be used with other initiated brethren. This name may be that of a great magician of the past, like John Dee (1527–1608), or it may even be a motto. (William Butler Yeats's name was "Daemon est Deus Inversus," which in translation means "the Devil is the reverse side of God.")

Secrecy is a vital part of the magician's lifestyle. It provides protection from a hostile world that does not understand magick and thrill seekers who are attracted to magick for shallow reasons, such as the chance to participate in an orgy. For most, however, secrecy is an element of the faith, which they believe is for the few. (The masses, being neither prepared nor intelligent enough, would misuse, degrade, and be unable to understand the teachings. Such vulgarization of the faith would destroy the power of the ritual.)

Secrecy is bolstered by a system of initiations and degrees. New members, after a probationary period, are given a basic initiation. Some groups have only one initiation, others may have three, ten, twenty-three, or even more. Initiation to each higher degree gives one access to a greater amount of secret material and presupposes an added proficiency in the magical arts.

The material that is kept secret is the magical knowledge of the group. This knowledge may consist of rituals, various incantations, metaphysical teachings, and the more powerful

Western Esoteric Family III: Magick Chronology

1801	Francis Barrett's *The Magus* marks the beginning of the post-Enlightenment magical revival.
1888	The initial lodge of the recent founded Hermetic Order of the Golden Dawn is opened in London.
1891	Arthur Edward Waite joins the Hermetic Order of the Golden Dawn.
1898	Aleister Crowley joins the Golden Dawn (at age 23).
1898	McGregor Mathers publishes *The Book of the Sacred Magic of Abra-Melin the Mage.*
1899	C. G. Leland publishes *Aradia, the Gospel of the Witches.*
1900	Crowley is expelled from the Golden Dawn.
1909–13	Crowley publishes semi-annual book-length periodical *The Equinox.*
1904	The *Book of the Law* is dictated to Aleister Crowley while in Cairo, Egypt.
1913	Eliphas Levi's *Histoire de la magie* (1860) is translated by Arthur Edward Waite and published as *The History of Magic.*
1920	Crowley founds the Abbey of Thelema.
1920s	Paul Foster Case founds the Builders of the Adytum.
1921	"The Witch Cult in Western Europe" by Margaret Murray is published.
1924	Founding of Lectorium Rosicrucianum.
1928	Dion Fortune founds the Fraternity (later Society) of the Inner Light.
1931	*The God of the Witches* by Margaret Murray is published.
1937–40	Israel Regardie publishes Rituals of the Order of the Golden Dawn.
1847	Crowley dies and is succeeded by Karl Germer.
1948	The first edition of *The White Goddess* by Robert Graves is published.
1949	The modern Wicca movement is traced to the publication of *High Magic's Aid* by Gerald Gardner (under his magical name, "Scire").
1951	The British Witchcraft Act is repealed and replaced by the Fraudulent Mediums Act. Witchcraft ceases to be illegal in the United Kingdom.
1954	*Witchcraft Today* by Gerald Gardner is published.
1957	Fred Adams forms Fereferia.
1962	Tim Zell and Robert Christie found the Church of All Worlds.
1963	Raymond Buckland starts first Gardnerian coven in North America.
	Modern Druid movement in North America is formed by students at Carlton College, Northfield, Minnesota.
1967	*The Julian Review*, an early Pagan periodical, begins.
1969	Psychedelic Venus Church formed in Berkeley, California.
1972	Susan B. Anthony Coven formed by Z. Budapest. The Church and School of Wicca formed by Yvonne and Gavin Frost receives tax exempt status.
1973	Raymond Buckland withdraws from the Gardnerian movement and founds Seax Wicca.
1974	Selena Fox forms Circle Sanctuary.
1977	Governor Michael Dukakis names Laurie Cabot the Official Witch of Salem, Massachusetts.
1979	Margot Adler publishes *Drawing Down the Moon.*
1979	Starhawk publishes *The Spiral Dance.*
1983	Circle purchases land in rural Wisconsin that becomes Circle Sanctuary.
1985	North Carolina senator Jesse Helms introduces legislation that would deny Witchcraft religious groups from gaining tax exemption. It does not pass.
1997	Wiccan priest Patrick McCollum becomes the statewide Pagan chaplain for the California Department of Corrections and Rehabilitation.
1999	Rep. Robert Barr introduces anti-Wiccan legislation into the U.S. House of Representatives. It is not enacted.
2007	U.S. Department of Veterans Affairs grants approval for Wiccan and Pagan veterans to have the pentacle symbol placed on their memorial markers.

magical formulas. There are also the particular group's secrets, such as the magical names of members.

Most magical worldviews include a belief in reincarnation, alchemy, the Atlantis myth, and astrology and the other divining arts. Many groups would argue that their tenets constitute not a religion but a philosophy with possible religious overtones. Most groups adopt a specific calendar and practice their ceremonies according to an astrological or Egyptian year. Some have begun to articulate their practices in Jungian archetypical terms.

Possibly as important as any characteristic shared by the magical groups is their common history. The works of the ancient mystery schools, the Gnostics, and, more recently, Francis Barrett (eighteenth–nineteenth century), Éliphas Lévi (1810–1875), Louis Claude de Saint-Martin (1743–1803), S. L. MacGregor Mathers (1854–1918), and Aleister Crowley appear in the histories of all the various magical subdivisions. This common history manifests not only a common effort, but also a consensus as to which issues are important enough to generate polemics, a consensus that is most important to the creation of a family group.

The differences between magical groups reflect those issues around which debate centers. Groups vary in particulars of ritual, in organization, in attitudes toward drugs, and in the specific calendar used. The major groups vary on the particular aspect of ancient wisdom with which they identify. Related to the particular ancient wisdom (Egyptian, Druidic, Hebrew, etc.) are varying ideas about deity. Some groups are close to Unitarian Christianity; others are unashamedly polytheistic.

A SHORT HISTORY OF MAGICK.

That magick was a common practice of the ancient and even prehistoric world is a truism today. The magical world of the shaman, the alchemist, the magi, the vodou cult, and the medieval witchcraft trials have been given ample treatment in historical, archaeological, anthropological, and psychological literature. Most modern magical groups take much inspiration from two magical groups that developed in the Middle Ages—the Knights Templar and the Kabbalists.

KNIGHTS TEMPLAR. The Knights Templar was formed in 1118 by Hugh de Payens (c. 1070–1136) and Geoffrey de Saint-Omer (c.1080.– c.1150). The group was sanctioned by the king of Jerusalem and by the pope in its primal mission to protect Jerusalem for Christian pilgrims. The order developed into a monastic and then a magical group, and much Gnostic-like theology was taught by Hugh and his followers. The group learned the "mysteries of true Christianity" from the Johannites, a magical sect operating in Jerusalem in the twelfth century. Caught in a power play with the king of France two hundred years after its founding, the wealthy and powerful organization was destroyed almost overnight, and Jacques de Molay (c.1244–1314), the leader, was burned at the stake. The charges of black magick leveled against them were never proved, but that they were a magical fraternity is little doubted.

The role of the Templars in occult history received new life in the years immediately after the French Revolution (1789–1799). Masonry arrived in France from Great Britain with a message that it was the product of knights who survived the fourteenth-century holocaust by quietly settling in England. Bernard-Raymond Fabré-Palaprat (1773–1838) arose out of these Masonic discussions of the Templars. In 1804 he announced that he had discovered documents proving that the old Templar order had continued, led by a succession of grand masters, the last of whom, Duke Louis Hercule Timoléon de Cross (1734–1792), was killed in 1792. Fabré-Palaprat thus was free to reconstitute the order and proclaim himself the new grand master. He also founded an associated esoteric Catholic "Johannine" church, and consecrated its first bishop, Ferdinand-François Chatel (1795–1857).

The activity of Fabré-Palaprat and his successors infused Templar terminology into the European occult community and provided a foundation in both French- and German-speaking lands upon which various "templar" organizations could be created. Among the groups that have roots in the neo-Templar worldview, if not direct organizational ties, are the German-based groups, the Ordo Templi Orientis (later made famous by Aleister Crowley) and the Ordo Novi Templi founded by Jörg Lanz von Liebenfels (1874–1954).

KABBALAH. Development of the Kabbalah from older Hebrew sources had begun in Babylon in the early Middle Ages. The most important book, the *Book of Zolar,* was a thir-

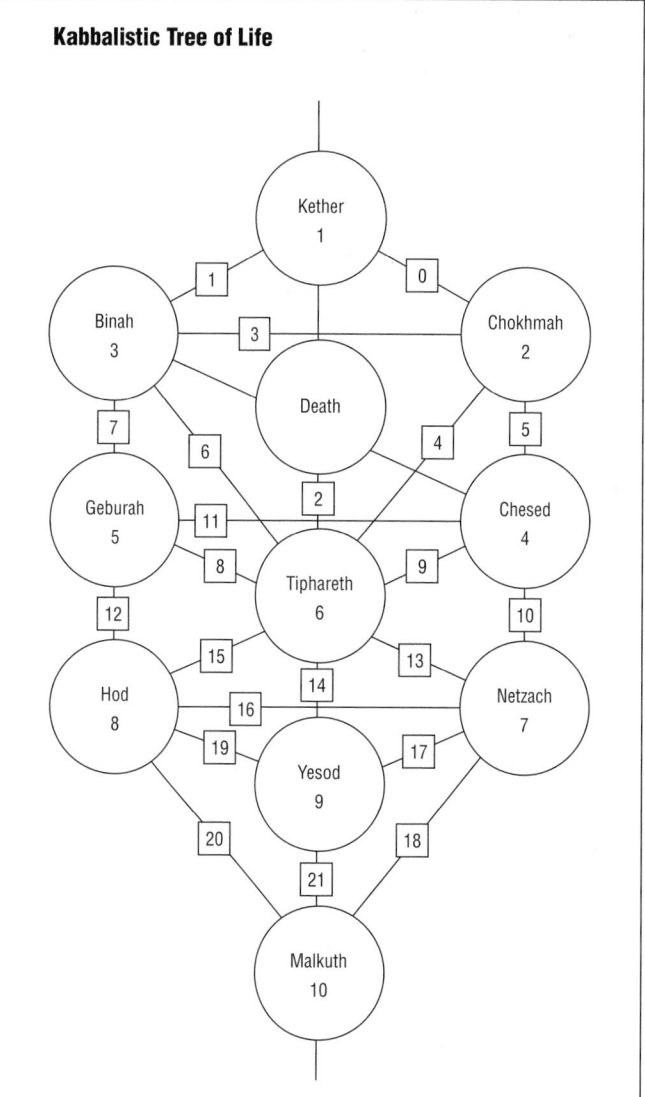

Kabbalistic Tree of Life

Adapted from www.byzant.com

teenth-century product of Moses de Leon (1250–1305). Kabbalists believe the world can be grasped through numbers and letters, and that their job is to discover the meaning hidden in the numbers and letters using traditional methods. The number "ten" is the basic organizing principle of the universe. Through the ten numbers (*sephirot*), the basic working principles of life are organized and are pictured in the Sephirotic tree. The Sephirot are emanations of God, who is at the top of the tree, and man climbs the tree, by means of magick, to the divine.

Each Sephirot represents an aspect of life as well as a realm of attainment for the Kabbalistic student. Above the first Sephirot is the Ein Soph, the ineffable ground of all being, that is, God. The Ein Soph emanates the ten Sephirot. Each Sephirot has a name and quality ascribed to it. They are as follows:

1. Kether—being or existence
2. Chochmah—wisdom
3. Binah—intelligence or understanding

4. Chesed—mercy or love
5. Geburah—strength and/or severity
6. Tiphareth—beauty
7. Netzach—firmness
8. Hod—glory
9. Yesod—foundation
10. Malkuth—kingdom

An eleventh Sephirot lies concealed behind and between Chochmah and Binah. It is Daath—knowledge (of the sexual kind, as spoken of in the opening chapters of Genesis). Daath often takes prominence in the systems of Kabbalistic groups that practice sex magick.

THE NINETEENTH CENTURY. Also developed in the Middle Ages (the fourteenth century) was the Tarot, though its present form is a nineteenth-century refinement of the work of such men as Éliphas Lévi (1810–1875), Aleister Crowley, and Arthur E. Waite (1857–1942). Each of the seventy-eight cards carries a complicated picture full of occult symbolism, much of it Kabbalistic. Today, the Tarot is one of the most popular forms of divination.

The modern history of magick begins in the late eighteenth century when magical groups, no longer fearful of persecution, began to emerge into the public eye concurrently with the rise of a dilettante interest in occultism in western Europe. In 1784 Ebenezer Sibley (1751–1799) published his *Celestial Sciences*, which contained a lengthy section on magick and necromancy. That same year, Antoine Court de Gébelin (1725–1784) published a book that connected the Tarot with the Egyptian *Book of Thoth*. At the turn of the century, Francis Barrett gathered a magical group around him, and in 1801 he published *The Magus*, which became that group's textbook on magic and alchemy.

The real impetus to the spread of magick came in the early 1800s when an ex-Catholic seminarian, Alphonse-Louis Constant, rediscovered the Kabbalah, the Tarot, and the entire magical tradition. He became familiar with Barrett's work and joined a group called the Saviours of Louis XVII. The group's leader, Ganneau, believed that he was the reincarnation of Louis XVII, and he preached a form of revolutionary royalism. Toward midcentury, Constant left the group and in the 1850s published his *Dogma and Ritual of High Magic*, followed by the *History of Magic* and *Key of the Great Mysteries*. In his writings, he claimed for magick both antiquity and potency and said it was the only universally valid religion. Constant, in publishing these books, took the Kabbalistic pen name Éliphas Lévi. Lévi was to become over the next decades the teacher of the many magical traditions that began to flourish. Rosicrucians, ritual magicians, and witches all would look to Lévi for direction, even as they formed highly differentiated groups.

RITUAL MAGICK. The rise of ritual magick (also known as ceremonial magick) is understandable only in light of the blending of several traditions that emerged forcefully in mid-nineteenth-century England. On the one hand, Spiritualism and what was to become Theosophy were having a major cultural impact. (Spiritualists claimed that they received messages from the world of the spirits, while Theosophist claimed contact with a group of advanced occult masters. By 1855 the *Yorkshire Spiritual Telegraph*, England's first Spiritualist newspaper, was founded.) This helped to stir popular interest in things supernatural. On the other hand, the magical writings of Lévi, the existence of the Societas Rosicruciana in Anglia (SRIA) and the continuing impact of speculative Freemasonry provided fertile soil in which new magical orders could grow. In the 1850s and 1860s, a group using Barrett's *Magus* gathered around the psychic Fred Hockley (d. 1885), trying to make use of magick formulas. In 1888 the two traditions merged to produce the Isis-Urania Temple of the Golden Dawn.

The founders of the temple and the Hermetic Order of the Golden Dawn (OGD) that it represented included the Reverend A. F. A. Woodford (d. 1887), Kenneth R. H. Mackenzie (d. 1886), William Robert Woodman (1828–1891), Dr. Wynn Westcott (1848–1925), and S. L. MacGregor Mathers. All except Woodford had been members of the SRIA, but Woodford had been the one to inherit, in 1885, the magical manuscripts owned by Fred Hockley, upon which the ritual of OGD would be built. Westcott decoded the manuscripts, and Mathers systematized them into a useful form. The material also contained the Nuremberg mailing address of the mysterious Anna Sprengel, who seemed to be a Rosicrucian of high degree. Mathers reportedly corresponded with her, receiving voluminous materials and the charter for the Isis-Urania Temple. Other temples were soon founded in Edinburgh, Weston-super-Mare, Bradford, and Paris.

In 1897 Westcott left the Order of the Golden Dawn, and Mathers took complete control. Mathers had already gained a wide reputation for his occult scholarship. He had reworked Barrett's texts and produced a grimoire, or magical text, of superior quality. He also published a book on the Kabbalah. By 1892 Mathers had moved to Paris. From there, he conducted the OGD.

Under Mathers's leadership, the order developed a ritual and worldview from which other groups would create variations. This system is generally termed *Western magick*. The basic idea was the hermetic principle of the correspondence of the microcosm (the human being) and the macrocosm (the whole, the universe). Any principle that exists in the universe also exists in humans. The trained occultist can become attuned to these cosmic forces. In the process, invocation and evocation become standard practices. Invocation is the "calling down" into the self of a cosmic force, with a purely psychological result. Evocation is the "calling up" of that same force from the depths of the self, and it may result in objective physical phenomena. The correspondences also include relationships between colors, shapes, Kabbalah, and so forth, and the universe. A second belief is in the power of the will. The trained will can do anything. Central to magick is the will—its training and activity.

The ritual magician also looks to other planes of existence, usually referred to as *astral planes*. These planes are inhabited by entities other than human beings, known as secret chiefs, Oliponthic forces, and the gods, among other names. Much magical work is in the astral. Finally, most ritual magicians have adopted a Kabbalistic initiation system wherein each grade is given a numerical symbol related to the Tree of Life. The numerical symbol uses two numbers, the number on the right being identical to the number of the Sephirot, and the number on the left being the opposite of that Sephirotic number. The names Zelator Adeptus Minor and Theoricus Adeptus Minor are simply two names for the same grade. The chart of the grades and their numerical symbols comes from *Ritual Magic in England* (1970) by Francis King.

• • •

FIRST ORDER

GRADE	NUMERICAL SYMBOL
Neophyte	0° = 0°
Zelator	1° = 10%
Theoricus	2° = 9°
Practicus	3° = 8°
Philosophus	3° = 8°

(The Link-Lord of the Paths of the Portal in the Vault of the Adepti.)

• • •

• • •

SECOND ORDER

GRADE	NUMERICAL SYMBOL
Zelator Adeptus Minor	5° = 6°
Theoricus Adeptus Minor	
Adeptus Major	6° = 5°
Adeptus Exemptus	7° = 4°

• • •

• • •

THIRD ORDER

(The Secret Chiefs)

GRADE	NUMERICAL SYMBOL
Magister Templi	8° = 3°
Magus	9° = 2°
Ipissimus	10° = 1°

• • •

All the founders of the OGD began as 7 degrees = 4 degrees, a degree conferred by Sprengel. (Mathers himself claimed to have contacted the secret chiefs in 1892.)

The most prominent member of the OGD was Aleister Crowley, whose magical thought has come to dominate modern magical practice. Reared in an Exclusive Plymouth Brethren home, Crowley had been introduced to magick in a book by Arthur E. Waite. His Kabbalistic studies led him in 1898 to the OGD. Crowley rose quickly in the order, but was refused initiation to Adeptus Minor because of his moral turpitude (in this case, homosexuality). However, Crowley went to Paris and was initiated (5° = 6°) by Mathers. His initiation led to a split in the order in London.

Table of Correspondences

Mystical and Spiritual Relationships

Traditional seven planets	Qabalistic Sephiroth	Qabalistic path	Hebrew double letters	Precious stone	Body center (planetary)
Saturn	Binah	32nd	Tau	Onyx	Base of spine
Jupiter	Chesed	21st	Kaph	Lapis Lazuli	Reproductive
Mars	Geburah	27th	Peh	Ruby	Solar Plexus
Sun	Tiphareth	30th	Resh	Crysoleth	Pineal
Venus	Netzach	14th	Daleth	Emerald	Heart
Mercury	Hod	12th	Beth	Agate	Thyroid
Moon	Yesod	13th	Gimmel	Moonstone	Pituitary

In 1904 Crowley received a communication in Cairo from the astral with instruction for the establishment of a new order, which he set up in 1907. It was called the Astrum Argentinum (silver star). In 1909 he began publishing the biannual book-size periodical, *The Equinox*, to spread his ideas.

Crucial to understanding Crowley and his followers is Crowley's Cairo revelation. At this time, an entity called Aiwass communicated a prose poem entitled *Liber al Vel Legis*, that is, *The Book of Law*. The Egyptian magick favored by Crowley is manifested in this cryptic work, which divides history into the aeon of Isis (or matriarchy) until 500 B.C.E., the aeon of Osiris (or patriarchy) until 1904, and the aeon of Horus beginning in 1904. The aeon of Horus, the son, is one of the dominance of Thelema or Will. From the book came Crowley's themes: "'Do what thou wilt' shall be the whole of the Law"; "Every man and every woman is a star"; and "Love is the Law, Love under Will." These three phrases constantly reappear in Crowley's writing. By them, Crowley meant that each person is to move in his true course through the cosmos as marked out by the nature of his position, the law of his growth, and the impulse of his past. One's duty is to be determined to experience the suitable event at each moment. Love is an art of uniting with a part of Nuit, the total possibilities of every kind. Each act must be willed so as to fulfill, not thwart, one's true nature.

Around the turn of the century, Carl Kellner (1850–1905) founded the Ordo Templi Orientis (OTO), a ritual magick group that taught sex magick. Crowley joined the OTO and was made the head of its British affiliate. OTO sexual magick seems to have arisen from the discussions of occult perspectives on sexuality that had been held in a number of different occult groups. Given the circulation of the Oriental sex manuals discovered, translated, and published by Sir Richard Burton (1821–1890), it is not surprising that in the late nineteenth and early twentieth centuries individuals began to explore the possibilities of sex magic. Crowley discovered sex magic in the process of working on some rituals and was aware of its potential prior to his encounter with the OTO.

Crowley immediately jumped into a leadership position in the OTO and led it during the last quarter century of his life. Upon his death in 1947, Karl Johannes Germer (1885–1962) succeeded to the outer headship of the order. Germer had been with Crowley in England, but returned to Germany in the 1930s. He was arrested in Hitler's purges of occult groups and spent some time in a concentration camp.

Germer was deported in 1941 and migrated to the United States. He died in 1962 without designating a successor. In continental Europe, Karl Metzger, a Swiss disciple, assumed leadership; in England, Kenneth Grant filled the vacuum. No leader was present in America for several years until the end of the 1960s when Grady McMurtry emerged, claiming authority from several letters he had been sent by Crowley in the 1940s that authorized him to act in the event of a lack of leadership.

RITUAL MAGICK IN AMERICA. Ritual magick was brought to America from Britain by Americans who had joined the OGD. However, the real beginning stemmed from Crowley's visits in 1905 and 1915. Shortly before World War I (1914–1918), Charles Stansfeld Jones (Frater Achad) (1886–1950) opened OTO branches in Vancouver, Los Angeles, and (possibly) Washington, D.C. Jones was Crowley's magical child, but the two soon split. Crowley visited the Vancouver lodge in 1915. He met Wilfred Talbot Smith (Frater 132) (1885–1957) while there, and gave Smith permission to open an OTO lodge, which he did. Smith later moved to Pasadena, California, and, upon Achad's fall from favor with Crowley, became head of the American OTO. Smith's move to Pasadena begins one of the most bizarre episodes in American religious history.

Once in Pasadena, Smith seduced Helen Parsons, the wife of Frater 210, known in public life as John W. (Jack) Parsons (1914–1952), an explosives expert and key man at the California Institute of Technology, who had joined Smith's OTO lodge in Pasadena. After Helen had a child by Smith, Parsons took Helen's younger sister, Sara Northrup, also known as Betty, as his mistress and magical partner. At this point, probably in 1945, a new frater in the person of L. Ron Hubbard (1911–1986) appeared on the scene, and two distinct accounts exist as to what happened between Parsons and his new "assistant."

According to accounts published by the OTO, Parsons developed an immediate liking for Hubbard and took him into the OTO work, though Hubbard never formally became a member, nor was he properly initiated. The two worked together on several magical operations, including an attempt to produce a moonchild. In this process, while Parsons engaged in ritual intercourse, Hubbard acted as a seer to describe the concurrent events on the astral plane. The act was supposed to induce a spirit into the child produced by the intercourse.

Early in 1946, Parsons and Hubbard had a parting of the ways. Parsons claimed that Hubbard had persuaded him to sell the property of the Agape Lodge in Pasadena, after which Hubbard, along with Parsons's sister-in-law Betty, absconded with the money. Hubbard's wife filed for divorce, and he reappeared on a newly purchased yacht off the Florida coast.

Parsons pursued him, and on July 5, 1946, a confrontation occurred. Hubbard had sailed at 5 p.m. At 8 p.m., Parsons performed a full invocation to "Bartzabel." At that same moment, a squall struck the yacht and ripped the sails, thus forcing Hubbard to port. Parsons was able to recover only a small percentage of the money, however.

Hubbard's account (and that of the present-day Church of Scientology that he founded), denies that Hubbard had any attachment to the OTO. Rather, the church claims that Hubbard was sent to investigate Parsons because the Pasadena headquarters of the lodge also housed a number of nuclear physicists who lived there while working at Caltech. These physicists were among 64 later dismissed from government service as insecure. Hubbard asserts that due to his efforts the headquarters were torn down, a girl rescued from the group, and the group ultimately destroyed.

Both stories stand and, in fact, may be genuine perceptions of the events, since Hubbard obviously did not make his "investigative" function known until some years later. Hubbard's story is consistent with the observation that the present Church of Scientology shows no direct OTO influence.

Though weakened by Hubbard's actions, the Agape Lodge was not destroyed by him. Parsons did that himself. In 1949 he took the oath of AntiChrist and adopted the magical name Belarion Armiluss Al Dajjal AntiChrist. Then in 1952, in a still unexplained occurrence, he was killed when his home laboratory exploded. According to Louis T. Culling, Parsons had been making bootleg nitroglycerine to sell to earn money to keep the work going after the loss of the Lodge's treasury.

Besides the Agape Lodge, several other lodges were formed in the years after World War I. One of these was the Choronzon Club, or Great Brotherhood of God (GBG), formed in Chicago in 1931. The head of the GBG was Cecil Frederick Russell (1897–1987), who had been with Crowley in Sicily; Russell later split with Crowley. Among the Choronzon Club's members was Louis T. Culling, who in 1969, published its ritual as the *The Complete Magick Curriculum of the Secret Order G.B.G.* Its three degrees were preceded by basic occult training. The sexual magick began with Alphaism, a discipline of complete chastity in thought, word, and deed; moved to Dianism, or Karezza, prolonged sexual congress without orgasm; and finished with Quodosch, similar to the completed heterosexual activity of the OTO ninth degree. Culling, head of the San Diego Lodge of the Great Brotherhood of God, left in 1938 to join the OTO.

Another derivative of the Order of the Golden Dawn was the Order of the Portal, a lodge headquartered in Boston in the late 1920s and early 1930s. It was headed by Aleta Baker and was the most overtly Christian of the various OGD offshoots, though it emphasized belief in the bisexuality of God and the equality of woman.

Little information is available on the present practices of ritual magick groups. They are secret materials, given in written form to only a few leaders and carefully guarded by the members. However, rituals used by a number of defunct lodges have become available. The publication of the OGD rituals resulted in the dissolution of two groups that were using them. The published rituals show a remarkable similarity; present rituals are almost certainly derivatives of these, with changes suitable to particular needs and uses. Almost all of the rituals of the OTO have also been published.

WITCHCRAFT/WICCA.

The growth of witchcraft (the craft of the Wicca or wise ones) can be dated to 1951, when the last of the British witchcraft laws was repealed, and to the subsequent publication in 1954 of *Witchcraft Today* by Gerald B. Gardner (1884–1964), a self-proclaimed witch from the Isle of Man in Britain. Gardner's book signaled to the world that witches still existed. His work was based upon the thesis of archaeologist Margaret Murray (1863–1963) that witchcraft had existed since pre-Christian times in small, scattered, occult groups practicing the old pagan religion and hidden in fear of persecution. Many contemporary witches accepted Murray's historical thesis, but the legitimacy of her conclusions is now a matter of intense debate in the occult community.

There can be little doubt that various, mostly agricultural, religions existed in Europe at the time that the Christian Church was in the process of becoming Europe's dominant religious form. There is also little doubt that in the 1500s the church turned its inquisitional powers on something called witchcraft. What was described as witchcraft was a mixture of the local religions, a number of practices the church wished to suppress, and many things that existed solely in the imaginations of the early inquisitors. It was during this era that various new images of witchcraft, particularly the one connecting it with Satan worship, were published.

Many men, women, and even children died in the witch scare that gripped Europe in the sixteenth and seventeenth centuries. In the face of the myth of satanic witchcraft, some genuine satanists and even genuine witches arose. The most famous incident was the Black Mass scandal that rocked the court of Louis XIV (r. 1643–1715) and led to the arrest of more than 300 persons. In the 1670s, Madame La Voisin, one of Louis XIV's mistresses, suspected she was losing Louis's affection and hired a priest to say Black Masses, hoping thereby to win back the king. Some of the masses included the killing of babies and some were offered on Madame LaVoisin's nude body. Louis imprisoned or banished the participants in the heinous affairs.

Contemporary witchcraft (or Wicca) bears little resemblance to the witchcraft described in the literature of the witchcraft trials. Going beyond the medieval image, modern witches try to separate themselves from any connection with satanism. Rather than reacting to Christianity (i.e., being anti-Christians), they see themselves as an alternative faith (like Buddhism or Islam). As magicians, they have selected the old faiths of Europe with which to identify.

Just what are the elements of Wiccan faith? This question is not an easy one to answer, there being a wide variety of definitions in the literature. First, witchcraft is a religion. There is much more to the adherents' faith than just magick. Witchcraft offers a worldview, a relationship to deity, a community for worship, and an ethical code. Of course, magick and psychic development are a part of the religion; much of the ritual and energy of witches is spent in their practice. "Witchcraft is the raising and manipulation of psychic power," says one witch.

Wicca is polytheistic, finding its pantheon in various European pre-Christian nature religions. The prime deities are the Goddess and God, usually represented as the Triple Goddess and Horned God. The triple aspects of the Goddess are maiden, mother, and crone. There are different explanations of the origin of these gods, although most agree that the Goddess is ascendant in modern cultic expressions. Psychic development, besides being training for magick, is also for communion with the deity. (The Horned God was connected with Satan by medieval witch hunters, and Satan has been pictured since with a goatee and cloven hoofs.)

The witch's two essential books are the grimoire and the book of shadows. The grimoire is the book of spells and magical procedures. The best-known grimoires are medieval: *Greater Key of Solomon the King* and *The Book of the Sacred Magic of Abra-Melin the Mage*, both translated and published in the late 1800s. The book of shadows is the traditional book of rituals. According to custom, it is copied by hand by each individual witch, and thus no two copies are alike.

The basic organization of witches is the *coven*, though there is also an associational tie between covens of like belief and practice, especially where one coven has broken off from another and owes its initiation to the other. Such a relationship exists in the Gardnerian covens; they each consist of thirteen people (an optimum number that may vary from four to twenty) who meet regularly to practice witchcraft. The regular meeting of the coven is called an *esbat*. Eight times per year there are seasonal festivals, the *sabbats*. The most famous festival is October 31, Halloween or Samhaim. Others include Candlemas or Oimelc (February 2), May Eve or Beltane (April 30), August Eve or Lammas (August 1), and the lesser sabbats—the two solstices (June 22 and December 22) and the equinoxes (March 21 and September 21). The eight festivals are reflected in the common practice of publishing witch-oriented periodicals eight times per year.

Most covens have both a basic initiation and higher initiations that are reserved for potential and actual priests and priestesses, who are the coven leaders. There are usually three degrees that require a year and a day between each initiation. Work within the coven is done with a magick circle, nine feet in diameter, drawn on the floor or ground. Magick is done within the circle, which functions both for protection and concentration. Within the circle are placed the various magical items. They include the athame (a ritual knife), the pentacle (a disc-shaped talisman), a chalice, and a sword. These items vary from coven to coven. The athame is most ubiquitous.

Many covens worship in the nude (i.e., skyclad), but in the majority of covens, street clothes or ritual robes are worn.

When the robe is worn it is bound with a cord, the color of which designates the degree of initiation. The work of the coven covers all religious practices (psychic healing and problem-solving playing a big part) and includes handfasting (marriage).

Witches share with all magicians a belief in reincarnation and the manipulative worldview. They also place belief in the power of spells. They cast spells for the healing of themselves and others, for their own betterment (financially, sexually) and, on rare occasions, against someone else. For most witches, the magical worldview is tempered by a poetic-mystical appreciation of nature. In their writings are numerous references to ecology, to living naturally, and, in a few cases, to vegetarianism. For most, acceptance of the gods is a poetic expression of attunement with the forces of life.

AFRICAN WITCHCRAFT. Vodou, the major folk religion of Haiti, is an African form of magick and witchcraft mixed with New World elements, complete with the ruling mother goddess, a pantheon of lesser deities (correlated to specific human needs), a psychic ritual, and a manipulative worldview. Vodou has a significant history in eighteenth- and nineteenth-century America, particularly in the Creole country. In the nineteenth century, Dr. John and, later, Marie Laveau (1801–1881), the vodou queen of New Orleans, openly flaunted their magical powers in public. They were followed by Dr. Alexander and Lou Johnson.

For a number of reasons, modern witchcraft practice has had little input from vodouism, apart from the romantic aura of the word. This lack of input can be traced to several elements, the same that have prevented many books on vodou from appearing. Vodou is not a literary religion; the source material must be gathered directly from practitioners. Practitioners are few in number and hard to find. They are mostly members of the black community or recent immigrants from the Caribbean. The latter often have a language barrier to overcome.

As the term *vodou* is found in popular American usage, it refers to at least four distinct phenomena. The first, vodou proper, is the magical religion brought from Haiti in the late 1700s. It is a mixture of French Catholicism and the religion of the Ibos, Magos, and Dahomeans. Its leading god is Damballah, the serpent. The second, Santeria, is a mixture of Iberian Catholicism and Yoruba religion. Its main god is Chango, the god of fire and stone. It is found throughout most of Latin America, and in Brazil is called Macumba. The third, the Conjure Man (or Root Doctor) in the southern United States, is an adoption by blacks of European magick but is associated with vodou because of the mystique of New Orleans. This phenomenon does not seem to produce groups, as such. The fourth, the Bruja (or Latin American witch), is often placed under the vodou label, but is more closely related to the folk witchcraft traditions. Besides the widespread practice of vodou and Santeria, as evidenced by the numerous botanicas (stores that sell magical ingredients) in most urban centers, there are at least three public vodoulike groups.

Vodou and its relatives exist in America today; its outward manifestations can be found in the black, Puerto Rican, and Cuban communities of major cities of the United States and in the occult supply shops that sell magical items. Such items include *yerbabuena* and *perejil*, herbs that, when used properly, are assumed to have powers to keep away evil. Other items, such as bat's blood and graveyard dust, are also available.

Since the nineteenth century, vodou in America has been centered in New Orleans, where it was brought from Haiti. After World War II (1937–1945), as New Orleans emerged as a tourist destination, several vodou leaders and aficionados arose in the French Quarter. Bookstores focusing on vodou and magick serviced a inquisitive public, and a couple of vodou temples made themselves accessible to the more persistent inquirer. The New Orleans scene was severely disrupted by Hurricane Katrina in 2005. Although the French Quarter was spared the major destruction of the hurricane and lay above the resulting flood, the drop in tourism over the next year led to the closing of many of the bookstores and the relocation of the vodou leaders. By 2008 the scene was being restored with several new bookstores replacing those that were lost. Reestablishing themselves after Katrina and continuing their leadership to the vodou community were priestesses Mariam Chamani, head of the Voodoo Spiritual Temple, and Sallie Ann Glassman, proprietor of the Island of Salvation Bookstore and head of La Source Ancienne.

WITCHCRAFT IN AMERICA. The history of witchcraft in America begins with the first settlers. As early as 1636, New England colonists felt a need to pass a law against witchcraft. In 1648 the first execution under this law occurred. (Note that there is little similarity between witches as defined by seventeenth-century Puritans and contemporary practitioners of the craft.) New England persecution of witches reached a climax at Salem in 1692. Spurred by confessions of occult practices by a Jamaican servant and the finding of vodou dolls at the home of Goodwife Rebecca Nurse (c. 1621–1692), the community launched a massive witch hunt that led to the deaths of a number of persons. In the wake of the killings, realization by the community of what it had done led to reaction against any belief whatsoever in the existence of witches. The history of American witchcraft then switches to Pennsylvania.

Among the Pennsylvania Dutch there is the survival of what seems to be a genuine "witchcraft-like" practice, known locally as *powwowing*. One must call it witchcraft-like because, while it involves magick and the psychic, it is theologically a Christian derivative with Kabbalistic elements. The practitioners are Bible believers, who feel themselves to be supernaturally endowed with their powers. The most obvious manifestations of the powwow power are the many colorful hex signs on farmhouses in eastern Pennsylvania. Each sign is a circle; within the circle are birds, hexagonal stars, and so forth.

Powwowers are, in essence, Christianized witches working in the agricultural society of the Pennsylvania Dutch. They have a grimoire (a book of spells and magical procedures),

The Long Lost Friend by John George Hohman, and they are as feared for their ability to hex as they are liked and sought after for their ability to heal. *The Long Lost Friend*, first published in 1819, is an eclectic compilation from the Kabbalah, Albertus Magus (a magician), German folklore, folk medicine, and other sources. No group of what could be called a powwow cult exists, but the power of powwow belief is demonstrated by the sporadic trials of people for murder and various lesser offenses because of "victims' beliefs that they were hexed."

The magical folklore that produced the powwow practices can be traced to medieval Germany and was brought to America by the Rosicrucians who settled in Germantown, Pennsylvania, in the 1690s. When their group, known as the Woman in the Wilderness, dissolved, its members passed its teaching on as a popular magical lore. The lore included a belief in astrology, amulets and charms, herbal medicine, and the psychic powers of gifted people.

Prior to the 1960s, there were only a few manifestations of witchcraft in America apart from the powwow men. There were isolated areas that had the equivalent of the powwower, but not in such strength or prominence. Such an area was the Shenandoah Valley in Virginia and Pennsylvania, where practitioners had a German heritage. Occasionally, there was a witchcraft trial such as the one that occurred in Omaha, Nebraska, in 1939. A woman accused a local "witch" of casting spells against her. The "witch" was found guilty and expelled from the community.

THE GARDNERIAN REVIVAL.

Many contemporary witches claim associations with witches, covens, or a faith that they can trace backward for many generations. However, little evidence to substantiate those claims has been brought forward and several have proved to be without any basis in fact. Most witches are converts who have come into the movement since 1960. While a few can trace their ancestry to individuals accused of witchcraft in the sixteenth and seventeenth centuries, there is no evidence of any survival of the practice within the families during the intervening centuries.

During the 1970s, a few active covens with a history predating 1960 were identified, but overwhelmingly, modern witchcraft can be traced to the work of Gerald B. Gardner (1884–1964), a retired British civil servant. Gardner had only a minimal amount of education and in his teen years moved to Ceylon (now Sri Lanka), where he worked on a plantation. During the next 39 years, he worked at various government and private jobs throughout India and Southeast Asia. He became an accomplished amateur anthropologist and authored the standard work on the *kris*, the Indonesian ceremonial weapon. In Palestine, he participated in the excavation of a site centered upon the worship of the goddess Astaroth.

Upon his return to England just before World War II, Gardner associated himself with the Corona Fellowship of Rosicrucians, founded by Mabel Besant-Scott (1870–1922), daughter of theosophist Annie Besant (1847–1933). Through the group, he met several witches, who introduced him to Dorothy Clutterbuck (1880–1951). According to Gardner, Clutterbuck initiated him into witchcraft. After the death of the priestess of the coven to which he belonged, he was allowed to describe some of the life of the group in a novel, *High Magic's Aid* (1949), published under his magical name, Scire. Then, in 1954, following the repeal of the witchcraft laws in England in 1951, he published *Witchcraft Today*, which gave a more detailed picture of what Gardner described as a dying religion. The book, however, initiated a revival of interest, and led to a new generation of witches who turned to Gardner for initiation.

Recent research has done much to discredit Gardner's account of the rise of modern witchcraft. Examination of his papers sold to "Ripley's Believe It or Not" by his daughter, and the publication of several sets of rituals that he and his associates gave to various initiates, have disclosed a radically different account of the origin of Gardnerian witchcraft. Rather than being initiated into a preexisting Wiccan religion, it appears Gardner created the new religion out of bits and pieces of Eastern religions and Western occult and magical material.

Basic rituals were adapted from ritual magic texts such as the *Greater Key of Solomon*, the writings of Aleister Crowley, and Freemasonry (into which Gardner had been initiated in Ceylon). Beginning with the eight ancient pagan Sabbats (agricultural festivals) as major holy days, he added regular biweekly gatherings at the esbats full and new moon. From the Malayan kris, he developed the athame (the witch's ritual knife). Having become a practitioner of nudism as a result of sunbaths taken while recovering from an illness, he ordained that rituals were to be done in the nude, or *skyclad* (a term used to describe the nude *sadhus* of India). He also incorporated several Eastern religious practices (ritual scourging) and beliefs (karma and reincarnation). In 1948 he published a novel, *A Goddess Arrives*, which described a Goddess-worshipping faith.

By 1954 Gardner and the small group he had gathered around him had created Wicca, a religion more accommodating to a popular audience than ritual magic could ever be. During the late 1950s and early 1960s, Wiccan initiates took Gardner's rituals and formed separate covens, and slowly the movement began to spread. One initiate, Alexander Sanders (1926–1988), revised the rituals slightly and began a new "Alexanderian" lineage of witchcraft. Though beginning entirely from Gardnerian rituals, Sanders created a fictionalized story of his having begun his career in witchcraft after being initiated as a child by his grandmother. Sybil Leek (1917–1982), another witch who began her practice with Gardnerian rituals, came to America in the late 1960s. Before becoming famous as a professional occultist, she formed several covens in different locations around the United States.

The Gardnerian origin of contemporary covens is often obscured by the adoption of designations such as "traditional" and "hereditary" to indicate their allegiance to a non-Gardnerian form of witchcraft and by implication their derivation from a pre-Gardnerian lineage of witchcraft.

However, while covens deviate at particular points, they all adhere to Gardner's original belief system, retain the unique elements of Gardnerian ritual, and perpetuate the overall pattern of practice that he originated. Certainly, numerous variations of his original rituals have been developed and a few entirely new sets of rituals composed, but all have proved to be products of the post-Gardnerian era, and follow the ritual pattern he established in the 1950s.

Witches may practice alone, but most are organized into covens, which meet biweekly at the new and full moon and eight times per year for the major holidays. Most covens have abandoned nudity and do their rituals in robes, though strict Gardnerians and Alexanderians retain the practice.

GARDNERIAN WICCA IN THE UNITED STATES.
Gardnerian Wicca or witchcraft was brought to the United States in the mid-1960s by Raymond Buckland (b.1934) and Rosemary Buckland. Longtime students of the occult, they heard of Gardner and traveled to the Isle of Man, where he operated a witchcraft and magic museum. There, they went through a intensive program in Gardner's witchcraft and were initiated into both the first and second degrees (which is contrary to standard practice, which requires a year and a day between initiations). Upon their return, they formed a coven on Long Island and became the center of a burgeoning movement. Much of the spread of the movement was due to the Bucklands' availability to the media, whose interest was sparked both by their witchcraft museum and their willingness to be interviewed and photographed as witches.

Soon after witchcraft spread across America, other people attracted to the Goddess faith began to create variations on it. One set of variations became known as Neopaganism. Donna Cole (d. 2004), a Chicago witch who had received her initiation in England in the late 1960s, composed a set of rituals similar to Gardner's but much more worshipful and celebrative and less focused on magic. These rituals circulated through the witchcraft community in the United States and became the basis of a set of Pagan Way temples, several of which served as outer courts for the more secret and exclusive witchcraft groups. The term *Neopaganism* was coined by Tim Zell (b. 1942) (now known as Otter Zell), who composed a set of alternative rituals and founded a new group, the Church of All Worlds.

Neopagan groups differ primarily from witchcraft groups by their rejection of the designation *witch*. They will also occasionally vary by their use of a term other than *coven* to designate groups (nest, grove, etc.) or by their adoption of a particular pre-Christian tradition (Druidic, Norse, Egyptian) from which to draw the inspiration and symbology of their ritual life. For the purposes of this encyclopedia, all witchcraft and Neopagan groups are treated as products of the Gardnerian revival, from which they are believed to have originated.

Of the many "new religions" to emerge in North America in the 1970s, the Wiccan and Neopagan groups have formed a distinct set. They draw on a rich mythology of ancient and medieval lore and have taken the witch hunts that culminated at Salem as their own prehistory. While other new religions have attained some level of fame due to the controversy and scandals that have dogged them, Wiccans have attracted media attention simply because of their accepting the designation *witch*, along with a willingness to speak up in defense of witches of past generations, whom they see as people wrongfully persecuted by an intolerant religious community that freely accused people of practicing a nonexistent Satanism.

Meanwhile, over a generation, young Wiccans attended universities and earned advanced degrees in religious studies and related fields and now exist as an intelligentsia ready to dialogue with many of their colleagues who have found in the Neopagan community a rich field for research. Unlike most groups in the Western esoteric family, the Wiccans have moved to establish their own school for the training of priests and priestesses, though the majority of leadership training is still done in more informal settings.

SATANISM.
Often confused with witchcraft (Wicca) is the worship of Satan; witches, however, are quick to protest such identification and to assert the strong distinction between the two. The basic distinction is the relation to Christianity. Witchcraft logically (if not chronologically) predates and is independent of Christianity. That is, it exists in its own right, much as other non-Christian religions. (There is some doubt that any religion can grow up in Western culture without direct reaction to Christianity, but the witches are certainly articulating the possibility.) Witchcraft exists as an alternative to the Christian faith, much as do Buddhism and Hinduism.

Satanism, on the other hand, is logically subsequent to Christianity and draws on it in representing an overthrow of the Christian deity in favor of its adversary. It stands in polemical relation to Christianity and, in both belief and ritual, uses Christian elements, which are changed and given new meaning. The most famous element used by satanists is the Black Mass, an obvious corruption of Christian liturgies.

Apart from their allegiance to Satan and resultant dislike for the Christian church, satanists do share the magical worldview of witches. Many satanists openly claim witchcraft (as the working of magick) as their own. Their most vocal exponent, Anton LaVey (1930–1997), titled one of his books *The Compleat Witch* (1971). Satanists have had an unwitting ally in the conservative Christian press, which has frequently branded "witches" as Satanists (and tends to lump all psychics in with them). They are also aided by a tradition stemming from the era of the great witch trials, when witchcraft was defined as the worship of Satan. One could easily make the case that contemporary Satanism is a product of Christian polemics. Paranoid perceptions of "the enemy" have led to irrational accusations concerning beliefs, obscenities, profanities, rituals, and behavior patterns. These accusations merely gave people new ideas; the antiwitch books became the textbooks for satanic practices.

Contemporary satanism seems to have little connection organizationally with earlier forms of satanism. Books on black magick, satanism, and the psychic in general seem to provide the source, and the contemporary psychic scene provided the setting from which satanic practices could emerge. The writings of Aleister Crowley provided significant content on the practice of magick.

Satanists do share a number of symbols (and ritual practices) with all magical religions, but several are unique and distinctive. The inverted pentagram, the five-pointed star with the single point down, is the most frequently used. The Horned God in the form of the goat of Mendes is common. The pentagram is often stamped upon the goat's forehead, or a goat is imposed on the pentagram with the goats beard filling out the downward point. Not seen as often as some might think is the black inverted cross. With the decline in power of the Roman Catholic Church (since the days of the Holy Roman Empire), from which most satanists come, the Black Mass is also not as prominent.

As one studies the contemporary satanist scene, two distinct realities emerge. On the one hand, there are those groups that are frequently termed the "sickies." These are disconnected groups of occultists who employ satan worship to cover a variety of sexual, sadomasochistic, clandestine, psychopathic, and illegal activities. They typically engage in grave robberies, sexual assaults, and bloodletting (both animal and human), and are characterized by a lack of theology, an informality of gatherings, an ephemeral life, and disconnectedness from other similar groups. Usually they are discovered only in the incident that breaks up the group.

On the other hand, there are the public groups that take satanism as a religion seriously and have developed articulate theologies that do not resemble in many ways what one might expect. Their systems closely resemble liberal Christian theologies with the addition of a powerful cultural symbol (Satan), radically redefined. There is a wide gulf between the second type of satanism and its "sick" cousin. While theologically the Christian might find both reprehensible, the behavior of the two groups is drastically different, and they should not be confused.

After enjoying a decade of marked growth beginning with the announcement of Anton LaVey that he was founding the Church of Satan, satanism experienced a significant decline through the late 1970s. The Church of Satan splintered, and several new but much smaller satanist groups appeared. The most stable of the new groups was the Temple of Set, which developed a unique satanic theology based on Egyptian motifs. By the mid-1980s, while satanism itself showed no sign of a revival, a new wave of anti-satanism began to emerge around charges that satanist groups were actually present in large numbers and that proof of their existence was in the process of coming forth. Some saw the emergence of satanic symbols in the youth culture as a sign that a heavy recruitment of teenagers was occurring. Evidence cited for satanic activity, though satanists were virtually invisible, included the overt satanic themes that had begun to be used in rock music and the popular fantasy game Dungeons and Dragons, as well as the testimony of former satanists converted to Evangelical Christianity.

More sinister satanist groups were reportedly centered upon the ritual abuse of children. Some law enforcement officials claimed to see an increase in ritually slaughtered animals. However, in spite of attempts to locate satanist groups by law enforcement officials, and despite widespread attention focused by anti-satanist groups, direct evidence of any significant new growth of satanism failed to materialize, and by the end of the 1990s, the accusations of widespread satanic activity had lost their credibility and largely disappeared. Many of the claims of ritual abuse of children and even the stories of some Evangelical Christian converts proved unfounded or even deliberate hoaxes. Successive attempts to locate any of the groups reputedly responsible for the illegal and immoral actions in the thousands of reports of satanic activity since the 1970s have repeatedly failed.

SOURCES

A large collection of materials on the revival of magical religion in the last half of the twentieth century can be found in the J. Gordon Melton American Religions Collection at Davidson Library at the University of California–Santa Barbara.

General Sources

Bonewits, P. E. I. *Real Magic: An Introductory Treatise on the Basic Principles of Yellow Magic.* Rev. ed. York Beach, ME: Weiser, 1989. 304 pp.

Green, Marian. *Magic for the Aquarian Age.* Wellingborough, U.K.: Aquarian Press, 1983. 160 pp.

Lewis, James, ed. *Magical Religion and Modern Witchcraft.* Albany: State University of New York Press, 1996. 423 pp.

Mauss, Marcel. *A General Theory of Magic.* Trans. Robert Brain. New York: Norton, 1972. 128 pp.

Melton, J. Gordon, and Isotta Poggi. *Magic, Witchcraft, and Paganism in America: A Bibliography.* 2nd ed. New York: Garland, 1992. 408 pp.

History of Magic

Cavendish, Richard. *A History of Magic.* New York: Taplinger, 1977. 180 pp.

Gilbert, R. A. *The Golden Dawn: Twilight of the Magicians.* Wellingborough, U.K.: Aquarian Press, 1983. 144 pp.

Howe, Ellic. *The Magicians of the Golden Dawn: A Documentary History of a Magical Order, 1887–1923.* London: Routledge and Kegan Paul, 1972. 306 pp.

———. *The Alchemist of the Golden Dawn.* Wellingborough, U.K.: Aquarian Press, 1985. 112 pp.

King, Francis. *Ritual Magic in England: 1887 to the Present Day.* London: Spearman, 1970. 221 pp.

McIntosh, Christopher. *Eliphas Lévi and the French Occult Revival.* New York: Weiser, 1974. 238 pp.

Starr, Martin P. *The Unknown God: W. T. Smith and the Thelemites.* Bolingbrook, IL: Teitan Press, 2003. 416 pp.

Thomas, Keith. *Religion and the Decline of Magic.* New York: Scribner's, 1971. 716 pp.

Webb, James. *The Occult Underground.* LaSalle, IL: Open Court, 1974. 387 pp.

———. *The Occult Establishment.* LaSalle, IL: Open Court, 1976. 525 pp.

Woods, Richard. *The Occult Revolution: A Christian Meditation.* New York: Herder and Herder, 1971. 240 pp.

Ritual Magick

Ashcroft-Nowicki, Dolores. *First Steps in Ritual: Safe, Effective Techniques for Experiencing the Inner Worlds.* Wellingborough, U.K.: Aquarian Press, 1982. 96 pp.

Conway, David. *Magic: An Occult Primer.* New York: Dutton, 1972. 286 pp.

Crowley, Aleister. *Magick in Theory and Practice* (1929). New York: Castle, 1965. 436 pp.

Crowley, Aleister. *Magick Without Tears.* Ed. Israel Regardie. St. Paul, MN: Llewellyn, 1973. 522 pp.

DuQuette, Lon Milo. *The Magick of Aleister Crowley: A Handbook of the Rituals of Thelema.* San Francisco: Weiser, 2003. 261 pp.

Gilbert, R. A. *The Golden Dawn: Twilight of the Magicians.* Wellingborough, U.K.: Aquarian Press, 1983. 144 pp.

Greer, Mary K. *Woman of the Golden Dawn.* Rochester, VT: Park Street Press, 1995. 489 pp.

King, Francis, and Stephen Skinner. *Techniques of High Magic: Handbook of Divination, Alchemy, and the Evocation of Spirits.* New York: Warner Destiny, 2000. 240 pp.

Lévi, Éliphas. *Transcendental Magic: Its Doctrine and Ritual.* Trans. Arthur Edward Waite. London: Redway, 1896. 438 pp.

———. *The History of Magic: Including a Clear and Precise Exposition of its Procedure, Its Rites, and Its Mysteries.* Trans. Arthur Edward Waite. London: Rider, 1913. 384 pp.

McIntosh, Christopher. *The Devil's Bookshelf: A History of the Written Word in Western Magic from Ancient Egypt to the Present Day.* Wellingborough, U.K.: Aquarian Press 1985. 208 pp.

Regardie, Israel. *Ceremonial Magic.* Wellingborough, U.K.: Aquarian Press, 1980.

Schreck, Nokolas, and Zeena Schreck. *Demon of the Flesh: The Complete Guide to Left-hand Path Sex Magic.* Washington, DC: Creation Books, 2002. 398 pp.

Sutin, Lawrence. *Do What Thou Wilt: A Life of Aleister Crowley.* New York: Saint Martin's Press, 2000. 483 pp.

Urban, Hugh B. *Magia Sexualis: Sex, Magic, and Liberation in Modern Western Esotericism.* Berkeley: University of California Press, 2006.

Witchcraft

Baroja, Julio Caro. *The World of the Witches.* Trans. O. N. V. Glendinning. Chicago: University of Chicago Press, 1965. 313 pp.

Berger, Helen A. *A Community of Witches: Contemporary Neo-Paganism and Witchcraft in the United States.* Columbia, SC: University of South Carolina Press, 1999. 148 pp.

Berger, Helen A., and Douglas Ezzy. *Teenage Witches: Magical Youth and the Search for the Self.* New Brunswick, NJ: Rutger University Press, 2007. 278 pp.

Boyer, Paul, and Stephen Nissenbaum. *Salem Possessed: The Social Origins of Witchcraft.* Cambridge, MA: Harvard University Press, 1974. 231 pp.

Clifton, Chas. S., ed. *Witchcraft Today.* Book 1: *The Modern Craft Movement.* St. Paul, MN: Llewellyn, 1992. 198 pp.

Hansen, Chadwick. *Witchcraft at Salem.* New York: New American Library, 1969. 318 pp.

Harvey, Graham. *Contemporary Paganism: Listening People, Speaking Earth.* New York: New York University Press, 1997. 250 pp.

Hutton, Ronald. *The Triumph of the Moon: A History of Modern Pagan Witchcraft.* Oxford: Oxford University Press, 1999. 486 pp.

Kieckhefer, Richard. *European Witch Trials: Their Foundations in Popular and Learned Culture, 1300–1500.* Berkeley: University of California Press, 1976. 181 pp.

Monter, E. William. *European Witchcraft.* New York: Wiley, 1969. 177 pp.

Russell, Jeffery Burton, and Brooks Alexander. *A History of Witchcraft: Sorcerers, Heretics, & Pagans.* 2nd ed. London: Thames and Hudson, 2007. 192 pp.

Afro-Caribbean Religion

Glassman, Sallie Ann. *Vodou Visions: An Encounter with Divine Mysteries.* New Orleans: Island of Salvation Botanica, 2007. 237 pp.

González-Wippler, Migene. *Santeria: African Magic in Latin America.* New York: Julian Press, 1973. 285 pp.

Langguth, A. J. *Macumba: White and Black Magic in Brazil.* New York: Harper & Row, 1975. 273 pp.

Long, Carolyn Morrow. *A New Orleans Voudou Priestess: The Legend and Reality of Marie Laveau.* Gainesville: University Press of Florida, 2006. 336 pp.

Murphy, Joseph M. *Santeria: African Spirits in America.* Boston: Beacon Press, 1993. 189 pp.

Ward, Martha. *Voudou Queen: The Spirited Lives of Marie Laveau.* Oxford, MS: University of Mississippi Press, 2004. 224 pp.

Modern Witchcraft and Paganism

Adler, Margot. *Drawing Down the Moon: Witches, Druids, Goddess-Worshippers, and Other Pagans in America* (1979). Rev. ed. New York: Penguin, 2006. 584 pp.

Berger, Helen A. *A Community of Witches: Contemporary Neo-Paganism and Witchcraft in the United States.* Columbia: University of South Carolina Press, 1999. 148 pp.

A Book of Pagan Rituals. New York: Weiser, 1978.

Bracelin, J. L. *Gerald Gardner: Witch.* London: Octagon Press, 1960. 224 pp.

Clifton, Chas. *Witchcraft Today.* 3 vols. St. Paul, MN: Llewellyn, 1992–1994.

Farrar, Janet, and Stewart Farrar. *Eight Sabbats for Witches, and Rites for Birth, Marriage, and Death.* London: Hale, 1981. 192 pp.

———. *The Witches' Way: Principles, Rituals, and Beliefs of Modern Witchcraft.* London: Hale, 1984. 350 pp.

Farrar, Stewart. *What Witches Do: The Modern Coven Revealed.* New York: Coward, McCann & Geohegan, 1971. 184 pp.

Fox, Selena, and Circle Staff. *Circle Guide to Pagan Groups: A Nature Spirituality Networking Sourcebook.* 14th ed. Barneveld, WI: Circle, 2005. 144 pp.

Gardner, Gerald. *Witchcraft Today* (1954). London: Jarrolds, 1968. 163 pp.

Harvey, Graham. *Contemporary Paganism: Listening People, Speaking Earth.* New York: New York University Press, 1997. 250 pp.

Kelly, Aidan A. *Crafting the Art of Magic.* St. Paul, MN: Llewellyn, 1991. 190 pp.

Leek, Sybil. *Diary of a Witch.* Englewood Cliffs, NJ: Prentice-Hall, 1968. 187 pp.

Luhrmann, T. M. *Persuasions of the Witch's Craft: Ritual Magic in Contemporary England.* Cambridge, MA: Harvard University Press, 1991. 382 pp.

Miller, David L. *The New Polytheism: Rebirth of the Gods and Goddesses.* New York: Harper & Row, 1974. 86 pp.

Pike, Sarah M. *Early Bodies, Magical Selves: Contemporary Pagans and the Search for Community.* Berkeley: University of California Press, 2001. 288p.

———. *New Age and Neopagan Religions in America.* New York: Columbia University Press, 2004. 256 pp.

Starhawk. *The Spiral Dance: Rebirth of the Ancient Religion of the Great Goddess.* San Francisco: Harper & Row, 1979. 288 pp.

———. *Dreaming the Dark: Magic, Sex, and Politics.* Boston: Beacon Press, 1982. 242 pp.

Valiente, Doreen. *An ABC of Witchcraft, Past and Present*. New York: St. Martin's Press, 1973. 416 pp.

———. *The Rebirth of Witchcraft*. Custer, WA: Phoenix, 1989. 136 pp.

Satanism

Ashton, John. *The Devil in Britain and America* (1896). Ann Arbor, MI: Gryphon, 1971. 363 pp.

Laver, James. *The First Decadent: Being the Strange Life of J. K. Huysmans*. New York: Citadel Press, 1955. 278 pp.

Lewis, James R., and Jesper Aagaard Petersen, eds. *The Encyclopedia Sourcebook of Satanism*. Amherst, NY: Prometheus, 2006. 991 pp.

Lyons, Arthur. *Satan Wants You*. New York: Mysterious Press, 1988. 192 pp.

Richardson, James T., Joel Best, and David G. Bromley. *The Satanism Scare*. New York: de Gruyter, 1991. 320 pp.

Somerset, Anne. *The Affair of the Poisons: Murder, Infanticide, and Satanism at the Court of Louis XIV*. New York: St. Martin's Press, 2004. 400 pp.

Wolfe, Burton H. *The Devil's Avenger*. New York: Pyramid, 1974. 222 pp.

❀ Intrafaith Organizations

Aleister Crowley Foundation

c/o Order of Thelemic Knights, PO Box 8052, Portland, OR 97280

The Aleister Crowley Foundation was founded in 1997 in Brazil by two members of the Thelemic Order of the Golden Dawn. The next year, David Cherubim, an American member of the Order, founded an American branch of the Foundation. For legal reason, the Brazilian organization was forced to change its name to the Aleister Crowley Institute. Shortly thereafter, the American branch, still bearing the name Aleister Crowley Foundation, became independent of the Brazilian organization.

The purpose of the Foundation was to promote unity within the larger Thelemic community, still divided into a number of orders. The Foundation's members join together in the tasks of perpetuating the teachings of Aleister Crowley and Thelema over the Internet and promoting the activities of contemporary Thelemites and Thelemic orders, magicians, and publishers.

In 2003 David Cherubim transferred leadership of the Aleister Crowley Foundation to Gerald del Campo, primate of the Thelemic Gnostic Church of Alexandria and head of the Order of Thelemic Knights (O.T.K.), a fraternal charitable organization operating on Thelemic principles. Previously, del Campo had worked with the Foundation in establishing its Supporting Membership program. Del Campo is also in the North American College of Gnostic Bishops. Currently, the O.T.K. hosts the Foundation's Web page.

Membership in the Foundation is open to all Thelemic organizations and individuals. The primary requirement is that the members have a Web site. Any new member must agree to promote Thelema on their Web site and put the Foundation's logo and Web link on their index page. The Foundation reciprocates by linking to the member's Web site.

Membership: In 2008 the Foundation listed 39 individuals and organizations as members.

Sources:

Aleister Crowley Foundation. www.thelemicknights.org/acfhome.html.

American Vinland Association (AVA)

537 Jones, PMB 165, San Francisco, CA 94102-2007

The American Vinland Association (AVA) is a fellowship of Heathens following the traditions of northern and central Europe. A very similar Paganism, popularly termed Norse (or Asatru), was practiced from Iceland across Scandinavia to Poland, Russia, and Siberia. They are united in following the same deities, the old gods of the Aesir and Vanir, but have a wide range of beliefs and practices and use some different terminology.

The association is headed by a board of directors, the Jafnhar. It functions as a licensing board for priests, priestesses, and elders. Regional coordinators have been appointed for California, Washington, Massachusetts, Wisconsin, Oregon, New Mexico, and parts of Canada.

Membership: In 2008 the AVA reported over 500 members with 42 congregations and 23 licensed clergy. They have affiliated work in Canada, Lithuania, Latvia, the United Kingdom, Sweden, Finland, Gemany, France, and Japan.

Periodicals: *Yogdrasil* • *Update* (occasional) • *Yarbok* (defunct; back issues available).

Sources:

American Vinland Association. www.freyasfolk.org/.

Fellowship of Isis

c/o Clonegal Castle, Enniscorthy, Wexford, Ireland

The Fellowship of Isis (FOI) is an international, multifaith organization dedicated to honoring the goddess in her many forms. It was founded at Clonegal Castle, Enniscorthy, Ireland, in 1976, by author and painter Olivia Robertson and the late Lawrence Durdin-Robertson (d. 1994) and Pamela Durdin-Robertson, to revive worship and communion with the feminine principle in deity and to promote knowledge of the world's matriarchal religions. Olivia and her brother Lawrence authored a number of books on goddess research and ritual. Olivia wrote the liturgy that is used by the independently run centers of the Fellowship of Isis.

The fellowship is organized democratically, and there are no vows of secrecy. It is religiously tolerant, and a wide variety of New Age thought coexists in the fellowship. The fellowship has no direct affiliations. Communication between members is maintained through literature and correspondence. The fellowship includes the College of Isis, through which lyceums offer structured courses in Magi degrees; the Spiral of the Adepti; initiate system of Iseum centers; the Noble Order of Tara, an order of chivalry that works to save the environment; and the Druid Clan of Dana, whose primary work is the development of psychic gifts.

Membership: In 2008 the loosely organized fellowship had a total combined membership of approximately 26,564 individuals in groups located in 122 countries. There are an estimated 3,000 centers of activity.

Educational Facilities:

College of Isis, Enniscorthy, Ireland.

Periodicals: *Isian News*.

Sources:

Fellowship of Isis. www.fellowshipofisis.com.

The College of Isis Manual. Enniscorthy, Ireland: Cesara Publications, n.d.

Durdin-Robertson, Lawrence. *The Goddesses of Chaldea, Syria, and Egypt*. Enniscorthy, Ireland: Cesara Publications, 1975.

———. *The Fellowship of Isis Directory for 1980*. Enniscorthy, Ireland: Cesara Publications, 1979.

Robertson, Olivia. *The Call of Isis*. Enniscorthy, Ireland: Cesare Publications, 1975.

———. *Dea: Rites and Mysteries of the Goddess*. Enniscorthy, Ireland: Cesara Publications, 1996.

———. *The Handbook of the Fellowship of Isis*. Enniscorthy, Ireland: Cesara Publications, 1996.

Frigga's Web Association

PO Box 701, Carlisle, MA 01741-0701

Frigga's Web, named after the Norse deity who is thought of as the spiritual mother of all heathen people, is an ecumenical organization founded in 1995 to further the cause of the heathen society and promote heathen solidarity. Founder Alissa Sorenson saw the Web as a fruitful space for pro-heathen interaction that focuses on commonalities rather than differences. She emphasized the fact that most of the issues that divide the Asatru folk do not affect the great majority of heathens.

Frigga's Web welcomes individuals who follow the faith known as Asatru, or heathenism. The association provides clergy accreditation to the heathen community. Asatru-U publishes courses for its members.

Membership: In 1997 Frigga's Web reported 70 members in the United States, two in Canada, and 10 in other countries.

Periodical *Lina: The Quarterly Journal of Frigga's Web.*

Sources:

Frigga's Web. www.friggasweb.org.

Pagan Federation/Fédération paienne—Canada (PFFC)

PO Box 876, Stn. B, Ottawa, ON, Canada K1P 5P9

The Pagan Federation/Fédération paienne—Canada (PFFC) was formed in 1994 on the model of the Pagan Federation (UK), founded in 1971 in the United Kingdom. Originally named the Pagan Front, the federation had functioned as an umbrella organization for the groups that emerged from the revival of pre-Christian paganism initiated by Gerald B. Gardner in the 1950s. Some of those who responded to the Gardnerian impulse called themselves witches or wiccans; others preferred the name pagan. The group functioned to provide communication between various British pagan groups and new seekers; contact between British pagans and those in other European countries; and information to the British public on paganism, which was often parodied and defamed in the press.

The need for a pagan federation in Canada emerged as many Canadian witches and pagans began to change their strategy of assuming a low profile in Canadian religious life to taking up a visible and recognizable place in the larger religious community. That change was prompted in part by the open acknowledgement of pagans by various government and religious authorities. In addition, some pagan leaders saw the need to provide religious services for pagans in various institutional settings (e.g., prisons, hospitals, the armed services) and hence the need for chaplaincy services. (Chaplains are usually appointed from recognized religious groups whose officials can interact with institutional authorities.) Finally, there remains a need to fight for the religious rights and freedoms of pagans and others in Canada's various new religions.

An opening for interaction with authorities was provided in 1994 when Lucie DuFresne of the Department of Religious Studies at the University of Ottawa was asked by the Canadian Association of Pastoral Education to lead a training session on wicca and goddess worship. While at the meeting, she realized some of the major problems that would arise as chaplains attempted to relate to hospitalized pagans.

Membership in the federation is open to anyone who accepts the pagan minimal principles: love for and kinship with nature; the pagan ethic ("That ye harm none, do what thou will"); and acceptance of deity as both male and female.

Membership: Not reported.

Periodicals: *Hecate's Loom.*

Sources:

Pagan Federation/Fédération paienne—Canada. www.pf-pc.ca.

Du Fresne, Lucie, Adrienne Slater, and Dave Slater. "Pagan Federation/Fédération Paienne—Canada." *Hecate's Loom* 27 (Imbolc 1995): 9–10.

Universal Federation of Pagans, Ltd.

PO Box 672125, Marietta, GA 30006-0036

Alternate Addresses: c/o Ines and John Mullins, Conradstrasse 4, 1000 Berlin 27, Germany; c/o Ellen Williams, BM Box 7097, London WC1N 3XX, England.

The Universal Federation of Pagans (UFP) was founded June 21, 1991, in Atlanta, Georgia, by Rhuddlwm Gawr and Otter G'Zell. They invited over 300 pagan leaders

from around the world to participate in creating a unified fellowhip. In December 1992 the federation was incorporated in the State of Georgia. It was founded as an international association of pagans promoting the cause of paganism in the world and the larger religious community and providing fellowship among pagans of varying beliefs and practices. It accepts members from paths (equivalent to a denomination in Christianity), circles (equivalent to a congregation), or individuals. Affiliated paths (which must be legally incorporated and have at least five circles) are granted two seats on the UFP Council of Elders and in the UFP General Assembly, which guide the work of the federation. Member circles are granted one seat in the Council of Elders and representation in the General Assembly. Individual members (remembering that many pagans operate as solitaires) are granted representation in the General Assembly.

Members of the federation are expected to be knowledgeable concerning pagans, to conduct themselves in an ethical manner, and to promote actively the cause and ideals of paganism in their daily life and in their relations with others. Members are generally expected to accept a basic consensus of pagan belief and be in general agreement with the "Declaration of a Global Ethic" as formulated and promulgated by the 1993 World's Parliament of Religions.

The federation is an umbrella organization for pagan leaders and organizations worldwide and is affiliated with the Church of Dynion Mwyn, Inc., the Church of Y Tylwyth Teg., Inc., the Association of Cymry Wicca, Camelot of the Wood, Inc., Gathering of the Tribes, Inc., and Camelot Press Group, Inc. In 2008 the federation had plans to revive the Bangor Institute, an educational facility that ceased operating in 1990.

In 2008 the leader was Lord Rhuddlwm Gawr, the author of over twenty-three books, including *The Quest, The Way, The Word*, on Welsh paganism and witchcraft.

Membership: In 2008 the federation reported 612 organizations and 5,179 individual members, two-thirds of who live in the United States and the rest around the world.

Sources:

Universal Federation of Pagans. www.dynionmwyn.net./ufp.html.

❊ Ritual Magick

Abbey of Thelema

Abbey of Thelema Headquarters, Box 666, Old Greenwich, CT 06870-0666

The Abbey of Thelema is an independently functioning initiatory magical group that provides a point of contact with the Order of the Silver Star (also known as the A. A., Astron Argon (Greek) or Argenteum Astrum (Latin), otherwise known as the Great White Brotherhood. The leader of the abbey, Gregory von Seewald, has in turn been delegated to the Authority of the Triad, which originally was conferred upon George Cecil Jones (D.D.S.), Aleister Crowley (O.M.), and George Stansfeld Jones (O.I.V.I.V.I.O.). The abbey provides for instruction in the A. A. following the magical practices and studies that were perfected by its foremost founder, Aleister Crowley (1875–1947). New members of the order are expected to show their serious intentions by acquiring and reading a number of books in magick and mysticism, including the entire set of *The Equinox*, the magazine Crowley began in 1909 as the official organ of the A. A. Following an exam on his or her basic knowledge of magick, the student may become a probationer and begin the path of magical training. There are 11 magical grades, or degrees.

The secret, and secret practice (long ago publicly revealed), of the Ordo Templi Orientis (the other magical group Crowley headed) was sex magick. It was taught in stages as members attained the seventh through ninth degrees. However, in the A. A. system as taught by the abbey, the probationer who has reached the zelator grade is invited to begin study in this practice. The sexual, magical practices constitute the essence of a second division of the abbey, namely, the Sovereign Penetralia of the Gnosis, to which those who desire to follow the practice adhere.

A. A. members who have attained a level referred to as *zelatores* may be invited to membership within the Order of Thelemites (also known as the Order of Thelema), which was conceived in the 1920s by Crowley. Various charters, in the form of constitutions, were conferred upon A. A. members of that era. These constitutions recently have been recognized and the order of Thelemites has emerged from dormancy. The order is not a mystical, magical, or occult order in the ordinary sense of these words. Its purpose is to enable its members to succeed in life by teaching them the correct attitudes toward life and how to avoid wasting time in lines of effort for which they are unsuited.

Because the Abbey of Thelema is a secret order, much of its teachings and practice are not revealed to outsiders. The leader of the abbey, Gregory von Seewald, serves as praemonstrator of the A.A., outer head of the Sovereign Penetralia of the Gnosis, and abbot of Thelema for the Order of Thelemites. The Abbey of Thelema is affiliated with the Holy Order of RaHoorKhuit (H.O.O.R.), the Holy Gnostic Catholic Church (H.G.C.C.), and the Ordem dos Cavaleiros de Thelema (O.C.T.) in Brazil.

The Abbey of Thelema has a second center, in Miami, Florida, the New Flesh Palladium Chapter, which is headed by Robert North.

Membership: In 2008 there were fewer than 50 active members reported.

Sources:

Abbey of Thelema. www.thelemicmagick.com.

Motta, Marcelo Ramos. *Calling the Children of the Sun*. Trans. Monica Rocha, ed. Gregory von Seewald. Sydney, Australia: Headland Press, 1999.

One Star in Sight. Old Greenwich, CT: Abbey of Thelema, n.d.

Yorke, Gerald J. *666: Sex and the OTO*. Intro. Gregory von Seewald. York Beach, ME: Weiser Antiquarian Books, 2005.

Astrum Sophia

For information: phanes@isd.net., Minneapolis, MN

The Astrum Sophia (Ordo Astrum Sophiae), founded in 2002, is a new initiatory magical order, but one that continues the Ogdoadic Tradition of the Western Mysteries as exemplified in the Aurum Solis. The Aurum Solis was originally founded in 1897, but became well known in the 1970s through the work of Melita Denning (d. 1997) and Osborne Phillips. The Aurum Solis provided the charter and hence the initiatory lineage for the Astrum Sophia.

The founder of the Astrum Sophia is William Stoltz, who began working with Denning and Phillips in 1980. Stoltz rose quickly in the Aurum Solis and in 1985 became the order's administrator-general. In 1987 the Aurum Solis became inactive for a period. In 1999, Stoltz resumed his Third Hall work and subsequently received a charter of succession from the Grand Master of the Aurum Solis, empowering him to establish and govern an autonomous Order of the Ogdoadic Tradition. This charter included the authority to administer all degrees, appoint all officers, and to establish or revise all rites.

The Astrum Sophia's magical teachings, which build on the system presented in Denning and Philip's five-volume work The Magical Philosophy, are presented to students in three stages. Following a period of probation, a new student will be introduced successively to the Lesser Mysteries in what are termed the First and Second Halls. These two "halls" constitute the Outer Order or the Order Astrum Sophia. Through the Third Hall, the Greater Mysteries are presented in what is termed the Inner Order or Stella Gloriosa. In the Inner Order, through mastery of the teachings and subsequent personal endeavor, an initiate may reach the grade of Adeptus Minor, and beyond.

The Astrum Sophia is guided by its Collegium Cathedrarum, or College of Thrones, consisting of the Grand Master, the Prior, and the Administrator-General. Under it are Commanderies and Citadels. A Commandery is an autonomous structure that, acting within the principles of the Astrum Sophia, is able to administer its own affairs, set its own curriculum, and establish Citadels. A Citadel is a work-ing group established by a Commandery, operating under the authority of that Commandery

A Commandery is empowered to transmit the first two grades of the Order; initiation to the Third Hall requires permission from the College of Thrones. These officers of the Collegium Cathedrarum operate as members of the Grand Commandery of the Winged Serpent.

The Astrum Sophia also has a consultative governing body called the Star Council, consisting of all Masters of Commanderies and all Third Hall initiates.

Membership in the Astrum Sophia is by invitation, usually extended in response to an application. Probationers become members after receiving the First Hall initiation.

Membership: Not reported. As of 2008, there are three Commanderies operating in the United States, one each in Minnesota, Washington, and California. There are also two in Europe, one in Belgium and one for Ireland and the United Kingdom.

Sources:

Ordo Astrum Sophiae. astrumsophia.org/.

Denning, Melita, and Osborne Phillips. *The Magical Philosophy*. 5 vols. St. Paul, MN: Llewellyn Publications, 1974-1981.

Builders of the Adytum

5105 N Figueroa, Los Angeles, CA 90042

Builders of the Adytum (B.O.T.A.) is a western mystery school whose teachings are based on the Holy Qabalah and sacred Tarot. According to B.O.T.A., the Holy Qabalah is the mystical (occult) wisdom teaching of ancient Israel. The great prophets of the Old and New Testaments (including Jesus of Nazareth) were versed in the Qabalah and received their spiritual training therefrom. The Holy Qabalah is based on a diagrammatical and symbolic glyph called the Tree of Life. It is a pictorial-symbolic representation of the One God and man's relationship to God and creation. The Tarot is a pictorial textbook on ageless wisdom.

B.O.T.A. was founded in 1922 by Dr. Paul Foster Case (1884—1954), one of the American members of the Hermetic Order of the Golden Dawn, for the study of practical occultism. A recognized world authority on the Tarot and Qabalah, Dr. Case was given the task by the Inner School of reinterpreting the ageless wisdom into terms understandable to the modern western mind.

The primary purpose of B.O.T.A. is to teach and practice the doctrine of the Oneness of God, the brotherhood of man, and the kinship of all life, patterned after the Ageless Wisdom mystery schools of spiritual training as particularly exemplified by the Holy Qabalah. Occult orders such as B.O.T.A. have as their major objective "the promotion of the welfare of humanity." The great masters of wisdom, from whom flow the inspiration and spiritual impetus of this work, refuse to have anything to do with any order that fails to recognize the primary importance of this great objective, for they devote all their energy and influence to that end. Their conception of the meaning of "the welfare of humanity" is embodied in the following seven-point program:

1. Universal Peace;
2. Universal Political Freedom;
3. Universal Religious Freedom;
4. Universal Education;
5. Universal Health;
6. Universal Prosperity; and
7. Universal Spiritual Unfoldment.

According to adherents of B.O.T.A., in order to promote the welfare of humanity, we need first to look to the units of which humanity is composed. Selfish personalities make their unhappy contribution to a selfish social structure. Chaotic thinking and immature emotions affect the mental and emotional levels of all humanity. We do not live unto ourselves alone. To the degree that the aspirant becomes a more effective unit in his personal environment, he brings spiritual powers into action for all humanity and prepares himself to serve life in ever greater measure.

Dedicated work with the Tarot techniques in the B.O.T.A. curriculum has as its aim the transmutation of personality. A transformed personality will bring with it the ability to change its environment, bringing it closer to the heart's desire. A fulfilled life becomes a positive radiating center, an effective channel through which the higher self can function, and a living example for others. The particular potency of the western mystery training system lies in its use of symbols, a universal language that directly instructs subconsciousness with its pictorial wisdom.

B.O.T.A. is the outer school behind which stands an inner mystery school offering instruction for students who wish to participate in the esoteric work. Qualified students may become members of a pronaos; many are found in the United States and various other countries, and members are referred to as *pronaons*. After initiation in a pronaos, members may participate in the group ritual work of B.O.T.A.

The external affairs of the order are managed by the board of stewards. The proculator general is the primary link between the outer and inner schools. Prior to 1976, the only groups open to the general membership were in Los Angeles. However, during the next decade approximately 50 study groups and working groups (pronaos) were formed in 19 states. Groups also appeared in Montreal and Toronto, Canada; Great Britain; the Netherlands; New Zealand; Colombia; and Aruba, in the Caribbean.

The B.O.T.A headquarters in France is in Perpignan; the B.O.T.A. headquarters in New Zealand is in Naenae.

Membership: Not reported.

Sources:

B.O.T.A. Builders of the Adytum. www.bota.org,

Case, Paul Foster. *The Book of Tokens*. Los Angeles: B.O.T.A., 1947.

————. *The Tarot*. Richmond, VA: Macoy, 1947.

————. *The True and Invisible Rosicrucian Order*. Author, 1928.

Davies, Ann. *Inspirational Thoughts on the Tarot*. Burbank, CA: Candlelight Press, 1983.

————. *This Is the Truth About the Self*. Los Angeles: Builders of the Adytum, 1960.

Frazer, Felix J. *Parallel Paths to the Unseen Worlds*. Los Angeles: Builders of the Adytum, 1967.

CIRCES International

PO Box 279, Plainfield, IN 46168

CIRCES International is the American (and English-language) affiliate of the Cercle International de Recherches Culturelles et Spirituelles (International Circle for Cultural and Spiritual Research). The International Circle was founded in 1988 in France as a New Age initiatic association inspired by the Templar tradition of inclusiveness. Integral to the understanding of the organization is the idea that each era is unique in the way the cosmos impacts the inner consciousness of humanity. New eras are defined by astrological ages. The previous age, the Age of Pisces, was keynoted by Jesus' admonition to "love ye one another." The keynote of the present Aquarian age is the desire for confluence of personal integration. In this age, the path formerly trod primarily by mystics and sages will become common to a large number of the human race.

CIRCES emphasizes two important truths regarding the discovery of a spiritual path that would lead to personal integration. First, each individual must find his/her own path, rather than slavishly attempting to follow a predetermined "true" path. Second, the discovery and treading of one's path can be greatly enhanced by modern psychological insights. In this light, CIRCES does not present doctrines and dogmas, but a variety of techniques that members are encouraged to use as they awaken to their own personal perspectives of truth.

CIRCES is open to all aspirants who are willing to live by the command, "love ye one another" and who are dedicated to the ideals of chivalry, world peace, and the reduction of human suffering. These goals are pursued by way of the practical integration of the spiritual and psychological technologies. Members are encouraged to discover the way they can most effectively express the various spiritual values, including unconditional love, in daily life.

New members of CIRCES are admitted into the Outer Circle and participate in its work on three levels: (1) in a general research council, members pursue studies on a particular subject and attempt to apply results in a practical context; (2) as part of a commission, work of the research councils on related topics is synthesized; (3) in the Academy, which organizes all the work of the Outer Order, the member may pursue research in one of several colleges—the College of Arcane Sciences, the College of Mundane Sciences, or the College of Creative Sciences.

After a three-year probationary period in the Outer Circle, members may also be invited to participate in the Inner Circle, where the traditional teachings of the Templars as understood by the order are presented. Involvement in the Inner Circle begins with the Order of Sovereign Templar Initiates (OSTI). Since all instruction of the Inner Circle is oral, attendance at the monthly gatherings of OSTI units is required of Inner Circle members. New members of the order may attend Inner Circle meetings but are not to participate verbally for the first year, a period of silence. Work in the Inner Circle progresses on a degree basis. There are three degrees in OSTI, which is followed by three degrees in the International Order of Pythagoreans. At the center of the order is the Universal Order of Melchisedech.

CIRCES International was initially headed by the founder, Fr. Raymond Bernard. Bernard passed away in January 2006, but his influence is still very much alive. CIRCES-USA has been completely independent since Bernard granted it full independence in 1992, and is now very much committed to the original version of its founder, which is universal fellowship, or the one human family, thereby, "materializing the spiritual."

Each country has been organized as a Grand Commandery under the direction of a Grand Commander appointed by the Sovereign Grand Master. Regional divisions within a country are organized into Grand Preceptories headed by a Grand Preceptor. A Grand Preceptor can operate in the absence of the Grand Commander. Local groups are variously designated commanderies or templar research circles.

Membership: At this time, May 2008, group reports that it is not in a position to determine with accuracy the number of members in CIRCES International. However, given the fact that CIRCES-USA has recently decided to initiate the integration of the French and Spanish languages into its activities, numbers could change dramatically. Therefore, in the not-too-distance future, CIRCES will be trilingual, and as time goes by, it will integrate other languages in all of the activities. At the moment, CIRCES estimates that membership numbers are in the low-to mid-hundreds.

Sources:

CIRCES International. Available from http//:www.circesinternational.org

Clan Invisible

Current address not obtained for this edition.

Clan Invisible is a small magical order that emerged in the larger context of the spread of thelemic magic articulated in *The Book of the Law*, revealed to Aleister Crowley (1875–1947) in 1904. *The Book of the Law* is often summarized in the statements, "Do what thou will shall be the whole of the law," and "Love is the law, Love Under Will." Along with respect for the Law of Thelema or Will, as revealed in the *Liber al vel Legis*, the clan promotes fitness of the mind and the body through the philosophies of Taoism and practice of the martial arts. It also practices a technique for gaining access to parallel dimensions utilizing dream walking, past-life regression, alchemy, divination, herbalism, holistic living, mysticism, and astronomy.

Unlike some thelemic groups, the clan does not use a grade structure; however, newer and more advanced aspirants are recognized, and the former will be referred to the latter for assistance in the development process. The clan is administered by the secretet.

Membership: Not reported.

Sources:

Clan Invisible. www.angelfire.com/ut/Invisible.

College and Temple of Thelema

PO Box 415, Oroville, CA 95965

Alternate Address: College Main Campus, 222 N Manhattan Pl., Los Angeles, CA 90004.

The College and Temple of Thelema are two interrelated structures that focus on the thelemic teachings as passed to Phyllis Seckler (Soror Meral), an early American member of the Ordo Temple Orientis and student of the magical system of Aleister Crowley (1875–1947). The College of Thelema was opened in 1973 as a magical and spiritual education program offering instruction in the basic teaching of the western esoteric tradition, especially in the thelemic mode as developed by Crowley. From 1976 to 1996 the college published *In the Continuum*, a journal featuring important (and rare) writings by Crowley, as well as other magical materials (copies of back issues are still available from the college). All teachers of the college are bound to the precepts and philosophy as revealed in *Liber AL vel Legis* (*The Book of the Law*) and Crowley's work as the prophet of the current Aeon of Horus.

In 1904 Crowley claimed to have received the channeled dictation of *The Book of the Law* from a praeterhuman intelligence who declared its name to be Aiwass and identified itself as "the minister of Hoor-paar-kraat," that is, the instrument of the Egyptian God of Silence. *The Book of the Law* announced the dawning of a new spiritual era for humanity. The primary message of the book is contained in the Greek words *thelema* (will), or True Will inherent in each person, and in *agape* (love), referring to the passionate love of the divine as a basis for authentic human love. For thelemites, the Great World is a matter of finding one's True Will and expressing loving within that context.

The curriculum of the College of Thelema is broken into four consecutive courses dealing with the practical application of psychology, thelemic philosophy, Qabalah, astrology, and magick. Once enrolled, the student has two years to complete the course. The college's main campus is located in Los Angeles, California, and there are smaller campus branches in San Francisco and in Vancouver, British Columbia.

The Temple of Thelema was established upon the principles and methods of the College of Thelema, of which it is a part. The temple is an initiating order, a modern mystery school that focuses on the systematic teaching and training of its members in the spiritual disciplines of magick and mysticism. The old grade ceremonies of the legendary Hermetic Order of the Golden Dawn have been recast to conform to thelemic symbols and principles. A "three ray" model of balanced development (wisdom, love, and power) includes intellectual training, meditation, and magical ritual at every stage of progress. Initiation rituals, other ceremonies, and the ongoing group healing work are also a central aspect of the curriculum. Although the actual content and ritual process taught is reserved for members of the order, a general understanding may be gained from reading Crowley's readily available magical writings.

Following a pattern set by the Hermetic Order of the Golden Dawn in the late nineteenth century, the work of the temple is divided into a series of steps based on a Qabalistic diagram called the Tree of Life. In each of these degrees of training, the member is given the opportunity and responsibility to explore himself/herself from a different point of view, climaxing in a stage of synthesis, or integration.

There are marked differences between the Temple of Thelema and the original Golden Dawn order. For example, at the temple, more practical instruction was added in the early degrees that incorporate much of what has been learned in the last century concerning personal transformation, and steps were taken to remove the remnants of the previous era's sexist assumptions.

Membership: Figures not reported. In 2008 there were seven centers of the Temple of Thelema in the United States and one temple in Toronto, Canada.

Periodicals: *Black Pearl*.

Sources:

College and Temple of Thelema. www.thelema.org.

Cor Lucis

222 N. Manhattan Pl., Los Angeles, CA 90004

Cor Lucis is a new magical order in the Thelemic tradition. It was formed and is headed by Anna-Kria King. Temple Number One is located in Los Angeles and the largest number of members resides in the Los Angeles metropolitan area. Those outside this area must be willing to come to Los Angeles for initiation and at least annually for further ritual participation. Membership is by invitation only, though seekers are invited to submit an application.

Cor Lucis operates out of the Golden Dawn and Thelemic magical traditions. It offers members a graded program combining group and private ritual, study, and meditation. Students work with material from the Golden Dawn, the Kaballah, and the Tarot. *The Book of the Law*, received by Aleister Crowley in 1904, provides the framework for all of the Cor Lucis's work.

Cor Lucis has attempted to strip the masculine bias from the Western magical tradition and honors both male and female participants. Learning the magical tradition and attaining a degree of self-mastery is seen as analogous to training for an Olympic event. Beginning students are expected to devote at least an hour a day to their own self-improvement and to attend group events every two weeks.

Membership: Not reported. There is one center, in Los Angeles.

Sources:

Cor Lucis. www.corlucis.org/.

Ecclesia Gnostica Universalis

For information: Tau Sir Hasirim (Allen Greenfield), bishop17@mindspring.com

The Ecclesia Gnostica Universalis was founded in 2000 by several bishops in the Thelemic Gnostic tradition of Aleister Crowley (1875-1947) and active with the Ecclesia Gnostica Catholica, which is closely tied to the Ordo Templi Orientis. Since its founding, the Ecclesia Gnostica Universalis has been joined by several other Thelemic bishops, who together form the College of Bishops that leads the organization. Tau Aleph, one of the founders who had been a bishop in the Ecclesia Gnostica Catholica, notes that he had concluded that the church's mass had lost is power in the concern to preserve its form as dictated by Crowley. The need to revise the mass and be open to changes that would bring it to life became a catalyst for the founding of the new church.

All of the bishops of the church have been consecrated in one (or more) of the lineages of apostolic succession that currently exist in the Gnostic and Thelemic community, primarily that passed to the Ordo Templi Orientis by Crowley from Jules-Benoit Doinel or Tau Valentin II (1842-1894). Tau Aleph had been consecrated by Grady McMurtry (d. 1985), who revived the Ordo Templi Orientis in America in the 1970s and led it for many years. Allen Greenfield (b. 1946), whose ecclesiastical name is Tau Sir Hasirim, was consecrated by Most Rev. Michael Paul Bertiaux of the Neo-Pythagorean Church based in Chicago and Tau Silenus of the Ecclesia Gnostica Catholica and Ordo Templi Orientis. Greenfield sits as a member of the North American College of Gnostic Bishops.

While clearly based in the Thelemic teachings initially articulated by Aleister Crowley, which emphasize the following of one's own unique will (or destiny) as the best path to supreme realization, the bishops of the Ecclesia Gnostica Universalis have been open to insights drawn from the larger Gnostic tradition as it has emerged through the late twentieth century to the present. The church believes in the continuing evolution of the Gnosis and as such, believes rituals should also change. It encourages the creation of new Gnostic Masses that draw on variant traditions. It also encourages members to create personal rituals that assist them in their individual situation and path to realization.

The church exists to assist people to remember the gnosis (knowledge) they already have but have forgotten. The church is led by its bishops, but they attempt to limit their duties to necessary administrative matters while encouraging the membership to assume active leadership in spiritual matters. The assumption of administrative duties by the bishops frees the priests and priestesses in the church to concentrate on ritual and spiritual matters.

Bishops and worshipping communities of the Ecclesia Gnostica Catholica are found in Atlanta, Georgia; Austin, Texas; San Francisco, California; Portland, Oregon; St. Louis, Missouri; and Moscow, Russia.

Membership: Not reported.

Sources:

Ecclesia Gnostica Universalis. www.egnu.org/wiki/Ecclesia_Gnostica_Universalis.

Eglise Gnostique Catholique Apostolique

c/o The Most Rev. Msgr. Robert M. Cokinis, Cathedral of the Four Holy Crown Martyrs, 5215 Randolph St. W, Bellwood, IL 60104

The Eglise Gnostique Catholique Apostolique (the Gnostic Catholic and Apostolic Church) was brought to the United States in 1970 with the appointment of Roger Victor-Herard as the primate of the church for North America, but it has its roots in the gnostic/mystical groups of eighteenth-century Europe. Through the centuries, gnostic Christianity (a form of Christianity considered heretical by the Roman Catholic Church) disappeared from public view. However, in the wake of the Reformation in the sixteenth century, groups such as the Rosicrucians claimed to possess the teachings of the ancient wisdom (i.e., the gnosis). By the end of the eighteenth century (in the relative freedom created by the French Revolution) attempts were made, initially by French Roman Catholic clerics, to reestablish the Gnostic church, and as early as 1800 a Msgr. Mauviel was consecrated as a bishop and established the Johannine Church of Primitive Christians.

A short time later, a second gnostic thrust was initiated by Eugene Vintras (1807–1875), whose gnostic movement ran into trouble with a revived Roman Catholic Church. In 1848 he claimed that in a vision Christ had consecrated him to the papal office and given him a new liturgy. After a brief period outside of France he returned to found, in 1865, the Sanctuary of the Interior of the Carmel of Elie in Lyon.

The Eglise Gnostique Catholique Apostolique, inspired by this growing gnostic milieu, can be traced to 1904 when Julius Houssaye (or Hussay) was consecrated by Paolo Miraglia-Gulotti, an Italian bishop who had been consecrated by Abp. Joseph Rene Vilatte of the American Catholic Church. Houssaye was a gnostic who under his ecclesiastical name Abbe Julio published several occult texts. He passed the leadership of the Gnostic Church to Louis Francois Giraud, whom he consecrated in 1911. Two years later, Giraud consecrated Jean Becaud, who took the ecclesiastical name Tau Jean II and later, as the first patriarch of the church, developed a considerable following in the city of Lyon. In 1918 he consecrated Victor Blanchard (Tau Targilius), who became head of the church in 1934. Blanchard, in part responding to pressures from the rise of Nazism, helped spread the Gnostic Church into Portugal, and on to Brazil. In 1945 Blanchard consecrated Roger Menard (Tau Eon II), who in 1946 consecrated Robert Ambelain (Tau Jean III). Ambelain consecrated Andre Mauer (Tau Andreas), who assumed the role of patriarch of the church.

It was Tau Andreas who named Pedro Freire primate of South America. Then in 1970, Dom Antidio Vargas, a bishop of the Brazilian Catholic Church, consecrated Pedro Freire as patriarch of the Eglise Gnostique Catholique Apostolique. As Mar Petrus-Johannes XIII, he succeeded Tau Andreas. Mar Petrus-Johannes XIII encouraged the spread of the church in the Americas and encouraged Roger Victor-Herard (d. 1989) to initiate work in the United States. In 1970 he named Herard (as Tau Charles) the primate of the North American branch of the church. In 1977 Mar Petrus-Johannes XIII died. The synod decided against naming a new patriarch. At that point the American branch became autocephalous (independent). The church is administered by the presiding bishop, Tau Charles Harmonius II, who has been president of the board of directors since 1984.

The Gnostic Catholic Church perpetuates a gnostic interpretation of Christianity and has instituted a sacramental ministry to that end. In the gnostic view, the world is the end product of successive emanations from God. Humanity is trapped in this material world. Through the gnosis (or secret wisdom), we may receive initiation and a way back to God. Christ, the logos, has been God's agent in salvation by his bringing the gnosis to us. The church is the custodian of the gnosis.

The church is divided into several dioceses in the United States, and the one in the Midwest (Illinois) serves as its national headquarters.

Membership: In 1995 the church reported approximately 3,000 members in the United States and 200 members in Canada.

Educational Facilities:

Athenea Theologica, Bellwood, Illinois.

Periodicals: *Journal of the Athenea Theologica*.

Franz Bardon Foundation

c/o Jim Bardon, 1344 High St., #1-FBF, Denver, CO 80218

Franz Bardon (d. 1958) was an Austrian teacher of hermetic initiatory magic. His important texts were published in the 1950s in Germany, shortly before his death, and translated into English in the 1970s. Bardon's three major books included a basic text on hermetic magic, a commentary on the Kabbalah (which he spelled Quabbalah), and a system of spirit evocation. These books found an audience among English-speaking readers, and the foundation was begun in 1986 to propagate Bardon's teaching, provide a network among students of the books, and offer instruction in his system.

Membership: Not reported.

Periodicals: *The Franz Bardon News*.

Sources:

Franz Bardon Foundation. geocities.com/franzbardon/

Bardon, Franz. *Initiation into Hermetics*. Wupperthal, Germany: Deiter Ruggeburg, 1970.

———. *Die Praxis der magischen Evokation*. Freiburg/Breisgau, Germany: Verlag Hermann Bauer, 1956. Trans. as *The Practice of Magical Evocation*. Wupperthal, Germany: Deiter Ruggeburg, 1970.

———. *Der Schkussel zur wahren Quabbalah*. Freiburg/Breisgau, Germany: Verlag Hermann Bauer, 1957. Trans. as *The Key to the True Quabbalah*. Wupperthal, Germany: Deiter Ruggeburg, 1971.

Fraternitas L.V.X Occulta

International Headquarters, Box 5094, Covina, CA 91723

The Fraternitas L.V.X. Occulta, Latin for the Fraternity of the Hidden Light, was founded in Covina, California, in 1982, but traces its lineage to the U.S. section of the Hermetic Order of the Golden Dawn (OGD). According to the present leadership of the fraternity, at one point in the early twentieth century the head and three other officers of the OGD reorganized the order as a mystery school and transitional order to assist in bringing in the New Age, or Age of Aquarius. The present heads of the fraternity inherited this tradition, and during the mid-1980s they assumed a more public profile.

The fraternity has three main objectives: to act as a modern-day repository of the ancient wisdom; to train members for selfless service to humanity through application of the ancient wisdom; and to promulgate the ancient wisdom. Teachings are drawn from the writings of Hermes Mercurius Trismegistus, the legendary Egyptian magus, and the Qabalah. Instruction is also given in Tarot, alchemy, astrology, and occult psychology.

The fraternity is organized in three levels. An outer level trains new initiates in the growth into wisdom, love, and power. The second order is composed of those initiates who have developed harmony and balance within themselves and have received illumination, and whose higher self is in control of their lives. The third level consists of the great adepts and masters of the ages who guide the fraternity from the inner realms.

Members work through a curriculum of graded instruction in the occult, as well as instruction in meditation and ritual. Rituals are used to invoke quantum changes in the consciousness (i.e., high magic). Probationers pass through a period of at least three months in which a basic knowledge of the occult must be acquired. They may then apply for full membership. In 2008 the head (steward) of the fraternity was Paul A. Clark.

Membership: In 1995 the fraternity reported five temples and members in 17 countries worldwide. The Grand Preceptory of Europe is located in Cambridge, England. The international affiliations are located in the United Kingdom, Spain, France, Japan, Canada, and Australia. There are study groups in Boston, Massachusetts; Dallas, Texas; Denver, Colorado; and several cities in California.

Periodicals: *The Hidden Light* • *The Threshold* • *The Path of Return* • *The Halls of Thoth* • *The Book of the Rose*.

Sources:

Fraternity of the Hidden Light. www.lvx.org.

Clark, Paul A. *The Book of the Rose*. Covina, CA: Fraternity of the Hidden Light, 1985.

Gnostic Alchemical Church of Typhon-Christ

For information: pelicanus@webtv.net.

The Gnostic Alchemical Church of Typhon-Christ is one of several magical Gnostic groups to arise in the wake of the dissemination of information in the 1980s of the 1976 discovery of what is termed the New Aeon English Qaballa (also spelled Cabala). The New Aeon refers to the period beginning in 1904, when Aleister Crowley (1875–1947), considered the founder of the Thelemic magical tradition, received a work, *The Book of the Law,* from a preternatural being named Aiwass. Interpreting the book and following its dictates has been integral to Thelemic practice through the years. The book, however, was by no means easily understood and in fact noted that neither Crowley, nor his magical child (Charles S. Jones, 1886–1950) would be able to fully interpret it, but that "one cometh after him [i.e., Jones], whence I say not, who shall discover the Key of it all" (III, 47). Over the years various people had attempted unsuccessfully to decipher it, but in 1976 the independent Thelemite Jim Lees discovered a new interpretive tool that uses the English language in a manner analogous to the Hebrew Kaballah. He and two associates, Jake Stratton-Kent and Carol Smith, subsequently announced his findings to the larger Thelemic community, to a mixed response. Over the succeeding years, Kaaba Publications, headed by Smith, began releasing books expanding on the techniques of the English Qaballa. While most Thelemites rejected Lees's work, some found it a very valuable tool in understanding *The Book of the Law*. Among the first groups to utilize the discoveries of the English Qaballa was the Hermetic Alchemical Order of the QBLH.

Founded as knowledge of the English Qaballa grew, the Gnostic Alchemical Church of Typhon-Christ has as its stated goal the spreading of knowledge/wisdom (*gnosis*) created through the application of the English Qaballa to the Holy Books of Thelema, especially *The Book of the Law*.

Membership is open to those interested in exploring Thelema, and individual initiations are arranged at astrologically determined times when the Sun is in conjunction with Venus, Mercury, and/or Jupiter.

The founders of the Gnostic Alchemical Church of Typhon-Christ have continued a relationship with Jim Lees and Carol Smith, who serve as editors of *The New Equinox: The British Journal of Thelema*, through which a variety of articles on

Thelema in general and the New Qaballa have been released. The church maintains electronic versions of older issues on its Web site. The church also maintains a relationship with Kiblah Publishing in the United Kingdom, which publishes *The New Equinox* and has released an edition of *The Book of the Law* with added materials on the English Qaballa.

The church is a supporting member of the Aleister Crowley Foundation.

Membership: Not reported. Members are found in France, England, Canada, and the United States.

Sources:

Gnostic Alchemical Church of Typhon-Christ. www.geocities.com/Area51/Stargate/7770/.

The Holy Books of Thelema. York Beach, ME: Samuel Weiser, 1988.

Hermetic Order of the Golden Dawn

PO Box 1757, Elfers, FL 34680

The Hermetic Order of the Golden Dawn is the European-headquartered Hermetic Order of the Golden Dawn (H.O.G.D.), an organization dedicated to the continued preservation of that body of knowledge known as hermeticism, or the western esoteric tradition. The order is rooted in the hermetic and Rosicrucian traditions that teach and practice the triad of spiritual disciplines known as the Trivium Hermeticum; theurgy (magic), astrology, and alchemy. The theurgy includes Qabalistic, Egyptian, Enochian, and Chaldaean magic. The order promotes the teachings of the original Hermetic Order of the Golden Dawn, the magical fraternity founded in London in 1888 by William Wynn Westcott (1848–1925), S(amuel). L(iddell). MacGregor Mathers (1854–1918), and R. Woodman.

The founders used certain documents known as the *Cipher Manuscripts*, which had been encrypted using the Trithemius cipher by Freemason scholar Kenneth MacKenzie (1833–1886). MacKenzie had been initiated as a Rosicrucian in Vienna by the Hungarian count Apponyi in 1850. This provides the link to Golden's Dawn's Rosicrucian lineage.

Upon his return to England, MacKenzie founded the esoteric society that later became the Golden Dawn under the original name *Fratres Lucis*, or Brethren of the Cross of Light. MacKenzie's temple was number one, the Bristol temple of F. G. Irwin was number two, and the Isis-Urania temple, where the Golden Dawn was founded, became number three.

During a visit to Paris in 1891 MacGregor Mathers reestablished contact with MacKenzie's continental European adepts, whom he referred to as the "secret chiefs." MacGregor Mathers founded the Second Order of the Golden Dawn's projected three-order system, Rosae Rubeae et Aureae Crucis, or R.R. et A.C. He eventually moved permanently to Paris to be close to his Rosicrucian teachers.

Following a rebellion of adepts in London in 1903 and a press scandal involving the Golden Dawn name, in 1906 MacGregor Mathers changed the name of the order to the Rosicrucian Order of Alpha et Omega, keeping the Hermetic Order of the Golden Dawn as its outer order.

According to the order's Web site, in 2002 Golden Dawn leaders Jean-Pascal Ruggiu and David Griffin met in Paris with representatives of MacKenzie and MacGregor Mathers's continental European secret chiefs, from whom they received the initiation rituals and curriculum for the Golden Dawn's projected third and final order. These materials allegedly include the secrets of Hermetic Inner Alchemy, which uses the physical body in a *prima materia*, first matter. According to the Golden Dawn, this *opus magnum*, great work, is a system that uses the subtle fires of the body, including love and sexuality, to transmute the physical body into higher and more refined forms of energy. The goal is to project consciousness into a solar body and the moment of death, thus rendering the alchemist consciously immortal.

As originally designed by its founders, the Golden Dawn was to be an hermetic society dedicated to the philosophical, spiritual, and psychic evolution of humanity. It was supposed to be a school and a repository of knowledge concerning the principles of occult science and the various elements of western philosophy and magic. Symbolism used within the H.O.G.D. came from a variety of religious sources, and people from very diverse esoteric religious paths found themselves at home with the Golden Dawn.

The order owns the Hermetic Order of the Golden Dawn trademark in the European Union and the Hermetic Order of the Golden Dawn International trademark in Canada. In the United States, they operate by legal agreement adopted by the U.S. District Court as the Hermetic Order of the Golden Dawn, an outer order of the Rosicrucian Order of Alpha et Omega. They also own the R.R. et A.C. trademark of their second order, Ordo Rosae Rubeae et Aureae Crucis and the Alpha et Omega trademark of their three-order superstructure founded by MacGregor Mathers in 1906, Ordo Rosae Crucis, Alpha et Omega.

Membership: In 2008, 4,215 members were reported.

Sources:

Hermetic Order of the Golden Dawn. www.hermeticgoldendawn.org; www.golden-dawn.com.

Howe, Elllic. *The Magicians of the Golden Dawn*. London: Routledge and Kegan Paul, 1972.

King, Francis. *Ritual Magic in England: 1887 to the Present Day*. London: New English Library, 1972.

Regardie, Israel. *The Golden Dawn*. 4 vols. Chicago: Aries Press, 1937–1940.

————. *What You Should Know about the Golden Dawn*. Phoenix, AZ: Falcon Press, 1983.

Wescott, Wynn. *History of the Societas Rosicruciana in Anglia*. n.d.

Hermetic Order of the Golden Dawn (Regardie)

270 N Canon Dr., Ste. 1302, Beverly Hills, CA 90210

The Hermetic Order of the Golden Dawn, outer order of the Rosicrucian Order of Alpha et Omega, is the U.S. jurisdiction of the European-headquartered Hermetic Order of the Golden Dawn, founded in the United Kingdom in 1888. The order has been credited with constructing a brilliant synthesis of mythical and magical material from varied sources of the western magical tradition. When the order was discontinued early in the twentieth century, its work was carried on by organizations founded by several of its members, and most of its materials have been published. A most important event was the publication of its main rituals by Israel Regardie (1907–1985).

In the early 1980s Regardie was considered by many in the occult world as the last contact point with the era of the Golden Dawn and Aleister Crowley (1875–1947). Regardie and his student, Cris Monnastre, resurrected the Hermetic Order of the Golden Dawn and the Ordo Rosae Rubeae et Aureae Crucis (R. R. et A. C.). In 1982, under Regardie's guidance, Monnastre founded the Osiris Khenti Amenti Temple in Los Angeles, California. Over the succeeding years, other temples were opened.

In 1988 Monnastre retired from the Golden Dawn, leaving the Golden Dawn adept David Griffin as his successor. In 1999 Griffin merged the order with the European-headquartered Hermetic Order of the Golden Dawn, forming a triad of chiefs with Ukrainian nobleman Marquis Nicholas Tereschenko and the reigning imperator of S. L. MacGregor Mathers Ahathoor Temple Number 7 in Paris, Golden Dawn adept Jean Pascal Ruggiu.

The Ordo Rosae Rubeae et Aureae Crucis operates temples of the Hermetic Order of the Golden Dawn around the world. The United Confederation of Independent and Autonomous Temples, officially known as the Confederatio Fraternitatis Rosae Crucis (C. F. R. C.), consists of temples from around the world, descending with initiatic and/or chartered lineage and affiliation from the Hermetic Order of the Golden Dawn, as reinstituted by Regardie and Monnastre. Within the confederation, it is believed, are reunited initiatic and/or chartered lineages deriving from the Hermetic Order of the Golden Dawn, the Ordo Rosae Rubeae et Aureae Crucis, and

the several groups formed from them early in the twentieth century, specifically the Stella Matutina, the Ordo Rosae Crucis, Alpha et Omega (Rosicrucian Order of Alpha et Omega), the Holy Order of the Golden Dawn (deriving from A. E. Waite), and the Order of the Sacred Word.

The order offers ritual initiation as well as instruction in the Rosicrucian system of ceremonial magic. It is claimed that this system facilitates personal as well as spiritual development through a systematic program of ritual initiation and the spiritual disciplines of ceremonial magic (a powerful tool for self-realization and transformation).

The order distinguishes itself from several other groups claiming roots in the Golden Dawn that engage in what the order views as dubious practices, in particular "initiation by proxy" or "astral initiation." All initiations marking the progress of the student are performed while the student is physically in the presence of the initiator, during which time, it is believed, the actual transmission of magical energies occurs.

The European-headquartered Hermetic Order of the Golden Dawn operates in the United States by a legal agreement adopted by the U.S. District Court as the Hermetic Order of the Golden Dawn, the outer order of the Rosicrucian Order of Alpha et Omega.

Membership: In 2008 2,130 members were reported.

Remarks: In 1982 Cris Monnastre was given a number of Israel Regardie's personal magical accoutrements, among which were Regardie's Elemental Weapons, a complete Rosicrucian chess set, and a Rose Cross that he had inherited from Elsa Barker (an important historical link in the Rosicrucian Order of Alpha et Omega between Mathers' Ahathor Mother Temple, No. 7, in Paris and the temples of the A. O. in the United States). She has donated these items to the R. R. et A. C.

Sources:

Golden Dawn F.A.Q. www.golden-dawn.info.

Regardie, Israel. *The Golden Dawn*. 4 vols. Chicago: Aries Press, 1937–1940.

————. *The Middle Pillar*. Chicago: Aries Press, 1938.

————. *My Rosicrucian Adventure*. [1936.] St. Paul, MN: Llewellyn Publications, 1971.

————. *What You Should Know about the Golden Dawn*. Phoenix, AZ: Falcon Press, 1983.

Hermetic Order of the Morning Star International (Golden Dawn–Canada)

4035 E Guasti Rd., Ste. 306, Ontario, CA 91761

The Hermetic Order of the Morning Star International Golden Dawn–Canada is the Canadian jurisdiction of the European-headquartered Hermetic Order of the Golden Dawn, founded in 1888. It is a worldwide fraternity dedicated to the "great work," the higher development of spiritual growth through the magical way of life. The order believes that magic is a powerful system of inner growth and spiritual development. As a mystery school, it is designed to take the student step-by-step to the door of adepthood. The adept in the making learns the "secrets" of listening and hearing to what is thought of as one's inner voice of light, often called the "higher genius" or "holy guardian angel."

The order owns the Hermetic Order of the Golden Dawn International trademark in Canada. They also own the Canadian R.R. et A.C. trademark of their Second Order, Ordo Rosae Rubeae et Aureae Crucis, and the Canadian Alpha et Omega trademark of their three-order superstructure founded by S. L. MacGregor Mathers in 1906, Order Rosae Crucis, Alpha et Omega.

Students are taught through a series of graded lessons from the starting point of neophyte. Each grade has a series of lessons, more than 175 of which constitute the lessons for the outer order (neophyte to philosophus). Students receive the lesson for their grade, and they work at their own speed. The student is tested on each grade before being passed into the next grade. The movement from grade to grade is marked with an initiation ceremony held in the Temple of Isis Mighty Mother in southern California, or if a person cannot come to the temple, initiations may take place through what is termed an "astral initiation."

The actual teachings of the order are given to members only, but they flow from the now generally well documented teachings of the western mystery tradition found in the material produced by and written about the Hermetic Order of the Golden Dawn. Almost all of the rituals and teaching materials of the lesser and outer schools originally produced for the Golden Dawn early in the twentieth century have been published, and during the 1980s several groups appeared that directly draw upon these materials. Lessons of the Morning Star include the study of mystical Christianity, Qabalah, Egyptian mysteries, philosophy, Tarot, Greek mysteries, alchemy, astrology, astral travel, clairvoyance, and ritual magic.

V.H. Frater T.D.L., the imperator, and V.H. Soror T.F., prae monstratrix, were the leaders of the order in 2008.

The order has established the Golden Dawn Forum, an email list with free discussion on subjects including Tarot, Qabalah, hermetics, healing, and initiation. A Western Mysteries Form was created as an Internet mailing list for serious discussion of hermetics, ritual, and alchemy. Sincere students are encouraged to join.

Membership: In 2008, 926 members were reported in Canada.

Periodicals: *Sword of Wisdom*.

Sources:

Golden Dawn Research Center. Golden-Dawn.org.

Hermetic Order of the Golden Dawn. www.golden-dawn.ca.

Esoteric Order of the Golden Dawn. www.esotericgoldendawn.com.

Holy Order of RaHoorKhuit

Box 24691, Tampa, FL 33623

The Holy Order of RaHoorKhuit (H.O.O.R), conceived in 1978 and founded in 1991, is an outer order of Thelema established to fulfill and teach the concepts and principles of the method of theurgy (magic) known as Thelema. The teachings of Thelema (from the Greek word for "will") derive from *Liber Al vel Legis* (*The Book of the Law*), a small volume dictated to the eminent magical theorist and practitioner Aleister Crowley (1875–1947) by a praeterhuman intelligence known as Aiwass in 1904. The teachings of Thelema are generally summarized in several of the statements from *Liber Al*: "Do what thou wilt shall be the whole of the Law" and "Love is the law, Love under will."

In essence, Thelema teaches that every human being is a complete, unique, and divine entity (a star). Each person has a unique purpose (destiny), which is the law. Each person's function is to follow one's destiny. Love serves as the agent, under the regency of will, that binds all things in their course. Thelemites see the law of Thelema as a law of freedom casting off the authority of priests and demanding that individuals learn to listen internally, by which method the will is discerned. The individual is thus empowered to decide upon the course of his or her own life—associations, movements, living arrangements, and so on. "Do what thou wilt..." does not mean "do anything you want"; rather, it suggests that having discovered one's destiny or purpose, that becomes the sole guide for action in the world. H.O.O.R. also teaches a method of theurgy that facilitates the discovery of the will and provides guidance for dealing with all aspects of life on planet earth.

The order was headed by Ray Eales (b. 1958), who took the lead in its formation. H.O.O.R. is organized in temples and lodges, and membership is open to men and women. Progress is through grades attained by study, accomplishment, and initiation. The lodges serve as instruments of fellowship, education, and the encouragement of society in the adoption of thelemic principles. The order is closely associated with the Abbey of Thelema, headed by Gregory von Seewald.

The order is administered by a council of generals chosen by the overseer, who holds the position for life. The overseer and the council of generals remain anonymous according to the order's constitution. In 2008 the overseer was identified as "Frater 939."

Membership: As of 1997 there were more than 100 members of H.O.O.R.

Periodicals: *Warriors LVX*.

Sources:

Holy Order of RaHoorKhuit. www.hoor.org.

Preliminary Thoughts on H.O.O.R. Old Greenwich, CT: Holy Order of RaHoorKhuit, 1994.

Monastery of the Seven Rays

Box 1554, Chicago, IL 60690-1554

The Monastery of the Seven Rays is the organizational umbrella given to the various magical activities focused in the person of Michael Bertiaux (b. 1935), a noted Chicago occultist-magician. Bertiaux is the inheritor of the French Martinist tradition, which he received through his magical training in Haiti and by his ordination and consecration as bishop of the Neo-Pythagorean Church.

Louis Claude de Saint-Martin (1743–1803) was a Roman Catholic raised in France. As a soldier, he met Martines de Pasqually, a disciple of Emanuel Swedenborg and Rosicrucianism. De Pasqually founded an occult order, the Order of the Elect Cohens, which Saint-Martin joined in 1768. After de Pasqually's death in 1774, Saint-Martin became the focus of a group of occultists. He began to write books (published posthumously), and a movement, the history of which is still known only in fragments, was born.

By the end of the eighteenth century, a branch of the Martinist Order had been established in Haiti. This group continued to function after Haiti gained its independence. It tended to blend with vodou. In the 1890s there was a revival movement in the Martinist Order, emphasizing a purist strain of Gnostic philosophy. In the years between the world wars the Gnostic Church was established in Leogane, Haiti, and was brought to the United States after World War II. In general, the Gnostic philosophy emphasizes a secret knowledge that humans can attain and denies the divinity of Christ.

The Monastery of the Seven Rays, which became widely known through its advertisements in *Fate Magazine* in the 1970s, is a magical order drawing upon modern Thelemic magick (derived from the writings of Aleister Crowley), vodou, and the nineteenth-century French Gnostic occult tradition. Bertiaux wrote the lessons, which teach a basic magical system and lead the student into the higher levels of magical working.

The Neo-Pythagorean Gnostic Church is the ecclesiastical structure which, along with six other fraternal and psychically oriented structures with which it is interlocked, focus the Martinist occult/mystical tradition in North America. The tradition began in France, was brought to Haiti, and from there came to the United States in the mid-1950s. Bertiaux was consecrated by Bishop Hector Francois Jean-Maine, a Haitian who had received orders from the Spanish Albigensian Church which in turn had orders from the French Gnostics. The famous French occultists Joseph-Antoine Boullan (1824–1893) and Eugene Vintras (1807–1875) are included in the lineage.

The Neo-Pythagorean Gnostic Church is a ritual theurgic body in which the Eucharist is the center of initiation. Through it, the invocation of angels and planetary spirits is made, and spirit communication often takes place during the mass. Purity of ritual is emphasized, and no tallow (i.e., nothing that carries the suffering of animals) is used in the candles. All members of the clergy are clairvoyant and often have visions during mass. Also, during worship a mystical language is intuitively (i.e., clairvoyantly) perceived and mystically spoken.

A Gnostic hierarchical system is headed by the Absolute, similar to the Kabbalist Ein Soph. The Absolute emanates a Trinity, which in turn is the source of Lucifer and Sophia, the basic male/female polarity. Lucifer is the morning star, inferior to Christ but not to be confused with Satan. Sophia is paid homage in the cult of the Virgin, the archetypical divine being. She is often revered as Our Lady of Mt. Carmel. Satanism and black magick are strongly opposed.

The church is subject to a supreme heliophant (in 1984, Dr. Hector Francois Jean Maine, residing in Madrid). The American jurisdiction is under Bishop Pierre-

Antoine Saint-Charles of Boston, who has direct authority over all Haitian American members. Michael Bertiaux in Chicago presides over the Caucasian American members and Bishop Marc Lully of Chicago heads overseas development in South America and the West Indies. In 1979 Bertiaux exchanged consecrations with Bishop Forest Barber of the Catholic Apostolic Church in America.

Associated with the church are the Ancient Order of Oriental Templars, the Arithmosophical Society, Zotheria, and the Esoteric Traditions Research Society. The Ancient Order of Oriental Templars is a lodge with credentials derived from the pre-Crowleyite Ordo Templi Orientis in Germany. It teaches a 16-degree system of magick. The Arithmosophical Society concentrates on Saint-Martin's philosophy of numbers. Numbers form a key to Saint-Martin's system of magical correspondences and tie Saint-Martin to Pythagoras. Both Zotheria and the Esoteric Traditions Research Society are outer courts of the various esoteric structures.

Membership: Not reported.

Periodicals: *Esoteric Ontology Newsletter*.

Sources:

Baca, Docteur Bacalou [Michael Bertiaux]. *Lucky Hoodoo*. Chicago: Absolute Science Institute, 1977.

Bertiaux, Michael. *Cosmic Meditation*. Edmonds, WA: Holmes Publishing Group, 2007.

———. *The Voudon Gnostic Workbook*. Exp. ed. Weirs Beach, ME: Weiser Books, 2007.

Grant, Kenneth. *Cults of the Shadow*. New York: Samuel Weiser, 1976.

McIntosh, Christopher. *Eliphas Levi and the French Occult Revival*. New York: Samuel Weiser, 1974.

Order of Napunsakas in the West (O.N.)

PO Box 1219, Corpus Christi, TX 78403-1219

The Order of Napunsakas in the West (O.N.) was founded in 1996 as a special interest group associated with the Servants of the Star and the Snake. It was inspired by the writings of the late Alain Danielou (1907–1994), the author of *The Gods of India: Hindu Polytheism* (1985), *Shiva and Dionysus*, and *While the Gods Play*. The Hindu word *napunska* designates some 16 categories of nonheterosexual gender variant types mentioned in the Sanskrit dictionary of V. S. Apte. Members of the O.N. seek to reestablish the natural, divine order found in pre-Aryan Shaivism, but the emphasis is on gay, lesbian, bisexual, and transgendered tantra. The outer order is open to all napunskas; affiliates are considered as associate members. An inner order, the Cultus Skanda-Karttikeya (C.S.-K.), is open to gay males only, and only upon formal, in-person *diksha*, or initiation. The focus of the C.S.-K. is on gay tantra, with special emphasis on the *sadhana* (worship, or more properly, adoration) of the Hindu deity Skanda, the patron of gays, in His many forms (Kumara, Marugan, etc.).

The current head of the O.N./C.S.-K. is Sahajananda Skanda-Das.

Membership: Not reported.

Periodicals: *Zibaq*. Available from Abrasax Publications, Box 1219, Corpus Christi, TX 78403-1219.

Sources:

Danielou, Alain. *The Gods of India: Hindu Polytheism*. Rochester, VT: Inner Traditions, 1985.

Order of the Lily and the Eagle

Center for Inner Initiative, attn: WS, PO Box 937, Littleton, CO 80160-0937

The Order of the Lily and the Eagle is a Western initiatic school working in the ancient lines of Judeo-Christian and Egyptian thought to the Hellenic mystery schools of Orpheus, Pythagoras, and Socrates. It also combines its teaching of St. Martin, alchemy, the Kaballah, contemporary science, and psychology.

The order's teachings deal with the transformation and liberation of personality. It guides those who seek to know themselves, so that their lives can be used to aid the well-being of others. The order, by means of enlightened advice, helps its members create their own understanding through experience, reasoning, meditation, and introspection.

Sources:

Order of the Eagle and the Lily. www.innerinitiative.org/history.php.

EON: The Path of Initiation: A Collection of Works from the Order of the Lily and the Eagle. Littleton, CO: Center for Inner Initiative, 1995. 240 pp.

Order of the Thelemic Golden Dawn

1636 N Wilcox Ave., Ste. 418, Los Angeles, CA 90028

The Order of the Thelemic Golden Dawn was founded in 1990 as the Thelemic Temple and Order of the Golden Dawn in Los Angeles by David Cherubim, its frater superior chief. It is a magical/religious/scientific order devoted to the teachings of Aleister Crowley and exists to assist in the initiation of persons into the magical life of Thelema. Thelema (or will) was the basic concept of Crowley's magical system. The order offers seven grades of initiation from neophyte to ipsissimus, each level representing one of the seven chakras of the human body in the Indian tantric system, one of the seven planets of traditional astrology, and one of the seven metals of alchemy.

The order has attempted to interpret Crowley's *Book of the Law* (1904), the basis of his proclamation of the new Aeon of Horus in which his followers now consider we are living. Regarding ritual, the order believes that the injunction "rituals shall be half-known and half-concealed" means that initiation rituals should be developed in response to the nature of each initiate. Thus each initiation of a member becomes a unique event.

The members of the order together constitute a religious body of free warriors who are seeking to extend the dominion of the Law of Thelema; that is, they are attempting to establish on earth the principles of *The Book of the Law*. The methods for accomplishing this task are occult research, practical mysticism, ceremonial magick, and tantric alchemy. The order also offers members a system of self-initiation based upon the Qabalah (Kabbalah) and the Tarot.

The order has been created in an environment in which the great majority of Crowley's writings (including the rituals of the Ordo Temple Orientis, which he headed) have been published and are readily available. It is assumed that members have or will gain a solid background in Crowley's thought.

Membership: In 1997 the group reported that there were 200 members in the United States, 20 in Canada, and 100 in Brazil. There were temples for initiation in the United States and Brazil.

Sources:

Cherubim, David. "Magick and the Way of the Empty Hand." Thelemic Golden Dawn, 1994. www.totse.com/en/religion/the_occult/163734.html.

Cherubim, David. "The History of the Thelemic Golden Dawn." Thelemic Golden Dawn, 2001. www.totse.com/en/religion/the_occult/163733.html.

Order of Thelema

PO Box 511, Chula Vista, CA 91912

The Order of Thelema is a Thelemic magick group that rejected the attempt by various branches of the Ordo Templi Orientis (OTO) to establish their authority by reference to a line of succession from Aleister Crowley (1875–1947). It was structured as a Crowleyan study group. There is no system of rituals except those ideas that members interpret from Crowley's revelatory bible, *Liber Al vel Legis* (*The Book of the Law*), each according to his own will. The group believes that Crowley still operates close to this plane of existence as a present and active force and that it is possible for him to reach the order by psychic means. The written words of Crowley are the only source of Thelemic Law. Strong support is given the perspective of *The*

Book of the Law. Headquarters of the Order of Thelema are in Chula Vista, California. The word *Thelema* means "will."

Sources:

Order of Thelema. www.orderofthelema.com.

Ordo Adeptorum Invisiblum

Current address not obtained for this edition.

The Ordo Adeptorum Invisiblum (OAI) is a British-based thelemicist order aligned to the Maatian magical "current." It grew out of the proclamation of the magical Aeon of Ma (or Maat) proclaimed in 1948 by Frater Achad (Charles Stansfeld Jones). Maat is the ancient Egyptian goddess of Truth and Justice. The order looks toward a planetary manifestation of the presence of Maat, whose coming has been heralded by three twentieth-century trends: the great liberation movements leading to the recognition of human rights; the attempts to balance male-dominated Western magic; and the nonelitist androgynous approach to magic practiced by Maatian groups. In recognition of their acceptance of feminist liberation concerns and the nonsexist nature of their magical workings, members of the OAI have dropped the use of common designations of male and female members as *frater* and *soror* in favor of the single designation *persona*.

The OAI began in England in 1979 in the informal workings of three Thelemic magicians (two women and one man). In 1980 they made a formal alignment to the Aeon of Maat and thus the OAI came into existence. At the end of the year, the three original members separated. One went to Fez, Morocco, and the following year, one came to Chicago, where the first members of the OAI were received.

The order has developed as a very loose confederation of otherwise independent magicians pursuing their own magical experiments in alignment to the Maatian Aeon. Periodically, members will gather for group rituals. New initiates are received after their successful performance of *Liber Samekh He*, a revised version of *Liber Samekh*, a Thelemic ritual designed to promote conversation with one's Holy Guardian Angel (higher self). The order is nonhierarchical. Leadership can be exercised by any member and teaching is a matter of sharing the results of individual ritual workings with the larger membership. All members have access to all materials possessed by the order.

Membership: In 1985 members of the order, reported to number less than 100, could be found in England, the Chicago metropolitan area, and California.

Sources:

Liber ANDANA. Chicago: Ordo Adeptorum, 1983.

Persona PVAD MASURUS 1043. *Liber Samekh He*. Chicago: Stellium Press, 1981.

Skia, Persona. *O.A.I. Manifesto: Origin, History, Organization*. Kenilworth, IL: Ordo Adeptorum Invisiblum, 1982.

Ordo Aurum Solis

1203 W Bryn Mawr Ave., Chicago, IL 60660

Ordo Aurum Solis, Gold of the Sun, is a magical and initiatory order founded in England in 1897 by George Stanton and Charles Kingold that claims descent from the Ogdoadic Tradition of the Western Mystery Tradition. Ordo Aurum Solis is a private and independent esoteric society rooted in neo-Platonist theurgy tradition. It is not affiliated to any other esoteric, religious, or political associations.

Like the Hermetic Order of the Golden Dawn, the Ordo Aurum Solis teaches a system of high magick, that is, a disciplined approach to self-transformation. Its system, much of which has been published in the five-volume set *The Magical Philosophy* by Melita Denning and Osborne Phillips, centers upon the myth of the sacred king (i.e., the magician) who chooses of his own free will the path of sacrifice, but subsequently rises again and passes into the light of attainment.

Melita Denning and Osborne Phillips are the pen names of Vivian Barcynski and Leon R. Barcynski, who until recently served as administrator general and grand master, respectively, of the order. Both had encountered the order while living in

England and participated in its reconstitution in 1971. They brought the order to the United States in 1978 when they moved to St. Paul, Minnesota. Under their pen names they authored numerous books on various occult topics. Phillips founded in 1997 the first French-language Masonic publication on the Internet, *La Parole Circule* (*Spread the Word*), and in 2008 he continued to publish it. It comprises a dissemination of materials pertinent to all degrees. The publication is sent to more than 1,500 subscribers worldwide. There are an estimated 3,000 readers worldwide.

The order is directed by a grand master. The Star Council is composed of eight officers. The location where members meet is called a house. Each state or country has one mother house. There are houses located in the United States, Brazil, Canada, Congo, Spain, France, Greece, and the Netherlands.

The official seal of the order is an eight-pointed star that includes an interlacing design. There is an octagon within the interlacing design and an equal armed cross in the center.

In 1957 three members of the Ordo Aurum Solis founded the Order of the Sacred Word for special studies and practices of the Holy Gnosis. This order was governed by the council of three members until 1959. After then, the initiates in charge were Earnest Page (1959–1966) and Leon Barcynski (1966–1971).

Membership in the order is by invitation only, though inquiries are invited. The order has three degrees preceded by pronaso, a probationary period that can last several months. The first degree is neophytos, or neophyte. The formal title is apprentice of the great world. The second degree is servitor, or server, and the formal title is servitor of the secret flame. The third degree is adeptos minor, or adept, and the formal title is priest of the gnosis.

The position of grand master has been held by George Stanton (1897–1914), Morris Greenberg (1914–1938), Charles Roughlett-Boch (1938–1952), Michael B. Foy (1952–1975), Thomas Maughan (1975–1976), Vivian Godfrey (1976–1987), Carl Weschcke (1987–1988), Vivian Godfrey (1988–1997), Leon Barcynski (1997–2003), and Jean-Louis de Biasi (2003–).

Membership: In 2008 it was reported there was affiliated work in 30 countries.

Sources:

Ordo Aurum Solis. www.aurumsolis.net.

Kabbalistic Order of the Rose+Cross. www.okrc.org.

De Biasi, Jean-Louis. *Planetary Harmonizations*. Calgary, Canada: Academia Platonica Publications, 2006.

Denning, Melita, and Osborne Phillips. *The Magical Philosophy*. 5 vols. St. Paul, MN: Llewellyn Publications, 1974–1981.

———. *The Magick of Sex*. St. Paul, MN: Llewellyn Publications, 1982.

———. *The Magick of the Tarot*. St. Paul, MN: Llewellyn Publications, 1983.

Ordo Templi Astarte

PO Box 40094, Pasadena, CA

Alternate Address: The Church of the Hermetic Sciences, PO Box 403, Silverado CA 92676.

The Ordo Templi Astarte (Order of the Temple of Astarte, or OTA), which also operates under the name Church of Hermetic Sciences, is a ritual magick group begun in 1970 to practice Kabbalistic magick in the Western tradition. Based upon Jungian psychology, the OTA defines magick as a "system of ritual hypnotic induction (conjuration) that calls upon archetypal forms from the unconscious (evocation) and allows them to be visualized (manifestation) whereupon they can be used for numerous purposes ranging from the frankly psychotherapeutic to the more abstract system research and development."

The OTA traces its history to Aleister Crowley through Louis Culling, who claimed to have had a charter from Crowley for an autonomous lodge. This charter was given after Culling left C. F. Russell, who was deviating from Crowley's teachings. Culling turned over the charter to the OTA leadership before his death. The group also claims to possess the "secret rituals of the Ordo Templi Orientis in Crowley's original holographs." Though operating with a Thelemic charter, the OTA does not consider itself fully Thelemic. In describing the order, founder Carroll R. Runyon Jr. has noted, "We operate a Collegium ad Spiritum Sanctum of the O.T.O. in our Philosophus Grade as a research and study program. In its own context, it is Thelemic; but we do not initiate or operate ceremonially under a Thelemic aegis. We have great respect for the works of Aleister Crowley, but we consider him a Master of the Art in much the same way that Sufis consider Jesus a Great Prophet—without calling themselves Christians." The OTA is centered in a lodge in Pasadena headed by Runyon, also known as Frater Thabion.

Membership: Not reported.

Periodicals: *The Seventh Ray.*

Sources:

Ordo Templi Astarte. www.templeofastarte.com.

Christensen, Cheryl JoAnne. "Magical Epistemic Communities: The Construction of Specialized Social Realities in Bunyoro, Uganda and Los Angeles, California." Ph.D. diss., Massachusetts Institute of Technology, 1975.

Ellwood, Robert S., Jr. *Mysticism and Religion.* Englewood Cliffs, NJ: Prentice-Hall, 1980.

Ordo Templi Baphe-Metis

PO Box 1219, Corpus Christi, TX 78403-1219

The Ordo Templi Baphe-Metis (OTB) was founded in January 1985. It is a Thelemic fraternal order "chartered" by fiat in Aleister Crowley's (1875–1947) *Khabs am Pekht,* though the OTB is in no way connected to any of the branches of the Ordo Templi Orientis (OTO) either in America or Europe. In common with other Thelemic organizations, members of the OTB must accept as a Holy Book *Liber Al vel Legis* (*The Book of the Law*), given to the prophet Ankh-f-n-Khonsu (Crowley) by Aiwaz, his holy Guardian Angel, in Cairo in 1904. Additionally, Knights of the Order (which may be of either sex) promulgate the Law of Thelema, together with the Thelemic Bill of Rights, Liber 77 (Liber Oz). Grand Master Ekagratanath trance-channeled the order's own Holy Book, *Liber Ba Neb Tet* (*Book of Baphomet*), available, with commentary, to members only. Members of the order practice ritual and ceremonial magick. A study manual, *The Way of the Warrior-Magus,* is given to members.

The order has operated the Invisible College, a home-study course in ritual and ceremonial magick, alchemy, divination, and Hermeticism. The OTB is closely related to the American Gnostic Church, with which it has shared an overlapping leadership and published a periodical, *Abrasax.*

Membership: Not reported.

Periodicals: *Abrasax • The Philosopher's Stone.*

Ordo Templi Orientis

JAF Box 7666, New York, NY 10116

The Ordo Templi Orientis (OTO), which had become disorganized following the death of Karl Germer (Frater Saturnus, 1885–1962), who had succeeded Aleister Crowley (1875–1947) as outer head of the order, was reborn in 1969 when Grady McMurtry (Hymenaeus Alpha, 1918–1985) asserted his authority as head of the OTO. McMurtry had been given two letters in 1946 from Crowley granting him authority to reform the order and act as Crowley's representative in the United States subject to the approval of Germer. Though these letters were originally intended to apply to the situation of the lodge in Pasadena, California, which Crowley had specifically asked McMurtry to investigate, they literally gave McMurtry broad emergency powers. After Crowley's death in 1947 the authorization was used with the Germer's cooperation and was never withdrawn. Germer's death in 1962 left McMurtry as the only person with power to act. McMurtry further held that he was carrying out Crowley's wishes; that Crowley had anticipated

Germer's succession problems; and that he had openly discussed them with McMurtry.

McMurtry had been initiated into the Agape Lodge of the OTO in Pasadena in the early 1940s and, during World War II while stationed in England, was the only American OTO member to be with Crowley. He rejected the claims of Kenneth Grant, the British leader of another OTO group, noting that Grant had been expelled from the order in 1955. (Grant later dropped some of his claims to OTO leadership.) McMurtry also rejected the claims of Hermann Metzger, head of a Swiss-based OTO organization, on the grounds of his "spurious" election by his own Swiss group, with no international representation.

During the 16 years of McMurtry's leadership, the OTO grew into a substantial body with chapters and lodges across the United States and Canada and ten countries overseas. Full membership in the OTO requires physical participation in the ceremonies of initiation and the payment of subscription costs and dues. A correspondence-only associate membership is available.

On July 14, 1984, the supervisor general of the Society OTO expelled McMurtry from the order for violating various duties that were detailed in the Constitution of the OTO, and he was replaced.

Integral to the OTO is the Ecclesia Gnostica Catholica (Gnostic Catholic Church). As part of his magical work, Crowley had been consecrated a bishop in the French Gnostic lineage of Jules Doinel (1842–1903) and he, in turn, passed that lineage to others in the order. Hymenaeus Beta, in addition to holding a consecration in the Antiochean succession of Abp. Joseph Rene Vilatte (1854–1929), was consecrated in the Doinel line. He is designated as patriarch of the Ecclesia Gnostica Catholica. Integral to the work of the OTO lodges is the regular performance of the Gnostic Mass composed by Crowley, and priests, priestesses, and bishops have corresponding rank in the OTO.

Membership: In 2008 the OTO reported 44 lodges and camps in the United States. Additional lodges and camps were to be found in 14 countries around the world.

Periodicals: *The Magical Link • The Oriflamme.*

Remarks: During the 1980s the legitimacy of the OTO as led by McMurtry and his successor was challenged in court by Marcelo Ramos Motta, head of the Society Ordo Templi Orientis in America. In federal court rulings in 1985 and 1988, McMurtry was found to be the outer head of the order of the OTO.

Sources:

U.S. Grand Lodge, Ordo Templi Orientis. www.oto-usa.org.

DuQuette, Lon Milo. *The Magick of Aleister Crowley: A Handbook of Rituals of Thelema.* San Francisco: Weiser Books, 2003. 261 pp.

Heidrick, Bill. *Magick and Qabalah.* Berkeley, CA: Ordo Templi Orientis, 1980.

The Holy Books of Thelema. York Beach, ME: Samuel Weiser, 1988.

Hymenaeus Beta, ed. *The Equinox* 3, no. 10. New York: Thelema Publications, 1986.

O.T.O. System Outline. San Francisco, CA: Stellar Visions, 1981.

Sacred Keltic Church of America

4 Favour Ct., Stafford, VA 22554

The Sacred Keltic Church of America is a Neopagan group that worships the deities of the ancient Celtic lands, popularly referred to as the Norse gods. The church was founded as the American Church of Teutonic Life in 1992 in Carthage, New York. It is headed by Senior Lord High Priest Eugene D. Kyle, who is also the president of the National Council of Elders.

Membership: In 1998 the church reported 135 members and seven clergy in the United States. They also had five clergy members in the military, stationed overseas.

Periodicals: *Sacred Keltic Church of America.*

Servants of the Light (SOL)

c/o Fran Keegan, PO Box 6563, Syracuse, NY 13217-6563

Alternate Address: International Headquarters: PO Box 215, St Helier, Jersey, Channel Islands, UK, JE2 3RD

Servants of the Light (SOL) is a contemporary Western Mystery school founded in 1965 by William E. Butler. Butler had begun his esoteric training in Dion Fortune's Fraternity of Inner Light, which in turn had developed from the Hermetic Order of the Golden Dawn (founded in the 1880s). He received further training from the psychic Robert King, who later served as director of studies for the Servants of the Light until his death in 1978. Dolores Ashcroft-Nowicki succeeded King in 1978 and became head of the school following Butler's death.

The purpose of the SOL is to assist in spreading esoteric knowledge in an ethical manner to all who want to receive it. It has a loose structure that allows for a great degree of independence and free thinking among the students. The SOL teaches through correspondence, and each student is assigned a personal tutor to assist him or her. The First Degree Course consists of 50 lessons of one month each. Each lesson includes written teachings, exercises, and meditations. Students keep a journal that is periodically sent in for assessment.

Lesson material is centered upon the Western esoteric tradition, and the early lessons include discussions of Kabbalah (and the related Tarot) as a basic system leading to numerous other topics. The SOL also claims direct psychic contact with the Inner Planes where the true directors, members of the Inner Hierarchy, of the school are believed to reside.

Membership: In 1998 the SOL reported 2,600 members in 23 countries. In 2008 the SOL Web site reported 6,000 students in 23 countries.

Sources:

Servants of the Light (SOL). www.servantsofthelight.org.

Ashcroft-Nowicki, Dolores. *First Steps in Ritual*. Wellingborough, Northamptonshire, UK: Aquarian Press, 1982. 96 pp.

————. *The Shining Paths: An Experimental Journey through the Tree of Life*. Wellingborough, Northamptonshire, UK: Aquarian Press, 1983. 240 pp.

Butler, William E. *Apprenticed to Magic and Magic of the Qabalah*. Wellingborough, Northamptonshire, UK: Aquarian Press, 1990.

————. *Magic: Its Ritual, Power and Purpose*. London: Aquarian Press, 1952. 76 pp.

————. *The Magician: His Training and Work*. London: Aquarian Press, 1959. 176 pp.

Servants of the Star and the Snake

Current address not obtained for this edition.

The Servants of the Star and the Snake (SSS) is a federation of ceremonial magicians, shamans, witches, neopagans, sorcerers, and tantrikas founded in the spring of 1994 for the purpose of networking and mutual respect. A Tantric-Thelemic organization, it has no degree system, no grades, no official reading list, no attainments, no hierarchy, no pope, no head, no soteriology, no holy books, no gurus, and no formal initiation. All of these accoutrements are regarded by the SSS as "Old Aeon" and more appropriate for Masonic orders or religious sects. The SSS evolved from the remnants of the Ordo Templi Baphe-metis (OTB). It is based upon the teachings of the cofounder of AMOOKOS (the Arcane Magical Order of the Knights of Shambhala), Shri Gurudev Mahendranath ("Dadaji," 1911–1991) and Alain Danielou (1907–1994) but retains the Thelemic character of the OTB. The federation is overseen by an administrater-general, a revolving office currently held by Bhaganatha AOM. Associated with the SSS is the Order of Napunsakas in the West.

Membership: Not reported.

Periodicals: *Lila* (occasional).

Sources:

Servants of the Star and the Snake. www.wild.net.au/sss/.

The Umbrazonule. groups.yahoo.com/group/umbrazonule/.

Freeman, Harvey. *Everything That Is . . . . Is Within: An Introduction to Dadaji*. Center Family Press, 1974.

Society Ordo Templi Orientis International

c/o David Bersson, PO Box 59326, Pittsburgh, PA 15210

Among those who made claim to the lineage of the Ordo Templi Orientis (OTO) following the death of Karl Germer (1885–1962), who had succeeded Aleister Crowley (1875–1947) as outer head of the order, was Marcelo Ramos Motta (1931–1987), a Brazilian member of the OTO. He claimed that Germer, on his deathbed, had appointed him outer head of the order. In the years following Germer's death he completed his initiatic work and assumed the magical status needed to become the leader. In 1975, through the Society of the Ordo Templi Orientis (SOTO), as his branch was known, he issued the first of four massive volumes of the *Equinox*, each issue of which contained his own writings along with those by Crowley and others. These were seen as a revival of the semiannual publication issued originally by Crowley (1909–1913). Other publications followed.

The SOTO immediately ran into a conflict with the Ordo Templi Orientis over the copyright to the writings of Aleister Crowley that had been left to the OTO in Crowley's will. The SOTO claimed to be that organization, and writers and organizations not associated with the SOTO who wrote about or published Crowley's writings were denounced in various issues of the *Equinox*. The tension between the OTO, SOTO, and Samuel Weiser (the publisher of the first issue of the new *Equinox*) led to several lawsuits. In 1985 a libel suit filed against Motta and the SOTO by Grady McMurtry (caliph of the OTO) and others, concerning remarks made in the *Equinox*, resulted in the awarding of all copyrights and trademarks to the OTO and turned back all claims by Motta to be the outer head of the order of the Ordo Templi Orientis. It is the belief of its members that the SOTO is the true OTO and to reject Motta is to reject Crowley.

Motta died two years later in 1987, and at the time of his death left responsibility for the SOTO in the hands of three people—Daniel Ben Stone, Claudia Canuto de Menezes, and William Barden. They, however, failed to follow through on selecting new leadership. At the higher levels the order ceased to operate. Following the withdrawal of de Menezes and Stone, and the death of Barden, Frater Sphinx (aka David Bersson) contacted another senior member, Frater KSK, and initiated correspondence concerning the future of the order. After reaching a consensus, Frater Sphinx assumed control of what was left of the order and began the process of reorganization and rebuilding. In 2007 Bersson published a revised Constitution and OTO Manifesto. According to the constitution, the purposes of the order are to promulgate *The Book of the Law* and promote the philosophy and the works of Edward Alexander Crowley (aka Aleister Crowley).

The order's curriculum includes the writings of Aleister Crowley and Marcelo Motta.

Membership: Not reported. The size and extent of the order, as is the identity of its national and international leadership, is a matter of internal secrecy

Periodicals: *Equinox*.

Sources:

Society Ordo Templi Orientis. www.castletower.org/society.html.

Motta, Marcelo. *Letter to a Brazilian Mason*. Nashville, TN: Troll Publishing Company, 1980.

————. *Manifesto*. Nashville, TN: Society Ordo Templi Orientis in America, 1978.

————. *The Political Aims of the O. T. O.* Nashville, TN: Ordo Templi Orientis in America, 1980.

————. *Thelemic Political Morality*. Nashville, TN: Society Ordo Templi Orientis in America, 1978.

Temple of the Holy Grail

PO Box 3816, Santa Cruz, CA 95063-3816

The Temple of the Holy Grail (THG) is an initiatory mystery school for individuals wishing to undertake private advanced esoteric training in order to anonymously serve human and planetary evolution. Training is offered by invitation to people already ordained or otherwise advanced in recognized groups, or to individuals who, having prepared themselves apart from organizations, manifest a devotion to the spiritual unfoldment of humanity and of the planet.

The THG teaches that the Grail mysteries existed in western Europe long before the advent of Christianity as the "Graded Path of Initiation," comparable to the Lam Rim of Tibetan Buddhism. The mysteries evolved into an esoteric Christian school through the work of the legendary Graalmeister Treverizent in the ninth century and were later associated with chivalric orders, and the alchemical and Gnostic schools.

According to THG history, in the late 1800s a secret English Templar order in possession of an ancient Jewish terra-cotta cup believed to be the true Eucharistic vessel of the Last Supper, now encased in gold, with two ancient silver auxiliary "grails," prepared to do the sacred Grail Rites that had been done once each century by the order and its predecessors in the year 88 (the mystical Christian Kabbalistic number). The purpose of the rite was to reempower a channel for Divine Blessing upon the planet for the coming century and protect humanity from being overwhelmed by dark forces. The abbot of the order was an elderly man with great concern that the Grail chalices would be stolen by people who wished to use them for magical purposes.

The chalices were secretly transported to London, where the centennial rite (a theurgical Eucharist) was performed, but in spite of all precautions, all three chalices were stolen and used for black magical purposes. After the chalices were retrieved from the thieves, the gold of the True Chalice was melted down, and the pottery cup smashed into the earth. One of the auxiliary chalices turned up at an antiquities auction in Antioch and was purchased by the Metropolitan Museum in New York; it is now exhibited as the "Chalice of Antioch" with legends of it having been the Holy Grail. The third chalice was never found.

In the 1980s, after two decades of spiritual training and progress, the unnamed person destined to become the Grailmaster of the THG, who knew nothing of these events, responded to interior guidance to construct a new chalice through white magical and theurgical preparations that required several years to complete. In August 1988 he was inspired to travel, without any knowledge of the final destination, over 1,000 miles to a sacred site in Canada, where he used the chalice for a theurgical Eucharist to bless the planet and humanity. While returning home, he heard an interior voice naming him the "Grailmaster," a term unfamiliar to him. He then received teachings telepathically in lucid dreams from a Tibetan lama, which eventually became the First Empowerment of the First Order of THG. Shortly after this he discovered a written account of the Grail Blessing that had been done in 1888. He then began to understand what had been occurring: he had been instrumental in preparing a new vessel for the 1988 centennial Grail Blessing and the blessing had then occurred as scheduled.

Soon after these events, he was contacted by Bp. George Boyer (d. 2008) of the Sanctuary of the Gnosis in London, who transmitted to the Grailmaster all of the charters, titles, and authorities necessary to preserve the esoteric European lineages deriving from the Grail traditions under the auspices of the Temple of the Holy Grail. Bishop Boyer also underwent the new initiations and contributed to the teachings that the Grailmaster began to bring forth in the 1990s.

THG writings state that part of the temple's authority resides in the apostolic authority of its leadership. Drawing on the community of independent bishops, all 18 historical apostolic and 22 European esoteric lineages flow by live transmission into temple orders. Additionally, the Grailmaster and temple are Keepers of the True

Grail, which is the Divine Royal Blood (San Greal in Christian esoteric tradition, often confused with the Grail chalice itself). The THG believes that the Grail is the normally invisible and intangible divine sacrificial energy that nurtures evolutionary unfoldment in the physical universe and among beings developing in this level of existence. The power sanctifies matter. It is the philosopher's stone that transforms the lower into the higher, expands contracted heart-consciousness, and mediates inspiration, guidance, selfless service, and divine love.

In the Liturgy of the Chalice, the essences of the Holy Grail are poured out as a potent blessing and nurture for the spiritual evolution of all beings in all worlds. Members of the order proceed through the mysteries it perpetuates in an ordered sequence.

Membership: Not reported.

Sources:

Temple of the Holy Grail. www.hometemple.org/THG.htm.

Temple of the Vampire

Box 3582-E, Lacey, WA 98509

Temple of the Vampire emerged in the late 1980s, paralleling elements of the Western Esoteric magical tradition and utilizing a vampiric metaphor. It practices what it terms the religion of Vampirism. Like many magical groups, its members tend self-consciously toward an elitism, and see themselves as above the mass of humanity by seeking authentic power, wealth, and worldly enjoyment as well as physical immortality. Members are described as Vampires. They believe that Vampires, people like themselves, created the world's religions to keep humankind docile and civilized.

Demythologized, the Vampiric perspective is a rational religion, but one that acknowledges the hidden natural laws that are referenced in order to work magic. Magic is real and the Vampire honors the results it produces. The religion is also focused on this life, and the active pursuit of physical immortality, both through the current scientific advances in medicine and bioengineering, as well as by pursuing the traditional teachings of the Vampire religion. The temple motto is "Test Everything. Believe Nothing"; the religion is based not on faith but on validated personal experience.

The Vampire pictures two realities. The Daylight self is a true skeptic who renounces superstition while maintaining an open mind to validated evidence. The Nightside self practices magic using techniques revealed to advanced members. The practice of magic can lead to appropriation of the powers traditionally associated with the vampire (hypnotic control, shapeshifting, and even physical immortality). It also leads to contact with the Undead Gods (the advanced members of the religion) and allows for the attainment of the transhuman condition.

The essential teachings of the temple are summarized in *The Vampire Bible*. Membership begins with the purchase of authorized copies of *The Vampire Bible* and acceptance of its basic perspective. Purchase of *The Vampire Bible* and a written agreement to not engage in criminal activity allows one to be registered as a lifetime member. However, to become a subscribing active member is to commit to achieving measurable success in wealth acquisition and survival techniques, as well as to progress through the various levels of experience of the Vampiric existence.

Adult members may join cabals, local groups of temple members. Cabals are now located internationally throughout the world. Past conclaves have been held in Washington, D.C., London, and Australia.

Membership: In 2008 the Temple reported cabals in all 50 states and approximately 40 countries, including most of the countries of Europe. In addition there were cabals in Australia, New Zealand, Brazil, South Africa, Malaysia, Japan, China, and Canada.

Periodicals: *Lifeforce: The International Vampire Connection to CABAL.*

Sources:

Temple of the Vampire. www.vampiretemple.com/.

Temple ov Psychick Youth (TOPY)

PO Box 163138, Sacramento, CA 95816

The Temple ov Psychick Youth (TOPY) is a loosely organized magical group that originated in 1981 out of the philosophical musings of musician Genesis P. Orridge. The beginning was marked by Orridge leaving a band, Throbbing Gristle, to start the temple as well as a new musical group, Psychic TV. He wished to explore the nature of human limitations, conditioning, and potential and saw performance art as a tool for his investigation. He soon concluded that he was doing magic. Early on, he reached the conclusion that humans possess an endless potential. He came to resent any constraints on this potential, a belief that echoed what Aleister Crowley maintained in *Book of the Law:* "The word of sin is restriction."

As TOPY developed, it ascribed the chief problem of society to the extreme narrowing of human choice down to a few freedoms and the sleep state in which most people exist, unaware of their vast potential. In this sleep state, society reaches a crisis as more and more increasingly zombie-like individuals are required to produce less. Religion and politics are the primary forces putting people to sleep. Temple membership consists of people who are awake to their possibilities and are constantly fighting constraints even as they realize their potentials.

The first realization in the wakening process is the individual's acceptance of mortality and a coming to terms with physical transience. The acceptance of mortality liberates. Also, temple members expect to come into a relationship with their True Will (in the Thelemic sense of "Do what thou wilt") and act in accordance with it. As Crowley expressed it, "Do what thou wilt shall be the whole of the Law." From such an approach to life, an intuitive way of acting, acting according to what one believes rather than from any public moral code, emerges.

Essential to developing such an approach is attention to one's sexuality. Rather than conforming to accepted public sexual norms, one should express sexuality according to one's own belief. Since sex is the basic and universal motivator of human action, it is the most appropriate tool for initially claiming self-control.

A logical extension of its belief about the power of sex, the Temple asserts that ritual sex magick is the best means of liberating the energy needed to progress. As one grows and transforms within the continuously changing environment, magical activity allows for constant adaptation. As one discovers and moves toward realizing one's True Will, ritual magick allows its actualization. Ritual magick pushes the individual to test his or her own limitations and often moves him or her outside accepted behavioral patterns. Ritual magick includes the mastering of altered states of consciousness that in and of themselves produce a new view of reality.

TOPY is unusual in the magical community in that it is not organized in a hierarchical fashion. Members are regarded as equals whose varying skills and interests complement each other. They are united in a visionary psychick alliance. TOPY also rejects the idea of secret rituals (a belief that grew out of, and was made possible by, the publication during the last generation of all of the secret Crowleyan magical rituals). While the rituals used and created by individual TOPY members vary considerably, the working of sigil magick, a practice especially associated with the late Austin Spare, is by far the most common practice. Sigils are symbolic representations of a magical goal that are created by writing out a sentence articulating one's goal and then reducing that sentence to a simple symbol. The symbol/sigil is then energized by an act of magick during which the sigil is anointed with a set of body fluids (spittle, blood, and sexual secretions) and the attachment of body hair. A basic belief of the Temple is that the visualization of a goal and the magick applied to that goal causes its realization.

Membership: Not reported. There are several centers of activity in the United States.

Sources:

The Temple ov Psychick Youth. www.ain23.com/topy.net/.

Burton, Tina. "'Intuitive Magick?': A Study of the Temple ov Psychic Youth, 1981–1989." Unpublished paper in the American Religions Collection, Davidson Library, University of California, Santa Barbara, 1989.

An Introduction to the Temple ov Psychick Youth. Brighton, UK: Temple Press Limited, 1989.

Thelemic Gnostic Church of Alexandria

c/o Sanctuary of the Golden Flower, PO Box 8052, Portland, OR 97280

The Thelemic Gnostic Church of Alexandria is the religious arm of the Order of Thelemic Knights (O.T.K.), a fraternal order in the Thelemic tradition of Aleister Crowley (1875–1947). The O.T.K. was founded in 1999 by Gerald del Campo, who serves as both the primate of the Thelemic Gnostic Church and head of the Order of Thelemic Knights.

The Church advocates the Thelemic magick espoused and taught by Aleister Crowley and separates itself from the popular Christian Gnosticisms that emerged in the late twentieth century. It posits in their stead the Thelemic interpretation of the individual's spiritual nature. The church teaches that spiritual insights are to be found in all the world's scriptures when properly interpreted, but that institutional religion tends to have a distorting effect on understanding.

> By Gnosticism, we do not mean the Christian revival that has become so popular today, but a true Gnostic interpretation of one's spiritual nature as informed by the tenets of Thelema. We posit that all sacred texts yield profound insights, and that much of the messages in these texts are lost when distorted by institutionalized religions. Our interpretation of religion is quite simple:
>
> The church does not concentrate on building a relation to God (an unknowable reality) or the afterlife, rather it emphasizes assisting members to live to the fullest in the present as they follow their True Will or destiny, which they feel will lead to positive social change.

The Church is led by its patriarch, under whom there are bishops, priests, and deacons. As a New Aeon church, the Thelemic Gnostic Church of Alexandria freely admits women to all levels of the priesthood. The church opposes any legislation that would ban gay marriage. It holds that for adults, how sexuality is lived out is a matter of personal choice, including the choice of celibacy.

The Thelemic Gospel Church of Alexandria is a member of the North American College of Gnostic Bishops. Gerald del Campo serves as the College's secretary.

Membership: Not reported.

Sources:

Thelemic Gnostic Church of Alexandria. www.thelemicknights.org/.

Thelemic Order and Temple of the Golden Dawn

c/o New Falcon Publications, 1755-A Purina Way, Sparks, NV 89431

The Thelemic Order and Temple of the Golden Dawn was established in 1989 by Christopher S. Hyatt and David Cherubim. In the early 1980s Hyatt, a student of the famous magician Israel Regardie (1907–1985) and founder of Falcon Press, conceived the idea of a new magical order inspired by the Hermetic Order of the Golden Dawn. The Golden Dawn, the original ceremonial magic organization founded in 1880 in England, had become the fountainhead of modern magical teachings. Regardie made many of the teachings of the order available to the general public in 1937–40 when he published *The Golden Dawn*, a multivolume reprint of the basic documents and rituals. Regardie also wrote a number of books that have become standard reading for anyone doing ceremonial magick. Falcon Press was also responsible for reprinting many of Regardie's books in the 1970s and early 1980s. David Cherubim, a ceremonial magician, met Hyatt shortly after Regardie's death in 1985. The first initiations for the order were made in March

1990. Since that time, initiation ceremonies have been held each equinox and solstice.

While inspired by the older Golden Dawn, the new order differs in several important aspects. The older Golden Dawn, for example, had a distinctly Christian cast. The new order is Thelemic. It accepts the revelation of the "new aeon" that began in 1904 with the giving of *The Book of the Law* to Aleister Crowley by the entity Aiwass. The new aeon is named for Horus, the son of Osiris and Isis, and is designated the Crowned and Conquering Church.

The Law of Thelema (or Will) as enunciated in *The Book of the Law* asserts the right of every person to be the god that they are rather than follow false gods and their outmoded commandments. There are no gods but man. Each individual has a duty to discover his or her true purpose in life, and to create and assert that purpose. The order initiates members into the truth of their godhood and supplies them with means (ceremonial magick, tantra, astrology, yoga, tarot, and the Qabalah) of realizing their true will. The goal of the order is to create a new race of free men and women who will in turn build a new civilization based upon the Law of Thelema.

Membership is limited to people over 18 years of age. The order has a correspondence course for members unable to attend lectures in either Phoenix or Los Angeles. Falcon Press publishes the writings of Hyatt, Regardie, and others in basic agreement with the Thelemic teachings. Associated with the order is the Israel Regardie Foundation in Los Angeles, originally established by Regardie's student Laura Jennings.

Membership: In 1993 the order reported approximately 200 members.

Periodicals: Newsletter.

Sources:

Crowley, Aleister, Lon Milo DuQuette, and Christopher S. Hyatt. *Enochian World of Aleister Crowley: Enochian Sex Magick*. Phoenix, AZ: Falcon Press, 1991. 162 pp.

DuQuette, Lon Milo, and Christopher S. Hyatt. *Aleister Crowley's Illustrated Goetia: Sexual Evocation*. Phoenix, AZ: Falcon Press, 1992. 222 pp.

Hyatt, Christopher, ed. *An Interview with Israel Regardie: His Final Thoughts and Views*. Phoenix, AZ: Falcon Press, 1985. 144 pp.

New Golden Dawn: Flying Roll. Parts 1–15. Phoenix, AZ: Thelemic Order and Temple of the Golden Dawn, 1990–1991.

Typhonian Ordo Templi Orientis

c/o Starfire Publishing, BCM Starfire, London, England WC1N 3XX

Kenneth Grant (b. 1924) emerged in the 1970s as the self-proclaimed leader of the British branch of the Ordo Templi Orientis (OTO). He had coedited *The Confessions of Aleister Crowley* (1969), late head of the order, and had even earlier (in the 1950s) under the direction and charter of Crowley's successor, Karl Germer, established the New Isis Lodge in London. However, Germer's charter had given Grant the charter to work only the first three degrees. Grant began to work all eleven, writing his own materials where they were unavailable. Germer expelled him from the OTO. However, when Germer died, and with the OTO almost extinct, there were few who could challenge Grant's leadership. In 1973 he published *Aleister Crowley and the Hidden God*, the first of six substantive books that began to explore the Qliphoth, the so-called backside of the Kabbalah, the mystical Tree of Life. His concentration on the magick of this shadowy realm of the consciousness gave his brand of magick a unique quality but also led other magicians, even Thelemites, to accuse him of tampering with black magick.

Except for the concentration on the Qliphoth in the experimental areas of magick, Grant's order follows much traditional OTO tradition and practice, the secret material of the order having become public during the 1970s through the access given to the Crowley papers deposited at the Warburg Institute in London. Like the other Thelemic groups, the Typhonian Ordo Templi Orientis has as its aim the establishment of the Law of Thelema. It does not undertake the training of novices and

accepts for membership only those who have submitted a record of nine months' magical practice. They must also publish or disseminate *Liber LXXVII*, a brief statement by Crowley of some major Thelemic principles.

Organizationally, this branch of the OTO has dropped the quasi-Masonic structures typical of most magical groups, and its ten degrees are no longer conferred in secret, elaborate rituals. There is no set course to study. Advancement beyond the third degree is subject to the invitation of the governing body. Each applicant is aided to discover the great work that is her or his own true will.

The Typhonian Ordo Templi Orientis came to the United States through individuals who contacted Grant after reading his several books. It grew and spread in the mid-1970s. For several years a periodical, *Mezla*, appeared. However, in the early 1980s, Soror Tanith (J. R. Ayers), head of the order in North America, resigned, and no successor was named.

Membership: Not reported. In 2008 there were no known lodges in the United States, and fewer than 100 members of the OTO branch headed by Kenneth Grant were thought to live here.

Sources:

Grant, Kenneth. *Aleister Crowley and the Hidden God*. New York: Samuel Weiser, 1974.

———. *Nightside of Eden*. London: Frederick Muller, 1977.

———. *Outside the Circles of Time*. London: Frederick Muller, 1980.

# Wiccan Religion and Contemporary Paganism

Alexandrian Wicca

Current address not obtained for this edition.

Most closely related to the older Gardnerian Wicca are the Alexandrians, followers of Alexander Sanders (1926–1988), termed by his biographer "The King of the Witches." According to Sanders, in 1933, as a seven-year-old, he surprised his grandmother, who was nude and standing in a circle in the kitchen. She ordered Sanders into the circle and had him strip and bend over with his head between his thighs. She took a knife, nicked his scrotum and declared, "You are one of us now." Sanders realized that he was a witch. He was later initiated by her as third-degree witch. In actual fact, all indications are that Sanders was an early member of one of the Gardnerian Wicca covens, and that he took the Gardnerian rituals, modified them slightly, and began his own work independently. In any case, in 1967, after the failure of several marriages, Sanders settled in London with his third wife, Maxine Sanders (b. 1951).

In 1969 a sensationalized article on Sanders in a Sunday London newspaper led to a meteoric rise. Other papers and media turned him into a celebrity, and his biography was released during the year. He also made a film, *Legend of the Witches*, which further boosted his popularity; he was a frequent guest on television talk shows. His text of the Witchcraft rituals were among the first to be published and become publicly available.

The Alexandrians ritually resemble the Gardnerians, upon whom they base their practices. Like the Gardnerians, their rituals are skyclad (i.e., in the nude), and the coven in London became one of the most photographed in all the craft. Alexandrians have become noted for the culmination of the third-degree initiation in the Great Rite, that is, sexual intercourse, also used at handfasting (marriage) ceremonies. Ideally the rite is held for two people about to leave and form a new coven. The rite may be symbolic or actual.

The situation of Alexandrian witchcraft as a distinct tradition has been greatly altered by attacks within the Witchcraft community questioning Sanders's credentials and by the defection of a leading member, Stewart Farrar (1916–2000), who, with his wife Janet Farrar (b. 1950), began an independent coven. He emerged as an important author and ritual innovator. Much of the attention that once came to

Sanders now flows to the neo-Alexandrian system of Farrar. However, rather than creating a new lineage of covens, Farrar's work has tended to be absorbed into the larger Pagan-Witchcraft community as another source for eclectic covens to draw upon.

Membership: In North America a few Alexandrian covens still exist, but their number has steadily decreased.

Sources:

The Alex Sanders Lectures. New York: Magickal Childe, 1980.

Farrar, Janet, and Stewart Farrar. *Eight Sabbaths for Witches*. London: Robert Hale, 1981.

————. *The Witches' Way*. London: Robert Hale, 1984.

Farrar, Stewart. *What Witches Do*. New York: Coward, McCann & Geoghegan, 1971.

Johns, June. *King of the Witches*. New York: Coward-McCann, 1970.

Algard Wicca

Current address not obtained for this edition.

Algard (from "Alexandrian" and "Gardnerian") Wicca was formed in 1972 by Mary Nesnick, an Alexandrian Wicca high priestess, in New York City. Nesnick was initiated into the craft in 1964 by a college professor. She was a freshman at the time. The intent of Algard was to lead to a more independent sect of Wicca that would allow more latitude in ritual and action. As the name implies, both Alexandrian and Gardnerian rituals were sources for Algard practices (Alexandrian Wicca and Gardnerian Wicca are discussed in separate entries). Combining the two was relatively easy, since they were similar and at many points even identical. Algard covens worship both skyclad and robed, at the coven's discretion. All initiation ceremonies are skyclad.

The Algard covens are governed by the grand high priestess (Nesnick) and a grand high priest, who oversee the covens and settle intercoven problems and who speak for the craft. Each coven is headed by a high priestess and high priest. Twenty elders assist the ten neophyte priestesses and priests in learning craft ways. A one-year waiting period is required before initiation. Homosexuality is grounds for rejection. Members must be 18 years of age. Screening before initiation was a point at issue with Alexander Sanders, who felt that the first degree was the place for strict screening. Worship is centered on the eight festivals and 13 esbats (full-moon observances). Only initiates attend.

The Algard Wiccans were one of the most highly organized bodies of covens. An *Algard Newsletter*, issued only to members, tied the leaders together. However, in the flux of the Wiccan community during the late 1970s, the tradition seems to have been largely dissipated.

Membership: Not reported. In 1973 there were a reported 48 covens with affiliated groups in England, Canada, and Greece. There was no verification of those claims, and there is good reason to doubt them. By the early 1980s, the tradition had been reduced to one or two covens in the New York area.

Ammonite Foundation

Current address not obtained for this edition.

The Ammonite Foundation is the modern expression of ancient Egyptian religion. Though recently becoming visible in western Europe and North America, it traces its origin to the reign of Pharaoh Tutankhamun and the city of Thebes. The current head of the foundation is Her Grace Sekhmet Montu. According to the foundation, the Ammonites were the original people of Egypt, and their religion, now commonly treated as simply "mythology," was the Ammonite Faith. It is, according to the foundation, the oldest still-practiced religion in the world, religion being considered the whole range of codes of conduct (morality, diet, dress) and the psychological and philosophical aspects of living in the world. Its approach has both a monotheistic and polytheistic theological perspective in that it affirms belief in one God as the root of faith, which finds expression in a multitudinous or multifaceted

God face—in other words, a polytheistic expression of belief. It is comparable to modern systems in which the work of the one God is carried out through angels and/or saints. The Ammonite Faith has many obvious parallels to Hinduism and Native American faiths but also to Christianity because, it is believed, Jesus Christ borrowed many of his teachings from Egypt.

Individual believers are urged to work out a personal code of behavior based upon their acquisition of facts and the exercise of their free will. There are no commandments. The foundation also rejects the practice of tithing (the payment of a designated amount of one's income to the religion's centers) but survives from the voluntary offerings of members.

A complete presentation of beliefs and practices is offered to prospective members through a correspondence course available from the foundation's headquarters. It is believed that after successfully restoring the deity Ammon (also spelled *Amon* or *Amun*) to his temples, Pharaoh Tutankhamun decreed that the ancient religion of Egypt be preserved intact so the worship of Ammon could continue throughout the ages. Thus it was that Horemheb (the last pharaoh of the 18th dynasty) created the Ammonite Way to preserve the knowledge for future generations. The Ammonite Foundation claims to possess the book commonly referred to as the *Book of Tehuti* or *Book of Thoth* in its complete form. The first half of that book, found on tomb walls and published as *The Book of the Dead*, is readily available to anyone. It deals with death and resurrection. The second half, that part not found in the tombs, deals with creation and life. It was kept secret to preserve the faith. The correspondence course prepares the believer for what is contained in the second part of the *Book of Tehuti*.

The foundation recommends a variety of books on Egyptian religion to those who wish to identify with the Ammonite Faith. The list includes the writings of E. A. Wallis Budge, Joan Grant's *Winged Pharaoh*, Isha Schwaller de Lubicz's *Her-Bak*, and Elizabeth Haich's *Initiation*.

Membership: In 1995 the foundation reported 50 lay members and four clergy members in the United States but 270,000 lay members and 9,000 clergy worldwide. Members are found in Egypt, Iran, Nigeria, India, Germany, and Great Britain.

Ancient Keltic Church

PO Box 663, Tujunga, CA 91043-0663

The Ancient Keltic Church is a pagan organization that is attempting to revive the ancient mystery faith of the Celtic peoples and integrate it into modern life. It began as an experimental group, the Roebuck, put together by Ann and David Finnin. The Roebuck included people from various Wiccan traditions. Of particular importance in the formation of the Roebuck were the writings of Robert Cochrane, the pseudonym of Roy Bowers (d. 1966). Cochrane was the head of the Clan of Tubal Cain, a Wiccan group in the Gardnerian tradition that emerged in England in the 1960s and became public through articles that appeared in various Wiccan and occult publications in the mid-1960s.

In 1976, the Finnins began a revival of the Clan of Tubal Cain. In 1982, they contacted William G. Gray and Evan John Jones, former members of Cochrane's original group. After two years of study, the Finnins were adopted into the clan by Jones who empowered them to lead the tradition in the United States and to teach the various methods of personal magical development. In 1989, the Roebuck incorporated and became the Ancient Keltic Church, a modern day Celtic mystery school. Membership is concentrated in a group of devotees who study the mysteries and an initiate priesthood who lead rituals, teach, and offer oracles. This core group guards the rites and teachings against anyone who might dilute or corrupt them.

While many of the teachings are not available to nonmembers, the church practices a form of magic that includes the invocation of unseen forces and the use of natural materials (stones, herbs, animals, etc.) to that end. It places spiritual development ahead of magic in its priorities. One method for spiritual development is contact with what are termed "inner plane guardians," also known as gods, shining ones, or fairies, which derive from the primordial forces of nature described in Irish, Welsh, and Gaelic folklore.

These guardians, along with the Father God and Mother Goddess, constitute the church's pantheon. The goal of spiritual and magical development is service to the people. Service by church members is offered in the form of healing, counseling, and rites of passage.

The church operates primarily in southern California, where the Finnins lead various public festivals and workshops that give an introduction to the church. The church differs from much of the pagan and Wiccan community in that it is self-consciously an elitist group that believes only a minority of pagans have "the intelligence, imagination and will to study the mysteries." This stance is opposed to the majority of the pagan and Wiccan community who espouse a more democratic and egalitarian approach. The church also differs in that it is, by its own ascription, antifeminist, meaning it does not focus upon women's (and, by extension, the earth's) fertility cycles, and homophobic, in that the church's teaching assumes the different ways of generating magical power in men and women and that does not change with sexual preferences. The church is also committed to traditional sexual mores concerning marriage and sexual behavior.

Membership: Not reported.

Sources:

Ancient Keltic Church. www.ancientkelticchurch.org.

Aquarian Tabernacle Church

48631 River Park Drive, PO Box 409, Index, WA 98256

The Aquarian Tabernacle Church was founded by the Rev. Pierre C. Davis and other pagans in 1979. Davis had been a pagan for several years when the decision was made to organize independently and incorporate the group as a church. The incorporation was completed in 1983. Since that time, the church has emerged as an aggressive and assertive proponent of neopaganism. In 1988, the church received tax exempt status from the Internal Revenue Service. Subsequently, in 1991, the church was granted a group exemption letter covering affiliated congregations. Davis and Deborah K. Hudson serve as the archpriest and archpriestess of the ATC tradition.

Paganism is defined by the church as the set of common beliefs held by most pagans. These include the following: the idea that divinity is both imminent and transcendent, and likely to be manifested as both male and female; a multiplicity of gods and goddesses; a respect for nature; a distrust of monolithic religious organizations; life as joyful, loving, and pleasurable; ethics based on the avoidance of harm to others; magic; celebration of the solar and lunar cycles; eclecticism; faith in the ability of people to solve their own problems; commitment to growth, evolution, and balance; human interdependence and the need for community cooperation; and the need for consistency between one's lifestyle and professed belief.

The church operates both a church and retreat house in the Cascade Mountains. The church's purpose is to re-treat the body, mind, and spirit. Near the church is the Moon Stone Circle, a ring of menhirs used for worship and meditation. They also have a shrine dedicated to the goddess Hecate located nearby. The church annually sponsors a Spring Mysteries Festival (Eostre), Hecate's Sickle Festival (Samhain), and the Pagan Church Conference. The church operates a phone service that features a two-to-three minute recorded message on some aspect of neopaganism. It is also affiliated with the Interfaith Council of Washington State. Davis was elected president of the Interfaith Council in March 1995, the first Wiccan priest ever to hold such a position in the United States. He served two terms. He also serves as a member of the Religious Advisory Commission of the Department of Corrections in Washington State.

Membership: In 1995 the church reported 1,894 members in 36 congregations in the United States, Canada, Ireland, South Africa, and Australia.

Educational Facilities:

The Woolston-Steer Theological Seminary, Index, Washington.

Periodicals: *Panegyria* • *Looking Upward* • *Hecate's Horn*.

Sources:

Aquarian Tabernacle Church. www.aquariantabernaclechurch.org/.

Ar nDraiocht Fein: A Druid Fellowship, Inc.

PO Box 17874, Tuscon, AZ 85731-7874

Ar nDraiocht Fein: A Druid Fellowship, Inc. is a neopagan druid community founded in the mid-1980s by Isaac Bonewits. The attempt to reconstruct and revive a form of druidism began at Carleton College during the 1962–1963 school year. It spread from there to become the Reformed Druids of North America (RDNA). Bonewits became a druid in 1969. The following year he attained some degree of fame when he graduated from the University of California at Berkeley with a degree in Magic. He published his survey of the field, *Real Magic*, in 1971. Through the 1970s, Bonewits took a prominent role in druid affairs. He published a newsletter and edited *The Druid Chronicles (Evolved)* (1976), but toward the end of the decade he withdrew from leadership and kept a low profile for several years.

Bonewits reasserted his position as an archdruid in 1984 with the publication of the first issue of *The Druids' Progress* and the announcement of the founding of Ar nDraiocht Fein as a specifically neopagan form of druidism. The order maintains a contemporary faith based upon the most current academic research and assessment of ancient druidism. While reviving the best aspects of the past, this approach advocates self-consciously living in a modern, scientific, artistic, ecological, and holistic context. Like other neopagan groups, it is a nature-worshipping, polytheistic faith.

Bonewits also designed the new druidism so that it was not limited to Celtic traditions but also included pan-Indo-European traditions to allow a broad intercultural participation. Though neopagan druidism is considered to be very close to Wicca, it is distinguished from Wicca by its emphasis upon polytheism rather than the two major Wiccan deities (the Sky God and the Earth Mother), its large group orientation as opposed to small covens, and its public, inclusionary character.

Neopagan druids are organized into groves that meet twice monthly and celebrate the common eight pagan festivals. Bonewits (with the assistance of other members) has written *The ADF Grove Organizers Handbook*, *The ADF Members' Guide*, *The ADF Study Manual*, and the *ADF Liturgical Manual*. Recently Bonewits retired and was named archdruid emeritus. Ian Corrigan was named acting archdruid in the interim before a new archdruid was designated. The current archdruid, Rev. Skip Ellison, was first elected in 2000, then reelected in 2004 and again in 2007.

Membership: As of 2002 there were 43 groves in the United States and one grove in Ontario, Canada.

Periodicals: *Oak Leaves*.

Remarks: It appears that most, if not all, of the various druid groups that were functioning in the 1970s and 1980s have disbanded with their work now surviving through the ADF. However, at last report there was a former group of the Reformed Druids of North America still functioning in California.

Sources:

Ar nDraiocht Fein: A Druid Fellowship, Inc. www.adf.org.

Adler, Margot. *Drawing Down the Moon*. Boston: Beacon Press, 1986.

Bonewits, Isaac. *Real Magic*. New York: Coward, McGann, and Goeghegan, 1971.

———. *What Do Neopagan Druids Believe?* Newark, DE: Mother Grove, 1991. Tract.

———. *What Is Ar nDraiocht Fein?* Newark, DE: Mother Grove, 1991. Tract.

Artemisian Order

c/o Oriethyia, PO Box 7184, Capitol Station, Albany, NY 12224

One expression of the feminist emphasis in Neopaganism in the 1990s, the Artemisian Order, founded by Oriethyia, a feminist poet, is a clan of sisterhood, a society of women who protect one another while serving nature. Oriethyia was a Dianic Wiccan who decided to start a new Wiccan tradition with the goddess Artemis (the Greek equivalent of the Roman Diana) at the center. Artemisian faith affirmed the female image of god in opposition to the primary male image with which she had grown up, and, unlike most Wicca, Oriethyia saw no need to balance male-female energies by providing the goddess with a consort. The balancing of energies comes from asserting the feminine in a masculine-dominated culture.

Artemisians see themselves as Amazons, the moon women, the fierce fighters whom even the bravest of male warriors fear and respect. In describing their roots, they state, "We are proud, capable women who firmly worship the goddess Artemis. We bow to no man for any reason. If you believe we are war-like and man-haters, consider that men of strictly patriarchal cultures persecuted and killed us for our beliefs. We refuse to submit to the loss of our freedom and rights; therefore, many consider us to be dangerous and unnatural." The modern Artemisian Order consists of the Sisterhood, Philos, and Gargareans. The Sisterhood maintains the workings of the order on a day-to-day basis; goddesses are seen as the order's patrons. The women form the council of the Sophias, who lead with their wisdom, the High Priestesses who keep the rituals, the Amazons who defend the way of life, and the Maidens who assist with their strength of mind and spirit. The new Initiates learn from their elder sisters. The Gargareans and Philos, males, assist the Sisterhood by protecting their sacred ways. Present-day Gargareans and Philos are descendants of the men who once existed solely to serve the Amazon women as mates and slaves. Only females may become Initiates. Males may apply, but they will only be allowed to follow the ranks of Gargareans and Philos.

Membership: Not reported.

Sources:

Hopman, Ellen Evert, and Lawrence Bond. *People of the Earth: The New Pagans Speak Out*. Rochester, VT: Destiny Books, 1996.

Avalon Isle/Order of the Royal Oak

PO Box 6006, Athens, GA 30604

Avalon Isle is the covenstead for the American branch of the Order of the Royal Oak, a chivalrous order established in 1660 by King Charles II to honor the men who had supported him during his exile from the throne. According to members, Charles II was widely regarded as sympathetic to the ways of the wise (witches), and he created the Order of the Royal Oak as a defiant gesture against the Puritans who had run the now discarded Commonwealth. The original symbol of this order was a young oak growing from the cut stump of the old. Members claimed that the old Pagan religion was kept alive for over 300 years, hidden from hostile eyes, and a new modern version of the order was revived.

Lady Amythyst, a direct ancestor of Sir George Carteret, a knight of the Order of the Garter and an original member of the Order of the Royal Oak, leads the new order. Amythyst's family came to America in 1663 from the Isle of Jersey. The High Priestess of Avalon Isle, she affirms that she has been a student of the Ancient Ways since her earliest childhood, and began to teach the Craft of the Wise (Wicca) in 1976.

Located in the hills of East Tennessee, on the edge of the Great Smoky Mountains, Avalon Isle provides a center for higher esoteric learning and a gathering point for Wiccans of all traditions. Avalon Isle has hosted the annual Highlands of Tennessee Samhain Gathering (HTSG) since 1991. It also offers workshops and programs throughout the year.

Lady Amythyst also operates one of the largest Wiccan-owned nonprofit charitable organizations in North America, a transitional home for men reentering the mainstream of life, and a shelter for battered women and children. These facilities admit residents regardless of race, creed, religion, or national origin.

Membership: Not reported.

Sources:

Avalon Isle. www.avalonisle.org/.

Brothers of the Earth

c/o Church of the Earth, Box 13158, Dinkytown Sta., Minneapolis, MN 55414

The Brothers of the Earth is a male-oriented Neopagan fellowship composed of groups and individuals interested in exploring, creating, and celebrating a positive male, earth-centered, life-affirming spirituality that is nurturing, nonhomophobic, and nonsexist. It was founded in 1983 by Gary Lingen (aka Earthkin), founding elder and priest of the Church of the Earth, a Neopagan aquarian age church of nature in Minneapolis-St. Paul, Minnesota.

Lingen saw the emergence of men who had developed a new consciousness in response to the emergence of the feminist movement of the previous decade, but who had become isolated in a world of dominant patriarchal male values. Such men sought not only support, but participation in spiritual consciousness-raising for healing and empowerment, and in rituals that celebrated a new vision of manhood. Earlier attempts at male-oriented groups had emerged in the Neopagan community through the Radical Fairies (a gay group) and in all-male activities at pagan festivals. Brothers of the Earth differs in that it seeks to involve gay, heterosexual, and bisexual men of all ages and cultures.

As pagan men, the Brothers of the Earth affirm their link to the Earth, sun, moon, and all the elemental forces. The feminine principle in nature is worshipped as the Goddess, and the male principle as the Horned God (One). The Horned God is worshipped as an aspect of Son, Lover, and Co-Creator and equal to the Goddess (who tends to take precedence in most Neopagan and witchcraft groups). The Horned God is neither effeminate nor a representation of machismo; he is the expression of positive male qualities of creativity and power within, rather than power over, and of natural regenerating potency inseparable from the Goddess, the prime and nurturing force.

Membership: In 1988 the fellowship reported 125 members in the United States, 8 members in Canada, and 12 in other countries. Membership in the fellowship network comes from all parts of the United States and includes several witchcraft and Neopagan groups.

Periodicals: *Brothersong*.

Church and School of Wicca

PO Box 297-IN, Hinton, WV 25951-0297

The Church and School of Wicca was founded in 1968 by Gavin Frost and his wife Yvonne Frost. It was among the earliest organizations to develop in the United States out of the Neopagan revival. In 1972 it earned IRS tax-exempt status, the first Wiccan organization so recognized. It became known internationally because of the widely advertised correspondence course it conducts. Since its founding, the church has received more than a half-million inquiries and accepted more than 50,000 students.

The church has eclectic teachings that draw on a variety of religious and magical beliefs and practices. It has what is described as a Celtic flavor because of the personal history of the founders in that tradition. The current teachings of the church rest on what are thought of as its five supports: 1) Old masters and new texts: the church members, many of whom possess specialized linguistic and scholarly skills, have examined its beliefs and have offered insights from many ancient and modern religious texts. 2) Experimental work: a continuous process of research on beliefs and practices, both undergoing change and modification. 3) Research into modern remnants of pre-technological cultures: especially as studies by social anthropologists continue, this research forms one of the expanding areas of new insight for the church. 4) Family traditions: the church began with a family tradition passed to Gavin Frost that has largely been discarded because if its patriarchal tone. 5) Students and other Wiccans and Pagans: as dialogue is had with Wiccans and Pagans outside the church, especially those who come to the church after years of practice elsewhere, new insights are brought into the church's teachings.

The church's present philosophy, called the Spiritual Path, can be summarized in five basic tenets resting on a central affirmation of an unnamable deity, postulated as an impersonal reality. From this affirmation other ideas flow, including: 1) The Wiccan Rede: "If it harm none, do what you will." 2) Reincarnation as an orderly system of learning: reincarnation is not so much an accounting of sins and punishments, as it is a means of guiding learning, with death regarded as a graduation. 3) The Law of Attraction: what I do to other living creatures, I will draw to myself. 4) Power through knowledge: it is assumed that each living creature has power or energy within its body and that the skill to direct that power can be taught and learned. 5) Harmony: it makes sense to live in harmony with the perceptible rhythms of the sun, moons, and seasons of the year.

Over the years, the church has chartered 28 subsidiary churches worldwide. All of these subsidiaries have completed their training period and have become independent entities.

The Church continually works for Wiccan rights and recognition in the public sphere. This has involved them in supporting religious freedom for incarcerated Wiccans and for gays, and in assisting the military in becoming informed about Wicca. The church also sponsors special interest groups for gay Wiccans, military Wiccans, solitary Witches, and other Wiccan groups founded around a particular interest or concern. A milestone in the church's history was *Dettmer v. Landon* (799 F.2d 929, 4th Cir. 1986), an appeals case involving an inmate in a Virginia prison who was a member of the School of Wicca. The United States Court of Appeals for the Fourth Circuit affirmed that Wicca was a religion, the first time a court had so ruled.

Members of the church adhere to a complex set of doctrines relating to the spiritual aspects of their lives. The church's teaching arm, the School of Wicca, offers a full range of courses on alternative topics, requiring considerable independent study and reading. Approximately 250 students graduate from the school annually.

Membership: The church reported that it limits its active student body (enrolled in correspondence courses) to 5,000.

Periodicals: *Survival*.

Sources:

Church and School of Wicca. www.wicca.org/.

―――――. *Good Witch's Bible*. New York: Berkley Publishing Company, 1976.

Frost, Gavin, and Yvonne Frost. *The Magic Power of Witchcraft*. West Nyack, NY: Parker Publishing Company, 1976.

―――――. *A Witch's Guide to Life*. Cottonwood, AZ: Esoteric Publications, 1978.

―――――. *Who Speaks for the Witch*. New Bern, NC: Godolphin House, 1991.

―――――. *The Witch's Magical Handbook*. Upper Saddle River, NJ: Prentice Hall, 2000.

―――――. *The Solitary Wiccan's Bible*. Newburyport, MA: Weiser, 2004.

Church of All Worlds

PO Box 758, Cotati, CA 94931

Among the largest and most influential of all Neopagan religious groups during the 1970s was the Church of All Worlds (CAW). The church traces its history to April 7, 1962, when a "water-brotherhood," called Atl, was formed by Tim Zell and Lance Christie at Westminster College in Fulton, Missouri. During the mid-1960s, the group was centered on the University of Oklahoma campus at Norman and operated under the name Atlan Foundation. A periodical, *The Atlan Torch* (later *The Atlan Annals*), was published from 1962 to 1968. Following a move to St. Louis, Missouri, in 1968, the Church of All Worlds was legally incorporated. In March of

that year, the *Green Egg* appeared. From its inauspicious beginnings as a one-page ditto sheet, it grew into a 60-page journal over 80 issues, becoming the most significant periodical in the Pagan movement during the 1970s and making Zell, its editor, a major force in Neopaganism (a term that Zell coined). It was also the major instrument in the church's expansion.

The Church of All Worlds took much inspiration from the science fiction classic *Stranger in a Strange Land* by Robert Heinlein. In the novel, the Stranger, Valentine Michael Smith, is an Earthman born on Mars and raised by Martians. Among his adventures after being brought to earth is the formation of the "Church of All Worlds." The fictional church was built around "nests," a combination of a congregation and an intentional community. A basic concept was "grokking" (literally, "drinking;" the ability to be fully empathic). CAW also emphasized the experience of nonpossessive love and the joyous expression of sexuality as divine union. The nests were places where this grokking and joyful sexual love could find expression. The common greeting was, "Thou art God," a recognition of divinity immanent in each person.

The nonfiction Church of All Worlds is organized around a central office where master records are kept. Autonomous nests are composed of at least three members of "2nd Circle" or "inner" located in the same area. There are nine circles of inward progression, named after the nine planets, divided into three RINGs (Seeker, Scion, and Beacon). Each circle includes study, writing, magical training, personal actualization work, connection to the CAW tribe, and service to the organization and the community. The clergy, consisting of legally ordained priests and priestesses, is separate from the RINGs training program, and is made up of longtime members of the church who have undergone personal and leadership development, religious training, and completed the church's other ordination requirements. The board of directors is elected by the Beacon Council from candidates recommended by the general membership. Communication between the church hierarchy and the broader membership is facilitated by annual, regional, and special curias, where membership feedback is sought and group consensus is gauged.

BELIEFS: The basic theology of the CAW is a form of pantheism that focuses on the Divine as being immanent in every human being, expressed, as in the Heinlein book, in the common greeting, "Thou Art God," or "Thou Art Goddess." The most important theological statement came in the form of revelatory writings by Zell in the years 1970 to 1973, on the theory that later came to be known as the Gaia thesis. This concept is a biological validation of an ancient intuition: that the planet is a single living organism—Mother Earth (Gaia).

As pantheists, CAW holds as divine the living spirit of Nature. Thus, the CAW recognizes Mother Earth, the Horned God, and other spirits of animistic totemism as the Divine pantheon. In this manner, the Church of All Worlds became an early forerunner of the Deep Ecology movement. Through its focus on Mother Nature as a goddess, its recognition and ordination of women as priestesses, CAW can also rightly be held to be the first Eco-Feminist church. CAW is "dedicated to the celebration of Life, the maximal actualization of Human potential, and the realization of ultimate individual freedom and personal responsibility in harmonious eco-psychic relationship with the total Biosphere of Holy Mother Earth."

With the third reincarnation of CAW in 2005, the church undertook the task of elucidating its doctrine by restructuring its old by-laws as religious canons. The new canons define the non-creedal doctrine established by long-held traditions of the church. That doctrine holds as central CAW's mission: "to evolve a network of information, mythology and experience to awaken the Divine within and to provide a context and stimulus for reawakening Gaea [Gaia] and reuniting Her children through tribal community dedicated to responsible stewardship and the evolution of consciousness." The other points of established doctrine are 1) the aforementioned theological position on imminent Divinity; 2) commitment to being a non-creedal, eclectic faith; 3) honor for dissent and respect for the value that "heretics" have to the examination of faith and spiritual growth; 4) reverence for the Earth; 5) the sacramental experience of "sharing water"; 6) nondiscrimination; and 7) affirmation of and support for the freedom of expression in intimacy and family.

Worship in the church involves weekly or monthly meetings held usually in the homes of nest members on a rotational basis, and often also includes the observation of Neopagan holidays such as the Wiccan Wheel of the Year. The basic liturgical form is based on a circle where members take turns sharing their creativity. A chalice of water is always shared around the circle either as the opening or closing of the ceremony. Other events are celebrated at festivals around the country, as well as at the church sanctuary, a 55-acre parcel of sacred land called Annwfn, in northern California. Annwfn has a two-story temple, a garden, an orchard, and a small pond. It has solar-powered electricity, propane hot water, and a cellular telephone. In addition to the eight seasonal festivals commonly associated with Wicca, the church holds handfastings (marriages), vision quests, initiations, workshops, retreats, work parties, and staff meetings.

HISTORY: Incorporated in 1968, CAW was the first of the Neopagan/Earth Religions to obtain full federal recognition. However, the church had some trouble being recognized as a legitimate religious body and was originally refused recognition by the Missouri Department of Revenue for purposes of state sales tax exemption. The rejection was on the basis of its lack of primary concern about the hereafter, God, the destiny of souls, heaven, hell, sin and its punishment, and other supernatural matters. The ruling was overturned as unconstitutional in 1971.

In 1974 the church reported nests located in Missouri, California, Illinois, Kansas, Wisconsin, Iowa, Wyoming, Minnesota, Pennsylvania, Tennessee, New Jersey, New York, and Ohio. It was publishing two periodicals, *Green Egg* and *The Pagan*. Two years later, Zell, having established the church, moved from St. Louis to northern California with his new wife, Morning Glory, an ordained Priestess, for a rural life more centered on writing, research in some areas of particular interest, and the practice of the religion he had developed. They left the administration and the publication of the *Green Egg* in the hands of other church leaders. After only a few more issues, the magazine ceased to appear and many of the church nests dissolved in the wake of intense internal conflicts.

By the mid-1980s, CAW survived only in California, focalized around the sanctuary land bequeathed to the church by its bard, the late Gwydion Pendderwen. On and around this rural retreat, a pagan homesteading community formed that included the Zells (Tim Zell had changed his first name to Otter in 1979 following a vision quest) and other long-time church members who moved to the community, as well as many new people. Two new clergy, Orion Stormcrow and Anodea Judith, were ordained and became significant leaders in the church; Anodea served as president for seven years.

In the late 1980s, following Otter and Morning Glory's emergence from eight years of living in the wilderness, the Church of All Worlds began a reorganization and revivification. The community on the land broke up as the other people moved back into civilization. The membership program was radically upgraded to include intensive training courses and new responsibilities, along with a new members-only newsletter, *The Scarlet Flame*.

The first issue of the revived *Green Egg (The Next Generation!)* appeared in May 1988 to commemorate the 20th anniversary of its original publication, and it once again rose to a position of prominence among the 500 or so Pagan periodicals then being published. In 1991, with 52 pages and a four-color glossy cover, *Green Egg* won the Silver Award from the Wiccan/Pagan Press Alliance for "Most Professionally Formatted Pagan Publication."

By February 1992 the church had six chartered nests in California, with others in Florida, Illinois, Arizona, and Minnesota, and was growing in other areas as well. Otter worked with other prominent pagans to form the Universal Federation of Pagans, a worldwide association that he hoped would unify the global Pagan community. A Grand Convocation was held in August of 1992 to mark the 30th anniversary of the church.

In September 1996 changes in the configuration of the board of directors initiated a series of events that led to radical changes within the group. Zell (now

Oberon Zell, another name change inspired by a spiritual experience), was replaced as editor of *Green Egg* and then underwent a one-year sabbatical from his duties as Primate. *Green Egg* experienced financial difficulties, and by 2001 the board of directors had decided to cease publication.

By late 1998 the central office had moved to Toledo, Ohio, and administrative operations were overseen by Jim Looman as executive operations manager. Over the next several years, conflicts intensified resulting in the resignation, retirement, or disassociation of many members, including Zell and a large portion of the clergy. During this period, in recognition of the many diverse paths developing out of the tradition of CAW, Liza Gabriel wrote a proposal defining the Church of All Worlds Tradition, an acknowledgment that CAW accepted this diversity. This proposal was endorsed by Oberon and Morning Glory Zell and many of the membership, but was rejected by the Ohio board of directors as violating CAW's "trademark" as an organization.

In September 2004 the Ohio board of directors, now headed by Looman as president, citing legal and financial problems as their justification, passed a "Resolution to Implement the Dormancy of CAW," which declared their intention to cease operations and resolve all business matters of CAW by June 2005. They also announced to the online membership that they had incorporated a separate organization named the International Church of All Worlds (iCAW) in 2000 in Ohio, and that they were cancelling all Church of All Worlds, Inc., memberships but would honor those memberships for any members who wished to leave CAW and join iCAW. The entire board then resigned before completing the actions outlined by this resolution. Jim Looman passed away, and all records of the organization, both physical and electronic, were reported by prior board members to have been "accidentally destroyed." CAW nests either associated with iCAW or disassociated with CAW and became independent CAW Tradition Nests.

In 2005 Zell and his co-founder, Lance Christie, along with other longtime members of the church, bonded together once again to initiate what they called the Third Phoenix Resurrection of CAW. They filed amended articles of incorporation to return the central office to California, appointed a new board of directors, and resumed operation of the original California religious nonprofit. The next few years were spent attempting to reconnect to the CAW nests, which had been dispersed in the years of turmoil. The Church of All Worlds now recognizes both formal nests (those formally associated with CAW, Inc.) and CAW Tradition nests as valid members of the Church of All Worlds tribe. As of 2008, the organization was being revived and restructured, and an organizational structure that was designed to honor both the consensus of the membership and the guidance of the Church Elders was being adopted in hopes of preventing future division.

Over the years, the Church of All Worlds has chartered a number of subsidiary organizations through which it practices and teaches its religion. These subsidiaries have continued to function even while the main body of the church went dormant. These subsidiary orders and addresses, as of 2008, are as follows:

Forever Forests: PO Box 559, Redwood Valley, CA 95470. Founded in 1977 by Gwydion Pendderwen. This is the ecology branch. Sponsors tree-planting events and rituals.

Lifeways: lifeways@caw.org. Founded in 1983 by Anodea Judith. The teaching branch. Offers workshops, classes, healing rituals, recovery programs, and training for the priesthood.

Nemeton: PO Box 758, Cotati, CA 94931. Founded in 1972 by Gwydion Pendderwen and Alison Harlow. The marketing branch. Tapes, records, songbooks, t-shirts, philosophical tracts, and books. Catalog available.

Ecosophical Research Assn. (ERA): PO Box 758, Cotati, CA 94931. Founded in 1977 by Morning Glory Zell. Branch devoted to research and exploration in the fields of history, mythology, and natural sciences. Produced the the New Guinea Mermaid expedition, a Peruvian Pilgrimage, a series of replicas of ancient God and Goddess votive figurines (sculpted by Otter), and the Living Unicorn project. The Zells claimed that their research showed that the unicorn was originally created by ancient pastoral people in the Middle East by means of an operation on baby goats. An animal that had undergone this surgery was temporarily leased by the Zells for exhibition by the Ringling Bros./Barnum & Bailey Circus.

Holy Order of Mother Earth (HOME): PO Box 758, Cotati, CA 94931. Founded in 1977 by the Zells and Alison Harlow. Magical and shamanic branch open only to trained initiates of this religious discipline. Creates and conducts the church's rituals and ceremonies.

Membership: In 2008, during restructuring, the church reported a membership of approximately 75.

Periodicals: *The Green Egg*. Available from www.greeneggzine.com/.

Sources:

Church of All Worlds. www.caw.org/.

Guiley, Rosemary. *Encyclopedia of Witches and Witchcraft*. New York: Facts on File, 1989.

Judith, Anodea. *Wheels of Life*. Illustrated by Otter Zell. St. Paul, MN: Llewellyn Publications, 1987.

The Living Unicorn. Los Gatos, CA: Living Unicorn, [1980].

Oberon and Morning Glory Zell-Ravenheart. *Creating Circles & Ceremonies: Rituals for All Seasons and Reasons*. New Page Books, 2006.

Zell, Tim. *Cataclysm and Consciousness: From the Golden Age to the Age of Iron*. Redwood Valley, CA: Author, 1977.

Church of Pan

114 Johnson Rd., Foster, RI 02825

The Church of Pan was founded in 1970 by Kenneth Walker (d. 1987) and members of a nudist campground in rural Rhode Island. The church's founding was occasioned by the request of two members to be married in the nude and the inability of the group to locate a minister to perform the ceremony. They decided to form a church, and Walker became the minister.

The Church of Pan espouses naturalist principles. Reverence and devotion is directed toward the Creator, and actions follow patterns discerned to be in concert with the Creator's designs and purposes. While engaged in altruistic actions that attempt to modify the harshness of nature, in line with the destiny of creation, the church denounces human actions that have destroyed life-supporting systems and polluted nature. Humans have the task of maintaining the balance of life on the planet. The church also opposes the distortion of human society by what it views as an erroneous treatment of sexuality. Forgetting the naturalness of sex, society tends to view it either as sinful or something to be marketed.

The church is headquartered at a nudist campground managed by Beulah A. Rathbun. Members are active in the promotion of environmental concerns. As might be expected from the nature of its beginning, the church has experienced difficulties over its status as a tax-exempt religious organization.

Membership: In 1988, the church reported 30 families, all members of the one "congregation" in Rhode Island.

Church of Seven Arrows

PO Box 185, Wheat Ridge, CO 80034-0185

The Church of Seven Arrows was founded in 1975 by the Revs. George Dew and Linda Hillshafer who serve as the shamans of the church. In 1977, the church was established in Wheatridge, Colorado, a Denver suburb, and began publishing the monthly periodical *Thunderbow*. While functioning within the larger neopagan movement, the Church of Seven Arrows derives its system of beliefs and practices from a variety of sources, including contemporary western occultism, Hinduism, and, most prominently, the traditions of the Hopi and Plains Indians as expressed in the writings of Frank Waters and Hyemeyohsts Storm. The basic worldview and

practices are described in two sets of books produced by the church, *Basics of Magic* and *Shaman's Notes*.

The beliefs of the church are expounded in terms of mythos, dogma, and doctrine. The church's mythos (its overall perspective on the nature of life and the universe) states that in the beginning, Creator existed as a State of Being. Creator acted, creating Nephew, who in turn created nine realms, one for Creator himself, and seven others. Spirits were created to populate the realms and the worlds. The world of humanity was given to the charge of "She Whom We Call Grandmother." She first created the body-forms of the animal and plant kingdoms and then the human species in which the spirit resides. The human spirit is special in that it is the only spirit that may choose whether or not to fulfill its place, and it is the only one that must learn its place. Humanity's function is to lead all the beings of Earth in raising a harmonious sound to the Creator's realm.

Eventually, the original harmony was lost and the sound arising from earth became a cacophony. At that point, Nephew and Grandmother cleansed the world with fire, and the first world gave way to a second. The second world proceeded like the first, but added to the growing cacophony was a mistreatment of the earth for purposes it was never intended for. A second cleansing by ice was followed by the third world, its disintegration, and a cleansing by means of water and a geologic shift. We now live in the fourth world, which is progressing toward the time of another cleansing cycle. Those in touch with the harmony of Earth, Grandmother, and the original purpose and function of humankind will survive and pass through the cleansing activity.

Among the dogmas of the church are the following affirmations: each being is a spirit and mirror of the Creator; a being cannot be destroyed; the universe exists in a state of patterned change; each being has a right to exist (but each form of existing may or may not be acceptable); bodies are masks of the spirit; no one path is proper for all people at all times; and the same basic principles are manifested in both the spiritual and material realms.

The more ephemeral beliefs of the church are called doctrine and summarized in nine statements as a "Guide for Daily Living on the Path of Seven Arrows." These statements call for members to know themselves, live in harmony, study the sciences (including the ancient science of magic), avoid self-destructive agreements, and live in such a way that joyous sounds arise to the Creator's ear. The ancient sciences should be used in a manner that avoids harm to anyone. The church offers a set of rituals for both personal and group use.

The church is headed by a board of directors. A variety of classes on basic magic and shamanism are taught at regular intervals. Most members live in the Denver metropolitan area, but the periodical has a national audience. Rituals follow the solar and lunar cycles. *Thunderbow*, a popular pagan periodical for a decade, was discontinued in 1987. Since 1990 the church has sponsored the Earth Home Society, which networks among holistic healers in the Denver metropolitan area.

Membership: As of 1997, approximately 50 participants attend church activities in the Denver area during any given period. Currently, approximately 500 "graduate-practitioners" of church training from around the country keep in communication and retain some informal ties with it.

Periodicals: *Earth Home Society Resource Directory*.

Sources:

Basics of Magic. 2 vols. Wheatridge, CO: Church of Seven Arrows, 1980.

Shaman's Notes. 3 vols. Wheatridge, CO: Church of Seven Arrows, 1983–1985.

Storm, Hyemeyohsts. *The Song of Heyoehkah*. San Francisco: Harper & Row, 1981.

Waters, Frank. *Book of the Hopi*. New York: Ballantine, 1963.

Church of the Eternal Source

PO Box 2778, Mission Viejo, CA 92690-0778

The Church of the Eternal Source, the most substantial of the several Egyptian neopagan bodies, was founded in 1970 by the late Donald D. Harrison (1931–2004) and Harold Moss. Harrison (a former Roman Catholic) and Moss were converted to paganism through the study of the Greek and Roman religions and their attraction to the fine arts of ancient Egypt. In 1967, Harrison founded the *Julian Review*, which became the organ of the Delphic Fellowship, an early pagan fellowship based upon Greek motifs. Moss organized a social group professing the Egyptian religion after seeing a movie, *The Egyptian*, that focused on Akhenaten. In 1963, the group held an Egyptian costume party. The Church of the Eternal Source combines aspects of a number of Egyptian temples. Each priest and priestess acts autonomously in supervising ritual and initiation procedures for his or her temple. The church currently has four consecrated temples and congregations in California, Idaho, and Oregon. Continuing its tradition of public rituals, in 2006 the CES drew a capacity crowd of over 250 (50 latecomers were turned away) at the Pantheacon in San Jose, California. The ceremony included recitations in the ancient Egyptian language and a number of reconstructed sacred wands and staffs.

The two basic principles of the Church of the Eternal Source are polytheism and authentic Egyptianism. The church teaches that divinity is a balance of distinct divine vectors. The diversity of the gods and their transactions produces reality. Man's task is to achieve balance in his soul in the divine vectors. Authentic Egyptian religion relates to the early period when Egypt was relatively untainted by non-Egyptian ideas. This period became a source for all later religious insights. The mastery of Egyptian history is stressed. Many of the church leaders have made pilgrimages to Egypt.

Religious practices center on personal shrines, the study of theology, divination, the fine arts, and personal worship with wide variations. Group worship is manifest in the festivals, which are dramatic reenactments of a holy myth. The Egyptian pantheon forms the basic content of faith. A typical myth is the story of the rebirth of Osiris. Osiris was killed by Set, the god of darkness. Isis, the wife of Osiris, sought him, her tears causing the Nile to overflow. She found the body and buried it, but not carefully. Set exhumed it, dismembered it, and scattered the pieces through the land. Isis then carefully sought and assembled each piece. Osiris was then resurrected. Osiris and Isis are accompanied in the pantheon by Horus, their son; Bast, the beneficent solar goddess represented as a cat; Thoth, the god of wisdom; and Ra, the sun god often represented as Khepera, the beetle (believed to be self-generated). The myths are described in ancient literature such as *The Egyptian Book of the Dead*.

Important festival days are held each full moon and during the equinoxes and solstices. The birthdays of the deities are also celebrated, generally in mid-July, although various temples may use different dates for the Egyptian new year. Ritual magick is performed and ancient texts are recited both in English and the ancient language, although no set ritual is prescribed. A typical Egyptian ritual is found in *Magic: An Occult Primer* by David Conway.

Membership: The church does not keep congregational membership records.

Periodicals: *Kephera*.

Remarks: The late Don Harrison, one of the church's founders, is the author of several novels emphasizing both ancient religions and sexual themes.

Sources:

Church of the Eternal Source. www.ceswebhq.org or
www.home.earthlink.net/~ceswebhq/.

Conway, David. *Magic: An Occult Primer*. New York: E. P. Dutton, 1972.

Frankfort, Henri. *Ancient Egyptian Religion: An Interpretation*. New York: Harper & Row, 1961.

Church of Universal Eclectic Wicca

PO Box 1, Center Valley, PA 18034

The Church of Universal Eclectic Wicca (CUEW) is a Web-based Wiccan community that began in 1997 as a means of helping solitary Wiccans find materials to assist them in learning about Wicca and pursuing their solitary rituals. It continues that basic purpose, but has matured and changed, especially in reaction to the ubiquity of the Internet, which was just beginning to permeate the Wiccan community in 1997.

The Church of Universal Eclectic Wicca operates out of a general Wiccan consensus, but with an emphasis on universalism (believing that truth exists in a multitude of places) and eclecticism (the practice of taking religious resources from many places). The CUEW believes that the solitary is central to the vitality of the Wiccan community, an essential concept behind its original structure, the Coven of the Far Flung Net.

Individuals may have a number of different relations to the CUEW. First, they may relate to the church as an unaffiliated solitary Wiccan. This is a person who reads Universal Eclectic Wiccan books and Web sites and practices what those Web sites and books teach, but keeps it to him or herself. Such a person has no standing in Universal Eclectic Wicca or the CUEW and is not authorized to teach Universal Eclectic Wicca to another person.

Second, an individual may join online teaching groups such as the Coven of the Far Flung Net, the Coven of Non-Fluffy Wicca, or Vircle, which all assume that their solitary contacts are practicing Wicca offline while also participating in lessons or activities.

Third, a person may actually join an offline group. Universal Eclectic Wicca allows for individuals to combine being a part of a coven or teaching circle with being a solitary.

Fourth, some solitaries may want to seek out a mentor who has gone through Universal Eclectic Wiccan training and who would vouch for the individual's accomplishments or assist in a person's instruction. Universal Eclectic Wicca is taught in three levels called *circles*. Most members are in or have completed the Second Circle. Most mentors are in the Third Circle.

Finally, some people, after completing their study, decide that they would like to be part of an offline group. As it has grown, the Church of Universal Eclectic Wicca has begun to found such groups.

The CUEW's view of Wicca is contained in its basic textbook, *All One Wicca* by Kaatryn MacMorgan-Douglas, available online at the church's Web site. That Web site also contains many other pieces of teaching material. One particular item unique to the CUEW is the Affirmation of Acknowledgment, which covers its relationship to other religions, especially Christianity:

> *I: I acknowledge the presence of other faiths on my planet, indeed, right here in my city/town/village. I acknowledge that the followers of these faiths feel as strongly, maybe more so, than I do about mine.*
>
> *II: I forgive the other faiths and wipe clean the slate between us. I cannot hold a person responsible for the acts of their faith, I cannot hold a faith at fault for individual practitioners. It is not my place to convert, or otherwise alter a person's religion. I invite discussion of beliefs without judgment of those holding them.*
>
> *III: I acknowledge that I may be wrong, and I have found comfort in the fact that I may be right.*

CUEW is led by the Association of Universal Eclectic Wiccan Clergypersons (AUEWC). Membership in AUEWC is open to elected Universal Eclectic Wiccan leaders, lay ministers, and ordained priests, and single representatives of egalitarian covens. Persons may attain clergy status through study with an accredited Universal Eclectic Wiccan teacher (either online or offline).

Membership: Not reported.

Sources:

Church of Universal Eclectic Wicca. www.cuew.org/.

Circle Sanctuary

PO Box 9, Barneveld, WI 53507

Circle Sanctuary (also known as Circle) began in October 1974 when Selena Fox (b.1949), its founder, received the central concept, logo, and name in meditation.

Shortly after this event, she and her partner at the time, Jim Alan, began to host informal gatherings of people interested in Paganism, Nature religion, Wicca, magic and mysticism in their home in Madison, Wisconsin. In June 1975 they moved to a farm near Sun Prairie, Wisconsin. This site, known as Circle Farm, was the meeting place for Circle's first group, a Wiccan coven, and later for the beginning of Circle's spiritual community, comprised of individuals and several groups. Through their writings and music, Fox and Alan began to meet and correspond with Pagans around the United States, Canada, and England. In 1977 their first book, a songbook, was published, as well as an album of their spiritual music. Fox also founded Circle Network that year. The following year Fox began to devote her efforts full time to the expanding Circle ministry which was incorporated as the Church of Circle Wicca in October 1978. In May 1979 Fox compiled and released the first Circle resource guide, a networking directory and sourcebook, which contributed to the growth of the developing Pagan movement.

In November 1979, after being evicted from their first farm because of their religion, which became known after Fox had received national media attention, Circle's headquarters moved first to a farm near Ashton, Wisconsin, and then to another rented farmstead outside of Black Earth. In 1983 the church relocated to a 200 acre site it purchased near Barneveld, Wisconsin. Circle changed its incorporated name to Circle Sanctuary and named its land Circle Sanctuary Nature Preserve. This site serves as church headquarters and it includes a variety of ritual sites and meditation places, including a stone circle, outdoor shrines, a cemetery, and an indoor temple.

Circle Sanctuary became the focus of an ever-widening network of contemporary Pagans, Wiccans, Witches, and other Nature religion practitioners throughout the United States and other countries. In 1980 Circle began publishing *Circle Magazine* (initially known as *Circle Network News*), in a quarterly newspaper format. Also that year, Circle began forming specialty networks within the larger Circle Network, including an international and interreligious Pagan friendship network. In 1981 the first of the annual week-long international Pagan Spirit Gatherings was held.

In 1985 Circle Sanctuary's Wiccan-Pagan religious freedom work became widely known through its leadership in a nationwide action that defeated anti-Wiccan legislation in the US Congress. This battle and victory led Fox to form the Pagan Strength Web which later became the Lady Liberty League. In 1988, after a four-year legal battle over the right to use its land for religious activities, Circle Sanctuary land won local zoning as a church, and Circle Sanctuary began being listed alongside churches of other faiths in worship directories in the greater Madison, Wisconsin area. Circle Sanctuary is active in local, regional, national, and global interfaith organizations, projects and conferences.

Rev. Selena Fox and others from Circle Sanctuary and the Lady Liberty League have continued to be in the forefront of Pagan religious freedom work. They have been consulted on a variety of cases involving discrimination against Pagans in schools, workplaces, child custody cases, prisons, and government. In 1999 they helped lead a nationwide campaign that defeated federal legislation and upheld the rights of Wiccans serving in the US Armed Forces relative to their practice of their religion at military installations. In 2007 Circle Sanctuary, represented by Americans United for Separation of Church and State, successfully concluded a decade-long battle on behalf of Pagan veterans and their families with the settlement of its lawsuit against the US Department of Veterans Affairs (VA) filed in the US District Court of Western Wisconsin in November 2006. On April 23, 2007, the VA finally added the Pentacle, symbol of faith for Wiccans and many Pagans, to its list of emblems of belief that can be included on government-issued grave markers for deceased veterans. VA pentacle grave markers are now at public and private cemeteries throughout the nation, including at Arlington National Cemetery and Circle Sanctuary's church cemetery.

The spiritual foundation of Circle Sanctuary is rooted in a form of shamanic Wiccan spirituality developed by Fox. Known as "Circle Wicca" in the 1970s and "Wiccan Shamanism" in the 1980s, it has evolved as the "Circle Craft Tradition." This synthesis of Wiccan spirituality, Pagan folkways, nature mysticism, multicultural shamanism, and transpersonal psychology, emphasizes communion with the "Divine in Nature." Since the 1990s, Circle Sanctuary has increasingly used the terms "Nature Spirituality" (a term coined by Fox in 1981) and Nature religion to describe its multifaceted networking and spiritual focus.

Circle Sanctuary has emerged as one of the most visible and public centers for ecospirituality, contemporary Paganism, and the Wiccan religion in the United States, and Fox is regularly called upon by the media, the government, and other churches to speak for the broader Pagan community. Through the variety of periodicals and festivals sponsored by Circle Sanctuary, it has built one of the largest networks currently existing within contemporary Paganism. It has also been the seedbed for other Pagan groups, festivals, and land projects, some of which have had their beginnings among those who have studied and worked at Circle Sanctuary headquarters.

Currently the church is headed by Fox, who serves as Senior Minister. The multifaceted local, regional, national, and global ministry of Circle Sanctuary is carried out by volunteers and full-time staff members. Fox, who is a professionally trained psychotherapist, does counseling and spiritual healing as part of her ministry. In 1995 Fox and her husband, Dr. Dennis Carpenter, a psychology professor, co-founded the Nature Religions Scholars Network, which a decade later became the Pagan Studies section of the American Academy of Religion. Fox and Carpenter supervise Circle Sanctuary's academic research and networking efforts, including the Pagan Academic Network, which has its national meeting each year at the Pagan Spirit Gathering. Circle Sanctuary sponsors Pagan groups at several universities and at military installations. In addition, Circle Sanctuary and its ministers are active in hospital and hospice chaplaincy work, prison ministries, and interfaith endeavors. Circle Sanctuary operates Circle Cemetery, a national Pagan cemetery and one of the first Green cemeteries in the USA.

Membership: In 2008 Circle Sanctuary reported a membership and constituency of 60,000 inclusive of the United States and internationally.

Educational Facilities:

Circle Sanctuary, Barneveld, Wisconsin, and online.

Periodicals: *Circle Magazine* (in-print) • *Circle Guide to Pagan Resources* (in-print) • *Circle Times* (e-bulletin) • *Community Circle News* (e-bulletin).

Sources:

Circle Sanctuary. www.circlesanctuary.org/.

Alan, Jim, and Selena Fox. *Circle Magick Songs*. Madison, WI: Circle Publications, 1977.

Carpenter, Dennis D. *Spiritual Experiences, Life Changes, and Ecological Viewpoints of Contemporary Pagans*. Mt. Horeb, WI: Circle Publications, 1994.

Fox, Selena. *Goddess Communion: Rituals & Meditations*. Mt. Horeb, WI: Circle Publications, 1989.

————. *When Goddess Is God: Pagans, Recovery, & Alcoholics Anonymous*. Mt. Horeb, WI: Circle Publications, 1995.

Fox, Selena, et al. *Guide to Pagan Groups*. Mt. Horeb, WI: Circle Publications, 2003.

Congregationalist Witchcraft Association

PO Box 2205, Clearbrook, BC, Canada V2T 3X8

The Congregationalist Witchcraft Association was founded in the late 1980s by members of several Neopagan Witchcraft covens across Canada, after several years of discussion regarding its bases of agreement and constitution. When it was finally chartered in 1992 by the Canadian government as a nonprofit corporation, the association began life as a confederation of self-governing groups (covens) in several Canadian provinces (initially in Ontario, British Columbia, and Nova Scotia; in 2008 it also has members in Alberta, Quebec, Manitoba, and Saskatchewan.). Groups share a common statement of belief and ethical principles, but member groups control their own administration and worship. The association was formed to accomplish tasks that member groups (all of which tend to be small covens) could not accomplish alone. For example, it represents members to the government, promotes festivals and gatherings, and assists the growth of Wicca.

The association holds that divinity is multifaceted, and as such can be given a variety of names by which the many gods and goddesses are known. There are also levels of divinity. Thus, it is appropriate to speak of lesser deities such as guardian spirits. The divine is primarily immanent rather than transcendent, and it is thus ever-present and active in the world. Every woman and man is an embodiment of divinity, and all acts of love and pleasure are acts of praise of the Goddess. All forms of sexual expression that are noncoercive are considered legitimate by the association. Members also practice magic and believe that through petition, action, and ritual the world may be changed according to their will.

Members of the association agree not to practice animal sacrifice, promote coercive activities, or charge fees either for teaching the craft or for initiation. Priests and priestesses are expected to keep pastoral confidences.

The association is headed by a national council of officers chosen by vote of the member covens.

Membership: In 1994 there were five full-member congregations (one each in British Columbia, Alberta, Ontario, Quebec, and Nova Scotia) and seven associate-members congregations (found in Alberta, Saskatchewan, Manitoba, and Nova Scotia). There were also 17 individual members.

Periodicals: *Duck Tales*

Covenant of Gaia Church of Alberta

PO Box 1742, Sta. M, Calgary, AB, Canada T2P 2L7

The Covenant of Gaia Church of Alberta (COGCOA) is a Neopagan Wiccan church founded in Calgary, Alberta, in 1989. The church is congregational in structure, being composed of autonomous covens and solitary practitioners. It honors a multiplicity of female and male deities and follows the worship cycle of the eight common Wiccan festivals by celebrating community cycles. The church offers many different clergy services to its community, such as weddings, funerals, and coming-of-age rites. The church is headed by a board of directors who are elected annually.

Membership: In 2002 the church reported having 30–60 members.

Sources:

Covenant of Gaia. www.cogcoa.ab.ca.

Covenant of Gaia. *What Is the Covenant of Gaia?* Calgary, AB: Covenant of Gaia, 1991. 5-page tract.

Covenant of the Goddess

PO Box 1226, Berkeley, CA 94701

The Covenant of the Goddess (CoG) was formed in 1975 by members of approximately ten covens in California. It is a confederation of autonomous covens whose purpose is to facilitate cooperation between covens and secure legal status and tax exemption for Witchcraft groups. Largely confined to California in its first years, by the end of the decade it had accepted covens in the East, and during the early 1980s it became a national organization and shifted a significant amount of its activity to the Midwest. The CoG now has covens in seven regional groupings across the country.

Membership is open to witches, both covens and individuals practicing as solitaries. New members must be recommended by two active CoG members and follow the worship of the Goddess and/or the Old Goddess and the Gods. A code of ethics binds members to the Wiccan Rede, "An ye harm none, do as ye will." It also espouses guidelines on finances, the sovereignty of the individual covens, secrecy, and respect for diversity.

Annually members of the Covenant of the Goddess gather for the MerryMeet, an annual festival at which the Grand Council meets and the officers are elected.

Where three or more covens exist in close geographic proximity, they may organize a local council for the accomplishment of specific projects and general cooperative endeavor.

Membership: In 1992 there were 65 covens.

Periodicals: *The Covenant of the Goddess Newsletter*.

Sources:

Covenant of the Goddess. www.cog.org.

Starhawk. *Dreaming the Dark*. Boston: Beacon Press, 1982.

———. *The Spiral Dance*. San Francisco: Harper & Row, 1979.

Covenant of Unitarian Universalist Pagans (CUUPS)

PO Box 3128, Durham, NC 27715-3128

The Covenant of Unitarian Universalist Pagans (CUUPS) emerged in the mid-1980s among some Unitarian Universalists who had come into contact with the Neopagan Movement and had concluded that the two had much in common and much of value to share with each other. At the 1985 Assembly of the Unitarian Universalist Association (UUA) in Atlanta, Georgia, a spontaneous and spirited summer solstice ritual led to an exploration of the possibility of an ongoing organization. A newsletter was begun, and Margot Adler a writer, scholar, and Wiccan priestess, was invited to address the 1987 assembly, at which time CUUPS was formally organized. The interim steering committee became the first board of directors.

The possibility of such a group within the UUA came about as the UUA shifted from a primarily liberal Christian body to one that sees itself as a confluence of the world's religious traditions and insights. The association also places a great deal of emphasis upon individual freedom of belief and worship, intellectual inquiry, and the toleration of differences. Religious pluralism has become an established way of life within the association.

CUUPS has developed a formal program of providing networking among Unitarian Universalists who identify themselves as Pagan, promoting dialogue among Pagans and those of the dominant western religious traditions, and serving as a liaison between Pagans and the larger UUA. In practice, CUUPS has provided the Pagan community with a means for Pagan clergy to gain a theological education and credentials, as well as a spiritual home for many Pagans who otherwise have no relation to the UUA. Thus, CUUPS operates as both a caucus within the association and as a growing and increasingly important Pagan grouping in its own right. In 1995 the UUA Assembly voted to acknowledge the "earth-centered spirituality" in the association by-laws as a major source of UUA beliefs, thus indirectly acknowledging the beliefs of CUUPS. It was the first such recognition of the significance of Neopaganism by a major American religious body.

CUUPs is headed by a board of directors cochaired by the Revs. Lesley Rebecca Phillips and Linda Sophia Pinti. It holds a national meeting in conjunction with the annual UUA Assembly, and numerous chapters have been formed around the United States and Canada.

Membership: Not reported. There are approximately 80 CUUP chapters in North America.

Periodicals: *Pagan NUUS*.

Sources:

Covenant of the Unitarian Universalist Pagans. www.cuups.org

Church of Y Dynion Mwyn

PO Box 672125, Marietta, GA 30006-0036

Originally known as Y Tylwyth Teg, the Church of Y Dynion Mywn is a Celtic traditional witchcraft group founded in 1967 in Washington, D.C., by Rhuddlwm Gawr. In 1966 founder Gawr was initiated in North Wales, and was given the name Rhuddlwm Gawr by the elders of the Welsh Tribe of Dynion Mwyn. The Church of Y Dynion Mywn received its laws and traditions from Great Britain through

Rhuddlwm. They are contained in eight volumes in manuscript form. In 1973 the group moved its headquarters to Georgia.

The Church of Y Dynion Mywn has three deities: the Goddess, the Horned God, and their son, the Child of Light (corresponding to the Egyptian Isis, Osiris, and Horus). Celtic names are employed by the Church of Y Dynion Mywn. Worship is both skyclad (naked) and robed, and both inside and outside the circle, depending on the occasion. Reincarnation is stressed. The major focus of the Church of Y Dynion Mywn is on becoming attuned to nature and its forces. Drugs are forbidden to members.

The Church of Y Dynion Mywn differs from other Wicca groups in that it is organized on seven levels. Each probationer is given a level name and a secret name, both in Welsh. Movement through the levels is occasioned by initiation ceremonies. The first level, the "naming," is coincidental with the members' identification with the coven. The church is organized into autonomous covens. There is no witch king or queen, but there are elders who render binding decisions on questions put to them.

Covens of the Church of Y Dynion Mywn were most active in the mid-1970s. In 1974 there were approximately 15 covens located in Georgia, Florida, Tennessee, North Carolina, Alabama, and Virginia. As of 2008, there were many sister covens throughout the world, including in Africa, Australia, and Western Europe. Rhuddlwm Gawr compiled two editions of the *Pagan/Occult/New Age Directory*, which includes broad segments of the American Wicca and Neo-Pagan community.

In 1968, in upstate Georgia, the group hosted the first of several Gatherings of the Tribes, a conclave of Witches and Neopagans from a wide variety of traditions and perspectives. In its early U.S. history in the late 1960s and early 1970s, the group focused on growing quietly, sometimes resorting to secrecy to avoid interference. Beginning in the latter half of the 1970s, public relations seems to have become a focus, resulting in stories in local newspapers, and the publication of the *Sword of Dyrnwyn Newsletter*. During this same period, the group received the first IRS Group Tax Exemption ever awarded to a Pagan or Witchcraft church assembly. (Senator Jesse Helms later attempted to take away federal church status from Wiccan churches.)

In the mid-1980s, another court case was heard over ownership of a church post office box in Athens, Georgia. As a result, the judge declared the Church of Y Tylwyth Teg a legal church, Rhuddlwm Gawr a legal minister of that church, and Witchcraft a bona fide religion. Beginning in the early 1990s, the group began to have an online presence, and branched out into numerous study groups on Yahoo. In February of 2003, Rhuddlwm Gawr retired as CEO of Y Tylwyth Teg, Inc. That same year, Dynion Mwyn and Y Tylwyth Teg diverged, with Y Tylwyth Teg falling under the leadership of Cerridwen Gawr and Dynion Mwyn falling under the leadership of Rhuddlwm Gawr. The group held its 40th Gathering of the Tribes in 2007.

Membership: Not reported.

Periodicals: *The Sword of Dyrnwyn*.

Sources:

Celtic Church of Dynion Mwyn: Who Is Rhuddlwm Gawr? www.tylwythteg.com.

Church and Coven of Dynion Mwyn. www.dynionmwyn.net/tylwyth.html.

Gawr, Rhuddlwm. *Pagan/Occult/New Age Directory*. Atlanta: Pagan Grove Press, 1980.

Gawr, Rhuddlwm, with Marcy Edwards. *The Quest*. Smyrna, GA: Pagan Grove Press, 1979.

Dianic Wicca

c/o Susan B. Anthony Coven No. 1, Box 11363, Oakland, CA 94611

Dianic Wicca is a name given to those Witchcraft covens that have developed a strong emphasis on feminism and the role of Witchcraft as the religion of females (wimmin). Whereas most Wiccans recognize their origins in the work of Gerald B. Gardner and the new form of Witchcraft he developed in the 1940s, the Dianics claim a tradition independent of Gardner, in the worship of Diana, the ancient Greek Goddess, from Central Europe. It is the belief of Dianic witches that the worship of the Goddess in a primeval past co-existed with a period of peace on earth that was destroyed by the rise of men and patriarchal deities. In Dianic covens, worship is focused on the mother Goddess as the Source of Life and as the Source of both sexes, and seen as including both sexes already. Individual covens vary from all-female separatist groups, to all female groups, to mixed male-female groups with a strong feminist emphasis.

Within the Dianic coven, the high priestess represents the Goddess and facilitates a ritual based on the circle. She is assisted by a maiden, and occasionally (where men are allowed) by a high priest. They represent the consort and the child. Some all-female covens operate in the nude, weather and inclination permitting, and some Dianic covens believe in parthenogenic birth, that is, birth not requiring male assistance.

Dianic Wicca began to emerge in the United States in 1971 when at least two different Dianic groups began. In southern California, Zsuzsanna Emese Budapest developed a coven associated with the Feminist Wicca, a matriarchial spiritual center in Venice, California. That original coven, known as the Susan B. Anthony Coven No. 1, continues under the leadership of Ruth Barrett, a High Priestess trained by Budapest. It has been renamed the Circle of Aradia. In the early 1980s, Budapest moved to Oakland, California, and began a second coven that eventually took the name abandoned by the first one. In Oakland, Budapest has led in the formation of the Women's Spirituality Forum, an organization dedicated to bringing Goddess consciousness into the mainstream of feminist, earth conservationist, and peace and justice work in the United States. It has held a number of conferences featuring leading feminist Wiccans, such as Merlin Stone, Starhawk, Diana Paxton, Margot Adler, and Budapest. It also holds a biannual Goddess festival.

Also in the early 1970s, in Dallas, Texas, a Dianic coven was founded by Morgan McFarland and Mark Roberts. High Priestess McFarland was a freelance photographer, writer, and feminist who began to explore the Craft in her early teens. She published a short-lived Neopagan periodical, *The Harp*, before going public in 1972. High Priest Roberts was also a freelance writer and photographer. Their group had originally been established as an occult group called the Seekers. In 1972 that group began to publish *The New Broom*. One of the articles published therein described the Dianic aspect as a blending of monotheism and pantheism. Dianic witches were monotheistic in that they worshipped the Goddess as the essential creative force. They were pantheists in their consideration of every creation in nature a child of the Goddess.

Withstanding attacks from those who complained that Dianic Witchcraft had lost the balance implied in the acknowledgment of the God and Goddess, the Dianics have become recognized as an important part of the Goddess tradition in North America. Besides the separate Dianic covens, Dianic Wicca has found strong advocates within otherwise non-Dianic groups. For example, Starhawk, the popular feminist Wiccan writer, is the leader of the Compost Coven, a coven within the larger fellowship of the Covenant of the Goddess (see separate entry), as is the Susan B. Anthony Coven No. 1.

"Dianic" is a designation describing a number of covens and Witchcraft groups. Their inclusion under that label does not imply any organizational connection or even mutual recognition. They are united only in their sharing and emphasizing a generally feminist perspective within the larger Neopagan community.

Membership: Dianic Wicca reports an estimated 20,000 Dianic Wiccans in the United States.

Periodicals: *Of a Like Mind*.

Sources:

Z Budapest. www.zbudapest.com/.

Budapest, Z. *The Feminist Book of Lights and Shadows*. Venice, CA: Luna Publications, 1976.

―――. *The Rise of the Fates*. Los Angeles: Susan B. Anthony Coven No. 1, 1976.

―――. *The Holy Book of Women's Mysteries*. Berkeley, CA: Wingbow Press, 1989.

―――. *Summoning the Fates: A Guide to Destiny and Sacred Transformation*. St. Paul, MN: Llewellyn Publications, 2007.

Christ, Carol P. *Diving Deep and Surfacing*. Boston, MA: Beacon Press, 1980.

Starhawk. *Dreaming the Dark*. Boston, MA: Beacon Press, 1982.

―――. *The Spiral Dance*. New York: Harper & Row, 1979.

Stone, Merlin. *When God Was a Woman*. New York: Harcourt Brace Jovanovich, 1976.

Discordian Society

Current address not obtained for this edition.

The Discordian Society appears to be a comic or satiric takeoff on the Neopagan movement. As described in *Principia Discordia*, the "bible" of the group, Discordians worship Eris, the goddess of chaos. The society's founder was one who called himself Malaclypse the Younger. In 1958, upon evoking the Lady in the Erisian aspect, he was told, "We Discordians must stick apart." Among the prominent Neopagans who identified themselves with the society was Robert Anton Wilson (1932–2007), also known as Mordecai the Foul. Wilson was a popular writer and advocate of the Illuminatus conspiracy. He coauthored, with Robert Shea, a three-volume fantasy novel *Illuminatus!*, describing the Discordian world, including its sister organization, the John Dillinger Died for You Society.

Members in the Discordian Society are initiated as popes. Being infallible, they have the power to excommunicate everyone. As pope, a member is in the Fifth House of Discordia, popularly known as the Out House. The member can then proceed to higher orders—bishop, knight, castle, priest, dupe, and finally clown.

The Discordian movement has not in fact functioned as an organization but rather has been perpetuated as an inside joke and means of relieving tension within Pagan groups. As stated at its Web site, "As you learn more you will understand less." Periodically, individuals publish material in the name of the Society. The most well-known literature, apart from *Principia Discordia* (which has been kept in print), was a periodical, *St. John's Bread*, that enjoyed a brief life in the mid-1970s.

Membership: Not reported.

Sources:

Discordian Society. discordiansociety.org/.

Malacylpse the Younger. *Principia Discordia*. Mason, MI: Loompanics Unlimited, 1978.

Divine Circle of the Sacred Grove

Box 1737, Fontana, CA 92334

The Divine Circle of the Sacred Grove was founded in 1985 by Janette Gordon, a priestess who has a long history of participation in Druidism as well as training in Wicca and a broad mastery of occultism in general. In 1965 she founded the Order of Druids, School and Church of Drunements, which was incorporated into the Divine Circle. The church holds weekly religious services and the school offers a full course of study on Wicca, magic, ritual, healing, occultism, and related topics. The school operates as a correspondence school under the tutelage of Janette and her husband, Norman Gordon. She has authored all of the curriculum and lesson material.

The church teaches the balance of nature affirmed in ritual activity, the polarity of Goddess and God, and a way of life based upon personal empowerment through magic. While operating out of a single center in Fontana, California, the church has extended its influence to Wiccans across the United States through its school, which offers master's and doctorate degrees to its graduates. It also offers special training for the priesthood and provides an opportunity for graduates to become initiates and priests of the church.

Membership: Not reported.

Egyptian Temple of Fitness

158 N Hill Ave., Pasadena, CA 91106-1950

The Egyptian Temple of Fitness was founded in the mid-1980s by Master Gamal Selim as a center of Egyptian religion, language, culture, and healing. It strives to teach the universal knowledge of the ancient Egyptians, which it believes can be of benefit to all. The temple offers a weekly round of activities, including worship services each Sunday afternoon. Ongoing classes are held on the Egyptian sacred sciences, hieroglyphics, natural healing techniques, exercise, and oracle reading (with an Egyptian version of the tarot cards).

Membership: Not reported.

ESP Laboratory

PO Box 2883, Durango, CO 81320-2883

The ESP Laboratory was founded in Los Angeles in 1966 by the late Al G. Manning (1927–2006). Manning was a certified public accountant who, during meditations, was contacted by a "Professor Reinhardt," his spirit teacher and guide. With Reinhardt's help, he wrote his first book and founded the ESP Laboratory, which functions as both a psychic interest center and a church. Manning became a minister of Spiritual Science and wrote several books. Manning's approach to the psychic focused on results. An early program made use of color to aid attunement to the living light in its differing shades, so as to attain personal goals of success, power, prosperity, and healing. Instruction in the mystic light was offered in a twenty-lesson correspondence course, and healing was also a major emphasis in his teaching.

Divination and the occult steadily became more important parts of the laboratory's work. In 1970 a course on the *I Ching* was first offered. In 1971 a course titled "White Magic and Witchcraft" was offered, and a new book, *Helping Yourself with White Witchcraft*, appeared the following year. Emphasis was placed not so much on the religion of Wicca but rather upon "magick," control, and the rituals to use for various purposes. One of the members of the laboratory who completed the course later formed the Astral Coven.

The ESP Laboratory moved its headquarters from Hollywood to Texas in the early 1980s. Members, via correspondence, are found in all 50 states and some foreign countries. Ordination as a minister is offered after the passing of required courses. A monthly newsletter contains announcements, reports on research, a monthly light exercise, and an astrology column.

Membership: Not reported.

Periodicals: *E.S.P. Laboratory Newsletter.*

Sources:

ESP Laboratory. www.esplab.com.

Manning, Al G. *Helping Yourself with White Witchcraft*. West Nyack, NY: Parker Publishing Company, 1972.

―――. *Helping Yourself with the Power of Gnostic Magic*. West Nyack, NY: Parker Publishing Company, 1979.

Fellowship of the Spiral Path

Box 5521, Berkeley, CA 94701

The Fellowship of the Spiral Path grew out of the early stages of the Goddess movement in the Bay Area of North California. In 1977 a small group of women, some of whom had a background in Neopaganism, gathered to perform a ritual for a friend who felt the need for a rite of passage into womanhood to complete the transition that had begun at puberty. That first ritual also proved to be a meaningful experience for the participants, who decided to continue meeting to explore goddess-centered worship and express their own developing sense of community. They began to meet each new moon and called themselves the Darkmoon Circle.

The group developed in stages but soon moved to a renovated carriage house in Berkeley, California, where they developed rituals to celebrate various events in women's lives, such as motherhood and the onset of menopause. In 1981 the Center for Non-Traditional Religion was opened to host various groups and activities, including the Darkmoon Circle. That same year, Diana Paxton authored the *Liturgy of the Lady*, which became the focus of a monthly open ritual for the public. In 1982 the first priestesses were consecrated. At about that same time, the circle joined the Covenant of the Goddess. In 1986 the center transformed into the Fellowship of the Spiral Path.

The Fellowship of the Spiral Path sees itself as a center of the Old Religion. The Old Religion includes the indigenous religions of tribal cultures from Africa to Europe and North America, which bear a close relationship to Hinduism and Shinto in the East. The fellowship views European and American Old Religionists as engaging in a process of reestablishing themselves after a millennia of disruption by Christianity.

Old Religionists believe that the purpose of life is to live in harmony with nature, and that creation is a continuum of consciousness from inanimate objects to the pantheons of gods and spiritual beings, which are all aspects of a single Divine principle. Since sacredness is in all things, no single form of deity can or should predominate. Old Religionists worship the Divine Energy as both male and female, Goddess and God. Life is essentially good, but evil results when natural processes are perverted or unbalanced. The moral life is based upon a reverence for all life, love and trust within the religious community, personal responsibility, respect for the free will of others, and an understanding that what is done to others will react upon the doer. Salvation is dependent upon one's own life-affirming decisions.

A respect for differences means that worship and leadership styles and forms will vary. Most traditions celebrate the rites of passage, and most acknowledge holidays marked by the astronomical and agricultural years, such as the solstices, the equinoxes, and the cross-quarter days halfway between the two.

In Berkeley, the fellowship sponsors several circles, a monthly celebration of the *Liturgy of the Lady*, and various outreach activities. There is also a fellowship center in Sacramento, California. Among the leading members of the fellowship is the popular fantasy novelist Marion Zimmer Bradley, many of whose novels reflect her own Neopagan beliefs.

Membership: Not reported.

Periodicals: Newsletter.

Sources:

Fellowship of the Spiral Path. www.thespiralpath.org.

Bradley, Marion Zimmer. *The Best of Marion Zimmer Bradley*. Chicago: Academy Chicago, 1985.

Feraferia

12318 Shady Ln, Nevada City, CA 95959-3255

Feraferia, one of the oldest Pagan groups in North America, derives from the Fellowship of Hesperides, founded by Fred Adams in 1957. As early as 1951, Adams had become involved in ritual magic and enactments of the Eleusinian mysteries, first studied at Stanford University and later at the University of Southern California. In 1956 Adams had a vision of the Goddess and became a staunch believer in the worship of her. By 1958 he had become fully paganized. He began to seek a purified paganism of the highly sacramental culture of Minoan Crete, and he believed that humankind could develop a utopian, paradisiac life on earth by basing its culture on horticulture. In 1959 he established an open-air temple in Sierra Madre.

Adams and Lady Svetlana met in 1963. Together, they delineated the foundations of Feraferia, which were in place by 1965. Feraferia was incorporated as a church in 1967. Svetlana and Fred met and conferred with Robert Graves, the author of *The White Goddess*, on the island of Majorca early in 1968. As the Pagan Movement developed, Adams became a significant leader as a poet and artist. His stylized presentations of the Goddess circulated widely through the movement, as did his calendars of archetypal ecosystems.

Feraferia is somewhat unique among Pagan groups in that it centers upon Kore, "the Maiden," rather than the Great Mother. Kore is also identified with Persephone in the Eleusinian mysteries, as well as with Aphrodite, the ruler of the Golden Age. Feraferia's Maiden Way includes an emphasis on earth mysteries; organic gardening; a reverence for all life, especially trees; a vegetarian diet; outside living; the realization that health, vitality, and rejuvenation are basic to spiritual growth; handicraft technology; the dissolution of coercive structures and the elimination of artificial conditions; natural safeguards against overpopulation; a maximum of free, creative play and erotic development in the tradition of refined and romantic love and devotion; the veneration of beauty, desire, and creativity; the affirmation of the divine mystery of sex as the central polarity of the cosmic process; and the ultimate fusion of the immortal soul with the transmuted body in the living landscape of paradise.

After being headquartered for many years in Southern California, Adams moved to Nevada City in Northern California in the early 1990s. In Nevada City, Adams's consort wife Svetlana conducts her versions of Feraferia ceremonies nine times a year. For many years, Adams published a newsletter, but it has been discontinued. Ten Feraferia texts were published as booklets in Holland in 2000 and 2001, with more to be published at some future time.

Membership: Feraferia reported 21 initiated members plus associates in 2002.

Sources:

Feraferia. www.phaedrus.dds.nl/fera.htm

Free Spirit Alliance

PO Box 94, Lambertville, NJ 08530-0094

The Free Spirit Alliance (FSA) is an association of Neopagan and Witchcraft groups that emphasize a shared belief in a pantheistic worldview. The alliance was founded in 1985. FSA member groups represent a wide variety of Pagan beliefs and practices, including traditional Wiccan traditions, non-Wiccan Pagans, and Druids. These groups accept a basic belief in the many deities of Paganism within the divine universe of nature. Most of the groups follow the eight festivals common to Paganism, and some meet biweekly (on the new and full moon) or monthly.

The alliance emphasizes the ethical standards for pantheist groups and has published a code of honor to which its members must ascribe. It asserts a belief in human freedom and the need to follow the Wiccan Rede ("An it harm none, do as ye will"). Members are admonished to consider their pledged word sacred, to respect the rights and freedoms of others, to respect all life on the planet, to seek to undo any harm done to another, and to value honesty. Each summer the FSA sponsors a Free Spirit Gathering, which is attended by approximately 700 people. It has other seasonal gatherings attended by 100–200 people.

Membership: The FSA has approximately 100 members and more than 1,500 "friends" on its local mailing list.

Sources:

Free Spirit Alliance. www.free-spirit.org.

Gardnerian Wicca

No central address.

Gerald B. Gardner (1884–1964) did more to revive modern Witchcraft than any single individual. With the assistance of a few others, including Doreen Valiente, he composed rituals that became the source of most rituals used by both Witches and Neopagans. Several members of his British covens (for example, Alexander Sanders and Sybil Leek) took copies of his rituals and published their own edited versions of them as the basis for a new form of Wicca. However, the single largest group of Wiccans are those who continue to use the rituals as finally developed by Gardner in the 1960s.

Gardnerian Wicca was brought to America in the 1960s. It came through several individuals who traveled to Great Britain for initiation in one of Gardner's covens. Most of these revised and rewrote the rituals upon their return. Such was not the case with Raymond Buckland (b. 1934) and his wife, Rosemary Buckland, who operated the Buckland Museum of Witchcraft and Magick on Long Island. Reared as good members of the Church of England, they began dabbling in occultism and were attracted to Gardner after settling in New York in the early 1960s. They corresponded with him and visited his home on the Isle of Man, where he operated a witchcraft museum. While there, the Bucklands went through a three-week crash program and were initiated in the second degree before they left. (The usual time between any of the three degrees of witchcraft is one year and a day.) Upon their return, they began to organize Gardnerian covens, which spread across the country. This growth was due in part to the widespread media coverage of the museum and the then unique religion espoused by the Bucklands.

Each Gardnerian coven is headed by a high priestess and a high priest. Without the former no ceremonies are held. Membership in the covens is primarily by couples, and the size of the coven is limited only by the space available in the nine-foot circle. New covens are usually formed by a witch's leaving a full-size coven and beginning a new one. The high priestess of the original coven becomes the "witch queen" of the new coven. Within Gardnerian covens there is a form of apostolic succession from Rosemary Buckland (who is no longer associated with the Gardnerian covens) through a lineage of witch queens to presently functioning priestesses.

Gardnerian witches worship in the nude, and by so doing have given to the craft a new word, "skyclad." The female witch does wear a necklace, a symbol of reincarnation. The high priest and priestess wear bracelets symbolic of rank, and the witch queen wears a crown and garter.

In 1973 the Bucklands, known in the craft as Robat and Lady Rowen, were divorced. They turned over the leadership of the Gardnerian covens to Judy Kneitel and her husband Tom Kneitel, known as Lady Theos and Phoenix; they published *Gardnerian Aspects* as a magazine within the *Green Egg*, but discontinued it with issue No. 63 (1974) in favor of an intracoven letter. *The Hidden Path*, begun by Lady Dierdre of the Coven of the Silver Trine in Louisville, Kentucky, continues as a semipublic periodical. Buckland developed an alternative Wicca system called Seax-Wica. On May 1, 1985, Judy Kneitel retired and turned over leadership to Roberta Faillace, known as Lady Rhiannon, and her partner Martin Fleischman, known as Theseus.

Membership: Membership in covens and numbers of people who consider themselves Gardnerian not reported.

Periodicals: *The Hidden Path*. c/o Windwalker, Box 934, Kenosha, WI 53141.

Sources:

Gardnerian Tradition. www.gardnerian.org/.

Proteus Coven. draknet.com/proteus/proteus.html.

Bracelin, J. L. *Gerald Gardner: Witch*. London: Octagon Press, 1960.

Gardner, Gerald B. *Witchcraft Today*. London: Karrolds, 1968.

Valiente, Doreen. *Natural Magic*. New York: St. Martins, 1975.

———. *Witchcraft for Tomorrow*. London: Robert Hale Limited, 1978.

A Witch. *The Devil's Prayerbook*. London: Mayflower, 1975.

The Georgian Church
1908 Verde St., Bakersfield, CA 93304

The Georgian Church—originally called the Church of Wicca of Bakersfield—was formed by George E. Patterson (d. 1984) in 1970. Patterson claimed to have been initiated in 1940 by a Celtic group. After World War II, he settled in California, and in the 1970s began to gather a coven. The group was eclectic, combining rituals from Gardnerian Wicca, Alexandrian Wicca, and other sources, and was termed "Georgian." In 1971 a charter was granted by the Universal Life Church, and Patterson obtained a doctor of divinity degree from the American Bible Institute.

As with most such groups, there is belief in the Gods and Goddesses, magick, the unity of life, and reincarnation. The group does not accept satanism, black

magicians, or groups organized only for sex. There are three degrees in Georgian Wicca. These degrees acknowledge attainment of knowledge and time devoted to the craft. The church publishes a periodical, noteworthy for its size, quality, and longevity. Jean M. Davis succeeded Patterson as president of the church.

Membership: Not reported, but in 1987 the *Georgian Newsletter* reported a circulation of 250 copies. By 1973, there were four affiliated covens in Southern California. By 1978 there were associated covens in Missouri, New York, and New Jersey. As of the mid-1980s, there are loosely affiliated covens (many of them led by priests and/or priestesses trained by Patterson) across the United States and in several foreign countries. According to the website there are covens found in British Columbia, California, Colorado, Florida, Maryland, Michigan, Oklahoma, Oregon, and Washington.

Periodicals: *Georgian Newsletter*.

Sources:

The Georgian Tradition. Melton's Encyclopedia of American Religions www.georgianwicca.com/index.htm.

Hawthorn Grove
Box 706, Monticello, NY 12701-0706

Hawthorn Grove is an independent congregation for witches, Druids, shamans, deep ecologists, and Neopagans. It was founded in 1990 and incorporated two years later. It serves people in the Upper Delaware and mid-Hudson river valleys. The grove is very eclectic in its beliefs and practices but it is united in the acceptance of the basic Pagan ethical principle, the Wiccan Rede, "An ye harm none, do what thou wilt." It also looks for inspiration to the "Charge to the Goddess," a passage from a modern sourcebook for Witchcraft, *Aradia: The Gospel of the Witches* (1899) by Charles Leland. It reads:

> Now when Aradia (the daughter of Diana) had been taught, taught to work all witchcraft, how to destroy the evil race (of oppressors), she (imparted to her pupils) and said unto him:
>
> When I shall have departed from this world, Whenever you have need of anything, Once in the month, and when the moon is full, Ye shall assemble in some desert place Or in a forest all together join To adore the potent spirit of your Queen My mother, great Diana. She who fain Learn all sorcery yet has not won Its deepest secrets, then my mother will Teach her, in truth, all things as yet unknown. And ye shall all be freed from slavery, And so ye shall be free in everything; And as a sign that ye are truly free, Ye shall be naked in your rites, both men And women also; this shall last until The last of your oppressors shall be dead.

In order to encourage its diversity, the Hawthorn Grove has remained organizationally independent of other Pagan groups. It is headed by a board of directors consisting of a Secretary, Pursewarden, and Summoner. There is no permanent designated High Priestess or Priest, and leadership in worship rotates among the members. There is a Council of Elders consisting of from 3 to 13 of the ordained clergy (elders). Elders are trained by the grove.

Membership: In 1995 the grove reported 50 members and 3 elders.

Periodicals: *The Hawthorn Spinner*.

Sources:

Hawthorn Grove. hawthorngrove.faithweb.com/toc.htm.

Leland, Charles G. *Aradia: The Gospel of the Witches*. 1899. Reprint, New York: Samuel Weiser, 1974.

Mental Science Institute
Current address not obtained for this edition.

Barney C. Taylor (known as Father Eli and Grandmaster Eli), the grand master for the United States of what is termed druidic witchcraft, was a descendant of

Thomas Hartley, a healer and herbalist who was burned at the stake for practicing witchcraft in England in the early 1550s. Others like Hartley fled persecution to settle in America in the mountain country of the Appalachians and the Ozarks, where Taylor grew up. The Mental Science Institute, founded in 1971, was designed to foster Taylor's brand of herbal magick. He traced his particular kind of witchcraft to the druid. It is also a robed tradition, in contrast to both the modern "naked ones" (i.e., the practitioners of Gardnerian Wicca), and the clothed ones who emphasize magick. The robed ones emphasize healing.

The membership of the Mental Science Institute is divided into covens of no more than twelve individuals, meeting under a wizard. Wizards in turn meet under a magi; the magis under a master magi; and the master magis under the grand master. Apprentices are those studying in order to join the group. There are three degrees in the craft: a first degree, a basic member; a second degree, a wise leader; and a third degree, the wise doctor.

Worship is conducted in regular esbats and the four grand sabbats. The institute is the most male-oriented of all the Wiccan groups and has a theology closely related to Christianity and to ritual magick. The universe is seen as a series of levels—celestial, terrestrial, and telestial. The celestial is divided into sublevels at the top of which is God the Father, followed by the Lord of Lights, archangels and angels. Man, animals, and plants are on the terrestrial level. At the lowest level, the telestial, are the mineral, chemical, and electrical elements and creative thought. Just as there is a Father, there is a Mother of all people.

In a concept very close to Mormonism, the institute teaches that God the Father was at one time a child. The children will, in like measure, become gods. Reincarnation is part of that process. A complete cycle lasts for approximately 142 years: from birth to death, a year in purgatory, 70 years to integrate the life experience, and a year waiting for rebirth.

Membership: Not reported.

Sources:

Mental Science Institute. www.geocities.com/Athens/4239/msi.html.

Eli [Taylor]. *The First Book of Wisdom*. Author, 1973.

————. *The Second Book of Wisdom*. N. p., n. d.

New, Reformed, Orthodox Order of the Golden Dawn

c/o *The Trine*, 48 Page St., San Francisco, CA 94102

The New, Reformed, Orthodox Order of the Golden Dawn (NROOGD) began in 1969 in the San Francisco, California, area when a group of friends assembled to help one of their number with a term project for a class on rituals. The original rituals were based on research in a variety of books by authors on witchcraft and magic such as Gerald B. Gardner and Margaret Murray and magical texts such as the *Greater Key of Solomon*. They decided to become a coven in late 1969, and by the early 1970s other covens had emerged, all governed by a Red Cord Council. During these years, NROOGD published a magazine, *The Trine*.

NROOGD disbanded as a formal order in May 1976, when the Red Cord Council decided that henceforth NROOGD would be a craft tradition rather than a general pagan religious society. It continued in this form, with covens in the San Francisco Bay area and along the West Coast. Because there is no longer any formal organization, it is unknown how many covens are practicing in the NROOGD tradition or where they are located. Over the years, a few thousand people have attended NROOGD events and many have incorporated NROOGD elements in their rituals.

The Bay Area covens hold biannual ingatherings for those belonging to the order. They hold rituals open to the Neopagan and craft communities, with responsibility rotating informally among them. Most of the eight sabbats are celebrated, and there is an annual September ritual based on the Eleusinian mysteries. Attendance ranges from 50 to 300. The esbats (held at the new and full moons) are closed, celebrated privately by individual covens and their invited guests. The rituals continue to evolve; sometimes old sabbat rituals are revised, sometimes completely new ones are written. The basic form of the esbat and many of the sabbat rituals are quite similar to the original ones written in 1968.

In July 2008 the NROOGD planned to celebrate its 40th anniversary with an ingathering at a retreat center north of Napa Valley.

Membership: Not reported.

Periodicals: *The Trine*.

Sources:

New Reformed Orthodox Order of the Golden Dawn. www.nroogd.org/.

Scott, Gini Graham. *Cult and Countercult*. Westport, CT: Greenwood Press, 1980.

New Wiccan Church International (NWC)

Box 162046, Sacramento, CA 95816

Established in 1973, the New Wiccan Church is an international association of individual members of British Traditional Wicca (Witchcraft). The NWC defines British Traditional Wicca as an initiatory Pagan Mystery faith, which has ancient roots that originated in the British Isles. The members of the NWC consist of an oath-bound priesthood, which differentiates the NWC from the popular Pagan/Wiccan movement that grew significantly in the late twentieth century.

MWC membership is open only to initiated witches of legal age who are in one or more of the following traditions: Kingstone, Silver Crescent, Daoine Coire, Majestic (all derived from Central Valley Wicca or CCW), Gardnerian, Alexandrian, Mohsian, and related traditions. The NWC limits itself to traditions that have similar structures and practices, some of which include a three-degree structure, cross-gender initiations, and the tenet that Wiccans are not permitted to charge money for initiating or teaching their religion. Wiccans also have an obligation to maintain the privacy of others who are initiates by not revealing the name, identity, or residence of another initiated witch without that individual's expressed permission. All members agree to observe and uphold the tenets and bylaws of the NWC, and all members are responsible for the common-sense application of the oaths of initiation that they took as members of their respective traditions.

The objectives of the New Wiccan Church are to preserve and sustain the Craft by: 1) Providing a communications and mutual aid network among members of British Traditional Wicca; 2) Providing avenues through which members may share teachings and other material, in a licit and honorable manner; 3) Allowing members to experience the different styles of practice that fall within the British Traditional Wicca; 4) Encouraging the teaching of British Traditional Wicca and aiding those who teach; 5) Preserving and maintaining the heritage of Wiccan traditions, and promoting study and research in all related fields; 6) Promoting and maintaining a high ethical standard within the Wiccan and Pagan community; and 7) Promoting mirth and reverence and joy in the activities of the members of the association.

As Wiccans, members acknowledge that all of creation stems from an unknowable Source, which is beyond human comprehension. Many members view this Source as both immanent and transcendent. Wiccans honor and worship the Old Gods of Nature: the Great Mother and her consort, the Horned God. Members also work with other additional deities as they see fit. Wiccans seek to experience and understand the cycles and tides of birth-life-death in their daily lives through a personal relationship and a direct connection with their Gods, their ancestors, and the local spirits of the land. They believe in the power of magic, and use both traditional and experimental techniques to achieve their personal goals as well as to help others in an ethical manner. Actual rites are confidential, but published accounts of Gardnerian or Alexandrian-derived rituals are similar. Teachings focus on the development of a personal relationship with Deity, and a keen awareness and attunement with the cycles of nature through ritual and daily life. Members use traditional Wiccan techniques to gain self-mastery and develop their skills as witches to help themselves and to help others. Experimental methods may be used, for their traditions provide them with a firm foundation on which to build and improvise.

The New Wiccan Church holds periodic meetings to discuss business and religious matters concerning the church and its members. Other events include various social gatherings, ritual events, and workshops. Some events are for members only, while others may be open by invitation. The church has a lending and research library of books available to members only.

The NWC works with other Pagan organizations such as Covenant of the Goddess. Various branches of the church have also been active in Pagan Bride Day and at various Pagan festivals. Educational materials about British Traditional Wicca area available at the NWC Web site or by mail.

Membership: Membership figures are confidential, but most members are in the western United States with some overseas.

Sources:

New Wiccan Church International. www.newwiccanchurch.com/.

Omphalos

Current address not obtained for this edition.

While Greek Neopagan groups were among the first such groups formed in the 1960s, Greek and Roman mythology have been a relatively minor theme in the developing Wiccan and Neopagan community, which has centered more on the ancient deities of western and northern Europe. Omphalos is a Neopagan organization established in the mid-1990s to bring together Pagans who find their inspiration and format in ancient Greek or Roman religion. It was formed by John Opsopaus, also known as Apollonius Omphalos.

At present, Omphalos has its primary existence on the Internet, where it has established a networking presence and a large group of informational links to publications, organizations, festivals, and relevant files on rituals, hymns, and other texts useful to Hellenic Neopagans. A major goal of Omphalos is providing contact information for Pagans living in the same geographic area, and a number of member homepages are listed on the Web site.

Membership: Not reported.

Sources:

The Stele: Home Page of the Omphalos. www.cs.utk.edu/~mclennan/OM.

Ordo Arcanorum Gradalis

c/o Ormus, PO Box 96, Clinton, IA 52732

The Ordo Arcanorum Gradalis (O.A.G.) is an eclectic fellowship drawing on Gnostic, Wiccan, and Arthurian themes. Members of the order seek wisdom (*gnosis*) and the enlightenment it brings. The roots of the church can be traced to ancient sites such as the caves at Liseaux, France, and Stonehenge, England, and it weaves a path through history to the Gothic cathedrals and Jewish Kabbalah to modern paganism. It is unique in its view of the legends of King Arthur, seen from both pagan and esoteric Christian perspectives, as serious teaching material relevant to worship, mysticism, and personal conduct. The heart of the Arthurian mythos is the Holy Grail, the focus of the order's spiritual quest. The grail is the orienting point that guides members through the complexities of the western mysteries.

The O.A.G. is a fellowship organized as a religious order, a union of assemblies and individuals, both lay and clerical, who gather for worship. Worship is centered on the Great Goddess and her consort, the God. The ritual cycle follows the seasons of the year with the eight major festivals common to Wiccans and the movements of the moon. The primary rite is the Grail Mass, also known as the Mass of the Goddess, in which the communion of bread and wine unites the worshipper with the Goddess. Participation in the mass is open to all, although the central mystery of the mass is reserved for the priests and priestesses.

The life of the order is summarized in its affirmation:

We embrace the primordial Unity of the Holy, and the eternal epiphany of the Ineffable, reflected in the revelation of Sophia and the Logos; through

Whom the ages were framed, the galaxies fashioned, and the world brought forth into being.

We adore the Mother of All Mysteries, Mistress of Magick and the Moon, crowned with the horns of Isis; and Her celestial Consort, the Lord of Light, clothed in the splendor of the Sun.

We worship the Great Goddess, Queen of Nature, adorned with the beauty of the Earth; and Her Son, the Dying and Rising God, Lord of the cycles of Life.

We affirm our reverence for the ancient rites, our respect for timeless Tradition, and our responsibility for the stewardship of the Sacred.

We proclaim our Quest for the Gnosis of the Numinous as a priesthood in the service of the Grail; seekers of the Spirit, Templars of the Truth.

So we have sworn, so shall it be.

The O.A.G. was originally organized in the late 1980s as the Tradition of Grail Quest Wicca. Rituals for the ordered are contained in the *Missale Mysteriorum*, a book published on the group's web site. The basic perspective of the order is contained in another book, *The Crafted Cup* (1994), authored by one of the group's founders, Rev. Shadwynn (Murray Johnston). Some of it is available on the web site, and a complete copy may be obtained from the order. It is required reading for all prospective members.

Membership: Not reported.

Sources:

Ordo Arcanorum Gradalis. www.geocities.com/Athens/Oracle/2310/Welcome.htm.

Plummer, John R. *The Many Paths of the Independent Sacramental Movement: A Study of Its Liturgy, Doctrine, and Leadership in America*. Dallas, TX: Newt Books, 2005.

Shadwynn. *The Crafted Cup: Ritual Mysteries of the Goddess and the Grail*. St Paul, MN: Llewellyn Publications, 1994.

Ossirian Temple Assembly

Current address not obtained for this edition.

The Ossirian Temple Assembly/Order of Osirus was founded in 1979 by Kara Apu, the Guardian-Chief of the Ossirian religion. The assembly is dedicated to the restoration of this ancient Egyptian religion, with the goal of creating a new age of harmony between deity, entity, and humanity. The religion is based upon the sacred law of *Mayet* (or *Maat*), which is carved upon the inner walls of pyramids and temple columns. The message of the religion was made available to the modern world through the instrument of the Rosetta Stone, which has allowed access to the ancient writings.

Ossirians believe in one eternally existing Creator God, Ra, who is identical to the same God recognized in all religions worldwide. Ra sent his message to humanity through the instrument of Lord Osiris, the same Son born in all ages to bring humanity back into fellowship with God. All who accept the Creator God become divine children of God, and all who seek to serve God receive his divine spirit, called Heru. Through Heru, who lives in the inner mind, each person can work toward the state of *Ka-djed*, a state of stability of mind and spirit. One must enter this state before entering the ultimate state of union with the Creator. Reincarnation affords additional opportunities to enter *Ka-djed*.

All people who worship the Creator and seek to follow *Mayet* (justice, truth, and cosmic order) will be acceptable to Ra. However, the Egyptian rites open the way of understanding the mysteries of God and applying the divine power to energize the inner mind. All people can become Ossirians.

Ossirians find meaning in the story of Osiris, who with Lady Isis ruled in ancient Egypt via *Mayet*. Osiris was killed by Set out of envy, and his body was cut up into 14 pieces. At Isis's imploring, Ra restored Osiris and made him Judge of all souls. Meanwhile, Isis had lost her throne and bore her son Horus in the marshes of the Nile. When Horus reached adulthood he fought and reclaimed the throne from Set, and he now rules with Isis at his side. Osiris, Isis, and Horus are a holy family serving as a contemporary model of harmony that will bring in a new age of peace and prosperity for body, mind, and spirit.

Members of the Ossirian religion agree to maintain a daily adoration of the Creator, share the concept of living according to *Mayet*, sacrifice a portion of their earnings to support the temple, and observe the teachings and rituals of the temple. Individuals wishing to join first become *shenit* (seekers) and then *shemsu* (full members). *Shemsu* may become either scribes of the temple or priests. The priesthood has three degrees, and there is also a high priesthood of four degrees. The temple/order is headed by a high council (consisting of scribes and priests) and a great council (consisting of some members, scribes, and priests).

Major festivals commemorate the death of Lord Osiris (November 13), his resurrection (December 26), the birth of Horus (December 25), the solstice of Ra (December 21), and Lady Isis's blessing of the sea (March 5). The temple also holds regular services at the full and new moons.

Membership: In 1985 there were 108 members.

Educational Facilities:

Ossirian Theological College Seminary

Periodicals: *New Horizons.*

Our Lady of Enchantment, Church of the Old Religion

39 Amherst St., PO Box 1366, Nashua, NH 03061

Our Lady of Enchantment, Church of the Old Religion was founded in 1978 in Danville, California, by Lady Sabrina. In 1980 the church and school moved to New Bern, North Carolina, and in 1982 it moved to the New England area. Our Lady of Enchantment offers public classes, regular worship services, and degree-training programs for priesthood and ministerial credentials. Our Lady of Enhantment is recognized by both the state of New Hampshire and the federal government as a legally established church and educational institution with nonprofit status.

Our Lady of Enchantment teaches various forms of Wicca, which it describes as not exclusively a religion, but rather as a teaching derived from a time when religion, art, science, and magic were part of an inclusive whole. Integral to Wicca is the practice of magic, a system of working with the powers of nature in order to bring about change and manifest desire.

The church is centered around a Wiccan Metaphysical Center, which houses the seminary, administrative offices, library, chapel, and a gift shop. Both church members and seekers gather for regular Friday night church services and campus classes. They also gather for a variety of other activities, mostly presided over by Lady Sabrina.

Membership: In 1997 Our Lady of Enchantment reported more than 25,000 students in more than 30 different countries and republics.

Periodicals: *Outer Court Communications.*

Sabaean Religious Order

Current address not obtained for this edition.

The Sabaean Religious Order is a continuation of an Afro-Mediterranean religion that dates back to ancient Sumer, Babylon, and Egypt in prehistoric times. Frederic M. de Arechaga (now Odun) and his mother opened the Sabaean Center and the Temple of Amn in Chicago in the late 1960s. The center's purpose is to study and research Sabaeanism, as well as to celebrate its festivals and rites as a means of preserving it. This was the first Sabaean temple to be opened since the Temple of the Moon, in the city of Harran, was closed in the sixth century by the reigning Islamic leaders.

Saba is both the name of an ancient city and an ancient Egyptian word found in hieroglyphics and in Arabic. The Arabic word *Sabaa* means "a star, rising or coming forth." The Egyptian hieroglyph means either "star" or "to emanate from a center point of light," like a star.

The Sabaeans believe in the concept of *Amn*, an idea that can be either plural or singular and implies the "hidden." Therefore, "divinity" to a Sabaean is both gender-

less and awesome. The religion is described as "henotheistic"—or rather, "kathenotheistic"—which is the belief in a "personal god without the exclusion of any other, sometimes emphasizing one supreme at a time without denying the rest."

In symbolic or poetic imagery, Amn is referred to in the feminine and in four different colors. It is also associated with the four races of humanity, the seasonal stations, and the major colors of the spectrum. Thus, in the winter Amn is the White goddess; in the spring, the Blue goddess; in the summer, the Yellow goddess; and in the fall, the Red goddess. There are two "new year's days" acknowledged by Sabaeans: the autumnal equinox, which is the pontifical beginning, and the vernal equinox, which is a secular celebration. Following the ancient Roman tradition, the common New Year's Day (January 1) is also celebrated, though not as the beginning of a new year, but rather as the ending of the Saturnalia that starts December 17 and continues through midnight, December 31.

Beside the main body of "four" symbols, there is also the image of the warriors, a trinity headed by the "trickster," the two-faced, Janus-like god who is the means of communication between gods and men, whose celebration always begins the year. The festival of this god is usually around January 6 during the perihelion of the Earth, when the planet is closest to the Sun.

Astronomy and astrology are very important to the Sabaean system, not so much as divinatory tools but as relevant positions. Sabaean temples and shrines are usually sidereal oriented, particularly with the rising and passing of the sun and the moon, but sometimes with other stars as well. The precession of the equinoxes is observed and the zodiacal calculations are corrected to this phenomena with true sidereal composition.

Like some other ancient religions, Sabaeanism still observes the ritual of animal sacrifice that originally served to supply food for a celebration, making the food ritually pure. But other offerings of fruits, vegetables, and grains are made to Amn, as well as incense and flowers, which are more frequently given.

Marriages are called "eclipses" and are designed to last for a specific period of time, at the end of which the couple can either re-eclipse or part ways. The standard marriage contract is considered a partnership of possessions, and it is imperative to sign a contract at an eclipse. However, if the couple part at the end of their eclipse, this contract must be fulfilled through courts of law.

Sabaeanism is inherently matriarchal. However, unlike its predecessors, it primarily identifies with brothers and sisters, as they are truly of the same blood. The mother is considered the matrix, or source, and is certainly honored for that function. However, it is easy to see who the mother of an individual is, but it is very difficult to prove who the father is.

The Sabaean Religious Order is headquartered is in Chicago, where the Temple of Amn is located. The group has run an occult store, El Sabarum, since 1968. For several years the group has also published a periodical, *Sabaean Chronicles*, which superseded previous periodicals titled *Iris* and *Janus*. The *Sabaean Chronicles* is usually printed on a quarterly basis, relative to the passing of the seasons.

The Sabaean Religious Order occasionally writes and produces pagan mystery plays, and the order sponsors and trains a troupe of dancers, called "hierodules" (temple servants), who perform different dances and pantomimes that use ancient Egyptian dance movements. There is also a small group of musicians that perform on drums, bata and other instruments at festivals.

Membership: Not reported.

Periodicals: *Sabean Chronicles.*

Sources:

Sabaean Religious Order. www.sabaean.org/index.htm.

Seax-Wica

PO Box 892, Wooster, OH 44691-0892

After his divorce in 1973, Raymond Buckland moved to New Hampshire, remarried, and emerged as the founder and spokesperson (along with his second wife, Joan

Buckland) of a new tradition, Seax-Wica. Seax-Wica differs from other Wicca groups in that it claims no relation to previously existing covens. A Saxon background has been adopted as an alternative to the Gardnerian Wicca tradition, with all new rituals written by Buckland. (Buckland and his first wife, Rosemary Buckland, brought Gardnerian Witchcraft to America in the early 1960s.) Woden and Freya are the names chosen for the male and female deities of Seax-Wica.

Seax-Wica covens are headed by a high priest and priestess, who are chosen annually by a vote of the coven, thus precluding any power plays or ego trips by the leadership. Members, including priests, are termed *Ceorl* before initiation and *Gesith* afterward. Those outside the craft are termed *Theow*. There is only one degree of initiation. The Book of Shadows, the traditional book of rituals, is called *The Tree*.

Seax-Wica differs from other groups in several ways apart from its new traditions. For example, the male deity and the high priest are raised to a level of equality with their female counterparts in Seax-Wica. In addition, ritual scourging and binding have no part in the rites. Worship is either skyclad or in a short simple tunic, and There is no sexual activity in the rituals. Finally, Seax-Wica accepts self-initiation and solitary practice, in addition to coven practice.

By 1974 autonomous covens had been established in New York, New Jersey, and Massachusetts. A decade later there were covens in most states and several foreign countries including Russia, South Africa, Great Britain, Australia, and New Zealand. Facilitating the rapid spread of Seax-Wica was a home study course in Saxon Witchcraft, which was written by Buckland. *Seax-Wica Voys* was published for several years as the official journal.

Membership: In 1992 Seax-Wica reported approximately 5,000 members in the United States, with an additional 2,000 members in foreign countries.

Sources:

Seax-Wica. www.seaxtradusa.org.

Buchland, Tara. *Beauty Secrets of the Ancient Egyptians*. Scottsville, VA: Taray Publications, 1982.

Buckland, Raymond. *The Tree*. New York: Samuel Weiser, 1974.

————. *Practical Color Magick*. St. Paul, MN: Llewellyn Publications, 1983.

————. *Scottish Witchcraft: The History and Magick of the Picts*. St. Paul, MN: Llewellyn Publications, 1991.

————. *Buckland's Complete Book of Witchcraft*. 2nd ed. St. Paul, MN: Llewellyn Publications, 2002.

————. *Buckland's Book of Saxon Witchcraft*. York Beach, ME: Red Wheel/Weiser, 2005.

SM Church

c/o SMC Sanctuary, PO Box 1335, El Cerrito, CA 94530

The SM Church emerged in the mid-1970s in Berkeley, California, among people who defined themselves as being interested in sadism and masochism and who also had come to believe in the ancient historical practices of Goddess worship (which had appeared in the previous decade throughout the San Francisco Bay area). Discussions of the SM experience led to questions of spiritual meaning associated with intense SM fantasy, beyond simple sexual gratification. Early positive explorations led to the establishment of the Temple of the Goddess of the SM Church.

The SM Church opposes the male father image that has dominated Western religion and encourages members to focus on the feminine aspects of God, which it seeks to uncover in ongoing research into periods and cultures that emphasized Goddess worship. The church differs from many other Neopagan groups in that it believes in a powerful female deity, equivalent to the male monotheistic God. The church is feminist in orientation and from the beginning excluded male dominant–female submissive patterns from its organization. It allows both homosexual and heterosexual patterns of female dominance within the church's philosophy.

The church believes that Western culture is undergoing great transition: society could collapse, and in that event females would have to take control. The church plans for that possibility.

Ritual life, initially adopted from other Neopagan group patterns, includes a unique emphasis on the use of controlled pain and mortification experiences as a sacrament of penance. On occasion, such rituals are designed to allow both males and females to experience the extremes of female dominance fantasies, though the church denies that female rule in the envisioned postmodern society would be vindictively harsh. Further, the sacramental atmosphere of the rituals attempts to separate them from any identification with commercialized exploitation of SM practices.

The church published a set of purposes that includes the following: the purchase and/or construction of church facilities; the continuance of the seminary, which trains women for the priesthood; the development of ordered communities as models of a matriarchal society; and assistance in improving the image of the SM community (through various charity projects).

Membership: Not reported.

Sources:

Budd, Russell. "Interview: The SM Organizations of San Francisco." *Woman/Slave* no. 14 (October–December 1982): 30–37.

Green, Gerald, and Caroline Green. *SM, the Last Taboo*. New York: Ballantine Books, 1974.

Scott, Geni Graham. *Erotic Power: An Exploration of Dominance and Submissions*. Secaucus, NJ: Citadel Press, 1983.

Temple of Isis

c/o Crow Haven Corner, 125 Essex St., Salem, MA 01970

The Temple of Isis is a Wiccan center founded in 1988 by Laurie Cabot (b. 1933), who became one of the more famous practitioners of Witchcraft in America when Governor Michael Dukakis of Massachusetts named her the "Official Witch of Salem" in 1977. She was introduced to Witchcraft in high school in Boston by a teacher who revealed herself as a witch. According to her own story, she was initiated in 1949, at the age of 16, but it was not until 1965 that she decided to live totally as a witch. Since that time she has dressed in black, and worn a pentacle (a five-pointed star) and heavy black eye makeup. A short time later, at the suggestion of a friend, she moved to Salem.

In Salem she began to teach a class called Witchcraft as a Science in local adult education programs. She also started to work as a psychic and tarot card reader. She opened The Witch Shop, which was soon succeeded by Crow Haven Corner, a book and supply house and teaching center. This shop became her center of activity in the 1970s. The Witchcraft as a Science classes were still being taught in 2008, with an emphasis on psychic development and elementary magic. In the advanced class, students are introduced to ritual.

Cabot has also added a class called The Religion of Witchcraft, in which students are prepared for initiation into the Temple of Isis. Cabot was ordained by the National Alliance of Pantheists, which also officially chartered the temple. The temple centers its teaching upon an understanding of a basic creative force underlying and permeating the universe, rather than the Goddess and God of Gardnerian Wicca.

Cabot is also the founder of the Witches League for Public Awareness and Project Witches Protection, activist groups that fights for the civil rights of Wiccans and increases public awareness of Witchcraft. The league was founded in 1986 as a forum to protest the film version of John Updike's novel *The Witches of Eastwick*, which Cabot felt misrepresented Witchcraft to the general public.

Membership: Not reported.

Sources:

About Laurie. www.lauriecabot.com/About_Laurie.html.

Cabot, Laurie, with Tom Cowan. *Power of the Witch*. New York: Delacorte Press, 1989.

Triskellion

Current address not obtained for this edition.

Triskellion is a traditionalist Wicca group, in the Gardnerian and Alexandrian traditions. It has incorporated elements of ritual magic, which are placed in the service of Wiccan theology. The divine energy is mediated by three principles: the Masculine (god), the Feminine (the goddess) and the Collective (the community). Ultimately, all three principles merge into one and serve the growth of sentient beings. They operate together, with ritual duties being passed through the group as different skills are needed. Triskellion rituals are based upon a cooperation between coven members, the Gods and Goddesses, and the particular energies raised in each ritual.

Triskellion sees itself as a second-genesis fertility religion. First-genesis fertility religions invoked divine energies for fecundity on the physical plane. Having no need of large families, Triskellion members leave the energies called forth on the astral plane and then draw upon them as needed for various creative activities.

Triskellion is located in Minneapolis, Minnesota, and offers a 29-week course in basic Wicca training, which may be followed by a 29-week course in ritual. The group is active in the Heartland Spiritual Alliance, a cooperative Wicca and Pagan fellowship in Kansas City, Missouri.

Membership: Not reported.

Sources:

Triskellion. www.usfamily.net/web/triskellion1/index.html.

Venusian Church

Box 95, Redmond, WA 98073-0905

The Venusian Church was formed in 1975 by Ron Petersen, a Seattle businessman, and chartered the following year by the Universal Life Church. During the 1960s and early 1970s Petersen, a former member of the Seventh-Day Adventist Church, followed a spiritual pilgrimage that centered on the release of sexual feelings repressed by the strict sexual code under which he was raised. He found assistance within the human potential movement and became an advocate of helping others who wished to confront their sexual feelings. Meanwhile, he had also become a professional pornographer.

Petersen gathered around him a group of interested people, including several sex therapists and human potential counselors, and began to explore the realm of sex and sexual experience in releasing human creativity and opening the realm of the spiritual. For a short while, the church operated a Temple of Venus in downtown Seattle that featured pornographic films and sexually explicit presentations that attempted to communicate the church's attitude about open sexuality to the general public. In 1977 a retreat center, Camp Armac, was opened and became the focus of church activities. A variety of seminars, workshops, and sexual experimentation was condoned and encouraged.

The leaders of the church resisted any attempts to systematically build a belief system or pattern of worship, and the life of the group slowly emerged out of the spontaneous experiences of various gatherings of the members. First came the worship of nature in the form of the Goddess and the acknowledgment of Her at communal feasts and in the celebration of the solar equinox and solstice. Then in 1979 church members discovered the preexisting Neopagan movement. Having found Neopaganism a larger movement that already possessed a complete religious system toward which the Venusian Church seemed to be heading, the church began to absorb both thought and practices from their new acquaintants, especially from the Church of All Worlds. In 1979 Camp Armac closed, and for several years the church conducted its programs in the homes of members. In 1981 the church purchased a large tract of land near Redmond, Washington. A former warehouse was converted into a church center named the Longhouse, and a stonehenge was erected for outdoor rituals.

Because of its strong opinion that sex was divine, the church began to provide public events in Seattle's First Avenue pornography district. The programs, some of which featured nudity and overt sex acts, placed the church in the center of a storm of controversy. Several members were arrested and a lengthy but futile battle with the Internal Revenue Service ensued. As a result, the facilities in Seattle were closed and all activity was restricted to members and their guests only. Later, the church sponsored workshops and seminars for its members and the public emphasizing personal growth and the aspects of consciousness that expand the wholeness of humanity. These programs were also offered to inmates in local penitentiaries and to several sex-offender programs.

The Venusian church describes its theology as centered on a unique sacred space technology, meaning it is a "spatial" system rather than a "conceptual" one. The church's focus is on achievement rather than attempting or trying to create sacred space to be experienced rather than sacred beliefs to which assent is given. Essential to the experience of this sacred place is both inner and outer freedom. The individual's divinity is experienced only in an environment where people have the freedom and the opportunity to be whole and complete. The presence of such an environment would make the experience of a Venusian Paradise possible.

The church has as its immediate concern several steps that will allow for the emergence of the Venusian Paradise. It attempts to realign members' attitudes toward their own sexuality so as to undo the damage that society and religion have caused by their repressive opinions and rules. This realignment is accompanied by efforts aimed at healing the individual's damaged spirit. The church also works to remove any present outside interference from either church or state with the member's religious freedom.

To implement its goals, the church launched a program called "Paradise Now" through the Internet, which according to the church has become a physical reality beyond simply a cybercommunity. Paradise Now presents a simulated version of a visit to the Isle of Eros. The Internet version of the Isle of Eros has become the basis for a correspondence curriculum called the "Apotheosis Course." Members are taken through the steps of preparation for entry into the Venusian Paradise under the leadership of a priest or priestess as a guide. The individual is led through several steps of purification, deconditioning, and pleasuring as a prelude to their induction into the spiritual/erotic arts (presented as the "Sacred Pleasures Course"); introduced to Venusian technology; and given knowledge on maintaining legal rights and living the spiritual life free of government interference.

Through the 1980s and 1990s, the church kept a low profile and limited its activities primarily to its members. However, the church developed greater visibility by means of the Internet.

Membership: Not reported.

Remarks: In the mid-1980s the church failed to reclaim its tax-exempt status; members who had contributed had their deductions disavowed. The resulting financial reverses greatly hindered the progress of the fragile group.

In January 1997 the Church of Ecstasy merged into the Venusian Church. The Church of Ecstasy was founded by its high priest, Rev. Michael, out of a vision he had experienced on June 27, 1992, on the beach in San Francisco. After having consumed a brownie laced with ganja (marijuana), he fell into a mystical oneness with the Earth and Universe and heard a voice within him say, "Cannabis is the sacrament, and your body is the temple." He interpreted his vision as a spiritual directive to become an advocate of sensually based spirituality through the sacraments of cannabis and nudism. He summarized the beliefs of the new Church of Ecstasy in statements affirming that nudity is a form of meditative yoga that assists in sensitizing people to their environment, that Nature is the highest Power and that humans should live in harmony with it; that the right to expand spiritual consciousness is limited only by the violation of the rights of others; that the primary goal of the spiritual path is the development of sensitivity, kindness, and love toward others; and that members celebrate the vast diversity of human form, culture, and experience. The church existed as a network of like-minded individuals who accepted its basic spiritual perspective and were tied together by *Ekstasis*, the church's periodical.

858

After leading the church for several years, Rev. Michael concluded that he lacked the resources to properly administer it and promote its vision. He took the lead in guiding the members of the Church of Ecstasy into the larger, better-organized Venusian Church, in which he became an active leader.

Sources:

Venusian Church. www.venusianchurch.us/.

Wiccan Church of Canada

c/o The Occult Shop, 109 Vaughan Rd., Toronto, ON, Canada M6C 2L9

The Wiccan Church of Canada is a Neopagan Witchcraft group incorporated in 1979 by High Priestess Tamara James and High Priest Richard F. James. They had their first contacts with Neopaganism in 1977 in California. In 1979 they moved to Toronto, where they founded the Wiccan Church and opened an occult store catering to witches and pagans. With the expansion of their network, in 1983 they organized the area's first Pagan festival. The following year, the first of several covens formed within the church.

The church believes that the universe is self-aware; portions of self-awareness within the universe have been differentiated and are properly designated gods. The number of gods is unknowable, since self awareness is without gender, and deity may be personified as male or female. There are greater and lesser orders; thus one may speak of the gods and goddesses and also of angels, nymphs, fairies, and spirits.

The Wiccan Church espouses the idea that much about the universe is unknowable. We are ignorant ultimately of the origin of the universe, life after death, or the mechanics of miracles and prayer. In the face of such ignorance, the church asserts that religious expressions are purely subjective. Tolerance and nonjudgmental attitudes should hold sway when approaching another's religious life. Awareness is also amoral. Morality is a human creation, and society has the right to assert itself and legislate so as to be protected from violence and outside forces. Among the things that are knowable is that human life is interrelated and linked by karmic ties. Such ties may carry into the future.

The church follows the eight annual festivals common to witches and pagans and also normally gathers on the new and full moon every two weeks. It has developed a full set of rituals to mark the rites of passage from wiccaning (the naming and blessing of a child), to handfasting (marriage), and passing the veil (funeral). They also mark the coming of age (physical maturity) of men and women, bless pregnancies at each trimester, and hold handpartings for couples who are separating.

The church is led by its priesthood council, which includes all of the church's priests and priestesses. The council members lead ritual, train new members, and set qualifications for the priesthood.

Membership: Not reported.

Sources:

Wiccan Church of Canada. www.wcc.on.ca/index.html.

James, Richard. *The WIC-CAN Handbook*. Toronto: Wiccan Church of Canada, 1987.

Marron, Kevin. *Witches, Pagans, and Magic in the New Age*. Toronto: Seal Books, 1989.

❧ Druid Neopaganism

Henge of Keltria

2350 Spring Rd. PMB-140, Smyrna, GA 30080-2630

The Henge of Keltria was established in 1987 (incorporated in 1995) by cofounders Sable Taylor and Tony Taylor, both former members of the Ar nDraiocht Fein (ADF). Keltrian Druidism is a spiritual path that reveres the nature spirits, honors the ancestors, and worships the ancient Irish deities. The Henge of Keltria provides information, training, and networking to those who practice or who are interested

in Keltrian Druidism, Druidism in general, and the evolution of mind, body, and spirit through an Irish Celtic context.

Special emphasis is placed on spiritual development fostered through study and practice of the Druidic arts and Celtic magick. Through training, networking, resource material, ritual participation, and meaningful communication, the group aims to provide a religious and spiritual framework through which people may reach their full potential.

Affiliated local groups are called groves. Each grove is free to compose and perform ritual and magick geared to its own particular focus, provided such work remains compatible with the beliefs, ethics, and ritual and structural framework of the Henge.

Members progress through three grades of initiation called rings, a symbolic name derived from the rings of a tree; the ring system measures the growth of its participants. The three rings are named for sacred trees: the Ring of the Birch, the Ring of the Yew, and the Ring of the Oak. Within the highest ring, the Oak, there are three tiers—Hawthorn, Rowan, and Mistletoe. Advancements are based on time, knowledge, and service to either a local grove or the Henge. Special provisions are made for those transferring from other Neopagan paths, so that those with several years of training and experience do not need to begin at the bottom.

Membership: In 2008 the Henge of Keltria reported 250 members. Groves are found in Georgia and New York and recognized study groups in California, Louisiana, New York, and Wisconsin.

Periodicals: *Keltria: Journal of Druidism and Celtic Magic* • *Henge Happenings*

Sources:

The Henge of Keltria. www.keltria.org/index.html.

The Henge: An Introduction to Keltrian Druidism and the Henge of Keltria. Smyrna, GA: The Henge of Keltria, 2004.

Hopman, Ellen Evert, and Lawrence Bond. *People of the Earth: New Pagans Speak Out*. Rochester, VT: Destiny Books, 1996.

IMBAS

PO Box 1215, Montague, NJ 07827-0215

IMBAS (an Irish word meaning "poetic inspiration" and pronounced "im-bus") is a Druid Neopagan group founded in the mid-1990s. It promotes what it terms "Celtic Reconstructionist Paganism" and the cultural heritage of the Celtic peoples. Celtic Reconstructionist Paganism is grounded in folk tradition, mythological texts, and the archaeological and historical records of the Celtic people, who include the modern peoples of Alba (Scotland), Breizh (Brittany), Cymru (Wales), E'ire (Ireland), Kernow (Cornwall), and Mannin (Isle of Man). IMBUS focuses on the home, the family, and the community or tribe in honoring the land, the ancestors, and the traditional Celtic gods and goddesses. Though Celtic in emphasis, IMBAS is open to people of all ethnic backgrounds.

In reconstructing the Celtic tradition, IMBAS members show a deep reverence for the pre-Christian Celtic deities. They attempt to make contact with both the ancestors and the land spirits, which in a modern context assumes a concern for family and a deep environmental awareness. Members are also students of history and strive to be as historically (and mythologically) accurate as the evidence allows. Gaps in the evidence often make it necessary to create something new, however. These new realities should nevertheless be as consistent as possible with what is known about the Iron Age Celts and their legacy. Thus, IMBAS represents a balanced approach to understanding early Celtic religion, relying on both sound scholarship and poetic inspiration, but without mistaking one for the other.

At the same time, IMBAS has distanced itself from ceremonial magick (and modern traditions influenced by it, especially Wicca), romantic Revival Druidism (that is, anything inspired by Iolo Morganwg or the Druidic movements of the eighteenth and nineteenth centuries), and eclecticism (the combining of early Celtic religion with other cultural traditions).

IMBAS publishes a quarterly journal and other material, charters local IMBAS groups, provides a training program for prospective Seanch i (traditional lore keepers), and attempts to provide the public with accurate information about Celtic culture and Celtic Reconstructionist Paganism.

Membership: Not reported.

Periodicals: *An Trbhs Mhr: The IMBAS Journal of Celtic Reconstructionism* (not currently being published).

Sources:

IMBAS. www.imbas.org.

Reformed Druids of North America (RDNA)

c/o Michael James Scharding, PO Box 353, Elmore, OH 43416-0353

The Reformed Druids of North America was formed in 1963 by a group of students at Carleton College in Northfield, Minnesota, as a protest against compulsory chapel attendance. In a conversation among David Fisher, Howard Cherniack, and Norman Nelson, the idea emerged to form a Druidic group involving no bloody sacrifices. If students were denied credit for attending its services, then they would claim religious persecution; if they received credit, the whole project would be revealed as a hoax, thus ridiculing the requirement. The requirement was dropped in the summer of 1964, and the Reformed Druids quickly claimed victory. The group decided that, since it benefited from the spiritual inquiry and enjoyed the practice of rituals, it would continue.

The group outlined two basic tenets of belief: 1) The object of the search for religious truth, which is a universal and a never-ending search, may be found through the Earth Mother, which is Nature, but this is one way, yea, one way among many. 2) And great is the importance, which is of a spiritual importance, of Nature, which is the Earth Mother, for it is one of the objects of Creation, and with it we do live, yea, even as we do struggle through life as we come face to face with it. The group, concluding that most Druids would not remember this, simplified the tenets to: 1) Nature is good. 2) Likewise, Nature is good.

The Reformed Druids came up with rituals that bore a resemblance to the Episcopal service, in addition to materials in anthropological literature, such as *The Golden Bough*, by Sir James Fraser. They built a fire-burning altar on nearby Monument Hill, where the first Protestant service in Minnesota had been held. Though frequently destroyed, the altar was constantly replaced, proving to be an inspiration to future Druids whenever persecuted. Later, prominent immovable boulders were used. Members often wore white robes made from bedsheets with various colored ribbons of office. They drew inspirational readings and concepts from the texts of all the world's religions, with a strong emphasis on Oriental and Celtic sources. The passing of the waters-of-life is a symbol of oneness with nature and each other. The eight major festival days are Samhain (Nov. 1), Mid-Winter, Oimelc (Feb. 1), Spring Equinox, Beltane (May 1), Mid-Summer, Lughnasadh (Aug. 1), and Fall Equinox. Most groves, or divisions of the Druids, retained the Celtic/Druidic gods and goddesses to help focus attention on nature; some groves used other pantheons or called the simple spirit of the Earth.

Autonomous groves are headed by an Arch-Druid, a Preceptor (for business matters), and a Server who assists the Arch-Druid. Three orders of priesthood are recognized, but the majority of members do not enter them. The RDNA is not a scripture-based religion, rather deriving wisdom from experience and inspiration. Many in the group refuse to acknowledge it as a religion, preferring to call it a philosophical form of inquiry. About half of even the most active members eventually join mainstream religious movements, since the lessons of Reformed Druidism are often seen as a catalyst to inquiry and compatible with nearly all faiths.

In the mid-1970s leadership of the Druid movement passed to Isaac Bonewits, who had made national headlines when he graduated from the University of California at Berkeley with a degree in magick. Many members of various groves were active protesters against the draft, which was seen as a target similar to the

chapel requirement of the Founding Days, and other prominent issues. Also during the mid-1970s a debate arose over whether the RDNA was part of the Neopagan movements of California that had blossomed early in the decade. In the resulting schism, Bonewits formed the New Reformed Druids of North America (NRDNA), which was amenable to Neopaganism; a further schism led to the formation of the Schismatic Druids of North America (SDNA), which was exclusively Neopagan.

After several years of publishing the *Pentalpha* (a national Druid periodical), trying to promote Druidism, and research into Indo-European religious origins, Bonewits formed a new organization called Ar nDraiocht Fein (ADF) (Our Own Druidism) in 1983. ADF was famous for a broad Indo-European source of inspiration, seminary training, intensive research into liturgical formation, church tax-status, and strong organization, and soon became one of the largest Neopagan groups in the country. In 1986 some members of ADF rebelled and formed the Henge of Keltria, based in Minneapolis, focusing on Celtic religion and more relaxed training methods (see separate entry). The bulk of Druids in America belong to one of these four members of the family of American Druism. Their only major rival in North America is the British organization, Order of Bards Ovates and Druids (OBOD).

During the 1990s, owing to easier communication and dissemination of materials through the Internet, grove formation surged. In addition to the four remaining groves of 1991, thirty-odd new groves were operating in 2002 on the West and East Coasts and in the Midwest, as well as in Japan and Canada. However, a majority of solitary members live apart from groves. Therefore, what happens in the groves should perhaps be seen as the exception to what is standard in the RDNA.

Membership: Not reported.

Periodicals: *Druid Missal-any.*

Sources:

"A Psuedo-Official Homepage of the Reformed Druids of North America." orgs.carleton.edu/druids/.

Bonewits, P. E. Isaac. *Authentic Thaumaturgy*. Albany, CA: The CHAOSium, 1978.

———. *Real Magic*. New York: Coward, McCann & Geoghegan, 1971.

The Druid Chronicles (Evolved). Berkeley, CA: Berkeley Drunemetom Press, 1976.

✿ Norse Heathensim

Asatru Alliance

PO Box 961, Payson, AZ 85547

One of the groups to emerge from the disbanding of the Asatru Free Assembly in 1987 was the Asatru Alliance, which followed the assembly in its basic teachings and in being a revived form of the ancient religion of the Northern European peoples. It formed as a free association of local Asatru groups called kindreds. The alliance promotes the growth of the faith on the national and regional levels by sponsoring meetings and publishing materials. The alliance is headed by the Allthing, its representative legislative body to which all the kindred send a delegate.

Membership: Not reported.

Periodicals: *Vor Tru.*

Sources:

Asatru Alliance. www.asatru.org.

Asatru Folk Assembly

PO Box 445, Nevada City, CA 95959

The Asatru Folk Assembly is one of several groups that emerged following the disbanding of the Asatru Free Assembly in 1987. Stephen A. McNallen, who had founded the original Viking Brotherhood that evolved into the Asatru Free Assembly, expressed his desire to step down as leader of the Asatru movement in

North America and bring the Asatru Free Assembly to an end rather than pass its corporate structure on to others. In the wake of that decision, a spectrum of Asatru groups emerged. In 1994, McNallen decided to return to an active leadership role in the Asatru movement, and he founded the Asatru Folk Assembly. He had previously, in 1992, begun to issue *The Runestone*, the periodical that had previously served the Asatru Free Assembly.

The Asatru Folk Assembly continues the beliefs and practices of the former AFA with its acknowledgment of the ancient Norse deities. Local groups have been organized and several special interest groups (guilds) have emerged. The Warrior Guild issues a periodical, *Wolf Age*.

An issue plaguing the Asatru community, arising from criticism of the group's ethnic basis in the peoples of northern Europe, has been the charge of racism. McNallen has strongly refuted the charge. He notes on the assembly's website, "We are not racists (unless being of European heritage and not hating yourself is racist). We are opposed to racial hatred and intimidation, regardless of who practices it. We salute honorable men and women of all racial, ethnic, and religious groups. The AFA sympathizes with the efforts of all cultural and racial groups to maintain their identity and promote their legitimate interests. We are opposed to all forms of totalitarianism, of the left and the right alike."

Membership: Not reported. Membership is estimated to be in the low hundreds.

Periodicals: *The Runestone* • *Bearclaw* • *Wolf Age*.

Sources:

Asatru Folk Assembly. www.runestone.org/home.html.

McNallen, Stephen A. *Rituals of Asatru*. 3 vols. Breckenridge, TX: Asatru Free Assembly, 1985.

The Runestone. www.runestone.org/articles/index.html.

Confederation of Independent Asatru Kindred (CIAK)
PO Box 85, Adamsville, AL 35005

The Confederation of Independent Asatru Kindred (CIAK) was founded in Alabama in 1996 as a pagan organization that facilitates following, in a nondogmatic manner, the gods of the northern tradition and fellowship. CIAK is led by a circle of elders. Early growth came as otherwise independent Asatru groups affiliated. Any group of three or more adult members may form a kindred (a local group) within CIAK.

At the time of its creation, the founders of CIAK dictated there would be several semi-independent guilds and halls that would be active as subsidiary organizations. They include the Ancestors Hall, to provide a focus on the religious importance of honoring one's ancestors and doing research in family history; the Clergy Hall, to facilitate the training of the clergy (the *gothi* and *gythia*) and encourage the continuing pursuit of knowledge by the leadership; and the Warriors Guild, which prepares members to cope with the enemies of the faith.

While it presents a loose format for the worship of the deities, CIAK has a strong ethical policy that members are asked to accept. It includes responsibility to the organization and its members; living in a manner that contributes constructively to the public image of Asatru and Asatru-like belief systems; honesty; and not acting in any manner that is unlawful or detrimental to the health and welfare of the public. Members are asked to refrain from attacks upon other Asatru or Norse tradition organizations.

CIAK has developed a reading program of clergy training for those preparing to assume leadership. It annually sponsors a national Asatru gathering, the Summer's End Moot. A variety of holidays are celebrated annually, including the anniversary of the founding of the original kindred in Alabama during yule of 1996. Among CIAK's goals are to offer an online library about the northern traditions and to locate land upon which a *hof* (a temple or church) can be built and around which an Asatru community can be created.

Membership: Not reported. Currently there are four kindreds associated with CIAK, estimated to contain fewer than 50 members.

Sources:

Confederation of Independent Asatru Kindred.
www.members.tripod.com/~SigTyr/Nordstrom.html.

Irminsul Aettir
PO Box 43, Renton, WA 98057-0423

Irminsul Aettir is an association of Ásatrúar (people who follow Ásatrú, the old Pagan religion of Iceland and Scandinavia) formed in the mid-1990s. It consists of actual (and fictive) kin, family members, friends of the Irminsul Aett, and those affiliated with the Aett to practice and promote the religion of Ásatrú. The organization is headed by Susan Granquist, who assumed full administrative duties during Yule 1995, when she was named Drottning (Queen). She is currently assisted by Andrew J. Cantrell, who was named Thule in 1997. The basic organizational unit of the Aett is the family, supported by extended family type organizations and associations such as kindreds. Both exist to encourage the growth of individuals in their faith.

Members also believe that everyone should be free to choose his or her own godhi/gydhia (leader), as well as one's fellow worshippers. Traditionally, a believer entered into a "Thing-agreement" (agreement of association) with the godhi or gydhia of choice. A godhi or gydhia is a person who serves the community and represents the people of his or her association at assemblies, holds meetings, and maintains meeting places and records (as well as performing other services). According to the ancient oath of office, holding the office of godhi involves perpetual dedication to the gods, folk, and other beings. Today, it is roughly equivalent to a community minister.

Given the nonhierarchical nature of the religion, the primary responsibility of the leader is to assist individuals in meeting their own spiritual needs through example, the provision of resources and information, and by organizing events at which individuals can meet with others in their community.

In 1994 Irminsul Aettir organized its first godhordh, which is similar to a church. It is designed to be actively involved in outreach programs, as is any other ministry. Members also sponsor Vinnuhoppurs and Felag groups, study groups, and fellowships, all of which focus on particular topics and allow for more intimate contact between members.

Membership: Not reported.

Sources:

Irminsul Aettir. www.irminsul.org.

Odin Brotherhood
Current address not obtained for this edition.

The Odin Brotherhood is a secret society that follows a polytheistic religion devoted to Odin, Thor, Sif, and the other deities of the Norse tradition. According to the brotherhood, Odinism is an ancient religion that acknowledges the gods by fostering thought, courage, honor, light, and beauty. It traces its existence to the fifteenth century; having survived in the face of Christian attempts to annihilate it, it has attempted to make itself known. The brotherhood has no buildings (temples or churches) but attempts to honor the gods everywhere, as long as outsiders are excluded; all words are "whispered," and all "abominations" (promiscuity and assassination) are avoided.

The central rite of the brotherhood is called the Glimpse-of-Extraordinary-Beauty, during which the celebrants believe they are "enveloped and penetrated by the thoughts of a god." Members do not have faith so much as they are taught to seek knowledge. The brotherhood does, however, believe in life after death and that there are three "Other-Worlds," one of which is called Valhalla or the White-Kingdom. It is reserved for those heroes who die violent deaths. The existence of the Christian hell is denied.

The brotherhood glorifies strength, asserting that "it is only by becoming stronger that a man can realize his divinity." Initiates to the brotherhood must cut themselves three times with a dagger and "devote, hallow, and sanctify" their blood to "the gods who live."

The brotherhood has distanced itself from the racism that infected Norse beliefs in the twentieth century and eschews the idea that there are either chosen peoples or master races.

Membership: Estimated at 1,000 members found in the United States, Canada, the United Kingdom, Argentina, Chile, Brazil, Spain, Italy, Germany, the Netherlands, Belgium, Scandinavia, and Mexico.

Sources:

Odin Brotherhood. www.odinbrotherhood.com/.

The Odin Brotherhood. www.geocities.com/odinbrotherhood/.

Mirabello, Mark. *The Odin Brotherhood*, 5th ed. Oxford, England: Mandrake of Oxford, 2003.

The Poetic Eddas: The Mythological Poems. Trans. Henry Adams Bellows. Mineola, NY: Dover Publications, 2004.

Sturluson, Snorri. *The Prose Edda: Tales from Norse Mythology*. Trans. Arthur Gilchrist Brodeur. Mineola, NY: Dover Publications, 2006.

Odinic Rite Vinland

PO Box 2022, Sandusky, OH 44871-2022

Odinic Rite Vinland (ORV) is the autonomous American branch of the Odinic Rite, an Odinist group based in Great Britain. The ORV worships the deities of ancient northern Europe in a manner similar to that of the European branches. It recognizes the spiritual leadership provided by the Court of Gothar in Great Britain, the head of the Odinic Rite, and Heimgest, its director. The American branch is led by the Witan ORV, a council of three individuals who are oathed in the realms of Gods and men to lead and advance the Holy Nation of Odin and the Odinic Rite Vinland. The council members are Osferth ORV, the High Wita; Heidrun ORV, the Witan Reeve; and Wulfgaest ORV, the Hofwarden.

The Odinic Rite Vinland has developed a gothi (clergy) training program for its members, and it publishes a range of Odinist materials, including *The Book of Blotar of the Odinic Rite: Authentic Rituals of the Odinic Rite*, which contains the 12 major monthly rituals of the ORV, as well as rites of passage, a healing ritual, and the other major rituals, such as sword naming, land reclamation, and banner consecration.

Membership: Not reported.

Periodicals: *ORBriefing-Vinland*.

Sources:

The Odinic Rite. www.odinic-rite.org.

Odinist Fellowship/Kirk of Odin

PO Box 1973, Parksville, BC, Canada V9P 2H7

The Odinist Fellowship is an international, Heathen organization intent on bringing back the pre-Christian beliefs and spirituality of northern Europe. The fellowship seeks to find isolated devotees of the Ásatrú faith and provide the means for a wider fellowship. The Odinist Fellowship is the functioning arm of the Kirk of Odin. It was founded by Else Christensen in 1969 and is headquartered on Vancouver Island, British Columbia.

Any three members of the fellowship, living in reasonable proximity, may form a Kindred. A Kindred holds a minimum of four celebrations annually, and the spokesperson for the Kindred has the title of Kirk Elder. The Kindred also appoints a Chronicler, who keeps records of its activities.

Membership: Not reported.

Ring of Thoth

PO Box 25637, Tempe, AZ 85285

The Ring of Thoth was founded shortly after the disbanding of the Asatru Free Assembly in 1987. It was established by Edred Thorsson and James Chisholm as an explicitly nonracist organization dedicated to the promotion of the religion of the Germanic peoples. (During the 1980s racism was a persistent charge leveled against groups promoting Norse Paganism.) It sees itself as taking a more liberal and scholarly approach than that taken by the other major group formed somewhat simultaneously, the Asatru Alliance. In other respects it continues the beliefs and practices of the former Asatru Free Assembly. Thorsson has authored a number of books on the Asatru traditions.

Membership: Not reported.

Periodicals: *Idunna*.

Sources:

Gundarsson, Kveldulf R Hagan, ed. *Our Thoth*. N.p.: Ring of Thoth, 1992.

Thorsson, Edred. *A Book of Thoth*. St. Paul, MN: Llewellyn Publications, 1989.

Skergard

1003 Cottonwood Ave., No. 53, Red Wing, MN 55066-1300

Skergard is a Pagan organization devoted to the deities of the old Norse religions generally referred to as Asatru and Vanatru. Included in this polytheistic faith is the worship of Odin, Thor, Freyr, Frigga, and Freyja, the gods and goddesses of the old Norse sagas. Religious gatherings, called blots, are held eight times a year.

Membership: Not reported.

 Vodou

African Theological Archministry

c/o Oyotunji African Yoruba Village, PO Box 51, Sheldon, SC 29941

In December 1973 a group of blacks from Harlem received national news coverage for their establishment of a "vodou kingdom" in Beaufort County, South Carolina. This kingdom was called the sacred village of Oyotunji, and it was headed by one of the founders, Oba (King) Efuntola Oseijeman Adelabu Adefunmi I (1928–2005), born Walter Eugene King. King had abandoned the Baptist Church of his family during his teens and begun a search for the ancient gods of Africa. He traveled to Haiti in 1954 and discovered vodou. Early in 1955 he traveled to Europe and North Africa, and upon his return to the United States he founded the Order of Damballah Hwedo Ancestor Priests. In 1959 he traveled to Cuba and was initiated in the Orisha-Vodou African priesthood by Afro-Cubans at Matanzas, Cuba. The Order of Damballah was then superceded by the Shango Temple, and in 1960 King incorporated the African Theological Archministry. The Shango Temple was then renamed the Yoruba Temple.

In 1970 King Efuntola moved with most of the temple members to rural South Carolina, where the Yoruba Village of Oyotunji was established. He began a complete reform of the Orisha-Vodu priesthood along lines of the Nigerian tradition. In 1972 he traveled to Nigeria and was initiated into the Ifa priesthood. Upon his return he was proclaimed oba-king (Alashe) of Oyotunji. He opened the first Parliament of Oyotunji chiefs and landowners and founded the priests' council (Igbimolosha) in 1973. These two groups make the rules for the community, and they attempt to adhere closely to African patterns in doing so.

Oyotunji was modeled on a Nigerian village, including a palace for the King and his wives (Efuntola had four in 1995) and children. There are also several temples dedicated to the various deities. Only Yoruban is spoken before noon each day. Efuntola was invited to a convention of Orisha-Vodum priests at Ile-Ife, Nigeria, in 1981, and on June 5 he was coronated by the King of Ife.

The Yoruba religion is considered to be the "rain forest version of the Ancient Egyptian Mystery System." It is the source for Afro-Cuban Santeria, but it makes no attempt to equate its gods with Christian saints. The Yoruba world is headed by Olorun, a universal energy without anthropomorphic characteristics. Olodumare, equated with Ifa, the God of Destiny and Divination, sets a destiny for everything in nature. It was Orishanla (Obatala), the Creator God, who created the solid land mass and the first earthlings. The pantheon also includes Eshu-Elegba, God of Luck and the personification of the unpredictable element in life; Ogun, God of Iron, or the violent element in life; Oshoun/osun/, Goddess of Sex and Beauty, or the sensuous element in life; and Shango, God of Lightening and Thunder, or the political element in life. Yoruba practices include animal sacrifice, polygamy, ecstatic dancing, and the appeasement of the gods by various offerings. Worship centers upon the veneration of the deities, and it is also directed toward the ancestors, the spiritual forces closest to individual humans.

Membership: In 2002 there were 51 residents of Oyotunji Villabe, 55 affiliated centers in the United States, and the Yoruba Temple reported that it had more than 10,000 members.

Educational Facilities:

African Theological Archministry, Sheldon, South Carolina.

Yoruba Theological Archministry, Brooklyn, New York.

Remarks: King Efuntola became a leader in the African Nationalist movement in the 1960s. After he moved to South Carolina, his village became a pilgrimage site for many blacks, irrespective of their acceptance of his religious stance.

Sources:

Oyotunjia Village. www.oyotunjiafricanvillage.org.

Adefunmi, Baba Oseijeman. *Ancestors of the Afro-Americans*. Long Island City, NY: Aims of Modzawe, 1973.

Adefunmi I, Oba Efuntola Oseijeman Adelabu. *Olorisha, A Guidebook into Yoruba Religion*. Sheldon, SC: Author, 1982.

Canet, Carlos. *Oyotunji*. Miami, FL: Editorial AIP, n.d.

Hunt, Carl M. *Oyotunji Village*. Washington, DC: University Press of America, 1979.

Mason, John. *Ebo Eje (Blood Sacrifice)*. New York: Yoruba Theological Archministry, 1981.

———. *Sin Egun (Ancestor Worship)*. New York: Yoruba Theological Arch-ministry, 1981.

———. *Usanyin*. New York: Yoruba Theological Archministry, 1983.

———. *Unje Fun Orisa (Food for the Gods)*. New York: Yoruba Theological Archministry, 1981.

Odunfonda I Adaramila. *Obatala, The Yoruba God of Creation*. Sheldon, SC: Great Benin Books, n.d.

Afro-American Vodoun

Current address not obtained for this edition.

Occasionally, a leader of a Vodou group will allow an outsider (such as a reporter) to have limited access to the organization. Such a leader was High Priestess Madam Arboo of Afro-American Vodoun. Born in Georgia, Madam Arboo was reared in Vodou and migrated to New York City, where she settled in Harlem. As described in a lengthy 1964 article that is the only source of information about her, she described Vodoun as an Afro-Christian cult centered on Damballah, the chief Vodou deity and god of wisdom, personified as a serpent. As a high priestess, she was his messenger. Her group differed from Haitian Vodou groups in that it reduced the remainder of the pantheon to the position of subdeities or spirits. Damballah was equated with the brass serpent that Moses made in the wilderness (Numbers 21:9).

Healing is a high priority of Afro-American Vodoun, and it includes both psychic and psychological counseling and (where permitted) the dispensing of folk remedies such as rattlesnake oil. Worship is held on the evening of the new moon and is centered around ecstatic dance accompanied by flute and drum and led by the papaloi (priest) and mammaloi (priestess). The members, as they dance, enter trance-like states, which become occasions for revelations and messages from the spirits.

Elements of Christianity survive in this form of Vodoun in the use of spirituals. The threefold way of Vodoun teaches faith, love, and joy as virtues. The pentagram (for females) and the Star of David (for males) are major symbols. Animals carry symbolic power: the goat represents fertility; the eagle, majesty; the turtle, caution; and the vulture is Damballah's "sanitation department."

Membership: No direct contact has been established with Madame Arboo, and the current status of her group is uncertain. Vodoun groups exist along the East Coast and are organized into gatherings of from 15 to 20 persons.

Sources:

Arboo, Madam, as told to Harold Preece. "What 'Voodoo' Really Is." *Exploring the Unknown* 4, no. 6 (April 1964): 6–19.

Church of Lukumi Babalu Aye
PO Box 22627, Hialeah, FL 33002

The Church of Lukumi Babalu Aye was founded in the early 1970s and incorporated in 1974 in Miami, Florida, by Ernesto Pichardo, its president, and his brother Fernando Pichardo in an effort to provide a public center for the largely secretive Santeria religion. Santeria has become a significant practice in the Cuban-American community of southern Florida, where it was introduced by refugees from the Cuban Revolution under Fidel Castro. The church existed in relative quiet for many years, with its main public appearance being in a class Pichardo conducted at Miami-Dade Community College. The practice of Santaria also featured in a series of cases in the city courts in which the church defended its members. Then, in the mid-1980s, a decision was made to open a Santeria church that would hold public services in the Miami suburb of Hialeah, and this helped make the religion more well known, though it also created controversy.

Santeria is based upon the worship of the *orishas*, African deities from the country of Nigeria. This worship was brought to the Americas by the many slaves transported to the region from the seventeenth to the nineteenth centuries. In Spanish colonies such as Cuba, the Nigerian religion took on a veneer of Roman Catholicism, and many of the orishas became identified with Catholic saints. The resultant New World practice became known as the "religion of the saints," or *Santeria*. Worship in the religion is built around the possession of the priest/priestess and the believer by an orisha. During this time of possession, the possessed person will take on the characteristic of the particular divinity involved. Integral to the worship of the deities, especially on special occasions such as a marriage ceremony, is animal sacrifice. This characteristic has made Santeria controversial in the otherwise very tolerant religious environments of Miami, New York, and Los Angeles, the three cities with the largest number of Santeria practitioners.

Shortly after announcing the opening of the church in the 1980s, the city of Hialeah passed four ordinances outlawing ritual animal sacrifice, ostensibly to protect residents from the spread of disease, to prevent cruelty to animals, and to prevent traumatizing any children who might witness the death of an animal. The case became the subject of a court battle that went to the U.S. Supreme Court, which struck down the ordinance in 1993.

Membership: Not reported.

Periodicals: *CLBA Journal.*

Sources:

Church of Lukumi Babalu Aye. www.church-of-the-lukumi.org.

Resnick, Rosalind. "To One City, It's Cruelty. To Cultists, It's Religion." *National Law Journal* (September 11, 1989).

Church of the Seven African Powers

PO Box 453336, Miami, FL 33245

The Church of the Seven African Powers is one of several churches founded during the 1980s through which the largely secretive Santeria community could reach out to the public at large, especially those who had become curious about it and wanted to experience it first hand. The church promotes the worship of the orishas, the African deities whose actions form the heart of the Santeria faith. The church offers a correspondence course for people wishing to become knowledgeable about the faith. Each lesson contains instructions for ebbos (spells) designed to aid the believer. The church also provides a means for seekers to come to Miami and to experience direct contact with the orishas through meetings with a Santeria priestess or priest.

Membership: In 2002 the church reported 100 to 200 members.

Sources:

Church of the Seven African Powers. geocities.com/athens/sparta/1332/.

Religious Order of Witchcraft

Current address could not be obtained for this edition.

The Religious Order of Witchcraft was incorporated in 1972 in New Orleans, Louisiana, by Mary Oneida Toups, its high priestess. A housewife and mother, she began her magical career in 1969 in a Kabbalistic system. In 1970 she opened the Witches'Workshop (now the Witchcraft Shop), a magick/witchcraft/vodou shop in the city. She continued her study in the ritual magick systems of Aleister Crowley and Israel Regardie and, in 1971, reached the point of mystical communion with her holy guardian angel. That communion led to the founding of the order. According to her textbook, *Magick, High and Low*, the order was focused on Kabbalistic magick with a strong emphasis on astrology, Egyptian mythology, and the Tarot. Members venerated the "God of the Witches" popularly known as the Goat of Mendes. They did not worship it, but rather what it symbolized: the magical light of universal intelligence always available to people when they learn how to use it, the belief that sacrifice must come before complete illumination, the balance between justice and mercy, eternal life, and the dual masculine-feminine nature of the body, among other things.

Prior to her death, Toups created several Wiccan priestesses who continue her lineage at different locations around the country. Among those who claim Toups's heritage is Rev. Samantha Corfield (a.k.a. Mambo Sam, b. 1956), who resides in Albuquerque, New Mexico. She and her husband operate Sheer Goddess and www.spellmaker.com, through which they keep in touch with believers. They also sponsor an annual Voodoo Convention.

The Witchcraft Shop Toups operated in New Orleans continued under new management, but did not survive the Katrina hurricane disaster of 2005.

Membership: Not reported.

Periodicals: *Universal Messenger*.

Sources:

Samantha Corfield. www.spellmaker.com/.

Toups, Oneida. *Magick, High and Low*. Jefferson, LA: Hope Publications, 1975.

Voodoo Spiritual Temple

828 N Rampart St., New Orleans, LA 70116

The Voodoo Spiritual Temple, located on the northern edge of the French Quarter in New Orleans, is an important center of Vodou. Its importance lies in its openness to people not of African lineage, especially visitors to New Orleans, and its willingness to introduce outsiders to the often secret world of Vodou

The term *Vodou* comes from the French word *Voudon*, which can mean "the power," "that who is invisible," or "the creator of all things." Originating in Benin, West Africa, and the Congo, Central Africa, Vodou is an earth-based religion that honors the forces of nature and the universe, as well as ancestral spirits that provide

guidance in the present. During the slave trade, Africans taken from these regions kept their traditional spiritual practices alive despite constant attempts to destroy the spirit and traditions of those who had been captured and sold into slavery.

Since its introduction in the Western Hemisphere, Vodou's opponents have depicted the religion as a sinister, even abominable, belief system, and the leaders of the Voodoo Spiritual Temple have noted that these characterizations are the result of both misunderstandings and deliberate misconceptions on the part of writers, anthropologists, scholars, and even Hollywood producers.

Vodou devotees believe in an Omnipresent Creator and the loas, or orishas (forces or saints of the universe). The loas act as intermediaries between the creator and the human world, comparable to saints in Catholicism. Each loa interacts with people and things to help create and maintain a spiritual balance.

The temple was founded in 1990 by Priestess Miriam Chamani (b. 1943) and her husband, Priest Oswan Chamani (1944–1995). A native of Mississippi, Miriam had experienced the power of mysterious forces since childhood, and she was led to various spiritual orders, culminating in the attainment of vast spiritual and metaphysical knowledge. In 1982 she was consecrated as a bishop at the Angel Angel All Nations Spiritual Church in Chicago. Oswan Chamani was born in Belize, Central America, where he studied Vodou (known as *Obeah* in Central America) under three teachers, two of whom were African Diviners.

Membership: Not reported.

Periodicals: *Voodoo Realist Newsletter*.

Sources:

Voodoo Spiritual Temple. www.voodoospiritualtemple.org.

Costonie, Toni. *A Brief History of Priestess Miriam & the Voodoo Spiritual Temple*. New Orleans: Voodoo Spiritual Temple, 2003.

 # Satanism

Church of Satan

PO Box 499, New York, NY 10101-0499

One story repeated continually in the media throughout the 1970s was how Anton LaVey (1930–1997) shaved his head on Walpurgisnacht (April 30) in 1966, proclaimed the beginning of the satanic era, and launched the Church of Satan. LaVey became a celebrity of the burgeoning occult movement and the object of front-page newspaper articles. His early fame came from news coverage of such events as a satanic funeral service for a Navy man killed in an accident at Treasure Island Navy Base, rituals performed with a nude woman on the altar in his black house in San Francisco, the revelation of the actress Jayne Mansfield's association with the church, and a bit part for LaVey (as the Devil) in the movie *Rosemary's Baby*.

LaVey had been a circus animal trainer and carnival organist. While he was with the carnival, he became intrigued by claims of paranormal phenomena and gained a reputation as a ghost-hunting debunker. Over the coming years, LaVey would write five books—*The Satanic Bible* (1969), *The Compleat Witch* (1971; reprinted in 1989 as *The Satanic Witch*), *The Satanic Rituals* (1972), *The Devil's Notebook* (1992), and *Satan Speaks* (1998). Each explores the philosophy of satanism he embodied in the Church of Satan, and the latter two works include much in the way of social commentary and wry observations on the human condition.

The basic themes of LaVey's satanism are carnality, self-assertion, anti-establishmentarianism, and the epicurean gratification of man's physical and mental nature. Satan is seen as a Promethean figure, representing indulgence, vital existence, undefiled wisdom, kindness to the deserving, vengeance, responsibility to the responsible, the notion that man is just another animal, and the so-called sins that lead to physical, mental, or emotional gratification when indulged in with moderation. In LaVey's view, Satan represents the source of these life-enhancing values. Rituals were conceived both as self-transformative psychodramas and as magical acts that focus emotional energy, with the goal being to plant thoughts in the minds of others, who will bring about the sorcerer's will.

Satanic philosophy is, at its base, atheistic. It embraces social Darwinism and skepticism, and it is meant to be a tool for getting the most out of life, since there is no belief in an afterlife. Each satanist is seen as living according to his own set of values. The Church of Satan opposes illegal acts that are at variance with laws established for the common good. Sex is viewed as the strongest instinct (next to self preservation) and natural in all forms between consenting adults. Drugs use is viewed as escapist and contrary to the realistic view of life as preached by the church.

The church celebrates three main holidays. For individuals, the most important day is one's birthday. For the group, Walpurgisnacht celebrates the climax of spring and the anniversary of the church's founding, while Halloween is an ancient harvest festival that now serves as a time to explore the often repressed sides of its celebrants through dressing in masks and costumes. The equinoxes and solstices are also celebrated as seasonal turning points..

Baptism is a ceremony of glorification of the one baptized. LeVey's works offer rituals for different magical goals (e.g., compassion, lust, destruction) as well as celebratory purposes. The Enochian Keys, which first appeared in print in 1659 in a biography of John Dee (and were later used by the Hermetic Order of the Golden Dawn) are employed in satanized versions in rituals. The text used for the traditional Black Mass ritual, "Le Messe Noir," is found in *The Satanic Rituals*). As performed by the church, it is meant to be not simply a blasphemous pageant against the Catholic Church, but a purging ritual that makes full use of psychodrama to rid individuals of the influence of any sacred cows. Satanic wedding and funeral rites were revealed in *The Satanic Scriptures* (2007) by High Priest Peter H. Gilmore.

Operating from the San Francisco headquarters, the Church of Satan spread to urban centers across the United States, with grottos in Miami, Florida; New Orleans, Louisiana; New York City; and throughout the Midwest. By 1977, one spokesperson claimed more than 10,000 members for the church (lifetime membership is available for a $200.00 registration fee). In the mid-1970s, administratively centralized grottos were deemed counterproductive and disbanded. A more cabal-like underground structure was instituted and continues today. Over the years, groups have emerged that use LaVeyan ritual and philosophy, but that may or may not give LaVey credit and are not affiliated in any way with the Church of Satan.

When LaVey died in 1997, Blanche Barton was High Priestess and succeeded him as the Church's administrative head. In 2001 Peter H. Gilmore was appointed High Priest, and in 2002 his wife Peggy Nadramia became High Priestess, with Barton remaining as the chairperson of the advisory board, the Council of Nine. In 2007 Gilmore wrote *The Satanic Scriptures*, which brings the philosophy of satanism up to date and explains the workings of the Church of Satan. The book also includes social commentary and important rituals. It is being translated to date into French, German, Portuguese, Russian, and Estonian.

Membership: Not reported. Church membership statistics are considered confidential. Church membership is granted for life to new members (who can be expelled if they do not live up to the philosophy), and there is no published account of active members (estimated to be several thousand). Internationally, the church reports concentrations of members in just about every nation in the Americas and Europe, as well as Australia and New Zealand, with newer members in the Middle and Far East as well as South Africa. *The Satanic Bible* has recently been translated into French, German, Danish, Swedish, Norwegian, Russian, Italian, and Spanish.

Periodicals: *The Black Flame* (officially endorsed) • *The Cloven Hoof.*

Sources:

Church of Satan. www.churchofsatan.com.

Barton, Blanche. *The Secret Life of a Satanist.* Los Angeles: Feral House, 1990.

LaVey, Anton Szandor. *The Satanic Bible*. New York: Avon, 1969.

———. *The Compleat Witch*. New York: Lancer Books, 1971.

———. *The Satanic Rituals*. Secaucus, NJ: University Books, 1972.

———. *The Devil's Notebook*. Los Angeles: Feral House, 1992.

———. *Satan Speaks*. Los Angeles: Feral House, 1998.

Lewis, James R., and Jesper Aagaard Petersen. *The Encyclopedic Sourcebook of Satanism*. Amherst, NY: Prometheus Press, 2008.

Wolff, Burton H. *The Devil's Avenger*. New York: Pyramid Books, 1974.

First Church of Satan
Current address not obtained for this edition.

The First Church of Satan was one of several small satanic groups to emerge in the 1990s as the Church of Satan experienced a shift of leadership from founder Anton LaVey (1930–1997) to Blanche Barton and the controversies accompanying that change. John Dewey Alle (b. 1951), known as Lord Egan, had been a member of the church of Satan in the 1970s but turned to other pursuits in the 1980s. In the mid-1990s he decided to reactivate his association with the milieu created by LaVey but quickly found himself in conflict with Barton. He charged the Church of Satan with having shifted its emphasis from a celebration of individualism (the primary message behind the Church of Satan's outward manifestation) into an assertion of elitism.

Alle founded the First Church of Satan as an instrument to champion the satanic spiritual path. Satanism was viewed as a path for freethinkers and individualists who wished to pursue truth through self-exploration and spiritual stimulation. The church did not center on a particular structure or belief system, but allowed individuals to seek their own way. The church tolerated all spiritual paths, discouraging any dogmatic approach to the spiritual life.

The church also discouraged debate over the existence of Satan. Rather, images of Satan as the promoter of freedom were seen as valid metaphors of the spiritual aspiration, and the *Satanic Bible* (with the additional teachings offered by LaVey through the Church of Satan) as tools encouraging individuals to develop their personal spirituality.

The church encouraged the creation of satanic covens (groups), though such local groups were considered strictly autonomous. The First Church of Satan did not issue charters for covens, though it did provide material to facilitate their operation. Membership was open to anyone who made a modest donation to the church.

Alle continued to evolve philosophically. In 2003, with the help of his wife, Lillee C. Alle, he created a new magical system based on Hermetics that he termed the Alle Shadow Tradition. The new "tradition" superseded and replaced the First Church of Satan.

Membership: The First Church of Satan was a small organization (low hundreds) that sought to influence people primarily through the Internet. The LaVey movement numbered in the low thousands. Many people were influenced by *The Satanic Bible*, which has remained in print since its first publication in the 1960s.

Sources:

Alle, John. www.myspace.com/crystalscryer

Alle Shadow Tradition. www.alleeshadowtradition.com

First Satanic Church
PO Box 475177, San Francisco, CA 94147

The First Satanic Church is one of several small satanic groups to emerge in the 1990s in the wake of the death of Anton LaVey (1930–1997), the founder of the Church of Satan, and the emergence of Blanche Barton to leadership. Karla LaVey, Anton LaVey's eldest daughter, did not accept Barton's leadership, and in 1999 she disaffiliated with the Church of Satan and founded the First Satanic Church in an attempt to recover what she felt had been lost. The church promotes and uses the writings of Anton LaVey.

The First Satanic Church sees itself as an elite organization designed to engage those few who wish to engage in a serious study of the occult realm, particularly satanism. The new church differs from the present Church of Satan in several aspects. Although sharing the teachings presented in *The Satanic Bible* and other writings of LaVey, the First Satanic Church engage in the recruitment of members. Those who become aware of the church and wish to affiliate take the lead in making contact. In addition, although it has several Internet sites, the church does not see itself as a cyberspace organization and demands that prospective members make contact by more traditional means. Prospective members must go through a screening process.

The First Satanic Church sees itself as the purveyor of individualism and self-interest. Satan is the symbol of opposition to the majority mindset that seeks to mold the individual into its image. As such, satanism is neither the inverse of Christianity, but presents another spiritual path. Nor is the church involved with illegal activities such as animal mutilation or sacrifice. The church has established an online community using a cyber address that parodies *The 700 Club*, the television show of popular Christian televangelist Pat Robertson. The church has also developed a radio outreach, *The Voice of Satan*. Karla LaVey holds an annual celebration of the Black Mass each year on Halloween.

Membership: Not reported. The church has less than 100 members.

Sources:

First Satanic Church. satanicchurch.com/content/.

Luciferian Light Group
PO Box 7207, Tampa, FL 33673

The Luciferian Light Group is an organization founded in the early 1990s that is dedicated to bringing forth the ancient teachings of Lucifer and hastening the establishment of the Satanic Empire. The order is organized as a secret society with an inner circle that is called the Church of Luciferian Light.

Membership: Not reported.

Periodicals: *Onslaught*.

Temple of Set
PO Box 470307, San Francisco, CA 94147

The Temple of Set was founded in 1975 by members of the international priesthood of the Church of Satan who had resigned from that institution because of what they considered to be its over-commercialism. A senior initiate, Michael A. Aquino, invoked the Prince of Darkness in quest of a new mandate to preserve and enhance what he held to be the more noble concepts which the Church of Satan had conceived. The mandate was given in the form of *The Book of Coming Forth by Night*, a statement by that entity in his most ancient semblance as Set. Set ordained the Temple of Set to succeed the Church of Satan. The temple describes itself as an initiatory institution dedicated to Set, an ancient Egyptian deity, the corrupted legends of whom became the basis for the Christian Satan.

Temple initiates do not consider Set an evil figure, nor do they consider the temple merely a refutation of conventional religion. According to temple philosophy, the universe is a nonconscious environment possessed of mechanical consistency. In contrast to the universe, and occasionally violating its laws, is Set. Set has, over a period of millennia, altered the genetic makeup of humans in order to create a species possessing an enhanced, nonnatural intelligence. The techniques and teachings of the temple are designed to identify and develop this higher evolutionary potential in appropriate individuals.

The temple is governed by the Council of Nine, which appoints the high priest of Set and the executive director. There are six initiatory degrees: Setian, Adept, Priest(ess) of Set, Master of the Temple, Magus, and Ipsissimus. The program is designed principally for individuals, although there are local Pylons of the Temple in several parts of the United States. International conclaves for the entire temple are held annually. The temple provides an annotated reading list containing material on a wide range of occult, scientific, and religious subjects. Topics covered include ancient Egypt, historical and contemporary occultism, psychology, ethics, and experimental science.

Membership: In 2002 the temple had approximately 500 members.

Periodicals: *Scroll of Set*.

Remarks: Among those who joined in the founding of the Temple of Set was Lilith Sinclair, leader of what had been known as the Spottswood (New Jersey) Grotto of the Church of Satan, the largest group of its kind on the East Coast.

Sources:

Temple of Set. www.xeper.org/

Aquino, Michael A. *The Crystal Tablet of Set*. San Francisco, CA: Temple of Set, 1985.

————. *Temple of Set Reading List XIX*. San Francisco, CA: Temple of Set, 1984.

Scott, Gini Graham. *The Magicians*. New York: Irvington Publishers, 1983.

Western Esoteric Family IV: Christian Science-Metaphysical

20

Developments of belief and practice within the larger esoteric community set the stage for the emergence of a uniquely American religious movement in the last quarter of the nineteenth century. The roots of Christian Science and New Thought are more complex than their being simply a new expansion of esoteric thinking; the primary heritage of these movements lies in the emphasis on alternative methods of healing that blossomed in Spiritualism and the new method of biblical interpretation advocated by Emanuel Swedenborg (1688–1772).

The nineteenth century proved a transition period for the medical community. In the United States, what would later become the dominant allopathic medical system (yet to be wedded to the separate practice of surgery) competed with homeopathy and what was termed the eclectic system of medicine but awaited the discovery of bacteria as a causative agent of disease before it would assume its present pervasive role. In the meantime, many found the practices of physicians to be more horrific than the diseases they were trying to cure. The state of nineteenth-century medicine, and the yet-to-appear discipline of psychology, provided a context in which the new practice of healing advocated by Franz Anton Mesmer (1734–1815) could flourish.

Mesmer suggested the existence of a universal cosmic energy, which he likened to the energy easily demonstrated in magnetic attraction, that could be manipulated for healing. He established a center for the practice of healing in Paris, and it flourished for a period prior to the French Revolution (1789–1799) until denounced by the French Academy of Science. But even in the face of official disapproval, Mesmer's success in treating people's problems allowed the movement he started to continue and spread. The theoretical aspects of Mesmer's thinking would provide a basis for the magical revival, with Éliphas Lévi (1810–1875) proposing that the cosmic energy discovered by Mesmer was the agent producing results for magical operations. The unusual trance states that mesmerists discovered they could produce in some people led directly to the mediumistic trance states that became the center of Spiritualist practice, as well as being reworked into the modern practice of hypnotism.

Often forgotten is the spread of mesmerism as entertainment. In the early nineteenth century, mesmerism became a popular movement built around traveling mesmerists who gave public demonstrations of magnetic healing and trance.

Though less known than the mediumistic trance state, the healing emphasis of mesmerism was also absorbed into Spiritualism, the realm of contact with spirits providing a new setting for speculation on how healing worked. While some accepted Mesmer's view of cosmic energy, others came to see the spirits of the deceased as playing a major role in healing, while others began to speculate about various mental processes in the patient as the key element. In the United States, the personal tragedies resulting from the Civil War (1861–1865) merely punctuated the drive for health that was evident in the many paths to health being offered to the American public.

The secularity of the American frontier contributed to the setting in which a broad speculation on spiritual matters was possible. The dominate Christianity was split into a variety of competing factions that together held the allegiance of only one-fourth of the public. New movements like the Latter-day Saints and the Unitarians had plenty of space to grow among both the unchurched and less-committed church members. The new Swedenborgian movement flourished for a time in the open religious climate. Emanuel Swedenborg's life of communication with angels would presage the Spiritualist medium's efforts to speak with spirits.

Swedenborg also introduced a new way of looking at the Bible. In contrast with the Protestant approach to the biblical text in search of its plain and simple meaning, Swedenborg proposed a more complex allegorical reading that sought a higher but more hidden spiritual interpretation. Among the Swedish seer's primary writings were lengthy biblical commentaries in which the real interpretation of the scriptures as taught him by the angels was laid out. The Swedenborgian approach to the Bible offered a distinct alternative to both Protestantism and Roman Catholicism. Swedenborg's interpretations never caught on outside the Swedenborgian movement, but his approach provided a method for those attached to the Bible to draw more from it than the mainstream Christian churches were providing.

While the growing esoteric community was providing a radical alternative to the burgeoning Protestant movement, Unitarianism was attacking Christian orthodoxy at its very heart. Unitarian leaders raised doubts about the central building block of orthodox Christianity, the doctrine of the Trinity. The Trinity provided the means of reconciling the many seemingly contradictory assertions in the Bible about the transcendent Father God, the divine nature of the man

Christian Science-Metaphysical Family Chronology

1749 and 1756	Emanuel Swedenborg publishes the *Arcana Coelestia*, a multi-volume commentary on Genesis and Exodus using his spiritual (allegorical) interpretation of scripture.
1836	Ralph Waldo Emerson's essay "Nature," marks beginning of Transcendentalism as a popular intellectual movement.
1838	Phineas Parkhurst Quimby takes up the practice of mesmerism (mesmeric sleep or hypnotism), after attending a lecture in Belfast, Maine, by a traveling French physician/mesmerist, Dr. Robert Collyer.
1863	New Thought precursor Warren Felt Evans (1817–1889) is healed by Quimby.
1866	Mary Baker Eddy finds healing from a realization of God as the only Reality.
1867	Ralph Waldo Emerson becomes the first member of the Free Religious Association.
1875	The foundational statement of the Christian Science movement, Mary Baker Eddy's *Science and Health*, is published.
1879	Eddy founds Church of Christ, Scientist, in Boston, Massachusetts.
1883	First issue of *The Christian Science Journal* appears.
	Julius and Annette Dresser accuse Eddy of plagiarizing Quimby. Eddy denies the charges and subsequently wins a court case in which she accuses one of her students of plagiarizing *Science and Health*.
1886	Former Eddy student Emma Curtis Hopkins opens the Emma Hopkins College of Metaphysical Science and begins training what will become New Thought teachers.
1888	Hopkins's student Malinda Cramer opens the Home College of Divine Science, precursor to the International Divine Science Association (1892). Hopkins's student Annie Rix Militz founds the Home of Truth in San Francisco.
1889	Hopkins's students Charles and Myrtle Fillmore found the Unity School of Christianity in Kansas City, Missouri.
1894	Orison Swett Marden's *Pushing to the Front* become the first of a series of successful books advocating prosperity consciousness.
1895	After ten years of active teaching, Hopkins retires to New York City and takes only a few students, among them Ernest Holmes.
1897	Ralph Waldo Trine's *In Tune with the Infinite* becomes New Thought bestseller.
1898	Elizabeth Towne launches *Nautilus*, the most widely read New Thought periodical, which will continue to appear for the next half century.
1903–07	New Thought writer William Walker Atkinson pens 13 books under the name of Yogi Ramacharaka.
1914	The International New Thought Alliance is formed as a tool for cooperation and fellowship among the many New Thought churches and organizations.
1927	Hopkins's student Ernest Holmes founds a metaphysical movement called Religious Science a year after publishing his most influential book, *The Science of Mind*.
1929	Frank Robinson founds Psychiana to offer New Thought lesson through the mail.
1930	Japanese convert of Religious Science, Masaharu Tanigichi, founds Seicho-No-Ie.
1937	Napoleon Hill revives prosperity consciousness themes in his very successful *Think and Grow Rich*.
1946	Christian Science practitioner Joel Goldsmith withdraws from the church and become an independent teacher of what he terms the Infinite Way.
1952	Norman Vincent Peale's *The Power of Positive Thinking* becomes an instant success and remains on the *New York Times* bestseller list for the next 186 weeks.
1955	The International Metaphysical Association is founded as a home for independent Christian Science practitioners and teachers.
1974	An African American female Unity minister, Dr. Johnnie Coleman, founds the Universal Foundation for Better Living, which in 1985 evolves into the Christ Universal Temple in Chicago.
1975	*A Course in Miracles* by Dr. Helen Schucman is published.
1987	*Science and Health with Key to the Scriptures* is found in court to be in the public domain.
1988	A group of New Thought scholars found the Society for the Study of Metaphysical Religion during a meeting of the American Academy of Religion.
1995	Unity School of Christianity holds first Unity World Conference in Birmingham, England.
2000	United Church of Religious Science begins a reevaluation process centered on revisioning the church's mission and purpose that leads to reorganization under a new name, United Centers for Spiritual Living.
2002	The Society for the Study of Metaphysical religion meeting in conjunction with the International New Thought Alliance celebrates the bicentennial of Phineas P. Quimby's birth.
2006	*The Secret* revives New Thought teachings on prosperity consciousness as television show and CD.

Jesus, and the role of the Holy Spirit. The understanding of Jesus as offering atonement for sin by his death on the cross rested on the concept of the Trinity. If the Trinity was abandoned, so were a host of Christian affirmations. Unitarians tended to replace Christian devotion with attention to public morality.

If the Trinity was abandoned, soon many additional elements of Christianity would be abandoned and then possibility Christianity itself. And among the more radical elements of Unitarianism, Christianity was up for grabs. The Unitarian emphasis on rationality in thought and morality in behavior opened the door for the Transcendentalists, who launched a new quest for spiritual reality in an inner search for communion with the divine spirit. They would find inspiration in a wide variety of new source material, from European Romanticism to newly translated writings from Asia like the Bhagavad Gita. In the process of finding a new path, they would place a great deal of reliance on their intuitive feelings, which would lead to an appreciation of the processes of the natural world and, among the more poetic, a form of nature mysticism. Ralph Waldo Emerson (1803–1882) would emerge as the most appealing and articulate of the Transcendentalist thinkers.

Mesmerism, Spiritualism, Swedenborgianism, and Transcendentalism would make possible the two new nineteenth-century American movements—Christian Science and

New Thought. Christian Science and New Thought are two movements whose adherents generally do not like to speak to or of each other. They are now two very distinct movements with a number of obvious differences. Yet while distinct, they also are related. They emerged within a few years of each other in the United States and then internationally. They shared historical roots both in the idealistic philosophy of the nineteenth century and in the search for alternative means for healing at a time when the healing arts were still in a primitive state. In combining these roots, they found some agreement concerning the role of "mind" as the agent in healing. As a matter of fact, it is the confusion between the movements, and the intense polemics concerning their separation, that led in large part to the mutual denial of their common roots.

The first movement to appear was Christian Science. It took its main embodiment in the Church of Christ, Scientist, founded by Mary Baker Eddy (1821–1910). However, within a few years of its launching, teacher-practitioners of Christian Science arose claiming to be true to the memory and teachings of Eddy, but not affiliated with the church she headed. While bearing little continuity from generation to generation, there has long existed a group of such independent Christian Scientists.

Also, from the first years of Christian Science, there appeared a growing number of teacher-practitioners who had started their careers with the Church of Christ, Scientist, or the writings of Eddy, but who differed with her on one or more important issues. The most important of these people was Emma Curtis Hopkins (1853–1925), a former student of Eddy. Around Hopkins, originally under the label of Christian Science, grew a movement that soon departed on an increasing number of points from Eddy. By the end of the century it had left the world of Christian Science and had become known as New Thought. Freed from its attachment to Eddy, New Thought quickly developed as a national movement in its own right.

THE FORERUNNERS.

Christian Science and New Thought brought together insights from several traditions in nineteenth-century America that had sought an alternative to the growing materialism that dominated both public discourse and religious thought. Although they frequently tried to appropriate the dominant Christianity of their culture, they also deviated at a number of important points, especially (in its New England context) from the larger Puritan worldview embodied in the Westminster Confession of Faith and the Cambridge Platform. The alternatives asserted the reality of a spiritual world, the importance of mystical experience, and the healing value of invisible forces operating on the mind and body. This tradition is often called the *metaphysical* tradition and is defined best by the ideas of the several writer-thinkers who dominated the tradition as it developed through the early nineteenth century: Mesmer, Swedenborg, Emerson, Phineas Parkhurst Quimby (1802–1866), and Warren Felt Evans (1817–1889).

Franz Anton Mesmer, an Austrian physician, discovered what he claimed was an amazing healing force. Astrology and the forces that made it work, an important element in eighteenth-century medical training and the subject of Mesmer's doctoral dissertation, became the launching point of his discovery. Asked to summarize his teachings for the French Academy of Science in the 1780s, he produced the "21 Propositions." In this brief statement, he described a subtle fluid universally diffused through nature. This fluid had the property of receiving and communicating impulses between material bodies. The fluid could be used for the cure of all diseases (those of the nerves immediately and others over a period of time) and could produce a somnambulistic state or trance.

Though rebuffed in his attempt to find acceptance within the academy, Mesmer's ideas found many disciples during the next decades. Scientists tried to refine his theory and discover convincing ways of demonstrating the existence of the magnetic force. Disciples of mesmerism appeared in America throughout the 1830s. Popular lecturers toured the country speaking about and demonstrating the unusual properties of animal magnetism. Eventually, the mesmeric sleep was separated from the rest of the phenomena and the theories about fluids discarded. The magnetic state survives today as the hypnotic state, an altered state of consciousness brought about primarily by suggestion. Spiritualism perpetuated the theories of mesmeric healing fluid or force. The theories survive, though slightly altered by reference to more recent science. The "fluid" has been transformed into electromagnetic energy, part of the invisible light spectrum.

An early contemporary of Mesmer, Swedish scientist Emanuel Swedenborg is most noted for his communications with angelic beings, the results of which filled many volumes of theological treatises and biblical commentaries. Systematized, his thought became the basis of the Church of the New Jerusalem. The church, founded in England shortly after Swedenborg's death, was brought to the United States just after the American Revolution (1775–1783) and spread throughout the Northeast. By the middle of the nineteenth century, it had reached the Midwest and one church had even been planted in San Francisco. (See the more complete discussion of Swedenborg and the movement that grew up around his teachings in chapter 18.)

It can be hard to understand Swedenborg's popularity in the nineteenth century in light of his being so ignored by the late twentieth century. However, one cannot understand Spiritualism without reference to his thought and his metaphysical assumptions, which would become major building blocks taken over by Mary Baker Eddy and her students. First, he championed the notion of the priority of the world of spirit over that of matter. Spirit was ultimately real, whereas matter was only a frail shadow of secondary existence. Matter assumed its reality only in its possession of a correspondence to the spiritual. Second, based upon the priority of spirit and the "law of correspondence" between the spiritual and the material, Swedenborg offered a true spiritual interpretation of scripture to enhance the more mundane literal (i.e., materialistic) interpretation. Often adding lengthy glossaries to his books, Swedenborg proposed a spiritual meaning to various individual concepts, people, and events in the Bible. Although differing in content, both Eddy and Hopkins would follow a similar method in interpreting scripture. Within New Thought, the method of metaphysical interpretation would lead to the monumental *Metaphysical Bible Dictionary* (1932) compiled by Charles S. Fillmore (1854–1948) of the Unity School of Christianity.

Among the people most affected by the mesmerist movement was Phineas P. Quimby. As a young clockmaker in Belfast, Maine, Quimby attended a mesmerist lecture-demonstration by Dr. Robert Collyer (d. 1844) in 1838. Fascinated, he began to experiment with mesmerism and found a suitable subject in Lucius Burkmer, a person who easily slipped into a trance state. While entranced, Burkmer would frequently diagnose and prescribe treatment for illnesses of people brought before him. Quimby noted on several occasions that people were healed by taking a prescribed medicine that had no real medicinal value. Gradually, Quimby discarded any hypotheses about magnetic fluid and attributed the healing agency to what he termed "mind."

Quimby equated God with wisdom, science, or first cause. Wisdom contains all truth, ideas, and knowledge. Wisdom, his favorite term, gives forth an essence that fills all of space, much as perfume fills a room with its odor. This essence is not wisdom, but has the character of wisdom. Matter is created out of this essence, and matter then condenses into the various forms and elements. Out of the most gross matter, human beings were created and breathed with the essence of God, or mind. Quimby compares the individual with a locomotive. The body is the locomotive itself. Mind is the steam that drives it forward. Wisdom is the engineer.

Quimby saw mind as a separate independent reality apart from matter. It is invisible and intelligent. Disease is a malfunction of mind caused by error (a false idea) condensing into the material. The major sources of error, in Quimby's opinion, were religion, reason, and medicine, and he frequently denounced clergy, teachers, and doctors who perpetuated the wisdom (or more correctly, the opinions) of the world and taught people they were sick and going to die. Such diseased ideas led to illness and eventual death. Through the use of the mind, however, Quimby could convince people of the error of false opinion and replace it with the truth of wisdom or science. Once the truth was implanted in the mind of the patient, it could operate directly upon the body to heal. This science was the same as that taught by Christ and could properly be called the science of the Christ.

Toward the end of his life, though Quimby took a few students, he could by no means be said to have started a movement. One of his students, Warren Felt Evans (discussed below), began a healing practice but did not take students of his own. Two of Quimby's students, Annetta and Julius Dresser, did little with what they had learned from him until some years later, after a fourth student, Mary Baker Eddy, had

begun a movement developing ideas concerning health and healing.

Though contemporaries, there is no evidence that Quimby and Ralph Waldo Emerson took note of each other. Their life's works moved in different arenas. Emerson had left the ministry to develop a kind of nature mysticism and to work as a writer and lecturer. In the process, he became the most noted spokesperson for the Transcendentalist movement. During the 1830s, having been inspired by Swedenborg (from whom he frequently drew his concepts), having absorbed some of the basics of Hinduism through the Bhagavad Gita, and having adopted the new Romanticism from Europe, he argued for a united worldview based upon the priority of mind. To Emerson, the world was the product of one mind (God) that is everywhere active (i.e., immanent in nature). Whatever opposes that one mind eventually comes to naught. Good is positive and real. Evil does not really exist, it is merely the privation of good, not an opposing reality in itself. All things proceed out of the same spirit-mind-good, and one's alignment with that good brings strength. The realization of this truth, concluded Emerson, awakens within humanity the religious sentiment.

Most people, even that vast majority who disagreed with his conclusions, read Emerson. In him, the metaphysical tradition found its most significant nineteenth-century propagandist, and through him and his colleagues reached a vast audience.

Warren Felt Evans had been a student of Quimby, but before that he had become a devotee of Swedenborg, so much so that he forsook his Methodist training and became a minister in the Church of the New Jerusalem. But Evans was a sickly man, and along the way he turned to Quimby, under whom he was returned to a degree of health. After Quimby's death, Evans moved to a Boston suburb and opened a healing practice. However, while acknowledging a certain debt to Quimby, he quietly discarded Quimby's ideas and methods. Instead, he found in the broader Swedenborgian worldview a more adequate framework to conduct his therapeutic work. In developing a Swedenborgian interpretation of healing and health, he expanded the tradition in a direction that Swedenborg had never explored. In the end, Evans returned to a mesmeric model, identifying Swedenborg's concept of the divine "influx" with the healing power.

The issue of the extent to which the major figures in the metaphysical tradition referred to or even knew about each other is a matter of intense scholarly debate. It is known, for example, that Emerson read Swedenborg, and Quimby absorbed the magnetist tradition. The well-read Evans seems to have taken ideas from numerous sources, including Hinduism. But there is little to link Mesmer and his contemporary Swedenborg, or Emerson and his contemporary Quimby. Together, however, Mesmer, Swedenborg, Quimby, Emerson, and Evans created a common language, a concern for healing, and an emphasis upon the reality and immanence of the spiritual, which undergirded the work of Mary Baker Eddy and the students who would come after her.

CHRISTIAN SCIENCE. As she launched her public career, Mary Baker Eddy asserted,

At the commencement of the study of Metaphysical science, we must acquaint ourselves with its Principle whereby to gain the demonstration of this Principle in healing the sick. For the sake of brevity, these first lessons are arranged in questions and answers.

"Question—What is God?

"Answer—Jehovah is not a person. God is Principle.

"Question—What is Principle?

"Answer—Principle is Life, Truth and Love, Substance and Intelligence.

"Question—Is there more than one Principle?

"Answer—There is not. The varied manifestations of science have but one Principle, for there is but one God. All science expresses God, and is governed by Principle"

Eddy, *The Science of Man by Which the Sick Are Healed*, 1879.

Mary Baker Eddy, the founder of Christian Science and the Church of Christ, Scientist, grew up in a devout New England Congregationalist home. Her early formal education had been limited by her poor health, but she recovered enough in her teen years to attend Holmes Academy. She married in 1843, but her husband died just months before the birth of their child, an event that signaled another period of poor health for her.

She married again in 1853. Her husband, George Patterson, joined the Union Army during the Civil War, during which he was captured. Meanwhile, Mary had heard of Quimby and in 1862 she traveled to Portland, Maine, to receive treatment. Within a month she was seemingly cured and wrote in praise of Quimby to the newspaper in Portland. Her first stay in Portland, which lasted for three months, began the most crucial and controversial period of her career. It is evident that Quimby had opened up a new direction for her and that she initially gave him enthusiastic credit for an improvement of health. In later years, Eddy's critics would quote her words of appreciation as a means of discrediting her own unique contributions. Hence her relation to Quimby bears close scrutiny.

Her years as a student-associate of Quimby were ones of fluctuating health. After an initial improvement, her health would fail, only to improve when she returned to Maine. Also, while obviously engaged in the study of Quimby's ideas, and enthusiastically using his methods on others, she was not an uncritical student. Like Evans, she had trouble accepting the concept of mind as spiritual matter, and she could not reconcile Quimby's hostility to religion with her own continuing Christian faith. In spite of these differences, Quimby helped her, and she continued her association with him until his death on January 16, 1866. A few days later, she wrote her oft-quoted poem in his memory, "Lines on the Death of P. P. Quimby, who healed with the truth that Christ taught, in contradistinction to all isms."

The death of Quimby, however, was to be immediately followed by events that were to move her into a distinct realm of thought and practice and separate her forever from Quimby's ideas and ways. On February 1, 1866, while visiting Lynn, Massachusetts, Eddy fell on the ice. The next day, she was found to be suffering from severe internal spasms. Taken back to her home in Swampscott, she was confined to her bed. Those in attendance varied in their opinion about her recovery, some even doubting its possibility. Then on February 4, given a Bible to read and left to meditate alone, she was overwhelmed with the conviction that her life was in God and that God was the only life, the sole reality of existence. In that discovery came her healing. She got out of bed, dressed, and walked into the next room to the astonishment of all present.

The next months and years would be ones of personal turmoil, punctuated by her divorcing her husband for desertion, and her growing comprehension of the implication of the insight received at the time of her healing. During the next decade, she would engage in intensive Bible study, struggling to understand the implications of God as healer versus Quimby's notion of mind as healer. In 1870 she formed a partnership with Richard Kennedy as a practitioner and teacher, and in August she held her first class. She also began writing what would eventually become *Science and Health, with Key to the Scriptures*, the first edition of which was published in 1875 (as simply *Science and Health*).

In 1876 the Christian Scientist Association was formed as a fellowship of Eddy's personal students, among whom was Asa Gilbert Eddy (d. 1882), whom she married in 1877. In 1879 the Church of Christ, Scientist, was organized, and two years later Eddy was ordained by her students as its pastor. In 1882 she moved from Lynn to Boston and opened the Massachusetts Metaphysical College. At the college, she taught the basic classes, the successful completion of which allowed students to become Christian Science practitioners. Students later opened Christian Science offices in Boston, in the nearby cities, and gradually in urban centers around the United States and Canada. Chicago quickly arose as the strongest center for Christian Science outside of New England.

As a result of the circulation of *Science and Health* and the work of Eddy's students, Christian Science began to blossom. Before it could establish itself, however, Eddy had to deal with a situation that has distorted the entire history of the Church of Christ, Scientist, and those movements derived from it. The events began with the resignation in 1880 of Edward J. Arens, a former student of Eddy, from the Christian Scientist Association. Before the year was out, he published a pamphlet titled *The Science of the Relation between God and Man and the Distinction between Spirit and Matter*. It seemed to rely heavily upon *The Science of Man*, a booklet originally used as Eddy's textbook, and *Science and Health*. Eddy considered filing suit, but at first rejected the notion.

Then, in 1882, another former student of Quimby, Julius Dresser (1838–1893), returned to Boston after having spent several years in California. He took a Christian Science class from Arens, and in February of 1883 launched an attack upon Eddy in the *Boston Globe* in which he accused her of stealing the thought of Quimby and presenting his ideas as her own under the new label of Christian Science. Eddy answered him. Dresser wrote a second article, which Eddy again answered. In the wake of the series, Eddy filed suit against Arens for plagiarism. Arens tried to refute the charge with a countercharge. Since Eddy had plagiarized from Quimby, he could not be held accountable for any copying from Eddy. He lost the case, and the court ordered the destruction of 3,000 copies of his pamphlet.

Though Eddy won the case, she did so in the absence of Quimby's unpublished papers, as Quimby's son refused to release them for the trial. As a result, Eddy's critics claimed that Arens lost only because he was unable to produce the crucial Quimby manuscripts. The lack of the manuscripts allowed Julius Dresser and his wife, Annetta Dresser, to continue the attack upon Eddy for the rest of their lives. And their son, Horatio Dresser (1866–1954), perpetuated the controversy for decades to come. He would in later years be called upon to write the history of New Thought, the movement that grew out of Christian Science, and in his 1919 work he would enshrine Quimby and largely bypass Eddy. A few years later, when the Quimby manuscripts finally became available, Dresser was chosen to edit the published version.

By the time that the *Quimby Manuscripts* were published, the controversy that began in 1883 had taken on proportions equal to the two parties involved. Christian Scientists frequently tried to argue that Eddy's connection to Quimby was inconsequential, while advocates of New Thought argued that she was totally Quimby's student who merely presented his ideas in a distorted version. Both positions have become untenable in the light of the publication of the Quimby papers and the subsequent historical work. On the one hand, it is impossible to dismiss the role of Quimby in giving direction to Eddy's thought and in providing her a language not otherwise available. At the same time, to equate Quimby's and Eddy's thought is to distort both. They had a profound disagreement on most issues vital to each, such as the existence of matter and the role of religion. More definitively, there is a basic distinction between the thoroughgoing idealism of Eddy as contrasted with the mind-material dualism of Quimby.

THE DEVELOPMENT OF THE CHURCH OF CHRIST, SCIENTIST. Surviving in spite of the Quimby controversy, Eddy built a national and international church. In so doing, she tried to create a body that adhered as far as possible to the Congregationalism of her childhood. Its tenets affirmed the inspired Bible as the sufficient rule leading to eternal life, the one supreme and infinite God, salvation through Christ, and the crucifixion and resurrection of Jesus. One oft-quoted summary of the basic perspective is called the Statement of Being:

> There is no life, truth, intelligence, nor substance in matter. All is infinite Mind and its infinite manifestations, for God is All-in-all. Spirit is immortal Truth; matter is mortal error. Spirit is the real and the eternal; matter is the unreal and

temporal. Spirit is God, and man is His image and likeness. Therefore man is not material; he is spiritual.

Ministers from more traditional Christian churches rejected her formulation of doctrine, arguing that she had poured such new meaning into the affirmations and placed them in such a foreign context as to make them say something completely different from traditional Christianity.

Christian Science progressed through the 1880s. The sale of *Science and Health* necessitated new printings that allowed for its constant revision. In 1883 the first issue of the *Journal of Christian Science* appeared. In 1884 Eddy added an advanced class to the Metaphysical College's curriculum. Graduates of these "normal" classes were certified not only to be practitioners, but to hold their own classes and train new practitioners. Many formed Christian Science institutes in cities across the United States. By 1886 these institutes had produced enough new practitioners to create the National Christian Scientist Association (the Christian Scientist Association being limited to personal students of Eddy).

Then, almost as soon as the organization was established, Eddy had second thoughts about attempts to organize the movement at all. In the fall of 1889, she took action by successively disbanding the Christian Scientist Association, the Massachusetts Metaphysical College, and the Church of Christ, Scientist. Earlier in the year, she had turned the journal over to the National Christian Scientist Association, but after its 1890 meeting its members did not gather. Around the country, however, Christian Science churches were being organized and buildings erected. While she reconsidered the structure of the movement, she worked on a major revision of *Science and Health*.

In 1892 the manifestation of the new direction for the organization of the movement began to be apparent. In 1892, in Boston, she formed the First Church of Christ, Scientist, generally known as The Mother Church. Twenty students became the first members. Tenets, rules, and bylaws were adopted. The Mother Church then assumed the central organizational role in the Christian Science movement. Around it the older remnants (branch churches, for example) of the movement would be reoriented, and from it new elements (the Board of Lectureship, for example) would grow. Membership in The Mother Church became essential for anyone wishing to be active in the movement, as it was a requirement for anyone wishing to take the basic Christian Science class. Local churches continued to exist as autonomously governed bodies, but followed the organizational rules and procedures as laid down in the *Church Manual* of The Mother Church. After 1892, The Mother Church and those in communion with it constituted the center of the Christian Science movement. However, there were always those who were attracted to the teachings and practice of the church but who rejected its organizational formation.

INDEPENDENT CHRISTIAN SCIENCE. Almost from the beginning, Eddy was faced with students who defected but who wished to continue practicing what she had taught them. In some cases, these were students who disagreed on one or two points of belief, but appreciated Eddy's teachings as a whole. More often, students rejected the demands of the organization or the lack of variance in belief it allowed. In any case, as early as 1880, former students of Eddy established offices and retained their previous designation as Christian Science practitioners.

The first significant former student to establish offices was Edward J. Arens, slowed but not stopped by the loss to Eddy in court. He founded the University of the Science of Spirit and authored his own textbook, *The Old Theology*. Even before the 1883 trial, Arens had been making Christian Science history in Chicago. One of his students, George B. Charles, was the first Christian Science practitioner active in Chicago. In 1882 Charles introduced Christian Science to the Sherman family. After their study with him, Bradford Sherman, his wife, Martha Sherman, and their son, Roger Sherman, traveled to Boston and in 1883 took the basic class in Christian Science directly from Eddy. After their return to Chicago, they operated for many years as her authorized representatives.

On October 23, 1881, eight students of the early Lynn group resigned from the Christian Scientist Association, among them Amanda Rice and Elizabeth Stuart. Both continued to practice what they had been taught. Rice introduced Christian Science on the West Coast, while Stuart taught throughout New England and is most remembered as the teacher of some of the most prominent of the New Thought leaders—Leander Whipple and Charles Brodie Patterson.

Throughout the 1880s, as the Church of Christ, Scientist, was spreading across the country and becoming a national church body, an increasing number of individual students defected. Possibly the greatest loss was Emma Curtis Hopkins, editor of the *Christian Science Journal*, who moved to Chicago and founded the Hopkins Metaphysical Association and the Christian Science Theological Seminary, the seed organizations from which New Thought emerged. Even before Hopkins arrived, both A. J. Swartz and Joseph Adams had established rival offices and begun publishing periodicals, *The Mind Cure Journal* and the *Chicago Christian Scientist*. Luther M. Marston, a graduate of Eddy's first normal class, remained in Boston as head of the Boston College of Metaphysical Science and editor of *Mental Healing Monthly*. Mary Plunkett, who had left for Chicago with Hopkins in 1885, moved to New York City several years later to form the International Christian Science Association and another rival journal.

Looking out to see all these independent organizations flourishing, Eddy turned in 1888 to face another mass defection of students in Boston. The occasion for the disruption was the case of Abby H. Corner, a practitioner who was working with her pregnant daughter. At the time of the delivery, both the daughter and the baby died. Corner was indicted for manslaughter. The Christian Scientist Association defeated a motion to contribute to the defense (Eddy preferred contributions come from individual Christian Scientists). In response, Sarah Crosse, a member of the association's

Committee on Publication and a relative of Corner, attacked Eddy and the association's leadership. She gained some support but not enough to take over the association, so with her supporters she withdrew and founded the *Boston Christian Scientist*. Crosse's defection was all the more devastating as it came on the heels of the loss of one of the most prominent Chicago practitioners, Ursula Gestefeld (1845–1921), who would later associate with the New Thought movement.

Among the last breaks between the church and a prominent student prior to Eddy's death was the case of Augusta Stetson (1842–1928). In 1886 Eddy had sent Stetson to New York to lead the work. The work grew under her able care, and around the turn of the century the members built a large Christian Science Institute (teaching facility) on Central Park West with an adjacent home for Stetson. Then, in 1902, Eddy limited the terms of first readers, the position Stetson formally held in New York, to three years. She resigned but remained the popular leader. In 1909 Stetson was accused of both deviating in her teachings and of building a personal following. She was dismissed from the church on Eddy's orders.

When Eddy died without reinstating her, Stetson turned the institute, of which she had remained in charge, into the headquarters of what was termed the Church Triumphant. She continued to preach, teach, and write for the rest of her life.

INDEPENDENTS IN THE TWENTIETH CENTURY. Eddy's death in 1910 created a new series of problems for the church and led to even more independent Christian Science organizations. This second set of groups grew out of the organizational crisis created by the *Church Manual*. The manual, which set the rules for The Mother Church and those individuals and organizations related to it, left many actions (such as filling vacancies in church offices) dependent upon the approval of the pastor (Eddy), who died without naming a successor. Eddy also left two separately created corporations that seemed to have overlapping jurisdictions.

Among the first publicly to discuss the problem of trying to operate the church according to the *Church Manual* was a British Christian Scientist, Annie C. Bill. She suggested a novel solution. The church must be dissolved and reorganized under a new manual (or constitution). She declared herself to be Eddy's successor, based in part upon her articulation of both the problem and the solution. At this time, Bill had been an ex-member of the church for several years, having resigned in 1909. Unsuccessful in having the board of directors of The Mother Church recognize her (though one former member of the board, John V. Dittemore, did join her), she formed the Christian Science Parent Church. Interestingly enough, after Bill's death, her church underwent a change of leadership similar to the one she had advocated for the Church of Christ, Scientist, and emerged as the Church of Integration, which survived into the 1950s.

Quite apart from Bill, in 1918 the organizational crisis in the church resulted in a legal case between the board of publication and the board of directors of The Mother Church. This period, known as the time of the Great Litigation, finally resulted in the court declaring the board of directors to be the ultimate authority in the church. The litigation also led to the dismissal of Herbert W. Eustace (d. 1957), a member of the board of publication, who went on to become a popular writer and practitioner among independents.

During the twentieth century, any number of practitioners left the church to develop their own work independently. Unlike Bill, they have generally refrained from attempting to organize anything resembling a church. Rather they have adopted a notion suggested by Geoffrey Hamlin in his 1922 booklet, *Notes on the Manual and Trust Deed.* Hamlin argued that since the organization of The Mother Church depended so heavily on Mary Baker Eddy, possibly she intended that the church should dissolve after her death. Henceforth, Christian Science should continue without the centralized structure, through the many autonomous churches and practitioners, tied together only by their mutual loyalty to Eddy. For many of the practitioners who became independent, that idea, coupled with a bad experience with the board of directors, served to prevent their creating large churchlike organizations. Most independents merely continued quietly as practitioners. Some privately published and circulated their own writings. A few formed small informal organizations that facilitated their personal (and necessarily limited) healing work, or they published and distributed independent Christian Science writings. Few of these organizations had any continuity from generation to generation, but as they died (with the retirement or death of the individual head), new ones arose.

Among the prominent practitioners asked to leave the Church of Christ, Scientist, have been Peter V. Ross, Alice L. Orgain, Glenn A. Kratzer, William W. Walter, and Lillian de Waters. Others who left, often in the midst of controversy, include Margaret Laird, Hugh A. Studdert-Kennedy, Edward A. Kimball, Bicknell Young, Arthur Corey, Frederick Dixon, John Doorly, and possibly the most famous outside of Christian Science circles, Joel Goldsmith (1892–1964). Goldsmith's work continues under the name Infinite Way. In 1955 the International Metaphysical Association was founded as an umbrella organization for many of the former Christian Scientists. It circulated the works of Ethel Schroeder, Peggy Brooks, Max Kappeler, and Gordon Brown. Closely related to the association was the Rare Book Company of Freehold, New Jersey, which continues to publish and distribute the books and writings of the independents.

After several decades with few new prominent independent centers being created, a new wave of independence began on October 11, 1975, when Reginald G. Kerry, a worker at the church center in Boston, sent a lengthy open letter to all the practitioners and branch churches listed in the *Christian Science Journal.* He noted with alarm the decline in membership during the previous two decades and a financial crisis resulting from overspending on a new center building. He charged gross mismanagement of funds in the

treasurer's office, abuse of authority in the Department of Branches and Practitioners, immorality among all levels of the church's staff at the center, and negligence on the part of the board of directors. He demanded membership action. Responses included further accusations of problems within the church and its center in Boston.

Practitioners who left the church came forward, and a court case ensued. In 1977 the Plainfield, New Jersey, congregation had its name removed from the listing in the *Christian Science Journal.* The Mother Church asked it to discontinue use of the name "Christian Science." It went to court and won the right to continue as an independent Christian Science church. Another group of independents organized as the United Christian Scientists and filed suit to have the textbook, long past its normal 56-year copyright allotment, declared in the public domain. They won the case. As the Kerry letters continued to arrive, Ann Beals, a practitioner from Pasadena, California, opened The Bookmark, a publishing and mail-order distributing company with a branch in England, to assist in the circulation of materials supporting the cause of the independent movement.

Kerry, The Bookmark, and the newer independents represent a new generation of independent Christian Scientists, many of whom have only a passing acquaintance with the earlier independent literature. The Bookmark largely distributes a distinct set of literature from that offered through the Rare Book Company. While lacking association with the earlier independents, the new wave has accepted the thesis concerning Eddy's desire to have The Mother Church dissolve and turn Christian Science into a decentralized movement.

Independent Christian Science has continued as a decentralized movement with different people and organizations taking the lead at various times. Among the prominent independent structures as the twenty-first century begins are Healing Unlimited, which sponsors the Christian Science Library and publishes the periodical *Our Holy Heritage*, and the Christian Science Endtime Center, an independent organization in Denver, Colorado. The Rare Book Company in Freehold, New Jersey, continues to serve the movement as publisher and distributor of unofficial literature.

NEW THOUGHT. By the mid-1880s, an array of healers, most of them in some manner related to Christian Science, were functioning in America, especially in the immediate vicinity of Boston, the other northern urban centers, and a few places in the Midwest, most notably Chicago. Itinerant healers reached almost every American community of any size at some point during the year. Among the large number of Christian Science practitioners radiating from the centers in Boston and Chicago, the independents ranged from those who tried to stick firmly to what they had been taught as members of the Church of Christ, Scientist, to those who merely used Eddy as a point of departure. Among the causes of their deviation was their interaction with other nonconventional religious healers, most notably Spiritualists (such as W. J. Colville), Theosophists (such as M. J. Barnett), and even a few Christian healers, such as Albert Benjamin Simpson

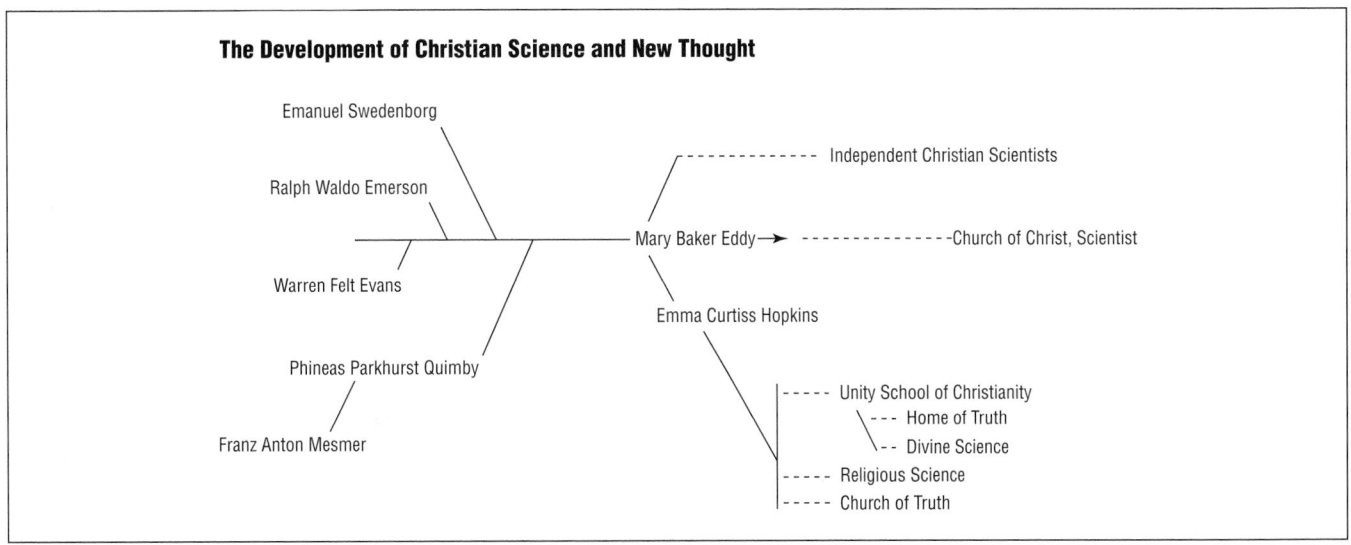

The Development of Christian Science and New Thought

Emanuel Swedenborg

Ralph Waldo Emerson

Warren Felt Evans

Phineas Parkhurst Quimby

Franz Anton Mesmer

Independent Christian Scientists

Mary Baker Eddy → - - - - - - - - - - Church of Christ, Scientist

Emma Curtiss Hopkins

Unity School of Christianity
Home of Truth
Divine Science
Religious Science
Church of Truth

(1843–1919) and Charles Cullis (1833–1892). Quimby student Warren Felt Evans practiced in a Boston suburb and authored a number of books, while the Dressers, making common cause with the independents, continued their attack on Eddy. Into this chaotic situation stepped Emma Curtis Hopkins.

Hopkins first encountered Christian Science in 1881 and two years later moved to Boston to study with Eddy. After taking Eddy's primary class, she was invited to assume editorial duties for the *Christian Science Journal* in early 1884 as Eddy was preparing for an extended trip to Chicago. Her work on the journal continued until November 1885, when she had a sudden break with Eddy, the church, and the Christian Scientist Association. She moved to Chicago and the next summer opened the Emma Hopkins College of Metaphysical Science (modeled on the Massachusetts Metaphysical College) and offered her first classes. Her work was an immediate success, and during the fall enough students had gathered to form the Hopkins Metaphysical Association.

As word spread about her work, students began to travel to Chicago to study with her, and she began to travel to other places—Milwaukee, San Francisco, New York City. By the end of 1887, she was bringing the scientists and students into a string of associated centers that stretched from Maine to California. Not yet content, in 1888 she transformed the college into the Christian Science Theological Seminary and offered advanced training for students planning to enter the Christian Science ministry. (At that time, Eddy was the only person ordained within Christian Science, and since her death the movement has continued to be led by lay people.) In January 1889 Hopkins held the first graduation ceremonies from the seminary, and assuming the office of bishop, she became the first woman to ordain others to the ministry in modern times.

The ordination service highlighted the unique innovation that Hopkins was making in the Christian Science milieu. First, Hopkins attracted primarily women to her school. Among the 22 graduates ordained in that first service

in 1889 only two were men, both husbands of women who were ordained. Second, the service highlighted Hopkins's innovative approach to Christian Science itself. Her theology now assigned women a key position in God's activity in history, especially notable in her consideration of the doctrine of the Trinity. She adopted a form of Trinitarian thought first articulated by Joachim of Fiore (c. 1135–1202) in the twelfth century. Joachim pictured God's distinct manifestation through the different periods of history. God the Father, the first aspect, exemplified the ancient patriarchal ideal. The second era, which began around the time of the birth of the Nazarene (i.e., Jesus), was a time for the masses to free themselves from oppression. The third period, that of the Spirit, the truth-principle, or the mother-principle, was the time for the rise of women. While Eddy has been cited as a woman who assumed a role usually denied women, and is credited with creating a new public role for women, Hopkins now articulated a thoroughgoing feminist theology and opened the Christian ministry to her female students. After ordaining her students, she sent them to create new churches and ministries around the country.

Thus Hopkins, somewhat reluctantly, created the very thing most independents eschewed, a growing organized movement. Then, having trained more than 100 ministers, in 1895 Hopkins retired, closed the seminary, and moved to New York City. She spent the rest of her years taking students on a one-on-one basis. Her former students scattered across the United States and Canada to establish their own variations on Hopkins's thought, just as she had made numerous alterations on Eddy's.

THE DEVELOPING MOVEMENT. As Hopkins's students established their own centers, they began to differentiate themselves from the Christian Science with which they had begun. The search for other institutional names began. Myrtle Fillmore (1845–1931) and Charles Fillmore (1854–1948) in Kansas City adopted the name Unity, possibly inspired by the Unity Publishing Company, the publishing arm of the International Christian Science Association.

Melinda Cramer (d. 1906), one of Hopkins's students in San Francisco, renamed her work Divine Science. Faculty member Helen Van Anderson (b. 1859) moved to Boston after the seminary closed to form the Church of the Higher Life. Faculty member Annie Rix Militz (1856–1924) established the Homes of Truth on the West Coast. George Burnell (1863–1948) and Mary Burnell formed the Burnell Foundation in Los Angeles. Clara Stocker introduced Albert C. Grier (1864–1941) to Hopkins, and he in turn founded the Church of the Truth. One of Hopkins's last students, Ernest S. Holmes (1887–1960), founded the Institute (later, the Church) of Religious Science. In the early twentieth century, these students passed their lineage to the next generation of students. Each ultimately derived their authority for ministry from Hopkins and Eddy, and they eventually found a modest degree of unity in the name of New Thought. First suggested in the 1890s, by the beginning of World War I (1914–1918) it was the generally accepted designation.

New Thought distinguished itself from Christian Science in a variety of ways. First, it came under the leadership of an ordained ministry, though many lay teacher-writers such as Clara Stocker and Harriet Emilie Cady (1848–1941) did yeoman service. Second, it developed a decentralized movement that celebrated its diversity of opinion. Third, almost from the beginning, it developed an emphasis upon prosperity. Without losing the healing emphasis of Christian Science, New Thought leaders reasoned that poverty was as unreal as disease and taught students to live out of the abundance of God. Fourth, while some of the groups, such as the Unity School of Christianity, retained a specifically Christian emphasis, the movement as a whole moved to what it saw as a more universal position that acknowledged all religious traditions as having value.

Significant in the developing presentation of New Thought was Thomas Troward (1847–1916). A retired judge who had served many years in India, Troward developed what amounted to a second career as a New Thought lecturer. His importance came in the introduction of new psychological concepts into the movement in the early twentieth century. Specifically, he argued for the differentiation of the mind into its objective (waking consciousness) and its subjective (unconscious) aspect. In so doing, he opened the movement to the new concept of the dynamic subconscious, a concept missing in both Eddy and Hopkins. Holmes would take Troward's main insights and use them in creating Religious Science.

After several abortive attempts to unite the various New Thought groups, the International New Thought Alliance was finally formed in 1914. It quickly moved to produce a statement of agreement that became its first Declaration of Principles. A revised statement was adopted in 1957. While showing some similarity to the idealistic thought of Eddy, it had moved considerably away from some of her ideas and made no specifically Christian affirmations. It affirmed the belief in God as universal wisdom, love, life, truth, power, peace, beauty, and joy, and the beliefs that the universe is the body of God, that human beings are invisible spiritual dwellers inhabiting bodies, and that human beings continue, grow, and change after death. This statement highlights what is often thought of as the main difference between Christian Science and New Thought. While not leaving the common idealism, New Thought has assigned a more positive role to the body and the material world. Matter is not mortal error; while the material is secondary, it is also the manifestation of spiritual reality. One can begin to see the distinctions by comparing the Christian Science Statement of Being (quoted above) with that of Divine Science:

> God is all, both invisible and visible.
> One Presence, One Mind, One Power is all.
> This One that is all perfect life, perfect love, and perfect substance.
> Man is an individualized expression of God and is ever one with this perfect life, perfect love, and perfect substance.

Both Christian Science and New Thought look to a manifestation of the truth they teach in the individual's life. That manifestation is usually referred to as *demonstration*. To move from sickness to health is to demonstrate healing. To move from poverty to wealth is to demonstrate abundance.

To aid in demonstration is the role of the practitioner, a professional who has been trained in the arts of healing prayer. While each church trains its practitioners in slightly different ways, and advocates slightly different techniques by which they are to work, all of the churches discussed in this chapter provide their membership with the assistance of healing prayer specialists. To pray for healing or some other concern is frequently spoken of as "treating" for health or the improvement of relationships or prosperity. In New Thought churches, some practitioners specialize in assisting the manifestation of abundance. (The Unity School of Christianity is a major exception. It has no practitioners, though it does have licensed Unity teachers, which are somewhat analogous.)

PROSPERITY CONSCIOUSNESS. While healing is the major thrust of both Christian Science and New Thought, the latter has been distinguished by the articulation of a secondary theme, that of god's abundance. Almost from the beginning of the movement, New Thought leaders reasoned that the same allness of God that was total health and healing was also total abundance and wealth. In God, as there was no illness, there also was no poverty.

This twofold emphasis on health and wealth would persist through the years within New Thought churches, but would also produce a more secularized presentation directed to young executives in the emerging corporate world of the 1890s. The first successful advocate of success was Orison Swett Marden (1850–1924), best known for his best-selling *Pushing to the Front* (1894). He would be succeed by the likes of Charles F. Haanel (1866–1949), Napoleon Hill (1893–1970), author of *Think and Grow Rich* (1937), Robert Collier (1885–1950), and insurance executive W. Clement Stone (1902–2002). Most people known for their work on spreading prosperity consciousness have been based in New Thought churches, such as Chicago pastor Johnnie

Coleman's megachurch or Unity's Catherine Ponder, though unlike Ponder, most New thought ministers have emphasized both themes of healing and wealth.

Periodically, prosperity consciousness becomes an object of public attention, such as occurred when Pentecostal evangelist Oral Roberts began to speak of it. His Christianized version of prosperity thinking gave birth to a new school of Pentecostalism, the Word Faith movement, which spread through a number of televangelists, such as Kenneth Hagin (1917–2003), Fred Price, and Kenneth Copeland. The Word Faith movement frequently produces best-selling books, the most recent being the phenomenally successful book and compact disc set, *The Secret* (2006), by Australian New Thought writer Rhonda Byrne.

The New Thought movement is a relatively small segment of the American religious community, the total membership being several hundred thousand. However, it has shown itself immensely influential among the wider public who are unaware or only vaguely aware of New Thought's existence, but who have regularly since the 1890s turned some of its books into best-selling volumes and created New Thought leaders like ministers Norman Vincent Peale (1898–1993) and Robert H. Schuller (b.1926), who have no outward connection to the movement, into religious superstars.

SOURCES

The study of the metaphysical groups is given focus by the Society for the Study of Metaphysical Religion, Box 37, New Port Richey, FL 34656-0037 (websyte.com/alan/ssmr.htm). It publishes *JSSMR: The Journal of the Society for the Study of Metaphysical Religion.*

Archives for Christian Science and related movements are located at the Church of Christ Scientist headquarters in Boston, Massachusetts. A significant collection of Christian Science material has been donated by William Braden to the Perkins School of Theology Library in Dallas, Texas.

There are several archives of New Thought material; among the most significant are those included in the archive of the New Thought movement at the International New Thought Alliance in Mesa, Arizona; the J. Gordon Melton American Religions Collection at the Davidson Library of the University of California–Santa Barbara; the library of the Unity of School of Christianity in Unity Village, Missouri; and the library at the headquarters of United Church of Religious Science (now the United Centers for Spiritual Living) in Burbank, California.

General Sources

Albanese, Catherine. *A Republic of Mind and Spirit: A Cultural History of American Metaphysical Religion.* New Haven, CT: Yale University Press, 2008. 640 pp.

Fuller, Robert C. *Mesmerism and the American Cure of Souls.* Philadelphia: University of Pennsylvania Press, 1982. 227 pp.

Harrington, Anne. *The Cure Within: A History of Mind-Body Medicine.* New York: Norton, 2008. 354 pp.

Judah, J. Stillson. *The History and Philosophy of the Metaphysical Movements in America.* Philadelphia: Westminster Press, 1967. 317 pp.

Meyer, Donald. *The Positive Thinkers: Popular Religious Psychology from Mary Baker Eddy to Norman Vincent Peale and Ronald Reagan.* Rev. ed. Middletown, CT: Wesleyan University Press, 1988. 426 pp.

Parker, Gail Thain. *Mind Cure in New England: From the Civil War to World War I.* Hanover, NH: University Press of New England, 1973. 197 pp.

Podmore, Frank. *Mesmerism and Christian Science: A Short History of Mental Healing.* London: Methuen, 1909. 299 pp.

Zweig, Stefan. *Mental Healers: Franz Anton Mesmer, Mary Baker Eddy, Sigmund Freud* (1932). Trans. Eden and Cedar Paul. New York: Ungar, 1962. 363 pp.

The Forerunners—Quimby and Evans

Clark, Mason Alonzo, ed. *The Healing Wisdom of Dr. P. P. Quimby.* Los Altos, CA: Frontal Lobe, 1982. 127 pp.

Dresser, Annetta Gertrude. *The Philosophy of P. P. Quimby.* Boston: Ellis, 1895. 114 pp.

Dresser, Horatio W. ed. *The Quimby Manuscripts.* New York: Crowell, 1921. 474 pp.

Evans, Warren Felt. *The Mental Cure.* Boston: Colby & Rich, 1869.

———. *Mental Medicine.* Boston: 1873. 15th ed., Boston: Carter, 1885. 216 pp.

———. *Soul and Body.* Boston: Carter, 1876. 147 pp.

———. *The Divine Law of Cure.* Boston: Carter, 1884. 302 pp.

———. *The Primitive Mind Cure.* Boston: Carter & Karrick, 1885. 215 pp.

———. *Esoteric Christianity and Mental Therapeutics.* Boston: Carter & Karrick, 1886. 174 pp.

Hawkins, Ann Ballew. *Phineas Parkhurst Quimby: Revealer of Spiritual Healing to this Age: His Life and What He Taught.* Los Angeles: DeVorss, 1951. 56 pp.

Quimby, Phineas Parkhurst. *Immanuel.* Mokelumne Hill, CA: Health Research, 1960. 109 pp.

Mary Baker Eddy and Christian Science

Baxter, Mary Niblack. *Open the Doors of the Temple: The Survival of Christian Science in the 21st Century.* New York: Hawthorn, 2004. 126 pp.

Beasley, Norman. *The Cross and the Crown.* New York: Duell, Sloan and Pearce, 1952. 664 pp.

———. *The Continuing Spirit.* New York: Duell, Sloan and Pearce, 1956. 403 pp.

Braden, Charles S. *Christian Science Today.* London: Allen & Unwin, 1959. 432 pp.

Christian Science: A Sourcebook of Contemporary Materials. Boston: Christian Science Publishing Society, 1990. 345 pp.

Eddy, Mary Baker. *Science and Health.* Boston: Christian Scientist Publishing, 1875. 456 pp. Authorized ed., *Science and Health, with Key to the Scriptures.* Boston: Trustees Under the Will of Mary Baker G. Eddy, 1906. 700 pp.

———. *The Science of Man by Which the Sick Are Healed.* Lynn, MA: Parker, 1879. 22 pp.

Gill, Gillian. *Mary Baker Eddy.* New York: Perseus Press, 1999. 714 pp.

Gottschalk, Stephen. *The Emergence of Christian Science in American Religious Life.* Berkeley: University of California Press, 1973. 305 pp.

———. *Rolling Away the Stone: Mary Baker Eddy's Challenge to Materialism.* Bloomington: Indiana University Press, 2005. 483 pp.

Knee, Stuart E. *Christian Science in the Age of Mary Baker Eddy.* Westport, CT: Greenwood Press, 1994. 158 pp.

Peel, Robert. *Christian Science: Its Encounter with American Culture.* Garden City, NY: Doubleday, 1965. 224 pp.

———. *Mary Baker Eddy.* 3 vols. New York: Holt, Rinehart and Winston, 1966–1977.

Schoepflin, Rennie B. *Christian Science on Trial: Religious Healing in America.* Baltimore, MD: John Hopkins University Press, 2002. 320 pp.

Studdert-Kennedy, Hugh A. *Christian Science and Organized Religion: A Plea for an Impartial Consideration and the Examination of a New Point of View.* Rev. ed. Los Gatos, CA: Farallon Foundation, 1961. 170 pp.

Swihart, Altman K. *Since Mrs. Eddy.* New York: Holt, 1931. 402 pp.

What Makes Christian Science Christian. Boston: Christian Science
   Publishing Society, 1982. 30 pp.

New Thought

Anderson, Alan. *Horatio W. Dresser and the Philosophy of New Thought.*
   Ph.D. diss., Boston University, 1963. 356 pp.

Anderson, Alan, and Deborah G. Whitehouse. *New Thought: A Practical
   American Spirituality.* New York: Crossroad/Herder & Herder, 1995.
   154 pp.

Beebe, Tom. *Who's Who in New Thought.* Lakemont, GA: CSA Press,
   1977. 318 pp.

Braden, Charles S. *Spirits in Rebellion: The Rise and Development of New
   Thought.* Dallas, TX: Southern Methodist University Press, 1963. 571
   pp.

Dresser, Horatio. *A History of the New Thought Movement.* New York:
   Crowell, 1919. 352 pp.

Harley, Gail M. *Emma Curtis Hopkins: Forgotten Founder of New Thought.*
   Syracuse, NY: Syracuse University Press, 2002. 176 pp.

Koopman, William. *Talking Lightly: Interviews with Leading Personalities of
   New Thought.* Rutland, VT: Tuttle, 1995. 363 pp.

Larson, Martin A. *New Thought: A Modern Religious Approach.* New York:
   Philosophical Library, 1939. 458 pp.

Maday, Michael A., ed. *New Thought for the New Millennium: Twelve
   Powers for the 21st Century.* Unity Village, MO: Unity Books, 1998. 235
   pp.

Martin, Darnise C. *Beyond Christianity: African Americans in a New
   Thought Church.* New York: New York University Press, 2005. 181 pp.

Mosley, Glenn. *New Thought, Ancient Wisdom: The History and Future of
   the New Thought Movement.* West Conshohocken, PA: Templeton
   Foundation Press, 2006. 176 pp.

Satter, Beryl. *Each Mind a Kingdom: American Women, Sexual Purity, and
   the New Thought Movement, 1875–1920.* Berkeley: University of
   California Press, 1999. 394 pp.

Shepherd, Thomas. *Friends in High Places: Tracing the Family Tree of New
   Thought Christianity.* New York: iUniverse, 2004. 228 pp.

Intrafaith Organizations

Affiliated New Thought Network (ANTN)

522 Central Ave., Pacific Grove, CA 93950

The Affiliated New Thought Network is a cooperative fellowship of independent
New Thought Centers formed in 1992. ANTN seeks to assist affiliated centers with
practical knowledge concerning their development as an organization designed to
provide mental, spiritual, emotional, and physical fulfillment. Although creedless,
the centers share an appreciation for the New Thought tradition as found in the
writings of the Transcendentalists, Ralph Waldo Emerson, and Ernest S. Holmes.

Membership: In 2008 the fellowship reported 42 affiliated centers in 17 states, as
well as 36 independent ministers in the United States and 1 in Australia.

Educational Facilities:

Emerson Institute.

Sources:

Affiliated New Thought Network. www.newthought.org.

International New Thought Alliance (INTA)

5003 E Broadway Rd., Mesa, AZ 85206

The International New Thought Alliance was founded in 1914 as an ecumenical
expression of the merging New Thought movement. It recognizes Phineas P.
Quimby (1802–1866) as the "Father of New Thought."

The alliance, a successor to some earlier attempts at developing the New
Thought, formed as an umbrella organization to further the work of numerous
groups and individuals and adopted a Declaration of Principles. Believers in the
New Thought have a primary mission to heal the sick through prayer. Individuals
affirm their faith through the "Divine Nature"—health, wisdom, love, life, truth,
power, peace, beauty, and joy. People are considered to be invisible spiritual
dwellers within human bodies and will unfold as spiritual beings beyond the
change called physical death.

Membership: In 2008 the alliance reported approximately 145 congregations in
the United States as well as six in Canada, one in Australia, one in Ghana, two in
the West Indies, one in New Zealand, one in the Philippines, and one in France.

Periodicals: *New Thought.*

Sources:

International New Thought Alliance. www.newthoughtalliance.org/.

 ## Christian Science

Church of Christ, Scientist

Christian Science Church Center, Boston, MA 02115-3195

Alternate Address: The First Church of Christ, Scientist, 210 Massachusetts Ave.,
Boston, MA 02115-3195.

The Church of Christ, Scientist, grew out of the experiences, work, and writings of
Mary Baker Eddy. Following her healing in 1866, which happened concurrently
with her discovery of God as the sole reality of life, Eddy began a period of Bible
study that involved testing the practicality of her new discovery, as well as questioning the earlier teachings on mental healing she had received from Phineas P.
Quimby. The result was the development of her thought, first expressed in a booklet, *The Science of Man* (1870), and later embodied in her textbook, *Science and
Health with Key to the Scriptures* (1875). Eddy began almost immediately to apply
the precepts of Christian Science to healing and to teach them informally to others. Her work led her to seek a letter of dismissal from the Congregational Church
in which she was raised, and in 1876 she founded the Christian Science
Association, the first organization for her students.

The next 16 years saw the development of a variety of organizational expressions, some temporary, some lasting. A final reorganization in 1892, and the
development of the church's by-laws in the *Church Manual* (1895), resulted in the
church as it is known today. These 16 years were punctuated by the formation of
the Church of Christ, Scientist, in 1879; Eddy's ordination in 1881; the dissolution
of the church in 1889; and its reorganization in 1892. This reorganization placed
the governance of the Christian Science movement in the First Church of Christ,
Scientist, of Boston, generally known as the Mother Church. The remainder of
Eddy's life was spent in perfecting the textbook of the movement, which went
through several revisions, and in completing by-laws as codified in the *Church
Manual.* The texts of these two volumes remain the prime sources of the church's
doctrine and polity.

The beliefs of the Church of Christ, Scientist, are summarized in a set of Tenets
printed in both *Science and Health* (p. 497) and the *Church Manual* (p. 15). The
Church defines itself as Christian in essence, a major difference between it and
most other "metaphysical" churches with which it is often compared. The Tenets
affirm the Church's allegiance to the inspired Word of the Bible as the sufficient
guide to Life, and belief in one God, God's Son, the Holy Ghost, and man as being
in God's likeness and image. Forgiveness for sin comes with spiritual understanding that casts out evil as having no God-ordained reality. Jesus is acknowledged as
the Way-shower. His atonement, as the evidence of God's love and salvation,
comes through the Truth, Life, and Love he demonstrated in his healing activity
and by his overcoming sin and death.

Healing activity following the principles laid down in the Bible and in *Science and Health* has been the keynote of the Christian Science movement. Christian healing is a normal practice among members—with some giving their full time to the ministry of spiritual healing. This is in accord with Eddy's experience of the allness of God. Spiritual healing is distinct from other forms of healing, especially psychic or magnetic healing.

Eddy is held in high regard by Christian Scientists. The church does, however, carefully distinguish Eddy's status and role as the discoverer of Christian Science from that of Jesus as the Savior of humanity. In like measure, while acknowledging the essential and central role of the Christian Science textbook, it does not understand *Science and Health with Key to the Scriptures* to be a second Scripture or a revelation equal in authority to the Bible. Rather, *Science and Health* is considered a tool for understanding the Bible.

The governance of the Christian Science movement is vested in the Mother Church, whose rules of operation are spelled out in the *Church Manual*. Administration is placed in a five-member, self-perpetuating board of directors. The board charters branch churches, which are run according to their own democratic control (apart from any matters covered in the *Church Manual*). Worship in all branch churches is conducted by elected readers, each of whom must be a member in good standing of the Mother Church. Services in the branch churches consist of readings from scripture and *Science and Health*. The exact passages for each week are delineated in *The Christian Science Quarterly*.

Publications of the Church are produced by the Christian Science Publishing Society and its board of directors. Included in its publications are its award-winning newspaper, *The Christian Science Monitor*; its prime foreign language periodical, *The Herald of Christian Science* (published in 12 languages and in braille for the blind); and numerous books and pamphlets. Eddy's writings are controlled and published by the Trustees Under the Will of Mary Baker Eddy. Under the board of directors of the Mother Church is a board of lectureship that approves speakers who travel the world offering free public lectures on Christian Science. The Committee on Publication is charged with correcting false information about the church and injustices done to Mrs. Eddy, the Mother Church, and Christian Scientists.

Headquarters of the church are in the Christian Science Church Center (also known as Christian Science Plaza), a large complex in Boston, Massachusetts, that has become one of the city's most-visited tourist stops. As of 2008 approximately 2,000 branch churches and societies exist in more than 80 nations of the world (though approximately 73 percent of the membership is in North America).

Membership: Not reported.

Educational Facilities:

Principia College, Elsah, Illinois. (Unofficial.)

Periodicals: *The Christian Science Monitor*. • *The Christian Science Journal*. • *Christian Science Sentinel*. • *The Herald of Christian Science*. • *The Christian Science Quarterly Bible Lessons (Study Edition)* (published in 12 languages).

Remarks: Since its founding, the Church of Christ, Scientist, has been the subject of intense controversy. Its healing emphasis brought criticism from a variety of perspectives, encompassing both those who shared the emphasis but followed a different set of teachings and practices, and those who disapproved of any form of spiritual healing. The most intense criticism found its way into various legal proceedings and has led to an extensive body of legal opinion defining the rights and limits of Christian Science practice. Courts have defined Christian Science healing as a form of worship and thus a legally protected activity of the church. Deductions for some Christian Science services are allowed by the U.S. Internal Revenue Service. Various state-level committees have issued handbooks defining the legal rights and obligations of Christian Scientists in some detail.

During the 1880s Eddy was accused of drawing her teachings from Phineas P. Quimby—first by Annetta Dresser and her husband, Julius Dresser, who, like Eddy, had been students of Quimby, and later by numerous members of what became known as the New Thought movement. An impartial examination of Eddy's writings and the publications of the Church of Christ, Scientist, however, reveals an essential difference between Eddy's teachings on healing and those of Quimby and shows that the major similarity lies in the area of terminology, and results from the attempt to struggle with some of the same questions of religion and health.

The Church of Christ, Scientist, has maintained over the years that there is a basic gulf between its teachings and those of the New Thought movement. This difference is highlighted in Eddy's rejection of Quimby's adherence to magnetic healing and the movement's abandonment of Eddy's essential Christian orientation. The Church also disapproves of the emphasis in the movement on prosperity and the openness to various psychic and occult practices most evident in some of the larger New Thought groups. Christian Science retains a focus on healing and has denounced Spiritualism and animal magnetism, the forms of the occult most evident in Eddy's lifetime, from its earliest years. Some obvious differences between New Thought and Christian Science can be seen by comparing the Tenets of the Church with the Declaration of the International New Thought Alliance (INTA). Despite these differences, the two movements are historically related. New Thought was, to a great extent, built upon the work of Eddy's early students, particularly Emma Curtis Hopkins, and used *Science and Health* as a major sourcebook. Today, New Thought groups vary considerably, from those who are close to Eddy's teaching to those who more closely follow Quimby while developing their own form of metaphysical thought.

Finally, over the years the Church has had to face formal and informal challenges to its authority, beginning with the various individuals and groups claiming to have inherited Mary Baker Eddy's authority. These challenges led to the formation of several movements, such as the Christian Science Parent Church, none of which prospered more than a few years. There is, of course, a small but steady stream of practitioners who have left the church and who continue to practice independently. Many have built a successful personal following (possibly the most prominent being Joel S. Goldsmith). Most, however, have been anti-organization and their following has continued only briefly after their retirement or death.

Sources:

Church of Christ, Scientist. www.churchofchristscientist.org.

Braden, Charles S. *Christian Science Today*. Dallas, TX: Southern Methodist University Press, 1958.

Christian Science: A Sourcebook of Contemporary Materials. Boston: Christian Science Publishing Society, 1990.

Eddy, Mary Baker. *Church Manual of the First Church of Christ, Scientist, in Boston, Mass*. Boston: Trustees Under the Will of Mary Baker Eddy, 1908.

———. *Science and Health with Key to the Scriptures*. Boston: Trustees Under the Will of Mary Baker Eddy, 1906.

Gill, Gillian. *Mary Baker Eddy*. Reading, MA: Perseus Books, 1998.

Gottschalk, Stephen. *The Emergence of Christian Science in American Religious Life*. Berkeley: University of California Press, 1973.

Peel, Robert. *Mary Baker Eddy*. 3 vols. New York: Holt, Rinehart, & Winston, 1971.

Swihart, Altman K. *Since Mrs. Eddy*. New York: Henry Holt & Co., 1931.

Infinite Way

PO Box 8260, Moreno Valley, CA 92552

The Infinite Way is the name given to the teachings of Joel S. Goldsmith (1892–1964), a nonpracticing Jew who encountered Christian Science as a young man. When Goldsmith's father was healed by a practitioner in 1915, Goldsmith began seriously to study Christian Science. Later, consulting a practitioner for help with a cold, he found himself cured not only of the cold, but also of smoking and drinking. The experience changed his life. He began to pray for people, and to his amazement, they were healed. He joined the Church of Christ, Scientist, and became a practitioner, a practice he pursued for sixteen years. In 1946, however, after having grown uncomfortable with the pressure of the organization, he withdrew from the church. He began working on a book, *The Infinite Way*, and then accepted invitations to teach and lecture, primarily on the West Coast and Hawaii.

In 1946, a year after withdrawing from Christian Science, he experienced a mystic "initiation" that lasted over several months and that has been described as lifting him to a new dimension of life, a God-experience. Most of the Infinite Way emphases derive from that incident. The Infinite Way represents a mystical form of Christian Science. Without rejecting healing or prosperity demonstration, Goldsmith centered his teaching on the experience of God, believing that the seeker of truth begins with solving problems and overcoming discord. When these endeavors become futile, he can then perceive that one can transcend them. Desiring to improve his human condition, he can move toward spiritual consciousness.

Spiritual consciousness is attained by contemplative meditation, the holding of spiritual truth in the consciousness. As posited by the Infinite Way, pure meditation is the state of complete silence within. God is within; people cannot make it so, they can only come to the realization. To establish a relationship with the God within is to be able to tap the ready supply of all that makes life worthwhile. As the Infinite Way stresses, God appears as the many, but appearance must not be confused with reality. Christ is the activity of truth within each individual consciousness. The revelation brought by Jesus is the revelation of the Christ.

Goldsmith rejected the idea of founding another organization, and during his lifetime the Infinite Way existed only as an informal circle of his students. However, he did offer regular classes that were taped and transcribed (and later became the bases for several books). A newsletter provided a means to keep the scattered students in regular contact. The first of several Infinite Way study centers appeared in Chicago in 1954. For several years after Goldsmith's death, his wife, Emma Goldsmith (1904–1986), continued to issue the newsletter from Hawaii, with the editorial assistance of Lorraine Sinkler, a longtime student. Emma Goldsmith moved to Arizona, and with the assistance of Thelma G. "Geri" McDonald, her daughter (by a previous marriage), continued to make available the tapes of his lectures. McDonald continued this work after her mother's death. The majority of Goldsmith's material has been edited by Sinkler and published in book form.

Membership: Because the Infinite Way is not an organization but rather a designation given to Goldsmith's teachings, there is no formal membership. In 2008 McDonald reported that she and her daughter, Sue Ropac, were available to conduct classes and give lectures upon invitation.

Periodicals: *The Monthly Letter*.

Sources:

The Infinite Way. www.joelgoldsmith.com.

Goldsmith, Joel S. *The Art of Spiritual Healing*. New York: Harper & Row, 1959.

————. *The Infinite Way*. San Gabriel, CA: Willing Publishing Company, 1961.

Sinkler, Lorraine. *The Alchemy of Awareness*. New York: Harper & Row, 1977.

————. *The Spiritual Journey of Joel S. Goldsmith*. New York: Harper & Row, 1973.

International Metaphysical Association

Current address not obtained for this edition.

Among the various independent Christian Science groups, the International Metaphysical Association (IMA), formed in 1955, is perhaps the largest and most influential. It was formed by a number of ex-members of the Church of Christ, Scientist, who saw that the often individual, fragmentary and undisciplined study of independent followers of Mary Baker Eddy was inadequate. The Association has as its purposes to bring to public notice Eddy's scientific revelation, and to encourage students of Christian Science to regard the teachings as a science and approach them in an orderly way.

To accomplish these goals, it sponsors television and radio work, lectures and special schools, and publishes a number of pamphlets and books. Closely associ-

ated is the independent Rare Book Company, which has reprinted the first three editions of *Science and Health* by Mary Baker Eddy and serves as a clearinghouse and distributor of much Christian Science literature.

The IMA is headed by a seven-member board of trustees which included Ethel Schroeder, a popular speaker and writer. In 1966, it sponsored its first international conference, which featured popular independent Christian Scientists from Europe: Peggy Brook, Max Kappeler, and Gordon Brown. A second conference was held in California in 1968. At the time of last publication, the mailing list of the IMA included students from around the United States, some of whom were banded into study groups that use IMA material.

Membership: Not reported.

Periodicals: *Independent Christian Science Quarterly*.

Sources:

Brown, W. Gordon. *Christian Science Nonsectarian*. Haslemere, Surrey, England: Gordon & Estelle Brown, 1966.

Kappeler, Max. *Animal Magnetism—Unmasked*. London: Foundational Book Company Limited, 1975.

Schroeder, Ethel. *Science of Christianity*. New York: International Metaphysical Association, n.d.

William Samuel Foundation

307 N Montgomery St., Ojai, CA 93023

William Samuel (1924–1996) was a writer and teacher in the field of religion, science, and metaphysics. In 1968 he began publishing *Notes from Woodsong* (originally *Notes from Lollygog*), sent to an unspecified number of students across the United States. Groups in several areas formed to study the letters and Samuel's books, most notably *A Guide to Awareness and Tranquillity*. Samuel professed a profound sense of well-being and a surprising ability to pass that well-being on to others. He asserted that tranquillity is acquired not through step-by-step methods but rather by simplicity and honesty in a childlike approach.

Periodicals: *The Child Within, A Journal*.

Membership: Not a membership organization. The foundation looks to a community of like-minded people who support the ideas articulated in Samuel's books and wish to communicate with each other about living with these ideas.

Sources:

William Samuel and Friends. www.williamsamuel.com/.

Samuel, William. *The Child within Us Lives!: A Synthesis of Science, Religion and Metaphysics*. Mountain Brook, AL: Mountain Brook Publications, 1986.

————. *A Guide to Awareness and Tranquillity*. Lakemont, GA: CSA Press, 1967.

————. *The Melody of the Woodcutter and the King*. Palo Alto, CA: Seed Center, 1976.

————. *2 Plus 2=Reality*. Lakemont, GA: CSA Press, 1963.

Truth Center

566 Crestview Dr., Ojai, CA 93023

Truth Center was founded in Los Angeles, California, in 1970 by W. Norman Cooper. Born in Winnipeg, Canada, in the 1920s, as a youth Cooper moved with his family to Los Angeles in 1939. He received his college degree from Chapman College and a Doctor of Divinity degree from Eastern Nebraska Christian College (associated with the Congregational Church of Practical Theology and now superceded by St. John's University, Ponchatoula, Louisiana). An active church worker, he withdrew from church life in 1965 and spent three years largely in meditation. After his years of withdrawal he began to hold one-day seminars to share his discoveries and later initiated Sunday services. This activity led to the organization of Truth Center.

Cooper's teachings emphasize two principal aspects. He teaches the Bible and Bible history (primarily the Gospels) as illustrative of the inner life. In this process he has come to believe that the apocryphal *Gospel of Thomas* provides the purest presentation of Jesus' teachings. Secondly, he emphasizes the inner search for one's divine Self. He advises daily meditation. The inward search should lead to a realization of the individual's oneness with the Source, i.e., God. Cooper also stresses the need for activity in the world as opposed to merely a self-centered mysticism.

Membership: At the time of last publication, there was one center in Los Angeles where most of Cooper's students resided. However, some of Cooper's students were scattered across the United States.

Sources:

Cooper, W. Norman. *Dance with God*. Marina del Rey, CA: DeVorss & Company, 1982.

————. *The Non-Thinking Self*. Marina del Rey, CA: DeVorss & Company, 1980.

Field, Filip. *W. Norman Cooper, a Prophet for Our Time*. Marina del Rey, CA: DeVorss & Company, 1979.

Witt, Roselyn. *W. Norman Cooper, A View of a Holy Man*. Marina del Rey, CA: DeVorss & Company, 1982.

United Christian Scientists
Current address not obtained for this edition.

United Christian Scientists was founded in 1975 in New Jersey by a group of independent students of Christian Science. The following year David James Nolan of San Jose, California, was elected to serve as chairman of the religious education foundation. The prime issue raised by the United Christian Scientists concerns the polity of the Church of Christ, Scientist. They filed a suit seeking to have the text of the writings of Mary Baker Eddy declared in the public domain and were successful. More recently they have begun a probe into the issues involved in the establishment of centralized control at the Boston, Massachusetts, headquarters of the Church of Christ, Scientist, in what they consider to be flagrant disregard of Eddy's instructions to dissolve such control at the time of her passing.

The United Christian Scientists operate within the context of the larger movement of independent Christian Scientists, continuing their work individually in much the same way as they did prior to leaving the Church of Christ, Scientist.

Membership: Not reported.

 New Thought

Antioch Association of Metaphysical Science
Current address not obtained for this edition.

The Antioch Association of Metaphysical Science is a metaphysical church founded in 1932 by Dr. Lewis Johnson of Detroit, Michigan. It serves a predominantly black membership.

Membership: Not reported. In 1965 there were 6 churches.

Christ Truth League
2409 Canton Dr., Fort Worth, TX 76112

The Christ Truth League was founded in 1938 by Alden Truesdell (d. 1985) and his wife, Nell Truesdell (d. 1971), as an independent ministry and fellowship of students seeking what they believed to be the right application of the law of life as taught and lived by Jesus Christ. The Truesdells were closely aligned with the teachings of Harley Bradley Jeffery (1872-1954).

Jeffery was a popular New Thought author and lecturer for most of the first half of the twentieth century. He had come into New Thought through the efforts of Charles Brodie Patterson and studied with Emma Curtis Hopkins, with whom he collaborated while she was writing her classic study, *High Mysticism*. He studied in England with Thomas Troward and was associated for a period with the Unity School of Christianity. During his mature years he produced a number of books developed out of the concepts of *High Mysticism*, including: *The Principles of Healing* (1939), *Coordination of Spirit, Soul, and Body* (1948), and *Mystical*

Teachings (1954). After Jeffery's death, the Truesdells acquired rights to his works and, for more than 30 years, carried on his ministry, published his books, and saw to their distribution. The Truesdells have been succeeded by Dr. Robert Applegate, the current minister and president of the league. The magazine *Spiriticity* has recently resumed publication. The league is a member of the International New Thought Alliance (INTA).

Membership: The league is a free fellowship with no formal membership. At the time of last publication, there was one center, in Fort Worth, Texas, where Sunday services and weekly classes were offered, with affiliated work in Benin, Nigeria, and the Philippines.

Sources:

Jeffery, H. B. *Coordination of Spirit, Soul and Body*. Fort Worth, TX: Christ Truth League, 1948.

————. *Mystical Teachings*. Forth Worth, TX: Christ Truth League, 1954.

————. *The Principles of Healing*. Fort Worth, TX: Christ Truth League, 1939.

————. *The Spirit of Prayer*. Cambridge, MA: Ruth Laighton, 1938.

Christian Assembly
PO Box 6120, San Jose, CA 95150

Among the most specifically Christian of the several New Thought groups is the Christian Assembly. It was founded by William Farwell in 1900 in San Jose, California, as a branch of the Home of Truth, the loose association of centers led by Annie Rix Militz. Around 1920 Farwell's congregation separated from the Home of Truth and took its present name. The Christian Assembly believes Christianity is founded upon the doctrines of Jesus Christ and the Bible, and these are used by the Assembly as a source of teaching. The Bible contains a spiritual sense within its historical/literal sense, and this spiritual meaning can be discerned by the Spirit of truth working upon the understanding.

Unlike many New Thought groups, the Christian Assembly has attempted to produce a summary statement of its beliefs. The fundamental principles of the teaching of the Christ include: God is Spirit, whose nature is love and wisdom; the kingdom of God is within; Jesus is the Christ, the son of the living God; he is divine and human (a perfect unity) and, as the risen Lord, he abides in his kingdom within; true faith comes from God and makes all things possible; evil has no power from God; love is the fulfillment of the law which is constitutional to man; Christian healing is properly a part of the gospel; the kingdom is known through works of faith and love. The work of the Christian Assembly is centered upon a weekly Sunday morning worship service, prayer groups, and Bible classes and truth lectures through the week. The sacraments have been discontinued so that concentration can be upon inner meaning.

Over the years, branches of the Christian Assembly were established in the San Francisco Bay area. At the time of last publication, ministers trained and ordained by the Christian Assembly were pastors of branch churches in Gilroy, Palo Alto, Oakland, Redwood City, and San Jose (2). Farwell was also a prolific writer, and the assembly has published much of his material.

Membership: Not reported. In 1971 there were 6 congregations.

Sources:

Farwell, William. *Be Thou a Blessing*. San Jose, CA: First Christian Assembly, 1936.

————. *The Paraclete*. San Jose, CA: Christian Assembly, 1928.

Church of the Fuller Concept
Current address not obtained for this edition.

The Church of the Fuller Concept is a New Thought group headed by Dr. Bernese Williamson, a doctor of metaphysical science. Dr. Williamson teaches that we live in the God dispensation. God is our Father and Mother, our natural parents being God caring for us. God has a body (I Cor. 11:30) and is manifested in body-form on earth. Man's body is the image and likeness of God. In recognizing God's body, man can have the blessing of a healthy, whole body. Members of the church do not carry insurance, because in God, where man lives and moves and has his being (which is the body of God), there can be no illness. Dr. Williamson teaches that every meal is a communion and that what one visualizes as he eats and drinks will materialize.

Headquarters of the church are at the Hisacres New Thought Center in Washington, D.C. Members live by a pledge to remember their spiritual nature. They greet each other with the word, "Peace." They adopt spiritual names, because they want to acquire the nature, characteristics and attributes of God. All students sign a pledge to give honest service to their employer for their pay, not accepting tips or vacation-with-pay, nor using intoxicants on the job. This pledge is given to the employers.

Membership: Not reported.

Church of the Trinity (Invisible Ministry)

Box 4608, Salem, OR 97302-8608

Friend Stuart (i.e., A. Stuart Otto) was a West Coast publisher who, in 1954, had a religious awakening that started his metaphysical search. Over the next few years, he was able to study with many of the outstanding New Thought leaders. In 1957, a series of additional enlightenment experiences began, culminating in 1963 with an inward ordination in what is called the invisible ministry. Three years later, Stuart began to conduct private metaphysical practice under the name "Invisible Ministry," and, in 1967, obtained a charter and began issuing *Tidings* as a quarterly bulletin. Work was primarily by mail at a distance, though classes were held at the Invisible Ministry center. In 1972, Church of the Trinity was established as an outgrowth of the healing ministry.

The theology of Church of the Trinity is based upon the work of James Allen, Henry Drummond, Emmet Fox, and Friend Stuart. The church is grounded in the faith that the Christian doctrine of the Father, Son, and Holy Spirit is the ultimate spiritual truth, and that all things proceed from these three aspects of almighty God. The church calls its theology the science of dominion, the Christ Jesus way. According thereto, man fulfills his destiny by achieving dominion and glorifies God in so doing. Jesus came to overcome death, and, as we recognize truth, we are freed of disease, disharmony, and lack. Those on the way are members of the fifth kingdom. The Church of the Trinity thus is similar to the Unity School of Christianity in its emphasis on specifically Christian tenets that are allegorized in a New Thought framework. However, the church is strictly trinitarian, an aspect not strongly emphasized by Unity.

The Church of the Trinity is purely spiritual and refrains from involvement in secular matters. It enjoins its members to obey the law and to be good citizens. Healing is the major concern, and the church sees itself as a balancing influence with Christ's church as a whole. Seven sacraments are practiced by members: baptism, confirmation, communion, matrimony, holy orders, cognition of divine life, and expiation. As of 1972, there was only one center of the Church of the Trinity, but others were imminent and a school of theology has been opened.

Membership: Not reported, but in 1992 the *Tidings* newsletter reported a circulation of 400 copies. The church considers all baptized Christians as members. In 1992 there were two ministers and one center with affiliated work in Nigeria and the Philippines led by lay members. Affiliated individuals and supporters of the ministry, especially those involved in the healing work, can be found across the United States. They stay in contact through the mail.

Educational Facilities:

Trinity School of Theology, San Marcos, California.

Periodicals: *Tidings* • *Theologia 21Master Thoughts* • *The Theologia 21 Encyclopedia*.

Divine Science Federation International

8084 Watson Rd., Ste. 236, St. Louis, MO 63119

Divine Science continues the merger of two streams of early metaphysical teachings, both of which began in the 1880s and both of which had derived from the initial work of Emma Curtis Hopkins, the founder of what today is termed New Thought. The first stream began in 1886 with Kate Bingham of Pueblo, Colorado. Bingham went to Chicago, Illinois, hoping to find some cure for her illness. She found that healing under the ministration of Mabel MacCoy, a student of Hopkins, who sent Bingham to her teacher for classes. Bingham would eventually complete the ministerial course at the Christian Science Theological Seminary and be ordained by Hopkins. Meanwhile, however, after completing her basic class work with Hopkins, Bingham returned to Colorado in 1887 to teach a class attended by two sisters, Nona Lovell Brooks (1862–1945) and Althea Brooks Small. Nona Brooks experienced a healing as a result of the class. At about the same time, MacCoy held a class in Denver, Colorado, which was attended by yet a third sister, Fannie Brooks James. By the summer of 1887 the Hopkins School of Christian Science was flourishing in Denver. It continued to be active until the mid-1890s, when Hopkins retired from her work in Chicago and moved into private work in New York.

At about the same time that Bingham was offering her class in Pueblo, Colorado, Hopkins traveled to San Francisco, California, and held a class in April 1887 attended by more than 200 people. Among those in attendance were Miranda Rice and Malinda Elliott Cramer (1844–1906). Miranda Rice had been an early student of Mary Baker Eddy but had left the Church of Christ, Scientist, moved to San Francisco, and opened the first Christian Science practitioners' office on the West Coast. Malinda Cramer had moved to San Francisco in 1870, hoping that the climate would be a cure for the ill health she had suffered for many years. She found that cure in 1885. Both women attended Hopkins's class. Malinda Cramer began sharing and healing, and in 1887 began teaching classes and then incorporated the Home College of Divine Science, with which Rice affiliated. Later that year Cramer began publishing *Harmony*, one of the most prominent early New Thought periodicals.

The Denver and San Francisco streams began to flow together in 1889 when William McKendree Brown, a student of Hopkins from Iowa, moved to Denver and became the local agent in charge of distributing *Harmony*. In early 1890, Cramer came to Denver and taught a number of classes that were well received. Nona Brooks attended the classes and discovered a close affinity with Cramer. In 1892 Cramer formed the International Divine Science Association, originally an attempt to build a fellowship association for the early New Thought centers in the West and Midwest. Annie Rix Militz of the Home of Truth served as the first vice president. The first convention was held in San Francisco in 1894. The association continued to hold meetings through the end of the century.

In the early 1890s Nona Brooks moved to Denver, where Fannie James had organized a separate metaphysical group. Over the years the sisters had developed several important differences with Kate Bingham and the ideas taught her by Hopkins. They also began to remold Hopkins's basic teaching around the central concept of the omnipresence of God. For example, they rejected any notion of prayer as supplication and centered their work on meditation as contemplation of God's omnipresence. They discarded any distinction between a mortal and immortal mind, present in both Eddy and Hopkins's thought, in favor of a simple reliance on omnipresence. They disagreed with the idea of *chemicalization*, passed on by Hopkins from Eddy, which explained what happened when some patients seem to get worse before getting better. They also rejected Hopkins's use of alternating denials and affirmations in treating patients, as well as the multiple six-day healing treatments that utilized them. They preferred a single-method treatment, which merely affirmed the omnipresence of God.

In the mid-1890s Althea Small also moved to Denver. Brooks and James were already holding classes and doing healing from the latter's home. However, by 1896 the work required them to open an office in downtown Denver. In 1898 they incorporated as the Divine Science College. Brooks received her ordination from Cramer that year, and on Sunday, January 1, 1899, Brooks opened the first church chartered by the college. James served as president of the college until her death during World War I, after which Brooks succeeded her. The formal organization of the work in Denver was vital to the survival of the movement, because the work in San Francisco was destroyed in the San Francisco earthquake and subsequent fire of 1906. Cramer herself died from injuries sustained in the disaster. Indeed, there have been many myths written about the beginnings of Divine Science, perhaps partly because much of Cramer's historic, prolific writings were lost in the earthquake and subsequent fire.

Following the demise of Cramer, Nona Brooks came to the forefront as the leader. In response to divine guidance in 1929, Brooks resigned from the church but returned to Denver in 1938 and continued to be a part of the community and church family until her death in 1945. She was ably assisted over the years by some of the most talented teachers in the New Thought field. During the early twentieth century, W. John Murray and Ernest S. Holmes (later to found Religious Science) were ordained by Divine Science. Emmet Fox, at one time the preacher for the largest New Thought congregation in America, was a Divine Scientist. More recently Joseph Murphy, who had the largest New Thought audience in Southern California, built up the Los Angeles church.

BELIEFS. Divine Science teachings explain that Divine Science is a wholly open spiritual yet scientific and practical religion based on the teachings of Christ Jesus. Divine Science acknowledges every advance in the world of natural science, art, and religion as the further expansion of God-consciousness in man, and proclaims the right of man to achieve—through right thinking and true living—health, wealth, happiness, and power. Divine Science teachings are based in the Statement of Being: "God is All, both visible and invisible. One Presence, One Mind, One Power is all. This One that is All is perfect Life, perfect Love, and perfect Substance. Man [later changed to I AM] is the individualized expression of God and is ever one with this perfect Life, perfect Love, and perfect Substance." The numerous expressions of the Statement of Being are all formulated to accord with the Law of Expression, the process by which the Creator reveals or produces creation. By this law it is seen that "like produces like, or that which is born of Spirit is Spirit." This law shows the relationship existing between cause and effect, between God the creator and God the creation. It works from the invisible to the visible, from principle to example, from the inner to the outer. Divine Science believes in the omnipresence of God and that evil comes from man's perception of the world and from man's inhumanity to man.

ORGANIZATION. The work of Divine Science grew rather informally; churches are autonomous and there is no creed other than the Statement of Being. Divine Science does not issue rules. In 1957 the Divine Science Federation International was formed to serve the churches and centers and to more closely link in fellowship these autonomous organizations. It is governed by a House of Delegates composed of representatives of the various churches. A board of officers consisting of nine members from across the country handles administrative matters between the meetings of the House of Delegates. The Federation licenses ministers and practitioners; charters churches, centers, and study groups; publishes a monthly newsletter, *Spirit in Action*, a bi-monthly daily studies booklet, *At-one-ment*, and print material for use in Divine Science churches, centers, and study groups; and pays for the printing and distribution of Divine Science print material.

Membership: Not reported. The churches, centers, and study groups are autonomous, join the federation by choice, and do not report statistics.

Educational Facilities:

Brooks Center for Spirituality, Denver, Colorado.

The Divine Science School, Washington, D.C.

United Divine Science School, San Antonio, Texas.

Periodicals: *At-one-ment* • *Spirit in Action*

Sources:

Divine Science Federation International. www.divinesciencefederation.org.

Brooks, Louise McNamara. *Early History of Divine Science*. Denver, CO: First Divine Science Church, 1963.

Cramer, Malinda E. *Divine Science and Healing*. San Francisco, CA: C. L. Cramer, 1907.

Dean, Hazel. *Powerful Is the Light*. Denver, CO: Divine Science College, 1945.

Divine Science: Its Principle and Practice. Denver, CO: Divine Science Church and College, 1957.

Gregg, Irwin. *The Divine Science Way*. Denver, CO: Divine Science Federation International, 1975.

McCrary, Joan Cline, ed. *Malinda Cramer's Hidden Harmony*. Denver, CO: Divine Science Federation International, 1990.

First Church of Divine Immanence
Current address not obtained for this edition.

The First Church of Divine Immanence was founded in 1952 by Dr. Henry Milton Ellis (d. 1970). Ellis was a journalist who studied at the College of Divine Metaphysics, from which he received a doctorate. He was for a while a Religious Science practitioner. He became aware that no New Thought group was serving the scattered believers not close to urban areas, so he founded the First Church of Divine Immanence as a mail order denomination. Ellis wrote *Bible Science: the Truth and the Way* as a textbook. At its height, before Ellis's death, the church numbered close to 1,000 members, but with a much larger constituency. Ellis sent a newsletter, *From the Pastor's Study*, regularly to the membership.

Teachings of the church and, *Bible Science,* draw heavily upon the works of Ernest S. Holmes, founder of the Church of Religious Science. Followers believe that God is Spirit, the original life-essence. "Infinite mind" is the life principle, and we think, decide and act with this omniscient mind. Further, believers hold that man is an expression of God in activity. The law of mind is the power of authority in the natural order of law. Man enters the kingdom of heaven by being "born again," in Greek, *metanoia*, changing the mind. That change occurs when man realizes his true nature.

Membership: Not reported.

Foundation for *A Course in Miracles* (FACIM)
41397 Buecking Dr., Temecula, CA 92590-5668

Among the prominent centers perpetuating *A Course in Miracles*, the work channeled by Dr. Helen Schucman from an entity she believed to be Jesus, is the Foundation for *A Course in Miracles,* established in 1983 by cofounders Kenneth Wapnick and his wife, Gloria Wapnick. Dr. Kenneth Wapnick, a clinical psychologist, was a close friend and associate of Helen Schucman and William Thetford, the two people whose joining together was the immediate stimulus for the scribing of *A Course in Miracles*. Together with Dr. Schucman he prepared the *Course* manuscript for publication and sits on the executive board of the Foundation for Inner Peace, the book's publisher. Gloria Wapnick is a former social studies instructor and high school dean of students who has been working with *A Course in Miracles* since 1977.

In 1984 the Foundation for *A Course in Miracles* (FACIM) evolved into the Teaching and Healing Center in Crompond, New York, which was quickly outgrown. In 1988 the Wapnicks opened the Academy and Retreat Center in upstate New York, and in 1995 began the Institute for Teaching Inner Peace Through *A Course in Miracles* (ITIP-ACIM), an educational corporation chartered by the New York State Board of Regents. The institute operates under the aegis of the foundation, administering workshops and academy courses. In 2001 the foundation moved to Temecula, California, and added an emphasis on electronic teaching.

The foundation's Statement of Purpose defines its goal as to foster spiritual development through the study and practice of *A Course in Miracles*, a set of three books channeled by Jesus, that teach that the way to remember God is by undoing guilt through forgiving others. The corporation has as its specific aims to teach the *Course*, helping those interested to integrate the principles into their personal lives, that they may better realize their true identity, shared with all people, as children of God; to teach and train those who wish to teach the *Course*, to others; to teach the *Course*'s reinterpretation of traditional Christian principles such as sin, suffering, forgiveness, atonement, and the meaning of the Crucifixion; to further understanding of the *Course* by means of educational and training programs, seminars, and publications.

As they worked with the *Course*, the Wapnicks concluded that it was not the simplest of thought systems to understand, not only in the intellectual grasp of its teachings, but in the application of these teachings to personal lives. Additionally, Dr. Schucman shared a vision of a teaching center that the Wapnicks understood to be a place where the person of Jesus and His message in *A Course in Miracles* would be manifest. Their thinking has always been inspired by Plato (and his mentor Socrates), and it is their hope that the foundation would function in a manner similar to Plato's Academy, a place where serious and thoughtful people studied his philosophy in an atmosphere conducive to their learning, and then returned to their professions to implement what they were taught by the great philosopher.

It is the Wapnicks' belief that Jesus gave *A Course in Miracles* at this particular time in this particular form for several reasons, including: 1) The necessity of healing the mind of its belief that attack is salvation; this is accomplished through forgiveness, the undoing of our belief in the reality of separation and guilt. 2) The needed emphasis on the importance of Jesus and/or the Holy Spirit as a loving and gentle Teacher, and developing a personal relationship with this Teacher. 3) A need to correct the errors of Christianity, particularly where it has emphasized suffering, sacrifice, separation, and sacrament as being inherent to God's plan of salvation.

The Wapnicks have traveled across the United States and around the world to conduct classes and workshops. They have appeared on several radio and television shows discussing the teachings of *A Course in Miracles* and the work of their foundation.

Membership: Not a membership organization. The FFCIM serves its nationwide constituency out of two centers in Temecula and La Jolla, California.

Periodicals: *The Lighthouse*.

Sources:

Foundation for *A Course in Miracles*. www.facim.org/.

The Message of A Course in Miracles, vol. 1: *All Are Called*; vol. 2: *Few Choose to Listen*. Temecula, CA: Foundation for *A Course in Miracles*, 1997.

Miller, Patrick. *The Complete Story of The Course: The History, the People and the Controversies Behind* A Course in Miracles. Berkeley, CA: Fearless Books, 1997.

Wapnick, Kenneth. *Absence from Felicity: The Story of Helen Schucman and Her Scribing of* A Course in Miracles. Temecula, CA: Foundation for *A Course in Miracles*, 1991.

Global Religious Science Ministries

4625 W. Broad St., Richmond, VA 23230

Global Religious Science Ministries (GRSM) is a recently formed New Thought association of ministers and churches in the Religious Science tradition developed by Ernest S. Holmes (1887-1960) in the early twentieth century. It was founded by Dr. Robert Karle, Rev. Dr. Thelma Smith, and other ministers who had formerly been affiliated with the Religious Science International. Global Religious Science Ministries follows the beliefs and practices of the Religious Science International, differing primarily only on issues of administration. Of particular concern was the development of an expanded understanding of ministry.

GRSM licenses and ordains ministers, and charters churches and personal ministries. It sponsors a seminary, which operates through the several GRSM churches.

GRSM is led collectively by its Commission of Ministers, which in 2008 consisted of Rev. Lisa Marks, its president, and Rev. Roberta Adair, Rev. Dr. Thelma Smith, Doug Kinney, Rev. Christine Coates, Rev. Dwight Smith, Joe Burcham, and Rev. Leo Mosely.

Members: In 2008 the GRSM reported 28 ministers serving several congregations and a variety of ministries in California, Illinois, Maryland, New York, and Virginia.

Educational Facilities:

GRSM Professional Seminary.

Sources:

Global Religious Science Ministries. www.grsm.org/.

Home of Truth Spiritual Center

1300 Grand St., Alameda, CA 94501

The Home of Truth Spiritual Center is the sole remaining congregation among the Homes of Truth, for several decades of the early twentieth century the largest New Thought group in the world. Founded by Annie Rix Militz (1856–1924) and her sister Harriet Rix in 1888, these congregations grew directly out of the early ministry of Emma Curtis Hopkins (1849–1925). In April 1887 Hopkins came to San Francisco, California, and held what was for many years the largest Christian Science class ever held. Annie Rix, a school teacher, was transformed by the class, believing she had found her role in life. She founded the first Home of Truth in San Francisco. A second one was started in Alameda, California, a few years later. Annie also accepted an invitation from Hopkins to join the faculty of her Christian Science Theological Seminary in Chicago, Illinois, where she met and married Paul Militz and came to know many of the early New Thought leaders, including Myrtle Fillmore (1845–1931) and her husband Charles S. Fillmore (1854–1948), who were also students at the seminary.

After the dissolution of the seminary and the retirement of Hopkins to New York City in the mid-1890s, Militz returned to California. Finding the work in the Bay Area stable, she moved to Southern California and opened a Home of Truth in Los Angeles. She also developed close ties to the Fillmores, who had started the Unity School of Christianity, and became one of the important contributors to their magazine, *Unity*. She wrote one of the first sets of Unity basic lessons, later republished as *Primary Lessons in Christian Living and Healing*, and an early volume on prosperity, which remained in print into the late twentieth century.

During the last two decades of her life, Militz traveled widely (including several around-the-world tours) on behalf of New Thought. She was an early and energetic supporter of the International New Thought Alliance (INTA). She developed the Homes of Truth along the Pacific Coast as well as in Chicago and Boston. At the time of her death, there were no less than twelve Homes of Truth. Militz also founded the Master Mind Publishing Company, which published New Thought books and, beginning in 1911, *The Master Mind*, one of the most prominent metaphysical magazines into the 1930s.

Militz, along with the Fillmores and other early New Thought leaders, had a strong belief in the possibility of physical immortality. At the time of her death, her closest disciples refused to bury her body; the city of Los Angeles intervened, an action that brought some unwanted press coverage to the movement. In spite of the loss of Militz, the movement remained vital for another generation but began to decline after World War II. By the 1970s there were only two congregations. One of these, the Boston Home of Truth, dissolved upon the death of its longtime leader, Eleanor Mel.

The Home of Truth Spiritual Center draws eclectically on and attempts to integrate a variety of New Thought systems, including Unity and New Age emphases such as *The Course in Miracles*.

Membership: In 2008 the Home of Truth Spiritual Center reported approximately two hundred members.

Periodicals: *The Channel*.

Sources:

The Home of Truth Spiritual Center. www.thehomeoftruth.org/.

Militz, Annie Rix. *Both Riches and Honor*. Kansas City, MO: Unity School of Christianity, 1945.

————. *Primary Lessons in Christian Living and Healing*. New York: Absolute Press, 1909.

————. *The Renewal of the Body*. Holyoke, MA: Elizabeth Towne, 1920.

Rix, Harriet Hale. *Christian Mind Healing*. Los Angeles: Master Mind Publishing, 1918.

International Alliance of Churches of the Truth

690 E. Orange Grove Blvd., Pasadena, CA 91104

The International Alliance of Churches of Truth was formed in 1987 out of the remnants of what had been a loose fellowship of congregations of the Church of the Truth, also known informally as the Church of Truth. The church was formed in 1913 when Albert C. Grier, pastor of a Universalist Church in Spokane, Washington, resigned from the church and, with most of his congregation, formed a new congregation which taught Divine Science or New Thought. Later that year he began *Truth*, for many years an important New Thought periodical. Grier had become converted to New Thought after reading a pamphlet written by Clara T. Stocker, a student of Emma Curtis Hopkins, who worked as a practitioner in Spokane and in Cascade, British Columbia. Grier's work expanded quickly as he became a popular lecturer and as other New Thought leaders were drawn into his fellowship. In 1914, work began in nearby Coeur d'Alene, Idaho, and within a few years affiliated centers spread across the Northwest.

Grier also developed close ties with Nona Brooks and the Divine Science Church in Denver, Colorado. He joined them, and along with Ernest S. Holmes of the Metaphysical Institute, they formed the Truth Association in 1918 as a competing ecumenical group to the recently formed International New Thought Alliance (INTA). After the alliance made changes in its declaration of principles to accommodate the association members, they dissolved the association and joined the alliance in 1921. Grier became an honorary president and, in 1922, a field lecturer, a duty that began to consume much of his time. In 1924 he was granted a year's leave of absence from his pulpit and spent the year traveling for INTA and organizing a new church in Pasadena, California. In 1925 he moved to New York to become pastor of the Church of the Healing Christ, a prominent independent New Thought congregation formerly headed by W. John Murray. Early in 1925, after only a few months in his new post (to be succeeded by Emmet Fox), he resigned and formed a new Church of the Truth congregation, for many years the church's largest. That church was later pastored for several decades by Erwin Seale.

Grier was succeeded in the Spokane pastorate by Erma Wells, who became the leader of the church after Grier's death in the 1930s. Wells, outstanding in her own right, founded the University of Metaphysics to train New Thought ministers, and was president for three years of the INTA. Her career was cut short by an automobile accident. The university was moved to Portland, Oregon, and the Spokane congregation eventually affiliated with the Association of Unity Churches. Leadership of the loosely organized group shifted to the Pasadena church. During its first generations the church produced a number of outstanding New Thought leaders such as Elizabeth Towne, James Dodds, and H. Edward Mills. However, after Wells's accident, much of the organizational glue was lost, the informal fellowship began to collapse, and many of the congregations became independent or were lost to other New Thought organizations.

BELIEFS. Grier brought little hostility toward organized religion with him in creating the new Church of the Truth, and showed no reluctance in composing statements of belief and church mission so evident in many New Thought circles. Almost immediately after the church was formed, he published a church covenant and a "Statement of the Truth" in which he affirmed the allness of God, the primacy of thought, Love as the essence of the Divine Omnipresence, and the ability to know and utilize the power of Divine Omnipresence through thinking God's

thoughts. While drawing heavily upon Divine Science, he hoped to build a broader, more universal faith capable of withstanding the ravages and changes of time. The intellectual thrust of his ministry was manifest in the University of Metaphysics created by Erma Wells and in the theological text written by his daughter, *Foundation Stones of Truth*.

ORGANIZATION. The Church of the Truth has always existed as a loose supportive association of like-minded ministers and churches tied together by *Truth* magazine. In recent decades, the fellowship dwindled to only a few churches. During the tenure of Pasadena pastor, Judi D. Warren, (1979–1989) the attempt was made to revive the church's common life and to breathe new vitality into the organization. While creating a broad program of activities, including a Wellness Center, at the Pasadena location, Warren opened a ministerial training school and developed a new generation of mission-oriented pastors. In 1987, she led in the founding of the International Alliance of Churches of Truth and launched an aggressive program of creating new congregations and inviting independent like-minded congregations into the alliance.

Unfortunately, following Rev. Warren's retirement from the Church of Truth in Pasadena in 1989, the International Alliance became dormant. Most recently, however, Rev. Deborah Coleman of the Deborah Coleman Ministries in Ontario, Canada, has assumed a leadership role and is reactivating the organization. In the meantime, Rev. Kathleen S. Myers, who succeeded Warren as pastor of the Church of Truth in Pasadena, has continued to nurture the Albert Grier Ministerial School which has a 3 1/2 year program to train people for the ordained ministry in the Church of Truth.

Membership: In 1988 the fledgling alliance had three congregations, Pasadena, California; Coeur d'Alene, Idaho; and Victoria, British Columbia; and reported approximately 1,000 members. In 1992, there were reported 11 congregations.

Educational Facilities:

Albert Grier School of Religious Studies, Pasadena, California.

Periodicals: *Open Heart*.

Sources:

Grier, Albert C. *Truth's Cosmology*. Spokane, WA: Church of the Truth, n.d.

Grier, Albert C., and Agnes M. Lawson. *Truth and Life*. New York: E. P. Dutton, 1921.

Grier, Gladys C. *Foundation Stones of Truth*. Los Angeles: Williang Publishing Company, 1948.

Seale, Ervin. *Ten Words That Will Change Your Life*. New York: William Morrow & Company, 1954.

Stocker, Clara T. *Realization through Concentrated Attention*. Pasadena, CA: Church of the Truth, n.d.

Life-Study Fellowship Foundation, Inc.

Dept. W, Noroton, CT 06820

The Life-Study Fellowship Foundation, Inc. was begun in 1939. It differs from other New Thought groups in that its members are related to each other and to the headquarters only through the literature sent out regularly. Recent literature carries no mention of the Foundation's founders or present leaders, but often quotes from testimonials of members who have been helped. Several of the more substantial early books were written by Herbert R. Moral. The basis of the Fellowship is the "new way of prayer," which, while simple, is believed to be able to open the power of prayer to all.

The new way is based on *Unity Prayer*, the thrice-daily prayer by all members for others in the Fellowship. The prayer to be used at each period is printed in the bimonthly *Faith* magazine. At 8:00 A.M., the prayer is for God's guidance; at 12:00 noon, it is for prosperity; and at 9:00 P.M., it is for healing. A second aspect of the "new way of prayer" is the use of special printed prayers that are sent to members with particular types of problems. These prayers articulate needs, requests for blessings, and affirmations. They are to be read daily at a regular prayer time. The third part of the new way is the special-help department devoted to short-term special problems. Members may write to headquarters for help at any time. Members of the Fellowship are urged to use the prayers as a means for problem-solving and obtaining particular goals. A golden key is distributed for good fortune. Each key has letters that can bring good luck when understood and used.

Membership in the Fellowship is solicited through numerous advertisements in the printed media. Members fill out a lengthy form. The work is supported by the offerings of the members. The Teachings Department has, since the mid-1960s, published a series of books and booklets containing prayers on particular themes, such as prosperity, healing, and peace of mind.

Membership: Not reported.

Periodicals: *Faith.*

Sources:

Life-Study Fellowship Foundation, Inc. www.lifestudyfellowship.org.

Moral, Herbert R. *How to Have Better Health through Prayer.* Noroton, CT: Life-Study Fellowship, n.d.

[Moral, Herbert R.?]. *"With God All Things Are Possible!"* Noroton, CT: Life-Study Fellowship, 1945.

Power for Peace of Mind. Noroton, CT: Life-Study Fellowship, n.d.

Miracle Distribution Center

3947 E La Palma Ave., Anaheim, CA 92807

The Miracle Distribution Center, founded in 1978 by Richard Hutchinson and Beverly Hutchinson (brother and sister), is a nonprofit organization that serves as a resource center for *A Course in Miracles,* a three-volume channeled textbook that offers a set of teachings very close to traditional New Thought metaphysics. The material in the *Course* was received by Dr. Helen Schucman (d. 1981), a psychologist at the Neurological Institute at Columbia University in New York City. Born into a Jewish family, Schucman had become an atheist, but in 1965 she began to receive the material for the *Course* as dictated by an inner voice. The dictations continued over a seven-year period, and the speaking voice claimed to be Jesus Christ.

In 1975 Dr. Schucman met Judith Skutch, a well-known leader in New York City's psychic-metaphysical community and head of the Foundation for Parasensory Information. During the next year Skutch read the material and was so impressed that she established the Foundation for Inner Peace. During that year she also met Saul Steinberg, owner of Coleman Graphics, a print shop on Long Island, who offered to print the book. It was published in 1976 without any mention of Dr. Schucman. Although given little fanfare and informally promoted, largely by word of mouth, it quickly found an audience. By 1977 groups studying *A Course in Miracles* had sprung up from New York to California. In addition to Coleman Graphics, Steinberg founded a publishing company, Miracle Life, Inc. (now Miracle Experiences, Inc.), and began a newsletter, *Miracle News,* which promotes the *Course* through conferences and workshops and has fostered the emergence of a network of study groups.

The movement that grew around the *Course* soon attracted leaders from among people already accepting New Thought metaphysics, including some medical and psychological professionals previously aligned with the human potential movement. Several of these professionals, most notably Dr. Gerald G. Jampolsky, founder of the Center for Attitudinal Healing in Tiburon, California, became national promoters and spokespersons for the *Course.*

As the movement grew, Saul Steinberg emerged as the national conference coordinator and national group coordinator for the *Course.* During the 1980s a national network of study groups emerged, and Miracle Experiences, Inc., headed by Steinberg, coordinated and promoted national and regional conferences. Numerous independent centers and teachers of the *Course* material formed a loosely connected Miracles community across North America and in Europe. Through the 1990s new teachers and centers continued to emerge. Prominent

teachers included Tara Sigh, Jon Mundy, and best-selling author Marianne Williamson. Coming to prominence as a nurturing and organizing center for the community was the Miracles Community Network. It publishes *Miracles Magazine,* provides coordination for the network of *A Course in Miracles* students and study groups, and sponsors conferences.

The Miracle Distribution Center distributes the *Course in Miracles* and related materials, fosters study groups, and serves as the nexus of the worldwide network of students of the *Course.*

Membership: In 2008 the Miracle Distribution Center reported 2,000 *Course in Miracles* study groups around the world. Over 100,000 copies of *A Course in Miracles* have been sold.

Periodicals: *The Holy Encounter.*

Sources:

Miracle Distribution Center: *A Course in Miracles* Resource Center. www.miraclecenter.org/.

A Course in Miracles. 3 vols. New York: Foundation for Inner Peace, 1975.

Koffend, John. "The Gospel According to Helen." *Psychology Today* 14 (September 1980): 74–78.

Miller, Patrick. *The Complete Story of the* Course: *The History, the People and the Controversies Behind* A Course in Miracles. Berkeley, CA: Fearless Books, 1997.

Ray, Sondra. *Drinking the Divine.* Berkeley, CA: Celestial Arts, 1984.

Skutch, Robert. "A Course in Miracles, the Untold Story." *New Realities* 4, nos. 1–2 (July/August, September/October 1984): 17–27; 8–15, 78.

———. *Journey without Distance.* Berkeley, CA: Celestial Arts, 1984.

Noohra Foundation

4480H S. Cobb Dr. Ste. H PMB 343, Smyrna, GA 30080-6989

The Noohra (Light) Foundation was founded in 1970 by Dr. Rocco A. Errico, a student of George M. Lamsa (1890–1975), an Assyrian-born Bible scholar and translator. The Noohra Foundation grew out of and supercedes the Aramaic Bible Society, founded by Lamsa in 1927. Lamsa had migrated to the United States in 1917. He attended Virginia Theological Seminary (Episcopal) and the University of Pennsylvania, and then began his career as a Bible translator. It was Lamsa's claim that Greek was not the original language of the Scriptures. He believed that Jesus and the Apostles spoke Aramaic, that they wrote in Aramaic, and that the Eastern Peshitta Bible was the original version. He argued that only by understanding the Aramaic background could the many idioms of the New Testament be understood. Most important, Lamsa claimed that the Assyrian (the modern form of Aramaic) language, customs, and manners of his home country, Assyria (present-day eastern Turkey), were unchanged since the time of Jesus and could be studied for direct light on Scripture.

Lamsa's scholarship was embodied in a series of translations of biblical literature and commentaries on the New Testament that deal with Aramaic customs. The Aramaic Bible Society was created to teach Lamsa's insights and distribute his writings. In 1970 Errico founded the Aramaic Bible Center in San Antonio, Texas (where Lamsa resided during the 1960s), as an educational organization to expand knowledge of Lamsa's work and do further work on Aramaic texts. At the time he was co-pastor of the Calvary Missionary Church, which served briefly as a "branch office" of the society, and co-editor of *Light for All,* the society's magazine. Two years later he resigned his position at the church to devote his full attention to the center.

During the 1960s and 1970s, Lamsa's work was increasingly identified with metaphysical movements, and his interpretation of Scripture leaned toward a more metaphysical worldview associated with New Thought. During this time he became a popular speaker for New Thought groups, especially the Unity School of Christianity and its affiliated churches. As Lamsa's health failed during the 1970s,

Errico became the spokesperson for his ideas. In 1970 the center took its present name, and in 1976 Errico moved its operations to Irvine, California; after seventeen years there, he moved it to Santa Fe, New Mexico, and in 2001 to its present location in Smyrna, Georgia. The foundation's stated purpose is to encourage humanity's potential through the study of the scriptural, mystical, and practical aspects of Truth, using the Lamsa translation of the Bible. Besides its regular ongoing classes at various locations, Errico is a popular speaker-teacher and has attracted members to the foundation from across the nation.

The Noohra Foundation is associated with other Aramaic study centers such as St. Ephrem's Institute in Solna, Sweden, and the Lamsa Foundation in Germany. Errico has also spoken frequently at the Church of Daily Living, an independent congregation that shares facilities with the foundation in Costa Mesa. The Center of Creative Living in Westminster, Colorado, pastored by Mary Beth Olson, is an affiliate branch of the foundation. Both the foundation and the center in Colorado are members of the International New Thought Alliance (INTA).

Membership: Not reported.

Periodicals: *Noohra Light.*

Sources:

Noohra Foundation. www.noohra.com/.

Alyes, Tom. *The Life of George Lamsa*. St. Petersburg, FL: Aramaic Bible Society, 1966.

Lamsa, George M. *The Kingdom on Earth*. Lee's Summit, MO: Unity Books, 1966.

————. *My Neighbor Jesus*. Philadelphia: Aramaic Research, 1932.

————. *New Testament Commentary*. Philadelphia: A .J. Holman, 1945.

Religious Science International

901 E 2nd Ave., Ste. 301, Spokane, WA 99202

Alternate Address: PO Box 2152, Spokane, WA 99210-2152.

Religious Science International (RSI) continues the original fellowship of Religious Science ministers and churches, the International Association of Religious Science Churches (IARSC), organized in 1949. In 1954, at the annual meeting, Ernest S. Holmes presented a plan for reorganizing the Religious Science movement, which involved disbanding the association and realigning each individual church as an affiliate church to the Church of Religious Science (the name assumed in 1953 by the Institute of Religious Science, which trained all Religious Science ministers). That church is now known as the United Church of Religious Science. A number of the ministers and churches chose to continue as the IARSC. The IARSC, now known as Religious Science International, is like the United Church in following the teachings and practice of founder Ernest Holmes; both use his textbook, *The Science of Mind®*, which was first published in 1926 and revised in 1938. The mission of Religious Science International, as a world religion with world concerns, is to create an environment that nurtures and celebrates the individualized, authentic expression of Spirit through the principles of the Science of the Mind®. The organization and its affiliated congregations support the International New Thought Alliance (INTA) and the Association for Global New Thought.

Membership: In 2002 the organization had 143 churches including 13,100 members in the United States and 15 churches and 1,270 members in Canada. In 2008 there were also churches and groups located in Australia, Jamaica, and South Africa, with contacts and activities in 35 countries worldwide.

Educational Facilities:

RSI Distance Learning.

Periodicals: *Creative Thought • RSI Reporter • Awakenings.*

Sources:

Religious Science International. www.rsintl.org.

Bitzer, Robert H. *How to Make Your Mental Computer*. Hollywood, CA: Author, 1963.

Keyhoe, Merle A., ed. *A Fountain of Truth*. Marina del Rey, CA: DeVorss & Co., 1980.

Whitaker, Claudine. *God Is in This Place*. Chicago: First Church of Religious Science, 1974.

Whitehead, Carleton. *Can You Keep a Secret?* Wakefield, MA: Montrose Press, 1955.

School of Truth

PO Box 62549, Marshalltown, Republic of South Africa2107

New Thought invaded the Union of South Africa in the 1930s through an influx of literature and the visits of various leaders. One person affected was Dr. Nicol C. Campbell, who, in 1937, founded the School of Practical Christianity in Johannesburg. This institution later changed its name to School of Truth. By the late 1960s, New Thought had saturated South Africa and moved into Rhodesia. In the early 1960s, a center was opened in Los Angeles.

The teachings of the School of Truth are more heavily drawn from the Bible than are those of many New Thought bodies. The basis principle is the necessity to "Seek first the kingdom of God" (Matt. 6:33). The kingdom of God is within. Jesus longed for the manifestations of the kingdom, which in latent form is within every person. The kingdom is found through a state of awareness, the consciousness of love's omnipresence. As we attune to love, we bring the kingdom into expression on earth. Love is the omnipresent law that rules supreme. To live the law we must think and feel good thoughts: love, health, happiness, peace, and goodwill to all men. Thinking and feeling these thoughts will allow us to reap their benefits in our own lives.

Literature and lectures of the School of Truth are offered without charge on its Web site. The two monthly periodicals are sent worldwide without the need to request a subscription. Members of the School of Truth are taught to tithe, and it is from their gifts and tithes that the work is sustained. Affiliated centers and study groups are found in England and several African countries. The school is a member of the International New Thought Alliance (INTA).

Membership: Not reported. As of 1985 there were no centers in the United States (the Los Angeles center having closed). Adherents keep in contact through periodicals, e-mail, and Web site resources.

Periodicals: *The Path of Truth • Young Ideas.*

Sources:

School of Truth. www.wjm.0catch.com/School_of_Truth.html.

Campbell, Nicol C. *My Path of Truth*. Johannesburg, South Africa: School of Truth, 1954.

Seicho-No-Ie Truth of Life Movement

United States Missionary Headquarters, 14527 S Vermont Ave., Gardena, CA 90247

New Thought was organized in Japan in 1930 through the efforts of Dr. Masaharu Taniguchi. Taniguchi (1893–1985) studied English literature at Waseda University, where he became a devotee of Omoto, one of the new religions of Japan. He took a job as an editor of Omoto's publications and used his leisure time to continue his education in Western philosophy, spirituality, Buddhism, and psychotherapy. In 1921 he left Omoto and, among other activities, edited a magazine on psychic phenomena. In 1928 he obtained a copy of *The Law of Mind in Action* by Fenwicke Holmes, brother of Ernest S. Holmes, founder of Religious Science. Putting the principles into practice, he was able to improve his financial situation and heal his daughter. He also had a mystical experience with an influx of a brilliant light.

In 1930 Taniguchi began publishing a magazine, *Seicho-No-Ie* (meaning "the home of infinite life, wisdom, and abundance"). Material from the magazine was later collected into a book, *Seimei No Jisso* (*Reality in Life*), comprising forty volumes. In 1931 the Holy Sutra, Nectarean Shower of Holy Doctrine, now recited by all the members, was given to Taniguchi by an angel. Seicho-No-Ie grew as a religion, interrupted only for a period after World War II when Taniguchi was prevented from teaching because of his expression of extreme Japanese nationalism during the war.

Seicho-No-Ie's teaching is similar to that of Religious Science, but it is unique in its use of Shinsokan, the art of prayerful meditation. Members gather together, or in the privacy of their own homes, to begin each day by reciting the Holy Sutra. It is described as a means of self-remembering to clear the mind so that the real man can shine forth. Shinsokan begins in a correct posture, sitting with the palms together in prayer and contemplating reality. A closing prayer ends the session. Elements from many sources that Taniguchi has encountered during his studies embellish the basic New Thought thrust.

Seicho-No-Ie came to the United States in 1938 when Masaharu Matsuda, Tsuruta Yojan, and Mrs. Taneko Shimaza began work among the Japanese Americans on the West Coast. These leaders had been through the 15-day training session, an intensive experience in the divine nature through which all leaders are trained. After the war a church was opened in Los Angeles, which was later moved to suburban Gardena, serving as its headquarters. Other churches were founded in Seattle, Washington; Honolulu, Hawaii; and San Jose, California. By 1974 approximately 7,000 members and 24 missionaries were under the leadership of Rev. Paul K. Kumoto, appointed by Dr. Taniguchi.

Membership: In 2008 Seicho-No-Ie reported nine Truth of Life centers in the United States and three in Canada.

Periodicals: *Seicho-No-Ie Truth of Life*.

Sources:

Seicho-No-Ie Truth of Life Centers. www.snitruth.org/.

Davis, Roy Eugene. *Miracle Man of Japan*. Lakemont, GA: CSA Press, 1970.

Taniguchi, Masaharu. *The Magic of Truth*. Gardena, CA: Seicho-No-Ie Truth of life Movement, 1979.

———. *Recovery from All Diseases*. Tokyo: Seicho-No-Ie Foundation, 1963.

———. *Seimei No Jisso*. Denver: Smith-Brooks Printing Company, 1945.

———. *Wondrous Way to Infinite Life and Power*. Gardena, CA: Seicho-No-Ie Truth of life Movement, 1977.

Today Church

504 Business Pkwy., Dallas, TX 75081

The Today Church was formed in 1969 as the Academy of Mind Dynamics by Bud Moshier and his wife, Carmen Moshier in Dallas, Texas. Bud Moshier was a former Southern Baptist minister who was influenced by New Thought ideas, particularly the secular ideas concerning success motivation. Carmen Moshier was a music teacher in the public school system and formerly a minister with the Unity School of Christianity. The present name of the Moshier's church was adopted in 1970.

The theology is like that of the Unity School of Christianity, and much Unity material is used in teaching. The oneness of God and the Christ within are affirmed. Man's problems are considered to be due to his having lost sight of his spiritual origin and of his dominion over thought and feelings. Man manifests oneness in three phases—spirit (Christ mind), soul (awareness), and body (vehicle of expression). Man is responsible for finding the inner awareness of God that leads to prosperity, peace, and health.

The Today Church is governed by the members while the program is implemented by the pastors and board of trustees. The group has developed a vigorous program of classes and book-publishing. The weekly periodical circulates around the country. A tape library of lessons and lectures has been established, and copies are available on request. The aim of the program is to help people help themselves. The Moshiers have developed a new liturgy and hymnology to express the work of the church. They have authored syllabi for the classes on some of the classic books of the New Thought tradition.

Membership: Not reported.

Periodicals: *The Voyager*.

Sources:

Moshier, Bud, and Carmen Moshier. *Freeing the Whole Self*. Dallas, TX: The Today Church, 1971.

Moshier, Carmen. *Success Programming Songs for You!* Dallas, TX: Academy of Mind Dymanics, 1970.

A Syllabus for the Study of "Science of Succeeding." Dallas, TX: Academy of Mind Dynamics, n.d.

United Centers for Spiritual Living

573 Park Point Dr., Golden, CO 80401

HISTORY. The United Centers for Spiritual Living, also known by its original name, the United Church of Religious Science, grew out of the work of Ernest S. Holmes (1887–1960), a metaphysical teacher in Los Angeles, California, during the early twentieth century. Born in rural Maine, where his family attended the Congregational church, he was educated in the public schools until the age of 15. Several years later he moved to Boston and soon enrolled in a school for public speaking. Continuing his own education through extensive reading, he discovered the realm of metaphysical thinking through the writings of both the philosopher Ralph Waldo Emerson and the founder of the Church of Christ, Scientist, Mary Baker Eddy. He became an avid student, consuming the writings of the leading metaphysical thinkers, such as Ralph Waldo Trine and Christian D. Larson.

In 1912 Holmes moved to California, where his brother Fenwicke Holmes had settled as the Congregational minister at Venice. Several years later, at a local metaphysical library, he discovered the writings of Thomas Troward, the British New Thought writer, whose approach freed Holmes to develop the mature perspective that would become known as the Science of Mind.

In 1916 Holmes organized the Metaphysical Institute, under whose umbrella he began to give public lectures, and with his brother started a magazine, *Uplift*. He received ordination for his work through the Divine Science Church in Denver, Colorado. For several years he cooperated with Divine Science and the Church of the Truth in Spokane, Washington, in the organization of the Truth Association, a short-lived New Thought ecumenical organization that had formed in opposition to the International New Thought Alliance (INTA). The Truth Association disbanded as soon as its objections had been met by the INTA, and the Metaphysical Institute affiliated with it. In 1919 Holmes published his first book, *Creative Mind*, and spent the next few years traveling as a lecturer.

In 1924 Holmes moved to New York, where he became the last student of Emma Curtis Hopkins (1853–1925), who introduced him to the mystical element that became so prominent in his later thought. In 1925 he returned to Los Angeles and the following year published his most important work, *The Science of Mind*, a textbook that systematically presented the fundamental teachings of Religious Science. In 1927 he founded the Institute of Religious Science and School of Philosophy, Inc., under whose banner he spoke each Sunday and taught classes during the week. In 1935 the organization incorporated as the Institute of Religious Science and Philosophy. Holmes was speaking to more than 2,800 people each Sunday.

Organized Religious Science proceeded through several stages. In the 1930s graduates of the Institute began to open teaching centers (chapters) and teach Religious Science. Soon, a few began to designate their centers as "churches," and the "ministers" began meeting as the Annual Conference of Religious Science Chapters and Churches. In 1949 the conference was transformed into a more permanent organization, the International Association of Religious Science Churches. The association, a representative body, established a working arrangement with the institute, which trained the ministers. Then in 1953 the Institute of Religious Science became the Church of Religious Science, and a new reorganization began. Designating the various centers as affiliated churches, the new church asked each center to resign from the association and formally affiliate with the church. This change led to the most severe opposition from some ministers, who refused to align themselves and their congregations with the new church. Many continued as the International Association of Religious Science Churches, eventually taking their present name, Religious Science International. Others simply became independent as leaders of nonaffiliated Science of Mind churches. The Church of Religious Science added the word "United" to its name in 1967.

BELIEFS. The church describes its teachings as a correlation of the laws of science, opinions of philosophy, and revelations of religion applied to human needs and the aspirations of man. The first four chapters of *The Science of Mind* textbook spell out the church's essential philosophy, built around the beliefs that people are made in the image of God and are thus forever one with infinite Life; that all life is governed by spiritual laws; and that people create their experiences by their thoughts and beliefs.

The teachings of Religious Science, or Science of Mind, as it is also known, featured two distinctions within the New Thought movement of the early twentieth century. While accepting the basic ideas of the International New Thought Alliance that Mind or Spirit was the one absolute and self-existent Cause (God) which manifested Itself through all of creation, Religious Science developed an emphasis on the understanding of "mind" as taught by Thomas Troward. Troward recognized a distinction between what he termed objective mind (waking consciousness) and subjective mind (or subsconscious, most clearly visible when a person was hypnotized). The subjective mind, when impressed with the images of healing and wholeness by the objective mind, could bring health to individuals. Practitioners are trained in the process of using the Universal Subjective Mind to bring healing to others.

The church also teaches a method of affirmative prayer called spiritual mind treatment. Integral to the treatment is a five-step process, developed by Holmes, of accomplishing the desired results. As outlined in his textbook, the five steps are: 1) recognition of God as Omnipotent, Omniscient, and Omnipresent; 2) unification with the One Reality; 3) realization and acceptance of the good one is seeking; 4) thanksgiving, even before a visible manifestation of healing, for the answered prayer; and 5) release, knowing that all is well. Going through these five steps in relation to specific concerns, which may include a variety of problems including physical sickness, financial distress, and tension in one's relations with others, is termed "treating" the problem. The purpose of the treatment is not to placate God or to persuade God to grant one's desires, but rather to change one's own beliefs to conform to Divine reality.

Integral to the ministry of the church are the many practitioners, individuals trained in the art of spiritual mind treatment, who make themselves available to assist members and the general public with their problems. Ministers are drawn from the ranks of practitioners.

ORGANIZATION. At the national level, the church is governed by a board of trustees, which is elected by delegated district business meetings at the annual convention. The annual convention serves primarily an advisory function in receiving reports from and making recommendations to the board of trustees. The board sets general policy, provides leadership in directing the church's mission and goals, and provides oversight to the management of the church. It also elects the ecclesiastical head of the church, the president, who serves a two-year term. The president acts as the ecclesiastical spokesperson for the church.

The day-to-day administration is delegated to a chief operating officer who is appointed by the board. The board provides for the ordination and regulation of ministers and licensed practitioners, and charters local churches. Member churches are governed congregationally in accord with an agreement signed at the time of affiliation. They own their own property and organize themselves locally as seems suitable.

The church oversees the World Ministry of Prayer, located at the church's headquarters, which offers 24-hour assistance to the ill and those in spiritual need through a toll-free telephone number. The educational program of the church is directed through the office of Growth Education and Ministries, which maintains the records of Science of Mind classes taught in local churches. Ministerial training

is conducted through the Holmes Institute, School of Consciousness Studies, which was founded in 1972 as the Ernest Holmes College School of Ministry. Science of Mind Publications produces books, periodicals, and audio materials for local churches and the general public. The principal publication is the magazine *Science of Mind*, which circulates more than 100,000 copies per issue and has been in continuous publication since 1927. United Church congregations remain among the major supporters of the International New Thought Alliance.

In 2000 a denominational review raised the idea of a new name for the church. The adoption of the name United Centers for Spiritual Living for use in all facets of the church's operations is an ongoing process.

Membership: In 2008 the United Churches reported approximately 170 churches and study groups across the United States and two in Canada.

Educational Facilities:

Holmes Institute, School of Consciousness Studies, Burbank, California; San Diego, California; Santa Rosa, California; and Denver, Colorado.

Periodicals: *Science of Mind*.

Sources:

United Centers for Spiritual Living. www.religiousscience.org/.

Armor, Reginald. *Ernest Holmes, the Man*. Los Angeles: Science of Mind Publications, 1977.

Awbrey, Scott. *Path of Discovery*. Los Angeles: United Church of Religious Science, 1987.

Holmes, Ernest. *The Science of Mind*. New York: Dodd, Mead, 1944.

Holmes, Fenwicke L. *Ernest Holmes, His Life and Times*. New York: Dodd, Mead, 1970.

Practitioner's Manual. Los Angeles: United Church of Religious Science, 1967.

United Church and Science of Living Institute
4140 Broadway, New York, NY 10033

The United Church and Science of Living Institute was formed in 1966 by the Rev. Frederick Eikerenkoetter II, a former Baptist minister, popularly known as Reverend Ike. After graduating from the American Bible School in Chicago in 1956, Reverend Ike worked in evangelism and faith healing and became influenced by New Thought. "Science of Living" is the term used to describe the teachings of Reverend Ike, which focus upon the prosperity theme in New Thought thinking. He believes the lack of money is the root of all evil.

Reverend Ike emphasizes the use of mind-power. Members are urged to rid the self of attitudes of "pie-in-the-sky," and postponed rewards. Instead, they should begin thinking of God as the real man in the self. Turning one's attention to the self allows God to work. Believing in God's work allows one to see the self as worthy of God's success. Visualization is a popular technique to project desires into the conscious mind as a first step to the abundant life. A prosperity "blessing plan" emphasizes believing, giving, and prospering. Reverend Ike developed an extensive media ministry and is heard over 89 radio and 22 television stations in the Eastern half of the United States and in California and Hawaii.

Membership: Not reported. In 1974 there were two congregations, one in New York (over 5,000 average attendance) and one in Boston. At the time of last publication, Rev. Ike's ministry was focused in the New York Center with outreach across America.

Periodicals: *Action*.

Sources:

Eikerenkoetter, Frederick. *Health, Happiness and Prosperity for You!* New York: Science of Living Publications, 1982.

Unity School of Christianity

1901 NW Blue Pkwy., Unity Village, MO 64065-0001

Alternate Address: Association of Unity Churches International, Box 610, Lee's Summit, MO 64063.

HISTORY. The Unity School of Christianity and the affiliated Association of Unity Churches International are two aspects of the Unity movement founded in the 1880s by Charles S. Fillmore (1854–1948) and his wife, Myrtle Fillmore (1845–1931). Unity originated with the attendance of the Fillmores, then living in Kansas City, Missouri, at a lecture by Eugene B. Weeks, a representative of the Illinois Metaphysical College, an independent Christian Science school founded by George B. Charles in Chicago, Illinois. At the time, Myrtle was afflicted with tuberculosis. She left the lecture remembering and frequently repeating a phrase used by Weeks: "I am a child of God and therefore do not inherit sickness." From this beginning, over a period of months, she made a thorough recovery. Myrtle Fillmore soon was using on other people the same techniques that had brought her health. In 1890 she had the idea of an organization to offer prayer for those in need and led in the formation of the Society of Silent Help. Skeptical at first, Charles Fillmore slowly accepted the new metaphysical ideas and in 1889 left the real estate business to devote himself full time to their pursuit and promulgation. He began a magazine, *Modern Thought*, and led gatherings of interested students in Kansas City. He also opened a lending library of metaphysical books. In 1890 he sponsored lectures by Emma Curtis Hopkins in Kansas City, after which both Fillmores traveled to Chicago to take classes at Hopkins's Christian Science Theological Seminary. Won over to Hopkins's presentation of metaphysics, he renamed his magazine *Christian Science Thought*. Then in June 1891, the Fillmores were ordained by Hopkins.

Over the years, the Fillmores had been searching for a name to tie together their various activities, and in the spring of 1891, while completing their studies with Hopkins, they chose the name Unity. A new magazine, *Unity*, was begun. The Society of Silent Help became Silent Unity, by which name it is known today. Publishing activity was placed under the Unity Book Company. The first steps toward expanding the organization came in late 1891 when the Fillmores called for local societies of Silent Unity to be formed by interested persons. By the mid-1890s more than 6,000 people had been issued memberships. As Silent Unity grew, the Fillmores instituted a free-will offering plan for those seeking assistance from Unity prayer, a plan that set them apart from many of the metaphysical groups whose practitioners charged a set fee for their healing assistance work.

During the 1890s, the demand for a more systematic presentation of the ideas taught by Unity led to the appearance in the magazine of the two most important teachers in the early years of Unity, Dr. Harriet Emilie Cady and Annie Rix Militz, both Hopkins's students. Cady published a series of articles later put together as a book, *Lessons in Truth*, which became Unity's introductory text. Militz began to write a Bible column commenting on the weekly International Sunday School Lessons that introduced most readers to the metaphysical interpretation of the Bible. She also wrote articles that became important Unity textbooks, *Primary Lessons in Christian Living and Healing* and *Both Riches and Honor*, on prosperity. In 1894, the advertisements placed in the magazine by various metaphysical healers were dropped in favor of a column listing approved teachers and healers with whom Unity was in basic agreement.

Through the years, Charles Fillmore had begun to teach locally, holding regular Sunday meetings and occasionally teaching classes. In 1905 he began to publish his own lessons in the magazine; these appeared the next year as his first book, *Christian Healing*, which joined Cady's text as the second definitive work outlining the Unity perspective. He turned soon afterward to writing a Unity correspondence course. About that same time, he reorganized the movement in Kansas City, and at a service in August 1906, the Fillmores and seven other students were ordained as Unity ministers.

In 1914 a most important organizational development in the Unity movement occurred when the literature distribution arm of the movement, the Unity Tract Society, and Silent Unity were incorporated together as the Unity School of Christianity. The following year a field department was organized, both as a liaison between the school and the teachers and healers around the country affiliated with it, and as a coordinating center for Unity groups. Out of the correspondence course, a training school for teachers and ministers developed. Originally a two week summer intensive course, by 1980 it had developed into the Unity School of Religious Studies, with a wide variety of programs for ministerial training, the education of teachers and lay people, and the conducting of national retreats.

In 1923 the first annual Unity convention was held. Attended by most Unity teachers and healers, it led to a growing awareness that all manners of teachings were occurring in the field. Concern about occult and spiritualist ideas being offered in Unity's name led to the formation, at the third annual meeting in 1925, of a Unity Annual Conference to govern teaching and regulate leaders of local Unity groups. Chartered in 1934, the conference would pass through several reorganizations to become the Unity Minister's Conference (1946) and eventually emerged in 1966 as a separate organization, the Association of Unity Churches. The Association, headquartered in nearby Lee's Summit, Missouri, now has charge of the training and oversight of all Unity ministers and the servicing of all Unity churches in the United States.

BELIEFS. Though offering a liberal degree of freedom of belief among its members, Unity teaches what it terms *practical Christianity*, a return to what is believed to be the primitive Christianity of Jesus and the Apostles. Unity teaches a belief in one God and in Christ, the Son of God, made manifest in Jesus of Nazareth. Jesus is believed to be divine, but divinity is not confined to Jesus. Because all people are created in the image of God, all are potentially divine. Jesus is regarded as the great example, the Wayshower, pointing the way to the regeneration of each person. Jesus created an "at-one-ment" between God and humanity and, through Jesus, each person can regain his or her estate as a son or daughter of God.

The authority of the Bible is accepted, but Unity follows a metaphysical interpretation of it (as exemplified in Charles Fillmore's *Metaphysical Bible Dictionary*), which offers a somewhat allegorical approach to Scripture. For example, the 12 apostles are seen as representing 12 powers in humans that can be used for the salvation of the world. The kingdom of God is seen as the harmony within each individual.

Unity has become identified with several practices within the larger context of New Thought metaphysics. It has long emphasized the form of prayer termed "entering into the silence," which begins with a quiet inwardness and establishment of a state of receptivity. Unity has also emphasized the use of affirmations, the repetition of positive statements that affirm the presence of a condition desired but not yet visible. In the development of the prayer life, in 1924, Unity began what has become its most widely circulated periodical, *Daily Word*, a devotional magazine that has readers far beyond the bounds of Unity or even the New Thought movement as a whole.

ORGANIZATION. Today Unity is headquartered at Unity Village, a 1,400-acre tract adjacent to Lee's Summit, Missouri, about 15 miles from Kansas City. It moved to that location permanently in 1949. Unity Village is the spiritual home and headquarters for Unity Worldwide, which encompasses Unity Institute, Silent Unity, Unity Village Chapel, the Unity School Library and Archives, a publishing arm, and more recently an inn, hotel and conference center, and gardens. Silent Unity offers a 24-hour-a-day prayer service. Within the Silent Unity building, a prayer vigil is kept without interruption. Unity Village is an incorporated municipality.

Unity is a major publisher of religious materials. *Daily Word* is now a monthly magazine and has been printed in seven languages and circulated in more than 175 countries. *Unity* magazine contains inspirational articles aimed at effective spiritually based living. Unity also publishes and produces a wide range of books, pamphlets, cassettes, CDs, and specialty products. Though the largest of the New Thought bodies in the United States, Unity has had only nominal relations with the organized New Thought movement. It briefly participated in early conferences organized by Divine Science in the 1890s. It was also a member of the International

New Thought Alliance (INTA) for a few years, but withdrew in 1923 because of Charles Fillmore's feeling that the INTA embraced too many beliefs that Unity could not support. Individual Unity churches have been free to affiliate, and many are staunch supporters of INTA.

Membership: In 2002, there were more than 1,000 Unity centers, churches, and study groups. About 230 of these ministries were outside the United States, Canada, and Puerto Rico.

Educational Facilities:

Unity Institute, Unity Village, Missouri.

Spiritual Education and Enrichment Distance Learning.

Periodicals: *Unity* • *Daily Word* • *USRS Newsletter* • *Children on the Quest* • *Minister Letter* • *Variety of Ministry Manuals* • *Contact*.

Sources:

Unity School of Christianity. www.unityonline.org.

Bach, Marcus. *The Unity Way of Life*. Unity Village, MO: Unity Books, 1972.

D'Andrade, Hugh. *Charles Fillmore*. New York: Harper & Row, 1974.

Freeman, James Dillet. *The Story of Unity*. Unity Village, MO: Unity Books, 1978.

A Manual of Special Unity Services. Unity Village, MO: Association of Unity Churches, 1976.

Witherspoon, Thomas E. *Myrtle Fillmore, Mother of Unity*. Unity Village, MO: Unity Books, 1977.

Universal Church of Scientific Truth

1250 Indiana St., Birmingham, AL 35224

The Universal Church of Scientific Truth is headed by its founder, Dr. Joseph T. Ferguson, and headquartered in Birmingham, Alabama. Ferguson also operates the Institute of Metaphysics, in Birmingham. It offers both resident and correspondence courses on a wide variety of metaphysical topics, including metaphysical healing, philosophy, sacred theology, and psycho-vaxeen. Dr. Ferguson authors the textbooks from which the lessons are taught. In 1970, the church had congregations in Birmingham and Harrisburg, Pennsylvania, and Dallas, Fort Worth, Brownsville, and Waco, Texas.

Metaphysical healing is the major thrust of the church's program. A basic course explains the laws and principles as well as the disciplines and techniques by which the individual attains the "superconscious mind" wherein all is attained. The church offers a Christ universal healing service that involves the sacrament of Christ healing. In the service, the inner light or divinity is released in the individual.

Membership: Not reported.

Educational Facilities:

Institute of Metaphysics, Birmingham, Alabama.

Sources:

Ferguson, Joseph T. *Manual on Metaphysical Healing*. Birmingham, AL: Institute of Metaphysics, 1959.

Universal Foundation for Better Living

21310 NW 37th Ave., Miami Gardens, FL 33056

The Universal Foundation for Better Living (UFBL) is an international association of New Thought Christian churches, centers, and study groups. UFBL was founded in 1974, but grew out of the ministry begun in Chicago, Illinois, in 1956 by Dr.

Johnnie Colemon, then a minister with the Unity School of Christianity and one of the first black New Thought ministers. In 1953, Colemon learned that she had an incurable disease. She moved to Kansas City, Kansas, and enrolled in the Unity School of Christianity. In a few months she was healed. Moving to Chicago, she founded the Christ Unity Temple, which first met in the Y.M.C.A. building on South Cottage Grove. She became a prominent Unity minister and was the first black to be elected president of the Association of Unity Churches. However, in 1974 she withdrew from the association and renamed her congregation Christ Universal Temple. In 1976 she founded the Johnnie Colemon Institute as an educational arm of the church for both lay and professional education. The first ministers were graduated and ordained in 1978. In 1981, she began a television ministry with *Better Living with Johnnie Colemon*, a show that aired on 13 stations across the United States.

In 1985, the growing ministry reached a major plateau with the opening of the Christ Universal Temple complex on the far south side of Chicago. Christ Universal Temple, which also served as headquarters for the foundation and institute, held 3,500 in its sanctuary, the largest in Chicago at the time. The building also housed the UFBL Bookstore and the Prayer Ministry, offering a 24-hour call-in service for those in need.

The beliefs of the foundation are in harmony with those of the Unity School of Christianity, the break being largely a matter of social policy, not doctrine. A statement of belief emphasizes that it is God's will for everyone to live a healthy, happy, and prosperous life and that such a life is attainable for each person. The kingdom within can be brought to visible expression by following the principles of Jesus Christ, the Wayshower. The key is right thinking followed by right action. Specifically cited is a belief that rather than making a primary effort to provide for the needy, the church should provide the teaching that will allow each person to provide for themselves.

As of 2008 Rev. Dr. Mary A. Tumpkin was the second president in the history of the foundation. Dr. Tumpkin is also the founding minister of the Universal Truth Center for Better Living (UTC), a UFBL affiliate in Miami Gardens, Florida. The foundation is a member of the International New Thought Alliance (INTA).

Membership: In 2008 the foundation had 38 member churches, study groups, discussion groups, and satellite locations in the United States, Canada, Trinidad, Jamaica, the Bahamas, and Guyana. In 1995 UFBL reported 20,000 members in the United States, 350 in Canada, and an additional 1,650 members worldwide.

Educational Facilities:

Johnnie Colemon Institute, Chicago, Illinois.

Johnnie Colemon Theological Seminary; UFBL Online Classes.

Periodicals: *The Daily Inspiration*.

Sources:

Universal Foundation for Better Living. www.ufbl.org.

Colemon, Johnnie. *The Best Messages from the Founder's Desk*. Chicago: Universal Foundation for Better Living, 1987.

————. *It Works If You Work It*. 2 vols. Chicago: Universal Foundation for Better Living, n.d.

Harrell, Allison D. *Follow Me*. Chicago: Universal Foundation for Better Living, 1981.

————. *Prosperity for Better Living*. Chicago: Universal Foundation for Better Living, n.d.

Nedd, Don. *Practical Guidelines for Better Living*. Chicago: CSA Press, 1983.

Middle Eastern Family, Part I: Judaism

21

When your son asks you in times to come, saying: What do the testimonies, and the statutes, and the ordinances, which the LORD our God hath commanded you, mean, then you shall say to your son:

We were Pharaoh's bondmen in Egypt; and the LORD brought us out of Egypt with a mighty hand.

And the LORD showed signs and wonders, great and sore, upon Egypt, upon Pharaoh, and upon all his house, before our eyes.

And He brought us out from there, that He might bring us in, to give us the land which He swore unto our fathers.

And the LORD commanded us to do all these statutes, to fear the LORD our God, for our good always, that He might preserve us alive, as it is at this day.

And it shall be righteousness unto us, if we observe to do all this commandment before the LORD our God, as He hath commanded us.

    Deuteronomy 6:20–25.

In this passage from Deuteronomy, the story of the origin of the Jewish people is briefly recounted. The expanded story would include an account of the life of Moses, an Israelite who became the adopted son of a pharaoh of Egypt. Reared a prince, Moses forsook his palace to lead his enslaved people out of Egypt, into the wilderness and to the very edge of their new home in Canaan, where he mediated to them the Covenant Law (Torah). These events and the subsequent movement into Canaan welded the nomadic tribes into a nation and made Moses the founder of one of the world's great faiths. While the story of the Jews begins in Genesis, with creation, and with Abraham and his descendents, it was the Exodus-Sinai event that made them a nation. The history of the Jewish people is found in the Torah, Prophets, and Writings, which together comprise the Hebrew Bible (what Christians call the Old Testament). Rabbinic literature, the other great body of Jewish sacred texts, includes exegetical commentary on scripture, traditions, and law. Its texts include the Mishnah (c. 200 C.E.) and the Talmud (c. 500 C.E.).

The next major event shaping Israel's history was the emergence of the Diaspora in Babylonia following the destruction of the First Temple in Jerusalem in 586 B.C.E. and the exile of the Jews to Babylon. After the fall of Babylon, some Jews returned to Jerusalem. From this point forward, Jewish communities existed simultaneously both within, in the land of Israel, and without, in Diaspora communities.

Later in the first century of the new millennium, during the Roman occupation of Judea, the Jews revolted. After four years of war, the Roman army destroyed Jerusalem and the Second Temple in 70 C.E. With the destruction of the Temple and the end of its sacrificial cult, Jewish religious life changed. Its new centers became the synagogue (congregation), and prayer, study of the ever-expanding body of Jewish law, and deeds of loving kindness became its chief attributes. Several centuries later in the wake of the decline of the Roman Empire, other Jewish communities, notably the Jewish community of the Neo-Persian Empire, became major centers of Jewish religious life

During the Middle Ages, Jews established communities throughout northern, western, and later eastern Europe. Times of tolerant acceptance were interspersed with persecution, attempts at forced conversion, expulsion, and the emergence of a few Jews as prominent moneylenders. Lending money for profit, an almost necessary practice in modern states, was denied Christians at this time, and became a stereotype associated with anti-Jewish animus.

In the modern era, Jews established major communities in important urban settings—including Berlin, Paris, London, and Warsaw. Modernity challenged Judaism and these Jewish communities. The challenges posed by emancipation from disabling anti-Jewish legislation and historic persecution led many to modify and some to reject the Judaism of the past. The result led to a plethora of varieties of Jewish expression and enabled some, among them Sigmund Freud (1856–1939) and Karl Marx (1818–1883), to become molders of Western culture.

Nonetheless, the anti-Judaism of the past morphed into racial anti-Semitism. One cannot understand contemporary Jewish life without grasping the reaction to the most brutal episode of the Diaspora: the Holocaust. During World War II (1937–1945), as the Nazis occupied Europe, they exterminated more than six million Jews—men, women, and children—in an almost successful attempt to eliminate them from the continent

Following the Holocaust, an independent Jewish state was finally established in Palestine, as the Romans had renamed the historic homeland of the Jewish people. The establishment of Israel in 1948 was the culmination of a national political movement called Zionism, which began in the late

---

Judaism Chronology

1492	Jews are expelled from Spain. Many are forced to convert and become known as conversos or New Christians.
1497	Jews expelled from Portugal, but most are forcibly converted prior to expulsion.
1500s–1700	Many conversos and their descendants flee the threat of the Inquisition. Some move to the Netherlands, and a few set off for Recife, Brazil.
1654	Portuguese Jews from Recife arrive in New Amsterdam. Soon after their arrival they found Congregation Shearith Israel (the first Jewish worshipping community in America).
1658	Jews in Newport, Rhode Island, form a Jewish community and establish a cemetery.
1730	Congregation Shearith Israel constructs the first synagogue in America in Manhattan.
1749	Following the British assuming control of Halifax, Nova Scotia, Jews, previously banned by the previous French government, organize a Jewish community and purchase a cemetery (1750).
1763	The second synagogue in America is built. Jeshuat Israel (Salvation of Israel), later known as the Touro Synagogue, is the oldest synagogue structure in the United States.
1790	President George Washington visits the synagogue at Newport and promises that the Unites States is a nation which "to bigotry gives no sanction, to persecution no assistance."
1802	Ashkenazi (Central European) Jews in Philadelphia create a second synagogue, Rodeph Shalom.
1824	First American experiment with reforming Judaism emerges in Charleston, South Carolina.
1838	Rebecca Gratz creates the first Hebrew Sunday school in Philadelphia.
1840	First ordained rabbi, Abraham Rice, comes to the United States.
1850	Jews migrate to California in response to the discovery of gold. They found two synagogues.
1851	In Albany, New York, Isaac Mayer Wise permits men and women to sit together during worship.
1860	Rabbi Morris Jacob Raphall becomes the first rabbi to pray at the opening of a session of the U.S. House of Representatives.
1862	First Jewish chaplain commissioned by U.S. Army.
1873	Reform Jews found Union of American Hebrew Congregations and two years later Hebrew Union College (Reform), the first seminary for the training of rabbis.
1881	Violent pogroms and anti-Jewish legislation follow the assassination of Russian czar. They spark the beginnings of what becomes a massive migration of Eastern European Jews. By 1924, more than two million arrive in the United States and 125,00 in Canada.
1886	Jewish Theological Seminary opens in New York City. It trains modern rabbis who establish Conservative Judaism.
1893	Jewish women found the first national Jewish women's organization, the National Council of Jewish Women.
1897	Theodor Herzl convenes the first Zionist Congress in Basel, Switzerland.
1898	The Union of Orthodox Jewish Congregations in America is founded.
1912	Henrietta Szold founds Hadassah, the Women's Zionist Organization of America.
1913	B'nai B'rith founds the Jewish Anti-Defamation League.
1920	Car manufacturer Henry Ford's *Dearborn Independent* begins publishing anti-Semitic articles drawn from the fraudulent *Protocols of the Learned Elders of Zion.*
1924	New immigration law severely limits immigration from Eastern Europe.
	Arnold Josiah Ford, an African American, founds Beth N'nai Abraham, a black Jewish congregation inspired by Marcus Garvey.
1929	Yosef Yitzchok Schneersohn, the Lubavitcher rebbe, visits his following in America and has a meeting with President Herbert Hoover. Schneersohn migrates in 1940 to escape the Nazis.
1933–38	After the Nazis come to power in Germany, they constrict Jewish life through anti-Semitic legislation and increasing violence.
1939–45	The Holocaust of European Jewry. By the end of World War II, the Nazis and their allies have murdered some six million Jews, many in the notorious death camp, Auschwitz.
1940	Mordecai Kaplan leads in the formation of the Jewish Reconstructionist Foundation.
1945	Yeshiva University (Orthodox) established in New York City. It incorporates institutions of advanced Jewish study that were originally established in 1886.
	Large migration of Hasidic Jews to United States begins.
1946	Yoel Teitelbaum, the Satmar rebbe, settles in Brooklyn, New York.
1948	State of Israel declares its independence.
1958	Atlanta's Hebrew Benevolent Society, known by all as The Temple, is bombed in retaliation for its rabbi's call for civil rights.
1962	SS-Oberstrumbannffführer Adolf Eichman tried in Israel for his role in the Holocaust. Following his conviction for the crime of genocide, he is executed.
1967	During the Six-Day War Israel re-unites the divided city of Jerusalem, bringing the Western Wall, the remnant of the ancient Jerusalem Temple, under Jewish sovereignty for the first time in almost 2,000 years.
1968	A group of black Israelites from the United States migrates to Israel.
1972	When Sally Priesand is ordained at Hebrew Union College, she becomes the first woman ordained as a rabbi in the United States. Women rabbis in Reconstructionist Judaism (1974) and Conservative Judaism (1985) follow.
1983	Jewish Theological Seminary (Conservative) accepts first women as rabbinical students.
2000	An Orthodox Jew, Sen. Joseph Lieberman, becomes the first Jew to run for vice-president on a major American political party ticket.
2004	American Jews celebrate 350 years of Jewish settlement in the United States.
2006	Havina Ner-David claims to receive traditional (Orthodox) ordination in Isreal.

---

nineteenth century. It rested on the ancient religious teaching that Zion, another name for Judea, remained the historic homeland of the Jewish people.

Jewish beliefs hark back to the Exodus. It was this event that initially called the community together and it is from this event that the community draws its life. Beliefs and morals, ritual and custom, are all ultimately derived from or inspired by the story of God's redemption of the Israelites from Egyptian bondage and the covenant made at Sinai. A central demonstration of these beliefs is the prayer known as the Shema, which is repeated in three daily synagogue services: "Hear O Israel, the Lord Our God is One Lord" (Deuteronomy 6:4).

Integral to the relationship of Israel and its God and God's law was the concept of the covenantal relationship. In the covenant, God promised the Jews that they would become a nation in the land of Canaan. In return, God asked that they offer him their obedience to his laws. These laws were far-ranging. They included what has popularly become widely known in the Christian community as the Ten Commandments, and covered basic religious commandments (from monotheism to Sabbath observance), basic ethical perspectives within the community (relative to murder, theft, and attitude to one's neighbor), and dietary restrictions (to eat food from only certain animals, to refrain from mixing milk and meat). Some laws govern civil relations (what to do if an ox destroys property), and others emphasize the welfare of the poor (care for the widow and the orphan). In the centuries following the giving of the law, a process of scriptural (and legal) interpretation (already evident in the prophetic writings) developed, which greatly assisted Judaism to survive for millennia by repeatedly adapting to new situations and circumstances.

WHAT JEWS BELIEVE.

While making creeds has never been a Jewish preoccupation, on a number of occasions in the nineteenth and twentieth centuries, attempts to summarize Jewish belief have been made. Many of these draw on the twelfth-century creed authored by Moses Maimonides (1135–1204), the most acceptable traditional summary of Jewish belief. In 13 statements, Maimonides affirmed belief in one God who is incorporeal and eternal, the only object of true prayer. The biblical Moses is cited as the greatest prophet due to his reception of God's law, which will never be changed or superseded. God acts in history to punish evildoers and reward the just. At some point in the future, a messiah will come. Also, there will be a resurrection from the dead.

Out of the encounter with modernity, the Reform, Conservative, and Reconstructionist branches of Judaism arose. (Orthodox Judaism has not escaped the challenges of modernity, as seen, for example, in the enhanced religious education that young Orthodox girls currently receive.) Each of these more liberal movements within Judaism, however, has produced statements summarizing its disagreements with traditional Judaism and setting forth its distinctive teachings. For example, the Columbus Platform of 1937, one of several statements issued by the ever-evolving Reformed Jewish movement, speaks to the issue of law (Torah), in which it differs from Orthodoxy, but then goes on to speak to issues of ethics, social justice, peace, and the nature of the religious life, not mentioned by Maimonides. (The texts of these various statements were compiled in J. Gordon Melton, ed., *The Encyclopedia of American Religions: Religious Creeds* [1988].)

Basic to Judaism is the concept of Torah. Narrowly, Torah is the Five Books of Moses (also included in the Christian Old Testament): Genesis, Exodus, Leviticus, Numbers, and Deuteronomy. It is the story of God's calling a nation. More broadly, however, Torah means teaching, a way of life based on the dictates of Israel's God given in the written Torah. At the heart of the Torah is the covenant God made with his people of Israel.

No description of Jewish life would be complete without mention of the notion of the chosen people: "For you are a people consecrated to the LORD your God: of all the peoples on the earth the LORD your God chose you to be His treasured people" (Deuteronomy 7:6). While the exact significance of this passage has been widely debated, it remains a controlling concept. The effect on Jewish life of this idea has been tremendous, both in keeping the Jews from too-ready assimilation in their many surrounding cultures and in making them easy targets for persecution.

Also important to Judaism are its holidays. The great pilgrimage festivals appear in the Torah, when in ancient times Jews were to make a pilgrimage to sacrifice at the Temple in Jerusalem. Passover, in early spring, is a commemoration of the Exodus from Egypt with specific reference to the Lord's passing over Jewish homes when he slew the first-born in each household in Egypt (Exodus 12). Shavuot, sometimes translated as Pentecost, follows in late May or early June, and commemorates the revelation at Mt. Sinai. Sukkot, or the Feast of Tabernacles, marks the Jewish wanderings in the desert for forty years after the Exodus (Exodus 23:14, 34:23). Other holiday celebrations include the Feast of Lights or Hanukkah, which celebrates the purification of the Temple in 164 B.C.E. by the Maccabees, who waged a war against the Greek/Syrian rulers who had defiled it. Purim honors the rescue of the Jewish people by Mordecai and Esther, as recounted in the biblical book of Esther.

The high holidays in the Jewish calendar begin with Rosh Hashanah, or New Year's Day, which is followed by 10 days of penitence. This period culminates in the single most important day of the Jewish year, Yom Kippur, the Day of Atonement, a day of fasting and prayer.

The basic organization of Judaism is the congregation or synagogue, which may be constituted wherever there are 10 males to form the prayer quorum known as a *minyan*. (Some liberal congregations include women in the minyan.) This is the basic governing body in Judaism, which is congregationally structured. The synagogue has as its spiritual leader a rabbi (teacher). The congregation usually sponsors an array of educational programming for all ages, including a school for children. Often its primary goal is to prepare children for Bar Mitzvah (Bat Mitzvah for girls), the coming-of-age ceremony for Jewish youth, which allows Jewish youth to take their places as adults in communal worship.

Number of Jewish Congregations by State (2000)

Rank	State	Value
1	New York	995
2	California	425
3	New Jersey	331
4	Florida	263
5	Massachusetts	201
6	Pennsylvania	197
7	Illinois	161
8	Ohio	114
9	Maryland	107
10	Texas	92
11	Connecticut	87
12	Michigan	71
13	Virginia	53
14	Georgia	52
15	Colorado	41
16	Arizona	38
17	Washington	36
18	Wisconsin	36
19	North Carolina	34
20	Missouri	33
21	Indiana	27
22	Minnesota	25
23	Nevada	23
24	Tennessee	19
25	Rhode Island	19
26	Alabama	18
27	Louisiana	17
28	Iowa	16
29	Oregon	15
30	South Carolina	15
31	Mississippi	14
32	Vermont	13
33	New Hampshire	12
34	West Virginia	11
35	Kentucky	11
36	Oklahoma	10
37	New Mexico	10
38	Maine	10
39	Arkansas	10
40	Kansas	10
41	Delaware	7
42	Nebraska	7
43	Utah	6
44	Montana	6
45	Alaska	5
46	Hawaii	4
47	South Dakota	3
48	Wyoming	2
49	North Dakota	2
50	Idaho	2

Adapted from Association of Religion Data Archives

JEWS IN AMERICA. The story of Jews in the Americas began in the fifteenth century with the arrival of Christopher Columbus (1451–1506). Several of the members of the crew were converted Jews, victims of Spanish persecution. Spanish and Portuguese Jews helped finance Columbus's voyages, and many early Jews in America were Marranos, forced converts who had, as a result of persecution, accepted Christian baptism but secretly practiced Judaism, a practice that could bring them before the Inquisition as heretics. Others were refugees, Jews exiled from Spain in 1492 and forcibly converted in Portugal after its edict of expulsion in 1497.

Many refugees fled to Holland and prospered there. That community produced the philosopher Baruch (Benedict de) Spinoza (1632–1677), but excommunicated him for his deviations from religious tradition. When the Dutch made war in Brazil and South America in the early 1600s, many Marranos there sided with them. The first openly Jewish community in the Americas—Kahal Kodesh, the Holy Congregation—was founded in Recife, Brazil, in the 1630s. Recife fell to the Portuguese in 1654, and the Jews had to emigrate. Many returned to Holland; others moved to new Dutch colonies. CuraÁao, a Dutch island off Venezuela, became the location of a congregation in 1656, the oldest still in existence in the New World.

Twenty-three Jews fled to New Amsterdam (later New York City), where they found a few Jewish traders. Peter Stuyvesant (c. 1612–1672), the governor, desiring religious conformity, tried to expel the Jews but was overruled by the Dutch West India Company, which owned the colony. Eventually, the community established a cemetery, a congregation, and a synagogue. A corner of its first cemetery still exists in Manhattan.

In 1682, sometime after New York had become English property, toleration was granted and a building was rented for use as a synagogue. In 1728 the group organized as Congregation Shearith Israel, the Remnant of Israel, and built its first synagogue. The next colonial Jewish community to emerge in what is now the United States was in Newport, Rhode Island. Religious toleration and the opportunity to trade attracted Jewish settlers. The cemetery, founded there in 1677, is older than the remaining one in New York. The synagogue, built in 1763, still stands, and is known as the Touro Synagogue, but its congregation dispersed during the American Revolution (1775–1783) when the British captured Newport.

Early America's Jews also settled in other port cities—Philadelphia, Charleston, and Savannah—and during the Revolutionary War, a community emerged in Richmond, Virginia. Perhaps 1,500 Jews lived in the United States by the eve of the Revolution. While most Jews were Patriots, some stood with the Loyalists. In any event, they shared in the founding of the nation, and the group has grown with the nation as an integral part of its history. In this respect, the Jews differ dramatically from other non-Christian religious communities that established their first organizations in America in the nineteenth century.

Although most of America's first Jews were Sephardim (that is, they came from Spain and Portugal or were descendants of Jews from the Iberian Peninsula), by the mid-eighteenth century, Ashkenazim (that is, Jews from Germany and elsewhere in Western and Eastern Europe) constituted the majority. Still, all six pre-nineteenth-century congregations followed the Sephardic religious ritual. There were differences of rite between the two groups, and there was also a feeling among the Sephardim that they were the elite of the Jewish community. Until the nineteenth century, the synagogue defined the community. Only after 1802 in Philadelphia and 1825 in New York City, when second synagogues emerged in each city, did the American Jews begin to become a community of synagogues. These immigrants started out as poor peddlers; in time, as some of them became merchants and storekeepers, they formed new Jewish communities in small towns and cities across the expanding American frontier.

Eastern European Jews had arrived in small numbers in the eighteenth century and, in 1848, the first Eastern European synagogue was formed in Buffalo, New York. But motivated by pogroms and Russia's anti-Jewish decrees, mass immigrations began in 1881. To the 250,000 Jews in the United States in 1880 were added almost two million from Eastern Europe. In 1880 there were 270 synagogues; in 1916, before World War I (1914–1918) halted the immigration, there were 1,902.

Contemporaneous with the arrival of the Eastern European Jews in America, a new issue arose within the Jewish community—Zionism. In contradistinction to German Jews, who tended to see Judaism as primarily a religion, Eastern European Jews tended to see it more as a total religious culture and nationality. Following the lead in 1896 of Viennese journalist Theodor Herzl (1835–1902), they began to clamor for a Jewish homeland. The first Zionist Congress was held in 1897, with four American Jews in attendance. Enthusiasm for the cause was slow to spread. The Central Conference of American Rabbis (Reform) reacted by unanimously condemning Zionism, while the large majority of Eastern European Jews who came to the United States manifested a decision to cast their lot with America rather than Zion. They were, by and large, poor and too concerned with making a living initially to pay much attention to Zionism.

The early recognition of the growth of Zionism came with the 1917 Balfour Declaration that committed England to the Zionist cause. The United States endorsed the declaration in 1922, along with its acceptance of the British protectorate of Palestine. These actions, and the dedication to the cause by outstanding Jewish leaders such as Louis D. Brandeis (1856–1941), finally swung the support of American Jews behind Zionism. When World War II ended, the great majority of American Jews favored a Jewish commonwealth in Palestine. The founding of Israel has turned Zionism mainly into a program of support for Israel, a program of fundraising and political lobbying.

During the twentieth century, the Jewish community in America grew from over four million in 1930 to around 6 million by 1970. Jewish life thrived in America, especially as anti-Semitism declined after World War II. Jews built an array of institutions to sustain Jewish life: synagogues and schools, including parochial schools; community centers and homes for the aged; and a network of social and cultural organizations designed to link American Jews to one another and to Jews all over the world. Various national fellowships of rabbis and congregations formed as divisions on ritual law and the nature of Judaism concretized. The main organizations were formed around the boundaries of Orthodox, Conservative, Reform and, more recently, Reconstructionist Judaism. Less well known was the development of a tiny Hasidic community

in Brooklyn after World War I, which grew after World War II as a result of large migrations of survivors of the Holocaust. The Hasidim, at one time a sizable minority of European Jewry (and the majority party in western Ukraine and eastern Poland), pulled the American Jewish community toward Orthodoxy in the last decades of the twentieth century. It grew significantly through both evangelistic efforts and a high birth rate.

From a tiny immigrant group, Jews found a home in America, where they were both influenced by the wider culture and played important roles in contributing to it. They became a part of American life, and yet stood apart from it to some degree. Jews are best known for their contributions to medicine, psychotherapy, law, entertainment, and business. Given their emphasis on education, Jews have excelled in every field in the academy. Their slow but steady entry into prominence in the national political scene reached a new peak in 2000 with the nomination of Senator Joseph Lieberman as the Democratic candidate for vice-president. Lieberman is an observant Orthodox Jew whose religious life has not been found by his predominantly non-Jewish Connecticut constituency to detract from his active role in the U.S. Senate, nor was it seen as a barrier precluding the possibility of his assuming the second highest office in the land.

JEWS IN CANADA. Though the first Jews in what is today Canada came there during the French era, they were officially banned by the French government from settlement in New France. Hence it was not until the British founding of Halifax in 1749 that a Jewish community became visible. A small Sephardic community organized very early in Halifax, and is known from its purchase of a cemetery in 1750. It was short-lived, however, and a more permanent settlement of primarily British Jews, most of whom were merchants, emerged at the end of the decade in Lower Canada (Quebec). Congregation Shearith Israel, modeled on the Sephardic congregation in London and on the one with the same name in New York City, opened as the first such synagogue in Canada. A building was erected in 1777. A second synagogue was founded at Three Rivers at the end of the century. The community grew slowly, and 50 years after the congregation was founded, there were still fewer than 100 Jews in the Canadian colonies.

The 1840s saw the emergence of a Jewish community in Toronto, Upper Canada (now Ontario). In 1849 the Toronto Hebrew Congregation was founded. It was followed in 1856 by the Sons of Israel congregation, organized by English Jews. These congregations merged in 1858 to become the Toronto Hebrew Congregation–Holy Blossom Temple. Other early congregations were founded in Hamilton and Kingston. Most of the Jews came to Canada from England, and few German Jews ventured that far north. As a result, a Reform Jewish community never developed there.

In 1881 Czar Alexander II (r. 1855–1881) was assassinated, and a pogrom against the Jews began that year. Russian Jews began a mass exodus to North America. During the 1880s, a string of congregations was established across Canada. Many of the newcomers went west into the newly opened territories, especially Winnipeg, which developed Canada's third-largest Jewish community. In 1881 there were only 2,393 Jews in Canada (more than 2,000 of whom were in Quebec and Ontario). By the end of the century, that number had grown to 16,000. By 1920 it had grown to more than 125,000. As the community grew, it continued to concentrate in the three cities of Montreal, Toronto, and Winnipeg.

The absence of the wave of German Jewish immigration that so altered American Jewry contributed to Canadian Jewry's more distinctively Orthodox cast. By 1953 there were but three Reform congregations, though 10 more were added by 1970. The majority of the nineteenth-century congregations have become Conservative in orientation, and by 1960 there were more than 20 such centers affiliated with the United Synagogues of America. In contrast, by 1970 there were approximately 175 Orthodox congregations, some affiliated with the congregational associations in the United States and some unaffiliated.

By 1981 there had been some shift in the community, including a consolidation of synagogues and the emergence of a stronger Conservative element, though the community remained decidedly Orthodox. Of 112 synagogues reported that year, 53 were Orthodox, 43 were Conservative, 14 were Reform, and 2 were Reconstructionist. At the end of the decade, among Canadian Jews who identified themselves religiously, the Orthodox represented about 19 percent (compared to 9 percent in the United States), the Conservatives about 37 percent (38 percent in the United States), Reform only 11 percent (43 percent in the United States), and 32 percent identified themselves as "other" (9 percent in the United States). As the twenty-first century began, Orthodoxy gave the appearance of being the most vibrant segment of the Canadian Jewish community.

As early as 1919, there was an attempt to organize a Canadian Jewish Congress, but it soon dissolved. It was revived in 1934, in the face of the Nazi threat, and is noteworthy in facilitating the immigration of over 40,000 Jews to Canada after World War II. Today, it is headquartered in Montreal.

HASIDISM.
The phenomenon of the mystic who reacts to formal religion by seeking a closer direct experience of the divine is common in religious history. Judaism has had a long mystical tradition. In the early modern period, the messianic claimant Shabbetai Zevi (1626–1676) offered such a direction. In the following century, a more stable style of mysticism would arise in Hasidism, a form of mystical pietism attributable to the efforts of Israel Baal Shem Tov (c. 1700–1760), a rabbi in Ukraine.

Hasidic teachings are plainly Orthodox in that they emphasize fulfillment of all Jewish precepts and ritual, but they incorporate the mystical. The Baal Shem Tov taught that all men were equal before God and that piety, devotion, purity, and devotion in prayer were more important than study, learning, or ascetic practices. In communing with God,

the virtues of *shiflut* (humility), *simcha* (joy), and *hitlahavut* (enthusiasm) were emphasized. The movement spread rapidly and, at its height, attracted large numbers of Jews in Eastern Europe, particularly those in Poland and Ukraine.

After the Baal Shem Tov's death, local charismatic leaders called *zaddikim*, or righteous ones, took over, and the movement diffused. Unlike the rabbi, or teacher, known for his scholarship and wisdom, the *zaddik*, who might also be a rabbi, was honored also for his mystical powers—miracle working, shamanism, and personal magnetism. Organizationally, zaddikim came to lead segments of the movement, and eventually created various Hasidic dynasties, passing on leadership to sons or followers. Thus schools or subsects, as in Sufism, were formed.

The Hasidic movement aroused the indignation of Jews who came to be called "opponents," and a lengthy, bitter era of polemic followed. Eventually, a modus vivendi was reached. The twentieth century brought new problems as pogroms began in Russia. Some Hasidim even migrated. The Holocaust, of course, all but wiped out European Hasidism. Fortunately, many of the rebbes, a common title for the zaddikim, escaped and sought new homes for their followers in Israel and America.

The first Hasidim in America were members of that initial wave of Eastern European immigrants to America that began in the 1880s. For lack of a Hasidic synagogue or zaddik (all of whom were still in Europe), they often became indistinguishable from other Orthodox Jews. Separated from their zaddik, they became discouraged in the attempt to perpetuate Hasidism. After World War I, several zaddikim came to the United States, including the Ukrainian Twersky Zaddik. They gathered followers, but did not begin to reach outward to seek new believers. The real era of Hasidic growth in the United States began after World War II. Led by the Lubavitcher Rebbe, Hasidic zaddikim, especially from Poland and Hungary, came to the United States after escaping from Adolf Hitler (1889–1945).

The Hasidim, as a group, settled in Brooklyn in the section designated as Williamsburg. There they created a social structure unique in all of American Judaism—an isolated urban religious culture. Williamsburg is a haven of "true" Judaism. They have been able not only to survive but even to prosper, in spite of an economic system that seeks to assimilate them. The vitality of Hasidism is shown in the emergence of new Hasidic groups among younger Jews. A strong emphasis on tradition, social service, celebration, communal life, and experiment with radical ideas is characteristic of their lifestyle. Though largely ignored by writers on American Judaism prior to the 1980s, in the last generation the Hasidim became the fastest growing segment of American Judaism. This growth comes from both proselytization within the wider Jewish community and a high birth rate.

BLACK JEWS.
Among the black population of the early nineteenth century were some individuals who became legends as regular worshipers at the local synagogues. Possibly the most famous was Old Billy, who in the first half of the

nineteenth century was a faithful attendant at the Charleston, South Carolina, synagogue. He described himself as a Rachabite (Jeremiah 35:2ff) and, accordingly, abstained from all wines and liquor. Other black members have been noted by various authors. To this day, and in growing numbers since the 1950s, there are black members of white Jewish congregations.

A real spur to African Americans to elect Judaism as an alternative to Christianity was the discovery in the nineteenth century by French explorer Joseph Halévy (1827–1917) of the Falashas, the Black Jews of Ethiopia. For centuries, a legend had circulated in Europe that Black Jews, descendants of the Queen of Sheba, had lived in Ethiopia, but most believed that if they ever existed they had long ago disappeared. Knowledge in the West of their present existence increased in the 1920s, when Jacques Faitlovitch (1881–1955) of the University of Geneva followed up previous pro-Falasha committee activities with a passionate revival of efforts to aid them. While African-American Jews like to identify with them, the Falashas have no direct connection with Judaism in the African-American community. As a matter of fact, much recent scholarship has concluded that the Falashas are probably not Negroid, though in addition to the Falashas, isolated pockets of African Black Jews, products of interracial marriages, have been identified.

While the African Jews supplied much inspiration for the American Black Jewish movement, the biblical faith of rural America supplied the content. Black Bible students were quick to identify with the Ethiopians and, in their search for identity and status in the white culture, began to see a special place for themselves as Jews. Proponents cite all the biblical references to the Ethiopians (such as I Kings 10; Isaiah 18:1–2; Amos 9:7; and Acts 8:26–40); attempts are also made to prove that the true Jews were black. Psalm 119:83, in which the author sees himself as becoming like a bottle (*King James Version*) in the smoke, is a passage popularly quoted as proof of the existence of Black Jews in biblical times.

The Christian biblical origin of the movement is made by the early leaders, who articulated its postulates. Warren Roberson, one of the first prophets of Black Jewishness, spoke of himself as a second Jesus Christ. Another called his group the Church of God and Saints of Christ. It would be hard to find a more Christian designation.

Along with Rabbi Mordica Herman's Moorist Zionist Temple, the contemporary Black Jewish movement is generally traced to three men who appeared in northern urban black centers at the turn of the twentieth century. Two of these, F. S. Cherry and William S. Crowdy, founded movements that still exist and are discussed in entries below. The third, the first of several New York City–based leaders, was Elder Warren Roberson. Roberson was a notorious charismatic leader who alternated between being messianic and being a sex-cult priest. He spent several terms in jail, which only added to his aura as a persecuted black savior.

Roberson's group and its several spin-offs, such as Rabbi Ishi Kaufman's Gospel of the Kingdom Temple, were swept up into the Garveyite movement. Coming from the West Indies, Marcus Garvey (1887–1940) instilled within his followers and admirers a dream of a black nation where black men would rule. Since white Christianity had enslaved and tamed black people, an alternative had to be found. Judaism provided one such alternative. With the encouragement of Arnold Josiah Ford (1877–1935), Garvey's choirmaster and a self-proclaimed Ethiopian Jew, a new phase of history began.

Ford tried to get Garvey to accept Judaism, but he refused, whereupon Ford organized the Moorish Zionist Church, in which he taught that all Africans were Hebrews. He also followed Garvey's nationalistic program. Ford united his efforts with another self-professed Jew, Mordecai Herman, but they soon parted ways. Ford then organized, in 1924, the Beth B'nai Abraham congregation. Both groups were able to obtain funds from white Jews, which allowed them to survive through the next decade. Additionally, elements of Islamic lore (possibly also from the Garvey movement) crept into Ford's theology.

The Beth B'nai Abraham came to an abrupt end in 1931 when Ford decided to sail for Europe. He gave his blessing to a new leader, Wentworth Arthur Matthew (1892–1973), whose career initiated the present phase of Black Judaism. Ford disappeared to Africa (he later died in Ethiopia), but had laid the groundwork for a widespread Black Judaism. Today, a number of independent synagogues are located in black urban areas around the country.

SOURCES

General Sources

For its size, the Jewish community is one of the most scholarly in North America. Study of Judaism is taught in American institutions of higher learning through the academic field of Jewish studies. The Association for Jewish Studies, a learned society with approximately 1,500 members, is located at the Center for Jewish History, 15 West 16th Street, New York, NY 10011. The study of the history and culture of American Jews is advanced through the American Jewish Historical Society, also headquartered at the Center for Jewish History in New York. The Society publishes *American Jewish History* (quarterly) and has established a network of local Jewish historical groups across North America.

Bamberger, Bernard J. *The Story of Judaism.* 3rd ed. New York: Schocken, 1970. 484 pp.

Baskin, Judith R., ed. *Jewish Women in Historical Perspective.* 2nd ed. Detroit, MI: Wayne State University Press, 1998. 384 pp.

Dosick, Wayne D. *Living Judaism: The Complete Guide to Jewish Belief, Tradition, and Practice.* San Francisco: HarperSanFrancisco, 1998. 400 pp.

Fishman, Sylvia Barack. *The Way into the Varieties of Jewishness.* Woodstock, VT: Jewish Lights, 2007. 262. pp.

Melton, J. Gordon, ed. *The Encyclopedia of American Religions: Religious Creeds: A Compilation of More than 450 Creeds, Confessions, Statements of Faith, and Summaries of Doctrine of Religious and Spiritual Groups in the United States and Canada.* Detroit, MI: Gale, 1988.

Robinson, George. *Essential Judaism: A Complete Guide to Beliefs, Customs, and Rituals.* New York: Pocket Books, 1999. 656 pp.

Rosenthal, Gilbert S. *The Many Faces of Judaism: Orthodox, Conservative, Reconstructionist, & Reform.* New York: Behrman House, 1978. 159 pp.

Seldin, Ruth. *Image of the Jews: Teachers' Guide to Jews and Their Religion.* New York: KTAV, 1970. 151 pp.

Skolnik, Fred, ed. *Encyclopedia Judaica.* 2nd ed. 22 vols. New York: Macmillan, 2006.

Solomon, Norman. *Historical Dictionary of Judaism.* 2nd ed. Lanham, MD: Scarecrow Press, 2006. 528 pp.

Steinberg, Milton. *Basic Judaism.* New York: Harcourt, Brace, 1947. 172 pp.

Werblowsky, R. J. Zwi, and Geoffrey Wigoder, eds. *The Encyclopedia of the Jewish Religion.* New York: Holt, Rinehart and Winston, 1965. 415 pp.

Judaism in America

Diner, Hasia R., and Beryl Lieff Benderly. *Her Works Praise Her: A History of Jewish Women in America from Colonial Times to the Present.* New York: Basic Books, 2002.

Farber, Robert Rosenberg, and Chaim Isaac Waxman, eds. *Jews in America: A Contemporary Reader.* Hanover, NH: University Press of New England, 1999. 439 pp.

Glazer, Nathan. *American Judaism.* 2nd rev. ed. Chicago: University of Chicago Press, 1989. 214 pp.

Hertzberg, Arthur. *The Jews in America: Four Centuries of an Uneasy Encounter: A History.* New York: Columbia University Press, 1998. 409 pp.

Karp, Abraham J. *A History of the Jews in America.* New York: Aronson, 1997. 504 pp.

Marcus, Jacob Rader. *United States Jewry: 1776–1985.* 4 vols. Detroit, MI: Wayne State University Press, 1993.

———. *The American Jew, 1585–1990: A History.* New York: Carlson, 1995.

Nadell, Pamela S., and Jonathan D. Sarna. *Women and American Judaism: Historical Perspectives.* Hanover, NH: Brandeis University Press, 2001. 322 pp.

Neuhaus, Richard John, ed. *The Chosen People in an Almost Chosen Nation: Jews and Judaism in America.* Grand Rapids, MI: Eerdmans, 2002.

Neusner, Jacob. *Understanding American Judaism.* 2 vols. New York: KTAV, 1975.

Papo, Joseph M. *Sephardim in Twentieth-Century America: In Search of Unity.* San Jose, CA: Pele Yoetz, 1987.

Raphael, Marc Lee. *Judaism in America.* New York: Columbia University Press, 2003. 234 pp.

———, ed. *The Columbia History of Jews and Judaism in America.* New York: Columbia University Press, 2008. 490 pp.

Sachar, Howard. *A History of the Jews in America.* New York: Knopf, 1992. 1051 pp.

Sarna, Jonathan D., ed. *The American Jewish Experience.* New York: Holmes and Meier, 1986. 303 pp.

———. *American Judaism: A History.* New Haven, CT: Yale University Press, 2004. 490 pp.

Shapiro, Edward S. *A Time for Healing: American Jewry since World War II.* Baltimore, MD: Johns Hopkins University Press, 1992. 313 pp.

Sklare, Marshall. *Observing America's Jews.* Hanover, NH: Brandeis University Press, 1993. 302 pp.

Wertheimer, Jack. *A People Divided: Judaism in Contemporary America.* New York: Basic Books, 1993. 267 pp.

Judaism in Canada

Abella, Irving. *A Coat of Many Colours: Two Centuries of Jewish Life in Canada.* Toronto, ON: Lester & Orpen Dennys, 1990.

Golick, Peter Samuel. *A Tribute to Freedom, 1832–1982: In Commemoration of the 150th Anniversary of the Declaration Granting Equal Rights and Privileges to Persons of the Jewish Religion.* Montreal, QC: Canadian Jewish Congress, 1982.

Gottesman, Eli, ed. *Canadian Jewish Reference Book and Directory, 1963.* Montreal, QC: Jewish Institute of Higher Research, 1963.

Rome, David. *70 Years of Canadian Jewish Life: 1919–1989.* Montreal, QC: Canadian Jewish Congress, 1989.

Rosenberg, Stuart E. *The Jewish Community in Canada: A History,* Vol. 1. Toronto, ON: McClelland & Stewart, 1970.

———. *The Jewish Community in Canada in the Midst of Freedom,* Vol. 2. Toronto, ON: McClelland & Stewart, 1971.

Tulchinsky, Gerald. *Canada's Jews: A People's Journey.* Toronto, ON: University of Toronto Press, 2008. 530 pp.

Jewish Thought

Barish, Louis, and Rebecca Barish. *Basic Jewish Beliefs.* New York: David, 1961. 222 pp.

Eisenstein, Ira. *Varieties of Jewish Belief.* New York: Reconstructionist Press, 1966. 270 pp.

Fackenheim, Emil L. *God's Presence in History: Jewish Affirmations and Philosophical Reflections.* New York: Harper & Row, 1970. 104 pp.

Gordis, Robert. *Judaism for the Modern Age.* New York: Farrar, Straus & Cudahy, 1955. 368 pp.

Heschel, Abraham Joshua. *God in Search of Man: A Philosophy of Judaism.* New York: New York: Farrar, Straus & Cudahy, 1955. 437 pp.

Neuser, Jacob. *Understanding Jewish Theology: Classical Issues and Modern Perspectives.* New York: KTAV, 1973. 280 pp.

Jewish Life and Customs

Greenberg, Irving. *The Jewish Way: Living the Holidays.* New York: Simon & Schuster, 1993. 463 pp.

Maslin, Simeon J., ed. *Gates of Mitzvah.* New York: Central Conference of American Rabbis, 1979. 165 pp.

Posner, Raphael, Uri Kaploun, and Shalom Cohon, eds. *Jewish Liturgy: Prayer and Synagogue Service through the Ages.* New York: Ameil, 1975. 278 pp.

Trepp, Leo. *The Complete Book of Jewish Observance.* New York: Behrman House, 1980. 370 pp.

Hasidism

Abelson, J. *Jewish Mysticism: An Introduction to the Kabbalah.* New York: Hermon Press, 1969. 182 pp.

Aron, Milton. *Ideas and Ideals of the Hassidim.* New York: Citadel Press, 1969. 350 pp.

Bokser, Ben Zion. *The Jewish Mystical Tradition.* New York: Pilgrim Press, 1981. 277 pp.

Buber, Martin. *The Origin and Meaning of Hassidism.* New York: Horizon Press, 1960. 254 pp.

Dresner, Samuel H. *The Zaddik: The Doctrine of the Zaddik According to the Writing of Rabbi Yaakov Yosef of Polnoy.* New York: Schocken, 1960. 312 pp.

Idel, Moshe. *Hasidism: Between Ecstasy and Magic.* Albany: State University of New York Press, 1995. 438 pp.

Mintz, Jerome R. *Hasidic People: A Place in the New World.* Cambridge, MA: Harvard University Press, 1992. 433 pp.

Rabinowitz, H. *A Guide to Hassidism.* New York: Yoseloff, 1960. 163 pp.

Rubenstein, Aryeh. *Hassidism.* Jerusalem: Ketter, 1975. 120 pp.

Anti-Semitism and the Holocaust

Bauer, Yehuda. *Rethinking the Holocaust.* New Haven, CT: Yale University Press, 2001. 335 pp.

Berenbaum, Michael. *The World Must Know: The History of the Holocaust as Told in the United States Holocaust Memorial Museum.* Boston: Little Brown, 1993.

Dawidowicz, Lucy. *The War against the Jews: 1933–1945.* New York: Holt, Rinehart, and Winston, 1975. 460 pp.

Engel, David. *Holocaust: The Third Reich and the Jews.* New York: Longman, 2000. 148 pp.

Friedländer, Saul. *The Years of Extermination: 1939–1945.* New York: Harper Collins, 2007. 870 pp.

Levin, Nora. *The Holocaust: The Destruction of European Jewry, 1933–1945.* New York: Crowell, 1968. 768 pp.

Littell, Franklin H. *The Crucifixion of the Jews.* New York: Harper & Row, 1975. 153 pp.

Mitchell, Joseph R., and Helen Buss Mitchell. *The Holocaust: Readings and Interpretations.* New York: McGraw Hill, 2001.

Poliakov, Léon. *The History of Anti-Semitism.* Trans. Richard Howard. New York: Vanguard, 1965. 340 pp.

Singerman, Robert. *Antisemitic Propaganda: An Annotated Bibliography and Research Guide.* New York: Garland, 1982. 448 pp.

Spector, Shmuel, and Geoffrey Wigoder, eds. *The Encyclopedia of Jewish Life: Before and During the Holocaust.* 3 vols. New York: New York University Press, 2001.

Black Judaism

ben-Jochannan, Yosef. *We the Black Jews.* New York: Alkebu-lan, 1983. 408 pp.

Goitein, S. D. *From the Land of Sheba: Tales of the Jews of Yemen.* Rev. ed. Trans. Christopher Fremantle. New York: Schocken, 1973. 142 pp.

Kaplan, Steven. *The Beta Israel (Falashas) in Ethiopia: From Earliest Times to the Twentieth Century.* New York: New York University Press, 1992. 231 pp.

Landing, James M. *Black Judaism: Story of an American Movement.* Durham, NC: Carolina Academic Press, 2002. 544 pp.

Rapoport, Louis. *The Lost Jews: Last of the Ethiopian Falashas.* New York: Stein and Day, 1980. 252 pp.

Winsor, Rudolph R. *From Babylon to Timbuktu: History of the Ancient Black Races Including the Black Hebrews.* New York: Exposition Press, 1969. 151 pp.

Pan-Denominational Jewish Organizations

International Federation of Secular Humanistic Jews

28611 W Twelve Mile Rd., Farmington Hills, MI 48334

The International Federation of Secular Humanistic Jews is a worldwide organization that was established in 1986 in Detroit, Michigan, to bring together secular and humanistic Jewish organizations across international boundaries. Secular humanistic Judaism offers a nontheistic approach to Jewish identity and culture, and has come into being as a distinct alternative to Orthodox, Conservative, Reform, and Reconstructionist Judaism. The organization exists through its regional structures (in North America, Latin America, Europe, and Israel) and its national branches currently located in Argentina, Australia, Belgium, Canada, France, Great Britain, Israel, the United States, and Uruguay. The North American region consists of two organizations, the Society for Humanistic Judaism and the Congress of Secular Jewish Organizations.

The International Federation is headed by its president Yehuda Bauer (b. 1926), a historian and Holocaust scholar at the Hebrew University in Jerusalem. Serving as honorary president is Albert Memmi (b. 1921), a sociologist at the University of Paris. The federation supports the International Institute for Secular Humanistic Judaism, an intellectual and training center in Jerusalem.

The federation has affirmed its belief in the value of human reason, human existence, and the power of human beings to solve their problems; Jewish identity and the survival of the Jewish people; and a secular humanistic democracy for Israel.

Membership: In 1995 there were nine national branches with a constituency of 30,000 people, approximately half of whom live in the United States.

Sources:

International Federation of Secular Humanistic Jews. www.ifshj.org/.

Goodman, Saul N. *The Faith of Secular Jews.* New York: KTAV Publishing House, 1976.

Ibry, David. *Exodus to Humanism: Jewish Identity without Religion.* Buffalo, NY: Prometheus Books, 1999.

Wine, Sherwin T. *Humanistic Judaism.* Buffalo, NY: Prometheus Books, 1978.

New York Board of Rabbis

136 E 39th St., New York, NY 10016-0914

The New York Board of Rabbis, founded in 1881, is the largest interdenominational rabbinic body in the world. The board consists of more than 800 rabbis—Orthodox, Conservative, Reform, and Reconstructionist—who serve 1.5 million congregants. The board furnishes chaplains for city, county, and state hospitals; nursing homes; and mental health and correctional institutions. It is involved in interfaith and interethnic dialogues with clergy of various faiths. It lobbies on behalf of Jewish religious interests on the city, county, and state levels. For example, it has called for kosher food to be served at public functions within the Jewish community; insisted on proper Jewish rites at funerals; enrolled rabbis to urge the issuance of a Get and the signing of a prenuptial agreement to obtain a Get; lobbied for Kashrut standards in public institutions and correctional facilities, including the distribution of Passover food and religious articles for patients and inmates; moved to protect the rights of Sabbath observers; prevented the administering of exams in the public universities on the Sabbath and holidays; and prevented the County Medical Examiner from forcing delays in burial. The Brith Milah Board, an affiliate of the New York Board of Rabbis, certifies Mohalim who satisfy halakic and medical requirements.

The board conducts television and radio programs and helps maintain the international synagogue at Kennedy Airport.

The New York Board of Rabbis has emerged as the voice of mainstream religious Jewry in the New York metropolitan area. It has been able to operate as rabbis have put aside their theological and religious differences and focused on mutual cooperation on the values and goals they share in common.

Though the New York Board is by far the largest, similar rabbinic boards are found in other urban areas across the United States.

Membership: In 2002 the board reported 800 members in the United States and 50 overseas.

Periodicals: *Bulletin.*

Sources:

New York Board of Rabbis. www.nybr.org/.

Rosenthal, Gilbert S. *Come Let Us Reason Together.* New York: New York Board of Rabbis, n.d.

Teplitz, Saul I. *The Rabbis Speak: A Quarter Century of Sermons for the High Holy Days.* New York: New York Board of Rabbis, 1986.

North American Coalition to Advance Religious Pluralism in Israel

c/o Nan Rich, National Council of Jewish Women, 820 2nd Ave., New York, NY 10017-4504

Efforts that led to the formation of the North American Coalition for the Advancement of Religious Pluralism in Israel began in 1996 following the disbanding of the Synagogue Council of America. The council, which had included Orthodox, Reform, and Conservative Jewish leaders, floundered on issues concerning the status of the Reform, Reconstructionist, and Conservative Jewish communities, particularly in Israel. Then in May 1996, as elections in Israel approached, six Reform organizations, eight Conservative agencies, one Reconstructionist group, the American Jewish Congress, Labor Zionist Alliance, NA'AMAT USA, and the New Israel Fund hastily formed a coalition and issued a letter to the leading candidates for prime minister concerning rumored concessions to the Orthodox majority that would negatively affect non-Orthodox communities in Israel. That letter was sent out under the name of the North American Coalition to Advance Religious Pluralism in Israel.

Following the elections, a second letter was sent to Prime Minister Benjamin Netanyahu that further expressed the coalition's concern that Reform and Conservative representatives would be denied any seats on the municipal religious councils, and that the Orthodox would be granted sole authority over issues involving people converting to Judaism.

Then in 1998, concern for what it saw as growing religious intolerance in Israel led the National Council of Jewish Women to convene a gathering of representatives from several Jewish organizations to establish an organization to address issues of religious pluralism. They named the resulting group the North American Coalition for the Advancement of Religious Freedom in Israel. It chose to focus initially on marriage in Israel, where civil marriage and marriage conducted by non-Orthodox clergy are prohibited.

In its first statement, issued in 1999, the coalition stated, "We support the right of full religious expression and worship for all streams of Judaism at public religious sites such as the Western Wall in Israel."

Membership: Not reported. The coalition includes a number of Reform, Reconstructionist, and Conservative organizations.

Sources:

National Council of Jewish Women. www.ncjw.org/.

Reform Judaism. rj.org/.

 # Conservative Judaism

Conservative Judaism

c/o The United Synagogue of Conservative Judaism, 155 5th Ave., New York, NY 10010

Alternate Address: The Rabbinical Assembly, 3080 Broadway, New York, NY 10027.

As Reform and Orthodox polemics began to polarize the Jewish community, there arose a middle group that advocated an allegiance to traditional Judaism, and simultaneously a willingness to balance tradition with change. In 1886, drawn together by an affront to tradition at the graduation of the first class at Hebrew Union College, the Reform college located in Cincinnati, Ohio, Rabbi Sabato Morais, Marcus Jastrow, and Henry Pereira Mendes formed a Jewish Theological Seminary Association to counteract the effects of the liberalizing Reform movement.

Although it was not a strong movement at that time, Conservative Judaism nevertheless found champions in Solomon Schechter and Cyrus Adler. The two revived the faltering Jewish Theological Seminary in the first decade of the twentieth century, and Schechter became the mainstay of a Judaism that respected tradition but was saturated with contemporary scholarship. The Conservative synagogue uses English as well as Hebrew, does not separate men and women, and emphasizes modern education. However, many Orthodox practices are retained, such as covering heads during worship.

The Jewish Theological Seminary in New York remains the educational center of Jewish Conservatism. In 1913 Schechter pulled together the United Synagogue of America, now the United Synagogue of Conservative Judaism, which serves as the association of Conservative congregations in North America. The Rabbinical Assembly, the association of Conservative rabbis, was founded six years later, growing out of the seminary's alumni association.

The United Synagogue is an association of congregations that accepts the Standards for Congregational Practice. A delegated convention meets biennially and elects the national officers and a board of directors. Congregations are grouped into 16 regions, each served by a regional office. National departments of educa-

tion, youth activities, extension activities, and leadership development, among others, provide guidance and materials for the congregations. Internationally, the Conservative movement finds expression through the World Council of Conservative/Masorti Congregations. The United Synagogue operates the Fuchsberg Center in Jerusalem. A Woman's League of Conservative Judaism also exists, as do several youth organizations.

During the twentieth century the Conservative movement found favor in Canada among the older congregations just as massive waves of Russian and Eastern European migration (primarily Orthodox in makeup) were remaking the Jewish community. By 1960 more than 20 congregations had affiliated with the United Synagogue. That number almost doubled over the next two decades.

Membership: In 2007 there were approximately 760 affiliated Conservative congregations and 1,500,000 affiliated members in North America.

Educational Facilities:

Jewish Theological Seminary, New York, New York.

University of Judaism, Los Angeles, California.

Periodicals: *CJ: Voices of Conservative/Masorti Judaism* (formerly *United Synagogue Review*) • *Conservative Judaism.*

Sources:

United Synagogue of Conservative Judaism. www.uscj.org/index1.html.

Rabbinical Assembly. www.rabbinicalassembly.org/indexfl.html.

Davis, Moshe. *The Emergence of Conservative Judaism.* Philadelphia: Jewish Publication Society of America, 1963.

Gillman, Neil. *Conservative Judaism: The New Century.* West Orange, NJ: Behrman House, 1993.

Karp, Abraham J. *A History of the United Synagogue of America, 1913–1963.* New York: United Synagogue of America, 1964.

Sklare, Marshall. *Conservative Judaism.* Glencoe, IL: Free Press, 1955.

Jewish Reconstructionist Federation

101 Greenwood Ave., Jenkintown, PA 19046

During the years following World War I, the Jewish community became prosperous and diffuse. In recognition of the not strictly religious nature of much of what was commonly labeled Judaism, in the 1930s Jewish Theological Seminary professor Mordecai M. Kaplan (1881–1983) proposed a new approach to Judaism that would take account of its diversity. In his *Judaism as a Civilization* (1934) he argued that Judaism was more than a religion; it was an evolving religious civilization. He called for a reconstruction of Judaism not around just the synagogue, but around the community as a whole. Jewish civilization would unite the disparate elements of the Jewish community—Reform, Conservative and Orthodox, Zionist, and others.

The ideas of Kaplan appealed especially to nonorthodox Jews who were nonetheless attached to "Jewishness," and eventually a new movement, Reconstructionism, emerged. In 1935 Kaplan began a periodical, *The Reconstructionist*, to propagate his ideas. Kaplan's approach to tradition, his rejection of the divine origin of the Torah, and his reevaluation of ritual in light of modern thought, however, proved a constant source of discord. After Kaplan retired from the Jewish Theological Seminary, his followers finalized the establishment of Reconstructionism as a distinct movement rather than simply an ideology influencing Conservatism. Conservatives were so upset by Kaplan's revisions of the prayer book that in 1945, he was excommunicated.

The Reconstructionist movement took incipient organizational form in 1940 with the founding of the Jewish Reconstructionist Foundation. Reconstructionist congregations appeared, and in 1954 the Federation of Reconstructionist Congregations and Havurot (now the Jewish Reconstructionist Foundation) was founded to coordinate the activities of the various centers. In 1968 a rabbinical college was established, and its graduates and rabbis founded the Reconstructionist Rabbinical Association.

Membership: In 2008 the federation reported 16,000 member households, 1,090 congregations, and some 300 rabbis in the United States, and 1,000 members, two congregations, and five rabbis in Canada.

Educational Facilities:

Reconstructionist Rabbinical College, Wyncote, Pennsylvania.

Periodicals: *The Reconstructionist* • *Raayonot*.

Sources:

Jewish Reconstructionist Federation. www.jrf.org/.

Alpert, Rebecca T., and Jacob J. Straub. *Exploring Judaism: A Reconstructionist Approach*. Elkins Park, PA: Reconstructionist Press, 2000.

Cohen, Jack J. *The Case for Religious Humanism*. New York: Reconstructionist Press, 1958.

Eisenstein, Ira. *Reconstructing Judaism: An Autobiography*. Elkins Park, PA: Reconstructionist Press: 1986.

Kaplan, Mordecai M. *Basic Values in Jewish Religion*. New York: Reconstructionist Press, 1948.

———. *The Future of the American Jew*. New York: Macmillan, 1949.

———. *The Meaning of God in Modern Jewish Religion*. New York: Reconstructionist Press, 1962.

Kohn, Eugene. *Religious Humanism*. New York: Reconstructionist Press, 1953.

Scult, Mel. *Judaism Faces the Twentieth Century: A Biography of Mordecai Kaplan*. Elkins Park, PA: Reconstructionist Press, 1993.

 # Orthodox Judaism

American Sephardi Federation
15 W 16th St., 6th Fl., New York, NY 10011

The Jewish community is usually seen as divided into two main segments, the Ashkenazi and the Sephardi. The Ashkenazi are that branch of the community that derived from the Jewish communities of northern and eastern Europe, and in the United States, the Ashkenazi are much the larger segment of the community, at more than 90 percent. The Sephardi are those Jews who, broadly speaking, come from the lands of the Mediterranean and western Asia. More narrowly, the Sephardi are Jews who derive from the prominent community of medieval Spain and Portugal. That community was disbursed in the 1490s, and many left Iberia for the Americas and the eastern Mediterranean. The Sephardi differ from the Ashkenazi primarily on matters of culture. They have developed a distinctive culture in Spain, and have various differences in their Sabbath and high holy days liturgy.

Sephardi from Brazil were largely responsible for the founding of the Jewish community in what is now the United States. They had emerged at Recife during the period of the Dutch occupancy of that city, but were forced to flee when Portugal regained control. The initial group arrived in New York (then New Amsterdam) in 1654 and went on to establish the first synagogue, Shearith Israel. Shortly thereafter, other participants in the same migration founded the first Canadian synagogue, in Montreal. Subsequently, synagogues were opened in Philadelphia, Newport (Rhode Island), Savannah (Georgia), and Charleston (South Carolina). The Sephardi constituted the majority of the American Jewish community until around 1720, when the Ashkenazi became the majority. A century later, they were completely overwhelmed by the first wave of German Jews that began to arrive following the fall of Napoleon (1815).

After the arrival of the massive numbers of Eastern European Jews in the 1880s, the Sephardi became an almost invisible minority, even though some 20,000

Turkish Sephardic Jews arrived early in the twentieth century, and later Jews from Iran and Iraq migrated from the Middle East.

Attempts to organize the Sephardic community in America began early in the twentieth century. The earliest association seems to have been in the New York area, a single urban area with several Sephardic synagogues. As early as 1912 the Federation of Oriental Jews was founded by the synagogues in New York, Montreal, and Philadelphia; it fell apart in 1918. Other attempts were made over the years, but it was not until 1972, with the founding of the American Sephardi Federation, that a permanent organization was effected. It drew strength from many immigrants of the Jewish communities of North Africa, Egypt, Lebanon, Iraq, and Iran, in particular. Although many Sephardi have joined Ashkenazi congregations, many others have formed their own congregations, a few nationally specific, and affiliated through the American Sephardi Federation.

Membership: As of the late 1980s, there were an estimated 150,000 Sephardic Jews in the United States, the largest percentage of which (60,000) live in the New York City area. There are organized Sephardic synagogues in 21 communities in all regions of the United States.

Periodicals: *Sephardic Connection*.

Sources:

Elazar, Daniel J. *The Other Jews: The Sephardim Today*. New York: Basic Books, 1989.

Congregation Bina—Indian Jewish Congregation of USA
c/o The Village Temple, 33 E 12th St., New York, NY 10023

In 1981 Congregation Bina was founded as a fellowship for Jews who had migrated to the United States from India. When Europeans began to invade India in numbers in the nineteenth century, they became aware of the existence of a small community of some 25,000 people who claimed that they were Jews descended from the 10 lost tribes of Israel, and who called themselves Bene Israel, Children of Israel. They traced their origin to the second century B.C.E., when they were shipwrecked off the coast of India near Bombay: Only seven families survived, and they were cut off from their fellow religionists for many centuries.

According to the accounts of Bene Israel historians, the survivors of the shipwreck lost their religious records and soon lost the Hebrew language, which they replaced with Marathi, a west India language. However, they retained the Sabbath, the practice of the Holy Days, the dietary regulations, circumcision, and the *Shema* (the confession of the Jewish faith). Other historians have suggested that the Bene Israel arrived in India much later, by way of Arabia or Yemen.

The Bene Israel seemed to have survived by becoming a separate caste within the complex caste system of India. They experienced a religious revival in the early 1800s when Christian missionaries, motivated by possible conversion of the Bene Israel to Christianity, translated the Bible into Marathi, created a Hebrew-Marathi grammar, and even hired members of the community to teach in their schools. However, few accepted Christianity, and the missionary efforts contributed more to the establishment of contacts between the Indian Jews and their fellow believers in Europe. European and American publications began to flow into India.

The Bene Israel were scattered throughout India until the modern era and they did not erect a synagogue until 1796 in Bombay. However, there are no rabbis; worship is in the hands of the membership.

In the years since the independence of India and the emergence of the state of Israel, the community in India has been decimated by migration. Though most have gone to Israel, during the 1970s a small number came to the United States. Thus in 1981 the Bene Israel in the United States came together and founded Congregation Bina. They seek to preserve the customs, liturgy, music, and folklore of the Indian Jewish community.

In addition to the Bene Israel, the largest of the Indian Jewish groups, the Indian Jewish community includes two additional groups. The Jews of Cochin originally settling in Cranganore and Malabar. After centuries in their adopted homeland, in the fifteenth century C.E. they were forced to flee to Cochin following attacks, first by the Moors and then later by the Portuguese. At one time they numbered about 2,500; in 2008 no more than 17 remain in Cochin.

In the nineteenth century a group of Jews from Baghdad and Syria who came to India as traders and refugees created communities in Bombay and Pune in western India and across the subcontinent in Calcutta. They initially settled in Surat, then the most important port on the west coast. They number around 5,000, but only about 200 now remain in India; the majority migrated through the British Commonwealth to the United Kingdom, Australia, and Canada.

Since 1993 the Jews of Indian origin in the United States have gathered annually for High Holy Days ceremonies, with representatives from all three Indian Jewish communities coming to New York from as far away as Minneapolis and Los Angeles. These annual gatherings were the precursor of the organization of the Indian Jewish Congregation of USA in 2005. The catalyst for the group's organization was the need to fundraise to restore the Beth El Synagogue in Panvel, India, which was severely damaged by a monsoon. Dating from 1849, the synagogue has persisted as an unitive structure for Indian American Jews.

In 2008 Cantor Romiel Daniel was the president of the Indian Congregation.

Membership: In 2008 the congregation reported 350 members scattered around the United States and one synagogue in New York City. Some 5,000 Indian Jews currently reside in India.

Periodicals: *Indian Congregation of USA Newsletter*.

Sources:

Jews of India web site. www.jewsofindia.org.

Strizower, Schifra. *The Bene Israel of Bombay*. New York: Schocken Books, 1971.

Yankovich, Iat. "Wandering Jews No More? Indian Jews in U.S. Struggle for Unity, Acceptance." *Jewish Press* (February 15, 2008): 62, 74. Available from www.jewsofindia.org/PDFs/The%20Jewish%20Press%20021508.pdf.

K'hal Adath Jeshurun

85 Bennett Ave., New York, NY 10033

K'hal Adath Jeshurun is an outpost of German Orthodox Judaism in the United States. In the 1880s Solomon Breuer (1850–1926) emerged as a staunch defender of Orthodoxy in Frankfurt, and in 1888 he founded Germany's Verbund orthodoxer Rabbiner (Association of Orthodox Rabbis), an ultra-Orthodox group in that it refused membership to Orthodox rabbis who cooperated with Reform Jewish rabbis on work for the Jewish community. Breuer was the son-in-law of Samson Raphael Hirsch (1808–1888), a great Orthodox leader who had defined what was later called "neo-Orthodoxy," a combination of strict Orthodox Jewish belief combined with an openness to the modern world and culture on secular matters.

In 1926 Breuer was succeeded as head of the congregation in Frankfurt by his son Joseph Breuer (1882–1980). In 1939, on the eve of World War II, Joseph Breuer migrated to the United States and became the spiritual leader of K'hal Adath Jeshurun. He saw himself as carrying on the work of his father in the United States. In 1944 he established a school, Yeshiva Rabbi Sampson Raphael Hirsh, named for a nineteenth-century German Orthodox leader who also happened to be his maternal grandfather. The school followed the pattern he had learned in Germany.

Breuer emerged as a respected rabbi, if somewhat extreme. He authored a number of books in both English and Hebrew. On his eightieth birthday he received a jubilee volume compiled in his honor.

Membership: Not reported.

Sources:

K'hal Adath Jeshurun. www.kajinc.org/.

National Council of Young Israel

3 W 16th St., New York, NY 10011

The Young Israel movement began in 1912 at the Jewish Theological Seminary. It was started by two professors, Israel Friedlander (1876–1920) and Mordecai M. Kaplan (1881–1983), and Rabbi Judah Magnes (1877–1948). The movement attempted to unite Orthodox Jewish youth of Manhattan's Lower East Side. It developed an English-language program and a supplementary program not generally available in other Orthodox centers. As the Conservative movement emerged and as the seminary became identified with it, in 1922 the Orthodox leadership of Young Israel repudiated Conservatism, but found that this practice did not fit well with other Orthodox groups.

Young Israel emerged as a powerful adult movement over the next decade. The group incorporated in 1926. Within a few years it expanded through the Jewish community in the United States and entered Canada. In 1939 it reported 35 affiliated synagogues, and by 1971 had reached 100. A variety of organizations were created to carry out its program. The American Friends of Young Israel in Israel promotes the formation of Young Israel synagogues in Israel. An Armed Forces Bureau counsels Orthodox Jews in the armed forces on various issues such as Sabbath observance and dietary behavior. The Mesilah Institute for Jewish Studies promotes Jewish education at all age levels. Young Israel Youth and Young Israel Collegiates and Young Adults are age-specific programs for young people.

Beginning at the more liberal end of Orthodoxy, Young Israel has with age become more conservative. It calls for attention to Sabbath laws, separates men and women in worship services, and attacks non-Orthodox Jews. It has become staunchly pro-Zionist.

Membership: In 2008 there were more than 200 Young Israel affiliated centers in the United States, Canada, and Israel.

Periodicals: *Viewpoint* • *Divrei Torah Bulletin* • *CYIR Newsletter*.

Sources:

National Council of Young Israel. www.youngisrael.org.

Rosenthal, Gilbert S. *Contemporary Judaism: Patterns of Survival*. New York: Human Sciences Press, 1986.

"Young Israel—Movement to Synagogue." In *The Jewish Directory and Almanac*, ed. Ivan L. Tillem. New York: Pacific Press, 1984.

Orthodox Judaism

Rabbinical Council of America, 305 7th Ave., New York, NY 10001

Alternate Address: Union of Orthodox Jewish Congregations of America, 333 7th Ave., New York, NY 10001.

The earliest divisions in American Judaism related to land of origin, and they came about as various national groups settled in the United States. Although all groups professed a similar Old World form of faith, they were differentiated by peculiarities of the various national cultures. Orthodox Judaism remains one of the major facets of the American Jewish experience. Orthodox Jews are distinctive within the Jewish community in their punctilious observance of the plethora of Jewish laws: strictly keeping the Sabbath, adhering to kosher food laws, and remaining deeply attentive to religious tradition. The learning and use of Hebrew is emphasized.

In the process of Americanization (and the demand for English in the service and other more radical changes), and with the importation of German-based Reform Judaism, there arose champions of tradition such as Rabbi Isaac Leeser (1806–1868) of the Mikveh Israel Congregation. Orthodoxy in the United States developed as a tradition-affirming segment of Judaism in reaction to both the Reform movement and the more moderate accommodations to modernity associated with the Conservative movement. Orthodox Jews were also traditionally the poorest. The Orthodox scattered into urban centers around the country and only formalized an organization at the end of the nineteenth century.

Preliminary efforts at cooperative endeavor began among Orthodox adherents in the 1880s, in reaction to Reform activities. In 1898 the Union of Orthodox Jewish Congregations of America was formed. Only two years earlier, the first rabbinical school, the Rabbi Elchanan Theological Seminary (now Yeshiva University) had been established. In 1902 the Union of Orthodox Rabbis was formed by the Eastern European rabbis who had come to control the congregational association. However, the English-speaking rabbis retained control of the seminary, which grew as the number of English-speaking Orthodox Jews grew, and in 1935 the English-speaking rabbis formed the Rabbinical Council of America.

The Rabbinical Council of America and the Union of Orthodox Jewish Congregations of America emerged as the primary organizations serving Orthodox Jews, with the exception of the Hasidic Jews, in the United States. Following the basic congregation-based organizational life of American Judaism, both rabbis and congregations are free in their associations, and the Union serves congregations whose rabbis are orthodox but not members of the Rabbinical Council.

Before the 1880s Canadian Jews were present in factions similar to those apparent in American Judaism. However, in Canada, the Orthodox segment remained the majority due to the significant wave of immigration at the turn of the twentieth century, supplemented by a second wave immediately after World War II, and in spite of the large advances of the Conservative movement, usually at the expense of Orthodoxy. Many Canadian Orthodox congregations are affiliated with the Union of Orthodox Jewish Congregations, though many others remain independent and unaffiliated with any association.

The Union carries on a far-reaching educational program through numerous publications, a Torah tape library, and materials for the deaf and developmentally disabled. It operates the National Orthodox Information Center and sponsors the National Conference of Synagogue Youth. Through its OU kashruth program it designates products as kosher. The Union and the Rabbinical Council cooperate in support of the Institute of Public Affairs, an advocacy think tank created to represent the American Orthodox Jewish community.

Membership: Not reported. In 1995 the Union of Orthodox Jewish Congregations reported about 1,000 congregations.

Educational Facilities:

Yeshiva University, New York, New York. (Its Isaac Elchanan Theological Seminary trains and ordains rabbis.)

Hebrew Theological College, Chicago, Illinois.

Ner Israel Rabbinical College, Baltimore, Maryland.

Mesivta Yeshiva Rabbi Chaim Berlin Rabinical Academy, New York, New York.

Periodicals: *Jewish Action* • *Tradition*.

Sources:

Rabbinical Council of America. www.rabbis.org.

Union of Orthodox Jewish Congregations of America. www.ou.org/.

Hapgood, Hutchins. *The Spirit of the Ghetto.* New York: Schocken Books, 1966.

Katz, Jacob. *A House Divided: Orthodoxy and Schism in Nineteenth-century Central European Jewry.* Brandeis University Press, 1998.

Mayer, Egon. *From Suburb to Shtetl.* Philadelphia: Temple University Press, 1979.

Schlossberg, Eli W. *The World of Orthodox Judaism.* Northvale, NJ: Jason Aronson, 1997.

Schwartz, Elkanah. *American Life: Shtetl Style.* New York: Jonathan David, 1967.

Union of Orthodox Rabbis of the United States and Canada
235 East Broadway, New York, NY 10002

The organization of Orthodox Judaism occurred very slowly in the United States but accelerated when waves of East European immigration brought more traditionalists at the close of the nineteenth century. Efforts at the municipal level met with varying degrees of success, but in 1898 the Union of Orthodox Jewish

Congregations was created. Two years later the Rabbi Elchanan Theological Seminary (the forerunner of Yeshiva University) was opened. Finally, the Union of Orthodox Rabbis of the United States and Canada, the oldest Orthodox rabbinical organization in North America, was founded in 1902.

The union, also known as the Agudat HaRabbonim, called together Yiddish-speaking rabbis. It rejected the graduates of the Jewish Theological Seminary (the primary school of what was emerging as Conservative Judaism) and backed the Rabbi Isaac Elchanan Theological Seminary. It demanded of its members that they possess the traditional *semikhah*, ritual ordination.

The founders and earliest members of the Agudat HaRabbonim were trained in Europe. As the graduates of Rabbi Isaac Elchanan Theological Seminary gradually Americanized, they began to lobby for more modern training and understood the need for proficiency in English more than Yiddish. Developing their strength through the school's alumni association in 1938, they organized the Rabbinical Council of America as a rival organization.

In 1997 the Agudat HaRabbonim issued a declaration claiming that the Reform and Conservative movements were illegal, heretical expressions of Judaism. Orthodox rabbis affiliated with the Rabbinical Council denounced the union's action.

Membership: Not reported.

Remarks: The Jewish historian Jerome Chanes described the Union of Orthodox Rabbis as consisting of "Yiddish-speaking, European-born-and-educated rabbis," who refused close association with rabbis trained and ordained by Yeshiva University. It still exists, but Chanes notes that it "is little more than a paper organization."

Sources:

Chanes, Jerome. "A Primer on the American Jewish Community." Jewish Living Publications. Available from www.ajc.org/site/apps/nl/content3.asp?c=ijITI2PHKoG&b=843137&ct=1044883.

Rosenthal, Gilbert S. *Contemporary Judaism: Patterns of Survival.* New York: Human Sciences Press, 1986.

❀ Reform Judaism

Reform Judaism
c/o Union for Reform Judaism, 633 Third Ave., New York, NY 10017

Alternate Address: Central Conference of American Rabbis, 355 Lexington Ave., New York, NY 10017.

Reform Judaism, the most liberal of the major movements within Judaism today, began in Germany in the early 1800s as Jews began to examine their religion with an eye toward rationality and decorum in the expectation that dignified worship would help justify their desire to become citizens. As a result, some congregations introduced changes in worship, including the use of the vernacular language for prayer and sermons, mixed seating, and organ music.

Although its roots were in Germany, Reform Judaism also flourished in the United States, where Jews had true freedom of religion due to the separation of church and state. As German Jews immigrated in the mid-1800s, Reform rapidly became the dominant belief system of American Jews.

The first congregation to identify itself as "Reform" was formed by individuals who had split from Congregation Beth Elohim in Charleston, South Carolina, in 1825, from Har Sinai Congregation in Baltimore in 1842, and from Emanu-El Congregation in New York in 1845. In 1846 Rabbi Isaac Mayer Wise, who is considered the leading institutional builder of Reform Judaism in North America, came to the United States from Bohemia. After spending eight years in Albany, New York, he moved to Cincinnati, Ohio, then the gateway to the West.

In Cincinnati Rabbi Wise founded *The Israelite*, an English-language weekly newspaper espousing the principles of Reform Judaism, and wrote the first prayer book for American worshippers, *Minhag American* (1857), which included both Hebrew and English readings.

At Wise's urging, delegates of 28 congregations gathered in Cincinnati in July 1873 and founded the Union of American Hebrew Congregations, with the primary objective of forming a seminary. In 1875 the Hebrew Union College opened in Cincinnati with Wise as its president. In 1889 Wise founded the third major institution of the Reform movement, the Central Conference of American Rabbis.

By 1880 over 90 percent of U.S. synagogues were Reform. Many Reform congregations of this time had rabbis wearing robes, pews with mixed seating, choirs, and hymnals. Yet, by 1935 Reform had already started on the path of return to a more traditional approach to Judaism—distinctly Jewish and distinctly American.

Reform Jews are committed to a Judaism that changes and adapts to the needs of the day. Since its earliest days, Reform Judaism has asserted that a Judaism frozen in time is an heirloom, not an evolving religion that encourages its members to be fully integrated into and involved in society. Reform differs from other major branches of Judaism in that it views the Torah as divinely inspired but a product of human hands.

Reform Judaism today is also committed to the absolute equality of women and the acceptance of gays and lesbians in all areas of Jewish life. It was the first movement to ordain women rabbis and to accept as Jews the children of only one Jewish parent—either the father or the mother—if they were raised as Jews. (Traditional Judaism stipulates that only a child born of a Jewish mother is a Jew.)

After World War II the Reform movement expanded rapidly as congregations were formed in the new suburban communities. Today it is the largest and fastest growing denomination of Judaism.

Membership: In 2008 there were approximately 1.5 million Reform Jews in the United States, and more than 900 congregations in North America affiliated with the Union of American Hebrew Congregations. More than 2,500 rabbis have been ordained by Hebrew Union College–Jewish Institute of Religion, which operates campuses in Cincinnati, New York, Los Angeles, and Jerusalem. It has more than 450 cantors.

Educational Facilities:

Hebrew Union College, Jewish Institute of Religion, Cincinnati, Ohio. There are HUC campuses in New York, New York; Los Angeles, California; and Jerusalem, Israel.

Periodicals: *Journal of Reform Judaism* • *Reform Judaism*.

Sources:

Union for Reform Judaism. urj.org.

Central Conference of American Rabbis. ccarnet.org.

Borowitz, Eugene B. *Liberal Judaism*. New York: Union of American Hebrew Congregations, 1984.

An Intimate Portrait of the Union of American Hebrew Congregations—A Centennial Documentary. Cincinnati: American Jewish Archives,1973.

Jacob, Walter, ed. *American Reform Responsa: Collected Responsa of the Central Conference of American Rabbis, 1889–1993*. Cincinnati, OH: Central Conference of American Rabbis, 1999.

Kaplan, Dana Evan. *Platform and Prayer Books: Theological and Liturgical Perspectives on Reform Judaism*. Lanham, MD: Rowan and Littlefield, 2002.

Meyer, Michael. *A Response to Modernity: A History of the Reform Movement in Judaism*. New York: Oxford University Press, 1988.

Olitzky, Kerry M., Lance J. Sussman, and Malcolm H. Stern, eds. *Reform Judaism in America*. Westport, CT: Greenwood Publishing Group, 1993.

Plaut, W. Gunther. *The Rise of Reform Judaism*. New York: World Union for Progressive Judaism, 1963.

Reform Judaism. Cincinnati, OH: Hebrew Union College Press, 1949.

Washofsky, Mark. *Jewish Living: A Guide to Contemporary Reform Practice*. New York: Union of American Hebrew Congregations, 2001.

 # Hasidic Judaism

Belz Hasidism

Belzer Yeshiva, 1779 51st St., Brooklyn, NY 11204

The Shapira are a Polish Hasidic family that established several Hasidic dynasties in the nineteenth century. One was established at Belz, a small town in Ukraine. By the beginning of the twentieth century the majority of the town's 6,000 residents were Jews.

The first Belzer rebbe was Shalom Rokeach of Belz (1779–1855), better known as the Sar Shalom. His lengthy career as head of the new dynasty began in 1817, and he started with good credentials, being a disciple of Rabbi Yaakov Yitzchak of Lublin (1745–1815) the famous Seer of Lublin, revered for both his humility and great intuitive powers. The Sar Shalom was succeeded by Yehoshua Rokeach of Belz (1825–1894), his youngest son, who had an equally long period in office (1855–1894); Yissachar Dov Rokeach (1854–1926); and Aharon Rokeach (1877–1957). Just ahead of the Nazis, Rabbi Aharon escaped from Belz to Hungary and then to Palestine.

Operating from headquarters in Tel Aviv after World War II, Rabbi Aharon began to rebuild his following, most of which had been destroyed in the Holocaust. When he died in 1957 his nephew and successor, Yissachar Dov, was only nine years old, so the movement operated without a leader for the next nine years until he was old enough to assume his duties. Among his major tasks has been the completion of a new synagogue, the Beis HaMedrash HaGadol (or Great Synagogue), the largest synagogue in Jerusalem and the movement's international headquarters.

As Belzer Hasidism has rebuilt, it has found a small following in New York, now centered on the yeshiva in the Williamsburg section of Brooklyn.

Membership: Not reported.

Sources:

Israel, Yosef. *Rescuing the Rebbe of Belz*. Brooklyn, NY: Mesorah Publications, 2005.

Shneider, Chaim. "The Belz'e Sect." HasidicNews.com. November 6, 2001. Available from hasidicnews.com/Belz.shtml.

Biala Hasidism

c/o Biala Institutions of America, 5809 13th Ave., Brooklyn, NY 11219

The Rabinowicz family has one of the most outstanding Hasidic lineages and is the source of several dynasties. The founder of the Biala dynasty was Yaakov Yitzchok Rabinowicz (1766–1813). As a wandering preacher, he was guided to Rabbi Jacob Isaac Horowitz, the father of Polish Hasidism, known for his psychic abilities and often referred to as the "sad-eyed Seer of Lublin." The Seer told him that he was a reincarnation of Patriarch Jacob Mordecai and Rabbi Jacob ben Meir Tam, a twelfth-century scholar. He quickly became known as a Talmudic scholar and a seeker of justice, then gradually separated himself from the Seer and established himself at Peshischa.

The emphasis of Yaakov Yitzchok was introspection, aimed at making an individual a good Jew. He thought it essential that one neither lies to himself nor lives in superficiality. The highest pinnacle of the love of God could be acquired only by painstaking personal striving. He insisted on *kavanah*, concentration and devotion in prayer. Peshishcha services were not always at the proper times; it was better to pray late than to pray without kavanah. Action and service, charity and loving kindness were seen as the measures of sincerity.

The lineage of Yaakov Yitzchok was passed down through Yerachmiel Rabinowicz of Peshischa (d. 1831) and Nathan David Rabinowicz of Shidlovtza (d. 1865) to Rabbi Yaakov Yitzchok Rabinowicz (1847–1905), who was known for his devotion to the Sabbath, a topic that fills most of his writings. The lineage then passed to Grand Rabbi Yechiel Yehoshua Rabinowicz, Biala Rebbe of Jerusalem (1900–1981). He survived the Nazis by fleeing to Siberia; then in 1947 he settled in Israel. He was known as a miracle worker, and he established a yeshiva (a school for Talmudic study) at B'nai Brak. From Rabbi Yechiel Yehoshua, the lineage passed to Grand Rabbi Dovid Matisyahu (Reb "Duv'tche") Rabinowicz (1928–1997) and then to Grand Rabbi Betzalel Simchah Menachem Ben-Zion Rabinowicz, the Biala rebbe of Jerusalem.

The Biala Hasidic tradition was brought to the United States in the early 1920s in the wave of Russian Jewish migration by Rebbe Joshua Hershal Rabinowicz (1860–1938). In 2008 it was headed by Grand Rabbi Aharon Shlomo Chaim Eleazar Rabinowicz, the son of Rabbi David Matisyahu, and the Biala rebbe of America. He resides in the Borough Park section of Brooklyn, New York.

Membership: Not reported.

Sources:

Biala Institutions. www.geocities.com/bialarebbe/.

Bobov Hasidism

c/o Hessi Halberstam, 4909 15th St., Brooklyn, NY 11219

The Halberstam family has contributed to the formation of several Hasidic groups. The Bobov dynasty originated with Rabbi Shlomo Halberstam (1847–1905), who opened the first yeshiva in Poland in 1881 in the town of Vishnitsa. He later moved the school to Bobov. The dynasty was then founded by his son, Rabbi Benzion Halberstam (1847–1941). He was a noted composer, and his *niggun* (melody) "Yah-Ribbon" ("God of the World") is still chanted on Sabbath evenings. The Bobov are known for their musical creativity. Under Rabbi Benzion's leadership, Hasidic education spread throughout Galicia in the Carpathian mountain region of southern Poland.

Rabbi Benzion, his family, and most of his following were killed in the Holocaust, but Rabbi Shlomo Halberstam (1905–2000) and his eldest son Naftali (1931–2005) escaped and found their way to the United States. There, Halberstam began to gather a new group of followers, many of whom had no Polish background; it grew steadily as Jewish families came to respect his mild-mannered pastoral approach. He founded a yeshiva that by 1985 had about 3,000 elementary students (many of whose families had no attachment to the Bobov organization); it became the largest religious school in the Borough Park area of Brooklyn. He also assisted displaced Jews in Europe and built followings in London and Antwerp, as well as in Canada and Israel. As Rabbi Shlomo aged, Naftali, his son and designated successor began to assume some of the leadership responsibilities. Unfortunately, Naftali died only five years after his father.

Membership: Not reported. Bobov Hasidism has centers in Brooklyn and Monsey, New York, and Miami, Florida. There are an estimated 50,000 Bobov Hasidim residing in Brooklyn. In Canada, centers are found in Montreal and Toronto. There are several centers in Israel, and in Europe in London and Antwerp, Belgium.

Remarks: Following the death of Rabbi Naftali Halberstam in 2005, the Bobov were divided over his successor. One group accepted Rabbi Mordechai Dovid Unger, Rabbi Naftali's son-in-law, and an almost equally large faction favored Rabbi Naftali's younger son, Rabbi Ben Zion Aryeh Leibish Halberstam. In 2008 the conflict remained unresolved, and the issue stood before a *Beth Din* (Jewish court).

Sources:

"A Brief Introduction to Hasidism." PBS Online. Available from
    www.pbs.org/alifeapart/intro.html.

Mintz, Jerome R. *Hasidic People: A Place in the New World*. Cambridge, MA: Harvard
    University Press, 1992.

Bostoner Hasidism

c/o New England Chasidic Center, 1710 Beacon St., Brookline, MA 02146

The Horowitz family has been a prominent Jewish family for many centuries, producing numerous rabbis. It was frequently divided between those supporting and those opposing Hasidism. Among the first Hasidic rebbes in the United States was Grand Rabbi Pinchas D. Horowitz (1876–1940), who settled in Boston in 1919. He came from a branch of the Horowitz family that had settled in Jerusalem several generations earlier. Rabbi Pinchas moved his court to Brooklyn in 1939.

Rabbi Pinchas died shortly after his move to Brooklyn. He was succeeded by his elder son, Rabbi Moshe Horowitz. Four years later, Rabbi Pinchas's younger son, Rabbi Levi Yitzchak Horowitz (b. 1921), left Brooklyn and established a second Bostoner court on Beacon Street, in suburban Boston at Brookline. Since then there have been two Bostoner rebbes, each heading his own court. Over the rest of the twentieth century, their practice diverged, though not enough to break their relationship.

Rabbi Moshe Horowitz resided for many years in a home adjacent to that of the Satmar rebbe, who heads one of the larger Hasidic communities in Brooklyn. The Bostoner Hassidim have been very much influenced by the more dominant Satmar group. Among the differences that have developed is that the Brooklyn Bostoners no longer light their pre-Sabbath candles 48 minutes before sundown as the group in Brookline does. The Brookline center has become known for social outreach in its community and has attracted a number of younger Jews interested in exploring their heritage through Hasidism.

In 2006 Rabbi Avrohom Horowitz, the current rebbe for the Brooklyn group, moved to Israel. Two years later, Rabbi Levi Yitzchak Horowitz also relocated to Israel. In recent years he had been spending more and more time there, and had advised his American following to move to Israel if possible.

Membership: Not reported. There are two centers in the United States and one in Israel. The movement serves several thousand members families worldwide and some 200 Jewish families residing in Brookline.

Sources:

Casper, Michael. "Leader of American Hasidic Dynasty Leaves the States." *Jewish Daily Forward*. April 17, 2008. Available from www.forward.com/articles/13176/.

Farber, Seth. "Between Brooklyn and Brookline: American Hasidism and the Evolution of the Bostoner Hasidic Tradition." *American Jewish Archives Journal* 52 (1999): 34–53.

Gil, Micah. "In the Court of the Bostoner Rebbe." Killing the Buddha web site. Available from
    www.killingthebuddha.com/critical_devotion/bostoner_rebbe.htm.

Shabbos, Zmiros, and Yom Tov. *From the Rebbe's Table*. Brookline, MA: New England Chasidic Center, 1983.

Bratslav (Breslov) Hasidism

c/o The Breslov Center for Spirituality and Inner Growth, 5014 16th Ave., Ste. 263, Brooklyn, NY 11204

Nachman of Bratslav (1772–1810) was a Ukrainian great-grandson of Baal Shem Tov. He became known, even as a child, for his asceticism. After he made a trip to the Holy Land, a group formed around him. He died at an early age, 38, and as he passed away he was heard to say, "My light will glow till the days of the Messiah." His followers interpreted his statement to mean that they would never need another rebbe. Unique in Hasidism as a group without a living rebbe, the Bratslav are referred to by other Hasidic groups as the "dead Hasidim." Rebbe Noson (1780–1844), who studied with Rebbe Nachman, recorded much of his work, and it is his record of Nachman's teachings that have survived for present study and reflection.

The outstanding follower of Rebbe Nachman in the twentieth century was Rebbe Avraham Sternhartz (1862–1955), who as a youth had studied Nachman's writings. He moved to Palestine in 1936, and over the next decade came to be revered as the outstanding Breslover elder of his generation. He trained a number of future Bratslav leaders, including Rebbe Zvi Aryeh Rosenfeld (1922–1978), Rebbe Shmuel Shapiro (1913–1989), and Rebbe Yaakov Meir Schechter (b. 1932).

The group's emphasis is on utter simplicity and warmth of feeling. Infusing prayer with devotion is of major importance. Teachings are found in the 13 stories of Rebbe Nachman, which emphasize that the trials of life are to be seen as preludes to new soarings of the spirit.

In the 1980s, a Bratslav group was headed by Rabbis Leo Rosenfeld and Gedaliah Freer, who gathered followers of the tradition primarily from young Orthodox Jews attracted to the Hasidic traditions. That work is continued by the Breslov Center for Spirituality and Inner Growth, founded in 1997 by HaRav Elazar Mordechai Kenig, the leader of the Breslov community of Tzefat, Israel. The center works closely with the Breslov Research Institute, the research and publishing arm of the movement (with facilities in Jerusalem, Monsey, New York, and the United Kingdom). It has assembled a team of scholars, and the Institute publishes their translations, commentaries, and general works on Bratslav Hasidism.

Membership: Not reported.

Sources:

Freer, Gedaliah. *Rabbi Nachman's Fire*. New York: Hermon Press, 1972.

Green, Arthur. *Tormented Master*. New York: Schocken Books, 1979.

Magid, Shaul. *God's Voice from the Void: Old and New Studies in Bratslav Hasidism*. Albany: State University of New York Press, 2002.

Sternharz, Nathan. *Eternally Yours (Alim LiTerufah): The Collected Letters of Reb Noson of Breslov*. Trans. Yaakov Gabel, ed. Moshe Schorr. Jerusalem: Breslov Research Institute. 1993.

The Tales of Rabbi Nachman. [Adapted by] Martin Buber. Trans. Maurice Friedman. London: Souvenir Press, 1974.

Chernobyl Hasidism

1520 49th St., Brooklyn, NY 11232

The Twersky family has given the world of Hasidism several dynasties. The oldest began with Menahem Nahum ben Zevi (1730–1787) of Chernobyl in the Ukraine, a contemporary of the Baal Shem Tov. Never a *tzaddik* ("righteous one") himself, he helped the initial spread of Hasidism in the Ukraine and laid stress on purification of moral attributes to make one worthy of the Torah. His son, Mordecai Twersky (1770–1837), was the first tzaddik and the real founder of the Chernobyl dynasty. Mordecai had eight sons. Aaron Twersky, the eldest, continued the dynasty, and the rest founded their own dynasties that dominated Ukrainian Hasidic Jewry in the nineteenth century. Most of these dynasties were destroyed by the Holocaust.

Grand Rabbi Yaakov Yisroel Twersky (1902–1983) was the last of the Chernobyl dynasty to reside in Chernobyl. He moved to the United States in 1938 and settled in the Borough Park section of Brooklyn. His son Rabbi Shlomo Twersky succeeded him.

In 2008 there were three Hasidic groups headed by members of the Twersky family in the United States.

Membership: Not reported.

Sources:

"Rabbi Menachem Nachum of Chernobyl." Nehora web site. Available from www.judaicaplus.com/Tzadikim/tz_viewer.cfm?id=107&page=menachemnachum.htm&t=Rabbi%20Menachem%20Nachum%20of%20Chernobyl.

Robinson, Ira. "Anshe Sfard: The Creation of the First Hasidic Congregations in North America." Conference on the Jewish Immigrant Experience in North America, Centre for American Studies, University of Western Ontario, 2005. Available from www.americanjewisharchives.org/journal/PDF/2005pp53-66%20Hasidic%20NA.pdf.

Congregation of New Square (Skver Hasidism)

N Main St., New Square, NY 10977

Isaac Twersky (1812–1895), the seventh son of Mordecai Twersky, the head of the Chernobyl Hasidic dynasty, settled at Skver, southwest of Kiev, Ukraine, and began a new dynasty in the 1830s. His successor, Rebbe Dovidl Twersky (1848–1919), moved to Kiev in 1914 and stayed there until his death in 1919. He passed his lineage through two of his sons.

First, Rebbe Yakov Yosef (1900–1968) moved to Belz, Ukraine, for a while before settling in Romania, where he remained through World War II. After the war he moved to the United States and established a synagogue in the Williamsburg section of Brooklyn. His repugnance of American urban materialism led him to establish a rural community in Rockland County, New York, which was named New Square. He moved there in 1956.

Reb Yakov Yosef was succeeded by his son, Rabbi Duvid Twerski, and under his guidance New Square prospered and a similar community was created in 1963 at Spring Glen, in upstate New York. Affiliated centers are found in Canada, the United Kingdom, and Israel.

Second, Rabbi Yitzchak Twersky (1888–1941), the grandson of Rebbe Dovidl's eldest son, Rabbi Mordechai (1866–1919), migrated to the United States in 1923. He settled in the Borough Park section of Brooklyn, New York, and opened a shul. He died, however, before his son Dovid (1922–2001) was ready to succeed him. In the late 1940s Dovid was taken under the tutelage of his uncle, Rabbi Yakov-Yosef, who had just arrived from Romania. When Dovid matured, he assumed leadership of his father's shul, which he led until his death in 2001. At that time, his son, Yechiel Michl Twersky, became the Skver rebbe of Borough Park.

Reb Yechiel Michl's community in Borough Park thrives and manages several key Hasidic instiutitions. including the Tomer Devorah Girls School and Bais Yitzchok, a school for boys.

Membership: Not reported. In 1988 the New Square congregation reported 20,000 members in 15 centers in the United States and 2,000 members in one center in Canada. There were another 3,000 members in centers in England, Belgium, and Israel.

Educational Facilities:

Rabbinical Seminary of New Square, New Square, New York.

Yeshiva of New Square, New Square, New York.

Sources:

Gould, Joan. "A Village of 'Slaves to the Torah.'" *Jewish Digest* (October 1967): 49–52.

Surkis, Leibel. *Reb Itzikl Skverer*. New Square, NY: Privately published, 1997.

Ger Hasidism

Yeshiva Yagdil Torah, 5110 18th Ave., Brooklyn, NY 11204-1534

The Ger Hasidic dynasty dates to the middle of the nineteenth century and to the town of Ger, Poland. The founder of the dynasty was Rabbi Yitzchak Meir Rothenberg Alter (1799–1866), better known as the Chiddushei HaRim. He came to his task in 1859 when the leader of another dynasty died and many of his followers chose Rabbi Meir as their new leader. After accepting the invitation to become the new rebbe of the Kotzker Hasidim, he settled in Ger and over the seven remaining years of his life created a new dynasty.

Rabbi Meir had been the student of Rabbi Menachem Mendel of Kotzk (1787–1859), who stood in stark contrast to the Baal Shem Tov. Rebbe Mendel became known for his strong belief that the enlightenment that was the goal of study and devotion could be attained by only the few most dedicated of individuals. Thus he sought out a small group of the elite with whom to work. The Ger, which would grow into one of the largest Hasidic groups, would become the children of Rebbe Mendel's demands for intensity, but infused by Rabbi Meir's warmth and desire to approach all Jews with the possibilities of accomplishment. Like his teacher, Rabbi Meir was also an accomplished scholar of the Talmud.

Rabbi Yitzchak Meir was succeeded by Rabbi Chanokh Heynekh HaKohen Levin (d. 1870), who died just four years later. He was then succeeded by Rabbi Yehudah Aryeh Leib (1847–1905), who despite his youth (he was in his twenties) quickly demonstrated his leadership abilities, and the Ger prospered under him. That prosperity continued under Rabbi Leib's son and successor Rabbi Avraham Mordechai Alter (1886–1948). Under his leadership, in 1926 the Ger established a yeshiva in Jerusalem.

By the end of the 1930s the Ger numbered almost 200,000, but by the end of World War II most of them were dead, victims of the Holocaust. Rabbi Avrohom Mordechai was able to escape to Palestine in 1940 with three of his sons, and he began the task of rebuilding the Ger after the war. He died in 1948 and the rebuilding was left to his three sons—Rabbi Yisrael Alter (1895–1977), Rabbi Simchah Bunim Alter (1898–1992), and Rabbi Pinchas Menachem Alter (1926–1996)—the next three leaders of the revived community. In 2008 the rebbe was the son of Rabbi Sincha Bunin, Rabbi Yaakov Aryeh Alter (b. 1939).

The Ger were among the first of the Hasidim in the United States. As early as 1903, Rabbi Yehudah Aryeh Leib encouraged Reb Shmulkeh Reichek and his family to settle in New York, where he opened the first Hasidic *shteibl* (synagogue) in the United States, Beth Hasidim de Palen, on Manhattan's Lower East Side. The shteibl became a gathering place for Polish Hasidim of various dynasties. Despite this early start for the Ger, however, the group almost died out due to assimilation, and was revived only by the arrival of Holocaust survivors after World War II.

In rebuilding the Ger, Rabbi Yisrael placed an emphasis on holiness and purity of life, two characteristics that have remained the keynotes of Ger existence. The Ger men are distinguished by their distinctive dark clothing and their habit of putting their trouser legs into their socks. Politically, the Ger were anti-Zionist in the early decades of the twentieth century, but emerged as pro-Zionists in the 1940s.

In 2008 the main community of the Ger was in Israel, where it has become the largest Hasidic group in the country. It also has centers (including two yeshivas) in the Borough Park section Brooklyn, New York, and a European presence in London and Antwerp.

Membership: Not reported.

Sources:

Alter, Judah Aryeh Leib. *The Language of Truth: The Torah Commentary of Sefat Emet*. Trans. Arthur Green. Philadelphia: Jewish Publication Society of America, 1998.

"Ger." Educational program on Yiddish Culture, YIVO Institute for Jewish Research web site. Available from epyc.yivo.org/content/8_2.php.

Reichek, Mort. "Earliest Hasidim in the U.S." PBS web site forum: *A Life Apart—Hasidim in America*. Available from www.pbs.org/netforum/static/alifeapart/11.html.

Karlin-Stolin Hasidism

Stolin Bet Midrash, 1818 54th St., Brooklyn, NY 11211

The Karlin-Stolin Hasidic dynasty began with Rebbe Aharon the Great, a disciple of the Maggid of Mezritch (c. 1710–1772), who in turn was a disciple of the Baal Shem Tov, the founder of Hasidism. Rebbe Aharon originally established his work in Karlin, in what is now Belarus. His followers became known for a distinctive custom of screaming while praying. Karlin-Stolin Hasidim settled in Palestine in the mid-nineteenth century, and the primary rebbe relocated in the twentieth century.

Possibly the first Hasidic rebbe to reach the United States was Rebbe Yaakov Chaim Perlow of Stolin (d. 1946). During his life there were four centers for prayer (*shtieblach*) in Brooklyn, New York, and one in Detroit. He frequently visited the Detroit center and was eventually buried in the city. By 1940 there were approximately 100 families under Rebbe Yaakov's leadership; holding the young adults was a major problem. In the meantime, the Stolin Hasidim in the Soviet Union suffered under the German onslaught, and four of Rebbe Israel's other sons were killed by the Nazis. Only one, Rebbe Yochanan Perlow (1900–1956), survived the war and made his way to Israel. Following Rebbe Yaakov's death, a delegation went to

Israel and persuaded Rebbe Yochanan to assume leadership of the U.S. group. Among his first efforts was the mobilizing of the community to create a yeshiva for the young men. Though not known for his public teachings, he was extolled for the miracles attributed to him.

After Rebbe Yochanan's death in 1956, the Stolin community was headed by two men designated by him because there was no male heir ready to assume the task. In 1967 the properties were signed over to the thirteen-year-old grandson of Rebbe Yochanan, and over the next decade, he gradually assumed his duties. In 2008 Rebbe Baruch Yaakov Meir Shochet (b. 1955) continues to lead the Stolin Hasidim in New York, though he has taken up residence in Israel, where he has gained notice for his efforts for Russian Jews and remains in contact with the small Stolin community that still exists in the Ukraine.

Membership: There are approximately 300 families associated with the Stolin Hasidim in the United States.

Sources:

Rabinowitsch, Wolf Zeev, ed. "Hasidim in Pinsk and Karlin." In *Pinsk Historical Volume, History of the Jews of Pinsk, 1506–1941*, vol. 1: *Belarus*. Trans. Ellen Stepak. Available from www.jewishgen.org/yizkor/Pinsk1/Pine12_005.html#Page9.

Mintz, Jerome R. *Hasidic People: A Place in the New World*. Cambridge, MA: Harvard University Press, 1992.

Klausenburg Hasidism

c/o Talmud Torah Chatzar Hakodesh, 1353 50th St., Brooklyn, NY 11219

The relatively new Klausenburg (also known as Sanz-Klausenburg) Hasidic dynasty was founded by Grand Rabbi Yekusiel Yehuda Halberstam (1905–1994), the first Klausenburger rebbe. He was a descendant of Grand Rabbi Chaim Halberstam (1793–1876) of Sanz (Nowy Są]cz), Poland. In 1927 Halberstam became the rabbi in the Romanian city of Klausenburg (also known as Cluj-Napoca, Romania), and soon developed a following. Both his community and his family were ravaged by the Holocaust, but he survived, and in 1947 he moved to the United States. After a decade of work, in 1956 he moved to Israel and founded the Kiryat Sanz community on the outskirts of Netanya. The community became well known for its hospital, the Laniado Hospital, where medical care strictly follows *halakha* (Jewish law).

Rabbi Yekutiel Jehudah died in 1994, but before he died he instructed his two sons (both of whom were born after his move to the United States) to each assume leadership of one section of the work and to develop them as two independent endeavors. Abiding by his guidance, his older son, Grand Rabbi Tzvi Elimelech Halberstam, became head of the work in Israel, and his younger son, Grand Rabbi Shmuel Dovid Halberstam, became the Sanz-Klausenburger rebbe in Borough Park.

Membership: Not reported. There are several centers in Brooklyn, one in Union City, New Jersey, and one in Montreal, Canada.

Sources:

Sanz-Klausenburg web sites. (Unofficial, in Hebrew.) www.klausenburg.org/;sanzusa.com/.

Lubavitch Hasidism

770 Eastern Pkwy., Brooklyn, NY 11213

By far the largest of the Hasidic bodies is the Lubavitch (also Lubavitcher). The arrival the Lubavitch rebbe Rabbi Joseph Isaac Schneerson (1902–1994) in New York in 1940 signaled the rebirth of Hasidism in the New World. Compared with most Hasidic groups, the Lubavitch are more open and evangelistic toward their non-Hasidic Jewish neighbors, and the group has established itself as a national body. Lubavitch Hasidism began in 1773 in Lithuania under the leadership of Rabbi Schneur Zalman (1745–1813), a child prodigy and student of Rabbi Dov Baer, an outstanding Hasidic scholar. Upon Dov Baer's death in 1772, Rabbi Zalman was sent to Lithuania as a Hasidic missionary. He spent the rest of his life in Lithuania and Russia, teaching and writing. His works include the *Likutic Amanan*, better known as the *Tanya*, the essential text of the Chabad, as his teachings became known.

A second Rabbi Dov Baer (1773–1827), the *mittler* (middle) rebbe, the son of Rabbi Zalman, succeeded as leader of the Chabad. After his father's death, he settled in White Russia's Lubavitch, the town that gave the dynasty its name. Rabbi Dov Baer was succeeded in turn by Rabbi Menachem Mendel Schneerson (1789–1866), son of Rabbi Zalman's daughter; Rabbi Samuel Schneerson (1834–1882), Rabbi Mendel's son; Rabbi Sholom Dov Baer (1860–1920), Rabbi Samuel's son, and Rabbi Joseph Isaac Schneerson (1880–1950), the son and secretary of Rabbi Dov Baer, who brought the movement to the United States.

The Lubavitch work began in the mid-1920s when Rabbi Joseph Isaac Schneerson formed the Agudas Chassidas Chabad of the United States of America and Canada. He visited the United States in 1929, during which time he met with President Herbert Hoover. He had settled in Warsaw after World War I. When his life was threatened by the Nazis, the rebbe was finally persuaded to migrate to the United States.

Schneerson's son Menachem Mendel Schneerson (1902–1994) had been living in Paris when World War II began. He escaped and in 1941 moved to the Lubavitcher headquarters in the Crown Heights section of Brooklyn, New York. Assuming the leadership in 1950, he began growing the relatively small movement and turning it into an influential force in the world of Jewish Orthodoxy. Over the next decades he aggressively recruited liberal and nonpracticing young Jews into the movement and founded more than 900 centers internationally. He built educational centers and developed programs of humanitarian aid and social services that reached beyond the Jewish community.

In the early 1990s Schneerson pointed to the fall of Communism in Central and Eastern Europe as the herald of an era of peace and tranquility for humankind. As he spoke of *Moshiach* (the messiah), his followers began to speculate about his relationship to the messiah and the messianic age, and some concluded that he himself was the messiah, especially in the years immediately before his death.

Schneerson's death in 1994 brought a fundamental split in the movement between those who believe Schneerson was/is the messiah and those who do not. One consequence of this conflict was that the group did not name a leader to succeed Schneerson. In 2008 the messianists appeared to be losing favor.

Chabad is an acronym for "*chochmah* (wisdom), *binah* (understanding), and *daath* (knowledge), the highest virtues in the Kabbalistic system. The three concepts reflect key aspects of God's manifestation in the world as described by Judaism's mystical teachings known as the Kabbalah. Faith and belief in God require intellectual study and understanding of religious truth. The emphasis on truth has made education basic to the Lubavitch program. The love of one's fellow Jew (*Ahavas Yisroel*), a second emphasis of Lubavitch, suggests an openness to the entire Jewish community, in contrast to the view of most other Hasidim, who generally hold a low opinion of their lax, nonpracticing brethren.

Music and dancing are important to Lubavitcher life. Dancing is the bodily manifestation of inward joy. It is always done by males separately from females, as mixed dancing is prohibited by Jewish law. There are two varieties: circle dancing, in which the hand is placed on the shoulder of the brother in front, and *rikkud*, jumping and skipping up and down. Dancing is a vital part of festivals such as Purim and the Hasidic historic anniversaries.

Lubavitcher headquarters are in Brooklyn, New York, where the Tomchoi T'mimim, the Lubavitcher yeshiva, is located. A year after Rabbi Schneerson arrived in the United States in 1941, he was placed in charge of the Merkos L'Inyone Chinuch, the educational arm of the Lubavitch movement; more than 67 educational institutions have since been founded. Rabbi Schneerson also guided the development of Merkos Publication Society, the major publisher of Hasidic literature in the United States, and the Ezrat Pleitim Vesidurom, a relief organization in 56 cities across the United States.

Membership: In 2007 there were approximately 200,000 adherents in some 3,300 Chabad centers located in 70 countries. Observers suggest that there is an additional constituency of up to a million persons.

Periodicals: *Talks and Tales* • *The Uforatzto Journal*.

Sources:

Chabad Lubavitch Global Network. lubavitch.com/; www.chabad.org/.

Challenge. London: Lubavitch Foundation of Great Britain, 1970.

Dalfin, Chaim. *The Seven Chabad-Lubavitch Rebbes*. Jason Aronson, 1998.

Fishkoff, Sue. *The Rebbe's Army: Inside the World of Chabad-Lubavitch*. New York: Schocken Books, 2003.

Mintz, Jerome R. *Hasidic People: A Place in the New World*. Cambridge, MA: Harvard University Press, 1992.

Schneerson, Menachem Mendel. *Anticipating the Redemption: Maamarim of the Lubavitcher Rebbe Rabbi Menachem M. Schneerson Concerning the Era of Redemption*. Brooklyn, NY: Sichos in English, 1997.

———. *I Await His Coming Every Day: Based on Talks of the Lubavitch Rebbe*. Brooklyn, NY: Kehot Publication Society, 1998.

———. *Letters by the Lubavitcher Rebbe*. Brooklyn, NY: Kehot Publication Society, 1979.

Novominsk Hasidism

1569 47th St., Brooklyn, NY 11220

The Novominsk dynasty was founded by Jacob Perlow (1847–1902), who as a young rabbi was advised to "go to Poland, raise a family, and establish a dynasty." He settled at Minsk-Mazowiech, not far from Warsaw. His fame and following grew, and he built a yeshiva and a large synagogue. Upon his death, his son, Alter Yisrael Shimon Perlow (1874–1933), succeeded him. Known for his intensity of prayer and passion while preaching, the young rabbi moved to Warsaw in 1917 and drew crowds to his Sunday discourses.

In 1925 Rabbi Yehuda Arye Perlow (d. 1960), brother of the rebbe of Novominsk, arrived in New York and established the Novominsk dynasty. He was succeeded by his son, Rabbi Nahum Mordecai Perlow (1896–1976), who had originally accompanied his father from Poland.

Membership: Not reported.

Satmar Hasidism

c/o Congregation Y L D'Satmar, 152 Rodney, Brooklyn, NY 11220

The Satmar Hasidic tradition is one of the newest, having been founded by Rebbe Yoel Teitelbaum (1887–1979) in the first decade of the twentieth century. Following the death of his father in 1904, Yoel, the second son, moved from Sighet, his birthplace, and founded his own group at Satmar in northeast Hungary. Zionism was a growing force in European Jewry in these formative years of Satmar, and from the yeshiva he had established at Orshovah, Yoel actively opposed Zionism. After the unexpected death of Rebbe Yoel's brother in 1926, the leadership of the dynasty passed to Yoel rather than the new rebbe of Sighet. Yoel's prestige grew steadily until 1944, when the Holocaust hit Hungary. The rebbe was saved, ironically, by his Zionist enemies, and he escaped to Switzerland.

In 1946 Rebbe Yoel settled in Williamsburg in Brooklyn, New York, with the Satmar's few survivors of the Holocaust. The congregation Yetev Lev D'Satmar, established in 1948, had 860 members by 1961. Many of these were converts. The anti-Zionist stand remains the distinctive feature of Satmar Hasidism. The Neturei Karta (Guardians of the City), an ultra-orthodox anti-Zionist group in Jerusalem, has placed itself under Satmar's care. Members believe that because only the Messiah can reestablish Israel, the attempt to set up a Jewish state is blasphemy. In 1965 Amram Blau, the leader of the Neturei Karta, was relieved of his position for marrying a divorced convert from Catholicism.

Headquarters of the Satmar movement are in Brooklyn, where there are a number of groups. They have purchased land at Monroe, New York, for the establishment of a Satmar community. Satmar groups are also found in Jerusalem and B'nai Brak, Israel; Antwerp, Belgium; London, England; Montreal, Quebec, Canada; Montevideo, Uruguay; São Paulo, Brazil; and Buenos Aires, Argentina.

Rabbi Yoel had a stroke in 1968 and was somewhat hampered in the performance of his duties during the last decade of his life. He died in 1979. His nephew, Rabbi Moshe Teitelbaum (1914–2006), then the rabbi of a small Sighet Hasidic congregation in the Borough Park section of Brooklyn and head of Sighet Hasidism, was designated his successor and installed in office in 1980.

Membership: Not reported. The Satmar community has an estimated 200,000 adherents worldwide. Of these approximately 70,000 reside in Williamsburg, 20,000 in Borough Park, about 20,000 in Kiryas Joel, and several thousand in Monsey, New York. The largest concentration of Satmar believers in Canada reside in Montreal. Tens of thousands live in Israel, and there are smaller but important communities in London, England, and Antwerp, Belgium.

Remarks: Since the recent death of Rabbi Moshe Teitelbaum, the Satmar community has been in some disarray. Four persons—three of Rabbi Moshe's sons and one of his sons-in-law—have each claimed all or part of his lineage and established their own independent groups with separate followers and institutions. Immediately after Rabbi Moshe's death, Rabbi Aaron Teitelbaum was declared his successor and the new Grand Rabbi of the Satmar dynasty. Rabbi Aaron's primary center is in Kiryas Joel, a Hasidic community in Monroe, New York.

Yet, as early as 1999, Rabbi Moshe had indicated his intention of placing his third son, Rabbi Zalman Leib Teitelbaum, in charge of the group's facilities in Williamsburg, where the group's wealth was centered. Rabbi Aaron remained in control in Kiryas Joel and in the Borough section of Brooklyn. Rabbi Zalman's followers declared that he was the new grand rabbi of the Satmar dynasty. Rabbi Zalman and Rabbi Aaron remain in charge of the two largest factions of the Satmar community.

In the meantime, Rabbi Lipa Teitelbaum assumed leadership of the small Zenta-Beirach Moshe Shul in the Williamsburg section of Brooklyn. He also does administrative work in the United Talmudical Academy of the Williamsburg Satmar School System. Finally, Chaim Shia Halberstam emerged as the Satmar rebbe in Monsey, New York.

As this encyclopedia goes to press in 2008, no resolution of the schismatic state of the community appears on the horizon.

Sources:

Gersh, Harry M., and Sam Miller. "Satmar in Brooklyn." *Commentary* 28 (1959): 31–41.

Mintz, Jerome R. *Hasidic People: A Place in the New World.* Cambridge, MA: Harvard University Press, 1992.

Rubin, Israel. *Satmar: Two Generations in an Urban Island.* New York: Peter Lang, 1997.

Weiss, Maud B., and Michael Neumeister. *The Challenge of Piety: The Satmar Hasidim in New York.* Munich, Germany: Gina Kehayoff, 1995.

Winson, Hella. *Unchosen: The Hidden Lives of Hasidic Rebels.* Boston: Beacon Press, 2006.

Talnoye (Talner) Hasidism

Talner Congregation, 64 Corey Rd., Brookline, MA 02146

David Twersky (1808–1882), the sixth son of Mordecai Twersky, established his dynasty at Talnoye, south of Kiev in Russia. It is said that he lived luxuriously and sat upon a silver throne engraved with the words "King David of Israel lives forever." Rabbi Nochum (another son of Rabbi Mordecai) succeeded Rabbi David in 1882, and was in turn succeeded by his son, Rabbi Meshulem Z. Twersky. In the mid-twentieth century Rabbi Yitzhak Twersky (1930–1997) became the Talner rebbe. He brought the lineage to the United States, and along with Rebbitzen M. Z.

Twersky was responsible for the founding and development of Beis Midrash in Brookline, Massachusetts.

Membership: Not reported.

Sources:

The Talner Beis Midrash. members.bellatlantic.net/~vze2nb56/talner/.

Even, Isaac. "Chasidism in the New World." *Jewish Communal Register of New York City, 1917–1918.* New York: Kehillah of New York City, 1918.

Vizhnitz Hasidism

c/o Vizhnitz Shul, 52 Francis Pl., Monsey, NY 10592

Vizhnitz Hasidism was founded by Rebbe Menachem Mendil Hager in the middle of the nineteenth century in the village of Vyzhnytsia, in what is now Ukraine. The leadership of the group was subsequently passed to Rebbe Baruch Hager of Vizhnitz and Rebbe Yisroel Hager of Vizhnitz. Rebbe Yisroel had two sons who reestablished the dynasty in Israel after World War II: Rebbe Baruch Hager of Seret-Vizhnitz, who settled in Haifa; and Rebbe Chaim Meir Hager of Vizhnitz, who settled in Bnei Brak. Under their leadership the Vizhnitz grew into one of the largest Hasidic groups in Israel, with sister centers in London and New York.

Rebbe Baruch passed his lineage to Rebbe Eliezer Hager of Seret-Vizhnitz, the present rebbe of Seret-Vizhnitz in Haifa. Rebbe Chaim Meir passed his lineage to his son Rebbe Moshe Yehoshua Hager of Vizhnitz, the present Vizhnitzer rebbe in Bnei Brak. Rabbe Moshe's brother, Rebbe Mordechai Hager, became the leader of the Vizhnitz Hasidim in Monsey, New York.

In the 1980s problems developed within the group in Bnei Brak. Rebbe Moshe removed his eldest son, Yisrael Hager, from any leadership in the group, and dismissed him as a Hasidic rabbi. His place was taken by the younger son, Rabbi Menachem-Mendel Hagar. Shortly after the beginning of the new century, pressure was brought upon the aging Rebbe Moshe to return his eldest son to a position within the community, an action favored by Rebbe Mordechai.

The return of the elder son led to a split in the Vizhnitz community, with the larger support going to Rebbe Yisrael. In 2005 supporters of Rabbi Menachem-Mendal broke into the Vizhnitz yeshiva in Bnei Brak and stole the computer that contained Rebbe Moshe's speeches. The situation was further exacerbated in 2006, when Rabbi Menachem-Mendal announced plans to open his own synagogue and yeshiva. He organized his following as the Ichud Chasidei Vizhnitz (Union of Vizhnitzer Chasidim). Meanwhile, members of the two factions were involved in fights with each other. The developments in Israel have had significant repercussions in the United States, especially in the Williamsburg section of Brooklyn, New York, where claims to ownership of the Bnei-Brak Vizhnitzer Shul have been made by both factions. The case was still being adjudicated in 2008.

Membership: Not reported.

Sources:

Sela, Neta. "So What Is Going On in Vizhnitz?" *Jewish World* (April 13, 2007). Available from www.ynetnews.com/articles/0,7340,L-3387142,00.html.

Shneider, Chaim. "The Two Viznitz's." *Hasidic News* (November 6, 2001). Available from hasidicnews.com/Viznitz.shtml.

African American Judaism

African Hebrew Israelites of Jerusalem

Washington, D.C. Community, 9185 Central Ave., Capitol Heights, MD 20743

The African Hebrew Israelites of Jerusalem (formerly known as the Original Hebrew Israelite Nation, and also sometimes called the Kingdom of Yah) emerged in Chicago in 1967 around Ben Ammi Carter (b. 1939), a black man who had studied Judaism with a rabbi, and Shaleah Ben-Israel. To the black Jewish ideas (which were espoused by several groups in Chicago at this time) Carter and Ben-Israel added the concept of black Zionism and held out the vision of a return to the holy land for their members. From their headquarters at the A-Beta Cultural Center on Chicago's south side, they began to gather followers. The somewhat anonymous group came into prominence in the late 1960s as a result of their attempts to migrate to Africa and then to Israel. The group moved first to Liberia, seen as analogous to the Hebrew children's wandering in the desert for 40 years to throw off the effects of slavery. Soon after their arrival, they approached the Israeli ambassador about a further move to Israel. They were unable to negotiate the move to Israel for members in Liberia. In 1968 Carter and 38 members from Chicago flew directly to Israel. Given temporary sanction and work permits, the group from Liberia joined them. By 1971, when strict immigration restrictions were imposed upon members of the group, more than 300 had migrated. Other members of the group continued to arrive, however, using tourist visas that were destroyed upon moving into the colony (which had been established at Dimona). By 2008 between 2,000 and 2,500 had settled in Israel.

The black Israelites feel they are descendants of the ten lost tribes of Israel and thus Jews by birth. They celebrate the Jewish rituals and keep the Sabbath. However, they are distinguished from traditional Jews by their practice of polygamy (a maximum of seven wives is allowed) and their abandonment of the synagogue structure.

The group is currently headed by Carter, the anointed spiritual leader, assisted by Prince Asiel Ben-Israel, the international ambassador. Under the princes are ministers responsible for providing education, distribution of food, clothing and shelter, economic assistance, transportation, sports, recreation and entertainment, life preservation, and sanitation. The group's publishing arm, Communicators Press, produces inspirational books and audiotapes.

In Israel, members of the group live what they describe as active and fruitful lives, founded on the laws, commandments, and prophecies of the Holy One of Israel. In addition to keeping the Sabbath and holy days as directed in the Old Testament, they eat a vegan diet, wear natural fabrics, circumcise males eight days after birth, and follow laws of purification for women.

Membership: In 2008 the organization reported more than 2,500 members residing in three communities in southern Israel: Dimona, Arad, and Mitzpe Ramon. In the United States there are an additional 2,500 living in communities in Washington, D.C.; Houston, Texas; Chicago; Atlanta, Georgia; St. Louis, Missouri; Cleveland, Ohio; Tallahassee, Florida; Charleston, South Carolina; and Vicksburg, Mississippi.

Remarks: In the wake of continuous immigration problems with the state of Israel during the 1970s, the group gained new prominence in 1980 when members in the United States were charged with the systematic theft of money, credit cards, and blank airline tickets, all of which were being used to support the group and assist members in their movement to Israel.

Sources:

Carter, Ben Ammi. *Everlasting Life: From Thought to Reality*. Washington, DC: Communicators Press, 1994. 190 pp.

————. *God, the Black Man, and Truth*. Washington, DC: Communicators Press. 1982.

Fish, H. Bashford, "Trouble among the Children of the Prophets." *The Washington Post Magazine*, February 7, 1982.

Gerber, Israel J. *The Heritage Seekers: American Blacks in Search of Jewish Identity*. Middle Village, NY: Jonathan David Publishers, 1977.

Whitfield, Thomas. *From Night to Sunlight*. Nashville, TN: Broadman Press, 1980.

Yehuda, Shaleak Ben. *Black Hebrew Israelites from America to the Promised Land: The Great International Conspiracy against the Children of the Prophets*. New York: Vantage Press, 1975.

Church of God and Saints of Christ
Temple Beth El, 3927 Bridge Rd., Suffolk, VA 23435

Elder William S. Crowdy (1847–1908), a black cook on the Sante Fe Railroad, claimed to have a vision from God calling him to lead his people to the true religion. He left his job and founded the Church of God and Saints of Christ in 1896 at Lawrence, Kansas. In 1900 he moved to Philadelphia, Pennsylvania, and the first annual assembly was held. Crowdy died in 1908, and Joseph N. Crowdy (1875–1917) and William H. Plummer (1868–1931) succeeded him as bishops. Joseph N. Crowdy died in 1917, the same year that the headquarters was moved to Belleville, Virginia, where the church had purchased a large farm. In 1931 Calvin S. Skinner (1847–1932), the last leader appointed by the founder, became bishop, but he lived only three months thereafter. He passed the leadership to Howard Z. Plummer (1899–1940), who held it for many years.

The doctrine of the Church of God is a complex mixture of Judaism, Christianity, and black nationalism. Members are accepted into the church by repentance, baptism by immersion, confession of faith in Jesus Christ, receiving communion of unleavened bread and water, having their feet washed by the elder, and agreeing to live by the Ten Commandments. They must also have been taught how to pray according to Matthew 6:9–13, and they must have been breathed upon with a holy kiss. They believe that black people are the descendants of the ten lost tribes of Israel. They believe in keeping the Ten Commandments and adhering literally to the teachings of both the Old and New Testaments as positive guides to salvation. The church observes the Jewish Sabbath and the use of corresponding Hebrew names. The church is a strong advocate of temperance.

The church is headed by its bishop and prophet, currently Rabbi Jehu August Crowdy Jr. (b. 1970), the great-grandson of the founder, who is divinely called to his office. He is believed to be in direct communion with God, to utter prophecies, and to perform miracles. The prophet presides over the executive board of twelve ordained elders. The church is divided into district, annual, and general assemblies. There are four orders of the ministry: bishops, missionaries, ordained ministers, and nonordained ministers. Deacons care for the temporal affairs of the church. Each local church bears the denominational name and is numbered according to its appearance in the state. The church at Belleville is communalistic, but other churches are not. The Daughters of Jerusalem and Sisters of Mercy is a women's organization whose duty is to look for straying members, to help the sick and needy, and to care for visitors from other local churches. A 52-unit senior housing community was built in 1989.

Membership: In 2008 the church reported 40 tabernacles in the United States, one in Jamaica, and more than 70 in Africa.

Sources:

Church of God and Saints of Christ—Temple Beth El. www.cogasoc.org

Directory of Sabbath-Observing Groups. Fairview, OK: Bible Sabbath Association, 1986.

Fauset, Arthur Huff. *Black Gods of the Metropolis*. Philadelphia: University of Pennsylvania Press, 1944.

Wynia, Elly M. *The Church of God and Saints of Christ: The Rise of Black Jews*. New York: Garland, 1994.

Church of God (Black Jews)
Current address not obtained for this edition.

The Church of God (Black Jews) was founded in the early twentieth century by Prophet F. S. Cherry, who claimed to have had a vision calling him to his office as prophet. He was sent to America and began the church in Philadelphia. A self-educated man, Prophet Cherry became conversant in both Hebrew and Yiddish. He became famous for his homiletic abilities, colloquialisms, and biting slang.

The Church of God is open only to blacks, who are identified with the Jews of the Bible. White Jews are viewed as frauds and interlopers. The church does not use the term synagogue, the place of worship of the white Jews (Rev. 3:9). The church teaches that Jesus was a black man. The first men were also black, the first white man being Gehazi, who received his whiteness as a curse (11 Kings 5: 27). The white man continued to mix with the blacks, and the yellow race resulted. Esau was the first red man (Gen. 25:25). God is, of course, black. Black people sprang from Jacob.

The New Year begins with Passover in April. Saturday is the true Sabbath. Speaking in tongues is considered nonsense. Eating pork, divorce, taking photographs, and observing Christian holidays are forbidden. The end of the period that started with creation is approaching, and the Black Jews were to return in 2000 C.E. to institute the millennium.

Membership: Not reported.

Commandment Keepers Ethiopian Hebrew Congregation of the Living God

PO Box 235, New York, NY 10027

The Commandment Keepers Ehtiopian Hebrew Congregation of the Living God emerged among West Indian blacks who migrated to Harlem, New York. The group began with the Beth B'nai Abraham Congregation founded in 1924 by Arnold Josiah Ford (1877–1935), an early black nationalist and leader in the Universal Negro Improvement Association (UNIA) founded by Marcus Garvey (1887–1940). Ford had repudiated Christianity, adopted Judaism, and learned Hebrew. During the years after the congregation began, Ford met Arthur Wentworth Matthew (1892–1973). Matthew was born in Lagos, West Africa, in 1892. His family moved to St. Kitts in the British West Indies and then, in 1911, to New York. Matthew became a minister in the Church of the Living God, the Pillar and Ground of Truth, a black Pentecostal church that had endorsed the UNIA. Then in 1919, with eight other men, he organized his own group, the Commandment Keepers: Holy Church of the Living God, over which he became bishop. In Harlem, he had met white Jews for the first time and in the 1920s came to know Ford. Possibly from Ford, Matthew began to learn Orthodox Judaism and Hebrew and began to acquire ritual materials.

Both also learned of the Falashas, the black Jews of Ethiopia, and began to identify with them. In 1930, Ford's congregation ran into financial trouble. Ford turned over the membership to Matthew's care and left for Ethiopia where he spent the rest of his life. The identification with Ethiopia merely increased through the years. In 1935, when Haile Selassie (1892–1975) was crowned emperor, Matthew declared himself leader of the Falashas in America and claimed credentials from Selassie.

The Commandment Keepers believe that the black men are really the Ethiopian Falashas and the biblical Hebrews who had been stripped of the knowledge of their name and religion during the slavery era. They believe it is impossible for a black man to conceive of himself as a Negro and retain anything but a slave mentality. With other black Jews, adherents believe the biblical patriarchs to have been black. Christianity is rejected as the religion of the Gentiles or whites.

An attempt has been made to align the Commandment Keepers with Orthodox Jewish practice. Hebrew is taught and revered as a sacred language. The Jewish holidays are kept, and the Sabbath services are held on Friday evenings and Saturday mornings and afternoons. Kosher food laws are kept. An Ethiopian Hebrew Rabbinical College trains leaders in Jewish history, the Mishnah, Josephus, the Talmud, and legalism. Elements of Christianity are retained such as foot washing, healing, and the gospel hymns.

Matthew also taught kabbalistic science, a practice derived from conjuring the folk magic of southern blacks. By conjuring, Matthew believed that he could heal and create changes in situations. The conjuring is worked through four angels. In order to get results, one must call upon the right angel.

Matthew was succeeded by Rabbi Chaim White, who died in 1997; Rabbi Yhoshua Yohanatan succeeded Rabbi White until his retirement in 2000. The current spiritual leader is Rabbi Zecharia Lewi. In April 2007 the congregation closed

its synagogue on 123rd Street in New York City and, as of 2008, is attempting to strategically position itself to carry on the mission and legacy set by its founder.

Membership: Not reported.

Sources:

Commandment Keepers Ethiopian Hebrew Congregation. commandmentkeeperscong.org

Brotz, Howard M. *The Black Jews of Harlem: Negro Nationalism and the Dilemmas of Negro Leadership*. New York: Schocken Books, 1970.

Ehrman, Albert. "The Commandment Keepers: A Negro Jewish Cult in America Today." *Judaism* 8, no. 3 (Summer 1959): 266–270.

House of Judah

Current address not obtained for this edition.

The House of Judah is a small Black Israelite group founded in 1965 by Prophet William A. Lewis. Alabama-born Lewis was converted to his black Jewish beliefs (which are similar to those of the Church of God and Saints of Christ) from a street preacher in Chicago in the 1960s. Throughout the decade he gathered a small following out of a storefront on the south side and in 1971 moved the group to a twenty-two-acre tract near Grand Junction, Michigan. The group lived quietly and little noticed until 1983 when a young boy in the group was beaten to death. The incident focused attention on the group for its advocacy of corporal punishment. The mother of the boy was sentenced to prison for manslaughter. By 1985 the group had resettled in Alabama.

The House of Judah teaches that the Old Testament Jews were black, being derived from Jacob and his son Judah, who were black (Jeremiah 14:2). Both Solomon and Jesus were black. Jerusalem, not Africa, is the black man's land. The white Jew is the devil (Rev. 2:9); he occupies the black man's land but will soon be driven out. The House of Judah awaits a deliverer, whom God will send to take the black man from the United States to Jerusalem. He will be a second Moses to lead his people to the promised land. The group lives communally.

Membership: In 1985 there were approximately 80 members living on the farm in rural Alabama. There is only one center.

Sources:

De Smet, Kate. "Return to the House of Judah." *Michigan, the Magazine of the Detroit News* (July 21, 1985).

Israelite Church of God and Jesus Christ, Inc.

1941 Madison Ave. (125th St.), New York, NY 10027

The Israelite Church of God and Jesus Christ Inc., formerly known as the Israeli Church of Universal Practical Knowledge, founded in New York City in the early 1990s is based in the identification of the biblical 12 tribes of Israel with the black and native people of North, Central, and South America. According to the church, black Americans are of the tribe of Judah. The remaining tribes include the indigenous people of the various areas of the Americas: Benjamin (Jamaica, Trinidad, Bahamas), Levi (Haiti), Simeon (Dominican Republic), Zebulon (Guatemala to Panama), Ephraim (Puerto Rico), Manasseh (Cuba), Gad (North America), Reuben-Seminole (Florida), Napthali (Argentina and Chile), Asher (Columbia to Uruguay), and Issachar (Mexico).

According to the church, nine of the 12 tribes left Assyria in the eighth century B.C.E. and sailed to the Americas. Three tribes—Judah, Benjamin, and Levi—were present in the holy land during the time of Christ. They were dispersed in 70 C.E. when Vespasian (9–79 C.E.) laid siege to Jerusalem, Israel. Some settled in West Africa. Here, Africans and Arabs sold them into slavery and eventually to the white men who brought them to America. This means that American blacks are Israelites, rather than Africans. Because Africans and Arabs sold the members of the tribes of Israel into slavery, American blacks were reluctant to affiliate with Africans and those from Islam.

In America, the church asserts, all of the Israelites have suffered at the hands of European Americans. White people are Edomites, the descendants of the biblical Esau (the son of Isaac and Rebecca). The Edomites are the enemy of God's people, Israel, and their end is destruction. Thus God's people should not integrate with the Edomites.

It is the goal of the Israelite Church to reunite the people of God now scattered across the Americas. According to the church, 1914 marked the beginning of the end of the Gentile age. Up until this time, the message of the Bible was sealed, but is now being revealed to the people of God. The Israelite Church uses only the King James Version of the Bible.

The Israelite Church of God and Jesus Christ Inc. broadcasts a television program in 15 states and radio programs over stations in Florida, New Jersey, and Pennsylvania.

Membership: In 2008 the church reported 27 congregations in 11 states.

Sources:

Chaa-Rask. *What You Need to Know about Islam and the Negroes*. New York: Israeli School of Universal Practical Knowledge, 1992.

The Holy Conception Unit: Homepage. www.theholyconceptionunit.org/portal/

Images of Israel in History. New York: Masha/Ahraya Iconographs, 1994.

Nation of Yahweh (Hebrew Israelites)

c/o P.E.E.S.S. Foundation, PO Box 520, Kirkland, QC, Canada H9H 0A6

The Nation of Yahweh, also known as the Hebrew Israelites or the Followers of Yahweh, is a movement founded by Yahweh ben (son of) Yahweh. Yahweh ben Yahweh (1935–2007) was born as Hulon Mitchell Jr., considered a slave name, and no longer used. He was the son of a Pentecostal minister who at one point joined the Nation of Islam, in which he became the leader of a mosque. Yahweh ben Yahweh began to call together the Followers of Yahweh in 1979.

Yahweh ben Yahweh taught that there is one God, whose name is Yahweh. God is black with woolly hair (Daniel 7:9; Revelation 1:13–15; Deuteronomy 7:21), and has sent his son, Yahweh ben Yahweh, to be the savior and deliverer of his people, the so-called black people of America. Those who believe in Yahweh ben Yahweh and his name are immortal. Blacks are considered the true lost tribe of Judah. They have been chosen by Yahweh, but have yet to be put into their destined office of rulership. Members of the Nation of Yahweh, upon joining, renounce their slave name and take the surname Israel. Many of them wear white robes as commanded in the Bible (Ecclesiastes 9:8). They believe that all people who oppose God are devils, regardless of race or color. A devil is one who is immoral and follows immoral teachings of wickedness and evilness. Many persons are capable of being and actually are devils.

While the Nation of Yahweh has a special place for the chosen blacks of America, and sees whites as especially used by Satan in exercising wicked rulership, in the end salvation is not a matter of color. Any person of any race or color can be saved by faith in Yahweh ben Yahweh.

Along with holding its particular religious beliefs, the Nation of Yahweh sees itself as establishing a united moral power to benefit the total community of America. It supports voter registration, education, self-help jobs, business opportunities, scholarships for children, health education, better housing, strong family ties, peace, love, and harmony among people regardless of race, creed, or color. Members are taught to practice charity and benevolence, to protect chastity, to respect the ties of blood and friendship, and revere the laws of Yahweh.

The Nation of Yahweh was headed by Yahweh ben Yahweh until his death in 2007. Under his leadership, the nation expanded, especially in the Miami area. By 1988 it owned, through its corporate entity, the Temple of Love, more than 42 businesses that were used to support the organization and its members.

Though the 1990s, the Nation of Yahweh was disrupted by accusations that acts of violence and murder had been committed by leaders between 1981 and 1986, against both former members and nonmembers. Concern about the group was heightened in 1986 when two residents of an apartment house were shot while members of the group were attempting an eviction. Then in 1988, a member of the group confessed to 4 murders and implicated the group's leadership in 12 more. Arrested in 1990, Yahweh ben Yahweh and several of his leaders were convicted in federal court of racketeering in 1992 and received lengthy prison terms. Yahweh ben Yahweh served 11 years and was released on probation in 2001. His movements were restricted and he was prevented from making contact with members of the continuing organization until a few months prior to his death.

In the meantime, the organization moved its headquarters from Miami to Quebec, Canada. The Nation of Yahweh currently is organized legally as the Abraham Foundation. Its publishing branch, the P.E.E.S.S. ("Politically, Economically, Educationally, Socially, Spiritually") Foundation, has offices in suburban Montreal and in Seguin, Texas. The collective leadership that emerged after Yahweh ben Yahweh's conviction has attempted to tone down the heightened racial rhetoric that the group became known for in the 1980s.

Membership: Not reported. In 1988, there were congregations in 37 North American cities and scattered followers in a number of other locations. The teachings had also spread to 16 countries.

Periodicals: *Yahweh Magazine*.

Sources:

Nation of Yahweh. www.yahwehbenyahweh.com/.

Mock, Bretin. "Rebirth of a Nation." *Intelligence Report* (Fall 2007). Posted at www.splcenter.org/intel/intelreport/article.jsp?aid=811.

Overcoming Saints of God

PO Box 879, Gainesville, FL 32601

The Overcoming Saints of God is a predominantly black Pentecostal church founded in 1959 by Anna Thompson Mobley (b. 1938). The original church, and still the lead congregation, is the Lethal Cathedral in Archer, Florida. Over the years other churches were founded along the Atlantic Coast as far north as Massachusetts, and missions were opened in Africa, the Virgin Islands, Haiti, and the Bahamas. The doctrine is similar to that of the Church of God and Saints of Christ. A youth convention is held annually during the third week in October.

Membership: In 1995 there were 10 churches and close to 1,000 members.

Sources:

DuPree, Sherry Sherrod. *African American Holiness Pentecostal Movement: An Annotated Bibliography*. New York: Garland, 1996.

Pan African Orthodox Christian Church (PAOCC)

Central Region, 7625 Linwood, Detroit, MI 48238

Alternate Address: Southwest Region, 5317 Martin Luther King Jr Blvd., Houston, TX 77021

The Pan African Orthodox Christian Church (PAOCC) dates to 1953 when 300 members of St. Mark's Presbyterian Church in Detroit, Michigan, walked out and formed the Central Congregational Church. In 1957 they moved into facilities at 7625 Linwood in Detroit and over the next decade became intensely involved in community issues, especially those impinging upon the black community. In 1967 the church's pastor, Albert B. Cleage Jr. (1911–2000), preached what has become a famous sermon, calling for a new black theology and a black church to articulate it. An 18-foot painting of a black Madonna was unveiled and the Black Christian Nationalist Movement was launched. The church building became known as the Shrine of the Black Madonna. In 1970 a book store and cultural center were opened. Cleage changed his name to Jaramogi Abebe Agyeman; following his death in 2000, Jaramogi Menelik Kimathi, also known as Card. Demosthene Nelson, became the holy patriarch and presiding bishop. The PAOCC reports that it is "committed to transform the spiritual emptiness, economic powerlessness, and social disorganization that plagues the black community."

The Black Nationalist Creed, printed below, spells out a position that identifies the black man and the Hebrew nation:

I Believe that human society stands under the judgment of one God, revealed to all, and known by many names. His creative power is visible in the mysteries of the universe, in the revolutionary Holy Spirit which will not long permit men to endure injustice nor to wear the shackles of bondage, in the rage of the powerless when they struggle to be free, and in the violence and conflict which even now threaten to level the hills and the mountains.

I Believe that Jesus, the Black Messiah, was a revolutionary leader, sent by God to rebuild the Black Nation Israel and to liberate Black People from powerlessness and from the oppression, brutality, and exploitation of the white gentile world.

I Believe that the revolutionary spirit of God, embodied in the Black Messiah, is born anew in each generation and that Black Christian Nationalists constitute the living remnant of God's Chosen People in this day, and are charged by him with responsibility for the Liberation of Black People.

I Believe that both my survival and my salvation depend upon my willingness to reject individualism, and so I commit my life to the Liberation Struggle of Black people and accept the values, ethics, morals, and program of the Black Nation defined by that struggle and taught by the Pan African Orthodox Christian Church.

During the 1970s the organization expanded significantly. Agyeman conducted seminary training and ordained over 100 ministers, who were given the title *mwalimu*, Swahili for *teacher*. Agyeman's own name means "liberator, blessed man, savior of the nation." Other congregations and centers have been established in Detroit; Atlanta, Georgia; and Calhoun Falls, South Carolina.

The PAOCC's social action minsitry participates in political forums, community outreach initiatives, and focus groups. A "feed my sheep" program distributes food and clothing to the homeless and destitute, while a health care ministry tends to people's health and physical needs. Teenagers ages 14 to 18 meet weekly in the Black Youth in Action ministry, which assists young people in attaining a balanced lifestyle by teaching etiquette, culture exploration, and team unity. A Shrine bookstore and cultural center are adjacent to the church at the location in Houston, Texas.

Membership: Not reported. In 2002 there were 10 institutions supporting the PAOCC.

Sources:

Shrine of the Black Madonna Pan African Orthodox Christian Church. www.blessingsoffaith.org

Boyd, Marsha Foster. *Self-Help in the Shrine of the Black Madonna #9 in Atlanta, Georgia: A Study of a Congregation and Its Leadership*. Berkeley, CA: Graduate Theological Union, 1995.

Cleage, Albert B., Jr. *Black Christian Nationalism: New Directions for the Black Church*. New York: William Morrow, 1972.

————. *The Black Messiah*. New York: Sheed and Ward, 1968.

Shrines of the Black Madonna of the Pan African Orthodox Christian Church: Thirtieth Anniversary. Detroit, MI: Mays Printing, 1983.

Ward, Hiley H. *Prophet of the Black Nation*. Philadelphia, PA: Pilgrim Press, 1969.

Rastafarians

Current address not obtained for this edition.

The Rastafarian Movement, a Jamaican black nationalist movement, grew out of a long history of fascination with Africa in general and Ethiopia in particular among the masses in Jamaica. The movement can be traced directly to the efforts of Marcus Garvey, founder of the Universal Negro Improvement Association, who, among other endeavors, promoted a steamship company that would provide transportation for blacks going back to Africa. In 1927 Garvey predicted the crowning of a black king in Africa as a sign that the redemption of black people from white oppression was near. The 1935 coronation of Haile Selassie as emperor of Ethiopia was seen as a fulfillment of Garvey's words.

Haile Selassie was born Ras Tafari Makonnen out of a lineage claimed to derive from the Queen of Sheba and King Solomon. He proclaimed his title as King of Kings, Lord of Lords, His Imperial Majesty the Conquering Lion of the Tribe of Judah, Elect of God. His name Haile Selassie means "Power of the Holy Trinity." Reading about the coronation, four ministers in Jamaica—Joseph Hibbert, Archibald Dunkley, Robert Hinds, and, most prominently, Leonard Howell—saw the new emperor as not only the fulfillment of the Garveyite expectation, but also the completion of biblical prophecies such as those in Revelation 5:2–5 and 19:16 that refer to the Lion of the Tribe of Judah and the King of Kings. The four, independently of each other, began to proclaim Haile Selassie the Messiah of the black people. Their first successes came in the slums of West Kingston, where they discovered each other and a movement began.

Howell began to proselytize around the island. He raised money by selling pictures of Haile Selassie and telling the buyers that they were passports back to Africa. He was arrested and sentenced to two years in jail for fraud. Upon his release he moved into the hill country of St. Catherine's parish and founded a commune, the Pinnacle, which, in spite of government attacks and several moves, became the center of the movement for the next two decades. At the Pinnacle, the smoking of ganga (marijuana) and the wearing of long hair curled to resemble a lion's mane (dread locks) became the marks of identification of the group.

As the Rastafarians matured, they adopted the perspectives of Black Judaism and identified the Hebrews of the Old Testament as black people. Their belief system was distinctly racial and they taught that the whites were inferior to the blacks. More extreme leaders saw whites as the enemies of blacks and believed that, in the near future, blacks would return to Africa and assume their rightful place in world leadership. Haile Selassie is believed to be the embodiment of God and, though no longer visible, he nevertheless still lives. Some Rastafarians believe Selassie is still secretly alive, though most see him as a disembodied spirit.

Relations with white culture have been tense, lived at the point of "dread," a term to describe the confrontation of a people struggling to regain a denied racial selfhood. Most Rastafarians are pacifists, though much support for the movement developed out of intense antiwhite feelings. Violence has been a part of the movement since the destruction of the Pinnacle, though it has been confined to individuals and loosely organized groups. One group, the Nyabingi Rastas, stand apart from most by their espousal of violence.

Rastafarians came to the United States in large numbers as part of the general migration of Jamaicans in the 1960s and 1970s. They have brought with them an image of violence, and frequent news reports have detailed murders committed by individuals identified as Rastafarians. Rastafarian spokespersons have complained that many young Jamaican-Americans have adopted the outward appearance of Rastafarians (dread locks and ganga smoking) without adopting Rastafarian beliefs and lifestyle.

A major aspect of Rastafarian life is the unique music developed as its expression. Reggae, a form of rock music, became popular far beyond Rastafarian circles, and exponents such as Bob Marley and Peter Tosh became international stars. Reggae has immensely helped in the legitimization of Rastafarian life and ideals.

In Jamaica the Rastafarian Movement is divided into a number of organizations and factions, many of which have been brought into the Jamaican community in America. Surveys of American Rastafarians have yet to define the organization in the United States though individual Rastafarians may be found in black communities across America, most noticeably Brooklyn, New York; Miami, Florida; and Chicago, Illinois.

Membership: There are an estimated 3,000–5,000 Rastafarians in the United States, though the figures are somewhat distorted by the large number of people who have adopted the outward appearance of Rastafarian life.

Periodicals: *Arise* • *Jahugliman*.

Sources:

Barrett, Leonard. *The Rastafarians*. Boston: Beacon Press, 1977.

Chevannes, Barry. *Rastafari: Roots & Ideology*. Syracuse, NY: Syracuse University Press, 1994.

Mulvaney, Rebekah Michele. *Rastafari and Reggae: A Dictionary and Sourcebook*. Westport, CT: Greenwood, 1990.

Murrell, Nathaniel Samuel, William David Spencer, and Adrian Anthony McFarlane, eds. *Chanting Down Babylon: The Rastafari Reader*. Philadelphia: Temple University Press, 1998.

Owens, Joseph. *Dread*. Kingston: Sangster, 1976.

Williams, K. M. *The Rastafarians*. London: Ward Lock Educational, 1981.

❋ Additional Jewish Groups

Congregation Kehillath Yaakov (Kehilat Jacob)

Carlebach Shul, 305 W. 79th St., New York, NY 10024

Among the most charismatic leaders to arise in the 1960s outside of the normal synagogue structures was Shlomo Carlebach (1925–1994). Born in Berlin, Germany, and raised in a traditional Hasidic family, Carlebach combined the neo-Hasidim of Martin Buber (1878–1965), the havurah (small group) movement in Judaism, and the counterculture lifestyle into a unique blend of traditional Judaism that has found a widespread audience among younger Jews.

Among the earliest structures that evolved out of Carlebach's work was the House of Love and Prayer, a Jewish community in San Francisco. It emerged in 1969 among Jews who had rediscovered their Jewishness in response to Carlebach's work in the drug culture. The emphasis of the house was placed on the shared life, Torah, and prayer. For several years Carlebach limited his travels to teach at the house's yeshivah. The San Francisco group published two periodicals, *Holy Beggars' Gazette* and *Tree*, and operated the Judaic Book Service. There were, in the mid-1970s, between 20 and 40 members at the house, an optimum number for a havurot. Services were held on Friday evenings, Saturday mornings, and each day at 6:30 a.m. Open classes were conducted in Hebrew and taught the Talmud. (The Talmud is an authoritative record of rabbinic discussions pertaining to Jewish law, ethics, customs, and history.)

While the San Francisco group flourished, similar groups emerged in New York and Jerusalem. By the early 1980s the San Francisco group had disbanded, and Carlebach transferred his headquarters to New York. There, he took over the synagogue his father, Rabbi Naphtali Carlebach (d. 1967), had founded in the 1940s. Shlomo Carlebach was considered both rabbi and rebbe, the leader of a Hasidic group. He traveled widely and was a popular speaker, storyteller, and musician. Since 2002, Naftali Citron has been the rabbi of Carlebach Shul; he has initiated new programs including the Rosh Chodesh Institute, Torah in the Park, Saturday morning shiurim, and a community-wide Lag Ba'Omer celebration.

A distinguishing characteristic of the Congregation Kehillath Yaakov is that it attempts to bring together and inspire a wide spectrum of the Jewish community, including traditional Chassid, modern orthodox, and the unaffiliated. The Carelbach Shul relies on two fundamental Torah teachings: Neshama Yesiera, a special soul received on Shabbos; and Lecham Mishnah, the two loaves of bread that commemorate the double portion of manna received in the desert for Shabbos.

Membership: Carlebach's following is national and international (especially in Israel). His following has continued to grow, though the structure containing it has evolved through the years.

Sources:

Carlebach Shul. www.carlebachshul.org

Hoffman, Edward. "Judaism's New Renaissance." *Yoga Journal* 61 (March/April 1985).

Jacobs, Susan. "A New Age Jew Revisits Her Roots." *Yoga Journal* 61 (March/April 1985).

Skir, Leo. "Shlomo Carlebach and the House of Love and Prayer." *Midstream* (February 1970).

Kabbalah Centre

1032 S Robertson Blvd., Los Angeles, CA 90035

Alternate Address: International Headquarters: 25 Burgrashov St., Tel Aviv 63342, Israel.

The Kabbalah Learning Centre, also known as the Research Centre of Kabbalah, was founded in 1922 by Rabbi Yehuda Ashlag (1886–1955), a mystic and scholar who hoped to open the teaching of the Kabbalah, the Jewish mystical system, to anyone who desired to study it. Traditionally, the Kabbalah was considered a subject for a few elite scholars. To accomplish his goal, Ashlag translated the entire Zohar, the basic Kabbalistic text, from Aramaic into modern Hebrew. He organized the text, breaking it into chapters and paragraphs. He also wrote an introductory text on the Zohar, which has been translated into English as *Ten Luminous Emanations*.

Ashlag was succeeded by his student, Rabbi Judah Brandwein, who continued translating the Aramaic Kabbalistic texts into Hebrew. Following his death in 1969, Brandwein was succeeded by Philip S. Gruberger, now known as Philip S. Berg. Berg, who in 2008 was the dean of the center, was an orthodox rabbi who met Brandwein in 1962 and became his close disciple. In 1965 Berg opened the first U.S. office of the center in New York City. He moved to Israel in 1974 with his wife, Karen Berg, who began teaching the Kabbalah in the early 1970s and later became the codirector of the center. The Berg's two sons, Yehudah and Michael, also assumed public leadership roles.

Under Berg's leadership the center expanded its program, opening offices across Israel, and in Europe, Canada, and Mexico. In 1981 Berg moved back to the United States. During his years leading the Kabbalah Centre, Berg has been a prolific author. His books in English have provided to be popular introductions to the Kabbalah and have attracted a wide following. Translations of his basic text, *Kabbalah for the Layman*, into Spanish, French, German, Russian, and Persian led the way for the center's spread in Europe and the Middle East, and his texts on reincarnation and astrology attracted Jews affected by the New Age movement. Berg suggested that Kabbalah is not simply a Jewish teaching, but one open to every person, and the center is focused in bringing Kabbalah to the world.

In the 1990s the growing movement became increasingly controversial. It attracted a number of celebrities, most notably the singer Madonna, comedian Rosanne Barr, and movie stars Winona Ryder, Ashton Kutcher, and Demi Moore. Berg's credentials were challenged by some Jewish leaders, some of whom questioned the legitimacy of his inheritance from Judah Brandwein and his lack of traditional rabbinical training. There also were complaints about the large cash flow that the movement generated. In Israel the orthodox rabbinate rejected Berg's claims to a role in Jewish leadership, and in the west some Jewish leaders have termed the group a "cult" in an attempt to separate themselves from its teachings. Many have objected to Berg's openness in sharing the secrets of the Kabbalistic teachings, and his receptiveness to other religions, especially those with a mystical bent. The center has largely dismissed these criticisms, and continued to defend its leadership and teachings and the direction its program is taking.

Membership: Not reported. In 2008 there were 32 centers and study group locations in the United States, and an additional 66 centers and study groups scattered around the world.

Periodicals: *Kabbalah Magazine*.

Sources:

Kabbalah Centre. www.kabbalah.com.

Ashlag, Yehuda. *Kabbalah: A Gift of the Bible*. Jerusalem, Israel: Research Centre of Kabbalah, 1994.

Berg, Philip, ed. *An Entrance to the Zohar*. Jerusalem, Israel: Research Centre of Kabbalah, 1974.

———. *Kabbalah for the Layman*. 3 vols. Jerusalem, Israel: Research Centre of Kabbalah.

———. *The Wheel of the Soul*. Jerusalem, Israel: Research Centre of Kabbalah, 1984.

Udovitch, Mim. "The Kabbalah Chronicles I–III." Radar Online web site, June 16, 2005. Available from www.radaronline.com/web-only/the-kabbalah-chronicles/2005/06/inside-hollywoods-hottest-cult.php.

Karaites

c/o KJA B'nai Israel, 1575 Annie St., Daly City, CA 94015

Karaites are Jews, originating in Iraq, who are distinguished by their refusal to acknowledge the authority of the Talmud, the commentary on Jewish law (the Torah), as on Jewish practice. In rejecting the authority of the Talmud, however, the Karaites do not consider it unlawful to consult it or to rely on it, but they deny its heavenly origin, considering it an original work of the sages in interpretation of the written Torah. As such, it is subject to the shortcomings inherent in any handiwork of mortals uninspired by heaven. The Karaites consider themselves the original pre-rabbinic Jews who follow only the Torah. The majority of the Jewish community is seen as having separated from them.

The Karaite community became visible in the eighth century C.E. in Babylonia (Iraq), where contemporary Kairaites insist that one Anan ben David had revitalized a lineage which had passed through a variety of earlier groups including the first century community at Qumran (which became famous in the twentieth century because of the Dead Sea Scrolls). Other modern historians have questioned Anan's role in Karaite origin, and argue that Karaites arose in the medieval period and later rewrote their history to include Anan.

The Karaite movement spread through that part of the Jewish community that resided in the Islamic Empire late in the ninth century and eventually found its way to Palestine. Its original Palestinian centers were wiped out by the first Christian crusade in 1099. Karaites moved to Byzantium (Constantinople). After the Ottomans conquered Constantinople in the fifteenth century, Karaites migrated northward to Poland, Latvia, and Lithuania and eastward to Crimea. Only a small Karaite community survived the Holocaust in Eastern Europe. By the middle of the twentieth century, the largest Karaite community was found in Egypt, but since the founding of Israel, most have moved there. The primary Israeli centers are at Ramla and Ashdod.

Karaites accept the authority of the Tanach (or Tanakh), the Hebrew Bible (called the Old Testament by Christians), but reject other writings such as the Apocrypha, the Pseudepigrapha, the Christian New Testament, and the Muslim Qur'an. They believe in the future arrival of a Davidic Messiah (Isaiah 11:1) who will be a human king filled with God's prophetic spirit. The Messiah will not be a divine or semi-divine in nature.

Karaites have rabbis, but reject the notion that they are the primary authority in interpreting the Torah; the individual is responsible for studying the Jewish Bible and reaching the best interpretation for their situation; in the end, it is the individual who will face judgment. This individual approach regularly introduces various interpretations into the community and insures a level of diversity.

Over the centuries, Karaites have developed several practices that contrast with those of the larger Jewish community, and their variant interpretations of Jewish law make intermarriage between Karaites and other Jews difficult. Karaites also calculate their calendar from actual observation of the new moon, and it varies slightly from the calendar now common in Judaism. They prohibit sexual relations on the Sabbath. Karaite synagogues do not have chairs and the liturgy is very different from that in other Jewish traditions. They do not recognize the post-biblical holiday Hanukkah.

More than 1,000 Karaites live in the San Francisco Bay Area. Most are associated with Congregation B'nai Israel in Daly City, led by Rav Joe Pessah. The founding members had fled from Cairo, Egypt, immediately after the Six-Day War in 1967.

Membership: In the early twenty-first century, there were some 30,000 Karaites in Israel, with smaller communities in Egypt, France, and the San Francisco Bay Area of California.

Sources:

The Karaite Korner. Available from http//:www.karaite-korner.org.

The Karaite Jews of America. Available from http//:www.karaites.org.

Astren, Fred. *Karaite Judaism and Historical Understanding*. Columbia: University of South Carolina Press, 2004.

Birmbaum, Philip, ed. *Karaite Studies*. New York: Sepher-Hermon Press, 1971.

Nemoy, L. Leon. *Karaite Anthology*. New Haven, CT: Yale University Press, 1952.

Schur, Nathan. *History of the Karaites*. New York: Peter Lang, 1992.

National Havurah Committee (NHC)

7135 Germantown Ave., 2nd Fl., Philadelphia, PA 19119-1842

During the 1960s, as part of the larger wave of communalism that swept America, a variety of primarily young Jews began to combine their exploration of Jewish roots with experiments in communal living. Havurot Shalom was one of the first such experiments. It was established as a traditional Jewish community in Boston in 1968. It was conceived as a core community around which a larger constituency would be oriented. It offered adult education courses in Torah, Hasidism, traditional arts such as challah baking, and more contemporary subjects.

At about the same time and in the years following, other havurot communities emerged within Jewish communities in such widely scattered locations as New York City; Phoenix, Arizona; Madison, Wisconsin; Ithaca, New York; Philadelphia, Pennsylvania; Washington, D.C.; Rochester, New York; and Austin, Texas. Some were attached to congregations; many were completely independent enterprises. The movement has tried to draw from each of the three dominant Jewish traditions rather than identifying with any one of them. Full equality of women has been a major commitment of the movement. In 1979, 350 havurot members held a conference at Rutgers University and organized the National Havurot Coordinating Committee, which immediately began planning programs to assist havurah communities to survive by gaining a greater knowledge of their Jewish heritage.

Administered by volunteers, the National Havurah Committee (NHC) is a network of diverse individuals and communities engaged in what they describe as a "joyful grassroots Judaism." A primary activity is the Summer Insititue, a weeklong event that includes prayer, conversation, and meditation, as well as activties such as singing, dancing, music sessions, and hiking. Rabbis and teachers are addressed by their first names during the event, and those who often are not in leadership roles are given the opportunity to instruct and contribute to the community. An annual three-day retreat, incorporating tradition and innovation, offers an opportunity for study, Jewish experience, and spiritual growth.

The NHC utilizes a five-person board of directors, currently headed by Sherry Israel, under which there are thirteen members at large and a managing director, assisted by a large advisory council.

Membership: Not reported.

Periodicals: *Havurah! Newsletter*, quarterly.

Sources:

National Havurah Committee—Homepage. www.havurah.org

Loeb, Laurence D. "Prayer and Community: The Havurah in American Judaism." *American Jewish History* 80, no. 2 (Winter 1991): 305–310.

Reisman, Bernard. "The Havurah: An Approach to Humanizing Jewish Organizational Life." *Journal of Jewish Communal Service* 52, no. 2 (Winter 1975): 202–209.

Neturei Karta of USA

Box 1315, Monsey, NY 10952

The Neturei Karta (Guardians of the City) emerged in 1935 as an ultra-Orthodox faction within the Agudat Israel, a movement that sought to focus Jewish attention on the Holy Land but was opposed to Zionism. Agudat Israel also had been a separatist movement in that it opposed cooperation with non-Orthodox Jews. In the early 1930s some members of Agudat Israel residing in the Holy Land demanded an independent Orthodox Jewish community separate from the "Zionist" community. When the larger membership of Agudat Israel opposed the demand, the organization split, and the group seeking the independent Orthodox community broke away and founded Hevrat ha-Hayyim, which eventually became Neturei Karta. Among the leaders of the breakaway group was Amram Blau (1895–1976).

After World War II Neturei Karta members opposed the creation of the Jewish state of Israel and Israel's control of Jerusalem. They claimed that the Talmud prohibits cooperation with any state not created by revelation from the heavenly realms. They worked, unsuccessfully, for the internationalization of the city. Today, many members of the Neturei Karta refuse to cooperate or even recognize the existence of the State of Israel, manifesting their opposition by refusing to vote, to accept an Israeli identity card, or to recognize the decisions of Israeli courts.

The Neturei Karta faced a severe test in 1966 when Blau married a convert, Ruth Ben-David; this led a number of members to leave the group. Members have established themselves in the United States and found an ally in the Satmar Hasidism, who share their anti-Zionist stance. The Satmar community contributes regularly to the support of the Neturei Karta.

Membership: Not reported.

Periodicals: *The Jewish Guardian*.

Sources:

Neturei Karta. www.nkusa.org/.

Domb, I. *The Transformation: The Case of the Neturei Karta*. Reprint. New York: Hachomo, 1989.

Lawrence, Bruce. *Defenders of God: The Fundamentalist Revolt against the Modern Age*. Columbia: University of South Carolina Press, 1995.

New Synagogue

Park West Church, 86th St. and Amsterdam Ave., New York, NY 10025

Hungarian-born Rabbi Joseph H. Gelberman was a leader of a Conservative congregation who left it to found the Little Synagogue (Congregation Tel Aviv), a "modern Hasidic community" located just north of Greenwich Village in Manhattan in New York City. After more than twenty years with the Little Synagogue, he continued his ministry with the New Synagogue. Gelberman's program combines elements of Hasidism, New Thought, and Eastern religious thought. Integral to the program is the Midway Counseling Center, specializing in psychological counseling and based upon the concept that learning to love is the key to growth on all levels of the self.

Rabbi Gelberman has become a popular figure in New Thought metaphysical circles and has often spoken at International New Thought Alliance (INTA) meetings and at the New York congregation of the Church of the Truth. Science of Mind lessons are a regular part of the weekly program. Over the years, Martin Buber's Hasidism has come more and more to the fore in Gelberman's thinking. The synagogue seeks, through Hasidic thought and techniques, to find personal growth and the joy of worship. Friday night Sabbath services include chanting, silent meditation, and spontaneous verbalization leading to mystical and metaphysical encounter. Interpretation of the Zohar is a central feature of the educational pro-gram. The synagogue also offers workshops on the Kabbalah and other aspects of Jewish experience.

Although a single congregation, the New Synagogue has immense influence through media coverage and Gelberman's lecturing and leading workshops around the United States. Gelberman also established, at age 87, the All-Faiths Seminary International, an institute that trains modern interfaith ministers who in turn provide community instruction, counsel, dedications, sermons, weddings, workshops, and memorials. Wisdom Press publishes Rabbi Gelberman's books and tapes, distributing them throughout the country.

Membership: Not reported. There is one center in Manhattan.

Educational Facilities:

All-Faiths Seminary International, New York, New York, www.allfaithseminary.org.

Sources:

All-Faiths Seminary International, Available from http//:www.allfaithseminary.org.

Gelberman, Joseph H. *Psychology and Metaphysics*. New York: Little Synagogue Press, n.d.

———. *Reaching a Mystical Experience: A Kabbalistic Encounter*. New York: Wisdom Press, 1970.

———. *To Be. . . Fully Alive*. Farmingdale, NY: Coleman Graphics, 1983.

———. "Kabbala for Moderns." *Hadassah Magazine* 54, no. 3 (November 1972).

Gelberman, Joseph H., with Lesley Sussman *Physician of the Soul: A Modern Kabbalist's Approach to Health and Healing*. Freedom, CA: Crossing Press, 2000.

P'nai Or Religious Fellowship

6445 Greene St., #A-401, Philadelphia, PA 19119

The P'nai Or Religious Fellowship evolved from the B'nai Or Religious Fellowship, founded in 1962 by Rabbi Zalman Schachter-Shalomi (b. 1924), one of the pioneers in the wave of Jewish spirituality that emerged among the youthful Jewish population in the 1970s. Schachter-Shalomi was born in Poland, but his family later moved to Belgium. There he became associated with Lubavitch Hasidism. After arriving in New York during World War II (1939–1945), Schachter-Shalomi trained for the rabbinate and was ordained in 1947. He served several Lubavitcher centers and took a master's degree in psychology of religion. Meanwhile, his personal mystical-religious quest led him to psychic and occult literature, non-Jewish forms of spirituality, and an early experimentation with psychedelic drugs. He found that his attachment to Judaism had deepened, but he also concluded that Judaism was not the only true religion. He believed truth expressed itself in all religions, especially in their mystical variations.

In the early 1980s the issue of the role of females within the fellowship was forcefully debated, and members committed themselves to make the fellowship more egalitarian (i.e., full participation at all levels for both men and women) and welcoming to gay and lesbian Jews. As part of this commitment, the name of the organization was changed from B'nai Or (sons of light) to P'nai Or (faces of light), a gender-free term derived from the Kabbalah. Rabbi Schachter-Shalomi departed for Colorado in 1995; the current rabbi is Marcia Prager.

P'nai Or is conceived of as a traditional Jewish center whose members pursue Judaism as a spiritual way of life. Its program centers upon traditional study of Torah, the mystical Kabbalah, Hasidic writings, and the celebration of traditional Jewish practices of ritual and worship. However, the traditional practices are set within an atmosphere of acceptance of modern spiritual practice, meditation, transpersonal psychologies, and the recognition of alternative spiritual paths, even for those born Jewish. In addition to a weekly Torah class, the program offers workshops such as Exploring Shabbat; festivals; high holy days; shofar blowing; service leadership; and writing a drash or D'var Torah.

Activities in Philadelphia have centered around the fellowship's house of study and prayer. It houses a library, a study area, administrative offices, and a space for weekly and seasonal celebrations. Increasingly, the group has developed an outgoing perspective and a commitment to *tikkun olam*, that is, a commitment to improve the world, using spirituality to fuel this work personally and socially. A national and international network, the Chai Network, consists of individuals and groups that support the fellowship and its program of revival within the larger context of Judaism. P'nai Or is a member of ALEPH: Alliance for Jewish Renewal, which advances vital Judaism as an ethical and spiritual path.

P'nai Or is supported entirely by members' annual dues and volunteer services; no one is denied membership for financial reasons.

Membership: There are seven affiliated centers in the United States and in two foreign countries, one each in Switzerland and the Netherlands.

Periodicals: *New Menorah*.

Sources:

P'Nai Or—Philadelphia. www.pnaior-phila.org

Schachter-Shalomi, Zalman. *Fragments of a Future Scroll: Hassidism for the Here and Now*. Germantown, PA: Leaves of Grass Press, 1975.

Schachter-Shalomi, Zalman, and Donald Gropman. *The First Steps to a New Jewish Spirit*. New York: Bantam Books, 1983.

Schachter-Shalomi, Zalman, and Edward Hoffman. *Sparks of Light: Counseling in the Hasidic Tradition*. Boulder, CO: Shambhala, 1983.

Schwartz, Howard, and Zalman Schachter-Shalomi. *The Dream Assembly: Tales of Rabbi Zalman Schachter-Shalomi*. Amity, NY: Amity House, 1987.

Weichselbaum, Lehman. "Reb Zalman Schachter-Shalomi, Rabbi to the Counterculture." *New Age* 7, no. 2 (September, 1981).

Sha'arei Orah
Current address not obtained for this edition.

Sha'arei Orah ("Gates of Light") is a neo-Hasidic congregation founded in 1982 by Rabbi David Din, a student of Rabbi Nachman of Bratslav (1772–1810). Following the death of Rabbi Nachman, his followers interpreted his words, "My light will glow till the days of the Messiah," as meaning that they would never need another rebbe, the traditional Hasidic leader. During the 1970s, Nachman's teachings enjoyed a revival. New English editions of his writings and stories appeared. Sha'arei Orah combines traditional Hassidic teachings with the newer movement of younger Jews for a close community of intense spirituality. There is one center, located in New York City.

Membership: Not reported.

Sources:

Hoffman, Edward. "Judaism's New Renaissance." *Yoga Journal* 61 (March/April 1985).

Kramer, Mordechai, ed. *The Thirteen Stories of Rebbe Nachman of Breslev*. Jerusalem: Hillel Press, 1978.

Society for Humanistic Judaism
28611 W Twelve Mile Rd., Farmington Hills, MI 48334

Within the American Jewish community, attempts have been made since the mid-nineteenth century to articulate a secular, humanistic, and even atheistic Judaism. Such efforts have resulted in structures such as the Ethical Culture Society (which, while predominantly Jewish in membership, did little to relate to the Jewish community) and a variety of Jewish agricultural communal experiments. Primarily, however, secular Jews were not related to synagogue life. In the 1960s there arose a group of rabbis who wished to combine the religious life and affirmation of their Jewishness within a humanist perspective. Rabbi Sherwin T. Wine (1928–2007) led the way in the formation of the first humanist congregation in 1963, the Birmingham Temple in suburban Detroit. He was joined by Rabbi Daniel Friedman who had led congregation Beth Or in Deerfield, Illinois, to adopt humanistic thought and practice. In 1969 they led in the formation of the Society for Humanistic Judaism and the Association for Humanistic Rabbis. Secular

Humanistic Judaism has since grown into an international movement with supporters on five continents.

Humanistic Judaism is a religion for Jews who value their Jewish identity but question the traditional view of Jewish history. It offers a non-theistic approach to the celebration of Jewish identity and Jewish culture. Humanistic Jews understand and appreciate the Jewish past and present in ways consistent with the best insights of modern enlightenment. Humanistic Judaism promotes certain important values in Jewish life that the traditional establishments have resisted. These values are rationality, personal autonomy, feminism, the celebration of human strength and power, and the development of a pluralistic world with mutual understanding and cooperation among all religions and philosophies of life.

Humanistic ethics assert that ethics and morality rest upon a human foundation, and that each person must be responsible for individual ethical decisions and their consequences. Humanistic ethics also assume that people must be treated noncoercively, with respect, and in such a way that their individuality and dignity are affirmed. Assisting others to assume responsibility for their own lives is a primary ethical activity.

The Society for Humanistic Judaism (SHJ) serves as a voice for Humanistic Jews. It publishes educational, philosophical, and celebrational materials, and helps to organize Humanistic Jewish communities and congregations in North America. As of 2008, there were 29 Humanistic congregations, communities, and havurot in the United States and Canada, plus affiliates in Israel, Australia, Belgium, France, Italy, Mexico, Russia, and Uruguay. The society is affiliated with the International Federation of Secular Humanistic Jews led by noted Holocaust scholar Yehuda Bauer, and is served by the International Institute for Secular Humanistic Judaism, based in Jerusalem and North America, which functions as the intellectual center and rabbinic seminary for Humanistic Judaism. The current SHJ president is Louis Altman, a member of the Florida congregation; its executive director is M. Bonnie Cousens. Rabbi Peter Schweitzer serves as a leader for The City Congregation for Humanistic Judaism in New York City and is also president of the Association of Humanistic Rabbis.

Membership: The society reports a membership of 10,000.

Educational Facilities:

Institute for Secular Humanistic Judaism, Jerusalem, Israel; Farmington Hills, Michigan.

Periodicals: *Humanistic Judaism*, quarterly.

Sources:

Society for Humanistic Judaism. Available from http//:www.shj.org.

Cohn-Sherbok, Dan, Harry T. Cook, and Marilyn Rowens, comp. *A Life of Courage: Sherwin Wine and Humanistic Judaism*. Farmington Hills, MI: The International Institute for Secular Humanistic Judaism/Milan Press, 2003.

Feldman, Ruth. "Beth Or Offers Alternative Form of Judaism, Maintains Low Profile, Earns Activists' Scorn." *North Shore* 2, no. 1 (January/February 1979): 56–59.

Goodman, Saul N. *The Faith of Secular Jews*. New York: KTAV Publishing House, 1976.

Weisman, Sidney M. "From Orthodox Judaism to Humanism." *The Humanist* 39, no. 3 (May/June 1979): 32–35.

Wine, Sherwin T. *The Humanist Haggadah*. Birmingham, MI: Society for Humanistic Judaism, 1979.

———. *Humanistic Judaism*. Buffalo, NY: Prometheus Books, 1978.

———. *Sherman T. Wine Papers, 1961–1999*. Available at the University of Michigan Bentley Historical Library, Ann Arbor, Michigan.

Society of Jewish Science
c/o Center for Applied Judaism, 109 E 39th St., New York, NY 10016

Jewish converts were mentioned in Christian Science literature in the 1890s. In the first decade of the twentieth century, substantial numbers in the still small Jewish community began to look to Mary Baker Eddy (who founded the Church of Christ, Scientist) for inspiration. In 1911 the California Grand Lodge of B'nai B'rith adopted a resolution denying membership to Jews adhering to Christian Science, and in 1912 the Central Conference of American Rabbis (Reformed) devoted a session at its annual meeting to a discussion of the issue. Of particular interest were those Jews who insisted that Christian Science only made them better Jews.

Out of this debate came Alfred Geiger Moses, a Reformed rabbi from Mobile, Alabama, who, in 1916, published his *Jewish Science*. Drawing upon Hasidic sources, he translated Chochmah (the Kabbalistic sephirot, generally translated as *wisdom*). He saw the Baal Shem Tov as the source of Eddy's thought and Christian Science as Hasidism with a veneer of Christology. He further emphasized "faith cure" as a genuinely Jewish tradition and recounted incidents of cures he had witnessed. Moses's position was actually nearer New Thought than Christian Science, inasmuch as he refused to deny the existence of matter. He emphasized thinking "right thoughts" and training the mind with affirmations (short statements "affirming" God and creation), following a proper diet, avoiding excesses, and refusing to become angered.

In 1922 the Lithuanian-born Rabbi Morris Lichtenstein gave organizational form to Moses's ideas, establishing the Society of Jewish Science in New York City. In 1925 he published *Jewish Science and Health* and, in subsequent years, several other books. From 1923 to the present, the society has published the *Jewish Science Interpreter* eight times per year. By 1938 there were nineteen practitioners. Rival groups had begun to emerge almost immediately: Rabbi Clifton Harby Levy organized the Center of Jewish Science in 1923. Levy published a series of lessons, *The Helpful Manual,* and a periodical, the *Jewish Life.* By 1929 he had six active groups in New York City and one each in Baltimore, Maryland; Rochester and Syracuse, New York; and Washington, D.C. The center continued until the late 1950s.

Rabbi Lichtenstein died in 1938 and was succeeded by his wife, Tehilla Lichtenstein, who occupied his pulpit until her death in 1973. She was the first woman to fill such a role uninterruptedly and for so long (more than three decades). She wrote the basic introductory booklet, "What to Tell Your Friends about Jewish Science." Ms. Lichtenstein draws the distinction between Jewish Science and Christian Science by noting that within Judaism are all the spiritual goals any Jew needs. Jewish Science is a way of life that puts into application all the spiritual, ethical, and moral principles of the Jewish faith, and thus enables one to attain health and happiness. That the cure of physical and mental illnesses can be effected by restoring one's mental processes to their natural condition is a central postulate.

Since the death of Tehilla Lichtenstein, the Society has been administered by non-rabbinic professionals; rabbis conduct religious services, High Holy Days, and Passover Seders, as well as teach Torah classes. Because the principles of Jewish Science are applicable to all Jews, some prefer to attend a local, usually movement-affiliated synagogue in addition to the Jewish Science synagogue.

Membership: Not reported. There are groups in New York City; Piscataway, New Jersey; Albuquerque, New Mexico; Los Angeles, California; and Netanya, Israel. Other adherents scattered across the country are affiliated through the society's literature.

Periodicals: *Jewish Science Interpreter*, eight per year.

Sources:

Society of Jewish Science. Available from http//:www.appliedjudaism.org.

Appel, John J. "Christian Science and the Jews." *Jewish Social Studies* 31 (April 1969): 100–121.

Levy, Charles Harby. *The Helpful Manual*. New York: Centre of Jewish Science, n.d.

Lichtenstein, Morris. *Jewish Science and Health*. New York: Jewish Science Publishing Company, 1925.

————. *Joy of Life*. New York: Jewish Science Publishing Society, 1938.

Lichtenstein, Tehilla. *What to Tell Your Friends about Jewish Science*. New York: Society of Jewish Science, 1951.

Trachtenberg-Alpert, Rebecca. *The Life and Thought of Tehilla Lichtenstein*. New York: Society of Jewish Science, n.d.

Umansky, Ellen M. *From Christian Science to Jewish Science: Spiritual Healing and American Jews*. New York: Oxford University Press, 2005.

United Israel World Union (UIWU)

200 East 10th St., Ste. 111, New York, NY 10003

Alternative Address: Editorial Offices: PO Box 561476, Charlotte, NC 28256.

The United Israel World Union (UIWU) was incorporated under the laws of the State of New York in 1944 by founder David Horowitz (1903–2002) who served as president until his death at age 99. The primary purposes of the UIWU are to represent a universal version of the Hebraic faith to the non-Jewish world, based primarily on the Hebrew Bible, as well as to provide a meeting place for Jews with non-Jews who are accordingly drawn to this message. The hallmark of the organization is Isaiah's prescription that "My house will become a house of prayer for all peoples." Central to this mission is the conviction that scattered among the Gentiles are untold numbers of descendants of the Lost Tribes of Israel who are discovering their identity and their kinship to the Jewish people. Membership is based on the simple declaration of faith in the One God of Israel and a commitment to live according to the principles of the Hebrew Bible. Members, accordingly, observe the Sabbath day, Jewish festivals, and a biblical "kosher" diet, although the manner and extent of such observances are left to one's individual conscience.

During the decades of the 1950s through the 1970s the movement flourished with centers in New York, Michigan, and West Virginia; members scattered through 30 states and 15 foreign countries; and the UIWU mantained an active mailing list of 9,000. Horowitz edited and published the triennial *United Israel Bulletin* from 1945 until his death. As an accredited member of the United Nations Press Corp since 1945, and serving twice as its president, Horowitz rubbed shoulders with many ambassadors and heads of state, forming a close friendship with the late Dag Hammarskjöld. He published a syndicated weekly column that appeared in 22 Anglo-Jewish newspapers, reflecting his Jewish perspectives on world events in the light of UIWU perspectives. Horowitz received many honors including Israel's Defender of Israel Medal presented by Prime Minister Menachem Begin. In the 1980s and 1990s operations of UIWU reached a low ebb due to the age and health of Horowitz.

Although it remains incorporated in New York, in 2004 the UIWU transferred most of its records, archives, and operations to Charlotte, North Carolina. Administered by Dr. James D. Tabor, the offices house the David Horowitz Memorial Library, which holds correspondence between Horowitz and various world leaders and celebrities including David Ben Gurion, Eleanor Roosevelt, and King Abdullah of Jordan; 60 years of back issues of the *United Israel Bulletin*; and a complete archive of Horowitz's weekly UN columns (1950–1998).

Membership: As of 2008 membership is at 300 with active surface and e-mail lists totaling 1,700.

Periodicals: *United Israel Bulletin*; this has ceased regular publication but archive and new materials are added regularly to the organization's Internet site, www.unitedisrael.org.

Sources:

United Israel World Union (UIWU). unitedisrael.org.

By-Laws of United Israel World Union, approved 1944, amended 2005.

Horowitz, David. *Thirty-three Candles*. New York: World Union Press, 1949.

Middle Eastern Family, Part II: Islam, Zoroastrianism, Baha'i

22

ISLAM. With only a few hundred thousand adherents in 1965 when the emigration barriers from predominantly Islamic countries were liberalized, Islam has grown to the point that it is challenging Judaism's position as the second largest religious community (Christianity being the largest) in America. Its growth has also propelled it from being the faith of a few ethnic enclaves to a powerful presence in national political debates and in every segment of urban society, due in no small measure to its association with oil and the turmoil of the Middle East. While not yet as well organized as the Jewish community, the Muslim community is rapidly gaining a high level of political sophistication.

Islam's upward trajectory in the United States suffered a severe setback on September 11, 2001, when terrorists crashed airplanes into the Pentagon building near Washington, D.C., and the World Trade Center in New York City. The terrorists were quickly identified as Muslims and adherents of an Islamic group called Al Qaeda, based in Afghanistan. American Muslims quickly moved to disassociate themselves from the actions of their fellow Muslims, much as Christian groups had earlier distanced themselves from the Branch Davidians and the People's Temple. However, the minority and less-known Muslim community had a more difficult task. While continuing to face critics, American Muslims—with the assistance of government officials, the Interfaith community, and the news media—have used the unique moment to communicate their desire to participate as Americans in the social, cultural, political, and religious life of the nation. It remains to be seen how successful they will be.

ORIGINS. "There is but one God and Muhammad is His messenger" is the great standard under which Islam has become the religion of one-seventh of the world's population. *Islam* means "submission," in this case submission to Allah, the creator-ruler God of the Muslim faith.

While Muslims believe that Islam started with Adam in the primal Garden of Eden, most scholars trace the origins of Islam to the experiences of Muhammad (c. 570–632), an Arabian, born and raised in Mecca. He married a widow named Khadijah, with whom he fathered a daughter, Fatima, and settled down to a mundane life. Muhammad's custom was to spend part of each year in the mountains meditating and fasting. Around the year 611, he began to have a series of encounters with the angel Gabriel. The angel spoke to him of the oneness of God (Allah) and of Allah's distaste of idolatry.

The message of the angel would later be written down in a book, the Qur'an (also spelled Koran). Muhammad began to teach in Mecca, but found few converts and a great deal of hostility from leaders of the various pagan tribes. Under persecution, in 622 Muhammad and his followers moved north to Medina, where they were offered refuge. This migration is known as the *hijra* or *hegira*. Muslims date their calendars from this time.

Muhammad himself is seen as the last of a series of prophets who have preached the unity of God and warned of the end-time judgment. The twenty-eight earlier prophets include Adam, Noah, Moses, John the Baptist, and Jesus. The judgment they described is a cataclysmic event when the trumpet will sound for humans to stand and be called to account. Paradise and hell wait to receive the just and the damned.

Belief in Allah, the supreme God, is the essential component of Islamic faith. Allah is seen as the transcendent being, creator and sustainer of the universe. He is the lawgiver, the arbiter of good and evil, and the judge at the end-time. The affirmation concerning Allah is amply captured in the opening lines of the Qur'an: "In the name of Allah, the Beneficent, the Merciful Praise be to Allah, Lords of the Worlds. The Beneficent, the Merciful. Owner of the Day of Judgment. Thee (alone) we worship; Thee (alone) we ask for help. Show us the straight path. The Path of those whom Thou has favored; who go astray" (Marmaduke Pickthall translation).

Existing with God are his angelic messengers. Chief among these is Gabriel, who communicated the Qur'an to Muhammad. (Opposing the angels are the satans or devils.) The Qur'an is the written revelation of God, accepted as transcribed by Muhammad. It is over 6,000 verses in length and is divided into 114 *suras* or chapters, which are arranged (with the exception of Sura I) in order of length, the longest first. These suras were given at various periods during the last 22 years of Muhammad's life.

Second only to the Qur'an as authority for Muslims is the Hadith, a collection of stories about and sayings of Muhammad that were gathered in the decades after his death. Muslim scholars had the task of sorting more genuine traditions from spurious ones. Al-Bukhari (d. 870) is remembered for his gathering a collection of some 7,000 believed to be genuine. His work is supplemented by that of al-Hajjah, a contemporary. Shi'a Muslims have a separate collection of traditions about Muhammad.

Islam Chronology

18th century	An estimated 15% of the African slaves brought to the British American colonies are of the Muslim faith.
1732	James Oglethorpe, founder of Georgia, frees Ayyub ibn Sulaiman Jallon, a Muslim slave in Maryland, and provides him transportation to England.
1807	Yarrow Mamout, an African Muslim slave, is freed. He later becomes a shareholder in the Columbia Bank, second bank chartered in the United States.
1828	President John Quincy Adams and Secretary of State Henry Clay arrange for the freeing of Abdulrahman Ibrahim Ibn Sori, a former prince from West Africa who resided as a slave in Georgia. He later becomes one of the most documented of African American former slaves.
1893	Alexander Russell Webb represents Islam at Parliament of Religions (Chicago).
1913	Noble Drew Ali establishes the Moorish Science Temple of America in Newark.
1915	Albanian American Muslims build a *masjid* in Maine and establish an Islamic association.
1917	Britain issues Balfour Declaration on Jewish settlement in Palestine (November).
1924	Shaykh Daoud Ahmed Faisal establishes the Islamic Mission of America, AKA the State Street Mosque, in New York City.
1933	Founding of the Nation of Islam under Elijah Muhammad.
1934	"Mother Mosque of America" completed in Cedar Rapids, Iowa.
1947	Washington Islamic Center founded.
1953	CIA aids coup against Iranian leader Mohammad Mosaddeq.
1963	Founding of the Muslim Students Association.
1965	Assassination of Malcolm X in New York City.
1975	Upon the death of Elijah Muhammad, founder of Nation of Islam, he is succeeded by his son, Warith Deen Mohammed.
1979	Iranian hostage crisis begins on November 4.
1981	Release of U.S. hostages in Iran on January 20.
1983	Attack on U.S. and French soldiers in Beirut on October 23.
1991	First Gulf War to liberate Kuwait from invading Iraqis.
1992	Imam Wallace D. Mohammed becomes the first Muslim to offer an invocation before the U.S. Senate.
1993	Bombing of the World Trade Center on February 26.
	Oslo Accords signed by Israel and Palestine Liberation Organization in Washington on September 13.
1994	Council on American-Islamic Relations (CAIR) founded.
1996	Osama bin Laden announces jihad against United States.
1998	World Islamic Front issues declaration against United States on February 23.
	American embassies in Kenya and Tanzania bombed on August 7.
2000	*USS Cole* attacked in Yemen on October 12.
	Breakdown of President Clinton's Israel-Palestine peace talks.
2001	Bombing of Pentagon and World Trade Center on September 11. American Muslims decry terrorist acts.
	United States invades Afghanistan and drives Taliban from power.
2003	U.S. forces invade Iraq in March.
2007	Yale Divinity School promotes Muslim-Christian dialogue.

THE FIVE PILLARS OF ISLAM. Islam (submission to Allah) has developed around five beliefs or practices known as the five *pillars*. The pillars symbolize the obligations owed to Allah by individuals. First, in performance and priority, is the *profession of faith*: "There is no God but Allah, and Muhammad is His messenger." These words state the Muslim's commitment to the supremacy of Allah, the one true God, and the singular role of his voice piece, Muhammad. The profession of faith also places the believer in the long tradition of Western monotheism and the previous prophets who proclaimed the one God.

Second, Muslims pray at five specified times each day. That prayer is made to Allah while facing toward Mecca, the Muslim holy city in Saudi Arabia. For the devout Muslim, prayer begins and ends the day and permeates all of life's undertakings.

Third, devout Muslims are required to tithe (*zakat*) a percentage of their income to the poor and needy. Depending upon where one lives, the zakat is left at the local mosque or, in a few countries, collected as a formal tax by the government. The zakat should be about 2.5 percent of one's net worth, and is used to support the poor and needy, especially in emergency situations.

Fourth, each year during the month of Ramadan (which because of the peculiarities of the Islamic calendar occurs at a different time each year on the Western calendar), Muslims engage in a fast by refraining from food, water, and sexual activity from sunrise to sunset. The ill and infirm are released from this obligation. Muslims use this time for spiritual reflection, consideration of the needs of others, and various pietistic practices, such as the reading of the Qur'an during the evening meal.

Fifth, at one time in their life, every Muslim attempts to make a pilgrimage to Mecca, the *hajj*, during Dhul Hijjah (the month for hajj). The object of the pilgrimage is the Ka'bah, "the House of God," which, according to the Qur'an, was built by Abraham (the same character whose activities were described in Genesis in the Jewish Bible).

Every year more than one million Muslim pilgrims make their way to Mecca. Only Muslims can enter the holiest of Muslim cities, and many report this as the most significant religious experience of their lives. Pilgrims come to Saudi Arabia by various means and walk the last distance to Mecca.

THE DEVELOPING COMMUNITY. The idea of submission to Allah as a basic maxim of Muslim life has led to a concentration on obedience to the law (*shariah*) as a means of embodying such submission. Fulfilling one's obligations are manifest in the adoption of the five pillars into one's life, and in the desire to propagate Islam worldwide (*dawah*) and in striving (*jihad*) in the cause of Islam. The efforts to spread Islam led to its rapid rise and, over several centuries, the establishment of Muslim-led governments in countries from Indonesia to Morocco.

From its home base in Saudi Arabia, Islam spread initially to Syria, Iraq, Jordan, and Egypt. These countries became the core lands of a new Arab religious culture. Subsequent expansion carried it west across North Africa into Spain, northward into Turkey, south along the eastern coast of Africa, and east into India and Central Asia. Further growth carried the faith into China and Southeast Asia, Indonesia being the most populous Muslim country as the twenty-first century begins. The movement into Europe in the fifteenth century was finally blocked at Vienna in 1521.

As Islam spread, it divided into various schools of thought around the interpretation of the law. Four commentators on the law would emerge as founders of major schools of interpretation—Abu Hanifah (699–767), Malik ibn Anas al-Asbahi (713–795), Muhammad ibn Idris al-Shafii (767–820), and Ahmad ibn Hanbal (780–855). These schools all agreed on basics, those items clearly taught and implied in the Qur'an and Hadith, but varied on larger issues in philosophy and secondary issues in law. Abu Hanifah, for example, suggested the use of analogical reasoning as a basic tool for reaching decisions, while Ahmad ibn Hanbal rejected such an approach. The variant schools had their greatest differences on matters of inheritance and the format of activities at the local mosque.

The Hanifite school became dominant in the Ottoman Empire that ruled over the largest block of Arab Muslims. The Malikite school is dominant in North and West Africa, and the Shafiite school is strongest in India and eastward to Indonesia. The Hanbalite school, the most conservative, dominates in Saudi Arabia and several adjacent countries. Mosques of these several schools of the dominant Sunni Islam often are found in close proximity and each have recognized the validity of the other.

However, within orthodox Islam, a major schism occurred in the seventh century among the followers of Ali, the fourth caliph of Islam and the son-in-law of Muhammad. Ali assumed the role of caliph, the spiritual and temporal ruler of Islam, in 656. He moved his capital to Kufa in present-day Iraq. While he was in Kufa, leadership in the Muslim community was focused there. But upon his death in 661, only five years later, political power shifted back to Syria, a development that the Iraqis disliked. Their political goals found religious expression in a new doctrine—the exclusive right of the house of Ali to the caliphate. In forming this doctrine, the house of Ali had to repudiate the first three caliphs: Abu Bakr, Omar, and Othman, three revered companions of Muhammad. The Arabs who held this doctrine are called *Shi'a* and are distinguished from the main body of orthodox or Sunni Muslims.

Shi'a Muslims recognize the leadership of twelve imams who descended from Ali through his two sons, al-Husayn and al-Hasan. These twelve leaders did not have an easy time and few died a natural death. In 878 the twelfth imam disappeared before his death. Rather than naming a new caliph, he became remembered as the hidden imam destined to return at the end of the age to usher in an era of true Islam. In contemporary Shi'a Islam, the highest spiritual leaders are known as *ayatollahs*, a title most famously connected to the Grand Ayatollah Ruhollah Musavi Khomeini (c. 1902–1989), who led Iran after the exile of the shah in 1979.

As the Shi'a community has spread and suffered its ups and down, a number of Shi'a subgroups have arisen. A set of them accept only seven of the twelve imams. They saw the lineage of the imam passing through Ismail al-Mubarakhad (d. 760), the son of the sixth imam, who died before his father. They are today known as Ismailis, the largest group of which is led by the Aga Khan, an honorific title. Prince Karim al-Hussaini became the leader of the Ismailis on July 11, 1957.

THE ISLAMIST MOVEMENT. The twentieth century has seen the rise of a new form of Islam, generally referred to as the movement but called *Islamic fundamentalism* by many in the West. This movement began as a reaction to the end of the Ottoman Empire in the years after World War II (1939–1945). For many, the center of the Muslim world had been the Arab Empire established in the decades following Muhammad's death, the lineage of which had been assumed by the Ottoman rulers in the Middle Ages. The final fall of the empire meant the loss of an Islamic theocracy and the necessity for all Muslims to face the realities of secularization and the dominance of modern nation states.

Fundamentalist Muslims often trace their modern ideological roots to the Wahhabi movement founded by Mohammad ibn Abd-al-Wahhab (c. 1703–1791), a reformer who assailed any Islamic practice not rooted clearly in the Qur'an and Hadith. His movement found a response among the more conservative Hanbalite Muslims of the Arabian Peninsula and long-lasting support from the Saud family that in the early twentieth century established the modern state of Saudi Arabia.

Militant Muslims also look to the Muslim Brotherhood and its founder al-Imam Hassan al-Banna (1906–1949) for ideological roots. Al-Banna advocated a revival of true Islam through Quranic emphasis and the development of social programs rooted in the Qur'an's call for justice. By the time of al-Banna's death at the hands of an assassin in 1949, his

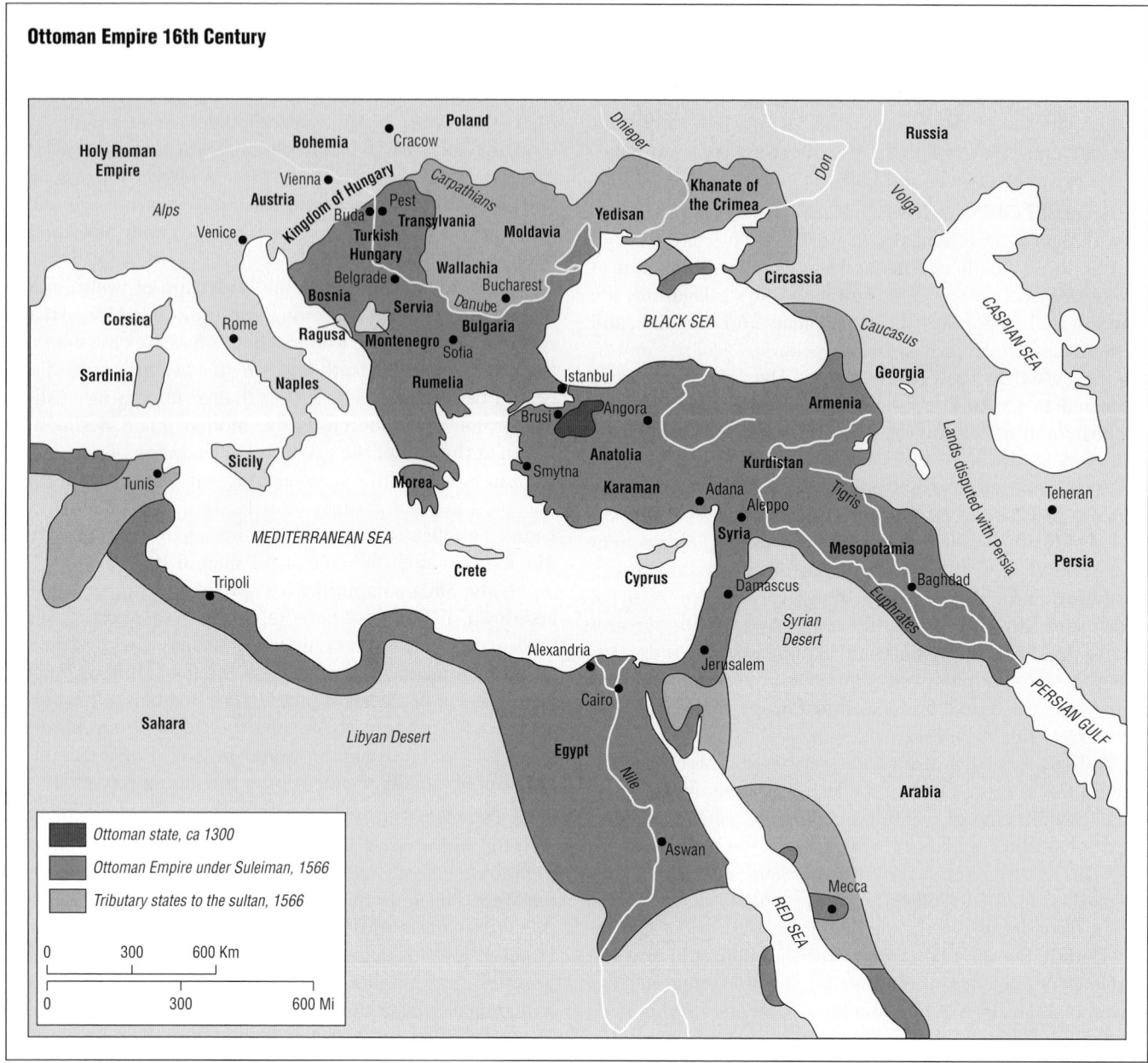

Ottoman Empire 16th Century

Legend:
- Ottoman state, ca 1300
- Ottoman Empire under Suleiman, 1566
- Tributary states to the sultan, 1566

ideas had found their way to India, where one of the most impressive of the modern Islamic theorists, Sayyid Abul A'la Mawdudi (1903–1979) would arise. Operating in the context of Indian independence and the separation of Pakistan as a Muslim nation, Mawdudi developed a broadly based program for the revival of Islam. In 1941 he founded the Jamaat-e-Islami to launch his program, which has, if falling far short of reforming Pakistan, brought many into a more devoted relationship with their faith.

Mawdudi's thought formed the basis of the ideas of al-Banna's intellectual successor, Sayyid Qutb (1906–1966). Qutb, having rejected a decadent American society and finding himself caught up in the secular world of Egyptian ruler Gamal Nasser (1918–1970), developed his own program to return his homeland to a truly Islamic state. He called for a revolutionary vanguard to rise up and take over the govern-

ment. His mature thought is given in his book, *Milestones (Ma'alim fi al-tariq)*. Qutb's radicalism earned him imprisonment in 1954 and execution on August 29, 1966.

During the Qutb years, the Muslim Brotherhood ideals would spread through the Middle East. In the changing scene of the Middle East, the use of violence would be among the most hotly debated of questions. Also, building on Qutb, many would ask about the role of the West in the falling away from Islam. Ruminations would lead in 1980s to the thought of Abd al-Salam Faraq (d. 1982), who redefined the nature of Islamic warfare. He suggested that the whole of the West was responsible for making cultural warfare on the Muslim world, and hence all of the West's citizens were legitimately subject to retaliatory action. Faraq's brief but significant pamphlet, "The Neglected Duty" (1980), laid the groundwork for subsequent terrorist activity against civilian populations that has become so much a part of one wing of the Islamist movement. It would lead directly to the rationale justifying the actions of Osama bin Laden (b. 1957) against the United States.

While acted upon by only a tiny minority of Muslims, the idea of bringing violence to civilian populations who support certain governments has had a dramatic effect in perpetuating the crisis in Palestine and Israel and in focusing attention on the United States and its European allies as enemies of Muslims. The actions of bin Laden's group, Al Qaeda, in attacking America facilities overseas and then on September 11, 2001—the bombing of the World Trade Center and the Pentagon—have altered the development of the Muslim world internationally, and the role of Islam in American society.

MUSLIMS IN AMERICA. There is probably no group whose presence in American history has been as well hidden as that of the Muslims. Like many minority groups, the Muslims appeared in the New World in the days of the colonies. Istfan the Arab was a guide to Franciscan explorer Marcos de Niya in Arizona in 1539. Nosereddine, an Egyptian, settled in the Catskills of New York in the 1500s and was burned at the stake for murdering an Indian princess.

In the seventeenth century, the possibility of Muslims settling in America was noted by Roger Williams (c. 1603–1683), founder of Rhode Island, who sought to create a colony that welcomed "even the Turks" and their unconventional (by Christian standards) worship. A number of Muslims did arrive in America in the eighteenth and early nineteenth centuries, but they did not come of their own accord. They were slaves captured from among the West African tribes that had converted to Islam. Once in America, however, their religion was as little welcomed as that of other Africans, and suffered the same destruction. The first Arab Muslims to arrive in America as the beginnings of the present-day Arab Muslim community came in the nineteenth century. One of the first of these Arab immigrants became a folk hero. His name was Haj Ali, and he assisted the U.S. Army with their experiments with breeding camels in the Arizona desert in 1850s. He is remembered today under his corrupted name, Hi Jolly:

Hi Jolly was a camel driver, long time ago.
He followed Mr. Blaine a way out West.
He didn't mind the burning sand,
In that God forsaken land,
But he didn't mind the pretty girls the best.
Hi Jolly! Hey Jolly!
Twenty miles today, by golly.
Twenty more before the morning light.
Hi Jolly, Hey, I
Gotta be on my way
I told my gal I'd be home Sunday night.

As early as the 1860s, Syrians and Lebanese, fleeing the invading Turks, came to the United States. But the first serious attempts to establish Islam in America followed the conversion of Muhammad Alexander Russell Webb (1846–1916) in 1888. Webb was the American consul in Manila at the time of his conversion, but he returned to New York in 1892. The following year, he opened the Oriental Publishing Company and began a periodical, *The Moslem World,* of which he was editor. He also wrote a number of booklets. In 1893 he was the only defender of the Islamic faith to be presented at the World's Parliament of Religions at Chicago.

Contemporaneous to Webb's activities was the beginning of large-scale immigration from the eastern Mediterranean—Syria, Lebanon, Iran, India, Turkey, and other predominantly Muslim countries. These immigrants fanned out across the United States and into the Upper Midwest. Three thousand Polish Muslims and a small community of Circassian (Russian) Muslims also settled in New York. The American Muslim community was distinguished by two characteristics: it was heavily male in population and extremely clannish. National and subnational communities formed in northern urban centers, particularly Detroit. Little effort either to keep records or to reach out toward non-Muslim neighbors was made.

Early organization attempts were made wherever large Muslim population centers developed, though the first mosque (after the one opened by Webb in New York City) was built in rural Ross, North Dakota. A second mosque appeared in Highland Park, Michigan (a Detroit suburb), in 1919, and within a few years centers were operating in Michigan City (Indiana), Chicago, Toledo, Cedar Rapids, Milwaukee, Akron, Philadelphia, and Baltimore. Within communities, divisions developed along national lines. About this time, with the arrival of Shakh al-Hajj Daoud Ahmad (1891–1980) from Bermuda in 1920, the story of African-American Muslims became intertwined with that of the Middle Eastern immigrants.

A major event in the American Muslim community was the dedication in 1957 of the Islamic Center in Washington, D.C. Built in part with money from 15 sponsoring countries with the idea of serving the diplomatic community, it also has served as a symbolic point of unity for the diverse Islamic community.

Through the 1970s and 1980s, the Muslim community, long confined to a few ethnic pockets, underwent a dramatic expansion. Spearheading the faith's rapidly expanding presence in the United States was large-scale immigration from predominantly Islamic countries (from Pakistan and Iran to Egypt and Turkey, with the Pakistani and Indian Muslims constituting a particularly large percentage of the American Muslim community). Seemingly overnight, mosques were springing up in every major urban area, with a strong concentration in the Midwest, southern California, and the New York metropolitan area. Assisting in this spectacular growth has been the discovery of Islam by many African Americans. While the primary attraction to Islam came in what the mainstream of the community considers a heretical form of the faith (that preached by the old Nation of Islam, with its intense racial teachings), as the Nation moved toward adoption of orthodox Islamic teachings, most of the members moved into the orthodox Muslim camp.

Estimates of the size of the Islamic community in America vary widely. On the low end of the scale, some suggest less than one million. They argue that even though many have moved to America from Muslim countries, a large percentage of these immigrants were Christians seeking a more hospitable religious climate. On the other end, some argue that Islam is already the size of the American Jewish community, five to seven million, and ready to outnumber them in the near future.

Given the significant Muslim presence in America, it was not surprising that several organizations arose to speak for the community on national issues. Most prominent of these are the American Muslim Council, the Council on Islamic American Relations, and the Islamic Circle of North America.

The importance of such groups was vividly demonstrated when they were called to respond to the events of September 11. They were able to mobilize Muslims nationwide to present the case for the majority perspective among American Muslims that decried the violent attacks and mourned the deaths of Muslims and others killed that day. They were also effective in gaining airtime on television and radio to present the basic teachings of Islam to a nation still largely ignorant of the tradition. They were able quickly to stem the reactionary tide of feeling that threatened to target American Muslims. In this endeavor, they found support from the national government, including the White House.

AFRICAN-AMERICAN MUSLIMS. No one knows when the first black Muslim came to America, but it is well known that Africans south of the Sahara had developed Islamic centers prior to the time of the slave trade, and that Muslims were among the first slaves in the United States. Morroe Berger notes that Muslim slaves tended to be viewed as superior by both themselves and other slaves; they were often educated, and they resisted acculturation and assimilation, thus retaining their faith longer.

Timothy Dwight (1752–1817), while in New York, recorded a visit with a slave from the South who told him stories of other Muslims. William B. Hodgson (1801–1871), an ethnologist, mentions five Muslim slaves in an 1852 work. One, Bul-Ali, was a slave driver on a Sapelo Island, Georgia, plantation. C. C. Jones (1804–1863), a missionary who authored *The Religious Instruction of the Negroes in the United States*, noted that Muslim slaves, under pressure from Christianizing forces, would try accommodation to the new faith by equating God with Allah and Jesus with Muhammad. Berger concluded that, while no definite connection can be made between twentieth-century black Muslims and those who might have survived the slave era, nevertheless, "It is quite possible that some of the various American Muslim groups of the past half century or so had their roots in these vestiges, that the tradition was handed down in a weak chain from generation to generation" (Berger, "The Black Muslims," 1964 , pp. 49–64).

A new era for Islam within the African-American community began in 1913 when Noble Drew Ali (born Timothy Drew, 1886–1929) initiated the Moorish Science Temple of America. Ali's thought was, to say the least, a very different version of what orthodox Muslims might consider Islam. For example, he published a Qur'an that he had put together from American occult literature, rather than issuing either a translated or edited version of the Muslims' Qur'an. Ali died in 1929 and while his movement continued, the thrust into the black community he began was picked up by a new group, the Nation of Islam. Also in the 1920s, the Ahmadiyya Muslims, a movement that originated in India, began a mission to proselytize Americans in 1921. As it turned out, their major successes were also in the African-American community, and the North American branch of the movement, through no prior intention, became largely a black movement.

Black Muslims are to be partly understood in terms of Black Nationalism, a movement to locate liberation from white oppression in the ownership and control of land, specifically a land that black people could call their own. Sometimes that aspiration was focused upon Africa, as expressed, for example, in the Universal Negro Improvement Association, the organization founded by Marcus Garvey (1887–1940) early in the twentieth century. It advocated a turn toward Ethiopia (symbolic of all of Africa) as a national homeland through which African Americans could shape their identity. The Nation of Islam took the idea even further and called for the establishment of a black nation in North America to be carved out of several southern states.

By 1960, Islam had spread through the black community, primarily because of the development of the Nation of Islam. During the 1960s and 1970s, the African-American Muslim community went through a disruptive and even violent era. This is noted most significantly in the assassination of Malcolm X (born Malcolm Little, 1925–1965). Following the death of Elijah Muhammad (1897–1975), longtime leader of the Nation of Islam in 1975, things began to change. Wallace D. Muhammad, Elijah Muhammad's son and successor, began to lead the movement into the orthodox Muslim camp. While losing some support, such as that of Louis Farrakhan, he was able to take most of the movement with him, and today many centers have been welcomed and integrated into the larger Islamic community.

SUFISM. The word *Sufism* is used to describe a wide variety of mystical and disciplined orders found throughout the Islamic world. No one knows the origin of the term, and several explanations vie for acceptance. Some relate the term to *suf*, or wool, denotative of the wool garments worn by some Sufis. Others see a connection to the Hebrew *en sof*, the name for the infinite divine in Jewish mysticism. Still others derive it from *safa*, the Arabic word for purity, or from *sophia*, the Greek word for wisdom.

Whatever the origin of their name, the Sufis appear to have developed from the ascetic pietism evident from the very first generation of the followers of Muhammad. From these early ascetics arose the *gussas* or storytellers, popular preachers of the Qur'an, and from the storytellers came the idea of the *madhi*, the divinely guided one who will help bring the ultimate victory of Islam by means of a cosmic event. In the eighth century, the ascetic movement began to take on a mystical aspect, and true Sufism emerged.

Once launched, Sufism became a popular religious movement that developed its own forms and peculiarities. The ecstatic experience offered the immediate knowledge of God, as compared to the secondhand knowledge of the theologians, who were replaced by the Sufi leaders, the *shaikhs*. These official teachers gained their position through charismatic authority. Outstanding shaikhs became founders of new schools of Sufism and were often regarded as saints after they died. Also, in contradistinction to the Qur'an, which looks down upon the unmarried state, many Sufi leaders practiced celibacy.

Sufism has often been an eclectic movement, drawing on Christian and Gnostic elements. A pantheistic theology sometimes emerged in various Sufi masters. More popular was a nontheological approach that accepted orthodoxy but included mysticism. The Sufi emphasis on God's love, epitomized in the poems of Rumi (1207–1273), is the best antidote to theories that Islam makes no room for confidence in God's care.

Sufism was in a constant battle for existence with the ruling orthodox religious leaders until the twelfth century. The change from persecution to acceptance is possibly attributable to the career of al-Ghazali (b. 1111), a man of marked intellectual acumen and religious insight. Beginning with a search for ultimate reality, he pursued a course through theology and philosophy and ended with the personal experience of God and Sufi mysticism. Al-Ghazali's greatest contribution seems to have been the creation of a religious synthesis through which Sufism could be accepted in an orthodox system, and orthodoxy could become an acceptable framework for the Sufis.

The changes that came with al-Ghazali allowed the development of the Sufi schools. He promoted the idea that disciples should move in close association to their shaikh, who then began to assume a status like that of a Hindu guru. Brotherhoods built around a shaikh grew, and initiation ceremonies were adopted. Initiates would often leave to found affiliated groups. A popular school thus could spread (and on occasion did) throughout the Islamic world. When the leader died, an initiate would inherit the former leader's role and prayer rug.

According to Sufi tradition, twelve orders were founded prior to the establishment of the Ottoman Empire. The first was the Uwaisi, founded by Uwais following a vision of the angel Gabriel in 659, less than forty years after the hegira. Uwais pulled all of his teeth out in memory of Muhammad, who lost two teeth in a battle. His imposition of that same sacrifice for members insured that the Uwaisi remained small in size. The remaining eleven schools or orders, most of which have taken the name of their founder, are: Illwani, Adhani, Sustami, Qadiri, Rifai, Nurbakhshi, Suharwardi, Qubrawi, Shazili, Mavlana, and Badawi. (Spelling of the names of the various Sufi orders varies from author to author as each tries

Number of Muslim Congregations by State (2000)

Rank	State	Value
1	California	163
2	New York	144
3	Texas	91
4	Illinois	79
5	New Jersey	68
6	Pennsylvania	57
7	Michigan	51
8	Ohio	41
9	Georgia	39
10	Florida	37
11	Maryland	31
12	North Carolina	29
13	Virginia	27
14	Massachusetts	25
15	Louisiana	23
16	Alabama	20
17	Connecticut	20
18	Indiana	20
19	Washington	18
20	Tennessee	16
21	Missouri	15
22	South Carolina	15
23	Wisconsin	14
24	Mississippi	14
25	Arizona	12
26	Colorado	12
27	Minnesota	11
28	Kentucky	10
29	Oklahoma	10
30	Kansas	9
31	Iowa	9
32	Oregon	7
33	New Mexico	7
34	Arkansas	6
35	Nebraska	5
36	North Dakota	4
37	Utah	4
38	West Virginia	4
39	Alaska	3
40	Rhode Island	3
41	Montana	3
42	Nevada	3
43	Delaware	3
44	Wyoming	2
45	Idaho	2
46	New Hampshire	2
47	Maine	2
48	Hawaii	1
49	South Dakota	1
50	Vermont	1

Adapted from Association of Religion Data Archives

to render the sound of the name into English. No standard spellings have yet been developed.)

Since the establishment of the Ottoman Empire and the subsequent spread of Islam from Indonesia to Albania, the number of orders has grown immensely and no catalog exists (though detailed lists for some countries do exist). The main orders in India at present are the Chishti, the Qadiri, the Suharwardi, and the Naqshbandi, two of which are of later origin. Other orders are prominent in other countries. Orders also have split into suborders. For example, both the Nizami and Sabiri suborders of the Chishti Order have a following in the United States, in the Chishti Order in America and the Sufi Order (headed by Pir Vilayat Khan [1916–2004]) respectively.

In their homeland, members of orders can frequently be distinguished by the peculiar clothes they wear. Apparel will vary in color and style, especially the headgear. Several of the orders have become famous for their peculiar ritual formats, which include the whirling dances of the Jerrahi and the howling of the Rifai.

The first Sufi group to become visible in America was the Sufi Order, founded in the early twentieth century by Hazrat Inayet Khan (1882–1927). During the 1970s, representatives of many Sufi groups migrated to the United States and set up their separate organizations. Also, since the end of World War II, the Middle East, like India, has become the site for pilgrimages by spiritual seekers looking for mystic teachers. Several who found their guru in a Sufi shaikh returned to the United States to found American branches of their shaikh's orders.

ZOROASTRIANISM.
Zoroaster (or Zarathustra) was a Persian prophet and religious teacher of the seventh century B.C.E. who worked a monotheistic revolution in his native land. According to tradition, Zoroaster, when he was about 30 years of age, was admitted into the presence of Ahura Mazda, the supreme being, and was personally instructed in the doctrines of the new faith. Over the next few years, he received visions of the six archangels, the chief attendants and agents of Mazda. After 11 years of frustrating work, he was able to convert Vishtapa (Hystaspes), one of the rulers of Iran, who aided Zoroaster in spreading the new faith with two holy wars.

Zoroaster's faith was monotheistic. Mazda is the all-wise creator and absolute sovereign. Mazda demands righteousness and promises to help those who follow truthfulness and justice and foster agriculture. The righteous will attain heaven. In the oldest Zoroastrian texts, Angra Mainyu appears as an evil spirit, but only in later years was he to arise as the evil counterpart of Mazda, thus transforming Zoroastrianism into a thoroughgoing dualism. The main representatives of this dualistic Zoroastrianism are the Parsees, many of whom have migrated to North America in recent decades.

BAHA'I WORLD FAITH.
Among the newest of the several religious traditions to grow beyond the country of its founding into an international movement, the Baha'i World Faith originated in Persia (now Iran) in the mid-nineteenth century. Baha'is generally date their founding to the work of Siyyad Ali Muhammad of Shiraz (1819–1850), a prophet who declared himself the Bab, that is, the Gate, through whom people would know about the advent of another messenger of God. His proclamations were made within the context of Islamic expectation of the *madhi*, the successor of the previous messenger, Muhammad, the founder of Islam. The Bab began his prophetic work in 1844, but after gaining a large following he encountered the opposition of the country's Muslim leaders. He was eventually imprisoned by the shah and, in 1850, executed.

Among the Bab's followers was Mirza Husayn-Ali (1817–1892). During the time of the Bab's imprisonment, at a conference of his followers, he assumed the title "Baha," and emerged as one of the principal figures in the Babi community. In 1852 Jinab-i-Baha, as he was then called, was imprisoned in another wave of anti-Babi persecution. While languishing in a Tehran jail, he received the first intimations that he was, in fact, the one of whom the Bab spoke, "Him Whom God shall make manifest." Soon released from prison, he gradually assumed the prime leadership role among the Babis. Finally, in 1863, to a small group of family and friends, he announced his conviction that he was the promised one foretold by the Bab.

Jinab-i-Baha's initial proclamation came just as a large segment of the Babi community was beginning an exile, first in Constantinople and then in Adrianople (now Edirne, Turkey). In Adrianople, he openly proclaimed his new role and new name, Baha'u'llah, "the Glory of God," through a series of letters, called tablets, sent to many world rulers and political leaders.

In 1868 Baha'u'llah and his family were further banished to Akka (now Acre) in Palestine, where he lived the remainder of his life, first at a penal colony and from 1879 in a residence in the city. During this period, he wrote his most important book, the *Kitab-i-Agdas* (Most Holy Book), the book of laws for Baha'is, as well as numerous shorter works, all now considered to have the authority of scripture.

Baha'u'llah was succeeded by his son, Abbas Effendi (1844–1921), who took the name Abdu'l-Baha, "the Slave of Baha." A devoted follower of his father even before the initial proclamation of his role in 1863, he followed Baha'u'llah into exile and wrote the first history of the movement in 1886. He assumed control of the movement under the authority of his father's will.

As the center of the covenant, Abdu'l-Baha directed the international spread of the movement. Following his confinement from 1901 to 1908 and the discontinuance of travel restrictions in 1911, he made the first of several foreign tours. A world tour the following year brought him to the United States, where he dedicated the grounds for the Baha'i temple in Wilmette, Illinois. Returning to Palestine just before World War I (1914–1918), he settled in Haifa, where Turkish authorities again confined him until the British took control.

As the interpreter of Baha'u'llah, Abdu'l-Baha summarized the major themes of the new faith revealed by his father. He emphasized its universal character: that all religions were essentially one and that all the prophets of God, the Great Manifestations, taught the same religion. He expounded the eleven principles of the Baha'i faith: (1) the independent investigation of truth; (2) the oneness of the human race; (3) that religion should be the cause of love and affection (not hate); (4) the conformity of religion to science and reason; (5) the abolition of religious, racial, political, and patriotic prejudice; (6) the equal opportunity to the means of existence; (7) the equality of persons before the law; (8) universal peace; (9) the noninterference of religion in politics; (10) the equality of the sexes; and (11) the power of the Holy Spirit as the means of spiritual development. He also advocated a universal language and universal compulsory education.

Abdu'l-Baha was succeeded by his nephew Shoghi Effendi (1896–1957), who did much to develop the international organization and administration of the faith. Under Shoghi Effendi, the Baha'is established a following on every continent. Since his death, a more collective form of leadership has emerged.

BAHA'IS IN AMERICA. The Baha'i faith was brought to America in 1892 by a Lebanese convert, Ibrahim Kheiralla (1849–1929). A former businessman, Kheiralla proved to be an energetic teacher and soon gathered groups of eager students. The first Baha'i groups were formed in Chicago, New York, Boston, and Kenosha, Wisconsin.

During the 1890s, there were almost no English translations of the writings of Baha'u'llah in print. In the absence of published volumes, Kheiralla taught a full course on the Baha'i faith, but presented what Baha'is soon discerned was a highly distorted version influenced by Kheiralla's occult speculations. Eventually, Kheiralla published his peculiar teachings in several books.

Kheiralla's deviations from Baha'i teachings reached a crisis during a pilgrimage by American Baha'is to meet Abdu'l-Baha during the winter of 1898 to 1899. Abdu'l-Baha's discovery of the content of Kheiralla teachings led to a heated argument and to Abdu'l-Baha's rejection of Kheiralla's speculative presentation of the faith. Kheiralla in turn rejected Abdu'l-Baha and, continuing in his own presentation of the faith, took supporters from the Chicago and Kenosha Baha'i groups and established a rival organization. The Behaists, as Kheiralla termed his followers, existed for several decades, but then disbanded. Kheiralla is now remembered as a covenant breaker, a term applied to individuals who attempt to establish rival Baha'i organizations.

In addition to the majority Haifa/Wilmette group, rival Baha'i groups include: (1) the Orthodox Baha'i Faith, following Joel B. Marangella: (2) Bahais Under Provisions of the Covenant (Leland Jensen); (3) Bahais Under Provisions of the Covenant (Neal Chase); (4) Tarbiyat Bahá'i Community (Rex King group); (5) Bahá'i Under the Living Guardianship (Donald Harvey as the third guardian and Jacques Soghomonian as the fourth guardian); and (6) the Reform Bahai movement, under the leadership of Frederick Glaysher.

BAHA'IS IN CANADA. Baha'ism in Canada began in 1898 when Gus Magee, a Chicago newspaperman who had interviewed an early Baha'i believer, passed on what he had learned to a niece who lived in London, Ontario. The niece told her mother, who traveled to Chicago with her two daughters for lessons in faith. The faith began in Quebec in 1902 when May Bolles (1870–1940), who had married Canadian architect William Sutherland Maxwell (1874–1952), moved to Montreal. The Maxwell home became the center of Baha'i activities, which received a boost in 1912 when Baha'u'llah

came to Montreal. Later, Shoghi Effendi, the guardian of the faith, married Mary Maxwell (1910–2000), their daughter.

Originally, the Baha'i work in Canada was incorporated under the care of the Spiritual Assembly, which was headquartered in the United States. It grew slowly until the 1930s, but in 1937 a seven-year plan was inaugurated that led to the formation of at least one Baha'i local assembly in every state and province of the country. In 1949 the work in Canada had grown to the point that it was set apart from the United States, and its own Spiritual Assembly was incorporated.

SOURCES

Islam: General Sources

The study of Islam in America has grown primarily in the religious studies departments of various universities, but it has been given focus in *The Muslim World*, a quarterly journal published by the Duncan Black Macdonald Center for the Study of Islam and Christian/Muslim Relations, c/o Hartford Seminary, 77 Sherman St., Hartford, CT 06105. Those seeking information on the American Muslim community may contact the American Muslim Council, 121 New York Ave. NW, Ste. 525, Washington, DC 20005.

Coulson, Noel J. *A History of Islamic Law.* Edinburgh, U.K.: Edinburgh University Press, 1964. 264 pp.

Esposito, John L. *Islam and Politics.* 4th ed. Syracuse, NY: Syracuse University Press, 1998. 393 pp.

———. *Islam: The Straight Path.* Rev. 3rd ed. Oxford: Oxford University Press, 2005. 304 pp.

Hallaq, Wael B. *A History of Islamic Legal Theories: An Introduction to Sunni Usul al-Fiqh.* New York: Cambridge University Press, 1997. 294 pp.

Küng, Hans. *Islam: Past, Present, and Future.* Trans. John Bowdon. New York: Continuum, 2007. 767 pp.

Lewis, Bernard. *Islam and the West.* Oxford: Oxford University Press, 1993. 217 pp.

Maududi, Sayyid Abul Ala. *Towards Understanding Islam.* Trans. Khurshid Ahmad. 14th ed. Lahore, Pakistan: Idara Tarjuman-Ul-Quran, 1974. 179 pp.

Rahman, Fazlur. *Islam.* 2nd ed. Garden City, NY: Doubleday, 1979.

Rippin, Andrew. *Muslims: Their Religious Beliefs and Practices.* 3rd ed. London: Routledge, 2005. 371 pp.

Schulze, Reinhard. *A Modern History of the Islamic World.* New York: New York University Press, 2000. 384 pp.

Watt, W. Montgomery. *Muhammad: Prophet and Statesman.* Oxford: Oxford University Press, 1961.

———. *The Majesty That Was Islam: The Islamic World, 661–1100.* New York: Praeger, 1974. 276 pp.

Muslims in America

Barrett, Paul M. *American Islam: The Struggle for the Soul of a Religion.* New York: Farrar, Straus and Giroux, 2007. 304 pp.

Ba-Yunus, Ilyas, and M. Moin Siddique. *A Report on Muslim Population in the United States of America.* New York: Center for American Muslim Research, 1998.

Elkholy, Abdo A. *The Arab Moslems in the United States: Religion and Assimilation.* New Haven, CT: College and University Press, 1966. 176 pp.

Haddad, Yvonne Yazbeck, ed. *The Muslims of America.* New York: Oxford University Press, 1991. 249 pp.

Haddad, Yvonne Yazbeck, and Adair T. Lummis. *Islamic Values in the United States: A Comparative Study.* New York: Oxford University Press, 1987. 196 pp.

Haque, Amber, ed. *Muslims and Islamization in North America: Problems and Prospects.* Beltsville, MD: Amana, 1999. 492 pp.

Khalidi, Omar, ed. *Indian Muslims in North America.* Watertown, MA: South Asia Press, 1989. 99 pp.

Koszegi, Michael A., and J. Gordon Melton. *Islam in North America: A Sourcebook.* New York: Garland, 1992. 414 pp.

Metcalf, Barbara Daly, ed. *Making Muslim Space in North American and Europe.* Berkeley: University of California Press, 1996. 264 pp.

Oren, Michael B. *Power, Faith, and Fantasy: America in the Middle East, 1776 to the Present.* New York: Norton, 2007. 778 pp.

Richardson, E. Allen. *Islamic Cultures in North America: Patterns of Belief and Devotion of Muslims from Asian Countries in the United States and Canada.* New York: Pilgrim Press, 1981. 64 pp.

Smith, Jane I. *Islam in America.* New York: Columbia University Press, 2000. 251 pp.

Waugh, Earle H., Baha Abu-Laban, and Regula B. Qureshi, eds. *The Muslim Community in North America.* Edmonton, AB: University of Alberta Press, 1983. 316 pp.

Williams, Raymond Brady. *Religions of Immigrants from India and Pakistan: New Threads in the American Tapestry.* Cambridge, U.K.: Cambridge University Press, 1988. 326 pp.

Shi'a Muslims

Fischer, Michael M. S., and Mehdi Abedi. *Debating Muslims: Cultural Dialogues in Postmodernity and Tradition.* Madison: University of Wisconsin Press, 1990. 564 pp.

Haddad, Yvonne. *Islamic Values in the United States: A Comparative Study.* New York: Oxford University Press, 1987. 196 pp.

Khomeini, Ruhollah. *Islamic Government.* New York: Manor Books, 1979. 154 pp.

Lalljee, Yousuf N. *Know Your Islam.* 6th ed. Elmhurst, NY: Tahrike Tarsile Qur'an, 2003. 255 pp.

Nasr, Vali. *The Shia Revival: How Conflicts within Islam Will Shape the Future.* New York: Norton, 2006. 287 pp.

Tabatabai, Allamah Sayyid Muhammad Husayn. *Shi'ite Islam.* Houston, TX: Free Islamic Literature, 1979. 253 pp.

ul-Amine, Hasan. *Shorter Islamic Shi'ite Encyclopedia.* Beirut, Lebanon: 1969. 355 pp.

Sufism

Arberry, A. J. *Sufism: An Account of the Mystics of Islam.* New York: Harper & Row, 1950. 141 pp.

Baldick, Julian. *Mystical Islam: An Introduction to Sufism.* London: Tauris, 1989. 208 pp.

Grisell, Ronald. *Sufism.* Berkeley, CA: Ross, 1983. 112 pp.

Nasr, Seyyed, ed. *Islamic Spirituality: Manifestations.* London: SCM, 1991.

Nicholson, Reynold A. *The Mystics of Islam.* New York: Schocken, 1975. 178 pp.

Rastogi, T. C. *Islamic Mysticism Sufism.* London: East-West, 1982. 126 pp.

Sedgwick, Mark. *Sufism: The Essentials.* Cairo: AUC Press, 2003.

Shah, Indries. *The Sufis.* Garden City, NY: Doubleday, 1971. 451 pp.

———. *The Diffusion of Sufi Ideas in the West: An Anthology of New Writings by and about Idries Shah.* Ed. L. Lewis. Boulder, CO: Keysign Press, 1972. 212 pp.

Shah, Sirdar Ikbal Ali. *Islamic Sufism.* New York: Weiser, 1971. 299 pp.

Subhan, John A. *Sufism: Its Saints and Shrines.* New York: Weiser, 1970. 412 pp.

Trimingham, J. Spencer. *The Sufi Orders of Islam.* London: Oxford University Press, 1971. 333 pp.

Williams, L. F. Rushbrook. *Sufi Studies: East and West.* New York: Dutton, 1974. 260 pp.

Islamicist Movement

Esposito, John, ed. *Voices of Resurgent Islam.* New York: Oxford University Press, 1983. 294 pp.

Jacquard, Roland. *In the Name of Osama bin Laden: Global Terrorism & the Bin Laden Brotherhood.* Trans. George Holoch. Durham, NC: Duke University Press, 2002. 293 pp.

Jansen, Johannes J. *The Neglected Duty: The Creed of Sadat's Assassins and Islamic Resurgence in the Middle East.* New York: Macmillan, 1986. 246 pp.

———. *The Dual Nature of Islamic Fundamentalism.* Ithaca, NY: Cornell University Press, 1996. 198 pp.

Juergenmeyer, Mark. *Terror in the Mind of God: The Global Rise of Religious Violence.* 3rd ed. Berkeley: University of California Press, 2003. 316 pp.

Mawdudi, Sayyid Abul. *A Short History of the Revivalist Movement in Islam.* Delhi: Markazi Maktaba Islami, 1972. 124 pp.

Moussallli, Ahmad S. *Radical Islamic Fundamentalism: The Ideological and Political Discourse of Sayyid Qutb.* Syracuse, NY: University of Syracuse press, 1994. 262 pp.

Qutb, Sayyid. *Milestones* (1965). Delhi, India: Markazi Maktaba Islami, 1995. (Many English-language editions are available.)

Rashid, Ahmed. *Taliban: Militant Islam, Oil, and Fundamentalism in Central Asia.* New Haven, CT: Yale University Press, 2001. 279 pp.

Wright, Lawrence. *The Looming Tower: Al-Qaeda and the Road to 9/11.* New York: Knopf, 2006. 469 pp.

Black Muslims

Austin, Allan D., ed. *African Muslims in Antebellum America: A Sourcebook.* New York: Garland, 1984. 759 pp.

Barboza, Steven. *American Jihad: Islam After Malcolm X.* New York: Doubleday, 1994. 370 pp.

Berger, Morroe. "The Black Muslims." *Horizon* 6 (January 1964): 49–64.

Craig, H. A. L. *Bilal.* London: Quartet, 1977. 158 pp.

Diouf, Sylviane A. *Servants of Allah: African Muslims Enslaved in the Americas.* New York: New York University Press, 1998. 254 pp.

Essien-Udom, E. U. *Black Nationalism.* New York: Dell, 1962. 448 pp.

Haney, Marsha Snulligan. *Islam and Protestant African-America Churches: Responses and Challenges to Religious Pluralism.* San Francisco: International Scholars Publications, 1999. 304 pp.

Lee, Martha F. *The Nation of Islam: An American Millenarian Movement.* Lewiston, NY: Mellen Press, 1988. 163 pp.

Lincoln, C. Eric. *The Black Muslims in America.* Boston: Beacon Press, 1961. 276 pp.

Mansour, Khalid Abdullah Taria Al, and Faissal Fahd Al Talal. *The Challenges of Spreading Islam in America.* San Francisco: Authors, 1980. 213 pp.

Turner, Richard Brent. *Islam in the African-American Experience.* 2nd ed. Bloomington: Indiana University Press, 2003. 312 pp.

Ahmadiyya

Ahmad, Mirza Bashiruddin Mahmud. *Ahmadiyyat or True Islam.* Washington, DC: American Fazl Mosque, 1951. 246 pp.

Dard, A. R. *Life of Ahmad: Founder of the Ahmadiyya Movement.* Lahore, Pakistan: Tabshir, 1948. 629 pp.

Hammann, Louis J. *Ahmadiyyat: An Introduction.* Washington, DC: Ahmadiyya Movement in Islam, 1985. 13 pp.

Khan, Muhammad Zafrulla. *Ahmadiyyat: The Renaissance of Islam.* Lahore, Pakistan: Tabshir, 1978. 360 pp.

Nafwi, S. Abul Hasan Ali. *Oadianism: A Critical Study.* Lucknow, India: Academy of Islamic Research and Publications, 1974. 167 pp.

Zoroastrianism

Bode, Dastur Framroze Ardeshir, and Piloo Nanavutty. *Songs of Zarathushtra.* Trans. Dastur Framroze Ardeshir Bode and Piloo Nanavutty. London: Allen & Unwin, 1952. 127 pp.

Dawson, Miles Menander. *The Ethical Religion of Zoroaster: Account of What Zoroaster Taught, as Perhaps the Very Oldest and Surely the Most Accurate Code of Ethics for Man, Accompanied by the Essentials of His Religion.* New York: AMS Press, 1969. 271 pp.

Hinnells, John R. *Zoroastrians in Britain.* Oxford: Claredon Press, 1996. 336 pp.

Kriwaczek, Paul. *In Search of Zarathustra: The First Prophet and the Ideas that Changed the World.* New York: Knopf, 2003. 248 pp.

Masani, Rustom P. *The Religion of the Good Life: Zoroastrianism.* London: Allen & Unwin, 1938. 189 pp.

Modi, Jivanji J. *The Religious Ceremonies and Customs of the Parsees.* New York: Garland 1979. 536 pp.

Baha'i Faith

The Baha'i center in Wilmette, Illinois, houses the American Baha'i Faith Archives and Library, which can be contacted for further information on the Baha'i faith. It is located at 535 Sheridan Road, Wilmette, IL 60091.

Balyuzi, H. M. *Edward Granville Browne and the Baha'i Faith.* London: George Ronald, 1970. 142 pp.

———. *'Abdu'l-Baha.* London: George Ronald, 1971. 560 pp.

Bjorling, Joel. *The Baha'i Faith: A Historical Bibliography.* New York: Garland, 1985. 168 pp.

Baha'u'llah: The King of Glory. London: George Ronald, 1980. 539 pp.

Collins, William P. *Bibliography of English-Language Works on the Babi and Baha'i Faith, 1845–1985.* Willmette, IL: Baha'i Publishing Trust, 1991. 550 pp.

Gayer, Jessyca Russell. *Baha'i Faith.* New York: Award Books, 1967. 222 pp.

Hatcher, William S., and J. Douglas Martin. *The Baha'i Faith.* San Francisco: Harper & Row, 1984. 226 pp.

Miller, William McElwee. *The Baha'i Faith: Its History and Teachings.* South Pasadena, CA: William Carey Press, 1974.

Perkins, Mary, and Philip Hainsworth. *The Baha'i Faith.* London: Ward Lock Educational, 1980. 96 pp.

Sears, William. *Release the Sun.* Wilmette, IL: Baha'i Publishing Trust, 1971. 250 pp.

———. *The Prisoner and the Kings.* Toronto ON: General Publishing, 1971. 240 pp.

Stockman, Robert S. *The Baha'i Faith in America.* Wilmette, IL: Baha'i Publishing Trust, 1985. 277 pp.

———. *The Baha'i Faith in America.* Vol. 2: *Early Expansion, 1900–1912.* London: George Ronald, 1994.

Van den Hoonaard, Will C. *The Origins of the Bahá'í Community of Canada, 1898–1948.* Waterloo, ON: Wilfrid Laurier University Press, 1996.

✺ Intrafaith Organizations

American Muslim Council (AMC)

2020 N California Ave., Chicago, IL 60657

The American Muslim Council (AMC) was founded in 1990 as a cooperative body serving the interests of the Muslim community in the United States. A nonprofit 501(c)(4) organization, its purpose, according to its Internet site, is to "provide a national structure within which American Muslims may express and act upon their shared concerns; promote, encourage and foster better understanding, in the United States, of Muslim culture, values and history; and enhance, encourage and foster the common good and general welfare of the people of the United States." The AMC has chapters in San Diego, California; Panama City, Florida; Atlanta, Georgia; and Honolulu, Hawaii. Its current national director is M. Ali Khan.

Sources:

American Muslim Council. amcnational.org.

As-Sunnah Foundation of America (ASFA)

G4417 S Saginaw St., Burton, MI 48529

The As-Sunnah Foundation of America (ASFA) was founded by a group of Muslims from various Islamic backgrounds who seek to promote the unity of Muslims. ASFA emphasizes a well-known Islamic principle: A believer may follow any school of thought (*fiqh*), and as long as she or he accepts the sunna and the shariah, she or he must be seen as living within the boundaries of the community (*ummah*) of the Prophet Muhammad. Experience has taught that the various schools of Islam have not been divisive but, in fact, have provided the basis of stability for the ummah.

ASFA has assembled a group of scholars and professors to teach, write, and translate from traditional sources of Islamic knowledge by authentic scholars of the various schools of *fiqh* and *'aqida*. The foundation has developed centers in the United States, Europe, the Middle East, South Asia, Africa, and East Asia. These offices are centers for scholarship, Islamic leadership training, and the development of Islamic character. ASFA is also connected to a number of associate and affiliate organizations specializing in Islamic scholarship. It has published several scholarly books that provide background on its beliefs. The current ASFA chairman is Shaykh Muhammad Hisham Kabbani.

Membership: Among ASFA's affiliate organizations are the al-Azhar al-Shariff, an Islamic university established in 972 C.E.; the Islamic Council of Singapore; the Idara Minhaj ul Quran, a university based in Lahore, Pakistan; Daar ul-Ehsaan, dedicated to providing vital information on Islam; the Abu Nour Insitutite of Islamic Studies; and the Institute of Arabic and Islamic Studies.

Educational Facilities:

Idara Minhaj ul Quran, Lahore, Pakistan; Al-azhar al-Shariff, Cairo, Egypt.

Sources:

As-Sunah Foundation of America Homepage. www.sunnah.org.

Hermansen, Marcia K. "Hybrid Identity Formations in Muslim America: The Case of American Sufi Movements." *Muslim World* 90 no. 1–2 (Spring 2000): 158–197.

Kabbani, Muhammad Hisham. *The Approach of Armageddon? An Islamic Perspective.* Washington, D.C.: Islamic Supreme Council of America, 2003.

Council of Islamic Organizations of America

676 St. Marks Ave., Brooklyn, NY 11216-3605

The Council of Islamic Organizations of America is a coordinating organization serving the many Muslim groups in the United States. It was founded in Saudi Arabia in 1973 by the representatives of different mosques who were in attendance at the Jeddah Unification meeting and was chartered in Washington, D.C., a short time later.

The council's main purpose is the propagation of Sunni Islam (as opposed to the Shi'a Islam that dominates in Iran and Iraq). It accepts the interpretation of Islam coming from Saudi Arabia. The council has a program of assistance for communities desiring to erect a mosque and provides financial assistance for activities that build and nurture the Muslim community as a whole (schools, summer camps, medical centers, etc.).

Membership: Members include a number of mosques across the United States and several cooperative associations such as the Muslim Students Association, the Federation of Islamic Associations, and the Islamic Society of North America.

Council of Muslim Communities of Canada (CMCC)

PO Box 2605, Sta. D, Ottawa, ON, Canada K1P 5W7

The Council of Muslim Communities of Canada (CMCC) was founded in 1971 by Dr. Ahmet Fuad Sahin to serve as a coordinating body for the numerous Canadian mosques established since the 1950s. The CMCC also works to improve relations between Muslims and their non-Muslim neighbors and to develop programs to pass Islam on to the second- and third-generation children of immigrants. To these ends, it published *The Quran, The Holy Book of God* (1982) and *My Book of Islam* in 1984, both for children, as well as a brochure, *The Question of Palestine*. The CMCC is affiliated with the Council of Islamic Organizations of America. In 1985 it established the International Development and Relief Foundation (IDRF) to help the destitute worldwide, regardless of race, religion, or color. The Council's current president is Hanny Hassan; the vice president is Aziz Khaki.

Membership: Not reported.

Periodicals: *Canada-Islam*.

International Association of Sufism (IAS)

14 Commerical Blvd., Ste. 101, Novato, CA 94949

The International Association of Sufism (IAS), founded in 1983 by Seyedeh Nahid Angha and Shah Nazar Seyed Ali Kianfar, operates as a general advocacy organization for Sufism. It seeks to introduce the various aspects of Sufism to the public; communicate the interrelation between Sufi principles and scientific principles; provide a forum for dialogue among the various schools of Sufism; and preserve and advance the study of Sufism and its goals. In furtherance of these objectives, the association has developed an extensive publication program, which brings Sufi masters together with writers, translators, editors, and other members of the English-speaking intellectual community. Association members have many articles, essays, and important Sufi works translated into English.

Among the more important IAS activities is an annual Sufism symposium. This international, multicultural festival brings prominent Sufi masters from around the world to the United States to share their wisdom with the largely English-speaking audience. Through the year, IAS also holds seminars, classes, gatherings, and conferences on such subjects as Sufism and psychology; Sufi poetry and literature; principles of Sufism; meditation; and Sufi music. IAS sponsors a social service and awareness program, the Sufism and psychology forum, the Sufi Women's Organization, and the Prison Social Service Project.

Membership: The IAS is a nonprofit organization supported by members and funded by private organizations and individual contributions. Membership is open to individuals and groups interested in furthering the goals of Sufism. There are four membership levels: sustaining, associate, friend, and benefactor.

Educational Facilities:

Institute for Sufi Studies, Novato, California.

Periodicals: *Sufism, an Inquiry Journal* (irregular) • *Insight* (quarterly) • *Psychology: Traditional, Spiritual, Contemporary* • *Sufi Women* (quarterly).

Sources:

International Association of Sufism. www.ias.org.

Hermansen, Marcia K. "Hybrid Identity Formations in Muslim America: The Case of American Sufi Movement." *Muslim World* 90, no. 1-2 (Spring 2000): 158–197.

Islamic Shura Council of North America

PO Box 38, Plainfield, IN 46168

Alternate Address: 6555 S 750 East, Plainfield, IN 46168

In 1993, through the initiative of Dr. Abdul Malik Mujahid, four major America Islamic associations—the Ministry of Imam W. Deen Mohammed, al-Ummah the community of Imam Jamil al-Amin, Islamic Circle of North America, and the Islamic Society of North America—founded the Islamic Shura Council of North America as a cooperative body.

Two years later the Shura Council made a significant impact on the American Muslim community when it agreed to assume authority over determining the Islamic calendar. The Islamic (Hijri) year consists of 12 (purely lunar) months: MuHarram, Safar, Raby' al-awal, Raby' al-THaany, Jumaada al-awal, Jumaada al-THaany, Rajab, SHa'baan, RamaDHaan, SHawwal, Thw al-Qi'dah, and Thw al-

Hijjah. For religious reasons, the beginning of a Hijri month is marked not by the start of a new moon, but by a physical (i.e., an actual human) sighting of the crescent moon at a given locale. Among the more important crescent sightings is the one that determines the beginning and end of the fast in the month of RamaDHaan (also spelled Ramadan). The traditional method of making this determination may be hampered by clouds or other obstructions; in addition, prior to 1995 several different methods had been used by American Muslims to determine the beginning of RamaDHaan.

Following considered review of the opinion of Muslim scholars, the Shura Council reached a decision to bring together the majority of American Muslims. "The beginning and end of Ramadan will be decided based on the evidence of actual crescent sighting in North America corroborated by the astronomical data. Therefore a confirmed crescent sighting report will be accepted as long as such a report in North America does not contradict indisputable astronomical information." The council also adopted a procedure for determining a crescent moon sighting. The decision was initially accepted only by the four member organizations, but has subsequently been accepted by most Muslim groups in North America. The current consultant and North American coordinator for the Shura Council is Dr. Mohib N. Durrani of the Islamic Society of North America (ISNA).

Membership: The council has four organizational members, which collectively include more than half of all American Muslims.

Sources:

Muhanna, W. A. "A Brief Introduction to the Islamic (Hijri) Calendar." www.fisher.osu.edu/~muhanna_1/hijri-intro.html.

Muslim World League

134 W 26th St., Box 1674, New York, NY 10001-6803

Alternate Addresses: International Headquarters: Box 537, Makkah al Mukarramah, Saudi Arabia. Canadian Headquarters: 2550 Argentia Rd. #220, Mississauga, ON, Canada L5N 5R1

The Muslim World League was founded in 1962 as a nongovernmental relief organization working in Muslim countries; it also had the aim of advancing Islamic unity and solidarity. The league coordinates the work of Islamic preachers, promulgates strategies for the spread of Islam in accordance with the Qur'an and Sunnah, conducts symposiums, and provides relief to Muslim victims of wars and natural disasters. Supported by the government of Saudi Arabia, the league has distributed grants for the erection of mosques around the world, including the United States. It includes within its structure the World Council of Mosques and the World Assembly of Muslim Youth. Its 60-member council has two representatives per nation. The current secretary-general is Dr. Abdullah bin Abdul Mohsin Al-Turki.

Sources:

Muslim World League, Canadian Office. www.mwlcanada.org.

 # Islam

al-Ummah

c/o Atlanta Community Mosque, 547 W End Pl., Atlanta, GA 30310

Al-Ummah is the official name of the association of mosques that have gathered around the person of Imam Jamil al-Amin (b. 1943), better known to the general public as civil rights activist H. Rap Brown. Imam Jamil was born Hubert Gerold Brown in Baton Rouge, Louisiana. In 1966 he became a field organizer for the Student Nonviolent Coordinating Committee (SNCC) in Greene County, Alabama, and in the following year he was named SNCC's new chairman following the ouster of Stokely Carmichael. In 1968, he became the minister of justice for the Black Panther Party.

In jail in 1971, Brown converted to Islam. Following his release in 1976, he went on pilgrimage to Mecca, Saudi Arabia, and then settled in the West End section of

Atlanta, Georgia, and opened the Atlanta Community Mosque. Meanwhile, another Islamic movement in the African-American community, Dar al-Islam, had been founded in 1963, and in 1980 had split into various factions. In 1983 some 30 of the Dar al-Islam mosques united with the Atlanta Community Mosque to form a coalition around Brown, now known as Imam Jamil al Amin. Imam Jamil is credited with moving the group into the Islamic mainstream. He reached out to those mosques that followed the ministry of Imam W. Deen Mohammed following the demise of the old Nation of Islam.

Though little known to the broader American public, Imam Jamil rose to a position of prominence in the Islamic world. In 1990 he became the vice president of the American Muslim Council. In 1993, his group became a charter member of the Islamic Shura Council of North America (along with the Islamic Society of North America, the Islamic Circle of North America, and the Ministry of Imam W. Deen Mohammed). He would later become the chairman of the Shura Council.

In 2001 Imam Jamil once again became the center of public attention when he was arrested in Atlanta for the murder of a police officer near the grocery store he had opened. Tried the following year, he was convicted, in spite of the confession of another man and support for him from the larger Muslim community. As of 2008 he remains in prison serving a life sentence, and members of al-Ummah continue to publicize what they believe is his unjust situation through fundraisers, rallies, and networking.

Membership: Not reported. In 2002 there were some 35 mosques affiliated with al-Ummah.

Sources:

Imam Jamil (unofficial). www.imamjamil.com/.

Amin, Imam Jamil al. *Revolution by the Book: The Rap Is Live*. Beltsville, MD: Writers Inc., International, 1993.

Brown, H. Rap. *Die Nigger, Die!* New York: Dial Press, 1969.

Visseer, Steve, and Lateef Mungin. "Al-Amin's Life Now on the Line: Jury Must Decide His Sentence for Murder." *Atlanta-Journal Constitution*, March 3, 2001.

Federation of Islamic Associations in the United States and Canada

25231 5 Mile Rd., Redford Township, MI 48239

Federation of Islamic Associations in the United States and Canada was established in 1952 at Cedar Rapids, Iowa, as a fellowship of mosques and Muslim communities, the oldest such association in North America. The immediate goals were to promote the spirit, ethics, and philosophy of Islam, to engage in cooperative activities, and to maintain contact with the rest of the Muslim world. They have subsequently enlarged their concerns to include the publication of Islamic materials and the development of media for the needs of local Muslim centers.

The federation has worked to enlighten non-Muslims about Islamic belief and practice and encourage cordial relations between Muslims and their neighbors of other faiths.

The federation holds an annual convention. It periodically tries to speak on issues of public interest for its constituency.

Membership: Not reported.

Sources:

Federation of Islamic Associations in the United States and Canada. www.islamerica.com.

His Highness Prince Aga Khan Shia Imani Ismaili Council for the United States of America

PO Box 77, Rego Park, NY 11374

The Shia Imami Ismaili Muslims, generally known as the Ismailis, belong to the Shia branch of Islam, one of the two major branches of Islam, the Sunni being the

other. The Ismailis live in more than 25 different countries, mainly in Asia, Africa, and the Middle East, as well as in the West.

As Muslims, the Ismailis affirm the fundamental Islamic Testimony of Truth, the *Shahada*, that there is no god but Allah and that Muhammad is His Messenger. They believe that Muhammad was the last and final prophet of Allah, and that the Holy Qur'an, Allah's final message to mankind, was revealed through him.

In common with other Shia Muslims, the Ismailis affirm that after the Prophet's death, Hazrat Ali, the Prophet's cousin and son-in-law, became the first imam—the spiritual leader—of the Muslim community and that this spiritual leadership (known as Imamat) continues thereafter by heredity through Ali and his wife Fatima, the Prophet's daughter. Succession to Imamat, according to Shia doctrine and tradition, is by way of *Nass* (designation), it being the absolute prerogative of the imam of the time to appoint his successor from among any of his male descendants whether they be sons or remoter issue.

His Highness Prince Karim Aga Khan is the 49th hereditary imam of the Shia Imami Ismaili Muslims. He was born on December 13, 1936, in Geneva, son of Prince Aly Khan and Princess Tajuddawlah Aly Khan, and spent his early childhood in Nairobi, Kenya. He attended Le Rosey School in Switzerland for nine years and graduated from Harvard in 1959 with a B.A. in Islamic history. He succeeded his grandfather Sir Sultan Mahomed Shah Aga Khan on July 11, 1957, at the age of 20.

Among the major contributions to the growth of Islamic civilization made by the Ismailis are the University of al-Azhar and the Academy of Science, Dar al-Ilm, in Egypt. Indeed the city of Cairo itself is a testimony to their contribution. Among the renowned philosophers, jurists, physicians, mathematicians, astronomers, and scientists of the past who flourished under the patronage of Ismaili imams are Qadi al-Numan, al-Kirmani, Ibn al Haytham (al-Hazen), Nasir-e-Khusraw, and Nasir al-Din Tusi. In more recent times, the 48th imam, Sir Sultan Mahomed Shah Aga Khan, has been recognized for his contribution to the Muslim world and his efforts to promote international understanding, especially as the president of the League of Nations (1937–1938), the forerunner of the United Nations.

Spiritual allegiance to the imam and adherence to the Shia Imami Ismaili *tariqa* (persuasion) of Islam, according to the guidance of the imam of the time, have engendered in the Ismaili community an ethos of self-reliance, unity, and a common identity. In a number of countries of their residence, the Ismailis have evolved a well-defined institutional framework through which they have, under the leadership and guidance of the imam, made notable progress in the educational, health, housing, and economic spheres, establishing schools, hospitals, health centers, housing societies, and a variety of social and economic development institutions for the common good of all citizens regardless of their race or religion. Programs and institutions established or expanded in recent years by the present Aga Khan, as imam of the Ismailis, include the Aga Khan Foundation, the Aga Khan University, the Aga Khan Education Services, the Aga Khan Health Services, the Aga Khan Fund for Economic Development, and the Aga Khan Trust for Culture, all of which seek to contribute to the progress and development of the many nations where the Ismailis live, as well as the third world generally.

The Aga Khan Foundation is a noncommunal development agency committed to promoting sustainable and equitable social development. The foundation provides grants and technical assistance to people and institutions that are evolving innovative approaches to pressing social and environmental problems. Its particular emphasis is on health, education, and rural development in the low-income countries of Asia and Africa. The foundation, which has affiliates in Canada and the United States, collaborates with more than 30 other national and international organizations in financing development programs, including the Canadian International Development Agency (CIDA), the Commission for European Communities, the Overseas Development Administration in the United Kingdom, UNICEF, the U.S. Agency for International Development (AID), and the World Health Organization (WHO).

The Aga Khan University, chartered in 1983 as the first private university in Pakistan, dedicates itself to the establishment and maintenance of internationally accepted standards of education while addressing itself to problems of particular relevance to developing countries. The Aga Khan University's Faculty of Health Sciences, which includes a Medical College and a School of Nursing located in Karachi, seeks through strong academic, clinical, and community health training to graduate doctors and nurses who are better equipped to respond to the primary health care needs of the third world. Clinical training facilities for the Medical College and the School of Nursing are located at the 650-bed Aga Khan University teaching hospital in Karachi which opened in November 1985. Formal agreements for collaboration by the Medical College have been concluded with three major universities—Harvard, McGill, and McMaster—underlining the commitment of the university toward a high standard of endeavor. The Aga Khan University will establish additional faculties in other countries and is currently exploring alternatives for developing the university's international dimensions.

The Aga Khan Education Services operates more than 300 institutions and programs from day care centers to university-level education, catering to some 50,000 students, the majority of whom are non-Ismaili. More than 5,000 students benefit from various Aga Khan scholarship programs.

The Aga Khan Health Services consists of more than 200 health care units and programs in the developing world, including maternity homes, primary care centers, diagnostic clinics, dispensaries, and five general hospitals. More than two million outpatients a year, the majority of whom are non-Ismaili, receive services through these institutions.

The Aga Khan Fund for Economic Development is committed to the support of economic development activities in the third world through the promotion of projects in the private sector, primarily through equity participation in third world enterprises, to increase productivity and raise standards of living. The fund also collaborates with national and international agencies in the promotion of development institutions. Since 1963, more than 100 new enterprises, ranging from building materials and textiles to mining and tourism which today employ some 10,000 people, have been established in East, West, and Central Africa, as well as in Asia.

The Aga Khan Trust for Culture focuses attention on contemporary expressions of the Islamic humanistic tradition, concentrating largely on the built environment. The triennial Aga Khan Award for Architecture and its associated program of seminars encourage architectural excellence in an effort to enrich the physical environment of the Islamic world, while the Aga Khan Program for Islamic Architecture at Harvard University and the Massachusetts Institute of Technology provide graduate education to a new generation of architects, planners, and researchers.

The Ismailis first arrived in the United States in the early 1960s. The majority were students from the developing world who in the post-independence years came to study at institutions of higher learning. In the 1970s, largely as a result of political instability in parts of Africa and Asia, the community's numbers in the United States increased significantly. Their education, linguistic, and professional skills have helped Ismailis to assimilate easily into the American social fabric. Today, Ismailis are settled throughout the country, and the community is administered by the Ismaili Council for the United States of America, based in New York. There are also local councils which operate under the direction of the national council in different regions of the country. Each council has portfolio members for community programs in such fields as education, health, youth and sports activities, economic development, and social welfare, who endeavor to secure continuing improvements in the quality of life of the community and assist it to make an effective contribution to the societies it lives among.

Membership: Not reported.

Periodicals: *The American Ismaili.*

Sources:

Daftary, Farhad. *A Short History of the Ismailis*. Princeton, NJ: Marcus Wiener Publishers, 1998.

Howell, Georgina. "The Story of K." *Vanity Fair* 51, no. 6 (June 1988): 100–108, 173–179.

Nanji, Azim. "The Nizari Ismaili Muslim Community in North America; Background and Development." In *The Muslim Community in North America*, Earle H. Waugh, Baha Abu-Laban, and Regula B. Qureshi, eds. Edmonton, AB: University of Alberta Press, 1883.

Williams, Raymond Brady. *Religions of Immigrants from India and Pakistan: New Threads of the American Tapestry*. New York: Cambridge University Press, 1988.

Islamic Assembly of North America (IANA)
3588 Plymouth Rd., No. 270, Ann Arbor, MI 48105

The Islamic Assembly of North America (IANA) was founded in 1993 by a group of American Muslims from various Muslim centers concerned with the propagation of Islam (*dawah*) in the United States. They shared a view that a combined effort was needed and that cooperative activity produced far greater results than did individual activity.

At the time of its founding, a set of goals were adopted that included work to unify and coordinate the efforts of the different dawah-oriented organizations in North America; to observe the current events in the Muslim world and analyze them in relation to the situation of American Muslims; to assist scholars, Islamic workers, and Muslim masses in any locality who were facing discrimination or persecution; to develop an effective media institute to serve North American Muslims; to direct dawah to youth; and to create programs and institutions for English-speaking Muslims.

Important to IANA is the application of what is considered the correct Islamic methodology as derived from the Book of Allah (Qur'an) and the sunnah (life and work) of the Messenger of Allah, according to the understanding and application of the early pious forefathers.

As part of its effort, IANA opened an office in Austin, Texas, from which to begin radio broadcasts. In 1999 it began live broadcasting through the Internet. The al-Hamdulillah program donated Islamic books to prison libraries. The assembly distributes a copy of the Qur'an especially to non-Muslims and, among other titles, has published a book on Jesus from a Muslim standpoint.

Membership: Not reported.

Periodicals: *Almanar.*

Sources:

Islamic Assembly of North America (IANA). www.iananet.org.

Abdullah, Misha'aliban ibn. *What Did Jesus Really Say?* Plymouth, MI: IANA, 1996.

Ibrahim, I.A. *A Brief Guide to Understanding Islam*. Houston, TX: Darussalem, 1997.

Islamic Circle of North America
166-26 89th Ave., Jamaica, NY 11432

Islamic Circle of North America (ICNA), founded in the mid-1970s, includes a number of mosques across the United States that have as their goal the establishment of the Iqamat-ud-Deen (the Islamic system of life) as defined in the Qur'an and the Sunnah (life and works) of the Prophet Muhammad. ICNA has its base in the American Pakistani community and draws its inspiration from the Islamic revivalist movement in Pakistan, especially the Jamaate-Islami and the Tablighi Jama'at. The circle has developed an outward-looking program for the propagation of Islam in North America that includes activities aimed at the increase of Islamic knowledge and the enhancement of the character and the skills of those associated with ICNA. To that end, ICNA supports efforts for civil liberties and socio-economic justice in the society and encourages programs that serve the needy both in North America and around the world.

To embody its concern for spreading Islam, ICNA has developed what is termed the "Why Islam?" project, developed by circle members in New Jersey, and produced a set of pamphlets that deal with the Islamic option over the many other competing philosophies, religions, and "isms." The project operates through a toll-free number, the Islamic Circle's website, an outreach to prison inmates, and the distribution of the pamphlets by various avenues.

Those associated with the circle are expected to study the Qur'an, the Hadith, and other Islamic literature regularly; to spend a minimum of four hours each month on dawah (propagation) work; to invite at least two persons to become ICNA members every year; to contribute in support of the group; and weekly to invite at least one Muslim to come to the weekly prayer service at the ICNA center.

The circle is headed by its ameer, Dr. Zulfiqar Ali Shah, the secretary general, Naeem Baig, and the entral shura (council). The sisters' wing (women's organization) of ICNA has founded the Institute of Islamic Learning in which women may be trained in Islam. The circle was one of the founding members of the Islamic Shura Council of North America, a cooperative organization that includes the ministry of Imam W. Deen Mohammed, al-Ummah (the community of Imam Jamil al-Amin), and the Islamic Society of North America.

Membership: Not reported.

Periodicals: *The Message*; *Noor*.

Sources:

Islamic Circle of North America. www.icna.org/icna/index.php.

Islamic Society of North America
PO Box 38, Plainfield, IN 46168

Islamic Society of North America, one of the largest Muslim bodies in the United States and Canada, is an outgrowth of the Indian/Pakistani phase of the twentieth-century Islamist revival that sought to call secularized Muslims back to a vision of Islam as a total way of life. The major organization of the movement, the Jamaat-e-Islami, was founded by Sayyid Abul A'la Mawdudi (1903–1979), who lived and work amid the Indian independence movement and the resultant separation of Pakistan as an Islamic state. Mawdudi emerged as a major commentator on the problems presented to Islam by Western culture Indian nationalism (which he saw as destructive of Muslim identity) and competing political ideologies. Based on his assessment of the situation, he began to reconstruct Islamic thought. He founded Jamaat-e-Islami in 1941, and subsequently moved to Pakistan to work for the formation of an Islamic state.

The spirit of Mawdudi's movement came to North America in the 1950s with the arrival of the Indian and Pakistani Muslims for college study. These students took the lead in founding the Muslim Student Association of the United States and Canada in 1963. MSA spawned a host of organizations to serve various segments of the American and Canadian Muslim community such as the North America Islamic Trust (NAIT), the Islamic Medical Association, and the Muslim Arab Youth Association (MAYA). In the 1980s, the maturing of the early leaders of MSA, the steady migration of Muslims to North America, and the many mosques that had appeared across the continent led to the organizing of the Islamic Society of North America (ISNA).

ISNA serves as a point of unity for many American Muslims and mosques, and sees as its primary task the nurturing of the American Muslim community. As an association of Muslim organizations and individuals it has established a unified platform of expression for Islam, encourages the development of educational, outreach, and social services, and is constructing an enhanced image of Islam in North American society.

ISNA's program is concentrated on the establishment of high-quality, full-time Islamic schools; the publication of outreach materials (especially for prisons and the military); the nurturing of strong and stable Muslim families; involvement in the social issues confronting North Americans; training Islamic workers, teachers, and imams; and assisting in the integration of Muslims into American political life.

ISNA has formed the Fiqh (law) Council that brings together a body of Islamic scholars who reside in the United States and Canada. The council receives and responds to inquiries from Muslims and makes itself available to resolve disputes between Muslim individuals and organizations following Muslim legal opinion. The council originated in the Religious Affairs Committee of the Muslim Students Association in the early 1960s. The committee evolved into the Fiqh Committee of the ISNA in 1980 and was transformed into the council in 1986. The Fiqh Council, as an affiliate of ISNA, advises it on matters relative to the application of Islamic lawn (*shari'ah*) in the individual and collective life of its membership. The council's membership includes a number of scholars who have earned the respect of the larger Muslim community.

ISNA is led by its Majlis Ash-Shura (council). ISNA was a founding member of the Islamic Shura Council of North America, a cooperative organization that includes the Islamic Circle of North America (with whom ISNA shares its heritage), the ministry of Imam W. Deen Mohammed, and al-Ummah (the community led by Imam Jamil al-Amin). It facilitated the founding of a variety of Islamic organizations that have since matured into autonomous groups in their own right, such as the Association of Muslim Social Scientists, the Association of Muslim Scientists and Engineers, and the Islamic Medical Association of North America.

Membership: Not reported.

Periodicals: *Islamic Horizons*.

Sources:

Islamic Society of North America. www.isna.net/.

Islamic Supreme Council of America (ISCA)
1400 16th St. NW, B-112, Washington, DC 20036
Alternate Address: 17195 Silver Pkwy., No. 201, Fenton, MI 48430.

Islamic Supreme Council of America (ISCA), an organization that seeks the cooperation of varied segments of the Muslim community, has its base of support in the Naqshbandi-Haqqani Sufi Order and its charismatic leader, Mawlana Shaykh Nazim Adil al-Haqqani, the council's founder. The goal of ISCA is to provide solutions to the problems faced by American Muslims based on the traditional Islamic legal rulings as provided by an international advisory board. The board is drawn from a group of high-ranking Islamic scholars. The council has pioneered an effort to integrate traditional scholarship to the challenges of maintaining Islamic belief in a modern, secular society.

The council attempts to facilitate individuals and organizations receiving legal advice from scholars and religious institutions around the world. At the same time, it tries to work proactively to present Islam as a religion of moderation, tolerance, peace, and justice. ISCA stresses the common heritage of Islam, Christianity, and Judaism in an effort to foster mutual respect and reshape the image of Islam in the West. To that end it supports peace efforts worldwide, condemns violations of human rights, denounces all types of terrorism (including intellectual, cultural, and ideological), favors the nonproliferation of nuclear, biological, and chemical weapons, and is committed to the values of charity, family love, education, and public responsibility in American life.

The ISCA program centers on a set of publications, meetings, seminars, and conferences whose purpose is the education of U.S. officials on Islamic culture and history. ISCA also works with the representatives of Muslim nations as a reliable source for traditional Islamic literature on a spectrum of topics.

The council is headed by its chairman, currently Shaykh Muhammad Hisham Kabbani, and a large advisory committee that includes a number of Muslim scholars and government officials. Kamilat, the affiliated women's organization, has built a cooperative network with various Muslim groups to assist Muslim widows, divorcees, and working mothers.

Membership: Not reported.

Periodicals: *The Muslim Magazine*.

Sources:

Islamic Supreme Council of America. www.islamicsupremecouncil.org.

Kabbani, Muhammad Hisham. *The Approach of Armageddon?: An Islamic Perspective.* Washington, DC: Isca Publications, 2003.

———. *Classical Islam and the Naqshbandi Sufi Tradition.* Washington, DC: Isca Publications, 2003.

———. *Naqshbandi Sufi Tradition Guidebook of Daily Practices and Devotions.* Washington, DC: Isca Publications, 2004.

Muslim American Society (MAS)

PO Box 1896, Falls Church, VA 22041

Muslim American Society (MAS) is one of several Muslim associations that has its roots in the Indo-Pakistani Islamist revival, the Muslim Student Association, and the Islamic Society of North America. Many of the people who founded MAS had previously been associated with the Islamic Society of North America. They saw themselves as particularly concerned with the changing dynamics of Islamic society in North America and a desire to construct a new foundation for the Islamic work perceived to be needed in the twenty-first century.

To that end, MSA has projected a six-point program for the mosques and individuals associated with it: to present the message of Islam to the public; to encourage Muslims in building a virtuous and moral society; to offer the Islamic alternative to society's major problems; to promote family values; to advocate for the human values of brotherhood, equality, justice, mercy, compassion, and peace; and to foster unity among Muslims and Muslim organizations.

Among MAS' major programs is the Muslim American Society Council of Islamic Schools, which as its educational branch offers several technical and support services and professional training programs for teachers and administrators of Islamic schools.

Membership: Not reported.

Educational Facilities:

Islamic American University, 17300 W. 10 Mile Rd., Ste. 2, Southfield, MI 48075.

Periodicals: *The American Muslim.*

Sources:

Muslim American Society. www.masnet.org.

Shi'a Muslims

c/o Islamic Center of America, 19500 Ford Rd., Dearborn, MI 48128

Alternate Address: Jaffari Islamic Centre, 7340 Bayview Ave., Thornhill, ON L3T 2R7

Of the two orthodox branches of the Muslim Community the Shi'a is by far the smaller. It includes some Iranian-Americans though Shi'as of other nationalities (Lebanese, Pakistani, Yemeni) are also present in significant numbers. The oldest and among the most prominent Shi'a centers is the Islamic Center of America, a Lebanese center that emerged as the Detroit Islamic community split into the traditional Sunni and Shi'a factions early in the twentieth century. Growth in the Shi'as was marked by its 1949 invitation to Imam Mohamad Jawad Chirri to become the community's spiritual leader and the establishment of the center in the 1960s under his guidance.

More typical of the Shi'a centers established since 1965 is the Islamic Society of Georgia, a Pakistani-American center in Atlanta founded in 1970. It is a major distributor of Shi'a publications from around the world and publishes *Islamic Affairs.* It has made a major priority of its program the circulation of Shi'a literature to "willing readers" at little or no cost. The Midwest Association of Shi'a Organized Muslims is a similar center in Chicago.

A step forward in the organization of the Shi'a community was the 1970 formation of the Shi'a Association of North America by families in New York and New Jersey. Through its newsletter, *Islamic Review,* and other publications, it has led in the establishment of traditional standards of belief and practice in the Shi'a community nationally. The Iranian Revolution under the Ayatollah Khomeini has had a marked effect of uniting the American Shi'a community, which has responded with strong support. In like measure, the American-Lebanese Shi'as have identified with the Shi'as of Lebanon, though they are somewhat divided in their support of the various factions that emerged in the 1970s.

While the majority of English-language Shi'a literature still originates from foreign presses, several publishing ventures have emerged in the United States. The Detroit center has published a number of works by Imam Chirri, an eminent Islamic scholar. It is joined by Free Islamic Literature, Inc. of Houston, Texas, and Mehfile Shahe Khorasan Charitable Trust of Englewood Cliffs, New Jersey.

Membership: Not reported. There are several dozen Shi'a centers scattered across the United States.

Educational Facilities:

The Islamic Seminary, New York, New York.

Periodicals: *Islamic Affairs* • *The Islamic Review* • *Husaini News*

Sources:

Islamic Center of America. www.icofa.com.

Chirri, Mohammad Jawad. *The Brother of the Prophet Mohammad.* 2 vols. Detroit: Islamic Center of Detroit, 1979–1982.

———. *Inquiries about Islam.* Detroit: Islamic Center of Detroit, 1965.

Iman Khomeini, Pope and Christianity. Tehran, Iran: Islamic Propaganda Organization, 1983.

The Life of Iman Husain. Englewood Cliffs, NJ: Mehfile Shahe Khorasan Charitable Trust, n.d. Tract.

Qazwini, Imam Hassan. *American Crescent: A Muslim Cleric on the Power of His Faith, the Struggle against Prejudice, and the Future of Islam in America.* New York: Random House, 2007. 282 pp.

Shariati, Ali. *Islamic View of Man.* Houston, TX: Free Islamic Literature, 1979.

Shiah Fatimi Ismaili Tayyibi Dawoodi Bohra (Daudi Bohras)

c/o Anjuman-e-Ezzi, Washington, DC, 18728 New Hampshire Ave., Ashton, MD 20861
Alternate Address: International headquarters: Dawat-e-Hadiyah, Administration of the 52nd al-Dai al-Mutlaq, His Holiness Dr. Syedna Mohammed Burhanuddin, c/o Saifee Masjid, Burhani Park, Lagos Road, City Centre, Nairobi, Kenya. Canadian headquarters: c/o Anjuman-e-Najmi, Toronto, 61 Queensmill Ct., Richmond Hill, ON L4B 1N2.

The Daudi Bohras constitute a worldwide religious group officially known as the Shiah Fatimi Ismaili Tayyibi Dawoodi Bohra, a community within the larger world of Orthodox Islam. This group follows a specific code of beliefs, doctrines, and tenets founded on the Qur'an and the Shariah, as taught and interpreted by their leader, the Dai al-Mutlaq. The Daudi Bohras traces its ancestry to the early conversions of Hindus in India in the eleventh century to the Ismaili branch of Shi'a Islam. These converts in turn gave their allegiance to the *dai mutlaq* in Yemen. They are named after their 27th dai, Daud ibn Qutubshah (d. 1612).

The Daudi Bohra community has largely been molded into its present form by the two dais who led the community in the twentieth century. The 51st dai, Dr. Sayyidna Tahir Saifuddin (1915–1965), was an accomplished scholar and capable organizer who revitalized the community during his half century of leadership and guided it through the tumultuous period of world wars and independence of nations. The present dai, H. H. Dr. Sayyidna Mohammed Burhanuddin, has continued his predecessor's endeavors with particular emphasis on strengthening the community's Islamic practices.

The religious hierarchy of the Daudi Bohras is headed by the dai mutlaq who is appointed by his predecessor in office. The dai appoints two others to the subsidiary ranks of *madhun* (licentiate) and *mukasir* (executor). These positions are followed by the rank of shaykh and mullah, both of which are held by hundreds of Bohras. An aamil (usually a graduate of the order's institution of higher learning, al-Jamiah al-Sayfiyah) leads the local congregation. The local organizations administer the activities of the local Bohras and report directly to the central administration of the dai, called al-Dawah al-Hadiyah.

At the age of puberty every Bohra believer takes the traditional oath of allegiance, which requires the initiate to adhere to the shariah and accept the leadership of the imam and the dai. This oath is renewed annually. The Bohras follow the Fatimid school of jurisprudence that recognizes seven pillars of Islam, the first of which is *walayah* (love and devotion) for Allah, the Prophets, the imam, and the dai. The other six are *tahrah* (purity & cleanliness), *salah* (prayers), *zakah* (purifying religious dues), *sawm* (fasting), *hajj* (pilgrimage to Mecca), and *jihad* (holy war). Pilgrimages to the shrines of the saints are also an important part of the devotional life of Bohras.

Within their community, Daudi Bohras speak an arabicized form of Gujrati, called lisan al-dawah, which is permeated with Arabic words and written in Arabic script. They also follow a Fatimid lunar calendar, which fixes the number of days in each month.

Dawat-e-Hadiyah, Allah's sovereignty over Heavens and Earth, is entrusted to the imam (who in the Ismaili tradition is known as the Hidden or Secluded Imam). In his absence, the Dawat-e-Hadiyah is headed by the Dai al-Mutlaq, the imam's representative and vicegerent, the supreme head of the Dawoodi Bohra community. Today, al-Dai al-Fatimi, His Holiness Dr. Syedna Mohammed Burhanuddin (TUS), is the 52nd Dai al-Mutlaq, the latest in a chain of succession that commenced in 1138 C.E. He succeeded to the throne of Dawat in 1965 as the successor to his father, H. H. Dr. Syedna Taher Saifuddin, the 51st Dai al-Mutlaq.

In the United States, the affairs of Dawat-e-Hadiyah are carried out in accordance with the wishes and direction of the Dai al-Mutlaq through the Dawat-e-Hadiyah (America). Members of the Daudi Bohra community migrated to the United States in the 1950s with the encouragement, permission, and blessings of the Dai al-Mutlaq. There are now a number of communities across the United States and Canada.

Membership: Not reported. Daudi Bohras number about a million and reside in India, Pakistan, the Middle East, East Africa (since the eighteenth century), and the West (since the 1950s).

Sources:

Shiah Fatimi Ismaili Tayyibi Dawoodi Bohra (Daudi Bohras). www.washingtondcjamaat.org.

Daftary, Farhad. *A Short History of the Ismailis*. Princeton, NJ: Marcus Wiener Publishers, 1998.

Sunni Muslims

c/o Islamic Center, 2551 Massachusetts Ave. NW, Washington, DC 20008

Alternate Address: The Council of Muslim Communities of Canada, PO Box 771, Station B, Willowdale, ON, Canada M2K 2R1.

The Islamic world, though concentrated in the Arab nations of the Middle East, stretches from Yugoslavia to Indonesia and includes not only a large part of the former U.S.S.R. but a growing community in Africa south of the Sahara. Since 1965, the Islamic community, which had been concentrated in the Midwest and a few eastern urban centers, has blossomed into a significant religious element of American life in every part of the United States. Literally millions of immigrants from Islamic Asia, Africa, and Europe have settled in North America and begun the generation-long process of building ethnic community centers and facilities for worship (often the same building).

Unlike much of Christendom, Islam is organized into a number of autonomous centers. Each center (which may be called a community center, a mosque, a *musjid*) tends to be dominated by one ethnic community, though outside the largest urban centers, where a variety of mosques can be found, centers have welcomed people of various nationalities into affiliation. Many of the major centers have periodicals, which have both a primary local audience and a national circula-

tion. The mosque, headed by the imam (minister-teacher), is the basic center of Islam.

Above the level of the local centers, a variety of national and continental organizations have been formed to mobilize the various local Islamic communities, provide the public (largely ignorant of Islam) with information, and coordinate the activities (particularly the propagation of the faith) of the community at large. These organizations, whose membership will come from a variety of ethnic backgrounds, tend to be divided politically. Each organization will be ideologically aligned to, for example, different factions in the Middle East, and/or attuned to a more-or-less activist role in support of various concerns of the land from which they emigrated. Political activism is particularly noticeable in those groups that serve the large Muslim community on the nation's campuses. Local centers often affiliate with several of the competing national associations.

Symbolic of Sunni Muslim presence in America is the Islamic Center in Washington, D.C. Begun in 1949, it took seven years to complete. It was officially opened in 1957. While begun as a center for diplomatic personnel, with financial support from seventeen countries, with the growth of Islam in North America it has become a place to which all American Sunnis look as a visible point of unity in the otherwise decentralized Islamic community. The importance of the center was dramatically underscored in the early 1980s when it was taken over by a group who supported the Iranian Revolution under the Ayatollah Khomeini and opposed the influence of the ambassadors from Saudi Arabia and other Islamic countries. The takeover disrupted the center for several years and led to the withdrawal of its prominent iman, Dr. Muhammad Abdul Rauf, a leading Islamic apologist in North America.

Among the oldest of the Canadian-United States organizations is the Federation of Islamic Organizations in the United States and Canada. It was founded in 1952, largely as a result of the efforts of Abdullah Ingram of Cedar Rapids, Iowa. He called a meeting attended primarily by Lebanese Muslims, representative of the older American Muslim centers, and formed the International Muslim Society, which two years later became the federation. The federation has as its goals the perpetuation of Islam and Muslim culture and the dissemination of correct information about Muslim society worldwide. It publishes a periodical, *The Muslim Star*, and holds annual conventions, usually in the Midwest. Federation accomplishments have been related to the fellowship of various Muslim centers across national and ethnic boundaries, and more activist groups, while acknowledging the contribution of the federation, saw the need for further organizations.

The Islamic Society of North America emerged in the early 1980s out of the Muslim Students Association originally founded in 1952. It represents a broadening focus of concern by former students who moved into roles of leadership in the Muslim, academic and professional communities in America. The society is headquartered at the Islamic Teaching Center, a large complex in suburban Indianapolis, from which it oversees the network of subsidiary organizations it has fostered and nurtured.

From its original goals, developed to assist graduate students temporarily in the United States for study to survive in a non-Muslim environment, the society has since 1975 refocused its attention on building Islamic structures among a permanent and growing North American Islamic population and actively propagating the faith among the non-Muslim public. To these ends, the society has established the Islamic Medical Association, the Association of Muslim Social Scientists, and the Association of Muslim Scientists and Engineers. It has published numerous books (including the proceedings of the many conferences it sponsors) and pamphlets (especially a set designed to introduce Islam to non-Muslims) and several periodicals, most prominently *Al-Ittihad* and *Islamic Horizons*. The Muslim Student Association continues as one department of the society. The Islamic Teaching Center is the main structure engaged in *dawah*, the propagation of the faith.

Possibly the most inclusive Islamic organization for Sunni Muslims is the Council of Islamic Organizations of America (both the Federation of Islamic Associations and the Islamic Society of North America are affiliates). The idea of the council emerged in 1973 at a meeting in Saudi Arabia. Then the Muslim World League, an international Muslim organization with offices in New York City, organized the first Islamic Conference of North America, which met April 22–24, 1977, in Newark, New Jersey. The council was organized at that gathering to meet primary needs for unity and coordination of the many Islamic centers in North America. In its lengthy list of goals, it set itself the task of fostering unity, establishing and propagating the faith in its fullness, perpetuating modest dress codes, assisting in building mosques and other facilities for Muslims, and funding various designated projects of broad Muslim interest.

Also in the 1970s, the Council of Imams in North America formed as a continentwide professional organization for the leaders of the various mosques and Islamic centers.

The several organizations mentioned above are but a few of the many new structures being established in the Muslim community. All of the organizations have been assisted by the development of Muslim publishing concerns, such as American Trust Publications, affiliated with the Islamic Society of North America; Kazi Publications in Chicago; and Crescent Publications, Tacoma Park, Maryland. As of the mid-1980s, however, the majority of English-language literature produced for the American Muslim community is still published overseas.

Membership: Estimates vary on the size of the Sunni Muslim community. As many as 400 mosques and centers have been counted. Approximately 3,000,000 immigrants from predominantly Muslim countries have come to the United States. Together with converts, including large followings in American black communities, the total number of Muslims approaches the size of the Jewish community.

Educational Facilities:

American Islamic College, Chicago, Illinois.

Periodicals: *Muslim Star* • *Islamic Horizons* • *al-Ittihad* • *The Minaret* • *Path of Righteousness* • *Al'Nourl* • *Islam Canada*

Sources:

Islamic Center. www.islamiccenterdc.com.

Abdalati, Hammudah. *Islam in Focus*. Indianapolis, IN: American Trust Publications, 1975.

Avdich, Kamal. *Outline of Islam*. Northbrook, IL: The Islamic Cultural Center, n.d.

Haneef, Suzanne. *What Everyone Should Know about Islam and Muslims*. Chicago: Kazi Publications, 1979.

Hussain, S. Mazhar, ed. *Proceedings of the First Islamic Conference of North America*. New York: Muslim World League, 1977.

Rauf, Muhammad Abdul. *Islam, Creed and Worship*. Washington, DC: Islamic Center, 1974.

Soddiqui, Moulana Mohammad Abdul-Aleem. *Elementary Teachings of Islam*. Tacoma Park, MD: Crescent Publications, n.d.

Tanzeem-e-Islami

c/o T.I.N.A. Center, 250 W. Saint Charles Rd., Villa Park, IL 62181-2430

Alternate Address: Tanzeem-e-Islami Pakistan, 67-A, Allama Iqbal Rd., Garhee Shahoo, Lahore.

Tanzeem-e-Islami grew out of the Indo-Pakistani branch of the Islamist revival of the twentieth century, which had as its keynote that the teachings of the Qur'an and those of the Sunnah (life and work) of the Prophet Muhammad must be implemented in their totality, especially in the public (social, cultural, juristic, political, economic) spheres of life. In India, the revival is traced to the works of Allama Muhammad Iqbal, Maulana Abul Kalam Azad, and most prominently Sayyid Abul A'la Mawdudi (1903–1979) and the Jamaat-e-Islami, which he founded in 1941. Following the creation of Pakistan (1947), Maududi and the Jamaat decided to take part in the country's secular electoral process, a change from its earlier revolutionary methodology. Many perceived that the result of this change was the

degeneration of the Jamaat from a revolutionary force into a mere political party. In 1975, Tanzeem-e-Islami was founded by Dr. Israr Ahmad (b.1932) to continue the original thrust of the Jamaat-e-Islami.

Ahmad, the son of a government employee, received his degree in Islamic Studies from the University of Karachi (1965). As a student he was influenced by Iqbal and Mawdudi, and later worked with the Jamaat-e-Islami. He resigned from the Jamaat in 1957 and continued to teach the Qur'an throughout Pakistan. A physician, Ahmad gave up his practice in 1971 in order to launch Tanzeem-e-Islami. He has authored more than 60 books, nine of which have been translated into English. In 1967, he wrote a tract, "Islamic Renaissance: The Real Task Ahead," to explain his basic ideas that the Islamic Renaissance necessarily implies the revitalizing of the imam (true faith and certitude) among the Muslims, particularly their intelligentsia, and the revitalization of imam is based on the propagation of the Qur'anic teachings in contemporary idiom, at the highest level of scholarship.

According to the Tanzeem-e-Islami perspective, the individual Muslim is obligated to develop real faith and conviction in his heart; to live a life of total obedience to the injunctions of the Islamic law (*shari'ah*); to propagate and disseminate the message of Islam; and to try his utmost to establish the ascendancy of Islam over all manmade systems of life. Tanzeem-e-Islami seeks to assist Muslims in carrying out these obligations.

In regard to propagating the faith, Tanzeem-e-Islami operates out of the spirit of Al-Deen Al-Naseeha (loyalty and sincerity toward each other) and organizes activity suggested by Al-Aqrabo Fal-Aqrab (i.e., one who is nearer should be given priority). Propagation extends from an individual to his family, his kith and kin, and then gradually his surroundings. Tanzeem-e-Islami seeks to supply the necessary religious teaching and training to this new generation. A most important task at the present moment is counteracting false beliefs and customs refuting the un-Islamic thoughts and philosophy of the modern age.

Tanzeem-e-Islam seeks the support of Sunni Muslims. Membership begins with the Baiy'ah or pledge of obedience (under the shari'ah) to the Ameer of Tanzeem-e-Islami, Dr. Israr Ahmad. At that time, the new member must promise to give up that which is considered disliked by Allah and will try to fulfill the obligations owed as a Muslim.

Tanzeem-e-Islami believes that the Western constitutional and democratic model is not suitable for the duty of struggling for the establishment of the Deen. In the baiyah system, one person gives a call that he is going to initiate the struggle for the Deen of Allah and invites people to join him. In this system, the leader (Ameer) is required to consult with his *rufaqa* (those who join him) but is not bound by any majority decisions. However, the Ameer is to be obeyed, though only within the bounds of the law.

Through the 1980s and 1990s, members of Tanzeem-e-Islami migrated to the United States and Canada. Offices are maintained in the Chicago and New York City metropolitan areas and in Montreal and Toronto, Canada. European centers are located in London and Paris. The organization has developed a radio and video broadcast through the Internet.

Membership: Not reported.

Educational Facilities:

Quran College Lahore of Arts and Science, Lahore, Pakistan.

Periodicals: *The Qur'anic Horizons.*

Sources:

Tanzeem-e-Islami. www.tanzeem.org.

Ahmad, Shagufta. *Dr. Israr Ahmad's Political Thought and Activities*. Montreal, Canada: McGill University, M.A. thesis, 1993. Rpt.: Lahore, Pakistan, Markazi Anjuman Khuddam-ul-Quran Lahore, 1996.

United American Muslim Association

5911 8th Ave., Brooklyn, NY 11220

Alternate Address: United Canadian Muslim Association. 182 Rhodes Ave., Toronto ON, Canada M4L 3A1; Islamic Culture Center of Rochester. 853 Culver Rd., Rochester, NY 14609

United American Muslim Association was founded in 1980 by a group of predominantly Turkish-American residents of Brooklyn, New York. The association was formed concurrently with the purchase of the building that has become Fatih Mosque, the parent mosque of the organization. Several other mosques were subsequently formed, including one in Canada that now serves as the headquarters of the Canadian affiliate, the United Canadian Muslim Association.

The association provides Islamic education for students (including study of Turkish history and geography), and since 1995 has organized a summer camp for its youth. It supports two foundations: the Turkish American Educational and Cultural Foundation and the American Turkish Islamic Cultural Foundation. Female members have organized the Fatih Turkish American Woman Assembly.

Membership: Not reported. UAMA has two branches on Long Island and one each in Boston; Rochester, New York; New Jersey; Chicago; Pennsylvania; Delaware; and Connecticut; and its Canadian affiliate has two in Toronto and one each in Montreal and Vancouver.

Sources:

United American Muslim Association. www.fatihcami.org.

United Submitters International

Box 43476, Tucson, AZ 85719

United Submitters International was founded by Rashad Khalifa (1935–1990), the imam (supreme leader) of a Muslim center in Tucson, Arizona. Born in Egypt, Khalifa was the son of a Sufi master in the Shadhili Order. He was trained in the natural sciences and moved to the United States in 1959 to study at the University of California at Riverside. He received a Ph.D. in biochemistry in the early 1960s. He married an American in 1963 and later became a citizen. While pursuing his career as an agricultural biochemist, he also conducted private research on the Qur'an, the Muslim bible. The results were first published in 1973 as *Miracle of the Quran: Significance of the Mysterious Alphabets*.

Khalifa was convinced of the miraculous nature of the Qur'an and his writing was a defense of this belief. His early writing was given broad coverage in the Islamic press because of his claims of scientific proof of the Qur'an's miraculousness. Using a computer, he discovered what he believed was a complex mathematical coding within the book. He concluded that it was organized around the number 19, that the organization was so complex that no human being could have worked it out (the keystone for his argument of its divine element), and that only with the arrival of the computer could we now see the mathematical sophistication of it. He expanded upon this basic notion in a second and more popular book in 1981, *The Computer Speaks: God's Message to the World.*

While defending the Qur'an, Khalifa also began to attack some basic Islamic affirmations. He suggested that two verses of the Qur'an were satanic insertions in the text. He attacked Muslims for their following the Hadith and the Sunna, both of which he saw as human inventions working against the Qur'an. He said it was idolatrous to venerate Muhammad and his writings. He also suggested that he was a messenger just as were Abraham and Muhammad. He claimed that on December 21, 1971, his soul was taken somewhere and introduced to all the prophets and they in turn designated him the "Apostle of the Covenant." His opinions concerning the Hadith and Sunna correlated with his notions of assimilation into Western society as he opposed the dress codes, the segregation of men and women, and other prohibitions they articulated. While many appreciated his work on the Qur'an, others denounced his ideas, questioning his authority and the unworthiness of the Hadith and Sunna. He was labeled a heretic and charlatan.

In the midst of the controversy, Khalifa found many supporters. Around 1979 he became the imam of a *masjid* (mosque) in Tucson, Arizona, and began a magazine, *Submitters Perspective.* He used his position to argue against the slavish adherence to what he saw as outdated Islamic practice. He was attacked by leading Muslim thinkers such as Ahmed Deedat of South Africa, Abu Ameenah Bilal Phillips, and Muzammil Saddiqi.

On January 31, 1990, Khalifa was murdered. James Williams, a member of an ultraconservative Muslim group, Al-Fuqra, was later arrested and convicted of Khalifa's murder. The center in Tucson has continued with a collective leadership and followers of its martyred imam can be found in Phoenix, Arizona, Southern California, and British Columbia.

Membership: Not reported.

Periodicals: *Submitters Perspective.*

Sources:

United Submitters International. www.masjidtucson.org.

Haddad, Yvonne Yazbeck, and Jane Idleman Smith. *Mission to America: Five Islamic Sectarian Communities in North America.* Gainesville, FL: University Press of Florida, 1993. 226 pp.

Hosenball, Mark. "Another Holy War: Waged on American Soil." *Newsweek* 123, 9 (February 28, 1994): 30–31.

Khalifa, Rashad. *The Computer Speaks: God's Message to the World.* Tucson, AZ: Renaissance Productions International, 1981. 263 pp.

———. *Miracle of the Quran: Significance of the Mysterious Alphabets.* St. Louis, MO: Islamic Productions International, 1973.

———. *Quran: The Final Testament.* Tucson, AZ: Islamic Productions International, 1989.

———. *Quran, Hadith, and Islam.* Tucson, AZ: Islamic Productions International, 1982.

Quran: The Final Scripture. Trans. by Rashad Khalifa. Tucson, AZ: Islamic Productions, 1981. 525 pp.

 # Sufism

Bawa Muhaiyaddeen Fellowship

5820 Overbrook Ave., Philadelphia, PA 19131

Bawa Muhaiyaddeen Fellowship was founded in 1971. Shaikh M. R. Bawa Muhaiyaddeen was a Sri Lankan Sufi teacher said to be over a hundred years old. In the 1930s he was discovered by pilgrims in the Kataragama Forest, and the Serendib Study Group was established in Colombo, the capital of Sri Lanka. He was first brought to Philadelphia in 1971 by a disciple, and as a group began to recognize him as their spiritual teacher, the Bawa Muhaiyaddeen Fellowship was organized. During the next years until his death in 1986 he traveled between Philadelphia and Sri Lanka.

Bawa saw himself not as the teacher of a new religion, but as dealing with the essence of all religion. He taught the unity of God and human unity in God. A Sufi is one who has lost the self in the Solitary Oneness that is God. It is the individual's sole duty to realize the 3,000 qualities of God within him or herself. The soul is that point of divine wisdom at which the consciousness of individuals is one with God. From contemplation of this point the individual realizes God.

The conditions leading to God realizations are the following: (1) the constant affirmation that nothing but God exists; (2) the continual elimination of evil from one's life; and (3) the conscious effort to embody God's qualities—patience, tolerance, peacefulness, compassion, and the assumption that all lives should be treated as one's own. Meeting these conditions leads naturally to the practice of *dhikr*, the remembrance of God.

The headquarters of the Bawa Muhaiyaddeen Fellowship is located in a large house in a residential section of Philadelphia where public meetings are held daily. Also on the grounds is the Shaikh M. R. Bawa Muhaiyaddeen Mosque, where the traditional five prayers a day and the Friday congregational prayers are held regularly. In addition, a house west of the Philadelphia center is the *mazaar* (tomb) of M. R. Bawa Muhaiyaddeen, which is open for visitation. Over the years, more than 20 books about Bawa Muhaiyaddeen's teachings have been published by the Fellowship Press. Also available are numerous audio and videocassette recordings of his discourses.

Membership: Not reported. In 1982 there were nine fellowship groups in the United States and two in Canada, and 3,000 members worldwide. There were four branches in Sri Lanka and one in Great Britain.

Sources:

Bawa Muhaiyaddeen Fellowship. www.bmf.org.

Muhaiyaddeen, M. R. Guru Bawa, Shaikh. *God, His Prophets, and His Children*. Philadelphia: Fellowship Press, 1978.

———. *The Guidebook*. 2 vols. Philadelphia: Fellowship Press, 1976.

———. *Mata Veeram, or the Forces of Illusion*. York Beach, ME: Samuel Weiser, 1982.

———. *Truth and Light*. Philadelphia: Guru Bawa Fellowship of Philadelphia, 1974.

———. *The Truth and Unity of Man*. Philadelphia: Fellowship Press, 1980.

Bektashi Order

21749 Northline Road, Taylor, MI 48180

The Bektashi Order of Sufis emerged in the Muslim community of Anatolia some 700 years ago. Over the centuries, it earned a reputation for its respect for other religions, for its inclusion of women, and for the beauty of its spiritual poetry. During the Ottoman period, the order gained a large following throughout the Balkan Peninsula. Bektashi clergy began to play a noteworthy role in the Albanian nationalist movement during the late nineteenth century. Like other Albanian religions, Bektashism was severely persecuted by the communist government after 1967. In 1991 the Bektashi Order of Sufis was able to reestablish itself in a newly democratized Albania. Today, there are still significant numbers of Bektashis in Albania, Macedonia, Kosovo, Bulgaria, and Turkey,

The Bektashi Order was brought to the United States by Baba (Father) Rexheb Beqiri (1901–1995), an Albanian refugee who escaped his homeland shortly before its communist takeover near the end of World War II. Rexheb was born and raised in Gjirokaster, a town in southern Albania. He completed studies in Islamic theology by age 16. In addition to his native Albanian language, he was fluent in Arabic, Turkish, and Persian. At the age of 21, he took the vows of celibate Bektashi dervish in his uncle's Sufi lodge. He was forced to flee Albania in 1944, owning to his opposition to communism. Following stays in Italy and Egypt, he finally made his way to the United States in 1952. With the help of the Albanian émigré community, he opened the first Albanian-American Bektashi Monastery in 1954. Baba Rexheb was the spiritual guide of this center until his passing in 1995. Today it is headed by Baha Arshi Bazaj. Over the years, the congregation has primarily been made up of Albanian-Americans, although in the last decade, a small number of people from other ethnic backgrounds joined the congregation.

Membership: In 2008 there were more than 1,000 members.

Educational Facilities:

The World Headquarters of the Bektashi Community, Tirana, Albania.

Sources:

The Bektashi Order of Sufis. www.bektashi.net.

Birge, John Kingsley. *The Betashi Order of Dervishes*. London: Luzac & Co., 1937.

Rexheb, Baba. *Islamic Mysticism and Bektashism*. Babagan Books, 2007.

Trix, Frances. *Spiritual Discourse: Learning with an Islamic Master*. Philadelphia: University of Pennsylvania Press, 1993.

Beshara School of Intensive Esoteric Education

Chisholme House, Roberton, Nr. Hawick, Roxburghshire, Scotland, UKTD9 7PH

The Beshara School of Intensive Esoteric Education (also known as the Beshara Foundation) was founded in 1971 at Swyre Farm in Gloucestershire, England. It is dedicated to the study of the writings of Muhyiddin Ibn'Arabi, a twelfth-century mystic born in Andalucia, Spain. Ibn'Arabi authored over 300 books, most growing out of his intense experience of God. He taught that there was only One Absolute Being, apart from which there is no other existence. He saw the unity of existence as the essence of all religion, a belief which causes many of his Islamic contemporaries and critics to judge him a pantheist.

The Beshara School has constructed a program which assists people in understanding their personal existence as an aspect of the One Reality. From the orginal center, other facilities were purchased throughout England. In the 1980s Sherborne House, which had served as the center of John Godolphin Bennett's work, was purchased and now serves as the international headquarters. Additional centers were opened in Canada, the Netherlands, and Australia. The Beshara School came to the United States when a center was opened in Berkeley, California in 1976. The American center has developed a study program, publishes the works of Ibn'Arabi, and holds a variety of workshops which apply his ideas to everyday life.

Membership: Not reported. There are contacts located in Australia, Brazil, Germany, Indonesia, Israel, Netherlands, and Spain.

Sources:

Beshara. www.beshara.org.

al-'Arabi, Ibn. *The Bezels of Wisdom*. New York: Paulist Press, 1980.

———. *Sufis of Andalucia*. Berkeley and Los Angeles: University of California Press, 1971.

Landau, Ron. *The Philosophy of Ibn 'Arabi*. London: Allen and Unwin, 1959.

Burhaniyya Sufi Order

Current address not obtained for this edition.

The Burhaniyya Sufi Order is a popular Sufi group in Egypt and the Sudan. In the 1980s members of this group moved to Canada and settled in Montreal. A center was formally organized in 1987, which now includes both first generation immigrants and some recent converts. Worship is held on Saturday evenings.

Membership: Not reported.

Sources:

McDonough, Sheila. "Muslims in Montreal." In *Muslim Communities in North America* by Yvonne Haddad and Jane Idleman Smith. Albany, NY: SUNY Press, 1994, pp. 321-22.

Chishti Order of America

PO Box 7249, Endicott, NY 13761

The Chishti Order of America is one of several Sufi groups in the United States which traces its origins to the Chisht Order, one of the four main branches of Sufism. The Chishti Order was founded by Khwaja Abu Ishaq Shami who settled at Chisht in Khurasan in what is present-day Iran during the tenth century. The lineage of leaders of the Chishti Order stayed in Persia until the succession of Khwaja Muinuddin Chishti (1142–1236), the most renowned saint in the order's history. He took the order to India and is regarded as the true founder of the modern order.

Khwaja Muinuddin was born in Sistan, Persia, and raised as a Sufi. The constant warfare he witnessed during his early life reinforced the mystic tendencies he inherited through his family. He studied with Hazrat Khwara Usman Harvani, a teaching master of the Chishti Order, for twenty years and was, upon his departure, granted the khalifat, or succession, of his teacher. He traveled to Lahore and Delhi before settling in Ajmer, then the seat of an important Hindu state. He became a major force in establishing Islam in India. His tomb in Ajmer is sacred shrine as well as the location of the international headquarters of the order.

Over the centuries, various leaders of the order have founded new branches. The two most important are the Nizami (founded by Nizamu'd-Din Mahbubiilahi) and the Sabiri (founded by Makhdum Ala'u'di-Din Ali Ahmad Sabiri). Both orders were started by students of Baba Farid Shakarganilj in the thirteenth century. The Chishti Order of America derives its lineage from the Sabiri branch of the Chishti Order. The Nizami branch is represented in America by the Sufi Order (see separate entry).

The Chishti Order of America was founded in 1972 by Hakim G. M. Chishti as the Chishti Sufi Mission, an affiliate of the Chishti Sufi Mission Society of India in Ajmer. Hakim was a student of Mirza Wahiduddin Begg who was the senior teacher at Ajmer during the 1970s. When Begg died in 1979, Hakim was granted his succession, a fact confirmed in a ceremony in Ajmer in 1980. At the same time, the Chishti Sufi mission was renamed the Chishti Order of America.

Khwaja Muinuddin stressed the essence of Sufism as the apprehension of Divine reality through spiritual means and the suppression of the lower self. He taught the need of devotion to one's spiritual master (Pir) as a necessity for salvation. He also stressed the obligation of humanitarian action in the face of the caste system

Membership: Not reported. In 1981 sheikhs of the order were to be found in New York, Chicago, and Los Angeles.

Sources:

The Chishti website. www.chishti.ru.

Begg, W. D. *The Holy Biography of Hazrat Khwaja Muinuddin Chishti*. Tucson, AZ: Chishti of Mission of America, 1977.

International Association of Sufism
14 Commercial Blvd., Ste. 101, Novato, CA 94949

The International Association of Sufism (IAS), founded in 1983 by Nahid Angha and Ali Kianfar, is a nonprofit, nongovernmental organization of the United Nations Department of Public Information. Its purpose is to promote Sufism to the general public, promote dialogue among Sufi schools, and publish educational material on Sufism. The IAS holds an annual symposium and publishes the journal *Sufism: An Inquiry*. The IAS has NGO/DPI status at the United Nations, to which Nahid Angha serves as the IAS representative.

Angha is the daughter and student of Moulana Shah Maghsoud, a Sufi master from the Uwaiysi School, born in Iran in 1916. Kianfar was also a student of Maghsoud, who gave Kianfar the title Shah Nazar (the Sight of the King). Angha and Kianfar are Masters of the Uwaiysi Tarighat, also based in Novato, California. The Uwaiysi School traces itself to the early Muslim saint Uwaiys-ibn-Amir Moradi-al-Gharani (d. 657 C.E.) of Yemen.

Membership: Not reported.

Educational Facilities:

Institute for Sufi Studies, Novato, California, and Redmond, Washington.

Periodicals: *Sufism: An Inquiry* • *Insight, IAS Newsletter.*

Sources:

International Association of Sufism. www.ias.org/.

Institute for Sufi Studies. instituteforsufistudies.org/.

International Mevlevi Foundation
Current address not obtained for this edition.

In 1995 Dr. Celalettin Celebi (1926–1996), international head of the Mevlevi Order, requested that an international Mevlevi foundation be established to bring the Mevlevis of the world under one roof. The Mevlevi Order continues the work of Mevlana Jalaluddin Rumi (1207–1273), an Islamic mystic poet and possibly the most famous Sufi among non-Muslims. The program of the foundation includes an annual international gathering of the heads of the various branches of the order, the sponsoring of seminars in different parts of the world, and the publication of a journal. An initial international gathering was held in Bodrum, Turkey, in June 1996. Attendees included representatives from Turkey, the United States, England, Germany, Switzerland, Austria, Chile, and Iran.

The foundation also assumes responsibility to inform everyone about actions and applications that are inconsistent with the moral and spiritual values of the Mevlevi tradition, which have been clarified in the last 700 years, preserving the spiritual teachings of Mevlana Jalauddin Rumi.

In modern secularized Turkey, Sufi organizations are illegal (though a law that is widely ignored). As a result of the law, however, common designation such as "Mevlevi Order" or "Mevlevi Tarikat" are avoided, and the Mevlevis are formally established as the International Mevlana Foundation (Uluslararasl Mevlânâ Vakfi), officially a cultural and educational foundation.

Following Dr. Celebi's death in April 1996, his son, Faruk Hemdem Celebi, succeeded him and now oversees the functioning of the International Mevlevi Foundation and other activities of the Mevlevi Order. The son has called for all Mevlevi groups to recognize his authority as the proper head of the order. Until recently, the Threshold Society operated as the American representative of the Mevlevi Order, but it now operates independent of the international order.

Membership: Not reported.

Sources:

International Mevlani Foundation. www.mevlana.net/ and www.dar-al-masnavi.org.

Hermansen, Marcia K. "Hybrid Identity Formations in Muslim America: The Case of American Sufism." Unpublished, undated paper in ISAR collection.

Ja'far-Shadhiliyya Sufi Order
Current address not obtained for this edition.

The Ja'far-Shadhiliyya Sufi Order made a significant impact on the American Sufi community in the 1980s. The group was founded by Shaikh Fadhlalla Haeri, an Iranian formerly affiliated with the Habibiyya Sufis. In 1980, he and a group of followers established Zahra Trust and began to build a community, Bayt al-Deen (home of religion) in Bianco, Texas. The community had as its model the original Muslim community in Medina. Haeri published a number of books through the associated Zahra Publications.

The community survived through the 1980s, but toward the end of the decade, Haeri decided to relocate to England, and the present state of the American membership is unknown.

Membership: Not reported.

Periodicals: *Nuradeen: An Islamic Sufi Journal.*

Sources:

Haeri, Shaykh Fadhlalla. *Beginning's End*. London: KPI/Zahra Publications, 1987.

———. *The Elements of Sufism*. New York: Penguin, 1997.

———. *The Journey of the Self: A Sufi Guide to Personality*. San Francisco: Harper, 1991.

———. *Living Islam*. Dorset, UK: Element, 1989.

Jerrahi Order of America
880 Chestnut Ridge Rd., Chestnut Ridge, NY 10977

The Jerrahi Order of America is the North American affiliate of the Halveti-Jerrahi Sufi Order headquartered in Istanabul, Turkey. The Halveti (also spelled Khalwati) is regarded as one of the original source schools of Sufism, and members attribute its founding to several thirteenth-century Muslim ascetics. The Halveti developed many branches, one of which was founded in the seventeenth century by Hazreti Pir Nureddin Jerrahi (d. 1733). Born in a prominent Istanbul family, Pir Nureddin studied law and at the age of 19 was appointed a judge for the Ottoman Empire's province of Egypt. Just as he was due to sail to his new post, he met Halveti Sheikh ali Alauddin and gave up his legal career to become a dervish. An accomplished student, he soon received *ijazat*, license to teach from his instructor.

The Halveti orders have been characterized by both a strict program of training and emphasis upon individualism (one cause of the continual branching). It has also invested great reverence in any of its leaders who could demonstrate power. Jerrahi is considered a *qutb*, a spiritual pole of the universe, and head of the hierarchy of saints. The order spread throughout the Ottoman Empire and beyond, from Yugoslavia to Indonesia.

The most distinctive practice of the Jerrahi Order is *dhikr* (or zhikr), literally the remembrance of God. Dhikr is the invocation of the unity of God and is performed by the dervishes with in a circle headed by their sheikh.

The Jerrahi Order of America is currently headed by Sheikh Tosun Bayrak al-Jerrahi, who resides in Istanbul. The order was established with in the American-Muslim community in the late 1970s. The Mosque of the Jerrahi Order of America, its main center, is located in Chestnut Ridge, New York.

Membership: As of 2001, four centers were active in America: New York, California, Illinois, and Washington. There are also centers in Buenos Aires, Sao Paolo, and Santiago. The Canadian center is in Toronto. European centers are found in Belgium, Germany, Greece, Italy, and Spain.

Sources:

Halveti-Jerrahi Order of Dervishes. www.jerrahi.org.

Al-Jerrahi, Shaykh Muzaffer Ozak. *Adornement of Hearts*. New York: Pir Press, 1991.

———. *Ashki's Divan*. New York: Pir Press, 1991.

———. *Blessed Virgin Mary*. New York: Pir Press, 1992.

———. *The Garden of Dervishes*. New York: Pir Press, 1992.

———. *Irshad: Wisdom of a Sufi Master*. New York: Pir Press, 1992.

———. *Love Is the Wine*. Monterey, CA: Threshold Books, 1987.

Al-Jerrahi, Muzaffer Ozak. *The Unveiling of Love*. New York: Inner Traditions International, 1981.

Al-Jerrahi al-Halveti, Shaykh Tosun Bayrak. *Divine Governance of the Human Kingdom*. Louisville, KY: Fons Vitae, 1997.

———. *Inspirations: On the Path of Blame*. Monterey, CA: Threshold Books, 1993.

———. *The Name and the Named*. Louisville, KY: Fons Vitae, 2000.

———. *Secret of Secrets*. Islamic Texts Society, 1992.

———. *Suhrawardi: The Shape of Light*. Louisville, KY: Fons Vitae, 1998.

———. *Sufi Chivalry*. Rochester, VT: Inner Traditions, 1991.

———. *The Tree of Being*. Los Angeles, CA: Archetype, 2005.

Al-Jerrahi al-Halveti, Shaykh Tosun Bayrak, and Rabia T. Harris. *What the Seeker Needs*. Monterey, CA: Threshold Books, 1992.

Birgivi, Imam. *The Path of Muhammed: A Book on Islamic Morals and Ethics*. Interpreted by Tosun Bayrak al-Jerrahi al-Halveti. Bloomington, IN: World Wisdom, 2005.

Frager, Robert. *Essential Sufism*. New York: HarperOne, 1997.

———. *Heart, Self & Soul: The Sufi Psychology of Growth, Balance, and Harmony*. Wheaton, IL: Quest Books, 1999.

Friedlander, Shems. *When You Hear Hoofbeats*. Costa Mesa, CA: Mazda Publishers, 1992.

———. *Whirling Dervishes*. Albany, NY: State University of New York Press (January 1992).

Harris, Rabia Terry. *Journey to the Lord of Power: A Sufi Manual on Retreat*. Rochester, VT: Inner Traditions, 1981.

———. *Sufi Book of Spiritual Ascent*. Chicago, IL: Kazi Publications, 1997.

Kebzeh Foundation

Kebzeh Foundation and Essentialist Church of Christ, 2001 45th Ave., Vernon, BC, Canada V1T 6N6

Ahmsta Kebzeh is an ancient spiritual tradition from the Caucasus Mountains that embodies elements of Sufism and Christian mysticism. It describes itself as an applied science of processing the human being by awakening and developing latent human faculties under divine grace and guidance. It is an oral teaching which has been passed on through story, song, and the way of being of the people who carry it.

Ahmsta Kebzeh can be thought of as the science of processing human beings to the level of enabling them to activate and use their utmost human faculties without limit. The life in this universe came to existence as a reflection of a creative power which is the source of everything, and which exists without beginning and without end. This power is electromagnetic in nature with an intelligence and will of its own.

Ahmsta Kebzeh teaches that once an entity comes to existence with a vibration peculiar to potential manifestation of self it enters the World of Creation and starts its cycle of evolution. Every entity which came to existence in creation evolves until ultimately the end of its evolution comes to be one with the very thing it originated from. Evolution takes place in two areas of existence: 1) Material Area, and 2) Mental Area. This cycle of evolution is taking place in everything existing in the world. Humans completed their material evolution some one million years ago and for the last million years have been in the process of evolving in consciousness. The destination of the evolution of human consciousness is ultimately Cosmic consciousness (Christ consciousness), and to such consciousness there is no limit.

The manifestation of this potential is the job of the science of Ahmsta Kebzeh. The application of Ahmsta Kebzeh consists of a long series of physical and mental exercises, somewhat reminiscent of the spiritual exercises brought to the West by Georgei Gurdjieff.

In this generation, Ahmsta Kebzeh has been transmitted orally by Murat Yagan, a Circassian elder who is thought to be the last known living light-holder of this particular tradition. He received it directly from the elders of his people and for the past 20 years has been teaching it to a small group of students in western Canada. The North American group began to work with Murat Yagan in 1975. His teaching work has included lectures, seminars, workshops, evening classes, and casual conversations while working and socializing. Many of these talks were recorded and have been transcribed and now constitute over 4,000 typed pages of material, the first written form the tradition has taken.

The Kebzeh Foundation includes departments and committees, such as The Essentialist Church of Christ and Sunday School, Kebzeh Publications, Distance Education, Application of Kebzeh to the Business of Contemporary Life (AOK), Leaping Committee (includes workshops and proposed Kebzeh School), Newsletter Publication, and Transcription. With in the Kebzeh tradition it is not allowed to receive money for the teaching and the overwhelming percent of all the work done by volunteers.

The Essentialist Church of Christ was founded in 1988 for the purpose of meeting for worship, i.e., showing a loving respect for a higher spiritual power or for someone who represents such a power. The church is based fully on the principles of Ahmusta Kebzeh and on Jesus' teachings under the light of Kebzeh. The church is not interested in proselytizing.

The church takes as guidance the essence of Christ directly. Such guidance is an essential component of mysticism: a faculty peculiar to humans, relating to the direct communion with God, or Ultimate Reality that is neither apparent to the senses nor obvious to the intelligence, but which can be experienced through developing the finest receptivity down in the deepest realm of the subconscious mind; communion with God.

The church affirms a relationship to God and Cosmic Mind and Jesus as the highest example of completed man. Humans' birthright is Christhood. To claim their destiny, human beings must work to awaken their latent human faculties and come to know who they are by discovering God within. The Second Coming of Christ consists of the elevation of the consciousness of all the people on the planet to Christhood.

Membership: Not reported.

Periodicals: *Kebzeh Review Newsletter*.

Sources:

Kebzeh Foundation. www.kebzeh.org.

Yagan, Murat. *Building Up a Kebzeh Community*. Vernon, BC: Kebzeh Publications, 1998.

————. *I Come from behind Kaf Mountain: The Spiritual Autobiography of Murat Yagan*. Putney, VT: Thresholds Books, 1984.

————. "Sufism and the Source." *Gnosis* 30 (Winter 1994): 40-47.

————. *The Teachings of Kabzeh: Essentials of Sufism from the Caucasus Mountains*. Vernon, BC: Kebzeh Publications, 1995.

Khanegah Maleknia Naser Ali Shah

Current address not obtained for this edition.

Khanegah Maleknia Naser Ali Shah is a small Nimatullahis Sufi Order headed by Naser Ali Shah, who moved between centers in Istanbul, Turkey, and Paris, France. Shah's nephew, who resides in Rhode Island, had been designated his kahalifa, and leaders (murids) are found in New York City; Boulder, Colorado; and North Carolina.

Membership: Not reported.

Sources:

Hermansen, Marcia K. "Hybrid Identity Formations in Muslim America: The Case of American Sufism." Unpublished, undated paper in ISAR collection.

Naqshbandi Sufi Order

PO Box 1065, Fenton, MI 48430

The Naqshbandi Sufi Order is an Islamic school of thought and practice that arose in Central Asia and India, spread through China and the Soviet Union in the twentieth century, and came into Europe and North America in the past generation. The word "Naqshband" includes two ideas: naqsh or "engraving" the name of Allah in the heart, and band or "bond" designating the link between the individual and the Creator. Ideally, the Naqshbandi followers practice their prayers and obligations according to the Qur'an and the Sunnah of the Prophet (Muhammad) and keep the presence and love of Allah alive through the personal experience of the link between themselves and Allah. The Naqshbandi Way holds as an ideal continuous worship in every action, both external and internal. It includes the maintenance of the highest level of conduct, keeping an awareness of the Presence of God, Almighty and Exalted, and a complete experience of the Divine Presence.

The Naqshbandi traces its life to one of the Caliphs, Abu Bakr as-Siddiq, who succeeded the Prophet Muhammad in his role of guiding the Muslim community, and takes its foundations and principles from the teachings and example of him and six other outstanding followers of Islam, and Salman al-Farisi, Jacfar as-Sadiq, Bayazid Tayfur al-Bistami, Abdul Khaliq al-Ghujdawani, and Muhammad Baha'uddin Uwaysi al-Bukhari. Of these, Abdul Khaliq formulated worship in the *dhikr* (remembrance of God), and in his letters he set down the code of conduct (*adab*) that the students of the Naqshbandiyya were expected to follow.

Muhammad Baha'uddin Uwaysi al-Bukhari, known as Shah Naqshband, the Imam of the Naqshbandi Tariqat (path), was born in the year 1317 C.E. He adopted a silent method of remembering God which would become a distinguishing feature of the Naqshbandiyya with in the larger Sufi community. Shah Naqshband made the Haj (pilgrimage to Mecca) on three occasions, after which he resided in Merv and Bukhara, and toward the end of his life he settled in his native city of Qasr al-carifan. His school and mosque remain as the largest Islamic center of learning in Central Asia. Shah Naqshband was buried in his garden as he requested, and the

succeeding kings of Bukhara care for his school and mosque. They were recently renovated and reopened after surviving 70 years of Communist rule.

The order is currently headed by Sheikh Muhammad Nazim al-Haqqani, the 40th in the chain of Naqshbandi Masters. He resides in Cyprus. His representative in the United States is Sheikh Hisham Kabbani, his son-in-law. Male followers of the group wear a distinctive dress that includes turbans and green robes.

Membership: Over 10,000 people in North America have been initiated into the Naqshbandi Order. In 1998 there were 18 Naqshbandi centers in the United States and two in Canada. Additional centers can be found in Great Britain, Spain, Sweden, France, Germany, Holland, Italy, Turkey, Cyprus, Egypt, Lebanon, Kenya, Syria, Argentina, Guadeloupe, Indonesia, Japan, Malaysia, Singapore, Pakistan, Brunei, Brazil, South Africa, and Venezuela.

Remarks: Among the disciples of Sheikh Nazim is the sultan of Brunei, reportedly the richest man in the world.

Sources:

The Naqshbandi-haqqani Sufi Order. www.naqshbandi.net.

Kabbani, Sheikh Hisham. *The Naqshbandi Way: History and Guidebook of the Saints of the Golden Chain*. Chicago: Kazi Press, 1995.

Naqshbandiyya-Mujaddidiyya Order of Sufism

c/o Golden Sufi Center, PO Box 428, Inverness, CA 94937

Naqshbandi Sufis, named after Bah ad-dn Naqshband (d.1389), are known as the "silent Sufis" because they practice the silent meditation of the heart. They consider God to be the silent emptiness who is most easily accessed in silence. They also attach great importance to dreams, which they consider to be a form of guidance along the Path. Unlike other Sufis, they do not practice *samac*, i.e., sacred music or dance, nor do they adopt a different dress. Their meetings consist of a period of silent meditation followed by dream work and discussion.

Sufi dream work combines both spiritual and psychological approaches, helping individuals to realize inner guidance and the inner processes of the Path as they are imagined in dreams. Dream work is regarded as the modern equivalent to the ancient Sufi teaching stories. Participants in dream meetings are encouraged to share their dreams, particularly those deemed to have a spiritual dimension.

The Naqshbandi Sufi movement was brought to the West in 1966 by Irina Tweedie, upon the death of her sheikh, Guru Bhai Sahib. He was a member of a family of Hindu Sufis that belonged to the lineage of the Naqshbandiyya-Mujaddidiyya, an Indian branch of the Naqshbandiyya Sufi order. Tweedie was the first Western woman to be trained in this particular form of Sufism. Tweedie retired in 1992, and died seven year later. Her work has been continued by Llewellyn Vaughan-Lee. In 1991 he was sent to northern California where he founded The Golden Sufi Center, whose purpose is to make the work and teachings of the Naqshbandiyya-Mujaddidiyya Order of Sufism available. Part of his work has been to integrate the traditional Sufi approach to dreamwork with the insights of modern psychology. He holds retreats and seminars in North American, Europe and Australia

Membership: In 2008 there were 500 members in American meditation groups operating in northern California; Los Angeles, California; New York City; Seattle; Boulder, Colorado; Minnesota; Chicago, Illinois; North Carolina; Boston, Massachusetts; New Hampshire, Michigan, and Vancouver, B.C. There were also meditation groups in a variety of locations in Germany, Switzerland, England, Spain, Australia, South Africa, and Argentina.

Sources:

The Golden Sufi Center. www.goldensufi.org.

Bancroft, A. *Weavers of Wisdom: Women Mystics of the Twentieth Century*. London: Arkana, 1989.

Rawlinson, Andrew. *The Book of Enlightened Masters*. La Salle, IL: Open Court, 1997.

Tweedie, Irina. *Chasm of Fire: A Woman's Experience of Liberation through the Teachings of a Sufi Master*. Tisbury, UK: Element Books, 1979. Expanded version as: *Daughter of Fire*. Inverness, CA: The Golden Sufi Center, 1986.

Vaughan-Lee, Llewellyn. *Sufism: Transformaion of the Heart. Inverness*. Iverness, CA: The Golden Sufi Center, 1995.

Nimatollahi-Gonabadi Erfan Foundation

23141 Verdugo, Ste. 200, Laguna Hills, CA 92653

The Nimatollahi-Gonabadi Erfan Foundation is a branch of the Nimatollahi Sufis headed by Sultan Husayn Tabandah, Rida al Sha (b. 1914), a resident of Iran. The majority of members in the United States are Iranian Americans. In 1960 he appointed his son as khalifa and successor.

Membership: Not reported. Centers are reported in Orange County, California; Washington, D.C.; Australia; and Toronto, Canada.

Sources:

Bonyad Erfan Gonabadi. www.erfan-gonabadi.com.

Hermansen, Marcia K. "Hybrid Identity Formations in Muslim America: The Case of American Sufism." Unpublished, undated paper in ISAR collection.

The Nimatullahi Sufi Order

306 W 11th St., New York, NY 10014

Khaniqahi-Nimatullahi (also known as Khaniqahi-Nimatullahi) is the Western representative of the Nimatullahi Order of Sufis, an Iranian Sufi order named after Nur addin M. Ni'matullah (1330–1431). Ni'matullah was born in Aleppo, in present-day Syria, the son of a Sufi master, and studied with several Sufi teachers before meeting his principal teacher, Abdullah al-Yafi-i, in Mecca. After Sheikh Yafi-i's death in 1367, Ni'matullah began a period of traveling, finally settling in Mahan, Persia (Iran), whence the order spread throughout Persia and India.

The present head of the order is Dr. Javad Nurbakhsh, former head of the Department of Psychiatry of the University of Teheran, Iran. Nurbakhsh brought the order to the West in the 1970s and by 1983 had established centers in London, England, and several United States cities. He also created Khaniqahi-Nimatullahi Publications as the publishing arm of the order, and it immediately began to generate English-language Sufi materials.

Nurbakhsh defines a Sufi as one who travels the path of love and devotion towards the Absolutely Real. Knowledge of the Real is accessible only to the Perfected Ones, the prime model being Ali, the son-in-law of Mohammad, to whom Iranian Shi'ite Muslims trace their authority. Ali traveled the path as a disciple of Mohammad and became not just a spiritual master, but the *qutb*, or spiritual axis, for his time. The head of the Nimatullahi Order continues in the succession of spiritual masters to whom disciples can look for knowledge.

Membership: The U.S. centers are in New York, Washington, Boston, San Francisco, Los Angeles, Santa Cruz, San Diego, Seattle, Chicago, and Santa Fe. Foreign centers are located in Great Britain, Canada, Mexico, Germany, France, the Netherlands, Spain, Sweden, Austria, Russia, Australia, Benin, Burkina Faso, Republic of Mali, and the Ivory Coast (Africa).

Periodicals: *Sufi: A Journal of Sufism.*

Sources:

Nurbakhsh, Javad. *Discourses of the Sufi Path*. New York: Khaniqahi-Nimatullahi Publications, 1996.

———. *In the Paradise of the Sufis*. New York: Khaniqahi-Nimatullahi Publications, 1979.

———. *In the Tavern of Ruin*. New York: Khaniqahi-Nimatullahi Publications, 1978.

———. *Masters of the Path*. New York: Khaniqahi-Nimatullahi Publications, 1980.

———. *Traditions of the Prophet*. New York: Kahniqahi-Nimatullahi Publications, 1981.

———. *What the Sufis Say*. New York: Khaniqahi-Nimatullahi Publications, 1980.

Osho Mevlana Foundation

26 Billin Rd., Myocum, NSW, Australia 2482

The Osho Mevlana Foundation was founded in 1976 by Reshad Feild, the first sheikh of the Mevlana school of Sufism to travel to the West. The Mevlana lineage was initiated by Mevlana Jelaluddin Rumi (1207–1272), the great thirteenth-century mystic poet. Raised as a Sufi, Rumi was an ecstatic and a visionary. He settled in Qonya, in present-day Turkey, and his tomb became the headquarters of his followers. They formally organized soon after his death.

Sufis share the basic beliefs of Islam but are organized around the leader, the sheikh, of the order who is considered the axis of the conscious universe. Rumi was especially devoted to music, and the Mevlana Order developed a musical emphasis. The order practices the *zhikr*, the remembrance of God, and became noted for its practice of the Turn, a dance in which individual Sufis attempted to establish a universal axis within themselves. For this practice the Mevlana became famous in popular folklore as the "whirling dervishes."

Reshad Feild was raised in London. He studied with a Gurdjieff/Ouspensky group, as well as with the Druids, and finally became a professional spiritual healer. In the early 1960s he met Pir Vilayat Khan, leader of the Sufi Order, and was initiated as a Sufi sheikh by him. In the fall of 1969, still on a spiritual pilgrimage, Feild encountered a man referred to simply as Hamid. As a result of this encounter, he traveled to Turkey to study. While there he met Sheikh Suleyman Dede, the head of the Mevlana Order.

In 1976 Feild left Turkey and moved to Los Angeles, where he became a Sufi teacher and healer. Shortly after the move, he assisted in Dede's visit to America. During this trip, Dede initiated Feild as the first sheikh in the West. Feild founded the Institute for Conscious Life, which later became the Mevlana Foundation.

Membership: Not reported. Groups affiliated with the foundation can be found in the United States, Canada, and England.

Sources:

Feild, Reshad. *Cooperation in the Three Worlds*. Los Angeles: Institute for Conscious Life, 1974.

———. *The Invisible Way*. San Francisco: Harper & Row, 1979.

———. *The Last Barrier*. New York: Harper & Row, 1976.

———. *I Come from behind Kaf Mountain*. Putney, VT: Threshold Books, 1984.

Qadiri Rifai Tariqa/Ansari Tariqa

PO Box 833, Nassau, NY 12123

The Qadiri Rifai Tariqa is a traditional Islamically based Sufi order that is a result of a merging of two Sufi orders. The Qadiri Tariqa was founded by the Sufi saint and scholar Es-Seyyid Es-Sheikh Abdul Qadir al Geylani (or Jilani) (1078–1166). The Rifa Tariqa was founded by another Sufi saint, Es-Seyyid Es-Sheikh Ahmed er Rifa'i (1120–1183). Both the Qadiri and the Rifai Tariqas continue to exist as separate Sufi orders.

Es-Seyyid Es-Sheikh Muhammad Ansari, who was born in Baghdad, moved to Erzincan in northeastern Turkey in the early 1900s. He was a sheikh of the Rifai order and a descendant of the Sufi saints Sheikh Abdul Qadir al Geylani and Sheikh Ahmed er Rifai. In Turkey he met Es-Seyyid Es-Sheikh Abdullah Hashimi, a Rifai, with whom he studied for many years. When Es-Seyyid Es-Sheikh Muhammad Ansari strengthened his connection to the Qadiri Order, Sheikh Abdullah Hashimi sent him to Istanbul to establish the Qadiri Rifai Tariqa.

Sheikh Muhammad Ansari headed the Qadiri Rifai Tariqa from 1915 until his death. His son, Es-Seyyid Es-Sheikh Muhyiddin Ansari, born in Erzincan, succeeded him. Sheikh Muhyiddin Ansari raised 56 *khalifas* (representatives) and many thousand of *murids* (students) in Turkey and the Balkans. Sheikh Taner Ansari took *biat* (initiation) with him during Ramadan in 1970, and continued to train with him until Sheikh Muhyiddin Ansari died in 1978. Sheikh Muhyiddin Ansari left the *tasarruf* (executive power) of the order to Sheikh Nureddin Ozal. The order affirms that while raising 10 khalifas, Sheikh Nureddin Ozal served everyone with whom he came in contact with humility and love.

In May 1993 Sheikh Nureddin Ozal passed away, leaving the *tasarruf* of the order to Es-Seyyid Es-Sheikh Taner Ansari Tarsusi er Rifai el Qadiri. Sheikh Taner Ansari is the current pir of the Qadiri Rifai Tariqa. The current headquarters of the Tariqa is in the state of New York where, under the behest of Sheikh Muhyiddin Ansari, Sheikh Taner Ansari founded the Ansari Tariqa, a new order of the Qadiri Rifai Tariqa.

The Ansari Tariqa is dedicated to serving humanity as it follows the traditional methods of Sufi instruction and worship. The intention of the Sufi murid is to embody the meaning of the Holy Qur'an in his or her daily life. The murid maintains *rabita* (heart connection) with his or her sheikh or sheikha (guide) and cleanses the *nafs* (ego) through *zikr* (remembrance of Allah). Each student has his or her own assignment prescribed by the guide. The goal of the Sufi path is to love Allah. Students are taught how to have a loving relationship with Allah in all phases of life.

Zikr and other Sufi practices are transmitted personally down through the generations to the present sheikhs and sheikhas of the Sufi Tariqas and their students. A Sufi sheikh is a teacher of these practices who has been appointed by his or her own sheikh in a line that recedes back to Prophet Muhammad.

Ansari Tariqa is an international order. Centers are located in South Africa, Tanzania, the United Kingdom, Bosnia, Australia, Turkey, and Mexico, as well as throughout the United States. Live classes open to the public are presented on the Internet.

Membership: Not reported. The main centers are in Berkeley, Marin County, and Los Angeles, California; and Santa Fe, New Mexico.

Periodicals: *Call of the Divine*.

Sources:

Qadiri Rifai Tariqa. www.qadiri-rifai.org.

Ansari, Taner. *Alternative Healing*. Nassau, NY: Ansari Publications, 2007.

———. *The Sun Will Rise in the West: The Holy Trail*. Nassau, NY: Ansari Publications, 2000.

———. *What about My Wood! 101 Sufi Stories*. Nassau, NY: Ansari Publications, 2006.

Rifa'i Marufi Sufi Fellowship/Universal Center of Light

PO Box 202, Chapel Hill, NC 27514-0202

The Rifa'i Marufi Sufi Fellowship is an international Rifa'i Sufi group, and thus part of a tradition that began with Ahmed er Rifa'i (1118–1181), a descendant of the Prophet Muhammad who was born and grew up in what is now Iraq. It has centers (*tekkes*) in Chapel Hill, North Carolina; New York City; Manisa, Turkey; and Baku, Azerbaijan. It is under the international leadership of Sheikh al-Hajj Sherif er-Rifa'i. American work began in 1992 when Sheikh Sherif Chatalkaya came to the United States following an invitation from the Jerrahi Order of America's center in New York City. He subsequently received an invitation to settle in North Carolina from a businessman who was a Sufi. The group's life is built around *dhikr* (remembrance of God), teaching sessions, and the performance of devotional songs.

Membership: Not reported. In 1995, there were 50 members in the United States. The organization is undergoing restructuring and renaming.

Sources:

Hilaamn, Hugh Talat. "A Silk Road Runs in the U.S." Unpublished paper presented at the Islam in America Conference, Chicago, Illinois, 1995.

School of Islamic Sufism (MTO Shahmaghsoudi)

PO Box 5827, Washington, DC 20016

The School of Islamic Sufism (Maktab Tarighat Oveyssi Shahmaghsoudi) is the present manifestation of the Oveyssi Sufi Order. It traces its roots through a lineage of Sufi masters to Amir-al Mo'menin Ali and Oveys Gharani, who lived in Yemen at the time of Muhammad. Amir al Mo'menin, also known as Hazrat Ali, represents the essence of the teachings of the School of Islamic Sufism. He was a close companion of Muhammad's and received the teachings of the Holy Prophet inwardly. On the other hand, Hazrat Oveys also received the teachings of Islam inwardly, and although he never physically met Muhammad, he lived by the Prophet's principles. According to the history of the school, the Prophet would say of Hazrat Oveys, whom he never met: "I feel the breath of the Merciful, coming to me from Yemen." Shortly before the Prophet died, he directed Omar (the second caliph) and Hazrat Ali (the first imam of the Shi'a) to take his cloak to Hazrat Oveys. This act confirmed the method of heart-to-heart communication through which Hazrat Oveys had received the essence of Islam.

The method of the passing of the cloak represents two significant elements in the teachings of the Holy Prophet that constitute the method of instruction of the School of Islamic Sufism: Cognition (understanding) must take place inwardly, and must be confirmed—as it was in the case of Hazrat Oveys, and Amir al-Mo'menin.

Since that time, the cloak and the methods of receiving knowledge through the heart (symbolizing divine illumination) and of recognizing the recipient have been handed down through an unbroken succession of Sufi masters. This process creates the only hierarchy within the School of Islamic Sufism. The designated Sufi master, called the *pir*, represents the essence of the Sufi Way.

The present master of the School is Molana-al-Moazam Hazrat Salaheddin Ali Nader Shah Angha (b. 1945), also known as Hazrat Pir. Hazrat Pir is the 42nd master in a lineage dating back 1,400 years. He was born in Tehran, Iran, and was tutored by his grandfather, who was the 40th Sufi master of the Oveyssi Order, and father, Molana Shah Maghsoud Sadegh Angha, the Order's 41st master.

Hazrat Pir's duties have included the designing and supervision of the construction of the Sufi Center known as Sufi Abad, located in Karaj (close to Tehran). Following his move to the United States (with his father) in 1979, Hazrat Pir took the lead in expanding the audience for the sacred teachings. He has authored more than 50 books.

Hazrat Pir's teaching includes the attempt to apply the knowledge of the sacred to tangible forms that become visible symbols of the creative power of the soul. One such symbol is a shrine near Novato, California, designed by Hazrat Pir as a memorial to his father. In accordance with the science of *jafr* (relation of letters and numbers), the dimensions of the building may be converted to letters that yield the name of his father. The shape of the roof structure represents Allah (in Arabic). All the sides of the roof join to form a summit representing the unification of the human being with God, signifying that God in the heavens can be known—in the heart, the pure elevated state of the human being.

Membership: In 1998 the school included some 400,000 adherents in a global network of centers encompassing the United States, Canada, Europe, Africa, Australia, New Zealand, and Asia.

Educational Facilities:

MTO College, London, England.

Sources:

School of Islamic Sufism (MTO Shahmaghsoudi). www.shahmaghsoudi.org.

Hermansen, Marcia K. "Hybrid Identity Formations in Muslim America: The Case of American Sufism." Unpublished, undated paper in ISAR collection.

Shadhiliyya-Miriamiyya

Current address could not be obtained for this edition.

Shadhiliyya-Miriamiyya is the name given to the group of students who gathered around author Frithjof Schoun (1907–1998), who studied with Sheikh Ahmad al-Awadi of the Shadhiliyya-Alawiyya Sufis in Algeria. Schoun was born in Basle, Switzerland, the son of a concert violinist. During his youth, he read the Upanishads and the *Bhagavad Gita*, and soon found the works of French esoteric philosopher Rene Guenon. As a young man he studied Arabic, and in 1932 made his first trip to Algeria, where he met the celebrated Sheikh Ahmad al-Alawi; six years later, he traveled to Egypt, where he met Guenon. Schoun served in the French Army during World War II, became a prisoner of the Germans, and finally sought asylum in Switzerland. He lived there until moving to the United States in 1980.

Through his many books and articles Schoun became known as the leader of the traditionalist or perennialist movement, which centered on a mystical monist view of the cosmos. After emigrating to the United States, he settled in Bloomington, Indiana, where he continued to live until his death in 1998. Known to his students as Sheikh Isa Nur al-Din, he offered an eclectic Islamic Sufi *tariqa* (path) that, though based in Islam, included insights from Native American teachings, Hinduism, and various forms of mysticism. Additionally, at some point he had had some visionary experiences of the Virgin Mary (also a figure in Muslim teachings), and his teachings (Tariqa Miriamiyya) had a special place for her.

Membership: Not reported.

Sources:

Borella, Jean. "Rene Guenon and the Traditionalist School." In *Modern Esoteric Spirituality*, ed. Antpoine Faivre and Jacob Needleman, pp. 330–358. New York: Crossroad, 1992.

Schoun, Frithjof. *The Essential Writings of Frithjof Schoun*. Ed. S. H. Nasr. World Wisdom Books, 1986.

———. *Islam and the Perennial Philosophy*. London: World of Islam Publications, 1976.

———. *Understanding Islam*. London: Allan & Unwin, 1963.

Shadhiliyya Sufism

c/o Shadhuli Sufi Center of Peace and Mercy, 2531 Jackson Rd., No. 169, Ann Arbor, MI 48103

The Shadhili Path of Sufism was founded in Egypt in the thirteenth century C.E. by as-Sheikh Ali Abu-I-Hasan as-Shadhili. Currently, leadership has passed to Sheikh al-Qutb al-Gawth, the Guide of the Shadhili Path. Since 1959, the sheikh has resided at the Mount of Olives in Jerusalem, and has been the imam at the Masjid al-Aqsa (the Dome on the Rock) for many years. The Dome on the Rock is sacred to the Holy House in Mecca for its place in the tradition of the al-Mi'raj (night journey) of the Prophet Muhammad from the Ka'ba in Mecca to the al-Aqsa Mosque and from there to the heavens. The sheikh is well known to many people both in Palestine and elsewhere in the world. In 1993 he decided that he should travel to other countries, and at the same time an order came to him from Allah to give teachings to all those in every part of the world who were sincerely seeking for the truth of their existence. Up until then the teachings had been offered only in Jerusalem.

An American following began to be created in the mid-1990s. The Sidi Muhammad Press prints materials representative of the group.

Membership: Not reported.

Sources:

Shadhuli Sufi Center of Peace and Mercy. www.sufiheart.com.

Society for Sufi Studies

c/o The Institute for the Study of Human Knowledge, Box 176, Los Altos, CA 94023

Alternate Address: Octagon Press, Box 227, London, U.K. N6 4EW.

Indries Shah (1924–1996) was a twentieth-century Sufi teacher who led a public career of note, but also became the focus of intense speculations about his true beliefs and affiliations. He was born in Simla, India, in 1924, to an Indian father and Scottish mother. Brought to England as a teenager, he would live most of his life in his adopted homeland. His father was a physician from Afghanistan (who met his mother while studying in Edinburgh), and Shah claimed a lineage that went back to the Prophet Muhammad. Shah was tutored by his father and after finishing his secondary education in England attended the Edinburgh Medical School for a period, though he did not finish his course of study.

In his thirties, he became the director of studies for the Institute for Cultural Research and began a process of teaching about Sufism. His first book on Sufism, *The Sufis*, appeared in 1964. It was the first of 20 on the subject. Shah was considered by his followers to be the greatest living exemplar of Sufism, but there was some debate over the source of his authority. Shah himself had to present a document to a prominent Western Sufi, John Godolphin Bennett, in support of a claim that he had been sent to the West by an esoteric school, possibly the same one that Georgei Gurdjieff represented. (Bennett was a student of Gurdjieff.) In his writings, Shah suggested that Gurdjieff was an amateur who had stumbled on some true Sufi knowledge, and by implication suggested that he (Shah) was the true inheritor of the tradition.

Ja'far Hallaji suggested that Shah was a Naqshbandi Sufi who also had the authority to initiate people in the lineage of several Sufi orders, but no acknowledged Sufi teacher emerged to back that claim. In any case, a number of people who encountered Shah's vast writings saw him as an authoritative teacher. Shah sees Sufism as only incidentally connected to Islam and hence a more attractive set of teachings for a Western audience. Among his leading disciples in North America is psychologist Robert Ornstein.

As the actual content of the teachings is secret, details are somewhat difficult to substantiate, as is the very organization of followers of the society who operate in small groups across North America and Europe. In an early book, *The Diffusion of Sufi Ideas in the West*, a training program was laid out. The potential Sufi learns about Sufism and then makes contact with some Sufis. After an interview, the aspirant will be assigned some initial reading. The aspirant joins a study group or other low-demand activity. The leader begins to guide the individual, who eventually may be sent on a pilgrimage to further stimulate development. Members of study groups receive regular mailings of "Sufi stories," which form the content of their discussions.

In the United Kingdom, Octagon Press served as a publisher and distributor of Shah's books. In the United States, the Institute for the Study of Human Knowledge (ISHK) has been the principal distributor for Shah's materials. Since the mid-1970s, ISHK has also been sponsoring research and educational programs on the human mind, and on the processes shaping one's beliefs, institutions, and experience.

Shah suffered two heart attacks in 1988, but continued to work and write until his death at the end of 1996.

Membership: Not reported.

Sources:

Lewis, L., ed. *The Diffusion of Sufi Ideas in the West*. Boulder, CO: Institute for Research on the Dissemination of Human Knowledge, 1972.

Shah, Indries. *Special Problems in the Study of Sufi Ideas*. Tunbridge Wells, U.K.: Society for the Understanding of the Foundation of Ideas, 1966.

———. *The Sufis*. New York: Jonathan Cape, 1964.

———. *The Way of the Sufis*. London: Octagon, 1968.

Williams, L. F. Rushbrook, ed. *Sufi Studies: East and West—A Symposium in Honour of Indries Shah's Services to Sufic Studies*. New York: Dutton, 1973.

Sufi Circle

St. Lawrence of Canterbury, 655 Old Country Rd., Dix Hills, NY 11746

The Sufi Circle is a small nonsectarian Sufi society started by Ned Gandevani, a stock trader and business teacher, on Long Island, New York, in 2004. The group meets one Sunday a month and introduces participants to major Sufi principles and teachers, including transpersonal psychologist Robert Frager, Sheikh Ragib of the Halveti-Jerrahi Order; Sheikh Kabir Helminski of the Mevlevi order and co-director of the Threshold Society; and Sheikhah Fariha al Jerrahi, the guide for the Nur Ashki Jerrahi Sufi Order. The group favors the teachings of the Halveti-Jerrahi Order (famous for the whirling dervishes).

The circle explores both Sufi traditions and other spiritual paths in an attempt to recognize the divine across multiple perspectives. It also runs the Rumi Sunday School for children. Members seek to serve others in need by taking part in food drives, raising funds for disaster victims, and collecting holiday toys for children.

Membership: Not reported.

Sources:

Sufi Circle. www.suficircle.com/index.html.

Haminski, Kabir. *The Knowing Heart: A Sufi Path of Transformation*. Boston: Shambhala, 2000.

Smith, Huston, Robert Frager, and James Fadiman. *Essential Sufism*. New York: HarperOne, 1999.

Sufi Foundation of America

50 Sufi Rd., Torreon, NM 87061

The Sufi Foundation of America was founded in the 1980s by Adnan Sardan, a Sufi master from Iraq who has studied and been recognized for his accomplishments in five Sufi Orders: the Qadri, Nashibandi, Rafai, Mevlevi, and Malamari. Sardan understands the term Sufism to have derived from the Arabic word *sufir*, to be clear. When the mind and body are pure, one can see the spirit within. Murky vision is caused by attachments to belief, family, traditions, and religion. The Sufi is free of such attachments and has nothing to do with the sense world of the physical, the ego, emotions, tension, and other problems.

The Sufi exercises, including music and dancing, chanting, drumming, and whirling, develop the person and teach self-reliance. The teacher merely assists the student on his or her own path to aloneness with god.

Sardan teaches at the center in New Mexico, the major program being a two-month camp each summer. Followers are found across North America and Europe.

Membership: Not reported.

Sources:

Sufi Foundation of America. www.sufifoundation.org.

Sarhan, Adnan. *The Human Chicken*. Torreon, NM: Sufi Foundation of America, 1989.

———. "The Sufi Path: Making Life Lovable and Love Livable." *Tantra* 4 (1992): 33–47.

Way of the Spirit with Adnan Sardan: Remarkable Experiences Told by His Students. Torreon, NM: Sufi Foundation of America, 1989.

Sufi Ruhaniat International (Sufi Islamia Ruhaniat Society)

PO Box 51118, Eugene, OR 97405

HISTORY The Sufi Ruhaniat International grew out of the work of Samuel L. Lewis (1896–1971), a Sufi teacher who was originally initiated by Pir Hazrat Inayat Khan in 1923 and is known by his religious name, Ahmed Murad Chisti. Following World War II, Lewis traveled to Africa and Asia, where he received initiations from several Sufi orders, as well as studying in Asia with a number of Buddhist and Hindu teachers. Returning to America in 1962, he began to teach and in 1966 initiated his first disciples. He found a responsive audience among the hippies of San Francisco, California, and began to teach them the spiritual dances and walks he

had developed. In 1968 he met Pir Vilayat Inayat Khan, son and successor to Hazrat Khan, and he and his disciples began to work with the Sufi Order.

After Lewis's death, his disciples continued to affiliate with the Sufi Order, but during the early 1970s issues emerged that led to their separation from Pir Vilayat and their continuance as a separate movement.

BELIEFS The teachings of the society draw upon the works of Pir Hazrat Inayat Khan and Murshid Samuel Lewis. The society has developed a central focus on the path of initiation and discipleship. The purpose of initiation is fulfilled in the realization of the One, within and without. The relationship between teacher and disciple is also stressed. It exists to provide the training that leads to realization of the divine essence believed to be in each human, and leads the disciple into a life of service to God and humanity.

Lewis is most remembered for his introduction of spiritual dances and walks in the late 1960s. The dances use motion to facilitate a change in the individual dancer's whole life, to make it whole. The dances usually combine simple dance motions with controlled breathing and a mantra (sacred words of power). They are usually done to simple rhythmic music and should lead to states of ecstasy and devotion to Allah. The first dances were derived from the dervish dances of the Middle East. The walks combined feeling, movement, and recitation of sacred phrases. Lewis also left a set of mystical writings that were published by the society. He is considered a true mystic.

ORGANIZATION The society is headed by a board of trustees. Centers have been established around the world to teach classes in various topics for the general public and the *mureeds* (those on the path of initiation), and to provide settings for the practice of the spiritual dances and walks. The Center for the Dances of Universal Peace has been created to facilitate the development of new dances and the training of dance leaders.

Membership: In 2008 the society reported approximately 2,000 members in 50 countries.

Periodicals: *Sufi Islamia Ruhaniat Society Newsletter*.

Sources:

Sufi Ruhaniat International. www.ruhaniat.org.

Lewis, Samuel L. *In the Garden*. New York: Harmony Books, 1975.

———. *Introduction to Spiritual Brotherhood*. San Francisco: Sufi Ismalia, 1981.

———. *The Jerusalem Trilogy*. Novato, CA: Prophecy Pressworks, 1975.

———. *Sufi Vision and Initiation*. San Francisco: Sufi Ismalia, 1986.

The Sufi Movement

Sufi Center of Washington, 1613 Stowe Rd., Reston, VA 22094-1600

Alternate Addresses: International Headquarters: 11 rue John Rehfous, 1208 Geneva, Switzerland. National Representative of Canada: 4432 John St. Vancouver, BC V5V 3X1.

The Sufi Movement emerged in 1927 following the death of Hazrat Inayat Khan (1892–1927), founder of the Sufi Order. Rabia Martin, a woman whom Khan had initiated and designated as his successor, was rejected by Khan's family and his European followers. Making use of an opening provided by Khan's not leaving a written will, the European members reorganized as the Sufi Movement and selected Maheboob Khan (1887–1948), Inayat's brother, as its leader. He was succeeded in 1948 by a cousin, Mohammad Ali Khan (1881–1958). Mohammad Ali Khan was in turn succeeded by Musharaff Khan (1895–1967) and Fazal Inayat Khan (1942–1990), who resigned in 1982.

Following Fazal Khan's stepping down, a collective leadership was formed, but it fell apart in 1985 and the movement split. The core of the Sufi Movement continued under the joint leadership of Hidayat Inayat Khan (b. 1917) and Murshida Shahzadi. Hidayat, a son of Hazrat Inayat, became the sole leader of the movement in 1993.

Hidayat Inayat Khan was only 10 years old when his father passed away in 1927. He later studied music in Paris at L'Ecole Normale de Musique and eventually became a professor in the Music School of Dieulefit, Drome, France, and conducted an orchestra in Haarlem in the Netherlands. He authored numerous compositions, including both secular music and a collection of Sufi hymns. He is a founding member of the European Composers' Union.

The movement closely resembles the Sufi Order, headed by Vilayat Inayat Khan, and is organized in five divisions to focus on universal worship, community, healing, symbology, and esoteric activity. The movement is based in the Netherlands, but has spread across Europe and to Canada and the United States. Members meet weekly for *dhikr* (worship) and classes.

Membership: Not reported. There are offices in New Zealand, South Africa, Switzerland, Mexico, Russia, India, Norway, Germany, and Canada.

Sources:

The Sufi Movement. www.sufimovement.org.

The Gathas. Katwijk, Netherlands: Servire, 1982.

Khan, Fazal Inayat. *Old Thinking: New Thinking*. New York: Harper & Row, 1979.

Khan, Hidayat Inayat. *Sufi Teachings: Lectures from Lake O'Hara*. Victoria, BC, Canada: Ekstasis Editions, 1994.

Sufi Order

Sufi Order International, 5 Abode Rd., New Lebanon, NY 12125

HISTORY Sufism was brought to the United States in 1910 by Pir Hazrat Inayat Khan (1881–1927). An Indian-born musician, he was initiated into the Nizami branch of the Chishti Order, one of the main Sufi schools of India. (The other main branch, the Sabiri, is represented in the United States by the Chishti Order of America.) The Chishti School was brought to India from Persia, and in its new home absorbed elements of Hindu Vedantic thought that gave it a distinctive position within the Sufi world. The idea in coming to the West was to westernize the Sufi path. By bringing together East and West, it was thought, a basis for unity in the religion of love and wisdom could be laid. Doctrinal bias would be replaced by the power of mysticism.

Khan's first initiate in the United States was Rabia Martin. Prior to World War I, Martin developed a center in San Francisco, which included among its members Samuel L. Lewis. Pir Inayat died suddenly in 1927 and succession was passed to his then 11-year-old son Vilayat. In the United States, Martin claimed the succession as the first initiate and *murshid* (minister). The European members and the family refused to recognize her, partly because she was female, and the American and European work separated. During the last years of her life, Martin (d. 1947) heard of and began to investigate a new Indian teacher, Meher Baba, but she died before completing her evaluation. Martin was succeeded by Ivy Oneita Duce, who became a disciple of Meher Baba and led the Sufi following entrusted to her under his care.

The Sufi Order was reintroduced to the United States in the 1960s by Pir Hazrat Vilayat Khan (b. 1916). His work on the West Coast was boosted by an encounter with Samuel Lewis. Lewis, a former member of Martin's group, did not accept Meher Baba. After World War II, Lewis traveled to Asia and received several independent initiations and recognition as a Sufi murshid. He founded a Sufic group in San Francisco in 1966 that he brought into the Sufi Order in 1968. (Eventually, much of that work was lost when in 1977 some of Lewis's students rejected some of Khan's regulations for the Order and withdrew to form the Sufi Islamia Ruhaniat Society.) Khan succeeded in building a stable national organization during the 1970s, and has become one of the most respected and popular teachers within the loosely organized New Age Movement.

BELIEFS The teachings of Inayat Khan have been summarized in 10 "Sufi Thoughts." The Thoughts affirm that there is but one God, Master, Holy Book (i.e., the sacred manuscript of nature), religion, law, brotherhood, moral principle, object of praise, truth, and path. Meditation and dervish dancing are the main means to induce mystic consciousness.

The activity headed by Khan has three aspects. The Sufi Order proper is an esoteric school into which individuals accepting Khan as their spiritual counselor are admitted by initiation (*Bayat*). Initiates follow a study program and follow a set of personal practices, including special breathing techniques and the repetition of a *wazifa* (or mantrum) usually delineated at the time of initiation. The more esoteric religious activity is called the Universal Worship of the Church of All. Universal Worship is built around a liturgy developed by Inayat Khan that attempts to emphasize what is perceived as the essence of religion with in all religions. Inayat Khan initiated the building of the Universel, a temple of all religions, in France shortly before his death. The Healing Order is built around the group healing ritual developed by Inayat Khan. Under Vilayat, the healing work has pushed the Sufi Order into the middle of the holistic health movement that became a prominent part of the larger New Age movement during the 1970s.

ORGANIZATION The American work of the Sufi Order is headed by Pir Khan and a board of trustees, which controls the property and assets of the Order. An Interstate Council, consisting of the trustees and representatives of all the branches of the Order, oversees financial transactions and coordinates programs. Center and branch leaders are appointed by Pir Khan. The on-going administration of the Order is in the hands of a secretary general. Internationally, the Sufi Order is headquartered in France, with national branches in England, the Netherlands, France, Germany, Austria, Italy, Switzerland, India, and Canada. Within the United States, the order is headquartered at the Abode of the Message, a community near Lebanon Springs, New York, located on the site of a former Shaker Village.

Membership: Not reported. There are centers across the United States and Canada.

Periodicals: *The Message • Under the Wings • Ziraat.*

Sources:

Sufi Order. www.sufiorder.org.

De Jong-Keesing, Elisabeth. *Inayat Khan*. The Hague, the Netherlands: East-West Publications Fonds B. V., 1974.

Initiation. Lebanon Springs, NY: Sufi Order, 1980.

The Sufi Order. New Lebanon, NY: Message, Sufi Order, 1977.

Toward the One. New York: Harper & Row, 1974.

Inayat Khan, Vilayat. *The Message in Our Time*. San Francisco: Harper & Row, 1978.

The Threshold Society

270 Quarter Horse Ln., Watsonville, CA 95076

The Threshold Society was founded by members of the Mevlevi Order, which emerged from the life and work of the great mystic poet Mevlana Jelaluddin Rumi (d. 1273), possibly the most famous Sufi among non-Muslims. The late Dr. Celalettin Celebi (d. 1996) of Istanbul, Turkey, the international head of the Mevlevi Tariqa (order) and a direct descendant of Rumi, appointed Dr. Edmund Kabir Helminski as a representative of the order in North America. Helminski is a Mevlevi sheikh, appointed to that position by Sheikh Suleyman Loras (d. 1985) of Konya, Turkey (whose son, Sheikh Jelaluddin Loras, was active in building a following for the order on the American West Coast). Helminski and his wife, Dr. Camille Helminski, have been working within the Mevlevi tradition for some two decades. They cofounded the Threshold Society, and the related Threshold Books, a publishing house focused on Sufi and related contemporary spiritual writings. Kabir Helminski is the author/translator of three books of Sufi poetry, and he and Camille Helminski have edited two collections of Rumi's writings.

The most distinctive aspect of Mevlevi Sufis is the Sema ritual, from which they have earned their popular designation as Whirling Dervishes. Just as the *kirtan* practiced by members of the International Society for Krishna Consciousness has often been the image people have of Hinduism, so too the whirling ritual of the Mevlevi, which can be traced back to Rumi, has become the image of Sufism for many. Mevlevis maintain that by revolving in harmony with all things in nature, the believer testifies to the existence and majesty of the Creator, thinks of him, gives thanks to him, and prays to him. It is their belief that revolving is the fundamental condition of our existence, as all beings are comprised of revolving electrons, protons, and neutrons in atoms, and human beings live by means of a set of revolutions—of these particles, of the blood in one's body, and ultimately of the stages of one's life.

The ritual attempts to unite the three fundamental components of human nature: the mind (as knowledge and thought), the heart (through the expression of feelings, poetry, and music), and the body (by activating life, by the turning). It represents the human being's spiritual journey, an ascent by means of intelligence and love to Perfection (*Kemal*). Turning toward the truth, the believer grows through love, transcends the ego, meets the truth, and arrives at Perfection.

The Threshold Society, as an outpost of the Mevlevi Order, has set as its purpose the facilitating of the experience of divine unity, love, and wisdom in the world. The society offers training programs, seminars, and retreats in North America and around the world. These are intended to provide a structure for practice and study within Sufism and spiritual psychology. The order is working to apply traditional Sufi principles to the conditions of contemporary life.

In May of 1994 at a conference in Konya, Turkey, on "Mevlana and Human Rights," a gathering of eminent cultural and spiritual figures declared the Threshold Mevlevi Center in Brattleboro, Vermont, "New Konya" in recognition of the work of the Threshold Society and Threshold Books in spreading Rumi's message of universal love. Following the death in 1996 of Dr. Celalettin Celebi, Faruk Hemdem Celebi, his son, succeeded him as leader of the Mevlevi Order. In 1999 Edmund and Carmille Helminski moved to California, where they now run the Threshold Society independently of Faruk Celebi.

Membership: Not reported.

Sources:

Threshold Society. www.sufism.org/.

Helminski, Kabir. *An Anthology of Translations and Versions of Jalaluddin Rumi.* Brattleboro, VT: Threshold Books, 1998.

———. *Jewels of Remembrance: A Daybook of Spiritual Guidance: Containing 365 Selections from the Wisdom of Rumi by Jalal Al-Din Rumi.* Brattleboro, VT: Threshold Books, 1996.

———. *The Knowing Heart.* Boston: Shambala, 2000.

———. *Living Presence: A Sufi Way to Mindfulness and the Essential Self.* Los Angeles: Jeremy Tarcher, 1992.

Helminski, Kabir, and Camille Helminski, trans. *Rumi: Daylight: A Daybook of Spiritual Guidance.* Brattleboro, VT: Threshold Books, 1995.

Tijaniyya Sufi Path

Current address could not be obtained for this edition.

The Tijaniyya Sufi Path is known as the "Muhammadan spiritual way" (Tariqa Muhammadiyya) because its practices are based on the Qur'an and Sunnah. The Tijani litanies consist of three principles mandated by the Islamic Revelation and widely reported sayings of the Prophet Muhammad: asking God for forgiveness (*astaghfirullah*), offering prayers to the Prophet (*salat 'ala-n-nabi*), and affirming the Oneness of God by saying "There is nothing worthy of worship but God." The Tijaniyya places special emphasis on the "Prayer of Opener," which provides access to the continued spiritual guidance of the Muhammadan Reality. But Tijanis do not value this more than the Qur'an, which they hold to be the best form of *dhikr*, or remembrance.

Tijaniyya was founded by Sheikh Abu Abbas Ahmad al-Tijani al-Hassani (1737–1815), a descendant of the Prophet (*sharif*) and a scholar known for his piety, generosity, and knowledge of the Islamic sciences. In his early years Sheikh Tijani traveled widely in Morocco, Algeria, Tunisia, Egypt, and the Hijaz in search of knowledge. He practiced the litanies of many Sufi orders in turn: various branches of the Shadhiliyya, the Qadiriyya, and the Khalwatiyya. After refusing to be invested with spiritual authority in any Sufi order, Sheikh Tijani eventually agreed to become an instructor of the Khalwatiyya under Egyptian Sheikh Mahmud al-Kurdi. In 1784, Sheikh Tijani received the first of many waking meeting with the Prophet Muhammad.

The Prophet told Sheikh Tijani to leave all his previous Sufi affiliations and ordered him to found a new Sufi order. All litanies of the order, both obligatory and supererogatory, were thus dictated to Sheikh Tijani directly from the Prophet, who told him that anybody who became initiated into the Tijani order would become a disciple of the Prophet Muhammad himself. By 1798, Sheikh Tijani had been so invested by God through the Prophet that he had attained the two highest positions in the Sufi hierarchy of saints: the Seal of Muhammadan Sainthood and the Pole of Poles. He required his followers to exalt the honor of all saints, and claimed no preeminence over the living companions of the Prophet. Doctrinally speaking, the Tijaniyya emphasizes classic Sufi doctrines such as thanksgiving, asceticism, subsistence in God, and kindness toward God's creation.

In the years since Sheikh Tijani died, the movement has been led by a succession of leaders, including Sheikh Umar Futi; Sheikh Muhammad al-Hafiz al-Tijani, a Mauritanian who brought the Tariqa to West Africa for the first time; Sheikh al-Hajj Abdullah Niasse, the father of Sheikh Ibrahim Niasse; Sheikh al-Hajj Malik Sy; and Sheikh Ibrahim Niasse (1990–1975), who was widely recognized as possessing *fayda*, the flood of spiritual grace enabling access to Divine gnosis foretold by Sheikh Tijani. A majority of Tijanis in the world today trace their initiation through Sheikh Ibrahim Niasse.

The Tijaniyya was introduced into the United States in 1976 by Alhamdulillah Sheikh Hassan Cisse (b. 1945), the grandson and spiritual heir of Sheikh Ibrahim Niasse. Sheikh Cisse holds degrees in Islamic studies and Arabic literature from Ain Shams University in Cairo, Egypt, and a master of philosophy from the University of London. His pursuit of a Ph.D. in Islamic studies at Northwestern University in Evanston, Illinois, was interrupted when his father, Sayyidi Ali Cisse, passed away, and he returned to Senegal to become the imam of Sheikh Ibrahim's community

Membership: Not reported. The Tijaniyya has major centers in New York; Atlanta, Georgia; Washington, D.C.; Chicago; and Memphis, Tennessee, with new communities in many other major cities. It has also spread to the Caribbean and South America in recent years.

Sources:

Tijaniyya Sufi Path. www.tijani.org.

Nasr, Jamil M. Abun. *The Tijaniyya.* London: Oxford, 1964.

Wright, Zachary. *On the Path of the Prophet.* New York: African American Islamic Institute, 2005.

❈ African-American Islam

African Islamic Mission

1390 Bedford Ave., Brooklyn, NY 11216

The African Islamic Mission emerged in the 1970s in Brooklyn, New York. It is an African-American orthodox Muslim organization that is headquartered in the Al Masjid Al Jaaami'a under the leadership of Imam Alhaji Obaba Muhammadu. The mission is most noted for its development of a black history publication series, which includes reprints of many rare and hard to find books on the origins of the Africans.

Membership: Not reported.

Sources:

African Islamic Mission, Inc.
www.inetmgrs.com/onepeoples/AfricanIslamicMission.htm.

Introduction to Islam: The First and Final Religion. Brooklyn, NY: African Islamic Mission, n.d.

Ahmadiyya Anjuman Ishaat Islam, Lahore, Inc.

1315 Kingsgate Rd., Columbus, OH 43221-1504

Alternate Addresses: International Headquarters: c/o Darus Salaam, 5 Usman Block, New Garden Town, Lahore-16, Pakistan. Canadian Headquarters: Box 964, Postal Station A, Vancouver, BC, Canada.

Following the death of Hazrat Mirza Ghulam Ahmad (1835–1908), founder of the Ahmadiyya Movement in Islam, a disagreement arose among his followers concerning the founder's status. Those who followed Ahmad's family proclaimed him a prophet. However, others, led by Maulawi Muhammad Ali, considered Ahmad the Promised Messiah and the greatest *mujaddid*, i.e., renewer of Islam, but denied that Ahmad had ever claimed the special status of "prophet." Ali asserted that Ahmad's use of that term was entirely allegorical. The claim of prophethood for Ahmad has resulted in the assignment of Ahmadiyya Muslims to a status outside of the Muslim community and has led to their persecution in several Muslim-dominated countries.

Members of the Ahmadiyya branch founded by Ali in 1914 came to America in the 1970s and incorporated in California.

Membership: Not reported. There are four centers in the United States and two in Canada. There are an estimated 100,000 people affiliated with the movement worldwide. Centers are found in Indian communities around the world.

Periodicals: *The Islamic Review.*

Sources:

Lahore Ahmadiyya Movement. www.muslim.org.

Ali, Muhammad. *The Founder of the Ahmadiyya Movement*. Newark, CA: Ahmadiyya Anjuman Ishaat Islam, Lahore, 1984.

Aziz, Zahid, comp. *The Ahmadiyya Case*. Newark, CA: Ahmadiyya Anjuman Ishaat Islam, Lahore, 1987.

Faruqui, Mumtaz Ahmad. *Truth Triumphs*. Lahore, Pakistan: Ahmadiyya Anjuman Ishaat-I-Islam, 1965.

Faruqui, N. A. *Ahmadiyyat in the Service of Islam*. Newark, CA: Ahmadiyya Anjuman Ishaat Islam, Lahore, 1983.

Ahmadiyya Movement in Islam

U.S. National Headquarters, 15000 Good Hope Rd., Silver Spring, MD 20905

The Ahmadiyya movement was not brought to the United States with the intention of its becoming an African-American religion. Ahmadiyya originated in India in 1889 as a Muslim reform movement. It differs from orthodox Islam in that it believes that Hazrat Mirza Ghulam Ahmad (1835–1908) was the promised Messiah, the coming one of all the major faiths of the world. It has, in the years since its founding, developed the most aggressive missionary program in Islam.

Ahmad had concluded, as a result of his studies, that Islam was in a decline and that he had been appointed by Allah to demonstrate its truth, which he began doing by authoring a massive book, *Barahin-i-Ahmaditah*. He assumed the title of *mujaddid*, the renewer of faith for the present age, and declared himself both Madhi, the expected returning savior of Muslims, and the Promised Messiah of Christians. He advocated the view that Jesus had not died on the cross, but had come to Kashmir in his later life and died a normal death there. The Second Coming is not of a resurrected Jesus, but the appearance of one who bore the power and spirit of Jesus.

Ahmadiyya came to the United States in 1921 and shortly after the first U.S. center was established in Chicago. Its founder, Dr. Mufti Muhammad Sadiq, began to publish a periodical, *Muslim Sunrise*. Though some immigrants were recruited, the overwhelming majority of converts consisted of American blacks. Only since the repeal of the Asian Exclusion Act in 1965 and the resultant emigration of large numbers of Indian and Pakistani nationals has the movement developed a significant Asian constituency in the United States.

A vast missionary literature demonstrating Islam's superiority to Christianity has been produced by the Ahmadiyya movement. Jesus is widely discussed. He is viewed as a great prophet who only swooned on the cross. He then escaped from his tomb to India and continued many years of ministry. He is buried at Srinagar, India, where the legendary Tomb of Issa (Jesus) is a popular pilgrimage site. The denial of the divinity of Jesus is in line with the assertion of Allah as the one true God. Christianity is seen as tritheistic.

Ahmadiyya Muslim Community U.S.A. has auxiliaries for various professions: the Ahmadiyya Medical Association (AMMA), the Ahmadiyya Scientists Association (AAMS), Ahmadiyya Computer Professionals (AACP), and Ahmadiyya Architects and Engineers (IAAAE). There are also chapters of these auxiliary organizations in other countries, which provide worldwide relationships for members and bring experience and knowledge to the organizations.

At present, the movement is small. Headquarters were moved to Washington, D.C., in 1950 after a quarter century in Chicago, and are now located in Maryland.

Membership: Not reported.

Periodicals: *The Ahmadiyya Gazette* • *The Muslim Sunrise*

Sources:

Ahmadiyya Muslim Community. www.alislam.org/.

Ahmadiyya Muslim Community U.S.A. www.ahmadiyya.us.

Ahmad, Hazrat Mirza Bashiruddin Mahmud. *Ahmadiyyat or the True Islam*. Washington, DC: American Fazl Mosque, 1951.

———. *Invitation*. Rabwah, Pakistan: Ahmadiyya Muslim Foreign Missions, 1968.

Dard, A. R. *Life of Ahmad*. Lahore, Pakistan: Tabshir Publications, 1948.

Khan, Muhammad Zafrulla. *Ahmadiyyat: The Renaissance of Islam*. London: Tabshir Publications, 1978.

Nadwi, S. Abul Hasan Ali. *Qadianism: A Critical Study*. Lucknow, India: Islamic Research and Publications, 1974.

Turner, Richard Brent. *Islam in the African-American Experience*. Bloomington: Indiana University Press, 1997.

American Muslims

c/o The Mosque Cares (Ministry of W. Deen Mohammed), PO Box 1061, Calumet City, IL 60409

Though there are a variety of Muslim groups functioning within the black community, when one reads in the media or hears mention of "Black Muslims," the most likely reference is to the Nation of Islam, founded by Master Wallace Fard Muhammad and headed for many years by its purported prophet, Elijah Muhammad (1897–1975). After Elijah Muhammad's death the organization's name was changed successively to the World Community of Islam in the West and, in 1980, the American Muslim Mission. It is the most successful of the Black Muslim bodies, having spread across the nation in the 1960s during the period of the black power movement. Its success and that of one dissident member, Malcolm X, led to numerous books and articles about it.

Following the death of Noble Drew Ali, founder of the Moorish Science Temple of America, there appeared in Detroit, Michigan, one Wallace D. Fard, a mysterious figure claiming to be Noble Drew Ali reincarnated. He proclaimed that he had been sent from Mecca to secure freedom, justice, and equality for his uncle (the Negroes) living in the wilderness of North America, surrounded and robbed by the cave man (the white man). (The white man was also referred to as the "Caucasian devil" and "Satan.") Fard established a temple in 1930 in Detroit. Among his many converts was Elijah Poole.

The 1930s was a time of intense recruiting activity and dispute for the Nation of Islam. Within its ranks discussion focused on Fard's divinity, legitimacy, and role. In 1934 a second temple was founded in Chicago, and the following year Fard dropped from sight. By this time, Poole, known as Elijah Muhammad, had risen to leadership.

Under Elijah Muhammad's leadership, the Black Muslims emerged as a strong, cohesive unit. Growth was slow, due in part to Muhammad's imprisonment during World War II as a conscientious objector. As the new prophet, he composed the authoritative *Message to the Blackman in America*, a summary statement of the Nation of Islam's position.

The central teaching of the Nation of Islam can be seen as a more sophisticated version of the Moorish Science study of the black man's history. According to Muhammad, Yakub, a mad black scientist, created the white beast, who was then permitted by Allah to reign for six thousand years. That period was over in 1914. Thus, the twentieth century was the time for the Nation of Islam to regroup and regain an ascendant position.

Education, economics, and political aspirations were major aspects of the Black Muslim program. The first University of Islam was opened in 1932, and parochial education (with many of the schools being named after Clara Muhammad, Elijah Muhammad's wife) has been a growing and effective part of the Nation ever since. Besides the common curriculum, Black Muslim history, Islam and Arabic have been stressed. Classes are offered through the twelfth grade. Economically, the Black Muslims have stressed a work ethic and business development. The weekly newspaper carries numerous advertisements from businesses owned by Black Muslims. Politically, Black Muslims looked to the establishment of a black nation to be owned and operated by blacks.

Black Muslims excluded whites from the movement and imposed a strict discipline on members to accentuate their new religion and nationality. Food, dress, and behavior patterns were regulated; a ritual life based on, but varying from, orthodox Muslim form, was prescribed.

Black Muslims instituted a far-reaching program in furtherance of their aspirations. An evangelizing effort to make the Muslim program known within the black community was sustained in a weekly newspaper, *Muhammad Speaks*. During the 1960s and into the 1970s, growth was spectacular. By the time of Elijah Muhammad's death there were approximately 70 temples across the nation, including the South, and over 100,000 members.

In 1975 Elijah Muhammad died and was succeeded by his son, Wallace D. Muhammad. During the decade of Wallace's leadership, a move toward both orthodox Islam and decentralization of the organization has occurred. These moves have been reflected in the name changes, a schism in which conservatives left to found movements continuing the peculiar emphases of the Nation of Islam prior to 1975, and the beginning of acceptance of the American Muslim Mission by orthodox Muslims. *Muhammad Speaks* was renamed *Bilalian News*.

In 1985 Wallace Muhammad, with the approval of the Council of Imans (ministers), resigned his post as leader of the American Muslim Mission and disbanded the movement's national structure. That move represents the establishment of a fully congregational polity by the Muslims whose local centers are now under the guidance of their imans rather than under the control of the Chicago headquarters. Wallace D. Muhammad, also known as Warith Deen Muhammad, now operates as an independent Muslim lecturer and a member of the World Council of Masajid, which is headquartered in Mecca, Saudi Arabia. His emphasis is upon the proper image of Muslims worldwide.

Membership: Not reported. There were approximately 200 centers in the mission at the time of its disincorporation. Foreign centers were located in Barbados, Belize, Guyana, Bermuda, Jamaica, the Bahamas, Canada, St. Thomas Island, and Trinidad.

Periodicals: *Muslim Journal*.

Sources:

The Mosque Cares. www.themosquecares.com.

Lincoln, C. Eric. *The Black Muslims in America*. Boston: Beacon Press, 1961.

Muhammad, Elijah. *Message to the Blackman in America*. Chicago: Muhammad Mosque of Islam, No. 2, 1965.

Muhammad, Wallace D. *Lectures of Elam Muhammad*. Chicago: Zakat Propagation Fund Publications, 1978.

Muhammad, Warith Deen [Wallace D. Muhammad]. *As a Light Shineth from the East*. Chicago: WDM Publishing Co., 1980.

———. *Religion on the Line*. Chicago: W. D. Muhammad Publications, 1983.

Ansaaru Allah Community

716 Bushwick Ave., Brooklyn, NY 11221

Members of the Ansaaru Allah Community, also known as the Nubian Islaamic Hebrew Mission, believe that the nineteenth-century Sudanese leader Muhammed Ahmed Ibn Abdullah (1845–1885) was the True Mahdi, the predicted Khaliyfah (successor) to the Prophet Mustafa Muhammed Al Amin. After his death, Al Mahdi was buried in the Sudan, and the group he founded (the Ansaars) continued under his successors—namely, As Sayyid Abdur Rahman Muhammad Al Madhi, As Sayyid Al Haadi Abdur Muhammad Rahmaan Al Madhi, and As Sayyid Al Imaan Isa Al Haadi Al Madhi. Presently, the third successor, who is also Al Mahdi's great-grandson, leads the mission.

The Community teaches from the Old Testament (Tawrah), the Psalms of David (Zubuwr), the New Testament (Injiyl), and the Holy Qur'an. The last testament, the Holy Qur'an, was given to the last of the prophets of the line of Adam, Mustafa Muhammad Al Amin. The group teaches that Allah is alone in his power, the All (*Tawhiyd*, "Oneness"), and does not use the term *God*. They believe that Jesus is the Messiah and that Ali (599–661 C.E.) and Fatima (610–633 C.E.) are the successors to Mustafa Muhammad Al Amin.

Adam and Hawwah (Eve) are believed to have been Nubians. After the flood, during the time of the prophet Nuwh (Noah), Nuwh's son Ham desired to commit sodomy while looking at his father's nakedness. This act resulted in the curse of leprosy being put upon Ham's fourth son, Canaan, thus turning his skin pale. In such a manner did the pale races come into existence, including the Amorites, Hittites, Jebusites, and Sidonites, who are all the descendants of Canaan. Mixing blood with these "subraces" (so-called because they are no longer pure Nubians), is unlawful for Nubians.

From the seed of Ibrahiym (Abraham), three nations were produced: the nation of Isaac, whose descendants later became known as Israelites, and whose lineage is through Abraham's son Jacob; the nation of Ishmael, whose descendants are called the Ishmailites; and the nation of Midian, whose descendents are known as Midianites and whose lineage stems from Ketura, Abraham's third wife. The Israelites were enslaved for 430 years in Egypt. The Ishmailites, it was prophesied, were to be enslaved in a land not their own for 400 years. The Nubians of the United States, the West Indies, and various other places around the world are the seed of Ishmael (and hence Hebrews). Al Madhi taught that all with straight hair and pale skin were Turks; however, this does not include people of color, such as Latinos, Japanese, Koreans, Cubans, Sicilians, and so on.

Under As Siddid Al Imaan Isa Al Haahi Al Madhi's guidance, the Nubian Islaamic Hebrew Mission was begun in the late 1960s in New York. In 1970, the prophesies of the "Opening of the Seventh Seal" (Revelation 8:1) began to come to fruition with the opening of the Ansaaru Allah Community and the publishing of literature to help remove the veil of confusion from Nubians. In 1972, communities were established in Philadelphia, Pennsylvania; Connecticut; Texas; and Albany, New York. The following year, centers were opened in Washington, D.C.; Baltimore, Maryland; North Carolina; South Carolina; Georgia; Michigan; Florida; and Virginia. In the Caribbean, centers were opened in Trinidad, Jamaica, Puerto Rico, Guyana, and Tobago. During the next decade, the movement spread to South America, Ghana, Hawaii, and other places around the world.

The symbol of the community is a six-pointed star (made from two triangles) in an inverted crescent. This is considered to be the seal of Allah.

Membership: Not reported. There are several hundred members in the United States.

Periodicals: *Ansar Village Bulletin*.

Sources:

Dietary Laws of a Muslim. Brooklyn, NY: Ansaru Allah Community, 1979.

Muhammad Ahmad: The Only True Madhi! Brooklyn, NY: Ansaru Allah Community, 1979.

Muhammad Al Madhi, Al Hajj Al Iman Isa Ibd'Allah, trans. *The Holy Qur'aan*. Brooklyn, NY: Ansaru Allah Community, 1977.

Muslim Prayer Book. Brooklyn, NY: Ansaru Allah Community, 1984.

Warner, Philip. *Dervish: The Rise of an African Empire*. New York: Taplinger, 1975.

What Is a Muslim? Brooklyn, NY: Ansaru Allah Community, 1979.

Hanafi Madh-hab Center, Islam Faith

7700 16th St. NW, Washington, DC 20012

HISTORY The Hanafi Madh-hab Center was first established in the United States during the late 1920s by Dr. Tasibur Uddein Rahman, a "Mussulman" (i.e., Muslim) from Pakistan. In 1947 Khalifa Hammas Abdul Khaalis (born Ernest Timothy McGee) met and became a student of Dr. Rahman, who gave him his new name and taught him the *sunnah* (the tradition and practice) of the Prophet Muhammad. In 1950 Dr. Rahman sent Khalifa Hamaas Abdul Khaalis into the Nation of Islam (now the American Muslim Mission) to guide the members into Sunni Islam (the faith and practice followed by the great majority of Muslims). By 1956 Khalifa Hamaas Abdul Khaalis was the national secretary of the Nation of Islam. He left the Nation of Islam in 1958, however, after unsuccessfully trying to convince its leader, Elijah Muhammad, to change the direction of the movement. He then established a Hanafi Madh-hab Center in Washington, D.C.

At the beginning of 1973, Khalifa Hamaas Abdul Khaalis wrote letters to the members and leaders of the Nation of Islam in which he once again asked them to change to Sunni Muslim belief and practice. On January 18, 1973, members of the Nation of Islam came into the center in Washington, D.C. (which also served as Khalifa Hamaas Abdul Khaalis's home) and murdered six of his children and his stepson. His wife was wounded. Subsequently, five members of the Philadelphia Nation of Islam group were convicted of the murders, only to receive relatively light sentences.

In 1977 Khalifa Hamaas Abdul Khaalis and other Al-Hanif Mussulmans, as members of the group are called, took action against the showing of a soon-to-be-released motion picture, *Mohammad, Messenger of God*, which they considered sacrilegious. They took over three buildings in Washington, D.C., and held people hostage for 38 hours. In the process, one man was killed. For this action Khalifa Hamaas Abdul Khaalis was sentenced to spend from 41 to 120 years in prison, and 11 of his followers were also convicted and sentenced. Because no believing Muslim was on the jury, Khalifa Hamaas Abdul Khaalis considers the jury to have lacked impartiality.

BELIEFS The Al-Hanif Hanafi Mussulmans uphold the two standards of Islam, the Holy Qur'an and the Hadiths, and are Sunni Muslims (obeying all things laid down by Allah to the Prophet Muhammad). They also follow the 124,000 prophets, major and minor, and believe in all holy books, from the perspective of Allah's knowledge. The Holy Qur'an is the final seal of all prophets and prophecy. The word *Hanafi* in their name means "unconditional" and "uncompromising."

The Hanafi Mussulmans have taken a special interest in presenting Islam to African Americans and in informing them that Islam is a religion that does not recognize distinctions of race or color.

ORGANIZATION Authority for Al-Hanif Hanafi Mussulmans is vested in the chief *iman* (teacher), Khalifa Hammas Abdul Khaalis, and each mosque is headed by an iman appointed by him.

Membership: Not reported. There are estimated to be several hundred Hanafi Muslims in the United States. Mosques are located in Washington, D.C.; New York City; Chicago, Illinois; and Los Angeles, California.

Periodicals: *Look and See*.

Sources:

Hanafi Madh-hab Center, Islam Faith. www.al-hanifhanafimdhbctr.com.

Khaalis, Hamaas Abdul. *Look and See*. Washington, DC: Hanafi Madh-hab Center, Islam Faith, 1972.

Lost-Found Nation of Islam

c/o Minister Ishmael Abdul-Salaam, 3040 Campbelton Rd., SW, Atlanta, GA 30311

The Lost-Found Nation of Islam emerged in 1977 under the leadership of Silis Muhammad, who had joined the original Nation of Islam in the 1960s. As a member of the Nation, he had developed a reputation for his promotion of the Nation's tabloid, *Muhammad Speaks*, and as a result was invited to the Nation's headquarters in Chicago to manage the paper's national circulation. He became a close confidant of Elijah Muhammad and eventually assumed a role as his spiritual son (there was no biological relationship).

Following Elijah Muhammad's death in 1975, Silis Muhammad rejected the changes instituted by the Nation's new leader, Warith Deen Muhammad, the son of Elijah Muhammad. In 1977 he charged Warith Muhammad with being a false prophet and demanded that he turn the property of the Nation back to his father's genuine followers. Soon afterward, Silis Muhammad left to reorganize the Nation of Islam under his own leadership with headquarters in the South. In 1982 he started a new edition of *Muhammad Speaks*, the name of the original having been changed. In 1985 he published an expanded book-length version of his attack upon Warith Deen Muhammad and an alternative program for the reorganized Nation.

Soon after Silis Muhammad attempted to resurrect the Nation of Islam, another prominent leader, Louis Farrakhan, also left and founded a rival Nation of Islam. Silis Muhammad and Farrakhan disagreed on the role of Elijah Muhammad in regards to Jesus. Farrakhan had interpreted some of Elijah Muhammad's statements as meaning that he had claimed to be the fulfillment of some of Jesus' prophecies. Silis Muhammad rejected that interpretation. In the wake of the disagreement the two have gone their separate ways.

The Lost-Found Nation of Islam headed by Silis Muhammad has established headquarters in Atlanta. The Nation has reaffirmed that Allah appeared in the person of Wallace Fard Muhammad in 1930 and that he spoke face-to-face with Elijah Muhammad from 1931 through 1933. Hence, Elijah Muhammad is Moses, and the biblical account (and the account in the Qur'an) is a prophetic and symbolic history of the African American of today.

Membership: In 2008, 13 temples associated with the Lost-Found Nation could be found across the United States.

Periodicals: *Muhammad Speaks*.

Sources:

Muhammad, Silis. *In the Wake of the Nation of Islam*. College Park, GA: Author, 1985.

Moorish-American National Republic

2530 N. Calvert St., Ste. 101, Baltimore, MD 21218

The Moorish-American National Republic is one of the groups rooted in the vision of Prophet Noble Drew Ali, aka Timothy Drew (1886–1929). Drew argued that blacks are an Asiatic people group known as Moors, descendants of the ancient Moabites who originally dwelt in Mecca, which is the site of the Garden of Eden. Drew started a temple in New Jersey in 1913 and moved to Chicago in the 1920s. The prophet's most famous text is the *Holy Koran of the Moorish Science Temple of America*, which serves as the holy book of the movement he founded.

After Drew's death the Moorish movement developed several factions. The Moorish-American National Republic traces its roots to the Moorish group led by John Givens El who was succeeded by Richardson Dingle-El and his brother Timothy. The current leader is Grand Sheik Joel Bratton-Bey while the National Secretary is Grand Sheikess Yumnah El. The group also refers to itself as the Moorish Science Temple and also as the Divine and National Movement of North America, Inc., #13.

Membership: Not reported.

Sources:

Moorish-American National Republic. www.moorishnationalrepublic.com.

The Moorish Orthodox Church in America
Diocese of New Jersey, Ongs Hat Rd. & Magnolia Ave., Pemberton, NJ 08068

The Moorish Orthodox Church is one of several groups to emerge from the original Moorish Science Temple founded by Noble Drew Ali. In the 1950s, in the Baltimore/D.C. area, some poets and jazz musicians encountered a remnant of the temple and individually acquired passports like the ones originally given to temple members, which were indicative of their new identity as Moors. They then formed the Moorish Orthodox Church of America, which they envisioned as partly Moorish Science and partly Eastern Orthodox. The latter element resulted from their acquaintance with various independent bishops with Old Catholic and Eastern Orthodox lineages.

In the early 1960s one of the church's original members, Warren Tartaglia (better known as Walid al-Taha), a musician and author of a now rare text, *The Hundred Seeds of Beirut*, initiated several people into the church and together they founded a new temple in Manhattan. The temple structure incorporated a head shop called the Crypt, and a Moorish Science reading room. The church also acquired a campsite in northern New York, where relationships were developed with the Ananda Ashrama. The campsite was eventually relocated to Millbrook, New York, where in the 1960s Timothy Leary (1920–1996) had established the headquarters of the League for Spiritual Discovery, and from which the psychedelic spiritual movement was launched.

During this period, the church dropped its ties to the Eastern Orthodox tradition and adopted a spirituality drawn from Sufism and Ismaili Islam. Over the years, it also absorbed elements of Advaita Vedanta, Tantrism, psychedelic mysticism, and Native American symbolism. When the community at Millbrook split up, the membership of the church scattered and through the 1980s interest lagged, though two small groups, one in Manhattan and one in Dutchess County (where Millbrook is located), preserved some form of community existence. At the end of the 1990s, however, some members began to work for a revived Moorish Orthodox Church. They restarted the church periodical, *The Moorish Science Monitor* (discontinued in 1967), and reprinted a basic Moorish Orthodox Church pamphlet, also out of print for three decades.

The church found early inspiration in the writing of Noble Drew Ali and has from the beginning attempted to explore the esoteric dimensions of those writings, especially the basic text, the *Circle Seven Koran*. The spiritual search conducted by the early members led not to a new belief system but to an individualized appropriation of spirituality tied together by what is thought of as a spiritual aesthetic. Members tend to share similar opinions of traditional religion (they are opposed to it) and toward a spectrum of "libratory teachings" (they accept them). They describe their perspective as a "rootless cosmopolitanism" that discovers a universal spirit hidden (occultized) anywhere, but available in all cultures. The Moorish Orthodox Catechism, then, centers on the "Six Pillars" of Moorish Science: Love, Truth, Peace, Freedom, Justice, and Beauty.

To symbolize this shared aesthetic, church members are encouraged to recreate their identity by taking a new name and some appropriate title (such as Moorish governor, metropolitan, deacon, vicar, exilarch, or imam). The Moorish hierarchy is self-appointed; anyone is free to print passports. Because all Moors have authority, they are entitled to titles.

Given the egalitarian nature of the church, as it has been revived a spectrum of new structures have appeared (on the Internet), including the Upper Left Temple of the Far West, based in Seattle, Washington (www.geocities.com/Heartland/Woods/4623/catechism.htm); the Moorish Fire Shrine, in Bisbee Arizona; and the Diocese of New Jersey (www.geocities.com/moorishorthodoxchurch/). The diocese of New Jersey maintains an online directory of church members.

Membership: Not reported.

Educational Facilities:

Hakim Bey Diocesan Theological College.

Periodicals: *The Journal of the Moorish Paradigm* • *The Moorish Science Monitor*.

Sources:

The Moorish Orthodox Church in America, Diocese of New Jersey. www.geocities.com/moorishorthodoxchurch/.

"History and Catechism of the Moorish Orthodox Church of America." www.deoxy.org/moorish.htm.

Moorish Science Temple of America
1445 Constitution Ave. NE, Washington, DC 20002

Timothy Drew (1886–1929), a black man from North Carolina, had concluded from his reading and travels that blacks were not Ethiopians (as some early black nationalists were advocating) but Asiatics, specifically Moors. They were descendants of the ancient Moabites and their homeland was Morocco. He claimed that the Continental Congress had stripped American blacks of their nationality and that George Washington had cut down their bright red flag (the cherry tree) and hidden it in a safe in Independence Hall. Blacks were thus assigned to the role of slaves.

As "Noble Drew Ali," Drew emerged in 1913 in Newark, New Jersey, to preach the message of Moorish identity. The movement spread slowly, with early centers in Pittsburgh, Pennsylvania; Detroit, Michigan; and several southern cities. In 1925, Ali moved to Chicago, where the following year he incorporated the Moorish Science Temple of America. In 1927 he published *The Holy Koran* (not to be confused with the Koran (or Qur'an) used by all orthodox Moslem groups). Ali's *Koran* was a pamphlet-sized compilation of Moorish beliefs that drew heavily on *The Aquarian Gospel of Jesus Christ*, a volume received via automatic writing by Spiritualist Levi Dowling in the 1890s. The *Koran* delineates the creation and fall of the human race, the origin of black people, the opposition of Christianity to God's people, and the modern predicament of the Moors.

It was Noble Drew Ali's belief that only Islam could unite the black man. The black race is Asiatic, Moroccan, hence Moorish. Jesus was a black man who tried to redeem the black Moabites and was executed by the white Romans. Moorish Americans must be united under Allah and his holy prophet. Marcus Garvey is seen as forerunner to Ali. Friday has been accepted as the holy day. Worship forms, particularly music, have been drawn from popular black culture and given Islamic content.

Ali died in 1919 and was succeeded by one of his young colleagues, R. German Ali, who still heads the movement. Shortly after Ali's death, one of the members appeared in Detroit as Wallace Fard Muhammad, the reincarnation of Noble Drew Ali, and began the Nation of Islam (now the American Muslim Mission). In spite of competition from the Nation of Islam, the Moorish Science Temple grew in the years after Ali's death, and during the 1940s temples could be found in Charleston, West Virginia; Hartford, Connecticut; Milwaukee, Wisconsin; Richmond, Virginia; Cleveland, Toledo, and Steubenville, Ohio; Flint, Michigan; Chattanooga, Tennessee; Indianapolis and Indiana Harbor, Indiana; and Brooklyn, New York. In more recent years, the movement has declined. During the 1970s, the headquarters were moved to Baltimore, Maryland.

Membership: Not reported. In 2008 there were 33 subordinate temples in the United States.

Sources:

Moorish Science Temple of America, Inc. www.moorishsciencetempleofamerica.com.

Ali, Noble Drew [Timothy Drew]. *The Holy Koran of the Moorish Science Temple of America*. [Baltimore: MD]: Moorish Science Temple of America, 1978.

————. *Moorish Literature*. Author, 1928.

Fauset, Arthur Huff. *Black Gods of the Metropolis*. Philadelphia: University of Pennsylvania Press, 1971.

Turner, Richard Brent. *Islam in the African-American Experience*. Bloomington: Indiana University Press, 1997.

Moorish Science Temple, Prophet Ali Reincarnated, Founder
Current address could not be obtained for this edition.

In 1975 Richardson Dingle-El, a member of the Moorish Science Temple of America in Baltimore, proclaimed himself Noble Drew Ali 3d, the reincarnation of Noble Drew Ali (1886–1929), the founder of the Moorish Science Temple of America. As such, he claimed succession to Noble Drew Ali 2d (d. 1945), who had claimed succession in the 1930s. The followers of Noble Drew Ali 3d have established headquarters in Baltimore and have several temples around the United States. A periodical is published by the temple in Chicago. In most ways, the temple follows the beliefs and practices of the Moorish Science Temple of America.

Membership: Not reported.

Periodicals: *Moorish Guide*.

Sources:

Turner, Richard Brent. *Islam in the African-American Experience*. Bloomington: Indiana University Press, 1997.

Nation of Islam (Farrakhan)
National Headquarters, 7351 South Stoney Island Ave., Chicago, IL 60649

Of the several factions that broke away from the American Muslim Mission (formerly known as the Nation of Islam and then as the World Community of Islam in the West) and assumed the group's original name, the most successful has been the Nation of Islam, headed by Abdul Haleem (Louis) Farrakhan. Farrakhan was born Louis Eugene Wolcott. He was a nightclub singer in the mid-1950s when he joined the Nation of Islam headed by Elijah Muhammad. As was common among Black Muslims at that time, he dropped his last name, which was seen as a slave name imposed by white society, and became known as Minister Louis X. His oratorical and musical skills carried him to a leading position as minister in charge of the Boston Mosque and, after the defection and death of Malcolm X, to the leadership of the large Harlem center and designation as the official spokesperson for Elijah Muhammad.

In 1975 Elijah Muhammad died. Though many thought Louis X, by then known by his present name, might become the new leader of the nation, Elijah Muhammad's son, Wallace, was chosen instead. At Wallace Muhammad's request, Farrakhan moved to Chicago to assume a national post. During the next three years, the Nation of Islam moved away from many of its distinctive beliefs and programs and emerged as the American Muslim Mission. It dropped many of its racial policies and began to admit white people into membership. It also began to move away from its black nationalist demands and to accept integration as a proper goal of its programs.

Farrakhan emerged as a leading voice among "purists" who opposed any changes in the major beliefs and programs instituted by Elijah Muhammad. Longstanding disagreements with the new direction of the Black Muslim body led Farrakhan to leave the organization in 1978 and to form a new Nation of Islam. Farrakhan reinstituted the beliefs and program of the pre-1975 Nation of Islam. He reformed the Fruit of Islam, the internal security force, and demanded a return to strict dress standards.

With several thousand followers, Farrakhan began to rebuild the Nation of Islam. He established mosques and developed an outreach to the black community on radio. He was only slightly noticed until 1984, when he aligned himself with the U.S. presidential campaign of Jesse Jackson, a black Christian minister seeking the nomination of the Democratic Party. Jackson's acceptance of his support and Farrakhan's subsequent controversial statements (some claimed by critics to be anti-Semitic) on radio and at press conferences kept Farrakhan's name in the news during the period of Jackson's candidacy and in subsequent months.

Since 1985 Farrakhan has been in the news continually, as he has proposed and created programs for the African-American community and led followers in establishing businesses. He has also periodically made public statements that critics charge evidence a continuing anti-Semitism. Farrakhan has spoken on several occasions of European American's history of involvement in the African slave trade and has taken pains to note the ownership of slaves by Jews.

In 1995 Farrakhan called a mass daylong demonstration by African-American males in Washington, D.C., called the Million Man March. This event attracted several hundred thousand men, and a number of prominent African-American leaders were included among the speakers. At the march Farrakhan, as he has done before, asked the Jewish community to institute a dialogue with him to resolve their differences, an offer Jewish leaders have said they will not accept until he publicly rejects comments of his they deem anti-Semitic. In 2000 Farrakhan convened the Million Family March, calling on humankind to unite.

Membership: Not reported. In 2008 there were regional centers in Atlanta, Georgia; Houston, Texas; Los Angeles; Miami, Florida; Washington, D.C.; New York; London; and Toronto.

Periodicals: *The Final Call*.

Sources:

Farrakhan, Louis. *Torchlight for America*. Chicago: FCN Publishing Co., 1993.

Gardell, Mattias. *In the Name of Elijah Muhammad: Louis Farrakhan and the Nation of Islam*. Durham, NC: Duke University Press, 1996.

Lee, Martha. *The Nation of Islam: An American Millenarian Movement*. Syracuse, NY: Syracuse University Press, 1996.

Muhammad, Elijah. *History of the Nation of Islam*. Cleveland, OH: Sectarius Publications, 1994.

————. *Our Savior Has Arrived*. Chicago: Muhammad's Temple of Islam No. 2, 1974.

Muhammad, Tynnetta. *The Divine Light*. Phoenix, AZ: H.E.M.E.F, 1982.

Turner, Richard Brent. *Islam in the African-American Experience*. Bloomington: Indiana University Press, 1997.

Nation of Islam (John Muhammad)
c/o Muhammad Temple of Islam #1, c/o Minister Sami Muhammad, 1448 E Outer Drive, Detroit, MI 48206

John Muhammad (1910–2005), brother of Elijah Muhammad (1897–1975), founder of the Nation of Islam, was among those who rejected the changes in the Nation of Islam, which led to its change into the American Muslim Mission. In 1978 he left the mission and formed a continuing Nation of Islam designed to perpetuate the programs outlined in his brother's two books: *Message to the Black Man* and *Our Savior Has Arrived*. According to John Muhammad, Elijah Muhammad was the last messenger of Allah and was sent to teach the black man a new Islam.

Membership: Not reported. John Muhammad had support around the United States, but there is only one congregation located in Detroit.

Periodicals: *Minister John Muhammad Speaks*.

Sources:

Supreme Minister John Muhammad.

www.webspawner.com/users/smjm/myhistoryaimspu.html.

Nation of Islam (The Caliph)

c/o Muhammad's Temple of Islam, 3217 Garrison Blvd., Baltimore, MD 21216-1320

As significant changes within the Nation of Islam, founded by Elijah Muhammad (1897–1975), proceeded under his son and successor Wallace D. Muhammad (b. 1933), the Nation of Islam became a more orthodox Islamic organization. It was renamed the American Muslim Mission and dropped many of the distinctive features of its predecessor. Opposition among those committed to Elijah Muhammad's ideas and programs led to several schisms within the organization in the late 1970s. Among the "purist" leaders, Emmanuel Abdullah Muhammad asserted his role as the caliph of Islam raised up to guide the people in the absence of Allah (in the person of Wallace Fard Muhammad [1877–1934]) and his messenger (Elijah Muhammad). One Islamic tradition insists that a caliph always follows a messenger.

The Nation of Islam under the caliph continues the beliefs and practices abandoned by the American Muslim Mission. A new school, the University of Islam, has been established and a new effort aimed at economic self-sufficiency has been promoted. Businesses have been created to implement the program.

Membership: Not reported. As of 1982, the Nation of Islam under the caliph had only two mosques, one in Baltimore, Maryland, and one in Chicago, Illinois.

Periodicals: *Muhammad Speaks*.

Sources:

None available.

Nation of the Five Percent/Nation of God and Earths

c/o Allah's Universal Development, PO Box 217, Albany, NY 12202-0217

The Nation of the Five Percent was founded in 1964 by Clarence 13X (1929–1969), a former member of the Nation of Islam. Clarence 13X was born Clarence Smith, and after joining the Nation of Islam in 1961 he took "X" as a last name, a practice within the nation indicating that African Americans' true names had been lost and they had been forced to take non-African slave names. Smith soon began to develop views divergent from those taught in the mosque in Harlem, New York. He believed that all blacks were Allah and rejected the teaching that Allah had appeared in 1929 in the person of Wallace D. Fard (1877–1934). In 1964 he was expelled from the Nation of Islam.

The idea undergirding the Nation of Five Percent was Smith's belief that only 5 percent of blacks understand the problem causing their condition and that these 5 percent are the only ones capable of leading the African-American community. He began to teach that all black men were Allah, and that black women were the earth, a teaching that earned the group a popular designation as the Nation of Gods and Earths. Women were to raise a nation; their children were seen as the salvation of the nation.

After settling its headquarters in New York, centers were soon established in neighboring Connecticut and New Jersey. In 1969 Clarence 13X was assassinated. The movement reorganized under a collective leadership and continued. In 1988 its Allah School in Mecca, its main outreach structure for Harlem, was burned to the ground. The organization has continued, however, though it still struggles to find its place in the African-American community as a whole.

Membership: Not reported.

Periodicals: *The Word; the Five Percenter*.

Sources:

The 5 Percent Network. www.allahsnation.net

Prince-A-Cuba, ed. *Our Mecca Is Harlem: Clarence 13X and the Five Percent*. Hampton, VA: U.B. & U.S. Communications Systems, 1995.

Sayyid Issa Al Haadi Al Mahdi. *The Book of Five Percenters*. Monticello, NY: Original Tents of Kedar, 1991.

Turner, Richard Brent. *Islam in the African-American Experience*. Bloomington: Indiana University Press, 1997.

United Nation of Islam

1608 N 13th St., Kansas City, KS 66102

The United Nation of Islam (UNOI), a splinter group from the Nation of Islam, was founded by Royall Jenkins. Born in South Carolina in 1942, Jenkins was raised first by his mother and then by foster parents in Maryland. He married Juanita Gattes when he was 16 and she was 13, and they had 10 children. He moved his family to Brooklyn, New York, where he discovered the teachings of Elijah Muhammad (1897–1975). The family subsequently moved to Chicago, where Jenkins worked for the Nation of Islam as a long-distance truck driver from 1970 to 1975.

Jenkins claims that in 1978 two angels took him on a spacecraft around the universe in order for him to learn his identity as Allah, the Supreme Being. Minister Louis Farrakhan (b. 1933), who had emerged as the leader of an independent Nation of Islam a year earlier, rejected Jenkins's claim. Jenkins now views Farrakhan as an enemy of Allah. Shortly after declaring that he was Allah, Jenkins and his wife divorced.

UNOI shares some of the ideology of the Nation of Islam in its earlier years under Elijah Muhammad. At first Jenkins taught that W. D. Fard, founder of the Nation of Islam, was the Allah of the Qur'an, but he revised this view when he asserted that he is the new and more powerful Allah. According to Jenkins, and in keeping with an older Nation of Islam belief, white people were created 8,000 years ago by a scientist named Yakub.

The UNOI was originally based in Temple Hill, Maryland, where Moreen, one of Jenkins's daughters, became a prominent leader in the movement. She was married to Joseph Kelly, who her father believed was the reincarnation of Elijah Muhammad. Moreen was called the "Mother of Civilization" within the group, until she withdrew in 2002. In 1993 Abbass Rassoull, one-time secretary to Elijah Muhammad, joined the UNOI.

The group runs a university and several businesses and owns farmland in several parts of the United States. It has been cited for its positive impact on urban life in Kansas City because of the group emphasis on a work ethic, drug-free living, and cleanliness.

Educational Facilities:

University of Islam.

Members: Not reported. Other sources estimate that there are 500 to 600 members as of 2008.

Remarks: Following her withdrawal in 2002, Moreen Kelly, along with other former UNOI members and members of the Cult Awareness movement, became a public critic of her father. They have criticized UNOI for its semi-communal aspects, with members drawing support checks from the government while working full-time for the organization. They have also raised concerns about Jenkins's sexual activities, which he compares to the polygamous practices of the biblical king Solomon.

Sources:

United Nation of Islam. unitednationofislam.com/.

Johnson, Allie. "Heaven Is Hell." *The Pitch* (March 37, 2003). Available from www.pitch.com/2003-03-27/news/heaven-is-hell/.

❀ Zoroastrianism

Mazdaznan Movement

Current address not obtained for this edition.

The first, and for many years the only, Zoroastrian group in the United States was the Mazdaznan movement founded by the Rev. Otoman Zar-Adusht Hanish (1844–1936). Hanish claimed to have been sent by the inner temple community of El-Khaman to bring Mazdaznan to the world. He began teaching around the early twentieth century and formally inaugurated the movement in New York in 1902. His headquarters was established in Chicago, Illinois, where he began a periodical, *The Mazdaznan*, published by the Sun Worshippers Press (later the Mazdaznan Press). The headquarters was later moved to Los Angeles, California, in 1916, and then to Encinitas, California, in the 1980s.

Mazdaznan emphasizes the monotheistic faith in the Lord Mazda, the creator. Man is in God and God in him. God is expressed as the holy family of father (male creative principle), mother (procreative female principle), and child (destiny/salvation). Man is on earth to reclaim the earth and to turn it into a paradise suitable for God to dwell therein. According to the movement, the means to reclaim the material, the body, and make it as perfect as one's spirit, is the power of breath. Mazdaznan teaches a discipline of breathing, rhythmic prayers, and chants. These are supplemented by a recommended vegetarian diet and exercises.

Mazdaznan quickly spread across America into Europe in its first decade of existence. By the time Hanish died in 1936, centers could be found in most urban areas. During the 1970s, centers were active in England (home to 13 congregations), as well as in Mexico, Belgium, Denmark, France, Germany, Holland, and Switzerland. In the mid-1980s, the longtime Los Angeles headquarters was abandoned for a new headquarters building that had been constructed in Encinitas, California. The movement is led by Alfonso R. Calderon.

Membership: There is no formal membership.

Periodicals: *Mazdaznan—Master Thot.*

Sources:

Hanish, O.Z.A. *Health and Breath Culture.* Chicago, IL: Sun Worshipper Publishing Co., 1902.

————. *Inner Studies: A course of 12 Lessons.* Mokelumne Hill, CA: Health Research, 1963.

————. *The Philosophy of Mazdaznan.* Los Angeles, CA: Mazdaznan Press, 1960.

————. *The Power of Breath.* Los Angeles, CA: Mazdaznan Press, 1970.

Hanish, O. Z. A., and O. Rauth. *God and Man United.* Santa Fe Springs, CA: Stockton Trade Press, 1975.

Mazdaznan, What It Teaches. Los Angeles, CA: Mazdaznan Press, 1969.

Federation of Zoroastrian Associations in North America

5750 S Jackson St., Hinsdale, IL 60521

Followers of the Zoroastrian faith began to migrate to North America from their native Iran and India, where they had been prominent in the business community in the 1950s. As their numbers have grown, they have spread across the continent.

The Zoroastrian faith is monotheistic. Its founder, Zoroaster (628–551 B.C.E.), taught of Ahura Mazda, the one Supreme God. Ahura Mazda created an ideal existence but as the world progressed, conflict between the opposing forces of good and evil emerged. Ahura Mazda gave humans the opportunity to choose between good and evil, as well as the responsibility to promote the good, vanquish evil, and move the world toward the final resurrection when all will be in a state of bliss and perfection.

Individual Zoroastrians are called to an ethical life based on good thoughts, words, and deeds. Humans should emulate the attributes of Ahura Mazda: *Vohu manah* (good mind) is the freedom to choose the good; *asha* (divine law) embod-

ies truth, wisdom, justice, and progress; *kshathra* (divine majesty) call humans to militantly promote good and fight evil; and *armaity* (benevolent spirit) elevates purity and devotion. The devout Zoroastrian can look forward to *haurvatat* and *ameratat* (perfection and immortality, respectively). The Zoroastrian is taught to lead an industrious active life characterized by honesty and charity. There is little room for asceticism. The generation of wealth is extolled as long as it is done honestly and used for charitable purposes. These teachings are contained in the Avesta, the ancient Zoroastrian texts, which include the hymns written by Zoroaster.

The life of the Zoroastrian is marked by three important ceremonies. A child is initiated into the faith through the Navjote ceremony in which the child is given (1) a *sudreh*, an undershirt made of white muslin with a pocket to remind the wearer to fill his or her life with good thoughts, words, and deeds, and (2) a *kusti*, a cord by which the wearer girds himself or herself to practice the teachings of Zoroaster. Getting married is a second blessed occasion. The death of a Zoroastrian is marked with extensive prayers that center upon the soul rather than the body. Each ceremony includes reading from the Avesta.

In the United States, Zoroastrians organized associations wherever a community of the faithful was located. In 1987 these associations created the Federation of Zoroastrian Associations of North America as an authorized body to represent Zoroastrians.

Membership: As of 2002 there were approximately 200,000 Zoroastrians in the world, 20,000 of them residing in North America. There are 22 local Zoroastrian associations (in major cities) in the United States and four in Canada. There are approximately 72,000 Zoroastrians in India, 90,000 in Iran, and lesser numbers in Europe, Pakistan, Africa, and Australia.

Educational Facilities:

Cama Oriental Institute, Bombay, India.

Periodicals: *Fezana Journal.*

Remarks: The Center for Zoroastrian Research in Bloomington, Indiana, has been actively gathering information on the American Zoroastrian community as well as actively participating in its ongoing self-examination.

Sources:

FEZANA: Home. www.fezana.org.

❀ Baha'i

Baha'i Faith

c/o National Spiritual Assembly of the Baha'is of the United States, 1233 Central St., Evanston, IL 60201

In Persia (present-day Iran), a predominantly Muslim country in the mid-1800s, the expectation that the coming of the Mahdi, the successor to Muhammad promised in Islamic writings, was strong. Into this environment was born Mirza Ali Muhammad (1819–1850), a Shi'a Muslim who declared himself the Bab, or gate, through whom people would learn of the imminent advent of another messenger of God. Many people accepted the messianic claims of the Bab who declaraed his station in 1844, and established the Babi religion. The initial enthusiasm of the movement quickly encountered fierce opposition eventually resulting in persecution. In 1850 the Bab was martyred.

Two years later, a Babi attempted to kill the shah, and persecution led to further imprisonments of Babis. Among those imprisoned was Mirza Husayn-Ali (1817–1892), who, while languishing in prison, came to understand himself as the Holy One whom the Bab foretold. In 1853 he and his family were exiled and left Tehran, Iran, for Baghdad, Iraq, where in 1863, he declared his station as a messenger of God.

During the following years, leadership of the Babi movement was in the hands of Mirza Yahya (1831–1912), Husayn-Ali's half brother, but gradually it shifted to

Husayn-Ali because of Mirza Yahya's incompetence. In 1863 Husayn-Ali revealed to a few close associates and members of his family that he was the messenger that the Bab had anticipated. From that time an increasing number of Babis accepted Baha'u'llah (as Husayn-Ali was called) and became Baha'is.

Baha'u'llah was exiled from Baghdad to Constantinople (now Istanbul), Turkey, and then later to Adrianople (now Edirne), Turkey. He then was exiled to the penal colony at Akka (now Acre) during 1868 in present-day Israel, where he spent the remainder of his life. While under house arrest there by the Turkish authorities, he produced the majority of his 15,000 works, considered scripture by his followers.

After his death in 1892, Baha'u'llah was succeeded by his eldest son, Abbas Effendi (1844–1921), known to the world by his religious name, Abdu'l-Baha (meaning servant of Baha). Abdu'l-Baha is considered the exemplar of the Baha'i teachings and served as head of the Baha'i community until his death. In 1902 he was confined by the Turkish authorities until the 1908 Young Turks Revolution brought a gradual easing of restrictions. Abdu'l-Baha then turned his attention to the spread of the Baha'i faith and traveled to Europe and North America in that effort. Upon his death in 1921, Abdu'l-Baha was succeeded by Shoghi Effendi (1897–1957), his grandson, as guardian of the faith.

The Baha'i faith was brought to America in 1892 by Ibrahim Kheiralla, though he later left the movement and founded a rival organization. Kheiralla founded a Baha'i group in Chicago, Illinois, in 1894 and several others sprang up as a result of his efforts. The first convert was Thornton Chase (1847–1912), who joined the faith in 1894. The first U.S. Baha'i convention would be held in 1907. In 1900, Agnes Baldwin Alexander (1875–1971) encountered the Baha'i religion in Rome, Italy, and took it to Hawaii.

In 1912 Abdu'l-Baha spent eight months in the United States and laid the cornerstone of the Baha'i house of worship in Wilmette, Illinois. The temple took 40 years to build and was completed in 1953. The temple's structure demonstrated the significance of the number nine. As the largest single digit, nine is a symbol of culmination and unity for Baha'is. The Wilmette temple, like all Baha'i temples, is nine-sided and capped with a dome.

The Baha'i teachings are contained in the writings of the Bab, Baha'u'llah, and Abdu'l-Baha, considered scriptures, and in the writings of Shoghi Effendi, which are considered infallible guidance. They teach the essential oneness of all revealed faiths, which have been given at different stages and ages. The Baha'i faith is considered the latest phase in the progressive unfolding of a single universal religion, of which all previous world religions are a part. Baha'is believe that God will continue to send messengers in the future.

The Baha'i faith teaches that God is, in essence, unknowable, though his word is known through his chosen messenger. Some Baha'i principles include the independent search for truth, the oneness of the human race, the unity of religion, the condemnation of prejudice, the harmony of science and religion, the equality of the sexes, compulsory education, the adoption of a universal language, the abolition of extremes of wealth and poverty, a world court, work in the spirit of service as worship, justice, and universal peace. Baha'i scriptures also stress the immortality and continuous progress of the soul. Baha'i writings also describe work done in a spirit of service as a form of worship and stress the immortality and continuous progress of the soul.

Baha'is gather regularly for weekly prayer and study of the sacred writings. There is an annual 19-day fasting period and nine holy days during which work is suspended. March 21 is also a holy day, celebrated as New Year's Day. Besides the temple at Wilmette, six others have been built around the world, with an eighth under construction in Chile.

After Shoghi Effendi's death in 1957, leadership of the faith passed to the Universal House of Justice, an international body headquartered in Haifa, Israel, where the Bab's shrine is located . Baha'u'llah indicated that there should be no clergy in the Baha'i faith, and instead ordained a system of elected councils at the local, national, and international levels to administer the affairs of the faith. The Universal House of Justice administers the affairs of the worldwide Baha'i community. It may enact laws and ordinances not expressly stated in the sacred Baha'i texts, but may not offer interpretation of scripture.

Members of the Universal House of Justice are elected every five years at an international convention composed of the members of the National Spiritual Assemblies, which are elected at annual conventions held in nearly every country in the world. The National Spiritual Assembly of the Baha'is of the United States is headquartered in Evanston, Illinois, near the house of worship and the Baha'i Publishing Trust in Wilmette.

Membership: In 2008 it was reported that 160,000 Baha'is resided in the United States. There were approximately 1,200 local spiritual assemblies. Worldwide there are more than 5 million Baha'is in close to 12,000 spiritual assemblies in more than 230 countries of the world. There were 182 national spiritual assemblies as of April 2001.

Periodicals: *World Order • Brilliant Star.*

Sources:

Baha'i Faith: United States Official Web Site. www.bahai.us.

Balyuzi, H. M. *Abdu'l-Baha: The Center of the Covenant of Baha'u'llah*. London: George Ronald, 1971.

———. *Baha'u'llah, The King of Glory*. Oxford, UK: George Ronald, 1980.

Miller, William McElwee. *The Baha'i Faith: Its History and Teachings*. South Pasadena, CA: William Carey Library, 1974.

Perkins, Mary, and Philip Hainsworth. *The Baha'i Faith (Living Religions)*. London: Ward Lock Educational, 1980.

Whitehead, O. Z. *Some Early Baha'is of the West*. Oxford: George Ronald, 1976.

Baha'is Under the Provisions of the Covenant (Leland Jensen)
PO Box 65, Missoula, MT 59806

Baha'is Under the Provisions of the Covenant was formed by Leland Jensen (1914–1996), a long-time adherent of the dominant Baha'i group based in Haifa, Israel. Jensen and his wife, Opal, were chiropractors. They served as missionaries to two small islands, Reunion and Mauritius, off the coast of India in the 1950s, as part of the Ten Year Crusade announced by Shoghi Effendi (1857–1957) in 1953. Through this work, Leland and his wife earned the title Knights of Baha'u'llah.

Jensen followed Baha'i leader Mason Remey (1874–1974) when the latter announced in 1960 that he was the new Guardian of the world wide Baha'i community. Remey was excommunicated by the Hands of the Cause, the top leaders in the Baha'i movement; he formed his own National Spiritual Assembly for what became known as the Orthodox Baha'i Faith. Jensen moved to Montana in 1964. He was sent to prison in 1969 following a conviction on charges of sexual assault against a female patient. He claimed to be innocent of the charges and also argued that his conviction and prison time fulfilled key passages in biblical prophecy.

He was released from prison in 1973. In 1979 he announced that there would be a nuclear holocaust on April 29, 1980. Jensen formed a Second International Baha'i Council in 1991, as a counterpart to the Haifa-based Baha'is. In 2001, five years after Jensen's death, his student Neil Chase announced that he was the Guardian in 2001. This led to a split over proper leadership. The majority, including Chase's wife, rejected his claims, leading to his leaving.

Membership: Not reported.

Sources:

Bahai's Under the Provisions of the Covenant (Leland Jensen). bupc.montana.com/.

Balch, Robert W., et al. "Fifteen Years of Failed Prophecy." In *Expecting Armageddon*, ed. Jon Stone, 269–282. New York: Routledge, 2000.

Baha'is Under the Provisions of the Covenant (Neal Chase)

248A North Higgins #126, Missoula, MT 59802

In 2001 Neal Chase claimed to be the true leader of Baha'is Under the Provisions of the Covenant (see separate entry), whose founder, Leland Jensen (1914–1996), had died without naming a successor. He also claimed to be the true head of the second International Baha'i Council (sIBC). Because his declarations were not accepted by the majority of the leaders of the Baha'is Under the Provisions of the Covenant, Chase left with his followers and reorganized under the same name as the parent body.

Chase claims to be the great-grandson of 'Abdu'l-Baha and also carries the title of Third President of the true Universal House of Justice of Baha'u'llah. The group believes that the Baha'i House of Justice in Haifa, Israel, is bogus and that it will be destroyed by a burning meteor. Chase has argued that both the Bible and the writings of Nostradamus predicted the exact date of the execution of Saddam Hussein. Chase also predicts that nuclear war will destroy one-third of the world's population.

Membership: Not reported.

Periodicals: *The Noonday Sun.*

Sources:

Baha'is Under the Provisions of the Covenant (Neal Chase). www.bupc.org/.

Stone, Jon R., ed. *Expecting Armageddon: Essential Readings in Failed Prophecy*. New York: Routledge, 2000.

Orthodox Baha'i Faith, National Baha'i Council of the United States

PO Box 3201, Roswell, NM 88202

Members of the Orthodox Baha'i faith, in contrast to most other Baha'is, believe that the Baha'i administrative order remains unchanged with all of its administrative institutions intact since the death of Shoghi Effendi (1897–1957), the first guardian of the faith. The Baha'i administrative order was dictated in the will and testament of Abdu'l-Baha (1844–1921), who was the son of Baha'u'llah (1817–1892), the author of the Baha'i Revelation. This document was characterized by Shoghi Effendi as divinely conceived, equal in sacredness and immutability to Baha'u'llah's most holy book, the *Kitab-I-Agdas*, and the charger of his world order. In his will, Abdu'l-Baha appointed Shoghi Effendi the first guardian of the Baha'i faith and stipulated that each guardian appoint his successor in his own lifetime. Under the terms of this document, the guardian is the head of the faith, the sole interpreter of Baha'i holy writ, and the sacred head of the Universal House of Justice, the supreme legislative body of the Baha'i administrative order.

Shoghi Effendi became guardian of the Baha'i faith in 1921 following the death of Abdu'l-Baha. For the next 30 years he painstakingly developed the Baha'i administrative order at the local and national levels. Based upon the fact that there were then nine functioning national administrative institutions, he established the first international Baha'i council, explaining that it was a temporary title given to what was to become the Universal House of Justice. Shoghi Effendi did not assume the presidency of the council. He appointed Charles Mason Remey (1874–1974), a leading American Baha'i who had been chosen by Abdu'l-Baha to design the Baha'i temple on Mount Carmel and who was the architect of other Baha'i temples. The council was never convened into a functioning body during Shoghi Effendi's lifetime, although he assigned tasks to individuals who had been appointed to it. Coinciding with the passing of Shoghi Effendi in 1957, Remey became the functioning president of the council. It is the belief of the Orthodox Baha'is that "president of the Universal House of Justice" (i.e., the International Baha'i Council) and "guardian of the faith" are synonymous terms; hence Remey became the second guardian of the faith. The majority of Baha'is refused to recognize the validity of the appointment and declared the office of the guardian terminated.

Members of the National Baha'i Council stated that Mason Remey elected to appoint his successor in the same manner that Shoghi Effendi had employed. He established the second International Baha'i Council and appointed as its president Joel B. Marangella (b. 1918). However, he reinforced the appointment in a letter addressed to Marangella, telling him to advise the Baha'is that he was the third guardian of the faith.

As it was impracticable for the second International Baha'i Council to function as a body, due to lack of support from national Baha'i administrative bodies, and as a majority of supporters of the guardian were to be found in the United States, Marangella established a national Baha'i bureau in New York City, New York. The bureau, which moved to New Mexico in 1972, administered the affairs of the faith in the United States on a provisional and limited basis.

In 1978 the bureau's functions were assumed and expanded by the local Baha'i council of Roswell, New Mexico, a body of nine believers designated by the third guardian as the National Baha'i Council of the Orthodox Baha'is of the United States. The council was assigned national Baha'i administrative jurisdiction pending the formation of a national Baha'i council when circumstances permit.

The council, in addition to propagating the faith through various media such as newspapers and magazines, inserted open letters and appeals by the guardian in newspapers in the United States and foreign countries in order to convince Baha'is that Shoghi Effendi provided for the continuance of the guardian's office. In 1995 the third guardian established an Internet site and in 1996 the Mother Baha'i Council established a site of its own.

In 2000 the guardian transferred the responsibilities for the direction of the faith in the United States to a provisional national Baha'i council. As was the case with the Mother Baha'i Council, the new administrative unit of the Orthodox Baha'i faith continues to declare aggressively that in terminating the guardianship, the other Baha'is have, in effect, negated the major provisions of the will and testament of Abdu'l Baha and hence are attempting to destroy the world order of Baha'u'llah.

Membership: Not reported.

Periodicals: *Herald of the Covenant* • *Friends in Touch* • *Star of the Covenant* (for Orthodox Baha'is only).

Remarks: The council is one of three groups that continue the guardianship and recognize Mason Remey as the second guardian. Donald Harvey claims to have a letter from Remey appointing him to be the third guardian. In the United States, Harvey's followers are affiliated in the Remey Society. The third group, an offshoot of the Mother Baha'i Council, is the Orthodox Baha'i Faith under the Regency.

Sources:

The Orthodox Baha'i Faith: An Introduction. Roswell, NM: Mother Baha'i Council of the United States, 1981.

The Reform Bahai Faith

PO Box 81842, Rochester, MI 48308

The Reform Bahai Faith traces its origins to events in the Baha'i world following the death in 1921 of Abdu'l-Baha, the son and successor of Baha'u'llah (1817–1892), the founder of the faith. Abdu'l-Baha's 1912 covenant and teachings contained no conception of a hereditary guardianship, and he repeatedly stated in public and in writing that the Baha'i faith could not be organized but was rather the "spirit of the age." Abdu'l-Baha's teaching of a universal religion inspired such early Baha'is as Ruth White to reject what she and others believed was a fraudulent will and testament, written apparently by the family of Shoghi Effendi, appointing him to the nondoctrinal position of "guardianship."

Following and seeking to revive Abdu'l-Baha's interpretation of the Baha'i Faith, Reform Bahais have rediscovered and returned to Abdu'l-Baha's covenant and emphasis on a universal religious movement. The Reform Bahai faith does not have officers, appointed administrative positions, or clergy, and operates primarily through its Web site, but refers to adherents as members. Abdu'l-Baha taught that the individual is responsible for her or his own spiritual growth. As the interpreter of Baha'u'llah's teachings and center of the covenant, he emphasized that the separation of church and state was the will of God, grounded in a spiritual democracy.

In common with other Baha'i denominations, Reform Bahais believe in the basic oneness of God, all religions, and humankind. It finds hope in Baha'u'llah's spiritual teachings and promised day of international peace and cooperation, through global institutions and consultation, uniting mankind in common faith.

Among declared members, Frederick Glaysher, a literary scholar and prominent critic of the larger Baha'i group based in Haifa, Israel, has been central to the revival of the Reform Bahai denomination. Glaysher and other Reform Bahais argue that the true, original Baha'i faith has been increasingly distorted since the death of Abdu'l-Baha.

In 2004 Glaysher created the Reform Bahai Web site. In 2008 the Reform Bahai Press published its first collection of Baha'i scripture, *The Universal Principles of the Reform Bahai Faith*. Glaysher has also published a volume documenting his personal Reform Bahai journey in *Letters from the American Desert*.

Reform Bahai ideology can be traced not only to the work of Ruth White, but also to the numerous works of Julie Chanler (1882–1961), and Mirza Ahmad Sohrab (1893–1958). These three argue, as does Glaysher, that Shoghi Effendi distorted the nature of Baha'u'llah's religion and that Abdu'l-Baha's purported will and testament was a fraudulent document. They believe this was proven independently through the work of Dr. C. Ainsworth Mitchell of the British Museum in 1930. White deposited Mitchell's *Report on the Writing Shown on the Photographs of the Alleged Will of Abdu'l-Baha* at the Library of Congress.

The Reform Bahai Faith has issued 95 Theses about what it views as proper Bahai views and conduct. The first thesis resolves "to witness the truth of the deviation of the organized, incorporated Baha'i Faith from the Path, and its imposition of manifest corruptions and innovations, over many lamentable decades, that have wrought ever-increasing alienation, fear, censorship, coercion, misrepresentation, distortion, and damage, all the stratagems of despots and dictators, political and religious, upon individual Bahais, their families, and the community of believers."

Membership: Not reported.

Remarks: In January 2008 Glaysher submitted documents on behalf of the Reform Bahai movement to the U.S. District Court of Northern Illinois in a civil case involving the use of Baha'i symbols. The National Spiritual Assembly (NSA) of Wilmette, Illinois, was the claimant against three minority Baha'i groups. The NSA argued that the smaller groups should be held in contempt for violation of a 1996 ruling about proper use of Baha'i symbols. The court ruled against the NSA, and the case is being appealed.

Sources:

The Reform Bahai Faith. www.reformbahai.org/.

Baha'u'llah, Abdu'l-Baha, and Frederick Glaysher. *The Universal Principles of the Reform Bahai Faith*. Reform Bahai Press, 2007.

Cole, Juan R. I. *Modernity and the Millennium: The Genesis of the Baha'i Faith in the Nineteenth-Century Middle East*. New York: Columbia University Press, 1997.

Glaysher, Frederick. *Letters from the American Desert: Signposts of a Journey, A Vision*. Rochester, MI: Earthrise Press, 2008.

Tarbiyat Baha'i Community

PO Box 1424, Las Vegas, NM 87701

The Tarbiyat Baha'i Community (formerly the Orthodox Baha'i Faith under the Regency) is one of three organizations of former members of the Baha'i Faith who accepted the claims of Charles Mason Remey (1874–1974) to be the successor of Shoghi Effendi (1897–1957), the first guardian of the Baha'i faith who died in 1957. Remey claimed to be the second guardian. After Remey's death in 1974, Joel B. Marangella was one of two men who claimed to have been appointed by Remey as the third guardian. In 1969, Marangella organized his followers as the Orthodox Baha'i Faith prior to Remey's death in 1974.

Among those appointed to a leadership role by Remey, Reginald B. (Rex) King (d. 1977) accepted Marangella as the third guardian but later came to the conclusion that both Remey and Marangella had taken actions that were contrary to Baha'i law, thus proving that they were not the guardian as claimed. He concluded that Remey, rather than being the second guardian, was but a regent who assumed control until such time as the second guardian from the bloodline of Baha'u'llah (1817–1892) appeared and took his rightful place. Upon reaching that conclusion, King withdrew from Marangella and claimed to be the second regent.

King died in 1977. In his will he appointed four members of his family— Eugene K. King, Ruth L. King, Theodore Q. King, and Thomas King—as the council of regents to succeed him. In 1993 Ruth L. King resigned from the council of regents. Maeny Whitaker was appointed to take her place. The Baha'is of the Tarbiyat Baha'i community follow the teachings of the Baha'i faith, differing only in that they do not accept the authority of the Universal House of Justice because of its rejection of the guardianship. Instead they accept the regency, which holds open the station of the guardianship until the appearance of the second guardian.

Membership: Not reported.

Sources:

Tarbiyat Baha'i Community. www.tarbiyatcenter.org/index.html.

World Union of Universal Religion and Universal Peace

Current address not obtained for this edition.

In the years after the death of Abdu'l-Baha (1844–1921) and the elevation of his grandson, Shoghi Effendi (1897–1957), to the guardian of the Baha'i faith, an American Baha'i, Ruth White (d. 1958), began to question Effendi's authority. In her first book, *Abdu'l-Baha and the Promised Age* (1927), she voiced her opposition to his attempts to develop the Baha'i organization by quoting Abdu'l-Baha. "The Baha'i Movement is not an organization," she quotes him as saying, "You can never organize the Baha'i Cause." More importantly, she began to voice opposition to Effendi's role as guardian, and in her 1929 work, *The Baha'i Religion and Its Enemy, the Bahai Organization*, she attacked the authenticity of the will and testament of Abdu'l-Baha, the document upon which Effendi's authority rested.

Though she lectured widely throughout the United States, her only success in recruiting supporters came in Germany where the Baha'i World Union was founded by Wilhelm Herrigel and other Baha'is, who were described as friends of Abdu'l-Baha. The Baha'i World Union continued until 1937 when the German government outlawed the Baha'i faith.

Simultaneously with White's attack upon Effendi, though separate from it, Mirza Ahmad Sohrab (1891–1958), a close friend of Abdu'l-Baha and an American Baha'i, Julie Chandler (d. 1961), formed an independent Baha'i network in New York City, New York. They felt that Effendi's increasing efforts to organize the faith were counterproductive. They established the New History Society, which offered lectures by Sohrab and other prominent guests (American physicist Albert Einstein [1879–1955] addressed it on one occasion) and opened a Baha'i bookshop. Members of the New History Society considered themselves participants in the Baha'i movement but separate from the organization headed by Effendi. In response, the Baha'i faith brought suit against Sohrab, Chandler, and the New History Society seeking to prevent their use of the name *Baha'i*. The court ruled against them, however, stating that no group of followers of a religion could monopolize the name of that religion or prevent other groups of followers from practicing their faith.

Like the Baha'i World Union, the New History Society found support in Europe and opened offices in Paris, France, in the 1930s, and Sohrab became the major spokesperson for the society. He spoke frequently and authored a number of books, including *Broken Silence*, a response to the 1941 court case.

White and Sohrab both died in 1958 and Chandler died in 1961. Since their deaths, their work and thought have been carried on by Hermann Zimmer of Stuttgart, West Germany. Zimmer had returned to Germany in 1948 after being released from a prisoner-of-war (POW) camp. He picked up the remnants of Herrigel's organization and formed the World Union for Universal Religion and Universal Peace. In 1950 he published *Die Wiederkunft Christi* (The Return of Christ) in which he equated Baha'u'llah (1817–1892) with Christ returned in his Second Advent. Though never a large organization, the World Union remains a rallying point for free Baha'is around the world.

Membership: Not reported. Estimates suggest that only a few hundred free Baha'is reside in the United States.

Sources:

National Spiritual Assembly of the Baha'i of the United States and Canada. *The Baha'i Case against Mrs. Lewis Stuyvesant Chandler and Mirza Ahmad Sohrab*. Wilmette, IL: Baha'i Publishing Trust, 1941.

Sohrab, Mirza Ahmad. *Broken Silence: The Story of Today's Struggle for Religious Freedom*. New York: Universal, 1942.

———. *The Will and Testament of Abdu'l-Baha: An Analysis*. New York: Universal, 1944.

White, Ruth. *Abdu'l-Baha and the Promised Age*. New York: J.J. Little and Ives, 1927.

———. *Baha'i Religion and Its Enemy, the Baha'i Organization*. Rutland, VT: Charles Tuttle, 1929.

Zimmer, Hermann. *A Fraudulent Testament Devalues the Baha'i Religion into Political Shoghism*. Waiblingen, Germany: World Union for Universal Religion and Universal Peace, 1973.

 # The Druze

American Druze Society

National Office, PO Box 291437, Davie, FL 33329

Alternate Address: American Druze Cultural Center, 2239 Merton Ave., Eagle Rock, CA 90024.

The Druze (or Duruz) community originated in Egypt in the eleventh century at a time when the Ismaili Shi'a Muslims had attained their greatest political success through the Fatimid dynasty. Some Ismailis began to view the caliph, al-Hakim, as a somewhat divine figure. He was considered the "imam" (leader) of the Ismaili movement. Among the leaders was Muhammad al-Darazi (d. 1020 C.E.). Following al-Darazi's death in 1020 C.E., leadership fell to Cairo Hamza ibn Ali in Persia (Iran). Hamza began to see himself as the imam and al-Hakim as the embodiment of the Godhead. He began to organize followers in expectation that al-Hakim would claim his position openly.

Al-Hakim disappeared in 1021. Hamza told the followers that al-Hakim had merely gone underground for a while and would reappear in all power. The following year Hamza also disappeared. The movement faded in Egypt, although it survived and actually took on new life in an isolated area of Syria under the leadership of al-Muqtana. Al-Muqtana wrote many letters that, with a few surviving writings

of al-Hakim and Hamza, would be compiled into the Druze scripture called *Rasa'il al-Hikma*, or the Epistles of Wisdom.

The Druze survived in the mountainous terrain and for centuries lived a rather closed and isolated existence. It emerged as a distinct social group with its own unique customs and beliefs. Converts are not accepted, and intermarriage is not allowed. The community is divided into the *djuhhal*, the ordinary members of the community, and the *ukkal*, the initiated religious members. The ukkals wear a special white turban. Leaders, drawn from among the ukkals, are termed *shaykhs*.

The religious life of the Druze is not wholly known to outsiders; even many of the faithful are not allowed to study the higher teachings of the faith. The Druze faith is a form of Islam with a mystical bent. There is a belief in reincarnation. However, Druze are most known for their strict moral code. The seven commandments include admonitions to (1) speak truth within the community; (2) defend and assist the community; (3) renounce any former religion; (4) dissociate from nonbelievers; (5) recognize the unity of "our Lord" in all ages; (6) be content with his actions; and (7) submit to his orders as conveyed through the community leadership.

Druze survival was frequently threatened over the centuries, because the Muslims treated them as heretics. During the twentieth century, as parcels of land changed hands, some Druze migrated to other parts of the Middle East and are now in Lebanon, Israel, and Saudi Arabia. Druze also moved to the United States in this century. By the end of World War II (1939–1945), enough had migrated to found the American Druze Society. In 1979 the society adopted a constitution that stated its purpose as the perpetuation of the Druze faith. Membership is open to any person of Druze descent.

The American Druze Society dates to a gathering in 1901 in Seattle, Washington, by a small group of Druze immigrants, which led to the 1911 incorporation of Al Bakourat Alderziet. A second branch was opened in Cleveland, Ohio, in 1916. Additional branches were established across the United States, primarily in the Midwest. In 1947, at a convention in Charleston, West Virginia, a more formalized organization, the American Druze Society, was created.

Membership: There are chapters in Massachusetts, Washington, D.C., North Carolina, Georgia, Florida, Ohio, Michigan, Illinois, Texas, Arizona, and California. There are more than 5,000 Druze in North America.

Educational Facilities:

Institute of Druze Studies, San Diego, California.

Periodicals: *Our Heritage* • *The Journal of Druze Studies*.

Sources:

American Druze Society National Web Site. www.druze.com.

Abu Izzedin, Nejla. *The Druze: A New Study of Their History, Faith, and Society*. Leiden, Netherlands: E. J. Brill, 1984.

Makarem, Sami Nasib. *The Druze Faith*. Delmar, NY: Caravan Books, 1974.

Swayd, Samy. *Historical Dictionary of the Druzes*. Lanham, MD: Scarecrow Press, 2006.

Eastern Family, Part I: Hinduism, Jainism, Sikhism

23

HINDUISM. What is Hinduism? Of no major religious community is this type of question more difficult to answer. It is without an individual founder, although the Vedas (c. 1500–800 B.C.E.), a set of orally transmitted and received revelatory texts in Sanskrit, are, strictly speaking, the authoritative scriptures of the tradition. While the Vedas are revered by almost all sects and groups within the Hindu tradition, they play a direct role in Hindu practice only rarely. Additionally, Hinduism has no single set of issues around which it can orient itself. Some writers, in the face of this frustration, have tried to turn these problems into a positive polemic for Hinduism by seeing its systematic anarchy as a sign of Hinduism's universal character. "Hinduism is absolutely indefinite ... It rejects nothing. It is all-comprehensive, all-absorbing, all-complacent," says one Hindu writer.

Yet on a second look, Hinduism is not so vague as might first appear. While there is a great diversity of opinion among Hindus, it is no greater than among Christians. While Hinduism has no founders, it has some mythological figures to which it relates. Despite a variety of ideas and emphases, Hindus possess certain ideas in common, such as a belief in reincarnation and karma, and they do practice certain disciplines, the most common of which is yoga. Hindus also relate to a common history, that of India. Certain writings have a great value for them, although the Vedas and Upanishads have only rarely functioned as has the Bible or Qur'an. Hinduism might thus be defined as a set of religions that positively relate to several mythological figures (Krishna, Rama, and Shiva are examples), some metaphysical ideas and practices (reincarnation, karma, yoga), the Vedic texts, and a people's history. That definition seems to describe justly the Hindus, while distinguishing them from other religious groupings, particularly the Jains and Sikhs (also discussed in this chapter).

Indian and Hindu history can be divided roughly into four periods. The first is defined as pre-Vedic. Prior to the arrival into India of the Aryans, or Indo-Europeans, a culture on a par with that of the ancient Mediterranean Basin existed, the artifacts of which have only recently and partially been uncovered. Although religious articles have been found, a clear picture of this people's religious faith has not yet emerged.

The second or Vedic period begins with the arrival into India of the Indo-Europeans. The waves of Aryan migration have been variously dated from 1500 B.C.E. to 1000 B.C.E. The primary document of this period is the Rig Veda, the oldest of India's existing sacred books. The Rig Veda actually comprises ten books of hymns and prayers to the gods, collected probably about 1000 B.C.E. The Vedas present a vigorous, worldly religion oriented to nature and a pastoral, agricultural life. The people of the Vedic period had a positive view of the world and saw their survival of death as a continuation of the good life. Along with the various gods, particular attention was paid to Soma, the deified intoxicant of the soma plant.

The third period of India's history begins in the several centuries following 1000 B.C.E. and represents a significant shift in religious outlook, which the Aryan influence must have brought to the previous Indian culture. The change in outlook is from a positive view of life to a pessimistic world-fleeing one. The two ideas that symbolized this change are transmigration or reincarnation and karma. Transmigration is the principle that asserts that all persons may undergo a succession of earthly lives, in some of which they may incarnate as animals (and in more extreme forms of Hinduism, as plants). All of life is on the wheel of rebirth, and the goal of life is to escape physical rebirth by reaching spiritual perfection. Part of the rationale for the rebirth theory is karma. Karma is the principle that the results of the deeds of this life will accrue in the next life or incarnation. The final goal of Hindu tradition, after the Vedic period, has almost always been to escape karma and break the cycle of birth and rebirth.

Escape from karma comes either through the grace of the Divine or through the realization of identity with the divine Reality, which can be expressed in theistic terms or as an uncharacterized Ultimate. How can realization be accomplished? Some groups advocate attention to ceremonies at the local temple; others emphasize the moral life. Among the more common answers within those Hindu groups that have a presence in North America is yoga, a spiritual discipline designed to lead the human being to self-integration and then to union with the Divine or Ultimate, Brahman. The best known of the several forms of yoga in the West (though not as widely practiced in India or among Indian Americans) is *hatha* yoga, which includes a series of body postures (*asanas*) designed to bring the body into a state of harmony. Hatha yoga is a discipline used in the East in development of the body as a spiritual instrument for health, longevity, and

---

Eastern Family, Part I: Hinduism, Jainism, Sikhism Chronology

1785   Charles Wilkins translates Bhagavad Gita into English.

1790   America's first Naturalization Law limits naturalization (citizenship) to aliens who are "free white persons."

1841   Yale University establishes chair in Sanskrit and Indology.

1845   Ralph Waldo Emerson reads the Bhagavad Gita and Henry Colebrooke's *Essays on the Vedas*.

1846   Henry David Thoreau's *A Week on the Concord and Merrimack Rivers* is heavily influenced by his having read Emerson's copy of the Bhagavad Gita.

1879   Helena P. Blavatsky and Henry Steel Olcott, co-founders of the Theosophical Society, move to India. The society subsequently becomes a major conduit of Indian religious ideas to the West.

1883   Protap Chunder Mozoomdar, the first Hindu teacher to come to America, delivers his first talk in the home of the late Ralph Waldo Emerson.

1893   Swami Vivekananda becomes star speaker at the World Parliament of Religions meeting in Chicago.

1894   Swami Vivekananda founds the Vedanta Society of New York, the first Hindu organization in America.

1903   New Thought teacher William Walker Atkinson begins to write books on yoga under the pen name Swami Ramacharaka.

1912   Anti-Indian riots in American Northwest target Sikhs, misidentified as "Hindoos."

1917   Asian Exclusion Act bars immigration from Asian Barred Zone, including India. Based on reading of 1790 Naturalization Law, many Indian Americans actually lose their citizenship.

1919   Sri Yogendra of Bombay introduces hatha yoga to America.

1920   Swami Paramahansa Yogananda becomes one of the last Indian religious leaders to enter the United States before immigration is fully curtailed.

1923   In *U.S. v. Thind*, the Supreme Court rules that immigrants from India, though rightly termed Caucasians, are not "white" and therefore are ineligible for naturalization.

1924   The Asian Exclusion provision of the new immigration law strengthens provisions against immigration from India.

1927   Best-selling *Mother India* by Katherine Mayo paints a very negative picture of India and Hinduism.

1934   Paul Brunton's *A Search in Secret India* introduces Westerners to Hindu gurus, especially Ramana Maharshi.

1946   Swami Yogananda publishes *Autobiography of a Yogi*.

1947   India gains independence from Great Britain, and immediately faces partition and the setting off of Pakistan.

1958   Maharishi Mahesh Yogi begins his public teaching of Transcendental Meditation.

　　　　Swami Vishnu Devananda founds headquarters for the Sivananda Yoga Vedanta Centers in Quebec.

1965   Asian Exclusion Law rescinded by the United States. Bhaktivedanta Swami Prabhupada, in the United States on a tourist visa, is able to obtain a residency visa and stays to found International Society for Krishna Consciousness.

1968   Haridas Chaudhuri founds the California Institute for Asian Studies, now known as the California Institute for Integral Studies, in San Francisco, California.

1969   Sikh teacher Yogi Bhajan attracts youthful students to his lessons on kundalini yoga in Los Angeles.

1970   The Hindu Temple Society of North America's new temple in Flushing, New York, is the first of over a hundred temples serving the Indian American community to open over the next two decades.

1971   Prem Rawat (better known as Guru Maharaj Ji), a Sant Mat teacher, brings the Divine Light Mission to California and becomes well known as the teenage guru.

　　　　Richard Alpert publishes his first book as Baba Ram Dass, *Be Here Now*.

1972   Maharishi Mahesh Yogi announces his World Plan for the complete renovation of human society via Transcendental Meditation and the science of Creative Intelligence.

1981   Federation of Jains in North America founded.

1994   World Vaisnava Association founded as a coalition of the various groups that grew out of the work of Bhaktivedanta Swami Prabhupada.

1996   Kirtanananda Swami Bhaktipada of New Vrindavan, West Virginia, pleads guilty to one count of racketeering and begins serving eight years of a 20-year term.

2001   70 million people gather for the Kumbha Mela, humanity's largest festival, at Allahabad, India.

2004   The Hindu American Foundation is founded to provide a voice for the estimated two million Hindus in the United States.

　　　　Hindu University of America, Orlando, Florida, holds first graduation ceremony.

　　　　Largest Sikh gurudwara in America opens in San Jose, California.

2005   The first Hindu Dharma Summit in North America, held at Rutgers University, leads to formation of the Hindu Collective Initiative of North America.

---

higher spiritual accomplishment. Some see hatha yoga as a preliminary to the four higher forms of yoga. In the West, hatha yoga has been put to a variety of uses in physical culture quite apart from Hindu notions.

The four paths to realization of the Divine or Ultimate by yoga are *bhakti* yoga (through devotion and/or love), *jnana* yoga (through knowledge), *karma* yoga (through work), and *raja* (royal) yoga (through meditative exercises). These four, more-advanced yogas are designed for the various types of people, according to Hindu analysis. Some people, being basically reflective, find the ideas and the philosophical, logical demonstrations of jnana yoga suited to their innate pat-

terns. By taking thought, students of jnana yoga can come to a realization that many levels of self are finite, and the students can discern their eternal selves beyond the finite qualities of size, shape, emotions, and so forth. In a person for whom feeling and emotion reveal more than the intellect, bhakti yoga directs one's emotional potential for love and redirects those potentials of love toward the Divine. A major feature of bhakti yoga is *japa*, the practice of repeating a sacred mantra. (A Christian form of this practice is the Jesus prayer in classical Russian Orthodoxy.) A physically active person can develop a realization of the Divine through work in the world. The smallest activity of life can be done wisely as a spiritual practice—karma yoga. Some believe that the highest path to the Divine is through raja yoga, the royal road to reintegration and realization. Through practice of the discipline of raja yoga, particularly meditation, the self penetrates the layers of the merely human until it reaches the beyond that is within. While bhakti yoga is most popular in India, raja tends to be the most popular in North America.

The collecting of the Upanishads (900 to 300 B.C.E.) became a watershed in Hindu history, as the Upanishads represent the end or culmination of the Vedic scripture to which Hindus give a more or less universal authority. From these writings the various schools of interpretation would arise, and to these writings later movements would react. Associated with the Upanishads were several subsidiary developments. The most important was the rise of the Brahmans, the priestly class, as the highest level of the caste system in India. The rule of the Brahmans would dominate Indian life and lead to reactions by later movements. The idea of *maya* or illusion developed at this period. Common to most Hinduism is the belief that outward life and suffering are mere illusion and that realization of this fact will lead to release from suffering. *Ahimsa* is one of the highest ethical precepts for Hinduism (it is also popular in several other religions) and is the vow of noninjury to life, nonkilling. Ahimsa is the foundation of the practice of vegetarianism.

LATER DEVELOPMENTS IN HINDUISM. Hinduism developed under significant political changes in the Indian subcontinent. Although Islam entered India in the 11th and 12th centuries, the subcontinent was ruled for almost 300 years by the Mughul Empire, beginning in the fifteenth century. After Mughul dominance, India experienced invasion and conquest by the British Empire in the early 1800s. The coming of the British marked the arrival of an alien culture and an alien religion, backed by political power. In the face of the development of a vigorous Christian mission, an initial defensive reaction was followed by a creative Hindu renaissance, which produced a number of outstanding leaders (such as Ram Mohan Roy and Sri Ramakrishna) and movements. These movements, in many cases, were important in the Indian nationalist drives of the twentieth century and in the dissemination of Hindu ideas and practices into North America.

Within Hindu circles, four figures are particularly important—*guru, swami, avatar,* and *chela.* A *guru* is a religious teacher who instructs the *chela* (pupil) on the basis of the knowledge the guru acquired either by inspired realization or years of practice of a spiritual discipline. The ideal of the guru is to become a *satguru,* or perfect master. The knowledge to be imparted by the guru to the chela is both technique and realization of the Divine (Brahman), which is the goal of the religious life. The guru may also be a swami (or monk) who functions both as teacher and religious leader. A guru may also be recognized as an avatar, that is, an incarnation of God, and thus properly an object of veneration and worship.

Increasingly, since the British made Christianity a force in India, the guru and swami have taken on a new function. In pre-Christian India, there was little or no congregational worship apart from the large seasonal festivals. The guru served primarily as a leader of an isolated *ashram* (retreat center) inhabited by only a few close disciples. Increasingly, the guru has become a resident of a population center and the leader of mass movements. Influenced by Christian worship, the urban ashram with regular gatherings of the guru's followers is becoming a significant mode of religious expression.

THE HINDU SAMPRADAYAS. Like American Christianity, Indian Hinduism is divided into a number of denomination-like groups, called *sampradayas*. Basic to Hinduism is the division of those groups in the northern part of India from those in southern India. Ritual calendars are different in the north and the south, which causes them to celebrate major festivals at different times. A second major division, roughly analogous to the Christian divisions of Catholic, Protestant, and Orthodox, separates Hindu groups into the Vaishnava, Shaiva, and Shakta. The Vaishnava, which emerged as a recognizable group around the fifth century B.C.E., worship Vishnu as the primary deity in the Hindu pantheon. In India, the majority of temples seen throughout the countryside are Vaishnava centers, and Vaishnava holy men, both monks and individual renunciates, can be seen in typical white robes and with vertical markings (*tilaks*) on their foreheads. Over the centuries, Vaishnavas have focused their attention upon a variety of Vishnu's incarnations; however, that of Krishna has been the most popular. The merger of Vishnu, the hero of the Hindu classic the *Mahabharata,* with Vasudeva-Krishna occurred over the period of the writing of the *Mahabharata* and becomes complete in the Bhagavad Gita, a late insertion into the text.

The Gita also introduces a prime emphasis of Vaishnava Hinduism, bhakti yoga or devotional service. The volume, a dialogue between the god Krishna and his human devotee Arjuna, discusses the more traditional approach to the deity through gifts, sacrifices, and austerities (i.e., jnana and raja yoga), and then points the reader to the truer path of devoted service as the means to really approach Vishnu-Krishna.

Over the centuries, four main Vaishnava sampradayas (denominations) have arisen. The Sri Vaishnavas, traditionally considered the oldest of the four, is said to have started with Vishnu and his wife Sri Lakshmi (hence the popular name of the group), but emerged as a distinct path under Ramanuja in the early twelfth century. Ramanuja most clearly established both the position of theistic worship as opposed to the allegiance to an impersonal divine reality of the Shaivites and the legitimacy of devotional service as the way of salvation.

The Nimbarki (or Sanat) Sampradaya was founded by Nimbarkacharya, who taught a theology that might be termed dualistic monism. Human souls (and the world in general) are seen as both different from God, being endowed with their own qualities and limitations, but at the same time not different, since God is omnipresent and souls depend upon him.

The Madhva Gaudiya Sampradaya was founded by the famous Bengali saint, Chaitanya Mahaprabhu (1486–1533). Centering his activity upon the Gita and the *Srimad Bhagavatam*, a voluminous devotional work on Krishna, Chaitanya taught the practice of *sankirtan*, the multiple recitation of the God's name, as the most acceptable form of devotional activity in the present age. His perspective became well known in America in the 1970s through the high visibility of the Hare Krishna movement, one of several representatives of the Madhva Gaudiya in the West.

The Madhva Sampradaya or Brahma Sampradaya, generally traced to Madhwacharya in the thirteenth century, centers it worship on Krishna and is a purely dualistic school of Hinduism, arguing that God is separate eternally from both the souls and the phenomenal universe.

Competing with the Vaishnavas for the loyalties of Hindus are the Shaivas, those who worship Shiva (or Siva) as the one great God. Shiva, under the name Rudra, appears very early in the Vedas and Upanishads as a principle deity, but the *Mahabharata* contains a full description of the popular Shiva. He is seen as both the great yogi who practices jnana and raja yoga in his mountain home and the creative deity symbolized by his lingam (phallus), a symbol centrally located in many Shiva temples (iconographically, the lingam is always surrounded by the yoni, the symbol of the Goddess's vulva).

Two figures stand out in Shaiva history, Patanjali and Shankaracharya. Patanjali, about whom almost nothing is known (including the century in which he lived), brought together the scattered teachings on yoga and organized them into a system of practice, the following of which constituted the major method by which an individual could become united or yoked to God. Within the Shaiva community, yoga is given varying degrees of emphasis from those who practice it as the major avenue of spiritual enlightenment, to those who integrate it into a larger slavific scheme, to those who discount its significance. The practice of hatha yoga postures (*asanas*) is much more prominent in the American Hindu community than in India.

The goal of Patanjali's system was *kaivalya* or "isolated liberation" reached through the practice of *samadhi*, a state of cosmic awareness reached through the control of body and mind. Practice begins with the negative discipline of *yama* (abstention from violence, falsehood, theft, incontinence, and acquisitiveness) and the positive observance of *niyama* (purity, contentment, austerities, study, and dedicated activity). Accompanying these overall disciplines was the practice of *asanas* (postures) of hatha yoga, *pranayama* (disciplined breathing), and *pratyahara* (detachment of the mind from senses by which it is connected to the outside world). Once the mind and body are suppressed, the yogi can progress to the ultimate three stages, *dharana* (contemplation), *dhayna* (meditation), and *samadhi*.

An important figure associated with Shaiva thought was the sage Shankaracharya (788–820). Shankaracharya became the major exponent of *advaita* (nondualistic or monistic) philosophy centered upon the sole reality of the impersonal Brahman. Brahman, the really real, is devoid of qualities. The phenomenal world with its qualities, designations, and forms is maya, illusion, believed to be real because of *avidya* (ignorance). If the world is illusion, so are most religious practices and beliefs, such as faith in a personal god. The avenue beyond ignorance is *jnana* (knowledge) resulting from withdrawal from maya and contemplation on Brahman.

Shankaracharya's perspective led in two directions. First and foremost, he had little concern for lay Hindus and believed that *jnana* could only truly be practiced by one living a life of renunciation. He thus gave a great impetus to the orders of renunciates, the *sannyasis*. On a practical level, he reorganized the sannyasis around four monastic centers (one in each part of India) and 10 orders, two or three of which were attached to each *math* (or monastery). The leaders of the four Sankara maths are among the most respected leaders in all of Hinduism, though their ultimate power is more informal than organizational. The four centers and the orders attached to each are as follows:

Badrinath in the foothills of the Himalayas (north)
Giri
Parwat
Sagar
Shringeri in Karnataka (south)
Saraswati
Bharati
Puri
Govardhan in Orissa (east)
Arayna
Van
Dvaraka in Gujarat (west)
Tirtha
Ashram

Kanchipuram in Tamil Nadu (also in the south) is recognized by some as a fifth math, but it is not contained in traditional literature.

A sannyasi renounces any connection with the world, including his family and any means of worldly occupation and support, and dons an orange (ochre) robe. He may be nomadic for part or all of his life. He may also engage in religious teachings, and many of the twentieth-century Hindu sampradayas have been formed by a sannyasi (or his Vaishnava counterpart) who gathers a personal following.

Along with the sampradayas, Hinduism has been structured through six orthodox schools of Hindu philosophy. Only one (Vedanta) has modern Western practitioners. Nondual (*advaita*) Vedanta looks to Shankaracharya as its founder. It has additional importance because it is a way of being Hindu that exists outside of the Shaivite, Vaishnavite, and Shakta sampradayas.

While Shankaracharya discounted most religious practice, he did recognize its possible value as a preparation for jnana and the renounced life. Thus, Sankara's philosophy mixed with the popular temple worship of Shiva and the associated deities in what is termed the Smarta tradition. Smartas follow the sutras or aphorisms of the Smriti, or memorized tradition. These detail the practices accompanying proper worship of the Vedic deities. The Smartas emphasize the *dharma* (duties) of *puja* (worship).

Typical of Smarta ritual is the puja of the five shrines, centered upon the worship of five deities: Shiva; Vishnu; Ganesh (Ganesa), the elephant-headed god who removes obstacles; Surya, the sun god; and Durga, the consort of Shiva. The Smarta tradition has been brought to the United States by Hindu immigrants beginning in the late twentieth century.

The third major group of Hindus, present in the United States in much greater proportion than in India, the Shaktas worship the feminine principle Shakti or the Goddess, one name of the female consort of Shiva. The practices of the Shaktas dramatize within the human the reunion of the passive Shiva with the dynamic Shakti, thus bringing enlightenment. This tradition emerged out of the Shaiva tradition around the fifth century B.C.E. with the production of a new set of ritual books called Agamas or Tantras.

The Shaktas worship the divinity in her female form. In one form of practice, associated with Tantrism, they emphasize the presence of the Shakti or female power within the human body. Commonly referred to as *kundalini*, a coil of power resting in potential at the base of the spine, it can be activated by specific practices and ritual procedures. Like a snake, kundalini awakens and springs upward.

Tantrics, who very often have a Shakta association, have also developed a unique view of the human body as possessing, in addition to the physical body, a subtle anatomy consisting of seven *chakras* (cosmic energy centers) located along the spine from its lower tip to the crown of the head, tied together by *nadis* (energy pathways). The practice of kundalini yoga releases the Shakti to rise through the chakras to the crown chakra. By thus bringing the dynamic Shakti back into union with the more passive Shiva, enlightenment is produced.

The Shaktas, when they have Tantric leanings, are also to be distinguished from other Indian traditions by their acceptance of the world. Enlightenment is to be received by using the world, not by denying it. The most controversial practice of the Shaktas has been the ritual use of the very items other Hindus avoid as most harmful to the person seeking spiritual progression, since they excite the outward senses. The so-called *panchamakara* (five m's) ritual involves the partaking of wine, meat, fish, grain (considered an aphrodisiac), and sexual intercourse (in Sanskrit each word begins with "m"). In the West, the word *Tantra* has become (though quite incorrectly) synonymous with any form of sexual magic.

HINDUISM IN AMERICA. The history of Hinduism in America begins long before any guru came to the United States to expound his tenets. During the seventeenth century,

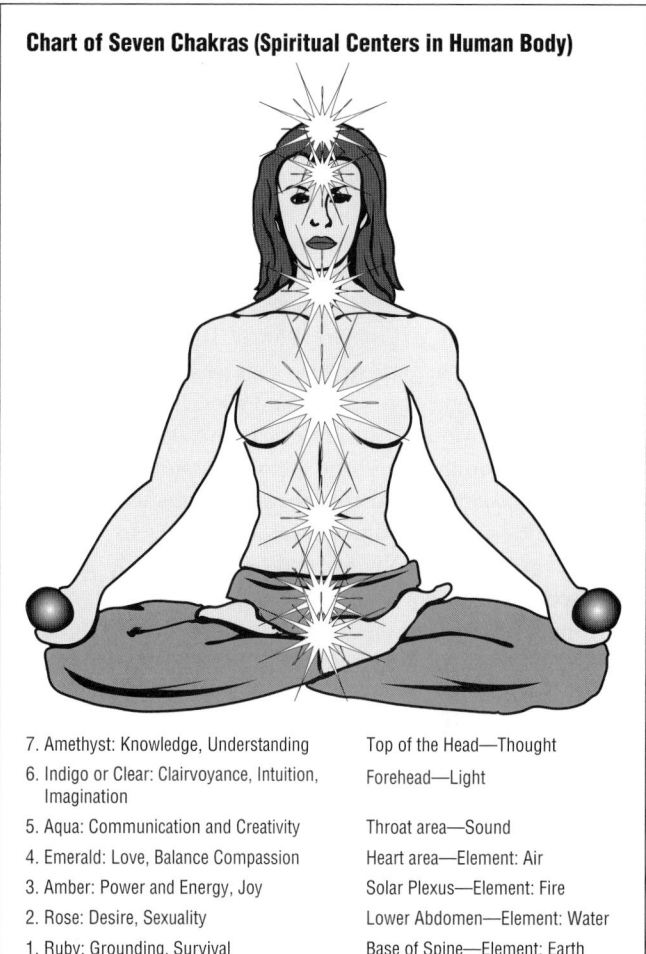

Chart of Seven Chakras (Spiritual Centers in Human Body)

7. Amethyst: Knowledge, Understanding — Top of the Head—Thought
6. Indigo or Clear: Clairvoyance, Intuition, Imagination — Forehead—Light
5. Aqua: Communication and Creativity — Throat area—Sound
4. Emerald: Love, Balance Compassion — Heart area—Element: Air
3. Amber: Power and Energy, Joy — Solar Plexus—Element: Fire
2. Rose: Desire, Sexuality — Lower Abdomen—Element: Water
1. Ruby: Grounding, Survival — Base of Spine—Element: Earth

colonists and missionaries began an active relationship with India that led to the translation into English of many of the Hindu sacred writings. Some of these, especially the Bhagavad Gita, had a direct and powerful influence upon New Englanders, particularly Ralph Waldo Emerson (1803–1882) and the other leaders of the Transcendentalist movement.

As the Transcendentalists absorbed the insights of Hindu literature, Hindus were responding to the impact of Christianity. Among the reformist movements that developed both as a positive response to Christianity and as a new presentation of Hinduism was the Brahmo Samaj, led by Ram Mohan Roy (1774–1832). The Brahmo Samaj was based upon the monotheism of the Upanishads and advocated the abandonment of all image worship. Roy's first book, *The Precepts of Jesus* (1820), reprinted in America in 1825, aroused a great deal of controversy but found some acceptance among early Unitarians. In the 1850s, Unitarian Charles Dall (1816–1886) and Brahmo Samaj leader Keshub Chunder Sen (1838–1888) developed a friendship that led to a relationship between the two organizations that is still active.

The first Hindu guru to come to America was a representative of the Brahmo Samaj. Protap Chunder Mozoomdar (1840–1905) delivered his first American address on

September 2, 1883, in the parlor of the widow of Ralph Waldo Emerson in Concord, Massachusetts. His brief tour was the only appearance by a Hindu teacher until the monumental events of 1893.

In 1893 Mozoomdar was one of several Hindus who traveled to Chicago for the World's Parliament of Religions. His addresses at this first international conclave between representatives of the major Eastern and Western faiths were eclipsed, however, by the appearance of Swami Vivekananda (1863–1902), the young flamboyant disciple of the late Bengali saint and priest Sri Ramakrishna (1836–1886). Vivekananda's impact was so great that he left the parliament to tour the country for two years and eventually founded the first Hindu movement in America, the Vedanta Society. Returning to India in 1895, he organized the scattered disciples of Ramakrishna and found two, swamis Abhedananda (1866–1939) and Turiyananda (1863–1922), to head the Vedanta groups already formed in New York and San Francisco, respectively.

A small wave of immigration from India beginning in the 1890s brought other teachers. Swami Rama Tirtha (1873–1906), a young sannyasi, arrived in 1902 and lectured throughout America for the next two years. That same year, Baba Premananda Bharati, a Bengali student of the teachings of Sri Chaitanya, began a five-year stay, during which time he organized the Krishna Samaj. He left behind disciples who carried his memory into the 1980s.

These early teachers from India were joined by westerners who adopted Hindu teachings and expounded them through writings and the formation of groups. No writer surpassed the popularity of William Walker Atkinson (1862–1932), who began to write books on Hindu teachings under the pseudonym of Swami Ramacharaka in 1903. His 13 books have remained in print since their initial appearance. Pierre Bernard (c. 1875–1955), known to his followers by his religious name, Oom the Omnipotent, founded the first U.S. Tantric organization, the Tantrick Order of America, in 1909. In spite of the several scandals that hit it, Bernard's group lasted for several decades, and his nephew, Theos Bernard (1908–1947), wrote classical texts on hatha yoga.

The growth of Hinduism was stymied in the decades during and after World War I (1914–1918). A growing anti-Asian sentiment, primarily directed against Chinese and Japanese Americans, included Indians in its attack, leading to the passing of the Asian Exclusion Act of 1917. This action effectively cut off Asian immigration for several generations and stymied what would have become, in all likelihood, the steady growth of Hinduism in the United States. Several years later, as the result of a lawsuit brought by Bhagat Singh Thind (1892–1967), an Indian Sikh, the U. S. Supreme Court ruled Indians ineligible for citizenship, an act that also revoked the citizenship of some who had already received it. Then, in 1927, Hinduism was viciously attacked in a best-selling volume, *Mother India*, by Katherine Mayo (1867–1940), a book credited with affecting Indian-American relations for a generation.

The Hindu community grew very slowly in the half century after the passing of the Asian Exclusion Act, but it did grow. A number of teachers were able to emigrate just prior to the passing of the law, and several stayed to found movements. For example, Basudeb Bhattacharya (1888–1949), a young playwright, migrated to New York, where he assumed the religious name Pundit Acharya and founded the Temple of Yoga, the Yoga Research Institute, and Prana Press. The most successful of the several gurus was Paramahansa Yogananda (1893–1952), who arrived in 1922 to attend an interfaith conference, but stayed to found the Yogoda-Satsang, known today as the Self-Realization Fellowship. His *Autobiography of a Yogi* (1946) was immensely popular and assisted the spread of Hinduism far beyond the fellowship.

Besides those mentioned above, other teachers who founded movements upon which modern American Hinduism is built were A. K. Mozumdar (1864–1953) (Messianic World Message); Swami Omkar (Shanti Ashrama); Sri Deva Ram Sukul (Dharma Mandal); Rishi Krishnananda (Para-Vidya Center, Sant Ram Mandal [Universal Brotherhood Temple and School of Eastern Philosophy]); and Swami A. P. Mukerji (Transcendent Science Society). Joining them were a number of teachers, such as Bhagwan Singh Gyanee (1882–1962) and Rishi Singh Grewal, who did not found their own groups but wrote books that enjoyed a circulation among those interested in Eastern and esoteric philosophies. Theosophy also contributed greatly to the growth of Hinduism through its continued dissemination of Indian books among the American occult community and its promotion of Jiddu Krishnamurti (1895–1986) as the vehicle for the coming world teacher.

Krishnamurti, a young Indian boy, had been picked out in the early twentieth century to be the cosmic figure predicted in Theosophical literature. He lectured through the 1920s on behalf of the Theosophical cause, while for health reasons he settled in Ojai, California. Then, in 1929, he renounced his messianic role and began a career as an independent teacher. Beginning with the remnants of his Theosophical following, he gradually attracted both an international audience and a following among academics. He became a forceful element in the buildup of interest in Hinduism noticeable after World War II (1937–1945), for which the most visible component, the spread of hatha yoga, was a far cry from Krishnamurti's emphases.

Just as 1893 and 1917 had become years of dramatic junctures in the history of American Hinduism, so was 1965. In the fall of that year, the Asian Exclusion Act was repealed and the immigration quotas from Asia were placed on a par with those of Europe. The number of Indian immigrants escalated. Also, during the years that the Exclusion Act was in force, Indian teachers who were not opposed to teaching Hinduism to westerners emerged in significant numbers. As quotas allowed, they came to America and began to build movements, primarily among young adults. Though Shaiva yoga teachers and Shakta Tantric teachers were most successful, Vaishnavas were also represented.

Most Indian immigrants have not been teachers motivated by goals of building an American following; rather, most have been Hindu lay people faced with the task of reestablishing traditional and familiar temple structures in the West. As their numbers have increased, they have banded together to erect both Shaiva and Vaishnava temples and have brought priests from India to lead ritual activities. The emergence of these traditional temples has completed the spectrum of Indian religion in North America. At present, the only significant element of Indian religious practice not evident in the larger Western Hindu community are the bands of holy men that roam the Indian countryside, some without clothes, living off the alms of the working people and regular pilgrimages to holy sites, all of which at present are within the country of India.

Since 1965, Hinduism has grown significantly by the immigration of Asian Indians to the United States who have proceeded to build Indian-style temples in urban centers across the nation. Several hundred Indian spiritual teachers (from Brahman priests to independent purveyors of spiritual wisdom) have arrived both to care for the spiritual needs of the Hindu community and to develop new centers of Hindu spirituality among Americans of other ethnic traditions. As the twenty-first century begins, the entire spectrum of Hindu thought had found a home in both the United States and Canada.

SIKHISM.
The early sixteenth century was a time of bitter conflict in North India. A series of invasions that culminated in 1526 established Muslim supremacy. The Punjab area was one of the most hotly contested regions, and it was here that Guru Nanak (1469–1539), the founder of Sikhism, was born. One day while bathing in a river, he had a vision of God's presence in which he was told to go into the world and teach the repetition of the name of God, the keeping of ritual purity through absolution, and the practice of charity, meditation, and worship.

According to tradition, after a full day of silence, he uttered the pronouncement, "There is no Hindu [follower of the native faith of India] and no Musselman [Muslim]." He adopted a unique garb, which combined both Hindu and Muslim features, and developed an eclectic faith that took elements from many religions, but mainly from Hindus and Muslims. From Islam he taught of one creator God, called the True Name to avoid such designations as Allah or Vishnu. From Hinduism he taught the ideas of karma, reincarnation, and the ultimate unreality of the world. Nanak also emphasized the unique role of the guru (teacher) as necessary to lead people to God. After Nanak's death, nine gurus followed him in succession.

The fourth guru, Baba Ram Das (1534–1581), began the Golden Temple of Amritsar, the present headquarters of the world Sikh community. The fifth guru, Arjan (1563–1606), completed the temple and installed the Sri Guru Granth Sahib, or Adi Granth, the collected writings of Nanak and the other gurus, within it.

The tenth guru, Gobind Singh (1666–1708), had the second most significant role in molding the Sikh community—second only to Nanak. Gobind Singh completed the Adi Granth, the main Sikh scripture, and militarized the Sikhs by forming the Khalsa, the Community of the Pure. Members were initiated by baptism in which they drank and were sprinkled with sweetened water stirred with a sword. They changed their name to Singh (Lion) and adopted the five K's: (1) *kesh*, or long hair, a sign of saintliness; (2) *kangh*, a comb for keeping the hair neat; (3) *kach*, short pants for quick movement in battle; (4) *kara*, a steel bracelet signifying sternness and restraint; and (5) *kirpan*, a sword of defense.

After Gobind Singh's death, the Adi Granth became the guru and no further human gurus were allowed. The military emphasis continued, however, and Sikhs served with distinction in British army units.

SIKHISM IN NORTH AMERICA. As early as 1790, some unnamed East Indian visitors, possibly Sikhs, were said to have landed in Salem, Massachusetts. They were much the exception, as Sikhs, mostly from northern and eastern India (the Punjab region), rarely traveled to the New World prior to the twentieth century. Sikhs were among the major religious groups not represented at the 1893 World's Parliament of Religions.

At the end of the nineteenth century, some Punjabis developed a wanderlust, seemingly occasioned by the 1897 diamond-jubilee celebration in London for Queen Victoria (r. 1837–1901). On their return journey, the Sikh regiment that played music at the event was taken across Canada. Members of the troop were impressed with the potential for farming in the prairie provinces. Traveling by way of Hong Kong, a few Sikhs reached Canada as early as 1903. In 1904 there were a reported 204 Sikhs in British Columbia. Most would arrive during the next four years. Of the several thousand who came into Canada, some settled in British Columbia; others headed immediately for the United States. Measures restricting Indian immigration into British Columbia and discriminatory legislation against the Indians by the government caused a shift of movement from Canada to the United States. Many Canadian Sikhs migrated southward. By 1915, there were approximately 7,000 Indians in America, the overwhelming majority being Sikhs and residents of California.

The first *gurudwara*, the Sikh's house of worship, where the copy of the scripture, the Sri Guru Granth Sahib, is enshrined and where housing for the needy is provided, was begun in Vancouver in the summer of 1906 and opened in January 1908. It was modeled on the gurudwara in Hong Kong. Four years later, a gurudwara opened in Stockton, California. During the early twentieth century, others were constructed in California and western Canada.

In 1917 the United States stopped almost all immigration from Asia, and the U.S. Sikh community, then numbering only in the thousands, stopped growing. The mostly male population found wives among their non-Indian neighbors, many of whom were Mexican. Immigration began to flow again after the 1965 change in immigration laws, and since then the Sikh community has grown considerably, with annual infusions of members moving to America from India. The North American Sikh community is no longer bound to the West Coast and has established gurudwaras across the continent. The development of an American consciousness has been assisted by organizations such as the Sikh Foundation, established in 1967 to promote Sikhism, pass its heritage to the next generation, and advance Sikh culture. The Sikh Communications Council, based in Menlo Park, California, assumed leadership in countering the attacks upon individual Sikhs following the September 11, 2001, attacks on the Pentagon and World Trade Center.

In 1984 American Sikhs hosted fellow believers from around the world in New York City, where the World Sikh Organization (WSO) was founded as a representative voice of Sikhs. There is currently both an American and a Canadian section of the WSO.

In the 1970s the Punjabi Sikh community was joined by a new organization, the Sikh Dharma, headed by Sri Singh Sahib Bhai Harbhajan Singh Khalsa Yogiji, popularly known simply as Yogi Bhajan (1929–2004). Bhajan concentrated his efforts on converting non-Indian Americans to the Sikh faith and was able to build a national organization during his first two decades of activity.

JAINISM. Jainism developed in the sixth century B.C.E. out of the teachings of Vardhamana Mahavira (599–527 B.C.E.) who, like his contemporary, the Buddha, was born into a kingly family, which he rejected to become an ascetic. After some twenty years of meditation and mortification, Mahavira discovered enlightenment and became a *jina*, a conqueror, from which the name of the community he founded took its name. By the time of Mahavira's death, his followers numbered about ten thousand.

Jain theology is atheistic. It poses the existence of two realities—*jivas*, eternal souls, and *ajivas*, eternal, nonliving, material elements. Humans are forced into cycles of reincarnation because their jiva has attached itself to ajiva. Attachment is by karma, the actions done in existence which inhere in the soul. Liberation occurs by directing one's life to reducing karma. Among the practices that aid liberation are: *ahimsa*—the nonhurting of any life (which implies strict vegetarianism); preservation—proper control over the mind, speech, and body; carefulness—proper care in walking, speaking, eating, lifting, and lying; ascetic observances; meditation; and right conduct. Among these, ahimsa is by far the most central to the Jain faith and the special feature by which Jains are recognized.

The austere practices required of Jains have led to some extremes. For example, the Digambara Jains reject the ownership of all property, including clothes, and encourage the practice of going naked. One visitor to the United States, Muni Sushil Kumarji, a Jain monk, made news because of the mask he wore (to prevent inhaling microscopic insects, thus harming them) and the brush he used (to gently sweep insects from his path so that he would not step on them).

In 1893 Virchand A. Gandhi (1864–1901) traveled to Chicago to address the World's Parliament of Religions, a most impressive endeavor. Like later Jain migrants, Gandhi was opposed by many coreligionists who felt that any travel, other than by foot, was morally wrong. From that time to 1972, only a few Jains, such as Champat Rai Jain, who ventured to England in the 1930s, found their way to the West. By 1975 a community of some 200 was reported in Chicago, with others scattered in various urban centers. By 1981 there were enough Jains in the United States and Canada to establish the Federation of Jains in North America. By the end of the century, the four original member groups had grown to 57.

SOURCES

General Sources

The largest archive of material relative to Hindus, Sikhs, and Jains in America can be found in the J. Gordon Melton American Religions Collection at the Davidson Library of the University of California–Santa Barbara.

Babb, Lawrence A. *Redemptive Encounters: Three Modern Styles in the Hindu Tradition.* Berkeley: University of California Press, 1987.

Dasgupta, Shashibhusan. *Obscure Religious Cults.* 2nd ed. Calcutta, India: Firma K. L. Mukhopadhyay, 1962. 436 pp.

Dell, David J. *Guide to Hindu Religion.* Boston: G. K. Hall, 1981.

Farquhar, J. N. *An Outline of the Religious Literature of India* (1920). Delhi: Moitilal Banarsidass, 1967. 451 pp.

Flood, Gavin. *An Introduction to Hinduism.* Cambridge, U.K.: Cambridge University Press, 1996.

Ghurye, G. S. *Indian Sadhus.* 2nd ed. Bombay, India: Popular Prakashan, 1964. 260 pp.

Griswold, Henry DeWitt. *Insights into Modern Hinduism.* New York: Holt, 1934. 288 pp.

Hopkins, Thomas J. *The Hindu Religious Tradition.* North Scituate, MA: Duxbury Press, 1971. 156 pp.

Johnson, Linda. *Daughters of the Goddess: The Women Saints of India.* St. Paul, MN: Yes International, 1994. 128 pp.

Jones, Constance A., and James D. Ryan. *Encyclopedia of Hinduism.* New York: Facts on File, 2007. 552 pp.

Klostermaier, Klaus K. *A Survey of Hinduism.* 3rd ed. Albany: State University of New York Press, 2007. 700 pp.

Knott, Kim. *Hinduism: A Very Short Introduction.* New York: Oxford University Press, 2000.

Pararignanar, Saiva Ilakkia. *The Development of Saiviam in South India.* Dharmapuram Adhinam, 1964. 359 pp.

Pereira, José. *Hindu Theology: A Reader.* Garden City, NY: Doubleday, 1976. 558 pp.

Renou, Louis. *The Nature of Hinduism.* Trans. Patrick Evans. New York: Walker, 1962. 155 pp.

Santucci, James A. *An Outline of Vedic Literature.* Missoula, MT: Scholars Press, 1976. 69 pp.

Sullivan, Bruce M. *Historical Dictionary of Hinduism.* Lanham, MD: Scarecrow Press, 1997.

———. *The A to Z of Hinduism.* Lanham, MD: Scarecrow Press, 2001.

Tripathi, B. D. *Sadhus of India.* Bombay, India: Popular Prakashan, 1978. 258 pp.

Uban, Sujan Singh. *The Gurus of India.* London: Fine Books, 1977. 175 pp.

Wilson, H. H. *Religious Sects of the Hindus.* 2nd ed. Ed. Ernst R. Rost. Calcutta, India: Susil Gupta, 1958. 221 pp.

Hinduism in America

Agarwal, Priya. *Passage From India: Post 1965 Indian Immigrants and Their Children.* Palos Verdes, CA: Yuvati, 1991.

Bromley, David, and Larry Shinn, eds. *Krishna Consciousness in the West.* Lewisburg, PA: Bucknell University Press, 1989. 295 pp.

Fenton, John Y. *Transplanting Religious Traditions: Asian Indians in America.* New York: Praeger, 1988.

Fisher, Maxine P. *The Indians of New York: A Study of Immigrants from India.* Columbia, MO: South Asia Books, 1980. 165 pp.

Forsthoefel, Thomas A., and Cynthia Ann Humes, eds. *Gurus in America.* Albany: State University of New York Press, 2005. 236 pp.

Jackson, Carl T. *The Oriental Religions and American Thought: Nineteenth-century Explorations.* Westport, CT: Greenwood Press, 1981. 302 pp.

Joshi, Khyati Y. *New Roots in America's Sacred Ground: Religion, Race, And Ethnicity in Indian America.* New Brunswick, NJ: Rutgers University Press, 2006. 240 pp.

Kamath, M. V. *The United States and India, 1776–1976.* Washington, DC: Embassy of India, 1976. 222 pp.

Kolapen, Mahalingum, and Sanjay Kolapen. *Hindu Temples in North America: A Celebration.* Orlando, FL: Hindu University of America, 2002. 320 pp.

Mann, Gurinder Singh, Paul Numrich, and Raymond Williams. *Buddhists, Hindus, and Sikhs in America: A Short History.* New York: Oxford University Press, 2007. 168 pp.

Pechilis, Karen. *The Graceful Guru: Hindu Female Gurus in India and the United States.* New York: Oxford University Press, 2004.

Riepe, Dale. *The Philosophy of India and Its Impact on American Thought.* Springfield, IL: Thomas, 1970. 339 pp.

Thomas, Wendell. *Hinduism Invades America.* Boston: Beacon Press, 1930. 300 pp.

Tweed, Thomas A., and Stephen Prothero. *Asian Religions in America: A Documentary History.* New York: Oxford University Press, 1999. 416 pp.

Sikhism

Cole, W. Owen, and Piara Singh Sambhi. *A Popular Dictionary of Sikhism.* Calcutta, India: Rupa, 1990.

Dhillon, Mahinder Singh. *A History Book of the Sikhs in Canada and California.* Vancouver, BC: Shromani Akali Dal Association of Canada, 1981. 519 pp.

Hawley, John Stratton, and Gurinder Singh Mann. *Studying the Sikhs: Issues for North America.* Albany: State University of New York Press, 1993.

Juergensmeyer, Mark, and N. Gerald Barrier, eds. *Sikh Studies: Comparative Perspectives on a Changing Tradition.* Berkeley, CA: Graduate Theological Union, 1979. 230 pp.

Kaur, Sardarni Premka. *Guru for the Aquarian Age.* Albuquerque, NM: Brotherhood of Life Books, 1972. 131 pp.

Kharak, Singh, G.S. Mansukhani, and Jasbir Singh Mann, eds. *Fundamental Issues in Sikh Studies.* Chandigarh, India: Institute of Sikh Studies, 1992.

Macauliffe, Max Arthur. *The Sikh Religion: Its Gurus, Sacred Writings, and Authors* (1909). New Delhi, India: Chand, 1978. 6 Vols.

McLeod, W. H. *The Sikhs: History, Religion, and Society.* Oxford: Clarendon Press, 1989.

———. *Who is a Sikh? The Problem of Sikh Identity.* Oxford: Clarendon Press, 1989.

Mann, Jasbir Singh, and Harbans Singh Saraon, eds. *Advanced Studies in Sikhism.* Irvine, CA: Sikh Community of North America, 1989.

Mathur, L. P. *Indian Revolutionary Movement in the United States of America.* Delhi, India: Chand, 1970. 169 pp.

Singh, Gopal. *The Religion of the Sikhs.* Bombay, India: Asia Publishing House, 1971. 191 pp.

Tatla, Darshan Singh. *Sikhs in America: An Annotated Bibliography.* New York: Greenwood Press, 1991.

Sant Mat

Fripp, Peter. *The Mystic Philosophy of Sant Mat.* London: Spearman, 1964. 174 pp.

Johnson, Julian. *With a Great Master in India.* Beas, India: Radha Swami Sat Sang, 1953. 200 pp.

———. *The Path of the Masters* (1939). Punjab, India: Radha Soami Satsang Beas, 1972. 572 pp.

Juergensmeyer, Mark. *Radhasoami Reality: The Logic of a Modern Faith.* Princeton, NJ: Princeton University Press, 1991.

Lane, David Christopher. *Radhasoami Parampara in Definition and Classification.* M.A. thesis. Berkeley, CA: Graduate Theological Union, 1981. 132 pp.

———. *The Radhasoami Tradition: A Critical History of Guru Successorship.* New York: Garland, 1992. 351 pp.

Jainism

Cort, John E. *Jains in the World: Religious Values and Ideology in India.* Oxford: Oxford University Press, 2001.

Dundas, Paul. *The Jains.* 2nd ed. New York: Routledge, 2002.

Gopalan, Subramania. *Outlines of Jainism.* New York: Halsted Press, 1973. 205 pp.

Jain, Muni Uttam Kamal. *Jaina Sects and Schools.* Delhi, India: Concept, 1975. 162 pp.

Jaini, P. S. *The Jaina Path of Purification* (1979). Delhi, India: Motilal Banarsidass, 1990.

Kumar, Bhuvanendra. *Jainism in America.* Fremont, CA: Jain Humanities Press, 1996. 221 pp.

Roy, Ahim Kumar. *A History of the Jainas.* New Delhi, India: Gitanjali Press, 1984. 179 pp.

Shah, Vikram V., ed. *Jain Heritage—Then, Now, and Forever: Pratishtha Mahotsav Souvenir.* Bartlett, IL: Jain Society of Metropolitan Chicago, 1993.

Singh, Narendra K., ed. *Encyclopedia of Jainism.* 30 vols. New Delhi, India: Anmol, 2001.

Stevenson, Mrs. Sinclair (Margaret). *The Heart of Jainism* (1915). New Delhi, India: Munshiram Manoharlal, 1970. 336 pp.

Tobias, Michael. *Life Force: The World of Jainism.* Berkeley: Asian Humanities Press, 1991.

❊ Intrafaith Organizations

Brahman Samaj of North America

PO Box 716, Belle Mead, NJ 08502

Though divided into several subgroupings, together the Brahmans constitute the dominant and highest caste of the four major castes in India. In the years immediately after the change of U.S. immigration law in 1965, large number of Brahmans immigrated to the United States and Canada. Many were engineers, physicians, professors, or other types of professionals. As their numbers grew, in 1979 Dr. Shri Kant Mishra made the initial suggestion that an association of Brahmans residing in North America would be desirable. That suggestion did not bear fruit, however, until the 1990s, when the need to pass on the tradition of their Brahman status became a major concern of some leading American Brahmans. By the middle of the decade, Dr. Shyam Narayan Shukla of Fremont, California, was involved in collecting names for a national directory of Brahmans, and Nirmalendu Choubey of Manlius, New York, had begun efforts to form a national organization. Shukla's directory was published in 1994, and the two men joined efforts to create a national association. The Brahman Samaj of North America (BSNA) was formally established in September 1994, at which time a constitution was adopted. Choubey was the first president and Shukla the first general secretary.

As communication and fellowship among Brahmans was a major goal, the organization immediately organized a first national convention (1995) and has held one annually since.

Essential to Brahman identity are the *samskars*, rituals that developed over several millennia and offer a context in which the Brahman is born, matures, and dies. The Hindu religious texts define 16 such *samskars*, which are to be observed by anyone wishing to become a refined Hindu. The first 10 concern aspects of birth and childhood, namely:

1. Impregnation
2. Pumsavana (ensuring the birth of a male child)
3. Simanta (hair-parting)
4. Jatakarma (birth)
5. Namakarana (naming ceremony)
6. Karnavedha (ear-boring ceremony)
7. Nishkramana (introducing the child to the community)
8. Annaprashana (first feeding of solid food)
9. Chudakarana (tonsure, haircut)
10. Vidyarambha (teaching of the alphabet)

The remaining 6 carry one through the adult years:

11. Upanayana (initiation)
12. Vedarambha (higher studies)
13. Keshanta or Godana (first shaving of beard)
14. Samavartana or Snana (completion of studies)
15. Vivaha (marriage)
16. Antyeshti (funeral rites)

The majority of the Hindu community no longer observe the *samskars* and their loss in the West is always threatened. The Brahman Samaj holds that "Religion, traditions, and above all the 'Samskar' are needed for being a Brahman." The Samaj attempts to build respect for the tradition while at the same time promoting a progressive outlook toward the wider culture.

The North American Samaj is in fraternal relations with similar organizations in India, Nepal, Australia, New Zealand, Fiji, the United Kingdom, Holland, and South Africa.

Membership: Not reported. The Samaj carries out its work through 22 chapters found across the United States and 2 in Canada.

Periodicals: *Brahma Bharati • Brahma-Vani • Brahmakulum.*

Sources:

Brahman Samaj of North America. www.bsna.org/.

Canadian Yoga Alliance

20 Bradmon Dr., Ste. 610, St. Catharines, ON, Canada L2M 3S5

The Canadian Yoga Alliance (CYA) is a cooperative fellowship and network of yoga teachers and centers serving groups and people across Canada. The alliance emerged in the 1990s with the growth of Hatha Yoga as a popular practice and the multiplication of classes being taught by people with very different backgrounds and qualifications. The alliance also wishes to affirm yoga's spiritual base in the context of the money economy in which it has emerged. The alliance attempts to remain unbiased relative to the many different schools of yoga and thus sees itself as primarily a network and a communication tool for the interaction of the various teachings, ideas, and fellowships.

The Alliance's manifesto affirms that "Yoga is about attaining 'Self-Realization' through Union. (Harmony of mind, emotions, body, spirit and breath)" and stands

against attempts to control or exploit the discipline for commercial gain. At the same time, independent yoga teachers often do rely on their classes for their personal income.

The Alliance draws members with no organizational ties as well as those who are affiliated with the larger national and international yoga associations. It offers individuals various forms of low-cost insurance especially designed to meet their particular needs (especially protection from any negative results for students resulting from the physical exercise element in yoga practice).

The CYA is a Canadian affiliate of the International Yoga Federation, the World Yoga Community (formerly the North American Yoga Federation), and the Yoga Alliance International.

Membership: Not reported.

Sources:

Canadian Yoga Alliance.
www.canadianyogicalliance.com/cya/canadianyogicalliance.cfm.

International Yoga Federation

c/o International Yoga College, PO Box 300, 2509 N. Campbell Ave., Tempe, AZ 85719

The International Yoga Federation (IYF) was founded in 1987. A rapid, worldwide expansion of yoga in the decade after World War II saw the emergence of many independent teachers and diverse offerings under the single label of yoga. In light of this, the federation attempts to provide leadership for the global yoga community in the setting of standards, fostering integrity, providing resources, and upholding the teachings of yoga. In 1989 another organization with similar goals and mission, the World Yoga Council, which was founded in 1980 by Bhagavan Krishna Kisore Das of New Delhi, India, became part of International Yoga Federation (and it also continues as an independent organization).

In western countries, yoga is most identified with the practice of *asanas* (postures) as a means to improving one's overall physical health, but the complete system of yoga includes a set of behavioral injunctions (*yamas* and *niyamas*), regulation of breathing, concentration, and meditation. The complete yoga system is a holistic practice that includes a spiritual element, which in the west gives it an inherent religious nature, though many eastern teachers refrain from calling their teachings religious.

Putting aside the religious question, the International Yoga Federation honors "authentic" yoga traditions in all their diversity, and finds within the diversity a harmony and unity. The federation promotes values of tolerance, friendship, sensitivity, and mutual support among its member organizations. It also supports minimum international standards for yoga teachers, and it established an International Yoga Teachers' Registry to recognize and promote yoga teachers whose training that meets those standards, which includes 200 to 500 hours of training.

Membership: Member groups in the United States include the International Yoga College, the American Yoga Foundation, the Institute of Holistic Yoga, the International Yogatherapy Conferences, the International Gurukulam Yogabhavan, the Yogsadhna Centre, the Traditional Yoga Academy, the Central Yoga Association, the Florida Vedic College, the Art of Zen Yoga Centre, the Sat Yoga Centres of San Francisco, and the North American Yoga Council. Member groups in Canada include the Canadian Yoga Alliance, the Francophone Yoga Federation, the Namaste Yoga British Columbia, the Prana Yoga College, the Kunda Yoga College, the Suddha Dharma Mandalam, the Yoga Satyam School of Quebec, Institut of Integral Yoga of Quebec, and the Yoga Centre of Quebec. In addition, a number of international organizations that have affiliated centers in Canada and the United States are among the organizations recognized by the International Yoga Federation.

Sources:

International Yoga Federation. www.internationalyogafederation.net/.

Vishwa Hindu Parishad of America

National Office Manager, PO Box 611, Iselin, NJ 08830

The idea of a cooperative world structure for Hindus was first proposed in 1964, and that proposal led to a gathering in India in 1966 at the time of the great Kumbha Mela festival. The first Hindu World Conference attracted some 25,000 attendees and included participants from the United States. An American branch of the Vishwa Hindu Parishad formed at that conference and was established in New York in 1970.

In the United States, the organization has focused upon a number of programs aimed at providing fellowship for Hindus of different ethnic and religious groups, cultural programs for children, cooperative celebrations of Indian festivals, and the furthering of Hinduism both within the Indian American community and among the public at large. It has also developed several relief projects and sponsors medical facilities in India.

The parishad holds an annual national conference. There are 19 local chapters in different locations around the country, which hold regular meetings.

Periodicals: *Hindu Vishwa.*

Sources:

Vishwa Hindu Parishad of America Inc. www.vhp-america.org.

World Vaisnava Association

No. 154 Gopeswar Rd., Mohala, Vrindavan, India 281 121

The World Vaisnava Association grew out of the global expansion of the Chaitanya form of Vaisnava Hinduism based on devotional service, which had been initiated by the International Society of Krishna Consciousness (ISKCON) in the mid-1960s. As ISKCON grew internationally, especially in the years immediately following the death of its founder Srila A. C. Bhaktivedanta Prabhupada (1896–1977), the organization splintered and new organization emerged in India out of the Gaudiya Math. The Gaudiya Math had been the organization with which Prabhupada was associated prior to his American sojourn.

Founded in 1994, the World Vaisnava Association hoped to overcome the many divisions that had formed from the Gaudiya Math and heal many of the hard feeling that had developed between some of the movement's branches. Various ISKCON groups had differed over issues of guru leadership. Members asked whether the gurus who succeeded Prabhupada should be venerated in the same manner that he had. Other gurus had problems with the governing body that assumed headship over the international movement. A few turned to teachers (gurus) associated with the Gaudiya Math for new leadership.

Efforts to found the World Vaisnava Association grew from initial meetings in Vrindavan, India, between several former ISKCON leaders and B. V. Tripurari, B. G. Narasingha, and B. A. Paramadvaiti—all revered Indian leaders in the Chaitanya community—to discuss the possibility of founding a new organization as an expression of unity. At one meeting in 1993, several decisions were made. They agreed to approach Srila B. P. Puri Maharaj, then 97 years old, the senior most Vaisnava then alive. He eventually agreed to become the first president of the proposed organization. They also decided to invite the leadership from all the different related groups to participate as founders of what would become the World Vaisnava Association.

In February 1994, they issued the first copy of the *World Vaisnava Association Newsletter* and sent it to all of the ISKCON-related groups. A founding meeting was held in November 1994. Among the 120 people present, 28 acaryas and sannyasis became the founding members. The founders saw the World Vaisnava Association as continuing the moribund Visva Vaisnava Raj Sabha that had been founded by Srila Jiva Goswami in the nineteenth century.

The World Vaisnava Association sees its task as promoting the true Hindu teachings, its theistic approach, and its answers to the problems of contemporary society. It also tries to build respect and fraternal relations between the several member organizations and does not seek to compete with them. Thus, it does not create ashrams (religious communities) nor facilitate the guru-disciple relationship. Any ISKCON-related organization may associate with the World Vaisnava Association.

Membership: Founding members of the association with centers in America include: Gaudiya Vaisnava Society, ISKCON, the Vrindavan Institute for Vaisnava Culture and Studies (VRINDA), Bhaktivedanta Ashram, Gaudiya Mission, Bhaktivedanta Institute, and Mantra Meditation Hawaii.

Periodicals: *WVA Journal.*

Sources:

VVRS—WVA World Vaisnava Association. www.wva-vvrs.org/.

Paramadvanti, Swami B. A. "Our Family the Gaudiya Math."
www.vrindavan.org/English/Books/GMconded.html.

World Yoga Community

Current address could not be obtained for this edition.

The World Yoga Community was founded as the North American Yoga Federation to be a fellowship of yoga groups and individuals in Canada, the United States, and Mexico. It sees itself as a community of individuals who are supportive of yogic, dharmic, holistic, and environmentally friendly living and who see such a lifestyle as an avenue for peace, beginning with individual peace and moving outward to ever more inclusive collectivities—family, neighborhood, nation, and world. It emphasizes yoga's role as a tool for personal and global enlightenment.

The World Yoga Community is part of a growing self-conscious community of yoga practitioners that emerged at the end of the twentieth century in the aftermath of the revival of yoga in India and its spread around the world. As such, the World Yoga Community includes several national yoga fellowships, such as the Canadian Yoga Alliance, as affiliates and is in turn affiliated with the Yoga Alliance International.

Jagat Guru H. H. Swami Buaji Maharaj, founder of the Indo American Vedanta Society, serves as the patron of the World Yoga community.

Membership: The World Yoga Community has member organizations in Canada, the United States, and Mexico. In Canada, these include the Canadian Yoga Alliance/Yoga in Niagara, Nitya Yoga, and the francophone Yoga Federation of Canada. Organizations in the United States include the International Gurukulam, the Indo-American Yoga Vedanta Society, Yogabhavan NYC, Sat Yoga of San Francisco, the New York Yoga Teacher's Association, and Central Yoga. In Mexico, members include the Yoga Alliance Mexico/Dharma Yoga Association of Mexico and the Purnoham Yoga Centre Mexico.

Sources:

World Yoga Community. www.nayf.org/.

 # Hinduism

Abhidhyan Yoga Institute

PO Box 1414, Nevada City, CA 95959-1414

Alternate Address: c/o Modern Seers Inc., PO Box 272, Fredonia, NY 14063

The Abhidhyan Yoga Institute was founded in 1991 by Anatole Ruslanov to prepare interested persons for what is termed *abhidhyan yoga* or *all-embracing yoga*, a form of tantric yoga that has survived through the centuries only in a few obscure Hindu and Buddhist tantric traditions.

Ruslanov completed a period of monastic training in Varanasi, India, with Shri Anandamurti (1921–1990), founder of the Ananda Marga Yoga Society. Following his monastic training, he continued his study with Anandamurti and eventually became a spiritual teacher and a bearer of the lineage. After his master's death, he founded his own teaching work. New students are expected to start a regular personal practice of meditation and *asanas* (body postures), adhere to a set of moral principles, and find a competent trustworthy teacher to follow.

Membership: Not reported. There are members in seven countries.

Periodicals: *The Tantrik Path*.

Sources:

Modern Seers: Authentic No-Nonsense Modern Nondual Tantra Yoga Meditation. www.abhidhyan.org/.

Adidam

12040 N Seigler Rd., Middletown, CA 95461

Adidam, formerly known as Free Daist Communion, was founded in 1972 by Franklin Jones (b. 1939). In 1960, after "a crisis of despair," he began a period of introspection that led him to study with Swami Rudrananda (1928–1973), an American disciple of Swami Muktananda (1908–1982). At Rudrananda's suggestion, he studied for a time in a Lutheran seminary. In 1968, he traveled to India to meet Muktananda. At Muktananda's ashram, he had his first adult experience of total absorption into transcendental consciousness. Later he was guided in the subtle form by Muktananda's guru, Swami Nityananda (1897–1961), and finally by the female personification of divine energy (Shakti).

On September 10, 1970, he entered what he has termed the permanent and unconditional state of sahaj samadhi, or "open eyes," which is coessential with the divine being consciousness itself. This is the condition that, according to his own confession, he consciously relinquished in his earliest years, and that he had been moved to recover throughout his life. Soon after this experience, he began to teach in order to transmit the God-realization he had attained. In 1973 he changed his name to Bubba Free John—*Bubba* denoting *brother*—and changed his method of teaching. He involved his students in the realms of experience that human beings are typically drawn to, including sexuality, the pursuit of material pleasure, and indulgence in spiritual and psychic phenomena. This method was aimed at showing the futility of seeking for any form of experience.

In 1979, Bubba Free John entered a new phase of work and adopted the name Da Free John—*Da* signifying *giver*. During this phase, he instructed his students in forms of sacramental worship and their relationship to him as spiritual master rather than brother. In 1986, his active teaching work came to an end, and he became known as Heart-Master Da Love-Ananda, or more formally Avadhoota Da Love-Ananda Hridayam. While he has continued to give instruction since 1986, he has been concentrating on the transmission of his divine condition.

He is now referred to as Avatar Adi Da Samraj. As Avatar Adi Da's work has grown and changed, so has the name of the body of practitioners from Shree Hridayam Satsang, to Dawn Horse Communion, to Free Primitive Church of Divine Communion, to Free Daist Communion, and most recently to Adidam.

The teachings of Avatar Adi Da have been termed, among other things, the "way of radical understanding." The foundation of this way is the relinquishment of the illusion of separateness of an individual existence, on the basis of the understanding that the apparent separateness is fundamentally an activity rather than a fixed entity. There is only the all-comprehensive reality: being consciousness bliss. This native condition of existence becomes obvious when all seeking and all activity of separation cannot be transcended (i.e., when radical understanding prevails). Enlightenment, thus, already exists: It cannot be attained by any strategy of individual effort. It must, however, be realized. To unlock the activity of seeking and separation is understood to be a matter of grace and revelation from Avatar Adi Da. Thus, the essence of his way is the devotional and spiritual relationship to him as spiritual master rather than any technique that one could apply to oneself.

Avatar Adi Da has created a definitive summary of his 30 years of teaching in a series of 23 books. One tool he has given, to enable one's understanding of other spiritual teachings and the progressive courses of realization, is the seven stages of life: Stage one begins at birth and focuses upon physical adaptation to the world; stage two, beginning around age seven, focuses upon socialization and emotional adaption to the world; stage three is a period of development of the mind, will, and emotional-sexual functions; stage four marks the beginning of spiritual awakening; stage five relates to the mystical inner search and the possibilities of subtle spiritual experience; stage six is the profound state of abiding as consciousness itself, but on the basis of excluding the awareness of the body, the mind, and the world; and stage seven is what Avatar Adi Da calls "divine enlightenment." It is the culmination of the entire spiritual process, in which the realizer exists entirely and permanently as "love bliss consciousness," regardless of whether any form of experience arises or not. Avatar Adi Da is recognized by his devotees as the final manifestation of the divine in human form. Thus, it is understood that the realization of the seventh stage of life is only possible for those who enter into a formal devotional relationship with him.

Membership: In 2002 there were approximately 1,200 members in the United States, 60 members in Canada, and more than 400 overseas. Some members now live at the resident retreat center in the Fiji Islands. Foreign centers are located in the United Kingdom, the Netherlands, Germany, Austria, Australia, New Zealand, Japan, South Africa, the Middle East, and India.

Educational Facilities:

Adidam Academy.

Periodicals: *Adidam Revelation Magazine*.

Sources:

Adi Da Samraj and the Spiritual Practice of Adidam. www.adidam.org.

Avatar Adi Da Samraj and the First 25 years of His Divine Revelation Work. Middletown, CA: Dawn Horse Press, 1997.

Feuerstein, George, ed. *Humor Suddenly Returns: Essays on the Spiritual Teaching of Master Da Free John*. Clearlake, CA: Dawn Horse Press, 1984.

Johannie Daist Communion. *The Next Option: An Introduction to the Teaching of the Adept Da Free John and the Johannie Daist Communion*. Clearlake, CA: Dawn Horse Press, 1984.

Jones, Franklin. *The Dawn Horse Testament of Heart-Master Da Free John*. San Rafael, CA: Dawn Horse Press, 1985.

———. *The Holy Jumping-Off Place: An Introduction to the Way of the Heart*. San Rafael, CA: Dawn Horse Press, 1986.

———. *The Knee of Listening*. Los Angeles, CA: Ashram, 1972.

———. *The Method of the Siddhas*. Los Angeles, CA: Dawn Horse Press, 1973.

———. *No Remedy: An Introduction to the Life and Practices of the Spiritual Community of Bubba Free John*. Lower Lake, CA: Dawn Horse Press, 1976.

Advaita Fellowship

PO Box 911-WS, Redondo Beach, CA 90277

The Advaita Fellowship was founded following Ramesh S. Balsekar's (b. 1917) 1987 visit to the United States. Balsekar is a disciple of Sri Nisargadatta Maharaj (1897–1981). Nisargadatta was a guru in a lineage that began with Saint Jnaneshwar (1275–1296), who lived in Maharashtra, India, in the thirteenth century and passed on a practice of *jnana* yoga, that is, the philosophical approach to spiritual enlightenment through *advaita vedanta* (the belief in nonduality). Maharaj was a popular teacher known for his ability to speak about profound thought so all could understand. He rarely gave lectures, but generally taught by holding conversations with those around him.

Balsekar was a graduate of London University who became a successful banker. He retired in 1970 and, at about the same time, met Maharaj. He became a close disciple and began to keep a record of his conversations, later the subject of several books. Meanwhile several Westerners came to know of Maharaj and began to spread his teachings in Europe and America. Maurice Frydman (1900–1976) transcribed and published the first book of his teachings, *I Am That: Talks with Sri Nisargadatta Maharaj*; and in 1982, author Peter Brent wrote of him in *Godmen of*

India. Jean Dunn, noting the relationship between Maharaj's teachings and those of Ramana Maharshi (1879–1950), published articles about Maharaj in *The Mountain Path*, the magazine from Maharshi's ashram (religious community). Dunn later edited the first books on Maharaj published in America.

In the years since Maharaj's death in 1981, Balsekar has been active in spreading the teachings of advaita Vedanta, and has traveled to the United States annually since his first visit in 1987. Advaita teaches that suffering comes from the mistaken idea that human beings are separate entities. It emphasizes that, in fact, the human soul (atman) and the universal soul (brahman) are one and the same. In the realization of that simple truth, ignorance and suffering are dispelled.

Membership: Not reported.

Sources:

Advaita Fellowship. www.advaita.org.

Balsekar, Ramesh S. *Experiencing the Teaching*. Redondo Beach, CA: Advaita Press, 1988.

———. *From Consciousness to Consciousness: Letters of Ramesh S. Balsekar*. Los Angeles, CA: Advaita Press, 1989.

Brent, Peter. *The Godmen of India*. Chicago: Quadrangle Books, 1972.

Dunn, Jean, ed. *Prior to Consciousness: Talks with Sri Nisargadatta Maharaj*. Durham, NC: Acorn Press, 1985.

———. *Seeds of Consciousness: The Wisdom of Sri Nisargadatta Maharaj*. New York: Grove Press, 1982.

Maharaj, Nisargadatta. *I Am That*. Bombay, India: Chetana, 1973.

Powell, Robert, ed. *The Blissful Life as Realized through the Teachings of Sri Nisargadatta Maharaj*. Durham, NC: Acorn Press, 1984.

Ajapa Yoga Foundation

c/o Shri Janardan Ajapa Yoga Ashram, PO Box 1731, Placerville, CA 95667

Ajapa yoga is a simple meditation and breathing technique believed by its practitioners to be the most ancient form of yoga, developed thousands of years ago by the *rishis* (seers) of India. Thus it is believed to be the original yoga, not a composite, abbreviation, or updated version of the forms of yoga. Ajapa yoga was rediscovered and given to the modern world by Guru Purnananda Paramahansa (1834–1928). He learned of the practice from Matang Rishi in a hidden monastery in Tibet, China. He created three ashrams in Bengal to spread the teachings that, while very old, had not been widely available until the last half of the nineteenth century. The work begun by Purnananda was continued by his disciple, Guru Bhumananda Paramahansa (1873–1958), who in turn passed the succession to Guru Janardan Paramahansa (1888–1980). Guru Janardan organized the World Conference on Scientific Yoga in New Delhi, which brought him into contact with many Westerners. Following the conference, he accepted an invitation to lecture in Czechoslovakia and expanded his Western tour to include Germany, Canada, and the United States. After being in the West for over a year, he returned to India.

Some of the Westerners he encountered upon his tour traveled to India in 1973. In 1974, upon their return to New York, they incorporated the Ajapa Yoga Foundation. Guru Janardan made visits in 1974, 1975, and 1976, establishing centers in Hamburg, Germany; Montreal, Quebec; Los Angeles, California; Baltimore, Maryland; Atlanta, Georgia; and Knoxville, Tennessee. *The Ajapa Journal* was begun in 1976, and a book summarizing the foundation's teachings was published. From this modest beginning, the foundation has steadily grown.

On January 6, 1966, Guru Paramahansa found a baby boy by the banks of the Ganges River, and named him Guru Prasad (b. 1966). He predicted that Guru Prasad would be a self-realized saint who would have a large role in helping suffering humanity. He trained him from birth for this purpose, and in 1980 Guru Prasad became the only living master of ajapa yoga. According to Guru Prasad, "A person has but to practice this technique and everything will be answered, naturally and automatically."

According to the foundation's teachings, humans have lost their true identities and are left in a world of pain, want, and illusion. True identity can be gained by the practice of ajapa yoga, beginning with the meditation on the mantra given by the guru at the time of initiation, accompanied by specific breathing techniques.

Membership: In 2008 there was only one ajapa yoga ashram in North America. Affiliated centers are also found in India, Germany, Poland, and Czechoslovakia. There were approximately 10,000 members worldwide.

Periodicals: *The Ajapa Journal*.

Sources:

Jai Guru: Ajapa Yoga Homepage. www.ajapa.org/.

Tattwa Katha: A Tale of Truth. New York: Ajapa Yoga Foundation, 1976–1979.

All World Gayatri Pariwar

c/o Gayatri Gyan Mandir, 5N 371 IL Route 53 (Rohwling Rd.), Itasca, IL 60143

All World Gayatri Pariwar was founded by Pandit Shriram Sharma Acharya (1911–1990) to deal with the human condition, which is characterized by ignorance, lack of righteousness and joy, insecurities, and infirmities, and to encourage the divinity in human beings and a heavenly atmosphere on earth. Sharma proposed a broad program that built on several means of spiritual awakening: *upasana* (contemplation on the divine virtues); *sadhana* (the practice of self-control for acquiring the divine virtues); *aradhana* (the utilization of acquired resources for the welfare of all of society); and the propagation of Gayatri (collective wisdom) and Yagna (cooperative virtuous demeanor). It was Sharma's belief that Indian culture was founded on the principles of Gayatri (the goddess of wisdom and pure intelligence and the protector of *prana*, vital life force) and Yagna (oblations made to the holy fire, symbolizing noble deeds).

Sharma was initiated into the worship of Gayatri, using the Gayatri Mantra, at age nine. In 1926 he met Swami Sarveshvaranandji, a Himalayan yogi, who appeared before him in an astral body. This experience clarified Sharma's understanding of his own divine origin and gave him a purpose in life. He devoted the next twenty-four years to a rigorous program of devotion, undertaking in each year a *mahapurashcharana*, in which he recited the Gayatri Mantra 2.4 million times, and pursuing altruistic activities without withdrawing from family life.

In 1943 he married Bhagwati Devi (1926–1994), a bhakti devotee. After completing the twenty-four mahapurashcharanas, in 1953 Sharma established Gayatri Tapobhumi at Mathura, India. Five years later, he organized a large Gayatri *yajna* (fire ceremony) to launch his Yug Nirman Yojna (mission for creation of a new era), a global movement for moral, cultural, intellectual, and spiritual revitalization. At Mathura he assembled a team of dedicated men and women to form a new organization, the Gayatri Pariwar, which superseded Yug Nirman Yojna. In 1971 the mission's headquarters at Shantikunj (Haridwar, India) was established as an academy for moral and spiritual awakening and training.

When Sharma died in 1990 his widow assumed leadership of the movement. Two years later she announced a plan for the global spread of the movement to be marked by a series of Grand Ashwamedha *yagyas* (ceremonies) to be performed in different locations, including Leicester, England, Toronto, Canada, and Los Angeles, California. Bhagwati Devi attended 18 of the ceremonies.

The present leaders of the worldwide movement are Rev. Dr. Pranav Pandya and Rev. Smt. Shailbala Pandya, the daughter of the founders. Centers are located in India, Thailand, Singapore, Australia, New Zealand, Japan, Brazil, Argentina, and across Europe. African centers are found in Tanzania, Uganda, South Africa, and Zimbabwe.

Membership: Not reported. In the United States there are four main centers (Los Angeles, Chicago, Atlanta, and New Jersey), and smaller centers across the country. Contacts in Canada are found in the Toronto and Montreal metropolitan areas.

Sources:

Gayatri Pariwar. www.awgp.org/.

Sharma Archarya, Shriram. *Divine Message of the Veds*. Mathura, India: Yug Nirman Yojna, 1997.

————. *Simple Ways for Peace and Happiness*. Chicago: Gayatri Pariwar Chicago, 2002.

American Meditation Society

2912 N Main St., Apt. #2, Flagstaff, AZ 62025

The American Meditation Society is the U.S. affiliate of the International Foundation for Spiritual Unfoldment founded in 1975 in Cape Town, South Africa, by Purushottan Narshinhran (b. 1932), whom his followers know by his spiritual name, Gururaj Ananda Yogi. As a child in his native Gujarat, India, he showed a distinct focus upon spiritual realities. When he was five years old he ran away from home to visit the temples in the neighborhood. When he was found, he explained to his parents that he had visited many temples, but had found to his frustration that "the Gods were lifeless and would not speak to me." His continued search for the divine culminated when he discovered that what he sought lay within himself. Having found the inner reality and having fully and permanently entered the self-realized state, he set himself to the task of becoming a spiritual teacher in the West.

He moved to South Africa and became a successful businessman. In 1975, following a problem with his heart, he retired from business and turned to full-time work as a spiritual teacher. He then founded the International Foundation for Spiritual Unfoldment. Within the first year it had spread to nine countries in the British Commonwealth and throughout Europe. In 1977 it was organized in California as the American Meditation Society.

Gururaj Ananda Yogi teaches not a religion, but the basis that underlies all religions. His task is seen as merely to awaken the individual to the same reality that he discovered and to lead him or her along the path of unfoldment. Meditation is the individual's major tool in turning inward, and it works best if individualized. The society offers basic meditation courses, which introduce the variety of ways to meditate. Narshinhran assists in the process of individualizing sound which is intoned during meditation. Individuals send their pictures to him; he meditates upon the picture and comes up with the sound he believes each person makes with the universe, then presents the distinct sound to each person as a unique personal mantrum.

Membership: Not reported. In 1984 the society had approximately 2,000 members in 30 centers. In 2008, the foundation had centers in Canada, Australia, Spain, Denmark, Germany, Belgium, Ireland, Great Britain, and South Africa.

Periodicals: *American Meditation Society Newsletter.*

Sources:

Anderson, V., and R. Morosani, eds. *From Darkness to Light: A Selection of Talks by Guruaj Ananda Yogi*. Farmingdale, NY: Coleman Publishing, 1987.

Taylor, Savita. *The Path to Unfoldment: An Introduction to the Teachings of Guruaj Ananda Yogi*. London: VSM Publications, 1979.

American Vegan Society

56 Dinshah Ln., PO Box 369, Malaga, NJ 08328-0908

The American Vegan Society was founded in 1960 at Malaga, New Jersey, by H. Jay Dinshah (1933–2000). The basis of the society is ahimsa, defined as "dynamic harmlessness." The six pillars of ahimsa (one for each letter) are abstinence from all animal products, particularly for food or clothing; harmlessness and reverence for life; integrity of thought, word, and deed; mastery over oneself; service to humanity, nature, and creation; and advancement of understanding and truth. Veganism is conceived as an advanced and comprehensive program for living and draws its inspiration from Donald Watson (1910–2005) and the Vegan Society, England, as well as from ahimsa and reverence for life as expressed by Mahatma Gandhi

(1869–1948), Albert Schweitzer (1875–1965), and other sages. Vegans are total vegetarians who only eat food from plants and exclude all animals (meat, fish, fowl) and animal products (milk, eggs, honey, and so forth) from their diet. They are also ecology-oriented because this lifestyle is economical of natural resources. Not just a matter of diet, the philosophy extends to clothing and toiletries, among other things.

The society is headquartered at Suncrest, which runs as a teaching center, at Malaga, New Jersey. An annual convention is held. The society is affiliated with the North American Vegetarian Society, headquartered at Dolgeville, New York, and the International Vegetarian Union in England.

Membership: The society reported a membership of more than 1,000 in 2002.

Periodicals: *American Vegan.*

Sources:

American Vegan Society. www.americanvegan.org.

Dinshah, Freya. *The Vegan Kitchen*. Malaga, NJ: American Vegan Society, 1970.

Dinshah, H. Jay. *Out of the Jungle*. Malaga, NJ: American Vegan Society, 1995.

American Yoga Association

PO Box 19986, Sarasota, FL 34276

The American Yoga Association was established in 1968 as the Light of Yoga Society by Alice Christensen. Christensen began her spiritual quest in 1953 when she had a visionary experience in which she was engulfed by a white light. She subsequently learned of Swami Sivananda Sivananda (1887–1963), the head of the Divine Life Society in India, and corresponded with him for many years. In 1964, the year after Sivananda's death, she traveled to India and met Swami Rama (1900–1972) of Hardwar, India, and became his student. Swami Rama (not to be confused with the person of the same name who founded the Himalayan International Institute of Yoga, Science, and Philosophy) had spent three years as a recluse in the Himalayas before settling in Hardwar as a teacher of yoga.

As Swami Rama's representative in the West, Christensen began to teach yoga in 1965 and six years later founded the Light of Yoga Society in Cleveland Heights, Ohio. At the time of Swami Rama's death in 1972, there were 11 yoga centers throughout India, Australia, and the United States that he had guided. The name American Yoga Society was adopted in 1982. More recently headquarters were transferred to Sarasota, Florida.

Swami Rama developed a simplified form of the wisdom of the Vedanta, and a form of hatha yoga especially for Western practitioners. Members of the society practice both hatha and meditation daily. They also consume a vegetarian diet, practice ahimsa (nonviolence), avoid alcohol, tobacco, and drugs, and are restrained in their use of sex.

Membership: Not reported. There are two centers in the United States and two affiliated centers in India.

Sources:

American Yoga Association. www.americanyogaassociation.org.

Christensen, Alice. *The American Yoga Association Beginner's Manual*. New York: Simon & Schuster, 1987.

Amrit Yoga Institute

PO Box 5340, Salt Springs, FL 32134

Amrit Institute was founded by Yogi Amrit Desai, a yoga teacher who began teaching in the United States in 1960. During the early 1970s, based upon the spontaneous flow of yoga postures he experienced during his daily practice, he began to develop a new form that he named Kripalu yoga, after his yoga teacher in India, Swami Kripalvanandaji (1913–1981). Over the next twenty years Desai taught hundreds of students his new form of yoga, and many went on to become yoga instructors and head of their own centers. He also founded and led the Kripalu Center for Yoga and Health.

In 1994 Desai resigned from the Kripalu Center and entered a period of retirement. After several years he began teaching again, and early in the new century founded Amrit Yoga Institute. He also continued to develop the unique form of hatha yoga he taught, which he now calls the Amrit method. The Amrit method attempts to integrate raja yoga (meditation) with hatha yoga to produce a practice that allows a convergence of inner stillness with effortless outer action.

The Amril Yoga Institute is located on Lake Kerr in the Ocala National Forest in Florida. The institute is designed to accommodate a core resident staff and provide a full set of events for students who come for workshops and retreats.

Membership: Not reported.

Sources:

Amrit Yoga Instituite. www.amrityoga.com/.

Desai, Yogi Amrit. *Amrit Yoga and the Yoga Sutras—Amrit Yoga and Its Roots in Patanjali's Ashtanga Yoga*. Salt Springs, FL: Yoga Network International, 2002.

———. *Amrit Yoga: Explore, Expand, Experience the Spiritual Depth of Yoga*. Salt Springs, FL: Yoga Network International, 2002.

In the Presence of a Master: Gurudev Yogi Amrit Desai. Lenox, MA: Kripalu Publications, 1992.

Amrita Foundation

PO Box 190978, Dallas, TX 75219-0978

The Amrita Foundation is an independent organization founded in 1976 and based upon the teachings of Swami Paramahansa Yogananda (1893–1952). The organization emphasizes the original nature of the material it uses, especially the original *praecepta* lessons (instructions by the teacher), the home study course through which the foundation presents Yogananda's teachings. The lessons detail the instructions for the practice of kriya yoga, including the practice of meditation, concentration, and physical exercises. It also includes teachings regarding diet and nutrition. Lessons are sent to students on a month-by-month basis. The foundation has reprinted the first edition of many of Yogananda's books, such as *Whispers from Eternity*, *Songs of the Soul*, and *The Second Coming of Christ* (two volumes).

Membership: Not reported.

Sources:

Amrita Foundation. www.amrita.com.

Yogananda, Paramahansa. *Whispers from Eternity: A Book of Unanswered Prayers*. Nevada City, CA: Crystal Clarity, 2008.

Ananda

14618 Tyler Foote Rd., Nevada City, CA 95959

The Ananda Church of Self-Realization and the Ananda World Brotherhood Village were founded by J. Donald Walters (b. 1926), also known as Swami Kriyananda. Both institutions are based on the spiritual principles set forth by yoga master, Paramhansa Yogananda (1893–1952), author of *Autobiography of a Yogi*.

Born of American parents in Romania in 1926, Kriyananda was educated in Romania, Switzerland, England, and the United States. At the age of 22, he became a disciple of Yogananda and lived with him until the master's death in 1952. As a minister and director of center activities for the organization that Yogananda founded, Self-Realization Fellowship (SRF), and later as vice president of SRF, he traveled and taught extensively in many countries. In 1962, he says God called upon him to serve his guru's mission in another capacity. He was separated from SRF to explore and expound, through writing, teaching, and lecturing, the implications of Yogananda's message for active yoga students and laypersons.

In 1968, Kriyananda founded Ananda Village near Nevada City, California, in response to inner guidance and to the oft uttered public plea of Yogananda: "Cover the earth with world-brotherhood colonies, demonstrating that simplicity of living plus high thinking lead to the greatest happiness."

Kriyananda has published more than 40 books, including *The Path: A Spiritual Autobiography*; *Rays of the Same Light*; and *The Essence of Self-Realization: The Wisdom of Paramhansa Yogananda*. He has also composed musical works including *Christ Lives*, an oratorio; a *Shakespeare Quartet*, composed for two violins, viola, and cello; an *Egyptian Suite*, written for harp, flute, and viola; and the *Divine Romance*, a piano sonata.

Ananda Village is situated at 2,600-foot elevation and on 750 acres of wooded and meadow land in the Sierra Nevada foothills of northern California. Members support themselves through a variety of businesses, some of which are privately owned and some of which are owned and operated by the community. Children are educated, from preschool through junior high, at the Ananda Education-for-Life School located within the village. High school students attend public school in Nevada City. The community and its branches includes approximately 600 people from many cultural, ethnic, and racial backgrounds. About 25 nationalities are represented among the residents. A village council is elected annually by Ananda members. The Expanding Light is Ananda's guest facility, open year-round, offering personal retreats, weeklong or four-week training courses, and special events and holiday programs.

Ananda members practice regular daily meditation using the techniques of kriya yoga, as taught by Yogananda. Resident members are all disciples of Yogananda. The group is also directly involved in a worldwide outreach to those interested in the teachings of Yogananda and his lineage of gurus.

Ananda's Church, established in 1990 in congregational form, has 2,000 members. The goal of the Ananda Church of Self-Realization is to provide fellowship and inspiration for those who want to find God; this is done through the practice of ancient raja yoga techniques for self-realization that were brought to the West by Yogananda. The church is open for membership for those who follow the teachings of Yogananda.

Membership: In 1997 there were 2,000 church members of Ananda worldwide; 250 people, including children, reside at the main community in Nevada City. Ananda Church has 150 ordained ministers, who serve in Ananda churches in the United States and abroad. Currently Ananda has seven residential spiritual communities located in Seattle, Washington; Portland, Oregon; Sacramento and Palo Alto, California; New Delhi, India; and Assisi, Italy. There is also a newly developed retreat center in Rhode Island. In addition, there are 50 centers and meditation groups throughout the world.

Periodicals: *Clarity Magazine* • Ananda Sangha Worldwide News

Sources:

Ananda: Source for the Teachings of Paramhansa Yogananda. www.ananda.org/.

Nordquist, Ted A. *Ananda Cooperative Village: A Study in the Beliefs, Values, and Attitudes of a New Religious Community*. Uppsala, Sweden: Religionist, 1978.

Walters, J. Donald. *Cities of Light: A Plan for this Age*. Nevada City, CA: Crystal Clarity, 1987.

———. *Cooperative Communities: How to Start Them, and Why*. Nevada City, CA: Ananda Publications, 1968.

———. *Crises in Modern Thought: Solutions to the Problem of Meaninglessness*. Nevada City, CA: Crystal Clarity, 1988.

———. *The Path: A Spiritual Autobiography*. Nevada City, CA: Ananda Publications, 1977.

———. *A Place Called Ananda*. Nevada City, CA: Crystal Clarity, 2001.

Ananda Ashrama

Yoga Society of New York, Inc., 13 Sapphire Rd., Monroe, NY 10950

Formerly known as the Intercosmic Center of Spiritual Associations (ICSA) and the International Center for Self-Analysis, Ananda Ashram was founded by Shri Brahamananda Sarasvati (d. 1993), also known as Dr. Rammurti Sriram Mishra, a student of Bhagavan Sri Ramana Maharshi. As a young yogi, Sarasvati was able to detach his consciousness from the transient world and experience transcendental reality. Upon returning to his physical body, he posed the question "Who am I?" The question was answered through a technique of self-analysis. The ashram seeks to help its adherents through a similar technique of analysis. Its stated goals are 1) to experience one's self as the cosmic center of vibrations; 2) to establish unity of all beings, especially all nations; 3) to promote global togetherness; 4) to promote a natural way of education, self-discipline and relations; 5) to promote the teaching of sanskrit; 6) to establish modern educational centers; 7) to promote natural, spiritual, and psychological methods of healing; 8) to experience automatic and spontaneous psychosynthesis and psychoanalysis; and 9) to assist the individual in realizing the God-hood that always resides within.

Membership: Not reported. In the United States the main centers are the Ananda Ashram in Monroe, New York; the Rochester Ashram; and the New York City yoga center (all sponsored by the Yoga Society of New York) and the Brahmananda Ashram, the teaching center of the Yoga Society of San Francisco in California.

Periodicals: *I Am News*.

Sources:

Ananda Ashrama. www.anandaashram.org.

Coble, Margaret. *Self-Abidance*. Port Louis, Mauritius: Standard Printing Establishment, 1973.

Mishra, Rammurti. *Dynamics of Yoga Mudras and Five Suggestions for Meditation*. Pleasant Valley, NY: Kriya Press, 1967.

———. *Fundamentals of Yoga*. New York: Lancer Books, 1969.

———. *Self Analysis and Self Knowledge*. Lakemont, GA: CSA Press, 1978.

Mishra, Rammurti S. *Isha Upanishad*. Dayton, OH: Yoga Society of Dayton, 1962.

Ananda Marga Yoga Society

97-38 42nd Ave., 1-F, Corona, NY 11368

The Ananda Marga Yoga Society was founded in 1955 in Bihar, India, by Prabhat Prabhat Ranjan Sarkar (b. 1921). From his early childhood in India, Sarkar attracted thousands of people by his deep love for humanity and by guiding them along the path of self-realization. Adjusting the ancient science of tantra yoga to meet the needs of the present, he developed a scientific and rational spiritual philosophy along with a system of practical disciplines for physical, mental, and spiritual development. Sarkar's path of tantra yoga begins with initiation, wherein the spiritual aspirant is privately taught the practice of meditation, and is given a two-syllable word or mantra along with a point of concentration, which are particular for that aspirant. In addition, the aspirant is taught the ancient moral codes of yama and niyama and is introduced to the pratika, an ancient tantric emblem with upward and downward triangles representing internal self-realization and external service to humanity. Recognizing him as a spiritually realized master, Sarkar's followers called him "Shrii Shrii Anandamurtii," which means "He who attracts others as the embodiment of bliss," or simply "Baba" (father). The society reports that those who followed his teachings found their lives transformed as they overcame the weaknesses and negative tendencies of the mind and experienced a deep peace and bliss within. Inspired by his example, they turned their energies to serving the society and elevating the oppressed and impoverished humanity.

In the 1960s Sarkar began training missionary monks and nuns to spread his teachings of "self-realization and service to humanity" all over India and later throughout the world. Reflecting the broadness of his vision, Ananda Marga has become a multifaceted organization with various branches, all dedicated to the upliftment of humanity through education, relief, welfare, the arts, ecology, intellectual renaissance, women's liberation, and a humanistic economy.

For the collective welfare of the entire society, Sarkar propounded a new economic theory that he named PROUT (Progressive Utilization Theory). PROUT states that no individual should be allowed to accumulate any physical wealth without the clear permission of the collective body. The theory also stands for the maximum utilization and rational distribution of all the resources and potentialities of the world (physical, mental, and spiritual) and the creation of a new, humanistic social order of harmony and justice for all.

In 1971 Sarkar was accused by a former follower of having conspired to murder some ex-members. Based upon the follower's testimony, Sarkar was arrested and jailed awaiting trial. His imprisonment lasted through the national emergency proclaimed by Indira Ghandi in 1975. Ananda Marga was one of the organizations she banned nationally. Meanwhile Ananda Marga had been involved in a number of violent incidents, some aimed at protesting Sarkar's imprisonment. Sarkar was finally brought to trial, under the conditions of the emergency, and convicted. He was unable to call any witnesses on his behalf. He was finally retried in 1978 and found not guilty. Thereafter he guided the rapid expansion of Ananda Marga worldwide until his death in 1990.

Ananda Marga is now established in more than 60 countries, and together with PROUT has become a force for global social change. Sarkar further created the concept of Neo-Humanism, which means that all created beings are the veritable expressions of the Supreme Consciousness. This concept will vibrate human sentiment in all directions, will touch the innermost recesses of the heart, and lead everyone to the final stage of supreme blessedness. Neo-Humanism will elevate human beings to universalism, which is the cult of love for all created beings of this universe.

On the practical level, Sarkar founded many branches of Ananda Marga, including ERAWS (Education, Relief, and Welfare Society), responsible for creating hundreds of primary and secondary schools worldwide; AMURT (Ananda Marga Universal Relief Team), registered as a United Nations Nongovernmental Organization, which carries out disaster relief work, conducts medical camps, and organizes food and shelter for victims of natural calamities; and RU (Renaissance Universal), dedicated to uplifting the downtrodden through the intellectual study of societal problems and their solutions.

Membership: In 2002 the society reported 5,000 members in the United States and two million worldwide.

Educational Facilities:

Ananda Marga Gurukul (University), Ananda Nagar, West Purulia, Bengal, India.

Periodicals: *Crimson Dawn* • *New Renaissance*.

Remarks: Acharya Vimalananda, who founded Ananda Marga in the United States, left the organization to found the Yoga House Ashram.

Sources:

Ananda Marga. www.anandamarga.org.

PROUT. www.prout.org.

Anandamurti, Shrii Shrii. *Baba's Grace*. Denver, CO: Amrit Publications, 1973.

———. *The Great Universe: Discourses on Society*. Los Altos Hills, CA: Ananda Marga Publications, 1973.

Nandita and Devadatta. *Path of Bliss, Ananda Marga Yoga*. Wichita, KS: Ananda Marga Publishers, 1971.

The Spiritual Philosophy of Shrii Shrii Anandamurti. Denver, CO: Ananda Marga Publications, 1981.

Sarkar, P. R. *Idea and Ideology*. Calcutta: Acarya Pranavananda Avadhuta, 1978.

Tadbhavananda Avadhuta, Acharya. *Glimpses of Prout Philosophy*. Copenhagen, Denmark: Central Proutist Publications, 1981.

Anasuya Foundation

Current address not obtained for this edition.

Alternate Address: International Headquarters: Sri Punitachariji, Girnar Sadhana Ashram, Bhavnath Taleti, Junagadh, Gujarat, India 362004.

The Anasuya Foundation dates to the 1975 experience of Indian teacher Swami Punitachariji (also called "Bapu") with Lord Dattatreya. The encounter occurred at Mount Girnar, a place sacred to Dattatreya in the Himalayan Mountains. Lord Dattatreya, one of the Hindu deities, is described as the divine essence behind all wisdom, all aspects of god combined. He is Brahma, Vishnu, and Shiva. He is usually pictured as a being with three heads and six arms with a minimal amount of clothing. He is satguru, and as such is capable of transmitting to others the power to understand life.

Prior to his encounter with Lord Dattatreya, Bapu had no physical guru, but had been a spiritual seeker wandering the forests and river banks for many years. He saw Lord Datta sitting on a rock being showered with flowers by saints and sages of past generations. He was chanting a mantra, "Hari Om Tatsat Jai Guru Datta." He gave this mantra to Bapu for the uplift of humankind.

It is the belief taught by Bapu that God created the world through sound. For every physical sound there is an equivalent sound on the subtle planes of creation. Thus by repeating certain charged sounds the creative plane is affected and those effects return to the physical plane and recreate it. Chanting the mantra of Lord Dattatreya brings his essence to the person doing the chanting and allows development without the need of an earthly guru.

Toward the end of the 1970s, the message of Bapu was brought to the West by Shantibaba, an early disciple. Centers were soon established in the United States, the United Kingdom, and Germany.

Membership: Not reported. Centers are located in California, New York, Colorado, New Jersey, Germany, and England.

Sources:

Matulay, Emily, and Shantibaba. *Spontaneous Meditation.* Basalt, CO: Anasuya Publications, 1983. 43 pp.

Anoopam Mission

Shree Swaminarayan Spiritual and Cultural Center, 2120 Clearview Rd., Coplay, PA 18037

Alternate Address: International Headquarters: Brahmajyoti, Yogiji Marg, Mogri-388 345 (Via Anand), Gujarat, India.

The Anoopam Mission was founded in 1977 as an independent branch of the Swaminarayan movement, a nineteenth-century Hindu religious movement most successful in the state of Gujarat but now known throughout the world. The Swaminarayan movement was founded by Shree Sahajanand Swami, popularly known as Swaminarayan (1781–1830). He championed the idea of theistic worship in opposition to the popular Vedanta idea of an impersonal divine reality. God manifests on earth through his incarnations and is ever present through his realized saints. The proper response of the believer is devotional service (bhakti yoga). Lord Swaminarayan declared himself to be the early manifestation of Narayan, the Supreme Being, and is so considered by his followers. Swaminarayan was succeeded by a series of leaders: Gunatitanand Swami, Bhagatji Maharaj, Jaga Swami, Krishnaji Ada, Shastriji Maharaj, and Yogiji Maharaj, all of whom espoused the Akshar Purushottam philosophy.

The Anoopam Mission was founded by a young aspirant named Jashbhai, born in Sokhada, Gujarat, in 1940. As a college student he met his guru, his Divine Holiness, Yogiji Maharaj, who called Jashbhai by a term of endearment, "Saheb," the name by which he has since been known. Saheb began to hold spiritual meetings among his fellow students. With the inspiration and blessing of Yogiji Maharaj, he founded a new order of dedicated young men who were commissioned to become holy men, *sadhus*, but without taking the traditional garb and vows of the *sanyassin*, the renounced life. They did not wear the saffron robe nor adopt a life dependent on alms. Instead, they continued their education and afterwards followed their chosen professions (karma yog).

Saheb's break with the larger AksharPurushottam movement came in 1965. Differences had arisen in the Swaminarayan movement over, among other issues, the place of women in the spiritual order. The conservative leaders in the movement did not want to allow women to take the sannyas vows, and being in control, they excommunicated those who supported the women. Saheb and his followers were viewed to be in the reform camp and were asked to leave. Saheb reorganized under the banner of Anoopam Mission, and eventually settled at Mogri, Gujarat, where the international headquarters of the movement, Brahmajyoti, has been constructed.

Anoopam Mission has rapidly expanded to develop other centers in India and elsewhere around the world. More than 100 sadhus now lead a life of austerity supported by their professional efforts. They have integrated their spiritual and secular life of bhakti and karma yoga to live a life of devotion to God and service to humanity. Charitable contributions of devotees are used to launch and sustain numerous humanitarian activities, comprising educational institutions, medical facilities, and relief organizations.

Followers of the Anoopam Mission began to migrate to the United States in the late 1960s, and their number has grown to well over 5,000. Saheb made his first visit to the West in 1973. He has regularly visited Europe, North America, and Africa since that time.

Membership: In 2008 there were around 50,000 members world wide. A major temple was dedicated in 2003 in Coplay, near Allentown, PA, and several smaller temples and shrines are located around the country.

Sources:

Anoopam Mission. www.anoopam-mission.org/.

Arcane Magical Order of the Knights of Shambhala (AMOOKOS)

c/o Shri Shyamanatha, PO Box 1425, Grand Central Station, New York, NY 10163

Alternate Address: Shambhala Nath, PO Box 661182, Los Angeles, CA 90066.

The Adinath Sampradaya is a tantric sect of yogis affiliated with the greater Natha tradition founded by Gorakhnath and Matsyendranath, two teachers credited with great magical powers. Matsyendranath (aka Macchagnanath) (c. 900 C.E.) is connected to the foundation of the Kaula school of tantra and the worship (puja) of the Goddess Kali. Gorakhnath (aka Gorakshanatha), the disciple of Matsyendranath, is credited with the foundation of laya or kundalini yoga and hatha yoga, and is revered by many of the Natha subsects as their founder.

Mahendranath (aka Dadaji) (1911–1992), the 23rd Adiguru (chief teacher) of the Adinathas, was born and grew up in London, where in his 20s he met magical teacher Aleister Crowley. After World War II, he traveled to his ancestral home and in Bombay he met his guru in the Natha tradition and initiated as a sadhu (holy man). For the next 30 years Dadaji wandered Southeast Asia as a penniless renunciate. In 1978 Dadaji initiated Lokanath Maharaj into the Adinath Sampradaya (sect), and he returned to England and initiated several people as Adinathas. He also founded AMOOKOS, or the Arcane Magical Order of the Knights of Shambhala, in 1982.

Dadaji had come to London in 1981, during which time he oversaw the writing of some papers by Lokanath for an organization that would act as a training ground for would-be magicians. These papers became the basis for AMOOKOS. Subsequently some of the papers were published, and over the next few years, international membership of AMOOKOS grew to over 200 individuals, several of whom started chartered lodges. One prominent member of AMOOKOS is Donald Michael Kraig, who ran a lodge in California in the 1980s.

The original material was presented to individuals for training purposes. Much of the material was and is tantric but presented in the English language for clarity and to avoid Indian words and jargon. Every individual who was initiated also became an initiate of the Adinath sect.

The Adinathas seek ultimate truth. They teach that a human being is already accomplished, a yogi or yogini. Conditioning and other factors prevent this yogic self from shining forth. In each individual, Shiva and Shakti coexist in equipoise. When they unite, the resulting bliss lights up the physio-psychological complex which is the Universe.

Much of the alchemy the Nathas used was based on the proposition that Breath is Time. According to the Nathas, a human being breathes 21,600 times during a 24-hour day. Half of these breaths are Sun (Shiva) breaths and half are Moon (Shakti) breaths. The out-breathing is Ha and the in-breathing, Sa. This is the so-called involuntary mantra Hamsah. One who has united the Solar and Lunar breaths is a Parama-hamsa (beyond Hamsa). The Natha aims to fight conditioning and to become free from Time.

A second aim is svecchacharya, or acting according to one's own will; in other words, independently. The secret teachings of the Adinathas also included teachings from the left-hand path (in which symbolism is actualized in physical acts) and described in some detail the use of sexuality in the process of seeking truth.

AMOOKOS is in the process of publishing much of Dadaji's and Lokanath's writings through Azoth Publishing. Also, from 1977 to 1985, Mike Magee published *Azoth Magazine* on behalf of the group. There is also a vast literature now available on the history of the Adinathas and the related Indian tantric groups.

Membership: Not reported.

Sources:

Dadaji. *The Amoral Way of Wizardry*. Stockholm: Tryckt I Sverige, 1992.

MacGee, Mike. *Rituals of Kalika*. New York: Azoth Publishing, 1985.

————. *Tantrik Astrology*. Oxford: Mandrake, 1989.

Arsha Vidya Pitham

PO Box 1059, Saylorsburg, PA 18353

Arsha Vidya Pitham was founded in the mid-1980s by Swami Dayananda Saraswati. Saraswati emerged in the 1970s as a leading disciple of Swami Chinmayananda and by the early 1980s was the heir apparent of the growing mission. Saraswati became the resident teacher at Sandeepany West, Chinmayananda's center in northern California. While associated with Chinmayananda, Saraswati taught several 30-month resident courses in Vedanta and Sanskrit. The graduates of these courses have gone on to become teachers themselves.

In 1982, however, after a long reappraisal of the direction of the growing work in America and his own likely future as head of it, Saraswati left Chinmaya Mission West to retain a more simple life as a teacher rather than an organizational director. Many of the people he had taught left the mission to keep their relationship with him.

Saraswati continued to teach and to write and, in 1986, purchased land in Pennsylvania for a new *ashram* (religious community). A temple to Lord Dakshinamurthi (a representation of the Hindu deity Shiva) was erected and a new 30-month resident course begun. Saraswati also continues his heavy schedule of travel and teaching around the United States and the world.

Membership: Not reported.

Sources:

Arsha Vidya Pitham. www.arshavidya.org.

Saraswati, Swami Dayananda. *Meditation at Dawn*. The Author, n.d.

Purbamadah Purnamidam. The Author, n.d.

The Sadhana and the Sadhya (The Means and the End). Rishikish, India: Sri Gangadhareswar Trust, 1984.

"Swami Dayananda Renounces Chinmaya Mission West: Changes and Challenges Ahead." *New Saivite World* (Fall 1983).

Art of Living Foundation

2401 15th St. NW, Washington, DC 20009

The Art of Living Foundation is the vehicle for the teaching activity of Sri Sri Ravi Shankar, a Hindu spiritual teacher from Bangalore, India. A precocious child, he memorized the *Bhagavad Gita* when he was four and began his studies of Indian literature at the age of eight. In the 1980s he began traveling the world teaching the Art of Living course, which emphasizes the uses of the ancient sciences in modern life. A major emphasis of Sri Sri's teaching is *sudarsha kriya*, a technique to restore the natural rhythms of the mental, emotional, and physical life. In 1995, the President of India at the *World Conference on Yoga* gave him the title of "Yoga Shiromani" (Supreme Flowering of Enlightenment).

He established Ved Vignan Maha Vidya Peeth in Bangalore, India, to engage in community services and spreading Vedic knowledge. It established centers across India. In Canada, England, and the United States, work is carried forth under the name "Art of Living" and in Europe as the Association for Inner Growth.

Membership: Not reported. In 1990 there were centers in 23 countries in all parts of the world.

Sources:

Art of Living Foundation. www.artofliving.org.

Shankar, Ravi. *Bang on the Door: A Collection of Talks*. Santa Barbara, CA: Art of Living Foundation, 1990. 101 pp.

Arunachala Ashrama

Bhagavan Sri Ramana Maharshi Center, 86-06 Edgerton Blvd., Jamaica Heights, NY 11432

Alternate Address: Canadian Headquarters: 1451 Clarence Rd., Bridgetown, NS B0S IC0; International Headquarters: Sri Ramanasramam, Tiruvannamalai 606 603, Tamil Nadu, India.

Inspired by the life and teachings of Sri Ramana Maharshi (1879–1950), Arunachala Ashrama was founded in New York City on December 7, 1966. For five years prior to this, weekly meetings had been conducted by those interested in Ramana Maharshi and his teachings.

At the age of 16, Ramana Maharshi absorbed himself in a singular inner quest for truth that resulted in his total abidance in God, or the "Self," as he called it. He then left home and resided on the slopes of the Arunachala Mountain, a sacred place of pilgrimage in South India. Living an exceedingly pure life, never touching money, and wearing only a coupina, he remained there for the next 54 years.

His most potent teachings, as attested to by his followers, were imparted in the silence of his presence, which conferred to mature souls the peace of Self-realization. Orally he taught the path of Self-inquiry and Self-surrender. He asked seekers to inquire where from the "I-consciousness" springs, to return to that source, and to abide there. To inquire "Who am I?" is the method of Self-knowledge he most often prescribed. He also taught seekers to throw all the burdens of life upon the Divine and to rest in perfect peace in the heart. He never interfered with outward religious practices or professions. Rather, he taught each person to seek his or her own source, as he believed there is only one source for all, the Supreme Self or God.

Arunachala Ashrama maintains a meditation center and office in New York City and a retreat center in Nova Scotia, Canada. A routine of prayer and meditation is followed at both locations. Arunachala Ashrama is affiliated with Sri Ramanasramam, Ramana Maharshis ashrama in India.

Membership: In 2008 the ashrama had 500 members in two communities and affiliated work in three3 countries, United States, Canada, and India. The ashrama is funded by unsolicited donations and the sale of literature on the life and teachings of Sri Ramana Maharshi.

Periodicals: *The Maharshi*.

Sources:

Arunachala Ashrama. www.arunachala.org.

Bhagawat, Arunachala Bhakta. *In Search of Self.* Jamaica Estates, New York: Arunachala Ashrama, n.d.

Mahadevan, T. M. P. *Ramana Maharshi, the Sage of Arunchala.* London: George Allen & Unwin, 1977.

Osborne, Arthur. *Ramana Maharshi and the Path of Self-Knowledge.* New York: Samuel Weiser, 1970.

— — —, ed. *The Teachings of Ramana Maharshi.* New York: Samuel Weiser, 1962.

Arya Samaj

Congress of Arya Samajs in North America Ved Niketan, 224 Florence, Troy, MI 48098
Alternate Address: International Headquarters: c/o Sarvdeshik Arya Pratinidhi Sabha, Dayanand Bhawan, Asaf All Road, New Delhi, India.

Founded in 1875 in colonial India, the Arya Samaj (noble soul) is a reformist Hindu sect representative of the nineteenth-century Hindu Renaissance that emerged in response to both the British and Christian presence in India. It synthesized Hindu ritual practice with new forms of social organization and interaction. It rejected much of traditional Hinduism (most notably idol worship and related animal sacrifice) and emphasized the role of the Vedas as sacred texts. They advocated ten basic principles: 1) God is the original source of all that is true; 2) God is a single, eternal, fully conscious being; 3) the Vedas are the books of all true knowledge; 4) all people should be ready to accept truth; 5) all acts should be performed with righteousness and duty; 6) Samajis should promote good to the whole world through physical, spiritual, and social progress of all humans; 7) all interactions should be regulated by love and due justice in accordance with the dictates of righteousness; 8) realization and acquisition of knowledge (vidyaa) should be promoted for all; 9) Samajis should strive for the upliftment of all and not be satisfied with only personal development; and 10) while the individual is free to enjoy individual well-being, everyone should dedicate themselves to overall social good. These principles support a program of anti-caste, universalizing, sentiment of social service.

The Arya Samaj also created a purification ceremony (shuddhikaran) for the conversion (or reconversion) of Hindus. Despite the organizations attack on the caste system, they discovered that many of their members have had difficulty forgetting the caste background of new adherents.

The Samaj was founded by Mul Shankara (1824–1883), who was born and raised in an orthodox Brahmin family in Gujarat. In 1848 he took the vows of sannyasin (the renounced life) and assumed the religious name, Dayananda Sarasvati. As the leader of the Arya Samaj, he argued for gender equality and social liberalism (strongly anti-caste). He had an abrasive and polemic style that led to frequent tension with traditional Hidu leaders, though many found his perspective refreshing. He found strong support in the Punjab, where it remains an important movement.

Members of the group spread its universalizing message throughout India and especially in the countries with prominent Indian minorities. In the twentieth century, members moved with the Hindu diaspora to North America though they emerged in strength only in the last quarter of the twentieth century. They have their strongest support in countries such as Guyana, Trinidad & Tobago, and Kenya where they have numerous, registered centers for worship. Trinidad is particularly notable for having its first woman to become a Hindu priest (pandit), Indrani Rampersad, a pandita of the Arya Parthinidhi Sabha.

Members of the Arya Samaj began to arrive in North America in measurable number following the change of laws in 1965 that allowed Asians to immigrate and settle. Through the 1980s branch centers were organized and the national organization took shape. By the end of the century, the Arya Samaj had formed branches in almost all the large cities of the United States and Canada; these branches are now related to each other through the Arya Pratinidhi Sabha America. Annually, members from across North America gather for the Arya Maha Sammelan, the main event on the Arya Samaj calendar. The first Sammelan was held in 1991 in Detroit.

Membership: Not reported. There are centers in 12 U.S. states, Canada, Great Britain, India, Pakistan, Bangkok, Singapore, Kenya, Australia, and Fiji.

Sources:

Arya Pratinidhi Sabha America. www.aryasamaj.com/.

Gupta, Shiv Kumar. *Arya Samaj and the Raj, 1875–1920.* New Delhi: Gitanjali Publishing House, 1991.

Lajpat Rai, Lala. *The Arya Samaj: An Account of its Origin, Doctrines, and Activities.* New Delhi: Reliance Publishing House, 1991.

Yoginder, S. S. "The Fitna of Irtidad: Muslim Missionary Response to the Shuddhi of Arya Samaj in Early Twentieth Century India." *Journal of Muslim Minority Affairs* 17: 1 (1997): 65-83.

Aurobindo, Disciples of Sri

c/o Sri Aurobindo Association, PO Box 163237, Sacramento, CA 95816
Alternate Address: International Headquarters: Bureau Central, Information Centre of Sri Aurobindo Ashram, Cottage Complex, 3, Rangapillai Street, Pondicherry 605001 India; Other United States centers: East West Cultural Center, 12392 Marshall St., Culver City, CA 90230; Wilmot Center, Box 2, Wilmot, WI 53192; Matagiri, HCI Box 98, Mt. Tremper, NY 12457.

Of the many Hindu religious leaders who have arisen in the last century, none remains as enigmatic as Sri Aurobindo Ghose (1872–1950). He was given an English education and began to make his mark as a literary figure. When Bengal, his native state, was the center of the independence movement, Aurobindo became a political activist. Thrown in jail on sedition charges, he turned to the Hindu scriptures and began to practice yoga. He had a vision of Krishna (the popular Hindu deity) that changed the course of his life. Released from jail, he soon fled to French-controlled Pondicherry as a refugee and continued his spiritual practice.

The next years were spent in writing, yoga, and the building of an ashram. Most of his famous books appeared in the sixteen years prior to what is referred to as "The Day of the Siddha," November 24, 1926. On that day he claimed that Krishna descended into the physical, thus preparing for the descent of the Supermind (the Divine) and Ananda (Bliss). His spiritual collaborator was Mira Richards (1878–1973), a French divorcee who met Aurobindo prior to World War I. She built up the ashram and, after 1926, when Aurobindo ceased to see people, she became the contact between him and his disciples. The "Mother," as she is known, had seen Aurobindo in her dreams before she came to Pondicherry in 1914. From 1950 to her death in 1973, she sustained the work of transformation.

Aurobindo's thought has often been compared with that of Teilhard de Chardin, as it was an evolutionary philosophy based upon man's growth in consciousness both individually and collectively. God—pure existence, will force—draws man to himself. Creation is the result of his "descent" and the evolution is as much a divine work as man's progress. It is believed that the supermental consciousness and its manifestation in 1956 will eventually bring about the evolutionary change from "man" to "superman."

The means to achieve the life divine is yoga. Aurobindo taught what is termed "integral yoga," based in part on vedenta and tantra. It includes the traditional forms of yoga and psychology of the internal psychic self, but worked primarily by a descent of the shakti into the mind.

In India, the Sri Aurobindo Society has established an international section to service centers outside of the country. In the United States, a number of more-or-less independent centers have arisen. Among the important centers are Matagiri in Mt. Tremper, New York, and Lotus Light in Wilmot, Wisconsin. In California, three prominent centers have survived for years. These include the East-West Cultural Center, founded by Judith Tyberg in 1953; the Cultural Integration Fellowship, founded by Haridas Chaudhuri; and the Atmaniketan Ashram, a residence center in Pomona, California. There are numerous smaller centers.

International headquarters remain at the ashram in Pondicherry. In 1972 the ashram published a 30-volume centenary edition of Aurobindo's works later superceded by a 20-volume set. More recently the Institute for Evolutionary Research in Mt. Vernon, Washington, has released a 13-volume set of the *Mother's Agenda, 1951–1973*.

Membership: Not reported.

Periodicals: *Collaboration*.

Sources:

Sri Aurobindo Association. www.collaboration.org/.

Chaudhuri, Haridas. *The Evolution of Integral Consciousness*. Wheaton, IL: Theosophical Publishing House, 1977.

Donnelly, Morwenna. *Founding the Life Divine*. Lower Lake, CA: Dawn Horse Press, 1976.

Kluback, William. *Sri Aurobindo Ghose: The Dweller in the Lands of Silence*. New York: Peter Lang, 2001.

McDermott, Robert, ed. *The Essential Aurobindo*. New York: Schocken Books, 1973.

————. *Six Pillars*. Chambersburg, PA: Wilson Books, 1974.

Minor, Robert N. *Sri Aurobindo: The Perfect and the Good*. Columbia, MO: South Asia Books, 1978.

Minor, Robert N. *The Religious, the Spiritual, and the Secular: Auroville and Secular India*. Albany: State University of New York Press, 1998.

Prasad, Narayan. *Life in Sri Aurobindo Ashram*. Pondicherry, India: Sri Aurobindo Ashram, 1968.

Badarikashrama

15602 Maubert Ave., San Leandro, CA 94578

Badarikashrama is a spiritual and cultural center that promotes a life of dedicated service based upon Vedic wisdom. Established in 1983, the ashrama conducts three worship services daily, Sunday school, Hindu rites for family occasions, and festival celebrations. It also offers instruction in music, philosophy, literature, yoga, Sanskrit, meditation, and *puja* (techniques of worship). Ongoing activities include concerts, festivals, retreats, weekend programs and children's programs.

Badarikashrama's work is inspired by the teachings of Sri Ramakrishna and Swami Vivekananda. It was established by Swami Omkarananda, who as a young seeker in India came into contact with the teachings of Sri Ramakrishna. He came to the United States in 1970 and after several years of work returned to India where he took his final vows of sannyasa from Mandaleswara Sri Swami Vidyananda Giri at Kailashashrama in Rishikish. He returned to the United States and founded Badarikashrama. Swami Omkarananda combines the renounced life with a life of service. He makes himself available for spiritual counseling, satsanga, and guidance in spiritual and cultural issues. He offers home worship throughout California and promotes Vedic teachings throughout the United States.

In 1984 an associate branch of Badarikashrama was begun in Madihalli, Karnataka, India. Ongoing activities there include evening devotional singing (*kirtan*), weekly music and Sanskrit classes, and yoga training camps. There is also an ayurvedic herbal garden. Accomodations are provided for individuals and groups wishing to visit Madihalli ashrama for short and long-term spiritual retreats. At present, a variety of programs are being developed including local community training in health and sanitation, an English tutorial service, provisions of nutritional supplements, and the establishment of a resident school. It continues to serve as a place for the residence and training of women and men interested in leading a monastic life of service. Swami Mangalananda currently directs the program at Madihalli.

Membership: In 1997 the ashrama reported 900 adherents at its American center and an additional 1,500 at its Indian center in Madihalli.

Periodicals: *Badarikashrama Sandesha* • *Sandesha*.

Sources:

Badarikashrama. www.badarikashrama.org/.

Barry Long Foundation International

Acorn Cottage, 218 Clove Rd., Salisbury Mills, NY 12577

Alternate Address: International Headquarters: PO Box 838, Billinudgel, NSW 2483, Australia.

Barry Long was a spiritual teacher who emerged in Australia in the 1970s and died in 2003. In 1965 Long had a realization of immortality or "mystic death," the first of a series that led to his realization of the master consciousness.

Long teaches that there is no duality between himself and the power. He eschews most religious forms and emphasizes the living of truth. His teachings are introduced through what is termed the "Course in Being." He also has authored books on self-discovery, meditation, and self-knowledge.

Membership: Not reported. There are centers of the foundation in England, Finland, Netherlands, Australia, and United States. It does not have formal membership.

Sources:

Barry Long Foundation International. www.barrylong.org

Long, Barry. *Barry Long's Journal*. Australia: Barry Long Books, 1994.

————. *Behind Life and Death; The Boundless Reality*. Australia: Barry Long Books, 2008.

Bhakti Marga Foundation

55 Marbella, Rancho Mirage, CA 92270

Bhakti Marga (literally, the path of devotion to god) is a spiritual society founded in 2004 as a teaching venue for Sri Swami Vishwananda. Bhakti Marga seeks to make God the focal point of one's life, to the point that each person becomes one with the love and omnipresence of God. It advocates the practices of prayer, meditation, repeating the divine names (japa yoga), studying holy scriptures (the Vedas), self-reflection, and selfless service as ways to become become more aware of God's presence.

Swami Vishwananda (b. 1978) was born on Mauritius. After completing his schooling he became a full-time spiritual teacher and traveled internationally. In 2001 Swami Vishwananda set up a chapel for the Holy Mother in Mauritius adjacent to a temple dedicated to the Indian saint Sri Shirdi Sai Baba. This was the first of his centers; others were established in Germany (2004) and South Africa (2006). He also developed followings in the United Kingdom, Poland, and the United States.

Membership: Not reported.

Sources:

Bhakti Marga Foundation. www.vishwananda.us/.

Blue Mountain Center of Meditation

PO Box 256, Tomales, CA 94971

The Blue Mountain Center of Meditation, founded by Indian teacher Eknath Easwaran in 1961, offers programs and publications presenting an Eight-Point Program of meditation and allied living skills. The center considers its approach as nondenominational, nonsectarian, and free from dogma and ritual, and the organization is not affiliated with any religious group or movement. Easwaran was a Professor of English at the University of Nagpur, India, when he came to the United States on the Fulbright exchange program in 1959. He has been writing and offering instruction in meditation and world mysticism in the San Francisco Bay Area regularly since 1965. The interest in meditation he encountered while at the University of California-Berkeley prompted him to find the Blue Mountain Center of Meditation. His class at the university in 1967 is believed to be the first academic course on meditation taught for credit on a major American campus.

The basis of the Eight-Point Program is meditation while the other points integrate meditation with daily life. The program includes: 1) Meditation: Going slowly and silently, in the mind, through inspirational passages from the world's great religions, for half-an-hour each morning. (Because of its universality, everyone is encouraged to begin with the Prayer of St. Francis ("Lord, make me an instrument of thy peace…"). 2) Mantram: Silent repetition in the mind of a holy name, mantram, or "prayer word" chosen from those hallowed by the world's great religions (the Jesus Prayer, Barukh attah Adonai, Allahu akbar, Om mani padme hum, Rama, Rama, etc.) whenever possible during the rest of the day. 3) Slowing Down: Simplifying activities and priorities so as to resist the pressure to hurry through the day. 4) One-Pointed Attention: Giving complete concentration to whatever one does. 5) Training the Senses: Undoing conditioned habits and learning to enjoy what is beneficial. 6) Putting Others First: Gaining freedom from self-centered thinking and behavior by focusing attention on the needs of the whole instead of dwelling on ourselves. 7) Spiritual Companionship: Spending time regularly with others who are following the same Eight-Point Program, for mutual inspiration and support. 8) Reading the Mystics: Filling the mind with inspiration from writings by and about the world's great spiritual figures and from the scriptures of all religions.

The Blue Mountain Center offers weekend and weeklong retreats in northern California near its headquarters in Tomales and one-day and weekend retreats at various sites around the country. Nilgiri Press, the center's publishing branch, publishes books and tapes on meditation and world mysticism. Eknath Easwaran has written 23 books that have been translated in 15 languages, in addition to translations of Indian scriptural classics (the Bhagavad Gita, the Upanishads, and the Dhammapada) and an anthology of passages for meditation from the world's major religions, *God Make the Rivers to Flow*.

Membership: The Blue Mountain Center is not a membership organization; however, approximately 25,000 people receive its newsletter.

Periodicals: *Blue Mountain*.

Sources:

Blue Mountain Center of Meditation. www.easwaran.org/.

Easwaran, Eknath. *The Bhagavad Gita for Daily Living*. Berkeley, CA: Blue Mountain Center of Meditation, 1975.

———. *Dialogue with Death*. Petaluma, CA: Nilgiri Press, 1981.

———. *Like a Thousand Suns*. Petaluma, CA: Nilgiri Press, 1979.

———. *A Man to Match His Mountains*. Petaluma, CA: Nilgiri Press, 1984.

———. *The Mantram Handbook*. Petaluma, CA: Nilgiri Press, 1977.

The Supreme Ambition. Petaluma, CA: Nilgiri Press, 1982.

Brahma Kumaris World Spiritual University

46 S. Middle Neck Rd., Great Neck, NY 11021

Alternate Address: International Headquarters: Post Office 3, Box 2, Mount Abu, Rajasthan, India 307501; Canadian Headquarters: 897 College St., Toronto, ON, Canada M6H 1A1.

The Brahma Kumaris World Spiritual University was founded in Karachi in 1936. Over a period of several months, the founder, Dada Lekhraj, who was a prosperous businessman, felt the need to invest more time in quiet reflection and solitude. Then one day, while in a meditative state, he felt a warm glow of energy surrounding him, filling him with light and exposing him to a series of powerful visions. These gave new insights into the innate qualities of the human soul, revealing the mysterious entity of God and explaining the process of world transformation. The intensity of the message they conveyed was such that Dada Lekhraj, now known as Brahma Baba, felt impelled to wind up his business and devote himself to

understanding the significance and application of this revealed knowledge. Brahma Baba left his body in 1969 at the age of 93 after entrusting leadership of the university to a group of young women. The university continues to be administered by women to the present day.

The program of the Brahma Kumaris is centered upon the practice of Raja Yoga, a method of meditation that develops a clear understanding of the relationship between soul and matter, mind and body, and the interplay between soul, God, and the material world. No mantras or special postures are required. Students gradually gain experience in calming a busy mind, creating positive thoughts, and forming a connection with God as the ultimate source of peace and happiness.

Membership: As of 2007, the Brahma Kumaris is located in over 100 countries with more than 5,000 centers and 800,000 regular members or "students." The United States has centers in New York, Boston, Austin, Milpitas, Sacramento, Washington (DC), Chicago, Los Angeles, Miami, San Antonio, San Francisco, Seal Beach, Seattle, Atlanta, Dallas, Tampa, and Honolulu. The centers in Canada are located in Toronto, Vancouver, Edmonton, Montreal, Quebec, and Winnipeg.

Educational Facilities:

Peace Village Learning and Retreat Center.

Periodicals: *The World Renewal* • *Purity Heart and Soul* • *Gyanamrit*

Sources:

Brahma Kumaris World Spiritual University. www.bkwsu.com.

Brahma Baba—The Corporeal Medium of Shiva Baba. Mount Abu, India: Prajapita Brahma Kumaris Ishwariya Vishwa Vidyalaya, n.d.

Illustrations on Raja Yoga. Mount Abu, India: Prajapita Brahma Kumaris Ishwariya Vishwa Vidyalaya, 1975.

Living Values: A Guidebook. London: Brahma Kumaris World Spiritual University, 1995. 110 pp.

Moral Values, Attitudes and Moods. Mount Abu, India: Prajapita Brahma Kumaris Ishwariya Vishwa Vidyalaya, 1975.

Visions of a Better World London. Brahma Kumars World Spiritual University, 1994. 205 pp.

The Way and Goal of Raja Yoga. Mount Abu, India: Prajapita Brahma Kumaris Ishwariya Vishwa Vidyalaya, 1975.

Chinmaya Mission West

PO Box 129, Piercy, CA 95587

Alternate Address: International Headquarters: Central Chinmaya Mission Trust, Powai Park Dr., Mumbai, 400072 India.

Swami Chinmayananda is an independent teacher of Vedanta who in 1949 was initiated into sannyas, the renounced life, by Swami Sivananda Saraswati at Rishikish, India. With Sivananda's blessing, Chinmayananda traveled into the Himalayan Mountains to Uttar Kasi to study with a learned teacher, Swami Tapovanam, known for his knowledge of the Hindu scriptures. He studied with Tapovanam for several years. In 1951 he began to share his knowledge with the public. As people responded the Chinmaya Mission evolved.

Chinmayananda first came to North America in the 1960s. As he periodically toured the country, groups of disciples came into existence. In 1975 Chinmaya Mission West was incorporated. Once formed, assisted by Chinmayananda's charismatic personality and drive, the Mission spread rapidly.

Chinmaya Mission has been distinguished both by its Vedantic teachings and its emphasis on knowledge of the Upanishads and the *Bhagavad Gita*, the two main Hindu scriptures. Chinmayananda has authored numerous books, including commentaries on the *Gita* and Upanishads, and his discourses are available on video.

Membership: In 2008 there were 250 centers in India and 50 outside India, including many in the United States. These are affiliated centers in India, Australia, Singapore, Hong Kong, and various locations across Europe.

Educational Facilities:

Sandeepany Sadhanalaya, Mumbai, India.

Periodicals: *Mananam • Mananam Quarterly Journal CMW Newsletter.*

Sources:

Chinmaya Dig Vijaya: H. H. *Swami Chinmayananda's 1991 Summer Tour of the Americas.* Piercy, CA: Chinmaya Mission West,1991.

Chinmaya Mission West. www.chinmaya.org.

Chinmayananda, Swami. *Kindle Life.* Madras: Chinmaya Publications Trust, n.d.

————. *A Manual for Self-Unfoldment.* Napa, CA: Chinmaya Publication (West), 1975.

————. *Meditation (Hasten Slowly).* Napa, CA: Family Press, 1974.

————. *The Way to Self-Perfection.* Napa, CA: Chinmaya Publications (West), 1976.

Church of the Christian Spiritual Alliance (CSA)

Lake Rabun Rd., PO Box 7, Lakemont, GA 30552-0001

The Church of the Christian Spiritual Alliance (CSA) was founded in 1962 by H. Edwin O'Neal, a Baptist; his wife, Lois O'Neal, an advocate of Religious Science; and William Arnold Lapp, a Unitarian. Its stated purpose was "to teach the fatherhood of God and brotherhood of man as interpreted in the light of modern-day experience." It emerged as a highly eclectic organization that combined Christian, psychic, and Eastern insights. It absorbed *Orion*, a popular independent occult monthly founded by Ural R. Murphy of Charlotte, North Carolina, and continues its publication, now as an annual.

In the late 1960s the church was joined by Roy Eugene Davis, a former student of Swami Paramahansa Yogananda and leader of the Self-Realization Fellowship (SRF) center in Phoenix, Arizona. Davis had left SRF and formed New Life Worldwide. He brought his organization and its periodical (which became *Truth Journal*) into CSA. Davis's traveling and speaking gave CSA a national audience.

CSA took a decisive turn in 1977 when O'Neal resigned as chairman of the board and president of the publishing complex and was replaced by Davis. The focus of CSA has in the ensuing years been that of Davis, who has established the church as part of the larger New Age movement with its concerns of astrology, holistic health, and meditation. The yoga teachings of Yogananda as presented through Davis have become the central core of the teachings. Davis keeps a year-round schedule of seminars around the United States. His ecumenical approach to religion is in keeping with the New Age emphases.

The educational arm of the church is the Center for Spiritual Awareness at Lakemont, Georgia. Meditation seminars are offered several times per year at the headquarters retreat center, focusing on teachings of the kriya yoga tradition. The Shrine of All Faiths Meditation Temple is part of the headquarters complex.

Membership: In 1991 the alliance reported 25 centers and meditation groups in the United States and five in foreign countries—Canada, Germany, Ghana, and South Africa.

Periodicals: *Truth Journal • Orion.*

Sources:

Center for Spiritual Awareness. www.csa-davis.org.

Davis, Roy Eugene. *An Easy Guide to Meditation.* Lakemont, GA: CSA Press, 1978.

————. *God Has Given Us Every Good Thing.* Lakemont, GA: CSA Press, 1986.

————. *The Path of Soul Liberation.* Lakemont, GA: CSA Press, 1975.

————. *The Teachings of the Masters of Perfection.* Lakemont, GA: CSA Press, 1979.

————. *The Way of the Initiate.* St. Petersburg, FL: New Life World-Wide, 1968.

————. *Yoga-Darshana.* Lakemont, GA: CSA Press, 1976.

Cross and the Lotus

c/o Cross and the Lotus Publishing, For information: contact@crossandlotus.com, Seattle, WA

The Cross and the Lotus continue the work of Rev. Mother Yogacharya Hamilton (1904–1991), a disciple of Paramahansa Yogananda (1893–1952), the founder of the Self-Realization Fellowship. Hamilton initially met Yogananda in 1925. She later was ordained by him and became one of only six persons—and the only woman—to whom he gave the title *yogacharya* (teacher, or master of yoga). He also commissioned her to initiate others into Kriya Yoga, the practice he had brought to the west that is passed from guru to *chela* (student) confidentially.

After Yogananda's death, Hamilton developed a relationship with Swami Ramdas and went to live in India at his ashram. She credited him with helping her to finally attain the complete realization of God. After returning to her hometown, Seattle, Washington, to resume teaching, in 1974 she met David R. Hickenbottom, who became her primary student. She ordained him in 1984 and subsequently gave him the title *yogacharya*. He has continued her work since her death in 1991.

The work of the Cross and the Lotus is based in Seattle and the surrounding region. The Cross and the Lotus publishing company issues a quarterly journal.

Membership: Not reported. There are groups in Seattle and Mount Vernon, Washington, and in Vancouver and Victoria, British Colombia.

Periodicals: *The Cross and the Lotus Journal* (archives available online).

Sources:

The Cross and the Lotus Publishing. www.crossandlotus.com/.

Datta Yoga Center

Moniteau Rd, RD 2, Box 2084, Sunbury, PA 16061

Alternate Address: International Headquarters: Sri Ganapati Sachchidananda Ashrama, Datta Peetam, Mysore Ooty Rd., 570 004, India.

Datta Yoga Center is an outpost of the international movement Avadhoota Datta Peetham built around His Holiness Sri Ganapati Sachchidananda Swamiji. Swamiji was born in Mekedati Village, Karnataka, in southern India. He became a postman, although as a youth he had been religiously inclined and a devoted practitioner of yoga. He became known for his healing powers and his ability to work miracles. During his early adulthood, Swamiji began to gather a following, and in 1966 he founded a spiritual center that was located in Mysore, India. He traveled widely around India and in the 1970s began to travel in Europe. He also traveled to the United States and the Caribbean, opening the first United States center in 1986 in Pennsylvania.

Swamiji is considered by followers to be an *avadhuta* (liberated one), in the tradition of Lord Dattatreya. His teachings are multifaceted and described as "universal and unconstrained by religious dogma." He teaches kriya yoga as a method to realize the One Reality as referred to in the teachings of advaita vedanta. The centers serve as temples at which *pujas* and *homas* (worship services) are performed. Always musically inclined, Swamiji has composed numerous *bhajans* (spiritual songs) and instrumental meditation music that are a major part of the gatherings of devotees. He is an advocate of ayurvedic medicine and sponsors a hospital for the underprivileged in India.

Membership: The Center is not a membership organization. There are several hundred devotees (as of 1992) in the United States. The center has constructed two temples, one in Louisiana and the other in Pennsylvania, that devotees are encouraged to visit. Associated centers can also be found in Malaysia, Switzerland, Belgium, Germany, England, and Trinidad.

Periodicals: *Bhakti Mala • Datta Mala.*

Sources:

Datta Yoga Center. www.dycusa.org.

Ganapati Sachchidananda, Swami. *Dattatreya the Absolute*. Trinidad: Dattatreya Yoga Centre, 1984.

————. *Forty-two Stories*. Trinidad: Dattatreya Gyana Bodha Sabha, 1984.

————. *Insight into Spiritual Music*. Mysore, India: Author, n.d.

————. *Sri Dattatreya Laghu Puja Kalpa*. Mysore, India: Author, 1986.

H. H. Sri Sri Ganapati Sachchidananda Swamiji: A Rare Jewel in the Spiritual Galaxy of Modern Times. Mysore, India: Sri Ganapathi Sachchidananda Trust, n.d.

Swamiji, Ganapati Sachchidananda. *Insight into Spiritual Music*. Mysore, India: Author, n.d.

Deva Foundation

336 S Doheny Dr., No. 7, Beverly Hills, CA 90211

The Deva Foundation was founded in Sweden in the early 1980s by Dr. Deva Maharaj (1948), a high caste Hindu and doctor of ayurveda and homeopathic medicine. Before leaving India, he had studied yoga and meditation at the Yoga Research Hospital in New Delhi, India. He came to the United States in the mid-1980s and established headquarters in Beverly Hills, California. The stated aim of the foundation is to bridge the gap between Western psychology and Eastern philosophy. It offers members a wide variety of approaches drawn from both Eastern and Western techniques for personal growth, transformation, and enlightenment. These include various health classes, self-hypnosis, nutrition, acupressure, massage, and *shaktipat*, the awakening of the kundalini, the latent energy believed to rest at the base of the spine. Members may also participate in the activities of the Tantra House operated by the foundation, an educational center that teaches the esoteric secrets of sexuality and spirituality.

Deva travels widely and has become a radio and television personality because of his clairvoyant abilities.

Membership: In 1987 the foundation reported two centers in the United States and one in Canada. There were approximately 100 members in the United States and 1,000 members internationally.

Educational Facilities:

Yoga Center, New Delhi, India.

Devatma Shakti Society

Current address not obtained for this edition.

Alternate Address: International Headquarters: Nawali, Dahisar PO vía Mumbai, Mumbai Panver Rd., Distrit – Thame, 400 612, Maharashtra, India.

The Devatma Shakti Society was formed in 1976 by Swami Shivom Tirth (b. 1924) for the practice of the *shaktipat* system of yoga, a system revived by Swami Gangadhar Tirth Maharaj. Little is known of this swami; he lived in solitude and initiated only one disciple, Kali Kishore Gangopadhyay, who became known as Swami Narayan Tirth Dev Maharaj (1870–1935). He founded a meditation center in Madaripur, Faridpur, India, and passed his succession to Shri Yoganandaji Maharaj (d.1959). Yoganandaji established an ashram in Rishikish. He initiated Swami Vishnu Tirth Maharaj (d.1969) who established the Narayan Kuti Sanyas Ashram at Dewas.

Swami Shivom Tirth was initiated by Vishnu Tirth in 1959 and took the vows of the *sannyasin* (the renounced life) in 1963. During the 1970s Shivom Tirth began to propagate the shaktipat system outside of India, first in Europe and Southeast Asia and then in America. The first ashram in North America was established in central Texas. Shivom Tirth occasionally visits America on lecture tours, visiting his disciples across the United States.

Shaktipat is the descent of the power of the guru upon the disciple, thus activating the disciple's own latent kundalini shakti, often pictured as a serpent sleeping coiled at the base of the spine. The awakening of the energy and its movement up the spinal column to the top of the head produces enlightenment. This way to enlightenment is through the guru's grace and bypasses the years of effort and discipline necessary in other forms of yoga.

Membership: Not reported.

Sources:

Devatma Shakti Society. www.par.org.ar/shaktipat/shivom.htm.

Tirth, Shivam. *A Guide to Shaktipat*. Paige, TX: Devatma Shakti Society, 1985.

Devi Mandir

5950 Hwy. 128, Napa, CA 94558-9632

Devi Mandir, also called the Temple of the Divine Mother, is a Hindu center established in a town in the San Francisco Bay Area by two people known by their religious names, Shree Maa and Swami Satyananda. Swami Satyananda is an American who in the 1960s traveled to India as a seeker of spiritual enlightenment. He remained there, receiving spiritual nurture from various teachers and activities until meeting Shree Maa in the 1980s. Shree Maa was born in Assam, India, and began to devote her life to spiritual practice as a teenager. She received many visions and became known throughout India as a spiritual teacher. She heads the Sanatan Dharma Societies in India with centers at Calcutta, Belur, and Gauhati. After their meeting, the pair became inseparable, and Swami Satynanda traveled with Maa as she held celebrations of worship. The two came to California in the mid-1980s and established the Devi Mandir as a center in Moraga (later relocated to Martinez and then to Napa) for the performance of the ancient Vedic fire worship.

The Devi Mandir is a traditional Hindu temple at which an annual round of Hindu festivals are celebrated. In the altar area, statues of many of the primary deities of Hinduism have been installed, including Shiva and Durga, Brahma and Saraswati, Vishnu and Lakshmi, Kali, and many others. Puja (worship) is offered daily. For three years at the end of the 1980s and into the 1990s, Shree Maa and Swami Satyananda devoted themselves to 1,000 days of continuous worship, during which neither left the temple. During this period they tended the fire inside the temple, making sure that it did not die out.

Shree Maa promotes devotion to the deities through the performance of *puja* (worship). Swami Satyananda has written and translated several books to assist attendees at the temple in their worship, including a beginner's guide to Sri Siva Puja. Shree Maa also promotes a behavior code that grows out of the devoted life. She advises attendees at the temple to be true, simple, and free. They should take refuge in God, cultivate wisdom, develop discrimination (or discernment), and allow their actions to manifest love. She notes that spirituality is simple, noting the saying of a sage—that God is everywhere and thus if one hurts any form, he is hurting himself. In like measure, if he raises any form to a higher level, he elevates himself.

Membership: Not reported. The temple serves both Indian Americans and American converts to Hinduism.

Sources:

Devi Mandir. www.shreemaa.org/drupal/.

Johnsen, Linda. *Daughters of the Goddess: The Women Saints of India*. St. Paul, MN: Yes International Publishers, 1994. 128 pp.

Satya Nanda, Swami, trans. *Kali Dhyanam: Meditation on Maha Kali and the Adya Stotram*. Martinez, CA: Devi Mandir, 1990. 28 pp.

————. *Saty Narayan Katha: The Vow to Speak and Act in Truth*. Martinez, CA: Devi Mandir, 1990. 16 pp.

————. *Sri Siva Puja: Beginner*. Martinez, CA: Devi Mandir, 1990. 40 pp.

Dhyanyoga Centers

PO Box 3194, Antioch, CA 94531

Indian yoga teacher Dhyanyogi Mahant Madhusudandasji Maharaj left home as a child of 13 to seek enlightenment. He spent the next 40 years as a wandering student, during which time he met and worked with his guru whom he discovered at Mt. Abu in Rajasthan State in northern India. From his guru he received *shaktipat*, a transmission of power believed to release the latent power of kundalini, pictured as residing at the base of the spine. The emergence of that power and the experience of its traveling up the spine to the crown of the head is considered by many Hindu groups to be the means of enlightenment.

In 1962 Dhyanyogi Madhusudandasji ceased his wanderings and began to teach. He established an ashram at Bandhvadi, Gujurat, the first of several in western India. He authored two books, *Message to Disciples* and *Light on Meditation*. During the 1970s followers moved to England and the United States. He made his first visit to his Western disciples in 1976 and began to build a following among American converts.

Dhyanyogi Madhusudandasji's teachings emphasize meditation (*dhyan*), or raja yoga, and kundalini yoga. The center offers shaktipat to *sadhuk*s (students). As the kundalini awakens the student is open to the guru's continuing influence and is able to shed past encumbrances and to move on the path of enlightenment. After Madhusudandasji's death in 1994, his teachings continued through his "spiritual heir," Shri Anandi Ma.

Membership: Not reported.

Periodicals: Monthly newsletter.

Sources:

Dhyanyoga Centers. www.dyc.org.

Madhusudandasji, Dhyanyogi. *Brahmanada: Sound, Mantra and Power*. Pasadena, CA: Dhyanyoga Centers, 1979.

————. *Death, Dying and Beyond*. Pasadena, CA: Dhyanyoga Centers, 1979.

————. *Light on Meditation*. Los Angeles, CA: 1978.

————. *Message to Disciples*. Bombay: Shri Dhyanyogi Mandal, 1968.

————. *Shakti, Hidden Treasure of Power*. Pasadena, CA: Dyanyoga Centers, 1979.

Divine Love Mission

c/o Kripalu Bhavanam, 17409 Durbin Park Rd., Edmond, OK 73003

Alternate Address: International Headquarters: Kripalu Kuteer, Village & Post Mangarh, District Pratapgarh, UP, India. • Canadian Headquarters: Sadhana Mandir, 30 Nantucket Blvd., Scarborough, Ontario, Canada.

The Divine Love Mission grew out of the work of the devotion inspired by Jagadguru Shri Kripalu Ji Maharaj (born in 1922 as Ram Kripalu Tripathi in Mangarth, near Allahabad, India). After completing his formal education, at the age of 16 he found his way to Vrindavan and the next year emerged as a guru known affectionately as Shri Maharaj Ji. He is remembered for leading devotees in a six-month continuous chanting of the Hare Krishna mantra when he was only 17 years old. He was 34 years old when given the title "Jagadguru" (world-teacher) on January 14, 1957, by the Kashi Vidvat Parishad, a group of Hindu scholars. As such, he is seen by his followers to stand in a lineage that includes Jagadguru Shankaracharya, Jagadguru Nimbarkacharya, Jagadguru Ramanujacharya, and Jagadguru Madhavacharya (all well-known figures from Hindu history).

The teachings of Shri Maharaj Ji were first spread in America by Siddheshvari Devi (Didi Ji). She led in the founding of the American branch of the Divine Love Mission in 1997. The mission teaches the bhakti yoga tradition of India, similar to the Krishna devotion made popular by the International Society for Krishna Consciousness (ISKON; see separate entry), but completely independent of that organization. Shri Maharaj Ji has taught that, "The essence of all doctrines is to love Lord Krishna, the Supreme Master, and to meditate on His Divine Form with an

increasing desire to serve Him. This is the true ultimate knowledge." He has summarized the tradition in his book of poems, *Bhakti Shatak: Hundred Gems of Divine Love*, posted on the Internet. He has also authored a number of books, English translations of which are being published by the mission.

Membership: Not reported. The mission operates out of three main centers in India, three in the United States (Oklahoma, Texas, Michigan), and one in Canada.

Dynastic Kriya Yoga

For information: kriyayoga.usa@gmail.com

Shibendu Lahiri (b. 1939), the great grandson of Yogi Lahiri Mahasaya (1828–1895), taught Kriya Yoga in India for many years, but in the 1990s he began to spread the teachings and techniques of Kriya Yoga throughout Europe and North America. Lahiri Mahasaya was introduced to the west through the writings of Paramahansa Yogananda (1893–1952), and the kriya yoga teachings that he brought to North America have been perpetuated by his students such as Daya Maya, Swami Kriyananda, and Roy Eugene Davis. Dynastic Kriya Yoga (also called Purna Kriya Yoga) offers the same teachings that Self-Realization Fellowship, Ananda, and the Center of Spiritual Awareness offer, presenting them directly from a physical descendant of Lahiri Mahasaya.

In 1999 Shibendi Lahiri toured the United States and was received so well that annual tours followed in subsequent years. Since then small groups of Dynastic Kriya Yoga practitioners have appeared, but they remain largely invisible in the United States because they have not opened stable centers and have produced little literature. Information on their gatherings is word-of-mouth or via impermanent Internet announcements, and contact with the group is by email and telephone. The largest groups are on the West Coast—Seattle, Los Angeles, San Diego.

Membership: Not reported.

Sources:

Dynastic Kriya Yoga. www.purnakriya.com/index.html; www.kriyayogalahiri.com/.

EnlightenNext

EnlightenNext, PO Box 2360, Lenox, MA 01240

EnlightenNext was founded in the late 1980s by Andrew Cohen (b. 1955). It was formerly known as the Moksha Foundation (California) from 1988 to1999 and the Impersonal Enlightenment Fellowship from 1999 to 2005. Cohen had been raised in a somewhat secular Jewish home. As a teenager, following the death of his father, he moved to Rome to live with his mother. There, at the age of 16, he experienced an extraordinary event of expanded consciousness that initiated a quest in search of someone who could explain the strange occurrence. Cohen's search led him to Swami Hariharananda Giri (a master of kriya yoga) and to the practice of martial arts and Zen meditation. Then in 1986, while in India, Cohen met Harivansh Lal Poonja, a disciple of Sri Ramana Maharshi and his teachings of advaita vedanta. Poonja taught that human beings are in reality pure consciousness in the absolute, here and now, always free. Since human beings are already free, there is no need to search for spiritual freedom, merely realize it.

Cohen felt he immediately understood Poonja's message and after only a short time with him, he left his presence to begin teaching, first in Lucknow, India, and then in England. Early in 1987 he taught classes in Holland and Israel and the following year returned to the United States. His work was centered upon a group that began to form in Cambridge, Massachusetts.

In 1989 he moved his work to Marin County, California, where a group of his closest disciples established an intensive communal life that attempted to live out the implication of the freedom they had begun to realize. The group is informally known as the Sangha. That same year Cohen published his first book, *My Master is My Self*, a volume that includes his diary about meeting with and letters to his guru.

Meanwhile, some problems began to become apparent between himself and Poonjaji (the name used affectionately by Poonja's close followers). As Cohen began to teach, he had come to understand that the initial Enlightenment experience served to reveal the Absolute and gave the student a glimpse of his/her potential for liberation. The purpose of the community he formed was to learn to live in such a way that their lives express the Enlightenment. To the contrary, Poonjaji had taught that Oneness had nothing to do with anything manifested in human life. Cohen came to feel that he had surpassed his teacher, a realization he asserts in his second book, *Autobiography of an Awakening* (1992). He now teaches independently of Poonjaji.

Membership: Not reported. As of 2008 EnlightenNext had two centers in Massachusetts, one in New York, six in Europe, and one each in Israel and India, with regional groups in the United States, Germany, and Australia.

Periodicals: *What Is Enlightenment?*

Sources:

EnlightenNext. www.enlightennext.org.

Cohen, Andrew. *Autobiography of an Awakening*. Corte Madera: Moksha Foundation, 1992.

———. *My Master Is My Self*. Moksha Foundation, 1989.

Fivefold Path Inc.

278 N White Oak Dr., Madison, VA 22727

Fivefold Path Inc. was founded in Madison, Virginia, in 1973 by Vasant Paranjpe, who had received a divine command to come to the United States and teach kriya yoga, the Fivefold Path. From the Virginia headquarters, Paranjpe began to visit and teach in neighboring cities—Washington, D.C.; Baltimore, Maryland; Philadelphia, Pennsylvania; and Riverton, New Jersey. A semimonthly periodical was begun, and a fire temple consecrated at Param Dham, the name given the headquarters.

The Fivefold Path is a system of kriya yoga which begins with purification of the atmosphere as a step leading to the purification of the mind. Its steps include the following: (1) *Agnihotra*, a fire ceremony done at sunrise and sunset each day; (2) *Daan*, sharing one's assets in a spirit of humility; (3) *Tapa*, self-discipline; (4) *Karma*, right action; and (5) *Swadhyaya*, self-study. The Fivefold Path, derived from the teachings of the Vedas, is also called the *Satya Dharma* (Eternal Religion). It respects all avatars and divine messengers and makes no distinction between them. Anyone of any religion may learn the teachings of the Fivefold Path. Vasant has stated that he has come to fulfill the biblical prophecy of Daniel 8:26: "This vision about the evening and morning sacrifices which has been explained to you (i.e., Agnihotra) will come true. But keep it secret now, because it will be a long time before it does come true" (*The Good News Bible* translation).

Membership: Fivefold Path Inc. is not a membership organization. As of 1995, the Fivefold Path had spread to all continents, and its literature has been translated into several languages.

Periodicals: *Satsang*.

Sources:

Fivefold Path Inc. www.agnihotra.org.

Paranjpe, Vasant V. *Grace Alone*. Madison, VA: Fivefold Path, 1971.

———. *Homa Farming, Our Last Hope*. Madison, VA: Fivefold Path, 1986.

———. *Homa Therapy: Our Last Chance*. Madison, VA: Fivefold Path, 1989. 79 pp.

———. *Light towards Divine Path*. N.p., n.d. 57 pp.

———. *Ten Commandments of Parama Sadguru*. Randallstown, MD: Agnihotra Press, 1976.

Foundation of Revelation

59 Scott St., San Francisco, CA 94117

The Foundation of Revelation was formed in 1970 in San Francisco by persons who recognized the existence of perfect knowledge and practical omnipotence in the form of a "beggar" then living in the village of Gorkhara near Calcutta, India. The man had been born of a ruling Brahmin family in 1913 and spent his early years as an avid student of various forms of modern knowledge. On the eve of June 14, 1966, he perceived that the illusions of these limited and disintegrating forms of modern knowledge were burned down by Agni, the fire of knowledge, and on September 19, 1966, the convergence of persisting cosmic existence, the luminous nature of consciousness, was concentrated in the person of this Yogi as Siva, the Destroyer. Thus 1966 is the first year of a new era of Siva Kalpa (meaning the period of time of Lord Siva's omnipotent imagination).

To the foundation, Siva is the creator of conscious life and the destroyer of ignorance, whose pure love of knowledge moves the forms of ego into intensifying contradictions of their own divisive natures to the point of spontaneous recoil toward the synthesis of body, life, and mind. He is considered the most accessible of powers. He never refused the request of a supplicant, perhaps his most dangerous attribute, and he surrounds himself with those from the extremes of the social spectrum whose natural penchant for truth, the power of self-expression, and the ability to manifest same, holds them apart from the world of mediocrity, always gravitating to the heights or depths of existence in the pull toward ultimate perfection.

The first Western contact with the holy man was in 1968 when he made an appearance at the Spiritual Summit Conference in Calcutta, India, sponsored by the Temple of Understanding of Washington, D.C. Several delegates followed him home and one, Charlotte P. Wallace, now president of the foundation, stayed to learn. Word spread of his work, and in 1969 he was invited to the United States to take up residence in San Francisco, which became the world headquarters of the foundation. Those from countries around the world who witnessed his revelations firsthand returned to their respective countries to organize themselves within the spirit and corporate structure of the foundation to create bases for international communication and activity, with the single purpose of breaking down the barriers of nationality, religion, and race and foster the mutually beneficial and harmonious relationships of nations.

The foundation is led by a governing body consisting of the president and seven officers. Each country has a president directly responsible to the world president. Each local leader is responsible to the national president.

Membership: In 1997 the foundation reported 5,000 members in the United States and 25,000 members in the world. There were 21 centers worldwide in 10 countries.

Sources:

The Foundation of Revelation. www.thefoundationofrevelation.org.

Gangaji Foundation

2245 Ashland St., Ashland, OR 97520

Harivansh Lal Poonja (1910–1998), affectionately called Poonjaji by his students, is a teacher of advaita vedanta, the Indian philosophy of nonduality. He was born in 1910 in Gujranwala, India (Pakistan), and grew up in what is now Pakistan. His mother was the sister of Swami Rama Tirtha (d. 1906), an early twentieth-century vedanta teacher who was one of the first Hindu gurus in America. He married and joined the army, but his only interest was in the spiritual life. In 1944 he met Ramana Maharshi (1879–1950) and stayed with him until he was forced to return to his family at the time of the partition of Pakistan. He cared for his family until the last child left home, and then in 1966, he retired and began a period of his life as one who had discovered absolute oneness. He wandered for many years, but finally settled in Lucknow, India.

Poonjaji emphasizes a simple message. Human beings are pure consciousness and hence absolutely free. The spiritual life is not a matter of attaining freedom, but of realizing that one is already free.

Poonjaji met many of the Americans who came to India on spiritual quests beginning in the 1960s. During the 1980s he made several trips to America to teach, but established no permanent work. Then in 1988, Andrew Cohen, one of his students, began teaching in Cambridge, Massachusetts. Cohen separated from Poonjaji and headed the Moksha Foundation (California), currently EnlightenNext (see separate entries).

In 1990 Antoinette Varner met Poonjaji. Confirming her Self-realization, Poonjaji gave her the name Gangaji and instructed her to carry this message of freedom to the West. Today, Gangaji travels throughout the world holding satsang, and has established Satsang Foundation & Press in Boulder, Colorado, to further the teachings of this lineage to all who are interested.

The Gangaji Foundation's purpose is to serve "truth of universal consciousness, and the potential for individual and collective recognition of peace, inherent in the core of all beings." It is to present the teachings and transmission of Gangaji through Sri Ramana Maharshi and Poonjaji.

Membership: Not reported.

Sources:

The Gangaji Foundation. www.gangaji.org.

Ingram, Catherine. "Plunge Into Eternity." *Yoga Journal* (September/October 1992): 56–63.

Poonja, H. W. L. *Wake Up and Roar*. Kula, Maui, HI: Pacific Center Press, 1992.

Grace Essence Fellowship

c/o Martin Lowenthal, 53 Westchester Rd., Newton, MA 02158

Grace Essence Fellowship was founded in the late 1970s by Lars Short, formerly a student of the late Swami Rudhrananda (1928–1973). Rudrananda, the founder of the Nityananda Institute, Inc., was among the first of the contemporary teachers of kundalini yoga in America. Lars Short trained with Rudrananda and in 1965 began his career as a yoga instructor. After Rudrananda's death, Short went on to study with His Holiness Dilgo Khyentse, a Tibetan master, and to absorb elements of Zen and Taoism into a synthesis that, he notes, Rudrananda had seen emerging as an all-encompassing Spiritual Work.

Short refers to his system as the Way of Radiance. The Way begins in the presupposition that it is possible to live life to the fullest rather than suffer, and to be an agent of grace rather than struggle. It proposes four principles: Life is a gift. All experience can nurture growth. We can live each moment so as to make our self-expression a celebration of life. If we commit ourselves to growth and freedom beyond any set agenda or identity, we can transcend present ways of relating to ourselves, others, and life itself. Short has adapted practices from his several teachers, including Tibetan mindfulness practices and tantric exercises.

Members of the fellowship have the opportunity to train to become practitioners and then seminarians, who take responsibility for passing on the Radiance teachings.

Membership: Not reported. There are eight study groups across the United States, two in Canada, and one in Venezuela.

Sources:

Lowenthal, Martin. "Grace Essence Fellowship: Supporting Growth and Freedom." *Tantra* 9 (1994): 64–65.

————. "A Spiritual Home in the Grace Essence Fellowship." *Tantra* 9 (1994): 65.

Haidakhan Samaj

Current address not obtained for this edition.

Alternate Address: International Headquarters: Haidakhan Ashram, P. O. Haidakhan, via Kathgodam. Dist. Nainital, Utter Pradesh 263126, India.

The Haidakhan Samaj was founded in 1980 to coordinate the activities of followers of Haidakhan Baba, also known as Babaji and Mahavatar Babaji. Babaji is believed to be an *avatar*, a physical incarnation of divinity, who has a history of incarnation over a period of thousands of years. He is known as an incarnation of Lord Shiva, who, in the Hindu tradition, is considered to be the Master Teacher. Babaji incarnates in human form from time to time to demonstrate and teach ways that can lead people to harmony and unity with the Divine.

Present-day disciples of Babaji look to several ancient scriptural references that may refer to him as well as several nineteenth and twentieth century accounts. The first, and still the major, book in the West about Babaji is *Autobiography of a Yogi* (1946) by Swami Paramahansa Yogananda, founder of the Self-Realization Fellowship. Yogananda wrote of his master's teacher's first encounter with Babaji in the Indian Himalayas in 1863. There are many stories of people's miraculous encounters with Babaji in the last half of the nineteenth century.

There are several books in the Hindi language detailing the incarnation of an avatar-saint known as Haidakhan Baba, who lived in the Kumaon foothills of the Himalayas from about 1890 to 1922. He was recognized then as an incarnation of Lord Shiva and as a form of Mahavatar Babaji. Some of the stories about this incarnation of Babaji were collected and translated by Baba Hari Dass of the Sri Rama Foundation of Davis, California, in a book titled, *Hariakhan Baba Known, Unknown*. When he left his body in 1922, Babaji is reported to have said that he would return to help humanity.

In 1949, an Indian saint named Mahendra Baba, who had seen Babaji several times in his childhood and youth, was blessed with a physical manifestation of Babaji in an ashram of Haidakhan Baba. From that time on, Mahendra Baba devoted his life to preparing for the return of Babaji. He wrote several books about Babaji, restored the old ashrams, and called upon people to be ready for his return. Mahendra died in 1969.

In June 1970 Babaji appeared again in Haidakhan Baba's ashram in the Kuaon village of Haidakhan. From then until his death on February 14, 1984, he traveled extensively in northern India and taught from several Babaji ashrams around the country, but spent the majority of his time in the remote village ashram in Haidakhan. Tens of thousands of Indians came to him, and hundreds came from Europe and America. Most of the time, he purposely avoided large crowds in order to perform the traditional guru's task of teaching and training people who were truly dedicated to the attainment of spiritual knowledge and growth. He taught them mostly by example, often on a mind-to-mind level rather than orally. He guided each devotee step by step through the experiences they needed for growth. Many people were brought to Babaji by miraculous experiences.

According to his own claim, Babaji came, in every incarnation, to restore the Sanatan Dharma—the eternal law of order under which the creation was manifested and operates in harmony with the Divine Will. He urged his followers to live in Truth, Simplicity, and Love, seeing all of creation as a manifestation of the Divine, and living in harmony with all. He respected all the established religions, and taught that each one can lead its devotees to unity and true devotion, renouncing the attachment to materialism which chains humankind to its lower nature. As an aid to keeping the Divine foremost in the followers' consciousness, he taught people to repeat the names of God at all times: the mantra which he taught to most people was "Om Namah Shivai," which may be translated as "I take refuge in God (Shiva)."

Babaji's followers worship him through a sung worship service called the *aarati*, morning and evening, and worship the formless Divine through an ancient fire ceremony, called the *yagya* or *hawan*. But the worship most advocated was that of selfless work, *karma yoga*, performed without ego for the benefit of all living beings, in harmony with the Divine Will.

There are Babaji ashrams and centers in Asia, Europe, Africa, Australia, and New Zealand. In the United States, there are ashrams in The Baca Grande, Crestone, Colorado; Mountain View, Hawaii; Malmo, Nebraska; and at Consciousness Village near Sierraville, California, as well as centers in many cities.

Membership: In 1995 the ashram reported 90 members in the United States and 10 in Canada. There were 15 centers in the United States and one in Canada. There were 8,000 members worldwide.

Periodicals: *American Haidakhan Samaj Newsletter*.

Sources:

Goodman, Shdema. *Babaji, Meeting with Truth at Hairakhan Vishwa Mahadham*. Farmingdale, NY: Coleman, 1986.

Hari, Dass Baba. *Hariakhan Baba Known, Unknown*. Davis, CA: Sri Rama Foundation, 1975.

Orr, Leonard [and Makhan Singh]. *Babaji*. San Francisco, CA: Author, 1979.

Teachings of Babaji. Nainital, India: Haidakhan Ashram, 1983–1984.

Yogananda, Paramahansa. *Autobiography of a Yogi*. Los Angeles, CA: Self-Realization Fellowship, 1946.

Hamsa Yoga Sangh

GSY (Gurunath Siddhanath Yoga), PO Box 930, Union City, CA 94587

Alternate Address: Siddhanath Forest Ashram, Sitamai Dara, Simhagadh, Pune, Maharastra, India.

The Hamsa Yoga Sangh was founded by Gurunath Siddhanath, a spiritual teacher of Kriya Yoga who has a lineage derived from his study with the Nath Masters of the Himalayan Mountains. The Nath lineage traces its origins to the deity Shiva and found its most important embodiment in Babaji, the mysterious master teacher originally introduced to the West by Swami Paramahansa Yogananda (1893–1952). Among the several Nath lineages, the one represented by Gurunath Siddhanath has been commissioned to bring Kriya Yoga teachings to the West. Siddhanath exercises his powers of *shakipat* to initiate the emergence of the kundalini power (believed to be latently existing) in each individual. Kriya Yoga is a form of Kundalini Yoga, exact teachings of which are reserved for initiates.

Gurunath Siddhanath had led in the construction of the Earth Peace Temple near Pune, Mahasharstra, India. It houses a unique alchemical Mercury Shiva linga (symbol of Shiva), whose radiations are believed to assist those who meditate there to realize Peace on Earth through Self Peace. Over the last decade, the Hamsa Yoga Sangh has spread internationally and developed centers across the United States and in the United Kingdom, Germany, Italy, and Switzerland.

Membership: Not reported. In 2008 there were 10 centers operating in the United States, of which 8 were on the West Coast.

Sources:

Hamsa Yoga Sangh. www.hamsa-yoga.org/.

Gurunath Siddhanath. *Dew Drops of the Soul*. Whitesboro, NY: Alight Publications, 2001.

————. *Earth Peace through Self Peace*. Whitesboro, NY: Alight Publications, 2003.

————. *Wings of Freedom*. Whitesboro, NY: Alight Publications, 2006.

Hanuman Foundation

223 N Guadalupe St., Santa Fe, NM 87501

The Hanuman Foundation, incorporated in 1974, is the focus of a number of activities that had their origin in the continuing career of Baba Ram Dass and were inspired by his guru, Neem Karoli Baba, popularly known as simply Baba. The foundation's purposes have been to further the spiritual well being of society through education, service, and spiritual training. Its major project has been to support the spiritual teaching of Baba Ram Dass. Ram Dass is the name taken by Richard Alpert, the former professor of psychology at Harvard University who was fired along with Timothy Leary because of their LSD experiments. Within a short time he became discouraged with drugs as a means to attain higher states of consciousness and he turned to India. There he met Bhagwan Dass, a young American guru, and his teacher, Maharaji, who lived in the foothills of the Himalayas. From Maharaji he learned raja yoga, the path to God through meditation. Ram Dass also developed a devotion to Hanuman, the monkey-faced deity of popular Hinduism. Maharaj taught him to serve and worship Hanuman, a practice which he has continued over the years, though many of his fans are unaware of it.

Upon returning to the West, Baba Ram Dass wrote and published *Be Here Now*, which emphasized his ideal of living in the present, other than being tied to the past or contemplating the future. He sees all people on a journey to enlightenment. Each person needs and has a guru to help his progress. Some gurus are on the physical plane, but such is not necessary since the relationship is spiritual. Each person is at a different place on his journey, and, thus, differing exercises are needed by each individual. Some might need yoga, renunciation, mantras, sex, or even psychedelic drugs. For Baba Ram Dass, yoga was the path to enlightenment.

During his first years back in the United States, Ram Dass traveled and spoke from a base in his residence in New Hampshire. Gradually, several organizations emerged to disseminate Ram Dass's teachings. The Orphalese Foundation controlled a tape library and the ZBS Foundation (also known as Amazing Grace) published several records. Ram Dass also found himself at the center of a network that included a variety of service projects. These included a prison-ashram library project and assistance to the Hanuman Foundation, an organization seen as perpetuating the spirit and teachings of Neem Karoli Baba. In the more than a decade of existence, several structures associated with the foundation have emerged as important aspects of the work.

The Hanuman Foundation Tape Library superseded the Orphalese Foundation. It currently distributes audio and video tapes of Ram Dass and several close associates such as Stephen Levine. The Prison Ashram project distributed spiritual literature to prison libraries and has created a manual specially designed for inmates who wished to learn to meditate and follow a spiritual path during their years of imprisonment. In recent years the project has expanded to include residents of halfway houses, mental hospitals, and drug abuse programs.

The Neem Karoli Baba Hanuman Temple is located in a renovated adobe building at Taos, New Mexico. It houses a 1,500-pound marble statue of Hanuman carved to Ram Dass's specifications. It serves approximately 300 Hindu families in a strip from Albuquerque to Denver. There is an annual and a weekly cycle of devotional services anchored in the singing and chanting services each Tuesday (Hanuman day). Hanuman's birthday is celebrated in April and Neem Karoli Baba's Mahasamahdi (death) is celebrated in September.

Seva Foundation, founded by Larry Brillant, a devotee of Baba, is an organization that began with a goal to end blindness in Nepal. Though independent of the Hanuman Foundation, Baba Ram Dass has given it his full support and the Hanuman Foundation Tape Library distributes recordings of Ram Dass's lectures promoting its work.

In 2006, the Hanuman Foundation established the New Mexico Water Initiative along with local citizens and businesses to support community water conservation efforts through public education programs.

Membership: The Hanuman Foundation is not a membership organization.

Sources:

Hanuman Foundation. www.hanumanfoundation.com

Dass, Baba Ram. *Grist for the Mill*. Santa Cruz, CA: Unity Press, 1977.

————. *Miracle of Love*. New York: E. P. Dutton, 1979.

————. *The Only Dance There Is*. New York: Jason Aaronson, 1976.

————. *Remember, Be Here Now*. San Christobal, NM: Lama Foundation, 1971.

Inside Out. Nederland, CO: Prison-Ashram Project, Hanuman Foundation, 1976.

Himalayan International Institute of Yoga Science and Philosophy
952 Bethany Tpke., Honesdale, PA 18431

Swami Rama (1925–1996) was a learned philosopher and master yogi who came to the United States to teach. As a child, he was adopted by an accomplished yogi from Bengal and raised in the tradition of the cave monasteries of the Himalayas. In 1949 he attained the position of Shankaracharya, an honor he relinquished in 1952 to further his own teaching goals. He came to the United States in 1969, where he served as research consultant to the Menninger Foundation Research Project on Voluntary Controls of External States. Working with psychologists Elmer Green and his wife Alyce Green, he demonstrated extraordinary physical feats of body-function control that offered significant material for the understanding of the mind/body connection. Swami Rama taught superconscious meditation, which is "a unique system to awaken the sleeping energy of consciousness, to raise its volume and intensity so that individual awareness becomes one with the Universal Self." It involves relaxation, posture, breathing, and mantras.

Swami Rama founded the Himalayan International Institute of Yoga Science and Philosophy in 1971 in Illinois. The institute headquarters moved to Honesdale, Pennsylvania, in 1977. Yoga, meditation, and holistic health are the main emphases of the institute. All levels of hatha yoga are taught, and raja yoga is emphasized as a means to balance body, mind, and spirit.

The Himalayan Institute publishes over 80 books on yoga science, meditation, health, psychology, and philosophy. It also publishes the bimonthly magazine *Yoga +*. Programs at the centers, especially at the headquarters campus, include a wide range of seminars, health programs, and residential programs. The Himalayan Institute partakes in a number of projects through its Global Humanitarian Projects program, which focuses on social regeneration, sustainable living, and empowerment of rural communities.

Membership: In 2002, the institute reported 37 branch and affiliated centers in the United States and abroad. Foreign work is conducted in Canada, India, Germany, Italy, Great Britain, Trinidad, Curacao, and Malaysia. In 2002, there were 1,500 members in the United States.

Periodicals: *Yoga +*.

Sources:

Himalayan Institute. www.himalayaninstitute.org.

Inspired Thoughts of Swami Rama. Honesdale, PA: Himalayan International Institute of Yoga Science and Philosophy, 1983.

Rama, Swami. *Lectures on Yoga*. Arlington Heights, IL: Himalayan International Institute of Yoga Science and Philosophy, 1972.

————. *Living with the Himalayan Masters*. Honesdale, PA: Himalayan International Institute of Yoga Science and Philosophy, 1978.

————. *Path of Fire and Light*. Honesdale, PA: Himalayan International Institute of Yoga Science and Philosophy, 1986.

————. *A Practical Guide to Holistic Health*. Honesdale, PA: Himalayan International Institute of Yoga Science and Philosophy, 1978.

Rama, Swami, Rudolph Ballentine, and Swami Ajaya [Allan Weinstock]. *Yoga and Psychotherapy*. Glenview, IL: Himalayan Institute, 1976.

Hohm Community
PO Box 4272, Prescott, AZ 86302

Hohm Community, known as Hohm Sahaj Mandir since 1996, was founded in 1975 by Lee Lozowick, a former meditation instructor and businessman who experienced a spontaneous spiritual awakening after some years of intense spiritual discipline. This event left him in what he has described as an abiding condition of God-realization that subsequently led to his teaching work and the establishment of the formal guru-disciple relationship with a small group of students. Shortly

after that, while traveling extensively in India, Lozowick met his spiritual teacher, Sri Yogi Ramsuratkumar (d. 2001), to whom he attributes his own awakening and who he calls the "source" of his teaching work. Beginning in 1976 Lozowick maintained a close and uniquely intimate relationship with Yogi Ramsuratkumar as his own guru and visited him annually at his ashram in Tiruvannamalai, India.

Lozowick adheres to an Eastern form within the lineage of Yogi Ramsuratkumar and his master Swami Papa Ramdas but also has called his school the Western Baul Way because of the deep resonance that his teaching and the *sadhana* (spiritual life) of his students have with the Bauls of Bengal. The Bauls of Bengal are an obscure sect of musicians and mystics who practice a form of bhakti yoga called *kaya sadhana*, or realization through the body. The tenets of the Baul path are based on a blend of Sahajiya Buddhism and Vaishnava Hinduism; the Bauls typically encode their teaching in poems, song, and dance rather than in written texts or treatises and often travel about Bengali villages singing and chanting for alms.

The Western Bauls of the Hohm Community live a life of disciplined spiritual practice, with daily meditation, a vegetarian diet, exercise, and study of spiritual/classic literature and comparative religion recommended as foundation-level preparation in the school. Other recommended aspects of sadhana are committed monogamous relationships, conscious child raising (completely nonabusive and child-centered), and mutual respect between sexes. As Western Bauls the community has two bands—a rock & roll band called "Atilla the Hunza," and a traditional blues group called "Shri"—both of which perform original music (lyrics by Lozowick) composed by his students on a professional basis.

Membership: The Holm Community maintains an ashram in Arizona and an ashram in central France. As of 2001 the Hohm Community includes about 150 members in the United States, Canada, and Europe. Lozowick travels extensively, teaching and giving seminars, and resides on the ashram in France four months out of the year and in Arizona the remainder of the year.

Periodicals: *Tawagoto*.

Sources:

A Basic Introduction of the Teachings and Practices of the Hohm Community. Prescott Valley, AZ: Hohm Community, n.d.

Lozowick, Lee. *Acting God*. Prescott Valley, AZ: Hohm Press, 1980.

————. *Beyond Release*. Tabor, NJ: Hohm Press, 1975.

————. *Book of Unenlightenment*. Prescott Valley, AZ: Hohm Press, 1980.

————. *The Cheating Buddah*. Tabor, NJ: Hohm Press, 1980.

————. *In the Fire*. Tabor, NJ: Hohm Press, 1978.

————. *Laughter of the Stones*. Tabor, NJ: Hohm Press, n.d.

The Only Grace Is Loving God. Prescott Valley, AZ: Hohm Press, 1984.

Holy Shankaracharya Order
6980 E River Rd., Rush, NY 14543

The Holy Shankaracharya Order had its beginning in 1968 when Swami Lakshmy Devyashram, a disciple of Swami Sivananda Saraswati, established the Sivananda Ashram of Yoga One Science. Through self-study and under Sivananda's spiritual inspiration, she found *samadhi* (a mystic state of altered consciousness) in 1963. In 1964, she had a vision of Swami Sivananda and was led by him to the Pocono Mountains of Pennsylvania and New York. The guidance continued in the building of the retreat/camp. In 1969, she was ordained by Swami Swanandashram in the Holy Order of Sannyasa Saraswati, the order in which Sivananda was ordained. In 1974, Swami Lakshmy was elected Mahamandaleshwari (Great Overlord) of the Holy Shankaracharya Order in the United States.

In 1974 property was purchased in Virginia and a second ashram-temple complex was begun. It was dedicated in 1977. In 1978, from her superior in the Shankaracharya Order—Jagadguru Shankaracharya Abhinava Vidyateertha Maharaj, headquartered at Sringeri, India, the holy seat of the Order—Swami

Lakshmy was requested to establish a *shakti peetham* (monastery), which was named Sri Rajarajeshwari Peetham. As the Swami gathered students around her, she ordained them, and they have become instructors in the various programs and activities. In the same year a Hindu Heritage Summer Camp was created. The response to this program led to the acceptance of the non-Indian, female swami by the Indian-American community.

In 1981, shortly before Swami Lakshmy died, Hindu priestly services were begun at the peetham. Swami Lakshmy was succeeded by Swami Saraswati Devyashram, one of her female students. Under her leadership the outreach to the Indian community has grown. A center has been opened in Tucson, Arizona, and a winter heritage camp initiated in 1982. The Holy Shankacharya Order has been a major traditional Saivite Hindu center. In 1983 Swami Saraswati Devyashram was initiated by the Jagadguru Shankaracharya at Sringeri. In 1984 it joined the ecumenical Council of Hindu Temples. It provides a full range of temple services at the peetham in the Poconos.

Membership: Not reported.

Periodicals: *Vedic Heritage Newsletter*.

Sources:

Sri Rajarajeswari Peetham. www.srividya.org.

Indo-American Yoga-Vedanta Society

30 W 58th St., Apt. 11-J, New York, NY 10019

The Indo-American Yoga-Vedanta Society was founded in New York City by His Holiness Sri Swami Satchidananda Bua Ji (b. 1896), popularly known as Swami Bua Ji. Swami Bua Ji had been crippled at birth, and because doctors were unable to treat him, he was not expected to survive into adulthood. However, he was turned over to Sri Yogeswar Ji Maharaj, a teacher who worked with him using yoga and herbal treatments. At the end of this period, the youthful Swami Bua Ji emerged as both healthy and an accomplished yogi. For many years he was associated with the Divine Life Society founded by Swami Sivananda Saraswati.

In the years after Indian independence (1948) Swami Bua Ji began to travel widely throughout Europe and North America giving popular demonstrations of yoga and allowing himself to become the subject of scientific investigations. In 1972 he settled in the United States and founded the Indo-American Yoga-Vedanta Society.

Membership: Not reported. There is one center in the United States and several others in Europe and India.

Institute of Advanced Mutuality

For information: info@awakenedmutuality.org.

Waking Down in Mutuality was cofounded by Saniel Bonder (b. 1950) a Jewish-American spiritual teacher, and his wife, Linda Groves-Bonder. Saniel Bonder began his spiritual seeking as a student at Harvard University at the end of the 1960s. He later discovered the writings of Ramana Maharshi, and then in 1973 joined the Daist community led by Adi Da (then known as Bubba Free John). He left the Daist community (now called Adidam) in 1992, complaining of an overemphasis on guru devotion, and entered a period of intense self-examination that led to what he described as an establishment in the "onlyness of being."

He called the new approach to spiritual awakening "Waking Down," as opposed to "waking up." He suggests that we err in trying to disassociate ourselves from the messy stuff of life, to escape the wheel of birth and death (reincarnation). Instead, he teaches that we should seek a liberation *into* the wheel of birth and death, but with our infinite spirit-consciousness intact: The purpose of life is not to escape life, but to be present more profoundly. Earth is seen as a very suitable place for the critical work of conscious evolution. Bonder and his students began to explore spiritual existence through combining infinite, unconditional conscious spirit and finite, mortal embodiment and relationships.

Bonder created several successive organizations to facilitate his teachings, including Mt. Tam Awakenings in the mid-1990s and, in 2005, the Institute for Advanced Mutuality. Meanwhile, he had begun to train and certify teachers of the Waking Down process; those teachers now are organized in the Waking Down Teachers Association. The institute sponsors programs throughout the United States, which is divided into seven regions administered by seven area teachers.

Membership: Not reported.

Sources:

Institute of Advanced Mutuality. www.wakingdown.org/; awakenedmutuality.org/; www.sanielandlinda.com/.

Bonder, Saniel. *Great Relief: Nine Sacred Secrets Your Body Wants You to Know about Freedom, Love, Trust, and the Core Wound of Your Life*. Petaluma, CA: Mt. Tam Empowerments, 2004.

———. *Waking Down: Beyond Hypermasculine Dharmas: A Breakthrough Way of Self-Realization in the Sanctuary of Mutuality*. Petaluma, CA: Mt. Tam Empowerments, 1998.

Integral Yoga International

c/o Satchidananda Ashram-Yogaville, 108 Yogaville Way, Buckingham, VA 23921

The Rev. Sri Swami Satchidananda, one of several disciples of Swami Sivananda Saraswati to carry his teaching around the world, founded the Integral Yoga Institute. Satchidananda, after years of spiritual seeking, met Swami Sivananda in 1947. In 1949, he was initiated as a *sannyasin* (monk) into a life of renunciation and selfless service and was given his name, which means Existence-Knowledge-Bliss. Because of Swami Satchidananda's mastery of all the branches of yoga, he was given the title "Yogiraj," or master of yoga. After 17 years of work with Sivananda's Divine Life Society, he came to New York on an intended two-day visit, but was asked to stay to become the founder-director of the Integral Yoga Institute (IYI) and the spiritual head of Integral Yoga International.

The IYI teaches all aspects of Integral Yoga including Hatha Yoga (to purify and strengthen the body and mind); Karma Yoga (selfless service); Bhakti Yoga (the path of love and devotion to God); Jnana Yoga (the path of wisdom); Japa Yoga (the repetition of a mantra); and Raja Yoga (the path of concentration and meditation).

Since 1975, Swami Satchidananda initiated disciples (both men and women) into the Holy Order of Sannyas. Sannyasins take the traditional vows to serve and to practice nonviolence toward all living beings. In 1980 the Integral Yoga Ministry was established. Integral Yoga ministers may be married or single; they take vows to live in the spirit of nonattachment, physical and mental purity, and obedience. In 1985, the headquarters of Integral Yoga International moved from the ashram in Connecticut to a new ashram in Virginia.

Sri Swami Satchidananda is known for his involvement in interfaith work. In 1986, at the Virginia ashram, the Light Of Truth Universal Shine (LOTUS) was dedicated to honor all the world religions. Here, people of all faiths can come to meditate and pray in the same place. A central column of light rises and divides into 12 rays to illuminate altars for individual faiths set within the petals of LOTUS. The LOTUS symbolizes the unity in diversity of all religions and reflects Satchidananda's teaching that "Truth is One—Paths are Many." Several yoga teacher training programs are in place at the Yogaville ashram.

Membership: There is no formal membership in IYI. In 1997 it reported 23 centers in the United States and four in Canada headed by 60 monks and ministers worldwide. There were 11 affiliated centers in various foreign countries.

Periodicals: *Integral Yoga Magazine*. • *IYI News*. Send orders to 227 W 13th St., New York, NY 10011.

Sources:

Integral Yoga International. www.iyiva.org.

Bordow, Sita, et al. *Sri Swami Satchidananda: Apostle of Peace*. Yogaville, VA: Integral Yoga Publications, 1986.

Satchidananda, Sri Swami. *A Decade of Service*. Pomfret Center, CT: Satchidananda Ashram-Yogaville, 1976.

———. *The Healthy Vegetarian*. Yogaville, VA: Integral Yoga Publications, 1986.

Satchidananda, Swami. *Integral Hatha Yoga*. New York: Holt, Rinehart and Winston, 1970.

———. *The Glory of Sannyasa*. Pomfret, CT: Satchidananda Ashram-Yogaville, 1975.

Satchidananda, Swami, et al. *Living Yoga*. New York: An Interface Book, 1977.

Weiner, Sita. *Swami Satchidananda*. New York: Bantam Books, 1972.

Inter Faith Center (IFC) Temple of Divine Love

Current address could not be obtained for this edition.

The IFC Temple of Divine Love was formed by Shri Param Eswaran, a Tamil Indian born in 1944 in Malaysia. Eswaran met Swami Sivananda (1887–1963) when he was only nine years old, and later studied with one of Sivananda's students, Swami Shantananda, and read widely in the writings of Paramahansa Yogananda (1893–1952). He emerged as a teacher in the mid-1970s and in 1976 moved to Australia. That same year Eswaran made his first tour of his adopted national home as a teacher of Tantric Yoga. In 1982, with the assistance of his students, he opened Param's Indian Restaurant and an associated healing center in Woollahra, Australia. Eswaran founded the IFC Temple of Divine Love in 1990.

The IFC Temple of Divine Love promulgates Inter Faith Tantra, tantric teachings it believes to be the most suited to the contemporary world (and similar to those perpetuated by the Self-Realization Fellowship). It does not see itself as a particular religion, but as a temple of God/Goddess All That Is that makes available knowledge of scientific techniques for attaining direct personal experience of Shakti, the Mother God within each person.

As part of his Tantric Yoga teaching, Eswaran also teaches what he terms *yoni healing*, a practice integrated with his understanding of astrology. Vedic astrology teaches that each person possesses 1 of 14 specific soul tendencies toward emotional involvement or entanglement within sexual relationships (known as *yoni kutas*), each personified as a different kind of animal. Using astrology, Eswaran determines the basic nature of each individual's *yoni kuta*. It is his belief that the placement of the planets at the time of birth gives each person an electromagnetic imprint highlighting the particular karmic obstacles that must be overcome to reach the goal of oneness. He believes that anyone may reach that goal in this life.

To carry out his work, Eswaran travels widely and has developed centers of activity in Canada, the United States, the United Kingdom, the Netherlands, Italy, Malaysia, and India. The IFC Temple has also developed an expansive Internet presence, through which it shares information on all aspects of tantra and vegetarianism.

Membership: Not reported. In the United States, support is concentrated in Maine, Texas, and California.

Sources:

Inter Faith Center (IFC) Temple of Divine Love. www.tantra-ifc-the-art-of-conscious-love.com/.

Intergalactic Culture Foundation

1569 Stonewood Ct., San Pedro, CA 90732

Alternate Address: International Headquarters: Sri Swami Shyam Paramahansa Ministry International, Enlightenment Connoisseur's Cozy Corner, Laxman Jhula 249302, Himalayas, India.

The Intergalactic Culture Foundation was founded in 1981 in Los Angeles by Sri Swami Shyam Paramahansa Mahaprabho, an Indian spiritual teacher. Originally known as the Intergalactic Lovetrance Civilization Center, in 1986 the organization created four divisions, each of which assumed a Sanskrit name: Sarvam Kalvidam Brahma Foundation, Aiem Hrem Kleem Chamundayai Vichche Foundation, Aum Naham Parvati Pate Foundation, and Aum Namo Bhagavate Vasudevay Foundation. Each of these divisions assisted aspirants from different intellectual and emotional backgrounds to attain the wisdom of Truth.

Sri Swami Shyam and the foundation have published more than 100 titles, 60 *Lovetrance World* journals, the *India Experience Newspaper*, the *Journey Back in Time* Correspondence Course, and more than 100 videos and 200 audio cassette tapes. Swami Shyam made annual lecture tours across the United States and in 1998 was responsible for planning the international Galactic Chronicles Lecture Tour. By 2002 he had produced 2,000 pages of his own Commentary on Srimad Bhagavatam and 1,500 pages on Yoga Vasistha, Vivek Chudamani, and Upanishads. In addition, 70 audio discourses on his Bhagavat Katha are available for order; several electronic books are available at no charge. The discourses may be heard on www.live365.com.

Membership: Not reported.

Periodicals: *Hindu Digest.* • *Golden India Enlightenment Connoisseur's Newsletter.*

Sources:

Paramahansa, Swami Prem. *What Is ILCC?*. Hawthorne, CA: Intergalatic Lovetrance Civilization Center, [1983].

Prem, Sri Swami. *Galatic Chronicles Lecture Program*. Harbor City, CA: Aum Namo Bhagavate Vasudevay, 1995. 37 pp.

Swami Prem Paramahansa and His Message. Hawthorne, CA: Intergalatic Lovetrance Civilization Center, 1983.

Who Is Swami Prem Paramahansa Mahaprabho? Hawthorne, CA: Intergalatic Lovetrance Civilization Center [1982].

International Babaji Kriya Yoga Sangam

14011 Mansa Dr., La Mirada, CA 90638

The International Babaji Yoga Sangam was founded in 1952 by Yogi S. A. A. Ramaiah. Yogi Ramaiah is the disciple of Kriya Babaji Nagaraj, the satguru of the order. Born and raised in Tamil, India, Nagaraj was initiated into Kriya Kundalini Pranayam by a sage named Agasthiya who resided at Kuttralam, India. He also traveled to Sri Lanka to study with another Siva Siddhanta teacher under whom he attained enlightenment. He eventually settled in the Himalayas, where he still lives. He has chosen to live quietly and allow his disciples to spread his teachings. The Babaji Yoga Sangam was founded under the guidance of Babaji Nagaraj. It is claimed that Nagaraj was born in 203 C.E. and lives on in defiance of the limitations of death.

Ramaiah became well known in the early 1960s as a result of his submitting to a number of scientific tests in which he demonstrated his control over several body functions, including the ability to vary his body temperature over a 15-degree range. He brought the movement he had founded in India to America in the 1960s. By the early 1970s, 15 centers had been opened across the country with headquarters in Norwalk, California. Sadhana centers, for more intense, live-in practice of kriya yoga, were established in several rural California locations. More recently the Yogi Ramaiah established the first shrine to Ayyappa Swami, a figure in the ancient Hindu holy books, the Puranas, in Imperial City, California. Each December, beginning in 1970, members of the sangam make a pilgrimage from the shrine, which also serves as the American headquarters of the group, to Mount Shasta, 800 miles away in the mountains of northern California. Ramaiah passed away in July 2006 at the age of 83.

Membership: Not reported.

Educational Facilities:

KBYS Holistic Hospital and Colleges of Yoga Therapy and Physiotherapy, Tamil Nadu, India.

Sources:

International Babji Yoga Sangam. www.kriyayoga.org.

Ramaiah, Yogi S. A. A. *Shasta Ayyappa Swami Yoga Pilgrimage*. Imperial City, CA: Pan American Babaji Yoga Sangam, n.d.

International Divine Realization Society

c/o Devanand Yoga Cultural Center, 2285 Sedgwick Ave., No. 102, Bronx, NY 10468

The International Divine Realization Society was founded by H. H. Swami Guru Devanand Saraswati Ji Maharaj, a spiritual teacher from India. Swami Devanand teaches a form of jnana yoga which is practiced by a form of meditation with the use of a mantra. It is Swami Devanand's claim that the use of mantra yoga meditation will give the practitioner a growth of goodwill and stability, improve memory and concentration, bring an awareness of the supreme being, and eliminate psychiatric disorders. The center in New York hosts a complete round of activities including meditation sessions, Sunday puja, hatha yoga classes, and special activities in stress management and natural medicine. Most programs are held in both English and Spanish.

Membership: Not reported.

International Gurukulam

114 E 28th St. #2A, New York, NY 10016

The International Gurukulam was founded by Yogacharya Yogabhaskara Yogiraj Yogashiromani Yogarshi Dileepkumar, popularly known simply as Guru Dileepji. It can be traced to an alternative healing clinic founded by Guru Dileepji's parents in Kottayam, India, in 1957. In 1979 Guru Dileepji expanded and renamed the center, now located in Tripunithura, as the International Gurukulam (A Divine Life Research Center for Yogic Arts, Sports, and Medicines). He later opened a second center at Kothamangalam, India.

Along the way, Guru Dileepji was joined by Yogacharini Mata Nanditaji, a Western yoga practitioner who had studied with a variety of teachers, including Indra Devi, Swami Satchitananda, Swami Vishnu-Devananda, and Swami Bua (who was reportedly 128 years old as of 2007). With Mata Nanditaji'a assistance, in 1999, Guru Dileepji opened the first International Gurukulam center in the West, the Yogabhavan in Brooklyn, New York. That center relocated to New York City in 2004. The same year, he opened an additional Yogabhavan in Cochin, Kerala, India.

The International Gurukulam offers a spectrum of classes in yoga, geared to the individual. Classes include *asanas* (postures and poses) that lead to a full practice of Raja Yoga, including work on breathing, concentration, and meditation.

The International Gurukulam is affiliated with the World Yoga Community and the International Yoga Federation and has strong fraternal ties to the Divine Life Society and the Ramakrishna Mission in India.

Membership: Not reported. There is one center in the United States, which serves as an outpost of the international movement.

Sources:

Yogabhavan International Gurukulam. www.yogabhavan.com/main.asp.

International Meditation Institute

Current address not obtained for this edition.

Alternate Address: International Headquarters: Kullu, H.P. 175 101, Himalayas, India.

The International Meditation Institute grew out of the work of Swami Shyam (b. 1924). As a young man, he realized a state which he termed "Shyam Space," described as a state of pure existence and pure consciousness in which one drops one's identification with the world and identifies with the pure self. This is a form of what is generally termed *advaita vedanta*. The future Swami Shyam was a government career worker when he began to teach out of his experience. In the 1970s he was discovered by two Canadian tourists who invited him to Toronto. His brief visit was extended to more than a year after his papers were stolen, and when he finally returned to India, he had a group of Canadians with him. They gave him the

unofficial title of "Swami". Officially, the title "Yog Shromani" was added to the title of "Swami" by the President of India, Giani Zail Singh, in 1987.

From the original Western center in Montreal, other centers have been founded in Canada, the United States, Europe, New Zealand, Israel, Japan, and Taiwan.

Membership: Not reported.

Sources:

International Meditation Institute. www.shyamspace.com.

Cushman, Anne, and Jerry Jones. *From Here to Nirvana: The Yoga Journal Guide to Spiritual India*. New York: Riverhead Books, 1998.

International Society for Krishna Consciousness (ISKCON)

c/o ISKCON International Ministry of Public Affairs, 1030 Grand Ave., San Diego, CA 92109

The International Society for Krishna Consciousness (ISKCON) is a major representative of that form of devotional Vaishnava Hinduism which grew out of the work of Chaitanya Mahaprabhu (1486–1534?), the famed Bengali saint. Chaitanya advocated a life of intense devotion centered upon the public chanting of the names of God, primarily through the chanting of the Hare Krishna mantra: Hare Krishna, Hare Krishna/Hare Hare, Krishna Krishna/Hare Rama, Hare Rama/Hare Hare, Rama Rama.

ISKCON developed out of the activity of A. C. Bhaktivedanta Swami Prabhupada (1896–1977). Prabhupada was a businessman. He was initiated into the revived Krishna Consciousness movement represented in the Guadiya Mission in 1932. In 1936 his guru told him to take Krishna worship to the West, but he was unable to fulfill his mission to spread the movement until the 1950s. In 1959 he took his vows for the renounced life in the sannyasin order. In 1965 he traveled to America, where he established a movement to spread Krishna Consciousness. ISKCON was founded the following year in New York City. A magazine was begun and a San Francisco center opened in 1967. Besides leading the movement and serving as the initiating guru to the several thousands of adherents, Prabhupada was a prolific translator/author. He produced two series of translations and commentaries on the main scriptures of Krishna Consciousness, *The Srimad Bhagavatam* and the *Caitanya-caritamrita*. His primary work, the one that most new members first encounter, was his translation of and commentary on the Bhagavad-Gita, *The Bhagavad-Gita As It Is*.

The movement grew, though never in the great numbers that its media coverage often suggested. It was a frequent object of media coverage because of its colorful appearance and strange, exotic beliefs and practices. During the 1970s it became one of the major targets for the anti-cult movement.

The central thrust of ISKCON is bhakti yoga, which with this organization takes the form of chanting the Hare Krishna mantra. The chanting is the process for receiving the pure consciousness of God (thought of in his prime incarnations of Krishna and Rama) and dispelling the *maya* or illusion in which the world is immersed. Devotion also includes the following: service to the deity statues found in all Krishna temples; *telok*, markings of the body with clay in 12 places, each representing a name of God; *kirtan*, the public chanting and dancing to Krishna; and eating and distribution of *prasadam*, food (vegetarian) offered to Krishna. Devotees also study much traditional Hindu lore (Vedic culture), the history of bhakti yoga, and the writings of the founder.

As the society has spread, it has gained fame for its festivals and feasts. Each summer one or more international festivals featuring a mass parade honoring Lord Jagannath are held, and everyone is fed a vegetarian meal. Weekly feasts (open to the public) are part of the normal activity of the local temple.

Prior to Prabhupada's death, he appointed a 22-member governing body commission (GBC) which had begun to function in the early 1970s and provided a smooth transition of power in 1977. Included in the GBC were the initiating gurus, that is, those within the movement with the power of initiating new disciples. The initiating gurus are looked to for maintaining high spiritual standards and inspiring others to do so. The GBC provides overall coordination and administrative oversight to the movement, which is divided into a number of zones. The various zones are further divided into different corporations, each independent and autonomous under the management of local teachers and the zonal GBC. There is no longer any central headquarters, although in the major cities and in Vrindavan, India, ISKCON temples are international centers for the movement as the destinations of mass annual pilgrimages. The decentralization has led to the formation of a variety of publishing programs in the several zones.

During the 1980s, ISKCON was hit with a serious controversy between the more conservative elements and those advocating reforms. Crucial to the disagreements were varying opinions on the *guru puja*, the veneration of the guru, which had been an integral part of the daily morning ISKCON ritual while Prabhupada lived. Reform-minded gurus began to question the legitimacy of the current initiating gurus receiving guru puja and began to discontinue it in their zones. Some of the call for reform came as a response to several gurus who had been disciplined for not living according to their vows. Most vocal in the cause of reform was Satsvarupa Dasa Goswami, who authored a number of books on the subject.

Most persistent in defending the guru puja was Kirtananda Swami Bhaktipada, head of the New Vrindaban community in West Virginia (see separate entry). This was one major issue in the 1987 excommunication of Bhaktipada and the reorganization of the temples under him into a separate organization.

Membership: In 2008, ISKCON reported 10,000 temple devotees and 250,000 congregational devotees, with 350 centers, 60 rural communities, 50 schools, and 60 restaurants worldwide.

Periodicals: *Back to Godhead*. Send orders to Box 18928, Philadelphia, PA 19119-0428. • *The ISKCON World Review*. Send orders to 3764 Watseka Ave., Los Angeles, CA 90034. *ISKCON Communications Journal*.

Remarks: In Hawaii, ISKCON experienced a temporary schism when a rival group under Sai Young emerged. Young's followers, known as the Haiku Meditation Center and Krishna Yoga Community, followed Bhaktivedanta's teachings but did not don the saffron robes or shave their heads. The group disbanded in 1971, and ISKCON inherited its members.

In 1983 a former member of the movement, Robin George, was awarded $9,700,000 in a lawsuit against the movement. The amount was later reduced on appeal, and ISKCON reached a settlement with George for an undisclosed amount in 1993.

Sources:

International Society for Krishna Consciousness. www.iskcon.com.

Goswami, Satsvarupa dasa. *Srila Prabhupada-lilamrta*. 6 vols. Los Angeles: Bhaktivedanta Book Trust, 1980–1983.

Judah, J. Stillson. *Hare Krishna and the Counterculture*. New York: John Wiley & Sons, 1974.

Knott, Kim. *My Sweet Lord*. Wellingborough, Northamptonshire: Aquarian Press, 1986.

Prabhupada, Swami A. C. Bhaktivedanta. *Bhagavad-Gita As It Is*. New York: Bhaktivedanta Book Trust, 1972.

Rocheford, E. Burke, Jr. *Hare Krishna Transformed*. New York: New York University Press, 2007.

Isha Foundation

Dhyanalinga Temple, Isha Yoga Center, Semmedu (PO), Coimbatore, India 641 114

The Isha Foundation is a yoga fellowship founded in 1992 by Satguru Jaggi Vasudev (b. 1957). Vasudev was born in Mysore, Karnataka, India, and as a young man graduated from Mysore University. He had also studied yoga since his childhood years under Shri Raghavendra Rao, also known as Malladihalli Swami. Then, at the age of 25, he had a mystical experience that he described as a spontaneous experience of the Self (Divine or Ultimate Consciousness). The experience altered his life and led

him to develop a new form of yoga that he called the Yoga of the Divine and offered as a spiritual science that could lead to a transcending of the body and mind. The ultimate goal was the awareness of the essential divine nature within all human beings. Along the way Vasudev authored four books: *Encounter the Enlightened*, *Dhyanalinga: The Silent Revolution*, *Eternal Echoes*, and *Mystic's Musings*.

Vasudev envisioned the Isha Foundation as an organization that would transmit inner sciences of universal appeal. The operative word in the foundation's name, *Isha*, is understood as the formless primordial source of creation. The foundation offers instruction in the new system of yoga developed by Vasudev, which he renamed Isha Yoga. Vasudev sees it as distilling ancient yogic methods for the modern person. Very early in learning Isha Yoga, the individual is introduced to a process of inner engineering, *Shambhavi Maha Mudra*, a powerful *kriya* (or inner energy process) designed to facilitate deep inner transformation.

The foundation has completed the erection of the Dhyanalinga Yogic Temple, located in a forest at the foothills of the Velliangiri Mountains. Within the temple is a Dhyanalinga. At 13' 9", it is the largest mercury-based *linga* (or stylized phallus, a common a symbol of the deity Shiva) in the world. Vasudev consecrated it in 1999 following three years of intense yogic practice. Believed to be alive, Dhyanalinga provides the spiritual seeker an opportunity to perform yogic practices in intimate proximity to what can be considered a guru.

Above and beyond its yoga teachings, the foundation also sponsors several large-scale human service projects in India aimed at rural revitalization, reforestation, and implementation of an education program designed to assist village schools. These are being carried out through a large volunteer program.

Membership: In 2008, the foundation reported 18 centers in the United States and 2 in Canada. The several programs initiated by the foundation are carried out by more than 250,000 volunteers from more than 150 city-based centers spread worldwide.

Sources:

Information on the Isha Foundation can be found on its various Web sites: www.dhyanalinga.org/about.htm, www.ishafoundation.org, www.ruralrejuvenation.org, www.projectgreenhands.org, www.ishavidhya.org, www.sadhguru.org.

Simone, Cheryl, and Satguru Jaggi Vasudev. *Midnights with the Mystic: A Little Guide to Freedom and Bliss*. Charlottesville, VA: Hampton Roads Publishing Company, 2008.

Vasudev, Satguru Jaggi. *Dhyanalinga: The Silent Revolution*. Coimbatore, India: Isha Foundation, 2000.

———. *Encounter the Enlightened: Conversations with the Master*. New Delhi, India: Wisdom Tree, 2004.

ISKCON Revival Movement

93 St. Marks Pl., New York, NY 10009-5141

Alternate Address: PO Box 1056, Bushey, Great Britain WD23 3XH.

The ISKCON Revival Movement (IRM) is a movement working for the revival and reordering of the larger International Society for Krishna Consciousness (ISKCON), founded by Hindu guru A. C. Bhaktivedanta Swami Prabhupada (1896–1977). The IRM was created in 1999 as a vehicle for ISKCON members who believe that the ISKCON movement has erred in the guru structure it adopted after the death of Prabhupada and thus needs to be exposed and reformed.

Born in in Calcutta, Prabbhupada studied at Scottish Churches' College, was married in 1918, and spent most of his life as a pharmacist and business manager. He was initiated as a disciple of Srila Bhaktisiddhanta Sarasvati Thakur in 1933. In 1965 Prabhupada traveled to the United States to bring the message of Krishna consciousness to the West. He attracted a significant number of followers in New York City, and the movement began to spread to other parts of the country and the world. He died in 1977 in India.

The ISKCON Revival Movement believes that ISKCON disobeyed the will and wishes of Prabhupada in adopting a zonal guru leadership after his death. The IRM has offered signed documents and papers arguing that the leadership in the movement was assigned to 11 gurus—Harikesa Swami, Jayatirtha dasa Adhikari, Hamsaduta Swami, Hrdayananda Gosvami, Ramesvara Swami, Bhagavan dasa Adhikari, Kirtanananda Swami, Tamala Krsna Gosvami, Satsvarupa dasa Gosvami, Bhavananda Gosvami, and Jayapataka Swami—instead of keeping Prabhupada as sole guru. In 2008 there were approximately 70 gurus in the worldwide ISKCON movement.

The IRM was formed through the efforts of longtime ISKCON devotee Krishnakant Desai, a British citizen of Indian ancestry. Krishnakant began researching the issue of guru succession in the late 1980s; his work resulted in initial publication of the *Back to Prabhupada* magazine in 1995. The book *The Final Order* was released the next year. After the governing body commission of ISKCON failed to accept Krishnakant's arguments, he started the ISKCON Reform Group (IRG) which was expanded into the IRM. The group's Web site contains extensive material on the issues related to guru succession.

Membership: In 2008 the movement reported approximately 500 members. The IRM is present in the United States, Canada, and 13 other countries, and has 10 centers.

Periodicals: *Back to Prabhupada.*

Sources:

ISKCON Revival Movement. www.iskconirm.com/.

Krishnakant. *The Final Order*. 1996. Available from www.iskconirm.com/tfo.pdf .

Jean Klein Foundation

Box 2111, Santa Barbara, CA 93120

Jean Klein (d. 1998) was an Eastern European teacher of *advaita*, a teaching of nonduality. According to the advaita, our essential being or consciousness is beyond subject/object duality, beyond the thought process. In the year following the end of World War II, Klein, a musicologist and medical doctor, traveled to India on a spiritual quest. He had been stimulated to go to India by reading some of the writings of Rene Guenon. Within weeks he met a teacher who initiated him into the teachings of advaita vedanta, a teaching shared by such Indian teachers as Ramana Maharshi, Sri Nisargadatta Maharaj, and Atmananda Krishna Menon. He returned to France in 1960 and held dialogues and yoga seminars. His first book, *L'Ultimate Realité*, was published in France in 1968. His first book in English, *Be Who You Are,* appeared in London, England, in 1978.

During the 1980s, Klein visited the United States for seminars and in 1989 he formed the Jean Klein Foundation to spread the teachings of advaita vedanta as presented by Klein. The foundation carries on an active teaching program through seminars held throughout the United States. Third Millennium Publications of Santa Barbara, California, is closely associated with the foundation and publishes Klein's books.

Membership: Not reported.

Periodicals: *Listening, The Jean Klein Foundation Newsletter.*

Sources:

Klein, Jean. *Be Who You Are*. London, England: Watkins, 1978.

———. *The Ease of Being*. Durham, NC: The Acorn Press, 1984.

———. *I Am*. Santa Barbara, CA: Third Millennium Publications, 1989.

Kali Mandir

c/o Kali Mandir Puja Shop, PO Box 4700, Laguna Beach, CA 92652-4700

Founded in 1993 by Elizabeth Usha Harding, author of *Kali the Black Goddess of Dakshineswar*, Kali Mandir was formed to facilitate worship of the Divine Mother in the form of Kali and to make worship available to all. The worship is modeled on the teachings and practice of Sri Ramakrishna and Sri Sarada Devi as established in the Dakshineswar Kali Temple in Calcutta, India. In adopting the Indian Hindu temple ideal, the leaders of the mandir are initially attempting to provide a place of worship for the seeker of God in the form of the Mother, especially in the form of Kali. Kali Mandir does not have a resident guru and is not based on any particular guru's teachings. Rather than seek to convert people away from previously held beliefs, the mandir simply welcomes all.

Daily *pujas* (worship ceremonies), monthly *amavasyas* (New Moon worship), and yearly festivals are led by temple priests Sri Haradhan Chakraborti and Sri Pranab Ghosal. The organization aims to create a tangible spiritual atmosphere through worship, ritual, singing, chanting, volunteer service, reading of scriptures, and spiritual discussions.

A new temple was under construction in Laguna Beach, California, in mid-2008. Each summer the mandir sponsors an annual Kali Puja in Laguna Beach, officiated by the priests from the Dakshineswar Kali Temple in India.

Membership: Kali Mandir has no membership. The organization is financially supported primarily by donations and in part by income from gift shop sales.

Sources:

Kali Mandir. www.kalimandir.org.

Kashi Church Foundation

11155 Roseland Rd., No. 10, Sebastian, FL 32958

The Kashi Church Foundation was founded by Ma Jaya Sati Bhagavati, a spiritual teacher who emerged as a result of an intense experience in the mid-1970s. She had been born Joyce Green into an orthodox Jewish family in Brooklyn, where she grew to adulthood. She married into a Roman Catholic family and settled into life as a housewife. Then in December 1972 she had a vision of someone whom she recognized as Jesus Christ. He subsequently reappeared three more times. Hesitantly at first, she turned for guidance to residents of a nearby Catholic seminary. Then in the spring of 1973 she had a second set of apparitions, this time of a person who called himself Nityananda.

As the apparitions began, she had no knowledge that such a person as Nityananda had actually lived. In fact, Swami Nityananda had been a prominent Hindu guru in India, had initiated a movement later headed by Swami Muktananda, and had an American disciple named Swami Rudrananda who initially brought his teachings to the United States. Nityananda, as he appeared to her, taught her about what he termed *chidakash*, the state in which love and awareness are one. He appeared to her almost daily for a year. He gave her a new name, *Jaya* (Sanskrit for "victory" or "glory"). Green, who began to call herself Joya Santanya, sought out Swami Rudrananda and shortly thereafter discovered Hilda Charlton, an independent spiritual teacher in Manhattan who encouraged her to become a teacher.

The final events in her transformation began on Good Friday 1974, when she began to bleed in a manner similar to Jesus' crucifixion wounds. On Easter Sunday morning, much to the consternation of her Roman Catholic in-laws, she bled profusely from both her hands and her forehead. The stigmata presaged a third set of apparitions, which began a few months later. An older man wrapped in a blanket appeared and introduced himself as her guru, and she was especially drawn to him as he seemed to share her devotion to Jesus. She would later see a picture of someone identified to her as Neem Karoli Baba (who had died the year before). This person had been a prominent Indian spiritual teacher who had deeply influenced Baba Ram Dass, who in turn had first introduced American audiences to his teachings.

Through the mid-1970s, 13 small communities that responded to Joya's teachings were founded. In July 1976 she moved to central Florida with a small group of disciples and founded Kashi Ashram. Over the next few years she regularly visited the several houses and expanded her teaching work to the West Coast. Then in 1978 she fell ill, and many thought she might die. Responding to her condition many of the people living in the cooperative houses moved to Florida. After she regained her health, the people decided to stay at what had become an expanded ashram.

TEACHINGS Ma Jaya Sati Bhagavati teaches a form of *advaita vedanta*, the traditional monistic worldview derived from the Indian scriptures, the Vedas and the Upanishads. Vedanta sees the diversity of the visible world and human experience dissolve in the perception of the Oneness of ultimate reality. This insight is common to mysticism and may be found in esoteric forms of the major faiths and thus provides a meeting ground for people of other faiths.

Residents at Kashi come from different backgrounds and are drawn more by their relationship to Ma as guru than the acceptance of any particular religious beliefs. They also bring varying foundations to the religions in which they were raised. No attempt is made to convert people; rather, the individual's devotion to a particular religion is recognized and nurtured as one expression of the mystical unity. In this manner Kashi is following the tradition of Neem Karoli Baba, who counted members of all the religions of India among his followers. Ma and members of the ashram assumed a prominent role at the centennial Parliament of the World's Religions gathering in Chicago in 1993 as well as the Parliament of World's Religions meeting in 1999 in Capetown, South Africa, and have been among those who arose to continue its work.

Through the 1990s Ma developed an impressive ministry to people affected by AIDS and HIV. Beginning with a small ministry in Los Angeles, southern Florida, New York, and Atlanta, the AIDS-related work has become a dominant element of ashram life. Ma regularly invites terminal AIDS patients to spend the last weeks of their life at the respite home at the ashram in Florida and enjoy the loving care it offers. The AIDS ministry grew out of Anadana into the River Fund, the ashram's community service organization, which facilitates the participation of Kashi members in a variety of service projects in their community, from delivering food for meals-on-wheels recipients to manning the local crisis hotline. As the ashram's ministries have grown and diversified, Ma established the River Fund as Kashi International, devoted to helping people in need. The community also has shown particular concern for ministering to children and has created a quality school to serve both the children of residents and the neighborhood.

ORGANIZATION Kashi is headed and tied together by Ma. The Florida ashram is organized on a semi-communal basis with each adult resident responsible for an equal share of the community's needed support. Most of the members hold jobs outside of the ashram. Residents follow a vegetarian diet. Narcotics, alcohol, and tobacco are forbidden. Family life is encouraged and married couples live together though celibacy is practiced except when couples are trying to have a child.

Members of the community gather daily for *puja* (worship ceremony) in the morning and for *darshan* (gathering with Ma) in the evening. Various different religious festivals are celebrated, especially Christmas and the Durga Puja (a major Hindu festival). Above community spiritual life, each individual is encouraged to follow personal devotional activities. Some are active in local churches.

In the early twenty-first century, Kashi has been developing some of its land in Sebastian, Florida, as a senior adult community called By The River, for adults age 62 years and older.

Membership: In addition to the Florida ashram, Kashi has centers in New York, New York, Los Angeles, California, and Atlanta, Georgia, each providing spiritual, educational, and service programs to its participants. Other programs and affiliated groups are located in the United States, Canada, and Africa. Through its network of thousands of volunteers, the Kashi Foundation touches the lives of 300,000 people worldwide annually.

Educational Facilities:

Kashi Center for Advanced Spiritual Studies.

Sources:

Kashi Ashram. www.kashi.org.

Ma Jaya Sati Bhagavati. *Bones and Ash*. Sebastian, FL: Jaya Press, 1995.

———. *The River*. Roseland, FL: Ganga Press, 1994.

Kripalu Center for Yoga and Health
57 Interlaken Rd., PO Box 309, Stockbridge, MA 01262

The Kripalu Center for Yoga and Health was founded in 1966 as the Yoga Society of Pennsylvania by Amrit Desai, who had learned yoga as a teenager in his native India. Desai came to the United States in 1960 and began teaching yoga while otherwise pursuing a secular career. In 1970, however, a significant moment in his developing work occurred as he was performing his daily yoga practices. He experienced a spontaneous flow of yoga postures in which the innate and autonomous intelligence of his body performed the postures without conscious or willful direction from his mind. Through repetition and study of his experience, he developed a technique by which others could experience the same spontaneous flow. He termed this new technique *Kripalu yoga* in honor of Swami Kripalvanandji, his yoga teacher in India.

In 1971 the first Kripalu residential community was established in Sumneytown, Pennsylvania, as a small retreat where Desai and his students could live the contemplative lifestyle. By 1974, the community had grown in number and became a nonprofit organization known as the Kripalu Yoga Fellowship. In 1975 a retreat center was founded on a 370-acre plot near Summit Station, Pennsylvania, and approximately 170 residents moved into the new facilities. Then in 1983 the community moved to Shadowbrook, a former Jesuit novitiate in Stockbridge, Massachusetts. The ashram offered a full range of yoga and related programs, and many teachers who trained there went forth to found affiliated yoga centers across the United States. By the mid-1990s there were some 2000 certified yoga teachers working in more than 130 affiliated support groups in North America and some 35 countries of Europe and Central America.

The work built around Yogi Desai was prospering. The 270 residents at the ashram in Lenox constituted the largest such yoga center in North America. Then in the fall of 1994 the center's board had to face the accusations of several women that Yogi Desai, who preached a celibate existence, had been forcing himself sexually upon them. In the face of the scandal, and following his admission of guilt, Desai was forced to resign as the spiritual director of the organization, which has since continued under the leadership of the center's board.

The following years led to a restructuring, and by 1999 Kripalu was organized as a nonprofit rather than a religious order. By 2004, the board hired current executive leaders Garrett and Ila Sarley, whose focus was to upgrade aging facilities and strengthen and revitalize programs and outreach. The main focus of Kripalu as it stands today is education and outreach for yoga practice, yoga teacher training, training in ayurvedic practice and massage, as well as the development of several formal schools and institutions.

The center offers yoga retreats, programs, and festivals year-round.

Educational Facilities:

Kripalu School of Ayurveda; Kripalu School of Massage; Institute for Integrated Leadership; Institute for Extraordinary Living; Institute for Integrated Healing.

Membership: Not reported.

Periodicals: *The Kripalu Experience*.

Remarks: Among other disciples of Swami Kripalvanandaji in the United States is Shanti Desai, brother of Yogi Amrit Desai, head of the Shanti Yoga Institute and Yoga Retreat in New Jersey.

Sources:

Kripalu Center for Yoga and Health. www.kripalu.org.

Desai, Amrit. *Guru and Disciple*. Sumneytown, PA: Kripalu Yoga Ashram, 1975.

Gurudev, Sukanya Warren. *The Life of Yogi Amrit Desai*. Summit Station, PA: Kripalu Publications, 1982.

Kripalvanandji, Swami. *Premyatra*. Summit Station, PA: Kripalu Yoga Fellowship, 1981.

———. *Science of Meditation*. Vadodara, Gujarat, India: Sri Dahyabhai Hirabhai Patel, 1977.

MacDowell, Andie, and Isabella Rossellini. "Bad Karma." *Boston* 87, 12 (December 1995): 66–71, 78–92.

Krishnamurti Foundation of America

Box 1560, Ojai, CA 93024-1560

The Krishnamurti Foundation of America was founded in 1969 to protect and disseminate the teachings of Jiddu Krishnamurti, a spiritual teacher who emerged into prominence early in the twentieth century and carried on a unique independent teaching mission until his death in 1986.

Krishnamurti was born May 12, 1895, at Madanapalle, Andhra Pradesh, India, into a Brahmin family. When he was 14 years old he was designated by Annie Besant and Charles W. Leadbeater of the Theosophical Society as the vehicle for the coming world teacher whose appearance they had come to expect in their lifetime. Besant adopted Krishnamurti and took him to England, where she saw to his education and groomed him for his messianic role. In 1911 he was made head of a newly formed organization, the Order of the Star of the East, and through the 1920s he traveled around the world speaking on its behalf.

In 1929, after several years of questioning himself and his role, he dissolved the order, repudiated its claims, and returned all of the assets given to him for its furtherance. Setting the perspective that would dominate his future, he declared, "Truth is a pathless land and you cannot approach it by any path whatsoever, by any religion, by any sect. Truth, being limitless, unconditioned, unapproachable by any path whatsoever, cannot be organized; nor should any organization be formed to lead or to coerce people along any particular path. My only concern is to set humanity absolutely, unconditionally free."

Renouncing any allegiance to caste, nationality, particular religion, or tradition, he spent the rest of his life traveling the world and lecturing until shortly before his death. He suggested that individuals had to free themselves from all fear, conditioning, authority, and dogma through self-knowledge, and that the gaining of such self-knowledge would result in order and psychological mutation. Only this psychological mutation by enough individuals, brought about by self-observation, not by a guru or organized religion, could transform the world. No social engineering would bring a world of goodness, love, and compassion.

His assertion that humans have to be their own guru and his rejection of all authority, including his own, attracted many people. A number of intellectuals and religious leaders engaged him in dialogue, and scientists discussed the bridging of science and mystical thought with him.

Krishnamurti was optimistic about the possibilities of education that emphasized the integral cultivation of the mind and heart and not just the intellect. Such education would allow students to discover the conditioning that distorts their thinking. To this end, he led in the founding of many schools in the United States, Great Britain, and India. The Krishnamurti Foundation of America supports the Oak Grove School in Ojai, California.

Krishnamurti also established foundations in those countries where support for his work was manifest. During his lifetime, the foundations provided a focus for his teaching work and assisted in the publication and dissemination of his teachings. In the years since his death their role of protecting and continuing the process of making his material available has come to the fore. Krishnamurti's lectures and dialogues became the sources of numerous books and booklets, and during the last year of his life his lectures were taped on both audio and video.

The Krishnamurti Foundation of America works cooperatively with other foundations around the world including: Krishnamurti Educational Centre of Canada, the Krishnamurti Foundation Trust, the Fundacion Krishnamurti Latinoamericana, and the Krishnamurti Foundation of India. The Krishnamurti Foundation of America houses a library and archives of Krishnamurti's talks and related materials. Krishnamurti's teachings are available via streaming video and audio presentations through www.kfa.org or jkrishnamurti.org.

Educational Facilities:

Oak Grove Teacher's Academy, Ojai, California.

Membership: In 1995 there were approximately 1,000 friends of the foundation who contribute to its work.

Periodicals: *Newsletter*.

Remarks: After Krishnamurti's death, the foundation announced that it would continue to facilitate the distribution of Krishnamurti's tapes and books and to channel support to Oak Grove School.

Sources:

Krishnamurti Foundation of America. www.kfa.org.

Alcyone [Jiddu Krishnamurti]. *At the Feet of the Master*. Adyar, India: Theosophical Publishing House, n.d.

Krishnamurti, Jiddu. *Commentaries on Living*. 3 vols. Wheaton, IL: Theosophical Publishing House, n.d.

Krishnamurti, Jiddu, and David Bohm. *The Ending of Time*. San Francisco, CA: Harper & Row, 1985.

Lutyens, Mary. *Krishnamurti, The Years of Awakening*. New York: Farrar, Straus & Giroux, 1975.

———. *Krishnamurti, The Years of Fulfillment*. London: J. Murray, 1983.

Kriya Yoga Centers

PO Box 924615, Homestead, FL 33092-4615

Alternate Address: International Headquarters: Nimpur, PO Jagatpur, Cuttack 754021, Orissa, India.

The Kriya Yoga Centers were founded by Swami Hariharananda Giri, a teacher of kriya yoga from the same lineage as Swami Paramahansa Yogananda, founder of Self-Realization Fellowship. Swami Yogananda was a disciple of Sri Yukteswar who settled in Puri in the state of Orissa, India, in 1906, and built an *ashram* (religious community). Yogananda succeeded Yukteswar as president of the ashram. He was succeeded in 1936 by Sreemat Swami Satyananda. In 1970 Satyananda was succeeded by Swami Hariharananda Giri (b. 1911), who had been associated with the ashram for many years. Hariharananda spread the work of the ashram through India and in 1974 made his first trip to the West, to Switzerland. By the end of the decade he had several ashrams in Europe and in New York City. He continued to travel to the West periodically until his death in 2002. Today, the organization is led by Hariharananda's successor, Paramahamsa Prajnanananda.

Kriya yoga is a technique imparted to disciples in initiation. It is based on breath control, which is believed to bring about God realization by turning attention from the outward to the inner self. It transforms the life force into divine force by magnetizing the psychic centers believed to exist along the human spine.

The organization has 10 centers in the United States and others in Canada, Australia, Brazil, and the United Kingdom.

Membership: Not reported.

Periodicals: *Soul Culture: A Journal of Kriya Yoga*. Available from PO Box 9127, Santa Rosa, CA 95404.

Sources:

Kriya Yoga Centers. www.kriya.org.

Hariharananda Giri, Swami. *Isa Upanishad*. Kriya Yoga Ashrams, 1985.

Kriya Yoga Tantra Society

633 Post St., Ste. 647, San Francisco, CA 94109

Amid the larger movement of Hinduism to North America, tantric forms have also come and a noticeable tantric movement has emerged around a set of independent tantric teachers. Several have established organizations propagating tantra, among them the Kriya Yoga Tantra Society. The society was founded by Andre O. Rathel, better known by his spiritual name, Sunyata Saraswati. Sunyata was a student of martial arts, the occult, and tantra. He traveled to India, where he studied with Satyananda Saraswati, the most important of the modern tantric teachers at his Bihar School of Yoga in Bengal. In the early 1980s he founded Beyond Beyond in Los Angeles, California. The Kriya Yoga Tantra Society supersedes Beyond Beyond.

While he has studied with additional tantric teachers, as well as Chinese Taoist masters in Hong Kong, Sunyata believes the kriya tantra tradition to be the purest and most elevating. This tradition is ascribed to Babaji, the legendary Himalayan teacher who Swami Paramahansa Yogananda first introduced to the West in his kriya yoga teachings, though Yogananda did not emphasize the left-hand tantrism as has Sunyata.

According to the society, the goal of tantric practice is to generate intense sexual energy through tactile sensations and yogic practices. That energy (usually termed *kundalini*) is then transmitted to the brain, and as the brain comes to life, the individual can perceive the Divine Order.

The society offers a wide variety of programs covering the range of tantric insight, and Sunyata travels the country giving workshops. Retreats are offered at a secluded center in Hawaii. He has also authored a basic text on the art of tantric union.

Membership: Not reported.

Periodicals: *Jyoti.*

Sources:

Rathel, Andre O., and Annette B. White. *Tantra Yoga: The Sexual Path of Inner Joy and Cosmic Fulfillment.* Hollywood, CA: Beyond Beyond, 1981.

Saraswati, Sunyata. *Activating the Five Cosmic Energies.* San Francisco: Kriya Jyoti Tantra Society, 1987.

Saraswati, Sunyata, and Bodhi Avinsha. *The Jewel in the Lotus: The Art of Tantric Union.* San Francisco: Kriya Jyoti Tantra Society, 1987.

Kundalini Research Foundation

Box 2248, Darien, CT 06820

Gopi Krishna (1903–1984) was a Hindu master of kundalini yoga. After 17 years of meditation, he experienced the kundalini at the age of 34. He spent the years since exploring the nature of kundalini and has produced 14 books on the subject. In 1970, American Gene Kietter organized the Kundalini Research Foundation to disseminate Gopi Krishna's books and writings and to continue his research.

Kundalini is the name given the divine energy believed to be lodged at the base of the spine. Often pictured as a coiled snake, the awakened energy travels up the spine and remolds the brain. It is identified with *prana*, the nerve energy which effects altered states of consciousness. The awakened energy is the biological basis of genius. Kundalini, according to Krishna, is concentrated in the sex energy. Awakening the kundalini redirects the prana from the sexual regions to the brain. In the awakening, a fine biological "essence" rises from the reproductive region to the brain through the spinal column. The flow can be felt behind the palate from the middle point of the tongue to the root and can be objectively measured.

In 2008 the foundation described its mission and purpose as promoting the scientific investigation of enlightenment, inspiration, genius, and the evolution of consciousness.

Membership: The foundation is not a membership organization. There are affiliated groups in India, Switzerland, and Canada.

Sources:

Kundalini Research Foundation. www.kundaliniresearch.org.

Irving, Darrel. *Serpent of Fire: A Modern View of Kundalini.* York Beach, ME: Samuel Weiser, 1954. 229 pp.

Krishna, Gopi. *The Awakening of Kundalini.* New York: E. P. Dutton, 1975.

———. *The Biological Basis of Religion and Genius.* New York: Harper & Row, 1972.

———. *The Goal of Consciousness Research.* Darien, CT: Friends of Gopi Krishna, 1998.

———. *The Riddle of Consciousness.* New York: Kundalini Research Foundation, 1976.

———. *The Secret of Yoga.* New York: Harper & Row, 1972.

———. *The Wonder of the Brain.* Noroton Heights, CT: Kundalini Research Foundation, 1987.

———. *Yoga, a Vision of Its Future.* New Delhi, India: Kundalini Research and Publication Trust, 1978.

Life Bliss Foundation

9720 Central Ave., Montclair, CA 91763

The Life Bliss Foundation is an international community that has grown up around the life and work of Paramahamsa Nithyananda. Nithyananda was born in 1978 in Tiruvannamalai in South India and as a youth showed an inclination toward spiritual practices. He engaged in meditation and yoga and studied the Tantra, Vedanta, and Shaivite philosophies. As a college student, he completed a degree in mechanical engineering. In the early and mid-1990s he freely wandered the sacred Arunchala Mountain (made famous in the West by its association with Ramana Maharshi [1879–1950]) and studied with a variety of teachers, including one of Maharshi's students. By the age of 22 he was considered to have gained the ultimate state of consciousness, termed *nithyananda* or eternal bliss. His inspiring and winsome personality soon drew followers to him, and Nithyananda extended his influence by allowing himself to be examined by scientists who were studying altered states of consciousness.

As Paramahamsa Nithyananda emerged as a teacher in the late 1990s, he founded the Life Bliss Foundation, which grew at a rapid rate in India. Early in the new century he began to travel the world, resulting in the formation of a number of meditation centers in different countries. In 2005 the Vedic Temple in Duarte (near Pasadena), California, was opened. This now serves as the Western headquarters for the foundation.

Nithyananda teaches that the goal of life is self-realization and that an effect of such realization is intense joy and bliss. To that end, he teaches his students the technique of Life Bliss Meditation (LBM), described as a simple and natural procedure through which to connect the meditator to their inner resources. Practice frees up creativity, energy, intelligence, and bliss. Nithyananda also teaches Nithya Yoga, a form of Ashtanga Yoga that he developed from his early study with Raghupati Yogi. He came to believe that Raghupati Yogi was a reincarnation of Patanjali (generally recognized as the founder of yoga).

Membership: Not reported. As of 2008, Life Bliss centers are found in 33 countries, including Canada, Mexico, New Zealand, Australia, Singapore, Taiwan, Kenya, France, and Italy. Centers are located across the United States.

Sources:

Life Bliss Foundation. www.lifebliss.org/.

Life Bliss Meditation. www.lifeblissmeditation.org/intro.htm.

Nithya Yoga. www.nithyayoga.org/.

Nithyananda (Glimpses from the Biography of Paramahamsa Nithyananda). Bangalore, India: Life Bliss Foundation, 2006.

Life Mission

c/o Kirit N. Shah, 936 Commons Rd., Naperville, IL 60563

Alternate Address: c/o Mehul H. Patel, 515 Merril Lane, Peachtree City, GA 30236.

Life Mission (or more fully, the Lakulish International Fellowship's Enlightenment Mission) was founded in 1993 by Swami Rajarshi Muni, a yoga teacher and a student of Swami Kripalvanandji (1913–1981), best known in the West as the teacher of Yogis Amrit and Shanti Desai. In the 1970s, Kripalvanandji focused his attention on the task, given to him by his guru, of reviving Indian culture, especially its cultural and moral values. He envisioned an expansive program of yoga education, and to that end Swami Rajarshi Muni drew up plans for a yoga institute, outlined its curriculum, and trained its first teachers. Kripalvanandji inaugurated the Lakulish Yoga Vidyalay (Lakulish Institute of Yoga) in 1976. Lakulish is the reputed ancient founder of the Pashupata sect of Shaivism; some see him as the real founder of yoga (rather than Patanajli).

Once the institute was set in motion, Swami Rajarshi Muni retreated into seclusion until 1993, when he had a vision of Lord Lakulish, who asked him to pick up the task left unfinished by Kripalvanandji. In response to this vision, Swami Rajarshi Muni established the Life Mission. The Mission has four objectives: to work for spiritual and cultural awakening around the globe; to promote the practice of yoga; to direct people toward the highest values; and to serve all humanity.

The Life Mission sees itself as an international fellowship that includes all who have received initiation from either Swami Kripalvanandji or Swami Rajarshi Muni; those who join and participate in the activities at the mission's centers; and those rendering services in the work of the Mission. It is organized into two basic wings: renunciates (monks) and non-renunciate (lay) members, all of whom follow a code of conduct that includes simple rules concerning goodness and devotion. Also enjoined upon members is a daily set of devotions built around the practice of *japa* (mantra) yoga, utilizing the mantra given during initiation. Renunciate members strive to live a life in seclusion and to pursue a more intensive form of the practice of yoga.

Since its founding, the Life Mission has spread outside India to Canada, Australia, the United Kingdom, and the United States.

Membership: Not reported.

Sources:

Life Mission. www.lifemission.org.

Rajarshi Muni, Swami. *Classical Hatha Yoga*. Gujarat, India: Life Mission Publications, 2007.

————. *Divine Body through Yoga*. Gujarat, India: Life Mission Publications, 2007.

————. *Yoga*. Gujarat, India: Life Mission Publications, 2005.

Light of Sivananda-Valentina, Ashram of

3475 Royal Palm Ave., Miami Beach, FL 33140

The Ashram of the Light of Sivananda-Valentina was established in the early 1960s by Sivananda-Valentina, a guru whose name came from the experience of merging her consciousness with that of her teacher, Swami Sivananda Saraswati (1887–1963), the famous guru from Rishikish, India. Sivananda taught integral yoga, a combination of the several aspects of yoga with some attention to hatha yoga, the physical postures (or *asanas*) as preparation for the higher disciplines of yoga.

Sivananda-Valentina followed the integral yoga tradition, stressing particular aspects. For example, she emphasized the mystical aspect of performing the yoga asanas which makes them more than a therapeutic exercise. She also concentrated on nada yoga, the yoga of sound, and the use of music—the singing of *bhajans* (devotional songs) forms an important part of *satsangs* (student gatherings with their guru).

A weekly round of yoga and meditation classes, informal prayer classes, and Wednesday evening meditation were undergirded with periodic celebrations, many observed from those of the world's religions (Wesak, Christmas, Chanukah, etc.).

Membership: Not reported.

Sources:

Light of Sivananda-Valentina. lightsv.org.

The Heart and Wisdom of Sivananda-Valentina. 5 vols. Miami Beach, FL: Light of Sivananda-Valentina, 1970–1973.

Sivananda-Valentina. *Meditations at Dawn*. Miami Beach, FL: Light of Sivanada-Valentina, 1977.

Wings of Sivananda-Valentina. Miami Beach, FL: Ashram of the Light of Sivananda-Valentina, 1976.

Lokenath Divine Life Fellowship

c/o Mr. Paul Juneja, 211 Gunther Ln., Belle Chase, LA 70037

Alternate Address: Lokenath Divine Life Mission, P-591 Purna Das Rd., Calcutta 700 029, India.

The Lokenath Divine Life Mission was founded in 1987 by Swami Shuddhananda (b. 1949), a swami who has become famous for his social service work in Calcutta, India. Frequently compared to Mother Teresa, he has led in the founding of a variety of schools and medical services, and a number of economic ventures aimed at improving the life of city residents. As a young man, he had had a series of visions of the nineteenth-century saint Baba Lokenath. In the meantime he had become a professor of business at Hyderabad University. He eventually quit his job, wandered in the Himalayas for several years, and then opened the mission, in which he combines the spiritual teaching with social outreach in a manner reminiscent of Swami Sivananda Saraswati of Rishikish, the founder of the Divine Life Society.

In the 1990s, Swami Shuddhananda traveled to the United States to share his spirituality and information about his work in India. A small number of American disciples have begun to appear.

Membership: Not reported.

Sources:

Cushman, Anne, and Jerry Jones. *From Here to Nirvana*. New York: Riverhead Books, 1998. 399 pp.

Lovers of Meher Baba

c/o Meher Spiritual Center, 10200 Hwy. 17 N, Myrtle Beach, SC 29572

Meher Baba (1894–1969) was an Indian spiritual master born Merwan Sheriar Irani of Zoroastrian parents living in Pune, India. Baba is believed by his followers to be the avatar of the age. As a young man, he met Hazrat Babajan (b. 1931), a Muslim woman considered by some to be one of the five *perfect masters* (i.e., spiritually enlightened or "God-realized" persons) of the age. From her he received what he described as self-realization. According to Baba, the five perfect masters are always responsible for unveiling the avatar when he comes. Thus, in 1921, the last master, Upasani Maharaj, folded his hands and said, "Merwan, you are the Avatar; I salute you."

That same year he gathered his first disciples, who began to call him Meher Baba, which means "compassionate father." In 1924 he opened a permanent colony near Ahmednagar, India, called Meherabad. There he established a free hospital and clinic for the poor, and a free school for students of all creeds and castes. In 1925, he began observing silence, which he maintained for the rest of his life. For many years he communicated by pointing to the letters of the alphabet painted on a wooden board. In the last period of his life, he relied on hand gestures alone. Baba asserted that he kept silent in order to speak the Word of God in every heart. He also said that enough words had been spoken and it was now time to live God's words.

Baba came to the West, including the United States, for the first time in 1931. Some of the Westerners he met on this and subsequent trips became disciples and went to live and work with him in India. His number of followers in the West grew steadily, spurred by his occasional visits (he made a total of six trips during his lifetime).

Baba said that he had not come to establish a new religion or sect, but rather to awaken people to the love of God. He declared himself the avatar, the same "ancient one" who has come age after age as Zoroaster, Rama, Krishna, Buddha, Jesus, and Muhammad, to renew divine love in the world. He also indicated that his advent required that he shed blood in both the East and the West, which, it is claimed, occurred in two automobile accidents: one in the United States (1952) and one in India (1956). He stated that suffering was a necessary part of his mission as avatar to bring about what he called a new humanity. He spent much of his life in service to others, especially the poor, the lepers, and those he termed *masts* or God-intoxicated. He considered these activities to be outward manifestations of transforming consciousness by awakening humanity to the oneness of all life. According to Baba, God was within every living thing and the goal of all life was to become one with God through love.

Because Baba said that his only message was of divine love, people who follow him are often called "lovers of Meher Baba." Over the years many have been inspired to become Meher Baba lovers though there is no formal organization or membership. In the 1950s, many Americans came into contact with Meher Baba during his three visits to Meher Spiritual Center in Myrtle Beach, South Carolina, a place he called "my home in the West." Today, the center and his tomb shrine in Meherabad, India, have become places of pilgrimage for thousands of Meher Baba lovers each year. Groups of followers gather informally throughout North America, India, Europe, and Australia. There are no set practices or creeds, and no formal organization to join. Meetings usually consist of sharing Meher Baba's love through film, music, discussion, and readings from his discourses.

Membership: Since there is no formal membership, estimates of the number of Meher Baba's followers varies widely. The number of newsletters and centers suggest that there may be some 10,000 in the United States, Europe, and Australia, and hundreds of thousands in India.

Periodicals: *Glow International*.

Remarks: With in the larger body of Baba lovers, there is one special close-knit group called Sufism Reoriented. This group derives from the original Sufi groups organized early in the century by Hazrat Inayat Khan (1882–1927), founder of the Sufi Order International. Khan appointed Rabia Martin of San Francisco, California, his successor, an appointment not recognized by members in Europe largely because Martin was female. Toward the end of her life, Martin heard of Meher Baba and began to correspond with him. She became convinced that he was the *Qutb*, that is, the hub of the spiritual universe in Sufi understanding. Though Martin never met Baba, her successor, Ivy Oneita Duce, did. He confirmed her succession, but more importantly, in 1952 during a trip to Myrtle Beach, South Carolina, Meher Baba presented the group with a new plan contained in a document titled "Chartered Guidance from Meher Baba for the Reorientation of Sufism as the Highway to the Ultimate Universalized."

Within Sufism Reoriented, the Sufi path begins in submission and obedience to the murshid as the arm of Baba. For the student, there must be a need to know that God exists, to be able to discriminate between the real and the unreal, to be indifferent to externals, and to be ready to gain the six mental attitudes: control over thoughts, outward control, tolerance, endurance, faith, and balance.

Sources:

Baba, Meher. *Discourses*. Myrtle Beach, SC: Sheriar Press, 1987.

———. *God Speaks: The Theme of Creation and Its Purpose*. New York: Dodd, Mead, and Company, 1973.

Davy, Kitty. *Love Alone Prevails: A Study of Life with Meher Baba*. Myrtle Beach, SC: Sheriar Press, 1981.

Duce, Ivy Oneita. *How a Master Works*. Walnut Creek, CA: Sufism Reoriented, 1975.

Hopkinson, Tom, and Dorothy Hopkinson. *Much Silence: Meher Baba, His Life and Work*. New York: Dodd, Mead, and Company, 1975.

Ma Yoga Shakti International Mission

114-41 Lefferts Blvd., South Ozone Park, NY 11420

The Ma Yoga Shakti International Mission was founded in 1979 by Ma Yoga Shakti Saraswati, an educator, reformer, philosopher, renunciate, and guru. Her followers have considered her primarily as a loving mother. Saraswati has traveled internationally and established centers in India, England, and the United States and now spends her time traveling between them. In her teachings, presented in a number of books she has written, she emphasizes the unity of *bhakti*, *gyaan*, *karma*, and raja yoga for self-unfoldment and the adaptability of the ancient wisdom to modern life. Her centers offer regular devotional services and yoga and meditation classes, workshops, and retreats.

Membership: In 2008 the mission reported centers in South Ozone Park, New York, and Palm Bay, Florida, as well as in the United Kingdom and India.

Periodicals: *Yoga Shakti Mission Newsletter*.

Sources:

Yogashakti Mission. www.yogashakti.org.

Chetanaschakti, Guru. *Guru Pushpanjali*. Calcutta: Yogashakti Mission Trust, 1977.

Yogashakti, Ma. *Yoog Vashishtha*. Gondia, India: Yogashakti Mission, [1970].

Yogashakti Saraswati, Ma. *Prayers & Poems from Mother's Heart*. Melbourne, FL: Yogashakti Mission, 1976.

———, trans. *Shree Satya Narayana Vrata Katha*. Melbourne, FL: Yogashakti Mission, n.d.

Mahayog Foundation

51 E 42nd St. #521, New York, NY 10017

The Mahayog Foundation supports the teaching of Mahayogi Pilot Baba. As a young man Babaji, as he is popularly known, joined the Indian Air Force and as a wing commander fought in India's 1965 and 1971 wars with Pakistan. His career in the air force led him to question his life, and after the 1971 war he resigned his commission and took up the renounced life of a yogi. He had concluded that no religion could give absolute peace, nor could any political organization impart peace.

In his search for peace he came to advocate inward exploration. The deeper one goes within, the purer the sources of consciousness that are found. When the center is reached, the individual reaches the center of the universe. Then and there wisdom unfolds and the individual become a realized one, and the self is liberated.

According to Babaji, his work is an enquiry into the ultimate truths that he teaches, including that the soul exists after death and transmigrates to another form of life or dissolves into the universe. He does not see himself as teaching a new religion but as showing his followers a path and offering himself as a bridge leading to the self's true destination, one's inner self. The path he outlines leads from "misery to happiness, from bondage to libration, from ignorance to enlightenment, and from this world to yourself."

Babaji established his primary center in northern India in the Himalayan Mountains. He has several centers in India and two overseas, one in Japan and one in New York, the latter being his one North American outpost.

Membership: Not reported. There is one center in New York City.

Sources:

Mahayog Foundation. www.pilotbaba.org/.

Mata Amritanandamayi Center

10200 Crow Canyon Rd., Castro Valley, CA 94552

Alternate Address: International Headquarters: Mata Amritanandamayi Mission Trust, Amritapuri P.O., Kollam DT., Kerala, India 690 525.

The Mata Amritanandamayi Center was established in 1987 as an outgrowth of the worldwide ministry of Mataji "Amma" Amritanandamayi (b. 1953), an Indian spiritual teacher. A devoted worshipper of Krishna from childhood, at the age of seven she began to compose *bhajans* (devotional songs) to him. She so completely identified with God, that she was able to manifest any aspect or form of the Deity and would assume the mood of Krishna or Devi (the Divine Mother) in order to facilitate devotion. Gradually during the 1970s, people began to recognize Amritanandamayi as a realized (enlightened) soul and her father gave her the family land upon which to build an *ashram* (religious community). Since 1988, she has built a number of temples, called Brahmastanams or the Abode of the Absolute, in which four deities are installed as part of a single image representing the principle of the Unity of God.

Amritanandamayi teaches a form of *bhakti*, or devotional practice, built around her singing and meditation. She believes that all religions lead to the same goal; hence, meditation upon any of the prominent deity figures, including Jesus, is acceptable.

In 1987 Amritanandamayi made her first trip to the West, a trip prepared by a small number of Western devotees who had encountered her in India. She tours the United States, Japan, and Australia.

Humanitarian efforts are central to the center and focus on care for the needy. The organization runs an orphanage as well as elderly care homes, and other efforts offer food and health care for those in need.

Membership: In 2008 there were three regional centers in the United States in California, New Mexico, and Michigan, with more than 80 affiliated satsang groups throughout the country. Additional centers are found in Canada, South America, India, Europe, Asia, Africa, Australia, and the Middle East.

Periodicals: *Immortal Bliss* (Published in the U.S.) • *Matruvani* (Published in the U.S.).

Sources:

Mata Amritanandamayi Center. www.amma.org.

Amritanandamayi, Mataji. *Awaken Children!* 2 vols. Vallickavu, Kerala, India: Mata Amritanandamayi Mission Trust, 1989ndash;1990.

————. *Bhajanamritam: Devotional Songs*. Vallickavu, Kerala, India: Mata Amritanandamayi Mission Trust, 1987.

Balagopal. *The Mother of Sweet Bliss*. Vallickavu, Kerala, India: Mata Amritanandamayi Mission Trust, 1985.

"Holy Woman Brings the Mother Spirit to the West." *Hinduism Today* 9, no. 4 (July 1987): 1, 15.

Matri Satsang

Current address not obtained for this edition.

Matri Satsang is an organization of devotees of Sri Anandamayi Ma (1896–1982), one of the most prominent gurus in twentieth-century India. Born Nirmala Sundari in a Bengali Brahmin family, she had little schooling and was married at the age of 13. Five years later she went to live with her husband. Her husband recognized her as an unusual person; as her mystical nature clearly emerged, he became her disciple. Her ecstatic state attracted others, and in 1929 her followers built an *ashram* (religious community) for her. She began to travel widely around India. A second ashram was built at Dehradun, India, in 1932. As the number of ashrams grew, Shree Shree Anandamayee Sangha was formed to administer them.

Anandamayi Ma did not lecture, but would answer questions put to her by seekers. Her writings consisted mainly of letters answering similar inquiries. Excerpts were later gathered into books. Anandamayi Ma supported traditional Hinduism and had no new message. Disciples seem to have been attracted to her because of the awakenings they had in her presence and the wisdom they attributed to her because of her answers to their questions.

Matri Satsang began in 1974 in Sacramento, California, as a point of focus for North American disciples of Anandamayi Ma. A small group, they see their task as supplying the world with materials, primarily those published in India by the Sangha, that communicate Anandamayi Ma's presence through her words and the books of those who knew her. Devotees of Anandamayi Ma are scattered around the world.

Sources:

Anandamayi Ma, Sri. *Matri Vani*. 2 vols. Varnasi, India: Shree Shree Anandamayee Charitable Society, 1977.

————. *Sad Vani*. Calcutta, India: Shree Shree Anandamayee Charitable Society, 1981.

Lipski, Alexander. *Life and Teachings of Sri Anandamayi Ma*. Delhi, India: Motilal Banaridass, 1977.

Matri Darshan: Ein Photo-Album Uber Shri Ananda Ma. Seegarten, Germany: Mangalam Verlag S. Schang, 1983.

Singh, Khushwant. *Gurus, Godmen, and Good People*. New Delhi, India: Orient Longman, 1975.

Metamorphosis League for Monastic Studies

4130 SW 117th Ave., Ste. 171, Beaverton, OR 97005

The Metamorphosis League for Monastic Studies was founded in 1987 by Kailasa Chandra Das (birth name, Mark Goodwin), formerly a member of the International Society for Krishna Consciousness (ISKCON; see separate entry). The league was established at a time of intense controversy within ISKCON over the role of the leadership status of those individuals who had been appointed initiating gurus by founder A. C. Bhaktivedanta Swami Prabhupada. The league provides guidance for aspirants so they can come to a point of understanding about the nature of the guru (teacher, spiritual guide) and decide who might be a genuine guru. A bona fide guru must be a self-realized Vaishnava, that is, a devotee of Vishnu, who has realized the Supreme Personality of Godhead (i.e., Krishna).

Members of the league are advised to avoid both the wild card guru, the charismatic figure whose own personality and personal attributes become the center of attention, and the institutional guru, who derives authority from the group in which s/he functions and operates as an agent of the governing body of that institution. The genuine guru, of which Swami Prabhupada is the prime example, derives authority from God, and that authority is manifest in the purity of his/her life.

The league follows the beliefs and practices as transmitted by A. C. Bhaktivedanta Swami Prabhupada. Members must be vegetarians and do not use any intoxicating substances. They cannot be associated with ISKCON or gurus or groups that are considered bogus. Kailasa Chandra Das has published several booklets covering the major emphases of the league.

Membership: In 1995 the league reported nine members.

Moksha Foundation

PO Box 2360, Lenox, MA 01240

The Moksha Foundation was founded in 1976 as the Self-Enlightenment Meditation Society by Bishwanath Singh, known by his religious name Tantracharya Nityananda. Nityananda began studying yoga at the age of seven. He became a student of Shri Anandamurti and eventually served as a monk with the Ananda Marga Yoga Society. In 1969 he realized that he was a siddha yogi in his previous incarnation and that he had been reincarnated in this life to teach meditation and yoga. He left the Ananda Marga Yoga Society and began independent work, eventually establishing centers in India and England. He also renounced his vows as a monk and married.

In 1973 Nityananda moved to Boulder, Colorado, and established the Self-Enlightenment Meditation Society. The center served as a residence for several of his closest students. He taught meditation, tantric yoga philosophy, and lathi, a martial art, and offered personal instruction and initiation for his followers. From his Colorado headquarters he regularly journeyed to meet with students in Chicago, Minneapolis, New York, and Los Angeles.

In 1981 Nityananda traveled to Europe on a speaking tour. While on the Continent, he was invited to lecture in Sweden. After leaving the plane in Stockholm, he disappeared. His body was found several months later; he had been murdered. Mira Sussman, a resident student at the Boulder center, succeeded to leadership of the foundation and has continued the program initiated by Nityananda.

Membership: Not reported. At the time of Nityananda's death in 1981 he had approximately 50 students in Boulder, with other groups in several U.S. cities. The centers previously founded in London and in Bihar, India, continued, and he regularly visited them.

Periodicals: *The Tantric Way.*

Mother Meera Society
C.P. 38, Ste-Justine-de-Newton, Quebec, Canada J0P 1T0
Alternate Address: International Headquarters: Mother Meera, Oberdorf 4a, 65599 Dornburg-Thalheim, Germany.

The Mother Meera Society was founded in Canada in the early 1980s by disciples of Mother Meera, an Indian spiritual leader believed by followers to be an incarnation of the Divine Mother, one of several currently present on earth. She was born Kamala Reedy in 1960 in a small village in Andhra Pradesh, in southern India. Her family were not religious people and she was given no religious training and had no guru. However, at the age of six she first entered that trance-like state called *samadhi*. When she was 14, her uncle and leading disciple, B. V. Reddy, noted her spiritual activities and took her to the ashram of Sri Aurobindo in Ponticherry. She told of receiving visionary guidance from Aurobindo and his colleague, the Mother. As might be expected, she was not accepted by many at the ashram, and she left after a short stay and began holding *darshan* (sessions in which she met with her followers) throughout India.

In 1979 she left India with her uncle for Europe and a side trip to Canada, where the initial Mother Meera Society was formed. In 1983, due to her uncle's illness, she settled in Thalheim, a small town near Frankfurt, Germany, where she has since resided. Her uncle died in 1985. She made her first trip to the United States in May 1989 to attend a conference at Hobart and William Smith Colleges.

Mother Meera describes her work as that of the Cosmic Shakti, to bring down the light of Paramatma to prepare humanity for spiritual transformation. Not known for a specific body of teachings, disciples revere her for the transformations and healings they have experienced in her presence. She offers a simple discipline to people: "Remember the Divine in everything you do. If you have time, meditate. Offer everything to the Divine. Everything good or bad, pure or impure. This is the best and quickest way." Devotion to Mother Meera has especially spread through the writing of Andrew Harvey, a professor at Hobart and William Smith Colleges, who has written a book about his encounter with her in the late 1970s.

Membership: Not reported.

Sources:
Mother Meera Darshan Calgary. www.mothermeeradarshancalgary.com.

Adilakshmi. *The Mother.* 2nd edition. Thalheim Germany: n.p., 1995.

Brown, Mick. *The Spiritual Tourist: A Personal Odyssey through the Outer Reaches of Belief.* London: Bloomsbury, 1998.

Cox, Christine, and Jeff Cox. "Germany's Meera." *Hinduism Today* 11, 4 (April 1989): 1, 18.

Harvey, Andrew. *Hidden Journey.* New York: Henry Holt, 1991.

———. Harvey, Andrew. *The Return of the Mother.* Berkeley, CA: Frog, 1995.

Mother Meera. *Answers.* 2 vols. Ithaca, NY: Meeramma Publications, 1991.

Narayanananda Universal Yoga Trust
c/o N. U. Yoga Ashram, W 7041 Olmstead Rd., Winter, WI 54869
Alternate Address: International Headquarters: N. U. Yoga Ashrama, Gylling, DK 8300 Odder, Denmark.

Narayanananda Universal Yoga Trust was founded by Sri Swami Narayanananda (1902–1988) in 1967 in Rishikesh, India. In 1929 he renounced the world, became a monk, and then went to the Himalayas in search of God-realization. After a mental struggle, he attained Nirvikalpa Samadhi (Cosmic Consciousness) in 1933. After this struggle, he remained in seclusion until 1947, when he witnessed the bloodshed between the Hindus and Muslims during the partition of India. He then focused his energies on writing books about religion, philosophy, mind-control, and Kundalini Shakti. He began to work and guide spiritual seekers during the 1950s and 1960s. In 1971 he went to Europe to visit his international headquarters in Denmark.

Narayanananda uses the term "The Universal Religion" for his teachings. This religion is based on his perception of Ultimate Truth and contains both philosophy and practical spiritual advice. It states that there is only one God, which can be compared to the center of a circle, while the many different religions of the world are like the radii of a circle—all ultimately reaching the same goal. With its motto: "Help a man from where he stands. Supplement but never supplant," it embraces all people irrespective of caste, creed, color, or sex.

The Universal Religion stresses the importance of a moral life, sex sublimation, and mind-control for spiritual growth. It also emphasizes the value of an education, which combines practical, intellectual, and ethical training, and it works to promote understanding between the different religions and ideologies of the world.

The religion is of a monastic order as well as lay disciples. The monks and nuns living in the same *ashramas* (monasteries) follow the teachings of the founder—they combine meditation and mind control with an active life in society and earn their own livelihood.

Membership: In 1998 the trust had approximately 30 centers in India, Denmark, Sweden, Norway, Germany, and the United States. There are approximately 5,000 members worldwide.

Periodicals: *Yogandash; Magazine for the Universal Religion.*

Sources:
Narayanananda, Swami. *The Mysteries of Man, Mind and Mind Functions.* N.p., n.d.

———. *A Practical Guide to Samadhi.* Rishikish, India: Narayanananda Universal Yoga Trust, 1966.

———. *The Primal Power in Man.* Rishikish, India: Narayanananda Universal Yoga Trust, 1970.

———. *The Secrets of Mind-Control.* Rishikish, India: Narayanananda Universal Yoga Trust, 1970.

———. *The Secrets of Prana, Pranayana, and Yoga-Asana.* Gylling, Denmark: Narayanananda Universal Yoga Trust & Ashrama, 1979.

New Vrindaban Community
International Society for Krishna Consciousness (ISKCON), R.D. 1, Box 319, Moundsville, WV 26041

This rural Hare Krishna Community was founded in 1968. One of its pioneering founders was Keith Ham, son of a Southern Baptist Minister; another was Howard

Wheeler, a friend of Ham. They were among an initial group of young American spiritual seekers who encountered A. C. Bhaktivedanta Swami Prabhupada (1896–1977) in New York in the late 1960s, after they had gone on a spiritual search to India. Prabhupada was beginning the task of establishing his worldwide mission. Believing that Prabhupada was genuine, the young Americans dedicated themselves to him. They received Vaisnava initiation from him, taking on the names Kirtananda Swami Bhaktipada and Hayagriva.

In 1968 Bhaktipada noticed an advertisement offering a lease on 100 acres to anyone willing to start a spiritual commune in West Virginia. He ventured out to Moundsville, eventually signed a lease, and began New Vrindaban, which in turn became part of ISKCON, founded by Prabhupada.

After Prabhupada's departure to India in 1977, Bhaktipada secured for himself a prominent role within the ranks of ISKCON. He was also the spiritual leader of New Vrindaban, by then a thriving community. The members of the community had turned an intended residence for Prabhupada into a memorial, attracting media coverage. Bhaktipada was New Vrindaban's de facto singular spiritual leader from the mid-1970s until the beginning of the 1990s, when legal difficulties caught up with him.

During the 1980s, several gurus were expelled and others resigned due to the organization's standards, particularly in the area of illicit sexual relations and the use of psychedelic drugs. The tension led to demands for reform, and the most intense debate centered upon the role of the guru in relation to Prabhupada. Some members of the governing body commission (GBC) called for a more democratic structure, a lessening of the status of the guru vis-a-vis his disciples, and an end to the acceptance of guru puja (worship) by the current society leaders.

The debate on reform, largely confined within the GBC, became public in 1986 with the publication of the *Guru Reform Notebook* by Satsvarupa Dasa Goswami, which demanded reform of the society's understanding of the guru, especially the elimination of any practices which tended to place current gurus on the same level as Prabhupada (as demonstrated in their receiving guru puja). Bhaktipada quickly emerged as the major antagonist in the debate, arguing that organization and structure must remain as Prabhupada left them. The argument reached a culmination point on March 16, 1987, when the GBC expelled Bhaktipada from ISKCON. The GBC cited four major reasons for the expulsion by claming that Bhaktipada (1) had minimized the position of Phadhupada; (2) had rejected the authority of the GBC (thus destroying the society's unity); (3) had established temples in areas assigned to other gurus; (4) had, while acting independently of the society's authority, misrepresented the society to the public.

Bhaktipada answered the charges by noting that he had been merely following the pattern of life established by Prabhupada and the particular mission to which he had been assigned. Further, he noted in his book, *On His Order*, an answer to the Satsvarupa, that it was the GBC that was guilty of deviating from Prabhupada's teachings through their reform movement and the re-editing of Prabhupada's commentary on the Bhagavad-Gita.

While Bhakipada was accusing ISKCON of deviating from the teachings and pattern of life established by Prabhupada, he was in turn accused of also deviating by his adoption of elements from the Christian tradition. He moved to have an organ installed in the temple at New Vrindaban, and members of the community began to wear, at times, brown monk-like habits. ISKCON leaders charged that these changes were far more drastic than those which they had been accused of making.

Except for the issues mentioned above, including those which led to Bhaktipada's expulsion from the society, New Vrindaban and its subsidiary temples follow the same pattern of worship and belief as the temples and centers of ISKCON. In the wake of the expulsion, New Vrindaban and its aligned centers (mostly in Ohio), having been founded originally as a separate corporation, merely reorganized as an independent entity under its corporate name, the International Society for Krishna Consciousness of West Virginia. Almost immediately, leaders from New Vrindaban were sent out to found new centers in such places as Philadelphia and New York City.

The year of Bhaktipada's leadership of the independent ISKCON of West Virginia was one of intense controversy. He tried to exert leadership in the interfaith community and initially attracted a number of people to New Vrindaban from various religious communities. He also initiated plans for the creation of a large community on the ISKCON property. However, he was continually distracted by controversy. Shortly after his expulsion from ISKCON, authorities raided the community searching for evidence supportive of allegations of fraudulent fund raising and information on the death of a former resident, Charles St. Dennis, killed in 1983, and in the 1986 murder of vocal critic Stephen Bryant. Earlier in 1985, Bhaktipada was almost killed when a former devotee attacked him.

A variety of court actions followed, including Bhaktipada being found not guilty of arson in a trial in which he was charged with setting fire to a building owned by the community in order to collect the insurance. And a follower, Thomas Dreshner, was found guilty in connection with the murder of St. Dennis. Finally, on August 28, 1996, Bhaktipada pled guilty to a racketeering charge that included conspiracy to murder (Stephen Bryant). Dreshner, who had previously denied Bhaktipada's involvement in any illegal acts, eventually turned and offered testimony against him. Bhaktipada began serving a 20-year prison term in September 1996, a sentence since reduced to 12 years. In the wake of his conviction, as well as revelation of his breaking his vows of sexual abstinence, there was a move to integrate ISKCON of West Virginia back to the International Society of Krishna Consciousness.

In 2000 the community was accepted again as part of ISKCON and allowed representation in the worldwide leadership council. New Vrindaban's management has focused on reintegrating the community into the global Hare Krishna network while working to rectify illegal activities and other mistakes of Bhaktipada's leadership. Current residents prefer to focus on the primary role that Swami Prabhupada played in bringing Krishna Consciousness from India to the West.

The reputation that New Vrindaban had enjoyed of being the first farming community in ISKCON has yielded to the community's function as a place for spiritual holiday among the community of Indian immigrants to the United States. The community claims to host more overnight staying guests than all the other temples in North America. A primary draw is the memorial to Swami Prabhupada, referred to as "The Palace of Gold." Replacing the previous central communal ownership of all property is a more natural system of individual or family ownership.

The community celebrates many festivals that are a distinct feature of India's 5,000-year-old culture. The community's festivals provide vegetarian feasts for which Hare Krishnas are famous; the community does not allow alcohol, tobacco, or nonvegetarian foods.

Membership: The community extends various categories of membership to persons not resident at New Vrindaban. Most contributing members are Indian professionals and businesspeople. There are approximately 7,000 individuals on the community mailing list.

Periodicals: *New Vrindaban Today.*

Remarks: Kirtanananda Swami Bhaktipada and New Vrindaban have been the object of intense controversy which began in the early 1980s, when charges of drug dealing and the stockpiling of weapons were published in newspapers and magazines across the United States. In October 1985, a fringe member of the society attempted to murder Bhaktipada with a lead bar. Then in 1986 a former member, Stephen Bryant, came to West Virginia and threatened Bhaktipada's life. In May, Bryant was murdered in Los Angeles. Following Bryant's murder, the local sheriff called for a federal probe of New Vrindaban. It was convened in September 1986, just a few weeks before two ex-members, Daniel Reed and Thomas Dreshner, went on trial for the murder of a man who raped Reed's wife. Both ex-members were convicted. Reed was allowed to plead guilty to manslaughter and he received one to five years. Dreshner, an accessory after the fact (he assisted Reed in burying the body), was given a life sentence. Later Dreshner was accepted back as a full member by Bhaktipada, who accepted him into the renounced or *sanyassin* order. Subsequently, Dreshner has frequently but incorrectly been cited in the press as a swami (teacher) and spokesperson for the group.

As a result of the federal investigation, Bhaktipada was indicted for setting fire to a building owned by the group in order to collect the insurance. At a trial in December 1987, he was acquitted of all charges.

Embarrassed by the events at New Vrindaban, the GBC included the accusations and subsequent federal probe as a secondary reason for Bhaktipada's expulsion.

Sources:

New Vrindaban Community. http://newvrindaban.com

Bhaktipada, Kirtanananda Swami. *Christ and Krishna*. Moundsville, WV: Bhaktipada Books, 1985.

———. *Eternal Love*. Moundsville, WV: Bhaktipada Books, 1985.

———. "A Community Struggles for Reinstatement." *Hare Krishna World* 5,5. (January/February1997).

———. *On His Order*. Moundsville, WV: Bhakti Books, 1987.

———. *The Song of God*. Moundsville, WV: Bhaktipada Books, 1984.

Shinn, Larry D. *The Dark Lord*. Philadelphia: Westminister Press, 1987.

Nityananda Institute, Inc.

PO Box 13310, Portland, OR 97232

Swami Rudrananda (1928–1973), born Albert Rudolph, was a spiritual seeker who had participated in groups following the methods of Georgei Gurdjieff and Subud, and later with the shankaracharya of Puri, prior to traveling to India. There, in 1958, he met Swami Nityananda (d. 1961) and his student Swami Muktananda (1908–1982). In these two swamis he found an end to his quest. He also arranged Muktananda's first visit to America in 1970 and helped launch his movement. However, after studying first with Nityananda and later with Muktananda for 15 years, he broke with Muktananda in 1971 and founded the Shree Gurudev Rudrananda Yoga Ashram. The teachings followed essentially the Saivite teachings of Nityananda and Muktananda, both of whom emphasized the role of the guru who gave *shaktipat* to awaken the kundalini. Kundalini is the cosmic power believed to be resting dormant like a coiled snake at the base of the spine. Its awakening allows the power to travel up the spine to the crown of the head, thus producing enlightenment.

Rudrananda founded a string of ashrams across the United States and Europe and wrote one book, *Spiritual Cannibalism*, published within months of his death in an airplane accident. The largest and most substantial remnant of Rudrananda's following was organized under Swami Chetanananda, head of the ashram in Bloomington, Indiana, in 1971. Several years later Chetanananda moved his headquarters to Cambridge, Massachusetts, and in 1993 to Portland, Oregon.

The ashram is a community of disciples living the practical spiritual life under the direction of Swami Chetanananda. The Nityananda Institute is a meditation center whose aim is to make the spiritual life accessible to westerners. The Rudra Press is the publishing arm of the organization.

Membership: In 2008 the institute was based in Portland, Oregon, with meditation centers in Santa Monica, California, New York City, Boston, Massachusetts, and Oslo, Norway. A retreat and research center was located in Kathmandu, Nepal. In 2002 there were approximately 2,000 people involved with the ashram and centers.

Periodicals: *Rudra. • Institute News.*

Sources:

Nityananda Institute. www.nityanandainstitute.org.

Chetanananda, Swami. *Songs from the Center of the Well*. Cambridge, MA: Rudra Press, 1983.

Hatengdi, M. U. *Nityananda, the Divine Presence*. Cambridge, MA: Rudra Press, 1984.

———, and Swami Chetanananda. *Nitya Sutras*. Cambridge, MA: Rudra Press, 1985.

Nevai, Lucia. "Rudi, The Spiritual Legacy of an American Original." *Yoga Journal* no. 65 (July/August 1985): 36–38, 68–71.

Rudrananda, Swami. *Spiritual Cannibalism*. New York: Links, 1973.

Oneness Movement North America

PO Box 35507, Monte Sereno, CA 95030

The Oneness Movement has grown from the vision of two Indian spiritual teachers, Sri Bhagavan and Sri Amma, a husband-wife team viewed by their followers as a single consciousness operating in two bodies. Their vision is to awaken humanity to our oneness and unity with the divine, and to elevate us to an altered state of consciousness—an awakened state of "oneness." To this end, they founded the Oneness University; the Oneness Movement consists of a group of independent but interconnected national affiliates of the Oneness University.

The primary means of spreading the experience of oneness is the Oneness Blessing (also known as Oneness Deeksha or Diksha), during which a transfer of divine energy occurs. Over time, that energy brings about a state of oneness and initiates a neurobiological change in the brain. Once the blessing is complete, the senses are freed from the interference of the mind, leading to new clarity of perception and feelings of joy, calmness, and oneness.

The Oneness Blessing is performed by people who have been trained at the Oneness University in India or Fiji, who are called Oneness facilitators or Oneness Blessing givers.

The Oneness Movement was brought to North America by Sri Raniji, a Malawian disciple of Sri Bhagwan and Sri Amma. As a young woman Sri Raniji met Anandagiri, one of Sri Bhagavan's Oneness facilitators, who gave her the Oneness Blessing. She later met Sri Bhagwan and Sri Amma, and impressed with their teachings, stayed in India to work with them. She eventually became a *dasa*, or lay monk, and Sri Bhagavan appointed her the spiritual leader of the Oneness Movement in North America, which includes not only the United States and Canada but also Australia, New Zealand, and Italy.

The Onenness Movement holds annual conferences that bring together large groups to pray for oneness. In 2008 a large Oneness temple in India, conceived as a temple for all religions, was nearing completion.

Membership: In 2008 the movement claimed more than 100 million members in more than 50 countries. In the United States there are more than 1,000 Oneness facilitators, and in Canada more than 200.

Sources:

Oneness Movement. https://www.onenessmovement.org/index.cfm.

Arjagh, Arjuna. *Awakening into Oneness: The Power of Blessing in the Evolution of Consciousness*. Boulder, CO: Sounds Good, 2007.

Windrider, Kara. *Deeksha: The Fire from Heaven*. Nocato, CA: New World Library, 2006.

Parmarth Niketan

c/o Hindu Jain Temple, 615 Illini Dr., Monroeville, PA 15146

Parmarth Niketan is an ashram in Rishikish, India, that serves as the headquarters of the Swami Shukdebanand Trust, an Indian spiritual community founded in 1942 by Pujya Swami Shukdevanandji Maharaj (1901–1965). In the twenty-first century, Parmarth Niketan extended its influence to the West through the activities of its president, H. H. Pujya Swami Chidanand Saraswatiji Maharaj. Trained in the ashram from childhood for his leadership role, at the age of 17 Chidanand was sent from Rishikish to complete his education. He emerged with master's degrees in Sanskrit and philosophy. After assuming leadership of the ashram, Swami Chidanand has emphasized his beliefs in the unity and harmony of reality, especially as they relate to the many paths to God that are available to humanity. His beliefs have made him a leader in interfaith work, and he has participated in a number of internationals conferences, such as the Parliament of World Religions gatherings (1993 and 1999), the Millennium World Peace Summit of Religious and Spiritual Leaders at the United Nations (2000), the World Council of Religious Leaders at the United Nations in Bangkok (2002), and the Global Youth Peace Summit at the United Nations in New York (2006).

In his many travels, Swami Chidanand has inspired the development of a number of temples in Australia, Europe, and North America, among the most notable being the first Hindu-Jain temple in America, located in suburban Pittsburgh, Pennsylvania. Swami Chidanand serves as the spiritual head of this temple, which is dedicated to providing a means for unity between Hindus and Jains across North America. Begun in 1981, the temple was constructed by the Hindu Temple Society of North America. Under Swami Chidanand's influence, the temple changed its name from Hindu Temple to Hindu Jain Temple in 1986. It was completed in 1990 and now serves the Indian American community in the Greater Pittsburgh Metropolitan Area.

Membership: Not reported.

Sources:

Hindu Jain Temple. www.hindujaintemple.org/.

Parmarth Niketan. www.parmarth.com/.

Prana Yoga Ashram

Yogalayam, 1723 Alcatraz Ave., Berkeley, CA 94703

The Prana Yoga Student Center was founded by Swami Sivalingam, formerly with the Yoga Vedanta Forest Academy. Swami Sivananda Saraswati established the academy at Rishikish on the Ganges River. Sivalingam began his stay at Sivananda's center in 1959. In 1962 he began his international work by bringing the yoga teachings first to Japan and then to Hong Kong, where he established several Sivananda Yoga Centers. He moved to the United States in 1973 and successively founded the Prana Yoga Foundation (1974), the Prana Yoga Ashram (1975), the Prana Yoga Center (1976), and the Ayaodhyanagar Retreat (1977). In 1975 he extended his work to Vancouver, British Columbia. As a result of this work and subsequent travels, he has established a string of centers that ring the globe from India to Japan, to North America to Denmark, and Spain.

Sivalingam follows the yogic teachings and practices of Sivananda with an emphasis upon hatha yoga *asanas* (positions) and the practice of *pranayama* (precise breath control). Through this practice, *prana*, or energy, is manifested and controlled and leads to purification of the nervous system and inner spiritual balance.

Membership: Not reported. In 1980 there were six centers in the United States and nine centers in other countries.

Periodicals: *Prana Yoga Life*. Send orders to Box 1037, Berkeley, CA 94701.

Sources:

Yogalayam Prana Yoga Ashram. www.yogalayam.org.

Sivalingam, Swami. *Wings of Divine Wisdom*. Berkeley, CA: Prana Yoga Ashram, 1977.

Pranayana Institute

PO Box 40731, Albuquerque, NM 87196

The Pranayana Institute was founded by Sankara Saranam, a writer, philosopher, and proponent of *pranayama* (sense introversion), a yoga practice that consists of various techniques of regulated breathing and concentration. Practicing pranayama is said to confer various positive results, including a calm, balanced, and focused mind, increased vitality, and longevity. Pranayama also is believed to awaken the brain and the cerebrospinal nerve centers to their limitless potential. Many of great spiritual and intellectual figures have been adept in pranayama, or something closely resembling it.

Saranam researched pranayana for many years and in 1997 produced a book, *Yoga and Judaism*, in which he claimed that asceticism and pranayama are evident in the practices of the early Hebrews. More recently he authored *God without Religion* (2005), which gets to the heart of the Pranayana Institute by offering an alternative to the divergent and divisive cultural views of God—one drawn from the experience of personal introspection and pranayana.

Saranam, an ascetic and mystic with a background in yoga, founded the Pranayama Institute to further his belief in pranayana and to make the basic techniques available to all at little or no cost. Complementing the institute is the Whirlwind Community, where people may come to study and practice pranayama in an environmentally friendly social context.

Membership: Not reported.

Sources:

Pranayana Institute. www.pranayama.org/.

Saranam, Sankara. *God without Religion: Questioning Centuries of Accepted Truths*. East Gillajay, GA: Pranyana Institute, 2005.

———. *Yoga and Judaism*. Astrologue, 1997.

Raj-Yoga Math and Retreat

Current address not obtained for this edition.

The Raj-Yoga Math and Retreat is a small monastic community formed in 1974 by Fr. Satchakrananda Bodhisattvaguru. Satchakrananda began the practice when he experienced the raising of the kundalini, an internal energy pictured in Hindu thought as a snake coiled and resting at the base of the spine that, upon awakening, rises to the crown chakra (psychic center at the top of the head). That event produced an awareness of Satchakrananda's divine heritage. Following that event, he spent a short time in a Trappist monastery, attended Western Washington University, then became coordinator for the Northwest Free University, where he taught yoga in the early 1970s.

In 1973 Satchakrananda was "mystically" initiated as a yogi by the late Swami Sivananda Saraswati (1887–1963), the founder of the Divine Life Society, through a trilogy of "female Matas" at a retreat he attended on the Olympic (Washington) Peninsula. The following year, with a small group of men and women, he founded the *math* (monastery). In 1977, he was ordained a priest by Abp. Herman Adrian Spruit of the Church of Antioch (see separate entry) and has attempted to use both Hindu and Christian traditions at the math. Spiritual disciplines include the regular celebrations of the mass, though the major practice offered is the Jaya Yoga Sadhana, consisting of the successive practice of *japa* (mantra) yoga, meditation, *kriyas* (cleansings), *mudras*, *asanas* (hatha yoga postures), and *pranayam* (disciplined breathing). Jaya yoga allows practitioners to become aware of their divine nature.

The math is located in the foothills of Mt. Baker overlooking the Nooksuck River near Deming, Washington. It accepts resident students for individual instruction but offers a variety of retreats/workshops for nonresidents. For those unable to travel to the math for instruction, Satchakrananda has put together a jaya yoga workshop packet.

Membership: The resident community at the math fluctuates between 2 and 12. Several hundred individuals are associated with the math through an oblate order of men and women.

Sources:

Letters to Satchakrananda. Deming, WA: Raj-Yoga Math & Retreat, 1977.

Satchakrananda, Yogi. *Coming and Going, The Mother's Drama*. Deming, WA: Raj-Yoga Math & Retreat, 1975.

———. *Thomas Merton's Dharma*. Deming, WA: Raj-Yoga Math & Retreat, 1986.

———. *To Create No Freedom*. Deming, WA: Raj-Yoga Math & Retreat, 1983.

Ramakrishnananda Yoga Vedanta Mission

96 Ave. B, New York, NY 10009

The Ramakrishanananda Yoga Vedanta Mission was founded in 2003 by Swami Ramakrishnananda, an American citizen of Indian heritage born in Chile in 1958. Ramakrishnananda's religious quest began with a spontaneous mystical experience that occurred when he was only eight years old. He was eventually led to VRINDA, an organization that followed the *bhakti* (devotional) yoga originally brought to the West by A. C. Bhaphktivedanta Swami Prabhupada (1896–1977), founder of the International Society for Krishna Consciousness. However, his search would later lead him to a number of the other Indian gurus working in the West, including Swami Vishnu Devananda (1929–1993), from whom he received his first initiation and was given the religious name Ramakrishna. Ramakrishnananda also studied Vishnu Devananda's integral yoga teachings and was recognized as a Yoga Acarya or Master Acarya of Yoga in 1989. He later studied with Brahmananda Sarasvati (d. 1993) of Ananda Ashram and Swami Jyotirmayananda (b. 1931), founder of the Yoga Research Foundation in Miami. In 1991, he was ordained as a *brahmana* by Kirtanananda Swami of the Divine Life Society in India. Four years later Swami Jyotirmayananda received him into the renounced life, as a *sannyasi*, under the name of Ramakrishnananda Swami.

In 1995, Ramakrishnananda met and received initiation from His Divine Grace Sri Baba Brahmananda Maharaja (b. 1931). It is from Brahmananda Maharaja that he received what he considers his primary lineage. Brahmananda Maharaja was a disciple of His Divine Grace Bhagavan Mastarama Babaji Maharaja (d. 1986), a renowned *siddha* yogi. In the end, however, the Vaishnava devotional yoga with which he started reasserted itself and Ramakrishnananda sought reconfirmation of his renounced monk vows from a *Vaishnava sannyasi* in the Ashram of VRINDA, His Divine Grace B. A. Paramadvaiti Swami Maharaja.

In 2000, Swami Ramakrishnananda moved to the United States, where three years later he founded the Ramakrishnananda Yoga Vedanta Mission and began accepting disciples for study in the ancient Vedic tradition. The center of the Mission is the Ramakrishnananda Mandir, a traditional Hindu Temple in New York City. The temple attempts to serve the needs of a broad range of Hindus. The central hall of the larger temple contains smaller temples for Lord Shiva, Lord Ganesha, Lord Hanuman, Durga Ma, Kali Ma, Lakshmi Ma, and Saraswati Ma and a separate hall with the temple to Lord Krishna. The temple celebrates all the major Hindu holidays and festivals.

Since the opening of the New York City temple, a second center has been opened in Monroe, New York, and there are also two affiliated centers in the Dominican Republic.

Membership: Not reported.

Sources:

Ramakrishnananda Yoga Vedanta Mission. www.ramakrishnananda.com/.

Ramakrishnananda has written several books, the texts of which are posted on the Mission's Web page.

S. A. I. Foundation

3491 Clover Oak Drive, San Jose, CA 95148

The first miracle related to Satya Sai Baba (b. 1926) concerned a mysterious cobra found under his bed, proclaiming, say his followers, Sai Baba's role as Sheshiasa, Lord of Serpents. As a child he worked miracles for his classmates, producing objects out of nowhere, a favorite practice still continued.

In 1940, he fell into a coma that lasted for two months. Upon awakening suddenly, he announced, "I am Sai Baba of Shirdi." Sai Baba of Shirdi (1856?–1918) was an Indian holy man who had left behind a large following who still venerated him and observed his teachings. Satya Sai Baba, by his statement, claimed to be his reincarnation. Followers assert his ability to recall conversations between individuals who were disciples of the original Sai Baba.

The thrust of the Sai Baba Movement is veneration of Sai Baba and recounting the miracle stories about him. Teachings are mainline Hinduism with emphasis on four aspects—Dharma Sthapana (establishing the faith on a firm foundation), Vidwathposhana (fostering scholarship), Vedasamrakshana (preservation of the Vedas), and Bhaktirakshana (protection of the devotees from secularism and materialism).

The Indian headquarters in Prasanthi Nilayam (Home of the Supreme Peace) are the focus of the Sai Baba movement. Here each Thursday devotees gather for a darshan or vision of Sai Baba. Special darshans are held during the Dasara holidays in October and his birthday celebration in November.

Interest in Sai Baba in America began with a set of lectures given in 1967 at the University of California at Santa Barbara. Movies of Prasanthi Nilayam were shown by Indra Devi, who had recently visited Sai Baba. The movement spread during the 1970s and groups have formed across the United States.

Membership: Not reported.

Periodicals: *Sathya Sai Newsletter*. Send orders to 1800 E Garvey Ave., West Covina, CA 91791.

Sources:

S.A.I. Foundation. www.thesaifoundation.org.

Brooks, Tal. *Avatar of Night*. New Delhi, India: Tarang Paperbacks, 1984.

Hislop, John. *Conversations with Sathya Sai Baba*. San Diego: Birth Day Publishing Company, 1978.

Lessons for Study Circle. Prasanti Nilayam, India: World Council of Sri Sathya Sai Organizations, n.d.

Manual of Sri Sathya Sai Seva Dal and Guidelines for Activities. Bombay: World Council of Sri Sathya Sai Organizations, 1979.

McMartin, Grace T., ed. *A Recapitulation of Sathya Sai Baba's Divine Teachings*. Hyderabad, India: Avon Printing Works, 1982.

Murphet, Howard. *Sai Baba, Man of Miracles*. New York: Samuel Weiser, 1976.

Sandweiss, Samuel H. *Sai Baba, The Holy Man . . . and the Psychiatrist*. San Diego, CA: Birth Day Publishing, 1975.

Sacha Dham Ashram

c/o Ganesh Foundation, 1750 30th St., PMB No. 137, Boulder, CO 80301

Alternate Address: International Center: Laxman Jhulla, P.O. Tapovan Sarai Pin 249192, Tehri Garhwal, U.P., India.

Sacha Dham Ashram was founded by Maharajji Hans Raj Swami (b. 1924), an advaita vedanta teacher. As a guru, like Ramana Maharshi, he gives few verbal teachings, inviting devotees merely to sit in his presence instead. In the silence they can surrender to the unconditional love of the guru and contact the limitless love of Being itself. The reality of Maharaj, as he is usually referred to by his disciples, was brought to the West in the early 1990s by Shantimayi (b. 1950), an American woman who discovered him and sat at his feet for seven years. These sessions were usually accompanied with a period of chanting and the singing of *bhajans* (holy songs). She was sent to the West as Maharaj's spiritual ambassador, and as a result a number of Europeans and Americans began to find their way to the Indian ashram, and from their visits a community of disciples has begun to appear in the West. These remain small, as the essence of the devotion is sitting in the presence of the guru, which can only be done at the ashram in India.

Membership: Not reported.

Sources:

Shanti Mayi. www.shantimayi.com/ashram/sachadham.html.

Cushman, Anne, and Jerry Jones. *From Here to Nirvana: The Yoga Journal Guide to Spiritual India*. New York: Riverhead Books, 1998. 399 pp.

Sacred Space Yoga Sanctuary

830 Bancroft Way, Berkeley, CA 94710

The Sacred Space Yoga Sanctuary was founded in 2001 by Swami Khecaranatha (born Steven Ott). Ott had been a student of Swami Rudrananda (1928–1973), the founder of the Nityananda Institute. After only a year of study, Rudrananda recognized Ott as a teacher in 1972. When Rudrananda died in 1973, Ott continued to live in the ashram through several relocations under Swami Chetananda, Rudrananda's successor. Ott left the ashram in 2001 and founded the new sanctuary as a independent center continuing Rudrananda's system of kundalini yoga.

In 2002 Ott took his *sannyasa* (renounced life) vows in the presence of Ma Yoga Shakti, a swami who heads centers in New York and Florida. She gave him the name Swami Khecaranatha ("moving in the fullness of the divine heart"). Recognizing that in most Hindu traditions sannyasa requires a divestment of worldly things and assuming the role of a monk, Khecaranatha noted that he took the vows as a tantric yogi, understanding renunciation to be an inner state that might take different manifestations. For Swami Khecaranatha, it means living as a householder.

Swami Khecaranatha continues the kundalini yoga teachings passed through Swami Muktananda (1908–1982) from Swami Nityananda (c. 1897–1961) to Rudrananda to him. He offers to his disciples *shaktipat*, a transmission of energy to awaken the kundalini energy. The main center at the sanctuary is the *rudramandir*, where spirit takes up residence and destroys all pain and suffering. Besides regular weekly meetings at the rudramandir, the sanctuary offers periodical retreats and workshops.

In 2008 there was one center of the Sacred Space Yoga Sanctuary, but Swami Khecaranatha had begun to train teachers to form new centers.

Membership: Not reported.

Sources:

Sacred Space Yoga. sacredspaceyogasanctuary.com/.

Sadhana Ashram

2414 Keystone Ct., Boulder, CO 80304-1936

The Sadhana Ashram dates to 1981 and a vision of the Divine Mother imparted to Shankar Das, an American yogi. Shankar Das spent several years in India as a seeker, and many of the teachers he met encouraged him to establish an ashram, originally in Tennessee, then California, and now Colorado.

Shankar Das teaches an eclectic spiritual outlook drawn from a variety of Indian religious traditions. He acknowledges inspiration from Sai Baba, Swami Muktananda, Sri Ramakrishna, and Sri Anandamayi Ma. He has stated that "Many are the Ways," and he holds that any one aspect of God represents all aspects. Shankar Das operates as a Mahashakti yoga master and practices *shaktipat,* the spiritual teacher's conferring a form of spiritual "power" or awakening on a disciple/student. In this case, the power is awakened through the stimulation of the *kundalini* (an unconscious, instinctive or erotic force or energy) believed to lie dormant at the base of the spine. When awakened, the kundalini travels upward along the spinal column and brings enlightenment.

The daily routine at the ashram begins early in the morning with chanting, meditation, and shaktipat. Sunday is dedicated to the Divine Mother (often seen as synonymous with the kundalini energy) and often includes a fire ceremony (*yajna*) and feast. During weekdays residents scatter to secular jobs in the area but begin and end the day in spiritual activity. The ashram's diet is vegetarian.

The Acharya Training Program is for formal practitioners of this order who have been with Shankaracharya for more than a year; it covers all aspects of teaching in this tradition, including philosophy, mantras, pujas/fire ceremony, biography/ashram history, teachers/psychology, shaktipat/kundalini (including diet and meditation aids), basic Hindu mythology, the worship of Chandi (the supreme Goddess of Devi Mahatmya), daily practice, holy days, spiritual texts and references, and the science of Tantra. There is no set time span for the course of study; the rate of completion varies with each student's pace of assimilation of the material.

Membership: Not reported.

Sources:

Sadhana Ashram. www.sadhanaashram.org

Saeejis Temple of Peace

5627 Lexington Ave., No. 6, Los Angeles, CA 90038-2232

The Saeejis Temple of Peace is a small Hindu organization founded in Los Angeles in 1977 by Govindram T. Lathi, an Indian American teacher known to his followers as Gurudev Saeeji or, simply, Saeeji. His goal is to fill the spiritual void of seekers left unfulfilled by the material blandishments and diversions of contemporary high-technology societies. He offers prayer, meditation, and yoga as the solutions to their needs.

Although his organization is small, Saeeji has developed plans for a large retreat center in southern California that will replicate the spiritual atmosphere available at the sacred ashrams of India.

Membership: Not reported.

Sahaja Yoga Center

4565 Sherman Oaks Ave., Sherman Oaks, CA 91403-3011

Alternate Address: 56 Cedars Ave., Walthamstow, London E17 7QN, England.

Among the fastest-growing Hindu-inspired movements in Europe and the United States is Sahaja Yoga, as taught by Shri Mataji Nirmala Devi. Born on March 21, 1923, into a Christian family in Chindawara, India, she is a direct descendant of the royal Shalivahana dynasty. She is married to the retired secretary general of the International Maritime Organization of the United Nations.

Devi's career as a guru grew from her disappointment with some of the other gurus who had come to the West from India. She knew she had been born a realized soul, and she sought a means to bring realization to masses of people. In her frustration, on the evening of May 5, 1970, she sat all evening under a bilva tree. During this time her crown *chakra* (believed to be at the top of the head) opened and the *kundalini* force (the cosmic power believed to be resting like a coiled snake at the base of the spine) began to rise. She then felt ready to begin her work.

Her followers believe that Nirmala Devi is connected with the power of the life source. She offers self-realization as the starting point rather than the end or goal of the practice of yoga or austerities. When one experiences self-realization, the kundalini energy rises. In her personal appearances Devi attempts to bring self-realization to her audiences. She also offers a meditation technique for those unable to be physically present. The meditation is done before one of her pictures.

Sahaja Yoga spread from centers in Delhi, India, and London, England, especially during the 1980s. This practice came to North America in the mid-1980s. Centers have opened across the United States and in Canada: in Toronto, Ontario, and Vancouver, British Columbia. In 1989 Devi made her first trip to Russia and Eastern Europe.

Membership: Not reported.

Periodicals: *Nirmala Yoga*. Available from 43 Banglow Rd., Delhi 110007, India.

Sources:

Devi, Shri Mataji Nirmala. *Sahaja Yoga*. Delhi, India: Nirmala Yoga, 1982.

Mathur, Rakesh. "The Russians' Love for Yoga: Nirmala Devi Shares Her Adventure." *Hinduism Today* 12, no. 10 (October 1990): 1, 7. Available from www.hinduismtoday.com/archives/1990/10/1990-10-03.shtml.

Sahaja Yoga Center. www.sahajayoga.org/

Saiva Siddhanta Church

107 Kaholalete, Kapaa, HI 96745

The Saiva Siddhanta Church, originally known as the Subramuniya Yoga Order, was founded by Master Satguru Sivaya Subramuniyaswami (1927–2001), a native of California who traveled to Sri Lanka and in 1949 was initiated by a guru, Jnaniguru Yaganathan, more popularly known as Siva Yogaswami. He returned to the United States and spent some years following his *sadhana* (spiritual discipline). In 1957 he founded the Subramuniya Yoga Order and opened the Christian Yoga Church in San Francisco. He founded a periodical, *Christian Yoga World*; developed a radio program, the "Christian Yoga Hour"; and authored a correspondence course. Other centers were founded in Redwood City, California, and Reno, Nevada, and an ashram was opened in Virginia City, Nevada. During the 1960s, all remnants of Christianity, which had earlier been woven into his teachings, were jettisoned in favor of the Saivite Hinduism of Subramuniya's guru. The Subramuniya Yoga Order became known as the Wailua University of Contemporary Arts; in 1973 its name changed again, this time to the Saiva Siddhanta Yoga Order, and in the late 1970s it took its current name, the Saiva Siddhanta Church.

The teachings of the church derive from the Vedas, the ancient Saivite scriptures: the Rig, Sama, Yajur, and Atharva. The church also draws on the Saiva Agamas (the authoritative practical scripture of Saivism) and the Tirumantiram, written by Saint Tirumulkar approximately 2,000 years ago. The latter volume is written in Tamil (not Sanskrit) and is a summary of Saivism. The teachings have been passed through a lineage of teachers (the Siva Yogaswami Guru Paramparai) to Yogaswami and Subramuniya; since November 12, 2001, the main bearer of the doctrine has been Satguru Bodhinatha Veylanswami.

The church is built around the worship of Siva, known as the only absolute reality, both immanent and transcendent. Siva is worshipped under the forms of the Siva Lingam, Ardhanarisava (as Siva/Sakti in whom all apparent opposites are reconciled), and Nataraja, the Divine Dancer. Siva created the other deities and the human soul, but not the essence of the soul, which is eternally one with God. This essence is the timeless, formless, spaceless Self—Parasivam. Realization of this self is the ultimate goal of existence. Dharma is Siva's divine law, which governs creation.

The soul is immortal but veiled by the bonds of ignorance (*anava*), the consequences of thoughts and deeds (*karma*), and illusions of matter (*maya*). In order to continue its spiritual evolution, the soul periodically reincarnates in a physical body. It is the human task to follow the established *dharma* (pattern) in his/her personal and social life. The doctrine also encourages good conduct, as summarized in the *yamas* (codes of conduct) and *niyamas* (observances or rituals) of classical yoga.

The communal life of Saivites centers on the temples of Siva, considered the abodes of the deity. One such temple has been constructed in Hawaii on a 458-acres estate that also houses the church's headquarters. Here *puja*, the invocation of Siva and the other deities and an expression of love for Siva, is offered daily. Most homes also have a home shrine where the deity is invoked.

The church is headed by Bodhinatha and the Saiva Swami Sangam, the ordained priesthood of 15 swamis, all of whom live at the Hawaiian monastery. Swamis train for 12 years before qualifying to join the order of sannyas by taking lifetime vows of poverty, purity (chastity), renunciation, confidence, and obedience.

In 1970 land was purchased in Hawaii on the island of Kauai for a temple and headquarters complex, which also houses the theological seminary. One education facility, the Himalayan Academy, distributes the San Marga Master Course, a correspondence course for new and prospective members, as well as the academy's periodical, *Hinduism Today*. In 1994 the Hindu Heritage Endowment was created to support Hindu institutions and projects worldwide. In 2002 it held funds in excess of $4 million. A daily chronicle of the church's activities is available at www.gurudeva.org.

Membership: In 2002 the church reported 700 tithing families as members, 7,000 students with various levels of commitment, and 125,000 readers of its magazine. There were 32 missions in eight countries: the United States, Canada, India, Sri Lanka, Mauritius, Malaysia, Singapore, and Germany.

Educational Facilities:

Himalayan Academy, Kauai's Hindu Monastery, 107 Kaholalele Road, Kapaa, Hawaii.

Periodicals: *Hinduism Today.*

Sources:

Saiva Siddhanta Church. www.himalayanacademy.com/ssc/

Saiva Dharma Shastras. Kappa, HI: Siddhanta Press, 1986.

Siva's Cosmic Dance. San Francisco: Himalayan Academy, [1983].

Subramuniya, Master. *Beginning to Meditate*. Kapaa, HI: Wailua University of Contemplative Arts, 1972.

————. *Raja Yoga*. San Francisco: Comstock House, 1973.

————. *The Self God*. San Francisco: Tad Robert Gilmore and Company, 1971.

————. *Yoga's Forgotten Foundation*. Kapaa, HI, n.d.

Subramuniya, Sr. *Gems of Cognition*. San Francisco: Christian Yoga Publications, 1958.

The Sambodh Society, Inc.

c/o Swami Bodhananda, Spiritual Director, 6363 N 24th St., Kalamazoo, MI 49004

The Sambodh Society is the American branch of the Sambodh Foundation, an Advaita Vedanta organization based in India and founded by H. H. Swami Bodhananda Saraswati, a teacher of Vedanta and meditation in the tradition of Shankaracharya. A graduate in economics at Christ College, Irinjalkuda, Kerala, India, Saraswati forsook graduate studies to wander the Himalayan Mountains on a spiritual quest. Upon finally settling down, he joined the Saraswati order, one of 10 *sannyasa* (monastic) orders established by Shankaracharya.

Bodhananda began his teaching work in 1978 and a decade later was offered the opportunity to establish a teacher training school called Sandeepani in Kerala. From that beginning he went on to found the Sambodh Foundation (1991), which serves as an umbrella organization for a set of ashrams and related organizations through which Bodhananda's students receive spiritual training and engage in service to the community at large.

Swami Bodhananda began his mission in America in 1997 with an initial visit to New York, Michigan, Illinois, and California. Before he returned to India, a group of devotees incorporated the Sambodh Society, established to teach meditation and Vedanta according to Swami Bodhananda's principles. Land outside Kalamazoo, Michigan, was purchased the next year for a temple and American headquarters. Bodhananda now visits America and Canada annually.

Drawing on his college work, Bodhananda has supplemented the traditional perspectives of Advaita Vedanta with some unique contemporary teachings that integrate traditional Vedantic values with modern economics and corporate management philosophy. Through these teachings he offers a means for students to hold to the Vedantic ideal of remaining inwardly detached even as one is active in the world.

Membership: The Sambodh Society has two centers: one in Michigan and one in California.

Sources:

Sambodh Society. www.sambodh.com/.

Bodhananda, Swami. *The Gita and Management*. New Delhi: Bluejay Books, 2003.

————. *Indian Management and Leadership*. New Delhi: Srishti Publishers & Distributors, 2007.

————. *Lectures on Vedanta Philosophy*. Whitefish, MT: Kessinger Publishing, 2007.

Sant Shri Asarmaji Ashram

c/o Shri Yoga Vedanta Ashram, 45 Texas Rd., Matawan, NJ 07747

The Sant Shri Asarmaji Ashram was founded in 1971 by Param Pujya Sant Shri Asaramji, generally referred to affectionately as Bapu. Bapu was born in the early 1904s in what is now Pakistan, but following the partition of India in 1947, he moved with his parents to Gujarat. As a youth he was drawn to meditation, at which he spent many hours. Following his father's death, he assumed financial responsibility for his family and was eventually married, though he wanted to live a life apart and to meditate. Bapu was still a young man when he renounced his family life and moved to the Himalayas as a wandering student. He eventually found a place at the ashram of Swami Shri Lilashahaji Maharaj at Rishikish, and later at the ashram of Shri Lalji Maharaj on the banks of the river Narmada at Moti Koral. Bapu was 23 years old when he finally attained *Samadhi* (control over consciousness) while sitting with Sad Gurudev Lilashahji Maharaj in Mumbai (Bombay).

After seven years of wandering, Bapu returned to Gujarat and settled at a spot at Motera on the Sabarmati River. A short time later, some devotees constructed a small room in which he could live. The reputation of this meditating renunciate spread, and hundreds and then thousands of people began to come to Motera to see him. The original room became the seed from which, beginning in 1971, a large ashram developed. By 2000, there were over a hundred affiliated ashrams operating across India. Some of the ashrams have *Maun Mandirs* (a temple for silent spiritual practice) that provide space for serious practitioners to enjoy complete seclusion for seven or more days at a time.

Bapu has emerged as a teacher of Kundalini Yoga and during gatherings will impart *shaktipat* to followers. Shaktipat is seen as a bestowing of divine love and the transmission of Divine Energy, allowing the student to begin to work with his own kundalini energy.

Bapu operates out of the pluralistic religious environment of modern India and emphasizes the existence of One Supreme Conscious in every human being. He downplays the differences between Hindu, Muslim, Jain, and Christian beliefs.

Through the 1990s, the movement spread across India and overseas to Singapore, Hong Kong, Dubai, the United Kingdom, Canada, and the United States. As it grew, Sant Shri Asarmaji Ashram developed a number of social programs to deal with hunger, disaster relief, education, and medical care. The group also supports a nursing home for the elderly.

Membership: Not reported. In 2008, Sant Shri Asarmaji Ashram had 21 centers of activity in the United States and 2 in Canada.

Periodicals: *Rishi Prasad*, Amdavad, Gujarat, India.

Sources:

Sant Shri Asarmaji Ashram. www.ashram.org/.

Sarada Ramakrishna Vivekananda SRV Associations of Oregon, San Francisco, and Hawaii

c/o SRV San Francisco, 465 Brussels St., San Francisco, CA 94134

The Sarada Ramakrishna Vivekananda SRV Associations of Oregon, San Francisco, and Hawaii are an independent West Coast parallel to the SRV Association of America originally established by the American poet, philosopher, spiritual practitioner, and teacher Lex Hixon (1941–1995). The Independent SRV Associations were founded in 1993 by Bob Kindler (b. 1950), a musician and a student of the Vedanta tradition as taught by Sri Ramakrishna Paramahansa, Sri Sarada Devi, and Swami Vivekananda. Kindler was initiated into Vedanta by Swami Aseshananda, a disciple of Sri Sarada Devi, Ramakrishna's wife and spiritual partner. He later received instruction from two additional teachers of the Ramakrishna Order—Swami Nityasvarupananda and Swami Damodarananda.

Kindler, known affectionately as Babaji, created Jai Ma Music, a sacred arts ensemble to express the teachings of India through devotional music. In this endeavor he was encouraged by Hixon, a friend and fellow believer. He toured with Jai Mai Music through the 1980s and 1990s.

The teaching of the ashrama is essentially the nondualistic form of Adavaita Vedanta popularized by Vivekananda and the Vedanta societies. Babaji's training in yoga, Vedanta, and music informed the teaching at the SRV ashramas, where the wisdom of India is integrated with devotional music from both East and West. Babaji visits the various centers approximately four times annually. He leads up to four retreats per year and a group pilgrimage to India every two to three years. Personal initiation into the SRV Association and individual guidance in spiritual life are offered to those who accept the universal teachings of Sanatana Dharma in the tradition of Sri Ramakrishna, Sri Sarada Devi, and Swami Vivekananda.

Membership: Not reported.

Periodicals: *Advaita Vedanta Journal*.

Sources:

Sarada Ramakrishna Vivekananda SRV Associations of Oregon, San Francisco, and Hawaii. www.srv.org.

Kindler, Bob. *Swami Vivekananda Vijnanagita: The Wisdom Song of Vivekananda*. Portland, OR: Sarada Ramakrishna Vivekananda, n.d.

———.*An Extensive Anthology of Sri Ramakrishna's Stories*. Portland, OR: Sarada Ramakrishna Vivekananda, n.d.

———.*The Avadhut and His Twenty-Four Teachers in Nature*. Portland, OR: Sarada Ramakrishna Vivekananda, n.d.

———.*The Ten Divine Articles of Sri Durga: Insights and Meditations*. Portland, OR: Sarada Ramakrishna Vivekananda, n.d.

Sarva Dharma Sambhava Kendra

Current address not obtained for this edition.

Sarva Dharma Sambhava Kendra was founded in the 1970s in India by Nemi Chand Gandhi (b. 1949), usually known by his religious name, Chandra Swami Maharaj. His family moved from his birthplace in Rajasthan to Hyderabad, where the young Chandra was involved in two popular social movements: one to save the Hindi language and the other to save the cows, which led to the assassination of a prominent political figure, Gulzarilal Nanda. Shortly afterward he began a spiritual search that took him to Kathmandu, where he met and studied with a tantric master. During this time he absorbed the worship of the Indian goddess Durga into his inherited Jain faith. After three years, in 1972, he returned as Chandra Swami. He is purported to be fluent in at least seven languages.

Soon after his return from Kathmandu, Chandra organized a *yagna* (an offering of praise, offering, or sacrifice) in Madhuban. The goddess Durga is one of the forms of the consort of Siva. Durga is pictured as the "delighter in blood" and is frequently worshiped with a yagna fire ceremony in which animals are sacrificed. (Before legal action by the British, the yagna often included a human sacrifice.) Since that first yagna Chandra has annually organized Durga Puja (worship) at various locations around India. Many of these are attended by famous people and political figures.

In the 1980s Chandra expanded his activities to a number of locations around the world, including Fiji, Canada, and the United States, where headquarters were established in Los Angeles, California.

Membership: Not reported.

Remarks: Chandra Swami Maharaj has become famous as the confidant and guru to the rich and powerful. In the United States he has had connections with tennis star John McEnroe, the actress Elizabeth Taylor, the actor George Hamilton, and U.S. House of Representatives majority leader James Wright. He is a frequent visitor to the multimillionaire Arab arms dealer Adnan Khashoggi (one of the participants in the Iran-Contra arms deal in 1986–1987), Prince Rainier of Monaco, and numerous political leaders in India. In 2004 Chandra Swami Maharaj was acquitted on charges of conspiracy in a St. Kitts forgery case. He has also been linked to political scandals and exercised considerable influence on former prime minister of India P. V. Narasimha Rao during his administration.

Sources:

Indo-Asian News Service (IANS). www.tribuneindia.com/

Sarvamangala Mission

c/o Srividya Center, 366 Grapevine Dr., Diamond Bar, CA 91765

The Sarvamangala Mission, established in California in the 1980s, is an outgrowth of the Hindu *shakti* (sacred force, power, or energy) tradition of Srividya. The mission is under the spiritual direction of Sri Rajagopala Anandanatha, a tantric saint and mystic. His followers claim that he was born by divine dispensation, was specially baptized by God, and attained spiritual perfection at the age of 38 following a period of testing and temptations and an interval of four years spent in prayer without food, drink, or sleep. According to his disciples, once he ascended to the higher levels of consciousness, he was commissioned by God to cure the sick and lead people to God.

Sri Rajagopala Anandanatha is a devotee of the Divine Mother and calls upon people to follow a path of realization through effort, self-surrender, and worship of the Divine Mother. He teaches that it is possible, no matter how many lifetimes a person has lived, to reach self-realization in this life. Vegetarian food is considered helpful in achieving mental concentration.

Membership: As of 1995 more than 50 families were contributing to the work of the mission.

Periodicals: *Shakti.*

Sources:

India Currents. www.indiacurrents.com/news/

Satsang with Robert

Current address not obtained for this edition.

Robert Adams (b. 1928) is a disciple of the Indian sage and guru Ramana Maharshi (1879–1950). At the age of 14, while preparing for a math test, Adams claims to have had a profound mystical experience, a realization that the world was not real; there was only the self, the immutable, all-penetrating, all-prevailing source of existence. The visible world was merely a set of images superimposed by the unchangeable self on reality. Some time after this life-changing event, he discovered Ramana Maharshi's book *Who Am I?* Upon seeing a picture of Maharshi, he recognized him as a little man he had seen standing at the end of his bed during his childhood years.

He soon became a disciple of Paramahansa Yogananda and became a monk at the monastery of the Self-Realization Fellowship in Encinatas, California. Yogananda advised him to go to Ramanashram, near Tiruvannamalai, India, and Adams remained with Ramana during the last three years of the guru's life.

For 17 years after Ramana's death, Adams traveled, met with other gurus, and discussed his enlightenment. Since 1967 he has traveled and taught, never staying in one place for very long. In the mid-1980s Adams had a vision of many great teachers coming together and merging like a mountain. He understood the vision as a sign to cease his traveling and take a group of students. He settled in the Los Angeles, California, where he has been teaching on a freelance basis.

Membership: Not reported.

Sources:

Adams, Robert. *There Is No Suffering, There Is No Death: Satsang with Robert.* Canoga Park, CA: Author, 1991.

————. *Silence of the Heart: Satsang with Robert Adams.* Atlanta, GA: Acropolis Books, 1999.

Satsang with Stuart

Current address could not be obtained for this edition.

Stuart Schwartz was a student of Robert Adams (1928–1997) in the 1990s. Adams in turn was a direct student of Ramana Maharshi (1879–1950) and perpetuated Ramana's teachings of Advaita Vedanta and his methods of sitting in silence and engaging with students based on the questions they posed to him.

In the years following Adams's death, Schwartz began his teaching career following the same model. Those drawn to Schwartz discover that being in his presence draws their attention inward and that their thoughts and mental activities are replaced by what is labeled the *no-thing*, which lies at the center of our being. To cease striving and abide in the Presence is the surest way to discover truth.

Schwartz maintains contact with students through his Internet Web page, where he publishes transcripts of his dialogue sessions.

Membership: Not reported. Most of Schwartz's dialogue sessions are offered from his hometown in Boynton, Florida, but he regularly visits several sites on the East (Philadelphia, New York City, Boston) and West (California and Arizona) Coasts.

Sources:

Satsang with Stuart. www.satsangwithstuart.com/.

Ramana Maharshi. *Talks with Ramana Maharshi: On Realizing Abiding Peace and Happiness.* Carlsbad, CA: Inner Directions, 2000.

Self-Realization Fellowship

3880 San Rafael Ave., Los Angeles, CA 90065-3298

The Self-Realization Fellowship (SRF) traces its beginning to 1861and the work of Mahavatar Babaji, who revived and taught *kriya yoga,* a system of meditation that purports to induce a deep state of tranquility and communion with God. He chose Swami Paramahansa Yogananda (1893–1952) to bring the teachings to the West. Born in India, Yogananda joined the strict Swami Order after his graduation from college and became the disciple of Sri Yukteswarji. In 1916 he discovered the techniques of Yogoda, a system of life-energy control for physical and spiritual development, which, combined with traditional yoga, became the central concern of his teachings.

Yogananda was trained by Swami Sri Yukteswar (1855–1936), who declared Yogananda his successor and left him his ashram properties. Yogananda founded the Yogoda Satsanga Society of India in 1917. In 1920 Swami Yogananda came to the United States to attend the Pilgrim tercentenary anniversary of the International Congress of Religious Liberals. Impressed by what he found in America, he decided to stay (one of the last Indians to come into America before the change in immigration laws stopped Asian migration to America). With the Americans who flocked around him he formed a small center of the Yogoda Satsang in Boston, Massachusetts. From that center he traveled throughout the eastern United States.

In 1924 he made his first transcontinental lecture tour of the United States, which culminated in the founding of a headquarters for his work on Mt. Washington in Los Angeles, California, in 1925. In the late 1920s he toured the principal cities of the United States as a lecturer and concentrated on compiling two volumes of inspirational writings: *Whispers of Eternity* (1929) and *Songs of the Soul* (1925). A magazine, *East-West* (now *Self-Realization*), and a course of printed lessons aided the rapid spread of the movement, but nothing was as effective as the personality of Yogananda himself. According to the reports of his followers, he was no less charismatic in death than in life. His demise was heralded by his disciples as an extraordinary event because of "the absence of any visual signs of decay in the dead body of Paramahansa Yogananda . . . even twenty days after his death," according to a notarized testimony from the Forest Lawn Mortuary in Glendale, California.

The spread of the work in America led, in 1935, to the incorporation of the Self-Realization Fellowship as an international society. In addition to the headquarters in Los Angeles, other California centers were opened in Encinatas, San Diego,

Hollywood, Long Beach, and Pacific Palisades; smaller groups were organized throughout the United States. The emphasis of the Self-Realization Fellowship is teaching the way to *ananda* (bliss), or self-realization or God realization. The way to bliss is through "definite scientific techniques for attaining personal experience of God." The technique is kriya yoga, a system of awakening and energizing the *chakras* or psychic centers believed to be located along the spinal column. The basic practice is regular deep meditation, which leads to a focusing of spiritual cosmic energies and a consequent direct perception of the divine. Yogananda's disciples believe that by the practice of kriya yoga, blood is decarbonized and recharged with oxygen, the atoms of which are transmuted into "life current" to rejuvenate the brain and spinal centers.

The essential unity of Eastern and Western religious traditions is also stressed by SRF; lecture services include interpretations of parallel scriptural passages from the New Testament and the *Bhagavad Gita*. Readings are also given from Paramahansa Yogananda's *Autobiography of a Yogi*, considered a modern spiritual classic; it has remained in print since its publication in 1946 and is widely used as a textbook and reference work in colleges and universities around the world. Worship centers on the inner communion (meditation) practices of Yogananda. Followers can study his teachings in depth through the many books of his lectures and writings that have been published as well as through a series of lessons designed for home study.

Yogananda was succeeded by Swami Rajarsi Janakananda (James J. Lynn). Lynn died in 1955 and was succeeded by Sri Daya Mata, the present head of the fellowship.

Membership: In 1998 the fellowship reported nine temples and ashram centers: six in California and one each in Phoenix, Arizona; Front Royal, Virginia; and Nuremberg, Germany. There are also an additional 172 centers and meditation groups in the United States and 220 in 47 other countries. The Yogoda Satsang Society of India had 100 centers and operated a variety of charitable facilities.

Educational Facilities:

There are four Yogoda Satsanga Society colleges in India: one each in Suraikhet and Palpara and two in Ranchi.

Periodicals: *Self-Realization*.

Sources:

Self-Realization Fellowship. www.yogananda-srf.org .

Mata, Sri Daya. *Only Love*. Los Angeles: Self-Realization Fellowship, 1976.

New Pilgrims of the Spirit. Boston: Beacon Press, 1921.

Self-Realization Fellowship Highlights. Los Angeles: Self-Realization Fellowship, 1980.

Self Realization Fellowship Manuel of Services. Los Angeles: Self-Realization Fellowship, 1965.

Yogananda, Paramahansa. *Autobiography of a Yogi*. Los Angeles: Self-Realization Fellowship, 1971.

———. *Descriptive Outlines of Yogoda*. Los Angeles: Yogoda Satsang Society, 1928.

———. *The Yoga of Jesus: Understanding the Hidden Teachings of the Gospels*. Los Angeles: Self-Realization Fellowship, n.d.

Self-Revelation Church of Absolute Monism

4748 Western Ave., Washington, DC 20816

Several movements have grown out of the work of Swami Paramahansa Yogananda's disciples. The Self-Revelation Church of Absolute Monism is an independent church founded by Swami Premananda, who was called from India by Yogananda in 1928. It now operates independently of the Self-Realization Fellowship. Besides the tradition of *kriya yoga* (self-realization) as taught by Premananda, the church highlights the life and work of Gandhi; the church oper-

ates the Mahatma Gandhi Memorial Foundation as an affiliate educational and cultural center.

Swami Premananda established the Swami Order of Absolute Monism for those who wish to follow the ideals of advaita vedanta. The current leader of the church and the Gandhi Memorial Center is Srimata Kamala. She was ordained a minister in the Swami Order in 1973 and a swami in 1978.

Membership: There is no formal membership. In 1995 there was one center in Washington, D.C., two other centers in the United States, and a mission in Midnapur, West Bengal. There are four ministers.

Educational Facilities:

The Gandhi Memorial Center administers a correspondence course on Mahatma Gandhi that is accorded independent-study credit at some American colleges. The course leads to a certificate from the Gujarat Vidyapith, the university founded by Gandhi in 1920. The Church of the Children, the original chapel, contains a small collection of books that began the Library of India; it contains more than 500 volumes of esoteric wisdom from the world's great religious traditions and a complete collection of Swami's own works.

Periodicals: *The Mystic Cross*. • *The Gandhi Message Self-Revelation*.

Sources:

Self-Revelation Church of Absolute Monism. www.self-revelationchurch.org.

Premananda, Swami. *Light on Kriya Yoga*. Washington, DC: Swami Premananda Foundation, 1969.

———. *The Path of the Eternal Law*. Washington, DC: Self-Realization Fellowship, 1942.

———. *Prayers of Self-Realization*. Washington, DC: Self-Realization Fellowship, 1943.

———. *Prayers of Soul*. Washington, DC: Self-Revelation Church of Absolute Monism, 1996.

Shanti Mandir

51 Mulktananda Marg, Walden, NY 12586

Alternate Address: International Headquarters: c/o Greenfield School, A/Z Safdarjung Enclave, New Delhi 110029, India

Before Swami Muktananda died in 1982 he picked a brother-and-sister team, Swami Nityananda and Swami Chidvilasananda, to succeed him. For three years they coadministered the large global organization, Siddha Yoga Dham, that Muktananda had built. The apparent smoothness of the transition was soon disrupted by controversy and accusations, and in 1985 Swami Nityananda withdrew from Siddha Yoga Dham, renounced his vows as a sannyasin, and entered private life as a teacher of meditation in California. In July 1987 he founded Shanti Mandir (Temple of Peace) and began holding meditation retreats and other programs in America, Europe, Australia, and India.

On December 26, 1989, with a dip in the near-freezing water of the Ganges River at Haridwar, India, Nityananda reaffirmed his sannyas vow and his commitment to Muktananda and to God's work. A lengthy period of conflict and harassment followed as members of Siddha Yoga Dham challenged his authority.

In May 1995 the Mahamandaleshwars, a network of spiritual leaders in Haridwar who act as advisors to the governing bodies of their respective regions, inducted Nityananda into their association in a ceremony at Suratgiri Bangla in Haridwar. Swami Nityananda, at the age of 32, became history's youngest Mahamandaleshwar.

Swami Nityananda continues to spread the teachings of Swami Muktananda, offering introductory meditation lessons while emphasizing chanting as a powerful meditation practice and encouraging his followers to see all life as a manifestation of God's energy.

Membership: Not reported. There are centers in India, Germany, Spain, United States, Mexico, and Australia.

Periodicals: *Eternally Blissful.*

Sources:

Shanti Mandir. www.shantimandir.com.

"Nityananda, One of Swami Muktananda's Successors, 'Retakes' Sannyasin Vows." *Hinduism Today* 12, 4 (April 1990). Available from www.hinduismtoday.com/archives/1990/04/1990-04-09.shtml.

Shanti Temple

43 S Main St., Spring Valley, NY 10977

The Shanti Temple is a Hindu center founded in the 1980s by Swami Shantanand Saraswati. Swami Shantanand teaches a simple way of regulation of the self, selfless service, and awareness. Awareness is attained through a seven-stage path of self-realization. The stages begin with *shubhechchha* (good desire), *suvicharana* (discrimination between the unreal and real), and *tanumansa* (steadfastness of mind). In the third stage the practice of concentration inaugurates the process of the development of detachment. In the fourth stage, *sattwapatti* (self-realization), one realizes the self as the light of pure awareness, the nonjudgmental observer of the mind. The fifth stage, *asansakti* (detachment), is a new level of detachment above ego, right and wrong, pride, and humility. The sixth stage, *padarthabjavni*, brings the ego into attunement with spirit and leads to the final stage, *turyaga*, in which the ego is completely immersed in spirit.

The Shanti Temple operates out of a single center in Spring Valley, New York. Swami Shantanand is the author of several books.

Membership: Not reported.

Sources:

Shantanand Saraswati, Swami. *The Challenge of Wisdom.* Spring Valley, NY: Shanti Temple, 1987.

Shanti Yoga Institute and Yoga Retreat

943 Central Ave., Ocean City, NJ 08226

The Shanti Yoga Institute and Yoga Retreat was founded in 1974 by Shanti Desai. Yogi Desai became a disciple of Swami Kripalvanandji at a young age and was initiated at age 15. He came to the United States to pursue graduate studies in chemistry at Drexel University, earning his master's degree in 1964. In 1972 he left his job as a chemist to devote his life to teaching yoga. He returned to India and received *shaktipat* (conferring of spiritual power on a student by a guru) initiation from his guru. On his return to the United States, he founded the Shanti Yoga Institute of New Jersey. In 1974 he opened the Yoga Retreat in Ocean City, New Jersey, and in 1981 he opened Prasad, a holistic health food store and restaurant. Shanti has published four books, an instructional yoga video, and a two-volume audio cassette, *Healing Mantra Chants*. Shanti designed his instruction of yoga for a Western audience and has trained several thousand students and a number of yoga teachers.

Membership: There was one center in New Jersey.

Remarks: Shanti Desai is the brother of Amrit Desai, founder of the Kirpalu Yoga Fellowship.

Sources:

Shanti Yoga Institute and Yoga Retreat www.yogishantidesai.com

Desai, Yogi Shanti. *The Complete Practice Manual of Yoga.* Ocean City, NJ: Shanti Yogi Institute, 1976.

———. *Hatha Yoga Practice Manual.* Ocean City, NJ: Shanti Yogi Institute, 1977. 72pp.

———. *Meditation Practice Manual.* Ocean City, NJ: Shanti Yogi Institute, 1981. 152 pp.

———. *Personal to Global Transformation.* Ocean City, NJ: Shanti Yogi Institute. 265 pp.

———. *Yoga, Holistic Practice Manual.* Ocean City, NJ: Shanti Yogi Institute, 1976. 260 pp.

Shiva-Shakti Kashmir Shavite Ashram

Current address not obtained for this edition.

The Shiva-Shakti Kashmir Shavite Ashram is a small Hindu group that emerged around the leadership of Swami Savitripriya. Beginning in 1968, Swami Savitripriya (b. 1930) had a series of mystical experiences that led her in the mid-1970s to proclaim herself a *siddha* (perfected master) guru of the highest level. She began to teach what she calls *maha siddha yoga* and to bring together a closely knit group of disciples who worked together as monks and nuns. During the 1980s they founded an ashram in Groveland, California.

The movement ran into problems in 1990 when the Siddha Yoga Dham challenged Swami Savitripriya's use of the term *maha siddha yoga*; a Siddha Yoga Dham claimed ownership of the term *siddha yoga*. The conflict was part of a larger conflict within Hindu circles over the trademarking of various terms common to Hinduism that had been pioneered in America by various organizations. At last report the issue remains unresolved.

Swami Savitripriya lives in her small private ashram and devotes her time to translating Hindu scriptures and original books.

Membership: Not reported.

Educational Facilities: Holy Mountain University, Groveland, California.

Sources:

Shiva-Shakti Kashmir Shavite Ashram. sanskritdocuments.org/sites/savitripriya/home.htm.

Palani, Sivasiva. "The Trademark Wars." *Hinduism Today* (November 1990): 1, 23. Available from www.hinduismtoday.com/archives/1990/11/1990-11-02.shtml.

Savitripriya, Swami. *From Darkness to Light: My Autobiography.* Sunnyvale, CA: New Life Books, n.d.

———. *Mysteries of the Cosmos Unveiled: Truths about the Universe, God and Man.* New Word Hinduism.

———. *Practice the Yoga Dharma at Home Workbook.* New World Hinduism.

———. *Psychology of Mystical Awakening.* Sunnyvale, CA: New Life Books, 1991.

Shri Krishna Pranami Association of U.S.A. and Canada

c/o Shree Krishna Pranami Mandir of Houston, 14303 FM 762, Richmond, TX 77469

The Shri Krishna Pranami Association of U.S.A. and Canada (formerly the Shri Krishna Association of the U.S.A.) is the North American representative of the Pranami religion, a form of Hinduism that originated in India in the sixteenth century during the midst of a Hindu-Muslim conflict. It was founded by Shri Devchandraji (1581–1655), a seeker who as a young man resided for a time at Jamnagar, where he was given a vision of Krishna during which the deity gave him the "Highest Knowledge" and initiated him with the Tartam Mantra. Shri Devchandraji was given the task of spreading this unique knowledge. He subsequently found an assistant in the person of Shri Prannathji (1618–1694), a government official in the state of Jamnagar who became a disciple of Shri Devchandraji's during the reign of Aurangzeb (r. 1658–1707), a Muslim. In response to an Islamic evangelistic campaign launched by Aurangzeb that was disrupting the Hindu community, Prannathji resigned his post and dedicated his life to saving Hinduism. He preached a monotheistic form of faith that rejected the many Hindu gods and goddesses in favor of Krishna, whom he believed to be the only god. Based upon this monotheism, he called for rapprochement between Hindus and Muslims.

The lineage of Shri Prannathji was continued into the twentieth century when it came to be held by Guruji Shri Mangaldasji (1896–1985). He spread the work to eastern India and founded the Guruji Pranami Mission Trust. He also oversaw the beginnings of the work in the West. Though he never came to the United States, his successor and the present head of the Trust, Guruji Shri Mohan Priyacharyaji, has on several occasions.

The Pranamis have a holy book, Tartam Sagar, composed of some 18,000 verses written by Prannathji. It draws on concepts from the Bhagavad-Gita, the Qur'an, and other scriptures. The movement took hold in Jamnagar and eventually spread across India into Nepal.

The Pranami religion was initially brought to the United States in the 1970s by immigrants. Followers can now be found in most major urban areas with a significant Indian-American population, including Los Angeles, Houston, Chicago, Detroit, and Atlanta. There are also followers in Canada. The current president of the Shri Krishna Pranami Association of U.S.A. and Canada, Ved P. Bhagat, resides in Washington, D.C.

Membership: Not reported. The movement claims some four million followers and 400 temples in India and Nepal.

Sources:

Guruji Pranami Mission Trust. www.pranami.org/pranami_mission.shtml.

Dongre, Archana. "Int'l Conference of Pranami Religion Held." *India-West*, July 3, 1992.

Priyacharya, M. *An Introduction to Krishna Pranami Religion.* Ed. D. Clinch. Detroit, MI: Shri Krishna Pranami Association, 1992.

Sharma, S. *Mahamati Prannath: The Saviour.* New Delhi, India: Shri Prannath Mission, 1984.

Shri Ram Chandra Mission

Rte. 1, Box 122-5, 5611 GA Hwy. 109, Molena, GA 30258

Alternate Address: International Headquarters: c/o Gayathri, 19 North St., Sri Ram Nagar, Madras, 600 018, India.

The Shri Ram Chandra Mission in India was established in 1945 by Sri Ram Chandraji Maharaj of Shahjahanpur; he is popularly known as "Babuji." The mission was founded in memory of Babuji's master, Samarth Guru Mahatma Shri Ram Chandraji Maharaj of Fatehgarh, who is affectionately known as "Lalaji." Its objectives are to educate and propagate among the masses the art and science of yoga, formulated to meet present-day conditions and needs; to promote the feelings of mutual love and universal brotherhood, irrespective of caste, creed, or color; and to conduct research in the field of yoga and establish research institutes for that purpose.

The son of a scholar, Ram Chandra was born to a Kayastha family on April 30, 1899, in Shahjahanpur. He was not an outstanding student but by his teen years had developed an interest in philosophy, literature, and geography. In his secular life, he joined the court and retired in 1954 after 30 years of service. He eventually found his way to Sri Ram Chandraji of Fategarh, who taught a forgotten method of *pranahuti* (divine transmission) used by yogis in ancient times. Ram Chandra commenced his spiritual training under the guidance of Sri Ram Chandraji and gave up the discipline of *pranayama* (lengthening of the *prana* or breath), which he had been practicing for the previous seven years.

When his guru died in 1931, Ram Chandra felt that his spiritual instruction had been completed. He had a sense of total convergence with his guru's spirit. In 1932 he received a further transmission from his guru but was not able to bear it fully, and he was overfilled with divine energy. He gave the guru credit in 1944, when he had the vision of a light like that which Moses saw and also Sri Krishna's viratsvarupa. The Sri Ram Chandra Mission was founded to carry out the mission of his master.

Sri Ram Chandraji Maharaj died on April 19, 1983. He was succeeded by his disciple, Sri Parthasarathi Rajagopalachari of Chennai, the current president of Shri Ram Chandra Mission. Also known as "Chariji," Sri Parthasarathi Rajagopalachari was born in 1927 in a village called Vayalur near Madras. He graduated from Benaras Hindu University with a B.S. degree and found employment with Indian Plastics Limited in chemical engineering. He rose to an executive position with the T. T. Krishnamachari group of companies in Bombay and stayed with this firm until his retirement in 1985. In the meantime, his conscious spiritual aspirations had been awakened at the age of 18 by a lecture on the *Bhagavad Gita*. He discovered Sri Ram Chandraji Maharaj in 1964, and both he and his father accepted him as their new guru after hearing about this system of raja yoga. In recent years Chariji has traveled extensively around the world, conducting public seminars in which he gives instruction on the *sahaj marg* system of meditation.

The way of sahaj marg is embodied in the 10 maxims, which lay out a daily schedule for the disciples. They rise before dawn to offer *puja* (worship) that begins with a prayer for spiritual elevation. Each day the disciples' goal is complete oneness with God. They strive to live a truthful, plain, and simple life and treat all people as their brothers and sisters. They eschew revenge and live out of gratitude, seeking to inspire feelings of love and piety in others. The day ends in a feeling of the presence of God and the asking for forgiveness for any wrongs committed.

Membership: The mission has several hundred centers in India and numerous countries around the world. The training is imparted by the president of the mission and more than 1,000 trainers (called preceptors) throughout the world.

Periodicals: *Sahag Marg Magazine*, SRCM Danmark, Vrads Sande, Vej4, 8654 Bryrup, Denmark.

Sources:

Shri Ram Chandra Mission. www.srcm.org.

Chandra, Ram. *Autobiography of Ram Chandra.* 3 vols. Shahjahanpur, India: Shri Ram Chandra Mission, 1974, 1986, 1997.

———. *Complete Works of Ram Chandra.* Vol 1. Pacific Grove, CA: North American Publishing Committee, 1989.

———. *Letters of the Master, Volumes I & II.* Shahjahanpur, India: Shri Ram Chandra Mission, 1992. Vol. 1, 363 pp.; Vol. 2, 338 pp.

———. *Letters of the Master, Volume III.* Shahjahanpur, India: Shri Ram Chandra Mission, 1996. 332 pp.

———. *Messages Universal, Volume I.* Shahjahanpur, India: Shri Ram Chandra Mission, 1986. 122 pp.

Shri Shivabalayogi International Maharaj Trust

PO Box 293, Langley, WA 98260

Alternate Addresses: Shri Shivabalayogi Maharaj Trust, J. P. Nagar, Bangalore 560 078, India. • 2 Olleff Rd., Langford Town, Bangalore 560 025.

The Shri Shivabalayogi Maharaj Trusts dates back to 1961, the year in which Bala Yogi completed a spiritual quest that led to his self-realization. Bala Yogi was born in 1935 to a poverty-stricken family in Adivarapupeta, a village in Andhra Pradesh, India. As a child he went to work as a weaver of sarees. His commercial endeavors were derailed when, at the age of 14, he had an intense experience of *jyoti*, the divine light, and he heard the sound of *om*, the basic generative sound of the universe. A person identified as Jangam Shiva, a Hindu deity, appeared before him, and he went into *samadhi*, a mystical state of consciousness.

The experience changed the course of Bala Yogi's life. He began a period of *tapas*, intensive meditation and austerity, that lasted for 12 years. On August 7, 1961, he emerged as a yogi. He began a mission that consisted of initiating students into the practice of meditation with the goal of *darshan* (vision of the realized person). He also gave consecrated *vibhuti* (ash) for healing of body and mind and trained disciples to achieve *bhava samadhi* (divine trance).

Shivabalayogi does not teach in words but through silence and experience. He gives *dhyana diksha* (initiation into meditation) to all who seek earnestly. His only verbal instruction is to meditate daily. Through our own meditation, we come to know the truth of who we are and our purpose in life. In the yogi's subtle body presence devotees often gather to sit in meditation, which is followed by *bhajans*, songs in praise of God; during this singing devotees may experience varying degrees of divine ecstasy.

Numerous ashrams were dedicated to Shavabalayogi in towns throughout India: Adivarapupeta, the location of the Mother Ashram; Bangalore, the site of the largest ashram; Dehradun, Sambhar Lake; Hyderabad; and Agra. In the late 1980s he established his first Western center in London and moved to the United States, establishing trusts in Portland, Oregon; Seattle, Washington; and Raleigh, North Carolina.

Membership: Not reported.

Sources:

Shri Shivabalayogi International Maharaj Trust. www.shiva.org.

Bala Yogi Maharaj, Shri Shiva. *Life and Spiritual Ministration.* Bangalore, India: Shri Shivabalayogi Maharaj Trust, n.d. 128 pp.

———. *Spiritual Essence and Luminescence.* Bangalore, India: Shri Shivabalayogi Maharaj Trust, n.d. 18 pp.

Palotas, Tom. *Divine Play: The Silent Teaching of Shiva Bala Yogi.* Twin Lakes, WI: Lotus Press, n.d. 290 pp.

"Shiva's Own Bala Yoga." *Hinduism Today.* 12, 8 (August 1990): 1, 25. Available from www.hinduismtoday.com/archives/1990/08/1990-08-01.shtml.

Shri Yoga Vedanta Ashram

45 Texas Rd., Matawan, NJ 07747

Alternate Address: International headquarters: Sabarmati, Motera, Ahmedabad-380005, Gujrat, India • Canadian headquarters: 2647 Crystalburn Ave. Mississauga, ON, Canada L5B 2N7.

The Shri Yoga Vedanta Ashram is the vehicle for the ministry of the Indian spiritual teacher Pujya Sant Sri Asaramji Bapu (b. 1942). He was born in what is now Pakistan; his family moved to Gujarat, India, following the partition of India. He was raised in a devout Hindu home. As a young man he made a pilgrimage to Vrindavan, the holy city, where he met Swami Sri Lilashahaji Maharaj. Upon his return home, he started a period of intensive spiritual practice at a site near the river Narmada at Moti Koral. His practice culminated in his meeting with SadGurudev Lilashahji Maharaj in Mumbai. He emerged from the experience as Swami Sri Asaramji Maharaj. He was instructed to continue to serve humanity by remaining a householder. Having attained a state of self-realization, he spent the next seven years in seclusion.

He chose to reside at a site in Motera, a village on the banks of Sabarmati River where some of his devotees constructed a small room for him. That room was the beginning of what became the first site of Shri Yoga Vedanta Ashram. His followers came to see him as the embodiment of an ancient Vedantic ideal of perfection, one who, after attaining liberation for himself, strives for the liberation of others. He is thus known as a *rishi*.

His message emphasizes traditional Hindu themes of Vedanta, yoga, divine love, *bhakti* (devotion), and *mukti* (salvation). He bestows "divine love" through *shaktipat* (the act of a guru or spiritual teacher conferring a form of spiritual "power" or awakening on a disciple/student), by which he releases *kundalini* (an unconscious, instinctive, or erotic force or energy) in his disciples. He has developed "Maun Mandirs," special temples for spiritual practices (primarily meditation) where adherents may stay in complete seclusion for seven days. These small structures (many in the shape of pyramids), available at all his ashrams, are reserved for those who wish to make rapid progress in the spiritual life.

After the formal establishment of the ashram in 1971, Pujya Bapuji began to travel and speak, first around India and then internationally. His popularity in the United States dates from his appearance in 1993 at the World's Parliament of Religions. Headquarters were established in New Jersey, and additional centers opened in Chicago, Boston, and California. There is one center in Canada.

An ashram for women was also established at Ahmedabad; there the residents devote their time to spiritual practices and performing services for the ashram. They are led by the honorable mother Laxmidevi. The ashram residents also mix and distribute various ayurvedic medicinal products. Their activity is part of a larger effort to assist people around India with ayurvedic medicine.

Membership: In 2000 there were 111 ashrams in India and 450 meditation centers around the world.

Periodicals: *Rishi Prasad.*

Sources:

Shri Yoga Vedanta Ashram. www.ashram.org/njashram.

Sivananda Yoga Vedanta Centers

673 8th Ave., Val Morin, QC, Canada J0T 2R0

Alternate Address: International affiliate: (unofficial) Divine Life Society, P.O. Shivanandanagar, Dist. Tehri-Garwal, Uttar Pradesh, India.

The first of the Sivananda Yoga Vedanta Centers was founded in North America in 1959 by Swami Vishnu Devananda (b. 1927), the North American representative of the late Swami Sivananda Saraswati (1887–1963), who was sent to the West in 1957.

Swami Sivananda Saraswati (born Kuppuswami Iyer) was one of several renowned twentieth-century Hindus who became revered as saints and holy men. Reared by devout parents who encouraged his education, he began to study medicine but interrupted his studies after the death of his father. He moved to Malaysia to work as a hospital administrator, but after 10 years, in 1923, he returned to India to pursue a spiritual quest. He was initiated as a *sannyasin*, a follower of a life of renunciation, and settled at Swargashram, near Rishikish, where many sannyasins lived. He began to write, teach, and make pilgrimages around India. He advocated a life of *bhakti yoga* (devotion) and *karma yoga* (service).

Unwilling to forget the life of service upon which he had embarked as a youth, he moved to Rishikish and established an ashram. As part of the ashram facility, he opened a medical dispensary to serve the local community. By 1936 the work had grown considerably. He formed the Divine Life Trust and the Divine Life Society, an open-membership auxiliary. The dispensary grew into a major medical facility, and the ashram became a major center for the propagation of yoga. It soon attracted many of the best teachers from various parts of India.

Sivananda's teaching is summarized in the motto "Serve, love, give, meditate, purify, realize." He led his students upon a *sadhana* (path to enlightenment) that included *bhakti* (practicing love) and *ahimsa* (constant striving to do no harm and cause no pain). He developed a synthesis of yoga that he called integral yoga; it included the four traditional forms of bhakti, jnana, karma, and raja, to which he added a fifth, *japa* (repetition of a mantra).

Sivananda never visited North America, but he sent several of his students. As early as 1959, Swami Chidananda, his successor as leader of the ashram in India, visited the United States. Even before Sivananda's death, his student began to establish work outside of India. Sivananda sent Swami Vishnu Devananda (1927–1993) to work in Canada and the United States. Although other students of Sivananda's have come to the United States, Vishnu Devananda is the teacher recognized by the Divine Life Society in India.

Swami Vishnu Devananda was originally attracted to Swami Sivananda by reading his books and formally became his disciple in 1947. In 1949, at the Sivanandashram in Rishikish, Sivananda initiated him into the ancient sannyasin order of the renounced life, and Vishnu Devananda, through his studies and practice of the rigorous spiritual disciplines, became one of Sivananda's most accomplished pupils. He came to the West in 1957 at Sivananda's direction. He founded several centers in the United States before settling permanently in Canada in 1958. He established his North American headquarters in Montreal.

Swami Vishnu Devananda follows the teachings of Sivananda. He emphasizes the benefits of a rigorous spiritual discipline and has focused upon raja and hatha yoga. He also purveyed the complete yoga doctrines of his teacher. The Sivananda Yoga Vedanta Ashrams are headed by Vishnu Devananda, and the various centers are headed by teachers trained by him. In 1962 he founded the Sivananda Ashram Yoga Camp in the Laurentian Mountains of Quebec; in 1967 he established the Sivananda Ashram Yoga Retreat in the Bahamas. Both provide intensive yoga training in a vacationlike setting. He has established ashrams (sanctuaries for the systematic practice of yoga for residents) in Val Morin, Quebec; Woodburne, New York; Grass Valley, California; and Trivandrum, India. Other centers are located in Austria, France, Germany, Great Britain, Israel, Spain, Switzerland, and Uruguay.

The True World Order, Vishnu Devananda's continuing world peace and brotherhood mission, was founded in 1969. To demonstrate his concern for peace and the importance of nonviolence, he has flown around the world dropping leaflets and organizing peace demonstrations at various trouble spots. He conducted one famous peace mission to Belfast, Northern Ireland, with the late actor Peter Sellers. He also has showered the Suez Canal and the Berlin Wall with leaflets and flowers.

Membership: There are four Ashrams and six centers located throughout North America. In addition, several thousand followers have been trained as yoga teachers and are now active in a wide variety of locations apart from the Sivananda Yoga Vedanta Centers.

Periodicals: *Yoga Life.* Available from Sivananda Yoga Vedanta Center, 243 W 24th St., New York, NY 10011.

Remarks: Among the disciples of Sivananda was Swami Venkatesananda, who did spiritual work in Australia and South Africa. During the 1980s the Chiltern Yoga Foundation was established in San Francisco, California, for the sole purpose of publishing and distributing Swami Venkatesananda's books in the United States and Canada.

Sources:

Sivananda Yoga Vedanta Centers. www.sivananda.org.

Behera, Sarat Chandra. *The Holy Stream: The Inspiring Life of Swami Chidananda.* Sivanandanagar, India: Divine Life Society, 1981.

Devananda, Swami Vishnu. *The Complete Illustrated Book of Yoga.* New York: Julian Press, 1960.

———. *The Hatha Yoga Pradhipika.* N.p., n.d.

———. *Meditation and Mantras.* New York: OM Lotus Publishing Company, 1978.

———. *The Sivananda Upanishad.* New York: OM Lotus Publishing Company, 1987.

Krishna, Copala. *The Yogi: Portraits of Swami Vishnu-Devananda.* St. Paul, MN: Yes International Publishers, 1995. 149 pp.

Sivananda, Swami. *Sadhana.* Sivanandanagar, India: Divine Life Society, 1967.

The Sivananda Yoga Center. *The Sivananda Companion to Yoga.* New York: Simon & Schuster, 1983.

Tawker, K. A. *Sivananda, One World Teacher.* Rishikish, India: Yoga-Vedanta Forest University, 1957.

Venkatesananda, Swami. *Gurudev Sivananda.* Durban, South Africa: Divine Life Society of South Africa, 1961.

SMVA Trust

14516 Rumfeldt, Austin, TX 78725

The SMVA Trust is the vehicle of the work and teaching of Sri Karunamayi (b. 1958), a female spiritual teacher from India who is generally known simply as Amma. Amma's spiritual and humanitarian inclinations manifested in her teen years, and

at one point she locked herself in the family meditation room for a month. She emerged with a new demeanor, which was described as intensely reflecting an impersonal, universal love. Soon afterward, she left home to spend a period in solitary meditation in the forest. She was 21 when she left home for good. She remained alone for the next 10 years, and through her spiritual practices during this time attained insights about which of the Vedic teachings and practices would be of greatest benefit to people in the modern world. She then returned to society to begin life as a teacher.

Amma initially settled in Bangalore, India, where an early disciple provided her a room in which to live and teach. Along with sharing her spiritual insights, she conducted ceremonies aimed at promoting world peace and universal well-being and worked toward the goal of supplying medical care for people living in the villages of the region. Out of this latter effort came the Sri Karunamayi Free Hospital.

Amma initially came to the United States in 1995 after accepting an invitation to present some public programs. She has subsequently returned annually for a national tour that has included lectures, classes, retreats, and *homa* (fire) ceremonies. Simultaneously, she began to develop a following in Europe.

Amma has emphasized the need for humans to cultivate inner beauty and ultimately reach spiritual liberation in order to reach a state in which they can provide selfless service to all. According to Amma, the purpose of human life is found in the development of a range of virtues, such as compassion, truthfulness, dispassionate wisdom, contentment, and selfless love. Manifesting such virtues leads to a peaceful state of mind that allows the deep meditation conducive to direct contact with the *Atman*, or divine inner self. Merging with the Atman is the destiny of all.

The international headquarters of the movement remains at the ashram in Bangalore. Humanitarian efforts have led to the development of the hospital and a Free School serving the surrounding region.

Membership: Not reported. In 2008 there were 15 *satsang* groups that met regularly at various locations across the United States.

Sources:

SMVA Trust. www.karunamayi.org/.

Karunamayi: A Biography. Bangalore, India: SMVA Trust, 2005.

Karunamayi, Sri. *Blessed Souls: The Teachings of Sri Karunamayi.* 2 vols. Bangalore: SMVA Triest, 1998, 2000.

———. *Sri Gayatri: The Inner Secrets Revealed.* I & II. Bangalore: SMVA Trust, 2005.

Society of Abidance in Truth (SAT)

1834 Ocean St., Santa Cruz, CA 95060

The Society of Abidance in Truth (SAT), founded in the mid-1970s, is consecrated to the teaching of nonduality, especially as revealed by Bhagavan Sri Ramana Maharshi, the south Indian sage who flourished (1879–1950) at the holy mountain called Arunachala. SAT is under the spiritual guidance of Nome, with a background influence of advaita Vedanta, Russell Smith, and nondual Ch'an (Zen) Buddhism.

The teaching of nonduality proclaims that the true nature of the self, one's own being or consciousness, is that of the absolute (i.e., God, Brahman, or Buddha nature). It proclaims that the self, undivided being-consciousness-bliss, is infinite and eternal, the one reality that pervades and transcends all. This teaching places special emphasis on self-knowledge attained by inquiring "Who am I?" Such self-questioning, it is believed, reveals the real self and overcomes the illusion of a separate ego to reveal the homogeneous, infinite presence of reality. The result is self-realization, characterized by permanent peace and happiness.

The teaching has its roots in the Upanishads, the wisdom portion of the Vedas, and scriptures of Hinduism (also called *sanatana dharma* [the way of eternal truth]). This outlook was also expounded by Sri Sankaracharya, the eighth-century Indian sage, as well as in numerous scriptures and sayings of many other sages and saints of this tradition. It also has roots in nondual Buddhism, as exemplified by the Zen master of China during the T'ang Dynasty.

SAT endeavors to preserve and disseminate the wisdom of this spiritual tradition. The group maintains a center in Santa Cruz, California, where seekers can learn about the teaching, practice it, and strive to realize self-knowledge. Other activities include the distribution of every book in English by or about Sri Ramana Maharshi; the distribution of Vedanta and Zen literature; and the translation and publication of books such as the *Ribbu Gita* (an ancient treatise on nondual truth), Sri Sankara's works, and teachings given by Nome and Russell Smith. SAT also conducts weekly *satsangs* (gatherings of persons who listen to, talk about, and assimilate the truth) and other holy events and retreats. It also sponsors performances of sacred music from around the world.

Membership: As of 2002, the SAT reported members scattered throughout the world, but most are concentrated in the area around Santa Cruz, California.

Periodicals: *Reflections.*

Sources:

Society of Abidance in Truth (SAT). www.satramana.org.

The Journey Home. Santa Cruz, CA: Avadhut, 1986.

Maharshi's Gospel. Tiruvannamalai, India: T. N. Venkataraman, 1957.

Spiritual Instruction of Bhagavan Sri Raman Maharshi. Tiruvannamalai, India: T. N. Venkataraman, 1939.

Maharshi, Sri Ramana. *The Collected Works of Sri Ramana Maharshi.* Thiruvannamalai, India: Sri Ramanasramam, 2007. 318 pp.

Nome. *The Four Requisites for Realization and Self-Inquiry.* Santa Cruz, CA: Society of Abidance in Truth, 2003. 32 pp.

————. *Ribhu Gita.* Santa Cruz, CA: Society of Abidance in Truth, 1995.

————. *Self-Knowledge.* Atma Jnana Publications, 2003.

Sankara, Adi. *Svatmanirupanam (The True Definition of One's Own Self).* Santa Cruz, CA: Society of Abidance in Truth, 2002.

————. *A Bouquet of Nondual Texts.* Santa Cruz, CA: Society of Abidance in Truth, 2006.

Source School of Tantra Yoga

PO Box 368, Kahului, HI 96733

Source School of Tantra Yoga was founded in 1978 by Charles Muir. Muir began to study yoga in 1965 and took his instructor training from Richard Hittleman. In 1974 he founded and directed the "Yoga for Health" Schools in California. In the meantime he became interested in tantra. Caroline Muir is a yoga instructor and massage instructor. The pair began working together in the early 1980s and now teach tantra as a means of physical, mental, and spiritual awakening.

The Muirs strive to facilitate their students to fully express themselves as both physical and spiritual beings and believe that sex and spirit are inextricably connected. Sexual activity thus becomes a means of profound meditation and sexuality a unifying, harmonizing, and spiritualizing force of the universe.

The school offers workshops and seminars in Hawaii, California, and Colorado, and the Muirs' teachings are spread through several tapes and one book.

Membership: Not reported.

Sources:

Source School of Tantra Yoga. www.sourcetantra.com

Muir, Charles, and Caroline Muir. *Tantra: The Art of Conscious Loving.* San Francisco: Mercury House, 1989.

Spiritual Realization Institute

c/o Sri Puri Dhama Vaishnava Community, PO Box 305, Lockport, NY 14095-0305

The Spiritual Realization Institute was founded by Geoffrey Giuliano (b. 1953), who has now legally changed his name to Jagannatha Dasa. As Geoffrey Giuliano he was well known for his books on popular music and various celebrities. He has written a number of books on the Beatles, including the controversial *Dark Horse: The Life and Art of George Harrison* and, more recently, *Two of Us: John Lennon and Paul McCartney Behind the Myth.* He also played the role of Ronald McDonald (the clown figure of the McDonald's fast food chain) in personal appearances for several years. As Jagannatha Dasa, he has been a student/practitioner of the Chaitanya devotional tradition of Hinduism and the founder of an ashram in Lockport, New York, the home of the Spiritual Realization Institute.

Giuliano initially became a devotee of Krishna consciousness in 1970, though only part time. After his graduation from college (with a degree in acting) in 1978, he took a job playing the Marvelous Magical Burger King and in 1980 began a two-year stint as Ronald McDonald in Canada. As he became more serious about his Krishna attachments and his belief in vegetarianism, he quit that job.

Giuliano joined the International Society for Krishna Consciousness (ISKCON) but left in 1980, when he found that "certain improprieties of my god-brothers came to light." That same year, while in Toronto, he met B. H. Mangal Niloy Goswami Maharaja, a Krishna-consciousness guru, and in 1982 both he and his wife took initiation and accepted their new spiritual names, Jagannatha Dasa and Vrndarani Devi. He eventually decided to follow the path of Krishna devotion. He recommitted himself to his religious faith in 1990. Three years later he and his wife established Sri Puri Dhama Vaishnava Community in Niagara County, New York. It was legally incorporated in 1996 as The Spiritual Realization Institute (SRI), which describes itself as an "international resource for those interested in the Vedic arts and sciences as well as a fully functioning educational and cultural institution." In the 1990s he also operated as an anti-McDonald's activist. SRI has become a member of the Food Bank of Western New York and, under the name Dasa Food For All, operates the only vegetarian food pantry in the area.

Membership: As of 1999 SRI had about 30 initiated disciples who have been given spiritual names and another 50 members from across western New York.

Sources:

Michelmore, William V. "Renowned Rock Biographer Reincarnates As Hindu Leader." www.vnn.org/usa/US9908/US30-4615.html.

Sree Rama Dasa Mission

Current address could not be obtained for this edition.

The Sree Rama Dasa Mission is the product of two extraordinary Indian spiritual teachers. The first, Brahmashree Neelakanta Gurupadar (1900–1965), was an original teacher who attained high states of consciousness without benefit of a teacher of his own. In 1920, as a young man, Gurupadar moved into a small ashram, after which he spent the next 45 years engaged in what is termed *Atmarama worship,* defined as a practice in which the worshipper and the worshipped attain absolute communion. He was watched by people and attained a reputation for leading a humble and disciplined life, as well as one filled with various manifestations of a variety of *siddhas,* or supernatural powers.

In 1962 Gurupadar formally established the Sree Rama Dasa Mission, consecrated the Rama-Sita-Anjaneya temple, and introduced regular worship. Three years later, he anointed his chosen successor, Jagadguru Swami Sathyananda Saraswathi (d. 2006). Swami Sathyananda shared many characteristics of his predecessor. Following Gurupadar's death, he engaged in 14 years of intense devotional practice based on a rigorous regime of conducting *pujas* (offerings to the divine) five times each day. He was believed to have attained a mystical union with the Divine Mother, at whose command he subsequently pursued an effort aimed at the comprehensive uplift of Indian society. Like his predecessor, he was also believed to have developed a number of *siddhas,* most notably the ability to bilocate. Sathyananda was also an advocate of the various paths of yoga.

Swami Sathyananda began his mission in the West in 2000. That year he was given the Hindu of the Year award by the Federation of Hindu Associations in Los Angeles. The next year he organized the first Kerala Hindu Convention of North America, which met at Dallas, Texas, in April 2001. Sathyananda subsequently took the lead in holding the Second and Third National Conventions of the Kerala Hindus of North America (2003 and 2005, respectively). His worldwide travels resulted in the formation of branch centers of the Mission in Malaysia, New Zealand, Switzerland, the Caribbean Islands, the United Kingdom, and the United States. The majority of affiliates are immigrants from Kerala State, India.

Membership: Not reported. As of 2008, American centers of the Sree Rama Dasa Mission were located in New York City, Boston, Philadelphia, Chicago, Richmond, Virginia, Dallas and Houston, Texas, and Los Angeles and San Jose, California.

Sources:

Sree Rama Dasa Mission. www.srdm.org/.

Sri Caitanya Sanga

Sri Chaitanya Saraswati Math, Kolerganj, PO Nabadwip, Dist. Nadia, West Bengal, India

The Sri Caitanya Sanga (formerly the Gaudiya Vaishnava Society) was founded in the mid-1980s by B. V. Tripurari Swami, previously a leader in the International Society for Krishna Consciousness (ISKCON). Tripurari Swami had met A. C. Bhaktivedanta Swami Prabhupada (1896–1977) in 1972, a year after he had joined ISKCON. Tripurari was initiated into *sannyas* (the renounced life) in 1975, two years prior to Prabhupada's death. In the years after Prabhupada's death, ISKCON was divided between reformists who denied the new initiating gurus (teachers) a status similar to that held by Prabhupada and the more conservative leaders who saw the new gurus as carrying on a guru lineage that made it proper to receive veneration much as Prabhupada had. Tripurari was among the reformists who left the organization and turned to Bhakti Rakshak Sridhara Maharaj (1895–1988), Prabhupada's godbrother. (The godbrother relationship exists when two or more are initiated by the same guru.) Remaining in India when Prabhupada went to America, Sridhara Maharaj based his work in the Sri Chaitanya Saraswati Math center in West Bengal. However, he slowly acquired a worldwide network of centers that had placed themselves under his guidance.

Tripurari and a small group of like-minded ex-ISKCON devotees placed themselves under Sridhara Maharaj's direction. The Gaudiya Vaishnava Society emerged as the organizational expression of the group's work in the United States. Almost immediately, the group ran into resistance from the city of San Francisco, California, which had passed an ordinance regulating the society's selling of their literature on the streets. In 1986 they took the city to court and won an injunction against the enforcement of the ordinance. For a number of years, beginning in 1988, the sanga issued a magazine, *The Clarion Call*.

The sanga is at one with ISKCON in belief and practice. The issues that divided them have largely been resolved with the dominance of the reform party in ISKCON in the 1980s. However, the society now flows out of the lineage of Sridhara Maharaj, a lineage not found in ISKCON. The sanga emphasizes a theistic Vaishnava Hinduism, follows a path of devotional service and temple worship (bhakti yoga), and emphasizes as a primary spiritual practice the repetition of the Hare Krishna Mantra:

> *Hare Krishna, Hare Krishna*
> *Krishna Krishna, Hare Hare*
> *Hare Rama, Hare Rama*
> *Rama Rama, Hare Hare.*

B. V. Tripurari Swami currently resides at Audarya, a retreat center near Philo, Mendocino County, California.

Membership: Not reported.

Sources:

Sri Caitanya Sanga. www.swami.org/.

"*Clarion Call*, a Classy New Journal from S. F. Gaudiyas." *Hinduism Today* 10, no. 9 (September 1988): 1, 17.

Sridhara Deva Goswami, Srila Bhakti Raksaka. *The Golden Volcano of Divine Love*. San Jose, CA: Guardian of Devotion Press, 1984.

———. *The Guru and His Grace*. San Rafael, CA: Mandala Publishing, 1983.

———. *The Hidden Treasure of the Absolute*. West Bengal, India: Sri Chaitanya Saraswati Math, 1985.

Thakur, Srila Bhaktivedanta. *Sri Chaitanya Mahaprabhu: His Life and Precepts*. Brooklyn, NY: Gaudiya Press, 1987.

Tripurari, Swami B. V. *Ancient Wisdom for Modern Ignorance*. Eugene, OR: Clarion Call Publishing, 1994.

Sri Chaitanya Saraswat Mandal

2900 N Rodeo Gulch Rd., Soquel, CA 95073

A. C. Bhaktivedanta Swami Prabhupada (1896–1977) was the founder-acharya of the International Society for Krishna Consciousness (ISKCON), the Hare Krishna movement in the West. Before he died, he informed his senior disciples that in his absence they should consult a higher authority. He instructed them to approach his trusted and revered godbrother (godbrother in the sense that they were both initiated by the same guru), Bhakti Raksaka Sridhara Deva Goswami. Both Prabhupada and Sridhara were initiated by Bhaktisiddanthanta Sarswati Thakur, the president-archarya of the Guadiya Math, which had been the main Krishna-consciousness organization in Bengal. In the wake of the disruption of the Guadiya Math in India, Sridhara was one of several disciples who founded an independent organization; his was called Sri Chaitanya Saraswati Math.

In the wake of Prabhupada's death, intense theological and organizational disputes emerged within the society and its governing board. Some of Prabhupada's disciples, following his instructions, turned to Sridhara for guidance and subsequently broke with the society and founded Sri Chaitanya Saraswat Mandal as an American branch of the math. Since its founding in the early 1980s, the Mandal has carried on an active publishing program through its Guardian of Devotion Press, which has issued many of Sridhara's books.

Membership: There is one temple affiliated with the mandal, with approximately 100 members. There are affiliated U.S. centers in California, Utah, Oregon, Oklahoma, New Jersey and Hawaii. There are also centers in England, Mexico, Brazil, Venezuela, South Africa, Italy, Netherlands, Hungary, India, Canada, Ireland, Malta, Portugal, the Czech Republic, Turkey, Thailand, Malaysia, the Philippines, Singapore, New Zealand, Fiji, Russia, Ukraine, Abkhazie, Ecuador, Mauritius, and Australia.

Sources:

Sri Chaitanya Saraswat Mandal. www.scsmath.com/centers.html.

Sridhara Deva Goswami, Bhakti Raksaka. *Parpanna Jivanamrta: Lifenectar of the Surrendered Souls*. Nabadwip Dham, West Bengal, India: Sri Chaitanya Saraswat Math, 1988.

———. *The Search for Sri Krsna: Reality the Beautiful*. San Jose, CA: Guardian of Devotion Press, 1983.

———. *Sri Guru and His Grace*. San Jose, CA: Guardian of Devotion Press, 1983.

———. *Srimad Bhagavad Gita*. 374 pp.

———. *Subjective Evolution of Consciousness: Play of the Sweet Absolute*. San Jose, CA: Guardian of Devotion Press, 1988.

Thakura, Bhaktivinoda. *The Bhagavat: Its Philosophy, Its Ethics, and Its Theology*. San Jose, CA: Guardian of Devotion Press, 1985.

Sri Chinmoy Centre

PO Box 32433, Jamaica, NY 11432

Sri Chinmoy Kumar Ghose was born in Bengal, India, in 1931. He entered the Sri Aurobindo Ashram at the age of 12. After two decades of intensive spiritual discipline, he responded to an inner command and came to the West in 1964 to be of service to seekers in that part of the world. He taught a path of yoga that directed the practitioner to conscious union with God. He also encouraged an active, dynamic life of service to the divine in humanity. His path called for a disciplined life involving regular meditation, living and working in the world, vegetarianism, and celibacy. Sri Chinmoy passed away on October 11, 2007, at his home in Queens, New York.

As a spiritual teacher Sri Chinmoy guided his students' meditative discipline and spiritual growth. He never charged any fee for his service and taught that the path of love, *bhakti* (devotion), and surrender to the divine is the easiest way to God, but he accepted all religions and had the utmost devotion for Christ, Buddha, Krishna, and the other great religious figures of the world. He encouraged athletics as a means to the illumination of the physical consciousness, and his centers around the world have sponsored many running events. Among other activities, his students sponsor the Sri Chinmoy Oneness—Home Peace Run, a 70-nation relay run for the cause of world peace that has been held every other year since 1987.

Sri Chinmoy was a prolific author, composer, and artist. He wrote more than 1,300 books of poetry, essays, and questions and answers, and he composed more than 13,000 devotional songs in English and his native Bengali. He also completed more than 4 million "soul-bird" drawings, depictions of the human spirit in the form of birds, which have been exhibited worldwide. Often described as an international ambassador of peace, he offered hundreds of meditative concerts to the cause of world peace and discussed peace with dozens of world leaders.

Inspired by his activities, authorities around the world have dedicated natural wonders or other sites to the cause of peace in his name. Collectively known as "Sri Chinmoy Peace—Blossoms," these have spread throughout the world, to Ottawa, Canada; Canberra, Australia; Auckland, Australia; the Swiss Matterhorn; Vietnam's Mekong Delta; Niagara Falls in Canada; Russia's Lake Baikhal; and various locations in the United States.

Membership: In 1995 the centers reported 5,000 members worldwide; 1,500 in the United States, and 1,000 in Canada.

Periodicals: *Anahata Nada*.

Sources:

Sri Chinmoy Centre. www.srichinmoycentre.org.

Chinmoy, Sri. *Arise! Awake!* New York: Frederick Fell, 1972.

————. *Astrology, the Supernatural, and the Beyond*. Hollis, NY: Vishma Press, 1973.

————. *My Lord's Secrets Revealed*. New York: Herder and Herder, 1971.

————. *A Sri Chinmoy Primer*. Forest Hills, NY: Vishma Press, 1974.

Madhuri [Nancy Elizabeth Sands]. *The Life of Sri Chinmoy*. Jamaica, NY: Sri Chinmoy Lighthouse, 1972.

Sri Premananda Center
For information: kachchi@hvc.rr.com

Sri Premananda (b. 1951) is an enlightened teacher from Sri Lanka who as a child was reported to be spiritually precocious, with abilities to materialize objects, to heal people, and to know the past and future. By age 14 he had realized that these abilities were not common to everyone and that he could use them to assist others. He subsequently dedicated his life to the divine and to helping people to know the truth and purpose of their existence. As a following developed, he took the vows of the renounced life and emerged as Swami Premananda.

At age 17 he started an ashram, Sarva Matha Shanti Nilayam (Abode of Peace for all Religions) in the Gandhi Hall, Matale, as an expression of his desire to find harmony in the different religious communities—Buddhism, Hinduism, Christianity, and Islam. He later adopted the more expressly Hindu name Poobalakrishna Ashram. That ashram was bombed in 1983 during conflict between Buddhists and Hindus in Sri Lanka. He relocated to Fathimanagar (near Trichy), Tamil Nadu, India, where he built a new ashram. The Sri Premananda Ashram formally opened in 1989. Here he was free to advocate his ideal: that people should see the divine in all religions. Foreigners came to India, discovered his ashram, and stayed to learn from

him, then went home and founded Sri Premananda centers in countries around the world.

Sri Premananda's global mission was blocked in 1994 when he was arrested and in 1997 convicted of the rape of several girls who lived in the orphanage he had founded. He received two life sentences and remains in jail in India. Many of his devotees around the world remain convinced that he was wrongly accused and convicted, and his movement continues in 19 countries.

Membership: Not reported. There are Sri Premananda centers in the United States and Canada.

Sources:

Sri Premananda Centers. www.sripremananda.org/.

Sri Rama Foundation
PO Box 2550, Santa Cruz, CA 95063

The Sri Rama Foundation was formed in 1974 as the vehicle for the teachings of Baba Hari Dass; the foundation claims to direct any profits to support homeless children in India. Baba Hari Dass was born in Almora District, India, in the Himalayan foothills. He left home at the age of eight to join a renunciate group in the jungle. He became a *mauni sadhu* (a person who accepts a vow of silence); nevertheless, he has led an active life managing ashrams and teaching yoga. He developed his own system of teaching the traditional *ashtanga* (eightlimbed) yoga. In 1971 some Western students persuaded him to come to the United States, and he began to hold regular *satsangs* (gatherings of persons who listen to, talk about, and assimilate spiritual truths) with a group of disciples who gathered around him.

Ashtanga yoga is the system of the legendary figure Patanjali; it was compiled from early teachings on yoga. Baba Hari Dass continues Patanjali's teachings of a process involving eight parts: *yama* (restraints); *niyama* (observances); *asana* (postures); *pranayama* (breathing); *pratyahara* (withdrawal of the mind from sense perception); *dharana* (concentration); *dhyana* (meditation); and *samadhi* (superconsciousness). His teaching is based on a strong foundation of Samkhya philosophy, a spirit of devotion, and a deep understanding of Vedantic nondualism.

The major center of Baba Hari Dass's students is the Mount Madonna Center for the Creative Arts and Sciences in Watsonville, California. In the mid-1970s a group of Babi Hari Dass's devotees In Vancouver, British Columbia, inaugurated the Dharma Sara series of publications, which included several books and a magazine, *Dharma Sara*, now discontinued. Another group formed the Ashtanga Yoga Fellowship in Ontario and sponsors annual events with Baba Hari Dass. In 1980 Baba Hari Dass founded Shri Ram Orphanage in the Himalayan foothills of northern India. The orphanage is home to 50 children. The foundation also supports a school for 300 children and a medical clinic in Haridwar, India.

Membership: Not reported.

Sources:

Sri Rama Foundation. sriramfoundation.org/sriramfoundation/.

Between Pleasure and Pain: The Way of Conscious Living. Sumas, WA: Dharma Sara Publications, 1976.

Dass, Baba Hari. *Ashtanga Yoga Primer*. Santa Cruz, CA: Sri Rama Publishing, 1981.

————. *Hariakhan Baba, Known, Unknown*. Davis, CA: Sri Rama Foundation, 1975.

————. *Silence Speaks*. Santa Cruz, CA: Sri Rama Foundation, 1977.

————. *Sweeper to Saint*. Santa Cruz, CA: Sri Rama Publishing, 1980.

SRV Association of America
c/o Interfaith Peace Temple, 20 Jennings Rd., Greenville, NY 12083

The SRV Association of America is an international fellowship the promotes the teachings of Advaita Vedanta as taught by Sri Ramakrishna, Sarada Devi, and

Swami Vivekananda. The group's outlook includes an affirmation of the "absolute oneness of all existence, the underlying harmony of all religions and cultures, and the practice of contemplative disciplines along the path of spiritual realization, not simply to benefit oneself but to benefit humanity."

The association was founded by Lex Hixon (1941–1995). As a young man Hixon was inspired to undertake a spiritual search through an encounter with the Zen Buddhist teacher Alan Watts and, later, with the Vedanta teacher Swami Nikhivananda, who encouraged his entrance into the Ph.D. program in comparative religion at Columbia University in New York City. In 1980 Hixon became a sheikh with the Khalwati-Jerrahi Sufi Order and assumed the care of four communities of Sufis. In 1983 he and his wife, Sheila, began a formal three-year study of the mystical theology of Eastern Orthodoxy at Saint Vladimir's Seminary, the American seminary of the Orthodox Church in America. In the last decade of his life, he tried to integrate the four spiritual traditions: Vedanta, Buddhism, Eastern Orthodoxy, and Jerrahi Sufism.

Hixon saw the key to life, however, in his encounter with Vedanta, a fact highlighted in his 1992 book, *Great Swan: Meetings with Ramakrishna*. He saw Ramakrishna as an inspiration for creating a global society based on the intuitive sense of the sacred. The SRV Association reflects this central concern.

Today the SRV Association is headed by an international board of directors. Although it provides guidance and teachings in the tradition of Advaita Vedanta, it emphasizes no single doctrinal or denominational affiliation. This outlook allows it to be open to all "authentic" religious practices and philosophical teachings as well as all forms of altruistic, nonpolitical activity.

The association's present endeavors are centered in the Upstate New York Interfaith Peace Temple/Center for Spiritual Living near Albany, New York, a place for meditation, reflection, and interfaith worship. The temple is dedicated to Sri Ramakrishna, Sri Sarada, and Swami Vivekananda as symbols of universal truth; it is modeled after the principles of "global education for human unity and world civilization" as presented by Swami Nityasvarupananda, a disciple of Sarada Devi.

Membership: Not reported.

Sources:

SRV Association of America. www.universaltemple.org/3version/alexsrv.html.

"Lex Hixon." www.srv.org/LexHixonBio.html.

Nityaswarupananda, Swami. "Global Education for Human Unity and World Civilization." www.members.global2000.net./~sarada/WC/WCC1.html.

Swami Kuvalayananda Yoga Foundation
339 Fitzwater St., Philadelphia, PA 19147

The Swami Kuvalayanananda Yoga (SKY) Foundation was founded by Dr. Vijayendra Pratap, who earned a Ph.D. in applied psychology in India at the Bombay University. Dr. Pratap was the student of Swami Kuvalayanandaji, the founder of Kaivalyadhama, the famous yoga center in Bombay, and served as its assistant director before coming to the United States.

The SKY Foundation offers classes in hatha yoga at all levels, trains teachers, and holds classes on yogic philosophy based on Patanjali (the ancient writer who put into simple, cogent language the theory and techniques of yoga). One of the purposes of the foundation is to research the older yogic traditions in the light of modern knowledge; it has sponsored several conferences on science and yoga. The Yoga Research Society was started in 1924 in order to help students and researchers better understand yoga through a scientific approach. The Philadelphia headquarters are above the Garland of Letters Bookstore, which is operated by the foundation. The foundation considers itself an educational organization rather than a religious or spiritual center.

Membership: Not reported.

Sources:

Swami Kuvalayananda Yoga Foundation. www.skyfoundation.org/home.asp • www.yogaresearchsociety.com/aboutYRS.asp.

SYDA Foundation
371 Brickman Rd., Box 600, South Fallsburg, NY 12779

Alternate Address: International headquarters, Gurudev Siddha Peeth, PO Ganeshpuri, Dist. Thoma, Maharastra, India.

Swami Muktananda Paramahansa (1908–1982) was the leading disciple of Bhagwan Nityananda (d. 1961), a Siddha master who in his later years settled in Ganeshpuri, India. Muktananda, or Baba, as he was called by his followers, left home at the age of 15 to wander through India studying philosophy and mastering the different branches of yoga. In 1947 he sought out Bhagawan Nityananda, whom he had met in his youth, and received *shaktipat* initiation (for the awakening of *kundalini*, the inner transformative energy) from him. After nine years of intensive spiritual practices under his guru's guidance, Muktananda attained self-realization. Before his death Nityananda transferred the power of the Siddha lineage to Muktananda. Following his guru's wishes, Muktananda established an ashram, Gurudev Siddha Peeth, in a small village called Gavdevi near the town of Ganeshpuri. It is considered the mother ashram of the movement.

In the 1960s, the first American seekers began to arrive. In 1970 some of these devotees requested Muktananda to undertake his first world tour, which lasted three months and included stops in Europe, New York, Dallas, Los Angeles, and Australia. Baba Ram Dass accompanied Muktananda on much of this tour. Soon after the tour the first centers began to appear in the United States. Also as a result of this visit, Westerners came in even greater numbers to Ganeshpuri; among them was Werner Erhard, the founder of Erhard Training Seminars (EST). At Erhard's invitation, Muktananda returned to the West in 1974, this time for two years. His final journey to the West, made in 1978, lasted for three years.

In 1974 the foundation was established to make the teachings of Siddha Yoga available to seekers around the world. SYDA oversees the Siddha Yoga curriculum, the publication of books and magazines, the production of audiovisuals, and the administration of the several educational and humanitarian projects, including the Muktabodha Indological Research Institute (in India), the PRASDA Project, and the Prison Project, sponsored by the practitioners. The foundation is headed by a board of directors.

The Muktabodha Indological Research Institute is dedicated to the preservation and dissemination of the scriptures and traditions of India through scholarly publications, research and study programs, and archival projects. The Vedashala Project preserves the mantras and rituals of the Vedas. The institute is accredited by the University of Pune, India, for postgraduate studies.

Before his death Swami Muktananda designated Swami Chidvilasananda, known as Gurumayi, as his successor. He had trained her since childhood to succeed him. At that time he also appointed another successor, Swami Nityananda, Chidvilasananda's brother, who retired from that position in 1985.

The path of Siddha Yoga is based upon shakipat initiation, or the awakening of the spiritual energy (kundalini) through the grace of the guru. The practice of the yoga includes meditation, chanting, selfless service, contemplation, and devotion to the guru.

Membership: There is no formal membership in Siddha yoga meditation. In 1997 there were more than 500 Siddha Yoga Meditation Centers throughout the world and residential centers in Australia, England, Mexico, and the United States.

Educational Facilities:

Muktabodha Indological Research Institute, South Fallsburg, New York.

Periodicals: *Darshan • Transformation Neeleswari • Siddha Yoga*. Both are available from Gurudev Siddha Peeth, PO Ganeshpuri, Dist. Thoma, Maharastra, India.

Remarks: During the 1980s the Siddha Yoga Dham had to weather two major scandals. Shortly after Swami Muktananda's death, several of his close associates left the movement and denounced him for taking sexual liberties with female disciples. The accusations became an occasion for widespread discussions of the nature and qualification of leadership in Indian-based movements in the West. Then, in 1986, the *Illustrated Weekly of India* published two stories concerning charges made by Subash Shetty, until his retirement in 1985 known as Swami Nityananda, about his sister, Swami Chidvilasananda. A defamation case was filed against the magazine, which resulted in a full retraction and apology in 1987. Neither incident significantly undermined the membership or influence of the group. Swami Nityananda, following his withdrawal from work with Swami Chidvalasananda, established a new organization, Shanti Mandir Seminars, and is continuing his work through it.

Sources:

SYDA Foundation. www.siddhayoga.org.

Brook, Douglas Renfrew, et al. *Meditation Revolution: A History and Theology of the Siddha Yoga Lineage.* South Fallsburg, NY: Agama Press, 1997. 709 pp.

Caldwell, Sarah. "The Heart of the Secret: A Personal and Scholarly Encounter with Shakta Tantrism in Siddha Yoga." *Nova Religio* 5, 1 (October 2001): 9–51.

Muktananda, Swami. *Guru.* New York: Harper & Row, 1981.

———. *Light on the Path.* Oakland, CA: SYDA Foundation, 1972.

———. *Play of Consciousness.* New York: Harper & Row, 1974.

———. *Reflections of the Self.* New York: SYDA Foundation, 1982.

Paramahansa, Muktananda. *Bhagawan Nityananda, His Life and Mission.* Ganespuri, India: Shree Gurudev Ashram, n.d.

Prajananda, Swami. *A Search for the Self.* Ganeshpuri, India: Durudev Siddha Peeth, 1979.

Tantrika International

PO Box 516, Loveland, OH 45140-3065

Tantrika International was founded by Bodhi Avinasha, a prominent tantric yoga teacher who began her spiritual career as a *sannyasin* (one who practices a renounced way of life) with Bhagwan Shree Rajneesh (Osho) and Osho International Commune. She later claimed mystical contact with the legendary Himalayan master known as Babaji (first introduced to the West by Pramahansa Yogananda). She gained initial fame as the coauthor of the best selling book *Jewel in the Lotus* (now available in seven languages). Through the 1990s she was a popular workshop and seminar instructor.

As an independent tantra teacher, Bodhi Avinasha developed Ipsalu Tantra, which she offers as an accelerated path for the mastery of sexual, emotional, and mental energies; she claims that this method safely activates the *kundalini* (a latent energy that tantrics believe resides at the base of the spine). Tantric practice traditionally aims at activating the kundalini, which, according to this teaching, travels up the spine and brings enlightenment. The key to this practice is the use of the cobra breath, a form of breathing that purportedly heightens the rise of kundalini.

Tantrika International bases its teachings on everyday experience (as opposed to abstract analysis or the search for absolute truth). It understands that one's perspective will continue to change throughout life. Individuals are invited to see the external world as a mirror of their internal states. They create their life experience. Freedom from the past comes from taking responsibility for the present. Then, as the individual identifies with his or her divine inner self, he or she can see the divine order in the totality.

Tantrika International offers a variety of events, including weekend intensive seminars, week-long retreats, and correspondence courses. Tantrika International also offers support and resources for the nurturing of Ipsalu Tantra communities around the world. Such communities begin with partnering with one of the Ipsalu-certified teachers and a couple who wish to share tantra with others in their hometown. Tantrika International teachers trained to offer Ipsula Tantra may be found in Germany, Slovenia, Austria, Hungary, Norway, Bulgaria, and New Zealand.

Membership: Not reported.

Sources:

Tantrika International. http://ipsalutantra.org

Avinasha, Bodhi, and Sunyata Sanaswati. *Jewel in the Lotus: The Tantric Path to Higher Consciousness.* Fairfield, IA: Sunstar Publishing, 2000.

———. *The Ipsalu Formula: A Method for TantraBliss.* Valley Village, CA: Ipsalu Publishing, 2006.

Temple of Cosmic Religion

174 Santa Clara Ave., Oakland, CA 94610

In 1966, while attending the Kumbha Mela (ritual bathing) Festival in the Ganges River, an independent Hindu teacher, later known as Satguru Sant Keshavadas (1934–1997), was told by a holy man named Lord Panduranga Vittala, "Go to the West; spread the cosmic religion." When Keshavadas returned to Delhi, the advice was reinforced in a vision. The following year he began a tour of Europe and the Middle East and arrived in the United States in May. In 1968 he founded a center in Washington, D.C., as the U.S. headquarters of the Dasashram International Center in India. In the mid-1970s the headquarters moved to Southfield, Michigan, near Detroit, and adopted the name of the Temple of Cosmic Religion, a title long used in the movement.

In bringing Hinduism to the West, Keshavadas envisioned the beginning of a world cosmic religion that would unite all faiths. According to this cosmic religion, truth is one, and all paths lead to the realization of God. Keshavadas teaches yoga, meditation, and devotion to God through chanting and singing (bhakti yoga, as discussed in the introductory material for this volume). The concepts of karma and reincarnation are central to the beliefs of the religion.

The world headquarters of the Temple of Cosmic Religion is located in Bangalore, India, at the Panduranga Temple. Five other temples have been established in India; there are additional temples in England, Trinidad, and the United States.

Membership: Not reported.

Sources:

Temple of Cosmic Religion. www.templeofcosmicreligion.org.

Keshavadasasji, Sadguru. *The Doctrine of Reincarnation and Liberation.* Bangalore, India: Dasasharama Research Publications, 1970.

Keshavadasji, Sant. *This Is Wisdom.* Privately printed, 1975.

———. *The Purpose of Life,* New York: Vantage Press, 1978.

———. *Sadguru Speaks.* Washington, DC: Temple of Cosmic Religion, 1975.

Life and Teachings of Sadguru Sant Keshavadas: A Commemoration. Southfield, MI: Temple of Cosmic Religion, 1977.

Mukundadas (Michael Allen Makowsky). *Minstrel of Love.* Nevada City, CA: Hansa Publications, 1980.

Temple of Kriya Yoga

2414 N. Kedzie, Chicago, IL 60647

The Temple of Kriya Yoga was founded by Goswami Kriyananda (born Melvin Higgins and not to be confused with the Swami Kriyananda, who founded the Ananda Ashrama). The temple is headquartered in a temple building on the north side of Chicago.

Kriyananda studied with a guru, spoken of only as Sri Sri Shelliji in the temple literature, who passed to him the kriya yoga tradition of Swami Paramahansa Yogananda, founder of the Self-Realization Fellowship. Kriyananda began teaching yoga in the 1940s and opened the temple in Chicago in the 1960s. Kriyananda, an accomplished astrologer, also opened the College of Occult Sciences, which offered classes in a variety of esoteric subjects.

During the late 1970s the temple abandoned its rented facilities in downtown Chicago for its new headquarters. Associated with the Chicago center is a retreat in South Haven, Michigan. In 1977 the Kriyananda Healing Center was established as a holistic health facility adjacent to the temple. There traditional Western medicine is supplemented by a program emphasizing yoga and meditation, fasting, biofeedback, and massage.

Kriyananda follows the yoga system of Yogananda, and over the years he has authored a variety of books elucidating kriya yoga, meditation, and astrology. In his view religion provides a deep personal understanding of the nature and purpose of God and the Universe. He teaches the oneness of law, spirit, and love and their identity with God. He affirms the meaningfulness of the universe and the possibility of attaining illumination and fulfillment (through the practice of kriya yoga) in this lifetime.

Membership: There are several hundred temple members and many more individuals who receive the benefits of the temple through its classes, programs and astrology services.

Periodicals: *The Flame of Kriya*.

Sources:

Temple of Kriya Yoga. www.yogakriya.org.

Kriyananda, Goswami. *The Bhagavad Gita, The Song of God*. Chicago: Temple of Kriya Yoga, n.d.

————. *The Blue Lotus Sutra*. Chicago: Temple of Kriya Yoga, n.d.

————. *Dictionary of Basic Astrological Terms*. Chicago: Temple of Kriya Yoga, n.d.

————. *Pathway to God-Consciousness*. Chicago: Temple of Kriya Yoga, 1970.

————. *Yoga: Text for Teachers and Advanced Students*. Chicago: Temple of Kriya Yoga, 1976.

Traditional Yoga Academy

6530 Annie Oakley Dr. #2825, Henderson, NV 89014

The Traditional Yoga Academy is the U.S. outpost of the Movement for Spiritual Integration in the Absolute (M.I.S.A.). M.I.S.A. was founded in 1990 in postrevolutionary Romania by Gregorian Bivolaru (b. 1952). As a child, Bivolaru had recurring dreams in which he was a Tibetan yogi who had attained a high level of spirituality. From these dreams he began to "remember" various yoga techniques that he began to practice on his own. His practice led to spiritual experiences that culminated in his attaining spiritual enlightenment when he was nineteen years old. He later was able to connect what he had experienced with the teachings he found in the books of several modern spiritual teachers, especially Ramakrishna (1836–1886), Sivananda (1887–1963), and Yogananda (1893–1952).

Bivolau, or Grieg, as he is generally called, started to teach yoga in Bucharest in 1978. Initially he was received warmly by the authorities with the Romanian Ministry of Health and the Association of Psychosomatic Medicine of Bucharest, but in the 1980s he fell victim to dictator Nicolae Ceausescu's negative opinions of transcendental meditation. Romania banned yoga as part of a general ban on all oriental teachings, and for several yeasr Bivolau was imprisoned.

It was not until 1990 that Grieg was allowed to resume teaching. Once opened, however, M.I.S.A. expanded rapidly, and soon Grieg's unique approach to yoga was being taught all over the country, and then expanded throughout Europe as accomplished students became teachers.

M.I.S.A. yoga is based in ancient teachings. Patanjali's ancient compendium of yoga, the "Yoga Sutras," provided a definition built around eight steps to perfection: *asthanga* (aspiration); *yama* (perfection in social morality) and *niyama* (perfection in individual morality); *asanas* (postures); *pranayama* (breathing exercises); *pratyahara* (withdrawing); *dharana* (concentration); *dhyana* (meditation); and

samadhi (sublime ecstasy). M.I.S.A. situates this practice in a larger context of tantra and meditation. Together, yoga, tantra, and meditation become a path for continuous transformation. In the tantric discipline, students learn to control and sublimate the creative potential of sexual energy, but tantra embraces all aspects of life, with applications for all.

The Traditional Yoga Academy is located in Henderson, Nevada. It offers regular classes and workshops in Las Vegas and Sandy Springs (suburban Atlanta), Georgia.

Membership: Not reported.

Sources:

Traditional Yoga Academy. www.traditionalyogacenter.com.

Truth Consciousness

c/o Sacred Mountain Ashram, 10668 Gold Hill Rd., Boulder, CO 80302-9716

Alternate Address: 68 Lulla Nagar, Pune 411040, Maharashtra, India.

Truth Consciousness was founded by Swami Amar Jyoti in 1974 and is devoted to a vision of what it perceives as truth and the transformation of human consciousness into divine consciousness. Prabhushri Swamiji, as he is called by his devotees, was born in northwest India in 1928. A few months before his graduation from college, he renounced his seemingly destined life of comfort and success to follow an inner dictum, "Know yourself and you shall know everything." After a decade of *sadhana* (spiritual practices) and meditation in the Himalayas, he achieved his goal. He then began traveling throughout India and in 1960, at the request of disciples, founded Jyoti Ashram in Pune, in the state of Maharashtra. In 1961 Prabhushri Swamiji visited the United States for the first time and then returned to Pune, concentrating for a decade on his work in India.

Prabhushri Swamiji's way is a classical path of spirituality based on the principles of dharma (living according to divine law). He stresses principles such as truthfulness, humility, purity, and devotion. With compassion, patience, and wisdom, the guru attempts carefully to guide each disciple toward a natural unfolding toward the divine.

Prabhushri Swamiji visited the United States again in 1973 and at that time founded his first ashram in the West, Sacred Mountain Ashram in Boulder, Colorado. Truth Consciousness is the nonprofit corporation that ties together the American centers. There are two ashrams (for renunciates) and two community centers for individuals, couples, and families who wish to live a spiritually oriented life under the direct guidance of the master.

The ashrams and community centers offer programs year round, and sincere seekers are welcome. *Satsang* (an assembly of persons who listen to and talk about spiritual truth) is held twice weekly and includes devotional music (chanting) and meditation. Other regular programs include *guru aarati* (morning prayers and worship), weekly group meditations, and weekend and extended retreats.

Membership: There is no formal membership. There are two Truth Consciousness ashrams in the United States: Sacred Mountain Ashram in Boulder, Colorado, and Desert Ashram in Tucson, Arizona. A community center is located adjacent to or near each Ashram. An estimated several hundred individuals are affiliated with the organization. In India, Ananda Niketan, the trust founded by Swami Amar Jyoti, maintains Jyoti Ashram in Pune, four hours from Bombay. There is also a center in New Zealand.

Periodicals: *Light of Consciousness—Journal of Spiritual Awakening* (USA). • *Chinmaya Jeevan—Conscious Living* (India).

Sources:

Truth Consciousness. truthconsciousness.org/TC_Ashrams.htm.

Frey, Kessler. *Satsang Notes of Swami Amar Jyoti*. Boulder, CO: Truth Consciousness, 1977.

Jyoti, Swami Amar. *Dawning: Eternal Wisdom Heritage for Today*. Boulder, CO: Truth Consciousness, 1991.

———. *Retreat Into Eternity*, Boulder, CO: Truth Consciousness, 1981.

———. *Spirit of Himalaya*. Boulder, CO: Truth Consciousness, 1985.

Vedanta Centre and Ananda Ashrama

130 Beechwood St., Cohassat, MA 02025

Alternate Address: Box 8555, La Crescenta, CA 91224-0555.

The Ananda Ashram of La Crescenta, California, and the Vedanta Centre of Cohasset, Massachusetts, continue the work begun in the early twentieth century by Swami Paramananda, a disciple of Swami Vivekananda and a monk of the Ramakrishna Order. Paramananda (1884–1940) was born Suresh Chandra Guha Thakurta. A pioneer swami of the Ramakrishna Order, he came to the United States in 1906 to assist Swami Abhedananda at the New York Vedanta Society. In 1909 he moved to Boston to open a Vedanta center there. He also established a monastic community for American women. His first disciple was Laura Glenn, better known by her religious name, Sister Devamata. She became his assistant in 1910 but is best remembered for her literary work. She wrote many books, edited both Swami Vivekananda's and Swami Paramananda's lectures, and was the chief editor of the *Message of the East*, a monthly periodical published without interruption for 52 years.

During his 34-year ministry in the United States, Paramananda lectured all over the United States and Europe. He established the Ananda Ashrama in La Crescenta in 1923 and a second ashrama in Cohasset in 1929. In 1931 Sri Ramakrishna Ananda Ashrama was established in his name in Dacca, now in Bangladesh. This ashrama was moved to Calcutta after the partition of the India and Pakistan. There are now two branches that serve destitute women, orphan children, and others in need. During Paramananda's lifetime all of these centers were part of the Ramakrishna Math (monastery) and Mission, whose headquarters are at Belur Math, near Calcutta.

After Paramananda's death in 1940, his centers were excommunicated from the parent order because he designated as his successor an Indian woman, Srimata Gayatri Devi (1906–1995). She came to the United States in 1926 and became the first Indian woman to teach Vedanta in the West. In 1952 she consolidated the eastern work by moving the Boston Vedanta Center to the ashrama in Cohasset, some 20 miles south of Boston.

The ashrama and center teach Vedanta. The essence of Vedanta's tenets are that truth or God is one without a second; that an individual's real nature is divine; that all paths lead to the same goal; and that the purpose of human life is to realize God within one's own soul. It shares these beliefs with the Ramakrishna Order (the break between the ashrama and the order being purely administrative).

For 55 years, until her death in 1995, Srimata Gayatri Devi was the spiritual mother of the several ashrams in the United States and India. She appointed an American woman, Srimata Sudha Puri Devi (Dr. Susan Schrager, b.1942) as her successor. The ashramas are home to monastic women. Associated with them are number of dedicated householders who consider them their spiritual home. Many others attend the weekly services and classes. Vedanta Centre (Cohasset) publishes the books of Swami Paramananda and several of the female leaders, including Sister Daya (Georgina Walton Jones) and Srimata Gayatri Devi. It also sells casettes and CDs of ashrama devotional music.

Membership: Neither the ashrama nor the center is a membership organizations. There are approximately 60 residents of the four ashramas (two in India and two in America). An estimated 1,500 persons look to the ashramas for spiritual guidance.

Sources:

Vedanta Centre and Ananda Ashrama. www.vedantacentre.org.

Devamata, Sister. *Swami Paramananda and His Work*. 2 vols. La Crescenta, CA: Ananda Ashrama, 1926–1941.

Devi, Srimata Gayatri. *One Life's Pilgrimage*. Cohasset, MA Vedanta Centre, 1977.

Hold Aloft the Light. La Crescenta, CA: Ananda Ashrama, 1973.

Levinsky, Sara Ann. *A Bridge of Dreams*. West Stockbridge, MA: Inner Traditions, 1984.

Paramananda, Swami. *The Path of Devotion*. Boston, MA: Vedanta Center, 1907.

———. *Vedanta in Practice*. Boston, MA: Vedanta Center, 1917.

Vedantic Center

3528 N. Triunfo Canyon Rd., Agoura, CA 91301

The Vedantic Center was founded in 1975 in Los Angeles by Alice Coltrane (b. 1937), an initiate of Swami Satchidananda, the founder of the Integral Yoga International, with whom she had journeyed to India and Sri Lanka. Raised in Detroit, Coltrane devoted her early life to music, as did her late husband, the jazz legend John Coltrane, and like him attained a high level of success and fame (Alice on the piano, John on the saxophone). In 1968, at the age of 31, she entered a period of both spiritual isolation and reawakening. She also received an initiation into the renounced order of sannyas but was instructed not to don the ochre robe, symbol of the renounced life, until 1975. During the early 1970s she released a series of albums expressing her spiritual pilgrimage and devotional life.

In 1975 Coltrane emerged as Swami Turiyasangitananda. A few months later she organized the Vedantic Center. She authored several books, including *Monument Eternal* and *Endless Wisdom*, and began to build a following. In 1983 the center purchased 48 acres of land in rural southern California, near the town of Agoura, and established a community, Sai Anantam Ashram, for the center's members.

The Vedantic Center is unique among Hindu organizations in being led by an African-American and in drawing members predominantly from the African American community. Although beginning with the yoga system passed to her by Swami Satchidananda, Turiyasangitananda has developed an eclectic blend of Eastern philosophy that draws on Western spiritual traditions as well. She teaches that the purpose of human life is to advance spiritually. The highest stage of life is devotional service (bhakti yoga), rendered unto the supreme lord (known in his three aspects as Brahma, Vishnu or Krishna, and Siva). In this light devotional singing has attained an important role at the ashram, and Turiyasangitananda has composed new music with a decidedly Western flavor for the traditional *bhajans* (devotional songs).

The weekly schedule at Sai Anantam Ashram begins with Sunday school for children. There is worship, including chanting and satsang discourses by Swami Turiyasangitananda, on Sunday afternoons. A prayer service occurs on Wednesday evening. The center operates a bookstore at the entrance to the ashram grounds.

Membership: As of 1995 approximately 30 people lived at Sai Anantam. A small number of nonresidents also attend the ashram's worship services.

Periodicals: *Sai Anantam*.

Sources:

Vedantic Center. www.saiquest.com.

Turiyasangitananda, A. C. *Endless Wisdom*. Los Angeles: Avatar Book Institute, 1981.

———. *Monument Eternal*. Los Angeles: Vedantic Book Press, 1977.

Vedic Society of America

PO Box 926, Pacific Palisades, CA 90272-0926

The Vedic Society of America was founded by Maha Guru Ji Dr. Pandit Bhek Pati Sinha, a Brahmin priest from Bihar, Bengal, India. He had studied at the Universities of Calcutta and Patna in India and eventually received his Ph.D. from Columbia University in New York City. Between 1948 and 1952 he lived in various parts of the world and then settled in the United States. Through the 1960s he taught political science in several institutions of higher learning on the East Coast.

Sinha founded the Vedic Society of America in New York City in 1950 at a time when there were very few Hindu options available to religious seekers. The society was designed to encourage spiritual disciplines, provide a sense of reverence for all life, promote brotherhood, and offer an awareness of the Vedas, the ancient scripture of India. A second center was opened in Pacific Palisades, California, in 1960. Sinha trained leaders who assumed ministerial duties at the two centers, leading the weekly worship services.

The society taught the 10 Vedic moral commandments of nonviolence (*ahimsa*), truthfulness, honesty, inhering in the consciousness of God, detachment, purity of body, contentment, perseverance in the consciousness of truth, study of the scriptures, and devotion to God. It taught that truth was God and true religion was the perception and realization of truth. Each individual is substantively divine and has the ability to realize that divinity. The society taught that humans are their own saviors and that growth in spiritual illumination and love and service to all is the only alternative in life.

The society operated a retreat center, Vedashram, and offered a correspondence course in its religious teachings. It published a periodical, *Lila*. Sinha authored several books, and the society members recorded two records of Vedic music and chants that were distributed through the Vedic Book and Gift Shop in Pacific Palisades.

The society continued to exist through the 1970s, but in recent years attempts to contact it have not been successful. Its present status is uncertain.

Membership: Not reported.

Sources:

Jayne, Linda. *The Vedic Society of America: New York and California*. Pacific Palisades, CA: Vedic Publishing House, 1968.

Veerashaiva Samaja of North America

PO Box 360380, Milpitas, CA 95036-0380

Veerashaiva Samaja of North America, founded in 1978, is an organization operating primarily among Indian Americans that seeks to perpetuate a form of Shaivite Hinduism known as Veerashaivism (or Lingayatism). Veerashaivism is traced to Shri Basaveshwar, a politician with a mystical temperament who lived in twelfth-century India. During his years in office (1157–1167), Shri Basaveshwar took leadership of a revitalization movement centered on worship of and devotion to Shiva as personified in a symbolic emblem known as the *Shiva linga* (hence the group's alternate designation as *Lingayats*). The distinctive mark of Veerashaivism is its advocacy of the wearing of the linga, an act that allows the believer's body to become a temple in which God dwells. The movement also stood out for its early attempt at egalitarianism, and made an effort to include untouchables.

Worship of Shiva is centered on the five *Panchacharas*, rules of conduct which when followed are believed to assist in making the body a suitable home for the deity. They call for daily devotion to one's personal Shiva linga; attention to one's vocation and duty; affirmation of Shiva as the single deity and of the equality of his devotees; humility; and defense of the community and its beliefs and practices. In addition to the *Panchacharas*, eight "shields" known as the *Ashtavaranas* guard believers from the things of the world that can pull them away from their devotion. Chief among these Ashtavaranas are the gurus (spiritual teachers). But the list includes the water used to wash both the *linga* and the guru's feet, the food offered to the deity (*prasad*), holy ash, holy beads, and the mantra (sacred words intoned during worship). The practice of Veerashaivism leads to heightened levels of attainment and eventually to the state of Aikya Sthala, in which the soul separates from the body and merges with Shiva. Veerashaivites tend to ascribe more authority to the Hindu writings known as the *agamas* than they do to the Vedas.

Veerashaiva Samaja of North America organizes U.S. and Canadian followers of Veerashaivism, many of whom belong to families that have lived outside of India since 1965, into chapters and holds an annual convention. As a whole, it has not built its own temples, and followers often attend local Shaivite temples built to serve the larger Hindu community.

Membership: Not reported.

Sources:

Veerashaiva Samaja of North America. www.vsna.org/.

Lord Shiva. www.shivayoga.net/veerashaiva/welcome.htm.

Vimala Thakar, Friends of

Current address not obtained for this edition.

Alternate Address: International address: Vimala Thakar Foundation, Huizerweg 46, 1261 Az Balricum, Holland.

Vimala Thakar (b. 1932) is a teacher in the tradition of Jiddu Krishnamurti (1895–1986). For several years she was a disciple of Vinoba Bhave (1895–1982). Bhave, a close associate of Mohandas Gandhi, initiated a voluntary land reform program in 1951. He traveled throughout India to solicit land from large landowners to give to the landless. The program failed, however, when it was recognized that the land actually transferred to new owners was almost worthless agriculturally. After graduating with a degree in philosophy from Nagpur University, Thakar traveled the country as an exponent of the Land Gift Movement.

A chance meeting with Krishnamurti in 1956 began to change Thakar's life. She encountered him several times over the next five years and absorbed his message of the need for total inward revolution or transformation. She resigned from the Land Gift Movement and began to travel, teaching and lecturing about her experience and its implications. She advocated the meditative life, which, in her view, begins with the observation and transcendence of mental processes. In her view meditation is not an activity but a state of total being in which there is no movement—a dimension of full life.

Thakar's travels in Europe and America during the 1960s drew followers who organized the Vimala Thakar Foundation (on the pattern of the Krishnamurti Foundation) in Holland and Friends of Vimala Thakar in California. The organizations facilitate lecture tours, publish and distribute books and tapes of Thakar's lectures, and organize conferences. Emulating Krishnamurti, she created a group with a minimal structure because she wishes to speak as an individual teacher rather than as the representative of an organization. Thakar resides in Mount Abu, in western India, and no longer travels outside her native land.

Membership: Not reported.

Periodicals: *Contact with Vimala Thakar*. Available from Vimala Thakar Foundation, Huizerweg 46, 1261 AZ Balricum, Holland.

Sources:

Vimala Thakar. www.ul.ie/~sextonb/vt.

Thakar, Vimala. *Mutation of Mind*.

———. *On an Eternal Voyage*. Ahmedabad, India: New Order Book Co., 1972.

———. *Totality in Essence*. Delhi, India: Motilal Banarsidass, 1971.

———. *Towards Total Transformation*. Berkeley, CA: Friends of Vimala Thakar, 1970.

"Vimala Thakar Speaks on Yoga." *Yoga Journal* (March/April 1977).

Why Meditation? Delhi, India: Motilal Banarsidass, 1977.

Vivekananda Vedanta Society

5423 W. Hyde Park Blvd., Chicago, IL 60615

Alternate Address: International headquarters: Ramakrishna Math and Mission, PO Belur Math, Dr. Howrah. W. Bengal 711 202, India.

A branch of the Ramakrishna Math and Mission, the Vivekananda Vedanta Society (formerly the Vedanta Society) is the only Hindu organization that was founded in the United States before 1900. In part because of its longevity, it has had a greater impact on the United States than any other Hindu group. The society grew out of the vision of Sri Ramakrishna (1836–1886) and the work of his best-known disciple, Swami Vivekananda (1863–1902).

Ramakrishna was a priest in a Calcutta temple of Kali, a branch of Hinduism in which God is worshiped as universal mother. Through long meditation and intense yearning for direct experience of the divine, Ramakrishna attained the state of *samadhi,* or God-consciousness. Continuous samadhi became his goal, and he followed a number of *sadhanas,* or paths to enlightenment, both within and outside the Hindu tradition. He became convinced that the divine mother wished him to remain on the threshold between the absolute and the relative in order to serve as an instrument for the spiritual uplift of humanity and that all religions (including Hinduism) are different paths to the same goal, all gods being different revelations of the same Godhead.

A number of disciples, some of them college-trained intellectuals, gathered around Ramakrisha. Before his death some revered him as an avatar, a divine incarnation. Vivekananda, commissioned by Ramakrishna, forged the younger disciples into a monastic brotherhood and gradually convinced them that, as Ramakrishna's followers, they had a mission not only to seek enlightenment but also to work to alleviate the suffering of humanity through spiritual ministration and social service.

In 1893 Vivekananda came to the United States to teach the universal religion realized by Ramakrishna. He took the World Parliament of Religions by storm, and for two years he lectured throughout the United States, gathering followers. In November 1894 the Vedanta Society of New York was formed, and in the next few years centers were added in San Francisco and Boston. Each is autonomous but works under the Ramakrishna Order. In 1897 Vivekananda returned to India and organized the Ramakrishna Mission, dedicated to serving humanity in a spirit of worship of the divine dwelling within each person.

The three central ideas of Vedanta monistic philosophy are as follows:

1. Brahman, or God, is the underlying unity manifested in all. Each person in essence is divine, and the goal of human life is to realize this divinity with oneself and in all others. This realization is the true basis of unselfishness; the divine unity is the basis of love.

2. Maya, the illusion of individual separateness, is an interpretation of the mind. One perceives variety rather than the underlying unity because of the condition of one's mind—its prejudices, desires, and fears. Absolute reality can be known even in this life through the purified mind: This possibility has been verified by the great mystics of all religions.

3. The mind may be purified by a variety of means, and each person's spiritual life evolves according to his or her mental makeup. Four basic yogas or spiritual disciplines have been codified by Vivekananda: devotion, intellectual discrimination, unselfish work, and psychic control. These correspond to the four basic aspects of the human mind: the emotional, intellectual, active, and reflective. The predominance of one or more of these in an individual determines what path that person should follow.

Vedanta differs from most other Hindu movements in stressing principles over personalities. Vivekananda and his successors have emphasized the universal teachings of Vedanta rather than the personality of Ramakrishna. At the same time freedom is given to the individual follower to worship Ramakrishna or any prophet of any religion as a means to enlightenment. Instruction by a qualified teacher is strongly recommended, although too much emphasis on the personality of the teacher is recognized as a danger. Vedanta's intellectual approach to Hinduism has found expression in the publication of numerous books, including popular editions of the Upanishads, the *Bhagava Gita,* and the *Yoga Aphorisms of Patanjali.* The dissemination of these words stimulated interest in Hinduism among many prominent Western intellectuals, including Gerald Heard, Aldous Huxley, and Christopher Isherwood.

Membership: In 2002 the society reported a membership of 250, plus approximately 2,000 contacts. The society has centers with additional members in California; Florida; Illinois; Maryland; Massachusetts; Missouri; New York and Stone Ridge, New York; Portland, Oregon; Providence, Rhode Island; Seattle, Washington; Buenos Aires, Argentina; Australia; Bangladesh; Sao Paulo, Brazil; Toronto, Ontario, Canada; Bourne End, Buckshire, England; Fiji; Gretz, France; Germany; Kanagawa ken, Japan; Malaysia; Mauritius; Amstelveen, Netherlands; Moscow, Russia; Singapore; South Africa; Sri Lanka; and Switzerland.

Periodicals: *Prabudda Bharata* (*Awakened India*). Send orders to 5 Dehi Entally Rd., Calcutta, India 700 014. • *Global Vedanta.* Send orders to Vedanta Society of Western Washington, 2716 Broadway E, Seattle, WA 98102.

Sources:

Vivekananda Vedanta Society. www.vedantasociety-chicago.org.

Gambhrananda, Swami. *History of the Ramakrishna Math and Mission.* Calcutta: Advaita Ashrama, 1957.

Isherwood, Christopher. *Ramakrishna and His Disciples.* New York: Simon and Schuster, 1965.

———, ed. *Vedanta for the Western World.* New York: Viking Press, 1945.

Johnson, Clive, ed. *Vedanta.* New York: Bantam Books, 1974.

Rolland, Romain. *The Life of Vivekananda and the Universal Gospel.* Calcutta: Advaita Ashrama, 1970.

VRINDA/The Vrindavan Institute for Vaisnava Culture and Studies
4138 NW 23 Rd. Ave., Miami, FL 33143

VRINDA (The Vrindavan Institute for Vaisnava Culture and Studies) was founded in 1984 by Srila Bhakti Aloka Paramadvaiti Maharaja (b. 1954). A German, Swami Paramadvaiti joined the International Society for Krishna Consciousness (ISKCON) in 1971 in Dusseldorf and eventually became a temple president. ISKCON's founder, Swami Prahbupada (1896–1977), sent him to South America to spread word of the society there. He found his greatest success in Colombia.

In the year following Prabupada's death, Swami Paramadvaiti developed an important relationship with Srila Sridhar Maharaja, a Vaisnava guru (and one of Prabhupada's godbrothers) in India, and took his *sannyas* vows (a pledge to lead a renounced life) from him. Having broken with ISKCON in 1984, he founded both ISEV (Instituto Superior de Estudios Vedicos) and VRINDA (The Vrindavan Institute for Vaisnava Culture and Studies). In Colombia, Chile, Brazil, Ecuador, Argentina, and Peru, he brought a variety of centers (ashrams, farms, cultural centers, and schools) into the new organization, which subsequently spread to countries in Central and North America and to Europe (Germany, Bulgaria, Hungary, and Switzerland). There are missions in Argentina, Bolivia, Brazil, Bulgaria, Chile, Colombia, Costa Rica, Ecuador, Germany, Guatemala, Hungary, India, Mexico, Panama, Peru, Spain, Switzerland, and the United States (Florida and Hawaii).

In 1990 VRINDA established its first center in India and later opened a world center in Vrinda Kunja. In Vrindavan VRINDA opened the first Gaudiya Vaisnava Bookstore, from which books and materials from all of the groups in the Krishna-consciousness tradition are distributed. VRINDA has committed itself to translating and publishing books in a variety of languages, especially German and Spanish.

VRINDA is a member of the World Vaisnava Association.

Membership: Not reported.

Sources:

VRINDA/The Vrindavan Institute for Vaisnava Culture and Studies. www.vrindavan.org.

Swami B. A. Paramadvaiti. *Our Family the Gaudiya Math.* www.vrindavan.org/English/Books/GMconded.html.

———. "The Temple President." www.vrindavan.org/bap/index.html.

World Community
Rte. 4, Box 265, Bedford, VA 24523

In 1970 Vasudevadas (also known as Shaykh Ahmed Abdur Rashid) and his wife, Devaki-Ma, founded Prema Dharmasala as a yoga ashram for dedicated lay disciples and renunciates; they also founded the World Community as a community of householders and families who looked to Vasudevadas/Rashid as their spiritual teacher. Throughout the 1970s Prema Dharmasala functioned as the main training center for those who had made a commitment to a life of renunciation and service to God and the human family. In the early 1980s, however, a shift of emphasis to the World Community occurred as the leaders embraced a vision of the community as a symbol of the oneness of truth and the transforming power of divine love. By 1984 Prema Dharmasala had been completely superseded by the World Community.

Rashid is a *pir* (master or leader) of five Sufi orders: Mujaddidiyya, Naqshbandiyya, Chishtiyya, Qadriyya, and Shadiliyya. He introduces innovative learning methods and helps to integrate Islamic values into mainstream curricula.

The World Community will be located on the acreage previously occupied by the Prema Dharmasala. Centered on a large Temple of All Religions will be a series of interrelated villages, an educational center, a holistic health clinic, and a research and training center for the New Age. The outlines of the emerging plan have remained open to allow for new insight as members become more attuned to truth.

Membership: In 2002 the community reported 150 members.

Sources:

World Community. www.circlegroup.org

Love Offerings at Thy Lotus Feet. Bedford, VA: Prema Dharmasala, 1975.

Vasudevadas. *Running Out of Time and Who Is Watching?* Bedford, VA: Prema Dharmasala Fellowship, 1979.

————. *A Time for Eternity.* Bedford, VA: Prema Dharmasala and Fellowship Association, 1976.

————. *Vasudevadas Speaks to Your Heart.* Bedford, VA: Prema Dharmasala and Fellowship Association, 1976.

World Community Service

3676 Delaware Dr., Fremont, CA 94538

The World Community Service was founded in 1911 in Madras, India, by Yogiraj Vethathiri Maharaj, a successful businessman and teacher of *kundalini* (an unconscious, instinctive, or erotic force) yoga. Vethathiri was born in southern India into a family of weavers. While still a child he placed himself under a spiritual teacher. Early in his development he rejected the impersonal monism taught by many forms of Hinduism and became a devotee of Vinayaka, a Hindu deity. His own reflections on his devotional activity led him to the conviction that God was without shape or form. At the age of eighteen, he moved to Madras to continue his education and, later, to start his own business manufacturing cloth.

After World War II Vethathiri met Swami Paranjothi, a teacher of kundalini yoga and founder of the Temple of Universal Peace in Madras. The practice of kundalini yoga brought together the religious speculations that had held much of his attention throughout his life. He soon discovered that he could project kundalini energy into others and thereby help them. In 1958 Vethathiri established the World Community Service in Madras. Three years later he moved the headquarters to his home town of Guduvancheri, whence it spread throughout India.

Vethathiri teaches simplified kundalini yoga (SKY), a process of arousing the kundalini latent in each individual; this force is often pictured as a coiled serpent at the base of the spine, waiting to uncoil and bring enlightenment. SKY claims to be able to bypass the laborious techniques traditionally considered integral to kundalini yoga and, through *shaktipat* (the act of a guru or spiritual teacher imparting a form of spiritual power or awakening on a disciple), arouse the kundalini and teach the student how to control the working of the energy, a process called *shanti yoga.* Once having mastered shanti yoga, the aspirant can have the kundalini fully aroused by Vethathiri through a process called *turiya* (a state of pure consciousness) yoga and experience a state of tranquility and bliss. Finally, the aspirant is led into a still higher state of consciousness, *turiyateetha* yoga, in which the individual consciousness is merged with the infinite.

Vethathiri made his first visit to the United States in 1972 at the invitation of the younger brother of the leader of the New Delhi World Community Service Centre. He resided in Bound Brook, New Jersey, where Vethathiri gave his first American lectures and organized the first American World Community Service Centre. The organization spread along the East Coast primarily through the Indian American community. Since the organization of the center, Vethathiri has made annual visits to the United States, and centers have been established across America and in other countries, including India, Indonesia, Malaysia, Netherlands, Norway, Oman, Singapore, Sri Lanka, the United Arab Emirates, and the United Kingdom.

Membership: Not reported

Sources:

World Community Service. www.vethathiri.org/Home.

Vethathiri, Yogiraj. *Atomic Poison.* Madras, India: Vethathiri Publications, 2002.

————. *Bio Magnetism.* Madras, India: Vethathiri Publications, 2003.

————. *Physical Transformation of Soul.* Madras, India: Vethathiri Publications, 1982.

————. *Sex and Spiritual Development.* Madras, India: Vethathiri Publications, 1982.

————. *The Story of My Life.* Madras, India: Vethathiri Publications, 1982.

World Plan Executive Council-US

139 Waldemere Rd., Livingston Manor, NY 12758

The World Plan Executive Council is one of several organizations that claim they are not religious groups and hence should not be included in an encyclopedia of religion. Critics of the council and of the technique it teaches to those affiliated with Transcendental Meditation (TM) have argued forcefully that it is a religion; some go so far as to charge the council with hiding its religious nature in order to deceive the public and gain some benefits available only to nonreligious organizations in the West. Some of these critics took their case to court; in 1978 the U.S. District Court in Newark, New Jersey, ruled that the practice of TM was religious in nature and banned the teaching of TM in the public schools of New Jersey. Subsequently, the teaching of TM was dropped from other programs supported by public funds.

In response the World Plan Executive Council has argued that the 1978 court decision was a mistake; it draws attention to the extensive scientific research on the efficacy of TM that has been completed and published in reputable journals. It also argues that its basic theoretical base, the Science of Creative Intelligence (SCI), was formulated as a scientific theory, not a religious teaching. It further notes the participation of people of many religions, even clergy, who not only practice TM but also teach it.

The argument between the council and its critics goes to the very heart of the discussion of the definition of religion in both the academic and legal uses of the term. TM emerged in the context of the growth of Eastern religious practice in the West. It is, in fact, impossible to tell the story of the rise of Hinduism in America without reference to TM, which helped to spur the initial wave of Indian teaching to come to America following World War II.

The founder of TM (or rather the modern rediscoverer) was Guru Dev (1870–1953), but its most influential exponent was Maharishi Mahesh Yogi (1917–2008), who spent 13 years in seclusion with Guru Dev and, upon Guru Dev's death, came forth in 1958 to tell the world about TM. Prior to his life of meditation, he had obtained a B.S. in physics at Allahabad University. In 1959 he made his first world tour, which brought him to the United States. His movement grew slowly until the mid-1960s, when some popular entertainers (including the Beatles, Mia Farrow, and Jane Fonda) identified with it.

In 1972 Maharishi announced his world plan, the overall strategy that guides the movement and from which the council takes its name. The goal of the world plan is to share the science of creative intelligence with the whole world. The immediate objective of the plan is to establish 3,600 world-plan centers (one for each million people on earth) and to staff each center with 1,000 teachers (one for each thousand people on earth.) The ultimate goal is to bring the age of enlightenment.

To carry out its agenda, the World Plan Executive Council has organized into five task-oriented structures. The International Meditation Society is the main structure for introducing the general public to TM. The Spiritual Regeneration Movement works with the "older" generation (people older than thirty), whereas the Student International Meditation Society targets the campus population. Maharishi International University is a four-year university that offers both bachelor's and master's degrees, with instruction based on presenting traditional material with a TM perspective. The university is in Fairfield, Iowa. The American Foundation for the Science of Creative Intelligence is working within the business community.

In 1976 Maharishi created the World Government of the Age of Enlightenment, described as a nonpolitical global organization that "enjoys sovereignty in the domain of consciousness" and "activity in the eternally dynamic silence of the unified field of all of the forces of nature." The World Government became an object of passing media attention in 1983, when Maharishi offered its services to the world's governments to assist them in solving their problems.

The essence of TM is a form of *japa* yoga—meditation with a mantra, a sound constantly repeated silently during meditation and upon which the meditator concentrates. Each individual begins his process of meditation with initiation. At that time he is given an individual mantra for his/her own use; it is not to be revealed to others. The mantra is most often given by a certified TM instructor. The initiation ceremony, during which members repeat a number of "prayers" to Hindu deities and offer veneration to a long line of gurus, became a cornerstone of the case built by critics claiming TM is a religious practice.

The overall perspective of the council is spelled out in Maharishi's book *The Science of Being and the Art of Living*, which presesnts a complete cosmology. According to Maharishi, underneath the universe is the absolute field of pure being, unmanifested and transcendental. Being is the ultimate reality of creation. The science of being teaches how to contact ultimate reality. TM is the tool. Once the meditation begins, one starts to "live the being," and the council offers instruction on correct thinking, speaking, acting, and health. The goal is God-realization. Maharishi's teaching is "the summation of the practical wisdom of the integrated life as advanced by the Vedic Rishis of ancient India." That is to say, the ultimate goal of TM is to "achieve the spiritual goals of mankind in this generation." At the time of his death in 2008, Maharishi had no legal affiliation to the World Plan Executive Council. He is looked upon as the founder of TM and the Science of Creative Intelligence. Through his books, taped lectures, and constant presence in picture and thought, his spirit still dominates the organization.

The council's encouragement of widespread research and documentation of its effects have helped to impart credibility and popularity to TM. More than 500 research studies have been completed at universities and colleges in more than 25 nations. Many of these have been published in academic journals and later reprinted and circulated by the movement. Such studies document the role of the practice of TM in (among other things) curbing alcohol and drug abuse, assisting in the rehabilitation of criminals and delinquents, increasing productivity on the job, producing a more healthy body, improving athletic performance, and raising intelligence.

The growth of TM during the early 1970s was rapid, and widespread media coverage helped provide openings in the business world, the U.S. Army, and the school system. Growth began to slow in the mid-1970s and decreased rapidly following the 1978 court decision. That same year TM announced its siddha program, a course in advanced techniques that allowed the student to gain various supernormal capacities, including levitation, invisibility, mastery over nature, and fulfillment of all desires. The overall goal was the creation of the Age of Enlightenment. Although many signed up for the course, it aroused attacks from many who argued that it was impossible to produce the advertised results. In 1987 a former TM instructor sued the organization over the siddha claims and was granted a $138,000 judgment.

During the 1980s the council has continued to extend its programs into broader areas of life. In the late 1980s a major promotional program for Ayurvedic medicine was launched, and the Maharishi Center for Ayur-Veda opened in Fairfield, Iowa. The center's directors have introduced "Maharishi Amrit Kalesh," an herbal supplement. It is being marketed by Maharishi Ayurvedic Products International. The council has sponsored the establishment of the Natural Law Party, a political party active in the United States and several European countries. The Natural Law Party offers the council's program to the electorate as an alternative to traditional political party platforms.

Membership: Not reported. By 2008 an estimated 6 million people had taken the basic TM course in the United States; many of those, however, are not continuing to practice TM. In 1978 the organization had more than 7,000 authorized teachers and 400 teaching centers. Researchers have noted that TM peaked in 1976, when it initiated 292,273 people. By the end of that year, however, it had begun a radical decline. In 1977 it initiated only 50,000.

Educational Facilities:

Maharishi International University, Fairfield, Iowa • Maharishi Open University • Maharishi University of Management • Maharishi School of the Age of Enlightenment • Maharishi Academy of Total Knowledge • Maharishi Spiritual University • and the Institute for Natural Medicine and Prevention.

Periodicals: *MIU World*. Send orders to 1000 N. 4th St., DB 1155, Fairfield, IA 52557-1155. • *Modern Science and Vedic Science*.

Sources:

World Plan Executive Council—US. www.tm.org/resources.

Bainbridge, William Sims, and Daniel H. Jackson. "The Rise and Decline of Transcendental Meditation." In *The Future of Religion*, eds. Rodney Stark and William Sims Bainbridge. Berkeley and Los Angeles: University of California Press, 1985.

Bloomfield, Harold H., Michael Peter Cain, and Dennis T. Jaffe. *TM: Discovering Inner Energy and Overcoming Stress*. New York: Delacorte Press, 1975.

Carrey, Normand J., and Lynn A. Suess. *TM and Cult Mania*. North Quincy, MA: Christopher Publishing House, 1980.

Ebon, Martin, ed. *Maharishi, the Guru*. New York: New American Library, 1968.

Goldhaber, Nat. *TM: An Alphabetical Guide to the Transcendental Meditation Program*. New York: Ballantine Books, 1976.

Lewis, Gordon R. *Transcendental Meditation*. Glendale, CA: G/L Regal Books, 1975.

Jefferson, William. *The Story of the Maharishi*. New York: Pocket Books, 1976.

Mahesh Yogi, Maharishi. *Life Supported by Natural Law*. Washington, DC: Age of Enlightenment Press, 1986.

———. *Love and God*. N.p., Age of Enlightenment Press, 1973.

———. *The Science of Being and Art of Living*. London: International SRM Publications, 1966.

Orme-Johnson, David W., and John T. Farrows, eds. *Scientific Research on the Transcendental Meditation Program: Collected Papers, I*. Seelisberg, Switzerland: Maharishi European Research University Press, 1977.

Patton, John E. *The Case Against TM in the Schools*. Grand Rapids, MI: Baker Book House, 1976.

Roth, Robert. *Maharishi Mahesh Yogi's Transcendental Meditation*. Maharishi University of Management Press, 1994.

Scott, R. D. *Transcendental Misconceptions*. San Diego, CA: Beta Books, 1978.

White, John. *Everything You Want to Know About TM, Including How to Do It*. New York: Pocket Books, 1976.

Yasodhara Ashram Society

Box 9, Kootenay Bay, BC, Canada V0B 1X0

The Yasodhara Ashram Society was founded by Swami Sivananda (1911–1995) (Sylvia Hellman, a German-born Canadian citizen). In her forties, while meditating, she saw the face of Swami Sivananda Saraswati in a vision. She traveled to India and was initiated as a *sannyasin* (renunciate) by Sivananda into the Saraswati (monastic) Order in 1956. At Sivananda's direction she returned to Canada to update Eastern teachings for a Western audience. From 1956 to 1963, the ashram was in Vancouver but then was moved to Kootenay Bay, in the mountains of southeastern British Columbia.

Swami Radha expanded the teachings of yoga to include Western psychology and symbolism in order to create a bridge of understanding between East and West. Swami Radha introduced numerous practical techniques that aim to enhance daily living and expand consciousness. She is one of the foremost authorities on *kundalini* (an unconscious, instinctive, or erotic energy) yoga. The ashram offers courses on various aspects of yoga, retreat packages for groups and individuals, and a three-month, personal-growth intensive course each winter. The Temple of Divine Light Dedicated to All Religions was completed in 1992. Connected with the ashram is the Association for the Development of Human Potential, also founded by Swami Radha, and the ashram's publishing arm, Timeless Books, both located in Spokane, Washington.

Membership: In 2002 the Ashram reported 108 members. There are also affiliated centers, called Radha Houses, across Canada and the United States, as well as in England.

Educational Facilities:

Yasodhara Ashram Society Centre, Kootenay Bay, British Columbia, Canada.

Periodicals: *Ascent.*

Sources:

Yasodhara Ashram Society. www.yasodhara.org.

Radha, Sivannada. *Gods Who Walk the Rainbow.* Porthill, ID: Timeless Books, 1981.

————. *Hatha Yoga, Hidden Language.* Port Hill, ID: Timeless Books, 1987.

————. *Kundalini: Yoga for the West.* Spokane, WA: Timeless Books, 1978.

————. *Light and Vibration: Consciousness, Mysticism, and the Culmination of Yoga.* Timeless Books. 176 pp.

————. *Mantras: Words of Power.* Porthill, ID: Timeless Books, 1980.

————. *Radha: Diary of a Woman's Search.* Porthill, ID: Timeless Books, 1981.

Yoga House Ashram

Current address not obtained for this edition.

The Yoga House Ashram was founded in the mid-1970s by Vimalananda (b. 1942), a former leader of the Ananda Marga Yoga Society. Dadaji, as he is affectionately known to his followers, was born to a Brahmin family in Badwel, in the south of India. At the age of six, he had an intense initiation experience of divine light filling his room and a voice instructing him on the path of enlightenment. He began to pursue the inner life, and at the age of sixteen, he became an instructor of meditation. In 1962 he met Sri Anandamurti, the founder of the Ananda Marga Yoga Society, and was impressed with both his spirituality and his program of service to humanity, especially the sick, the elderly, and the poor. Anandamurti was equally impressed with his young disciple and quickly elevated him to the status of teacher of yoga. In 1966 Dadaji left India to spread Ananda Marga. He was responsible for starting centers in Thailand, Singapore, Indonesia, Malaysia, Hong Kong, and the Philippines. The government and the United Nations honored him for his efforts on behalf of the victims of the 1968 earthquake that struck Manila.

In 1969 Dadaji came to the United States and assisted in the spread of Ananda Marga. In the mid-1970s, however, he left Ananda Marga and founded the Yoga House Ashram. Since that time he has spent his time creating his own following in the San Francisco Bay area of California. Dadaji came to the United States with a strong desire to bridge the gap between East and West. He teaches a traditional yoga but has retained the emphasis on social action he found in Ananda Marga. He teaches his students to keep their role in society as they strive for God.

Membership: Not reported. The work of the Yoga House Ashram is confined to northern California, where Dadaji Vimalananda teaches yoga at a variety of locations in the greater San Francisco Bay area.

Sources:

Vimalananda, Dadaji. *Yogamritam (The Nectar of Yoga).* San Rafael, CA: Yoga House Ashram, 1977.

Yoga in Daily Life

National Center, 2402 Mount Vernon Ave., Alexandria, VA 22301

Yoga in Daily Life is the name of the organization and the system of yoga created by Paramhans Swami Maheshwarananda, affectionately known as Swamiji. As a youth in India, Swamiji met his teacher Paramhans Swami Madhavananda (generally referred to as "Holy Guruji"), under whom he gained self-realization when he was seventeen years old. In 1972 Swamiji moved to Europe to teach yoga. As he contemplated the pervasive problems faced by individuals struggling in the modern world, he developed the system he called Yoga in Daily Life, emphasizing the ancient yoga tradition recast to speak to modern civilization.

Yoga in Daily Life is built around a few basic principles: the building of physical, mental, and spiritual health; respect for life; tolerance for all religions, cultures, and nationalities; global peace; protection of human rights and values; and the protection of the environment and preservation of nature. The principles find expression in a variety of humanitarian projects sponsored and supported by Yoga in Daily Life, including several in Rajasthan, the area of India in which Swamiji was raised.

Membership: Not reported. There are centers in twenty-six countries worldwide; the American Association includes three centers, one each in Alexandria, Virginia, Atlanta, Georgia, and New York City.

Sources:

American Association of Yoga in Daily Life. www.yoga-in-daily-life-usa.com/.

Maheshwarananda, Paramhans Swami. *Meetings with a Yogi.* Columbia, MO: South Asia Books, 1994.

Maheshwarananda, Paramhans Swami. *Yoga in Daily Life: The System.* Korneuburg, Germany: Ueberreuther, 2000.

Yoga Research Foundation

6111 SW 74th Ave., Miami, FL 33143

Alternate Address: Indian headquarters: International Yoga Society, Lal Bagh, Loni–201 102, Ghaziabad, U.P., India.

Swami Jyotirmayananda (b. 1931) began his religious pilgrimage as an ascetic, emerged into teaching and editing, and became a leading figure at Swami Sivananda Saraswati's Yoga Vedanta Forest Academy. He came to the United States in 1962 and founded the Sanantan Dharma Mandir, with headquarters in Puerto Rico. The headquarters were moved to Miami under the present name in 1969. Jyotirmayananda teaches integral yoga. The foundation offers classes in yoga philosophy, ancient Hindu texts from India (the *Bhagavad Gita*, the Vedas, Puranas, Yoga Vasistha, Srimad Bhagavatam), hatha yoga, and meditation. He has developed a vast publishing program centered on his many books, cassettes, study courses, and monthly magazine.

Membership: In 1995 the foundation reported approximately 2,000 active members. There is one center in Miami and one near Delhi, India. The foundation considers the subscribers to the magazine and recipients of the *International Yoga Guide* to be members.

Periodicals: *International Yoga Guide.* • *Integral Light.*

Sources:

Yoga Research Foundation. www.yrf.org.

Jyotir Maya Nanda, Swami. *The Way to Liberation*. Miami, FL: Swami Lalitananda, 1976.

———. *Yoga Can Change Your Life*. Miami, FL: International Yoga Society, 1975.

———. *Yoga in Life*. Miami, FL: Swami Jyotir Maya Nanada, 1973.

———. *Yoga of Sex-Sublimation, Truth, and Nonviolence*. Miami, FL: Swami Lalitananda, 1974.

———. *Yoga Vasistha*. Miami, FL: Yoga Research Society, 1977.

Dharma Mittra Yoga

297 3rd Ave. at 23rd St., New York, NY 10010

Yogi Gupta, born in Kanpur in the north of India, was a lawyer who left his profession to become a monk in the *sannyasa* (renunciate) order in Banaras. At that time he was renamed Swami Kailashananda and became a major teacher of yoga. He also founded the Kailashananda Mission at Rishikesh. Basic to Yogi Gutpa's teaching is *hatha yoga*, with its various postures (*asanas*). Hatha is the entrance into various other disciplines, including psychic development, vegetarianism, and yogic philosophy. Proponents of this variant of yoga claim that it promotes self-mastery, self-fulfillment, success, and freedom. Yogi Gupta first came to the United States in 1954. He founded a center in 1974 in New York City. Shri Dharma Mittra, who studied under Swami Kailashananda, now runs the studio and yoga center; he speaks throughout the United States about yoga and philosophy.

Membership: Not reported.

Sources:

Dharma Mittra Yoga. www.dharmayogacenter.com.

Gupta, Yogi. *Shradha and Heavenly Fathers*. New York: Yogi Gupta New York Center, n.d.

———. *Yoga and Long Life*. New York: Dodd, Mead, & Company, 1958.

———. *Yoga and Yogic Powers*. New York: Yogi Gupta New York Center, 1963.

Mittra, Dharma. *Askanas*. Novato, CA: New World Library, 2003.

❧ Indian-American Hindu Temples

Bharatiya Temple

6850 Adams Rd., Troy, MI 48098

The Bharatiya Temple grew out of an informal meeting held by a group of first-generation Indian Americans in Detroit, Michigan, in January 1975. (*Bharata* is the ancient name for India.) An ad hoc committee prepared a constitution, which was adopted two months later. The group elected a board of trustees, created an organization to erect a temple, and purchased land in Troy, a Detroit suburb. During the years of construction, biweekly religious meetings were held at the Unitarian Church in Southfield, Michigan. The temple was dedicated in July 1981. Swami Chinmayananda, head of the Chinmaya Mission West, and Sant Keshavadas of the Temple of Cosmic Religion participated in the dedication ceremonies. The temple has become a gathering place for Detroit's Hindus and is used by many other Hindu organizations for public programs. The yoga center offers beginner-level classes.

The temple has a board consisting of 15 trustees (12 elected and 3 appointed). The Executive Committee consists of a president, president-elect, secretary, joint secretary, treasurer, joint treasurer, and committee coordinator; these members are appointed annually.

Membership: Not reported.

Periodicals: *Chetana*.

Sources:

Bharatiya Temple. www.bharatiya-temple.org/home/index.shtml.

Bochasanwasi Swaminarayan Sanstha

43-38 Bowne St., Flushing, NY 11355

The Bochasanwasi Swaminarayan Sanstha, also known as Bochasanwasi Shri Akshar Purushottam Swaminarayan Sanstha, is the American branch of an international Hindu movement that originated in western India at the beginning of the nineteenth century. Its founder, Shree Sahajanand Swami (1781–1830) (popularly known as Swaminarayan), was born in Uttar Pradesh, India. He followed the teachings of the Vaishnava leader Sri Ramanuja, who in the twelfth century advocated theistic worship as opposed to the idea of an impersonal divine reality espoused by Shankaracharya; he also taught the necessity of *bhakti yoga* (devotional service) as a means to salvation.

Swaminarayan emphasized Ramanuja's teaching that God manifests himself on earth through both his incarnation and his fully realized saint. Swaminarayan was named the successor to his guru, Swami Ramanand. Shortly after assuming the mantle of his guru, he proclaimed that he was Lord Swami Narayan, the supreme being, manifest on earth, and he is so considered to this day by members of the movement. Worship of Swaminarayan is central to the life of the movement. His work, concentrated in the Indian state of Gujarat, led to a revival of religious life and the establishment of centers throughout western India. Since his death the movement has been led by a succession of high priests, through whom Swami Narayan's presence continues to reside in the world. The movement remained small during the nineteenth century and into the twentieth but has grown rapidly under the vigorous leadership of the present high priest, Pramukh Swami Maharaj (b. 1921).

The Swami Narayan movement was brought to the United States by the immigration of devotees in the late 1960s. In 1970, the high priest, Yogi Maharaj, toured England, where a center had been created. While he was there, an American devotee traveled to England and requested that the movement be organized in America. In response the high priest sent four monks to America with a list of known devotees. Touring the country, they established centers wherever they found a small concentration of devotees. A correspondence network was established around the center in Flushing, New York. In February 1972 the group in New York incorporated. The following year property was purchased, and in 1974 the high priest Pramukh Swami Maharaj (on the first of his many tours to include the United States) visited America for the installation of deities. Some 1,500 people attended the ceremony.

Since that time the movement has spread across the United States. There are major centers in Flushing, New York; Piscatway and Edison, New Jersey; Boston, Massachusetts; Erie, Pennsylvania; Chicago, Illinois; Dallas and Houston, Texas; Atlanta, Georgia; and San Francisco, San Jose, and Los Angeles, California. Deity statues were installed in the Chicago and Los Angeles temples during the 1984 visit of the high priest; in Houston, Dallas, Atlanta, and Toronto, Canada, during the 1988 visit; and in Edison, New Jersey, and San Jose, California, during the 1991 visit. Internationally, there are major across India and in Kenya, Tanzania, Uganda, South Africa, Australia, Belgium, Germany, England, Canada (Toronto and Kitchener, Ontario), Singapore, and Thailand. The international headquarters are in Ahmedabad, India.

Membership: In 1991 there were an estimated 60,000 devotees in the United States organized around nine main temples and 43 other centers. The temples are in New York, Edison, Boston, Chicago, Los Angeles, San Jose, Houston, Dallas, Atlanta, and Toronto. Membership is largely confined to the Gujarat Indian American community. B.S.S. has a worldwide following of millions of devotees with 450 saints and more than 3,000 centers.

Educational Facilities:

Pramukh Swami Institute of Electronics, Vidyanagar, Gujarat State, India • School of Architecture, S. P. University, Vidyanagar, Gujarat State, India • Pramukh Swami Science College, Kadi, Gurjarat State, India •

Akshardham-Centre for Applied Research in Social Harmony (AARSH), Gandhinagar, Gujarat State, India.

Remarks: The fellowship encountered strong local opposition from residents of Independence Township, near Washington, New Jersey, where it had purchased land for a large religious-educational complex. Residents were concerned about the negative impact on the area by the development of the group's land.

Sources:

Bochasanwasi Swaminarayan Sanstha.
www.swaminarayan.org/globalnetwork/america/newyork.htm.

Dave, H. T. *Life and Philosophy of Shree Swaminarayan.* London: George Allen & Unwin, 1974.

Fisher, Maxine P. *The Indians of New York City.* Columbia, MO: South Asia Books, 1980.

Priyadarshandas, Sadhu. *Pramukh Swami Maharaj: An Introduction.* Gujarat, India: Swaminarayan Aksharpith, 1995. 54 pp.

Vivesagardas, Sadhu. *The Immortal River.* Gujarat, India: Swaminarayan Askharpith, 1997. 95 pp.

Williams, Raymond Brady. *A New Face of Hinduism: The Swaminarayan Religion.* Cambridge, UK: Cambridge University Press, 1984.

Hindu Temple of Greater Chicago
10915 Lemont Rd., Lemont, IL 60439

The Hindu Temple of Greater Chicago was founded in 1977. It is one of several such associations within the larger Indian American community of Chicago. In 1980 it purchased 17 acres of land near Lemont, Illinois, and began construction of the Shri Rama Temple and Community Center. The groundbreaking ceremony for the temple was held in June 1984; the next year the temple was dedicated and opened for public worship. In 1990 an additional five acres of adjoining land was purchased. In 1991 a new youth branch was founded.

Membership: Approximately 13,000 families.

Periodicals: *Newsletter.* Send orders to Box 697, Lombard, IL 60148.

Sources:

Hindu Temple of Greater Chicago. www.htgc.org/test.

Hindu Temple Society of North America
45-57 Bowne St., Flushing, NY 11355

The Hindu Temple Society of North America was founded January 26, 1970, and has centered its activity on the construction and maintenance of the first Indian-style temple built in the United States according to strict Vedic standards. It was dedicated on July 4, 1977, by Sri La Sri Pandrimalai Swamigal of Madras, India. The central shrine of the temple is dedicated to Ganesha (Maha Ganapati), the deity known to be the remover of obstacles. Other shrines are dedicated to Siva (and his consort Parvati), Shanmukha (and his consorts Valli and Devayani), Vishnu-Venkateswara, and Lakshmi.

The temple was designed to serve all segments of the Indian American community. The temple supports a number of charities in India and the United States. The temple runs a school, Ganesa Patasala, on the weekends to teach religion, languages, Hindi, Sanskrit, and advanced English.

The Temple has an active youth club that is involved in organizing various seminars and other activities. Construction of a community center was completed in June 1998.

Membership: In 2001 the society reported 17,500 members.

Sources:

Hindu Temple Society of North America. www.nyganeshtemple.org.

Ehrlicher, C. C. "The New Hindu Temple: India Comes to Flushing." *The New Sun* 1, no. 9 (September 1977).

Hindu Temple Society of Southern California
1600 Las Virgenes Canyon Rd., Calabasas, CA 91302

The Hindu Temple Society of Southern California was formed in July 1977 by a group of Indian Americans to fulfill the religious needs of the Hindu Indian Americans in the metropolitan Los Angeles area. The group decided to construct a temple dedicated to Sri Venkateswara, the popular deity and incarnation of Vishnu. After an extensive search the society purchased a site near Malibu, California, in December 1979. Construction of the temple began in 1980, and the shrine to Lord Genesh—the son of Siva who is often worshipped as the remover of obstacles—was completed before the end of the year. Construction was immediately begun on the main shrine to Sri Venkateswara, and in May 1984 the shrine was completed, and the deity's statue was installed with appropriate ceremonies under the direction of the Brahman priest Varadaraja Bhattar. Other shrines have been added, including one dedicated to Krishna (installed October 1985), another incarnation of Vishnu, and construction continues.

Although the Sri Venkateswara Temple is primarily a Vaishnava worship center, shrines have been constructed immediately adjacent to the main temple for Saivite worship in recognition of the temple's function within the Indian American Hindu community. Ceremonies are scheduled daily at the temple, with special services on weekends and in observance of major Hindu holy days.

Membership: In 1994 membership was reported to be over 1,000. Current membership not reported.

Periodicals: *Newsletter.*

Sources:

Hindu Temple Society of Southern California. www.hindutemplesoutherncalifornia.org.

Hindu Temple Society of Texas
4533 Larch Ln., Bellaire, TX 77401

In 1974 Hindus in Houston, Texas, formed the Hindu Temple Society of Texas. Land was purchased in suburban Bellaire, and construction of a temple begun. That same year a monthly newsletter was begun by one of the members, Dr. Lal Sardana. Members of the temple follow traditional Hinduism, which they interpret as a monotheistic religion. *Om*, the word chanted by many Hindus, is considered the symbol of the one universal monotheistic God, who is formless. That god is also symbolized in its three dimensions as creator (Brahma), sustainer (Vishnu), and changer (Siva), the main deities in the traditional Hindu pantheon.

Membership: In 1984 there were approximately 2,000 members of the temple, most residing in southeast Texas. Current membership not reported.

Periodicals: *Hindu Jyoti.*

Sri Meenakshi Temple Society of Houston
17130 McLean Rd., Pearland, TX 77584-4630

The Sri Meenakshi Temple Society of Houston was initiated in October 1977 by a group of some 30 Indian American families in Houston, Texas. Over the next year they adopted a constitution, incorporated, and formed committees to pursue the construction of a traditional temple dedicated to the worship of Sri Meenakshi, a *Shakti* (the dynamic energy of a Hindu god personified as his female consort) deity form. Land was purchased in suburban Pearland, and the first phase, the construction of the temple dedicated to Sri Ganesh (the popular elephant-headed deity considered to be the "remover of obstacles" by Hindus) was begun. That small temple was completed and the deity installed in 1979.

The second phase, the building of the main temple to Sri Meenakshi, commenced immediately. Beside the main sanctum housing the statue of Sri Meenakshi there are two other sanctums housing the prominent Hindu deity forms Lord Venkateswara (Vishnu) and Sri Sundareswara (Siva, the consort of

Shakti). Dedication of the temple and installation of the deity statues were completed in an elaborate week-long ceremony in June 1982.

Integral to traditional shakti worship is the spreading of knowledge through *yantras,* mystic diagrams. The installation of the yantras, inscribed on thin metal plates, was an important part of the dedication services at the temple. This temple was the first important temple for tantric worship established among Indian Americans in the United States.

Radio broadcasts can be heard every Sunday between 10:30 and 11:00 A.M. on KBRZ AM 1460 in Houston, Texas.

Membership: By 1992 the society had enrolled approximately 200 families.

Periodicals: *Temple Times.*

Sources:

Sri Meenakshi Temple Society of Houston. www.meenakshi.org/index.php.

"Inaugural Ceremonies Held for Sri Meenakshi Temple in Houston, Texas." *The New Saivite World* 4, no. 2 (August 1, 1982): 1, 11.

Sri Venkateswara Temple
1230 S. McCully Dr., PO Box 17289, Penn Hills, PA 15235

Among the first temples to be envisioned by the emerging Indian American community in the 1970s was the Sri Venkateswara Temple in Pittsburgh, Pennsylvania. Planning for the temple began in January 1972, and construction was initiated four years later on a site in Penns Hills, east of Pittsburgh. The main deities were installed in November 1976.

The temple is modeled on the Tirupathi Shrine in South India. The main deity is Sri Venkateswara, an incarnation of Vishnu. One enters the temple through a massive Rajagopuran (entrance tower). There are also statues dedicated to Padmavathi (an incarnation of Lakshmi, Vishnu's consort) and the mother earth goddess Andal (or Bhooma Devi). Members of the temple, although following a full round of deity worship, view the idols (deities) as symbols of the one invisible spirit (God). Manavala Iyengar is the priest in charge of temple worship.

Membership: Not reported.

Periodicals: *Saptagiri Vana.* • *Indian Youth Review.* Both publications are available from Box 17280, Pittsburgh, PA 15235-0280.

Sources:

Sri Venkateswara Temple. www.svtemple.org/temple/index.shtml.

United Hindu Temple of New Jersey
1 CeCamp Ct., West Caldwell, NJ 07006

The United Hindu Temple of New Jersey was founded in the mid-1970s by representatives of a variety of Indian American organizations who wished to provide a place for traditional Hindu temple worship at a nonsectarian site. A coordinating council was selected, and by 1978 the first issue of a periodical, *Konarak,* appeared. The council took inspiration from Konarak, a town in Orissa, India, renowned for its beautiful temples.

Membership: Not reported.

Periodicals: *Konarak.*

 Jainism

Dada Bahgwan Foundation
For information: gv@dadabhagwan.org

Dada Bhagwan Foundation is the vehicle for the teaching of Shri Ambalal Muljibhai Patel, fondly known as Dadashri or Dada Bhagwan. Patel is considered by his followers to be a *gnani purush*—"one awakened to the self," or "enlightened being." He teaches the path to realization called Akram Vignan (science without steps), which is viewed as a shortcut for attaining self-realization. A contractor by profession, without particular religious training, Patel was sitting on a railway bench in 1958 when a spontaneous and natural phenomenon occurred: Dada Bhagwan, the Lord within Ambalal Patel, began to manifest. At the end of the process he was a self-realized person, and he began to teach others the spiritual science of Akram Vignan, which provides ultimate salvation—the acquisition of freedom from the cycles of birth and death.

Akram Vignan is described as the science of the *tirthankars* (divine omniscient lords, the twenty-three men and one woman who are believed to have been the founders of the Jain movement). Dadashri describes his teachings as simply the collective knowledge of the tirthankars, and himself as merely the instrument through which this knowledge flows. During his spontaneous enlightenment, Dadashri noted that he made a connection with the living tirthankar Lord Shri Simandhar Swami, who lives in Mahavideh Kshetra, a world outside this galaxy where Jains believe that tirthankars are still being born. He made his communication with Simandhar Swami through his astral body and received answers to his questions. According to Dadashr, direct liberation from planet Earth is no longer possible due to the negative conditions here, but it is possible from Mahavideh Kshetra. Having acquired self-realization in this life, the soul will be reborn in Mahavideh Kshetra, where it will experience the *darshan* (presence) of Lord Simandhar and begin its final journey to *moksha* (liberation).

Dadashri teaches through *satsangs* (spiritual discourses), with students asking questions that he answers. Many of these have been transcribed and published.

Since the 1990s support for Dadashri has grown quietly throughout the Indian diaspora community. There are groups of followers in Malaysia, Australia, New Zealand, Singapore, the United Arab Emirates, Kenya, and the United Kingdom. In North America groups have appeared in New Jersey, Florida, Kansas, Texas, and Los Angeles, and in Toronto and Montreal, Canada. The movement's international headquarters is located at a *trimandir* constructed on land between Ahmedabad and Gandhinagar, Gujarat State, India, which features a 13-foot statue of Shri Simandhar Swami.

Membership: Not reported.

Sources:

Dada Bahgwan Foundation. www.dadabhagwan.org/.

Federation of Jain Associations in North America (JAINA)
PO Box 700, Getzville, NY 14068

In the nineteenth century the Jain community, until then largely confined to Persia (Iran) and India, began to disperse around the world. Of those who left their homelands, the largest percentage moved to England. A few moved to North America, though large-scale immigration did not occur until after the change in immigration laws in 1965. As the number of Jains increased, organization was possible. The first such organization, founded in 1973, was the Jain Center of Greater Boston.

Subsequently centers were founded across North America, and the Boston center published a directory in 1979. In the meantime, two Jain organizations had been started by Acharya Sushil Kumar Ji and Gurudev Chitrabhanu Ji. Both were active in 1981, when an initial meeting was held by four of the Jain centers and the Federation of Jain Associations in North America (JAINA) was organized. The organization expanded rapidly.

JAINA provides a united voice for the Jain community in North America and has been able to provide religious activities and educational materials that no one center could provide. In addition, it promotes two important opinions of the group that are shared by many non-Jains: vegetarianism and *ahimsa* (nonviolence). Finally, through JIANA Jains stay in touch with the Jain international diaspora and the base communities in India and Iran.

JAINA conventions are held biennially. The organization was active in response to the January 2001 earthquake in Gujarati, India. JAINA is led by its president, Dr. Bipin D. Parikh, and an executive committee consisting of national officers and regional representatives.

Membership: There are 62 Jain organizations representing over 100,000 individuals in the U.S. and Canada.

Periodicals: *Jain Digest* • *JAINA Spectrum*.

Sources:

Federation of Jain Associations in North America. www.jaina.org.

International Nahavir Jain Mission

Acharya Sushil Jain Ashram, 722 Tomkins Ave., Staten Island, NY 10305

Since 1965 Jains began to immigrate to the United States, along with Hindus and Sikhs. Because of restrictions on travel over water, Jains did not arrive in numbers that rivaled those of other Indian religious groups. Among the immigrants were individuals associated with the International Mahavir Mission. The mission had been founded in India in 1970 by Guruji Muni Sushul Kumar (b. 1926). As a teenager Guruji entered the Sacred Order of Jain Munis, receiving from his guru two traditional symbols of nonviolence: the *mukh-patti*, a white mask worn over the face to keep the wearer from accidentally swallowing an insect and thus killing a living soul, and an *augha*, a broom for sweeping surfaces before sitting lest a living entity be harmed. The mission was brought to Europe and North America by its members. Guruji traveled to the United States in 1975 to visit the Jain communities.

The mission emphasizes the Jain tenets of vegetarianism, *ahimsa* (nonviolence), and *anekantavada* (the many-faceted nature of truth). It teaches hatha yoga, *pranayama* (breath control), *japayoga* (the use of mantric words of power), ayurvedic medicine, and chanting.

In the United States an urban ashram was opened in Staten Island and a rural center, Muni Sushil Yogville, was opened in upstate New York. Centers have also been opened in England, France, Germany, and Canada. The international headquarters are in New Delhi, India. Guruji has been active in interreligious work (growing out of the Jain belief in anekantavada) and organized the World Fellowship of Religions, which periodically sponsors international interreligious conferences. In 1977 Guruji also participated in the first North American Jain Conference held at Berkeley, California, in 1981.

Membership: Not reported.

Periodicals: *News from Jain Ashram*.

Sources:

International Nahavir Jain Mission. www.acharyasushilmuni.org.

Kumar, Acharya Sushil. *Song of the Soul*. Blairstown, NJ: Siddhachalam Publishers, 1987.

Jain Meditation International Center

Box 230244, Ansonia Sta., New York, NY 10023-0244

Gurudev Sri Chitrabhanu (b. 1922) had been a Jain *muni* (monk) for 29 years. During that time he had become widely known and respected in his native India and had, in 1965, founded the Divine Knowledge Society in Bombay. Then, in 1971, he gave up his monastic existence and rejected the millennia-long taboo on traveling over water and by means other than foot so that he could travel to the United States at the invitation of the Temple of Understanding to lecture at a conference at Harvard University. Following that conference he stayed in North America and lectured widely to other Jains who, like him, had immigrated to America. In 1974 he founded New Life Now, an organization dedicated to the spiritual illumination of the West. New Life Now evolved into the Jain Meditation International Center. Chitrabhanu defines a Jain as one who "speaks of a personal responsibility for his own deeds, regards a person as a master of his own destiny, and refrains from violence."

The center is headquartered in New York City and teaches meditation, yoga, vegetarianism, and tai chi. While moving among Jains who have immigrated to the United States, Chitrabhanu has had great success among people outside the Indian American community as well. Groups have been established in Boston, Pittsburgh, Philadelphia, West Orange, and Toronto. He has also worked in Brazil.

The associated Jain Peace Fellowship is headquartered in South Norwalk, Connecticut. Chitrabhanu participated in the first North American Jain conference, held in Berkeley, California, in 1981.

Membership: Not reported.

Periodicals: *Newsletter*.

Sources:

Jain Meditation International Center. www.jainmeditation.org.

Baakza, A. H. A. *Half-Hours with a Jain Muni*. Bombay: Jaico Publishing House, 1962.

Chitrabhanu, Gurudev. *The Philosophy of Soul and Matter*. New York: Jain Meditation Center, 1977.

———. *The Psychology of Enlightenment*. New York: Dodd, Mead & Company, 1979.

———. *Realize What You Are*. New York: Dodd, Mead & Company, 1978.

———. *Twelve Facets of Reality*. New York: Dodd, Mead & Company, 1980.

Osho Commune International

80 Fifth Ave., Ste. 1403, New York, NY 10011

Alternate Address: International headquarters: Osho Commune International, 17 Koregoan Park, Poona, India 411001 %bul; Osho International, 304 Park Ave. S., Ste. 608, New Yor, NY 10010.

Osho, formerly known as Bhagwan Shree Rajneesh, was born Rajneesh Chandra Mohan in a small town in Madhya Pradesh, India, in 1931. He became one of the most controversial spiritual mystics to travel to the West and establish his teachings there. Born of Jain parents, Osho, even as a child, began to question the wide variety of traditional religious beliefs to which he was exposed as a young man— Hindu, Christian, Mohammedan, or Jain—and asserted that individual spiritual experience was the only true value and that such experience could not be organized into any belief system.

At the age of 21, during his college days, he had what he termed an experience of *samadhi*, or spiritual awakening. Nevertheless, he decided to continue his academic studies, earning a master's degree in philosophy and sharpening his skills as a speaker by debating at universities all over India. In 1966 he resigned his post as professor of philosophy at the University of Jabalpur in order to share his understanding of religious experience and to conduct experimental "meditation camps" using his own unique methods.

In the early 1970s he began to initiate people into "neosannyas," a radical departure from the traditional Hindu form of sannyas in which the spiritual seeker renounces home, family, wealth, sex, and the material life. Instead, Osho taught that the real challenge for the sannyasin is to remain in the world, enjoying life to the full, but not being attached to it—"to be in the marketplace but not of it." Initiates were asked to dress in orange, wear a *mala* (a necklace of 108 wooden beads containing a locket with Osho's picture), receive a new name, and meditate for at least one hour a day.

In 1972 the first Westerners visited Osho while he was living in Bombay. Many of these newcomers were therapists from the Western humanistic psychology movement who were attracted by Osho's teachings that self-expression and emotional release are useful preparations for meditation. In 1974 a group of disciples purchased property in Poona, near Bombay, and this spot quickly became an international ashram attracting thousands of visitors from around the world. Daily activities included a 90-minute discourse by Osho, a regular program of meditation, a wide variety of therapy groups, and work in the commune. The best-known of Osho's spiritual disciplines is dynamic meditation, which lasts one hour and has five stages:

1. deep, rapid, chaotic breathing through the nose;
2. emotional catharsis, allowing free expression of anger, sadness, joy, and so on;

3. jumping, with arms raised, while saying the mantra "hoo!";

4. complete silence and stillness;

5. celebration through dance.

In his daily discourses Osho commented upon all of the major religious traditions and the sayings of many enlightened mystics, including Jesus, Buddha, Lao Tzu, Krishna, Mahavira, and Bodhidharma. He explained this as his way of "gathering his people," who would otherwise have remained involved with other religious disciplines.

Osho came to the United States in 1981. After a short stay in New Jersey, he moved to a 64,000-acre ranch in Central Oregon. Within a year a city named Rajneeshpuram had been incorporated on the ranch, with a population that rose to 5,000 people. The community aroused mounting opposition from local ranchers, Christian fundamentalists, the Oregon state government, and the Reagan Administration; much of the antagonism to the city centered on Osho's fleet of 93 Rolls-Royces and acts such as inviting thousands of homeless people to live at the ranch and vote in local elections.

In 1985 Osho, who had remained silent from 1981 to 1984, publicly revealed that his secretary, Ma Anand Sheela, had been involved in a number of crimes against his disciples and people in Oregon, and he invited the police to investigate. A few weeks later Osho himself was arrested by federal agents, jailed, and charged with immigration fraud. Although insisting on his innocence, Osho agreed to a plea bargain with federal prosecutors and was deported from the United States. With Osho no longer in residence, the Oregon commune was no longer an economically viable proposition, and the residents departed, turning Rajneeshpuram into a ghost town. Sheela and a small group of close associates arranged plea bargains with state and federal prosecutors and served jail sentences.

Osho returned to India, staying briefly in the Himalayas. Then, in 1986, he embarked on a world tour, during which he was refused entry by 21 countries, partially because of pressure from the Reagan Administration. He went back to India once more and in January 1987 returned to his old ashram in Poona, which quickly revived as a large international commune. At about this time Osho advised his disciples to drop their distinctive clothing and the mala because the Indian authorities were making it difficult for them to enter the country.

In 1988 he dropped the name Bhagwan Shree Rajneesh and assumed the name Osho, a Japanese term of reverence and endearment used by disciples to address their spiritual masters. During this time Osho's body became very weak, and he suffered from a variety of puzzling symptoms, including severe bone pain, hair loss, and impaired vision, which led his disciples to believe that he had been poisoned while in the custody of the U.S. government. He died on January 19, 1990, and a sacred grave was made for his ashes inside the commune. Before his death Osho had guided a group of 21 disciples into assuming control of the worldwide activities of his movement. This group is known as the Inner Circle.

In the United States, after Osho's departure, the movement decentralized and returned to its pre-1986 state—a loose association of meditation centers and small communes scattered around the country. A bimonthly news magazine for sannyasins, *Viha Connection*, is produced by the Osho Viha Meditation Center in Marin County, California. An English-language edition of *Osho Times International* is available online at www.osho.org. In 1995 about 500 sannyasins living in the United States gathered at an Osho center in Fairfax, California, to commemorate the tenth anniversary of Rajneeshpuram.

Meanwhile, legal actions growing out of events at Rajneeshpuram continue. Sannyasin attorneys have been challenging the U.S. government under the Freedom of Information Act in the hope of gathering enough evidence to prove that the Reagan Administration acted illegally and unconstitutionally in destroying the Oregon commune. The U.S. Justice Department is also pursuing cases against Sheela and her associates. In 1995 two former Osho disciples were extradited from England to Portland, Oregon, and convicted of conspiracy to murder former U.S. Attorney Charles Turner, who led the Reagan Administration's efforts to shut down Rajneeshpuram. The two disciples served short prison terms and are now back in England.

Through the 1990s Osho Commune International in Poona has expanded greatly and has become one of the world's largest centers for spiritual-growth activities; it offers a wide variety of classes, workshops, and training. Visitors still come from Europe and America, and increasingly from Japan, Korea, Taiwan, Russia, and Israel. Osho International has opened a New York headquarters, which oversees the publication of Osho's books; those works are increasingly available from commercial publishing houses in England, Germany, and North America. Osho International also prepares videotapes of Osho's discourses for relay through a number of Asian commercial satellite-television channels. In India Osho's books and audiotapes can be found in stores nationwide.

The Osho International Foundation is located in Zurich, Switzerland.

Membership: There are Osho centers in more than 60 countries. In the United States, as of 1997, there were 50 centers serving approximately 10,000 people and 20 centers serving some 4,000 people in Canada. There are a reported 900,000 people related to the 750 centers worldwide.

Educational Facilities:

Osho Multiversity, Poona, India

Periodicals: *Viha Connection.* • *Osho Times International.*

Sources:

Osho Commune International. www.osho.com.

Belfrage, Sally. *Flowers of Emptiness*. New York: Dial Press, 1981.

Bharti, Ma Satya. *Death Comes Dancing*. London: Routledge & Kegan Paul, 1981.

Braun, Kirk. *The Unwelcome Society*. West Linn, OR: Scout Creek Press, 1984.

Goldman, Marion. *Passionate Journeys: Why Successful Women Joined a Cult*. Ann Arbor, University of Michigan Press, 1999.

Gordon, James S. *The Golden Guru*. Lexington, MA: Stephen Greene Press, 1987.

Mehta, Gita. *Karma Cola*. New York: Simon & Schuster, 1979.

Milne, Hugh. *Bhagwan, The God That Failed*. New York: St. Martin's Press, 1986.

Osho. *Osho: Autobiography of a Spiritually Incorrect Mystic*. New York: St. Martin's Press, 2000.

Prasad, Ram Chandra. *Rajneesh: The Mystic of Feeling*. Delhi: Motilal Banarsidass, 1978.

Rajneesh, Bhagwan Shree. *The Great Challeng:, A Rajneesh Reader*. New York: Grove Press, 1982.

———. *I Am the Gate*. New York: Harper & Row, 1977.

———. *The Orange Book*. Rajneeshpuram, OR: Rajneesh Foundation International, 1983.

———. *Tantra, Spirituality, and Sex*. San Francisco: Rainbow Bridge, 1977.

Rajneesh, the Most Dangerous Man Since Jesus Christ. Zurich, Switzerland: Rebel Publishing House, 1987.

Rajneeshism. Rajneeshpuram, OR: Rajneesh Foundation International, 1983.

Strelley, Kate. *The Ultimate Game*. San Francisco: Harper & Row, 1987.

 Sikhism

Sikh Council of North America

95-30 118th St., Richmond Hill, NY 11419

Alternate Address: International Sikh Organization, 2025 Eye St. NW, No. 109, Washington, D.C. 20006 • International Sikh Organization, 238 Davenport Rd., Ste. 125, Toronto, ON Canada M2R 1J6.

The Sikh Council of North America attempts to provide communication and coordination for Sikh congregations and temples across the United States; its members are predominantly Indian American Sikhs. Since 1965 the number of Sikhs has risen dramatically, doubling between 1975 and 1985.

The beginning of Sikh organization in America traces to the arrival of Jawala Singh and Wisakha Singh, two advocates of Indian independence who came to California in 1908. They owned a ranch on the Holtville River, near Sacramento, where they practiced Gurbani Kirtan (singing the songs from *Sri Guru Granth Sahib*). Then, in 1912, a lot was purchased at Stockton, California, and the *Sri Guru Granth Sahib* was installed in a gurdwara (place of worship). The Pacific Coast Khalsa Diwan Society was organized to raise money for a temple. A wooden temple was constructed in 1916 but was replaced with a brick structure in 1929. For several decades it was the only Sikh center in the United States, and large gatherings were held there four times a year.

The temple in Stockton was closely associated with the Ghadar Party, an organization established in 1913 in San Francisco and financed in large part by Jawala Singh; the group advocated Indian independence from British rule. Though largely destroyed during World War I because of its ties to German supporters, it continued into the 1940s, and its building has been turned into a memorial to the struggle for Indian independence. In more recent years the Stockton temple has become identified with those Sikhs in the Punjab seeking independence from Indian rule.

After World War II and India's gaining of independence in 1948, there was an additional spurt of migration of Punjabis, enough to support the construction of a second temple at El Centro, California. In 1969 the largest Sikh temple in the world was erected in Yuba City, California. By 1974 there were close to 100,000 Sikhs from the Punjab in the United States. Centers can now be found in cities and towns across the United States.

In the 1970s the Sikh Foundation emerged as a public voice for East Indian Sikhs in the United States. From its headquarters in Redwood City, California, it published the quarterly *Sikh Sandar* and *Sikhs in the U.S.A. and Canada*, a directory. The foundation was later superseded by the council.

Membership: By the early twenty-first century there were an estimated 500,000 Sikhs in the United States.

Sources:

Sikh Council of North America. www.sikh.net/Gurdwara/SCSNY/index.htm.

Singh, Wadhawa. *Introduction to the Sikh Temple, Stockton, and the Ghadar Party*. Stockton, CA: Sikh Temple, 1983.

————. *Introduction to Sikhism and Its Holy Scripture: Sri Guru Granth Sahib*. Stockton, CA: Sikh Temple, 1981.

Sikhs in the U.S.A. & Canada. Redwood City, CA: Sikh Foundation, 1972.

Sikh Dharma

PO Box 35330, Los Angeles, CA 90035
Alternate Address: Dr. Sat-kaur Khalsa, Secretary of Religion, 409 E Coronado Rd., No. 3, Santa Fe, New Mexico 87505.

The chief religious and administrative authority for the Sikh Dharma in the United States and the rest of the Western Hemisphere is Yogi Bhajan, who arrived in the United States in 1969 and founded the Healthy, Happy, Holy Organization (better known as 3HO Foundation), the nonsecular educational affiliate of the Sikh Dharma. Siri Singh Sahib Bhai Sahib Harbhajan Singh Khalsa Yogiji, popularly known as Yogi Bhajan, is a priest of the Sikh Dharma, which is headquartered in Amritsar, India. The teachings are based upon those of the Ten Sikh Gurus (the first being Guru Nanak, about whom the organization has published a book) and center on the praise of God's name and the practice of *kundalini* (primal spiritual or erotic force or energy) yoga (a practice that has earned the Sikh Dharma some criticism from other orthodox Sikhs).

As Sikhs (literally "students of truth"), members follow the admonition of the Ten Sikh Gurus to rise before sunrise, bathe, and meditate upon God's name. These individual practices are followed by gathering together with the congregation and singing the guru's hymns (known as *gurbani kirtan*). Sikhs bow to the word of God contained in *Siri Guru Granth Sahib* (the scriptures compiled from the original teachings of the ten gurus), which now serves as the "living" guru. A copy of *Siri Guru Granth Sahib* is enthroned in every Sikh gurudwara (place of worship).

Members of the Sikh Dharma may be baptized and accept traditional Sikh practice. A baptized member is called an Amritdhari Sikh. Others affiliated with the group are called Sahajdhari. Members are vegetarian, and every gurudwara has a free kitchen. Several members have even opened vegetarian restaurants and grocery stores. Alcohol, tobacco, and intoxicating drugs are forbidden.

Leadership of the Sikh Dharma is vested in the Khalsa Council, which functions under Yogi Bhajan. It consists of the administrative and regional ministers, known as the Mukhia Singh Sahibs (men) and Mukhia Sardarni Sahibas (women), who oversee the local centers and local ministers.

Aside from the center in Los Angeles, there is a second headquarters complex in Espanola, New Mexico, where Yogi Bhajan resides part of the time. It is also the site of the semiannual international gatherings on the summer solstice and of summer camps for women and children. There is also a women's auxiliary, the GGMWW (Grace of God Movement of the Women of the World), based on a body of teachings dealing with the evolving role of women. Women are viewed as *shakti*, or manifested divine power, and are accorded equal opportunities at all levels of leadership in the organization. In addition, the Kundalini Research Institute gathers data on the effectiveness of kundalini yoga and publishes much of the movement's literature.

Kundalini yoga, an energetic yoga of awareness, incorporates traditional hatha yoga postures and regulated breathing techniques. The goal of this practice of yoga is enable the practitioner to remain centered and neutral in the face of adversity; it also seeks to enhance one's ability meditate on God's name.

Membership: In 1995 there were more than 139 ashrams and/or teaching centers in the United States, 11 in Canada, and 86 additional centers in 26 countries of the world. There are approximately 500,000 Sikhs in North America, of whom over 10,000 reside in or near Sikh Dharma ashrams and community centers.

Periodicals: *The Science of Keeping Up*. Order from 3HO Foundation, 1620 Preuss Rd., Los Angeles, CA 90035.

Sources:

Sikh Dharma. www.sdministry.org/Acrobat/procedure.pdf

Kaur, Sardarni Premka. *Guru for the Aquarian Age*. San Rafael, CA: Spiritual Community, 1972.

Kundalini Yoga/Sadhana Guidelines. Pomona, CA: KRI Publications, 1978.

Singh, Sahib Harbhajan [Yogi Bhajan]. *The Experience of Consciousness*. Pomona, CA: KRI Publications, 1977.

————. *The Teachings of Yogi Bhajan*. New York: Hawthorn Books, 1977.

Sant Mat

Ancient Teachings of the Masters (ATOM)

PO Box 68322, Oak Grove, OR 97268

Darwin Gross, previously the leader of the religious movement Eckankar, began teaching independently in 1983. Sounds of Soul (SOS Publishing), used by Gross to identify his writings, was phased out in 1989. He has characterized his teaching as the Ancient Teachings of the Masters (ATOM); in his view the individual soul is an atom. Gross became active in Eckankar in 1968, quickly rising to a position of leadership in disseminating the teachings of Paul Twitchell, the founder of Eckankar. Gross was selected as the new ECK master when Twitchell died in 1971. The appointment was confirmed by a formal passing of "the rod of power" in October of that year. Gross married Twitchell's widow in 1973; they were divorced in 1977.

In 1981 Gross nominated Harold Klemp as his assistant but continued to serve as president of Eckankar Corporation. In 1983 Klemp took the position that Gross was no longer an ECK master and terminated his membership in Eckankar and all agreements between him and the corporation. Gross responded by declaring that by these actions Klemp lost the "rod of power" nomination previously accorded to him. Gross emphasized that he was not founding a separate path or teaching but maintaining the original teachings of Paul Twitchell. Retaining the copyrights on his previously published books and musical compositions, he reissued them for his students. Though Gross is known as the "972nd living master" in the line of masters described by Paul Twitchell, by agreement he has avoided terms trademarked by Eckankar Corporation, including *ECK* and *Eckankar*.

Membership: Not reported.

Sources:

Ancient Teachings of the Masters (ATOM). www.atomshop.org

Gross, Darwin. *Awakened Imagination* Oak Grove, OR: SOS Publishing, 1987.

————. *Be Good to Yourself*. Oak Grove, OR: Author, 1988.

————. *The Golden Thread Discourses*. Oak Grove, OR: Author, 1987.

————. *My Letter to You Discourses*. Oak Grove, OR: Author, 1987.

————. *Treasures*. Oak Grove, OR: Author, 1988.

Divine Knowledge Meditation Center
1434 Willow St., Denver, CO 80220

The Divine Knowledge Meditation Center was founded by Mahatma Rama Nand, a disciple of Param Hansji Maharaj, the Indian Sant Mat teacher and founder of the Divine Light Mission. Following Sri Hans Ji's death, Rama Nand left the mission and, beginning in 1973, traveled through the United States teaching the way to divine knowledge he had learned. The Divine Knowledge Meditation Center is a direct outgrowth of his work in the United States.

Rama Nand teaches the *surat* ("soul") *shadba* ("word") *yoga* ("union") common to Sant Mat groups. The center offers a 10-week aspirant program designed to prepare people to learn the specific techniques for the practice. Preparatory practice includes simple hatha yoga, breathing, and meditation.

Rama Nand teaches that the purpose of existence is the realization of our spiritual nature and God, accomplished through surat shabda yoga. The immediate effect of meditation is a release of stress and the reduction of physical symptoms—reduced hypertension, nervousness, and insomnia.

Membership: Not reported. Rama Nand's work is concentrated on a single center in Denver.

The Divine Science of Light and Sound
Current address not obtained for this edition.

The Divine Science of Light and Sound was formed in 1980 by Jerry Mulvin (b. 1936), formerly a leader in the Eckankar religious movement. The Divine Science of Light and Sound is described as the study of the inner worlds through the movement of one's inner consciousness (attention/viewpoint) from the outer physical world into the soul. It purports to be the safe and natural way to travel into the inner worlds, beyond the known limits or boundaries of one's known universe. In order to travel out of the body, one must first learn the spiritual techniques that enable the individual to gather up inner attention and shift it to the spiritual eye center.

Mulvin believes that by practicing the techniques of the divine science, one can rediscover one's childlike innocence, the attitude that will propel one out of the body and into the direct experience of the inner realms. Truths encountered in this state begin to set one free spiritually.

Mulvin has authored two books. The first describes his early life, when he raised his *kundalini* (life force or energy believed to be located at the base of the spine) and mastered it through out-of-body exploration. It also describes his past lives,

which played an important role in his spiritual development in this life; the disciplines, teachers, and masters (such as Fubbi Quantz, a master first introduced in the writings of Paul Twitchell) that shaped his outlook; and the spiritual techniques that led to his current state of spiritual mastership.

In his later writings Mulvin has stressed the goal of leaving one's body to travel beyond what humans call time and space. Mulvin claims that his students can have a direct experience of freedom and truth through travel in the soul body; he believes that his techniques will prove the existence of reincarnation and karma. The movement in the soul body is also sharply distinguished from what is commonly called astral or mental projection.

Mulvin teaches students outwardly through personal discourses and weekly out-of-body workshops. He teaches them inwardly via the dream state, while they are traveling outside their body.

Membership: Not reported. There is one center in Marina del Rey, California.

Sources:

Mulvin, Jerry. *The Annals of Time*. Manhattan Beach, CA: Divine Science of Light and Sound, 1982.

————. *Out-of-Body Exploration*. Marina del Rey, CA: Divine Science of Light and Sound, 1986.

Eckankar
PO Box 2000, Chanhassen, MN 55317-2000

Eckankar proclaims itself to be the religion of the light and sound of God. It was founded in 1965 by ECK (divine spirit) Master Paul Twitchell (d. 1971). Twitchell, a former journalist, had been a student of various spiritual teachers, among them Sant Mat master Kirpal Singh, the founder of Ruhani Satsang and teacher of "the divine science of the soul." In 1964 Twitchell moved to San Francisco, California, and began to teach what was then considered an advanced form of *surat shabda* yoga, which emphasized attuning the "Soul to the Sound and Light emanating from God."

At that time Twitchell also emphasized bilocation (later called "soul travel"), the ability of the conscious soul to leave the body and travel in the invisible realms. In 1965 Twitchell announced that he was the "living ECK master" and formed the first public Eckankar group. He is considered by members of Eckankar to be the 971st mahanta and living ECK master of the Vairagi Order, taking his place in a line that began before recorded history. Twitchell is believed to have studied Eckankar under Sudar Singh in India and the ECK master Rebazar Tarzs in the Himalayas.

In many of its basic concepts, Eckankar appears to follow the Sant Mat teachings of Kirpal Singh and the Western writer Julian Johnson, a disciple (like Kirpal Singh) of Sawan Singh, the head of the Radha Soami Satsang Beas. Eckankar, however, holds that the original teachings of the light and sound had been presented in various forms throughout history and that Paul Twitchell reunited them in a single modern teaching. As presented by Twitchell and the current Mahanta and living ECK master Sri Harold Klemp, Eckankar differs from the Sant Mat tradition in significant ways. Eckankar, for example, teaches that the ultimate state for each individual is that of a coworker with God, not oneness with God; inner techniques are more active spiritual exercises than yogic practices; and Eastern austerities (vegetarianism, extended meditation) are not espoused. Twitchell also presented a different vocabulary than that of Sant Mat teachings.

Eckankar considers the Shariyat-Ki-Sugmad to be its ancient scripture residing in the inner worlds. According to the ECK teachings, the original works are located in various Temples of Golden Wisdom, which can only be reached in the "soul body." Two volumes copied and translated by Twitchell have been published. The primary body of Eckankar writings was authored by Sri Harold Klemp, the spiritual leader of Eckankar since 1981.

Eckankar teaches that all life flows from God (Sugmad) downward to the physical universe. The divine life current (ECK) can be perceived as light and sound. This current may be identified with the Sanskrit Nam and the Christian Holy Spirit. A central ECK belief is that each individual is soul, an eternal spark of God. Soul reaches higher spiritual states of wisdom and love through lessons learned via reincarnation over many lifetimes.

The spiritual exercises of Eckankar teach adherents (called ECKists or chelas) to expand their consciousness toward two successive states: self-realization and God-realization. There are more than 100 spiritual exercises given by the living ECK master to aid ECKists in their spiritual development. Basic techniques involve singing sacred words such as HU, which is regarded as an ancient name for God. Others feature putting attention upon the light and sound or the spiritual form of the Mahanta, the living ECK master.

Eckankar considers itself a living religion rather than an orthodox religion because it follows a living spiritual teacher and guide, the Mahanta, the living ECK master. The living ECK master is respected but not worshipped. It is believed that the living ECK master links the chela with the ECK current, leading the soul to total spiritual freedom. The Mahanta guides the chela personally through the lower astral and spiritual realms to the true God worlds and delivers the soul from the wheel of reincarnation. This guidance comes both outwardly—through printed discourses, books, and talks—and inwardly, through direct interaction. Spiritual travel of the soul body (*atma aarup*) through dreams, imaginative techniques, and direct projection is regularly reported by followers of Eckankar.

The international headquarters of Eckankar is in Minneapolis, Minnesota. It provides its members with study materials, local Eckankar classes, and international conferences that feature the living ECK master. After Paul Twitchell's death in 1971, he was succeeded by Darwin Gross. Gross married but later divorced Gail Twitchell, Paul Twitchell's widow. He passed on his position as living ECK master to Harold Klemp in 1981. Since 1984 Gross has not been associated with Eckankar, which no longer considers him an ECK master.

Harold Klemp, as the present Mahanta, the living ECK master, is responsible for the continued evolution of the ECK teachings and Eckankar as a modern religion. For example, Klemp has emphasized that an individual cannot reach the highest spiritual realms without giving divine love and service to others in everyday life. In 1990 he oversaw the completion of a Temple of Golden Wisdom, the temple of ECK in Chanhassen, Minnesota. The temple is the spiritual home of the religion, and the building and its surrounding grounds are regarded as having special spiritual significance.

Klemp was raised on a Wisconsin farm and trained at a divinity school. He then enlisted in the U.S. Air Force, where he served as a language specialist. He first encountered Eckankar during his Air Force service. Klemp has authored more than 40 books as well as 12 year-long discourse series for members of Eckankar. The group offers some 70 videocassettes and DVDs and more than 100 audiocassettes and CDs of his public talks. He speaks at Eckankar seminars in the United States and in Europe and the South Pacific. In July 1991 he spoke to a gathering of more than 10,000 people at the ECK African Seminar in Lagos, Nigeria.

Membership: In 2002 there were 164 centers in the United States and 367 worldwide. Members are located in more than 130 countries. Major ECK seminars in the United States routinely draw from 2,000 to 6,000 participants.

Periodicals: *ECK Spirituality Today* • *Eckankar Journal.*

Remarks: In the early 1980s Eckankar became the center of a controversy when the religious-studies scholar David Christopher Lane charged that Paul Twitchell had plagiarized materials, especially the writings of the Sant Mat teacher Julian Johnson. He also charged that Twitchell had fabricated a spiritual career out of his reading of and study with such teachers as L. Ron Hubbard, Kirpal Singh, and Swami Premananda. He presented evidence that articles that originally acknowledged his reliance upon these and other teachers were later republished with the names of former ECK masters substituted instead. The present ECK organization and current ECK Master Harold Klemp have acknowledged this problem in Twitchell's writings but insist that they do not detract from the value of his work as an ECK master.

Sources:

Eckankar, www.eckankar.org.

Klemp, Harold. *Ask the Master*. 2 vols. Minneapolis: Eckankar, 1993–1994.

————. *Soul Travelers of the Far Country*. Minneapolis, MN: Eckankar, 1987.

————. *The Spiritual Exercises of ECK*. Minneapolis, MN; Eckankar, n.d.

————. *The Temple of ECK*. Minneapolis, MN: Eckankar, 1991. 149 pp.

————. *What Is Spiritual Freedom?* Minneapolis, MN: Eckankar, 1995.

————. *The Wind of Change*. Menlo Park, CA: IWP Publishing, 1980.

Lane, David Christopher. *The Making of a Spiritual Movement*. Del Mar, CA: Del Mar Press, 1983.

Twitchell, Paul. *All About ECK*. Las Vegas, NV: Illuminated Way Press, 1969.

————. *Eckankar: The Key to Secret Worlds*. New York: Lancer Books, 1969.

————. *The Shariyat-Ki-Sugmad*. 2 vols. Menlo Park, CA: IWP Press, 1971–1972.

————. *The Tiger's Fang*. New York: Lancer Books, 1969.

Eureka Society/Elan Vital School of Meditation
PO Box 3117, Montrose, CO 81402-3117

The Eureka Society and Elan Vital School of Meditation were founded in 1969 in Eureka, California, by Bruce K. Avenell. After a near-fatal experience he was told, while sitting in meditation, that if he did not become a teacher, there was no reason to stay in his body. Since he was the father of five children, he decided to become a teacher. Having been a student of the Sant Mat teachers Bhagat Singh Thind and Kirpal Singh, Avenell began to teach his own version of *surat shabda* yoga, the yoga of the sound current.

Avenell acknowledges his roots in the Sant Mat tradition of India and the similarity of his teaching to that school of practice; he states, however, that the practices of Elan Vital also draw on advanced techniques from ancient Egypt and, as such, are unique. The Elan Vital system teaches students to reach to the spiritual realms that are termed "heaven." The group claims that one can reach these realms either by detaching from the physical body or by becoming attached to a spiritual master. Having attained this initial state, one is free to choose whether or not to pursue more advanced techniques.

Members are initiated by Avenell and practice the techniques he teaches through a series of correspondence lessons. There are semiannual gatherings in Texas and Mt. Shasta, California.

Membership: Not reported. There are an estimated several hundred students in the Eureka Society.

Periodicals: *Spectrums & Dimensions.*

Sources:

Eureka Society/Elan Vital School of Meditation. www.eurekasociety.com.

Avenell, Bruce. *A Reason for Being*. La Grange, TX: Eureka Society, 1983.

———— *Colors of Love*. La Grange, TX: Eureka Society, 2003.

———— *Escape to Immortality*. La Grange, TX: Eureka Society, 1994.

———— *Journeys of Ascension*. La Grange, TX: Eureka Society, 1998.

———— *Lights and the Gateways to Heaven*. La Grange, TX: Eureka Society, 2003.

———— *Mt. Shasta: The Vital Essence*. La Grange, TX: Eureka Society, 1999.

———— *Road to Life and Vortexes*. La Grange, TX: Eureka Society, 2003.

Kirpal Light Satsang
Lighthouse Center New York, 109 Merwin Lake Rd., Kinderhook, NY 12106

Following the death of Kirpal Singh (1894–1974) in 1974 (see biographical sketch in the entry on the Sawan Kirpal Ruhani Mission), Darshan Singh (1981–1989), Kirpal Singh's son, who most thought would succeed his father, was rejected by Madam Hardevi, who had been chosen the temporal chairman of the Sawan

Ashram and the Ruhani Satsang in India. She supported Thakar Singh (1929–2005), a leading disciple who had, in the months following Kirpal Singh's death, developed a growing belief in his commission to serve as the movement's guru. Madam Haedevi died in 1979, and Thakar Singh took complete control of the ashram. After Thakar Singh's death in 2005, the leadership of the movement was assumed by Baljit Singh.

In the wake of the refusal of the directors of the American corporation, the Ruhani Satsang–Divine Science of the Soul, some American followers who recognized Thakar Singh reorganized as the Kirpal Light Ashram and established headquarters in the Bay Area of northern California. The small group has grown in the wake of several visits by Thakar Singh to America, but it does not yet approach the size of the Sawan Kirpal Ruhani Mission. The movement has established a presence in Australia, Canada, India, New Zealand, the United Kingdom, and the United States.

The goal of Sant Mat is for individuals to become true human beings, to know the self as soul, and to realize oneness with the creator.

Membership: Not reported. In 1994 there were 45 satsang and meditation groups.

Periodicals: *Kirpal Light Satsang International Newsletter* • *Sat.*

Sources:

Kirpal Light Satsang. www.santmat.net.

Singh, Thakur. *Gospel of Love*. Delhi, India: Ruhani Satsang, 1984.

Manavta Mandir

Current address not obtained for this edition.

Alternate Address: International headquarters: c/o Be Man Temple, Sutehri Rd., Hoshiarpur, 146001 Punjab, India.

Manavta Mandir ("Be Man" Temple) is a Sant Mat/Radhasomi group that was founded in 1962 at Hoshiarpur, Punjab, India, by Faqir Chand (1886–1981), a spiritual teacher in the lineage of Shiv Brat Lal. Faqir saw Manavta Mandir providing a more ecumenical and nonsectarian approach to the Radhasoami tradition. Faqir also offered a different interpretation of guru-based spirituality. Faqir suggested that spiritual teachers were mostly unaware of the real cause of the miraculous events and visionary phenomena often attributed to them. This ignorance frequently led, unjustifiably, to the guru gaining power, attention, and devotion from followers who incorrectly imputed vast powers to such masters.

Faqir's guru, Shiv Brat La, was an initiate of Rai Salig Ram, who in turn was the chief disciple of Shiv Dayal Singh, generally viewed as the founder of Radhasoami. Faqir succeeded Lal in 1939 and afterward established his main center at Hoshiarpur.

Faqir traveled widely and made annual trips throughout India and abroad preaching his version of the Radhasoami teachings. He emphasized points shared with other Sant Mat teachers (vegetarianism, sexual purity, no drugs/alcohol, and daily meditation). He was notable for his confession of ultimate unknowingness. After 70 years of meditation, he still told people that he did not know what would happen to him after death and whether God really existed.

Faqir died in Pittsburgh, Pennsylvania, in 1981 while touring the United States. He was 95. Only a short time earlier, he had appointed his spiritual successor, Dr. I. C. Sharma, a philosophy professor residing in the United States. He also designated several other people (both male and female) as initiating gurus in his lineage. Sharma backtracked from Faqir and emphasized more traditional Radhasoami themes on shabd yoga and spirituality. Sharma appointed Shoonyo Maharaj as his spiritual successor; following Sharma's death, Shoonyo, who resides in India, became the chief resident guru for Manavta Mandir.

Membership: Manavta Mandir reports more than 100,000 followers worldwide. It has a small following in the United States and Canada.

Educational Facilities:

Shiv Dev Rao Senior Secondary School

Periodicals: *Manav Mandir*, c/o Be Man Temple, Sutehri Rd., Hoshiarpur, 146001 Punjab, India.

Sources:

Manavta Mandir. www.manavtamandir.com.

Juergensmeyer, Mark. *Radhasoami Reality*. Princeton, NJ: Princeton University Press, 1991.

Lane, David C. *The Radhasoami Tradition*. New York: Garland, 1992.

The Unknowing Sage: The Life and Work of Baba Faqir Chand. Walnut, CA: MSAC, 1993.

Master Ching Hai Meditation Association

PO Box 730247, San Jose, CA 95173

Alternate Address: Supreme Master Hai Meditation Association, PO Box 9, Hsi Hu, Miao Li Hsien, Taiwan, R.O.C.

The Master Ching Hai Meditation Association is built on the multireligious teachings of Master Ching Hai Wu Shang Shih, a teacher of shabd yoga of the sound current. Master Ching Hai was born in Vietnam, the daughter of Roman Catholic parents. She was introduced to Buddhism by her grandmother. When she was 18, she moved to England to study and then traveled to France and Germany. In Germany she married a physician, a Buddhist, and settled down to the mundane life of a housewife. During her married years, however, a long time spiritual quest came to the fore, and she sat at the feet of many teachers, both Buddhist and Hindu. Eventually she left home in pursuit of spiritual enlightenment. She had reached the conclusion that the best way to assist others was to first attain total realization herself.

In the Buddhist *Surangama Sutra*, she read of the quan yin method, purportedly the surest path to enlightenment, but it was not described, and she could locate no one was familiar with it. At length her quest led her to northern India, where she was initiated into the surat shabd yoga of the sound current by one of the masters of the Radha Soami tradition. This yoga, she concluded, was identical to the quan yin method. Along with practicing the method, she moved to Taiwan and was ordained. In Taiwan a group of devotees of Avalokitesvara (quan yin) sought her out and asked that she teach them her method.

Master Ching Hai taught in Taiwan through the 1980s and by the end of the decade was reaching out with her teachings worldwide; an initial network was established through Vietnamese refugee communities. Initiates are asked to follow the five precepts, which involve refraining from taking the life of sentient beings, speaking what is not true, taking what is not offered, sexual misconduct, and the use of intoxicants. Among the implications of the five precepts is the adoption of a vegan or lacto-vegetarian diet by initiates.

By the early 1990s the movement had spread worldwide, with followers in South Africa, Latin America (Argentina, Brazil, Chile, Costa Rica, Mexico, Panama, and Salvador), 11 countries of Europe, and the Asian Pacific Rim (Korea, Japan, Australia, and New Zealand). Writings by and about the teachings have been translated into a number of languages and are supplemented with both CDs and DVDs.

Membership: Not reported. As of 1993 there were 35 centers in the United States and an additional 73 centers worldwide.

Periodicals: *The Supreme Master Ching Hai News,* The Supreme Master Ching Hai Meditation Association in China, No. 39, Dongsanhu, Sanhu Village, Hsihu Shiang, Miaoli Hsien, Taiwan, R.O.C.

Sources:

Master Ching Hai Meditation Association.

www.godsdirectcontact.com/quanyin/bio.html.

Ching Hai Wu Shang Shih. *The Key to Enlightenment.* 2 vols. Miaoli Hsien, Taiwan, R.O.C.: Meditation Association in China, 1991.

MasterPath

PO Box 9035, Temecula, CA 9258-9035

MasterPath was founded in the mid-1980s by Gary Olsen. Olsen had been an associate of Darwin Gross, the former ECK master of Eckankar. Gross left Eckankar in 1983 to found Sounds of Soul (SOS). Olsen was associated with Sounds of Soul for a short while but left to found MasterPath.

MasterPath teaches the way to truth through the reactivation of the sound current within. That reactivation is accomplished by the living master. The goal is to become a coworker with Anami, a name for the deity. The first step on the path is self-realization, a realization of one's true self and place in the universe. The soul body, or true self, can travel the sound current to the higher spiritual worlds through the assistance of the shabda master, the inner teacher, who works through the living master.

Membership: Not reported.

Sources:

MasterPath. www.masterpath.org.

Holtje, Dennis. *From Light to Sound: The Spiritual Progression.* Glendora, CA: MasterPath, n.d.

Olsen, Gary. *Introduction to Master Path: The Master Responds to Common Seeker Inquiries.* Glendora, CA: MasterPath, n.d.

———. *MasterPath.* Glendora, CA: MasterPath, 1988.

A Profile of the MasterPath. Glendora, CA: MasterPath, n.d.

Movement of Spiritual Inner Awareness (MSIA)

3500 W Adams Blvd., Los Angeles, CA 90018

The Movement of Spiritual Inner Awareness (MSIA) was founded by John-Roger Hinkins and incorporated as a church in 1971. MSIA teaches Soul Transcendence, a means to become aware of oneself as a soul and, more than that, as one with the Divine.

The focal point of MSIA is the consciousness of the Mystical Traveler, a spiritual consciousness that exists throughout all levels of creation, resides within each person, and is a guide into the higher levels of the Spirit. The MSIA believes that in December 1963 John-Roger received the spiritual mantle as the physical anchor point of the Mystical Traveler Consciousness; in 1988 this passed to John Morton. John-Roger remains the spiritual wayshower for those he has initiated. The traveler can assist a person in working through karma (balancing past actions) on all the levels of consciousness, and the traveler's work with students is done inwardly, on the spiritual levels. In 2008 John Morton was the Spiritual Director of MSIA, and church president Paul Kaye was the administrative head.

Students of MSIA read a 12-year series of monthly Soul Awareness Discourses. (After the series has been completed, study continues through the Soul Awareness Tape Series.) Students are also encouraged to do spiritual exercises (silent meditation) for two hours each day. Nothing else is required for a student in MSIA, although there are many videotapes, audiotapes, and books by John-Roger and John Morton that can support a person's study. Students may gather together to listen to or view a taped seminar by John-Roger, and he has a nationally syndicated television program, *That Which Is,* that also shows his seminars. MSIA services include aura balancing, which helps to clear imbalances in the aura, the energy field around the body.

After two years of study, a person may apply for initiation, and levels of initiation in MSIA correspond to levels of consciousness both within and outside of each person: astral (imagination), causal (emotions), mental (mind), etheric (unconscious), and soul. The soul realm is considered our true home to which we seek to return. Through continued study and spiritual exercises, a person may be initiated to successive levels. After studying for two years in MSIA and receiving the first initiation, a person may apply for ordination. Ministers are ordained to minister to all, regardless of race, creed, color, situation, circumstance, or environment. The ministry is primarily spiritual, and the focus of the ministry is on service—to God, others, and self.

MSIA does not have rules and regulations governing behavior. Guidelines in MSIA are to take care of yourself so you can help take care of others, do not hurt yourself and do not hurt others, and use everything for your advancement and uplifting. Basic precepts include the following: Out of God come all things; God loves all of Its creations; not one soul will be lost; the kingdom of heaven is within; and each person is an heir to that kingdom.

Membership: Though there is no formal membership, in 2008 MSIA reported about 5,000 subscribers to Soul Awareness Discourses. About 2,700 are in the United States, and about 2,300 are in foreign countries, including approximately 30 students in Canada.

Educational Facilities:

Peace Theological Seminary and College of Philosophy, Los Angeles, California.

Periodicals: *The New Day Herald.*

Remarks: Prior to the founding of MSIA, John-Roger was affiliated with several other groups, including the Church of Jesus Christ of Latter-day Saints and Eckankar. Today MSIA has incorporated strong elements that resemble the sound-current teachings of Eckankar along with a significant element of Christian piety.

Sources:

Movement of Spiritual Inner Awareness. www.msia.org/.

Beck, Sanderson, and Mark T. Holmes, eds. *Across the Golden Bridge.* Los Angeles: Golden Age Education Publications, 1974.

Hinkin, John-Roger. *The Christ Within & the Disciples of Christ with the Cosmic Christ Calendar.* Los Angeles: Mandeville Press, 1994.

———. *Psychic Protection.* Los Angeles: Mandeville Press, 1976. Revised 1997.

———. *Forgiveness—The Key to the Kingdom.* Los Angeles: Mandeville Press, 1994.

———. *The Sound Current.* New York: Baraka Press, 1976.

———. *The Spiritual Family.* Los Angeles: Mandeville Press, 1976. Revised 1997.

Interviews with John Morton and John Roger: Religious Scholars Interview the Travelers. Los Angeles: Mandeville Press, 1999.

An Introduction to the Movement of Spiritual Inner Awareness. Los Angeles: Peace Theological Seminary & College of Philosophy, 1999.

Lewis, James R. *Seeking the Light.* Los Angeles: Mandeville Press, 1997.

Nirankari Universal Brotherhood Mission

1 Ball Ave., Carpentersville, IL 60110

The Nirankari Universal Brotherhood Mission is one of several Sant Mat groups that traces its lineage to Jaimal Singh, the founder of the Radha Soami Satsang Beas. It was founded by Boota Singh (1873–1943), a tattoo artist who, in 1929, received a succession from Kahn Singh. Boota Singh became known for his opposition to the rigid conventions and rituals of the Sikhs; he opposed all taboos, castes, creeds, and divisions based on external habits and appearances. He discarded all dictates concerning what one eats, drinks, or wears.

Boota Singh was succeeded by Avtar Singh (1899–1969). After the partition of 1947 (which established Pakistan as a separate state), Avtar Singh moved the headquarters of the Nirankari Mission to Delhi and formally established the Sant Nirankari Mandal. He wrote a constitution and gave the group its present organizational structure. He authored *Avtar Baani,* which is the holy book of the movement. Under Avtar Singh, the mission flourished, and a colony was established on the Januma River in Delhi. In 1969 Avtar Singh was succeeded by Gurbachan Singh, who in 1968 had traveled to Europe to establish the work there. By 1973 there were 354 branches outside of India—in England, Hong Kong, Canada, and the United States.

The spread of the Nirankari Mission to the West began in 1955, when Bhag Mal, a member, moved to England. The mission was formally organized in 1962. Soon after becoming head of the mission, Gurbachan Singh, who had helped develop the work in the West, formed a foreign section to focus on growth outside of India. In 1971 he made his first trip to North America. Beginning in Vancouver, he moved to San Francisco, where he appointed Dr. Iqhaljeet Rai as president of the Nirankari Universal Mission in the United States. He continued his journey across the United States and visited Toronto and Montreal before returning home. In 1972 the headquarters were moved to Madison, Wisconsin.

Internationally, the mission is headed by the "seven stars," seven men picked by the guru to serve for life. The mission in India, after undergoing persecution, organized the Sant Nirankari Seva Dal, a defense force to protect the group against acts of violence directed against it.

Essential to the life of the mission is *gian*, the giving of the knowledge by the guru to each member. This process, the exact nature of which is held confidential within the group, establishes the relationship of guru to disciple. As the mission has grown, certain disciples have been appointed to represent the guru in the giving of knowledge. Members of the mission agree to live by the five principles:

1. Nothing is ours. All possessions—physical, mental, material—are a divine loan that we must use only as trustees and not as masters.

2. There is no discrimination based on caste, creed, color, religion, or worldly status.

3. There is no criticism of anyone's diet or dress because such acts breed conflict and hatred.

4. There is no renunciation of the world. One should continue performing one's normal vocations and functions of life and be always righteous.

5. There is no divulgence of the divine secret of the gian except with permission of the true master.

Membership: Not reported. There are 250 branches located in the United States, United Kingdom, Germany, Australia, and India.

Periodicals: *Sant Nirankari*. Send orders to Nirankari Colony, Delhi 1100009, India • *Ek-Nazar* • *Nirankari Journal* • *Universal Target*.

Sources:

Nirankari Universal Brotherhood Mission. www.nirankari.com.

Chugh, J. S. *Fifty Years of Spiritual Bliss: Commemorative Souvenir on the Golden Jubilee Nirankari San Samagam, November 6–10, 1997.* Delhi, India: Sant Nirankari Mandal, 1997.

Gargi, Balwany. *Nirankari Baba.* Delhi, India: Thomson Press, 1973.

Joshi, Nirmal, and Bhupender Bekal, eds. *Salvation Tours (1995–96).* Delhi: Sant Nirankari Mandal, 1997.

Order of the Blue Star

1952 Glencove Ave., Palm Bay, FL 32907

The Order of the Blue Star was founded by Christopher Tims, a spiritual teacher who experienced a broad range of spiritual training in yoga, reiki healing, martial arts, and the *surat shabd* yoga of the sound current. Members think of him as a spiritual traveler who resides on the inner planes. He accompanies his students as they make their journeys into spiritual realms, in a manner similar to that of the ECK master in Eckankar. New members are presented the work of the order in a workshop on light and soul healing. A second workshop introduces the idea of spiritual traveling in the inner planes. The inner teachings of the order are presented in a set of lessons called discourses; one must pass a test on the discourses in order to be admitted to the inner circle of the order.

Membership: Not reported.

Sources:

Order of the Blue Star. www.soundhealing.org.

Radha Soami Satsang, Beas

Science of the Soul Study Center, 2415 E Washington St., Petaluma, CA 94954-9274
Alternate Address: International headquarters: Dera Baba Jaimal Singh, Dist. Amritstar 143 204, Punjab, India; RSSB-Canada, 2934–176th Street, Surrey, British Columbia, V3S 9V4, Canada.

Several groups presently operating in North America derive their existence from the spiritual movement begun in 1861 by Param Sant Soami Ji Maharaj, born Seth Shiv Dayal Singh (1818–1878), at Agra, India. It is reported that Soami Ji, as he is popularly called, began to expound on spiritual topics from an early age. The substance of his teaching were later gathered in his two books, both with the same title, *Sar Bachan*, one written in prose and one in poetry. His teachings were not new; rather they continued the Bhakti Nam (devotion to the name of God) teachings previously expounded by people such as Kabir Singh, Guru Nanak (1469–1539), Tulsi Singh (1763–1843?), and Guru Ravi Das. But the unique element in Soami Ji's presentation was the simple and lucid manner of his teachings on the practice of Nam Bhakti, also known as surat shabd yoga, or the yoga of the sound current. During his lifetime he initiated more than 4,000 people into the path.

Soami Ji designated Rai Salig Ram (1829–1898) as his successor at Agra. Rai Salig Ram in turn appointed Pandit Brahmanand Shankar Misra as his successor. When Misra died, a controversy arose over the designation of the next leader. This resulted in a split into two groups at the Radha Soami Satsang headquartered at Agra. Neither has known representatives in North America. At the same time that Soami Ji designated Rai Salig Ram as his successor at Agra (1877), he delegated Baba Jaimal Singh (1838–1903) to spread the teachings in the Pubjab. Baba Ji, as he is popularly called, was initiated by Soami Ji, who advised him to join the army rather than live a life as a recluse. During most of his army career Baba Ji was stationed at Agra and thus had frequent direct access to Soami Ji. He was still in the army when Soami Ji died, and thus did not even begin to teach and initiate until 1884. In 1889 he retired from the army and settled near Beas on the river at a place known as Dera Baba Jaimal Singh. He remained there for the last years of his life, giving satsang and meditating.

Shortly before his death, Baba Jaimal Singh appointed Maharaj Sawan Singh (1858–1948) as his successor. Like Baba Ji, he was a soldier, having served for 28 years. Initiated in 1894, he remained in the army until 1911 and then devoted the remainder of his life to teaching Sant Mat. He settled at the Dera and resided there the rest of his life. Sawan Singh built the Radha Soami Beas into the largest of the Radha Soami movements. During his leadership, the facilities at the Dera greatly expanded. He traveled widely through the Punjab and India spreading the message to all parts of the land among people of all castes. During this period the number of initiates increased from 2,343 to 125,375.

It was also during the time of Sawan Singh that the teachings reached the United States. One of his disciples, Kehar Singh Sasmus, passed them to Dr. H. M. Brock and his wife at Port Angelus, Washington, and initiated them in 1911. The Brocks in turn were authorized to initiate others. Julian P. Johnson (d. 1939) was attracted to the movement in the 1920s and in 1931 was initiated. His book, *The Path of the Masters* (1939), became a classic presentation of the teachings for English-speaking audiences. Brock was succeeded as the master's representative by Harvey Myers and he by Roland de Vries. There are currently three additional representatives in the United States: H. F. Weekly, Roy E. Ricks, and Gene Ivash. There are two in Canada: J. Khanna and R. S. Davis.

Sawan Singh appointed Maharaj Jagat Singh (1884–1951) as his successor. In only three years as leader, he initiated more than 18,000 people and gained a reputation as a practical mystic. The day before his death he designated Maharaj Charan Singh (1916–1990) as his successor. Charan Singh, the grandson of Sawan Singh, was largely raised at the Dera. Well educated, he became a lawyer in 1942 but gave up a flourishing practice in 1951 to assume leadership of the movement. He developed the movement in areas far beyond those envisioned by his predecessors, undertaking extensive tours of India and traveling to many foreign lands. Before his death, Charan Singh appointed Baba Gurinder Singh (b. 1954) as his successor. Raised in a traditional agricultural community in the Punjab, India, Baba Gurinder Singh in 2008 continued to lead the organization, which has become larger than all the other Sant Mat groups combined.

The Radha Soami philosophy is very much like the Gnostic and Manichean beliefs of the ancient Mediterranean Basin. (These religions believed matter to be evil, and only spirit to be good.) The Radha Soami cosmology begins with Radha Soami Dayal, the Supreme Spiritual Being, from whom emanated all existence in His *Mauj* (literally, wave). It is the divine sound (*shabd*, or the "word") from which emerged creation. As it descended into the lower realms of matter, maya, and mind, it became imprisoned beyond any possibility of escape by itself. To teach individuals the way of escape is the purpose of the incarnations of the Supreme Being in the human form of living masters, or *sant satgurus*.

Surat shabd yoga, it is believed, is the only way of return of the soul to its source. It consists of three parts: *simram*, the repetition of the five holy names; *dhyan*, contemplation of the form of the master; and listening to the divine melody (*shabd*), which enables the student to become attuned to the sound and the light emanating from it. The practical guidance of a living master, who is believed to be the "Word made flesh," is indispensable. The divine sound is like a radio wave that guides the soul back to its eternal home, where it merges and becomes liberated from the cycle of births and rebirths. Students on the path are required to be vegetarians, refrain from alcohol, and be of good moral character. Students are asked to devote two and a half hours a day to meditation, preferably in the morning.

International headquarters are in the Punjab. The movement internationally was headed in 2008 by the living master, Baba Gurinder Singh, also designated as patron. The movement is organized as a trust society (similar in India to a nonprofit corporation). The society consists of 11 members nominated by the patron, from which is drawn a five-member governing body, the executive committee.

In North America the movement is very decentralized, with four initiating representatives in various parts of the United States and two more in Canada. The movement's periodical, *Radha Soami Greetings*, is published in Kansas, and books centers are located in Washington, D.C., and Gardena, California.

Membership: In 2008 Radha Soami Satsang Beas reported centers in more than 90 countries. In the United States and Canada, more than a hundred small groups, usually meeting in informal and rented facilities, gather regularly for study and meditation. There are three Science of the Soul Study Centers in the United States and two in Canada that oversee these many local centers.

Periodicals: *Radha Soami Greetings*. Send orders to 18 Countryside Dr., Hutchinson, KS 67501.

Sources:

Radha Soami Satsang, Beas. www.rssb.org/.

Fripp, Peter. *The Mystic Philosophy of Sant Mat*. London: Neville Spearman, 1964.

Johnson, Julian P. *The Path of the Masters*. [1939]. Beas, India: Radha Soami Satsang, Beas, 1985.

Radha Soami Satsang Beas and Its Teachings. Beas, India: Radha Soami Satsang, Beas, n.d.

Radha Soami Satsang Beas, Origin and Growth. Beas, India: Radha Soami Satsang, 1981.

Singh, Huzur Maharaj Sawan. *Philosophy of the Masters*. 5 vols. Beas, India: Radhasoami Satsang, Beas, 1963–1967.

Singh, Maharaj Charan. *Light on Sant Mat*. Beas, India: Radha Soami Satsang, Beas, 1958.

———. *The Path*. Beas, India: Radhasoami Satsang, Beas, 1969.

Sant Bani Ashram

30 Ashram Rd., Sanbornton, NH 03269-2227

Among the early and more important centers of the followers of Kirpal Singh (1894–1974) was the Sant Bani Ashram in Franklin, New Hampshire, founded in 1963. Headed by Russell Perkins, the center had handled much of the publishing for the movement over the decades. Among the significant titles are several volumes of Kirpal Singh's collected works. After the death of Kirpal Singh in 1974, Perkins refused to recognize Darshan Singh, the candidate popularly supported as Kirpal Singh's successor. Having heard of Ajaib Singh, he visited his ashram in the Rajasthan desert and eventually recognized him as Kirpal Singh's successor. Joining Perkins was Arran Stephens, Kirpal Singh's Canadian representative and head of Kirpal Ashram in Vancouver. Stephens had been the first westerner to hear of Ajaib Singh and had raised the possibility of his being Kirpal Singh's successor in an issue of the movement's magazine, *Sat Sandesh*.

Ajaib Singh Ji Maharaj (1926–1997) was initiated in 1967 by Kirpal Singh. Ajaib Singh had his major following in North America and visited his American disciples on a number of occasions, including in the year before his death. He adopted the name of the New Hampshire center as that of his own work in India. Since his death in 1997, no successor has been named.

Membership: Not reported.

Periodicals: *Sant Bani: The Voice of the Saints*.

Remarks: After promoting Ajaib Singh for several years, Arran Stephens withdrew his support, claiming that Ajaib Singh contradicted many of Kirpal Singh's teachings and had on several occasions misrepresented events that had happened to him and his own relationship to Kirpal Singh.

Sources:

Sant Bani Ashram. www.santbaniashram.org.

Sant Ajaib Singh Ji. www.ajaibbani.org.

Singh, Ajaib, and Russell Perkins. *Streams in the Desert*. Tilton, NH: Sant Bani Ashram, 1982.

Singh, Kirpal. *Morning Talks*. Franklin, NH: Sant Bani Ashram, 1974.

———. *The Way of the Saints*. Sanbornton, NH: Sant Bani Ashram, 1976.

Singh, Kirpal, Ajaib Singh, and Sawan Singh. *The Message of Love*. Sanbornton, NH: Sant Bani Ashram, n.d.

Sawan Kirpal Ruhani Mission

4S175 Naperville Rd., Naperville, IL 60563

Alternate Address: International headquarters: Sawan Kirpal Ruhani Mission, Kirpal Ashram, Sant Kirpal Singh Marg, Vijay Nagar, Delhi 110009, India.

The Sawan Kirpal Ruhani Mission is one of three organizations that claim to continue the work of the Ruhani Satsang founded in 1951 by Kirpal Singh (1896–1974). In 1917 Kirpal Singh had a vision of a "Radiant Form" whom he took to be Guru Nanak (the founder of Sikhism). In 1924, however, he met Sawan Singh (1858–1948, head of the Radhasoami Satsang, Beas) and recognized him as the one in the vision. He stayed with Sawan Singh for the last 24 years of his life.

When Jagat Singh received the succession from Sawan Singh, Kirpal Singh left Beas and began the independent Sawan Ashram in Delhi. In 1951, at the time Maharaj Charan Singh Ji (1916–1990) succeeded Jagat Singh, he formed the Ruhani Satsang. In 1949 T. S. Khanna, a disciple of Kirpal Singh, migrated to Canada and established the Ruhani Satsang in Toronto. Several years later he moved to the Washington, D.C., suburb of Alexandria, Virginia.

The growth of the work was accelerated by Kirpal Singh's visits in 1955 and 1963, during which time he toured cities in North America and initiated many individuals. As a result, a national association of members and centers was incorporated in California as the Divine Science of the Soul. Kirpal Singh, however, had initiated people without regard for their affiliations and religious background.

Some preferred to create informal groups, and became tied together very loosely under the Ruhani Satsang, incorporated by Khanna in Washington, D.C. In 1972 Kirpal Singh ordered the merger of the U.S. work, and the California and Washington, D.C. corporations were dissolved. Khanna was elected chairman of the board of the merged body, Ruhani Satsang–Divine Science of the Soul.

Kirpal Singh died in 1974. The movement divided again as various centers became aligned to the several claimants to Kirpal Singh's succession. In both India and the United States, the largest number of initiates and centers followed Darshan Singh (1921–1989), Kirpal Singh's son. Led by T. S. Khanna and other longtime disciples such as Olga Donenberg and Sunnie Cowen, these members reorganized as the Sawan Kirpal Ruhani Mission. (Meanwhile, the broad of the Ruhani Satsang–Divine Science, the continuing corporate structure, refused to recognize any successor to Kirpal Singh.) Darshan Singh made his first visit to the United States in 1978. Having lost control of Sawan Ashram because he had been rejected by Madam Hardevi, who had been chosen temporal chairman of the Ruhani Satsang in India, he established a new center, Kirpal Ashram, also in Delhi. Following his 1978 tour, he also opened a free kitchen and medical dispensary at the ashram complex. Like his father, Darshan Singh continued to promote interfaith work and authored a number of books.

Darshan Singh was succeeded by the present (2008) spiritual head of Sawan Kirpal Ruhani Mission/Science of Spirituality, Sant Rajinder Singh Ji Maharaj. Like his predecessor, he travels widely and has been active in interfaith work. Most notably, he addressed the 1993 Parliament of the World's Religions in Chicago, then appeared at the 1994 World Conference on Religion and Peace in Italy. He presided over the Seventh World Religions Conference (1994) in Delhi, India, and the Sixteenth International Human Unity Conference (1996) and its successive gatherings, up to and including the twenty-fifth session in 2007.

Outside of India, disciples of Darshan Singh can be found in more than 25 countries of the world. Sawan Kirpal Publications is the publishing arm of the movement, and several structures have emerged to handle various audiovisual materials.

Membership: In 2008 members were found in numerous small groups scattered across the United States and Canada. These were grouped around five regional meditation centers in the United States and one regional center in Canada.

Periodicals: *Sat Sandesh* • *Sawan Kirpal Ruhani Mission Newsletter*. Send orders to Rte. 1, Box 24, Bowling Green, VA 22427.

Sources:

Sawan Kirpal Ruhani Mission/Science of Spirituality. skrm.sos.org/main.aspx.

Science of Spirituality (USA). www.sos.org/index.html.

A Brief Biography of Darshan Singh. Bowling Green, VA: Sawan Kirpal Publications, [1983].

Chadda, H. C., ed. *Seeing Is Above All*. Bowling Green, VA: Sawan Kirpal Productions, 1977.

Portrait of Perfection, a Pictorial Biography of Kirpal Singh. Bowling Green, VA: Sawan Kirpal Publications, 1981.

Sena, Bhadra. *The Beloved Master*. Delhi, India: Ruhani Satsang, 1963.

Singh, Darshan. *The Secret of Secrets*. Bowling Green, VA: Sawan Kirpal Productions, 1978.

Singh, Kirpal. *Godman*. Delhi, India: Ruhani Satsang Sawan Ashram, 1967.

———. *The Jap Ji*. Bowling Green, KY: Sawan Kirpal Productions, 1981.

Sserulanda Foundation

Current address not obtained for this edition.

The Sserulanda Foundation is the U.S. affiliate of the Sserulanda Nsulo Y'obulamu Spiritual Foundation, founded in 1957 by Dr. Jozzewaffe Kaggwa Kaguwa Kaggalanda Mugonza, known by his followers as Bambi Baaba (b. 1937), a spiritual teacher from Uganda. Mugonza was born in Bugere village in Uganda, the son of Roman Catholic parents. Two serpents were said to have appeared at the moment of his birth; they symbolize his power and his mission of emancipating humanity from disease and the vicious cycle of birth and rebirth. Mugonza showed signs of a religious bent early in life, assuming the role of a priest in playing with other children. He also had experiences of bilocation and had encounters with flying saucers, traveling in them to higher dimensional levels.

In 1969 he journeyed to India, where he apparently met a variety of spiritual teachers, including some in the Radha Soami lineages. Although Bambi Baaba's teachings are largely identical to the Radha Soami Path of the Master, Bambi Baaba claims that he did not receive the teachings in India, but used his relationship with an Indian master to gain the acceptance of the people in Uganda with whom he initially worked. Upon his return, with his brothers he founded Kaliisoliiso Star, a company to study scientific and esoteric phenomena. He was arrested by the government on three occasions, the first time in 1972, when he was accused of bringing into Uganda a new religion that prevented members from eating meat and drinking alcohol (he was found innocent two years later). He was arrested again in 1974 and 1985, but again was released after a short while. In 1975 he discovered a cave that he had seen in a vision in 1949. There he established Sseesa-mirembe (Generator of Peace) and began building a future spiritual city for studying and practicing the Path of the Masters.

The teachings of Bambi Baaba are quite similar to those of Radha Soami. Humans are seen as sparks of God who have for years associated with the alien nature of this life. To escape this life one needs a Perfect Living Saint and Master. The Master guides people through a process of initiation, termed *Okutendeka* (training). The soul must travel from the lower body centers to the higher body centers to the various physical realms (astral, causal, and spiritual) to the fifth level, the natural home of souls. The true Master initiates people into the sound current (*shabd*) that the soul will follow to the higher realms. He will also explain the colors that the soul will see at each level of development. The Master will meet the student as they travel the inner planes and assist them. Initiates are asked to eat a vegetarian diet and refrain from the consumption of alcohol, tobacco, and narcotics.

The Sserulanda Nsulo Y'obulamu spread to other locations in Uganda, and in 1985 a center was opened in Geneva, Switzerland. The first North American center opened in Montreal the next year. The New York community opened in 1987.

The Sserulanda Spiritual Foundation of Sseesamirembe, Rakai was legally registered in Uganda as the Sserulanda Development Association by the Registrar of Companies on April 27, 2000. Its high-ranking officials are the owners of the Lake Victoria Free Trade Zone Ltd., which was registered by the Uganda Registrar of Companies on October 29, 2003, with the objective of building, owning, managing, and developing free zones and special economic zones at strategic geopolitical locations in Africa and elsewhere in the world. The registered directors of Sserulanda Development Association are Njuba (the current president of the association); Princess Nkwine Kobuhamizo, sister to Prince John Barigye, the crown prince of Ankole and wife to Bhuka Bijumiro-jummiro; Mugonza's disciple and biographer; and Kasiimwe Ssemyanjo, the resident leader of Sserulanda Spiritual Foundation. Among the stated objectives of the Sserulanda Development Association are to pool resources for the purpose of fostering material, financial, social, and spiritual growth and development of the members and their families. According to their memorandum of association, members must follow a vegetarian diet and must never cut down trees or clear thickets in the company's area of operation or its estates without permission from the company management.

In 1992 Bambi Baaba released a petition to the world reflecting upon what he saw as the planetary dilemma of viceful behavior and worldwide discord that threatens human self-annihilation. He offered a message from the Ansenserenical adepts, those divine beings who had evolved and transcended to the higher planes of the spiritual world: It is now imperative that all of humanity institute a cooperative activity of sharing all knowledge and physical resources to accomplish planetary purification by means of an economic and cultural rejuvenation. The first step is the reconnection between the people of the world and the Ansenserenical beings.

Membership: Not reported.

Sources:

Bambi Baaba. *The Golden Advent of the Wisdom of the Ansenserenical of Planet Earth*. Unpublished paper, 1992.

Bijumiro-jjumiro, Bhuka B. M. *Bambi Baaba: Redeemer of the New Age*. Montreal, Canada: Sserulanda Spiritual Planetary Community, 1986.

Eastern Family, Part II: Buddhism, Shinto, Japanese New Religions

24

BUDDHISM. Buddhism can be traced to the experiences of Siddhartha Gautama, born a prince around 563 B.C.E. at Lumbini near the capital of the kingdom of Shakya, India. Gautama is often called Shakyamuni, after his birthplace. According to traditional accounts of his life, Gautama grew up in the court and was shielded from contact with the real mundane world of the people he would someday rule. He married at 17 and fathered a child. However, his life changed dramatically in 529 B.C.E. when he departed from the palace, abandoned his worldly existence, and began a career as a wandering seeker for the meaning of life. Gautama spent the next six years visiting various Indian religious groups, sitting with several teachers of renown, and experimenting with many religious practices, such as asceticism and meditation. His search ended in 523 B.C.E., while he was in meditation and contemplation at the foot of a tree, a "Bodhi tree," located at Sarnath, a site still considered a hallowed Buddhist shrine. As this period of meditation began, Gautama is said to have made the following vow: "Let my body be dried up on this seat, Let my skin and bones and flesh be destroyed So long as Bodhi is not attained ... My body and thought will not be removed from this seat."

He attained the "Bodhi," or enlightenment, in 523 B.C.E., and as a result became known as Gautama the Buddha or the Enlightened One. After this enlightenment, Buddha began to preach and teach, and a group of disciples gathered around him. A movement began to grow, particularly in northwest India. Buddha died of dysentery about 480 B.C.E.

Much of the essence of Buddhism is found in the teachings of the Buddha, which outline the Dharma, the true way of life. The Dharma is remarkably simple, for all its profundity, and lends itself easily to a brief summary. All Buddhists share a belief in the Buddha's Dharma, which centers upon the "four basic truths" and the "noble eightfold path." The four basic truths are: (1) all existence entails suffering; (2) the cause of suffering is desire, that is, the thirst for pleasure, prosperity, and continued life (it is this thirst for continued life that begets rebirth); (3) the way to escape suffering, existence, and rebirth is to rid one's self of desire; and (4) to be emancipated from desire, one must follow the eightfold path.

The noble eightfold path is pictured in the eight-spoked wheel, a symbol second only to the seated Buddha as a sign of Buddhist faith. The path consists of:

1. right understanding
2. right resolve
3. right speech
4. right conduct
5. right livelihood
6. right effort
7. right attention
8. right concentration

Various Buddhist groups would accept the eightfold path but disagree on their interpretation of it and the emphasis on, and priority of, certain aspects of it. This difference will often be manifest in the words that English Buddhist groups use to translate the language of the eightfold path in their literature.

For example, some groups, leaning toward a more intellectualized Buddhism, will translate the first step of the path as right belief or knowledge. Zen Buddhists, pointing to the mystic and indescribable nature of Buddhist experience, will often translate it as right vision. Interpretations of right concentration, or the goal of nirvana, range from the present-mindedness of mystic Buddhism, which finds nirvana in the mystical experience, to the otherworldliness of various groups of Buddhists. Some of the variations will become evident below.

The basic scriptures of Buddhism, the *Tripitaka* or *Three Baskets*, are divided into the Vinaya, the Sutras, and the Abhidhamma. The Vinaya consists basically of rules for the monks and information on Buddha's life. The Sutras are a collection of material attributed to the Buddha and his close disciples. How much is actually Buddha's words is a matter of debate. The Abhidhamma is composed of discourses of Gautama. Other scriptures have been added to the *Tripitaka* by various national Buddhist bodies, and each particular group has its own interpretive material.

SPREAD OF BUDDHISM. Buddhism arose as a reformist sect of Hinduism and included many elements of Hindu thought within it, although it modified greatly certain ideas, such as the transmigration of the soul. After the crisis of Buddha's death, a council, which has become known in Buddhist history as the First Council, was held under the leadership of Kashyapa, a disciple of Buddha. Some basic decisions about doctrine and discipline were made that enabled the Buddhist movement to be organized and to spread. The Second Council was held in 377 B.C.E. after a

Spread of Buddhism in Asia

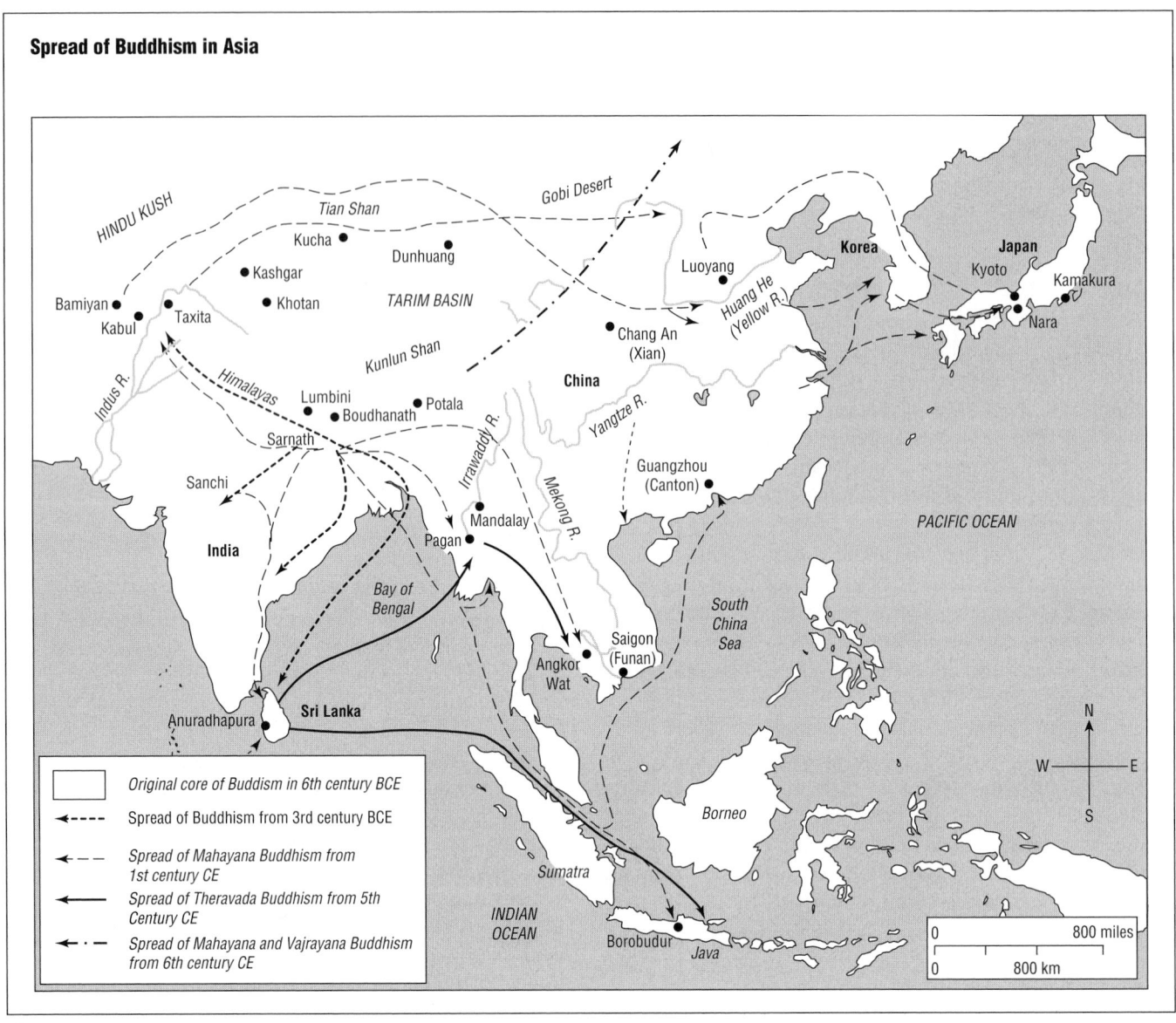

Adapted from Irons, Edward A. Encyclopedia of Buddhism. *Facts on file, 2008.*

group of monks revolted against the strict rules of the order and decided to reinterpret them. The Vaishali Council decided in favor of the strict interpretation, and the lax monks seceded from the order. They represent the first major schismatic school.

The next significant date in Buddhist history is 270 B.C.E. This year saw the emergence of the Indian Empire with its ruler Asoka (c. 304–232 B.C.E.), the man who did more for the spread of Buddhism than anyone since its founder. In remorse and regret produced by his wars of conquest, Asoka was led to become a Buddhist monk while still the emperor. Until Asoka, Buddhism was a local Indian sect, but with Asoka's help it was spread throughout his kingdom, to all of India, and into Ceylon, Nepal, and central Asia. Asoka had inherited an intensely missionary understanding of his faith from Buddhist scripture and implanted it within the movement. This missionary zeal has distinguished Buddhism from almost all other indigenous faiths of southern Asia.

By the time of Asoka, Buddhism had begun to develop an extensive literature. First steps toward the development of a canon were probably made during Asoka's time at the so-called Third Council. This council was called to deal with the problems created by the large increase in nominal members, a result of the extensive growth following Asoka's missionary endeavors.

After Asoka's death, the center of Buddhism shifted to the northwest (Kashmir, Kabul, Bactria, etc.), where a Greek king friendly to Buddhism had established himself in power. The role of the Greek king, Menander (c. 342–291 B.C.E.), was doubly important. He provided a haven for Buddhists from Asoka's successors, who were less than devoted admirers of the growing faith. He also provided the influence that led to Buddhist art, particularly statues of Gautama. No representations of the Buddha survive prior to this period.

In the centuries before and after Asoka, the two main schools of Buddhism began to take a more pronounced form.

American Buddhism/Shintoism Chronology

1850	Buddhists and practitioners of traditional Chinese folk religion arrive in San Francisco in response to the discovery of gold.
1868	Buddhists are among Japanese immigrants who begin arriving in Hawaii.
1882	Chinese Exclusion Act stops further immigration from China and excludes Chinese Americans from becoming citizens.
1889	Honpa Hongwanji priest Soryu Kagahi arrives in Honolulu and builds first Buddhist temple.
1893	Horin Toki, Zitsuzen Ashitsu, Soyen Shaku, Anagarika Dharmapala, and Sugao Nishikawa are among 12 Buddhists and two Shintoists who address the Parliament of the World's Religions gathering in Chicago.
	Following the Parliament, Dharmapala formally administers the Taking of the Buddhist vows to C. T. Strauss, the first Westerner to become a Buddhist in the West.
1897	Publisher Paul Carus begins a decade of collaboration with D. T. Suzuki, leading to the first wave of popularly available Buddhist publications in America.
1898	The first Shinto shrine in America is erected at Hilo, Hawaii.
1899	Honpa Hongwanji priests Shuyei Sonoda and Kakuryo Nishijima arrive in San Francisco and launch what will become the Buddhist Churches of America.
1903	Rev. Senyai Kawahara builds the first Soto Zen temple in America in Honolulu, Hawaii.
1906	Sokatsu Shoku leads a group of six Zen teachers to the United States and initiates the history of Renzai Zen.
1907	In the Gentlemen's Agreement, the United States agrees not to negatively cite Japan in any anti-immigration law and Japan agrees to severely limit immigration to the United States.
1924	Asian Exclusion Act bars immigration from most predominantly Buddhist countries including Japan, China, Laos, Siam, Cambodia, Singapore (then a British colony), Korea, Vietnam, and Burma. This law effectively violates the Gentleman's Agreement of 1907.
1929	Bishop Yemyo Imamura and American Ernest Hunt found the first American chapter of the International Buddhist Institute in Hawaii.
1930	Sokei-an Sasaki founds First Zen Institute in America in New York City. He later marries Ruth Fuller Everett, the first Western female to study Zen in Japan.
1942	Japanese cite the United States's breaking of the Gentleman's Agreement as part of justification for attacking Pearl Harbor.
1952	World Fellowship of Buddhist (WFB) organized as umbrella groups for all Buddhists. Several American groups are designated as WFB regional headquarters.
Late 1950s	Members of the "Beatnik" subculture appropriate Zen Buddhism.
1959	American students gather at Sokaji Temple to study with Shunryu Suzuki and form what becomes the Zen Center of San Francisco.
	Chinese occupy Tibet, leading to the Dalai Lama and thousands of Tibetans moving into exile.
1960	First chapter of Soka Gakkai formed during visit of the movement's president Daisaku Ikeda. It will become one of the largest Buddhist groups in North America.
1963	World takes notice of growing conflict in Vietnam following immolation of Buddhist monk Thich Quang Duc.
1965	New Immigration Law rescinds Asian Exclusion Act and places Asian countries on same immigration quotas as Western European nations. As a result, Chinese immigrants from Hong Kong, Taiwan, and Southeast Asia will come to constitute the largest segment of the North American Buddhist community.
1967	Students of Taizan Maezumi Roshi form Zen Center of Los Angeles.
1972	Korean Zen teacher Seung Sahn founds first center of what will become the Kwan Un School of Zen.
1973	The Thalmahsa Buddhist Monastery and Temple open in Los Angeles and become organizational center for Korean American Buddhists.
1975	The first wave of immigration following the Vietnam War leads to formation of the Congregation of Vietnamese Buddhists in the U.S. Vienamese form second largest Buddhist community in North America.
1981	Naropa Institute in Boulder, Colorado, hosts first conference on the role of women in Buddhism. The conference is a sign both of the emerging leadership role of women Buddhists and their protest of traditional patriarchal structures.
	Grand Master Sheng-yen Lu, head of the True Buddha School, establishes his headquarters in Seattle, Washington.
1986	American Buddhist Congress founded in Los Angeles.
1987	Dalai Lama presents his Five Point Peace Plan for Tibet to members of the U.S. Congress. American women support formation of Sakyadhita, the International Association of Buddhist Women, and attend its first International Conference on Women in Buddhism.
1988	The Taiwanese Buddhist group Foguangshan completes the His Lai Temple complex in Hacienda Heights, California, the largest Buddhist center in the West.
1989	Dalai Lama awarded Nobel Peace Prize.
1997	Buddhists from across the spectrum of American traditions gather in Boston on January 17–19 for a Conference on the Future of Buddhist Meditative Practices in the West.
2007	Buddhist monks in Burma assume a leading role in criticizing the government and make headlines around the world during the repression of demonstrations.
2008	Tibetan monks protest human rights in China on eve of Beijing Olympic Games.

The first of the schools to emerge was called Theravada. Theravada looked to the writings of Sariputra, an early disciple of Buddha whose method of interpreting Buddha's teachings was very conservative and emphasized the role of the monk and the monastic life as the way to nirvana. In reaction to the monk-oriented faith of Theravada, there arose Mahayana Buddhism, which dates itself to Ananda and other early disciples of Buddha who did not accept the interpretations of Sariputra. Mahayana was much more open to the role of nonmonks in the faith and held as a goal the ultimate salvation of all living beings. This universalist tendency made it a more efficient vehicle in which to carry the faith across Southeast Asia to Japan. As Buddhism spread, it not only took upon itself the national characteristics of each country but also generally related itself to one of the two major schools.

The term *Theravada* applies to the *Tripitaka* or *Pali Canon* of Buddha's writing. The Tripitaka was finally put into writing during the first century B.C.E. The Theravada Buddhists accepted it, but the Mahayanists accepted only part of it and developed their own canon, which included various Sutras that have become the basis of the widely differing Mahayana groups. Included would be such writings as the *Lotus Sutra* (used by Nichiren), the *Diamond Sutra* (used by some Zen groups) and the *Sukhavati-Vyuha* (used by the Pure Land groups).

SOUTHEAST ASIAN (THERAVADA) BUDDHISM. Asoka's son, Prince Mahinda, took Buddhism to Ceylon (Sri Lanka) in the third century B.C.E. Although the exact details of the conversion process are buried in legendary material, there is no doubt that Mahinda's activity established Buddhism in Anuradhapura, the capital, and among the royal family. Asoka sent to the new converts a scion of the sacred Bodhi tree, which is still preserved and venerated, and the monastery Mahinda established became a center from which the stricter Theravada could be spread.

Burma (Myanmar), like Ceylon, probably first heard of Buddhism as a result of Asoka's missionaries. For a period, a small Buddhist community established by Mahayanists vied for the allegiance of the people, but Theravada became firmly established as the dominant faith in the sixth century C.E. following the spread of a Theravada revival emanating from Madras in India.

Thailand, formerly Siam, represents the other main center of the Theravada school. The origin of Buddhism in Thailand has been lost, but early in the Christian era, Mahayana forms of Buddhism were coexisting with Brahmanism (Hinduism). Mahayana could possibly have entered from Cambodia during the era that the Cambodians ruled most of Indochina. (The Cambodians had received Buddhism from Indian merchants and settlers, just as they had received Brahmanism.) The Siamese began their rise to power in the eleventh century C.E. and controlled the country by the end of the thirteenth century. In the complexity of war and its resulting chaos, Theravada entered the country and in a relatively short time had supplanted both Mahayana and Brahmanism. As Theravada grew in Thailand, it spread also to neighboring Cambodia. Hinduism was already yielding to Mahayana there, and both then gave way to Theravada.

By the modern era, Theravada Buddhism had a firm control from Ceylon, along the southern coast of Asia, to Indochina. This growth, while impressive, was eclipsed by that accomplished by Mahayana with its more universal appeal. Several cases have been noted in which Theravada came into a country only after Mahayana had been present for some time.

CHINESE BUDDHISM. China received Buddhist missionaries possibly as early as 200 B.C.E. and quickly became the great center of Mahayana Buddhism. As Buddhism interacted with the religions of China, numerous variations of it (including what was to become Zen) sprang up. But over the centuries, the various Buddhist groups have evolved into what is usually the eclectic mixture of Buddhism, Confucianism, and Daoism that had been popularized throughout mainland China. The faith is a form of Buddhism centered on bodhisattvas, who function somewhat like saints in Roman Catholicism. Religious structures, temples, are dedicated to a particular bodhisattva; Guanyin (also known as Kwan Yin), the goddess of mercy, is a popular one. Other bodhisattvas

have lesser positions, and a temple thus gives the appearance of having a pantheon represented in the statuary. The most popular form of Buddhism in China (as in Japan) centers on Amitabha Buddha (known in Japan as Amida Buddha) with his promise of a Pure Land, or the Lotus Heaven, to which men are brought by faith in the Buddha.

Confucius, the Latinized name given Master Kong (K'ung), born in China in 551 B.C.E., was the great teacher of morals, practical religion, and philosophy. During his early twenties, he entered a time of seclusion to mourn his mother's death and found it a time of deep thought. By the age of 30, he was a teacher and later became chief judge of his own district of Lu. After a life of success and failures, he died in 479 B.C.E. His teachings—emphasizing family (including ancestor worship), morality, and respect for authority—became part of the Chinese way of life.

Laozi (Lao-tzu), the reputed founder of Daoism, was an early contemporary of Confucius. His name, which means "little old child," derives from a legend that he was born an old man. We know little about him beyond his retirement from public life and his composition of the *Daodejing* (Tao Te Ching), the chief religious book of the Daoists. A disciple, Zhuang Zhou (Chuang-tse), wrote a commentary on his master's work, which is also a part of the sacred writing. The teachings center on the nature of the Dao or Way. The Way is mystical, natural, and highly ethical, but vague and open to wide interpretation. The influence of Daoism has largely survived through the sacred writings, which are widely read, and a folk religion that merged the mystical faith of Daoism with the ancient polytheistic, magical religion of pre-Daoist China.

The common practice of presenting Chinese religion as a separate topic in itself is legitimate. Yet, in its American manifestations, Chinese religion should be considered within a Chinese Buddhism context. John F. Mulholland, in his survey *Hawaii's Religions*, reflects upon the Buddhist affiliation of many members of America's Asian community:

> When the Chinese immigrants prospered, the children went to private schools. If the school was Catholic or Episcopal and required or expected all students to be baptized, the children were baptized. The second and third generations found that in Hawaii they were expected to have a religion, and since the lack of religious designation in China was confusing, many Chinese simply said they were Buddhist. There were no organized Buddhist groups and no membership requirements as Christian churches had. The temples were privately owned or existed in connection with Chinese societies. As the Japanese Buddhists built temples which related them to Japan, so the Chinese began to emphasize the Buddhist part of their multiple religion.
>
> Mulholland, *Hawaii's Religions*, 1970.

KOREAN BUDDHISM. From China, Buddhism spread to Korea. Buddhism in Korea differs markedly from Buddhism in other Asian societies in that, during the modern era, the various schools of Buddhist thought began to emphasize their commonality over their differences. As a result, the several organizations were able not only to reverse the process of splintering but finally, in 1935, to unite into a single organization, the Chogye sect, from which most contemporary groups derive.

Buddhism entered what is today called Korea in 372 C.E., when it was brought from China to the kingdom of Koguryo, a state covering the northern portion of the peninsula. From there it spread southward to the kingdoms of Paekche and Silla. It flourished in the united kingdom created by Silla in 668 C.E., during which time Zen was introduced along with the original Mahayana (called Chiao in Korea) forms. Nine schools of Zen developed around nine outstanding masters, and six schools of Chiao emerged.

Through the next centuries, Buddhism waxed and waned, always remaining in competition with Confucius's thought and popular folk religion. Zen experienced a revival in the twelfth century when Master Pojo (1158–1210) advocated a union of thought that found favor with the varying Zen schools. A century and a half later, in 1356, under Master T'aego (1301–1382), a merger of all the Zen schools into the Chogyejong was accomplished. Master T'aego was one of several priests who had risen to prominence in the land and had been given the title "national teacher" by the king.

The Yi dynasty (1392–1910) became a time of great suffering for Korean Buddhism, as the ruling powers generally assumed a hostile posture toward it. Buddhism was suppressed and Zen almost died out, though in the face of opposition, Buddhism became more united. In 1424 two of the Chiao sects united with the Chogyejong to form the Sonjong, while the remaining Chiao sects united into the Kyojong. Only in the late eighteenth century did government policies toward Buddhism relax. King Kojong (r. 1864–1907) began to lift negative government regulations, and in the nineteenth century Buddhism began a revival, further spurred in the 1890s by the arrival of many Japanese Buddhist priests. In 1904, for the first time, the government ended its control of Buddhist temples. The revival of Buddhism, the cooperation with the Japanese priests, and the new freedom, however, came to an abrupt halt in the second decade of the twentieth century after Japan occupied Korea in 1910. The occupation government reclaimed control of the temples. Nationalistic feelings led to a new sense of unity by Korean Buddhists over against the Japanese. The growth of those sentiments led in 1935 to the merger of the Sonjong and Kyojong into the single Chogye sect, which dominates Korean Buddhism to this day.

JAPANESE BUDDHISM. From China, Buddhism spread to Korea and then to Japan. Japanese Buddhism is critical to an understanding of North American Buddhism, as the overwhelming majority of North American Buddhists were, at least prior to the 1970s, followers of one of the Japanese Buddhist traditions. When it first entered Japan, Buddhism was not attractive enough to win many converts from Shinto, the national religion of Japan, but Buddhism was granted toleration by the emperor. The building of the new capital at Nara in 710 C.E. marked the turning point in Japanese Buddhist history. During the Nara period, the emperor accepted Buddhism and made it the state religion. A number of the Chinese Buddhist sects, including Jojitsu, Sanron, Hosso, Kusha, Ritsu, and Kegon, were introduced (most of these are now represented in North America). In 807 the Tendai sect was brought to Japan. It was more open to the laity than the Nara sects, which tended to be rather exclusive. Esoteric (Tantric) Buddhism was introduced in the following century.

In the twelfth century, Honen (1133–1212) and his disciple Shinran (1173–1263) brought the Pure Land sect from China to Japan. Long before Honen organized the Jodo, or Pure Land sect, there had been a belief in the Amitabha (Amida), a benevolent deity who dwells in a western paradise to which men may gain access by calling upon his name. But it was Honen who gave the idea an independent form, thereby establishing a new school of thought. Various groups whose beliefs derive from Honen and Shinran are called the Shin groups.

Honen's basic disagreement with most Buddhists of his day was over whether one gained salvation by *jiriki*, one's own strength, or by *tariki*, another's strength. He believed firmly in tariki, in this case the power of the bodhisattva Amida acquired by calling upon his name. The practice of calling upon Amida is known as *nembutsu*. Those who repeat the nembutsu are promised rebirth into the western paradise. In the Pure Land, all enjoy powers and bliss. It is a step toward nirvana. The nembutsu, according to Honen, should be repeated often and with sincerity, deep belief, and longing.

The most important of Honen's students was Shinran, a monk and friend of Honen. The innovative Shinran abolished monasticism, permitted priests to marry, and promoted the worship of Amida and, to a lesser extent, Shakya (Shakyamuni, Gautama Buddha). Only the relics and images of Amida are allowed. Salvation is attained through faith alone, as a gift of Amida. Honen believed that man is saved by faith, but that ritual and working for others help.

The central act of all Shin groups is the repetition of the nembutsu: "Namu Amida Butsu" (to bow or submit to the one who is enlightened) is repeated often and is said before the statue of Amida Buddha. To repeat the nembutsu is to be one with Amida.

After Shinran's death, the Shin group gradually split into the Jodo (or Jodo-shu) and Shinshu groups. The Jodo look more to Honen, and the Shinshu more to Shinran. The Shinshu grew slowly, and in the medieval period fell victim to the various political upheavals and wars. Shinran's daughter supervised construction of the Hongwanji, or Temple of the Original View, in Kyoto, which became the headquarters of the True Pure Land sect. In 1496 a temple that became the new Shinshu center was founded at Yamashina. Yamashina was destroyed in 1532, and the headquarters were moved to Ishiyama.

In 1570 Oda Nobunaga (1532–1582), a feudal lord who was spreading Christianity to counteract Buddhism's power, attacked Ishiyama and eventually (after 10 years) destroyed it. Oda Nobunaga defended Christianity in conjunction with the missionary work of Francis Xavier (1506–1552), but Nobunaga's aim was less to spread Christianity than to destroy Buddhism. He considered the Buddhists a threat to his power. As a result of the evacuation by the chief abbot from Ishiyama, a disagreement arose among his sons as to how long the Shinshu should have fought Oda Nobunaga, and a split developed.

Ieyasu (1543–1616), the shogun of Japan, fearing the growth of the Shinshu among the people, took advantage of the split to divide the group. He sided with the elder son and gave him a tract of land upon which to build a Hongwanji. The supporters of the younger son are now known as the Honpa Hongwanji, and the supporters of the elder as the Higashi Hongwanji. Their differences were largely administrative, but, as time has passed, the Honpa groups have been the more progressive and adaptive to change.

The thirteenth century saw the appearance of Nichiren (1222–1282), another outstanding Buddhist teacher who began as a reformer and Buddhist ecumenist but became the founder of the Nichiren-shu (*shu* means "religion"). Nichiren believed that in the teachings known as the *Lotus Sutra* he had found the primitive, true Buddhism that could unite the many sects. He attacked the other sects' beliefs and won many followers as he traveled around Japan.

One of the central ideas in Japanese Buddhism, usually associated with Nichiren, is *mappo*, or end of the law. Nichiren divided history into three millennia, the first of which began with Buddha's death. The last phase or mappo, began in 1050 C.E. In this last period, salvation is to be obtained through belief in the *Lotus Sutra*.

ZEN BUDDHISM. Zen was also introduced into Japan about this time. Zen is the mystical school of Buddhism. It stands in relation to Buddhism much as Sufism does to Islam and contemplative Catholicism does to Christianity. It arose in the interaction of Buddhist philosophy with Daoist meditative techniques. The actual founder was Daosheng (Tao-sheng) (360–434), who added to Buddhist meditative techniques the doctrine of instantaneous enlightenment—the attainment in one single act of illumination of the goal of mystical truth in both its objective and subjective aspects.

Recognized by many Zen students as the legendary founder of Zen is Bodhidharma (d. 534 C.E.), who came from his native India to teach Zen in China during most of his mature life. He is termed the first patriarch and is credited with the addition of "wall-contemplation" to Zen practice. He was followed by five other patriarchs—Hui Ke (c. 487–c. 593), Jianzhi Sengcan (d. 606), Dao Xin (580–621), Hong Ren (601–674), and Hui Neng (638–713). Hui Neng is ranked next to Bodhidharma as the second (and actual) founder of Zen.

As Zen continued to develop in China, it went through the familiar process of schism and adoption of new ideas and practices. Among the new practices developed was the use of the *koan*. The koan is an anecdotal event or utterance of the masters given to disciples as problems. It is used as a means to enlightenment. The koan led to the development of the two

major schools of Zen that still exist. One school, Linji, accepted the koan and used it extensively. In reaction, a second school, Caodong, emerged and was characterized by its doctrine of silent illumination. Caodong saw the koan as "gazing on the word." Transported to Japan, the Linji sect became Rinzai Zen, and Caodong became Soto Zen. These two schools were both transferred to the United States. In pure Rinzai Zen, people use the koan; in pure Soto Zen, people do not. Most groups are neither pure Rinzai or Soto but lie between those two extremes.

One popular koan often used as the first exercise for Rinzai students is the *mu* koan. *Mu*, meaning "no" or "nothing" in Sino-Japanese, is understood as the nothing that contains everything. Mu is to be experienced, not intellectualized.

Dogen (1200–1253), the founder of Japanese Soto, is the originator of the typical Zen method of meditation, zazen. As described by Dogen, *zazen* proceeds thus:

If you wish to attain enlightenment, begin at once to practice zazen. For this meditation a quiet chamber is necessary, while food and drink must be taken in moderation. Free yourself from all attachments, and bring to rest the ten thousand things. Think of neither good nor evil and judge not right nor wrong. Maintain the flow of mind, of will, and of consciousness; bring to an end all desires, all concepts and judgments. Do not think about how to become a Buddha.

In terms of procedure, first put down a thick pillow and on top of this a second (round) one. One may chose either a full or half cross-legged position. In the full position one places the right foot on the left thigh and the left foot is placed on the right thigh. In the half position only the left foot is placed upon the right thigh. Robe and belt should be worn loosely, but in order. The right hand rests on the left foot, while the back of the left hand rests in the palm of the right. The two thumbs are placed in juxtaposition.

The body must be maintained upright, without inclining to the left or to the right, forward or backward. Ears and shoulders, nose and navel must be kept in alignment respectively. The tongue is to be kept against the palate, lips and teeth are kept firmly closed, while the eyes are to be kept always open.

Now that the bodily position is in order, regulate your breathing. If a wish arises, take note of it and then dismiss it. In practicing thus persistently you will forget all attachments and concentration will come of itself. That is the art of zazen. Zazen is the Dharma gate of great rest and joy.

Dumoulin, *A History of Zen Buddhism*, 1963, p. 161.

The essence of zazen is to achieve the full and perfect equilibrium of the organism.

Next to Dogen, Hakuin (1685–1768) was the greatest Zen master and was the one who revived Rinzai Zen in Japan. Hakuin described the tension of the disciple when confronted with the koan. This tension is the "great doubt." Hakuin also described *satori*, the great enlightenment, which is a central concern of Zen. In the various reports of *satori*, one again finds the range of reflections on mystical experience, this time described in Buddhist categories.

The *roshi* is the prime official in Zen. The roshi is the master, the one who has attained the goals of Zen meditation and has the knowledge and maturity to aid others in attaining them. There is a tendency toward a Buddhist version of apostolic succession in Zen, with the roshis seeing themselves in a lineage of Zen masters and in a school formed by a succession of patriarchs.

In America, most Zen is derived from Jito Gasan (1727–1797), a Japanese Zen master and head of Engaku Temple. He passed on the Rinzai tradition to Imakita Kosen (1816–1892), a Japanese master who was fascinated with Western culture and among whose students was Soyen Shaku (1859–1919), the first Zen teacher to visit the United States.

TIBETAN BUDDHISM. The last place that Buddhism entered as a conquering missionary faith was Tibet. The date traditionally given is 747 C.E., when Padmasambhava brought Tantric Buddhism to Tibet. In the mountainous terrain, Buddhism mixed with Bon, the native religion, the aim of which was the magical control of evil spirits and the use of cosmic powers. Tibetan Buddhism thus emerged as a somewhat magical faith, distinct from either Chinese or Indian Buddhism.

The older sects still emphasize the magic Tantra and make wide use of the *mantra* and the *mandala*. The mantra is a phonetic form (the most popular being "om" and "om mani padme hum," meaning the jewel in the heart of the lotus, the center of truth). The very sound of the mantra has a psychological effect and is aimed at producing deep mystical experience. A mandala is a circular drawing representative of the universe, a cosmogram whose center is thought to be the metaphysical center of the universe. It is used as an aid in worship.

Tantric Buddhism is based on the belief that everything is permeated by a single power (*Shakti*) emanating from God. This force manifests itself in three ways: positive masculine, negative feminine, and, most important, the union of the two. What is true on a cosmic level is considered true on a human, individual level. The union of opposites, a major goal in Tantric practice, is accomplished by the disciplines of yoga, the most controversial aspect of which includes ritual sexual intercourse.

Tantric sexual ritual involves the male practitioner's partaking of the 5 M's (True Things)—*madya* (wine), *mamsha* (meat), *matsya* (fish), *mudra* (parched grain), and *maithuna* (coitus). Tantric rituals can be practiced in three modes. The Sattvio Sadhana, or symbolic school, has spiritualized Tantra. The Rajasic Sadhana uses material substitutes for the 5 M's. The Kaula Sadhana practices a literal partaking of the 5 M's. The symbolic and substitutionary partaking of the 5 M's is usually termed "right-hand" Tantra. Such practice is typical of the Japanese Shingon sect. The literal school, which performs ritual sexual intercourse, is generally said to practice "left-hand" Tantra. The object of Tantra is twofold: the union of the individual with the divine, and the gaining of magical power that can be used to do miraculous works.

After the initial establishment of Buddhism in Tibet, a period began in 838 C.E. in which rulers inimical to Buddhism halted its progress. Also, toward the end of the tenth century, government instability created opportunities for the development of Buddhism. Atisha (982–1054), who arrived from India in western Tibet in 1042, was in the forefront of the religion's resurgence. His efforts were bolstered by a new generation of Buddhist leaders that included Marpa (1012–1096) and Naropa (1016–1100). Out of their work a new wave of Buddhist schools was created and over the next few centuries, Tibet became a Buddhist country.

Tibetan Buddhism is divided into several major schools that are split into subsects. The Nyingma or Old Ones are constituted by those who trace their lineage to the first transmission of Buddhism under Guru Rinpoche (Padmasambhava), who the Nyingma see as the manifestation of the god Avalokiteshvara and even the equal of Buddha. They also claim Guru Rinpoche hid his teachings in texts to await times when people would be ready for them. These Nyingma texts are considered treasures, and prominent lamas (priests) who possess such texts are honored.

The Kadam or Bound to Command school traces its existence to Atisha and emphasizes the building of monasteries noteworthy for their disciplined life and guru devotion. This group has been absorbed into the Gelugpa as a subsect.

The Sakya school derives from the work of Konchog Gyalpo (1034–1102), a disciple of Drogmi (992–1072), a later contemporary of Atisha. Their integration of Sutra (written text) and Tantra is designed to produce liberation in a single lifetime.

The Kagyu or Transmitted Command school traces its lineage to Naropa, Marpa, and Marpa's chief disciple, Milarepa (1052–1135). It places great emphasis on practical mysticism and the speedy attainment of enlightenment. The Kagyu has been among the least monastic of the schools and requires neither celibacy nor association with a monastery from its members.

A reform, led by Tsong Khapa (1357–1419) at the turn of the fifteenth century, created an additional major Buddhist school in Tibet. It attempted to tighten the monastic discipline, insisted on celibacy, reduced the emphasis on magic, and effected strong organization. Tsong Khapa also founded a monastery, Ganden, east of Lhasa, which grew into a large monastic university. In 1416 and 1419, two similar monasteries were created. These became the leading centers of learning for Buddhism and assisted the Gelugpa school in becoming the dominant Buddhist school in the land.

Tsong Khapa's reforms were accomplished at the time when the newer schools were teaching that the head of the chief monasteries were bodhisattvas. When a *lama*, or monastery ruler, died, a search was made for a new incarnation of him born at the time of his death. As the Gelugpa school became a dominant force, its leader became the chief lama of Tibet. The Dalai Lama is still the nominal head of

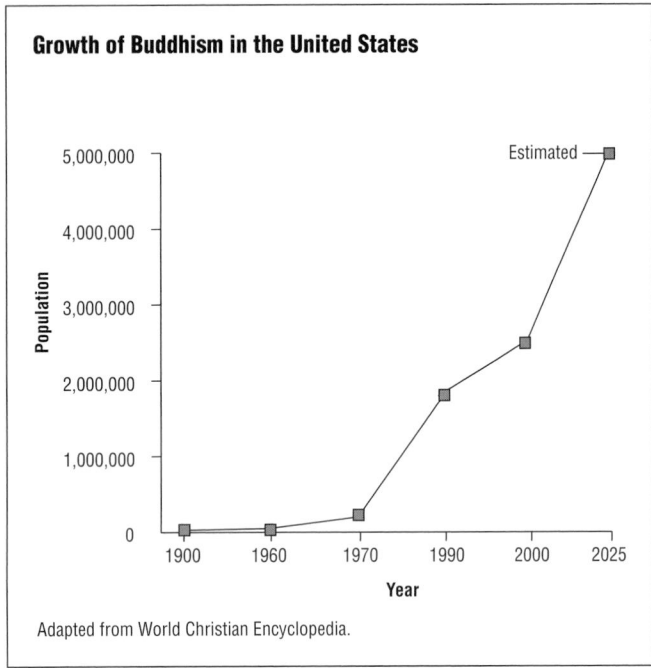

Growth of Buddhism in the United States

Adapted from World Christian Encyclopedia.

Tibet's Buddhists. Second only to the Dalai Lama is the Panchen Lama, head of the monastic complex of Tashihunpo.

Tibetan Buddhism was thoroughly disrupted by the Chinese invasion of Tibet in 1959. Many of the leading teachers, including the Dalai Lama, fled the country in order to preserve Tibetan traditions and practice in the face of what they feared would be hostile and destructive new rulers. Their fears were to a large extent realized. Most of the great monasteries were leveled, many monks were killed and those who survived were forced into secular labor, and many texts (some irreplaceable) were torched. In the wake of the institution of Chinese control in Tibet, the center of Tibetan Buddhism moved to northern India in the kingdoms of Nepal and Bhutan, and to the West. Here, an attempt to keep pre-1950s Tibetan culture and religion alive was launched, including the preservation and translation of all the texts smuggled out of Tibet into Western languages. Integral to the survival of Tibetan Buddhism has been the contact with the Western world. Many teachers came to the West and established teaching centers that attracted a new generation of believers among non-Tibetans. The growth of their Western community has been crowned by the recognition of several westerners as the reincarnation of prominent lamas.

BUDDHISM IN NORTH AMERICA.
Buddhism came to America in several waves beginning with Chinese immigrants attracted by the discovery of gold in California. A second wave came with the Japanese entry into Hawaii and California in the last two decades of the nineteenth century. Buddhist growth in the United States was blocked in the first half of the twentieth century by anti-Asian immigration laws. A third wave of immigration began in 1965 following the pass-

ing of a new immigration law favorable to Asians. This last wave revitalized Buddhism in America.

Buddhism in North America is best understood in the context of its international spread. In spite of valiant attempts to create an American Buddhism, most Buddhist bodies in the United States still represent transplanted forms of the many varied Asian schools of thought and practice. The community is also still structured by its immigration patterns. Overwhelmingly, Buddhists have come to the United States from Asia and entered the country through one of the West Coast ports, usually Los Angeles. As the twentieth century came to a close, 40 percent of all Buddhists in America resided in southern California, and the Los Angeles metropolitan area became unique in the Buddhist world as the one place where representative organizations of every major school of Buddhism can be found in a single urban center.

SOUTHEAST ASIAN (THERAVADA) BUDDHISM IN NORTH AMERICA. Prior to 1965, the story of Buddhism in America was largely the story of the emigration of Japanese Buddhists to Hawaii and the West Coast and the spread of Japanese forms of Buddhism in the Caucasian population. The presence of Theravada Buddhism was limited to a few intellectuals and the diplomatic mission personnel from the several Southeast Asian countries in New York City and Washington, D.C. The situation changed dramatically after the beginning of the Vietnam War (1957–1975) and its spread to surrounding countries and the replacing of the Asian Exclusion Act by the new immigration regulations of 1965. During the 1970s, a great wave of immigrants from Vietnam (increased by special legislation passed after the withdrawal of U.S. forces from the country), Cambodia, Laos, and Thailand moved to the West Coast and the northern American urban centers. Slowly, they have organized congregations, established temples, and developed national associations. The Theravada centers consist almost entirely of first-generation, non-English-speaking Asian Americans.

In 1980 language was the major barrier to the spread of Theravada Buddhism to the Caucasian population, though initial signs of its spreading began to emerge around the followers of the few English-speaking Theravada teachers. Over the next two decades, this barrier was erased as the immigrant community from Southeast Asia (especially Vietnam) grew in size and Americanized, as major works on *vipassana* mediation were translated into English (and other Western languages), and as the Internet made Theravada teachings readily available to all.

CHINESE BUDDHISM IN NORTH AMERICA. The Chinese came to the United States before the Japanese, their major immigration occurring between 1854 and 1883, when a law stopping further Chinese migration was passed. By 1880, more than 100,000 Chinese had settled in America, primarily on the West Coast.

The 1850s saw the arrival of the first large groups of Chinese laborers in the United States. Although the majority were Christians, having been recruited from the mission stations in China, many were not. Those who remained loyal to traditional religious patterns set up family altars and shrines. They soon became the source of numerous complaints about "heathen Mongolians," and were targeted by a reinforced Christian missionary movement.

As early as 1878, a Chinese monk brought statues of two bodhisattvas, Guanyin (Kwan Yin) and Guandi (Kwan Tai), to Honolulu and built a temple, or joss house, centered on the veneration of Guanyin. (Guandi was a military hero of the third century B.C.E. who was later canonized.) By 1887, three joss houses were reported. During World War II (1937–1945), one observer reported seven temples on Oahu and another on Kauai. Chinese joss houses appeared on the West Coast before 1900. Much of the Chinese faith is centered on these joss houses, particularly the small family shrines still found throughout Chinese American communities in California and Hawaii.

A modern revival of Buddhism in a Chinese mode has resulted in the establishment of a number of centers across the country, many of which have been formed by expatriates from the Maoist revolution and immigrants from Taiwan and Southeast Asia. Most Chinese Buddhist temples in America serve Chinese Americans, primarily first- and second-generation immigrants from Hong Kong, Taiwan, Malaysia, Singapore, and other Southeast Asian countries. A very few have been formed by American converts or by Americans who found themselves in China as missionaries or soldiers and were converted abroad. Independent Chinese Buddhist associations have formed to bring the temples into larger fellowships.

Most Chinese Buddhist centers are located in the metropolitan areas of Honolulu, San Francisco, Los Angeles, San Diego, Seattle, Vancouver, Chicago, and New York City. The existence of these centers, often only blocks apart but administratively independent, manifest the variety within Chinese Buddhism, as well as the distinctions formed by migration at different times and from different counties.

Chinese began to arrive in Canada at the time of the gold rush on the Fraser River in 1868. Approximately 2,000 came during the first two years. Several thousand more seemed to have arrived during the 1870s. In 1881 there were an estimated 4,300 Chinese in Canada (almost all in British Columbia). Three years later the number had grown to 10,000, most recruited to build the Canadian Pacific Railroad. After the railroad was constructed, they found jobs in the fishing industry. Lesser numbers continued to enter Canada until immigration was blocked in 1923. At the same time, Chinese were encouraged and assisted in living in the country.

Only a minority of the Chinese in British Columbia were Buddhist, a large percentage being either Confucian or Christian. For Buddhists, joss houses were established similar to the pattern in California, and over the years temples have been erected to serve the Buddhist community.

While a small Buddhist community dating to the nineteenth and early twentieth centuries continues to exist, it has been totally eclipsed by the new Chinese Buddhist community that has developed since 1965. That community is built around the migration of Chinese from Taiwan, and to a lesser extent Hong Kong, who have attempted to reestablish contemporary Buddhist practice in the West. The most visible sign of the new Chinese presence is Hsi Lai Temple in Hacienda Heights, California, the largest Buddhist temple complex outside of China. His Lai serves as the American headquarters of the Foguangshan order, one of the major Taiwanese Buddhist communities, and home to a thriving Buddhist university. The translation of Chinese Buddhist material into English lagged behind that of Japanese Buddhism into the 1970s but since then has been accelerated by several organizations, most notably the Corporate Body of the Buddha Education Foundation organized by the disciples of master Chin King, a Taiwanese leader.

KOREAN BUDDHISM IN NORTH AMERICA. Korean migration since 1965 has been proportional to that of other Asian countries, but a majority of the new Korean Americans are Christians. However, a few Korean Buddhist priests have come to the United States and at least one Zen priest, Master Seung Sahn Sunim, has been able to create a national organization with a primary appeal to westerners.

The majority of Korean Americans who are Buddhists are members of the Chogye order, the largest Buddhist community in Korea. Chogye is a relatively new Buddhist community that formed in 1935 but emerged in prominence in the last half of the twentieth century as Buddhist traditions in Korea joined in efforts of the nation attempted to throw off centuries of Japanese dominance and the effects of the Korean War.

JAPANESE BUDDHISM IN NORTH AMERICA. Japanese immigration began with the arrival of large numbers of laborers in Hawaii on June 19, 1868. Further Japanese immigration was encouraged until 1907, when limits were placed upon it. At present, approximately one-third of the Hawaiian population is Japanese. Because the early Japanese came to Hawaii as plantation laborers, the work of establishing Buddhism began in the countryside, usually on a plantation, and then moved to Honolulu as plantation life soured for the Japanese. Buddhist settlements in California came only a short time after those in Hawaii, as Japanese immigrants also settled on the West Coast. In many cases, the Buddhist missionary from Japan would stop in Hawaii on his way to California. The growth of the community, however, was stymied by the 1907 law.

The name of the first Buddhist in Hawaii is lost to history, but in 1889 Soryu Kagahi (1855–1917) of the Honpa Hongwanji arrived in Honolulu to minister to Buddhists on the plantations. Under his leadership a temple, the first in Hawaii, was built in April 1889 in Hilo, where he had found many former Buddhists ready to reactivate their faith. In the fall, he returned to Japan and soon disappeared from history. For the next 10 years, things did not go well for Hawaiian Buddhists. They were frequently visited by renegade Buddhist priests who took their hard-earned wages and left town. Such practices left the adherents of Japanese Buddhism open to the active Christian mission.

Pleas for help were finally heard by Buddhists in Japan, who sent official representatives to Hawaii: Jotei Matsuo, a Jodo-shu priest (1894), and Ejun Miyamoto of the Honpa Hongwanji (1897). Within a decade, followers of four more of the Buddhist sects—the Higashi Hongwanji, the Shingon, the Nichiren, and the Soto Zen—arrived. In 1899 Yemyo Imamura, the bishop who was to dominate Buddhism in Hawaii until his death in 1932, took up residence in Honolulu.

As early as 1898, the Honpa Hongwanji sent two priests to survey possibilities for an American mission. A mission in San Francisco was established after the arrival of the Reverends Shuyei Sonoda and Kakuryo Nishijimi in September 1899. These two men organized the Young Men's Buddhist Association and, by 1905, had consecrated a church, which became the mainland headquarters of the Jodo Shin Buddhists.

Japanese migration to Canada began in 1877 and proceeded slowly until the mid-1890s. Between 1895 and the beginning of World War I (1914–1918), almost 30,000 Japanese came into Canada, though over half of these soon moved on to the United States. Migration dropped after the war and did not pick up again until the mid-1960s, though it has never reached the level of the first decade of the twentieth century.

The Honpa Hongwanji, or Shin Buddhists, were the primary group to take responsibility for the Japanese-Canadians and, answering a request from the community, the Reverend Senju Sasaki arrived in Vancouver in 1904. The first church was constructed in 1911. During the initial phase of organization and growth, the Canadian work was placed under the American Buddhist Mission headquarters in San Francisco. It became independent in 1933, but both the American and Canadian work retained the same bishop. Like the Buddhist work in the United States, the work in Canada was totally disrupted by World War II. After the war, the work was reorganized and prospered with renewed immigration. In 1968 the Honpa Hongwanji work in Canada was fully separated from that in the continental United States. Throughout the years since the renewal of immigration, other Japanese Buddhist groups have also colonized in Canada, and a diverse religious community is emerging.

In the early twentieth century, the Japanese Buddhist community had arisen as the Chinese community declined. It established itself, especially in Hawaii and the America West Coast, in the years prior to World War I and, after recovering from the effects of World War II, developed an impressive presence as a successful minority community. In the decades since 1965, however, it has found itself overwhelmed by the influx of Buddhists and now finds itself no longer the largest Buddhist community, but one among many. It has remained somewhat aloof from the new Buddhist communities and has been notable for its absence in Buddhist ecumenical circles, including the American Buddhist Congress.

ZEN BUDDHISM IN NORTH AMERICA. Zen came to America in 1893 when a Renzai monk, Soyen Shaku (1859–1919), addressed the World's Parliament of Religions in Chicago. A graduate of the Western-oriented Keio University, he traveled, despite strong opposition, to the land of the "barbarians" to speak on "The Law of Cause and Effect, as Taught by the Buddha." After his brief visit, during which he did not make the impact of either the Hindu Swami Vivekananda (1863–1902) or Theosophist Annie Besant (1847–1933), he returned to Kamakura. In 1905 he again came to the United States as the guest of the Alexander Russells in San Francisco. After a year of hospitality, he ended his stay with a national and then a world tour. The remainder of his life was spent as a leader in Japanese Zen.

Soyen had been a student of Imakita Kosen (1816–1892), renowned in nineteenth-century Buddhism as one who took Western thought and culture seriously. After Kosen's death, his students came to the West and became the real founders of American Zen. One of these students was Daisetz Teitaro Suzuki (1870–1966), a lay scholar, who, through his books, has done more to enlighten American audiences about Zen than any other person. Another of Kosen's students, Sokatsu Shaku (1869–1954), became a teacher in Tokyo. In 1906 he migrated to America with six disciples. The group settled in Berkeley but soon moved to a farm in Hayward, California. After discovering their inability to farm profitably, they moved to San Francisco. Gradually, each returned to Japan, leaving no visible organization behind. The last of the group to return was Shigetsu Sasaki (1882–1945), who completed his Zen training in Japan and came again to the United States as a roshi with the new name of Sokei-an. His settlement in New York in 1928 marked the beginning of a continuous Rinzai history in America.

Soto Zen came to the United States in 1903. It began in Hawaii when the Reverend Senyei Kawahara came to Honolulu and erected a temple on the West Loch side of Pearl Harbor. Within a few years, Ryuki Hirai, another Soto priest, joined him and built a temple at Waialua to the north of Oahu. Other temples were added on Maui and Kauai as later priests arrived. Then, in 1913, Bishop Hosen Isobe (1870–1959) was sent to Honolulu, where a temple was built under his direction the following year. The mission spread to Kona on the largest island, Hawaii, in 1916. (Soto Buddhists look upon the arrival of Bishop Isobe as the beginning of Soto Zen in America.)

After beginning the work in Hawaii, Bishop Isobe brought Soto to California. He organized the Zenshuji Mission (now called the Soto Mission) in the home of Toyokichi Nagasaki in Los Angeles in 1922. The history of Soto Zen in America is continuous from that time.

The history of Zen in America, like the history of Buddhism, would be incomplete without mention of those non-Asian Americans who played a significant role in its spread and influence. Notable is Ruth Fuller Everett Sasaki (1893–1967), possibly the first American student of Zen in Japan. She came to New York in 1938 after work in a Japanese monastery and became a prime supporter of the First Zen Institute and editor of *Cat's Yawn*, its first magazine. In 1944, after four years of widowhood, she married Sokei-an Sasaki Roshi (Shigetsu Sasaki), a move that stabilized the institute during the final year of the war. Widowed a second time, she moved to Japan, where she became the first non-Asian priest and abbess of a temple, the Ryosen-an, and spent her life translating her late husband's work.

Chester F. Carlson (1906–1968), who discovered the process of xerography, was typical of several wealthy benefactors of Zen Buddhism. He was the first founder of the Zen Mountain Center of Tassajara Springs, California, but kept his support of Buddhist causes quiet during his lifetime.

The American Zen community, unlike the other Buddhist groups with their basis in Japan, has been largely composed of non-Japanese practitioners, and by the end of the twentieth century had freed itself from even the need of Japanese-trained Zen masters. The community is now led by westerners who emerged as the more competent students of the wave of Zen teachers who came into the United States beginning in the later 1960s. They have carried Zen to every part of the United States, though it remains a form of Buddhist life for the elite few.

TIBETAN BUDDHISM IN NORTH AMERICA. Since the Chinese occupation of Tibet in 1959, each of the major Tibetan Buddhist sects and subsects has arrived in the United States, and their representatives have established a number of separate organizations. Unlike Southeast Asian Buddhism, language has not been as significant a factor in slowing the spread of Tibetan Buddhism in the Caucasian population, and by the mid-1980s, Caucasian disciples far outnumbered Tibetan American Buddhists.

Much support for Tibetan Buddhism was generated by American sympathy for their plight in the face of the Chinese. Organizations such as the Tibetan Friendship Group, headquartered in Ojai, California, combined efforts with the Dalai Lama's Office of Tibet in New York City to focus attention upon the political and humanitarian side of the Tibetans' situation.

Since the 1990s, Tibetan Buddhism has become one of the significant growing edges of the North American Buddhist community. Numerous new centers covering the spectrum of Tibetan Buddhist thought have been opened. Buddhists have also been among the most organized and ecumenical of religious communities and are noteworthy for their networking and their presence on the Internet. In the United States, Tibetan Buddhists were prominent in the formation of the American Buddhist Congress, modeled somewhat on the National Council of Churches.

Notable in the rise of Tibetan Buddhism has been the Fourteenth Dalai Lama. Tenzin Gyatso, born Llhamo D^ndrub in 1935, has emerged as a skillful leader of the Tibetan community in exile as well as an articulate and personable exponent of Vajrayana Buddhism to non-Tibetans. He moves freely from academic settings to leadership of ritual occasions and informal conversations with seekers. His emergence as a prominent world religious and political leader, though the total Tibetan Buddhist community now numbers only a few million, has been punctuated by his receiving the Nobel Peace Prize (1989), honorary Canadian citizenship (2006), and the U.S. Congressional Gold Medal (2007).

WESTERN BUDDHISTS. The growth of Buddhism in America as a result of Japanese emigration, coupled with the increase of world religious studies in American universities, set the stage for a number of Americans to become Buddhists. They were largely attracted by Buddhist philosophy and ethics, but followed their studies with full identification with the faith. Often gaining their understanding from books instead of Buddhist religious teachers, they found like-minded believers and formed Buddhist study societies. Typical of the Western-led Buddhist societies, such as the English-language groups founded by Ernest Hunt (1876–1967) after World War I in Hawaii, has been a desire to transcend the sectarian rivalries within Buddhism.

Among the first Westerners attracted to Buddhism, though never a professing Buddhist, was Paul Carus (1852–1919) of the Open Court Publishing Company in LaSalle, Illinois. Attracted to Zen Master Soyen Shaku at the World's Parliament of Religions in 1893, he saw Buddhism as a worthy nontheistic alternative to the Christianity he had already rejected. In 1894 he published his compilation of Buddhist texts, *The Gospel of the Buddha*, and sent it to Soyen Shaku in Japan, who gave it to Daisetz Teitaro Suzuki to translate into Japanese. Carus later brought Suzuki to Illinois, and from their collaboration came one of the first major thrusts of American Buddhist history.

Central to the rise of Buddhism in America has been the work of a number of non-Asians who were attracted to the philosophy of Buddhism and became articulate spokespeople to an audience never reached by the Asian priests. Such a person was Dwight Goddard (1861–1939), who formed the Fellowship Following Buddha, which operated out of his home in Thetford, Vermont. Ernest Hunt, who became a Buddhist on the eve of taking his orders as an Anglican priest, settled in Hawaii in 1915 and became head of the English Department of the Honpa Hongwanji in 1927. He was the main interpreter to the English-speaking Hawaiians for the next 40 years. Mary Elizabeth Foster (1844–1930), a Honolulu heiress, was typical of several wealthy converted Buddhists who contributed financially to its promulgation. The Fosters had become interested in Buddhism through Dr. Wilhelm Hillebrand (1821–1886) of Germany, and they became heavy investors in the Banaras excavations in India at the place where Buddha was enlightened. (The Soto Temple in Honolulu is built on an Indian model.) The botanical gardens in Honolulu are named for Mary Foster.

Like many non-Christian religions, Buddhism profited greatly from participation in the 1893 World's Parliament of Religions in connection with the Columbian Exposition in Chicago, Illinois. In all, seven papers on Buddhism were presented, two by Anagarika Dharmapala (1864–1938) of Sri

Lanka. They covered the basics of Buddha's life, the Hinayana (of Siam), the Mahayana (of Japan), and Buddha's teaching. Dharmapala particularly tried to show Buddhism's superiority, and the several Japanese speakers tried to counter what they believed to have been unjust criticism of Buddhism by non-Japanese. "There are very few countries in the world so misunderstood as Japan," began Kinza Riuge Hirai in his address ("What Buddhism Teaches of Man's Relation to God, and Its Influence on Those Who Have Received It," 1894, p. 395). The special program on Buddhism to the whole congress on the evening of September 26 featured addresses by Hirai, Soyen Shaku, Jitsuzen Ashitzu, and Swami Vivekananda, a Hindu who offered his own appreciation of Buddha. Of significance was the absence of any representative of Buddhism from China.

Buddhist groups in America are of three kinds. Most are transplanted Chinese, Japanese, and other Asian sects that keep more or less close contact with a parent body. This contact may be formal and organizational, or may be merely by the continuation of a teaching. The second kind are schismatic groups. Schisms have occurred over differences of practice and emphasis, beliefs, and race. A common pattern in Buddhist groups is for a basically Asian body to grow by addition of Caucasians, only to find itself splintering along racial, ethnic, or linguistic lines as soon as the Caucasian members are a large enough group. The third type of body is the philosophical Buddhist center formed usually around one or more leaders who have settled in the United States after studying in Japan.

SHINTO.

Shinto, "the way of the gods," is the indigenous religion of Japan. Its polytheistic *kami* were, by and large, essentially the patronal deities of the *uji*, or clans, of ancient Japan. They were also associated with nature since their worship was often conducted in beautiful locations that engendered a great sense of natural awe, such as waterfalls.

Shinto holds to a strong sense of purity, as against ritual pollution. Hence, its shrines are often located outside the human community or on its fringes, away from the pollutions of blood, sickness, and death, and amid the natural purity of nature. Even those shrines now located in the midst of modern cities are situated, if possible, in a parklike setting amid a few stately trees. Shintoists ritually purify themselves before worship.

Most Shinto kami are of mythological background and are rooted in local communities. Some Shinto myths, especially those important to the imperial house, are contained in two of Japan's oldest books, the *Kohiki* (712 C.E.) and the *Nihonshoki* (720 C.E.). They tell of the generation of the Japanese Islands and the kami by the primal parents Izanagi and Izanami, and of the goddess Amaterasu, associated with the sun and the ancestress of the imperial family. Some figures in historical times have been enshrined as kami after their deaths, including the Meiji emperor (1852–1912), whose shrine is the most prominent in Tokyo.

Shinto *jinja*, or shrines, are typically modest buildings of simple but graceful lines, demarcated by the distinctive *torii*,

or Shinto gate. A few, influenced by Chinese styles of architecture, are ornate and colorful. A shrine is essentially the symbolic home of its kami. The kami-presence is indicated by such signs as a mirror and *gohei* (zigzag pieces of paper on a stick). Worshippers often approach shrines individually for brief moments of worship, clapping their hands twice before praying.

Shinto public worship centers around *matsuri*, or festivals. They are generally scheduled in accordance with the agricultural cycle, at seed time in the spring, midsummer, or harvest. On these occasions, and more often at larger shrines, priests present offerings, most often vegetables, fruit, rice, rice wine, and seafood, in a solemn and decorous manner, placing them on a table before the shrine's main sanctuary. Then a *norito*, or solemn prayer, is read. After the offerings are removed, other activities involving the participation of the community may occur: *kagura* (sacred dance), processions, carnival-like fairs, even sacred horse races or boat races. These will depend upon the traditions of the community; matsuri are often occasions of local distinctiveness and pride.

Shinto, as the way of the kami, was not thought of as a distinct religion until after the introduction of Buddhism in the sixth century C.E. made it necessary to distinguish it from the imported faith. During the medieval and early modern periods, Shinto shrines were frequently in close association with Buddhist temples, the kami being often thought of as guardians, students, or even alternative expressions of Japan's rich pantheon of Mahayana buddhas and bodhisattvas. After the Meiji Restoration of 1868 commenced Japan's modernization, however, the government forced a draconian separation of shrines and temples, the situation that still generally greets the visitor today.

The increasingly nationalistic regime of 1868 to 1945 also put Shinto under direct state control and used it as a symbol and vehicle of its ideology, emphasizing Shinto's legitimization of the divine authority of the sovereign, in whose name wars were fought and sacrifices demanded. After 1945, Shinto was separated from the state and generally reverted to its local bases, though the emperor still performs certain Shinto rituals in his personal capacity, and the Daijosiai, or Shinto accession rite, was celebrated by Emperor Akihito (b. 1933) in 1990. Most shrines are owned and administered by local organizations. There are also some "sectarian" Shinto groups, registered as such by the prewar government, promoting particular doctrines, practices, or places of pilgrimage. Some of Japan's "new religions," such as Tenrikyo, Konkokyo, and Omoto, have Shinto roots and employ some typically Shinto forms of worship, though they intend worship to be for a monotheistic rather than a polytheistic deity.

Most Japanese maintain a relationship to both Shinto and Buddhism, having traditional ties to both a shrine and a temple. Characteristically, funerals are conducted in temples and weddings are conducted in shrines, since the religion of kami is popularly felt to deal especially with the joyous family and community occasion of this life.

Shinto came to America with the Japanese immigration of the late nineteenth century. A shrine was constructed in Hilo, Hawaii, in 1898, and others followed on both the big island of Hawaii and Oahu. Shinto prospered there until the 1930s, when growing concern over Japanese imperialism led to criticism of Shinto priests as agents of a foreign power. After the Japanese attack on Pearl Harbor in 1941, the shrines were confiscated and their priests interned. However, most of the shrines were either recovered or rebuilt after the war. There have been few Shinto shrines in the mainland United States, apart from tiny altars in homes or places of business. (This section on Shinto was prepared with the cooperation of Robert S. Ellwood.)

JAPANESE NEW RELIGIONS.

There has been a significant amount of literature devoted to studying what have come to be called the Japanese new religions. These are religions that have been founded since 1800, but made their impact in the twentieth century, particularly since religious freedom was declared in Japan after World War II. These religions share a number of characteristics, the most important being their inroads into the membership of the older Buddhist and Shinto faiths.

However, the new religions do not share a common heritage, thought-world, or lifestyle. Groups such as Nichiren Shoshu and Rissho Kosei Kai are clearly variations on Buddhism. A second set of groups, such as Tenrikyo and Konkokyo, are clearly Shinto in basic faith. Seicho-No-Ie is an example of a third grouping, members of which are psychic and metaphysical. This third group has shown in America a movement toward psychic and New Thought advocates. A fourth grouping is made up of a few miscellaneous bodies, of which only one, Perfect Liberty Kyodan, has found its way to the United States.

Characteristic of many of the new groups is the influence of Christianity, though different groups have picked up different elements. "Church," the idea of group worship, has been adopted by many Buddhists. As in India, with the ashram, "church" has shown itself to be a powerful concept. Konkokyo seems to have been influenced by the Roman Catholic confession in its *toritsugi,* a form of group confession and meditation. In no case, at least in those that have come to America, has Christianity become the dominant element.

Since the end of World War II, there has been a steady growth of independent religious life in Japan, signaled by the appearance of several new religions annually. The most recent of these religions have drawn their converts primarily from people born and raised to adulthood after the war; observers of Japanese religion have dubbed these the "new new" religions. A few have had remarkable success in inserting themselves into Japanese life. One such group, the Aum Shinrikyo, a separatist Buddhist group, became the object of intense news coverage following the accusation that its members released a poisonous gas in Tokyo's subway system in 1995.

The appearance of so many new religions in post–World War II Japan became a significant element in subsequently alerting Western scholars to their rise in the West. Japanese observers initially saw the new religions as a particular phenomenon of the postwar situation, but have increasingly regarded them more simply as the product of secular legislation relative to religious freedom, a phenomenon now seen in free countries globally.

SOURCES

General Sources

Buddhist studies have proliferated in religious studies departments in American universities, and Buddhists have themselves established institutions of higher learning, including Naropa University (Boulder, Colorado), the University of the West at Hsi Lai Temple (Hacienda heights, California), Soka University of America (Aliso Viejo, California), Dharma Realm Buddhist University (Talmage, California), and the Institute of Buddhist Studies (Berkeley, California). The work of Buddhist scholars is given focus through the International Association of Buddhist Studies, which may be contacted c/o Section de langues et civilisations orientales, Université de Lausanne, B.F.S.H. 2, CH-1015 Lausanne, Switzerland. The largest collection of materials by and about American Buddhist groups is found in the J. Gordon Melton American Religions Collection at the Davidson Library of the University of California–Santa Barbara.

Ch'en, Kenneth K. S. *Buddhism: The Light of Asia.* Woodbury, NY: Barron's, 1968. 297 pp.

Conze, Edward, trans. *Buddhist Scriptures.* Baltimore, MD: Penguin, 1959. 250 pp.

———. *Buddhism: Its Essence and Development.* New York: Harper & Row, 1959. 223 pp.

Dutt, Nalinaksha. *Buddhist Sects in India.* Delhi, India: Motilal Banarsidass, 1978. 297 pp.

Haga Hideo. *Japanese Folk Festivals Illustrated.* Trans. Fanny Hagin Mayer. Tokyo: Miura, 1970. 223 pp.

Harvey, B. Peter. *An Introduction to Buddhism: Teachings, History, and Practices.* New York: Cambridge University Press, 1990. 374 pp.

Hirai Kinza Riuge. "What Buddhism Teaches of Man's Relation to God, and Its Influence on Those Who Have Received It." In *The World's Congress of Religions: The Addresses and Papers Delivered Before the Parliament,* ed. J. W. Hanson. Chicago: Monarch, 1894. 1,196 pp.

Irons, Edward A. *Encyclopedia of Buddhism.* New York: Facts on File, 2008. 634 pp.

Jayatilleke, K. N. *The Message of the Buddha.* Ed. Ninian Smart. New York: Free Press, 1974. 262 pp.

Kalupahana, David J. *Buddhist Philosophy: A Historical Analysis.* Honolulu: University Press of Hawaii, 1976. 189 pp.

Law, Bimala Churn. *Women in Buddhist Literature* (1927). Varanasi, India: Indological Book House, 1981.

March, Arthur C. *A Buddhist Bibliography.* London: Buddhist Lodge, 1935. 257 pp.

Mulholland, John F. *Hawaii's Religions.* Rutland, VT: Tuttle, 1970. 344 pp.

Robinson, Richard H., and Willard L. Johnson. *The Buddhist Religion: A Historical Introduction.* Belmont, CA: Wadsworth, 1997. 342 pp.

Saunders, E. Dale. *Buddhism in Japan.* Philadelphia: University of Pennsylvania Press, 1964. 328 pp.

Schumann, Hans Wolfgang. *Buddhism: An Outline of Its Teachings and Schools.* Trans. Georg Feuerstein. Wheaton, IL: Theosophical Publishing House, 1973. 200 pp.

Snelling, John. *The Buddhist Handbook: A Complete Guide to Buddhist Schools, Teaching, Practice, and History.* Rochester, VT: Inner Traditions, 1991. 337 pp.

Strong, John S. *The Experience of Buddhism: Sources and Interpretation.* Belmont, CA: Wadsworth, 1995. 367 pp.

The Teaching of Buddha. Tokyo: Bukkyo Dendo Kyokai, 1966. 300 pp.

Buddhism in North America

Coleman, James William. *The New Buddhism: The Western Transformation of an Ancient Tradition.* New York: Oxford University Press, 2001. 272 pp.

Dresser, Marianne, ed. *Buddhist Women on the Edge: Contemporary Perspectives from the Western Frontier.* Berkeley: North Atlantic, 1996. 321 pp.

Fields, Rick. *How the Swans Came to the Lake: A Narrative History of Buddhism in America.* 3rd ed. Boulder, CO: Shambhala, 1992.

Friedman, Lenore. *Meetings with Remarkable Women: Buddhist Teachers in America.* Rev. ed. Boston, MA: Shambhala, 2000. 362 pp.

Hunter, Louise H. *Buddhism in Hawaii: Its Impact on a Yankee Community.* Honolulu: University of Hawaii Press, 1971. 266 pp.

Kalbacker, Catherine Elmes. *Zen in America.* Ph.D. diss. Lansing: University of Michigan, 1972. 213 pp.

Keshima Tetsuden. *Buddhism in America: The Social Organization of an Ethnic Religious Institution.* Westport, CT: Greenwood Press, 1977. 272 pp.

Layman, Emma McCoy. *Buddhism in America.* Chicago: Nelson-Hall, 1976. 342 pp.

Lorie, Peter, and Julie Fookes, comp. *The Buddhist Directory: The Total Resource Guide.* Rutland, VT: Tuttle, 1997. 424 pp.

Melton, J. Gordon. *A Bibliography of Buddhism in America, 1880–1940.* Santa Barbara, CA: Institute for the Study of American Religion, 1985. 13 pp.

Morreale, Don, ed. *The Complete Guide to Buddhist America.* Boston: Shambhala, 1973. 403 pp.

Peiris, William. *The Western Contribution to Buddhism.* Delhi, India: Motilal Bonarsidass, 1973. 287 pp.

Prebish, Charles S. *American Buddhism.* North Scituate, MA: Duxbury Press, 1979. 220 pp.

———. *Luminous Passage: The Practice and Study of Buddhism in America.* Berkeley: University of California Press, 1999. 345 pp.

Prebish, Charles S, and Kenneth K. Tanaka, eds. *The Faces of Buddhism in America.* Berkeley: University of California Press, 1998. 350 pp.

Rapaport, Al, comp. *Buddhism in America: Proceedings of the First Buddhism in America Conference.* Rutland, VT: Tuttle Co., 1998. 566 pp.

Seager, Richard Hughes. *Buddhism in America.* New York: Columbia University Press, 2000. 336 pp.

Sidor, Ellen S., ed. *A Gathering of Spirit: Women Teaching in American Buddhism.* Cumberland, RI: Primary Point Press, 1987. 156 pp.

Tamney, Joseph B. *American Society in the Buddhist Mirror.* New York: Garland, 1992. 191 pp.

Tsomo, Karma Lekshe, ed. *Buddhism through American Women's Eyes.* Ithaca, NY: Snow Lion, 1995. 184 pp.

Tweed, Thomas A. *The American Encounter with Buddhism, 1844–1912: Victorian Culture and the Limits of Dissent.* Chapel Hill: University of North Carolina Press, 2000. 280 pp.

Williams, Duncan Ryuken, and Christopher S. Queen, eds. *American Buddhism: Methods and Findings in Recent Scholarship.* Richmond, U.K.: Curzon Press, 1999. 328 pp.

Theravada Buddhism

Dhiravamsa, V. R. *The Way of Non-Attachment: The Practice of Insight Meditation.* New York: Schocken, 1975. 160 pp.

Dutt, Sukumar. *Buddhism in East Asia: An Outline of Buddhism in the History and Culture of the Peoples of East Asia.* New Delhi: Indian Council for Cultural Relations, 1966. 225 pp.

Hamilton-Merritt, Jane. *A Meditator's Diary: A Western Woman's Unique Experiences in Thailand Temples.* New York: Harper & Row, 1976. 155 pp.

Hein, Jeremy. *From Vietnam, Laos, and Cambodia: A Refugee Experience in the United States.* New York: Twayne, 1995. 193 pp.

Jumsai, M. L. Manich. *Understanding Thai Buddhism.* Bangkok, Thailand: Chalermnit Press, 1973. 124 pp.

Numrich, Paul David. *Old Wisdom in the New World: Americanization in Two Immigrant Theravada Buddhist Temples.* Knoxville: University of Tennessee Press, 1996. 181 pp.

Japanese Mayahana Buddhism

Anesaki, Masaharu. *Nichiren: The Buddhist Prophet.* Cambridge, MA: Harvard University Press, 1949. 160 pp.

Buddhist Denominations and Schools in Japan. Tokyo: Bukkto Dendo Kyokai, 1984. 127 pp.

Earhart, H. Byron. *Religion in the Japanese Experience: Sources and Interpretations.* 2nd ed. Belmont, CA: Wadsworth, 1997. 312 pp.

———. *Japanese Religion: Unity and Diversity.* 4th ed. Belmont, CA: Wadsworth, 2004. 299 pp.

Ketelaar, James Edward. *Of Heretics and Martyrs in Meiji Japan: Buddhism and Its Persecution.* Princeton, NJ: Princeton University Press, 1990. 285 pp.

Murthy, K. Krishna. *Buddhism in Japan.* Delhi, India: Sundeep Prakashan, 1989. 132 pp.

Nakai, Gendo. *Shinran and His Religion of Pure Faith.* Kyoto, Japan: Shinshu Research Institute, 1937. 260 pp.

Suzuki, Beatrice Lane. *Mahayana Buddhism.* 3rd ed. New York: Macmillan, 1969. 158 pp.

Yanagawa, Keiichi, ed. *Japanese Religions in California: A Report on Research within and without the Japanese-American Community.* Tokyo: University of Tokyo, 1983.

Zen Buddhism

Becker, Ernest. *Zen: A Rational Critique.* New York: Norton, 1961. 192 pp.

Dumoulin, Heinrich. *A History of Zen Buddhism.* Trans. Paul Peachey. New York: Pantheon, 1963. 335 pp.

Humphreys, Christmas. *A Western Approach to Zen: An Enquiry.* Wheaton, IL: Theosophical Publishing House, 1972. 212 pp.

Kraft, Kenneth, ed. *Zen: Tradition and Transition.* New York: Grove Press, 1988. 240 pp.

Storlie, Erik Fraser. *Nothing on My Mind: An Intimate Account of American Zen.* Boston: Shambhala, 1996. 244 pp.

Suzuki, D. T. *Zen Buddhism.* Garden City, NY: Doubleday, 1956. 294 pp.

Tworkov, Helen. *Zen in America: Five Teachers and the Search for an American Buddhism.* New York: Kodansha, 1994. 271 pp.

Watts, Alan. *The Way of Zen.* New York: Pantheon, 1968. 236 pp.

Chinese Buddhism

Ch'en, Kenneth. *Buddhism in China: A Historical Survey.* Princeton, NJ: Princeton University Press, 1964. 576 pp.

———. *The Chinese Transformation of Buddhism.* Princeton, NJ: Princeton University Press, 1973. 345 pp.

Gernet, Jacques. *Buddhism in Chinese Society: An Economic History from the Fifth to the Tenth Centuries.* Trans. Franciscus Verellen. New York: Columbia University Press, 1995. 435 pp.

Pachow, W. *Chinese Buddhism: Aspects of Interaction and Reinterpretation.* Washington, DC: University Press of America, 1980. 260 pp.

Thompson, Laurence G. *Chinese Religion: An Introduction.* 5th ed. Belmont, CA: Wadsworth, 1996. 182 pp.

Yu, David C., with Laurence G. Thompson. *Guide to Chinese Religion.* Boston: G. K. Hall, 1985. 200 pp.

Yu Lu K'uan (Charles Luk). *Practical Buddhism.* Wheaton, IL: Theosophical Publishing House, 1973. 167 pp.

Korean Buddhism

Brief Introduction to Korean Buddhism. Los Angeles: Korean Buddhist Sangha Association of Western Territory of the U.S.A., 1984. 38 pp.

Grayson, James Huntley. *Korea: A Religious History.* Oxford: Oxford University Press, 1989. 320 pp.

Kim Duk-Whang. *A History of Religions in Korea.* Seoul, Korea: Daeji Monoonwha-sa, 1988. 487 pp.

Korean Buddhism. Seoul, Korea: Korean Buddhist Chogye Order, 1996.

Lancaster, Lewis R., and C. S. Yu, eds. *Introduction of Buddhism to Korea: New Cultural Patterns.* Berkeley: Asian Humanities Press, 1989. 240 pp.

———. *Assimilation of Buddhism in Korea: Religious Maturity and Innovation in the Silla Dynasty.* Berkeley, CA: Asian Humanities Press, 1991. 250 pp.

Seo, Kyung-Bo. *A Study of Korean Buddhism Approached through the Chidangjip.* Walnut Creek, CA: Walnut Creek Zendo, 1960?. 411 pp.

Shin-yong, Chun, ed. *Buddhist Culture in Korea.* Seoul, Korea: Si-sa-yong-o-sa, 1982. 134 pp.

Tibetan Buddhism

Anderson, Walt. *Open Secrets: A Western Guide to Tibetan Buddhism.* New York: Viking, 1979. 230 pp.

Blofeld, John. *The Tantric Mysticism of Tibet: A Practical Guide.* New York: Causeway, 1970. 257 pp.

Dasgupta, Shashi Bhushan. *An Introduction to Tantric Buddhism.* Boulder, CO: Shambhala, 1974. 211 pp.

Hoffman, Helmut. *The Religions of Tibet.* New York: Macmillan, 1961. 199 pp.

Johnson, Sandy. *The Book of Tibetan Elders: The Life Stories and Wisdom of the Great Spiritual Masters of Tibet.* New York: Riverhead, 1996. 282 pp.

Lopez, Donald S., Jr. *Prisoners of Shangri-La: Tibetan Buddhism and the West.* Chicago: University of Chicago Press, 1999. 283 pp.

Paine, Jeffrey. *Re-Enchantment: Tibetan Buddhism Comes to the West.* New York: Norton, 2004. 278 pp.

Payne, Richard K., ed. *Tantric Buddhism in East Asia.* Boston: Wisdom, 2006.

Powers, John. *Introduction to Tibetan Buddhism.* Rev. ed. Ithaca, NY: Snow Lion, 2007.

Sopa, Lhundup, and Jeffery Hopkins. *Practice and Theory of Tibetan Buddhism.* New York: Grove Press, 1976. 164 pp.

Thurman, Robert A. F. *Inside Tibetan Buddhism: Rituals and Symbols Revealed.* San Francisco: Collins, 1995. 110 pp.

Shinto

Aston, W. G. *Shinto: The Way of the Gods.* London: Longmans Green, 1905. 390 pp.

Ballou, Robert O. *Shinto: The Unconquered Enemy.* New York: Viking, 1945. 239 pp.

Bocking, Brian. *A Popular Dictionary of Shinto.* New York: McGraw-Hill, 1997.

Breen, John, and Mark Teeuwen, eds. *Shinto in History.* Richmond, U.K.: Curzon Press, 2000. 368 pp.

Hardacre, Helen. *Shinto and the State, 1868–1988.* Princeton, NJ: Princeton University Press, 1991. 224 pp.

Littleton, C. Scott. *Shinto: Origins, Rituals, Festivals, Spirits, Sacred Places.* New York: Oxford University Press, 2002. 112 pp.

Ross, Floyd Hiatt. *Shinto: The Way of the Gods.* Boston: Beacon Press, 1965. 187 pp.

Sectarian Shinto (The Way of the Gods). Tokyo: *Japan Times & Mail,* 1939. 62 pp.

Taoism

Blofeld, John. *Taoism: The Road to Immortality.* Boulder, CO: Shambhala, 1978. 195 pp.

Cleary, Thomas S. *Vitality, Energy, Spirit: A Taoist Source Book.* Boston: Shambhala, 1991. 281 pp.

Kohn, Livia, ed. *The Taoist Experience: An Anthology.* Albany: State University of New York Press, 1993. 404 pp.

———. *Daoism and Chinese Culture.* Boston: Three Pines Press, 2001. 228 pp.

Legge, James, trans. *I Ching Book of Changes.* New Hyde Park, NY: University Books, 1964. 448 pp.

Miller, James. *Daoism: A Short Introduction.* Oxford: OneWorld, 2003.

Pas, Julian F. *Historical Dictionary of Taoism.* Lanham, MD: Scarecrow Press, 1998. 480 pp.

Robinet, Isabelle. *Taoism: Growth of a Religion.* Stanford, CT: Stanford University Press, 1997. 320 pp.

Waley, Arthur. *The Way and Its Power: Study of the* Tao Te Ching *and its Place in Chinese Thought* (1934). London: Routledge, 2005. 262 pp.

Welch, Holmes. *Taoism: The Parting of the Way.* Boston: Beacon Press, 1965. 194 pp.

Confucianism

Chai, Ch'u, and Winberg Chai. *Confucianism.* Woodbury, NY: Barron's, 1973. 202 pp.

De Bary, William, ed. *Sources of Chinese Tradition.* 2nd ed. 2 vols. New York: Columbia University Press, 1999. 656 pp.

Lopez, Donald, ed. *Religions of China in Practice.* Princeton, NJ: Princeton University Press, 1996. 472 pp.

Taylor, Rodney L. *The Way of Heaven: An Introduction to the Confucian Religious Life.* Boston: Shambhala, 1986. 37 pp.

The Wisdom of Confucius. New York: Books, Inc., 1960. 236 pp.

Yao Xizhong. *Introduction to Confucianism.* Cambridge, U.K.: Cambridge University Press, 2000.

New Religions of Japan

Clarke, Peter B. *Bibliography of Japanese New Religious Movements.* Richmond, U.K.: Japan Library, 1999. 276 pp.

———, ed. *Japanese New Religions in Global Perspective.* Richmond, U.K.: Curzon Press, 2000. 321 pp.

Clarke, Peter B., and Jeffrey Somers, eds. *Japanese New Religions in the West.* Richmond, Surrey, UK: Curzon Press, 1994. 180 pp.

Ellwood, Robert S., Jr. *The Eagle and the Rising Sun: Americans and the New Religions of Japan.* Philadelphia: Westminster Press, 1974. 224 pp.

McFarland, H. Neill. *The Rush Hour of the Gods: A Study of New Religious Movements in Japan.* New York: Macmillan, 1967. 267 pp.

Offner, Clark B., and Henry van Straelen. *Modern Japanese Religions, with Special Emphasis upon Their Doctrines of Healing.* New York: Twayne, 1963. 296 pp.

Thomsen, Harry. *The New Religions of Japan.* Rutland, VT: Tuttle, 1963. 268 pp.

❀ Intrafaith Organizations

American Buddhist Congress

3835R E Thousand Oaks Blvd., Ste. 450, Westlake Village, CA 91362

The American Buddhist Congress grew out of an informal meeting of American Buddhist leaders in Boulder, Colorado, on August 24, 1986. They signed a declaration calling for the formation of such an organization and issued a call to all of the Buddhist organizations in the country to join them in its formation. They took as their common ground the essential teachings of Sakyamuni Buddha, especially the Four Noble Truths. The group formed an ad hoc committee, which in turn appointed two chairpersons, the Ven. Dr. Havanpola Ratanasara (1920–2000) and Rev. Karl Springer, to facilitate the arrangement of a convocation in 1987. At that convocation, hosted by the Kwan Um Sa Temple (Korean) in Los Angeles, the American Buddhist Congress was initiated and a constitution adopted.

The congress attempts to bring Buddhists together in projects for the common good, to promote understanding between the various Buddhist traditions, to educate the American public about Buddhism, and to carry out social, educational, cultural, and humanitarian projects.

The congress operates through an advisory council, which sets policy, and an executive council, which implements policy. There are several standing committees, including an education and promotion committee and a humanitarian committee. The congress in 2008 was headed by its executive president, Rev. Henry Shinn, who was assisted by two vice presidents (Ms. Ramya Gunesekera and Rev. Glenn Hughes).

Membership: In 1995 the congress reported 136 affiliated organizations.

Periodicals: *Journal of the American Buddhist Congress.*

Sources:

American Buddhist Congress. www.americanbuddhistcongress.org.

American Zen Teachers Association

For information: office@americanzenteachers.org

The American Zen Teachers Association (AZTA) is a fellowship of second-generation American Buddhist teachers from the Japanese Zen, Chinese Chan, and Korean Son traditions. It began informally in the late 1980s as the Second Generation Teachers Group, from the small group of westerners who had received either teaching authorization or dharma transmission from the pioneering Asian Zen teachers operating in the United States beginning in the 1960s. Through the 1990s the number of second-generation teachers grew dramatically, and a third generation, of their students, began to emerge. In the following decade more than 100 teachers affiliated with the AZTA.

The AZTA exists to facilitate contact and the exchange of information among authorized teachers in recognized Zen lineages; it does not itself issue any credentials. Membership is limited to approved teachers. Members may attend the annual meetings at which they discuss issues ranging from ethics to leading ceremonies to fundraising. The web site maintains a list of centers under the care of the affiliated members.

Membership: In 2008 there were approximately 100 members.

Sources:

American Zen Teachers Association. www.americanzenteachers.org/.

Buddhist Council of the Midwest

1812 Washington St., Evanston, IL 60202

The Buddhist Council of the Midwest (BCM) is an organization for all Buddhist groups in Chicago and the U.S. Midwest. The BCM was officially incorporated as a nonprofit religious organization by the State of Illinois on October 21, 1987, but it had its origin in the spring of 1984. At an American Buddhist Association meeting, Rev. Sunnan Kubose mentioned the desirability of getting all local Buddhists together in fellowship. One of the attendees at this meeting was Wayne Jones, who mentioned this idea to Phra Sunthorn Plamintr, a monk at the Thai Buddhist Temple. This led to the first informal meeting, which was held at the Buddhist Temple of Chicago on July 26, 1984.

Those in attendance were: Rev. Sunnan Kubose (Buddhist Temple of Chicago); Rev. Bunsei Ito (Nichiren Buddhist Temple); Wally Muszynski (Chicago Zen Center); Phra Sunthorn Plamintr (Thai Buddhist Temple); Rev. Hong-Sun Oh (Korean Buddhist Temple); Rev. Shunjo Takahashi (Chicago Jodo-shu Buddhist Temple); Achan Sobin S. Namto and Dhananjay Joshi (Chicago Meditation Center); Rev. Thich Thien Quany and Bang Nguyen (Vietnamese Buddhist Association); Ray

Kayano and Ted Miyata (Midwest Buddhist Temple); and Lilly Gleich and Jeanine Wieder (Dharmadhatu).

This initial meeting was followed by further meetings, and with the initiative of Dr. Sunthorn, all groups were invited to participate in an International Visakha '85 Celebration held at the Thai Temple. Because Gautama Buddha's birthday is a major holiday common to all Buddhist traditions, the participants decided that this celebration would be an annual unifying event. The second annual Visakha was sponsored by the Buddhist Temple of Chicago and was held at Northeastern Illinois University on May 17, 1986. The third annual Visakha was a joint organizational effort by all the participating groups and was held at Truman College on May 30, 1987.

Since then, similar regional councils have been formed in California and in New York. A national organization (American Buddhist Congress) has also been established.

The Buddhist Council of the Midwest promotes the spread of the Dharma by fostering the learning and practice of Buddhism in the United States, inclusive of all three Buddhist traditions. Its mission is to be a vehicle of mutual aid and fellowship for Buddhist organizations throughout the Midwest, to celebrate the diversity of Buddhist philosophy and culture, and to represent and advocate for the Buddhist community in the public realm, confronting misunderstandings or misrepresentations of the Dharma and engaging in interreligious dialogue. The founding purposes as stated in the Articles of Incorporation are: to foster the learning and practice of Buddhism; to represent the Midwest Buddhist community in matters affecting its membership; and to pool resources and coordinate efforts by its membership to create an atmosphere of fellowship and cooperation.

Sources:

Buddhist Council of the Midwest. www.buddhistcouncilmidwest.org.

Directory of Midwest Dharma Centers. Evanston, IL: Buddhist Council of the Midwest, annual.

Buddhist Sangha Council of Southern California

1847 Crenshaw Blvd., Los Angeles, CA 90019

The Buddhist Sangha Council of Southern California emerged out of the experiences of the thousands of Buddhists who migrated to the United States following the 1965 change in U.S. immigration laws relative to Asia. Buddhists from across Asia—Sri Lanka, Tibet, Burma, Cambodia, Vietnam, China, Taiwan, and Korea—settled in the United States, with the largest concentrations in Los Angeles, Orange County, and adjacent counties of southern California. Many of these groups experienced the same problems in adjusting to a new land and new language. They also found an entrenched Buddhist establishment already thoroughly Americanized.

The Buddhist Sangha Council grew out of a need to give expression to Buddhist unity in a predominantly Christian country and to provide assistance to newly arriving immigrants, thousands of whom settled annually in southern California. The council sponsors an annual community-wide celebration of Buddha's birthday each spring and has represented the Buddhist community to the government, in community activity, and in the media. In 1986 it became an official regional center of the World Fellowship of Buddhists.

The Sangha Council set as its primary goals greater communication, understanding, and cooperation among Buddhist groups in southern California and support and promotion of Buddhism and Buddhist activities. Dr. Havanpola Ratanasara spearheaded the early efforts with the close assistance of the Late Ven. Dr. Thich Thien-An, the late Ven. Dr. Faitana Khampiro, and Ven. Phra Thepsopon, who later returned to Bangkok. Other founding members included Vens. Subhadra Goldwater, Thich Man-Giac, Kim Do Anh, Walpola Piyananda, Pannila Ananda, Karuna Dharma, and 10 other Sangha members, both Asian- and U.S.-born.

The council headquarters, first located at Lao Wat Buddhagodom, moved in 1981 to Dharma Vijaya Buddhist Vihara, and then in 1985 to the College of

Buddhist Studies. Although the membership has grown slowly (but consistently), the council has been very active in many different areas.

Membership: Membership in the council is open only to ordained clergy; it includes representatives of most of the ethnic Buddhist communities in southern California. In 1997 the council reported 50 members.

Sources:

Buddhist Sangha Council of Southern California.
www.urbandharma.org/ratana/ratana2/sanghacouncil.html.

Hawaii Buddhist Council

c/o N&K CPAs Inc., 1001 Bishop St., Pacific Tower 1760, Honolulu, HI 96813-3696

Buddhists in Hawaii, one of the two places in the United States where a significant number of Buddhists have settled, first organized ecumenically in the 1930s through the International Buddhist Institute, which worked to spread a spirit of Buddhist unity in the face of its divisions into a variety of sectarian bodies. That effort was largely ended by the appearance in 1935 of a Buddhist leader with the Honpa Hongwanji, the largest of the Japanese groups, who rejected the ideals of the institute. The whole of organized Buddhism on the Hawaiian islands was disrupted following the 1941 bombing of Pearl Harbor. After World War II, in the 1950s a second effort at Buddhist cooperative activity was made with the formation of the Hawaii Buddhist Council, which was modeled on the councils of Christian churches that had been established across the United States.

The council has facilitated communication between the various Buddhist bodies and has provided the Buddhist community with a united voice to speak to the larger community of non-Buddhists. Among its first actions, the council in 1963 proposed that April 8 be designated Buddha's Day, a state holiday in Hawaii. The council argued that such a designation would exemplify American tolerance and acceptance of religious freedom and provide an opportunity for Japanese Americans to educate the general public about Buddhism. After a statewide debate, a compromise bill did pass the state senate naming April 8 as Buddha Day, but not in such a way as to designate it a state holiday.

The council sponsors a variety of educational programs on Buddhism and Hawaiian Buddhist history and culture.

Membership: Members of the council include the Higashi Hongwanji Mission of Hawaii, Honpa Hongwanji Mission of Hawaii, Jodo Mission of Hawaii, Nichiren Mission of Hawaii, Shingon Mission of Hawaii, Soto Mission of Hawaii, and Tendai Mission of Hawaii.

Korean Buddhist Sangha Association of Western Territory in U. S.A.

Current address not obtained for this edition.

Korean Buddhism became established in the United States in the 1970s when Buddhists arrived in large numbers following the 1965 changes in the laws regulating immigration from Asia. Members and priests of different Korean Buddhist traditions settled across the United States, though the largest numbers were in California, New York, and Illinois. The Sangha Association emerged in the early 1980s and became known during its participation in the Korean Cultural Exhibition as part of Korea Expo 84. It has published a directory of all of the Korean Buddhist centers in the United States and Canada.

Sources:

Brief Introduction to Korean Buddhism. Los Angeles: Korean Buddhist Sangha
Association of Western Territory in U.S.A., 1984.

Los Angeles Buddhist Church Federation

2203 W Jefferson Blvd., Los Angeles, CA 90018

Participants in the Los Angeles Buddhist Church Federation include the Higashi Honganji Betsuin, Jodoshu Betsuin Temple, Koyasan Betsuin Temple, Long Beach Buddhist Church, Nichiren Buddhist Temple, Nishi Hongwanji Betsuin, and Zenshuji Soto Mission, most of which are located in the section of Los Angeles known as Little Tokyo.

Remarks: In the 1970s Buddhists from across Asia—Sri Lanka, Tibet, China, Kampuchea, Vietnam, Cambodia, Burma, Korea—arrived in California. They organized the Buddhist Sangha of Southern California and became the basis for the more recent organization of the American Buddhist Congress. As a whole, the Japanese, who represent a community of older immigrants to the United States, have remained cordial but organizationally aloof from the latest generation of Buddhists to settle in southern California.

Sources:

Kokoro no Kate. 7 vols. Los Angeles: Los Angeles Buddhist Church Federation,
1981–1988.

Soto Zen Buddhist Association

For information: info@szba.org

Though introduced into North America in the 1890s, Soto Zen Buddhism did not experience real growth in the United States until the 1960s. In the following generation, it emerged around a group of teachers from Japan who in turn trained and gave dharma transmission to non-Asian, second-generation teachers. As the original masters finished their careers, many from the second generation became organizationally independent, founding new Zen centers and associations.

As the number of associations multiplied, the leadership of the Soto Shu in Japan (to which many of the new American Soto groups attempted to relate) recognized a need to bring some unity to the burgeoning tradition, and in 1996 they communicated their desire that a organization of Soto priests be created in North America. In response, the Soto Zen Buddhist Association (SZBA) in America was founded by Bernard Tetsugen Glassman, Chozen Jan Bays, Daido John Loori, Genpo Merzel, Jakusho Bill Kwong, Keido Les Kaye, Sojun Mel Weitsman, and Tenshin Reb Anderson. Glassman was named the first president.

The organization grew slowly for several years, but then took off in 2000. It currently includes most of the Zen teachers in North America. It held its first national meeting in 2004. Its major accomplishment was the development of the Soto Zen Training Institute for priest disciples.

The SZBA attempts to speak nationally for the Soto tradition and to build a spirit of cooperation among the various teachers and associations. It especially honors six pioneering Zen teachers—Shunryu Suzuki (1904–1971), Jiyu Kennett (1924–1996), Taizan Maezumi (1931–1995), Kobun Chino (1938–2002), Dainin Katagiri (1928–1990), and the still living Tozen Akiyama Roshi.

Membership: Not reported.

Sources:

Soto Zen Buddhist Association. www.szba.org/.

White Plum Asanga

c/o Zen Mountain Monastery, PO Box 197, South Plank Rd., Mount Tremper, NY 12457

The White Plum Asanga is an association of the successors in the lineage of Soto Zen teacher Baian Hakujun Daiosho. The stated purpose of the asanga is to promote and maintain harmony among the various Dharma successors in the lineage, many of whom are currently leaders of otherwise independent Zen centers. It provides a forum for conflict resolution, study and training, and the promotion of communication among its members as well as the leaders of other Buddhist schools and traditions.

Membership in White Plum Asanga is of several kinds. Voting members are those who are Shiho Dharma successors in the lineage of Taizan Maezumi Daiosho, best known as the founder of the Zen Center of Los Angeles, by whom most of the members were initially trained. Honorary membership is extended to the successors of Baian Hakujun Daiosho, and participating membership is drawn from Shiho Dharma transmission, denkai, Dharma holders, or other senior students of the Dharma successors.

In 2008 the White Plum Asanga's web site listed 58 practice centers in the United States.

Membership: Current honorary members include Kojun Kuroda, Koshinji, Japan; Takeshi Kuroda, Zenkoji, Japan; and Junyu Kuroda, Kirigayaji, Japan. Officers are retired president Bernard Tetsugen Glassman (Zen Community of New York); president Dennis Genpo Merzel (Kanzeon Zen Center); vice president John Daido Loori (Zen Mountain Monastery); secretary Susan Myoyu Andersen (Northwest Chicago Zen Group); and treasurer Gerry Shishin Wick (Great Mountain Zen Center).

Voting members include Jan Chozen Bays (Zen Community of Oregon); John Tesshin Sanderson, Mexico; Alfred Jitsudo Ancheta, California; Charles Tenshin Fletcher (Zen Mountain Center, Mexico); Nicolee Jikyo Miller-McMahon (Three Treasures Zen Community); William Nyogen Yeo, California; and Charlotte Joko Beck (Ordinary Mind Zen School).

Sources:

White Plum Asanga. www.whiteplum.org.

World Fellowship of Buddhists

616 Benjasiri Park, Soi Medhinivet off Sukhumvit 24, Sukhumvit Rd., Bangkok, 10110 Thailand

The World Fellowship of Buddhists (WFB) was founded in 1950 in Colombo, Sri Lanka, by 129 delegates representing 27 countries of Asia, Europe, and North America, as well as representatives of the major schools of Buddhism—Theravada, Mahayna, and Vajrajana. Five aims and objectives were incorporated into the constitution:

1. To promote, among the members, strict observance and practice of the teachings of the Buddha;

2. To secure unity, solidarity, and brotherhood among Buddhists;

3. To propagate the sublime doctrine of the Buddha;

4. To organize and carry on activities in the field of social, educational, cultural, and other humanitarian services; and

5. To work for happiness, harmony, and peace on earth and to collaborate with other organizations working for the same ends.

In particular, the WFB refrains from involving itself directly or indirectly in any political activity.

The WFB's highest decision-making body is the general conference, held every two years, which determines strategic direction and policy planning at the headquarters and at regional centers. The general council is the administrative body; it supervises assets and funds, establishes committees and their personnel, and organizes meetings after the general conference. Decisions of the general conference are implemented by the executive council, in which the WFB president presides over an auxiliary body that assists in the execution of WFB responsibilities. The executive council conducts regular sessions every six months for monitoring and evaluation.

Nine standing committees implement decisions of the general council: the finance committee; the publication, publicity, education, cultural, and art committee; the dhammaduta activities committee; the humanitarian services committee; the unity and solidarity committee; the youth committee; the socio-economic development committee; the women's committee; and Buddhist Pancasila Samadana. In addition, the WFB's World Fellowship of Buddhist Youth promotes peace and solidarity (including the practices of dhamma) among young Buddhists, and the liaison unit of UNESCO and other UN organizations coordinates activities that promote education, science, and culture.

Headquarters of the WFB were in Colombo until 1958 and in Rangoon from then until 1963, when permanent headquarters were established in Bangkok. In 1988 the general conference met at the large Hsi Lai Temple complex in Hacienda Heights, California, the first time the meeting had been held in North America.

Phan Wannamethee has served as president of the WFB since 1999.

Membership: In 2002 the WFB reported more than 140 regional centers in 37 countries worldwide, including the Temple of California, Sonoma Mountain Zen Center, Tibetan Nyingmapa Meditation Centre, Universal Buddhist Fellowship, the Union of Vietnamese Buddhist Churches in the United States of America, Vajradatu, Vietnamese Buddhist Renovation Committee, Vietnamese Theravada Buddhist Sangha Congregation, WFB, Hawaii Regional Centre, and Zen Center of San Francisco. Some of these centers are headquarters of different Buddhist organizations, some local centers of a larger Buddhist fellowship, and some headquarters of ecumenical organizations.

Educational Facilities:

World Buddhist University.

Periodicals: *WFB Newsletter*. • *WFB Journal*. • *WFB Review*.

Sources:

World Fellowship of Buddhists. www.wfb-hq.org/main.html.

The 16th General Conference of the World Fellowship of Buddhists/The Grand Opening of Fo Kuang Shan Hsi Lai Temple, U.S.A., Souvenir Magazine. Hacienda Heights, CA: Fo Kuang Shan Hsi Lai Temple, 1988.

Theravada Buddhism

Abhayagiri Buddhist Monastery

16201 Tomki Rd., Redwood Valley, CA 95470

Alternate Address: International Headquarters: Amaravati Buddhist Centre, Great Gaddesden, Hemel Hempstead, Hertfordshire HP1 2BZ, United Kingdom.

Abhayagiri Buddhist Monastery is a branch of the Amaravati Buddhist Monastery, a Thai Theravada Buddhist organization based in the United Kingdom which in turn is related to the Wat Pah Pong and Wat Pah Nanachat, two forest monastic communities in northeast Thailand. International leadership is provided by the Ven. Ajahn Sumedho (b. 1934), an American who studied with the legendary Thai monk Ajahn Chah.

Sumedho had originally encountered Buddhism while in the U.S. Army in Japan. After completing his college work, he went as a teacher to Thailand, where he became a student of Ajahn Chah. In 1974 he founded Wat Paa Nanachat, which like the other wats influenced by Chah emphasizes the whole lifestyle as practice above a special emphasis on meditation. In 1977 he visited England with Chah and remained there. Two years later he founded the Chithurst Forest Monastery in rural Sussex, from which other similar centers have arisen.

Abhayagiri Monastery is the first monastery in the United States to be established by followers of Ajahn Chah, a respected Buddhist master of the ancient Thai Forest Tradition of Theravada Buddhism.

The origin of the monastery can be traced to Sumedho's visits to northern California in the early 1980s. Over the next 10 years Sumedho developed a devoted following of students. In 1988 they formed the Sanghapala Foundation with the mission of creating a branch monastery of Ajahn Chah's lineage. In 1990 Ajahn Amaro accompanied Ajahn Sumedho to California and thereafter became the central teacher for the California students.

Efforts to establish the California monastery moved slowly until 1995. Before his death, Ven. Master Hsüan Hua, abbot of the City of Ten Thousand Buddhas located in Ukiah, California, instructed his disciples to deed over to Ajahn Chah's disciples 120 acres of forest in Redwood Valley, 15 miles north of the City of Ten Thousand Buddhas. On several occasions Master Hua had made a point of stating that it had been the dream of his life to bring the northern and southern traditions of Buddhism back together again. His offering was one of openhearted, ecumenical friendship. It enabled the communities to be physically close and to relate in an atmosphere of mutual respect and harmony.

In choosing a name for the monastery it seemed appropriate to reflect on the kindness of this offering and the spirit in which it was intended. It also felt important to use a name in the Pali language to confirm the sense of allegiance to the Theravada tradition. The name that was finally settled upon, *Abhayagiri*, means "Fearless Mountain." The original Abhayagiri Monastery was in ancient Sri Lanka at Anurādhapura. That monastery was most notable for welcoming practitioners and teachers from many different Buddhist traditions. They lived there amicably alongside one another, distinct in their particular practices but not separate as communities. During the fourth century Abhayagiri housed 5,000 monks.

While primarily a monastic community, visitors may stay at Abhayagiri for brief periods, especially if attending a retreat, if prior arrangements are made. Once a month, the monks go into San Francisco for public teaching sessions. There is also an affiliated sitting group in Berkeley.

Membership: Not reported.

Sources:

Abhayagiri Buddhist Monastery. www.abhayagiri.org.

Amaravati Buddhist Centre. www.amaravati.org.

Cummings, Joe. *The Meditation Temples of Thailand: A Guide*. Bangkok, Thailand: Wayfarer Books, 1990.

Kornfield, Jack. *A Still Forest Pool*. Wheaton, IL: Theosophical Publishing House, 1985.

Sumrdho, Ajahn. *The Path to the Deathless*. Hemel Hempstead, U.K.: Amaravati, 1985

———. *Teachings of a Buddhist Monk*. Totnes, U.K.: Buddhist Publication Group, 1990.

Ambedkar Mission

9-850 Tapscott, Scarborough, ON, Canada M1X 1N4

The Ambedkar Mission, founded in Toronto in 1979, is an Indian-based Buddhist mission that follows the ideology and social reform program enunciated by Indian reformer Dr. Bhim Rao Ambedkar (1891–1956). Born into a family of untouchables, the lowest caste of Indian society, he rose in 1947 to a prominent position in the government of the newly independent India. During his younger days he had suffered the humiliation and discrimination common to life as an untouchable and campaigned against it. Following India's freedom, he was the country's first minister for law and chair of the committee to frame a new constitution, which he largely wrote and defended once it was presented for adoption in 1948. One passage of the constitution dealt with the issue of untouchability, at least in the eyes of the law.

Before leaving government service Ambedkar began in 1950 to consider Buddhism as a path to help his people. He attended the Buddhist Conference in Ceylon (now Sri Lanka) in 1950 and shortly thereafter decided to become a Buddhist. In so doing he felt he was showing the way away from confusion while necessary changes were made in the economic and political life of the nation. Buddhism was an Indian faith. To deal with the problem of untouchability, a way that did not harm Indian culture or history had to be selected (hence his choice to stay away from Islam and Christianity). He formally embraced Buddhism at a ceremony on October 14, 1956. Unfortunately, he died two months later.

The Ambedkar Mission originally began in Vancouver in 1978 as Ambedkar Memorial Association. After one year Darshan Chaudhary moved from Vancouver to Toronto in June 1979, and Ambedkar Mission was started in the same year with the main objective of propagating the religion and social philosophy of BabaSaheb Dr. Bhim Rao Ambedkar. Yogesh Varhade was the chief organizer at that time. Nasib Sallan was its first president, Ram Parkash Rahul its secretary, Mohan Verdi its treasurer, Jit Lal Jhamat its cultural secretary, and Darshan Chaudhary its joint secretary. Gian Kaura, Mark Vaharade, and Banta Ram Jakkhu were other founding members of the mission. Weekly Buddha *puja* (service) started at the Toronto Maha Vihara in Scarborough because the mission did not have its own place of worship.

The centers of the mission host monks from India several times annually.

Membership: Not reported. There is an affiliated Ambedkar Memorial Association in Vancouver.

Sources:

Ambedkar Mission Canada. ambedkarmission.com.

Dr. Ambedkar Mission International. www.ambedkarmission.org.

Morreale, Don. *The Complete Guide to Buddhist America*. Boston: Shambhala, 1998.

Bhavana Society

Rte. 1, Box 218-3, Back Creek Rd., High View, WV 26808

The Bhavana Society is an independent Theravada Buddhist organization in the Sri Lankan tradition. The forest monastery was established on May 13, 1982, by the Ven. Bhante Henepola Gunaratana and Matthew Flickstein, offering both novices and advanced meditation students the opportunity to study with Gunaratana and his associate, Bhante Yogacacara Rahula. A variety of retreats are offered monthly, and provisions are made for men and women who wish to eventually take monastic vows.

Gunaratana, the author of *Mindfulness in Plain English*, has become a popular Theravada teacher, and associated centers have been established as a result of his speaking tours.

Membership: Not reported. There are associated centers in Largo, Florida, and Fairfax, Virginia.

Periodicals: *Bhavana Society Newsletter*.

Sources:

Bhavana Society. www.bhavanasociety.org.

Gunaratana, Henepola. *Mindfulness in Plain English*. 2nd ed. Somerville, MA: Wisdom Publications, 2002.

Buddhasasananuggaha Association

c/o The Loka Chantha Temple and America Burma Buddhist Association, The Universal Peace Buddha Temple of New York, 619 Bergen St., Brooklyn, NY 11238

The Venerable Mahasi Sayadaw (1904–1982) was born in northern Burma and as a child was recognized for his mastery of Pali Buddhist texts. While still a teenager he was ordained as a *bhikkhu* (monk). As a monk he pursued further intellectual mastery of the Buddhist texts, to which he added his determination to apply the texts to the practice of meditation. He began a search for an appropriate meditation teacher, which he found in the person of the Most Venerable Mingun Jetavan Sayadaw of Thaton. In 1938 Sayadaw began his own career as a teacher of the intensive practice of *satipatthana* (mindfulness), directing his work towards lay people, who had had little opportunity to learn the rigorous meditation technique.

He began teaching meditation at a monastery in a village known as Maha-Si Kyaung because of a large (*maha*) drum (Burmese: *si*) located there. Those whom he taught gave him the name by which he since has been known, Mahasi Sayadaw (*Sayadaw* is Burmese for "Great Teacher"). In 1944 Sayadaw completed his best known treatise, *The Method of Vipassana Meditation*, in which he summarized his view of the process of meditation, in which a consciousness of bodily functions is used to help focus awareness. This type of meditation leads to insight (*vipassana*) into the impermanent (*anicca*), unsatisfactory (*dukkha*), and unsubstantial (*anatta*) nature of all conditioned (i.e., non-*nibbana*) phenomena.

Sayadaw died from a heart attack on August 14, 1982. Some years earlier (1947), several Burmese Buddhists had founded the Buddhasasananuggaha Association in Rangoon. Sir U Thwin, its first president, donated a plot of land for the erection of a meditation center and proposed that Mahasi Sayadaw be invited to teach there. The Buddhasasananuggaha Association became the vehicle for the dissemination of the Mahasi Sayadaw meditation technique around the world, and especially in North America since the mid-1960s.

Sayadaw's approach to Theravada Buddhism and the practice of meditation has been picked up by a number of vipassana centers in the United States, and there are groups of centers especially related to the Buddhasasananuggaha Association, including the Dhammananda Vihara (Half Moon Bay, California), Jetavana Vihara Ky Vien Tu (Washington, D.C.), and the Myanmar Monastery (Columbia, Maryland).

Membership: Approximately one million people worldwide have received formal training in the Mahasi Sayadaw Vipassana technique. There are an estimated several thousand people practicing it in North America. In addition, affiliated centers are found in 39 countries in Asia and Europe.

Sources:

Mahasi Sayadaw. *Insight through Mindfulness*. Kandy, Sri Lanka: Buddhist Publication Society, 1990.

———. *Practical Insight Meditation*. Kandy, Sri Lanka: Buddhist Publication Society, 1971 (Excerpt from *The Method of Vipas-sana Meditation*, 1944).

Nyanaponika Thera. *The Heart of Buddhist Meditation*. York Beach, ME: Samuel Weiser, 1973.

U Sulananda Sayadaw. *The Four Foundations of Mindfulness*. Boston, MA: Wisdom Publications, 1990.

Cambodian Buddhism

Khmer Buddhist Society of New England, 178 Hanover St., Providence, RI 02907

Significant numbers of Cambodians first arrived in the United States in the wake of the terrors of the Khmer Rouge regime of the mid-1970s, when Buddhism was systematically attacked. Reportedly, of 80,000 monks alive at the beginning of the 1980s, only 800 survived. More than 3,600 temples were destroyed, and more than one-half million Cambodians fled the country. The immigration of Cambodian refugees to the United States peaked around 1982 but continued through the decade.

Most instrumental in the formation of the American Cambodian Buddhist community was the Ven. Maha Ghosananda (b. 1924), a disciple of the former head of the Cambodian Buddhist Sangha, the late Samdech Prah Sangha Raja Chuon Noth. Maha Ghosananda happened to be in Thailand when the worst of the troubles in his homeland began. He had completed his studies and adopted the life of a rural ascetic, when refugees began to flood the quiet area in which he had been living. In 1978 he began to establish Buddhist temples in the refugee camps. In 1981 he went to the United States to head the Cambodian Buddhist community in Rhode Island, which became the base for establishing Buddhist temples in refugee communities around the world. A second office was established in Thailand to bring Buddhist monks to the United States. Between 1983 and 1986 more than 80 monks came to Providence, Rhode Island, and were sent to the 41 temples that were opened in the United States and Canada. Ghosananda personally started 30 of these temples. Some of the temples have prospered, such as the one serving the Washington, D.C., area.

In Cambodia, Buddhism was the religion of the state before the rise to power of the Khmer Rouge, and the chief of state was the head of the Buddhist religious leadership. In the United States the organization of the Buddhist community is undergoing transition as it attempts to reorganize without state support and the larger direct cultural support of the community.

Membership: Not reported.

Sources:

Hein, Jeremy. *From Vietnam, Laos and Cambodia: Refugee Experience in the United States*. New York: Twayne Publishers, 1995.

Whitaker, Donald P., et al. *Area Handbook for the Khmer Republic (Cambodia)*. Washington, DC: U. S. Government Printing Office, 1973.

Center for Buddhist Development

c/o Arizona International Buddhist Meditation Center, 432 S Temple, Mesa, AZ 85204

Alternate Addresses: Calm Village Buddhist Temple, 726 W Baseline, Phoenix, AZ 85041; Los Angeles Buddhist Union, c/o Venerable Bhante Chao Chu, Rosemead Buddhist Monastery, 7833 Emerson Pl., Rosemead, CA 91770.

The Center for Buddhist Development (originally called "Meditation Friends") began in 1995 with the initiation of meditation sessions for faculty and students of Arizona State University in Tempe, Arizona. A following developed that included both campus residents and those from the surrounding community, and various sites were occupied until the spring of 1998, when the group moved to its present center, the Calm Village Buddhist Temple in Phoenix. The founder and director of the community is Rev. Kennard-Dhammapala. The widely traveled Dhammapala was ordained as a priest and a monk in the Theravada tradition. He and other leaders in the center have attempted to transcend any particular ethnic Buddhist traditions (e.g., Sri Lankan, Burmese, etc.) in order to focus upon what is considered the "Universal Truths of Sakyamuni Buddha's Teachings as recorded in the Pali Canon." In this regard, they are attempting to create an authentically American Buddhism.

The center promotes a program that includes practice in meditation, mindfulness, Dhamma study, and community engagement. Services and classes are offered in English.

Rev. Dhammapala currently serves as a Buddhist minister, ordained by the Sangha Council of Southern California. He leads meditation and discussion groups for English speakers at the Arizona International Buddhist Meditation Center in Mesa and the Calm Village Buddhist Temple in Phoenix. He is a member of the executive committee of the World Buddhist Sangha Council.

Membership: There are three cooperating meditation centers of the Center for Buddhist Development: the Arizona International Buddhist Meditation Center in Mesa, Arizona, the Calm Village Buddhist Temple in Phoenix, Arizona, and the Vipassana Buddhist Church in Jefferson City, Missouri.

Sources:

Center for Buddhist Development. aztec.asu.edu/worship/buddhist/.

Dhammakaya International Society of California

865 E Monrovia Pl., Azusa, CA 91702

Dhammakaya International Meditation Center (also known as the Dhammakaya International Society of California) is a Theravada center connected with the Sister of Dhammakaya Foundation of Thailand. It was founded in California in 1992. Since its founding, nine additional branch centers have opened across the United States.

Periodicals: *The Light of Peace.*

Sources:

Dhammakaya International Meditation Center. www.dimc.net.

Morreale, Don. *The Complete Guide to Buddhist America*. Boston: Shambhala, 1998.

Dharma Dena

c/o Desert Vipassana Center, HC-1, Box 250, Joshua Tree, CA 92252

Ruth Denison emerged in the 1980s as one of the leading Buddhist teachers in North America, and one of the very few female vipassana teachers. She learned meditation in the tradition of Burmese teacher Sayagyi U Ba Khin (1899–1971) and founded the Desert Vipassana Center, where she leads a regular schedule of retreats of varying lengths. The center is also open for individual retreats. As a result of her teaching, additional centers have been opened around the United States, including Rocky Mountain Insight in Colorado Springs, Colorado, whose leader Lucinda Green received dharma transmission from Denison.

Dhamma Dena Desert Vipassana Center, located in the Mojave Desert in Joshua Tree, southern California, was founded by Denison in 1977. The desert meditation center was blessed by Mahasi Sayadaw and his monks and has served as a zen and vipassana meditation center since the 1970s. Over time, additional buildings and land were acquired. The center has rustic accommodations with a 360-degree view of the mountains and high desert. Students and meditation practitioners come for both formal and self-retreats. Women's retreats are offered in the spring and fall.

Membership: Not reported.

Sources:

Dharma Dena. dhammadena.googlepages.com.

Dhiravamsa Foundation

1660 Wold Rd., Friday Harbor, WA 98250

The Dhiravamsa Foundation, formerly the Vipassana Fellowship of America, was formed by Dhiravamsa, a Thai monk who went to England in 1964 as chief incumbent monk of the Buddha-padipa Temple. He eventually gave up his monk's robe, finding it too confining in his work with westerners. In 1969 he went to the United States and began to teach vipassana meditation, the form of meditation traditional to Thai Buddhism. An initial center was established in New England. Dhiravamsa regularly tours the United States speaking, teaching meditation, and holding retreats. Dhiravamsa's students can also be found in Thailand, Canada, Sweden, Switzerland, Australia, and New Zealand.

Membership: Not reported.

Sources:

Dhirvamsa. *The Way of Non-Attachment*. New York: Schocken Books, 1977.

Insight Meditation Society

Pleasant St., Barre, MA 01005

The Insight Meditation Society began offering meditation retreats rooted in the Theravada Buddhist tradition in 1976. The founding teachers were Jack Kornfield, Sharon Salzberg, and Joseph Goldstein, all of whom had spent many years in India and Southeast Asia studying and practicing Vipassana (insight) meditation under the guidance of meditation masters such as Ajahn Chaa, Anagarika Munindra, Goenka, and Dipa Ma, and more recently, several Burmese masters such as Sayadaws U Pandita, Pa Auk, and U Tejaniya. The Insight Meditation Society consists of two centers, the Retreat Center and the Forest Refuge. The Retreat Center offers a yearly schedule of meditation retreats lasting in duration from a weekend to three months. The Forest Refuge is open to experienced meditators for sustained, long-term personal retreats. Stays at the Forest Refuge last from one week to a year or more.

Membership: The society is not a membership organization. In 2008 the society reported 19,000 adherents in the United States, 1,183 in Canada, and an additional 1,157 worldwide.

Educational Facilities:

Barre Center for Buddhist Studies, Barre, Massachusetts.

Periodicals: *Insight Newsletter*.

Sources:

Insight Meditation Society. dharma.org/ims/.

Fronsdal, Gil. "Insight Meditation in the United States: Life, Liberty, and the Pursuit of Happiness." In *The Faces of Buddhism in America*, ed. Charles S. Prebish and Kenneth K. Tanaka. Berkeley: University of California Press, 1998.

Goldstein, Joseph. *The Experience of Insight*. Boulder, CO: Shambhala, 1976.

———. *One Dharma: The Emerging Western Buddhism*. New York: HarperCollins, 2002.

Kornfield, Jack. *Living Buddhist Masters*. Santa Cruz, CA: Unity Press, 1977.

Kornfield, Jack, and Paul Brieter. *A Still Forest Pool*. Wheaton, IL: Theosophical Publishing House, 1985.

Salzberg, Sharon. *Lovingkindness: The Revolutionary Art of Happiness*. Boston: Shambhala, 1995.

———. *Faith: Trusting Your Own Deepest Experience*. New York: Penguin Putnam, 2002.

———, ed. *Voices of Insight*. Boston: Shambhala, 1999.

International Organization of Burmese Buddhist Sanghas

c/o Burmese Buddhist Association, 15 W 110 Forest Ln., Elmhurst, IL 60657

Throughout the 1970s, people from Myanmar (formerly known as Burma) began to arrive in the United States. The visit of the Ven. Taungpupu Kaba-Aye Sayadaw and several monks, who were on a goodwill tour in 1979, played an important role in the organization of these new U.S. residents. U. Silananda, one of those monks, decided to remain in the United States to provide leadership for Burmese Buddhists. He founded the Dhammananda Vihara in Daly City, California (serving primarily Burmese Americans), and the Berkeley Vipassana Center (serving primarily non-Asian students). Throughout the 1980s a number of teaching centers emerged, such as the Burmese Buddhist Association in suburban Chicago, founded in 1987. These centers associated with each other in the International Organization of Burmese-Buddhist Sanghas.

Membership: Not reported.

International Buddhist Meditation Center

928 S New Hampshire, Los Angeles, CA 90006

The International Buddhist Meditation Center was founded in 1970 by Thich Thien-An (1926–1980), a Vietnamese monk and scholar who had come to the United States in 1966 as a visiting professor of languages and philosophy at the University of California Los Angeles. Although he had intended to return to Vietnam in 1967, he stayed at the request of a group of students who wanted him to become their teacher. In 1973 he started the College of Oriental Studies as an education enterprise adjacent to the center. Following the fall of Saigon and the end of the Vietnam War in 1975, as one of the few Vietnamese scholars in the United States, Thien-An was called to serve a unique function. His energies began to be directed toward meeting the needs of the masses of war refugees, especially those resettling in the United States. He provided, in part through bilingual monks he had trained, both secular and religious services for the new immigrants. He was especially known for having founded most of the Vietnamese Buddhist temples established in the 1970s in the United States, and was recognized during the last years of his life as the patriarch of Vietnamese Buddhism in America.

Thich Thien-An was of the Lieu-Quan Zen School, which dates to its founder Thiet-Dieu Lein-Quan (d. 1743) in the eighteenth century. It is one of several popular Buddhist schools in Vietnam. However, in the United States, Thien-An began to emphasize a nonsectarian approach to Buddhism that slowly moved toward an indigenous American expression of Buddhist life and thought. As an expression of the nonsectarian approach, Buddhist leaders from a wide variety of national backgrounds and diverging lineages have been invited to teach at the center, and different Buddhist groups have been granted use of the center facilities for their own retreats and teaching sessions. The training of monks has followed a similar pattern, with monks from various traditions serving as preceptors for those in training, and with ordination services borrowing from several traditions.

The Sunday worship service reflects the syncretic nature of Buddhism practiced at the center. Chanting in English, along with the more common chanting in Pali, Sanskrit, and Japanese, forms part of the daily service. Special chantings in Pali, Japanese, and Vietnamese are done in special ceremonies, and then repeated in English. Wedding ceremonies are a blend of eastern and western elements.

The center was conceived as a place where practice and education would integrate to produce the total practitioner. It strives to be one location that combines Sunday services, daily meditation, monthly retreats, and a full range of evening classes to provide both spiritual and educational experiences for the devotee.

The center serves as a residence for 40 members and a training center for both males and females leading to full ordination in the Order of Bhiksus and Bhiksunis. In this regard, it has been the site of a number of historic events in the Buddhist community: the first Grand Ordination Ceremony for Bhiksus in July 1974, the first Grand Ordination for Bhiksunis in August 1976, and the first traditional Grand Ordination in the English language in August 1981. It provided all of the monks who worked as Buddhist chaplains in the three major U.S. refugee camps set up to process Southeast Asian refugees after the Vietnam War. During the five years when the American Vietnamese Buddhist community and the immigrant community functioned as one, the center itself housed 60 refugees and raised the funds to purchase and renovate properties to establish two Buddhist temples in Los Angeles, California.

Thien-An trained and ordained seven monks who are leaders in Buddhist work around the world. Leadership of the center passed to Dr. Karuna Dharma, who has by her own accomplishments during the 1980s emerged as one of the most important leaders in the American Buddhist community. She was one of the moving forces in the foundation and maintenance of the Buddhist Sangha Council of Southern California, and one of the major organizers of the American Buddhist Congress founded in 1987 (she served as a national president of the congress). And she has been the spokesperson for Sakyadhita, the International Association of Buddhist Women, whose headquarters were originally at the center.

In 1994 the center held the first ordination where they ordained *bhiksunis* in both the Theravada and Tibetan forms of Buddhism.

Membership: In 2002 the center reported approximately 300 members in one center served by seven priests.

Educational Facilities:

Thien-An Institute of Buddhist Studies, Los Angeles, California. • College of Buddhist Studies, Los Angeles, California.

Periodicals: *Monthly Guide*.

Sources:

International Buddhist Meditation Center. www.urbandharma.org/ibmc/.

Like a Lotus, Thich Thien-An. Los Angeles: International Buddhist Meditation Center, [1981].

Thien-An, Thich. *Buddhism and Zen in Vietnam*. Rutland, VT: Charles E. Tuttle, 1975.

————. *Zen Philosophy, Zen Practice*. Berkeley, CA: Dharma Publishing, 1975.

International Meditation Center—USA

4920 Rose Dr., Westminster, MD 21158

The International Meditation Center—USA, founded in 1988, is the U.S. branch of the International Meditation Centers, a worldwide Theravada Buddhist organization that grew out of the teachings and practice of Burmese lay teacher Sayagyi U Ba Khin (1899–1971), who started teaching in 1951 while still working as an accountant. From 1948 to 1953 he was the accountant general of Burma, and the year before his retirement he founded the International Meditation Center in Rangoon. His teachings emphasized intense practice over theoretical understanding as the road to enlightenment. The International Meditation Centers are currently under the guidance and leadership of Sayamagyi Daw Mya Thwin, chief disciple of Sayagyi U Ba Khin.

Membership: In 2008 the IMC-USA reported 150 members and two resident teachers for the center in Westminster. There are five affiliated centers in Burma, Austria, Australia, and the United Kingdom.

Sources:

International Meditation Center—USA. www.ubakhin.org.

Coleman, John E. *The Quiet Mind*. London: Harper and Row, 1971.

Sayagyi U Ba Khin. *Dhamma Texts*. Rev. ed. Heddington, U.K.: Sayagyi U Ba Khin Memorial Trust, 1999.

Webu Sayadaw. *The Way to Ultimate Calm*. Kandy, Sri Lanka: Buddhist Publication Society, 2001.

Lao Buddhist Sangha of the U.S.A.

c/o Wat Lao Boubpharam of San Diego, 205 South 65th St., San Diego, CA 92114

Like other Southeast Asians, Laotians have come to the United States in significant numbers since 1965, and particularly since the end of the Vietnam War. The number of new immigrants quadrupled during the period from 1980 to 1985, and the religious scene was in great flux with new work only beginning to become stabilized in each Laotian community. Temples have been established in Los Angeles, Chicago, and Washington, D.C.

Membership: Not reported.

Sources:

Hein, Jeremy. *From Vietnam, Laos, and Cambodia: Refugee Experience in the United States*. New York: Twayne Publishers, 1995.

Stuart-Fox, Martin. "Laos: From Buddhist Kingdom to Marxist State." In *Buddhism and Politics in Twentieth-Century Asia*, ed. Ian Harris. London: Pinter, 1999.

Van Esterik, Penny. *Taking Refuge: Lao Buddhists in North America*. Tempe, AZ: Arizona State University, 1992.

————. "Ritual and the Performance of Buddhist Identity among Lao Buddhists in North America." In *American Buddhism: Methods and Findings in Recent Scholarship*, ed. Duncan Ryuken Williams and Christopher S. Queen. Richmond, U.K.: Curzon Press, 1999.

Mid-America Dharma Group

455 E 80th Terr., Kansas City, MO 64131

The Mid-America Dharma Group is an umbrella organization uniting members of vipassana sitting groups in Missouri, Kansas, and Iowa. Though independent, it has close relationships with the Insight Meditation Society, from which it borrows teachers.

The organization's web site contains a variety of practice resources, including listings for retreats throughout North America and local practice groups. It also offers a number of study resources and a newsletter to keep people up to date on its offerings.

Periodicals: *Mid America Dharma News*.

Membership: In 1997 there were three groups in Missouri, four in Kansas, and one in Iowa.

Sources:

Mid-America Dharma Group. www.midamericadharma.org.

Morreale, Don. *The Complete Guide to Buddhist America*. Boston: Shambhala, 1998.

Order of Interbeing

Community of Mindful Living, c/o Deer Park, 2499 Melru Ln., Escondido, CA 92026

Among the best known figures to emerge during the Vietnam War was Thich Nhat Hanh (b. 1926), a Buddhist monk who has traveled the world in his advocacy of peace. Nhat Hanh has been a Buddhist monk since his teenage years. He became a professor at Saigon University, where he was located when the Vietnam War developed. As the war heated up through the 1960s, he became the leader of a group of Buddhists committed to ending the conflict and bringing peace to their land. His efforts were recognized in 1967 when he was nominated for the Nobel Peace Prize.

In moving out of their isolation into the public sphere, Nhat Hanh and his monastic associates began to articulate what they termed "Engaged Buddhism." Engaged Buddhism is an attempt to bring Buddhism into contemporary issues— issues that range from helping the victims of war to critiquing government war policies. In this endeavor, at the beginning of 1966 Nhat Hanh founded the Tiep Hien Order and developed its guidelines. The first members were received on Wesak, the Buddha's birthday.

Nhat Hanh called for members of the order to loosen their attachment to particular doctrines and views, concentrate on realization drawn from direct experience, center themselves on appropriate teaching, and employ skillful means to guide people in their practice of Buddhism. The 14 precepts of the order called upon members to find means of assisting those who suffer, to avoid the accumulation of wealth, and to separate from anger, discord, and untruth. At the same time, he encouraged them to remain centered and not allow the chaos of their environment to dissipate their efforts.

Immediately after the order was founded, Nhat Hanh began to travel the world promoting the peace process in Vietnam. He found ready acceptance among antiwar activists in the United States, an early expression of which was his dialogue in 1975 with the Catholic priest Daniel Berrigan (b. 1921). He also attracted many people who wanted to begin practicing his form of Buddhism, developed from traditional Vietnamese Buddhism that brought together Theravada and Zen in a complex mixture.

Through the 1980s especially, numerous groups sprang up as a result of people being inspired by Nhat Hanh; they exist as a loose network of Buddhist sitting groups and communities. Meanwhile, Nhat Hanh continued to travel throughout the United States and Europe conducting lectures and retreats that directed at both English-speaking and Vietnamese audiences. Exiled from Vietnam for many years, he was allowed to return for trips in 2005 and 2007.

Membership: Groups are found across the United States and in various countries of Asia and Europe, including Norway, France, and Switzerland. There is a core community of approximately 400, of whom 250 live in the United States and 25 in Canada. The larger fellowship includes some 10,000 persons, of whom 8,000 live in the United States and 1,000 in Canada.

Educational Facilities:

Buddhist Institute at Plum Village, Loubes-Beancec, France.

Periodicals: *The Mindfulness Bell*.

Sources:

Order of Interbeing. www.orderofinterbeing.org.

Berrigan, Daniel, and Thich Nhat Hanh. *The Raft Is Not the Shore*. Boston: Beacon Press, 1975.

Kotler, Arnold, ed. *Engaged Buddhist Reader*. Berkeley, CA: Parallax Press, 1996.

Nhat Hahn, Thich. *Interbeing: Commentaries on the Tiep Hien Precepts*. Berkeley, CA: Parallax Press, 1987.

————. *The Miracle of Mindfulness*. Boston: Beacon Press, 1975.

————. *Zen Keys*. Garden City, NY: Doubleday, 1974.

Ordinary Dharma

c/o Manzanita Village, PO Box 67, Warner Springs, CA 92086

Ordinary Dharma, founded by Caitriona Reed in 1982, is an independent organization that grew out of the "Engaged Buddhism" generally associated with the Vietnamese teacher Thich Nhat Hanh (b. 1926), from whom Reed received Dharmacarya transmission. Practice is in the Vietnamese tradition, which combines vipassana and Zen traditions. Practitioners are also called upon to engage in socially relevant activity, especially around issues of peace, deep ecology, and mindfulness in everyday life. Informal relations are maintained with the Spirit Rock Center and the larger vipassana community. Ordinary Dharma, located in Santa Monica, California, maintains Manzanita Village, a rural retreat center.

The Santa Monica center regularly schedules monthly one-day retreats, classes, meditation sessions, study groups, and classes in aikido. Manzanita is home to three annual 10-day retreats and a variety of retreats of shorter duration.

Membership: In 2002 the organization reported 500 members.

Periodicals: *Ordinary Kind*.

Sources:

Ordinary Dharma. www.manzanitavillage.org.

Morreale, Don. *The Complete Guide to Buddhist America*. Boston: Shambhala, 1998.

Resources for Ecumenical Spirituality

RES Main Office, PO Box 85, Forest Lake, MN 55025-0085

Resources for Ecumenical Spirituality (RES) is a Theravada Buddhist group that was begun to spread interfaith understanding through shared spiritual practice and dialogue. RES offers several retreats, all of which are inspired by the teachings of the Carmelite mystic St. John of the Cross. The retreats integrate Theravadan Buddhist Insight Meditation (vipassana) techniques with St. John's teachings as a way to practice contemplative prayer. RES sponsors retreats, colloquia, workshops, publications, meditation classes, and other projects related to spiritual practice and study.

Major retreat offerings include Buddhist-Christian Insight Meditation, 12-step Program Insight Meditation, and Loving-kindness (Metta).

Membership: Not reported. In 2008 RES's web site listed nine active teachers.

Sources:

Resources for Ecumenical Spirituality. resecum.org/default.aspx.

Morreale, Don. *The Complete Guide to Buddhist America*. Boston: Shambhala, 1998.

Saddhamma Foundation

350 Sharon Park Dr. R-1, Menlo Park, CA 94025

The Saddhamma Foundation is a Buddhist nonprofit organization formed in the early 1990s to support the Ven. Sayadaw U Pandita in his efforts to encourage and support the teachings of the Dhamma throughout the world. Sayadaw U Pandita is considered to be one of the leading authorities in the practice of Satipatthana as taught by his instructor, the late Ven. Mahasi Sayadaw. He possesses extensive knowledge in both the theory and practice of samatha and vipassana meditation.

Sayadaw U Pandita serves as the spiritual advisor to retreat centers, monasteries, and Buddhist organizations throughout the world. Since 1951 he has traveled to many countries to lead meditation retreats. Formerly the head "abbot" of Mahasi Sasana Yeiktha, in 2008 he was the Ovadacariya Sayadaw (head "abbot") of Panditarama monastery in Yangon, Myanmar.

The Saddhamma Foundation has facilitated retreats for Sayadaw U Pandita in the United States and Myanmar (Burma) and since 1995 has developed the Panditarama Forest Meditation Center outside Yangon, Burma. These efforts culminated in the 1998 International Inaugural Retreat. There is a 60-day winter retreat given each year at the center.

Each year, more than 100 meditators from more than 20 countries attend the annual retreat.

Membership: Not reported.

Sources:

Saddhamma Foundation. www.saddhamma.org.

Morreale, Don. *The Complete Guide to Buddhist America*. Boston: Shambhala, 1998.

Sri Lanka Sangha Council of North America

c/o Dharma Vijaya Buddhist Vihara, 1847 Crenshaw Blvd., Los Angeles, CA 90019

The Sri Lanka Sangha Council of North America (also called the Sri Lanka Buddhist Sangha Council of the United States and Canada) was formed in 1987 by a group of Sri Lankan monks. It grew out of the needs of the burgeoning Sri Lankan Buddhist community that had developed quickly in North America during the 1980s. The American-Sri Lankan community continues the tradition first introduced in the United States by Anagarika Dharmapala, a Ceylonese Buddhist who addressed the World's Parliament of Religion in 1893. Inspired by his visit, a U.S. chapter of the Maha Bodhi Society was organized, but no permanent Ceylonese Buddhism was established.

Then in 1964, while visiting the United States, the Most Ven. Madihe Panneseeha, Maha Nayake Thera of Ceylon, became aware of an interest in Buddhism and the lack of a center for Theravada Buddhism in the United States. (At that time there was only one small U.S. Theravada Buddhist center, a Thai-inspired center in California headed by Douglas Murray Burns.) Acting upon his suggestion, the Sesana Sevaka Society of Maharagama, Ceylon (now Sri Lanka), sent the Ven. Thera Bope Vinita to Washington, D.C., in 1965. The Washington Buddhist Vihara Society was founded that year with assistance from the Ceylonese embassy. In 1967 Vinita was succeeded by the Ven. Pandita Mahathera Dick-wela Piyananda, who was succeeded in turn in 1968 by his assistant, the Ven. Mahathera Henepola Gunaratana, the present (2008) head of the vihara. For many years, it was the only Ceylonese Buddhist center in the United States.

Since 1965, and especially since the late 1970s, Buddhists from Sri Lanka have moved to the United States and settled along both coasts. Monks have arrived to provide leadership for the growing number of Buddhist temples that have emerged. Among the most prominent centers are the Dharma Vijaya Buddhist Vihara in Los Angeles, California, the California Buddhist Vihara Society in Berkeley, California, and the American-Sri Lanka Buddhist Association in New York City. Among the most important of the scholarly leaders of the American-Sri Lankan community is David J. Kalupahana, a professor of philosophy at the University of Hawaii. Sri Lankan Buddhism in North America remains primarily an ethnic religion, though the number of non-Sri Lankans is growing. Assisting in that growth, which is common to Buddhist communities, are the very popular writings of Walpola Rahula, especially his basic introductory text to Ceylonese Buddhism, *What the Buddha Taught* (1974).

Membership: Not available.

Periodicals: *Washington Buddhist*. • *New York Buddhist*.

Remarks: During the twentieth century the Ceylonese Buddhists have been among the most open to potential converts from Western countries, and they have placed considerable emphasis upon the publication of English-language books on Buddhism. Important to any collection of English-language Buddhist literature are the Wheel Publications of the Buddhist Publication Society of Candy, Sri Lanka. Beginning in the 1950s, several hundred titles have appeared and have had a measurable effect in spreading Buddhism in North America.

Sources:

Buddha Vadana. Los Angeles: Dharma Vijava Buddhist Vihara, 1985.

Gunaratana, Henepola. *Come and See*. Washington, DC: Buddhist Vihara Society, n.d.

————. *The Path of Serenity and Insight*. Delhi, India: Banarsidass, Motilal. 1985.

Kalupahana, David J. *Buddhist Philosophy, A Historical Analysis*. Honolulu: University of Hawaii Press, 1976.

Maha Sthavira Sangharakshita. *Flame in Darkness, the Life and Sayings of Anagarika Dharmapala*. Pune, India: Triratna Grantha Mala, 1980.

Rahula, Walpola. *What the Buddha Taught*. New York: Grove Press, 1974.

Taungpulu Kaba-Aye Monastery

18335 Big Basin Hwy., Boulder Creek, CA 95006

The Taungpulu Kaba-Aye Monastery is a center for the teaching of Burmese Buddhism; it was founded in 1981 by the Ven. Taungpulu Kaba-Aye Sayadaw, a Burmese monk then on a goodwill tour of the United States. Dr. Rina Sircar, a long-time student of Taungpulu Kaba-Aye Sayadaw and cofounder of the monastery, serves as the resident meditation teacher. The monastery offers periodic retreats for those already versed in vipassana meditation, the form of meditation most common to Theravada Buddhism. Sircar is also a member of the faculty in the Department of Philosophy and Religion at the California Institute for Integral Studies in San Francisco. There is also a second center, Taungpulu Kaba-Aye Meditation Center, in San Francisco.

Membership: Not reported.

Educational Facilities:

The center has a cooperative arrangement with Antioch College, Yellow Springs, Ohio, by which it accepts students in a quarterly or semester work-study program.

Sources:

Sayadaw, Mahasi. *Purpose of Practising Kummatthana Meditation*. Silver Spring, MD: Burma-America Buddhist Association, n.d.

Thai-American Buddhist Association

c/o Council of Thai Bhikkhus in the U.S.A., 110 Rustic Rd., Centereach, NY 11720

Alternate Address: Wat Thai of Los Angeles, 12909 Cantara St., North Hollywood, CA 91506.

The general unrest in Southeast Asia and the rescinding of the Oriental Exclusion Act in 1965 combined to increase immigration from Thailand to the United States in the late 1960s. Significant Thai-American communities emerged on the West Coast and in several urban areas further inland. Assisted by leadership from Thailand, the new immigrant communities began to organize their predominantly Buddhist religious life. In 1970, at the invitation of the American Thais, the Ven. Pharkhru Vajirathammasophon of Wat Vajirathamsathit toured the United States. During his visit, the Thai-American Buddhist Association was formally organized in Los Angeles, and plans were initiated to build the Wat Thai of Los Angeles, a temple complex that would serve the largest of the Thai communities in the West. Later that year, three priests arrived to take up permanent residence.

The 1971 visit by the Ven. Phra Dhammakosacharn, a leading Thai Buddhist priest, was followed by the incorporation of the Wat Thai as the Theravada Buddhist Center and the beginning of a fund-raising drive. In 1972 the U.S. government invited the supreme patriarch, Phra Wannarat of Wat Phra Jetuphon, and a group of Thai priests to make an official state visit. During this visit, the presentation of the land-title deed for the future site of the Wat Thai was held in the office of the consul general in Los Angeles. The cornerstone was laid and construction commenced. The wat was finished in stages, and in 1980 the statue of Buddha in the main temple was consecrated.

While work on the complex in Los Angeles proceeded, other wats were being organized in other cities, from San Francisco and Denver, Colorado, to Houston, Texas, Washington, D.C., and New York. In June 1976, monks from the several existing Thai temples in the United States gathered in Denver and organized the Council of Thai Bhikkhus in the U.S.A. The Council is assigned the tasks of keeping the monastic practices of the member monks up to standards and of building a sense of unity between monks in the United States and those in Thailand. The Council meets annually.

A major practice of Theravada Buddhism is *insight meditation*, described as the practice of mindfulness. Mindfulness is the observation point arrived at by the meditator from which he or she can truly understand mental and physical phenomena as they arise. In general, Theravada Buddhists are among the most conservative of Buddhists in their adherence to the oldest traditions. They use the Pali-language texts of early Buddhism, as opposed to the Sanskrit texts used by the Mahayana Buddhists.

Membership: There are approximately 150,000 Thais in the United States, of whom some 50,000 reside in southern California. As of 2008, there were 93 Thai temples/wats scattered across the United States, along with 7 in Canada.

Periodicals: *Duangpratip*.

Sources:

Council of Thai Bhikkhus of the U.S.A. www.thaitemple.org/.

Hamilton-Merritt, Jane. *A Meditator's Diary*. New York: Harper & Row, 1976.

Jumsai, M. L. Manich. *Understanding Thai Buddhism*. Bangkok: Chalermit Press, 1973.

Narasapo, Phra Maha Singhathon. *Buddhism: An Introduction to a Happy Life*. Bangkok: Preacher's Association, Wat Phrajetubon, 1969.

Tiep Hien Order

c/o Parallax Press, PO Box 7355, Berkeley, CA 94707

Alternate Address: International Network of Engaged Buddhists, PO Box 1, Ongkharak, Nakhorn Nayok, Thailand.

Among the more well-known figures to emerge during the Vietnam War was Thich Nhat Hanh (1926–), a Buddhist monk who traveled the world in his advocacy of peace. Nhat Hanh had been a Buddhist monk since his teenage years. He was a professor at Saigon University as the Vietnam War developed. As the war heated up through the 1960s, Nhat Hanh became the leader of a group of Buddhists committed to ending the conflict and bringing peace to their land. His efforts were recognized in 1967 when he was nominated for the Nobel Peace Prize.

In moving out of their isolation and into the public sphere, Nhat Hanh and his monastic associates began to articulate what they termed "Engaged Buddhism." Engaged Buddhism is an attempt to bring Buddhism into contemporary issues— issues that range from helping the victims of war to critiquing government war policies. In this endeavor, at the beginning of 1964, Nhat Hanh founded the Tiep Hien Order and developed its guidelines. The first members were received on Wesak, the Buddha's birthday.

Nhat Hanh called for members of the order to lose their attachment to particular doctrines and views, to concentrate on realization drawn from direct experience, center themselves on appropriate teaching, and employ skillful means to guide people in their practice of Buddhism. The 14 precepts of the order called upon members to find means of assisting those who suffer, to avoid the accumulation of wealth, and to separate from anger, discord, and untruth. On the other hand, he encouraged them to remain centered and not allow the chaos of their environment to dissipate their efforts.

Immediately after the order was founded, Nhat Hanh began to travel the world on behalf of the peace process in Vietnam. He found a ready acceptance among antiwar activists in the United States, an early expression of which was his dialogue with Catholic priest Daniel Berrigan in 1975. He also attracted many people who wanted to begin practicing his form of Buddhism developed from traditional Vietnamese Buddhism that brought together Theravada and Zen in a complex mixture.

Through the 1980s, numerous groups formed as a result of people being inspired by Nhat Hanh, and now exist as a loose network of Buddhist sitting groups and communities. Meanwhile, Nhat Hanh travels through the United States and Europe in a constant series of lectures and retreats that are directed at both English-speaking and Vietnamese audiences. Worldwide, work is carried on through the International Network of Engaged Buddhists, headquartered in Thailand.

Membership: Not reported. Groups are found across the United States and in various countries of Europe, including Norway, France, and Switzerland.

Periodicals: *Mindfulness Bell.* • *Seeds of Peace.* Available from the International Network of Engaged Buddhists, PO Box 1, Ongkharak, Nakhorn Nayok, Thailand.

Sources:

Berrigan, Daniel, and Thich Nhat Hanh. *The Raft Is Not the Shore.* Boston, MA: Beacon, 1975.

Nhat Hahn, Thich. *Interbeing: Commentaries on the Tiep Hien Precepts.* Berkeley, CA: Parallax, 1987.

———. *The Miracle of Mindfulness.* Boston, MA: Beacon, 1975.

———. *Zen Keys.* Garden City, NY: Doubleday, 1974.

Viet Nam Buddhists

c/o Congregation of Vietnamese Buddhists in the U.S., 863 S Berendo, Los Angeles, CA 90005

Because of the resettlement of the many Vietnamese Buddhists who entered the United States after the Vietnam War, Vietnamese temples far outnumber the temples of other Southeast Asian groups, and they may be found in all sections of the United States. The temples serve first-generation Vietnamese Americans, and services are conducted in Vietnamese. Vietnamese Buddhism is distinctive in the way it has merged Theravada and Zen. Among the leading spokespersons for Vietnamese Buddhism is Thich Nhat Hanh (b. 1926), who became known to Americans during the Vietnam War as a peace advocate. He works closely with the Fellowship of Reconciliation.

Membership: Not reported. There are an estimated 900,000 Vietnamese in the United States, concentrated in southern California. Although a large number of them are Roman Catholics, the majority are Buddhists. Centers are found across the United States, including several located in Los Angeles and Orange County in California.

Sources:

Barber A. W., and Cuong T. Nguyen. "Vietnamese Buddhism in North America: Tradition and Acculturation." In *The Faces of Buddhism in America*, ed. Charles S. Prebish and Kenneth K. Tanaka. Berkeley: University of California Press, 1998.

Fields, Rick. *Taking Refuge in L.A.* New York: Aperture Foundation, 1987.

Hanh, Thich Nhat. *The Miracle of Mindfulness.* Boston: Beacon Press, 1976.

———. *Zen Keys.* Garden City, NY: Doubleday, 1974.

The Presence of Vietnamese Buddhists in America. Los Angeles: Vietnamese Buddhist Temple, 1981.

Vipassana Meditation Centers

386 Colrain-Shelburne Rd., Shelburne, MA 01370-9672

The Vipassana Meditation Centers have grown out of the teachings and practices of the Buddha as taught by Satya Narayan Goenka (b. 1924), a prominent Burmese meditation teacher. Formerly a businessman, Goenka had turned to vipassana meditation as a means to cure migraine headaches. The meditation not only cured him but also led him to drop his business career and become the student of Sayagyi U Ba Khin (1899–1971), with whom he studied for 14 years. In 1969 he moved to India and conducted his first classes that same year. He established the Vipassana International Academy near Mumbai, India, in 1976.

The first U.S. center, in Shelburne, Massachusetts, was founded in 1982, and subsequently 11 other centers have been opened, in the United States, Canada, and Mexico. Goenka's work has spread around the world with 80 centers in 25 countries.

Membership: Not reported. In 2008 there were 10 Vipassana Centers found across the United States and Canada and one in Mexico.

Sources:

Vipassana Meditation Center Dhamma Dharā. www.dhara.dhamma.org.

Vipassana Meditation International. www.dhamma.org.

Goenka, S. N. *The Gracious Flow of Dharma.* Igatpuri, India: Vipassana Research Institute, 1994.

Hart, William. *The Art of Living Vipassana Meditation as Taught by S. N. Goenka.* San Francisco: Harper and Row, 1993.

Morreale, Don. *The Complete Guide to Buddhist America.* Boston: Shambhala, 1998.

❀ Japanese Buddhism

Agon-shu

14518 S Western Ave., Gardena, CA 90247

Alternate Address: International Headquarters: Agon-shu Head Temple, 607 Kitakazan Omine-cho, Yamashina, Kyoto, Japan. • Canadian Headquarters: Toronto Agon-shu Buddhist Association, 16 Burch Ave., 2nd Fl., Toronto, ON M4V 1C8 Canada.

Agon-shu is a form of Japanese Buddhism founded in 1978 by Seiyu Kiriyama (b. 1921), who serves as its *kancho*, or leader. He had been a member of several different Buddhist groups, and in 1954 he founded Kannon Jijei-Kai, a small religious group superseded by Agon-shu. The great impetus for the founding of the new organization was the belief that emerged in the 1970s that the Agon (or *Agama*, in Sanskrit) sutras contain the original teachings concerning the path to Buddhahood (enlightenment) and ultimate salvation as given by Buddha. The emergent organization incorporated insights from all three major schools of Buddhism: Mahayana, Hinayana, and the esoteric Buddhism of Tibet. The esoteric practices represent the final stage of development in Buddhist practice. There are also elements of Shinto incorporated in the rites.

While acknowledging that there is great value in all Buddhist groups, Agon-shu believes that it alone has the full teachings of true and genuine Buddhism. It teaches and practices Jobutsu-ho, the teachings and methods required to attain enlightenment and full salvation, which includes release from karma, the accumulated burden of cause and effect that has decisive influence on one's present life.

Even prior to his founding of Agon-shu, Kiriyama in 1970 held the first Dai-saito-goma rite, an esoteric Buddhist ceremony centered on prayers offered up in a large outdoor bonfire. Today, the major ceremony of Agon-shu is the Hoshi Matsuri—literally, the "Combined Shinto-Buddhist Fire Rites Festival"—held near the group's main temple at Kyoto. It is concerned with the destiny of each individual and the reading of the future of each individual's birth star (esoteric astrology).

Agon-shu teachings are grounded in three principles: the Buddha, the Dharma, and the sangha. The Buddha, or object of worship, is found in the *shinsei-busshari*, a bone fragment from Shakyamuni Buddha that is preserved in a gold shrine. The Dharma is the actual training members undergo. It consists of the Jobutsu-ho (Buddha's method for attaining enlightenment), the Nyoi Hoju-ho (the esoteric teachings), and the Gumonji Somei-ho (which incorporates elements of Taoism and Tantrism, including kundalini yoga).

Kiriyama has carried on a worldwide program in support of world peace and the spread of true Buddhism. He established centers in Cambodia, Mongolia, Sri Lanka, Brazil, and eventually the United States (Hawaii and California). In 1989 he opened the Japanese American Agon Friendship Foundation in Washington, D.C.

Membership: Not reported. Agon-shu has only a small following in the United States. It has offices in Japan and in 1990 became the first foreign-based religion to open an office in mainland China, in Beijing.

Remarks: The Agon-shu received some unwanted publicity when it was discovered that Soko Asahara, the founder of Aum Shinrikyo, and one of that group's leaders, Tomomitsu Niimi, had gotten their early training in Agon-shu. In fact, it appears that Asahara began Aum with an assertion that he had surpassed Kiriyama in enlightenment, a fact demonstrated by his levitating before several of the members. This fact accounts for the similarity of teachings between Agon-shu and Aum, but it should be noted that there is no hint of a connection between Agon-shu and the crime allegedly perpetrated by the leaders of Aum—the 1995 sarin gas attack in the Tokyo subway system.

Sources:

Agon-shu. www.agon.org/us/.

Agon-shu and Its Activities. Tokyo: Agon-shu Public Information Division, 1990.

The Agon-shu: The Original Teachings of the Lord Buddha. Tokyo: Agonshu, 1989.

A Short Introduction to the Hoshi Matsuri. N.p.: Agon-shu, n.d.

Bodaiji Mission

1251 Elm, Honolulu, HI 96814

The Bodaiji Mission was founded in 1930 by Nisshyo Takao, the Holy Interpreter. It is continued by Roy S. Takakuwa as an independent congregation teaching "True Buddhism." Takakuwa is a baker in Honolulu, but he also serves as the mission's sole teacher and priest. The bakery provides the total support for the mission because no donations are allowed. The teaching of the mission is described as empirical, moving from fact to the source of facts.

The basic concept of Bodaiji teachings is *dai-o-kyo*, filial piety, the lack of which is a great cause of discord and trouble. Filial piety begins in *yojomanjo*, the unconditional salvation of true motherhood. Just as motherhood was the source of our nurture, so cooperation, coexistence, and right living lead us to universal salvation. True Buddhism teaches how to live rightly. An acceptance of the law of cause and effect underlies the teachings; where there is something wrong, one finds the cause and changes it. Thus, when one adopts a program of right living, salvation will come.

Healing, too, is a concept basic to right living. Each person who comes for healing must stick to a rigid diet and must learn to breathe properly. Holy water is also used. Fifteen minutes of meditation each day is advised for all to replenish energy.

Membership: In 1982 there were approximately 100 members. There is only one congregation, and no membership roll is kept.

Gedatsu Church of America

7850 Hill Dr., South San Gabriel, CA 91770

The Gedatsu Church was formed by Gedatsu Kongpo (the posthumous title of Shoken Okano), a priest in the Shugendo sect of Shingon Buddhism. Born in 1881, he rose to the rank of archbishop. In 1929 he founded the Gedatsu movement in his own town. A student of comparative religion, Gedatsu Kongpo borrowed freely from Shinto and Christianity to produce an eclectic Buddhist teaching.

According to Gedatsu, man desires wealth, fame, sex, food, and rest. Man runs into trouble whenever the search for these five desires (which are necessary for survival) becomes directed solely to self-satisfaction. He then falls into the tragedies of life and suffers from ignorance of karmic law, hereditary problems, and selfish thoughts. The object of religion is to move from the problems and suffering of the present to the state of enlightenment—calm resignation and complete peace of mind. (By the law of karma, a person must experience the consequences of his or her actions.)

Gedatsu offers a method of attaining enlightenment through the development of wisdom, the purification of emotion, and the improvement of willpower. Wisdom is developed by meditation on the symbol *AJI*. The emotions are purified by service to the souls of ancestors and other spiritual entities. Willpower is improved by the Way of the Holy Goho, a progressive method of disciplining the mind and spirit that can dissolve the bonds of karma.

Underlying the Gedatsu doctrine is the concept of universal law and universal truth. The universal law is the power of nature, absolutely unchangeable and indestructible. It is seen in the regular cycles of nature. This law also functions to bring to enlightenment those who follow the path.

The center of Gedatsu worship is the Goreichi Spiritual Sanctuary. This shrine is the resting place of all spirits and houses the Tenjinchigi, the spirit of the supreme creator, the source of the universal law. The shrine also contains a statue of Fudo Myo-Oh, who has the power to conquer all evil. Other bodhisattvas are also represented. A semiannual Thanksgiving Festival is observed in the spring and fall, and the annual Roku Jizo Festival is observed in June. All are noteworthy for their ceremony. Central to all worship is *kuyo*, the act of humbly repaying by absolute gratitude all the sources to which one is indebted. Kuyo is ritualized in the Nectar Service, during which spirits in a state of unrest are brought to rest.

Gedatsu was brought to the United States in the late 1940s and incorporated in 1951. It has headquarters in San Francisco, and it maintains three churches, in Sacramento, San Jose, and Honolulu. The Goreichi Shrine is in Mayhew, a Sacramento suburb.

Membership: Not reported.

Sources:

Gedatsu Church of America. gedatsu-usa.org/index2.html.

Gedatsu Ajikan Kongozen Meditation. San Francisco: Gedatsu Church of America, 1974.

Kishida, Eizan. *Dynamic Analysis of Illness through Gedatsu.* N.p., 1962.

Manual for Implementation of Gedatsu Practice. San Francisco: Gedatsu Church of America, 1965.

Yanagawa, Keiichi. *Japanese Religions in California.* Tokyo: Department of Religious Studies, University of Tokyo, 1983.

Hawaii Council of Jodo Mission

c/o Jodo Mission of Hawaii, 1429 Makiki St., Honolulu, HI 96814

Alternate Address: International Headquarters: 4-7-4 Shibakoen, Minato-ku, Tokyo, Japan 105-0011.

From the landing of the first 153 Japanese immigrants in 1868 until 1894, almost 30,000 Japanese arrived in Hawaii, most to work on the extensive plantation being developed there. They lived a demoralizing existence working 12-hour days, often at hard labor, and with no fixed days off. Gradually, news of the living conditions made its way back to Japan and, given that most of the Japanese laborers were Buddhists, the major Buddhist denominations decided to respond. In 1894 Jodo Shu sent two clergymen, Revs. Matsuwo Taijyo and Okabe Gekuwo, to comfort and reconstruct the lives of the demoralized workers.

For his efforts, Rev. Matsuwo caught tuberculosis and died a few years later while attempting to construct a temple at Kapaa on the island of Kauai. Rev. Okabe worked on the big island of Hawaii and succeeded in founding the first Jodo mission at Hamakua in 1896. In subsequent years additional clergymen came to work and built additional temples. Eventually there were 15 temples, on Oahu, Maui, Kauai, and Hawaii. The Jodo movement celebrated its 100th anniversary, dated from the arrival of its first two clergymen, in 1994. In 2008 the movement was led by Chikai Shibamura.

In 1969 a nonprofit U.S. religious entity was incorporated as the Hawaii Council of Jodo Missions. The council is an autonomous organization but cooperates with and receives guidance from Jodo Shu, headquartered in Japan. There are two Jodo missions on continental North America, the Jodoshu North America Buddhist Missions, which operates an extension school of the Buddhist University of Kyoto, Japan, and the Chicago Jodu Shu Temple.

The Pure Land Institute was established by the Hawaii Council of Jodo Missions in 1986. Its purpose is to spread the teachings of the Buddha by providing reliable and accessible English translations of important works in the Pure Land tradition.

Membership: In 2008 there were 14 temples in Hawaii. There also is a temple in Los Angeles and another in Chicago.

Periodicals: *Jodo Mission of Hawaii.* • *Hawaii Buddhism.*

Sources:

Hawaii Council of Jodo Mission. www.jodo.us.

Jodo Shu Headquarters. www.jodo.org/index.html.

Fung, Gordon L., and Gregory Fung. "Adapting Jodo-Shinshu Teaching for the West: An Approach Based on the American Work Ethic." *Pacific World* new series 9 (Fall 1993): 24–31.

Light of Asia. Honolulu: Hawaii Jodo Mission, 1962.

Matsunami, Kodo. *Introducing Buddhism.* Honolulu: Hawaii Jodo Mission, 1965.

Tabrah, Ruth. *Buddhism, A Modern Way of Life and Thought.* Honolulu: Hawaii Jodo Mission, 1969.

Higashi Hongwanji Buddhist Church

Current address not obtained for this edition.

Just behind the Buddhist Churches of America, the largest of the Shin Buddhist groups, was the Higashi Hongwanji. However, since it has done little to westernize, it has been slower to spread. In 1899 Shizuka Sazanami began to work on Kauai in Hawaii, where a temple was constructed in Waimea. It was 1916 before a temple appeared in Honolulu. On the mainland, the Higashi Honganji began with Rev. Junjyo Izumida, who in 1904 established the Los Angeles Buddhist Mission as an outpost of the Honpa Hongwanji. Two other churches were formed in Los Angeles, and soon a rivalry developed between them. In 1917 a merger of the three congregations was ratified, but Izumida opposed the merger, and in a court suit won the property of the congregation he had led. In 1921 he joined the Higashi Honganji and brought the congregation with him. Shortly after the establishment of the Higashi Honganji in Los Angeles, a second temple was opened in Berkeley, California. A third was added in Chicago after World War II. The Chicago temple, under the leadership of Gyomay Kubose, also sponsors a Zen center. Kubose, who serves as both a Shin priest and Zen master, follows in the pattern of the late Daisetz Teitaro Suzuki, the most famous member of the Higashi Honganji (at least to Western audiences). The U.S. branch of the Higashi Honganji is presided over by Gyoko Saito, the priest in Los Angeles.

Membership: In 1982 there were 1,800 members in six churches in Hawaii. There are three temples in the continental United States and several branch churches attached to the Los Angeles temple.

Periodicals: *The Way.*

Sources:

Akegarasu, Haya. *The Fundamental Spirit of Buddhism.* Trans. Gyomay M. Kubose. Chicago: Buddhist Temple of Chicago, 1977.

———. *Shout of Buddha.* Trans. Gyoko Saito and Joan Sweany. Chicago: Orchid Press, 1977.

Higashi Hongwanji Dedication—1976. Los Angeles: Higashi Hongwanji Buddhist Church, 1976.

Jodo Shinshu. Tokyo: Otani University, 1961.

Kiyozuma, Manshi. *December Fan.* Trans. Nobuo Haneda. Kyoto, Japan: Higashi Hongwanji, 1984.

Suzuki, Beatrice Lane. *Mahayana Buddhism.* New York: Macmillan, 1969.

Suzuki, D. T. *Shin Buddhism.* New York: Harper and Row, 1970.

Honpa Hongwanji Buddhism

c/o Buddhist Churches of America, 1710 Octavia St., San Francisco, CA 94109

Alternate Addresses: Honpa Hongwanji Mission of Hawaii, 1727 Pali Hwy., HI 96813; Buddhist Churches of Canada, 11786 Fentiman Place, Richmond BC V7E 6M6 Canada.

The Honpa Hongwanji sect, one of the major representatives of Jodo Shinshu Buddhism in Japan, is represented in North America by three separate organizations that report directly to the international headquarters in Kyoto. Shinshu Buddhists began to arrive in Hawaii, the U.S. mainland, and Canada in the 1880s. Through the twentieth century a Buddhist mission spread through the immigrant Japanese community, easing the cultural transition to American ways. The Honpa Hongwanji is one of three primary groups teaching Pure Land Shin Buddhism.

The Buddhist Churches of America has headquarters in San Francisco. Congregations in the United States are divided into seven administrative districts: four on the Pacific Coast, and one each for the Northwest, the Mountain states, and the East. Since 1996 Bp. Hakubum Watanabe has presided over the organization, assisted by a board of directors and a representative national council that oversees administrative functions.

The Honpa Hongwanji Mission of Hawaii, headquartered in Honolulu, is headed by Bp. Chikai Yosemori. Until World War II, the bishop was appointed from the international headquarters, but since then the Hawaiian members elect their bishop, who serves three-year terms.

The Jikoen Hongwanji Temple in Honolulu was built in 1938 as a center for Okinawan Shinshu immigrants who had come to Hawaii during the 1920s and 1930s. It functions as a member of the Honpa Hongwanji.

In Canada the first Shinshu church was organized in 1904. The work in Canada gradually separated from the U.S. organization in a process culminating a short time after the end of World War II.

Membership: In 1997 the Buddhist Churches of America reported 16,000 members in 61 independent churches and six branches served by 60 ministers. There were 35 branches throughout the Hawaiian Islands. There were 10 million members worldwide.

Educational Facilities:

Institute for Buddhist Studies, Berkeley, California. • American Buddhist Academy, New York, New York.

Periodicals: *Horin* (in Japanese). • *Pacific World*. • *Wheel of Dharma* (in English).

Sources:

Honpa Hongwanji Mission of Hawaii. www.hongwanjihawaii.com.

Buddhist Churches of America. buddhistchurchesofamerica.org.

Buddhist Churches of Canada. www.bcc.ca.

Buddhist Churches of America, 75 Year History, 1899–1974. 2 vols. Chicago: Norbet, 1974.

Buddhist Handbook for Shin-shu Followers. Tokyo: Hokuseido Press, 1969.

Shin Buddhist Handbook. Honolulu: Honpa Hongwanji Mission of Hawaii, 1972.

Traditions of Jodoshinshu Hongwanji-Ha. Los Angeles: Senshin Buddhist Temple, 1982.

Karuna Tendai Dharma Center

1525 Rte. 295, East Chatham, NY 12060

The Karuna Tendai Dharma Center is a single outpost of the Japanese Tendai tradition, a significant element of Japanese Buddhism that has but few followers in North America. The temple was founded in 1994 by Monshin (Paul) Naamon and his wife Tamani Naamon, who had gone to Japan for study in 1988. Monshin returned as the Dharma son of Ichishima Shoshin, who occasionally travels from Japan to teach.

The temple is located on a former Shaker farmstead, the barn having been converted into a zendo. It was the desire of the Naamons to create a village-style temple in a rural area suggestive of the mountainous areas of Asia, and to integrate the life of the temple into that of the larger community. There is no convent or monastery.

Tendai is a Vajrayana Buddhist school, one of the oldest introduced into Japan. As such it became a root school for many of the modern Japanese Buddhist groups. Tendai believers, however, treat the three vehicles (Mahayana, Hinayana, and Vajrayana) as one. Activities at the temple center on the Wednesday evening meditation service, which includes a Dharma talk and potluck dinner. Order of Interbeing meditations (based on the teachings of Thich Nhat Hanh) are held twice monthly. Also, a wide range of classes, lectures, festivals, and retreats are sponsored. A vegetarian diet is preferred. The temple also operates the Bodhi Tree Inn, a bed and breakfast facility open to the public.

After an official visit by Tendai-shu Jigyodan in 2001, the Karuna Tendai Dharma Center was designated the first *betsu-in* (branch temple) of Enryaku-ji in North America.

Membership: In 1998 there were approximately 30 members affiliated with the temple.

Sources:

Karuna Tendai Dharma Center. tendai.org.

Morreale, Don. *The Complete Guide to Buddhist America.* Boston: Shambhala, 1998.

Kofuku no Kagaku (Institute for Research in Human Happiness)

350 S Crenshaw Blvd., Ste. A205, Torrance, CA 90503

Alternate Address: International headquarters: 1-2-38 Higashi Gotanda, Shinagawa-ku, Tokyo 141-0022 Japan.

Kofuku no Kagaku, known in the United States as the Institute for Research in Human Happiness (IRH), is a Japanese "new, new religion" (*shin shin shukyo*), a designation of religious groups that have grown up among those generations born after World war II. Kofuku no Kagaku began in Tokyo in 1986 and was established in the United States in August 1993. Its founder, Okawa Ryuho (b. 1956), studied law at Tokyo Imperial University, during which time he came to believe that he was the incarnation of a spirit being known as El Cantare (the title by which he is known in the movement today). In his key book, *The Laws of the Sun* (1990), Okawa described his role as the one who reveals the "rising of the Sun of God's Truth." He thus provides human beings with essential light and energy that is often prevented from reaching them by "dark clouds."

During its first decade, the movement grew phenomenally. Just four years after its founding, Okawa announced a new program, "Sunrise 90," to raise the Sun of Truth, that is, to spread the name of the movement throughout Japan. In the next year some 77,000 people joined the movement. Sunrise 90 was followed by the "miracle three-year project," a program directed to make Kofuku no Kagaku the largest and most influential religion in Japan. In 1994 a coordinated missionary program initiated to establish the movement in countries outside Japan quickly led to the first overseas offices being opened, in London and New York.

In spite of its use of high-tech mass communications, including the production of several feature films, growth overseas has not followed the early success in Japan, though some moderate growth was experienced in Brazil, where there is a large Japanese expatriate community.

Okawa has written a number of books. The best known is *The Laws of the Sun*, which provides a summary of the movement's teachings and has assumed the status of a sacred text. Other popular titles include *The Laws of Gold* (1991) and *The Laws of Eternity* (1991). He has also written about an imminent apocalypse to be followed by a utopia in which everyone can declare without any reservations that they are happy. Happiness comes from living with a mind and heart full of love and compassion. This, according to Okawa, begins in the minds and hearts of believers who then transmit it to others. There are four basic principles of happiness: love, knowledge, development, and self-reflection. The practice of these principles is said to enable an individual to acquire the right-mindfulness that is a necessary precondition for happiness. Of the four, the most important is love, whose essence is giving. The practice of love is the beginning of happiness. At the same time, Kofuku no Kagaku also emphasizes its Buddhist roots and the three Buddhist treasures: the Buddha, the Dharma, and the sangha (community).

Kofuku no Kagaku's headquarters are in Tokyo, but two additional centers, the Shoshin-Ken (House of the Right Mind) and the Mirai-kan (House of the Future) in Utsonomyia (northeast of Tokyo) are also regarded as the Shoshin-Kan or main temple. Members began to migrate from Japan to North America (as well as Europe and South America) in the 1970s, and the earliest centers were established in the 1980s.

Membership: Not reported. U.S. centers are found in San Francisco, Los Angeles, and Pasadena, California; New Jersey; and Honolulu, Hawaii. Canadian centers are found in Toronto. Besides centers across Japan, additional centers are found in the United Kingdom, Brazil, Taiwan, Australia, and Korea. There are some 3,000 members in Brazil.

Periodicals: *Utopia*.

Sources:

Kofuku no Kagaku. www.kofuku-no-kagaku.or.jp/en/. http://irhla.org/

Institute for Research in Human Happiness, Los Angeles. irhla.org/.

Masaki Fukui. "Kofuku no Kagaku" The Institute for Research in Human Happiness (IRH)." In *A Bibliography of Japanese New Religions*, ed. Peter B. Clarke. Eastbourne, Kent, U.K.: Japan Library, 1999.

Okawa, Ryuhu. *The Laws of Eternity*. Tokyo: IRH Press, 1991.

———. *The Laws of Gold*. Tokyo: IRH Press, 1991.

———. *The Laws of the Sun: The Revelations of Buddha That Enlightens the New Age*. Tokyo: IRH Press, 1990.

Trevor. Astley. "The Transformation of a Recent Japanese New Religion: Okawa Ryuhu and Kofuku no Kagaku." *Japanese Journal of Religious Studies* 22, nos. 3–4 (1995): 343–380.

Nichiren Mission

33 Pulelehua Way, Honolulu, HI 96817

Alternate Address: International headquarters: Nichiren-shu, 1-32-15 Ikegami, Ota-ku, Tokyo, Japan. Mainland United States headquarters: Nicheren Order of North America, 2801 4th St., Los Angeles, CA 90033.

Nichiren (1222–1282) was a famous Buddhist reformer who began in 1253 to preach a new doctrine—that salvation lay in the Lotus Sutra, the most famous Buddhist Sanskrit text. The theme of the Lotus Sutra is the nature of Buddha's manifestations. Nichiren believed that the Lotus Sutra taught a combination of the methodologies of the other Buddhist groups—the ways of transformation, bliss, and law. Rather than call upon the Amida Buddha, as in Shin Buddhist practice, one should call upon the Lotus Sutra. Daimoku, a repetitive chant of "Namu myoho renge kyo" (reverence to the wonderful law of the Lotus), became and remains the distinctive practice of the Nichiren Buddhists. Nichiren believed that the teachings known as the Lotus Sutra constituted pristine, true Buddhism and could unite the many Buddhist sects.

Nichiren divided history into three millennia: *shobo*, the period of the true law, which was the first millennium beginning at Buddha's death; *zobo*, or image law, the second millennium; and *mappo*, or end of the law, which is to last 10,000 years. During mappo, which began in 1052 C.E., the Lotus was the way of salvation. Since the Lotus was perfect, all Japanese should yield to it and allow it to spread. According to Chinese figuring, Buddha died in 949 B.C.E. (By western figuring, he died in 486 B.C.E., but Nichiren followed the Chinese date.) The first millenium was the period of Hinayana Buddhism; the second, Provisional Mahayana Buddhism; the third, the True Mahayana Buddhism treated in the Lotus Sutra.

The worship of the Nichiren Buddhist is centered upon the repetition of the Lotus chant. This act is performed in front of the *gohonzon*, a mandala upon which the chant is inscribed along with the names of Buddhas, bodhisattvas, and other Buddhist deities and personalities.

Nichiren was an ardent advocate of his new cause; so dogmatic were his polemics that he angered other Buddhists. He died seeking the union of his ideas with Japan's national policy. The Nichiren Buddhists never reached their goal, but they have become one of the five largest Japanese Buddhist denominations.

Members of the Nichiren-shu (Nichiren religion) built a temple on the island of Hawaii at Pahala in 1902. This temple served the Japanese immigrants who had come to work on the plantations. In 1912 another was added on Oahu; today it serves as the headquarters of the Nichiren Mission of Hawaii under the leadership of Bp. Senchu Murano.

An independent Nichiren congregation was established on Oahu in 1931 by a priest of the Kempon Hokke sect (one of the Japanese Nichiren groups) under the name "Honolulu Myohoji." This temple joined the Nichiren Mission in 1979. It enshrines part of the relics of the Buddha. The Pahala Nichiren Temple ceased to exist in 1959 because of the evacuation of the Japanese people from the district, and it has recently been transferred to a Tibetan Buddhist group. Other temples have been added on the various islands. The Hawaiian temples are under the leadership of Bishop Murano.

Nichiren Buddhism came to California with the early Japanese immigrants, and in 1914 the first temple was organized. It subsequently spread to Japanese communities across the United States. After World War II national headquarters was established in Chicago, Illinois, and it later moved to San Jose, California. It is under the leadership of Bp. Ryusho Matsuda.

Membership: In 2008 there were 6 temples in Hawaii and 15 in the continental United States and Canada. Affiliated temples were located in Japan, Korea, and Brazil.

Educational Facilities:

Rissho University, Tokyo, Japan.

Minobusan Junior College, Minobu, Yamanashi-ken, Japan.

Periodicals: *The Newsletter*.

Sources:

Nichiren Mission of Hawaii. www.nichiren-shu.org/hawaii/index.htm.

Anesaki, Masaharu. *Nichiren, the Buddhist Prophet*. Cambridge, MA: Harvard University Press, 1949.

Hasu No Oshie (*The Teachings of the Lotus*). Honolulu, HI: Nichiren YBA of Honolulu, 1962.

A History of Nichiren Buddhism in Hawaii. Honolulu, HI: Nichiren Mission of Hawaii, 1982.

Murano, Senchu. *An Outline of the Lotus Sutra*. Minobu-San, Japan: Kuonji Temple, 1969.

Nichiren-Buddhist Service Companion. Chicago: Headquarters of the Nichiren Buddhist Temple of North America, 1968.

Nichiren Shoshu Temple

c/o Myohoji Temple, 1401 N Crescent Heights Blvd., West Hollywood, CA 90046

"The Orthodox School of Nichiren," Nichiren Shoshu is the 750-year old denomination following the teachings of Nichiren Daishonin (1222–1282), whom the school reveres as the True Buddha for this time period, the Latter Day of the Law. Its head temple, known as Taisekiji, was founded in 1290 and is located at the foot of Mt. Fuji near Fujinomiya City in Shizuoka Prefecture, Japan.

Shortly after Nichiren Daishonin died, his followers divided into several factions. There were disagreements over a number of issues, including sharing the responsibility for the upkeep and vigil over Nichiren Daishonin's tomb. Most important were disagreements over basic doctrinal issues. In 1290 one of the six main disciples of Nichiren, Nikko Shonin (1246–1332), separated from the other five in a dispute over the upkeep of Nichiren's tomb. But the dispute also had a doctrinal element. Nikko Shonin taught that Daishonin was the Eternal True Buddha from the infinite past who appeared in the Latter Day of the Law to reveal the True Teaching by which all humanity could attain enlightenment. Most of the other disciples regarded Shakyamuni Buddha as the True Eternal Buddha, and considered themselves to be priests loosely connected to the Tendai school. There were also disagreements over the correct object of worship and the correct interpretation of the Lotus Sutra and its two main sections, the Theoretical Gate Teaching (Jp Shakumon), which constitutes the first 14 chapters, and the True Gate Teaching (Jp Honmon), which constitutes the second 14 chapters, and their respective rank of superiority.

Nikko Shonin left the main temple at Mt. Minobu and took with him Nichiren Daishonin's ashes, various writings and sacred treasures, and the Dai-Gohonzon, inscribed in the form of a camphor wood mandala. In 1290 Nikko Shonin founded the head temple Taisekiji and enshrined the Dai-Gohonzon there, where it remains today.

Nichiren Shoshu upholds a principle called the Lifeblood Heritage of the Law. This doctrine teaches that Nichiren Daishonin transferred the mystic entity or essence of his enlightened life to Nikko Shonin, the second high priest, who passed it down to Nichimoku Shonin, the third high priest. This Heritage of the Law has been passed down face to face by each successive high priest to the next in an unbroken line for 750 years. In 2008 the high priest was Nikken Shonin, the 67th successor to the Heritage of the Law from the True Buddha. The high priest is considered to be the undisputed master of this school.

The high priest is the only person authorized to transcribe the Dai-Gohonzon. From his transcription, individual Gohonzons are made. They are issued by the priests at local temples to the believers of Nichiren Shoshu throughout the world so that they can conduct their daily practice in their homes. The doctrines of the True Buddha, the Heritage of the Law, and the Dai-Gohonzon are the most important teachings that distinguish Nichiren Shoshu from other Nichiren sects such as Nichiren-Shu.

The daily practice of a Nichiren Shoshu believer involves the essential practice of chanting "Nam-Myoho-Renge-Kyo" to the Gohonzon with faith. This is called chanting Daimoku. Also, twice per day, a recitation of part of the second chapter and all of the sixteenth chapter of the Lotus Sutra is conducted in front of the Gohonzon. This is the supporting practice, and is called Gongyo. All Nichiren Shoshu local temples have a resident chief priest who conducts daily Gongyo and Daimoku, and many ceremonies and activities. Most believers have a Gohonzon enshrined in an altar in their homes where they can conduct their practice.

Nichiren Daishonin taught that when the entire world takes faith in his teachings and believes in the Dai-Gohonzon, the world will become purified and tranquil, and all people will enjoy living happy lives together. A state of world peace and harmony will be achieved. This is called *Kosen-rufu*, and it is the ultimate goal of Nichiren Shoshu Buddhism. For this reason, the believers are encouraged to actively engage in propagating the teaching. This evangelistic practice is called *shakubuku*.

Nichiren Shoshu came to the United States through the immigration of its members to Hawaii and the mainland West Coast after World War II. However, the organization of work was largely the result of the arrival of leaders from Soka Kyoiki Gakkai (Creative Education Society), a Nichiren Shoshu lay movement founded in Japan in 1930. Repressed prior to World War II, it experienced growth in the decades after the war. In 1957 the Soka Gakkai leader Masayasu Sadanaga moved to the United States, and in the following year began holding meetings in Washington, D.C. The American Chapter of Soka Gakkai was organized in 1960 following the visit of Soka Gakkai International's president Daisaku Ikeda.

In 1965 the group built the first U.S. Nichiren Shoshu temple, which was constructed in Etiwanda, California. Over the next decade additional temples were opened in Chicago, San Francisco, Honolulu, suburban New York City, and Washington, D.C.; each location was in an urban center with a large Japanese ethnic community, and each temple was headed by one or more priests sent from Japan. Through the 1980s the temples and the lay organization worked closely together, though Soka Gakkai had numerous additional centers across North America, most of which were not geographically close to one of the 6 temples and most of whose members were not trained in temple worship.

During the late 1980s tension between the Soka Gakkai and the Nichiren Shoshu in Japan began to emerge. In 1991 Nichiren Shoshu excommunicated President Ikeda and cast the Soka Gakkai out of the Nichiren Shoshu organization. As a result, the six temples in the United States and the Soka Gakkai went their separate ways. A polemic and legal war continued between the two groups, and in 1997 the Nichiren Shoshu ordered all of its members to disassociate themselves from the Soka Gakkai by November 30, 1997, or face losing their membership status.

Membership: In 2002 Nichiren Shoshu reported more than 700 local temples in Japan, 6 temples in the United States, and temples in Europe, Brazil, Africa, and Taiwan. There are 21 temples, propagation centers, and offices outside of Japan. There are an estimated 350,000 believers worldwide, including approximately 7,000 in the United States, Canada, and Central America.

Periodicals: *Nichiren Shoshu Monthly*.

Remarks: Since World War II, as Soka Gakkai has grown in Japan, it has been strongly opposed by other Buddhist groups. First, Nichiren Shoshu articulated the doctrine of *obutsu myogo*, that is, a government essentially aligned with Buddhism. It called for the unification of imperial authority and Buddhism as well as the designation of Buddhism as the state religion. To this end it entered the field of politics, and by 1955 it had manifested a remarkable ability in getting its candidates elected. In 1964 a political party, the Komei Kai, was organized, and it soon became the third largest party in the Japanese Upper House; in 1965 the party elected 20 members. Second, in its evangelical efforts Soka Gakkai taught the practice of *shaku-buku*, literally "bend and flatten," the name given to the high-pressure recruitment tactics used on potential converts. The organization's opponents claimed that the tactics include bullying and badgering, applying pressure to the vulnerable, and, occasionally, physical assault. (Such practices have not been evident or reported in relation to the movement in the United States.) However, disturbed by Nichiren Shoshu's success, 96 Japanese religious bodies united in 1965 to fight it as a political entity. During the 1970s its political influence waned considerably, though it remains a powerful force.

In 1979 Soka Gakkai International was briefly affected by a scandal that erupted when some members accused Ikeda of personal misconduct. When tried, those who had brought the accusations were found guilty of libel. Meanwhile, the organization lost the support of some members, and a few Nichiren Shoshu priests resigned, but the organization quickly recovered.

Sources:

Nichiren Shoshu Temple. www.nst.org.

Ikeda, Daisaku. *Guidance Memo*. Tokyo: Seikyo Press, 1966.

Kirimura, Tasiji. *Fundamentals of Buddhism*. Tokyo: Nichiren Shoshu Center, 1977.

The Liturgy of Nichiren Shoshu. Etiwanda, CA: Nichiren Shoshu Temple, 1979.

Soka Gakkai. Tokyo: Soka Gakkai, 1983.

Williams, George M. *Freedom and Influence*. Santa Monica, CA: World Tribune Press, 1985.

Palolo Kwannon Temple (Tendai Sect)
3326 Paalea St., Honolulu, HI 96816

The Palolo Kwannon Temple in Honolulu is a small center of worship for Kwannon, the Japanese equivalent of Kwan Yin, the goddess of mercy.

The temple was founded in 1935 as an outpost of a large Kwannon temple in southern Japan. Kwannon is thought of in much the same way that Amida is thought of in Shin Buddhism, that is, as a bodhisattva, one who appears spiritually to people to enlighten them. A statue of Juzo Busatsu, another popular bodhisattva and patron of fishermen, had been placed on the southern shore of Oahu. It was cast into the sea and broken during World War II. After the war, the statue was found and repaired, and it now rests in the dooryard of the temple.

The founders of the temple, Rev. Kokan Matsumoto and Rev. Myosei Matsumoto, both immigrants from Kumamoto, Japan, started the Palolo Kwannon Temple in a humble residence in Palolo Valley before 1935, but as membership grew they saw the need for a larger building, so in 1935 the Palolo Kwannon Temple was dedicated.

In 1935 Rev. Kokan Matsumoto, through the kind guidance of Abp. Kyojun Shimizutani of Asakusa Kwannon Temple, was introduced to Abp. Kocho Chida of the Aira Kwannon Temple, Tendai Sect, in Kumamoto, Japan. Reverend Matsumoto received his religious training and ordination at Aira Kwannon Temple and returned to Hawaii. The following year Rev. Myosei Matsumoto received her training and ordination at Aira Kwannon Temple.

After the death of Rev. Kokan Matsumoto in 1944, Rev. Myosei Matsumoto served the temple until the return of her son, Bp. Chiko Matsumoto, in 1958, and in 1959 Reverend Myosei passed away. From 1958 Bishop Matsumoto ministered through his faith in Kwannon Bosatsu until his death in August 1986. Reverend Eshin Matsumoto, his wife, succeeded as the fourth head priest of Palolo Kwannon Temple.

Membership: Not reported.

Sources:

Palolo Kwannon Temple. http://tendai.org/i_around_the_world/hawaii/palolo-kwannon-temple-honolulu.html

Reiyukai America

20 N Raymond Ave., Ste. 200, Pasadena, CA 91103

Alternate Address: San Diego Office: 3142 E Plaza Blvd, Ste. I, National City, CA 91950. International Headquarters: 7-8, Azabudai 1-chome, Minato-ku, Tokyo 106-8644, Japan; Reiyukai Canada Office, 8833 Selkirk St., Vancouver, BC, V6P 4J6 Canada.

Reiyukai derives from the attempts of Kakutaro Kubo (1892–1944), a young Buddhist layman, to find a new way of Buddhism to replace what he considered the dead, formal Buddhism of 1920s Japan. Born near the birthplace of Buddhist prophet-reformer Nichiren (1222–1282), Kubo developed an early interest in the Lotus Sutra. Nichiren had taught his followers to emphasize the teachings of the Lotus Sutra, one of a number of Buddhist texts. Moving to Tokyo at a still youthful age, he was adopted by a childless family who encouraged his spiritual explorations. Kubo's study of the sutra led him to reject the Buddhism he saw practiced in the local temples and to emphasize the need to incorporate the practices and principles of the Lotus Sutra into daily life.

Following an admonition in the Lotus Sutra, he began to urge others to accept, read, recite, expound, and copy the Lotus Sutra. Following the teachings of an earlier Nichiren reformer, Mugaku Nishida (1850–1918), he advocated the lay practice of Buddhism over control of Buddhist life to the priesthood, and followers were taught to practice in their homes rather than at the temples.

In 1928 Kubo composed Reiyukai's Blue Sutra, bringing together materials mainly from the Threefold Lotus Sutra. Members were encouraged to recite the Blue Sutra daily in the morning and in the evening (it takes approximately 30 minutes to complete the recitation).

The first attempt to form a group following Kubo's teachings was in Tokyo in 1924. On July 13, 1930, Reiyukai was officially inaugurated in a ceremony held in Tokyo, when Baron Taketoshi Nagayama, a Japanese nobleman, was named president. Baron Nagayama's presence in such a prominent position helped Reiyukai gain social credibility and probably protected Reiyukai from some of the government persecution experienced by similar groups during World War II. Kakutaro Kubo was named chairman of the board, and Kimi Kotani (1901–1971), his sister-in-law and later Kubo's successor as the president of Reiyukai, was named honorary president. The work grew tremendously during the war, and by 1950 there were more than one million members. Kotani inaugurated the Youth Group Society in 1954. In 1964 she established Mirokusan in Shizuoka Prefecture, a training center primarily for youth, dedicated to the practice of the teachings of Buddha and the realization of world peace.

After the death of Kimi Kotani on February 9, 1971, Tsugunari Kubo, son of Kakutaro Kubo, served as president until 1993, when he was succeeded by Yae Hamaguchi. After her death in 2000, Ichitaro Ogata, a survivor of the atom bomb on Hiroshima, was elected president.

By the 1970s the organization had begun to expand abroad to America, Asia, and Europe. In order to implement the ideas of Reiyukai among young people, an International Youth Speech Festival, with national phases in each country, was conducted during the 1980s and 1990s. In 2008 Reiyukai had centers in more than 20 countries and regions worldwide.

Reiyukai also inaugurated a political research center to provide information about political affairs to Reiyukai members. Although Reiyukai has not entered directly into partisan politics, unlike the Soka Gakkai, another Nichiren-inspired lay Buddhist group, it does encourage members to participate in the political process and to promote democratic ideals.

Reiyukai America was established on October 26, 1972, with its headquarters in Los Angeles, California. Although work was initially concentrated among Japanese Americans, the practice had begun to attract the English-speaking public. To promote communication among the family members, Reiyukai America promoted various speech contests, such as the Letter to My Parents Contest. Currently, groups of Reiyukai America members are located in Los Angeles and San Diego, California; Honolulu, Hawaii; Weston, Connecticut; and Chicago, Illinois. It is also expanding to the Hispanic community.

Reiyukai promotes one's personal development for the benefit of all humanity. Reiyukai's practice, which includes daily recitation of the Blue Sutra (various portions of the Threefold Lotus Sutra), can create awareness and appreciation of the vertical line of "past-time" interconnection extending from one's ancestors through one's parents to oneself. It also can create awareness and appreciation of the horizontal line of "current-time" interconnection extending throughout all of one's daily-life relationships. The culmination of practice is the sincere motivation to demonstrate to others, through one's own personal attitude, action, and example, effective ways of living together in harmony. Reiyukai believes that by enhancing awareness and actions as individuals, one can effect a better inner self, a better family, a better community, a better nation, and a better world.

Membership: In 2008 there were more than 4.2 million Reiyukai members worldwide.

Periodicals: *Reiyukai America News.* (Monthly newsletter available in English, Spanish, and Japanese.)

Sources:

Reiyukai America. www.reiyukai-usa.org.

Reiyukai Headquarters. www.reiyukai.org.

Reiyukai Canada. www.canada.reiyukai.org.

The Development of Japanese Lay Buddhism. Tokyo: Reiyukai, 1986.

Follow the One Genuine Path—A Collection of Speeches by Mrs. Kimi Kotani, Co-Founder of Reiyukai. Tokyo: Reiyukai, 2002

Mizuno, Taiji. The Life of Kakutaro Kubo. Tokyo: Reiyukai, 1998.

Ogata, Ichitaro. *Thus Have I Heard—Encountering, Learning from and Living by the Influence of Mrs. Kimi Kotani.* Tokyo: Reiyukai, 2008

Reiyukai: Awareness, Action and Development. Tokyo: Reiyukai, 1997.

Rissho Kosei Kai

c/o Rissho Kosei-kai Buddhist Church of Los Angeles, 2707 E 1st St., Los Angeles, CA 90033

Rissho Kosei Kai (the Society for the Establishment of Righteous and Friendly Intercourse) is one of the new Nichiren bodies that arose as World War II was beginning. The movement was founded by Nikkyo Niwano, a farmer's son, and Naganuma Myoko. Niwano (b. 1906), a self-taught man, was a member of Reiyukai, a Nichiren sect formed in 1922. Naganuma (1899–1957) was the wife of an iceman in Tokyo, and for many years suffered from a serious disease. On Niwano's advice, she joined Reiyukai and was healed. Together they left the organization and in 1938 began Rissho Kosei Kai. The motivation seemed to be Niwano's desire for independence as well as a greater leadership role.

Rissho Kosei Kai follows Nichiren's interpretation of Buddhism. Attention is focused on the three Hokke Sutras (the Muryogi Sutra, the Lotus Sutra, and the

Kanfugen Sutra). The Daimoku, the repetition of the mantra "Namu myoho renge kyo," is used. Unlike Nichiren Shoshu, Rissho Kosei Kai does not use the Daimoku for its power; instead, it is an expression of gratitude and faith. Man is bound by the laws of reincarnation and cause and effect. The consequences of these laws can be broken only by repentance and perfect living. The goal of Rissho Kosei Kai is the attainment of perfect Buddhahood through faith and repentance.

Dharma worship takes place in instruction halls and includes chanting of the Lotus Sutra and the Daimoku and a sermon. After the service, *hoza*, or group counseling, begins. The congregation divides into small groups for discussions of personal problems and of the deeper aspects of faith. Divinatory practices are often incorporated. There are three annual festivals: the Foundation Festival on March 5; the Flower Festival on Buddha's birthday, April 8; and the Grand Festival on October 13.

Although Rissho Kosei Kai has grown strong in Japan, it has penetrated the United States slowly. It began in 1959 when Tomoko Ozaki opened her home in Kealakekua, Kona, Hawaii, for a gathering of members who had migrated from Japan. The occasion was the visit of Rev. Kazue Yukawe. During the 1960s the movement spread to Honolulu and then to California and Chicago. The group consists mainly of Japanese Americans. Members are also located in Korea, Hong Kong, Thailand, and Brazil.

The Buddhist Center—Rissho Kosei-kai International of North America (RKINA) was founded in 2008 in Irvine, Orange County, California, to help support Dharma development in the United States. The center has inherited the founder's spirit of creating unity in the world.

Membership: In 1984 the Rissho Kosei-Kai reported 10 centers serving 1,200 families in the United States. There were four priests. It reported more than 5 million members worldwide. In 2008 Rissho Kosei-Kai's web site listed 17 centers in the United States and one in Canada.

Periodicals: *Shan Zai*. Available from www.rk-world.org. • *Dharma World*.

Sources:

Rissho Kosei-kai. www.rk-world.org.

Rissho Kosei-kai Sangha of America. www.buddhistcenter-rkina.org.

Niwano, Nichiko. *My Father, My Teacher*. Tokyo: Kosei Publishing, 1982.

Niwano, Nikkyo. *Lifetime Beginner*. Tokyo: Kosei Publishing, 1978.

Rissho Kosei-Kai. Tokyo: Kosei Publishing, 1966.

Shingon Mission

c/o Koyasan Shingon Mission, North America, 342 E 1st Street, Los Angeles, CA 90012

Shingon Buddhism is a Japanese esoteric right-hand tantric sect. It places great emphasis on ritual, imagery, and ceremony, as well as occultism. The central practice is the use of mantras as magical formulas. *Mantra* means "true word," and its use emphasizes the need for the correct formula to accomplish the end. The incorporation of popular magical practices is one secret of Shingon's success. The man who integrated the elements that became Shingon was a monk named Ku Kai, or as he is most popularly known, Kobo Daishi. A student of Chinese religion, he was initiated by the Chinese into esoteric studies. He returned to Japan and began Shingon in 808 C.E.. In 816 he received a grant of land, Koyasan, a mountain near Osaka, upon which a collection of temples and monasteries were built. It remains the international Shingon headquarters.

Shingon's right-hand tantrism specializes in the worship of masculine gods. The pantheon shows numerous Hindu deities. A central solar divinity is Vairochana, from whom emanates the world. Vairochana is represented by graphic forms—the mandala, a cosmological form that artistically represents the essence of the universe. Art is an important facet of Shingon; Ku Kai believed that only art could convey the inner meaning of the Buddha's teaching. Also seen on the mandalas are the Buddhas and bodhisattvas who personify the godhead, including Amida, Shakyamuni (Gautama Buddha), and Kannon (Kwan Yin). Practices of the Shingon

include meditation (often with the mantra), *mudras* (symbolic gestures), postures, and handling of ritual instruments.

Shingon was brought to the United States in 1902 by Hogen Yujiri, an immigrant laborer who opened a preaching hall in Hawaii on the island of Maui. He claimed to have been cured of an eye ailment by the "limitless compassion of Kobo Daishi." In 1903 Kodo Yamamoto gathered a Shingon following and built on Kauai the "Eighty-eight Holy Places of Hawaii's Garden Isle," modeled on a Japanese shrine. Before the decade was out, temples had been founded in Honolulu and on the Big Island (Hawaii). The movement spread quickly through the plantations.

In 1914 Eikaku Seki came to Honolulu as an official representative from Koyasan. He considered deplorable the chaotic condition of the popularized manifestation of his faith. He set up headquarters and built a detached temple of the Kongobuji, the main temple on Koyasan. Shingon continued to grow and gradually came under Seki's control.

Shingon reached its peak in the years before World War II. Since then, it has declined. It had only thirteen temples in 1972, half of the number reported in 1926. Headquarters are in Honolulu where Bp. Tetsuei Katoda oversees 12 ministers.

Membership: Not reported. Beside the dozen temples in Hawaii, there is also a Shingon temple in Los Angeles, California.

Sources:

Light of Buddha. Los Angeles: Koyasan Buddhist Temple, 1968.

Shinnyo-En

3910 Bret Harte Dr., Redwood City, CA 94061

Alternate Address: Shinnyo-en Grand Head Temple 1-2-13 Shibasaki-cho, Tachikawa, Tokyo 190-0023 Japan.

Headquartered in Japan, Shinnyo-en is a lay Buddhist order founded in 1936 by Shinjo Ito (1906–1989) and his wife Tomoji Ito (1912–1967). Shinjo Ito mastered the traditional esoteric teachings of Shingon Buddhism at Daigoji Temple in Japan, where he became a successor to the Buddhist Dharma stream. There he was bestowed with the rank of Great Acharya ("Great Master"). As an ordained priest, he continued his studies in traditional Buddhism with the wish to make salvation available to a wide scope of people. Toward that end, he adopted the Mahaparinirvana Sutra (Buddha Shakyamuni's last teaching) as the main scripture of Shinnyo-en. In addition, he and his wife perfected a meditation training known as *sesshin* to help trainees understand the teachings of the Buddha and apply them in their immediate surroundings (family, workplace, school, and community). Followers are encouraged to become well-rounded members of society who can show the spirit of Buddhism through their own examples. It is believed that active involvement in society helps one to understand the theoretical principles of Buddhism and to recognize the inherent beauty and order of all things.

During the 1960s Shinjo and Tomoji Ito made several trips to foster religious exchange and goodwill. In 1966 they traveled to Thailand to attend the eighth International Conference of the World Fellowship of major religions. Included in this trip was an audience with Pope Paul VI at the Vatican. As a result of these travels, congregations developed in various parts of Asia (Taiwan, Hong Kong, Singapore, Thailand, and Sri Lanka), Australia, and Europe (France, Italy, Belgium, the United Kingdom, and Germany).

Sinjo Ito first came to the United States in 1970; the first Shinnyo-en temple was established in Hawaii in 1973. Since then, other congregations have been founded in San Francisco, Los Angeles, Seattle, White Plains (New York), and Chicago. Shinnyo-en USA administers the temples in the continental United States and has its head temple in Redwood City, California.

After Sinhjo Ito's death, his daughter formally succeeded him as the new head of Shinnyo-en.

The Shinnyo-en Foundation, established in 1994, helps build more caring communities by supporting educational programs that engage and inspire young people in meaningful acts of service.

Membership: In 2001 Shinnyo-en reported 796,477 members worldwide. Congregations can also be found in France, Belgium, Germany, Singapore, Hong Kong, Thailand, and Australia. In 2008 the Shinnyo-en USA web site listed 12 training centers and temples in the United States.

Educational Facilities:

Shinnyo-En Foundation, San Francisco, California.

Periodicals: *Nirvana* (English). • *Nagai Jiho* (Japanese). • *Kangi Sekai* (Japanese).

Sources:

Shinnyo-en USA. www.shinnyoenusa.net.

Global Shinnyo-en web site. www.shinnyo-en.org.

Shinnyo-en Foundation. www.sef.org.

Ito Shinjo. *Tomoshibi Nen Nen: Buddha's Light Everlasting.* Tokyo: Shin-nyo-En, 1976.

Nagai, Michiko. "Magic and Self-Cultivation in a New Religion: The Case of Shinnyoen." *Japanese Journal of Religious Studies* 22, nos. 3–4 (1995): 301–321.

Sakashita, Jay. "Shinnyoen and the Transmission of Japanese New Religions Abroad." Ph.D. diss., University of Stirling (Scotland), 1998.

The Way to Nirvana. Tokyo: Shinnyo-En, 1977.

Shinshu Kyokai Mission of Hawaii

1631 S Beretania St., Honolulu, HI 96826

The Shinshu Kyokai Mission of Hawaii is a Shinshu congregation in Honolulu that is independent of both the Honpa Hongwanji and the Higashi Hongwanji. As a congregational project, the group maintains a dormitory for students and working men.

Shinshu Kyokai Mission of Hawaii was founded on April 14, 1914, in Pawaa as a fledgling independent group of Jodoshinshu faithful. Twenty-five founding members met at Seisuke Yamashita's home in Liliha to form a charter and bylaws. They determined that their group would be called Shinshiyu Kiyokai. Its membership was comprised of *issei* immigrants primarily from Hiroshima who were deeply devoted to the life and teachings of Shinran Shonin, who taught the life of gratitude and reverence based on the truth of Amida Buddha's Primal Vows and Sacred Name that is the basis of Universal Salvation for all sentient beings, not only man.

Membership: In 1982 there were 800 members in one center.

Sources:

Shinshu Kyokai Mission. www.shinshukyokai.org.

Soka Gakkai International–USA (SGI–USA)

606 Wilshire Blvd., Santa Monica, CA 90401-1427

Alternate Address: Soka Gakkai International Headquarters, 15-3 Samoncho, Shinjuku-ku Tokyo 160-0017, Japan.

Soka Gakkai International–USA (SGI–USA) is a U.S. Buddhist organization that responds to the need for individual happiness and empowerment and the values of peace, culture, and education. Its exclusively lay membership adheres to the teachings of the Nichiren school of Mahayana Buddhism. The name *Soka Gakkai* literally means "society for the creation of value."

The philosophical origins of SGI–USA can be traced to the teachings of the historical Buddha known as Shakyamuni, who lived some 2,500 years ago in what is modern-day Nepal. Born Gautama Siddhartha, he renounced his royal birthright and set out in search of a solution to the suffering related to the inescapable experiences of birth, aging, sickness, and death. He spent the last years of his life engaging followers in dialogue and teaching his disciples to continue his work. After his death, Buddhism spread throughout southern and eastern Asia and, from the nineteenth century onward, to other continents.

SGI–USA believes that Shakyamuni's teachings culminate in the inference to a universal law (Sanskrit: Dharma) described in the Lotus Sutra and in his enlightenment as a human being. The thirteenth-century Buddhist teacher Nichiren Daishonin declared that this universal law is expressed in the phrase "Nam-myohorenge-kyo" and underlies the interdependent workings of all life. Accordingly, Nichiren's teachings affirm respect for all life and the potential to achieve happiness and global peace and prosperity. He first inscribed the object of devotion known as the Gohonzon to depict enlightenment within the context of all human conditions of life.

The Buddhist practice of SGI–USA members involves chanting "Nam-myoho-renge-kyo" and reciting portions of the Lotus Sutra before the Gohonzon. Typically, the Gohonzon is enshrined in a home altar.

Tsunesaburo Makiguchi (1871–1944) used the term *Soka* to encapsulate his theory of value creation and first applied it to his thoughts on education. The 1930 publication of his work, *The System of Value Creating Pedagogy*, marks the founding of the Soka Gakkai society as an educators' colloquium interested primarily in educational reform and secondly in the application of Buddhist principles to educational theory. During the 1930s it attracted more members with a primary interest in the religious practice of Nichiren Buddhism and its significance to their lives and the society in which they lived. The organizations' religious beliefs were at odds with State Shinto, the national religion of Japan from 1868 to 1945 used by the militarist government during World War II to rally the nation behind its war efforts and aggression against other Asian countries. For his opposition to wartime policies Makiguchi was sent to prison, where he died. Among others, Makiguchi's closest associate, Josei Toda (1900–1958), was also imprisoned. After Toda's release near the end of the war, he set about rebuilding the Soka Gakkai, determined to increase the membership to 750,000 households from its 1945 base of 3,000 households. He accomplished this goal before his death in 1958.

The Buddhist practice of the Soka Gakkai was brought to the United States by Japanese war brides who had married American military personnel during the Occupation. The U.S. chapter was formally established during a visit by the third Soka Gakkai president, Daisaku Ikeda, in 1960. The Soka Gakkai in the United States developed a diverse following under the name Nichiren Shoshu Soka Gakkai of America (NSA). In 1975 the Soka Gakkai International (SGI) association was formed, naming Ikeda as its president.

Simmering tensions between the SGI association and the Nichiren Shoshu clergy—dating back to the Soka Gakkai's opposition and Nichiren Shoshu's capitulation to State Shinto during World War II—erupted into public controversy in 1990. The SGI membership charged that Nichiren Shoshu exerted unreasonable control over its range of activities. In November 1991 Nichiren Shoshu ultimately responded by "excommunicating" the SGI. NSA changed its organizational name to Soka Gakkai International–USA, effectively severing all ties with Nichiren Shoshu.

The central activity of SGI–USA is the neighborhood discussion meeting. At these informal gatherings, usually held in members' homes, members pray together, share their experiences in faith, and study and discuss ways Buddhism can best apply to the everyday challenges of life. The organization also sponsors youth activities, educational seminars, cultural events, and exhibits that invite dialogue on common concerns such as human security, children's rights, the environment, and nuclear disarmament. These include Victory Over Violence, a youth-driven campaign to raise community awareness of kinds of violence and their potential causes and solutions; participation in interreligious dialogues and conferences; Treasuring the Future: Children's Rights and Realities, a traveling exhibit; conferences in support of the Earth Charter Initiative; and an educational project that collected and shipped more than 14,000 books to schools and colleges in Ghana.

Affiliated institutions include the Boston Research Center for the Twenty-first Century, Toda Institute for Global Peace and Policy Research, Soka University of America, Soka University of Japan, Institute of Oriental Philosophy, Tokyo Fuji Art Museum, and Minon Concert Association.

Membership: In 2002 SGI–USA reported 350,000 members, with 70 centers in the United States. The organization is part of the Soka Gakkai International, whose membership is more than 12 million in 180 countries and territories.

Educational Facilities:

Soka Gakkai University, Calabasas, California.

Periodicals: *World Tribune • Living Buddhism*

Sources:

SGA–USA. www.sgi-usa.org.

Soka Gakkai International (SGI). www.sgi.org.

Eppsteiner, Robert. *The Soka Gakkai International: Religious Roots, Early History, and Contemporary Development*. Cambridge, MA: Soka Gakkai International—USA, 1997.

Hamond, Philip, and David Machacek. *Soka Gakkai in America: Accommodation and Conversion*. Oxford, U.K.: Oxford University Press, 1999.

Ikeda, Daisaku. *Guidance Memo*. Tokyo: Seikyo Press, 1966.

Machacek, David, and Bryan Wilson, eds. *Global Citizens: The Soka Gakkai Buddhist Movement in the World*. Oxford, U.K.: Oxford University Press,2000.

Rawlinson, Andrew. *The Book of Enlightened Masters: Western Teachers in Asian Traditions*. Chicago: Open Court, 1997.

Seager, Richard Hughes. *Encountering the Dharma: Daisaku Ikeda, Soka Gakkai, and the Globalization of Buddhist Humanism*. Berkeley: University of California Press, 2006

Voices of Protest: Priests Speak Out for the Reformation of Nichiren Shoshu. Tokyo: Soka Gakkai International, 1993.

Williams, George M. *Freedom and Influence*. Santa Monica, CA: World Tribune Press, 1985.

Wilson, Brian, and Karel Dobbelaere. *A Time to Chant: The Soka Gakkai Buddhists in Britian*. Chicago: Open Court, 1997.

Tendai Buddhist Institute

1525 Rte. 295, East Chatham, NY 12060

Tendai Buddhism traces its history to the ninth century and the discovery of Chinese Tian Tai Buddhism by a Japanese Buddhist priest named Saicho (767–822). Having read some of the works of Zhi Yi (or Chih-i, 538–597), the founder of Tian Tai, Saicho traveled to China to study and returned in 805 C.E. with a number of Tian Tai texts. Finding the favor of the Japanese emperor, he settled on Mt. Hiei and developed the Japanese form of Tian Tai which we know as Tendai.

Tian Tai has developed a system to classify the many Buddhist texts and schools in a hierarchy of worthiness. The Lotus Sutra was ranked at the top of its consideration. Based upon his understanding of the Lotus Sutra, Saicho came to believe that all people could reach Buddhahood. Most Buddhist teachers in Japan at the time taught that only some people could become enlightened, and only a few reach full Buddhahood.

Saicho's disciples Ennin (794–864) and Annen (c. 841–c. 901) developed the esoteric potential that had manifested in the Tian Tai texts. They studied the two mandalas, the Diamond Realm and Womb World, and tended to see the magical practices associated with them (participation in the spiritual realms they picture) to be even superior to the Lotus Sutra. Ennin also brought the practice of invoking the name of the Buddha Amitabha (Amida) back to Japan.

Tendai believers came to the United States in the nineteenth century. The first temple, the Fudo-son temple, was opened in Hawaii in 1918 and survived until 1950, and then was reopened in 1973 with Rev. Ryokan Ara as its first bishop. Subsequently, several other Tendai temples were opened on various islands.

The Rev. Jikai Clark Choffy, who studied and was ordained at Mount Hiei in 1975, has recently opened a small private pilgrimage, Mitsugon-an, at his residence in Austin, Texas.

The Ven. Masao Shoshin Ichishima, who worked with Bp. Ara in Hawaii, trained two Americans: Joshin Jonathan Driscol and Daishin David Hall. Driscol completed training at Mount Hiei and returned to the United States in 1982, settling in New Mexico.

The Ven. Monshin Paul Naamon, another American student of the Venerable Ichishima, received ordination in 1992 and subsequently practiced as a priest in Japan. In 1995 Monshin and his wife, Shumon Tamami Naamon, opened the Karuna Tendai Dharma Center in Canaan, New York, modeled after a Japanese village temple. It is home to more than 100 families from New York and Massachusetts. Branch sanghas have also been formed in Great Barrington, Massachusetts; Albany and Buffalo, New York; and Germany and Denmark.

In 2001 an official visit by Tendai-shu Jigyodan to the Karuna Tendai Dharma Center led to its being designated a *betsuin*, or branch temple, of Enryaku-ji (the monastery on Mount Hiei) in North America.

Membership: Not reported. In 2008 there were seven Tendai centers in the United States, of which four were in Hawaii. Besides the large following in Japan, there were branch temples in Brazil, Denmark, Germany, England, and India.

Sources:

Groner, Paul. *Ryogen and Mount Hiei: Japanese Tendai in the Tenth Century*. Honolulu: University of Hawaii Press, 2002.

Pruden, Leo M., and Paul L. Swanson, trans. *The Essentials of the Vinaya Tradition: The Collected Teachings of the Tendai Lotus School*. Berkeley, CA: Numata Center for Buddhist Translation and Research, 1996.

Saso, Michael R. *Tantric Art and Meditation: The Tendai Tradition*. Honolulu, HI: Tendai Educational Foundation, 1990.

Tendai Buddhist Institute. www.tendai.org/.

Todaiji Hawaii Bekkaku Honzan

426 Luakini St., Honolulu, HI 96814

The Kegon sect was introduced into Japan from China in the eighth century and was one of the so-called Nara sects. Its basic text was the Avatamsakasutra. The sutra tells of the visit of Sudhana to some Buddhist worthies in order to realize the principle of *dharmadhatu*, the realization of the domain of Buddha's law. Basic is the idea of mutual interdependence and causation of all that exists. Symbolic of this interdependence is a figure known as Indra's Net, a huge net that bears a jewel at each point of intersection. Each jewel bears the image of all the others.

In Kegon, a traditional form of Buddhism, nature is seen to exist in a set of polarities—universality/specialization, integration/differentiation, and similarity/diversity. Ancestor worship is of prime importance and is coupled with the offering of food and drink in a gesture of belief in the nondying of spiritual being. The mutual interaction of this life and the next is a strongly held belief.

There is only one Kegon center in the United States—the Todaiji Hawaii Bekkaku Honzan. The Todaiji was organized in Honolulu by Bp. Tatsusho Hirai, who claimed to be the only female Buddhist bishop in the world. After an unsuccessful marriage to a second-generation Japanese immigrant to Hawaii, she returned to Japan and entered the Todaiji Temple as a nun. After years of study, she returned to Hawaii as a missionary and, after the war, organized the Branch Temple (officially recognized in 1948). Construction of the present temple began in 1950 and was finished in 1958.

Bishop Hirai faced opposition from the Buddhist clergy, who claim that she is incapable of expounding Kegon teaching. Nevertheless, she has persisted, aided by her adopted daughter, Kaeko Hirai, whom she trained and ordained.

Membership: In 1982 the center in Hawaii reported 30,000 adherents (i.e., the number who had received either a healing blessing and/or special amulet from the center).

Sources:

Hirai, Tatsusho. *Todaiji of Hawaii*. Honolulu: Todaiji Hawaii Bekkaku Honzan, n.d.

 # Zen Buddhism

Association Zen Internationale (AZI)

c/o New Orleans Zen Temple, 748 Camp St., New Orleans, LA 70130

Alternate Address: International Headquarters: Association Zen Internationale, 175, rue Tolbiac, 75013 Paris, France.

The Association Zen Internationale (AZI) was founded in 1970 by Taisen Deshimaru Roshi (1914–1982) in Paris, France, and brought to the United States in 1983 by Robert Livingston Roshi (b. 1933), who founded the American Zen Association, its U.S. affiliate. Born into an old Samurai family, Taisen Deshimaru rejected both the Shinshu Buddhism of his mother and the Christianity that had captured his attention as a youth. He eventually found his way to Zen and to the Soto Master Kodo Sawaki.

Kodo Sawaki was a wandering monk. As a teenager he had joined the army, and after almost dying as a result of a wound, he returned to Japan as a war casualty with neither family nor friends. He eventually found his way to Eiheiji monastery, where he stayed for several years. After leaving the monastery, he wandered the land and met Soto Master Koho Roshi, from whom he eventually received Dharma transmission. Over the years, a few disciples attached to him, including Taisen Deshimaru. They remained together until Deshimaru began his period of service in the Japanese Army during World War II. When the war was finally over, Deshimaru rejoined his master and remained by his side until the latter's death. He received the monastic ordination shortly before the master fell ill, and he received the transmission (the *Shiho*) in 1965 while Kodo Sawaki was on his deathbed. The master also commissioned Deshimaru to go to the west "so that Buddhism may again flourish."

Two years later Deshimaru entrusted the care of his family to his son, settled his business affairs, and took the Trans-Siberian rail to France, with no money and no knowledge of a single word of French. He was 53. He began sitting in the storage area of a food store. As the work grew he opened a dojo, founded other dojos throughout France, and eventually built the Gendronnire Temple, the biggest dojo in the west. In recognition of his accomplishment, he was recognized by the Soto authorities in Japan and named Kaikyosokan, responsible for Zen for all of Europe.

Deshimaru fell ill at the beginning of 1982 but continued teaching *zazen* each day. In the spring he left France for Japan, where he died on April 30.

Deshimaru's lineage was brought to the United States by Robert Livingston Roshi, who had practiced with him in Europe for 10 years. Livingston had grown up in New York, California, and Texas, and graduated from Cornell University. He spent two years in Japan and Korea in the U.S. army in the early 1950s, and became a businessman in Europe. He retired in the early 1970s and began practicing Zen with Master Deshimaru in Paris. Deshimaru authorized Livingston to teach and asked him to go to the United States to spread the teachings of true Zen. So in 1983 Livingston Roshi opened the New Orleans Zen Temple.

The New Orleans Zen Temple continues the Soto Zen practices established in France. Members of the New Orleans community practice *zazen* and *samu* (work practice) together, and Livingston Roshi conducts *sesshin* (retreats) every month. From the initial efforts in New Orleans, centers have been opened in other cities.

AZI was brought to Canada by Philippe Duchesne, who opened work in Sutton, Quebec. Subsequently, centers were opened at several locations in Quebec and in New Brunswick.

Membership: In 2002 the association reported 328 members. In 2008 affiliated centers were operating in New Orleans; New York; Mt. Pleasant, Michigan; and Miami, Florida. AZI centers are found around the world in 36 countries.

Periodicals: *Zen Magazine*. • *Here and Now*.

Sources:

Association Zen Internationale. www.zen-azi.org.

Morreale, Don. *The Complete Guide to Buddhist America*. Boston: Shambhala, 1998.

Atlanta Soto Zen Center (ASZC)

1167 C/D Zonolite Pl., Atlanta, GA 30306

The Atlanta Soto Zen Center (ASZC) was founded in the early 1970s under the leadership of Abbot Zenkai Taiun Michael Elliston, who was a disciple of Rev. Dr. Soyu Matsuoka-Roshi (d. 1997) in Chicago during the 1960s. In 2008 Elliston Sensei was the Zen Center's spiritual leader.

The ASZC provides a group (*sangha*) to sit with, a place to sit together with a full *zazen* schedule, a lending library, and experienced teachers to respond to any questions that arise. The Zen Center also operates a prison outreach program and offers meditation instruction to prisoners throughout the state of Georgia.

Membership: Not reported. In 2008 the ASZC had affiliated groups in Athens, Georgia; Chattanooga, Tennessee; Emory University in Atlanta, Georgia; Huntsville, Alabama; Statesboro, Georgia; and Wichita, Kansas.

Sources:

Atlanta Soto Zen Center. www.aszc.org.

Morreale, Don. *The Complete Guide to Buddhist America*. Boston: Shambhala, 1998.

Berkeley Zen Center

1931 Russell St., Berkeley, CA 94703

The Berkeley Zen Center is one of several organizations that originated in the Zen Center of San Francisco during the years of its leadership by Shunryu Suzuki Roshi (1901–1971). The Berkeley center was founded in 1967 and was at one in belief and practice with its parent body. However, following Suzuki Roshi's death, and the issues raised concerning the conduct of his successor, the Berkeley center became independent under Suzuki Roshi's student, Sojun Mel Weitsman. Emphasis is on lay practice.

In September 1979 Berkeley Zen Center moved to its present location on Russell Street, where a new *zendo* was constructed and officially named Shogakuji, in honor of Shogaku Shunryu Suzuki Roshi. There is a small residential community living at the center that includes priests, lay students, and children. Its general membership numbers more than 100, most living in Berkeley and the surrounding area. It is supported by the dues, donations, and strong work practice of members and friends who come from all walks of life and different age groups.

Membership: There is one center.

Periodicals: *Newsletter*.

Sources:

Berkeley Zen Center. www.berkeleyzencenter.org.

California Bosatsukai

5632 Green Oak Dr., Los Angeles, CA 90068

The California Bosatsukai shares the traditions of both Soen Nakagawa Roshi and Nyogen Senzaki (1876–1958), two Japanese Zen Buddhist pioneers in the United States. A Rinzai Zen monk, Senzaki came to California in 1905, and in 1928 established his own *zendo* in San Francisco. He started another in 1929 in Los Angeles. He was the Zen master of these two independent *zendos* until he died in 1958. The California Bosatsukai continues the tradition of Senzaki in Los Angeles.

In the early 1960s Hakuun Yasutani Roshi, who was a student of Soen Nakagawa Roshi and had been trained on both the Rinzai and Soto Zen traditions, came to the United States. Hakuun Yasutani accepted the role of Zen master for the California Bosatsukai along with his duties at other centers. He continued working with the California Bosatsukai until his death in 1973. Besides the Los Angeles center, there are branches in Hollywood, Del Mar, Los Gatos, and San Diego, California.

Membership: Not reported. There are approximately 100 members.

Sources:

Nordstrom, Louis, ed. *Namu Dai Bosa*. New York: Theatre Arts Books, 1976.

Senzaki, Nyogen, and Ruth Stout McCandless, eds. *Buddhism and Zen*. New York: Philosophical Library, 1953.

Senzaki, Nyogen, and Salidin Reps, trans. *Ten Bulls*. Los Angeles: DeVorss, 1935.

Cambridge Buddhist Association

75 Sparks St., Cambridge, MA 02138

The Cambridge Buddhist Association (CBA), a nonsectarian center for lay Buddhist practice and studies, grew out of an interest in Zen Buddhism that developed in the 1950s at Harvard University. It first took shape during the 1957 visit to Cambridge, Massachusetts, of the noted Buddhist scholar Daisetz Teitaro Suzuki (1870–1966) and Dr. Shinichi Hisamatsu, professor emeritus of Kyoto University, the first scholar to give a series of lectures on Buddhism at the Harvard Divinity School. A group headed by Mr. and Mrs. John Mitchell persuaded the two scholars to remain in Cambridge for a while to establish a western-style *zendo* (meditation center). Suzuki became the first president of the new association, a position he held until his death. For a period, Shunryu Suzuki Roshi of the Zen Center of San Francisco served as the spiritual advisor until the selection of a second president, the Rev. Chimyo Horioka, a Shingon Buddhist priest.

In 2008 the president and spiritual teacher of the association was Maurine Myoon Stuart, who received her permission to teach from the late Soen Nakagawa Roshi of Kyoto, Japan. Stuart is also a musician, an instructor in Buddhism at Phillips Exeter Academy in New Hampshire, and a popular teacher at other Buddhist centers around the United States. Other directors and advisors of the association have included Dr. Masatoshi Nagatomi of Harvard University and the late Dr. Holmes Welch, author of a variety of books on Chinese Buddhism. Because the association was for many years the only Zen center in the Boston area, it served as a central locus for Buddhist-interfaith dialogue. The results of a particularly significant early Christian dialogue session were published as *Conversations: Christian and Buddhist* (1968).

The association's zendo is in an old house in a residential neighborhood of Cambridge. Though the association does not publish a periodical or handbooks, it does have an extensive library of books and periodicals on Buddhism and related topics that it makes available to members. There is a daily (Thursdays excepted) meditation period open to the public, as well as monthly *sesshin* retreats, occasional lectures, and private interviews. There are no communal living facilities at the temple or any shared *sangha* dwellings nearby. A single resident, usually chosen from among the students, serves the temple for a short designated period. The emphasis of instruction at the temple is on *zazen* practice (sitting meditation). Local universities and other schools bring classes and groups to the center for instruction on Buddhism and *zazen* practice.

CBA's house on Sparks Street is open for use by Buddhist groups in the Boston area. All groups wishing to use the space must be approved by and make arrangements with the board of trustees. Throughout the years, a number of Buddhist groups have met at the Cambridge Buddhist Association: Tibetan groups, a Sri Lankan Theravada group, Zen groups, the Sakya Institute, Buddhist Peace Fellowship, and Boston Old Path Sangha in the tradition of Thich Nhat Han, among others.

Membership: In 1988 the association reported approximately 150 members and include a group from the Vietnamese-American community.

Sources:

"Cambridge Buddhist Association." The Pluralism Project at Harvard University web site. www.pluralism.org/research/profiles/display.php?profile=74856.

Cambridge Buddhist Association. Cambridge, MA: Cambridge Buddhist Association, 1960.

Fujimoto, Rindo. *The Way of Zazen*. Cambridge, MA: Cambridge Buddhist Association, 1969.

Graham, Aelred. *Conversations: Buddhist and Christian*. New York: Harcourt, Brace and World, 1968.

Renfrew, Sita Paulickpulle. *A Buddhist Guide for Laymen*. Cambridge, MA: Cambridge Buddhist Association, 1963.

Suzuki, Daisetz T. *The Chain of Compassion*. Cambridge, MA: Cambridge Buddhist Association, 1966.

Chozen-ji Kyudo

Daihonzan Chozen-ji/International Zen Dojo, 3565 Kalihi St., Honolulu, HI 96819

Alternate Address: Chozen-ji Betsuin/International Zen Dojo of Wisconsin, 301 S Bedford St., Ste. 219, Madison, WI 53703.

The Chozen-ji lineage of Zen emphasizes the integration of traditional Rinzai Zen training with instruction in the martial and fine arts. It was developed by Omori Roshi (b. 1904), who in 1975 was recognized as a Dharma successor of the Tenryu-ji Zen lineage. That same year he established Seitaiji Monastery. Three years later he was named president of Hanazono University, where he had previously taught.

In 1972 Omori Roshi transmitted a new Zen lineage to the United States in 1972 with the establishment of Chozen-ji, International Zen Dojo in Hawaii. Subsequently a center was opened in Wisconsin. The U.S. centers place an emphasis on kyudo, Zen archery, the oldest of Japan's traditional martial arts. Archery was neglected in the twentieth century with the new emphasis on firearms in the armed services. However, it was preserved by Honda Toshizane, a kyudo instructor at Tokyo Imperial University who developed an eclectic style known as the Honda Ryu. After the war, all other martial arts instruction was banned, but kyudo was allowed. The Zen Nihon Kyudo Federation (All Japan Kyudo Federation) was established in 1953. Omori Roshi is noted to have said, "Zen without the accompanying physical experience is nothing but empty discussion. Martial Ways without truly realizing the mind is nothing but beastly behavior."

Chozen-ji developed in the years after Japan's defeat in World War II, and the problems of war and peace weighed heavily on the consciousness of Omori Roshi. Out of that concern, in 1982 the Hawaiian members of Chozen-ji initiated the Institute of Zen Studies. It is their understanding there is an urgent need for Zen practitioners to introduce their perspective on human beings and the world to the west as part of the solution to ongoing international tensions.

Membership: Not reported. There are two centers in the United States, one in Hawaii and one in Wisconsin.

Periodicals: *The Journal, Institute of Zen Studies*.

Sources:

Daihonzan Chozen-ji/International Zen Dojo. www.chozen-ji.org.

Chozen-ji Betsuin/International Zen Dojo of Wisconsin. www.cbizdw.org.

Dogen Hosokawa. *Omori Sogen*. London: Kegan Paul International, 1997.

The Institute of Zen Studies. institutezenstudies.com.

Sogen Omori. *An Introduction to Zen Training*. London: Kegan Paul International, 1996.

Veary, Nana. *Change We Must*. Honolulu, HI: Water Margin Press, 1989.

Dharma Rain Zen Center

2539 SE Madison, Portland, OR 97214

Dharma Rain Zen Center is a Soto Zen Temple established in 1973 for lay practice under the direction of Kyogen Carlson and Gyokuko Carlson, a married couple who are Zen priests formerly associated with the late Juyi Kennett Roshi (d. 1996) and the Order of Buddhist Contemplatives. Subsequently, additional satellite centers have been formed. Meditation workshops are offered several times each month at no charge. One-day sittings and longer *sesshins* are held during the year.

During most of the year, the center operates a daily schedule of morning and evening meditation periods, as well as offering classes, workshops, and residential practice. The priests are available by appointment for counseling on spiritual matters.

Dharma Rain is nationally known for its children's programs, especially the Dharma School. The manual "Sharing the Dharma with Children" explains in depth the history, philosophy, structure, and curriculum of the school. The center in Eugene, Oregon, has created SAFE (Stop All Female Excision), a project aimed at educating African females.

While Dharma Rain is primarily a temple for lay practice, several monks reside there and provide support to the work of the temple. There are also lay teachers who have been recognized as having achieved a high level of integrated practice.

An elected board of directors oversees the temple and keeps the center responsive to the community.

Membership: Not reported. Four related groups are found in Portland, Eugene, Salem, and Pendleton, Oregon.

Periodicals: *Still Point Newsletter*.

Sources:

Dharma Rain Zen Center. www.dharma-rain.org.

Morreale, Don. *The Complete Guide to Buddhist America*. Boston: Shambhala, 1998.

Dharma Sangha

c/o Crestone Mountain Zen Center, 2000 Dreamway (PO Box 130), Crestone, CO 81131

After leaving the Zen Center of San Francisco, California, Richard Baker–Roshi continued to teach independently for several years. He retained the loyalty of some of his students from earlier days and gained a new following. In early 1985 he announced the formation of a new group, Dharma Sangha. The group purchased a building in San Francisco as a center and also opened a graduate seminary in Santa Fe, New Mexico. The San Francisco center contains a lecture and meditation hall. The Santa Fe center is for the training of senior students. Dharma Sangha is conceived as a lay-centered organization.

Membership: Not reported.

Sources:

"Baker Roshi Forms New Group." *Vajradhatu Sun* (March 1985): 4.

Diamond Sangha

Honolulu Diamond Sangha, 2747 Waiomao Rd., Honolulu, HI 96816

Diamond Sangha is a Zen Buddhist society based in Hawaii and founded by Robert Aitken and his wife, Anne Aitken. It is part of the Sanbo Kyodan (Order of the Three Treasures), a lay stream of Soto Zen wthat includes aspects of Rinzai Zen (the two main schools of Japanese Zen). The Sanbo Kyodan, headquartered in Kamakura, Japan, is based on the teachings of Harada Dai'un Roshi and was founded by Harada Roshi's successor, Hakuun Yasutani Roshi (1885–1973), in the mid-1950s.

In 1962 Yasutani Roshi began periodic visits to Hawaii to guide the Diamond Sangha in Zen practice. The current abbot of the Sanbo Kyodan, Yamada Ko'un Roshi, visited the Diamond Sangha annually during the 1970s and early 1980s.

Robert Aitken began his Zen practice in California with Nyogen Senzaki Sensei in 1947 and continued his training with Soen Nakagawa Roshi and other teachers in Japan before establishing a bond with Sanbo Kyodan. In 1974 Yamada Roshi authorized him to teach, and in 1984 gave him full transmission with the name Chotan Gyo'un Ken Roshi.

Robert Aiken Roshi retired in 1996 and was succeeded by Nelson Foster, who is also the teacher for the Ring of Bone community in Nevada City, California. Aitken lives near his son on the island of Hawaii and continues to write and consult with other Buddhist leaders. He has published eight books on Buddhism. Foster gladly bowed out so that Michael Kieran could serve the community. Kieran was authorized to teach by Foster in 1999, received transmission in 2004, and ascended the Mountain Seat in 2006.

The Honolulu Diamond Sangha has one center on the island of O'ahu. Palolo Zen Center (PZC) is nestled in a wooded 13-acre site at the back of Palolo Valley. The Palolo Zen Center comprises a zendo, teacher's quarters, and a residential wing. Activities at Palolo Zen Center include daily *zazen*, *samu*, one- to eight-day *sesshins* (retreats), and opportunities for residential practice. Several *sesshins* are offered each year at the Palolo facility, and more extended residences are also available there. There are 20 practice groups around the world officially affiliated with Diamond Sangha.

Membership: Not reported. In 2008 the group listed 11 centers in the United States and 19 centers worldwide.

Periodicals: *Blind Donkey*. • *California Diamond Sangha Newsletter*.

Sources:

Honolulu Diamond Sangha. www.diamondsangha.org.

Aitken, Robert. *The Mind of Clover*. San Francisco, CA: North Point Press, 1984.

————. *A Zen Wave*. New York: Weatherhill, 1978.

Not Mixing Up Buddhism: Essays on Women and Buddhist Practice. Fredonia, NY: White Pine Press, 1986.

Rawlinson, Andrew. *The Book of Enlightened Masters: Western Teachers in Asian Traditions*. Chicago: Open Court, 1997.

Tworkov, Helen. "Robert Aitken." In *Zen in America: Profiles of Five Teachers*. San Francisco: North Point Press, 1989.

First Zen Institute of America

113 E 30th St., New York, NY 10016

The First Zen Institute of America was founded in New York in 1930 by Sokei-an Sasaki Roshi, who came to the United States in 1906 with a missionary group from Ryomokyo-kai Zen Institute of Tokyo. Their effort to establish a center in San Francisco, California, was not successful, and all the members returned to Japan in 1910. Sokei-an settled in New York in 1916 and founded the institute there in 1930. It was incorporated the following year under the name the Buddhist Society of America; it assumed its present name in 1944. Ever since its founding, regular meetings have been conducted. A periodical, *Cat's Yawn*, was published from 1940 to 1941, and later was published in book form. Sokei-an, interned for a period after the beginning of World War II, in 1944 married Ruth Fuller Everett (d. 1967), one of the most active members of the institute and former editor of *Cat's Yawn*. Sokei-an died the following year.

Sokei-an left no successor, but his students continued to meet and practice what he had taught them. Ruth Fuller moved to Daitoku-ji to continue her study, and was the first woman to become a Zen priest at that temple. She also organized the First Zen Institute of America in Japan to receive American students who wished to study abroad.

In 1954 the institute began a second periodical, *Zen Notes*, which included the writings of Sokei-an and other Zen masters. In 1963 the institute moved into its present headquarters in Manhattan. A regular schedule of *zazen* meetings is held for members, and a weekly Wednesday evening session is open to newcomers. Still lay led, the institute periodically invites guest roshis to lead *sesshins* and extended meditation retreats.

Governance of the institute is by its members through a council drawn from its senior members.

Membership: Not reported.

Periodicals: *Zen Notes*.

Sources:

Cat's Yawn. New York: First Zen Institute in America, 1947.

Sasaki, Ruth Fuller. *Zen, A Method for Religious Awakening*. Kyoto, Japan: First Zen Institute of America in Japan, 1959.

Hazy Moon Zen Center

1651 S Gramercy Pl., Los Angeles, CA 90019

Alternate Address: Centro Zen Maezumi Kuroda in Mexico City, Fuente de Nezahualcoyotl 20B Casa 3, San Miguel Tecamachalco, Edo. De México.

The Hazy Moon Center is a Zen Buddhist congregation founded by William Nyogen Yeo Sensei, a Dharma successor of Hakuyu Taizan Maezumi Roshi (1931–1995), the founder of the Zen Center of Los Angeles. The sangha encompasses two practice centers, the Hazy Moon Zen Center (also known as Koun-ji Soto Zen Temple) in Los Angeles and the Centro Zen de Maezumi-Kuroda in Mexico City. Each center offers a variety of programs supporting seasoned practitioners as well as beginners.

The sangha's spiritual heritage is grounded in the Soto Zen tradition but also includes a thorough integration of koan practice (associated with Rinzai practice) introduced to the tradition by Maezumi Roshi's teachers, Hakuun Yasutani Roshi and Koryu Osaka Roshi.

Nyogen Sensei received Dharma transmission (authorization to teach) from Taizan Maezumi Roshi in 1995 after 26 years of intense practice and study. Following the Japanese Soto Zen way, in 1996 Sensei did his *zuise* ceremonies at the training monasteries of Eiheiji and Sojiji in Japan and thus completed the traditional Soto rites of recognition as a Zen teacher (*sensei*). Following Maezumi Roshi's death in 1995, Nyogen Sensei served for two years as the acting abbot of the Zen Center of Los Angeles before assuming his current role as the spiritual head of the Hazy Moon Sangha.

Membership: Not reported.

Sources:

Hazy Moon Zen Center. www.hazymoon.com.

Centro Zen Maezumi Kuroda. www.centrozen.net.

Morreale, Don. *The Complete Guide to Buddhist America*. Boston: Shambhala, 1998.

International Zen Institute of America (IZIA)

1760 Pomona Ave., No. 35, Costa Mesa, CA 92627

The International Zen Institute of America was founded by the Ven. Roshi Gesshin Prabhasa Dharma (1931–1999). Gesshin Roshi was an artist and poet. In 1967 she met the Japanese Zen Master Joshu Kyozan Sasaki Roshi, with whom she studied for the next 15 years. In 1968 she was ordained in the Rinzai Zen lineage of Myoshin-ji, and among her duties was supervising the development of an affiliated center at Mt. Baldy, California. She was ordained a teacher in 1972 and spent the next year and a half in Japan studying Zen with Hirata Roshi at Tenryu-ji Monastery and learning Japanese and calligraphy.

Upon her return from Japan, Gesshin Roshi became head priest at Rinzai-ji Zen Center. She began to travel to Europe and teach independently of the Rinzai-ji Center, and in 1983 she formally resigned from the lineage altogether. During this period Gesshin Roshi started to associate with the growing Vietnamese community centered in the International Buddhist Meditation Center in Los Angeles. In 1985 she received the Dharma Mind Seal Transmission from the Ven. Thich Man Giac of the United Vietnamese Buddhist Churches of America. She founded the International Zen Institute of America as an organizational umbrella for her work.

After her death in 1999 Prabhasa Dharma appointed her Dutch disciple Jiun Hogen as her successor.

Though she was headquartered in Los Angeles, Gesshin Roshi traveled widely and developed affiliated centers in Florida, Germany, the Netherlands, and Spain.

Membership: In 2002 the institute reported 250 members in the United States and 1,700 additional members at the centers in Europe.

Sources:

Friedman, Lenore. *Meetings with Remarkable Women: Buddhist Teachers in America*. Boston: Shambhala, 1987.

Kanzeon Zen Center

1274 E South Temple, Salt Lake City, UT 84102

Kanzeon Zen Center is a training center for both traditional Zen and Big Mind practice, under the guidance of Genpo Merzel Roshi. Dennis Genpo Merzel Roshi (b. 1944) was born in Brooklyn, New York, and grew up in Long Beach, California. He attended California State University at Long Beach (B.A., 1966) and the University of Southern California (M.A., 1968). He taught school in Los Angeles and Long Beach from 1966 to 1971.

Genpo Roshi started formal Zen training under Taizan Maezumi Roshi at the Zen Center of Los Angeles in 1972. He was ordained by Maezumi Roshi in 1973 and given the title *hoshi* (Dharma holder) after completing koan study in 1979. In 1980 Genpo Roshi received *shiho* (Dharma transmission) from Maezumi Roshi, followed by *zuisse* (another step toward full recognition as a teacher) in Japan in 1981. In the following year he began to conduct sesshins in several European countries, and in 1984 he left Los Angeles to devote himself completely to the international community of students he named the Kanzeon Sangha.

In 1988 Genpo Roshi completed *shinsanshiki* (installation as abbot) at Hosshinji Temple in Bar Harbor, Maine. In 1991 he moved to Oregon, and in 1993, at the invitation of the Wasatch Zen Group, he relocated Hosshinji (Kanzeon Zen Center) to Salt Lake City, Utah. Genpo Roshi received the certificate of Dendokyoshi Kenshuso in 1995 at Green Gulch Farm in California. In October 1996 he received *inka* (formal recognition in the Rinzai Zen school) from his elder Dharma brother, Tetsugen Glassman Roshi, in New York City. Tetsugen Roshi had received inka from Maezumi Roshi shortly before the latter's death in May 1995.

To date, Genpo Roshi has 12 Dharma successors: Catherine Genno Pages, John Shodo Flatt, Anton Tenkei Coppens, Malgosia Jiho Braunek, Daniel Doen Silberberg, Nico Sojun Tydeman, Nancy Genshin Gabrysch, Diane Musho Hamilton, Michael Mugaku Zimmerman, Richard Taido Christofferson, Michel Genko Dubois, and Tammy Myoho Gabrysch. Genpo Roshi has given inka to seven Zen teachers: John Daido Loori, Catherine Genno Pages, Anton Tenkei Coppens, Jan Chozen Bays, Charles Tenshin Fletcher, Nicolee Jikyo McMahon, and Susan Myoyu Andersen. For 10 years, until 2007, Genpo Roshi was the president of the White Plum Asanga, the worldwide community comprising all the Dharma heirs of Taizan Maezumi Roshi, their successors, and the many groups they lead.

The Kanzeon Center in Salt Lake City (named for the Buddhist embodiment of compassion, also known as Kwan Yin) provides an extensive training program that emphasizes the traditional combination of sitting meditation (*zazen*) and individual interviews with the teachers (*dokusan* and *daisan*). In addition to a daily schedule, full-time training sessions (*sesshins*) that last from three to nine days are held throughout the year. In 1999 Genpo Roshi created the Big Mind process, a more effective way to teach Zen to modern westerners. It blends western psychology and Zen tradition, enabling students to rapidly experience the many different aspects of the mind. Kanzeon offers both Big Mind practice and traditional Zen training methods such as zazen, koan study, and dharma talks. In 2008 the vice abbots were Diane Musho Hamilton Sensei and Michael Mugaku Zimmerman Sensei.

Membership: In 2008 the sangha had several thousand members in the United States and Europe. European centers were founded in France, England, Germany, Holland, Poland, Belgium, Portugal, England, and Malta.

Sources:

Kazeon Zen Center. www.kanzeonzencenter.org.

Merzel Roshi, Dennis Genpo. *Beyond Sanity and Madness—The Way of Zen Master Dogen*. Rutland, VT: Charles E. Tuttle Co., 1994.

———. *Big Mind, Big Heart: Finding Your Way*. Salt Lake City, UT: Big Mind Publishing, 2007.

———. *The Eye Never Sleeps—Striking to the Heart of Zen*. Boston: Shambhala, 1991.

———. *The Path of the Human Being*. Boston: Shambhala, 2003.

———. *24/7 Dharma*. Boston: Tuttle Journey Editions, 2001.

Kanzeonji Non-Sectarian Buddhist Temple

951 Terrrace 49, Los Angeles, CA 90042

The Kanzeonji Non-Sectarian Buddhist Temple was founded in the 1980s by the Rev. Ryugen Watanabe, also known as Swami Premananda. Born in Japan, Reverend Watanabe was inspired by Kanzeon Bosatsu (also known as Bodhisattva Kannon or Kwan Yin), the Buddha of compassion, to bring Buddhism to the United States. He is the sixty-second patriarch (counting from Bodhidharma) in his line of transmission in the Soto Zen tradition. He is the abbot of Kanzeonji and founder of the Siva Ashram Yoga Center, where he holds the title swami.

The temple offers daily zazen meditation and chanting. Classes in hatha yoga are taught, and Rev. Watanabe offers his services as a practitioner of Zen energy healing (popularly called acupressure or shiatsu). Rev. Watanabe practiced shiatsu in Japan and began his work in the United States as an alternative to drug-oriented medicine.

Watanabe understands Zen as the form of meditation practiced by Gautama Buddha. It has as its object the forcing of the practitioner beyond the sphere of words to an immediate encounter with ultimate truth.

Membership: There is a single center in Los Angeles, which in 2002 served approximately 1,500 participants.

Sources:

Kanzeonji Non-Sectarian Buddhist Temple. www.zenyoga.org.

Guideline to Kanzeonji. Los Angeles: Zen Center of Kanzeonji Non-Sectarian Buddhist Temple, n.d.

Living Dharma Centers

PO Box 9513, Bolton, CT 06043

Alternate Address: PO Box 304, Amherst, MA 01004

The Living Dharma Centers were founded by Richard Clarke (b. 1933), a psychotherapist who met Philip Kapleau (1912–2004) in 1967 and became his student at the Rochester Zen Center in New York. In 1980, he dropped his relationship with Kapleau after 14 years of intensive Zen training and founded a center in Bolton, Connecticut, and Amherst, Massachusetts. The stated goal of the centers is the awakening of the true self to be manifest in all of life. The teachings and practice of the centers combine elements from both the Soto and Rinzai traditions.

Membership: There are approximately 100 members.

Periodicals: *Sangha News*. • *Living Dharma Center Journal*.

Sources:

Living Dharma Center: Zen Buddhist Training and Practice. www.livingdharmacenter.org/

Clark, Richard. *Hsin Hsin Ming: Verse on the Faith-Mind by Sengtsan*. Buffalo, NY: White Pine Press, 1984.

Rawlinson, Andrew. *The Book of Enlightened Masters: Western Teachers in Eastern Traditions*. Chicago, IL: Open Court Press, 1997. 650 pp.

Middlebar Monastery

2503 Del Dio Dr., Stockton, CA 95204

One of the earliest Zen centers led by an American, Middlebar Monastery was founded with the expressed purpose of bringing traditional methods of Zen training to Americans without using Japanese or Chinese language and culture. The primate of Soto Zen in Japan, Rosen Takashina, certified the monastery in 1956 at Soto Zen headquarters. Middlebar was founded by Doki MacDonough, an American disciple of Hodo Tobase of the Sokoji Soto Mission of San Francisco. MacDonough was elevated to the rank of *roshi* by Rosen Takashina in 1962 and appointed to head Middlebar Monastery.

Abbot MacDonough follows a Soto approach to Zen Buddhism, using traditional methods that are modified to suit Americans. Soto Zen finds its expression through the humanities and arts, rather than through martial arts. Monks are trained to come to know themselves, recognize their own individual identity, and find their own expression for the benefit of society.

Applicants for admission must be unmarried, free of financial obligations, have graduated from high school, never been convicted of a felony, and be in good mental and physical health. There are no dietary practices for monks. Unlike their counterparts in Christian monastic life, the monks at Middlebar take no vows of any kind and maintain control of their assets. Some leave the monastery after a period of training to resume a worldly life, whereas others choose to remain and make a career of the religious life.

Membership: Not reported.

Sources:

Rawlinson, Andrew. *The Book of Enlightened Masters: Western Teachers in Eastern Traditions*. La Salle, IL: Open Court Press, 1997. 650 pp.

Minnesota Zen Meditation Center

3343 E Calhoun Pkwy., Minneapolis, MN 55408

The roots of the Minnesota Zen Meditation Center (MZMC) can be traced back to the 1960s, when a group of people in Minneapolis, Minnesota, started to practice *zazen*, or Zen meditation. These practitioners developed an association with the San Francisco Zen Center and its assistant priest, Dainin Katagiri Roshi (1928–1990), who visited them on several occasions. In 1972, the group extended an invitation to Katagiri Roshi to become the leader of a new Zen center they were establishing. He accepted, and the Minnesota Zen Center was formed in January 1973.

Katagiri Roshi was born in Japan and became a Zen monk in 1946. He trained at Eiheji Monastery, the original center of the Soto Shu Sect. He came to the United States in 1963 to work with the Japanese-American Soto Buddhists and was assigned to their Los Angeles, California, temple. After five months, however, he was sent to San Francisco, California, to assist Shunryu Suzuki Roshi in both the San Francisco temple (Sokoji) and the independent Zen Center of San Francisco. While there, he assisted in the opening of the Tassajara Zen Mountain Center.

After coming to Minneapolis, Katagiri Roshi attracted students throughout the Midwest, and affiliated centers emerged. In 1978 the center purchased 280 acres in southeastern Minnesota; it began construction of a year-round facility for intensive Zen practice. This developed into Hokyoji Zen Practice Community, which was incorporated as a self-sustaining entity in 2007.

The center is governed by a board of directors that is elected at the annual meeting of members.

Membership: In 2008 the center reported 100 members. The head teacher is Zentetsu Tim Burkett, an early student of Suzuki Roshi's who was ordained by Katagiri Roshi in 1979 and later received dharma transmission from Karen Sunna

(MZMC head teacher from 1995 to 2002). Seven ordained men and women study with Burkett and assist with teaching, lecturing, and other duties.

Periodicals: *MZMC Newsletter*.

Sources:

Minnesota Zen Meditation Center. www.mnzencenter.org.

Morgan Bay Zendo

532 Morgan Bay Rd., Surry, ME 04684

One of the oldest existing Zen centers in the United States, what is today known as Morgan Bay Zendo, was founded in 1969 as the Moonspring Hermitage by Walter Nowick (b. 1922). A professional pianist, Nowick initially practiced Zen at the First Zen Institute of America in New York City, New York. Then, shortly after World War II (1939–1945), he went to Japan for further study with Zuigan Goto Roshi (1879–1965) at the Daitokuji temple in Kyoto, Japan (where Zen pioneer Ruth Fuller Sasaki [1892–1967] also traveled). Seventeen years of work led to his being named roshi, the first Westerner in the Rinzai lineage. He returned to the United States and founded the hermitage. He retired in 1985.

Since Nowick's retirement, the hermitage reincorporated and has continued as the leaderless and independent Morgan Bay Zendo. Nowick and the hermitage were the subject of a book by a Dutch disciple of Goto Roshi, Janwillem van der Wetering (1931–2008).

The zendo offers meditation each Sunday throughout the year and Wednesday evenings during the summer. Retreats are frequently offered.

Zendo practice includes elements from Zen, Chan and vipassana schools of Buddhism.

Membership: About 100.

Periodicals: *Morgan Bay Zendo*.

Sources:

Morgan Bay Zendo. www.morganbayzendo.org

Rawlinson, Andrew. *The Book of Enlightened Masters: Western Teachers in Eastern Traditions*. Chicago, IL: Open Court Press, 1997. 650 pp.

Van der Wetering, Jan. *A Glimpse of Nothingness: Experiences in an American Zen Community*. London: Routledge and Kegan Paul, 1975. 184 pp.

Mountain Moon Sangha

No. 6, 939 Avenue Rd., Toronto, ON, Canada M5P 2K7

Mountain Moon Sangha is the name given to the students of Sei-un An Roselyn Stone, a teacher within the Sanbo Kyodan Buddhist lineage. In 1977, Stone went on sabbatical from the University of Toronto to Japan, where she spent most of the next 14 years in the San'un Zendo. The late Zen master Ko'un Yamada, of the San'un Zendo in Kamakura, confirmed her awakening in 1978. Seven years later, she became an authorized Zen master in the Sanbo Kyodan Zen lineage, with the teaching name of "Sei'un An" ("Clearing Away the Clouds").

In 1992 Stone established zendos in both Toronto, Canada, and Brisbane, Australia, and she now divides her time between the two centers. Stone appointed Mervyn Lander Gô'un Ken, Cecilie Lander Gô'en An, Li-yea Bretz Sei'un An (II), Matthew Love, Garry Cam, and Jean Wilson as teachers in the Mountain Moon Sangha.

New students are invited to attend a set of introductory lectures, which include basic instruction in meditation, and are then invited to join the regular meditation program.

Membership: In 2002, thirty-three members were reported.

Sources:

Mountain Moon Sangha. www.beruriahandrabia.com.

Morreale, Don. *The Complete Guide to Buddhist America*. Boston: Shambhala, 1998.

The Mountains and Rivers Order (MRO)

c/o Zen Mountain Monastery, PO Box 197, South Plank Rd., Mount Tremper, NY 12457

The Mountains and Rivers Order (MRO) is an organization of associated Zen Buddhist temples, practice centers, and sitting groups in the United States and abroad. Inspired by Zen Master Dogen's thirteenth-century Mountains and Rivers Sutra, MRO was founded by Abbot John Daido Loori, a Dharma heir of Hakuyu Taizan Maezumi Roshi (1931–1995), best known as the founder of the Zen Center of Los Angeles. Loori has received transmission in both the Rinzai and Soto lines of Zen Buddhism, from which he has developed a distinctive style, involving both monastic and lay practitioners in a program of study that embraces every aspect of daily life. Loori is also president of Dharma Communications, which is devoted to making Buddhist moral, ethical, and social teachings widely available through the production of videotapes, books, and meditation supplies.

MRO's function is maintaining the practice integrity of its member organizations. The main house of the order is Zen Mountain Monastery, a residential retreat center in the Catskills of New York State. The order also operates Dharma Communications, a media company supplying resources for home practice. Through the Society of Mountains and Rivers, groups of students around the world are joined in the MRO training program.

Zen Mountain Monastery is an American Zen Buddhist monastery and training center for monastics and lay practitioners. Each month an introductory weekend of Zen training is offered, as well as a weeklong silent intensive meditation retreat (*sesshin*). Throughout the year, the regular daily schedule is supplemented with retreats focusing on the Zen arts, martial arts, Buddhist studies, and other areas thought to be relevant and helpful to practitioners. Students can pursue training through either full-time or part-time residencies or as nonresidents whose practice at home is fueled by periodic visits to the monastery. Nonresidents may also find support by joining together with others in one of the centers or groups affiliated with an international umbrella organization, the Society of Mountains and Rivers Order.

Practice in Zen Mountain Monastery is based in what is termed the *Eight Gates*. Loori observed that most Western practitioners come to Zen with virtually no background in Buddhism. Thus, he felt it necessary to employ a broader spectrum of skillful means than just the traditional meditation and teacher-student relationship. As a result, he developed the "Eight Gates" of training, each of which is pursued over 10 stages of spiritual development.

The first gate, *zazen* (meditation), is followed immediately by the development of a strong teacher-student relationship during the face-to-face teachings that comprise the second gate. The third gate, academic study, explores—in addition to the particularly Zen Buddhist sutras—other schools of Buddhism, along with Buddhist history, philosophy, and psychology. The remaining five gates include liturgy, the Precepts, art practice, body practice, and work.

The Zen Environmental Studies Institute is a not-for-profit religious corporation that provides training and education focused on Zen Buddhism's relationship to the environment. It conducts and sponsors workshops, training, and research on the environment and the teachings of the insentient.

Membership: Not reported. The Mountains and Rivers Order includes the Zen Center of New York City, Fire Lotus Temple; Providence Place Zendo, Albany, New York; Zen Affiliate of Vermont (ZAV), Burlington; and the Zen Institute of New Zealand (with sitting places at Auckland, Christchurch, Nelson, Wellington, and Manawatu). Prison affiliates and groups include Green Haven Correctional Facility, Shawangunk Correctional Facility, Woodbourne Correctional Facility, Great Meadow Correctional Facility, Elmira Correctional Facility, Wende Correctional Facility, Wallkill Correctional Facility, and Arthur Kill Correctional Facility.

Periodicals: *Mountain Record*.

Sources:

Mountains and Rivers Order. www.mro.org/mro.html.

Loori, John Daido. *The Eight Gates of Zen*. Mt. Tremper, NY: Dharma Communications, 1992.

————. *The Heart of Being*. Rutland, VT: Charles E. Tuttle Co., 1996.

————. *Liturgy Manual*. Mt. Tremper, NY: Dharma Communications, 1998.

————. *Mountain Record of Zen Talks*. Boston: Shambhala, 1988.

————. *Still Point*. Mt. Tremper, NY: Dharma Communications, 1995.

————. *Two Arrows Meeting in Mid-Air: The Zen Koan*. Rutland, VT: Charles E. Tuttle, 1994.

One Drop Zendo

c/o Tahoma One Drop Zen Monastery, 6499 Wahl Rd., Freeland, WA 98249

One Drop Zendo was founded in 1989 in Seattle, Washington, by Shodo Harada Roshi (b. 1940), the abbot of Sogenji, a Rinzai Zen monastery in Okayama, Japan. Harada began his Zen training in 1962 when he entered Shofuku-ji monastery in Kobe, Japan, where he trained under Yamada Mumon Roshi for 20 years. He was then given dharma transmission and was made abbot of Sogenji monastery.

Since 1982 Sogenji has been one of those Japanese centers most open to students from the West. In the years since the zendo's founding, Harada Roshi has made annual trips to Seattle to lecture and lead retreats. In 1996, the zendo purchased a tract of land on Whidbey Island and built a monastery. The monastery maintains a daily schedule of morning and evening meditation, monthly weekend retreats, and intensive meditation training twice a year. Members provide retreats for caregivers and operate Enso House, a home for people who are dying.

One Drop Zendo groups include three other monasteries (in Germany, India, and Japan), 17 sitting groups (including ones in Denmark, Germany, Hungary, India, Italy, Mexico, Poland, and Switzerland), and three affiliated groups (in Oregon, New Mexico, and California).

Membership: Not reported.

Sources:

One Drop Zendo. www.onedropzendo.org.

Morreale, Don. *The Complete Guide to Buddhist America*. Boston: Shambhala, 1998.

Open Gate Sangha

PO Box 112107, Campbell, CA 95011-2107

Open Gate Sangha was founded in 1996 by the Zen teacher Adyashanti (born Steven Gray, 1962). Attracted to meditation early in his life, Gray studied with Arvis Joen Justi, herself a student of Soto Zen Master Taizan Maezumi Roshi (1931–1995), a pioneer Zen instructor in the United States who taught for many years at the Zen Center of Los Angeles. When he was 25 Gray began experiencing a series of spiritual awakenings. In 1996 Arvis began to encourage Gray to start teaching, and Gray founded Open Gate Sangha in Cupertino. A short time later he took the name "Adyashanti," a Sanskrit word meaning "primordial peace."

Asyashanti's teaching draws on the Soto Zen he was taught, but it has the distinct flavor of Adavaita Vedanta, a Hindu teaching that emphasizes the oneness of everything (nondualism). He calls it "a realization of the underlying connectedness and oneness of all beings." One awakens "when s/he realizes that common awareness is nothing more than a dream, and moves on to a perception of the underlying unity of all things. Awakening at first tends to be temporary. Enlightenment is when the awakened state remains permanent."

Open Gate Sangha supports Adyashanti's teaching work based in talks, weekend intensives, and five-night silent retreats. He also travels widely, speaking and leading meditation at various locations around the United States. He has authored several books, and many of his talks have been put on tapes. As support for his work has grown, the Sangha has organized gatherings—groups that meet regularly to meditate, listen to the audio tapes of Adyashanti's talks, and discuss his teachings.

Membership: Not reported. In 2008 the Sangha reported more than 50 gatherings taking place in 23 states and 4 countries.

Periodicals: *Adyashanti*.

Sources:

Open Gate Sangha. www.adyashanti.org/.

Adyashanti. *The Impact of Awakening: Excerpts from the Teachings of Adyashanti*. Campbell, CA: Open Gate Sangha, 2002.

————. *Emptiness Dancing*. Boulder, CO: Sounds True, 2006.

————. *True Meditation: Discover the Freedom of Pure Awareness*. Boulder, CO: Sounds True, 2006.

Saunders, Luc, and Sy Safransky. "Who Hears This Sound: Adyashanti Speaks on Waking Up from the Dream of Me." *The Sun* 384 (December 2007). Available from www.thesunmagazine.org/issues/384/who_hears_this_sound.

Order of Buddhist Contemplatives

c/o Shasta Abbey, 3724 Summit Dr., Mount Shasta, CA 96067-9102

The Order of Buddhist Contemplatives was founded by the Rev. Jiyu-Kennett Roshi (1924–1996), a British-born Buddhist who spent most of her early years studying Theravada Buddhism. She was a member of the council of the London Buddhist Society and gave lectures there. She began her study of Buddhism with Ven. Saddhatissa. In 1962, she was ordained in Malaysia in the Chinese Rinzai Zen tradition before traveling to Japan to study at Dai Hon Zan Soji-ji, one of the two main temples of the Soto Zen Church. She became the personal disciple of the Rev. Chisan Koho Zenji, the temple's abbot, from whom she received her dharma transmission. After several years at the temple, she became head of its foreign guest department and was placed in charge of instructing Westerners who came to Japan to learn Zen. She eventually became abbess of Unpuku-ji Temple in Mie Prefecture. In 1969, after completing her studies and following the death of Zenji, she moved to San Francisco, California, and established the Zen Mission Society. In 1970, the society moved to Mount Shasta, California, where a monastery and seminary were created. The society has more recently taken its current name: the Order of Buddhist Contemplatives.

Jiyu-Kennett Roshi had a commission to train and ordain others, and the prime thrust of the order has been to train both women and men for the Soto Zen priesthood. A Western environment is evident in the religious practice of the order. A complete course of study in Soto Zen Buddhism is offered, which includes religious music and temple administration skills. The order is among those Zen groups that place the most emphasis upon their Buddhist heritage. Along with *zazen* and the teachings of Soto Zen, a study is also undertaken in the teachings of the Buddha according to Theravada and Mahayana Buddhism. Priest trainees live full-time at the Mount Shasta monastery. Celibacy is required for all priests.

The publication of Kennett Roshi's several books, her lecture tours, and the development of trained teachers at Mount Shasta have contributed to the growth of several affiliated centers. Monasteries, priories (local temples), and affiliated meditation groups of the Order of Buddhist Contemplatives are located in California, Oregon, Washington, Idaho, Montana, and South Carolina; Alberta and British Columbia, Canada; the United Kingdom; the Netherlands; Germany; and the West Indies. Following the death of Rev. Jiyu-Kennett in 1996, Rev. Daizui MacPhillamy (1945–2003) was elected to succeed her as head of the order and Rev. Eko Little was elected to succeed her as abbot of Shasta Abbey. He was succeeded by the current head of the order, Rev. Master HaryoYoung (b. 1951).

Membership: As of January 2002, the order reports having 95 active priests and 150 lay ministers.

Educational Facilities:

Shasta Abbey, Mount Shasta, California; Throssel Hole Buddhist Abbey, Northumberland, England.

Periodicals: *The Journal of the Order of Buddhist Contemplatives.*

Sources:

Order of Buddhist Contemplatives. www.obcon.org/

Friedman, Lenore. *Meetings with Remarkable Women: Buddhist Teachers in America.* Boston, MA: Shambhala, 1987.

Jiyu-Kennet, P. T. N. H. *How to Grow a Lotus Blossom, or, How a Zen Buddhist Prepares for Death.* Mount Shasta, CA: Shasta Abbey, 1993.

————. *The Wild, White Goose: The Diary of a Female Zen Priest.* 2 vols. Mt. Shasta, CA: Shasta Abbey, 2002.

————. *Zen is Eternal Life.* Emeryville, CA: Dharma, 1976.

Jiyu-Kennett, P. T. N. H., and Daizui MacPhillamy, eds. *Buddhist Writings on Meditation and Daily Practice: The Serene Reflection Meditation Tradition,* trans. Hubert Nearman. Mount Shasta, CA: Shasta Abbey, 1994. 382 pp.

"Shasta Abbey, 1970—1995." Special issue, *The Journal of the Order of Buddhist Contemplatives* 10, no. 3-4 (Autum/Winter, 1995).

Zenji, Keizan. *The Denkoroku; or, The Record of the Transmission of the Light.* Mount Shasta, CA: Shasta Abbey, 1993. 303 pp.

Order of the Prairie Wind

c/o Nebraska Zen Center, 3625 Lafayette Ave., Omaha, NE 68131

The Order of the Prairie Wind is a Soto Zen community founded by Rev. Nonin Chowaney, an American Zen master. He did his training at several Zen centers in the United States and Japan and was ordained in 1984 by Dainin Katagiri Roshi (1928–1990), the abbot of the Minnesota Zen Meditation Center in Minneapolis. He received formal dharma transmission from Katagiri and has been certified to teach by him and by the Soto Zen headquarters in Japan.

Chaowaney serves as abbot of the Nebraska Zen Center in Omaha. The center was established in 1975 but became independent of the Minnesota Zen Meditation Center in the 1990s after Katagiri Roshi's death. Subsequently, other affiliated meditation centers have been created, including one in Pittsburgh, Pennsylvania (established in 1999), and another in Lincoln, Nebraska. There are also sitting groups in three Nebraska prisons, collectively known as the White Lotus Sangha.

Chowaney has emerged as a popular Zen leader nationally and is a frequent guest speaker at events throughout the United States. He is also active in both the American Zen Teachers Association and the Soto Zen Buddhist Association.

Membership: Not reported. There are three centers and three sitting groups affiliated with the Order of the Prairie Wind.

Sources:

Order of the Prairie Wind. www.prairiewindzen.org/.

Ordinary Mind Zen School

c/o Zen Center of San Diego, 2047 Felspar, San Diego, CA 92109

The Ordinary Mind Zen School was founded by Charlotte Joko Beck (b. 1917), who in the early 1980s had been named one of the four Dharma heirs of the Zen Center of Los Angeles. Since her separation from the Los Angeles center, Beck has become recognized as an important Soto Zen teacher in her own right and the author of several widely read books.

The Ordinary Mind Zen School manifests and supports practice in what has come to be called "the Awakened Way." It is composed of Charlotte Joko Beck, her Dharma successors, and the teachers and successors they, as individuals, have formally authorized. There is no affiliation between the Ordinary Mind centers and other Zen groups or religious denominations; however, individual membership does not preclude individual affiliation with other groups.

The Awakened Way is thought of as universal; the medium and methods of realization vary according to circumstances. Each Dharma successor in the school may apply diverse practice approaches and determine the structure of any organization that he or she may develop to facilitate practice. Within the school there is no hierarchy of Dharma successors. The successors acknowledge that they are ongoing students, and that the quality of their teaching derives from the quality of their practice. As ongoing students, teachers are committed to an openness and fluidity of practice, whereby the wisdom of the absolute may be manifested in/as our life. An important function of this school is the ongoing examination and development of effective teaching approaches to ensure comprehensive practice in all aspects of living.

Dharma successors Elihu Genmyo Smith and Diane Eshin Rizzetto reside at the Prairie Zen Center in Champaign, Illinois, and the Bay Zen Center in Oakland, California, respectively. Beck is an active member of the White Plum Asanga.

Membership: Not reported. There are centers related to the school in San Diego and Oakland, California; Champaign, Illinois; Philadelphia, Pennsylvania; Portland, Oregon; and New York City.

Sources:

Beck, Charlotte Joko. *Everyday Zen: Love and Work.* San Francisco: Harper, 1989. 224 pp.

————. *Nothing Special: Living Zen.* Ed. Steve Smith. San Francisco: Harper, 1994. 288 pp.

Ordinary Mind Zendo. www.ordinarymind.com/biography_4.html.

Rinzai-Ji, Inc.

c/o Rinzai-Ji Zen Center, 2505 Cimarron St., Los Angeles, CA 90018

Rinzai-Ji, Inc., is an association of Zen centers in the Rinzai tradition that began in 1968 with the founding of the Cimarron Zen Center in Los Angeles by Kyozan Joshu Sasaki Roshi (b. 1907). Sasaki Roshi had received his *inka,* or acknowledgment of his accomplishments as a student, from Joten Miura, later to become leader of the Myoshinji sect of Rinzai Zen in Japan. Sasaki Roshi left the monastery he headed in Japan to come to America in 1962. Rinzai-Ji began as a gathering of students who had responded to his several years of teaching in Southern California. In 1970 a second center was begun in Redondo Beach, California, and that same year the main training center was opened on Mt. Baldy, east of Los Angeles. Sasaki Roshi continued an active schedule of visiting centers, training students, and lecturing around the United States, and other centers developed in the East and in Puerto Rico (1983). A Canadian center in Vancouver can be traced to a group that formed in response to talks given by Sasaki Roshi in 1967. A set of lectures in Austria in 1979 led to the first European affiliated center being formed. Each Rinzai-Ji center offers an intensive program of *zazen* ("sitting with the master") and periodic *sesshin* ("extended sitting meditations"). All are headed by individuals trained by Sasaki Roshi.

Membership: Not reported. In 2007 there were 20 Rinzai-Ji Zen centers in the United States, all managed by priests trained by Joshu Roshi. There also are centers in Puerto Rico, Canada, Austria, and Germany.

Sources:

Rinzai-Ji, Inc. www.rinzaiji.org/.

Sasaki, Joshu. *Buddha Is the Center of Gravity.* San Cristobal, NM: Lama Foundation, 1974.

Rochester Zen Center

Seven Arnold Pk., Rochester, NY 14607-2082

The Rochester Zen Center grew out of the experience of Philip Kapleau. Kapleau had encountered Zen while in Japan as a war crimes trial court reporter. Further spurred by the lectures of lay scholar Daisetz Teitaro Suzuki at Columbia University, he returned to Japan and studied under Soen Nakagawa, Roshi, who assigned the "Mu" koan discussed elsewhere in this volume. Kapleau later trained for three years at the Soto monastery at Hosshinji under Daiun Harada Roshi. After five years in Japan, Kapleau experienced *kensho* or enlightenment under Hakuun Yasutani Roshi. This was followed by eight more years of training. In 1966 Yasutani Roshi sanctioned him as a teacher of Zen.

At this same time, Kapleau published one of the most influential English-language Zen books, *The Three Pillars of Zen*. This has a strong emphasis on koan work, as well as on the *zazen* meditation of his Rinzai training (enlarged by elements of Soto). *Zazen* means sitting still with a one-pointed, stabilized mind. The center in Rochester was founded in 1966 and under Kapleau's leadership grew steadily. In 1968, *Zen Bow* began as a quarterly publication.

In 1987 Kapleau appointed one of his Dharma heirs, Sensei Bodhin Kjolhede, as the spiritual director of the Rochester Zen Center. Bodhin Kjolhede had trained under Kapleau for 16 years before being sanctioned by him to teach in 1986. Currently, the Rochester Zen Center has an affiliate group in Madison, Wisconsin. Sensei Kjolhede has sanctioned six teachers, who direct their own affiliated centers in Chicago; Stockholm, Sweden; Helsinki, Finland; Mexico City, Mexico; Berlin, Germany; and Auckland, New Zealand.

Membership: In 2008 there were approximately 411 members in the United States and an additional 41 members worldwide.

Periodicals: *Zen Bow*.

Sources:

Zen Center. www.rzc.org/.

Kapleau, Philip. *Three Pillars of Zen*. Garden City, NY: Doubleday, 1980.

————. *To Cherish All Life*. San Francisco: Harper & Row, 1982.

————, ed. *The Wheel of Death*. New York: Harper & Row, 1971.

————. *Zen: Dawn in the West*. Author, 1981.

Low, Albert. *The Iron Cow of Zen*. Wheaton, IL: Theosophical Publishing House, 1985.

San Francisco Zen Center

300 Page St., San Francisco, CA 94102

The Zen Center of San Francisco dates to 1959, when students began to gather around the newly arrived Shunryu Suzuki Roshi (1904–1971), head of the Sokoji Temple, the Soto Zen Mission in San Francisco, at that time primarily a temple for the Japanese-American community. After Suzuki Roshi arrived, American students began to sit and study with him. Eventually, this group emerged as a distinct organization.

In 1967, the group purchased Tassajara Hot Springs outside of Carmel Valley, California, as the site for a mountain center more accommodating to traditional monastic Zen practice. Since this time the Tassajara Center has offered a monastic training period in the winter and a four-month guest season, as well as workshops and retreats in the summer. In 1969, a large building in San Francisco was purchased to serve as a city temple and a residence that also provides guest accommodations. The third practice place, Green Gulch Farm, was founded in 1972. Those who live at the farm follow the training schedule (as do residents at each of the other centers), as well as growing organic produce and caring for the many guests and retreatants who visit yearly.

Branching Streams, a network of Dharma centers in the tradition of Suzuki Roshi, are located in California, Florida, Idaho, Illinois, Montana, North Carolina, New Jersey, New York, and Texas. Numerous related groups are located across the country and in Canada, England, Germany, Italy, Northern Ireland, and Japan.

Suzuki Roshi was succeeded as abbot of Zen Center by his student Richard Baker Roshi (b. 1936). During the next decade the center prospered, adding members as well as developing several businesses (a bakery, a restaurant, etc.) as means of self-support. In 1983, Baker Roshi resigned. After a period of transition, Tenshin Reb Anderson (b. 1943) was installed as abbot of Zen Center, to be joined two years later by co-abbot Sojun Mel Weitsman (b.1929). Zoketsu Norman Fischer served as co-abbot of Zen Center from 1995 to 2000. Jiko Linda Cutts received Dharma transmission from Tenshin Reb Anderson in 1996 and was co-abbess of

Zen Center from 2000 to 2007. Paul Haller became co-abbot of Zen Center in 2003, and Myogen Steve Stücky became co-abbot in February 2007.

The center's outreach activities include food distribution to homeless people, street outreach, activities with children and families, mindfulness training in prisons and rehabilitation centers, Buddhist prison correspondence, and sitting and discussion group for people in recovery.

There are currently approximately 650 members of the San Francisco Zen Center, about half of whom are voting members. A voting member is one who has been a member for three years or more and is thus eligible to vote in the annual election for the center's governing board of directors. Many non-members also join the community for meditation, workshops, classes, and retreats or in a hospice volunteer program and other forms of community outreach. All programs are open to the public.

Membership: In the 2002 approximately 650 people were associated with the city center in San Francisco. Approximately 50 lived at Green Gulch.

Sources:

San Francisco Zen Center. www.sfzc.org/.

Brown, Edward Espe. *The Tassajara Bread Book*. Boulder, CO: Shambhala, 1970.

Butler, Katy. "Events Are the Teacher." *COEvolution* 40 (Winter 1983): 112–123.

Suzuki, Shunryu. *Zen Mind, Beginner's Mind*. New York: Weatherhill, 1970.

Sonoma Mountain Zen Center

6367 Sonoma Mountain Rd., Santa Rosa, CA 95404

The Sonoma Mountain Zen Center was founded in 1973 by Jakusho Kwong Roshi (b. 1935), a student of Shunryu Suzuki Roshi. A former commercial artist, Kwong Roshi began practicing at the Sokoji Temple, a Soto Zen temple serving the Japanese American community in San Francisco, and in 1970 was ordained by Suzuki Roshi (1904–1971). Kwong Roshi founded the Sonoma Center to honor his teacher and to perpetuate his Zen lineage. He also continued his study in Japan and in 1978 completed his Dharma transmission through Hoitsu Suzuki Roshi in Rinsoin, Japan. By this act he shared in a lineage that was traced back through 91 generations to Shakyamuni Buddha.

After relocating to Sonoma County, California, Kwong Roshi taught at Sonoma State University and laid plans for the development of a residential community for the practice of Zen. Within a short time, the center had a full program of *zazen* (meditation), *sesshin* (extended retreats), and one-day programs (seminars and sittings). Kwong Roshi has extended his teachings internationally and now oversees three centers in Poland and one in Iceland.

Membership: In 2008 there were 130 members in the single center in California. There were 60 members in Iceland and 123 members in three centers in Poland.

Periodicals: *Mountain Wind*.

Sources:

Sonoma Mountain Zen Center. www.smzc.net/.

Kwong-roshi, Jakusho. *No Beginning, No End: The Intimate Heart of Zen*. Ed. Peter Levitt. New York: Harmony Books, 2003.

Morreale, Don. *The Complete Guide to Buddhist America*. Boston: Shambhala, 1998.

Soto Mission

c/o Zenshuji Soto Mission, 123 S Hewitt St., Los Angeles, CA 90012

Zenshuji Soto Mission was founded in July 15, 1922, by Rev. Hosen Isobe (b. 1874), and its first temple was built at the mission's current location in October 1923. During World War II, the temple was closed due to the internment of American Japanese in relocation camps; afterward, Rev. Daito Suzuki (d. 1959) reestablished the temple upon his return from the camp. The Zenshuji as it exists today was built in 1969 by Rev. Reirin Yamada and Rev. Togen Sumi.

In 1932 the Zenshuji was appointed a subsidiary of the two main temples in Japan (Eiheiji and Sojiji), and in 1937 the general head office was established at the zenshuji in order to manage the administration of Soto Zen Buddhism in North America. From its inception, the Zenshuji has been the center of Zen Buddhism in America.

Although it has historically operated primarily among the Japanese-American community, Zenshuji Soto Mission is open to any person interested in Zen Buddhism and Japanese culture. The Mission's education center, established in 1997, works to propagate true Zen Buddhism to the Western world; its activities extend to Europe and South America. In 2008, 53 Soto Zen temples and centers in the United States were registered by the head office. The head office and education center also publish and distribute material about Soto Zen Buddhism, including an English translation of the main sutras for daily reading.

Membership: Not reported.

Periodicals: *Soto Zen Journal.*

Sources:

Soto Zen. www.sotozen-net.or.jp.

Zenshuji Soto Mission. www.zenshuji.org/.

Buddha's Seeds Taking Firm Roots in North America. Los Angeles: Activity Committee of the Association of Soto Zen Buddhists, 1997.

Hunt, Ernest. *Gleanings from Soto-Zen.* Honolulu, HI: Author, 1953.

A Short Manual of Soto Zen Buddhism. Tokyo: Evangelization Department of the Soto Zen Sect, 1962.

Springwater Center

7179 Mill St., Springwater, NY 14560

Springwater Center came into being in 1981 as the Genesee Valley Zen Center when Toni Packer (b. 1927) and a group of friends left the Rochester Zen Center. Packer had been a student of Roshi Philip Kapleau there and became a teacher before leaving. As a teacher, Packer's concern with the problems of tradition and authority led her to question her affiliation with formal Zen Buddhism: "Don't all present and past influences have to stop interfering in order to attend fully, immediately, now?" The new center was founded out of this need to see through the raw material of our everyday lives rather than grapple with traditional koans and practices. The center acquired the Springwater property, built a facility, and since 1985 has held retreats, with no rituals or ceremonies of any kind. In 1986 it changed its name to Springwater Center. Packer is involved in exploring how thought constructs images of self and other, how authority is created, how separation and conflict come into being, and what happens when there is awareness and insight.

Born in Germany, Packer has lived most of her adult life in western New York. She has led retreats since 1976. Besides her work at Springwater, Packer travels to Europe and California to give retreats and talks each year. She is the author of several books, including *The Work of This Moment, The Light of Discovery,* and *The Wonder of Presence.* Packer no longer calls herself a teacher, and makes no special claim to authority. Her approach is at once simple, radical, and ordinary. She is open to meeting with those who wish to work with her.

Membership: The center has 255 members.

Sources:

Springwater Center. www.springwatercenter.org.

Packer, Toni. *Seeing without Knowing: Writings on Zen Work.* New York: Genesee Valley Zen Center, 1983.

————. *What Is Meditative Inquiry?* Springwater, NY: Springwater Center, 1988.

————. *The Work of This Moment.* Boston: Shambhala, 1990.

Rawlinson, Andrew. *The Book of Enlightened Masters: Western Teachers in Eastern Traditions.* La Salle, IL: Open Court Press, 1997. 650 pp.

Three Treasures Zen Community

PO Box 720896, San Diego, CA 92172

The Three Treasures Zen Community consists of a set of centers founded by Nicolee Jikyo McMahon Roshi, who had received her Dharma transmission from Taizan Maezumi Roshi (1931–1995) of the Zen Center in Los Angeles. She and Barry Kaigen McMahon Sensei guide the North San Diego site. McMahon Roshi is a Zen priest and marriage and family therapist. She experiments with traditional Japanese Zen forms to find practices that resonate with Westerners. She developed the Practice of Immediacy (PI), which integrates the visual arts, writing, music, and movement into retreats. She also originated a Turning the Dharma Wheel Practice that is used in and outside of retreats. McMahon Roshi encourages students to deepen their practice by attending retreats offered throughout the year. She is certified in the Big Mind training developed by Genpo Merzel Roshi, head of the White Plum.

McMahon Roshi has Dharma successors at the Santa Monica Zen Center, the Zen Community of Oak Park in Illinois, the Vista Zen Center, and the Heart Circle Sangha in New Jersey.

Barry Kaigen McMahon Sensei is a Dharma successor of Charles Tenshin Fletcher Sensei. Both are part of the White Plum Sangha lineage.

The Three Treasures Zen Community strives to create an open and compassionate environment in which the Zen teaching can be transmitted to both lay and monastic students. A broad program includes both koan practice and sitting meditation, as well as art, sacred dance, the development of communication skills, and social concerns. There is a regular schedule of retreats.

Membership: Not reported. There are 19 sister and affiliated centers.

Sources:

Three Treasures Zen Community. www.ttzc.org/.

Morreale, Don. *The Complete Guide to Buddhist America.* Boston: Shambhala, 1998.

Toronto Zen Centre

33 High Park Gardens, Toronto, ON, Canada M6R 1S8

The Toronto Zen Centre was established in 1968 by Philip Kapleau Roshi, the founder of the Zen Center of Rochester and a number of affiliated centers. The Toronto center remained tied to the Rochester center for 18 years but became autonomous in 1986. Though autonomous, the center follows the belief and practices of its parent body. The associated Vermont Zen Center in Shelburne was founded in 1988.

In 1996, the Toronto Zen Centre came under the direction of Sensei Sunyana Graef, the abbot of the Vermont Zen Center and a Dharma heir of Kapleau Roshi. Sensei Taigen, a disciples of Sensei Sunyana Graef, was ordained as a priest in 2004. The following June he was sanctioned as a Dharma heir of Sensei Graef and was installed as the abbot of the Toronto Zen Centre.

The center conducts daily zazen meditation periods and offers private instruction in the practices of Zen Buddhism. The center also offers sutra recitation, study groups, Buddhist ceremonies, all-day sittings, and talks by senior members. Intensive retreats two to seven days in duration are periodically conducted in both Toronto and Vermont.

Membership: The center reports 114 members. Casa Zen in Costa Rica is affiliated with it.

Sources:

Toronto Zen Centre. www.torontozen.org/.

Morreale, Don. *The Complete Guide to Buddhist America.* Boston: Shambhala, 1998.

Udumbara Zen Center

501 Sherman Ave., Evanston, IL 60202

The Udumbara Zen Center was founded in the 1980s as an outpost of the Zen Center of San Francisco but has subsequently become independent, even though a fraternal relationship continues. The Udumbara center has remained a Soto center but has incorporated elements of both Hinayana (Theravada) and Vajrayana (Tibetan) tradition into its practice.

Sojun Diane Martin started her training at the San Francisco Zen Center in 1970, studying with Shunryu Suzuki (1904–1971). She began studying with Dainin Katagiri Roshi (1928–1990) in 1979 and was lay ordained in 1985. Yvonne Rand ordained her as a priest in 1995, and she received Dharma transmission from Karen Sunna, abbess of the Minnesota Zen Meditation Center, in 2001.

Udumbara chaplaincy programs focus on the areas of hospice care, prison work, social welfare, and mental health.

Udumbara Zen Center has affiliates in Waukegan, Illinois; Mequon, Milwaukee, and Palmyra, Wisconsin; Cleveland and Mansfield, Ohio; and Cupertino, California. It also runs a country retreat center in Ottawa, Illinois.

Membership: Not reported.

Periodicals: *Central Flower.*

Sources:

Udumbara Zen Center. www.udumbarazen.org/.

Morreale, Don. *The Complete Guide to Buddhist America*. Boston: Shambhala, 1998.

Valley Zendo

263 Warner Hill Rd., Charlemont, MA 01339

The Valley Zendo started in Northampton, Massachusetts, in 1970 as an outpost of Antaiji, a Soto Zen center in Japan. Kosho Uchiyama Roshi, then abbot at Antaiji, sent his students to serve as resident teachers. In 1975, the members moved the zendo to its current home in Charlemont, Massachusetts. They have maintained a strict schedule of zazen practice and retreats, following Uchiyama Roshi's approach of sitting without chanting, talks, zendo monitors, or formalities. The resident teacher is Eishin Ikeda.

Membership: In 2008, the Valley Zendo had 20 members.

Sources:

Valley Zendo. www.valleyzendo.org/home.htm.

Morreale, Don. *The Complete Guide to Buddhist America*. Boston: Shambhala, 1998.

Uchiyama, Kosho. *Opening the Hand of Thought*. Wisdom Publications, 2004.

White Wind Zen Community (WWZC)

c/o Zen Centre of Ottawa, 240 Daly Ave., Ottawa, ON, Canada K1N 6G2

The White Wind Zen Community (WWZC) is a Soto Zen organization founded by the Ven. Anzan Hoshin Roshi, a teacher who received his training at Hakukaze-ji Monastery in Japan. During the early 1980s Hoshin Roshi gathered a group of students in the Ottawa, Canada, area. In 1985 the original center was christened White Wind Zazenkai, after the name of the Soto Zen lineage stream that Hoshin Roshi had inherited. *Zazenkai* means "gathering together for zazen." Two years later the center was relocated to larger facilities and was then able to provide morning and evening zazen, along with regular classes and monthly sesshin and residential training for a few students. In 1988 Joan Shikai Woodward became the first student to receive postulant vows as a monastic.

In 1989, the Zazenkai was renamed White Wind Zen Community and relocated to Ottawa's Chinatown area. In 1990 two branch centers were formed, one in Wolfville, Nova Scotia, and the other in Harrow, England. A sub-temple, Jomyo-in, was established in Ottawa in 1993; this allowed for residential training and provided an auxiliary practice space (*dojo*).

In September 1996 the WWZC purchased a 9,700-square-foot mansion previously owned by the Brothers of the Sacred Heart (a Roman Catholic order) to serve as its permanent training monastery. It was given the temple name Honzan (meaning "root mountain" or "main center") Dainen-ji ("great mindfulness" or "vast mind moment") in honor of Hoshin's late master, Yasuda Joshu Dainen daiosho.

The WWZC transmits the practice and teachings of Hakukaze Soto Zen, and provides a formal environment and intensive schedule for monastic and lay training.

Membership: Not reported. There are three centers in Canada and one in England.

Periodicals: An electronic newsletter, *eMirror*, is sent out weekly.

Sources:

White Wind Zen Community. www.wwzc.org/.

Lorie, Peter, and Julie Foakes. *The Buddhist Directory*. Rutland, VT: Chares E. Tuttle Co., 1997. 424 pp.

World Zen Fellowship

c/o Potomac Zen Sangha, 1014 King St., Ste. #2, Alexandria, VA 22314

Alternate Address: PO Box 2739, Alexandria, VA 22301

The World Zen Fellowship was founded in 1994 by Korean Ven. Zen Master Pohwa Sunim. He teaches what is termed "lineage Zen," a special transmission from Buddha to lineage masters that occurs outside of doctrinal teachings. Zen Master Pohwa Sunim received this mind-to-mind teaching from lineage holders in Korea and brought it to the United States.

Originally settling in New York City, Pohwa Sunin founded what became the Patriarchal Zen Society. He later relocated to the Washington, D.C., area and founded the Potomac Zen Sangha, which now functions as the headquarters for the fellowship. Over the years, Pohwa Sunin trained teachers who now head the various centers associated with the fellowship.

The fellowship sponsors a television show, *Zen Dharma Exchange*, which appears on a community-access channel in Virginia.

Membership: Not reported. There are four Zen centers affiliated with the World Zen Fellowship.

Sources:

World Zen Fellowship. www.worldzen.org/index.php.

Zen Buddhist Temple of Chicago

PO Box 176, Northbrook, IL 60065-0176

Alternate Address: Street Address: 608 Dempster St., Evanston, IL, 60202.

The largest Zen center in the Midwest is the Zen Buddhist Temple of Chicago, a Soto center established by Soyu Matsuoka Roshi (1912–1997) in the late 1950s. The major activity of the group is its meditation service, which includes a lecture by one of the priests. Matsuoka Roshi was sent to the United States from Japan and served as a priest in California before coming to Chicago. Matsuoka Roshi passed the leadership of the temple to Kongo Langlois Roshi (born Richard Valentine Langlois, 1935–1999). Since Langlois Roshi's untimely death from complications of an operation, the work has been led collectively by the Revs. Zenku Jerry Smyers, Suirin Ray Witham, Tessen Stuart Ericksen, and Kozan Jim Matson. Small groups associated with the Chicago Temple can be found in the states surrounding Lake Michigan. Matsuoka Roshi opened a center in Detroit, Michigan, in 1973. Other temples founded by students of his include the Atlanta Soto Zen Center and the Zen Center of Las Cruces (New Mexico), both now independent of the Chicago temple.

Membership: Not reported.

Periodicals: *Diamond Sword.*

Sources:

Zen Buddhist Temple of Chicago. www.zbtc.org/.

Zen Center of Los Angeles

923 S Normandie Ave., Los Angeles, CA 90006-1301

The Zen Center of Los Angeles was formed in 1967 by a group of students under the leadership of Hakuyu Taizan Maezumi Roshi (1931–1995), a Zen master formerly with the Zenshuji Soto Mission in Los Angeles. Maezumi Roshi was a seminal figure in the development of Zen Buddhism in the West and the teacher of many who went on to found new (and independent) Zen centers across the United States. In the years since his death, many of these teachers have formally associated in the White Plum Sangha, an organizational acknowledgement of their shared origin and the essential sameness of their practice.

The inspiration for the Los Angeles center came from Hakuun Yasutani Roshi's visits in the early 1960s. The Los Angeles center supports a variety of activities, including daily zazen, weekly lectures, and beginning classes. Center members also attend *dokusan* (master/student interviews) and monthly *sesshin* (extended "sitting" meditations). A residence program allows a few students to live at the center.

During the 1970s, the center developed a vigorous publishing program and Maezumi Roshi built a following across the United States. In 2008 there were five affiliated groups, four in California and one in New Jersey. The Kuroda Institute develops programs aimed at the academic community. Internationally, affiliated centers have emerged in England, Mexico, and the Netherlands.

Wendy Egyoku Nakao Roshi has served as abbot and head teacher since 1999, when she succeeded Abbot Emeritus Bernie Glassman Roshi.

Membership: In 1988, there were approximately 1,000 members in more than 20 centers in the United States. Affiliated centers with an additional 1,000 members are located in England, Holland, Poland, and Mexico. There are approximately 20 members in Canada, but no center has yet been organized.

Educational Facilities:

Kuroda Institute, Los Angeles, California.

Periodicals: *The Waterwheel.*

Sources:

Zen Center of Los Angeles. www.zencenter.org/.

Buksbazen, John Daishin. *To Forget the Self.* Los Angeles: Zen Center of California, 1977.

Maezumi, Hakuyu Taizan, and Bernard Tetsugen Glassman, eds. *The Hazy Moon of Enlightenment.* Los Angeles: Zen Center of Los Angeles,1977.

———. *On Zen Practice.* 2 vols. Los Angeles: Zen Center of Los Angeles, 1976.

Zen Center of Oak Park

163 N Humphrey Ave., Oak Park, IL 60302

The Zen Center of Oak Park, Illinois, follows the lineage of Hakuyu Taizan Maezumi Roshi (1931–1995), best known as the founder of the Zen Center of Los Angeles. Their Zen practice includes *zazen*, samu work practice, study, koans, classes, workshops, and sesshins (retreats).They practice in both Soto and Rinzai traditions.

Sensei Robert Joshin Althouse, abott of the Zen Community of Oak Park Empty Sound Temple, established the center in 2004. He received his transmission from Roshi Jikyo Nicolee McMahon in 1999 and is an ordained priest and fully empowered Zen teacher in the White Plum lineage.

His teacher, Taizan Maezumi Roshi, is best known as the founder of the Zen Center of Los Angeles. Althouse was ordained as a Soto Zen Buddhist priest by Maezumi Roshi in 1973 and spent 12 years working as an artist in Los Angeles. Besides Zen, he has also studied in the Tibetan tantric tradition with Trungpa Rinpoche and Gyaltrul Rinpoche. As of 2008, he teaches "inner disarmament" workshops, which integrate nonviolent communication skills with Zen practice. He is a member of the Buddhist Peace Fellowship Board of Directors.

The center has an affiliate group on the island of Hawaii in Holualoa, which offers weekly zazen. Weekly hula classes are offered at the Oak Park center.

Membership: Not reported.

Sources:

Zen Center of Oak Park. www.zencommunity.org/

Morreale, Don, ed. *The Complete Guide to Buddhist America.* Boston, MA: Shambhala, 1998.

Zen Community of New York

Greyston Foundation, 21 Park Ave., Yonkers, NY 10703

The Zen Community of New York was founded in 1979 by Tetsugen Bernard Glassman, who had been named a dharma heir of Taizan Maezumi Roshi (1931–1995), founder of the Zen Center of Los Angeles. Over the years, the community became independent of the work in California. It has also developed into one of the more unique Zen communities in America by developing an outward-looking program that views its ministry primarily in terms of social work. For example, members hold retreats on the street with the local homeless community or in such locations in the local community as to bear witness to the social and economic problems of society.

Glassman developed the Greyston Mandala, a network of for-profit and non-profit organizations that improve the lives of people in southwest Yonkers. The Greyston Mandala provides jobs, workforce development, low-income housing, supportive services, child care, after-school programs, community gardens, and a bakery facility that supplies the ice cream industry with brownie chips. The Maitri Center, opened in 1997, serves 150 people with AIDS-related illnesses. Several additional centers are associated with the community, and Glassman is an active leader in the White Plum Asanga.

As of 2007, the Greyston Mandala hired 175 people and served at least 1,200 people annually. Glassman left it in 1996. He had also founded the Zen Peacemaker Order in 1980 to promote initiatives for social change that are grounded in Buddhist teaching and practice. In 2004, Glassman began developing a training campus to teach people the skills of spiritually based social enterprise and peacemaking called the Maezumi Institute, located in Montague, Massachusetts.

Membership: Not reported. Affiliated centers are found in New York City, Brooklyn, East Hampton, and Sagaponack, New York; and Boca Raton, Florida.

Sources:

Greyston Foundation. www.greyston.org/

Glassman, Bernard, and Rick Fields. *Instructions to the Cook: A Zen Master's Lessons in Living a Life That Matters.* New York: Bell Tower, 1996.

Maezumi Institute. www.zenpeacemakers.org/mi/

Morreale, Don, ed. *The Complete Guide to Buddhist America.* Boston, MA: Shambhala, 1998.

Zen Community of Oregon

PO Box 188, Clatskanie, OR 97016

The Zen Community of Oregon was founded in 1975 by Hakuyu Taizan Maezumi Roshi (1931–1995), who also founded the Zen Center of Los Angeles. The Oregon community has been led by Jan Chozen Bays Roshi (b. 1945) and her husband, Zen Teacher Hogen Bays, since 1984.

Chozen Bays was ordained by Maezumi Roshi in 1979 and was named his fourth Dharma heir in 1984. She is a mother and pediatrician, but most of her time is devoted to teaching and writing about Zen Buddhism.

Hogen Bays began practice in 1968 with Philip Kapleau Roshi, and was ordained by Maezumi Roshi in 1990. He has a doctorate in naturopathic medicine and a master's degree in psychology and works full time for the Zen Community of Oregon. Both Chozen and Hogen have continued their advanced Zen training with Shodo Harada Roshi (b. 1940), abbot of Sogenji Monastery in Japan.

The Zen Community of Oregon sponsors urban meditation and classes in Portland, Oregon. It has founded Great Vow Monastery, which holds meditation retreats (*sesshin*) monthly and a wide variety of classes for both ordained and lay Buddhists, along with about 70 days of intensive meditation per year. Great Vow Monastery also sponsors Buddhist speakers and offers workshops. There is a core program leading to ordination as a Zen Buddhist priest available for those who meet the criteria. Great Vow Monastery is located in the country near Portland.

Membership: In 2008, the community reported approximately 110 active members. In residence at the monastery are the two teachers, two ordained priests, and three ordained novice priests, as well as a number of lay people. It also has many visitors from all areas of the United States, who participate in their events.

Educational Facilities:

Great Vow Zen Monastery.

Periodicals: *Ink on the Cat.*

Sources:

Zen Community of Oregon. www.zendust.org/.

Rawlinson, Andrew. *The Book of Enlightened Masters: Western Teachers in Eastern Traditions.* La Salle, IL: Open Court Press, 1997. 650 pp.

Sidor, Ellen, ed. *A Gathering of Spirit: Women Teaching in American Buddhism.* Cumberland, RI: Primary Point Press, 1987.

Zen Studies Society

c/o Dai Bosatsu Zendo Kongo-Ji, 223 Beecher Lake Rd., Livingston Manor, NY 12758-6000

The Zen Studies Society was founded in 1956 to assist the work of Daisetz Teitaro Suzuki (1870–1966). Suzuki came to the United States in 1949 and settled at Columbia University in 1951. His lectures at Columbia lay behind much of the public interest in Zen in the United States, one visible result being the establishment of the Zen Studies Society. When Suzuki moved on to Harvard in 1957, the group continued its studies without the presence of a Zen master. Then in 1965 Eido Tai Shimano, formerly a monk at the Ryutaku-ji (Dragon Temple) headed by Soen Nakagawa Roshi (1907–1984), moved to New York. He assumed leadership of the Zen Studies Society and shifted it from its more intellectual study to the practice of *zazen* (Zen meditation). He established the New York Zendo Shobo Ji (Temple of True Dharma) in Manhattan in 1968 and then turned his attention toward the establishment of a rural Zen monastery. In 1971 land was purchased in the Catskill Mountains of upstate New York for the International Dai Bosatsu Zendo Kongo Ji (Diamond Temple), dedicated in 1976. In 1972 Eido Shimano Roshi received *inka*—Rinzai Zen Dharma transmission in the Hakuin/Torei lineage—from Nakagawa Roshi. Shimano Roshi serves as abbot of the Zen Studies Society and as the spiritual teacher at it two centers.

The New York Zendo Shobo Ji provides a place for Zen practice to residents of New York City. Beginners are invited to Thursday evening meetings. Otherwise, the Zendo is open at various times each week for zazen. There are weekend *sesshin* (zazen intensives) five times annually and periodic all-day zazen sessions. Monthly Dharma studies sessions are held. After a period of regular attendance and practice, one may apply for full membership.

Dai Bosatsu Zendo was dedicated on July 4, 1976, partially to commemorate America's bicentennial. Here, twice annually in the spring and fall, a three-month traditional monastic training is held, which attracts students from around the world. Students follow a rigorous schedule that includes zazen, chanting, and physical labor. They also follow a vegetarian diet. A monthly sesshin is also held, during which time the zazen retreat population at the monastery swells.

Membership: In 1996 the society reported a constituency community of 5,000, though there are only several hundred members and students regularly engaged in zazen. There are related Zen centers in Syracuse, New York; Jacksonville, Florida; and Zurich, Switzerland.

Periodicals: *The Newsletter of the Zen Studies Society.*

Sources:

Zen Studies Society. www.zenstudies.org/.

Daily Sutras for Chanting and Recitation. New York: New York Zendo of the Zen Studies Society, n.d.

Shimano, Eido T. *Golden Wind.* Tokyo: Japan Publications, 1979.

———, ed. *Like a Dream, Like a Fantasy.* Tokyo: Japan Publications, 1978.

———. *Points of Departure: Zen Buddhism with a Rimzai View.* Livingston Manor, NY: Zen Studies Society Press, 1991.

Shimano, Eido T., and Kosetsu Tani. *Zen Ward, Zen Calligraphy.* Boston: Shambhala, 1995.

Chinese Buddhism

Amitabha Buddhist Societies

650 S Bernardo Ave., Sunnyvale, CA 94087

Alternate Address: International headquarters: c/o The Corporate Body of the Buddha Educational Foundation, 11 Fl., No. 55, Hang Chow S Rd., Sec. 1, Taipei, Taiwan Republic of China

The Ven. Master Jing Kong, a teacher of Pure Land Buddhism, was born in China in 1927. In Taiwan following World War II (1939–1945), he studied toward ordination, which was granted in 1959. He has subsequently spent his time as a teacher and founder of Buddhist centers both in Taiwan and around the world. He founded a series of organizations that form the nexus of the network of Amitabha Buddhist societies, including the Hwa Dzan Society of Propagating Teachings, Hwa Dzan Monastery, Hwa Dzan Buddhist Library, Hwa Dzan Lecture Hall, and the corporate body of the Buddha Educational Foundation. He pioneered the publication of Buddhist materials on audio and video tapes and, through the educational foundation, has distributed millions of pieces of Buddhist literature, including his own writings.

Jing Kong has seen Buddhism as an educational endeavor and defined authentic Buddhism as the "education of understanding the true face of life and the universe" as originally put forth by Shakyamuni Buddha. Pure Land Buddhism is most identified with the popular practice of invoking Buddha Amida's name with the intention of it being the means of allowing the individual to be born in the heavenly realm called the "pure land of bliss." The Pure Land is the central tradition of Chinese Buddhism.

The Pure Land teachings are derived primarily from five Buddhist texts: *The Sutra of Amitabha's Purity, Equality, and Understanding; A Principle Explanation of the Amitabha Sutra; The Chapter of Universal Worthy Bodhisattva's Conduct and Vows; The Sutra on Contemplating Amitabha and His Pure Land;* and *The Chapter on the Foremost Attainment of Great Strength Bodhisattva through Buddha Recitation.* These are among the materials regularly reprinted by the Educational Foundation.

The texts also have given rise to four courses offered at the Amitabha centers that lead to an understanding of Buddhism and how to embody it in one's life. The basic course teaches a set of moral principles and the basic practice of reciting the Amida Buddha's name. Subsequent courses emphasize harmony and self-discipline. A final course centers upon the 10 great vows of bodhisattva conduct: respect for all people, praise for the virtues and kind practices of others, giving, repentance and reform of all one's faults, rejoicing in the virtuous deeds of others, promoting the broad spread of Buddhist teachings, seeking the guidance of the societies' teachers, holding the Buddha's teachings in one's heart, seeking accord with the wishes of people in one's environment, and dedicating the peace gained from practicing to all living beings.

Centers began to appear in the United States in the 1980s, primarily within the Chinese American community. The Amitabha Buddhist Society of U.S.A. was founded in 1989 to advocate the Pure Land Study of Buddhism. With the publication of an English-language translation of Master Jing Kong's writing, centers began to spread to the wider society in the 1990s.

Membership: Not reported. There are 20 centers in the United States and 3 in Canada. Additional centers are located in Taiwan, Australia, Singapore, Malaysia, and Hong Kong.

Sources:

Amitabha Buddhist Society of U.S.A. www.amtb-usa.org/eindex.htm

Jing Kong. *Buddhism: The Wisdom of Compassion and Awakening*. Taipei, Taiwan: The Corporate Body of the Buddha Educational Foundation, n.d.

————. *To Understand Buddhism*. Taipei, Taiwan: The Corporate Body of the Buddha Educational Foundation, 1998.

Jy Din Sakya. *Empty Cloud: The Teachings of Xu Yun*. Taipei, Taiwan: The Corporate Body of the Buddha Educational Foundation, n.d.

Buddha's Universal Church

720 Washington St., San Francisco, CA 94108

The largest of the Buddhist organizations centered upon the San Francisco, California, Chinese community is Buddha's Universal Church, founded during the late 1920s in Chinatown. The church is currently housed in a million-dollar temple begun during the 1950s, built by volunteers, and dedicated in 1963. It is one of the largest in the continental United States and contains a unique mosaic image of the Buddha.

Among the founders of Buddha's Universal Church was the late Dr. Paul F. Fung, a physician, a doctor of the Dharma, and vice president of the World Fellowship of Buddhists. Currently the church is led by Dr. Frederick Hong. A focus on scholarship enabled the church to become an American Buddhist intellectual center that now houses a fine library and research facility. A project of translating Buddhist texts led in 1964 to the publication of *The Sutra of the Sixth Patriarch on the Pristine Orthodox Dharma*, the first of several projected volumes. *The Pristine Orthodox Dharma*, Volume I, was published in 1977.

Public services are held every second Sunday at 11:15 A.M. and include a lecture and tour. On the fourth Sunday of each month at 10:30 A.M., meetings on the books of Buddhism are held for church members only. Members and visitors are invited to listen to the choir and then to a lecture given in both Chinese and English. The topics of these lectures include the history and teachings of the Buddha, classical stories and narratives, and lessons drawn from present-day circumstances. Tours of the church are given immediately after lectures and start with the golden image of the Buddha at the main altar. On the roof is a garden with a Bodhi tree, grown from a cutting of the tree under which Buddha is believed to have sat, and a lotus-shaped pool. A yearly bilingual (Chinese-English) costumed musical production depicting ancient China is presented by the young people of the church.

Membership: There are approximately 400 members of the church at the single center in San Francisco.

Sources:

Buddha's Universal Church. www.bucsf.com.

Fung, Paul F., and George D. Fung, trans. *The Sutra of the Sixth Patriarch on the Pristine Orthodox Dharma*. San Francisco: Buddha's Universal Church, 1964.

Hong, Frederick, and George D. Fung, trans. *Pristine Orthodox Dharma*. San Francisco: Buddha's Universal Church, 1977.

Buddhist Association of Colorado

8965 W Dartmouth Pl., Lakewood, CO 80227

The Buddhist Association of Colorado is a Chinese Pure Land organization (analogous to the Buddhist Churches of America, the Japanese Pure Land Buddhist

organization) established in 1990 under the direction of the Rev. Pat Leong. The majority of members are of Chinese descent, but all are welcomed. The primary gathering is a Sunday service at which the chanting of Buddha's name (Namo Amitabha) is a primary element.

Affiliated with the association is the Nan Hua Zen Buddhist Society of Las Vegas founded by two American teachers, Chaun Yuan Shakya and Chaun Chang Shakya, both of whom traveled to the People's Republic of China to be ordained at the monastery originally founded by Hui Neng, the Sixth Patriarch (of Zen Buddhism).

Membership: Not reported.

Sources:

Morreale, Don. *The Complete Guide to Buddhist America*. Boston: Shambhala, 1998.

Buddhist Association of the United States

c/o Temple of Enlightenment, 3070 Albany Cres., New York, NY 10463

The largest of the Buddhist organizations centered in the Chinese community of the New York area is the Buddhist Association of the United States, formed in 1964. The association attempts to synthesize various Buddhist trends, the two most important of which are Ch'an, the Chinese form of Zen, and Pure Land Buddhism, which focuses on the worship of Amida Buddha.

The association's Sunday schedule includes meditation, a lecture, and discussion. The association was led until recently by President Lok To and Vice President Chia Theng Shen (1913–2007). Shen, a popular author and lecturer, passed away on November 29, 2007.

The association's Great Buddha Hall, located at Chuang Yen Monastery in Carmel, New York, was dedicated in May 1997. Inside the hall is a 37-foot statue of the Buddha Vairocana—the largest Buddha statue in the Western hemisphere. Encircling the large statue are 10,000 small statues of the Buddha on a lotus terrace. Surrounding the pedestal of the Buddha statue are 12 bas-reliefs of Bodhisattvas. A mural covers the wall of the lotus terrace and depicts scenes from the "Pure Land" or "Western Paradise" of Amitabha Buddha. At the back of the terrace is another mural with paintings.

The Woo-Ju Memorial Library at the monastery contains more than 70,000 books, the bulk of which are Buddhist reference works, including sutras in Pali, Sanskrit, Mongolian, Chinese, Japanese, Korean, Vietnamese, French, and German. Ancient documents from the Duan Hwang Cave, contained in the original microfiche, are stored in this library, along with Tibetan holy books

Also at the monastery is Kuan Yin Hall, which contains the largest colored porcelain statue of Kuan Yin Bodhisattva in the world. It is believed to date back to the Ming Dynasty, and is about 700 years old. The monastery also is home to a six-foot wooden statute of Kuan Yin that is more than 1,000 years old.

The association's BAUS Prison Program provides free books and, when available, tapes about Buddhism to prisoners who request them and seeks to answer questions prisoners may have about Buddhism or Buddhist practice.

Membership: The association reports approximately 800 members.

Periodicals: *BAUS Wisdom Journal*. Available from www.bauswj.org.

Sources:

Buddhist Association of the United States. www.baus.org/.

Associated Content. www.associatedcontent.com/article/410773/visit_the_chuang_yen_monastery_in_carmel.html?cat=16.

The Enlightenment Sutra with Annotations. Bronx, NY: Buddhist Association of the United States, 1955.

Hsu, T'an. *On Amidism*. Bronx, NY: Buddhist Association of the United States, 1973.

Shen, C. T. *A Glimpse of Buddhism*. Taipei, Taiwan: Torch of Wisdom, 1970.

————. *What We Can Learn from Buddhism*. Taipei, Taiwan: Torch of Wisdom, 1975.

Thera, Narada. *An Outline of Buddhism*. Bronx, NY: Buddhist Association of the United States, n.d.

Buddhist Compassion Relief Tzu Chi Association

USA National Headquarters, 1100 S Valley Center Ave., San Dimas, CA 91773

Alternate Address: International Headquarters: 21, Kang Leh Village, Shin Cheng Shiang, Hualien County, Taiwan.

The Buddhist Compassion Relief Tzu Chi Association is the largest Buddhist organization in Taiwan. It was founded in 1966 by a female Dharma master, Cheng Yen (b. 1937), along with five disciples and some 30 followers. The organization has contributed greatly to the rise of a humanistic/this-worldly approach to Chinese Mahayana Buddhism in Taiwan (and Chinese overseas communities). This approach was developed in the decades prior to World War II by Tai Hsu (1890–1947) in mainland China, and then after the war by Yin Shun (b. 1906), his disciple, in Taiwan. Tai Hsu emphasized the importance of the laity (as opposed to priests and monks) and charitable activities (as opposed to religious services) in the propagation of the Dharma. For more than three decades, Tzu Chi has concentrated its activities in the four major missions of charity, medicine, education, and culture. Tzu Chi has built hospitals, colleges, and research centers, as well as developing educational, social, and cultural programs for its local communities. Cheng Yen became known for speaking in Minnanhua, the local Taiwanese language, rather than in Mandarin. She has also earned the admiration of the media, which has called her the "Mother Teresa of Taiwan." Master Cheng Yen was awarded the Eisenhower Medallion for her contributions to world peace. In 1996, she was nominated for the Nobel Peace Prize for her dedication to a renewed vision of compassion in action. In a July 2000 issue of *Business Week*, she was named one of 50 "Stars of Asia"—leaders at the forefront of change.

Cheng Yen's teachings have been summarized in a series of aphorisms that emphasize the performance of good deeds. Cheng Yen, now in her seventies, has led her followers to create an expansive program dedicated to providing relief services and free health care to the poor and vocational education for nurses. A notable campaign to create a bone marrow registry helped make this program widely respected, and reflected Cheng Yen's goal of "helping the poor and educating the rich."

Tzu Chi is notable for its female leadership. In Chinese Buddhism, only nuns can initiate women; thus, the small monastic community in which Cheng Yen resides is exclusively female. The majority of the membership at every level is female.

Members of the organization began to arrive in the United States in the 1970s, and centers emerged in the 1980s. Originally composed of first-generation emigrants from Taiwan, the association now counts many people who are not ethnic Chinese as adherents. The community in Los Angeles gained some publicity for the assistance it provided to victims of the 1991 cyclone in Bangladesh. Today, Tzu Chi centers in America support relief efforts worldwide.

Four American Tzu Chi offices are found in California; there also are offices in Illinois, Hawaii, New York, Texas, and Virginia. Canada has offices in Vancouver, British Columbia, and Markham, Ontario.

Membership: There is a core monastic community of 110 nuns. As of 2008, Tzu Chi is an international organization with more than 5 million supporters and more than 30,000 certified commissioners around the globe. As of August 2005, more than 57 countries in five continents have received Tzu Chi's aid. With offices in more than 20 countries, the Tzu Chi Foundation is one of the largest charity organizations originating from Taiwan.

Educational Facilities:

Tzu Chi College of Nursing, Hualien, Taiwan.

Tzu Chi College of Medicine, Taiwan.

Publications: *The Tzu-Chi World*. • *The Tzu Chi Quarterly*.

Sources:

Tzu Chi Foundation. www.tzuchi.org/global/. (In English).

Tzu Chi Foundation. www.tzuchi.org.tw/. (In Chinese).

Tzu Chi Foundation, Northern California Chapter. www.northerncal.us.tzuchi.org/.

Ching, Yu-ing. *Master of Love and Mercy: Cheng Yen*. Nevada City, CA: Blue Dolphin Publishing, 1995. 278 pp.

Jones, Charles Brewer. *Buddhism in Taiwan: Religion and the State, 1660–1990*. Honolulu: University of Hawaii Press, 1999.

Laliberte, Andre. *The Politics of Buddhist Organizations in Taiwan, 1989–1997*. Vancouver, BC: University of British Columbia, Ph.D. dissertation, 1999.

Chinese Buddhist Association of Hawaii-Hsu Yun Temple

42 Kawananakoa Pl., Honolulu, HI 96817

The Chinese Buddhist Association of Hawaii-Hsu Yun Temple, established in 1955 at the suggestion of the Hong Kong Chinese Buddhist Association, invited and received Abbot Sic Tse Ting (Abbot Sakya Jy-Din) the following year. The name of the temple was named in memory and honor of one of the greatest Buddhist monks in mainland China in the last century, Ven. Hsu Yun. There is a main temple for worship and two memorial halls for paying respect to ancestors. The temple has three 10-foot, gold-leaf statues of Buddha as the center of worship; the life of Buddha is depicted on its walls.

Membership: In 2002 there were about 1,500 members in one center, and about 500 are current members.

Chung Tai

c/o Buddha Gate Monastery, 3254 Gloria Terr., Lafayette, CA 94549

The Chung Tai Chan (Zen) Buddhist movement is the lengthened shadow of Ven. Wei Chueh, who began his career as a Buddhist teacher under Master Lin Yuan at the Shi Fan Da Jue ("Great Enlightenment") Chan Monastery in Keelung, Taiwan. Several years after his ordination (1963), he entered into a retreat in the mountains near Taipei that lasted a decade. There, in the early 1980s, he was sought out by disciples who increasingly asked him to leave his retreat and become a public teacher. He did so in the mid-1980s and subsequently assembled the resources to construct the Lin Quan Chan Monastery (1987), located on the site of his lengthy retreat. As the original center became too small for his disciples, he led in the building of Chung Tai Chan Monastery in the town of Puli in central Taiwan (completed in 2001).

By that time Grand Master Wei Chueh had become a well-known leader in Taiwanese Buddhism. The monastery nurtured the development of meditation centers around Taiwan and then among the Taiwanese diaspora community abroad in the United States, Australia, the Philippines, Thailand, and Hong Kong. The movement became quite expansive and developed programs around its notion of the "Five Modern Approaches of Propagating Buddhism" through academic research, education, culture and the arts, science, and daily living. Disciples are expected to created a well-rounded Buddhist life based on the integration of three disciplines—the cultivation of merit (through good works), scriptural understanding through study, and regular meditation.

The first center in the United States emerged in the 1990s as the Buddha Gate Monastery, now located in the San Francisco Bay area. Subsequently several more centers were founded in California, and one each in Texas and Oklahoma. Programs are offered in both Chinese and English.

Membership: Not Reported. There are five centers in the United States.

Sources:

Chung Tai. www.ctworld.org/english-96/html/index.htm.

Dharma Realm Buddhist Association
City of Ten Thousand Buddhas, 4951 Bodhi Way, Ukiah, CA 95482

The Dharma Realm Buddhist Association was founded as the Sino-American Buddhist Association in 1959 by disciples of Tripitaka Master Xuan Hua (1918–1995). In 1962, he moved from Hong Kong to San Francisco, California, and in 1968 established the Buddhist Lecture Hall as a center for the study and practice of Orthodox Buddhism in the West. Originally founded by Chinese Americans, the center quickly attracted a large Caucasian membership. The organization expanded rapidly. The Gold Mountain Monastery in San Francisco was opened in 1970; the Buddhist Text Translation Society (International Translation Institute) was founded in 1973; and the City of Ten Thousand Buddhas, an international study center for Western Buddhists, opened in 1976. In the Hall of Ten Thousand Buddhas there is a nearly 20-foot-high wooden statue of the thousand-handed, thousand-eyed Guanshiyin (Avalokiteshvara) bodhisattva carved by Layman Wang Taisheng, a master carver of wooden Buddhist statues from Hong Kong. The walls are lined with a grid of compartments, each containing a statue of a Buddha. There are a total of 10,000 Buddha statues of various sizes.

Among the many other temples, monasteries, and retreat centers established by Master Hua are the Gold Wheel Monastery in Los Angeles, California (1976); the Gold Summit Monastery in Seattle, Washington (1984); the Gold Buddha Monastery in Vancouver, British Columbia (1984); Long Beach Monastery in Long Beach, California; Avatamsaka Monastery in Calgary, Alberta; the Berkeley Buddhist Monastery and Institute of World Religions in Burlingame, California; the administrative headquarters and International Translation Institute also in Burlingame, California; the City of the Dharma Realm in West Sacramento, California; and the Blessings, Prosperity, and Longevity Monastery in Long Beach, California.

Master Xuan Hua had been a longtime student of Master Xu Yun (1840–1959) in China. He moved to Hong Kong after the Maoist revolution in 1949. In accepting the invitation to come to the West, he did so with the intention of establishing Buddhism in its entirety (Chan meditation, Pure Land, esoteric, Vinaya [moral discipline], and doctrinal studies). Among the young converts to Buddhism attracted to the lecture hall, he accepted some into monastic vows. In 1969, five disciples went to Taiwan to receive final ordination as *bhikshus* (monks) and *bhikshunis* (nuns), and by 1972 there were 10 fully ordained monks and several novices preparing for ordination. The first full ordination of disciples in the United States occurred in 1976 at the City of Ten Thousand Buddhas. Since that time, the association has held such ordinations every three or four years.

The Dharma Realm Buddhist Association, though based in the Chan (Zen) school of Chinese Buddhism, teaches all five main varieties of Chinese Buddhism. New members accept Chinese Buddhist names. Lay members add "Kuo" as part of their name; those destined for the priesthood who received their novice vows from Master Xuan Hua have "Heng" added to their name; and the fully ordained monks receive the surname *Shih*, the first character of the Chinese word, Sakyamuni (Gautama Buddha). Each new member takes the Three Refuges (a ceremony similar to Christian confirmation, by which the new member promises to take refuge in the Buddha, the dharma or teachings of Buddha, and the *sangha*).

The association has emphasized the development of a Buddhist monastic community, an element of Buddhist life frequently missing in Western Buddhist organizations. More than 50 persons have entered the orders. Members of monastic communities lead a very disciplined life of practice and study. They are sexually celibate, are strict vegetarians, and do not eat after noon. The program emphasizes Sutra study (including language studies and translation, lectures, and chanting) and meditation.

The Dharma Realm Buddhist University was the first Buddhist university to be established in the Western world. It offers degreed courses in Buddhist studies, letters and science, and the creative and applied arts. It is located in the City of Ten Thousand Buddhas in Talmage, California. Through the sangha (or clergy) training and laity training programs, the Buddhist equivalent of seminary education is offered for Buddhist leaders. Since its founding in 1973, the International Buddhist Text Translation Society has become a major publisher of Buddhist literature. Managed by both sangha and lay scholars under the guidance of Xuan Hua, it had by 1980 published translations of more than 100 volumes of Chinese Buddhist writings in various Western languages.

Membership: In 1992 the association reported 25,000 members in five centers served by 50 ministers in the United States and 5,000 members, two centers, and five ministers in Canada.

Educational Facilities:

Dharma Realm Buddhist University, Talmage, California.

Periodicals: *Vajra Bodhi Sea*. Available from the Gold Mountain Monastery, 800 Sacramento St., San Francisco, CA 94108. • *The Proper Dharma Seal*. Available from City of Ten Thousand Buddhas, PO Box 217, Talmage, CA 95481.

Sources:

Dharma Realm Buddhist Association: History. www.advite.com/sf/drba/drba2.html

Biographical Sketch of the Elder Master Venerable Xuan, Noble Hua. Talmage, CA: Dharma Realm Buddhist Association, 1996.

City of Ten Thousand Buddhas. www.cttbusa.org/

Hua, Xuan. *Buddha Root Farm: Pure Land Talks*. Burlingame, CA: Buddhist Text Translation Society, 1976.

———. *Out of the Earth Emerges: Wonderful Enlightenment Mountain. Celebrating 40 Years of Dharma in the West—as Transcribed by the Venerable Xuan Hua and the 25th Anniversary of the City of Ten Thousand Buddhas*. Burlingame, CA: Buddhist Text Translation Society, 2001.

———. *The Ten Dharma Realms Are Not Beyond a Single Thought*. San Francisco, CA: Sino-American Buddhist Association, 1976.

World Peace Gathering. San Francisco: Sino-American Buddhist Association, 1975.

Yin, Heng. *Records of the Life of the Venerable Master Xuan Hua*. 2 vols. San Francisco, CA: Committee for the Publication of the Biography of the Venerable Master Xuan Hua, 1973–1975.

Eastern States Buddhist Association of America
64 Mott St., New York, NY 10013

The Eastern States Buddhist Association of America was founded in 1963 as the first New York–area Chinese temple with a priest in attendance. Largely through the help of Mrs. James Ying, the program has grown and developed. In 1971 Dharma Master Bhikshu Hsi Ch'en, who had escaped China when the Communists took over, was brought to the United States to head the Temple Mahayana, an Association retreat center in the Catskill Mountains in New York.

The Eastern States Buddhist Association follows the T'ien-t'ai school founded by Chih-i (558–597), a monk at Mount T'ien-t'ai in China. The members emphasize the Lotus Sutra as inclusive of all of Buddha's teachings. Meditation, the study of the Sutras, repeating the name of Amitabha Buddha, and living a disciplined life are emphasized.

Membership: Not reported.

Falun Gong (Falun Dafa)
Falun Dafa Information Center, 331 W 57th St., Ste. 409, New York, NY 10019

Falun Gong (or Falun Dafa, the "Great Way of the Law Wheel") is one of a number of new spiritual disciplines that rose to prominence in China following the end of the Cultural Revolution in 1976. It was founded in 1992 in Changchun, in northeastern China, as a qigong practice group. Qigong is a popular indigenous health practice that uses movement and meditation to harness subtle energies such as qi, an energy believed to underlay the cosmos and which is basic to the practice of Chinese medicine. Founder Li Hongzhi (b. 1952) is regarded as a master of qigong and the sole instructor of Falun Gong. Prior to the founding of Falun Gong he served in the army and worked for a grain corporation. He is said to have studied with several Daoist and Buddhist masters over the course of four decades.

Through the rest of the 1990s, the practice spread across China and to Chinese diaspora communities in Hong Kong, Taiwan, Japan, and the United States. Falun Gong first caught the attention of the West when on April 25, 1999, some 10,000 adherents appeared in front of government offices in Beijing, where they peacefully, but boldly, petitioned the government over alleged mistreatment and a general ban on the group's publications. Subsequently Falun Gong became subject to ongoing suppression by the Communist Chinese state.

The group's name denotes a spiritual/meditation practice (*gong*) that implements a metaphysical wheel (*falun*) familiar to Buddhist doctrine. Falun Gong teaches members to lead a life of moral rectitude in which the abandonment of selfishness and problematic "attachments" figure centrally. It includes two components, described as "practice" and "self-cultivation." Practice consists of five qigong and meditation exercises, usually done each morning. Self-cultivation aims at removing negative tendencies of thought and behavior in pursuit of a higher state of purity and rectitude. Good health and inner calm are commonly cited benefits.

Adherents seek to align their life and being with what are understood to be the most basic qualities of the universe, that is, *zhen shan ren*—truth, compassion, forbearance. These properties inhere in all life and matter but are imperceptible to the average person, who cannot know other planes of existence. Selfish desires, attachments, and various notions formed in a person over the course of life distance him or her from *zhen shan ren* and hasten the accrual of karma, which further insulates a person from these higher qualities, creating a vicious cycle of spiraling alienation. Suffering and ordeals are given positive valuation in the practice insofar as they can diminish one's karma. The ultimate promise of the practice is a state of higher awakening, or enlightenment.

Falun Gong's teachings are found in *Falun Gong* and *Zhuan Falun* (*Turning of the Law Wheel*), as with additional books that collect talks given by the founder, Li. A collection of poetry authored by the founder, *Hong Yin* (*The Grand Verses*), is also available. All of Falun Gong's texts can be found online at the group's main Web site.

Falun Gong's community and organization in China have been drastically altered by official persecution. Outside of China it continues to be organized around practice groups, with a set of more formal national organizations that provide coordination and a flow of information. Li Hongzhi, who has resided in the United States since 1996, remains the recognized leader. Adherents gather annually for "experience sharing" conferences at which individuals reflect upon their progress in the practice and efforts to counteract state suppression in China. In Taiwan, a democracy, the practice is legal and enjoys widespread appeal.

Membership: It is not known how large the group is internationally, owing to its loose organization. According to an April 27, 1999, *New York Times* report, official Chinese sources once put the number practicing at 70 million. That number is thought to have since diminished after close to a decade of suppression and rights abuses. Falun Gong groups may now be found throughout the Chinese diaspora worldwide (especially in Southeast Asia) and are reaching out to the indigenous populations of those countries. Numbers of adherents outside China are hard to establish, though some 400,000 practitioners reportedly live in Taiwan. There are groups in most cities across the United States and Canada, and volunteer contacts can be found in some 80 countries.

Remarks: Falun Gong was officially banned in China on July 22, 1999. Subsequently many members have been arrested and tortured in police custody, with human rights groups documenting over 3,000 wrongful deaths. It has also been the subject of a government media campaign that has presented the group in a most negative light. In response, Falun Gong members have labored to document rights abuses perpetrated in China and raise public and government awareness. In this effort they have developed an extensive Internet presence. The

campaign to "eradicate" Falun Gong continues in China in spite of international criticism and following a change in China's leadership in 2002.

On the Internet are numerous sites on Falun Gong in a variety of languages, though with varying degrees of reliability. Especially good starting points are some of the official sites such as the Falun Dafa Information Center and the Falun Dafa (Falun Gong) sites. For a learned appraisal and periodically updated bibliography, see the site maintained by the Sinological Institute at the University of Leiden. An additional source is historian David Ownby's scholarly 2008 account.

Sources:

Falun Dafa Information Center. www.faluninfo.net.

Falun Dafa (Falun Gong). www.falundafa.org.

Li Hongzhi. *Falun Buddha Law (Lectures in the United States)*. Hong Kong: Falun Fo Fa Publishing, 1999.

Ownby, David. *Falun Gong and the Future of China*. Oxford: Oxford University Press, 2008.

Sinological Institute, University of Leiden. "Falun Gong." website.leidenuniv.nl/~haarbjter/falun.htm.

Wong, John, and William Ti Liu. *The Mystery of China's Falun Gong: Its Rise and Sociological Implications*. Singapore: World Scientific Publishing / Singapore University Press, 1999.

Hawaii Chinese Buddhist Society

1614 Nuuanu Ave., Honolulu, HI 96817

In 1953, a number of Chinese-American residents in Hawaii decided to take advantage of the movement of many Buddhist monks into Hong Kong after the Maoist revolution by establishing work under their leadership. The initial Hawaiian group divided between those who wished to choose the monks from among their acquaintances and those who wished the Hong Kong Chinese Buddhist Association to select the most qualified.

The Hawaii Chinese Buddhist Society chose to make its own selection and brought the Rev. Chuen Wai from Hong Kong to head the temple in Honolulu. He was joined in 1957 by Dharma Master Tsu Yin. These two men emphasize the Buddhist nature of the Society, as opposed to the strong Taoist influence found in some Chinese temples. All the statues are of traditional Buddhist bodhisattvas: Omito (Amida); Kwan Yin; Wei Ton (sometimes called General Wei Ton), who was asked by Buddha to protect Buddhist teachings; and Tay Chong Wong, the god of wisdom.

Membership: In 1982 there were 1,000 members in one center in Honolulu.

Hsu Yun Temple

42 Kawananakoa Pl., Nu'uanu, Honolulu, HI 96817

Hsu Yun Temple, a Chan Buddhist temple serving the Chinese-American community in Honolulu, Hawaii, was founded in 1956 by Jy Din Shakya (1917–2003). Shakya was born in China. At age thirty he encountered the aging Zen master Hsu Yun (1839–1959), the most outstanding Chan master of the twentieth century, credited with reviving what had been a declining tradition. Shakya studied with Hsu Yun at the Nan Hua Monastery in Guangdong Province, the home of Hui Neng (638–713), the sixth patriarch of Chan Buddhism.

Shakya was ordained in 1937. He later was asked to bring Chan Buddhism to Hawaii and began that mission in 1949 with a move to Hong Kong. From there it took another seven years to get to Honolulu. A year later, he was able to build the temple located on Kawananakoa Place. He retired in 1987 and passed the leadership to Fat Wei Shakya, who also heads the sister temple in San Francisco.

Hsu Yun Temple and its sister temple in San Francisco serve primarily Chinese-speaking residents of its community. In 1997 Jy Din Shakya authorized the development of an English-based Internet outreach, the Zen Buddhist Order of Hsu Yun, and in 1998 he elevated his disciple and dharma heir, Chuan Zhi Shakya, to become the order's Abbot. While developing an expansive Internet presence, the Zen Buddhist Order of Hsu Yun has become the basis of a new Zen community that continues to value its spiritual ties to Jy Din Shakya and Fat Wei Shakya.

Membership: Unreported.

Sources:

Zen Buddhist Order of Hsu Yun (Chan).
www.hsuyun.org/Dharma/zbohy/Home/home-index.html.

Shakya, Jy Din. *Empty Cloud: The Teachings of Xu Yun and a Remembrance of the Great Chinese Zen Master*. Hong Kong: H.K. Buddhist Book Distributor, 1996.

Wright, Walter. "Jy Din Sakya, Hsu Yun Temple Abbot, Dead at 85." *Honolulu Advertiser* (March 21, 2003). Available from
the.honoluluadvertiser.com/article/2003/Mar/21/ln/ln46a.html.

Il Bung Zen Society

c/o Zen Center of Huntsville, 1412 Randolph St., Huntsville, AL 35801

The Il Bung Zen Society was founded by Zen Master Don Gilbert (1909–2006), also known as Ta Hui. In 1968, he was initiated into the Chogye Order of Korean Zen Buddhism by Seo Kyung-bo (1914–1996), one of the first Korean Zen teachers who settled in the United States. In 1973, Gilbert was named Kyung-bo's dharma heir. Gilbert held services in three widely separated temples in Arcata and Carmel, California, and Huntsville, Alabama. He authored two cartoon books on Zen whose featured characters are a bloodhound and a canine Zen master.

Membership: Not reported.

Sources:

Gilbert, Don. *Jellyfish Bones: The Humor of Zen*. Oakland, CA: Blue Dragon Press, 1980.

————. *The Upside Down Circle: Zen Laughter*. Nevada City, CA: Blue Dolphin, 1988.

International Buddhist Progress Society

PO Box 5248, Hacienda Heights, CA 91745

Alternate Address: 3456 S Glenmark Dr., Hacienda Heights, CA 91745; International Headquarters: Foguangshan, Tashu, Gaoxiong 84010, Taiwan.

The International Buddhist Progress Society is an organization adhering to Chinese Buddhism in America. It was originally founded in 1967 in Taiwan by the Ven. Xingyun (b. 1926), the 48th patriarch of the Japanese Rinzai line of chan. When he was 12 years old he became a monk and received a monastic education. He was ordained in 1941. In 1949, in the wake of the Communist emergence as the ruling force in the country, Xingyun left for Taiwan. It was there in 1967 that he established Foguangshan, a forest monastery, said to be the largest in China.

During his life, Xingyun developed a great incentive to propagate "humanistic Buddhism," and the society became the launching pad for his evangelistic endeavors to create a pure land here on earth. Entering America in the early 1980s, the society began building Xilai Temple, a monastic complex in Hacienda Heights, California, the largest such complex in the West. Xilai Temple was built to serve as a spiritual and cultural center for those interested in learning more about Buddhism and the Chinese culture. The temple's objectives are to nurture Buddhist missionaries through education, to propagate Buddhism through cultural activities, to benefit society through charitable programs, and to edify the populace through Buddhist practices. Completed in 1988, it became the sight of the first meeting of the World Fellowship of Buddhists in North America.

This Buddhism is built around the teachings of the Venerable Xingyun, which emphasize the role of the monastic leadership in the Buddhist community and the presence of bodhisattvas (those who have attained enlightenment and have chosen to assist in the enlightenment of others) to assist Buddhists in their progress. The Hacienda Heights temple houses a large Buddhist cultural museum and sees itself as a focus for all of North American Buddhism.

Membership: In 2002 the society reported approximately 30,000 members in the United States and 10,000 members in Canada. By 2008, the society had established more than 100 temples worldwide. More than 1,300 monks and nuns serve in the Foguangshan Buddhist order. There are temples in Hacienda Heights, San Diego, and San Francisco, California; Las Vegas, Nevada; Phoenix, Arizona; Leawood, Kansas; Edmond, Oklahoma; Denver, Colorado; Dallas, Arlington, Austin, and Houston, Texas; Godeffroy and Flushing, New York; Miami and Orlando, Florida; Honolulu, Hawaii; Cambridge, Massachusetts; Edison, New Jersey; and Guam. Canadian temples are found in Vancouver, Edmonton, Ottawa, Montreal, and Toronto. Internationally there are four in Germany, three in Australia, two in Brazil, two in Britain, and one in Paraguay, Argentina, Sweden, Holland, Belgium, France, Switzerland, Austria, Spain, and Africa.

Educational Facilities:

Chinese Buddhist Research Institute; Eastern Buddhist College; Daipei Women's Buddhist College; Fu Shan Buddhist College; Gaoxiong, Taiwan; Hsi Lai University, Rosemead, California; Construction of a new Buddhist college in India has begun as of 2008; and the foundation-laying ceremony of Nantian University in Australia also took place.

Periodicals: *Merit Times Newspaper*. • *Buddha's Light Newsletter*.

Sources:

IBPS. www.ibps.org/

The Buddhist Liturgy. Monterey Park, CA: International Buddhist Progress Society, n.d.

Chandler, Stuart. *Establishing a Pure Land on Earth: The Foguang Buddhist Perspective on Modernization and Globalization*. Honolulu: University of Hawaii Press, 2004.

Fujiying. *Handing Down the Light: The Biography of Venerable Master Xingyun*, trans Amy Lui-Ma. Hacienda Heights, CA: Buddha's Light, 2004. 500 pp.

Xilai Temple. www.hsilai.org/

Xingyun. *How to Be a Foguang Buddhist*. Gaoxiong, Taiwan: International Buddhist Progress Society, 1987.

————. *Two Talks on Buddhism*. Gaoxiong, Taiwan: International Buddhist Progress Society, 1987.

Institute of Buddhist Studies/Chan Meditation Center

90-56 Corona Ave., Elmhurst, NY 11373

The Institute of Buddhist Studies/Chan Meditation Center was founded by Chan Master Sheng-yan (b. 1931), who came to the United States from Taiwan in 1975. Chan is the Chinese word for Zen. Master Sheng-yan was born in China and became a Buddhist monk at age 13. During his years of practice he became deeply committed to the propagation of Buddhism. In the late 1940s, as communism was spreading through China, he fled to Taiwan. He continued his practice in Taiwan and spent six years in solitary retreat on a mountain. After the retreat, Sheng-yan saw the need to improve the quality of Buddhist education and felt that in this way the spread of Buddhism would be assured. He therefore went to Japan and received a doctorate in Buddhist studies from Rissho University. He received dharma transmission (affirmation of his enlightenment and the special qualification to guide others in Buddhist teaching) from both the Rinzai and Soto Chan Buddhist lineage.

After moving to the United States, Sheng-yan settled in the Bronx, New York, where he became affiliated with the Buddhist Association of the United States, a predominantly Chinese Buddhist organization. He organized a Chan meditation class and began to hold meditation retreats that attracted many non-Chinese students. The Chan Meditation Center, in Queens, New York, is also a small monastery where fully ordained monks and nuns live and practice traditional precepts, including spiritual harmony, celibacy, and purity of mind. Sheng-yan also founded the Dharma Drum Retreat Center, whose current resident abbot is the Ven. Guorun Fashi, dharma heir of Sheng-yan.

In 1977 he started the *Chan Magazine*, and two years later formally founded the Institute of Buddhist Studies/Chan Meditation Center. He has been active in spreading Buddhism in the United States ever since. He now divides his time between the Chan centers in New York and Taipei, Taiwan.

Chan center affiliates are located in California, Florida, Georgia, Illinois, Michigan, New Jersey, New York, North Carolina, Ohio, Texas, Virginia, and Washington. International affiliates are located in Hong Kong, Malaysia, Singapore, Taiwan, Australia, Toronto, Vancouver, Croatia, Luxembourg, Poland, Sweden, Switzerland, the United Kingdom, and Mexico.

Membership: In 2006, Sheng-yan had 3,000 students in the United States and more than 300,000 students in Taiwan.

Educational Facilities:

The Zhong Hwa Institute of Buddhist Studies, Taipei, Taiwan.

Periodicals: *Chan Magazine*.

Sources:

Dharma Drum Mountain. www.chan1.org/

Hu, Muin. *Sharing Dharma Drum Mountain: A White Paper on Happiness*. Taipei, Taiwan: Dharma Drum, 2005.

Sheng-yen. *Dharma Drum: The life and Heart of Chan Practice*. Elmhurst, NY: Dharma Drum, 1996.

————. *Faith in Mind: A Guide to Chan Practice*. Elmhurst, NY: Dharma Drum, 1987.

————. *Getting the Buddha Mind: On the Practice of Chan Retreat*. Elmhurst, NY: Dharma Drum, 1982.

————. *Ox Herding at Morgan's Bay*. Elmhurst, NY: Institute of Zhong Hwa Buddhist Culture, 1988.

Tilling the Soil, Planting Good Seed: The 20th Anniversary of Zhong Hwa Institute of Buddhist Studies. Jinshan, Taipei County, Taiwan: Zhong Hwa Institute of Buddhist Studies, 2001.

Kuan Yin Temple

170 N Vineyard Blvd., Honolulu, HI 96817

The oldest Chinese temple in America is the Kuan Yin Temple begun by Leong Dick Ying, a monk who in 1878 brought to Hawaii two gold-leaf statues—the Taoist Kwan Tai and the Buddhist Kuan Yin, the goddess of mercy. A temple was built in Chinatown in Honolulu and, after several moves, in 1921 found a permanent home on Vineland Boulevard in Honolulu. Along with the statue of Kuan Yin, there are many statues of Buddha, bodhisattvas, and other deities.

The festival year that regulates the life of the various temples is followed at the Kuan Yin Temple. The Chinese New Year is the biggest festival, but throughout the year there are may festivals honoring the Buddha, bodhisattvas, and deities, including the Chinese Moon Festival (August 15) and the winter solstice.

Membership: In 1982 the temple reported 850 members.

Shaolin Buddhist Meditation Center

3165 Minnesota St., Los Angeles, CA 90031

The Shaolin Buddhist Meditation Center is part of a complex of structures founded in the late 1980s by Jefferson Chan, a teacher in the Chinese Shaolin tradition (the tradition made famous by the television series *Kung Fu*). The center of the complex is the California Buddhist University, opened in 1988, which offers a full curriculum (at the doctoral level) in Buddhist studies. The university sponsors the Kewanee Mountain Zen Center, the Bodhi bookstore, and a Zen garden.

Membership: Not reported.

Educational Facilities:

California Buddhist University, Los Angeles, California.

Periodicals: *The Shaolin Monastery*.

Sources:

Morreale, Don. *The Complete Guide to Buddhist America*. Boston: Shambhala, 1998.

Shaolin Temple

Overseas Headquarters, 132–11 41st Ave., Flushing, NY 11355

The Shaolin Temple, located in the Song Mountains of China, has attained legendary status as the originating point of kung fu, a practice intimately connected with the Chan Buddhism of its founder, the historically illusive character Bodhidharma (c. 470–c. 534). One of the many stories about Bodhidharma concerns his journey into the Song Mountains to the Shaolin Temple. Observing the poor physical condition of the monks there, he helped them by creating a program of physical techniques that strengthened their bodies, allowing them to endure both the rigors of their isolated existence and the concentrated Chan meditation program he had established. Those original techniques evolved into modern kung fu (*gongfu*), the first martial art.

The Shaolin Temple is the birthplace of martial arts and of Chan Buddhism. It has endured through the centuries, enduring the wrath of hostile governments. It was destroyed on several occasions, only to be rebuilt and continue. Having survived China's Cultural Revolution of the 1960s, its future is bright under its present abbot, Ven. Shi Yongxin.

In 1995 an outpost of the Shaolin Temple was started in Flushing, Long Island, New York, where many first-generation Chinese Americans reside. The Flushing temple, designated the foreign headquarters of the Shaolin Temple in China, offers a program of instruction in Chan Buddhism and in kung fu. It has spawned additional centers in Manhattan and Brooklyn. The Venerable Shi Goulin, a thirty-fourth–generation Shaolin monk, is the leader the Temple's Overseas Mission.

Membership: Not reported. There are three centers of the Shaolin Temple in the United States.

Sources:

Shaolin Temple. www.shaolin-overseas.org/home.html.

Demasco, Steve. *An American's Journey to the Shaolin Temple*. Valencia, CA: Black Belt Communications, 2001.

Guariglia, Justin, Shi Yong Xin, and Matthew Polly. *Shaolin: Temple of Zen*. New York: Aperture Foundation, 2007.

James, Andy. *The Spiritual Legacy of Shaolin Temple: Buddhism, Daoism, and the Energetic Arts*. Boston: Wisdom Publications, 2005.

True Buddha School

c/o Ling Shen Ching Tze Temple, 17012 NE 40th Ct., Redmond, WA 98052

The True Buddha School, a Vajrayana Buddhist movement operating in the Chinese-speaking community of the United States and Canada, was founded by Grand Master Sheng-Yen Lu, born in Taiwan in 1945. Following an awakening experience in 1969, Lu became a student of Buddhism and had frequent conversation with a spectrum of the Buddhas and Bodhisattvas that make up the Vajrayana Buddhist pantheon. In several steps, he reached a stage of enlightenment that has led his students to consider him a Living Buddha (Enlightened One).

Lu had already built a following in Southeast Asia when in 1981 he moved to the United States and built a large temple in suburban Seattle. In 1984 he reorganized his following as the True Buddha School. Through the rest of the century, he traveled widely and founded numerous centers, designated chapters, and temples.

Lu has assumed the role of a Tibetan lama and offers initiation and empowerments to those who wish to take refuge with him, either in his personal presence or through "remote initiation empowerment" offered twice monthly. He teaches a path to enlightenment very much like that offered in the Gelugpa Tibetan tradition. Lu's primary lineage comes through a Mongolian Gelugpa tradition, though he also claims lineages through all four of the major Tibetan schools, as well as the

Japanese Shingon tradition. Beginning in the middle of the first decade of the new century, Lu led a number of large gatherings at which he performed the Tibetan Kalachakre ceremony.

After receiving initial personal empowerment, the True Buddha School student receives a picture of the master and instruction in beginning practice. The master advises students to set up a personal shrine as a place for daily practice and offerings to the Buddhas and Bodhisattvas. Daily practice consists of meditation, chanting, the repetition of mantras, and visualization of one's personal deity. Many practitioners also attend weekly group meditations at the local chapter or temple.

Membership: As of 2008, some five million people are alleged to have sought instruction from Lu, overwhelmingly by writing him for a distant empowerment. There were some 300 temples and chapters worldwide, the majority in Malaysia, Indonesia, and Taiwan. There were seven temples, nine chapters, and eight meditation centers in the United States, and an additional five temples, four chapters, and four meditation centers in Canada. The majority of the several thousand core members in the United States are Chinese Americans.

Periodicals: *Enlightenment.* • *True Buddha News.*

Sources:

True Buddha School. www.tbsn.org/.

Casey, Noah. "The True Buddha School: A Field Research Report on the Chan Hai Lei Zang Temple." Montreal Religious Sites Project. www.mrsp.mcgill.ca/reports/html/ChanHai/.

Lu Sheng-Yen. *A Complete and Detailed Exposition on the True Buddha Tantric Dharma.* Union City, CA: Purple Lotus Society of USA, 1996.

————. *The Inner World of the Lake.* San Bruno, CA: Amitabha Enterprise, 1992.

————. *An Overview of the Buddhadharma.* Union City, CA: Purple Lotus Society of USA, 1996.

Tam Wai-lun. "Integration of the Magical and Cultivational Discourses: A Study of the New Religious Movement Called the True Buddha School." *Monumenta Serica* 49 (2001): 141–169.

U.S.A. Shaolin Temple

446 Broadway, 2nd Fl., New York, NY 10013

The U.S.A. Shaolin Temple is one of several structures in the United States that perpetuate the traditions of the Shaolin Temple founded 1,500 years ago in the Song Mountains of central China. The U.S.A. Temple originated from the defection in 1992 of Shifu Shi Yan Ming, a thirty-fourth–generation Shaolin Temple fighting monk, one of the monks taking part in an American tour sponsored by the Chinese government. Unable to speak English, he made his way to San Francisco's Chinese American community. A short time later, he moved to New York City. Once his political status was secured there, he founded the U.S.A. Shaolin Temple as a center to teach authentic Shaolin martial arts and Chan Buddhism, the two being somewhat indistinguishable in the temple program.

At the temple, Shifu teaches Chan Buddhism, thought to be the core of the Shaolin martial arts and understood as action meditation, and kung fu (*gong fu*), tai chi (*tai ji*), and chi kung (*qi gong*).

Membership: Not reported. There are three branch temples in the United States and five satellite branches internationally in Austria, South Africa, Trinidad, Chile, and Mexico.

Sources:

USA Shaolin Temple. www.usashaolintemple.com/.

Saunders, Nicole. "Inside the Shaolin Temople." *Fierce* 1, 3 (2003–2004): 41–43.

Shi Yan Ming. *The Shaolin Workout: Twenty-Eight Days to Transforming Your Body and Soul the Warrior's Way.* Emmaus, PA: Rodale Books, 2006.

Zen Buddhist Order of Hsu Yun (ZBOHY)

42 Kawananakoa Pl., Nu'uanu, Honolulu, HI 96817

In 1997 Grandmaster Jy Din Shakya (1971–2003), the founding abbot of Hsu Yun Temple in Honolulu, Hawaii, established the Zen Buddhist Order of Hsu Yun (ZBOHY), a web-based effort to broaden the outreach of his work, which had been confined largely to Chinese Americans. The next year he named his dharema heir, Chuan Zhi Shakya (b.1960), a European American, as the abbot for the new Internet ministry.

In 1998 Jy Din Shakya took Chuan Zhi Shakya to China, where he participated in a month-long full ordination ceremony at Hong Fa Temple. Before founding ZBOHY, he had created a Zen site on the Internet that became the seed from which the present ZBOHY site developed. Following Jyn Din Shakya's death in 2003, his successor Master Fat Wai Shakya assumed spiritual leadership of ZBOHY.

At its founding, ZBOHY's mandate was to make Zen accessible through the web with a westernized approach to the Chan (Zen) tradition, and to make themselves available to teach interested persons. They also received guidelines to refrain from participating in conflicts within the larger Chan/Zen community and to stay clear of political issues and discussions.

ZBOHY was able to draw a number of Western practitioners to its cause, both from a few who had studied like Chuan Zhi, earlier studied with Jy Din Shakya, and many more who studied with and were ordained through ZBOHY. They also brought to the Order skills in a variety of Western languages from French and Spanish to Polish. While the majority work primarily on the multiple Internet sites, some offer workshops on a periodic basis, and some have become leaders of a growing number of local Zen communities.

ZBOHY sees as its mission the presentation of classical but contemporary Chan teachings, methods, and principles in the tradition of Hsu Yun but in the Western idiom. The teachings are offered as a guide to individuals as they pursue their path. No attempt is made to push believers into a rigid conformity.

Membership: Not reported. In 2008, ZBOHY reported 22 ordained priests and 9 affiliated centers, 5 in the United States and 1 each in Venezuela, Sweden, Cuba, and Sweden.

Sources:

Zen Buddhist Order of Hsu Yun (Chan). www.hsuyun.org/Dharma/zbohy/Home/home-index.html.

Shakya, Jy Din. *Empty Cloud: The Teachings of Xu Yun and a Remembrance of the Great Chinese Zen Master.* Hong Kong: H.K. Buddhist Book Distributor, 1996.

Korean Buddhism

American Buddhist Shim Gum Do Association

203 Chestnut Hill Ave., Boston, MA 02135

The American Buddhist Shim Gum Do Association was founded in 1978 by Korean Zen master Chang Sik Kim (b. 1944). At age 13, Kim began studying under Zen master Seung Sahn Lee (1927–2004) at Hwa Gye Sa in Seoul, Korea. At age 21, Kim went on a retreat, during which the forms of shim gum do (mind sword path) were revealed to him. Shim gum do concerns the attainment of clear mind, thought, action, and enlightenment through martial art training. Students undergo bimonthly tests, marking their progress through 33 black belt levels. Daily, weekly, and monthly classes are offered, with separate classes available for children starting at age 5. Kim hosts a free public meditation class and dharma talk on the first Friday of each month.

Kim followed Sahn to Rhode Island where he established the Kwan Um School of Zen in Cumberland. Kim established his own school in 1976. Only the Brighton center in Massachusetts houses students. The American center is also the international headquarters of the World Shim Gum Do Association.

Membership: In August 2007, there were about 150 active members, including 10 live-in residents. Daily classes usually have between five and 15 students, and workshops will have about 50. Schools have opened in Providence, Rhode Island, and Ottsville, Pennsylvania, as well as Italy, Japan, Korea, and Poland.

Periodicals: *Universal Light Newsletter*

Sources:

Shim Gum Do—Mind Sword Path. www.shimgumdo.org/

Center Profile: Shim Gum Do Association. www.pluralism.org/research/profiles/display.php?profile=74829

Diaz, Johnny. "They Live by the Sword: Students of Shim Gum Do Seek Enlightenment through Martial Art in Brighton," *Boston Globe*, September 16, 2006.

American Zen College

16815 Germantown Rd. (Rte. 18), Germantown, MD 20767

Zen Master Gosung Shin, Ph.D, founded the American Zen College in 1976 for the purpose of studying and practicing religion and philosophy. Gosung Shin was ordained a priest of the Chogye Sect of Korean Buddhism by Zen Master Sul-Bong in 1956. He arrived in the United States in May 1969 from South Korea, where he had been the abbot of three Zen Buddhist temples. Since his arrival, he has established Zen schools and centers in Virginia, Pennsylvania, New York, and the District of Columbia.

In 1976, Gosung Shin settled on the 12-acre farm near Germantown, Maryland. There, a 7,000 square foot zendo and dharma hall has been erected. The building houses a library, kitchen, dining room, offices, and guest quarters. Other buildings on the farm have been renovated for dorm and resident space and an art gallery. An azalea garden surrounds a 30-foot pagoda of carved Indian limestone that houses Buddha Sakyamuni's Saria, pearl-like remains of the historic Buddha Sakyamuni. The Saria were donated to the college by the national treasury of South Korea and are the only Saria in the United States.

Membership: Not reported. In 1984 the American Zen College reported 2,500 members in three centers.

Periodicals: *Buddha World*.

Sources:

American Zen College. www.americanzencollege.org.

Shin, Gosung. *Zen Teachings of Emptiness*. Washington, DC: American Zen College Press, 1982.

Buddhist Society for Compassionate Wisdom

297 College St., Toronto, ON, Canada M5T 1S2

Alternate Address: c/o Zen Buddhist Temple, 1710 W Cornelia Ave., Chicago, IL 60657-1219; 1214 Packard Rd., Ann Arbor, MI 48104.

The Buddhist Society for Compassionate Wisdom, formerly known as the Zen Lotus Society, was officially founded in 1975 in Toronto, Ontario, but its roots date from the arrival in the United States in 1967 of an independent Korean Zen monk, Samu Sunim (b. 1941). Orphaned as a child, Sunim entered the monastery at the age of 17. After completing his three-year novice training and ordination, he began Zen meditation training under the guidance of Zen Master Solbong (1890–1969). While in training, he was drafted into the army (as required of all Korean youth) and, after serving in the military for one year, deserted it to honor his pacifist beliefs. Sunim then resumed his Zen training under Master Solbong while hiding out from the army in the Pomosa monastery in the mountains near Pusan, Korea. In the winter of 1966, he fled to Japan. In 1967, with the aid of friends, he immigrated to New York City and began to conduct meditation for the public.

In 1968, circumstances forced Sunim to move to Montreal, Canada, where he taught meditation while perfecting English and learning French. He was married for a short time and became a Canadian citizen. In 1972, he moved to Toronto,

Canada, where a Korean community existed, but his plans to pursue an academic career or form a temple were frustrated by a serious illness. After a three-year solo retreat in his basement apartment, he resumed his religious duties in 1975.

By 1979, support had grown to the point where a building could be purchased, and the society was formally incorporated. The name was subsequently changed to the Buddhist Society for Compassionate Wisdom. A sister temple was founded in Ann Arbor, Michigan, in 1981 and incorporated as the Zen Buddhist Temple—Ann Arbor. The temple conducts a peace camp for children aged 3 to 15; the camp emphasizes peace, cooperation, mindfulness, and fun. Inspired by children attending the camp, composer and camp teacher Nathaniel Needle has written and produced two audio tapes, "Dharma Moon" and "Bottom of the Ocean," collections of American Buddhist songs. Since 1983, the society has also maintained a growing community of members in Mexico City, Mexico.

A third temple of the Buddhist Society for Compassionate Wisdom opened in Chicago, Illinois, in June 1992. The society purchased a building formerly used by a Pentecostal church on the north side of Chicago and renovated it as a Buddhist temple. The top floor has been transformed into a year-round urban meditation retreat center. Sunim had the idea for this center years before, when he was spending a weekend in the society's Ann Arbor temple. A woman asked to stay the night. It turned out she lived a short distance away but needed to get away from the chaos of her family and household, with all its telephones and televisions and computers. She stayed two nights. Sunim resolved to have space for such a center if he ever started another temple. The urban meditation retreat center is designed for people who are effectively trapped by their living circumstances and need a place for peace and contemplation.

The temples conduct daily Buddhist religious services and meditation sessions, instruct beginners in basic and advanced meditation, and hold regular weekend meditation retreats. The Chicago and Ann Arbor temples hold children's services every Sunday. The children do simple yoga, a little meditation, and (if they are old enough) light candles and incense on the altar.

The society also holds quarterly three- to five-day Yongmaeng Chongjin (intensive retreats) and a biennial precept-taking ceremony in which more than 100 people participated in 2001. Temple members are active in promoting social affairs, environmental awareness, and right livelihood, that is, earning one's living in a way that does not harm other beings.

In 1986, the society organized and hosted the first Second Generation Zen Teachers Conference at the Ann Arbor temple. The following year, the society hosted an eight-day Conference on World Buddhism in North America. This conference was also the first of its kind and provided a special opportunity for encounters between ethnic and Western Buddhist teachers in both the Theravada and Mahayana traditions. Teachers from the United States, Canada, and England were represented. On that occasion, Sunim began the Buddhist Movement for Justice and Peace, an initiative to express a committed Buddhist concern for social injustice and human rights abuses.

The first national Conference on World Buddhism in Canada was held in Toronto in 1990 with monks, nuns, priests, and lay teachers from ethnic and Western Buddhist organizations across Canada. In July 1995, the society hosted an inaugural Conference for Academics Drawn to Buddhism in Toronto. These conferences represent a strong and ongoing commitment to the cause of Pan-Buddhism and are seen as the first of many such activities.

In 1993, in Chicago, Sunim attended the Centennial Parliament of the World's Religions as a member of the assembly of religious and spiritual leaders. Since then, he has served as a member of the board of trustees on the Council for a Parliament of the World's Religions.

Through the 1980s, the society published a journal, *Spring Wind: A Buddhist Cultural Forum*. It began a new series in 2002, with an issue on war and peace inspired by the September 11, 2001, attacks on the United States and resulting war in Afghanistan. In 1985, Sunim inaugurated a priest training program that has now evolved into the Maitreya Buddhist Seminary run by the Buddhist Society for

Compassionate Wisdom. The program offers a three- to five-year training for dharma teachers, junior priests, and monks. In 2002, a total of 24 students were enrolled. There is also a dharma guardian program for professionals wishing to improve the quality of their life and the life of their clientele.

Membership: The Buddhist Society for Compassionate Wisdom has four mission operations: Zen Buddhist temples are located in Ann Arbor, Michigan; Chicago; Toronto; and Mexico City. These temples serve as mission centers to advance the meditation movement and to train dharma workers to promote a culture of enlightenment and green spirituality. The society is starting a new temple in New York City. In 2002, the society reported approximately 500 members in the United States, 250 in Canada, and 50 in Mexico.

Educational Facilities:

Maitreya Buddhist Seminary, Toronto, Ontario.

Periodicals: *Spring Wind: A Buddhist Cultural Forum*. Available from Zen Buddhist Temple, 1710 W Cornelia Ave., Chicago, IL 60657. • *Temple News*. Available from Ann Arbor Zen Buddhist Temple, 1214 Packard Rd., Ann Arbor, MI 48104.

Sources:

Buddhist Society for Compassionate Wisdom. www.zenbuddhisttemple.org/

Hanmaum Zen Center

7852 N Lincoln Ave., Skokie, IL 60077

Alternate Address: Hanmaum Zen Center: 101-60, Seosku-dong, An Yang-si, Gyunggi-do, 430-040, Korea.

The Hanmaum Zen Center was founded in 1972 by Dae Haeng Sunim (b. 1927), an ordained Buddhist woman, in a small town south of Seoul, South Korea, on the side of Kwanak-san Mountain. Dae Haeng spent much of her childhood wandering alone in the mountains south of Seoul. She was ordained in 1950, and in the late 1950s she settled in a small hut near Sangwon Temple on Mount Chiak. Many people called on her to assist them in their sufferings. Eventually, Sunim became determined to teach others how to solve their problems for themselves. In 1972, Sunim moved to Anyang, just south of Seoul, and established the first Hanmaum Zen Center. There she began to teach people about their own true nature and how to rely on that nature. She drew inspiration from the Chogye sect, the main group of Korean Buddhism, to which she has added material drawn from the Zen teachings of Hui-neng (638–713 C.E.), the sixth patriarch of Chinese Zen, and her own original insights.

From the center in Korea, Dae Haeng leads the residents into the practice of Zen meditation in a schedule that begins at 4:00 A.M. each morning with chanting and meditation before breakfast. The goal of the meditation is enlightenment, which includes the attainment of *hanmaum*, or "one mind," a realization of the interrelatedness of all things. Residents at the center are also vegetarians.

In 1989, a first text containing teachings by Dae Haeng was translated into English. In 1991, the Hanmaum Zen Center in the Chicago region was established. As of 2004, 15 branches have been established within Korea, and nine Hanmaum Zen centers have been established in other countries. Dae Haeng Sunim is also the teacher of more than 150 sunims, many of whom help maintain the centers and assist people who come to the centers.

Membership: Not reported.

Periodicals: *Hanmaum Journal*. • *Hyundae Bulkyo* (newspaper).

Sources:

Hanmaum Zen Center. www.hanmaum.org/

Haeng, Dae. *In Search of the Genuine "I,"* ed. Haewon. Seoul, Korea: Lotus Flower Publishing Company, 1989.

Hanmaum Zen Center of Chicago. www.buddhapia.com/hmu/chi/index.html

Korean Buddhist Bo Moon Order

Current address not obtained for this edition.

The Bo Moon Order is one of the 18 registered Buddhist Orders in Korea. It came to the United States in 1979 when the Bul Sil Sa Temple was organized in Chicago. A second temple was organized in the Los Angeles suburb of Garden Grove in 1980.

Membership: Not reported.

Korean Buddhist Chogye Order

c/o Kwan Um Sa Temple, 4265 W 3rd St., Los Angeles, CA 90020

Not until the 1970s did significant numbers of Korean Buddhists migrate to the United States. Most of these were affiliated with the Chogye Order, the largest in Korea. In February 1973 the Thalmahsa Buddhist Monastery and temple was established in Los Angeles. It was soon followed by a second Los Angeles temple and by others established in various California locations and in Chicago; New York City; Tacoma, Washington; Detroit, Michigan; and Honolulu. During the 1980s the number of new temples continued to grow. These temples are to be distinguished from those of the Kwan Um Zen School (from which they are organizationally separate) as they primarily serve first-generation Korean Americans.

Membership: Not reported. In 1984 there were 23 Chogye Order temples in the United States and 3 in Canada.

Periodicals: *Buddhist Times & Society*. Available from 4267 W 3rd St., Los Angeles, CA 90020.

Sources:

Kwan Um Sa Temple. www.kwanumsa.com/. (In Korean.)

Har, Baba Moo, ed. *Brief Introduction to Korean Buddhism*. Los Angeles: Korean Buddhist Sangha Association of Western Territories in U.S.A., 1984.

Korea Buddhism. Seoul: Korea Buddhist Chogye Order, 1986.

Kwan Um School of Zen

99 Pound Rd., Cumberland, RI 02864-2726

The Kwan Um Zen School was founded in 1983 to connect the various temples and centers previously founded by Seung Sahn (1927–2004). Sahn is the 78th patriarch in his line of succession in the Chogye order. As a young man in Korea, he became deeply involved in radical politics but turned to Buddhism during World War II (1939–1945). He became a student of Zen Master Ko Bong (1890–1962) and eventually abbot of two temples. After the war, he became a leader in the effort to revive the Chogye sect, which had suffered much damage in the final years of Japanese occupation. In 1965 he traveled to Japan and founded three temples during his stay. In 1972 he came to the United States and began a small temple in Providence, Rhode Island. This temple became the headquarters from which he traveled around New England and across the United States. Early branch centers were established in New Haven, Connecticut; Cambridge, Massachusetts; New York City, New York; and Los Angeles and Berkeley, California.

Master Seung Sahn came to the United States with a missionary zeal to plant a new Buddhist tradition in the West. He emphasizes that the purposes of Zen are, first, to understand the true self (i.e., attain truth), and, then, to assist other people to attain the same heightened awareness. Most people have a significant amount of karma that forms an obstacle to enlightenment—hence the necessity of masters and centers. Like the Japanese Rinzai masters, Seung Sahn used the koan as a major teaching device. (A koan is a subject for meditation that is used to force people to abandon their dependence on reason and force them into gaining sudden intuitive enlightenment.) Besides the main practice of daily sitting meditation, each center associated with the school sponsors a silent three- or seven-day meditation retreat called Yong Maeng Jong Jin (to leap like a tiger while sitting), equivalent to the *sesshin* or extended meditation sessions at Japanese Zen centers.

The growth of the center in Providence led to its purchase of a tract of land in rural Rhode Island upon which it developed a residential community and to which it eventually moved its headquarters. Throughout the early 1980s, Sahn extended his travels and developed centers in South America and Europe, with special success in Poland and Germany. By the early 1990s, major centers had been established in Spain, Russia, and most of the newly opened countries of eastern Europe.

Primary Point Press offers books, videos, and audio on the teaching of Zen master Sahn and the Kwan Um School of Zen.

Membership: In 2008, the Kwan Um School of Zen has more than 100 centers and groups in the Americas, Asia, the Middle East, and Europe.

Periodicals: *Primary Point.* • *Providence Zen Center Newsletter.*

Sources:

Kwan Um School of Zen. www.kwanumzen.com

Kwang, Dae, ed. *Ten Gates: The Kong-an Teaching of Zen Master Seung Sahn.* New York: Random House, 2007.

Mitchell, Stephen, ed. *Dropping Ashes on the Buddha: The Teaching of Zen Master Seung Sahn.* New York: Grove Press, 1976.

————. *Only Don't Know.* San Francisco, CA: Four Seasons Foundation, 1982.

Prebish, Charles S. *Luminous Passage: The Practice and Study of Buddhism in America.* Berkeley: University of California Press, 1999.

Sahn, Seung. *Bone of Space: Zen Poems.* San Francisco, CA: Four Seasons Foundation, 1982.

Seager, Richard. *Buddhism in America.* New York: Columbia University Press, 1999.

Soeng, Mu. "Korean Buddhism in America: A New Style of Zen." In *The Faces of Buddhism in America,* eds. Charles S. Prebish and Kenneth A. Tanaka. Berkeley: University of California Press, 1998.

Sunim, Mu Soeng. *Thousand Peaks, Korean Zen: Tradition and Teachers.* Berkeley, CA: Parallex Press, 1987.

Sixth Patriarch Zen Center

133 Halsey Ct., Hercules, CA 94547

The Sixth Patriarch Zen Center is an independent Korean center in the Chogye tradition founded in Vancouver, British Columbia, in 1986 by the Ven. Hyunoong Sunim, a Buddhist monk and herbalist. Sunim trained for 10 years under Taoist Master Chong San. In 1982 Sunim was given sanction as a Taoist master.

The Sixth Patriarch Zen Center moved to Berkeley, California, in 1991. It has a dual emphasis on traditional Zen practice and health care through the use of correct diet, herbs, and a form of Korean Taoist breath meditation called *Sun-do.* The center is unique in that it offers both a regular schedule of sittings and retreats and a full program of health counseling and classes.

Membership: Not reported. There is one center in Berkeley and one in Seattle, Washington.

Sources:

Sixth Patriarch Zen Center. www.zenhall.org/

Morreale, Don, ed. *The Complete Guide to Buddhist America.* Boston, MA: Shambhala, 1998.

Won Buddhism

Won-Buddhism of New York, 143-42 Cherry Ave., Flushing, NY 11355

Alternate Address: International headquarters: 344-2 Singyong-Dong, Iksan City, Chollabuk-do, South Korea; Canadian headquarters: 123 Lanyard Rd., Toronto, Ontario, M9M 1Z1, Canada.

Won Buddhism (Won Pulgyo) is a form of Korean Mahayana Buddhism founded by Pak Chungbin (1891–1943) in 1916. Best known by his pen name Sot'aesan, Pak sought a way to transcend the three traditional religions of East Asia (that is, Confucianism, Taoism, and Buddhism), which he found in his enlightenment experience. At a later date, however, after reading the Diamond Sutra, he concluded

that Buddhism was the best vehicle for communicating his understanding of truth. Sot'aesan represented his enlightened vision of ultimate reality in a perfect circle, known as the "one-circle figure" (Irwonsang), which he equated to the concept of Dharmakaya (the body of the law or teaching) of conventional Buddhism. No images of Buddha are found in Won Buddhist temples.

According to Sot'aesan, the Dharmakaya Buddha finds embodiment in the "four graces": heaven and earth, parents, brethren (fellow creatures), and the law (religious, moral, and civil). Rejecting traditional concepts of deliverance or liberation, he pointed to a path of realization of a paradise on earth achieved by helping others to develop their own abilities, wisdom, education, and altruism. The path to enlightenment (represented in the one-circle figure) is the threefold learning through *samadhi* (meditation), prajna (wisdom), and sila (morality). Sot'aesan saw these traditional ways as the cultivation of spirit, the study of facts and principles, and choice of conduct. Thus, the adherent to Won Buddhism centers his life on worship of the one-circle figure (rather than any images of Buddha), by calling out the name of the Buddha Amitabha, seated meditation, repentance and prayer, and the study of scripture. Won Buddhism seeks to bring ancient Buddhist truth into contemporary society, revitalized and modernized, so Buddhist teachings can be used for practical purposes. Practitioners seek a balance between the spiritual and the material life.

Sources for Won Buddhist teachings are found in *The Canon of Won Buddhism* (*Wonbulygo Kyojon*). The canon has two parts, the principle book (*Chongjon*), written by Sot'aesan, and the records (*Daejonggung*), which chronicle his sayings and actions. Of slightly lesser importance is the *Religious Discourses of Master Chongsan* (*Chongsan Chongsa Pobo*), that record the words of Song Kyu (1900–1962), who succeeded Sot'aesan as head of the group in 1943. The current head of the order is Ven. Chwasan (b. 1936).

Won Buddhism came to the United States in the years following the Korean War (1950–1953), especially after the change of immigration laws in 1965 allowed more Asian residents to move into the country.

Membership: In 2008, there were 15 branch temples in the United States and two in Canada. Worldwide, there were 20 dioceses, about 600 temples, and 189 organizations reaching 1.4 million followers.

Educational Facilities:

WON Institute, Glenside, Pennsylvania; Wonkwang University, Chollabuk-do, South Korea.

Periodicals: *Living Buddha The Won-Buddhism Review*

Sources:

Won Buddhism: Buddhism, Meditation. www.wonbuddhism.info

Chung, Bongkil. *The Sacred Books of Won Buddhism.* vol. 6. Honolulu: University of Hawaii Press, 2001.

Park, Kwangsoo. *The Won Buddhism (Wonbulgyo) of Sot'aesan: A Twentieth-Century Religious Movement in Korea.* San Francisco, CA: International Scholars Publications, 1997.

Zen Wind

Current address not obtained for this edition.

Zen Wind is a radical lay Buddhist movement initiated by Tundra Wind, a former student of Korean Zen Master Seung Sahn, the head of the Kwan Um Zen School. Under his given name, Jim Wilson, he was given permission to teach by Seung Sahn, but was having problems with his sexuality. According to his account, when questioning his Master about his problems with remaining celibate, Seung Sahn said that he should simply satisfy his sexual desire and forget about it. Wilson rejected the idea, which seemed to imply that sex was merely physical.

He broke with Seung Sahn and, following a dream in which his new name—Tundra Wind—was bestowed on him, he began to teach and to reformulate what he had been taught in a manner he believed more culturally suitable for the West.

Included in his reformulation was a transformation of the precept not to misuse sex to a more positive admonition, "Express the sacredness of sexuality." His reformulation also made provision for Tundra Wind's own gay sexuality.

Among his students he has eschewed temples, monasteries, professional clergy, and even centers. Meetings are held in members' homes. He regularly offers introductory lectures, invites those who respond into ongoing meditation groups, and provides individual instruction for any who wish it. He leads two retreats annually.

Membership: Not reported.

Sources:

Discordian Zen. www.spiralnature.com/spirituality/discordianism/disczen.html.

Morreale, Don. *The Complete Guide to Buddhist America*. Boston: Shambhala, 1998.

 # Tibetan Buddhism

Amitabha Foundation

8246 Garibaldi Ave., San Gabriel, CA 91775

The Amitabha Foundation, is a Tibetan Buddhist organization of the Drikung Kagyu school founded in 1986 by H. E. K. C. Ayang Rinpoche. He began traveling in the West in general and the United States in particular in the early 1980s at the request of several Tibetan leaders primarily for the cause of Tibetan culture and the Tibetan peoples now residing outside of their homeland. He discovered that he could not separate the more secular cultural and political concerns from his presentation of Buddhism, and Buddhism was, for many supporters of the Tibetan cause, Tibet's most attractive asset.

The Drikung Kagyu lineage looks to Kyoba Jigten Sumgon, in the middle of the twelfth century C.E., as its founder. Jigten Sumgon, the recipient of secret oral transmissions from his teacher, Phagmodrupa, composed a set of teachings and instructions for practice, which he in turn passed on to his chief disciple, Gurawa Tsultrim Dorje. All these enlightened energies, blessings, and teachings have been handed down through the great spiritual masters to the present 37th and 36th lineage holders, His Holiness Drikung Kyabgon Chetsang Rinpoche and His Holiness Drikung Kyabgon Chungtsang, from whom Ayang Rinpoche receives his authority to teach.

Ayang Rinpoche was born to a nomadic family in Tibet, but as a child he was recognized as a lama by a delegation of important lamas and subsequently raised to assume his role as a teacher. He studied at a Drikung monastery and eventually became a master of Phowa, or the "transference of consciousness at the time of death." This teaching centers on a method for attaining enlightenment after bodily death. It includes a combination of breath, mantra, and visualization techniques used as one is dying. It is believed that the individual consciousness is ejected from the body and subsequently avoids reincarnation.

Leaving Tibet after the Chinese takeover, Ayang Rinpoche settled in India, where he founded two monasteries. He currently resides at the refugee community he assembled in Bylakuppe, Karnataka State.

The foundation sees itself as carrying out a twofold mission and has created programs designed both to spread Buddhist teachings and to raise money to preserve the Tibetan culture. Thus it works with many people who do not consider themselves Buddhists but have a concern for the Tibetan people.

Membership: Not reported. In 2008 the foundation reported centers in Los Angeles, New York City, and Vancouver, British Columbia. Additional centers were found in France, Germany, Australia, and Taiwan.

Sources:

Ayang Rinpoche / Amitabha Foundation. http://ayangrinpoche.org/

Amitabha Foundation Los Angeles. amitabhafoundationla.blogspot.com/.

Aro Gar

PO Box 3066, Alameda, CA 94501

Alternate Address: PO Box 724, Kila, MT 59920.

Aro Gar (known as Sang-Ngak-Cho-Dzong in Great Britain) is a Western representative of the Tibetan Aro gTer (or Mother Essence) Nyingma lineage, a lineage that traces its origin to a succession of enlightened women culminating in the visionary Khyungchen Aro Lingma (1886–1923), and her son Aro Yeshe (1915–1951). Aro Lingma received transmission from Yeshe Tsogyel, an enlightened female tantric. Aro Gar and Sang-Ngak-Cho-Dzong are headed by Ngak'chang Rinpoche (Ngapka Chogyam) and Khandro Dechen, the current holders of the Aro gTer lineage.

Rinpoche was born in Germany in 1952 and raised in England. He developed an interest in Tibetan Buddhism at the age of 13 and went on to become an art teacher, with a particular interest in thangka painting (tantric iconography). At age 19 he went to the Himalayas to study with some of the living tantric Buddhist teachers in a nonsectarian manner, though with particular attention to Nyingma teachers, and completed four years of solitary retreat in a cave. He was eventually recognized as the incarnation of Aro Yeshe, the son of Khyungchen Aro Lingma. In this life Ngak'chang Rinpoche, together with his wife Khandro Dechen, are the holders of the lineage of "treasure-teachings" given in vision to Aro Lingma by Yeshe Tsogyel, the enlightened consort of the tantric Buddha Padmasambhava.

Ngak'chang Rinpoche began to teach in the West in 1979. In 1989 he was awarded a doctorate from the University of West Bengal. He is the author of numerous books, including *Rainbow of Liberated Energy* (rewritten with Khandro Dechen and republished as *Spectrum of Ecstasy*), *Journey into Vastness* (rewritten with Khandro Dechen and republished as *Roaring Silence*), and *Wearing the Body of Visions*. He has been a lecturer at the Institute of Transpersonal Psychology in California and has contributed articles to several books, journals, and magazines on the subject of tantric psychology and its interface with therapy.

Khandro Dechen was born in 1960 and has been a committed Vajrayana practitioner since the age of 21. She is the spiritual wife of Ngak'chang Rinpoche, who describes her as his most important teacher. She specializes in sKu-mNye, the Dzogchen Long-de psycho-physical practices which generate profound experiences of the inner elements. She teaches primarily through "personality-display" and is known for her Mirror-transmission; a powerful method of giving direct introduction to the nature of the mind. She is writing a book with Ngak'chang Rinpoche on the path of romantic love and relationship in Tibetan Tantra, entitled *Entering the Heart of the Sun and Moon*.

The Aro gTer is a nonliturgical, nonmonastic tradition that specializes in the teaching and practice of Dzogchen, a practice that offers direct experience of mind. It emphasizes the importance of everyday life as practice. It is unique in the emphasis it places on integration with everyday working life, sexual equality, and the spiritual dimension of romantic relationships and artistic creativity.

Membership: Not reported. Practitioners in the Aro tradition reside in Great Britain, the United States, Canada, Austria, Germany, Switzerland, the Netherlands, Sweden, and Finland.

Sources:

Aro Buddhism. www.arobuddhism.org/.

Morreale, Don. *The Complete Guide to Buddhist America*. Boston: Shambhala, 1998.

BodhiPath

c/o Santa Barbra BodhiPath Center, 113 West Gutierrez St., Santa Barbara, CA 93101

BodhiPath is an international community of meditation centers founded by the fourteenth Kunzig Shamar Rinpoche (b. 1952), a leading teacher of the Karma Kagyu school of Tibetan Buddhism Karma. He is a nephew of the sixteenth Gyalwa Karmapa (1924–1981) and holder of the Shamarpa lineage, which dates to the fourteenth century. The close relationship between the Sharmapa and the

Kermapa is symbolized by the identical red crowns they wear at official functions. The Sharmapa's crown was a gift of the third Karmapa to the first Sharmapa.

In 1994 Shamar Rinpoche, in his role as the second highest lama of the Karma Kagyu lineage, officially recognized the seventeenth Gyalwa Karmapa Trinley Thaye Dorje (b. 1983). In succeeding years Sharmar Rinpoche was one of the young Karmapa's most important instructors.

The fourteenth Shamarpa Mipham Chokyi Lodro was born in Tibet and was formally recognized by the sixteenth Karmapa in 1956 and by the Dalai Lama in 1961. Meanwhile, in 1959 the young lama fled Tibet for Sikkim. He completed his studies at Rumtek Monastery and in the 1980s undertook the task of overseeing the reprinting of the *Tengyur*, a multivolume set of books by Indian and Tibetan masters. He later founded the Karmapa International Buddhist Institute in New Delhi and the Shri Diwakar Vihara Institute in Kalimpong, India.

In the 1990s he traveled extensively, founding the BodhiPath Buddhist centers. The centers follow the common beliefs and practices of Karma Kagyu Buddhism. The fourteenth Shamarpa has recruited a number of Tibetan teachers (rinpoches and khenpos) and has been joined by some American students who have become Dharma teachers. The BodhiPath now consists of a worldwide network of centers under the general oversight of the fourteenth Sharmapa.

Membership: Not reported. Centers in the United States are located at Natural Bridge, Virginia; Martha's Vineyard, Massachusetts; Washington, D.C.; Chicago, Illinois; Eugene, Oregon; and Buena Park, Pasadena, Santa Barbara, San Luis Obispo, and Menlo Park, California. Additional centers are located in India, Nepal, Australia, and across Europe.

Sources:

BodhiPath. www.bodhipath.org/; www.bodhipath-west.org/.

Coleman, Graham, ed. *A Handbook of Tibetan Culture*. Boston: Shambhala, 1994.

Center for Dzogchen Studies

17 Tour Ave., New Haven, CT 06515

The Center for Dzogchen Studies constitute a worldwide community of practitioners dedicated to the teachings and practices of the Nyingma lineage centered at the Pukang Monastery in Kham, Tibet. The center teaches what is known as the Nine Yanas of Nyingma Tibetan Buddhism. Such practices gradually introduce a nature of mind to the practitioner. The view from which one approaches the Nine Yanas teaches that the awakened state already exists within. Through continued use of the practices, direct experiences of one's Great Completeness (Dzogchen) becomes possible.

The Center for Dzogchen Studies was established in New Haven in 1993 after three practitioners invited Lama Padma Karma Rinpoche (b. 1952) from Asia to act as the center's spiritual guide. Raised as a Christian in the Virgin Islands, Rinpoche had a diverse religious background that culminated in his initial study of Buddhism beginning in 1985 after settling in China as a teacher. He was given the titles of Vajra Master and Rinpoche in 1992 by Ksertok Padma Dorje Tulku with the authorization to teach under the auspices of the Nyingma and Kagyu schools of Tibetan Buddhism and, more specifically, within the Longchen Nyingthig lineage of Kalsang Monastery, Tibet. Lama Padma Karma Rinpoche continued studies with H. H. Chadral Sangye Dorje in Pharping, Nepal, and Serdok Tulku in Albuquerque, New Mexico.

After settling in New Haven, Lama Padma Karma established a teacher training program and thangka (Tibetan sacred art) painting program. The center is also visited by a Tibetan herbalist every month.

Membership: Not reported.

Sources:

Center for Dzogchen Studies. www.dzogchenstudies.com.

Chagdud Gonpa Foundation

PO Box 279, Junction City, CA 96048

Chagdud Gonpa Foundation was established in 1983 by Chagdud Tulku Rinpoche (1930–2002), a meditation master, artist, and Tibetan physician born in eastern Tibet. As the abbot of Chagdud Gonpa monastery, established in 1131, Rinpoche received extensive instructions in all aspects of Tibetan Buddhism. He then fled Tibet at the time of the Chinese occupation in 1959 and helped to establish and administer several refugee camps in India and Nepal.

He was contacted by Americans who made pilgrimages to northern India, and at the request of several American students he came to the United States in 1979. From his American headquarters he concentrated on developing Padma Publishing for the translation and printing of sacred texts and teachings of Buddhist masters, for the founding of centers for practicing and preserving Vajrayana teachings, and for the training of students in Vajrayana philosophy, practices, and rituals.

The foundation's headquarters, Rigdzin Ling, located in the mountains north of Redding, California, is home to the Mahakaruna Foundation, a nonprofit organization devoted to supporting Tibetan practitioners in Nepal, India, and Bhutan. Also based there are Padma Publishing and Tibetan Treasures, which distributes videotapes, DVDs, and MP3s of Rinpoche's talks. Among the projects of Padma Publishing is the translation of the Tibetan teacher Longchenpa's *Seven Treasuries*. The Stupa Project at Rigdzin Ling undertook the construction of eight Tibetan *chortens*.

Membership: In 2008 the foundation reported 31 centers and practice groups in the United States and one in Canada, with additional centers and practice groups in Brazil, Uruguay, and Chile.

Sources:

Chagdud Gonpa Foundation. www.chagdud.org/.

Chagdud Tulku Rinpoche. *Gates to Buddhist Practice*. Junction City, CA: Padma Publishing, n.d.

———. *Life in Relation to Death*. Junction City, CA: Padma Publishing, n.d.

———. *The Lord of the Dance*. Junction City, CA: Padma Publishing, n.d.

Chokling Tersar Foundation USA (CTF)

66000 Drive Through Tree Rd., Leggett, CA 93585-0162

The Chokling Tersar Foundation (CTF) was established in 1996 as the American center of the Chokling Tersar, a lineage of Tibetan Buddhism within the Gelugpa school (the largest of the four main Tibetan schools of Buddhism). The foundation, presently the only center of the tradition in North America, was founded by Tulku Urgyen Rinpoche (1920–1996). The organization's spiritual heads are Tsikey Chokling Rinpoche and Chokyi Nyima Rinpoche, the abbot of Ka-Nying Shedrub Ling, one of Nepal's largest monasteries. In 1998 the foundation established the Rangjung Yeshe Gomde retreat center in northern California, nestled along the Eel River in Mendocino County. Gomde offers practice and study group meetings, individual retreats, and religious celebrations in a beautiful, peaceful location. It also provides an annual summer program that hosts masters of the Chokling Tersar tradition. The foundation's material is published by Rangjung Yeshe Publications.

Chokling Tersar literally means the "new treasures of Chokgyur Lingpa" and owes its name to the nineteenth-century Tibetan Buddhist master Chogyur Dechen Lingpa (1829–1870), whose teachings are widely practiced by both the Kagyu and Nyingma schools of Tibetan Buddhism. The collection of teachings from Chokgyur Lingpa is contained in the Chokling Tersar, a body of literature filling more than 40 large volumes. The connected teachings included in these 40 volumes were written over the last 150 years, chiefly by his contemporaries Jamyang Khyentse Wangpo and Jamgon Kongtrul the Great, as well as by the subsequent upholders of the lineage down to the present day.

The Chokling Tersar literature is meant to be studied and practiced as an addition to the traditional canonical scriptures of Tibetan Buddhism. These are found in the Kangyur and Tengyur, the written words of Buddha Shakyamuni, and their commentaries by learned Indian Masters. These two collections occupy 104 and 273 large volumes, respectively. In these scriptures are found detailed instructions on how to take full advantage of human life and imbue it with its fullest meaning. These revealed scriptures were concealed by the ninth-century Buddhist saint Padmasambhava with the expressed wish to be uncovered at specific times in the future. Many of them contain predictions for those times and for which particular spiritual practices would be most beneficial for the people of those times.

The independent American branch of the Chokling Tersar tradition is concerned with preserving, translating, and disseminating these teachings in the most authentic and principled way possible. CTF aims at doing so by inviting learned and authentic holders of the Chokling Tersar lineage to lecture and provide appropriate spiritual counsel corresponding to the current public demand in North America.

Periodicals *Chokling Tersar Times.*

Membership: Not reported.

Sources:

Chokling Tersar Foundation. www.choklingtersar.org/.

Rangjung Yeshe Gomde–Dzogchen Buddhist Meditation and Retreat Center. www.gomdeusa.org/.

Morreale, Don. *The Complete Guide to Buddhist America*. Boston: Shambhala, 1998.

Deer Park Buddhist Center

4548 Schneider Dr., Oregon, WI 53575

The Deer Park Buddhist Center grew out of the Ganden Mahayana Center, which was formed in the mid-1970s by a group of students who had gathered around Geshe Lhundup Sopa, a professor in the Buddhist Studies Program at the University of Wisconsin at Madison. Sopa had been a teacher at the monastery at Sera until the Chinese invasion of Tibet. He fled to India but was sent to Labsum Shedrub Ling, a monastery in New Jersey, in 1965 as a tutor for young monks. In 1968 he joined the faculty at the University of Wisconsin. Once formed, the center created Deer Park, a grove named after the place near Benares, India, where Buddha first taught, three miles from the university campus.

A full program of academic instruction in Buddhist, Tibetan, and related subjects, under the guidance of a resident monastic community, is offered at the center, as well as facilities for the practice of traditional Tibetan Buddhism. The center follows the branch of Tibetan Buddhism taught by the Dalai Lama and has on numerous occasions hosted the Dalai Lama, including his first American visit in 1979. In 1981, prior to the Dalai Lama's visit, the center purchased acreage near Oregon, Wisconsin, and transferred its program to the new center. This was the site of the first performance in the West of the Kalachakra ceremony for world peace by the Dalai Lama. The Kalachakra tantric path is a method of practicing Buddhist meditation for those who wish to progress speedily through intense meditational activity.

In July 2008 the Dalai Lama returned again to Deer Park to consecrate the center's new $6.1 million temple, which also includes facilities for display of the center's collection of Tibetan art and artifacts and housing of its extensive library of sacred literature.

Membership: Not reported.

Sources:

Deer Park Buddhist Center. www.deerparkcenter.org/.

Gyatsho, Tenzin, the 14th Dalai Lama. *The Opening of the Wisdom-Eye*. Wheaton, IL: Theosophical Publishing House, 1972.

———. *The Buddhism of Tibet and the Key to the Middle Way*. New York: Harper & Row, 1975.

Kalachakra Initiation, Madison, 1981. Madison, WI: Deer Park, 1981.

Keegan, Marcia, ed. *The Dalai Lama's Historic Visit to North America*. New York: Clear Light Publications, 1981.

Sopa, Geshe Lhundub. *The Wheel of Time*. Madison, WI: Deer Park Books, 1985.

Sopa, Geshe Lhundup, and Jeffrey Hopkins. *Practice and Theory of Tibetan Buddhism*. New York: Grove Press, 1976.

Dharma Centre of Canada

1886 Galway Rd., Kinmount, ON, Canada K0M 2A0

The Dharma Centre of Canada was founded in 1966 by the renowned pioneering Canadian Buddhist leader the Ven. Kyabje Namgyal Rinpoche (1931–2003). Namgyal Rinpoche was born G. Leslie Dawson in Ontario, Canada, to Irish parents. In his mid-20s he went to Bodh Gaya, India, the traditional site of the Buddha's enlightenment, and on October 28, 1958, took the vows of a novice monk. Two months later he was ordained a *bhikshu*, or full Buddhist monk, in Rangoon. Following a period of intensive meditation, he was recognized by His Holiness the Gyalwa Karmapa, head of the Kagyu School of Tibet, as the reincarnation of the famous Tibetan lama Mipham Namgyal Rinpoche, one of the first Westerners so recognized. Returning to the West, he founded Johnstone House as a contemplative community in Scotland. Later, through the auspices of Chogyam Trungpa Rinpoche, founder of Vajradhatu International, Johnstone House was converted into Kagyu Samye Ling, one of the first Tibetan monasteries to be established in Europe.

The Dharma Centre of Canada and its associated centers offer instruction and opportunity for the practice of meditation in order for individuals to develop awareness of the nature of mind and matter and to develop compassion and wisdom. Instruction is also offered in comparative religion, philosophy, and the arts and sciences. Both Western and Eastern spiritual insights are acknowledged.

Membership: In 2008 the Dharma Centre reported 10 affiliated centers in Canada, 1 in the United States, 2 in England, and 1 in New Zealand, with informal groups in France, Switzerland, Norway, Guatemala, Germany, and Japan.

Sources:

Dharma Centre of Canada. www.dharmacentre.org/.

Morreale, Don. *The Complete Guide to Buddhist America*. Boston: Shambhala, 1998.

Diamond Way Buddhist Centers

Diamond Way Buddhist Centers, USA, 110 Merced Ave., San Francisco, CA 94127

The Diamond Way Tibetan Buddhist tradition grew out of the efforts of Lama Ole Nydahl (b. 1941) and his wife, Hannah Nydahl (1946–2007), the first Western students of the 16th Gyalwa Karmapa. He recognized them as protectors of his lineage and asked them to work for him. Beginning in 1969, they spent three years training in the Himalayas, and then initiated teaching activity in the West, initially in Europe. Their work spread to America in the 1980s, and there are now centers across the United States. Teachings and practice are similar to those found in the centers of the Karma Triyana Dharmachakra (KTD) but are administratively separate.

Diamond Way centers recognize the spiritual authority of the 17th Karmapa, Thaye Dorje, who resides in New Delhi, India. They have a democratic structure, and members share the responsibility for guiding meditations, answering questions, and giving teachings. In addition, Lama Ole has trained some 30 students who are now traveling and teaching internationally.

The Karma Kagyu school offers a variety of methods for people to develop the mind's inherent richness and clarity in one's daily activities through the three emphases of (1) verifiable nondogmatic teachings; (2) meditation; and (3) the means to solidify the levels of awareness that have been attained. The Diamond Way is considered the most "skillful" method of the Buddha. As a lineage of direct oral transmission, Karma Kagyu treasures meditation and interaction with a qualified teacher. The teachings are traced to the historical Buddha Shakyamuni and his closest students. They were later passed on through the Indian Mahasiddhas: Padmasambhava, Tilopa, Naropa, and Maitripa, and the famous Tibetan yogis Marpa and Milarepa. In the twelfth century, the monk Gampopa gave the teachings to the first Gyalwa Karmapa, who is believed to have regularly reincarnated to the present.

Periodicals *Buddhism Today*.

Membership: There are more than 500 meditation centers around the world associated with the Karma Kagyu tradition. In 2008 Diamond Way reported 38 centers and groups in the United States.

Sources:

Diamond Way Buddhist Centers. www.diamondway.org/.

Nydahl, Ole. *Entering the Diamond Way: My Path among the Lamas*. Grass Valley, CA: Blue Dolphin Press, 1990. 251 pp.

———. *Mahamudra: Boundless Joy and Freedom*. Grass Valley, CA: Blue Dolphin Press, 1991. 96 pp.

———. *Riding the Tiger: Twenty Years on the Road: Risks and Joys of Bringing Tibetan Buddhism to the West*. Grass Valley, CA: Blue Dolphin Press, 1992. 512 pp.

Drikung Kagyu Order

Drikung Kagyu Institute, PO Kulhan, Sahastradhara Road, 248001 Dehra Dun, UA, India

The Drikung Kagyu Order is one school within the Kagyupa Tibetan Buddhist sect (which dates to Milarepa, the famous teacher). The order is unusual in that the lineage is carried by two heads simultaneously. In the early 1960s one of the heads, His Holiness Drikung Kyabgon Chetsang Rinpoche, left Tibet for India. Unable to leave Tibet, His Holiness Chungtsang, the other head of the order, was separated from his colleague for almost twenty-five years, their first meeting being in India in 1985. The first American Drikung center was founded under the auspices of the Drikung Kyabgon in 1978.

In 1985 H. H. Drikung Kyabgon Chetsang founded the nonprofit organization Drikung Kagyu Institute (DKI) in Dehra Dun, India, which strives to preserve, promote, and develop Buddhist philosophy and culture. The institute is made up of four institutions: Jangchubling Monastery, Samtenling Nunnery, Songtsen Library, and Kagyu College.

The Drikung Order is noted for its teachings on meditation, particularly the Drikung Phowa Meditation, a meditation intimately connected with the experience of death. Traditionally the Phowa Benediction was given every 12 years.

Membership: In 2008 the order reported 99 Drikung Kagyu centers worldwide. Of these, 32 were in the United States and 1 in Canada.

Sources:

Drikung Kagyu. www.drikung-kagyu.org/.

Dzogchen Foundation

PO Box 734, Cambridge, MA 02140

The Dzogchen Foundation was organized in March 1991 by Lama Surya Das and a small group of Dzogchen practitioners. Lama Surya Das was born Jeffrey Miller (1950) in New York and graduated from SUNY Buffalo (1971). He traveled throughout India and Nepal studying with various spiritual teachers. He was given the name Surya Das by the Indian Hindu teacher Maharajji (Neem Karoli Baba), and he lived and practiced in Tibetan monasteries under the guidance of Ven. Lama Thubten Yeshe, Ven. Kalu Rinpoche, and H. H. Gyalwa Karmapa. During 1977–1980 he lived in Woodstock, New York, establishing the Karmapa's monastery, Karma Triyana Dharmachakra (KTD). In 1980 he joined the first Nyingmapa retreat center in Dordogne, France, where he completed two traditional three-and-a-half-year retreats under the guidance of Dudjom Rinpoche and

Dilgo Khyentse Rinpoche, with Tulku Pema Wangyal and Nyoshul Khenpo Rinpoche. During this time he became a lama in the Nonsectarian Practice lineage of Tibetan Buddhism. Surya Das is a member of the International Padmakara Translation Committee and the organizer of the Western Buddhist Teachers Network and its Teachers' Conferences with the Dalai Lama in Dharamsala, India.

The foundation has set as its mission the preservation of the teachings of Dzogchen and their transmission to Westerners in an accessible form. It accomplishes this mission by offering opportunities to receive the guidance of Dzogchen teachers and by fostering the activities and emergence of Dharma teachers in both the East and the West. It also promotes nonsectarian dialogue, understanding, and cooperation between the various traditions of Buddhism.

The foundation believes that the Buddhism of Tibet represents the last extant wisdom culture to survive intact from ancient times. As an isolated cloister land, Tibet preserved all the teachings of the Buddha, which include the Theravadin, Mahayana, and tantric Vajrayana traditions of Buddhadharma. Many Buddhist sutras and commentaries in the Sanskrit language, which were lost in India during the Muslim invasions of northern India, were later discovered intact in Tibetan monastery libraries.

Dzogchen, practiced mainly by the Nyingma lineage, is seen as the consummate practice of Tibetan Buddhism. It is also considered an advanced and secret teaching.

The foundation conducts an annual month-long intensive meditation retreat, publishes a newsletter and schedule of the activities of Lama Surya Das and other lamas, engages in the translation and publication of texts and oral teachings, and brings venerable lamas to America to teach.

Membership: In 2008 the foundation reported practice groups led by Dzogchen Center practitioners in Cambridge, Massachusetts; Orange County and Los Angeles, California; Brooksville and Portland, Maine; Concord, New Hampshire; Plainfield and Roselle Park, New Jersey; Rochester and New York, New York; Portland, Oregon; Philadelphia, Pennsylvania; Austin, Texas; and Putney, Vermont.

Sources:

Dzogchen Foundation. www.dzogchen.org/.

Surya Das, Lama. *Awakening the Buddha Within: Eight Steps to Enlightenment*. New York: Broadway Books, June 1997. 320 pp.

Ewam Choden Tibetan Buddhist Center

254 Cambridge Ave., Kensington, CA 94708

Ewam Choden was the first center of the Sakyapa sect of Tibetan Buddhism founded in the United States. Its founder, Lama Kunga Thartse Rinpoche, came to the United States in the 1960s and settled in Kensington, California. He opened Ewam Choden in 1972. The Sakyapa sect was the last great reform movement in Tibetan Buddhism. It was founded in 1071 C.E. by Khon Konchok Gyalpo, who taught a "reformed" tantra that still retained parts of the older tantra practices (which contained significant magical and sexual aspects). Present head of the sect is Sakya Trizin, who paid his first visit to America, and Ewam Choden, in 1977.

Ewan Choden means the integration of method and wisdom, compassion and emptiness, and possessing the dharma (the true way of life taught by the Buddha). The center was established to practice and study Tibetan religion and culture. Lama Kunga established a program of meditation, classes, and ceremonial observation of holy days. Several students work to translate Tibetan texts into English, and the center periodically offers a Tibetan language class. The center administers the Tibetan Relief Fund. Public meditation services are held on Sunday mornings.

Membership: Not reported. There is one urban center in Kensington, California.

Sources:

Ewam Choden Tibetan Buddhist Center. www.ewamchoden.org/.

"His Holiness Sakya Trizin, An Interview." *Wings* 1, no. 1 (September–October 1987): 36–38, 51–53.

Foundation for the Preservation of the Mahayana Tradition (FPMT)

1632 SE 11th Ave., Portland, OR 97214-4702

The Foundation for the Preservation of the Mahayana Tradition (FPMT) is a worldwide association of Tibetan Buddhist centers founded by Lama Thubten Yeshe and Lama Thubten Zopa Rinpoche, both trained in the Gelugpa tradition of Tibetan Buddhism (the tradition associated with His Holiness the Dalai Lama). They met in 1959 when, as refugees from Tibet, they both settled in Buxaduar, India. The young Zopa Rinpoche was sent to Thubten Yeshe for further instruction. In 1965 the pair met Zina Ruchevsky, a Russian American who was ordained as a nun in 1967. The three established the Kopan Monastery near Kathmandu in 1969.

The center in Nepal began to attract Western students, and in 1973 the International Mahayana Institute, an organization of Western nuns and monks, was established at Kopan Monastery. The first Indian outpost, Tushita Retreat Center, opened in Dharmasala in 1972. That same year, the Mount Everest Center for Buddhist Studies opened at Lawudo, Nepal, to educate Nepalese children.

In 1974 the two lamas were invited to tour the West by C. T. Shen of the Institute for the Advanced Study of World Religions in New York. They toured the United States and spoke at most of the Tibetan Buddhist centers and several universities. These lectures, along with an American publication, brought them more students and the eventual development of several centers. In 1977 students donated 30 acres of land near Boulder Creek, California, for the development of a retreat center called the Vajrapani Institute, and in 1980 one student donated 270 acres in rural Vermont which became the Milarepa Center.

In 1984 Lama Thubten Yeshe passed away in Los Angeles and was cremated at the Vajrapani Institute. One year later, on February 12, 1985, a boy was born in Spain who was later identified as Lama Yeshe's reincarnation. This boy, named Tenzin Osel Rinpoche (Osel Hita), was enrolled in Sera Monastery in India. He later attended a private high school in Victoria, British Columbia, and continued his studies in Europe, thereby receiving both a traditional Tibetan education and a modern Western education to prepare him for his future role as the spiritual head of the FPMT.

FPMT has become a worldwide movement, with its world headquarters in the United States. Wisdom Publications, located in Boston, Massachusetts, distributes a wide array of books and CDs on Buddhism and related topics; these materials can be found for sale on the FPMT Web site. A line of English-language books on Tibetan Buddhism have appeared as the Wisdom Basic Books (Orange Series), Intermediate Books (White Series), and Advanced Books (Blue Series). FPMT is also active in translating Tibetan Buddhist texts into English.

In 2005 FPMT established an international organization, the Foundation for Developing Compassion and Wisdom (FDCW), whose mission is to attain world peace through a program of "Essential Education" (EE), which helps individuals reach their potential to be compassionate and wise. EE facilitates a more profound understanding of the nature of the mind and of its power to shape the way we live and relate to others.

Membership: In 2008 the foundation reported 150 centers, projects, and services in 33 countries worldwide. Of these, 32 were in the United States and 2 in Canada.

Periodicals: *Mandala*.

Sources:

Foundation for the Preservation of the Mahayana Tradition. www.fpmt.org.

Amipa, Lama Sherab Gyaltsen. *The Opening of the Lotus*. London: Wisdom Publications, 1987.

Hopkins, Jeffrey. *The Tantric Distinction*. London: Wisdom Publications, 1984.

MacKenzie, Vicki. *The Boy Lama*. San Francisco: Harper & Row, 1989.

Rabten, Geshe. *The Essential Nectar*. London: Wisdom Publications, 1984.

Rabten, Geshe, and Geshe Ngawang Dhargyey. *Advice from a Spiritual Friend*. New Delhi, India: Publications for Wisdom Culture, 1977.

Yeshe, Thubten, and Thubten Zopa. *Wisdom Energy*. Honolulu, HI: Conch Press, 1976.

Kampo Gangra Drubgyudling

200 Balsam Ave., Toronto, ON, Canada M4E 3C3

Kampo Gangra Drubgyudling was founded in 1973 as the Canadian center of the Tibetan Buddhist teacher Vajra Acharya Lama Karma Thinley Rinpoche. Karma Thinley Rinpoche (b. 1931) was born in Tibet and recognized at the age of two and a half as the reincarnation of Beru Shaiyak Lama Kunrik, a Sakya master, by Sakya Trizin, the head of the Sakya School of Tibetan Buddhism. At a later date he was also recognized by His Holiness the 16th Gyalwa Karmapa, head of the Kagyu tradition, as the fourth Karma Thinleypa, a highly realized bodhisattva of the Kagyu lineage. In addition to his position as a master of the Kagyu and Sakya schools, Rinpoche is also widely learned in the Nyingma and Gelug traditions. In 1974 the Gyalwa Karmapa appointed him a Lord of Dharma of the Karma-Kagyu lineage. Karma Thinley Rinpoche resides in Toronto.

The Marpa Gompa Meditation Society (Tibetan: Marpa Gompa Changchub Ling) was founded in 1977 as the Alberta center of Thinley Rinpoche's work. It has as a resident dharma teacher Choge Susan Hutchison (Jetsun Rigdzin Khandro). In addition to his centers in Canada, Thinley Rinpoche has followers in England, whom he has placed under the care of Lama Jampa Thaye as his Dharma regent. Teaching is primarily from the Kagyu tradition.

Membership: Not reported. Canadian centers are in Toronto, Ontario, and Calgary, Alberta; the U.K. center Kagyu Dechen Dzong is in Harrogate, Yorkshire.

Sources:

Lama Karma Thinley Rinpoche. www.karmathinleyrinpoche.com/cdn.html.

Morreale, Don. *The Complete Guide to Buddhist America*. Boston: Shambhala, 1998.

Karma Triyana Dharmachakra (KTD)

335 Meads Mountain Rd., Woodstock, NY 12498

Karma Triyana Dharmachakra (KTD) was founded in 1976 by His Holiness the 16th Gyalwa Karmapa, the head of the Karma Kagyu lineage. The Kagyu lineage is one of the four major lineages of the Tibetan Buddhism, and the Karma Kagyu is one of its main branches. Led by the Gyalwa Karmapas since the twelfth century, the lineage includes generations of scholars and mahasiddhas who devoted their lives to the realization of the truth of experience and the perfection of compassion for all beings. Before his passing in 1980 the 16th Karmapa named the KTD as his principal seat in North America and planned that from this monastery the Buddha's teachings would be introduced and disseminated in the West.

In 1985 H. H. Ogyen Trinley Dorje, the 17th Gyalwa Karmapa, was born to nomadic parents in the Lhathok region of Tibet. He was discovered in 1992 by a predicted letter written by the 16th Karmapa, and his identification was confirmed by H. H. the 14th Dalai Lama. In 2000 he fled from Tibet to India, where he began preparing for his role as leader and primary teacher of the Karma Kagyu lineage.

The KTD's authentic Tibetan temple building, which is said to be one of the largest in North America, is surrounded by residences for monastic and lay students. KTD hosts the Karma Kagyu Institute, which preserves Tibetan arts. Construction is under way to complete a large library, gallery space, and recording facility on the grounds. Ven. Khenpo Karthar Rinpoche and Ven. Bardor Tulku Rinpoche jointly hold the primary responsibility for fulfilling His Holiness's wishes with regard to KTD's activities. They conduct regular teachings at KTD and at affiliated centers around the country. KTD also maintains a traditional three-year, three-month meditation retreat center in Delhi, New York, and a stupa at Karma Thegsum Tashi Gomang in Crestone, Colorado.

Membership: In 2002 the KTD reported 37 centers in the United States, 3 in Canada, and 3 in South America.

Periodicals: *Densal.*

Sources:

Karma Triyana Dharmachakra. www.kagyu.org.

Karthar Rinpoche, Khenpo. *Dharma Paths.* Edited by Laura M. Roth. Ithaca, NY: Snow Lion Publications, 1992.

Kathok Gonpa

Tibetan Buddhist Temple and Retreat Center, 2800 Grafton St., Qualicum Beach, BC, Canada V9K 2968

Kathok Gonpa is the center established by Lingtrul Rinpoche (Lama Kadag Chöying Dorje; b. 1955). A teacher of the Kathok lineage within the Nyingma School of Tibetan Buddhism, Lingtrul Rinpoche is also the abbot of the Tra Ling Monastery in Tibet, which houses approximately 2,000 monks. He is the lineage-holder of what are termed the Great Perfection Teachings of the Ancients (Dzogchen), and is believed by his followers to be a reincarnation of an emanation of the fourteenth-century Tibetan teacher Gwalwa Longchenpa, known as the author of a book published in the West as *Kindly Bent to Ease Us.*

Lingtrul Rinpoche was born in Amdo-Golok, Tibet, and was recognized to be an incarnation of Ling Lama Dorje, a high lama of Eastern Tibet, at the age of three. Ling Lama Dorje had earlier been recognized as the incarnation of the daughter of King Trisong Detsun, and of Longchenpa. However, due to the Chinese occupation of Tibet, the recognition and subsequent enthronement of Lingtrul Rinpoche occurred in secret, and as a young tulku, he was forced to work in labor camps and serve the needs of the Chinese government.

Lingtrul Rinpoche studied under his root teacher, the great Khenpo Munsel, Thubten Tsultrim Gyatso, who passed on the lineage of the Clear Light Great Perfection that began with Dharmakaya Buddha Kuntuzangpo and was passed to Longchenpa and eventually to Khenpo Munsel. Lingtrul Rinpoche received all the transmissions of Clear Light Great Perfection, Dzogchen, and Ati-yoga, and over many years in retreat accomplished all the stages of development. He also received an extensive transmission of the Seven Treasures of Longchenpa, all other important Longchen Nyingthig transmissions, and a number of additional teachings from key Tibetan Buddhist masters.

Membership: Not reported.

Sources:

Kathok Gonpa. www.kathokgonpa.ca/.

Morreale, Don. *The Complete Guide to Buddhist America.* Boston: Shambhala, 1998.

Kunzang Palyul Choling (KPC)

18400 River Rd., Poolesville, MD 20837

Alternate Address: KPC of Arizona, 835 Andante Dr., Sedona, AZ 86336.

Kunzang Palyul Choling (KPC) is a Tibetan Buddhist organization in the Nyingmapa tradition formed in 1982 as the World Prayer Center. It was founded by Jetsunma Ahkon Lhamo and offers a full program of teachings in Buddhism and practice sessions in Buddhist meditation. It conducts weekly classes and lectures in its locations in Poolesville, Maryland, and Sedona, Arizona, and sponsors periodic retreats and workshops. Members are active in sponsoring Tibetan refugee children and youth as well as abused and neglected animals. KPC owns a 65-acre wildlife refuge.

Membership: Not reported. In 1993 there were approximately 150 members.

Educational Facilities:

Migyur Dorje Institute, Poolesville, Maryland.

Sources:

Kunzang Palyul Choling. www.tara.org/.

Ligmincha Institute

313 2nd St., SE, Ste. 307, Charlottesville, VA 22902

The Ligmincha Institute is a contemporary Western center of the ancient Bon (pre-Buddhist) religion of Tibet. It was founded in 1992 by Tenzin Wangyal Rinpoche. The transmission of the Bon religion to the West began in 1961 when Tenzin Namdak (b. 1926), the head of the Bon religious community, moved to London, England. Namdak became *lopon* (head) of the group in 1953 but had to flee Tibet in 1959 following the Chinese invasion. He moved to London two years later and cooperated with David Snellgrove in the translation and publication of *The Nine Ways of Bon*, a basic text on the Bon tradition. Upon his return to India in 1964, he founded New Menri as a center for the Bon community in exile. He made his first trip to the United States in 1989 and on that occasion founded the Tibetan Bon Temple Foundation in Signal Hill, California.

The Bon religion was founded by Tonpa Shenrab Miwoche, and as the teachings were passed and developed, they emerged into what is termed the Dzogchen teachings. The master practitioner is termed a *shen.* Shenrab's teachings are classified in the nine ways, or vehicles, to relieve sufferings. The initial four are termed the causal ways: Chashen (the Way of the Shen of Prediction), Nangshen (the Way of the Shen of the Visible World), Trulshen (the Way of the Shen of Magical Illusion), and Sichen (the Way of the Shen of Existence). These include various healing, divinatory, and astrological practices; purification rituals; practices to subdue spirits; and work with the souls of the living and dead. Bon practitioners share all of these practices with Tibetan shamanism.

Bon is unique in its practice of the five resultant vehicles, which are built upon a universal compassion and deal most directly with the life beyond death. These teachings are generally passed on orally from teacher to student. The founder passed the teachings on to the first nine masters, most of whom were from Zhang Zhung, an ancient land located in what is now western Tibet, near Mt. Kailash. The next masters, 24 in number, taught what is known as the oral transmissions of Zhang Zhung, which are contained in the *Zhang Zhung Nyn Gyud*, a multivolume text of Dzogchen teachings.

Dzogchen is described as a path of self-liberation. Human problems are located in the five poisons—attachment, anger, ignorance, pride, and jealousy. These are creations of the mind and do not exist in the true condition of the mind. The goal is to return to the true condition of the mind. Rather than attempt either to renounce the five poisons or to somehow transform them, Dzogchen suggests that we examine our problems. In the process we discover that they have no roots; they vanish. We are freed into a state where there are no passions.

Tenzin Wangyal Rinpoche received his transmission directly from Lopon Tenzin Namdak Rinpoche. The Ligmincha Institute offers the Bon tradition in a manner Tenzin Wangyal Rinpoche feels can communicate with Western audiences and also provides a spiritual home for Tibetan residents in the United States. The institute's library houses a number of rare Tibetan texts, and work has begun on translations. Of special interest is Tibetan medicine. Students may enter a seven-year program, focused in three-week summer retreats at the Serenity Ridge Retreat Center, through which they can be trained in the Bon religion and the spiritual exercises it perpetuates.

Membership: The institute is not a membership organization.

Periodicals: *The Voice of Clear Light.*

Sources:

Ligmincha Institute. https://www.ligmincha.org/.

Wangyal Rinpoche, Tenzin. *The Essence of Dzogchen in the Native B'n Tradition of Tibet.*

———. "The Way of Dzogchen: The Great Perfection." *Tantra* 5 (1992): 76.

———. "Shamanism in the Native B'n Tradition of Tibet." *Tantra* 8 (1994): 50–53, 79.

MahaSiddha Dharma

PO Box 1689, Soquel, CA 95073

MahaSiddha Dharma was founded in 1999 by a Buddhist teacher called Kali Ma and by her students and her husband Derrick Pawo. Kali Ma was ordained as a yogini in the *gö kar chang-loî dé* lineage, the white-skirt, long-haired, noncelibate lineage of the Nyingma tradition. This lineage was passed to her by Ngak'chang Rinpoche and his wife, Khandro Dechen, the lineage holders of the Aro Ter lineage, which traces back to Khyungchen Aro Lingma (1886–1923), a female master, and her son Aro Yeshe (1915–1951). She received transmission directly from Yeshe Tsogyal (757–817), the legendary female student of Padmasambhava, who introduced Buddhism to Tibet.

Kali Ma's spiritual career began as a young woman when she met a wisdom master and former student of Trungpa Rinpoche named Isa. From him she received her first initiations and empowerments, and after completing her training with him, she began her teaching work. She later met Ngak'chang Rinpoche and Khandro Dechen and received the Aro Ter lineage, then studied with Kali Ma Troma Rigtsal Rinpoche, another female teacher who works in the unorthodox style of the MahaSiddhas, the pioneering tantric teachers from India who supported the transmission of Buddhism to Tibet.

In founding MahaSiddha Buddhism, Kali Ma began to build an esoteric school that offered both beginning and advanced classes for students. Instruction includes classes in hatha yoga and in ayurveda medicine.

Kali Ma has concentrated her teaching in India, Nepal, and California, where she founded the Trigug Retreat in Santa Cruz, the MahaSiddha Center in Berkeley, and more than a dozen residential-practice communities. She also opened two clinics that offer ayurveda and panchakarma (ayurveda's purification therapy). The teachings of MahaSiddha Dharma are organized in stages that allow personal engagement with the practices, a relationship to a spiritual community, and a relationship with Kali Ma. Students may be community members (beginner), practitioner members (intermediate), or Vajra Sangha (advanced); each stage is offered in a way to meet the student's specific needs, maturity, and commitment levels.

Membership: Not reported. There are approximately 15 centers in the United States, all in California.

Sources:

MahaSiddha Dharma. www.mahasiddhas.org/.

Mahasiddha Nyingmapa Center

47 East Rd., Hawley, MA 01339

The Mahasiddha Nyingmapa Center is a small Nyingma center under the direction of Kyabje Dodrupchen Rinpoche. Students carry out a daily schedule of meditation and chanting.

Membership: In 2008 the center reported 50 members.

Sources:

Mahasiddha Nyingmapa Center. www.mahasiddha.org.

Thondup, Tulku. *Buddhist Civilization in Tibet.* Cambridge, MA: Mahasiddha Nyingmapa Center, 1982.

Namgyal Monastery Institute of Buddhist Studies

PO Box 127, Ithaca, NY 14851

Namgyal Monastery Institute of Buddhist Studies is the American headquarters of the Dalai Lama in his role as head of the Gelugpa School of Buddhism and nominal head of the Tibetan Buddhist community. The Gelugpa tradition is traced back to Lama Tsongkhapa (1357–1419), popularly known as Jetsun Tsongkhapa or Je Rinpoche in Tibet. He is thought to be a major reformer of Tibetan Buddhism. In his mature years, Je Rinpoche wrote a collection of texts on Buddhist doctrine and other related subjects, among them the Lam-Rim Chenmo, a study of the graduated path to enlightenment, which is considered by believers as the most authoritative volume on Buddhist teachings.

Je Rinpoche and his disciples founded the Gandan Monastery in 1409. His followers became known as the Gelugpas ("virtuous"), and his teachings spread throughout Tibet and to Mongolia, where almost the entire population became Gelugpa followers. The teachings also spread through China, influencing a succession of emperors who supported the spread of Buddhism.

The leader of this largest of Tibetan Schools is termed the Dalai Lama. The first Dalai Lama was Tsongkhapa's nephew. The Second Dalai Lama established the original Namgyal Monastery in the sixteenth century, and over the centuries it has served as the private monastery of each of the successive Dalai Lamas. In Tibet, this prestigious but relatively small monastery was located in the Potala in the capital city of Lhasa.

The present Dalai Lama, Tenzin Gyatso (b. 1935), was recognized as the new Dalai Lama at the age of two and in 1939 taken to Lhasa from his home in eastern Tibet. Though only 16, in 1951 he assumed his responsibilities in order to deal with the perceived threat that the new Chinese government posed for the country. When the country was finally overrun in 1959, he fled, and since that time he has worked both to regain the autonomy of Tibet and to care for the 100,000 Tibetan refugees, including numerous religious leaders who fled with him. His worldwide travels on behalf of these two causes have given him status as a prominent world religious leader similar to the Ecumenical Patriarch (Eastern Orthodox Christianity) or the Pope. The Dalai Lama established his headquarters (both a government-in-exile and Tibetan Buddhist center) in Dharmasala, India, and re-created Namgyal Monastery in a building immediately adjacent to his residence. Today a large community of monks pursues research and studies there.

In 1992 the monastery established a North American branch in Ithaca, New York, in conjunction with an innovative institute of study and practice for the benefit of lay as well as ordained Western women and men. With the approval of the Dalai Lama, the Administrative Committee of Namgyal Monastery in Dharmasala composed the charter for the Ithaca branch monastery and its institute and selected monks for its staff. Namgyal Institute has a program of bringing to the West both the program designed by the Dalai Lama and additional supplementary coursework. The institute hosts special events and guided pilgrimages, weeklong summer retreats, and a three-year curriculum of study in Tibetan language and Buddhist practices. The monks of the Namgyal Monastery Institute have also become well known for their intricate and beautiful sand mandalas, which have been exhibited in museums all over the world.

The Dalai Lama has written a number of books and overseen the translation of numerous Tibetan texts into Western languages. Snow Lion Publications was established in 1980 as an English-language publisher of books and other materials on Tibet, Tibetan culture, Tibetan Buddhism, and His Holiness the 14th Dalai Lama. As a publishing house it has been dedicated to the preservation of Tibetan culture and has become a major force in spreading Tibetan Buddhism in the West.

Remarks: During the 1990s, amid his broad work with the Tibetan Buddhist community, the Dalai Lama became involved in two international controversies that have particular significance for Gelugpa Buddhists. The first concerns the Panchen Lama. The Panchen Lama is the second most important religious figure in Tibet. The Fifth Dalai Lama, who became the sovereign ruler of Tibet in 1642, gave Tashi Lhunpo Monastery to the 15th abbot of the monastery, Lobsang Choekyi Gyaltsen, and officially conferred the title *panchen* (great scholar) upon him. Since his death, Lobsang Choekyi Gyaltsen's reincarnations have been recognized and known as the Panchen Lama.

Dalai Lamas and Panchen Lamas have enjoyed a unique and supportive relationship. Over the centuries, the adult Dalai Lama has been the person to recognize the new incarnation of the Panchen Lama, and vice versa. Thus it came about that in May 1995 (in the wake of the death of the 10th Panchen Lama in 1989), the present Dalai Lama recognized a six-year-old boy, Gedhun Choekyi Nyima, as the reincarnation of the Panchen Lama. However, shortly thereafter, the Chinese authorities detained Gedhun Choekyi Nyima and his parents and neither have been seen since. Then in November 1995, the Chinese government declared its recognition of another young boy, Gyaltsen Norbu, as the new Panchen Lama. The issue has become an important one in the ongoing relations between the Chinese government and the Dalai Lama, especially because the 10th Panchen had been severely treated in an effort to have him denounce the Dalai Lama, but he remained loyal.

The second issue has involved an internal struggle within the Gelugpa community. In 1978 the Dalai Lama gave a talk in which he spoke harshly of veneration ascribed to Dorje Shugden, a Tibetan Buddhist deity who has enjoyed popular support among Tibetan Buddhists. The Dalai Lama's words led to the suppression of worship in the community in India and Nepal and some discrimination against those who continued the practice. This was largely an internal matter little known outside of the inner circle of believers. But the Dalai Lama heightened controversy in 1996 when, in the wake of his problems with the Chinese over the Panchen Lama, he publicly declared Dorje Shugden to be an evil Chinese spirit who was harmful to Tibetan independence and to the Dalai Lama's life. He then took the extraordinary step of banning the worship of Dorje Shugden and initiating its forcible suppression within the exile Tibetan communities. This action infuriated many who felt forced to choose between the Dalai Lama and their own traditional spiritual practice.

Among the major supporters of Dorje Shugden veneration were the leaders and members of a rival Gelugpa branch, the New Kadampa Tradition (NKT), which has its center in a monastery in England. Members of the NKT demonstrated against the Dalai Lama during his European visit in the summer of 1996. Then in February 1997, three of the Dalai Lama's close disciples were murdered near Dharmasala. Again, on May 3, 1998, followers of Dorje Shugden (including NKT members) demonstrated against the Dalai Lama in New York during his visit there.

Neither the Panchen Lama controversy nor the Dorje Shugden controversy appears to be nearing a resolution. In each case, those opposed to the Dalai Lama are out of his reach, either in the controlled environment of Tibet or in the free religious environment of the modern West. He has no power to locate and free his designated candidate as the Panchen Lama or to force the followers of Dorje Shugden in various branches of Tibetan Buddhism to discontinue their veneration. The Dalai Lama will probably have to live with both issues for a number of years in the future.

Sources:

Namgyal Monastery Institute of Buddhist Studies. www.namgyal.org.

Snow Lion Publications. www.snowlionpub.com.

Batchelor, Stephen. "Letting Daylight into Magic: The Life and Times of Dorje Shugden." *Tricycle: The Buddhist Review* 7, 3 (spring 1998): 60–66.

Dalai Lama. *My Land and My People*. New York: Potala Corporation, 1983.

———. *Freedom in Exile: The Autobiography of the Dalai Lama*. San Francisco: Harper, 1991. 320 pp.

———. *Opening of the Wisdom Eye*. Wheaton, IL: Theosophical Publishing House, 1986.

———. *The Way to Freedom*. San Francisco: Harper, 1994. 192 pp.

Kay, David. "The New Kadampa Tradition and the Continuity of Tibetan Buddhism in Transition." *Journal of Contemporary Religion* 12, no. 3 (October 1997): 277–293.

Lopez, Donald S., Jr. "Two Sides of the Same God" *Tricycle: The Buddhist Review* 7, no. 3 (spring 1998): 67–69.

Snelling, John. *The Buddhist Handbook: A Complete Guide to Buddhist Schools, Teachings, Practice, and History*. Rochester, VT: Inner Traditions, 1991. 337 pp.

Namo Buddha Seminar

1390 Kalmia Ave., Boulder, CO 80304

Alternate Address: International Headquarters: Thrangu Tashi Choeling-Monastery, Namo Buddha Retreat Centre, PO Box 1287, Kathmandu, Nepal. Canadian Headquarters: Karma Tashi Ling, 10792 82nd Ave., Edmonton, AB T6E 2A8.

The Namo Buddha Seminar was established by the Ven. Khenchen Thrangu Rinpoche, a Tibetan lama of the Kagyu sect in 1988. In the fifteenth century, the seventh Gyalwa Karmapa, Chodrak Gyatso (1454–1506), visited the region of Thrangu in Tibet, and he established the Thrangu Monastery. He also enthroned Sherab Gyaltsen as the first Thrangu Rinpoche and asserted that he was the reestablished emanation of Shubu Palgyi Senge, one of the 25 great siddha disciples of Guru Padmasambhava, the eighth-century saint who brought Buddhism to Tibet.

Thrangu Rinpoche was born in Tibet in 1933 and was recognized by the age of five by H. H. the 16th Karmapa and Tai Situpa to be the ninth reincarnation of the famous Thrangu Tulku. He was forced to escape from Tibet when the Chinese invaded in 1959, and he found his way to the Karmapa's monastery in exile in Sikkim, India. Because of his great scholarship and unending diligence, he was given the task of preserving the teachings of the Kagyu lineage, with its long history of notable personages such as Marpa, Gampopa, and Milarepa, so that this lineage of 1,000 years of profound Buddhist teachings would not die out.

At the age of 23 he received ordination from H. H. Karmapa, along with Chogyam Trungpa Rinpoche (the founder of Vajradhatu International) and Surmang Garwang Rinpoche. He was introduced to the Absolute Nature by Lama Khenpo Gangshar Wangpo. Thrangu Rinpoche studied in Buxalor and in a few years achieved the highest Geshe Lharampa degree, and upon returning to Rumtek he was given the highest Khenchen degree. Because all the Buddhist texts were destroyed in Tibet, Thrangu Rinpoche helped begin the recovery of these texts from Tibetan monasteries outside of Tibet. He became abbot of the Nalanda Institute in Rumtek and, along with Khenpo Tsultrim Gyamtso, was one of the principal teachers in the Nalanda Institute, training all the younger tulkus of the lineage. Thrangu Rinpoche was also the tutor for the four major regents and established the fundamental curriculum of the Karma Kagyu lineage. Today he is the holder of the Zhentong lineage handed down by Jamgon Kongtrul the Great.

In 1976 Thrangu Rinpoche founded a small monastery in Boudhanath, Kathmandu, and also a retreat center in Namo Buddha (both in Nepal), and began giving authentic Buddhist teachings in the West and in the Far East. He has taught in more than 25 countries and has 17 centers in 12 countries. Additionally, he maintains a free medical clinic in an impoverished area of Nepal, Tara Abbey, which trains Tibetan women to become khenpos (teachers), and an elementary school for training Tibetan children in Western subjects as well as Buddhist topics.

In the United States, Thrangu Rinpoche established centers in Maine and California and often visits and teaches in centers in New York, Connecticut, and Seattle. In Canada he teaches in Vancouver, has a center in Edmonton, and is abbot of Gampo Abbey (a Buddhist monastery) in Nova Scotia. Thrangu Rinpoche conducts annual Namo Buddha seminars in the United States, Canada, and Europe, as part of a meditation retreat. In 2006 the Vajra Vidya Retreat Center in Crestone, Colorado, was completed. Under the guidance of Lama Wangdu and Khenpo Jigme, the center offers both short-term and long-term retreat packages as well as a summer program of study and meditation.

The Namo Buddha Seminar supports the activities of Thrangu Rinpoche and concentrates on publishing the authentic Buddhist teachings from a realized teacher. Namo Buddha Publications has collected an audio library of more than 800 tapes of Thrangu Rinpoche and has published many of these in 28 books, which are available from the online bookstore. It is planned that his works will be digitized and available for download on the Internet; a Cyber-sangha, which will present his teachings in a long-distance learning format, will also be available. A bimonthly Internet newsletter is sent to approximately 600 subscribers.

Membership: In 2002 an estimated 400 to 450 people attended Rinpoche's seminars, which are open to anyone.

Educational Facilities:

Thrangu Tashi Choling, Boudhanath, Kathmandu, Nepal.

Periodicals: *Namo Buddhist Seminar.*

Sources:

Khenchen Thrangu Rinpoche. www.rinpoche.com.

Vajra Vidya Retreat Center. www.vajravidyaretreatcenter.org.

Nechung Dorje Drayang Ling

PO Box 250, Pahala, HI 96777

In 1972 the head of the Nyingmapa branch of Tibetan Buddhism visited Hawaii. Inspired by his visit, a group of students initiated efforts to bring a teacher to live on the islands permanently. One of them consulted with the Dalai Lama concerning that possibility. The students had acquired the Woods Valley Temple, a Nichiren Buddhist temple five miles outside of Pahala, Hawaii, which had been abandoned when Japanese workers moved out of the area. They found a teacher, Nechung Rinpoche, in 1975. He was an accomplished master of both the Gelug and older Nyingma branches of Tibetan Buddhism. Shortly after his arrival, a second center was opened in Honolulu, and periodically meetings are held on the other islands. Nechung Rinpoche attempts to integrate the practices and teachings of all the branches of Buddhism, and the center has been host to a wide variety of Tibetan Buddhist teachers who have come to Hawaii. In 1994 the Woods Valley Temple hosted the Dalai Lama, who attracted more than 3,500 people.

The center has a full schedule of lectures, daily meditation sessions, and ceremonies. It has become a retreat facility that can accommodate approximately 20 people and has hosted numerous retreats with head and lineage lamas of all schools of Tibetan Buddhism. Contact is maintained with the Nechung Dorje Drayang Ling Monastery in Dharmasala, India, considered the mother of the Hawaiian work. There is also a Nechung Monastery in Lhasa, Tibet, which has about 25 monks in residence.

Membership: In 1988 four people lived at the Woods Valley temple, though during retreats the population may swell to around 25. Approximately 40 monks live at the monastery in Dharmasala.

Periodicals: *Newsletter.*

Sources:

Nechung Orje Drayang Ling. www.nechung.org.

New Kadampa Tradition (NKT)

Kadampa Meditation Center New York, Sweeney Rd., Glen Spey, NY 12737

Alternate Address: International Headquarters: NKT-IKBU, Conishead Priory, Ulverston, Cumbria, UK LA12 9QQ.

The New Kadampa Tradition of Tibetan Buddhism originated in the mid-1970s with the movement of the Ven. Geshe Kelsang Gyatso (b. 1931) to the West. He had been born in Tibet but left after the Chinese takeover. He trained for 19 years in the Tibetan monasteries of Jampaling and Sera under his spiritual guide, the Ven. Trijang Rinpoche, before entering into a meditation retreat in the Himalayas for almost 20 years. In 1977 he was invited to England as the resident teacher at the Manjushri Mahayana Buddhist Centre (now the Manjushri Kadampa Meditation Centre) in England, where he has remained ever since.

The Kadampa Tradition is traced to Atisha (982–1054 C.E.), who brought Buddhism to western Tibet (1042) from India. He emphasized guru devotion and the need for a monastic disciple. His work was carried on by his disciple Dromton (1088–1164), who largely shaped the tradition. It was eventually passed to Je Tsong Khapa (1357–1419), who helped revive Buddhism across Tibet during a time it was at a low ebb. In more recent centuries the Kadampa tradition has become a branch of the Gelugpa Tibetan Buddhist school.

The New Kadampa Tradition was created to present the old teaching in a manner that communicates with modern Westerners. To that end, Geshe Kelsang has published some 21 books ranging from volumes for beginners to detailed and lucid expositions of the profundities of Buddhist philosophy. He proposes the following of Atisha's instructions, called "Lamrim" or "Stages of the Path," which combines study and spiritual practice. These books are published by Tharpa Publications and are available for purchase through the company's Web site.

Membership: Not reported. In 2008 the NKT reported 1,100 Kadampa Buddhist centers and branches in 40 countries.

Remarks: The New Kadampa tradition has become widely known for its involvement in a controversy internal to the Gelugpa school headed by H. H. the Dalai Lama. On July 13, 1978, in exile, the Dalai Lama gave a talk in which he attempted to discredit the worship of Dorje Shugden, a Tibetan Buddhist deity who was enormously popular among the people of Gelugpa School. The worship of Dorje Shugden was also a practice of the Dalai Lama's own principal spiritual teacher, Kyabje Trijang Rinpoche.

The continued discrediting of Dorje Shugden led to the suppression of worship and some discrimination against those who continued the practice. The Dalai Lama raised the controversy to a new level in 1996 when, in the main Thekchen Choeling Temple near Dharamsala, he publicly declared Dorje Shugden to be an evil Chinese spirit who was harmful to Tibetan independence and to the Dalai Lama's life. He then took the extraordinary step of banning the worship of Dorje Shugden and initiating its forcible suppression within the exile Tibetan communities. This action infuriated many who felt forced to choose between the Dalai Lama and their own traditional spiritual practice.

The New Kadampa Tradition has been the main supporter of Dorje Shugden among practitioners of Tibetan Buddhism in the West. The controversy, which pitched the Dalai Lama against the New Kadampa Tradition, was further escalated by an NKT campaign during the Dalai Lama's European visit in the summer of 1996. Then, in February 1997, three of the Dalai Lama's close disciples were murdered near Dharamsala, India. Again, on May 3, 1998, followers of Dorje Shugden (including NKT members) demonstrated against the Dalai Lama in New York during his visit there, and no end of the controversy is in sight. It is thought that the ban on the worship of Dorje Shugden has resulted in the persecution of many of his followers, and practitioners in the West continue to protest the ban.

Sources:

Kadampa Meditation Center New York. www.kadampanewyork.org.

New Kadampa Tradition—International Kadampa Buddhist Union. kadampa.org/.

Tharpa Publications. www.tharpa.com.

Batchelor, Stephen. "Letting Daylight into Magic: The Life and Times of Dorje Shugden." *Tricycle: The Buddhist Review* 7, no. 3 (spring 1998): 60–66.

Kay, David. "The New Kadampa Tradition and the Continuity of Tibetan Buddhism in Transition." *Journal of Contemporary Religion* 12, no. 3 (October 1997): 277–293.

Lopez, Donald S., Jr. "Two Sides of the Same God." *Tricycle: The Buddhist Review* 7, no. 3 (spring 1998): 67–69.

Padmasambhava Buddhist Centers

Padma Samye Ling Retreat Center and Monastery, 618 Buddha Hwy., Sidney Center, NY 13839

The Padmasambhava Buddhist Centers (named for the eighth-century Tibetan saint) comprise a set of Nyingma Buddhist practice groups tied together by the teaching activity of Khenpo Tse-wang Dongyal Rinpoche and Khenchen Palden Sherab Rinpoche, both students of H. H. Dudjom Rinpoche, head of the Nyingma lineage within Tibetan Buddhism. The members gather annually for a summer retreat at Padma Samye Ling Retreat Center and Monastery, a retreat center in upstate New York. The rest of the year the teachers travel between their centers, which are found across the United States, and in Puerto Rico and Russia.

Membership: Not reported. As of 1998 there were nine centers in the United States and one in Puerto Rico.

Periodicals: *Tashi Deleg!*

Sources:

Padmasambhava Buddhist Centers. www.padmasambhava.org/.

Morreale, Don. *The Complete Guide to Buddhist America*. Boston: Shambhala, 1998.

Palyul Changchub Dargyeling

Box 1514, Mill Valley, CA 94941

Palyul Changchub Dargyeling was established in 1996 by Khenpo Tsewang Gyatso Rinpoche, the American representative of the Palyul branch of the Nyingma tradition of Tibetan Buddhism. The Palyul Nyingma date to 1665 C.E. in Eastern Tibet. The supreme head of the Palyul Buddhists is H. H. Padma Nornu ("Penor") Rinpoche, the eleventh throne holder of Palyul. His seat is currently at the Namdroling Monastery in Byla-Kuppe, India.

In February 1997, H. H. Penor Rinpoche recognized actor Steven Seagal as a *tulku*, the reincarnation of Chungdrag Dorje of Palyul Monastery. Later that year he toured the United States to formally open his newly established centers.

Membership: Not reported. There are several centers in the United States.

Sources:

Palyul Changchub Dargyeling. www.palyul.org/.

Morreale, Don. *The Complete Guide to Buddhist America*. Boston: Shambhala, 1998.

Rigpa Fellowship

Rigpa U.S. Headquarters, 9540 Waples St., Ste. A, San Diego, CA 92121

Rigpa Fellowship is an association of Tibetan Buddhist meditation centers under the direction of Sogyal Rinpoche. Rinpoche is an incarnate lama of the Dzogchen lineage who studied first under Jamyang Khyentse Chokyi Lodro. In the mid-1970s he accompanied the Dalai Lama on his first trip to the West, remaining behind to attend Cambridge University. He founded Orgyen Choe Ling in London and attracted students in France and the United States and later in Australia. Rinpoche teaches Dzoghen meditation, believed to be the final and ultimate teaching of Buddha, which brings the precise experience of the awakened state.

Tapes and booklets by Rinpoche can be ordered through the Rigpa Store Web site. Radio shows consisting of interviews with Rinpoche are distributed to stations by New Dimensions Radio in San Francisco. Rinpoche resides in England but makes regular visits to the United States and conducts an annual weeklong retreat for students. These retreats are complemented by a year-round program of courses in Rigpa centers and groups. An online curriculum, the Rigpa Distance Learning Program, offers individuals who do not live near a Rigpa center the opportunity to study Rigpa's graduated course program and deepen their understanding of Rinpoche's teachings.

Membership: In 2008 Rigpa reported 14 centers and groups in the United States and 4 in Canada. There were several thousand members in centers around the world, including France, Ireland, Germany, the Netherlands, Switzerland, Australia, New Zealand, Japan, and India.

Sources:

Rigpa Fellowship. www.rigpaus.org/.

Rigpa International. www.rigpa.org/.

The Rigpa Store. zamamerica.stores.yahoo.net.

Rinpoche, Sogyal. *Face to Face Meditation Experience*. London: Orgyen Choe Ling, 1978.

————. *View, Meditation and Action*. London: Dzogchen Orgyen Choe Ling, 1979.

————. *The Tibetan Book of Living and Dying*. Edited by Patrick Gaffney and Andrew Harvey. San Francisco: Harper San Francisco, 1992.

Rigpe Dorje Foundation

c/o Jan Puckett, Rigpa Dorje Center, 28 Eton Green Circle, San Antonio, TX 78257

Alternate Address: Rigpe Dorje Center (Centre Rigpe Dorje), 503 5th Ave., Verdun, QC, Canada H4G 272.

The Rigpe Dorje Foundation was founded by His Eminence Jamgon Kongtrul Rinpoche (1954–1992), a Tibetan teacher believed by his followers to be the mind incarnation of Lodro Thaye, Jamgon Kongtrul the Great (1813–1899), pioneer of the nineteenth-century Rime movement (an effort to overcome the differences among the major schools of Tibetan Buddhism). He also is believed to be the incarnation of Taranatha and Khyungpo Naljor, founders of the Jonangpa and Shangpa lineages. When he was but six years old, the 16th Gyalwa Karmapa enthroned him, and while growing up he lived and studied under the Karmapa's guidance at Rumtek Monastery in Sikkim.

Continuing the activity of the previous Kongtrul incarnations, he established retreat centers in Nepal and India. In his belief that Eastern wisdom and Western knowledge can combine to understand and resolve many contemporary problems, he initiated the Buddhism and Psychotherapy Conference in New York. He also funded the Paramita Charitable Trust and the Rigpe Dorje Foundation in the United States, Canada, and Europe through which his followers have supported projects of educational, medical, social, and cultural development, mainly in India.

Jamgon Rinpoche was killed in Siliguri, India, in 1992 in a car accident. His work was assumed by Khenpo Tsultrim Gyamtso Rinpoche. In October 1997, recognition of the fourth Jamgon Kongtrul reincarnation, Jamgon Lodro Chokyi Nyima Tenpe Dronme, was announced. He was born in Tibet on November 26, 1995, and recognized by His Holiness the 17th Gyalwa Karmapa, Orgen Trinley Dorje. Jamgon Kongtrul Rinpoche currently resides at Pullahari Monastery, on a hilltop overlooking the Kathmandu valley.

Membership: In 2008 the San Antonio center reported 15 members. Members participate in the annual Treasury of Knowledge retreat with the Dzogchen Ponlop Rinpoche.

Sources:

Rigpe Dorje Center (Centre Rigpe Dorje). centrerigpedorje.org/.

Jamgon Kongtrul Labrang. www.jamgonkongtrul.org/.

Morreale, Don. *The Complete Guide to Buddhist America*. Boston: Shambhala, 1998.

Rime Foundation

5900 N Kenmore, Ste. C1, Chicago, IL 60660

The Rime (or "nonpartisan") tradition within Tibetan Buddhism began in in eastern Tibet in the nineteenth century, when some scholars saw the need to overcome sectarian bias in evaluation of the doctrinal traditions of the various schools and to accept each tradition on its own merits. The movement was initiated by the Sakyapa teacher Jamyang Khyentse Wangpo (1820–1892). Among his students the most important were Chogyur Dechen Lingpa (1829–1870) and Jamgon Kongtrul the Great (1811–1899), who compiled the "Five Great Treasures," a compendium of teachings and practices of the various Tibetan traditions. The movement's fundamental attitude of unbiasedness was most evident in the person and work of Jamgon Kongtrul's recent incarnation, Jamgon Kongtrul Rinpoche (1954–1992), a Karma Kagyu teacher who established the Rigpe Dorje Foundation.

The Rime teachers and their students restructured doctrinal and practical materials, based on the example of the Gelugpa school. The process within the Rime movement of reviving transmissions of teachings that had been thought lost and providing them with fresh commentary also embraced the traditions of the other schools. Works of the Kagyupa, Sakyapa, Kadampa (a.k.a. Gelugpa) and Chod lineages are also found in the Rime collection of texts. Additionally, the Rime teachers advocated revival of the Tibetan Bon teachings.

The Rime Foundation, formerly the Chicago Rime Center, is a Western outpost of the Rime tradition that supports the development, practice, and integration of the various schools of Tibetan Buddhism. While exploring the richness unique to each lineage, the Rime Foundation honors the unity inherent within the vast spectrum of Tibetan Buddhist teachings. The center offers activities including weekly practice sessions and dharma talks and works to provide access to traditional teachings by notable masters within the larger Tibetan Buddhist tradition.

Membership: Not reported.

Sources:

www.geocities.com/RimeFoundation/.

Sakya Monastery of Tibetan Buddhism

108 NW 83rd St., Seattle, WA 98117

Sakya Monastery of Tibetan Buddhism is a place to learn from highly qualified Tibetan lamas in a traditional setting. The monastery, located in the Greenwood district of Seattle, Washington, occupies a beautiful renovated building that houses a pristine example of a Tibetan Buddhist shrine, one of only a few in North America. Although called a monastery, it is primarily a lay community of practitioners, with various levels of experience in the Buddhist tradition.

The head lama of Sakya Monastery is H. H. Jigdal Dagchen Sakya (called Rinpoche, meaning "Precious One" in Tibetan). He is a head lama of the Sakya school, one of Tibetan Buddhism's four main schools. The term *Sakya* derives from Rinpoche's family name and spiritual lineage and ultimately from the original Sakya Monastery in Sakya, Tibet, built by one of Rinpoche's ancestors in 1073. It received the name "Sakya" because it was constructed on a patch of earth (*sa*) that was pale (*kya*). The monastery in Seattle, while a seat of the Sakya school of Tibetan Buddhism in North America, is also a nonsectarian religious center and hosts visits and teaching from leading lamas of all four schools of Tibetan Buddhism.

The purpose of the monastery is to share and preserve Tibetan Buddhism and Tibetan culture. It does this through the promotion of Buddhist teachings and practices and by upholding Tibetan customs and traditions. Since the purpose of the Buddha's teaching, as practiced in Tibet, is to develop loving kindness and compassion, the main meditation practices at the monastery focus on the cultivation of these qualities. In keeping with the emphasis in Buddhism (and especially in the Sakya school) on education and learning, Sakya Monastery offers a variety of educational programs to foster a better understanding of the teachings of the Buddha.

The Seattle monastery was featured in Bernardo Bertolucci's 1993 film *Little Buddha*.

Membership: In 2008 the monastery had three lamas and reported approximately 1,000 members and congregants in the United States and Canada. There are a number of affiliated Sakya centers around the world.

Educational Facilities:

Virupa Ecumenical Institute, Seattle, Washington.

Sakya College, Rajpur, India.

Sources:

Sakya Monastery of Tibetan Buddhism. www.sakya.org/.

The Excellent Path Bestowing Bliss. Seattle, WA: Sakya Monastery of Tibetan Buddhism, 1987.

Shambhala International

1084 Tower Rd., Halifax, NS, Canada B3H 2Y5

Shambhala International, which comprises more than 170 meditation centers worldwide, was founded by Chogyam Trungpa Rinpoche (1939–1987) and is currently led by his eldest son and spiritual heir, Sakyong Mipham Rinpoche. Shambhala, the largest of the Tibetan Buddhist groups in the United States, is a representative of the Kagyupa sect founded by Marpa Lotsawa in the eleventh century. Chogyam Trungpa Rinpoche, the Vidyadhara, is believed to have been the 11th incarnation of the Trungpa *tulkus* (emanation of a bodhisattva) and was

abbot of Surmang Monastery, a center of the Kagyupa tradition, until the takeover of Tibet by the Chinese in 1959.

The Vidyadhara fled Tibet that year and settled in England. While attending Oxford University, he established a small Buddhist center in Scotland, Samye Ling. Two years later he left the center, dropped his monastic orders, and became a layperson. In 1970 he married and migrated to the United States, where he founded the meditation center Karme Choling in Vermont. He traveled, lectured, and established several more centers over the next few years. In 1973 he created an umbrella organization, Vajradhatu, for his expanding activities. He had by this time moved to Colorado. In 1985 he moved to Nova Scotia to establish Vajradhatu International, which, after his passing in 1987 and his son's succession as leader of the organization in 1990, became Shambhala International.

Under Shambhala proper are all the centers around the United States and Canada, called "dharmadatus." Karme Choling in Vermont and the Shambhala Mountain Center (formerly Rocky Mountain Dharma Center) in Colorado are used primarily for retreats, study programs, and training sessions. Shambhala Training, a series of contemplative workshops, provides a secular approach to the practice of meditation in everyday life.

In 1974 Trungpa had created the Nalanda Foundation to direct several outreach programs. Of these the educational arm, Naropa Institute, now the fully accredited Naropa University in Boulder, Colorado, is the most notable. It has long been an important center for Buddhist scholarship in the West through its varied and creative programs. Shambhala has also established prison outreach programs to serve the spiritual needs of inmates. In addition, it has organized an annual summer camp for young people, weekend seminars, and the Mipham Academy, a month-long intensive program of study for advanced practitioners. The organization's Web site provides information on the wide range of programs available to interested parties.

Membership: In 2008 Shambhala International reported more than 4,000 members worldwide in 170 dharmadatus, including major centers in Vermont, Colorado, Canada, and Europe.

Educational Facilities:

Naropa University, Boulder, Colorado.

Periodicals: *The Shambhala Sun*. • *The Dot*. • *Buddhadharma*.

Sources:

Shambhala International. www.shambhala.org/.

Clark, Tom. *The Great Naropa Poetry Wars*. Santa Barbara, CA: Cadmus Editions, 1980.

Guenther, Herbert V., and Choegyam Trungpa. *The Dawn of Tantra*. Berkeley, CA: Shambhala, 1975.

Tendzin, Osel. *Buddha in the Palm of Your Hand*. Boulder, CO: Shambhala, 1982.

Thinley, Karma. *The History of the Sixteen Karmapas of Tibet*. Boulder, CO: Prajna Press, 1980.

Trungpa, Chogyam. *Cutting through Spiritual Materialism*. Berkeley, CA: Shambhala, 1973.

———. *Born in Tibet*. Boulder, CO: Shambhala, 1976.

———. *Shambhala: Sacred Path of the Warrior*. Boulder, CO: Shambhala, 1985.

Tara Mandala

PO Box 3040, Pagosa Springs, CO 81147

Tara Mandala, a Tibetan Buddhist retreat center located in southwestern Colorado, offers a variety of Buddhist retreats year-round, particularly in the summer months. Lama Tsultrim Allione founded Tara Mandala in 1993, inspired by the vision of a western retreat center that she had had while living in the Himalayas and by the need to create a place for what she describes as the reemergence of the sacred feminine. Bordered by the San Juan National Forest and Ute tribal land near Pagosa Springs, the center sees itself as being rooted in the Buddhist tradition of partnership with earth, animals, family, and respect for all wisdom traditions. The focal point of Tara Mandala's 700 acres is a breast-shaped peak surrounded by four valleys. A new residence hall was completed in 2007, and the three-story, 14,000-square-foot Tara Temple has been scheduled for completion in December 2008.

The land, lying at an elevation of 7,400 feet, offers deep silence and vast views that the center hopes will inspire both spiritual and ecological awareness. The sacred space of Tara Mandala has to do with the shape and power of the landscape itself, which has been recognized by Tibetan lamas as the body of Tara, female Buddha of compassion.

Membership: Not reported.

Periodicals: *Tara Mandala Newsletter*.

Sources:

Tara Mandala Buddhist Retreat Center. www.taramandala.org/.

Allione, Tsultrim. *Women of Wisdom*. New York: Penguin, 1988.

————. *Feeding Your Demons: Ancient Wisdom for Resolving Inner Conflict*. New York: Little, Brown, 2008.

Thubten Dhargye Ling

PO Box 90665, Long Beach, CA 90809

Thubten Dhargye Ling Tibetan Center for Buddhist Studies was founded in 1979 by Geshe Tsultim Gyeltsen (b. 1924), a teacher in the Gelugpa tradition of Tibetan Buddhism. The center's name, which means "Land of Increasing Buddha's Teachings," was given by the Dalai Lama. Geshe Gyeltsen was educated at Ganden Monastic University in Tibet. He completed a 23-year course of study and was awarded the title of Lharampa Geshe. Continuing his studies, he graduated from Gyuto Tantric College. In the 1960s he was sent by the Dalai Lama to Great Britain as the director of Tibet House in Sussex, England. In 1976 he came to America, where he taught at the University of California—Santa Barbara and the University of Oriental Studies in Los Angeles, California.

In America, Geshe Gyeltsen has continued his close relationship with the Dalai Lama and on several occasions has hosted his visits to Los Angeles. Besides the Los Angeles center, Geshe Gyeltsen has also founded two affiliated centers: Mahakaruna Tibetan Buddhist Meditation Center in Fairbanks, Alaska, and a small center near Paonia, Colorado. Activities at the center in Los Angeles include weekly Sunday services, special monthly ceremonies, meditation courses, and weekend seminars. The center's Web site also offers a wide variety of books and DVDs for students and practitioners as well as online teachings from Geshe Gyeltsen on Sunday mornings.

Membership: Not reported.

Periodicals: *TDL Newsletter*.

Sources:

Thubten Dhargye Ling. www.tdling.com.

Tibetan Buddhist Learning Center

93 Angen Rd., Washington, NJ 07882-9767

The first Tibetan Buddhist group to arrive in America came in 1951 and settled near Howell, New Jersey. It included 200 members of the Kalmuck tribe of Mongolia who had fled Soviet authorities wishing to convert them to communism. In 1955, with the aid of Church World Service (a Christian ecumenical group), the Ven. Geshe Ngawang Wangyal (d. 1983), a Kalmuck-Mongolian lama who received his training at the Drepung Gomang Monastery near Lhasa, Tibet, came to America from Tibet. In 1958 he founded the Lamaist Buddhist Monastery of America (in Tibetan, Labsum Shedrub Ling) in Howell Township in central New Jersey, which he headed for the rest of his life. In 1968 the center was moved to its present location in Warren County. In 1984, the year after Geshe-la died, at the advice of His Holiness the 14th Dalai Lama, the English name of the center was changed to Tibetan Buddhist Learning Center.

The center takes its name from its main task of teaching Tibetan Buddhism. Over the years it has sponsored many Tibetan scholars to come to the United States and served as residence for both monk-scholars and American students. It has assisted in attending to the spiritual needs of the original Kalmuck community as well as a growing American Buddhist group attracted to the center by Wangyal. Among other services, the center nurtures the religious life of its students by providing the regular cycle of Tibetan Buddhist ceremonies and rituals.

The center attempts to convey to its students a basic knowledge of the many facets of Tibetan Buddhism. The study of the teachings is stressed as most important for the new Western Buddhists and is followed by putting the principles learned into practice. Many of the students have deepened their appreciation of Buddhism by learning the Tibetan language. Instruction at the center is given in English by both the resident Tibetan monk-scholars and associated American scholars. This joint teaching, which makes the subject matter easier to assimilate, is seen as essential for the center to accomplish its main aim—to develop a Buddhism that is culturally American but, at its heart, not different from the Buddhism that traveled from India throughout Asia to Tibet and from there to twentieth-century America.

Succeeding Geshe Wangyal at the center are executive directors Joshua W. C. Cutler, who trained with Geshe-la for 13 years, and his wife, Diana Cutler, who trained with Gesha-la for 11 years.

Membership: In 2008 the center reported that approximately 2,500 people participate to some degree in center activities.

Sources:

Tibetan Buddhist Learning Center. www.labsum.org.

Gonzalez, Arturo F., Jr. "New Jersey's Buddhist Shangri-La." *Coronet* (April 1950).

Wangyal, Geshe. *The Door of Liberation*. New York: Maurice Girodias Associates, 1973.

Tibetan Nyingma Institute

1815 Highland Pl., Berkeley, CA 94709

The Nyingma Institute was founded in Berkeley, California, in 1969 by Tarthang Tulku Rinpoche (b. 1935), a lama from eastern Tibet who left his homeland in 1959 when the Chinese assumed control. His father was a Nyingmapa lama, and as a youth Tarthang received instruction in each of the four major schools of Tibetan Buddhism. He later taught at the Sanskrit University in Varanasi, India, and began a project of reprinting Tibetan texts.

In Berkeley, drawing on the unreformed Nyingma tradition, Tarthang built a community centered on meditation, the recitation of the mantra of Padmasambhava, *Om Ah Hum Benza Guru Pema Siddhi Hum*, and the ideal of the *ngags-pa*, or householder-yogi, a dedicated religious practitioner living with family rather than in a monastery. He purchased a former fraternity house near the University of California campus and transformed it into a teaching center.

Continuing the work pursued in India, in 1970, Tarthang Tulku created Dharma Publishing, through which he has printed a number of books on Tibetan art, Buddhist teachings, and spiritual practice. Dharma Publishing has emerged as a major Buddhist publishing house that has an ongoing program to release copies of translations of Tibetan classics. Among its notable publications is the entire Kanjur and Tanjur, the basic Tibetan Buddhist canon, which has been reprinted in 128 Western-style volumes, and more than 600 additional volumes containing almost 80,000 texts retrieved from monasteries and libraries around the world. In 1975 he led the development of a rural retreat center, Odiyan. His community emerged as one of the earliest stable non-Japanese Buddhist organizations in North America.

Tarthang became known for his success at presenting the rather complicated insights of the Tibetan path in a contemporary format and language. He focused upon the application of Nyingma Tibetan Buddhist spirituality. Several of his books, such as *Gesture of Balance*, *Skillful Means*, and *Time, Space and Knowledge* (on meditation) and *Kum Nye Relaxation* (Tibetan yoga), found a readership far beyond Tarthang's students.

Through the 1980s and 1990s Tarthang founded additional centers in Europe and Latin America, the principal ones being in the Netherlands, Germany, and Brazil (two). In 1969 Tarthang also founded the Tibetan Aid Project to supply relief to Tibetan refugees exiled in India and the Himalayas. In more recent years the project has broadened its activity to include Tibetan monks and nuns in Tibet, India, Bhutan, Nepal, and Sikkim, rebuilding monasteries in Tibet, and making the public aware of the current situation inside Tibet.

Among Tarthang's most impressive accomplishments is the 1975 creation of Odiyan, in rural Sonoma County, California, which now serves as an international center focused on traditional Buddhist studies, the preservation of Tibetan culture, and providing space for the meeting of Eastern and Western knowledge. Odiyan's central temple was inspired by the monastery of Samye, founded in Tibet in 762 by Shantarakshita, Guru Padmasambhava, and the Dharma King Trisong Detsen. Northeast of the temple is the first large-scale stupa built in the United States, the seven-story golden Enlightenment Stupa.

The institute offers a variety of programs to enrich understanding of Buddhist teachings and Tibetan culture. Volunteers with the Nyingma work-study program live onsite and work with the Tibetan Aid Project, the Prayer Wheel Project, or the institute's volunteer staff. The institute hosts a four-month Human Development Training Retreat, which provides an intense period of study and practice of Nyingma teachings. State-authorized certification programs in meditation, psychology, and Nyingma teachings and practices are offered, as well as classes and workshops for lawyers and behavioral science workers. Interested practitioners can also participate in the Sacred Works Project, which prepares sacred Tibetan texts for Western eyes.

Membership: Not reported.

Sources:

Nyingma Institute. www.nyingmainstitute.com/.

Odiyan Buddhist Retreat Center. www.odiyan.org/.

Fields, Rick. *How the Swans came to the Lake*. 3rd ed. Boston, MA: Shambhala, 1992.

Tarthang Tulku. *Kum-Nye Relaxation*. Emeryville, CA: Dharma Publishing, 1978.

————. *Skillful Means*. Emeryville, CA: Dharma Publishing, 1978.

Unfettered Mind

264 La Cienega Blvd., Ste. 1083, Los Angeles, CA 90211

Ken McLeod was senior student of Kalu Rinpoche (1904–1989), the Tibetan Kagyupa master who established a number of the Kagyu Dharma centers in the United States. After his teacher's death, McLeod pioneered an approach to teaching that he hoped could effectively address spiritual development in a modern urban culture such as Los Angeles. Unfettered Mind, founded in 1990, follows much of the Kagyu tradition (supplemented with practices drawn from Mahayana Buddhism) and emphasizes McLeod's making himself available for private consultations with his students. His book *Wake Up to Your Life* (2001) presents the curriculum of practice and philosophy in which students of Unfettered Mind are trained. Much of McLeod's teaching is available on podcasts.

Unfettered Mind is now a loosely organized network of students and teachers in the United States and Canada who use a variety of methods to communicate, interact, and disseminate teaching.

Membership: In 2008 membership was estimated to be approximately 250 people.

Sources:

Unfettered Mind. www.unfetteredmind.org/.

McLeod, Ken. *Wake Up to Your Life*. San Francisco: HarperCollins, 2001.

Morreale, Don. *The Complete Guide to Buddhist America*. Boston: Shambhala, 1998.

United Trungram Buddhist Fellowship

155 Buff Rd., Cochecton, NY 12726

The United Trungram Buddhist Fellowship was founded in 1992 as a vehicle for the teaching of His Eminence Trungram Gyaltrul Rinpoche, a prominent Karma Kagyu monk. Trungram Gyaltrul is the lineage holder of the Trungram tradition, a specialized meditation tradition of the Kagyu School of Tibetan Buddhism. Trungram Gyaltrul is recognized as an emanation of the great yogi Milarepa.

After his recognition as the reincarnation of the third Trungram Gyaltrul Rinpoche (1894–1959), Rinpoche was given special tutoring by prominent Kagyu leaders, including the sixteenth Karmapa. He is also a practitioner of the Rimé teachings that had been transmitted from Dilgo Khyentse Rinpoche. He taught for the first time when he was only eleven years old. Later he traveled widely, which helped him to develop a large following beyond the Tibetan community in exile. Along with teaching Buddhism, he has developed strong interests in preserving the Tibetan heritage and in developing structures for humanitarian relief and educational service. Hence the founding of the United Trungram Buddhist Fellowship.

Trungram Gyaltrul Rinpoche works from Sankhu Monastery, located in the Sankhu, Nepal. There the Trungram Monastic Institute was founded in 1979 as a training center for monks who would represent the sangha around the world. The fellowship also has established dharma centers throughout the world as bases for teaching, group practice, and coordinating humanitarian efforts. They offer attendees a graduated course in meditation. There are also a number of small study groups that meet in members' homes to practice and discuss the teachings and work of the fellowship.

Dharmakaya, an affiliated organization of the United Trungram Buddhist Fellowship, has been charged with overseeing all dharma teaching activities for UTBF in the United States. The primary resident teacher for Dharmakaya is Ven. Khenchen Trinley Paljor Rinpoche, himself one of the chief lineage holders of the Kagyu school.

The fellowship has established centers in Nepal, Singapore, Hong Kong, Malaysia, and Indonesia. The largest number are in Taiwan.

Membership: Not reported. There are three centers in the United States, one each in Boston, New York City, and Seattle.

Sources:

United Trungram Buddhist Fellowship. utbf.org/en/.

Vajrakilaya Centers of North America

c/o Dudul Nagpa Ling, 7436 Sea View Pl., El Cerrito, CA 94530

The Vajrakilaya Centers were established by H. H. Orgyen Kusum Lingpa, a Dzogchen meditation master and renowned doctor of Tibetan medicine. He is also the supreme abbot of Thupten Chokor Ling, a monastery located in Golok, Eastern Tibet, and a Nyingma lineage holder with over 100,000 students worldwide.

It is believed by his followers that in a previous lifetime as Lhalung Palgyi Dorje, he was one of the 25 principal students of Padmasambhava, the eighth-century saint who brought Buddhism to Tibet, and that sealed in his mind are the teachings and transmissions received directly from Padmasambhava which are revealed today in the form of "mind treasures." Orgyen Menla, or Medicine Buddha, is one such treasure.

The centers are named for a Tibetan deity, Vajrakilaya, the supreme destroyer of obstacles to the attainment of enlightenment. His fierce form is looked upon as the embodiment of commitment to the development of wisdom, clarity, and compassion. Kusum Lingpa teaches meditation on this form by reciting the appropriate mantra with unwavering concentration. He has noted that the practice of Vajrakilaya is crucial now in order to overcome the many kinds of inner and outer upheavals so prevalent in this age.

Centers in the West have been established since Kusum Lingpa's initial visit in 1992.

Membership: Not reported. In 2008 there were 18 centers in the United States.

Sources:

Vajrakilaya Centers. www.omura.com/k_lingpa/kilaya1.htm.

Vajrayana Foundation

c/o Peme Osel Lilng, 2013 Eureka Canyon Rd., Corralitos, CA 95076

The Vajrayana Foundation is a Nyingma Tibetan Buddhist organization founded in 1987 by Lama Tharchin Rinpoche. Headquarters are at Peme Osel Ling, a 102-acre retreat center in the Santa Cruz Mountains south of San Francisco. Pema Osel Ling is the primary residence for Lama Tharchin Rinpoche, Tulku Thubten Rinpoche, and Khenpo Orgyen Thinley Rinpoche and serves as the administrative headquarters for Vajrayana Foundation.

Membership: Not reported. Vajrayana centers are located around the United States.

Periodicals: *Lotus Light*.

Sources:

Vajrayana Foundation. www.vajrayana.org/.

Morreale, Don. *The Complete Guide to Buddhist America*. Boston: Shambhala, 1998.

Yeshe Khorlo USA

2282-A Happy Day Overlook, PO Box 87, Crestone, CO 81131

Yeshe Khorlo is the name assumed by the contemporary followers of the fourteenth-century Bhutanese Buddhist master Padma Lingpa, who constitute the Drugpa branch of the Kagyu school of Tibetan Buddhism. His lineage holders have held the throne of Gangteng Gonpa Monastery in Bhutan, and the ninth and present throne holder is Gangteng Rinpoche. The Yeshe Khorlo center in Denver was founded in 1995. The Yeshe Khorlo centers around the United States have established a retreat center in Crestone, Colorado, known as Choying Dzong, which is recognized as the main center of Yeshe Khorlo in the United States.

Membership: Not reported. Yeshe Khorlo has six regional sanghas, in Los Angeles, California; Seattle; Washington; Santa Fe, New Mexico; Austin, Texas; and Boulder and Aspen, Colorado.

Periodicals: *Yeshe Khorlo*.

Sources:

Yeshe Khorlo. www.yeshekhorlo.org/.

Morreale, Don. *The Complete Guide to Buddhist America*. Boston: Shambhala, 1998.

Yeshe Nyingpo

19 W 16th St., New York, NY 10011

Yeshe Nyingpo was founded in 1976 by Dudjom Rinpoche, believed to be a reincarnation of one of Buddha's personal disciples and of Cheuchung Lotsawa, a disciple of Padmasambhava, who brought Buddhism to Tibet. Yeshe Nyingpo is envisioned as the instrument for the transmission of the pure Nyingmapa teachings and practice to the West. In 1980 Dudjom Rinpoche established a 50-acre spiritual retreat center, Orgyen Cho Dzong, in the Catskills under the guidance of Shenphen Dawa Rinpoche. The retreat center includes a traditional shrine room, an extensive library, meeting areas, and isolated retreat cabins for private meditation. The facilities are also open to other spiritual groups for retreats. Affiliated centers have been established across the United States and in Europe.

Membership: Not reported.

Sources:

Yeshe Nyingpo. www.tersar.org/YesheNyingpoNYC.html.

Yongey Buddhist Center

682 Carlsbad St., Milpitas, CA 95035

The Yongey Buddhist Center is the U.S. organization supporting the teachings and work of the seventh Yongey Mingyur Rinpoche (b. 1976). It came into being as the result of the fortuitous meeting of Mrs. Mei Yen Chen Ladle, a Chinese-American lay Buddhist, with Yongey Mingyur Rinpoche.

In 1998 Mrs. Ladle and her husband decided to build an enlightenment stupa on their property in northern California. As they enlisted the aid of friends in this endeavor, it was brought to their attention that placing the stupa on private property would greatly limit its access to the public. Therefore, Mrs. Ladle and others formed and incorporated the Buddhist Society for Supreme Enlightenment (BSFSE). When the stupa was completed in 2000, Mrs. Ladle invited H. E. Tai Situ Rinpoche to consecrate it. Tai Situ Rinpoche was unable to come, so at his suggestion, the invitation was passed to Yongey Mingyur Rinpoche.

As a child, Yongey Mingyur Rinpoche was identified as the reincarnation of Yongey Mingyur Dorjee (an eighteenth-century Buddhist master) by the sixteenth karmapa, the head of the Karma Kagyu School of Tibetan Buddhism. The karmapa gave him the name Karma Gyurmey Tenzin Chokyi Dorjee, and he was enthroned at age 12 by H. E. Tai Situ Rinpoche (b. 1954) at Sherib Ling, his monastery in northern India. Yongey Mingyur became an accomplished student and meditation master. In 1996, when he was twenty years old, Situ Rinpoche asked him to become his representative at the monastic seat Sherib Ling. He held this post from 1997 to 2002; since then he has traveled around the world teaching.

During his visit to consecrate the stupa, Mrs. Ladle asked Yongey Mingyur Rinpoche to return to northern California annually to teach and assume the role of BSFSE's dharma teacher for retreat and meditation. Rinpoche consented. A short time later, Mrs. Ladle attended a retreat given by Rinpoche in Taiwan, which deeply impressed her, and she led the society's board of directors to offer the nonprofit organization as a dharma center for Yongey Mingyur Rinpoche. When Rinpoche accepted, the organization was renamed Yongey Buddhist Center. It now serves as the outpost for Yongey Mingyur Rinpoche's global teaching work.

Membership: The center is not a membership organization. It is the sole U.S. center related to Yongey Mingyur Rinpoche.

Sources:

Yongey Buddhist Center. www.yongey.org/en/home.htm.

Yun Lin Temple

2959 Russell St., Berkeley, CA 94705

The Yun Lin Temple was founded in 1968 by Prof. Thomas Lin-Yun. It is a center of Black Sect tantric Buddhism of Tibet (the various major forms of Buddhism being distinguished by association with a color). The Black Sect traces its origins to the ancient Bon religion, which was dominant in Tibet at the time Buddhism was introduced in the eighth century C.E. Of the several sects of Tibetan Buddhism, the Black Sect retains most of the older Bon practices, and as it has grown and spread into China, it has incorporated elements of Chinese folk religion, healing practices, magic, and philosophy. A very eclectic system, it has encountered modern scientific thinking, and within the Yun Lin Temple attempts are made to reinterpret the tradition in modern forms.

Prof. Lin-Yun was born and raised in Beijing and even as a child began to study Buddhism with Lama Da-De, a teacher in the Black Sect tradition. He left mainland China as a teenager and relocated to Taiwan, where he found other members of the Black Sect school. He became a recognized authority on Feng Shui, the art of placement, a valued part of Chinese philosophy concerning the proper placement of objects such as houses to make beneficial use of the spiritual forces of the environment. The organization's Web site features a section on his Feng Shui teachings, written by Katherine Metz, known as "The Art of Placement." He came to the United States in 1980 and held teaching posts at the University of San Francisco, Stanford, and Seton Hall prior to his founding the temple, the first Black Sect center in the West. The temple offers regular classes taught by Prof. Lin-Yun on topics ranging from Ch'i, *I-Ching*, Feng Shui, Tang Dynasty poetry, calligraphy, holistic healing, folkloric cultures, and various meditation methods and also sponsors teachings and initiations given by high lamas and Buddhist masters. In 1993 Prof. Yu-Lin established the Cultural Center of the Yun Lin Temple in Berkeley. A year later he opened a second temple, the Lin Yun Monastery in Long Island, New York, which moved into its present eight-acre site in 1996.

Membership: Not reported.

Sources:

Yun Lin Temple. www.yunlintemple.org/.

 # Western Buddhism

American Buddhist Movement
301 W 45th St., New York, NY 10036

The American Buddhist Movement, also known as the Association of American Buddhists, was founded in 1980 as an independent Buddhist order to promote Buddhism in America and to ordain Buddhist monks. Rather than following any particular school of Buddhism, the movement respects all traditions as equal and encourages the unity of Buddhist thought and practice. Theravada, Mahayana, and Vajrayana Buddhists participated in the movement's founding. In defining its role, the movement asserts that an American form of Buddhism is possible and that Westerners do not have to adopt Asian cultural forms to be Buddhists.

The movement has established a variety of structures to perpetuate its program. Classes are offered on a variety of Buddhist concerns, including introduction to the several distinctive national traditions. Membership is open to all, and activities have been designed to serve those primarily affiliated with the movement as well as those affiliated with other groups. Kevin R. O'Neil has served as the movement's president since its inception.

Membership: In 2002 the movement reported 12,000 members in 535 centers. Most of these centers have their primary affiliations with the other Buddhist organizations discussed in this volume.

Educational Facilities:

Buddhist College, New York, New York.

Periodicals: *American Buddhist Newsletter*.

Sources:

American Buddhist. www.venkevinoneil.name/.

The American Buddhist Directory. New York: American Buddhist Movement, 1985.

Center for Timeless Wisdom
555 Bryant St., No. 302, Palo Alto, CA 94301

The Center for Timeless Wisdom was established in 1992 to provide Westerners access to nondualistic Asian wisdom (primarily Buddhism and Taoism). The center was founded by Dr. Peter Fenner, a Buddhist scholar who has taught and written in Buddhist studies, Asian philosophy, and East-West psychology in Australia and the United States for more than two decades. Through the 1980s and 1990s he also developed a form of inquiry that he espouses as a way to efficiently transmit the liberating wisdom of Buddhism and other nondualistic traditions in a pure and direct form.

The center views its work as being at the forefront of cross-cultural translation and productive of a refined synthesis of Eastern and Western wisdom. The distance of the average Westerner both in space and time from the ancient Eastern texts tends to communicate the impossibility of attaining enlightenment. However, Fenner attempts to combine perspectives found in Zen, Taoism, and the Buddhist Middle Path with an understanding of group dynamics in such a way that a simple and precise process for disclosing and releasing emotional and intellectual fixations emerges, and participants are meaningfully assisted in their spiritual progress.

The center's work is presented through dialogues, workshops, and retreats in Europe, the United States, and Australia. The Radiant Mind course is its core pro-

gram. The course presents the liberating essence of Asia's most profound wisdom traditions through an interactive process that opens up a way of being in which nothing more is needed to be complete and fulfilled. The course offers participants an opportunity to cut through blockades to spiritual progress and experience a state of "natural meditation" that is not disturbed by interpersonal activities and that dissolves the boundaries between practice and daily life. The participant is given skills for infusing all activities with peacefulness and clarity. In contrast to more traditional forms of spirituality, Living Wisdom is not based on ritual or present beliefs and practices. Instead it offers a method that responds to the emotional and intellectual rhythm of each participant.

Membership: In 2008 the center reported approximately 120 members. Besides its work in the United States, the center has maintained a presence in India, Canada, France, Germany, Spain, Australia, and Israel.

Sources:

Center for Timeless Wisdom. www.wisdom.org/timeless/center.htm.

Fenner, Peter. *The Ontology of the Middle Way*. Norwell, MA: Kluwer Academic Publishers, 1990.

———. *The Edge of Certainty: Dilemmas on the Buddhist Path*. Berwick, ME: Nocolas-Hays, 2002.

———. *Radiant Mind: Awakening Unconditioned Awareness*. Boulder, CO: Sounds True, 2007.

———. *Reasoning into Reality: A System-Cybernetics Model and Therapeutic Interpretation of Buddhist Middle Path Analysis*. Sommerville, MA: Wisdom Publications, 1995.

Fenner, Peter, and Penny Fenner. *Intrinsic Freedom: The Art of Stress-Free Living*. Agoura, CA: Millennium Books, 1994.

Chan Nhu Buddhist Pagoda
7201 W Bayaud Pl., Lakewood, CO 80226

The Chan Nhu Buddhist Pagoda is a significant center seeking a new way for American Buddhists, especially females. It was founded in 1985 by Ayya Chan Nhu, a Vietnamese nun, later assisted as codirector by Dharmapali (Martha Sentnor). Though begun as a Vietnamese center, Chan Nhu came to believe that the temple would be of more use as an open Buddhist space. Thus it has come to house a Chinese Pure Land group, a Tibetan Vajrayana group, and a Vipassana meditation group. In addition, other groups may use the facilities for classes, retreats, or weekly meditation sessions.

Dharmapali began in Theravada Buddhism in the Sri Lankan community in Washington, D.C., but rejected what she saw as the inherent sexism in the rules regarding monastics. However, she went on to become a nun, taking her vows first with the Thai-based community led by Ajahn Sumedho in England and then with the Sri Lankan community in New York City. She has a goal of creating a nunnery which combines Thai and Sri Lankan practice with some elements of Mahayana Buddhism.

Membership: Not reported.

Periodicals: *Newsletter*.

Sources:

Bucher, Sandy. *Turning the Wheel: American Women Creating the New Buddhism*. San Francisco: Harper and Row, 1986.

Rawlinson, Andrew. *The Book of Enlightened Masters: Western Teachers in Eastern Traditions*. La Salle, IL: Open Court Press, 1997. 650 pp.

The Frederick P. Lenz Foundation for American Buddhism
1901 Avenue of the Stars, Ste. 1100, Los Angeles, CA 90067

Rama Seminars was founded by Tantric Zen Master Rama (Frederick Lenz) in 1985 to carry on and supersede Lakshmi, an organization he had formed in the 1970s.

Lenz is a former English professor and disciple of Sri Chinmoy, with whom he studied for 11 years. Under the name Atmananda, given him by Chinmoy, he taught yoga in New York and Europe. He left Chinmoy and, moving to California in 1979, founded Lakshmi. During the early years of his work in California, his students began to report a number of extraordinary experiences. According to the reports, Lenz would levitate, disappear completely, and/or radiate intense beams of light during group meditations. Soon after these reported experiences, at a gathering of approximately 100 students, Lenz announced that eternity had given him a new name, "Rama."

Rama taught that humanity is at the end of a cycle. The present period, Kali Yuga, is a dark age. At the end of each cycle or age, Vishnu (a deity of the Hindus) is due to take incarnation. While Rama made no claim to be the same conscious entity as the historic Rama, a previous incarnation of Vishnu, he did claim to be the embodiment of the "particular octave of celestial light which was once incarnated as Rama."

By 1985 there were approximately 800 full-time students in Lakshmi. Branches had been formed in Los Angeles, San Diego, San Francisco, and Boston. Lakshmi seemed inadequate to the growing task. Rama Seminars was formed to provide a "more sophisticated format…to aid persons seeking enlightenment." Rama describes the teaching of Rama Seminars as Tantric Zen. He claimed to have been a Zen master in previous incarnations. Tantric Zen was described as a formless Zen, closely related to Chan (Chinese Zen), Tibetan Vajrayana Buddhism, Taoism, and jnana yoga.

During the 1990s, amid a controversy centered upon accusations of his misconduct by former members, Lenz relocated to New York and disbanded his organization. He taught computer science and founded a successful computer company, Advanced Systems, Inc., and authored two best-selling books titled *Surfing the Himalayas* (1994) and *Snowboarding to Nirvana* (1997). In 1995 he was cited by *New York* magazine as one of the "100 Smartest New Yorkers." He died at the age of 48 in April 1998 in an accident at his home in Long Island, New York. The exact circumstances of his death remain unclear.

The Frederick P. Lenz Foundation for American Buddhism was organized after Lenz's death to continue to promote his teachings on Buddhist practices, primarily through sales of the founder's books, audiotapes, and music.

Membership: Not reported.

Periodicals: *Self-Discovery*.

Sources:

The Frederick P. Lenz Foundation for American Buddhism.
  www.fredericklenzfoundation.org.

The Last Incarnation. Malibu, CA: Lakshmi Publications, 1983.

Lenz, Frederick. *Life Times*. New York: Fawcett Crest, 1979.

Rama [Frederick Lenz]. *The Wheel of Dharma*. Malibu, CA: Lakshmi Publications, 1982.

Friends of the Western Buddhist Order (FWBO)
c/o Aryaloka Buddhist Center, 14 Heartwood Cir., Newmarket, NH 03857

The Friends of the Western Buddhist Order (the FWBO) was founded by the Ven. Maha Sthavira Sangharakshita (b. 1925) as an instrument of a new Buddhist tradition for the West that would draw upon the whole Buddhist tradition while emphasizing its central principles in order to meet the spiritual needs of the modern world. Sangharakshita was born Denis Lingwood in South London, United Kingdom. Largely self-educated, he developed an interest in Eastern teachings as a youth and at the age of 16 realized that he was a Buddhist.

He went to India during World War II and stayed on to become the Buddhist monk Sangharakshita ("protected by the spiritual community"). He studied in the Theravada, Mahayana, and Vajrayana Buddhist traditions under eight primary teachers during a particularly formative time in the 1950s. Sangharakshita became

an accomplished teacher, a much-requested speaker, and author of more than 40 books. Sangharakshita worked for the revival of Buddhism in India, particularly through his work with the former Untouchables. He knew Dr. Bhim Rao Ambedkar (1891–1956), the Buddhist leader among the Untouchables, and after Ambedkar's death he continued to work for their conversion to Buddhism, which Ambedkar had started.

The FWBO is committed to presenting Buddhism in a way felt to be relevant to the modern world. The modern environment of industry, technology, and communications is a world away from the conditions under which traditional Buddhism evolved and thrived. While some of the forms through which Buddhism has been expressed need change, the FWBO believes that the essence of Buddhism is universal and unchanging, and it is this essence that it is trying to communicate. As heirs to the whole of Buddhism through Sangharakshita's several teachers, the FWBO emphasizes the unity of Buddhist teachings. Practitioners study and apply teachings from each of the three phases of Buddhist expression. Everyone learns to meditate and practice the five precepts and to reflect on fundamental principles that lead to Enlightenment. Going for Refuge to the Three Jewels is emphasized as the central act of being a Buddhist.

At the heart of the FWBO is the Western Buddhist Order, a body of men and women who have committed themselves to following the Buddhist path to enlightenment and made that commitment the central point of their lives. At the time of their ordination all order members undertake to practice the traditional set of ten precepts guiding actions of body, speech, and mind. Four "acceptances" are also part of the ordination, committing order members to practice for the attainment of enlightenment for the sake of all beings, with respect to the sangha and the teachers.

The order offers an alternative to the model found in some forms of Eastern Buddhism where everyone is either a monk or a lay person. It is open to any man or woman who is sincerely committed to the Buddhist path, not just to those who want to live a monastic lifestyle. Although order members aim to lead a 100 percent Buddhist life, they are not monks or nuns. The emphasis is not on the lifestyle but on the spiritual commitment. Some order members live a monastic life in a retreat center while others live with their families and pursue careers. Some work with a team of other Buddhists in a right livelihood business; still others are supported in order to work at their local FWBO center.

Membership: In 2008 the FWBO reported 1,500 members in 150 urban centers, retreat centers, and activities in more than 20 countries. The FWBO is one of the principal Buddhist movements in the United Kingdom, India, and Australasia and is well established in western Europe and the United States. It is also active in Canada, Mexico, Venezuela, and South Africa. Around the globe, tens of thousands of people attend sitting groups, discussion groups, classes, and retreats and work together in businesses, dharma outreach, and social projects.

Sources:

Friends of the Western Buddhist Order. www.fwbo.org.

Free Buddhist Audio. www.freebuddhistaudio.com.

Subhuti, Dharmachari (Alex Kennedy). *Buddhism for Today: A Portrait of a New Buddhist Movement*. Glasgow: Windhorse Publications, 1988. 234 pp.

Great Western Vehicle
PO Box 41795, Tucson, AZ 85717-1795

The Great Western Vehicle was founded by Sotopanna Jhanananda (the religious name of Jeffrey S. Brooks), a self-ordained western Buddhist monk. He describes the Great Western Vehicle as a Fourth Wheel Buddhist tradition, meaning it lies outside the major Theravada, Mahayana, or Vajrayana traditions. He sees the new tradition as an engaged ecstatic and contemplative tradition that seeks to emphasize Buddhist philosophy and contemplative practices so that they can be contextualized within any culture or religious tradition. Jhanananda brings to his presentation of Buddhism the study of mystic teachers from the broad spectrum of the world's religions. His study convinced him that enlightenment is available to anyone at any time.

Having completed his family obligations, Brooks quit his job, withdrew from society, and became a full-time contemplative monk. Through three years of practice he had many of the inner experiences reported in the mystic literature and accomplished many of their spiritual attainments. Based upon his attainments, Jhanananda offered himself as a teacher who is capable of interpreting the Buddhist texts, but his speaking of his own experiences became a matter of tension between himself and other Buddhist leaders, especially those in the monastic community.

Jhanananda primarily works with the texts of thepali canon, which he believes to be the least culturally determined practice strategy (*magga*) and philosophy (*dhamma*) and thus accessible to the largest number of people, especially those not raised as Buddhists. Janananda is currently attempting to produce a new translation of some of the pali texts.

The Great Western Vehicle began to provide support for contemplatives who had found gnosis (wisdom) through meditation. It initially reached out by forming an Internet support group that went online on April 9, 2003. By 2006 it had more than 650 members. The original support group soon multiplied into several groups focused on particular traditions. At the same time, an archive of useful texts and of personal stories of experience with meditation was created.

As the support groups grew, Jahnannada created a teacher-training and ordination program and started holding meditation retreats that focused on the attainment of gnosis in meditation, a subject he felt was missing from most meditation programs. Most of these programs were held in California and Arizona and included wilderness meditation retreats at the Inyo National Forest, where Jhanananda resides. Most recently, he has been joined by two meditation teachers, Michael Hawkins and D. Ernest Wachter.

Membership: Not reported.

Sources:

Great Western Vehicle. www.greatwesternvehicle.org/index.html.

Hoa Hao Buddhism

PO Box 3048, Santa Fe Springs, CA 90670

Hoa Hao Buddhism (Phat Giao Hoa Hao, or PGHH) is a reformist Buddhist movement combining elements of Vietnamese Buddhism with the popular veneration of ancestors. It is considered by its followers to be a "reform" branch of Buddhism and has abandoned an institutionalized priesthood while rejecting many of the ritual aspects of the more popular Vietnamese Buddhism. For instance, Hoa Hao altars display not Buddha statues but a piece of brown cloth.

Hoa Hao followers see their movement as an extension of the Buu Son Ky Huong (literally, "Strange Fragrance of Precious Mountains"), a Vietnamese group established in 1849. However, Hoa Hao Buddhism was formally launched in 1939 by Huynh Phu So (1919–1947), a charismatic youthful visionary. He taught basic Buddhist ideas coupled with the concept of the "Four Debts"—traditional duties owed to one's ancestors and parents, the fatherland, and one's compatriots—and Buddhist values. He launched the movement at Hoa Hao village in Tan Chau district, Chau Doc province, in the Mekong Delta near the Cambodian border. Hoa Hao was his birthplace. Within a few months the movement spread across Vietnam, and over the next two years Huynh Phu So composed four volumes that contained the basics of Hoa Hao doctrine. The movement distributed some 800,000 copies.

In 1945 Vietnam declared its independence, and Huynh Phu So allied with the Viet Minh to resist the French. On September 21, 1946, he established the Social Democrat Party of Vietnam (Viet Nam Dan Chu Xa Hoi Dang, also known as Dan Xa). But the alliance between the Hoa Hao and Viet Minh fell apart, and in 1947 he was executed by the Communists. Believers still hope that Huynh Phu So will soon descend back to earth and reappear among them. The group suffered persecution in the 1950s under the Ngo Dinh Diem regime. Only in 1963, after the fall of the

Diem government, was the movement able to reorganize and select a new administrative body. However, after the reunification of Vietnam in 1975, government authorities again moved against the organization by confiscating Hoa Hao properties, abolishing its organizational structure, and banning its public celebrations. The group was no longer allowed to distribute its sacred scriptures.

Beginning in the 1970s, Hoa Hao followers began to move to the United States as part of the postwar migration. Subsequently the international authority of the movement was reestablished in America. Membership is concentrated largely in Vietnam and the United States, the greatest number in the former. Followers are concentrated in the Mekong Delta region. Leadership is provided by a Central Council of Administrators under which a set of provincial and local administrative committees operate.

In 1999 the Vietnamese government officially recognized the Hoa Hao community, and in May of that year a group of 160 Hoa Hao delegates was able to convene a congress in An Giang province with government approval. However, the new organization has not been able to gain control of the movement because many followers both inside and outside the country view it as a government-dominated organization. The Hoa Hao community in Vietnam has continued to report incidents of religious persecution at the hands of the government.

Periodicals: *HHB Today.*

Membership: In 2002 the organization reported more than 3,000 centers of activity across Vietnam and some 2 million members. There were some 10,000 preachers. The much smaller membership in America was not reported.

Sources:

Hoa Hao Buddhism. hoahao.org.

Biography and Teachings of Prophet Huynh Phu So. Santa Fe Springs, CA: Hoa Hao Buddhist Overseas Office, 1983.

Tai, Hue-Tam Ho. *Millenarianism and Peasant Politics in Vietnam*. Cambridge, MA: Harvard University Press, 1983.

Phoenix Buddhist Network

PO Box 5076, Scottsdale, AZ 85261

The Phoenix Buddhist Network includes a diverse set of Buddhist centers and activities among Buddhists in the greater Phoenix area and across Arizona. It includes the Arizona Buddhist Temple, Arizona Zen Buddhist Society, Phoenix Buddhist Association, and Drikung Kagyu Buddhist Center, among others. An emphasis is placed on both meditation and mindfulness and service in the community. Also associated with the centers in Arizona is the Rosemead Buddhist Monastery in Rosemead, California, and Bhante Chao Chu, the abbot who serves as the spiritual head of the network.

Membership: Not reported. In 2008 the network's Web site listed 31 centers and groups.

Periodicals: *Common Sense.* • *Phoenix Buddhist Network Newsletter.*

Sources:

Phoenix Buddhist Network. www.phoenixbuddhists.org.

Morreale, Don. *The Complete Guide to Buddhist America*. Boston: Shambhala, 1998.

 # Shinto

Church of World Messianity

960 S Kenmore Ave., Los Angeles, CA 90006

Sekai Kyusei Kyo, generally known by its English name, the Church of World Messianity, is also known as Johrei Fellowship. It was originally founded by Mokichi Okada (1882–1955), usually referred to by his honorific title, Meishu-sama. Raised in poverty and beset with illness and business failure, Okada in the 1920s turned to religion and joined Omoto, one of the newer religions of Japan. In

1926, however, he began to receive revelations, as a result of which he began to see himself as a channel for the Light of God. He understood his mission to be the transmission of *Johrei*, the Light of God for the purification of the spiritual body. Such purification would lead to the elimination of spiritual clouds, resulting in health, prosperity, and peace, ultimately creating an ideal world, a paradise on earth.

In 1934 Okada left Omoto and founded Dai Nihon Kannon Kai (Japan Kannon Society). As World War II approached, innovative religious groups were suppressed, and Okada had to give up the practice of *Johrei* until after the war, though the movement continued to grow. During the war, Okada moved to Hakone and constructed a "paradise," a model of a future paradise on earth. A second such model was built in Atami a few years later. After a series of name changes, the church assumed its present name, Sekai Kyusei Kyo, in 1957, two years after Okada's passing, which occurred on February 10, 1955. Okada was succeeded by his wife, Yoshi, who served as spiritual leader until she passed away in 1962. Their daughter, Itsuki Fujieda, took over at that point and is still serving as the church's spiritual leader.

In the years after the war, members of the church immigrated to the United States. Okada sent Rev. Kiyoko Higuchi and Rev. Henry Ajiki to the United States to organize the church. The first center outside of Japan was incorporated in 1953 in Honolulu, Hawaii, followed by the second one in Los Angeles, California, in 1954.

Membership: During the past 40 years, more than a dozen centers have been established in many states, including several on the East Coast. Internationally, the church has spread to nearly 40 countries, including Brazil, Korea, and Thailand.

Periodicals: *Johrei Newsletter*.

Sources:

Clarke, Peter B. "Modern Japanese Millenarian Movements: Their Changing Perception of Japan's Global Mission with Special Reference to the Church of World Messianity in Brazil." In *Japanese New Religions: In Global Perspective*, ed. Peter B. Clarke. London: Curzon Press, 2002.

Introductory Course of World Messianity and Joining the Church. Los Angeles: Church of World Messianity, 1976.

The Light from the East: Mokichi Okada. Atami, Japan: MOA Productions, 1983.

Members' Handbook. Atami, Japan: Church of World Messianity, n.d.

M. Okada, A Modern-Day Renaissance Man. New York: M. Okada Cultural Services Association, 1981.

Teachings of Meishu-Sama. 2 vols. Atami, Japan: Church of World Messianity, 1967–1968.

Hawaii Kotohira Jinsha

Hawaii Ichizuchi Jinga, 2020 S King St., Honolulu, HI 96817

The Rev. Shina Miyake founded the Hawaii Ichizuchi Jinga in Honolulu in 1913. In 1963, on the occasion of the group's fiftieth anniversary, a rebuilt shrine building was dedicated.

Membership: Not reported. There is one shrine in Honolulu, Hawaii.

Healing Society Movement

2450 W Broadway, No. 108, Mesa, AZ 85202

The Healing Society Movement utilizes Dahnhak, a movement that originated in Korea based upon the ancient Eastern practice of qigong. While related to ancient traditions, the modern Dahnhak movement was founded by Seung-Han Lee, who opened the first center in Seoul, South Korea, in 1985. Following an enlightenment experience at Mo Ak mountain in South Korea, he took the spiritual name Ilchi (literally "a finger pointing to the truth"), by which he is now known. Lee had engaged in a process of spiritual seeking and development that led him to explore older approaches to spirituality. He modernized what he had discovered to create Dahnhak. The movement has subsequently spread to North and South America.

The practice of Dahnhak centers upon the appropriation and use of ki (also known as chi), the life force, a common element in various Eastern meditation systems, exercise formats, and martial arts. Dahnhak defines ki as the cosmic energy that circulates throughout the universe, which is the true essence of every living entity. Dahnhak practice follows a five-step program in which qigong exercises are introduced successively in order to introduce the individual to ki energy, to allow the accumulation of ki in the body's lower energy center (the Dahnjon), and the awakening and development of the Middle Dahnjon. The result of basic practice should be a state of habitual joy and peace. At a more advanced stage, the body energy meridians (the same energy paths identified in acupuncture systems) are opened so that the body is fully aligned to the energy flow of the universe. The goal of Dahnhak practice is Human Perfection in which the illusion of the ego is released and one identifies with the True Self, at which point there is a mystic realization of one's unity with all that exists.

Lee moved to the United States in 1994 and in 1997 established the Sedona Dahn Institute, now known as Healing Society in Action, which has become the center of the movement in the West. The many centers are headed by Dahnhak master teachers trained by Lee.

The Healing Society Movement also utilizes the practice of Brain Respiration, which is a five-step self-improvement program designed to help people both physically and mentally by repairing the brain energy circuits, awakening and developing one's brain potential, and maximizing one's own natural healing power. It also teaches its philosophy of "Peaceology," which regards the Earth as the living maternal source of all human life and the homeland of all human beings. This philosophy promotes the idea that we are "Earth-Humans" not separated from each other by nation, religion, or race.

In 2000 Lee joined together with Neale Donald Walsch, who had channeled the popular New Age volumes *Conversations with God*, to establish the New Millennium Peace Foundation, which has as its goal the building of a lasting world peace by raising human awareness. The group's Web site offers online consultations and classes as well as messages, meditations, and healing tips.

Membership: Not reported. More than 300 Dahnhak centers worldwide are in Korea, Japan, the United States, Canada, Brazil, and the United Kingdom.

Sources:

Healing Society in Action. www.healingsociety.org/.

Lee, Seung-Heun. *Dahnhak: The Way to Perfect Health*. Seoul, Korea: Dahn Publications, 1999.

———. *Healing Society: A Prescription for Global Enlightenment*. Charlottesville, VA: Hampton Road Publishing, 2000.

Honkyoku Shinto

Honkyoku-Daijingu Temple, 61 Puiwa Rd., Honolulu, HI 96817

Honkyoku Shinto bases its beliefs on the ancient Shinto text the *Kojiki* and sees itself as the Way of Nature, the spontaneous manifestation of the order of being taking form in human life. Worship is centered upon Amenominakanushi no kami (The Deity Who Is Lord of the Center of Heaven), the primary source of all. On the altar of the Honkyoku shrine are a mirror and a ball, which symbolize God. This absolute deity gives rise to two other deities: Takamimusubi no kami and Kamimusubi no kami. The world arises from the interaction of these two very different deities. From them arise other deities, the Japanese Imperial family, and the Japanese people. Through the ancestors of those now living, the people are tied to the divine as a great spiritual body. Shinto faith is best expressed in practice, reverence to the gods and one's ancestors, devotion to the Imperial family, and patriotism.

Honkyoku Shinto prospered during the first half of the twentieth century. On the eve of World War II it could report over 3,300 centers and 1.2 million members in Japan. It was also the earliest Shinto group to establish itself in Hawaii. The Daijingu Temple in Honolulu was founded around 1906 by Rev. Masasato Kawasaki. Because of its intense Japanese nationalism, it was closed, and the property confiscated, during World War II. A new temple was built after the war. In 1949 a statue of one of the Shinto goddesses confiscated and sent to Japan by the U.S. government was returned and enthroned at the Honolulu temple, then located on Buckle Street.

The Honkyoku temples in Hawaii hold monthly public services, but most worship is individual and private. There are annual festivals on New Year's Day and the second Sunday of September. As of 2003 Bishop Kazoe Kawasaki was head of the Honolulu temple.

Membership: There are two Daijingu temples, one in Honolulu and one in Hilo, Hawaii. In 2003 the Honolulu temple was reported to have 4,000 members.

Honmichi (Original Way)
4431 Wilshire Blvd., Los Angeles, CA 90010

Honmichi (Original Way) was established in 1925 as Tenri Association for the Study of Heavenly Truth (Tenri Kenkyukai) by Onishi Aijiro (1881–1958). Onishi, a former leader in Tenrikyo, believed that the founder of Tenrikyo, Nakayama Miki (1798–1887), was a mediator of divine truth to the Tenrikyo movement but that her mission had ended in August 1913, at which time the kami of truth, *Kanrodai-Sama*, chose him as the *tenkeisha* (revealed one) and appointed him to replace her.

Onishi established his independent work after being expelled from Tenrikyo in 1924. However, he quickly ran into trouble with the government when in 1928 he and several members were arrested for having distributed a pamphlet, *Kenkyu Shiryo* ("Research Materials"), that denied the divine status of the emperor and prophesied war and national crisis. Onishi spent seven years in jail. In 1939, after being freed, he distributed the pamphlet again and he and his members were again arrested for the same crime. His group was disbanded and he spent the rest of World War II in jail. In March 1946, under the new freedoms of the postwar era, Onishi restarted his movement under its new name, Tenri Honmichi (Original Way of Heavenly Truth), later dropping the first half of the name.

Honmichi's movement derives many of its beliefs from Tenrikyo and its scriptures—the *Ofudesaki* (Tip of Divine Writing Brush) and the *Migakura-uta*—which had been revealed to Nakayam Miki. Honmichi worship centers on the veneration of a group of ten *kami* or gods, of whom the most prominent is Tenri-O-no-Maced (God of Heavenly Reason). These kami form the core of the universe. Honmichi also emphasizes the Tenrikyo notion of *hinokishin* (voluntary activity of a mental and physical kind), which calls on members to combine the movement's teachings with selfless service to others.

Honmichi considers "right-mindfulness" to be the key to health, happiness, and peace. Right-mindfulness may be attained with the assistance of *Kanrodai-Sama*, the proper state of mind, and upon aligning the mind with the will of God. A lack of right-mindfulness correlates with misfortune, sickness, and unhappiness—evil forces that obstruct God's efforts to assist humankind. Honmichi members hope to create a paradise on earth in which humans can live in peace and harmony. However, they also believe that a world war and other catastrophes will afflict humanity prior to the manifestation of the paradise state.

Honmichi members began migrating to the United States in the 1970s and have recently formed the single overseas branch of the movement in Los Angeles. After Onishi's death in 1958, he was succeeded by his grandson, Onishi Yasuhiko (b. 1960), who is viewed as Aijiro's reincarnation and thus the new *Kanrodai-Sama*.

Membership: As of 2008, the membership of Honmichi in Japan is estimated to stand at 320,000. There are several hundred adherents associated with the center in Los Angeles.

Sources:

Clarke, Peter B., ed. *A Bibliography of Japanese New Religions*. Eastbourne, Kent, U.K.: Japan Library, 1998.

Shimazono, Susumu. "The Development of Millennialistic Thought in Japan's New Religions: From Tenrikyo to Honmichi." In *New Religious Movements and Rapid Social Change*, ed. James Beckford, pp. 55–87. London: Sage, 1986.

Konko Churches of North America (KCNA)
PO Box 221130, Sacramento, CA 95822

The Konko Churches of North America (KCNA) is an organization of several churches in the United States, Canada, and Japan that practice the Konkokyo tradition. Konkokyo was founded in 1859 by Bunjiro Kawate (1814–1883) (later given the title Konko Daijin), a Shinto farmer, who after years of misfortune and illness had a revelation of God as Tenchikane no kami, the parent God of the universe. God revealed to him that the prosperity of men is the ultimate purpose of creation and that God without that purpose realized is morally imperfect. In 1885 Konkokyo was recognized as one of the thirteen approved forms of sectarian Shinto in Japan, but in 1900 it was finally recognized as a separate religion.

The interrelation of God and man is the key to Konkoyo teaching. Man cannot exist apart from God, and God's work can only be complete through man. Konko Daijin was the mediator who informed humankind of this fellowship. Priests continue to function as mediators, just as Konko Daijin functioned. The process of mediation (*toritsugi*) is quite similar to Roman Catholic confessions.

Rites and ceremonies follow Shinto practice but are demythologized. Konkokyo is monotheistic and does not practice divination or magic. Much more emphasis is placed on the sermon, piety, and social concern. Belief in God with sincerity and a pious life are cardinal virtues. Social concerns have led to the founding of a hospital, a public library, museum, leper missions, and prison work.

Konkokyo was established in the United States in 1919 by Mr. and Mrs. Bunjiro Hirayama, who founded the Konko Kyo Association of Seattle, Washington. A second center was opened in Tacoma in 1923. Three years later the Rev. Kokichi Katashima, a Konko official from Japan, visited the Washington centers and, on his return route to Japan, organized believers who had recently migrated to Los Angeles and Honolulu. The work grew until the disruption of World War II and the internment of most of the leadership. The San Francisco headquarters were reestablished in the fall of 1945. The post–World War II freedom of religion in Japan has allowed Konkokyo to grow and spread as a vigorous movement.

Membership: Not reported. In 2008 the organization reported 12 churches in the United States (apart from Hawaii), 2 in Canada, and 1 in Japan. The Konko Missions of Hawaii (KMH) comprises an additional six churches.

Periodicals: *Konko Review*.

Sources:

Konko Churches of North America. www.konkofaith.org/.

Daily Service Book. San Francisco: Ministerial Staff of Konko Churches of America, 1971.

Fukuda, Yoshiaki. *Outline of Sacred Teaching of Konko Religion*. San Francisco: Konko Missions of North America, 1955.

Hombu, Konkokyo, ed. *The Sacred Scriptures of Konkokyo*. Konko-cho, Japan: Konkokyo Hombu, 1933.

Konko Daijin, A Biography. San Francisco: Konko Churches of America, 1981.

Konko Kyo's 50 Years in America. San Francisco: Konko Churches of America, 1976.

Ryugu, U.S.A.
11958 Hartsook St., North Hollywood, CA 91607

Ryugu, U.S.A., is a Shinto organization headed by Himiko Fujita, known among her followers as Mother Otohime, and revered as a living Shinto goddess. She was born near Mt. Aso at Kumamoto, Japan. Her followers claim that her birth was heralded in the writings of Degichi Onisabuo (1871–1948), the founder of Omoto, and Yoshisane Tomokiyo, founder of Tenkokyo Shinto, two Japanese new religions. As a child she had experiences of the ancient "holy spirits." Then in 1949 she was spiritually awakened and came to know the great love of Mother Deity.

In 1958 she felt led by Heaven to go to the Kansai district and began training herself for spiritual perfection at the sacred area on Ohmine Mountain. Her various spiritual experiences climaxed on October 7, 1973, as she stood before a great stone, Ama-no-Iwato (the Heavenly Gate of the Rock Cave), at Himuki, Kumamoto Province. As she looked at the stone, it suddenly opened and the Shinto deity Amaterasu Omikami (the Sun Goddess) appeared to her in the form of a mermaid. Striking Himiko on the forehead, the goddess said, "I have lain hidden behind the Great Rock Gate for twelve thousand years, but I have now come back to life again in thy soul in order to prevent the world from extinction." These words gave Mother Otohime her mission in life.

In 1981 Mother Otohime had a dream. A snow white horse carried her on a flight over a Shinto shrine at the foot of a mountain. A short time later she was taken by a friend to the Izumo Great Shrine in Tamba Province. It was the shrine of her dream. She decided to remain and serve Amaterasu as a shrine maiden. As part of her duties, she left the shrine on a tour of 46 countries, including the United States, to bring to each a special stone with divine energy from Ryugu Kai (the Sea Goddesses). Ryugu, U.S.A., was formed as a result of her visit.

Ryugu is an expression of the maternal love of the goddess and comes as a blessing on the world. Mother Otohime offers the opportunity to all human beings to have their inner Rock Gate opened, which will bring to consciousness old memories of the love of Amaterasu and a merger of God and Human into a state of oneness.

Membership: Not reported.

Shinreikyo

c/o Kameo Kiyota, 310C Uulani St., Hilo, HI 96720

Shinreikyo is a post–World War II Japanese healing group based on Kami-no-michi, the Way of God. Shinreikyo was founded by Master Kanichi Otsuka (1891–1972), viewed by his followers as the great sage (who was to appear as Buddhism lost its power) and the messiah that Christians expected at the Second Coming. The message of Shinreikyo is that Kami-no-michi is the way to happiness and prosperity. It is identified with Nippon Seishin, the Japanese spirit, common to all Japanese since ancient times and based on the laws of the universe. Such intense nationalism is typical of much Shinto.

At the center of Shinreikyo is its belief in healing miracles. Master Otsuka is said to attack disease in the three existences of past, present, and future. Accounts of healings of serious illnesses fill Shinreikyo literature. Shinreikyo came to the United States in 1963 when Kameo Kiyoto established a branch in Hilo, Hawaii. Literature in English is distributed by the Metaphysical Scientific Institute in Japan.

Membership: Not reported.

Sources:

Koepping, Klaus-Peter. "Ideologies and New Religious Movements: The Case of Shinreikyo and Its Doctrines in Comparative Perspective." *Japanese Journal of Religious Studies* 4/2–3 (June–September 1997): 103–149.

Sukyo Mahikari

23151 Camino Altozano, Rancho Santo Margarita, CA 92688
Alternate Address: International Headquarters: 2-956-1 Kamiokamoto-michi, Takayama City, Japan 506-0055.

Mahikari is the Japanese word for Divine True Light, believed to be a spiritual and purifying energy. Mahikari began in 1959 when Kotama Okada (1901–1974), at the time a member of the Church of World Messianity, received a revelation from God explaining how the use of the Divine Light of the Creator could produce health, harmony, and prosperity. Mahikari is viewed as a cleansing energy sent by Sushin, the Creator of Heaven and Earth, that both spiritually awakens and tunes the soul to its divine purpose. In 1960 he organized what became known as the Sekai Mahikari Bunmei Kyodan (Church of World True Light Children). Okada soon became known as Sukuinushisama (Savior).

God also revealed to Okada the existence of a Divine Plan. According to his teachings, all of the phenomena of the universe have been controlled by the Plan of the Creator. Under this plan, human souls are dispatched to Earth for the specific purpose of learning to utilize its material resources in order to establish a highly evolved civilization governed by spiritual wisdom. These revelations and teachings are to be found in the Mahikari scriptures *Goseigen, The Holy Words*, an English-language edition of which was published in 1982.

Okada dedicated his life to teaching the art of the Divine Light to anyone desiring to be of service to the Creator. Today it is taught in a three-day session at which attendees may learn to radiate the Light through the palm of the hand, a process known as Mahikari no Waza. At the time of initiation, new members receive an *omitama*, a pendent used to focus the light.

Just prior to his death in 1974 Okada passed the mission to his daughter, Seishu Okada, the present spiritual leader. Under her guidance, a new headquarters complex has been established at Suza, Takayama City, Japan. In 1985, a research center, the Civilization Research Institute (CRI), was established to bring science and spirituality together to examine pressing world issues. To that end, the institute hosts a series of seminars, international conferences, lectures, forums, and symposia on a number of topical subjects. Practitioners of Sukyo Mahikari have been active in the community, especially in the area of preservation and conservation of the environment and planting millions of trees around the world.

Membership: Not reported. In 2008, Sukyo Mahikari reported 18 centers in the United States, 1 in Puerto Rico, and 3 in Canada. There are associated centers in 14 countries.

Periodicals: *True Light*.

Remarks: It should be noted that the Church of World Messianity, of which Okada was a member prior to his revelations concerning Mahikari, has a similar teaching concerning what it calls *johrei*, God's healing light.

Also, after Okada's death, the leadership of his daughter was challenged by a prominent member, Sekiguchi Sakae. He filed a lawsuit and, upon winning, took possession of the former headquarters of the group. His son now leads a second Mahikari group in Japan.

Sources:

Sukyo Mahikari. www.sukyomahikari.org/index.html.

Davis, Winston. *Dojo*. Stanford, CA: Stanford University Press, 1980.

Goseigen, The Holy Words. Tujuna, CA: Sekai Mahikari Bunmei Kyodan, 1982.

Tebecis, A. K. *Mahikari, Thank God for the Answers at Last*. Tokyo: L. H. Yoko Shuppan, 1982.

Taishakyo Shinto

215 N Kukui St., Honolulu, HI 96817

Izumo Taishakyo Shinto, also known as Izumo Oyashirokyo, was one of the original 13 religious Shinto sects (as distinguished from the Shrine Shinto) in existence before World War II. It was founded in 1882 by Takatomi Senge at the ancient Grand Shrine of Izumo, located at Taishamachi, Shimane, Japan. The divinity that is enshrined there is one of the three Creator Gods, Okuninushi-no-Mikoto, the god of the spiritual and physical world, who settled the world and created the foundation upon which mankind and the rest of the universe exists. The group's teachings are set forth in the "Great Way," a catechism published in 1881. Man is to act in a sincere, virtuous, and trustworthy manner and must maintain proper relationships with his family, society, the leader of his country, God, and his environment. Man has a soul, born without sin, and upon death, the soul returns to the divine world.

The Hawaii Izumo Taisha was founded in 1906 by the Rev. Katsuyoshi Miyao as an affiliate of the Taishakyo sect. In 1923 a master shrine builder was brought from Japan to construct a shrine in Honolulu, Hawaii. Katsuyoshi Miyao died in 1935 and was succeeded by his son, the Rev. Shigemaru Miyao. During World War II, the shrine property was taken over by the city, due to the forced relocation of the Rev. Shigemaru Miyao, his family, and other leaders of the shrine organization. After release from the relocation camp, Miyao resumed church work at a temporary structure and reorganized and reincorporated the shrine organization in July 1952.

After over 10,000 petitions were gathered in 1953 and lengthy hearings were held, first by the city's board of supervisors and then by the court, the shrine property was finally returned in 1962. The original shrine built in 1923 was soon thereafter moved to its present site due to redevelopment of the original site. The shrine was finally repaired and restored in 1969. In 1996, the shrine observed its ninetieth anniversary celebration.

Membership: In 2001, Taishakyo Shinto had approximately 200 members.

Tenrikyo

Tenrikyo Mission Headquarters in America, 2727 E First St., Los Angeles, CA 90033

Of the various groups termed "new religions" in Japan, Tenrikyo is one of the largest, with more than two million members. The teachings of Tenrikyo had their origin in 1838, when Miki Nakayama, the wife of a well-to-do farmer in central Japan, began to go into trances and spoke as if God were speaking through her. Shortly after that she began to give away her family's possessions, finally reaching the depths of poverty. For a period of nearly 50 years she taught what had been revealed to her in trances to an ever increasing number of followers attached to her initially by her spiritual healing. According to the teachings of Tenrikyo, which Nakayama gave to the followers, the world is completely sacramental: everything is God; there is nothing but God, and all human beings were originally created by God with the intent that they live a life of joy, in peace with one another, being all brothers and sisters and of God. Nakayama committed the teachings to a book called the *Ofudesaki* ("Tip of the Writing Brush"), and instructed followers in several means of attaining the life of joy. The *Ofudesaki* is considered the Tenrikyo book of scriptures.

Tenrikyo teaches that human beings are essentially good but that during one's daily life "mental dust" is accumulated. The various kinds of dust identified are miserliness, covetousness, hatred, self-love, grudge-bearing, anger, greed, stinginess, and arrogance. These dusts cloud the mind, preventing one from truly seeing and understanding God's intent for human beings. By working to sweep this dust away, the mind will be opened to God's intent and thus to a joyous life, which Tenrikyo equates to salvation.

Of the several means of sweeping away this constantly accumulating dust, the most important is the service, to be performed with music, song, and dance. The service is performed monthly at every Tenrikyo church and mission worldwide. The principal part of the service is the repeated prayer "Ashiki o harote tasuku tamae, Tenri-O-no-Mikoto" (Sweeping away evils, please save us, Tenri-O-no-Mikoto), accompanied by hand motions symbolic of dust being brushed away from the mind. Tenri-O-no-Mikoto, or Lord of Divine Wisdom, is the formal name of God in Tenrikyo; another name more commonly used by followers is Oyagami-sama, or God the Parent, alluding to the father and mother nature of God as taught by Nakayama.

The rise of Tenrikyo coincided with a period of popular revolt in Japan. Because of the nature of its teachings, Tenrikyo is a strongly missionary religion, which brought it into conflict with the Japanese authorities in its early days. During the last 20 years of her life, Nakayama (called Oyasama, or "beloved parent," by her followers) and many ardent followers were severely persecuted by Japanese authorities, both civil and religious. It was not until after World War II that Tenrikyo as an independent religion was freed of government control.

Nakayama died in 1887. Her followers believe that she continues to reside and work, in spirit, for world salvation at the *jiba* (sanctuary) of Tenrikyo's main shrine in Tenri, Japan.

In its missionary activities, Tenrikyo spread to Korea and China in the first decades after receiving government recognition as a sect of Shinto in 1906. In 1927, at the time of Tenrikyo's fortieth anniversary, two missionaries, Yone Okazaki and Rinzo Torizawa, were sent to Seattle and began to work among members already living in the Pacific Northwest. By the beginning of World War II, churches and parishes had been established along the West Coast from San Diego to Vancouver, and by 1973 congregations had spread eastward to Chicago and New York.

Membership: In 2001 the North American headquarters reported 62 churches, 67 fellowships, and 5 mission centers in the United States, mostly in California. There are 800 *yoboku* (missionaries), and an estimated membership of 3,000.

Educational Facilities:

Tenri University

Tenri Seminary Schools

Tenri Language Institute (a school for missionaries going to countries overseas). All are located in Tenri City, Japan.

Periodicals: Tenrikyo Newsletter (English). • *Progress* (New York; English). • *Ichiretsu* (Japanese). • *Seijin* (New York; Japanese).

Sources:

Tenrikyo Mission Headquarters in America. www.tenrikyo.com.

The Life of Oyasama, Foundress of Tenrikyo. Tenri, Japan: Tenrikyo Church Headquarters, 1982.

Nishiyama, Teruo. *Introduction to the Teachings of Tenrikyo*. Tenri, Japan: Tenrikyo Overseas Mission Department, 1981.

Oyasato Research Institute, Tenri University. *The Theological Perspectives of Tenrikyo*. Tenri City, Japan: Tenri University Press, 1986.

Takano, Tomoji. *The Missionary*. Trans. by Mitsuru Yuge. Tenri, Japan: Tenrikyo Overseas Mission Department, 1981.

Tensho-Kotai-Jingu-Kyo

Hawaii Dojo, 888 N King St., Honolulu, HI 96817

Tensho-Kotai-Jingu-Kyo is a religion built around a remarkable charismatic figure, Sayo Kitamura (1900–1967), usually referred to as "Ogamisama" (The Great God) by her followers. A Japanese woman married to a farmer, Kitamura had no particular religious convictions until 1943, when a series of divine revelations began. She reported that the Absolute God, Tensho-kotai-jin, had descended into her body and told her to be the founder of the "Kingdom of God on Earth." The new religion spread rapidly and was registered with the government in 1947.

Tensho-kotai-jin is seen as the Absolute God of the universe, the heavenly Father (as in Christianity), and the eternal Buddha. The almighty God is a male-female pair, who by possessing Ogamisama (Kitamura) formed a trinity. Ogamisama's followers (like Ogamisama herself) described her in deific terms. She was seen to have powers of prophecy and healing. Ogamisama proclaimed 1946 as the first year of the New Era.

Ogamisama's sermons were sometimes "sung" while in a state of ecstasy and were always delivered spontaneously. Ogamisama taught her followers the prayers she received from God for the redemption of negative spirits and for world peace. As one way to express inner joy and gratitude, followers perform a dance (an ecstasy dance) in a state of non-ego.

Ogamisama's role is to establish the kingdom here and now by spreading God's teaching to humanity. The individual's responsibilities include a focus on purifying the world of the six roots of evil (regret, desire, hatred, fondness, love, and being loved excessively), redeeming evil spirits, severing personal karma, and continuing to improve the state of the soul with sincerity and courage.

Ogamisama made her first trip to Hawaii in 1952. She advised her listeners to burn the relics of Shinto and Buddhism, because they belonged to the past. The result of her trip was the establishment of eight branches of her religion. In October 1964, she began a nine-month worldwide tour that brought her to America for the last time. The movement had become worldwide by the time of her death in 1967. She was succeeded by her granddaughter, Kiyokazu Kitamura (b. 1950), revered as "Himegamisama."

The Tensho-Kotai-Jigu-Kyo's active evangelistic program is supported by a number of publications. The central document is *Prophet of Tabuse*, which introduces very briefly the life and teachings of Ogamisama. A periodical is published in Japanese, English, and Spanish, and other literature is available in 10 different languages. In the United States, there is an annual gathering of members (*doshi*) for a conference in each of the three divisions of the work—Hawaii, Northern California, and Southern California.

Membership: Not reported. In 1992, there were 13 Tensho-Kotai-Jingu-Kyo branches in Hawaii. Most of the mainland U.S. membership is located in several California communities, as well as in Seattle, Washington; Chicago, Illinois; and Bound Brook, New Jersey. Worldwide, centers are found in 76 countries.

Periodicals: *Voice from Heaven.*

Sources:

Clarke, Peter B. "Modern Japanese Millenarian Movements." In *Japanese New Religions: In Global Perspective*, ed. Peter B. Clarke, pp. 129–182. Richmond, Surrey, U.K.: Curzon Press, 2000.

Hamrin, Tima. "Illness and Salvation in Tensho Kotai Jingukyo." In *Japanese New Religions: In Global Perspective*, ed. Peter B. Clarke, pp. 240–257. Richmond, Surrey, U.K.: Curzon Press, 2000.

Lebra, Takie Sugiyama. "Logic of Salvation: The Case of a Japanese Sect in Hawaii." *International Journal of Social Psychiatry* 16, no. 1 (winter 1969/1970): 45–53.

Nishiyama Shigeru, and Fujii Takashi. "The Propagation and Spread of Tensho Kotai Jingukyo within Japanese American Society on Hawaii Island." *New Religions: Contemporary Papers in Japanese Religions*, ed. Nobutaka Inoue. Tokyo: Kokugakuin University, 1991.

Ogamisama Says . . . . Tabuse, Japan: Tensho-Kotai-Jingu-Kyo, 1963.

The Prophet of Tabuse. Tabuse, Japan: Tensho-Kotai-Jingu-Kyo, 1954.

Taoism

Da Yuan Circle

2633 Telegraph Cir., No. 305, Oakland, CA 94612

Da Yuan Circle is a modern Western group exploring the Daoism of Laozi—*wuwei-dao* (with references to *wuwei* interpretations found in Chan Buddhism and Dzogchen). The group's focus is the practice of *zuowang* (nonconceptual meditation) and is led by Liu Ming (born Charles Belyea). Teachings such as Chinese astrology, medicine, hygiene, and *neigong* (a breathing and meditation discipline) are also offered.

Membership: Not reported.

Sources:

Da Yuan Circle. www.dayuancircle.com.

Belyea, Charles. *Dragon's Play*. Berkeley, CA: Great Circle Lifeworks, 1991.

"The Shamanic Roots of Orthodox Daoism." *Tantra* 8 (1994): 54–57, 76.

Fung Loy Kok Institute of Taoism

International Taoist Tai Chi Society, 134 D'Arcy St., Toronto, ON, Canada M5T 1K3

Alternate Address: Fung Loy Kok Taoist Temple, Sam Tip Tem, Cheun Wan, New Territories, Hong Kong, China.

Fung Loy Kok Institute of Taoism was founded in Hong Kong in 1968 by the Taoist priest Mui Ming-to, his wife, Mui Tang Yuanmay, and the Taoist master Moy Lin-shin. The particular Taoist tradition can be traced to the Earlier Heaven Wu-chi Sect founded by the patriarch Tien Lung, who in turn had received the teaching of the Tao from Chen His I. Chaotic conditions in early-twentieth-century China led Taoist teachers to bring the teachings out of the monastic context to a lay public. In 1981 Master Moy and Mr. Mui established an institute in Toronto, the first of several additional branches to be opened in Canada and the United States. In 2007 construction was completed on the Quiet Cultivation Centre, which functions as an international training center and place for quiet contemplation of Taoist teachings.

The institute is dedicated to the teaching and practice of Taoism through the Taoist arts such as chanting, meditation, qigong, book discussions, internal exercises, and the promotion of charity for others through community service. An associated Taoist Tai Chi Society also teaches the art of tai chi, leading to an increase in humility, quietude, and compassion.

Membership: Not reported. In 2008 the institute reported branches throughout Canada, the United States, Australia, and New Zealand.

Sources:

International Taoist Tai Chi Society—Fung Loy Kok. www.taoist.org.

Wong, Eva, trans. *Seven Taoist Masters: A Folk Novel of China*. Boston: Shambhala, 1990. 178 pp.

Living Tao Foundation

PO Box 846, Urbana, IL 61803-0846

The Living Tao Foundation was founded in 1976 by Chungliang Al Huang, a Chinese artist and Taoist teacher who migrated to the United States in the 1960s. Following a year in China as a Ford Foundation scholar (1966–1967), he spent four years in Urbana, Illinois, as a postdoctorate fellow with the Center for Advanced Study and as artist-in-residence at the Krannert Center for the Performing Arts. He headed the Oriental Institute at York University for two years (1972–1974) and spent three years as the director of the Lan T'ing Institute for the Alan Watts Society for Comparative Philosophy. While at the institute he worked on finishing Watts's last book, *Tao: The Watercourse Way*, published several years after Watts's death in 1973. He is also the author of the classic *Embrace Tiger, Return to Mountain*.

The Living Tao Foundation emphasizes a synthesis of Eastern and Western ways through Taoist principles and uses various inner growth techniques. Huang is best known as a master of tai ji (or tai chi), the Chinese form of body movements believed to develop the natural coordination of body and mind. The foundation jointly sponsors the Lan Ting Institute, a cross-cultural study and conference center, with the government of the People's Republic of China. Huang is especially concerned with the recovery of Chinese culture, which suffered a severe blow from the Cultural Revolution in the 1970s; the institute sponsors trips to China to assist in that recovery. The foundation holds intensive study seminars on the Oregon coast.

Membership: Not reported.

Sources:

Living Tao Foundation. www.livingtao.org/.

Huang, Chungliang Al. *Embrace Tiger, Return to Mountain*. Moab, UT: Real People Press, 1973.

———. *Living Tao: Still Visions and Dancing Brushes*. Millbrae, CA: Celestial Arts, 1976.

"Tai Ji: The Dance of Life. An Interview with Chunglaing Al Huang." *Empty Vessal: A Journal of Contemparary Taoism* (spring 1994): 4–12.

Watts, Alan, with Chungliang Al Haing. *Tao: The Watercouse Way*. New York: Pantheon, 1975.

George Ohsawa Macrobiotic Foundation

1999 Myers, Oroville, CA 95966

Closely related to Taoism is macrobiotics, a philosophy developed by George Ohsawa (Yukikazu Sahurazawa, 1893–1966) drawing on Zen, Taoism, and Chinese wisdom philosophy. Macrobiotics is based on the concept of yin and yang. All things are differentiated apparatus of one Infinity. Yin and yang are the poles of the Infinity's bifurcation. Everything changes. Yin is centrifugal and yang centripetal. By their attraction and repulsion, energy and all phenomena are produced. All things are made of unequal proportions of yin and yang. All physical forms are yang (male) at the center and yin (female) at the surface.

The object of macrobiotics, for the individual, is to balance the yin and yang as far as possible in one's life. One ideally eats foods that are balanced; cereals and brown rice are good examples. One also learns to live in harmony with the environment.

Macrobiotics was introduced into the West in France by Ohsawa in the 1920s, and it gradually spread through Europe. By the time of his death in 1966 macrobiotic centers in Europe could be found in Belgium, England, Germany, Italy, Spain, and Sweden. From the center in Japan, work had also spread to Brazil and Vietnam. Macrobiotic teachings spread to America after World War II. During the 1950s Herman Aihara, a student of Ohsawa from Japan, migrated to the United States. He founded the Ohsawa Foundation, since renamed the George Ohsawa Macrobiotic Foundation. It was the first macrobiotic organization in North America and in 1961 began a periodical, *Yin Yang*. The foundation, through its publications and sponsoring of lecturers, became the focus of the early spread of macrobiotic teachings and continues as one of two national associations of people devoted to macrobiotic principles. It also sponsors the Fresh Meadows Summer Camp, which offers classes on macrobiotics, meditation classes, and exercise.

Membership: In 1997 the foundation reported 1,500 members in the United States, 60 members in Canada, and an additional 120 members worldwide. There is one center; it serves as a nexus of a network of independent macrobiotic centers around the United States and Canada.

Periodicals: *Macrobiotics Today*.

Sources:

George Ohsawa Macrobiotic Foundation. www.gomf.macrobiotic.net.

Aihara, Herman. *Seven Macrobiotic Principles*. San Francisco: George Ohsawa Macrobiotic Foundation, 1973.

Ohsawa, George. *The Book of Judgment*. Los Angeles: Ohsawa Foundation, 1966.

———. *Guidebook for Living*. Los Angeles: Ohsawa Foundation, 1967.

———. *Practical Guide to Far Eastern Macrobiotic Medicine*. Oroville, CA: George Ohsawa Macrobiotic Foundation, 1976.

———. *Zen Macrobiotics*. Los Angeles: Ohsawa Foundation, 1965.

One Peaceful World

Kushi Institute, Box 7, Becket, MA 01223

Michio Kushi (b. 1926), a student of George Ohsawa (1893–1966), the founder of the macrobiotic movement, came to the United States in 1949 and became active in the spread of its philosophy. Initially working through the Ohsawa Foundation (now the George Ohsawa Macrobiotic Foundation) headquartered in California, Kushi developed an independent following in New England. After Ohsawa's death Kushi founded the Order of the Universe Publications and in 1967 began to issue a periodical of that name. In 1972 Kushi founded the East West Foundation to oversee the spread of the work of presenting macrobiotics to the public and nurturing the growing number of people who had accepted macrobiotic principles and practice. In 1978 the Kushi Institute was founded to train leaders in the movement, known as the Macrobiotic Leadership Program. The institute also hosts the annual Summer of Healing conference, which brings together macrobiotic chefs, experts, authors, nutritionists, doctors, and teachers in order discuss the latest breakthroughs and techniques in natural healing.

Kushi's teachings are summarized in a set of theorems and principles that define the nature of yin and yang, the prime differentiation within the universe. All phenomena are composed of a complex of these two polar opposites, and macrobiotics defines and assists individuals in relating to the yin-yang composition of the universe. While a major component of macrobiotic philosophy relates to developing a balanced diet, the philosophy encompasses every area of life, as spelled out in numerous publications by Kushi and others.

Through the 1990s Kushi nurtured a network of people devoted to the twin issue of macrobiotics and peace, which became the One Peaceful World.

Membership: Not reported. In 1998 the institute functioned through national offices in 20 countries. A directory of the larger macrobiotic movement listed more than 400 individuals, businesses, and centers promoting the teachings, and the institute estimates that more than 800 people go through its courses every year.

Educational Facilities:

Kushi Institute, Beckett, Massachusetts.

Sources:

Kushi Institute. www.kushiinstitute.org/index.html.

Kohler, Jean Charles, and Mary Alice Kohler. *Healing Miracles from Macrobiotics*. West Nyack, NY: Parker Publishing, 1979.

Kushi, Michio. *The Teachings of Michio Kushi*. 2 vols. Boston, MA: East West Foundation, 1971.

———. *The Book of Macrobiotics*. Tokyo: Japan Publications, 1977.

Kushi, Michio, with Stephen Blauer. *The Macrobiotic Way*. Wayne, NJ: Avery Publishing Group, 1985.

Shrine of the Eternal Breath of Tao

117 Stonehaven Way, Los Angeles, CA 90049

The Shrine of the Eternal Breath of Tao was founded by Master Ni Hua-Ching, who began his study of Taoism as a child in China. After the Chinese Revolution, Ni moved to Taiwan and continued his studies. Eventually he became a teacher of Taoism and its related martial and healing arts. During the 1970s he moved to the United States and began to teach in Los Angeles.

Master Ni teaches the universal law of subtle energy response. Everything in the universe is a manifestation of energy in either its grosser or its more subtle states. Understanding and developing the proper response to the energies of one's environment will bring harmony to one's life. The practice of Taoist meditation, martial arts (kung fu and t'ai chi ch'uan), and medical practices (acupuncture and herbs) assist in attaining a balanced relationship to life. The universal law of response is basic to all spiritual practices.

Membership: Not a membership organization. The Center for Taoist Arts in Alpharetta, Georgia, is an affiliate of the Shrine.

Educational Facilities:

College of Tao, Santa Monica, California.

Yo San University of Traditional Chinese Medicine, Santa Monica, California.

Sources:

Ni, Hua-Ching. *Tao, the Subtle Universal Law and the Integral Way of Life*. Malibu, CA: Shrine of the Eternal Breath of Tao, 1982.

Taoist Sanctuary of San Diego

4229 Park Blvd., San Diego, CA 92103

Alternative address: Taoist Institute, 10630 Burbank Blvd, North Hollywood, CA, 91601.

The Taoist Sanctuary of San Diego traces its beginning to the Taoist Sanctuary founded in Los Angeles by Share K. Lew (b.1918) and Khigh Alx Dhieh (born Kenneth Dickerson, 1910–1991). Lew was born in China and lived for many years at the Yellow Dragon Monastery near Luofu Shan (one of the country's sacred mountains), where he learned the bread beliefs and practices of Taoism. He left China in 1948 to move to the United States. He began teaching in San Francisco. Though an ardent student of taioism and the *I Ching*, by the 1980s, Dhiegh was better know to television audiences as a popular character actor, frequently appearing on the heralded crime series *Hawaii 5-0*.

Formed in 1970, the Taoist Sanctuary became the first Taoist group to receive federal tax status as a religious organization. At the end of the 1970s, Lew moved to San Diego and Dhiegh to suburban Phoenix, and by the mid 1980s there were four affiliated sanctuaries, one each in North Hollywood, San Diego, and Santa

Barbara, California, and Tempe, Arizona. Following Dhiegh's death in 1991, the Santa Barbara center dissolved and the other three would follow separate paths. Lew trained a number of people who went on to assume teaching roles in the larger American Taoist community

Lew's organization in San Diego continues as the Taoist Sanctuary of San Diego with a focus upon the preservation and dissemination of information on traditional Chinese healing and martial arts and the teaching of Taijiquan (Tai Chi Chuan) and Qi Gong/Taoist Meditation. It is led by Bill and Allison Helm. Bill Helm was one of Lew's students. The Helms also studied with Grandmaster Chen Xiaowang, a master of Taijiquan and current representative of the Chen Family that created the practice. Chen now visits San Diego annually to offer seminars to the Sanctuary's constituency. Lew, now in his 80's, also continues to teach.

The original Taoist Sanctuary now exists as the Taoist Institute of Los Angeles. Its new incarnation was established by Taoist priest Carl Totton, now a member of the *United States Martial Arts Hall of Fame*. The Institute also offers a range of courses in Taijiquan and Qi Gong with an emphasis on the martial arts.

The Taoist Sanctuary in Tempe also continues as an independent center.

The Institute draws its inspiration from the philosophy of Lao-Tzu, an older contemporary of Confucius. A lower government official, he became discouraged and abandoned his post. According to tradition, as he was about to leave China, he was asked to write down his teachings. The result was the *Tao Te Ching*, the chief scripture of Taoism.

Tao (the Way of the universe) is harmony. When events and things are allowed to move naturally, harmony is the result. The chief aim of human existence is to attain fullness of life by attaining harmony with the Tao. The result of Taoist thinking is *wu-wei*, a quietistic, noninterfering style of life. Politically, *wu-wei* finds its best expression in laissez-faire and the ideal self-contained village state. The balance of the two forces into yin and yang, encompassing the basic polarities of the universe, is also crucial. As Taoism developed, divination emerged as a major practice. The most popular form of divining the future was the *I Ching*.

The *I Ching* is built upon a series of trigrams, each a combination of two primary forms: the *yang-hsiao*, a straight line, the symbol of the male or positive principle, and the *yin-hsiao*, a broken line, the symbol of the female or negative principle. The two symbols can be arranged into eight different trigrams, and the trigrams can form 64 hexagrams. Each hexagram has been ascribed symbolic meanings, correlating with the eight fundamental elements or factors in the universe and 64 phenomena in the universe. Together the hexagrams represent symbolically all the possible situations of creation. They may tell a person to do something or not to do it; to change or not to change. Dr. Dhiegh wrote a modern commentary on the *I Ching*, *The Eleventh Wing*.

Membership: Not reported.

Sources:

Taoist Sanctuary. http://www.taoistsanctuary.org/

Taoist Institute. www.taoistinstitute.com.

Dhiegh, Khigh Alx. *The Eleventh Wing*. New York: Delta Books, 1973.

Meyers, Robert. "Khigh Dhiegh Digs I Ching." *TV Guide* (February 20, 1971): 45–48.

Tian Dao (Yiguandao)

4050 Temple City Blvd., Rosemead, CA 91770

Alternate Address: Providence Maitreya Buddha Missionary Institute, 12th Fl., No. 31, Ming-Sheng E Rd., Sec. 3, Taipei, Taiwan.

Tian Dao (or Yiguandao) is a new religious movement that emerged in the 1930s in China, though it has its roots in the late-nineteenth-century Taoist movement the Way of Pervading Unity (Yiguandao).

In 1930 Zhang Tianran (1889–1947) assumed leadership of Yiguandao and initiated a set of reforms including the allowance of meat eating (though vegetarianism remained the preferred diet), dropping celibacy requirements, and simplifying rituals. He also emphasized proselytization. Yiguandao spread throughout urban China, frequently by absorbing previously existing temple networks. It experienced a growth spurt during World War II but fell victim to suppression after the Communists came to power in the 1950s. Many members fled to Taiwan, Hong Kong, and elsewhere in East Asia, and the movement experienced a period of turmoil as different leaders arose to assume leadership of various factions.

As new leaders emerged, recruiting proceeded anew. However, because of the group's history of cooperation with earlier governments in China, the Taiwanese feared it and began a period of suppression. It was outlawed from 1963 to 1987. In spite of persecution, it spread among the population and emerged as Taiwan's largest religious group. It has been especially strong among the new class of entrepreneurs and found its strength among factory workers and management.

When the movement became legal again, in 1987, Yiguandao's followers were organized into eight major groups, the four largest of which identified with different Yiguandao temples in China. Together they had established some 1,200 temples in Taiwan by 1991. In 2008 there were an estimated 5 to 10 million adherents of the tradition worldwide, the movement having by this time also permeated the diaspora communities of Chinese in North America and Europe. An umbrella organization, the Tian Dao General Assembly, was established in Taiwan in 1987, but only some 70 percent of the Taiwan-based groups have joined. Many Tian Dao groups still view rival organizations with a degree of suspicion.

Distinguishing the various Tian Dao groups remains a problem for Western scholars, as most are confined to Asia and operate exclusively in Chinese communities. Those that have arrived in America have only begun to reach out beyond the Chinese-speaking communities. One such group operates out of the Taiwan-based Providence Maitreya Buddha Missionary Institute, founded by His Holiness Gao Shan Yu Ren (d. 2000). It publishes the English-language periodical *Golden Voice of Maitreya*.

Worship in Tian Dao focuses upon veneration of the Ancient Mother (Lao Mu, also called Wusheng Laomu, "The Unborn Ancient Mother"). Seeing her human children lost in materiality, she sent Maitreya to Earth to save the lost and thus allow them to enter Heaven and be in her presence. The Ancient Mother is represented by a flame in the oil lamp placed at the center of the altar. Other deities on the altar are the smiling, seated Maitreya Buddha and Guan Yin, the bodhisattva of compassion. Also, there may be figures of Zhang Tianran and his third wife, Sun Yuehui (who escaped to Taiwan after World War II). An elaborate ritual is performed regularly before the altar.

Joining Tian Dao provides release from the cycles of reincarnation and entry into Heaven, a fact symbolized by the gift of a small passport. Proselytization by members is encouraged by allowing them to transfer merit from their work to the salvation of family members.

Tian Dao is eclectic, drawing from Buddhist, Daoist, and Confucian writings and traditions. It also includes a place for contemporary spirit writing, similar to what is termed "channeling" in the West. Members, often young teen females, believed to be under the influence of a deity, write messages in Chinese in sand with the use of a stylus. Such writings are then recorded, and the messages disseminated.

Membership: Not reported.

Periodicals: Golden Voice of Maitreya.

Sources:

Introduction to Dao. Taipei, Taiwan: Tsu Kwang Publishing, n.d.

Irons, Edward. "Yiguandao White Yang Drama: Repackaging the Emotional Message in a Contemporary Chinese Religion." Paper presented at the Annual Meeting of the American Academy of Religion, Nashville, Tennessee, November 18–12, 2000.

Jordan, David D., and Daniel L. Overmyer. *The Flying Phoenix: Aspects of Chinese Sectarianism in Taiwan*. Princeton, NJ: Princeton University Press, 1986.

Song Guanyu. *Tiandao Gouchen: Yiguandao Diaocha Baogao* (Fishing in the depths of the celestial way: a report of investigations into the unity sect). Taipei, Taiwan: Privately published, 1983.

————. *Tiandao Chuan Deng-Yiguan yu Xiandai Shehui* (The celestial way passes the torch-yiguan and modern society). Taipei, Taiwan: San Yang Printing, 1996.

Universal Healing Tao

c/o Taoist Esoteric Yoga Center and Foundation, PO Box 1194, Huntington, NY 11743

Alternate Address: International Headquarters: Tao Garden of Healing Tao, 274 Moo 7, Doi Sakep, Chiang Mai, Thailand 50220.

Universal Healing Tao, formerly known as the Healing Tao Centers, is a worldwide network of teachers and centers that have emerged around the work of Mantak Chia (b. 1944) and his wife Maneewan Chia. Born and raised in Thailand, Mantak Chia studied Buddhism from an early age. After moving to Hong Kong as a young man, he studied the martial arts. More importantly, Chia met the Taoist Master White Cloud Hermit, who imparted to him an understanding of the human body as conceived by Taoism. This understanding pictures the body as the container of a variety of energies that, in health, flow freely through it. Chia combined his instruction from the Hermit with a Western education in anatomy. This led to his producing the healing Tao system, a synthesis of traditional Taoism with Western science.

Maneewan Chia, trained as a medical technician, brought to the Universal Healing Taoist system an emphasis on healthful nutrition and cooking from her native China. After moving to New York, in the early 1980s the Chias founded the Universal Healing Tao center and began to spread their Taoist perspective. Mantak Chia's first book, *Awaken Healing Energy through the Tao*, appeared in 1983. Others soon followed. As Mantak Chia trained instructors, the movement spread across the United States and into Europe. In the mid-1980s the Chias established the Taoist Esoteric Yoga Center and Foundation in Huntington, New York.

In addition to his dozens of books and booklets, Mantak Chia has created videos and CDs describing the theory and methods of the Universal Healing Taoist system. Over the past 40 years, he has taught hundreds of thousands of students the principles of Taoist internal practice. In addition, he has trained and certified hundreds of instructors and practitioners. Students can download his teachings directly from the Universal Tao Web site or order books and CDs through his publishing company, Universal Tao Publishers. Mantak Chia also offers annual seminars and retreats for intensive study and practice at his centers worldwide.

Membership: Not reported. Universal Healing Tao has centers and groups in North America, Europe, South America, Asia, Australia, and Africa.

Educational Facilities:

Santa Fe Acupuncture College, Santa Fe, New Mexico.

Periodicals: *Universal Tao Journal.*

Sources:

Universal Healing Tao. www.universal-tao.com/.

Chia, Mantak. *Awaken Healing Energy through the Tao*. New York: Aurora Press, 1983.

————. *Taoist Ways to Transform Stress into Vitality: The Inner Smile/Six Healing Sounds*. New York: Aurora Press, 1985.

Chia, Mantak, and Maneewan Chia. *Healing Love through the Tao: Cultivating Female Sexual Energy*. Huntington, NY: Healing Tao Books, 1986.

Chia, Mantak, with Michael Winn. *Taoist Secrets of Love: Cultivating Male Sexual Energy*. New York: Aurora Press, 1984.

Yi Guan Dao (I-Kuan Tao)

Great Tao Foundation of America, 11645 Lower Azusa Rd., El Monte, CA 91732

Alternate Address: Taiwan Headquarters: 11th Floor, No. 2 Chien 8 Road, Chung Ho City, Taipei Hsien, Taiwan, R.O.C.

Yi Guan Dao (I-Kuan Tao) is one branch of a religious movement that emerged in China in the 1930s. It is variously known as the Way of Pervading Unity (Yiguandao) or the Way of Heaven (Tian Dao). In 1930 Zhang Tianran (1889–1947) assumed leadership of a previously existing Yiguandao Taoist movement and transformed it with a set of reforms that included dropping requirements for complete vegetarianism and celibacy. His emphasis on proselytization led the movement to spread through China's cities. After his death in 1947 and the Communist takeover in 1949, a number of leaders, including his third wife, assumed leadership of different factions among members who had fled to Taiwan, Hong Kong, and elsewhere in East Asia.

Growth in Taiwan, the main center for Yiguandao, was hampered by its division into several rival branches and suppression by the Taiwanese government, which outlawed it for a period (1963–1987). Once legalized, however, it was discovered that it had flourished, and through the 1990s it spread rapidly both in Taiwan and in other diaspora communities worldwide. Among the several branches, one, known in North America as Yi Guan Dao or I-Kuan Tao, established its international headquarters in the United States in 1996 (though the bulk of the membership remains in Taiwan). It has also developed several English-language Web sites.

Yi Guan Dao emphasizes the Tao as the cosmic power that creates and dominates all things visible and audible, and the harmonious order. It is the sum of the parts, the soul of the universe. The spirit of I-Kuan Tao is within each of us, and releasing it will lead to a clear self-understanding of our role in promoting harmony throughout the universe. It is awakened through acts of kindness and leads to an acceptance of individual responsibility for others. I-Kuan Tao is in essence one with the faith and practice of the other Yiguandao branches, as differences are largely administrative.

The movement is led by Senior Master Chang Pei-ching, chairman of the World I-Kuan Tao Headquarters in California, and other Yi Guan Dao senior masters. Senior Master Chang had come to Taiwan from mainland China in 1947. I-Kuan Tao supports nursing homes, hospitals, clinics, nursery schools, and some 30 publishing houses in Taiwan. In 1993 I-Kuan Tao initiated a program against the use of illicit drugs and tobacco.

Membership: In 2008 I-Kuan Tao claimed some 2 million members in Taiwan affiliated with 200 temples and an additional 15,000 family shrines. Followers may be found in 40 countries, including the United States, Canada, Australia, South Africa, France, Italy, Argentina, Brazil, Chile, Hong Kong, Singapore, South Korea, and Malaysia.

Sources:

Yi Guan Do (I-Kuan Tao) Worldwide Information. www.yiguandao.com.

World I-Kuan Tao Headquarters. www.with.org/.

Jordan, David D., and Daniel L. Overmyer. *The Flying Phoenix: Aspects of Chinese Sectarianism in Taiwan*. Princeton: Princeton University Press, 1986.

Unclassified Christian Churches

Body of Christ (Jim Roberts)

Current address not obtained for this edition.

The nomadic group called the Body of Christ was founded by Jimmie T. Roberts, a former U.S. Marine. The group generated a number of news stories in the late 1970s as its existence became known and several members were deprogrammed. Roberts, the son of a part-time Pentecostal minister, grew up in the South in a religious family. He came to feel that the mainline churches had become too carnal, and he wanted to create a following similar to that of the disciples who moved around the countryside with Jesus, who traveled as he preached. He found support for the idea in Bible passages calling believers to separate themselves from worldliness. Around 1970 he began to recruit members for his group in Denver, Colorado, and in California. As the leader of the group, Roberts was generally known as Brother Evangelist.

As the group took shape, a hierarchical structure was formed, headed by an elder (one of the oldest members). The hierarchy was comprised of the older brothers and the middle brothers (the positions were related to their seniority in the group). Women cared for the children and assisted the male members. During the 1970s group members wore a distinctive, monk-like garb that made them highly visible when they gathered as a group.

It was common practice for the Body of Christ to gather periodically, divide into groups of two or three, and travel by separate routes to the next designated gathering place. During gatherings members would listen to Brother Evangelist preach, sing, welcome new members, and have fellowship with each other. The time on the road was for witnessing and preaching to any who would listen.

The existence of the group was first brought to the public's attention in 1975 when several members were involved in an accident in Fayetteville, Arkansas. Several members were kidnapped and deprogrammed. For the rest of the decade the group was the focus of sporadic attention as parents of young adult members attempted to contact their children. In 1979 a book-length story of a former member, Rachel Martin, was published. Since then the group has dropped out of sight, and little has been heard of its members, possibly a response to the growing amount of negative publicity. Its present whereabouts and status are unknown.

The group was known for its practice of raiding garbage bins behind restaurants and grocery stores to find free food. This practice earned them the label "garbage eaters." Group members bathed infrequently and refused medical treatment.

Membership: At one time the group had as many as 100 members. The most recent reports, from the early 1980s, suggest membership is approximately 40.

Sources:

Martin, Rachel, as told to Bonnie Palmer Young. *Escape.* Denver, CO: Accent Books, 1979.

Brotherhood of the Cross and Star

1544 W Jarvis Ave., Chicago, IL 60626

Alternate Address: International headquarters: c/o Leader Olumba Olumba Obu, the Sole Spiritual Head, Brotherhood of the Cross and Star, 34 Ambo St., PO Box 49, Calabar, Cross River State, Nigeria.

The Brotherhood of the Cross and Star is one of numerous new religions that developed in post–World War II Africa. It was founded in Nigeria in 1954 by Leader Olumba Olumba Obu, designated as its sole spiritual head. Obu was born in 1918 in Blakpan, Nigeria. Though not a member of any church, at age five he began to manifest extraordinary and mysterious spiritual behavior, and he asked to be addressed as "teacher" and "leader." Things he had predicted soon came to pass. People began to bring their problems to him. By 1954 he already had a large following. In establishing the Brotherhood, it is believed that the kingdom of God has been established.

His followers believe that the appearance of Obu is the coming of the Holy Spirit, the comforter, whom Jesus promised in John 14:16, and who is mentioned in the book of Revelation as the Word made flesh (Rev. 12:5, 19:13–14). His message is to repent and refrain from sin because the kingdom of God is now with humanity.

The Brotherhood began to expand rapidly in 1981 when it sent out some 200 missionaries to various locations around the world, including the United States, but with special attention to the United Kingdom. The Brotherhood's youth fellowship sponsored 40 missionaries to the United Kingdom, and the next year 50 women, all ordained priests of the order, arrived in England and began to organize centers, especially among African immigrants. In August 1982 the youth fellowship sponsored a tour of 65 missionaries to the United Kingdom and the United States. They were joined by seven members of the Brotherhood's Christ Servants Fellowship in September, and they organized meetings along the East Coast from Atlanta to New York City. Early centers were established in New Jersey, New York, and Georgia.

Membership: In 2008 the Brotherhood reported eight church centers (called "bethels") in the United States and one in Canada.

Sources:

Brotherhood of the Cross and Star. www.ooo-bcs.org/.

Alexander-Reindorf, Carl. *The Five Mysteries in the Brotherhood of the Cross and Star.* New York: iUniverse, 2006.

"The Brotherhood of the Cross and the Star: The Story of a New Kingdom." *New York Times* (September 5, 1983): 18.

Mbon, Friday M. *Brotherhood of the Cross and Star: A New Religious Movement in Nigeria.* New York: Peter Lang, 1992.

Christ Community Church of Zion

2500 Dowie Memorial Dr., Zion, IL 60099

Christ Community Church of Zion, formerly known as the Christian Catholic Church, was founded by John Alexander Dowie (1847–1907). He was born in Scotland, and as a teenager migrated with his family to Australia. A short time later, he was healed of chronic dyspepsia. Dowie became a Congregationalist minister but was dissatisfied with his life until he discovered the healing power of God during the plague of 1876 in Australia. In 1882 he founded the International Divine Healing Association and, as its president, was a champion of God's healing power and an avowed foe of liquor, tobacco, and drugs. In 1888 he left Australia to attend an International Healing conference in England. However, he got only as far as the United States, where for several years he toured the country as an independent evangelist. In 1891 he settled in Chicago and launched a ministry in a mission to the city. Three years later he opened Zion Publishing House.

In 1896 Dowie founded the Christian Catholic Church in Chicago. Headquarters remained there until 1901, when 6,600 acres were purchased on Lake Michigan. The city of Zion was established there and became a communal economic enterprise of church members for many years. Extensive industry and businesses were developed and controlled by an established theocratic order.

The flamboyant Dowie, recuperating from a stroke that had partially paralyzed him, lost control of the church in 1906 to Wilbur Glenn Voliva (1870–1942), whom he had appointed to run the church in his absence. Voliva, finding the church near bankruptcy, led a revolt that saw Dowie deposed just a year before his death. Voliva was succeeded in 1942 by Michael J. Mintern (d. 1961), who in 1959 was succeeded by Carl Q. Lee. In 1976 Roger W. Ottersen was installed as the fifth general overseer of the Christian Catholic Church worldwide fellowship. He served through most of 1994, after which the office of general overseer was discontinued. In 1995 the headquarters church in Zion was without a senior pastor.

The Christian Catholic Church is rooted in evangelical Protestantism, though it has borrowed from several traditions. The Bible is accepted as the rule of faith and practice. Church members also believe in the necessity of repentance and personal trust in Christ for salvation, and other basic evangelical doctrines.

At the end of September each year the annual convocation is held at the headquarters in Zion. Since 1935 the church has sponsored the presentation of the Zion Passion Play, a live drama featuring a cast of more than 200. During the years of Dowie's leadership, the church founded the Zion Conservatory of Music, which enrolls more than 190 pupils. Foreign work is sponsored in Canada, Guyana, Israel, Jamaica, Japan, the Philippines, Malawi, and South Africa with the Amazoni people. Domestic ministries include Camp Zion in Ellison Bay, Wisconsin; Zion Gospel Chapel, Michigan City, Indiana; Inscription House Navajo Mission, Tonalea, Arizona; and Liberty Community Church, Lindenhurst, Illinois. In 1975 the church joined the National Association of Evangelicals.

Membership: In 2008 the church reported 100 members in the United States and mission partners operating in South Africa, Japan, the Philippines, Guyana, Palestine, Indonesia, and among the Navajo in the American West.

Sources:

Christ Community Church of Zion. www.ccczion.org.

Cook, Philip L. *Zion City, Illinois: John Alexander Dowie's Theocracy*. Zion, IL: Zion Historical Society, 1970.

Lindsay, Gordon. *John Alexander Dowie*. Dallas, TX: Christ for the Nations, 1980.

————. *The Sermons of Alexander Dowie, Champion of the Faith*. Dallas, TX: Voice of Healing, 1951.

Newcomb, Arthur. *Dowie, Anointed of the* Lord. New York: Century Company, 1930.

Christ Family

Current address not obtained for this edition.

The Christ Family was founded in the early 1960s by Charles Franklin Hughes, whose religious name is Lightning Amen. According to the group, Hughes went through a period of fasting for 40 days in the Arizona desert before making a public appearance as Lightning Amen. He began gathering disciples who assumed new names, all with "Christ" as their surname. The disciples have adopted a nomadic lifestyle that keeps them moving around the United States preaching and accepting more converts. Members of the group generally dress in white, wear a

headband, and, when not barefoot, wear shoes that are made of materials other than leather or other animal products.

The Christ Family claims to follow the teachings of Jesus and sees Lightning Amen as the messiah returned to earth. Members of the Family live the Bible, emphasizing nonviolence, abstinence from sex, and separation from materialism. Members are strict vegetarians and do not drink alcohol. They do, however, smoke tobacco and marijuana, natural weeds given by God.

The Family is organized very informally. A farm near Hemut, California, serves as the headquarters of the group, though most members travel throughout the United States the greater part of the year.

Membership: Not reported.

Remarks: Because of their nomadic, unconventional lifestyle and the associated difficulty of staying in contact with individual members of the group, families who have relatives in the Christ Family have termed it a cult. The group publishes little material, and the only substantive publication on the Christ Family is a booklet published by an anticult organization. The group has been the target of a number of deprogramming attempts.

Sources:

Long, Estelle. *The Christ Family Cult*. Redondo Beach, CA: Citizens Freedom Foundation, Information Services, 1981.

Christian Union

c/o Christian Union Bible College, PO Box 27, Greenfield, OH 45123

The Christian Union was formed in 1984 in Columbus, Ohio by a group of likeminded men who had a "desire for a more perfect fellowship in Christ and a more satisfactory enjoyment of the means of religious edification and comfort." The theology is conservative and evangelical. There is no creed to which allegiance must be paid, but seven cardinal principles are considered essential:

1. the oneness of the church of Christ;
2. Christ, the only head;
3. the Bible, the only rule of faith;
4. good fruits, the only condition of fellowship;
5. the Christian Union without controversy;
6. each local church governing itself; and
7. the discountenance of partisan political preaching.

These principles are set within a context of general Protestant affirmations.

The Christian Union, as can be implied from its principles, is congregational in government. Congregations are organized into state councils and a triennial General Council. Councils exist in the states of Oklahoma, Missouri, Iowa, Arkansas, Indiana, and Ohio. Missions are supported in Africa, Japan, and the Dominican Republic. Missionaries serve with various faith-mission organizations. The Macedonian Society raises money to support needy students preparing for a full-time Christian vocation. The Christian Union Extension Bible School offers training via correspondence to students around the United States.

Membership: In 1984 the union reported 114 congregations, 6,000 members, and 114 ministers.

Educational Facilities:

Christian Union Bible College, Greenfield, Ohio.

Periodicals: *The Christian Union Witness*.

Church for the Fellowship of All Peoples

2041 Larkin St., San Francisco, CA 94109

The Church for the Fellowship of All Peoples is a single congregation founded in 1943 by a group under the leadership of Presbyterian clergyman Dr. Albert G. Fisk, then chairman of the Department of Psychology and Philosophy of San Francisco State College. With a building and modest monthly stipend donated by the

Presbyterian Church, the group began to meet for worship and in 1944 called as its copastor Dr. Howard Thurman (1900–1981), the internationally known black minister and chaplain at Howard University. The original purpose of the group was to establish an interracial fellowship at all levels of the congregation's life. Under Thurman's leadership the congregation expanded, and eventually all ties to the Presbyterian Church dropped. Thurman remained pastor for nine years and was succeeded by a series of pastors primarily from liberal Protestant backgrounds: Dr. Dryden Phelps (1953–1955), Francis Geddes, (1955–1963), John D. Magnum (1963–1967), and H. Don Guynes (1965–1967). After five years without a pastor, the church was headed by Daniel Panger and Marvin Chandler, Timothy T. Malone, and Dorsey Blake.

The church is interreligious, with a commitment to see all people as children of God and to seek a vital experience of God as revealed in Jesus of Nazareth and other great religious spirits. The church members are also committed to an ethical awareness of and a bringing into fellowship of people of varied national, cultural, racial, and creedal heritages.

The memory of Howard Thurman is kept alive through the Howard Thurman Convocation held annually on the third Sunday of October.

Membership: In 2002 the church reported 112 members.

Periodicals: *The Growing Edge*.

Sources:

Church for the Fellowship of All Peoples. www.fellowshipsf.org.

Footprints of a Dream: The Story of the Church for the Fellowship of All Peoples. New York: Harper and Brothers. 1959.

Smith, L. E. *Howard Thurman: The Mystic as Prophet*. Richmond, IN: Friends United Press, 1991.

Thurman, Howard. *Disciplines of the Spirit*. New York: Harper and Row, 1963.

———. *The First Footsteps*. San Francisco, 1975.

———. *Illuminous Darkness*. New York: Harper and Row, 1965.

———. *The Inward Journey*. New York: Harper and Row, 1961.

———. *With Heart and Head*. New York: Harcourt Brace Jovanovich, 1979.

Young, Henry James, ed. *God and Human Freedom*. Richmond, IN: Friends United Press, 1983.

Church of Bible Understanding

Box 841, Radio City Station, New York, NY 10019-0841

The Church of Bible Understanding was founded in Allentown, Pennsylvania, in 1971 by Canadian-born Stewart Traill (b. 1936). An atheist at the time of his marriage in 1959, Traill turned to the study of religion after the birth of several children, and decided that Christianity was the true faith. He began attending an independent Pentecostal church in Allentown in 1970, held Bible meetings in the church's gymnasium, and frequented a coffeehouse sponsored by a Presbyterian congregation. Eventually, both the church and coffeehouse evicted Traill, citing his creation of doctrinal dissension. With a few followers, he began to hold meetings in several locations in Allentown. The group organized as the Forever Family. Although they never associated with the larger Jesus People movement that had come to the East Coast from California, the Forever Family adopted many of his characteristics.

The Forever Family grew quickly throughout the East, Midwest, and even Canada. At its peak it was reported to have as many as 10,000 adherents and 110 communal fellowships scattered as widely as Montreal, Charleston, South Carolina, and eastern Michigan. However, in the mid-1970s the media began to attack the group as a cult, and several members were deprogrammed. At this time the church adopted its present name. Internal dissension grew when in fall 1976 Traill divorced and remarried within a few weeks.

Traill's teachings, which follow a conservative evangelical theology on most points, have two emphases that set them apart from other Christian bodies. First,

Traill teaches that the Bible is a figurative book. He developed a simplified method of Bible interpretation called the "Colored Bible Method" that breaks down the light of understanding into 10 important subject areas. This method uses the Bible's own method of true interpretation, "the only real one!" Second, members of the group are aggressive in their evangelism and separatist in their lifestyle. The church is seen as a flock called together under Jesus, the Good Shepherd. Members are His sheep. New members are generally referred to as "lambs."

Organizationally, the church has adopted a communal lifestyle built around fellowship groups that live together in single residences. Each fellowship is headed by a male leader. All fellowships in a single area are grouped into "centers" overseen by leaders responsible to Traill. The group has developed a number of businesses to support its fellowships and ministry.

Membership: It was estimated that by 1980 the church had approximately 700 members in 13 fellowships. In 2008 its main centers were in New York and Philadelphia. It supports an active ministry in Haiti.

Periodicals: *Lamb Ledger*.

Sources:

Church of Bible Understanding. www.cbuhaiti.org.

Duffy, Joseph. "The Church of Bible Understanding, A Critical Expose." *Alternatives* (New York) 4, no. 6 (April/May 1977).

Traill, Stewart. *The Gospel of John in Colors*. Worcester, MA: Church of Bible Understanding, 1976.

Church of Interfaith Christians

c/o Rev. Ed Crabtree, CEO, PO Box 924, Nixa, MO 65714-0924

The Church of Interfaith Christians is a Christian church that uniquely affirms and embraces all "positive spiritual paths"—from the major world religious traditions, such as Buddhism and Islam, to smaller paths such as shamanism and earth-based religions like Wicca. It was founded in 2002 by Ernest A. Steadman.

The church affirms many traditional Christian beliefs, though they are stated in such a way as to banish exclusivity and open Christianity to other religious worldviews that are also believed to have been inspired by God. Interfaith Christians believe that God is the force of life itself and that His Son, Jesus Christ, unveiled the mystery of the Creator by identifying the Holy Spirit and that which dwells in every human child and allows him or her to be in constant communion with the Father. It teaches that Jesus Christ brought the message of salvation to all of mankind, which consists of doing God's will in all things and forever eliminating the written law, doctrine, and dogma that had been polluted by man's flesh. This message allows humankind to fellowship directly with the Father through the Holy Spirit.

The church draws its authority from the Bible, which it believes to be the inspired Word of God, while at the same time noting that the Bible is not the exclusive source of all knowledge of our Savior, nor is it entirely accurate in its present state of interpretation. It also rejects the idea that the present Holy Bible is complete, noting that the so-called "Lost Books of the Bible" derive from the same period of time and should still be relied upon as sound Scripture for reference purposes.

As with many liberal Christians, the church affirms that there will be many in Heaven who do not worship the Son or follow His Church on earth. This perspective has become the basis of the Church of Interfaith Christians' reworking of Christian theology and of their affirmation of peoples following other religions.

Steadman has enlarged on the basic ideal of the Church of Interfaith Christians in a book, *Pathway to the Stars*, which now serves as a basic text for new members and ministers. On its Web site, the church invites people who agree with its perspective to join and declares its willingness to ordain as ministers any who meet the very minimal requirements. One of the church's leaders, Rev. Ed Crabtree, has written a small volume entitled *Beginning Ministry* to assist the newly ordained.

Along with *Pathway to the Stars* and applications for ordination, it is available for reading through the Internet site.

The church sponsors the Interfaith Christian Radio Network, an Internet radio station that may be accessed through www.live365.com, a popular Internet site for Web-based radio. The church has an African affiliate, the Universal Interfaith Christian Church, Nigeria. It actively supports a number of interfaith organizations, including the Council for the Parliament of the World's Religions, the International Association for Religious Freedom, the Temple of Understanding, the United Religions Initiative, and the World Conference on Religion and Peace.

Membership: Not reported. The church has ordained and licensed more than 250 people to the Christian ministry, most in the United States, with a minority scattered around the world in some 14 countries. Some ministers have formed congregations, but most work with a noncongregational ministry.

Sources:

Church of Interfaith Christians.

    www.crabtreeinternet.com/church_of_interfaith_christian/index.php.

Steadman, Ernest A. *Pathway to the Stars*. Hawthorn, FL: Steadman & Associates, 2001. Posted at www.crabtreeinternet.com/church_of_interfaith_christian/ reference_library/PATHWAY_TO_THE_STARS.pdf.

Church of Ishtar

c/o Billy Rojas, PO Box 282, Eugene, OR 97440

The Church of Ishtar was founded in 1988 by Billy Rojas, the church's prophet, teacher, and leader. The church was inspired by faith in the goddess Ishtar, who was worshipped in ancient Sumer. According to Rojas, Ishtar was a historic person, the wife of Dumuzi, the king of Sumer around 2500 B.C.E. She came to be worshipped as the goddess of love and war, and as the female principle of creation, the creatrix.

The worship of Ishtar is a tolerant faith. It begins with a spiritual rebirth, a genuine change of heart by the individual member. Such rebirth means finding a new purpose in life, redirecting one's energies to become the best person one can be, and making no compromise with falsehood, especially that embedded in outdated religious traditions. It also means finding the path that is right for you as an individual, which should have a social/ethical dimension and not leave out others (who choose different paths). The Ishtar faith also acknowledges that spirituality has a sexual dimension and that the fundamental religious sacrament is *hieros gamos*, the sacred sexual union of a king (male) and high priestess (representing the goddess).

In announcing the formation of the Church of Ishtar in 1988, Rojas predicted the formation of a large national organization. The building blocks of that organization would be autonomous local church centers at which the worship of Ishtar would be celebrated. Among the functionaries at the local centers would be the *hierodules*, sacred prostitutes who would offer counseling to church members and on occasion serve as sexual surrogates. The church recognizes two ancient covenants: Abraham's covenant with God (El Shaddai, not to be confused with the monotheistic God of later Judaism) as recorded in Gen. 17, and Ishtar's covenant with her husband Dumuzi that she would rescue him from death—that is, she would rescue men from death-in-life, from loveless, sexless lives. The resurrected male, no longer lonely, would then restore the good life on earth.

To become a follower of Ishtar it is essential to become a student of the teachings of the faith, to learn about the goddess and the covenants, and to pledge oneself to Ishtar, El Shaddai, and the goal of becoming a better person. One should also pledge to help the church and other church members.

Membership: Not reported.

Sources:

Rojas, Billy. *The Church of Ishtar*. Eugene, OR: Author, 1988.

Church of the Living God

632 Mokauea, Honolulu, HI 96819

The Church of the Living God (known in Hawaiian as Ka Makua Mau Loa Hoomana O Ke Akua Ola) was formed shortly after the erection of the Honolulu branch of the Hoomana Naauao O Hawaii. Twelve members of the Hoomana Naauao O Hawaii left that church and founded an independent congregation, dedicating their first building in 1911. Prominent members of the church are the Wise family. In 1937 long-time pastor Rev. John Wise was succeeded by his daughter, Ella Wise Harrison. During Rev. Harrison's leadership of 41 years the membership continued to grow. After her death in 1978 Rev. Jacob K. Naweli succeeded her.

The church is organized congregationally and generally follows the Reformed theology of its parent body, though it has added some distinctly Hawaiian ideas. For example, the church has adopted elements of Hawaiian healing practices such as *ho'oponopono* and conflict resolution through prayer and forgiveness.

Membership: In 2002 the church reported six congregations, one on each of the major Hawaiian islands and two on the island of Hawaii.

Sources:

Mulholland, John F. *Hawaii's Religions*. Rutland, VT: Charles T. Tuttle, 1970.

Disciples of the Lord Jesus Christ

c/o Rama Behera, Shawano, WI 54166

Disciples of the Lord Jesus Christ is the unofficial name of a small evangelical Christian group gathered around Rama Behera. The group has no name, has not incorporated, and has grown slowly over the few years of its existence. Behera came to the United States from India in 1962 and earned a master's degree in nuclear engineering at Columbia University. According to his account, Behera met God in 1966 and converted from Hinduism to Christianity. He became an evangelist and traveled throughout the United States and Jamaica. In 1974, with a few people who had been converted under his ministry, he settled in Shawano, Wisconsin, and established headquarters for his following.

The Disciples of the Lord Jesus Christ are a conservative, evangelical, non-Trinitarian Christian group. They affirm that Jesus Christ is the only true and living God and that sinful humans can be saved only by repenting and being born again by the "Spirit of the Living God, Jesus Christ our Lord." The disciples are set against the compromises of the worldly church and have adopted a stringent moral code that centers upon becoming a servant of Jesus in all thoughts and desires and with all one's mind and heart. Discouraged activities include watching television, listening to popular music, dressing immodestly, and attending motion pictures. The church is the body of believers established for worship and the comfort of the faithful.

Membership: Membership is scattered throughout Wisconsin and Minnesota. Gatherings are regularly held at Shawano, Wisconsin, and Rochester, Minnesota. In 1985 there were approximately 150 in regular attendance.

Remarks: The group has been an object of controversy since its emergence in the 1970s. Families of people associated with the group complained of the rigid lifestyle they adopted, their unorthodox theology, and the control Behera seemed to have over their lives. At least three members were kidnapped and deprogrammed and became the subjects of major lawsuits. As a result of the deprogrammings, media coverage, and what the group considered undue harassment, the group developed a strong polemic against the Roman Catholic Church and the Lutheran Church, which are viewed as agents of persecution.

First Church of the Doors

Berkeley, CA

Social science observers have noted the similarities between religious devotion and the veneration of movie and music superstars. That observation was given support in early 1984 by the formation of the First Church of the Doors, a church built around the memory of rock musician Jim Morrison. Morrison, the leader of a band, the Doors, died in 1971 at the age of 27 of a heart attack, but like Elvis Presley, he still has a large and faithful following. According to the church's founder, Tony Spurlock (b. 1958), members "worship their potential to be as wise as Jim Morrison." Followers saw Morrison as a symbol of anyone who wants to defy the laws of reality.

Members paid annual dues of $110.00. They gathered annually to commemorate Morrison's death, to watch videos, and to sing Morrison's songs. The church was headed by Spurlock, the "high mojomuck" and editor of the church's semiannual newsletter. He gathered a collection of Morrison artifacts that he keeps in trust for the unincorporated church.

Membership: In 1992 the church reported approximately 50 members.

Periodicals: *The Deadly Door Knell*.

Sources:

Slonaker, Larry. "First Church of the Doors Lights Some Fires Among Fans." *Wichita Eagle* (July 25, 1992).

Spurlock, Brian Anthony. "The Founding of the First Church of the Doors." Available from at www.pictdom.org/Mojomuk1.html.

Followers of Christ

Current address not obtained for this edition.

The Followers of Christ is a small Bible-believing group founded by a Mr. Riess. Riess went to Oklahoma when it was opened to white settlers, and took up residence at Ringwood. He passed the leadership of his group to Elder Morris by the laying on of hands for imparting and consecrating in the Holy Spirit. Elder Morris was succeeded by his son, Elder Marion Morris. The group believes in the necessity of following Jesus, taking their lead from Matt. 4:19. If a person is to be saved, he will repent, and God will grant time for following Christ. The King James Version of the Bible is used by the followers.

The Followers of Christ believe in repentance, baptism, receiving the Spirit, and following Christ's commands. Baptism is for adults and by immersion. Children are sanctified by the faith of their parents. Footwashing and fasting are also practiced. No medicine is used; rather, members pray for the sick. For nonbelievers, deathbed repentance of sin is believed to be insufficient to assure salvation, for there must be a period of following Christ.

Membership: There is only one congregation, but members believe that there are Followers of Christ scattered around the world.

Full Salvation Union

Current address not obtained for this edition.

The Full Salvation Union was formed in 1934 at Lansing, Michigan, by James F. Andrews, a former minister of the Free Methodist Church. Later that year he was joined by his father, E. A. Andrews, who was appointed general pastor. The first General Council meeting occurred the following year. The founding principles included a general protest against politics and human manipulation in the church, and a plea that "all of the Lord's children have a voice and that decisions be made through prayer and counsel."

The union developed at a number of points some distinctive doctrines. It adopted a dispensational view of Christian history, which it sees as divided into three dispensations: Father, Son, and Holy Ghost. The Son's dispensation occurred during Jesus' 30 years on earth. The union teaches that some parts of the Bible are more relevant today than others. It is seen as a stream from the fountain; it is not the fountain itself, it is secondary, deriving its excellence from the Holy Spirit. Experimental religion, the witness of the Spirit, and the inward consciousness of God are stressed, but no absolute distinction between conversion and sanctification is made. The believer moves from conversion to the more abundant life, but holiness is not attained in a single experience only. The union also teaches that eventually everyone will have the opportunity to accept God.

It is the union's belief that during the dispensation of the Holy Ghost, no ceremonies, including the sacraments, should be observed. The Jewish practices were continued in the early church for a time, but only as a concession to custom. Baptism was considered a sign of the confession of faith, yet the union stresses that the apostle Paul preached a baptism of the Spirit rather than of water. The union's main attribute is believed to be its unity of spirit, as manifested in its lack of artificial divisions by age and gender and in its making decisions without majority vote. The group believes in tithing and healing.

The union is governed by a general council and the elders. The general pastor is head of the union. Elders are those who have been recognized as eligible to govern. There are both ordained and unordained ministers.

Membership: Not reported.

Hoomana Naauoa O Hawaii
910 Cooke St., Honolulu, HI 96813

Hoomana Naauoa O Hawaii was formed in 1853 when Rev. J. H. Poliwailehua and other Hawaiian members of the Kalahikiola Church, the Congregational Church congregation at Kohala, Hawaii, formed an independent congregation. The Kohala congregation was predominantly Hawaiian in membership. Friction had developed in these congregations because the nineteenth-century missionaries had been, to some degree, insensitive in their work; as they converted individuals the missionaries left them isolated from their larger family units, which in Hawaii included grandparents, aunts, uncles, and cousins.

Hoomana Naauoa O Hawaii spread through the Hawaiian islands as several large extended families affiliated with it. By the end of the century a group from the Kohala congregation relocated in Honolulu and built a parish. Other congregations were located in Hilo, Koae, and Lanai.

Membership: In the 1970s there were four congregations.

Sources:

Mulholland, John F. *Hawaii's Religions*. Rutland, VT: Charles T. Tuttle, 1970.

International Community of Christ, Church of the Second Advent
643 Ralston St., Reno, NV 89503

The International Community of Christ, Church of the Second Advent, is an independent Christian denomination that offers a distinctive, alternative presentation of Christian teachings and a new authoritative dispensation that it believes fulfills the messianic church under Jesus. The church functions primarily as a religious order known as the Order of the Holy Child (Jamilians). Originally organized in 1959 as the American Philosophical Institute of Cosolargy in New Smyrna Beach, Florida, it relocated to Peru, and in 1962 was renamed the Interdenominational Christian Church. The organization was subsequently known for a decade as the Mystery School of the Andes until a permanent center was established in Reno, Nevada, in 1972.

The church maintains that Jesus was an Essene master teacher who, as earthly messiah and interpreter of God's law, came to announce the appearance of the Sun of Righteousness (Mal. 4:1–2) for the redemption of the human family. He came not only to restore the True Mosaic Law for Israel, but also to unify the religious Orders of Light who held to a common solar teaching known in different forms throughout the ancient world and who were expecting his coming. With Jesus' death and the martyrdom of his disciples, the new covenant of God was rejected and the redeeming force of the First Advent Sun of Righteousness was withdrawn from the world. However, it was prophesied that in the end-times of the earth, God would again manifest as Christ through the Light of the Second Advent Sun of Righteousness (Matt. 24:27–31).

The church teaches that the long-awaited Second Coming is the appearance of the New Sun of Righteousness. which has been manifesting since 1962. This cosmic event, in which God has incarnated His presence in divine light, ushers in a dynamic and unprecedented age on earth, bringing forth universal Christ-consciousness into the world on a level never before experienced in human history. The advent of the Second Sun of Righteousness was announced by Jamil (1959–1962), a wondrous child seer whose birth had been predicted by the prophets of many traditions and whose life fulfilled the scriptural requirements of the one to come as God's final human messenger.

Fundamental to the Second Advent teaching is that people can participate in the manifesting cosmic Christ and commune with God by developing personalized Christ consciousness through spiritual regeneration and self-transformation by means of a sacred process. This process, which was taught by Jesus and his immediate disciples and is the "secret" gospel, was lost to the established churches but has been repossessed by the Second Advent Church through revelation. It is a highly advanced spiritual system by which the individual spirit is brought into contact with God's Word through light and made a living soul. The sacred represents a living theology that the church calls cosolargy (a word created from *cosmic*, *solar*, and *logos*).

A synthesis of scientific, metaphysical, and religious principles for modern men and women, cosolargy is not restricted to the individual living the ascetic life. On the contrary, it is a cosmopolitan teaching that is available to anyone living in the modern world. Cosolargy teaches that solar light-energy is the carrier of intelligible information that, when properly applied by means of specialized solar techniques and other techniques of transcendence, activates latent psycho-physical and spiritual faculties (e.g., force centers and fields) in the individual, which leads to development of the spiritual light body for ultradimensional participation in worlds of light while in the present time-space continuum. Cosolargy thereby provides the individual the means of achieving immortality of the spirit/soul and transcendence from lower dimensional existence.

The church holds that the world is in the end-times, a period prophesied by all the great religions, in which God's divine light will bring about a spiritual golden age that will restore a universal religion of light and eventually bring about the restoration of the creation to its original state. The church believes that a new solar epoch has dawned with the advent of the Sun of Righteousness. It teaches that man must learn to process the spiritual forces inherent within the heightened cosmic/solar energy streaming down upon the earth for the survival of the human species and for its continued evolution under a new state of the universe. Cosolargy restores and supplements the ancient spiritual systems of the past for the emergence of a highly developed, spiritually evolved modern individual. The arts, sciences, and technologies of cosolargy constitute a new religious system made available to help the human species adapt to and survive new and increased levels of cosmic/solar radiation that are producing new life conditions on earth. In the broadest sense, cosolargy represents the ideal ecological system because the perpetuation of the planet and the human species is dependent upon harmonious coexistence in accord with a changing environment. The marriage of science and religion becomes reality in cosolargy because physiological, psychological, and spiritual attributes are involved directly with natural and supranatural laws. The Second Advent Church Community, the precursor for the restoration of the great religions of the world, has been established to instruct humankind of this transforming condition and is under mandate to revive and renew the Sacred Teachings of Light for those who seek illumination in the Second Advent Age.

Associated with the church are the American Cosmic-Solar Research Center, the Order of the Holy Child, Advocates for Religious Rights and Freedoms, and Project "X"—Search for the Secrets of Immortality.

Leading the International Community of Christ for more than three decades was Douglas Eugene "Gene" Savoy (1927–2007), who served as head bishop from 1971 until his death. He also served as president of the Jamilian University of the Ordained, chancellor of the Sacred College of Jamilian Theology, and president of the Advocates for Religious Rights & Freedoms. Savoy was the author of most of the books published by the church that present its views on the Essenes, Christianity, and the child Jamil, Savoy's son. Collectively, these texts, which are used as the church's curriculum material, present what Savoy saw as the real teach-

ings of the Essenes and communicate how the recovery of this information can assist in bringing religious enlightenment to today's world. The Second Advent Church refers to said restoration and renewal as the "emerging new Christianity."

Educational Facilities:

Jamilian University of the Ordained, Reno, Nevada.

Sacred College of Jamilian Theology, Reno, Nevada.

American Philosophical Institute of Cosolargy, Reno, Nevada.

Membership: In 2008 the church reported a fellowship nearing 2,000 worldwide (primarily in North America), 108 members of the Jamilian Order, and approximately 100 students enrolled in the Jamilian University of the Ordained.

Periodicals: *Community Communiqu.*

Sources:

International Community of Christ. www.communityofchrist.org.

Jamilian University of the Ordained. www.jamilian.org.

Savoy, Gene. *The Essaei Document Secrets of an Eternal Race: Codicil to The Decoded New Testament. The Sacred teachings of light, codex 7.* Reno, NV: International Community of Christ, 1980.

———. *Image and the Word. The Secret Sayings of Jamil.* Reno, NV: International Community of Christ, 1976.

———. *Jamil the Christ Child.* Reno, NV: International Community of Christ, 1976.

———. *The Lost Gospel of Jesus: The Hidden Teachings of Christ.* Reno, NV: International Community of Christ, 1984.

Ka Hale Hoano Hou O Ke Akua

1760 Nalani, Honolulu, HI 96819

Ka Hale Hoano Hou O Ke Akua (Hallowed House of God, King of Kings and Lord of Lords) is a 1948 schism of the Hoomana Naauoa O Hawaii. Lt. Com. W. H. Abbey was its early leader, and he was succeeded by Rev. Edward Ayau, pastor of the headquarters church on Molokai. A second congregation is at Kahili.

Membership: In the 1970s there were two congregations.

Sources:

Mulholland, John F. *Hawaii's Religions.* Rutland, VT: Charles T. Tuttle, 1970.

Kealaokamalamalama

1207 Prospect, Honolulu, HI 96822

The Kealaokamalamalama (Way of the Light) was formed by former members of the Kawaiahao Church, a Congregational church parish and the oldest Christian church in Hawaii, in reaction to the death of Rev. Akaiko Akana. Akana had served 25 years as pastor of the Kawaiahao Church, and the new independent congregation was established in 1935 in his honor. Rev. Akana's brother, Rev. Francis K. Akana, was the first pastor of the new church. In 1970 he was succeeded by his son, Rev. Francis K. Akana Jr. A second congregation is located in Honolulu.

Membership: There are two congregations.

Sources:

Mulholland, John F. *Hawaii's Religions.* Rutland, VT: Charles T. Tuttle, 1970.

Megiddo Church

481 Thurston Rd., Rochester, NY 14619

L. T. Nichols (1844–1912) was an independent Bible student who became a minister, believing that he had discovered religious truths obscured since the fourth century. The key truth was that every man is responsible for his sins and that "No man could be saved apart from knowing and keeping the Commandments of God." First in Oregon in 1880 and then in Minnesota in 1883, Nichols proclaimed this truth and gathered followers. He was spurred in his work by a belief, based on a study of Bible chronology, that the end-time was near. In the 1890s he conceived the idea of building a mission boat to bring the followers together in a common home. This boat, the *Megiddo*, a Mississippi River steamer, was launched in 1901 and gave the movement its name.

The boat traveled the Mississippi and Ohio rivers and their tributaries. It was sold in 1903 and the group moved to new mission fields. In 1903 a community was established in Rochester, New York. Nichols died in 1912. He was succeeded by Maud Hembree, a former Roman Catholic. She developed an active mission program with several boats on the Great Lakes and in 1914 began the church's periodical, the *Megiddo Message*, which is still published today.

The community in Rochester, previously known as the Megiddo Mission, worships in a building on the church's estate and carries on an active educational program. From their facilities a large literature ministry is carried on in the United States. Through direct-mail advertising of their monthly periodical and their set of eleven booklets on Bible teachings, they support a major evangelistic effort to encourage people to believe, study, and live by the Bible.

The crusade of the Megiddo Church is based upon the members' belief in the imminence of the Second Coming of Jesus. Its imminence is heralded, they say, by contemporary signs and political corruption, the craze for pleasure, universal fear, the armaments race, and the peace movement. Elijah the prophet will return to signal Christ's return as king. The judgment will lead to a revolt by all who will not acknowledge him. This revolt is the great Battle of Armageddon mentioned in the Bible. The millennium will follow the battle.

Members of the Megiddo Church deny the Trinity. Jesus is considered God's son, and the Holy Spirit is seen as a divine power, not a person. Man is mortal; immortality comes only as God's reward for a life of righteous living. There is no eternal hell, only death for the wicked. Distinctive is their belief that man did not fall in Adam—each person is responsible only for himself. If a person follows Christ's example, he will be saved.

Membership: In 1997 there were approximately 100 members worldwide. More than 16,000 receive the *Megiddo Message*.

Periodicals: *Megiddo Message*.

Sources:

Megiddo Church. megiddo.com.

Hembree, Maud. *The Known Bible and Its Defense*. 2 vols. Rochester, NY: Author, 1933.

History of the Megiddo Mission. Rochester, NY: Megiddo Mission Church, 1979.

An Honest Man: The Life and Work of L. T. Nichols. Rochester, NY: Megiddo Press, 1987.

Millennium Superword. Rochester, NY: Megiddo Mission Church, 1980.

Patzwald, Gari-Anne. *Waiting for Elijah: A History of the Megiddo Mission*. Knoxville, TN: University of Tennessee Press, 2002.

New Apostolic Church

3753 N Troy, Chicago, IL 60618

Alternate Address: International Headquarters: Box 532, CH 8044, Zurich, Switzerland.

The New Apostolic Church is a variant of the Catholic Apostolic Church, a movement that began in England in 1830. By the beginning of the 1860s a crisis had developed within the Catholic Apostolic Church. The church was led by a group of "apostles," and in the expectation that their generation was in its last days, they had established no system to appoint new apostles as they were needed. In 1860 Heinrich Geyer, a member in Germany recognized by many as having the gift of prophecy, was moved to call two men to the apostleship, though he knew the British leadership would disapprove. Immediate schism was averted by the appointment of the two men as "coadjutors" for Germany's Catholic Apostolic Church. However, Geyer then went on to appoint a third man as an apostle, Elder Rosochacky of Knisberg. Although acknowledged as an apostle by Angel (Bishop) F. W. Schwarz, Rosochacky later repented of accepting the office. In 1863 Schwarz and Geyer were excommunicated from the Catholic Apostolic Church. Geyer again

called Schwarz to the apostleship and a new structure, duplicating the Catholic Apostolic Church, was initiated.

The New Apostolic Church spread across Europe and, in the twentieth century, around the world, though it was hindered for some years when it fell victim to Nazi persecution. It believes that it is the Church of Christ corresponding to the apostolic churches in the days of the first apostles, and that it teaches the true doctrine of Christ and His apostles. It was set up following the revival of the apostolate, and now addresses itself to one task—the care of souls and the preaching of the Gospel. In carrying out its task, the church refrains from all political activities, in compliance with Jesus' words, "My kingdom is not of this world." However, it expects its members to discharge their duties as citizens of the state, following Jesus' words, "Render unto Caesar the things which are Caesar's." A member of the New Apostolic Church can play an active part in public life, and the church takes it for granted that members of the church will discharge the duties incumbent upon them in public life, in their families, and in the profession they follow, with all due efficiency and a sense of responsibility.

BELIEFS. Members of the New Apostolic Church believe in

the omnipotent God who created the world and rules in eternity;

the immortality of the soul;

free will that permits humans to decide for and against God;

the availability of God's salvation to all people;

the divine plan of redemption that aims at saving a fallen humanity;

God's incarnation in Jesus;

the sacrificial death of the son of God upon the cross, which enabled humans to be reconciled to God;

Christ's resurrection and ascension, and the mission on which He sent His apostles to preach the gospel to all nations;

the necessity of being endowed with the Holy Spirit by an apostle in order to have fellowship with God, the Father and Son;

the second coming of Christ at the First Resurrection when He will take unto Himself "all those who have accepted his teachings" (John 14:30);

the idea that Jesus will set up the millennium, during which period the evil one will have no power over humankind, all human beings on earth and the beyond will be offered grace and redemption;

the Last Judgment, at which those who did not have a part in the First Resurrection will be judged according to their works; and

the promise that the redeemed will enjoy everlasting fellowship with God.

ORGANIZATION. The church consists of all the New Apostolic congregations worldwide, united to form one body. The head of the church is the chief apostle, who is the supreme authority in all church affairs. His official seat is in Zurich, Switzerland. The congregations in a district or region constitute an apostolic district, over which a district apostle serves. Apostles, bishops, and district rectors are appointed by the district apostles to care for the congregations in their respective territories.

A rector in a priestly ministry is in charge of each congregation. The ministers discharging priestly functions are a bishop, an elder, a shepherd, an evangelist, and a priest. They are assisted by deacons and subdeacons in pastoral work undertaken for the benefit of each member. Special attention is paid to the requirements of children and youth. As in the early church, the ministers are laymen. They come from all walks of life and have not been trained in theology. Nearly all of them serve in an honorary capacity.

Expenses incurred by churches (e.g., the building and maintenance of churches, missionary work, etc.) are covered by voluntary contributions made by church members. The church does not charge dues, ask for donations or pledges, or require members to sign church mortgages.

The church dispenses three sacraments, as was in the case of the first apostles. They are: Holy Baptism, Holy Sealing, and Holy Communion. Holy Baptism is the first step toward fellowship with God. This sacrament is dispensed by a priestly minister authorized by an apostle. Holy Sealing is dispensed by the laying on of hands and prayer by an apostle. Holy Communion is celebrated every Sunday. It is preceded by the absolution pronounced in the name of Jesus by an apostle.

In addition, the church solemnizes the following events with a special blessing: confirmation, engagement, marriage, and wedding anniversaries. These blessings are pronounced by priestly ministers authorized for that purpose. Funeral services are also conducted by such ministers. A prenatal blessing is pronounced at the parent's request.

Membership: In 2008 the church reported more than 10 million members worldwide. In the United States there are some 500 congregations scattered across the country.

Periodicals: *Our Family Magazine.*

Sources:

New Apostolic Church. www.newapostolicchurch.org/.

New Apostolic Church International. www.nak.org/en/nac-around-the-world/north-america.

Guide for the Administration Brothers of the New Apostolic Church. Frankfurt am Main, Germany: Apostles College of the New Apostolic Church, 1967.

Kraus, M. *Completion Work in the New Apostolic Church.* Waterloo, ON: New Apostolic Church, 1978.

Questions and Answers Concerning the New Apostolic Church. Frankfurt am Main, Germany: J. G. Bischoff, 1978.

Social Brethren

c/o Rev. Earl Vaughn, Moderator, R.R. 2, Flora, IL 62839

The Social Brethren emerged in Saline County, Illinois, in the wake of the U.S. Civil War. Some former members of the Methodist and Presbyterian churches, among them the Revs. Frank Wright and Hiram T. Brannon, were concerned with the reconciliation of Christians who had been split over the issue of slavery in the decades prior to the war. The members of the Social Brethren suggested that the biblical position was to have fellowship with all believers in Christ regardless of their positions on the slavery issue, a somewhat unpopular view in the postwar Northern states.

The Social Brethren hold to the essential affirmations of Protestant Christianity, including the sufficiency of the scriptures in matters of faith and salvation through Jesus Christ. They affirm the possibility of a believer falling into apostasy (here they differed with the Presbyterians). They practice two ordinances (rather than sacraments): the Lord's Supper and baptism. Baptism may be by any mode: sprinkling (preferred by Methodists), pouring (preferred by Presbyterians), or immersion. They also believe, in keeping with their reconciling mission, that ministers should refrain from preaching on politics or any other subject outside of the central affirmations of the gospel.

Rather than following the presbyterial or episcopal polity of the Presbyterians and Methodists, the Social Brethren are organized as a loose congregational fellowship. Church fellowships are based on three associations; each of the associations—the Midwestern, Illinois, and Union—meet annually. There is also an annual general assembly to elect a moderator. There is no general headquarters.

Membership: Not reported. In 1975 there were 40 churches, 1,784 members, and 47 ministers.

Sources:

Piepkorn, Arthur C. *Profiles in Belief: The Religious Bodies of the United States and Canada.* Vol. 4. San Francisco: Harper and Row, 1979.

Summum

707 Genesee Ave., Salt Lake City, UT 84104

Summum was founded in 1975 by Claude Rex Nowell (b. 1944), who claimed to have received direct instruction from advanced beings concerning the underlying principles (Natural Laws) that establish and maintain the universe. These principles were given as a never-ending story and form the foundation for Summum philosophy. The purpose of Summum is to allow those searching for a comprehension of Creation to receive the keys to that understanding, and to use these keys to reconcile the many bits of religious, philosophical, and scientific knowledge they may have already acquired. The principles, as presented in 1975, have always existed as a continuum and cannot be accredited to any one person or human source, for they are considered to represent the workings of Creation itself. It is left to individuals to apply these principles to themselves in their reconciling of all religion, science, and philosophy.

The basic knowledge of Summum is the esoteric teachings of every race and religion. Despite the many diverse teachings that have evolved over the centuries, a basic similarity and correspondence remains. The Summa individuals, beings who untiringly work the pathways of spiritual evolution, and who were referred to as Neters in the ancient Egyptian hieroglyphs, have restored these principles to their original purity.

The Summum philosophy embodies what are considered the principles of Creation itself and is able to explain the Grand or First Cause. The principles are formulated through nature and are nature, and cannot be ascribed to a god or humans but are the cause of gods, humans, and all that exists. Summum stresses that the Law of Knowledge must be applied to all the principles in order for one to achieve real understanding, as opposed to mere faith or belief.

Nowell, whom for purposes of the work later changed his name to Summum Bonum Amen Ra, was instructed to construct pyramids and produce "Nectar Publications": wine specially created within a pyramid that initiates transform through psychokinesis and imbue with knowledge. This liquid is consumed in small amounts just prior to meditation. There are no incorrect forms of meditation; it is taught that individuals become what they meditate on—or, in other words, that where their attention is, is where they are.

One of Summum's key meditations is the Meditation of Sexual Ecstasy. Summum views the basis and foundation of all creation as copulation between two subjective states referred to as the "Grand Opposites," and accordingly maintains that everything is an effect of this grand copulation. As such, Summum holds sexuality as a divine and integral part of spiritual evolution and defines "ecstasy" as "the state of Union with God." From the smallest subatomic particle to the highest forms of life, every element, at its level of consciousness, experiences sexual ecstasy in its bond-making and bond-breaking, its copulation. This meditation, along with the other meditations taught at Summum, awakens the individual to the recognition, realization, and manifestation of the spirit, essence, or soul within. This is considered by Summum to be the veracity of genuine religion. As the beliefs of the group have continued to evolve, Nowell has identified them with Gnostic Christianity.

During the mid-1980s, Summum reintroduced the art of mummification, which according to Summum was practiced by most cultures at the pinnacle of their civilizations and as practiced by Summum is a science that culminates in permanent body preservation. The preserved body serves as a base from which the essence of the departed can be guided by means of an esoteric art known as Transference. Summum teaches that the departed being can be assisted in its progression by guidance from both physical and nonphysical assistants who work the pathways of spiritual evolution. Summum offers mummification and Transference to interested individuals from all religions and walks of life. Ceremonies connected to the transference are given. Afterward, the mummiform is placed in a permanent sepulcher.

Membership: In 2002 Summum reported 175,000 members in the United States (who are served by 400 ministers), 6,200 members in Mexico, 5,000 members in Canada, 1,900 members in France, 1,300 members in the United Kingdom, and 1,700 members in various Central and South American communities. Summum groups are also reported in 34 other countries.

Sources:

Summum. www.summum.us/summum.shtml.

Summum Bonum Amen Ra. *Summum: Sealed Except to the Open Mind*. Salt Lake City, UT: Summum, 1994.

———. *Sexual Ecstasy from Ancient Wisdom*. Salt Lake City, UT: Summum Press, n.d.

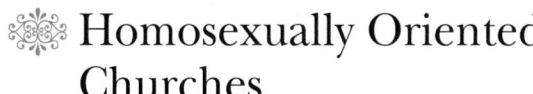

Homosexually Oriented Churches

American Ecumenical Catholic Church

c/oDiocese of Connecticut, Most Rev. Dr. Lorraine Bouffard, Bishop, 30 Woodland St., Unit 10, Hartford, CT 06105

Early in the twenty-first century, Rev. Lorraine Bouffard, who had been ordained in 1994 by Abp. Mark Shirilau for the Ecumenical Catholic Church, was consecrated as a bishop by Bp. Richard Cardarelli of the American Apostolic Catholic Church. Bouffard subsequently led in the founding of the American Ecumenical Catholic Church based in the Mission of the Sacred Hearted, in Windsor Locks, Connecticut. The new jurisdiction is similar to the Roman Catholic Church (in which Bouffard was raised), and follows it theologically and in its sacramental emphasis. It is, however, administratively independent and has developed a special concern for those that older church bodies have not welcomed or sacramentally affirmed due to gender issues, divorce/remarriage, sexual orientation, or physical, psychological, or mental challenges. The church is friendly to gays and welcomes women to all levels of the priesthood.

The small jurisdiction has two dioceses, the one in Connecticut headed by Bishop Bouffard and one in Dennis, Massachusetts, headed by Bp. John French. It has affiliated with the National Council of Community Churches, through which it claims membership in the World Council of Churches. The church supports a television broadcast ministry, "Voices in the Wilderness."

Membership: Not reported. In 2008, the church oversaw two parishes and several chaplaincy ministries.

Sources:

American Ecumenical Catholic Church.

http://americanecumenicalchurch.com/index.html.

Ancient British Church in North America (The Autocephalous Glastonbury Rite in Diaspora)

9–47 Marion St., Toronto, ON, Canada M6R 1E6

The Ancient British Church in North America is a small Western Rite Orthodox body founded by Bp. Jonathan V. Zotique (Mar Zotikos), its presiding bishop. Mar Zotikos was a Franciscan monk who received consecration through Old Catholic sources. The church's ministry, which is built around a small group of independent Franciscans, both priests and lay brothers, is directed to the sexual minorities of Toronto (homosexuals, transsexuals, transvestites, prostitutes) and others (e.g., drug addicts) who feel rejected by the Eastern Orthodox communions and the Roman Catholic Church. As independent Franciscans, the group sees itself as being "for, of, and by gay Christians holding hope that in good faith we can touch the charity of the Church of Christ as a whole."

The clergy of the church are self-employed, and ministers are worker-clerics. Both men and women are accepted for ordination to the priesthood. The church is

headed by its presiding bishop and a governing synod. Those affiliated with the church in the ordered life are organized as the Celtic-Catholic Culdee Community of Orthodox Monks, Hermits, Missionaries, and Evangelists of the Old Church of the Blessed Virgin, St. Mary of Glastonbury (Our Lady of Avalon), in Diaspora. Future plans call for the establishment of a rural retreat center (Avalon Abbey) for meditation and contemplation retreats.

Membership: Not reported.

Apostolic Catholic and Spiritual Church

3377 Bethel Rd. SE, Port Orchard, WA 98366

The Apostolic Catholic and Spiritual Church traces its beginning to the Old Catholic Church of India founded in southern India in 1890 by Bp. Matthew A. Grimes. The church subsequently transferred its operations to the United States and adopted its present name. It is currently headed by the fifth apostolic archbishop, W. E. Haley, who traces his succession directly to Bishop Grimms.

The church adopted an Old Catholic perspective, by which it means that it is in substantial theological agreement with the Roman Catholic Church while being administratively independent of it. The Roman Church considers Old Catholic orders valid but irregular. Unlike many Old Catholic bodies, the Apostolic Catholic and Spiritual Church is essentially accepting of the developments in doctrine and practice promulgated by Vatican II.

The Apostolic Catholic and Spiritual Church has one important difference with the Roman Church. It has adopted a pastoral view regarding a set of contemporary ethical issues and rejects what it sees as the legalistic approach to issues such as abortion, sexual orientation, divorce and remarriage, birth control, and various complex medical issues. It encourages members to reach decisions on these questions by searching their own conscience in the light of their understanding of the central Gospel principles of truth, justice, compassion, and love. In addition, the Church allows priests to marry, and welcomes women, lesbians, and gays into the ordained ministry.

In line with many Old Catholic churches, the Church asks its priests to support themselves through outside employment, rather than drawing salaries as parish priests.

Membership: Not reported. Parishes are located in Washington, California, Nevada, and New Mexico.

Sources:

Apostolic Catholic and Spiritual Church. acschurch.org.

Brotherhood of Mithras

Box 94, Uniontown, OH 44685-0094

Alternate Address: International headquarters: 11 Ellswood Ct., Lovelace Rd., Surbiton, Surrey, London KT6 6NQ, United Kingdom.

The Brotherhood of Mithras was founded in 1980 in Surrey, suburban London, by a group of men who wished to reconstruct and revive the ancient religion of Mithras. It is their belief that Mithras was a real person who lived some 3,500 years ago in Persia, and that the gods decided to make him a god like unto themselves. What is commonly known is that the religion of Mithras spread through the Roman Empire and competed for many centuries with Christianity. Statues of Mithras have been found in Roman ruins, many of which included Mithraic worship centers. The god is often depicted nude and entwined with a snake or in the act of plunging a knife into a bull (a statue of the latter type, called a *tauroctonous*, graces the inter sanctum of Mithraic temples).

According to the ancient story, Mithras was set a task by the gods to prove his worthiness. He was sent a messenger in the form of a raven who told him to slay a bull. After meditating on the instructions, he herded a bull into a cave and there slew it with his knife. With this act Mithras became an object of worship for his bravery, virility, and manliness.

The brotherhood has attempted to reconstruct the worship of Mithras in the context of phallic worship and the contemporary revival of sex magick. Worship takes place in the nude in a temple that, like the original story's cave, is void of any natural source of light. It is believed that during the sex act men create more energy than women, so an all-male circle creates more energy than a mixed group would. The energy thus raised is used for various worthy ends.

The brotherhood is open to all men over the age of 21. Initiation is an arduous ordeal that involves corporal punishment, humiliation, and subjugation. Personal limits are respected, but it is expected that they will be extended in order to reach a new level of experience.

Membership: Not reported. There are centers in England and the United States.

Sources:

Speidel, M. P. *Mithras-Orion: Greek Hero and Roman Army God*. Leiden, Netherlands: Brill, 1984.

Catholic Church of the Americas
c/o Office of the Presiding Bishop, 1201 W Esplanade Ave., Ste. 1709, Kenner, LA 70065

The Catholic Church of the Americas was founded in 1996 by a group of clergy, many with Roman Catholic backgrounds. Its purpose was to establish a community of faith that was open to all people without regard to race, color, gender, sexual orientation or preference, nationality, or socioeconomic status. This goal sets them apart from the Roman Catholic Church, which condemns homosexuality and does not admit women to the ministry. Founders included Fr. Benjamin Evans, Deacon Daniel Little, Bp. Denis Martel, Bp. John Reeves, and Fr. Jerry Wood. Bishop Martel was named the first presiding bishop.

The church continues the sacramental worship of the western Catholic tradition. It affirms the centrality of the seven sacraments (as redefined in the post–Vatican II context). It affirms the need of apostolic succession. and its bishops were consecrated in several lineages available in independent Catholic circles, though it emphasizes its lineage from Bp. Carlos Duarte Costa (1888–1961) and the Brazilian Catholic Apostolic Church. It dissents from Roman Catholic doctrine of transubstantiation, but holds to the real presence of Christ in the Eucharist. The church differs from the Roman Catholic Church in that it has opened the sacrament of marriage to all adults, and thus is willing to oversee same-gender unions. In addition, it sanctions the remarriage of individuals who had a previous marriage otherwise legally dissolved. Divorce also is not seen as preventing one from receiving the sacraments. As with the reception of the Eucharist, the church does not view gender, sexuality, and present marital status as barriers to receiving any of the sacraments, including ordination. The church sanctions the ordination to the priesthood of women, married persons, and members of sexual minorities, if they are otherwise qualified. In its sacramental liturgy, the church seeks to use inclusive language.

The church is headed by its Synod of Bishops and the National Synod of clergy and laity. It is the desire of the church, however, that decisions be made by consensus rather than by any part of the church, including the bishops, acting unilaterally.

Membership: Not reported. In 2008 there were three centers for worship, one in Louisiana and two in Massachusetts.

Sources:

Catholic Church of the Americas. www.thecca.org.

Christianbrunn Brotherhood
The Hermitage, RR1, Box 149, Pitman, PA 17964

The Christianbrunn (Christianspring) Brotherhood is a gay spiritual community that asserts as its purpose the worship of life. It is an all-male ordered community that existed in the eighteenth century in the Moravian Church. Most especially, they look to Christian Renatus Graf von Zinzendorf (1827–1752), the homosexual son of Count Nicolas Ludwig von Zinzendorf, the Moravian leader whose efforts led

to the community's revival. As early as 1728, a group of 26 unmarried men moved into a common household. During the last eight years of his life, Christian Renatus had been in charge of the single brothers' choirs of the Moravian Brethren.

In 1749 in the American colonies the Moravians established Christianspring, a community west of Nazareth, Pennsylvania. It was occupied entirely by unmarried men for the next 50 years. However, by the end of the eighteenth century it was caught up in the larger changes in the church, and early in the nineteenth century it merged into the community at Nazareth.

The attempt to reestablish Christianbrunn as an openly gay community began in 1987 with the founding of an ordered community. Brother Johannes Renatus Zinzendorf was the chief councilman.

The brotherhood believes that life is all there is—there is nothing else before, beyond, or after this life, and all morality, aesthetics, and ethics derive from that fact. Stewardship is critical—the earth is finite, so members of the brotherhood assume the role of caretakers for wise management of its limited resources to meet basic needs of food, shelter, education, and freedom for all. As gay men, they look upon semen as the essence of life and the erect phallus as the giver of semen.

The brotherhood called themselves spiritual atheists because they embrace the mystery of life without a belief in a higher power. Good works, which enhance and respect all life forms, is the spiritual value that raises consciousness into a godlike form and can make the doers stewards and the guiding force on the planet. They can also reveal ways in which individuals are all parts of one great wholeness rather than isolated entities.

These attributes are incorporated into the Hermitage, a working farm and retreat center where people come for limited periods to contemplate the meaning of their existence. Summer residences are free in exchange for a limited amount of daily work, which is part of the stewardship. The brotherhood describes the Hermitage as one of the few places for such contemplation, free of theological and ideological conformity and allowing freedom of inquiry into one's nature and the meaning of life itself.

As a working farm, the Hermitage stresses self-reliance, and is sustained by crafts, livestock, and the raising of crops, in addition to donations.

Membership: In 2002 the community had 100 associates and two full-time residence members.

Periodicals: *The Flaming Faggot*.

Sources:

Hamilton, J. Taylor, and Kenneth G. Hamilton. *History of the Moravian Church*. Bethlehem, PA: Interprovincial Board of Christian Education, Moravian Church in America, 1967.

Church of Universal Love (Washington)
PO Box 1620, Stanwood, WA 98292

The Church of Universal Love (Washington) was founded in the mid-1980s by Rev. Barbara Allen as a New Age fellowship. Although open to all, it has a special mission within the homosexual community of the Pacific Northwest. The church considers itself omnidenominational. It has no creed and draws inspiration from all the master teachers, especially Jesus and Buddha. It sponsors workshops on metaphysics, parapsychology, world religions, and holistic healing techniques, as well as retreats on a variety of subjects. On most Sundays the church sponsors a circle of love meeting that includes guided meditation, group sharing at an intensive level, Sufi dancing, and a potluck supper.

The church welcomes people from different spiritual paths and believes that each individual must develop his or her own individual way. The church attempts to help individuals in their spiritual searches and avoids proselytization to a particular view. Interaction between members is based upon the Golden Rule, nonjudgmental attitudes, and unconditional love.

Church activities are held throughout the Puget Sound area at various locations, and are led by Allen and her associates. The church sponsors an annual New Year's retreat.

Membership: Not reported.

Remarks: The Church of Universal Love is not connected with a church of the same name headquartered in El Paso, Texas.

Church of Zeus and Ganymede (CZG)
Current address not obtained for this edition.

The Church of Zeus and Ganymede (CZG) takes its name from the ancient Greek tale of Ganymede, a prince of the house of Troy who was so loved by Zeus that the mighty deity changed himself into a great eagle, took the youth away, and made him immortal. Ganymede became his cup bearer. While believing that there is only one religion, and striving to come into greater harmony with the Almighty (Zeus, Yahweh, God, Allah, or any of the other names used by various groups over the centuries) and to achieve a greater knowledge of creation, the church particularly celebrates loving relationships on the model of Zeus and Ganymede—that is to say, it sanctions and promotes man-boy sexual relationships.

The CZG describes itself as more a disorganization than an organization, in that it has no hierarchy, no property, no bank accounts, and no schedule of meetings (because many of the activities it promotes are illegal in the countries of North America and Europe). Thus the church is somewhat diffuse and ephemeral. It exists to provide spiritual support for its members. Its basic principle and rule is love, which is defined as a deep caring for the happiness and well-being of someone else. The CZG asserts that loving relationships (sexual or otherwise) between males, regardless of their ages, are a gift from the Almighty.

Considering the social disapproval of the primary idea behind the church, the CZG articulated a "Boylove Code of Ethics" that draws upon the nature of the practice in ancient Greece. Noting the sexual aspect of most man-boy love relationships, it calls for participants to deal with the issue of sex "in a mature and responsible way." However, the code does not address the dominant cultural view that boylove relationships are by their very nature manipulative and exploitative of the younger party, who because of his age cannot deal with the relationship in a mature manner.

Though the church has an Internet presence, it is unlikely that it will develop a more visible and formal structure given the nature of its beliefs and practices.

Membership: Not reported.

Community of the Love of Christ (Evangelical Catholic)
Current address not obtained for this edition.

Community of the Love of Christ (Evangelical Catholic) is one of the oldest church organizations that developed a specific ministry to the homosexual community and openly identified with its concerns. The organization was founded in 1959 as the Primitive Catholic Church (Evangelical Catholic) by Mikhail (Michael) Francis Itkin (1936–1989). Itkin began his work as a minister in the gay community in 1955 when he was licensed by George A. Hyde (b. 1923), later the presiding bishop of the Orthodox Catholic Church in America. Hyde had founded the Eucharistic Catholic Church in the 1940s as a church for homosexuals. Itkin was ordained in 1957 and continued to work with Hyde and the Eucharistic Catholic Church for two more years, then left in 1959 at the same time that Hyde was moving his work into the American Holy Orthodox Catholic Apostolic Eastern Church. Itkin accused Hyde of backing away from an openly gay ministry and "moving back into the closet."

Itkin gathered those members who agreed with him and for more than a year led them as an episcopal administrator until he was consecrated by Abp. Christopher Maria Stanley in November 1960. Stanley had orders to consecrate Itkin from Hugh George de Willmott Newman of the Catholicate of the West, which carried a variety of lines of episcopal succession. Among those lines was the Syro-

Chaldean succession of the Church of the East brought to the west by Ulric Vernon Herford (Mar Jacobus), founder of the Evangelical Catholic Communion.

The new church first chose the name Primitive Catholic Church (Evangelical Catholic), but after Itkin's consecration the name was changed to Gnostic Catholic Church (Evangelical Catholic). The new name led to confusion, as some thought the church emulated the gnostic heretics. Then the members called themselves "Free Catholics," but learned of a British fascist group using that designation. Again the church adopted a new name—Western Orthodox Catholic (Anglican Orthodox). During this period, the church members became aware of Ulrich Vernon Herford (1866–1938) and the Evangelical Catholic Communion. They began to see Herford's lineage as the primary line of the historical episcopate received from Stanley. Itkin began to correspond with some European bishops who were attempting to carry on Herford's work, and from them he received permission to reformulate the Evangelical Catholic Communion in the United States. In 1978 Mar Anthony (W. Martin Andrew), the British successor to Herford, recognized Itkin's work in the United States as "the sole jurisdiction actually carrying on the work of Mar Jacobus and the original Evangelical Catholic Communion."

A short time after the development of the Evangelical Catholic Communion, Itkin and Stanley broke communion due in large part to the strong social activism advocated by Itkin. Among Itkin's first actions as a bishop was the consecration of a woman to the priesthood. Stanley, although open to female deacons, was opposed to their admission to the priesthood. In 1963 the communion underwent an internal reorganization, transforming itself into a religious order that originally called itself the Brotherhood of the Love of Christ: Evangelical Catholic Communion. That name was changed in 1970 to the Community of the Love of Christ (Evangelical Catholic), its present name, to eliminate the sexist connotations of the word *brotherhood*.

During the 1960s the church attracted a number of able leaders such as John Perry-Hooker, a psychologist working with a youth ministry in Boston. The church became deeply involved in civil rights and antiwar crusades. Itkin, heralding what would be termed "liberation theology" in the 1970s, articulated a revolutionary Christian theology that emphasized pacifism, freedom from oppression, and civil rights for minorities. He advocated gay liberation and the role of Christianity as a means for creating a universal androgynous community. The work suffered a severe setback in 1968 when more conservative elements in the church, including those who rejected female priests, split the communion and took most of the property with them. They reorganized as the Evangelical Catholic Communion. Itkin and his followers continued their efforts as the Community of the Love of Christ.

In the late 1980s it became known that Itkin was suffering from AIDS. He passed away in 1991 and was succeeded by Bp. Marcia Herndon (d. 1997), whom he had consecrated in 1985.

The community adopted a distinct position within the Syro-Chaldean tradition, as it also considers itself a part of the Mennonite-Radical Reformation heritage. From the Church of the East, it draws an apostolic liturgical heritage. It accepts only the first three Ecumenical Councils, which includes an acceptance of the Nicene Creed. However, because of its Radical Reformation heritage, it takes a "low church" approach to the sacraments. Only three, not seven, are acknowledged. The church also accepts, for historical purposes only, the December 1903 Pastoral Letter to the Syro-Chaldean Christians in India authored by Herford.

Following its own statement of faith that acknowledges Christ as sovereign and liberator, the community is fully committed to a liberation theological praxis that includes a struggle against sexism, heterosexism, racism, classism, imperialism, and violence. It strongly supports and works for Christian gay/lesbian liberation, feminism, racial integration, civil rights, economic mutuality, democracy, universal citizenship, and nonviolence. The community does not consider itself a gay or homosexual church, but rather "a Christian covenant-community for all people, preaching the inclusive love of God to everyone." "Everyone" includes, specifically, gay and lesbian individuals.

Membership: Not reported.

Remarks: For a period beginning in 1971, Itkin held joint membership in the Metropolitan Community Church (MCC). He saw MCC as committed to his own belief of "unity in diversity," but concluded by 1984 that such was not the case. He withdrew his affiliation with MCC as a member, though he retained status as a "friend."

In *The Old Catholic Sourcebook* by Karl Pruter and J. Gordon Melton, Bishop Itkin was confused with another bishop who had also taken the ecclesiastical title Mar Mikhail and who resides in the San Francisco Bay area. The other Mar Mikhail is the leader of the Holy Apostolic–Catholic Church of the East (Syro-Chaldean).

Sources:

Faith and Practice of the Brotherhood of the Love of Christ. New York: Pax Christi Press, 1966.

Itkin, Michael Francis. *The Hymn of Jesus.* New York: Pax Christi Press, n.d.

Itkin, Michael Francis Augustine. *The Spiritual Heritage of Port-Royal.* New York: Pax Christi Press, 1966.

Itkin, Mikhail. *The Radical Jesus and Gay Consciousness.* Hollywood, CA: Communiversity West, 1972.

Ecumenical Catholic Church

20 Lincoln, Irvine, CA 92604-1947

The Ecumenical Catholic Church (ECC) was founded by Mark Steven Shirilau. Shirilau was born in 1955 as Mark Steven Shirey. In 1984 he "married" Jeffery Michael Lau, and both assumed the last name Shirilau. The church is a liturgical body that draws upon Catholic, Episcopal, and Lutheran traditions, but is distinguished by its direct and open ministry to the gay and lesbian community as well as to women, the divorced, and others disenfranchised by the mainline church. Shirilau was raised a Lutheran but joined the Episcopal Church. He was consecrated to the episcopacy by Bp. Donald Lawrence Jolly of the Independent Catholic Church International on Pentecost in 1991. Shirilau is one of the more educated Independent Catholic leaders, having graduated from both the Episcopal Theological School at Claremont (Bloy House) and the School of Theology at Claremont and having earned his Ph.D. from the University of California at Irvine.

The Ecumenical Catholic Church was designed to operate within the space between the very Protestant Universal Fellowship of Metropolitan Community Churches (with whom it maintains cordial relations) and Roman Catholic, Episcopal, and Lutheran churches that had not updated their social ethics stances regarding the gay and lesbian community.

The ECC expanded in 1995 when the four regional deans—Richard John Cardarelli of Hartford, Connecticut; Michael Robert Frost of Plattsburgh, New York; Denis Armand Martel of New Orleans, Louisiana; and Robert Wayne Martin of Oklahoma City, Oklahoma—were consecrated bishops (though several later left the church). In 2008 the church had bishops in New York, Iowa, North Carolina, and Oklahoma.

Membership: In 2002 the church reported 1,000 members in 12 churches in the United States and Australia.

Educational Facilities:

Holy Apostles Seminary, Irvine, California (correspondence seminary).

Periodicals: *The Tablet.*

Sources:

Ecumenical Catholic Church. www.ecchurch.org.

Shirilau, Mark. *Apostolic Succession in the Ecumenical Catholic Church.* Irving, CA: Healing Spirit Press, 1998.

———. *Formative Documents of the Ecumenical Catholic Church: From the Marriage of Mark and Jeffrey Shirilau to the Monsignor Appointment of Robert Hall.* Irving, CA: Healing Spirit Press, 2001.

———. *History and Overview of the Ecumenical Catholic Church: The First Ten Years: 1985–95.* Ville Grand, CA: Healing Spirit Press, 1995.

Eucharistic Catholic Church

Current address not obtained for this edition.

The very first ministry to the homosexual community was begun in Atlanta, Georgia, in 1946 by the Rev. George A. Hyde (b. 1923). Eleven years later, Hyde was consecrated by Abp. Cyril John Clement Sherwood (1895–1969) and began to move his ministry into Sherwood's American Holy Orthodox Catholic Apostolic Eastern Church. As he worked under Sherwood, he moved to Washington, D.C., a prelude to his forming the Orthodox Catholic Church of America in 1960. He backed away from an identification of his new church with the homosexual community, but continued an interest in ministering to gay people.

One ministry authorized by Hyde was a new Eucharistic Catholic parish in New York City's Greenwich Village, begun in 1970 by Fr. Robert Mary Clement (b. 1925). Clement stayed with Hyde for several years, seeing ordination in an apostolic liturgical church outside of independent Old Catholic circles. Unable to locate a bishop who would accept his gay congregation, he turned finally in 1974 to Abp. Richard A. Marchenna (1911–1982), then head of the Old Roman Catholic Church (Marchenna), who consecrated him. Clement reorganized his work as a separate episcopal jurisdiction independent of the Orthodox Catholic Church of America.

Membership: There is one congregation of several hundred members.

Gay and Lesbian Atheists and Humanists (GALAH)

PO Box 34635, Washington, DC 20043

The Gay Atheist League of America (GALAH) was formed in 1978 as the Gay Atheist League of America by Daniel Curzon and Tom Rolfsen, both former members of the Roman Catholic Church. Both had come to feel that there is a direct relationship between the doctrines of religion and social discrimination against homosexuals. The formation of GALAH was occasioned by an exchange of letters between Rolfsen and John Raphael Quinn (b. 1929), the Catholic archbishop in San Francisco. Rolfsen concluded that the church had developed a tradition of persecuting homosexuals. Curzon had come to feel that all religions were oppressive, especially Catholicism, born-again Protestantism, and Orthodox Judaism. The new organization rejected the attempts of gay religious organizations to seek accommodation with the church.

GALAH teaches that each person must discover the moral basis of life, without reference to what it considers self-appointed religious experts. They also support separation of church and state and oppose attempts by religionists to impress their antigay moral codes on legislation. They also believe that churches should be taxed, that is, treated as businesses. GALAH has assumed an activist role, demonstrating in opposition to antigay legislation.

Membership: Not reported. There are monthly meetings in San Francisco, Washington, D.C., and Los Angeles.

Periodicals: *GALAH Newsletter.*

Sources:

Gay and Lesbian Atheists and Humanists. www.galah.org/

Curzon, David. *Something You Do in the Dark.* New York: Putnam, 1971.

Independent Catholic Christian Church

c/o Bishop Timothy Cravens, 721 Melon Terr., Unit A, Philadelphia, PA 19103

The Independent Catholic Christian Church is a small autonomous Catholic jurisdiction led by its presiding bishop, Most Rev. Timothy Cravens. In 2004, not long after the church's founding, Cravens accepted the Episcopal oversight of the Augustinians of the Immaculate Heart of Mary, a previously existing religious community. The latter was founded in 1993 by Joseph Augustine Menna and a small group of friends, as an Augustinian Association of the Christian Faithful to pray, minister, and build spiritual friendship together. The new associations sought to live the Rule of Augustine in a more inclusive manner. They were unsuccessful in obtaining a home within the Roman Catholic Church and thus, after some years of seeking, found their way to Bishop Cravens. The parishes led by the Augustinian Association currently constitute the majority of work in the Independent Catholic Christian Church.

The Church is a traditional sacramental Catholic jurisdiction that affirms the authority of the Bible, the sufficiency of the Nicene Creed as a statement of Christian faith, and salvation through Jesus Christ. It administers the seven sacraments—baptism, the Eucharist, confirmation, marriage, anointing of the sick, reconciliation, and ordination. It leadership is vested in a threefold ministry of bishops, priests, and deacons who exist in a lineage of apostolic succession. The church differs from Roman Catholicism primarily in its inclusivist policy of ordaining men and women—as well as gay, lesbian, bisexual, and transgendered people—to all levels of the priesthood. It also sanctions the marriage of same-sex couples as sacramentally valid.

Both its Catholic affirmations and its inclusivist policies dictate the church's ecumenical relations. It has found communion with three churches: the Free Episcopal Church, the Diocese of Rumney Marsh, and the United American Catholic Church.

Membership: Nor reported. The Augustinian Association oversees Parishes in Media, Pennsylvania, and Durham, North Carolina.

Sources:

Independent Catholic Christian Church. www.forministry.com/USPAINDPTICCCI/.

Gay Buddhist Fellowship

2215-R Market St., PMB 456, San Francisco, CA 94114

The Gay Buddhist Fellowship, like similar groups in other cities, exists to support Buddhist practice in the San Francisco gay community. Membership includes practitioners who identify with all of the various Buddhist traditions, and a broad program is conducted to accommodate a spectrum of needs and desires. Offered on a regular basis are dharma talks, classes, time for sitting meditation, retreats, and a variety of workshops and classes on topics of interest to the gay community, from personal relationships to HIV to social action.

The fellowship was founded in 1990. It is a single center operating out of rented facilities in San Francisco and has analogous structures such as the Lesbian Buddhist Group and the Gay Zen Group, both of which are semiautonomous groups sponsored by the International Buddhist Meditation Center in Los Angeles. Buddhism has expressed no particular animus toward homosexuality like that found in many Christian and Jewish circles, and thus the actual number of explicitly gay and/or lesbian Buddhits groups is relatively small.

Membership: Not reported.

Periodicals: *Gay Buddhist Fellowship Newsletter*.

Sources:

Gay Buddhist Fellowship. www.gaybuddhist.org/index.html.

Morreale, Don. *The Complete Guide to Buddhist America*. Boston: Shambhala, 1998.

Hermetic Order of the Silver Sword

2483 Gerrard St. E, Scarborough, ON, Canada M1N 1W7

The Hermetic Order of the Silver Sword, founded in 1982 in Toronto by Ian Young and James Perry, is a ceremonial magical order whose rituals are based on those of the Hermetic Order of the Golden Dawn. The Silver Sword attempts to unify elements of Cabbalistic, Rosicrucian, and pagan traditions into a workable magical system, a modern science of mental power and self-knowledge. The order sees magic as utilizing ceremonial acts and images deeply rooted in the human consciousness. Ritual actions and the manipulation of symbols produce changes in the magician that affect the world.

The order promotes communication among groups attempting to revive and explore Western spiritual and magical traditions and sees itself as working toward the healing of the Earth through enlightenment and friendship. Membership is by invitation.

Membership: Not reported.

Inclusive Celtic Church

PO Box 31486, San Francisco, CA 94131-0486

The Inclusive Celtic Church is an independent, sacramental, and inclusive Christian church that has adopted a British Celtic heritage largely defined by a liturgy derived from the Book of Common Prayer, the Iona Abbey Worship Book, and the Celtic primer by Brendan O'Malley. The church draws inspiration from the pre-Roman Christianity of the Celtic peoples but tries to operate out of a contemporary worldview. The church operates as an inclusive community, a keynote being the welcoming of lesbian, gay, bisexual, and transgender persons into the life and leadership of the church. Priests stand ready to bless unions for gay and lesbian couples.

The church originated with the establishment of the Church of St. Savior in San Francisco in 2002. Following the election of a bishop, the congregation assumed the name New Church–Inclusive Anglican Reform. Over the next three years, members discovered an affinity for contemporary Celtic Christian spirituality. At the same time, the church developed beyond San Francisco. In 2007 the church, now grown into a new denomination, adopted a new name—Inclusive Celtic Episcopal Church. It later dropped the word Episcopal.

Church members have committed themselves to be present where those of other churches will not or have forgotten to go, especially where they can show their support of the LGBT community, victims of crime, indigenous peoples, and the homeless. The membership of the cathedral congregation goes out of its way to welcome the homeless to their services and to offer hospitality. They especially attempt to create safe spaces for those who visit their community.

The church is led by its bishop, Rt. Rev. Rusty Clyma. It has developed a policy of not entering into intercommunion agreements, as these tend to limit inclusivism. Thus, the church posits that all communities and individuals of faith who live out the All Inclusive Love of God are in communion with them.

Membership: Not reported.

Sources:

Inclusive Celtic Church. inclusivecelticchurch.com/default.aspx.

O'Malley, Brendon. *Celtic Blessings and Prayers: Making All Things Sacred*. New London, CT: Twenty-Third Publications, 1999.

National Catholic Church of America

c/o Priory of St. Martin de Porres, 166 Jay St., Albany, NY 12210-1806

The National Catholic Church of America traces its history to 1994 and the founding of the Order of Saint John the Divine, an order religious community that accepted both men and women into a life of prayer and apostolic service in the world. The order was founded by then Fr. Richard G. Roy, and was distinctive in its admitting otherwise qualified candidates to membership and to Holy Orders without reference to their gender, marital status, sexual orientation, race, or any physical disabilities. Roy believed that an inclusive spirituality would be the keynote of the Catholic Christian community in the third millennium.

In 1997 Roy, who had served as abbot of the Order of Saint John the Divine, was consecrated as a bishop. He received several of the lines of apostolic succession available in the independent Catholic world, but primarily acknowledges that from former Brazilian Roman Catholic bishop Carlos Duarte Costa, and the independent Brazilian Catholic Apostolic Church. Several months later, on New Year's Day 1998, he led in the founding of the National Catholic Church of America. Previously, he had been active in the ministry to people with AIDS. In 2008 Roy was residing in Albany, New York, with Br. Stephen K. Peterson, OSJD, his life partner since 1975.

The church follows the faith and practice of the Western Catholic tradition but draws a line between the essential teachings of the faith (as summarized by the seven Ecumenical Councils and the Nicene Creed) and various matters of church discipline and its historic development and application. The church affirms the equal role of women in the life of the church and will ordain otherwise qualified females to the priesthood. It also celebrates "the love which can exist between persons of the same gender and advocate[s] justice and equality before the law for those who are gay or lesbian."

Membership: In 2008 the church listed three parishes, two in New York and one in Colorado.

Sources:

National Catholic Church of America. members.aol.com/NatCathCh/.

Orthodox Episcopal Church of God

Box 1528, San Francisco, CA 94101

The Rev. Ray Broshears (d. 1982), founder of the Orthodox Episcopal Church of God, was one of the most controversial of all gay ministers of the 1970s. Headquartered in that section of San Francisco popularly called the Tenderloin, the residence of the largest gay community in the United States, Broshears became a national figure through his radical activism on behalf of civil rights for gay people. He opened and operated the Helping Hands Gay Community Service Center for political action on behalf of pro-gay politicians and to facilitate legal counseling and assistance, drug rehabilitation, and gay-oriented activities. He ran for Congress, unsuccessfully, on several occasions. Possibly his most controversial activity was starting the Lavender Panthers, a group he formed to prevent youth gangs from invading the Tenderloin and beating up gay people. The members were trained in judo and karate.

Broshears was reared in the Cumberland Presbyterian Church but became a Pentecostal at an early age. He attended school at the White Wing College (of the Church of God of Prophecy) at Cleveland, Tennessee. He left the Pentecostal movement and in 1966 founded the Orthodox Episcopal Church of God. It was not until 1969 that he and the church began to be involved in the gay community.

The Orthodox Episcopal Church, now apparently defunct, was eclectic, combining elements of traditional Catholicism with liberation theology and psychic/New Age thinking. Its program was mainly expressed in social activism. Congregations were centered in the gay communities of California (Los Angeles and San Jose) and El Paso, Texas. Broshears edited several Gay Alliance periodicals, including *Gay Pride Quarterly* and the *Gay Crusader*.

Membership: Not reported.

Periodicals: *The Light of Understanding*.

Pride Church International

Current address not obtained for this edition.

Pride Church International emerged in 2001 from the remnants of the American Orthodox Catholic and Apostolic Church, Holy Synod of the Americas, formerly the Diocese of Florida of the American Catholic Church. After becoming independent, the Synod had adopted an Eastern Orthodox theology and liturgy, but retained the American Catholic Church's inclusive stance toward women and gays and lesbians, who were welcomed into all areas of church life and leadership. However, on December 31, 2000, Met. Abp. Vladimir Sergius II (b. 1946), the Synod's primate, resigned and dissolved the corporation, and in 2001 he reorganized his own ministry as the Pride Church International, with a primary relationship to the gay/lesbian/bisexual/transgendered (GLBT) community. Bp. John Columba continued the former Holy Synod as the Orthodox Christian Fellowship of Mercy.

The church is Orthodox in faith and practice. It uses the Divine Liturgy of Bishop Serapion, a mid-fourth-century Egyptian liturgy, as the standard liturgy of the new church, though the primate made some alterations to adapt it to Orthodox demands. It added "holy union" of gay and lesbian couples to its list of seven sacraments beside marriage of heterosexual couples. A list of GLBT "saints" was added to the church calendar for annual commemoration. As the only national Eastern

Orthodox church openly identified with the GBLT community, the church has grown rapidly as GBLT people with Orthodox backgrounds discover its existence. The church actively recruits Orthodox clergy. In 2002 there were four bishops assisting the primate.

Educational Facilities:

Holy Wisdom Seminary.

Membership: Not reported.

Remarks: Pride Church International has cordial relations with the Russian Orthodox Church in America (not to be confused with either of the large Russian Orthodox jurisdictions, the Orthodox Church in America or the Russian Orthodox Church Outside of Russia).

Sources:

Pride Church International. http://pridechurch.faithweb.com

Reformed Catholic Church

c/o St. Sebastian Catholic Church, PO Box 2, Worthington, OH 43085

The Reformed Catholic Church was founded in 2000 by Robert J. Allman. In 1995, Allman had led in the founding of the American Catholic Church, which continues through several splinters groups. Like the American Catholic Church, the Reformed Catholic Church was established as a church that continues the beliefs and practices (especially the liturgical tradition) of Roman Catholicism but has opened its doors to those who have had difficulties in participating fully in the Roman Catholic Church. Most importantly, the Reformed Catholic Church is welcoming to women, the divorced, and those who self-identify as gay, lesbian, bisexual, or transgender. Women and gay people are accepted into the ordained ministry as every level.

In 2005 Archbishop Allman resigned as the presiding bishop of the Reformed Catholic Church and leadership fell to Philip Zimmerman, whom Allman had consecrated to the episcopacy a year earlier. Under Zimmerman's leadership, the church has prospered. In 2006 Zimmerman consecrated four additional bishops: Patrick Batuyong, David Frazee, Joshua Alekzandor, and G. Peter Posthumus. Most Rev. Mother Raelynn Scoot, the first female bishop, was consecrated in 2007. The church is currently divided into seven dioceses that cover the United States (including Hawaii and Alaska). In addition, there are several ordered communities representative of the Jesuit, Franciscan, Benedictine, and Dominican traditions. The church has appointed nuncios to Ireland, Australia, Africa, and South and Central America.

The church has developed a radio program, *Reformed Catholic Church Radio*, which is delivered by podcast.

Membership: Not reported. In 2008, there were 39 parishes, missions, and monastic centers in the United States and two in Ontario, Canada.

Periodical: *The Pax Press Newspaper*.

Sources:

Reformed Catholic Church. www.reformedcatholicchurch.org/.

Sarum Episcopal (Old Catholic) Church

1757 North D St., San Bernardino, CA 92405-4015

The Sarum Episcopal Church was founded in 1989 in Riverside, California, by two priests ordained as independent Old Catholics. The church exists to provide a sacramental ministry to gay men and lesbians. The first parish, St. Aelred's, originated in a private home but soon moved to its present facilities in San Bernardino, California. There the church operates a coffee house (no alcoholic beverages served) and houses a number of services for the gay community in the area, and has a special ministry for people with AIDS.

The church took its name from Sarum, the old name of Salisbury, a city in England that was an important center of English Catholicism before the

Reformation of the sixteenth century. The liturgy used throughout England, the "Sarum Rite," took its name from this city.

The church is headed collectively by its priests because the jurisdiction has not yet designated a bishop. The church annually hosts a conference of independent Catholic bishops, priests, and laity for a day of discussions and worship.

Membership: In 2008 there was a single independent parish of about 100 members.

Sources:

St. Aelred's Chapel of the Sarum Episcopal Church (Old Catholic). www.geocities.com/staelreds/page1html.

Breton, J. E. Paul. *Papers Presented at the First Annual Gathering of Independent Catholic Christians, September 15, 1990*. San Bernadino, CA: Sarum Episcopal Church, 1991.

Daily and Sunday Eucharist from the Book of Common Prayer of the Sarum Episcopal Church. San Bernadino, CA: Sarum Episcopal Church, 1990.

Temple of Priapus

PO Box 1164, Stn. H, Montreal, QC, Canada H3G 2N1

Priapus was a Greek god of Dionysus and Aphrodite, guardian deity of gardens, vineyards, and herbs. He personified male procreative power. Worship of Priapus spread to Greece in the fourth century B.C.E., during the time of Alexander. Groups devoted to his worship, and similar groups in other cultures also involved in erotic worship practices—often in the nudeand including ritual intercourse—survived throughout Europe, never having been completely suppressed.

Priapus worship reemerged in North America in the 1970s due to the efforts of a Reverend Jackson who had been ordained during a visit to Italy and subsequently, in 1973, incorporated the church in California. The year before, a dentist in Calgary, Alberta, had incorporated the church in Canada. He remains as a high priest.

The affairs of the Temple of Priapus (also known as the Church of St. Priapus) are administered by a governing council that meets every four years. In 1984 D. Francis Cassidy was elected the new pontifex, a position he has held since. Membership in the temple consists primarily of gay and bisexual men, though some temples have heterosexual gatherings. A greater variation of members can be found in temples in Europe, some of which (such as those in Switzerland) include families. There are four levels of membership in the temple.

Members acknowledge the power and beauty of the phallus and see it as their path to truth and wisdom; a source of joy and pleasure whose power can destroy evil. Sex is a vital part of the services, which may also involve sex magick and other forms of magick (candle, ceremonial, and so on). Semen is regarded with reverence and is considered a sacrament of the Most Holy Seed. High priests are ordained following the rites of Mary Magdalen in the west and similar rites in the east.

The church has formed an alliance with the American Gnostic Church.

Membership: Not reported. In 1997 there were six temples in Canada and 11 in the United States.

Periodicals: *Cock.*

Sources:

Temple of Priapus. www.templepriapus.org.

United Independent Catholic Church

c/o Bp. John Reeves, 1603 Old Creal Springs Rd., Marion, IL 62959

The United Independent Catholic Church is a small Old Catholic jurisdiction founded in 2002 by Bp. John Reeves, formerly of the Catholic Church of the Americas, and bishop of the Diocese of St. Petersburg (Florida), and other bishops, all with an independent Catholic background. The church follows the Old Catholics in belief and practice. It does not recognize the administrative authority of the pope but recognizes the authority of the Bible, and administers the seven traditional sacraments.

The church differs primarily in its emphasis on the belief that God created all humans equal and that believers are called upon to love all without judgment. From this idea it has structured itself to welcome women to all levels of church leadership and has created a community that accepts all who believe in Jesus' call to love one another without regard to race, sexual orientation, economic status, or nationality.

The church is headed by its three bishops who head the three dioceses—the Diocese of St. Peter, the Diocese of St. Raphael, and the Diocese of St. Nicholas.

Membership: Not reported. In 2008 the church had fewer than 10 small communities that gathered weekly for worship.

Sources:

United Independent Catholic Church. uicchurch.homestead.com/index.html.

United Order of the Family of Christ

Current address not obtained for this edition.

The United Order of the Family of Christ was founded in 1966 by David-Edward Desmond of Denver, Colorado, as a Mormon-inspired communal group whose membership was entirely gay men. All of the members had been raised in the Church of Jesus Christ of Latter-day Saints, known for its strong stand against homosexual practice. The Order accepted the basic beliefs and practices of the Latter-day Saints, but rejects its leadership and their stance on self-affirming the gay life.

The Order was organized as a commune in which all the members' assets were held in common in a savings and checking account. At the time of its founding, membership consisted of young men between the ages of 18 and 30. Officers, called *keys*, led the group. One of their number is designated the first key, a position initially held by Desmond. The keys obtain guidance by holding council with the Heavenly Father and attempt to direct the group, thought of as a family, in such a way that it will bring union and peace among the members and with the Father.

Desmond has had a prophetic role within the group. It is believed that he has a special communion with God the Father, and members report seeing a golden halo around his head as he teaches.

Membership: Not reported.

Sources:

Shields, Steven L. *Divergent Paths of the Restoration*. Los Angeles: Restoration Press, 1990.

Universal Fellowship of Metropolitan Community Churches

8704 Santa Monica Blvd., 2nd Fl., Los Angeles, CA 90069

Alternate Address: MCC of Toronto, 115 Simpson Ave., Toronto, ON M4K 1A1, Canada.

The largest of the several churches serving the homosexual community is the Universal Fellowship of Metropolitan Community Churches, founded in 1968 in Los Angeles by Pentecostal minister Troy Perry. In his popular autobiography *The Lord Is My Shepherd and He Knows I'm Gay* (1978) Perry recounts the story of his early religious and sexual awakenings. After discovering that he was homosexual, he repressed his desires and became a relatively happy married father and the pastor of a Church of God of Prophecy congregation in Santa Ana, California. Certain events, however, led to the revelation of his homosexual life, and he left the ministry. He then began the Metropolitan Community Church with a few friends and an ad placed in *The Advocate*, a popular gay periodical.

Perry carried his Pentecostalism into the Metropolitan Community Church. But as the church grew, primarily by the addition of other ministers who acknowledged their homosexual orientations and subsequently joined the church, a wide variety of worship and belief emerged. The church developed a theology of love in which the central affirmation is God's acceptance of all people, including homosexuals. The church's theology treats the Apostle Paul's statements about homosexuality in the Bible as cultural accretions much as his statements against women speaking in church. In line with this theology, Perry has blessed the union of gay couples living in "married" relationships.

Growth has continued in spite of continued resistance to gay concerns in the general population, the burning of several congregational buildings (four in 1973 alone), and the deaths of several members. It is headed by a seven-person Board of Elders elected by the General Conference, which meets annually. In 1973 the first woman, Freda Smith, was elected to the board. In 1984 a majority of the board members were women.

In 1985, as the AIDS crisis was beginning, the Metropolitan Community Churches began a programmed response that included a major education program, and attempted to focus the attention of the larger religious community on the problem of AIDS. In 1987 they began a new newsletter, *Alert*, aimed at keeping the church informed of the ongoing crises and providing resources for those affected.

The church is organized into 17 regions/districts, 8 of which are located outside the United States and oversee churches in Africa, New Zealand, Australia, Great Britain, Denmark, Canada, Mexico, and the Philippines.

Membership: In 2008 there were 185 congregations in the United States, 6 in Canada, and and additional number scattered around the world.

Educational Facilities:

Samaritan College, Los Angeles, California.

Periodicals: *Journey*. • *Alert*.

Sources:

Metropolitan Community Churches. www.mccchurch.org/.

Burns, Stephanie. *The Universal Fellowship of Metropolitan Community Churches (UFMCC): History and Governance*. Washington, DC: Wesley Theological Seminary, 2000.

Enroth, Ronald M., and Gerald E. Jamison. *The Gay Church*. Grand Rapids, MI: William B. Eerdmans, 1974.

Perry, Troy D. *The Lord Is My Shepherd and He Knows I'm Gay*. New York: Bantam Books, 1978.

Perry, Troy, and Thomas L. P. Swicegood. *Don't Be Afraid Anymore: The Story of Reverend Troy Perry and the Metropolitan Community Churches*. New York: St. Martin's Press, 1992.

Unclassified Religious Groups

All-One-God-Faith, Inc.

Box 28, Escondido, CA 92025

All-One-God-Faith, Inc., is not a church; it is a soap company. However, the products of the company have become the means of informing people of the religious vision of Rev. Henry Corey, a retired U.S. Marine, and Dr. E. H. Bronner (1908–1997), the soap maker. Their ideas are based upon the Dead Sea Scrolls, a group of Jewish religious writings from the first century B.C.E., discovered in 1948. The writings, which include texts of the Jewish Bible (the Old Testament), were found in a cave near the Dead Sea. Bronner termed their discovery the "Second Coming of God's Law."

All-One-God-Faith, Inc. (originally called the All-One-Faith-in-One-God State) was founded in 1959. It unites all persons through the teachings of Confucius's absolutes, Hippocrates's ABCs of perfect health, Hillel's moral ABCs, Jesus' Manual of Discipline, Mohammad's love, and Thomas Paine's army of principles for the brotherhood of man. The teachings are printed in fine print on the labels of each of the products produced by the soap company.

Membership: In the 1970s there were four congregations, in Cardiff-by-the-Sea, Modesto, and Oceanside, California, and Indianapolis, Indiana.

Sources:

Dr. Bronner's Magic "All-One!" www.drbronner.com/.

Ares Pilgrims

Current address not obtained for this edition.

Alternate Address: International headquarters: Frère Michel Potay, Maison de la Revelation, B.P. 16, 33740 Ares, France.

The Ares movement grew out of revelations received by a French prophet, Michel Potay (b. 1929). Potay was originally trained as an engineer, but in 1964 became a professional occultist. He converted to Orthodoxy and in 1969 was ordained a deacon in the Eglise Catholique Orthodoxe de France (Orthodox Catholic Church of France), an independent Western-rite Orthodox jurisdiction. Two years later he affiliated with the Living Church, a Russian Orthodox schism that had emerged in the Soviet Union with a decidedly pro-Soviet allegiance. Then in 1974 Potay and his family settled in Ares, not far from Bordeaux.

Soon after his arrival in Ares, he claimed that Jesus appeared to him and dictated what would become *The Gospel Delivered in Ares*. It was published that same year. In 1977 Potay received further revelation from God through a stick of light, the contents of which were included in a second volume, *The Book*. The two texts constitute *The Revelation of Ares*.

Potay placed the new revelation within the Abrahamic tradition that includes the Bible (with the exception of some books) and the Qu'ran, though both now are seen as less significant than the *Revelation of Ares*. The community that has grown from the revelations affirms a belief in monotheism but rejects the Trinitarian perspective, and does not affirm that Jesus is God. Their goal is to transform the world in order to realize the Eden originally planned by God for humankind. This goal can be reached if a "small remnant of just people" decides to adopt a different behavior; the Ares Pilgrims, that "small remnant," are called upon to effect that change, which will occur only several generations from now. Ares Pilgrims often engage in grassroots activism, uniting their efforts with others'.

The Ares Pilgrims are scattered mainly in France and other French-speaking regions (including Quebec). There is a core group of a few hundred who gather for missionary activities and various projects. An annual pilgrimage to Ares offers opportunity for gathering. Pilgrims may visit the spot where God is believed to have spoken to Potay, which is open during three periods of two weeks every summer. When approaching the House of the Saint's Word, the pilgrims wear white tunics and prostrate themselves on the ground while chanting self-selected passages from the Bible, the Qu'ran, or the *Revelation of Ares*. Potay often addresses the gathered pilgrims. Apart from the pilgrimage, the group has only a few ritual practices, primarily the reciting of the prayer "Father of the Universe" (a revised version of the Lord's Prayer) four times per day.

Membership: There is a core group consisting of several hundred members, and several thousand more people who identify themselves with Potay's message. The majority are in French-speaking countries (France, Switzerland, and Belgium). The *Revelation of Ares* appeared in English only in 1995, and the number of adherents in the North America remains minuscule, with most in Quebec.

Sources:

Ares Pilgrims. www.adira.net/facts+witness.html.

Mayer, Jean-Francois. *Michel Potay et la Revelation d' Ares*. Fribourg, Switzerland: Les Trois Nornes, 1990.

Mayer, Jean-Francois. "La' Revelation d' Ares': naissance d' un pelerinage dans la France contemporaine." *Social Compass* 48, no. 1 (2001): 63–75.

The Revelation of Ares. French-English bilingual ed. Ares, France: Maison de la Revelation, 1995.

Church of God Anonymous (CGA)

PO Box 100, Gowen, MI 49326

The Church of God Anonymous (CGA) was created over a period of 17 years at the end of the twentieth century by a group of recovering alcoholics, drug addicts, and veteran addiction activists in Michigan. They had been helped by Alcoholics Anonymous (AA), the famous alcoholic recovery program that emerged in the 1930s, and had come to feel that its formation was the greatest positive event of the twentieth century. They seek to "bring the spiritual program and living lessons of Alcoholics Anonymous to all who seek serenity and real meaning in their lives." They see the acknowledgment of God as conceived in AA ("God as you understand Him") to be a point of unity between people. All people can be helped by AA's God.

For many in the AA program, the trappings of religion—prayers, ceremonies, music, creeds, doctrines, and so on—have little meaning. "Real religion is centered upon the simple act of doing good!" Church founders have suggested that the pure clear light of God has been manipulated by a professional class of priests and other religious spokespersons to the point that it seems encased in a lantern, with the light filtered entirely by false and irrational dogmas. In contrast, the Twelve-Step God is the light clearly visible, with no dogma. It is expressed through the twelve-step experience of love and service.

The church differs from AA, in that it offers a variety of perspectives on various religious, ethical, and moral questions not related directly to the recovery process. Ethical statements are offered to members as suggestions, and individuals may disregard them, improve them, or accept them, as they see fit.

The church has its headquarters at the World General Service Office in Michigan and finds expression in churches and small groups across the country. Leadership is assumed by the president and Table of Twelve who manage the church's affairs, make policy, and attempt to discern the group conscience on issues that come before it. Consensus is established by reference to the CGA's steps, traditions, and principles (all derived from AA). Neither the president nor the Table of Twelve are to dictate to any church or church group. The church ordains ministers (deacons). All must be familiar with twelve-step programs, but are not necessarily program participants.

As might be expected, the church approves and uses an array of materials associated with twelve-step programs. Jim K., one of the church's founders, prepared *A Guide To The Twelve Steps of the Church of God Anonymous*.

Membership: Not reported. In 2002 the church reported related groups in Pennsylvania, Louisiana, New York, California, Florida, Massachusetts, Michigan, Texas, and Illinois.

Sources:

Narcotics Anonymous. Van Nuys, CA: World Service Offices, 1989.

Peck, M. Scott. *The Road Less Traveled*. New York: Touchstone, 1978.

Church of the New Song

1465 Exeter Rd., Bluffs, IL 62621

The Church of the New Song emerged in 1970 as an expression of a new rights movement among inmates of penitentiaries in the United States. It was begun by Bp. Harry W. Theriault, a convicted bank robber, in the federal prison at Atlanta, Georgia. The name of the church refers to the new song mentioned in Rev. 5:9 and 14:3, which church members believe is the sound of the new era and also the new song sung by the youth. Theriault, his cofounder Jerry M. Dorrough, and others immediately began to agitate for recognition within the prison system. In February 1972 a federal court recognized the church as a legitimate body and ordered prison officials to permit it to meet and hold services. After that decision the church spread rapidly and became the focus of controversy. It was accused of causing a work strike at San Quentin, and its sincerity was questioned because of a claimed specification that porterhouse steak and Harvey's Bristol Cream were its communion elements. Theriault was soon transferred to the federal prison at La Tuna, Texas.

According to the church, *Eclat* is the "new name" of the divinity referred to in Rev. 3:2, hence the church is also termed the Eclatarian movement. Eclatarianity is the highest fulfillment of Christian prophecy. The end of the Christian era, the era of grace, is the beginning of the Eclat era. The church considers the U.S. government and bureaucracy to be so corrupt that there is no more time for grace. The message of the Church of the New Song is the word of life. The law of nature is to act and have power. Man's basic needs are said to be shelter, food, and someone to love; when these have been attained, man should busy himself with helping others attain their basic needs. The teachings of the church are summarized in Holy Mizan, termed a "paratestament"—a third testament coming after the first (Old Testament) and the second (New Testament).

The church is episcopal in polity, operating within the boundaries of prison existence. Theriault, the bishop of Tellus, is assisted by Dr. Stephen S. Fox, S.R.M. (sealed revelation minister), the international chancellor of information. Fox is also a professor of psychology at the University of Iowa. Other officers include Dr. Richard Tanner, S.R.M., prime coadjutor; Dr. Becky Hensley, envoy international;

Robert Copeland, redactor international; and Jerry Dorrough, coadjutor of Tellus. Male Eclatarians are referred to as "maverites," and females as "sporades."

By 1972 the church had 27 chapters in state prisons and 16 in federal prisons. The church has grown in recent years both inside and outside the prison system, despite Theriault's isolation at La Tuna, and has pursued a militant program concerning religious freedom in the prison system. In 1972 Theriault took a Nazarite vow, which included a refusal to cut his hair (a primary requirement in most prisons). He also began to question the government's subsidy of religion through its salaries to prison chaplains.

Membership: Not reported.

Remarks: Church has survived in the prison system for a generation. As recently as 2004, officials in Iowa filed suit asking the court to remove any religious recognition from the church, claiming that it was sham religion.

Sources:

Lightbringer Shiloh [Harry W. Theriault]. *Holy Mizan, Supreme Paratestament of the New Song*. Bend, OR: Sacred Text Press, 1982.

[Theriault, Harry W.]. *Grass Roots of the New Song*. Millington, TN: Book University of the New Song, 1979.

Congregation de l'Aumisme

c/o Monastere de Ste-Lucie Ste-Agathe, Ste-Lucie Ste-Agathe, QC, Canada J8C 2Z8

The Congregation de l'Aumisme is the Canadian center of the Aumist religion, a new religion founded by Gilbert Bourdin (1923–1998), better known by his religious name, Lord Hamsah Manarah. Bourdin was raised in France in a Catholic family but was attracted to mysticism as a young man and sought wisdom in various ancient wisdom and magical orders (Rosicrucians, Martinism, etc.). At one point he traveled to India to study with Swami Sivananda Saraswati, who in 1961 received him into the sannyasin order (the renounced life) and gave him the name Hamsananda Saraswati. During his travels in Asia Bourdin also explored and received initiations into Jainism, Sufism, and various forms of Buddhism. Several of the teachers he met bestowed titles upon him in recognition of his accomplishments.

Upon his return to the West, L. Hamash Manarah emerged as an accomplished master of both Eastern and Western initiatic traditions. In the winter of 1962 to 1963 he resided in a cave in the mountains of southeastern France and subjected himself to the ascetic practices of the early Christian fathers. During this time an inner voice told him that he was destined to create an initiatic order teaching spiritual liberation while avoiding the pursuit of psychic powers or passing satisfactions.

Manarah then created the Order of the Knights of the Golden Lotus and established a monastery in the Alps of Haute-Province that grew into the Holy City of Mandarom, constructed by the members of the order. Since that time the order spread through French-speaking Europe and during the 1980s to Quebec, Canada. In the late 1980s plans were made for building a Pyramid Temple of Unity. At about the same time, the order came under attack from the anticult movement, represented in France by the Association pour la Défense de la Famille de l'Individu (ADFI). As of 2008, the building permit for the temple had not been obtained.

In 1967 Manarah established the Association of the Knights of the Golden Lotus (replaced in 1995 by the current Association of the Triumphant Vajra) and two years later founded the holy city of the Mandarom. Over the next years he revealed himself to be the messiah, the Lord Hamsah Manarah, and in 1990 was publicly acknowledged as such in a ceremony. He also hoped to add a larger Temple-Pyramid to the Mandarom's huge statues and existing temples that represent all the great religions of the world.

But the anticult campaign that emerged against the group became even more intense following the deaths associated with two other groups, the AUM Shinrikyo in Japan and the Solar Temple in Switzerland and Canada. The campaign against the Mandarom was orchestrated largely by ADFI, the largest French anticult organization. The Mandarom was raided repeatedly between 1992 and 1995 by tax and police officers. Then in 1994 a former member filed a complaint against Bourdin, based upon a recovered memory, that he had molested and raped her. Bourdin and several members were arrested. He was released pending the trial, but in 1998 he died. Although the case against him died with him, a new controversy immediately arose concerning his burial.

The prefet of the French Alpes de Haute-Provence denied the permission needed under French law to bury Bourdin at the Mandarom as he had requested. The burial finally took place in Castillon on April 6, 1998, under the protests of both the Aumists and local residents (who did not want their town to become a pilgrimage site). The Aumists continue to seek Bourdin's reburial at the Mandarom.

It is not expected that the Aumists will designate a new leader. They believe that the Lord Hamsah Manarah will be reincarnated, and that they will be able to detect the male infant who will be the next leader as the reincarnated lord (a process similar to the practice of Tibetan Buddhists in discovering a new lama). Once the boy is found, elder Aumists will guide him in assuming his duties as the reincarnated lord. In the meantime, a college of high priests governs the movement.

Membership: By 2008 membership of the Aumist movement internationally had dwindled to a few hundred. The North American membership is less than 50.

Sources:

Aumism: Universal Religion of the Unity of the Faces of God. www.aumisme.org/gb/.

Namsah Manarah, S. *Aumism: The Doctrine of the Golden Age*. Castellane, France: Le Mandarom, 1999.

Daheshism

c/o Dahesh Heritage, 304 W 58th St., New York, NY 10019-1107

Daheshism is the name given to the teachings of Saleem Moussa Ashi (1909–1984), a twentieth-century Lebanese author, philosopher, religious teacher, and miracle worker who at age 21 adopted the name *Dahesh*, Arabic for "inspiring wonder." He was born in Jerusalem but grew up in Lebanon, where he received little formal education but became known as a healer. In his teen years he began to speak of the return of Christ and of the need for people to prepare for his appearance and to purify themselves. In 1930 Dahesh was granted an honorary doctorate in psychic research by the Sage Institute in Paris.

On March 23, 1942, Dahesh believed that he had received the divine command to proclaim his mission to the people of the world. Already in the early 1930s a group of followers had begun to form around him. His activity increased, and proportionately, opposition emerged. In 1944 Dahesh and several of his closest followers were arrested, and a short time later, without a trial, he was stripped of his Lebanese citizenship and expelled from the country. He secretly returned to Lebanon and began to publish a series of "black" books and pamphlets denouncing his accusers. On June 28, 1947, without identity papers he entered Azerbaijan, where a revolution was taking place. He was arrested on July 1, 1947, and reportedly executed and buried. The Iranian government, which was then in control of Azerbaijan, issued a formal statement of his death, and his picture appeared in the newspapers in Beirut. On that same day, however, his followers attest that Dahesh reappeared in Beirut. His citizenship was reinstated in 1953, following a change of government in 1952. Afterward, Dahesh continued his work in public.

Dahesh first came to the United States in 1969. It was not until the 1990s that his books began to be translated into English. The majority of his followers are still found in the Arabic-speaking Lebanese-American community.

Daheshists believe that Dahesh fulfilled the yearning in all religions for a redeeming messenger, most prominently symbolized as the returning Jesus Christ or the Mahdi spoken of by Muslims. They believe that Dahesh was the coming Christ who in his person unites the personalities of all of the promised messengers of the world's faiths.

Dahesh taught belief in God as the Creator and compassionate Father. Creation began with the worlds of spirits—the origin of every creature. *Sayyals* (spiritual fluids, i.e., conscious entities of different levels) emanated from the worlds of spirits, forming the universes with all the physical beings, including humans. Therefore, humans and other beings need to strive for purity and freedom from materialism through many and different reincarnations so that they can return to the heavenly worlds. Dahesh performed his miracles to instill belief in God and the heavenly realms where absolute truth, goodness, beauty, strength, and true happiness lie.

Dahesh taught belief in the Christ, the spiritual divine force constituting the highest level of heavens. Union with this force is the only way of returning to God. This force extends itself into the material world in the form of spiritual fluids. These fluids are incarnated in certain people known as prophets (Moses, Jesus of Nazareth, Muhammad) and divine or spiritual guides (Lao Tzu, Confucius, Buddha, Socrates, and Gandhi).

Membership: There is no official count; however, the number of members is estimated to be more than 20,000 worldwide as of 2008.

Sources:

Daheshism. www.daheshism.com.

Brax, Ghazi. *Lights Upon Dr. Dahesh and Daheshism*. New York: Daheshist, 1986.

Haykal, Mohammad Husein. *The Correspondence Between Dr. Dahesh and Dr. Mohammad Husein Haykal*. Comp. Farid Abou Suleiman. Beirut, Lebanon: Al-Nisr al-Muhalliq, 1981.

Onbargi, Salim. *Born Again with Doctor Dahesh*. New York: Daheshist, 1993.

Shahin, Iskandar. *Dr. Dahesh, Man of Mystery*. New York: Daheshist, 2001.

Embassy of Heaven Church

8777 Basl Hill Rd. SE, Strayton, OR 97383-9630

The Embassy of Heaven Church was founded in 1987 following what some believed to be a revelation from Jesus Christ. The church considers itself a corporation of the Kingdom of Heaven and thus refuses to incorporate under any government of the world. The members believe that all world governments are illegitimate. There is only one legitimate government, the Kingdom of Heaven established by Jesus Christ during the Lord's Supper (Luke 22:24–30). The church promotes separating from the systems of the world and giving allegiance to God's government with Jesus Christ as head.

Drawing their authority from various biblical passages, members of the church promote the Kingdom of Heaven as a holy nation that exists outside of the jurisdictions of state and federal governments. Pr. Paul Revere and other church leaders see themselves as ambassadors for Christ, living under the laws of the Kingdom of Heaven. Out of that belief, the church issues Kingdom of Heaven passports, driver licenses, and vehicle plates for ambassadors using the Kingdom of Heaven highways.

The church provides sanctuary to anyone who repents and sins no more. In 1993 the church received broad publicity when it was raided by the federal government in search of a man who had been given asylum.

The church came to public attention again on January 31, 1997, when its headquarters was raided military style by a SWAT team and tank. Members were locked out of their 34 acres and the property was sold at auction because the church had not paid property taxes. The church continues to function from mobile headquarters, using buses, motor homes, and trailers. The church plans to take back the land peacefully, based on truth and without court intervention.

Church leaders have appeared as guests on televisions and radio talk shows, and have been featured in newspaper and tabloid articles. The church publishes numerous books and tapes and a bimonthly newsletter that follows the situation of the 400 ambassadors for Christ.

Membership: In 1997 there were about 400 ambassadors for Christ. The newsletter circulates approximately 1,000 copies per issue.

Periodicals: *Midnight Rider*.

Sources:

Embassy of Heaven Church. www.embassyofheaven.com.

"Embassy of Heaven Says It's Above the Law." *Register Guardian* (Eugene, Oregon) (August 6, 1993).

Revere, Paul. *What Is the Embassy of Heaven Church?* Sublimity, OR: Embassy of Heaven Church, 1991.

———. *Would Jesus Register with Caesar?* Sublimity, OR: Embassy of Heaven Church, 1991.

The Emin

Current address not obtained for this edition.

The Emin was founded by Raymond Armin (b. 1924 as Raymond Schertenlieb). In his youth Armin began a search for the meaning of life. He had an early enlightenment experience in the 1940s. In 1972 some chance encounters brought him into contact with several others who were on spiritual quests. They began the Emin (Arabic for "faithful one") and the movement gradually expanded. The seekers found that Armin's prior researches and findings had great meaning for their own lives. Armin became known as Leo. From less than 100 adherents in England in 1975, the movement grew to include some 2,000 people scattered around the world at the beginning of the twenty-first century.

The group has experienced periods of focused exploration of metaphysical and ethical questions, beginning with a search in several previously existing systems of thought and practice. Beginning in 1977, under the name "Eminent Way," they began to focus on internal searching, primarily through meditation. The following year, Leo published *The Poem of the Church of Emin Coils* and projected a strictly religious structure to be developed in the United States. However, the group soon abandoned the idea.

In 1993 all of the "research" to that date was collected into a cohesive body of data known as the "Emin Loom of Research Starters." As they have worked together, Leo and his associates have arrived at a set of basic philosophical principles based on the assertion that creation is ordered by natural law and has evolved toward completeness. Human life is the high point of that evolution. Individual humans also are striving toward their own completeness. The human imperative is to upgrade the mental faculty and other potential according to natural law. Life continues after death, and individuals must prepare for that transition. The basic principles lead to a life that is spent realizing one's potentials and keynoted by pathfinding—living so as to expand the present boundaries of understanding. From this progressive viewpoint, Leo's writings are seen more as helpful tools than as sacred scripture.

Those just beginning to participate in the Emin endeavor spend much time in an encounter with Leo's writings, and are said to be "in the Emin Stream." The more advanced members follow one of two streams of endeavor known as the Gemrod and the Acropolis, the former more practical, the latter more theoretical, an exploration of the potentials of human evolution. Members usually take a new name reflecting their goal at the moment and change it occasionally as they themselves go through changes.

Over the years, as Leo aged and retired to a home in Florida, a new leadership team arose, each member of whom had participated in the work for at least two decades. Their job is to ensure the work continues at a high level and to pioneer new methods and perspectives drawn from the spectrum of research and discovery. Each has his or her own specialty. For example, one of the leaders, Mark Ballabon, is in his secular life the managing director of a publishing company. His Emin concerns the exploration of the roots, causes, and meanings of language and the development of new applications in music. Hana Grinboim, another of the six, is a specialist in working with children with learning difficulties. In Emin, she is especially concerned with understanding teamwork and developing methodologies in education.

The result of their "research" has led to the emergence of a eclectic perspective drawing upon many religious and philosophical impulses, from the Human Potentials movement to the work of G. I. Gurdjieff. The group stands on the edge of religious boundaries, having adopted an abstract religious foundation from which various religions may be pursued (and some claim to do just that). At the same time, there is a strong emphasis on personal ethics, a demand to live in conformity to the law of the land, and a disparagement of the group's becoming involved in partisan politics.

Now widely scattered, the Emin groups are located in various countries of Europe and North America. In 1986 some members established a settlement in Israel that by the mid-1990s had some 130 families in residence.

Membership: Not reported. There are approximately 2,000 adherents scattered in Emin groupings located in 15 countries in North America, Europe, and the Middle East, as well as in New Zealand and Australia.

Sources:

The Emin. www.emin.org.

Barrett, Bavid V. *The New Believers: Sects, Cults and Alternative Religions*. London: Cassell and Company, 2001.

Shaw, William. *Spying in Guru Land: Inside Britain's Cults*. London: Fourth Estate, 1994.

Freedom Church

13211 Myford Rd., No. 332, Tustin, CA 92782

Freedom Church is the religious arm of a larger movement developed to mobilize people who consider themselves to be freedom-loving, self-responsible, and committed to living apart from "oppressive" control and taxation by government while freely pursuing their own happiness. Freedom Church seeks to restore "natural law," which it sees as a natural goal based upon the sinderesis that exists within each person. It understands natural law to be a rule of conduct that arises by the "natural relations of human beings, established by the Creator," which have existed prior to any human law-making. Natural law can be discovered by the use of right reason assisted by divine revelation. It applies equally to individuals and national entities. A rule of conduct arises out of the natural relations of human beings, established by the Creator, and exists prior to any positive precept. The foundation of this law is placed by the best writers in the will of God, discovered by right reason, and aided by divine revelation; and its principles, when applicable, apply with equal obligation to individuals and to nations.

Sinderesis is viewed as the natural power of the soul that moves the soul toward the good, and leads to an abhorrence of evil. Sinderesis was placed in humans by God and is sometimes called the "law of reason." It is in every person by nature. Freedom Church teaches that no person or entity (such as a nation) is above the natural law, and no human sanction can rightfully override or negate the natural law.

Freedom Church looks to the Western legal tradition to provide a basis for its assertion of natural rights, which its defines as "those rights which grow out of the nature of man and depend upon personality, as distinguished from such as are created by law and depend upon civilized society; or they are those which are plainly assured by natural law; or those which, by fair deduction from the present physical, moral, social, and religious characteristics of man, he must be invested with, and which he ought to have realized for him in a jural society, in order to fulfill the ends to which his nature calls him."

Once individuals become knowledgeable of the present law (and of natural law) and join together with other freedom-loving people residing in close proximity, individuals can force governments to concentrate on controlling crime rather than unduly regulating law-abiding citizens.

One may join the Freedom Church simply by declaring agreement with its basic principles. Joining the church is seen as nonexclusive, and members may be members of other churches at the same time.

The church supports the Freedom Law School, founded in 1996 by Peymon Mottahedeh, an Iranian Jew who became a U.S. citizen in 1989. Some of his Iranian relatives had been tortured and executed by the Iranian government. In the United States he became concerned with possible mistreatment of citizens by the Internal Revenue Service. Thus Freedom Law School originated as part of an effort to empower people and educate them to oppose "oppressive taxation and control" exercised by the IRS.

Membership: Not reported.

Educational Facilities:

Freedom Law School, Phelan, California.

Periodicals: *Freedom News*.

Sources:

Freedom Church. www.freedomchurch.org/.

Humanity Benefactor Foundation

University of Lawsonomy, 4529 Hwy. 41, Sturtevant, WI 53177

The Humanity Benefactor Foundation and the University of Lawsonomy are the two institutions that grew out of the thinking of Alfred William Lawson (1869–1954), whose work includes a system of philosophy and theology, as well as extensive writings on science, health, and economics. Lawson, one of the more creative thinkers in American history, was simultaneously hailed by some as a genius and reviled by critics as a crackpot.

Lawson was born in London, England, but his parents moved to Canada when he was three weeks old, and then to Detroit, Michigan, in 1874. He attended public school, but dropped out and in 1888 began a career in baseball as a pitcher and a manager. He is credited with introducing night baseball in 1901 with a portable electric light system that he carried from city to city. He was both a right- and left-handed pitcher. He organized more clubs, leagues, and mergers than any other man. A 1908 newspaper wrote: "As an organizer, Lawson perhaps stands without a peer, as history records that he was the father of the Central League and Interstate League, which are now in existence and which are two of the strongest circuits in organized baseball.... When Lawson floated the Atlantic League last winter the matter was looked upon as a joke, but Lawson showed his master hand by steering the organization through the season. He managed the Reading (Pennsylvania) club, and in addition to winning the pennant for that city he successfully bucked the invasion of the Tri-State League and cleared up $12,000 profit on the season."

In 1908 he entered the world of aviation and began the first aeronautic magazine, *Fly* (1908–1909), succeeded by *Aircraft* (1910–1914). He began flying in 1910. At the beginning of World War I he became the general manager of a small aircraft company and designed several training planes for the government. As early as 1909 he had conceived of the idea of a passenger airliner, and after the war he found backing to build such a plane. He became president of the Lawson Airplane Company. During 1919 he built and demonstrated the practicality of a passenger plane. His work on the passenger plane was probably his most lasting contribution, but he continued to work in aviation and transportation through the 1920s.

During his years in aviation, Lawson had begun to think about economics and the injustices of the capitalist system. The Great Depression became the occasion for his pulling his thoughts together and developing the direct credits alternative system, the outlines of which first appeared in a book, *Direct Credits for Everyone*, in 1931. In essence, Lawson saw three players in the economic system: labor, capital, and the financiers. He saw the financiers as the problem and called upon labor and capital to make common cause against them. He also proposed a new understanding of money as nothing of value in itself, but as a measure of wealth and of one's ability to facilitate trade. He proposed doing away with interest and placing control of money in the hands of the government. The government would then make available credits to people in the form of grants and interest-free loans to nurture wealth-producing activities.

Lawson gave organizational form to his new economic system through the Direct Credits Society, and through the 1930 he gained a large following. Popular support for the direct credits idea waned during the years of World War II and never regained its prewar level. Lawson continued to expand his thought into other areas, and gradually created a whole system of knowledge that came to be known as Lawsonomy, the basic ideas of which were summarized in a three-volume work, *Lawsonomy* (1935–1939). In 1943 he purchased the campus of the former Des Moines University and renamed it the Des Moines University of Lawsonomy.

The volumes on Lawsonomy treated some of Lawson's theological ideas. Further elucidation of his religious thought led in 1948 to the establishment of the Lawsonian religion, the basic principles of which were laid down more definitively in a 1949 work, *Lawsonian Religion*. Lawsonian religion builds upon Lawsonomy, the knowledge of life and the basic laws that govern physical, mental, moral, and spiritual manifestations. It includes the highest understanding of God, the omniparent who created humanity and is its benefactor. It espouses a pure birth, clean life, honest dealings, kind treatment of all people (especially people of different religions), provable education, and perpetual improvement. It is the ultimate goal to bring all humans together for the worship of the one God.

Lawson died in 1954. Later the university moved to rural Wisconsin, south of Milwaukee. The Humanity Benefactor Foundation was founded as the publishing arm of the Lawsonomy movement. Students of Lawsonomy may participate by reading Lawson's many books and taking correspondence courses offered by the school. Resident students engage in self-guided reading and study of Lawson's writings, punctuated by a monthly gathering of the students. Worship services are held at noon on the last Sunday of each month, and include the singing of songs specially geared to the movement.

Membership: Membership is not counted but is national and international. People acquire the Lawson literature and become voluntary students without legal requirements. Associated centers include the Humanity Benefactor Foundation Inc., the Direct Credits Society, Inc., and Lawsonian Religion Inc., all in Melvindale, Michigan; the Chapel at the of University of Lawsonomy, Sturtevant, Wisconsin; and the Lawsonian churches in Detroit, Michigan; Wichita, Kansas; and Murrieta, California.

Periodicals: *Benefactor*.

Sources:

Farrell, V. L. A. *Lawson: From Bootblack to Emancipator*. Detroit, MI: Humanity Benefactor Foundation, 1934.

Henry, Lyell, Jr. *Zig-Zag-and-Swirl: Alfred W. Lawson's Quest for Greatness*. Iowa City: University of Iowa Press, 1991.

Lawson, Alfred W. *Direct Credits for Everybody*. Detroit, MI: Humanity Benefactor Association, 1931.

————. *Lawsonian Religion*. Detroit, MI: Humanity Benefactor Foundation, 1949.

————. *Lawsonomy*. 3 vols. Detroit, MI: Humanity Benefactor Association, 1935–1939.

Taylor, Margaret C., and Arlene Osmun. *Songs of Lawsonomy*. Detroit, MI: Humanity Benefactor Foundation, 1961.

Iglesia ni Cristo (Church of Christ)

1617 Southgate Ave., Daly City, CA 94015

Alternate Address: International headquarters: 1, Central Ave., New Era, Diliman Quezon City, 1107 Philippines.

The Iglesia ni Cristo (Church of Christ) was founded in the Philippines by Felix Manalo Isugan (1886–1963), who was born a Roman Catholic but later became a member of several Protestant churches. In 1913, however, he felt a call from God to establish a new church. The Iglesio ni Cristo was incorporated in 1914 as World

War I began. Filipinos began to refer to it as the "Manalists," after its leader. Growth was slow until after World War II, but then membership began to expand rapidly.

The Iglesia ni Cristo has adopted a traditional Protestant Christian view, but its modifications at several points have produced a serious barrier between it and other churches. The church rejects the doctrine of the Trinity (which it considers polytheistic) and views Jesus not as God but as the messiah. The founder is viewed as a messenger—*sugo*, the last messenger of God. Members reject the immortality of the soul and have adopted a sectarian view called *conditionalism* (in agreement with the Adventists) that suggests that the dead remain in their graves until called forth at the last judgment. The church has become quite controversial, having drawn attacks with its own persistent denouncing of the Roman Catholic Church.

Among their more unusual views is their acceptance of the biblical command to not drink blood (a view similar to that of the Jehovah's Witnesses). In the Philippines this belief has a cultural implication because there is a popular dish prepared with cooked animal blood, dinuguan, that church members refuse to consume.

The church located its headquarters for international missions in the United States. Its views and obvious success have brought it to the attention of Christian countercultists who oppose its doctrinal differences with orthodox Protestantism.

Membership: According to the Philippine census of 2000, the number of Filipinos who declared themselves members of the Iglesia ni Cristo was 1,762,845. There are some 5,300 members in Europe, and several thousand in North America.

Periodicals: *God's Message*.

Sources:

Tuggi, A. Leonard. *Iglesia ni Cristo: A Study in Independent Church Dynamics*. Quezon City, Philippines: Conservative Baptist Publishing, 1976.

—————. "Iglesia ni Cristo: An Angel and His Church." In *Dynamic Religious Movement: Case Studies of Rapidly Growing Religious Movements Around the World*, ed. David J. Hesselgrave, pp. 85–101. Grand Rapids, MI: Baker Book House, 1978.

Initiatives of Change

1156 15th St. NW, Ste. 910, Washington, DC 20005-1704

Initiatives of Change, formerly known as Moral Re-Armament, is a worldwide network of people who are committed to transformation in society based on change in individuals.

Dr. Frank N. Buchman (1878–1961) was an American Lutheran minister from Pennsylvania who, early in his ministerial career, started a hostel in Philadelphia for underprivileged boys. A fight with his trustees led to his separation from the hostel, leaving him personally exhausted. In 1908, while traveling in Great Britain, he experienced a change of heart in a Keswick chapel. Buchman began to share his experience of release from resentment with others and became the center of an international fellowship, the First Century Christian Fellowship. The fellowship emerged in the early 1920s and included many students from Cambridge University and Oxford University. The group was later dubbed the Oxford Group.

Buchman taught that God could become real to anyone who was willing to believe in Him. Estrangement from God is man's fault, and is caused by moral compromise. People need to examine their lives against the standards of absolute purity, unselfishness, and love. The recovery of personal morality proceeds and leads to the recovery of social morality. Buchman emphasized the need for sharing and guidance. Sharing consists of the confession of one's sins and failures to another member of the group. Guidance could come directly from God during quiet moments when individuals record their inner thoughts. During the 1930s the Oxford Group became known for its "house parties," group settings in which sharing was promoted. These house parties also became a source of controversy, with critics charging that participants indulged in embarrassing confessions.

During the late 1920s many Princeton University students became affiliated with the Oxford Group. However, because of opposition aroused by the nature and content of the sharing sessions, the university kicked the movement off campus. An investigation by a university commission found that the charges were without merit and not only invited the group back on campus but also gave it credit for the high moral standards. The president of the school invited Buchman to conduct a chapel service with him.

In 1938, as Europe armed, Buchman reached the firm conviction that the next great world movement must be one for moral and spiritual rearmament. The Oxford Group's program for Moral Re-Armament (MRA), the name by which the group then became known, was launched that year. Many of those trained by the program enlisted in the several armies or took part in resistance movements. In the United States a group was deferred by the Selective Service that they might undertake a patriotic, morale-building program, "You Can Defend America." Gen. John J. Pershing lent strong support to the effort and wrote the foreword for the program's handbook.

After the war a group of Swiss acquired a large hotel above Montreux, in the village of Caux, to offer a European platform for MRA's work of healing and reconciliation. Likening their efforts to an ideological equivalent of the Marshall Plan, MRA established a program that brought together those who had been on different sides of the war. The first group of Germans allowed to leave Germany by the Allied Occupation Forces came to Caux for meetings. In like measure the Japanese came. In 1986 Prime Minister Nakasone publicly underlined the important role MRA played in building modern Japan.

After Buchman's death in 1961, MRA continued under an informal international leadership committed to the ideals of seeing the world governed by people who were governed by God. They also continued Buchman's emphasis on the discipline of spending time in quiet each morning to listen for God's guidance and accepting the fact that change begins with oneself.

In the United States during the 1960s, Up With People, a program developed under MRA auspices, began to gain some fame because of a touring singing group made up of youth members. In 1968 the individuals associated with Up With People and the affiliated Pace Publications severed all connections with MRA; in 1999 Up With People was disbanded.

In 2001 MRA changed its name to Initiatives of Change (IC) and established for the first time an international body, under the name Initiatives of Change—International. It is headquartered in Switzerland and chaired by Cornelio Sommaruga. IC continues to function as a network of independent national organizations, each organized as a charity or appropriate body in its own land. A similar training center is located in Panchgani, India, with smaller facilities in Australia, Brazil, Zimbabwe, Japan, and Great Britain. IC is registered in more than 40 countries.

Membership: Initiatives of Change is not a membership organization. It has a small staff, but most of its work is carried out around the world by volunteers.

Periodicals: *Breakthroughs*. • *For a Change*.

Remarks: Buchman was accused by his detractors of being sympathetic to Nazism. In the 1985 biography *Frank Buchman—A Life*, author Garth Lean suggested that although Buchman may have been naive about the prospect of "changing" Hitler, he was also, equally, the victim of a smear campaign. Much of that campaign was spearheaded by journalist Tom Driberg, who was later discovered to have been an agent of the KGB. Several decades of observation of IC have revealed no alignment to Nazism either ideologically or in its policies and program.

Sources:

Buchman, Frank N. *Remaking the World*. London: Blandford Press, 1961.

Driberg, Tom. *The Mystery of Moral Re-Armament*. New York: Alfred A. Knopf, 1965.

Eister, Allen W. *Drawing-Room Conversion*. Durham, NC: Duke University Press, 1950.

Entwistle, Basil, and John McCook Roots. *Moral Re-Armament, What Is It?* Los Angeles: Pace Publications, 1967.

Howard, Peter. *The World Rebuilt*. London: Blandford Press, 1951.

Lean, Garth. *Frank Buchman: A Life*. London: Constable, 1985.

————. *On the Tail of a Comet*. Colorado Springs, CO: Helmes and Howard, IA.

Williamson, Geoffrey. *Inside Buchmanism*. New York: Philosophical Library, 1955.

Integrative Spirituality

Sausalito, CA 94966

Emerging in a period of widespread religious pluralism and the immediate availability of information about the world's religions, Integrative Spirituality is a spiritual community that collects, synthesizes, and then uses what it considers to be the most useful, effective, and life-affirming spiritual wisdom and practices of humanity's traditional spiritual groupings. It operates out of a belief that the process of synthesizing spiritual wisdom and practices filters out religious pathologies and gives birth to new and transcending repetitions of wisdom. The active reworking of spiritual traditions is believed to move beyond the limited gains of mere interfaith dialogue.

Integrative Spirituality also operates out of a belief that all individuals have a right to determine what is spiritual truth for themselves and that all should have access to the humanity's common storehouse of spiritual wisdom. The integrative spirituality community exists to assist individuals in maximizing their spiritual growth and advancement in what becomes a personalized spiritual path, seen as a lifelong endeavor.

Integrative Spirituality does not put its stamp of approval on every religious pursuit. It seeks a spiritual approach that is dynamically transformative, leading to a more inclusive, nonauthoritarian approach to life.

Spiritual growth is equated somewhat with the ability to act from love while finding inner personal empowerment and transformative personal healing. These goals are met as individuals learn to expand their direct spiritual experience and relationship with the absolute integrative spirit/consciousness (which some call God, Buddha, Brahman, etc.), their own highest self/spirit, and the highest selves/spirits of others.

The ultimate goal of the Integrative Spirituality movement is the creation of a group of spiritually mature individuals who could create a new form of evolutionary, pantheistic spirituality (based on the idea that God is both immanent in all things and transcends the created order) that would perform the many functions traditionally assigned to religion, including promoting service and unselfish fellowship; answering the questions of ultimate concern; conserving morality; promoting family life; providing counsel and guidance; and encouraging group meditation and worship—all without the failings of older religious communities.

The Integrative Spirituality Movement is headed by Lawrence Wollersheim, who gained some fame from his lengthy court battle with the Church of Scientology. Wollersheim continues to strongly oppose the Scientologists and other groups he considers to be destructive cults, extending his criticism to all authoritarian religions. His understanding of religious pathologies has been shaped by his leadership role in the cult awareness movement.

The Integrative Spirituality movement is based on a boat that generally is anchored in San Francisco Bay at Sausalito, California. The boat has a worship and meditation chapel at which regular events are held several times a week. The floating center serves as the spiritual research center for the movement, a spiritual teacher-training seminary and monastery, and a retreat center for members and visitors. The boat also serves as a site for the celebration of various life events such as weddings.

Membership: Not reported.

Sources:

Integrative Spirituality. www.integrativespirituality.org/.

Heron, John. *Participatory Spirituality: A Farewell to Authoritarian Religion*. N.p.: Lulu.com, 2006.

JeungSanDo

936 S Crenshaw Blvd., No. 307, Los Angeles, CA 90019

Alternate Address: International headquarters: Jeung San Do International Dept., Jeung San Do Culture and Education Center, 409–1 Jungri-dong, Daedeok-gu, Daejeon 306-824, Korea. Canadian center: Toronto Doh-jahng, 153 Spalding Rd., Toronto, ON M3K 1K3, Canada.

JeungSanDo (or Jeung Sanh Doh) is a new Korean religious movement, a tao or way that embodies the teachings of Kang Ilsun Sah-ok (1871–1909), better known as SangJeNim, who is believed by members to be the incarnation of the Lord God who ruled with the Triune God. He came from heaven to fulfill both the Buddhist prophecy of the coming Maitreya and the Christian prophecy of the Second Coming of Jesus Christ. JeungSanDo teachings identify Shang-ti (Confucianism), the Jade Emperor (Taoism), Maitreya (Buddhism), and God (in Western traditions), and SangJeNim is the embodiment of this entity.

Kang is believed to have experienced sudden enlightenment in 1877, though he waited until 1894 to begin his work of saving and enlightening the world. In 1901, working in invisible realms, he defeated all evils, opened the Great Gate of Spirituality, and began the work of reconstructing heaven and earth. At that time he also began to call a group of disciples around him. He designated the first disciple, Kim Hyong-yol, the keeper of the way of JeungSan-Do. SangJeNim suggested that a new world would arise in the relatively near future.

Having proclaimed that men and women were equal, in 1907 SangJeNim was called Ko Pam-lye (1880–1935) and Sabu, the Head of all Women. After his death in 1909, Lady Ko then known as Tae-mo-nim (Holy Mother), succeeded him as leader of the movement. She (rather than Kim Hyong-yol) assumed the task of propagating the faith. She taught the new T'aeulju mantra, the chanting of which is believed to provide a lifeline to the enlightening and healing energy of T'aeul Heaven, the womb of the universe. Along with the mantra, she also taught a set of 16 tai chi movements (slow, controlled, and synchronized with the breath) that correspond to the sound symbols of the mantra. The movements are believed to activate the healing energy (*chi*) from the universe and to expel the toxic energies from the body. Each movement is also correlated to the function of one or more internal organs.

JeungSanDo experienced sporadic growth through the disruptions of life in Korea in the middle of the twentieth century, then gained new life in the decades after the Korean War. It initially spread throughout South Korea and then internationally, becoming visible in North America in the 1990s. The 1995 publication of an English-edition of the account of the founder's supernatural work *JeungSanDo DoJeon* has facilitated its movement into English-speaking lands.

Membership: Not reported. In 2008 there were seven centers in the United States and one in Canada. Additional centers are found in Japan, Taiwan, Indonesia, the Philippines, New Zealand, Germany, and the United Kingdom.

Sources:

Jeung San Do. www.jeungsando.org.

JeungSanDo DoJeon. Seoul, Korea: Daewon, 1995.

Kennedy Worshippers

Current address not obtained for this edition.

Shortly after the death of the charismatic U.S. president John F. Kennedy (1917–1963), people began to claim contact with his spirit and to ascribe healings of many serious diseases, some congenital or terminal, to that spirit. By 1970 more than 100 such reports were on file. Coincidental with these accounts of miracles was the emergence of a loosely organized movement that elevated Kennedy as an object of worship. The first manifestations were home shrines featuring pictures of Kennedy. In 1972 Farley McGivern organized a John F. Kennedy Memorial

Temple in Los Angeles to provide headquarters for the movement. To believers, Kennedy is a god. McGivern believed that Kennedy gave his life for his people to warn them of the evil around them.

The existence of the movement was known only through the occasional contacts journalists made with people who claimed to be a part of it. To most people involved in it, their belief is a very private matter that is rarely shared with others, even close friends. Hence, little information about it exists.

Membership: In the 1970s 2,000 adherents around the United States were reported.

Mandeans
c/o Lamea Abbas Amara 5757, Lake Murray Blvd., No. 50, La Mesa, CA 91942-2212

The Mandeans, a group that can be traced to the ancient Gnostics, was rediscovered by Western scholars in the seventeenth century. The Gnostics (from the Greek *gnosis*, or wisdom) were believed for many centuries to have completely disappeared, but were found in Iraq, where there are major centers in Baghdad and Basra and smaller communities located in the towns along the Tigris and Euphrates Rivers. Early Christian missionaries in the region saw them as surviving remnants of the followers of John the Baptist mentioned in the biblical book of Acts, and Muslim referred to them as "baptizers." This latter term, which appears in the Qu'ran, has allowed the Mandeans to survive in the years since Islam has dominated the land.

The Mandeans appear to have originated in Palestine as a Jewish sect in the first century B.C.E. They later absorbed beliefs and practices (including baptism) from both the John the Baptist movement and the early Christians. They left Palestine probably toward the beginning of the second century C.E. They settled in Mesopotamia, but much of their early history was lost during the third century as Zoroastrianism gained the ascendancy. Once the Muslims conquered Mesopotamia in the seventh century, they were recognized as a "people of the Book" and received official toleration.

The Mandeans are traditionally led by their *ethnarch* ("the head of the people"), who oversees the hierarchy of bishops and priests. The office of ethnarch, however, has remained vacant since the beginning of the twentieth century, and today the community is led by a community of clergy and laity. It appears that most of the clerical leadership was killed in an epidemic in 1830 and that educated laypeople assumed a significant leadership role that they have retained.

Mandean teachings divide the cosmos into the world of light (the north) and the world of darkness (the south). A ruler leads each realm. The world has emerged as a consequence of the battle between light and darkness (good and evil). Humans, a product of darkness, possess a soul, a core of light. The soul is freed at death and begins a pilgrimage to the light realm.

There is a set of sacred books used by the Mandeans, but the Ginza Rba ("Great Treasure") is the central book; its centerpiece is the mass for the dead (*masiqta*), a ceremony marking the release of the soul from the body and its "ascent" on its afterlife journey. The Mandean Jewish heritage is marked by dietary laws that include the ritual slaughtering of animals and alms giving. Worship occurs in a sanctuary (*mandi*), a fenced-in area usually built adjacent to a river, the water of which is diverted to provide a baptismal pool with flowing water. Baptism is central to Mandean worship and integral to each Sunday's worship service. Every member participates several times per year. Mandean baptism, unlike its Christian equivalent, it is not a once-in-a-lifetime event.

Membership: In 2002 an estimated 15,000 to 20,000 Mandeans were found in southeastern Iraq. There is one small community in Khuzistan, Iran. There are several hundred Mandeans in the United States, the result of migrations that began in the 1980s. Small communities also exist in Canada, Australia, New Zealand, and various locations in Europe (including the United Kingdom, Sweden, and Holland).

Periodicals: *Mandaee*.

Sources:

The Australian Mandeans. www.mandaean.com/au/index.html.

Foerster, Werner. Gnosis: *A Selection of Gnostic Texts*, vol. 2: *Coptic and Mandean Sources*. London: Clarendon Press, 1974.

The Gnostic Society Library. www.webcom.com/~gnosis/library/mand.htm.

Mandean World. www.geocities.com/usamandaean/who.html.

Rudolph, Kurt. *Gnosis: The Nature and History of Gnosticism*. San Francisco: Harper and Row, 1983.

Yamauchi, E. M. *Gnostic Ethics and Mandaean Origins*. Oxford, U.K.: Oxford University Press, 1970.

New Enlightened Inspired Living
Current address not obtained for this edition.

New Enlightened Inspired Living is the name given the program and the movement inspired by Neil Howard Brandt (b. 1946), who eventually assumed the name David Neil and announced that he is the Messiah, the King of Kings, and NEIL (the New Enlightened Inspired Leader).

According to Neil, he first came to know of his messiahship in 1973 when he was given a vision of the future. He saw himself surrounded by a group of reporters who were shouting "The Messiah! The Messiah!" Two years later he had a second vision, of newspapers with dates from the future proclaiming him the Messiah in bold headlines accompanied by his picture. The first story on his claims ran in 1975 in the *Marin Independent Journal*. However, few were aware of Neil's claims until he published his autobiography and began a campaign to announce his mission.

Neil claims that he has been both King David and Jesus Christ, but that he is not a perfect person, only an instrument of God. As he put it, "I cohabit my actual thinking mind with another consciousness." This God force resides within him. The ability to access God's energy means that he is able to influence major world events.

The messianic program is termed NEIL Deal. It includes a new government with a global rather than a national base and an international peace-keeping army, navy, and air force. Economically, it calls for a balanced national budget, new housing starts, and reduced federal income tax.

Membership: Unknown.

Sources:

Neil, David. *I Am the Messiah!*. Novato, CA: Author, 1992.

Nudist Christian Church of the Blessed Virgin Jesus
Current address not obtained for this edition.

The Nudist Christian Church of the Blessed Virgin Jesus grew out of a revelation received by the church's founder, Zeus Cosmos. During 1985, while a student at Iowa State University, he asked direction from God and the Spirit of Jesus Christ was sent to him, directing him to the West, where he would meet God. He journeyed to the Canaan Wilderness (which he renamed the Zeus Cosmos Nudist National Wilderness) near the Utah-Arizona border. God and the angel Ephygeneia, both naked, appeared to him, directing him to a cave on a nearby ridge. While engaged in a fast and living in the cave, Zeus Cosmos again met "God the Almighty the Triune God" and an angel. God gave him an additional revelation to be added to the Bible, the Book of Zeus, to be placed next to the Book of Revelation.

The Book of Zeus begins with an admonishment to the Mormon polygamists to give up their adulterous pagan practices and their belief in the inferiority of the black race. Zeus Cosmos was told of the holy land of the Nudist Christian people northwest of the Grand Canyon where a city, Cosmos, would be built. There men and women would have godly respect for each other, their nakedness, and the wholesome natural body.

It is the belief of the church that the human body is God's creation. Nudity means cleanliness, honesty, family atmosphere, modesty at its best, freedom, and goodliness. Life with nudity reduces sexual hang-ups, problems caused by undue expectations of one's body, pornography, and crime. The church actively seeks the establishment of clothes-optional public areas across the United States.

Though he has gained few adherents, Zeus Cosmos actively seeks converts to nudism. In that cause he was arrested in Washington, D.C., in 2002, and in Colorado City, Arizona, the center of the Fundamentalist Church of Jesus Christ of Latter-day Saints, the polygamist group, where he was accused of leaving nude photos of himself in the mailboxes of residents.

Membership: Not reported.

Perfect Liberty Kyodan

700 S Adams St., Glendale, CA 91205

Perfect Liberty Kyodan was founded in Japan in 1946 by Tokuchika Miki (1900–1983), but it originated in 1912 when Kanada Tokumitsu (1863–1919), an Osaka cutlery dealer, founded the Shinto-Tokumitsu-Kyo ("the divine way taught by Tokumitsu"). The original group used elements of both Shingon Buddhism and Shintoism, drawing from them an emphasis on art and nature. Tokuchika's father, Tokuharu Miki (1871–1938), a Zen priest, joined Tokumitsu's group and brought to it an emphasis on meditation. In 1919 Tokuharu inherited the leadership. The group grew and changed its name several times before being suppressed by the government during the 1930s. Tokuchika, who became the *oshieoya* (patriarch) in 1936, spent the final years of World War II in prison. Perfect Liberty was permanently established after his release from prison during the Allied occupancy. Perfect Liberty became the only one of the postwar Japanese religions to adopt an official English name—Tokuchika wanted the faith's cosmopolitan nature to be reflected in its name.

The teachings of Perfect Liberty are summarized in its "Twenty-One Precepts." The first and most important is that "life is art," by which Tokuchika means that it is all-important to see one's life as a total pattern, a single unified work of art. Art is a striving to overcome limitation, and a molding of what is outside of oneself into a form that is both true to itself and an expression of the artist. Life itself becomes a work of art by the artist's self. The remaining precepts provide guidelines for the artistic life.

The center of worship in Perfect Liberty is the *asamairi*, a daily morning service that starts before 5 A.M. and lasts about an hour. During the service each member pledges himself to lead an artistic life during the day. Leading the service is an appointed leader who is able to give *mioshie*, or divine instruction. Worship is directed to Mioya-okami, the parent god.

The artistic nature of Perfect Liberty is expressed in worship and festivals. On August 1 each year a giant Founder's Day festival is held at the Perfect Liberty Seichi. Oshieoya's birthday is celebrated on April 8. These are times for massive displays of art, dance, fireworks, and music. The Perfect Liberty Peace Tower is a large modern sculpture at the headquarters in Osaka, where there are also modern buildings, a golf course, a memorial garden, baseball grounds, and other works of art.

Perfect Liberty came to the United States in 1960 when several immigrants began missionary work. A minister arrived in 1961. By 1972 the group had expanded, and a center modeled on the one in Japan was constructed in the Santa Monica Mountains above Los Angeles.

Membership: In 1974 Perfect Liberty had approximately 5,000 members in 6 churches and 15 missions in the United States, all on the West Coast. Approximately 25 percent of the membership is drawn from black and Spanish-speaking communities. In 2008 Perfect Liberty Kyodan reported 10 congregations in the United States and 1 in Canada. The primary membership remains in Japan, but churches are found also in Australia, France, Portugal, Argentina, Brazil, Paraguay, and Peru.

Sources:

Perfect Liberty Kyodan. www.perfectliberty.org/

Bach, Marcus. *The Power of Perfect Liberty*. Englewood Cliffs, NJ: Prentice-Hall, 1971.

Yashima, Jiro. *An Essay on the Way of Life*. N.p., 1950.

This appendix provides information on organizations that have become defunct, listed according to their religious family in the order in which those chapters appear in the Encyclopedia.

1. Interfaith & Ecumenical

CHRISTIAN ECUMENICAL ORGANIZATIONS

Federal Council of the Churches of Christ in America

The Federal Council of the Churches of Christ in America was the dominant ecumenical structure in American Christianity during the first half of the twentieth century. Prior to its formation, there had been much cooperative work on the part of various Protestant church groups, but none had moved to the national level to organize an official cooperative body backed by the respective denominations. The need for such a cooperative body grew out of the desire to have a more influential voice in solving the new urban problems that had resulted from the dramatic expansion of cities in the 1880s and 1890s.

In 1898 the National Council of the Congregational Churches called for a gathering to consider the creation of such a structure. Then, in 1900, an unofficial National Federation of Churches and Christian Workers formed, with the purpose of planning a conference of church representatives to strategize about building closer working relationships. Elias B. Sanford (1843–1932), corresponding secretary of the Open and Institutional Church League, took the lead in advocacy for the new federation. In 1901 Sanford gained the signatures of 25 prominent church leaders in support of his plan to issue a call for a national federation. In 1902 plans for a national conference of official delegates were initiated, and a conference date was set for 1905. Later in 1902, the Methodist Episcopal Church, South, became the first to offer a positive response.

In 1905 a total of 29 denominations sent delegates to a planning conference in New York City, where a "Plan of Federation" was developed looking toward the creation of the Federal Council. As it was assumed that the denominations were in substantial agreement theologically, little mention was made of doctri-

nal divergences (at that point, the most acrimonious phase of the fundamentalist-modernist controversy was still two decades in the future). The American Unitarian Association, a nontrinitarian group, did not attend.

At the conference, a proposed plan was submitted to the various denominations. The council was designed as a delegated body centered on the common witness of its denominational members. Each denomination was apportioned members according to size, but each group had a minimum of four delegates. The council was to be an advisory body that would facilitate communication among the different churches and allow them to speak with a common voice on important issues. Committees were appointed to work on various aspects of church life, such as evangelism, Sunday observance, temperance, and so on, though they had little financial support or power to act. The Federal Council also sought to build regional and local ecumenical councils around the country to implement the National Council's work.

Thirty-three denominations were represented in 1908 at the gathering held in Philadelphia to inaugurate the Federal Council of Churches. The council immediately had to confront the competition it posed for older cooperative organizations that specialized in single areas of church life, such as Sunday schools, foreign missions, and youthwork. Thus, the council moved first into an as-yet poorly addressed area, social concerns. From the Methodists it borrowed a social statement that it reworked as "The Social Ideals of the Churches." This statement set the Federal Council on a course that would, in the next decades, clearly identify it with the more liberal and "social gospel" theological perspectives that became such an important part of what was being termed "modernist" theology. Several of the smaller, more conservative denominations soon dropped out of membership because of what they perceived as too much emphasis on social issues.

Because the ecumenical movement owed much of its inspiration to concerns in the mission field over competing missionary programs, the council spoke to the need for spreading to foreign lands the spirit of cooperation expressed by the existence of the council in America. This perspective would lead to a later shift of emphasis on the part of American churches, which moved funds away from the sending of missionaries

to the undergirding of indigenous churches in former mission fields.

The Federal Council held together during the World War I era and joined in rebuilding efforts after the war. It survived the fundamentalist-modernist controversy and saw the organization of two competing groups during World War II, the American Council of Christian Churches representing separatist fundamentalists and the National Association of Evangelicals representing more mainline conservative Protestants.

After World War II the growing ecumenical movement, signaled by the efforts to organize the World Council of Churches, also gave voice to those who wished that a more centralized agency, bringing together all of the concerns now spread out among a number of ecumenical structures, could be created. While the Federal Council was such an agency in name, in fact it did not operate effectively in areas such as foreign missions, religious education, or women's concerns. Therefore, a plan was drawn up to unite the Federal Council with a number of other agencies, and on January 1, 1951, the Federal Council was superseded by the National Council of the Churches of Christ in the U.S.A.

Sources:

Cavert, Samuel McCrea. *The American Churches in the Ecumenical Movement*, 1900–1968. New York: Association Press, 1968.

National Fraternal Council of Negro Churches

The National Fraternal Council of Negro Churches was a pioneering African-American ecumenical organization founded in Chicago, Illinois, in 1934 as the Negro Fraternal Council of Churches. Bp. Reverdy C. Ransom (1861–1959) of the African Methodist Episcopal Church was the first president of the council. From the original seven-member organization, the council grew to encompass 12 organizations. The council was somewhat modeled on the Federal Council of Churches and represented the most liberal Protestant denominations. It divided its work into 12 areas that largely paralleled those of the Federal Council, though with some specialized work areas such as race relations, Africa, and peace. The Fraternal Council maintained a Washington, D.C., office to monitor legislation of special interest to the African-American community.

The council functioned well for a generation. Among its accomplishments was the founding of the Interdenominational Theological Center in Atlanta, Georgia. However, as the civil rights movement gained steam, the council's leadership role passed to other, newer organizations, and it gradually faded in importance.

The 12 members of the council were the African Methodist Episcopal Church, the African Methodist Episcopal Zion Church, the African Orthodox Church, the Bible Way Church of Our Lord Jesus Christ World Wide, the Central Jurisdiction of the Methodist Episcopal Church, the Christian Methodist Episcopal Church, the Church of God in Christ, the Church of God and Saints of Christ, the Metropolitan Community Church of Christ, the National Baptist Convention, U.S.A., Inc., the National Baptist Convention of America, and the United American Free Will Baptist Church.

Sources:

Guzman, Jessie Parkhurst. *Negro Yearbook*. Tuskegee, AL: Department of Records and Research, Tuskegee Institute, 1947.

2. Western Liturgical

INDEPENDENT AND OLD CATHOLIC CHURCHES

American Catholic Church (Syro-Antiochean)

In the late 1930s, Abp. Daniel C. Hinton, the third primate of the American Catholic Church, resigned in favor of Bp. Percy Wise Clarkson (d. 1942). Clarkson was the founder-pastor of the jurisdiction's most successful parishes in Laguna Beach, California. However, he had strong theosophical leanings, and strengthened the tendency to move the American Catholic Church into theological alignment with the Liberal Catholic Church. Among those who strongly opposed the direction in which Clarkson was leading the church was Ernest Leopold Peterson (d. 1959), a black man who had been consecrated in 1927 by the former primate, Abp. Frederick E. J. Lloyd. Peterson had authored the liturgy used by the church prior to Clarkson's leadership.

Peterson withdrew from Clarkson's jurisdiction and formed the American Catholic Church (Syro-Antiochean), which continued in the faith and practice of the American Catholic Church. In 1950 Peterson consecrated Herbert F. Wilkie, who succeeded as primate in 1959.

The church reported 40 churches, 4,663 members, and 66 clergy in 1961, but by 1979 only 3 churches, 501 members, and 8 clergy remained.

American Orthodox Catholic Church, Archdiocese of Ohio

The American Orthodox Catholic Church, Archdiocese of Ohio was a short-lived religious organization established by the Most Rev. Charles T. Sutter. He had been pastor of St. Jude's parish, now a part of the Orthodox Catholic Church of North and South America, but was consecrated in 1979 by Abp. Richard B. Morrill (Mar Apriam) of the Holy Orthodox Catholic Church, Eastern and Apostolic. Sutter established his see in Zanesville, Ohio, and by early 1982 had established parishes in Miami and Pompano Beach, Florida; a religious order in Coconut Creek, Florida (the Missionary Order of Saint Jude the Apostle); and a school in Rogers, Arkansas (the University of the Holy Transfiguration). However, in the summer of 1982, Sutter dissolved the corporation and retired from his priestly and episcopal offices. Information on the subsequent fate of the several parishes is not available.

Apostolic Old Catholic Church

The Apostolic Old Catholic Church was a small jurisdiction founded in the 1980s in Los Angeles, California, by Bp. Hans Kronenburg, formerly of the American Hebrew Eastern Orthodox Greek Catholic Church. Kronenburg was ordained by Ronald I. Bessler and then in 1979 consecrated by Bp. David Voris. Though consecrated in an Eastern Orthodox tradition, he followed a Western Roman rite. The jurisdiction was centered on a congregation in Los Angeles.

Sources:

Ward, Gary L. *Independent Bishops: An International Directory*. Detroit, MI: Apogee Books, 1990.

Archepiscopate Ordinariate of Healing Arts Missionaries and Chaplains in America

The Archepiscopate Ordinariate of Healing Arts Missionaries and Chaplains in America was a small Catholic jurisdiction founded by Dr. Arthur J. Garrow, who is a chiropractor and founder of the Southern California College of Chiropractic. After many years as a chiropractor, Garrow was ordained to the priesthood in 1985 by Bp. Paul G. W. Schultz (1931–1995) and consecrated as a bishop the following year. The jurisdiction served as a home for priests who wished to work as chaplains or to bring a spiritual element into healing activity.

Catholic Christian Church

Wallace David de Ortega Maxey began his episcopal career on January 2, 1927, when he was consecrated by William Montgomery Brown, a bishop in the Old Catholic Church in America, at that time headed by Abp. W. H. Francis Brothers. Maxey functioned in various capacities during the next two decades, including a period as general secretary of the Temple of the People, an international theosophical body headquartered in Halcyon, California. During the 1940s he became associated with the Apostolic Episcopal Church founded by Arthur Wolfort Brooks. He traveled to England at the close of World War II and was consecrated again by Hugh George de Willmott Newman and named Supreme Hierarch of the Catholicate of the Americas. Upon Maxey's return to New York, Brooks, who had previously accepted the title of hierarch of the Catholicate of the United States, reconsecrated Maxey and placed him in charge of the Apostolic Episcopal Church on the West Coast. Maxey served the two intertwined bodies, and for a period following Brooks death in 1948, he headed them. However, in 1951, he resigned his episcopal positions and joined the Universalist Church.

In 1977 Maxey again assumed authority as an archbishop and founded the Catholic Christian Church. With the assistance of Archbishop Joachim of the Western Orthodox Church in America, he consecrated Alan S. Stanford as his coadjutor. Through the 1980s, Stanford, also known as Metropolitan Abp. Joseph Thaddeus, headed ministries in San Francisco, California, operating out of the church's chapel, the Holy Order of the Society of St. Jude Thaddeus. During the same period, he also ran the National Catholic Street Ministry Project. In 1991, however, Stanford, pled no contest to five counts of child molestation and was sentenced to a prison term of 13 years.

Catholic Life Church

The Catholic Life Church was founded in 1971 by the Revs. A. L. Mark Harding and Peter A. Tonella. Tonella, a former Roman Catholic priest who had married in the 1950s, had earlier joined the Protestant Episcopal Church but soon left it to become bishop of St. Petersburg, Florida, under Bp. Peter A. Zhurawetsky of the Christ Orthodox Catholic Patriarchate. The Catholic Life Church grew quickly, ministering to Latinos in Denver, Colorado, where the church had gathered several congregations. Mark Harding, who was consecrated bishop by Tonella and Walter X. Brown of the Archdiocese of the Old Catholic Church, supported the small denomination with funds he earned as the owner and operator of four pornographic bookstores in Denver. The church virtually disappeared when Harding, who had become its patriarch, was arrested and sentenced to prison. After his confinement ended in the fall of 1981, Harding resumed his ministry as patriarch and presiding bishop.

Evangelical Catholic Communion

The Evangelical Catholic Communion was formed in 1960 by Michael A. Itkin (1936–1989) and other members of the Eucharistic Catholic Church. The new organization took its name from the group formed in England in 1902 by Ulric Vernon Herford (1866–1938), following his consecration by Mar Basilius of the Syro-Chaldean Church in India, Ceylon, Socotra, and Messina, a small Orthodox Church headquartered in southern India. Itkin's second consecration by Christopher Maria Stanley (1902–1976) carried the apostolic lineage from Herford through

British Abp. Hugh George de Willmott Newman (1905–1979). In 1968 the Itkin-led group split. Itkin founded the Community of the Love of Christ, while the remaining members reorganized under Marlin P. B. Ballard.

The communion described itself as an independent body of believers, Catholic in faith, standing for social justice, peace, and goodwill among men. It emphasized the love of God and neighbor; the communion of man with man; the living of a sacramental life; and the uniting of humanity into one sacramental faith. It was governed by a Holy Synod.

The several bishops and their dioceses tended to follow an independent course. Most congregations were small and led by ordained worker/priests who earned their livelihood in secular pursuits. Occupations within the helping professions were preferred. Bishop Ballard died in 1994.

Independent Ecumenical Catholic Church (Shotts)

The Independent Ecumenical Catholic Church was formed in 1976 by Rev. John Michael Becket, a former Universalist minister, and Bp. David E. Shotts. Father Becket was placed in charge of Saint Jude Abbey and the Brothers of the Sacred Rosary. However, the year after its founding, Father Becket left the church and placed himself under the Ecumenical Catholic Communion headed by M. P. B. Ballard.

The Independent Ecumenical Catholic Church followed the Tridentine Roman Catholic liturgy but used the English translation of 1951. Its doctrine was Catholic, and all seven sacraments were served. No excommunication was recognized. Due to its commitment to ecumenicity, members of a variety of Christian groups, including some Protestant churches, were allowed to take communion.

In 1977 the church reported four churches, 200 members, and eight ordained clergy. However, in 1979 Shotts, who had been charged in a child molestation case, abandoned the church and placed himself under Abp. Edward Stelik of the North American Old Catholic Church, Ultrajectine Tradition, headquartered in Necedah, Wisconsin. Following this, the Independent Ecumenical Catholic Church dissolved.

Old Roman Catholic Church, Archdiocese of Chicago (Fris)

In 1970 Abp. Robert A. Burns (d. 1974) of the Old Roman Catholic Church (English Rite), now the Old Roman Catholic Church in North America, consecrated Howard Fris, giving him the right to succession. However, three years later he removed Fris and replaced him with Andrew G. Johnston-Cantrell. Fris proceeded to found his own church and took some of Burns's small following with him. After Burns's death, the corporation of the Old Roman Catholic Church (English Rite) lapsed, as no one filed the annual reports during the bickering and infighting of that

period. Fris revived the corporation and had it assigned to himself.

It is unknown if Burns knew of Fris's personal problems at the time of the consecration in 1970, but there is no doubt that they led to his deposition. They did not stop his continuing to function as the leader of his small flock, however. Though an alcoholic himself, in the late 1970s Fris opened St. Teresa's Manor, described as a home for alcoholics and wayward men. Because of Fris's ecclesiastical connections, social service agencies in the city began to refer men to the Manor. Then in 1979 Fris was arrested for contributing to the sexual delinquency of a child and the theft of credit cards. In the publicity accompanying his arrest and conviction, it was discovered that both of the priests working with him at the Manor also had long records of arrest and conviction for felonies. Fris died in 1981, reportedly of cirrhosis of the liver.

Fris's conviction and the public scandal accompanying it did not destroy his jurisdiction, and he continued to lead his diocese. He performed at least one consecration, and after his death, his coadjutor John Kenelly succeeded him. St. Teresa's Manor was closed, but Bishop Kenelly continued to head the Missionaries of St. Jude, who ministered to the residents of a private hotel for the mentally disturbed, alcoholics, and elderly, located on the north side of Chicago.

In 1979 the archdiocese claimed 13 clergy and two parishes. It considered the residents of the hotel to be lay members.

Sources:

Old Catholic Church (Utrecht Succession). Chicago: Old Catholic Press of Chicago, [1980].

Old Roman Catholic Church in the U.S. (Hough)

Joseph Damien Hough, while under the jurisdiction of Bp. Richard A. Marchenna of the Old Roman Catholic Church, formed a congregation of Oblates of St. Martin of Tours and was designated bishop-elect in 1964. However, following a dispute with Marchenna in 1966, Hough obtained Marchenna's permission to withdraw, and founded the Old Roman Catholic Church in the U.S. In early 1969 Hough was consecrated by Bp. Robert Raleigh of the American Catholic Church (Malabar Succession) with right of succession. Following Raleigh's death, Hough, being the only ultrajectine bishop in California, gathered the faithful into his reorganized church, which combined both Marchenna and Raleigh's traditions. The ultrajectine element predominated, and worship and belief followed the ultrajectine tradition. Headquarters were established in Venice, California, and all members of the church resided in the state. Both Roman and ultrajectine Catholics were admitted to the services and Holy Communion. Bishop Hough was in communion with the Old Catholic Church in England, then under Bp. Gerard George Shelley. Hough retired in the early 1980s, and the jurisdiction he headed dissolved.

Polish Catholic Church

The Polish Catholic Church existed throughout most of the twentieth century as one remnant of the organization begun by independent Polish Bp. Stephen Kaminski (d. 1911) that did not join with the Polish National Catholic Church. Kaminiski died without designating a successor or consecrating a bishop for his jurisdiction. Several of his priests, however, continued to serve their parishes, awaiting a new opportunity to reestablish Kaminski's diocese. One such priest was Francis Ignatius Boryszewski (1873–1957). During the 1920s, Boryszewski initially worked under Abp. Carmel Henry Carfora (1878–1958) of the North American Old Roman Catholic Church (Rogers), but in 1927 he affiliated with the American Catholic Church, headed by Abp. Frederick E. J. Lloyd (1859–1933). Like Kaminski, Lloyd had been consecrated by Abp. Joseph Rene Vilatte (1854–1929). In 1928 Boryszewski began a new parish in New York City, the St. Peter and St. Paul Polish Catholic Church. The following year Bishop Lloyd, assisted by Bps. Gregory Lines (d. 1940) and Daniel C. Hinton, consecrated Boryszewski to head an independent Polish Catholic Church in communion with the American Catholic Church. (It appears that Polish Mariavite Bp. J. M. P. Prochniewski consecrated Boryszewski a second time in a separate ceremony in 1930.)

The Polish Catholic Church followed Roman faith and practice but rejected the authority of the Roman Catholic Church. The jurisdiction never grew very large, but Bishop Boryszewski continued to pastor the church in New York City until his death in the 1970s.

Sources:

Church Directory and Year Book. New York: St. Peter and St. Paul Polish Catholic Church, 1933.

Fifth Year Book. New York: St. Peter and St. Paul Polish Catholic Church, 1933.

Polish Old Catholic Church in America

The Polish Old Catholic Church in America derived from the Polish Mariavite Church. The Mariavite movement dates from 1893, when Sister Felicia (Maria Franciska Kozlowska), a member of the Third Order of St. Francis, a Roman Catholic order, claimed to have had a vision of the Blessed Virgin. In the vision she was told to establish a mixed order of men and women dedicated to the Blessed Virgin. Thus Sister Felicia founded the Mariavite order, which soon spread, carried by its strong mystical element. Polish Roman Catholic bishops denounced the vision and labeled it hallucinatory. They ordered the disbanding of the Mariavites, but the members refused to obey. They were excommunicated in 1906. They found support from the Russian Church and were eventually able to obtain priestly orders from the Old Catholic Church at Utrecht. Denied a place in the Roman Catholic Church, the order transformed into a large denomination. Freed from Roman authority, they made several changes to traditional Roman Catholic practices. They ordained females to the priesthood and episcopacy and placed a great emphasis on the veneration of the Virgin. It is estimated that over a half million Mariavites can be found in Poland.

During the first decades of the twentieth century, Mariavites began to migrate to the United States. Many joined the Polish Old Catholic Church of America, founded in 1913 by Joseph Zielonka, a former priest of the Polish National Catholic Church. Zielonka sought consecration from Paolo Miraglia Gulotti, an independent Italian bishop. In 1925 Zielonka brought his jurisdiction into the Old Catholic Church in America, headed by Abp. W. H. Francis Brothers. After 15 years with Brothers, Zielonka left the Old Catholic Church in America and established the Old Catholic Archdiocese for the Americas and Europe. In 1960 the church had 22 parishes and 7,200 members.

In 1961 Zielonka died and was succeeded by his suffragan, Peter A. Zhurawetsky, a Ukrainian by birth. Zhurawetsky's leadership was immediately questioned by Fr. Felix Starazewski, pastor of the parish in South River, New Jersey, who claimed to be Zielonka's true successor. Many of the Polish parishes, opposed to Zhurawetsky's attempt to make the Church more inclusive, followed Starazewski in founding the Polish Old Catholic Church in America.

Consisting originally of a few parishes in the northeast (primarily in New Jersey and Massachusetts), the church struggled to resist the forces of Americanization. Over time, however, the parishes declined in strength and eventually ceased to exist.

Traditional Catholics of America

In the late 1970s, Fr. Francis E. Fenton encountered opposition from some of the leadership of the Orthodox Roman Catholic Movement, due in large part to his membership in, and vocal support of, the John Birch Society. While approving the anti-Communist attitude of Father Fenton, his critics disapproved of the manner in which he had chosen to express it. As the issue became more and more contentious, Fenton moved to Colorado and began to reorganize those loyal to him, forming the Traditional Catholics of America. Their beliefs and practices were similar to those of the Orthodox Roman Catholic Movement. The church published a periodical, *The Athanasian*.

Sources:

Fenton, Francis E. *The Roman Catholic Church: Its Tragedy and Its Hope*. Stratford, CT: Orthodox Roman Catholic Movement, 1978.

Traditional Christian Catholic Church

The Traditional Christian Catholic Church was founded by Abp. Thomas Fehervary (1917–1984) and was built around a group of immigrants of Austro-Hungarian heritage who came to Quebec, Canada, in 1965 following the failure of the Hungarian revolt. Fehervary had been consecrated in 1945 by Abp. R. M. J. Prochniewski of the Polish Mariavite Church, and he had served an independent Hungarian church since 1939. The faith and practice of the group were in accordance with that of the Roman Catholic Church before the Second Vatican Council of the 1960s, and the church opposed the innovations of that Council. Priests were unsalaried, but (unusually for Old Catholics) they were university-trained.

In 1972 the church reported one parish in Canada, three missions in the United States, three missions in Western Europe, two missions in Eastern Europe, and one mission in Hong Kong. One mission in New York City became independent in 1976 as the Tridentine Catholic Church, currently headed by Abp. Leonard J. Curreri.

United Old Roman Catholic Church (Whitehead)

The United Old Catholic Church resulted from the 1963 merger of three independent jurisdictions: the Catholic Episcopal Church and two other churches. The archbishop and head of the new merged body was Armand C. Whitehead, who had been consecrated in 1960 by Michael A. Itkin (1936–1989) but who had soon left Itkin's jurisdiction to found the Catholic Episcopal Church. Whitehead was consecrated a second time by James E. Burns in 1970.

In general, doctrine and practice conformed to the seven ecumenical councils held between 325 C.E. and 787 C.E. and the canons of the Roman Catholic Church prior to 1880. Distinctive features of the church included a vernacular liturgy, non-obligatory use of the sacrament of penance, and recognition of the primacy (though not the supremacy or infallibility) of the pope. None of the newer doctrines of the Virgin Mary, such as her bodily assumption into heaven, were accepted. Also, "individual bodily parts of our Blessed Lord," such as the "Sacred Heart," were not held in special veneration.

In 1967 the United Catholic Church reported three parishes and approximately 100 members. Starting in 1984, Archbishop Whitehead began living in semi-retirement.

Universal Episcopal Communion

The Universal Episcopal Communion was organized in 1930 by James Christian Crummey (d. 1949), a Chicago theosophist, with the hope of uniting the various small and divided Old Catholic jurisdictions of North America and eventually other continents. During the 1920s, Crummey became a priest under Abp. Carmel Henry Carfora (1878–1958) of the North American Old Roman Catholic Church. On March 19, 1931, Carfora consecrated him as a bishop. As a step toward uniting the Old Catholics, Crummey conceived of an additional organization in which bishops could coordinate activity but which would not attempt to control them in their independent ministries. This second body, hardly distinguishable from the first, was called the Universal Christian Communion. Crummey headed both bodies and kept them within Carfora's jurisdiction until 1944, when he withdrew. At that point, the Universal Episcopal Communion and the Universal Christian Communion became independent entities. Joining him in leaving Carfora were Bps. Mather W. Sherwood and Murray L. Bennett. The two communions lasted until Crummey's death but dissolved soon afterward, neither having attained any significant support from their targeted constituency.

Sources:

Anson, Peter. *Bishops at Large*. London: Faber & Faber, 1964.

Brandreth, Henry R. T. *Episcopi Vagantes and the Anglican Church*. London: Society for Promoting Christian Knowledge, 1947.

3. Anglicanism

ANGLICAN CHURCHES

Anglican Church, Inc.

The Anglican Church, Inc., founded in the 1980s as the Anglican Church, U.S., was a small independent jurisdiction affiliated with the Continuing Church movement, which in the previous generation had rejected the direction in which the Episcopal Church was heading. In 1988 the Anglican Church, U.S., was joined by the former Diocese of the South of the Anglican Episcopal Church. This new body was under the leadership of Bp. Frank H. Benning, who, unlike most of the leaders of the independent Anglican movement, had never been a priest in the Episcopal Church. Benning was ordained in 1968 as a priest by James Parker Dees (1915–1990) of the Anglican Orthodox Church, and in 1972 he went into the Anglican Episcopal Church of North America. In 1973 he was elected suffragan bishop and consecrated by Walter Hollis Adams, assisted by James George and Orlando J. Woodward. In 1975 he was elected coadjutor for the Anglican Episcopal Church. As the Anglican Episcopal Church grew, it was subdivided into dioceses, and Benning was elected bishop of the Diocese of the East in 1980.

For a number of years, Walter Adams had promoted the cause of unity among the several independent Anglican factions. To further this unity, the bishops of the Anglican Episcopal Church, including Benning, were consecrated *sub conditione* by Philippine Independent Church bishops Francisco Pagtakhan, Sergio Mondala, and Lupe Rosete in 1981. This action gave each bishop the unquestionably valid orders of the Philippine Church. It also promoted the union of the Anglican Episcopal Church and the American Episcopal Church in 1982. Benning participated wholeheartedly in the merger, and his diocese was renamed the Anglican Diocese of the South. He served in that position for six years. In 1988 he withdrew because of administrative canonical changes and joined the Anglican Church, U. S., with his diocese, now renamed the Anglican Episcopal Diocese South. The new jurisdiction retained the same doctrine and practice.

In 1993 the name of the Anglican Church, U.S. was changed to Anglican Church, Inc. In 1994 Benning became presiding bishop of the Anglican Church, Inc., while remaining ordinary of the Anglican Episcopal Diocese South.

Prior to its dissolution, the church was affiliated with the St. Georges School of Theology in San Antonio, Texas.

Sources:

Nones, Jane. *1994/95 Directory of Traditional Anglican and Episcopal Parishes*. Tulsa, OK: Fellowship of Concerned Clergymen, 1995.

Ward, Gary L. *Independent Bishops: An International Directory*. Detroit, MI: Apogee Books, 1990.

Anglican Episcopal Church

The Anglican Episcopal Church was founded in 1994 by Bp. Robert H. Hawn and the majority of churches and missions of the former Diocese of the West and Missionary District of the Southwest of the United Episcopal Church in North America. Hawn had been a leader in the charismatic renewal within the Episcopal Church. He was the first president of the Episcopal Charismatic Fellowship and the original editor of *Acts 29*, the fellowship's magazine. However, he left the Episcopal Church, joined the United Episcopal Church in North America, and in 1992 was consecrated to the episcopacy by Bps. Ogden Miller, Albion Knight, and John Gramley. He was assigned as bishop of the Diocese of the West and had oversight of the Missionary District of the Southwest. By the end of 1993, Hawn had become dissatisfied with what he termed the lack of leadership at the national level within the United Episcopal Church.

As a part of the Continuing Church Movement, the Anglican Episcopal Church adhered to the 1928 edition of the Book of Common Prayer and accepted the Thirty-nine Articles of Religion as its doctrinal standard. The church believed that the Episcopal Church had left the Apostolic Faith and Order. It was most favorable to charismatic congregations and members but was inclusive of noncharismatic Evangelicals and Anglo-Catholics in its membership. It maintained a policy of openness to relationships with the other churches, consisting largely of former members of the Episcopal Church constituting the Continuing Church movement.

Anglican Episcopal Church of North America

The Anglican Episcopal Church of North America was founded in 1972 by Walter Hollis Adams, a veteran of the British Foreign Office who had retired in California.

That same year, Adams was consecrated by William Elliot Littlewood of the Free Protestant Episcopal Church. He was consecrated *sub conditione* later that year by Herman Adrian Spruit of the Church of Antioch, and the next year by Frederick Littler Pyman of the Evangelical Orthodox (Catholic) Church in America (Non-Papal Catholic).

Adams spearheaded efforts in the 1970s to bring together a number of traditional Anglican groups that, by the end of the decade, had either disappeared or merged into the Anglican Episcopal Church. These included, among others, the Anglican Church of America, the Episcopal Church (Evangelical), and the United Episcopal Church. In 1981 intercommunion was established with the American Episcopal Church (later revoked) and the Holy Catholic Church, Anglican Rite Jurisdiction of the Americas. On September 26, 1981, Adams was the first of several bishops to be consecrated (in his case, *sub conditione*) by Bps. Francisco Pagtakhan, Sergio Mondala, and Lupe Rosete of the Philippine Independent Church as part of an effort initiated by Pagtakhan to promote unity among Anglican traditionalists.

In May 1982, the Anglican Episcopal Church and the American Episcopal Church met in Seattle, Washington, to discuss steps toward unity. This effort failed for a variety of reasons (Adams was undergoing emergency surgery at the time of the meeting). However, Anglican Episcopal Church Bps. John M. Hamers and Frank H. Benning withdrew from the church and, taking some of their respective dioceses with them, joined the American Episcopal Church.

In 1983, the Anglican Catholic Church (ACC) initiated discussions with Adams looking toward the merger of the two jurisdictions. At separate synods in 1985, the two formally approved a merger in which the Anglican Episcopal Church would retain its identity as the non-geographical Diocese of St. Paul within the ACC. This union was short-lived, for on July 14, 1986, with the backing of the clergy and parishes, Adams announced the withdrawal of the diocese and the reconstitution of the Anglican Episcopal Church of North America. In a manifesto published two weeks later (July 29, 1986), he accused the ACC hierarchy of intending, contrary to their previous agreement, to eliminate the special status of the Diocese of St. Paul, its bishop, and its clergy.

The Anglican Episcopal Church was traditionally Anglican, with roots deeply embedded in the Church of England. It used the King James Version of the Bible and the 1928 Book of Common Prayer. It believed the Holy Bible to be the inspired Word of God. It accepted the Apostles, the Nicene and Athanasian Creeds, and the Thirty-Nine Articles of Religion as found in the Book of Common Prayer. The church permitted a broad spectrum of ceremonial practice (encompassing both high and low emphases). It also took the lead in supporting the efforts of the Bishop of London

and the Archbishop of Sydney, Australia, to establish a worldwide unity of faith among traditional Anglicans.

The church had two dioceses, each headed by a bishop. Bishop Adams was the ordinary for the Diocese of St. Paul. In January 1987, Robert Henry Voight, a former priest of the Protestant Episcopal Church in the U.S.A., was consecrated bishop for the Diocese of the Southwest. In that service, Adams was joined by four bishops from the United Episcopal Church of North America and the Anglican Rite Jurisdiction of the Americas.

The United Episcopal Church had been founded in 1973 by former members of the Anglican Orthodox Church under the leadership of Bps. Troy A. Kaichen, Thomas Kleppinger, and Russell G. Fry. Under Kleppinger's leadership the church joined the Anglican Episcopal Council and subsequently merged with the Anglican Episcopal Church. Kleppinger served as suffragan to Bishop Adams and continued to edit the periodical *Episcopal Tidings*, which he had begun several years before. Kleppinger later transferred to the Anglican Catholic Church.

During its existence, the Anglican Episcopal Church was affiliated with an educational facility in Deming, New Mexico, the Laud Hall Anglican Episcopal Seminary.

Anglican Fathers of the Corpus Christi

The Anglican Fathers of the Corpus Christi was a small Anglican jurisdiction operating in the American South that described itself as a community of bishops, priests, deacons, and subdeacons faithful to traditional Anglican beliefs and practices—especially as related to the affirmation that grew out of the convention of traditionally oriented Episcopalians that met in St. Louis, Missouri, in 1976. The jurisdiction was led by its two bishops: the Rt. Rev. Kenn Duley, who served St. Francis parish in Spartanburg, South Carolina, and oversaw the adjacent St. Anselm Seminary Center (also home to the Anglican Guild of Scholars and the Parish Resource Center), and the Rt. Rev. Arthur Rushlow, who also served as rector of St. George's Church in Ocala, Florida. Together Duley and Rushlow constituted the pontificate and had the power to assign parish priests and to choose their own successors.

The church represented the Anglo-Catholic or high-church wing of Anglicanism that emphasizes the church's affinity with Roman Catholicism. It was committed to the 1928 edition of the Book of Common Prayer and rejected the more recent revisions of the Book that are now commonly used in the parishes of the Episcopal Church.

The episcopate of the Anglican Fathers of the Corpus Christi developed a relationship with Mt. Rev. A. Donald Davies, the retired conservative Episcopal Church bishop of Forth Worth, Texas, who later became the primate archbishop of a Canadian branch of the Continuing Church movement, the Christian Episcopal Church of Canada.

Anglican Rite Synod in the Americas

The Anglican Rite Synod in the Americas was founded in 1989 by David Marion-Davis, William C. Thompson, and Rt. Rev. Larry L. Shaver (b. 1936), formerly a bishop with the Holy Catholic Church, Anglican Rite Jurisdiction, and the American Episcopal Church. Shaver began his pastoral career as a Methodist minister but was led first to the Lutheran and then to the Anglican tradition by his discovery of and love for Apostolic Faith and sacramental theology. He was elected and consecrated a bishop by Abp. Frederick Littler Pyman (d. 1993) of the Evangelical Orthodox (Catholic) Church in America (Non-Papal Catholic) while still a Lutheran pastor (1972); following his retirement from the Lutheran Church (1980), he emerged as Pyman's coadjutant.

In 1985 Shaver was reconsecrated *sub conditione* by Abp. Gerald Wayne Craig, Abp. Robert Q. Kennaugh, and Bp. Ogden Miller of the Holy Catholic Church, Anglican Rite Jurisdiction. That same year, he began to build a congregation (ProCathedral of St. Andrew) in Merrillville, Indiana. In late 1987 he and St. Andrew Church left the Anglican Rite Jurisdiction. In 1989, with the permission of the Philippine Independent Catholic Church (PICC), he led the founding of the Anglican Rite Synod as an independent church body in full communion with the PICC. Cofounders in this effort were Bps. Davis and Thompson, both formerly of the PICC. Shaver was reconsecrated *sub conditione* by Philippine Abp. Francisco Pagtakhan and Abp. Maximo Macario V. Ga. He was elevated to the rank of archbishop with full vote and voice in the Sacred Council of Bishops of the PICC in November 1994 by Abp. Ga.

The Anglican Rite Synod in the Americas was at one with several other traditional Anglican jurisdictions, its differences being more administrative than doctrinal. It was in full communion with the Reformed Episcopal Church and in 2007 became affiliated with the Missionary Society of St. John. It supported a mission in Haiti. It also ran an educational facility, the Geneva Theological College, in Merrillville, Indiana.

At the beginning of the twenty-first century, the Anglican Rite Synod moved to affiliate with the Anglican Province of America, into which it eventually was absorbed. It initially became the Diocese of St. Augustine, a nongeographical diocese of the Province, and then in 2007 completed the merger by becoming the Diocese of the Midwest of the Anglican Province of North America. Archbishop Shaver continues to head the Diocese of the Midwest.

Sources:

Anglican Diocese of Mid America (formerly Anglican Rite Synod in the Americas).
www.saintaugustinediocese.org/.

"Profile: Bishop Shaver." *The Evangelist* 3, no. 4 (June 1985).

Ward, Gary L. *Independent Bishops: An International Directory*. Detroit, MI: Apogee Books, 1990.

Diocese of the Southwest

The short-lived Diocese of the Southwest was originally formed in 1978 as a constituent part of the Anglican Catholic Church (ACC). In 1982 it left the ACC and for several months existed as an independent jurisdiction. In December 1983 it merged into the American Episcopal Church. It no longer exists as a separate body.

Ecumenical Anglican Catholic Church

The Ecumenical Anglican Catholic Church was formed at the end of the 1990s as an independent jurisdiction representative of the Continuing Church movement, which held that the Episcopal Church had departed from the Anglican tradition insofar as it had made revisions to the 1928 Book of Common Prayer and had begun to ordain females to the priesthood. The church was led by its bishops: Mt. Rev. Howard E. Stark, the presiding bishop; Rt. Rev. Adolphus C. Howard II, the bishop coadjutor; and Mt. Rev. Daniel C. Williams, the general secretary. Their several lines of apostolic succession came through the independent Old Catholic churches. The primary consecrator of Bishop Stark was Stephen I (Gary Stephen Trivoli-Johnson) of the Reform Catholic Church.

Though possessing Old Catholic orders, the church was Anglican in belief and practice. Like other Continuing Church movement jurisdictions, it accepted the 1928 Book of Common Prayer, but recognized the validity of more modern liturgical forms. The church had a broad ecumenical approach to Anglican, Orthodox, and Catholic communions that also shared an apostolic succession in their episcopacy. It also accepted clergy from other such communions and attempted to remove the red tape that often hinders the acceptance of clergy and the formation of new parishes and missions. The church viewed itself as nondiscriminatory, nonpolitical, and nonrestrictive, and it rejected what it saw as ecclesiastical hypocrisy and bigotry among church officials.

Though relatively small, the church sponsored two national conferences annually. There were work centers in the New York metropolitan area.

Holy Catholic Church, Anglican Rite Jurisdiction of the Americas

In the several years following the 1977 St. Louis congress, the Anglican Movement grew to encompass more than 200 congregations. However, as it grew, it splintered into several factions due to administrative disagreements, as well as the issue of the domination of the Anglican Catholic Church by the Anglo-Catholic (high-church) perspective. Some congregations remained outside of the various diocesan structures altogether. Bp. Francisco Pagtakhan of the Philippine

Independent Church, who had participated in the original consecrations of the four Anglican bishops in 1978, became increasingly disturbed at the splintering and lack of unity in the Anglican Movement. In 1980, asserting his role as the ecumenical and missionary officer for the Philippine Independent Church, Pagtakhan decided to create an "umbrella" for those in the Anglican Movement who were searching for a home where they could "belong to a genuinely canonical part of the One, Holy, Catholic and Apostolic Church." Thus in March 1980, in Texas, he initiated the incorporation of the Holy Catholic Church, Anglican Rite Jurisdiction of the Americas.

On September 26, 1981 (with the permission of the supreme bishop of the Philippine Independent Church, the M. Rev. Macario V. Ga), Bishop Pagtakhan, assisted by retired bishops Sergio Mondala and Lupe Rosete, consecrated Robert Q. Kennaugh, F. Ogden Miller, and Gerald Wayne Craig, all former priests in the Anglican Catholic Church. Kennaugh became head of the Diocese of St. Luke, centered in Corsicana, Texas, and archbishop for the jurisdiction. Miller was named bishop of the Diocese of St. Matthew, with headquarters in California. Craig became bishop of the Diocese of St. Mark, with headquarters in Columbus, Ohio. In 1982 Herman F. Nelson was consecrated as bishop for the Diocese of St. John the Evangelist, with headquarters in Venice, Florida. Shortly thereafter, Kennaugh retired as archbishop, and Craig was named to that post. In 1985 the Anglican Rite Jurisdiction received Bp. Harold L. Trott into the church as the Bishop of the Missionary Diocese of Reconciliation. Trott had left the American Episcopal Church in 1979 and had formed the Pro-Diocese of Reconciliation (consisting of several congregations in California and New Mexico) while waiting for a larger body with which to affiliate.

In 1986 the jurisdiction accepted Rt. Rev. Lafond Lapointe, a Haitian-born bishop who had been exiled from his homeland for political reasons. In the intervening years Lapointe had worked in the Haitian-American community in Chicago, Illinois. After the fall of the dictatorship in Haiti he was able to return as the bishop of the Anglican Diocese of Haiti. He reconstituted L'Iglise Orthodox Apostolique Haitienne, an independent church established in 1874 by Bp. James Theodore Holley with the approval and backing of the Protestant Episcopal Church. Holley died in 1911, and his church was absorbed into the Episcopal Missionary Diocese in 1913.

In addition to accepting Lapointe, the Anglican Rite Jurisdiction of the Americas established close ties to Los Hermanos Franciscanos de la Providencia, a Franciscan order in Puerto Rico. Retired archbishop Robert Q. Kennaugh became the bishop-protector of the order. The church also maintained an education facility, the Anglican Theological Collegum, in Columbus, Ohio.

Sources:

Dibbert, Roderic B. *The Roots of Traditional Anglicanism*. Akron, OH: Dekoven Foundation, 1984.

Official Directory of Bishops, Clergy, Parishes. Akron, OH: Holy Catholic Church, Anglican Rite Jurisdiction of the Americas, Office of the Secretary of the ARJA Synod, 1985.

The Prologue. Akron, OH: DeKoven Foundation, 1984.

Independent Anglican Church (Canada Synod)

The Independent Anglican Church (Canada Synod)—also known as the Archdiocese of Canada, the Anglican Church, Canada Synod (Independent)—traced its origins to the 1930s and the founding of the Independent Anglican Church by William H. Daw (1902–1986), a former priest in the Anglican Church of Canada. The church went through several changes of name and administration over the next half century, before emerging in 1984 as the Anglican Church of North America. In 1978 Daw, assisted by Abp. Joseph Edward Neth and Bp. William Vincent (Paul) Hains-Howard, consecrated Peter Wayne Goodrich to the episcopate. The body that was to become the Independent Anglican Church (Canada Synod) first served as the Canadian affiliate of the Anglican Church of North America. In the 1990s that relationship was severed and the Canada Synod became an independent church in its own right, with Goodrich as the presiding archbishop.

The Canada Synod identified itself with the Continuing Church movement, a loose network of jurisdictions, the first of which emerged in the 1970s. The movement rejected what it saw as the liberal trends in the Episcopal Church and strongly affirmed traditional Anglican standards of doctrine. The Canada Synod saw itself as conservative in policy. It retained use of the 1938 edition of the Book of Common Praise and also published both its own version of the Book of Common Prayer (1991) based directly on Archbishop Cranmer's Prayer Book of 1549, and the Anglican Chant for the Psalms and Canticles (1991). All clergy were required to subscribe to the Thirty-Nine Articles of Religion. Women were not accepted into the ordained priesthood, though they could be admitted to the deaconate.

Congregations in the church ranged across the traditional Anglican spectrum from low-church Evangelical to high-church Anglo-Catholic, though most followed the middle ground between the two.

The church ran a training facility, St. Matthew's Cathedral College, which granted diplomas or certificates for future ministers, as well as honorary doctorates of divinity.

International Communion of Christian Churches

The International Communion of Christian Churches (ICCC) was founded in 1998 by Rev. Dr. Daniel Williams. Williams is the pastor of Christ the Redeemer Church, in Ponte Vedra, Florida (founded in 1992). Associated with several Evangelical organizations, Williams is also the founder and president emeritus of Calvary International (a missionary sending agency), a trustee of the Association of International Mission Services (AIMS), and the chairman of the board of Teen Mania Ministries.

William was consecrated to the bishopric in 1999 by Abp. Paul Wayne Boosahda and several bishops of the Communion of Evangelical Episcopal Churches. The Communion of Evangelical Episcopal Churches remained in communion with the ICCC, both having grown out of the "convergence movement" (a term referring to the "convergence" of various streams of renewal that shared an understanding of the church as one body with a variety of diverse but contributing parts). This movement is generally traced to Robert Webber, a professor of theology and Bible studies at Wheaton College who developed the concept of convergence in two books, *Common Roots* (1978) and *Evangelicals on the Canterbury Trail* (1985), the latter recounting his own pilgrimage to Anglicanism. Webber saw the Anglican Church as having a three-fold essence: It was Catholic in relation to its emphases on "incarnation and creation," Protestant in its emphasis on "biblical proclamation and conversion," and Orthodox/Pentecostal in its relation to "the mystical and the Holy Spirit."

Like the Communion of Evangelical Episcopal Churches formed earlier, the ICCC accepted the Chicago-Lambeth Quadrilateral of 1886 and affirmed the authority of the Holy Scriptures of the Old and New Testaments, the Apostles' Creed, and the Nicene Creed. It practiced two sacraments (baptism and the supper of the Lord) and held to the historic episcopate.

Sources:

Webber, Robert. *Common Roots*. Waco, TX: Word Publishing, 1978.

————. *Evangelicals on the Canterbury Trail: Why Evangelical Christians Are Attracted to the Liturgical Church*. Waco, TX: Word Publishing, 1985.

National Anglican Church

The National Anglican Church was a small jurisdiction created in the late 1980s by Bp. Montgomery Griffith-Mair. A former priest in the Episcopal Church, Griffith-Mair was consecrated in 1987 by Donald Lee West, a bishop of the Evangelical Catholic Communion. He served as premier bishop of the church and ordinary for the Anglican Diocese of the Eastern United States.

Old Episcopal Church

The Old Episcopal Church was a small diocese in the Southwest headed by Rt. Rev. Jack C. Adam, Bishop of Arizona. A former Protestant Episcopal Church priest, Adam left the Episcopal Church and was consecrated by Abp. Walter A. Propheta of the American Orthodox Catholic Church in 1972. His Old Episcopal Church grew to encompass several parishes in Arizona and New Mexico.

Old Episcopal Church of Scotland (OECS)

The Old Episcopal Church of Scotland (OECS) traced its heritage to the pre-Roman Celtic Christian community, which is believed to have existed in the British Isles as early as the first century. This tradition continued in the Celtic monastic communities through the centuries until the Reformation of the sixteenth century, when the state-sanctioned Church of Scotland became Presbyterian—that is, reorganized as a church led by an assembly of elders (the presbytery) rather than by bishops. Those who retained the reformed Catholic faith and polity reorganized as the Episcopal Church of Scotland. Problems developed in the Episcopal Church of Scotland in the mid-eighteenth century when King William of Orange and the Church of England attempted to install English bishops over the Scottish church. Those nonjurors opposed to the new policy, who also refused to swear allegiance to the deposed monarch, left and formed the Old Free Episcopal Church of Scotland. Later, members of the Old Free Episcopal Church of Scotland migrated to Canada. A small community continued through the years and experienced a revival in the 1970s.

In 1983 the Rt. Rev. Fredrick R. O'Keefe, O.S.B., succeeded Brian G. Turkington as leader of the church. Turkington, who went on to join the Federation of St. Thomas Christian Churches, had been voted out of office by the church's leadership. O'Keefe had been a priest in the Old Catholic Church of North America. He was loaned to the OECS, which needed additional leadership. In 1981 O'Keefe was consecrated by Abp. Charles V. Hearn of the Old Catholic Church in North America as a bishop for both jurisdictions. An increasing amount of his time was spent with the OECS, and in 1983 he was chosen as its primus, though he still retained his formal ties to the Old Catholics. He was assisted by Bp. Fonzy J. Broussard. In cooperation with several other small Old Catholic jurisdictions, the church sponsored a Benedictine monastic community, Incarnation Abbey, in Clearwater, Florida.

The church had no property and all worship was conducted in the homes of members or in rented facilities. Altogether, there were fewer than 50 members and six priests. Ministers were unsalaried and usually worked at a secular occupation. Both the 1928 and the 1979 Episcopal Prayer Books were used, as well as the Eastern Orthodox Peshitta Bible, translated from the Aramaic by George M. Lamsa.

During the 1970s and early 1980s, in an attempt to move away from their singular ethnic identification, a number of names for the church were used by different leaders. These included Free Anglican Church, Free Anglican Church (Iona Conference), Free Anglican Church in America, Free Anglican Church in America and the British Isles, Free Anglican Communion,

United Anglican Communion, and United Anglican Communion in America (and the British Isles). The use of such diverse names led to a great deal of confusion, with observers seeing several churches where, in fact, there was only one. The OECS was also confused with other small jurisdictions that used identical or similar names. Eventually, the use of divergent names ceased.

The relationship of the OECS to the movement founded in the eighteenth century is not entirely clear. At one time it was claimed that the lineage had passed through Bp. Cowan King, the last of the OECS bishops in Great Britain. Supposedly, King consecrated Harry Edwin Smith in 1970, and Smith passed the lineage to Brian G. Turkington. However, that story has been challenged by O'Keefe.

Primitive Episcopal Church

The Primitive Episcopal Church was founded in 1997 as the Diocese of the Holy Spirit. On May 28 of that year, its presiding bishop, Steven Murrell, was both ordained as a priest and consecrated as a bishop. The later name was adopted in 2001. The church described itself as Evangelical, Anglican, and Catholic. It accepted the absolute authority of the Bible; traditional Anglican liturgy and belief; the threefold ministry of bishop, priest, and deacon; the apostolic succession of episcopal leadership; and participation in the historical lineage of the Christian church. Though conservative in its approach, it was not particularly identified with the Continuing Church Movement (the loose network of jurisdictions that emerged in the 1970s in opposition to "liberal" trends in the Episcopal Church).

The church had two congregations in the continental United States and one parish in Puerto Rico. Its missionary outreach in Puerto Rico was centered in Dorado at Christ the King of Glory Church, which was pastored by the Very Rev. Juan Cepero.

Protestant Anglican Bible Church

The Protestant Anglican Bible Church, originally known at the Evangelical Episcopal Church, was founded in the 1980s by Bp. Edward Marshall. The name change took place in July 2001. The church was associated with the Continuing Church Movement among Anglicans who rejected the changes in the Episcopal Church during the previous generation. Marshall arrived at his position by a distinct route, as he was never an Episcopal minister. As a young man, he had become a published poet of some note. He was also a lay reader in the Episcopal Church. Then in 1965 he accepted ordination from Abp. Richard A. Marchenna of the North American Old Roman Catholic Church. Marshall was consecrated in 1976 by Bp. James E. Burns of the United Episcopal Church (1945) Anglican/Celtic. Finally in 1989 he was reconsecrated by Francisco Pagtakhan, the bishop of the Philippine Independent Church, from whom many in the Continuing Church Movement have their orders.

The Evangelical Episcopal Church had fraternal ties to several other small Anglican jurisdictions of similar faith and practice, especially the Traditional Protestant Episcopal Church and the United Anglican Church.

Sources:

Ward, Gary L. *Independent Bishops: An International Directory*. Detroit, MI: Apogee Books, 1990.

Provisional Diocese of St. Augustine of Canterbury

The Provisional Diocese of St. Augustine of Canterbury was formed in 1978 by Canon Albert J. duBois (1906–1980), former head of the American Church Union, and the members of five former parishes of the Diocese of the Holy Trinity (a diocese of what is now the Anglican Catholic Church). It was the desire of the parishes to unite with the Roman Catholic Church, though they wished to retain their own liturgy and forms of piety and their traditional lay involvement in the life of the Church. The group was led by its senior priest, Canon duBois; the Rev. John Barker, head of the Clericus, a priests' conference; and Dr. Theodore L. McEvoy, head of its Laymen's League.

In 1980 John Raphael Quinn, the Roman Catholic archbishop of San Francisco, announced a plan by which Anglicans could come into the Roman Catholic Church and keep their own priests, an approved Anglican liturgy, and a common identity. In 1981 James Parker became the first priest to move from the Protestant Episcopal Church to the Roman jurisdiction. By 1985, a total of 23 married priests had been reordained as Roman priests. Five parishes had been received by the Vatican.

Traditional Episcopal Church

The Traditional Episcopal Church was founded in 1991 by Most Rev. Richard G. Melli, its presiding bishop. In the mid-1970s, Melli was a lay-reader at the St. Edward the Confessor Episcopal Church in Mt. Dora, Florida, a congregation of the Protestant Episcopal Church in the U.S.A. He also studied with the Diocesan Deacon Training Program. Following the formation of the Anglican Catholic Church, a conservative body of former Episcopal priests and laypeople, he assisted in the founding of new congregations in central Florida. He was ordained a deacon in 1980 and the following year as a priest by Bp. Frank Knutti.

Melli initially served as the diocesan administrative officer and soon was named canon. During these years the Anglican Catholic Church largely established itself as an Anglo-Catholic high church and developed some intolerance for the evangelical wing of the conservative Continuing Church movement. Following Knutti's death, Melli left the church and joined the Anglican Episcopal Church of North America under Bp. Walter Hollis Adams.

Melli found himself in charge of four parishes and a mission, an ordered community, the Order of Oblates of the Holy Spirit (founded in 1983), and Laud

Hall Seminary, an in-house school to provide training for the church's clergy.

When Adams died and the AECNA moved into a period of instability, Melli and the parishes under his leadership began to seek another jurisdiction that was similarly nonpolitical, Christ-centered, spirit-filled, and serving God. Finding no jurisdiction to their liking within the Continuing Church movement, in 1991 they decided to form the Traditional Episcopal Church. To ensure the validity of his orders, Melli sought consecration by bishops in three different lineages: Bps. Howard Russell (Anglican), Peters (Orthodox), and Roberto Toca (Old Catholic).

As the church grew, a Diocese of the Mid-Atlantic, anchored on the St. Charles the Martyr parish in Annapolis, Maryland, was also formed, as well as overseas dioceses in Colombia and India. An Abbot of the Order of the Oblates of the Holy Spirit was consecrated as the fifth bishop sitting in the College of Bishops. The church maintained the Anglican College of Chaplains in Palaka, Florida, and issued an Internet periodical, *The Traditional Episcopalian*.

United Episcopal Church of America

The United Episcopal Church of America started in 1970 as an independent Anglican parish meeting in the home of Howard Love of Columbia, South Carolina. The congregation decided to affiliate with the American Episcopal Church (AEC) and called former Protestant Episcopal priest Richard C. Acker (d. 1985) to the pulpit. Acker was installed in 1971 by Abp. Anthony F. M. Clavier, head of the American Episcopal Church. In 1973 the congregation withdrew from the AEC. Over the next few years Acker became acquainted with Bp. James E. Burns of the United Episcopal Church (1945) Anglican/Celtic. Burns's consecration of Acker in 1976 led to the formation of the United Episcopal Church of America, over which Acker served as archbishop. Acker was succeeded as head of the church by Charles Edward Morley, whom he consecrated in 1984. Morley disbanded the church, which was superseded in 1986 by the Traditional Protestant Episcopal Church.

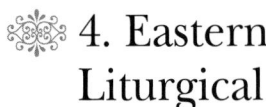

4. Eastern Liturgical

EASTERN LITURGICAL FAMILY

Celtic Christian Communion

The Celtic Christian Communion (CCC) was an ecumenical association of independent Catholic and Orthodox jurisdictions that in turn were composed of small faith communities, many of which met as either house churches or small chapels. The communion was united in the affirmation of the teachings of the first seven Ecumenical Councils of the undivided Christian Church as summarized in the Nicene Creed. Member jurisdictions, which included the Anamchara Celtic Church, the Church of the Culdees, and St. Ciaran's Fellowship of Celtic Christian Communities, celebrated the seven sacraments (also called Mysteries) and believed in the real presence of Christ in the Eucharist.

Christians from every denomination were welcome at services of the communion's member churches, and it was not necessary to give up one's denominational affiliation to participate in their services.

While the communion was particularly attractive to persons of Celtic heritage, it did not set any kind of ethnic limitation on membership or participation. Priesthood was open to both men and women, married or celibate. Bishops were elected by church members. The communion had a presiding archbishop who was also elected. Episcopal jurisdictions were based not on geography, as dioceses are, but on spiritual "spheres of influence." Thus, bishops were those who were elected by the people they served spiritually, regardless of location, and there could feasibly be several bishops near each other.

There were some in the communion, both married and single, who were members of religious communities (not unlike the Third Orders of the Roman Church) and who had added the discipline of monastic prayer to their lives. Personal prayer was strongly encouraged for everyone.

INTRAFAITH ORGANIZATIONS

Federated Independent Catholic and Orthodox Churches

The Federated Independent Catholic and Orthodox Churches was a short-lived ecumenical organization founded by Bp. Antoine Joseph Aneed (1881–1970) of the Byzantine Universal (Catholic) and Orthodox Church of the Americas. The federation was apparently formed around 1944 following Aneed's consecration by Lowell Paul Wadle of the American Catholic Church and E. R. Verostek of the North American Old Roman Catholic Church—Utrecht Succession. The federation, never very active, did not survive Aneed's death.

Federation of Orthodox Catholic Churches (FOCC)

The Federation of Orthodox Catholic Churches (FOCC) was founded in the mid-1990s. Taking the lead in its formation was Abp. Seraphim MacLennan of the Holy Orthodox Catholic Church; other founding members included Abp. Donald William Mullen of Christ Catholic Church International, Archbishop Melchizedek of the Free Orthodox Church International (Eparchy of Lincoln), and Archbishop Ingram of the American Orthodox Catholic Church.

The FOCC grew out of an expressed need among some of the smaller Orthodox Catholic jurisdictions to have a meeting place where each group could find recognition and succor without the fear of any challenge to its particular expression of the Orthodoxia (correct way, right theology). The word *Orthodox* in

the FOCC's name did not refer to Eastern Orthodoxy, but to the true teachings of Orthodoxia and Orthopraxis (correct practice). Members believed themselves to be Orthodox Catholics in belief and practice.

The FOCC also provided a synodical covering for those Orthodox Catholic jurisdictions that for one reason or another did not have one. Thus, the FOCC existed as a synod of synods that both allowed jurisdictions with an active synod to meet without abandoning that synod and permitted jurisdictions with no synod to participate without losing their identity. Member churches sought to acknowledge and strengthen the core similarities of member jurisdictions without limiting diversity among members. Members included the Holy Orthodox Catholic Church, Christ Catholic Church International, the Free Orthodox Church International (Eparchy of Lincoln), and the American Orthodox Catholic Church.

Holy Synod of the Orthodox Catholic Churches of the Americas and Europe

The Holy Synod of the Orthodox Catholic Churches of the Americas and Europe was a short-lived ecumenical endeavor organized in 1967 by Abp. Peter A. Zhurawetsky (1901–1994), then head of the Christ Catholic Church of the Americas and Europe. The synod grew out of a dispute between Zhurawetsky and Abp. Cyril John Clement Sherwood (1895–1969), who had succeeded Joseph Klimovich as head of the Orthodox Catholic Patriarchate of America. Zhurawetsky, who had cofounded the patriarchate with Klimovich, claimed that Sherwood stole the patriarchate. The new synod included Zhurawetsky and the heads of the Autocephalous Greek Orthodox Church of the Americas and Europe (Abp. Joachim Souris), the Greek Orthodox Diocese of America (Archbishop Theoklitos), and the Universal Shrine of Divine Guidance (Abp. Mark Karras).

The synod dissolved in 1975, by which time Sherwood had died and the original charter had become inactive. Zhurawetsky seized the opportunity to assume corporate control of the patriarchate and revived it around the core of the Orthodox Catholic Churches of the Americas and Europe.

Synod of Autonomous Canonical Orthodox Churches in North America

The Synod of Autonomous Canonical Orthodox Churches in North America was founded in the 1990s as a fellowship of independent Orthodox jurisdictions committed to the faith and gifts given by Christ and the Holy Spirit to the Undivided Church (the Christian community prior to the Great Schism of 1054 C.E. between the Roman Catholic Church and Eastern Orthodoxy). The synod believed it was built on the true faith and the right administration of the sacraments, and stood against the apostasy and paganism it perceived to be the hallmarks of the present age.

ORTHODOXY

African Orthodox Church of New York and Massachusetts

The African Orthodox Church of New York and Massachusetts was founded in the mid-1930s by Reginald Grant Barrow (1889–1979), a bishop in the African Orthodox Church. Barrow had been born in Barbados but migrated to the United States, where he became one of the founding members of the African Orthodox Church in 1921. In 1925 Barrow became the fourth bishop of the church. In 1934 Abp. George A. McGuire (1866–1934) died and was succeeded by Bp. William E. J. Robertson (1875–1962). Robertson resided in Miami, Florida, where the church was incorporated. Church affairs in New York, where the church had its greatest strength, were placed in the hands of Frederick A. Toote, the vicar general. Barrow, Toote, and two bishops, Arthur Stanley Trotman and Robert Arthur Valentine, moved to take control of the church in the northeast by founding a separate jurisdiction, which they called the African Orthodox Church of New York and Massachusetts.

A short time after the founding of the new church, Barrow had a falling out with Trotman, who left to found the African Orthodox Church, Inc. Archbishop Robertson moved legally against both Barrow and Trotman, and in 1938 the court ruled that they were illegitimately using the name African Orthodox Church. Trotman renamed his group the Holy African Church. Barrow soon patched up his differences with Trotman, and his jurisdiction was absorbed into the Holy African Church, which eventually reunited into the African Orthodox Church in 1964.

Sources:

Terry-Thompson, A. C. *The History of the African Orthodox Church*. Author, 1956.

African Orthodox Church of the West

In 1984 Bp. G. Duncan Hinkson, a physician and pastor of St. Augustine's African Orthodox Church, on the south side of Chicago, left the African Orthodox Church and formed a new jurisdiction. Though it followed the teachings and ritual of its parent body, the new jurisdiction was administratively independent. Bishop Hinkson consecrated Bp. Franzo King to lead work in San Francisco.

In 1992 the church had two parishes: one in Chicago, and one in California with several hundred members. The church published a periodical, *Expression*.

Albanian Orthodox Archdiocese in America

The Albanian Orthodox Archdiocese in America can be traced to 1908, when the first Albanian parish in the United States was established in Boston. In the same year, an Albanian-American immigrant, Fan Stylin Noli (1882–1965), was ordained to the priesthood by Metropolitan Platon of the Russian Orthodox Church in America. In 1920 Father Noli returned to Albania, where he had a prominent political career, eventually becoming prime minister. He became a bishop in 1923, but in 1930 returned to the United States and organized the American parishes into the Albanian Orthodox Archdiocese in America. The archdiocese remained in communion with the church in Albania until after World War II, when a Communist government hostile to the church took control of the country, and, in the eyes of the archdiocese, subverted the leadership of the church. While retaining orthodox belief and practice, the Archdiocese became independent. Noli was succeeded by Bp. Stephen Lasko, who led the Archdiocese into the Orthodox Church in America in 1971. Since merging into the Orthodox Church in America, the Albanian work has lost its identity as a separate organization and has been thoroughly integrated into the larger work.

Sources:

Orthodox Church in America. www.oca.org.

All Faiths Ecumenical Diocese of the South and Southwest

The All Faiths Ecumenical Diocese of the South and Southwest was founded by Bp. Leo E. Rondeau, who was consecrated in 1985 by Bp. Francis Joseph Ryan of the Ecumenical Orthodox Catholic Church-Autocephalous. Rondeau had originally been consecrated by Charles David Luther of the Western Orthodox Church. Rondeau was assisted by Bp. Raymond Hefner, his auxiliary, also ordained by Luther and consecrated by Ryan.

Sources:

Ward, Gary L. *Independent Bishops: An International Directory*. Detroit, MI: Apogee Books, 1990.

American Eastern Orthodox Catholic Church

The American Eastern Orthodox Catholic Church was founded in 1977 by a group of clergy and laity who were Orthodox in faith but who wished to escape the national and political bigotry that they felt characterized the life of the older ethnic Orthodox churches. The group constituted a synod and elected Fr. Martin de Porres as their bishop. De Porres was consecrated on January 29, 1977, by Most Rev. Thomas Ephraim (the ecclesiastical name of Bp. Dennis Smith) of the Reformed Orthodox Catholic Church and Bp. R. Michael Chaffee of the Byzantine Ecumenical Catholic Church. The church was incorporated in 1980 as the Christist Orthodox Catholic Church, but officially changed its name in 1982. The same year, the church sent a letter and papers to the ecumenical Patriarch Demetrios I, the spiritual head of the Eastern Orthodox communion, seeking to come under his jurisdiction. A Holy Antimensia (blessing) was received in return, but no action was taken on the church's request for union with the ecumenical patriarch.

In 1984 the American Eastern Orthodox Catholic Church aligned itself with the Western Orthodox Catholic Church of California headed by Metropolitan Martin J. Hill. Later that year, after concerns were raised about the consecration of de Porres by only two bishops (instead of the usual three demanded in Orthodox lineages), de Porres was consecrated *sub conditione* by Patriarch Andre Barbeau (Andre I; 1912–1994), head of the Catholic Charismatic Church of Canada, with the assistance of Bps. Andre Letellier and Bruce Rodgers. In 1990 the union between the Western Orthodox Catholic Church of California and the American Eastern Orthodox Catholic Church came to an end.

The American Eastern Orthodox Catholic Church was Orthodox in faith and practice. It accepted the teachings of the seven ecumenical councils. There were two dioceses, one in Michigan, where Bishop de Porres resided, and one in southern California under the leadership of R. Michael Cullinan. Besides its parishes in southern California, the church established St. Francis of Assisi Orthodox Mission and the Queen of Peace Orthodox Center, an ecumenical project devoted to promoting world peace and brotherhood, in Alger, Michigan (near Flint). There was also a parish in Detroit, Michigan, and a mission in Seattle, Washington, with a ministry to people with AIDS. The church published a periodical, the *Queen of Peace Orthodox Newsletter*. Women were welcomed into the ministry of the church, which ordained them to the office of deacon.

Sources:

The American Eastern Orthodox Catholic Church: A Brief History. Alger, MI: American Eastern Orthodox Catholic Church, 1994. 50 pp.

American Eastern Orthodox Church

Since the second century, India has had Eastern Orthodox churches, which call themselves Mar Thomas churches based on the claim that St. Thomas the Apostle founded them. In the 1930s the Church of England was India's state church. When the Christian Missionary Society of the Church of England attempted to convert members of the Mar Thomas churches, a controversy arose. One of its results was that Bp. Anthony Devan left India and came to the United States to locate members of the Mar Thomas churches residing there. He succeeded in locating a few families, and he ordained four priests, thus establishing the American Eastern Orthodox Church. This church continued the tradition of the Mar Thomas Christians, and was one in faith and practice with the Orthodox churches. St. Thomas was honored on the Sunday after the Resurrection (Easter), on July 19 (his birthday), and on October 19 (the anniversary of his martyrdom). The Liturgy of St. Basil was used. In 1973 the church had five parishes, five mission stations, and 1,240 members.

Sources:

Following Christ in the American Eastern Orthodox Church. Las Vegas, NV: St. George Monastery, 1967.

American Hebrew Eastern Orthodox Greek Catholic Church

The American Hebrew Eastern Orthodox Greek Catholic Church was a small Orthodox jurisdiction founded by Bp. Gregory Voris following his consecration by Bp. Robert Marshall of the Evangelical Catholic Church on December 21, 1963. Marshall had originally consecrated Voris in 1957, but in 1963 the two men participated in a ceremony in which they mutually exchanged consecrations. Also associated with Voris were Bps. David R. Vashon, James Griffis, Ronald I. Bessler, and Kenneth L. Hite.

Sources:

Ward, Gary L. *Independent Bishops: An International Directory*. Detroit, MI: Apogee Books, 1990.

American Holy Orthodox Catholic Eastern Church

The American Holy Orthodox Catholic Eastern Church was incorporated in 1933 under the leadership of Cyril John Clement Sherwood (1895–1969), popularly known by his ecclesiastical name, Clement I. His Holiness Clement I had previously belonged to the Benedictine community founded by Abp. W. H. Francis Brothers (1887–1979) of the Old Catholic Church in America. In 1927, however, he received priestly orders from Abp. Frederick E. J. Lloyd (1859–1933) of the American Catholic Church, and three years later he was consecrated by Bp. William F. Tyarks of the African Orthodox Church. He was then reconsecrated in 1932 by Bp. George A. McGuire (1866–1934) of the American Catholic Orthodox Church, and throughout the rest of his life he considered this latter consecration as his true one.

The American Holy Orthodox Catholic Eastern Church followed Eastern Orthodox faith and practice but was established as a completely autocephalous jurisdiction, autonomous of all foreign bishops and church bodies. Headquarters of the church were established in Sts. Peter and Paul Church in New York City. For a while Clement issued a periodical, *The Voice of the Community*. Clement founded a coalition of various independent Orthodox and Catholic bishops, the Orthodox Catholic Patriarchate of America. Clement died in 1969. Following his death, leadership of the patriarchate passed to Abp. George A. Hyde of the Orthodox Catholic Church of America. In succeeding years, the already weakened organization ceased to exist (though it was eventually reestablished by Abp. Alfred Louis Lankenau, who succeeded Hyde as head of the Orthodox Church in America). At the same time, the American Holy Orthodox Catholic Apostolic Eastern Church was received into the Orthodox Catholic Church in America as its Eastern Rite Diocese and ceased to exist as a separate body.

American National Catholic Church (Bridges)

The American National Catholic Church was founded in 1976 by Richard W. Bridges, whose episcopal orders were conferred in 1980 by Bps. Gregory Voris, C. Engel, and Hans Kroneberg. It adhered to the faith of the Seven Ecumenical Councils and the Three Ecumenical Creeds and was designed to use both Eastern and Western rites. Though not open to ordaining females to the priesthood, it was open to receiving homosexuals into Holy Orders. Through the 1980s, the church was known as the American Independent Orthodox Church; it adopted its later name around 1990. Archbishop Bridges attained some fame in 1990 when he consecrated Fr. George A. Stallings as the bishop of the African-American Catholic Congregation.

American Orthodox Catholic and Apostolic Church

The American Orthodox Catholic and Apostolic Church was founded in 1922 by Abp. Vladimir Sehorn, formerly a bishop of the Holy Eastern Orthodox Catholic and Apostolic Church in North America. Sehorn had been consecrated in 1987 by Abp. Dennis Garrison, then THEOCACNA's primate-metropolitan. The new church followed Orthodox faith and practice, the issues involved in its establishment being administrative.

American Orthodox Catholic Church (Healy)

One of several jurisdictions of the same name formed by clergy belonging to Abp. Walter A. Propheta's American Orthodox Catholic Church, this jurisdiction was formed by Bp. Lawrence Pierre, formerly the auxiliary bishop for New York and the Eastern States. It continued the beliefs and practices as well as the name of Propheta's church, being bi-ritualistic (i.e., it allowed both Eastern and Western liturgies to be used in its parishes' worship services). Archbishop Pierre was succeeded as primate by Abp. Patrick J. Healy. Upon the death of Healy in 1984, the jurisdiction dissolved.

American Orthodox Catholic Church (Irene)

The American Orthodox Catholic Church (Irene) was founded in 1962 and incorporated three years later. Its presiding head was a female bishop known only as Archbishop Irene, whose consecrators are unknown. The spokesperson for the church was Bp. Emeritus Milton A. Pritts, who had been consecrated by Abp. Walter A. Propheta (1912–1972) of the American Orthodox Catholic Church.

The church was Orthodox in faith and practice, accepting as it did the forms presented in the *Service Book* edited by Isabel Florence Hapgood, and the principles enunciated in such standard orthodox volumes as Fr. John Meyendorff's *The Orthodox Church*. The Revised Standard Version of the Bible was used. It differed from mainstream orthodoxy in two ways, however: (1) It was willing to consider otherwise qualified women and homosexuals for the priesthood; and (2) it believed that apostolic succession was not necessary to the establishment of a valid church or ministry. A resolution passed by the grand synod of the church on January 6, 1979, stated, "We now hold with the Churches of England, Sweden, Congregational, Presbyterian, Lutheran, Methodist, Christian Scientists, and others who are determined to revive lay selection and authority of the congregation to avoid the further creation of hierarchies."

Although renouncing the necessity of apostolic succession and the idea of building further hierarchies, the church claimed to have a ministry with valid apostolic episcopal orders and claimed to have built an elaborate hierarchy. The jurisdiction was reportedly divided into 53 dioceses and spread over all of North America. Apart from Bishop Pritts, however, the names of church officers and bishops and the addresses of their diocesan headquarters were not made available for publication. Because of the unverifiable nature of the church's claims, there is some doubt as to what size the church attained, in part because no parishes associated with Bishop Pritts or Archbishop Irene were independently identified.

American Orthodox Church (Maryland)

The American Orthodox Church was founded in 1992 by four former bishops of the Holy Eastern Orthodox Catholic and Apostolic Church in North America. Two of the bishops, Dennis Garrison and Paul Vincent Dolan, had, at one time, been primate-metropolitan of THEOCACNA. The new denomination was Orthodox in faith and practice, and continued the vision of an American Orthodoxy first enunciated by Abp. Aftimios Ofiesh (1889–1966).

The church had four dioceses: Baltimore (Maryland), headed by Archbishop Garrison; Philadelphia (Pennsylvania), headed by Archbishop Dolan; Hickory (North Carolina), headed by Bp. D. Michael Martinat; and the Diocese of the Ozarks, headed by Bp. Victor Prentice.

American Orthodox Church (Philippines)

The American Orthodox Church was established in 1981 by Harold Donovan as the Orthodox American Catholic Church, Diocese of the Ozarks, under a charter from the Orthodox Church of the Philippines. Donovan was originally consecrated by Bps. Howard Fris and John Kenelly of the Old Roman Catholic Church, Archdiocese of Chicago. However, in 1982 Donovan was reconsecrated by Abp. John A. Christian of the American Orthodox Catholic Church (Propheta) in order to establish formal continuity with the original American Orthodox Church established by Abp. Aftimios Ofiesh in the 1920s. Donovan took the religious name of the late archbishop and became known as Abp. Aftimios Donovan. In January 1983 Archbishop Christian, in cooperation with the Orthodox Church in the Philippines, established an exarchate known as the North American Synod of the Holy Eastern Orthodox Catholic and Apostolic Church (shortened to its later name the following year).

The church followed Eastern Orthodox belief and practice. The liturgy of St. Germain was used and sacraments were administered according to the American Rite of St. Germain, an abbreviated and modified formula based on the Byzantine Rite.

The exarchate retained formal ties to both the Orthodox Church in the Philippines and the American Orthodox Catholic Church headed by Archbishop Christian. Its parish work included two missions in Los Angeles: one to Asian-Americans and one to Hispanic-Americans. The church ran a seminary in Manila, named the Seminary of the Orthodox Catholic Church in the Philippines, and published a periodical, *The Orthodox Catholic*.

Sources:

The Liturgy. Springfield, MO: American Orthodox Church, 1983.

American Orthodox Exarchate: Archdiocese of North America

The American Orthodox Exarchate: Archdiocese of North America was founded in 1989 by the Most Rev. Donald L. Locke (b. 1930), who became its metropolitan archbishop. Archbishop Locke was ordained to the priesthood by James F. Mondok, who had left the Western Orthodox Church in America the previous year and founded Christ Catholic Orthodox Church. Locke was consecrated as a bishop in Christ Catholic Orthodox Church in February 1988. In December 1988 he was elevated to archiepiscopal status by the Most Rev. Andre Barbeau (1912–1994) of the Catholic Charismatic Church of Canada.

The exarchate existed as an autocephalous and autonomous jurisdiction under a mandate from the Moscow patriarchate of the Russian Orthodox Church. Locke was open to relationships with sister Orthodox churches and invited bishops from the Ukrainian Eastern Orthodox Church (Most Rev. Ignatius Cash), Apostolic Orthodox Church of Canada (Most Rev. Renee Bergeron), and the Catholic Charismatic Church of Canada (Most Rev. Walter G. Allard).

The exarchate included parishes with both Eastern and Western orientations, and congregations were allowed to use either the Orthodox liturgy of St. John Chrysostom (in English) or the modified Roman Catholic liturgy. Priests were permitted to use both Eastern- and Western-style liturgical garments as the occasion demanded. The church ran an educational facility in Maine, the St. Clement's School for Theological Studies.

Sources:

Ward, Gary L. *Independent Bishops: An International Directory*. Detroit, MI: Apogee Books, 1990. 524 pp.

American Synod: Holy Orthodox Catholic Church

The American Synod: Holy Orthodox Catholic Church was established in 1969 in Denver, Colorado, by bishops of the earlier existing American Orthodox Catholic Church. The metropolitan from the time of the church's inception was the Most Rev. Colin James Guthrie. The church underwent a reorganization in 1984 and, for a brief while, took the name Holy Synod of Denver (1984–1986).

The church had congregations and ministries in a number of western and midwestern states. During the 1970s, it counted among its members Abp. Bartholomew Cunningham, who was noted for his efforts to extend Orthodoxy among Americans at large and for his positive and friendly contacts with ethnic Orthodox hierarchs.

The American Synod was organized into two dioceses, the Archdiocese of Denver and the Diocese of Berkeley. The latter followed the Old Calendar observance. The church traced it episcopal orders to the independent Old Calendar Greek archbishop Christopher Contogeorge and to the Albanian archbishop Theophan Noli, who in the 1940s established Orthodoxy in New England among people not traditionally or ethnically Orthodox. In 1992 the Synod had parishes in California, New Mexico, and Washington, D.C.

Sources:

Guthrie, Colin J. *A Brief History of the American Synod, Holy Orthodox Catholic Church*. Denver, CO: Office of the Metropolitan Archbishop, 1991.

Autocephalous Greek Orthodox Church of the Americas and Europe

The Autocephalous Greek Orthodox Church of the Americas and Europe was founded in 1934, according to the church seal. Its bishop was Joachim Souris, who was consecrated in 1951 by Abp. Joseph Klimovich (1880–1961) of the Orthodox Catholic Patriarchate of America, with the assistance of several others. At that time, Souris also joined Klimovich as a member of the Holy Synod of the Orthodox Catholic Patriarchate of America. In 1967 he associated with the rival Holy Synod of the Orthodox Catholic Churches of the Americas and Europe founded by Peter A. Zhurawetsky (1901–1994).

By the mid-1970s, the church had a single diocese, the Diocese of Brooklyn and New Jersey, which consisted of one small parish/mission, the Church of St. Fanourios and Sts. Anargyroi, located in Newark, New Jersey.

Autocephalous Slavonic Orthodox Catholic Church (in Exile)

The Autocephalous Slavonic Orthodox Catholic Church (in Exile) dated its existence to the coming of Saint Cyril and Saint Methodius to Moravia in the ninth century. Worship was established according to that of the Greek Orthodox Church, and in 1620 a jurisdiction of the Podcarpathian Church was founded. It was always a small jurisdiction in a predominantly Roman Catholic land. Following World War I, when Czechoslovakia declared its independence, Orthodox believers asked for their own independent church. This church was organized in 1921 under the Serbian Orthodox patriarch, and a bishop, Gorazd Pavlik, was consecrated. However, in early 1923, the ecumenical patriarch consecrated a rival archbishop named Sabbazd. Both churches existed side by side until the Nazi occupation and World War II, during which they both disappeared. In 1946 the church reappeared under the patriarch of the Russian Orthodox Church in Moscow, who appointed an exarch to head the small group.

Some perceived the action of the Russian patriarch to be a takeover of the Czechoslovakian church, and in 1946 a group of priests and laity formed an underground church movement. In 1968 one of the leaders of this movement, Bishop Filotej, fled the country and settled in America, where he founded the Slavonic Orthodox Church. In 1968 he consecrated Bp. William Andrew Prazsky as his coadjutor archbishop, and after Archbishop Filotej's death in 1970, Archbishop Andrew became the head of the church.

Archbishop Andrew soon established communion with the Ukrainian Autocephalous Orthodox Church in the United States of America and in 1969 accepted provisional reconsecration from Abp. Hryhorij Osijchuk (1898–1985) and Archbishop Hennadij. In 1980, the episcopal leadership of the two churches united their efforts into a single *sobor*, or synod, which had oversight of both churches. Archbishop Andrew stepped aside at that time in favor of Archbishop Hryhorij. In 1985, following the death of Archbishop Hryhorij, Archbishop Andrew was elected metropolitan archbishop of the united sobor.

Metropolitan Andrew Prazky passed away on December 16,1990. The bishop of New York, Alexis Nizza, was elected and enthroned as archbishop metropolitan primate on May 19, 1991. Leadership was shared with His Grace Efthimious Kontargiris, who was elected as archbishop coadjutor the same day. The sobor of bishops withdrew from the Ukrainian Autocephalous Orthodox Church, though the Slavonic Orthodox Church, now a completely independent body, remained in communion with it. A dialogue with the ecumenical patriarch began in hopes of attaining the eventual union of the Slavonic Orthodox Church with the mother see in Constantinople.

The Slavonic Church was Orthodox in faith and practice. The church's strength was in the Bronx, where it ministered to Slavic Americans of various national backgrounds, many first-generation immigrants.

Sources:

Clarke, Boden. *Lords Temporal and Lords Spiritual*. San Bernardino, CA: Borgo Press, 1986.

Byzantine Universal (Catholic) and Orthodox Church of the Americas

The Byzantine Universal (Catholic) and Orthodox Church of the Americas was founded in 1942 by Antoine Joseph Aneed (1881–1970), a Lebanese-American. Though never a large jurisdiction, the Byzantine American Church played an important role among independent Catholic and Orthodox churches because of Aneed's having possessed Roman Catholic episcopal orders. As a young man, Aneed was ordained as a priest in the Roman Catholic Church (in 1909) and served for a short time as secretary of the archbishop of the Melkite-Greek Catholic Patriarchate of Antioch and All the East, one of the uniate Eastern-rite churches within Roman Catholicism. He then moved to the United States and was there in 1911 when Melece Sawoya defied Pope Pius X and came to the United States on a pastoral visit to some of the Melkite parishes.

Aneed was consecrated by Sawoya on October 9, 1911, to serve as his assistant bishop. However, the Vatican did not recognize that consecration. The consecration was recognized by Sawoya's successor and by Abp. S. G. Messmer (1847–1930) of Milwaukee, who allowed Aneed to use the title *exarch*. During the 1920s, while working within the Syrian community in San Francisco, Aneed began to associate with some of the independent Catholic and Orthodox bishops on the West Coast, especially E. R. Verostek of the North American Old Roman Catholic Church—Utrecht Succession and Lowell Paul Wadle of the American Catholic Church. In 1929 he moved to New London, Connecticut, to serve St. Ann's Church. He remained as St. Ann's until 1937, but left the Roman Catholic Church at some point and in 1942 formed a separate jurisdiction.

The situation became muddled in 1944 when Aneed, in spite of carrying Roman Catholic orders, was consecrated *sub conditione* by Wadle and Verostek. He engaged in a second important service in 1945 when he exchanged consecrations with Wadle, Henry Joseph Kleefisch, Charles Hampton, and Wallace David de Ortega Maxey. Kleefisch, an independent Orthodox bishop, then became a bishop in Aneed's church. In 1946 Aneed was named patriarch of his church. In 1949 Aneed consecrated Nicolas Urbanovitch and assigned him as bishop of Canada.

The Byzantine Universal Church survived until Aneed's death in 1970 but dissolved soon afterward. Aneed's influence remains in those bishops who claim to derive their apostolic authority from him.

Sources:

Aneed, Antoine Joseph. *A Brief History of he Catholic Church of St. George in Milwaukee, Wis., and a Sketch of the Eastern Church*. Milwaukee, WI: Author, 1919.

Ward, Gary L. *Independent Bishops: An International Directory*. Detroit, MI: Apogee Books, 1990. 524 pp.

Eastern Orthodox Catholic Church in America

Among the several bodies claiming to carry on the mission of Abp. Aftimios Ofiesh (1889–1966), the Eastern Orthodox Catholic Church in America can make one of the strongest cases for being the real antecedent body of Aftimios's independent jurisdiction. The first bishop consecrated by Aftimios was Bp. Sophronius Bishira (1888–1934) in 1931. Aftimios's retirement and Bishop Joseph Zuk's unexpected death just months after his consecration by Ofiesh left Sophronius in charge. He turned to Metropolitan Benjamin Fedchenkov of the Moscow Exarch (later the Patriarchal Parishes of the Russian Orthodox Church in the United States and Canada), one of several warring Russian Orthodox factions, and with his blessing, consecrated John More-Moreno (d. 1958) in 1933. Sophronius soon left the United States, and More-Moreno took up the task of creating an American Orthodox church, in 1951, by forming the Eastern Orthodox Catholic Church in America.

The church followed the practice of Orthodoxy in both liturgy and theology. For many years it published the influential monthly periodical the *American Review of Eastern Orthodoxy* (suspended in 1980).

Though the church is now defunct, in 1974 it reported four churches, 13 clergy, and 315 members.

Greek Orthodox Church of America

The Greek Orthodox Church of America was formed on December 1, 1971, at a meeting held in Miami, Florida, for the purpose of forming a federation of independent Greek Orthodox Churches. Many of these churches had grown out of local schisms and were headed by priests who had left the jurisdiction of Archbishop Iakovos (1911–2005). Members objected to what they saw as a movement "to Catholicize and Protestantize the church." They hoped to preserve Greek faith, language, and traditions. They believed in local control of property, not archdiocesan ownership. By 1974 the church was without episcopal supervision but was seeking it from various sources.

During its active period, Fr. Theodore Kyritsis was a moving force in the Greek Orthodox Church of America. He was defrocked by Archbishop Iakovos and went under the jurisdiction of Bishop Petros of the Hellenic Orthodox Church in America. Bishop Photios of the Greek Orthodox Diocese of New York was installed as archbishop in Memphis in St. George's Greek Orthodox Church which Kyritsis pastored, and became a vocal opponent of Archbishop Iakovos.

In the mid-1970s the church had 10 parishes scattered around the United States in states such as Miami, Rhode Island, Pennsylvania, Michigan, and Tennessee. It now appears to be defunct.

Greek Orthodox Missions to the Americas

The Greek Orthodox Missions to the Americas was founded in 1963 as a loose confederation of independent Greek parishes. In 1976 Fr. Garasimos Vlosoplos was consecrated as the metropolitan for the church, and the following year it was incorporated. Metropolitan Garasimos headed the small jurisdiction from the church in Astoria, New York. At the time the church was active, both Greek- and English-language liturgies were used.

Sources:

Clarke, Boden. *Lords Temporal and Lords Spiritual*. San Bernardino, CA: Borgo Press, 1985.

Holy African Church

The Holy African Church emerged around 1937 under the leadership of Bp. Arthur Stanley Trotman, formerly a bishop of the African Orthodox Church. Following the death of Abp. George A. McGuire (b. 1866) in 1934, leadership of the church passed to Abp. William E. J. Robertson, then head of the church's work in Miami, Florida. The primary membership of the church was in New York and the northeast, and Trotman joined Bps. Reginald Grant Barrow, Robert Arthur Valentine, and Vicar General Frederick A. Toote in the founding of a new church, the African Orthodox Church of New York and Massachusetts, to continue the church apart from the Miami jurisdiction. The new church soon had its own problems as Barrow and Trotman disagreed and Trotman left to found the rival African Orthodox Church, Inc. In the meantime, Robertson filed suit against both churches, claiming that they should not be able to take the name of the African Orthodox Church and confuse people by establishing a rival organization. The court agreed and in 1938 ruled against both Barrow and Trotman. Trotman moved quickly to reorganize his jurisdiction as the Holy African Church. A short time later Barrow and Trotman reconciled, and Barrow merged his work into the Holy African Church.

Trotman was succeeded as head of the church successively by Robert Arthur Valentine (1945), Frederick A. Toote (1954), and Gladstone St. Clair Nurse (1959). Once all the people involved in the schisms of the 1930s were dead, Nurse was able to work out an agreement with the African Orthodox Church by which in 1964 the Holy African Church merged into its parent body.

Sources:

Terry-Thompson, A. C. *The History of the African Orthodox Church*. N.p.: the author, 1956.

Holy Apostolic Orthodox Catholic Church

The Holy Apostolic Orthodox Catholic Church was founded in the mid-1960s with headquarters in Fort Lauderdale, Florida. During the 1970s it claimed to have a seminary and an elaborate hierarchy, including two archbishops and one bishop in the United States, and additional archbishops in West Germany, the Canal Zone, Hong Kong, and Switzerland. Since the 1980s, no manifestation of the church or its founder Abp. Mark Cardinal Evans has been seen. During the time it was active, the church professed the Orthodox faith as based in the Nicene Creed without the *filoque* clause (a heavily disputed clause added to the Nicene Creed in 589) and used the Liturgy of St. John Chrysostom without alteration.

Sources:

Ecclesiatical Proclamation, Divine Liturgy. Home Missions Department of the Holy Apostolic Orthodox Catholic Church, 1965.

Holy Orthodox Church, Diocese of New Mexico (Cunningham)

The Holy Orthodox Church, Diocese of New Mexico was formed by Abp. Bartholomew Cunningham, a former priest of the Roman Catholic Church and seminary professor. Cunningham was consecrated by Bps. Colin James Guthrie and Robert S. Zeiger of the American Orthodox Catholic Church on June 23, 1968, and served under Guthrie until the Holy Orthodox Church, Diocese of New Mexico, was established in 1970. The church was Orthodox in faith and practice. It was open to the ordination into the priesthood of otherwise qualified homosexuals but rejected females for holy orders.

In the early 1980s, the church reported 15 parishes and a few hundred members, primarily in New Mexico and Illinois. Archbishop Bartholemew died in 1984, and the Diocese now appears to be defunct.

Hungarian Greek Catholic Church

The Hungarian Greek Catholic Church was a short-lived Orthodox jurisdiction that grew out of attempts to extend the influence of Eastern Orthodoxy into Hungary. During the chaos of World War I, the patriarch of the Serbian Orthodox Church announced the extension of his jurisdiction into Hungary, a predominantly Roman Catholic country. The action gave an idea to Istvan Theodosius de Nemeth, a Roman Catholic priest, who decided that an independent Hungarian Orthodox church would have a following. However, it would be 20 years before the idea came to fruition.

In 1933 de Nemeth founded the Greek Oriental Hungarian Orthodox Church. He was consecrated as bishop of that church the following year by Moran Mor Ignatius Ephrem I, Patriarch of the Syrian Patriarchate of Antioch and All the East. The small jurisdiction continued through the years. In 1968 de

Nemeth consecrated a man named de Nagy as his successor.

The Hungarian Greek Catholic Church was brought to America at some point after World War II by Stefan Boros, a priest who migrated to America from Hungary. For a period he functioned as a priest in the American Catholic Church, but by the early 1960s had established the Hungarian Greek Catholic Church in New York.

Sources:

Ward, Gary L. *Independent Bishops: An International Directory.* Detroit, MI: Apogee Books, 1990.

Mercian Orthodox Catholic Church

The Mercian Orthodox Catholic Church (formerly known as Mercian Right Catholic Church) viewed itself as the continuing church body originally established in the United States by Apb. Joseph Rene Vilatte (1854–1929). Archbishop Vilatte was consecrated in Ceylon (now Sri Lanka) in 1892 by Mar Julius I of the Malankara Syrian Orthodox Church. He returned to the United States to establish the American Catholic Church. Vilatte was succeeded by Frederick E. J. Lloyd (1859–1933), and Lloyd by Daniel C. Hinton. When Hinton died, an era of confusion began in the small, but widely scattered, American Catholic Church. There were several claimants to the leadership, though the corporation eventually fell into the hands of Lowell Paul Wadle, a theosophically oriented bishop who took the American Catholic Church into the orb of the Liberal Catholic Church.

For a time, the Mercian Orthodox Catholic Church continued the Eastern or Catholic Orthodox thrust initiated by Vilatte. In this respect, they regarded Abp. Joseph G. Sokolowski as the rightful inheritor of Vilatte's leadership. Sokolowski was consecrated in 1970 by Abp. Joseph John Skureth. He served as a bishop for several years under Francis Xavier Resch in the Archdiocese of the Old Catholic Church in America. However, he broke with Resch's successor, Walter X. Brown, in 1975. Sokolowski founded an independent jurisdiction, St. Paul's Monastery Old Catholic Church. In the late 1970s the jurisdiction began to use the name Orthodox Catholic and gradually added the name Mercian. In 1987 Sokolowski consecrated Stephen Robert Thomas, announced his retirement (at 84 years old), and named Thomas as his successor.

The Mercian Orthodox Catholic Church was a Western Rite Orthodox Church. It adopted the Liturgy of St. Germain for use throughout the church under the leadership of Sokolowski. Through the 1970s and 1980s revisions of the liturgy were undertaken, resulting in a new Mercian Liturgy that was approved in 1987 for the church's worship. The term *Mercian* was adopted by the church in the late 1970s and identified the jurisdiction with Christ the Merciful while keeping it free from any association with a particular ethnic or national group.

The church was Orthodox in faith and practice. There were seven sacraments, and in Orthodox fashion (as opposed to Roman Catholic practice) the church separated the service of Holy Unction (for the ill) from the service of Last Rites (for the dying). When it was active, the church also issued the periodical *Mercian Messenger.*

The Mercian Church experienced significant growth through the 1980s and spread into Canada, Malaysia, Mexico, West Africa, Belgium, and Japan. Two dioceses were initially established in the United States: the Primatial Diocese (Colorado Springs, Colorado) and the Diocese of St. Michael (La Porte, Indiana). Later the Missionary Diocese of St. Gregorios was designated in California and the Diocese of St. Peter the Apostle in Minnesota. Besides St. Paul's Monastery in Indiana, the church established several schools, including Notre Dame de Lafayette University in Aurora, Colorado. Then in 1994, the upward progress of the church was halted when the State of Colorado's Commission on Higher Education moved against the university and its administration. It was charged with engaging in deceptive business practices in that it was offering degrees in nonreligious subjects beyond the authorizations of its charter and implying to its students, primarily correspondents, that it was an accredited institution.

The action of the state led to a process of adjudication against the church and Abp. Stephen Thomas.

Sources:

Thomas, Stephen R. *The Mercian Rite Church: A Catholic Alternative.* Colorado Springs, CO: SCM Publications, 1988. Brochure.

———. *The Mercian Rite of the One, Holy, Catholic, and Apostolic Church.* Colorado Springs, CO: SCM Publications [1988].

Old Orthodox Catholic Patriarchate of America

Not all of the independent Polish Catholic Churches founded in the late nineteenth and early twentieth centuries joined with the Polish National Catholic Church. Some of these parishes had associated with independent Old Catholic bodies which had grown out of the work of Abp. Joseph Rene Vilatte (1854–1929) and his American Catholic Church, especially the Old Catholic Church in America headed by Abp. W. H. Francis Brothers (1887–1979) and the Polish Catholic Church of Bp. Stephen Kaminski (d. 1911). In 1937 some of these churches joined with several parishes of Slavic (Lithuanian) background and came together to form the Polish Old Catholic Church. They incorporated in New Jersey and elected Bp. Joseph Zielonka as their leader. Zielonka had been consecrated some years previously by Paolo Miraglia-Gulotti and had served as a bishop under Brothers.

Under Zielonka's capable leadership the church grew and by the time of his death in 1961 consisted of 22 parishes. Most were located in New Jersey with others in Pennsylvania and Massachusetts. The growth phase under Zielonka, however, was completely reversed under his successor, Peter A. Zhurawetsky (1901–1994). Zhurawetsky, Zielonka's suffragan, had been consecrated in Springfield, Massachusetts, in 1950. Participating in the consecration service were Patr. Joseph Klimowicz of the Orthodox Catholic Patriarchate of America; Abp. Konstatin Jaroshevich (a Byelorussian prelate who had been consecrated by Abp. Fan Stilian Noli [1882–1965] of the Albanian Orthodox Church); Archbishop Zielonka; Metropolitan Nicholas Bohatyretz of the Ukrainian Orthodox Church; and Old Catholic Bp. Peter M. Williamowicz.

Among his first acts, Zhurawetsky changed the name of the Church to Christ Catholic Church of the Americas and Europe, an expression of a desire to move beyond ethnic and language barriers in his jurisdiction so that all nationalities might feel welcome. The future looked promising, but problems began to plague the newly named church almost immediately. First some churches and clergy did not accept Archbishop Peter's leadership. They also did not like the name change. Second, Fr. Felix Starazewski asserted a claim to be the legitimate successor of the late Bishop Zielonka, and he and his church in South River, New Jersey, refused to honor the jurisdiction of Archbishop Peter. His defection led the way, and other congregations departed for either the Polish National Catholic Church or one of the other independent Catholic or Orthodox bodies.

Third, and most importantly, Zhurawetsky shifted his attention away from building his jurisdiction through expanding parishes and membership to growth by uniting with other independent Old Catholic and Eastern Orthodox bodies. He thus brought into his jurisdiction the divisiveness that had led to the splintering of these independent groups in the first place, and he exacerbated the situation by assuming the title of Patriarch in America. Gradually all of his time and energy were poured into the actualization of a dominating vision, an American Patriarchate. At the same time, his churches, consisting largely of Eastern European ethnic parishes, were being further reduced by the inevitable processes of Americanization.

By 1965, the church having been reduced to a handful of communicants and clergy, a new possibility emerged. Rev. Karl Pruter, who had come from the Free Catholic Movement in the Congregational Church, was ordained by Archbishop Peter and organized a nonethnic congregation in Boston, out of which a second congregation emerged. The Church of St. Paul was organized in Hobbs, New Mexico, by Fr. Daniel Smith. Zhurawetsky moved to enlarge the patriarchate. Assisted by Abp. Uladyslau Ryzy-Ryski (1925–1978), he consecrated Pruter, who consented to the consecration only on the condition that they be set aside as an independent jurisdiction to be called Christ Catholic Church, Diocese of Boston, now known simply as Christ Catholic Church. Then Smith was consecrated, but after a short while in Hobbs, he moved to Denver and withdrew from Archbishop Peter's jurisdiction altogether. Another briefly successful venture was the establishment of the Monastery of Our Lady of Reconciliation at Glorieta, New Mexico, in 1969. Fr. Christopher William Jones was a successful author and minister to many of the disenchanted youth of the late 1960s and early 1970s. However, shortly after Archbishop Peter consecrated him, he too left to form an independent, self-governing jurisdiction.

During its active period, the church issued a periodical called *Our Missionary*. By the mid-1980s Archbishop Peter had no congregations in his jurisdiction but continued his efforts to build the patriarchate. He maintained a chapel at Vineland, New Jersey, and a home in Chicago.

Turkish Orthodox Church

The Turkish Orthodox Church was established in 1926 when the excommunicated priest Pavlos Karahisarithis claimed to have had his sentence of excommunication lifted by two members of the Holy Synod of the Greek Orthodox Church and that Bishops Cyril of Erdek and Agathangelos of Prinkipo consecrated him. Karahisarithis, who later changed his name to Zeki Erenerol, became popularly known as "Papa Eftim." The new church grew out of a controversy begun by Papa Eftim's demand for a Turkish Church independent of the Greek Orthodox ecumenical patriarch in Constantinople. In 1933 Papa Eftim introduced a Turkish-language version of the Divine Liturgy. In 1962 his son Turgut Erenerol assumed the title Eftim II and succeeded his ailing father as head of the church. Papa Eftim died in 1968. Papa Eftim's other son, Selcuk Erenerol, in turn succeeded his brother as Eftim III, and Selcuk's son, Pasa Umit, succeeded him as Eftim IV. The relations of the Turkish movement and the ecumenical patriarch remained shaky and very much tied to Turkish-Greek relations.

On December 6, 1966, the Turkish Orthodox Church came to the United States with the appointment of the Most Rev. Civet Kristof (a.k.a. Christopher M. Cragg) as metropolitan archbishop of New York and patriarchal exarch and primate of the Turkish Orthodox Church in America. Cragg, a well-educated black American of Ethiopian ancestry, had been consecrated by Abp. Christopher Maria Stanley in 1965 and named auxiliary bishop of New York for the American Orthodox Catholic Church headed by Abp. Walter Propheta. He edited the jurisdiction's periodical, the *Orthodox Catholic Herald*, which became the first periodical for the Turkish Orthodox Church. Kristof issued the first copies of *Orthodoks Mustakil*, the new periodical for the Turkish Orthodox Church, in 1969. At this time, the Turkish Orthodox Church reported 14 churches and six mission parishes.

In 2008 the daughter of Papa Eftim III and sister of primate Papa Eftim IV, was arrested for alleged links to a Turkish underground group with nationalist tendencies. While the Turkish Orthodox Church continues to exist in Turkey, its existence in the United States is doubtful. It has not been manifest for several decades and is presumed defunct.

Sources:

Kristof, Most Reverend Metropolitan. *A Brief History of the Turkish Orthodox Church in America (Patriarchal Exarchate)*. New York: Turkish Orthodox Church in America, Exarchal Office [1967].

Ukrainian Autocephalic Church of North and South America

The Ukrainian Autocephalic Church of North and South America was founded by Abp. Wasyl Sawyna. Sawyna had reportedly been consecrated in 1959 by independent Ukrainian Bp. Evhen Batchynskiy, then a resident of Switzerland. Sawyna came to public attention when in 1964 he participated in the consecration of James Parker Dees (1915–1990), founder and primate of the Anglican Orthodox Church. Subsequently, efforts to obtain information about Sawyna and his jurisdiction, then headquartered in Allentown, Pennsylvania, proved fruitless. While his consecration probably occurred as reported, it also seems likely that his jurisdiction was a paper organization which had no active parishes and is now totally defunct.

Sources:

Piepkorn, Arthur C. *Profiles in Belief*. New York: Harper & Row, 1977.

NON-CHALCEDONIAN ORTHODOXY

Afro-American Orthodox Church

The Afro-American Orthodox Church was a small liturgical church founded in the late 1930s by Bp. George A. Brooks, who had been consecrated by Reginald Grant Barrow of the African Orthodox Church of New York and Massachusetts. It was similar in faith and practice with the African Orthodox Church. In the 1930s, the church was superseded by the Holy African Church, which in the 1960s merged into the African Orthodox Church.

Sources:

Trela, Jonathan. *A History of the North American Old Roman Catholic Church*. Scranton, PA: Author, 1979.

Coptic Orthodox Church Apostolic

The Coptic Orthodox Church Apostolic was chartered in New York City in 1942 by John Hickerson (also spelled Hickersayon). Hickerson, an African American, had one of the more interesting careers in American religion. Little is known of his origin. He first emerged as a preacher in a Pentecostal church in Boston, Massachusetts, shortly after the turn of the century. Around 1908 he associated himself with Samuel

Morris, the leader of a small African-American movement in Baltimore, Maryland. Morris had proclaimed himself God and taken the name Father Jehovia. He was assisted by a man named George Baker, known as the Messenger, later to reappear as Father Divine.

Around 1911, the team split up. Hickerson had challenged Morris's leadership by arguing that the Spirit of God resided in everyone. Hence all could claim some godhood. Hickerson went to New York and founded a congregation called the Church of the Living God, located on 41st Street. He offered what appeared to be a mixture of Pentecostalism and New Thought. He believed that God lived in everyone and hence none could die. However, the church seems to have disintegrated. Hickerson was also an early advocate of Ethiopianism, the idea that Africans were the true Jews and that Jesus was an African. He is credited with preparing the way for the emergence of Ethiopianism among blacks in the 1920s in New York City.

In any case, Hickerson was consecrated in 1938 by Bp. Edwin Macmillan Jack, known as Bishop Yakob, head of the Episcopal Orthodox Church (Greek Communion), a small, independent Eastern orthodox jurisdiction with orders from the African Orthodox Church. He had founded his church in 1921 in Cuba and been consecrated a bishop two years later. Bishop Yakob moved to New York in 1938.

Hickerson incorporated the Coptic Orthodox Church Apostolic in 1942. He seems to have corresponded with His Holiness Abuna Basilios, the head of the Ethiopian Coptic Orthodox Church, but was never received into communion.

Among Hickerson's actions as head of the Coptic Orthodox Church Apostolic was the consecration of Mar Lukos (Denison Quartey Arthur) in 1947. Mar Lukos operated primarily in the Caribbean area but was responsible for passing along Hickerson's apostolic order to several independent Old Catholic bishops, including Primate Hugh George de Willmott Newman (Mar Georgius), who subsequently passed them to a number of others.

Sources:

Anson, Peter. *Bishops at Large*. London: Faber and Faber, 1964.

Harris, Sara. *Father Divine*. New York: Collier, 1971.

Newman, Richard. *Black Bishops: Some African-American Old Catholics and Their Churches*. New York: The Author, 1992.

Holy Apostolic Catholic Church, Syro-Chaldean Diocese of Santa Barbara and Central California

The Holy Apostolic Catholic Church, Syro-Chaldean Diocese of Santa Barbara and Central California was founded by Michael Djorde Milan d'Obrenovic (1926–1986). In 1971, d'Obrenovic became the head of a small group in Cornville, Arizona, consisting of former Roman Catholics, Old Catholics, and Serbian Orthodox. Having been chosen the group's pastor, he sought ordination from Christ Catholic Church. The attempt was unsuccessful, and he was later ordained by Abp. Gerret Munnik of the Liberal Catholic Church, Province of the United States. After a few years he left the Liberal Catholics and was consecrated by Bps. John Marion Stanley (b. 1923), of the Orthodox Church of the East, and Elijah Coady, of the Christian Orthodox Church (now the Catholic Apostolic Church at Davis) in 1977. The Holy Apostolic Catholic Church follows the practice and belief of the Church of the East, without the charismatic-pentecostal emphasis introduced by Stanley and accepted by Coady.

Quite apart from his ecclesiastical career, d'Obrenovic developed a second identity under his birth name, George Hunt Williamson. D'Obrenovic claimed to be a descendent of the Yugoslavian royal family of d'Obrenovic (the last member of which was supposed to have been assassinated in 1903) and he used the name Williamson because it was easier for Americans to pronounce. As George Hunt Williamson, he became one of the first people in the early 1950s to claim direct contact with the entities inhabiting flying saucers. He was present when George Adamski made his initial contact with the Venusian in the California Desert, and eventually as Brother Philip, founded the Brotherhood of the Seven Rays.

The church had only one parish located in Santa Barbara, California. No evidence of that parish has been found since d'Obrenovic's death in 1986.

Sources:

Philip, Brother [George Hunt Williamson]. *The Brotherhood of the Seven Rays*. Clarksburg, WV: Saucerian Books, 1961.

Williamson, George Hunt. *Other Tongues—Other Flesh*. Amherst, WI: Amherst Press, 1953.

―――. *Road in the Sky*. London: Neville Spearman, 1959.

―――. *The Saucers Speak*. London: Neville Spearman, 1963.

―――. *Secret Places of the Lion*. London: Neville Spearman, 1959.

Holy Orthodox Catholic Church, Eastern and Apostolic

The Holy Orthodox Catholic Church, Eastern and Apostolic (HOCC) was established in the 1970s by Mar Apriam (Richard B. Morrill; d. 1994), formerly a bishop of the American Orthodox Catholic Church. He was enthroned as Metropolitan by Patriarch Christian I (John A. Christian or Chiasson) and also named Deputy Patriarch of the American Orthodox Catholic Church (AOCC).

In July 1974, Mar Apriam resigned as Deputy Patriarch of the AOCC and on December 23, 1974. He moved to Nigeria, where the AOCC had some work,

and assumed leadership of the Nigerian AOCC. In 1976 (following some internal turmoil in the AOCC), following consultation with the AOCC's new Patriarch Lawrence Pierre, Mar Apriam renounced any claim to a position in the AOCC and founded the Holy Orthodox Catholic Church, Eastern and Apostolic.

In 1977 Mar Apriam merged the HOCC with the North American Orthodox Catholic Church under the direction of Mar Markus I (Mark I. Miller). He assumed the ecclesiastical name Patriarch James VI as head of the merged church. The merger lasted only two years as disagreements arose over the charismatic nature of Mar Apriam's ministry. He was deposed and excommunicated, but left to reestablish the HOCC. In 1984 Mar Apriam and Mar Markus I again reunited their work as the Byzantine Catholic Church. In June of that year he reconsecrated Mar Markus I *sub conditione*.

After only a few months, Mar Apriam and Mar Markus I again went their separate ways. On Christmas Day 1984, Patriarch Christian I died. In the wake of his passing, Mar Apriam reasserted his role as Apostolic Administrator of the AOCC and assumed the role of Metropolitan and Primate of the American Orthodox Catholic Church, Holy Synod of the Americas with headquarters in Sacramento, California. He died there in 1991 and the present status of his jurisdiction is unknown.

During the church's active period, it operated the Orthodox Academy of Education in Tarzana, California, and issued the periodical *Maranatha*.

Orthodox Catholic Synod of the Syro-Chaldean Rite

The Orthodox Catholic Synod of the Syro-Chaldean Rite was formed in 1970 by Bp. Bashif Ahmed and is one of several bodies to continue the tradition of Mar Jacobus (Ulric Vernon Herford), who brought the Syro-Chaldean Church to the West in 1902. Raised a Unitarian, Herford journeyed to the Orient on a quest to find a means of uniting East and West. In 1902 he was consecrated by Mar Basilius Soares, bishop of Trichur, and head of a small body of Indian Christians called the Mellusians. Mar Basilius had been ordained to the priesthood by Julius Alvarez (who had consecrated Joseph Rene Vilatte) and had been consecrated to the episcopacy by Mar Antonius Abd-Ishu of the Nestorian linage. Upon his return to England, Herford founded the Evangelical Catholic Communion.

The Orthodox Catholic Synod of the Syro-Chaldean Rite derived from a schism of the Evangelical Catholic Communion, an American church founded by Michael A. Itkin, who had led his organization to take a positive activist stance in support of homosexuals. Rejecting Itkin's leadership, Ahmed founded an independent jurisdiction within the same tradition.

Western Orthodox Church

The Western Orthodox Church was one of several small jurisdictions which grew out of the ministry of Most Rev. David Stanns (Mar David), an independent

bishop who founded the American Coptic Orthodox Church. That church was continued by Abp. Richard B. Morrill (Mar Apriam; d. 1994) of the Holy Orthodox Catholic Church, Eastern and Apostolic. Joseph Russell Morse established the Western Orthodox Church and its Diocese of the Pacific Coast in 1972. In 1973 he was consecrated bishop and elevated to archbishop in 1974.

The Western Orthodox Church was described as Western because it used the English language in its worship. It was Coptic in that Archbishop Morrill, who succeeded Archbishop Stanns, gave permission for the establishment of the church with an English-speaking Coptic liturgy. It was charismatic in that the gifts of the spirit were recognized and used in the worship of the church. During its active period, it was orthodox and acknowledged the Nicene Creed.

5. Lutheran

INTRAFAITH ORGANIZATIONS

American Lutheran Conference

The American Lutheran Conference was a short-lived ecumenical body founded in 1930 soon after the formation of the American Lutheran Church (1930-1960). The American Lutheran Church took the lead in inviting the Augustana Synod, the United Danish Evangelical Lutheran Church (later the United Evangelical Lutheran Church), the Norwegian Lutheran Church in America (later known as the Evangelical Lutheran Church), and the Lutheran Free Church into an associated relationship. Many saw the new structure as designed to facilitate eventual union.

The several member groups quickly moved toward establishing doctrinal consensus and pulpit fellowship, and by the 1950s all but the Augustana were engaged in serious merger negotiations. In the light of these negotiations, the purpose of the conference had been served, and it was disbanded in 1954. The merger in 1960 produced the American Lutheran Church (1960-1988), now a constituent part of the Evangelical Lutheran Church in America. During most of its active period, the conference published *Lutheran Outlook* (originally the *Journal of the American Lutheran Conference*).

Sources:

Dolvin, O. E. *The American Lutheran Conference*. Minneapolis, MN: Augsburg Press, 1935.

Stavig, L. M. "The Genius of the American Lutheran Conference." *AL Conference Report* (1944): 100-115.

Wiederaenders, Robert C., and Walter G. Tillmans. *The Synods of American Lutheranism*. St. Louis, MO: Lutheran Historical Conference, 1968.

Lutheran Council in the U.S.A.

The Lutheran Council in the U.S.A. was founded on January 1, 1967, at which time it superseded the

National Lutheran Council. The National Lutheran Council had been founded in 1918, growing out of the successful cooperative activity of the Lutheran Church in America (then split into a number of autonomous synods) during World War I. Over the next two decades, it provided a nexus for cooperative activities and fellowship and a context in which mergers could and did occur, the primary one being the formation of the American Lutheran Church (1930–1960) in 1930.

World War II led to heightened action in the area of relief efforts, work with refugees, and—after the war—the reestablishment of relations with European Lutheran churches through the formation of the Lutheran World Federation. The Lutheran Church–Missouri Synod, though not a member of the council, cooperated with its relief efforts. In the 1960s formal talks were opened with the Missouri Synod on the occasion of their joining with the National Lutheran Council. After some years of discussion, there was a decision to disband the National Lutheran Council in favor of a structure to which the Missouri Synod could relate: the Lutheran Council in the U.S.A.

Throughout the 1980s events conspired to cause the disbanding of the Lutheran Council in the U.S.A. Most importantly, the Association of Evangelical Lutheran Churches, which had split from the Missouri Synod in 1967, joined with the American Lutheran Church and the Lutheran Church in America to form the Evangelical Lutheran Church in America. That merger was consummated on January 1, 1988. It brought all of the major Lutheran bodies other than the Missouri Synod into a single ecclesiastical organization. In the meantime, the Missouri Synod had taken a more conservative stance, having lost most of its prominent liberal voices in the 1976 split. Thus there no longer seemed to be a need to continue the Lutheran Council, and it was disbanded.

Sources:

Bonderud, Omar, and Charles Lutz, eds. *America's Lutherans*. Columbus, OH: Wartburg Press, 1955.

Wiederaenders, Robert C., and Walter G. Tillmans. *The Synods of American Lutheranism*. St. Louis, MO: Lutheran Historical Conference, 1968.

Synodical Conference

The Synodical Conference was formed in 1872 by the more conservative synods of American Lutherans—Missouri, Ohio, Wisconsin, Minnesota, Illinois, and the Norwegian. The synods opposed liberalizing trends in some of the other Lutheran bodies, which were looking toward union, and opposed to Freemasonry. Their initial ambitious plans for cooperation were interrupted in the 1880s by a major doctrinal controversy over predestination, which caused the Ohio Synod to withdraw permanently and others to withdraw for a brief period. Others joined soon after the turn of the century.

In 1950, by which time the majority of American Lutherans were moving toward the mergers that would produce the American Lutheran Church (1960), the Lutheran Church in America (1962), and eventually the Evangelical Lutheran Church in America (1988), the Synodical Conference consisted of the Lutheran Church–Missouri Synod, the Wisconsin Evangelical Lutheran Synod, the Norwegian Synod, the Slovak Church, and a set of African-American parishes that had emerged from a missionary effort in the American South beginning in the 1980s. The conference had also established a mission in Nigeria and welcomed the fellowship of several independent conservative Lutheran churches in Europe.

In the wake of the mergers of 1960 and 1962, the several larger Lutheran bodies, including the Lutheran Church-Missouri Synod, entered into discussions that led to the creation of the Lutheran Council in the U.S.A. In 1963, during the process of approval of this plan, the more conservative members of the conference felt that they could no longer be in fellowship with the Missouri Synod, and the Norwegian (now known as the Evangelical Lutheran Synod) and Wisconsin Synods withdrew from the Synodical Conference, an action which effectively disbanded it.

Sources:

Meyer, Carl S. *The Synodical Conference–The Voice of Lutheran Confessionalism*. St. Louis, MO: Concordia Publishing House, 1956.

Wiederaenders, Robert C., and Walter G. Tillmans. *The Synods of American Lutheranism*. St. Louis, MO: Lutheran Historical Conference, 1968.

LUTHERAN CHURCHES

Concordia Synod of the West

The Concordia Synod of the West (also known as the German Evangelical Lutheran Concordia Synod of America) was founded in 1862 by four Lutheran pastors who had left positions in the Ohio, Buffalo, and Missouri Synods: L. F. E. Krause of Winona, Minnesota; F. W. Wier of Washington, Minnesota; C. F. Jung of New Oregon, Iowa; and D. J. Warns of Bethalto, Illinois. The synod apparently met in 1862 and 1864, but afterward it disappeared and no record of it being received into another Lutheran body has been located to date.

Sources:

Wiederaenders, Robert C., and Walter G. Tillmans. *The Synods of American Lutheranism*. St. Louis, MO: Lutheran Historical Conference, 1968.

Evangelical Lutheran Church in America

Elling Eielsen was a young Norwegian immigrant who was ordained in America. He led the formation of the Evangelical Lutheran Church in America, the first Norwegian Lutheran synod in the New World, in 1846. Growth of the synod was slow partly due to the demand for proof of conversion prior to admission to

membership. Controversy arose as some clergy demanded the admission of all who accepted the Christian faith and led a moral life. In 1876 a constitution revised along these lines was accepted and the name changed to Hauge's Norwegian Evangelical Lutheran Synod (which became part of the American Lutheran Church). At this time Eielsen and his supporters withdrew and formed the Evangelical Lutheran Church in America according to the Old Constitution. Eielsen himself died in 1883, but the synod continued as a small body for period after his death. During its active period, doctrine was at one with other Lutheran bodies. Liturgy was simple. During his leadership of the church, Eielsen had also protested domination by university-trained clergy, clerical garb, and a too formal liturgy.

Thought it is now defunct, in 1997 the church reported having two congregations with a total membership of 50. At that time there was one ordained minister, Truman L. Larson, ordained in 1986.

Federation for Authentic Lutheranism

The Federation for Authentic Lutheranism was formed in 1971 by members of the Lutheran Church–Missouri Synod. They had signaled their intention to withdraw prior to the 1971 meeting of the Missouri Synod if it did not stop fellowship relations with the liberal American Lutheran Church, withdraw from the Lutheran Council in the U.S.A. (which included both the Lutheran Church in America and the American Lutheran Church), and discipline "errorists" in the synod. (An attempt at the latter action resulted in controversy in the Missouri Synod.) Seven congregations formed the original federation. Eleven more joined within two years.

Theology was extremely conservative and pulpit fellowship was immediately declared with the Wisconsin Evangelical Lutheran Synod and the Evangelical Lutheran Synod. Positions have been taken against women's suffrage, the ordination of women, the Boy Scouts, and military chaplaincies. The federation was congregational in polity and run by a board of directors (half lay and half clerical) elected by the entire federation.

In the late 1970s, after less than a decade of existence, the federation disbanded, and its congregations joined either the Wisconsin Evangelical Lutheran Synod or the Evangelical Lutheran Synod. During its brief existence, it published a periodical, *Sola Scriptura*.

Immanuel Synod

The Immanuel Synod (of the Evangelical Lutheran Church in North America) is an independent Lutheran body that emerged among German Lutherans in Pennsylvania in the early 1870s. In 1874, the *Lutheran Almanac* reported the existence of an organization called the Bruderbund, with 12 pastors. No Bruderbund is reported in 1875, but in 1876 the Immanuel Synod suddenly appears in the church history with six of the pastors of the Bruderbund among its leadership. It appears that the Immanuel Synod evolved out of the Bruderbund. It also appears that at some point in the mid-1880s the Immanuel Synod disbanded and was superseded by a new Immanuel Synod. A report from 1885 indicated that the synod was the result of a desire of several ministers and churches to have greater freedom in church life than was then possible in many other Lutheran synods.

Having survived a generation, the synod took steps to disband, but Pastor J. Frederick was able to garner the necessary support from member churches to keep the doors open. Upon Frederick's death in 1921, however, no one arose to provide further leadership and the synod soon disbanded.

Jehovah Conference

Hesse is a state in central Germany where Reformed and Lutheran elements vied for ultimate control, but neither obtained it. It was here in the nineteenth century that trends toward the union of Reformed and Lutheran churches were supported by the political rulers. In this climate, a Free Lutheran movement emerged which identified with the traditional Lutheran Confessions and opposed unionism. It found a champion in J. W. G. Vilmar (1804–1884), one of the leading theologians of the day, pastor at Melsungen, and head of the Lower Hessian Mission Association.

In 1886 Rev. Wilhelm C. F. Hartwig (1854–1927) came to America as a representative of the Mission Association and began work around Detroit, Michigan. He was soon joined by several other pastors. About 1893 they organized the Jehovah Conference, over which Hartwig presided for many years. It was distinctive in holding to the Augsburg Confession as the only true confession of the Lutheran Church. The synod was small and in 1926 still had only six congregations and less than 1,000 members affiliated with it. Hartwig died in 1927, and the synod seems to have disbanded a short time later.

Sources:

Lueker, Erwin, ed. *Lutheran Cyclopedia*. St. Louis, MO: Concordia Publishing House, 1975.

Wiederaenders, Robert C., and Walter G. Tillmans. *The Synods of American Lutheranism*. St. Louis, MO: Lutheran Historical Conference, 1968.

Synod of Evangelical Lutheran Churches

Lutherans from Czechoslovakia began to migrate to the United States in the 1870s and early congregations were formed at Streator, Illinois; Freeland, Pennsylvania; and Minneapolis, Minnesota. Attempts to organize began in the 1890s, and the Slovak Evangelical Lutheran Synod was finally established at Connellsville, Pennsylvania, in 1902. Theologically, it declared itself at one with the Lutheran Synodical Conference. The move into the synodical conference proved the first step toward full merger with the

Missouri Synod, which was accomplished in 1971. Thus the Synod of Evangelical Lutheran Church ceased to exist as a separate denomination and became a district within the Missouri Synod.

6. Reformed-Presbyterian

REFORMED

Orthodox Reformed Church

In the late 1960s within the Protestant Reformed Churches, charges of sin against some members of the First Protestant Reformed Church of Grand Rapids resulted in the excommunication of some of its members. Feeling the excommunication to be unjust and to be a denial of their rights, members of the First Protestant Reformed Church of Grand Rapids organized the Orthodox Reformed Church (unaffiliated) in the fall of 1970. In doctrine and polity the church was like its parent body though it did not "subscribe to the church political policies of the Protestant Reformed Churches after the year 1965." Worship was simple and expressed a love of decency and order.

Rev. Gerald Vanden Berg, the leader of the church until his death in 1984, had previously been the stated clerk of the Protestant Reformed Church. He had been active in forming the Fellowship of Reformed Churches, an ecumenical group of independent reformed congregations. Vanden Berg was succeeded by the Rev. Peter J. Breen. The church supported missionary activity in India and Pakistan. The Orthodox Reformed Publishing Society, an independent organization, was informally associated with the church. During its active phase, the church published the periodical *The Reformed Scope*. While the church is now defunct, at the beginning of the 1990s, the church consisted of a single congregation of 61 members. In 1992 it voted to disband, and the members joined other Reformed Congregations of their choice.

Sources:

VandenBerg, Gerald. *Why Orthodox Reformed?* Grandville, MI: Orthodox Reformed Publishing Society, n.d.

PRESBYTERIAN

Presbyterian Church of the Lower Provinces

The Presbyterian Church of the Lower Provinces no longer exists as a separate entity. It became a constituent part of the United Church of Canada and the Presbyterian Church in Canada. The Presbyterian Church of the Lower Provinces (1817–1875) grew out of the Seceders, a faction of Scottish Presbyterianism which emerged during the revivals that swept the Scottish church in the early 1700s. The Seceders were united in their attack upon the patronage system of

the established Church of Scotland and its lack of spiritual awareness. They divided into two factions, usually termed Burgher and anti-Burgher, which resulted from the demand of an oath as part of the requirement to hold office in Scotland; the anti-Burgher party refused the oath, claiming it legitimized the established church.

Members of both parties arrived in Canada in the late 1700s. Three members of the Burgher Synod, Daniel Cook, David Smith, and Hugh Graham, organized the Presbytery of Truro in 1786. Almost contemporaneously, James McGregor and two other anti-Burgher ministers began work which culminated in the formation of the Presbytery of Pictou in 1795. Attempts at reconciliation in the new setting eventually led to the merger of the two presbyteries, the creation of a third presbytery (Halifax), and the formation of the Synod of Nova Scotia in 1817.

In 1825 the Church of Scotland organized the Glasgow Colonial Society, which sent missionaries to Canada. Those who settled in Nova Scotia and other Eastern Provinces refused to join the Synod of Nova Scotia. In 1833 the Presbyterian Synod in Connection with the Church of Scotland was organized. This synod prospered until 1843 when the Church of Scotland went through a period of turmoil which led to a number of ministers resigning and forming the Free Church of Scotland. In Canada, the Presbyterian Synod sided with the Free Church faction in the homeland. In 1860 this Free Church Synod merged with the Synod of Nova Scotia to form the Presbyterian Synod of the Lower Provinces.

In the disruption of 1843, one faction of the Presbyterian Church in Connection with the Church of Scotland, the Presbytery of New Brunswick (which had grown to become the Synod of New Brunswick), remained loyal to the established Church of Scotland. It became independent of the Free Synod. Three of its members in New Brunswick then withdrew and formed The (Free) Presbyterian Synod of New Brunswick, which in 1866 became a part of the Presbyterian Synod of the Lower Provinces.

In 1875 the Presbyterian Church of the Lower Provinces merged with three other Presbyterian churches to form the Presbyterian Church in Canada. In 1925 most of that church merged with the Methodist Church, Canada and the Congregational Union of Canada to form the United Church of Canada.

Sources:

Reed, R. C. *History of the Presbyterian Churches of the World*. Philadelphia: Westminster Press, 1912.

Silcox, Claris Edwin. *Church Union in Canada*. New York: Institute of Social and Religious Research, 1933.

Presbyterian Church of the Maritime Provinces

The Presbyterian Church of the Maritime Provinces no longer exists as a separate entity. It became a constituent part of the United Church of Canada and the Presbyterian Church of Canada. The Presbyterian Church of the Maritime Provinces (1868–1975) traces its history to the arrival in Canada of ministers of the Church of Scotland in the 1820s. In 1833 the Presbyterian Synod in Connection with the Church of Scotland was organized by a group of ministers, many of whom had been sent to Canada by the Glasgow Missionary Society. At the same time, a Presbytery of New Brunswick had been designated as one of the synod's constituent units. During the next decade the Presbytery of New Brunswick had grown into the Synod of New Brunswick. In 1943 the Church of Scotland had been disrupted by a dispute involving government powers in the appointment of ministers. Those who disagreed with the court's decision in the controversy left the Church of Scotland and formed the Free Church of Scotland. In Canada, the Presbyterian Synod in Connection with the Church of Scotland sided with the Free Church and broke its relation with the established Church of Scotland. The Synod of New Brunswick, however, remained loyal to the established church and became independent. Some members of the new Free Synod wished to return to their connection with the established church and in 1854 established the Synod of Nova Scotia and Prince Edward Island. These two groups merged in 1868 to form the Church of the Maritime Provinces.

In 1875, the Church of the Maritime Provinces united with three other Presbyterian churches to form the Presbyterian Church in Canada. In 1925 the majority of that church merged with the Methodist Church, Canada and the Congregational Union of Canada to form the United Church of Canada.

Sources:

Reed, R. C. *History of the Presbyterian Churches of the World*. Philadelphia: Westminister Press, 1912.

Silcox, Claris Edwin. *Church Union in Canada*. New York: Institute of Social and Religious Research, 1933.

Synod of the Canada Presbyterian Church

The Synod of the Canada Presbyterian Church no longer exists as a separate entity. It became a constituent part of the United Church of Canada and the Presbyterian Church of Canada. The Synod of the Canada Presbyterian Church (1861–1875) can be traced to 1832 with the arrival of three missionaries into Western Canada as representatives of the independent United Associate Synod of Scotland, one of the factions of Scottish Presbyterianism not connected with the established Church of Scotland. The church offered the missionaries the opportunity to join one of the two existing synods (the Presbyterian Church in Connection with the Church of Scotland or the United Synod of Upper Canada). However, the missionaries turned down the offer upon discovering that these already existing synods were quite willing to accept government support for their work, a position directly

opposing that of the United Associate Synod. Therefore, in 1834 the ministers formed the Missionary Presbytery of the Canadas. In 1843 the Presbytery split into three presbyteries and organized the Missionary Synod of Canada.

In 1843, 26 ministers of the Presbyterian Church in Connection with the Church of Scotland left the church to found the Synod of the Free Church of Canada. This was done in reaction to ministers in the Church of Scotland who, in protest of governmental influence in clerical matters, resigned from the established church to form the Free Church of Scotland. In 1861 the Synod of the Free Church of Canada and the Missionary Synod of Canada merged to become the Synod of the Canada Presbyterian Church.

In 1875 the Synod of the Canada Presbyterian Church merged with three other Presbyterian churches to form the Presbyterian Church in Canada. The majority of the Presbyterian Church in Canada merged with the Methodist Church, Canada and the Congregational Union of Canada, forming the United Church of Canada.

Sources:

Reed, R. C. *History of the Presbyterian Churches of the World*. Philadelphia: Westminister Press, 1912.

Silcox, Claris Edwin. *Church Union in Canada*. New York: Institute of Social and Religious Research, 1933.

Synod of the Presbyterian Church in Connection with the Church of Scotland

The Synod of the Presbyterian Church in Connection with the Church of Scotland no longer exists as a separate entity. It became a constituent part of the United Church of Canada and the Presbyterian Church of Canada. The Synod of the Canada Presbyterian Church (1861–1875) began with the arrival of Presbyterians in the eighteenth century into that part of Canada which was termed the Western Provinces (presently Quebec and Ontario). As early as 1796, Rev. John Bethune (1750–1815) organized a Presbyterian congregation in Montreal. However, it was not until 1818 that enough growth and development had occurred to organize a presbytery. In that year the Revs. Robert Easton, William Stuart, William Bell, and William Taylor organized the Presbytery of the Canadas. These ministers were associated with the Burgher faction of Scottish Presbyterians who had seceded from the established Church of Scotland. Within a few years the presbytery reorganized and took a new name, the United Presbytery of Upper Canada, which grew into the United Synod of Upper Canada in 1831.

As the United Synod was taking shape, ministers associated with the established church formed the Presbyterian Church in Connection with the Church of Scotland. In 1840 these two groups merged to become the Synod of the Presbyterian Church in Connection with the Church of Scotland. In 1875 the Synod of the Presbyterian Church in Connection with

the Church of Scotland merged with three other Presbyterian Churches to form the Presbyterian Church in Canada. The majority of the Presbyterian Church in Canada merged in 1925 with the Methodist Church, Canada and the Congregational Union of Canada to become the United Church of Canada.

Sources:

Reed, R. C. *History of the Presbyterian Churches of the World*. Philadelphia: Westminister Press, 1912.

Silcox, Claris Edwin. *Church Union in Canada*. New York: Institute of Social and Religious Research, 1933.

Westminster Biblical Fellowship

Following the 1969 meeting in which Dr. Carl McIntire was removed from his responsibilities with the American Council of Christian Churches (ACCC), several former leaders of the McIntire-led Bible Presbyterian Church also withdrew support from him. These included J. Phillip Clark, former General Secretary of the Independent Board of Presbyterian Foreign Missions and pastor of Calvary Bible Presbyterian Church in Glendale, California. After the 1969 ACCC meeting, Clark announced the formation of the Westminster Biblical Fellowship in order to provide a vehicle for Bible Presbyterians to remain with the ACCC. Other Bible Presbyterian leaders—Richard E. Smitley, Jack Murray and Arthur Steele—joined Clark. The Westminster Biblical Fellowship continued the faith of the Bible Presbyterian Church in general, but it objected to the strong crusading stance of Carl McIntire.

Sources:

McIntire, Carl. *A Letter to Bible Presbyterians*. Collinwood, NJ: Bible Presbyterian Church, 1969.

CONGREGATIONALISM

Congregational Union of Canada

The Congregational Union of Canada no longer exists as a separate entity. It became a constituent part of the United Church of Canada. The Congregational Union of Canada was formed in 1906 by the merger of the Congregational Union of Nova Scotia and New Brunswick and the Congregational Union of Ontario and Quebec. Together they represented the Congregational Church tradition which entered Canada from the United States in the eighteenth century.

Congregational beginnings in Canada awaited the British takeover of Nova Scotia in 1748. At the invitation of the government, shiploads of settlers arrived from New England to establish towns and begin farming. The first Congregational Church was organized in Chester in 1759; others followed, and two years later a second one was formed in Liverpool. Though never a large and growing movement, these churches passed a generation in peace until, in the 1780s, they were disturbed by the independent revivalistic efforts of Henry Alline (1748–1784), whose preachings led to a split in many congregations. The new congregations, though remaining officially Congregational during Alline's lifetime, eventually became the core of Canadian Baptists in the area. Concurrently, the Methodists began their period of growth under William Black, Jr. (1760–1834). The competition between the Baptists and Methodists, coupled with the difficulties of obtaining ministers after the American Revolution, effectively hampered the future growth of Congregationalism.

At the same time settlements were being established in Nova Scotia, New Englanders traveled to New Brunswick. The first Congregational Church emerged in 1766 at Maugerville. Newfoundland's first congregation came a decade later at St. John's.

Organization of the scattered congregations awaited events in England. In the 1830s the Congregational Union of England and Wales was formed, thus consolidating Congregational efforts in Britain. In 1834 fraternal delegates were sent to Canada. They reported their findings, which led to the formation of the Colonial Missionary Society in 1836. This society, whose purpose was to aid churches through the British Empire, assisted the work in Canada and facilitated the formation of the Congregational Union of Nova Scotia and New Brunswick in 1846.

Congregationalism in Quebec and Ontario grew out of two separate movements. In the years after the American Revolution, settlers from New England began to move northward across the border into Canada. A church was founded at Stamstead as early as 1798. As other churches were founded, ministers were drawn from Vermont. In the 1840s, the Congregationalist-sponsored American Home Missionary Society initiated work in Canada and organized several predominantly black congregations among former slaves who had fled to freedom.

As early as 1801 the British Congregationalists sent a representative of the London Missionary Society to Quebec. Most of that work was lost to the Presbyterians, and the New England–based church was all that survived. British settlers organized a joint Congregational-Presbyterian Church in Elgin County, Ontario, in 1819. It survived to become fully congregational, the first in that province.

As with the churches in the Maritime Provinces, those in Quebec and Ontario received a boost from the 1834 delegation from England. Unions were organized in each province, and in 1853 they merged into the Congregational Union of Ontario and Quebec.

In 1807 the Congregational Union of Canada received the Canadian Conference of the United Brethren in Christ into its membership. This German body had become predominantly English-speaking in the late nineteenth century. Rather than becoming another small independent sect after breaking with

the American branch, they chose to unite with the Congregationalists.

In 1925 the Congregational Union of Canada joined with the Methodist Church, Canada and the Presbyterian Church in Canada to form the United Church of Canada.

Sources:

Dunning, Albert E. *Congregationalists in America*. New York: J. A. Hill & Co., 1894.

Silcox, Claris Edwin. *Church Union in Canada*. New York: Institute of Social and Religious Research, 1933.

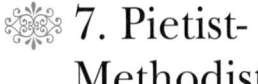

7. Pietist-Methodist

NON-EPISCOPAL METHODISM

Cumberland Methodist Church

The Cumberland Methodist Church withdrew from the Congregational Methodist Church in 1950 because of a disagreement on both polity and doctrine. It was organized at Laager, Grundy County, Tennessee, in the mountainous country near Chattanooga. Membership never reached beyond the several counties in southeastern Tennessee. Since its founder's death, no trace of the existence of the Cumberland Methodist Church has been found.

Reformed New Congregational Church

The Reformed New Congregational Methodist Church was organized in 1916 by the Rev. J. A. Sander and the Rev. Earl Wilcoxen, a minister in the Congregational Methodist Church. A large following was built in southern Illinois and Indiana; however, no data has been located since 1936 when there were eight churches.

BRITISH METHODISM

Methodist Church, Canada

The Methodist Church, Canada no longer exists as a separate entity. It is now a constituent part of the United Church of Canada. The Methodist Church, Canada (1884–1925) was formed by the merger of the Methodist Church of Canada with three smaller Methodist bodies, two of which had been transported to Canada by representatives of the various divisions of British Methodism (the Primitive Methodist Connection of Canada and the Bible Christian Church), the third a product of a schism within Canadian Methodism in 1833 (the Methodist Episcopal Church of Canada [1833–1884]). The Methodist Church of Canada was formed in 1874 by the merger of several Methodist bodies, the result of American and British Methodists who had completed their efforts to unite.

Methodism in Canada had been taken under the guidance and leadership of the Methodist Episcopal Church as soon as that church emerged as a separate

entity in 1784. Itinerants were initially sent to Nova Scotia, but in 1791 William Losee (1757–1832) was sent to Kingston, Ontario, by the New York Conference and work developed in the Western Provinces under the New York and later the Genesee (Western New York) Conferences. In 1828 this work became independent as the Methodist Episcopal Church in Canada (1828–1833). In 1833 a merger of the Methodist Episcopal Church in Canada (1828–1833) and the British Wesleyan Connection, then still directly tied to the British headquarters, was accomplished. A minority of those formerly associated with the Methodist Episcopal Church in Canada (1828–1833) rejected the merger and reorganized as the Methodist Episcopal Church in Canada (1833–1884). They wanted an independent Canadian church, free of control from England, and they wanted to keep the episcopal polity. (The British had not developed an episcopacy, while the American Methodists had.)

An initial conference of the dissenting ministers was held in 1834, and a general conference was held the following year. It was at the general conference that a bishop was selected and the new jurisdiction formally organized. Since most of the meeting halls and members had been lost in the merger, the new church began with almost nothing, but by 1837 reported over 3,500 members. By 1843 there were over 8,000 members, and the single conference was divided into two conferences. A third conference was designated in 1875.

The Primitive Methodist Church of Canada had roots similar to those of the Primitive Methodist Church in the United States, begun in the 1820s. It grew out of the Primitive Methodist Connection in England, a group of Methodists attached to revival and camp meetings and generally known for the emotional displays at their gatherings. In 1829, at about the same time the Primitive Methodist Church began work in New York and Pennsylvania, William Lawson and his family arrived in Toronto. Lawson had been a local preacher in the Wesleyan Methodist Connection, but had been expelled and joined the Primitive Methodists. In Toronto, Lawson organized a class and preached to a small gathering. In 1830 Rev. William Watkins was sent from England to assist in the work. He was replaced a year later by William Summersides, one of the original missionaries sent to America. The Primitive Methodists in Canada formed their conference in 1854. Lawson became the first secretary. The church grew slowly but steadily through the next generation but welcomed the prospect of union with the rest of Canadian Methodism.

The Bible Christians began in England in the second decade of the nineteenth century out of the work of William O'Bryan (1778–1868), a Methodist local preacher, who continually found himself at odds with his superiors and was twice expelled from the Wesleyan Connection for his operating outside of the discipline of the church. He was an effective preacher, and raised a following in some areas of Cornwall and Devon not otherwise touched by Methodism. O'Bryan organized the first Bible Christian society in October 1815. The first quarterly conference in January 1816 reported 11 societies in the fellowship. At the first conference of the Connection in 1819, 16 male and 14 female itinerant preachers were reported, with a following of 2,000.

In 1831 the Connection sent two missionaries to Canada to work among Cornish immigrants: John Hicks Eynon to Upper Canada and Francis Metherall to Prince Edward Island. From these small beginnings, other missionaries came and the church grew rapidly. There were over 1,000 members at the first district meeting in 1844. The church slowly became self-supporting and, by the time the Canadian conference was organized in 1855, had freed itself from British support. From the time of the formation of the conference until the merger in 1884, the church more than doubled its membership.

At the time of their merger in 1884, the four uniting churches reported as follows: Methodist Church in Canada, 128,644 members; Methodist Episcopal Church in Canada, 25,671 members; Primitive Methodist Church, 8,090 members; Bible Christian Church, 7,398 members.

Sources:

Centennial of Canadian Methodism. Toronto: William Briggs, 1891.

Davies, Rupert, A. Raymond George, and Gordon Rupp, eds. *A History of the Methodist Church in Great Britain.* Vol. 2. London: Epworth Press, 1978.

Sanderson, J. E. *Methodism in Canada.* 2 vols. Toronto: William Briggs, 1910.

Shaw, Thomas. *The Bible Christians, 1815-1907.* London: Epworth Press, 1965.

Silcox, Claris Edwin. *Church Union in Canada.* New York: Institute of Social and Religious Research, 1933.

Methodist Church in Canada

The Methodist Church in Canada no longer exists as a separate entity. It is now a constituent part of the United Church of Canada. The Methodist Church in Canada was formed in 1874 by the merger of the Wesleyan Conference of Eastern British North America, the Conference of the Wesleyan Methodist Church in Canada, and the Methodist New Connexion Church in Canada.

The Wesleyan Conference of Eastern British North America continued the earliest Methodist work in Canada. In 1772 a group of Methodists from Yorkshire settled in Cumberland County, Nova Scotia, an area familiar with revivals. In the 1780s it became the site of a revival initiated by Congregationalist minister Henry Alline (1748–1784), which had split the older Congregational churches and produced a set of rival Separatist congregations. Among the Methodists, 19-

year-old William Black, Jr. (1760–1834) emerged as a preacher who began to travel through the county and then all of Nova Scotia, organizing small groups of believers. In 1784 he traveled to Maryland to attend the founding conference of the Methodist Episcopal Church and to ask their assistance in the work he had begun. The prospects for Methodism in the Maritime Provinces were enhanced by the migration of many American colonists still loyal to the British government. The first conference was held in 1786.

The work in Nova Scotia and New Brunswick came under the care of the New York Conference of the Methodist Episcopal Church, which appointed ministers throughout the 1790s. However, these ministers experienced open rebuke for their disloyalty to the British government, and the last departed in 1799. That same year Black traveled to England and appealed to the Wesleyan Connexion for ministers. Four returned with him in 1800; others followed. The work spread through the Maritime Provinces. In 1790 a mission in Bermuda was inspired by the efforts of John Stephenson. Until 1855 the work was under the direct supervision of the English Wesleyans and was administered by its London Missionary committee. In that year the work was organized into affiliated conferences and designated the Wesleyan Methodist Connexion of Eastern British America. The British Connexion, besides continuing financial support, retained the right of ratifying the election of the conference president and vetoing actions of the conference. This relationship (tied to the British but independent of efforts further west) remained until 1874.

The Wesleyan Methodist Church in Canada originated with the movement of Methodism into what is today Quebec and Ontario (designated Upper and Lower Canada in the late 1700s). Methodist work began in 1780 with the arrival of a British officer by the name of Tuffey in Quebec. Tuffey was also a Methodist preacher. Six years later Major George Neal, also a Methodist preacher, began preaching in the Niagara area. Their work was taken into an area of Canada organized by former American colonists still loyal to the British government. Among the immigrants were Paul Heck (d. 1795) and his wife Barbara Heck (1734–1804), loyalists who had been instrumental in the founding of Methodism in New York prior to the Revolution. They formed a class in Augusta (Ontario) in 1788. The first itinerant, William Losee (1757–1832), arrived in 1790, and in 1791 he led in the organization of a number of classes.

A decade later the Canadian work had grown to become a separate district. In 1810, western New York was separated from the New York Conference and designated the Genesee Conference. The Canadian work was transferred to the Genesee Conference and was also divided into two districts, Upper and Lower Canada. The work was disrupted during the War of 1812, when the area became a battlefield. After the

war, the work resumed. The New England Conference developed two charges across the border in Quebec. In 1824 the General Conference separated the Canadian work from the Genesee Conference and created a new Canada Conference. By this time many of the ministers, including leading minister and presiding elder Henry Ryan (1775–1833), were firmly convinced that full independence of the Canadian Methodists was in order. They worked for that independence during the next four years, and in 1828 the General Conference granted it: the Canadian Conference became the Methodist Episcopal Church in Canada. No bishop was ever elected to head the church, which existed only five years.

As the War of 1812 was drawing to a close, the British Methodists appointed a missionary to Canada. John B. Strong arrived in Quebec in 1814 to begin the growth of a rival to the American-based effort. Its growth was augmented by the movement of many Methodists with anti-American sentiments into the new jurisdiction. Competition between and duplication of efforts by the two conferences were somewhat lessened in 1820, when a division of territory was agreed upon. The Americans concentrated on Upper Canada, the British on Lower Canada. In 1833, five years after the Methodist Episcopal Church conference had become independent, a merger between the two was finalized. The new Canadian Wesleyan Conference remained in close relationship with the British Methodists, and its polity (which had no bishop) was accepted. The union proved unsatisfactory to many; those committed to an episcopal polity withdrew and formed the Methodist Episcopal Church in Canada (1833–1884).

Of intense concern after the 1833 merger was the reception by the British Methodists of Canadian government funds which were to be used to underwrite Indian missions and to stop the political activities of the Canadian Methodists. The Canadian Methodists were, on the other hand, opponents of state aid to religion. The issues led to a break between the groups in the 1840s. As that break proceeded, some independent efforts developed in Quebec as the Eastern District Meeting. This independent effort merged with the reunited Wesleyans to form the Wesleyan Methodist Church in Canada in 1854. That church continued until 1874. The Methodist New Connexion emerged after the death of John Wesley (1703–1791) in a dispute over the status of Methodism as a dissenting movement. Under Wesley and his immediate successors, Methodists considered themselves Anglicans. They would not schedule meetings to conflict with parish worship, advised their members to have their babies baptized by the local Anglican priest, and encouraged members to receive their sacrament at the local Church of England. William Thom (1751–1811) and Alexander Kilham (1762–1798) disagreed and argued that Methodism should become a dissenting movement and offer the sacraments directly to its members. They also argued for a variety of lay rights in the choice of class leaders (then exclusively the prerogative of the preachers) and representation at the annual conference. In 1797 they led in the formation of the Methodist New Connexion.

The Methodist New Connexion Church in Canada began in the 1820s after a wealthy layman, William Ridgeway, visited it and reported its needs to the British Connexion. A short time later a retired minister settled there and began to preach. In 1832 Joseph Clementson traveled to Toronto, only to return and report on the continued needs of the population. Finally, in 1837 John Addyman (1808–1887) was sent to formally institute a mission. He was followed two years later by Henry O. Crofts. The work made an immediate advance by its encounter and subsequent merger in 1841 with a small group, the Canadian Wesleyan Methodist Church.

The Canadian Wesleyan Methodist Church was formed in 1829 by Rev. Henry Ryan (1775–1833). Ryan had been a presiding elder working in Canada in the Genesee Conference of the Methodist Episcopal Church. After the War of 1812, he was among the loudest voices appealing for independence for Canadian Methodism from American control. Impatient with the slow process, Ryan became a severe critic of the conference, so much so that after independence was declared in 1828, he led a schismatic movement of several hundred members to the formation of the Canadian Wesleyan Methodist Church. It had grown to approximately 2,000 members when it united with the New Connexion.

The merged church became known as the Canadian Wesleyan Methodist New Connexion, with a direct link to the New Connexion Missionary Society in England through a superintendent appointed by the British leaders. In 1843 the Connexion absorbed the small body of Methodist Protestants, a Canadian conference affiliated with the Methodist Protestant Church which had been organized in 1836. At that time the Methodist Protestants had less than 600 members. In 1864 the Connexion changed its name to the Methodist New Connexion Church in Canada, the name it carried into the union of 1874.

In 1884, the Methodist Church of Canada merged with the Bible Christian Church, the Methodist Episcopal Church in Canada, and the Primitive Methodist Church in Canada to become the Methodist Church, Canada.

Sources:

Centennial of Canadian Methodism. Toronto: William Briggs, 1891.

Davies, Rupert, A. Raymond George, and Gordon Rupp, eds. *A History of the Methodist Church in Great Britain*. Vol. 2. London: Epworth Press, 1978.

Sanderson, J. E. *The First Century of Methodism in Canada*. 2 vols. Toronto: William Briggs, 1908.

Silcox, Claris Edwin. *Church Union in Canada*. New York: Institute of Social and Religious Research, 1933.

 ## 8. Holiness

NINETEENTH CENTURY HOLINESS

Christ's Sanctified Holy Church (Louisiana)

In 1903 members of Christ's Sanctified Holy Church (South Carolina) came to West Lake, Louisiana, and proselytized a group of blacks, who in 1904 organized the Colored Church South. Among the leaders were Dempsey Perkins, A. C. Mitchell, James Briller, Sr., and Leggie Pleasant. The church soon changed its name to Christ's Sanctified Holy Church Colored. Over the years the church members dropped the word "Colored" from their title and returned to using the same name as their parent body, Christ's Sanctified Holy Church. The parent body was predominantly white and had headquarters in South Carolina, whereas the church under discussion here was headquartered in Louisiana. Organization and doctrine were the same as the parent body, except that the ministers in Christ's Sanctified Holy Church (Louisiana) were salaried. Though the church is now defunct, in 1957, there were approximately 600 members in 30 churches.

Church of God (Northern Indiana Eldership)

The Church of God (Northern Indiana Eldership) originated as a schism from the Churches of God General Conference, which was generally known in the later nineteenth century as the Churches of God in North America (General Eldership). It resulted from the influx of holiness experience and theology into the Churches of God. Among its prominent members was Daniel Warner, who served as editor for its newspaper. In 1880 Warner left the group, taking many members with him, and they became the core of the Church of God (Anderson, Indiana). The Church of God (Northern Indiana Eldership) was little heard of after that date and is presumed to have slowly dwindled away.

Sources:

Jones, Charles Edwin. *A Guide to the Study of the Holiness Movement*. Metuchen, NJ: Scarecrow Press, 1974.

Evangelical Christian Church (Wesleyan)

The Evangelical Christian Church was born in the holiness revival that occurred spontaneously in various parts of the United States during the latter part of the nineteenth century. In 1882 L. Frank Haas, along with four others, conducted open-air and hall meetings in the city of Philadelphia, Pennsylvania. These efforts resulted in the conversion of many people. Haas and his coworkers assumed spiritual leadership for this rapidly growing fellowship of new Christians.

While the organization of a church was not the original plan, the necessity of organizing was soon apparent. The converts needed to be established in holiness of heart and life and opportunities were opening for the expansion of the work into other communities. The name Heavenly Recruit Association was chosen and the new organization was granted a charter by the city of Philadelphia in 1884.

The evangelistic ministry spread rapidly into the areas surrounding Philadelphia. Churches were soon established in Chester and West Conshohocken, Pennsylvania, and Wilmington, Delaware. New missions were organized at other locations in eastern Pennsylvania and in the state of Indiana. At the Annual Conference held at Linwood, Pennsylvania, in 1889, resolutions were passed to establish an itinerant ministry, elect a presiding elder, and station pastors. Haas, president of the association was elected the first Presiding Elder.

Articles of Faith and Bylaws were adopted by the Annual Conference of 1892, which convened at Reading, Pennsylvania. At this time the publication of a church paper was approved. It was called *The Crown of Glory*, and it was first published in Pennsylvania but later was moved to Indiana and was succeeded in 1906 by a new publication, *A Voice from Canaan*. Previous to these publication efforts, *Good News* and *The Heavenly Recruit* had been printed and circulated by the association.

At the tenth Annual Conference, held at West Conshohocken, Pennsylvania, in 1894, the denomination, which had outgrown the limitations of the original charter, voted to reorganize. At this time the church at Philadelphia withdrew, claiming the original charter and name. The conference then adopted the name Holiness Christian Association, elected Rev. C. W. Ruth as Presiding Elder and continued their sessions as the first Annual Conference of the reorganized denomination.

The Annual Conference of 1896, held at Reading, Pennsylvania, authorized the organization of a second Annual Conference in Indiana and a General Conference. The Indiana Conference was duly constituted that same year at Tipton, Indiana, under the direction of Rev. Jonas Trumbauer, the Presiding Elder. The first General Conference convened at Reading, Pennsylvania, in 1897. At this conference the organization modified its name to Holiness Christian Church.

In the period of 1907–1908, the Pennsylvania Conference considered consolidating with the Pentecostal Church of the Nazarene (the word "Pentecostal" was dropped in 1919). Release was requested from the General Conference and was granted. In 1908 several of the churches and ministers did unite with the Church of the Nazarene, forming the nucleus for their Philadelphia District. About an equal number of churches and ministers declined merger, reorganized, and continued as the Pennsylvania Conference of the Holiness Christian Church. In 1916 this conference reunited with the general church then centered in Indiana.

In 1919 at the General Assembly convened in Cincinnati, Ohio, the Holiness Christian Church, with the exception of the Pennsylvania Conference, voted to merge with the International Apostolic Holiness Church. The Indiana Conference, which provided much of the strength of the new organization, was joined by the Kansas and Oklahoma Conference and the Illinois and Missouri Conference in the union, which selected the name International Holiness Church. A subsequent merger with the Pilgrim Church formed the Pilgrim Holiness Church, which in 1968 united with the Wesleyan Methodist Church to become the Wesleyan Church. The Pennsylvania Conference continued as the Holiness Christian Church.

Annual camp meetings were conducted at various locations throughout the church's history. In 1921 a camp meeting ground was purchased at Seyfert, near Reading, Pennsylvania. This also served as the Conference Center for the denomination. The growth of the church led to the development of congregations beyond the original boundaries of the conference. At one time there were churches in Pennsylvania, Maryland, Delaware, New York, and Virginia, as well as Jamaica. A denominational camp meeting was also held at Fruitland, Maryland, beginning in 1950. Publication of a church periodical, first called *The Holiness Christian Messenger*, and later *The Christian Messenger*, began in 1937.

The church was incorporated under the laws of the Commonwealth of Pennsylvania in 1945. The corporate name, Holiness Christian Church of the United States of America, was changed to Holiness Christian Church in 1969. The name Evangelical Christian Church (Wesleyan) was approved by the Annual Conference in 1976 and was legally authorized on January 1, 1977.

The Evangelical Christian Church was a member denomination of the Christian Holiness Association and the National Association of Evangelicals. Supportive and cooperative ministries were also addressed through affiliation with the Evangelical Wesleyan Fellowship, an association of similar holiness denominations.

Throughout its history, the church was involved in missionary endeavors. Work was conducted in Central and South America, Africa, and other world regions. In 1945, a movement which had begun in Jamaica 20 years previously, united with the Holiness Christian Church. The Jamaican church was incorporated in 1949 and was the focus of evangelistic and missionary activity through the years. Recognized as a District Conference in 1969, the Holiness Christian Church in Jamaica continues its ministry under that name while remaining fully a part of the Evangelical Christian Church.

During its active phase, the church endorsed Circleville Bible College in Circleville, Ohio, and Kentucky Mountain Bible College in Vancleve, Kentucky. Missionary outreach has also been accomplished through cooperation with selected international mission organizations. Through its present affiliation with World Gospel Mission, the Evangelical Christian Church is part of a global thrust to bring Christ's love to the nations. In 1995 the church reported 1,200 members, 25 churches, and 54 ministers in the United States. At that time there were 2,800 members worldwide.

Sources:

The Manual of the Evangelical Christian Church (Wesleyan). Birdsboro, PA: Evangelical Christian Church (Wesleyan), 1987.

Missionary Christian and Soul Winning Fellowship

The Missionary Christian and Soul Winning Fellowship was formed in 1957 by Rev. Lee Shelley, a minister of the Christian and Missionary Alliance. It continued the evangelistic and missionary interests of the Christian and Missionary Alliance (CMA), but its doctrinal statement deleted any reference to healing, a particular interest of CMA founder A. B. Simpson.

A missionary program was once active in 19 countries. In the United States there was a single congregation (Christian in Action Chapel) at Long Beach, California. A school provided vocational training for Christian workers. Within the United States a Jewish ministry in Los Angeles led by Abe Schneider was supported, as was an Apache Indian Mission.

Missionary Church of Canada

In 1987 the Canadian conferences of the Missionary Church separated and reorganized as an independent church. The separation followed a pattern of several of their American-based denominations with work in Canada; it was amicable, and the two organizations continued to work closely together. One stream of Missionary Church history can be traced to the 1869 conversion of a Canadian Mennonite minister, Solomon Eby (1834–1929), of Ontario. The people affected by his message and experience became known as the Reformed Mennonites. In 1894 this group, known as the Mennonite Brethren in Christ, after several mergers, spread to Alberta. Eventually two districts emerged, one centered in Ontario and Quebec and the other in Alberta and British Columbia.

The Missionary Church of Canada and the Evangelical Church in Canada merged in 1993 to become the Evangelical Missionary Church of Canada (EMCC). Though the Missionary Church in Canada is now defunct, in 1987 there were 92 churches, 6,431 members, and 129 ministers.

Sources:

Lageer, Eileen. *Merging Streams: Story of the Missionary Church*. Elkhart, IN: Bethel Publishing, 1979.

Peniel Missions

The first Peniel Mission was founded by T. P. Ferguson and his wife Manie Ferguson in Los Angeles in 1886. Ferguson had been influenced by the preaching of Charles G. Finney, an early nineteenth-century holiness theologian and evangelist. In 1880 he experienced sanctification under some holiness evangelists. Given the success of the Los Angeles work, he established rescue missions in the urban areas of the West Coast in attempts to win the urban masses to Christ. The missions have been marked by intense evangelistic endeavor, spiritual guidance, and stress on sanctification and sinlessness. For a short time, Phineas Bresee, founder of the Church of the Nazarene, worked at the Los Angeles center. By 1900 work had spread north along the West Coast and in Alaska, Hawaii, and Egypt. In 1949 responsibility for the Egyptian mission was assumed by the National Holiness Missionary Society, currently known as the World Gospel Mission, located in Winona Lake, Indiana.

Standard Church of America

Ralph G. Horner (1854–1921) had been an evangelist in both the Methodist Church in Canada and the Wesleyan Methodist Church, which in the late nineteenth century became a constituent part of the Wesleyan Church. Horner later left them to found his own organization, the Holiness Movement Church, in 1895. As its bishop, he ruled with all the authority of both a bishop and a charismatic personality, and within five years there were 118 places of worship. Churches were planted across Canada, into New York, with foreign work in Ireland, Egypt, and China. In 1918 the aging bishop was asked to retire. Not satisfied with the request of the church, he, with his supporters, left and founded the Standard Church of America, incorporated at Watertown, New York, in 1919. (The Holiness Movement Church eventually merged with the Free Methodist Church, which accounts for that church's large membership in Egypt.)

Like the Holiness Movement Church, the Standard Church of America was Methodist in doctrine with a strong emphasis on holiness and evangelism. Polity were episcopal. Pastors were stationed by the annual conferences for four-year terms. There were four conferences: Western, Kingston, New York, and Egyptian. A Bible School and printing establishment were maintained adjacent to the headquarters. During its active period, the Standard Church of America issued a periodical entitled *Christian Standard,* and operated the Brockville Bible College located in Brockville, Ontario, Canada. The church was also involved in missionary work in China and Egypt.

Undenominational Church of the Lord

The Undenominational Church of the Lord was founded at Placentia, California in 1918 by Pastor Jesse N. Blakeley, a holiness minister. Previously, he had helped form the Pentecost Pilgrim Church at Pasadena (which merged into what became the

Pilgrim Holiness Church, later a constituent part of the Wesleyan Church). Blakeley became pastor of the Independent Holiness Mission in Placentia following a revival in Santa Ana. He felt the Holy Spirit leading him south and discovered the pastorless congregation in Placentia praying for the Lord to send them the right person. The Independent Holiness Mission became the Undenominational Church of the Lord.

A second branch of the church was founded in 1920 in Anaheim and became the headquarters. In 1922 the Placentia church was consolidated with the Anaheim church. In 1930 Blakeley was succeeded by Elsie Heughan, and in 1941 the headquarters returned to Placentia.

Doctrine of the Undenominational Church of the Lord was holiness, and evangelism, especially by the printed word, was emphasized. Mission churches were established in Nigeria, India, and Korea, all of which eventually became autonomous. In the 1970s, there were reportedly fewer than 100 members in three congregations in Placentia, California; Chillicothe, Ohio; and Sheridan, Oregon. During its active period, the church issued a periodical called *The Second Comforter*. The church is now defunct.

TWENTIETH CENTURY HOLINESS

Church of the Gospel

The Church of the Gospel was formed in 1911 in Pittsfield, Massachusetts, by the Rev. and Mrs. C. T. Pike and members of the Advent Christian Church. In 1912 the group incorporated as the Church of God but adopted its present name in 1930 to avoid confusion with other groups. Basic doctrinal perspective was drawn from the Wesleyan holiness tradition. The members practiced baptism by immersion and believed in the imminent Second Coming. During its active period, the church distributed "Narrow Way" tracts by the thousands across the country.

Never a large body, in the 1940s there were only four or five churches. In 1971 there was only a single congregation in Virginia and scattered remnants in New England.

BLACK HOLINESS

Evangelical Church of Christ (Holiness)

The Evangelical Church of Christ (Holiness) was founded in 1947 by Bp. William C. Holman, formerly a minister of the Church of Christ (Holiness). As the break was administrative, the doctrine and practice were the same as that of the parent body. While the church is now defunct, in 1990 there were approximately 500 members in four churches in Washington, D.C.; Los Angeles, California; Omaha, Nebraska; and Denver, Colorado, as well as two missions in Los Angeles.

Sources:

DuPree, Sherry Sherrod. *African American Holiness Pentecostal Charismatic: Annotated Bibliography*. New York: Garland Publishing, 1992.

GLENN GRIFFITH MOVEMENT

Bible Holiness Church

The Bible Holiness Church was a small group that separated from the Bible Methodist Connection of Tennessee. The members included a statement on healing among their beliefs, which otherwise were staunchly conservative in content. While the church is now defunct, in 1968 there were 9 congregations and approximately 200 members in Tennessee and Virginia.

Bible Methodist Connection of Tennessee

Protesting both the centralization of authority and the lack of holiness for years in the Wesleyan Methodist Church was D. P. Denton, editor of the *Evangelist of Truth*, an independent monthly out of Knoxville, Tennessee. On October 17, 1966, Denton led a meeting in Knoxville with representatives of the various factions opposed to the merger of the Wesleyan Methodist Church and the Pilgrim Holiness Church into the Wesleyan Church, a merger finally effected in 1967. At the Knoxville meeting, representatives opposed to merger decided to organize a new "connection," a new association of churches. The new group would continue the use of Wesleyan Methodist *Discipline* (a book of church order), with the exception that each church would be completely autonomous. The new connection would be formed as the merger was consummated. After the negotiations were completed and those who stayed out of the merger settled on the price of buying their property from the new Wesleyan Church, three new bodies emerged: the Bible Methodist Connection of Tennessee, the Bible Holiness Church, and the Bible Methodist Connection of Churches.

From the former Wesleyan Methodist Church, the members of the Tennessee Conference led by Denton became the Bible Methodist Connection of Tennessee. Denton was elected president. The former conference paper, *Tennessee Tidings*, became the new church's organ. A campground outside of Knoxville served the church, and the *Evangelist of Truth* was issued as an independent monthly. In 1987, following the death of his wife, Denton retired and was succeeded as president of the Connection by Earl Newton. Though the church is now presumed defunct, in 1987 there were 45 churches and 110 ministers.

 ## 9. Pentecostal

INTRAFAITH ORGANIZATIONS

United Fellowship Convention of the Original Azusa Street Mission

The United Fellowship Convention of the Original Azusa Street Mission was an association of Holiness Pentecostal churches, all of which traced their lineage back to William J. Seymour (1870–1922) and the beginnings of Pentecostalism in Los Angeles, California, at the Azusa Street Mission. Seymour, formerly a member of the African Methodist Episcopal Church, had entered into the Pentecostal experience in Houston, Texas, under the ministry of Charles Parham, but left to pastor a church in Los Angeles in 1905. Kicked out of his first parish because of his Pentecostal teachings, he began independent work on Azusa Street which became the center of a worldwide movement during the years 1906–1909. Around 1909 Seymour and Charles H. Mason (1866–1961), founder of the Church of God in Christ, held a series of revival meetings in Washington, D.C. Among those converted in the meetings was Charles W. Lowe of Handsom, Virginia. He went on to found the Apostolic Faith Church of God which, over the decades of the twentieth century, grew and became the source of a number of other churches. In 1987 these churches held a gathering to affirm their shared heritage and common belief. Members of the fellowship include Apostolic Faith Church of God, Apostolic Faith Church of God and True Holiness, Apostolic Faith Church of God Live On, Apostolic Faith Churches of God, and Church of Christ Holiness unto the Lord.

Sources:

Payne, Wardell J., ed. *Directory of African American Religious Bodies: A Compendium by the Howard University School of Divinity*. Washington, DC: Howard University Press, 1991.

WHITE TRINITARIAN HOLINESS PENTECOSTALS

Church of God House of Prayer

Harrison W. Poteat joined the Church of God (Cleveland, Tennessee) in its early years and was an overseer in the Northeast for more than 20 years. In 1933, he established churches on Prince Edward Island. In 1939, he broke with the Cleveland headquarters and founded the Church of God House of Prayer. At the time of the split, many of the churches which Poteat had established went with him. A suit was brought by the parent body, which was able to recover occupancy in many of the church properties, and the loss of the property cut deeply into Poteat's support. Some congregations withdrew from the Church of God House of Prayer and became independent. During its active phase, the church's doctrine followed that of the parent body. The church was also affiliated with the Markleysburg Bible Institute in Markleysburg, Pennsylvania. H.W. Poteat remained as Overseer of the Church of God House of Prayer until 1932, when he was succeeded by his sons George Poteat (1952–1955) and Paul E. Poteat (1955–1961). The next general superintendents were Evan Hedglin (1961–1965), Charles McNevin (1965–1991), and Arnold Culleton (b. 1991).

Church of God of the Original Mountain Assembly

In 1939 Steve N. Bryant, longtime leader of the Church of God of the Mountain Assembly, died. He was succeeded by A. J. Long, who led the Church in a reorganization in 1944. However, in 1946, Long was not reelected as moderator. That same year, with his supporters, he left and founded the Church of God of the Original Mountain Assembly. Approximately one-fourth of the membership (15 ministers, eight deacons, and approximately 300 people) established the new church on the original structure of the parent body. The church was headed by a general overseer and a council of 12. The first meeting of the Church of God of the Original Mountain Assembly was held at Williamsburg, Kentucky. The doctrine of the parent body was adopted, from the covenant originally made when it was incorporated in 1917, but articles were added on the need for harmony between pastors and deacons (lay leaders), the subordinate role of women and opposition to snake handling. Though the church is now defunct, in 1967 there were 11 churches and 17 ministers.

Pentecostal Fire-Baptized Holiness Church

The enforcement of discipline in the Pentecostal Holiness Church, now the International Pentecostal Holiness Church, led to a 1918 schism by those who wanted stricter standards concerning dress, amusements, tobacco, and association between the sexes. In the Pentecostal Fire-Baptized Holiness Church, the schismatic church, women's dresses are to be at least mid-calf in length; women are not to bob or wave their hair, or wear jewelry, gold, or costly apparel. Men are not to wear neckties. Attending fairs, swimming pools, and theaters is forbidden. The strict group was joined by a few who never approved the 1911 merger of the Pentecostal Holiness Church and the Fire-Baptized Holiness Church. The pre-1911 name was adopted and the word *Pentecostal* added. The group also was joined in 1921 by the North Carolina Conference of the Pentecostal Free Will Baptist Church.

The church had 1,929 members in 85 churches in 1952. However, the next year more than half the members left to form the Emmanuel Holiness Church. That schism began a period of unabated decline.

The polity was connectional. During the church's active period, a general convention met biennially, with power to legislate. A seven-member board of missions, elected at the general convention, oversaw

work in Haiti and Mexico. A campgrounds and printing establishment were owned at Toccoa Falls, Georgia, where the church headquarters were located.

By 1981 the church had decreased to 298 members; it is now defunct.

Romanian Apostolic Pentecostal Church of God

The Romanian Apostolic Pentecostal Church of God had its origins in the influx of the Pentecostal awakening within the Romanian-American community in the early twentieth century. The first congregation was founded in Detroit, Michigan, in 1922. Eventually more than 40 congregations were part of a loose fellowship. However, in 1981, the majority of these congregations joined the Church of God (Cleveland, Tennessee), and five more joined the Assemblies of God. Some For some time, one congregation of about 50 members in California continued to use the name of the older fellowship.

The Church of God congregations worked together as the Romanian Pentecostal Ministries and published a periodical, *Propovaduitorul*. The Rev. Ioan J. Buia, pastor of the original Detroit congregation (once located in Dearborn Heights, Michigan), conducted a Romanian radio ministry, Maranatha, that was heard over one station in Michigan and one in Kitchner, Ontario. When the church was active, there was also an annual convention of the Romanian Pentecostal congregations. In 1987, it met in Detroit and in 1988, in Portland, Oregon.

Sources:

Buia, Ioan J. *Pine Pe Unde* (Bread on Waves). Detroit, MI: Romanian Pentecostal Church of God, 1987.

Romanian Pentecostal Church of God, 1937–1987, Semicentinar. Detroit, MI: Romanian Pentecostal Church of God, 1987.

WHITE TRINITARIAN PENTECOSTALS

Apostolic Church

The Apostolic Church grew out of the Apostolic Faith Church founded in England in 1908 by W. O. Hutchinson (1864–1928). The Apostolic Faith Church was one of the first Pentecostal bodies in England, and it had roots both in the Azusa Street revival in Los Angeles, and the Welsh Revival led by Evan Roberts (1878–1951) that began in 1904. Distinctive of the Apostolic Faith Church was to give precedence to the Holy Spirit in everything, and an accompanying belief that one of the primary purposes for the exercise of spiritual gifts is to bring a revelation from God, through either prophecy or speaking-in-tongues and the accompanying interpretation. Prophecy could then be used in matters such as the selection of church officers and the making of various decisions. To some people, the practice produced only fanaticism and intolerable excesses. Thus the Rev. Daniel Powell Williams led a group of members out of the Apostolic

Faith Church to found what in 1916 became the Apostolic Church. From its headquarters in Wales, within a decade it had circled the globe, especially in British colonial lands.

The group came to North America in 1924 when a church was founded in Canada. From that original congregation, churches were formed in Pennsylvania and California, which operated as two separate districts. The Canadian churches supported missions in Brazil, Barbados, and Jamaica, but the North American churches remained part of the worldwide church headquartered in Wales.

Sources:

Worsfold, James E. *The Origins of the Apostolic Church in Great Britian*. Wellington, New Zealand: Julian Literature Trust, 1991.

Calvary Pentecostal Church

The Calvary Pentecostal Church was formed in 1931 by a group of Pentecostal ministers in the northwestern United States who were dissatisfied by what they regarded as "a sad departure from the entire dependence on the power of God that had brought the Pentecostal revival." They formed a ministerial fellowship in Olympia, Washington, which was the following year named the Calvary Pentecostal Church. What was originally intended as an interdenominational fellowship became a denomination as churches began to affiliate.

The doctrine was like that of the Assemblies of God. Healing was emphasized. Adult baptism by immersion was practiced, but when parents requested it, infants were dedicated to God (not baptized). The literal Second Coming was awaited. The church was governed in a loose presbyterial system headed by a presbyterial board and the general superintendent. A general meeting of all ministers and local church delegates was held annually. The local churches were governed by the minister, elders, and deacons. The church supported a home for the aged in Seattle and foreign work in Brazil and India.

By the early 1970s, there were 22 churches and 8,000 members; however, internal problems disrupted the church and led to its disbanding.

DELIVERANCE PENTECOSTALS

International Deliverance Churches

Among the deliverance evangelists associated with William M. Branham was W. V. Grant (1913–1983). After several years as an active evangelist, he settled in Dallas because of health problems and became a prolific writer of deliverance literature. He became pastor of the Soul's Harbor Church in Dallas and the leading force in the International Deliverance Churches.

From the Dallas Center, annual conventions were held each summer beginning in 1962. During this period, classes were held for two weeks, and ministers were ordained. The church was also affiliated with the Eagle Bible Institute in Dallas, Texas. Following his death Grant was succeeded by his son, W. V. Grant, Jr. Grant emerged as one of the better known healing ministers among Pentecostals with his national radio and television broadcasts.

During its active period, the church was involved in foreign work in Haiti, Ghana, Nigeria, and India. It also issued the periodical *Where Eagles Fly*.

Sources:

Grant, W. V. *Faith Cometh*. Dallas: The Author, n.d.

———. *The Grace of God in My Life*. Dallas: The Author, 1952.

———. *The Truth About Faith Healers*. Dallas: Faith Clinic, n.d.

Kathryn Kuhlman Foundation

Kathryn Kuhlman (1907–1976) emerged in the 1970s as the most famous and sought-after spiritual healer in the country. Born in Concordia, Missouri, and reared in the Methodist Church, she could not preach for the Methodists because she was a woman, so she became a Baptist and was ordained by the Evangelical Church Alliance. While she pastored a church in Franklin, Pennsylvania, spontaneous healings began to occur. These were coincidental with some personal mystical/psychical experiences of Mrs. Kuhlman, experiences that included a trancelike state in which her consciousness left her body. From that time on, spectacular healing activity was characteristic of her services. She was reported to have cured such illnesses as muscular dystrophy, emphysema, terminal cancer, and blindness. In 1947, she moved to Pittsburgh, where her work was later institutionalized as the Kathryn Kuhlman Foundation. She died in 1976.

Kuhlman was pastor of a congregation in Pittsburgh and once a month held Sunday morning services in Los Angeles. She was a popular speaker for the Full Gospel Businessmen's Fellowship International. In 1970, the Foundation was subsidized by approximately 21 churches in countries around the world. The Foundation operated a vigorous radio and television ministry, a food assistance program, and a college scholarship program.

Sources:

Hosier, Helen Kooiman. *God Can Do It Again*. Englewood Cliffs, NJ: Prentice-Hall, 1969.

———. *Kathryn Kuhlman*. Old Tappan, NJ: Fleming H. Revell, 1971.

Kuhlman, Kathryn. *I Believe in Miracles*. Englewood Cliffs, NJ: Prentice-Hall, 1962.

———. *Nothing Is Impossible with God*. Englewood Cliffs, NJ: Prentice-Hall, 1974.

Spraggett, Allen. *Kathryn Kuhlman, the Woman Who Believes in Miracles*. New York: New American Library, 1970.

APOSTOLIC PENTECOSTALS

God's House of Prayer for All Nations

God's House of Prayer for All Nations Inc. was founded in 1964 in Peoria, Illinois, by Bishop Tommie Lawrence, formerly of the Church of God in Christ. The group's doctrine was "oneness" Pentecostal, identifying Jesus with the Father, and the polity was strongly episcopal. Great stress was placed on healing as one of the signs of the spirit, and the group maintained close fellowship with the churches of the Miracle Revival Fellowship founded by Asa Alonzo Allen (1911–1970).

United Church of Jesus Christ

The United Church of Jesus Christ withdrew from the Church of Jesus Christ (Kingsport) in 1948. The occasion for the split was a controversy over baptism. The United Church believed that not only should baptism be in the name of Jesus Christ, but that the words should be said over the candidate while the person is under the water. In referring to ministers, the word *bishop* was not used, but the term *reverend* was employed. Also, the church mixed water and wine (not grape juice) in the Lord's Supper. Otherwise, the church followed the belief and practice of the parent body. The church was under the leadership of a chairman, elected at its annual convention. In the 1980s the church reported approximately 1,250 members, 100 ministers, and 25 congregations.

BLACK TRINITARIAN PENTECOSTALS

Azusa Street Apostolic Faith Mission of Los Angeles

The Pentecostal movement, begun in Topeka, Kansas, under the leadership of Charles Parham (1873–1959), was brought to the West Coast by William J. Seymour (1870–1922), a black holiness minister and former member of the Church of God (Anderson, Indiana). He established work in a renovated building on Azusa Street in Los Angeles, California, from which the movement would spread across the North American continent and into many foreign lands between 1906 and 1909. Before the first year was out, however, Parham charged Seymour with distorting the teachings and practices of the movement and the two broke. Seymour reorganized the mission under his sole leadership.

During the next few years, Seymour personally spread the movement across the nation, especially in black communities. On trips to the East, his evangelistic activities led to the founding of a number of congregations that associated with the Los Angeles mission. Others who visited Azusa Street took the revival back home with them. Then, in the midst of the spreading movement, several events led the initially interracial work to split along racial lines. In 1907 Florence L. Crawford took the mailing list of the mission's newspaper with her to Oregon, where she

established an independent organization, the Apostolic Faith Mission of Portland, Oregon, Inc. In 1909 Seymour broke with William H. Durham over the issue of sanctification, and most of the remaining white members left.

Seymour had inherited a Wesleyan holiness approach to Pentecostalism. He taught a succession of three major spiritual experiences for the believer: justification, sanctification, and baptism in the Holy Spirit. The first brought the new believer into a relationship with God. The second infused perfection in love, while the third brought the indwelling of the Holy Spirit. This three-experience approach was denied by Durham, who taught that the baptism of the Holy Spirit was for any believer and that holiness of life came gradually through Christian living.

Seymour led the congregation in Los Angeles and the several affiliated congregations around the country. The revival quickly burst beyond his Azusa Street Mission. People who received the baptism of the Holy Spirit there returned to their homes to found numerous new churches never organizationally tied to Azusa Street. Seymour continued to lead the Los Angeles congregation for the rest of his life, but few looked to him for leadership around the United States, and his organization folded soon after his death in 1922.

Sources:

The Doctrine and Discipline of the Azusa Street Apostolic Faith Mission of Los Angeles. Los Angeles: W. J. Seymour, 1915.

Lovett, Leonard. "Black Origins of the Pentecostal Movement." In *Aspects of Pentecostal Charismatic Origins*. Edited by Vinson Synan, 123–213. Plainfield, NJ: Logos International, 1975.

Nelson, Douglas J. *For Such a Time As This: The Story of Bishop William J. Seymour and the Azusa Street Revival: A Search for Pentecostal/Charismatic Roots*. Ph.D. diss., University of Birmingham, England, 1981.

Tinney, James S. "Black Origins of the Pentecostal Movement." *Christianity Today* 16 (October 8, 1971): 4–6.

Free Church of God in Christ

The Free Church of God in Christ dates from 1915 when J. H. Morris, a former pastor in the National Baptist Convention of the USA, and a group of members of his church experienced the baptism of the Holy Spirit and spoke in tongues. The group, mostly members of Morris's family, founded a Pentecostal group that they called the Church of God in Christ. They chose as their leader the founder's son, E. J. Morris, who believed he was "selected" for the role. In 1921 the group united with the larger body led by Bishop Charles H. Mason, which had the same name. The union lasted for only four years, and Morris's group adopted its present name when it again became independent in 1925. It has the same doctrine and polity as the Mason body. By the late 1940s the church had 20 congregations. No direct contact has been made with the church since then, and it is thought to be defunct.

Mt. Zion Spiritual Temple

King Louis H. Narcisse (1921–1989), founder of Mt. Zion Spiritual Church, was one of the most colorful of the Spiritual Church leaders. Baptized in Mt. Zion Baptist Church, his singing abilities made him a choir soloist and the winner of five radio auditions. During World War II he moved to San Francisco, California, and found an $85-a-week job as an electrical worker in a shipyard. He also spent some time as a bank janitor, living in the Hunter housing project in South San Francisco.

In 1945 Narcisse had a vision that impelled him to found the Mt. Zion Spiritual Temple, which began as a simple prayer meeting among a handful of people. It soon grew to a large church on 14th Street in Oakland, through a combination of his personal charisma and the success of his radio program, *Moments of Meditation*, which developed a national audience of as many as 1.5 million. He further increased his visibility with a number of single records, such as "Without the Lord" and "Jesus, I Can't Forget You," cut for such labels as Jaxyson, Modern, Hollywood, Music City, Veltone, and Peacock. His signature theme song and church motto was "It's Nice to Be Nice."

King Narcisse maintained his "international headquarters" in Oakland, California, and his "East Coast headquarters" in Detroit, Michigan. In addition to these two temples, the association had seven other congregations, including a second temple in Detroit and temples in Sacramento and Richmond, California; Houston, Texas; Orlando, Florida; New York City; and Washington, D.C.

On March 9 each year, he held a mass prayer meeting in Oakland Park with city officials and citizens, and the mayor of Oakland proclaimed it Prayer Day. In September 1955 a coronation ceremony was performed at the municipal auditorium by the Rt. Rev. Frank Rancifer in which he was officially given the title "His Grace, the King of Spiritual Church of the West Coast."

For those occasions when King Narcisse could not be with his flock at the King Narcisse Michigan State Memorial Temple, a large picture of "His Grace" faced the congregation, reminding its members of their spiritual leader. A sign below the picture read as follows:

GOD IS GREAT AND GREATLY TO BE PRAISED IN THE SOVEREIGN STATE OF MICHIGAN IN THE KING OF "HIS GRACE KING" LOUIS H. NARCISSE, DD, WHERE "IT'S NICE TO BE NICE, AND REAL NICE TO LET OTHERS KNOW THAT WE ARE NICE."

Part of his appeal was his flamboyant style; he was literally treated as royalty. He wore a crown, diamond rings, and other jewels, and wherever he went in his Rolls-Royce, a red carpet was rolled out in front. He lived in a 24-room palace in Oakland's Piedmont district, known as "The Light on the Hill," with numerous personal attendants. He often received followers in a "throne room," with a copy of federal income tax regulations sitting nearby. Narcisse explained that all the finery was not just for himself but was a means of attracting those who were not yet ready for the purely spiritual. It also served as a symbol of the earthly achievements and prizes to which he called his followers. His church was also known for its many charity functions in the community.

Sources:

Baer, Hans A. *The Black Spiritual Movement: A Religious Response to Racism*. Knoxville, TN: University of Tennessee Press, 1984.

"His Grace King: The West Coast's Most Colorful Religious Leader." *Sepia* 9 (February 1961): 4247.

Robinson, Louie. "The Kingdom of King Narcisse." *Ebony* 18 (July 1963): 112–118.

Sought Out Church of God in Christ

The Sought Out Church of God in Christ and Spiritual House of Prayer Inc. was founded in 1947 by Mother Mozella Cook. Mother Cook was converted in a service led by her physical mother, an ecstatic person who was once hauled into court to be examined for lunacy because of her mystical states. Mother Cook's mother seemed to go into trances and was "absent from this world while she talked with God." Mother Cook moved to Pittsburgh, Pennsylvania, and there became a member of the Church of God in Christ founded by Charles H. Mason. She left it to found her own church in Brunswick, Georgia, after feeling a divine call. In 1949 the church had four congregations and 60 members.

True Fellowship Pentecostal Church of God of America

The True Fellowship Pentecostal Church of God of America was formed in 1964 by the secession of the Rev. Charles E. Waters Sr., a presiding elder in the Alpha and Omega Pentecostal Church of God of America Inc. Doctrine was like that of the Church of God in Christ, differing only in the acceptance of women into the ministry as pastors and elders. Bishop Waters and his wife operated a mission for those in need in Baltimore.

LATTER RAIN PENTECOSTALS

Community Chapel and Bible Training Center

Community Chapel and Bible Training Center grew out of the Charismatic movement of the late 1960s. Some individuals with a variety of denominational backgrounds began to meet in the home of the Pentecostal minister Donald Lee Barnett for Bible study. The study led to the formation of a church in 1967. Meeting at first in members' homes, the group outgrew available facilities and in 1969 began construction of a church building. At about the same time, a Bible college was begun. Within a decade the church facility, expanded to seat over a thousand, had become inadequate, and in 1979 a new sanctuary with seating for 2,200 was completed. Enrollment in the Bible college grew to approximately 900. The center had a lengthy statement of faith that affirmed belief in the authority and inerrancy of the Bible; God as Father and Creator; Jesus Christ as fully God and fully human; the Holy Spirit; the necessity of repentance; water baptism by immersion for the remission of sins; the Lord's Supper as a memorial feast; strict church order led by pastors, elders, and deacons; tithing; divine healing for the body; the gifts of the Holy Spirit; and a premillennial eschatology. There was no clear affirmation of the Trinity.

The center was led by the pastor, who had complete authority in spiritual matters. Administratively the center was led by a four-member board of senior elders. More than 125 paid staff worked at the center, which included the college, a Christian school (kindergarten through high school), a music program, recording studios, and a number of evangelical and social outreach ministries in the greater Seattle area. Members were encouraged to participate in one or more of the 150 active ministries. Community Chapel Publications published a number of booklets by Barnett and a periodical titled *Balance*; it also produced a set of cassette tapes reflecting the center's music program.

During the early 1980s Community Chapel faced a variety of widely publicized charges from former members. These included accusations that Barnett asked members to shun the businesses of former members, that former longtime members suffered mental problems related to their association with the church and its understanding of demon possessions, and that marriage relations were disrupted because of the encouragement of close "spiritual connections" (which did not include any sexual liaison) between men and women apart from their spouses. The latter charge was directly related to the church practice of dancing with one's spiritual connection during church services. Some members of the center staunchly defended the pastors and church leaders from such charges and from additional charges by leaders from other churches that the group was a "cult." Several lawsuits ensued, and Barnett was expelled by the remaining elders in 1988. The church and college facilities were eventually sold to the State of Washington for use as its Criminal Justice Training Center, while Barnett went on to found, with several hundred of his followers, the Church of Agape in Renton, Washington.

Independent Assemblies of God International

Among the many independent Pentecostal churches that did not join the Assemblies of God in 1914 were congregations consisting primarily of Scandinavian immigrants, converts of the Scandinavian Pentecostal movement. Petrus Lewi Johansson of Stockholm, Sweden, and Thomas Ball Barrett of Oslo, Norway, were the dominant figures in the Scandinavian Pentecostal movement. The Scandinavians were extreme congregationalists and believed that all discipline, even of ministers, should be vested in the local level.

In the United States, extreme congregationalism worked for a while, but gradually loose federations began to develop. In 1918 a Scandinavian Assemblies of God in the United States, Canada and Other Lands was formed in the northwestern states. In St. Paul, Minnesota, in 1922, a fellowship of independent churches was formed. A third group, the Scandinavian Independent Assemblies of God, was formed around Pastor B. M. Johnson, who had founded the Lakeview Gospel Church in Chicago in 1911, and A. A. Holmgren, who published the *Scanningens Vittne*, a periodical for Scandinavian Pentecostals. In 1935 the latter group dissolved its corporation, and the three groups united to form the Independent Assemblies of God. They began to Americanize and to move beyond their ethnic exclusiveness.

In 1947–1948 the Independent Assemblies of God divided over participation in the Latter Rain movement, a revival that swept western Canada and became known for extreme doctrine and practices in some phases. The words "Latter Rain" refer to the end of the world when God will pour out his Spirit upon all people. One group accepted the revival as the present movement of God, as God's deliverance promised in the Bible. This group, under the leadership of A. W. Rasmussen, became the Independent Assemblies of God International. It published a periodical, *The Mantle*, and supported missions in 17 countries around the world.

Sources:

Rasmussen, A. W. *The Last Chapter*. Monroeville, PA: Whitaker House, 1973.

Maranatha Christian Churches

Maranatha Christian Churches began in 1972 as a campus ministry. It founders were Bob Weiner, a former youth pastor for the Assemblies of God, and his wife, Rose Weiner. Bob Weiner had dropped out of Trinity College, the school of the Evangelical Free Church at Deerfield, Illinois, and joined the U.S. Air Force. However, a chance encounter with Albie Pearson, a former baseball player turned evangelist-pastor, led to his receiving the baptism of the Holy Spirit. Weiner finished his commitment to the Air Force and soon became involved with a coffeehouse

ministry. With Bob Cording he formed Sound Mind Inc. to evangelize youth and in 1971 began to tour college campuses as an evangelist. He eventually settled at the Christian Life Center in Long Beach, California. In 1972 he moved to Paducah, Kentucky (where his wife's father was a minister in the United Methodist Church), and began a campus ministry at Murray State University.

As campus minister, Weiner sought to convert students and train them in the fundamentals of the Christian faith. While focusing on Murray State, he continued to travel as an evangelist and develop other ministries. By the end of the decade 30 Maranatha Campus Ministries had been established. As national ministries grew and members finished their college careers, Maranatha Campus Ministries became part of the larger work, which was named Maranatha Christian Churches, based in Gainesville, Florida.

The doctrine and practice of Maranatha followed the common affirmations of Protestant Christianity and Pentecostalism but developed a few distinctives of practice. Weiner emphasized a "scriptural pattern" for church organization based upon Ephesians 4:11 and attempted to build each center as a strong fellowship and training ground for practical discipleship. In earlier years each center had a dorm in which converts could live while attending college, but that practice ceased. General meetings of the fellowship were held weekly, and most members also participated in small group fellowships. Prophecy was an important practice in Maranatha and was seen as ongoing confirmation of God's present activity in the church.

Maranatha's work was focused on the campus ministry, and all the congregations were adjacent to a college or university. The Weiners wrote a series of books published by Maranatha Publications, which were used as textbooks in the discipleship training work; they also published a periodical, *The Forerunner*. Maranatha Leadership Training School, often featuring a variety of charismatic leaders not otherwise associated with Maranatha, offered more advanced training for people on a national basis.

There was a world leadership conference every two years. In 1985 Maranatha began a satellite TV network show as a televised prayer meeting in which 60 churches, tied together for the broadcast, prayed for specific requests phoned in by viewers.

During the early 1980s Maranatha became the focus of a variety of accusations centered around its intense program for training new members. Many of these accusations proved unfounded, and in other cases program adjustments were made. A program of parent-student contact was broadly implemented in order to reduce the problems that had arisen because of lack of knowledge by parents of Maranatha and the life shared by new members, most of whom were students. By 1988 the churches reported 5,000 members, 150 churches (campus outreach locations), and 300 ministers in the United States, with one Canadian cen-

ter, work in 17 foreign countries, and 7,000 members worldwide. Nevertheless, in November 1989 the Maranantha board decided to disband the organization as a federation of churches, citing its member churches' wishes for a less denominational-style structure. Many of these churches continued their work independently or with new affiliations.

Sources:

Andrews, Sherry. "Maranatha Ministries." *Charisma* 7, no. 9 (May 1982).

Frame, Randy. "Maranatha Disbands as a Federation of Churches." *Christianity Today* (March 19, 1990).

Weiner, Bob, and Rose Weiner. *Bible Studies for a Firm Foundation*. Gaineville, FL: Maranatha Publications, 1980.

————. *Bible Studies for the Life of Excellence*. Gainesville, FL: Maranatha Publications, 1981.

————. *Bible Studies for the Lovers of God*. Gainesville, FL: Maranatha Publications, 1980.

OTHER PENTECOSTALS

Church of Jesus and Watch Mission

The Church of Jesus and Watch Mission was a small Pentecostal church founded in the home of Bp. George A. Luetjen in Long Island City, New York. Luetjen had been converted, according to his own account, in 1910 following a period of depression and guilt brought on by some family problems. One day in December of that year, while walking the streets of New York smoking a cigar, he tossed his cigar away, found his new relationship to God, and received the baptism of the Holy Spirit.

Luetjen began preaching some 12 years later, and by the mid-1940s his mission reported ministers in eight states and Canada. He published a tract recounting his conversion and a periodical, *Prophetic Age*. Closely associated with the group was the Mizpah Mission of Taft, Florida, and the Israel Gospel Church, also of Long Island City.

In recent years no sign of the small mission has been found and it is presumed defunct.

Sources:

Clark, Elmer T. *The Small Sects of America*. Nashville, TN: Abingdon Press, 1949.

Gospel Assemblies (Jolly)

In 1952 Elder Tom M. Jolly became pastor of the Gospel Assemblies (Sowders) congregation in St. Louis, Missouri, succeeding Dudley Frazier. In 1965 Jolly led supporters to separate from the older, larger Gospel Assemblies group. Under his leadership there was a marked tendency to centralize congregations in or near major urban areas, followed by centralization of funds in preparation for the purchase of land upon which the congregations could settle away from the evil influences of contemporary cities. Twice yearly, members gathered for pastoral conferences, fellowship meetings, and youth rallies. Doctrine followed that of the parent body. The number of congregations (originally 12) more than doubled in the first five years: in 1970 there were approximately 30 congregations and 4,000 members.

Grace Gospel Evangelistic Association International Inc.

The Grace Gospel Evangelistic Association International Inc. was formed in the mid-1930s by Pentecostals of a Calvinist (predestinarian) theological background who rejected the Arminian (free will) theology of the main body of Pentecostals. The association was organized congregationally. By the early 1970s it had approximately 70 ministers and missionaries, and foreign congregations could be found in Canada, Jamaica, Colombia, Formosa, Japan, and India. A periodical, *Grace Evangel*, was published. In the late 1980s, however, the association disbanded and many of the formerly affiliated congregations merged into other Pentecostal groups or became independent churches.

Jesus People Church

The Jesus People Church (JPC) of Minneapolis, Minnesota, grew out of a "discipleship ministry" led by Dennis Worre, Roger Vann, and four other young men who created a Christian home in order to become better established in the Christian life. Beginning in 1969, Worre and Vann led weekly Bible study meetings for what became formally known as Disciple Homes, one for men and one for women. As the ministry grew, a church building was purchased for Sunday services and, with fifty charter members, Jesus People Church was established. The church grew steadily through the 1970s, and by the early 1980s two Sunday services, now being held at the large State Theatre in downtown Minneapolis, were required to serve the congregation. Over 7,000 received the monthly bulletin, and a number of smaller churches began in the Minneapolis–St. Paul area.

The Jesus People Church was Pentecostal in belief. Its statement of faith affirmed belief in the Bible as infallible and authoritative; the Trinity; the Deity of Christ; healing from the redemptive work of Christ on the cross; the present-day reality of the baptism of the Holy Spirit as recorded in Acts 2; and the Resurrection.

The Jesus People Church created a variety of outreach programs. Worre, a former actor, organized the Academy of Christian Theatre Sciences, which put on periodic professional drama for the public. Jesus People Institute was a lay educational program conducted through the week. A radio show, *Today's Walk in the Spirit*, aired over several area stations. The church owned a retreat center, Shepherd's Inn, located ninety miles north of Minneapolis, and operated Hesed and Fishnet, ministries to high school and junior high students. Foreign missionaries were supported in Canada, Germany, Haiti, Mexico, the Philippines, South Africa, and Thailand. There was also

a missionary in Hawaii and a domestic mission among Cambodian refugees.

In the early 1980s the JPC's pastors became the center of a scandal involving improper sexual activity. Dennis Worre himself admitted to several indiscretions with women (which did not include adultery), and he was asked to step aside from his leadership role, though he soon returned to active duty as senior pastor. The State Theatre was sold in 1985, and the remaining Minneapolis JPC leaders and members went on to form new churches and congregations in the area. By 2007 Dennis Worre had become senior pastor of a "new" Jesus People Church in Rogers, Minnesota.

Pentecostal Fellowship of Churches and Ministers of Canada

The Pentecostal Fellowship of Churches and Ministers of Canada was founded in 1988 as YES International Ministries by Mark Woodley as a corporate home for his music and evangelism. Associates in other independent ministries soon asked to affiliate with the corporation, including Rusty Crozier, Geoff Smith, and Marie Smith of Project Russia and Paul Sharrow of Head East. The name Pentecostal Fellowship was assumed in the late 1990s. In subsequent years, Fear of God (an alternative Christian band) and Catacombs (a young adult ministry in Hamilton, Ontario) also affiliated.

The fellowship was a Trinitarian Pentecostal organization whose beliefs included the infallibility of the Bible, affirmation of the Triune God, baptism of the Holy Spirit with the accompanying sign of speaking in tongues, and divine healing. It also attempted to implement the fivefold ministry of Ephesians 4:11 with apostles, prophets, pastors, evangelists, and teachers.

The fellowship offered ordination to independent Pentecostal ministers in Canada and charters for churches and ministries. Ministerial credentials were offered for licensed ministers and for ordained ministers who had demonstrated their abilities over a period of time. A credentials committee considered and approved the issuance of all licenses.

Woodley, the fellowship's president and also pastor of Shiloh Pentecostal Church in Hamilton, Ontario, died in 2006. With the loss of his leadership, the fellowship's board disbanded the organization in September 2007.

Sources:

Pentecostal Fellowship of Churches and Ministers of Canada Inc.

www.bigchurch.cc/pfchurches/ordained.html.

10. European Free-Church

QUAKERS (FRIENDS)

The Rogerenes

The Rogerenes were a small religious group that began as Baptists but were strongly influenced by members of the Society of Friends. They were originally led by John Rogers (1648?–1721). James Rogers, John's father, had settled in New London, Connecticut, in 1656 and soon became one of the wealthiest men in the colony. Then in 1674 John and his wife, Elizabeth, withdrew from the Congregational Church and joined the Seventh-Day Baptist Church in Newport, Connecticut. Soon afterward, Elizabeth's father persuaded her to leave her husband and return home, a separation that became permanent. But other members of the family joined John, and they began a Baptist congregation in New London. John Rogers became the pastor. He actively attacked the state-supported Congregational Church, especially its support of infant baptism and the forced payment of church taxes. As Rogers's ideas became more radical, the congregation also broke its ties to the Baptists in Newport around 1677. One of the radicalizing influences was the meetings John and members of the congregation had held with William Edmundson, a Quaker from Ireland visiting America, in 1675. Out of these discussions, the Rogerenes, as they were soon to be known, dropped the Sabbatarian beliefs. But though they worshipped on Sunday, they felt that all days were alike. Rogers especially attacked idolatry, which for him included many of the practices of the Congregational Church, such as a salaried ministry and the use of elaborate titles of respect. The group adopted plain clothes, refused to use oaths, and opposed war and violence. Rogers became a shoemaker as a means of demonstrating the belief that ministers should make their own living. They also opposed contemporary medical practice, replacing it with clean living, good nursing, homemade remedies, and prayer. The group continued to disagree with the Quakers on the issue of sacraments. They baptized new members and celebrated the Lord's Supper annually.

Almost from the beginning the group was persecuted, and John Rogers seems to have spent as much as one-third of his life in jail for his religious beliefs. It should be noted that the group did little to decrease the tension with the state church. Members refused to pay church taxes. They traveled on Sunday to attend meetings in defiance of state regulations. They periodically staged demonstrations against idolatrous practices. For example, they attended the Congregational services and brought work with them. They interrupted and contradicted the minister. Gordon Saltonstall, the Congregational minister in New

London and later governor of Connecticut, led the persecution until his death in 1724. A final period of intense persecution occurred in the mid-1760s.

John Rogers was succeeded in leadership of the group by his son John Rogers, Jr. (d. 1853), and he by John Walterhouse, John Bolles, Samuel Whipple, and Jonathan Whipple (1794–1877). Bolles was an early abolitionist who had freed his slaves in the 1720s. In 1735 a group of Rogerenes moved to Morris County, New Jersey, and established a colony. Three years later they moved to Monmouth County, New Jersey, near present-day Ocean City. The settlement died out by the end of the century. During the 1740s land was purchased near Groton and Mystic, Connecticut, and over a generation the group migrated westward. Its prosperity in spite of difficulties during the Revolution and the War of 1812 is shown by the erection of a large new meetinghouse in 1815 and an even larger one in the post–Civil War era.

The twentieth century saw the decline of the church. Some families had moved west before the turn of the century, and others drifted to other churches. By the 1940s only a small group was left in Mystic and a smaller group in California. A generation later, some descendants of former Rogerene families still identified themselves with the group, but it seems to have ceased to exist as a church body.

Sources:

Brinton, Ellen Starr. "The Rogerenes." *New England Quarterly* (March 16, 1943): 3–19.

Randolph, Corliss Fitz. "The Rogerenes." In *Seventh Day Baptists in Europe and America*. Plainfield, NJ: Seventh Day Baptist General Conference, 1910.

 11. Baptist

CALVINIST MISSIONARY BAPTISTS

Christian Unity Baptist Association

The Christian Unity Baptist Association traced its beginnings to 1901, when the Mountain Union Regular Association passed a resolution dropping from membership all churches that practiced open communion. Those who opposed the action walked out and for many years functioned as independent congregations. Over the years, only two ministers, F. L. Sturgill and Eli Graham, and three churches survived. In 1932 these churches organized as the Macedonia Baptist Association. In 1935 they were joined by other churches that had left the Mountain Union Regular Association, and the Christian Unity Baptist Association was organized.

Doctrinally, a mild Calvinism prevailed. The article on the security of the believer was amended to read that all who are saved and endure to the end shall be saved. Foot washing and open communion were practiced. The polity was congregational, and the association acted in an advisory role.

Independent Baptist Church of America

The Independent Baptist Church of America dates to the 1870s, when Swedish Free Baptists emigrated to the United States and settled in the Midwest. In 1893 an annual conference began to be held under the name Swedish Independent Baptist Church, later changed to Scandinavian Independent Baptist Denomination of America. In 1912 a split occurred when part of the group incorporated. The incorporated group called itself the Scandinavian Independent Baptist Denomination in the United States of America. The unincorporated group continued as the Scandinavian Free Baptist Society of the United States of America. In 1927 the two groups reunited at a conference in Garden Valley, Wisconsin, and adopted the name Independent Baptist Church of America.

Doctrinally the churches were pietistic and evangelical. Like the Six-Principle Baptists, they practiced the laying on of hands at the time a member was received into the church. Members believed in the authority of and obedience to the civil government in all of its demands except those contrary to the Word of God, such as participation in war. The church had two congregations and 70 members in 1965 (down from 13 congregations in 1926) and within the next few years reportedly ceased to exist.

Orthodox Baptists

The Orthodox Baptists grew out of the most conservative fundamentalist element of the Southern Baptist Convention in the 1940s. The movement was founded by W. Lee Rector (1883–1945), a former professor at Baylor University who in 1931 had become pastor of the First Baptist Church of Ardmore, Oklahoma. In the early 1940s he resigned from the Southern Baptist Convention and organized the first Orthodox Baptist Church in Ardmore, and he was soon joined by several like-minded ministers and congregations. In 1944 he opened the Orthodox Bible Institute to train ministers. The church remained staunchly fundamentalist, and members refrained from association with apostasy, liberalism, neo-evangelicalism, and compromise on doctrinal matters.

In the 1960s the Orthodox Bible Institute closed and a new Orthodox Baptist College, located in Dallas, Texas (now the Independent Baptist College), succeeded it. The Texas school was founded by James L. Higgs, then pastor of Trinity Baptist Temple. In the early 1970s there were approximately 300 congregations associated with the Orthodox Baptists.

Sources:

Dollar, George W. *A History of Fundamentalism in America*. Greenville, SC: Bob Jones University Press, 1973.

 12. Independent Fundamentalist

FUNDAMENTALISTS AND EVANGELICAL CHURCHES

Association of Torah-Observant Messianics

The Association of Torah-Observant Messianics was formed 1994 to provide a home for Messianic Jews and non-Jews to live a life in observation of the Torah (i.e., the biblical law), which association members believed was given by the Creator as a perfect standard for his people. While it is clear from the Scriptures that salvation is an undeserved and unearned gift from the Creator through his grace, and that human works and effort cannot earn salvation, the Scriptures also teach that the Creator is a righteous and just deity who never changes.

Taking its cue from Matthew 5:17–19, the association was based on the belief that the Torah as given to the Jewish people has never been abolished and thus stands as a true test of humanity's love for Him. Thus, without judging other believers, the association provided a fellowship link for observant Messianic believers.

The association was founded by Yeshayahu Heiliczer, who became a popular teacher within the Messianic Jewish community through the 1990s. Along with his wife, he headed a small congregation, Knesset HaShuvim, in Bowie, Maryland. His continued studies of the Jewish roots of Christianity, however, led him to conclude that the New Testament was not reliable history and that Jesus/Yeshua was not the promised Jewish Messiah. These conclusions led him to the belief that the Torah and normative Judaism is the only truth and that the Hebrew Bible is the Creator's only guidebook for humanity. He subsequently left Knesset HaShuvim and disbanded the Association of Torah-Observant Messianics. In 2005 he and his wife emigrated to Israel and have since resided in Jerusalem.

Ecumenical Fellowship of Ministers International

The Ecumenical Fellowship of Ministers International was an Evangelical association of churches, ministers, and laypeople founded in 1996 by Bps. Joe Huff, Harold Brinkley, and Gordon Barrett. The fellowship provided ordination for those seeking to become ministers and charters for congregations.

The fellowship had a very basic statement of faith affirming "the Bible as God's written revelation that is verbally inspired, authoritative, and without error in the original manuscripts; one God eternally existent in three persons: Father, Son, Holy Spirit; the deity of Jesus Christ, His virgin birth, sinless life, miracles, death on the cross to provide for our redemption, bodily resurrection and ascension into heaven, present ministry of intercession for us, and His return to earth in power and glory." Further, "Regeneration by the Holy Spirit is essential for salvation of the lost, and results in the new birth whereby sinful man becomes a new and different person, and humans as created in the image of God, but because of sin, were alienated from God. That alienation can be removed only by accepting through faith alone God's gift of salvation that was made possible by Christ's death."

The fellowship was headed by an executive council that included but was not limited to its bishops. It sponsored an annual convention.

Evangelical Ministers and Churches International Inc.

Evangelical Ministers and Churches International Inc. was formed in 1950 by a group of independent ministers who were evangelical and fundamentalist in belief. Government was congregational, but the fellowship was headed by an executive board elected by the national convention. The group founded a college, Colorado Bible College and Seminary, and published the *EMCI Herald*. In the 1970s there were approximately 150 affiliated ministers, and missions were conducted in South Korea, Portugal, and Spain.

International Ministerial Federation Inc.

The International Ministerial Federation was founded in 1930 by Dr. J. Kellog and Dr. W. E. Opie as a fellowship of independent ministers. Its purpose was to give "ministerial status and authorization to whoever wants it without affiliating with a specific denomination." There was a strong antidenominational bias. Members were to be "Evangelical believers in the basic Christian concepts," but there was no statement of doctrine by which that concept could be made specific. Dr. Sidney Cornell of St. Petersburg, Florida, served as the federation's president and Dr. Opie, of Fresno, California, as its executive director. In 1968 there were more than 400 members, all ministers.

GRACE GOSPEL MOVEMENT

Last Day Messenger Assemblies

Nels Thompson, born in Denmark, immigrated to the United States in the early 1900s and in 1912 was converted in a meeting of the Plymouth Brethren (Grant Brethren) under the leadership of Harry A. Ironside (1876–1951), later pastor of Moody Church. Thompson became an evangelist, but a conflict arose with the Brethren over the control of his evangelical activity. He also accepted the Grace Gospel position and dropped water baptism (as of the Jewish dispensation). He founded an assembly in Oakland, California, and soon others were formed.

Gospel Tract Distributors was founded as an independent, but associated, publishing concern and began publishing *Outside the Camp* (later titled *Last Day Messenger*) as a nondenominational dispensational periodical. Each issue carried a seven-point

statement of belief in the verbal inspiration of the Bible, the Trinity and the deity of Christ, total depravity, redemption by grace, the security of the believer, the personality and punishment of Satan, and the pretribulation Second Coming. The group did not practice baptism and was opposed to celebrating Christmas and Easter. Headquarters for Gospel Tract Distributors were in Portland, Oregon. The assemblies were disbanded in the mid-1990s.

OTHER BIBLE STUDENTS

Witness and Testimony Literature Trust and Related Centers

Theodore Austin-Sparks (1888–1971), a former member of the Baptist Church, left to found an independent meeting place in the Honor Oak suburb of London, England, for Christians who wished to fellowship together around the Lord Jesus Christ and not men. That ministry was conceived to be apart from and above traditional denominational barriers. The nondenominational approach manifested the influence of the Plymouth Brethren. Austin-Sparks was also influenced by Jessie Penn-Lewis (1861–1927), a popular speaker and writer on the "deeper Christian life." The group that gathered under Austin-Sparks's ministry became known as the Honor Oak Christian Fellowship. The fellowship's distinctive emphasis, partially derived from Penn-Lewis, was upon the subjective work of the Cross in the Christian's life, an emphasis that many evangelical Christians saw as distracting from the primary work of witnessing to the faith. In 1923 Austin-Sparks began the publication of a periodical, *A Witness and a Testimony*, and later established the Witness and Testimony Literature Trust. The magazine was discontinued in 1971. Over the years he published a number of books and pamphlets, most compiled from his spoken ministry. In 1939–1940 he discovered his close agreement with Watchman Nee (1903–1972), Chinese founder of an evangelical movement popularly called the Little Flock or the Local Church. Nee spent 18 months with Austin-Sparks while the first edition of Nee's most important books, *The Normal Christian Life* and *Concerning Our Mission* (reissued as *The Normal Christian Church Life*), were translated with the assistance of the fellowship's members. While Austin-Sparks's ministry was never merged into that of Watchman Nee, the groups remained on cordial terms for many years. Austin-Sparks shared many of Nee's emphases, such as those of the twofold expression of the church (local and universal) and the importance of the local assembly, which are reflected in his writings. However, Austin-Sparks saw himself as part of an even more loosely organized movement of God that had many centers of like-minded Christians. Over the years such centers were tied together filially and distinguished by their circulation of the literature of an informally "approved" set of teachers. When in England, these teachers would speak at the Honor

Oak Centre, and Austin-Sparks would speak at their centers when traveling around the world, but no direct responsibility was shared for the separate ministries. The ministries also circulated the literature produced by Austin-Sparks and other associated writers. Some of these teachers, such as Bakht Singh, the popular Indian leader, were associated with Watchman Nee but not with Witness Lee, the recognized leader of the largest segment of Nee's movement.

Austin-Sparks's materials began to reach America soon after the fellowship was organized, and he made his first visit to the United States in 1925. Among the early centers of his support was Hephzibah House in New York City and the Almquist Christian Book Nook in Northfield, Minnesota, which distributed Austin-Sparks literature. By the 1960s the trust regularly recommended three American centers that distributed its literature: MORE (Mail Ordering Religious Education), the Westmoreland Chapel in Los Angeles, California, and Convocation Literature Sales in Norfolk, Virginia. MORE was headed by Dean Baker of Indianapolis, Indiana. It absorbed the Northfield work as well as a periodical, *The Ultimates*, edited by DeVern Fromke, an early friend and supporter of Austin-Sparks. MORE was supported by the Sure Foundation. Westmoreland Chapel was an independent congregation in Los Angeles, pastored for a decade by C. J. B. Harrison, formerly of the Honor Oak Centre. Convocation Literature Sales (later Testimony Book Ministry) was headed by Ernest L. Chase, who also organized the Atlantic States Christian Convocation, held annually from 1966 to 1972 at Camp Wabanna in Mayo, Maryland. The Testimony Book Ministry reprinted some 40 Austin-Sparks titles. More loosely affiliated was the Rev. John Myers and Voice Christian Publications of Northridge, California. During the 1960s and 1970s Myers edited a quarterly, *Voice in the Wilderness*. The *Voice* (after 1970, *Recovery*) promoted the views of both Nee and Austin-Sparks but was not limited to supporting them.

Although Austin-Sparks was in fellowship with Nee for years, he did not follow Nee's ideas completely on the local church. He broke off relations with Witness Lee's followers in 1958. In later years literature was reprinted primarily by Christian Fellowship Publishers of Richmond, Virginia. Testimony Book Ministry also distributed the books of Bakht Singh. In England, a longtime associate of Austin-Sparks, Harry Foster, published the periodical *Toward the Mark* until 1989.

Those congregations and centers most closely associated with Honor Oak and the Witness and Testimony Literature Trust were distinguished from the local church founded by Watchman Nee in that the former generally did not accept the writings and teachings of Witness Lee.

Sources:

The Online Library of T. Austin-Sparks.
http://www.austin-sparks.net/

Austin-Sparks, T. *The Battle for Life*. Washington, DC:
Testimony Book Ministry, n.d.

———. *The Centrality and Supremacy of the Lord
Jesus Christ*. Washington, DC: Testimony Book
Ministry, n.d.

———. *The Recovery of the Lord's Testimony in
Fullness*. Washington, DC: Testimony Book Ministry,
n.d.

———. *The Work of God at the End Time*.
Washington, DC: Testimony Book Ministry, n.d.

Myers, John. *Voices from Beyond the Grave*. Old Tappan,
NJ: Spire Books, 1971.

No Other Foundation. Indianapolis, IN: Sure Foundation,
1965.

Roberts, Frances. *Dialogues with God*. Northridge, CA:
Voice Christian Publications, 1968.

Singh, Bakht. *David Recovered All*. Bombay: Gospel
Literature Service, 1967.

———. *"This Ministry": Messages Given at Honor
Oak, London*. 2 vols. London: Witness and Testimony
Literature, n.d.

 # 13. Adventist

SEVENTH DAY ADVENTISTS

Seventh-Day Adventist Reform Church (Rowenite)

The Seventh-Day Adventist Reform Church (Rowenite) was founded out of the visionary experiences of Margaret Rowen, a member of the Seventh-Day Adventist Church in Los Angeles. Her initial vision of coming events occurred on June 22, 1916. Her visions attracted more attention than they otherwise might have because the Seventh-Day Adventist Church had given great authority to the visions of its founder, Ellen G. White, who died the previous year. Some who witnessed the early visions suggested that God had chosen another prophetess to guide the church. Several church leaders, especially Dr. B. E. Fullmer, became active supporters. They were affected by Rowen's sincerity, her striving for moral uprightness, and the sufferings she seemed to be enduring.

Concerned, the Southern California Conference conducted an initial investigation of her claims. The report was inconclusive but did note that some of the teachings were out of harmony with the Bible and the message of Ellen G. White. In 1918 Adventist Church official A. G. Daniells reported that those who had investigated Rowen had unanimously concluded that her visions did not come from heaven. In 1919 Rowen and Fullmer were disfellowshipped. Meanwhile, a periodical, the *Reform Advocate and Prayer Band*

Appeal, was launched to create a network of followers of Rowen's visions.

The next year, in order to legitimize her role, Rowen created a document that she signed with Ellen G. White's signature and slipped into the files at White's northern California home. The document, dated 1911, would have placed White's authority on Rowen. However, when examined, the poorly produced document was immediately recognized as a forgery.

Rowen's visions led to some doctrinal innovations. She suggested that Christ had been created as an angel and later elevated as the Father's son. She predicted a worldwide famine in 1916 and in 1923 predicted the end of the world for 1925. The latter prediction led to actions by followers to prepare for the end-time. The failure of the prediction led to a falling away of followers. Even Fullmer, her strongest supporter and editor of the movement's periodical, fell away. In the March 1926 issue he declared his belief that Rowen was a charlatan and apologized for his role in attracting people to her claims. In the most bizarre event in the movement's history, Rowen conspired to murder Fullmer. The attempt was botched, however, and she and her coconspirators were arrested and convicted of assault with attempt to injure. The movement, which had peaked at around a thousand followers, died away.

Sources:

Fullmer, B. E. *Bearing Witness*. Los Angeles: Reform
Press, 1923.

Rowen, Margaret W. *A Stirring Message for the Time*.
Pasadena, CA: Grant Press, 1918.

White, Larry. "Margaret W. Rowen: Prophetess of Reform
and Doom." *Adventist Heritage* 6, no. 1 (Summer
1979): 28–40.

CHURCH OF GOD ADVENTISTS

A Candle

A Candle was a small Sabbatarian body that became known in the 1960s for its wide circulation of a number of one-page tracts that detailed its theological perspective. The group's beliefs were similar to those of the Worldwide Church of God and advocated the observance of the Old Testament law, the seventh-day Sabbath, and the Hebrew feast days. A Candle opposed evolution, voting, healing by medicine, the Good Friday hoax, Christmas, and Easter. Members believed that hell is the grave, baptism is necessary for salvation, and parts of the Bible (specifically those books mentioned in the Old Testament but not preserved) are missing. Headquarters of A Candle were in Lehigh Valley, Pennsylvania.

Fountain of Life Fellowship

The Fountain of Life Fellowship was organized in 1970 by James L. Porter, a former member of the Worldwide Church of God. Five years previously he had published a study of the feast days of the Old

Testament and the seventh-day Sabbath. The study began with a discussion of his discovery of what he felt to be the proper method of entering the Kingdom of God, calling directly upon the name of Jesus in prayer. (This method of prayer had led to his being disfellowshipped from the Worldwide Church of God in 1958.) In 1972 Porter began a study of the doctrine of the baptism of the Holy Spirit which led him to believe in the necessity of Christians having the baptism of the Holy Spirit with the accompanying sign of speaking in tongues. He placed an emphasis upon the centrality of all nine gifts of the Spirit (I Corinthians 12) and the fruits of the Spirit (Galatians 5:22–23).

Porter's group was organized as a fellowship of believers. He began a radio program but soon dropped it in favor of printing and circulating a periodical. The fellowship was headed by a board. No membership roll was kept, but supporters gathered annually for the Feast of Tabernacles. Believers met locally in fellowship groups. Teachings followed Church of God emphases. Worship was weekly on the Sabbath, and the Old Testament festivals were celebrated annually. Porter traveled around the United States to meet with the several hundred believers.

Sources:

Porter, James L. *Knowing the Father through the Spring
Feasts*. Valley Center, KS: Fountain of Life, 1985.

———. *The Sabbaths of God*. New York: Exposition
Press, 1965.

Porter, Virginia. *The Gifts of the Spirit*. Valley Center, KS:
Fountain of Life Fellowship, 1984.

———. *Man's Substitute Gifts of the Spirit*. Valley
Center, KS: Fountain of Life, 1985.

Global Church of God

The Global Church of God grew out of the doctrinal changes that began to occur in the Worldwide Church of God in the months immediately after the death of church founder Herbert W. Armstrong in 1986. Among its founders were Roderick C. Meredith and Raymond McNair, both prominent leaders in the Worldwide Church. They opposed the changes initiated by Joseph W. Tkach, Armstrong's successor, who dropped many of the church's distinctives, especially during the 1990s. The Global Church of God retained the doctrines and practices of the Worldwide Church prior to 1986.

In 1998 an internal conflict developed between Meredith and the church's board. Unable to resolve the conflict, Meredith left and the great majority of the church's 7,000 members left with him. The loss of so many members left the Global Church heavily in debt. It subsequently moved into bankruptcy. The remaining membership reorganized as the Church of God, a Christian Fellowship (CGCF).

Sources:

Barrett, David V. *The New Believers*. London: Sassell, 2001.

BIBLE STUDENT GROUPS

Back to the Bible Way

Roy D. Goodrich, a longtime pioneer for the International Bible Students Association and the Jehovah's Witnesses, was excommunicated in 1944. To put his case before the public and to provide a rallying point for other "free" Bible Students, he began publishing a periodical, *Back to the Bible Way*, in 1952. Goodrich departed from the main body of Bible Students at two points. He denied that Charles Taze Russell, founder of the Bible Student movement, was to be considered the "wise and faithful servant" of Matthew 25: 45–47. He also rejected Russell's thinking relative to the ransom and to the significance of 1914. Headquarters were established in Fort Lauderdale, Florida, from which a large amount of literature was distributed to a mailing list of as many as 3,000.

Goodrich died in 1977 and the movement centered upon him dissolved.

Christian Bible Students Association

Gradually separating from the Dawn Bible Students Association in the late 1960s was the Christian Bible Students Association, headquartered in Warren, Michigan. This group began publication of the periodical *Harvest Message* in 1969 and subsequently published several booklets and tracts. Like the Dawn Bible Students Association and the Pastoral Bible Institute, the group emphasized the writings of Pastor Charles Taze Russell (1852–1916) and carried the same statement of beliefs. A radio program, *The Harvest Message Broadcast*, aired in Chicago, Nashville, and Detroit. The group disbanded in 1978 and members were absorbed back into the Dawn and other Bible Student groups.

SACRED NAME GROUPS

Assemblies of Yah

The Assemblies of Yah was a small Sacred Name group headquartered in Albany, Oregon. Its aims were to present Yah's name to the world; to teach the laws, statutes, and judgments of the Most High; and to foster growth of the Assemblies throughout the world. During the 1960s it published a periodical, *The Word*.

House of Yahweh (Odessa, Texas)

The House of Yahweh of Odessa, Texas, was founded in in 1975 by Jacob Hawkins (d. 1991), an American who had gone to Israel in 1967 to work on a kibbutz in the Negev. (A second House of Yahweh, located in Abilene, Texas, and founded by Jacob's brother Yisrayl [Buffalo Bill] Hawkins in 1980, became a separate entity owing to a falling-out between the brothers and was still extant in 2008.) While he was in Israel,

Jacob Hawkins learned of the discovery in 1973 of an ancient sanctuary dating to the first century that had "House of Yahweh" engraved over its entrance in Hebrew. In his own study of Scripture, he had determined that the name of the people called out by Yahweh was the "House of Yahweh." Thus he was led to found Yahweh's House anew.

Members of the House of Yahweh in Odessa directed their worship to Yahweh the Father, whose title is Elohim, and his son Yeshua, whose title is Messiah. Yahshua's shed blood cleanses believers from sin if they keep the Ten Commandments, Yahweh's law. Members tithed one-tenth of their income to the support of the ministry. They were sabbatarians.

The House of Yahweh observed the Old Testament feast days as mentioned in Leviticus 23. Further, it taught that all believers must come together for the feasts of Passover, Pentecost, and Tabernacles, and members traveled from around the United States and the world for these events. In like measure, holidays such as Christmas, Easter, Halloween, and Sunday as a day of worship were condemned as pagan and un-Biblical. Yahshua was born in the spring (around Passover), not in December.

The House of Yahweh was organized on a biblical pattern with twelve apostles and seventy elders. They met to conduct business each new moon. The group founded the Ministers Training School in Odessa and published a periodical, the *Prophetic Watchman*. In 1980 the group reported congregations in the United States, Israel, India, South Africa, West Africa, Burma, Australia, and Belgium. Jacob Hawkins died from cancer in 1991.

Sources:

Directory of Sabbath-Observing Groups. Fairview, OK: Bible Sabbath Association, 1980.

New Life Fellowship

The New Life Fellowship was formed by nine ministers, representing four Sacred Name congregations, who gathered at Van Buren, Arkansas, and drew up the doctrinal statement "A Declaration of Those Things Most Commonly Believed among Us." This group differed from most other Sacred Name organizations in its adoption of a Pentecostal perspective that places strong emphasis upon the gifts of the Spirit as outlined in Corinthians 1:12 and initially evidenced by speaking in tongues. Its members also believed in the organization of the church under the fivefold ministry as outlined in Ephesians 4:11: apostles, prophets, evangelists, pastors, and teachers lead the church fellowship as a whole; locally, elders and deacons lead individual congregations.

At the time of the fellowship's formation, a 260-acre tract of land near Natural Dam, Arkansas, was purchased for the purpose of establishing an intentional community. The New Life Community was attached to the congregation at Van Buren. The New Life Fellowship accepted the Sacred Name emphases

and acknowledged Yahweh as the Father Creator and Yahshua as his son and humanity's savior. Weekly worship was on the seventh-day Sabbath (Saturday), and the Old Testament feasts were kept. The annual feast of tabernacles was a time for members of the fellowship to gather from around the United States. Missionary work was supported in Haiti and Europe. The fellowship disbanded in 1986.

Sources:

Directory of Sabbath-Keeping Groups. Fairview, OK: Bible Sabbath Association, 1980.

OTHER ADVENTISTS

Leatherwood God, Followers of the

The story of the man who came to be known as the Leatherwood God began in August 1828, in the small community of Salesville, Ohio. He quietly joined a group that had gathered for a camp meeting and—during a pause in the proceedings, when the preacher had called for repentance—he interrupted the service with a loud shout of "Salvation!" People turned to look at the strangely dressed man. He wore a black silk beaver hat. He seemed to be approximately 50 years old. The people later learned his name was Joseph C. Dylks. During the next few weeks he moved through the town as a rather mysterious personage. At times he preached and on occasion interrupted others with his shout.

As days passed, he revealed his claim that he was the true messiah and that he had arrived to establish the millennial kingdom. He further claimed that he was immortal, that his kingdom would never end, and that all who joined him would not die. He had a decisive encounter with the devil after which he declared his work done and never again shouted. He also appointed a man named McCormick as his associate leader. Within a short time the majority of the village had become adherents and taken control of the local church building, rededicating it for the use of Dylks' followers. At the service Dylks proclaimed, "I am God, and there is none else. I am God and the Christ united." Angry detractors now challenged Dylks, demanding a miracle. He promised one but did not deliver. Finally, someone grabbed him and pulled a handful of hair from his head. (He had said that not a hair on his head could be touched.) He was arrested, but a judge could find no crime with which to charge him.

In October 1828, a mere three months after his appearance, he announced that Philadelphia, not Salesville, would be the center of the New Jerusalem. He would depart, and while he was away preparing the new site, the faithful should remember him by facing east (toward Philadelphia) when they prayed. He left with McCormick and two other disciples. However, several miles from Salesville, Dylks parted with his disciples and said that they would meet again in Philadelphia when the New Jerusalem began to appear. However, Dylks did not reappear. The men searched in vain for him in Philadelphia and finally returned to Ohio to tell their story to the congregation.

The disappointment at Dylks's departure without actually founding the millennium did not deter the congregation, and most of the members remained faithful. Some seven years after the journey to Philadelphia, one of the three men, a former minister, told the church members that he had recently seen Dylks ascend to heaven and that he would soon return to set up his kingdom. The next day the man disappeared. McCormick remained faithful through the rest of his life, dressing in a manner similar to that of Dylks when he first appeared. The church slowly dissolved as the members died off, there being few new converts. Around 1850, a man named Moses Hartly appeared in the neighborhood and claimed that he had seen Dylks and that Dylks would reappear before the end of the century. Dylks, however, was never seen again.

Sources:

Kummer, George. Introduction to *The Leatherwood God*, by Richard H. Taneyhill. Gainesville, FL: 1966.

Taneyhill, Richard H. *The Leatherwood God*. Cincinnati, OH: N.p., 1870.

Matthias, Followers of

There appeared in Albany, New York, in 1830 a man calling himself Matthias who declared that he was the Christ and had come to judge the world. Matthias had been born Robert Matthews, but little is known of his life before assuming his religious persona. He dressed in unusual, expensive clothes—pontifical robes lined with silk and velvet—carrying a rule in one hand and a sword in the other. He claimed the sword was the Sword of Gideon, but it was identified by onlookers as merely a common U.S. Army issue. He identified himself with Matthias, the apostle chosen to take the place of Judas (Acts 1:21–26). The new Matthias was the Spirit of Truth that had disappeared from the earth with the death of the first Matthias. With his sword he would pronounce judgment and with his rule he would measure the New Jerusalem.

Soon after his appearance, he declared that Albany would be destroyed and warned residents to flee. He left on what became a grand apostolic tour (though Albany was not destroyed) and made his way west toward the Ozark Mountains. He then went into the South through Tennessee and Georgia. He soon returned to New York, having gathered a small following. He became a public figure walking around New York City in his apostolic costumes. At one point, around 1833, he was briefly committed to Bellevue Hospital for the insane. A short time later, when his wife became pregnant, he announced that a holy son would be born. The child turned out to be a girl.

He left New York and was last seen visiting with Joseph Smith, Jr., and the members of the Church of Jesus Christ of Latter-day Saints in Kirtland, Ohio. When he explained his message, Smith had him ejected from their community. From that time on the fate of Matthias and his small following is unknown.

Remnant Church

The Remnant Church originated in the early 1950s in the visions of Mrs. Tracy B. Bizich of Sewickley, Pennsylvania. In 1951 Ellen G. White, founder of the Seventh-Day Adventist Church, reportedly appeared and told her that that church had backslid beyond recovery. She was also told that her spiritual name was "The Bee" and that she would soon be joined by a man whose spiritual name would be "The Fly." Together they would begin to gather the 144,000 mentioned in Revelation 14:1–3, who would be the only ones to enter the new earth after its (imminent) destruction.

In 1957 Bizich met Elsworth Thomas Kaiser (b. 1901), a railroad worker from Rochester, New York. He too had had many visionary experiences, which Mrs. Bizich was able to interpret for him. She recognized him as "The Fly" and designated him an elder and the first minister of the Remnant Church. That same year, a congregation was founded in Rochester.

According to the Remnant Church, 1957 marked the beginning of the end of the world. In 1962 the first angel blew his trumpet (Rev. 8:7); 1965 brought a foretaste of the burning up of all the green grass. The Remnant Church was very strict. Members were required to be obedient to superiors, observe the Sabbath, dress modestly, share a community of goods, live in sinless purity, eat without question the food placed before them, clean their quarters, be diligent in study, and wear uniforms (gray for women and tan for males). Members were forbidden to go to physicians (although the use of herbs and leaves was permitted, since these are for the healing of the nations); take others to court except in defense of the Remnant; make distinctions on the basis of race; use drugs, alcohol, or tobacco; or attend other church services. The Lord's Supper was celebrated annually. Baptism was by immersion, and full baptism included baptism with the Spirit.

The church believed that the 144,000 will perform active spiritual work in the world until they are all caught up in the Spirit, and that some souls have already risen from their graves and have preached in the spirit to friends and relatives. Membership in the church was not reported, but when last encountered in the mid-1970s, it had only a few members.

Star of Truth Foundation

The Star of Truth was the ministry of Ruth H. Lang and V. Jean Mallatt of Galena, Kansas. It was their belief that the fullness of time had come (Eph. 1:10, Mk. 16:7), and a new age was upon us. Each new age (or period of administration) is initiated by God's representatives giving birth to the Christ. The previous age was begun by Mary, who conceived and brought forth

the Son of the most high God. This Son was not a physical birth but a spiritual being she conceived within the consciousness of her own being. As God's representative, Mary was told to go and tell the brethren (Matt. 28:7), and a new pattern was set for the age.

It was the foundation's belief that this period was the day for a new birthing of the Christ. The representative of God for this new birth would be Ruth Lang. In the passing dispensation, the Comforter was given; in the new age, the Spirit of truth which will abide forever would be given. Paul ran ahead of time and saw this new age. He is thus the establisher of it. At one time, Ruth thought of herself as a reincarnation of Paul. She then came to see him as the resurrected one in Christ, who had come in her to resurrect her also.

The Star of Truth Foundation published *The Sparkler* bimonthly. Lang also wrote a number of pamphlets. The publications tied together the small band of believers, who were scattered across the United States. The Star of Truth Foundation was disbanded in the early 1980s.

True Church

The True Church began in 1930 in the home of Mina Blanc Orth in Seattle, Washington. Orth, the daughter of Baptist home missionaries in Julian, California, had opened her home to George J. Sherwin (b. 1879) to teach a Bible class. In 1937 she took over leadership of the group, becoming the author of a dozen books and pamphlets that contain the basics of the True Church's teaching. Beginning in 1950, she engaged in an extensive radio ministry.

The beliefs of the True Church were based upon an allegorical (spiritual) interpretation of Scripture. The church taught that God's Word is understood in "God's three-way light": the literal light, the historical light, and the symbolic, or spiritual, light. Numbers were a focus of the interpretation, which held that the Bible is "formed over a numeric system divisible by seven," the number of perfection. Typical elucidation of texts is seen in the Song of Solomon 6:8, an allegorical description of churchianity: "There are sixty queens (Catholicism) and eight concubines (Protestantism) and maidens without number (Modernism). God is Father and Son. The personhood of the Holy Spirit is denied."

There was a strong expectancy of the imminent return of Christ. During the 1940s, a date between 1950 and 1967 seemed a possible time for that return. World War III, the third War of Revelation 11:14, would begin in the near future. Churchianity would be destroyed; only a remnant of Anglo-Saxon nations (Israel) and the Jews in Palestine would survive. Upon Christ's return, he would destroy all systems of men in opposition to him and set up a new government, symbolized by Job's seven new sons (Job 43:13) to rule during the millennium.

The True Church was organized into small groups meeting in homes. There were an estimated 600 such centers in the United States and Canada in 1968. Headquarters were in Seattle.

BRITISH ISRAELISM

Covenant, the Sword and the Arm of the Lord

The Covenant, the Sword and the Arm of the Lord (CSA) was founded in the mid-1970s by James D. Ellison, an Identity minister in San Antonio, Texas. He had had a vision of the coming collapse of the American society and decided to flee the city and establish a survivalist community in the Ozark Mountains. He moved to Elijah, Missouri, and then in 1976 purchased a 224-acre tract of land in Arkansas, adjacent to the Missouri border, near Pontiac, Missouri. The commune, called Zarephath-Horeb, was viewed as a purging place, the name having been adopted from its biblical counterpart.

The CSA taught the Kingdom Identity message; that is, it identified the white Anglo-Saxon race as the literal descendents of Ancient Israel and hence the heir to the covenants and promises God made to Israel. The Anglo-Saxons have been called to be the light of the world, and black people were created for perpetual servitude. The CSA also believed the Bible teaches that the two-edged sword of God's Spirit is coming soon in judgment to the earth, and God's Arm will be manifest to administer that judgment. The CSA would be that Arm of God. In preparation for the difficult times ahead, the community stored food and stockpiled weapons and ammunition.

In line with Ellison's vision, the CSA expected the imminent collapse of America, the sign of judgment, and an ensuing war. In that war (Armageddon), whites would be set against Jews, blacks, homosexuals, witches, satanists, and foreign enemies. At that point, the settlement in Arkansas would have become a Christian haven.

The community was largely self-supporting. A farm produced much of the food. Education and medical services were provided internally, and most families lived without electricity or plumbing.

Since its founding, the CSA had been a matter of concern for law enforcement officials. Following a revelation in 1978, the group began to acquire sophisticated weaponry adequate for modern warfare. In 1981 it opened a survival school and gave training to the public in the use of firearms and survivalism. In 1984 a warrant was issued for Ellison's arrest when he failed to appear before a grand jury investigating the murder of an Arkansas state trooper. A gun found in the possession of the accused was registered to Ellison. In spite of a splintering in the winter of 1981–1982 over the continuance of paramilitary training and the departure of those most in favor, the tension that grew out of the CSA's potential for violence remained an unresolved concern.

In April 1985 FBI agents surrounded the CSA compound and arrested Ellison and several members on federal racketeering charges. Following the raid, the group disbanded. Subsequently, four members of CSA were sentenced to prison terms. Ellison received 20 years for racketeering. Others receiving lesser terms were Kerry Noble, Kent Michael Yates, and William Thomas.

Sources:

Schwartz, Alan M., et al. "The 'Identity Churches': A Theology of Hate." *ADL Facts* 28, no. 1 (Spring 1983).

Ministry of Christ Church

The Ministry of Christ Church was a national ministry headed by William Potter Gale (1917–1988). It held a prominent place in the larger Identity movement because of Gale's activism and involvement with several associated organizations. A retired army officer, Gale served on General Douglas MacArthur's staff during World War II. After his retirement Gale became associated with several groups, including the Church of Jesus Christ–Christian founded by Wesley Swift. In 1960 he organized the California Rangers, a paramilitary group condemned by the office of that state's attorney general. During the 1970s he started his own church in Glendale, California, and later moved it to Mariposa, California. While the church was centered on the small congregation at Mariposa, which only numbered around 30, the major work of the church was in the distribution of tapes and literature across the country to members of the church and the Identity movement, including the periodical *Identity*.

The church followed the consensus of beliefs of the Identity movement. It was segregationist and strongly opposed to interracial marriage. It had a survivalist orientation and circulated tapes condemning the Internal Revenue Service and the idea of income tax. Gale was a member of the Posse Comitatus, a tax protest group with strong ties to the Identity movement.

The work of the Ministry of Christ Church was slowed by the conviction in 1987 of Gale and Fortunato Parrino, a minister of the church, on 10 counts of attempting to interfere with the administration of internal revenue laws and the mailing of threatening communications to IRS agents and a state judge. These convictions arose out of Gale's involvement with a tax protest group called the Committee of the States.

Sources:

Gale, William P. *Racial and National Identity*. Glendale, CA: Ministry of Christ Church, n.d.

Schwartz, Alan M., and Gail L. Gans. "The Identity Churches: A Theology of Hate." *ADL Facts* 28, no. 1 (Spring 1983).

National Association of Kingdom Evangelicals

The National Association of Kingdom Evangelicals arose out of the ministry of C. O. Stadsklev in the 1930s. Stadsklev had been a minister with the Christian and Missionary Alliance but left that organization when he came to accept the perspective of British Israelism, the idea that the Anglo-Saxon, Celtic, Nordic, and related peoples of northern and western Europe were the literal descendants of the ancient nation of Israel, the 10 tribes that formed a separate kingdom from the tribe of Judah and who were lost to history after the nation was conquered and its leaders deported. As with most British Israel leaders in the United States, Stadsklev also saw the United States, like the nations of Europe, as having a special scheme in the prophetic plan of God.

Stadsklev emerged as one of the most prominent proponents of British Israelism in the years after World War II. He saw the former Soviet Union as the primary enemy of God's people, the standard-bearer of communism, and believed that at some point it would attack the United States. He opposed what he saw as the "Babylonian money system" that undergirded the current economy. He advocated a system in which money could be loaned interest free and backed by the nation rather than by gold. Among the many British Israel ministers, some wished to associate with Stadsklev's special emphases, and thus the National Association of Kingdom Evangelists was founded, though Stadsklev's writings circulated within the larger movement far beyond the association.

The association was generally conservative and orthodox in its belief. It affirmed the Trinity (a doctrine not held by many who believe in British Israelism). It varied from Evangelical emphases by its belief that God has chosen an earthly servant race through whom he works in a special way to bless humankind and its disavowal of a doctrine of a hell of eternal torment.

The association was a loose fellowship of autonomous congregations that met annually in a national conference. For many years Stadsklev had a radio show, *America's Hope*, and the association published a periodical, *Truth and Liberty Magazine*. The Gospel Temple, which Stadsklev served for most of his adult life, circulated his writings and tapes.

Sources:

Piepkorn, Arthur C. *Profiles in Belief: The Religious Bodies of the United States and Canada*. Vol. 4. San Francisco, CA: Harper & Row, 1979.

Stadsklev, C. O. *Our Christian Beginnings*. Hopkins, MN: America's Hope Broadcasts, n.d. 15 pp.

————. *Personal Salvation*. Hopkins, MN: America's Hope, n.d. 18 pp.

————. *What Happened at Calvary*. Hopkins, MN: America's Hope, n.d. 27 pp.

Prophetic Herald Ministry

The Northwest has been a center of British-Israelite activity partly because of a strong concentration of believers in Vancouver, British Columbia, Canada. Bethel Temple in Spokane, Washington, was one of the most active British-Israel centers, serving as headquarters of the Prophetic Herald Ministry and its leader, Alexander Schiffner (b. 1900). Founded in 1933, the ministry concentrated on anticommunism and anti–Roman Catholicism as major themes in its British-Israel message.

Schiffner taught that the United States is "branded as God's servant nation, Israel." Jacob gave his name "Israel" to both Ephraim and Manasseh, making 13 tribes instead of the original 12. The number 13 is prominent in the history and founding of the United States. The monthly *Prophetic Herald* proclaimed the new consummation of history, at which time true Israel and true Judah (Romans 2:28–29) will be restored as the terrestrial kingdom and head of nations over unrepentant Gentiles and heathen nations. The ministry also advocated the celestial restoration of true Israel to be joint heir with Christ. In an emphasis missing in other British-Israel ministries, Schiffner taught that "only those who receive God's Holy Spirit through repentance and faith in the Lord Jesus Christ" can be a part of the "chosen people" and that a consecrated life is essential to celestial glorification.

In 1970 approximately 40 radio stations carried the Prophetic Herald broadcasts from coast to coast. Schiffner also wrote a variety of pamphlets and booklets. His death ended the ministry, and in 1973 Bethel Temple was sold.

14. Liberal

INTRAFAITH ORGANIZATIONS

Congress of Religion

The Congress of Religion was founded in 1895 in Chicago, Illinois, as the American Congress of Liberal Religious Societies. It was a direct outgrowth of the World's Parliament of Religions held two years earlier in Chicago. The congress provided a meeting ground for liberal leaders among Reform Jews, Unitarians, Universalists, Ethical Culturalists, and others in more conservative denominations who were beginning to feel the changes in thought brought about by the new science, critiques of denominationalism, biblical criticism, and a faith in progress.

A moving force in the organization was the Unitarian minister Jenkin Lloyd Jones, who for some years had published a periodical, *Unity*, and had led in the planning of the Unitarian participation at the parliament. The idea of a congress of religious liberals had first been broached during the planning for that gathering.

Some 200 attended the first meeting of the congress in 1895. Many members expressed concern about the group's name—American Congress of Liberal Religious Societies—and it became a topic of consideration for the next several meetings. It was finally changed in 1900 to Congress of Religion, which dispelled any suggestion that it was a delegated congress or looking toward the formation of a new denomination.

The congress met for the first time in the South in 1897 in Nashville, Tennessee. By the early twentieth century, the need for the congress seemed to have faded. Most of the Jewish members joined the American Ethical Union. National meetings were discontinued, and only a few state meetings persisted, primarily in the Midwest. *Unity* was published into the early 1920s but survived on its own merit, not in connection to the congress. By 1909 the thrust of the congress had been picked up in the East by the National Federation of Religious Liberals.

Sources:

Miller, Russell E. *The Larger Hope: The Second Century of the Universalist Church in America, 1870–1970.* Boston, MA: Unitarian Universalist Association, 1985.

National Federation of Religious Liberals

The National Federation of Religious Liberals was formed in Philadelphia, Pennsylvania, in 1908 by a coalition of Unitarians, Universalists, Reform Jews, liberal Quakers, Ethical Culturalists, and a few members of some mainline Christian denominations. The organization picked up the thrust of the Congress of Religion, which had operated primarily in the Midwest in the 1890s, and could be seen as a national expression of the International Council of Unitarian and Other Liberal Religious Thinkers and Workers (later the International Council of Religious Liberals). The International Council held its second American meeting in Boston, Massachusetts, in 1907, and the National Federation was in large part an attempt to consolidate the gains and good feeling generated by it.

The purpose of the federation was "to promote the religious life by united testimony for sincerity, freedom, and progress in religion, by social service, and with a fellowship of spirit beyond the lines of sect and creed." Those who participated represented the most liberal wing of the religious community, who had become positively influenced by science, were committed to a social ethic of reform, and had little use for the confines of denominational strictures.

The first gathering of the federation was held in 1909 in Philadelphia. Many who had formerly supported the Congress of Religion (which still had a formal existence) attended and became active in the federation's work. In 1913, following some communication with the Federal Council of Churches of Christ in America, which represented the more liberal wing of Protestant Christianity, the federation adopted the

council's social program as its own. The federation continued to meet biannually until 1932. Along the way it absorbed the Mid-Southern Federation of Religious Liberals, which it had fostered following World War I.

The federation disbanded in 1933. Having lost most of its money at the time of the national bank closing, it was broke. Also, the two groups that supplied the largest amount of support, the Universalists and Unitarians, had adopted a plan under which they organized the Free Church, a cooperative arrangement in which the two churches operated in fellowship while remaining autonomous as to governance and creed. The Free Church idea took most of the wind from the federation's sails.

Sources:

Miller, Russell E. *The Larger Hope: The Second Century of the Universalist Church in America, 1870–1970.* Boston, MA: Unitarian Universalist Association, 1985.

National Federation of Religious Liberals. Seventh Congress: Program, Proceedings, and Papers. Boston: National Federation of Religious Liberals, 1919.

Wendte, Charles W. *The Unity of the Spirit: Proceedings and Papers of the First Congress of the National Federation of Religious Liberals.* Boston: National Federation of Religious Liberals, 1909.

LIBERAL

American Rationalist Federation

The American Rationalist Federation, formed in 1955 by a number of rationalist groups and individuals, continued the organized rationalist movement in America, which dates to the middle of the nineteenth century. As early as 1857 (St. Louis), German American rationalists had begun to organize local societies. (That early St. Louis group may have grown out of an even earlier group called Lichtfreunde, formed in 1832.) In 1859 several such societies came together to form the Bund der deutschen Freien Gemeinden von Nordamerika (Federation of German Free Communities of North America). At the time of the second national convention in 1871, societies could be found in Hoboken, New Jersey; New York City; Milwaukee, Painesville, and Maryville, Wisconsin; Frankfurt, Missouri; and New Ulm, Minnesota. Organization of the German American rationalists was followed by that of the Czechs and a number of English-speaking groups such as the Friendship Liberal League. These groups seemed to thrive in the late nineteenth century but by the time of the formation of the federation had dwindled noticeably.

In 1947 many of the surviving rationalist groups had banded together in the United Secularists of America. However, members began to protest the secretive financial policies adopted by the Secularists, and in 1955 most of the local societies in the United

States withdrew and reorganized as the American Rationalist Federation. Representatives of 12 societies gathered in Chicago, in the building owned by the Czech Rationalist Federation (and previously used as the address of the United Secularists) for the organizing convention.

Rationalism is defined as the mental attitude that "unreservedly accepts the supremacy of reason and aims at establishing a system of philosophy and ethics verifiable by experience and experiment and independent of all arbitrary assumptions of authority." The federation believed in the complete separation of church and state, in free public education, and that the improvement of civilization can come only by combating all forms of political, social, religious, and economic tyranny.

At the organizing meeting of the American Rationalist Federation, delegates from Chicago and St. Louis formed the Rationalist Association Inc., whose main task was the publication of the *American Rationalist*, a bimonthly periodical, and the circulation of rationalist/atheist books and literature. Through the years the magazine, though completely independent, became closely associated in the public mind with the federation and was often mistakenly seen as its official organ.

Included within the American Rationalist Federation were several surviving German groups and the Czech Rationalist Federation of America, centered in Chicago, where a monthly periodical, *Vekrozumu*, was published. Local organizations of rationalists were also found in San Francisco, Chicago, and Cleveland (Czech). In the early 1980s there were 11 independent rationalist/freethought organizations and 20 state organizations in the federation.

Sources:

Capek, Thomas. *The Czechs in America*. Boston: Houghton Mifflin, 1920.

School, Eldon, and Walter Hoops. "Going Back to the Beginning: Twenty-five Years Ago." *American Rationalist* 25, no. 1 (May–June 1980): 17–19.

American Secular Union

The American Secular Union, one of the most prominent freethought/atheist organizations at the beginning of the twentieth century, grew out of the efforts of Francis Ellingwood Abbot (1836–1903), who in 1872 published "The Nine Demands of Liberalism" in his paper, *The Index*, then published in Toledo, Ohio. The "Demands" virtually defined freethought's agenda at the time and called for the complete separation of church and state and the total secularization of tax-supported institutions. Abbot's call for separation implied doing away with chaplains, dropping the Bible from school curricula, withdrawing support for religious holidays, ending Sunday blue laws, and ending tax exemption for religious organizations.

Several "liberal" societies were formed by Abbot's readers, and in 1875 delegates met in a convention in Philadelphia, Pennsylvania, and chose Abbot as their president. That meeting also issued a call for a national convention to be held the following year for the purpose of creating a national organization. The convention gathered in Philadelphia on July 1, 1876, and formed the national Liberal League.

The league met annually and chartered chapters across the United States. It was soon hit by a controversy over the enforcement of the so-called Comstock Laws, aimed against trafficking in obscene literature. Postal official Anthony Comstock expanded the scope to include antireligious materials. In 1878 he conspired to have D. M. Bennett, editor of *The Truth Seeker*, arrested. Some liberals began to agitate for the repeal of the Comstock Laws. Abbot argued for their revision. The debate, in which the majority stood for repeal, led to Abbot's pulling out of the organization. In 1879 Robert G. Ingersoll (1833–1899) championed a proposal in defense of Bennett that called for rewriting the Comstock Laws while decrying obscene literature; many included the Bible on their list of obscene materials. The league also called for the complete separation of church and state.

At the convention in 1883 the league changed its name to National Secular Union. Ingersoll was elected president of the organization and served for two years.

In 1892 Samuel P. Putnam (1838–1896), a prominent freethinker, called for the formation of a national organization that would push for the liberal program in a political arena. The result was the formation of the Freethought Federation of America. Two years later it merged into the National Secular Union, and Putnam was named president of the merged organization, which became known as the American Secular Union. It had little success in gaining legislative support for its views. The union continued into the 1920s.

Sources:

Putnam, Samuel P. *400 Years of Freethought*. New York: The Truth Seeker, 1894.

Warren, Sidney. *American Freethought, 1860–1914*. New York: Gordian Press, 1966.

Americans First Inc.

Kent Meyer was a member of the Society of Separationists, now known as the American Atheists Inc., but he resigned in 1969 and formed his own organization. The small group operated within the state of Oklahoma as an atheist/freethought organization. Within weeks of the founding of Americans First, Meyer made national headlines for his instigation of a lawsuit to have a 50-foot lighted cross removed from the state fairgrounds in Oklahoma City. He charged that the presence of the cross was a violation of the state constitution. No recent information

on Americans First has been forthcoming, and it has been reported defunct.

Bund der deutschen Freien Gemeinden von Nordamerika

During the mid-nineteenth century, several freethought organizations were formed in German-speaking communities in the United States. Among the earliest was one called Lichtfreunde (Light Friends), of St. Louis, Missouri. During the 1850s it was suggested that a national organization be created. Thus at a gathering of German freethought leaders in Philadelphia, Pennsylvania, the Bund der deutschen Freien Gemeinden von Nordamerika (Federation of German Free Communities of North America) came into existence. The Philadelphia Freie Gemeinde became the organizational center of the group, and seven of its members were the first directors.

The start of the Civil War largely curtailed the new organization's work; however, Friedrich Schuenemann-Pott, the editor of *Blaetter fuer freies-religioeses Leben* (Sheets for a Free-Religious Life), authored a widely distributed pamphlet, *Die freien Gemeinden*, for the new organization in 1861. Chapters appeared along the East Coast and as far west as Milwaukee and Sauk City, Wisconsin. Among the early accomplishments were the appointment of several "secular" chaplains in the Union Army and the development of a corresponding relationship with European freethought groups.

The first national convention was held in 1866, and contact was established with the Free Religious Association. The national organization continued to be active into the twentieth century. By the end of the 1920s only three centers remained: Chicago, Milwaukee, and St. Louis. The St. Louis center finally closed in 1970 and deeded its assets to the St. Louis Ethical Society.

Sources:

Hempel, Max. *Was sind die Freien Gemeinde?* St. Louis, MO: 1902.

Stein, Gordon. *Encyclopedia of Unbelief*. 2 vols. Buffalo, NY: Prometheus Press, 1985.

Canadian Secular Union

The Canadian Secular Union emerged from the Toronto Free-thought Association, the earliest organized expression of freethought in Canada. It was formed in 1873 by a small group of rationalists, secularists, and atheists who dedicated themselves to challenging Christian beliefs, removing Sabbath laws, and promoting evolution. In 1877 the association was reorganized under the leadership of J. Ick Evans, and a periodical, the *Freethought Journal*, was launched, though it folded after only a few issues. The organization's name was changed in 1881 to Toronto Secular Society. Some have argued that the name change suggested an emphasis on Sabbath laws, which might serve to mobilize members of the public who had shown little interest in freethought philosophy.

In 1884 the society's president, Alfred Piddington, invited the freethought lecturer Charles Watts, newly arrived from England, to address the citizens of Toronto. Watts had been one of the founders of the National Secular Society in England in 1866. The lectures were a great success, and eventually Watts settled in the city. In 1885 the society was again reorganized, this time by William Algie, and emerged as the Canadian Secular Union, following the English model. The growth in the society allowed branches to form in neighboring towns and the revival of a periodical, *Secular Thought* (which ran through some 30 volumes).

The union, according to its prospectus of 1887, affirmed a "constructive Secularism," which found expression in agnosticism, the destruction of the influence of the errors "born of priest-craft, dogmatism, and perpetuated prejudice," and the championing of free speech and inquiry.

The union seems to have run out of steam around the beginning of World War I.

Sources:

Putnam, Samuel P. *400 Years of Freethought*. New York: The Truth Seeker, 1894.

Stein, Gordon. *Encyclopedia of Unbelief*. 2 vols. Buffalo, NY: Prometheus Press, 1985.

Christian Universalist Church of America

The Christian Universalist Church of America was founded in 1964 by Universalists with a Christian emphasis. Headquarters of this small organization were in Deerfield Beach, Florida. In 1967 the group reported an estimated 200 churches and missions (some of which were also affiliated with the Unitarian Universalist Association) located in 21 states, with more than 15,000 members. The subsequent disappearance of the church has cast some doubts on the reported figures.

Church of Eternal Life and Liberty

The Church of Eternal Life and Liberty was a libertarian church founded on June 2, 1974, by Patrick A. Heller, Anna Bowling, and James Hudler. It had no creed but espoused a noncoercive libertarian philosophy. Confirming its strong belief in individual freedom, the church offered support for tax protesters, draft resistance, and alternative schooling for children in the home and published a periodical, *Live and Let Live*. The church also had a strong interest in cryogenics, the practice of freezing the body at death in hopes of its being brought back to life at a future point in time when science has conquered physical death and disease.

The church cooperated with other libertarian churches, particularly the Church of Nature, with which it held regular joint meetings. Beginning in the early 1980s, the church was engaged in a constant battle with the U.S. Internal Revenue Service, which questioned the group's legitimacy as a church body and moved to deny it tax-exempt status.

Sources:

Heller, Patrick A. *As My Spirit Beckons*. Pontiac, MI: Church of Eternal Life and Liberty, 1974.

————. *Because I Am*. Oak Park, MI: Church of Eternal Life and Liberty, 1981.

Church of Nature

The Church of Nature was founded in 1979 in Dryden, Michigan, by Rev. Christopher L. Brockman. It was a libertarian humanist church that espoused a naturalistic philosophy. The church placed a high value upon individual freedom and believed that "living up to one's best nature as a human being is the standard of goodness." Freedom was seen as essential to goodness. The church established two sacraments: marriage and affirmation. The latter consisted of providing a ceremonial context in which an individual (or group of individuals) could offer an affirmative statement of some truth or concern to members of the church.

The church attempted to provide an ethical and religious context within the larger libertarian movement and cooperated with organizations such as the now disbanded United Libertarian Fellowship and the American Humanist Association to encompass libertarianism and humanism under a single, consistent ethical philosophy. (Its periodical was titled *Exegesis*.) In 1988 the church reported 150 members in two congregations (Michigan and Virginia) served by two ministers.

Church of the Humanitarian God

The Church of the Humanitarian God was founded in 1969 in St. Petersburg, Florida, as an alternative to yielding to the prevailing military-industrial complex. The church taught that it is man's purpose in this life to aid his fellow man as best as he can. Such service to others establishes man's status in the life hereafter. Sustaining life is the natural law of God. Therefore, members of the church could engage only in self-defensive aggression. Nonviolent change was part of the new direction in which the church wished to lead people.

The church believed that introspection is man's means of facing himself and allowing his conscience to guide him. Thus, questions of sex, nudity, divorce, drinking, and smoking were largely left to individuals. Drug use was disapproved. Ministers had to be 18 years old, but there were no other restrictions of age, sex, or marital status.

Deistical Society of New York

The Deistical Society of New York was the first expression, other than the very ephemeral Universal Society of Philadelphia, Pennsylvania, of what was to become a tradition of organized freethought in the United States. It was formed in 1794 by a group of liberal thinkers who responded to a lecture given by Elihu Palmer (1764–1806). A former Presbyterian and Baptist minister, Palmer had become a deist, a fact he announced publicly in Philadelphia in 1791 with a lecture before the newly formed Universal Society attacking the divinity of Jesus Christ. That lecture sealed the society's fate. Palmer was forced out of the city. He left the ministry, read law for several years, and traveled about. He was on his way to Connecticut when prevailed upon to lecture in New York.

The Deistical Society of New York espoused the religion of nature and opposed all forms of what it termed fanaticism and superstition. It affirmed the existence of One God, worthy of adoration, and believed that humans possess the moral and intellectual faculties sufficient for the improvement of life. It also believed that the religion of nature emerges out of the moral relationships in society and is aligned with progressive improvement and the common welfare. It opposed religious persecution and championed civil and religious liberty.

The society barely survived for the next few years but found new life with the election of Thomas Jefferson, himself a deist, to the presidency of the United States. It launched a periodical, the *Temple of Reason*. By this time Palmer was lecturing every Sunday evening at a hall on Broadway. The society became Palmer's headquarters for the rest of his life, but he also traveled south to Philadelphia and Baltimore to lecture and raise funds. The society died soon after Palmer passed away in 1806.

Sources:

Gay, Peter. *Deism: An Anthology*. Princeton, NJ: Van Nostrand, 1968.

Koch, G. Adolf. *Republican Religion*. New York: Henry Holt, 1933. Reprinted as *Religion of the American Enlightenment*. New York: Thomas Y. Crowell, 1968.

Free Religious Association

The Free Religious Association (FRA) emerged at the end of the Civil War in reaction to the solidification of Unitarianism into a denomination as the American Unitarian Association (AUA) and its affirmation of the supernatural lordship of Jesus (though the association had repudiated the doctrine of the Trinity and the deity of Jesus). The more radical elements among the Unitarians looked for an alternative to denominationalism and the theological boundaries such an organized life represented. Thus it was in October 1866 that eight Unitarian leaders gathered in the home of Cyrus A. Bartol (1813–1900) in Boston, Massachusetts, to discuss the situation. At a second gathering a few weeks later, William Potter (1829–1893), Francis Ellingwood Abbot (1836–1903), and Edward C. Towne (1834–1911) presented a draft constitution for a Free Religious Association. A public meeting was held on May 30, 1867, at which a constitution was presented and accepted. Octavius Brooks Frothingham (1822–1895) was elected president and Potter secretary. Ralph Waldo Emerson was the first member enrolled. Other officers included Robert Dale Owen (1801–1877) and the liberal Rabbi Isaac Mayer Wise.

The Free Religious Association was designed as a home for theistic radicals, people who believed in God but who held opinions that often put them at odds with other institutions with which they were in association. It was designed especially to assist the more left-wing Unitarians who did not want to break with the AUA but found it impossible to accept its doctrinal guidance. Initially the FRA affirmed its allegiance to what was termed "pure religion," defined as the worship of God. This definition of pure religion was challenged in 1872 and theism dropped as a core idea. At this time Felix Adler (1851–1933) (who later left to form the Society for Ethical Culture) and Benjamin Franklin Underwood (1839–1918) joined the FRA. Underwood spearheaded the organization's decision in 1885 to drop any reference to pure religion. Thus the FRA was committed to "the scientific study of religion and ethics," its goals being "to advocate freedom in religion, to increase fellowship in the spirit, and to emphasize the supremacy of practical morality in all of the relations of life." The change, an attempt to reconcile the goal of defining a rationalistic religion with the infinite divergences among radical free speculative theologians, was in the latter's favor.

The FRA was continually threatened with dissolution from the very different souls who constituted its membership. Its survival through the nineteenth century was largely credited to the organizational zeal of William Potter. Potter died in 1894, by which time the FRA had seemingly run its course and been left behind by developments in the larger religious community. It continued to operate into the twentieth century but slowly dwindled into nonexistence.

Sources:

Persons, Stow. *Free Religion*. New Haven, CT: Yale University Press, 1947. Reprint, Boston: Beacon Press, 1963.

Freethinkers of America

The Freethinkers of America was a small freethought group founded in New York in 1915. Around 1920 Joseph Lewis (1889–1968), an atheist who would later become one of the leading exponents and popularizers of atheism in the United States, moved from his home in Alabama to New York. He joined the group and became its leader. During the next decade he wrote several classic statements of the atheist position, all published by the Freethought Press Association, which he had founded: *The Tyranny of God* (1920); *The Bible Unmasked* (1926) and *Atheism and Other Addresses* (1930). During this period he also became interested in the study of sexuality, and in the early 1930s he initiated a second publishing concern, Eugenics Publishing Company, which pub-

lished low-cost books on sexology written by specialists.

Lewis's books addressed a host of major atheist concerns. He attacked religion, particularly the Judaism he had forsaken early in life. He denied the necessity of religion as a basis for either the individual moral life or social order. He argued for the separation of church and state. He publicized the life of America's founding fathers as a means of arguing for the patriotic role of freethought.

Lewis continued to write into the 1950s. Possibly his two most important books appeared after World War II, *The Ten Commandments* (1946) and *An Atheist Manifesto* (1954). The Freethinkers of America were headquartered in New York, though Lewis lived in Miami for a brief period (and frequently appeared on local radio programs to speak on atheist themes). In the 1960s there were branches in San Diego and Milwaukee and as many as several thousand members. The group shrank significantly after the exclusion of the Communists, rejected because they tended to dominate meetings with their own brand of atheism. The Freethinkers had close relations with the American Association for the Advancement of Atheism for many years, but differed in that it did not demand members to be atheists. The Freethinkers published a periodical, *Age of Reason*, which ceased publication after Lewis's death in 1968. The organization persisted after Lewis's death for only a few years.

Sources:

Howland, Arthur H. *Joseph Lewis—Enemy of God*. Boston: Stratford, 1932.

Lewis, Joseph. *An Atheist Manifesto*. New York: Freethought Press Association, 1954.

———. *The Bible Unmasked*. New York: Freethought Press Association, 1926.

———. *The Ten Commandments*. New York: Freethought Press Association, 1926.

———. *The Tyranny of God*. New York: Freethought Press Association, 1921.

Goddian Organization

The Goddian Organization was formed in 1965 by Lawrence A. Whitten of Portland, Maine. It was begun as a back-to-God movement because other religious organizations, in Whitten's view, were not doing their work of bringing people back to God. Whitten consolidated all religious belief into one affirmation—God as the creator. He sought the union of all people in one brotherhood of man. That union could be achieved if each person stopped insisting that those who differ from him must believe as he does.

There were no ministers or churches. Whitten attempted to unite all Goddians through the headquarters in Portland around a mutual allegiance to the program of good works. In a monthly periodical, *The Goddian Message*, an attack on Christianity and the Bible followed traditional free thought ideas.

Although people from around the country responded to ads about the organization, it never received enough support to make it a viable concern. After a few years, it was discontinued.

Society of Evangelical Agnostics

The Society of Evangelical Agnostics was founded in 1975 by William Henry Young. Young had called himself an agnostic for several years and had harbored a hope that an agnostic organization would emerge. After developing the idea of the society, he placed ads in a number of liberal, religious journals such as *The Humanist* and mass circulation periodicals such as *the Nation* and the *Saturday Review*. He also began to champion the cause of agnosticism, frequently speaking to audiences on the subject and writing letters to periodicals whenever he thought agnosticism had been misrepresented. He also began a newsletter, *The SEA Journal*.

The society defined agnosticism by reference to a tradition of outstanding freethinkers who called themselves by that label, most notably Thomas Henry Huxley (who coined the term), Bertrand Russell, and Robert G. Ingersoll. Its principles consist of three statements: (1) One should approach all questions and issues with an open mind; (2) One should avoid advocating conclusions without adequate or satisfactory evidence; and (3) One should accept not having final answers as a fundamental reality in one's life. According to Young, agnosticism was to be distinguished quite strongly from atheism. The latter flatly denies the existence of God while the former affirms that God is both unknown and an unknowable factor. Atheism, like Christianity, violates the second principle of agnosticism by advocating conclusions without adequate evidence.

The society was headed by Young and a board of directors. Young was also the librarian of the Cedar Springs Library, in Auberry, California, which had developed a special collection of freethought literature. The library was the official archive of the society and distributed numerous inexpensive items related to the society's concerns. The society reprinted many classic statements of agnosticism as well as original material written by its members. Membership was open to all who considered themselves agnostics and who contributed a modest annual membership fee. Members were also encouraged to form chapters and hold meetings in their local neighborhoods. The society was dissolved in 1987 at the request of its founder after enrolling more than 1,150 members.

Sources:

Huxley on Agnosticism. Auberry, CA: Cedar Springs Library, n.d.

Ingersoll, Robert G. *Ingersoll's Greatest Lectures*. New York: Freethought Press Association, 1944.

Stephen, Leslie. *An Agnostic's Apology*. New York: G. P. Putnam's Sons, 1903.

Young, William Henry. "The Agnostic as Prophet." *Faith and Thought* 1, no. 2 (Summer 1983): 27–31.

United Libertarian Fellowship

The United Libertarian Fellowship was incorporated in 1975 in Los Altos, California, by William White, Kathleen J. White, and C. Douglas Hoiles. The fellowship was organized as a religious order espousing libertarian ideals of individual freedom and responsibility within a religious context. It offered a broad framework within which libertarians could develop religiously by following their own initiative and perspectives.

The fellowship had a simple statement of beliefs. God was acknowledged as the fundamental force in the universe. Human beings possessed the capacity to think and act. That capacity placed a duty on people to search for truth and to act in accord with that truth. Individuals, being capable of influencing their own destiny, also accepted responsibility for their actions and the consequences that flow from them. The guidance of personal conduct began in refraining from the initiation of the use of force or fraud on another person and the general assumption that others are free and should be allowed that freedom to develop their own religious nature.

The fellowship described worship as "focusing the mind in search for truth." Five sacraments were observed as outward manifestations and public observances of the sacred realm in human life. Affirmation, parallel to confirmation in other churches, was a declaration of adulthood and acceptance of adult responsibility. Marriage was contracted to share lives. Consecration was the dedication of a person or property to sacred purposes. The final two sacraments attempted to integrate religious ideals into everyday life by infusing otherwise mundane activity with sacred worth. Transformation was the act of changing physical materials into a new form with more utility and/or value than the original materials possessed. Exchange was the voluntary giving and receiving of objects or labor.

The direction of the fellowship was in the hands of a three-person board of elders, officers, and its ministers. The board appointed the officers: a president who directed the religious work, a secretary-treasurer who kept the records, and bishops who managed the temporal affairs. The board also appointed and ordained ministers who had sacramental functions and could, if they chose, establish churches. In keeping with libertarian principles, neither bishops nor ministers were assigned tasks; rather, they were encouraged to work in accordance with libertarian beliefs and spread its fellowship as their individual creativity dictated. After functioning for several years, the fellowship ran into problems with the Internal Revenue Service. It was declared nonreligious, and eventually its elders were tried and convicted of tax evasion.

Sources:

The United Libertarian Fellowship, A Religious Order. Los Altos, CA: United Libertarian Fellowship, 1982.

United Moral and Philosophical Society for the Diffusion of Useful Knowledge

The United Moral and Philosophical Society for the Diffusion of Useful Knowledge was founded in 1836 at Saratoga Springs, New York, as the response of a convention of freethinkers to the call for the establishment of a national organization. Prominent among its supporters were Abner Kneeland and Benjamin Otten. Kneeland (1774–1844) was a former Universalist minister turned atheist and beginning in 1830 the editor of an atheist journal, the *Boston Investigator*, and lecturer for the First Society of Free Inquirers. The society lasted for five years and held annual conventions. After its demise, a second attempt at a national organization was made with the formation of the Infidel Society for the Promotion of Mental Liberty, which lasted from 1845 to 1848.

Sources:

Post, Albert. *Popular Freethought in America, 1825–1850*. New York: Columbia University Press, 1943. Reprint, New York: Octagon Books, 1974.

United Secularists of America

The United Secularists of America was formed in 1946 as an anti-God, anti-religion organization by William McCarthy. It was the secularists' belief that religion is a great hoax; the organization opposed the "dangerous" encroachments of religion in education and other areas of life. Among the group's outstanding members was ex-priest Joseph M. McCabe (1867–1955), one of the major popularizers of atheism in the twentieth century. He wrote more than 200 books against the church and translated 30 others. Titles include *The Sources of Morality of the Gospel, Crime and Religion*, and *A Rationalist Encyclopedia*.

The United Secularists of America advocated the complete separation of church and state; the right not to believe as part of freedom of religion; the exclusion of all religion from public schools; and the taxation of church property. Opposing all supernaturalism and superstition, the United Secularists of America believed in the free intellectual growth of man and the advancement of society toward a rational civilized existence.

During its first decade the United Secularists were among the largest of the rationalist/atheist bodies, drawing support from many independent rationalist and secularist societies. In 1947 they had begun a magazine *Progressive World*. However, in the early 1950s, protests against secretive financial policies led most of the groups to withdraw and in 1955 form the American Rationalist Federation. After that year the United Secularists lacked support even to hold an annual meeting. By 1970 there were only three centers, 1,000 active members, and 1,000 at-large members. Over the decade the United Secularists steadily lost their remaining support. In 1981 they disbanded and the magazine ceased publication.

Universal Society

The Universal Society was the first organization in America to give expression to the deist/freethought religious-philosophical perspective. It was founded in Philadelphia, Pennsylvania, in 1791. Philadelphian Benjamin Franklin was a deist theologically, but his prominence did little to assist the young society.

Elihu Palmer (1764–1806), a blind Baptist minister in the city, was fired from his position for holding and preaching heretical views. At about that same time, John Fitch (1743–1798), the inventor of the steamboat, had organized the Universal Society to which Palmer and his few supporters adhered. Palmer became the minister of the society and in one of his first discourses broached the subject of the divinity of Jesus, which he proceeded to deny. Bp. William White, the Episcopal Church authority in the city, then applied pressure to the society's landlord to refuse to rent to the group and mobilized public hostility against Palmer. Palmer left town and the society collapsed.

Thus the first freethought organization in the United States came to an end in a matter of weeks. It became the foundation, however, upon which a more successful organization, the Deistical Society of New York, would be built in the early years of the nineteenth century.

Sources:

Koch, G. Adolf. *Republican Religion*. New York: Henry Holt and Company, 1933. Reprinted as *Religion of the American Enlightenment*. New York: Thomas Y. Crowell, 1968.

MAIL ORDER AND INTERNET CHURCHES

Brotherhood of Peace and Tranquility

The Brotherhood of Peace and Tranquility was a fellowship of semi-autonomous churches that included local autonomous congregations and a "Church of the Brotherhood," a single worldwide congregation of individuals. Individual churches varied widely in belief and practice. The brotherhood operated the Academy of the Brotherhood, its teaching arm, which offered training to ministers as well as courses for members who wished merely to improve their religious knowledge. It offered both resident and nonresident instruction, and the curriculum was slanted toward the psychic. Both the academy and the church were headquartered in Costa Mesa, California.

The Church of Holy Light

The Church of Holy Light was a small mail-order church that ordained ministers and chartered congregations. The church asked only that candidates felt called to preach and required an initial $50.00 offering from new applicants.

Church of Universal Brotherhood

The Church of Universal Brotherhood, founded by Michael Valentine of Hollywood, California, aimed to help people become aware that they are in charge of their own beliefs. It offered (for $10.00) a kit that included an ordination certificate, a doctor of divinity certificate, and complete instructions on forming a church. Ordinations were seen as a means of releasing power for good. The church admonished members to love themselves, to love their brothers and sisters as they loved themselves, and to take control of their lives. The church stressed that all is one and taught that the goals of life are best attained by getting high and staying there, raising the vibes, cherishing the world, and praising God for his grace. Freedom was a keynote: members of the church expressed the belief that people are in prison and deserve to be free. They viewed the prime virtue as the constant striving for self-mastery, for which three tools were available to aid the seeker: mirrors, waterbeds, and hypnosis.

Hilltop House Church

On November 1, 1971, newspapers across the United States carried pictures of Sadie, a Labrador retriever in Terre Linda, California, who had been ordained a minister in the Hilltop House Church by Archbishop Ben F. Gay, its founder. Gay, former president of Holiday Magic, Inc., a cosmetics firm founded by the late William Penn Patrick, founded the Hilltop House Church in 1970 in San Rafael, California. He had formerly been ordained by the Missionaries of the New Truth, a Chicago-based group. The guiding precepts of the Hilltop House Church were the golden rule and John 8:32, "Ye shall know the truth and the truth shall set you free."

Inherent within the Hilltop House Church was a certain cynicism toward religion as a whole. Ministers were ordained for $15.00 and a registration form. They were then promised promotions for recruiting other ministers. The church's stated goal was to ordain 48 bishops, 24 monsignors, and 12 vicars. Ministers were offered ordination simply because of all the benefits ordination brings.

On January 8, 1973, after a year of protesting tax shelters offered to churches, Gay, in a letter to the U.S. Internal Revenue Service, asked that the tax-exempt status of his church be canceled. This act was a protest against the large, nonreligious, tax-free holdings of other churches.

Life Science Church

The Life Science Church, formed by Abp. Gordon L. Cruikshank, was similar to the Universal Life Church. He offered to ordain "those gifted people that have been called to the ministry and for various reasons have been denied the right to fulfill their mission because of lack of formal education and/or college or seminary training." Ministers could be ordained by sending in $25, an application form, and a short thesis on "what the Ministry means to me and how I can serve." All ministers received an ordination certificate and a doctor of divinity degree from the Life Science College. Churches were chartered for $35.00. Ministers could become bishops by recruiting others for ordination.

Cruikshank believed that the science of life consists of learning to live to the fullest. Freedom is the most important part of life, especially freedom of religion. Although the church was not doctrinally oriented and stressed freedom of belief, each minister made a "nondenominational affirmation of faith."

In the 1970s the Life Science Church became associated with the Posse Comitatus, a right-wing tax protest group in the Midwest. Ministers were accused of using the church as a tax dodge and of involvement in several violent confrontations between members of the Posse and legal authorities.

Missionaries of the New Truth

The Missionaries of the New Truth was formed in 1969 by Frederich W. Zurndorfer and David A. Muncaster of Chicago. The organization immediately began to advertise, offering respondents ordination and a doctor of divinity degree. Advantages offered included the right to ordain others in the church's name, the authority to conduct weddings, tax exemption, cash grants for doing missionary work, draft exemption, and reduced rates for ministers at hotels and theaters and on public transportation. The church urged its ministers and members to seek truth, recognizing that subjective truth will differ from person to person. The higher truth is synonymous with God. By 1971 the Missionaries of the New Truth had ordained 7,000 ministers, signifying the church's success. However, the organization was beset with problems. Following an expose in the *Chicago Tribune*, the Illinois state attorney general filed suit, charging the group with fraud in soliciting funds to establish schools and churches that never materialized. In addition, Muncaster and several leaders of the church were seized in a drug raid and were accused of running the largest hallucinogenic drug factory in the Midwest. Following their conviction, the church dissolved.

Universal Free Life Church

The Universal Free Life Church was formed in 1969 by the Rev. Dr. Arthur H. Fox, assisted by the Rt. Rev. Richard H. Kerekes and the Rev. Diane Fox. There was no doctrine; the church recognized the individual's right to his own beliefs. In 1970 the church reported 1,100 centers in the United States (912 on college campuses) and 43,000 members. These reports were never verified, and no activity by the church has been located since the 1970s.

Universal Life Mission Church

The Universal Life Mission Church, also known as the General Council of the Apostolic Sabbatarian Baptist Churches of America, Inc., was founded by Kenneth Russell Lyons, its bishop. The church, originally chartered by the Universal Life Church, was independently incorporated in 1977. As a sabbatarian group, the church believed in the Bible as its only guide, preferring the New International or World Version published by the Jehovah's Witnesses.

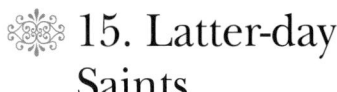

15. Latter-day Saints

UTAH MORMONS

Church of Christ (Brewster)

The Church of Christ (Brewster), a Latter-day Saint–inspired communal group, was founded by James C. Brewster (b. 1826) in 1848 soon after the martyrdom of Mormon prophet Joseph Smith, Jr. (1805–1844), the resulting disruption of the Mormon community at Nauvoo, Illinois, and the movement of the majority of the saints to Utah. Prior to the founding of the church, Brewster had a lengthy career as a would-be prophet. In 1836, a few years after the founding of the Church of Jesus Christ of Latter-day Saints, Brewster, then 10 years old, claimed that he had communicated with the Angel Moroni (from whom Smith claimed he had originally obtained the Book of Mormon). Church leaders disfellowshipped Brewster.

Two years after his being put out of the church, Brewster began writing a book that he finished and published in 1842 as *The Words of Righteousness to All Men*. Over the next few years, Brewster wrote additional books criticizing Smith's new revelations and the direction taken by the church he headed. Brewster was not far away when the Mormon settlement was disrupted, and in 1848 he began to work directly among those members who had not joined the exodus westward. As the church was being organized, a periodical, *The Olive Branch, or, Herald of Peace and Truth to All Saints*, began to appear from Kirtland, Ohio, where the church's headquarters had been established. Brewster claimed that by 1842 Smith had been led astray and that a reorganization of the church was needed.

Among the first converts to Brewster's cause was Hazen Aldrich, a former member of the First Council of Seventy in the church at Nauvoo. When the church was formally organized, Aldrich was named president, with Brewster and Jackson Goodale as counselors. Other members filled out the remaining hierarchy of the church. Brewster guided the church with a series of communications from the spirit world. Brewster designated an area in the Rio Grande Valley as the gathering place for the saints, and he and Goodale migrated there while Aldrich remained behind in Kirtland.

The church held together for several years, but in 1851 Aldrich proclaimed his belief that Brewster had misconstrued the writings from Esdras. Brewster answered Aldrich's charges with a revelation suggesting that Aldrich had improperly usurped authority. Meanwhile, Goodale was found guilty of a transgression and put out of the church. In the midst of the infighting, the church fell apart. A short time later, Brewster moved to California and became a lecturer for Spiritualism, which found strong support among California Mormons. He remained a Spiritualist for the rest of his life.

Sources:

Brewster, James C. *An Address to the Church of Christ, and Latter Day Saints*. Springfield, IL: Author, 1848.

————. *A Warning to the Latter Day Saints, Generally Called Mormons. An Abridgement of the Ninth Book of Esdras*. Springfield, IL: Author, 1845.

————. *The Words of Righteousness to All Men, Written from One of the Books of Esdras, Which Was Written by the Five Ready Writers, In Forty Days, Which Was Spoken of by Esdras, in His Second Book, Fourteenth Chapter of the Apocrypha, Being One of the Books Which Was Lost, and Has Now Come Forth, by the Gift of God, In the Last Days*. Springfield, IL: Ballad and Roberts, Printers, 1942.

Shields, Steven L. *Divergent Paths of the Restoration*. Los Angeles: Restoration Press, 1990.

Church of Christ (Whitmer)

David Whitmer (1805–1888) was one of the original witnesses to the authenticity of the Book of Mormon, and during the early years of the Church of Jesus Christ of Latter-day Saints was a close associate of the church's founder, Joseph Smith, Jr. (1805–1844). However, as a result of disagreements with Smith in the 1830s he separated from the main body of the church. In the late 1840s he refused to assume the leadership of a group of Mormons who did not move to Utah, and little was then heard from him for many years. In the years after the Civil War he gathered a small following and by the mid-1870s formed an independent church organization. He commissioned missionaries who went out to preach and assemble groups of believers. He remained active until his death in 1888.

Among Whitmer's last activities was the writing and publication of a booklet, *An Address to All Believers in Christ* (1887). In this work he not only attested to his belief in the authenticity of the Book of Mormon but expressed his opinion that, though Joseph Smith, Jr., was called to translate it and to preach the restored gospel, he was never called to receive revelations or to lead a church.

After Whitmer's death, the movement appears to have been headed by John J. Snyder. In 1889 Ebenezer Robinson began to edit a periodical, *The Return*, which was published intermittently until 1900, when it was superseded by *The Messenger*. A hymnal was issued in 1890 as well an edition of the Book of Mormon, under the title *The Nephite Record*, in 1899, and the Book of Commandments in 1903. The church seems to have continued until 1925, when Snyder led the membership of several hundred members in Missouri, Iowa, and Kansas, to unite with the Church of Christ (Temple Lot).

Sources:

Brown W. P. *Defense of the Church of Christ; and Exposure of the Errors of Mormonism*. Newton, KS: Democrat Publishing House, 1887.

Shields, Steven L. *Divergent Paths of the Restoration*. Los Angeles: Restoration Press, 1990.

Snyder, John J. *The Solution to the Mormon Problem*. Independence, MO: Zion's Advocate, 1926.

Whitmer, David. *An Address to All Believers in Christ. By a Witness to the Divine Authenticity of The Book of Mormon*. Richmond, MO: Author, 1887.

Church of Jesus Christ of Israel

The Church of Jesus Christ of Israel was founded in 1936 by J. H. Sherwood, a former member of the Church of Jesus Christ of Latter-day Saints residing in Los Angeles, California. Sherwood had come to believe that he was a literal descendant of the biblical Aaron, the older brother of Moses, and the first high priest of Israel. Because of his relation to Aaron, Sherwood demanded that the church give him the office of presiding bishop. The church refused. He then proclaimed that on September 13, 1936, the priesthood authority was withdrawn from the LDS Church, and all ordinances performed by the church's priests after that date were invalid. Sherwood was excommunicated and founded the Church of Jesus Christ of Israel. His small but dedicated following persisted quietly over the next few decades.

The Church of Jesus Christ of Israel followed the basic beliefs and practices of its parent body. Sherwood's allegiance to Latter-day Saint practice was demonstrated in 1954, at which time he briefly emerged from obscurity to request the use of the facilities of the temple in Salt Lake City for a service of baptism for the dead. His request was denied, and he performed the service at a lake near Ventura, California. The service consisted of a proxy baptism for all of the dead, which Sherwood claimed would do away with the necessity of putting so much time and energy into genealogy.

The church was organized around two levels of membership. Members of the church partaking in celestial glory were required to live communally according to the united order. All the members of the priesthood were of the celestial order. Those of the lesser glory, the terrestrial, were required merely to tithe.

As nothing was heard from the church through the remainder of the twentieth century, it is presumed to be defunct.

Sources:

Shields, Steven L. *Divergent Paths of the Restoration*. Los Angeles: Restoration Press, 1990.

Church of Jesus Christ of Latter-day Saints (Walter Murray Gibson)

Among the most colorful leaders in Latter-day Saints history is Walter Murray Gibson (1822–1888). He arrived in Hawaii in 1861 for a stopover on his way to Japan as a missionary for the Church of Jesus Christ of Latter-day Saints. There he found the remnant of a small Mormon mission that had succeeded in getting the Book of Mormon translated into Hawaiian in 1855 and had since turned its attention to converting the native Hawaiians. Unfortunately, the missionaries had been withdrawn in 1858 because of the impending War Between the States (the Civil War). Gibson stayed in Hawaii rather than continuing his journey. He reorganized the remaining Mormons and established headquarters on Lanai, which he saw as the future center of the kingdom of God. He designated himself "Chief President of the Islands of the Sea and the Hawaiian Islands for the Church of Latter-day Saints." He raised money for his various concerns through simony (the selling of church positions). One of his concerns was building a temple, and he chose a site on the island for its future erection.

In 1864 a delegation of Mormon leaders arrived from Salt Lake City to investigate Gibson's mission. As a result, they decided to excommunicate him. Initially, most of his followers stayed with him, and Gibson continued on his course. His plans for expansion, however, were shattered by the lack of necessary water on the area of the island he owned. After a number of unsuccessful schemes to develop his property on Lanai, his following dwindled away and Gibson moved to Honolulu.

His church leadership career over, Gibson turned to politics and in 1882 became prime minister of Hawaii. For the next five years he was the most powerful white man in the islands, an articulate spokesperson for the cause of keeping "Hawaii for the Hawaiians." He was toppled in the revolution in 1887 and fled to California. He died there the following year.

Sources:

Adler, Jacob, and Robert M. Kamins. *The Fantastic Life of Walter Murray Gibson: Hawaii's Minister of Everything*. Honolulu: University of Hawaii Press, 1986.

Gibson, Walter Murray. *The Diaries of Walter Murray Gibson, 1886, 1887*. Edited by Jacob Adler and Gwynn Barrett. Honolulu: University Press of Hawaii, 1973.

Joesting, Edward. *Hawaii: An Uncommon History*. New York: Norton, 1972.

Shields, Steven L. *Divergent Paths of the Restoration*. Los Angeles: Restoration Research, 1990.

Church of Jesus Christ of Saints of the Most High

The Church of Jesus Christ of Saints of the Most High, a short-lived Mormon group of the 1860s, was founded by Joseph Morris (1824–1862). Morris converted to the Church of Jesus Christ of Latter-day Saints in 1848 and moved to Utah in 1853. Previously he had lived in St. Louis and was affiliated with the Congregation of the Presbytery of Zion, another Mormon splinter. He became known for his piety, which some considered excessive. In 1857 he had a revelation in which he was told he was a prophet of God. In a series of letters written to Brigham Young, president of the Church of Jesus Christ of Latter-day Saints, Morris proclaimed God's rejection of the church leaders and His desire that the saints unite around Morris. Morris believed he was a reincarnation of the biblical Seth and Moses. He identified himself with the seventh angel of the Book of Revelation. He also opposed the Mormon practice of polygamy.

In 1860 Morris moved to South Weber, Utah, and began to attract a few followers, including the bishop of the South Weber Ward. In 1861, along with 17 followers, Morris was excommunicated, a rebuff that led to the formal organization of the Church of Jesus Christ of the Most High in April 1861. The following month Morris issued a call for people to move to his settlement on the Weber River, predicting the imminent appearance of Jesus. In the meantime, the group would live communally; over 300 responded.

In 1862, in the midst of a legal dispute, the militia was ordered to Morris's settlement. In a brief skirmish, Morris was killed. Following his death, the church splintered into several factions as new prophets arose. It is believed that the largest group became a part of the Church of the First Born (Prophet Cainan), a faction led by George Williams, also known as the Prophet Cainan.

Sources:

Morris, Joseph. *The Spirit Prevails*. San Francisco, CA: George S. Dove and Company, 1886.

The Church of the First Born (Dove)

The Church of the First Born (Dove) was a short-lived Mormon group founded in the mid-1870s by George S. Dove. Dove was a follower of George Williams (1814–1882), the Prophet Cainan, who founded the Church of the First Born (Prophet Cainan). In the early 1870s Dove, whose father, James Dove, had been an active worker on behalf of Cainan, began receiving revelations. He did not claim to be a prophet, but he assumed pastoral functions and baptized five people, including his father. He began to proselytize among the former followers of Joseph Morris (1824–1862) and over the next several decades gathered a small following, primarily in California and Montana. With his father, Dove also published many of the revelations of Joseph Morris.

The beliefs of the Church of the First Born were outlined in its Articles of Religion. They followed the beliefs of the Church of Jesus Christ of Latter-day Saints in many areas, but also made several important departures. The Godhead was believed to consist of God and Jesus Christ, the Holy Ghost being identified with angels of God. The church advocated a second chance for sinners through reincarnation, rather than through punishment in hell.

This small faction seems to have existed into the 1890s, fading by the end of the century.

Sources:

Anderson, C. Leroy. *For Christ Will Come Tomorrow: The Saga of the Morrisites*. Logan, UT: Utah State University Press, 1981.

Dove, George S., and James Dove. *A Voice from the West*. San Francisco, CA: Church of the Firstborn, 1879.

Dove, James. *A Few Items in the History of the Morrisites*. San Francisco, CA: Church of the Firstborn, 1892.

Church of the First Born (Prophet Cainan)

George Williams (1814–1882), a pious Mormon, participated in the religious revival that swept Utah in 1857; he had been rebaptized as a sign of his commitment. In April 1862 he received a revelation telling him to prepare to follow the ministry of Joseph Morris, a prophet who had established a colony on the Weber River in Utah. Morris had been receiving and publishing revelations for several years. He rejected the leadership of the Church of Jesus Christ of Latter-day Saints and, after founding his settlement near South Weber, Utah, was excommunicated. In spite of official disapproval, over 300 joined him in his new church, the Church of Jesus Christ of Saints of the Most High. In June 1862 the militia attacked his settlement, and Morris was killed in the battle.

At the time of Morris's death, Williams was not involved with the Church of Jesus Christ of Saints of the Most High. Then in the fall of 1862, he began to circulate a manuscript entitled, "A Description of Interviews with Celestial Beings." Subsequently, he was ordained by two spiritual beings, Elias and Enoch. Williams was identified as a reincarnation of an angel, Cainan, and of the Old Testament priest, Melchisedec (or Melchizedek). He assumed the title and became known as the Prophet Cainan.

From his home in Salt Lake City, Cainan began to visit the Morrisite settlement. Some of those who accepted his revelations moved to Montana and settled at Deer Lodge Valley. In 1868 Cainan announced his intention of joining them. After only a year, however, he appointed William James as leader of the church, and returned to England, his birthplace. Cainan led the group in Montana through his letters, until his death in 1892. The group remained in existence into the twentieth century. James was eventually suspended from membership in the church for

rebelling against its teachings. He was succeeded by George Thompson (d. 1894) and Andrew Hendrickson, one of the church's bishops. Hendrickson served as president until his death in 1921. The last leader was George Johnson (d. 1954). By the 1940s less than a dozen members were reported.

Sources:

Anderson, C. LeRay. *For Christ Will Come Tomorrow: The Saga of the Morrisites*. Logan, UT: Utah State University Press, 1981.

Eardley, J. R. *Gems of Inspiration*. San Francisco, CA: Joseph A. Dove, 1899.

Church of Zion

The Church of Zion was a short-lived, but important, movement that grew out of a major disagreement over economic policy in post–Civil War Utah. In late 1868 William S. Godbe (1833–1903), Elias L. T. Harrison, and some associates began to receive revelations, confirmed by various spiritual manifestations, that instructed them to oppose some of the new policies being introduced by church president Brigham Young (1801–1877). The revelations represented a direct challenge to Young's power. The focus of the dissent by Godbe was the newly organized Zion's Cooperative Mercantile Institute (ZCMI), a structure to coordinate the economic resources of Utah Mormons. All Mormon business were ordered to join, and faithful Mormons were to do their buying through it. Young saw ZCMI as a step in building a self-sufficient Mormon community.

Godbe and the Church of Zion members believed in an open economy of free enterprise and opposed the controlled economy exemplified by ZCMI. Godbe looked to the future integration of Utah into the United States as a whole and argued for industrialization, the bringing of Gentile (non-Mormon) culture to Utah, and an openness to non-Mormons in general. Godbe had no doctrinal quarrel with the Church of Jesus Christ of Latter-day Saints, including its doctrine of plural marriage.

The Godbeite movement flourished for only a few years. A periodical, the *Utah Magazine*, lasted for two years (January 1868 to December 1869); Godbe continued to publish into the early 1870s. However, it soon became evident that his views were not shared by a significant minority of Utah residents, and the church disbanded.

Sources:

Godbe, William S. *Manifesto from W. S. Godbe and E. L. T. Harrison*. Salt Lake City, UT: Authors, 1869.

———. *Polygamy; its Solution in Utah: A Question of the Hour*. Salt Lake City: Salt Lake Tribune, 1871.

Shields, Steven L. *Divergent Paths of the Restoration*. Los Angeles: Restoration Research, 1990.

Walker, Ronald W. "The Commencement of the Godbeite Protest: Another View." *Utah Historical Quarterly* 42 (summer 1974): 216–244.

Kingdom of Heaven

The Kingdom of Heaven, one of the most unusual groups in Mormon history, was established by William W. Davies (b. 1833). Davies was a British Methodist who converted to the Church of Jesus Christ of Latter-day Saints and migrated to Utah in 1847. He became dissatisfied with the church leadership, and in 1861 joined the Church of Jesus Christ of Saints of the Most High, founded by the prophet Joseph Morris (1824–1862). Davies was present at the Morrisite settlement on the Weber River in June 1862 when Morris was killed by the militia. In subsequent years he associated himself with the Church of the First Born (Prophet Cainan) and migrated to Montana. Eventually he settled at Deer Lodge Valley, where a number of the followers of George Williams (1814–1882; also known as the Prophet Cainan) resided.

When Williams moved to Montana in 1868, Davies had departed. In 1866 Davies had a vision that convinced him that he had been chosen as an instrument through which God would speak His will to humanity. He was directed to begin the millennial Kingdom of Heaven near Walla Walla, Washington. With 40 followers, Davies migrated there in 1867, purchased 80 acres, and established a communal life. The group was joined over the next few years by a few additional converts, including John Livingston, one of the original apostles of the Church of Jesus Christ of Saints of the Most High.

In the Kingdom of Heaven, reincarnation and the designation of the true identity of some of the more illustrious residents became central to the life of the group. Davies claimed to be Michael the Archangel, a reincarnation of Adam, Abraham, and King David. Following the birth of his son Arthur on February 11, 1868, Davies revealed that he (Arthur) was Jesus Christ returned. Soon after the announcement, the size of the community doubled. A second child, David, was revealed to be none other than "God, the Eternal Father of Spirits." Both children were believed to be incarnate members of the Godhead, which, among various factions of the Morrisites, consisted only of God the Father and Jesus Christ.

The colony survived for a decade, but a series of events in 1879–1880 led to disaster. First, Davies's wife died. Then, in the winter of 1880, both of the divine children died of diphtheria. The disgruntled members of the community turned on Davies; one sued him and received a $3,200 judgment. The Kingdom's land was sold to satisfy the judgment and court costs. The loss of the land effectively destroyed the Kingdom of God. Davies moved to Mill Creek, Washington, with a few followers, remarried, and proclaimed that the daughter born to his second wife was the reincarnation of his first wife. A short time later he abandoned all semblance of rebuilding the Kingdom and moved to San Francisco, where he died in obscurity.

Sources:

Anderson, C. Leroy. *For Christ Will Come Tomorrow: The Saga of the Morrisites*. Logan, UT: Utah State University Press, 1981.

LDS Scripture Researchers

Also known as the Believe God Society and Doers of the Word, the LDS Scripture Researchers was a small group headed by Sherman Russell Lloyd, a music teacher in Salt Lake City. Members believed that the present age is the time for the promised return of Joseph Smith, Jr., in the flesh reincarnated. He was believed to be a member of their group. While accepting the basic Mormon scripture, they also read the writings of Emanuel Swedenborg. The group was organized under the authority of the one spoken of in Third Nephi 20:23, who would come forth with fabulous information. The group published several pamphlets.

United Outcasts of Israel

The United Outcasts of Israel was a small, short-lived Mormon group that emerged in the 1950s under the leadership of Noel B. Pratt, a descendant of Parley Pratt, a first-generation leader of the Church of Jesus Christ of Latter-day Saints. Noel Pratt left that church and joined the polygamy-practicing Church of the First Born of the Fullness of Times soon after its founding in 1955. In 1957 he became the editor of *The Rolling Stone*, a periodical for the Church of the First Born. However, by the end of 1958 Pratt's opinion of the church's founder, Joel LeBaron, had changed dramatically, and in the December 1958 issue of *The Rolling Stone* he attacked LeBaron and his brothers, who were working with him. As a result, Pratt was excommunicated from the church. With a small following, he founded the United Outcasts of Israel, headquartered in Alexandria, Virginia.

Pratt emerged as the champion of a barter system of economics and advised people to put all of their money into tangible assets, especially in real estate. He founded a credit association, a bank, and a political party to further embody his ideals. Then, as quickly as he had emerged, Pratt quit, for reasons not altogether clear, but possibly from a lack of support. In November 1960 he announced, "My records and books are burned, as a testimony that I no longer shall seek to set myself up as a light unto the world." The United Outcasts of Israel was dissolved.

Within a year, however, Pratt developed a new cause, the restoration of Native Americans—in his view the present outcasts and rightful heirs of Israel—to their proper place in the world. In this regard he founded American Indians Restoration Enterprises, an organization dedicated to the organization of American Indians into a self-governing body. In that effort he published a new edition of the Book of Mormon under the title *The Indian Bible*. In the introduction he presented the book as a history of Native Americans. He suggested that in the near future Native Americans would be restored to their white skin and would subsequently build a great city centered on a temple to the Great Spirit. In so doing the Indians would save the present white people from self-destruction. Like the United Outcasts, American Indian Restoration Enterprises lasted only a few years.

Pratt pursued at least two further efforts to find a following. In the mid-1960s he emerged in Independence, Missouri, and called attention to his preaching through advertisements in the local newspaper. His presence was noted because of his prediction that the leadership of the Reorganized Church of Jesus Christ of Latter-day Saints would be killed by lightning. His prediction was not fulfilled, and he returned to a period of obscurity. In the mid-1980s he emerged in Salem, Massachusetts, as the head of Praetorian Press. After several years, the Press was relocated to Maine.

Sources:

Pratt, Noel B. *An Apology of Conscience*. N.p.: Author, 1959.

Shields, Steven L. *Divergent Paths of the Restoration*. Los Angeles: Restoration Press, 1990.

POLYGAMY-PRACTICING

Church of the First Born

When Joel LeBaron (d. 1972), founder of the Church of the First Born of the Fullness of Times, claimed Patriarchal Priesthood for himself, his brother, Ross Wesley LeBaron, rejected Joel's claim in favor of himself. He thus left his brother's church and formed the Church of the First Born. The statement of beliefs published by Ross LeBaron emphasized belief in Michael, the Eternal Father, and in his Son, Jesus Christ, and in Joseph Smith, the witness and testator. The Church of the First Born, said to be established originally by Adam and restored in Joseph Smith, firmly held a belief in One Mighty and Strong to come. LeBaron disincorporated the church in the early 1980s.

Sources:

LeBaron, Ross. *The Redemption of Zion*. Colonia LeBaron, Chih., Mexico: Church of the First-Born, [1962].

LeBaron, Verlan M. *The LeBaron Family*. Lubbock, TX: Author, 1981.

Perfected Church of Jesus Christ Immaculate Latter-Day Saints

Among the most unusual of the polygamy-practicing churches was the Perfected Church of Jesus Christ Immaculate Latter-Day Saints, founded by William C. Conway, D.D., of Redondo Beach, California, who claimed to be "the scribe and goodwill ambassador for 500,000 Indians," members of the Perfected Church. Conway claimed that when the Church of Jesus Christ of Latter-day Saints rejected the six commandments given to Joseph Smith (concerned with the united order and plural marriage primarily), Jesus Christ walked out of the church to Walker Lake, Nevada. There, in the spring of 1890, directed by visions and dreams, several hundred Indians had assembled. Jesus reestablished the kingdom as it was in pre-Edenic days and gave Joseph Smith's authority to one of their members, a young white Indian from Yu-ka-tan, named Eachta Eacha Na. He is identified with the One Mighty and Strong, the prophetic personage mentioned in the Mormon scriptures, the Doctrines and Covenants 85. The reincarnated Joseph Smith and Angel Moroni (an angel mentioned in the Book of Mormon) are with the One Mighty and Strong.

In 1930 additional keys of authority were transferred by Lorin C. Woolley, founder of the United Order Effort, the largest of the Mormon fundamentalist groups. Woolley was supposedly one of the five authorized to continue plural marriage by President John Taylor of the LDS Church.

Conway also claimed that Moroni "succeeded in perfecting a plan of instruction that abolished menstruation among the woman folk," and that Jesus had explained the technique of immaculate conception, by which babies stay for 12 months in the womb and are immune to all disease.

MISSOURI MORMONS

Church of Christ, Nondenominational Bible Assembly

The Church of Christ, Nondenominational Bible Assembly, grew out of a splintering movement among former members of the Reorganized Church of Jesus Christ of Latter Day Saints and the Church of Christ (Temple Lot) in the 1940s. The church was founded and led in its first generation by Pauline Hancock, the daughter of a leader in the Reorganized Church. In the mid-1920s she sided with those church members who protested the realignment of authority in the Reorganized Church into the church president's hands, and in 1926 she joined the Church of Jesus Christ (Protest Group). She was the church's secretary for most of the years of its existence but also worked within a congregation of the Church of Christ (Temple Lot). In 1931, when the Protest Church disbanded, she followed the majority of members in joining the Church of Christ (Temple Lot). Hancock continued as a powerful figure and teacher in the congregation of the former Protest group.

Over the years Hancock began to absorb the idea of the single Godhead, a more orthodox Christian understanding of God, as opposed to the generally accepted Mormon understanding of God as being several personages. Some Mormons held this view of God, but it was not generally taught within the church. During

the 1940s she also began to lead a Friday evening study group that researched apparent discrepancies in the Bible, the Book of Mormon, and the Doctrine and Covenants (the third Mormon scripture). Gradually, the group began to believe that the Reorganized Church taught a number of ideas that contradicted the Bible and the Book of Mormon.

Underlying her teaching role, Hancock had experienced several visions. In January 1950, responding to one of these visions, she baptized a number of the people attending her church. She began to assume the full duties as pastor of the congregation, including leadership of the Sunday meetings. She cited Joseph Smith's "ordination" of Emma Smith, his wife, as precedent for her assuming the pastoral role. When the Church of Christ was asked to leave the property, the church purchased a lot at Crysler and Linden Streets in Independence, Missouri, where it established itself as the Church of Christ (Bible and Book of Mormon Teaching). Over the next decade Hancock and the church departed from numerous doctrines held by most Mormons.

The early 1970s became a critical period in the history of the group. During 1973 the group discovered and accepted as factual evidence that Joseph Smith, Jr., was a fraud. At that point the group decided it must discontinue any use of the Book of Mormon. On November 24, 1973, the church issued a statement that appeared in the local newspaper to the effect that the Book of Mormon was not of divine origin and that the group would henceforth rely solely on the Bible.

In subsequent years the church moved toward an orthodox evangelical Christian position. It taught the exclusive authority of the Bible, the Trinity, the deity of Christ, and the destiny of humanity in an afterlife in heaven or hell. Dissenting from Mormon beliefs, the church denied that the gospel was ever taken from the earth; hence there has been no need for a restoration. Baptism by immersion was retained. After a generation of activity, the church disbanded in the early 1990s and its members moved into other evangelical churches.

Sources:

Correspondence between Israel Smith and Pauline Hancock on Baptism for the Dead. Independence, MO: Church of Christ, [1955].

Hancock, Pauline. *The Godhead, Is There More Than One?* Independence, MO: Church of Christ, n.d.

————. *Whence Came the Book of Mormon?* Independence, MO: Church of Christ, [1958].

Wood, Samuel. *The Infinite God*. Fresno, CA: Author, 1934.

Church of Christ/Order of Zion

The Church of Christ/Order of Zion was organized in Kansas City, Missouri, in 1918 by John Zahnd, a former member of the Reorganized Church of Jesus Christ of Latter Day Saints. Zahnd emerged during World War I

as a critic of church organization. He rejected the idea of a First Presidency, seeing it as an umbilical office, and suggested that the church should be headed by the Twelve Apostles. His conclusions led him to believe that Joseph Smith, Jr., the prophet to whom Mormons look as their founder, should never have taken the authority to assume the presidency of the church, though he was undoubtedly a prophet of God. Equally important, Zahnd believed that the entire church should be living according to the united order, that is, communally.

The church was organized in September 1918. He began a periodical, *The Order of Zion*. The next month Zahnd received a revelation designating him an apostle (elder) and naming several men as priests and apostles. Two men were also named as bishops to handle the temporal affairs of the church. At the annual meeting, 12 men among the elders were chosen by casting lots as the Twelve Apostles to head the church.

The church seems to have survived approximately a decade in the Kansas City area.

Sources:

Zahnd, John. *All Things Common*. Kansas City, MO: Church of Christ/Order of Zion, 1919.

————. *The Old Paths*. Kansas City, MO: Church of Christ/Order of Zion, 1920.

————. *The Order of Zion*. Kansas City, MO: Order of Zion, n.d.

Church of Jesus Christ of Latter-day Saints (William Smith)

William Smith (1811–1893) was the brother of Joseph Smith, Jr. (1805–1844), the prophet and founder of the Church of Jesus Christ of Latter-day Saints. Following the deaths of both Joseph and Hyrum Smith (another brother; 1800–1844), William emerged as the leading member of the family in the church. However, he had significant disagreements with Brigham Young (1801–1877), who succeeded Joseph Smith as the new president of the church following Smith's assassination in 1844. When Young demoted William Smith, who had been the church's patriarch, Smith responded by publishing a statement comparing Young to Pontius Pilate. On October 19, 1845, Young excommunicated Smith.

Cut off, Smith then associated for a time with James Jesse Strang (1813–1856). He reappeared in 1847 with the announcement that he was the church's new president. He excommunicated the leadership that had acknowledged Young. Smith's actions, occurring as Young was moving with a large group of the Saints to Utah, were intended to call together those who had remained behind in the Midwest. He called for a gathering in Lee County, Illinois. He was assisted by Aaron Hook, whom he had appointed his counselor. A second center developed in Covington, Kentucky, but was lost in the controversy following

Smith's acknowledgment that he was open to the practice of polygamy. In 1849 Smith gained the support of Lyman Wight (1796–1858), and his colony in Texas came into Smith's church.

Smith's following never stabilized and within a few years dissolved. The majority of the membership, including Smith, joined the Reorganized Church of Jesus Christ of Latter Day Saints, which had been organized in 1852.

Sources:

Shields, Steven L. *Divergent Paths of the Restoration*. Los Angeles: Restoration Research, 1990.

————. *The Latter Day Saint Churches: An Annotated Bibliography*. New York: Garland Publishing, 1987.

Church of Jesus Christ (Protest Movement)

The Church of Jesus Christ (Protest Movement) was founded in 1926 by Thomas W. Williams (1975–1931) and others who protested the actions of Frederick M. Smith, then president of the Reorganized Church of Jesus Christ of Latter Day Saints. In 1924, in what became known as the "Supreme Directional Control Controversy," Smith asked for more direct managerial authority over the programs of the church. Many saw his request as a move to gain power at the expense of members and other leaders. Several hundred members signed and presented to the 1925 church general conference a formal document opposing the governmental changes. When their protest was rebuffed and further attempts to be heard seemed lost, they held a conference in February 1926 to form a new church. The group survived for several years, but at the end of the decade Williams, the acknowledged leader, moved to Los Angeles, California. After his death in 1931 the church was disbanded. The largest number of protest group members joined the Church of Christ (Temple Lot).

Church of Jesus Christ Restored

The Church of Jesus Christ Restored began in 1979 when a group of members from the Reorganized Church of Jesus Christ of Latter Day Saints separated from that church and began to hold independent meetings. They called Stanley M. King to lead the restored church, which began a vigorous outreach program. King had received a number of revelations that became part of the church's scripture. A mission in Independence, Missouri, was opened in the mid-1970s, as well as churches in India and the Netherlands.

The church believed that it is necessary for Christians to be a part of the true church on earth and that both the Church of Jesus Christ of Latter-day Saints and the Reorganized Church of Jesus Christ of Latter Day Saints had apostatized. The Church of Jesus Christ Restored was God's chosen church to preach the fullness of the gospel. The church was organized under a First Presidency, a Council of Twelve Apostles,

the Standing High Council of the Church, a Presiding Bishopric, and a Presiding Patriarch.

The purpose of the church was the perfection of its human members. In order to reach perfection, life must be lived in the stakes of God. Stakes are communities built around a central temple, the place for the performance of the high ordinances of the church. Each member's task was to become independent of, and above, every creature and system of this world.

The church accepted the Book of Mormon (the inspired version of the Bible as revised by Joseph Smith, Jr.), the Doctrines and Covenants, and the additional prophecies received by King.

Following King's death in 1987, church members kept his body out of the ground for three days, hoping it would be resurrected. It was then buried. Subsequently, the leadership of the group collapsed and the church soon dissolved. The majority of members affiliated with the Restoration Church of Jesus Christ of Latter Day Saints.

Church of Jesus Christ (Williams)

The Church of Jesus Christ emerged out of what was called the "Supreme Directional Control" controversy within the Reorganized Church of Jesus Christ of Latter Day Saints. The controversy flared in 1924 when Frederick M. Smith (1915–1946), president of the Reorganized Church, requested more managerial authority in directing the program agencies of the church. Some members, including Thomas W. Williams (1875–1931), immediately objected as they saw in the request a dangerous move to centralize power in the president's hands with a resultant loss of democratic controls by the members. Leaders of what became known as the protest held a prayer meeting that lasted for 10 days prior to the 1925 general conference at which the request would be considered.

At the close of the prayer meeting, approximately 25 people signed a statement protesting what they saw as granting "supreme directional control" that would "fundamentally change the established order of the church." The conference sustained Smith's request, and many of the protest leaders left the church. While the largest group that withdrew transferred their membership to the Church of Christ (Temple Lot), others called a conference to meet in Independence, Missouri, in April 1926, at which they organized the Church of Jesus Christ. Williams was among the several men elected to the executive committee that headed the new church.

The Church of Jesus Christ generally followed beliefs and practices of the Reorganized Church, though the church issued its own statement of doctrine. The church moved away from acceptance of the Doctrine and Covenants and replaced it with the older Book of Commandments. More important, in reaction to the centralized structure of the Reorganized Church, the new church had an extremely loose organization. Biennial church conferences were held regularly for a

few years, but the issue that called the church into existence faded in prominence, and the leadership's commitment to the church declined. Williams, the church's primary leader, moved to California before the end of the decade, and his death in 1931 seemed to seal the fate of the new church. It soon disbanded, and the majority of the members went into the Church of Christ (Temple Lot).

Sources:

Shields, Steven L. *Divergent Paths of the Restoration*. Los Angeles: Restoration Press, 1990.

Williams, T. W. *The Protest Movement: Its Meaning and Purpose*. Independence, MO: Church of Jesus Christ, 1926.

Lundgren Faction

In 1983 Jeffrey Lundgren (1950–2006), born in Independence, Missouri, and raised there as a member of the Reorganized Church of Jesus Christ of Latter Day Saints, was ordained a priest in the church (a ceremony through which most male members pass). In 1984 he moved to Kirtland to work at the Kirtland Temple, the original temple constructed by Joseph Smith, Jr., the prophet on whose writings the church is based. The Kirtland Temple is a popular tourist site, especially for Mormons, and Lundgren served as a tour guide.

Within a few years Lundgren gave voice to several ideas at variance with the teachings of the Reorganized Church. He formed a study group of church members with whom he shared his ideas. During 1987 officials in the church became aware of his heterodox notions and began to monitor his work with the tourists. In 1988 the church stripped him of his priesthood, silenced him, and fired him from his position at the temple. On October 21, he and his wife formally withdrew from the church and, with approximately 30 followers, organized separately. Lundgren proclaimed himself a prophet and established a communal living arrangement.

Over the next several months Lundgren claimed to have found a chamber holding the golden plates from which the Book of Mormon was written and a sword of Laban spoken of in that book. He believed that Kirtland was to be the center of the new Zion and developed plans to gather several hundred followers, take over the Kirtland Temple, and from there await the return of Christ.

Before the group could take over the temple, however, Lundgren decided to pursue purifying and ritual cleansing actions, including a period in the wilderness. On April 17, 1989, five people, Dennis and Cheryl Avery and their three children, were executed as an act of cleansing. Some 20 people were involved in some way with the murders, though Lundgren himself pulled the trigger. After the murders the group moved to Davis, West Virginia, and then to Chillowee,

Missouri. The group then appears to have split up over disagreements as to Lundgren's status as a prophet.

The murder of the Averys came to light in January 1990 when the five bodies were discovered. Within a few days, most of those involved were arrested. Lundgren and his wife, found in San Diego, California, were convicted at a trial later that year. Lundgren was sentenced to death and his wife to life imprisonment. Other members of the group received lesser sentences. By these legal proceedings, the remnant of the group was effectively disbanded. Lundgren was executed on October 24, 2006.

Sources:

Earley, Pete. *Prophet of Death*. New York: Morrow, 1991.

New Jerusalem Church of Jesus Christ

The New Jerusalem Church of Jesus Christ was founded in Independence, Missouri, in 1975 by Barney Fuller, a former member of the Reorganized Church of Jesus Christ of Latter Day Saints. For more than a decade Fuller had been protesting the spread of liberalism in the reorganized church and as early at 1967 had published a book, *Have You Received the Holy Ghost?*, in which he and his co-authors argued that the Holy Ghost had been withdrawn from the church. In 1969, together with others in protest against what they agreed were unwelcome trends in the Reorganized Church, he formed World Redemption. At this time the church was experiencing some dissent over changes in church school curricula, the attendance at a Methodist seminary of some ministerial leaders, and the promotion of the cause of female ordination.

Fuller and the other leaders of the group were silenced by the church leadership but made their views known through a periodical, *Zion's Warning* (1970–75). World Redemption continued until 1975 when it was superseded by the New Jerusalem Church. The new church adopted the Book of Mormon, the Book of Commandments, and the Inspired Version of the Bible as scripture and gained some popular support from conservative members of that church. However, in 1976 Fuller renounced the Latter Day Saint scriptures, and the majority of his supporters withdrew. A short time later, the church was disbanded.

Sources:

Fuller, Barney R. *Stick of Joseph*. Pasadena, CA: Tri Tech Publications, 1969.

———, Glen Stout, and William Spilsbury. *Have You Received the Holy Ghost?*. La Mirada, CA: Authors, 1967.

Shields, Steven L. *Divergent Paths of the Restoration*. Los Angeles: Restoration Press, 1990.

OTHER MORMONS

Church of the Messiah

The Church of the Messiah was formed in 1861 in Springfield, Massachusetts, by George J. Adams (c. 1811–1880). Adams had become a follower of Mormon prophet Joseph Smith, Jr., in 1840. During the 1840s, the Nauvoo, Illinois, years of the Church of Jesus Christ of Latter-day Saints, he took several mission journeys to England and Massachusetts. He was in Nauvoo when Smith was assassinated, an event that deeply affected him. Discouraged, Adams soon fell into conflict with Brigham Young, who had emerged as the new president of the church. In 1845 Young excommunicated Adams. Adams then associated for a time with James Jesse Strang. He put his theatrical knowledge to the task of staging the coronation of Strang as "King of the Kingdom of God." Then in 1856 he was excommunicated from the Strangite church.

Adams emerged from obscurity in 1860 and began to identify himself as a minister of the Church of the Messiah. He published a short work on a traditional Mormon theme, *Lecture on the Destiny and Mission of America and the True Origin of the Indians*. However, his essential message was the imminent return of Jesus Christ and the redemption of Israel. To that end, he founded the Church of the Messiah in 1861 and issued a Church Covenant signed by 43 people. The next year he began a periodical, *The Sword of Truth*, issued from his home in South Lebanon, Maine.

In summer 1865 Adams acted on revelations he had received and moved to the Holy Land. The following year 156 church members joined him in the attempt to establish a colony. The effort failed in a few years from lack of local government cooperation and scarce water resources. By 1870 Adams and his following had returned to the United States. He reestablished his Church of the Messiah in Philadelphia, Pennsylvania, and pastored it for the rest of his life. After his death in 1880, the church soon dissolved.

Sources:

Holmes, Reed M. *The Forerunners*. Independence, MO: Herald Publishing House, 1981.

Shields, Steven L. *Divergent Paths of the Restoration*. Los Angeles: Restoration Research, 1990.

Congregation of Jehovah's Presbytery of Zion

The Congregation of Jehovah's Presbytery of Zion was founded in 1847 by Charles Blanchard Thompson (1814–1890s), a former member of the Church of Jesus Christ of Latter-day Saints. Blanchard, among the first to respond to the message of Mormon prophet Joseph Smith, Jr., joined the Mormons in the 1830s in Kirtland, Ohio. After Smith's murder, he joined the Church of Jesus Christ (Strangite), a Mormon faction led by James Jesse Strang, but left it

and moved to St. Louis. He soon began to receive revelations which became the basis of his new church.

On New Year's Day, 1848, Thompson issued a revelation that accused the Latter-day Saints of failure in God's eyes for not completing the temple abandoned at Nauvoo, the Mormon settlement in Western Illinois. The Congregation of Jehovah's Presbytery of Zion was to be a temporary substitute for the real Zion to be established in Independence, Missouri. A few weeks later he denounced the polygamy practices instituted among the saints. Because of Smith's actions, Thompson's progeny could not inherit the keys to the kingdom, which had been transferred to him. By 1853 approximately 50 families had affiliated with the congregation. They purchased a tract of land in Monona County, Iowa, and began to build Preparation, a communal settlement. The settlement failed in 1857, just after Thompson had issued his collection of revelations. Thompson was also accused of mismanaging funds. Driven from the community, he returned to St. Louis to reestablish the congregation there and developed a small following. During this time he published another book, *The Nachash Origin of the Black and Mixed Races*. It was an elaborate anthology that included a defense of slavery. But his hopes of rebuilding were dashed by the lawsuit over the Iowa property, which was awarded to the former members in 1867. Thompson moved to Philadelphia, where, for the third time, he rebuilt the congregation and began a newspaper, *Cyips Herald*. In 1888 this group also disintegrated as the result of an internal dispute. Thompson died in obscurity a few years later.

Sources:

Arbaugh, George Bartholomew. *Revelation in Mormonism*. Chicago: University of Chicago Press, 1932.

Thompson, Charles Blanchard. *The Nachash Origin of the Black and Mixed Races*. St. Louis: George Knapp & Co., 1860.

Primitive Church of Jesus Christ (Bickertonite)

In 1914 a schism occurred in the Church of Jesus Christ (Bickertonite). A schismatic group, led by James Caldwell, formed the Primitive Church of Jesus Christ at Washington, Pennsylvania. They were joined shortly by another Bickertonite schism, the Reorganization Church, which had formed in 1907 under the leadership of Elder Allen Wright. Caldwell was succeeded by his nephew, Lawrence Dias. The Primitive Church largely followed the beliefs and practices of the parent body but held that the institution in 1830 of the office of the first presidency was an introduction of an alien institution. The members opposed polygamy, plurality of gods, and baptism for the dead.

By the 1970s the church has dwindled to a single congregation in Erie, Pennsylvania. The congregation later disbanded; some of the members rejoined the parent group.

Reorganized Church of Jesus Christ (Wright)

The Reorganized Church of Jesus Christ (Wright) was founded in 1907 by Allen Wright, formerly a member of the Twelve Apostles of the Church of Jesus Christ (Bickertonite). At the Bickertonite general conference in 1907, Wright's pamphlet, in which he expressed dissenting opinions on the millennium and the return of Jesus Christ to earth, was publicly condemned. The conference passed a resolution suspending any who believed in Wright's ideas. Wright and five other church apostles refused to sustain the conference actions and as a result were removed from office and excommunicated. Several months later, with their supporters, Wright and the other apostles held a conference and founded a reorganized church. Except for the issue that occasioned the split, the Reorganized Church followed the beliefs and practices of its parent body. One of the former apostles, William T. Maxwell, was named as president. The church seems to have continued into the mid-1930s, when it disintegrated and its members returned to either the Bickertonite church or other Mormon bodies.

Sources:

Armburst, J. L. *Reformation or Restoration, or Which Is the Church? Jesus Christ Established but One Visible Church*. N.p.: Reorganized Church of Jesus Christ, 1929.

Maxwell, W. T. *A Statement Issued by the Re-Organized Church of Jesus Christ, July 4th, 1908*. Youngwood, PA: Re-Organized Church of Jesus Christ, 1908.

Shields, Steven L. *Divergent Paths of the Restoration*. Los Angeles: Restoration Press, 1990.

Wright, Allen. *A Conversation on the Thousand Years' Reign of Christ*. St. John, KS: The County Capital, 1907.

 # 16. Communal

COMMUNAL–BEFORE 1960

Adonai-Shomo

Adonai-Shomo was an Adventist communal group founded in 1861 at Athol, Massachusetts, by Frederick T. Howland, a Quaker who had accepted the Adventist perspective on the imminent Second Coming of Jesus. Among the beliefs Howland taught the group of some 30 members was Sabbatarianism (worship on Saturday, then becoming a popular perspective within Adventist circles) and the equality of men and women. Howland also believed in physical immortality. The group faced a major crisis when Howland was killed in an accident a few years after the group was formed.

A short time after Howland's death, a man named Cook arrived and announced that God had sent him to become the new leader of the group. He was accepted as leader, but when he tried to institute some unconventional sex practices, the group revolted; he was indicted by a local grand jury. The next leader, a man named Richards, headed the group for many years. Under Richards, the group prospered for a generation, and the colony moved to a large house on an 840-acre tract of land near Petersham, Massachusetts.

By the 1890s the group had dwindled, with many of the original members having died and the younger members moved away. The end of Adonai-Shomo came in 1896 when a group of young ex-members sued Richards in an attempt to gain some equity in the property. They won, but when the land was sold there was nothing left after the community's debts and legal fees were paid. The charter that had been granted in 1876 was dissolved, and the group formally disbanded.

Sources:

Communities of the Past and Present. Newllano, LA: Llano Cooperative Colony, 1924.

Webber, Everett. *Escape to Utopia: The Communal Movement in America*. New York: Hastings House Publishers, 1959.

Altruria

Altruria was a communal experiment that grew out of an attempt to merge liberal Protestantism with the vision of an ideal society as expressed by William Dean Howells (1837–1920) in his utopian novel *A Traveler from Altruria* (1894). The novel inspired the thinking of Rev. Edward Biron Payne, a Unitarian pastor in Berkeley, California, who had been advocating a form of Christian socialism in his sermons. Of the essence of Christian socialism was the idea of the immanence of God in the social context and a program of saving people by reorganizing society in such a way that the sinful structures perpetuated by capitalism would be discarded. Humanity would improve by learning to live in a more just society that emphasized brotherhood, cooperation, and good will.

Payne and a small group of idealists met in 1894 to draft plans for a cooperative colony based on democratic suffrage and equality of community goods with some retention of private ownership of personal possessions. A site was selected near Fountain Grove, California, and in October, 18 adults and 6 children moved onto the land. A community periodical, the *Altrurian*, kept the larger community of supporters informed of its progress and promoted the formation of Altrurian clubs across the state. Clubs emerged in San Francisco, Oakland, Berkeley, San Jose, Pasadena, and Los Angeles. The clubs began to establish cooperative ventures and served as screening agencies for people desiring to move into the colony.

Although it attracted a number of new members, Altruria suffered from undercapitalization and poor financial planning. Within a year bankruptcy was imminent, and in June 1895 a reorganization plan was announced. The colony's assets were liquidated and the entire effort restructured into several smaller units. Sixteen members moved to a new colony near Cloverdale, a second group moved to Santa Rosa, and a few remained at the original site. However, the restructuring only postponed the inevitable, and the next year all three of the subunits disbanded.

Sources:

Hine, Robert V. *California's Utopian Colonies*. San Marino, CA: Huntington Library, 1953.

Association of Beneficents

In 1953 John Murray Spear and a group of Spiritualists established the Association of Beneficents at Kiantone, New York, in Chautauqua County in the western part of the state. Three years earlier, a blacksmith at Kiantone had gone into a trance in which information came forth that the area around a spring in the community had once been the site of a perfect society. Free love was one element in that perfection. The blacksmith sent samples of the water, which he believed had special magnetic and healing properties, to various prominent Spiritualists, including Spear. A former Universalist, Spear had received communication from the spirit world instructing him to initiate some radical changes in society. He was told to inaugurate a model community and was even given the location, the design for domiciles, and a program for social reform. He decided that the site at Kiantone conformed to the information he had been given and would be an ideal location for building a city of universal harmony. In the spring of 1893 he constructed 10 small oval and octagonal homes, each approximately 10 feet by 14 feet, and attracted upward of 40 members, though most wintered away from the site. The colony was also known as the Domain, Harmonia, and the Kiantone Community.

Those attracted were feminists and believers in Spiritualism and free love. These were all espoused in a large convention held on the site by Spiritualists in 1858.

In 1859 the colonists abandoned the site and headed down the Mississippi River to promote a "planetary congress" to bring peace on earth. At the beginning of their journey, they reorganized as the Sacred Order of Unionists. Their journey was interrupted by a side trip to Patriot, Indiana, where in early 1860 they established a second colony that survived until 1863.

Sources:

Duino, Russell. "Utopian Themes with Variation: John Murray Spear and His Kiantone Domain." *Pennsylvania History* (April 1962).

Fogarty, Robert S. *Dictionary of American Communal and Utopian History*. Westport, CT: Greenwood Press, 1980.

Bethel-Aurora Communities

The communities of Bethel (Missouri) and Aurora (Oregon) were the result of the leadership of William Keil (1812–1877), a former Methodist minister who launched his first communal experiment in 1844. Keil, an Austrian by birth, arrived in the United States as a young man. He became a tailor and then a Methodist preacher at Phillipsburg, Pennsylvania. Along the way he came to see himself as one of the end-time witnesses mentioned in the biblical book of Revelation. In the early 1940s some former members of the Harmony Society, at the time headquartered not far away at Economy, Pennsylvania, left and joined Keil's church. From them he possibly developed the idea of forming a community.

In the spring of 1844, with his congregation of 200 members (all German-speaking), Keil moved onto a 2,560-acre tract in northern Missouri. He named the new community Bethel, after the old biblical town. The town tripled in size over the next three years. The colonists built a church in which Keil preached a simple Christianity that centered on primary Christian affirmations and the Golden Rule. Keil preached at the monthly church services.

A first branch colony was founded at Nineveh, Adair County, Missouri, in 1847. At its height it housed some 150 people on 2,000 acres. In 1856 a second group left Bethel for the far West. They settled in the Willamette River Valley about 30 miles from Portland and built another town, Aurora. Keil chose to move with the group to Oregon.

The Bethel and Aurora communities prospered through the 1870s. However, Keil died in 1877, and soon afterward both groups dissolved their communal structures. Historic museums survive at both sites today to interpret the history to visitors and tourists, and many descendants of the colonists still live in the two towns.

Sources:

Hendricks, R. J. *Bethel and Aurora*. 1933. Reprint, New York: AMS Press.

Hinds, William Alfred. *American Communities and Cooperative Colonies*. Chicago: Charles H. Kerr & Company, 1908.

Bishop Hill

Bishop Hill was a pietistic Christian community that originated in the independent preaching of Eric Janson (1808–1850) in the 1830s in Sweden. Janson had rejected the writings of Luther and professed to preach the Bible alone. Members of his group refused to attend their parish church, a fact that brought them (and their leader) to the attention of the authorities. The Church of Sweden showed little patience toward

Janson and charged him with spreading heresy. In the face of continuing repression, the group commissioned one of their number, Olaf Olson, to search out possibilities of a new life in America. He arrived in 1845 and purchased land in Henry County, Illinois. Janson also came that year (to avoid a jail term in Sweden), and the group, 1,200 strong, arrived the next year.

In 1850 Janson was shot by a disgruntled former member of the community who had been prevented by Janson from marrying a community member. The community continued without him. In 1853 they finally surmounted the legal difficulties surrounding organizing as a corporation and formally established the community. Loosely organized, the community was led in its business dealings by a board of trustees, and several foremen organized the work. There were several preachers among them who shared the Sunday preaching duties but otherwise labored with the rest of the men through the week. Two worship services consisting of hymn singing, prayer, Bible reading, and preaching, were held each Sunday.

The simple community life continued until a significant number of youth reached adulthood and complained of boredom with the life and disbelief in the religion. In several steps during 1861 and 1862, the communal organization was abandoned and the property divided among the members. The church gave way to two new congregations, the members becoming either Methodists or Adventists.

Today, the Bishop Hill State Historic Site offers self-guided tours of several surviving buildings of the old Bishop Hill community. A historical museum interprets the story of Bishop Hill to tourists and visitors.

Sources:

Nordhoff, Charles. *The Communistic Societies of the United States*. 1875. Reprint, New York: Schocken Books, 1965.

Brotherhood of the New Life

The Brotherhood of the New Life was the collective name given to the followers of prophet and visionary Thomas Lake Harris (1823–1906), whose movement took on a number of different organizational forms during his lifetime. Born in England, Harris was raised a strict Baptist but as a young man became a Universalist. At some point he migrated to the United States and in 1844 emerged as the pastor of the Fourth Universalist Church of New York City. While serving that church, however, he read the writings of the Swedish philosopher Emanuel Swedenborg (1688–1772) and converted to the Church of the New Jerusalem, an ecclesiastical organization founded by Swedenborg's followers. In 1847 he became pastor of a Swedenborgian congregation in New York. Swedenborgianism led him into Spiritualism, which was spreading across the nation at that time. In 1851 he became involved in the short-lived Spiritualist Mountain Cove Community in Fayette County, Virginia.

In the years after the failure of the Mountain Cove experiment, Harris became a writer and editor and a champion of Christian Spiritualism (the Spiritualist community having been divided into Christian and non-Christian factions). He founded the Brotherhood of the New Life in 1861 in Wassaic, New York. The community moved to nearby Amenia, New York, in 1865, then to Brocton, in western New York, in 1868, and to Santa Rosa, California, in 1875. The Brocton community remained active through 1881 and became a screening place for people before moving to Fountain Grove, as the California center was called.

Harris's teachings evolved out of Swedenborgianism and Spiritualism. In the attempt to live out of the spiritual world, two ideas came to the fore. Harris believed himself to have been singled out as the core person to be the priest/king of a new society. His community would consist of people who had learned to breathe in harmony with himself, the "pivotal man." They would then become the vortex of divine power. The special breathing techniques enabled people to inhale what was believed to be a divine vapor and to repel evil spirits seen as pervasive in the atmosphere.

Harris became best known for his doctrines on sexuality. God, he taught, was bisexual, and he found sexuality expressed throughout nature. However, Harris called for a spiritualized sex life. Harris believed that one came closest to God when united with one's sexual counterpart. One's true counterpart existed in the spirit world and was able temporarily to inhabit a human body, but rarely did it inhabit the body of one's earthly spouse. Union with the counterpart could be obtained only in exalted states of consciousness reached through the breathing technique he taught.

In keeping with his arcane doctrine, spouses lived separately in the community and maintained celibacy. Harris fathered two children by his first wife but lived a celibate life with his second and third wives. However, Harris's writings were filled with sexual language that could be easily misunderstood by a reader unfamiliar with the metaphysical system out of which Harris operated. On several occasions, the community life was disturbed by accusations of sexual improprieties.

Harris came under strong attack in 1891 when Margaret Oliphant, whose cousin Laurence Oliphant (1829–1888) had been a member of the Brotherhood, and Alzire A. Chevaillier both published accounts of the community. Oliphant accused Harris of sexual immorality and improper financial maneuvering. Chevaillier centered her attack on Harris's strong control over the community, but also hinted at sexual wrongdoing. Harris left and settled in New York, attempting to manage the community from across the country. It continued after Harris's death in 1906. Gradually, the spiritual teachings of the group died out, and in the 1920s the property reverted to

Kanaye Nagasawa, the last of the community members.

Sources:

Fogarty, Robert S. *Dictionary of American Communal and Utopian History*. Westport, CT: Greenwood Press, 1980.

Hine, Robert V. *California's Utopian Colonies*. San Marino, CA: Huntington Library, 1953.

Celestia

Celestia was a nineteenth-century communal group that grew out of the Adventist excitement over the predicted imminent return of Christ. Among those affected by the preaching of Christ's return were Peter E. Armstrong and his wife Hannah Taylor Armstrong, who together operated a paper store in Philadelphia. Armstrong became convinced that Christ had been rejected during his life on earth because the people had not been prepared for his arrival. In his study of the Bible, he was drawn to Isaiah 40:3, "In the wilderness prepare ye the way of the Lord." He saw this passage as a personal message to himself and began to act on it literally. In 1850 he purchased a tract of land in Sullivan County, Pennsylvania, and began to lay plans for the building of a city modeled on the one described in Revelation 21:6. Eventually other pieces of land were added, bringing the total to some 600 acres by 1860.

Celestia (the new city) was to be on a mountain top and to be laid out in a set of squares. The people attracted to the new city would live in a theocracy apart from human law. The theocracy included a communal lifestyle. Armstrong moved onto the property in 1860, and Celestia was formally organized in 1863. The group was supported by farming and the operation of a few businesses. In 1864 Armstrong, in his most remembered action, deeded the land to God. Armstrong also created a second village that served as a probationary stopover for people inquiring about joining Celestia.

The community survived through the 1870s, though it never prospered. In 1876 the local county treasurer demanded the back taxes from God's property. The land was sold; Armstrong's son became the legal owner. Armstrong died in 1887 and the community faded away. His widow settled in Philadelphia.

Sources:

Bender, D. Wayne. *From Wilderness to Wilderness: Celestia*. Dushore, PA: Sullivan Review, 1980.

Miller, Timothy. *American Communes, 1860–1960: A Bibliography*. New York: Garland Publishing, 1990.

Chapter of Perfection

The Chapter of Perfection, frequently referred to as the Woman in the Wilderness community, was a pietistic Rosicrucian group founded in Germany in the seventeenth century by Johannes Jacob Zimmerman. The original members were primarily Lutheran scholars ready to delve into the inner mystical mysteries of life. Zimmerman had also been affected by two female seers who, drawing on their personal psychic visions, had published their speculations about the return of Jesus, possibly in 1694.

Zimmerman proposed that the members of the chapter leave the relatively hostile atmosphere of Germany and accept the offer of land tendered by William Penn, should they migrate to the new colony of Pennsylvania. There they would await the Second Coming. Zimmerman died in 1693, before the group's departure, and was succeeded by Johannes Kelpius. The group arrived in Philadelphia on June 24, 1694, just in time to celebrate the summer solstice on St. John's Eve.

The group settled in Germantown, which had been settled by other German colonists in 1683, on the Wissahickon Creek, north of Philadelphia. There they constructed a headquarters building, shaped as a cube, each side being 40 feet in length. Numerologically, 40 was believed to be a perfect number. The building had a sanctuary, study room, and meditation room. On the roof they established their astronomical laboratory, where during the evenings they scanned the sky for evidence of the imminent appearance of Christ. In the meantime, the brothers (all the members were male) founded a school for the neighborhood children, served as doctors for the community, and did astrological work for any who requested it.

The community lived through a series of disappointments when Christ did not return in 1694 or in 1700. Matthias died in 1708 after a lengthy illness, and the chapter began to disintegrate. The surviving members remained in the area as individual healers and psychic practitioners. Their work seems to have led directly to the practice of the hexen-meisters, magical practitioners who can still be found in rural southeastern Pennsylvania.

Sources:

Holloway, Mark. *Heavens on Earth: Utopian Communities in America, 1680–1880*. London: Turnstile Press, 1951.

Melton, J. Gordon. "Pioneers … in Land, in Knowledge, in Astrology!" *American Astrology* 41, no. 10 (December 1973): 18–21.

Christian Commonwealth Colony

Among the more important experiments in Christian socialism, the Christian Commonwealth was formed by the merger of two previously existing efforts, the Willard Cooperative Colony and the Christian Corporation. It was organized for the purpose of demonstrating to the world the desirability of Christian cooperative activity as a means to building a Christian civilization. The Willard Cooperative Colony had been formed in 1895 at Harriman, Tennessee, by a group of some 50 prohibitionists who sought an alternative to capitalist society. Frances Willard (1839–1898), then the prominent president of the Women's Christian Temperance Union, lent her name and support to the project. After its founding, the colonists settled on land near Andrews, North Carolina. The Christian Corporation was founded in 1896 by George Howard Gibson. The colony was located in Lincoln, Nebraska, and included some 26 members.

Both colonies experienced some instability, but in 1896 merged their efforts into a new colony in Muskogee County, Georgia, and were united by a vision of Christian brotherhood, a belief in making Christianity practical, and the desire to continue the cooperative life. Members of the two older colonies were joined by new members attracted by accounts of its plans in *The Kingdom*, a socialist magazine. The colonists began their own periodical, *The Social Gospel*.

The colony was supported by the Right Relationship League, a socialist group headquartered in Chicago, which advanced it some initial capital. The colonists began a textile mill and publishing concern. By 1898 the mill was producing and selling towels, but in 1899 the colony ran into trouble. The textile business failed, and several ex-members began to voice charges of mismanagement. In 1900 the Right Relationship League took steps to secure its investment. By the summer of 1900 the corporate assets went into receivership and the colony dispersed. At its height, some 90 people resided in the community.

Sources:

Hinds, William Alfred. *American Communities and Cooperative Colonies*. Chicago: Charles H. Kerr & Company, 1908.

Church of Jesus Christ of Latter-day Saints (Wight)

Lyman Wight (1796–1858) was one of the Twelve Apostles of the Church of Jesus Christ of Latter-day Saints during the Nauvoo, Illinois, years in the 1840s. With the formation of Texas as a new independent republic, Mormon prophet Joseph Smith, Jr. (1805–1844), had considered it a possible place of refuge for the embattled Saints. He commissioned Wight as the leader of a company to explore the opportunities in Texas, but the plan was postponed while Smith campaigned for president of the United States. It was further delayed by Smith's assassination in 1844. Brigham Young (1801–1877), who succeeded Smith as president of the church, disapproved of the plan. Nevertheless, Wight felt he had a commission from Smith and led a group of approximately 150 church members to Austin, Texas. The group settled near Fredericksburg and built a new town, Zodiac, in 1847. In 1848 Wight issued his sole statement relating his position to that of the church as a whole and defending himself against accusations made by

Young. On January 1, 1849, the group formally organized a new church and elected Wight as its president. Young excommunicated Wight a month later. A temple was dedicated on February 17, 1849, though little is known of how much of the temple ceremony from the Nauvoo period was carried over. A communal life was adopted.

In 1845, after a falling out, Young had excommunicated William Smith, the brother of Joseph Smith, Jr., and patriarch of the church at the time of the assassination. In 1847 Smith had emerged as the president and patriarch of a new church, and by 1849 he was looking toward Texas as a place of refuge. In 1850 he attempted to consolidate his work with that of Wight. As the two groups merged, Wight was named as Smith's counselor. Smith, because of his fraternal relationship to Joseph Smith, Jr., was granted the leadership of the church.

The church that Smith had created in the Midwest was never stable and had suffered a major controversy because of Smith's openness to polygamy. In the months following the merger, the organization completely fell apart and most of the membership, including Smith, moved into the Reorganized Church of Jesus Christ of Latter Day Saints, which had been constituted in 1852. With the disintegration in the Midwest, Wight's colony simply returned to its pre-merger organization.

Wight's colony prospered through the 1850s. Forced to move because of flooding in 1851 and 1853, the group eventually settled near Bandera, Texas. After Wight's sudden death in 1858, no new leader arose, and a short time later the colony united with the Reorganized Church.

Sources:

Hunter, J. Melvin. *The Lyman Wight Colony in Texas*. Bandera, TX: Author, n.d.

Shields, Steven L. *Divergent Paths of the Restoration*. Los Angeles: Restoration Research, 1990.

Wight, Lyman. *An Address by Way of an Abridged Account and Journal of My Life from February 1844 up to April 1848, with an Appeal to the Latter Day Saints, Scattered Abroad in the Earth*. Austin, TX: Author, 1848.

Church of the Covenant

The Church of the Covenant was one name for the religious community that arose in the larger community founded in the 1870s at Preston, California, under the leadership of Emily Preston. It was also referred to as the Church of Heaven or the religion of inspiration. The church began soon after Emily's husband, H. L. Preston, moved to land he purchased several miles north of Cloverdale, California, in 1869. Over the next few years he purchased some 1,500 acres. After the railroad was extended to Cloverdale, people began to arrive in the area and settled on or near the Preston land. A church building was erected and a town arose,

centered on Emily Preston's work as a healer and preacher.

As people moved to the community, attendance at the Sunday and Thursday church services was one requirement. Emily Preston had learned some of the secrets of herbal medicine during her youth, and in the years before her marriage, she had worked as a healer in San Francisco. She gave up her healing work after her marriage, but her husband saw a need for it and encouraged her to begin again after they moved to Preston. Many were drawn to Preston for either a brief visit or as residents following their receipt of some healing potions sent to them through the mail.

Preston seems to have preached a simple, practical faith built around the worship of God and the Golden Rule. She believed that how one led one's life determined whether one would go to heaven or hell after death. Worship consisted of a time of singing, quiet meditation, and Preston's preaching. She taught that verbal prayer was not needed as God knew what to do better than any humans did. It was proper to be thankful to God at all times. Her thoughts on religion were gathered in a book, *The Hell and the Heaven*, published in 1902. Preston had a peculiarity in generally referring to God as a Man (rather than a spirit). She referred to Christ as the Son of Man.

H. L. Preston died in 1887 and Emily in 1909. At the time of her death some 100 people lived at Preston, either on the Preston land or adjacent property. For several decades through the early twentieth century, people continued to gather at the church for periods of singing and silent meditation. Many of the structures at Preston continued to stand and be used into the 1980s. In 1988 a fire swept through the area and destroyed many of the buildings.

Sources:

Miller, Timothy. *American Communes, 1860–1960: A Bibliography*. New York: Garland Publishing, 1990.

Preston, Mrs. H. L. *The Hell and the Heaven*. Author, 1902.

Votruba, M. J. "The Preston Story." Unpublished paper in the collection of the Institute for the Study of American Religion, 1971.

Dorrilites

One of the first of the nonconventional religions founded among the European colonists in North America arose in New England in the years after the American Revolution (1775–1783). A former British Army officer named Dorril claimed to be a prophet of God and to be receiving revelations from him. He worked in Massachusetts and Vermont and gathered groups of followers during the 1790s. At its height, membership was approximately 40.

Dorril organized his followers communally. There was no private property, vegetarianism was strictly observed, and leather shoes were not allowed. It also appears that the group did away with marriage vows

and practiced a form of free love, though the records of their exact patterns of behavior have not survived. They were attacked for their sexual license by one contemporary minister, the Rev. Joseph Lathrop of Springfield, Massachusetts, who also noted that they disregarded the laws of the land and worked on the Sabbath.

The end of the small band is reported to have been brought on by a confrontation between Dorril and a local unbeliever. Dorril had told his followers that he was immune to pain. He was challenged by a man who proceeded to hit him several times. The man did not stop until Dorril announced not only his pain, but also promised not to make any further supernatural claims. The group dispersed shortly after the incident.

Sources:

Ludlum, David M. *Social Ferment in Vermont, 1791–1850*. New York: Columbia University Press, 1939.

Fruitlands

Fruitlands was a communal experiment established as a visible expression of the Transcendentalist Movement in nineteenth-century New England. Transcendentalism was an idealistic spiritualized philosophy, the end product of the questioning of Christian orthodoxy that began in Unitarianism. Whereas Unitarianism had found its base in rational thought, Transcendentalism was based more clearly in the nonrational. Its main exponent was Ralph Waldo Emerson (1803–1882), who admonished the readers of his many essays to embrace the spiritual realities that stand behind the visible world and to come to a comprehension of the oneness of spiritual reality. His thoughts would, in the late nineteenth century, lead directly to Christian Science and New Thought.

Fruitlands began in the idealism of A. Bronson Alcott (1799–1888), the father of the author Louisa May Alcott (1832–1888) and an associate of Emerson. In 1842 Emerson lent the financially strapped Alcott money to visit England, where a school had been established on a model of the school Alcott had established in Boston. While in England, Alcott met three men who shared his ideals and his vision of an ideal society. When he returned to America, two of them, Henry Wright and Charles Lane, along with Lane's son William, accompanied him. They also brought a large occult library. Charles Lane (1800–1870) put up the initial capital to obtain the land on which the community could be founded. The young idealists and the Alcott family moved to Fruitlands, a 90-acre farm about two miles from Harvard, Massachusetts.

The first goal of the Fruitlands program was personal reform through a number of behavior changes. The group accepted a strict vegetarian diet that disallowed even milk and butter. They did not drink coffee, tea, or alcoholic beverages and existed on a diet of apples, bread, cereal, herbs, and roots. The life at

Fruitlands was to be a simple one that allowed for the nurturing of culture. However, the group rejected the idea of using animals to assist in farming and soon found that their leisure time was taken up in the realities of farm life. Culture soon was limited to after-meal conversations. No form of religion was adopted, Transcendentalism being best expressed in individual mystical appropriation of a spiritual vision.

A communal dress was adopted. It consisted of linen tunics and shoes made of cork and canvas (rather than leather). The men had trousers and hats; the women wore bloomers. Daily baths were taken in unheated water.

While many came to see what Alcott had established, few joined and remained. They were unwilling to don the strange dress and accept the rigid diet. In the winter after the first year, the capital was used up and the community was forced to close. The land was sold at the beginning of 1844. At its height it had approximately 20 members.

Sources:

Hinds, William Alfred. *American Communities and Cooperative Colonies*. Chicago: Charles H. Kerr & Company, 1908.

Lawson, Donna. *Brothers and Sisters All Over This Land: America's First Communes*. New York: Praeger, 1972.

Webber, Everett. *Escape to Utopia: The Communal Movement in America*. New York: Hastings House, 1959.

Harmony Society

The Harmony Society was a prominent communal group that originated in the pietistic preaching of a farmer, George Rapp (1757–1847), who began to preach to his neighbors in a rural area of Württemburg, Germany. He was one of a number of unofficial preachers and Bible teachers who had emerged as purveyors of a popular pietistic religious faith to supplement the rather dry and ritualistic experience many had in the local Lutheran parish church. The Lutherans viewed such movements, such as those led by Rapp, as challenges to authorities rather than the natural outgrowth of faith. Rapp and some of his followers were fined, imprisoned, and subjected to various attempts to discourage their assembling. Such activity merely led to the group's expansion.

In 1803 Rapp left for America in an attempt to find land where the group could settle. He initially purchased land north of Pittsburgh in southwest Pennsylvania, and the next summer the group of more than 700 people migrated. They survived on their own through the winter of 1804–1805, but in 1805 they assembled on the land Rapp had purchased and formally organized the Harmony Society. At this time the group adopted a communal order that included a common purse, a simple form of dress, and a plan to care for the elderly and the children. They

then turned to the task of building a community based on farming and some related industries: a sawmill, a tannery, a distillery, and a winery. Following a wave of religious fervor that swept the community in 1807, they adopted celibacy (though not nuclear family life) and gave up tobacco.

In 1814 the community bought 30,000 acres of land along the Wabash River in southern Indiana, and the following year the entire community in Pennsylvania moved and founded the town of New Harmony. In 1818 the group renewed their communal commitment, signaled by their burning all the records of what each person and family had originally contributed to the group more than a decade earlier. However, New Harmony, while a great success financially, was less than what the group had hoped, and in 1824 and 1825 the group moved back to Pennsylvania on land near their earlier location and created the town of Economy. Robert Owen (1771–1858) purchased New Harmony and built his own community there. Economy prospered, as had the previous communities, and was disturbed only by a schism in 1832 when several hundred members were drawn away by a rival leader.

The community was built around the pietistic Lutheran faith espoused by George Rapp, usually called Father Rapp by his followers. He was ably assisted by an adopted son, Friedrich Rapp (d. 1832), who handled much of the practical business and administrative affairs of the group. When Father Rapp died in 1847, he was succeeded by Romelius Baker and Jacob Henrici. In the late nineteenth century John Duss became the leader; during his tenure in the 1890s, the community suffered from a number of bad investments. Their economic problems led to a series of lawsuits and severe internal disputes that finally resulted in the colony disbanding in 1898.

After the end of the communal life, many of the colonists continued to reside in Economy and perpetuated the group's religious life into the first decades of the twentieth century. By World War I, however, almost all signs of the group had faded away.

Sources:

Arndt, Karl J. R. *George Rapp's Harmony Society, 1785–1847*. Philadelphia: University of Pennsylvania Press, 1965.

———. *George Rapp's Successors and Material Heirs, 1847–1916*. Rutherford, NJ: Fairleigh Dickinson University Press, 1972.

Duss, John. *The Harmonists: A Personal History*. Pennsylvania Book Service, 1943. Reprint, Philadelphia, PA: Porcupine Press, 1973.

Holloway, Mark. *Heavens on Earth: Utopian Communities in America, 1680–1880*. London: Turnstile Press, 1951.

Heaven City

Heaven City was a communal group founded by Albert J. Moore (d. 1963) in 1923 in Harvard, Illinois. Moore was born in Wales and migrated to Chicago as a young man. Claiming miraculous powers to assist people, he founded an organization called the Life Institute. In 1922 he was convicted on charges of fraud, but his case was overturned on appeal. Shortly thereafter, he and 28 followers established a community on a 130-acre farm near Harvard. The colony practiced a community of consumption, but was largely financed by the jobs held by some members who worked outside it. In the 1930s Heaven City moved to Mukwonago, Wisconsin, where the group operated a motel, restaurant, and bar. Membership reached a peak of 75 in the mid-1930s.

Along with a strict communalism, the group started its own school. Sexual relationships were rather free, though marriages did occur. Moore believed that the sex instinct was the creative force of the world. Heaven City continued until Moore's death, though it had begun to decline. The motel was managed by his secretary Shirley P. Talcott, who died in 1978 at the age of 95. She willed the motel to two of its employees, who continued to manage it as a business.

Following Talcott's death, some of Moore's family tried to lay claim to the motel property, and even briefly reorganized the Heaven City religion, but their effort failed in court.

Sources:

Zahn, Michael. "Heaven City Dies with Founder." *Milwaukee Journal* (August 14, 1979).

Holy City Brotherhood

The Holy City Brotherhood was founded in 1914 in Los Angeles as the Perfect Christian Divine Way by William Edward Riker (1873–1969). Riker, a native Californian who moved to San Francisco as a young man, was an avid reader of occult and New Thought metaphysical literature, out of which he began to develop his own metaphysical world. Soon, he began to think of himself as The Comforter, the biblical name for the Holy Spirit sent by God to humankind. He started to travel the country preaching what he called the Perfect Christian Divine Science. In 1914, with a core of five close disciples, Riker established headquarters of the Perfect Christian Divine Way in Los Angeles. A second group emerged in San Francisco. Incorporation followed in 1918. Among his unique ideas was a racial understanding of humanity on the analogy of the human body, with Jews representing the mind (head) and Christians the heart (chest). Black people made up the legs and Oriental races the arms. He felt humanity's great sin was race mixing.

In 1991 Riker purchased some 200 acres in the Santa Cruz Mountains and moved there with his followers, who set about building Holy City. They created a self-sufficient community complete with an electric generator, barber shop, laundry, and cafe. They raised much of their own food and built a soft drink bottling company. Holy City itself was built on the road from San Jose to Santa Cruz and became a popular tourist stop. Riker ran for governor on several occasions.

Through the 1930s, Holy City prospered with 38 permanent members and up to several hundred who passed through for short stays. It began a long process of decline in the years after World War II as members moved away and few new members took their place. By 1956 only eight members (seven males and one female) remained. That year Riker sold the property to Maurice Kline, but the members were allowed to stay on the property. Riker and Kline soon disagreed over the future of the community; Riker sued to regain control of the property but lost in court in 1958. Meanwhile, he passed the leadership of the Perfect Christian Divine Way to Robert Clougher. The property finally passed into the hands of the H. C. Development Company. In the late 1950s several fires destroyed much of the community. Finally, in 1966 the few remaining disciples were thoroughly alienated from Riker when he suddenly converted to Roman Catholicism. He died three years later, still a member of the Catholic Church.

Sources:

"Holy City Brotherhood." *Fortnight* (March 2, 1955): 1617.

Plate, Harry. "Riker: from Mechanic to Messiah." *California Today* (August 30, 1978).

Jerusalem

Jerusalem was a religious community founded in 1788 near Seneca Lake, New York, by Jemima Wilkinson (1752–1819), known to her followers as the Public Universal Friend. Wilkinson, raised as a Quaker, was deeply affected by the preaching of traveling evangelist George Whitefield (1714–1770) and by the New Light Baptists. Around 1774 Wilkinson became ill and fell into a coma. When she came out of the coma she claimed that Jemima Wilkinson had died and her soul had ascended to heaven. In its place was the "Spirit of Life" sent by God to warn the world, as the Methodists were preaching, to flee from the wrath to come. She told everyone that she was now to be called the Public Universal Friend and would no longer answer to her birth name. She began to preach to all who would listen.

Soon after her change, she acquired a small band of followers, and with them toured Rhode Island and Connecticut. She traveled on a white horse and wore men's clothes over which she draped a flowing robe. Work was slow during the years of the American Revolution, but by 1782 she had three churches. As her evangelistic endeavors continued, she became a controversial figure when one member of a family who joined her was not followed by the rest of the

household. In 1788 she obtained land in western New York to build a community. A faithful vanguard began to clear the land and prepare it for the movement of the main body of members. Jerusalem grew and prospered through the 1790s and by 1800 had some 250 residents. It survived peacefully into the 1820s, but began a rapid decline after Wilkinson's death in 1819.

Sources:

Holloway, Mark. *Heavens on Earth: Utopian Communities in America, 1680–1880*. London: Turnstile Press, 1951.

Kraybill, Donald B., and Carl F. Bowman. *On the Backroad to Heaven: Old Order Hutterites, Mennonites, Amish, and Brethren*. Baltimore, MD: Johns Hopkins University Press, 2001.

Joyful

Joyful, a Christian utopian community, was funded in 1884 by Isaac B. Rumford and his wife, Sara Rumford, in Kern County, California. As early as 1880 Rumford had a visionary dream in which he pictured a heaven-like land where Christian love ruled. Already involved in a variety of reformist efforts, the Rumfords now felt inspired to create a community that would express their ideals of a simple Christian life. Integral to their vision was a new "Edenic" diet, a vegetarian diet based on the consumption of raw foods. Rumford had concluded that cooking destroyed the vital life of food substances. The Rumfords adopted the Edenic diet in 1881 and ascribed to it their continuing good health.

The Rumfords took steps to realize their communal vision in 1884 with the publication of the *Joyful News Co-operator*. "Joyful" was the name they had already given their fruit farm near Bakersfield, California. They also published a constitution for what they termed the Association of Brotherly Co-operators, the corporate name for the colony. Recruitment meetings were held in San Francisco, and a small number of converts moved to the farm. However, the movement never really got off the ground, and by the end of the year the experiment was discontinued. The Rumfords remained active as reformers and advocates of the raw food diet.

Sources:

Hine, Robert V. *California's Utopian Colonies*. San Marino, CA: Huntington Library, 1953.

Koreshan Unity

The Koreshan Unity was formed in 1888 in Chicago by the followers of Cyrus Read Teed (1839–1906), a physician and metaphysician who developed a religious system called cellular cosmology. The group was organized as a celibate religious organization. The followers of Koresh (Hebrew for Cyrus) moved into a home, and the next year they began to publish the *Guiding Star*, which after six months became the *Flaming Sword*. In 1894 a colony was established in

Estero, Florida, where the climate was mild and communal living was tolerated. In 1903 the entire group arrived from Chicago. At its height the organization had more than 300 resident members living on 6,000 acres, with more than 4,000 other followers throughout the United States. A press was established, and numerous books, pamphlets, and periodicals were produced up until 1949, when the press was destroyed by fire.

Cellular cosmology is based upon the belief that the earth's surface is concave and that man lives on the inside of a sphere, not on a ball in space. The earth is not 4.5 billion years old, but eternal. God is an eternal being, both male and female, dwelling in the central brain cells of aggregate humanity. Jesus Christ is God perpetuating himself in an individual person formed by parthenogenesis (virgin birth).

Cellular cosmology contains theories on the macrocosm and the microcosm. The macrocosm is viewed as a cosmic, hollow egg. The inside of the "eggshell" is the surface of the earth, and in the hollow center of the egg floats the sun, which provides light, heat, and gravity. The shell of the earth limits the effects of the sun, which are expressed in the materialization of metallic and mineral substance. In a reciprocal relationship, the shell of the physical cosmos gives forth the energies, decomposed from material substance, which move toward the sun by Levic force (the opposite of gravity). Through this reciprocity, eternal perpetuity is ensured. Mankind, in this view, is a microcosm of the macrocosm. God, the central sun, has his eternal habitation in the environmental circumference of humanity. From God flow truth and love, which are reciprocated by worship, which comprises the highest and purest moral thoughts.

The membership of the Koreshan settlement in Florida peaked soon after the turn of the century, and the departure of 30 members in 1906 signaled the beginning of a long period of decline. By 1940 the Unity had been reduced to 36 members. In 1960 the presidency of the group passed to Hedwig Michel, a Jew who had escaped from the Holocaust and joined the Unity in December 1941. She reorganized the small band of worshipers and led in the deeding of 300 acres of the group's land to the State of Florida in 1961. The land became the Koreshan State Historic Site in 1967, and it was later designated a national historic site.

In 1965 Michel revived the periodical, *The American Eagle*, and on the small amount of land the Koreshans still had, she started the Koreshan Unity Foundation. She led in the building of a library and museum to house and preserve the community publications and artifacts. She died in 1982 and is considered to be the last Koreshan. The foundation, now called the College of Life Foundation, has continued to preserve the property and opened it to scholars and the general public.

Sources:

Koresh (Cyrus R. Teed). *Cellular Cosmology, or, the Earth a Concave Sphere*. Estero, Lee County, FL: Guiding Star Publishing House, 1922.

Koreshanity, the New Age Religion. Miami, FL: Koreshan Foundation, 1971.

Landing, James E. "Cyrus R. Teed, Koreshanity, and Cellular Cosmology." *Communal Societies* 1 (Autumn 1981): 117.

Teed, Cyrus R. *The Alchemical Laboratory of the Brain*. Chicago: Eta Company, n.d.

The Lord's Farm

The Lord's Farm was founded in 1877 by Mason T. Huntsman. At some point in the 1870s, Huntsman, who had been raised an orphan, underwent a religious conversion. He took the name Paul Blandin Mnason and settled in Westwood, New Jersey. He assumed some messianic pretensions and was known to his followers as the "New Christ." Members of the Lord's Farm lived communally and supported themselves by raising crops on their 23 acres of land and operating a furniture-moving business. They had a policy of welcoming anyone to their farm and inviting them to partake of the community's activities and resources (food and shelter).

Mnason came to public attention in 1887 after he launched a vocal assault on the nearby village of Park Ridge, New Jersey, which he accused of being a corrupt and evil place. Residents, unappreciative of his words, manifested their disgust by attacking Mnason and cutting off his beard and long hair. Their actions did not stop Mnason, however, and he continued to preach and gather a following. However, he now faced a series of community reactions to his efforts. Between 1890 and 1893, Lord's Farm members were subjected to a series of court actions on charges ranging from violations of Sabbath laws to fraud. In 1893 Mnason was imprisoned for running a disorderly and immoral house, and in 1899 he was convicted under New Jersey blasphemy laws for "impersonating the Saviour" and abducting two young girls (two of his early followers).

The group continued until around 1910. At its height, it had 35 adult resident members, although there were always others living on the farm for longer or shorter periods. The group was vegetarian, celibate (in spite of continued charges of nudity and sexual misconduct), and sought to live a simple life following their inner guidance. Mnason referred to the colony as "The City of God, Land of Rest and Peace, State of Eternal Bliss." In the end, Mnason's brother took control of the property and evicted the group.

Sources:

Fogarty, Robert S. *Dictionary of American Communal and Utopian History*. Westport, CT: Greenwood Press, 1980.

Hinds, William Alfred. *American Communities and Co-operative Colonies*. Chicago: Charles H. Kerr, 1908.

Miller, Timothy. *American Communes, 1860–1960: A Bibliography*. New York: Garland, 1990.

Mountain Cove

The Mountain Cove community was a commune founded in 1851 at Mountain Cove, Virginia, by James L. Scott (b. 1814) and Thomas Lake Harris (1823–1906). The original members of the community came from Auburn, New York, and the idea seems to have originated with the spread of Spiritualism out of western New York, where it had emerged in the mid-1840s. Spiritualism and idealism were combined to create the possibility of founding a perfect Edenic society. Among the circle of Spiritualists was Ira S. Hitchcock, who made the trip to Virginia and found the land at Mountain Cove. He believed that the spot was the site of the original Garden of Eden and that no humans had set foot on it since Adam and Eve were driven from the garden. An open letter dated December 14, 1851, called people to participate in the new community, which was described as a place of refuge where one could escape the vales of death. Among the participants at Mountain Cove was Thomas Lake Harris, who would, a decade later, found the Brotherhood of the New Life as a Spiritualist communal movement.

The Mountain Cove community was led by Scott and Harris, who acted as mediums and professed direct communication and inspiration from God. They gave guidance to the movement from their "channelings" of the divine. Members were required to donate their real property to the community and live from the community treasury. The temporal life of the colony was based upon agriculture.

In spite of the claims of divine guidance, the community soon found itself divided by internal bickering. Some rejected the arbitrary nature of leadership provided by Scott and Harris, suggesting that members had become the equivalent of slaves to work the community farm. Others complained about the financial and property arrangements. As a result of the discord, the experiment collapsed in 1853.

Sources:

Hinds, William Alfred. *American Communities and Co-operative Colonies*. Chicago: Charles H. Kerr, 1908.

Noyes, John Humphrey. *History of American Socialisms*. 1870. Reprint, New York: Dover, 1966.

New Jerusalem

New Jerusalem was a communal group established near Cairo, Illinois, in the mid-nineteenth century. It was founded by Cyrus Spragg, who had been a member of the Church of Jesus Christ of Latter-day Saints. Expelled from a congregation (or stake) in Michigan, he gathered a few followers and led in the founding of a commune noted for its disavowal of polygamy and its practice of nudism. The experiment reportedly failed because of the bitter winter weather.

Following the collapse of his community in Michigan, Spragg led the remnant of his following to Illinois and organized New Jerusalem near Cairo. He had come to believe himself to be the Messiah, and he had an ark built to save group members from a flood that was predicted to occur in the near future and overrun Cairo. In fact, a heavy rain brought a flood, but it did not do the damage or reach the extent predicted. A short time later, Spragg moved into the ark, announcing that he was the "Invisible Presence of God" and would never be seen again. He remained in touch with the members of the group through a window cut in the side of the ark. He received food, and each evening he was visited by a virginal member of the group, one of whom, it was predicted, would become a Madonna, the mother of a messiah.

The new arrangement worked for some months, and several children were born to the young women who visited Spragg. Then a man who had fallen in love with one of the sacred virgins broke into the ark and, he claimed, shot Spragg before fleeing the community. That night, the young woman appointed to visit the leader reported that he had not been shot but was very much alive. The community resumed its normal course until Spragg's daughter-in-law accused her husband, Obadiah Spragg, and his brother, Jared Spragg, of having gone into the ark, disposed of their father's body, and assumed his role each evening. Members of the community then went into the ark and discovered that Spragg was not there. The revelation led to the collapse of the community.

No contemporary records of New Jerusalem exist. The site of the community is unknown, and the main account, which appeared in the 1920s, was a "biography" of Spragg's daughter written in the form of a novel. Some have suggested that the story of New Jerusalem is a folk account derived from the account of James Jesse Strang, the Mormon leader on Beaver Island, Michigan. The parallels in the lives of Spragg and Strang are indeed striking. Presently, however, there is no way to resolve the issue.

Sources:

Bromfield, Louis. *Strange Case of Miss Annie Spragg*. New York: Frederick A. Stokes Co., 1928.

Muncy, Raymond Lee. *Sex and Marriage in Utopian Communities: 19th Century America*. Bloomington: Indiana University Press, 1973.

Randolph, Vance. *Americans Who Thought They Were Gods: Colorful Messiahs and Little Christs*. Girard, KS: Haldeman-Julius Publications, 1943.

Webber, Everett. *Escape to Utopia: The Communal Movement in America*. New York: Hastings House, 1959.

Oneida Community of Perfectionists

The Oneida Community of Perfectionists was a religious community founded in 1841 in Putney, Vermont, by John Humphrey Noyes (1811–1886). It was inspired by the spread in early nineteenth-century America of both Methodist perfectionist thought and communal idealism. Although he had become something of a religious skeptic during his college days, Noyes was soundly converted in a revival in 1830 and a short time later felt a call to preach. He attended a seminary but found the atmosphere cold and uninviting, so he turned to personal Bible study. He concluded that Christians were called to be perfect. He also believed that Christ had made perfection humanly possible and, as part of that perfection, had taken away the need to observe earthly laws. He graduated from seminary, but the Congregationalists took back his license to preach.

During the next few years Noyes wandered around Vermont and New York and gathered a small following. He began a periodical, *The Witness*, and in 1837 he began an informal Bible study group in Putney. He instituted the practice of mutual criticism he had learned at the seminary. In a very structured atmosphere, members would allow the community to freely censure them and offer suggestions for change and improvement. All members underwent such criticism. Among the ideals that Noyes slowly espoused to the group was a new sexual order that put aside regulations against fornication and adultery. His wife, Harriet, and his converts also accepted the concept of a community of wives.

Noyes was greatly affected by the painful experiences of his wife, who had several miscarriages. He thought that celibacy would be the only way to prevent her further distress from unwanted pregnancies, but he then discovered what he called "male countenance." This was actually an old technique widely practiced in some Asian cultures by which males were able to engage in lengthy sexual intercourse without reaching a climax. The technique, also called *coitus reservatus* and *karezza*, would later become the basis of the Oneida community's new sexual order.

In 1841 the group was formally organized as the Putney Society. Noyes's goal to initiate the establishment of the kingdom of God on earth, and he restructured the group by the imposing a system of complex marriage. Briefly stated, Noyes assumed (as did most of his contemporaries) that monogamous marriages would be abolished in the heavenly society. However, he departed from most other Christian thinkers by assuming that sexual relations would continue. For this to occur, sexual relations would have to continue without the benefit of marriage. Thus, in the heavenly society, all the men would be "married" to all the women. The attempt to actualize such a situation, however, presented new problems. How would one keep from falling into mere libertinism? How did one regulate the random pregnancies and children that would result? To deal with these problems, Noyes developed the system of complex marriage.

In Noyes's system, the men and women of the community regularly changed partners, but they did not make random choices based upon momentary attractions. Instead, partners were assigned each month according to the women's menstrual cycles. Men requested their partner for the next month, but the actual choices were made by the older women. Thus, during any one month, a woman would have relationships with only one man. In case of an accidental pregnancy, the father would then be known. Under this system, every person in the community had a new sexual partner each month, and pains were taken to see that no exclusive relationships developed that would distract individuals from their commitments to the community.

In 1848, under pressure from legal authorities in Putney who complained about the immoralities among the group, the community moved to Oneida, New York, where they built one of the most successful community experiments. The economy of the community was based on the sale of traps, silk, and horticultural products. In the 1870s the community started a silverware industry that became their most successful business, and which continues to the present day.

At Oneida the practice of complex marriage was so successful that only a very few unplanned pregnancies occurred. The success led to further speculation on sexuality and the development of a new eugenics program called "stirpiculture," which involved children being produced by the union of two "scientifically selected" parents. Some 51 children were born following the implementation of the stirpiculture plan.

The community at Oneida lasted for more than three decades. Its long and successful existence is credited to Noyes, who became an astute student of the communal life and wrote one of the first books describing America's communal experiments, *History of American Socialisms* (1870). Through most of its existence it averaged some 300 residents members. In 1851 it founded a second community in Wallingford, Connecticut. However, for reasons still not fully understood, on January 1, 1881, the community came to an end and reorganized the economic segment of the community as a joint stock company. Many of the former members then settled in Oneida in nuclear families.

Sources:

Carden, Maren L. *Oneida: Utopian Community to Modern Corporation.* Baltimore, MD: John Hopkins University Press, 1969.

Foster, Lawrence. *Women, Family, and Utopia: Communal Experiments of the Shakers, the Oneida Community, and the Mormons.* Syracuse, NY: Syracuse University Press, 1991.

Noyes, John Humphrey. *History of American Socialisms.* 1870. Reprint, New York: Dover, 1966.

Noyes, Pierrepont B. *A Godly Heritage.* New York: Rinehart, 1958.

Robertson, Constance Noyes, ed. *Oneida Community: An Autobiography, 1851–1876.* Syracuse, NY: Syracuse University Press, 1970.

The Pilgrims

The Pilgrims were a small group that arose in the Canadian province of Quebec, just north of the Vermont border, in 1816. The group was founded by Isaac Bullard, who recovered from a long illness with a determination to follow Christ. He began to preach and gathered a following, which he organized along what he saw as a primitivist pattern. The group lived communally out of a common purse and became known for their constant prayer and frequent fasts. However, the most remembered characteristic by those who encountered them was their refusal to bathe. They also discarded their civilized "manufactured" clothing and donned animal skins. Their clothing—coupled with their refusal to bathe—led to their exuding an offensive smell.

In the summer of 1817, Bullard received a revelation instructing him to migrate toward the American Southwest in a pilgrimage to a Promised Land. Meanwhile, Bullard had married and named his first child, a boy, Christ. When the pilgrimage began, the Pilgrims numbered approximately 55. As they traveled across New England, they were heard to mutter a prayer, "My God, My God, What wouldst thou have me do? Mummyjum, Mummyjum." As a result they were often dubbed the Mummyjums.

The pilgrimage took the better part of a year, as the Pilgrims journeyed through New York, New Jersey, Ohio, and Missouri. As they traveled, members dropped out, some because they fell ill, others because they came to reject the message preached by Bullard. Still others left to join the Shakers. When the group reached Arkansas in 1881, only about 10 people were left. They settled on an isolated island, and the Pilgrims soon passed into obscurity.

Sources:

Fogarty, Robert S. *Dictionary of American Communal and Utopian History.* Westport, CT: Greenwood Press, 1980.

Ham, F. Gerald. "The Prophet and the Mummyjums: Isaac Bullard and the Vermont Pilgrims of 1817." *Wisconsin Magazine of History* 56 (1973): 290–299.

Societas Fraternia

The Societas Fraternia was a communal group founded in 1878 by George Hinde on land he had purchased near Fullerton, California. Hinde settled on the land in 1876, but the beginning of the community followed the arrival of a Spiritualist, Dr. Louis Schlesinger, two years later. The major beliefs and practices seem to have been derived from those of Isaac B. Rumford and the Joyful Community. Rumford had advocated a form of Christian Spiritualism and a diet of raw food. In addition, buildings were erected in a circular pattern to allow the better circulation of air.

In 1879 Schlesinger was forced into court to answer charges that a child at the farm was being starved to death on a diet of apple, rice, and barley water. The case (in which Schlesinger was convicted and then later acquitted) initiated a period of controversy that led him to leave the colony in 1882. Hinde vanished the following year. Leadership of the group was then assumed by Walter Lockwood, who led the group for almost 40 years until his death in 1921. During its years of existence, the colony's dietetic commitments led to its participation in the development of the fruit and vegetable industry in southern California. The colony dissolved a short time after Lockwood's death.

Sources:

Hine, Robert V. *California's Utopian Colonies.* San Marino, CA: Huntington Library, 1953.

The Society of the Separatists of Zoar

The Society of the Separatists of Zoar originated in a dissenting religious movement led by George Bimeler (originally Bäumeler), a German weaver. The group, which grew up around the unofficial preaching of Bimeler, ran into conflict with state church authorities because they refused to send their children to the local schools, which were controlled by the Lutheran Church, and because the young men in the group refused to serve in the army. Further, they refused to recognize the authority of government officials. Thus, they soon found themselves on the receiving end of church and government repression.

In 1817, with some money contributed by British Quakers, Bimeler was able to purchase 5,600 acres in northeast Ohio, and the group settled there in 1818. They had no plans to establish a communal society, but in 1819 they formally adopted a new corporate structure as a means of improving the group's survival. They struggled until 1827, when many of the men were employed to work on the new canal that was being built through their county. The money their labor brought in provided the necessary capital to lift them out of poverty. In 1832 the group was incorporated as the Society of the Separationists of Zoar, and leadership was invested in a three-man board of trustees.

The Zoarites practiced a simple, quietist faith based upon the Sermon on the Mount. They did not use audible prayer, did not baptize or celebrate the Eucharist, and tended to avoid all ceremony. They had no religious functionaries except for Bimeler, who delivered "discourses" (not sermons) at the Sunday gatherings. Hymns and music seem to have been their chief form of entertainment. Like the Quakers, they tended to address people in the familiar tense with "thou." Originally celibate, they began to marry and have children in the 1830s, although the Bimeler

(who was married) contended that celibacy was the better way.

The Zoarite experiment lasted into the 1890s, when internal disputes among the aging group led to its dissolution; there were some 221 adult members at the time. Some have attributed the dissolution to a lessening of religious faith and zeal among the leaderless members, Bimeler having died in 1853.

Sources:

Holloway, Mark. *Heavens on Earth: Utopian Communities in America, 1680-1880.* London: Turnstile Press, 1951.

Randall, E. *History of the Zoar Society, from its Commencement to its Conclusion: A Sociological Study in Communism.* 3rd ed. Columbus, OH: F. J. Heer, 1904. Reprint, New York, AMS Press, 1971.

Straight Edge Community

The Straight Edge Community was a Christian Socialist community founded in 1899 in New York City by Wilbur F. Copeland and his wife. Its rather unusual name was derived from the fact that Jesus had been a carpenter, and that a carpenter's rule is a "straight edge." Chapman placed an ad in the *New York Herald* asking for responses from any who might want to take the teachings of Jesus Christ seriously and work in a cooperative endeavor based upon the Golden Rule.

The Golden Rule became the constitution of the group, and a set of bylaws were adopted from applicable Bible verses: (1) Thou shalt love thy neighbors as thyself; (2) In honor preferring one another; (3) Lay not up for yourself treasures upon earth; (4) I am in the midst of you as he that serveth; (5) Take heed that ye do not let your righteousness before men to be seen of them; and (6) Whatsoever things are true, honest, just, pure, of good report, virtuous, praiseworthy, think on these things.

The Straight Edge Community emerged as a school of methods for the application of the teachings of Jesus to business and society. A periodical, *The Straight-Edge,* was initiated, the Copelands' home became the center of the community, a farm was purchased on Staten Island, and several small industries were begun in Manhattan. The community averaged some 18 people at any one time, but more than 200 people passed through it during the years of its existence. Many entered out of poverty but left possessing a skill and ready for financial independence. Workers were not paid a salary, but they shared in the earnings of the corporation according to a complex point system that provided some incentive for improving work skills and staying with the community. The community continued for more than a decade, but it seems to have disbursed soon after the turn of the century.

The Straight Edgers also developed a school and camp program for the children of its member-workers, which provided a place for young people to learn the simple life without paying large sums of money.

These children received a practical education that prepared them for work in industry.

Sources:

Hinds, William Alfred. *American Communities and Cooperative Colonies.* Chicago: Charles H. Kerr, 1908.

WFLK Fountain of the World

Francis H. Pencovic (1911–1958) was born in obscurity, but as Krishna Venta, the leader of the Fountain of the World, he died a martyr's death among his followers, who thought of him as the reincarnated Christ. Pencovic spent part of his early life in Utah, where he married his second wife, Ruth, and became enamored of Joseph Smith and the *Book of Mormon.* According to his followers, as Krishna Venta he landed in America from the Himalayas in 1932. He had been sent from heaven to work among the Indians 144 years previously. Venta established his group in Box Canyon in the San Fernando Valley of California, where it gained a reputation for fire-fighting activities. He was rumored to have developed an openly promiscuous sexual lifestyle, which seems to have been his downfall, for on December 10, 1958, two dissident sexual partners of Venta set off an explosion in the group's administration building, killing themselves, Venta, and seven others.

Members of WFLK (Wisdom, Faith, Love, Knowledge) Fountain of the World believed that Venta was the latest in a series of "saviors" of mankind who came down from heaven. Preceding him were Adam, Enoch, Methuselah, Noah, Abraham, Moses, Elijah, Jesus, Constantine, Abraham Lincoln, and Joseph Smith. One by one, each gave up in disgust as the sins of men overcame them, both spiritually and physically. Fountain of the World members lived communally, turning over any prior possessions to the group. Thus, they became united with one another spiritually, mentally, and through sharing their belongings. They were called upon to practice the virtues of wisdom, knowledge, faith, and love. The Fountain was headed by Krishna Venta and 12 apostles.

Venta's death in 1958 was a setback, but it did not destroy the group. Mother Ruth Pencovic assumed leadership of the Fountain of the World, which survived into the early 1980s near Canoga Park, California. There was also a second center near Homer, Alaska, set up by Krisha Venta before his death.

Sources:

Mathison, Richard R. *Faiths, Cults, and Sects of America: From Atheism to Zen.* Indianapolis, IN: Bobbs-Merrill, 1960.

Orrmont, Arthur. *Love Cults & Faith Healers.* New York: Ballantine Books, 1961.

Woman's Commonwealth

The Woman's Commonwealth was a communal society organized by Martha McWhirter (1827–1904) in Belton, Texas, in the late 1860s. In the years immediately after the Civil War, the Holiness Movement, which offered to believers the possibility of entire sanctification, spread through all parts of Methodism. The movement was initially carried by informal prayer bands, many of which were led by women. Thus it was that McWhirter, a life-long Methodist, called together a few women to meet for prayer, Bible study, and an exploration of the meaning of the sanctified life. They soon experienced sanctification, and, as occurred elsewhere, their experience and the resulting censure they made of unsanctified church members split the local congregation. It also split families, McWhirter's included, and many of the women were cut off from any financial support. The idea of living together communally then arose and was adopted.

To keep themselves together financially, the women began several businesses, including a boarding house and a laundry. Initially, many of the women worked at day jobs until the community businesses were prosperous enough to support all of them. As they prospered, hostile opinions of the group gave way to more favorable ones. By the 1890s they had become an economic force in the small community, and McWhirter was elected to the town council.

In 1898 the entire group relocated to Washington, D.C. In 1902 the group, consisting of approximately 24 members, was incorporated as the Woman's Commonwealth of Washington, D.C. McWhirter died in 1904 and was succeeded by Fannie Holtzclaw.

The group followed a Methodist Holiness theology. Believers could receive the Holy Spirit and be sanctified, and as most of the women had experienced sanctification prior to the community's establishment, the group lived as a community of the sanctified and were frequently referred to as Sanctificationists, a designation members did not find inappropriate. They believed that communal living produced the important virtues of honesty, sobriety, spirituality, happiness, and justice, and they tried to organize their life according to the Golden Rule. There were no men in the community, so celibacy was a way of life for all members. They also lived separate from involvement in local churches, though they had a positive view of the role and work of government.

In the end, because of their celibacy and reluctance to take in new members, the group died out, though remnants survived on their farm in rural Montgomery County, Maryland, into the 1930s. One member, Martha Scheble, lived on the farm until her death in 1983.

Sources:

Fogarty, Robert S. *Dictionary of American Communal and Utopian History*. Westport, CT: Greenwood Press, 1980.

Hinds, William Alfred. *American Communities and Co-operative Colonies*. Chicago: Charles H. Kerr, 1908.

Miller, Timothy. *American Communes, 1860–1960: A Bibliography*. New York: Garland, 1990.

COMMUNAL—AFTER 1960

Circle of Friends

The Circle of Friends was a small New Age communal group built around the teachings of George Jurcsek. Born in Hungary around 1920, Jurcsek migrated to America in 1950. Over the years he absorbed a variety of Eastern and occult teachings from the writings of Rudolf Steiner and Edgar Cayce and a trip to India. He came to believe that a catastrophe would overwhelm the earth in the near future and that civilization would end. Jurcsek began lecturing in the late 1960s, and the Circle of Friends was formed in 1973. At its height in the late 1970s, there were approximately 75 members. Group members believed they would emerge as leaders in the New Age.

Soon after its formation, the Circle came under attack by anticult groups for its intensive lifestyle. The charges focused on the group's communal life, which required members to live on a minimal allowance (above their room and board) and pool their money for investments for the group. There were also charges that Jurcsek manipulated the lives of people, such as dictating members' marriage partners. Several deprogrammings occurred, with mixed success. In 1979 Jurcsek dropped out of sight, but he reappeared several years later in central North Carolina, where the group had purchased property.

The Circle encountered severe problems a few years later when Jurcsek and Mary O'Rourke, one of the group's leaders, were indicted for fraud involving student loans. Both were convicted in 1988 and given seven-year prison sentences. They both appealed their convictions, but O'Rourke then renounced the group, withdrew her appeal, and applied for a reduced sentence.

Information on members of the Circle of Friends since Jurcsek's conviction has been difficult to attain. In the following years, the group kept a low profile and published little. Media coverage generally centered on the claims of former members, most of whom were associated with anticult networks, which made it difficult to objectively assess their testimony.

Katharsis

Kartharsis was established in 1971 by a group wishing to establish an alternative community with an emphasis on harmony and spiritual growth. In 1974 the members purchased 20 acres near Nevada City, California, for their community and research center. The goals of Katharsis included the following: (1) spiritual growth and self-realization through the study of yoga and related sciences, (2) the development of a natural lifestyle based on diet, (3) cooperative living, and (4) promotion of the practice of astrology as an aid to a fuller life. The group published an annual "Solar Lunar Calendar," as well as a line of related astrology products. After several years Katharsis disappeared, and no sign of their existence has surfaced since then.

Mu Farm

Mu Farm was named for the ancient continent of Lemuria, or Mu, made famous in theosophical lore. It was begun in 1971 when Fletcher Fist and two other people purchased land near Yoncalla, Oregon. A goat farm was established, and the sale of goat's milk provided an economic base. In 1988 there were approximately 30 resident members.

The beliefs of Mu Farm were eclectic and derived from the many psychical and mystical teachings that developed in the 1960s. Sources of belief included the Bible, the I Ching, the *Aquarian Gospel of Jesus Christ* by Levi, and the writings of Martin Buber, Swami Yogananda, Einstein, and others. The Golden Rule was emphasized rather than a set of specific rules and regulations.

Renaissance Church of Beauty

The Renaissance Church of Beauty (and the Renaissance Community) was founded by Michael Metelica (1950–2003) in 1969 as the Brotherhood of the Spirit. While he was still in his teens, and having just returned from California, Metelica built a tree house near Leyden, Massachusetts. He moved into the structure and was soon joined by eight friends. They all began to work for farmers for wages of food or goods instead of money. When vandals burned down the tree house, they moved into a cottage on the land of a farmer for whom they had been working. The Brotherhood was born there.

Metelica, who chose the name Michael Rapunzel, was greatly influenced by the Spiritualist medium Elwood Babbitt, who also introduced him to *The Aquarian Gospel of Jesus the Christ* (1908) by Levi Dowling, a major source of the group's beliefs. Babbitt specialized in psychically providing information about an individual's previous incarnations on earth.

The beliefs of the Renaissance Community were centered upon the seven immutable laws: order within the universe; balance of the mind (positive) and brain (negative); harmony (a direct alignment with all vibration of electrical energy); growth from carnal to celestial; God-perfection; spiritual love; and compassion. In its early days the community was devoted to vegetarianism and abstinence from alcohol, but a less strict diet was eventually adopted.

During the first years of the 1970s the group expanded rapidly, numbering 365 by 1973. By 1972, the movement had decentralized and moved into new centers near four northwestern Masschusetts towns. To provide an economic base, several businesses were created. Most of these eventually failed, but some were successful, including Rockets, which outfitted buses for touring musicians, and Renaissance Builders and Renaissance Excavating. By 1974 two separate organizational structures had emerged. The Renaissance Church of Beauty was created so that all residents and nonresidents could participate in the support of the beliefs and practices of the former Brotherhood of the Spirit. The Renaissance Community, comprising the resident members, was then created for church members who wished to practice the church's beliefs on a full-time basis.

In 1975 a 80-acre tract in Gill, Massachusetts, was purchased. The group began to reassemble there and construct the 2001 Center, conceived in part as a haven against the time of troubles Edgar Cayce said would occur as the twentieth century came to an end. An organic farm was started on the property, and the group produced the

Renaissance Community Newsletter. The community slowly dwindled away through the 1980s, as some members rebelled against Rapunzel's leadership. By 1988 it had essentially disappeared, although some of the businesses continued to exist. Rapunzel died of cancer in 2003.

Sources:

Borowski, Karol. *Attempting an Alternative Society*. Norwood, PA: Norwood Editions, 1984.

Brown, Daniel A. *The History of the Brotherhood of the Spirit/Renaissance Community: 1968–1988*. Ahmerst: University of Massachusetts, Amherst. Available from http://www.library.umass.edu/spcoll/galleries/brown/history.htm

Hapgood, Charles H. *Voices of Spirit: Through the Psychic Experience of Elwood Babbitt*. New York: Delacorte Press, 1975.

Popenoe, Cris, and Oliver Popenoe. *Seeds of Tomorrow: New Age Communities That Work*. San Francisco: Harper & Row, 1984.

Shiloh Youth Revival Centers

Shiloh Youth Revival Centers was one of the most successful movements to emerge out of the Jesus People Revival of the 1970s. The movement originated in a vision of John J. Higgins, Jr., to extend the Jesus People Movement, then centered in California, into Oregon. Higgins was a drug addict who had converted to Christianity in the mid-1960s. He began attending Calvary Chapel in Costa Mesa, California. In 1968, with others like himself, he founded a Jesus People commune called the House of Miracles. His work attracted followers, and soon a string of similar houses sprang up around southern California.

In April 1969, Higgins and some 30 other young people moved to Pleasant Hill, Oregon, where the first house to bear the name Shiloh was opened. The new name reflected a belief that Shiloh (Jesus) would soon return. Over the summer the group tripled in size and purchased 70 acres of land near Dexter, Oregon, where they built a discipleship training center. They incorporated as the Oregon Youth Revival Centers, which was later changed to Shiloh Youth Revival Centers. From that point forward they centered their life work on building the center, evangelizing, and founding centers across the country. By 1974 they had

founded some 163 Shiloh centers, though most were short-lived, and only half that number were in existence at any one time.

Shiloh was communal in nature. Members made a commitment to Christ to forsake all and follow him. The movement took care of the basic needs of the members. The group also believed in working to support themselves rather than asking for donations. They built a number of very successful businesses, including canning, construction, printing, and carpet cleaning operations. Eugene, Oregon, became their second central focus of activity, and they opened the Shiloh Fellowship there for regular public worship services.

The organization went through a severe upheaval when the board questioned Higgins's autocratic leadership and fired him. A period of turmoil followed, and many members left the movement. Higgins left to become a pastor with Calvary Chapel. Meanwhile, the Internal Revenue Service began to question the tax status of the group and its numerous business ventures. The group reorganized and began a lengthy fight with the IRS. Slowly, the many communities around the country closed, and by 1986 none were left. The first trial on tax charges occurred in 1986, and the following year the court ruled that the businesses were not tax exempt, and that taxes were therefore owed. That decision effectively bankrupted the organization, and two years later it formally disbanded. A final reunion was held in the summer of 1987, but by then most of the members had drifted into other similar movements.

Sources:

Peterson, Joe V. *Jesus People: Christ, Communes and the Counterculture of the Late Twentieth Century in the Pacific Northwest*. Master's thesis, Northwest Christian College, 1990.

Richardson, James T., Mary W. Stewart, and Robert B. Simmons. *Organized Miracles: A Study of a Contemporary Youth, Communal, Fundamentalist Organization*. New Brunswick, NJ: Transaction Books, 1979.

The Synanon Church

The Synanon Church began in 1958 as Synanon Foundation, Inc., a therapeutic group for alcoholics and drug addicts. Charles E. Dederich (1913–1997), a former member of Alcoholics Anonymous, began the organization informally in his apartment in Ocean Park, California. As the group grew and began to experience some benefits, it rented a clubhouse and incorporated. The following year it moved to Santa Monica, and over the next few years the group gained a reputation for re-educating drug addicts. From its base in Santa Monica, Synanon communities formed along the West Coast during the 1960s, particularly in San Francisco, Marin County, and Oakland. Outposts also opened in the East, the Midwest, and Puerto Rico. Residents totaled 1,400 by decade's end. In 1968

Dederich moved to Marin County, and within a few years three rural Synanon communities developed near the town of Marshall.

The religious nature of Synanon, coming as it did out of another religious organization, Alcoholics Anonymous, had been tacitly recognized from almost the beginning of its existence. However, Dederich also recognized that many of the people Synanon was attempting to assist had rejected organized religion; therefore, Synanon was not formally called a religion. Those outside Synanon tended to view it as another therapeutic community, but as the group's community life developed, its religious nature could not be denied. Discussions of Synanon's role as a religion led to a change in its Articles of Incorporation in January 1975. The new articles designated the Synanon Foundation as the organization through which the Synanon religion and church was manifest. On November 17, 1980, The Synanon Church, was formally adopted as the organization's name.

Synanon derived its theological perspective from Eastern thought (particularly Buddhism and Taoism), and from those Western mystics who had absorbed a prominent Asian religious component in their teachings, most notably Ralph Waldo Emerson and Aldous Huxley. As a community, Synanon sought to manifest the basic principles of oneness, and members sought to manifest that integration (or oneness) in themselves and in their relations with each other. The Synanon Game, described as the group's central sacrament, was the principal tool utilized in adherents' search for unity. Similar to encounter groups, the Synanon Game was "played" by a small group of people who met together as equals to share in an intense and emotionally expressive context. When successful, the game led to mutual confession, repentence, and absolution, while providing overall pastoral care.

Synanon residents followed the Golden Rule, and helping others was a basic part of the practical philosophy that all residents attempted to follow. Residents also believed that the most effective way to redeem humanity from alienation and achieve unity and integration was to form religious communities based upon the beliefs of the Synanon religion and church.

The Synanon Church was organized hierarchically. It was headed by an eight-member executive committee of the board of directors, which was composed of the ministers of the church. These ministers oversaw the communities, schools, and offices of the church, in addition to performing their normal ministerial functions.

Since its earliest days, Synanon had been subject to controversy. In December 1961, Dederich went to jail for the first time, charged with a zoning code violation. Synanon was also attacked in articles by individuals who disagreed with its practices and techniques. One such attack, considered particularly defamatory, led to a libel suit against the *San Francisco Examiner*. Synanon received not only a large cash settlement in the case, it won an additional $2,000,000 in damages from the Hearst Corporation, the newspaper's publisher, for, among other things, burglarizing the Synanon offices.

Possibly the most controversial event affecting Synanon occurred in 1978 when an attorney, representing a person suing The Synanon Church, was bitten by a rattlesnake. In the year following this incident, Dederich, who along with two church members had been charged with intentionally placing the snake in the lawyer's mailbox, suffered three strokes. As the trial date approached, and with Dederich in failing health and unable to pursue the defense of the case, he and the other two members settled the case by pleading no contest.

Eventually, over 40 people associated with The Synanon Church were indicted on various charges by grand juries. None of these well-publicized indictments went to trial, however, as charges were dropped in each case for lack of evidence. Further, The Synanon Church always held that, had Dederich's health permitted a trial, he and the others charged in the rattlesnake incident would also have been found innocent. Nonetheless, in 1982 the Internal Revenue Service revoked the church's tax-exempt status, and after a lengthy legal battle its properties were confiscated and sold.

Sources:

Dederich, Charles E. *The Tao Trip Sermon*. Marshall, CA: Synanon Publishing House, 1978.

Endore, Guy. *Synanon*. Garden City, NJ: Doubleday, 1968.

Garfield, Howard M. *The Synanon Religion*, Marshall, CA: Synanon Foundation, 1978.

Gerstel, David U. *Paradise Incorporated—Synanon: A Personal Account*. Novato, CA: Presidio Press, 1982.

Janzen, Rod. *The Rise and Fall of Synanon: A California Utopia*. Baltimore, MD: Johns Hopkins University Press, 2001.

Mitchell, Dave, Cathy Mitchell, and Richard Ofshe. *The Light on Synanon*. New York: Seaview Books, 1980.

Olin, William F. *Escape From Utopia: My Ten Years in Synanon*. Santa Cruz, CA: Unity Press, 1980.

Yablonsky, Lewis. *The Tunnel Back: Synanon*. New York: Macmillan, 1965.

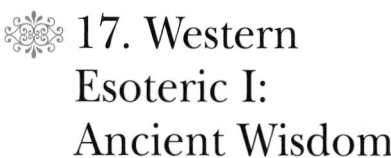

17. Western Esoteric I: Ancient Wisdom

INTRAFAITH ORGANIZATIONS

Synod of Independent Sacramental Churches

The Synod of Independent Sacramental Churches was founded in 1984 following a disruption in the Federation of St. Thomas Christian Churches, an organization which had served as an ecumenical home for many of the smaller independent liturgical churches that had developed an esoteric, gnostic, or theosophical perspective, many of which had a lineage tracing back to either the Liberal Catholic Church or the American Catholic Church. Much of the motivation for the formation of the new group came from Bp. Michael G. Zaharakis of the Mesbarim Fellowship, though Zaharakis died suddenly before the synod was fully organized.

The synod served as a point of unity for independent churches with a valid apostolic succession for the purpose of mutual aid and education. It imposed no doctrinal unity. The synod was fully in accord with the acceptance of women into all levels of the ministry and selected as its first chairperson Bp. Rosamonde Miller of the Ecclesia Gnostic Mysteriorum. While based in sacramental Christianity, it professed acceptance of the authenticity and validity of other religions and the ongoing nature of revelation.

Also included among the original member churches were the Independent Church of Antioch, the Independent Catholic Church International, the New Church of the East, the Johannine Catholic Church, the New Church Universal, the Church of the Seven Seals, the Apostolic Order of the Christos, and the Mesbarim Fellowship. During its active period, the synod issued a periodical entitled *SISCOM*.

ROSICRUCIANISM

Holy Rosicrucian Church

The Holy Rosicrucian Church was a small short-lived Rosicrucian body known primarily through a single literary remain, a booklet, *Rosikrucianism*, published in 1915. The church and its associated orders were founded by a person known only as Sergius Rosenkruz and headquartered in Los Angeles. The church and brotherhood taught a method of liberation, the awakening to the knowledge of unity with the One. The church advocated a series of preparatory methods which included study, twice-daily baths, the practice of charitable works, the avoidance of frivolous activities, and the adoption of a variety of occult meditative techniques. The church was associated with the Order of the Knights of the Golden Circle which through rites and ceremonies prepared members for either a favorable reincarnation or safety in the beyond.

Sources:

Rosenkruz, Sergius. *Rosikrucianism*. Los Angeles: The Author, 1915.

Rosicrucian Anthroposophical League

The Rosicrucian Anthroposophical Society was formed in 1932 by Samuel Richard Parchment (b.1881), a former leader in the San Francisco Center of the Rosicrucian Fellowship. Parchment, continuing the astrological emphasis of the fellowship, wrote a classic textbook, *Astrology, Mundane and Spiritual*, and even before leaving the Fraternity began writing the books which were to guide the League: *The Just Law of Compensation*, *The Middle Path, the Safest*, *Ancient Operative Masonry*, and *Steps to Self-Mastery*. Early centers were in California and New York. (In the late 1970s the surviving New York City center broke away to become the Ausar Auset Society.)

The principles of the League committed it to an investigation of occult laws, the brotherhood of man, the dissemination of spiritual truth, and the attainment of self-conscious immortality. There has been no recent contact with the league, and its present status is presumed to be defunct.

Sources:

Parchment, S. R. *Ancient Operative Masonry*. San Francisco: San Francisco Center-Rosicrucian Fellowship, 1930.

———. *Astrology, Mundane and Spiritual*. San Francisco: Anthroposophical Rosicrucian League, 1933.

———. *The Just Law of Compensation*. San Francisco: San Francisco Center-Rosicrucian Fellowship, 1932.

———. *Steps to Self-Mastery*. Oceanside, CA: Fellowship Press, 1927.

OCCULT ORDERS

Christian Fellowship Organization

Among the most outstanding of the occult-metaphysical teachers in Southern California in the decades immediately before and after World War II was Edward Lewis Hodges, a San Diego physician. He claimed to be the representative and earthly head of the Secret Order of the Christian Brotherhood and School of Christian Initiation. The order consisted of those evolved beings who had in ages past spiritualized their body, perfected their wisdom and understanding, and had been given the keys to the Kingdom Universal to rule the earth (similar to what other groups term the Great White Brotherhood). Hodges, as an initiate of the order, was given its teachings and told to propagate them. He founded the Christian Fellowship Organization and in 1938 published the *Teachings of the Secret Order of the Christian Brotherhood*.

According to Hodges, the order taught how to achieve liberation from death through the restoration and spiritualization of the body. Further, knowledge of the spiritualization processes was held to be as old as humanity, but periodically almost forgotten. The group believed that at one point Jesus, head of the order, appeared to teach that the great secret of life was God the Universal. All of this was thought to be expressed through the Christ which was simply the mortal body. The Christ within the human form was what saves. The first step on the path of initiation was realizing oneness with that Christ within.

New students of the Christian Fellowship Organization were invited to place themselves under the "cultural condition of the Christian Brotherhood" by invoking its presence. They were also taught a series of formulas, (i.e. affirmations) to bring about health, prosperity, and eventually the spiritualization of the body. Hodges claimed that the use of the formulas would lead to a rejuvenation of the body and ultimately to a state in which the individual could take his/her body to the heaven worlds, capable of returning to earth as situations warrant.

Hodges continued to publish into the early 1950s, but no evidence of the persistence of the Christian Fellowship Organization has been uncovered in recent years.

Sources:

Hodges, Edward Lewis. *Be Healed...A Remedy That Never Fails*. San Diego: Christian Fellowship Organization, 1949.

————. *Teachings of the Secret Order of the Christian Brotherhood*. Santa Barbara, CA: J. F. Rowney Press, 1938.

————. *Wealth and Riches by Divine Right*. San Diego: Christian Fellowship Organization, 1945.

THEOSOPHY

Aquarian Foundation

Not to be confused with the presently existing Spiritualist reorganization of the same name, the theosophical Aquarian Foundation was established in 1927 by Edward Arthur Wilson. The previous year, Wilson reported that he had been "translated in spirit to the higher realms in order to meet the eleven masters of Wisdom." As head of the foundation, Wilson assumed the name "Brother XII." Wilson initially placed his work in the context of the major program of the Theosophical Society of the time, the announcement of the arrival of the World Teacher in the person of Jiddu Krishnamurti. Brother XII denied Krishnamurti's assigned role and suggested instead that preparation for the coming World Teacher would be made through the foundation. A community was established in British Columbia, Canada. Over 100 theosophists left England with him at the beginning of 1927 to become the community's initial residents. Brother XII authored several books detailing the foundation's basic theosophical teachings and perspective.

The foundation was planted near Nanaimo, on Vancouver Island. Residents turned over their worldly possessions, and many friends of the work contributed additional sums. The colony flourished in spite of the introduction of some new teachings not otherwise disclosed in Brother XII's books. The immediate goal of the foundation was to give birth to a new generation of advanced human beings. To accomplish

this end, each of the colony females, no matter what their present marital status, was to have sexual relations with Brother XII, and the resultant children raised by the colony were to be the individuals who would actually receive the coming World Teacher in 1975. Brother XII also designated one colonist, Myrtle Baumgartner, as the mother of the World Teacher. Baumgartner did not produce a male child, however, and was soon replaced by Mabel Skottowe, known to her fellow colonists as Madame Zee.

The work continued until 1934, when two former members filed suits claiming that Wilson had treated them harshly and had misused the funds entrusted to him. The trials, which received sensational coverage in the press, were both decided for the plaintiffs, who were awarded both property and money. Wilson and Madame Zee soon disappeared, and the colony dissolved.

Sources:

Brother XII. *Foundation Letters and Teachings*. Akron, OH: Sun Publishing Co., 1927.

————. *The Three Truths*. Akron, OH: Sun Publishing Co., 1927.

Oliphant, John. *Brother Twelve: The Incredible Story of Canada's False Prophet*. Toronto: Mc Clelland & Stewart, 1992.

————. "The Teachings of Brother XII." *Theosophical History* 4, 6/7 (April/July 1993): 194–219.

Santucci, James. "The Aquarian Foundation." *Communal Societies* 9 (1989): 39–61.

Wilson, Herbert Emmerson. *Canada's False Prophet*. Richmond Hill, ON: Simon & Schuster, 1967.

International Group of Theosophists

The International Group of Theosophists is a small group which grew out of the American Theosophical movement in southern California. It was founded in the 1940s by Boris Mihailovich de Zirkoff (1902–1981), the grand-nephew of Helena Petrovna Blavatsky. Its objectives were to uphold and promote the original principles of the modern Theosophical movement and to disseminate the teachings of the esoteric philosophy as set forth by Blavatsky and her teachers. The group has tried to operate outside of the disagreements of the more established lodges and has cooperated with them in Zirkoff's major life work, the editing and publishing of Blavatsky's collected writings. For over 30 years it published *Theosophia*, a quarterly journal (1944–1981), but issued a final volume in the summer of 1981 as a tribute issue to its founder.

ALICE BAILEY GROUPS

School of Light and Realization (Solar)

The School of Light and Realization (Solar) dates to 1969, when the concept of the school emerged in a conversation between Hamid Bey of the Coptic

Fellowship in America and Norman Creamer, the founder of Solar. Following the conversation, Creamer, who had been searching for the right course for his life, and his wife, Katy Creamer, purchased a farm north of Traverse City, Michigan. The vision of Solar emerged largely out of a reading of the works of Alice Bailey and Theosophy. There was a strong belief in the imminent reappearance of the Christ and coming of the Aquarian Age. Solar was conceived to be one of the "New Group of World Servers" that would create the new society on the principles of goodwill and basic human character.

Solar's program was centered upon training men and women for life in the new age and training them to raise the level of consciousness in order to come in touch with the world of ideas and intuition. Solar taught the growth of the communal ideal; the coming of the one Christ; the removal of limitations and the development of potentials; that there was no original sin; that each individual had his own set of liabilities, assets and responsibilities; that to give the soul its freedom was the goal of human life; that discipline was self-imposed; and that Eastern philosophy was useful for Western man.

A school for both children and adults was established on the farm near Traverse City. The first session of the adult training school was held in the summer of 1972.

Centers for the dissemination of Solar concepts were also being established across the United States; the first was in St. Petersburg, Florida. Solar also offered correspondence lessons in its teachings. During its active period, the group also issued a periodical entitled *The Solarian*.

Sources:

Creamer, Norman. *The Aquarian Cosmic Vision*. Suttons Bay, MI: School of Light and Realization, n.d.

————. *Song of Solar*. Suttons Bay, MI: School of Light and Realization, 1972.

LIBERAL CATHOLIC CHURCHES

Canadian Catholic Church

The Canadian Catholic Church was a short-lived Liberal Catholic jurisdiction founded in 1948 by Odo Acheson Barry as an independent sister church of the American Catholic Church. A priest of the Liberal Catholic Church, Barry was originally consecrated by Antoine Joseph Aneed of the Byzantine Universal (Catholic) and Orthodox Church of the Americas on July 26, 1946. He was consecrated again three days later by Charles Hampton, a liberal Catholic bishop, assisted by several other bishops, including Lowell Paul Wadle of the American Catholic Church. In 1948 he was consecrated *sub conditione* by Wadle.

A short time after establishing the Canadian Catholic Church, Barry moved to Sri Lanka (Ceylon). He also lived for a while in New Zealand and England and only returned to Canada in 1960. Little was heard of his jurisdiction during the years he was away, and it did not develop any substantial membership after his return. Barry died in 1968, and the church folded afterward.

Sources:

Ward, Gary L. *Independent Bishops: An International Directory*. Detroit, MI: Apogee Books, 1990. 524 pp.

Independent Catholic Church International

The Independent Catholic Church International was formed in 1981 as both a new jurisdiction out of the Anglican heritage and an ecumenical body which related a variety of independent episcopal bodies, some out of the theosophical Liberal Catholic tradition. The first primate was Peter Wayne Goodrich. Goodrich resigned in 1983 and was succeeded by R. V. Bernard Dawe (b.1925), who had been consecrated in 1980 and had served as the church's international legate.

As constituted, the small jurisdiction had freely developed interchanges with a variety of Old Catholic and Anglican jurisdictions and remained open to theosophical currents. During its active period it was a member of the Synod of Independent Sacramental Churches.

Sources:

Ward, Gary L. *Independent Bishops: An International Directory*. Detroit, MI: Apogee Books, 1990.

International Liberal Catholic Church

The International Liberal Catholic Church was founded in 1966 by Bp. Edmund Walter Sheehan and others who left the Liberal Catholic Church branch led by Bp. Edward M. Matthews. He had previously served as an auxiliary bishop under Bp. Charles Hampton. His disagreement with Matthews concerned administrative matters.

Sheehan linked the International Liberal Catholic Church to the Brotherhood of the Blessed Sacrament, a Dutch group which had broken with the British headquarters of the Liberal Catholic Church. The Brotherhood had originally sided with Matthews but had broken relations with him in 1962.

The International Liberal Catholic Church followed the Matthews faction in doctrinal and liturgical matters. While reporting 9 bishops, 25 clergy, and 3,000 members in 1969, the International Church dwindled to only a few parishes during the 1970s and in the early 1980s was disbanded.

Sources:

International Liberal Catholic Church, Origins, Principles, Worship, Theology, Sacraments. Ojai, CA: St. Raphael's Printing Guild, 1968.

Sheehan, Edmund. *Teaching and Worship of the Liberal Catholic Church*. Los Angeles, CA: St. Alban Press, 1925.

Order of St. Germain, Ecclesia Catholica Liberalis

The Order of St. Germain, Ecclesia Catholica Liberalis was founded in 1969 as the Order of St. Germain. Its more recent name was adopted two years later. Its founder was James A. J. Taylor, also known as James Matthews, a former member of the Holy Order of MANS, an esoteric-metaphysical group modeled on the structure of a Roman Catholic religious order. Like traditional orders, the Order of St. Germain had no lay members, but was made up entirely of priests, ministers and "practitioners." Taylor asserted that although he "was consecrated by a Bishop (unnamed) of the Liberal Catholic Church, the Order claims no genetic connection with that Church."

The Order existed to forward the work of the Masters, the Christs, in the world. It was a sacramental church but differed in that it attempted to offer the widest latitude in matters of intellectual liberty and respect for individual conscience. Theologically it was Liberal Catholic in perspective.

The small order was headed by the Archbishop, assisted by other bishops appointed to administer state jurisdictions. A board of directors assisted in administrative matters. The order never grew beyond northern California.

Order of the Americas

The Order of the Americas is a Gnostic religious jurisdiction founded in 1994 by Bp. Michael von Stambach Bruce. The order can be traced to a series of lectures offered by Bruce in 1992 at several locations in Atlanta, Georgia. Out of the positive response to his lectures, the Gnostic Academy, a school of Gnostic studies in Atlanta, Georgia, was formed. In the meantime, Bruce became a seminarian at Sophia Divinity School, the seminary of the Church of Antioch, and in 1993 he attended the American College of Seminarians, the school of the Federation of St. Thomas Christian Churches. He was ordained by Abp. Joseph Vredenburgh on October 31, 1993. He was consecrated on April 25, 1994 by Bp. Louis S. Keizer of the Independent Church of Antioch, and the following day founded the Order of the Americas. On January 1, 1995, he participated in a service of cross-consecration with Bp. Russell Hill of the Ecclesia Gnostica Spiritualis and the NeoPythagorean Church. He was elevated to the office of archbishop in April 1995.

The Order of the Americas was a noncreedal Gnostic church. The Gnostic perspective rejects the God of Judaism and Christianity, which it considers a tribal deity. The highest expression of God to the Gnostic is an impersonal God as Ineffable, i.e., consciousness at rest, one that has not thought of itself. The faith held that God cannot be expressed in images but can be experienced. Salvation was considered to be an act of awakening from the dream of life in matter and remembering who one really is, a spiritual being. Jesus was seen as the personification of the

Logos, an impersonal principle of reason. The group held that, as a person awakens, Logos operated to translate the new knowledge of the self.

The Order of the Americas, as an independent episcopal jurisdiction, was organized as a chivalric order and offered a course in religious knighthood. Knighthood was considered an archetypal role model. Through the Gnostic academy, ministers were trained for the orders of deacon and priest. Priests were also eligible for consideration for the office of bishop. Ministers organized study groups and led Sunday worship services. Services were conducted on a democratic basis and included meditation, readings from Gnostic scriptures, communion, and healing. The primary worship center was at the Gnostic shrine of Sophia in Atlanta. Worship services were open to all. During its active period, the Order of the Americas issued the periodical *Gnostica*. Though it is now presumed defunct, in 1995 the order reported approximately 300 members and eight clergy. The great majority of members were in the United States, but there were members in Great Britain, New Zealand, and Canada.

Sources:

Gregorious, Tau, Russell Slay Hill, and Michael von Stambach Bruce. "European Esoteric Lineages." *Gnostic* 1, 9 (February 1995): 1–5.

"Questions and Answers." Atlanta, GA: Order of the Americas, 1995.

Paracletian Catholic Church

The Paracletian Catholic Church was founded in 1982 by Leonard R. Barcynski and Vivian Barcynski, two bishops in the Church of Antioch. The Barcynskis had become well known during the 1970s for their many books on magick and the occult written under their pseudonyms, Melita Denning and Osborne Phillips. They have been leaders for over a decade in the Aurum Solis, a ritual magick organization which they helped reconstitute in 1971.

In 1978 the Barcynskis moved to the United States and soon after met Abp. Herman Adrian Spruit, who in June 1982 consecrated them and established a Diocese of St. Paul (Minnesota) which the Barcynskis jointly administered. However, in October of that year, they broke with the Church of Antioch and established an independent jurisdiction. The church never became firmly established, however, and several years later they abandoned any further effort to establish its parishes.

The articles of association of the Paracletian Catholic Church indicated that the church's main purposes were "to spread the love and knowledge of Christ, to administer the sacraments of the Catholic and Apostolic tradition in their plenitude, and to perform charitable works." The church was an attempt to give expression through the forms of the Catholic liturgical tradition to the teachings of Western

Occultism as transmitted through the Aurum Solis. As defined by the Aurum Solis, the purpose of life in this world is to discover one's True Will and to do it. God is envisioned as the Divine Spark within, which motivates people to search out their true Vocation or Will.

I AM GROUPS

Ascended Master Fellowship

The Ascended Master Fellowship was founded in 1972 by the Rev. Theodore M. Pierce, a former minister in the Cosmic Church of Life and Spiritual Science. In 1954, he had been called by Ascended Master Saint Germain through a vision in which he was shown the word "Freedom" written across the universe. The basic teachings of the church are found in two volumes written by A.D.K. Luk, *Law of Life*. The volumes are a variation on the original "I AM" teachings as presented by Guy Ballard, founder of the "I AM" Religious Activity. Volume II includes a minute description of the spiritual hierarchy and the personages that fill the positions. The Fellowship worked especially under Saint Germain, the Chohan of the Aquarian Age, but also was in cooperation with Ascended Masters Jesus and Mother Mary.

The Reverend Pierce entered the realm of spiritual healing and practiced cosmic surgery through several spirit doctors. According to the Fellowship, in January, 1969, during a healing session, he was taken out of his body and taken back in time so as to be able to release "misqualified energy" (karma) from the individual. Pierce subsequently became a karmic eraser, one who can remove the consequences of evil that was done in former incarnations.

Regular services were held at the headquarters at Yarnell, Arizona. Affiliated groups were located in South Carolina, North Carolina, and Phoenix; Arizona; and individual members were found across the United States and in Canada, New Zealand, and Saudi Arabia. For a number of years, Pierce published a periodical, *Temple Notes*. The fellowship was discontinued when the demand on Pierce for past life readings began to take all of his time.

Sources:

Luk, A. D. K. *Law of Life*. 2 vols. Baltimore, MD: The Author, 1959-60.

Pierce, Ted M. *Healer Extraordinaire*. Yarnell, AZ: Top Publishers, 1987.

The Foundation of Love

The Foundation of Love was an independent "I AM" organization established in Livingston, Montana, in 1990 by Bill Guillot, its director. Based upon the teachings of the Ascended Masters who have spoken through the Messengers of the "I AM" Religious Activity and the Church Universal and Triumphant, the foundation emphasized the one path, that is, the Path of Love, the only way to God. Sacrifice, service, surrender, and selflessness were believed to be the four essential "sure" ways to find true meaning and purpose in life.

The foundation's goals were to help people realize that they can be healthy, happy, and whole, to assist them toward a higher consciousness of divine love, and to work together in a cooperative Christ relationship.

Sources:

The Master Book of Health, Happiness, and Higher Consciousness. Livingston, MT: The Foundation of Love, 1993. 50 pp.

Joy Foundation, Inc.

The Joy Foundation, Inc., was founded in Santa Barbara, California, in 1977 by the Rev. Dr. Elizabeth Louise Huffer assisted by Richard Huffer and Donald Cyr. Dr. Huffer was raised a Roman Catholic but passed through an extensive and eclectic program of metaphysical/occult education after leaving the church. She studied astrology with renowned astrologer Carroll Righter and with the First Temple of Astrology in Los Angeles. She then studied with Dr. D. J. Bussell, founder of the Chirothesian Church of Faith; Dr. Fletcher Harding of the United Church of Religious Science in Tarzana, California; and Dr. Henry Cairns of the College of Divine Metaphysics, from which she received her doctorates in divinity and psychology. She was ordained in the Universal Church of the Master (UCM) in 1969 and in 1974 chartered the Joy Church as a congregation of the UCM. The Joy Foundation emerged as an independent body from the church in 1977.

The teachings and practice of the Joy Foundation reflected the eclectic background of the founder. Huffer drew upon the teachings of Alice Bailey, Ann Ree Colton, and Corinne Heline, but was also herself a channel for the Ascended Masters. She understood that planet earth was receiving the Rays of Light. Besides the seven rays commonly spoken of in "I AM" Religious Activity literature, Huffer described 12 rays, 5 additional rays related to humanity's inherent possibilities of awareness and the entire 12 rays related to the signs of the zodiac. These rays were of particular colors and were related to the work of particular masters, as were the first seven. The work of the foundation consisted of being aware of the rays and qualifying (or directing them to particular tasks) by the process of decreeing and by meditation. (Decrees are invocations to the masters spoken in a forceful directive manner.) By using decrees and spending time in meditation, members were able to balance their physical and spiritual selves and thus become prepared to enter the New Age, the Age of Aquarius. Members used a variation of the Violent Flame Decree daily; this was first popularized by the I AM Movement. A book of Invocations and Decrees offered decrees for all 12 rays to be used throughout the year.

Huffer described a spiritual hierarchy consisting of chohans, elohim, archangels, and angels. The chohans (or lords) were individuals who have lived many lifetimes during which they have mastered the energies of the rays, but especially mastered the energy of one ray. They were known as Ascended Masters. The elohim were cosmic beings with a more depersonalized and planentary influence. Archangels presided over the seasons of the years. Angels assisted all humanity and planetary life.

Centers of the foundation were found in Sedona, Arizona, and Santa Barbara, California. The three festivals popularized by Alice Bailey consisting of Easter, Wesak, and Goodwill were celebrated by foundation members, and additional celebrations were held to mark the solstice and equinox.

While the group is presumed defunct, in 1992 the foundation reported 35 members in two centers led by two ministers. During its active period, it issued two periodicals entitled *Prisms of Joy* and *Waves of Joy*. Donald Cyr, co-founder of the foundation, operates a printing shop in Santa Barbara, California, and is the editor of *Stonehenge Viewpoint*, a popular magazine which attempts to discern the significance of Stonehenge and the other megalithic sites of Europe, North America, and elsewhere.

Sources:

Huffer, Elizabeth Louise. *Spiral to the Sun*. Santa Barbara, CA: Joy Foundation, 1976.

Invocations and Decrees. Santa Barbara, CA: Joy Foundation, 1982.

Law of Life Activity

A. D. K. Luk is an independent interpreter of the I AM teachings who wrote and published the *Law of Life*, a popular variant treatment of I AM themes. The *Law of Life* was also a comprehensive summary of the information scattered through the discourses given by the masters through Guy W. Ballard (1878–1939), founder of the "I AM" Religious Activity. During the 1960s a number of independent groups such as those advocated in the first volume of Law of Life formed to study, meditate, and decree. In 1971 Luk issued an instruction manual for group leaders to guide their efforts. Beliefs and practice follow those of the I AM Activity and the original Bridge to Freedom Activity. A. D. K. Publications issued a wide variety of materials for use by related groups. The books by Guy W. Ballard issued by the I AM Activity were also used, but there was no organizational affiliation. Besides the writings of Ballard, the Law of Life Activity also used the works of Geraldine Innocente, who received messages for the Bridge to Freedom in the 1950s.

The *Law of Life* was not established formally as an organization and there was no accounting of members. The publications have been distributed to many countries of Western Europe and Africa, as well as to Australia and New Zealand. During its active period, the group issued a periodical entitled Law of Life Enlightener.

Sources:

Luk, A. D. K. *Law of Life*. 2 vols. Oklahoma City, OK: A. D. K. Luk Publications, 1959–60.

———. *Law of Life Instruction for Group Directors*. Oklahoma City, OK: A. D. K. Luk Publications, 1983.

Ruby Focus of Magnificent Consummation

The Ruby Focus of Magnificent Consummation, Inc. was founded in the mid-1960s by Garman Van Polen and Evangeline Van Polen, both former students of the "I AM" Religious Activity and the Bridge to Freedom, now the New Age Church of Christ. Evangeline eventually became a channel of the ascended masters and in the late 1950s began to issue discourses under the aegis of the New Age Clinic of Spiritual Therapy in Phoenix, Arizona. Influential in the emergence of the Magnificent Consummation were the writings of Dr. C. H. Yeang. Yeang agreed with the Bridge to Freedom that over the years a number of changes had occurred in the makeup of the spiritual hierarchy. Specifically, he noted that in 1955, Gautama Buddha replaced Sanat Kumara as Lord of this World, that Lord Maitreya, formerly the World Teacher, now held the office of Buddha, and that Jesus and Koot Hoomi, formerly Chohans (ascended masters) of the Sixth and Second Rays, respectively, jointly functioned as the World Teacher. Yeang also believed that Saint Germain had been elevated and that Godfre-Ray King and Lotus King (i.e., Guy Ballard and Edna Ballard) had replaced him as Chohan of the Seventh Ray. St. Germain, in 1965, proclaimed himself as Eolia, now radiating the Golden Liquid Snow of Eolian Consciousness, the Light of the Central Sun. From that position, he continued to direct the Seventh Ray and its new Chohan.

The Magnificent Consummation was the particular child of the Ruby Light of the Sixth Ray. Sananda and Lady Nada, Chohans of the Sixth Ray, were the directors. (Sananda is so labeled on all the literature.) The special work was to aid the descent of the Ruby Light of freedom, justice, peace, confidence, balance, and magnificence into the physical world. Almost all of the literature of the Ruby Focus was on pink paper, usually with red ink.

In the early 1970s, new additions to the hierarchy were recognized in the persons of Ruby and Christos, two additional Rays of Light. Ruby's color was iridescent ruby and Christos's was iridescent mother of pearl. They represented the negative and positive electric polarities and, together, were said to be the perfect laser beam of light. The thought was that they would bring in the Magnificent Consummation of all seven colors plus themselves as the Rainbow Ray Consciousness and thus usher in the Aquarian Age.

From its headquarters, the Ruby Focus issued a variety of books. An order of service was built around a call upon one of the Seven Rays (plus the Eighth and Ninth Rays daily), songs, a message from one of the masters, and the taking in and radiation of light into the country and the world. Decrees were used extensively. The channeled messages received each Sunday were printed in the periodical *Open Letter*.

Ruby Focus was not a membership organization.

Sources:

Van Polen, Garman, and Evangeline Van Polen. *Catechism of Light*. 2 vols. Sedona, AZ: Magnificent Consummation, 1965.

Van Polen, Garman, and Theresa Martin. *A Treatise on Father-Mother Light as Golden Experiences*. The Author, 1966.

Yeang, C. H. *Who Am I? I Am That I Am*. Privately published, [1965].

Sacred Society of the Eth, Inc.

The Sacred Society of the Eth, Inc. is the creation of Walter W. Jecker, known by his celestial name, Jo'el of Arcadia. During the 1960s, he went into the Siskiyou Mountains (a range in California and Oregon) and for seven years compiled volumes of words regarding love, light, and life. The words were published in 1967. He also founded the Sacred Society of the Eth, Inc. His particular contact was with Jesus the Christ, known as the Ascended Master Sananda.

According to Jo'el, man is an emanation (sun) of God. While living in a body, man must know that he is the God of his being. Basic to man is Breath. The intelligence, says Jo'el, is in the Breath. Breath is thought and breathing is mind. Through Breath is the constant flow of the water of life. The etheric body is the fallen Breath of life. The Breath is creational. Man's life is determined by the hate or love within his mind.

During its active period, literature was distributed to study groups and individuals around the United States.

Sources:

Jecker, Walter W. *God in Man Alive*. Forks of Salmon, CA: Sacred Society of the Eth, 1972.

———. *God Speaks, I Hear His Voice*. Forks of Salmon, CA: Sacred Society of the Eth, 1967.

———. *The Words of Light*. Forks of Salmon, CA: Sacred Society of the Eth, 1967.

Sanctuary of the Master's Presence

The Sanctuary of the Master's Presence was closely related to other I AM groups. The Sanctuary was formed in the 1960s, but the public manifestation was not made until 1966 with the appearance of *The Mentor*, a periodical which carried the messages from the ascended masters. The Mentor was one of the entities from the spirit world who spoke through Mary Myneta, the principal percipient and teacher.

According the Mentor, man is evolving to a greater awareness of his creator. The present age is a time of man's becoming aware of a truth and awakening to a reality previously unknown. This step was thought to be precipitated by the powerful radiations of spiritual light from ascended masters' spheres of activity. The masters were thought to project a golden radiance into earth to stir up our awareness.

Originally, the Sanctuary was headquartered in New York City and its periodical, edited by the Rev. Wayne Taylor, was published from Melbourne, Florida. However, in 1968, both were moved to Scarsdale, New York. From 1965 to 1968 Taylor had been president of Sologa, Inc., for whom his wife Grace Taylor was a channel. However, in 1968 the Taylors moved to Columbus, New Mexico, to found Christ's Truth Church and School of Wisdom. Besides the group in Scarsdale, there were a few classes and group meetings, though they popularity waned after the 1960s.

The Sanctuary peaked in support in the 1960s and ultimately trickled down to only one group in Scarsdale and few students around the United States. It is now presumed defunct.

Sources:

The Order of the Service. New York: Sanctuary of the Masters' Presence, [1969].

Shasta Student League Foundation

The Shasta Student League Foundation, active in the 1930s from its headquarters in Long Beach, California, was a Christian theosophical group in the "I AM" tradition. According to the teachings of the foundation, creation was generated out of the Central Sun, the center of the universe, located beyond the Lyra section of the constellation Sagittarius. The Central Sun was thought to contain the Three-Fold Life-Flame and the Form Concept of Cosmic Creation, the pattern from which all forms were created. Creation began as the Three-Fold Life-Flame projected into expression. The Basic Elements of the Flame—Life (energy), Light (intelligence), and Substance—are incorporated in all individual creations. The first level of manifestation was thought to be the band of the Macrocosmic Forms and the second that of the White Light Forms of the Angels or Celestial Beings. The White Light Forms were the individual expressions of God that came into being when God said, "Let there be Light." Angels were thought to exist in interstellar space, outside the segment of space with stars and planets.

As the belief system goes, the White Light of the Central Sun travels into the realm of solar systems and planets. When it hits the atmosphere of a planet, such as Earth, it breaks into the seven bands of the light spectrum. The violet ray forms around the outermost atmosphere, the red band is closest to the planet. All manifestation in form occurs through the seven rays. Chief among the manifestations are human beings. Humans result from the projection of the Life Flame of the Cosmic Christ Beings (Angels) into the blue light band (the second band) in the planet's atmosphere. The projected flame became a human ego, which then took its bodily substance from the blue light. This human then decided to experience life on the planet's (in this case Earth's) surface. It assumed a flesh body and became like an animal, with one important difference. The animal evolved as an expression of red ray, while humans were projections from the celestial realms into red ray existence.

The seven color bands form a ladder that the human must climb in order to return to its celestial origin. Through various lifetimes (reincarnations) humans search the various levels, and the dominant thoughts and feelings of a person at present indicate the levels explored in previous lives. As each level is explored and its vibrations absorbed, the individual enlivens the next body it inhabits. As the process nears completion, the rate of vibration of the body is so transformed that it is capable of transmutation into an etheric body and can rise to the higher realms of light never to incarnate again. Eventually each individual will ascend and return to the White Light Plane.

As with all "I AM" groups the members of the Foundation utilized decrees—the declaration of spiritual truth in the form of affirmative statements. Among the key decrees used was the Shasta Declaration of Being:"I Am the Individualized Focus of God Mind, thinking my way back to my Source, the Great Central Sun, from which I was projected at the beginning of this Cosmic Day, and to which I must return at its end."

Sources:

Lyra (Lucy Simms Thompson). *The Shasta Cosmic Key Message*. Long Beach, CA: Shasta Student League Foundation, 1937. 37 pp.

Sologa, Inc.

Sologa, Inc., was established in 1959 by Dr. Ruth Scoles Lennox and included among its members Wayne Taylor, who succeeded to the presidency of the group upon Lennox's death in 1965, and Grace Taylor, his wife, a channel for the masters. In 1968, Taylor left Melbourne, Florida and Sologa, Inc., for New Mexico, where he founded Christ's Truth Church and School of Wisdom and the City of the Sun Foundation.

In 1968 there were two Sologa groups, one in Miami and one in Melbourne, Florida. The group is presumed defunct.

University of the Christ Light with the Twelve Rays

In the 1970s, Dr. Mary L. Myers, who had been trained for the previous 40 years by the Angelic Host, established a training center to pass on the material she was receiving to the world. The center existed under various names, each reflective of the new rise in consciousness: Essene Teachings (1977), University of the Twelve Rays of the Great Central Sun (1982), and the Path of Light (1986). Most recently the center took the name University of the Christ Light with the Twelve Rays. Beginning in 1982, intensive weekly lessons were distributed, allowing students to progress to ever higher states of consciousness and make direct contact with the Angelic Host and the Oneness of the Christ Light.

Myers's work was directed toward the beginning of the New Age as Angelic Beings were thought to have entered the earth's atmosphere. The work focused on pioneering new knowledge, raising the consciousness of members and leaders, and clearing them of their DNA and RNA genetic codes, thus enabling them to enter interdimensional levels through cleansing activities, as each individual established the advanced truth within themselves, their own spirits, and received into conscious awareness, their own souls.

According to Myers, Jesus the Christ was the World teacher who had become One with the Universal Light of the Creator, who created our earth. He represented three great Rays—the Rays of Truth, Wisdom, and Love. He was the perfect interpreter of every portion of the Bible. He was also Yahweh, who had mastered the 12 Rays of the Great Central Sun of our Universe. Yahweh, the Ancient of Days, was considered the administrator of the Path of Light. He was also known as Sanat Kumara. His divine complement is Lady Master Venus Kumara. Yahweh's body was considered so vast that it included the entire earth and all of humankind.

As of the late 1980s, the organization of Myers's students had decentralized as the leaders she trained took her teachings around the world. Affiliated teachers could once be found in Canada, England, France, Germany, Italy, Africa, Singapore, Malaysia, and Australia.

Sources:

Myers, Mary. *Here Comes the Sun!* N.p, n.d.

————. *My Truth*. Nurnberg, Germany: The Author, 1965.

Myers Kumara, Mary. *The Path of Light*. N.p., n.d.

OTHER THEOSOPHICAL GROUPS

Bodha Society of America

The Bodha Society of America was incorporated in 1936 by its president, Ms. Violet B. Reed. She described it as a movement fostering spiritual consciousness through self-realization and world service. Spiritual virility could be attained only through a better outlook on life and a deeper realization of the spiritual realm. According to the society, the Bodha movement was begun in 1907 under the direction of the Sanctuaries of Tibet and Sikkim and assumed "the full responsibility which once rested in the Theosophical Society, this organization being no longer patronized by its founders, inspirers and real leaders: the masters." The Bodha Society was seen as the vehicle of the Great Brotherhood, the ascended masters who were once humans and who now as spirits teach people about spiritual realities.

The Society kept the three spiritual festivals associated with Buddhism, particularly Wesak. Associated centers were opened in France and Cuba; world headquarters were claimed to be in Tibet. National headquarters were in Long Beach, California. *Sun Rays*, a periodical, was published.

Lighted Way

The Lighted Way was described as a "New Age School for Discipleship Training." It was founded in 1966 by Muriel R. Tepper (known as Muriel Isis), under the direction of Master D.K. of the White Brotherhood. It was guided and inspired by the cosmic mother Isis. Muriel was the outer symbol of the mother principle—truth and inspiration. The mother as Isis revealed the cosmic laws and pure truths for the building of the immortal light body and the resurrection of the physical form. These laws included the laws of light radiation, magnetism, cause and effect, polarity, and correspondence.

The Lighted Way was seen as the highway back to divinity. To help the members in their return, a variety of services was offered. Light Radiation Circles allowed each person a chance to gain direct awareness of the Universal Mind. Individual counseling in Akashic records, in the aura, and in personal soul evolvement were offered by Muriel, either in person or by mail on cassette tape. (Akashic records were the recordings on the "universal ethers" of all thoughts and actions; psychics could "tap into" these records. The auras were psychic emanations from the human body; psychics could see and interpret auras.) Full moon meditations were held monthly. Classes were offered in meditation, Yoga and the lessons of Isis on metaphysical truths. Healing services were held weekly.

Though the group is now presumed defunct, in 1973 centers were functioning in Los Angeles, Pacific Palisades, Costa Mesa, and Hollywood, California.

Sources:

Tepper, Muriel R. *The Lighted Way Road to Freedom*. Los Angeles: Lighted Way Press, n.d.

————. *Mechanisms of the Personality through Personology*. Pacific Palisade, CA: Lighted Way Press, n.d.

Oasis Fellowship

The Oasis Fellowship began in the home of George White and his wife, Alice White. While meditating, they began to make contact with several spirit entities named Elawa, Malala, and Yeban, believed to be teachers from a higher plane of evolvement. As messages began to come through, friends of the Whites began to attend the sessions. Healing prayer was a major concern. As time passed, the Whites disposed of their business and went in search of a place for a center to which those dedicated to the program could gravitate. After a year of searching, such a spot was located near Florence, Arizona, and the Oasis Fellowship began.

At Florence, on the 17.5 acres, members of the fellowship led a communal-like existence in separate mobile homes and travel trailers. Many left during the summer months. Soon after the establishment in Arizona, weekly "lessons in living" began to come through the channels. The lessons were taped, transcribed, and sent out, on request only, across the United States. Early in the experiment, the teachers specified that no charge was ever to be made or money solicited. If ever there were insufficient voluntary "love gifts" to cover cost of production and mailing the lessons, they should be stopped, accepting the lack as "evidence that the power had gone out of them." From the beginning, adequate financial support had always been received.

Beliefs of the fellowship followed the teachings of Jesus and the lessons were frequently comments by the spirit teachers on a Bible passage. There was strong emphasis on the spiritual evolvement of the individual. Both psychic communication, if on a spiritual level, and reincarnation were accepted. God was seen as the center of life and a Spirit shining within.

Other than the small group residing at the Oasis in Florence, Arizona, between 120 and 150 at one time regularly received the lessons. Some of these in turn shared them with others as the leaders of study groups. The lessons were sent out across the United States and Canada, as well as to several foreign countries, most notably Nigeria.

Open Way

The Open Way was a New Age group centered in Celina, Tennessee, and headed by Lovie Webb Gasteiner. There was a close affinity with Mary L. Myers of the Essene Teachings. The Open Way taught that God manifests as Father and Mother and lives in all. According to the belief system, God was the source of life, love, peace, strength, and abundant life. Man's goal was a return to God in self-realization. The law of life was giving and receiving, and the Open Way taught exercises on giving and receiving divine energy. The secret was tensing and relaxing the muscles, nerves, and tissues of the body in combination with the human voice, used in speaking, chanting, humming, and singing.

Philo-Polytechnical Center

The Philo-Polytechnical Center of Los Angeles had aims similar to those of the Bodha Society of America. It was headed by Ronald Clifton and published *The Bodha Renaissance*.

Sun Center

The Sun Center was a theosophical group formed in Akron, Ohio, in the 1920s which developed a uniquely Christian emphasis. It took its name from the theosophical concept of God as the Great Central Sun. Much of the inspiration for the center came from Joseph S. Benner (d. 1941), author of the popular mystical/occult volume, *The Impersonal Life*. The small book, penned prior to World War I, was directed to what was considered to be the true self, the imper-

sonal self, the spirit within, also identified with the "I AM," the Christ Self, and God's Holy Spirit. Beginning in the 1920s, Benner also developed a series of lessons to assist students to understand and progressively work with the ideas presented in *The Impersonal Life*. *The Way Out* and *The Way Beyond*, the first of these booklets, provided training for the development and discipline of the mind. *The Inner Life Course* dealt with the awakening of the soul. A final set of lessons led students to the unfolding of the spirit.

Through its magazine, *The Inner Life*, begun in 1933, the Sun Center solicited support for its work as a group of followers of Christ to bring the Light of Christ to every soul ready to receive it. As a first step, those related to the center were asked to serve in the cause of brotherhood by entering into the silence each day at noon. During these silent moments, each person would see himself as a center of Love's Light and Power and would pour that Love out upon the world. Noon was chosen as the moment when the earth received the greatest downpouring of the light (wisdom), heat (love), and energy (power) of the sun (the visible expression of Father-God).

The Sun Center continued to operate through the 1930s but eventually dissolved. There is no record of the size of the center's support, though in the mid-1930s there were more than 30 groups across the United States and in Australia, Canada, England, France, and New Zealand. After Brenner's death, the publishing rights of his books were eventually turned over to Willing Publishing Company, which was in turn absorbed by DeVorss Publishing Company, which keeps *The Impersonal Life*, in print to this day. The Sun Publishing Company, intimately connected with the Sun Center, was publisher of the books of the Aquarian Foundation, a short-lived theosophical group in the 1920s.

Sources:

The Impersonal Life. San Gabriel, CA: Willing Publishing Co., 1971.

Morgan, Elise Nevins. *Your Own Path*. Akron, OH: Sun Publishing Co., 1928.

The Way Beyond Course. Akron, OH: Sun Publishing Co., n.d. [193–].

The Way Out. Akron, OH: Sun Publishing Co., 1930.

The Way Out Course. Akron, OH: Sun Publishing Co., [193–].

Universal Religious Fellowship

The Universal Religious Fellowship was founded by Harriette Augusta Curtiss (1855–1932), also known by her religious name Rahmea, and Frank Homer Curtiss (1875–1946), also known by his religious name Pyrahmos. Homer Curtiss, a physician and graduate of the University of Pennsylvania, married Harriette in 1907. They began to head a study group which formally began its work on January 1, 1908.

Originally known as the Order of The 15, a name derived by numerological reference, it soon took its more descriptive title, the Order of Christian Mystics, by which it was known through the 1920s. The Curtisses formed a corporation, the Universal Religious Fellowship in 1928, and that name gradually came to denominate their efforts through the 1930s. For a brief period in the 1920s, the name Church of the Wisdom Religion was also used. The order was founded in Philadelphia, Pennsylvania, but moved its headquarters to California prior to World War I. Around 1925 it moved to Washington, D.C., where it remained until after Homer Curtiss's death in 1946; at that point it moved to Hollywood, California, where its remained during its final years.

The Curtisses were former theosophists who originally established the Order of The 15 for the purpose of correlating advanced philosophical teachings (i.e., theosophy) with orthodox Christian teachings, and changed its original name to the Order of Christian Mystics so it could more easily approach members of Christian churches. Its particular concern for expressing the universal principle in Christian terms and by using Christian scriptures (instead of eastern holy books) separated it from the main body of theosophists (the Liberal Catholic Church not having been created at the time of the order's founding). The order also saw itself as anti-organizational and for many years did not incorporate.

Teachings of the order (and fellowship) were put forth in the numerous books (more than 20) written by the Curtisses, though their central teachings were summarized in *The Voice of Isis*, *The Message of Aquaria*, and *Letters from the Teacher*. In addition to their books, the Curtisses published a monthly lesson for order members, who were encouraged to form study groups and to use the "Prayer for World Harmony," printed in one of the textbooks. The order emphasized personal self-mastery and offered personal counsel via correspondence with the Curtisses.

The order followed theosophical teaching in general but developed its own special emphases. The Curtisses advocated a middle way on most issues within the occult community. It did not advocate vegetarianism or celibacy, though it strongly advocated reincarnation. It offered an occult interpretation of the Bible which the Curtisses believed had been lost due to emphases upon literal and historical interpretations. Psychic awakening, as a natural part of spiritual unfoldment, was emphasized and the use of special techniques for the development of psychic powers discouraged. Most importantly, the order was preparing for the advent of the Coming World Teacher, the Avatar. However, they sought to keep their pupils from being led astray by personality, i.e., from the Theosophical Society, which was at that time promoting Jiddu Krishnamurti as the World Teacher. The order trained its pupils to recognize and respond to the teacher on the spiritual planes. Finally, the order emphasized the important theosophical teachings of the oneness of truth and universal brotherhood.

The order survived only a few years after the death of the Curtisses, though several of their books were kept in print for many years.

Sources:

Curtiss, F. Homer. *Reincarnation*. Santa Barbara, CA: J. F. Rowney Press, 1949.

Curtiss, Harriette Augusta, and F. Homer Curtiss. *The Message of Aquaria*. San Francisco: Curtiss Philosophic Book Company, 1921.

———. *Letters from the Teacher*. 2 vols. Hollywood, CA: Curtiss Philosophic Book Co., 1918.

———. *The Voice of Isis*. Los Angeles: Curtiss Philosophic Book Co., 1912.

The Fellowship of the Order of Christian Mystics. Washington, DC: Order of Christian Mystics, n.d.

White Lodge

Lady Elizabeth Carey was an agent of the White Eagle Lodge, a British New Age group, who was sent to the United States to open the work. In 1941, while in Los Angeles, she became aware that she was being guided by spirits, and, on Grouse Mountain near Vancouver, a group became aware, through her, of the imminent return of Christ. In 1943, a tract of land near Del Mar, California, was purchased as a site for a sacred shrine. The guidance was received from the Great White Brotherhood, a group of elder brothers identical to the Buddhist bodhisattvas or the Theosophical ascended masters. These brothers have often incarnated in the past and have existed as a group since the first godman walked the earth. Roselady, as Ms. Carey was known, was in contact with a Great White Brotherhood initiate, Azrael.

Through the shrine at Del Mar called the White Lodge, the message of Azrael began to be published through a monthly periodical, *Angelus*. Growing popularity led to the publication in the 1960s of four *Books of Azrael* containing collections of Azrael's messages. Advertising in such psychically oriented periodicals as *Chimes* made the shrine well known throughout the United States.

The teachings of Azrael were concerned with the work of the White Brotherhood and its role in bringing in the New Age of Aquarius. Azrael was helping to create a new humanity by raising the consciousness of those who receive the teachings. The content of Azrael's message was summed up in two words, "love" and "light." Love was the cohesive force of the universe, the principle by which God acts, judges, and heals. Light was the symbol of man's path back to God. The Brotherhood dwelled in the light and taught the path to illumination through prayer and meditation. Reincarnation and karma were strongly held beliefs, and prayer for healing through the white light was a major practice. Healing prayer was accompa-

nied by a "linking in," during which members scattered across the United States joined in prayer at the same hour.

In the late 1960s, tension arose among the supporters of the shrine. On Easter Sunday, 1969, Eloise Mellor, the guardian of the shrine, asserted that she was the channel for Azrael and St. John the Beloved. According to the fourth *Book of Azrael*, a special work by St. John was directly to precede the coming of Jesus, the world teacher. Eloise also replaced members of the shrine's board of trustees. These changes were made with the claimed blessing of White Eagle, a guide from the spirit world, but without going through Roselady. Almost immediately, two factions arose and, in 1971, open schism appeared.

After Easter of 1969, Joseph E. Hall, deposed vice president of the shrine at Del Mar, California, called the White Lodge, continued to receive the communications from Azrael and to circulate them among former supporters of the work. Then, in 1970, Philip Schraub of Corpus Christi, Texas, was confirmed by the aging Roselady as her successor as the channel of Azrael and the one to be used to carry forward the New Age teachings of John the Beloved. In the spring of 1971, public announcement of Philip's role, as well as a denouncement of Eloise, was made by Mr. Hall and nine other leading supporters of the Shrine in the first issue of a new monthly, *The New Angelus for the New Age*. A letter from the White Eagle Lodge denied support of Eloise. Through Philip, the Brotherhood announced its temporary withdrawal from the Shrine and the relocation of the work to Corpus Christi.

Efforts began to recover the Shrine, at first through negotiation with Eloise, Mari Mae Napier, and her husband, who at that time constituted the Shrine's board. In the midst of these negotiations, Eloise fell ill. During her convalescence, she repented of her activity and began to support Philip. She was also deposed as guardian of the Shrine, and five trustees were appointed in her place. *Rays of Wisdom* replaced the Angelus as the periodical.

Upon her recovery, a court fight was initiated by Eloise to regain her guardianship, but she died in 1974, before the matter could be resolved. Several years later, the trustees turned the work and the property over to Elizabeth Clare Prophet and the Church Universal and Triumphant, into which it was completely absorbed.

Philip Schraub continued to publish The New Angelus for the New Age first in Corpus Christi and then in West Sedona, Arizona, until 1983, after which the work was discontinued.

Sources:

Book of Azreal. 4 vols. Santa Barbara, CA: J. F. Rowny Press, 1965–67.

Eloise [Mellor]. *Youth: Open the Door*. Los Angeles: DeVorss & Co., 1969.

 # 18. Western Esoteric II: Spiritualism & New Age

SPIRITUALISM

Aquarian Fellowship Church

The Aquarian Fellowship Church was formed in 1969 by the Reverend Robert A. Ferguson, who until that time was president of the Universal Church of the Master, one of the larger Spiritualist organizations. Ferguson founded the new church as a result of inspiration received through dreams. He also felt a growing concern about the doctrine of reincarnation, which most ministers in the Universal Church of the Master accepted, but which he, their leader, denied.

The Aquarian Fellowship Church centered its teachings upon the Bible, the writings of Andrew Jackson Davis (1826–1910), the founder of modern Spiritualism, and the writings of Ferguson as primary sources of belief. Ferguson initiated a project of reprinting Davis's works. Like Davis, Ferguson rejected the Christian beliefs in the Trinity and the deity of Christ, but he considered Jesus the most perfect of men and a pattern for all to copy. He believed that this life is the beginning of a process of continual growth. After death, individuals go to one of seven heavens, to which they gravitate according to their earthly character, and where they continue to work out their salvation. Communication with those in "summerland" (the afterworld) was emphasized. There were no sacraments, although infant dedications did occur.

The headquarters of the Aquarian Fellowship Church were in San Jose, California, and in 1972, there were three congregations, one in Los Angeles, one in San Jose, California, and one in Dayton, Ohio. Lessons in Spiritualism were offered on a correspondence basis. Ferguson authored several books on psychic themes. The church seems to have dissolved sometime during the 1980s.

Sources:

Ferguson, Robert A. *Adventures in Psychic Development*. London: Regency Press, 1972.

———. *Universal Mind: New Way to Mystic Power and Prosperity*. West Nyack, NY: Parker Publishing Company, 1979.

Ferguson, Walter F., as told to Robert A. Ferguson. *The Celestial Telegraph (A Message from Beyond)*. New York: Carlton Press, 1974.

Church of Cosmic Science

The Church of Cosmic Science was a small Spiritualist body formed in 1959 in Rialto, California, by Rev. William Dickensen, Reginald Lawrence, and

Josephine Dickensen. For many years, the associated Cosmic Light Press issued the monthly *Cosmic Light*, which was widely circulated among the independent Spiritualist churches, which used it for advertising. The group also circulated *Awareness for Cosmic Truth*, a periodical containing lessons in psychic development. The headquarters, in Jamul, California, granted ordinations, healer's certificates, and church charters to otherwise autonomous ministers. In 1970 there were 500 members and seven churches, but by the 2000s the church's headquarters had been closed and its activities had ceased.

Churches of Spiritual Revelation Association

The Churches of Spiritual Revelation Association was a small fellowship of Spiritualist churches and mediums functioning in the 1970s. Although the association had a loosely organized structure, it had an episcopal polity. Most of the churches were in the Northeast and the headquarters were in Reading, Pennsylvania, at the residence of Bishop Edward M. Leighton. There has been no evidence of the continuance of the association since around 1980.

Cosmic Church of Life and Spiritual Science

The Cosmic Church of Life and Spiritual Science was a small Spiritualist body headed by Rev. M. Russo of San Francisco, California. Ordinations and healing certificates were granted, but little else is known about the church or what became of it.

Foundation for Science of Spiritual Law

The Foundation for Science of Spiritual Law was founded in 1968 at Tonopah, Arizona, by Dr. Alfred Homer and Rev. Gladys A. Homer. From Tonopah, the Homers toured the country as Spiritualist mediums, teaching and speaking to small groups of followers. They spent the winter in Tonopah, and the foundation headquarters were only a short distance from the Sun Spiritualist Camp, which is still in existence. The foundation also published a newsletter.

Hallowed Grounds Fellowship of Spiritual Healing and Prayer

The Hallowed Grounds Fellowship of Spiritual Healing and Prayer was established in 1961 by the Reverend George Daisley, a British medium who settled in Santa Barbara, California. Beginning with a mailing list of 1,500 names accumulated while on previous lecture tours, Daisley traveled around the country teaching Spiritualism. He also issued *The Witness*, a small quarterly journal. Only one center was opened, but adherents and supporters were found across the country. *The Witness* ceased with the December 1973 issue.

The emphasis of Daisley's teachings was a form of Christian Spiritualism that had a particular focus on the nature of the next life. Daisley's insights were derived from material received in spirit communication, and the Bible was interpreted in Spiritualist ter-

minology. He believed that the next life is a discarding of the physical body and a manifesting of its duplicate spiritual body. After death, the soul continues on several planes of existence, each of a higher vibration, and hence invisible. Those with a gift of discerning spirits can communicate with them. Daisley believed that spirit life is much like this life. The fellowship dissolved in 1994 following Daisley's retirement due to ill health.

Holy Grail Foundation

The Holy Grail Foundation was founded in Fresno, California, in the early 1940s by the Reverend Leona Richards, who was one of a group of 12 who sat in meditation, seeking guidance. The messages they received were recorded, and the foundation grew out of this shared experience. In the early 1960s the headquarters were moved to Santa Cruz, California.

The messages received by the group emphasized man's essential divinity and the awareness of the divine as a part of one's life. Classes, which used the messages received from spirits, taught self-development through spiritual enlightenment. The goal was for each member to know the presence of God within, the Holy Grail, and his or her own personal guardian angel. At its height, the foundation had three centers, in Fresno, Santa Cruz, and Portland, Oregon.

Independent Associated Spiritualists

The Independent Associated Spiritualists was incorporated in 1925. It was headquartered in New York City but had churches across the country. Notable among its members was the late psychic surgeon Tony Agapoa of Bagio City, Philippines.

Sources:

Valentine, Tom. *Psychic Surgery*. Chicago: Henry Regnery Company, 1973.

Metaphysical Episcopal Church

The Metaphysical Episcopal Church was founded as an independent Episcopal jurisdiction in 1974 in Titusville, Florida, by Fr. R. D. Finzer II, its bishop primate. The church described itself as "metaphysical" in philosophy and theology. It also believed in the unity of religion and that all religious paths eventually lead to God. The creedal statement included in the church's liturgy affirmed a belief in the fatherhood of a God and the brotherhood of man.

The church followed the teaching of the Master Jesus and the guidance of angels, and its Spiritualist influence was manifested in the affirmation of communication with those who have passed through the experience of death and the future progress of the soul after death. The church was decidedly Christian and followed a liturgy derived from the Book of Common Prayer.

Sources:

Fenzer, F. D. *The Missal of the Metaphysical Episcopal Church*. Titusville, FL: Metaphysical Episcopal Church, 1975.

National Federation of Spiritual Science Churches

The National Federation of Spiritual Science Churches was a Spiritualist association founded in 1927. Member churches were primarily on the West Coast. In the 1930s, a periodical, *Spiritual Science Magazine*, was inaugurated. In the 1940s, associated churches were to be found in the states of California and Washington. The federation taught a form of Christian Spiritualism and affirmed a belief in God revealed in Nature, the teaching of Jesus the Christ, and the worthiness of the Bible as a source of inspirational truth (to be tested by reason and the Laws of God). Spiritual healing was emphasized, as was spirit communication. The small federation granted ordination and church charters and offered study preparatory courses for the ministry. The mother church was in Los Angeles, but no sign of its continuance has been observed in recent years, and it is presumed to be defunct.

Sources:

Textbook of Spiritual Science. Los Angeles: National Federation of Spiritual Science Churches, 1932.

National Spiritual Aid Association

The National Spiritual Aid Association, Inc., was formed in 1937 and incorporated at Springfield, Illinois. It functioned as a central office to certify and hold certification credentials for otherwise independent Spiritualist ministers. Beliefs were not specified beyond the insistence that Spiritualism is the true religion that God sent Christ to teach. The association was headquartered in St. Petersburg, Florida.

Order of the White Rose

The Order of the White Rose was a Spiritualist organization founded in Chicago, Illinois, in the 1890s by Jesse Charles Fremont Grumbine (1861–1938). Around 1900, Grumbine moved the headquarters to Boston, Massachusetts, where it was to remain for the next two decades. Around 1921, Grumbine moved to Cleveland, and two years later he relocated again, this time to Portland, Oregon. The order was described as mystical and Rosicrucian in nature, or as pure Spiritualism. There were two branches, the Spiritual Order of the Red Rose, which was the exoteric or outer branch, and the Spiritual Order of the White Rose, which was the esoteric or inner branch. Both branches led members to the celestial branch of the order.

Grumbine began his understanding of Spiritualism by distinguishing universal spirit and personal individual spirits. Universal spirit does not exist as a God outside of the universe, but is the radiant center from which spirits draw life. Matter is the substance of form, and form defines and limits spirits, which are temporal, relative, and finite. Spiritualism is the revelation of the being of God within each person. The message of excarnate spirits through mediums is the divinity of each spirit. Psychic abilities such as clairvoyance, telepathy, healing, and prevision were seen as innate divine powers that, when properly used and controlled, could check evil and produce a divine manhood and womanhood.

The primary task of the order was the establishment of the Universal Spiritual, as defined in Grumbine's many books. Members were organized into chapters around the United States, but no estimate of the size of the order seems to have ever been made. Grumbine wrote a number of books, which continued to appear into the mid-1920s. The order appears to have gone out of existence following Grumbine's death in 1938.

Sources:

Grumbine, J. C. F. *Clairaudience*. Boston, MA: Order of the White Rose, 1911.

————. *Clairvoyance*. Boston, MA: Order of the White Rose, 1911.

————. *Melchizedek, or the Secret Doctrine of the Bible*. Boston, MA: Order of the White Rose, 1919.

Pyramid Church of Truth and Light

The Pyramid Church of Truth and Light was formed in 1941 by the Reverends John Kingham and Emma Kingham in Ventura, California. They continued to head the church until 1962, when the leadership passed to Dr. Steele Goodman. During the pre-1962 era, four churches were chartered, but none of them have survived. The teachings of the church centered upon individual unfoldment. According to the church's teaching, the basic principle of the universe is vibration or love, which is manifest in many laws. In 1973 there were two churches, the main church in Sacramento and a second one in Phoenix, headed by the popular medium Isaiah Jenkins.

Society of Christ, Inc.

The Society of Christ was a small Spiritualist body founded by Bishop Harriette Leifeste and Bishop Dan B. Boughan, who served as president. Teachings were derived from the Bible and the "wisdom teachings of all the great religions," which were interpreted esoterically. God was seen as infinite intelligence manifested in nature and as love and goodness. Members believed in the moral responsibility and free choice of the individual; that science and religion have proved the continuity of life after death, as demonstrated through mediumship; that the highest morality is the Golden Rule; that the possibility of reformation is never closed; and that man can unfold and manifest the gifts of the spirit. The church granted ordinations, healing certificates, and church charters. In the 1980s

there were 2 congregations and 4 ministers, but it is not known what became of the society.

Spiritual Prayer Home, Inc.

The Spiritual Prayer Home was incorporated in 1939 in California as a Spiritualist organization. The home issued ordinations and charters and offered training courses for students. The president during the 1970s was Norman C. Fredriksen, and the headquarters were in San Dimas, California. Recent attempts to locate the church have failed.

Spiritual Science Mother Church

Mother Julia O. Forrest, a former Christian Science practitioner, became a Spiritualist and in 1927, with Dr. Carl H. Pieres, organized a new body modeled on the Christian Science Mother Church in Boston. The Spiritual Science Mother Church was headquartered in New York City. Its ruling ecclesiastical council issued charters and ran the Spiritual Science Institute, which trained ministers.

The church retained a number of concepts from Christian Science. These included the idea of the mother church, as well as the concepts of the demonstration of spiritual realities through preaching; of messages (received via clairvoyance) that give to each knowledge of what God has for him to do; of communications from other realms; and of healing through the channeling of healing power. The church affirmed that Jesus Christ is Lord and affirmed the Trinity of God the Father and creator, the virgin-born Son, and the Holy Spirit.

In 2008 it was reported that the Spiritual Science Mother Church had been folded into the National Spiritual Science Center (see separate entry in main body).

Universal Christ Church, Inc.

The Universal Christ Church was formed in 1970 by the coming together in fellowship of several Spiritualist churches in the Los Angeles area. Doctrine was Spiritualist, and reincarnation was accepted. There was an element of ritualism in the church's worship; for example, the clergy wore clerical vestments. The Rev. Anthony Benik was the head of the church.

In 1971 there were five churches, all in the Los Angeles area, and one 500-member congregation in Australia. The church published a periodical, the *U.C.C. Spokesman*.

CHANNELING

Anthropological Research Foundation

In 1967 William Ralph Duby, the leader and channel for the Organization of Awareness (see Cosmic Awareness Communications in main body), died. Over the several years following his death, his organization splintered into several groups. One of these was the Anthropological Research Foundation, which was founded in the early 1970s in San Diego by Jack T. Fletcher and Pat Fletcher. Among the members of the

group was Danton Spivey, a trance medium who claimed to be a continuing voice for "Cosmic Awareness," the universal mystical voice who spoke through Duby. In 1972 the foundation began to issue a magazine, *Aware*, and announced plans for the creation of an organization based on the messages given through Spivey.

The foundation saw itself as composed of ordinary people who had been exposed to extraordinary information. It viewed its task as exposing those forces that divide humans from each other and from the divine, and discovering the new culture that is characterized by wholeness. To this end it proposed projects that looked at ancient cultures, especially those of Atlantis and Lemuria.

The foundation did not survive for more than a few years.

Association for the Understanding of Man

The Association for the Understanding of Man (AUM) was formed in 1971 as an organization focused on the psychic accomplishments of Ray Stanford (b. 1938). Stanford is the brother of noted parapsychologist Rex Stanford. Ray Stanford began to manifest psychic abilities in his youth. In 1960, while meeting with a meditation group, he slipped into an unconscious trance-like state during which he was able to accurately answer questions from group members. The next year he began giving readings to the general public. Over the years, five types of readings evolved: self-help, question-and-answer, dream-interpretation, group-help, and research readings. The self-help readings included reflections on past lives, while the research readings explored various issues in depth. In 1972 a book containing the research readings on the Fatima prophecy was published. The book discusses the significance of the appearance and words of Mary, the mother of Christ, at Fatima, Portugal, in 1917.

The "source" of the Stanford readings was not considered to be a disincarnate entity, but rather was described as the unconscious and superconscious of Stanford, which contacted the object of the reading (the person the reading concerns). Recordings of all the readings were kept. Though no creed or dogma was established around Stanford's readings, a consistent world-view did emerge. It included Hindu concepts. The basic nature of man and the universe was viewed as psychic/spiritual. Various spiritual regions, including the lower astral and causal planes and, at the top, the "Abode of the Most High," were thought to transcend the earth plane. From the higher planes, it was believed, there emanates Aum, the great sound, and the music of the spheres, the audible life stream that underlies and sustains all creation, called by Hindus, *Nam*. Among the inhabitants of the high planes are the Great White Brotherhood, beings advanced beyond the need of reincarnation.

Man was thought to be a spiritual entity, spirit individualized. Soul was regarded as the enduring vehicle of individual form that records all past experiences. The component parts of the self were believed to be the seven psychic centers (*chakras*), which serve as contact points between soul and body. The third-eye center (in the forehead, above the nose) was considered to be a point of contact with higher levels of consciousness.

The headquarters of AUM were established in Austin, Texas. Members could be found across the country and were of two kinds: recipient and full-participant members. Both a newsletter and the *Journal of the Association for the Understanding of Man* were published, as were a number of books and booklets. AUM was disbanded in the early 1980s.

Stanford also possessed a lifelong interest in UFOs (Unidentified Flying Objects). As teenagers in the 1950s, both he and his brother had professed contact with space beings. Associated with AUM during its years of existence was Project Starlight International (cofounded by Ray Stanford), which operated a sophisticated UFO detection system in Austin, Texas. This organization published the short-lived *Journal of Instrumented UFO Research*.

Sources:

McCoy, John, Ray Stanford, and Rex Stanford. *Ave Sheoi: From Out of This World*. Corpus Christi, TX: Authors, 1956.

Speak, Shining Stranger. Austin, TX: Association for the Understanding of Man, 1975.

Stanford, Ray. *Fatima Prophecy: Days of Darkness, Promise of Light*. Austin, TX: Association for the Understanding of Man, 1974.

———. *The Spirit unto the Churches*. Austin, TX: Association for the Understanding of Man, 1977.

———. *What Your Aura Tells Me*. Garden City, NY: Doubleday, 1977.

Church of Universal Love (Texas)

The Church of Universal Love (Texas) was a New Age organization founded in 1968 and chartered in 1972. It was built around the channeling of Rev. Linda Forman, its founder. Forman channeled from the Cosmic Masters, believed to be extraterrestrials. Some of the channeled material was published for church members in a bimonthly newsletter, *Cosmic Channelings*. Members were scattered around the country and had access to the Powers through private channelings, which were recorded and sent to members via mail. The single church center in El Paso, Texas, offered a weekly schedule of worship and healing services, classes, and study groups.

The Church of Universal Love (Texas) had no connection with the church of the same name headquartered in Washington State.

Circle of Inner Truth

Marshall Lever was a Presbyterian seminarian who developed the ability of trance mediumship. As a medium, he began to receive messages from a guide, Chung Fu. Chung Fu is viewed as a spirit last incarnated as a student of Lao Tzu in China. The Circle of Inner Truth was begun in 1970 by Marshall and his wife, Quinta Lever, as an instrument for the expression of Chung Fu's work and teaching. Through counseling in trance, Chung Fu offered help to individuals on personal problems, particularly health, and worked with groups to teach spiritual truths. Health readings resembled those given through Edgar Cayce, the founder of the Association for Research and Enlightenment.

Lever taught that man has an immortal spirit within, which has evolved through many life forms and previous incarnations. This spirit is continually reincarnating until it breaks the cycle of reincarnations; man must identify with his spiritual self or God Force during an earth cycle, after which he is spiritually free, eternal and universal, and will not again incarnate. To aid its members, circles were developed for inner awareness through affirmative meditation, nutrition and health, and direct lessons from Chung Fu.

During the 1970s, the Levers had no home and spent all their time traveling among the several groups of the Inner Circle, which were widely scattered across the United States. One was located in London, England. A monthly, *Our News and Views*, was issued from San Francisco and mailed to approximately 600, of whom 400 were in the United States. During the 1980s the Circle ceased to exist, and the Levers moved into other psychic endeavors.

Sources:

Fu, Chung. *Evolution of Man*. San Francisco: Circle of Inner Truth, 1973.

Cosmerism

Cosmerism was the name of a short-lived group that began in September 1972, when the *Book of Cosmer* was channeled by seven angels, the most important of whom was named "Ashram." Receiving the communications was a couple simply known as Luke and Mark (the latter of whom was female). In accordance with the entities' instructions, an original group of 13 was collected and each member received a Cosmerite name: Matthias, Matthew, Judas Secarius, Josephus, Ananda, Peter, James the Elder, Thomas, Paul, Thaddeus, John the Beloved, and Luke and Mark. In the summer of 1974 the first circle devoted to the formal study of the *Book of Cosmer* was held, and the first issue of *The Moon Monk*, a periodical, was issued.

Cosmerites termed their message "the Way" of Cosmer, the creative force innate in all things and the source of creation. They believed that the power of Cosmer focuses in small groups and goes out with them into the world. The Way is a beginning toward peace, both external and internal. Under the oversight of Cosmer, man is on a path toward final absorption, or the building into oneness of the creative forces of men and angels.

In 1974 the headquarters of the Cosmerites was located at Winter Park, Florida; the small group of followers was drawn from eastern Florida and Canada. Plans included the building of Ichikama, a wilderness *ashram* (or secluded retreat) of peace and tranquility. A brief time later, however, the group's address became obsolete and its periodical was discontinued. No sign of the group has been seen since the mid-1970s, and it is presumed to have disbanded.

Father's House

Ralph F. Raymond (d. 1984) was a channel for spirit teachers who in the late 1960s operated a Universal Link group, the Los Angeles–based Universal Link Heart Center. In 1968 he was directed by the "Master" to visit the various Universal Link centers, first in the United States and then in England and Scotland. His findings were published in a booklet, *The Universal Link Concept*. Upon his return to the United States, he established the Father's House. The original seven-person board of trustees included several prominent Universal Link personalities.

The Father's House published *The Father's House Quarterly*, which had several hundred subscribers. A plan was initiated in 1973 to acquire a Center for Healing and Meditation. Brother Francis, as Raymond was commonly known, was joined in this endeavor by Carole Freeman. These plans had not materialized at the time of Brother Francis's death. By that time, however, foreign affiliated groups were to be found in New Zealand and England.

The thrust of Brother Francis's efforts was to provide guidance and leadership as the earth moved into the Aquarian Age. Though the Father's House was independent of other Link groups, informal contact was frequent. Selections of writings from other Link writers appeared in each issue of the quarterly. For example, Tarna Halsey regularly submitted articles channeled from the space people (beings in outer space), and almost every issue carried material from Illiana of New Age Teachings. Brother Francis also circulated *The Three Day Scene*, one of the books of Jakob Lorber, whose American followers founded the Divine Word Foundation.

Sources:

[Raymond, Brother Francis Ralph]. *Universal Link Concept*. Los Angeles: Universal Link Heart Center, 1968.

Freewill Foundation

The Freewill Foundation was founded to facilitate the public's exposure to the channeling activity of Gerry Bowman and the channeled teachings of the entity John. Bowman's channeling dates to the evening of January 22, 1976, when a group of people gathered to contact the spirit world through a ouija board. During the evening, members of the group had their previous lives described and were told how those lives affected their present life. Bowman, one of the people in attendance, was told that in the future he would become verbal and have no more need of the ouija board. It was some five years later, on August 2, 1981, that Bowman first went into a light trance and John announced his presence with the words, "We are known as John. We are here to assist you, and any who are willing to listen, to discover who, and more importantly, what you are." John was believed to be identical to the biblical apostle John, the brother of James and follower of Jesus.

Bowman was assisted by Joe Albani, a former radio talk show host, who transcribed what became weekly sessions with Bowman and John. Albani also contacted Los Angeles radio station KIEV and in 1984 arranged for a weekly talk show, *The Out-of-the-Ordinary Show*, which aired each Sunday evening at midnight. The show, during which people called in and talked to John, was a success, and Bowman and Albani went on to create a series of workshops/seminars at which John periodically made public appearances.

Within a general New Age framework, John's teachings centered on attaining a means to personal power through compassion, humility, and confidence. John also taught a simple technique to enhance the natural healing powers of the body through relaxation and concentration.

The foundation was composed of Bowman, Albani, and John. People who wished to relate to John were able to arrange private sessions with him or to attend group sessions. Tapes and transcripts of the seminars were also circulated by the foundation.

International Organization of Awareness

In 1967 William Ralph Duby, leader of the Organization of Awareness (see Cosmic Awareness Communications in the main body), died. Within a short time, his organization splintered into a number of factions. The International Organization of Awareness, founded in Honolulu by Edward Young, was one of these. This small body survived into the 1970s.

Light of the Universe

The Light of the Universe (L.O.T.U.) group was formed in the early 1960s as a psychic interest group in Tiffin, Ohio. Its investigations included research on ESP, health foods, and UFOs. Gradually, a more formal organization emerged, and a teacher, Helen Spitler, known publicly as "Maryona" (one who has received teachings of light from a higher source), became the leader. In 1965 Maryona published a book, *The Light of the Universe I*, and in 1966, a quarterly periodical began publication. In December 1969 the first branch of the group was formed in Cortland, Ohio. Others were subsequently organized. Correspondence lessons were mailed to students around the country.

Behind the L.O.T.U. group lay a number of books that influenced both members and teacher. These books included *The Aquarian Gospel* by Levi Dowling, *The Life and Teachings of the Masters of the Far East* by Baird Spalding, and *Breathing Your Way to Youth* by Edwin John Dingle (of Mentalphysics). A strong emphasis was placed on helping those dissatisfied with false and outmoded traditions and on teachings that included a focus on problems in translating the Bible, information on the hidden years of Jesus, and corrections to Christian teachings, especially several previously asserted in the *Aquarian Gospel*.

Strong emphasis was placed on the great cosmic law of reincarnation. It was Maryona's teaching that as a soul progresses through various experiences and lessons, it never goes backward; progress is ever upward. Each person is a master within himself, possessing unlimited power and potential. The god within is pointed to in the words of the Old Testament, "Ye are Gods." This power within, a shining inner presence, man's true self, the divine soul, rules the universe. As man leaves the mud and filth in which he is mired, he can turn to the light and claim his divine birthright. To accomplish this turning, a series of cleansing exercises and meditation techniques was offered to students.

In 1988 the Light of the Universe had two ministers. Members were scattered around North America, and a few were located in Europe and Africa. A periodical, *The L.O.T.U.S.*, was published in Tiffin.

Sources:

Maryona. *The Light of the Universe I and II*. Tiffin, OH: Light of the Universe, 1965–1976.

———. *Mini-Manual for Light Bearers*. Tiffin, OH: Light of the Universe, 1987.

Lighting the Way Foundation

In an early book about Jeanne Dixon, Ruth Montgomery's *A Gift of Prophecy*, Dixon reported having had a vision on February 5, 1962, from which she learned that an exalted master had been born somewhere in the Middle East. That same vision was given to Helena Elizabeth Ruhnau, a New Age channel. In 1969 Dixon, under heavy pressure from critics—primarily conservative Christian ministers—reversed her earlier claim. In her book *My Life and Prophecies* she suggested that the vision concerned the advent of the Anti-Christ. In the wake of Dixon's retraction, Ruhnau, who claimed that Dixon had allowed her human consciousness and lower mind to hold sway and create a new interpretation, emerged as a champion of the original vision. Ruhnau asserted her role as the "Messenger of the New World Avatar," and founded the New World Avatar Link in Colorado Springs, Colorado.

In 1951 Ruhnau had an experience during which she felt someone tap her on the shoulder and heard a voice (later identified as that of the Christ) say, "Come, follow Me." Three years later she had the experience of dying and leaving her body, after which she was returned to her body by the Christ. Ruhnau spent the next 15 years studying theosophy and metaphysical writings and became a channel. She channeled the Spirit of God, the masters of the Great White Brotherhood, and her own God Self. Her first book, *Light on the Mountain*, appeared in 1966. Along the way it was revealed to her that she had been, in one of her past lives, Akhenaten, the Egyptian pharaoh who brought the religion of the one God to his people.

After her own vision of the new avatar born in 1962, Ruhnau was given a picture of him, taken when he was four years old. She reported that as the child grew older, the image in the picture changed. It was not until 1970, however, that she was told what her mission in life would be and why she had been returned to her body in 1954. Having been related to the new avatar in a previous life, it would be her task to explain to the world who he really was.

According to Ruhnau, an avatar comes whenever evil increases and law and order break down. The new avatar's coming was marked by the great conjunction of sun, moon, and planets in the sign of Aquarius in 1962. He would set affairs in order and teach the brotherhood of man to all nations. This brotherhood would be based on the knowledge of the one God. Ruhnau believed there was only one true religion: the worship of the one God and the keeping of right relations with all.

Over the next few years Ruhnau was given information on forthcoming catastrophic earth changes. In 1974 she began publishing a newsletter, *Lighting the Way*, in which she recorded the information she was receiving. All of this material was compiled in 1978 in her book *The Return of the Dove*. Ruhnau declared that the avatar would make his appearance prior to the coming catastrophes, giving people time to move away from those portions of the planet that would be most adversely affected.

During the 1980s, Ruhnau relocated from Colorado City to Ava, Missouri, and the New World Avatar Cosmic Link was superseded by the Lighting the Way Foundation.

Sources:

Ruhnau, Helena Elizabeth. *Let There Be Light: Living Water of Life for the New Age*. Ava, MO: Lighting the Way Foundation, 1987. 171 pp.

———. *Light from the Fifth Dimension (The Heaven World)*. Colorado Springs, CO: Colleasius Press, 1982. 171 pp.

———. *Light on a Mountain*. Riverside, CA: Author, 1966. 168 pp.

———. *Mirror of a Soul*. Colorado Springs, CO: Colleasius Press, 1981. 80 pp.

———. *Reappearance of the Dove*. Colorado Springs, CO: Colleasius Press, 1978. 203 pp.

Morse Fellowship

The Morse Fellowship was founded in 1959 by Louise Morse of Silver Springs, Maryland, and was named for Elwood Morse, her husband, who had died the year before. In 1961 the headquarters were moved to Alamogordo, New Mexico. Two years prior to the founding of the fellowship, Mrs. Morse had begun to publish lessons, mostly based on material that had been channeled through her. With the creation of the fellowship, she also began to travel and teach. In 1967 she met and married James Spence, and, in 1968, they moved to Richardson, Texas (a suburb of Dallas).

The "Portals of Light" was the name given to the ministry of Mrs. Morse, who was seen as a channel for the Holy Spirit. Her ministry was also seen as a fulfillment of biblical prophecy concerning the last days, when the spirit of truth would be poured out on all flesh. The whole range of psychic issues was dealt with in the lessons given to Mrs. Morse by the celestial teachers. The teachers, who spoke through Mrs. Morse while she was in a trance, were never identified, but were of both sexes.

According to the teachings, man has been alienated from his God nature. Disobedience in the Garden of Eden had lowered man's consciousness and allowed sin to take root. The race of man entered the kingdom of Satan. In Jesus, man is given the chance to enter God's kingdom through obedience. By consciously identifying with Jesus, man is drawn back into the nature of God. The way back is through love. The reorientation toward God's will allows one to become aware of the still, small voice within. As this voice becomes clearer and one follows it, one moves closer to God's will.

Mrs. Morse gave weekly trance sessions with a more or less stable group of sitters from the 1950s into the 1970s. The lessons were made available on tape and in printed form. By 1968, approximately 250 persons were receiving the lessons regularly. During the last years of her work, Morse was able to receive messages from the spirit world without going into trance.

Sources:

The Living Water. Richardson, TX: Morse Fellowship, 1970.

New Age Teachings

New Age Teachings was established in 1967 in Brookfield, Massachusetts, by Anita Afton (b. 1922), better known as Illiana, the name she uses as a channel. Illiana is referred to as the "soul which is in this body." In the beginning of her work as a channel, she reports, entities from a planet called Jamal spoke through her, but after a few years, as her own consciousness was "uplifted," the "I AM THAT I AM" was and remains the only voice that speaks through her.

Illiana had become influenced by Eastern philosophy while attending a Unitarian Church. She later joined the Self-Realization Fellowship of Par-

amahansa Yogananda (discussed in the chapter on Hinduism) and went through the entire set of lessons in Kriya Yoga. She learned of her past lives in India and how to meditate. In 1965, while in meditation, she received her first message as a channel. It was a rather mundane message concerning a lecture topic. A second, later message was a complicated code-like message drawn from several languages. Messages began to be received regularly from then on.

At the request of the cosmic being who issued messages through her, Illiana began to publish regular bulletins under the name *New Age Teachings*. They carry the messages from the cosmic hierarchy, the "I AM THAT I AM," which emphasizes the increasing Light coming into earth as a result of the New Age vibrations being poured forth upon the planet.

From the headquarters in Massachusetts, the bulletin and other publications are mailed to followers across the United States and around the world to every continent. Some members have formed study groups and centers from which the bulletins can be circulated locally. The bulletin is considered a "Universal Organ for World Upliftment though study and spiritual understanding." In 1976, a Spanish edition of the bulletin appeared and segments of the messages are regularly translated into several languages. Headquarters for the Spanish-language work are in Houston, Texas.

In the mid-1980s, a music ministry was begun. It is believed that music is a Universal Vibrational Aspect of the LIGHT and can assist in bringing people "in tune" with their higher selves. Each person, it is believed, has his or her own keynote, which, when sounded, brings harmony, peace, and openness. Individuals using the ministry receive a chart, a cassette tape of a complete life song, and a composition based upon the life song channeled by Illiana. The chart is based upon the person's birth data and birth name.

In 1992, approximately 2,000 people in the United States received *New Age Teachings*. There are 30 study groups who use the material channeled by Illiana. It is mailed to some 3,500 followers in 35 countries around the world.

Open Channel Resources, Unlimited

Open Channel Resources, Unlimited, was an organization that facilitated the channeling work of Katar Schoenstadt, a channel of various ascended masters, collectively referred to as the Guides. The primary entities who spoke through her included Tsen Tsing of the Council; Ariana, the Goddess of Truth; Clark; Seth; and Favor. These entities brought a message concerning the basic divinity of each human being. In sessions students were linked to a network of energies that allowed the acceleration of the individual's growth as limiting ideas and other blockages were removed. Ariana, the goddess of Truth, provided special contact with feminine energies.

Katar began channeling in the early 1970s and developed into a full-body trance medium. During sessions, her consciousness departed and the various entities spoke through her. She was assisted by her husband Darryl Schoenstadt, who conducted the channeling sessions, led students in discussions of the Guides' teachings, and helped share their techniques for personal development. Primary in the techniques were the mastery of breath and learning to use of the "Sword of truth," which each person carries in their hand, "to cut the strings of attachment that cause us to feel separate from our Creation."

Open Channel Resources, Unlimited, offered a wide variety of classes, "playshops," and personal sessions during which individuals were able to talk with the Guides. Cassette tapes of the Guides' teachings were also available, and a periodical, *Open Channel: A Journal with Spirit*, was published.

Organization of Awareness (Calgary)

In 1967 the Organization of Awareness, which had formed in the early 1960s, splintered when its main leader and spiritual channel, William Ralph Duby, died. Three branches retained the name of the original group, among them a small group in Calgary, Alberta, headed by Nick Chwelos. This branch survived into the 1970s.

Organization of Awareness (Federal Way)

The Organization of Awareness (Federal Way) was one of several groups that splintered off from the original Organization of Awareness after the death of that group's leader and spiritual channel, William Ralph Duby, in 1967. It was headed by Frances Marcx and headquartered in Federal Way, Washington. A small body, it survived into the 1970s.

Organization of Awareness (Olympia)

One of several splinters of the original Organization of Awareness formed in the early 1960s (see Cosmic Awareness Communications, which retained the name under which the organization operated until the death of its main spiritual channel, William Ralph Duby). This small branch was formed in 1967 and headed by David DeMoulin. Headquartered in Olympia, Washington, it survived into the 1970s.

Radiant School of Seekers and Servers

The Radiant School of Seekers and Servers was founded at Mt. Shasta, California, in 1963 by Kenneth Wheeler and a small group of followers, who moved to the village at the mountain's base. That same year, the Radiant School began channeling from an entity known as Phylos the Tibetan, knowledge of whom had drawn them to Mt. Shasta. In the 1890s, Phylos had begun to speak through Frederick Spencer Oliver, his amanuensis. The material conveyed by Phylos was collected into a book, *A Dweller on Two Planets*, published in 1899. It described the existence of a mystic brotherhood of survivors from Atlantis, who live inside Mt. Shasta. The existence of Phylos was further highlighted in 1940 by the appearance of *An Earth Dweller Returns*, a second book based on his transmissions.

Members of the Radiant School were offered the material from Phylos in lesson form. Phylos advocated belief in God's divine plan, which is for all and is enwrapped in the "folds of every life pattern." Each life pattern is interwoven into a great universal pattern, and each person is expected to unfold his plan in full. There is opportunity to meet all others with whom we have interfered and created karma. Each divine plan includes the rights to health, happiness, and prosperity.

The physical body in which man resides is a "Temple" and is the means of contacting the higher self. The self is overshadowed by angels and is thus never alone. Prayer is the expression of desires. Abundance comes from longing to know the great love of God. Being patient, willing, forgiving, and enduring is the key to the soul's progress toward perfection.

The School, which disbanded in the early 1980s, was run by a six-person board of directors, a president, a bishop, and an assistant bishop. Members received monthly lessons from Phylos.

Sources:

Phylos the Tibetan [Frederick Spencer Oliver]. *A Dweller on Two Planets*. Los Angeles: Borden Publishing Co., 1899.

Van Valer, Nola. *My Meeting with the Masters on Mount Shasta*. Mount Shasta, CA: Radiant School, 1982.

Servants of Awareness

In 1967, following the death of William Ralph Duby, the Servants of Cosmic Awareness (see Cosmic Awareness Communications) split into several groups. One of those groups was the Servants of Awareness, formed by David E. Worcester and headquartered in Seattle. At its height, the Servants of Awareness had several branches located around the United States. It continued into the 1970s.

Seth-Hermes Foundation

Seth is a spirit entity who was originally channeled through Jane Roberts, a New York housewife. Roberts's channeled material, which appeared in a host of books beginning with the 1966 volume *How to Develop Your ESP*, stood at the fountainhead of the modern New Age movement in America and is generally seen as one beginning point of modern channeling (mediumship). Among the people who responded to Seth was Thomas Massari. As early as 1972, Massari also began to channel Seth. Born and raised in Chicago, Massari moved to Los Angeles as a musician. A short time later, unplanned, he began to channel.

Seth first began to speak through Massari in 1972, but Massari eventually came to understand that prior to his present incarnation he had made an agreement with Seth to be his voice. During the mid-1970s

Massari taught in the ESP school managed by his sister in Milwaukee, and then founded his own organization, the Parapsychology Center. He moved back to Los Angeles in 1977 and in 1981 formed the Seth-Hermes Foundation. Through the foundation, individuals were able to relate to Seth, who gave lectures and classes, led retreats, and made himself available for private consultations. A monthly master class was held for advanced students.

The Seth-Hermes Foundation viewed itself as dealing with the realities people create for themselves. It contended that most people simply create a world without knowing what they are doing or taking responsibility for it. Seth called attention to the potentials humans possess for creating their world and the need to take action to make that world as positive as possible.

Seth Network International

Seth Network International was a network of people who followed and promoted the teachings articulated by "Seth," a spirit entity who spoke (was channeled) through Jane Roberts (Mrs. Robert Butts). The network was founded in 1979 as the Austin Seth Center by Dr. Maude Caldwell. Following her death in 1992, the headquarters were moved to Eugene, Oregon, and the later name was adopted. The new head of the network was Lynda Dahl.

Seth described himself as an "energy personality essence." Jane Roberts (1929–1984) was a housewife and writer who began her career as a channel following some experiments with a ouija board in 1963. Seth first spoke through the board, but was soon speaking through an entranced Roberts, whose husband taped the sessions. Three years later, the first of what would become 22 books based on Seth's words was published as *How to Develop Your ESP Power* (1966); it was later retitled *The Coming of Seth* (1976). In this and the later books, Seth taught a metaphysical system that included among its basic ideas the following: People form their experience through their thoughts, feelings, expectations, and focus; each individual is a multidimensional whole; together, human beings are cooperating in forming our present reality.

The network had as its goal the bringing of the Seth ideas into the mainstream of global consciousness. It hosted an annual conference, SethNet, which centered on the reform of world society in accordance with the agenda discussed in Roberts's book *Psychic Politics* (1976). Human Journeys was a project to make Seth's teachings available in countries where the books were not yet distributed and in languages into which they had not yet been translated. *Reality Change: The Global Seth Journal* was the network's periodical. In 1993 members of the network were found in 17 countries.

Though the Seth Network International became inactive in 1999, its Web site and database are still maintained, and conferences organized by former

members are still held. The network's bookstore, Brass Ring Bookstore, was taken over by former members and continues to operate.

Sources:

Seth Network International. http://www.sethnet.org/

Melton, J. Gordon. *Religious Leaders of America*. Detroit, MI: Gale Research, 1991.

Roberts, Jane. *Adventures in Consciousness: An Introduction to Aspect Psychology*. Englewood Cliffs, NJ: Prentice-Hall, 1975.

―――. *Dreams, "Evolution," and Value Fulfillment: A Seth Book*. 2 vols. Englewood Cliffs, NJ: Prentice-Hall, 1986.

―――. *The God of Jane: A Psychic Manifesto*. Englewood Cliffs, NJ: Prentice-Hall, 1981.

―――. *How to Develop Your ESP Power*. New York: Frederick Fell, 1966. Rept. as: *The Coming of Seth*. New York: Pocket Books, 1976.

―――. *The Nature of Personal Reality: A Seth Book*. Englewood Cliffs, NJ: Prentice-Hall, 1974.

―――. *Seth: Dreams and Projection of Consciousness*. Walpole, NH: Stillpoint Publishing, 1986.

―――. *The Seth Material*. Englewood Cliffs, NJ: Prentice-Hall, 1970.

―――. *Seth Speaks: The Eternal Validity of the Soul*. Englewood Cliffs, NJ: Prentice-Hall, 1972.

Watkins, Susan. *Conversations with Seth: The Story of Jane Roberts's ESP Class*. 2 vols. Englewood Cliffs, NJ: Prentice-Hall, 1980–1981.

Sisters of the Amber

As the message of the Universal Link spread in the United States, a number of informal centers developed. Some evolved into independent teaching organizations built around a single teacher/spiritual channel, whose writings were published independently, though the teachings remained similar to those of the Universal Link. During the 1970s, the name most connected with the Universal Link operation in North America was that of Merta Mary Parkinson (d. 1983). Like Liebie Pugh, the British leader of the Link, Parkinson was a journalist and writer. Her interest in metaphysics led Parkinson to become an early devotee of the Link.

Parkinson created two more-or-less informal organizations to tie together students. The first, the Dena Foundation, supplied material to a more general audience. A second group, called the Sisters of the Amber, consisting of many of the female members, was established by Parkinson after an inner light called for its creation. Parkinson had become intrigued with amber after a friend asked for help in locating some for healing purposes. The Sisters were linked to each other by their dedication to mutual loving service and by the amber each has been given by Parkinson.

Spiritual Research Society

Edwin Cain Sr. was the son of a Spiritualist medium. Shortly after his marriage, he and his wife, Nellie Cain, detected some spirit rappings (rhythmic noises made by spirits to communicate messages), which led to the formation of a "developing circle" around them and the emergence of Mr. Cain's mediumship in the early 1940s. Mrs. Cain also began to develop spiritual abilities and was soon in contact with a group of "Masters" from the White Brotherhood (a group of once-human spirits who evolved to levels of spiritual excellence and teach humans about spiritual reality). She was accepted by them as a novice and was presented with the robe of the initiate. The Cains founded the Spiritual Research Society, which evolved from the original circle.

The teachings that came through the Masters were centered on the evolution and progression of life and the soul. The universe is organized on an upward spiral, ascending from electronic and mineral to vegetable, animal, and human, to Christ-Buddhic or divine. The levels can be likened to the rising frequency of the musical scale. The soul also evolves to higher levels of consciousness. The universe is organized on seven-fold structures and according to the universal laws of vibration, correspondence, cause and effect, rhythm, polarity, and gender.

When the Cains's first book on the Masters was published, a copy was sent to Merta Mary Parkinson of the Sisters of the Amber, who was an American representative of the Universal Link. Parkinson then forwarded a copy to Liebie Pugh, of the Universal Link in England. Subsequent correspondence brought the Cains into close association with Parkinson and Pugh.

The Cains were both disappointed by the nonoccurrence of the momentous event predicted for Christmas of 1967. They soon came to view the period since 1967 as a time of great siftings in every area of man's life, a time of renewal and reevaluation and spiritual discoveries. In 1971 they received a message that the Linking had been completed on the outer levels, after which they conceived their work as one of radiating light in a collective "Nuclear Evolution" Operation.

Sources:

Cain, Nellie B. *Exploring the Mysteries of Life.* Grand Rapids, MI: Spiritual Research Society, 1972.

————. *Gems of Truth from the Masters.* Grand Rapids, MI: Spiritual Research Society, 1965.

Trilite Seminars

Trilite Seminars was an organization that facilitated the work of a channel known as Shaari. Shaari was described as a "walk-in"—that is, a soul that had moved into the body of a person who had decided to leave their body. The personality who inhabited Shaari's present body before the walk-in took place had been a trance medium who channeled two entities, named Abraham and Malaya. Shaari continued to channel these two entities.

Shaari described herself as an extraterrestrial entity from Star Command, with conscious memory of interdimensional and universal knowledge. She also operated as a "holographic" healer. She integrated into the body of the former trance medium in 1989 after that person had requested to leave her body following an automobile accident. Following her integration, Shaari worked to understand the complexities of communication between humans and the Star Command.

Abraham, whom Shaari channeled, was described as a member of the Light Brotherhood and the Intergalactic Command, whose teachings provide a practical understanding of individuals as dynamic beings in the Universe. Malaya, a feminine entity, brought forth a New Ray of Consciousness, and assisted individuals in integrating the new information into their lives. Together, Shaari, Abraham, and Malaya formed the triad of the Trilite Seminars.

Shaari held regular workshops around the United States and Canada, triennial four-day retreats, and private sessions with individuals. Once or twice a year she offered journeys to places considered sacred power sites, such as the pyramids in Egypt or Machu Picchu, the Inca center in Peru. These journeys had a twin focus on healing the planet and individual growth.

Universal Link

The Universal Link and the Universal Foundation were two closely related British organizations that traced their history to a vision experienced on April 11, 1961, by Richard Grave of Worthing, England. While working on a newly rented house, Grave saw "a bearded Christlike figure" who blocked his path. Pointing to a picture, the figure touched the glass covering it, causing an explosion that drove fragments of the pulverized glass into the picture. The being then disappeared in a blaze of orange light. The picture, a representation of an angel announcing the birth of Jesus, soon gained renown as the "Weeping Angel of Worthing" as salty drops of moisture formed on its surface.

The being, who called himself "Truth," visited Grave often after that and left him a series of apocalyptic messages. These suggested mankind was on the brink of disaster, and concentrated on the imminent Second Coming of the Christ. The messages and the events surrounding them were described in a May 4, 1961, article in the *Psychic News*. Liebie Pugh, an English artist, heard of Grave through the articles. After meeting Pugh, Grave realized that the spiritual being that had visited him was the one portrayed in a sculpture by Ms. Pugh, which she called "Limitless Love."

Ms. Pugh is regarded as the architect of the "Universal Link," a linking of a number of individuals and groups to the Highest, who in this period is ever increasingly breaking through. The Link developed as an informal fellowship of like-minded individuals centered on a number of "channels." These channels were delivering revelations of the cosmic operation ushering in the new age.

The critical period of the revelation was from 1961 to 1967. An early revelation received through Grave declared the following: "No one can know the day nor the hour of MY COMING, or when the great Universal Revelation will be enacted; however by Christmas morning 1967, I will have revealed myself through the medium of nuclear evolution. This is MY PLAN which is absolute."

During the six years between 1961 and 1967, a major effort was made to spread the message and tie together other channels, primarily through the travel and work of Anthony Brooke. Brooke was a descendant of Sir James Brooke (1803–1868), the first "White Rajah of Sarawak," and himself ruled that land (now part of Brunei) before it became a British colony in 1946. In the middle and late 1960s, Brooke traveled widely, locating and tying together individuals and groups. In England, the Universal Foundation was formed, with Brooke and Monica Parish at its head.

As December 1967 approached, a great feeling of expectancy pervaded the movement. There was hope for an objective event, a spectacular changeover in universal thinking, which would signal the coming new age. When no event occurred, a spiritualized explanation was sought. Brooke focused his attention on the purpose of Liebie Pugh. Liebie had become identified with the entity known as Limitless Love, and, as early as 1964, the hypothesis had been put forth that Limitless Love was Liebie herself in the form of a constellated fragmentation of her own personality. Liebie was, reasoned Brooke, "an extension or a projection—a secondary personality, if you like—of Truth or Limitless Love." In January 1966, Liebie was given a prophecy of her death in December of that year. After she died in December, members of the Universal Link groups discovered that Limitless Love was "appearing with ever greater frequency in the actions and to the vision of more and more people."

Thus, the work of the Universal Foundation became the linking together of groups and individuals who were working toward the spiritual evolution of mankind around the world. These people formed a vanguard attuned to the cosmic lights and awaited the yet-to-appear day of manifestation that will mark the Christing of the whole earth and the beginning of the Golden Age.

The Universal Link was brought to the United States in the late 1960s, primarily through the visits of Anthony Brooke. Initial centers were formed in Elkins, Pennsylvania; Grand Rapids, Michigan; Kansas City, Missouri; Brookfield, Massachusetts; Denver, Colorado; and Los Angeles, California. During the 1970s several of these centers died out, but others became independent centers in their own right, publishing their own books and newsletters. In effect, their work superseded that of the Foundation for North America, though they remained more or less loosely affiliated with the work in England and acknowledged their debt to it. In Grand Rapids, Nellie Cain and Edwin Cain Sr. developed the Spiritual Research Society. In Kansas City, Merta Mary Parkinson began to issue material under the names of the Sisters of the Amber and the Dena Foundation. In Brookfield, Illiana (Anita Afton) developed an international network receiving her New Age Teachings. Brother Francis (Ralph F. Raymond) moved the Universal Link Heart Center in Los Angeles to Santa Monica, where it was renamed the Father's House, and then later in the decade to Santa Clara, California, where it existed for many years. Each of these centers is covered elsewhere in this chapter. There is currently no direct affiliate of either the Universal Foundation or the Universal Link currently functioning in America.

Sources:

Brooke, Anthony. *The Universal Link Revelations*. London: Universal Foundation, 1967.

Pugh, Liebie. *Nothing Else Matters*. St. Anne's-by-the-Sea, Lancashire, U.K.: Author, 1964.

[Raymond, Brother Francis Ralph]. *The Universal Link Concept*. Los Angeles: Universal Link Heart Center, [1967].

FLYING SAUCER GROUPS

Brotherhood of the Seven Rays

Among the early flying saucer contactees was George Hunt Williamson (1926–1986), an archeologist and student of Theosophical literature. He and his wife were among those who watched from a distance as George Adamski made his first contact with a Venusian in the California desert on November 12, 1952. Then, in 1953, Williamson published his own story, *The Saucers Speak*, in which he claimed contact with Martians by way of automatic writing (writing what a spirit dictates) as early as August 2, 1952. The messages were, initially, from Kadar Laqu, the head of the Interplanetary Council-Circle. They called for cooperation, in order to prevent the death of human civilization. Following his receipt of these messages, the Telonic Research Center was established by Williamson to study the new science of space-visitation.

All of Williamson's interests were brought together in the Brotherhood of the Seven Rays. Besides his contact with the space beings, Williamson had been in touch with the ascended masters, those mysterious beings first described by Guy Ballard, founder of the "I AM" Religious Activity. As early as 1955, Lake Titicaca had been mentioned as a sanctuary of the Great White Brotherhood, the hierarchy of ascended masters who were once human and who now, as spirits, teach

humans about spiritual realities. In 1956 it was decided that an outer retreat of the Lake Titicaca sanctuary (and of the other sanctuaries around the world) would be established by dedicated individuals. The inner sanctuaries for full-fledged members of the Great White Brotherhood date to the submergence of Lemuria, when the secrets of that advanced civilization were deposited in secluded centers the world over. Araru-Muru, now an ascended master in the spirit world, was in charge of Titicaca. The outer retreat, or abbey, was to be located near the inner sanctuary on the Peruvian side of Lake Titicaca, and was to have priories at spots around the world, to serve as contact points with the general populace.

In December 1956, Williamson, under his religious name, Brother Philip, and others made a trip to Peru to establish the Abbey of the Seven Rays, Lord Muru's primary outer retreat. The expedition extended through most of 1957. The ruins of the area were viewed as partially the result of contact and cooperation between the Great White Brotherhood and the space masters. This contact has continued and is focused in the Brotherhood of the Abbey. It was Williamson's belief that "the space confederation has a gigantic base there near the remains of the lost cities," which survived from the time of the original contacts.

The Brotherhood of the Seven Rays, the name of which refers to the spectrum of light rays administered by the ascended masters, was established at the time of the destruction of Lemuria between 10,000 and 12,000 B.C.E., but not until 1956 did it have outward expression in a monastic system in which students could come together. Because individual students would be most attuned to one of the seven rays, the grouping of students would bring a harmony of the seven colors symbolic of the spiritual life of the monastery. The monastery was established in the 1960s and continued into the 1970s. Students who came to live at the center in Peru had to accept the cosmic Christ as one who came to earth and who is due to return in the near future. The Essene way of life—meditation, fasting, and contemplation—was followed. The communal meal, or supper, of the Essenes was observed daily. Novices underwent water-baptism by immersion before becoming friars and were anointed with oil before becoming monks. No narcotics or stimulants (including chocolate) were used, and monks were vegetarians. Hair was worn long. Both sexes were welcome to all levels, and marriage was acceptable.

Two orders were associated with the Brotherhood. The Order of the Red Hand was dedicated to the preservation of the arcane knowledge handed down through the ages, particularly through building up and maintaining the scriptorium at the monastery in Peru. The Ancient Amethystine Order was the prime group associated with the Brotherhood; its name referred to the vibrations of the seventh ray of violet, into which the earth is moving. Its hoped-for goals

were to cure humanity of its ills and the earth of its drunken state. The U.S. headquarters of Williamson's small following was located in Corpus Christi, Texas.

Williamson claimed that his real name was Michael d'Obrenovic and that he was a descendent of a Yugoslavian royal family. During the last years of his life, Williamson reasserted that claim and, as Michael Djorde Milan d'Obrenovic, was consecrated to the episcopacy by an unnamed bishop claiming orders from the Nestorian (Syro-Chaldean) Church. Williamson moved to Santa Barbara, California, and established an independent jurisdiction called the Holy Apostolic Catholic Church, Syro-Chaldean Diocese of Santa Barbara and Central California. There was but one small parish, which existed for several years in the early 1980s.

Sources:

McCoy, John. *They Shall Be Gathered Together*. Corpus Christi, TX: Author, 1957.

Williamson, George Hunt [Brother Philip]. *The Brotherhood of the Seven Rays*. Clarksburg, VA: Saucerian Books, 1961.

———. *Road in the Sky*. London: Neville Spearman, 1959.

———. *The Saucers Speak*. London: Neville Spearman, 1963.

———. *Secret Places of the Lion*. London: Neville Spearman, 1959.

Last Day Messengers

The Last Day Messengers was a small group centered in Fort Lauderdale, Florida, headed by Dave W. Bent. After becoming interested in psychic phenomena, Bent had begun to develop his psychic consciousness. During this process, he encountered material from the Mark-Age Meta Center and other groups in contact with the spiritual hierarchy. He subsequently became a channel for the White Brotherhood, and formed the Last Day Messengers. Bent claimed that we are in the last days prior to Christ's physically cleansing the earth. Man must cleanse his consciousness before that time. The Messengers point to positive signs of the New Age: technological progress, the youth who are seeking love and simplicity in life, the spread of psychic development and healing, and the growth of belief in reincarnation and flying saucers.

Ministry of Universal Wisdom

Among the most important of the 1950s flying saucer contactees was George Van Tassel (1910–1970). A former employee of Howard Hughes, in 1957 Van Tassel moved to Giant Rock, California, and started an airport to service the burgeoning postwar air industry. Beginning in 1949 he and his wife, Doris Van Tassel, held weekly meditation sessions during which he would go into an altered state and channel messages. In January 1952 he began to receive channeled messages from several entities who identified themselves as space commanders, entities from outer space. Among these entities was one named Ashtar, commandant quadra sector, patrol station Schare. By this time flying saucers had become an item of popular national interest and the first people were coming forward to claim contact with beings inside the saucers, which they believed to be spacecraft from other worlds. Ashtar and his colleagues revealed their mission as one of saving humanity from self-destruction, which loomed closer with the discovery of atomic power.

A record of Van Tassel's initial contacts was published in the booklet *I Rode a Flying Saucer*. Van Tassel also received information on constructing a building in which people would be able to be rejuvenated through a process that would cause their aging to stop or be significantly reduced. This building was dubbed the Integratron. There was also some hope that the devices in the building would be able to turn cosmic energy into useful electricity, would allow time travel, and would supply a means to nullify gravity. Beginning in the 1950s, Giant Rock became the site of a popular annual flying saucer convention.

Through the channeled messages, Van Tassel developed a theological perspective. God was continuously creating the universe. Man had been a part of that creation (humans did not evolve), but was created on another planet. Adam, or more properly the Adamic race, came from outer space to inhabit this planet. God finished his creative work on humans and rested. Then another entity, called "Lord God" in the Bible, entered the picture. According to Van Tassel, the Lord God was a member of the Adamic race. He created Eve, a female counterpart of the all-male Adamic race. Eve was an animal, not a human. One of the Adamic race mated with Eve and created the hybrid "hu-man." Thus, each of us has an Adamic constructive aspect and a destructive physical aspect. We have degenerated from following our bestial tendencies. The space brothers, pure Adamic beings, have some concern for us because we were created through one of their number having sexual relations with Eve. Ashtar and his colleagues operated from a space station called Schare; together, they constituted what was known as the Council of Seven Lights.

Van Tassel founded the Ministry of Universal Wisdom as the corporate form through which he disseminated the messages of the space brothers. He also established an associated College of Universal Wisdom that controlled the research conducted within the Integratron.

Van Tassel died in 1970, and for a while his work was carried on by his widow. However, he had leased the land used by the ministry and it was eventually reclaimed by the government, which also took possession of the items inside the Integratron. The ministry was continued by Doris Van Tassel into the 1980s but eventually died out. A number of channels have claimed continued contact with Ashtar.

Sources:

Van Tassel. George. *The Council of Seven Lights*. Los Angeles: DeVorss & Co., 1958. 156 pp. Reprinted as: *Religion and Science Merged*. Yucca Valley, CA: Ministry of Universal Wisdom, 1968. 156 pp.

———. *Into This World and out Again*. Yucca Valley, CA: Author, 1956. 94 pp.

———. *I Rode a Flying Saucer*. Los Angeles: New Age Publishing Co., 1952. 44 pp.

———. *When Stars Look Down*. Los Angeles: Kruckeberg Press, 1976. 198 pp.

Star Light Fellowship

The Star Light Fellowship was founded in 1962 in New York City by Sterling Warren and Jackie Altisi as a "continuing Spiritual Education Program, initiated, directed and transmitted by Etheric Master Teachers of this and Other Planets, Galaxies and Realms of the Universe." Mrs. Altisi functioned as Jackie White Star and was the main direct-voice channel of messages from the spirit world but was assisted by Phyllis Veronica. Messages were received from departed spirits, the ascended-master hierarchy, and the space brothers, including Gloria Lee (discussed elsewhere in this volume). One of the central communications was from Christopher, aide to the King of the Moon and spokesman for the Luna Moon Government Headquarters of United Cosmic Planets. Christopher described the moon as a "complete authority in itself, but working with an interplanetary confederation."

Within the context of emphasis on communication with the space brothers, the general "ascended master" theology was accepted, and there was much correspondence with the "I AM" ascended master groups (discussed elsewhere in this volume). Ascended masters were once human and now, as spirits, teach humans about spiritual realities. During the 1970s, activities of the Fellowship were centered in New York City, where regular meetings were held and a semiannual periodical, *The Star Light Messenger*, was published.

Universariun Foundation

The Universariun Foundation was formed in 1958 in Portland, Oregon, where it was headquartered for many years. Two of the small group, Zelrun Karsleigh and his wife, Daisy Karsleigh, then still in her teens, had begun to receive telepathic material. Meetings were held regularly in their home, and the work grew steadily. For several decades, the Karsleighs remained the primary channels of messages from the spirit world; eventually, though, others within the group developed into channels as well.

Messages were received from both the ascended masters and the masters from outer space. The principle communicators have been Sri Soudah, Koot Hoomi, and Lord Michael. The material followed the perspective of the "I AM" Religious Activity and was

aimed at the illumination and emancipation of earth from its fear, chaos, and confusion.

The Universariun Foundation was governed by a board of seven directors elected by the membership at an annual meeting. The board oversaw publication of the monthly periodical, *The Voice of Universarius*. A sanctuary for weekly meditation and telepathic channeling and a bookstore were maintained in Tucson, Arizona. A recommended reading list of books, sold on a mail-order basis, included a wide variety of metaphysical works.

Sources:

How the Forces of Love Can Overcome the Forces of Hate. Portland, OR: Universariun Foundation, n.d.

Khul, Djwhal. *The Prophecies of the Tibetan*. Tucson, AZ: Universariun Foundation, 1983.

Oh! Urantia. Portland, OR: Universariun Foundation, [1967].

Prins, Ethera. *Miracle of Love and Life*. Portland, OR: Universariun Foundation, 1974.

Universarius as Given in Space Messages of 1960. Portland, OR: Sadhana-Western Publishers, 1961.

World Understanding

Daniel Fry, an explosives technician and employee of Aerojet General Corporation, became one of the most famous of the flying saucer contactees following an experience that occurred on July 4, 1950. Out walking on a hot evening near the Organ Mountains and White Sands Proving Grounds, New Mexico, he saw an "ovate spheroid about thirty feet in diameter." He encountered a space being, A-Lan, and took a ride in the saucer. The trip, to New York and back, took less than an hour. The purpose of the visit was to determine the basic adaptability of the earth race when confronted with concepts completely foreign to its customary mode of thinking. Fry was judged to be open. The entire visit was discussed in a book, *The White Sands Incident*, published in 1954. The following year, Understanding, Inc., was founded.

Understanding, Inc., was one of the most eclectic of UFO groups but was very much shaped by the teachings of A-Lan, as transmitted through Daniel Fry. A major thrust was the charting of the areas of worldwide agreement among branches of "spiritual" science and the identification of those tenets accepted as valid by all races and creeds, with the goal of working toward a guide for the behavior of man. Hypnotism, as long as it was properly used, was highly recommended. The group promoted the UFO cause generally, and Fry was a popular speaker in psychic circles. A periodical, *Understanding*, helped spread the group's message.

During the 1970s the headquarters of Understanding, Inc., were moved from Oregon to Tonapah, Arizona, where the Universal Faith and Wisdom Association, founded by the Rev. Enid Smith (and centered on several saucer-shaped buildings adjacent to the Sun Spiritualist Camp), was absorbed into Understanding, Inc. Subsequently, the headquarters were moved again, to New Mexico. The organization was administered by its officers, who were elected during the annual membership meeting. During the 1970s, there were approximately 60 units worldwide.

Sources:

Fry, Daniel W. *Alan's Message: To Men of Earth*. Los Angeles: New Age Publishing Co., 1954.

————. *Atoms, Galaxies, and Understanding*. El Monte, CA: Understanding Publishing Co., 1960.

————. *The Curve of Development*. Lakemont, GA: CSA Printers and Publishers, 1965.

————. *To Men of Earth*. Alamagordo, NM: El Cariso Publishing Co., 1973.

————. *The White Sands Incident*. Los Angeles: New Age Publishing Co., 1954.

DRUG-RELATED GROUPS

The Church of Sunshine

The Church of Sunshine was founded in 1980 by Jack McCall and his wife, Mary Jo McCall. The McCalls, who had been members of the Neo-American Church through most of the 1970s, rejected the leadership style of that church's founder, Art Kleps. His autocratic rule, in their opinion, had led to the creation of dogma and tended to isolate Kleps behind his close associates.

Furthermore, Jack McCall disagreed with Kleps's belief in solipsistic nihilism. Kleps and McCall both believed that the psychedelic experience led to the conclusion that life was a dream. However, Kleps maintained that ultimately life was a very personal dream, which he spoke of as "my dream" and thus not a shared dream that could be spoken of as "our dream." McCall thought it was meaningless to speak of the nature of the dream.

In establishing the Church of Sunshine, the McCalls limited their beliefs to two items. The church affirmed that psychedelic substances, primarily LSD and related psychoactives, bring salvation—that is, liberation from ignorance and illusion and a sense of deliverance from danger. Hence the peak psychedelic experience is the most profound experience imaginable. Second, the church affirmed that it was under the authority of no person, group of persons, or special writings, but rather derived its authority solely from the logical analysis of experience. Thus, while McCall served as an administrative focus, he did not dictate policy or particular beliefs.

Initially, congregations of the Church of Sunshine were established in Whittier, California, by the McCalls, and in Frankfurt, Germany, by Peter Akwai. Members were invited to become ministers and to establish additional congregations, but were required to go through a period of "seminary" training at one of the churches. A periodical, *The L Train*, was published.

The church was always quite small (with fewer than 100 members), in part because of the numerous judicial rulings against psychedelics that occurred in the years following the church's founding.

Church of the Awakening

The Church of the Awakening was formed in 1963 by John W. Aiken and Louisa Aiken, both retired physicians. The Aikens lost their sons in 1951 and 1957 and were led into the realm of the psychic to seek an answer to why their sons were taken from them. They also began to experiment with peyote, which they used as early as 1955. The year after the Church of the Awakening was formed, they sold their home and became active in speaking to psychic and psychedelic groups around the country.

The church had no formal statement of doctrine, but six affirmations formed a common core of accepted ideas: the unity of mankind, the reality of man's spiritual nature, the importance of experiencing that reality, the importance of the properly directed psychedelic sacrament as a means of achieving the unitive experience, the practical application of the unitive experience in everyday life, and the extension of the awareness of the reality as a factor in the solution of both personal and world problems. A great deal of control was exercised over the taking of the sacrament. Members were required to make an application, after which an experienced monitor was secured, and a proper environment arranged.

The church was a loosely organized fellowship. Ten or more members of the church in a given area could apply for a charter to operate as a branch. Among the outstanding members were Dr. Huston Smith, professor of religion at Massachusetts Institute of Technology, and Dr. Walter Houston Clark, professor emeritus of the psychology of religion at Andover-Newton Theological Seminary. Clark remained a major advocate of the religious psychedelics until his death in 1994.

The church suffered heavily from the 1966 ruling that made psychedelic drugs illegal. In 1969, hoping for a status like that of the Native American Church, the group had a hearing with the Bureau of Narcotics, but received a negative verdict. In 1970 the church had 400 members nationwide, but further rulings against it eventually proved fatal.

Sources:

Clark, Walter Houston. *Chemical Ecstasy: Psychedelic Drugs and Religion*. New York: Sheed & Ward, 1969.

————. "What Light Do Drugs Throw on the Spiritual and the Transpersonal?" *Journal of Religion and Psychical Research* 4, no. 2 (April 1981): 131–137.

Church of the Psychedelic Mystic

The Church of the Psychedelic Mystic was founded in 1978 by a small group of people who described themselves as mystics and used psychedelic drugs in their search for a direct personal experience of the Divine. The church was founded at a time when the use of psychedelic drugs for any purpose, religious or otherwise, was illegal, and the church did not use illegal substances at any church function. However, the church was dedicated to overturning those drug laws that prevented their use of psychedelics for religious purposes. The church at the same time recognized that many individuals, including church members, might continue to use psychedelics regardless of their legal status. It opposed the use of consciousness-altering drugs administered without the consent of the individual for the purpose of social control.

The church considered its members to be mystics and as such taught them to seek the Divine in very individualized ways. There was no external authority in the church, no sacred books, and no church buildings. Though aware of the vast literature on psychedelic mysticism, the church recognized the individuality of interpretations of psychedelic experiences and the new syntheses of knowledge that result from continued use of drugs. The church proposed its own four "noble truths":

1. God is One; Praise the Lord;
2. The kingdom of God is within us, perceived through our individual selves;
3. It is possible for any of us to directly experience this divinity within;
4. It is desirable for us to do so.

The church was originally chartered by the Universal Life Church. In the early 1980s, it was headquartered in Encinitas, California, from which its periodical, *Mystic Vibes*, was published. Through the 1980s, no progress was made in liberalizing laws governing the use of drugs by psychedelic mystics. Nothing has been heard from the church since then, and it is likely that the church is now defunct.

Church of the Tree of Life

Apart from the Native American Church, the only psychedelic church to survive into the 1980s with its legal status intact was the San Francisco–based Church of the Tree of Life, formed in 1971. It was a nondogmatic church that believed that each person is the sovereign of his or her own mind and body and must have the right to do with himself or herself, or with any consenting adults, whatever he or she pleases, as long as those actions do not violate the rights of others. For the church, this sovereignty included the use of psychedelic drugs.

It was the belief of the church that all substances are God's gifts, to be used as one elects. However, because LSD and marijuana were illegal, they were not "officially" embraced as sacraments; rather, a number of alternative legal mind-altering substances were listed instead. These included nutmeg, kava, soma, peyote, ginseng, and calamus. The church felt a responsibility to impart information to members and published *The First Book of Sacraments* as a guide to legal mind-alterants. It also published a periodical, *Bark Leaf*. Ritual was practiced in connection with the individual's taking of psychedelic substances as a means of organizing and thus gaining the most from the experience. In 1972 the church reported 1,500 members.

Sources:

Mann, John, ed. *The First Book of Sacraments of the Church of the Tree of Life*. San Francisco: Church of the Tree of Life, 1972.

OTHER PSYCHIC NEW AGE GROUPS

The Aquarian Academy

The Aquarian Academy was founded in 1972 by Robert E. Birdsong (b. 1912) to assist people through what was believed to be the transition period into the Aquarian Age and to teach the principles of what it termed *Adamic Christianity*, a form of gnostic wisdom.

According to the academy's teachings, the first act of creation occurred when God emanated an image of Its own nature as the first Adam of Life, Spirit, Soul, and Body of the Creator. The first human beings were microcosmic replicas of the first Adam. A second group of human entities, this time differentiated into male and female, were created in order to balance the activity of Spirit (wisdom) and Soul (Love). Some of these human entities became trapped in the gross material plane of animal existence, resulting in the earthly humans we know today.

The divine plan calls for the eventual extraction of the humans from their material captivity. The Lord God ordained that those humans so trapped would have to undergo a period of training and would be released from the body when the lessons of physical experience were mastered. The supervision of the plan was turned over to the divine emanations personified as "male" and "female." The female Divine Soul assumed responsibility for the reproduction, growth, and emotional stability of humanity, whereas the male Divine Spirit (Wisdom) was assigned responsibility for the education and mental stability of humanity. Individual humans would progress through a series of human embodiments until the lessons were mastered. The Divine Soul maintained her mission as the constantly present Mother Nature, and the Divine Spirit periodically reappeared as an avatar/teacher. The last avatar was Jesus. The crucifixion of Jesus represented the reunion of Divine Spirit and Divine Soul and the appearance of the androgynous Christ as the Indwelling Spirit of Earth.

It was the belief of the Academy that the teachings of the various avatars, while not lost, have been obscured by the religious leaders of the world. Adamic

Christianity is a restatement of the avataric truth in language suitable to the present generation.

In the beginning, humans were divided into five races (brown, yellow, red, white, and black), each of which lived on one of five great continents isolated from each other. The first avatars brought a message of guidance to each continent. However, these messages were largely ignored. On the continent of Mongolia, where the Gobi Desert is now located, a remnant of the people who accepted and lived by the message of the avatars built a retreat, Shambhala (later relocated to Tibet), to keep the truth alive. The divine powers assigned to this group of advanced humans the task of perpetuating the truth and recruiting initiates into it. The group at Shambhala later became known as the Great Brotherhood of Light. The brotherhood established wisdom schools on each of the five continents. These schools gave way to a set of 12 wisdom centers, described as vibratory vortexes or spheres of influence. In addition, there was a 13th center, the central hub, to which the other wisdom centers owed allegiance. It brought together all of the specialized wisdom of each of the other centers into a single body of truth. That 13th center, located near Mt. Shasta, California, was the Aquarian Academy.

As part of its work, the Academy published a set of books written by Birdsong, which embody the truths of Adamic Christianity and cover the wide range of subjects embraced by its teachings, the basic text being *The Revelations of Hermes*. It also published a set of monographs that explore selected subjects in great detail. No classes or correspondence lessons were given, as Birdsong believed that each person is responsible for searching out the truth.

Membership in the Academy was open to all who asked. As individuals read the literature and progressed in their understanding of its truth, Birdsong offered his guidance. Members were encouraged to establish discussion groups, both as a means of spreading the teachings and in order to become more established in the truths.

Sources:

The Aquarian Academy. Eureka, CA: Sirius Books, 1978. 12 pp.

Birdsong, Robert E. *Fundamentals of Adamic Christianity*. San Francisco, CA: Sirius Books, 1974. 30 pp.

———. *Mission to Mankind: A Cosmic Autobiography*. Eureka, CA: Sirius Books, 1975. 122 pp.

———. *The Revelation of Hermes: An Exposition of Adamic Christianity*. Eureka, CA: Sirius Books, 1974. 278 pp.

———. *Steps on the Path: Daily Words of Wisdom*. Eureka, CA: Sirius Books, 1975. 64 pp.

Astrological, Metaphysical, Occult, Revelatory, Enlightenment Church

The Astrological, Metaphysical, Occult, Revelatory, Enlightenment Church (AMORE) was formed in 1972 by the Rev. Charles Robert Gordon, formerly a minister of the African Methodist Episcopal Zion Church. His father was Bp. Buford Franklin Gordon of the AMEZ Church. The church was Bible-based and viewed Jesus as the embodiment of cosmic consciousness. The AMORE Church believed in using the occult arts as a means to enlightenment in the coming Aquarian Age. Headquarters for the AMORE Church were established in Meriden, Connecticut. During the 1980s church headquarters were relocated, but the church soon dropped out of sight.

AUM Temple of Universal Truth

The AUM Temple of Universal Truth was founded by Elizabeth Delvine King (1858–1932) as the Church Truth Universal—Aum in 1925 in Los Angeles. A metaphysician for many years, she received, in 1907, as an answer to prayer, "the infilling of the Holy Spirit, which is the New Birth." Three days after her experience, the "Voice of the Infinite" spoke to her, saying, "Child, thy ministry is to be among what is called advanced thinking people." Over the next seven years, she wrote five books, which formed the basic texts of the movement. In 1912 she directed a center for Practical Christianity in Manhattan Beach, California, and in 1916 she moved to Los Angeles and began a ministry of "Primitive Christian Teachings." In 1925, the first Sunday services were held.

Work progressed, and, by 1930, a total of 22 ministers had been ordained. In 1929 construction began on a temple in the La Crescenta Valley outside Los Angeles. An ashram was also built as an adjunct of the temple. At the time of Dr. King's death, there were two centers in Los Angeles and one in the Valley. Dr. King was succeeded by Dr. E. W. Miller, and Miller in turn was succeeded by Nina Fern Brunier (Dennison), who became the temple's leader in 1940. Under her guidance, the later name of the church was adopted. In 1956 she relocated the temple to the Mojave Desert, where she had found a site for a new sanctuary and retreat complex. In 1964 the move was made to Newberry Springs, California, the La Crescenta Temple having previously been sold. A new temple was completed in 1967. The center at Newberry Springs served the group through the 1970s, but in the early 1980s, the AUM Temple was disbanded.

The AUM Temple taught Esoteric Christianity as transmitted by the Great White Brotherhood, of which Jesus Christ is the active head. Truth is the light and wisdom divine, given to assist men to the kingdom of God. To enter the kingdom, the self must be cleansed and purified through scientific prayer, renunciation of carnal beliefs, and meditation. Through cleansing, not bodily death, one escapes the cycle of reincarnation in the dense material world and the law of cause and effect.

Aum is God's own name for himself, is God in unmanifested and manifested form. The repetition of the name of God attunes one to the vibration of the spirit. In speaking the word, one wields the power of the universe. The word is but part of the "Secret Heart Way," the discipline of mind, body, and spirit through which one attains union. The Way is the path of Bhakti Yoga, first taught in the United States by Baba Premanand Bharati, a Krishna devotee who worked in the United States from 1902 to 1907. Healing is an integral aspect of the work.

The sanctuary and retreat in Newberry Springs housed a self-contained community of disciples, who lived their love and devotion and kept an organic garden, beehives, goats, and chickens. Besides the disciples, there were a few members of the Temple who did not reside at Newberry Springs, but supported the work and frequently attended the weekly services on Sunday and Thursday. At various times two periodicals, *The Greeting Messenger* and *AUM: The Cosmic Light*, were published.

Sources:

Althma, Leh Rheadia. *The Garden of the Soul*. Newberry Springs, CA: AUM Temple of Universal Truth, 1943.

Brunier, Nina. *The Path to Illumination*. Highway Highlands, CA: Author, 1941.

King, Elizabeth Delvine. *The Flashlights of Truth*. Los Angeles: AUM Temple of Universal Truth, 1918.

———. *The Lotus Path*. Los Angeles: J. F. Rowny Press, 1917.

New Age Songs. Newberry Springs, CA: AUM Temple of Universal Truth, 1972.

The Awakened, A Fellowship in Christ

The Awakened, A Fellowship in Christ, was founded on Easter Sunday of 1932 in Los Angeles, California, by Melvin L. Severy. Severy had been a student of popular religious literature, including books about the Great Pyramid of Egypt and the possible prophetic significance of its architecture. Concerned about the state of the world, he began to envision an organization for human betterment, an idea that matured over several decades. Finally, in 1932, he was invited to view a new painting of Christ done by Los Angeles artist Charles Sindelar. Deeply impressed by the picture, Severy became convinced that the picture should be used as a standard around which to rally the people of the earth into a Christ-minded fellowship. Severy enlisted Sindelar to design a membership button and a membership certificate, and called together an initial group.

The fellowship was designed to ready the world for the coming new dispensation promised in the Bible, revealed by the Great Pyramid, and foretold by more recent prophets and seers. Rallying around the portrait was seen as a way to hasten the advent of the new age. Once the body of believers was formed, it was to await a sudden call, the time and nature of which Severy never divulged. Indeed, much of the future of the fellowship was to be revealed through further revelation as it matured. Unfortunately, the group never matured, as the thrust of its program was assumed by another organization soon after the formation of the initial group and the publication of a small pamphlet calling for other groups to form.

In the mid-1930s Guy Ballard, founder of the "I AM" Religious Activity, visited the Sindelar Studios and was equally impressed with the portrait of Christ, identifying it with the same Master Jesus with whom he had been in communication. Sindelar, equally impressed with Ballard, offered the resources of his artistic establishment to the "I AM" movement. His studio on Hoover Street, which had served as the headquarters of the fellowship, became the "I AM" movement's West Coast headquarters. Sindelar did the art work and published the magazine for the "I AM." The fellowship, for its part, survived only a brief time and most of its resources were absorbed into the newer movement.

Sources:

The Awakened. Los Angeles: Awakened, [1933].

Christ Ministry Foundation

The Christ Ministry Foundation was established in 1935 by Eleanore Mary Thedick (1883–1973) of Oakland, California, following a series of visions. Thedick received her initial vision in 1926, when she was told that she would be a channel for a "spiritual broadcasting station." The purpose of the ministry was to illustrate the Christ-Light within. Its outer foundation was to have 48 dual sects, each to be named for the Christ-qualities displayed in persons. Over the years, Thedick wrote several books. In 1970 she merged her efforts with those of one of her students, Woods Mattingley. Mattingley had been involved in psychic/spiritual work for many years and had founded the Seeker's Quest. Within the new, merged work, the Seeker's Quest Ministry was seen as having an exoteric role, and the Foundation as having an esoteric one.

The Christ Ministry Foundation taught a form of esoteric Christianity. Christ is the great teacher who brought love into the world. The soul was envisioned as growing slowly toward "at-onement" with the Father. This process takes many incarnations, but, as with the prodigal, all souls will eventually return. During incarnation, we attempt to overcome character weakness, pay karmic debts, and bear witness to the Light of God. Healing is achieved by channeling the Light of God, often envisioned as the Triune Ray (Father, Son, and Holy Spirit). In 1970 Ms. Thedick retired from active work, and the ministry was then headed by Mattingley. In 1972 Thedick gave two students, Genevah D. Seivertson and her husband, Wayne Seivertson, charge over the Foundation, and Mattingley's Seeker's Quest Ministry in San Jose became independent, though affiliated. Mattingley continued to publish his quarterly periodical, *The Seeker's Quest Newsletter*.

Sources:

Seivertson, Genevah D. *The Christ Highway*. Marina del Rey, CA: DeVorss & Company, 1981.

Thedick, Eleanor. *The Christ Highway*. Oakland, CA: Christ Ministry Foundation, n.d.

———. *Jewels of Truth and Rays of Color*. Oakland, CA: Christ Ministry Foundation, n.d.

———. *Light on Your Problems*. Oakland, CA: Christ Ministry Foundation, n.d.

Christian Institute of Spiritual Science

The Christian Institute of Spiritual Science, founded by Hanna Jacob Doumette, functioned in the Los Angeles area in the early 1960s. It taught a form of esoteric Christianity that included attention to mystic and occult philosophy. The institute believed in one God, considered as the Creator and Heavenly Father, the Spirit of Life. God is experienced by human consciousness as a Trinity—as Father, Mother, and Son and/or as Creative Spirit, Holy Spirit, and Christ Spirit. The Trinity lives in humans as their true identity. The Divine Father Principle is a person's spirit, the Mother Principle is the soul, and the Christ Principle is the mind and consciousness. Humans are the idea of God manifest in creation.

Humans possess all the powers of God. Individuals may receive the Gift of the Holy Spirit (a spiritual experience). It is attained by faith, purity of heart, renunciation of all negation, fervent devotion, and constant concentration and meditation upon the indwelling Christ Self. Thus, the individual attains spiritual transformation (resurrection), which in turn brings a quickening and mastery of spiritual and psychic powers, especially the power of healing. In this state of Divine Presence there are no negatives, only life, righteousness, immortality, and goodness.

The institute was headquartered in Santa Monica, California. There is no information on its size or the years of its existence. Doumette authored a number of books and booklets expounding the institute's teachings.

Sources:

Doumette, Hanna Jacob. *After His Living Likeness*. Santa Monica, CA: Christian Institute of Spiritual Science, n.d. 12 pp.

———. *Jesus the Man*. Santa Monica, CA: Christian Institute of Spiritual Science, n.d. 12 pp.

———. *The Sun of Higher Understanding*. Author, n.d.

Church of Basic Truth

The Church of Basic Truth was founded in 1961 in Phoenix, Arizona, and was headed by Dr. George H.

Hepker. It taught *huna* (power), the belief system of the pre-Christian religious leaders of Hawaii, with an emphasis on healing via "Meda-Physical Dynamics." This therapy was developed on the theory that any disorder the mind can allow to develop can be controlled and often cured.

In addition to the church's center in Phoenix, a second center was located in Gary, Indiana.

Church of Eductivism

Jack Horner (b. 1927) worked from 1950 to 1965 with L. Ron Hubbard, founder of the Church of Scientology. A prominent member of the church, he was awarded the first Doctor of Scientology degree. Then in 1965, he left the church over what he considered an authoritarian ethics policy. After a period of nonassociation with Scientology, he began to develop Dianology, viewed as an improved Scientology drawing from a number of sources. In 1970, Horner moved to Los Angeles and founded the Personal Spiritual Freedoms Foundation. In 1971 he changed the name Dianology to Eductivism, with emphasis placed on "educing" latent potentials and uncovering what is hidden. The Church of Eductivism, originally called the Church of Spiritual Freedoms, was the religious adjunct to the Foundation; both were aspects of the umbrella corporation, the Association of International Dianologists.

Eductivism is an applied philosophy aimed at evoking the individual's infinite spiritual potentials. Individuals (usually referred to as "life sources") are infinitely capable of total creation and total cessation, simultaneously. But individuals do not use that potential. Through classes and exercises, the potentials can be released in a meaningful context.

The creed of the church emphasized the freedoms believed to be implicitly denied in the Church of Scientology—to seek God, however he may be perceived; to create alternatives; to possess opinions, thoughts, and sanity; to communicate freely with others; and to join voluntary associations. Like Scientology, Horner taught that humans are basically "well disposed" and that "occlusions which mar and blemish the human spirit can be removed by the application of Spiritual technology."

Horner had an immediate response to his efforts, and associated centers were established and independent clearing consultants trained. Horner was a leader in the California Association of Dianetic Auditors, a fellowship of independent consultants.

Sources:

Horner, Jack. *Clearing*. Santa Monica, CA: Personal Creative Freedoms Foundation, 1982.

————. *Dianology*. Westwood Village, CA: Association of International Dianologists, 1970.

————. *Eductivism and You*. Westwood, CA: Personal Creative Freedoms Foundation, 1971.

Horner, Jack, and J. Rey Geller. *What an Eductee Should Know*. Santa Monica, CA: Personal Creative Freedoms Foundation, 1974.

Church of General Psionics

The Church of General Psionics was founded by John L. Douglas and Henry D. Frazier. Douglas was an amateur hypnotist and student of the psychic. Over the decade preceding the church's founding in 1968, Douglas had been evolving a pragmatic view of "psi"—the psychic. "Does it work?" became his criterion for things psychic. Then, in a visionary experience in 1968, a new understanding of the nature and purpose of humanity was given and a group was formed by those who were of like mind.

The purpose of Psionics is to help a person develop his own philosophy. General Psionics aids the individual on the path to enlightenment, which is loaded with obstacles, by offering training to help him to become aware of his immortality. Man is a soul inhabiting a body, as it has inhabited other bodies previously. The various techniques of becoming aware are termed *psionic engineering*. New members of the church, before they were introduced to psionic engineering, were asked to agree to the "code of an immortal." The code acknowledges the dignity of all entities, quite apart from the body, and the fight of each entity to self-determination. From the church's sole center, located in Redondo Beach, California, a program of classes, workshops, and counseling was offered during the 1970s.

Church of Mercavah

Mercavah was a small New Age church founded in 1982 by Rev. James R. Montandon. Montandon had a decade-long background in metaphysical and spiritualist training. He graduated from the International Spiritualist University, and finished a course of study with a variety of educational structures: the University of Metaphysics, the Neotarian Fellowship, the New England Academy of Hypnosis, and the Natural School of Healing. He had also been a member of a variety of metaphysical and spiritualist organizations and had lectured widely in meditation and spirituality. He served as a chaplain at one of the Louisiana state prisons.

The church was headed by a board of deacons, composed of 10 ministers who served for life. A wide spectrum of opinion was encouraged in the church concerning matters of belief. The church's doctrinal statement centered upon a belief in the spiritual nature of human beings. As spiritual beings, individuals must find their path to self-knowledge. Emphasis was placed on allowing individual freedom in the search for truth. The openness of the church allowed it to cooperate locally with a variety of esoteric organizations.

Ministers in training and other members were able to study with the church via correspondence. In 1992, students studying with the church's College of Applied Arts included several from neighboring states and one in London, England.

Sources:

Book of Service: The Book of Guided Group Worship for the Church of Mercavah. Baton Rouge, LA: Church of Mercavah, n.d. 99 pp.

Church of the Gentle Brothers and Sisters

Frank Douglas was a trance medium in New York City who moved to London to continue his work. While in London in January of 1971, he received messages through other mediums that Mexico was an ideal place to begin a spiritual center and healing group. He arrived at Puerto Angel and there met Martin Myman, who agreed to join forces in forming a center. Healing work commenced, and the center's fame spread throughout both Mexico and California. A community formed around Douglas, who died in 1986. Healing work was a combination of spiritual healing, zonal therapy, counseling, massage, and even drugs. After two years, the Mexican government began to suppress the efforts, and the center moved to San Francisco, where it incorporated as the Church of the Gentle Brothers and Sisters. Because of legal restrictions on some of the church's healing methods, the laying-on of hands became the main method employed in healing following the move. Prior to healing, palm readings were done on patients. The group was Theosophic in outlook and studied the Alice Bailey books. Emphasis was placed on spiritual unfoldment (religious growth), as opposed to psychic development (through telepathy, clairvoyance, etc.).

Church of the Gift of God

The Church of the Gift of God was a nonsectarian group whose prime manifestation occurred through the New England Conservatory of Health headquartered in Magnolia, Massachusetts. There, the Conservatory operated a retreat house that offered a program "dedicated to restoring your natural and spiritual good health." The church was headed by Prof. James A. Dooling II, who based church doctrine and practice on the teachings of St. Luke, St. Benedict, and St. Dorothy. It was Dooling's belief that good health is within the reach of all who will merely abide by the laws of the creator of nature.

Various healing techniques were offered at the Conservatory. They ranged from the more accepted medical and physical therapy practices to less orthodox approaches, such as medical astrology, color therapy, and psychic healing. Emphasis was placed on natural diet and exercise and on "human ecology"—the correct ordering of the total environment of physical and spiritual man. The church seems to have dissolved in the early 1980s.

Church of the Lord Jesus Christ (Ishi Temple)

The Church of the Lord Jesus Christ (Ishi Temple) was founded by Bp. Robert N. Skillman, known to his followers as the Prophet Saoshyant. The church was described as Christoid, that is, in the image of Christ. It honored the holy name of God, Ishi (Hosea 2:16), meaning "My Husband." It was a church that recognized the necessity of having living prophets to govern it: "Saoshyant" is the name in Avestan (Zoroastrian) literature of the great coming Prophet. The church also taught that miracles were needed to demonstrate the power of God in extraordinary ways and that revelation was needed as a vehicle for bringing greater truth to the world today. Finally, the church taught the truth of the Latter Rain, concerning the movement from the divine light of the Sixth Ray to the Seventh Ray (a reference to theosophical teaching on the light that emanates from the divine).

Skillman was assisted in the Ishi Temple by Archdeacon Robert S. Kimball. Headquarters were established in Brisbane, California, from where a periodical, *The Christoid Evangel*, was published irregularly. The church offered correspondence lessons in "prosperity" and distributed talismans for a variety of needs. Saoshyant authored several booklets: *The Grand Affirmation*, *The Healing Affirmation*, and *The Sayings*.

Essene Center

The Essene Center was founded in 1972 in Hot Springs, Arkansas, by the Rev. Walter Hagen. In 1970 Hagen had a vision of Christ, and the stigmata (marks similar to those on Jesus' hands after the crucifixion) were placed on his hands as a sign of his acceptance of his mission. In other visions, he was given the power to work miracles. Hagen also acted as a prophet and regularly made predictions of coming events.

According to Hagen, Jesus was an Essene, and the order of Essenes actually dates to the time of Moses. The House of Prophets on Mt. Carmel was the center of the order. Essenes were characterized by abstinence from slavery, communal living, disdain for commerce and industry, longevity, belief in reincarnation, healing by God's power, and psychic abilities. As modern-day Essenes, Hagen's followers were taught to believe that war is wrong, that waste is a misuse of what God had given, that all religions are acceptable to God, that respect for the rights of all men includes disdain of slavery, and that it is a duty to help other Essenes. Hagen accepted the validity of the Dead Sea Scrolls and believed that the coming messiah would arise from among the Essenes.

During the 1970s there was only one Essene group, the one associated with the center at Hot Springs, but members were located around the country. They were tied together by *The Guide*, a monthly periodical. Hagen's workshops and a variety of services were offered through the center. No evidence of the continuance of the center into the 1980s has been found.

Etherian Religious Society of Universal Brotherhood

The Etherian Religious Society of Universal Brotherhood was formed in 1965 in California by its director, the Rev. E. A. Hurtienne, and had its source in the mental visions given Mr. Hurtienne earlier in his life. No being or form was seen in these visions; rather, Hurtienne sensed waves of love and a universal consciousness. The purpose of the society was to minister through love so as to insure dignity, equality, and justice for all throughout the universe and to help establish the future root races (developmental stages) of mankind on earth and thus assure the entrance of earth into our solar system's Planetary Federation of Light.

The basic philosophy of the society recognized a consciousness that is divine and manifested in the four principles of omnipresence, omnipotence, omniscience, and love. It further held that all men are brothers throughout the universe; all forms of life on all planes are related; all religions, though under the direction of God, are man-made; love is the unifying force and must become a living reality, for only through it can eternal life by achieved; karma and reincarnation are universal laws; man is divine and is entitled to free thought and action; man is a spiritual being with seven complete bodies; and all life is to be held in reverence. Behavior should center on sincerity, tolerance, integrity, kindness, and affection.

The society had among its immediate goals the establishment of primary classes in metaphysics and esoteric studies and the formation of light and meditation groups devoted to healing, unity, and harmony between nature and mankind. Membership was open to all; after a year, members were able to become a part of the Brotherhood of Light, an inner group with the society. The group circulated copies of *Man, Know Thy Divinity*, published by the Living Christ Movement of New Zealand, and also published a periodical, *The Etherian Bulletin*. The society's long-range goals included the establishment of a university, a healing center, and a religious community of advanced spiritual beings.

Sources:

Man, Know Thy Divinity. Auckland, NZ: Living Christ Movement, n.d.

First Century Church

The Rev. David N. Bubar was a Southern Baptist minister and graduate of New Orleans Baptist Theological Seminary. After a seven-year pastorate during which he became more and more aware of his psychic abilities, he resigned his parish and, in 1969, opened the Spiritual Outreach Society (later renamed the First Century Church). During the 1970s, Bubar developed a national reputation as a clairvoyant, prophet, and psychic counselor, and he kept a heavy schedule of lectures around the country.

In 1975 Bubar was implicated in a fire at the Sponge Rubber Plant in Shelton, Connecticut. Plant owner Charles Moeller had been a longtime client of Bubar's and Bubar had predicted a plant "disaster" shortly before it was bombed. Bubar was convicted as a participant in the arson and served a prison term.

There was only a single congregation of the First Century Church, but it had a significant outreach through its nationally circulated periodical, *Flaming Sword*. Weekly services and classes were held at the church, which survived only a short time after Bubar began his long sentence.

Future Foundation

The Future Foundation was formed in 1969 in Steinauer, Nebraska, by Gerard W. Gottula, a member of an associated group that had been meeting for several months. The history of the group actually dates to the 1950s and the healing work of Jennings Ruffing, who lived in a small Wyoming town. Ruffing discovered that one of his patients was clairvoyant and, under the direction of Ruffing, could give psychic readings. The eight members of the original foundation group, formed by Ruffing, gathered for a reading from Ruffing and his associate, at which time the formation of the Future Foundation was announced to them.

The first issue of the *Future Foundation*, a newsletter, appeared in 1969. A board of 12 members was formed to govern the work, which consisted of giving health, life, and guidance readings.

The foundation grew throughout the 1970s and 1980s; however, it faced continual conflict due to new regulations from the Food and Drug Administration (FDA) and in 1991 disbanded.

Sources:

Prophecies of Cyrus. Steinauer, NE: Future Foundation, 1970.

Haikim International Meditation Society

The Haikim International Meditation Society was a small group headquartered in Houston, Texas, and headed by Mary Beatrice Gunn, its director/counselor. Its world headquarters were in Zurich, Switzerland. No sign of its continuance into the 1980s has been observed.

Holy Order of Ezekiel

The Holy Order of Ezekiel was founded in 1969 by Dr. Daniel Christopher. Dr. Christopher was a student of Dr. Judith Tyberg, who had been a disciple of Sri Aurobindo and later taught at the East-West Cultural Center in San Francisco, California. Christopher graduated from the Center and later studied in Europe at the Prasura Institute and the Guggenheim Academy. The Order, founded upon Christopher's return to the United States, was composed of two parts: the

Celestial and Terrestrial Circles. The Celestial Circle, composed of three masters, seven practitioners, and other initiates, was the center of guiding light that radiated celestial illumination to every attuned being. The masters were the spiritual gurus of all members. Christopher was the First Master. The Terrestrial Circle consisted of the scribes, secretaries, and members and was to be the growing branch of the Order. Members who manifested assimilation of and dedication to the precepts of the Order were welcomed as initiates.

The Order's basic teachings centered on the knowledge of God's power and the techniques of achieving personal success and fulfillment through that power. The Divine Life Lessons distributed by the Order prepared the seeker to receive the power promised by Christ. These include instruction in meditation, breathing, the use of "Aum" (a mantra), mystical symbolizing, spiritual healing, and numerology. There was a strong belief in reincarnation and karma. The masters were seen as helpful in the student's progress. The Order taught that God assumes one-half of the student's burden and the master, one-fourth. The members needed to generate the initial spark themselves.

In the 1970s, headquarters of the Holy Order were in Glendale, California. From there, the lessons were sent out to students across the country.

International Church of Spiritual Vision, Inc. (Western Prayer Warriors)

The International Church of Spiritual Vision, Inc., was formed by Dallas Turner, who as "Nevada Slim" became a country-music star in the 1960s. In 1959 Turner received the Pentecostal "baptism of the Holy Spirit" and spoke in tongues, reportedly in an actual foreign language. A long-time student of psychical metaphysics, numerology, and hypnotism, Turner built an eclectic system of belief that combines elements of the psychic, Pentecostalism, and Sacred Name Adventism in a blend called Aquarian Metaphysics.

The church's essential beliefs are summarized in the Yahwist Creed: "I believe in Yahweh the Father Almighty, creator of all things. And in Yahoshua—whom the world knows as Jesus Christ—Yahweh's only begotten Son our Savior; who was conceived by the Holy Ghost, born of the blessed virgin, suffered under Pontius Pilate, was crucified, died and was buried. He descended into hell; preached to the spirits in prison. The third day He arose from the physical dead. He ascended into the World of Spirit, sits at the right hand of Yahweh the Father Almighty; from there He shall come to judge the living and the so-called dead. I believe the original message of our Saviour and Wayshower. I accept the Scriptural and Metaphysical Truths of all religions. I give no place to the devil. I believe that Yahweh is the only power that exists. I believe in the Holy Ghost, the nine gifts of the Spirit, the communion of believers, the resurrection of

the spiritual body, and life everlasting. Amen." Members related to the church through the mail. After their concerns were solicited, members were sent blessed cloths (Acts 19:12) and were included in metaphysical healing prayers. Turner also offered lessons in Aquarian Metaphysics.

Lorian Association

The Lorian was an association of people dedicated to a vision of the New Age, defined as the spirit of wholeness upon the earth. Members believed that humanity was striving for a new level of completeness expressed in a new sense of partnership with creation, the emergence of a holistic spirit within individuals, and a new covenant between God and the godliness in each person.

The catalyst for the formation of the Lorian Association was the return of David Spangler (b. 1945) to the United States in 1973 after three years in northern Scotland as the codirector of the Findhorn Community, a New Age community founded by Peter Caddy, his wife, Eileen Caddy, and Dorothy McLean. Along with the Universal Link, Findhorn was one of the most important groups fostering the larger New Age Movement. Spangler led in the founding of the association soon after his arrival in America. Over the next few years, he authored several books that for many people provided the definitive statements of the New Age vision. From the 1960s, Spangler had been in contact with a spiritual entity named "John," and he viewed much of his literary production as a synthesis of John's insight and his own words.

The beliefs of the association were summarized in their 15-part "Statement of Interdependence," which committed members to a dedication to sacred, cooperative decision making, the process of growth, one world, harmless interaction with the environment, the building of a planetary village, conservation and wise use of energy, diversity in cultural expressions, an open social order, and communication with and learning from preterhuman intelligences who also inhabit the earth.

In the mid-1980s, the association moved from Wisconsin to a new center in Washington. An active program was built around educational events for the public, publication of New Age literature, encouragement of music and the arts, and networking with people who shared one or more common concerns. The association was a small and dedicated community that encouraged the development of like-minded groups over its own growth. It disbanded in the late 1980s.

Sources:

Spangler, David. *Festivals in the New Age*. Forres, Moray, Scotland: Findhorn Publications, 1975.

———. *Reflections on the Christ*. Forres, Moray, Scotland: Findhorn Publications, 1977.

———. *Revelation: The Birth of a New Age*. San Francisco: Rainbow Bridge, 1976.

———. *Towards a Planetary Vision*. Forres, Scotland: Findhorn Foundation, 1977.

———, ed. *Conversations with John*. Elgin, IL: Lorian Press, 1980.

Mahanaim School of Interpretation

The Mahanaim School of Interpretation was founded around 1900 in Chicago, Illinois, by George Chainey (b. 1851). Prior to founding the school, Chainey had had a long ministerial career, first as a Methodist and then, after 1877, as a Unitarian. He spent much of the 1880s touring the world as an independent author and lecturer on religion and mysticism. Chainey settled in Chicago during the 1890s and devoted himself to writing an interpretation of the Bible. In 1901 he began publishing *The Interpreter*, a monthly magazine through which he announced the school's programs and publicized its teachings. The first volumes of his projected 30-volume occult-metaphysical commentary on the scriptures, *The Unsealed Bible*, were published in 1902.

As the school's "conductor," Chainey identified three main teachings: (1) the knowableness of God, who is manifest in revelation; (2) the true relation between God and humanity; and (3) the law of immortal life. Chainey viewed his role to be that of interpreter of God's language of revelation. Revelation was of the essence or *amrit* of God. Present living revelation was to be appropriated through the interpretation of past revelation—hence Chainey's efforts to compose interpretative volumes on the various books of the Bible.

In the formative years of the school, Chainey conducted worship weekly on Sunday mornings and public classes on most weekdays. He also accepted a few private students who did more intense study in a resident home situation, the summer being spent in a resort center in Wisconsin. Chainey's work continued over the next two decades, during which the school's center was moved to Burnett, California, and then in the 1920s to Long Beach, California. By this time, Chainey had established Amrita University, which consisted of the Mahanaim School of Interpretation, which Chainey personally headed; the School for Parents, under the direction of Walt de Noir Church; the Emersonian Delsarte School of Life and Expression; and the School of Metaphysics, Psychology, and Healing, headed by Dr. Fredoon C. Birdi. The majority of Chainey's students studied through his correspondence course, though some did reside at the school in order to work under his personal direction.

Sources:

Chainey, George. *Deus Homo*. Boston: Christopher Publishing House, 1927.

———. *Time's Garland of Grace*. San Diego, CA: Charles Gardner, 1918.

———. *The Unsealed Bible*. London: Kegan Paul, Trench, Truebner & Co., 1902.

Mindstream Church of Universal Love

The Mindstream Church of Universal Love began in 1979 with a charter from the Universal Life Church of Modesto, California. It was headed by the Rev. Kenneth Donabie-Dixon and Wendie Gilmour Donabie-Dixon. The church had no set doctrine. Its prime mission was to assist members in discovering their own path in life. God was seen as a living part of all that is. Man's purpose is to return to the Godhead. This may be accomplished by living the Law of Love. This Law, the basic truth of existence, is "God is Law, Law is Love, and Love is God." Love for humans means providing the opportunity for others to do for themselves.

The church provided practical tools to assist members. These tools took the form of classes and individual sessions on dream study, development of psychic skills, meditation, spiritual healing, relaxation, goal setting, age regression and reincarnation, and motivation. Age regression was done without hypnosis. Under the direction of the church, monies were set aside to assist the development of self-sufficient communities across North America. The church published a periodical, *Spiritual Growth and Psychic Awareness*.

New Age Church of Truth

Gilbert N. Holloway (b. 1915) began his career as a lecturer and metaphysical teacher in the 1930s. He became aware, as a result of studies in Rosicrucianism and Theosophy, that he had psychic powers. In the 1960s, he became prominent as a psychic on radio and television, and large audiences flocked to hear his lectures and to obtain readings (the statements he uttered while in a psychic state). In 1967, he received a Pentecostal experience and spoke in tongues. In the mid-1960s Holloway established a community and center in Deming, New Mexico. After his conversion, this center became the Christ Light Community.

Through the 1970 and 1980s, Holloway and his wife, June Holloway, who specialized in healing work, continued to travel, lecture, and give psychic demonstrations. They built the Deming community into a New Age center. There was free movement in the programming between Pentecostal and psychic categories. Holloway wrote books and booklets and published a monthly newsletter for members and friends of the church. He was particularly adept at prophecy; predictions of future events composed much of the content of his publications.

Sources:

Holloway, Gilbert N. *E.S.P. and Your Super-Conscious*. Louisville, KY: Best Books, 1966.

———. *Let the Heart Speak*. Los Angeles: DeVorss & Co., 1951.

———. *New Ways of Unfoldment*. Deming, NM: New Age Truth Publications, n.d.

———. *Seven Prophetic Years*. Deming, NM: New Age Truth Publications, 1969.

———. *This Way Up*. Deming, NM: New Age Church of Truth, 1975.

New Age Samaritan Church

The New Age Samaritan Church was incorporated in 1961 by the Rev. Ruth McWilliams of Everett, Washington. The doctrine was eclectic, a combination of material from the New Testament, New Thought, metaphysical beliefs, Theosophy, Zen, and Spiritualism. The church espoused no system of beliefs, but professed to help its students and members to discover for themselves the spiritual laws. Its goals included helping the poor in body and spirit, relieving the suffering in the world, eliminating prejudice, and teaching the interrelation of all creatures. It practiced the various psychic arts, including "treasure mapping" as a means to achieving the heart's desire. This involved visualizing what one wanted as a means of obtaining it.

In 1967 there were four study groups and students engaged in correspondence across the United States. Attempts at contact have not been successful for several years and the church is presumed defunct.

The Only Fair Religion

The Only Fair Religion was founded by Saint Kenny and a group of his followers. Neither the identity of Saint Kenny, nor any of his group, is disclosed in the literature. During its active period, the group taught modern reincarnationism. Within this belief system, the universe is in constant flux, governed by natural laws. Souls progress through lower life-forms to higher ones. When a being evolves to a point of gaining a sense of awareness, it simultaneously acquires an immortal soul. It then moves through a series of incarnations which are necessary for its development. It eventually evolves to become a planetary ruling spirit. The system was known as the "Only Fair Religion" because it assured a balance of woe and happiness, explained evil and promised eventual salvation for all.

When the group was flourishing, new groups would form for the discussion of issues in light of modern reincarnationism. Members sought to unite in their concept of God and in their concern for justice, and true communion results. During this process, telepathy and psychic phenomena often occurred. While the group is now presumed defunct, in 1972, the Only Fair Religion claimed 10,000 members in Southern California, a figure based on the number of people successfully qualified to be group leaders.

People's Temple Christian (Disciples) Church

The People's Temple Christian (Disciples) Church was formed in 1955 in Indianapolis by the Rev. Jim Jones. (Though formally a member congregation in the Christian Church [Disciples of Christ], the People's Temple, in the 1970s, developed beliefs and practices that were very much different than those of its parent body.) Jones emerged in the 1960s as a charismatic leader who cared for the poor and the blacks of the city and preached a message of equality, brotherhood and socialism.

In 1965, a year after being ordained in the Christian Church (Disciples of Christ), he migrated with his following to Ukiah, California. From there the People's Church became a communal group modeled on the Peace Mission of Father Divine, whom Jones had known and revered. Though white himself, Jones gathered a largely black following who came to view him as a prophet and miracle worker. By 1972 Jones claimed that over 40 people had been raised from the dead. Church services featured psychic readings and healings by Jones, spirited singing, testimonies, and sermons. A wide range of social services was supported.

By 1972 congregations flourished in San Francisco, Los Angeles, and Indianapolis and there were followers in cities around the United States. That same year Jones leased land in Guyana which became a farming community, Jonestown. Jones became a prominent, controversial, but powerful figure in the California religious community, but also became an object of government investigation because of reports of violence directed toward ex-members and abuse of children under his care. Coincidental with the publication of several major media reports on the church and with the filing of several lawsuits, Jones moved with many of his members to Guyana.

By 1977 when Jones moved to Guyana, Jonestown had swelled to 1,000 residents. This town was the scene, in 1978, of the murder of Congressman Leo J. Ryan and several of his party, who came to Jonestown to investigate the charges which had been brought against it. Immediately following Ryan's murder was the mass suicide/murder of over 900 of the town's residents, including Jones. In 1978 the church was formally disbanded by the remaining members in California.

In the years since the deaths in Guyana, the People's Temple and its leader have become symbols of the possibilities inherent in religious groups and have frequently been invoked as the end result of cultic practice. As most of the papers assembled for the investigation of Congressman Ryan's death remain unpublished, the likelihood of substantive future revelations about Jones, the temple, and the deaths in Guyana remains high.

Sources:

Feinsof, Ethan. *Awake in a Nightmare*. New York: W. W. Norton & Co., 1981.

Klineman, George, and Sherman Butler. *The Cult That Died*. New York: G. B. Putnam's Sons, 1980.

Maaga, Mary McCormick. *Hearing the Voices of Jonestown: Putting a Human Face on an American Tragedy*. Syracuse, NY: Syracuse University Press, 1998.

Mills, Jeanne. *Six Years With God*. New York: A & W Publishers, 1979.

Reiterman, Tim, with John Jacobs. *Raven*. New York: E. P. Dutton, 1982.

Yee, Min S., and Thomas N. Layton. *In My Father's House*. New York: Holt, Rinehart & Winston, 1981.

Planetary Light Association

The Planetary Light Association was founded by Jann Weiss, a psychic medium who, in January 1983, began to channel messages from a spirit entity named Anoah. Anoah is considered to be a member of the Melchizedek Order of the White Brotherhood. His work was to assist in a smooth transition from the old age into the new. Under Anoah's direction, Golden Circle sessions were initiated. Each session consisted of a planetary meditation, a dissertation that Anoah delivered through Weiss, and a question and answer period. In July 1983 the Planetary Light Association was formed. It was dedicated to uplifting the planet through positive thought, word, and activity. By the fall of 1983 the association had a program that included psychic development workshops, books by Anoah, and a line of "Be Your Light and Be in Peace" products. A regular schedule of events in Texas and Washington was established. Through the cassette tapes and literature derived from the Golden Circle sessions, the organizations spread throughout the country. During its active period, the group issued the periodical *Planetary Beacon*. By 1986 "Anoah Material" was being communicated internationally.

Though the group is now presumed defunct, in 1987 the association reported 2,700 members in the United States and an additional 500 internationally.

Sources:

Achad, Frater. *Melchizedek Truth Principles*. Phoenix, AZ: Lockhart Research Foundation, 1963.

Weiss, Jann. *Reflections by Anoah*. Austin, TX: Planetary Light Association, 1986.

Process Church of the Final Judgment

The Process Church dates to 1963, when a group began to gather around the charismatic Robert de Grimston, then a resident of London. The group was primarily psychologically oriented to begin with, but its search led to a spiritual quest. In 1966, members spent several months at Xtul, Yucatan, which is viewed as a place of miracles and shared religious experiences. Those who went formed a closely knit group. Over the next seven years, a theology-in-process developed, primarily through the continued revelations of de Grimston. Development was rapid; significant changes could be noted annually and with each issue of the irregularly issued *Process*.

As the theology appeared in 1973, the central emphasis was a dualism of Christ and Satan overcome by a reconciliation expressed in the formula "The Unity of Christ and Satan is Good News for You. If that conflict can be resolved, then yours can be too." Behind this theme was a belief in the four deities: Jehovah, Lucifer, Christ, and Satan—each representative of a personality-type and a spiritual path. All doctrine was set within the context of a biblical apocalypticism.

To perpetuate the teaching, a strong hierarchical organization was established. Topping the hierarchy with de Grimston was a twelve-member Council of Masters. Ministers were called messengers. Initiated lay members were disciples and joined the ranks of the Inside Processeans, as opposed to the Outside Processeans who lived according to process teaching without initiation. Inside Processeans dressed in the black uniform and wore the cross with a snake entwined upon it.

The Process Church was dealt a fatal blow in 1974 when the majority of the Council of Masters rejected de Grimston's prophetic leadership (particularly his emphasis on satanic themes) and reorganized as the Foundation Church of the Millennium (now the Foundation Faith of God). Most of the members, including de Grimston's wife, aligned themselves with the new church.

The Process Church did not die completely with the schism. De Grimston reorganized the Process in a loose fashion and attempted to gather the remnant of followers into a very loose organization. He sent an open letter to his followers from his new home in New Orleans, encouraging them to form local autonomous groups around his teachings. Chapters formed in Boston and Toronto and smaller groups in Chicago, New Orleans, New York City, San Francisco, and London, England. A periodical, *The Process*, was published from the Boston headquarters. After several years it became evident that the organization could not be rebuilt, and de Grimston returned to England and obscurity. All signs of the Process disappeared before the end of the decade.

After a period without public manifestation, a remnant of the Process Church reappeared in the late 1980s. It was composed of a small number of former Process members who had remained believers in spite of the reverses of the 1970s. They attempted to establish contact with other members scattered around the country, but then again disappeared from public sight. Their present status is unknown.

Sources:

Assemblies and Hymns. Process Church of the Final Judgment, n.d.

Bainbridge, William Sims. *Satan's Power*. Berkeley and Los Angeles: University of California Press, 1978.

de Grimston, Robert. *Exit*. Letchworth, Herts., England: Garden City Press, 1968.

————. *The Gods and Their People*. Chicago: Process Church of the Final Judgment, 1970.

Facts and Figures, Some Questions and Answers about the Process Church. Chicago: Process Church, 1973.

Theocentric Foundation

The Theocentric Foundation was founded in 1959 in Phoenix, Arizona, but was the successor to a series of prior structures dating to the 1920s: the Shangrila Missions of Ojai, California, the Eden Foundation, the Manhattan Philosophical Center and the Theo-centric Temple. The basic teachings of the Foundation were Hermetic, based on the writing of Hermes Mercurious Trismegistus. The Bible and other metaphysical books were also used.

The Theocentric Foundation taught a doctrine of basic truth, the understanding of the divine self. In this understanding, the 73 "Gods of the walking dead," such as anger, fear, grief, domination, limitation, prejudice, etc., and the five basic questions (What am I? What is my origin? Why am I here? Where do I go? and What am I doing about it?) could be dealt with. According to this belief system, before man could recognize his divine origin, he must become fully human and possess attributes such as affection, discrimination, enthusiasm, justice, kindness and tenderness. These attributes would lead into the attributes of pure awareness, possessed by the self-governing identity. The self-governing identity was one that had conquered the outside forces that would dominate a person and embodied love, certainty, consideration, understanding, empathy, and admiration.

The headquarters of the Theocentric Foundation were in Phoenix. It had also established branch centers around the country, and classes were offered in Hermetic theology. Degrees were issued after completion of the courses. Inner-order courses of 10 degrees were also offered to students.

Sources:

Orpheus. *The Poimandres of Hermes Mercurius Trimegistus*. Phoenix, AZ: Theocentric Foundation, 1960.

True Church of Christ, International

The True Church of Christ, International, was formed by Christian Weyand of Buffalo, New York. It was described as the "nonprofit establishment of religion authorized by ecclesiastical authority of the True Bible Society International" (also headed by Weyand) and "the only existing Christian Church founded upon and teaching the *True Complete Christian Bible* and the *True Complete Teachings and Scriptures of God and Christ.*" The church published the *True Complete Bible*, which contained the Old and New Testaments translated from Aramaic; the *True New Testament*, containing the secret unwritten teachings of Jesus; the *Lost Books of the Bible* and the *Forgotten Books of Eden*, a collection of apocryphal writings, and the *Apocrypha*.

The True Church taught psychic development and mediumship, holding that the reason why no miracles occur in contemporary churches is because churches limit themselves to the Old and New Testament. The True Church believed Jesus taught hypnosis, miracle power and ESP. Further, the church held that man's soul, his life spirit, is part of God, the great creative intelligence. Psychic powers were believed to be natural to the soul and it was through these powers that all miracles were wrought. The church believed also that the water baptism of John was replaced with spirit baptism.

During its active period, the True Church advertised widely and offered its members around the country correspondence courses in the True Scriptures, hypnotism, and the psychic. The church also formed the World Roster of Psychic Contact, a prayer group.

Universal Brotherhood

The Universal Brotherhood was an occult group headquartered in New York City and headed by the Rev. Ureal Vercilli Charles. The Order was under the guidance of the Great White Brotherhood and offered lessons on the "Seven Immutable Laws of the Universe," man's key to health, success, and happiness. These laws were the laws of gender, cause/effect, rhythm, polarity, vibration, correspondence, and mentalism. Mr. Charles ran the First Church of Spiritual Vision in New York City. Other centers of the Brotherhood were in Jamaica, New York City, and the Bronx. *Lessons from the Great Masters* was a correspondence course taken by students across the United States. The Brotherhood also published *Wake Up and Learn!*, a series of pamphlets by Krishnahara, a Master of the Great Lodge who dictated through Elizabeth Dean. During its active period, the Universal Brotherhood also issued a periodical entitled *The Light Beyond*.

World Catalyst Church

The World Catalyst Church sought to be a catalyst in moving from old ideas to new. The church believed that there is an inner light that is beyond ourselves in wisdom, power and scope. The church's job was to lead men from their ignorant state to the eternal something within. Further, man's forward movement could be accomplished through his own efforts. Man was bound, however, by natural law and by his oneness with others. No man would enter eternal perfection until all were able to. Man was a microcosm of the macrocosm. He was reincarnated in any given dimension long enough to learn the necessary les-

sons. Prayer and meditation were considered useful tools in learning to live.

The World Catalyst Church had members around the United States, drawn from those who had taken the basic correspondence study course, "That Man May Find Himself." The course was also introductory material for any who wished to become teachers for the church. The church refused to put money into religious edifices. There was no charity assistance of a material nature. All monies went into communities. The church was formed in 1967 at Butte, Montana, by Helen Muschell (author of *Wells of Inner Space*), Margot Jones, Ese Jasper, Ernest Hanson, Ruth Adams, Beata Kamp, and Matt Gleason.

19. Western Esoteric III: Magick

INTRAFAITH ORGANIZATIONS

Alliance of the Phoenix

The Alliance of the Phoenix is an umbrella organization of independent houses (centers/groups) dedicated to the Netjer (Egyptian gods). Alliance was formed in the mid-1990s to provide a supportive forum for all who worship the Netjer by promoting fellowship and encouraging ongoing education. It is closely associated with the House of the Open Eye, a San Francisco-based Egyptian Neopagan group.

American Council of Witches

While several Pagan-wide ecumenical fellowships formed in the early 1970s, there was a need felt by some Neopagan witches for a similar group based in the Gardnerian witchcraft or Wiccan movement. Taking the lead in building such a structure was Carl Weschcke, owner of Llewellyn Publications and publisher of *Gnostica* magazine. In 1974 he called together a meeting of Wiccan leaders and members to be held in Minneapolis, Minnesota. At that meeting the council was formed and officers elected. Weschcke was chosen to head the council.

Possibly the most important work of the council was that it issued a lengthy statement, the "Principles of Wiccan Beliefs," which summarized the consensus of belief of those groups that had emerged out of the Gardnerian Witchcraft revival. It affirmed witchcraft as a nature-oriented religion based in rites attuned to the natural rhythms of life, exemplified in the phases of the moon and the seasonal movement of the sun. Wiccans sought to live in harmony with nature. They believed the Creative Power of the universe was manifested in polarity, male and female, and they valued sex as pleasure, the symbol and embodiment of life, to be utilized as a source of energy in worship and magical practice. The statement went on to emphasize the nonhierarchical nature of the Wiccan move-

ment and their nonbelief in "absolute evil" or the concept of "Satan" or the "devil."

The council immediately ran into the fierce independency of Wiccans, many of whom saw any attempt to organize above the coven level as an attempt to control. While many gave tacit approval to the council, it was never able to function as it was designed. It survived into the early 1980s.

Council of Themis

The Council of Themis was an early attempt to form a cooperative ecumenical organization among the new Neo-Pagan groups which were emerging around the United States. It was founded by Fred Adams and Richard Stanewick of Feraferia in January 1969. They had previously received correspondence about such an organization from Tim Zell, the founder of the Church of All Worlds (CAW) and editor of possibly the most popular Pagan periodical at the time, *Green Egg*. Feraferia and CAW jointly administered the council. Among the early members of the council were the Dancers of the Sacred Circle, the Ordo Templi Astarte, the Delphic Fellowship, the Psychedelic Venus Church, the Church of the Eternal Source, a variety of Wiccan covens, and the Hellenic Group, a member of the council in the United Kingdom.

The council, named for the Aegean goddess Themis, conceived of itself as a trans-sectarian council of Nature religions and had as its goal to serve as a forum for the exchange of information. It accepted as a common basis of association a belief in polytheism, worship of Nature focusing on the goddess and god as divine lovers, and reincarnation. It advocated freedom of worship, an openness to eroticism, nonviolence, and a mythic approach to reality.

The council prospered for several years. Most of the member groups were located in Southern California, but its active leadership was offered by the St. Louis, Missouri–based Church of All Worlds, the largest Pagan group in terms of membership. In 1972 the council moved to expel two members, the Psychedelic Venus Church and the Hellenic Group. The former was accused of public advocacy of the use of illegal drugs and the public exploitation of sexual practices. The Hellenic Group had advocated a public "bloody sacrifice" of a lamb. The actions provoked intense debate within the council, which led to its splitting; those members who left formed the Pagan Ecumenical Council. While the Council of Themis survived for several more years, it was an ineffective organization and for all practical purposes had ceased to exist.

An account of the Council of Themis, highly disputed as to its accuracy, appeared in *The New Pagans* by popular occult writer Hans Holzer (Doubleday, 1972). More accurate information can be found in the several official publications of the council and the pages of the *Green Egg*.

Pagan Ecumenical Council

The Pagan Ecumenical Council was an early, short-lived Pagan ecumenical association founded in 1972 following a split in the Council of Themis. The council, possibly the earliest of the Neo-Pagan efforts to build a cooperative body, expelled two members for un-Paganlike activities. Both the method and legality of the expulsion were questioned by various members of the Council of Themis, some of whom accused co-founder Fred Adams of Fereferia of assuming dictatorial powers. They left and founded the rival Pagan Ecumenical Council. Leading members of the new council included the Church of All Worlds, Church of the Eternal Source, the Rainbow Coven (a Wiccan group), the Dancers of the Sacred Circle, and popular writer Ed Fitch, associated with the Pagan Way. The new council was to be democratically organized and within the first year grew to include some five member groups.

The council continued to function for a few years but soon died as the Pagan movement, especially in Southern California.

RITUAL MAGICK

American Gnostic Church

The American Gnostic Church was founded in 1985 by Rev. James M. Martin. It served as an umbrella organization for several closely related spiritual movements, each claiming some form of illumination by stellar-gnosis. The church's ministry had a special concern for connections and cognate deities in both the Gnostic systems and the Oriental religions. The latest groups with which it maintained a relationship were the Servants of the Star and the Snake, a tantric-thelemic "federation" of magicians, sorcerers, witches, pagans, shamans, Natha yogis who network online and through several periodicals, and an S.S.S. SIG or special interest group, the Order of Napunsakas in the West (O.N.) which maintained an Outer Order for all nonheterosexual tantrikas and an Inner Order open only to males, known as the Cultus Skanda-Karttikeya (C.S.-K.). Both Tantra and Thelema (the system developed by Aleister Crowley) had sex magick as an essential component in their magical teachings.

Sources:

Crowley, Aleister. *The Law Is for All*. Phoenix, AZ: Falcon Press, 1985.

————. *Magick in Theory and Practice*. New York: Dover Publications, 1976.

King, Francis, and Stephen Skinner. *Techniques of High Magick*. New York: Destiny Books, 1976.

Bavarian Illuminati

The Bavarian Illuminati was founded in 1776 by the infamous Dr. Adam Weishaupt, a professor of canon law at the University of Ingoldstadt in Germany. The group associated with the Masons and gained a reputation as a secret revolutionary body. The group was present in England as the Hell-Fire Club headed by Sir Francis Dashwood. (This English group is supposedly the source of a flirtation with Masonry by the founding fathers of the United States, who allegedly placed the Illuminati pyramid and the Eye of Horus on the Great Seal of the United States.)

A modern version of the Order of the Illuminati was established during the 1970s with headquarters in San Francisco, California, and Nantes, France. It was one of a variety of half-serious/half-joking organizations created by magician-author Robert Anton Wilson, more recently a resident of Ireland. Wilson has authored a series of books on magick and occult philosophy using the Illuminatus metaphor but drawing its content from the twentieth-century Thelemic magick of Aleister Crowley and modern psychical and consciousness studies. Since Wilson's departure from the United States there are no formal representatives of the modern order, though it could be seen to have continued informally among Wilson's large reading audience. Even in the 1970s, the order existed only as a loose confederation of independent but like-minded magicians. It existed primarily to pursue Thelemic magick, as Wilson thought of Aleister Crowley as the twentieth-century inventor of the Illuminati tradition. Adherents were also devotees of Eris, the goddess of chaos and discord. The order was a confederation of like-minded magicians who helped each other through any problematic times in magical practice.

Sources:

Holmes, Donald. *The Sapiens System: The Illuminati Conspiracy*. Phoenix, AZ: Falcon Press, 1987.

Wilgus, Neal. *The Illuminoids*. New York: Pocket Books, 1978.

Wilson, Robert Anton. *Cosmic Trigger*. Berkeley, CA: And/Or Press, 1977.

————. *The Illuminati Papers*. Berkeley, CA: And/Or Press, 1980.

————. *Masks of the Illuminati*. New York: Pocket Books, 1981.

————. *Schroedinger's Cat*. 3 vols. New York: Pocket Books, 1980–1981.

Bennu Phoenix Temple of the Hermetic Order of the Golden Dawn

A short-lived attempt to revive the Hermetic Order of the Golden Dawn (HOGD) emerged in the early 1970s, led by John Phillips Palmer. The Bennu Phoenix Temple continued the tradition of the HOGD prior to the revelations of its secrets by Aleister Crowley. Crowley was viewed as a former member "impervious to discipline ... consequently degraded to the Paths of the Portal in the Vault of Adepti and expelled." The group also followed the tradition which rejected S. L. MacGregor Mathers's leadership. He is believed to have fallen to the dark powers of the left-hand path.

The Bennu Phoenix Temple followed the ten rituals of the Order of the Golden Dawn and used forms of the rituals published by Israel Regardie. Sex magick was allowed if practiced within the context of marriage. Sex magick outside of marriage with a homosexual partner or as a mystic masturbation was strictly condemned. Homosexual behavior was regarded as impure. Drugs and animal sacrifice were also forbidden.

Sources:

Regardie, Israel. *The Golden Dawn*. St. Paul, MN: Llewellyn Publications, 1969.

Fellowship of Ma-Ion

In 1904, Aleister Crowley received *The Book of the Law*, which became the new revelation for Thelemic magicians. The revelation included the prediction of a "child" who would "discover the key of it all." In 1915 Crowley carried out a series of sex magick workings with Jane Foster. Nine months later Charles Stansfeld Jones (d. 1950), known within thelemic circles as Frater Achad, proclaimed his assumption of the magical grade of Master of the Temple. Crowley accepted Achad as a magical child, i.e., a product of his own magical workings. Over the next 18 months, Achad worked out the kabbalistic formulas which allowed Crowley to interpret some of the obscure passages of *The Book of the Law*.

In spite of Crowley's acceptance of Achad as the child, in 1919 they broke relations, never to be associated again (though they periodically corresponded.) Achad wrote several books based upon his speculations on the kabbalah (qabala), but his interpretations never gained wide acceptance. Achad moved to London in the late 1920s. He initiated a period of intense self-reflection which issued forth in a new perspective which he termed the "arising of the Silver Star," artistically depicted as a silver pentagram in a blue circle. In 1932 he composed a set of magical rituals and in the spring opened the Immanual Lodge. The work of the lodge bore magical fruit 16 years later when Achad proclaimed the arrival of the Aeon of Ma, the manifestation of Truth and Justice. (Maat was the ancient Egyptian goddess of Truth and Justice.) The Aeon of Ma superseded the Aeon of Horus proclaimed by Crowley in 1904. The Aeon was never announced publicly, but communicated to a few magicians in private letters.

According to some sources, a small following who responded to the proclamation of the Aeon of Ma and who followed Achad's unique interpretation of the kabbalah formed an informal Fellowship of Ma-Ion which had members in both England and America. No verification of the existence of this group has been located. In the 1970s, in the wake of the publication of much of Aleister Crowley's materials and material on the Aeon of Ma(at), several groups have arisen which have developed a Maatian perspective, but these have arisen without any connection with or even knowledge of a Fellowship of Ma-Ion. (See separate entry on Ordo Adeptorum Invisiblum.)

Sources:

Achad, Frater [Charles Stansfeld Jones]. *The Anatomy of the Body of God*. New York: Samuel Weiser, 1969.

Achad, Frater. *The Egyptian Revival*. New York: Samuel Weiser, 1969.

King, Francis. *Ritual Magic in England*. London: Neville Spearman, 1970.

Foundation, A Hermetic Society

The foundation was organized in 1971 by W. E. Stone, Jr., for the purpose of establishing a definite procedure for the study of ritual magick. Study was based upon the work of the Hermetic Order of the Golden Dawn. Insights of such magicians as William E. Butler, William G. Gray, Gareth Knight, and Israel Regardie were utilized. Membership in the foundation was not solicited, but the leadership was quite open in sharing its findings with a wider audience through published articles and open lectures. In 1972, there were fewer than 20 members. The organization lasted only a few years.

The foundation offered students a method of ceremonial magick as a "determined effort to establish a working relationship through himself between his lower and higher selves." The form was modernized in line with what was viewed as the natural evolution of the art. Group work was stressed; several working together increase the power available. Beginning as a neophyte, the student passed through four degrees to the portal series. Along the way, he learned the basics of occultism, meditation, astrology, Tarot, Kabbalah, various forms of divination, and psychic development. The portal series was training in pure magick. Headquarters were in Houston, Texas.

Fraternity of Light

The Fraternity of Light was formed in Philadelphia by a small group of Qabalistic magicians. It drew on the tradition of the Hermetic Order of the Golden Dawn but has no organizational connection. The fraternity taught that individuals are essentially a spark of divine consciousness which exists eternally and periodically clothes itself in a series of sheaths or bodies, the most dense of which is the physical. At death, the spark and its several bodies leave the physical and three days later the less dense bodies separate from the more dense. The spark may be attracted to a vortex created by two individuals during the sex act. If conditions are right and the woman's egg is fertilized, then the spark will begin to build a new set of bodies which enter the baby's physical body at the time of birth.

This evolutionary process which repeats itself many times was termed reincarnation. The fraternity held that when the spark evolves enough, it no longer needs a physical body. Eventually everyone would complete the evolutionary process. The work of the fraternity was toward assisting people to speed the normal course of evolving. To this end the fraternity offered a set of lessons and involvement in ritual practice.

The lessons of the fraternity consisted of a philosophy course in two levels. Probationers, after completing the course, could join the fraternity as neophytes and were accepted into either the Order of the Holy Grail or the Coven of Diana. The order offers course work in a Celtic approach to magic. The coven explores witchcraft, mysticism, and moon magic. Membership in both groups was prohibited. After completion of either the coven's or the order's study course, the initiate was able to become a full member of the fraternity through the Order of the Golden Sword. Membership began with a 20-lesson series in ritual magic. Members at all levels were required to agree to refrain from the use of any illegal drugs.

The fraternity also scheduled a regular series of rituals, both weekly and quarterly; additional rituals at the solstices and equinoxes; and individual initiations. As members become involved in the ritual life, they were introduced to the Scroll of Daath, the fraternity's holy book. Copies were available only to fraternity members who received them on loan. Members leaving the fraternity were asked to return their copy.

The Fraternity of Light differed from many magical orders by its focus upon the All-Mother in its rituals. Integral to this focus was the importance of the high priestess as the chief spiritual guide and ritual leader of the group. Women participated fully at all levels of the fraternity.

The fraternity was headed by the Group Guide, the High Priest, and the High Priestess. Within the core of the fraternity were two secret circles. The Circle of the Pentacle was an elite group which managed the fraternity and did advanced work and study. The Brotherhood of the Cup was engaged in esoteric (magical) work under the direction of the Group Guide and the Inner Plane Adepti (i.e., those advanced sparks who have evolved beyond a need for a body and who guide the work of the fraternity from their present elevated state).

Sources:

Gerber, Jack. "Paganism Is Where? In Philadelphia." *Gnostica* 4, no. 9 (July 1975).

The Path of Light. Philadelphia: Fraternity of Light, 1974.

International Academy of Hermetic Knowledge

The International Academy of Hermetic Knowledge was founded in 1991 as the outer court of an older magickal group, the Holy Order of the Winged Disk. The Holy Order was inspired by the predynastic teaching of ancient Egypt and its teachings were given only by oral instruction. Its teachings were secret and shared only with members.

The International Academy was the organization through which the teachings of the Holy Order were released to the public. The occasion of its formation was the observed development of a growing popular interest in alternative spirituality (Wicca, New Age, Eastern philosophy, and Magic). The Academy's curriculum concentrated on practical techniques for spiritual development.

Through the Academy, the esoteric knowledge of the Holy Order was written down in a book, *The Practical Arcanum*, and a series of monographs that were distributed to the Academy's students. The monographs were written by Phaedron, the Hierophant of the Holy Order. People were invited to Academy membership initially for a year. They were tested on their mastery of the information in the monographs. Those who passed the tests and wished to continue were allowed to pursue a second year and third year. Work in the Academy put its students in contact with the Holy Order and opened the possibility for membership in that organization.

New England Institute of Metaphysical Studies

The New England Institute of Metaphysical Studies was founded in the early 1970s by Ron Parshley and Mark Feldman as a correspondence school dedicated to the pursuit of occult knowledge. It was the Institute's perspective that Aleister Crowley placed magick in a system open to all. Through its own P-F Publications, it published the five-volume *Theorems of Occult Magick* by Feldman and Parshley as a study in Crowley's teachings. It also offered 17 courses in occultism, divination, witchcraft, and magick. A quarterly newsletter was sent to all students. Also associated was *Tamlacht*, published three times a year by Victor Boruta of Linden, New Jersey. Headquarters were in Methuen, Massachusetts.

Sources:

Feldman, Mark, and Ron Parshley. *Theorems of Occult Magick*. 10 vols. Methuen, MA: P-F Publications, 1971.

Ordo Lux Kethri

The Ordo Lux Kethri (the Order of the Kethric Light) was formed in 1982 by April Schadler Bishop and Michael Albion Macdonald, both former initiates of the Builders of the Adytum, through which they claim lineage from the Hermetic Order of the Golden Dawn. The order is similar in structure to the Rosicrucians and considers itself a fraternal order. Studies include Qabala (kabbalah), alchemy, hermetic meditation, and ritual magick. The initiatory grades, 10 in number, of the Golden Dawn system are followed. The hermetic teachings of Franz Bardon are used, especially his techniques of visualization and astral travel.

Though the order is now presumed defunct, in 1987 it had 14 members in one group. At that same time, there was a second group, the Persephone

Lodge, in the process of formation in London, England.

Sources:

Bardon, Franz. *The Key to the True Quabbalah.*
  Wuppertal, West Germany: Deiter Rueggeberg, 1971.
————. *The Practice of Magical Evocation.*
  Wuppertal, West Germany: Deiter Rueggeberg, 1970.
Macdonald, Michael-Albion. *The Secret of Secrets.*
  Berkeley Heights, NJ: Heptangle, 1986.

Ordo Templi Orientis (Roanoke, Virginia)

The Ordo Templi Orientis headquartered in Roanoke, Virginia, had claimed to be the true Ordo Templi Orientis (OTO). It rejected the claims of the other groups which had emerged in the 1970s based on a charter or lineage dating to Aleister Crowley. Its head was Robert E. L. Shell, who saw the mission of the OTO as preventing "hard-won knowledge from being lost in the upheavals and birth pangs of the Aeon Horus [the new era announced by Crowley in 1904]...." One must validate claims by proving allegiance to the law of Thelema, or the Will, the primary principle guiding thought and action for Crowley's disciples. The goal is the Great Work, the ultimate lifting of all humanity to the status of gods. Shell claimed contact with the secret chiefs, the entities (much like the theosophical Great White Brotherhood), who guided the order from the inner planes of existence.

Shrine of Sothis

The Shrine of Sothis made its appearance in 1973 by way of some ads in psychic/occult periodicals. It taught a system of practical theurgy (magick) as the highest and most efficient mode of communication between man and his inner self. A complete set of lessons, which could be obtained on a correspondence basis, took the student step-by-step through the magical disciplines. The student was taught about the pentagram (a disc-shaped talisman), the gods, initiation, reincarnation, black magick, divination, the construction of talismans, and invocation. The goal of the lessons was to lift the student into the realization of the "great concealed one," God. Students practiced daily devotions and orations in their own homes. Members joined by paying an initiation fee. Headquarters were in San Francisco. After several years of operation, the order dropped out of sight.

WICCAN RELIGION AND CONTEMPORARY PAGANISM

American Order of the Brotherhood of Wicca

The American Order of the Brotherhood of Wicca was an eclectic traditional Wiccan group headed by Lady Sheba (Jessie Wicker Bell). American Celtic was the name given the covens, which combined Lady Sheba's Celtic heritage and American Indian magical tradition. Lady Sheba was initiated into the craft in the 1930s.

She became the focus of controversy in the early 1970s for publishing her *Grimoire* and *Book of Shadows*, thus making public secret rituals and practices. These rituals turned out to be slightly revised versions of the Gardnerian rituals. She also referred to herself as a Witch Queen, a title used in Gardnerian Wicca for a priestess who has raised coven members to the third degree and sent them out to form a new coven. The title was rejected by many of the more individualistic craft members.

Lady Sheba defined witch as "the wise one" and witchcraft as "magick," denying that it was nature worship or a fertility cult. To her, witchcraft was learning to manipulate and use the natural laws. Nature was the physical manifestation of the creator, who appeared as Mother-Father. Astrology was also an important aspect of witchcraft. Lady Sheba's rituals adhered to the traditional Gardnerian Wiccan forms—the circle, the rituals, the three degrees, the eight festivals and covens of 13 or fewer persons. They differed primarily in espousing a robed tradition (Gardnerian rituals are done in the nude). Couples and family relations were emphasized.

The American Order was organized into dependent covens tied together by their relationship to Lady Sheba, who was recognized as having come from a long line of witches. Covens were located across the United States, and there were a few overseas.

During the 1970s, at the time Lady Sheba's books were being published, the American Order was among the most active groups in promoting interaction and cooperation among witches of various traditions. Much of the organizational leadership was assumed by Carl Weschcke, owner-publisher of Llewellyn Publications, who had been initiated by Lady Sheba. In 1973, the Twin Cities Area Council of the American Order of the Brotherhood of Wicca was formed as a council of coven leaders, and all traditions were invited to participate. In 1974, the Order was a strong force behind the formation of the short-lived ecumenical organization, the Council of American Witches. In more recent years the Order has assumed a much lower profile, and its current status is uncertain. During its last known active period, there were only a few covens associated with the order.

Sources:

Sheba, Lady [Jessie Wicker Bell]. *The Grimoire of Lady Sheba.* St. Paul, MN: Llewellyn Publications, 1974
————. *Witch.* St. Paul, MN: Llewellyn Publications, 1973.

Church of Aphrodite, Goddess of Love

The Church of Aphrodite, Goddess of Love, was founded in 1939 on West Hempstead, Long Island, New York, by Gleb Botkin (1900–1969). Born and raised in Russia, the son of the tsar's personal physician, he trained for the Russian Orthodox Church priesthood, but prior to ordination he had a change of

heart. He decided that Aphrodite, the ancient Greek goddess of love, was a more appropriate object of his worship. Before Botkin was able to start a church in Russia, the 1917 revolution began. He fled to Japan and finally came to the United States in 1923. During the following years Botkin provided for his family by writing about his homeland. However, he never gave up his belief and he finally founded his church in his Long Island home. He acquired a copy of the life-sized statue *Venus de' Medici* as a worship center.

By the time the church was formally chartered, it had some 50 members. Botkin was a monotheist of the feminine principle and believed the "Eternal Feminine" was a truer personal symbol of the Divine than its masculine counterpart. The church's creedal statement affirmed a belief in Aphrodite, described as "the flower-faced, sweetly-smelling, laughter-loving Goddess of Love and Beauty." He was committed to the ideal of love as a primal virtue and advocated the concept of love both as ethical goodwill toward the neighbor and as an affinity with a beloved individual. He also favored greater freedom between the sexes as a means of reducing passion. Sex was seen as an ideal, divine and wonderful. Botkin believed in conditional immortality; one could gain immortal life by coming into a relationship with Aphrodite. Worship was held four times weekly, on Sunday morning and afternoon and on Friday and Saturday evenings.

Botkin lived in New York for a number of years but at some point moved to Charlottesville, Virginia, where he died in 1969. The church ceased to exist at that time.

Sources:

"Church of Aphrodite." *Newsweek* (November 27, 1939): 32.
"Church of Aphrodite, Goddess of Love Is Chartered in New York." *Life* (December 4, 1939): 101.

Church of the Most High Goddess

The Church of the Most High Goddess was a Neo-Pagan organization founded in 1986 by Mary Ellen Tracy and her husband, Wilbur Tracy. According to Wilbur Tracy, the church grew out of a 1984 revelation enabling him to discover the existence of a priestess with a lineage back to ancient Egypt. She could not publicly assume her religious functions, but she ordained him. Mary Ellen Tracy soon had a similar revelation and was trained and ordained as a priestess by her husband.

The church taught and practiced a form of hedonism, a philosophy that sees the search for pleasure as the goal of life. The church drew its inspiration from ancient Egypt, which it also saw as the originating point of Christianity. Thus, members considered themselves Christian but denied any relation to Judaism. They believed that Mary Magdalene was a priestess of Isis (or Eastar) and that it was to her that Jesus first appeared after his resurrection (also an old

Egyptian belief). Jesus entrusted the church to Mary Magdalene, but the apostles later wrestled control away from her.

The essence of the church's practice was found in the rituals, the ordinances of the Goddess. The nature of these rituals was only hinted at in the church's few pieces of literature. Participation in the series of rituals was deemed necessary for individual progress. They began with confession, a personal acknowledgment of one's spiritual state. Dedication (or commitment) was an act of devotion that led to a higher order of hedonism. A sacrifice, or offering, was required as a sign of dedication. Immersion was the preparatory ritual for the communication through the Goddess, represented by the priestess.

In 1989 the Tracys were arrested for prostitution. The State of California charged that the church was merely a cover for their operating a house of prostitution and that the rituals, which involved oral sex (dedication), the payment of a sum of money (sacrifice), and intercourse (immersion) constituted simple sex for money. The Tracys were convicted and pursued an appeal, claiming interference with their right to freely practice their religion.

Sources:

Bush, G. M. "Priestess or Prostitute? Municipal Court to Consider Freedom-of-Religion Defense." *Los Angeles Daily Journal* (July 12, 1989).

"The Church of the Most High Goddess." N.p., 1987. Tract.

Church of the Wyccan Rede

The Church of the Wyccan Rede was a Celtic traditional Witchcraft group headed by Lady Cybele and headquartered in Madison, Wisconsin. The Goddess and Horned God were worshipped, the former taking slight precedence. The Goddess was thought to rule from Yule to Midsummer's Eve and the God the other half of the year. The eight sabbats were also celebrated. Midsummer's Eve was the most important. The sabbats were concluded with a shared meal. There were also regular esbats.

Worship was within the circle. Members took turns in being the coven leader and conducting the ceremonies. There were no overt sexual activities involved in the rituals. Oneness with nature was the prime goal. Members were pacifistic and charitable, and they refused reward for their services. Black magic and satanism were strongly condemned.

For several years, Lady Cybele managed the Cauldron, an occult supply store and center. It offered lectures on occult topics, psychic readings, books, and health food. Lady Cybele, an herbalist, incorporated her knowledge of herbs into her teachings. Associated with the Church of the Wyccan Rede was a coven in Milwaukee headed by Frederic A. Buchholtz, who was the operator of Sanctum Regnum, an occult supply and bookshop.

Church of Universal Forces

The Church of Universal Forces was a Neopagan nature-oriented religion founded in Columbus, Ohio, in 1980 by Lady Isis and Lord Adonis. It taught a system of pantheism that emphasized freedom, joy, and self-worth. The church emphasized the right and privilege of religious freedom and championed a "live and let live" philosophy. At the same time, the church was opposed to those forms of religion that are preoccupied with sin and suffering to the extent that followers are not allowed to develop their own individuality.

The Church of Universal Forces acknowledged the Godhead of the Divine as the root of humanity. The Godhead, known under many names of gods and goddesses, is both male and female in equal portions. The Godhead was to be worshipped daily. Members were encouraged to have daily devotions in their homes and to raise their children in the knowledge of the deities.

Ethically the church followed the Rede, "That ye harm none, do what you will." It also encouraged members to develop a spirit of brotherly love toward one another and to watch over other members, especially in times of illness. Members were advised to be slow to take offense and quick to seek reconciliation with any members with whom they had differences.

The church developed its own variation on the Neo-Pagan rituals. It taught development of psychic ability and affirmed a belief in astrology. It offered a course on magick and magical religions whose graduates were ready to form their own groups. The church also operated an occult supply house and offered a course to the general public on various occult and related topics.

Congregation of Aten

A growing split within the Pristine Egyptian Orthodox Church led in 1974 to a schism and the withdrawal of Milton J. Neruda, who then formed the Congregation of Aten. At least one issue in the schism was the method of approaching the dominant American Christian faith. Neruda argued that Christianity was heavily reliant on Egyptian religion for such concepts as the Trinity, the virgin birth, Christmas, and resurrection. He took a highly polemical stance with respect to the Christian faith. The Egyptian faith of the congregation of Aten offered answers "to one who is not blinded by prejudice and ignorance. Knowledge is the only path to true salvation!" The Pristine Egyptian Orthodox Church had taken a much milder stance. Neruda's congregation existed for several years in Chicago.

Dancers of the Sacred Circle

Closely related to Feraferia were the Dancers of the Sacred Circle, founded in the early 1970s by Richard Stanewick. Stanewick was one of the founders of Ferefeira and served as its secretary until he moved to the San Francisco area and formed an autonomous group. Headquarters for the Dancers were near Redway, California, on a 40-acre nature sanctuary.

The Dancers attempted to build a total life based on the central figure of the Maiden divinity. Devotions were daily and seasonal and had both aesthetic and erotic emphases. Included were wilderness mysteries, henge rites (a henge is an open-air ring temple), and work in the maintenance and creation of gardens, orchards, and wilderness shrines. The group was small, consisting of Richard, his wife, Phyllis Stanewick, and a few adherents. It disbanded in the early 1980s.

Delphic Coven

Among the early Goddess-worshipping groups in the United States was the Celtic traditional Delphic Coven founded by Bonnie Sherlock, who operated from a small town in Wyoming. According to Sherlock, the tradition had been handed down through the family, which migrated from Scotland in 1570, first to Ireland and later to America. Sherlock was taught the craft by her great-grandmother, who imparted the first two initiations. The third was received from a Sioux medicine man.

The group claimed Celtic origins "in that we take our muse from the Cauldron of the Kerridwen, and will at length become as the radiant browed Taliesin." Egyptian and American Indian elements were added, though a basic dualistic cosmology remained. "The dragon of darkness is the great fetter of ignorance which we must overcome through educational enlightenment, communication, and involvement with others who are likeminded." Included in the group's beliefs were reincarnation and karma (the consequences of good and bad actions from former incarnations). Creative expression, primarily through arts, was a major theme; ecology and love of nature, especially as expressed in reverence of the mountain environment, were also emphasized. "The earth is a living, breathing thing to be reverenced and looked after, as are all the lesser creatures." Even the Horned God was visualized as a "Big Horned Sheep." Several issues of a periodical, the *Medicine Wheel*, were published. The coven dissolved following Sherlock's death in the late 1970s.

Delphic Fellowship

The Delphic Fellowship originated in 1967 when Michael Kinghorn and Donald D. Harrison began to publish the *Julian Review* as a forum of discussion of the Pagan religion. The fellowship was formed the following year with the intent of restoring the heritage of Greece and rightful homage to the gods. The group initiated a program to acquaint people of Christian, Jewish, and agnostic/atheistic backgrounds with the Pagan option.

The Delphic Fellowship took its inspiration from the ancient oracle at Delphi. It worshipped the Greek pantheon, headed by Zeus. The Delphian Affirmations asserted belief in the plurality of Gods; in the experience of the wholeness of nature; in the sacred character of the Cosmos (and the denial of its fall); in man as a child of Holy Earth; in moral freedom; and in the beauty, purity, and holiness of man's sexuality. It was further affirmed that the instinct to survive is natural and pleasing to the gods and that man's posture toward nature should be one of reverence and joyous participation. Central to the fellowship's beliefs were the Sacred Precepts of Elder Delphi, especially his admonition "Know Thyself; Nothing in Excess."

The Delphic Fellowship was small and largely superseded by the Church of the Eternal Source, an Egyptian Pagan group that Harrison helped found. The headquarters of the Delphic Fellowship were in Los Angeles.

Earthstar Temple

The New York Coven of Welsh Traditionalist Witches was a group headed in the early 1970s by Ed Buczynski, better known by his ritual name, Hermes, who had taken the Celtic rituals used by Gwen Thompson of the New England Traditionalist coven and adapted them for use by a group in Brooklyn, New York. The form of Wicca the group followed is called Gwyddoniaid and is traced to the mixture of Celtic (male deity) and Pictish (female deity) religions in Wales. Followers worship the Earth Mother in her ninefold aspects and the Horned God.

Covens are limited to 13 male and female members, chosen alternately. Each coven is under the guidance of a high priest and high priestess. (Each coven is autonomous but is tied to others by similar rituals and laws.) The high priestess is ascendent, in keeping with the matriarchal orientation. There are weekly and monthly (on the full moon) rituals as well as the eight sabbats. No magick is worked at the latter. Power usually raised for magick is "given directly to the god in loving sacrifice." Worship is done within a nine-foot circle. Identical red robes are worn, emphasizing the equality of individuals before the gods.

The New York coven came into prominence in the early 1970s when Buczynski and Herman Slater became public advocates for the Craft. They presented awards to the Inquisitional Bigot of the Year through Friends of the Craft, an affiliated organization. They also operated the Warlock Shop, an occult supplies store in Brooklyn, and for several years published *Earth Religion News*. In the late 1970s Slater, who had absorbed some elements of ritual magick into his practice, assumed leadership of the group and store. He moved both to Manhattan. The group was renamed Earthstar and the store named the Magickal Childe. Slater periodically sponsored large festive gatherings of Neo-Pagans, witches, and magicians in New York City.

Buczynski died in 1989 and Slater in 1992. After Slater's death, friends continued operating the Magickal Childe until it finally closed its doors in 1999.

Sources:

Buczynski, Edmund M. *Witchcraft Fact Book*. New York: Magickal Childe, n.d.

Slater, Herman, ed. *The Magickal Formulary*. New York: Magickal Childe, 1981.

First Occult Church

The First Occult Church was an eclectic Pagan church formed in the early 1990s. It welcomed all who shared an interest in occultism and magick from the range of possible perspectives, including Wicca, ritual magick, vodou, Norse Paganism, and other related systems. Members of the church condemned the idea that there is only one way to spiritual truth but also saw patriarchal monotheism (which would include Judaism, Christianity, and Islam) as outside the realm of their belief—teachings that produce self-hatred, sexism, racism, and homophobia.

Distinct from most groups that operate in the Wiccan/Neo-Pagan context, the First Occult Church was open to satanic religious expressions. "Manifesto 13," their statement of belief, noted that members were not to equate dark with "evil" and light with "good" and that magick is neither black nor white but varies with the intent of the practitioner.

Organizations within the church included the Coven of the Blue Candle, a traditional Wiccan group; the Temple of Aradia, a relatively new form of Witchcraft created by Lady Ygraine and based upon *Aradia: The Gospel of the Witches* by Charles Leland; and the Order of the Infernal Grotto, a satanic order headed by a former agent of the Church of Satan. The order had an inner circle called the Order of the Apocalypse. It followed what is termed "Infernal Paganism," which merged satanic thought with pre- and post-Christian Pagan theories and practices.

Manifesto 13, whose first command was "Thou shalt not bore the gods," articulated the church's stance as a group of socially aware Pagans. They believed that magick should not become a means of escaping the world. Members were to engage in activities that benefited the whole and avoid those activities that hurt it. Thus members were called upon to support Pagan neighbors, avoid scapegoating, work to change unjust laws, and keep up a program of learning.

The church's board of directors, called the Cauldron, was led by Rev. Lady Ygraine as president and high priestess, and her husband, Rev. William Gidney, vice president and high priest. Board members included Lady Dymphna Reynard, Sabre Wilde, Vulcan Lupus, and the church guardian, Snow Eagle. William and Ygraine Gidney produced several occult documentaries, including *The War against God: Occultism in Your Backyard*, and published a periodical, *A Taste from the Cauldron*. The church did not report membership statistics but indicated that members were found across the United States and in several foreign countries.

First Wiccan Church of Minnesota

The First Wiccan Church of Minnesota grew out of the Camelot of the Star of the North Coven of the American Order of the Brotherhood of Wicca, a Wiccan group founded by Lady Sheba. The church was formed by Carl Weschcke (Gnosticus) and his wife Sandra Weschcke (Kashta) in 1973. Carl is head of Llewellyn Publications, which during the 1970s published Lady Sheba's books and the *Gnostica News*, which was a major voice within the Wicca/Pagan community. Though following much of the material of Lady Sheba, the First Wiccan Church also developed its own practices.

Three foci of coven activity were recognized. Worship occurred at the esbats held during the full moon and at the sabbats on the solstices and equinoxes. It was an effort to tune into the natural rhythms of the sun and moon. Magick is seen as the ceremonial work that brings people-integration. The ritual of the craft focuses on practical mundane success, the use of mind power to gain an object of desire. Like Lady Sheba, this group opposed the secrecy that has traditionally surrounded the craft. The church was dissolved in the late 1970s.

Sources:

Sheba, Lady. *The Grimoire of Lady Sheba*. St. Paul, MN: Llewellyn Publications, 1974.

Sheba, Lady [Jessie Wicker Bell]. *Witch*. St. Paul, MN: Llewellyn Publications, 1973.

Hollywood Coven

The Hollywood Coven was formed as a Celtic traditional Wiccan group in 1967 by E. Tanssan of Hollywood, Florida. Tanssan had formerly been a member of a coven in Birmingham, Michigan. The Birmingham coven, headed by T. Milligan, had been established in the early part of the century. Tanssan had succeeded his teacher as leader in Birmingham shortly before the coven was disbanded because of police harassment. He and some of the members moved to Florida and established the new coven. Emerging as spokesperson for the coven was Kitty Lessing, who edited its periodical, the *Black Lite*.

Worship was in the circle. No drugs were allowed. It was a robed tradition. Initiation was allowed only after a year of study of occultism and witchcraft. Initiates were eligible to become a coven lady or grand master. There were no priests or priestesses.

The basic deities were the Great One, the Horned God, and the Lady of Silver, the earth mother. The God was considered the father of all gods and guide to the afterlife. Nature was seen as the creation of the gods, hence sacred. Only four sabbaths—Halloween, Yule, Candlemas (February 2), and Lammas (August 1)— were celebrated. The solstices and equinoxes were not formally celebrated. Esbats were held weekly or biweekly. In 1972 two covens were being operated in Hollywood, the main coven and a student coven.

During the mid-1970s Lessing moved to California, and shortly afterward the Hollywood Coven dropped out of sight. This may have been one of the few genuine pre-Gardnerian covens in the United States.

Holy Order of Briget

The Holy Order of Briget was a Wicca group formed in the late 1960s in Denver by Michael Myers. For several years the group operated a co-op book store, Spell, Book and Candle, in Denver, but it closed in November 1973. Land was purchased in rural Colorado, and Craftcast Farm was begun as a "monastic" focus within American Wicca.

Craftcast was run during the brief period of its existence on a communal basis and set aside as a place where ritual would be continual. A deep love for the Mother was the motivating force. Witchcraft, viewed as seeking wisdom by changing knowledge into understanding, was practiced. The monastic ideal allowed "one spiritual goal" to become dominant. According to Myers, other covens in various locations throughout the West were affiliated with the Holy Order of Briget; however, since the dissolving of the farm in the late 1970s, considerable doubt has been cast upon Myers's claims.

House of the Open Eye

House of the Open Eye was a Neopagan group in the San Francisco Bay Area headed by Rev. Paula Ashton which drew its inspiration from ancient Egyptian religion and was intent upon revitalizing it. The group built upon the knowledge of the Netjer (Egyptian pantheon) from history and archeology and offered strong support to believers gaining all the knowledge of the past. However, members also understood that a significant period of time had passed and that just as culture evolved, so should the Egyptian religious tradition and the practices associated with it. Thus, they proposed a method of serving and honoring the Netjer in ways that were relevant to the modern psyche and environment.

The House of the Open Eye offered a course in Egyptian religion which included a broad understanding of the Egyptian deities, ancient Egypt, the important concepts of theology and ritual, magick, divination, daily devotional disciplines, and the priesthood.

During its active period, the group participated in the larger Neopagan community in the Bay Area, and maintained a web site on the Internet.

Lady Sara's Coven

Sara Cunningham was an Episcopalian who turned witch. During the late 1960s she operated the Albion Training Coven and, in 1970, became one of the founders of the Church of the Eternal Source. She separated from that group in 1971 over eclecticism (which she expounded) versus a pure Egyptian religion. She founded the First Temple of Tiphareth, which combined elements of Western ritual magick, Egyptian religion, and Wicca. The temple was located in Pasadena, where she also ran Stonehenge, an occult supply house. She also met Hans Holzer, who wrote about her psychic abilities in several of his books. In 1973 she moved to Wolf Creek, Oregon, where she formed Lady Sara's Coven, an eclectic Wicca group. She published "A Course in Wicca," a year-and-a-day study course offered to students around the country. Her coven has dropped out of sight in recent years.

Sources:

AUM, The Sacred Word. Glendale, OR: First Temple of Tiphareth, 1975.

The Hermetic Art. Glendale, OR: First Temple of Tiphareth, 1975.

Sara [Cunningham]. *Candle Magic*. Hollywood, CA: Phoenix House, 1974.

Sara, Lady [Cunningham]. *Questions and Answers on Wicca Craft*. Wolf Creek, OR: Stonehenge Farm, 1974.

Neo-Dianic Faith

W. Holman Keith came to Paganism early in the 1940s. He attended the Church of Aphrodite, an early Pagan group founded in the 1920s by Gleb Botkin and, in the late 1960s, emerged as head of his own Neo-Dianic Faith. Keith described the revival of Paganism as the recovery of the ancient spirituality embodied in the prehistoric nature religion and Mother Goddess worship. Though the Neo-Dianic Faith was confined to a small group in the Los Angeles area, as Paganism grew through the 1970s, Keith emerged as an elder brother for many just discovering its precepts.

Keith thought of the divine, the great mover, as eternal desire, ideally embodied in woman. Man's and woman's oneness with life and nature is expressed in a primal piety that includes an ethic of pleasure, beauty, subordination of the drive for power and its resulting machinations of control, and worship of the feminine. The Greco-Roman pantheon is favored, but not exclusively. The active participation in the experience of being alive, in worshipping the Goddess, brings its own assurance of immortality, the moment in time being identical with the eternal now.

After Keith's death in the late 1970s his small following dissolved.

Open Goddess

The Open Goddess was an eclectic Wicca group that drew on Alexandrian Wicca revised with insights from a broader perspective on Western occultism. The Kabbalistic symbolism of balance was predominant; both the Goddess (my Lady) and God (my Lord) were worshipped. In this view the Goddess is identified with the sephirot Binah and the god with Chokmah. These are the first emanations from Kether, the unseen Godhead. The God is the solar principle, the king to be enthroned. The Goddess is the lunar principle, veiled in the mysteries of nature and the universe. The group's name was derived from the belief that the various names of the Goddess are all equally valid.

At one point in the mid-1970s, the Open Goddess claimed over 50 affiliated covens scattered from New Hampshire to Florida. Headquarters were in Woodbridge, New Jersey, where High Priestess and Priest Pennie Robbins and Kevin Robbins resided.

Order of Osirus

According to Samuel R. Graves, who in the 1970s led a contemporary version of this storied group, the Order of Osirus dates from 1572, with Edward Wharton, a Cambridge graduate and schoolteacher who had early become interested in divination and the occult. During his last year at college, he became interested in witchcraft. He started his first coven in the 1510s, but it was disbanded. The first covens of the new order in 1572 had seven members (to avoid the accusation of being a parody on the 12 apostles). The order considered these the first "white covens," as opposed to popular "black" covens that were involved with satanism and black magic. It was also Wharton's belief that the smaller, more intimate body could generate unlimited power.

The Osirian Order, wrote Graves, spread to Massachusetts in the seventeenth century. In 1676 Mary Austin and Anne Brintone arrived in Boston. They were apprehended by Richard Bellingham, who accused them of witchcraft. They were released, however, upon paying 10 pounds sterling and promising to leave Boston. To Simon Newell, who paid the money, credit is due for preservation of the rituals, spells, and incantations. They moved to Salem and began the first Osirian coven. By 1692 there were 37 covens in New England. The order then went underground for 200 years.

Graves was introduced to witchcraft by Chris Newell of North Bristol, Massachusetts, a descendant of Simon Newell. Chris gave Simon's journals to Graves, who in turn led a contemporary revival of the order and published several books. For the order, witchcraft had to do with the mastering of the power of the mind, the strength of individual will, and the power of suggestion. The group was primarily concerned with spells and incantations toward some positive goal. Work was done in a circle. Symbol of the Osirian Order was the goat skull, associated with the Horned God, Pan, and the love of nature.

Headquarters of the order were established in Kearney, Nebraska. Membership was open to all after payment of the five-dollar fee. A bimonthly newsletter was published. No recent evidence of the continuance of the order has been available.

Sources:

Graves, Samuel R. *Witchcraft: The Osirian Order*. San Francisco: JBT Marketing, 1971.

Potions and Spells of Witchcraft. San Francisco: JBT Marketing, 1970.

Pristine Egyptian Orthodox Church

The Pristine Egyptian Orthodox Church was founded in 1963 in Chicago by Milton J. Neruda and Charles Renslow. It grew out of a small group in suburban Chicago Heights, Illinois. The original name was the Egyptian Holy Church. The source of its tradition was Pharoah Amenhotep IV (Akhenaten). The church saw itself as the heir to the original (Pristine), authentic (Orthodox) Egyptian doctrines.

High priority was placed upon individuality and the right of the individual to reason toward belief. Salvation was equated with knowledge. All religions are man-made as outward expressions of God-given faith. The church believed in one creator (Khepera) but venerated the many gods as physical examples of the attributes of the creator. These found expression in the basic Egyptian pantheon. The church also taught living in harmony with nature, the equality of all humans, and the spiritual (magical) powers. It sought not to judge individuals but to leave questions of adultery and murder, as well as homosexuality, to civil rather than church authority. (Neruda was an activist in the Chicago homosexual community.) There were four major Holy Days: Easter (March, spring), the Unity of Hator (June 22), the Seb and Mut Festival (September 22), and the Festival of Lights (December 28). There was but a single congregation of the Egyptian Church, in Chicago. It was headed by the Rev. Charles Renslow, arkon of North and South America. There were three priests. *The Egyptian Bible*, composed of ancient Egyptian materials, formed the scriptures of the church. The church split following a disagreement between Renslow and Neruda over its stance in regard to Christianity. Neruda was more actively against the Christian faith and believed that the church should be vocal in its criticism. He left to found the Congregation of Aten. Neither group survived to the end of the decade.

Psychedelic Venus Church

The Psychedelic Venus Church was formed in 1969 partly as an outgrowth of a former body, the Shiva Fellowship. As its name implies, it combined elements of sexual freedom and psychedelic drugs. The Shiva Fellowship began in November 1967, when Willie Minzey went to India and was dedicated and marked in the traditional way as a worshipper of Shiva. The practice of the religion includes the smoking of hashish. Minzey returned to the United States and established a temple to Shiva in his home in San Francisco. He also began to hold public services in Golden Gate Park. On April 16, 1969, Minzey was arrested and in 1971 was sentenced to prison for a term lasting from 10 years to life. The Shiva Fellowship disintegrated into other groups.

The Psychedelic Venus Church was founded by Jefferson Poland. As a pagan fellowship dedicated to the worship of the Hindu goddess Kali, who was equated with Venus, the church drew together elements implicit in the Sexual Freedom League, the Gay Liberation Front, emerging paganism, the Shiva Fellowship, and various other radical activist groups in the Berkeley/San Francisco area. The Psychedelic Venus Church described itself as a "pantheistic nature religion, humanist hedonism, a religious pursuit of bodily pleasure through sex and marijuana."

Worship in the Psychedelic Venus Church focused upon its celebrations. Until the conviction of Minzey, these were held regularly and openly. Afterward, they were held irregularly. Typical indoor celebrations would begin with the sacrament—smoking marijuana—during which time a liturgy would be held. After the liturgy, sensitivity sessions and partying in the nude would conclude the evening. Public celebrations would center upon the smoking of marijuana and participation in sexual activity. At one such ceremony, Jefferson Poland was arrested.

The church was governed by a board of directors (four females and three males) elected annually by the membership. The board appointed officers. The president through the late 1970s was Mother Boats. *Intercourse*, a magazine, and *Nelly Heathen*, appeared as occasional periodicals. At its height in 1971, there were 1,000 members, but the church steadily lost support through the 1970s. By 1974 the group reported only 250 members. By the end of the decade the group had disappeared.

Temple of Bacchus

The Temple of Bacchus was formed in 1978 by Bishop H. Carlisle Estes, the temple's pastor. Bacchus, also known as Dionysus, was the ancient Greek god of food and drink. Estes claimed in 1975 that Bacchus revealed to him the temple's teachings, which were published in a pamphlet, *The Book of Bacchus*. The Temple believed that there is one God, known by many names, and that Bacchus is his disciple. Bacchus decreed that Estes should form a church to worship God and ordered that it be a place of joy and celebration. Bacchus taught that everything God created is good and that humans should enjoy the pleasures of the body—food, wines, music, creative activity, and the arts. However, all should be enjoyed in moderation. Excess in any area leads to illness and pestilence and the disfiguring of bodily form.

According to the revelation, Bacchus decreed daily worship with feasting and dancing. Six days of bacchanals were followed by a day of fasting and rest. Priests, bishops, and cardinals of the church assisted in the preparation of the daily feast with a primary responsibility of preventing the rituals from becoming repetitious and stereotyped.

Almost from its founding, the temple was a subject of controversy. Critics charged Bishop Estes and his

assistant, Cardinal Vincent Morino, with operating a restaurant under the guise of a temple in order to circumvent local zoning laws that had previously denied them permission to open a restaurant in the building occupied by the temple. They further charged that the nightly bacchanals (in which those in attendance were asked to contribute a stated donation and in return received a full meal) were in fact not religious events at all. The controversy led to several lawsuits.

The temple was one of several religious bodies chartered by the Universal Life Church of Modesto, California. In 1979 the temple reported 125 members of the single congregation in Maine, with new congregations beginning in Honolulu, Hawaii, and in Wiltshire, England.

Temple of the Goddess Within

The Temple of the Goddess Within was formed by Ann Forfreedom in the 1970s. Raised in the Jewish faith, Forfreedom rejected Judaism for being "too male-dominated." She was drawn into Witchcraft, or Wiccecraeft, through her activity in various feminist causes where she met other female Wiccans. Originally from Sacramento, California, she moved to Oakland in 1984. It was the teaching of the temple that the proper name for the religion of Witchcraft is Wiccecraeft or Wicce (Craft of the Wise). Wiccecraeft is the Old English feminine form of Witchcraft used by some feminist witches as the proper name of their religion.

As publisher/editor of the *Wise Woman*, Ann Forfreedom (a name assumed to accentuate her feminist concerns) became a leading spokesperson for Dianic Witchcraft, a term coined by Morgan McFarland and Mark Roberts to describe those traditions which focus mainly or totally on the Goddess. Forfreedom did not believe, however, that the Dianic tradition was necessarily equated with either female separateness or antimale attitudes. In the Dianic tradition worship is more Goddess- than God-oriented, but the male deities serve a complementary role. The Goddess is seen as an expression of the life force of the universe. Among the basic principles of the temple, it was said that "All Goddesses are one Goddess; all Gods are one God." Members were encouraged to act both collectively and individually upon their feminist goals.

Like other Wicce groups, the Dianics attend to lunar and solar cycles, gathering in the evenings for times of work (magic) and feasting (celebration). Wicce is a religion of love. Initiation into Wicce is an important step and should be preceded by a period of study. It should be entirely voluntary on the part of the initiate, and the initiator should perform his/her duties without monetary compensation. The temple was an autonomous coven. Unlike Gardnerian Wicca, Feminist Wicce does not have a single leader such as a witch queen or a single sourcebook such as the Book of Shadows. Rituals are eclectic and variable.

In 1982 the temple sponsored a major conference, "Goddess Rising," which brought together many leading Goddess worshippers and feminists. As a result of the conference, a second organization, Goddess Rising, was founded and incorporated to educate men and women about Feminist Wiccecraeft and to explore Goddess lore. Goddess Rising was discontinued by 1992. Ann Forfreedom served as the California director of the Witch's Anti-Discrimination Lobby, a coalition founded by Leo Louis Martello that sought to educate the mass media and public about Witchcraft.

Sources:

Forfreedom, Ann. *Feminist Wicca Works*. Sacramento, CA: The Author, 1980.

————. *Mythology, Religion and Woman's Heritage*. Sacramento, CA: Sacramento City Unified School District, [1981].

Forfreedom, Ann, and Julie Ann, eds. *Book of the Goddess*. Sacramento, CA: Temple of the Goddess Within, 1980.

Temple of the Pagan Way

The Temple of the Pagan Way dates from 1966 and the formation of an occult study and worship group led by Herman Enderle and Virginia Brubaker. The group became associated with the British Pagan Front and began to use the rituals written by Donna Cole. However, divergences developed within the temple over the ascendancy of the Mother Goddess, a prominent theme in the Pagan Way rituals. A system incorporating a balanced view of deity, both male and female, was adopted, with prominent elements from the Kabbalah. Enderle, who was a student of ritual magick, advocated a strong emphasis on magick in addition to "just worshipping the Goddess."

During the 1970s the temple was the motivating force in the formation of a number of other Neo-Pagan bodies. Most of the currently existing Neo-Pagan and Wicca groups in the Chicago area derive from it. They include the Calumet Pagan Temple, Epiphanes, and the First Temple of the Craft of WICA (all now independent organizations). The Temple of the Sacred Stones, an eclectic witchcraft coven headed by Donna Cole, had a long association with the temple, and it later met in the building that formerly housed the temple.

After several years as the Temple of the Pagan Way, the group adopted a new name in the spring of 1974, Uranus Temple. During this period, its emphasis upon ritual magick was at its height. Uranus was an initiatory temple with its basis in Western occultism and paganism. Members attended regular services associated with the full and new moon as well as the eight festivals. New members began with a series of ethics classes that introduced them to the basic perspective of the temple. They were then prepared for a Ritual of Dedication, where a public declaration of the acceptance of paganism was made. The next step was initi-

ation. There were five degrees, each of which corresponded to the classical elements of the ancients and entailed approximately one year of study.

The first degree was Earth, in which students were taught to gain control over themselves and introduced to basic occult material and exercises. The second degree was Water, with emphasis on exploring the psychic and emotional self. The third degree was Fire, which dealt directly with self-change through magick. The fourth degree was Air, which expressed the use of what had been learned and the ability to function easily as a magician and pagan. The fifth degree, Spirit, was the completed use of the first four degrees.

The temple was headed by a high priest and high priestess elected annually from among the priests and priestesses. Members in the second degree could choose studies leading to the priesthood. A General Council consisting of all members was the highest authority, and there was a Council of Elders, composed of senior members of the community, to which the high priest and priestess were responsible.

In 1975 the high priest (Enderle) and high priestess (Brubaker) of the Uranus Temple had sufficient irreconcilable differences that the group split. The majority (and hence the name) followed Brubaker. Enderle went on to form Earthstar Lodge. After using the name Uranus for a short while, Brubaker's group discarded it for the original name. The group later became a witchcraft coven, though retaining many of the unique ritual and magical emphases from the 1970s. The temple took an active role in the Covenant of the Goddess.

Temple of the Pagan Way

One of the most important groups spreading Neo-Paganism (as opposed to Witchcraft) was the Pagan Way, a loosely associated set of Neo-Pagan groves that emerged in the late 1960s. The group had several sources. Donna Cole, a witch in Chicago, had traveled to England in the 1960s and was initiated into Gardnerian Wicca. Upon her return to the United States, she made contact with Herman Enderle and Virginia Brubaker, who had formed an occult study group. Together they established a Pagan temple. Cole also composed a set of Pagan rituals that were less magical and more celebratory than the Gardnerian ones. During this period she met Ed Fitch, a California Pagan. Fitch later composed a second set of rituals similar in perspective to Cole's. During the early 1970s Cole and Fitch circulated the Pagan Way rituals around the United States with the result that a number of Pagan Way temples (groves) emerged.

One early grove was in Philadelphia and had among its leaders Penny Novack, Michael Novack, and Thomas (a pseudonym). Thomas became the editor in 1970 of the original pagan journal *Waxing Moon* (later the *Crystal Well*) when its founder, Joseph Wilson, moved to England. Wilson began a British *Waxing Moon*, thus precipitating the name change in

America. The *Crystal Well* was never the official organ of the Pagan Way, but it had a close informal connection and functioned as a means whereby Pagan Way groups could stay in contact.

The Pagan Way was a celebratory nature religion dedicated to the growth in understanding of the sacred quality of the seasonal rounds and the holy, mystic qualities of everyday life. Unlike most pagan groups, it was not a "magical" group and has no secret rituals. (The rituals were published in book form as *A Book of Pagan Rituals*.) While many individuals practiced magick, the group came together for celebration only. The Goddess was, of course, the central theme of the celebrations.

Pagan Way study centered on three basic steps: first, study of the myths and history of paganism; second, practice of rituals for both individuals and groups; and third, in-depth working in the craft (for those who desired it). In many areas the Pagan Way served as an outer portal to the more secretive craft.

In 1973 Pagan Way groves were functioning in Philadelphia, Pennsylvania; New York City; Wilmington, Delaware; Huron, South Dakota; Louisville, Kentucky; San Bernardino, California; Passaic, New Jersey; and Chicago, Illinois. There were also numerous small Pagan Way groups scattered across the country. Ed Fitch headed the California Grove. In 1974 the Chicago Pagan Way became the Uranus Temple (later changed back to the Temple of the Pagan Way). There were between 30 and 60 members in Philadelphia. By 1980 the Pagan Way had largely died. Some groups had been destroyed by internal dissension. Most were simply superseded by numerous Neo-Pagan and witchcraft groups under the leadership of those trained in the groves, coupled with the retirement of many of the original leaders. The original rituals, which were not copyrighted, have been published in several editions and remain popular among Neo-Pagans in North America and England.

Sources:

Fitch, Ed. *Magical Rites from the Crystal Well*. St. Paul, MN: Llewellyn Publications, 1984.

Slater, Herman, ed. *A Book of Pagan Rituals*. New York: Samuel Weiser, 1978.

Witches International Craft Associates (WICA)

Witches International Craft Associates (WICA) was the public structure of the Sicilian Strege tradition headed in America by Dr. Leo Louis Martello (1930–2000). It was formed in 1970. Prior to that time Martello had been an active Spiritualist. In 1955 he was ordained and became the head of the International Guidance Temple of Bible Spiritual Independents, Mother Church & Seminary, in New York City. He served the church for five years. He was also a national officer of the American Graphological Society, a hypnotist, and a popular writer on occult subjects.

According to Martello, Witchcraft teaching and practice was passed through his family and was initiated in 1951. During the 1960s he returned to Sicily (from America, where his parents had immigrated) and reestablished contact with the Strege. In 1969 he published his first book on Witchcraft, and the following year he founded WICA.

Martello emerged as one of the earliest spokespersons of the new Witchcraft. His organization led in the formation of a number of necessary structures serving the emerging community in the early 1970s: the Witches Encounter Bureau (to aid witches in contacting each other), the Witches Liberation Movement (which published the "Witch Manifesto"), and the Witches Antidefamation League. He initiated two periodicals, *Witchcraft Digest* and the *W.I.C.A. Newsletter* and circulated his many books through WICA's publishing arm, Hero Press.

According to Martello, the actualities of Strege Wicca have never been revealed, though Charles Leland's book *Aradia* comes close to revealing them. *Aradia* was meant to be a study of Strege. The basic deity is Diana, the first created before all creation. She divided into darkness and into light (Lucifer). Desiring the light, she tricked Lucifer into lying with her and thus became the mother of Herodias (Aradia). She also became the Queen of the Witches. The basic ritual is the conjuration of Diana and the invocation of Aradia. Cubes of meal, salt, and honey in the shape of a crescent moon are consecrated and eaten. The climax of the ritual, performed at the full moon, is dancing and "love in the darkness." The ritual is skyclad (performed in the nude).

One point at which Sicilian Wicca differs from most traditions is its use of spells and incantations that threaten the deity. For example, Diana is addressed: "Or I may truly at another time So conjure thee that thou shalt have no peace Or happiness, for thou shalt ever be In suffering until thou grantest that Which I require in strictest faith from here!" Threats are a recognition of the essential divinity in each person, a sense of personal power that even the gods and goddesses cannot undermine.

Strege continues to function as an ethnic branch of the craft in the United States. Martello retired from public life in the early 1990s but continued to serve the community in an advisory capacity until his death in 2000.

Sources:

Leland, Charles Godfrey. *The Mystic Will*. New York: Hero Press, 1980.

Martello, Leo Louis. *Weird Ways of Witchcraft*. New York: HC Publishers, 1969.

————. *Curses in Verses*. New York: Hero Press, 1971.

————. *Witchcraft, The Old Religion*. Secaucus, NJ: University Books, 1973.

————. *How to Prevent Psychic Blackmail*. New York: Samuel Weiser, 1975.

————. *What It Means To Be a Witch*. New York: The Author, [1975].

DRUID NEOPAGANISM

Temple of Truth

One of the prime movers in the founding of the Ordo Templi Astarte was Nelson H. White, who served as its vice-president and, under his magical name, Frater Khedemel, served as its major apologist. In 1973, however, he left the Ordo Templi Astarte and he and his wife, Anne White (Soror Veritas) began the Temple of Truth (T.O.T.). The Temple differed from other occult orders in that it had no grades and no fixed curriculum. It has also dispensed with many of the ceremonial trappings of traditional ritual magick; emphasis was placed on individual independent study and spiritual development. Students adopted an individualized course after an initial series of classes. The teachings were basically Kabbalistic and followed the teachings in the Whites' books. As of 1988, the Whites had written and published more than 40 books on magick and the occult.

The T.O.T. was the magical order sponsored by the Light of Truth Church, a licensed corporation in California. The church was neither evangelistic nor fundamentalistic and recognized the subjectivity of what most people call "Truth." Membership in both the church and the order was open to all persons, though periodically both groups would refrain from accepting new members if the Whites's teaching time was filled.

Headquarters of the church were in Pasadena, California, where the Whites operated a church-sponsored bookstore, The Magick Circle. *The White Light*, which began publication in the fall of 1974, had become one of the oldest continuously published magical magazines in the country.

Membership was not reported, but in 1987 the newsletter reported a circulation of 200 copies. There was one center located in Pasadena, California. Individual students using the Whites' material could at one time be found in approximately 15 foreign countries, as well as Hawaii, Alaska, and Canada.

Sources:

White, Nelson, and Anne White. *Collected Rituals of the T.O.T.* Pasadena, CA: Technology Group, 1982.

————. *Secret Magick Revealed*. Pasadena, CA: Technology Group, 1979.

————. *The Wizard's Apprentice*. Pasadena, CA: Technology Group, 1982.

————. *Working High Magick*. Pasadena, CA: Technology Group, 1982.

NORSE HEATHENISM

Angelseaxisce Ealdriht

The Angelseaxisce Ealdriht (Anglo-Saxon Eldright) was a structured, closely knit society which sought to understand and live the beliefs and values of Anglo-Saxon and other Germanic Heathens (or Pagans) in the context of modern life. Most of the group's deities, values, and beliefs were like those of other Norse Heathen/Asatru organizations and groups. Its deities were those termed the Aesir and the Vanir, including among others Woden (Odin), Frige (Frigg), Thunor (Thor), Tiw (Tyr), Ing Frea (Freyr), and Freo (Freya).

The word "Ealdriht" refers to the common-law rights, customs, and moral values that belong to people by ancient tradition and precedent, those rights and customs that have been earned, established, and held firm through many generations, the Magna Carta (1217 C.E.) being a worthy example. Building on the ancient Heathen ways, the modern Heathens sought to reestablish the enduring customs, values, and ways in the modern world. As modern Heathens, the Angelseaxisce Ealdriht valued thoth (beliefs), which included loyalty to the gods and goddesses, ancestors, and other Heathens. Thoth was strengthened through the swearing of holy oaths and vows.

The Angelseaxisce Ealdriht was organized on a Heathen Anglo-Saxon model. Social rankings were termed "arungs," and these were earned by demonstrating learning, skill, community service, and a level of acceptance of responsibility. The important decisions together were voted upon democratically during the quarterly maethelings (assemblies or Things). Ranks were conferred by democratic vote of the maethels (social units).

The following were three categories of membership in the Eldright: the Folgere, an associate or a "friend of the Eldright" (without oath); the Laet, an apprentice preparing for full membership (requiring a provisional oath); and the full, oathed permanent members who had full voting rights and ranks. Members affiliated with "maethels," and each full member of the Eldright belonged to one and only one maethel. Incoming members were required to be accepted by a maethel which would sponsor and teach them and promote their growth and well-being in the Eldright. The maethel leaders, either Maethelgerefa (with a temporary term of leadership, renewable by vote) or Maethel Ealdor (elected permanent leader), were elected from within each maethel and served on the Witangemot, the governing council of the Eldright. Maethel officers included the Heargweard (priest) if available, Hordere (hoarder/treasurer), and Stigeweard (steward).

Ideally, a maethel was composed of people who lived relatively close together, who could physically gather and get to know one another face to face. However, since Eldright members were scattered across the country, and it was often not possible to have enough members in one place to form a maethel locally, modern maethels often included members who were geographically distant from one another.

The governing body of the Eldright as a whole was the Witangemot, the Eldright council. It was comprised of the leaders of all the maethels, plus the Eldright's Thyle (the counsellor or rede-giver, who was also the educational coordinator) and the leader of Haligwaerstow, the Eldright's Priest Hall or Guild. The Witangemot and the whole voting body of the Eldright elected the leader of the Witangemot and the Eldright—the Eldright Ealdor. The Witangemot was required to approve the establishment of new maethels or guilds (independent social units, each focused on some defined area of skill, knowledge, and service).

Asatru Free Assembly

The Asatru Free Assembly was formed in 1972 from the Viking Brotherhood by Stephen A. McNallen, then a student at Midwestern University in Wichita Falls, Texas. McNallen had been a follower of the Norse deities for several years as an individual and he decided that the time had come for him to speak publically about them. He began to publish *The Runestone*, a quarterly periodical. Shortly after forming the brotherhood, McNallen went into the army and served as an officer with NATO in Europe. During this period *The Runestone* continued to appear, and other groups of Norse Pagans appeared. Upon returning to civilian life in 1976, McNallen began to refine the brotherhood's ritual and doctrine. This refinement led to the adoption of a new name, the Asatru Free Assembly. This change emphasized the great value placed on individualism, courage, integrity, and independence, and the general opposition to all collective ideologies (including fascism) within the assembly (which was home to a wide variety of belief and practice within its general framework). It also set itself apart from "Odinism" (the popular name for Norse Paganism) in that the assembly was looking to revive the "cults" of all the Norse deities, not just Odin.

Worship was viewed as a contradiction of the spirit of ego centrality in the Viking religion. However, basic rituals were devised to celebrate certain events and to recognize the gods, who epitomized certain values. New members were initiated, and name-givings and burials were also occasions for ritual. Adherents celebrated Yule (December 22); Ragnar's Day (March 28), in commemoration of Viking Ragnar Lodbrok, who sailed up the Seine River in 845 and sacked Paris, France; Lindisfarne Day (June 8); and Midsummer Day (summer solstice). *The Runestone* regularly carried a calendar of ritual and remembrance days.

Local groups of the brotherhood were called "Skeppslags" or "ship's crews," and they consisted of from two to 15 members. Each Skeppslag operated under the chieftain of the brotherhood. Also becoming active during the early 1980s were a variety of guilds, groups built around a particular interest. These varied from sewing guilds to warriors' and brewers' guilds. Some guilds published their own newsletters. In November 1987, McNallen announced the dissolution of the assembly in the wake of a failure to reorganize. Its periodical, *The Runestone*, was discontinued. At its height in the mid-1980s, the assembly had approximately 200 members.

Within the larger Pagan community, the Norse groups have, as a whole, been condemned for their overt racism. The Asatru Free Assembly was largely free of racist expression and continued to be accepted by non-Norse Pagans.

Sources:

Hundingsbani, Heigi. *The Religion of Odin-A Handbook*. Red Wing, MN: Viking House, 1978.

McNallen, Stephen A. *Rituals of Asatru*. Breckenridge, TX: Asatru Free Assembly, 1985.

Atlantion Wicca

Atlantion Wicca, though originating in the 1960s, was based upon the teachings (and dedicated to the memory) of Elizabeth Sawyer, the witch of Edmonton, England. Ms. Sawyer was hung at Tyburn, England, on April 19, 1621, for supposedly killing, by witchcraft, a neighbor, Agnes Ratcleife. She had been known in the town as a healer, a midwife, and for helping farmers with their crops. The founding high priest was Don Sawyer, a descendant.

Rituals and teachings of Atlantion Wicca were found in its own *Book of Shadows*, which drew heavily upon Gardnerian Wicca practice. Esbats were held at both the full and new moons, and the sabbats were celebrated. Work was conducted within the circle. Reincarnation was a central belief. The group forbade the use of drugs, orgies, sacrifice, public nudity, and any behavior which might reflect poorly upon the craft.

The Atlantion witches were headquartered in Syracuse, New York, and in 1977 they had three covens. For several years they engaged in vigorous activity to establish in the public's mind the image of Witchcraft as a serious religion and to destroy the negative images which connected Wicca to violence, black magic, and the worship of Satan. No sign of the survival of the covens into the the the mid-1980s and beyond has been manifest.

Runic Society

The Runic Society was formed in 1974 by N. J. Templin. It advocated Wotanism, or Odinism, viewed as the oldest religion in the world and the religion of the Aryans since the late Stone Age. The society believed that the Nordic Race is the "Chosen Race of Nature" and that only through Odinism can Nordics be true to nature. The Norse gods were worshipped and thought of as manifestations of nature. Religion was considered a personal matter, so there were no religious services. There were, however, religious festivals —termed "blots"—and priests, whose function it was to perform marriages and funerals. The family unit, self-respect, and loyalty to the ancestral heritage were promoted. The Odinist faith is opposed to Christianity. Odinism is seen as this-worldly; immortality is given through the improvement of the future generation. The society sought to establish a true economic, racial, and spiritual community (not as a separate nation but within the nation).

The Runic Society was governed by the supreme council, made up of several Wotanist priests, a secretary, treasurer, and advisory personnel. It published *Einherjar*, a quarterly. The associated House of Odin sold Odinist jewelry and articles. Headquarters were in Milwaukee, with a second group in Chicago. Around 1980 the group dissolved after a period of internal dissension.

During its years of existence, the Runic Society kept close association with Da-America (in Pittsburgh), which published the journal *New America*, and with Die Artgemeinschaft (The Old Religion) in Germany. Also closely related to the Runic Society was the Odinist Movement headquartered in Toronto. It was formed in 1971 and published two periodicals, *The Sunwheel* and *The Odinist*.

Teutonic Temple

In Dallas, Oregon, the Teutonic Temple functioned as a polytheistic religion derived from the folk customs and festivals of the English, German, and Scandinavian peoples. Members believed in a supreme God and a pantheon of lesser deities including Tiw, the sky father; Wodan; Thunar; Fria; and Frua, goddess of fertility and magick. The eight pagan festivals were celebrated. Yule, the winter solstice, marked the beginning of the Teutonic year. The Teutonic Temple was a conservative religion against free love, perversion, pornography, drugs, draft dodging, and permissiveness. No evidence of its continuance beyond the 1970s has been located.

VODOU

Chamber of Holy Voodoo

The Chamber of Holy Voodoo emerged in the 1970s as a semi-public vodou organization that offered to teach vodou to students via correspondence. While the specific teachings were revealed only to students, the Chamber offered to introduce those who joined to the world of Holy Spirits and to teach them how to invoke them for various purposes. After a basic course, students could prepare themselves for the priesthood and learn the secrets of healing, exorcism, and the process of spirit possession. The Chamber also had a special section devoted to dealing with the problems of its members, the Room of Blessing, in which vodou was used to assist individuals in overcoming obstacles and reaching goals. Marriage counseling was a particular concern.

First Church of Voodoo

Robert W. Pelton, a freelance journalist, made an extensive study of vodou in the early 1970s, traveling around the United States visiting magicians, conjure men and women, and vodou practitioners. His research led to a number of books surveying the topic. He also decided to organize a vodou church, which began meeting in the home of Francis Torrance and Candy Torrance, a vodou priest and priestess in North Knoxville, Tennessee, who taught a course in vodou magic at the University of Tennessee evening school. The church was incorporated in 1973. Its teachings combined elements of vodou, conjureman (hoodoo), and Christianity. Ordination was available by mail.

Sources:

Pelton, Robert W. *The Complete Book of Voodoo*. New York: G. P. Putnam's Sons, 1972.

———. *Voodoo Charms and Talismans*. New York: Drake Publishers, 1973.

———. *Voodoo Secrets from A to Z*. South Brunswick, NJ: A. S. Barnes, 1973.

———. *Voodoo Signs and Omens*. South Brunswick, NJ: A. S. Barnes, 1974.

SATANISM

Brotherhood of the Ram

Operating from the early 1960s into the 1970s, the Brotherhood of the Ram established a book store in Los Angeles. Satan was to this group a god of joy and pleasure. Some traditional aspects of satanism, such as the "pact," were accepted. Members made a pact with Satan renouncing all other devotion and their Christian baptism, and then signed the pact with their own blood. Membership was confined to Southern California. By the 1980s the store had been closed and the group reportedly disbanded.

Church of Satanic Brotherhood

In the early 1970s, controversy began to develop among the Midwestern grottoes of the Church of Satan. Among those involved were Wayne West of Detroit and John DeHaven of Dayton, Ohio. The dissolution of the Stygian Grotto of the Dayton area of the Church of Satan occurred on February 11, 1973. Anton LaVey had revoked the grotto's charter, accusing it of "having been acting in violation of the law." With members from Ohio, Indiana, and Michigan, the Church of Satanic Brotherhood was formed in March 1973 by John DeHaven, Joseph Daniels, Ronald E. Lanting, and Harry L. Booth.

The church followed the practices of the Church of Satan with several exceptions that grew out of the controversy. Only those people who "can get along with others" were allowed in the Brotherhood. *The Satanic Rituals* by LaVey was viewed as a collection of butchered rites as used in their original form at the Central Grotto. An intense polemic against LaVey was launched.

After its founding, the Brotherhood spread rapidly. Grottoes were established in St. Petersburg, Florida; Dayton-Centerville, Ohio; Indianapolis, Indiana; Louisville, Kentucky; New York City; and Columbus, Ohio. A Council of the Churches was headed by the bishops (fourth degree). The priesthood made up its third degree. Each grotto was headed by a magister. A periodical, the *True Grimoire*, was published monthly.

The Church of Satanic Brotherhood lasted only a short period. In 1974 John DeHaven publically renounced satanism and proclaimed his conversion to Christianity. He made his announcement in the midst of a gathering of the church in St. Petersburg, during which he smashed many of the altar implements.

Order of Dionysus/Sabazios

The Order of Dionysus/Sabazios was founded in 1990 as the Church of Satanic Youthfulness by Joseph E. Aufricht. Originally Aufricht enjoyed a good relationship with the Church of Satan, whose perspective inspired him to start his separate work, but the two groups eventually pulled apart over disagreements on specific teachings.

The order was essentially atheistic in belief but allowed its members a belief in the existence of spiritual entities. Aufricht argued that if a supreme creator exists, the creator would be responsible for both good and evil. God would have created Satan with the ability to rebel and, being all-knowing, would have known that Satan would rebel. Aufricht believed the basic philosophy of the Christian Bible to be mere myth written by very fallible human beings for the purpose of controlling the masses in one form or another. The order stood staunchly against forms of social control and for the destruction of Christianity and other forms of spirituality. It disseminated these views in its periodical, *Rejuvenation*.

The order basically followed the teachings presented by Anton LaVey, the founder of the Church of Satan, in his various books and writings. It differed primarily in its advocacy of the rights of teenagers, who, according to the order, exist in a state of "slavery" wrought by parents and other authorities. The order believed that teens are essentially adults and should be so treated. Members of the order asserted that teenagers should have the same freedom of choice, especially in matters of sexuality, as legal adults and that they should fight for legal changes that would allow such freedom to become operative. Included in the freedoms the order advocated was the freedom of teenagers to engage in sexual relationships with adults.

Order of the Black Ram

The Order of the Black Ram was a satanic organization based on belief in Aryan racial superiority and closely associated with the National Renaissance Party, a neo-Nazi organization. Adherents believed that each race is the embodiment of a racial soul that is expressed in its culture and philosophy. Individuality

is stressed. The Order of the Black Ram was eclectic, drawing on the writings of Anton LaVey (founder of the Church of Satan); Robert Heinlein's novel *Stranger in a Strange Land*, and Neo-Paganism. It was headquartered in suburban Detroit, Michigan, where its grand magister, Rev. Seth Klippoth, resided. *Liber Venifica* was an irregular periodical.

Ordo Templi Satanas

Closely associated with the Church of Satanic Brotherhood was the Ordo Templi Satanas (OTS). Some OTS members were former members of the Brotherhood. Practices, beliefs, and organization were similar. There were two temples of the OTS, one in Indianapolis, Indiana, and one in Louisville, Kentucky (headed by Clifford Amos). Leader of the OTS was Joseph Daniels, known as Apollonius, priest of Hermopolis. He was also one of the founders of the Brotherhood. This minuscule group disbanded after a few years.

Our Lady of Endor Coven

Existing for many years prior to the establishment of the Church of Satan was Our Lady of Endor Coven, the Ophite Cultus Satanas, founded by Herbert Arthur Sloane of Toledo, Ohio, in 1948. Satanas (the Horned God) appeared to him first when Sloane was a child. Later Sloane saw him as the figure pictured on the dust jacket of Margaret Murray's *The God of the Witches*. The Lord Satanas appeared again when Sloane was 25 years old.

The system of Our Lady of Endor Coven was based heavily on Gnosticism; *The Gnostic Religion* by Hans Jonas was a highly recommended book. The Christian God, the creator, was identified with the Gnostic Demiurge. The Demiurge is the God beyond the creator God, an emanation of the transcendent God. Satanas is the messenger of the remote God who brought Eve the knowledge that there was a God beyond the God who created the cosmos. The God beyond takes no part of "this world," except as he is concerned with the return of his spirit, now entrapped in matter as the divine within humanity. The return of the divine within humanity to the God beyond is accomplished through Gnosis, occult knowledge that people can attain.

The coven believed satanism to be the oldest religion, dating to the worship of the Horned God found in the prehistoric cave paintings in Europe. Satanism differs from witchcraft in not turning the Horned God into a fertility god and thus retaining his spiritual significance. (For a brief period of time Sloane was a member of the Church of Satan, but his membership did not visibly alter the coven he led.) Organization of his group followed a pattern similar to witchcraft, covens being the prime structure. The organization was headed by a priest but had no extra-coven structure.

Our Lady of Endor was the only coven led by Sloane. It dissolved after his death in the early 1980s.

Thee Satanic Church

In 1974 Thee Satanic Church of Nethilum Rite divided, and a second organization was established by Dr. Evelyn Paglini, one of the original cofounders. Its belief and structure were identical to those of the parent church. The Satanic Church opened a book and occult supply store in a Chicago suburb, and Paglini began an occult periodical, *Psychic Standard*, which did not carry any satanic material. Paglini's group slowly dropped their satanic trappings. In one of their last public actions, they gathered at Comiskey Park prior to a Chicago White Sox baseball game to do a magical ritual to aid the faltering team.

The *Psychic Standard* ceased publication in 1980. Shortly after that time Paglini moved away from Chicago.

Thee Satanic Orthodox Church of Nethilum Rite

Centered in Chicago was Thee Satanic Orthodox Church of Nethilum Rite headed by High Priest Terry Taylor. Headquarters were at the Occult Book Shop in Chicago. The church went public in 1971. It was opposed to the satanism of Anton LaVey and the Church of Satan. Members believed in God as the creator of the universe and in Satan as the creature of God. Satan is the apex of creation who possesses all the power and knowledge of the universe. Members tried to acquire as much of Satan's knowledge and power as possible. This acquisition was to be achieved through magical rituals and psychic development and through the elders, described as an "international group of high ministers in the private end of Thee Satanic Church." The church disappeared in the mid-1970s.

Only one center, in Chicago, was ever established. It claimed 538 members in 1973. Weekly Saturday night meetings were held including songs, prayers, a ritualistic mass, and introduction of new members. Recruitment was through evening public discussion sessions, the store, and classes given by Taylor.

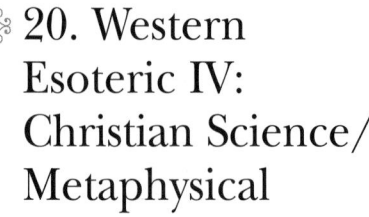

20. Western Esoteric IV: Christian Science/ Metaphysical

CHRISTIAN SCIENCE

Church of Integration

The Church of Integration was founded in 1935 as the Society of Life, but its roots went back to 1912 and the formation in London, England, of a small group of former members of the Church of Christ, Scientist around Annie C. Bill (1865?–1937). Bill, a member of the Third Church of Christ, Scientist, resigned after a friend named R. L. Rawson was excommunicated. The

church took exception to Rawson's book, *Life Understood*, which Bill had a hand in writing. Rawson would later found a prominent British New Thought group, the Society for the Propagation of True Prayer. In the meantime, a few months after Bill resigned, Mary Baker Eddy, the founder of the church, died and left no successor. Bill became convinced that she was the true successor, and in 1912 she organized what became known as the Christian Science Parent Church. After World War I she moved to the United States, and in 1924 she established the church in America.

Around the time that Bill became active in America, the Church of Christ, Scientist was involved in an intense controversy surrounding the varying interpretations of Eddy's instruction to the church once she had died. Bill's church acquired members from among the losers in that battle, the most prominent being John V. Dittemore. About the same time, she made a most significant convert, A. A. Beauchamp, who turned over the services of his publishing house, including his magazine, *Watchman of Israel*, to the new church. Bill's church grew steadily, and in the 1926 *Census of Religious Bodies* it reported 29 churches and 582 members in the United States. By 1928 there were 44 branches, including churches in Great Britain, Australia, and Canada, with approximately 80 branches and 1,200 members by 1930.

The last major development of Bill's church occurred around 1930. During the 1920s, Bill had become convinced that many of the criticisms leveled by Eddy's critics were true. In particular, she came to believe that Eddy had been a frequent user of morphine and that she had derived many of her teachings from Phineas P. Quimby, the healer and mesmerist who had been her teacher in the 1860s. Bill concluded that Eddy no longer deserved the central role the parent church had accorded her and that Eddy's textbook, *Science and Health, with Key to the Scriptures*, was no longer a valid textbook. She authored a new textbook, *The Science of Reality* (1930), which replaced *The Universal Design of Life* (1924), the older volume that had acknowledged Eddy's authority. She also reorganized the parent church into the Church of Universal Design, and *The Watchman* became *The Universal Design, A Journal of Applied Metaphysics*.

Two ideas dominated the new church. First, Bill suggested the possibility of conscious spiritual evolution by direct intention and in accordance with a universal design of life that impels periodic transformations. This design is based upon the prior recognition that Mind is God and that the universe unfolds from Mind. This unfoldment would follow a sevenfold pattern. Second, a response to this universal design was built into the new organization. When the church's recognized leader died, the church entered an interim period during which church directors appointed deputy leaders to carry on the services of the church until a new leader emerged. The next

leader would be one who demonstrated that she or he had made the discovery of the next successive step in the design of Life.

Bill adopted several controversial ideas that took prominence in the church's beliefs. A. A. Beauchamp had been an advocate of British-Israelism, the idea that the modern Anglo-Saxon people of northern and western Europe and North America were the descendants of the ancient 10 tribes of Israel. His magazine, published on behalf of British-Israelism, became the magazine of the parent church and the central perspective adopted by Bill. She also came to believe in pyramidology, the idea that the measurements and geometric design of the Great Pyramid in Egypt had religious and prophetic significance.

The transition from the Church of Universal Design to the Church of Integration occurred following Bill's death in 1937 in a manner quite similar to the pattern she had proposed. In 1934, Francis J. Mott (b. 1901), who had been with Bill since 1922, withdrew from the Church of Universal Design. Claiming to have found a new light on the spiritual process, he organized The Society of Life. Following Bill's death he presented his new findings and new organization to the leaders of the Church of Universal Design, who gave him their support. They voted to dissolve the church and urged all its members to join the Society of Life. Most of the members did so, although there were a few exceptions, such as Dittemore, who wrote a letter to the Church of Christ, Scientist, recanting his association with Bill.

The society evolved over the next decade, and after several years it emerged as the Church of Integration, which saw itself as still being in continuity with the Church of Christ, Scientist. Its tenets acknowledged one God who creates according to One Plan. Particular reverence was given to the "Seed in the Church," or the discoverer of the new, who is often looked upon at first as a heretic but is actually the bearer of a new birth for the church. Mott also believed that the new Seed need not wait until the death of the present leader before addressing the mind of the church.

Mott initially published his views in a several books (published by A. A. Beauchamp), and over a decade at least four editions of the covenant of the new church were issued. The British branch of the church was destroyed in the chaos of World War II. In America, however, the church survived and was briefly revived after the war. A new magazine, *Integration*, was issued from the church's headquarters in Washington, D.C., beginning in 1946. Eventually, however, the church, which was never numerically strong, dissolved.

At least one follower of Bill who opposed Mott's leadership, Mary Sayles Atkins, continued to write about Bill. She wrote under her pen name, Mary Sayles Moore, and during the 1950s she published several volumes with A. A. Beauchamp, who had left the Church of Integration in the 1940s. Her most important volume was *Conquest of Chaos* (1954), which reviewed Bill's career and the rise of Mott.

The organization headed by Annie C. Bill frequently changed names, a fact that can be confusing to anyone seeking information on the church. Founded originally as the Central Assembly of the Church of Christian Science in 1913 in England, it became the New Church of Christ, Scientist, the Mother Church in 1916. The following year the name became the New Church, the Leading Christian Science Church. In the United States in 1922, it was briefly known as the New Community of Christian Scientists, the Parent Community. In 1924 it became the Christian Science Parent Church of the New Generation, though it was also known as the Church of the Transforming Covenant. It eventually became known as the Church of Universal Design, which remained the official name until Bill died.

Sources:

Bill, Annie C. *The Universal Design of Life*. Boston: A. A. Beauchamp, 1924.

Church of Integration. *Spiritual Organization*. New York: Integration Publishing Company, 1946.

Mott, Francis J. *Christ the Seed*. Boston: A. A. Beauchamp, 1939.

————. *Consciousness Creative*. Boston: A.A. Beauchamp, 1937.

————. *The Universal Design of Birth*. Philadelphia: David McKay Company, 1948.

Swihart, Altman K. *Since Mrs. Eddy*. New York: Henry Holt, 1931.

Margaret Laird Foundation

Margaret Laird was a practitioner at the First Church of Christ, Scientist, in Evanston, Illinois. In the late 1930s, she was accused of erroneous teachings. These charges led to a decade of negotiations between Laird and the board of directors of the Mother Church, and in the end her name was removed from the list of practitioners. In 1957 she resigned from the Mother Church, but she continued to teach and operate as an independent Christian Science practitioner. Then, in 1959, she incorporated the Margaret Laird Foundation in California.

The stated purposes of the foundation were to conduct research into the science of being and disseminate the results of this research. A worldwide fellowship with other independent Scientists was established and centers were opened in Liverpool and Bombay. The British group published *The Liverpool Newsletter of the Margaret Laird Foundation*, a bimonthly periodical.

Among the former Christian Scientists associated with Laird was Harold Woodhull Lund of Bridgeport, Connecticut. In 1963 Lund began publishing *The Lund Re-View* and he authored a number of pamphlets as well. Lund maintained a cordial relationship with the Margaret Laird Foundation, and each distributed the other's writings.

After Laird's Death in 1982, the foundation became the Institute of Metaphysical Science, now located in La Jolla, California. The institute continued to do research in the manner laid out by Baird.

Sources:

Laird, Margaret. *Christian Science Re-explored: A Challenge to Original Thinking*. Rev. ed. Los Angeles: Margaret Laird Foundation, 1971.

————. *The Personal Concept*. Los Angeles: Margaret Laird Foundation, 1969.

Lund, Harold Woodhull. *Four Steps in the Evolution of Religious Thought*. Bridgeport, CT: Author, 1964.

NEW THOUGHT

Altrurian Society

The Altrurian Society was founded by L. A. Fealy in 1911 in Birmingham, Alabama. In 1892, Fealy had had a vision in which he was told to "go heal the sick" and to seek, through laws that would be revealed, a plan in which all might know the "freedom from the bonds of matter and have Health, Happiness, and Abundance." Following this inspiration, he studied the hidden and latent forces of the inner self and became a successful healer. His success led to an "Initiation into Apostolic Powers," and as a bishop he was able to establish churches and commission others as ministers and healers. By 1902 he was actively traveling, preaching, and healing.

The goals of the Altrurian Society were to "Heal, Teach Abundance and Happiness, and otherwise perform the ordinances of God." The society taught a belief in One God. By strict obedience to law, individuals could become conscious of God within. According to this teaching, every person has the potential to follow in the footsteps of Jesus, the Son of God. Christ healed the sick and did other mighty works as a demonstration of the way of salvation, and what he did, anyone can do. Healing the sick and abundance from God are a part of the Christian's inheritance.

The society followed seven ordinances: belief, faith, repentance, baptism, remission of sin through confession and work, divine consciousness, and the transmission of the power of the Holy Ghost by the laying on of hands. The Kingdom of God is present when persons comply with the law of God in belief, acceptance, faith, intention, contemplation, meditation, and conviction.

The Altrurian Society was administered by a board of trustees with a president, vice president, secretary, and treasurer. Spiritually, it was led by a hierarchy of apostles, bishops, ministers, deacons, and disciples. The members were called upon to demonstrate healing, happiness, and opulence.

The society was hindered in its work by the arrest of Fealy in 1916 for violating the medical practice acts of the state of Alabama. While his conviction slowed the society, it did not prove fatal. Nonetheless, the Altrurian Society seems to have disappeared in the 1930s, and it is known today primarily through several pamphlets that have survived.

Sources:

Fealy, L. A. *Love's Way*. Birmingham, AL: Altrurian Society, 1927.

McCulloch, Bonnie. *Fealy Aphorisms*. Birmingham, AL: Altrurian Society, 1913.

Rubenstein, I. H. *A Treatise on the Law on Cults*. Chicago: Ordain Press, 1981.

American School of Mentalvivology

The American School of Mentalvivology was founded in the 1960s by Dr. Merle E. Parker. It grew out of the Foundation for Divine Meditation, which was founded by Parker in 1949 and headquartered in Santa Isabel, Calfornia. Mentalvivology was devised as a science of mind and a practical application of the law of mind. The goal was to produce whole men and women. The basic course involved teaching the student to produce any sensation at will, the use of mind to effect "faith healing," the use of the inner mind to set goals and accomplish them, and the practical application of mind. Advanced courses dealt with mysticism and the ritual magic of the ancient wisdom. These advanced lessons were originally published by the now defunct Aquarius School of the Masters, also located in Santa Isabel. All of the courses were done by correspondence. It is not known how many students took these courses, however.

Sources:

Parker, Merle E. *Instant Healing Now!* Santa Isabel, CA: Foundation for Divine Meditation, 1955.

————. *The Mentalvivology Story*. Thornfield, MO: Author, 1969.

Applied Power

Applied Power was the name given to the metaphysical ministry of Jane Hanford Hopkins and Charles Henry Hopkins, two metaphysical teachers during the 1920s. C. H. Hopkins had been a successful businessman, while his wife had been a teacher of oratory and drama. When they retired, they forsook urban life and moved to Les Cheneaux Islands, Michigan, for a life centered on nature and self-expression. In this rustic setting, revelations began to flow through Jane Hopkins. Applied Power grew out of these revelations, which the Hopkinses compiled into a book, *Applied Power*, in 1926.

Leaving behind the conception of an anthropomorphic deity, the Hopkinses began with God, whom they described as Pure Spirit, Perfect Life, Love, Truth, Law and Harmony, All Wise, Knowing, Powerful, Perfect, and Immanent. They viewed humans as threefold beings consisting of body or matter, mind or soul, and spirit. They felt that while most individuals acknowledged their physical and mental aspect, most people only partially acknowledged their spiritual aspect. While everything in the universe is an expression of Spirit, humans are only vaguely aware of that fact. As an expression of God, humans are conceived in power (not sin), and there is virtually no limit to a human's power short of the infinite.

In the Applied Power view, the universe operates under three great laws: love, the creative force in the universe; life, the expression of cooperation between God and man; and liberty, or freedom from limitations as one comes into a realization of God. Success depends upon the full harmonious working of the whole human being.

Jane and Charles Hopkins lived in Cedarville on Les Cheneaux Islands. Theirs was a personal ministry, rendered through one-to-one relationships with pupils. They invited their students to gather at Cedarville each summer for intensive study based upon their textbook. The rest of the year they spent touring the country, teaching and lecturing.

Sources:

Hartman, William C. *Who's Who in Occultism, New Thought, Psychism and Spiritualism*. Jamaica, NY: Occult Press, 1927.

Hopkins, Jane Hanford, and Charles Henry Hopkins. *Applied Power*. Cedarville, MI: Authors, 1926.

The Aquarian Ministry

The Aquarian Ministry, founded by George B. Brownell (d. 1945) and Louise B. Brownell (d. 1967) in 1918 in Brookline, Massachusetts, was a major force within the larger New Thought metaphysical community for half a century. Organized around a magazine, *The Aquarian Age*, and correspondence lessons, it gathered members from across the United States and around the world. Shortly after its founding, the ministry moved to California, finally settling in Santa Barbara in 1920. The heart of the ministry was a daily prayer time each morning, during which the Brownells prayed for individuals who wrote them asking for help on matters of either health or financial distress. The prime teaching work was done through a 52-part correspondence course. The Prosperity League (later the Mutual Blessing League), an integral part of the ministry, was organized by the Brownells to assist members in financial and career goals.

The ministry established itself on the left wing of the emerging New Thought metaphysical community, and it freely included various theosophical and occult teachings. The Brownells believed strongly in reincarnation, and astrology was also given a special emphasis. However, the ministry departed from theosophy in its main work of healing. (Healing was the central work of the Brownells' ministry. They believed that, in light of each person's Divine heritage, healing is an immediate possibility, and anyone can rise above hereditary, environmental, and karmic influences.) In particular, the Brownells opposed the theosophic admonitions against healing work as interfering with an individual's karma. During the early years of the ministry, a special emphasis was placed upon assisting young mothers during their pregnancy and childbirth.

Following the death of her husband in 1947, Louise Brownell enlisted the help of James Dodds (d. 1951), a pastor of the Church of the Truth in Portland, Oregon—and a noted author in his own right—to head the ministry and edit the magazine. Under his leadership, the magazine, heretofore written primarily by the Brownells, featured articles by many of the leading New Thought authors. In addition, the emphasis on astrology, so prominent in the Brownells' ministry, virtually disappeared. Following his untimely death four years later, there was a succession of editors. Finally, Lionel Kenworthy, also a pastor in the Church of the Truth, assumed control in 1958. In 1963 Kenworthy moved the ministry headquarters to Atascadero, California, but it survived only a few years after this final relocation.

Sources:

Brownell, George B. *Reincarnation*. Santa Barbara, CA: Aquarian Ministry, 1946.

Brownell, Louise B. *Life Abundant for You*. Santa Barbara, CA: Aquarian Ministry, 1928.

————. *Your Destiny in the Zodiac and Its Mastery*. Santa Barbara, CA: Aquarian Ministry, 1925.

Brownell, Louise B., and George B. Brownell. "Lessons in Truth from the Aquarian Ministry." *The Aquarian Age* 37 (April 1927).

Dodds, James E. *Conscious Immortality*. Santa Barbara, CA: Aquarian Ministry, 1942.

Association of Independent Ministries (AIM)

The Association of Independent Ministries (AIM) was a fellowship of independent New Thought ministers and churches founded in 1984 under the leadership of Dr. Margaret Stevens, the pastor of the Santa Anita Church in Arcadia, California. Stevens was ordained in 1966 by the Church and School of Christian Philosophy in Phoenix, Arizona, and she became the pastor of the Santa Anita Church the following year. In 1977 she founded the Santa Anita Center for Ministerial Studies, a school and seminary.

At its initial meeting in 1984, a newsletter, *On Target*, was planned, and future conferences were slated to be held semiannually. In addition, AIM provided a home for New Thought ministers in noncongregationally oriented chaplaincy ministries. AIM also established a speakers bureau and a prayer ministry. By the end of the decade, however, two of the leading ministers had retired, and in the absence of fresh leadership, the association disbanded.

Sources:

Stevens, Margaret. *Prosperity Is God's Idea*. Marina del Rey, CA: DeVorss, 1978.

Church of Hakeem

The Church of Hakeem was founded by Clifton Jones, better known to his followers as Hakeem Abdul Rasheed, in Oakland, California, in January 1978. Jones, a Detroit-born black man, attended Purdue University as a psychology major. In the mid-1970s he ran a weight-reduction clinic, which was closed in 1976 when the state Board of Medical Quality Assurance reported that he was using "psychology" rather than diet and exercise to treat clients. This meant that he was practicing psychology without a license.

Jones then turned from weight reduction to religion and assumed his new name. Like his colleague, Rev. Frederick Eikerenkoetter II (Reverend Ike), the founder of the United Church and Science of Living Institute, Hakeem built upon New Thought emphases that health, wealth, and happiness came from positive mental attitudes put into positive action. He emphasized positive action as a means to wealth. In contrast to Reverend Ike, however, Hakeem implemented his teachings through a variation of what is known as the Ponzi scheme, a standard confidence game. Members paid into the church with the promise of a 400 percent return within three years. Members would, in turn, recruit further investors. In such schemes, early investors receive their promised return, but those who join later receive nothing, not even their original investment. Such schemes are illegal.

In May 1979, Hakeem was indicted and later convicted on six counts of fraud. In addition, a group of members signed a class action suit against the church, and the Internal Revenue Service moved against the church to collect back taxes. The cummulative effect of these actions paralyzed the Church of Hakeem, which by then had been established in San Diego, Los Angeles, San Francisco, and Sacramento, California, with an estimated 5,000 to 10,000 members.

Church of Inner Wisdom

The Church of Inner Wisdom was founded in San Jose, California, in 1968 by a metaphysician, Dr. Joan Gibson. Prior to 1968, she had been a member of the Rosicrucians (Ancient Mystic Order of the Rosy Cross) and had studied with Clark Wilkerson, the founder of the Institute of Cosmic Wisdom. The church combined the teachings of New Thought with a major secondary emphasis on the psychic. The teachings were described as "macro-ontology" and focused on the nature of a child of God, forgiveness, the expansion of awareness, Jesus and the major religious prophets as examples for living, and sharing received truth. The psychic was viewed as a tool in expanding awareness. However, without the perspective of metaphysics, this approach became a means of mere ego gratification.

Lessons, which could be taken in classes or by correspondence, were the main means of disseminating the church's teachings. The church was governed by a board of directors, with Gibson as the permanent chairman. The church's annual business meeting was open only to officers, directors, and ministers. Total membership was never reported, but in 1972, ministers of the church were at work in Alameda, Alhambra, Concord, and Burlingame, California; Phoenix, Mesa, and Wickenburg, Arizona; Chicago, Illinois; Erie, Pennsylvania; and Atlanta, Georgia. The church also published a periodical called *The Voice*.

Church of the New Civilization

The Church of the New Civilization was founded by Julia Seton (1862–1950), who emerged as one of the most energetic exponents of New Thought metaphysics during the early twentieth century. Her early bouts with tuberculosis led her into medicine, and she became a doctor, doing postgraduate work at Tufts Medical College in Boston, Massachusetts. She also became a theosophist and was briefly married (1903–1914) to the New Thought lecturer and writer F. W. Sears, during which time her books appeared under her married name, Julia Seton Sears. Her healing practice led her to concentrate first on preventive medicine, but in 1905 she left her medical work to pursue a career in metaphysical healing. Her teachings blended theosophy (represented in her books on numerology, the aura, and the emanation on body) and more traditional New Thought metaphysical themes (e.g., healing and prosperity).

The Church of the New Civilization was founded in Boston in 1905. In 1907 Seton moved to New York City and began a second congregation, called the New Thought Church and School. Within a few years there were affiliated centers in Brooklyn, Hempstead, and Buffalo, New York; Boston, Salem, and Brockton, Massachusetts; Cleveland, Ohio; Chicago, Illinois; Denver, Colorado; and California. Classes were taught in healing, abundance, graphology, the tarot, and numerology. As World War I was beginning, Seton began a period of travel to England (where an affiliate center had developed soon after the first Boston work) and Australia. Upon her return to America she settled in Kansas City, Missouri. Around 1937 she purchased land near Ocala, Florida, and began to build the New Civilization school, known as the Ocala Post-Graduate School of Metaphysics. Unfortunately, the location was commandeered by the army during World War II, and the day after she reclaimed her property all but one of the buildings burned in a massive fire. Seton, then in her 80s, retired from active leadership in the movement she had led, and it dwindled away after her death in 1950.

The basic perspective of the church was presented systematically in the students' manual, *Fundamental Principles of the New Civilization*. Seton proposed a reordering of human life around the basic principle that "God Is All." She taught that humans are Individualized God on a self-imposed pathway. Seeing life as a whole, people can see themselves as part of the larger system and know that there is no evil, for what people call evil is simply undeveloped good.

Sources:

Seton, Julia. *Fundamental Principles of the New Civilization*. New York: Edward J. Clode, 1916.

———. *The Key to Health, Wealth and Love*. New York: Edward J. Clode, 1917.

———. *The Mystic's Goal*. London: William Rider & Son, 1924.

———. *The Science of Success*. New York: Edward J. Clode, 1914.

———. *Western Symbology*. Chicago: New Publishing Company, 1929.

Church of the Science of Religion

The Church of the Science of Religion was founded in 1922 by Rev. Carolyn Barbour Le Galyon, a former practitioner with the Church of Christ, Scientist, who had been healed of a broken wrist. She became a student of various New Thought leaders, including Charles S. Fillmore, Ernest S. Holmes, and others. The Church of the Science of Religion taught an eclectic New Thought perspective drawn from numerous early metaphysical teachers. It was headquartered in Cleveland, Ohio, at the New Thought Temple of Christ. The church dissolved following Le Galyon's death in the 1970s.

Sources:

LeGalyon, Carolyn Barbour. *All Things New: The Science of Religion Textbook*. New York: Analysts' Publisher, 1963.

Comforter League of Light

The Comforter League of Light grew out of the intense religious experience of Florence Gloria Crawford, who, around 1913, was "given the Comforter message." The Comforter is a reference to one of the last sayings of Jesus to his disciples: "It is expedient for you that I go away; for if I go not away, the Comforter will not come unto you" (John 16:7). Traditionally, the Comforter has been interpreted by Christians as the Holy Spirit. Crawford interpreted both the Holy Spirit and the Comforter as the Christ Consciousness. From the time of her experience, Crawford acted as one entrusted with a message for the entire world. She opened the Irvington Center of Truth in Portland, Oregon, which became the core congregation of the Comforter League of Light. A major step in the emergence of the league occurred in the months following the begin-

ning of World War I, when Crawford was led to focus upon the work of the Christ Consciousness as bringing a message of love, peace, and comfort to the world. Thus, in December 1914, she issued the first copies of a new magazine, *The Comforter*.

Crawford taught the central New Thought affirmations. God was defined as the great life-power, substance, and intelligence, while humans bring God into active expression. Crawford believed that she was in regular contact with Jesus, from whom she received teachings. Included in her revelatory writings were her commentaries on Jesus' parables and a lengthy book on peace. She also placed an emphasis on prosperity, which she believed to be immediately available to people as they expressed their highest ideals following universal laws.

During the years of her ministry, Crawford was a popular speaker at ecumenical New Thought gatherings. In 1921 the league moved to San Francisco, California, where it continued for another decade. Integral to the league's work was the Comforter Healing Circle. Each morning at 10 a.m. Crawford and others at the San Francisco headquarters prayed individually for those requesting their assistance. Members and readers of the magazine around the country were invited to join them for a half hour of silence at that time. Following the healing prayers, members were invited to participate in the Comforter Study Hour, for which materials were published in the magazine. Healing groups were formed along the West Coast.

Among the members of the Comforter League of Light was Baird Spalding, the author of the multivolume occult classic *The Life and Teachings of the Masters of the Far East*, the first chapters of which were originally published in *The Comforter* in 1922.

(Florence Gloria Crawford should not be confused with Florence L. Crawford, the founder of the Pentecostal denomination the Apostolic Faith, which was also headquartered in Portland, Oregon, during the years of the Comforter League of Light.)

Sources:

Crawford, Florence Gloria. *The Christ Ideal for World Peace*. San Francisco: Comforter League of Light, 1925.

Disciples of Faith

The Disciples of Faith, based in Nashville, Tennessee, was a prayer fellowship similar in nature to the Life-Study Fellowship. Like that fellowship, no mention of the leadership was made in the group's literature. Members were linked through mailings and printed testimonials. The group was focused on a united worldwide prayer fellowship. Members were asked to rate themselves according to health, prayer life, use of time, faith, and relation to God, and they worked on receiving the full abundance of God.

Central to the Disciples of Faith were lessons designed to train members to prepare the prayer-time, to understand the power of prayer, and to know the laws of abundant living, faith, and spiritual healing. The mystical teachings of Jesus on the necessity of prayer as "holy communion" were stressed, and the group believed that miracles would happen for people after their prayers were offered in Jesus' name.

Dispensable Church

The Dispensable Church was founded in 1985 as an instrument to facilitate the teaching work of Hugh Prather (b. 1938). Prather had been raised as a Christian Scientist, and for a year he attended Principia College. As his thought developed, however, he found himself more in tune with the teachings of a New Age spiritual text called *A Course in Miracles*. Through the 1970s, Prather issued a series of books containing reflections on his inner explorations and pilgrimage, and these became popular metaphysical and New Age texts. The first, *Notes to Myself* (1970), became a best-seller and was followed by *I Touch the Earth, the Earth Touches Me* (1972) and *Notes on Love and Courage* (1977). Each book offers a set of brief entries from Prather's diary, which comprise seemingly random reflections upon his reactions to mundane events. However, for many readers, the numerous brief entries led to an understanding of the nature of the world and provided advice on a way of existing in the world.

Prather, by his example, made note of an underlying spiritual reality and projected a means of living at peace with that reality. He sought to be in touch with his feelings as a means of living in the present. He felt that spending too much time reflecting on the past or projecting oneself into the future was dehumanizing and a way of holding on to unhappiness. He also asserted that a major problem with society was the tendency to continually analyze events in life, rather than simply experience and learn from them.

Prather's vision was subjective in the extreme. He saw the need for self-exploration and self-knowledge as a means to freedom and happiness. He saw body states, especially illness, as the projection of inner states and attitudes into visible expression. As he became intimate with his own inner state and conscious of his actions and reaction in community, he began to develop a series of games and exercises that could assist others in the same explorations, with a goal of producing a life of consistent happiness. Happiness, to Prather, is consistent with a life of simplicity, peace, gentleness, forgiveness, humor, trust, and fearlessness.

The Dispensable Church provided a means for Prather to interact with the people who had been attracted by his writings. Prather spoke and led attendees in the mental exercises he had developed. The name of the church indicated that attendance was not a necessary activity, but that gatherings might be useful for a while. Tapes of Prather's sessions were recorded and distributed to people across the country and around the world.

Sources:

Prather, Hugh. *A Book of Games: A Course in Spiritual Play.* Garden City, NY: Doubleday, 1981.

———. *I Touch the Earth, the Earth Touches Me.* Garden City, NY: Doubleday, 1972.

———. *Notes on How to Live in the World . . . and Still Be Happy.* Garden City, NY: Doubleday, 1986.

———. *Notes on Love and Courage.* Garden City, NY: Doubleday, 1977.

———. *Notes to Myself: My Struggle to Become a Person.* Lafayette, Ca: Real People Press, 1970.

ESP Picture Prayers

ESP Picture Prayers was headed by Murcie P. Smith of Gary, Indiana. Like the Life-Study Fellowship, ESP Picture Prayers offered printed prayers based upon the idea of God as a loving father. The organization also offered private ESP readings to members as an added incentive. Included in the prayers were special ones for those in the armed services, a "Blessed Sacred Heart of Jesus Christ Prayer" (with a picture of the Sacred Heart included), and a "Blessed Sacred Eyes of Jesus Christ Prayer" (with a picture of the sacred eyes included).

Inner Powers Society

The Inner Powers Society was founded by Alfred Pritchard, its president, in the 1950s. A metaphysician, Pritchard contacted prospective members through advertisements in metaphysical and psychic publications. The society was organized by members living near the home office in Yucca Valley, California. It offered courses that Pritchard constructed on a wide variety of New Thought topics.

Pritchard taught that one must become attuned to the "inner environment" of "cycling cosmic forces." As these forces of inner powers flow through mankind, the distortions of past reversals of truth will be eliminated, and a new age of super-intelligence will be established. Pritchard believed that humanity was entering a new age, an occurrence that is repeated every 2,155 years.

Sources:

Pritchard, Alfred W. *Man—God's Helpmate.* Los Angeles: Inner Powers Society, 1958.

Institute of Esoteric Transcendentalism

Dr. Robert W. C. Burke is a New Thought teacher in Los Angeles. In 1956, he founded the Robert Burke Foundation. In 1969 his interest in Christology, combined with his New Thought beliefs, led him to found the Institute of Esoteric Transcendentalism. The institute had no formal statement of belief, and the right to hold divergent religious tenets was acknowledged.

The basis of the institute's teachings was Christology, the science of the knowledge of Christ, which rests solely upon the words credited to Jesus. All else in the Bible is considered history and stories for guidance and inspiration. Jesus is described as the man who spoke the illumined Word, Christ, and laid before mankind a foundation for spirituality. Mankind is a creature of divinity, and thus "of God." He has within him the divine power that moves the universe, but man misuses the abundant gift of God. In this tradition, intellectual awareness is the first step in building toward a spiritual consciousness. When spiritual consciousness is put into action, complete self-awareness occurs. Meditation is also emphasized as a way to spiritual consciousness.

The institute was headquartered at the William Penn Hotel in Whittier, California, where a full program of lectures, classwork, and individual counseling was offered. The institute produced *The Christext* and *The Transcendentalist* both of which followed a lesson format and were mailed to people several states.

Institute of Infinite Science

Dr. Roman Ostoja was a Polish nobleman who discovered as a teenager that he was telepathic. After finishing his medical degree, he traveled to India and Tibet to learn yoga and improve his psychic skills. He returned to the West and offered himself to many psychical researchers for testing. In these tests he demonstrated his psychic abilities and yogic austerities, including being buried alive for several hours without air, lying on a bed of nails, and sticking a nail through his hand.

Ostoja traveled to America in the 1920s and worked with Dr. William McDougall, a professor of psychology at Harvard University. He also studied in the early 1920s with Swami Paramahansa Yogananda, the founder of the Self-Realization Fellowship. Shortly thereafter he opened the Institute of Infinite Science in Los Angeles, California. Ostoja offered a variety of nonmedical forms of healing at the institute, and he became known for the cures he facilitated. However, he primarily thought of himself as a Westernized yogi, and he combined the teachings of the East with the new Western psychology, thus providing a form of Hinduism acceptable to modern Westerners. He shared his multiple healing techniques with students as an integral part of his spiritual and metaphysical teachings.

The teachings of Ostoja combined the yoga teachings of Yogananda with New Thought metaphysics. The object was to produce both self-mastery and the identity of the deepest level of the self with the Infinite One, Mind, Self of All, God. The primary method used to achieve these goals, in Ostoja's teachings, is concentration and will power. He taught the yoga disciplines, especially *pranayama* (breathing) for the development of the will, as well as the use of suggestion and autosuggestion as a means of projecting ideas into the mind. Once in the mind, ideas could be a force for good, such as controlling the body in the cure and prevention of disease.

Ostoja continued to head the institute into the late 1940s, but in the ensuing years he died and the institute dissolved. Former students can still be found in southern California.

Sources:

Ostoja, Roman. *Body and Mind Control*. Santa Barbara, CA: J. F. Rowney Press, 1949.

————. *Mind Made Visible*. Santa Barbara, CA: J. F. Rowney Press, 1928.

Interfaith Fellowship

The Interfaith Fellowship was founded in New York City in 1977 as Interfaith, Inc., by Rabbi Joseph H. Gelberman of the New Synagogue, Rev. Jon Mundy (a United Methodist minister), and Swami Satchidananda of Integral Yoga International. As originally conceived, Interfaith provided a meeting ground where people from various faiths could meet together for dialogue, sharing, and mutual worship and celebration. It was built upon the idea that the experiences of joy, love, serenity, wisdom, and healing, which all religions share in common, was more important than those elements of theology and ritual that divided people. The mystical relationship to transcendent reality was emphasized. Interfaith, Inc., held a meeting one Sunday afternoon each month until 1993. Interfaith Fellowship emerged out of this experience as a church where weekly worship services were held.

Taking the lead in Interfaith Fellowship have been Revs. Mundy and Diane Burke. Both have a longtime involvement with *A Course in Miracles*, a metaphysical text channeled by Dr. Helen Schucman. The perspective of the Course is strongly evident in the fellowship's literature. Also growing out of Interfaith, Inc., was the New Seminary, which was established to carry the spirit of the evolving fellowship into the training of ministers, counselors, and practitioners for work in local communities. Joining Rabbi Gelberman and Rev. Mundy in the creation of the seminary was Fr. Giles Spoonhour. Graduates of the seminary have banded together in the Association of Interfaith Ministers.

The Interfaith Fellowship was built upon the idea that inclusiveness is better than exclusivity, and people of all religious and spiritual backgrounds were welcomed. In addition, the literature and wisdom of all faiths were utilized in worship. There was neither a creed nor a set of beliefs to which members had to subscribe. Emphasis was placed upon each person having a direct loving relationship to God, humanity, and all creation. Members sought an understanding and appreciation of all different kinds of people, confident that the process would bring them closer to the Spirit within each person.

As of 1995, there was only one congregation left, with approximately 250 members. The New Seminary, located in New York City, continues the tradition, and over 2,000 individuals have graduated from the two-year training program and been ordained as Interfaith Ministers.

Sources:

About Interfaith Fellowship. Monroe, NY: Interfaith, 1992.

New Thought Science

New Thought Science was a New Thought organization founded by Dr. Crist V. Bass in Los Angeles. Described as a worldwide metaphysical movement, it was very close to the Church of Religious Science and used the writings of Ernest S. Holmes and Frederick Beals as primary texts.

As with most New Thought churches, New Thought Science affirmed that all phenomena of nature, both physical and spiritual, are the expression of one Infinite Intelligence. Members believed that the basic truth of all religions is similar, and that if understood and applied in daily life, truth will bring health and prosperity to the individual. They also adhered to the teachings of Christ found in the New Testament, especially that the kingdom of Heaven is within us, that we are one with the Father, that we should not judge, that we should love each other, that we should return good for evil, that we should minister to each other, and that we should be perfect as the Father is perfect. New Thought Science was open to all and existed as a racially integrated fellowship.

Founded in Nevada, New Thought Science was reincorporated in California in 1954. Bass also founded and led Searchlight University, the church's ministerial training school. The university offered instruction leading to a designation as a practitioner, master metaphysician, minister, or bishop. New Thought Science also offered home study courses.

"Now" Folk

"Now" Folk was formed by people drawn to Henry Harrison Brown (1864–1918), a New Thought leader in San Francisco, California, at the beginning of the twentieth century. Brown, a Civil War veteran and former Unitarian minister, had become an independent lecturer in the 1890s, and in 1900 he launched *Now*, a New Thought periodical, in San Francisco. It was his belief that the most important task to be accomplished in his day was teaching humanity to know itself as an expression of Infinite Energy (i.e., everything theologians mean by God and everything scientists mean by energy). The key to knowledge of humanity's real essence was, according to Brown, suggestion, by which anyone could direct his or her subconscious (the real self) and thereby control the outward expression of the self and produce life according to present desire. Brown's belief was expressed in an affirmation that became the group's

motto: "Man is spirit here and now, with all the possibilities of Divinity within him, and he can consciously manifest these possibilities Here and Now."

Brown developed a broad program of what he termed "soul culture," which involved the education of people in the use of their spiritual faculties. In this regard, he produced a series of booklets that became the basis of a variety of correspondence courses. These courses covered such topics as suggestion, the art of living, psychic development, self-healing, concentration, and psychometry. Brown lectured regularly in San Francisco and organized home meetings throughout the Bay Area.

Brown also offered a critique of turn-of-the-century society, which he saw as characterized by "competition through concentration." He felt that individuals were lost within various social structures, whose members saw fellow members as brothers and all outsiders as aliens. To this competitive society he offered a vision of brotherhood and cooperation through the practical application of the Golden Rule. To that end, in 1906 he organized a short-lived cooperative community in Glendale, California.

Brown died in 1918, and the "Now" Folk did not survive his death. However, *Now*, the magazine he founded, continued for many years as a prominent independent New Thought periodical under its new editor, Sam E. Foulds.

Phoenix Institute

The Phoenix Institute was founded in 1966 in San Diego by the metaphysician Kathryn Breese-Whiting, its president. It had three stated purposes: to teach the inner creative action of science, art, and religion; to encourage an intercultural atmosphere; and to provide a place for those who wished to live a life of dedicated service. It implemented these goals through a basic course in mind science and through its affiliated structures: the School of Man, the International Friendship Club, and the Church of Man. The Church of Man was the specifically religious aspect of the institute, and its statement of belief formed the basis for the Institute's ideals.

The Church of Man taught that there is only one presence, God; that God and man cannot be separated; that man hungers for oneness with the self of his own being; that this "one" acts reciprocally and man is the evidence of this action; that man experiences the finding of himself; that every man is the church; and that the principle "Ye are Gods" is verified by both esoteric and exoteric experience.

Sources:

Breese-Whiting, Kathryn. *Miracle of the Phoenix*. San Diego: Phoenix Institute, 1995.

————. *The Phoenix Rises*. San Diego: Portal Publications, 1971.

Psychiana

Psychiana, one of the first mail-order religious groups, was founded by Frank Bruce Robinson (1886–1948), the son of a Baptist minister and a former Baptist minister himself. His bad experiences with what he termed "orthodox" churches led Robinson away from his Baptist faith, while concurrently spurring his search for God. While working in a pharmacy in Portland, Oregon, he had an encounter with God, which became a life-changing event for him. Shortly after that event, he enrolled for the 1915–1916 school year at the College of Divine Metaphysics, an early New Thought school in Indianapolis. Around 1928 he moved to Moscow, Idaho, where he worked in a pharmacy and began to teach metaphysics. He authored a series of correspondence lessons, and in 1929 he founded Psychiana as a new religion. Developing a national advertising campaign, he gathered students who took his lessons by mail.

The lessons quickly became a success, and within a few years they were being sent out to all 50 states and to some 70 countries. During the peak of the movement, Robinson was receiving more than 1,000 letters daily. Periodically, he would travel around the country to lecture. In the late 1930s he began to establish offices in other countries to facilitate the distribution of his writings, but he lost most of them during World War II. He also founded the *Psychiana Quarterly* magazine. As the work grew, Robinson, as founder and teacher of the organization, appointed himself archbishop. By the late 1940s he was assisted by four bishops in leading the organization. Members became a part of the Psychiana Brotherhood.

Robinson's lessons expounded a naturally revealed religion that rejected all supernaturalism. To Robinson, God worked through immutable Law and was identical with that Law. Rather than a personal deity, Robinson described God as the Spiritual Law (usually referred to as the God-Law). This Law was equated with the invisible power and intelligence behind the physical universe, and matter is a visible expression of that power. By understanding and using the Law, he believed, people can rid themselves of poverty, sickness, and unhappiness. Thought was considered the manifestation of God in human life.

Robinson was also opposed to the deification of Jesus, a popular subject in several of his books. He denounced a religion based upon the life of a "crucified God." Rather, he felt that an emphasis should be placed on the message of Jesus: that the power of the God-Law is real, and the Life Spirit can be used to produce health, wealth, and happiness. The evil in the world can be attributed to humanity's ignorance of the God-Law.

Robinson died in 1948. His son carried on the work for several years, but eventually it dissolved. During the last years of his life, Robinson encouraged the formation of Psychiana groups, something he had actively discouraged during most of his years as a writer. During the 1970s there was a brief attempt to revive Psychiana by a former student in California, but it lasted only a brief time.

Sources:

Bach, Marcus. *He Talked with God*. Portland, OR: Metropolitan Press, 1951.

Braden, Charles Samuel. *These Also Believe: A Study of Modern American Cults and Minority Religious Movements*. New York: Macmillan, 1949.

Robinson, Frank B. *The God Nobody Knows*. Moscow, ID: Psychiana, 1941.

———. *The Pathway to God*. Moscow, ID: Psychiana, 1943.

———. *The Strange Autobiography of Frank B. Robinson*. Moscow, ID: Psychiana, 1949.

Psychophysics Foundation

The Psychophysics Foundation was headed by Ingra Raamah and dedicated to teaching the science of abundant living. Psychophysics teachings were centered upon the great laws of being that, when known and practiced, lead to healing, success, and fulfilled dreams. In the most ancient times, during the Golden Age, humanity lived in direct contact with God and in accord with his laws. Since that time, human history has been one of losing interior contact with the Word. Truth has remained alive, however, in every age, and it was to be made available through psychophysics. The mid-twentieth century was seen as the time immediately preceding the return of a second Golden Age, just at the very time when humanity seemed to have lost hope of such an event.

Psychophysics was a mixture of metaphysics and concern for bodily health. New students were given exercises and adjustments in diet right from the beginning of their affiliation. The basic law of the universe was seen to be love. The headquarters of the Psychophysics Foundation were in Glendora, California.

Sources:

Raamah, Ingra. *The Science of Abundant Life*. Glendora, CA: The Psychophysics Foundation, n.d.

———. *The Science and Fine Art of Creative Living*. Glendora, CA: The Psychophysics Foundation, n.d.

School of Esoteric Christianity

The School of Esoteric Christianity was a coalition of independent Science of Mind (Religious Science) churches based around Denver, Colorado. The school offered classes for both interested lay students and those seeking licenses as practitioners and ministers at several churches in metropolitan Denver. Among the leading ministers was Dr. Helen V. Walker, pastor of the Esoteric Truth Center in suburban Englewood and publisher of *The Esoterian News*. In the 1970s there was one church in Englewood, one in Pueblo, and three in Denver. Although the school no longer exists, the participating congregations continue as independent churches.

Society of Pragmatic Mysticism

The Society of Pragmatic Mysticism was formed by Mildred Mann (1904–1971), a metaphysical teacher in New York City. Mann was the author of several books, lesson pamphlets, and tracts. When she died, in 1971, she was succeeded by a group that carried on her work and teaching. The society was originally called the Society of Religious Pragmatism and had a meeting center in New York City, where a library, bookstore, and offices were located. After the name was changed, the society relocated to Vermont. Teaching work was centered upon a textbook, *How to Find Your Real Self*, and several lesson series. There were also members located around the country who stayed connected through correspondence.

The Society of Pragmatic Mysticism focused on teaching metaphysics, the combination of science and religion. Metaphysics teaches that man is a child of God, the great mind, and has been given everything he needs for complete self-expression and dominion over his own life. The only issue in life is the self's dealing with its own acceptance and belief. Love and fear are the two emotions from which other issues derive. The task of humans is to express love and overcome fear. Fear arises from the belief that one will lose. When one changes this belief to love and acts on that belief and on self-acceptance, then one finds that God is life.

In 1995 the society reported 30,000 members worldwide with the majority residing in Nigeria.

Wisdom Institute of Spiritual Education

The Wisdom Institute of Spiritual Education (WISE) was founded by Frank and Martha Baker in Dallas, Texas. Martha Baker, the institute's president, was a prolific writer and poet. From the Dallas headquarters, lessons and books were distributed locally and nationally through correspondence courses and mail order. The nonprofit Allison Press published the church's materials.

WISE taught the "life message," which was aimed at perfection of the spirit, mind, and body, and it offered techniques to accomplish this perfection. Self-knowledge of the power within was stressed. In classes, pupils were taught to control their thoughts and feelings and to locate their inner selves and God.

Sources:

Baker, Martha. *Sermonettes in Rhyme*. Dallas, TX: Allison Press, 1960.

———. *Wake Up the God In You and Live*. Dallas, TX: Allison Press, 1958.

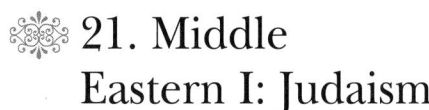

21. Middle Eastern I: Judaism

PAN-DENOMINATIONAL JEWISH ORGANIZATIONS

American Association of Rabbis

The American Association of Rabbis was a professional organization of rabbis who ministered in a congregation, an educational setting, or the chaplaincy. It published a quarterly bulletin.

Synagogue Council of America

The Synagogue Council of America was founded in 1926 for the purpose of providing the several branches of Judaism with a common voice and making the synagogue the center of Jewish spiritual influence. It served as a coordinating body for several of the rabbinical and congregational associations, especially in speaking to the president of the United States and members of Congress. Members of the council included the Central Conference of American Rabbis (Reform), Rabbinical Assembly (Conservative), Rabbinical Council of America (Orthodox), Union of American Hebrew Congregations (Reform), Union of Orthodox Jewish Congregations of America, and United Synagogue of America (Conservative).

Sources:

Rosenthal, Gilbert S. *Contemporary Judaism: Patterns of Survival.* 2nd ed. New York: Human Sciences Press, 1986.

ORTHODOX JUDAISM

Association of American Orthodox Hebrew Congregations

The Association of American Hebrew Congregations was an early attempt to organize Orthodox Jewish synagogues. It was founded in 1887 by lay leaders in some 15 congregations. They advertised in Europe for a rabbi to come to America and serve as a chief rabbi. Jacob Joseph of Vilna came over the next year. His task was to supervise the congregations, establish a Beth Din (Jewish court), see to the proper observance of dietary regulations in the preparation of kosher food, and administer the religious schools.

Chief Rabbi Joseph met fierce opposition from other rabbis (none of whom were consulted by the association earlier), and people were displeased by the attempt to establish kosher regulations. He died in 1902, by which time the association had been abandoned and new structures of a more permanent nature arose.

Sources:

Rosenthal, Gilbert S. *Contemporary Judaism: Patterns of Survival.* New York: Human Sciences Press, 1986.

HASIDIC JUDAISM

Sighet Hasidism

Rebbe Moses Teitelbaum of Ujhely, Hungary, was the founder of the Teitelbaum Hasidic dynasty. The third in the succession, Rebbe Zalmen Leib Teitelbaum, established the center of the work at Sighet (now in northern Romania). Until 1926 Sighet was a prominent Hasidic center, but the sudden death of Rebbe Hayin Hersch Teitelbaum in that year left his 14-year-old son, Zalmen Leib Teitelbaum, as heir to the succession. Because Hasidism is built on the charisma of the rebbe, the Sighet center never regained its former authority. After the Holocaust, the Sighet Hasidic community was disrupted. Finally it was reestablished in Zenta, Yugoslavia, by Rebbe Zalmen Leib's brother, Rebbe Moses Teitelbaum. Rebbe Moses moved to the United States and became leader of the surviving Sighet members from Brooklyn. In 1980, after the death of his uncle, Joel Teitelbaum, he became grand rebbe of the much larger community of Satmar Hasidim, and the two lines were merged under his leadership.

Work of the Chariot

The Work of the Chariot was a Jewish mystical group active during the 1970s whose main objective was the translation, publication, and distribution of Jewish, Christian, and Islamic mystical material, particularly Hasidic/Kabbalistic source materials. The work was centered in three groups that met to practice the principles of practical mysticism. Two were in Los Angeles and one in Hollywood. Affiliate groups were located in England and Israel, and a number of distinguished scholars served as consultants in the translation work.

The Work of the Chariot published its own translation of Kabbalistic texts such as the *Book of Formation*, *Book of Splendor*, and *Tree of Life* by Rabbi Yitzaq Luria, Ha-Ari. The group was heavily Kabbalistic. The Chariot of God of Ezekiel is a major theme in Kabbalistic literature. Its authors attempted to know not the unknowable Ein Soph but the Throne of God on its Chariot. Such knowledge is one of the "secrets" of God, to be obtained by theurgic (magical) means.

Sources:

Book of Formation (Sepher Yetzirah): The Letters of Our Father Abraham. Hollywood, CA: Work of the Chariot, 1971.

Book of Names. Hollywood, CA: Work of the Chariot, 1971.

Work of the Chariot, Ezekiel, Isaiah, II Kings. Hollywood, CA: Work of the Chariot, 1971.

Work of the Chariot, Introduction. Hollywood, CA: Work of the Chariot, 1971.

AFRICAN-AMERICAN JUDAISM

United Hebrew Congregation

The United Hebrew Congregation was the name of about a half dozen congregations of black Jews that, during the mid-1970s, were centered upon the Ethiopian Hebrew Culture Center in Chicago, headed by Rabbi Naphtali Ben Israel. It was this group's belief that Ham's sons were black. Included were the Hebrews of which one reads in the Bible. Abraham came from Chaldea, and the ancient Chaldeans were black. The congregation members believed Solomon was black (Song of Solomon 1:5). Sabbath services were held on Saturday. No sign of their continuance into the 1980s has been found.

ADDITIONAL JEWISH GROUPS

Community of Micah (Fabrengen)

The Community of Micah was one of several radical, left-oriented groups that emerged from the wave of social consciousness in the late 1960s. Members attempted to relate all action to the goal of human liberation. A major concern was the survival of Judaism, and the group was involved in Jewish consciousness-raising. The community was an urban communal structure but in 1972 attempted to establish Kibbutz Micah as an experiment in Jewish rural communal living in central Pennsylvania. It did not survive.

The community developed an active study program that included Hasidic literature (especially the books of Martin Buber), mysticism, yoga, and radical Jewish politics. The group was disowned by the Washington (D.C.) Jewish Community in 1971. The community published the *Voice of Micah* and other Jewish and political action material.

Sources:

Waskow, Arthur I. *The Bush Is Burning.* New York: Macmillan, 1971.

Society of the Bible in the Hands of Its Creators Inc.

The Society of the Bible in the Hands of Its Creators Inc. was formed in 1943. The inspiration for the society was the work of Moses Guibbory, the Ukrainian-born international president and organizer of the group. He was assisted by the British-born radio commentator and Jewish convert Boake Carter and by David Horowitz, founder of the United Israel World Union, who met Guibbory in Jerusalem. The object of the society was to publish and spread the ideas of *The Bible in the Hands of Its Creators* by Guibbory and both a Hebrew and an English Bible as perfected by Guibbory's research. It also sought to develop and maintain places of devotion and spiritual guidance for members of the society.

The Bible in the Hands of Its Creators is a massive volume, the chief ideas of which center upon defining the nature of Jehovah, the one God, besides whom there is no other. Jehovah, while one, is also many. He is both male and female, the terrible God, the creator, the merciful and gracious God, the forgiving and long-suffering one. The prophetic day of Jehovah began in 1929 (5689 A.M.) and has since continued.

Guibbory, as the international president, controlled the society, assisted by an executive board of from 5 to 13 members. Missionary work began, but Guibbory stopped it. In the late 1970s, the society closed its New York office, and the only known gathering of members was at Guibbory's South Norwalk, Connecticut, home for the major Jewish holidays. Gentile converts were included.

Sources:

Guibbory, Moses. *The Bible in the Hands of Its Creators.* New York: Society of the Bible in the Hands of Its Creators, 1943.

 ## 22. Middle Eastern II: Islam, Zoroastrianism, Baha'i

ISLAM

Al Qaeda

Al Qaeda (literally, "the base," also spelled Al Qa'ida, or Al-Qa'idah) was founded in 1989 by Osama bin Laden (b. 1957), a wealthy Arabian. While enjoying some support in the United States in the 1990s, its status was called into question when it was implicated by U.S. government officials in a series of terrorist actions culminating in the attacks on American embassies at Kenya and Tanzania in 1998. Then on September 11, 2001, agents connected to Al Qaeda carried out the bombings of the Pentagon in suburban Washington, D.C., and the World Trade Center in New York City, New York. In response, the American president, George W. Bush (b. 1946), moved to activate a coalition similar to the one that supported the Persian Gulf War a decade earlier. In October 2001, the United States and its allies opened military operations against Al Qaeda, then based in Afghanistan, and its allies, the Taliban, who then ruled Afghanistan. This operation has brought down the Taliban government and disrupted the Al Qaeda network, though the current status of the organization remains a matter of some speculation. There is no evidence that Al Qaeda has existed in the United States as more than small cells of operatives sent into the country for temporary missions. Given the impact of the events of September 11, 2001, on both the secular and religious community, it has been deemed important to summarize information concerning Al Qaeda.

The development of Al Qaeda has depended in a large part on the career of bin Laden. He was born the son of a wealthy Saudi businessman and his Syrian wife. While attending King Abdulaziz University, he met Abdullah Azzam (1941–1989), a Jordanian who had joined the university faculty, and Muhammad Qutb, the brother of Sayyid Qutb (1906–1966). Both were leading figures in the Islamist movement, a reactionary Muslim movement that had developed in Egypt following the final collapse of the Islamic Empire in the years after World War II (1939–1945) and the division of its territories into various independent countries. They looked toward the reestablishment of the empire and placed the blame for its fall on the West. Islamists also staunchly opposed the rise of the state of Israel and the occupation of Afghanistan by Soviet forces. Azzam and Qutb introduced Islamist thought to bin Laden.

In 1980, bin Laden relocated to Afghanistan, where he raised money for the forces resisting the Soviets. In 1984, he established the House of the Faithful (*Beit-al-Ansar*) in Peshawar, Pakistan, that served as a base of operation for the anti-Soviet forces. He traveled widely and created a large international network of support. In 1989, the same year the Soviets pulled out of Afghanistan, he founded Al Qaeda.

In 1991, bin Laden made common cause with Hassan al-Turabi (b. 1932), the leader of the National Islamic Front (NIF), an Islamist political party that had assisted the military takeover of Sudan. Bin Laden would move to Sudan to expand and establish Al Qaeda as an organization dedicated to bringing the Islamic ideal to fruition. He created a number of businesses to support his program that gradually expanded to include centers for the training of people in guerilla warfare and terrorism. In 1996, bin Laden returned to Afghanistan, where he would enjoy the approbation of the new ruling force: the Taliban. He supplied the Taliban with funds for a spectrum of activities from the arming of its forces to the building of new mosques.

In 1996, bin Laden also issued the first of his legal rulings (called a *fatwa*) highlighting aggressive actions directed against the Muslim world. He was particularly concerned with the United States and directed particular animus at his home country (Saudi Arabia) and America for their mutual role in the Persian Gulf War and the subsequent stationing of American troops in Saudi Arabia in the years after the war. Bin Laden himself stated the following:

> The latest and the greatest of these aggressions incurred by the Muslims since the death of the Prophet (Allah's blessings and salutations be upon Him) is the occupation of the land of the two Holy Places, the foundation of the house of Islam, the place of revelation, the source of the message and the place of the noble Ka'ba, the Qiblah of all Muslims, by the armies of the American Crusaders and their allies.

Two years later, bin Laden, speaking for Al Qaeda and the World Islamic Front, a network of groups aligned with it, activated the core of its network for issuing the now famous manifesto: the ruling against the Jews and crusaders (Americans). He charged the United States with various sins related to its support for Israel and other meddling in Middle East affairs: "For over seven years the United States has been occupying the lands of Islam in the holiest of places, the Arabian Peninsula, plundering its riches, dictating to its rulers, humiliating its people, terrorizing its neighbors."

The World Islamic Front includes the jihad movement in Egypt, Jamiat-ul-Ulema-e-Pakistan (an Egyptian Islamic group), and the jihad movement in Bangladesh. Their cause is what had variously been termed *Islamism*, or popularly in the West, *Islamic fundamentalism*. Islamists have as their goal the removal of Western influence (both politically and culturally) in the Muslim world and the restoration of Islamic law in Muslim countries. The World Islamic Front has been distinguished from other Islamist groups in the Indo-Pakistani region by its adoption of a platform that includes a justification for undertaking violence (including terrorism) in the pursuit of their cause.

Bin Laden and the World Islamic Front have called upon Muslims everywhere to join their fight against the Americans (and their allies):

> The ruling to kill the Americans and their allies—civilians and military—is an individual duty for every Muslim who can do it in any country in which it is possible to do it, in order to liberate the al-Aqsa Mosque (in Jerusalem) and the holy mosque (in Mecca) from their grip, and in order for their armies to move out of all the lands of Islam, defeated and unable to threaten any Muslim.

Al Qaeda is headed by bin Laden, its amir. Following a common Muslim organizational pattern, the amir is assisted by a consultative council called the Majlis-e-Shura. Among the members of this council is Ayman al-Zawahiri (b. 1951), a former leader of the Egyptian jihad, the group linked to the assassination of Egyptian president Anwar Sadat (1918–1981).

The activity of Al Qaeda, its amir, and its council was disrupted late in 2001 following the operation begun by the United States and its allies in response to the events of September 11. The Taliban leadership in Afghanistan came to an abrupt end, and its leadership along with that of Al Qaeda went into hiding. Al Qaeda has claimed responsibility for several terrorist acts since then, including an attack on the London underground that resulted in 53 deaths and 700 wounded in 2005. The organization has also been linked to a 2003 car bomb explosion in Riyadh, Saudi Arabia, a bombing of a Mombasa hotel and an Indonesian nightclub in 2002, synagogue bombings in Istanbul, Turkey, in 2003, and a train station explosion in Madrid, Spain, in 2004. The present status of the leaders of both organizations and their level of activity remains questionable. As of 2008, Bin Laden and the council of Al Qaeda are international fugitives sought by a number of governments.

Sources:

Bergen, Peter L. *Holy War, Inc.: Inside the Secret World of Osama bin Laden*. New York: The Free Press, 2001.

Jansen, Johannes J. *The Neglected Duty: The Creed of Sadat's Assassins and Islamic Resurgence in the Middle East*. New York: Macmillan, 1986. 246 pp.

The Jihad Fixation: Agenda, Strategy, Portents. Delhi, India: Wordsmiths, 2001. 424 pp.

Juergenmeyer, Mark. *Terror in the Mind of God: The Global Rise of Religious Violence*. Berkeley: University of California Press, 2000.

Kramer, Martin. "Fundamentalist Islam at Large: The Drive for Power." *Middle East Quarterly* 3, no. 2 (June 1996).

Rashid, Ahmed. *Taliban: Militant Islam, Oil, and Fundamentalism in Central Asia*. New Haven, CT: Yale University Press, 2000.

World Islamic Front Statement Urging Jihad against Jews and Crusaders. 1998. www.fas.org/irp/world/para/docs/980223-fatwa.htm

Taliban

The Taliban, the "Students of Islamic Knowledge Movement," was in control of the largest part of Afghanistan as the twenty-first century began. The movement originated among youth who attended religious schools (*madrasas*) established in the 1980s by refugees from the Afghan War who moved to neighboring Pakistan during the 1980s. Most of the refugees were ethnic Pashtuns. Pashtuns traditionally followed the Hanafite school of Sunni Islam. The new Taliban movement, however, assumed an extreme and conservative interpretation in their tradition, making them natural allies of the equally conservative Wahhabi movement based in Saudi Arabia.

The Taliban quickly evolved into a more formal organization and as is common in Islam created a leadership council (called a *ulema*, literally, a community of learned men) and selected a leader, Mullah Muhamad Omar. The movement found support throughout the Pashtun region of Afghanistan. Joining in the struggle to throw off the ruling forces in Kabul (the capital), and in 1996 it replaced the former ruling elite, many of whom were drawn from the ethnically Uzbek and Tajik minorities and represented either Shi'a Islam or secular Marxism. The defeated leadership reorganized and formed an alliance against the Taliban regime and were able to retain control of a small territory in the northern part of the country. During this period, neither the United States nor the United Nations recognized the Taliban government; Afghanistan was considered to be a land devoid of a government. They recognized the leadership of Burhanuddin Rabbani and the Northern Alliance as the rightful rulers of Afghanistan, while also aware of their inability to exercise government powers. Only Pakistan, Saudi Arabia, and the United Arab Emirates recognized the Taliban.

In Kabul, Taliban leaders instituted a strict interpretation of the *shariah*, the unique Islamic law. They demanded traditional dress for women, imposed restrictions on female education and movement, and prevented their receiving medical treatment by male physicians. The Taliban leaders also reintroduced various forms of punishment for crimes that had largely been abandoned elsewhere (including flogging, amputation of limbs, and executions by stoning). They found support for these practices, especially in those areas of the country plagued by chaos and lawlessness during the previous decade.

Internationally, the Taliban were unpopular but tolerated. However, their destruction of some large Buddhist statutes in March 2001 brought widespread denouncement from around the world, both from the interfaith religious community and from the international artistic community.

In 1996, the leaders of the Taliban had invited Osama bin Laden (b. 1957) to move the headquarters of his organization, Al Qaeda, to Afghanistan. Through the 1990s, Al Qaeda was charged with a series of attacks upon United States citizens and property culminating in the bombing of the Pentagon and the World Trade Center in the United States on September 11, 2001. The United States held the Taliban responsible for harboring Al Qaeda and bin Laden in Afghanistan.

In October 2001, the United States began military action in Afghanistan aimed at capturing bin Laden and his associates and destroying Al Qaeda. As a secondary consequence of that action, the Taliban was brought down and its leader disappeared into the countryside. Both Omar and bin Laden remain fugitives.

During the 1990s, the Taliban found support internationally, and a community that identified themselves with the Taliban developed in the United States. The American Taliban operated quite openly within the larger Islamic community and developed a presence on the Internet. All of that ended in September 2001. Shortly after the bombings, the Internet site restricted access to the general public and then in 2002 disappeared altogether. While it is likely that remnants of the groups continue in the United States, no outward manifestation has been apparent since the Internet site was taken down.

Sources:

The Jihad Fixation: Agenda, Strategy, Portents. Delhi, India: Wordsmiths, 2001. 424 pp.

Maley, William, ed. *Fundamentalism Reborn? Afghanistan and the Taliban*. New York: New York University Press, 1998. 253 pp.

Matinuddin, Kamal. *The Taliban Phenomenon: Afghanistan, 1994-1997*. Karachi: Oxford University Press, 1999.

Parfrey, Adanm, ed. *Extreme Islam: Anti-American Propaganda of Muslim Fundamentalism*. Los Angeles: Feral House, 2001. 317 pp.

Rashid, Ahmed. *Taliban: Militant Islam, Oil and Fundamentalism in Central Asia*. New Haven, CT: Yale University Press, 2001. 279 pp.

SUFISM

Habibiyya-Shadhiliyya Sufic Order

The Habibiyya-Shadhiliyya Sufic Order originated with Shaikh Muhammad Ibn al-Habib, termed Perfect Shaikh and Gnostic of Allah. The Shadhiliyya Order originated in the thirteenth century with Shaikh Al Shadhili of Fez, Morocco, and subsequently divided into a number of sub-orders of which the Habibiyya is one. Al-Habib is designated the Qutb (head of the spiritual hierarchy of saints) and is venerated as the Light of the Messenger. Followers are urged to annihilate themselves in him. He is the author of the *Diwan*, a poetic presentation of his teachings.

Al-Habib speaks of God as the beloved; the goal of life is immersion in him. The way of the world is "Jahiliyya," pride and arrogance. Islam's way is submission and the recognition of our place in the harmonious whole. The main practice of the Habibiyya is Dhikr'Allah (or zhikr), the invocation, remembering, and calling upon Allah.

The Habibiyya came to the United States in 1973 and opened a center in Berkeley, California. In 1977 the order claimed 5,000 American members. However, no work in the United States has been visible since then and its present status is unknown.

Sources:

The Sufic Path. Berkeley, CA: Privately printed, n.d.

AFRICAN-AMERICAN ISLAM

Calistran

The Calistran was a short-lived splinter group of the original Nation of Islam (now the American Muslim Mission) which came to public attention in the early 1970s, a period of heightened tension and internal violence within the black Muslim community. On October 7, 1973, two members of the Calistran who had reportedly "stepped out of line" were shot in Pasadena, California, by a "disciplinarian." No sign of the Calistran has been seen since the 1980s.

Muslim Mosque, Inc.

The Muslim Mosque, Inc., was founded in 1964 by Malcolm X (1925–1965), who, at the time, had just announced his departure from the Nation of Islam, then headed by Elijah Muhammad. Malcolm X had become the most prominent spokesperson of the Nation of Islam in the early 1960s, and in 1963 he was made the nation's first national minister. A short time after Malcolm X assumed his new position, news broke that Elijah Muhammad was the object of two paternity suits filed by former secretaries. Malcolm X received the news as a word of betrayal by the leader he so respected.

A major incident then occurred in November 1963, following the assassination of President John F. Kennedy. Elijah Muhammad had ordered a three-day period of silence on any comment on the death. During this time, however, Malcolm X was approached by a group of reporters following a speech in New York. Pressed for a comment, he said simply that the assassination appeared to be a case of the "chicken's coming home to roost." The comment was reported widely and in the wake of the negative publicity, Elijah Muhammad silenced Malcolm X for 90 days. Malcolm X soon found other Muslims shunning him and learned that a contract had been put out on his life.

In the controversial atmosphere, on March 1964, Malcolm X resigned from the Nation of Islam. The new Muslim Mosque was created to act as a spiritual force behind the social action to eliminate the oppression of African Americans. As a first action, Malcolm X decided to make the obligatory pilgrimage to Mecca, one of the basic requirements of a Muslim. While in the Middle East, he was impressed with the lack of racism among the pilgrims and among Muslims in general. The experience forced him away from the previously held belief that all white people were evil. He also became directly aware of the difference between the Nation of Islam's beliefs and the teachings of orthodox Islam.

Upon his return he began to build the program of the Muslim Mosque, but on February 21, 1965, he was shot and killed by several members of the Nation of Islam who were later tried and convicted for the murder. The Muslim Mosque did not survive Malcolm X's death for very long.

Sources:

Breitman, George. *The Last Year of Malcolm X: The Evolution of a Revolutionary*. New York: Schrocken Books, 1969.

Clark, John Henrik, ed. *Malcolm X: The Man and His Times*. New York: Macmillan, 1969.

Goldman, Peter Loomis. *The Death and Life of Malcolm X*. Urbana, IL: University of Illinois Press, 1979.

"Organizations and Leaders Campaigning for Negro Goals in the United States." *New York Times,* August 10, 1964.

Turner, Richard Brent. *Islam in the African-American Experience*. Bloomington: Indiana University Press, 1997.

BAHA'I

Faith of God

The Faith of God grew out of the work of Jamshid Ma'ani, a Persian prophet known to the public as simply "The Man," a title used to signify the coming of maturity to humanity and that the real station of man is a spiritual station. The Man announced his mission in 1963 in Israel and then in Iran. He began to gather followers in various nations around the world to the Faith of God. The Faith emerged following the death of Shoghi Effendi, the guardian of the Baha'i World Faith, and the failure of another guardian to emerge as his successor. Among the early converts to The Man's cause was John Carre, a lifelong Baha'i, who traveled extensively on his behalf and organized the House of Mankind, the administrative aspect of the Faith, in several countries.

The Man continued the Baha'i belief in progressive revelation to mankind through the various mediators or teachers from Zoroaster to Baha'u'llah and saw himself as the latest in this series. Evolution was also a key notion. The universe and its various parts are in continuous evolution. The universe is alive. The culmination of material creation is man's moving toward spiritual man. This evolutionary process is part of a divine plan leading creation toward unity.

The overall evolution of humanity is toward perfection on all levels. This goal was the reason for all the prophets. Their teachings are one. All forms of worship are acceptable except those contrary to wisdom or detrimental to others. We must strive to give all persons the attributes of the saintly ones. The individual's progression is aided by thorough meditation and prayer, but they must become effective in our thoughts and actions.

The House of Mankind was initially established in each of five areas of the world. Like the Baha'i Faith, there was no clergy. Pictured for the future was the development of the Universal Palace of Order, which would bring to realization the aspirations of mankind for the unity and oneness of government. The House of Mankind functioned for a period of approximately ten years in the United States from its headquarters in the residence of John Carre in Mariposa, California. However, during the 1970s, The Man lived with Carre for a number of months, during which time Carre came to know Ma'ani personally and as a result withdrew his support. The movement, which had only several hundred members, ceased to exist in America soon after.

Sources:

Carre, John. *An Island of Hope*. Mariposa, CA: House of Light, 1975.

The Man [Jamshid Ma'ani]. *Heaven*. Mariposa, CA: John Carre, 1971.

———. *The Sun of the Word of the Man*. Mariposa, CA: John Carre, 1971.

———. *Universal Order*. Mariposa, CA: John Carre, 1971.

Remey Society

The Remey Society was one of three organizations of former members of the Baha'i Faith who accepted Charles Mason Remey (1874–1974) as the Second Guardian of the Faith. Remey was a prominent Baha'i for many years. He authored a number of books, designed several Baha'i temples, and served as president of the International Baha'i Council. In 1951 he was one of nine people named by Shoghi Effendi as a hand of the cause.

In 1957 Shoghi Effendi died without having fathered a child, leaving a will, or naming a successor. Remey then joined with the other hands in proclaiming the formation of a Baha'i World Centre made up of nine hands of the cause to assume temporarily the function of the guardian. Remey was one of the nine. However, during the next few years, Remey dissented from the position of the other hands. He argued that the guardianship was a necessary feature of the structure of the faith. He also asserted that, as the president of the International Baha'i Council (a position assigned Remey by Shoghi Effendi), he was the only one in a position to become the Second Guardian. He waited two years for the hands to accept his position. Then, in 1959, he left Haifa, Israel, where the Baha'i Faith has its international headquarters, and came to the United States. In 1960 he issued a proclamation to the Baha'is of the World and circulated it at the annual gathering of the American Baha'is that year. He also issued a pamphlet, "A Last Appeal to the Hands of the Faith," asking them to abandon plans to elect members of the International House of Justice in 1961. The hands continued to reject his claims and expelled him from the faith.

Throughout the 1960s Remey insisted upon his right to be designated the Second Guardian. Finally, in 1968 he appointed the first five Elders of the Baha'i Epoch and announced the organization of his followers under the name The Orthodox Abha World Faith. He retired to Florence, Italy, and lived out the last decade of his life in virtual retirement.

After Remey's death in 1974, Donald Harvey and Joel B. Marangella each claimed that Remey had appointed him as the Third Guardian of the Faith. The Remey Society united the American followers of Donald Harvey. The society was organized by Francis C. Sparato and published a periodical, the *Remey Letter*. Following Harvey's death in 1991, Jacques Soghomonian became the new Guardian of the Faith. In 1995 the society reported 400 members in the United States, 150 in Canada, and 200 in two European centers in Italy and France.

Sources:

Remey, Charles Mason. *The Baha'i Movement*. Washington, DC: J. D. Milans & Sons, 1912.

❀ 23. Eastern I: Hinduism, Jainism, Sikhism

HINDUISM

Center of Being

The Center of Being was a short-lived movement founded in 1979 by Baba Prem Ananda, also known as Anandaji (b. 1949), and Her Holiness Sri Marashaam Devi, affectionately known as Mataji, an African-American woman considered by her followers to be an avatar (a self-realized master of the highest order). Mataji was believed to have been born fully enlightened and to have retained that state for the first 12 years of her life. At the age of 12 she began to regress in order to experience the separation from the divine and the path to reunion. During the 12-year period of regression, she retained some communion with the divine and experienced many unusual powers, among them an ability to see Lord Shiva (a prominent Hindu deity), who functioned directly as her guru. At the age of 24 she regained the state of Enlightenment and began to teach privately. One of her first disciples, Anandaji, assisted her in the formation of the Center of Being and in her public teaching activity. Anandaji also attained the enlightened state.

Mataji taught a path of Enlightenment, a spontaneous way of being beyond intellectual rules and answers. Mataji, as a divine personage, was able to bestow this grace, which leads to Enlightenment. She offered herself in weekly darshans—sessions in which disciples sat in her presence—and in "grace intensives" (thrice annually). Darshan sessions included lectures by Mataji and question-and-answer periods. Devotional worship services directed to the deities and to Mataji were held quarterly.

At the Center of Being's height in the mid-1980s, there was one center in Los Angeles and a journal, *Lila*, was published.

Divine Awareness Center

The Divine Awareness Center was founded in 1989 by Yogi Kamal, an Indian teacher and disciple of Siddha Guru Swami Yogiraj Nanak, an enlightened master, the founder of the Adhyatmic Sadhana Sangh in India. Yogiraj Nanak was the spiritual heir of the famous sixteenth-century saint and poet Malukdasji Maharaj, also looked upon as an enlightened master, who worked from his residence in Kara, Allahabad, India. The center taught the full range of yoga but concentrated upon a new technique developed by Yogiraj Nanak, de-hypnotic meditation, a way of meditating that combined older yogic insights and metaphysics with new scientific discoveries.

According to Yogi Kamal, the modern world produced a peculiar heightened environment of tension, turmoil, unrest, and social destruction. The individual affected by the social disintegration manifested a variety of symptoms, including shallow breathing, improper diet, degeneration of the nervous system, decreased energy, anxiety, and mental instability. As the mind and body were believed to be closely intertwined, human problems were intensified, with the health of the mind affecting the body and the health of the body affecting the mind. It followed that what hurt one hurt the other, and curing one meant curing the other. The mind often retained the effects of illness and caused reoccurrences of illness when not cared for.

De-hypnotic meditation consisted of six steps: bodily relaxation, proper breathing, thought of the brilliant light, concentration on the organ of the sixth sense (pineal gland), concentration on the sound wave (symbolized in the word "om"), and quietness. It was believed that the practice of de-hypnotic meditation led to the reduction of stress, self-healing, the harmonization of mind and body, the breaking of old habits, and the production of healthy vibrations. Those who practiced it learned how to keep negative thoughts away, to command the subconscious mind, to tap the divine power, and to develop the divine magnetic aura.

The initial Divine Awareness Center was opened in Los Angeles as a base for founding centers in other cities. In 1998 Yogi Kamal abandoned his work and closed the center.

Hindu Yoga Society

The Hindu Yoga Society was begun in the 1920s by Sri Deva Ram Sukul (d. 1965), an Indian residing in Chicago. In 1927 he started *Practical Yoga*, a quarterly journal, and issued a 10-part course in what he termed "Yoga Navajivan." From his Chicago base he toured the United States lecturing. He later settled in California, where he incorporated his work as the Yoga Institute of America. The institute continued to function until Sukul's death. Among his disciples was actress Mae West.

Sri Sukul taught the various forms of yoga (hatha, bhakti, jnana, karma, and raja), following the teachings presented in the classic work by Patanjali (compiler of the yoga sutras) but with a distinct emphasis upon raja yoga, with additional insights gleaned from tantra. He also taught students the subtle anatomy of the chakra system and the means to raise the *kundalini* (the power believed to reside in latency at the base of the spine). The rise of the kundalini along the spine to the crown chakra at the top of the head brings enlightenment. Integral to Sri Sukul's tantric teachings was the Gayatri Mantram, which was believed to contain the sevenfold planes of vibration of the soul's ascent (corresponding to the seven chakras).

Sources:

Krishna Samaj

The Krishna Samaj was formed by Surendranath Mukerji (d. 1914), better known by his religious name, Baba Premanand Bharati. Baba Bharati was among the first Hindu teachers to come to America, arriving in the United States around 1902 from Bengal. He was a student of Swami Brahmanand Bharati and follower of the Krishna Consciousness movement which had been revived in Bengal in the nineteenth century (and which became well known in America and the West in the 1970s through the International Society for Krishna Consciousness [ISKCON], also known as the Hare Krishna movement). The Krishna Consciousness movement originated with Chaitanya Mahaprabhu (1486–1534?), a *bhakti* (devotional) yogi, who spread the practice of repeating the Hare Krisha mantra as the way to enlightenment and release from the wheel of karma and reincarnation.

Bharati, the nephew of a prominent Bengali judge, formed the Krishna Samaj in New York City and lectured to popular audiences in other eastern cities. He eventually moved to Los Angeles, where a temple was constructed and he had his greatest following. In 1909 he returned to India, where, with a few of his American disciples, he opened a mission in Calcutta. The mission failed for lack of financial support, and he and his followers returned to America. He died in Calcutta in 1914. The temple dissolved in America soon after Bharati's death.

In the years immediately after his death, Bharati was attacked by people opposed to the growth of Hinduism in America, such as Elizabeth A. Reed, whose study of Bharati and the other early gurus was a significant factor in building public support for the anti-Asian Immigration Act of 1917. The strength and devotion of Bharati's disciples, however, kept his memory alive over the years. In the 1930s members of the Order of Loving Service, a California metaphysical group, dedicated the book *Square* as follows: "To Baba Premanand Bharati, who by his love, patience, and continued watchfulness has led me out of darkness into *Light*, out of weariness into *Rest*, out of confusion into *Understanding*, out of continuous striving into *Perfect Peace*." In the 1970s members of the AUM Temple of Universal Truth, founded in the 1920s, were reprinting Bharati's writings in their periodical and selling pictures of "Our Beloved Baba Bharati."

Sources:

Bharati, Baba Premanand. *Krishna*. New York: Krishna Samaj, 1904.

———. *American Lectures*. Calcutta: Indo-American Press, n.d.

Farquhar, J. N. *Modern Religious Movements in India*. New York: Macmillan, 1915.

Lalita [Maud Lalita Johnson]. *Square*. Laguna Beach, CA: Order of Loving Service, 1934.

Reed, Elizabeth A. *Hinduism in Europe and America*. New York: G. P. Putnam's Sons, 1914.

Mahavidhya, Inc.

Mahavidhya, Inc., was a small Hindu group which operated in the Midwest from the 1920s through the 1940s. Its leader was Mahasiddha Satchidananda, identified only as a master-teacher and a resident of Kansas City, Missouri. Little is known of the group, only a set of private lessons on *The Mahavidhya Philosophy* having survived. The course consisted of 15 lessons on rejuvenation. In addition to a discussion of various points of Hindu philosophy, the lessons offered exercises for the student in breathing, nutrition, concentration, and psychic development.

Sources:

Satchidananda, Mahasiddha. *Private Class Lessons in the Mahavidhya Philosophy*. 5 vols. Kansas City, MO: The Author, 1945.

Para-Vidya Center

The Para-Vidya Center was founded in Los Angeles, California, in the 1930s by Rishi Krishnananda, who migrated to America around 1920, just prior to the United States ending immigration from India. He taught small numbers of students for a number of years and opened a center in Los Angeles prior to World War II. The center was later relocated to New York City.

Krishnananda tried to adapt Hindu teachings to a Western audience without losing their essence in the translation. While teaching hatha yoga postures, he also tried to communicate the complete system of yoga as contained in the Upanishads, the Hindu holy books. As part of this belief system, the goal of life is seen as self-realization, beginning with a conscious awareness of the Universal Life Principle (i.e., God) which animates life and ending in a union with the Principle. A process of controlled breathing

(*pranayama*) and a vegetarian diet was recommended.

There is no indication of how long the center lasted after its move to New York.

Sources:

Krishnananda, Rishi. *The Mystery of Breath*. New York: Para-Vidya Center, n.d.

———. *Yoga Science of Eating*. Los Angeles: Para-Vidya Center, 1941.

Nivenanda, Darha. *Strange Journey*. Los Angeles: Para-Vidya Center, 1941.

Real Yoga Society

The Real Yoga Society was founded in 1973 by Swami Shiva, a high-caste Hindu teacher from Calcutta, India. In India he had been the editor of a magazine, *Atma-Darshan* (Self-Realization) and a popular speaker on yoga. He was invited to the United States by Dr. J. M. Patel, an Indian American resident of Chicago, and he began the society shortly after his arrival. A master of hatha yoga, Swami Shiva also taught all of the main forms of yoga—raja, karma, jnana, and bhakti. Yoga is seen as a means to self-realization and enlightenment.

The society florished in the late 1970s and had centers in Chicago, Oak Park, and Wheaton, Illinois. Its status since that time is unknown.

Sources:

Shiva, Swami. *Dawn of Life through Yoga*. Oak Park, IL: Real Yoga Society, 1975.

Satyananda Ashrams, U.S.A.

Swami Satyananda Saraswati (b. 1893), a former disciple of Swami Sivananda Saraswati (1887–1963), founder of the Divine Life Society, pioneered the modern opening of yoga to all, both sannyasins and householders, regardless of sex, nationality, caste, or creed. After working with Sivananda for 12 years, he wandered India for nine more. In 1964, the year after his guru's death, Satyananda founded the Bihar School of Yoga. He built the Sivananda Ashram on the banks of the Ganges and the Ganta Darshan on a hill overlooking the river valley. Satyananda continued Sivananda's broad approach, which integrated the various yogic techniques, but gave particular emphasis to tantra. Also, like Sivananda, he actively spread his teachings, first throughout India, and beginning with a world tour in 1968, to the West. During the 1970s he established 10 ashrams and many centers within, and outside of, India; followers could be found in Australia, Indonesia, Columbia, Greece, France, Sweden, England, and Ireland. As the movement spread, he organized the International Yoga Fellowship.

Satyananda's teachings came to the United States via two paths. First, in 1975 Llewellyn Publications, an occult publisher in St. Paul, Minnesota, released a major work by Swami Anandakapila (a.k.a. John

Mumford), a leading disciple of Satyananda's in Australia. The publication of *Sexual Occultism* was followed by a United States tour in 1976 and feature articles in *Gnostica*, a major occult periodical. Concurrently with the publication of Anandakapila's book, a New York publisher released *Yoga, Tantra and Meditation* by Swami Janakananda Saraswati, a teacher for Satyananda in Scandinavia. Second, during the 1970s many students of Satyananda migrated to the United States from India, and as their numbers increased, they formed small yoga groups. In 1980 Swami Niranjanananda Saraswati (b. 1960), a leading teacher with Satyananda who had traveled extensively and organized ashrams for the International Yoga Fellowship, arrived in the United States. On October 28, 1980, he organized Satyananda Ashrams U.S.A., the American affiliate of the International Yoga Fellowship. Niranjanananda remained in the United States teaching and organizing local centers. In the summer of 1982, Swami Amritananda, visited the United States. Her visit was followed immediately by Satyananda's first tour of North America.

While it was not the main emphasis of his teachings, Satyananda became known as an exponent of the so-called left-hand path of tantric yoga. Tantra is built upon the blending and exchange of male and female sexual energies and consciousness. In left-hand tantra, sexual intercourse is utilized as a means of reaching ananda (or bliss).

The International Yoga Fellowship was one of the largest yoga groups worldwide. Its extensive membership in the United States was somewhat hidden, being once largely confined to the Indian-American community. Membership was estimated to be in the thousands as ashrams and centers could be found across the United States and Canada. The Bihar School of Yoga still publishes the periodical *Yoga*, available from Bihar School of Yoga at www.yogavision.net/pubs/intro.htm

Sources:

Janakananda Saraswati, Swami. *Yoga, Tantra & Meditation*. New York: Ballantine Books, 1975.

Mumford, John [Swami Anandakapila]. *Sexual Occultism*. St. Paul, MN: Llewellyn Publications, 1975.

Satyananda Saraswati, Swami. *Sure Ways to Self-Realization*. Munger, Bihar, India: Bihar School of Yoga, 1983.

———. *Taming the Kundalini*. Munger, Bihar, India: Bihar School of Yoga, 1982.

Teachings of Swami Satyananda Saraswati. Mongyar, Bihar, India: Bihar School of Yoga, 1981.

Sonorama Society

The Sonorama Society was formed after Maharishi Mahesh Yogi's first trip to the United States in 1959 and was devoted to the Maharishi's guru, the late

Swami Brahmananda Saraswati Maharaj, the illustrious Jagad-Guru Bhagawan of Jyotir-Math, Bhadrikashraman, India. At the age of nine, Swami Saraswati Maharaj began a 40-year exploration of inner consciousness that allowed him to rediscover the mental technique of transcendental meditation and become leader of the Shankaracharya Order. Within this order, he was seen as the perfect master.

The Society was formed as an association of persons who were practicing transcendental meditation. Sonorama Society members were united by correspondence lessons and irregular contact with those who had mastered the techniques. Headquarters were established in Los Angeles under the leadership of R. Manley Whitman, the sponsor-director. The society lasted only a few years; its work was superseded by the growth of the transcendental meditation (TM) movement, now organized by the World Plan Executive Council.

Tantrik Order in America

The Tantrik Order was one of the first Hindu groups founded in the United States, and possibly the first created by a Western student of the Eastern teachings. It was founded in New York City by Pierre Bernard (born as Peter Coons) (1875–1955), better known by members of the order as Oom the Omnipotent. The order superseded the Bacchante Academy, whose California operation had ceased in the San Francisco earthquake of 1906. Associated with the order was the New York Sanskrit College.

Bernard taught a form of Tantric Hinduism combined with hatha yoga. The sexual aspects of tantra were included as integral aspects of the instruction, and Bernard came under scrutiny during the early days of the order's operation as police began to suspect him of trying to seduce his pupils. He survived several early scandals, however, and in 1924 moved to an estate in Nyack, New York, on Long Island, and continued as leader of the order for the next three decades (closed only briefly during World War II when the estate was used as a center for refugees from Nazi Germany). His clientele included many wealthy people, including several members of the Vanderbilt family. Bernard became a wealthy and influential citizen. He donated a zoo to the community and eventually became president of the bank in nearby Pearl City.

The order apparently died with founder Pierre Bernard. There are reports of the existence of an offshoot, the New York Sacred Tantrics, which functioned during the 1960s. However, reports have not been confirmed and if the group existed, it was disbanded by the late 1970s.

Pierre Bernard had several famous relatives. He was the cousin-by-marriage of Mary Baker Eddy, founder of the Church of Christ, Scientist. In the early years of his work in New York, he was the guardian of his half-sister, Ora Ray Baker, who became the wife of Hazrat Inayat Khan, founder of the Sufi Order. Bernard's

nephew, also named Pierre Bernard, wrote what is a classic text on yoga as his thesis at Columbia University, *Hatha Yoga: The Report of a Personal Experience*.

Sources:

Boswell, Charles. "The Great Fume and Fuss over the Omnipotent Oom." *True* (January 1965): 31-33, 86-91.

"In Re Fifth Veda" in *International Journal of the Tantrik Order*. New York: Tantrik Order in America, n.d. [1909].

Sann, Paul. *Fads, Follies, and Delusions of the American People*. New York, 1967.

Temple of Yoga (Acharya)

The Temple of Yoga was founded by Besudeb Bhattacharya (d.1949), an Indian poet, playwright, and yoga teacher who came to America just prior to World War I. Under the name "Sree Besudeb" he authored several plays but some time in the 1920s turned his attention to teaching yoga and Hinduism. He founded the Yoga Research School in New York City but later moved to Long Island. Nyack became the center of his activities, which included Prana Press, Hope, Inc., and the Temple of Yoga. He wrote a number of books under his religious name, Pundit Acharya, though some of them were published posthumously by his students.

Integral to Pundit Acharya's approach to yoga was his attempt to reinterpret yoga in scientific terminology, in light of "neuro-bio electronics." He developed the Acharyan Method of yoga, which involved a number of exercises to release the life force and bring relaxation. He believed that sleep was a great rejuvenator, as it was the time for recharging the brain from the energy reservoirs of the infinite universe.

Sources:

Acharya, Pundit. *Breath, Sleep, the Heart, and Life*. Clearlake, CA: Dawn Horse Press, 1976.

———. *Mukti*. Nyack, NY: Prana Press, 1967.

———. *The Saffron Veil*. New York: Prana Press, 1963.

———. *A Strange Language*. Nyack, NY: Yoga Research School, 1939.

Transcendent-Science Society

The Transcendent-Science Society was founded in Chicago, Illinois, by Premel El Adaros, also known as Swami Brahmavidya, around 1920. The society is known by one book on its teachings written by its founder and several by Swami A. P. Mukerji, a prominent South Indian yogi. Brahmavidya claimed to be the United States representative of the same order, the South India Brotherhood, to which Mukerji belonged. Transcendent-science, the science of self-knowledge, was designed to lead to a knowledge of the self, union with the divine, and liberation or *mukti*. The practices

of transcendent-science consisted of strict moral living, yoga postures, breathing exercises, concentration, and meditation.

Mukerji presented a course in yogi philosophy and practice based on concentration, meditation, and thought control. He included instructions on breath control (*pranayama*), hatha yoga exercises, diet (vegetarianism was advised), and various body cleansing techniques. He was among the earliest Hindus to introduce the concept of guru worship (reverence for the teacher, who is a person of high spiritual attainment), a most controversial idea for Western audiences. Equally controversial was the concept of worshipping the terrible, i.e., becoming one with the negative, which he taught as a means of seeing its ultimate unreality.

The society survived only a brief time; however, the writings of A. P. Mukerji continue to be circulated, having been kept in print by the Yogi Publication Society.

Sources:

Brahmavidya, Swami. *Transcendent-Science or the Science of Self Knowledge*. Chicago: Transcendent-Science Society, 1922.

Mukerji, A. P. *The Doctrine and Practice of Yoga*. Chicago: Premel El Adaros, 1922.

———. *Spiritual Consciousness*. Chicago: Yogi Publication Society, 1911.

Universal Brotherhood Temple and School of Eastern Philosophy

The Universal Brotherhood Temple and School of Eastern Philosophy was an early American Hindu organization founded Yogi Sant Rama Mandal in San Francisco in the 1920s. During the 1930s it was headquartered in Santa Monica, California and is known today only through Mandal's surviving publications. Mandal taught a system of yoga for self-development and self-realization which included hatha yoga, meditation, the repetition of mantras, diet, and practical exercises. He also taught a method to awaken the *kundalini*, the latent energy believed to be located at the base of the spine which, upon awakening, travels up the spinal column to bring enlightenment. No information on Mandal's early years or the eventual fate of the temple has been available.

Sources:

Mandal, Sant Rama. *Course of Instruction in Mystic Psychology*. Santa Monica, CA: Universal Brotherhood Temple and School of Eastern Philosophy, n.d.

———. *Gems of Aryan Wisdom*. San Francisco, CA: Universal Brotherhood Temple and School of Eastern Philosophy, 1931.

———. *The Self and the Not-Self*. San Francisco, CA: Universal Brotherhood Temple and School of Eastern Philosophy, 1927.

Vedantic Cultural Society

The Vedantic Cultural Society was formed in 1983 by Hansadutta Swami (a.k.a. Hans Kary), a former initiating guru with the International Society for Krishna Consciousness (ISKCON). During the late 1970s, Hansadutta had been the subject of strong criticism by the other gurus in ISKCON because of his unorthodox fundraising, administrative, and recruiting activities. In the spring of 1980, he was arrested for possession of illegal firearms. While the charges were later dropped, his advocacy of survivalism and his possession of a number of weapons led to his being sent to India for a year. After consideration of the sacred nature of the relationship of an initiating guru and his disciples (which constituted most of the Berkeley temple), the governing council reinstated him. However, his return to Berkeley did not ease the tension, and in 1983 ISKCON excommunicated Hansadutta. He left and took most of the Berkeley temple with him, forming the Vedantic Cultural Society. Hansadutta's troubles did not end with the break from ISKCON. In September of 1983, he was arrested and accused of shooting out several store windows in Berkeley. Several weapons and empty shells were found in his car. Following this incident, Hansadutta assumed a low profile. The Berkeley temple returned to ISKCON, and the rural center was sold. Hansadutta has applied for reinstatement in ISKCON.

Sources:

Hansadutta, Swami. *The Book, What the Black Sheep Said*. Berkeley, CA: Hansa Books, 1985.

————. *The Hammer for Smashing Illusion*. Berkeley, CA: Hansa Books, 1983.

————. *Kirtan*. Berkeley, CA: Hansa Books, 1984.

Yoganta Meditation Center

The Yoganta Meditation Center was a small eclectic community based upon the concept of spiritual growth through a variety of meditative and yogic techniques. The center provided residential facilities where adherents could practice their own discipline for an extended time. There was no guru; the belief was that the exchange of personal experiences would benefit all.

Seminars were irregularly offered on such topics as mantras, hatha yoga, meditation, and miscellaneous psychic topics. A quarterly journal, *The Yoganta Center Newsletter*, was published. During the 1970s there were approximately 10 to 15 residents at the center located at Nederland, Colorado.

Yogiraj Sect

Swami Swanandashram was born in Calcutta in 1921 and in his youth became a yogi. In college he was a student of philosophy, mathematics, and Sanskrit. In 1950, however, he renounced all possessions and for 20 years lived in a cave at Gangotri. He was initiated in the Shankaracharya Order and became head of the Yogiraj Sect. In 1970, Swanandashram emerged from his cave and began a public ministry to teach a way of oneness with God through yoga. According to his teaching, the essential reality of the unchangeable God was held up as that which was to be seen behind the transitory illusions of commonplace life. The erroneous identification of the body as the real self was the root of all evil, suffering, and death. Yoga was the means to overcome the false identification. During the early 1970s there was one American center of Swanandashram's followers in Easton, Pennsylvania. It was absorbed into the Holy Shankaracharya Order.

SANT MAT

Divine Light Mission

The Divine Light Mission was founded in India in the 1920s by Shri Hans Ji Maharaj but became well known in the West in the 1970s after being brought to Europe and North America by his son Guru Maharaj Ji (b. 1957). Guru Maharaj Ji, then still a teenager, had assumed the leadership of the mission following the death of his father. The mission spread rapidly after its introduction into North America and by 1973 it had more than 40 centers and was publishing two periodicals: a magazine, *And It Is Divine*, and a tabloid, *The Divine Times*.

A former member of the eclectic Brahmo Samaj, Shri Hans Ji Maharaj had met a guru in the Sant Mat tradition, identified only as Dada Guru, who initiated him into *surat shabda yoga* (the yoga of the sound current) through four techniques, or *kriyas*, which were to become the trademark of the Divine Light Mission. In the 1920s, following the death of his guru, Shri Hans began to travel in north India and around 1930 first arrived in Delhi. His work grew informally for many years, spreading across the northern half of India from Bombay to Calcutta. In 1950 he commissioned the first mahatmas, assistants who had the authority to initiate as his representative, and a short time afterwards he issued the first copies of a monthly magazine, *Hansadesh*. His following was formally organized in 1960 as Divya Sandesh Parishad, i.e., the Divine Light Mission.

Shri Hans was considered a *sat guru*, or perfect master, by his followers. His death in 1965 was experienced as a great loss. However, at his funeral, in the midst of the mourning crowd, the youngest of Shri Hans four sons, then only eight years old, arose and addressed the crowd, stating, "I feel that Maharaji is alive and will always remain." Afterwards, this eight-year-old was acknowledged by both his family and the followers of Shri Hans as his father's successor and he became known as Maharaji.

Maharaj Ji had been an unusual child. He began meditating at the age of two and gave discourses when he was six. He entered his teen years with a blend of normal childhood urges and the meditative life of a sat guru. On November 8, 1970, at the India Gate in Delhi, he proclaimed the dawn of a new era, and his followers answered his call to mission. Early in 1971 he made his tour of the United States, mixing normal teenage activities (a visit to Disneyland) with meetings with prospective disciples. A second visit in the summer of 1972 centered upon a massive gathering of disciples at Montrose, Colorado. Each trip was accompanied by broad coverage in the media.

Following the Sant Mat tradition, Maharaj Ji was considered a perfect master and, as such, an embodiment of God. He offered initiation (termed the giving of knowledge) into the truth of life technique. Initiation involved instruction in the four yoga techniques taught to Shri Hans by his guru. They were taught to a *premie* (follower of the guru) by a mahatma (personal representative of the guru). These techniques were practiced daily by premies and were seen as allowing the premie to become attuned to the sound and light current emanating from the divine.

In the early 1970s the mission suffered greatly from its Millennium 73 program, which proved unable to attract enough people to fill (and pay for) the Houston Astrodome. This disaster was followed by an internal dissent within Maharaj Ji's family. A month after the Houston event, Maharaj Ji turned 16 and took personal administrative control of the mission. A short time later he married without parental approval, and his mother reacted by asserting control of the Indian branch of the mission and declaring an older brother the new guru. A later agreement gave the family the older mission in India, while Maharaj Ji continued to lead his following internationally. All through this period, the mission was a major target of the anti-cult movement. In 1986, it was reported that several hundred people supported the work of Divine Light Mission monthly and approximately 4,000 periodically. Supporters were once found on every continent and most European countries.

In the early 1980s, Maharaj Ji moved to disband the Divine Light Mission and he personally renounced the trappings of Indian culture and religion. After disbanding the mission, he founded Elan Vital, an organization to facilitate his future role as a teacher.

Elan Vital is a nonprofit organization established by people who wanted to make available the teachings of Maharaji (the current spelling). Funded by voluntary contributions, Elan Vital holds events at which Maharaji is invited to speak and offers video and audio material of his talks to interested people.

Over the last decade Maharaji has emphasized a central premise that the source of contentment and happiness is within each individual. He continues to offer the set of four techniques as a means to access that inner experience which he calls Knowledge. Offered without charge, these techniques help individuals to focus their awareness inside of themselves. Kim Knott, who studied Elan Vital in the late 1980s, found that those now involved in Maharaji's teaching process described the experience as one of being more in harmony with themselves. Maharaji has made every attempt to abandon the traditional Indian religious trappings in which the techniques originated and to make his presentation acceptable in all the various cultural settings in which his followers live. He sees his teachings as independent of culture, religion, beliefs, or lifestyles, and regularly addresses audiences in places as culturally diverse as India, Japan, Taiwan, the Ivory Coast, Slovenia, Mauritius, and Venezuela, as well as North America, Europe, and the South Pacific.

Elan Vital, Inc. may be contacted at PO Box 2220, Agoura Hills, CA 91376. More information on Elan Vital, Inc, can also be found at www.elanvital.org/.

Sources:

Cameron, Charles, ed. *Who Is Guru Maharaj Ji?* New York: Bantam Books, 1973.

Collier, Sophia. *Soul Rush.* New York: William Morrow and Company, 1978.

Downton, James V., Jr. *Sacred Journeys.* New York: Columbia University Press, 1979.

An Introduction to the Divine Light Mission. London: Shri Hans Production, [1972].

Light Reading. Miami, FL: Divine Light Mission, 1980.

Maharaji. *Listen to the Cry of Your Own Heart. Something Wonderful Is Being Said.* Visions International, 1995.

Maharaj Ji, Guru. *The Living Master.* Denver, CO: Divine Light Mission, 1978.

Satgurudev Shri Hans Ji Maharaj. Delhi, India: Divine Light Mission, n.d.

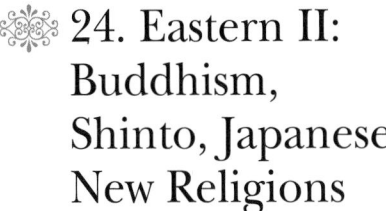

24. Eastern II: Buddhism, Shinto, Japanese New Religions

INTRAFAITH ORGANIZATIONS

International Buddhist Institute

The International Buddhist Institute (IBI) emerged in the late 1920s out of the realization of the spread of Buddhism around the world. In 1929, Abbot Tai Hsu of the Lin Yin Temple in Hangchow, China, made a world tour promoting the cause of a united Buddhism and the breaking down of sectarian barriers. Early branches of the institute were founded in New York, New York; Chicago, Illinois; and Honolulu, Hawaii. Soon other branches appeared in Los Angeles, San Francisco, and Oakland, California, with an additional branch appearing in Idaho.

The Honolulu branch, under the guidance of Bp. Yemyo Imamura and British convert Ernest Hunt, became the most active of the American branches of the movement. Hunt found it a perfect vehicle for reaching non-Japanese people with the message of Buddhism, for lessening tensions between the

Japanese and white populations of the islands, and for slowing competition between the various branches of Buddhism operating in the Hawaiian Japanese community. Hunt believed that the practice of active goodwill was the surest way to Enlightenment, and he put his ideas into the institute's program, especially in its social service activities centered upon visitation to hospitals and prisons.

Hunt helped vitalize the Buddhist youth program, wrote books, and worked to spread understanding of Buddhism in the larger non-Buddhist community. He also published, beginning in 1930, four issues of and IBI *Annual* and a magazine, *Navayana.*

Unfortunately, much of what Hunt did was undone following the death of Bishop Imamura in 1932. Hunt succeeded Imamura as president of the IBI. He carried on under the brief leadership of his immediate successor, but in 1936 Gikyo Kuchiba was appointed the new bishop of the Hongwanji Buddhists in Hawaii (the group over which Imamura was bishop). He was the exact opposite of his predecessor. Imamura had been an able leader who operated with tact and goodwill in the difficult situation on the islands. He openly tried to build bridges between the Japanese Hawaiians and their neighbors. By contrast, Bishop Kuchiba was a staunch Japanese nationalist who had little tolerance for other forms of Buddhism or making converts among non-Japanese people. He drove Hunt away and without the support of the Hongwanji, the largest of the Buddhist groups, the IBI quickly ceased to exist as a viable organization on the islands.

What little remained of the IBI both nationally and internationally after the disruption of the Hawaiian branch was completely destroyed by World War II.

Sources:

Hunt, Ernest, ed. *Hawaii Buddhist Annual.* Honolulu: International Buddhist Institute, 1932.

Hunter, Louise. *Buddhism in Hawaii: Its Impact on a Yankee Community.* Honolulu: University of Hawaii Press, 1971.

THERAVADA BUDDHISM

Neo-Dharma

Dr. Douglas Murray Burns was a psychiatrist born in Boston and raised in Oregon. As a high school student, he became interested in Buddhism. In 1960, he published his first work, *The Principles of Buddhist Philosophy.* He moved to California in 1961 and gathered around him a group interested, as he was, in a rational Theravada form of Buddhist faith, which he called Neo-Dharma. (Buddha's teachings outline the Dharma, the true way of life. Theravada Buddhism also called Hinayana, is a conservative, monastic Buddhism.) In 1965, Burns went to Thailand with the intent of entering a monastery but was prevented by his induction into the Army. After his service in the Army, he continued to travel, write, and lecture. On one of his travels in 1976, he disappeared while in the

jungle and has not been heard from since. He is presumed dead.

Burn's ideas can be summarized in a few statements, which obviously represent a neo-Buddhist or modernist approach: 1) The universe is regulated by impartial and unchanging laws. 2) Knowledge of these laws is acquired by insight and by unprejudiced reasoning in the light of one's experiences, not by faith in scriptures or mystical revelations. 3) Moral law, like physical law, is inherent in the workings of nature. Greed, hatred, and egotism result in proportionate amounts of unhappiness for one who is responsible for such motivations. 4) This three-dimensional realm of space, time, and matter is not the only level of existence. The concrete world of sense perception is a reality, but it is not the only possible dimension of reality. His rational modern approach found an audience in Thailand, Ceylon, and the United States. For many years, the American membership, concentrated in California, published a newsletter, *Neo-Dharma Notes.*

Sources:

Burns, Douglas. *Buddhism, Science and Atheism.* Bangkok, Thailand: World Fellowship of Buddhists, 1965.

———. *Nirvana.* Bangkok, Thailand: World Fellowship of Buddhists, 1967.

Stillpoint Institute

The Stillpoint Institute was founded in 1971 as the Susana Yeiktha Meditation Center and Buddhist Society. The founder, an American now known by his Buddhist name, Anagarika Sujata, was a college dropout who went to Ceylon and took training as a monk in Theravada Buddhism. He was ordained in 1967, returned to the United States, and, in 1970, founded the Buddhist Society of Clearwater. In 1971, he moved to Denver. From there, Sujata developed his Theravada Buddhist perspective in lectures, in teaching meditation, and in leading retreats. Around him a small community developed.

The goal of the institute was the "integration of body awareness techniques with the Satipatthana Vipassana Insight Meditation," in which the mind is trained to be more observant while refraining from comment on or judgment of what it views. In the mid-1970s the institute moved to San Jose, California.

The emphasis of Sujata's teaching, as manifested in his book, *Beginning to See,* is on present-mindedness and detachment. Buddhist insight meditation is the key to the laying down of anger, attachment, and selfishness and to the attainment of loving kindness, compassion, sympathetic joy, and equanimity.

Sources:

Sayadaw, Mahasi. *The Satipatthana Vipassana Meditation.* Elgin, AZ: Unity Press, 1957.

Sujata, Anagarika. *Beginning to See.* Denver: Sasana Yeiktha Meditation Center, 1973.

JAPANESE BUDDHISM

Aleph

Formerly known as AUM Supreme Truth and also known by its Japanese name, AUM Shinrikyo, Aleph is a Japanese Buddhist group that became known internationally in 1995 after an incident in which nerve gas was released in a Tokyo subway station and was traced to members of the group. During the summer and fall of 1995, more than 100 members of the group, including most of its leadership and its founding leader, Master Shoko Asahara, were arrested and a lengthy judicial process was begun. In the accompanying investigation, a variety of additional capital crimes were tied to the group's officials as were other incidents of suspected gassings. In the wake of these events, the organization was totally disrupted in Japan and the organization became unstable.

Aleph was founded by Asahara (born Chizuo Matsumoto in 1955) in Japan in 1987, though it was rooted in another organization that published books and taught yoga. It brought together the teachings he had acquired from his study of tantric yoga, Buddhism, and Taoism, through which he developed a unique training method to bring students to their own enlightenment, a realization of One's True Self. Asahara was most impressed by the Theravada and Tibetan Buddhist writings, which he considered more authentic than those Buddhist scriptures most used by Japanese Buddhists—one of several opinions held by Asahara that contributed to his isolation from other Japanese Buddhist leaders.

According to Asahara's teachings, the world consists of the gross world of everyday experiences, the astral world of images that we experience in our dreams, and the causal world of ideas. Above these three is the world of truth, Maha-Nirvana. Asahara held that Aleph practice led to emancipation, the ability to move freely at will from one world to the next. Further, supreme bliss and freedom were experienced in Maha-Nirvana (death).

Asahara directed students to the spiritual path called *tantrayana*, the goal being to become a buddha (enlightened one) in a single lifetime. The path demands total devotion to the guru and his initiations. New members were trained in yoga and meditation, and there was a stringent program of psychic development reminiscent of some of the austerities of Hindu sadhus.

Master Asahara offered three initiations. An earthly initiation included oral instructions on ethics, yoga, meditation, the use of mantras, and other matters leading to a purification of one's consciousness in regards to the gross world. The astral initiation via *shukufuku* (blessing) and *shaktipat* (awakening the kundalini energy) purified one's consciousness, relative to the astral world. The causal initiation purified one's superconsciousness and included the transfer of energy from the master to the trainee. The causal initiation led directly to emancipation and enlightenment. Ritual accompanying the initiations included the consumption of some of the bath water of the guru (a rite derived from an incident in Gautama Buddha's life in which followers consumed water from a pond in which he had washed) and some of his blood.

Those who passed through the three initiations were considered more spiritually advanced, and many were admitted into the ordered life. The monastic community, which included approximately 10 to 15 percent of the Japanese membership, lived at Aleph facilities. The development of the ordered community, not a prominent part of Japanese Buddhist life, further separated Aleph from the mainstream of Japanese Buddhism and also led to protests by many parents of Aleph members who felt that Aleph was disruptive of family units.

Organizationally, Aleph was modeled after the Japanese government. It was divided into various departments each headed by a minister. Ministries included Health and Welfare, Science and Technology, Intelligence, Medical, Home Affairs, and Construction. Aleph was headquartered at a rural center called Kaikuishiki, Yamanashi Prefecture near Mount Fuji. The organization operated a hospital in Tokyo and members formed many businesses aligned to the group's program.

Along with the Buddhist theology and psychic development program, Master Asahara had a fascination with prophecy and was a student of the Christian New Testament book of *Revelation* and the writings of Nostradamus. Through the early 1990s, he made a variety of predictions concerning the future of Japan, including World War III/Armageddon in the latter half of the 1990s. The public's awareness of these predictions was heightened following the unsuccessful bid by Asahara and the 24 other candidates who ran as members of Aleph in the 1990 national elections. The various enterprises organized by AUM were in part designed to survive the apocalypse and emerge unscathed in the aftermath of the destruction of social order.

The first American branch of the Aleph was opened in 1987 in New York City. While it survived for a period after the gas incident, it has subsequently disappeared. The period of instability that followed the gas incident and the subsequent arrest of Asahara and most of the group's leadership continued as the time-consuming process of adjudicating the charges against the principles proceeded. During the litigation period, additional crimes committed by those in custody were revealed. The government moved to disincorporate the group, its properties were seized, and it was forced into bankruptcy. In the wake of these actions, and the arrest of the last of the major leaders, Fumihiro Joyu, who had become the group's spokesperson in the months after the gassing, many predicted the group's disappearance. However, in 1996, the court ruled that, with the accused in jail, the group (the overwhelming majority of members having no involvement or knowledge of the acts of its leadership) AUM Shinrikyo no longer posed a public threat and allowed it to continue.

In the wake of the court's ruling, the group which had been completely decimated by the government's action against it, began to rebuild. As of early 1998, it appeared to have approximately 2,000 members in Japan (about 20 percent of its size in 1995). Its activities remained under close observation of the police, but activities were centered on the previous religious practices. Asahara's sons were designated the official gurus of the group until such time as Asahara might be released (the prospect of which is highly unlikely).

The number of crimes, including the deaths of various people not connected to the gassing, has never been revealed. Together, the crimes committed by Aleph's leadership constitute the most destructive serial crime wave ever in the country's history. The national trauma that the Japanese experienced led to the passing of a new law that tightens government control of religious groups.

Prior to the arrests in the summer of 1995, Aleph reported some 50,000 members worldwide, of which 10,000 were in Japan and 40,000 in Russia. Several hundred members were also found in New York City, Sri Lanka, and Germany. During its active period, the Aleph issued a periodical entitled *Truth Monthly*.

Sources:

Asahara, Shoko. *Supreme Initiation*. New York: AUM, U.S.A., 1988.

———. *Disaster Approaches the Land of the Rising*. Hitoana Fujuinimiya, Shizuyoko, Japan: AUM Shinrikyo Publishing Co., 1995.

———. *Tathagata Abhidhamma: The Ever-Winning Law of the True Victors*. 2 vols. Hitoana, Fujuinimiya, Shizuoka, Japan: AUM Shinrikyo Publishing Co., 1991–92.

———. *The Teaching of Truth*. 5 vols. Hitoana, Fujuinimiya, Shizuoka, Japan: AUM Shinrikyo Publishing Co. 1991–92.

———. *Your Daily Practice. A Book of Esoteric Teachings: The Tantra Vajrayana System of Practice*. Japan, AUM Shinrikyo, n.d.

Reader, Ian. *A Poisonous Cocktail? AUM Shinrikyo's Path to Violence*. Nordic Institute of Asian Studies, 1996. 116 pp.

———. *Religious Violence in Contemporary Japan: The Case of Aum Shinrikyo*. London: Curzon Press/Honolulu: University of Hawaii Press, 2000.

Chowado Henjo Kyo

Chowado Henjo Kyo was a Buddhist healing body founded by the Rev. Reisai Fujita, a former priest in the Shingi Shingon Chizan (a Shingon group without representatives in America). The worship and temple arrangement was typical of Shingon practice, and Kobo Daishi was worshipped. However, the healing experience and resultant teaching of the Reverend Fujita were the essential aspects of Chowado. Fujita, in spite of his success as a Shingon priest, was afflicted by chronic stomach and intestinal trouble that led to tuberculosis and paralysis. He tried unsuccessfully the method of Hakuin, the Zen priest, but soon discovered that he needed physical exercise as well as spiritual healing. Beginning with the practice of breathing, he developed a system which led to his cure. In 1906, he decided to devote his life to helping others as he had been helped.

Fujita's physical exercises, which were mastered by church members, included regulated breathing and harmony exercises of various parts of the body. The stomach, the most important part of the body, was singled out for special consideration; the correctly exercised abdomen was, according to Fujita, "gourd-shaped."

As part of his evangelistic endeavors, Fujita went to Hawaii in 1929 en route to California. In Hawaii he found both a need and an audience ready to listen. He sent his student companion on to California and ministered to the Japanese community in Hawaii, instead of going on to California. The mission flourished during the 1930s but was severely hurt by the war. After the war, Fujita moved to Honolulu and operated from a two-story church in Honolulu. The single congregation dissolved in 1990.

Kailas Shugendo

The Kailas Shugendo was founded by Dr. Neville G. Pemchekov-Warwick, known to his followers as Ajari. Shugendo was an old Buddhist tradition that borrowed from pre-Buddhist Japanese shamanism and mountain religion. Ajari had been conducting Shugendo practices since 1940 and was termed Dai Sendatsu, which allowed him to start his own movement. His background was Russian Buddhist, and he immigrated to America in the 1960s.

Central to the Shugendo was fire worship. Twice a day, members observed Goma, the fire ceremony. During the practice, the ritual master conducted while the members chanted. Once a week Hiwatari, fire purification, was performed. Members walked the sacred fire but were not burned. At intervals, members went to the mountains for ascetic practices—shugyo (climbing the mountain while chanting mantra), going under ice-cold waterfalls, and hanging people off rocks. Music was also a part of daily life. Headquarters of the ashram were in San Francisco, California, where it offered musical and cultural presentations to the Bay Area community and performed emergency community services.

Kongosatta-In Tendai Buddhist Temple

The Tendai Sect of Japanese Buddhism originated in a monastery in China in the T'ien T'ai mountains. It was developed by Chih K'ai (538–597). Chih K'ai believed the Lotus Sutra to contain the essential embodiment of Buddhism. Buddhism had progressed through several periods leading up to the Lotus Sutra. The teachings flourished over the next few centuries, and the T'ien T'ai movement became quite prominent in China. However, in the middle of the ninth century it came under heavy persecution and rapidly declined.

At the beginning of the ninth century, Dengyo Dhashi introduced T'ien T'ai Buddhism into Japan, where it became known as the Tendai school. A center was established near Kyoto, Japan, on Mt. Hiei. Dengyo Dhashi taught that Buddha was the historical manifestation of a more primordial Buddha-nature, which could appear at any time. The appearance would assist in the universal attainment of Buddhahood. Gautama Buddha attained such Buddhahood in its fullness. Further, the goal of individual life was the attainment of Buddhahood; all other activity was ultimately in vain except for striving for such.

The Tendai was among the most recent of the Japanese schools to come to America. Its first center was opened in Missouri in the 1980s.

During its active period, there were approximately 20 members of the single Tendai center. There were three million Tendai Buddhists worldwide, including a strong following in Brazil.

Sources:

A Dictionary of Buddhism. New York: Charles Scribner's Sons, 1972.

CHINESE BUDDHISM

Buddha's Universal Church and Ch'an Buddhist Sangha

Buddha's Universal Church was founded in the 1960s by the Rev. Dr. Calvin C. Vassallo, in Houston, Texas. The church was eclectic and drew upon all of the Buddhist traditions, though the Chinese was preferred. According to Vassallo, the church taught truth, the common denominator of all religion and philosophy. Truth is universal and is to non-Buddhists equated with "God." Truth is your father; from truth you were born and from the truth you must go unto your savior, the Buddha. Great emphasis was placed on the four basic truths, the noble eightfold path, and a codified presentation of Buddha's teachings.

During the 1970s the church carried on an active program. Worship was centered upon the daily family worship before the family shrine. Sunday services were adopted from the Buddhist Churches of America (Japanese Shin). Adjacent to the Houston headquarters was a nunnery headed by Mother Superior Samma Yasodhara. A Department of Buddhist Education offered courses in T'ai Chi Chuan (Chinese yoga), Buddhism, and Kung-Fu; in addition, there was an active social program reaching the needy in Houston through the city's welfare agencies.

Sources:

Truth: An Outline of the Buddhist Churches and Sangha. Houston, TX: Buddha's Universal Church, 1971.

TIBETAN BUDDHISM

American Buddhist Society and Fellowship Inc.

One of the earliest Tibetan Buddhist centers in the United States was the American Buddhist Society and Fellowship, founded in 1945 (incorporated in 1947) by Robert Ernest Dickhoff. The French-born Dickhoff migrated to the United States in 1927. He became involved in the occult and claims that "Out of the Invisible Realm of the Spirit of Tibet" he was given recognition by several spiritual entities, including Maha Chohan K. H. (i.e., the ascended master Koot Hoomi, first brought to the attention of the West by the Theosophist Helena Petrovna Blavatsky). He was given the titles "Red Lama" and "Most Reverend" and instructed to gather the Buddhists in American into a society. In 1950, according to Dickhoff, he was given the title of Grand Lama of the White Lodge of Tibet, See of New York, by the Dalai Lama. The society consisted of one center in New York City.

During the 1960s Dickhoff became known in UFO circles for his advocacy of the theory that UFOs were hostile. He believed that the UFOs are winged garudas (a birdlike demon in Buddhist thought), capturing humans and killing them for food.

Sources:

Dickhoff, Robert E. *Agharta*. Mokelumne Hill, CA: Health Research, 1964.

———. *Behold . . . the Venus Garuda*. New York: The Author, 1968.

———. *The Eternal Fountain*. Boston, MA: Bruce Humphries, 1947.

Arya Maitreya Mandala

German-born Lama Anagarika Govinda (b.1898) began to think of himself as a Buddhist while still a teenager. Working as an archeologist, he was able to travel freely in southern Asia and also worked for the promotion of an ecumenical Buddhism in Europe. In 1931 he traveled to Tibet and studied under Tomo Geshe Rinpoche. In 1933, in honor of his guru, he founded the Arya Maitreya Mandala as a Buddhist order. (Maitreya, it is noted, was the only bodhisattva [saint] acceptable to all Mahayana Buddhist groups.) Centers of the order were first established in Germany and throughout Europe.

The Home of the Dharma was founded in San Francisco 1967 by the Rev. Iru Price as the American branch of the Arya Maitreya Mandala. The order was held together by a common acceptance of the ideal of the awakening of our innermost spirit, the "Buddha-nature" within us. This ideal was expressed by making Buddhism a way of life, assisting those wishing to understand the Buddha's teaching, and developing methods of religious practice suitable to Western psychology. Lama Govinda made his first visit to the United States in 1969. He lectured and exhibited his paintings at the Zen Center of San Francisco. Subsequently, he made several tours teaching meditation.

The Home of the Dharma held regular meetings and conducted an annual Wesak celebration in the spring to honor Buddha. The Kwan Yin Free School for refugee children was also supported in Hong Kong.

Sources:

Govinda, Anagarika. *Creative Meditation and Multi-Dimensional Consciousness*. Wheaton, IL: Theosophical Publishing House, 1976.

————. *Foundations of Tibetan Buddhism*. New York: Humanities Press, 1959.

————. *The Psychological Attitude of Early Buddhist Philosophy*. London: Rider & Company, 1961.

"Special Meditation Issue." *Human Dimensions* 1, no. 4 (1972).

Chakpori-Ling Foundation Sangha

The Chakpori-Ling Foundation was a Nyingmapa Tibetan Buddhist center founded in the 1970s by Dr. Norbu L. Chen, formerly physician of Dharma Chakra Monastery in Kathmandu, Nepal. He received his basic instruction in Buddhism and Buddhist healing practices from refugees who had fled Tibet to Nepal following the 1959 Chinese invasion. He subsequently came to the United States and established Chakpori-Ling, named for a famous healing center just outside Lhasa, the capital of Tibet.

The foundation operated a college that offered courses in Buddhism for prospective monks and nuns and training in Oriental medicine. There was also a clinic for those who wished to receive treatment from an Oriental physician.

Enlightened Heart Meditation Center

Enlightened Heart Meditation Center was a Dzogchen center and part of the network of centers under the spiritual guidance of Khenchen Palden Sherab Rinpoche. Dzogchen meditation is traced to an enlightened yogi saint known as Sri Pramodavajra, who came from the mountains of northern Pakistan (the Swat valley) and taught at Bodh Gaya, in India, in the seventh century C.E. His teachings, as transmitted through a line of male and female saints, are concerned with enabling individuals to discover their true nature, and the real meaning of life, through the direct experience of meditation.

Khenchen Palden Sherab Rinpoche was born in Tibet and lived as a yogi and wandering mystic in the highlands of Tibet, meditated in caves in the Himalayas, and dwelled in temples throughout India. He subsequently moved to the United States with his brother, Khenpo Tsewang Dongyal Rinpoche. In 1989 the brothers founded Padmasambhava Buddhist

Center (PBC) in New York, with chapters and monasteries in the United States, Canada, Russia, and Puerto Rico.

The Enlightened Heart Meditation Center in San Francisco was headed by a resident teacher and British-born lama, Kunzang Palden Rinpoche, who studied not only with Khenchen Palden Sherab Rinpoche but with a number of other Buddhist teachers, especially the renowned Canadian lama Tenzin Dorje Namgyal Rinpoche, founder of the Dharma Centre of Canada. In his teaching Kunzang Palden Rinpoche was concerned with the emergence of a distinctly American form of Buddhism that nevertheless is drawn from pure sources of Eastern wisdom. In particular, he extolled Western culture (art, music, architecture, literature, medicine, science, and democratic principles) as an incomparable treasure that should not be rejected. He also emphasized an appreciation for the spiritual teachings of other religious traditions by honoring the world's great religious saints and revering the universal truths taught through the ages by divine messengers such as Moses, Zarathustra, Lao-tse, Krishna, Jesus, Mani, and Mohammed. Kunzang Palden Rinpoche assumed leadership of the Enlightened Heart Meditation Center in the early 1990s. After five years he retired from active teaching and became administrative head lama of the Dharma Fellowship of His Holiness the Gyalwa Karmapa, a nonprofit religious organization active in the Bay Area.

Jetsun Sakya Center

Jetsun Sakya Center was a small Sakyapa center founded in 1977 by Dezhung Rinpoche. Like Ewam Choden, it was under the Sakya Trizin, the head of the Sakyapa Order who resides in India, but was organizationally separate.

Kagyu Dharma

Kagyu Dharma was the collective name given the several centers established by Kalu Rinpoche, a teacher of the Kargyupa sect of Tibetan Buddhism. Rinpoche studied at the Palpung Monastery in eastern Tibet. He left Tibet in 1957 to establish a monastery in Bhutan, at the request of the queen. He then settled at Sonada, Darjeeling, India, and established his own center, Samdup Tarjeyling Monastery. He trained a number of monks especially to head centers in the West, and during the 1970s he started centers in Europe and North America. Focus of the European work was in Belgium at the urban center in Antwerp and the rural retreat at Huy. Each center carried on a regular format of worship and meditation which followed a daily, weekly, and lunar month schedule.

Among the American centers, Kagyu Droden Choling in San Francisco was most active. It was headed by Lama Lodo, the author of several books, and administered a publishing arm, KDK Publications, which published books in both Tibetan and English. Khawachen Dharma Center in Anchorage, Alaska, was an eclectic Buddhist center under the direction of N.

Paljor, and it received guidance from one of Rinpoche's students, Lama Karma Rinchen of Hawaii.

Rinpoche died in 1989. Several years later a young child born in 1990 was recognized by both the Dalai Lama and Tai Situ Rinpoche as the reincarnation of Rinpoche. The child was raised as Kalu returned and travelled to perform official ritual functions. During its active period, the group published a periodical entitled *Dundrub Yong* (Song of Fulfillment).

Sources:

Dorje, Kakhyab. *A Continuous Rain to Benefit Others*. Vancouver, BC: Kagyu Kunhyab Chuling, n.d.

Lodo, Lama. *Bardo Teachings*. San Francisco: KDK Publications, 1982.

Lodru, Lama. *Attaining Enlightenment*. San Francisco, CA: Kagyu Droden Kunchab Publications, 1979.

McLeod, Kenneth, trans. *The Total Flowering of Activity to Help Others*. Vancouver, BC: Kagyu Kunchab Chuling, 1975.

————. *The Chariot for Traveling the Path to Freedom*. San Francisco, CA: Kagyu Dharma, 1985.

Palzang, Rikzin, trans. *Prayers for Generating Guru Devotion*. San Francisco, CA: Kagyu Droden Kunchab Publications, 1979.

Longchen Nyingthig Buddhist Society

The Longchen Nyingthig Buddhist Society was founded in New York City by the Venerable Tsede Lhamo, Rhenock Chamkusho. The Longchen Nyingthig lineage extended unbroken to Padmasambhava, the famous teacher recognized as the founder of the Nyingmapa branch of Tibetan Buddhism. The teachings, which required intensive practice and close contact between student and teacher, offered the possibility of attaining permanent Buddhahood in a single lifetime. Its last known leader, a female, Rhenock Chamkusko, was the daughter of Kyungtrul Pema Wangchen, a Nyingmapa rinpoche. Following the death of her father when she was only three years old, she was taken to study with another female guru, Jetsun Lochen Rinpoche. This guru's monastery was on White Brow Mountain, where centuries earlier Nyingma Lama Gwalwa Longchenpa had founded the Longchen Nyingthig lineage.

In 1948 Chamkusko married Sonam Kazi, and in 1956 went with him to establish a monastery in Sikkim. Discovered by American pilgrims, they were invited to move to the United States, which they did in 1969. They established the Longchen Society. In 1972 the Dzogchen Pema Choling Meditation Center was opened in Philadelphia. A retreat center, which also served as headquarters, was added in 1975.

Pansophic Institute

The Pansophic Institute was founded in 1973 in Reno, Nevada, by Simon Grimes (Simon Theurgos, Choskyi Palden Konchog Chopel). One of its main goals was to bring the concepts of Tibetan Vajrayana (tantric)

Buddhism into the mainstream of Western thought. The Pansophic Institute was most closely related to the Gelugpa sect of which the Dalai Lama is the head. In the eleventh century, Atisha Dipankara came from India and began a great reformation of the Tibetan practices. Atisha's work was followed up in the fifteenth century by Tsong Khapa. He introduced strict discipline and the practices of the mendicant monks. Vajradhara was the Buddha, and there was a strong belief in Maitreya, "the coming Buddha." The strong discipline was based on the authority of the Dalai Lama. By the seventeenth century, the Gelugpa sect became the established religion of Tibet.

One of the leading monasteries of the Gelugpa was Tashi Lhunpo Monastery near Shigatse. The successive reincarnations of its hierarch, beginning with the scholar Kas Grub-Je, were, according to tradition, installed as the Panchen Rinpoche. The sixth Panchen Rinpoche was Choskyi Nyima (1883–1937). It was prophesied that the line of the Panchen Rinpoche would disappear from Asia and reappear in the West with the mission of unifying Eastern and Western thought as the foundation of world culture. Many came to believe Simon Grimes, the founder of the Pansophic Institute who was born in North China, was the reincarnation of the sixth Panchen Lama.

According to the Pansophic Institute, the most important concept of Vajrayana Buddhism was "Mahamudra," total awareness of one's consciousness. It contained the seed of enlightenment and was the goal of meditation. A seven-point ethical code was adhered to: abstain from injury to other beings, from taking what is not given, from sexual obsessions, and from making false claims and slandering others; work to maintain conscious, seek clear awareness in oneself and others; and cultivate this ethical code in oneself and in mankind.

The institute developed branch centers throughout the United States and in Canada, Australia, India, Nepal, and several countries in West Africa. It functioned through its School of Universal Wisdom (Reno, Nevada) and Church of Universal Light. The curriculum included Tibetan religion and culture, meditation, spiritual healing, parapsychology, comparative religion, esoteric (gnostic) cosmologies, and the four types of theurgy (tantra as adapted to the West). The institute also promoted planetary understanding, peace, and unity. During its active period, the institute also issued the periodical *Clear Light*. After two decades of activity, the institute ceased its operations in the early 1990s.

Sources:

The Graduated Path to Liberation. Reno, NV: Pansophic Institute, 1972.

Grimes, Simon. *The Flaming Diamond*. Reno, NV: Pansophic Institute, 1974.

WESTERN BUDDHISM

Buddhist Fellowship of New York
The Rev. Boris Erwitt, an American ordained to the Buddhist priesthood in Japan, began the Buddhist Fellowship of New York in 1961. The original group consisted of eight friends of the Reverend Erwitt who banded together to practice, study, and propagate Buddhism and to provide a gathering for Buddhists of non-Buddhist background. The fellowship's program was centered on bimonthly meetings with a service conducted according to the Pure Land practice and a lengthy discussion in which all participated. A number of pamphlets, along with a periodical, *Kantaka*, were published and distributed.

The membership was small and drawn largely from the intellectual and artistic community. Some first became interested in Buddhism through the "beat" generation's emphasis on Zen. Project Sujata (named after the girl who saved Buddha's life) practiced the virtue of *ooana* (giving) by sponsoring the education of an indigent Native American child and providing scholarships for "untouchables" in India.

Buddhist World Philosophical Group
The Buddhist World Philosophical Group was a small Buddhist fellowship headquartered in Three Rivers, Michigan. Its leader, Marie Harlow (b. 1902), took over the longstanding Chicago-based occult periodical *The Occult Digest* in the 1940s and began almost immediately to emphasize Eastern religion, particularly Buddhism, over occult topics. In 1944 she renamed the magazine *World Philosophy*, and later moved its editorial office to Three Rivers. In 1962 *World Philosophy* became *Buddhist World Philosophy*, and Harlow announced a set of four aims for the magazine: to promote universal brotherhood, to proclaim the sanctity of life, to destroy the "limitations of the negative Semitic religious God-concept," and to turn America toward Buddhism. A small group of people inspired by Harlow's ideals congregated together and continued to meet until her death.

Church of One Sermon
The Church of One Sermon, located in Lemon Grove, California, was formed in the 1970s to aid in "the Full Awakening in all people of that special Reality knowledge first testified to by Guatama Siddhartha, the Buddha." Its founder and director was Leonard Enos. An eclectic approach centered on Mahayana Buddhism, but including Tantra and Zen and even some Sufism, was taught, with particular interest being given to research in psychology on the meditative states of consciousness. The program consisted largely of meditation, exercise, and discussion sessions. In 1973, the church had one center.

Davachan Temple
Davachan Temple, established in 1980 in the health resort town of Eureka Springs, Arkansas, helped pio-

neer the emergence of American Buddhism. Over two decades, the temple's leader, Bhikkhuni Miao Keang Sudharma (Alexa Roy), studied, mastered, and was ordained in three distinct Buddhist traditions: Soto Zen (through Juyi Kennett Roshi, 1963), Sri Lankan Theravada (1973), and Chinese Pure Land (1983). Her religious name indicated her varied background.

Devachan Temple was an eclectic center with practices taken from the Soto, Theravada, Ch'an (Chinese Zen), and Pure Land traditions, and chanting was done in both Pali and Chinese. The temple invited Buddhists from all traditions to use its facilities for personal retreats (for which there was no charge) and to participate in its varied activities. The resulting practice constituted a new unique Buddhism that was female-friendly.

Sources:

Rawlinson, Andrew. *The Book of Enlightened Masters: Western Teachers in Eastern Traditions*. La Salle, IL: Open Court Press, 1997. 650 pp.

Friends of Buddhism–Washington, D.C.
Alabama-born Robert Stuart Clifton became interested in Buddhism as a student at Columbia University in the 1920s. He moved to San Francisco and lived in the Japanese community. In 1933 he was ordained as a priest in the Honpa Hongwanji Mission, now the Buddhist Churches of America, and began English language work along the West Coast. In 1934 he traveled to Japan and while there became a Higashi Hongwanji priest. Upon his return to America, he lectured widely and organized a number of Friends of Buddhism societies, mostly in the East.

The Washington Friends of Buddhism was formed in the home of Mr. and Mrs. Lee Sirat at a gathering of persons Clifton had interested in Buddhism. There were 11 in the original group. The program centered on lectures and discussion of Buddhism, but meditation and worship also were included. Wesak, the spring festival honoring Gautama Buddha, was celebrated.

Besides the Washington group, the only Friends of Buddhism group to survive through the 1960s was the Friends of Buddhism of New York, founded in the early 1950s. In the late 1960s, following the retirement of its leader, Frank E. Becker, the New York group merged with the Washington group. Kurt F. Leidecker, who succeeded Clifton as head of the Washington group, died in 1991, and the society is thought to be defunct.

Sources:

Leidecker, Kurt F. *History of the Washington Friends of Buddhism*. Washington, DC: United States Information Service, 1960.

Harmony Buddhist Mission
The Harmony Buddhist Mission was founded in 1953 by Frank Newton. It was centered on Buddhist ethical

and philosophical teachings. Self-responsibility and attunement to fact were stressed. Leaders in the mission (called preceptors) were not allowed to receive any income for their religious duties. Frank Newton gained a reputation as a writer and translator of Buddhist literature. Some 1,500 people reportedly came into Buddhism through his efforts.

Shivapuram

Shivapuram was founded in 1963 by Radha Appu (also known as Rakshasi) in the Catskill Mountains of New York. While on a retreat and doing vigorous breathing and concentration exercises to raise his *kundalini* (creative energy), Radha Appu became aware of the Master Vijaya Bhattacharya, who appeared to him. Over a period of time, the master gave instructions and told Radha Appu to "Go forward" and found Shivapuram. Radha Appu remained the master's sole contact, though sporadic appearances were made to the *shivas* (the members of the Shivapuram). In 1967 Radha Appu was given instructions to found a worldwide Crusade of the Spirit to save humanity from self-destruction.

Though borrowing from Hinduism, the Shivapuram was basically Mahayana Buddhist with large portions of Tantra. Adherents did not believe in escape into nirvana, but in accepting the world and using it as a means of liberation. They sought *Buddhatva*, the quality of being enlightened. They used chants and mantras and meditative yoga.

The Shivapuram members were largely drawn from California. In 1971 there were 3 priests, 10 lecturers, and approximately 300 members. Though committed to spreading the movement, members were not openly evangelistic and were highly selective about who was invited to join or even attend meetings. There has been no evidence of a continuing movement in recent years.

Universal Buddhist Fellowship

The Universal Buddhist Fellowship was formed in 1951 by the Venerable H. H. (Tissa) Priebe of Ojai, California. It was described as autonomous and nonsectarian. Its purpose was dissemination of the Western Dharma (the true way of life taught by Buddha). The fellowship published a periodical, *Western Bodhi*.

SHINTO

Inari Shinto

In Hawaii the Inari have departed from the Inari deities common to the group in Japan. The Hawaiian Inari worship a main deity, Shoichii Shi Sha. The Wakamiya Shrine in Honolulu was founded in 1912 by the Rev. Yoshio Akizaki. Following his passing in 1951, he was succeeded by his son, the Rev. Takeo Akizaki. Takeo Akizaki assumed the role of pastor and the temple conducted regular worship services. A second temple was located on Molokai.

Society of Johrei

The Society of Johrei was formed in 1971 by former leaders of the Church of World Messianity who felt that it had departed from the teachings of founder Mokichi Okada. They began to work independently of the church and then organized the society. Their following included people in Korea and Brazil. An American office was opened in the 1980s and began to publicize the society through distribution of an edited volume of Okada's writings.

Sources:

Okada, Mokichi. *Johrei: Divine Light of Salvation*. Kyoto, Japan: Society of Johrei, 1984.

Third Civilization

The Third Civilization was one of the "new religions" of Japan and represented a twentieth-century form of Shinto based upon the work of Sen-sei Koji Ogasawara. Ogasawara retranslated the *Kojiki* and *Nippon-Syoki* (*Nihongi*), the Shinto scriptures, in such a way as to lift the veil of symbolic mythology and in order to put the name of God into sound. The Third Civilization was involved in the study of the Kototama principle. Kototama was equated with the biblical *Logos* and the Chinese *Tao*, and was considered the underlying life-principle that is the source of all.

According to the Third Civilization, history can be divided into three periods. Ten thousand years ago, our human ancestors perfected the Kototama principle and lived as one family in a peaceful society. This perfect society was the First Civilization and is equated with the Garden of Eden. About 5,000 years ago, the Kototama principle was hidden from society and a new principle guiding society toward the material-scientific or Second Civilization emerged. During this time, man divided into tribes and nations and became competitive. Basic to the Second Civilization is the division between physical and spiritual. The present time, in which the pollution of the planet is monumental, is the hellfire prophesied in prior ages. Our only hope is the "messiah," the capacity of the human soul that has been dormant, the Kototama principle. With this principle, the Third Civilization will emerge.

In addition to the Third Civilization centers in North America, European centers were located in Paris and Uppsala, Sweden. A periodical, *Third Civilization Monthly*, was published.

Sources:

Nakazono, Masahilo. *Kototama*. Santa Fe, NM: Third Civilization, 1976.

———. *Messiah's Return: The Hidden Kototama Principle*. Santa Fe, NM: Third Civilization, 1972

———. *My Past Way of Budo*. Santa Fe, NM: Kototama Institute, 1979.

 # 25. Unclassified Christian

UNCLASSIFIED CHRISTIAN CHURCHES

Assembly of Christian Soldiers

The upsurge of the Ku Klux Klan in the American South during the 1960s led in 1971 to the formation of a Klan-based church, the Assembly of Christian Soldiers. Its founder and leader, Jessie L. Thrift, was a former Grand Wizard of the Original Knights of the Ku Klux Klan, one of several Klan schismatic groups. The assembly began a program of assisting the all-white segregated academies that had been established in reaction to the desegregation of public schools in the South. Money from tax-exempt church funds was used to subsidize the schools so that parents could transfer children from public schools without extra cost. There was an affiliated organization, "The Southerners," which organized mass rallies.

In 1972 there were 10 churches in Alabama, 6 in Georgia and Mississippi, and approximately 3,000 members.

Bible Christians

The Bible Christians, not to be confused with the Bible Christian Church (the Canadian body with Methodist roots), dated from the independent efforts of former Church of England minister William Cowherd (1763–1816), a popular preacher in Manchester, England. Cowherd had left the Church of England due to its sectarianism and eventually established an independent meetinghouse in Salford, England. He felt that all members should take their life patterns from the Bible. He refused to draw a salary and earned his living as a physician. Members simply called themselves Bible Christians.

The group held the Bible as its only creed and emphasized the doctrines of the Trinity, the incarnation of Christ, the revelation of God to the prophets and apostles, and the church. The Bible Christians also taught that the true church was composed of those who had responded to the truth, and that the order of the church should center on prayer, preaching, and worship. As the movement developed, Cowherd began to advocate and then impose upon his very large following the ideals of vegetarianism and abstinence from alcohol. He supplemented his biblical support for these ideas with the latest findings of the scientific study of the human body.

In 1817 two Bible Christian leaders, the Revs. James Freeman Clarke and William Metcalfe, migrated to Philadelphia, Pennsylvania. Clarke proceeded to the western United States and was lost to the movement, but Metcalfe established a congregation in Philadelphia, which by 1823 was strong enough to purchase land upon which a church building was erected. Under Metcalfe's leadership, the church survived for a number of decades. In 1847 it reported around 75 members in the single congregation.

Metcalfe is generally remembered as the first prominent vegetarian in the United States. He authored the first vegetarian tract published in America and in 1850 became the first corresponding secretary of the American Vegetarian Society. The Bible Christian Church was a center of the society during the years of Metcalfe's life.

Sources:

Metcalfe, William. "History of the Bible Christians." In *History of All the Religious Denominations in the United States*. Harrisburg, PA: John Winebrenner, 1848, pp. 123–129.

Numbers, Ronald L. *Prophetess of Health*. New York: Harper & Row, 1976.

Trall, Russell T. *The Scientific Basis of Vegetarianism*. St. Catherine's, ON, Canada: Provoker Press, 1970.

Catholic Apostolic Church

The outpouring of charismatic gifts in 1906 at the Azusa Street mission in Los Angeles, California, led to the modern Pentecostal movement. But prior sporadic charismatic events in the Western world figure in Pentecostal history as precursors of the twentieth-century movement. One such outpouring in England led to the founding of the Catholic Apostolic Church. In 1828 the Rev. John McLeod Campbell, a Presbyterian who believed in the universal love of Christ and drew great crowds of people to hear of it, began to notice "supernatural" happenings in his parish. The first event was the deathbed conversion of James Grubber, remarkable for the change in his countenance from anxiety to peace, and for his words about Christ's imminent return. A Mr. Johnstone had a similar death the next year, and Isabella Campbell followed in the same fashion.

In 1830 Margaret MacDonald, weak and near death, began to experience visions of God's mercy and of heavenly hosts; two months later she was healed. In the excitement that followed the gathering at Margaret's house for prayer meetings, George MacDonald, and then James MacDonald, began to speak in tongues and to prophesy. A small group gathered around the MacDonalds and eventually a small chapel was rented to hold services. News spread to all corners of the British Isles.

One group that heard of the MacDonalds was composed of clergy and laymen gathered at the country estate of Henry Drummond to study the signs of the end of the world. Delegates were dispatched to investigate the occurrences associated with the MacDonalds and, upon their return, reported favorably. Greatly influenced by the report was the Rev. Edward Irving, a Presbyterian minister who had been impressed with John McLeod Campbell. Irving published the delegates' account, claiming that they had heard languages that were indeed unknown tongues.

Irving became a prolific exponent of charismata. He was removed from the Presbyterian Church, and, from this split, the Catholic Apostolic Church dates.

As the new church took shape, a non-Presbyterian polity began to develop. Members believed that they were in community with the biblical church and should possess a biblical government. Apostles arose to lead the new church order, and other biblical offices, such as that of prophet, came into existence. The church grew and spread.

Members of the Catholic Apostolic Church came to America in the 1840s and organized a church at Potsdam, New York. In 1851 a society was organized in New York and three years later a church was purchased. Early congregations were established in Enfield and Hartford, Connecticut, and in Boston. Members were largely drawn from New England Congregationalist and Episcopalian churches. The leader of the new church was William Watson Andrews, a former Congregational minister.

The Catholic Apostolic Church was at variance with its parent Presbyterian, Congregational, and Episcopal bodies in its acceptance of and belief in the necessity of all the charismatic gifts and in its polity. Among the gifts it sought were healing, speaking in tongues, and prophecy. However, at its formation, the church did not stress speaking in tongues as the sign of the Holy Spirit's indwelling. The church was not the first church within the Pentecostal movement, because it did not initially describe the gift of tongues. The Catholic Apostolic Church accepted the Nicene Creed and closely followed the Church of England, largely in its doctrine. It retained the sacramental view of baptism and the Lord's Supper. It revived the sacrament of the laying-on-of-hands for the gift of the Holy Spirit. Sacraments of the second order included sealing and marriage. The church believed in the premillennial Second Coming of Jesus. One aim of the Catholic Apostolic Church was to reestablish the church in its apostolic order. In 1832, a new restoration of the college of "apostles" was begun in the call of John Bate Cardale. Also included among the 12 were Henry Drummond, Thomas Carlyle, and Henry Hilton. When these men died, the apostles' office was dissolved. Under the apostles were the servants (Luke 10:1). The three-fold ministry of angel (bishop), priest (or elder), and deacon functioned at the local church level. Members of the ministry were exclusively called, appointed, and ordained by the apostles. The last of the 12 apostles died in 1901. Following that, there were no more ordinations.

The thrust of the Catholic Apostolic Church was directed totally toward awakening other churches to its concerns. This program, often seen as a proselytizing endeavor, was successful in the nineteenth century. Soon after the death of the apostles, however, growth stopped. The 13 churches reported in 1916 were reduced to 7 by 1936, and then to a single

church. Since then, the Catholic Apostolic Church has ceased to exist in the United States.

Sources:

Dallimore, Arnold. *Forerunner of the Charismatic Movement: The Life of Edward Irving*. Chicago: Moody Press, 1983.

Drummond, Andrew Landale. *Edward Drummond and His Circle*. London: James Clarke, 1934.

Shaw, P. E. *The Catholic Apostolic Church, Sometimes Called Irvingite: A Historical Survey*. New York: King's Crown Press, 1946.

Christian Survival Fellowship

The Christian Survival Fellowship was formed as the Fellowship of Christian Men by its founder, Julius Rose. It was Rose's opinion that humanity was living in the last days and that atomic war was inevitable. He also believed that Christianity was essentially a white man's religion, given to the Western world and authoritarian in character. He proposed the establishment of several survival towns (hence the change of name in the 1970s) as the only effective civil-defense strategy. Each town would be nominally populated at all times, have a vast supply of food and other necessities on hand, and be run on a semi-communal basis. These towns would then be able to offer hospitality to all in times of crises.

In the 1960s Rose moved to Richland, New Jersey, and began to clear land for a prototype survival town. He also created the General Development Company to manufacture and market low-pollution, high gas mileage (over 100 m.p.h.) vehicles. In the center of the town, called Survival Town, was Fellowship Park, a place for Christians to meet and spend weekends together.

Church of the Christian Crusade

Billy James Hargis was ordained as a minister in the Christian Church (Disciples of Christ). While pastoring a congregation at Supulpa, Oklahoma, in 1948, he founded the Christian Crusade, and by 1950 he was devoting his full-time efforts to the Crusade. The Crusade opposed modernism, liberal theology, and the social gospel. It advocated a fundamental Christian faith centered in Christ, premillennial eschatology, and belief in the existence of Satan.

In 1955 the Crusade hired L. J. White, Jr., a public relations man who began to build the renown of Hargis and the Crusade. Anticommunism came to the forefront of the Crusade's program. A project to balloon copies of the Bible behind the Iron Curtain made Hargis a leader in the right-wing political movement that climaxed in Barry Goldwater's 1964 presidential campaign. From that point on, the Crusade expanded and a variety of subsidiary structures emerged.

In 1966 the Church of the Christian Crusade was established as a single congregation in Tulsa, Oklahoma; weekly services were held each Sunday.

Some members of the Crusade, following Hargis's lead, withdrew from their "denominational churches" and transferred their membership to the new organization. As groups of members emerged in different locations, independent Bible churches affiliated with the Tulsa church were formed.

In the mid-1970s, Hargis suffered a nervous breakdown, and the ministry foundered during his absence of almost a year. Upon his return Hargis reassumed the reins of the church and began to revive and expand its ministries. A variety of organizations conducting many specialized ministries became associated with the Church of the Christian Crusade. The David Livingstone Missionary Foundation and the Good Samaritan Children's Foundation conducted a large foreign missionary outreach program, the most developed in India. An antiabortion crusade was conducted through Americans Against Abortion. Quarterly conferences were held at the church-owned Christian Crusade Log-School Cabin in the Ozark Mountains. The Christian Echoes National Ministry ran the Crusade, published the weekly periodical, and organized conferences and rallies around the United States. Other associated ministries included the Billy James Hargis Evangelistic Association and Evangelism in Action.

Over 4,000 people belonged to the Church by Mail, a ministry to homebound individuals. A monthly sermon and other tapes were sent to these individuals. The tape ministry also produced sets of teaching tapes on a variety of topics. In addition, a weekly television show, *Pray for America*, was added to the longstanding radio ministry. Over 200,000 people supported the ministries of the Christian Crusade, though most were not members of the church. The monthly newspaper, *Christian Crusade*, had a circulation in excess of 250,000.

In the mid-1970s, the Church of the Christian Crusade and its associated ministries suffered a severe setback when Hargis was charged with having had sexual relations with students of the American Christian College, a college founded by Hargis and affiliated with the church. Confronted with the testimony of the students in October 1974, the board of the college asked for Hargis's resignation as president and his retirement from the church and associated ministries. Six months after Hargis came out of retirement, he regained control of the church and all the allied ministries except the college. In 1976, when the charges became public, Hargis denied the accusations and attributed his split with David Noebel, who had succeeded him as president of American Christian College, to doctrinal differences.

Sources:

Hargis, Billy James. *Christ and His Gospel*. Tulsa, OK: Christian Crusade Publications, 1969.

———. *The Far Left*. Tulsa, OK: Christian Crusade, 1964.

———. *My Great Mistake*. Green Forest, AR: New Leaf Press, 1985.

Hargis, Billy James, and Bill Sampson. *The National News Media, America's Fifth Column*. Tulsa, OK: Crusader Books, 1980.

Hargis, Billy James, and Jose Hernandez. *Disaster File*. Tulsa, OK: Crusader Books, 1978.

Church of What's Happening Now

Among the responses to the death of Martin Luther King, Jr., was the founding by Imagene Stewart of the Church of What's Happening Now in Dublin, Georgia. Her ministry included a radical attack on institutional religion and denominationalism. After a short time, headquarters of the church were moved to Washington, D.C., where a street ministry was begun and a weekly radio show developed. The ecumenical commitment of Stewart led her to seek ordination from an interfaith group of clergy and laity on Reformation Sunday, 1974. This act was considered an identification with King's break with denominationalism, man-made doctrine, and educational requirements for ministers.

In the mid-1970s, the church had congregations in Washington, D.C.; Chicago; and Dublin, Wrightsville, and Atlanta, Georgia.

Reverend Stewart encountered some conflict with authorities because her church's name was the same as that of a fictitious church mentioned in a routine by popular black comedian Flip Wilson. In 1972 she was denied authorization to perform marriages in the District of Columbia.

Dawn of Truth

The Dawn of Truth was the name given to the teaching ministry of Mikkel Dahl, a Canadian who described himself as a nondenominational Christian. In his early life Dahl had pursued a spiritual pilgrimage that led him through a number of esoteric and metaphysical movements and finally culminated in his acceptance of Christianity. He then devoted his life to the "proving" of Christ to the masses. He often offered his teachings to those in the movements he had once investigated and frequently took out advertisements in metaphysically oriented periodicals, such as *Fate* magazine. His literature and correspondence lessons were mailed out across North America and to many countries overseas. These writings covered a wide range of biblical, prophetic, and current events–related topics; among them was an attempt to explain Christianity to those who followed esoteric and metaphysical teachings.

In his autobiographical testimony, *The Land of Mist Illusion*, he declared: "But now is our Christ demonstrated, while the challenge is flung in the teeth; refute the proof! Believe nothing is my counsel, but receive that which defies refutation. Reject the God of those who preach tomorrow and the sweet by and by. God is today, while the arena of His power is Here in the Present World, and right now! That is the great joy I have to preach, teach and also demonstrate! A Christ who lives Now in the Here in jubilant defiance of life's every storm; a Savior not for tomorrow, but for Now and for our Here."

Such statements led to his being described as a "doubting Thomas," or "one from Missouri."

Dahl retired in 1978, but several groups that saw themselves as aligned with Dahl's thinking continued to publish and distribute his material.

Sources:

Dahl, Mikkel. *The Coming New Society*. Windsor, ON, Canada: Dawn of Truth, n.d.

———. *God's Master Plan of Love for Man*. Windsor, ON, Canada: Dawn of Truth, 1961.

———. *Have You Heard, the Great Pyramid Speaks*. Fulton, MO: Shepherdsfield, 1986.

Free Church of Berkeley

The Free Church of Berkeley was one of a number of free, or liberated, churches that first emerged in the 1960s. Factors that contributed to the formation of such churches included a renewed emphasis on social activism, the emergence of a counterculture with its "hippies" and flower children, and the reluctance of members of institutionalized churches to support ministries among people who wished to significantly alter worship patterns, associate with drug users, aid unchurched youth, and meet the needs of people outside the church. The liberated churches were based on liberal Protestant theology that defined the church *as* a mission, rather than the more traditional idea that conceived of the church as having a mission to fulfill. According to this new perspective, the church was equated with those groups that do the work of the church—struggle against war, violence, racial injustice, male dominance, and pollution, to name but a few. The liberated churches aligned themselves with the late 1960s "movement," those involved in radical political activism.

One free, liberated church developed in Berkeley, California, adjacent to a locus of much radical political thought, the University of California. The Free Church of Berkeley began in 1968 as the South Campus Community Ministry, sponsored by several Berkeley congregations. Dick York, a priest in the Protestant Episcopal Church, was appointed to an experimental youth ministry. His work expanded and additional space became necessary, as did medical and psychiatric services, food, and clothing. People both outside and inside the church community organized to meet those needs, taking the name "Free Church." York's home became the center of their activity. After months of work, the Free Church began supplying people's needs for worship and opportunities to learn about Jesus. A radical liturgy developed, and the notion of a "Radical Jesus" emerged. The Free Church was transformed into a "radically involved ecumenical church made up of youth, street people, students, church dropouts, hippies, and activists." It followed the ideal of liberal Protestant social activism to its logical conclusion.

Illustrative of the Free Church lifestyle was its experimental liturgy. Baptism was seen as "going through the waters" in much the same way as Moses led the Hebrew children through the Red Sea. The Lord's Supper became the "Freedom Meal." Jesus was pictured as the Liberator of people, who, though killed by his oppressors, led his people out of the house of exploitation.

The Free Church movement spread across the United States in the 1970s, though it was largely absorbed by the mainline churches in the 1980s. During the 1970s, the Berkeley Church published *A Directory of the Liberated Church in America, Win with Love*. The directory included listings for "movement" groups, as well as for specifically Christian organizations that were theologically aligned. There was also a periodical, *Radical Religion*, published quarterly.

Sources:

Moody, Jess. *The Jesus Freaks*. Waco, TX: Word Books, 1971.

Harvest House Ministries

Harvest House Ministries was one of the most successful and important of the Jesus People groups to emerge in the early 1970s. It grew out of David Abraham's conversion to Christianity in 1970. Abraham had been the editor of the *Oracle*, one of the prominent underground newspapers of the 1960s. From its San Francisco offices, the paper reached a circulation of over 100,000 with its coverage and promotion of the drug revolution, Eastern religion, and sexual freedom. It ceased publication in 1969 as the hippie community disintegrated. A short time later, Chris D'Alessandro met Alexander and became the force leading to his conversion. Abraham, a Jew, turned the rights of the *Oracle* over to D'Alessandro, who became the new editor. *Oracle* was reborn in 1971 as the organ of Harvest House Ministries, then five communes in the Haight-Ashbury district of San Francisco.

Harvest House Ministries was started by Oliver Heath and his wife, Mary Louise Heath, who had moved to San Francisco from Alabama in 1970. Oliver was a Baptist who had experienced a charismatic renewal. He established Harvest House to offer a Pentecostal-charismatic alternative to the popular psychic-mystical-Eastern teachings of Stephen Gaskin, Edgar Cayce, Meher Baba, Swami Satchidananda, and groups such as the Self-Realization Fellowship and the Vedanta Society. D'Alessandro, formerly a member of the International Society for Krishna Consciousness, led members of the Ministries to Krishna Consciousness group meetings to distribute literature and engage in evangelical activity.

Heath appointed an elder, assisted by one or more deacons, to supervise each of the Harvest House communal residences, which housed between 15 and 18 residents. Supervisors were supported by the income of the residents. While there was not a specific teaching program, each person was encouraged in Bible study and members met together for worship. There is no recent evidence of the survival of the Ministries, and it is assumed that, like most of the Jesus People revival groups, Harvest House Ministries was absorbed into one of the larger Pentecostal churches.

Jesus People International/International Christian Ministries

Jesus People International began in October 1969, when Duane Pederson, then an entertainer and Assemblies of God college dropout, noticed a *Los Angeles Free Press* hawker on Sunset Boulevard in Hollywood. He conceived the idea for a free Christian paper, and within three days had published the first issue of the *Hollywood Free Paper*. He distributed 10,000 copies, and circulation climbed with subsequent issues. As people were converted, a variety of ministries developed: coffee houses, emergency switchboards, Bible study groups, rock festivals, and drug counseling activities. In 1972 the first issue of the *Jesus People Magazine*, a Bible study monthly, was issued. At the same time Jesus People International was formally organized. A few years later, Jesus People International changed its name to International Christian Ministries.

The *Hollywood Free Paper* was distinctive in its use of cartoons with simple and direct Christian messages. A line of Jesus People posters and bumper stickers were also developed. In 1972, a record and a book telling Pederson's story were issued, and groups around the country began to look to Peterson for leadership. Affiliated groups were founded in 11 California cities, as well as in Tucson, Arizona; Denver, Colorado; Detroit, Michigan; Minneapolis and St. Paul, Minnesota; Kansas City, Kansas; Chicago, Illinois; Cleveland, Ohio; and Raleigh, North Carolina. Pederson ordained pastors to lead these groups. Over the years, as the Jesus People Revival was absorbed into the mainline evangelical and Pentecostal churches, the national ministry gave way to a set of ministries, primarily in the Los Angeles area. A focus on social projects assumed a place beside the evangelistic concerns. The Ministries supplied housing, clothing, and other assistance to the poor, and developed two widely publicized programs for intercity children, "Christmas for Kids" and "Camp for Kids."

In the 1980s the headquarters of the Ministries was located in the Venice Community Church that Pederson pastored. He resigned that position in 1985 and returned to Hollywood. The Ministries then changed its name to Duane Pederson Ministries and ceased being a church-forming organization. It continued its social service programs, but placed a renewed emphasis on cooperation with other street and prison ministries. Ex-prisoners and other converts were channeled into established congregations, many of which were served by longtime associates of Pederson. Pederson released three issues of the *Hollywood Free Paper* in 1987 before ceasing publication. In 1989 Pederson joined the Antiochean Orthodox Christian Archdiocese of North America and was ordained as a priest.

Sources:

Pederson, Duane. *Jesus People*. Pasadena, CA: Compass Press, 1971.

Streiker, Lowell D. *The Jesus Trip*. Nashville, TN: Abingdon Press, 1971.

Williams, Don. *Call to the Street*. Minneapolis, MN: Augsburg Publishing House, 1972.

Osgoodites

The Christian sectarian movement, known as the Osgoodites after its founder, Jacob Osgood (1777–1844), was founded around 1818 in Warner, New Hampshire. Osgood, a farmer, was a member of the choir of the Congregational Church. However, he developed an aversion to both Calvinism and Universalism (the two theological perspectives that were warring for control of Congregationalism). Calvinism was Trinitarian in faith with a strong emphasis on predestination. Unitarians denied the doctrine of the Trinity. Osgood's own individual approach led to a break with the Congregational Church. He joined the Free Will Baptists, who preached an Arminian perspective (opposed to predestination), but, not feeling at home there, soon withdrew.

Osgood's own church began with the conversion of Thomas Hackett and soon developed a small congregation. Among Osgood's peculiar ideas was a belief in the laying-on of hands for healing of the sick. He also argued against the hiring of either lawyers or preachers. Most importantly, the group refused to vote, continually complained of taxes, and refused to train for the militia or to pay the fines coincidental with such refusal. The first members of the group were arrested and jailed in 1819. The following year Osgood was also arrested and incarcerated. During this time he began to write his autobiography, the major source of information about him and his group.

Through the 1820s, the movement spread. A second congregation was organized in Canterbury, New Hampshire, and disciples could be found in many of the nearby towns. They built no church buildings, being content to meet in private homes. Dress was nonconforming, the men wearing out-of-style clothes and keeping their hair long and unkempt. The women cut their dresses straight and plain, and wore a white kerchief around the neck with a bonnet on the head.

Following his death in 1944, Osgood was succeeded in leadership by Nehemiah Ordway and Charles H. Colby. They did not have the enthusiasm and ability of the founder and the movement slowly died away. It had entirely disappeared by 1890.

Sources:

Osgood, Jacob. *The Life and Christian Experience of Jacob Osgood, with Hymns and Spiritual Songs*. Warner, NH: 1873.

Scott, Kenneth. "The Osgoodites of New Hampshire." *New England Quarterly* 16 (1943): 20—40.

Shalom Ecumenical Church

The Shalom Ecumenical Church was founded by Bp. Joergen Koch Larsen (1914—1989). Larsen was born in Denmark and raised in the Lutheran Church of Denmark, his father being a dean in the church. He was serving in the Danish Army when World War II erupted. After Hitler overran Denmark, Larsen was arrested, escaped, and served in the Danish underground. He migrated to Canada after the war and served in the Royal Canadian Army Medical Corps in the Korean War.

Larsen claimed to have been in possession of a rare manuscript, a "fifth Gospel," possibly the book of Jesus' sayings that many scholars believe stood behind and was a source for the four gospels in the Christian Bible. His father had brought the manuscript to Denmark from the Holy Land around 1920. The original manuscript was destroyed by the Gestapo but not before Larsen made a copy of it. He claimed to have brought the copy with him to Canada.

Larsen was consecrated as a bishop by Peter Wayne Goodrich of the North American Episcopal Church. Shortly thereafter he founded the Shalom Ecumenical Church in Hamilton, Ontario. Though possessing apostolic orders, the church differed considerably from the tradition from which he assumed his authority. Larsen articulated what he considered a scientific approach to Christianity. The church was non-Trinitarian. Jesus was accepted as Messiah, Son of Man, and Son of God, but all of God's children were also considered sons and daughters of God. One became a child of God by keeping the Ten Commandments and the strictures of the Sermon on the Mount (Matthew 6—8). The church disavowed belief in purgatory, hell, or the devil. Evil exists, but not the Evil One. There were only two sacraments: baptism and the eucharist.

Church groups met in private homes, there being no church buildings. Membership was limited to those with one or more college or university degrees. In 1988 the church claimed approximately 200 members in Canada, the United States, and Scandinavia.

Sources:

Ward, Gary L. *Independent Bishops: An International Directory*. Detroit, MI: Apogee Books, 1990. 524 pp.

United Christian Church of America

The United Christian Church of America was begun in 1893, but was reorganized in the 1940s by Bp. Alexander A. Lowande, who is considered its founder. In 1944 Lowande was a partner in the promotion of a fraudulent "National Day of Prayer." After receiving the cooperation of numerous governors, congressmen, and even the White House, Lowande was exposed and the project fell through.

Upon Lowande's death, he was succeeded by the Rev. Herbert J. Elliott of Brooklyn, New York. For a short period of time in the 1940s, the church was a member of the American Council of Christian Churches.

HOMOSEXUALLY ORIENTED CHURCHES

The National Gay Pentecostal Alliance (NGPA)

The National Gay Pentecostal Alliance (NGPA) was an Apostolic Pentecostal church with a special outreach to the gay/lesbian community. It was founded on July 28, 1980, in the city of Schenectady, New York, by William Carey and Sister Schwarz. Carey, a 22-year-old ministerial student in the United Pentecostal Church International, was forced out when his homosexuality became public. Schwarz, a woman from the same congregation in which he worshipped in Schenectady, left with him. Unable to locate a Pentecostal church that did not oppose gay and lesbian sexual orientations, they formed the Gay Pentecostal Alliance.

In the spring of 1981, a second similar congregation was founded in Omaha, Nebraska, occasioning the addition of the word *National* to the church's name. The first ordination occurred in August of 1981 in Omaha. Carey, E. Samuel Stafford, and Frances Cervantes were the first ordained ministers.

NGPA's belief was similar to that of the United Pentecostal Church. It believed that the Bible in its original languages was the inspired word of God and affirmed that there was only one God, the God of Israel, who took on human form and was born of the Virgin Mary, to save sinful humanity. Salvation was available through repentance, through water baptism by immersion, and through receiving the Holy Ghost, as evidenced by speaking in tongues. The alliance extolled the nine Gifts of the Spirit (I Cor. 12:8—10) and the living of a holy and moral life. It expected the imminent return of Jesus to claim his church. Thus, like the United Pentecostal Church, the alliance did not accept the doctrine of the Trinity as traditionally held within Christianity, and had a second significant divergence in its belief that homosexuality was not sinful. It accepted the view, common to all of the churches serving the homosexual community, that the scriptures fail to condemn homosexuality.

In 1990, a presbyterial form of church government was instituted. The church was then led by two presbyters, appointed by district elders. The two presbyters were Carey and Sister LaDonna C. Briggs. Lighthouse Ministries served as the outreach and evangelism department of the alliance and was responsible for the printing and distribution of literature and cassette tapes. The Home Missions Department, operating out of Niagara Falls, New York, oversaw the founding of new congregations in the United States, and the Foreign Missions Department performed the same function elsewhere. Home Missions also operated a Division of Prison Ministries, centered in West Monroe, Louisiana. The alliance published a periodical, *The Apostolic Voice*, and was affiliated with an educational facility in Schenectady, the Pentecostal Bible Institute.

Tayu Fellowship

The Tayu Fellowship was organized in the 1970s by Daniel Inesse and others and was open to gay men and women who wished to follow and teach the Path of Truth, a spiritual life based upon the wisdom of the ancient Greeks. According to the fellowship, the gods of Greece began as the Guides to humanity. Each deity represents a basic personality facet of the universe and as such is a key to the inner life of humankind. A *Tayu* (true human) is one who has first understood an initial Guide, who symbolizes the basic theme of his or her life, and then moved on to integrate 11 other perspectives to a point that he or she becomes complete.

According to the fellowship, history evolves in cycles or eons of 2120 years each. Each eon is under one of the Guides. The last eon was under Poseidon. The present eon, begun in mid-1987, is under Athene, the Guide of Openness, symbolized astrologically by the constellation Aquarius, the water bearer. The water bearer is Ganymede, the most beautiful of mortal youths, taken as a favorite lover by the god Zeus.

Though organized in the 1970s, the fellowship considered itself to possess "roots dating back thousands of years." Members were expected to follow six precepts, which admonished them, among other things, to seek understanding, create a fulfilling existence, harm nothing, and love themselves and others. Membership was concentrated in the San Francisco Bay area, with other members scattered along the Pacific coast. A correspondence program in Tayu Wisdom allowed the fellowship a larger outreach. During the late 1970s, the fellowship operated a center in San Francisco, the Tayu Institute. A Grand Council met in the summer at the time of the solstice, and winter solstices and equinoxes were also major days for gatherings and ceremonies. The fellowship published a periodical titled *Ganymede*.

Sources:

Wright, Ezekiel, and Daniel Inesse. *God Is Gay*. Santa Rosa, CA: Tayu Press, 1982.

26. Unclassified

UNCLASSIFIED RELIGIOUS GROUPS

Church of the Bride of Christ

The Church of the Bride of Christ was founded in 1903 in Corvallis, Oregon, by Edmund Franz Creffield. Born in Germany around 1867, Creffield had studied for the priesthood. Before ordination, however, he migrated to Portland, Oregon, around 1902, then joined the Salvation Army and moved to Corvallis as an Army representative. In 1903 he had a sudden revelation from which he emerged with a new name, Joshua Elijah (the names of two prophets in the Hebrew Bible). He allowed his hair to grow freely.

Joshua Elijah founded the Church of the Bride of Christ and immediately began to recruit members from among the women in the town. The goal was to find the woman who would become the mother of a new Christ child. He began to hold meetings in which he and the female recruits would engage in some of the ecstatic practices associated with revival meetings, frequently in a state of nudity. As word circulated through the neighborhood of the activities, husbands and fathers began to pull their wives and daughters out of the church and in January 1904, they tarred and feathered Creffield. He remained in the neighborhood, was caught in bed with a married woman, and was eventually arrested for adultery. He was sentenced to two years in prison, and that seemed to end the church. However, following his release in December 1905, Joshua Elijah began to correspond with his former members. He proposed the founding of a community on the Oregon Coast, as a haven against the curse he had placed on the cities of the West Coast, including San Francisco. In April 1906, as members began to gather, San Francisco suffered and was largely destroyed by an earthquake and fire, prompting some to say Creffield's prophetic curse had come true.

The Prophet's vision of a new Garden of Eden came to an abrupt end a month later. Joshua Elijah was assassinated in Seattle, Washington, on May 7, by the brother of Esther Mitchell, one of his devoted followers. Tried for murder, George Mitchell was found not guilty. Several days later he was shot by his sister at the Seattle rail station as he was journeying back to Corvallis. Joshua Elijah's small band of followers reportedly continued on for several years.

Sources:

Holbrook, Stewart H. "Oregon's Secret Love Cult." *American Mercury* (February 1941): 167–174.

Pintarich, Dick, and J. Kingston Pierce. "The Strange Saga of Oregon's Other Guru." *The Oregonian*, January 7, 1986.

The New Church

The New Church was founded by N. N. New in the first decade of the twentieth century, but grew out of the previous work of John Fair New, a nineteenth-century religious lecturer who had previously founded the New Life Society and the New Life Church. John Fair New had become convinced early on that Christianity was a life, that this life must begin at birth, and that a new birth initiated a new life. This new life is based on the understanding that Jesus is essentially identical with God the Father, and that the divinity and humanity of God are one, and hence God and man are the same being. Jesus is the highest example of the divine man. This discovery of the new life principle led to the further discovery of the power of prayer to heal all illnesses.

John Fair New passed along his teachings to his son N. N. New, who established headquarters in San Francisco and London, England, and continued his father's work. N. N. New published his father's lectures in 1909 and shortly afterward issued his own version of the teachings as a booklet, *Newology: The New Bible*.

Essential to the movement was its emphasis on healing. Newological medicine centered on conscious cooperation with God, promised reconstruction of the human body, perpetual youth, and even physical immortality. Adherents were discouraged from wearing black, the color of sin, poverty, despair, disease, and death. The use of alcoholic beverages was forbidden. New also believed that hair was the last remnant of horns and will disappear as Man evolves. All races will lose their hair as they grow white, intellectual, and spiritual. The New Church also advocated vegetarianism.

New's efforts met with some response within the larger metaphysical movement. Operating under the label of Newthot Science, New proposed the establishment of a Newthot church (over which he would be the archbishop), printing plant, and university. He began to enroll people in the university for a $10 fee, for which he was indicted for fraudulent use of the mails. Convicted in 1917, New was found by the court to be an imposter who regularly indulged in the very actions that he forbade his followers. His conviction effectively ended the church.

Sources:

New, John Fair. *The New Life Theology*. New York: J. F. New, 1909.

New, N. N. *Newology: The New Bible*. San Francisco: Newthot Publishers, n.d.

Rubenstein, I. H. *Law on Cults*. Chicago: Ordain Press, 1981.

The Truth

The Truth was an organization founded by Peter Crames (b. 1957) in September 1983 in Cambridge, Massachusetts. Crames, born into the Jewish faith, had a deep spiritual crisis that precipitated a spiritual quest. The quest climaxed in November 1982 when Crames realized he was a machine controlled by God. During the next year he composed an essay that explained this basic truth and published it as a booklet entitled *The Truth That Will Make You Free*. While writing the essay, Crames claimed that God informed him that he was the messiah, the one who was to fulfill Christ's mission of establishing God's kingdom on earth. Crames circulated the essay locally and nationally through magazine advertisements.

The essence of "The Truth" was that "the universe is one large mechanical machine whose movements, including Human thoughts and actions, are planned and caused by one God." The universe began with God's first cause, the Big Bang. Everything was determined from that initial thrust. God does have a plan for the universe, though it is as yet unknown to humankind. The state of sin was equated with our ignorance of the Truth, and the state of salvation with our knowledge of it. At the time of salvation, individuals would be born again with God's personality.

For many years, Crames circulated copies of his essay, some 2,500 in all, but by the mid-1990s he had still made no converts. In the meantime, he had concluded that the essay was not as accurate as the Bible. He abandoned the essay and became a Bible student.

Sources:

Crames, Peter. *The Truth That Will Make You Free*. Cambridge, MA: Author, 1984.

This appendix arranges the organizations in the directory listings by country, subarranged by state, then city. The United States appears first, followed by Canada, and then various countries outside of North America.

United States

Alabama

Confederation of Independent Asatru
  Kindred (CIAK)
PO Box 85
Adamsville, AL 35005

Apostolic Faith Mission Church of God
3344 N Pearl Ave.
Birmingham, AL 36101

Fellowship of Christ International
801 4th Ave. N
Birmingham, AL 35204

Universal Church of Scientific Truth
1250 Indiana St.
Birmingham, AL 35224

Upper Cumberland Presbyterian Church
172 CR 1564
Cullman, AL 35055-1426

Bible Methodist Connection of Churches
1216 Taylor Rd.
Glencoe, AL 35905

Il Bung Zen Society
1412 Randolph St.
Huntsville, AL 35801

Apostolic Overcoming Holy Church of God
2257 St. Stephens Rd.
Mobile, AL 36617

Integrity Communications (and Related
  Ministries)
Box Z
Mobile, AL 36616

General Association of Six-Principle Baptist
  Churches, Inc.
88 Lee Rd. 419
Opelika, AL 36804

Traditional Protestant Episcopal Church
Scenic Hwy 98
Point Clear, AL 36564-0916

First Congregational Methodist Church of
  the U.S.A.
PO Box 427
Rainsville, AL 35986

Assembly of Yahvah
PO Box 89
Windfield, AL 35594

Alaska

New Testament Holiness Church
PO Box 100
Ashdown, AK 71822

United Orthodox Church
202 International Ave.
Hyder, AK 99923

Arizona

Order of Nazorean Essenes (Sons Ahman
  Israel)
HC 65-535
Canebeds, AZ 86022

Ashtar Command
PO Box 328
Clarksdale, AZ 86324

Blue Rose Ministry
Box 332
Cornville, AZ 86325

American Meditation Society
2912 N Main St., Apt. #2
Flagstaff, AZ 62025

Antioch Network
9524 W Camelback Rd.
Glendale, AZ 85305-3104

Peyote Way Church of God
30800 W Klondyke Rd.
Klondyke, AZ 85643

Anglican Churches of America and
  Associates
2402 Usery Pass Rd.
Mesa, AZ 85207

Center for Buddhist Development
432 S Temple
Mesa, AZ 85204

Healing Society Movement
2450 W Broadway, No. 108
Mesa, AZ 85202

International New Thought Alliance (INTA)
5003 E Broadway Rd.
Mesa, AZ 85206

New Testament Association of Independent
  Baptist Churches
8856 E Fairfield St.
Mesa, AZ 85207-5124

Holy Eastern Orthodox Catholic and
  Apostolic Church in North America
733 Tick Rd.
Mountain View, AZ 72560

Essene Order of Light
PO Box 1080
Patagonia, AZ 85624

Asatru Alliance
PO Box 961
Payson, AZ 85547

The Bridge to Spiritual Freedom, Inc.
PO Box 753
Payson, AZ 85547

Ministers for Christ Assembly of
  Churches/Ministers for Christ Outreach
7549 W. Cactus Rd. No. 104-207
Peoria, AZ 85381

Bethany Bible Church and Related
  Independent Bible Churches of the
  Phoenix, Arizona, Area
6060 N 7th Ave.
Phoenix, AZ 85013-1498

Church of Essential Science
PO Box 62284
Phoenix, AZ 85082

Gospel Ministers & Churches
  International/Gospel Alliance Church
2501 W Dunlap, Ste. 185
Phoenix, AZ 85021

Hall Deliverance Foundation
9840 N 15th St.
Phoenix, AZ 85020-1810

Independent Episcopal Church (Anglican
  Rite, Old Catholic Church)
5414 W Pierson St.
Phoenix, AZ 85031

Miracle Life Fellowship International
11052 N 24th Ave.
Phoenix, AZ 85029

New Age Community Church
6418 S 39th Ave.
Phoenix, AZ 85041

Royal Priest Research
PO Box 30973
Phoenix, AZ 85046

University of Life Church
5600 6th St.
Phoenix, AZ 85040

Hohm Community
PO Box 4272
Prescott, AZ 86302

Evangelical Catholic Church
PO Box 26824
Scottsdale, AZ 85255-0160

Phoenix Buddhist Network
PO Box 5076
Scottsdale, AZ 85261

Teleos Institute
7119 E Shea Blvd., Ste. 109, PMB 418
Scottsdale, AZ 85254

Trinity Foundation
11827 E Cannon Dr.
Scottsdale, AZ 85259

Anglican Diocese of Arizona
PO Box 870
Sedona, AZ 86339-0870

International Yoga Federation
2509 N. Campbell Ave.
Tempe, AZ 85719

Ring of Thoth
PO Box 25637
Tempe, AZ 85285

Ar nDraiocht Fein: A Druid Fellowship, Inc.
PO Box 17874
Tuscon, AZ 85731-7874

EarthStar Alliance
1163 N Thunder Ridge Dr.
Tucson, AZ 85745-3378

Great Western Vehicle
PO Box 41795
Tucson, AZ 85717-1795

River of Crazy Wisdom
PO Box 65870
Tucson, AZ 85728

United Episcopal Church (1945)
  Anglican/Celtic
PO Box 1931
Tucson, AZ 85702

United Submitters International
Box 43476
Tucson, AZ 85719

Arkansas

Christian Research
PO Box 385
Eureka Springs, AR 72632-0385

Worldwide Missionary Evangelism (WME)
1285 Millsap Rd.
Fayetteville, AR 72701

Kingdom Identity Ministries
PO Box 1021
Harrison, AR 72602

Church of God in Christ, International
125 N Fisher St.
Jonesboro, AR 72401

Baptist Missionary Association of America
PO Box 30910
Little Rock, AR 72260-0016

The Registry
Box 180
Marshall, AR 72650

Old Catholic Communion in North America
181 Baywood Ln.
Monticello, AR 71655

Free Christian Zion Church of Christ
1409 S Mill St.
Nashville, AR 71852

Church of the Little Children
89 Home Place Tr.
Pocahontas, AR 72455

Pilgrim Nazarene Church
504 Valley Dr.
Rogers, AR 72756

Fellowship of Christians
1680 Sparksford Dr.
Russellville, AR 72802

Biblical Apostolic Organization (BAO)
716 S Maple St.
Siloam Springs, AR 72761

Christian Catholic Church (Old Catholic) in
the United States of America
1205 Thomas Blvd.
Springdale, AR 72762

Shiloh Trust and Church
309 Griffin Ave.
Sulphur Springs, AR 72768

California

Vedantic Center
3528 N. Triunfo Canyon Rd.
Agoura, CA 91301

Aro Gar
PO Box 3066
Alameda, CA 94501

Home of Truth Spiritual Center
1300 Grand St.
Alameda, CA 94501

Triumph Prophetic Ministries (Church of
God)
PO Box 292
Altadena, CA 91003

The (Local) Church
1853 W Ball Rd.
Anaheim, CA 92804

Miracle Distribution Center
3947 E La Palma Ave.
Anaheim, CA 92807

True Jesus Church
314 S Brookhurst St. #104
Anaheim, CA 92804

Dhyanyoga Centers
PO Box 3194
Antioch, CA 94531

Fellowship of Friends
Apollo, CA

Apostolic Episcopal Church—Order of
Corporate Reunion
PO Box 2401
Apple Valley, CA 92307

Holy Celtic Church
PO Box 2401
Apple Valley, CA 92307

Esoteric Fraternity
PO Box 37
Applegate, CA 95703

Universal Church of Metaphysics
PO Box 4505
Arcata, CA 95518

Berean Bible Fellowship
9325 El Bordo Ave.
Atascadero, CA 93422

Dhammakaya International Society of
California
865 E Monrovia Pl.
Azusa, CA 91702

Believers' Circle
7437 Bear Mt. Blvd.
Bakersfield, CA 93313

The Georgian Church
1908 Verde St.
Bakersfield, CA 93304

Lectorium Rosicrucianum
Box 9246
Bakersfield, CA 93389

General Assembly of the Korean
Presbyterian Church
17200 Clark Ave.
Bellflower, CA 90706

Tridentine Old Roman Community Catholic
Church (Jones)
10446 Highland Ave.
Bellflower, CA 90706-4123

Berkeley Area Interfaith Council
2340 Durant Ave.
Berkeley, CA 94704

Berkeley Zen Center
1931 Russell St.
Berkeley, CA 94703

Chaplaincy Institute for Arts and Interfaith
Ministries (ChI)/Interfaith Congregation
for Creative and Healing Ministries
2138 Cedar St.
Berkeley, CA 94709

Church of Divine Man
2018 Allston Way
Berkeley, CA 94704

Covenant of the Goddess
PO Box 1226
Berkeley, CA 94701

Fellowship of the Spiral Path
Box 5521
Berkeley, CA 94701

First Church of the Doors
Berkeley, CA

General Assembly Churches
1521 Derby St.
Berkeley, CA 94703

Nyingma Institute
1815 Highland Pl.
Berkeley, CA 94709

Prana Yoga Ashram
1723 Alcatraz Ave.
Berkeley, CA 94703

Sacred Space Yoga Sanctuary
830 Bancroft Way
Berkeley, CA 94710

Tiep Hien Order
PO Box 7355
Berkeley, CA 94707

Yun Lin Temple
2959 Russell St.
Berkeley, CA 94705

Deva Foundation
336 S Doheny Dr., No. 7
Beverly Hills, CA 90211

Great Among the Nations, Inc.
8306 Wilshire Blvd., Ste. 2021
Beverly Hills, CA 90211

Hermetic Order of the Golden Dawn
(Regardie)
270 N Canon Dr., Ste. 1302
Beverly Hills, CA 90210

Gnostic Orthodox Church of Christ in
America
Borrego Springs, CA

Independent Church of Antioch
350 Santa Cruz St.
Boulder Creek, CA 95006

Religious School of Natural Hygiene
PO Box 1011
Boulder Creek, CA 95006

Sunburst (formerly Solar Logos Foundation)
PO Box 2008
Buellton, CA 93427

Missionary Dispensary Bible Research
Box 5296
Buena Park, CA 90622

Universal Church of God
PO Box 10752
Burbank, CA 91510-0752

The Colony
Burnt Ranch, CA 95527

Hindu Temple Society of Southern California
1600 Las Virgenes Canyon Rd.
Calabasas, CA 91302

Church of Jesus Christ (Bulla)
95 E Hwy. 98, D-107
Calexico, CA 92231

Universal Shrine of Divine Guidance
PO Box 1771
Camarillo, CA 93011

Open Gate Sangha
PO Box 112107
Campbell, CA 95011-2107

Society of Novus Spiritus
1700 Winchester Blvd., Ste. 100
Campbell, CA 95008-3001

Universal Church of the Master
100 W Rincon Ave., Ste. 101
Campbell, CA 95008

Interplanetary Connections
7210 Jordan Ave., Ste. B53
Canoga Park, CA 91301

Pre-Nicene Gnosto-Catholic Church
23301 Mobile St.
Canoga Park, CA 91307-3322

American Fellowship Church
225 Crossroads Blvd., No. 345
Carmel, CA 93923

Mata Amritanandamayi Center
10200 Crow Canyon Rd.
Castro Valley, CA 94552

School of Natural Science
PO Box 1115
Cedar Ridge, CA 95924

International Evangelism Crusades
21601 Devonshire St., No. 217
Chatsworth, CA 91311-8415

Philippine Independent Catholic Church in
the Americas
14373 Shady Hollow Ln.
Chino Hills, CA 91709

Philippine Independent Church
14373 Shady Hollow Ln.
Chino Hills, CA 91709

Most Holy Church of God in Christ Jesus
502 Anita St. #21
Chula Vista, CA 91911

Order of Thelema
PO Box 511
Chula Vista, CA 91912

Mennonite World Conference
2529 Willow Ave.
Clovis, CA 93612

Vajrayana Foundation
2013 Eureka Canyon Rd.
Corralitos, CA 95076

International Zen Institute of America (IZIA)
1760 Pomona Ave., No. 35
Costa Mesa, CA 92627

Church of All Worlds
PO Box 758
Cotati, CA 94931

Christian Presbyterian Church (Korean)
4741 N Glen Arden Ave.
Covina, CA 91724

Fraternitas L.V.X Occulta
Box 5094
Covina, CA 91723

Missionary Church of the Disciples of Jesus
Christ
15906 E San Bernardino Rd.
Covina, CA 91722

Transformation Ministries (Baptist)
970 S Village Oaks Dr., Ste. 101
Covina, CA 91724-0609

Arcana Workshops
3916 Sepulveda Boulevard, Suite 107
Culver City, CA 90230

Prosperos
PO Box 4969, Dept. E
Culver City, CA 90231

Iglesia ni Cristo (Church of Christ)
1617 Southgate Ave.
Daly City, CA 94015

Karaites
1575 Annie St.
Daly City, CA 94015

Catholic Apostolic Church at Davis
921 W 8th St.
Davis, CA 95616

Filipino Assemblies of the First Born Inc.
(FAFB Inc.)
614 13th Ave.
Delano, CA 93215

Sarvamangala Mission
366 Grapevine Dr.
Diamond Bar, CA 91765

Johannine Catholic Church
18372 Highway 94
Dulzura, CA 91917

Mexican National Catholic Church
4011 E. Brooklyn Ave.
East Los Angeles, CA 90022

Unarius—Science of Life
143 S Magnolia
El Cajon, CA 92022

SM Church
PO Box 1335
El Cerrito, CA 94530

Vajrakilaya Centers of North America
7436 Sea View Pl.
El Cerrito, CA 94530

Yi Guan Dao (I-Kuan Tao)
11645 Lower Azusa Rd.
El Monte, CA 91732

All-One-God-Faith, Inc.
Box 28
Escondido, CA 92025

Christward Ministry
20560 Questhaven Rd.
Escondido, CA 92029-4810

Order of Interbeing
2499 Melru Ln.
Escondido, CA 92026

American Exarchate of the True (Old
Calendar) Orthodox Church of Greece
PO Box 398
Etna, CA 96027-0398

Divine Circle of the Sacred Grove
Box 1737
Fontana, CA 92334

Loving Hands Institute
639 11th Ave.
Fortuna, CA 95540-2346

World Community Service
3676 Delaware Dr.
Fremont, CA 94538

Fundamental Evangelistic Association
1476 W Herndon, Ste. 104
Fresno, CA 93711

World Christianship Ministries (WCM)
PO Box 8041
Fresno, CA 93947

General Assemblies and Church of the
First Born
200 N. Lawrence Ave.
Fullerton, CA 92832

Agon-shu
14518 S Western Ave.
Gardena, CA 90247

Seicho-No-Ie Truth of Life Movement
14527 S Vermont Ave.
Gardena, CA 90247

United Spiritualist Church
813 W 165th Pl.
Gardena, CA 90247

Ann Ree Colton Foundation of Niscience,
Inc.
336 W Colorado St.
Glendale, CA 91209

Armenian Evangelical Union of North
America
616 N Glendale, Ste. 23
Glendale, CA 91206-2407

Community Churches of America
333 E Colorado St.
Glendale, CA 91205

Fellowship of Universal Guidance
1524 Glenoaks Blvd.
Glendale, CA 91201

Independent Catholic Clergy Association
Box 6903
Glendale, CA 91205

Perfect Liberty Kyodan
700 S Adams St.
Glendale, CA 91205

Universal World Church
PO Box 4545
Glendale, CA 91222

Apostolic Orthodox Catholic Church
PO Box 1834
Glendora, CA 91740

Reformed Church in the United States
407 W Main St.
Grass Valley, CA 95945

International Buddhist Progress Society
PO Box 5248
Hacienda Heights, CA 91745

Temple of the People
906 South Halcyon Road
Halcyon, CA 93421

International Church of Ageless Wisdom
PO Box 194
Half Moon Bay, CA 94019

Pentecostal/Charismatic Churches of North
America
1027 W Tennyson Rd.
Hayward, CA 94544

Sixth Patriarch Zen Center
133 Halsey Ct.
Hercules, CA 94547

Christian Biblical Church of God
PO Box 1442
Hollister, CA 95024-1442

Aetherius Society
6202 Afton Pl.
Hollywood, CA 90028

Atheists United
4773 Hollywood Blvd.
Hollywood, CA 90027

The Inter-American Old Catholic Church
7561 Center Ave., Ste. 49
Huntington Beach, CA 92647

International Missionary Society—
Seventh-day Adventist Reform
Movement
2877 E Florence Ave.
Huntington Park, CA 90255-5751

Naqshbandiyya-Mujaddidiyya Order of
Sufism
PO Box 428
Inverness, CA 94937

Ecumenical Catholic Church
20 Lincoln
Irvine, CA 92604-1947

Sold-Out Discipling Movement Churches
601 Marinella
Irvine, CA 92606

Dharma Dena
HC-1, Box 250
Joshua Tree, CA 92252

Institute of Mentalphysics
59700 29 Palms Hwy.
Joshua Tree, CA 92252

White Star
Box 307
Joshua Tree, CA 92252

Chagdud Gonpa Foundation
PO Box 279
Junction City, CA 96048

Church of Cosmic Origin and School of
Thought
Box 257
June Lake, CA 93529

Mandeans
Lake Murray Blvd., No. 50
La Mesa, CA 91942-2212

International Babaji Kriya Yoga Sangam
14011 Mansa Dr.
La Mirada, CA 90638

Chung Tai
3254 Gloria Terr.
Lafayette, CA 94549

American Catholic Church (Laguna Beach,
California)
430 Park Ave.
Laguna Beach, CA 92652

Kali Mandir
PO Box 4700
Laguna Beach, CA 92652-4700

Old Catholic Church (Anglican Rite)
489 Jasmine St.
Laguna Beach, CA 92651

American Catholic Church—Old Catholic
5230 Clark Ave., Ste. 9
Lakewood, CA 90712

Eagle Rock Fellowship
PO Box 151
Lakewood, CA 90714-1051

Vision of Hope Christian Fellowship
PO Box 365
Lathrop, CA 95330

Chokling Tersar Foundation USA (CTF)
66000 Drive Through Tree Rd.
Leggett, CA 93585-0162

Churches of Christ (Non-Instrumental, Non-
Class, One Cup)
1147 Sherry Way
Livermore, CA 94550

Christ's Apostolic Church of North America
316 Hullett St.
Long Beach, CA 90805-3424

Community of St. James the Just
PO Box 92497
Long Beach, CA 90809-2497

Morningland Community of the Ascended
Christ
2600 E 7th St.
Long Beach, CA 90804

Thubten Dhargye Ling
PO Box 90665
Long Beach, CA 90809

Harmony of Life Fellowship
1434 Fremont Ave.
Los Altos, CA 94022

Society for Sufi Studies
Box 176
Los Altos, CA 94023

Aspects of Light
12540 Braddock Dr., Ste. 218B
Los Angeles, CA 90066

Associated Churches of Christ (Holiness)
1302 E Adams Blvd.
Los Angeles, CA 90011

Buddhist Sangha Council of Southern
California
1847 Crenshaw Blvd.
Los Angeles, CA 90019

Builders of the Adytum
5105 N Figueroa
Los Angeles, CA 90042

California Bosatsukai
5632 Green Oak Dr.
Los Angeles, CA 90068

Christ Faith Mission
6026 Echo St.
Los Angeles, CA 90042

Church of Scientology
6331 Hollywood Blvd., Ste. 1200
Los Angeles, CA 90028-6329

Church of Utrecht in America
2103 S. Portland St.
Los Angeles, CA 90007

Church of World Messianity
960 S Kenmore Ave.
Los Angeles, CA 90006

The Church Which Is Christ's Body
PO Box 42021
Los Angeles, CA 90042

Concilio Olazabal de Iglesias Latino
Americano
1925 E 1st St.
Los Angeles, CA 90033

Coptic Catholic Church
2701 Newell St.
Los Angeles, CA 90039

Cor Lucis
222 N. Manhattan Pl.
Los Angeles, CA 90004

Ecclesia Gnostica
3363 Glendale Blvd.
Los Angeles, CA 90039

Fellowship of Inner-City Word of Faith
Ministries (FICWFM)
7901 S Vermont Ave.
Los Angeles, CA 90044

Gnostic Association of Cultural and
Anthropological Studies
4885 Melrose Ave.
Los Angeles, CA 90029

Hazy Moon Zen Center
1651 S Gramercy Pl.
Los Angeles, CA 90019

Honmichi (Original Way)
4431 Wilshire Blvd.
Los Angeles, CA 90010

Institute of Divine Metaphysical Research
PO Box 19877
Los Angeles, CA 90019

International Buddhist Meditation Center
928 S New Hampshire
Los Angeles, CA 90006

International Church of the Foursquare
Gospel
1910 W Sunset Blvd., Ste. 200
Los Angeles, CA 90026-0176

JeungSanDo
936 S Crenshaw Blvd., No. 307
Los Angeles, CA 90019

Kanzeonji Non-Sectarian Buddhist Temple
951 Terrrace 49
Los Angeles, CA 90042

Kingdom and World Mission of Our Lord
Jesus Christ
PO Box 3600
Los Angeles, CA 90078-3600

Kingdom of God on Earth Within Man
PO Box 77659
Los Angeles, CA 90007

Korean Buddhist Chogye Order
4265 W 3rd St.
Los Angeles, CA 90020

Light of the World Church/Iglesia la Luz del
Mundo
4765 E 1st St.
Los Angeles, CA 90022

Los Angeles Buddhist Church Federation
2203 W Jefferson Blvd.
Los Angeles, CA 90018

Movement of Spiritual Inner Awareness
(MSIA)
3500 W Adams Blvd.
Los Angeles, CA 90018

Order of the Thelemic Golden Dawn
1636 N Wilcox Ave., Ste. 418
Los Angeles, CA 90028

Oriental Missionary Society Holiness Church
of North America
3660 S Gramercy Pl.
Los Angeles, CA 90018

Philosophical Research Society
3910 Los Feliz Blvd.
Los Angeles, CA 90027

Rinzai-Ji, Inc.
2505 Cimarron St.
Los Angeles, CA 90018

Rissho Kosei Kai
2707 E 1st St.
Los Angeles, CA 90033

Saeejis Temple of Peace
5627 Lexington Ave., No. 6
Los Angeles, CA 90038-2232

Self-Realization Fellowship
3880 San Rafael Ave.
Los Angeles, CA 90065-3298

Shaolin Buddhist Meditation Center
3165 Minnesota St.
Los Angeles, CA 90031

Shingon Mission
342 E 1st Street
Los Angeles, CA 90012

Shrine of the Eternal Breath of Tao
117 Stonehaven Way
Los Angeles, CA 90049

Sikh Dharma
PO Box 35330
Los Angeles, CA 90035

Soto Mission
123 S Hewitt St.
Los Angeles, CA 90012

Sri Lanka Sangha Council of North America
1847 Crenshaw Blvd.
Los Angeles, CA 90019

Superet Light Doctrine Church
2516 W Third St.
Los Angeles, CA 90057

Tenrikyo
2727 E First St.
Los Angeles, CA 90033

Unfettered Mind
264 La Cienega Blvd., Ste. 1083
Los Angeles, CA 90211

United Church of the Living God, The Pillar
and Ground of Truth
Los Angeles, CA

United Lodge of Theosophists
245 W 33rd St.
Los Angeles, CA 90007

Universal Fellowship of Metropolitan
Community Churches
8704 Santa Monica Blvd., 2nd Fl.
Los Angeles, CA 90069

Viet Nam Buddhists
863 S Berendo
Los Angeles, CA 90005

Zen Center of Los Angeles
923 S Normandie Ave.
Los Angeles, CA 90006-1301

Church of Revelation (Hawaii)
21475 Summit Rd.
Los Gatos, CA 95030

Saddhamma Foundation
350 Sharon Park Dr. R-1
Menlo Park, CA 94025

Adidam
12040 N Seigler Rd.
Middletown, CA 95461

Heart Consciousness Church and New Age
Church of Being
PO Box 82
Middletown, CA 95461

Palyul Changchub Dargyeling
Box 1514
Mill Valley, CA 94941

Veerashaiva Samaja of North America
PO Box 360380
Milpitas, CA 95036-0380

Yongey Buddhist Center
682 Carlsbad St.
Milpitas, CA 95035

Church of the Eternal Source
PO Box 2778
Mission Viejo, CA 92690-0778

Universal Life Church
601 3rd St.
Modesto, CA 95351

Life Bliss Foundation
9720 Central Ave.
Montclair, CA 91763

Oneness Movement North America
PO Box 35507
Monte Sereno, CA 95030

Old Catholic Orthodox Church
PO Box 3221
Montebello, CA 90640

Infinite Way
PO Box 8260
Moreno Valley, CA 92552

Ascended Master Teaching Foundation
PO Box 466
Mount Shasta, CA 96067

Association of Sananda and Sanat Kumara
PO Box 197
Mount Shasta, CA 96067

Essene New Life Church
515 Pony Trail Dr.
Mount Shasta, CA 96067-9063

Order of Buddhist Contemplatives
3724 Summit Dr.
Mount Shasta, CA 96067-9102

The Church of Gnosis (Ecclesia Gnostica
Mysteriorum)
1965 Latham St.
Mountain View, CA 94040

Devi Mandir
5950 Hwy. 128
Napa, CA 94558-9632

Abhidhyan Yoga Institute
PO Box 1414
Nevada City, CA 95959-1414

Ananda
14618 Tyler Foote Rd.
Nevada City, CA 95959

Asatru Folk Assembly
PO Box 445
Nevada City, CA 95959

Feraferia
12318 Shady Ln
Nevada City, CA 95959-3255

Institute for the Development of the
Harmonious Human Being (IDHHB)
Box 370
Nevada City, CA 95959

Ryugu, U.S.A.
11958 Hartsook St.
North Hollywood, CA 91607

International Association of Sufism (IAS)
14 Commerical Blvd., Ste. 101
Novato, CA 94949

Apostolic Episcopal Church, Diocese of
California/Nevada
1933 73rd Ave.
Oakland, CA 94621

Da Yuan Circle
2633 Telegraph Cir., No. 305
Oakland, CA 94612

Dianic Wicca
Box 11363
Oakland, CA 94611

Temple of Cosmic Religion
174 Santa Clara Ave.
Oakland, CA 94610

Essene Foundation/Neo-Essene Community
399 Compass Rd.
Oceanside, CA 92054

Rosicrucian Fellowship
2222 Mission Ave.
Oceanside, CA 92058

Ecumenical Ministry of the Unity of All
Religions
107 N Ventura St.
Ojai, CA 93023

Krishnamurti Foundation of America
Box 1560
Ojai, CA 93024-1560

Liberal Catholic Church, Province of the
United States
1502 E Ojai Ave.
Ojai, CA 93024

Meditation Groups, Inc.
Box 566
Ojai, CA 93024

Truth Center
566 Crestview Dr.
Ojai, CA 93023

William Samuel Foundation
307 N Montgomery St.
Ojai, CA 93023

Hermetic Order of the Morning Star
International (Golden Dawn—Canada)
4035 E Guasti Rd., Ste. 306
Ontario, CA 91761

Diocese of Ecumenical and Old Catholic
Faith Communities
1111 W. Town and Country Rd.
Orange, CA 92868

Michael Educational Foundation
10 Muth Dr.
Orinda, CA 94563

College and Temple of Thelema
PO Box 415
Oroville, CA 95965

George Ohsawa Macrobiotic Foundation
1999 Myers
Oroville, CA 95966

Affiliated New Thought Network (ANTN)
522 Central Ave.
Pacific Grove, CA 93950

Pastoral Bible Institute
1425 Lachman Ln.
Pacific Palisades, CA 90272

Vedic Society of America
PO Box 926
Pacific Palisades, CA 90272-0926

Center for Timeless Wisdom
555 Bryant St., No. 302
Palo Alto, CA 94301

American Orthodox Catholic Church
(Kochones)
810 E Walnut St.
Pasadena, CA 91101

Church of God, Philadelphia Era
PO Box 371
Pasadena, CA 91102

Egyptian Temple of Fitness
158 N Hill Ave.
Pasadena, CA 91106-1950

International Alliance of Churches of
the Truth
690 E. Orange Grove Blvd.
Pasadena, CA 91104

Ordo Templi Astarte
PO Box 40094
Pasadena, CA

Reiyukai America
20 N Raymond Ave., Ste. 200
Pasadena, CA 91103

Theosophical Society
PO Box C
Pasadena, CA 91109-7107

World Insight International
PO Box 35
Pasadena, CA 91102

Worldwide Church of God
300 W Green St.
Pasadena, CA 91129

Inner Light Foundation
Box 750265
Petaluma, CA 94975

Radha Soami Satsang, Beas
2415 E Washington St.
Petaluma, CA 94954-9274

Chinmaya Mission West
PO Box 129
Piercy, CA 95587

Christian Prophets of Jehovah
PO Box 3900
Pinedale, CA 93650-3900

Ajapa Yoga Foundation
PO Box 1731
Placerville, CA 95667

Lemurian Fellowship
17201 Highway 67
Ramona, CA 92065

Eastern Catholic Archdiocese (Chaldean-
Syrian)
PO Box 610
Rancho Cordova, CA 95741-0610

Apostolic Assembly of the Faith in Christ
Jesus
10807 Laurel St.
Rancho Cucamonga, CA 91730

Astara
10700 Jersey Blvd., Suite 450
Rancho Cucamonga, CA 91730

Praise Chapel Christian Fellowship Churches
and Ministries International
PO Box 1769
Rancho Cucamonga, CA 91729

Bhakti Marga Foundation
55 Marbella
Rancho Mirage, CA 92270

Sukyo Mahikari
23151 Camino Altozano
Rancho Santo Margarita, CA 92688

Advaita Fellowship
PO Box 911-WS
Redondo Beach, CA 90277

Shinnyo-En
3910 Bret Harte Dr.
Redwood City, CA 94061

Abhayagiri Buddhist Monastery
16201 Tomki Rd.
Redwood Valley, CA 95470

Tian Dao (Yiguandao)
4050 Temple City Blvd.
Rosemead, CA 91770

Aurobindo, Disciples of Sri
PO Box 163237
Sacramento, CA 95816

New Wiccan Church International (NWC)
Box 162046
Sacramento, CA 95816

Progressive Universal Life Church (PULC)
PO Box 276265
Sacramento, CA 95827

Russian Orthodox Church Outside of Russia
(Vitaly)
PO Box 191363
Sacramento, CA 95819

Temple ov Psychick Youth (TOPY)
PO Box 163138
Sacramento, CA 95816

North American Old Roman Catholic
Church—Utrecht Succession
19230 Mallory Canyon Rd.
Salinas, CA 93907

Sarum Episcopal (Old Catholic) Church
1757 North D St.
San Bernardino, CA 92405-4015

Church of Reality
754 Glenview Dr. #201
San Bruno, CA 94066

Assemblies of God International Fellowship
(Independent/Not Affiliated)
PO Box 22410
San Diego, CA 92192-2410

Free Catholic Church
1010 University Ave., No. 158
San Diego, CA 92103

Global Ministry Resource Network
5663 Balboa Ave., #416
San Diego, CA 92111

Inner Circle Kethra E'Da Foundation, Inc.
Box 121722
San Diego, CA 92112-1722

International Society for Krishna
Consciousness (ISKCON)
1030 Grand Ave.
San Diego, CA 92109

Lao Buddhist Sangha of the U.S.A.
205 South 65th St.
San Diego, CA 92114

Liberal Catholic Church International
741 Cerro Gordo Ave.
San Diego, CA 92102

New Psychiana
4069 Stephens St.
San Diego, CA 92103

Ordinary Mind Zen School
2047 Felspar
San Diego, CA 92109

Rigpa Fellowship
9540 Waples St., Ste. A
San Diego, CA 92121

Taoist Sanctuary of San Diego
4229 Park Blvd.
San Diego, CA 92103

Teaching of the Inner Christ, Inc.
2834 N Park Way
San Diego, CA 92104

Three Treasures Zen Community
PO Box 720896
San Diego, CA 92172

Universal Catholic Church
741 Cerro Gordo Ave.
San Diego, CA 92102

Western Orthodox Catholic Church of
California
4109 Louisiana St.
San Diego, CA 92104-1691

Buddhist Compassion Relief Tzu Chi
Association
1100 S Valley Center Ave.
San Dimas, CA 91773

Ancient Church of the East
2064 Fifth St.
San Fernando, CA 91340

American Vinland Association (AVA)
537 Jones, PMB 165
San Francisco, CA 94102-2007

Anglican Province of Christ the King
2725 Sacramento St.
San Francisco, CA 94115

Buddha's Universal Church
720 Washington St.
San Francisco, CA 94108

Christian Orthodox Catholic Church
795 La Playa St., No. 1
San Francisco, CA 94121-3258

Church for the Fellowship of All Peoples
2041 Larkin St.
San Francisco, CA 94109

Church of Amron
2254 Van Ness
San Francisco, CA 94109

Diamond Way Buddhist Centers
110 Merced Ave.
San Francisco, CA 94127

Ecclesia Catholica Traditionalis "Conservare
et Praedicare"
Box 26414
San Francisco, CA 94126-6414

First Satanic Church
PO Box 475177
San Francisco, CA 94147

Foundation of Revelation
59 Scott St.
San Francisco, CA 94117

Gay Buddhist Fellowship
2215-R Market St., PMB 456
San Francisco, CA 94114

Gurdjieff Foundation
85 St. Elmo Way
San Francisco, CA 94127

Honpa Hongwanji Buddhism
1710 Octavia St.
San Francisco, CA 94109

Inclusive Celtic Church
PO Box 31486
San Francisco, CA 94131-0486

Kerista Commune
PO Box 410068
San Francisco, CA 94141-0068

Kriya Yoga Tantra Society
633 Post St., Ste. 647
San Francisco, CA 94109

Molokan Spiritual Christians (Postojannye)
841 Carolina St.
San Francisco, CA 94107

New, Reformed, Orthodox Order of the
Golden Dawn
48 Page St.
San Francisco, CA 94102

Orthodox Catholic Church
544 Oak St.
San Francisco, CA 94127

Orthodox Episcopal Church of God
Box 1528
San Francisco, CA 94101

Sarada Ramakrishna Vivekananda SRV
Associations of Oregon, San Francisco,
and Hawaii
465 Brussels St.
San Francisco, CA 94134

Temple of Set
PO Box 470307
San Francisco, CA 94147

United Religions Initiative
PO Box 29242
San Francisco, CA 94129-0242

West Coast Communities
866 Potero
San Francisco, CA 94110

White Robed Monks of St. Benedict
Box 27536
San Francisco, CA 94127

American Temple
PO Box 953
San Jose, CA 95108

Ancient and Mystical Order of the Rosae
Crucis
1342 Naglee Ave.
San Jose, CA 95191

Christian Assembly
PO Box 6120
San Jose, CA 95150

Congregation of God (Biblical Church of
God)
PO Box 612440
San Jose, CA 95161

Evangelical Orthodox (Catholic) Church in
America (Non-Papal Catholic)
1213 N San Pedro St.
San Jose, CA 95110-1436

Gnostic Order of Christ
PO Box 8660
San Jose, CA 95155-8660

Master Ching Hai Meditation Association
PO Box 730247
San Jose, CA 95173

S. A. I. Foundation
3491 Clover Oak Drive
San Jose, CA 95148

Badarikashrama
15602 Maubert Ave.
San Leandro, CA 94578

Evangelical Anglican Church in America
(EACA)
Park Western Dr., Ste. 329
San Pedro, CA 90732

Intergalactic Culture Foundation
1569 Stonewood Ct.
San Pedro, CA 90732

Norwegian Seaman's Church (Mission)
1035 Beacon St.
San Pedro, CA 90731

Calvary Chapel
3800 S. Fairview Rd.
Santa Ana, CA 92704

BodhiPath
113 West Gutierrez St.
Santa Barbara, CA 93101

Jean Klein Foundation
Box 2111
Santa Barbara, CA 93120

Spiritual Education Endeavors—The Share
Foundation
1556 Halford Ave., No. 288
Santa Clara, CA 95051

Concordant Publishing Concern
15570 Knochaven
Santa Clarita, CA 91330

Foundation Church of Divine Truth, Inc.
PO Box 802694
Santa Clarita, CA 91380-2694

Federation of St. Thomas Christians
134 Dakota Avenue, No. 308
Santa Cruz, CA 95060

Society of Abidance in Truth (SAT)
1834 Ocean St.
Santa Cruz, CA 95060

Sri Rama Foundation
PO Box 2550
Santa Cruz, CA 95063

Temple of the Holy Grail
PO Box 3816
Santa Cruz, CA 95063-3816

Hoa Hao Buddhism
PO Box 3048
Santa Fe Springs, CA 90670

New Age Bible and Philosophy Center
1139 Lincoln Blvd.
Santa Monica, CA 90403

Soka Gakkai International—USA (SGI—USA)
606 Wilshire Blvd.
Santa Monica, CA 90401-1427

Sonoma Mountain Zen Center
6367 Sonoma Mountain Rd.
Santa Rosa, CA 95404

Tayu Meditation Center
Box 11554
Santa Rosa, CA 95406

Traditional Orthodox Christian Church
(TOCA)
306 Mendocino Ave., Apt. 314
Santa Rosa, CA 95401

Universal Industrial Church of the New
World Comforter (One World Family
Commune, Galactic Messenger Network)
PO Box 1241
Santa Rosa, CA 95402-1241

Ukrainian Orthodox Church–Western Rite
Metropolia
PO Box 1303
Seaside, CA 93955

Sahaja Yoga Center
4565 Sherman Oaks Ave.
Sherman Oaks, CA 91403-3011

MahaSiddha Dharma
PO Box 1689
Soquel, CA 95073

Sri Chaitanya Saraswat Mandal
2900 N Rodeo Gulch Rd.
Soquel, CA 95073

Gedatsu Church of America
7850 Hill Dr.
South San Gabriel, CA 91770

Middlebar Monastery
2503 Del Dio Dr.
Stockton, CA 95204

Amitabha Buddhist Societies
650 S Bernardo Ave.
Sunnyvale, CA 94087

Foundation for *A Course in Miracles* (FACIM)
41397 Buecking Dr.
Temecula, CA 92590-5668

MasterPath
PO Box 9035
Temecula, CA 9258-9035

Blue Mountain Center of Meditation
PO Box 256
Tomales, CA 94971

Kofuku no Kagaku (Institute for Research in
Human Happiness)
350 S Crenshaw Blvd., Ste. A205
Torrance, CA 90503

Ancient Keltic Church
PO Box 663
Tujunga, CA 91043-0663

Freedom Church
13211 Myford Rd., No. 332
Tustin, CA 92782

Hamsa Yoga Sangh
PO Box 930
Union City, CA 94587

Universal Pantheist Society
PO Box 3499
Visalia, CA 93278

GAF International/Adamski Foundation
Box 1722
Vista, CA 92085

Interdenominational Ministries International
(IMI)
PO Box 2107
Vista, CA 92085-2107

Liberty Foundation (Twentieth Century
Church of God)
PO Box 2900
Vista, CA 92085

New Covenant Ministries International
1920 Brea Canyon Cutoff Rd.
Walnut, CA 91789

Ordinary Dharma
PO Box 67
Warner Springs, CA 92086

The Threshold Society
270 Quarter Horse Ln.
Watsonville, CA 95076

Nichiren Shoshu Temple
1401 N Crescent Heights Blvd.
West Hollywood, CA 90046

American Buddhist Congress
3835R E Thousand Oaks Blvd., Ste. 450
Westlake Village, CA 91362

Korean American Presbyterian Church
8500 Bolsa Avenue
Westminster, CA 92683

Christ's Church of the Golden Rule
16200 N Hwy. 201
Willits, CA 95490

The Byzantine Catholic Church, Inc.
(Independent Jurisdiction)
19818 Hart St.
Winnetka, CA 91306

Dharma Realm Buddhist Association
4951 Bodhi Way
Ukiah, California 95482

Colorado

Faith Bible Chapel International
12189 W 64th Ave.
Arvada, CO 80004

American Old Catholic Church
3138 S Parker Rd.
Aurora, CO 80014

Ecumenical Communion of Catholic and
Apostolic Churches
14100 E Jewell Ave.
Aurora, CO 80012

Assembly of YHWHHOSHUA
PO Box 278
Boone, CO 81025

Namo Buddha Seminar
1390 Kalmia Ave.
Boulder, CO 80304

Sacha Dham Ashram
1750 30th St., PMB No. 137
Boulder, CO 80301

Sadhana Ashram
2414 Keystone Ct.
Boulder, CO 80304-1936

Truth Consciousness
10668 Gold Hill Rd.
Boulder, CO 80302-9716

Universal Faithists of Kosmon, Inc.
3439 Grand Valley Canal Rd.
Clifton, CO 81520

Alliance World Fellowship
8595 Explorer Dr.
Colorado Springs, CO 80920

Christian and Missionary Alliance (C&MA)
8595 Explorer Dr.
Colorado Springs, CO 80920

Continuing Episcopal Church (CEC™)
PO Box 50824
Colorado Springs, CO 80949-0824

Emmanuel Association
2713 W Cucharas
Colorado Springs, CO 80904

Evangelical Episcopal Church (GRIDER)
17275 E Goshawk Rd.
Colorado Springs, CO 80908

International Coalition of Apostles
PO Box 63060
Colorado Springs, CO 80962

Dharma Sangha
2000 Dreamway (PO Box 130)
Crestone, CO 81131

Yeshe Khorlo USA
PO Box 87
Crestone, CO 81131

Colorado Reform Baptist Church
Box 12514
Denver, CO 80212

Divine Knowledge Meditation Center
1434 Willow St.
Denver, CO 80220

Franz Bardon Foundation
1344 High St., #1-FBF
Denver, CO 80218

General Conference of the Church of God
(Seventh-Day)
PO Box 33677
Denver, CO 80233

House of Prayer for All People
Box 837
Denver, CO 80201

Rocky Mountain Yearly Meeting
4575-B Eliot St.
Denver, CO 80211

ESP Laboratory
PO Box 2883
Durango, CO 81320-2883

Federation of Ministers and Churches
International
PO Box 40042
Grand Junction, CO 81504

Buddhist Association of Colorado
8965 W Dartmouth Pl.
Lakewood, CO 80227

Chan Nhu Buddhist Pagoda
7201 W Bayaud Pl.
Lakewood, CO 80226

Evangelistic Missionary Fellowship
5405 W 1st Ave.
Lakewood, CO 80226

LaPorte Church of Christ
3206 E Country Rd. 52
LaPorte, CO 80535

Christian Outreach Centre
6657 W. Ottawa Ave., A11-B
Littleton, CO 80128

Order of the Lily and the Eagle
PO Box 937
Littleton, CO 80160-0937

CBAmerica
3686 Stagecoach Rd., Unit F
Longmont, CO 80504-5660

Emissaries of Divine Light
100 Sunrise Ranch Rd.
Loveland, CO 80538

Eureka Society/Elan Vital School of
Meditation
PO Box 3117
Montrose, CO 81402-3117

Tara Mandala
PO Box 3040
Pagosa Springs, CO 81147

Brotherhood of the White Temple
7830 Oak Way, Dept. A
Sedalia, CO 80135

Church of Seven Arrows
PO Box 185
Wheat Ridge, CO 80034-0185

New Order of Glastonbury
Box 285
Yellow Jacket, CO 81335

Connecticut

Living Dharma Centers
PO Box 9513
Bolton, CT 06043

United Catholic Church
PO Box 603
Cheshire, CT 06410

Kundalini Research Foundation
Box 2248
Darien, CT 06820

Universal Life: The Inner Religion
PO Box 651
Guilford, CT 06437

American Ecumenical Catholic Church
30 Woodland St., Unit 10
Hartford, CT 06105

Christian Millennial Fellowship
307 White St.
Hartford, CT 06106

Arica School
10 Landmark Ln., PO Box 645
Kent, CT 06757

Kingdom Life Network of Ministries
597 Naugatuck Ave.
Milford, CT 06461

Orthodox Roman Catholic Movement
15 Pepper St.
Monroe, CT 06468

Center for Dzogchen Studies
17 Tour Ave.
New Haven, CT 06515

Life-Study Fellowship Foundation, Inc.
Dept. W
Noroton, CT 06820

Abbey of Thelema
Box 666
Old Greenwich, CT 06870-0666

Northeast Atheist Association of
    Connecticut (NAA)
PO Box 63
Simsbury, CT 06070

Independent Old Roman Catholic Hungarian
    Orthodox Church of America
Box 290261
Weatherfield, CT 06129-0261

Delaware

African Union First Colored Methodist
    Protestant Church
1106 E 16th St.
Wilmington, DE 19802

Union American Methodist Episcopal
    Church
3101 N Market St.
Wilmington, DE 19802

District of Columbia

Alliance of Baptists
1328 16th St. NW
Washington, DC 20036

Art of Living Foundation
2401 15th St. NW
Washington, DC 20009

Church of the Saviour
2025 Massachusetts Ave. NW
Washington, DC 20036

Ethiopian Catholic Church
415 Michigan Ave. NE, Ste. 65
Washington, DC 20017

The Family International
PMB 102
Washington, DC 20006-1846

Foundation Church of the New Birth
Box 996, Benjamin Franklin Sta.
Washington, DC 20044

Gay and Lesbian Atheists and Humanists
    (GALAH)
PO Box 34635
Washington, DC 20043

Gospel Spreading Church
2006 Georgia Ave. NW, Ste. 300
Washington, DC 20001

Hanafi Madh-hab Center, Islam Faith
7700 16th St. NW
Washington, DC 20012

Highway Christian Church of Christ
436 W St. NW
Washington, DC 20001

Initiatives of Change
1156 15th St. NW, Ste. 910
Washington, DC 20005-1704

Inner Peace Movement
PO Box 499
Washington, DC 20008

Islamic Supreme Council of America (ISCA)
1400 16th St. NW, B-112
Washington, DC 20036

Moorish Science Temple of America
1445 Constitution Ave. NE
Washington, DC 20002

National Spiritual Science Center
276 Carroll St. NW
Washington, DC 20012

Progressive National Baptist Convention, Inc.
601 50th St. NE
Washington, DC 20019

Roman Catholic Church
3211 4th St. NE
Washington, DC 20017-1194

Self-Revelation Church of Absolute Monism
4748 Western Ave.
Washington, DC 20816

Subud
4101 Legation St. NW
Washington, DC 20015

Sunni Muslims
2551 Massachusetts Ave. NW
Washington, DC 20008

True Grace Memorial House of Prayer
205 V St. NW
Washington, DC 20001

The United House of Prayer for All People of
    the Church on the Rock of the Apostolic
    Faith
601 M St. NW
Washington, DC 20001-3620

Way of the Cross Church of Christ
819 D. St. NE
Washington, DC 20002

Florida

Rex Humbard Ministry
Box 3063
Boca Raton, FL 33431

Gospel Crusade Ministerial Fellowship
    (GCMF)
1200 Glory Way Blvd.
Bradenton, FL 34212

Evangelical Marian Catholic Church
PO Box 10317
Brookville, FL 34603

International Free Catholic Communion
PO Box 3454
Clearwater, FL 33767

Mount Zion Overcoming Body of Christ—
    The True Bride
Rte. 1
Crescent City, FL 32012

United Biblical Church of God
PO Box 547
Crystal River, FL 32623

American Druze Society
PO Box 291437
Davie, FL 33329

International Apostolic Ministries (IAM)
225 N Dover Rd.
Dover, FL 33527

Hermetic Order of the Golden Dawn
PO Box 1757
Elfers, FL 34680

Independent Catholic Churches
3460 Powerline Rd.
Fort Lauderdale, FL 33309

Reformed (Slavonic) Orthodox Church
808 W Sunrise Blvd.
Fort Lauderdale, FL 33311

Laodicean Home Missionary Movement
9021 Temple Rd. W
Fort Myers, FL 33912

Esoteric Interfaith Church
7257 NW 4th Blvd., #78
Gainesville, FL 32607

Holy Temple of God
1220 NE 23rd Ave.
Gainesville, FL 32609

Overcoming Saints of God
PO Box 879
Gainesville, FL 32601

Global Cause Network
27 W Hallandale Beach Blvd.
Hallandale, FL 33009

Church of Lukumi Babalu Aye
PO Box 22627
Hialeah, FL 33002

African Universal Church, Inc.
2336 SW 48th Ave.
Hollywood, FL 33023

Essenes of Arkashea
21450 SW 240th St.
Homestead, FL 33031

Kriya Yoga Centers
PO Box 924615
Homestead, FL 33092-4615

Spiritual Life Concepts, Inc.
PO Box 94
Indian Rocks Beach, FL 33785

Primitive Church of Jesus Christ
Hwy. 19 N
Inglis, FL 34449

Afro-American Social Research Association
Box 2150
Jacksonville, FL 32203

The Church (Gene Edwards)
PO Box 3450
Jacksonville, FL 32206

Church of God by Faith
2409 Old Middleburg N
Jacksonville, FL 32210

Vision International Ministerial Association
PO Box 744
Jupiter, FL 33468

United American Free Will Baptist Church
    General Conference
207 W Bella Vista St.
Lakeland, FL 33805

International Ministerial Association
5201 W Homosassa Tr.
Lecanto, FL 34461

Bible Teachers International (BTI)
2005 Johns Ave.
Leesburg, FL 34748

Logos Christian Fellowship
8839 CR 44
Leesburg, FL 34788-9201

Ecumenical Old Catholic Church
7451 NW 23 St.
Margate, FL 33063

United Catholic Church
5017 Bellflower Ct.
Melbourne, FL 32940

Southeastern Yearly Meeting
PO Box 510795
Melbourne Beach, FL 32951-0795

United Spiritual Church of the Spiritual
Advisory Council
115 Cygnet Ln.
Melrose, FL 32666

Universal Religion of America
295 N Tropical Trl.
Merritt Island, FL 32952

Light of Sivananda-Valentina, Ashram of
3475 Royal Palm Ave.
Miami Beach, FL 33140

Universal Foundation for Better Living
21310 NW 37th Ave.
Miami Gardens, FL 33056

Church of the Seven African Powers
PO Box 453336
Miami, FL 33245

Church of Transition
200 NE 48th Terr.
Miami, FL 33137

Churches of Christ in the Apostles Doctrine
9501 SW 175th Ter.
Miami, FL 33157

REMAR International
664-668 NE 61st St.
Miami, FL 33137

Soldiers of the Cross of Christ, Evangelical
International Church
636 NW 2nd St.
Miami, FL 33128

VRINDA/The Vrindavan Institute for Vaisnava
Culture and Studies
4138 NW 23 Rd. Ave.
Miami, FL 33143

Yoga Research Foundation
6111 SW 74th Ave.
Miami, FL 33143

Ethiopian Zion Coptic Church
PO Box 1161
Minneola, FL 34755-1161

Epiphany Bible Students Association
PO Box 97
Mount Dora, FL 32757

Holy Gospel Church IV, Inc.
2812 Blue Finch Way
New Port Richey, FL 34653-6510

National Fellowship Churches of God
300 Park Ave. N
Orange Park, FL 32073

Liberal Catholic Church-Theosophia Synod
1606 New York Ave.
Orlando, FL 32803

Anglican Province of America
3348 W State Rd. 426
Oviedo, FL 32765

Order of the Blue Star
1952 Glencove Ave.
Palm Bay, FL 32907

Old Roman Catholic Church
(Shelley/Humphreys)
5501 62nd Ave.
Pinellas Park, FL 33565

Reformed Catholic Church of America
PO Box 3165
Pinellas Park, FL 33780

G12 Vision International
1490 N Flamingo Rd.
Plantation, FL 33323

Lotus Ashram
264 Mainsail
Port St. Lucie, FL 33452

Amrit Yoga Institute
PO Box 5340
Salt Springs, FL 32134

Christian International Ministries Network
177 Apostles Way
Santa Rosa Beach, FL 32459

American Yoga Association
PO Box 19986
Sarasota, FL 34276

International Alliance of Messianic
Congregations and Synagogues
PO Box 20006
Sarasota, FL 34276-3006

Shrine of the Master, Church of
Metaphysical Christianity
2717 Browning St.
Sarasota, FL 34237

Kashi Church Foundation
11155 Roseland Rd., No. 10
Sebastian, FL 32958

Universal Harmony Foundation
5903 Seminole Blvd.
Seminole, FL 33772

Charismatic Orthodox Church
110 Masters Dr.
St. Augustine, FL 32086

National Primitive Baptist Convention of
the U.S.A.
PO Box 7451
Tallahassee, FL 32314

Apostolic Messianic Fellowship
7911 N 40th St.
Tampa, FL 33604

The Catholic Church of the Antiochean Rite
PO Box 8473
Tampa, FL 33674

Holy Order of RaHoorKhuit
Box 24691
Tampa, FL 33623

Luciferian Light Group
PO Box 7207
Tampa, FL 33673

Old Catholic Church of North America
PO Box 260473
Tampa, FL 33685

Orthodox Church of the West—USA
W. Henry Ave.
Tampa, FL 33604

Churches of Christ (Non-Instrumental,
Conservative)
119 N. Glen Arven Ave.
Temple Terrace, FL 33617

Orthodox Christian Fellowship of Mercy
PO Box 1107
Thonotosassa, FL 33592

American Evangelistic Association
PO Box 121000
W Melbourne, FL 32912-1000

Alliance of Divine Love
PO Box 19612
West Palm Beach, FL 33416

Georgia

Southern Congregational Methodist Church
Alma, GA

Anglican Catholic Church
PO Box 5223
Athens, GA 30604-5223

Avalon Isle/Order of the Royal Oak
PO Box 6006
Athens, GA 30604

al-Ummah
547 W End Pl.
Atlanta, GA 30310

American Anglican Council
2296 Henderson Mill Rd. NE, Ste. 406
Atlanta, GA 30345-2739

Anglican Church of North America
1906 Forest Green Dr. NE
Atlanta, GA 30329

Atlanta Soto Zen Center (ASZC)
1167 C/D Zonolite Pl.
Atlanta, GA 30306

Cooperative Baptist Fellowship
PO Box 450329
Atlanta, GA 311-0329

First Deliverance Church of Atlanta
65 Hardwick St. SE
Atlanta, GA 30315

First Interdenominational Christian
Association
1061 Memorial Dr. SE
Atlanta, GA 30316

Karin Society
2531 Briarcliff Rd. NE, Ste. 217
Atlanta, GA 30329

Lost-Found Nation of Islam
3040 Campbelton Rd., SW
Atlanta, GA 30311

Triumph the Church and Kingdom of God
in Christ
2571 Browntown Rd. NW
Atlanta, GA 30318

Fellowship of Vineyard Harvester Churches
in the United States
1890 Rome Hwy.
Cedartown, GA 30125

International Communion of Charismatic
Churches
PO Box 687
Cedartown, GA 30125

Celtic Rite Orthodox Diocese
PO Box 350
Clarkdale, GA 30020

World Changers Church International
2500 Burdett Rd.
College Park, GA 30349

Victory Unto Victory Revivals, Inc.
230 Creekview Blvd.
Covington, GA 30016

Primitive Baptists—Progressive
PO Box 69
Culloden, GA 31016

Church of God of the Union Assembly
PO Box 1323
Dalton, GA 30722-1323

Network of Kingdom Churches
4650 Flat Shoals Rd.
Decatur, GA 30034-5095

Asbury Bible Churches
PO Box 1021
Dublin, GA 31021

Congregational Holiness Church
3888 Fayetteville Hwy.
Griffin, GA 30223

Miracles Ministries Fellowship (MMF)
PO Box 21
Griffin, GA 30224

First International Church of the Web
4202 Windsor Spring Rd., No. 131
Hephzibah, GA 30815

International Alliance of Web-Based
Churches
4202 Windsor Spring Rd., No. 131
Hephzibah, GA 30815

Church of Tzaddi
PO Box 308
Kennesaw, GA 30156

Congregation of God, Seventh-Day
2751 S Main St., PO Box 2345
Kennesaw, GA 30156

Church of the Christian Spiritual Alliance
(CSA)
PO Box 7
Lakemont, GA 30552-0001

Presbyterian Church in America
1700 N Brown Rd., Ste. 105
Lawrenceville, GA 30043-8122

Healing Temple Church
660 Williams St.
Macon, GA 31201

Cymry Wicca
PO Box 672125
Marietta, GA 30006-0036

Universal Federation of Pagans, Ltd.
PO Box 672125
Marietta, GA 30006-0036

Nationwide Independent Baptist Fellowship
850 Mill Rd.
McDonough, GA 30253

Shri Ram Chandra Mission
Rte. 1, Box 122-5, 5611 GA Hwy. 109
Molena, GA 30258

Church of God General Conference
(Abrahamic Faith)
PO Box 100,000
Morrow, GA 30260

Praise Christ Ministries
PO Box 71514
Newnan, GA 30271

Christ's Sanctified Holy Church (Georgia)
CSHC
Perry, GA 31069

Fellowship of Churches and Ministers,
International (FCMI)
PO Box 2165
Reidsville, GA 30453

Church of Christ Holiness unto the Lord
PO Box 1642
Savannah, GA 31401

Holy Church of God
707 Little Neck Rd.
Savannah, GA 31419

Southern Appalachian Yearly Meeting and
Association
330 Goebel Ave.
Savannah, GA 31404

Henge of Keltria
2350 Spring Rd. PMB-140
Smyrna, GA 30080-2630

Noohra Foundation
4480H S. Cobb Dr. Ste. H PMB 343
Smyrna, GA 30080-6989

Oratory of Saint Jerome
114 Deluxe Cir.
Thomaston, GA 30286

United Evangelical Churches
PO Box 1175
Thomasville, GA 31799

Hawaii

Shinreikyo
310C Uulani St.
Hilo, HI 96720

Apostolic Faith (Hawaii)
1043 Middle St.
Honolulu, HI 96819

Bodaiji Mission
1251 Elm
Honolulu, HI 96814

Celtic Evangelical Church
PO Box 90880
Honolulu, HI 96835-0880

Chinese Buddhist Association of Hawaii-Hsu
Yun Temple
42 Kawananakoa Pl.
Honolulu, HI 96817

Chozen-ji Kyudo
3565 Kalihi St.
Honolulu, HI 96819

Church of the Living God
632 Mokauea
Honolulu, HI 96819

Diamond Sangha
2747 Waiomao Rd.
Honolulu, HI 96816

Door of Faith Church and Bible School
1161 Young St.
Honolulu, HI 96814

Ecumenical Catholic Church of America
98-1277 Kaahumanu St. PMB 345
Honolulu, HI 96701

Hawaii Buddhist Council
1001 Bishop St., Pacific Tower 1760
Honolulu, HI 96813-3696

Hawaii Chinese Buddhist Society
1614 Nuuanu Ave.
Honolulu, HI 96817

Hawaii Council of Jodo Mission
1429 Makiki St.
Honolulu, HI 96814

Hawaii Kotohira Jinsha
2020 S King St.
Honolulu, HI 96817

Honkyoku Shinto
61 Puiwa Rd.
Honolulu, HI 96817

Hoomana Naauoa O Hawaii
910 Cooke St.
Honolulu, HI 96813

Hsu Yun Temple
42 Kawananakoa Pl., Nu'uanu
Honolulu, HI 96817

Inclusive Orthodox Church (IOC)
1750 Kalakaua Ave., No. 103-183
Honolulu, HI 96826-3795

Ka Hale Hoano Hou O Ke Akua
1760 Nalani
Honolulu, HI 96819

Kealaokamalamalama
1207 Prospect
Honolulu, HI 96822

Korean Christian Missions of Hawaii
1832 Liliha St.
Honolulu, HI 96817

Kuan Yin Temple
170 N Vineyard Blvd.
Honolulu, HI 96817

Lamb of God Church
612 Isenberg St.
Honolulu, HI 96826-4532

Nichiren Mission
33 Pulelehua Way
Honolulu, HI 96817

Shinshu Kyokai Mission of Hawaii
1631 S Beretania St.
Honolulu, HI 96826

Taishakyo Shinto
215 N Kukui St.
Honolulu, HI 96817

Tendai Buddhist Institute
3326 Paalea St.
Honolulu, HI 96816

Tensho-Kotai-Jingu-Kyo
888 N King St.
Honolulu, HI 96817

Todaiji Hawaii Bekkaku Honzan
426 Luakini St.
Honolulu, HI 96814

Zen Buddhist Order of Hsu Yun (ZBOHY)
42 Kawananakoa Pl., Nu'uanu
Honolulu, HI 96817

Source School of Tantra Yoga
PO Box 368
Kahului, HI 96733

United Reform Catholic Church International
PO Box 1058
Kane'ohe, HI 96744-1058

Saiva Siddhanta Church
107 Kaholalete
Kapaa, HI 96745

Nechung Dorje Drayang Ling
PO Box 250
Pahala, HI 96777

Alpha and Omega Christian Church
96-171 Kamehameha Hwy.
Pearl City, HI 96782

Huna International
PO Box 223009
Princeville, HI 96722

Idaho

Seventh-Day Church of God
PO Box 804
Caldwell, ID 83606-0804

Church of Jesus Christ Christian, Aryan
Nations
PO Box 2016
Coeur d'Alene, ID 83816

General Council of the Churches of God
1827 W 3rd St.
Meridian, ID 83642-1653

Illinois

Plymouth Brethren (Tunbridge Wells
Brethren)
PO Box 649
Addison, IL 60101

Baptist General Conference
2002 S Arlington Heights Rd.
Arlington Heights, IL 60005

Church of Christian Liberty
502 W Euclid Ave.
Arlington Heights, IL 60004

Eglise Gnostique Catholique Apostolique
5215 Randolph St. W
Bellwood, IL 60104

Ukrainian Evangelical Baptist Convention
6751 Riverside Dr.
Berwyn, IL 60402

Church of the New Song
1465 Exeter Rd.
Bluffs, IL 62621

Evangelical Church Alliance International
205 W Broadway
Bradley, IL 60915

American Muslims
PO Box 1061
Calumet City, IL 60409

Nirankari Universal Brotherhood Mission
1 Ball Ave.
Carpentersville, IL 60110

American Muslim Council (AMC)
2020 N California Ave.
Chicago, IL 60657

Brotherhood of the Cross and Star
1544 W Jarvis Ave.
Chicago, IL 60626

Catholic Apostolic National Church
7030 W. Diversey Ave.
Chicago, IL 60707

Cosmic Circle of Fellowship
4857 N Melvina Ave.
Chicago, IL 60630

Ecumenical Institute (Institute of Cultural
Affairs)
4750 N Sheridan Rd.
Chicago, IL 60640

Evangelical Covenant Church
5101 N Francisco Ave.
Chicago, IL 60625

Evangelical Lutheran Church in America
(1988)
8765 W. Higgins Rd.
Chicago, IL 60631-4101

Independent Evangelical Catholic Church
PO Box 178388
Chicago, IL 60617-8388

Jesus People USA
920 W Wilson Ave.
Chicago, IL 60640

Lithuanian Evangelical Reformed Church
3542 W 66th Pl.
Chicago, IL 60629

Lutheran World Federation
8765 W Higgins Rd.
Chicago, IL 60631

Monastery of the Seven Rays
Box 1554
Chicago, IL 60690-1554

Moody Church
1630 N Clark St.
Chicago, IL 60614

Nation of Islam (Farrakhan)
7351 South Stoney Island Ave.
Chicago, IL 60649

New Apostolic Church
3753 N Troy
Chicago, IL 60618

North American Old Roman Catholic Church
(Schweikert)
4200 N. Kedvale
Chicago, IL 60641

Ordo Aurum Solis
1203 W Bryn Mawr Ave.
Chicago, IL 60660

Temple of Kriya Yoga
2414 N. Kedzie
Chicago, IL 60647

Temple of Universal Law
5030 N Drake
Chicago, IL 60625

Thee Orthodox Old Roman Catholic Church
Box 49314
Chicago, IL 60649

U.S. National Committee for the Lutheran
World Federation
8765 W Higgins Rd.
Chicago, IL 60631

Urantia Foundation
533 Diversey Pkwy.
Chicago, IL 60614

Vivekananda Vedanta Society
5423 W. Hyde Park Blvd.
Chicago, IL 60615

Christian Believers Conference
5930 W 29th St.
Cicero, IL 60650

Church of St. Joseph
2307 S. Laramie
Cicero, IL 60650

Independent Spiritualist Association of the
United States of America
5130 W 25th St.
Cicero, IL 60650

Berean Bible Fellowship (Illinois)
PO Box 6
Collinsville, IL 62234

Church of God in Christ, Congregational
6939 Marine Rd.
Edwardsville, IL 62025

Church of the Brethren
1451 Dundee Ave.
Elgin, IL 60120

International Churches of Christ (ICOC)
655 W. Grand Ave., Ste. 220
Elmhurst, IL 60126

International Organization of Burmese
Buddhist Sanghas
15 W 110 Forest Ln.
Elmhurst, IL 60657

Syro-Malabar Catholic Church
372 S Prairie Ave.
Elmhurst, IL 60126

Old Roman Catholic Church (English Rite)
1722 N 79th Ave.
Elmwood Park, IL 60635-3505

Baha'i Faith
1233 Central St.
Evanston, IL 60201

Buddhist Council of the Midwest
1812 Washington St.
Evanston, IL 60202

Reba Place Fellowship and Associated
Communities
737 B Reba Pl.
Evanston, IL 60204

Udumbara Zen Center
501 Sherman Ave.
Evanston, IL 60202

Christian Conservative Churches of America
PO Box 575
Flora, IL 62839

Social Brethren
R.R. 2
Flora, IL 62839

International Council of Community
Churches
21116 Washington Pky.
Frankfort, IL 60423-3112

Federation of Zoroastrian Associations in
North America
5750 S Jackson St.
Hinsdale, IL 60521

All World Gayatri Pariwar
5N 371 IL Route 53 (Rohwling Rd.)
Itasca, IL 60143

Hindu Temple of Greater Chicago
10915 Lemont Rd.
Lemont, IL 60439

United Independent Catholic Church
1603 Old Creal Springs Rd.
Marion, IL 62959

Anchor Bay Evangelistic Association
PO Box 406
Maryville, IL 62062

Universal Ministries
PO Box 31
Milford, IL 60953

Apostolic Catholic Assyrian Church of the
East, North American Diocese
8908 Birch Ave.
Morton Grove, IL 60053

Life Mission
936 Commons Rd.
Naperville, IL 60563

Sawan Kirpal Ruhani Mission
4S175 Naperville Rd.
Naperville, IL 60563

Zen Buddhist Temple of Chicago
PO Box 176
Northbrook, IL 60065-0176

Concordia Lutheran Conference
Central Ave. at 171st Pl.
Oak Forest, IL 60452-4913

Lithuanian Evangelical Lutheran Church in
Diaspora
9000 S Menard Ave.
Oak Lawn, IL 60453

Fellowship of Lutheran Congregations
320 Erie St.
Oak Park, IL 60302

North American Baptist Conference
1 S 210 Summit Ave.
Oakbrook Terrace, IL 60181

Salem Acres
7419 E Brick School Rd.
Rock City, IL 61070

Bible Missionary Church
PO Box 6070
Rock Island, IL 61204-6070

General Association of Regular Baptist
Churches
1300 N Meacham Rd.
Schaumburg, IL 60173

"I AM" Religious Activity
1120 Stonehedge Dr.
Schaumburg, IL 60194

Hanmaum Zen Center
7852 N Lincoln Ave.
Skokie, IL 60077

International Lutheran Fellowship
1124 S Fifth St., LL-C
Springfield, IL 62703

Living Tao Foundation
PO Box 846
Urbana, IL 61803-0846

Tanzeem-e-Islami
250 W. Saint Charles Rd.
Villa Park, IL 62181-2430

Free Episcopal Church
2100 Manchester Rd., Ste. 900
Wheaton, IL 60187

National Association of Evangelicals
Box 28
Wheaton, IL 60187

Theosophical Society in America
1926 N Main St.
Wheaton, IL 60187

World Evangelical Alliance
Box WEF
Wheaton, IL 60189-8004

Christ Community Church of Zion
2500 Dowie Memorial Dr.
Zion, IL 60099

Indiana

United Christian Ministries International
(UCMI)
2401 South 425 West
Albion, IN 46701

Central Yearly Meeting of Friends
Rte. 1, Box 226
Alexandria, IN 46001

Church of God (Anderson, Indiana)
Box 2420
Anderson, IN 46018

Pilgrim Holiness Church of the Midwest
6402 Ridgeview Dr.
Anderson, IN 46013

Orthodox Catholic Church of America
5355 CR 35
Auburn, IN 46709-9717

Padanaram Settlement
PO Box 334
Avoca, IN 47420

Faith Mission Church
1817 26th St.
Bedford, IN 47421

Apostolic Church of Jesus Christ
5019 N Lakeview Rd.
Bloomington, IN 47404

Old German Baptist Brethren
Rte. 1, Box 140
Bringhurst, IN 46913

Gospel Revelation, Inc.
PO Box 52
Connersville, IN 47331

Apostolic World Christian Fellowship
11 W Iowa St.
Evansville, IN 47711

American Association of Lutheran Churches
Augustine Hall, #13
Fort Wayne, IN 46825-1551

Calvary Ministries, Inc., International (CMI)
PO Box 11228
Fort Wayne, IN 48656-1228

Lutheran Churches of the Reformation
4014 Wenonah Ln.
Fort Wayne, IN 46809

Missionary Church, Inc. (U.S.)
PO Box 9127
Fort Wayne, IN 46899-9127

Evangelical Christian Church
3534 S. Shelby 750 W
Franklin, IN 46131

Pentecostal Church of Zion
Box 110
French Lick, IN 47432

National Association of Holiness Churches
351 S Park Dr.
Griffith, IN 46319

Church of the United Brethren in Christ USA
302 Lake St.
Huntington, IN 46750

American Coalition of
    Unregistered Churches
Box 11
Indianapolis, IN 46206

American Evangelical Christian Churches
PO Box 47312
Indianapolis, IN 46247-0312

Bethel Ministerial Association (BMA)
7055 Marker St.
Indianapolis, IN 46227

Byzantine Orthodox Catholic Church (St.
    Peters)
6329 E 55th Pl.
Indianapolis, IN 46226-1647

Church of the Living God, the Pillar, and
    Ground of the Truth Which He Purchased
    with His Own Blood, Inc. [McLeod
    Dominion]
PO Box 55090
Indianapolis, IN 46205

Evangelical Methodist Church
PO Box 17070
Indianapolis, IN 46217

Free Methodist Church of North America
PO Box 535002
Indianapolis, IN 46253

Lutheran Ministerium and Synod—USA
2837 E. New York St.
Indianapolis, IN 46201

Pentecostal Assemblies of the World
3939 N Meadows Dr.
Indianapolis, IN 46205

Universal Christian Church
2140 Martindale Ave.
Indianapolis, IN 46202

Wesleyan Church
Box 50434
Indianapolis, IN 46250-0434

Branham Tabernacle and Related
    Assemblies
Box 325
Jeffersonville, IN 47130

Christ Gospel Churches International
2614 Hwy. 62
Jeffersonville, IN 47130

Truth for Today Bible Fellowship
Box 6358
Lafayette, IN 47903

Midwest Congregational Christian
    Fellowship
8009 N CR 500 West
Muncie, IN 47304

Universal Spiritualist Association
4905 W University Ave.
Muncie, IN 47304-3460

CIRCES International
PO Box 279
Plainfield, IN 46168

Islamic Shura Council of North America
PO Box 38
Plainfield, IN 46168

Islamic Society of North America
PO Box 38
Plainfield, IN 46168

Friends United Meeting
101 Quaker Hill Dr.
Richmond, IN 47374

Faith Assembly
2214 E Winona Ave.
Warsaw, IN 46580

Fellowship of Grace Brethren Churches
PO Box 576
Winona Lake, IN 46590

Iowa

Avalonian Catholic Church
437 Ninth Ave. S
Clinton, IA 52732

Ordo Arcanorum Gradalis
PO Box 96
Clinton, IA 52732

Gospel Assemblies (Sowders/Goodwin)
7135 Meredith Dr.
Des Moines, IA 50322

Kingsway Fellowship International
3707 SW 9th St.
Des Moines, IA 50315-3047

Open Bible Standard Churches, Inc.
2020 Bell Ave.
Des Moines, IA 50315-1096

Evangelical Mennonite Church
1633 N 29th St.
Fort Dodge, IA 50501-7937

Augsburg Lutheran Churches
PO Box 332
Greenfield, IA 50849

The Living Word Fellowship
PO Box 3429
Iowa City, IA 52247-3429

Amana Church Society (Community of True
    Inspiration)
PO Box 103
Middle Amana, IA 52307

Iowa Yearly Meeting of Friends
    (Conservative)
PO Box 657
Oskaloosa, IA 52577

Union of Nazarene Yisraelite Congregations
PO Box 556
Ottumwa, IA 52501

Kansas

Apostolic Faith (Kansas)
335 W 10th St.
Baxter Springs, KS 66713

Catholic Church (Pope Michael I)
PO Box 74
Delia, KS 66418-0074

United States Conference of Mennonite
    Brethren Churches
PO Box 220
Hillsboro, KS 67063-0220

Congregational Bible Churches International
PO Box 165
Hutchinson, KS 67501

Bible Holiness Church (1995)
304 Camp Dr.
Independence, KS 67301

Fundamental Baptist Fellowship Association
1916 Central Ave.
Kansas City, KS 66102

United Nation of Islam
1608 N 13th St.
Kansas City, KS 66102

Church of God in Christ, Mennonite
420 N Wedel
Moundridge, KS 67107

Christian Brethren (Open or Plymouth
    Brethren)
PO Box 3831
Olathe, KS 66063-3831

Church of God (Holiness)
7407 Metcalf
Overland Park, KS 66204

Churches of God, Holiness
PO Box 4220
Overland Park, KS 66204

Dunkard Brethren Church
Quinter, KS 67752

Kentucky

International Circle of Faith
115 Hwy. 42 E
Bedford, KY 40006

Aquarian Christine Church Universal
348 E. Lexington Ave.
Danville, KY 40422

Associated Brotherhood of Christians
PO Box 1112
Henderson, KY 42419

Continuing Apostolic United States
    Episcopacy
1718 Moseley Dr.
Hopkinsville, KY 42240

Union of Traditional Apostolic Churches
    (UTAC)
1718 Moseley Dr.
Hopkinsville, KY 42240

Council of Old Roman Catholic Bishops
704 Old Harrods Creek Rd.
Louisville, KY 40223

Independent Catholic Church of America
8701 Brittany Dr.
Louisville, KY 40220

International Fellowship of United Apostolic
    Churches
PO Box 11763
Louisville, KY 40251-0763

Old Roman Catholic Church in North
    America
1207 Potomac Pl.
Louisville, KY 40214

Pentecostal Churches of Apostolic Faith
723 South 45th St.
Louisville, KY 40211

Presbyterian Church (U.S.A.)
100 Witherspoon St.
Louisville, KY 40202

Sanctified Church of Christ
1141 S. 2nd St.
Louisville, KY 40203

Sovereign Grace Baptist Churches
6088 Zebulon Hwt.
Pikeville, KY 41501

Kentucky Mountain Holiness Association
75 Mill Creek Lawson Rd.
Vancleve, KY 41385

Louisiana

World Evangelism Fellowship
PO Box 262550
Baton Rouge, LA 70826-2550

Lokenath Divine Life Fellowship
211 Gunther Ln.
Belle Chase, LA 70037

Independent Church of Jesus Christ of Latter
Day Saints
22 Homas Pl., Apt. C
Destrehan, LA 70047

Catholic Church of the Americas
1201 W Esplanade Ave., Ste. 1709
Kenner, LA 70065

New Christian Crusade Church
Box 25
Mandeville, LA 70470

AEGA (Association of Evangelical Gospel
Assemblies) International
2149 Hwy. 139
Monroe, LA 71203

Association Zen Internationale (AZI)
748 Camp St.
New Orleans, LA 70130

Full Gospel Baptist Church Fellowship
2240 Simon Bolivar St.
New Orleans, LA 70113

Voodoo Spiritual Temple
828 N Rampart St.
New Orleans, LA 70116

Congregational Church of Practical Theology
31916 University Cir.
Springfield, LA 70462

Maine

Morgan Bay Zendo
532 Morgan Bay Rd.
Surry, ME 04684

Maryland

New Covenant Churches of Maryland
804 Windsor Rd.
Arnold, MD 21012

Shiah Fatimi Ismaili Tayyibi Dawoodi Bohra
(Daudi Bohras)
18728 New Hampshire Ave.
Ashton, MD 20861

Church of God in Christ Jesus, Apostolic, Inc.
PO Box 29276
Baltimore, MD 21205

Evangelical Bible Church
2444 Washington Blvd.
Baltimore, MD 21230

Grace and Hope Mission, Inc.
4 S. Gay St.
Baltimore, MD 21202-4007

Greater Grace World Outreach
6025 Moravia Park Dr.
Baltimore, MD 21206

Nation of Islam (The Caliph)
3217 Garrison Blvd.
Baltimore, MD 21216-1320

Savitria
2405 Ruscombe
Baltimore, MD 21209

United Church of Jesus Christ (Apostolic)
5150 Baltimore National Pke.
Baltimore, MD 21229

Scripture Research Association
14410 S. Springfield Rd.
Brandywine, MD 20613

Seventh Day Pentecostal Church of the
Living God
3722 41st Ave.
Brentwood, MD 20722

African Hebrew Israelites of Jerusalem
9185 Central Ave.
Capitol Heights, MD 20743

Independent African American Catholic Rite
4105 Alton Street
Capitol Heights, MD 20731

United Holy Church of America
825 Fairoak Ave.
Chillum, MD 20783

Portal Enterprises
PO Box 1449
Columbia, MD 21044

Free Gospel Church of the Apostle's Doctrine
4703 Marlboro Pke.
Coral Hills, MD 20734

American Catholic Church in the United
States
PO Box 119
Frederick, MD 21705-0119

Sovereign Grace Ministries
7505 Muncaster Mill Rd.
Gaithersburg, MD 20877

American Zen College
16815 Germantown Rd. (Rte. 18)
Germantown, MD 20767

Anglican Independent Communion
PO Box 262
Lothian, MD 20711

Bible Brethren
17904 Binkley Ave.
Maugansville, MD 21767

Kunzang Palyul Choling (KPC)
18400 River Rd.
Poolesville, MD 20837

Ahmadiyya Movement in Islam
15000 Good Hope Rd.
Silver Spring, MD 20905

Body of Christ Movement
16819 New Hampshire Ave.
Silver Spring, MD 20905

Seventh-Day Adventist Church
12501 Old Columbia Pke.
Silver Spring, MD 20904

International Evangelical Church (IEC)
13901 Central Ave.
Upper Marlboro, MD 20774

International Evangelical Church and
Missionary Association
13901 Central Ave.
Upper Marlboro, MD 20772

International Meditation Center—USA
4920 Rose Dr.
Westminster, MD 21158

Massachusetts

Insight Meditation Society
Pleasant St.
Barre, MA 01005

One Peaceful World
Box 7
Becket, MA 01223

Reformed Congregational Fellowship
14 McKinley Ave.
Beverly, MA 01915-3430

American Buddhist Shim Gum Do
Association
203 Chestnut Hill Ave.
Boston, MA 02135

Church of Christ, Scientist
Boston, MA 02115-3195

Mount Calvary Holy Church of America
PO Box 236
Boston, MA 02121

Unitarian Universalist Association of
Congregations
25 Beacon St.
Boston, MA 02108

Church of Greece
50 Goddard Ave.
Brookline, MA 02140

Melkite Catholic Church
158 Pleasant St.
Brookline, MA 02446

Talnoye (Talner) Hasidism
64 Corey Rd.
Brookline, MA 02146

Cambridge Buddhist Association
75 Sparks St.
Cambridge, MA 02138

Dzogchen Foundation
PO Box 734
Cambridge, MA 02140

United Pentecostal Council of the
Assemblies of God (UPCAG)
211 Columbia St.
Cambridge, MA 02139

Frigga's Web Association
PO Box 701
Carlisle, MA 01741-0701

Valley Zendo
263 Warner Hill Rd.
Charlemont, MA 01339

Vedanta Centre and Ananda Ashrama
130 Beechwood St.
Cohassat, MA 02025

Twelve Tribes
92 Melville Ave.
Dorchester, MA 02124

The Eloists, Inc.
Drawer O
Duxbury, MA 02321

National Alliance of Pantheists
PO Box 484
Groton, MA 01450

Mahasiddha Nyingmapa Center
47 East Rd.
Hawley, MA 01339

International Communion of the Holy
Christian Orthodox Church
207 Main St.
Indian Orchard, MA 01151

National Spiritual Alliance
RFD 1
Lake Pleasant, MA 01347

EnlightenNext
PO Box 2360
Lenox, MA 01240

Moksha Foundation
PO Box 2360
Lenox, MA 01240

Old Roman Catholic Church-Utrecht
Succession
21 Aaron St.
Melrose, MA 02176

Anglo-Saxon Federation of America
PO Box 177
Merrimac, MA 01860

Grace Essence Fellowship
53 Westchester Rd.
Newton, MA 02158

New England Evangelical Baptist Fellowship
40 Bridge St.
Newton, MA 02158

General Convention of the New Jerusalem
11 Highland Ave.
Newtonville, MA 02460

Holy Orthodox Church in North America
1476 Centre St.
Roslindale, MA 02131-1417

Temple of Isis
125 Essex St.
Salem, MA 01970

Vipassana Meditation Centers
386 Colrain-Shelburne Rd.
Shelburne, MA 01370-9672

Sirius Community
72 Baker Rd.
Shutesbury, MA 01072

World Bishops Council
PO Box 2302
Springfield, MA 01101

Slaves of the Immaculate Heart of Mary
PO Box 1000
Still River, MA 01467

Kripalu Center for Yoga and Health
PO Box 309
Stockbridge, MA 01262

Michigan

Islamic Assembly of North America (IANA)
3588 Plymouth Rd., No. 270
Ann Arbor, MI 48105

Lower Lights Church
Ann Arbor, MI

Shadhiliyya Sufism
2531 Jackson Rd., No. 169
Ann Arbor, MI 48103

Church of Daniel's Band
4832 S Bard Rd.
Beaverton, MI 48612

Israelite House of David
PO Box 1057
Benton Harbor, MI 49023

Israelite House of David as Reorganized by
Mary Purnell
PO Box 187
Benton Harbor, MI 49023-0187

As-Sunnah Foundation of America (ASFA)
G4417 S Saginaw St.
Burton, MI 48529

Lutheran Congregations in Mission to Christ
7000 Sheldon Road
Canton, MI 48187

Shi'a Muslims
19500 Ford Rd.
Dearborn, MI 48128

Apostolic Assemblies of Christ, Inc.
8425 Fenkell Ave.
Detroit, MI 48238

Church of Universal Triumph the Dominion
of God
1651 Ferry Park
Detroit, MI 48206

Metropolitan Spiritual Churches of Christ,
Inc.
8747 Fenkell St.
Detroit, MI 48238

Nation of Islam (John Muhammad)
1448 E Outer Drive
Detroit, MI 48206

National Baptist Evangelical Life and Soul
Saving Assembly of the U.S.A.
441-61 Monroe Ave.
Detroit, MI 48226

Pan African Orthodox Christian Church
(PAOCC)
7625 Linwood
Detroit, MI 48238

Pentecostal Church of God
9244 Delmar
Detroit, MI 48211

Universal Hagar's Spiritual Church (UHSC)
PO Box 07071
Detroit, MI 48207-7071

Full Gospel Truth, Inc.
304 3rd St.
East Jordan, MI 49727

Assembly of Yahweh
1017 N Gunnell Rd.
Eaton Rapids, MI 48827

Spiritual Episcopal Church
141 Frost St.
Eaton Rapids, MI 48827

International Federation of Secular
Humanistic Jews
28611 W Twelve Mile Rd.
Farmington Hills, MI 48334

Society for Humanistic Judaism
28611 W Twelve Mile Rd.
Farmington Hills, MI 48334

Naqshbandi Sufi Order
PO Box 1065
Fenton, MI 48430

Church of God Anonymous (CGA)
PO Box 100
Gowen, MI 49326

Christian Reformed Church in North
America
2850 Kalamazoo Ave. SE
Grand Rapids, MI 49560

Free Reformed Church of North America
950 Ball Ave. NE
Grand Rapids, MI 49503

Grace Gospel Fellowship
1011 Aldon SW
Grand Rapids, MI 49509

Heritage Netherlands Reformed
Congregations
540 Crescent St. NE
Grand Rapids, MI 49503

Reformed Ecumenical Council
2050 Breton Rd. SE, Ste. 102
Grand Rapids, MI 49546-5547

Robin's Return
1008 Lamberton St., NE
Grand Rapids, MI 49505

Strict Baptists
1710 Richmond NW
Grand Rapids, MI 49504

IFCA International
3520 Fairlanes
Grandville, MI 49468-0810

Protestant Reformed Churches in America
(PRC)
4949 Ivanrest SW
Grandville, MI 49418

American Apostolic Catholic Church
124 S Lafayette
Greenville, MI 48838

Anglican Diocese of the Great Lakes
2415 McCann Rd.
Hastings, MI 49058

Romanian Orthodox Episcopate of America
2535 Grey Tower Rd.
Jackson, MI 49201-9120

The Sambodh Society, Inc.
6363 N 24th St.
Kalamazoo, MI 49004

Christadelphians—Amended Fellowship
14676 Berwick St.
Livonia, MI 48154

Evangelical Presbyterian Church
17197 N Laurel Park Dr., Ste. 567
Livonia, MI 48152-7912

Illinois Lutheran Conference
2969 David Rd.
Midland, MI 48640

Church of God (Sabbatarian)
PO Box 37349
Oak Park, MI 48237

Federation of Islamic Associations in the
United States and Canada
25231 5 Mile Rd.
Redford Township, MI 48239

The Reform Bahai Faith
PO Box 81842
Rochester, MI 48308

Chaldean Catholic Church
25603 Berg Rd.
Southfield, MI 48034

Word of Faith International Christian Centers
20000 W 9 Mile Rd.
Southfield, MI 48075

Bektashi Order
21749 Northline Road
Taylor, MI 48180

Arya Samaj
224 Florence
Troy, MI 48098

Bharatiya Temple
6850 Adams Rd.
Troy, MI 48098

Mariavite Old Catholic Church—Province of
North America
2803 10th St.
Wyandotte, MI 48192-4994

Coptic Fellowship of America
1735 Pinnacle Dr. SW
Wyoming, MI 49509-1339

Spiritual Israel Church and Its Army
501 Eugene St.
Ypsilanti, MI 48198

Minnesota

Plymouth Brethren (Ames Brethren)
Box 1052
Anoka, MN 55303-1052

Eckankar
PO Box 2000
Chanhassen, MN 55317-2000

Syro-Russian Orthodox Catholic Church
5907 Grand Avenue
Duluth, MN 55807

Church of the Lutheran Brethren of America
1020 Alcott Ave. W
Fergus Falls, MN 56537

Resources for Ecumenical Spirituality
PO Box 85
Forest Lake, MN 55025-0085

Laestadian Lutheran Church
279 N Medina St., Ste. 150
Loretto, MN 55357

Evangelical Lutheran Synod
6 Browns Ct.
Mankato, MN 56001

Astrum Sophia
Minneapolis, MN

Brothers of the Earth
Dinkytown Sta.
Minneapolis, MN 55414

Evangelical Church of North America
9421 West River Rd.
Minneapolis, MN 55444

Evangelical Free Church of America
901 E 78th St.
Minneapolis, MN 55420

International Ministerial Fellowship
PO Box 32366
Minneapolis, MN 55432

Association of Free Lutheran Congregations
3110 E Medicine Lake Blvd.
Plymouth, MN 55441

Skergard
1003 Cottonwood Ave., No. 53
Red Wing, MN 55066-1300

Christ's Household of Faith
355 Marshall Ave.
St. Paul, MN 55102-1898

Heartland Old Catholic Church
1624 Luella St. N.
St. Paul, MN 55119-3017

Association of Faith Churches and Ministries
(AFCM)
PO Box 1918
Willmar, MN 56201

Minnesota Baptist Association
PO Box 527
Willmar, MN 56201

Mississippi

International Council of Christian Churches
PO Box 2453
Collins, MS 39428-2453

Methodist Protestant Church
722 Hwy. 84W
Collins, MS 39428

Congregational Methodist Church
Box 9
Florence, MS 39073

Association of Independent Methodists
405 Marquis St.
Jackson, MS 39206

Church of Christ (Holiness) U.S.A.
329 E. Monument St.
Jackson, MS 39202

Fellowship of Independent Reformed
Evangelicals
PO Box 8055
Laurel, MS 39441

Celtic Anabaptist Communion
Rte. 1, Box 114-E
Tillatoba, MS 38961

Missouri

Huna Research, Inc.
1760 Anna St.
Cape Girardeau, MO 63701-4504

Bible Way Association
PO Box 370
Doniphan, MO 63935

United American Orthodox Catholic Church
1000 Lake Maurer Rd.
Excelsior Springs, MO 64024

Davidian Seventh-day Adventist Association
Bashan Hill
Exeter, MO 65647

Shepherdsfield Community
777 Shepherdsfield Rd.
Fulton, MO 65251-9473

United Pentecostal Church International
8855 Dunn Rd.
Hazelwood, MO 63042

Christ Catholic Church
405 Kentling Rd.
Highlandsville, MO 65669

Center Branch of the Lord's Remnant
709 W Maple
Independence, MO 64050

Church of Christ (Fetting/Bronson)
1138 E Gudgell
Independence, MO 64055

Church of Christ (Temple Lot)
PO Box 472
Independence, MO 65051

The Church of Christ "with the Elijah
Message," Established in 1929 Anew
PO Box 1134
Independence, MO 64051

Church of Jesus Christ (Cutlerite)
807 S Cottage St.
Independence, MO 64050

Church of Jesus Christ (Zion's Branch)
108 S Pleasant
Independence, MO 64050-3605

Community of Christ
1001 W Walnut
Independence, MO 64050-3562

Restoration Branches Movement
915 E 23rd St.
Independence, MO 64055

Restoration Church of Jesus Christ of
Latter-day Saints
PO Box 2027
Independence, MO 64055

Pentecostal Church of God
PO Box 850
Joplin, MO 64834

Anglo-Lutheran Catholic Church
1200 NE 81st Terr.
Kansas City, MO 64118-1361

Association of Fundamental Ministers and
Churches
8605 E 55th St.
Kansas City, MO 64129

Association of Gospel Rescue Missions
1045 Swift St.
Kansas City, MO 64116-4127

Augustana Evangelical Catholic Communion
1200 NE 81st Terr.
Kansas City, MO 64118-1361

Church of the Nazarene
6401 The Paseo
Kansas City, MO 64131

Mid-America Dharma Group
455 E 80th Terr.
Kansas City, MO 64131

Missouri Valley Friends Conference
4405 Gillhan Rd.
Kansas City, MO 64110

Church of God, in Truth
PO Box 1120
Kimberling City, MO 65686

Yahweh's New Covenant Assembly
PO Box 50
Kingdom City, MO 65262

Zion's Order, Inc.
Rte. 2, Box 104-7
Mansfield, MO 65704

Church of Interfaith Christians
PO Box 924
Nixa, MO 65714-0924

Church of Christ (David Clark)
PO Box 126
Oak Grove, MO 64075

Society of St. Pius X
11485 N Farley Rd.
Platte City, MO 64079

General Association of General Baptists
100 Stinson Dr.
Poplar Bluff, MO 63901

Yahweh's Assembly in Messiah
401 N Roby Farm Rd., No. 1
Rocheport, MO 65279

Church of Christ at Halley's Bluff
Schell City, MO 64783

Church of Israel
PO Box 62 B3
Schell City, MO 64783

Baptist Bible Fellowship International
PO Box 191
Springfield, MO 65801

Evangelical Old Catholic Communion
1420 S. Catalina Ave.
Springfield, MO 65804

Fundamental Methodist Conference
1034 N Broadway
Springfield, MO 65802

General Council of the Assemblies of God
1445 N Boonville Ave.
Springfield, MO 65802-1894

Divine Science Federation International
8084 Watson Rd., Ste. 236
St. Louis, MO 63119

International Lutheran Council
1333 S. Kirkwood Rd.
St. Louis, MO 63122-7295

Lutheran Church—Missouri Synod
1333 S Kirkwood Rd.
St. Louis, MO 63122-7295

Newfrontiers
St. Louis, MO

North American Interfaith Network (NAIN)
4910 Valley Crest Dr.
St. Louis, MO 64128-1829

Spiritual Human Yoga (SHY)
7321 S Lindbergh Blvd., Ste. 209
St. Louis, MO 63125

Universal Great Brotherhood
6002 Pershing
St. Louis, MO 63112

Unity School of Christianity
1901 NW Blue Pkwy.
Unity Village, MO 64065-0001

Interfaith Church of Metaphysics (ICOM)
163 Moon Valley Rd.
Windyville, MO 65783

Montana

Agasha Temple of Wisdom
PO Box 80483
Billings, MT 59108

Church Universal and Triumphant
10 East Gate Rd.
Gardiner, MT 59030

Baha'is Under the Provisions of the
Covenant (Leland Jensen)
PO Box 65
Missoula, MT 59806

Baha'is Under the Provisions of the
Covenant (Neal Chase)
248A North Higgins #126
Missoula, MT 59802

Hutterian Brethren-Dariusleut
Stanford, MT 59479

Hutterian Brethren-Lehrerleut
Wolf Creek, MT 59648

Nebraska

Emmanuel's Fellowship
8345 Crown Point Ave.
Omaha, NE 68134-1905

Fellowship of Evangelical Bible Churches
3339 N 109th Plz.
Omaha, NE 68164-2908

Order of the Prairie Wind
3625 Lafayette Ave.
Omaha, NE 68131

Nevada

Traditional Yoga Academy
6530 Annie Oakley Dr. #2825
Henderson, NV 89014

Albanian Orthodox Diocese of America
6455 Silver Dawn Ln.
Las Vegas, NV 89118

Institute of Cosmic Wisdom
3528 Franciscan Ln.
Las Vegas, NV 89121

Restoration Church of God
2375 E Tropicana Ave., Ste. 158
Las Vegas, NV 89119

Rose Ministries
3675 S Rainbow Blvd., Ste. 107–601
Las Vegas, NV 89103

United States Raelian Religion
Topaz Station
Las Vegas, NV 89108

Thelemic Order and Temple of the Golden
Dawn
1755-A Purina Way
Sparks, NV 89431

New Hampshire

Catholic Charismatic Church
240 School St.
Berlin, NH 03570

Foundation for Biblical Research
43 Paris Ave.
Charlestown, NH 03603

Our Lady of Enchantment, Church of the Old
Religion
PO Box 1366
Nashua, NH 03061

Friends of the Western Buddhist Order
(FWBO)
14 Heartwood Cir.
Newmarket, NH 03857

Sant Bani Ashram
30 Ashram Rd.
Sanbornton, NH 03269-2227

New Jersey

Societas Rosicruciana in America
PO Box 1316
Bayonne, NJ 07002-6316

Brahman Samaj of North America
PO Box 716
Belle Mead, NJ 08502

Holy United Orthodox Catholic and
Apostolic Church
PO Box 703
Browns Mills, NJ 08015

Bible Presbyterian Church
1115 Haddon Ave.
Collingswood, NJ 08108

International Association of Reformed and
Presbyterian Churches
756 Haddon Ave.
Collingswood, NJ 08108

Dawn Bible Students Association
199 Railroad Ave.
East Rutherford, NJ 07073

American Catholic Church International
38 Prince St.
Elizabeth, NJ 07208

Mt. Zion Sanctuary
21 Dayton St.
Elizabeth, NJ 07202

Russian Orthodox Autonomous Church
of America
95 Elm St.
Elmwood Park, NJ 07407-1610

Antiochian Orthodox Christian Archdiocese
of North America
358 Mountain Rd.
Englewood, NJ 07631

Ecumenical Catholic Church USA
23 Atrium Way
Englishtown, NJ 07726

Gospel Mission Corps of the American
Rescue Workers
Box 175
Hightstown, NJ 08520

Syro-Malankara Catholic Church
670 Hulses Corner Rd.
Howell, NJ 07731

Deliverance Jesus Is Coming Association of
Churches
43 Harrison Pl.
Irvington, NJ 07111

Vishwa Hindu Parishad of America
PO Box 611
Iselin, NJ 08830

Coptic Orthodox Church
427 West Side Ave.
Jersey City, NJ 07304

Free Spirit Alliance
PO Box 94
Lambertville, NJ 08530-0094

American Vegan Society
56 Dinshah Ln., PO Box 369
Malaga, NJ 08328-0908

Sant Shri Asarmaji Ashram
45 Texas Rd.
Matawan, NJ 07747

Shri Yoga Vedanta Ashram
45 Texas Rd.
Matawan, NJ 07747

Fellowship of Fundamental Bible Churches
284 Whig Ln.
Monroeville, NJ 08343

IMBAS
PO Box 1215
Montague, NJ 07827-0215

Celebrant USA Foundation and Institute
93 Valley Rd., 2nd Fl.
Montclair, NJ 07042

Deliverance Evangelistic Centers, Inc.
826 S 10th St.
Newark, NJ 07108

Universal Church of Christ
491 Orange St.
Newark, NJ 07107

Catholic Apostolic Church International
925 Felix Palm Ave.
North Las Vegas, NJ 89032

Shanti Yoga Institute and Yoga Retreat
943 Central Ave.
Ocean City, NJ 08226

American Association for the Advancement
of Atheism (AAAA)
PO Box 5733
Parsippany, NJ 07054-5733

American Atheists, Inc.
PO Box 5733
Parsippany, NJ 07054-6733

Hungarian Reformed Church in America
220 4th St.
Passaic, NJ 07055

The Moorish Orthodox Church in America
Ongs Hat Rd. & Magnolia Ave.
Pemberton, NJ 08068

Ukrainian Orthodox Church of the USA
PO Box 495
South Bound Brook, NJ 08880

Syrian Orthodox Church of Antioch
(Patriarchal Vicariates of the United
States and Canada) (Jacobite)
260 Elm Ave.
Teaneck, NJ 07666

Syrian Orthodox Church of Malabar
260 Elm Ave.
Teaneck, NJ 07666

Anglican Rite Catholic and Orthodox Church
in America
9 Abaco St.
Toms River, NJ 08757-3736

Syrian Catholic Church
502 Palisade Ave.
Union City, NJ 07087-5213

Orthodox Catholic Patriarchate of America
66 N Brookfield St.
Vineland, NJ 08360

Restored Israel of Yahweh
468 Wheat Rd.
Vineland, NJ 08360

Tibetan Buddhist Learning Center
93 Angen Rd.
Washington, NJ 07882-9767

United Hindu Temple of New Jersey
1 CeCamp Ct.
West Caldwell, NJ 07006

Pillar of Fire
10 Chapel Dr.
Zarephath, NJ 08890

New Mexico

Church of Light
2119 Gold Ave. SE
Albuquerque, NM 87106-4072

Independent Greek Orthodox Church of the
United States
1814 Slate NW
Albuquerque, NM 87104-1320

Pranayana Institute
PO Box 40731
Albuquerque, NM 87196

Union of Messianic Jewish Congregations
529 Jefferson St. NE
Albuquerque, NM 87108

City of the Sun Foundation
Box 370
Columbus, NM 88029

Aggressive Christianity Missions Training
Corps
HR 60, Box 11
Fence Lake, NM 87315

Light Institute
HC-75, Box 50
Galisteo, NM 87540

Apostolic Ministerial Alliance
1530 E Arizona Ave.
Las Cruces, NM 88001

Contemporary Catholic Church
1300-G, El Paseo Blvd.
Las Cruces, NM 88001

Christ's Church Fellowship
PO Box 67
Roswell, NM 88202

Orthodox Baha'i Faith, National Baha'i
Council of the United States
PO Box 3201
Roswell, NM 88202

Russian Orthodox Church in America
1105 W Deming St.
Roswell, NM 88203

Lama Foundation
Box 240
San Cristobal, NM 87564

Church of Antioch/Catholic Apostolic Church
of Antioch
111 W Cordova Rd.
Santa Fe, NM 87505-3623

Hanuman Foundation
223 N Guadalupe St.
Santa Fe, NM 87501

Quimby Amenti Foundation
41 Verano Loop
Santa Fe, NM 87508

Sufi Foundation of America
50 Sufi Rd.
Torreon, NM 87061

New York

Artemisian Order
Capitol Station
Albany, NY 12224

Nation of the Five Percent/Nation of God
and Earths
PO Box 217
Albany, NY 12202-0217

National Catholic Church of America
166 Jay St.
Albany, NY 12210-1806

Pilgrim Holiness Church of New York
32 Cadillac Ave.
Albany, NY 12205

American Humanist Association
7 Harwood Dr., Box 8188
Amherst, NY 14226-7188

Council for Secular Humanism
PO Box 664
Amherst, NY 14226-0664

Institution for the Secularization of Islamic
Society (ISIS)
3965 Rensch Rd.
Amherst, NY 14228

Association of Independent Evangelical
Lutheran Churches
14th St. and 27th Ave.
Astoria, NY 11102

Church of the True Orthodox Christians of
Greece (Synod of Bishop Gregory)
26-37 12th Street
Astoria, NY 11102-3723

American Orthodox Catholic Church
(Propheta)
2004 Esprit Glade
Baldwinsville, NY 13027

Our Lady of the Roses, Mary Help of
Mothers Shrine
Box 611052
Bayside, NY 11361

Malankara Orthodox (Syrian) Church
80-84 Commonwealth Blvd.
Bellerose, NY 11426

Grail Movement of America
2081 Partridge Ln.
Binghamton, NY 13903

The Assembly of Christian Churches, Inc.
722 Prospect Ave.
Bronx, NY 10454

Bible Church of Christ
1358 Morris Ave.
Bronx, NY 10456

Church of the Lord (Aladura)
505 E 183rd St., Apt. #2
Bronx, NY 10458

Damascus Christian Church
170 Mt. Eden Pkwy.
Bronx, NY 10473

Holy Temple Church of the Lord Jesus Christ
of the Apostolic Faith
2075 Clinton Ave.
Bronx, NY 10457

International Divine Realization Society
2285 Sedgwick Ave., No. 102
Bronx, NY 10468

Reformers Ministries International (RMI)
PO Box 743
Bronx, NY 10462

African Islamic Mission
1390 Bedford Ave.
Brooklyn, NY 11216

Ansaaru Allah Community
716 Bushwick Ave.
Brooklyn, NY 11221

Ausar Auset Society
140 Buckingham Rd.
Brooklyn, NY 11226

Belarusan Autocephalous Orthodox Church
in the U.S.A.
401 Atlantic Ave.
Brooklyn, NY 11217

Bible Way Church of Our Lord Jesus Christ
World Wide, Inc.
261 Rochester Ave.
Brooklyn, NY 11213

Bratslav (Breslov) Hasidism
5014 16th Ave., Ste. 263
Brooklyn, NY 11204

Buddhasasananuggaha Association
619 Bergen St.
Brooklyn, NY 11238

Council of Islamic Organizations of America
676 St. Marks Ave.
Brooklyn, NY 11216-3605

Jehovah's Witnesses
25 Columbia Heights
Brooklyn, NY 11201

Maronite Catholic Church
109 Remsen St.
Brooklyn, NY 11201

National Conference for Community and
Justice (NCCJ)
PO Box 402
Brooklyn, NY 11217

People's Christian Church
777–779 Schenectady Ave.
Brooklyn, NY 11203

Pilgrim Assemblies International
9202-14 Church Ave.
Brooklyn, NY 11236

Sabian Assembly
279 President St.
Brooklyn, NY 11231

Tridentine Catholic Church Traditional
Catholic Archdiocese in America
1740 W. 7th St.
Brooklyn, NY 11223-1301

United American Muslim Association
5911 8th Ave.
Brooklyn, NY 11220

Federated Orthodox Catholic Churches
International
407 Donovan Rd.
Brushton, NY 12916

Christ Apostolic Church of America
(Obadare)
PO Box 117
Cambria Heights, NY 11411

Holy Cross Anglican Communion
6 Jefferson
Castile, NY 14427

Servant Catholic Church
50 Coventry Ln.
Central Islip, NY 11722

Jerrahi Order of America
880 Chestnut Ridge Rd.
Chestnut Ridge, NY 10977

United Trungram Buddhist Fellowship
155 Buff Rd.
Cochecton, NY 12726

Ananda Marga Yoga Society
97-38 42nd Ave., 1-F
Corona, NY 11368

Karuna Tendai Dharma Center
1525 Rte. 295
East Chatham, NY 12060

Tendai Buddhist Institute
1525 Rte. 295
East Chatham, NY 12060

Chishti Order of America
PO Box 7249
Endicott, NY 13761

Bochasanwasi Swaminarayan Sanstha
43-38 Bowne St.
Flushing, NY 11355

Hindu Temple Society of North America
45-57 Bowne St.
Flushing, NY 11355

Shaolin Temple
132–11 41st Ave.
Flushing, NY 11355

Won Buddhism
143-42 Cherry Ave.
Flushing, NY 11355

Federation of Jain Associations in North
America (JAINA)
PO Box 700
Getzville, NY 14068

Church of South India
PO Box 40278
Glen Oaks, NY 11004

New Kadampa Tradition (NKT)
Sweeney Rd.
Glen Spey, NY 12737

Brahma Kumaris World Spiritual University
46 S. Middle Neck Rd.
Great Neck, NY 11021

SRV Association of America
20 Jennings Rd.
Greenville, NY 12083

American Catholic Church (Hampton Bays,
New York)
PO Box 725
Hampton Bays, NY 11946

Universal Healing Tao
PO Box 1194
Huntington, NY 11743

Namgyal Monastery Institute of Buddhist
Studies
PO Box 127
Ithaca, NY 14851

Orthodox American Church
33-11 89th St.
Jackson Heights, NY 11372

Islamic Circle of North America
166-26 89th Ave.
Jamaica, NY 11432

Sri Chinmoy Centre
PO Box 32433
Jamaica, NY 11432

Tabernacle of Prayer for All People
Jamaica, NY

Ukrainian Orthodox Church in America
(Ecumenical Patriarchate)
9034 139th St.
Jamaica, NY 11435

Arunachala Ashrama
86-06 Edgerton Blvd.
Jamaica Heights, NY 11432

Kirpal Light Satsang
109 Merwin Lake Rd.
Kinderhook, NY 12106

National Spiritualist Association of Churches
PO Box 217
Lily Dale, NY 14752

Elim Fellowship
1703 Dalton Rd.
Lima, NY 14485-9516

World Plan Executive Council-US
139 Waldemere Rd.
Livingston Manor, NY 12758

Zen Studies Society
223 Beecher Lake Rd.
Livingston Manor, NY 12758-6000

Spiritual Realization Institute
PO Box 305
Lockport, NY 14095-0305

Fraternite Blanche Universelle (FBU—USA)
PO Box 932
Locust Valley, NY 11560

Embassy of the Gheez-Americans
Box 53
Long Eddy, NY 12760

International Communion of the
Charismatic Episcopal Church
50 St. Thomas Pl.
Malverne, NY 11565

American Orthodox Catholic
Church—Western Rite Mission, Diocese of
New York
318 Expressway Dr. S
Medford, NY 11763

Ananda Ashrama
13 Sapphire Rd.
Monroe, NY 10950

Neturei Karta of USA
Box 1315
Monsey, NY 10952

Hawthorn Grove
Box 706
Monticello, NY 12701-0706

The Mountains and Rivers Order (MRO)
South Plank Rd.
Mount Tremper, NY 12457

White Plum Asanga
South Plank Rd.
Mount Tremper, NY 12457

Qadiri Rifai Tariqa/Ansari Tariqa
PO Box 833
Nassau, NY 12123

Sufi Order
5 Abode Rd.
New Lebanon, NY 12125

Advent Sabbath Church
255 W 131st St.
New York, NY 10027

African Orthodox Church, Inc.
122 W 129th St.
New York, NY 10023

Agni Yoga Society
319 W 107th St.
New York, NY 10025

American Buddhist Movement
301 W 45th St.
New York, NY 10036

American Ethical Union
2 W 64th St.
New York, NY 10023

American Sephardi Federation
15 W 16th St., 6th Fl.
New York, NY 10011

Arcane Magical Order of the Knights of
Shambhala (AMOOKOS)
Grand Central Station
New York, NY 10163

Arcane School
120 Wall St., 24th fl.
New York, NY 10005

Armenian Apostolic Church of America
138 E 39th St.
New York, NY 10016

Armenian Catholic Church
110 E 12th St.
New York, NY 10003

Buddhist Association of the United States
3070 Albany Cres.
New York, NY 10463

Bulgarian Eastern Orthodox Diocese of the
USA, Canada, and Australia
550-A W 50th St.
New York, NY 10019

Chosen People Ministries
241 E 51st St.
New York, NY 10022

Church of Bible Understanding
Radio City Station
New York, NY 10019-0841

Church of Our Lord Jesus Christ of the
Apostolic Faith
2081 Adam Clayton Powell Blvd.
New York, NY 10029

Church of Satan
PO Box 499
New York, NY 10101-0499

Commandment Keepers Ethiopian Hebrew
Congregation of the Living God
PO Box 235
New York, NY 10027

Congregation Bina—Indian Jewish
Congregation of USA
33 E 12th St.
New York, NY 10023

Congregation Kehillath Yaakov (Kehilat
Jacob)
305 W. 79th St.
New York, NY 10024

Conservative Judaism
155 5th Ave.
New York, NY 10010

Daheshism
304 W 58th St.
New York, NY 10019-1107

Dharma Mittra Yoga
297 3rd Ave. at 23rd St.
New York, NY 10010

Diocese of the Armenian Church of America
630 2nd Ave.
New York, NY 10016

Eastern States Buddhist Association
of America
64 Mott St.
New York, NY 10013

Eclesia Catolica Cristina
2123 Grand Ave.
New York, NY 10453

Episcopal Church
815 2nd Ave.
New York, NY 10017

Falun Gong (Falun Dafa)
331 W 57th St., Ste. 409
New York, NY 10019

First Zen Institute of America
113 E 30th St.
New York, NY 10016

Greek Orthodox Archdiocese of America
8-10 E 79th St.
New York, NY 10021

Hermetic Society for World Service, United
States
423 W 50th St.
New York, NY 10019-6502

Indo-American Yoga-Vedanta Society
30 W 58th St., Apt. 11-J
New York, NY 10019

Inter Religious Federation for World Peace
481 8th Ave.
New York, NY 10011

International Gurukulam
114 E 28th St. # 2A
New York, NY 10016

Israelite Church of God and Jesus Christ, Inc.
1941 Madison Ave. (125th St.)
New York, NY 10027

Jain Meditation International Center
Box 230244, Ansonia Sta.
New York, NY 10023-0244

K'hal Adath Jeshurun
85 Bennett Ave.
New York, NY 10033

Latin-American Council of the Pentecostal
Church of God of New York
115 E 125th St.
New York, NY 10035

Mahayog Foundation
51 E 42nd St. #521
New York, NY 10017

Muslim World League
Box 1674
New York, NY 10001-6803

National Council of Churches of Christ in
the U.S.A.
475 Riverside Dr.
New York, NY 10115-0050

National Council of Young Israel
3 W 16th St.
New York, NY 10011

New Synagogue
86th St. and Amsterdam Ave.
New York, NY 10025

New York Board of Rabbis
136 E 39th St.
New York, NY 10016-0914

The Nimatullahi Sufi Order
306 W 11th St.
New York, NY 10014

North American Coalition to Advance
Religious Pluralism in Israel
820 2nd Ave.
New York, NY 10017-4504

Ordo Templi Orientis
JAF Box 7666
New York, NY 10116

Orthodox Catholic Church in America
(Verra)
238 Mott St.
New York, NY 10012

Orthodox Judaism
305 7th Ave.
New York, NY 10001

Osho Commune International
80 Fifth Ave., Ste. 1403
New York, NY 10011

Patriarchal Parishes of the Russian Orthodox
Church in the U.S.A.
15 E 97th St.
New York, NY 10029

Ramakrishnananda Yoga Vedanta Mission
96 Ave. B
New York, NY 10009

Reform Judaism
633 Third Ave.
New York, NY 10017

Reformed Church in America
475 Riverside Dr.
New York, NY 10115

Russian Orthodox Church Outside of Russia
75 E 93rd St.
New York, NY 10028

Salvation and Deliverance Church
37 W. 116 St.
New York, NY 10026

Seventh-day Christian Conference Inc.
252 W 138th St.
New York, NY 10030

Society of Jewish Science
109 E 39th St.
New York, NY 10016

Standing Conference of Canonical Orthodox
Bishops in the Americas
10 E 79th St.
New York, NY 10075

Temple of the True Inner Light
New York, NY

Temple of Understanding
211 E 43rd St., Ste. 1600
New York, NY 10017

U.S.A. Shaolin Temple
446 Broadway, 2nd Fl.
New York, NY 10013

Unification Movement
4 W 43rd St.
New York, NY 10036

Union of Orthodox Rabbis of the United
States and Canada
235 East Broadway
New York, NY 10002

United Church and Science of Living
Institute
4140 Broadway
New York, NY 10033

United Israel World Union (UIWU)
200 East 10th St., Ste. 111
New York, NY 10003

United Wesleyan Methodist Church of
America
270 W 126th St.
New York, NY 10027

Urantia Book Fellowship
Grand Central Station
New York, NY 10163

World Conference of Religions for Peace
(WCRP)
777 United Nations Plz.
New York, NY 10017

World Council of Churches
425 Riverside Dr.
New York, NY 10115

World Council of Independent Christian
Churches (WCICC)
PO Box 76
New York, NY 10274-0076

Yeshe Nyingpo
19 W 16th St.
New York, NY 10011

Evangelical Wesleyan Church
219 Fox Hill Rd.
Northville, NY 12134

American World Patriarchates
19 Aqueduct St.
Ossining, NY 10562

Society of St. Pius V
8 Pond Pl.
Oyster Bay Cove, NY 11771

American Traditional Catholic Church (ATCC)
104-11 95th Ave.
Ozone Park, NY 11416-1808

Holy Orthodox Church in America
PO Box 192-B
Preston Hollow, NY 12469

Apostolic Episcopal Church
80-46 234th St.
Queens, NY 11427

His Highness Prince Aga Khan Shia Imani
Ismaili Council for the United States of
America
PO Box 77
Rego Park, NY 11374

Sikh Council of North America
95-30 118th St.
Richmond Hill, NY 11419

Church Communities International (formerly
Bruderhof Communities in New York)
Woodcrest, 2032 Rte. 213
Rifton, NY 12471

General Assembly of Spiritualists
27 Appleton St.
Rochester, NY 14611

Latin-Rite Catholic Church
Box 16194
Rochester, NY 14616

Megiddo Church
481 Thurston Rd.
Rochester, NY 14619

The Word Foundation, Inc.
PO Box 17510
Rochester, NY 14617

Holy Shankaracharya Order
6980 E River Rd.
Rush, NY 14543

Barry Long Foundation International
218 Clove Rd.
Salisbury Mills, NY 12577

Padmasambhava Buddhist Centers
618 Buddha Hwy.
Sidney Center, NY 13839

Russian-Ukrainian Evangelical Baptist Union
of the U.S.A., Inc.
52 Steele Ave.
Somerville, NY 08876

SYDA Foundation
371 Brickman Rd., Box 600
South Fallsburg, NY 12779

Ma Yoga Shakti International Mission
114-41 Lefferts Blvd.
South Ozone Park, NY 11420

Shanti Temple
43 S Main St.
Spring Valley, NY 10977

Springwater Center
7179 Mill St.
Springwater, NY 14560

North American Old Roman Catholic Church
(Rogers)
118-09 Farmers Blvd.
St. Albans, NY 11412

International Nahavir Jain Mission
722 Tomkins Ave.
Staten Island, NY 10305

Italo-Albanian Catholic Church
51 Redgrave Ave.
Staten Island, NY 10306

Worldwide Pentecostal Church of Christ
292 Vanduzer St.
Staten Island, NY 10304

Greek Orthodox Missionary Archdiocese of
Vasiloupolis
44-02 48th Ave.
Sunnyside/Woodside, NY 11377

Orthodox Church in America
PO Box 675
Syosset, NY 11791

Macedonian Orthodox Church
5073 Onondaga Rd.
Syracuse, NY 13215

Servants of the Light (SOL)
PO Box 6563
Syracuse, NY 13217-6563

Confraternity of the Rose Cross
PO Box 304
Tillson, NY 12486-0304

Shanti Mandir
51 Mulktananda Marg
Walden, NY 12586

Institute for Religious Development
7 Chardavogne Rd.
Warwick, NY 10990

Zion Fellowship International
PO Box 79
Waverly, NY 14892

World Pantheist Movement
PO Box 103
Webster, NY 14580

Ecumenical Catholic Diocese of America
151 Regent Pl.
West Hemstead, NY 11552

Karma Triyana Dharmachakra (KTD)
335 Meads Mountain Rd.
Woodstock, NY 12498

Mount Hebron Apostolic Temple of Our Lord
Jesus of the Apostolic Faith
27 Vineyard Ave.
Yonkers, NY 10703

Zen Community of New York
21 Park Ave.
Yonkers, NY 10703

North Carolina

International Christian Community Churches
PO Box 6787
Asheville, NC 28816

School for Esoteric Studies
345 S French Broad Ave., Ste. 300
Asheville, NC 28801

Convention of Original Free Will Baptists
Box 39
Ayden, NC 28513

Universal Gnostic Fellowship
507 Old Toll Cir.
Black Mountain, NC 28711

Emmanuel Holiness Church
PO Box 818
Bladenboro, NC 28320

Rifa'i Marufi Sufi Fellowship/Universal
Center of Light
PO Box 202
Chapel Hill, NC 27514-0202

Advent Christian General Conference
PO Box 690848
Charlotte, NC 28227

African Methodist Episcopal Zion Church
3225 Sugar Creek Rd.
Charlotte, NC 28269

Carolina Evangelistic Association
7700 Wallace Rd.
Charlotte, NC 28212

Church of the Great God
PO Box 471846
Charlotte, NC 28247-1846

Living Church of God
PO Box 3810
Charlotte, NC 28227-8010

Missionary Methodist Church of America
318 Ballard St.
Cherryville, NC 28021

Pentecostal Free Will Baptist Church
PO Box 1568
Dunn, NC 28335

Covenant of Unitarian Universalist Pagans
(CUUPS)
PO Box 3128
Durham, NC 27715-3128

Christian Spirit Center
Box 114
Elon College, NC 27244

United Gospel Fellowship Covenant
Ministries
2400 Murchison Rd.
Fayetteville, NC 28302

Fundamental Brethren Church
424 Griffith Rd.
Green Mountain, NC 28740

North Carolina Yearly Meeting of Friends
(Conservative)
PO Box 4591
Greensboro, NC 27404

Shiloh True Light Church of Christ
Rte. 1, Box 426
Indian Trail, NC 28079

World Methodist Council
Box 518
Lake Junaluska, NC 28745

Orthodox Anglican Church
464 N. County Home Rd.
Lexington, NC 27292

Upper Triad Association
PO Box 825
Madison, NC 27025

Church of God, Body of Christ
159 Parker Rd.
Mocksville, NC 27028-1074

Societas Rosicruciana in Civitatibus
Foederatis
406 Harris Ln.
Monroe, NC 28112

Anglican Orthodox Church
PO Box 128
Statesville, NC 28687

United Episcopal Church of North America
614 Pebblestone Ct.
Statesville, NC 28677

Apostolic Faith Church of God Giving Grace
Rte. 3, Box 111G
Warrenton, NC 27589

New Beginnings
PO Box 228
Waynesville, NC 28786

Apostolic Church of Christ
2044 Martin Luther King, Jr., Dr.
Winston-Salem, NC 27107

Apostolic Church of Christ in God
1217 E 15th St.
Winston-Salem, NC 27105

Church of God Apostolic, Inc. (COGA)
PO Box 12187
Winston-Salem, NC 27107

True Vine Pentecostal Holiness Church
500 Kinard Dr.
Winston-Salem, NC 27101

Ohio

Beth-El Fellowship of Visionary Churches
1650 Diagonal Rd.
Akron, OH 44320

Celtic Orthodox Christian Church
Box 72102
Akron, OH 44372

Orthodox Catholic Church of North and
South America
PO Box 1213
Akron, OH 44309

Brethren Church (Ashland, Ohio)
524 College Ave.
Ashland, OH 44805

International General Assembly of
Spiritualists
5403 S Ridge W
Ashtabula, OH 44004

Ohio Yearly Meeting of the Society of
Friends, Conservative
108 Fowler Ave.
Barnesville, OH 43713-1176

Global Independent Baptist Fellowship
4431 Tiedeman Rd.
Brooklyn, OH 44144

World Harvest Church
4595 Gender Rd.
Canal Winchester, OH 43110

Evangelical Friends Church—Eastern Region
5350 Broadmoor Cir. NW
Canton, OH 44709

Evangelical Friends International
5350 Broadmoor Cir. NW
Canton, OH 44709

Romanian Greek Catholic Church
1121 44th St. NE
Canton, OH 44714

Friends Catholic Communion
PO Box 60
Chesapeake, OH 45619-0060

Church of the Blessed Hope
7450 Wilson Mills Rd.
Chesterland, OH 44026

Christ Catholic Orthodox Church
2079 Harkness Ave.
Cincinnati, OH 45225

Christian Churches and Churches of Christ
110 Boggs Ln., Ste. 330
Cincinnati, OH 45246

Church of the Living God (Christian Workers
for Fellowship)
434 Forest Ave.
Cincinnati, OH 45229

Churches of Christ in Christian Union
1426 Lancaster Pke.
Circleville, OH 43113

Church of God (O'Beirn)
13022 Kingston Way
Cleveland, OH 44133

Church of Reason
3359 W 58th St.
Cleveland, OH 44102-5670

House of F.A.M.E. Mansions of Glory
3846 W 133rd St.
Cleveland, OH 44111

Joint College of African American
Pentecostal Bishops
10515 Chester Ave.
Cleveland, OH 44106

United Church of Christ
700 Prospect Ave.
Cleveland, OH 44115-1100

Old Order (Reidenbach) Mennonites
Rte. 1
Columbiana, OH 44408

Old Order (Wenger) Mennonites
Rte. 1
Columbiana, OH 44408

Old Order (Wisler) Mennonite Church
Rte. 1
Columbiana, OH 44408

Ahmadiyya Anjuman Ishaat Islam, Lahore,
Inc.
1315 Kingsgate Rd.
Columbus, OH 43221-1504

Emmanuel Tabernacle Baptist Church
Apostolic Faith
329-333 N Garfield Ave.
Columbus, OH 43203

Great Commission Association of Churches
PO Box 29154
Columbus, OH 43229

Ohio Bible Fellowship
3865 N High St.
Columbus, OH 43214-3797

Separate Baptists in Christ
14470 S. Jonesville Rd.
Columbus, OH 47201

International Ministers Forum
PO Box 1717
Dayton, OH 45401-1717

Apostolic Christian Church of America
14834 Campbell Rd.
Defiance, OH 43512

Reformed Druids of North America (RDNA)
PO Box 353
Elmore, OH 43416-0353

Original Glorious Church of God in Christ
Apostolic Faith
995 Foster Ave.
Elyria, OH 44035

Churches of God, General Conference
PO Box 926
Findlay, OH 45839

Christian Nation Church, U.S.A.
10059 Pleasant Renner Rd.
Goshen, OH 45122

Christian Union
PO Box 27
Greenfield, OH 45123

Conservative Mennonite Fellowship
(Nonconference)
PO Box 36
Hartville, OH 44632

Conservative Mennonite Conference
9910 Rosedale-Milford Center Rd.
Irwin, OH 43029

Assembly of God in Christ Jesus
PO Box 770537
Lakewood, OH 44107

Association of Free Reformed Churches
14030 Radcliffe Rd.
Leroy Township, OH 44077

International Pentecostal Church of Christ
(IPCC)
2245 U.S. 42 SW
London, OH 43140

Ipsalu Tantra
PO Box 516
Loveland, OH 45140-3065

Alliance for Renewal Churches
365 Straub Rd. E
Mansfield, OH 44903-8434

The Way International
PO Box 328
New Knoxville, OH 45871

SOL Association for Research
Box 2276
North Canton, OH 44720

Bulgarian Eastern Orthodox Church (Diocese
of North and South America)
519 Brynhaven Dr.
Oregon, OH 43616

Beachy Amish Mennonite Churches
9650 Iams Rd.
Plain City, OH 43064

Allegheny Wesleyan Methodist Connection
2291 Depot Rd.
Salem, OH 44460

Interdenominational Holiness Convention
Salem, OH

Odinic Rite Vinland
PO Box 2022
Sandusky, OH 44871-2022

Anointed Word Ministries and Fellowships
International
PO Box 3006
Springfield, OH 45502

Autocephalous Traditional Orthodox
    Catholic Church
Box 17105
St. Bernard, OH 45217

Apostles Anglican Church
1375 Syvania Ave.
Toledo, OH 43612

Brotherhood of Mithras
Box 94
Uniontown, OH 44685-0094

Restored Church of God
PO Box 23295
Wadsworth, OH 44282

Seax-Wica
PO Box 892
Wooster, OH 44691-0892

Reformed Catholic Church
PO Box 2
Worthington, OH 43085

Oklahoma

Church of God (Anadarko)
900 W Alabama Ave.
Anadarko, OK 73006

International Fellowship of Bible
    Churches, Inc.
PO Box 1222
Bethany, OK 73008

Divine Love Mission
17409 Durbin Park Rd.
Edmond, OK 73003

Philadelphia Church of God
PO Box 3700
Edmond, OK 73083-3700

Church of God (Guthrie, Oklahoma)
304 E. Lakeview Rd.
Guthrie, OK 73044

Deaf Ministries Worldwide Fellowship
PO Box 10833
Midwest City, OK 73140

Pentecostal Faith Assemblies
PO Box 6054
Moore, OK 73153

Elohim City
Muldrow, OK 74948

Bible Churches (Classics Expositor)
1429 NW 100th St.
Oklahoma City, OK 73114

Church of God (Which He Purchased with
    His Own Blood)
1628 NE 50th
Oklahoma City, OK 73111

International Pentecostal Holiness Church
7300 NW 39th Expressway
Oklahoma City, OK 73157-2609

Pentecostal World Fellowship
PO Box 12609
Oklahoma City, OK 73157

Light of Christ Community Church
11 Summit Ridge Dr.
Tahlequah, OK 74464-9215

Azusa Interdenominational Fellowship of
    Christian Churches
8621 S. Memorial Dr.
Tulsa, OK 74133-4312

Church of God of Apostolic Faith
PO Box 691745
Tulsa, OK 74169-1745

Churches of God (Independent Holiness
    People)
PO Box 472202
Tulsa, OK 74147

Churches of God Outreach Ministries
PO Box 54621
Tulsa, OK 74155-0621

Faith Christian Fellowship International
PO Box 35443
Tulsa, OK 74153-0443

Full Gospel Evangelistic Association (FGEA)
1400 East Skelly Dr.
Tulsa, OK 74105-4742

Rhema
PO Box 50126
Tulsa, OK 74150-0126

St. Matthew's Churches
PO Box 3036
Tulsa, OK 74101-3036

Victory Fellowship of Ministries (VFM)
7700 S Lewis
Tulsa, OK 74136-7700

Oregon

Gangaji Foundation
2245 Ashland St.
Ashland, OR 97520

Metamorphosis League for Monastic
    Studies
4130 SW 117th Ave., Ste. 171
Beaverton, OR 97005

Zen Community of Oregon
PO Box 188
Clatskanie, OR 97016

North Pacific Yearly Meeting of the Religious
    Society of Friends
3311 NW Polk
Corvallis, OR 97330

Federation of Independent Catholic and
    Orthodox Bishops
32378 Lynx Hollow Rd.
Creswell, OR 97426

Bible Study Association
28877 Summerville Rd.
Eugene, OR 97405

Church of God (Reinertsen)
33738 McKenzie Vw. Dr.
Eugene, OR 97401

Church of God, the Eternal
PO Box 775
Eugene, OR 97440-0775

Church of Ishtar
PO Box 282
Eugene, OR 97440

Sufi Ruhaniat International (Sufi Islamia
    Ruhaniat Society)
PO Box 51118
Eugene, OR 97405

Foundation of Human Understanding
Box 1000
Grants Pass, OR 97528

Northwest Yearly Meeting of Friends Church
200 N Meridian St.
Newberg, OR 97132-2714

Ancient Teachings of the Masters (ATOM)
PO Box 68322
Oak Grove, OR 97268

Chirothesian Church of Faith
PO Box 1264
Port Orford, OR 97465

Aleister Crowley Foundation
PO Box 8052
Portland, OR 97280

The Apostolic Faith Mission of Portland,
    Oregon, Inc.
6615 SE 52nd Ave.
Portland, OR 97206-7660

Associates for Scriptural Knowledge
PO Box 25000
Portland, OR 97298-0990

Dharma Rain Zen Center
2539 SE Madison
Portland, OR 97214

Faith Tabernacle Council of Churches,
    International
7015 NE 23rd Ave.
Portland, OR 97211

Foundation for the Preservation of the
    Mahayana Tradition (FPMT)
1632 SE 11th Ave.
Portland, OR 97214-4702

Full Gospel Pentecostal Association
1032 N Sumner
Portland, OR 97217

Ministers Fellowship International (MFI)
9200 NE Fremont
Portland, OR 97220

National Black Evangelistic Association
5736 N Albina Ave.
Portland, OR 97217

Nityananda Institute, Inc.
PO Box 13310
Portland, OR 97232

Thelemic Gnostic Church of Alexandria
PO Box 8052
Portland, OR 97280

Divine Word Foundation
1999 Pine Grove Rd.
Rogue River, OR 97537

Church of the New Covenant in Christ
Box 3910
Salem, OR 97302

Church of the Trinity (Invisible Ministry)
Box 4608
Salem, OR 97302-8608

Science of Man Church
52501 E Sylvan Dr.
Sandy, OR 97055

Soulcraft Enterprises, Inc.
PO Box 1410
Silverton, OR 97381

Union of Independent Catholic Churches of
    the North American Old Catholic Church
135 Fiske St.
Silverton, OR 97381-2012

Church of the Culdees
2665 C St.
Springfield, OR 97477

Embassy of Heaven Church
8777 Basl Hill Rd. SE
Strayton, OR 97383-9630

Solar Light Retreat
7700 Avenue of the Sun
White City, OR 97503

Pennsylvania

Assemblies of Yahweh
PO Box C
Bethel, PA 19507

American Council of Christian Churches
PO Box 5455
Bethlehem, PA 18015

Moravian Church in North America
PO Box 1245
Bethlehem, PA 18016-1245

Reformed Episcopal Church
260 Second Ave.
Blue Bell, PA 19422

The Lord's New Church Which Is Nova
    Hierosolyma
PO Box 7
Bryn Athyn, PA 19009

The New Church/General Church of the New
    Jerusalem
PO Box 743
Bryn Athyn, PA 19009

Celtic Christian Church
PO Box 299
Canadensis, PA 18325-0299

Association of Reformed Baptist Churches of
America (ARBCA)
401 E Louther St.
Carlisle, PA 17013

Church of Universal Eclectic Wicca
PO Box 1
Center Valley, PA 18034

Laymen's Home Missionary Movement
1156 St. Matthews Rd.
Chester Springs, PA 19425-2700

United Christian Church
523 W Walnut St.
Cleona, PA 17042

Full Gospel Assemblies International
PO Box 1230
Coatesville, PA 19320-1230

Anoopam Mission
2120 Clearview Rd.
Coplay, PA 18037

United Zion Church
181 Hurst Dr.
Ephrata, PA 17522

Parkville Bible Church
800 Whisler Rd.
Etters, PA 17319

Free Gospel Church, Inc.
PO Box 477
Export, PA 15632

The Peace Mission Movement
1622 Spring Mill Rd.
Gladwyne, PA 19035-1021

World Reformed Fellowship
430 Montier Rd.
Glenside, PA 19038

Brethren in Christ
PO Box A
Grantham, PA 17027-0290

Apostolic Orthodox Church (Harrisburg,
Pennsylvania)
2410 Derry St.
Harrisburg, PA 17111-1141

Primitive Methodist Church USA
730 Preston Ln.
Hatboro, PA 19040

Himalayan International Institute of Yoga
Science and Philosophy
952 Bethany Tpke.
Honesdale, PA 18431

Delval UFO, Inc.
948 Almshouse Rd.
Ivyland, PA 18974

Church of Spiritual Humanism
PO Box 180
Jenkintown, PA 19046

Jewish Reconstructionist Federation
101 Greenwood Ave.
Jenkintown, PA 19046

American Carpatho-Russian Orthodox Greek
Catholic Church
312 Garfield St.
Johnstown, PA 15906

Weaver Mennonites
1259 Scalp Ave.
Johnstown, PA 15904

Reformed Mennonite Church
602 Strasburg Pke.
Lancaster, PA 17602

DOVE Christian Fellowship International
(DFCI)
11 Toll Gate Rd.
Lititz, PA 17543

Congregational Bible Church
PO Box 180
Marietta, PA 17547

Voice of the Nazarene Association of
Churches
PO Box 606
Meadow Lands, PA 15347-0606

God's Missionary Church
125 N Main St.
Middleburg, PA 17842

Church of Jesus Christ (Bickertonite)
6th & Lincoln Sts.
Monongahela, PA 15063

Evangelical Congregational Church
100 W Park Ave.
Myerstown, PA 17067

Lutheran Orthodox Church
PO Box 74
Neffs, PA 18065

Antioch International Ministries (AIM)
PO Box 169
New Wilmington, PA 16142

Twentieth Century Church of God
(Pennsylvania)
PO Box 25
Nineveh, PA 15344

Sri Venkateswara Temple
PO Box 17289
Penn Hills, PA 15235

Alliance of Confessing Evangelicals
1716 Spruce St.
Philadelphia, PA 19103

American Presbyterian Church
1647 Dyre St.
Philadelphia, PA 19124-1340

Anglican Church in America
PO Box 37635 #54594
Philadelphia, PA 19101-0635

Aquarian Research Foundation
5620 Morton St.
Philadelphia, PA 19144

Bawa Muhaiyaddeen Fellowship
5820 Overbrook Ave.
Philadelphia, PA 19131

Calvary Holiness Church
3415-19 N Second St.
Philadelphia, PA 19140

Church of the Lord Jesus Christ of the
Apostolic Faith (Philadelphia)
701 S 22nd St.
Philadelphia, PA 19146

Deliverance Evangelistic Church
2001 W. Lehigh Ave.
Philadelphia, PA 19132

Freedom Worldwide Covenant Ministries
6100 W Columbia Ave.
Philadelphia, PA 19151

Friends General Conference
1216 Arch St., 2B
Philadelphia, PA 19107

Friends World Committee for Consultation
1506 Race St.
Philadelphia, PA 19102

Independent Catholic Christian Church
721 Melon Terr., Unit A
Philadelphia, PA 19103

Mount Sinai Holy Church of America, Inc.
1469 N Broad St.
Philadelphia, PA 19122-3327

National Havurah Committee (NHC)
7135 Germantown Ave., 2nd Fl.
Philadelphia, PA 19119-1842

P'nai Or Religious Fellowship
6445 Greene St., #A-401
Philadelphia, PA 19119

Shiloh Apostolic Temple
1516 W Master
Philadelphia, PA 19121

Swami Kuvalayananda Yoga Foundation
339 Fitzwater St.
Philadelphia, PA 19147

Christianbrunn Brotherhood
RR1, Box 149
Pitman, PA 17964

Kodesh Church of Emmanuel
2601 Centre Ave.
Pittsburgh, PA 15219

Reformed Presbyterian Church of North
America
7408 Penn Ave.
Pittsburgh, PA 15208

Ruthenian Catholic Church
66 Riverview Ave.
Pittsburgh, PA 15214-2253

Society Ordo Templi Orientis International
PO Box 59326
Pittsburgh, PA 15210

Atheist Alliance International (AAI)
PO Box 234
Pocopson, PA 19366

Fraternitas Rosae Crucis
Beverly Hall
Quakertown, PA 18951

Holy Catholic Church (Anglican Rite)
44 S. 8th St.
Quakertown, PA 18951-5334

Arsha Vidya Pitham
PO Box 1059
Saylorsburg, PA 18353

Polish National Catholic Church
1006 Pittston Ave.
Scranton, PA 18505

Independent Baptist Fellowship of North
America (IBFNA)
754 E Rockhill Rd.
Sellersville, PA 18960-1799

Christian Missionary Anglican Communion
PO Box 228
Slatington, PA 18080

Datta Yoga Center
Moniteau Rd, RD 2, Box 2084
Sunbury, PA 16061

Plymouth Brethren (Reunited Brethren)
PO Box 261
Sunbury, PA 17801

General Council of Christian Church of North
America (CCNA)
1294 Rutledge Rd.
Transfer, PA 16154

Association of Evangelicals for Italian
Missions
314 Richfield Rd.
Upper Darby, PA 19082

American Baptist Churches in the U.S.A.
PO Box 851
Valley Forge, PA 19481

Bible Fellowship Church
3000 Fellowship Dr.
Whitehall, PA 18052

American Rescue Workers (ARW)
25 Ross St.
Williamsport, PA 17701

North American Presbyterian and Reformed
Council (NAPARC)
607 N Easton Rd., Bldg. E, Box P
Willow Grove, PA 19090-0920

Orthodox Presbyterian Church
607 N Eastern Rd., Bldg. E, Box P
Willow Grove, PA 19090-0920

Schwenkfelder Church in America
Valley Forge Rd.
Worcester, PA 19490

(Original) Church of God
220 S 11th St.
Wytheville, PA 24382

Puerto Rico

Defenders of the Faith
PO Box 2816
Bayamon, PR 00621-0816

La Iglesia de Dios, Inc.
PO Box 72
Caguas, PR 00725

Mita's Congregation
Calle Duarte 235
Hata Rey, PR 60919

Iglesia Evangelica Congregacional, Inc., de
Puerto Rico
Box 396
Humacao, PR 00792

Rhode Island

Kwan Um School of Zen
99 Pound Rd.
Cumberland, RI 02864-2726

Church of Pan
114 Johnson Rd.
Foster, RI 02825

Cambodian Buddhism
178 Hanover St.
Providence, RI 02907

South Carolina

Called to All Nations Ministries, Inc.
790 E Pine Log Rd.
Aiken, SC 29803

Episcopal Missionary Church
Box 1294
Aiken, SC 29802

Revival Fellowship International
PO Box 1007
Beaufort, SC 29901

Reformed Methodist Union Episcopal
Church
1136 Brody Ave.
Charleston, SC 20407

Missionary Church International
PO Box 1761
Columbia, SC 29202

Progressive Church of our Lord Jesus Christ
2222 Barhamville Rd.
Columbia, SC 29204-1203

Associate Reformed Presbyterian Church
1 Cleveland St., Ste. 110
Greenville, SC 29601-3646

Associated Gospel Churches
209 Pine Knoll Dr., Ste. B
Greenville, SC 29609

Fire-Baptized Holiness Church of God of the
Americas
901 Bishop W. E. Fuller Sr. Hwy.
Greenville, SC 29601-4103

South Carolina Baptist Fellowship
3931 White Horse Rd.
Greenville, SC 29611

Church in the Lord Jesus Christ of the
Apostolic Faith
2449 Calvary Rd.
Hartsville, SC 29550-7167

Southwide Baptist Fellowship
1607 Greenwood Rd.
Laurens, SC 39360

Lovers of Meher Baba
10200 Hwy. 17 N
Myrtle Beach, SC 29572

Southern Methodist Church
425 Broughton St.
Orangeburg, SC 29115

Anglican Mission in the Americas
PO Box 3427
Pawleys Island, SC 29585

General Association of Davidian Seventh-
Day Adventists
Box 450
Salem, SC 29676

African Theological Archministry
PO Box 51
Sheldon, SC 29941

Kingdom Life Fellowship International
1221 Good Hope Church Rd.
Starr, SC 29684

Fundamental Baptist Fellowship
500 W Lee Rd.
Taylors, SC 29687

Free Will Baptist Conference of the
Pentecostal Faith
868 Puddin' Swamp Rd.
Turbeville, SC 29162

General Conference Evangelical Protestant
Church/Evangelical Lutheran Protestant
Church
PO Box 5184
West Columbia, SC 29171

South Dakota

Hutterian Brethren-Schmiedeleut
Olivet, SD 57052

Orthodox Lutheran Confessional Conference
of Independent Congregations
1200 N. Lily Pl.
Sioux Falls, SD 57103

Tennessee

Church of the Holy Monarch
4656 Dowdy Dr.
Antioch, TN 37013-2746

National Association of Free Will Baptists,
Inc.
PO Box 5002
Antioch, TN 37011-5002

Every Nation
PO Box 1787
Brentwood, TN 37024

Church of God (Cleveland, Tennessee)
PO Box 2430
Cleveland, TN 37320-2430

Church of God (Jerusalem Acres)
1826 Dalton Pke. SE
Cleveland, TN 37364-1207

Church of God of Prophecy
PO Box 2910
Cleveland, TN 37320-2910

United Christian Church and Ministerial
Association
Box 700
Cleveland, TN 37311

Christian Holiness Partnership
263 Buffalo Rd.
Clinton, TN 37716

Evangelistic Messengers' Association (EMA)
100 Charity Ln.
Huntingdon, TN 38344

Church of God/Mountain Assembly
PO Box 157
Jellico, TN 37762

Central Baptist Association
309 Lebanon Rd.
Kingsport, TN 37663

Church of Jesus Christ (Kingsport)
5836 Orebank Rd.
Kingsport, TN 37662

Evangelical Methodist Church of America
Box 751
Kingsport, TN 37662

Antiochian Catholic Church in America
2001 Middlebrook Pike
Knoxville, TN 37921

Archdiocese of the Antiochian Catholic
Church in America / St. Demetrios
Antiochian Catholic Church
2001 Middlebrook Pke.
Knoxville, TN 37921

Messianic Israel Alliance (MIA)
PO Box 3263
Lebanon, TN 37088

Reformed Presbyterian Church General
Assembly
PO Box 356
Lookout Mountain, TN 37350

People of the Living God
366 Cove Creek Rd.
McMinnville, TN 37110-9512

Assemblies of the Lord Jesus Christ, Inc.
(ALJC)
PO Box 22366
Memphis, TN 38122

Christian Methodist Episcopal Church
4466 Elvis Presley Blvd.
Memphis, TN 38116-7100

Church of God in Christ
938 Mason St.
Memphis, TN 38126

Cumberland Presbyterian Church in America
1978 Union Ave.
Memphis, TN 38104

African Methodist Episcopal Church
500 8th Ave. S
Nashville, TN 37203

Church of God (Sanctified Church)
PO Box 281615
Nashville, TN 37207

Churches of Christ (Non-Instrumental)
Box 150
Nashville, TN 37202

Holy Orthodox Church, American
Jurisdiction
355 Tusculum Rd.
Nashville, TN 37211-6101

National Baptist Convention of
the U.S.A., Inc.
1700 Baptist World Center Dr.
Nashville, TN 37207

Southern Baptist Convention
901 Commerce St., Ste. 750
Nashville, TN 37203

Southern Episcopal Church
234 Willow Ln.
Nashville, TN 37211

United Methodist Church
810 12th Ave. S
Nashville, TN 37203

World Convention of Churches of Christ
PO Box 41487
Nashville, TN 37204-1487

Mark-Age, Inc.
PO Box 10
Pioneer, TN 37847

The Farm
100 The Farm
Summertown, TN 38483

First Church of Jesus Christ
1100 E. Lincoln St.
Tullahoma, TN 37388

Texas

House of Yahweh (Abilene, Texas)
Box 2498
Abilene, TX 79604

Full Gospel Church Association
PO Box 265
Amarillo, TX 79105

Christ's Holy Sanctified Church of America
PO Box 120574
Arlington, TX 76012

International Convention of Faith Ministries
(ICFM)
5500 Woodland Park Blvd
Arlington, TX 76013

Liberty Fellowship of Churches and
Ministers
5229 Kelly Elliott Rd.
Arlington, TX 76017

World Baptist Fellowship
3001 W Division
Arlington, TX 76012

Old Catholic Church in America (Brothers)
1905 S. 3rd St.
Austin, TX 78704

Original Kleptonian Neo-American Church
(OKNeoAC)
Box 3473
Austin, TX 78764

SMVA Trust
14516 Rumfeldt
Austin, TX 78725

Branch Davidians
PO Box 144
Axtell, TX 76624

Friends Catholic Episcopate of the
Resurrection
1212 N. Major Dr. #27S
Beaumont, TX 77706

Hindu Temple Society of Texas
4533 Larch Ln.
Bellaire, TX 77401

Church of the Golden Rule
6507 Ranch Rd. 32
Blanco, TX 78606

Apostolic Orthodox Church (Boerne, Texas)
248 Deer Creek
Boerne, TX 78006

Quartus Foundation for Spiritual Research
PO Box 1768
Boerne, TX 78006

Church of Seven Planes
PO Box 294
Cooper, TX 75432

Covenant Connections International
916 W Hwy. 190
Copperas Cove, TX 76522

Order of Napunsakas in the West (O.N.)
PO Box 1219
Corpus Christi, TX 78403-1219

Amrita Foundation
PO Box 190978
Dallas, TX 75219-0978

Ancient Rosae Crucis (ARC)
PO Box 4764
Dallas, TX 75208

Full Gospel Holy Temple
39727 LBJ Fwy.
Dallas, TX 75237

Holy Orthodox Catholic Church
5831 Tremont
Dallas, TX 75214

National Baptist Convention of America, Inc.
777 S R Thornton Freeway, Ste. 210
Dallas, TX 75203

National Missionary Baptist Convention of
America
6925 Wofford Dr.
Dallas, TX 75227

Today Church
504 Business Pkwy.
Dallas, TX 75081

World Bible Way Fellowship (WBWF)
PO Box 70
DeSoto, TX 75123-0070

Church of the First Born of the Fullness of
Times
5854 Mira Serana
El Paso, TX 79912

Christ Truth League
2409 Canton Dr.
Fort Worth, TX 76112

Independent Baptist Fellowship
International
724 N Jim Wright Fwy.
Fort Worth, TX 76116

School of the Prophets
PO Box 820882
Fort Worth, TX 76182

Timely Messenger Fellowship
1450 Oak Hill Rd.
Fort Worth, TX 76112-3017

Redeemed Church of God
PO Box 1061
Greenville, TX 75403

The Pure Truth
Lock Box 126
Hamilton, TX 76531

Apostolic Catholic Orthodox Church
1900 St. James Pl., Ste. 880
Houston, TX 77056

Association of Independent Ministries
(A.I.M.)
1535 Greensmark Dr.
Houston, TX 77067

Berachah Church
2815 Sage Rd.
Houston, TX 77056

Grace International
PO Box 591876
Houston, TX 77259-1876

New Light Christian Center Church
1535 Greensmark Dr.
Houston, TX 77067

Saraydarian Institute
915 Franklin St., 9B
Houston, TX 77002

Sharon Fellowship Churches of North
America
13503 Creek Springs
Houston, TX 77083

Worldwide Assembly of YHWH
PO Box 841689
Houston, TX 77284-1689

Full Gospel Fellowship of Churches and
Ministers International
1000 N Belt Line Rd., Ste. 201
Irving, TX 75061-4000

Global Network of Christian Ministries
PO Box 154747
Irving, TX 75015

Remnant of Israel
PO Box 142633
Irving, TX 75014-2633

World Healing Fellowship (Benny Hinn)
Box 163000
Irving, TX 75016-3000

Evangelical Lutheran Diocese of North
America
718 HCR 3424 E
Malone, TX 76660

Free Liberal Catholic Church
Rt.1, PO Box 153
Manor, TX 78653-9801

Victory New Testament Fellowship
International
PO Box 850146
Mesquite, TX 75185-0146

Churches of Christ (Pentecostal)
Box 457
Missouri City, TX 77459

Church of the White Eagle
2615 St. Beulah Chapel Rd.
Montgomery, TX 77316

Confederation of Reformed Evangelical
Churches
8784 FM 226
Nacogdoches, TX 75961

Sri Meenakshi Temple Society of Houston
17130 McLean Rd.
Pearland, TX 77584-4630

World Ministry Fellowship
6000 Custer Rd., Bldg. 3
Plano, TX 75023-5100

Anglican Rite Old Catholic Church
PO Box 5787
San Antonio, TX 78201

The Eastern Orthodox Catholic Church,
North American Synod (EOCC)
PO Box 15302
San Antonio, TX 78212-8502

Family of Abraham
Box 690070
San Antonio, TX 78269

Holy Catholic Church (Western Rite)
4851 Anacacho St.
San Antonio, TX 78217

Infant Jesus of Prague Traditional Roman
Catholic Chapel and Shrine
3442 W. Woodlawn St.
San Antonio, TX 78228

Mayan Order
731 Fredericksburg Rd.
San Antonio, TX 78201

Rigpe Dorje Foundation
28 Eton Green Circle
San Antonio, TX 78257

Independent Christian Churches
International
507 Willard Ave.
Spur, TX 79370-2347

Association of Vineyard Churches
PO Box 2089
Stafford, TX 77497

Unity of the Brethren
1612 S 43rd St.
Temple, TX 76504

American Baptist Association
4605 N. State Line Ave.
Texarkana, TX 75501

Church of God, International
Box 2525
Tyler, TX 75710

Intercontinental Church of God (ICG)
PO Box 1117
Tyler, TX 75710

Church of God Evangelistic Association
908 Sycamore St.
Waxahachie, TX 75165

Anamchara Celtic Church
432 W High St.
Wills Point, TX 75169

Foundations of the Apostles and Prophets:
    School of Ministry and Local Assemblies
    International
PO Box 8073
The Woodlands, TX 77387

Utah

Confederate Nations of Israel
Long Haul, Box 151
Big Water, UT 84741

Apostolic United Brethren
3139 W 14700 S, No. A
Bluffsdale, UT 84065

Foundation Faith of God
5001 Angel Canyon Rd.
Kanab, UT 84741-5000

Aaronic Order
Box 57095
Murray, UT 84157-0095

The Church of Jesus Christ of Latter-day
    Saints
47 E. South Temple
Salt Lake City, UT 84150

Kanzeon Zen Center
1274 E South Temple
Salt Lake City, UT 84102

Summum
707 Genesee Ave.
Salt Lake City, UT 84104

Vermont

Conservative Grace Brethren Churches
    International
PO Box 1275
Morrisville, VT 05661

Apostolic Light Fellowship
PO Box 311
St. Albans, VT 05478-0311

Virginia

Church Universal and Global
PO Box 7512
Alexandria, VA 22307

Reformed Presbyterian Church (Hanover
    Presbytery)
PO Box 10015
Alexandria, VA 22310-5432

Salvation Army
PO Box 269
Alexandria, VA 22313

Volunteers of America
1660 Duke St.
Alexandria, VA 22314

World Zen Fellowship
1014 King St., Ste. #2
Alexandria, VA 22314

Yoga in Daily Life
2402 Mount Vernon Ave.
Alexandria, VA 22301

World Community
Rte. 4, Box 265
Bedford, VA 24523

Integral Yoga International
108 Yogaville Way
Buckingham, VA 23921

Ligmincha Institute
313 2nd St., SE, Ste. 307
Charlottesville, VA 22902

Baptist World Alliance
405 N Washington St.
Falls Church, VA 22046

Muslim American Society (MAS)
PO Box 1896
Falls Church, VA 22041

North American Baptist Fellowship (NABF)
405 N Washington St.
Falls Church, VA 22046

Anglican Church of Virginia
582 Simons Way
Front Royal, VA 22630

Fellowship of Independent and Global
    Churches and Ministries
PO Box 112
Garrisonville, VA 22463

New Life Church and Ministry
PO Box 1268
Hillsville, VA 24343

Apostolic Faith Church of God Live On
2300 Trenton St.
Hopewell, VA 23860

Liberty Baptist Fellowship
PO Box 10174
Lynchburg, VA 24506

Fivefold Path Inc.
278 N White Oak Dr.
Madison, VA 22727

True Vine Pentecostal Churches of Jesus
931 Bethel Ln.
Martinsville, VA 24112

American Unitarian Conference
6806 Springfield Dr.
Mason Neck, VA 22079

Messianic Bureau International (MBI)
701B Industrial Park Dr.
Newport News, VA 23608

Calvary Alliance of Churches and Ministries
5833 Poplar Hall Dr.
Norfolk, VA 23502

The Sufi Movement
1613 Stowe Rd.
Reston, VA 22094-1600

Global Religious Science Ministries
4625 W. Broad St.
Richmond, VA 23230

Redeemed Assembly of Jesus Christ,
    Apostolic
2200 Fairfax Ave.
Richmond, VA 23224

Seventh Day Adventist Reform Movement
PO Box 7240
Roanoke, VA 24019

Reformed Zion Union Apostolic Church
416 South Hill Ave.
South Hill, VA 23970

Sacred Keltic Church of America
4 Favour Ct.
Stafford, VA 22554

Church of God and Saints of Christ
3927 Bridge Rd.
Suffolk, VA 23435

Association for Research and Enlightenment
Box 595
Virginia Beach, VA 23451

Fellowship of the Inner Light
620 14th St.
Virginia Beach, VA 23451

The Rock Church
640 Kempsville Rd.
Virginia Beach, VA 23464

United American Catholic Church
612 Crows Nest Ct.
Virginia Beach, VA 23452

Washington

United Apostolic Church International
PO Box 1452
Aberdeen, WA 98520

Bible Sabbath Association
802 NW 21st Ave.
Battle Ground, WA 98604

United Anglican Church
1640–167th Ave. NE
Bellevue, WA 98008-2909

United Crusade Fellowship Conference
14250 SE 13th Pl.
Bellevue, WA 98008

International Fellowship of Ministries
18706 North Creek Pky., Ste. 104
Bothell, WA 98011

Association for Christian Development
PO Box 4748
Federal Way, WA 98063

Bethel Temple/Bethel Fellowship
    International
2919 SW 312 Pl.
Federal Way, WA 98023-7860

One Drop Zendo
6499 Wahl Rd.
Freeland, WA 98249

Dhiravamsa Foundation
1660 Wold Rd.
Friday Harbor, WA 98250

African-American Catholic Congregation
10911 194th St., Ct. E
Graham, WA 98338-8142

Aquarian Tabernacle Church
PO Box 409
Index, WA 98256

Michael Teachings
PO Box 5459
Lacey, WA 98509-5459

Temple of the Vampire
Box 3582-E
Lacey, WA 98509

Shri Shivabalayogi International Maharaj
    Trust
PO Box 293
Langley, WA 98260

SHEM Ministries International
25016 Maple Valley Hwy.
Maple Valley, WA 98038

Calvary Fellowship, Inc.
302 56th Ave. W
Mountlake Terrace, WA 98043-4718

Cosmic Awareness Communications
PO Box 115
Olympia, WA 98507

Universal Matrix Church
4102 Meadowsweet St.
Pasco, WA 99301

Apostolic Catholic and Spiritual Church
3377 Bethel Rd. SE
Port Orchard, WA 98366

True Buddha School
17012 NE 40th Ct.
Redmond, WA 98052

Venusian Church
Box 95
Redmond, WA 98073-0905

Irminsul Aettir
PO Box 43
Renton, WA 98057-0423

Apostolic Catholic Church in America
425 23rd Ave. S, Ste. A204
Seattle, WA 98144

Aquarian Foundation
315 15th Ave. E
Seattle, WA 98112

Cross and the Lotus
Seattle, WA

Sakya Monastery of Tibetan Buddhism
108 NW 83rd St.
Seattle, WA 98117

Crown of Life Fellowship
PO Box 9048
Spokane, WA 99209

Pentecostal Evangelical Church
1028 W Rosewood Ave.
Spokane, WA 99208

Religious Science International
901 E 2nd Ave., Ste. 301
Spokane, WA 99202

True Catholic Church
PO Box 133
Springdale, WA 99173

Church of Universal Love (Washington)
PO Box 1620
Stanwood, WA 98292

Amica Temple of Radiance
763 S 53rd St.
Tacoma, WA 98408

Conservative Lutheran Association
PO Box 7186
Tacoma, WA 98407

Church of Christ (Restored)
4717 NE 15th Ave.
Vancouver, WA 98663

Ramtha's School of Enlightenment (RSE)
Box 519
Yelm, WA 98587

West Virginia

Claymont Society for Continuous Education
667 Huyett Rd.
Charles Town, WV 25414

Bhavana Society
Back Creek Rd.
High View, WV 26808

Church and School of Wicca
PO Box 297-IN
Hinton, WV 25951-0297

http://newvrindaban.com
R.D. 1, Box 319
Moundsville, WV 26041

Church of God (Seventh-Day, Salem, West
Virginia)
79 Water St.
Salem, WV 26426

Primitive Advent Christian Church
1640 Clay Ave.
South Charleston, WV 25312

Wisconsin

Church of Jesus Christ (Drew)
35315 Chestnut
Burlington, WI 53105

Church of Jesus Christ of Latter-day Saints
(Strangite)
1320 Spring Valley Rd.
Burlington, WI 53105

Lifelight University
4030 Dodd Dr.
Cable, WI 54821

Orthodox Catholic Church in America
409 N Lexington Pky.
DeForest, WI 53532

Church of the Lutheran Confession
501 Grover Rd.
Eau Claire, WI 54701

International Congregational Fellowship
400 West Capitol Dr.
Hartland, WI 53029-1921

Universal Oneness United (UOU)
500-B Prairie Ln.
Hudson, WI 54016

Seventh Day Baptist General Conference
USA and Canada
3120 Kennedy Rd., PO Box 1678
Janesville, WI 53547

Metropolitan Church Association
323 Broad St.
Lake Geneva, WI 53147

Fellowship of Christian Assemblies (FCA)
4909 East Buckeye Rd.
Madison, WI 53716-1898

Freedom from Religion Foundation, Inc.
PO Box 750
Madison, WI 53701

Latvian Evangelical Lutheran Church in
America
1853 N. 75th St.
Milwaukee, WI 53213

Wisconsin Evangelical Lutheran Synod
2929 N Mayfair Rd.
Milwaukee, WI 53222-4398

For My God and My Country
W5703 Shrine Rd.
Neceda, WI 54646-7916

National Association of Congregational
Christian Churches
PO Box 288
Oak Creek, WI 53154-0288

Native American Church
Rte. 1, Box 67
Osseo, WI 59758

Disciples of the Lord Jesus Christ
Shawano, WI 54166

Humanity Benefactor Foundation
4529 Hwy. 41
Sturtevant, WI 53177

Narayanananda Universal Yoga Trust
W 7041 Olmstead Rd.
Winter, WI 54869

Canada

Alberta

Apostolic Lutheran Church of America
R.R. 1
Bentley, AB, Canada T0C 0J0

Apostolic Church of Pentecost of Canada,
Inc. (ACOP)
119-2340 Pegasus Way NE
Calgary, AB, Canada T2E 8M5

Covenant of Gaia Church of Alberta
PO Box 1742, Sta. M
Calgary, AB, Canada T2P 2L7

Life Links International Fellowship of
Churches
287 Prestwick Landing SE
Calgary, AB, Canada T2Z 3W2

United Reformed Churches of North
America
5824 Bowwater Cr. NW
Calgary, AB, Canada T3B 2E2

Victory Churches International
Box 65077, North Hill
Calgary, AB, Canada T2N 4T6

Canadian National Baptist
Convention/Convention Nationale
Baptiste Canadienne
100 Convention Way
Cochrane, AB, Canada T4C 2G2

Orthodox Church of Canada—Orthodox
Church of the East and West (Canada &
USA)
5824-118 Ave.
Edmonton, AB, Canada T5W 1E4

The Universal Church Triumphant of the
Apathetic Agnostic (UCTAA)
531 10 St. SE
Medicine Hat, AB, Canada T1A 1R4

British Columbia

Congregationalist Witchcraft Association
PO Box 2205
Clearbrook, BC, Canada V2T 3X8

Christian Community and Brotherhood of
Reformed Doukhobors (Sons of
Freedom)
Site 8, Comp. 42
Cresent Valley, BC, Canada V0G 1H0

Union of Spiritual Communities of Christ
(Orthodox Doukhobors in Canada)
Box 760
Grand Forks, BC, Canada V0H 1H0

Yasodhara Ashram Society
Box 9
Kootenay Bay, BC, Canada V0B 1X0

Canadian Atheist Society
923 12th St.
New Westminster, BC, Canada V3M 6L1

International Spiritualist Alliance
201—317 Columbia St.
New Westminster, BC, Canada V3L 1A7

Odinist Fellowship/Kirk of Odin
PO Box 1973
Parksville, BC, Canada V9P 2H7

Kathok Gonpa
2800 Grafton St.
Qualicum Beach, BC, Canada V9K 2968

Christian Episcopal Church of Canada
4300 Corless Rd.
Richmond, BC, Canada V7C 1N2

Church of God, a Christian Fellowship
Box 1480
Summerland, BC, Canada V0H 1Z0

Bible Holiness Movement
PO Box 223, Sta. A
Vancouver, BC, Canada V6C 2M3

Canadian Ecumenical Action
1420 West 12th Ave.
Vancouver, BC, Canada V6H 1M8

Glad Tidings Missionary Society
3456 Fraser St.
Vancouver, BC, Canada V5V 4C4

Kabalarian Society
5912 Oak St.
Vancouver, BC, Canada V6M 2W2

Old Catholic Church of British Columbia
715 E. 51st Ave.
Vancouver, BC, Canada V5X 1E2

Traditional Roman Catholic Church in the
Americas
425 E. 11th Ave., Apt. 215
Vancouver, BC, Canada V5T 4K8

International Conference of Reformed
Churches
8586 Harbour Heights Rd.
Vernon, BC, Canada V1H 1J8

Kebzeh Foundation
2001 45th Ave.
Vernon, BC, Canada V1T 6N6

Bold Bible Living
PO Box 75120
White Rock, BC, Canada V4B 5L3

Manitoba

Reinland Mennonite Church
PO Box 96
Rosenfeld, MB, Canada R0G 1X0

Chortitzer Mennonite Conference
479 Hanover St.
Steinbach, MB, Canada R5G 1M7

Evangelical Mennonite Conference
440 Main St.
Steinbach, MB, Canada R0A 2A0

Old Colony Mennonite Church
PO Box 601
Winkler, MB, Canada R6W 4A8

Brunstad Christian Church (Smith's Friends)
470 Ediron Ave.
Winnipeg, MB, Canada R2G 0M4

Evangelical Lutheran Church in Canada
302—393 Portage Ave.
Winnipeg, MB, Canada R3B 3H6

Evangelical Mennonite Mission Conference
Niakwa PO
Winnipeg, MB, Canada R2M 5P9

Lutheran Church—Canada
3074 Portage Ave.
Winnipeg, MB, Canada R3K 0Y2

Lutheran Council in Canada
1512 St. James St.
Winnipeg, MB, Canada R3H 0L2

Ukrainian Catholic Church
233 Scotia St.
Winnipeg, MB, Canada R2V 1V7

Ukrainian Evangelical Baptist Convention of
Canada
PO Box 2437, Station Main
Winnipeg, MB, Canada R3C 4A7

Ukrainian Orthodox Church of Canada
9 St. John's Ave.
Winnipeg, MB, Canada R2W 1G8

Newfoundland

Pentecostal Assemblies of Newfoundland
and Labrador (PAONL)
PO Box 8895, Sta. A
St. John's, NF, Canada A1B 3T2

Nova Scotia

Shambhala International
1084 Tower Rd.
Halifax, NS, Canada B3H 2Y5

Ontario

Old Order Amish Mennonite Church
Rte. 4
Aylmer, ON, Canada N5H 2R3

Associated Gospel Churches (Canada)
1500 Kerns Rd.
Burlington, ON, Canada L7P 3A7

Canadian and American Reformed Churches
PO Box 62053
Burlington, ON, Canada L7R 4K2

Presbyterian Reformed Church
PO Box 82
Chesley, ON, Canada N0G 1L0

Presbyterian Church in Canada
50 Wynford Dr.
Don Mills, ON, Canada M3C 1J7

Markham-Waterloo Conference
(Mennonite)
Rte. 2
Elmira, ON, Canada N3B 2Z2

Christ Catholic Church International
5165 Palmer Ave. Niagara
Falls, ON, Canada L2G 1Y4

Old Catholic Churches
1307 Bethany Ln.
Gloucester, ON, Canada K1J 8P3

Independent Holiness Church
1564 John Quinn Rd.
Greely, ON, Canada K4P 1J9

Fellowship of Evangelical Baptist Churches
in Canada
PO Box 457
Guelph, ON, Canada N1H 6K9

Christadelphians
4 Mountain Park Ave.
Hamilton, ON, Canada L9A 1A2

Church of the Universe
544 Barton St. E
Hamilton, ON, Canada L8L 2Z1

Dharma Centre of Canada
1886 Galway Rd.
Kinmount, ON, Canada K0M 2A0

Conservative Mennonite Church of Ontario
RR 2
Kippen, ON, Canada N0M 2E0

Evangelical Missionary Church of Canada
130 Fergus Ave.
Kitchener, ON, Canada N2A 2H2

Christian Church (Disciples of Christ) in
Canada
PO Box 25087
London, ON, Canada N6C 6A8

Evangelical Fellowship of Canada
MIP Box 3745
Markham, ON, Canada L3R 0Y4

Canadian Baptist Ministries (CBM)
7185 Millcreek Dr.
Mississauga, ON, Canada L5N 5R4

Old Catholic Church of Canada
Mississauga, ON, Canada

Pentecostal Assemblies of Canada
2450 Milltower Court
Mississauga, ON, Canada L5N 5Z6

Anglican Catholic Church of Canada
Unit 4, 190 Colonnade Rd.
Nepean, ON, Canada K2E 7J5

A Case of Faith Ministries (ACOFM)
7580 Donlee Dr.
Niagara Falls, ON, Canada L2H 2N5

Independent Catholic Church of Canada
4520 Huron St., Apt. 602
Niagara Falls, ON, Canada I2E 6Y0

Council of Muslim Communities of Canada
(CMCC)
PO Box 2605, Sta. D
Ottawa, ON, Canada K1P 5W7

Humanist Association of Canada
PO Box 8752, Station T
Ottawa, ON, Canada K1G 3J1

Pagan Federation/Fédération paienne—
Canada (PFFC)
PO Box 876, Stn. B
Ottawa, ON, Canada K1P 5P9

White Wind Zen Community (WWZC)
240 Daly Ave.
Ottawa, ON, Canada K1N 6G2

Ambedkar Mission
9-850 Tapscott
Scarborough, ON, Canada M1X 1N4

Hermetic Order of the Silver Sword
2483 Gerrard St. E
Scarborough, ON, Canada M1N 1W7

United Apostolic Faith Church
92 Bathgate Dr.
Scarborough, ON, Canada M1C 3G7

Canadian Yoga Alliance
20 Bradmon Dr., Ste. 610
St. Catharines, ON, Canada L2M 3S5

Ancient British Church in North America
(The Autocephalous Glastonbury Rite in
Diaspora)
9—47 Marion St.
Toronto, ON, Canada M6R 1E6

British-Israel-World Federation
(Canada) Inc.
313 Sherbourne St.
Toronto, ON, Canada M5A 2S3

British Methodist Episcopal Church
of Canada
460 Shaw St.
Toronto, ON, Canada M6G 3L3

Buddhist Society for Compassionate
Wisdom
297 College St.
Toronto, ON, Canada M5T 1S2

Canadian Council of Churches
47 Queen's Park Crescent E
Toronto, ON, Canada M5S 2C3

Estonian Evangelical Lutheran Church
(Abroad)
383 Jarvis St.
Toronto, ON, Canada M5B 2C7

Fung Loy Kok Institute of Taoism
134 D'Arcy St.
Toronto, ON, Canada M5T 1K3

Kampo Gangra Drubgyudling
200 Balsam Ave.
Toronto, ON, Canada M4E 3C3

Mountain Moon Sangha
No. 6, 939 Avenue Rd.
Toronto, ON, Canada M5P 2K7

The Peoples Church
374 Sheppard Ave. E
Toronto, ON, Canada M2N 3B6

Toronto Zen Centre
33 High Park Gardens
Toronto, ON, Canada M6R 1S8

United Church of Canada
3250 Bloor St. W, Ste. 300
Toronto, ON, Canada M8X 2Y4

Wiccan Church of Canada
109 Vaughan Rd.
Toronto, ON, Canada M6C 2L9

Association of Regular Baptist Churches
(Canada)
17 Laverock St.
Tottenham, ON, Canada L0G 1W0

Prince Edward Island

Free Church of Scotland on Prince Edward
Island
Box 4907
Crapaud, PE, Canada C0A1J0

Quebec

Army of Mary (Armee de Marie) / Centre
International de l'Armee de Marie Spiri-
Maria
626 Rte. du Sanctuaire
Lac-Etchemin, QC, Canada G0R 1S0

Catholic Charismatic Church of Canada
11,141 Rte. 148, RR 1
Mirabel, QC, Canada J0N 1S0

Catholic Church of the Apostles of the Latter
Times
PO Box 4478
Mont-Tremblant, QC, Canada J8E 1A1

Canadian Assemblies of God
6724 Fabre St.
Montreal, QC, Canada H2G 2Z6

Temple of Priapus
PO Box 1164, Stn. H
Montreal, QC, Canada H3G 2N1

Congregation de l'Aumisme
c/o Monastere de Ste-Lucie Ste-Agathe
Ste-Lucie Ste-Agathe, QC, Canada J8C
2Z8

Sivananda Yoga Vedanta Centers
673 8th Ave.
Val Morin, QC, Canada J0T 2R0

Mother Meera Society
Ste-Justine-de-Newton
Quebec, Canada J0P 1T0

Reformed Church of Quebec
844, rue de Contrecoeur
Quebec, QC, Canada G1X 2X8

Saskatchewan

Old Protestant Episcopal Church
Cathedral District Post Office
Regina, SK, Canada S4T 7X2

Australia

Temple Society
152 Tucker
Bentleigh, Australia

Osho Mevlana Foundation
26 Billin Rd.
Myocum, NSW, Australia 2482

Traditional Anglican Communion
PO Box 746
Blackwood, SA, Australia 5051

England

Anglican Consultative Council
16 Tavistock Crescent
London, England W11 1AP

International Association for Religious
  Freedom
1-6 Essex Street
London, England WC2R 3HY

International Humanist and Ethical Union
1 Gower St.
London, England WC1E 6HD

Order of the Cross
10 De Vere Gardens
London, England W8 5AE

Typhonian Ordo Templi Orientis
BCM Starfire
London, England WC1N 3XX

Fellowship of Independent Evangelical
  Churches
39 The Point
Market Harborough, England LE16
  7QU

Germany

Leuenberg Church Fellowship
Jebensstrasse
Berlin, Germany 3 D-10623

India

Isha Foundation
Semmedu (PO)
Coimbatore, India 641 114

Drikung Kagyu Order
PO Kulhan, Sahastradhara Road
Dehra Dun, UA, India 248001

World Vaisnava Association
No. 154 Gopeswar Rd.
Mohala, Vrindavan, India 281 121

Church of North India
16, Pandit Pant Marg
New Delhi, India 110 001

Ireland

Fellowship of Isis
Enniscorthy, Wexford, Ireland

Israel

Church of God (Jerusalem)
PO Box 10184
Jerusalem, Israel 91101

Workers Together with Elohim
Box 14411
Jerusalem, Israel

The Netherlands

Theosophical Society (Hartley)
De Ruyterstratt 74
The Hague, The Netherlands 2518 AV

Republic of South Africa

School of Truth
PO Box 62549
Marshalltown, Republic of South Africa
  2107

Scotland

Beshara School of Intensive Esoteric
  Education
Roberton, Nr. Hawick
Roxburghshire, Scotland TD9 7PH

Sweden

International Federation of Free Evangelical
  Churches
Box 6302
Stockholm, Sweden SE-113 81

Switzerland

World Alliance of Reformed Churches
150 route de Ferney, PO Box 2100
Geneva, Switzerland 1211

Semjase Silver Star Center
Schmidrueti, Switzerland CH-8495

Thailand

World Fellowship of Buddhists
Sukhumvit Rd.
Bangkok, Thailand 10110

Bold page numbers refer to the main entry on the subject. Italic page numbers refer to illustrations.

CMI Connect (periodical), 349
CMI Newsletter (periodical), 349
Coachman, George, 764
Coady, Albert Ronald, 210
Coates, C. A., 528
Coates, Christine, 884
Coates, Gerald, 403
Cobb, C. E. "Buddy," 402
Cobb, Clarence, 762
Cochrane, Robert, 841
Cock (periodical), 1137
Cockeram, Alban, 127
Codde, Peter, 82
Coe Colelge, Cedar Rapids, Iowa, 260
Coffeehouse ministries, 349
Cohen, 349
Cohen, Andrew, 984–985
Cohen, Henry, 597
Cohn, Leopold, 544
Coitus reservatus, 1203
Coke, Daniel, 289
Coke, Thomas, 274, 278
Colby, Charles H., 1268
Cold War, 61
Cole, Bruce, 629
Cole, Donna, 822, 1240
Cole, Raymond C., 582
Colegio Biblico, Eagle Pass, Texas, 510
Coleman, Deborah, 885
Coleman, Johnnie, 876–877
Coleman, Michael A., 537
Coleman Graphics, 886
Colemen, Gilbert, 386
Colemon, Johnnie, 891
Colgan, C. W., 533
Colgate Rochester/Bexley Hall/Crozer, Rochester, New York, 484
Coll, Francisco, 801
Collaboration (periodical), 980
College and Temple of Thelema, **829**
College of Applied Arts, 1228
College of Buddhist Studies, Los Angeles, California, 1062
College of Cardinals, 98
The College of Idaho, Caldwell, Iaho, 260
College of Isis, Enniscorthy, Ireland, 825
College of Life Foundation, 1201
College of Ministry, 386
College of Occult Sciences, 1019
College of Religious Education, 767
College of Seminarians, Santa Cruz, California; Atlanta, Georgia, 722
College of Tao, Santa Monica, Caliornia, 1120
College of the Ozarks, Point Lookout, Missouri, 260
College of the Scriptures, Louisville, Kentucky, 510
The College of Wooster, Wooster, Ohio, 260
Collegia pietatis, 269
Collegiate Association for the Research of Principles, 809
Colley, W. W., 477
Collier, Robert, 876
Collin, Michael, 109, 113
Collin, Rodney, 734
Collins, Arthur H., 358
Collins, Mabel, 695

Collins, Martin, 582
Collins, Sarah E., 305
Collyer, Robert, 870
Colonia Hermosa Provincia, 396
Colonial America
    Baptists, 472
    Church of the Brethren, 455
    Congregationalism, 243, 266
    Cumberland Presbyterian Church, 254
    Dorrilites, 1199
    Episcopal Church, 158
    Free Will Baptists, 504
    Freemasonry, 691
    Judaism, 896
    Lutheranism, 219–220
    Methodism, 274–275
    Moravianism, 271
    Presbyterianism, 259
    Reformed Church, 251
    Reformed-Presbyterian family, 242
    The Rogerenes, 1177–1178
    Roman Catholic Church history, 96
    Shakers, 673
Colonial Missionary Society, 35, 1167
Colonial Tabernacle of Long Beach, California, 353
Colonial Village Pentecostal Church of the Nazarene, **421**
Colonialism
    Anglicanism, 142
    India, 965
    Roman Catholic Church history, 96
    world religions, 51
The Colony, **676**
Color, 796–797
Color Awareness, **737**
Colorado Bible College and Seminary, 1179
Colorado Reform Baptist Church, **504**
Colored Fire-Baptized Holiness Church at Anderson, South Carolina, 386
Colored Methodist Episcopal (CME) Church, 15, *277. See also* Christian Methodist Episcopal Church
Colored Methodist Society, 289
Colton, Ann Ree, 737
Coltrane, Alice, 1020
Coltrane, John, 1020
Columba, John, 1136
Columbia College, Columbia, Missouri, 508
Columbia College, Columbia, South Carolina, 284
Columbia Theological Seminary, Decatur, Georgia, 259
Columbia Union College, 577
Columbian Exposition, 53
Columbus Platform of 1937, 895
Columbus, Christopher, 5, 896
Colver, Mervin, 775
Colville, W. J., 874
Combs, Paul, 128
"Come out" movement, 300, 306, 562
The Comforter (periodical), 1247
Comforter League of Light, **1247**
Comingo, Bruin Romkes, 29–30
Commandment Keepers Ethiopian Hebrew Congregation of the Living God **913**
The Commission (periodical), 496
Committee for Skeptical Inquiry, 616

Committee for the Scientific Investigation of the Claims of the Paranormal. *See* Committee for Skeptical Inquiry
Committee of the States, 1183
Common Sense (periodical), 1114
Common Sense Wholesome Food Store and Restaurant, 684
Communal family, **661–686,** *664,* 1196–1207
Communalism
    Aaraonic Order, 644
    Aggressive Christianity Missions Training Corps, 529
    Christ Faith Mission, 419
    Church of the New Covenant in Christ, 648
    Endtime Body-Christian Ministries, Inc., 402
    Havurot Shalom, 917
    history, 661–665
    Kingdom of Heaven, 1192
    Moravian Church, 281
    1960's, 665
    Oasis Fellowship, 1212–1213
    People's Temple Christian (Disciples) Church, 1230
    River of Life Ranch and Ministry of Truth, 543–544
    Shaker sites, 662
    successful, 665–666
    Tony Alamo Christian Church, 357
    Yearning for Zion Ranch, 650
    Zarephath-Horeb, 1183
    Zion's Order, Inc., 646
The Communicator (periodical), 193, 534, 575, 579
Communion, 512, 543. *See also* Eucharist
Communion of Evangelical Episcopal Churches, **156–157**
Communism, 199
COMMUNITIES Magazine (periodical), 731
Community Chapel and Bible Training Center, **1175–1176**
Community Chapel Publications, 1175
Community Churches, 262–263
Community Churches of America, **535**
Community Circle New (periodical), 848
Community Communique (periodical), 1128
Community Fellowship Pentecost Church. *See* Bible Way Association
Community of Catholic Churches, **114**
Community of Christ, **655–656.** *See also* Reorganized Church of Jesus Christ of Latter-day Saints
    antipolygamy stance, 641
    Fishel, Paul, silencing of, 652
    formation of, 638
    ordination of women, 651, 654
    Restoration Branches Movement, 656
    Restoration Church of Jesus Christ of Latter-day Saints, formation of the, 657
    Smith translation of the Bible, 639
    temple lots possession controversy, 653
    Walton, Eugene O., excommunication of, 659
Community of Micah (Febrengen), **1251**
Community of St. James the Just, **188**

Community of the Good Shepherd, 208
Community of the Love of Christ (Evangelical Catholic), **1133–1134**
Community of the Sons and Daughters of Mary, 107
Community of True Inspiration, **667**
Comparat, Bernard, 607
Comparative theology, 51–53, 612–613
Comparet, Bertrand L., 608
Compass (periodical), 403
Compese, Louis, 151
Compton-Caputo, Peter A., 151
Comstock, Anthony, 1185
Comstock Laws, 1185
Comte, Auguste, 616
Concilio Latino-Americano de la Iglesia de Dios Pentecostal de New York, Incorporado. *See* Latin-American Council of the Pentecostal Church of God of New York
Concilio Olazabal de Iglesias Latino Americano, **394–395**
Concord Press, 713
Concordant Publishing Concern, **549–550**
Concordats of Intercommunion, 105
Concordia College, Ann Arbor, Michigan, 233
Concordia College, Austin, Texas, 233
Concordia College, Bronxville, New York, 233
Concordia College, Moorhead, Minnesota, 229
Concordia College, Portland, Oregon, 233
Concordia College, St. Paul, Minnesota, 233
Concordia College, Selma, Alabama, 233
Concordia College, Seward, Nebraska, 233
The Concordia Lutheran (periodical), 227
Concordia Lutheran Conference, **227**
Concordia Lutheran Seminary, Edmonton, Alberta, Canada, 232
Concordia Lutheran Theological Seminary, St. Catharines, Ontario, Canada, 232
Concordia Seminary, St. Louis, Missouri, 232, 233
Concordia Seminary in Exile, 228
Concordia Synod of the West, **1165**
Concordia Theological Institute for Biblical Studies, 231
Concordia Theological Seminary, Ft. Wayne, Indiana, 233
Concordia Theological Seminary, Oak Forest, Illinois, 227
Concordia University, Irvine, California, 233
Concordia University, Mequon, Wisconsin, 233
Concordia University, River Forest, Illinois, 233
Concordia University College of Alberta, Edmonton, Alberta, Canada, 232
Condron, Barbara, 803
Condron, Daniel R., 803
Confederate Nations of Israel, **648–649**
Confederation of Independent Asatru Kindred (CIAK), **861**
Confederation of Reformed Evangelical Churches, **249**
Conference of United Mennonite Brethren of North America, *442*

H

Nashotah House, Nashotah, Wisconsin, 159
Nasorean Orthodoz Qahal, **546–547**
Nasser, Gamal, 924
Nast, Wilhelm, 299
Nath lineages, 987
Natha tradition, 977
Nation of God and Earths, **955**
Nation of Islam, 48, 926, 950–951, 1253
Nation of Islam (Farrakhan), **954**
Nation of Islam (John Muhammad),
   954–955
Nation of Islam (The Caliph), **955**
Nation of the Five Percent/Nation of God
   and Earths, **955**
Nation of Yahweh (Hebrew Israelites), **914**
National Academy of Metaphysics, West
   Toluca Lake, California, 793
National Alliance of Pantheists, **625–626**
National Anglican Church, **1155**
National Apostolic Bible College/Colegio
   Biblico Apostolic Nacional, Ontario,
   California, 366
National Association of American Churches.
   See Churches of Christ in Zion
National Association of Congregational
   Christian Churches, **263–264**
National Association of Evangelicals,
   70–71
   American Council of Christian Churches,
      opposition by, 69
   establishment of, 63
   Evangelical Fellowship of Canada
      compared to, 70
   fundamentalism, 20
   Great Commission Association of
      Churches, 538
   inclusiveness, 523
   National Council of Churches, dialogue
      with, 64
   Pentecostalism, 46
   Twenty-first Century, 22
   United Fundamentalist Church, 358
National Association of Free, Autonomous
   Christian Churches, **514**
National Association of Free Will Baptists,
   Inc., *476,* **505–506**
National Association of Holiness Churches,
   322–323
National Association of Kingdom
   Evangelicals, **1183**
National Baha'i Council of the United States,
   958
National Baptist Convention, 15, 477
National Baptist Convention of America,
   Inc., *476,* **501–502,** 502
National Baptist Convention of the U.S.A.,
   Inc., *476,* 477, 501, **502,** 503
National Baptist Evangelical Life and Soul
   Saving Assembly of the U.S.A., *476,* **502**
National Baptist Publishing Board, 502
National Baptist Voice (periodical), 502
National Bible Institute, 570
National Black Evangelistic Association, **71**
National Camp Meeting Association for the
   Promotion of Holiness, 299, 300, 302
National Catholic Church of America,
   1135–1136
National Christian Scientist Association, 872

National Colored Spiritualist Association of
   Churches, **762**
National Conference for Community and
   Justice, **67**
National Conference of Christians and Jews.
   See National Conference for Community
   and Justice
National Conference of Unitarian Churches,
   615
National Congress, 501
National Council of Bible-Believing
   Churches in America, 61, 254
National Council of Churches
   Antiochian Orthodox Christian
      Archdiocese of North America,
      withdrawal of the, 183
   Bible Presbyterian Church, opposition
      by the, 253
   data collection, 42
   Evangelical Lutheran Church in
      America, 220
   Fundamental Brethren Church,
      opposition of the, 457
   overview, 64
   Twenty-first Century, 22–23
   Upper Cumberland Presbyterian Church,
      opposition of the, 262
National Council of Churches of Christ in the
   U.S.A., **71–72**
   establishment of, 63–64
   Federal Council of the Churches of Christ
      in America, supersession of the, 1149
   International Council of Christian
      Churches, opposition by, 70
   non-Chalcedonian churches, 177
National Council of Jewish Women, 902
National Council of the Congregational
   Churches, 1149
National Council of the People's Community
   Churches, 263
National Council of Young Israel, **904**
National Evangelistic Center, 409
National Federation of Churches and
   Christian Workers, 1149
National Federation of Religious Liberals,
   1184
National Federation of Spiritual Science
   Churches, **1215**
National Fellowship Churches of God,
   389–390
National Fellowship Churches of God, Inc.,
   389
National Fraternal Council of Negro
   Churches, **1149–1150**
The National Gay Pentecostal Alliance
   (NGPA), **1268**
National Havurah Committee (NHC),
   917–918
National Holiness Association, 302
National Holiness Camp Meeting
   Association for the Promotion of Holiness,
   21
National Holiness Missionary Society. *See*
   World Gospel Mission
National Inter-Religious Conference on
   Peace, 56, 68
National Investigations Committee on
   Unidentified Flying Objects, 426

National Liberal League, 615
National Lutheran Commission for Soldiers'
   and Sailors' Welfare, 223
National Lutheran Council, 220, 223, 1165
The National Message (periodical), 603
National Missionary Baptist Convention of
   America, *476,* **502–503**
National Negro Evangelical Association. *See*
   National Black Evangelistic Association
National Pentecostal Missionary Union, 343
National Presbyterian church. *See*
   Presbyterian Church in America
National Primitive Baptist Convention of the
   U.S.A., **500**
National Renaissance Party, 1243
National Secular Union, 1185
National Society of Clinical Hypnotherapists,
   795
National Spiritual Aid Association, 758
National Spiritual Alliance, **762**
National Spiritual Assembly, 38
National Spiritual Association. *See* National
   Spiritualist Association of Churches
National Spiritual Science Center, **762–763**
National Spiritual Temple of Christ Church
   Union (Inc.) U.S.A., 392
National Spiritualist Association of
   Churches, 749, 762, **763**
The National Spiritualist Summit
   (periodical), 763
National Spritual Aid Association, **1215**
National States Rights Party, 609
National Trust for Historic Preservation, 248
Nationalism, 132, 176
The Nationalist Spiritualist Reporter
   (periodical), 762
Nationwide Independent Baptist
   Fellowship, **493**
Native American Bible College, Shannon,
   North Carolina, 353
Native American Church, 16, 752,
   789–790, 791
Native Americans
   American Indian Evangelical Church,
      345
   Canada, 27–28, 34, 35
   Church of Jesus Christ (Cutlerite), 658
   European colonization, 4–5
   Lumber River Annual Conference of the
      Holiness Methodist Church, 316
   Methodism, 278
   Moravianism, 272
   pre-European contact, 1–2
   restoration of, 1192
   Twenty-first Century, 24
   westward expansion and spread of
      Christianity, 16
Natural hygiene, 806
Natural Law Party, 1024
Natural Rights (periodical), 679
Naturally, the Hygiene Way (periodical), 806
Nature Orders, 703
Nature's Eternal Religion (Klassen), 623
Nauhunty Association, 475
Nauvoo, Illinois, 637
Nauvoo Expositor (periodical), 637
Nava, Antonio Castaqeda, 366
Navarro, Juan, 366

Navayana (periodical), 1259
Naweli, Jacob K., 1126
Nazarene Publishing Company, 308
Nazarene Theological Seminary, Kansas City,
   Missouri, 313
Nazim al-Haqqani, Muhammad, 943
Nazir Order of the Purple Veil. *See* Nahziryah
   Monastic Community
Nazorean Christianity, 650
Nazrey, Willis, 291
Neal, Eli N., 366, 370
Neal, Major George, 1169
Neal A. Maxwell Institute for Religious
   Scholarship, 640
Nebraska Christian College, Norfolk,
   Nebraska, 510
Nebraska Methodist College, Omaha,
   Nebraska, 284
Nebraska Wesleyan University, Lincoln,
   Nebraska, 284
Nebraska Yearly Meeting, 459, 462
Necedah, Wisconsin, 117
Nechung Dorje Drayang Ling, **1106**
Nechung Rinpoche, 1106
Nee, Watchman, 552–553, 1179
Needed Truth, **527**
Needed Truth (periodical), 527
Neem Karoli Baba, 987
Neeser, Julius A., 150
"The Neglected Duty" (Faraq), 924
Negro General Conference, 503
Neihof, J. Eldon, 316
Neil, David, 1146
Nelly Heathen (periodical), 1239
Nelson, Arlene, 775
Nelson, Buck, 752
Nelson, Herman F., 1154
Nelson, Norman, 860
Nelson, Thomas, 183
Nembutsu, 1045
Nemeton, 845
Nemkovich, Robert M., 132
Neo-American Church, 751
Neo-atheists, 617
Neo-charismatic movement, 46
Neo-Dharma, **1259**
Neo-Dharma Notes (periodical), 1259
Neo-Dianic Faith, **1238**
Neo-Essene Community, **797**
Neo-evangelicalism, 71, 118, 523
Neo-Hasidim, 916, 919
Neo-Humanism, 976
Neo-Pentecostalism, 331
Neopaganism
   Adams, Fred, 852
   American Council of Witches, 1232
   Aquarian Tabernacle Church, 842
   Ar nDraiocht Fein: A Druid Fellowship,
      Inc., 842
   Artemisian Order, 843
   Brothers of the Earth, 843
   Church and School of Wicca, 843
   Church of All Worlds, 844
   Church of the Eternal Source, 846–847
   Church of Universal Forces, 1236
   Council of Themis, 1232
   Free Spirit Alliance, 852
   history, 822